American Men & Women of Science™

23rd Edition

American Men & Women of Science™

23rd Edition

A Biographical Directory of Today's Leaders in Physical, Biological and Related Sciences

Volume
4
J-L

Katherine H. Nemeh
Project Editor

Detroit • New York • San Francisco • New Haven, Conn. • Waterville, Maine • London

American Men & Women of Science, 23rd edition

Project Editors
Katherine H. Nemeh

Editorial
Jeffrey Muhr, Bridget Travers

Imaging and Multimedia
Lezlie Light, Christine O'Bryan

Product Design
Pamela A. E. Galbreath

Composition and Electronic Prepress
Gary Leach

Manufacturing
Lori Kessler

© 2007 Thomson Gale, a part of the Thomson Corporation.

Thomson and Star logo are trademarks and Gale is a registered trademark used herein under license.

For more information, contact
Thomson Gale
27500 Drake Rd.
Farmington Hills, MI 48331-3535
Or you can visit our internet site at
http://www.gale.com

ALL RIGHTS RESERVED
No part of this work covered by the copyright herein may be reproduced or used in any form or by any means—graphic, electronic, or mechanical, including photocopying, recording, taping, Web distribution, or information storage retrieval systems—without the written permission of the publisher.

This publication is a creative work fully protected by all applicable copyright laws, as well as by misappropriation, trade secret, unfair competition, and other applicable laws. The authors and editors of this work have added value to the underlying factual material herein through one or more of the following: unique and original selection, coordination, expression, arrangement, and classification of the information.

For permission to use material from the product, submit your request via the Web at http://www.gale-edit.com/permissions, or you may download our Permissions Request form and submit your request by fax or mail to:

Permisssions Department
Thomson Gale
27500 Drake Rd.
Farmington Hills, MI 48331-3535
Permissions Hotline:
248-699-8006 or 800-877-4253, ext. 8006
Fax 248-699-8074 or 800-762-4058

While every effort has been made to ensure the reliability of the information presented in this publication, Thomson Gale does not guarantee the accuracy of the data contained herein. Thomson Gale accepts no payment for listing; and inclusion in the publication of any organization, agency, institution, publication, service, or individual does not imply endorsement of the editors or publisher. Errors brought to the attention of the publisher and verified to the satisfaction of the publisher will be corrected in future editions.

LIBRARY OF CONGRESS CONTROL NUMBER 89-6454236

ISBN-13 978-1-4144-0086-0 (8 vol. set)
ISBN-13 978-1-4144-0087-7 (vol. 1)
ISBN-13 978-1-4144-0088-4 (vol. 2)
ISBN-13 978-1-4144-0089-1 (vol. 3)
ISBN-13 978-1-4144-0090-7 (vol. 4)
ISBN-13 978-1-4144-0091-4 (vol. 5)
ISBN-13 978-1-4144-0092-1 (vol. 6)
ISBN-13 978-1-4144-0093-8 (vol. 7)
ISBN-13 978-1-4144-0094-5 (vol. 8)

ISBN-10 1-4144-0086-1 (8 vol. set)
ISBN-10 1-4144-0087-X (vol. 1)
ISBN-10 1-4144-0088-8 (vol. 2)
ISBN-10 1-4144-0089-6 (vol. 3)
ISBN-10 1-4144-0090-X (vol. 4)
ISBN-10 1-4144-0091-8 (vol. 5)
ISBN-10 1-4144-0092-6 (vol. 6)
ISBN-10 1-4144-0093-4 (vol. 7)
ISBN-10 1-4144-0094-2 (vol. 8)

ISSN 0000-1287

Printed in the United States of America
10 9 8 7 6 5 4 3 2 1

CONTENTS

Advisory Board VI

Introduction VII

Major Honors & Awards IX

Statistics XIII

Sample Entry XIX

Abbreviations XXI

Biographies 1

ADVISORY BOARD

James E. Bobick (Retired)
Former Department Head, Science and Technology Department
Carnegie Library of Pittsburgh, Pennsylvania

K. Lee Lerner
Lerner & Lerner, LLC

David A. Tyckoson
Director of Public Service
Henry Madden Library, California State Univeristy, Fresno

INTRODUCTION

American Men & Women of Science (*AMWS*) remains without peer as a chronicle of scientific endeavor and achievement in the United States and Canada. The present work is the twenty-third edition, and was first compiled as *American Men of Science* by J. McKeen Cattell in 1906. In its one hundred year history, *AMWS* has profiled the careers of more than 300,000 people in various scientific fields. Since the first edition, the number of U.S. and Canadian scientists and the fields they pursue has grown immensely. This edition alone lists 133,340 people in science, approximately 4,000 of which are listed for the first time and approximately 80,000 updated entries. Although the book has grown, our stated purpose is the same as when Dr. Cattell first undertook the task of producing a biographical directory of active American scientists. It was his intention to record educational, personal and career data which would make "a contribution to the organization of science in America" and "make men [and women] of science acquainted with one another and with one another's work." It is our hope that this edition will fulfill these goals.

CONCEPT AND SCOPE

The biographies of people in science constitute seven of the eight volumes of the current edition and provide the following information, if available and applicable: birthdate, birthplace, citizenship, name of spouse, name(s) or number of children, field of specialty, education, honorary degrees, professional experience, honors and awards, memberships, research information, addresses, facsimile numbers, and e-mail addresses for each entrant. These sections are preceded by subheads in boldface for easier reference. The eighth volume, the discipline index, organizes entrants by field of activity. This index, adapted from the National Science Foundation's Taxonomy of Degree and Employment Specialties, classifies entrants by 192 subject specialties listed in the table of contents of Volume 8. The index lists entrants by state or province within each subject specialty, allowing the user to easily locate a person in science in a given geographic area. Also included are statistical information and charts showing the distribution of *AMWS* entrants by age and discipline and an annotated listing of the recipients of the Nobel Prizes, the Crafoord Prize, the Charles Stark Draper Prize, the National Medal of Science, the Fields Medal, the National Medal of Technology, and the Alan T. Waterman Award since the previous edition.

While the scientific fields covered by *AMWS* are comprehensive, no attempt has been made to include all U.S. and Canadian scientists. Entrants are meant to be limited to those who have made significant contributions in their field. The names of new entrants were submitted for consideration at the editors' request by current entrants and by leaders of academic, government and private research programs and associations. Those included met the following criteria:

1. Distinguished achievement, by reason of experience, training or accomplishment, including contributions to literature, coupled with continuing activity in scientific work;

or

2. Research activity of high quality in science as evidenced by publication in reputable scientific journals; or, for those whose work cannot be published due to governmental or industrial security, research activity of high quality in science as evidenced by the judgement of the individual's peers;

or

3. Attainment of a position of substantial responsibility requiring scientific training and experience.

EDITORIAL PRACTICES

This edition profiles living persons in the physical and biological fields, as well as public health scientists, engineers, mathematicians, statisticians, and computer scientists. The information is collected by means of direct communication whenever possible. All entrants received forms for corroboration and updating. The information submitted by entrants is included as completely as possible within the boundaries of editorial and space restrictions. If an entrant does not return the form and his or her current location can be verified in secondary sources, the full entry is repeated. Entrants known to be deceased are noted as such and a reference to the previous edition is given. Entrants who are not citizens of the United States or Canada are included if a significant portion of their work was performed in North America. Also, in the first Gale edition, the editors have combined the former current and concurrent position sections of entrants' profiles into the professional experience section, in order to create a more accessible chronological portrait of a scientist's contributions to his or her field. However, the scientist's current position(s) is presented as capitalized text for those users only seeking to quickly locate this information. Gale editors have also fully expanded and bolded the rubrics in each profile to aid users in navigating text.

ACKNOWLEDGMENTS

A project as large as publishing *AMWS* involves the efforts of a great many people. The editors' appreciation is expressed to the many scientific societies that provided their membership lists for the purpose of locating former entrants whose addresses had changed, and to the tens of thousands of people around the world who took time to provide us with biographical information.

AVAILABLE IN ELECTRONIC FORMATS

Licensing. *American Men & Women of Science* is available for licensing. The complete database is provided in a fielded format and is deliverable on such media as disk or CD-ROM. For more information, contact Thomson Gale's Business Development Group at 800-877-GALE, or visit our website at www.gale.com/bizdev.

SUGGESTIONS ARE WELCOME

Comments, suggestions, and nominations of entrants for the twenty-fourth edition are encouraged and should be sent to The Editors, *American Men & Women of Science,* Thomson Gale, 27500 Drake Rd., Farmington Hills, MI 48331-3535 [telephone: 248-699-4253; toll-free: 800-347-4253; facsimile: 248-699-8062; e-mail: amws@thomson.com].

MAJOR HONORS & AWARDS

NOBEL PRIZES

Nobel Foundation, Royal Swedish Academy of Sciences & Nobel Assembly at Karolinska Institutet

The Nobel Prizes were established in 1900 (and first awarded in 1901) to recognize those people who "have conferred the greatest benefit on mankind."

2005 Recipients
CHEMISTRY
Yves Chauvin, Robert H. Grubbs & Richard R. Schrock
Awarded "for the development of the metathesis method in organic synthesis."

PHYSICS
Roy J. Glauber
Awarded "for his contribution to the quantum theory of optical coherence."
John L. Hall & Theodor W. Hänsch
Awarded "for their contributions to the development of laser-based precision spectroscopy, including the optical frequency comb technique."

PHYSIOLOGY OR MEDICINE
Barry J. Marshall & J. Robin Warren
Awarded "for their discovery of the bacterium Helicobacter pylori and its role in gastritis and peptic ulcer disease."

CRAFOORD PRIZE

Royal Swedish Academy of Sciences

The Crafoord Prize was introduced in 1982 to award scientists in disciplines not covered by the Nobel Prize, namely mathematics, astronomy, geosciences and biosciences.

2005 Recipients
James E. Gunn, P. James E. Peebles & Martin J. Rees
Awarded "for contributions towards understanding the large-scale structure of the Universe."

CHARLES STARK DRAPER PRIZE

National Academy of Engineering

The Draper Prize, awarded biennially, was introduced in 1989 to recognize engineering achievement.

2005 Recipients
Minoru S. Araki, Francis J. Madden, Edward A. Miller, James W. Plummer & Don H. Schoessler
Awarded "for the design, development, and operation of Corona, the first space-based Earth observation system."

2006 Recipients
Willard S. Boyle & George E. Smith
Awarded "for the invention of the Charge-Coupled Device (CCD), a light-sensitive component at the heart of digital cameras and other widely used imaging technologies."

NATIONAL MEDAL OF SCIENCE

National Science Foundation

The National Medals of Science were established by the United States Congress in 1959 and have been awarded by the President of the United States since 1962. The National Science Foundation's selection criteria are based on the "total impact of an individual's work on the present state of physical, biological, mathematical, engineering, behavioral, or social sciences."

2003 Recipients
J. Michael Bishop
G. Brent Dalrymple
Carl R. de Boor
Riccardo Giacconi
R. Duncan Luce
John M. Prausnitz
Solomon H. Snyder
Charles Yanofsky

2004 Recipients
Kenneth J. Arrow
Norman E. Borlaug
Robert N. Clayton
Edwin N. Lightfoot
Stephen J. Lippard
Phillip A. Sharp
Thomas E. Starzl
Dennis P. Sullivan

FIELDS MEDAL

International Mathematical Union

The Fields Medals were established in 1936 by Canadian mathematician John Fields to acknowledge outstanding research by young mathematicians. The medals are awarded every four years at the International Congress of Mathematicians.

2006 Recipients
- Andrei Okounkov
- Grigori Perelman
- Terence Tao
- Wendelin Werner

Awarded to Okounkov for his contributions bridging probability, representation theory and algebraic geometry. Awarded to Perelman for his contributions to geometry and his revolutionary insights into the analytical and geometric structure of the Ricci flow. Awarded to Tao for his contributions to partial differential equations, combinatorics, harmonic analysis and additive number theory. Awarded to Werner for his contributions to the development of stochastic Loewner evolution, the geometry of two-dimensional Brownian motion, and conformal field theory.

NATIONAL MEDAL OF TECHNOLOGY

U. S. Department of Commerce

The National Medals of Technology were created as part of the 1980 Stevenson-Wydler Technology Innovation Act and were first awarded in 1985. They are bestowed by the President of the United States to recognize individuals and companies for their development or commercialization of technology or for their contributions to the establishment of a technologically-trained workforce.

2003 Recipients
- Jan D. Achenbach
- Watts S. Humphrey
- Robert M. Metcalfe
- Ronald M. Lewis
- Irwin M. Lachman
- Rodney D. Bagley
- UOP LLC
- Wisconsin Alumni Research Foundation

2004 Recipients
- Ralph H. Baer
- Roger L. Easton
- Gen-Probe Inc.
- IBM-Microelectronics Division
- Industrial Light and Magic
- Motorola Inc.
- PACCAR Inc.

ALAN T. WATERMAN AWARD

National Science Foundation and National Science Board

Established by the United States Congress in 1975, the Waterman Award is given annually to an outstanding researcher, aged 35 or younger, in any field of science or engineering supported by the National Science Foundation.

2005 Recipient
Dalton Conley

Awarded "[f]or his contribution to the field of sociology as a research scientist and published author exemplified by his research on how socio-economic status is transmitted across generations. He brings methodological rigor and sophistication to deep social questions."

DIAGRAM OF GEOGRAPHIC DEFINITIONS

XII

STATISTICS

Statistical distribution of entrants in *American Men & Women of Science* with U.S. and Canadian mailing addresses is illustrated on the following pages. The regional scheme for geographical analysis is diagrammed in the map on the preceding page. A table enumerating the geographic distribution can be found below. The statistics are compiled by tallying all occurrences of a major index subject. Each entrant may choose to be indexed under as many as four categories; thus, the total number of subject references is greater than the number of entrants in *AMWS*.

GEOGRAPHIC DEFINITIONS

Northeast
Connecticut
Indiana
Maine
Massachusetts
Michigan
New Hampshire
New Jersey
New York
Ohio
Pennsylvania
Rhode Island
Vermont

Southeast
Alabama
Delaware
District of Columbia
Florida
Georgia
Kentucky
Maryland
Mississippi
North Carolina
South Carolina
Tennessee
Virginia
West Virginia

North Central
Illinois
Iowa
Kansas
Minnesota
Missouri
Nebraska
North Dakota
South Dakota
Wisconsin

South Central
Arkansas
Louisiana
Texas
Oklahoma

Mountain
Arizona
Colorado
Idaho
Montana
Nevada
New Mexico
Utah
Wyoming

Pacific
Alaska
California
Hawaii
Oregon
Washington

Canada
Alberta
British Columbia
Manitoba
New Brunswick
Newfoundland
Northwest Territories
Nova Scotia
Nunavut
Ontario
Prince Edward Island
Quebec
Saskatchewan
Yukon Territory

GEOGRAPHIC DISTRIBUTION OF SCIENTISTS BY DISCIPLINE

Discipline	Northeast	Southeast	North Central	South Central	Mountain	Pacific	Canada	Total
Agricultural & Forest Sciences	1,139	1,585	1,009	494	595	877	640	6,339
Biological Sciences	11,169	8,716	4,683	2,658	2,057	5,159	2,526	36,968
Chemistry	8,005	4,938	2,469	1,434	1,164	2,646	1,087	21,743
Computer Sciences	1,708	1,097	498	333	322	883	226	5,067
Engineering	7,513	4,857	2,159	1,623	1,584	3,578	1,066	22,380
Environmental, Earth & Marine Sciences	2,414	2,186	873	903	1,280	1,900	812	10,368
Mathematics	2,884	1,972	1,040	647	599	1,333	522	8,997
Medical & Health Sciences	6,330	4,796	2,238	1,390	759	2,383	979	18,875
Physics & Astronomy	5,328	3,591	1,469	879	1,668	3,158	983	17,076
Other	3,009	2,761	954	587	650	1,309	398	9,668
Total	**49,499**	**36,499**	**17,392**	**10,948**	**10,678**	**23,226**	**9,239**	**157,481**

AGE DISTRIBUTION OF AMERICAN MEN & WOMEN OF SCIENCE

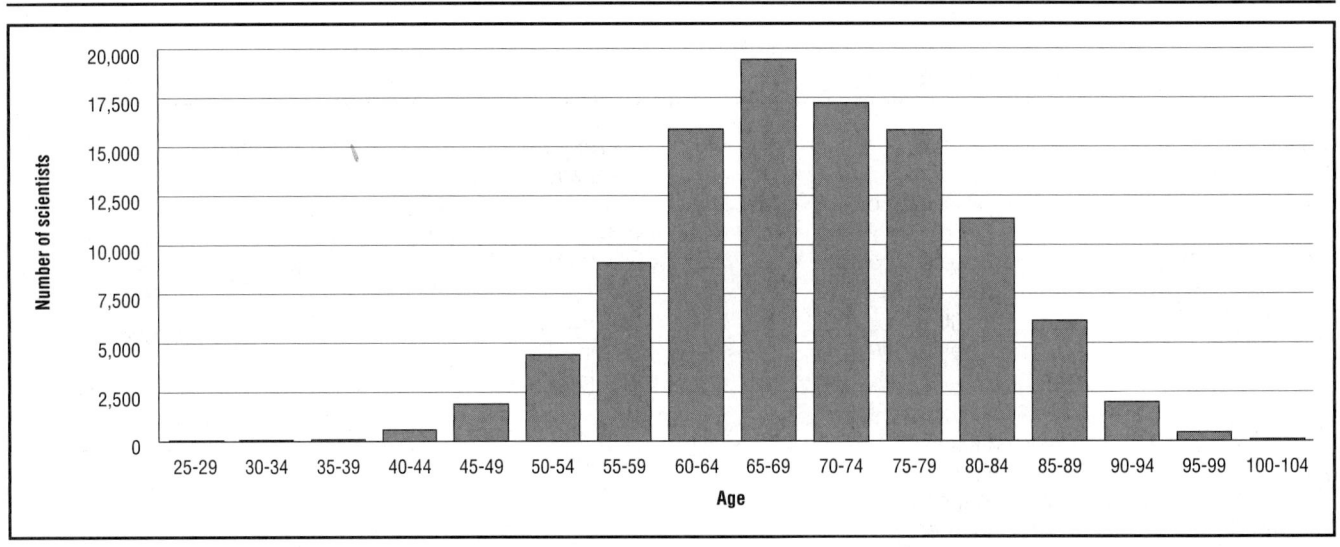

NUMBER OF SCIENTISTS IN EACH DISCIPLINE OF STUDY

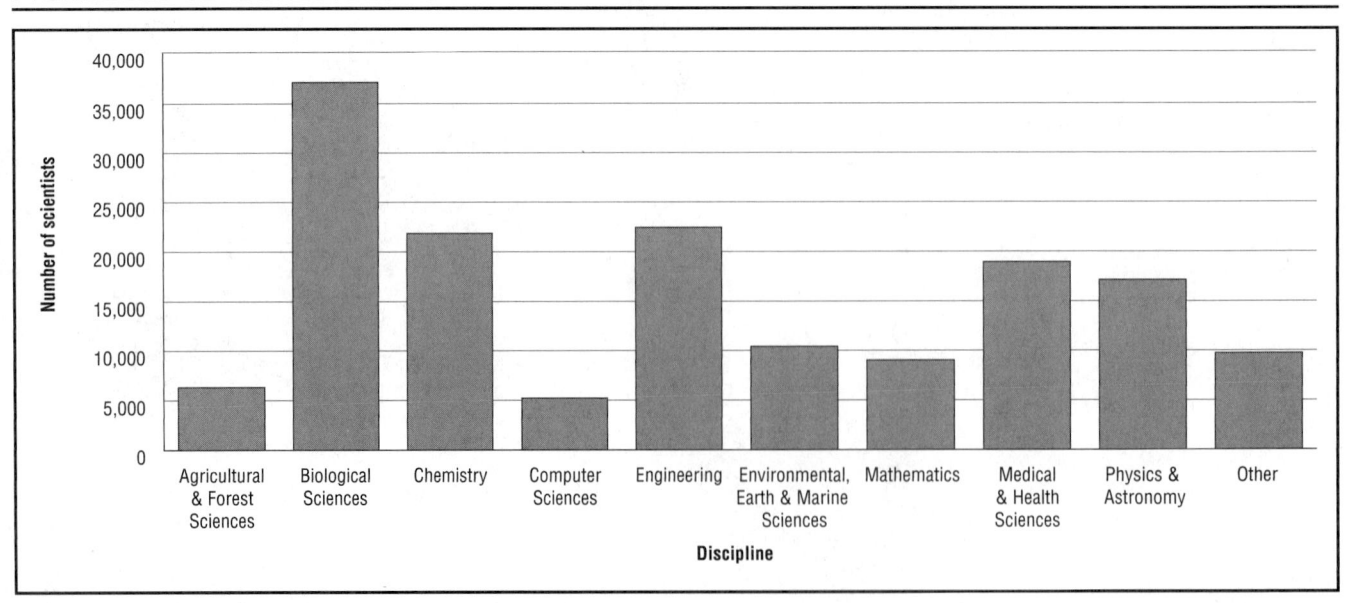

ALL DISCIPLINES

Region	Number	Percent
Northeast	49,499	31%
Southeast	36,499	23%
North Central	17,392	11%
South Central	10,948	7%
Mountain	10,678	7%
Pacific	23,226	15%
Canada	9,239	6%
Total	157,481	100%

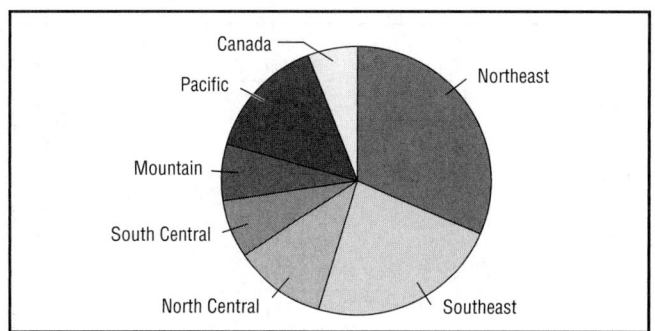

AGRICULTURAL & FOREST SCIENCES

Region	Number	Percent
Northeast	1,139	18%
Southeast	1,585	25%
North Central	1,009	16%
South Central	494	8%
Mountain	595	9%
Pacific	877	14%
Canada	640	10%
Total	6,339	100%

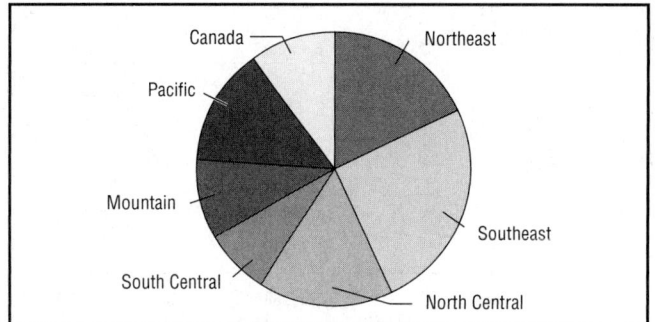

BIOLOGICAL SCIENCES

Region	Number	Percent
Northeast	11,169	30%
Southeast	8,716	24%
North Central	4,683	13%
South Central	2,658	7%
Mountain	2,057	6%
Pacific	5,159	14%
Canada	2,526	6%
Total	36,968	100%

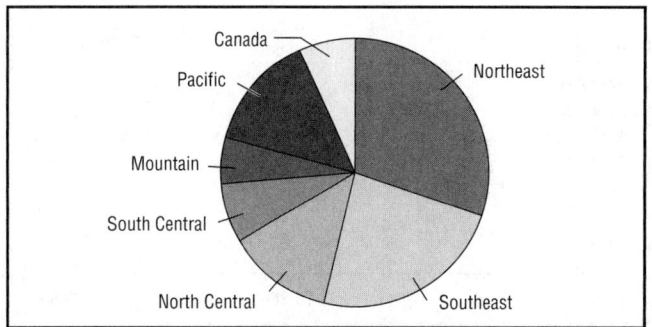

CHEMISTRY

Region	Number	Percent
Northeast	8,005	37%
Southeast	4,938	23%
North Central	2,469	11%
South Central	1,434	7%
Mountain	1,164	5%
Pacific	2,646	12%
Canada	1,087	5%
Total	21,743	100%

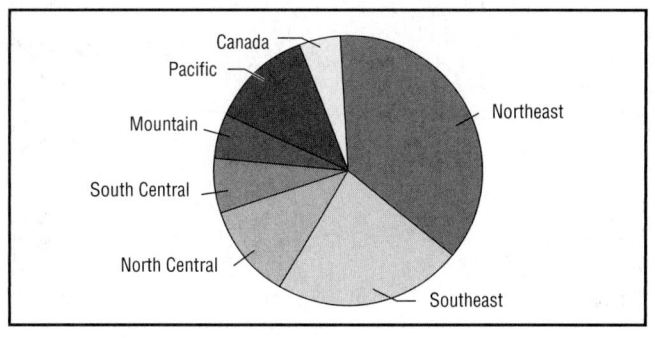

COMPUTER SCIENCES

Region	Number	Percent
Northeast	1,708	34%
Southeast	1,097	22%
North Central	498	10%
South Central	333	6%
Mountain	322	6%
Pacific	883	18%
Canada	226	4%
Total	5,067	100%

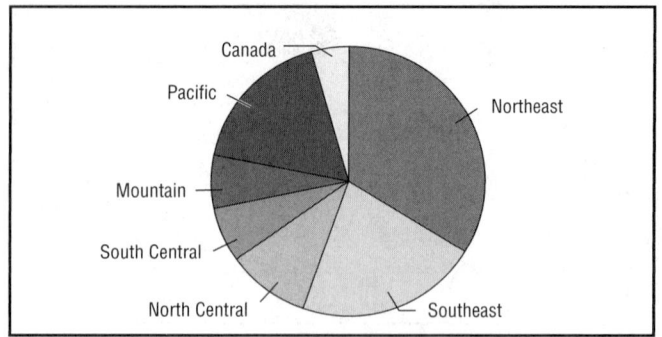

ENGINEERING

Region	Number	Percent
Northeast	7,513	33%
Southeast	4,857	22%
North Central	2,159	10%
South Central	1,623	7%
Mountain	1,584	7%
Pacific	3,578	16%
Canada	1,066	5%
Total	22,380	100%

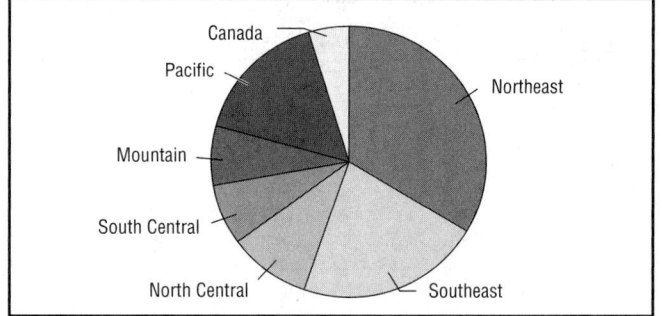

ENVIRONMENTAL, EARTH & MARINE SCIENCES

Region	Number	Percent
Northeast	2,414	23%
Southeast	2,186	22%
North Central	873	8%
South Central	903	9%
Mountain	1,280	12%
Pacific	1,900	18%
Canada	812	8%
Total	10,368	100%

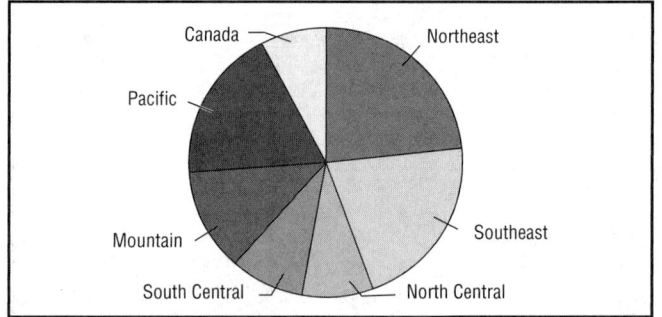

MATHEMATICS

Region	Number	Percent
Northeast	2,884	31%
Southeast	1,972	22%
North Central	1,040	12%
South Central	647	7%
Mountain	599	7%
Pacific	1,333	15%
Canada	522	6%
Total	8,997	100%

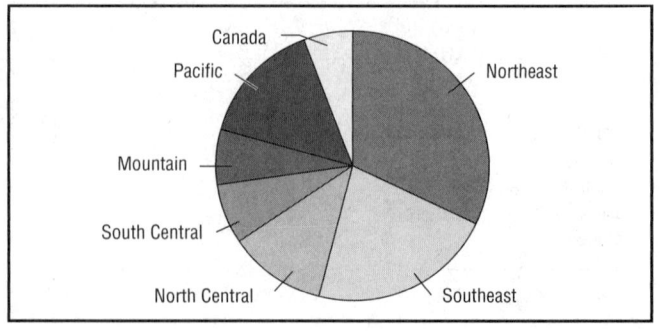

MEDICAL & HEALTH SCIENCES

Region	Number	Percent
Northeast	6,330	34%
Southeast	4,796	25%
North Central	2,238	12%
South Central	1,390	7%
Mountain	759	4%
Pacific	2,383	13%
Canada	979	5%
Total	**18,875**	**100%**

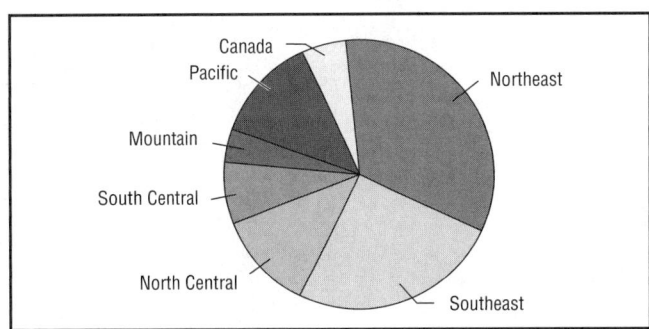

PHYSICS & ASTRONOMY

Region	Number	Percent
Northeast	5,328	31%
Southeast	3,591	21%
North Central	1,469	8%
South Central	879	5%
Mountain	1,668	10%
Pacific	3,158	19%
Canada	983	6%
Total	**17,076**	**100%**

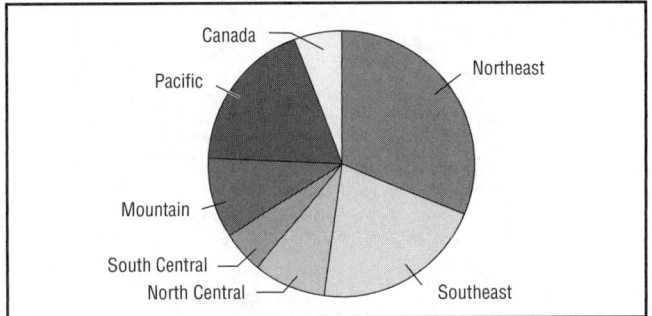

OTHER PROFESSIONAL FIELDS

Region	Number	Percent
Northeast	3,009	31%
Southeast	2,761	29%
North Central	954	10%
South Central	587	6%
Mountain	650	6%
Pacific	1,309	14%
Canada	398	4%
Total	**9,668**	**100%**

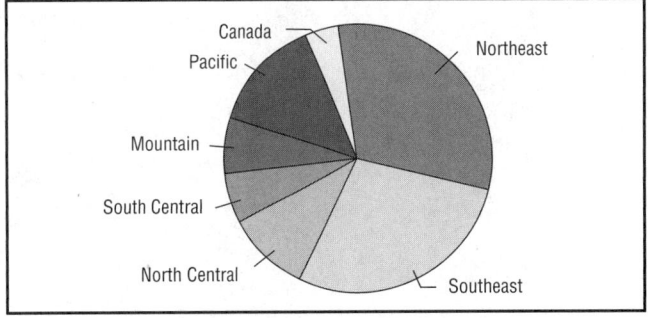

SAMPLE ENTRY

American Men & Women of Science (*AMWS*) is an extremely useful reference tool. The book is most often used in two ways: to find more information about a particular scientist and to locate a scientist in a specific field.

To locate information about an individual, the biographical section is most helpful. It encompasses the first seven volumes and lists people in scientific fields alphabetically by last name. The fictitious biographical listing shown below illustrates every type of information an entry may include.

The Discipline Index, volume 8, can be used to easily find an entrant in a specific subject specialty. This index is first classified by area of specialty; within each specialty entrants are divided further by geographical location.

Name ─── **RATINER, LEIGH A(NN)**, OCEANOGRAPHY, MARINE BIOLOGY. ─── Field of Specialty

Personal Data: b New York, NY, November 9, 1951; ─── Birthplace/Birth date

Marriage date/Spouse Name ─── m 1976, Mark Smith;

c Stephen E & Mary J. ─── Names of Children

Education ─── **Education:** Univ Mich, BS, 1973, MS, 1975; Purdue Univ, PhD(oceanog), 1980.

Honorary Degrees: DSc, Univ Calif, San Diego, 1998. ─── Honorary Degrees

Honors & Awards ─── **Honors & Awards:** Henry Bryant Bigelow Medal, Oceanog Soc, 1992.

Professional Experience: Vis lectr, Wash Univ, 2000; consult, New England Aquarium, 1989-1999; ASSOC PROF OCEANOG & BIOL, HARVARD UNIV, 1986-; asst prof oceanog, Harvard Univ, 1982-1986. ─── Professional Experience

Memberships ─── **Memberships:** AAAS; Am Soc Naval Engrs; Sigma Xi; Oceanog Soc.

Research Statement & Publications: Ocean pollution prevention, water treatment and analysis, ecology of marine plankton and sponges; author of 13 publications. ─── Research Statement & Publications

Mailing Address ─── **Mailing Address:** 1 Avery Place, Cambridge, MA 02138.

Fax Number ─── **Fax:** 617-555-5939;

E-Mail: laratiner@harvard.edu ─── E-mail Address

XIX

ABBREVIATIONS

A

AAAS: American Association for the Advancement of Science
abnorm: abnormal
abstr: abstract
acad: academic, academy
acct: account, accountant, accounting
acoust: acoustic(s), acoustical
ACTH: adrenocorticotrophic hormone
actg: acting
activ: activities, activity
addn: addition(s), additional
adj: adjunct, adjutant
adjust: adjustment
Adm: Admiral
admin: administration, administrative
adminr: administrator(s)
admis: admission(s)
adv: adviser(s), advisory
advan: advance(d), advancement
advert: advertisement, advertising
AEC: Atomic Energy Commission
aerodyn: aerodynamic
aeronaut: aeronautic(s), aeronautical
aerophys: aerophysical, aerophysics
aesthet: aesthetic
AFB: Air Force Base
affil: affiliate(s), affiliation
agr: agricultural, agriculture
agron: agronomic, agronomical, agronomy
agrost: agrostologic, agrostological, agrostology
agt: agent
AID: Agency for International Development
Ala: Alabama
allergol: allergological, allergology
alt: alternate
Alta: Alberta
Am: America, American
AMA: American Medical Association
anal: analysis, analytic, analytical
analog: analogue
anat: anatomic, anatomical, anatomy
anesthesiol: anesthesiology
angiol: angiology
Ann: Annal(s)
ann: annual
anthrop: anthropological, anthropology
anthropom: anthropometric, anthropometrical, anthropometry
antiq: antiquary, antiquities, antiquity
antiqn: antiquarian
apicult: apicultural, apiculture
APO: Army Post Office
app: appoint, appointed
appl: applied
appln: application
approx: approximate(ly)
apt: apartment(s)
aquacult: aquaculture
arbit: arbitration
arch: archives
archaeol: archaeological, archaeology
archit: architectural, architecture
Arg: Argentina, Argentine
Ariz: Arizona
Ark: Arkansas
artil: artillery
asn: association
assoc(s): associate(s), associated
asst(s): assistant(s), assistantship(s)
assyriol: Assyriology
astrodyn: astrodynamics
astron: astronomical, astronomy
astronaut: astronautical, astronautics
astronr: astronomer
astrophys: astrophysical, astrophysics
attend: attendant, attending
atty: attorney
audiol: audiology
auth: author
AV: audiovisual
Ave: Avenue
avicult: avicultural, aviculture

B

b: born
bact: bacterial, bacteriologic, bacteriological, bacteriology
BC: British Colombia
bd: board
behav: behavior(al)
Belg: Belgian, Belgium
Bibl: Biblical
bibliog: bibliographic, bibliographical, bibliography
bibliogr: bibliographer
biochem: biochemical, biochemistry
biog: biographical, biography
biol: biological, biology
biomed: biomedical, biomedicine
biomet: biometric(s), biometrical, biometry
biophys: biophysical, biophysics
bk(s): book(s)
bldg: building
Blvd: Boulevard
Bor: Borough
bot: botanical, botany
br: branch(es)
Brig: Brigadier
Brit: Britain, British
Bro(s): Brother(s)
byrol: byrology
Bull: Bulletin
bur: bureau
bus: business
BWI: British West Indies

C

c: children
Calif: California

Can: Canada, Canadian
cand: candidate
Capt: Captain
cardiol: cardiology
cardiovasc: cardiovascular
cartog: cartographic, cartographical, cartography
cartogr: cartographer
Cath: Catholic
CEngr: Corp of Engineers
cent: central
Cent Am: Central American
cert: certificate(s), certification, certified
chap: chapter
chem: chemical(s), chemistry
chemother: chemotherapy
chg: change
chmn: chairman
citricult: citriculture
class: classical
climat: climatological, climatology
clin(s): clinic(s), clinical
Co: County
Co: Companies, Company
co-auth: co-author
co-dir: co-director
co-ed: co-editor
co-educ: co-education, co-educational
col(s): college(s), collegiate, colonel
collab: collaboration, collaborative
collabr: collaborator
Colo: Colorado
com: commerce, commercial
Comdr: Commander
commun: communicable, communication(s)
comn(s): commission(s), commissioned
comndg: commanding
comnr: commissioner
comp: comparitive
compos: composition
comput: computation, computer(s), computing
comt(s): committee(s)
conchol: conchology
conf: conference
cong: congress, congressional
Conn: Connecticut
conserv: conservation, conservatory
consol: consolidated, consolidation
const: constitution, constitutional
construct: construction, constructive
consult(s): consult, consultant(s), consultantship(s), consultation, consulting
contemp: contemporary
contrib: contribute, contributing, contribution(s)
contribr: contributor
conv: convention

coop: cooperating, cooperation, cooperative
coord: coordinate(d), coordinating, coordination
coordr: coordinator
corp: corporate, corporation(s)
corresp: correspondence, correspondent, corresponding
coun: council, counsel, counseling
counr: councilor, counselor
criminol: criminological, criminology
cryog: cryogenic(s)
crystallog: crystallographic, crystallographical, crystallography
crystallogr: crystallographer
Ct: Court
Ctr: Center
cult: cultural, culture
cur: curator
curric: curriculum
cybernet: cybernetic(s)
cytol: cytological, cytology
Czech: Czechoslovakia, Czech Republic

D

DC: District of Columbia
Del: Delaware
deleg: delegate, delegation
delinq: delinquency, delinquent
dem: democrat(s), democratic
demog: demographic, demography
demogr: demographer
demonstr: demontrator
dendrol: dendrologic, dendrological, dendrology
dent: dental, dentistry
dep: deputy
dept: department
dermat: dermatologic, dermatological, dermatology
develop: developed, developing, development, developmental
diag: diagnosis, diagnostic
dialectol: dialectological, dialectology
dict: dictionaries, dictionary
Dig: Digest
dipl: diploma, diplomate
dir(s): director(s), directories, directory
dis: disease(s), disorders
Diss Abst: Dissertation Abstracts
dist: district
distrib: distributed, distribution, distributive
distribr: distributor(s)
div: division, divisional, divorced
DNA: deoxyribonucleic acid
doc: document(s), documentary, documentation
Dom: Dominion

Dr: Drive

E

E: East
ecol: ecological, ecology
econ(s): economic(s), economical, economy
economet: econometric(s)
ECT: electroconvulsive or electroshock therapy
ed: edition(s), editor(s), editorial
ed bd: editorial board
educ: education, educational
educr: educator(s)
EEG: electroencephalogram, electroencephalographic, electroencephalography
Egyptol: Egyptology
EKG: electrocardiogram
elec: electric, electrical, electricity
electrochem: electrochemical, electrochemistry
electroph: electrophysical, electrophysics
elem: elementary
embryol: embryologic, embryological, embryology
emer: emeriti, emeritus
employ: employment
encour: encouragement
encycl: encyclopedia
endocrinol: endocrinologic, endocrinology
eng: engineering
Eng: England, English
engr(s): engineer(s)
enol: enology
Ens: Ensign
entom: entomological, entomology
environ: environment(s), environmental
enzym: enzymology
epidemiol: epidemiologic, epidemiological, epidemiology
equip: equipment
ERDA: Energy Research & Development Administration
ESEA: Elementary & Secondary Education Act
espec: especially
estab: established, establishment(s)
ethnog: ethnographic, ethnographical, ethnography
ethnogr: ethnographer
ethnol: ethnologic, ethnological, ethnology
Europ: European
eval: evaluation
Evangel: Evangelical
eve: evening
exam: examination(s), examining
examr: examiner

except: exceptional
exec(s): executive(s)
exeg: exegeses, exegesis, exegetic, exegetical
exhib(s): exhibition(s), exhibit(s)
exp: experiment, experimental
exped(s): expedition(s)
explor: exploration(s), exploratory
expos: exposition
exten: extension

F

fac: faculty
facil: facilities, facility
fed: federal
fedn: federation
fel(s): fellow(s), fellowship(s)
fermentol: fermentology
fertil: fertility, fertilization
Fla: Florida
floricult: floricultural, floriculture
found: foundation
FPO: Fleet Post Office
Fr: French
Ft: Fort

G

Ga: Georgia
gastroenterol: gastroenterological, gastroenterology
gen: general
geneal: genealogical, genealogy
geod: geodesy, geodetic
geog: geographic, geographical, geography
geogr: geographer
geol: geologic, geological, geology
geom: geometric, geometrical, geometry
geomorphol: geomorphologic, geomorphology
geophys: geophysical, geophysics
Ger: German, Germanic, Germany
geriat: geriatric
geront: gerontological, gerontology
Ges: Gesellschaft
glaciol: glaciology
gov: governing, governor(s)
govt: government, governmental
grad: graduate(d)
Gt Brit: Great Britain
guid: guidance
gym: gymnasium
gynec: gynecologic, gynecological, gynecology

H

handbk(s): handbook(s)
helminth: helminthology
hemat: hematologic, hematological, hematology
herpet: herpetologic, herpetological, herpetology
HEW: Department of Health, Education & Welfare
Hisp: Hispanic, Hispania
hist: historic, historical, history
histol: histological, histology
HM: Her Majesty
hochsch: hochschule
homeop: homeopathic, homeopathy
hon(s): honor(s), honorable, honorary
hort: horticultural, horticulture
hosp(s): hospital(s), hospitalization
hq: headquarters
HumRRO: Human Resources Research Office
husb: husbandry
Hwy: Highway
hydraul: hydraulic(s)
hydrodyn: hydrodynamic(s)
hydrol: hydrologic, hydrological, hydrologics
hyg: hygiene, hygienic(s)
hypn: hypnosis

I

ichthyol: ichthyological, ichthyology
Ill: Illinois
illum: illuminating, illumination
illus: illustrate, illustrated, illustration
illusr: illustrator
immunol: immunologic, immunological, immunology
Imp: Imperial
improv: improvement
Inc: Incorporated
in-chg: in charge
incl: include(s), including
Ind: Indiana
indust(s): industrial, industries, industry
Inf: Infantry
info: information
inorg: inorganic
ins: insurance
inst(s): institute(s), institution(s)
instnl: institutional(ized)
instr(s): instruct, instruction, instructor(s)
instrnl: instructional
int: international
intel: intelligence
introd: introduction
invert: invertebrate
invest(s): investigation(s)
investr: investigator
irrig: irrigation

Ital: Italian

J

J: Journal
Jct: Junction
jour: journal, journalism
jr: junior
jurisp: jurisprudence
juv: juvenile

K

Kans: Kansas
Ky: Kentucky

L

La: Louisiana
lab(s): laboratories, laboratory
lang: language(s)
laryngol: laryngological, laryngology
lect: lecture(s)
lectr: lecturer(s)
legis: legislation, legislative, legislature
lett: letter(s)
lib: liberal
libr: libraries, library
librn: librarian
lic: license(d)
limnol: limnological, limnology
ling: linguistic(s), linguistical
lit: literary, literature
lithol: lithologic, lithological, lithology
Lt: Lieutenant
Ltd: Limited

M

m: married
mach: machine(s), machinery
mag: magazine(s)
maj: major
malacol: malacology
mammal: mammalogy
Man: Manitoba
Mariol: Mariology
Mass: Massachusetts
mat: material(s)
mat med: materia medica
math: mathematic(s), mathematical
Md: Maryland
mech: mechanic(s), mechanical
med: medical, medicinal, medicine
Mediter: Mediterranean
Mem: Memorial
mem: member(s), membership(s)
ment: mental(ly)
metab: metabolic, metabolism
metall: metallurgic, metallurgical, metallurgy

metallog: metallographic, metallography
metallogr: metallographer
metaphys: metaphysical, metaphysics
meteorol: meteorological, meteorology
metrol: metrological, metrology
metrop: metropolitan
Mex: Mexican, Mexico
mfg: manufacturing
mfr: manufacturer
mgr: manager
mgt: management
Mich: Michigan
microbiol: microbiological, microbiology
micros: microscopic, microscopical, microscopy
mid: middle
mil: military
mineral: mineralogical, mineralogy
Minn: Minnesota
Miss: Mississippi
mkt: market, marketing
Mo: Missouri
mod: modern
monogr: monograph
Mont: Montana
morphol: morphological, morphology
Mt: Mount
mult: multiple
munic: municipal, municipalities
mus: museum(s)
musicol: musicological, musicology
mycol: mycologic, mycology

N

N: North
NASA: National Aeronautics & Space Administration
nat: national, naturalized
NATO: North Atlantic Treaty Organization
navig: navigation(al)
NB: New Brunswick
NC: North Carolina
NDak: North Dakota
NDEA: National Defense Education Act
Nebr: Nebraska
nematol: nematological, nematology
nerv: nervous
Neth: Netherlands
neurol: neurological, neurology
neuropath: neuropathological, neuropathology
neuropsychiat: neuropsychiatric, neuropsychiatry
neurosurg: neurosurgical, neurosurgery
Nev: Nevada
New Eng: New England

New York: New York City
Nfld: Newfoundland
NH: New Hampshire
NIH: National Institute of Health
NIMH: National Institute of Mental Health
NJ: New Jersey
NMex: New Mexico
No: Number
nonres: nonresident
norm: normal
Norweg: Norwegian
NS: Nova Scotia
NSF: National Science Foundation
NSW: New South Wales
numis: numismatic(s)
nutrit: nutrition, nutritional
NY: New York State
NZ: New Zealand

O

observ: observatories, observatory
obstet: obstetric(s), obstetrical
occas: occasional(ly)
occup: occupation, occupational
oceanog: oceanographic, oceanographical, oceanography
oceanogr: oceanographer
odontol: odontology
OEEC: Organization for European Economic Cooperation
off: office, official
Okla: Oklahoma
olericult: olericulture
oncol: oncologic, oncology
Ont: Ontario
oper(s): operation(s), operational, operative
ophthal: ophthalmologic, ophthalmological, ophthalmology
optom: optometric, optometrical, optometry
ord: ordnance
Ore: Oregon
org: organic
orgn: organization(s), organizational
orient: oriental
ornith: ornithological, ornithology
orthod: orthodontia, orthodontic(s)
orthop: orthopedic(s)
osteop: osteopathic, osteopathy
otol: otological, otology
otolaryngol: otolaryngological, otolaryngology
otorhinol: otorhinologic, otorhinology

P

Pa: Pennsylvania
Pac: Pacific
paleobot: paleobotanical, paleobotany
paleont: paleontology

Pan-Am: Pan-American
parasitol: parasitology
partic: participant, participating
path: pathologic, pathological, pathology
pedag: pedagogic(s), pedagogical, pedagogy
pediat: pediatric(s)
PEI: Prince Edward Island
penol: penological, penology
periodont: periodontal, periodontic(s)
petrog: petrographic, petrographical, petrography
petrogr: petrographer
petrol: petroleum, petrologic, petrological, petrology
pharm: pharmacy
pharmaceut: pharmaceutic(s), pharmaceutical(s)
pharmacog: pharmacognosy
pharmacol: pharmacologic, pharmacological, pharmacology
phenomenol: phenomenologic(al), phenomenology
philol: philological, philology
philos: philosophic, philosophical, philosophy
photog: photographic, photography
photogeog: photogeographic, photogeography
photogr: photographer(s)
photogram: photogrammetric, photogrammetry
photom: photometric, photometrical, photometry
phycol: phycology
phys: physical
physiog: physiographic, physiographical, physiography
physiol: physiological, physiology
Pkwy: Parkway
Pl: Place
polit: political, politics
polytech: polytechnic(s)
pomol: pomological, pomology
pontif: pontifical
pop: population
Port: Portugal, Portuguese
Pos: Position
postgrad: postgraduate
PR: Puerto Rico
pract: practice
practr: practitioner
prehist: prehistoric, prehistory
prep: preparation, preparative, preparatory
pres: president
Presby: Presbyterian
preserv: preservation
prev: prevention, preventive
prin: principal
prob(s): problem(s)
proc: proceedings

proctol: proctologic, proctological, proctology
prod: product(s), production, productive
prof: professional, professor, professorial
prog(s): program(s), programmed, programming
proj: project(s), projection(al), projective
prom: promotion
protozool: protozoology
Prov: Province, Provincial
psychiat: psychiatric, psychiatry
psychoanal: psychoanalysis, psychoanalytic, psychoanalytical
psychol: psychological, psychology
psychomet: psychometric(s)
psychopath: psychopathologic, psychopathology
psychophys: psychophysical, psychophysics
psychophysiol: psychophysiological, psychophysiology
psychosom: psychosomatic(s)
psychother: psychoterapeutic(s), psychotherapy
Pt: Point
pub: public
publ: publication(s), publish(ed), publisher, publishing
pvt: private

Q

Qm: Quartermaster
Qm Gen: Quartermaster General
qual: qualitative, quality
quant: quantitative
quart: quarterly
Que: Quebec

R

radiol: radiological, radiology
RAF: Royal Air Force
RAFVR: Royal Air Force Volunteer Reserve
RAMC: Royal Army Medical Corps
RAMCR: Royal Army Medical Corps Reserve
RAOC: Royal Army Ordnance Corps
RASC: Royal Army Service Corps
RASCR: Royal Army Service Corps Reserve
RCAF: Royal Canadian Air Force
RCAFR: Royal Canadian Air Force Reserve
RCAFVR: Royal Canadian Air Force Volunteer Reserve
RCAMC: Royal Canadian Army Medical Corps
RCAMCR: Royal Canadian Army Medical Corps Reserve
RCASC: Royal Canadian Army Service Corps
RCASCR: Royal Canadian Army Service Corps Reserve
RCEME: Royal Canadian Electrical & Mechanical Engineers
RCN: Royal Canadian Navy
RCNR: Royal Canadian Naval Reserve
RCNVR: Royal Canadian Naval Volunteer Reserve
Rd: Road
RD: Rural Delivery
rec: record(s), recording
redevelop: redevelopment
ref: reference(s)
refrig: refrigeration
regist: register(ed), registration
registr: registrar
regt: regiment(al)
rehab: rehabilitation
rel(s): relation(s), relative
relig: religion, religious
REME: Royal Electrical & Mechanical Engineers
rep: represent, representative
Repub: Republic
req: requirements
res: research, reserve
rev: review, revised, revision
RFD: Rural Free Delivery
rhet: rhetoric, rhetorical
RI: Rhode Island
Rm: Room
RM: Royal Marines
RN: Royal Navy
RNA: ribonucleic acid
RNR: Royal Naval Reserve
RNVR: Royal Naval Volunteer Reserve
roentgenol: roentgenologic, roentgenological, roentgenology
RR: Railroad, Rural Route
Rte: Route
Russ: Russian
rwy: railway

S

S: South
SAfrica: South Africa
SAm: South America, South American
sanit: sanitary, sanitation
Sask: Saskatchewan
SC: South Carolina
Scand: Scandinavia(n)
sch(s): school(s)
scholar: scholarship
sci: science(s), scientific
SDak: South Dakota
SEATO: Southeast Asia Treaty Organization
sec: secondary
sect: section
secy: secretary
seismog: seismograph, seismographic, seismography
seismogr: seismographer
seismol: seismological, seismology
sem: seminar, seminary
Sen: Senator, Senatorial
ser: serial, series
serol: serologic, serological, serology
serv: service(s), serving
silvicult: silvicultural, silviculture
soc(s): societies, society
soc sci: social science
sociol: sociologic, sociological, sociology
Span: Spanish
spec: special
specif: specification(s)
spectrog: spectrograph, spectrographic, spectrography
spectrogr: spectrographer
spectrophotom: spectrophotometer, spectrophotometric, spectrophotometry
spectros: spectroscopic, spectroscopy
speleol: speleological, speleology
Sq: Square
sr: senior
St: Saint, Street(s)
sta(s): station(s)
stand: standard(s), standardization
statist: statistical, statistics
Ste: Sainte
steril: sterility
stomatol: stomatology
stratig: stratigraphic, stratigraphy
stratigr: stratigrapher
struct: structural, structure(s)
stud: student(ship)
subcomt: subcommittee
subj: subject
subsid: subsidiary
substa: substation
super: superior
suppl: supplement(s), supplemental, supplementary
supt: superintendent
supv: supervising, supervision
supvr: supervisor
supvry: supervisory
surg: surgery, surgical
surv: survey, surveying
survr: surveyor
Swed: Swedish
Switz: Switzerland
symp: symposia, symposium(s)
syphil: syphilology

syst(s): system(s), systematic(s), systematical

T

taxon: taxonomic, taxonomy
tech: technical, technique(s)
technol: technologic(al), technology
tel: telegraph(y), telephone
temp: temporary
Tenn: Tennessee
Terr: Terrace
Tex: Texas
textbk(s): textbook(s)
text ed: text edition
theol: theological, theology
theoret: theoretic(al)
ther: therapy
therapeut: therapeutic(s)
thermodyn: thermodynamic(s)
topog: topographic, topographical, topography
topogr: topographer
toxicol: toxicologic, toxicological, toxicology
trans: transaction(s)
transl: translated, translation(s)
translr: translator(s)
transp: transport, transportation
treas: treasurer, treasury
treat: treatment
trop: tropical
tuberc: tuberculosis
TV: television
Twp: Township

U

UAR: United Arab Republic
UK: United Kingdom
UN: United Nations
undergrad: undergraduate

unemploy: unemployment
UNESCO: United Nations Educational Scientific & Cultural Organization
UNICEF: United Nations International Childrens Fund
univ(s): university, universities
UNRRA: United Nations Relief & Rehabilitation Administration
UNRWA: United Nations Relief & Works Agency
urol: urologic, urological, urology
US: United States
USAAF: US Army Air Force
USAAFR: US Army Air Force Reserve
USAF: US Air Force
USAFR: US Air Force Reserve
USAID: US Agency for International Development
USAR: US Army Reserve
USCG: US Coast Guard
USCGR: US Coast Guard Reserve
USDA: US Department of Agriculture
USMC: US Marine Corps
USMCR: US Marine Corps Reserve
USN: US Navy
USNAF: US Naval Air Force
USNAFR: US Naval Air Force Reserve
USNR: US Naval Reserve
USPHS: US Public Health Service
USPHSR: US Public Health Service Reserve
USSR: Union of Soviet Socialist Republics

V

Va: Virginia
var: various
veg: vegetable(s), vegetation
vent: ventilating, ventilation

vert: vertebrate
Vet: Veteran(s)
vet: veterinarian, veterinary
VI: Virgin Islands
vinicult: viniculture
virol: virological, virology
vis: visiting
voc: vocational
vocab: vocabulary
vol(s): voluntary, volunteer(s), volume(s)
vpres: vice president
vs: versus
Vt: Vermont

W

W: West
Wash: Washington
WHO: World Health Organization
WI: West Indies
wid: widow, widowed, widower
Wis: Wisconsin
WVa: West Virginia
Wyo: Wyoming

Y

Yearbk(s): Yearbook(s)
YMCA: Young Men's Christian Association
YMHA: Young Men's Hebrew Association
Yr(s): Year(s)
YT: Yukon Territory
YWCA: Young Women's Christian Association
YWHA: Young Women's Hebrew Association

Z

zool: zoological, zoology

AMERICAN MEN & WOMEN OF SCIENCE

J

JA, WILLIAM YIN, ANALYTICAL CHEMISTRY. **Personal Data:** b March 5, 1936; American citizen. **Education:** Univ Calif, Berkeley, BS, 1960. **Professional Experience:** RES ASSOC, RICHMOND RES CTR, STAUFFER CHEM CO, 1966-; anall chemist, Philadelphia Quartz Co, Calif, 1964-1966; anal chemist, Hyman (Julius) Labs Inc, 1962-1964; chemist, Qual Assurance Tech Agency, US Army Chem Corps, 1960-1962. **Memberships:** Am Chem Soc; Am Soc Testing & Mat; Assoc Official Anal Chem. **Research Statement & Publications:** Analytical methods development; trace analysis; separations and purification techniques, especially preparation of high-purity pesticide standards and metabolites by large-scale, high-speed column chromatography. **Mailing Address:** 145 Windward Ct, ValleJo, CA 94591-6938.

JAANUS, SIRET DESIREE, PHARMACOLOGY, OCULAR PHARMACOLOGY. **Personal Data:** b Tallinn, Estonia, American citizen; m 1973, Jaak Jurison. **Education:** City Col NY, BS, 1960; Hunter Col, MS, 1966; State Univ NY Downstate Med Ctr, PhD (pharmacol), 1970. **Honorary Degrees:** LHD, Southern Calif Col Optom. **Honors & Awards:** Paul Yarwood Award, 1979. **Professional Experience:** VIS PROF & CHMN, DEPT BIOL SCI, STATE UNIV NY COL OPTOM, 1994-; vis prof, Pa Col optom, 1991-1994; Assoc ed, Clin Ocular Pharmacol, 1984, 1989 & 1995; chmn, Dept Basic & Visual Sci, Southern Calif Col Optom, 1978-1981; prof basic sci, Dept Basic & Visual Sci, Southern Calif Col Optom, 1973-1993; chmn dept, State Univ NY Col Optom, 1972-1973; asst prof basic sci, State Univ NY Col Optom, 1971-1972; path, State Univ Downstate Med Ctr, 1970-1971; res asst, NIH fel pharmacol, 1966-1970; res asst, State Univ Downstate Med Ctr, 1964-1966; Res asst pharmacol, Albert Einstein Col Med, 1960-1964; Consult. **Memberships:** Am Optom Asn; Am Soc Pharmacol & Exp Therapeut; Am Acad Optom; Asn Res Vision & Opthal. **Research Statement & Publications:** Autonomic and endocrine pharmacology. **Mailing Address:** 65 Cent Park W, New York, NY 10023. **Fax:** 212-780-5176. **E-Mail:** sjaanus@scco.edu

JABALPURWALA, KAIZER E, INORGANIC CHEMISTRY, PHYSICAL CHEMISTRY. **Personal Data:** b Surat, India, m 1960, Sharifa Ahmadi; c Sheila & Inez. **Education:** Univ Bombay, BSc, 1954, MSc, 1956, PhD (coord chem), 1960. **Professional Experience:** TECH DIR, JABALPUR INDUST INC, 1983-; partner, G H Chem Ltd, 1974-1983; tech mgr, Zochem Ltd, 1974; tech dir, Zinc Oxide Co Can Ltd, Hudson Bay Mining & Smelting Co, Montreal, 1968-1974; chief chemist, Zinc Oxide Co Can Ltd, Hudson Bay Mining & Smelting Co, Montreal, 1964-1968; res assoc inorg chem, Boston Univ, 1961-1964; res asst phys chem, Inst Sci, Univ Bombay, 1958-1961. **Memberships:** Am Chem Soc; Brit Chem Soc; Sigma Xi; Chem Inst Can. **Research Statement & Publications:** Light scattering by colloid systems; solution stabilities of complex ions; electrophotography related to photoconductivity of zinc oxide; technology of zinc oxide; zinc dust. **Mailing Address:** Mcic, Box 36505, St Lambert, PQ J4P 1Y5, Can. **Fax:** 514-671-1197. **E-Mail:** kaizerj@axess.com

JABARIN, SALEH ABD EL KARIM, POLYMER CHEMISTRY. **Personal Data:** b Haifa, Israel, February 7, 1939; m 1969, c 1. **Education:** Dartmouth Col, BA, 1966; Polytech Inst Brooklyn, MS, 1968; Univ Mass, PhD (polymer sci & eng), 1971. **Professional Experience:** DIR, POLYMER INST, UNIV TOLEDO, as of 2003; PROF, CHE & ENVIRON ENG, UNIV TOLEDO, as of 2003; SR SCIENTIST, OWENS-ILLINOIS TECH CTR, 1971-. **Memberships:** Am Chem Soc; Soc Plastics Engrs. **Research Statement & Publications:** Studies of thermal, mechanical and optical properties of polymers and polymer crystallization using light scattering, x-ray diffraction, infra-red dichroism and birefringence; molecular orientation and solution characterization. **Mailing Address:** Polymer Inst, Col Eng, Univ Toledo, W Res Annex Toledo, Holland, OH 43606-3390. **Fax:** 419-530-5019. **E-Mail:** sjabari@utnet.utoledo.edu

JABBOUR, J T, PEDIATRIC NEUROLOGY. **Personal Data:** b Tiptonville, Tenn, August 5, 1927; m 1957, Helen Block; c 5. **Education:** Univ Tenn, Martin, BS, 1948; Univ Tenn, Memphis, MD, 1951; Am Bd Pediat, dipl, 1960. **Professional Experience:** CONSULT, 1985-; prof pediat & neurol & head child div child neurol, Univ Tenn, Memphis, 1967-1975; consult, Ment Retardation Br, Bur Chronic Dis, USPHS, 1966-1969; chief pediat neurol, Child Develop Ctr, Med Units, Univ Tenn, Memphis, 1965-1968; asst prof, Univ Tenn, Memphis, 1965-1967; consult, Oklahoma City Speech & Hearing Ctr, 1961-1965; consult, Oklahoma City Children's Ctr, 1961-1965; asst prof pediat & neurol & assoc dir clin study, Ctr Birth Defects, 1961-1965; co-dir pediat neurol & seizure clin, Sch Med, Univ Okla, 1959-1961; Fel neurol, Univ Minn, Minneapolis, 1958-1961; res assoc pediat, Col Med, Univ Tenn, Memphis, 1957; resident, Col Med, Univ Tenn, Memphis, 1956-1958; gen pract, Tenn, 1953-1956; Rotating intern, Baylor Univ Hosp, Dallas, 1952-1953. **Memberships:** AMA; Am Acad Pediat; Am Acad Neurol; Am Acad Cerebral Palsy; Child Neurol Soc. **Research Statement & Publications:** Subacute sclerosing panencephalitis; behavioral neurology. **Mailing Address:** 680 S Mclean Blvd, Memphis, TN 38104. **Fax:** 901-572-5090.

JABBOUR, KAHTAN NICOLAS, ENGINEERING. **Personal Data:** b Safita, Syria, August 26, 1934. **Education:** Damascus Univ, cert math, 1953 & 1954; Sch Advan Eng, Beirut, BS, 1957; Purdue Univ, MS, 1960, PhD (struct), 1962. **Professional Experience:** ACTG SEC CHIEF, PROJ DIRECTORATE II, DIV LICENSING PROJ MGT, OFF NUCLEAR REACTOR REGULATION, US NUCLEAR REGULATORY COMN, as of 2002; sr proj mgr, Us Nuclear Regulatory Comn, beginning 1980; sr mech engr, US Nuclear Regulatory Comn, 1973-1980; aerospace engr, Goddard Space Flight Ctr, NASA, 1969-1973; staff engr, Fairchild Hiller Corp, 1967-1969; NSF res grant, 1965-1966; assoc prof eng sci, Tenn Technol Univ, 1963-1967; asst prof eng, Kans State Univ, 1962-1963; design engr, El-Ghab Proj, Syria, 1958-1959; field engr, Arabian Am Oil Co, Saudi Arabia, 1957-1958. **Memberships:** Am Soc Eng Educ. **Research Statement & Publications:** Structural mechanics and engineering; perforated plates. **Mailing Address:** Div Licensing Proj Mgt, US Nuclear Regulatory Comn, Washington, DC 20555.

JABBOUR, KAMAL, HIGH SPEED COMPUTER NETWORKS, COMPUTER APPLICATION TO POWER SYSTEMS. **Personal Data:** b Chemlan, Lebanon, August 10, 1957; m Marla; c Randa, Marc & Paula. **Education:** Am Univ Beirut, Bachelor Eng, 1979; Univ Salford, UK, PhD (elec eng), 1982. **Professional Experience:** Chmn, dept Elec & Comput Eng, 1990-1993; ASSOC PROF ELEC ENG, SYRACUSE UNIV, 1988-; prin investr, Niagara Mohawk Power Corp, 1985-1990 & Int Bus Mach, 1988-1991; asst prof elec eng, Syracuse Univ, 1982-1988. **Memberships:** Sr mem Inst Elec & Electronics Engrs. **Research Statement & Publications:** Modeling and performance evaluation of high-speed computer networks and in the application of artificial intelligence to power systems. **Mailing Address:** Dept Comput Eng, Syracuse Univ, 2-222, 121 Link Hall, Ctr Sci & Technol, Syracuse, NY 13244-4100. **Fax:** 315-443-4745. **E-Mail:** jabbour@syr.edu

JABINE, THOMAS BOYD, APPLIED STATISTICS. **Personal Data:** b Brooklyn, NY, January 26, 1925; m 1950, Marian; c Thomas P, William T, Ann B & Leslie N. **Education:** Mass Inst Technol, BS & MS, 1949. **Honors & Awards:** Roger Herriot Award Innovation in Fed Statistics, Am Statistical Assoc, 1999. **Professional Experience:** STATIST CONSULT, 1980-; statist policy expert, Energy Info Admin, US Dept Energy, 1979-1980; chief math statistician, Soc Sec Admin, 1973-1979; chief statist res div, US Census Bur, 1969-1973; var pos, US Census Bur, 1949-1968; Const mem, Inter-Am Statist Inst. **Memberships:** Fel Am Statist Asn; Int Statist Inst. **Research Statement & Publications:** Survey methodology; sampling; quality control. **Mailing Address:** 3231 Worthington St NW, Washington, DC 20015-2362. **E-Mail:** tjabine@nas.edu

JABLON, SEYMOUR, BIOSTATISTICS, EPIDEMIOLOGY. **Personal Data:** b New York, NY, June 2, 1918; m 1941, c 2. **Education:** City Col NY, BS, 1939; Columbia Univ, MA, 1940. **Honors & Awards:** Order of Sacred Treasure, Govt of Japan, 1987. **Professional Experience:** RETIRED; expert, Radiation Epidemiol Br, Nat Cancer Inst, 1987-1993; dir med follow-up agency, Nat Res Coun, 1975-1987; mem, Nat Comn Radiation Protection, 1974-1987; assoc dir, Nat Res Coun, 1971-1975; chief dept statist, Atomic Bomb Casualty Comn, 1970-1971; assoc dir, Med Follow-up Agency, Nat Res Coun, 1963-1970; chief dept statist, Atomic Bomb Casualty Comn, 1960-1963; prof assoc, Med Follow-up Agency, Nat Res Coun, 1948-1960. **Memberships:** Fel Am Statist Asn; Am Epidemiol Soc; Radiation Res Soc; Biomet Soc; Health Physics Soc; fel AAAS. **Research Statement & Publications:** Late effects of radiation; epidemiology of cancer. **Mailing Address:** 6813 Persimmon Tree Rd, Bethesda, MD 20817.

JABLONER, HAROLD, polymer chemistry, organic chemistry; deceased, see previous edition for last biography

JABLONSKI, DANIEL GARY, MICROWAVES & COMMUNICATIONS. **Personal Data:** b Washington, DC, 1954; m 1982, Elizabeth. **Education:** Mass Inst Technol, BS, 1976, MS, 1977; Cambridge Univ, PhD (physics), 1982. **Professional Experience:** PHYSICIST, JOHNS HOPKINS UNIV APPL PHYSICS LAB, 1991-; res staff mem, Supercomput Res Ctr, 1986-1991; Adj prof, Capitol Inst Technol, 1985-; Res physicist, Naval Surface Weapons Ctr, 1981-1986. **Memberships:** Am Phys Soc; Inst Elec & Electronics Engrs. **Research Statement & Publications:** Spacecraft mission engineering, microwave properties of superconducting devices; properties of materials at millimeter wavelengths; phase-locked loops; supercomputing; theory of computation; microwave systems, electronic seniors; satellite navigation. **Mailing Address:** 7905 Greentree Rd, Bethesda, MD 20817. **E-Mail:** dan.jablonski@jhuapl.edu

JABLONSKI, DAVID, PALEONTOLOGY. **Personal Data:** b New York, NY, June 23, 1953. **Education:** Columbia Univ, BA, 1974; Yale Univ, MS, 1976, PhD (geol), 1979. **Honors & Awards:** Paleont Soc Schuchert Award, 1988. **Professional Experience:** Hon res fel, Nat Hist Mus, London, beginning 1993; Am Rev Ecol Syst, 1989-1994 & Geol, 1991-1993; PROF PALEOBIOL, COMT EVOLUTIONARY BIOL, UNIV CHICAGO, 1995-; assoc ed, Conserv Biol, 1986-1995; assoc prof, Dept Geophys Sci, 1985-1989; assoc ed, Evolution, 1984-1986; assoc ed, Paleobiol, 1983-1985 & 1986-1988; asst prof evolutionary biol, Dept Ecol & Evolutionary Biol, Univ Ariz, 1982-1985; Miller res fel paleobiol, Dept Paleont, Berkeley, 1980-1982; asst res geol, Univ Calif, Santa Barbara, 1979-1980.

Memberships: Paleont Soc; Soc Study Evolution; Int Paleont Union; Soc Syst Biol; Am Soc Naturalists. **Research Statement & Publications:** Evolutionary patterns and processes above the species level, in living and fossil organisms; marine inverts, particularly mollusks; published over 50 articles. **Mailing Address:** Dept Geophys Sci, Hinds 213, Chicago, IL 60637. **Fax:** 773-702-9505. **E-Mail:** djablons@midway.uchicago.edu

JABLONSKI, FRANK EDWARD, ELECTROOPTICS. **Personal Data:** b Brooklyn, NY, February 2, 1915; m 1949, Dorothy E Condor; c Timothy, Michael & Daniel. **Education:** Fordham Univ, BS, 1936; NY Univ, MS, 1940; Harvard Univ, MS, 1946. **Professional Experience:** RETIRED; consult physicist, Chief Naval Opers, 1973-1987; tech adv, Chief Naval Opers, 1963-1973; physicist off long range plans & progs, Goddard Space Flight Ctr & NASA Hq, 1961-1963; physicist, Goddard Space Flight Ctr & NASA Hq, 1959-1961; res adv comt control, guid & navig, NASA, 1959-1960; physicist, Nat Security Agency, 1958-1959; ord engr, Spec Projs Off, 1957-1958; mem, Polaris Re-entry Body Coord Comt, 1957-1958; active duty, US Navy, 43-46 physicist influence devices, US Naval Ord Lab, 1946-1957; physicist bur ord, US Dept Navy, 1940-1943. **Memberships:** Fel AAAS; Am Phys Soc; Wilderness Soc. **Research Statement & Publications:** Degaussing of ships; proximity exploders and fuzes; warheads for missiles; communications; space electronics; sonar; infrared; lasers. **Mailing Address:** 9916 Julliard Dr, Bethesda, MD 20817.

JABLONSKI, WERNER LOUIS, ORGANIC CHEMISTRY. **Personal Data:** b Frankfurt, Ger, May 6, 1924; m 1954, c 5. **Education:** Univ Toronto, BA & MA, 1949; McGill Univ, PhD (org chem), 1953. **Professional Experience:** RETIRED; chemist, Foster Grant Inc, 1971-1985; chemist, US Plywood Champion Papers Inc, 1969-1971; chemist, Dow Chem Co, 1950-1969; chemist, Can Indust Ltd, 1949-1950. **Memberships:** Soc Plastics Engrs; Am Chem Soc; Sigma Xi. **Research Statement & Publications:** Polymers. **Mailing Address:** 404 Woodberry Dr, Chesapeake, VA 23320.

JACCARINO, VINCENT, SOLID STATE PHYSICS. **Personal Data:** b Brooklyn, NY, May 12, 1924; m 1965, c 2. **Education:** Brooklyn Col, BS, 1948; Mass Inst Technol, PhD (physics), 1952. **Professional Experience:** USA chmn, magnetism sect, Int Union Pure & Appl Physics, 1991; chmn, Int Conf Magnetism, beginning 1985; DIR, QUANTUM INST, 1985-; Yamada Found fel, Japan, 1980; Lady Davis fel, 1979; Guggenheim Found fel, 1973-1974; chmn dept, Quantum Inst, 1969-1972; PROF PHYSICS, UNIV CALIF, SANTA BARBARA, 1966-; head solid state phys res dept, Bell Tel Labs, 1963-1966; mem tech staff, Bell Tel Labs, 1954-1963; res assoc, Mass Inst Technol, 1952-1954. **Memberships:** Fel Am Phys Soc. **Research Statement & Publications:** Magnetic resonance in solids; magnetism; superionic conductors; critical phenomena. **Mailing Address:** Dept Physics, Division Mathematical, Life, & Physical Scis, Broida Hall 3019, Santa Barbara, CA 93103. **Fax:** 805-893-3307. **E-Mail:** ugrad@physics.ucsb.edu

JACH, JOSEPH, PHYSICAL CHEMISTRY. **Personal Data:** b SAfrica, December 15, 1929; m 1964, c 2. **Education:** Univ Cape Town, BSc, 1950, MSc, 1952; Oxford Univ, PhD, 1955. **Professional Experience:** RETIRED; staff mem, Lawrance Radiation Lab, Calif, 1969-1970; assoc prof eng, State Univ NY, Stony Brook, 1963-1991; res assoc, Brookhaven Nat Lab, 1956-1963; lectr chem, Univ Cape Town, 1953. **Research Statement & Publications:** Solid state chemistry, particularly thermal decomposition of solids and Szillard-Challmers reactions and chemical reactivity at defect sites in solids. **Mailing Address:** 46 Bay Rd, Patchogue, NY 11772.

JACHE, ALBERT WILLIAM, INORGANIC CHEMISTRY, FLUORINE CHEMISTRY. **Personal Data:** b Manchester, NH, November 5, 1924; m 1948, Lucy Hauslein; c Ann Gail (Smiley), Ellen (Hoium), Philip W & Heidi (Houtl). **Education:** Univ NH, BS, 1948, MS, 1950; Univ Wash, PhD (chem), 1952. **Honors & Awards:** Outstanding Serv, Div, Fluorine Am Chem Soc. **Professional Experience:** EMER PROF CHEM, MARQUETTE UNIV, 1990-; scientist in residence, Argonne Nat Lab, 1985-1986; chmn, Div Flourine Chem, Am Chem Soc, 1982; assoc vpres acad affairs, Grad Sch, 1977-1985; Consult, Allied Chem Corp, 1977-1978; assoc acad vpres health sci, Grad Sch, 1974-1977; dean, Grad Sch, 1972-1977; prof, Dept Chem, Marquette Univ, 1967-1990; Consult, Olin Corp, 1967-1975; chmn, Dept Chem, Marquette Univ, 1967-1972; sect mgr, Olin Mathieson Chem Corp, 1965-1967; sr res assoc, Olin Mathieson Chem Corp, 1964-1967; assoc res dir, Ozark Mahoning Co, 1961-1964; from asst prof to assoc prof chem, Agr & Mech Col Tex, 1955-1961; res assoc physics, Duke Univ, 1953-1955; Sr chemist, Air Reduction Co, Inc, 1952-1953. **Memberships:** Fel AAAS; Am Chem Soc; Sigma Xi; fel Am Inst Chem. **Research Statement & Publications:** Fluorine chemistry; halogens; nonaqueous solvent systems; environmental problems. **Mailing Address:** 301 Ohio St, Marietta, OH 45750. **Fax:** 740-376-9107. **E-Mail:** albert@jache.com

JACHE, ANN, SOCIOLOGY. **Professional Experience:** ASST PROF SOCIOL, UNIV ALASKA ANCHORAGE, as of 2004. **Mailing Address:** Dept Sociol Univ Alaska, 3211 Providence Dr, Anchorage, AK 99508. **E-Mail:** jache@uaa.alaska.edu

JACHENS, ROBERT C, MINING GEOPHYSICS. **Personal Data:** b San Francisco, Calif, June 4, 1939. **Education:** San Jose State Univ, BS, 1962; Columbia Univ, MS, 1968, PhD (geophys), 1972. **Professional Experience:** RES GEOPHYS, US GEOL SURV, as of 2000; reg, Crustel Dynamics Sect, US Geol Surv Off Mineral Resources & Geophys BR, beginning 1988; chief, Crustel Dynamics Sect, US Geol Surv Off Mineral Resources & Geophys Br, 1985-1988; res geophysicist, Crustel Dynamics Sect, US Geol Surv Off Mineral Resources & Geophys Br, 1975-1985; res assoc, Lamont Doherty, Geol Observ, Columbia Univ, 1972-1976. **Memberships:** fel Geol Soc Am; AAAS; Am Geophys Union. **Research Statement & Publications:** Solid earth geophysics and tectonics; mining geophysics; published over 20 atricles. **Mailing Address:** US Geol Surv, 345 Middlefield Rd MS 989, Menlo Park, CA 94025. **E-Mail:** jachens@usgs.gov

JACHIMOWICZ, FELEK, PHOTOCHEMISTRY, POLYMER CHEMISTRY. **Personal Data:** b Poznan, Poland, July 2, 1947; American citizen; m 1971, c 2. **Education:** Univ Basel, Switz, dipl, 1971, PhD (phys org chem), 1975. **Professional Experience:** VPRES RES & DEVELOP & CHIEF TECH OFFICER, WR GRACE & CO; mem, Grace team, 1978-. **Memberships:** Am Chem Soc. **Research Statement & Publications:** Physical chemistry; Polymer chemistry; Inorganic chemistry; Synthetic chemistry; radical ions chemistry; analytical chemistry; spectroscopy; Colloid chemistry. **Mailing Address:** 36 Cypress St, Brookline, MA 02445. **E-Mail:** felek.jachimowicz@grace.com

JACHOWSKI, RICHARD LEO, MANAGEMENT RESEARCH SUPPORTING WILDLIFE CONSERVATION, SCIENTIFIC ADVICE SUPPORTING ECOSYSTEM MANAGEMENT. **Personal Data:** b Washington, DC, January 18, 1944; m 1974, Martha Herrin; c David. **Education:** Univ Md, BS, 1965, PhD (zool), 1970; Univ Miami, MSc, 1967. **Honors & Awards:** Dishigvished Serv Award, US Dept of the Interior, 2000; Resolution Appreciation, Am Asn Zool Parks & Aquariums, 1985; Governors Salute to Excellence, State of Md, 1994. **Professional Experience:** Center dir, USGS Northern Rocky Mountain Sci Center, 2000-; CHIEF RES, PATUXENT WILDLIFE RES CTR, US GEOL SURV, 1996-; co-chair, Res Working Group, Partners in Flight, 1995-1996; spec asst to regional dir, Nat Biol Surv, 1993-1994; mem mgt bd, Black Duck Joint Venture, 1991-1997; Chief, Off Mgt Authority, US Fish & Wildlife Serv, 1987; chief, Br Migratory Bird Res, 1985-1996; chief, Off Sci Authority, 1980-1985; gen biologist, Fed Wildlife Permit Off, US Fish & Wildlife Serv, 1976-1980; Mgr, Smithsonian Inst-Peace Corps Environ Prog, Smithsonian Inst, 1971-1972. **Research Statement & Publications:** Leadership of a research program supporting management of natural resource in the Northern Rocky Mountains through the development of partnerships and other working relationships among institutions. **Mailing Address:** USGS Northern Rocky Mountain Sci Center, PO Box 173492, Bozeman, MT 59717-3492. **Fax:** 406-994-6556. **E-Mail:** richard_jachowski@usgs.gov

JACK, HULAN E, PHYSICS. **Personal Data:** b New York, NY, May 6, 1935; c 4. **Education:** NY Univ, BS, 1960, MS, 1964, PhD (physics), 1971. **Professional Experience:** PROF PHYSICS, KANS STATE UNIV, 1971-; instr, Finch Col, 1970-1971; lectr, Wash Sq Col, NY Univ, 1968-1970; instr physics, NY inst Technol, 1961-1966 & Eng Sch, Pratt inst, 1966-1968. **Memberships:** AAAS; Am Asn Physics Teachers; Am Phys Soc; Asn Comput Mach. **Research Statement & Publications:** Solid state and atomic physics. **Mailing Address:** 9832 57th Ave Apt 8D, Flushing, NY 11368. **E-Mail:** hjack@ksu.edu

JACK, JOHN JAMES, ANALYTICAL CHEMISTRY, PLASTICS MARKETING & PROCESSING. **Personal Data:** b Trenton, NJ, January 11, 1943; m 1967, c 2. **Education:** Princeton Univ, AB, 1965; Mass Inst Technol, PhD (anal chem), 1971. **Professional Experience:** BUS CONSULT, EI DUPONT DEL NEMOURS & CO INC, 1997-; mgr, nylon prod progs, Dupont eng polymers, 1993-1997; res chemist & tech mgt plastics mkt, Polymer Prod Dept, 1970-1993. **Research Statement & Publications:** Development of instrumental methods of analysis, especially spectroscopic, and application to industrial analytical problems; automation of laboratory testing and efficient use of newly developing mini- and micro-computers. **Mailing Address:** 27 Stirrup Run, Newark, DE 19711.

JACK, ROBERT CECIL MILTON, BIOCHEMISTRY. **Personal Data:** b St Vincent, WI, October 10, 1929; m 1959, c Valerie & Marcy. **Education:** McGill Univ, BSc, 1956; Columbia Univ, PhD (plant biochem), 1964. **Professional Experience:** RETIRED; chmn, Dept Biol, 1977-1980; prof biol, arts & sci, 1976-1990; assoc prof, St John's Univ, 1967-1976; assoc biochemist, Boyce Thompson Inst, 1967; asst biochemist, Boyce Thompson Inst, 1964-1966; chemist, Cent Exp Sta, WI, 1958-1960. **Memberships:** Am Chem Soc; Am Soc Biochem Molecular Biol; AAAS; NY Acad Sci. **Research Statement & Publications:** Lipid chemistry and metabolism; lipids; biological membranes; biomed applications of computers. **Mailing Address:** 97 Mohican Park Ave, Dobbs Ferry, NY 10522-2308.

JACK, THOMAS RICHARD, PETROLEUM MICROBIOLOGY, INORGANIC CHEMISTRY. **Personal Data:** b Toronto, Ont, March 4, 1947; c 1. **Education:** Univ Toronto, BSc, 1969, PhD (chem), 1975. **Professional Experience:** NOVA RES & TECHNOL CTR, as of 2004; RES SUPVR, NOVACOR RES & TECHNOL CORP, DIV NOVACOR CHEM, 1992-; mgr appl sci, Div Nova Corp, 1987-1992; group leader, NOVACOR Res & Technol Corp, 1983-1987; res scientist, NOVACOR Res & Technol Corp, Calgary, 1981-1983; indust assoc, Arctic Inst NAm, Univ Calgary, 1981-1983; petrol microbiologist, BC Res, 1980-1981; asst prof, Scarborough Col, Univ Toronto, 1977-1979; vis asst prof chem, Scarborough Col, Univ Toronto, 1976-1977; fel Bioengineering, Fac Eng Sci, Univ Western Ont, 1975-1976; fel, Nat Res Coun Can, 1975; chmn, Biominet Steering Comt. **Memberships:** fel Chem Inst Can; Am Soc Microbiol; Am Chem Soc. **Research Statement & Publications:** Interface between inorganic chemistry and microbiology; biotechnology and inorganic chemistry in energy production; environmental research spanning air, water and soil; concerns related to petrochemical operations. **Mailing Address:** NOVA Res & Technol Ctr, 2928 16th St NE, Calgary, AB T2E 7K7, Can.

JACKANICZ, THEODORE MICHAEL, REPRODUCTIVE ENDOCRINOLOGY. **Personal Data:** b Chicago, Ill, October 6, 1938; div, c 1. **Education:** Northwestern Univ, BA, 1959; Mich State Univ, PhD (biochem), 1965. **Professional Experience:** SR SCIENTIST REPRODUCTION, POP COUN, NY, as of 2003; scientist reproduction, Pop Coun, NY, beginning 1974; staff scientist, Pop Coun, NY, 1970-1974; proj specialist pop, Ford Found, 1969-1970; NIH fel, Harvard Med Sch, 1965-1967 & Karolinska Inst, 1967-1968; res fel endocrinol, Harvard Med Sch & Karolinska Inst, Sweden, 1965-1968. **Memberships:** Sigma Xi; AAAS; NY Acad Sci. **Research Statement & Publications:** Reproductive endocrinology and contraceptive development. **Mailing Address:** Ctr Biomed Res, Pop Coun, 1230 York Ave, New York, NY 10021. **Fax:** 212-327-7678.

JACKEL, LAWRENCE DAVID, MACHINE LEARNING, KNOWLEDGE DISCOVERY. **Personal Data:** b New York, NY, June 16, 1948; m 1969, c 2. **Education:** Brandeis Univ, BA, 1969; Cornell Univ, MA, 1972, PhD (physics), 1976. **Honors & Awards:** Paul Rappaport Award, Inst Elec & Electronics Engrs Electron Device Soc, 1985. **Professional Experience:** DEPT HEAD, AT&T LABS RES, as of 2003; adaptive info serv res, AT&T Labs, beginning 1996; head, Adaptive Systs Res Dept, AT&T Bell Labs, NJ, 1990-1995; head, Device Struct Res Dept, AT&T Bell Labs, NJ, 1984-1990; mem tech staff exp solid state physics, 1975-1984; res assoc, Sch Appl & Eng Physics, Cornell Univ, 1975; res asst, Sch Appl & Eng Physics, Cornell Univ, 1971-1975. **Memberships:** Fel Am Phys Soc; fel Inst Elec & Electronics Engrs. **Research Statement & Publications:** Machine learning methods are applied to problems in pattern recognition and knowledge discovery; published over 150 papers in professional journals and granted 10 US patents. **Mailing Address:** AT&T Labs Res, 100 Schultz Dr Rm 3-140, Red Bank, NJ 07701-7033. **E-Mail:** ldj@research.att.com

JACKELS, CHARLES FREDERICK, QUANTUM CHEMISTRY. **Personal Data:** b St Paul, Minn, November 3, 1946; m 1970, Susan; c Elizabeth. **Education:** Univ Minn, BChem, 1968; Univ Wash, PhD (phy chem), 1975. **Professional Experience:** PROF, COMPUT & SOFTWARE SYSTS & INTERDISCIPLINARY ARTS & SCI, UNIV WASH, BOTHELL, 2000-; ACTG DIR, COMPUT & SOFTWARE SYSTS PROG, UNIV WASH, BOTHELL, 2000-; vis prof, Lib Studies, Univ Wash, 1995-1996; vis res prof chem, Lab Donald G Truhlar, Univ Minn, 1993-1994; prof chem, Wake Forest Univ, 1990-1995; from asst prof to assoc prof, Wake Forest Univ, 1977-1990; fel theoret chem, Battelle Mem Inst, 1975-1977; vis Scholar Atmospheric Chem, Lab James G Anderson, Harvard Univ, 1985-1986; fel Chem Physics, Battelle Mem Inst, Columbus, Ohio, 1975-1977; teaching asst, Chem Dept, Univ Wash, Seattle, Wash, 1971-1972; NDEA fel, 1971-1973. **Memberships:** AAAS; Am Chem Soc; Asn Comput Mach; Inst Elec & Electronics Engrs Comput Soc; Am Asn Univ Professors; Sigma Xi. **Research Statement & Publications:** Ab initio quantum chemical investigations of small molecules; potential energy surface calculations using self-consistent-field and configuration-interaction methods; applications to atmospheric chemistry. **Mailing Address:** Comput & Software Systs Prog, Univ Wash-Bothell, 18115 Campus Way NE, Bothell, WA 98011. **Fax:** 425-352-5216. **E-Mail:** jackels@u.washington.edu

JACKELS, SUSAN CAROL, INORGANIC CHEMISTRY, BIO-INORGANIC CHEMISTRY. **Personal Data:** b Wichita, Kans, July 12, 1946; m 1970. **Education:** Carleton Col, BA, 1968; Univ Wash, PhD (inorg chem), 1973. **Professional Experience:** Sabbatical leave, Univ Cent Am Managua & Catholic Relief Serv/Nicaragua, Matagalpa, NI, 2003-2004; chair, Chem Dept, Seattle Univ, Seattle, WA, 1997-2003; PROF CHEM, SEATTLE UNIV, SEATTLE, WA, 1996-; affil Staff Scientist, Battelle Pac Northwest Lab, Richland, WA, 1994-1996; sabbatical leave, Univ Minn & Battelle Pac Northwest Lab, 1993-1994; prof chem, Wake Forest Univ, Winston-Salem, NC, 1990-1995; res assoc prof Radiol, Bowman Gray Sch Med, Winston-Salem, NC, 1986-1995; Sabbatical leave, Mass Gen Hosp, Harvard Univ, 1985-1986; res fel, Dept Radiol, Bowman Gray Schl Med, Winston-Salem, NC, 1985; from assoc prof to asst prof chem, Wake Forest Univ, 1977-1990; Res biochem, Univ Wash, 1973-1975 & inorg chem, Ohio State Univ, 1975-1977; fel, Biochem, Univ Wash, 1973-1975. **Memberships:** Am Chem Soc; Sigma Xi. **Research Statement & Publications:** Design, synthesis and study of transition metal complexes relevant to biological systems; macrocyclic complexes; electrochemistry of transition metal complexes. **Mailing Address:** Dept Chem, Seattle Univ Broadway & Madison, Seattle, WA 98122-4460. **E-Mail:** sjackels@seattleu.edu

JACKIEWICZ, ZDZISLAW, MATHEMATICS. **Education:** Univ Gdansk, Poland, PhD (Math), 1980. **Professional Experience:** LECTR, DEPT MATH, ARIZ STATE UNIV, as of 2006. **Mailing Address:** Math Dept, Ariz State Univ, Tempe, AZ 85287-0001. **Fax:** 602-965-8119. **E-Mail:** jackiewi@math.la.asu.edu

JACKIW, ROMAN WLADIMIR, THEORETICAL PHYSICS, HIGH ENERGY PHYSICS. **Personal Data:** b Lublinec, Poland, November 8, 1939; American citizen; m 1981, So; c Simone Ahlborn, Roman Nicholas & Stefan. **Education:** Swarthmore Col, AB, 1961; Cornell Univ, PhD (physics), 1966. **Honorary Degrees:** Dr (Hon Causa), Univ Turin, Italy, 2000, Univ Uppsala, Swededn, 2000, Bogolyubov Inst, Kyiv, Ukraine, 2003. **Honors & Awards:** D Heineman Math Phys Prize, Am Phys Soc & Am Inst Physics; Dirac Prize & Medal, ICTP, Trieste, Italy. **Professional Experience:** From Assistant Professor to Jerrold Zacharias Prof Physics, MIT 1969 - present; Columbia Univ, 1989-1990; group leader, Inst Theoret Physics, Univ Calif, Santa Barbara, 1980; Univ Calif, Los Angeles & Santa Barbara, 1980; J S Guggenheim Mem Found fel, 1977-1978; vis prof, Rockefeller Univ, 1977-1978; consult, Los Alamos Nat Lab, 1974-1984; A P Sloan Found res fel, 1969-1971; Soc Fels jr fel physics, Harvard Univ, 1966-1969. **Memberships:** Am Phys Soc; Am Acad Arts & Sci, US Nat Acad of Sci; Nat. Acad. Sci. Ukraine (fgn.mem.). **Research Statement & Publications:** Theoretical and mathematical physics with specialization to particle, condensed matter and gravitational physics. **Mailing Address:** Ctr Theoret Physics Mass Inst Technol NE 25-4085, 77 Mass Ave, Cambridge, MA 02139-4307. **Fax:** 617-253-8674. **E-Mail:** jackiw@lns.mit.edu

JACKLET, JON WILLIS, NEUROPHYSIOLOGY, ANIMAL BEHAVIOR. **Personal Data:** b Springfield Gardens, NY, April 16, 1935; m 1962, Alice; c 3. **Education:** Univ Ore, BS, 1962, MA, 1964, PhD (biol), 1966. **Honors & Awards:** Fel AAAS. **Professional Experience:** Vis scientist, Alta Heritage Found, 1992; chmn, dept Biol Sci, 1985-1991; PROF BIOL SCI, UNIV ALBANY, STATE UNIV NY, 1981-; from asst prof to assoc prof, State Univ NY Albany, 1968-1980; USPHS res fel neurophysiol, Calif inst technol, 1967-1968. **Memberships:** Soc Neuroscience; Am Physiol Soc; AAAS. **Research Statement & Publications:** Neurophysiology of behavior; Nitric oxide as transmitter and neuromodulator; cellular and molecular aspects of circadian rhythms. **Mailing Address:** Dept Biol Sci, Univ Albany, State Univ NY, Albany, NY 12222. **Fax:** 518-442-4767. **E-Mail:** jwj74@albany.edu

JACKMAN, DONALD COE, INORGANIC CHEMISTRY, ANALYTICAL CHEMISTRY. **Personal Data:** b Cleveland, Tenn, November 29, 1940; m 1981, Jane; c 3. **Education:** Maryville Col, BS, 1962; Univ Tenn, Knoxville, PhD (inorg chem), 1966. **Professional Experience:** CHMN, DEPT CHEM & PHYSICS, 1990-; dept energy grant, 1987 & 1988; Celanese grant, 1985-1986; PROF CHEM, PFEIFFER COL, 1980-; NSF res grant, 1971; from asst prof to assoc prof inorg & anal chem, dept chem & physics, 1966-1980. **Memberships:** Am Chem Soc; Int Union Pure & Appl Chem. **Research Statement & Publications:** Electron exchange mechanisms in Cobalt-III and Chromium-II systems; immobilized liquid membrane; ruthenium polypyridyls. **Mailing Address:** Dept Chem, Pfeiffer Univ, Harris 302, Misenheimer, NC 28109. **Fax:** 704-463-1363. **E-Mail:** djackman@pfeiffer.edu

JACKMAN, LLOYD MILES, ORGANIC CHEMISTRY. **Personal Data:** b Goolwa, SAustralia, April 1, 1926; m 1950, c 3. **Education:** Univ Adelaide, BSc, 1945, Hons, 1946, MSc, 1948, PhD (chem), 1951. **Professional Experience:** PROF EMER CHEM, PA STATE UNIV, UNIVERSITY PARK, as of 2001; Wilsmore fel, 1988; Humboldt fel, 1977-1978; Guggenheim Found fel, 1973; prof chem, Pa State Univ, University Park, beginning 1967; consult, Esso Res & Eng Co, 1967-1970 & Smith, Kline & French Labs, 1967-; NSF sr foreign fel, 1965; vis prof, Iowa State Univ, 1962 & Univ Tenn, 1965; prof, Univ Melbourne, 1962-1967; reader org chem, Univ, 1961-1962; consult, Monsanto Co, UK & Australia, 1960-1967; Royal Commonwealth Soc bursary, 1960; lectr, Imp Col, Univ London, 1953-1961; asst lectr chem, Imp Col, Univ London, 1952-1953; Beit fel, Univ London, 1951-1952. **Memberships:** Am Chem Soc; The Chem Soc; fel Royal Australian Chem Inst; fel AAAS. **Research Statement & Publications:** Applications of nuclear magnetic resonance spectroscopy in organic chemistry; structures and mechanisms of reactions of organic compounds of lithium. **Mailing Address:** Dept Chem, Pa State Univ, 152 Davey Lab, University Park, PA 16802.

JACKMAN, THOMAS EDWARD, INTERFACE SCIENCE, ION-SOLID INTERACTIONS. **Personal Data:** b Thamesville, Ont, March 16, 1951; m 1977, c 2. **Education:** Univ Guelph, BS, 1972, MS, 1974, PhD (physics), 1979. **Professional Experience:** DIR MAT TECHNOL, NAT RES COUN CAN, 1994-; actg dir technol, Nat Res Coun, 1993-1994; mem, Grant Selection Comt, Nat Sci & Eng Res Coun Can, beginning 1990; adj prof eng physics, MacMaster Univ, 1988-; secy & treas, Surf Sci Div, Chem Inst Can & Can Asn Physicists, 1987-1990; res off, Nat Res Coun, 1986-1994; res officer, Chalk River Nuclear Labs, Ont, 1980-1986; vis fel, Chalk River Nuclear Labs, Ont, 1980; resident vis, Bell Labs, Murray Hill, NJ, 1977-1978; res asst, Dept Physics, Univ Guelph, Ont, beginning 1976; guest scientist, Max Planck Inst, Stuttgart, 1974-1975. **Memberships:** Chem Inst Can; Can Asn Physicists; Boehmische Phys Soc; Sigma Xi. **Research Statement & Publications:** Fundamental interactions between MeV ion beams and solids and their application in material science; the growth and characterization of two-dimensional, multilayer semiconductor structures. **Mailing Address:** Inst Microstruct Sci, Nat Res Coun Can, Rm 167A, Build M-50, 1200 Montreal Rd, Ottawa, ON K1A 0R6, Can. **Fax:** 613-957-8734. **E-Mail:** tom.jackman@nrc-cnrc.gc.ca

JACKNOW, JOEL, PHYSICAL CHEMISTRY, GENERAL ENGINEERING. **Personal Data:** b New York, NY, December 15, 1937. **Education:** City Col NY, BChE, 1959; Univ Utah, PhD (phys chem), 1963. **Professional Experience:** PROG ANALYST & MGR, ENG PROG MGT, RES & DEVELOP SERV, FED AVIATION ADMIN, 1989-; proj mgr & sr scientist, Habitat Resources Prog, US Fish & Wildlife Serv, 1979-1986; environ & energy consult, 1975-1979; sr prog mgr, Environ Qual Systs Inc, 1974-1975; phys sci adminr, Environ Protection Agency, Off Planning & Eval, 1971-1974; sr staff mem, Int Res & Technol, 1968-1971; sr physiologist, Bioelectronics Br, Instrumentation Lab, NASA Electronics Res Ctr, 1967-1968; res assoc med sch, Tufts Univ, 1966-1967; res assoc & fel chem, Polytech Inst Brooklyn, 1965-1966; res chemist, Fundamental Res Sect, Texaco Inc, 1963-1965. **Memberships:** Am Chem Soc; Wildlife Soc; Asn Sci Technol & Innovation; Technol Transfer Soc. **Research Statement & Publications:** Sources of water pollution; economic and technical analysis of environmental alternatives; research and progammatic strategic guidance; resource allocation; environmental contaminant impacts on fish and wildlife; airport safety and aviation weather development. **Mailing Address:** 8110 Timber Valley Ct, Dunn Loring, VA 22027.

JACKO, MICHAEL GEORGE, TRIBOLOGY, CHEMISTRY. **Personal Data:** b Windsor, Ont, October 11, 1938; m 1963, Mary. **Education:** Assumption Univ, BSc, 1961; Univ Windsor, PhD (phys chem), 1964. **Professional Experience:** CONSULT, 1997-; mem staff, Allied Signal Friction Mat, 1996-1997; mem staff, Allied Signal Braking Systs, 1993-1996; mem staff, Allied Automotive Tech Ctr, 1983-1992; prin chemist, Bendix Mat Ctr, 1981-1982; sr prin chemist, Bendix Advan Technol Ctr, 1979-1980; res assoc chem, Univ Windsor, 1973-1974; phys chemist, Bendix Res Lab, 1966-1979; phys chemist, Imp Oil Res Dept, Sarnia, Ont, 1964-1966. **Memberships:** Am Chem Soc; Soc Automotive Engrs; fel Am Chem Inst. **Research Statement & Publications:** Gas kinetics; radical reactions; gas chromatography; petroleum products; polymers; thermal analysis; friction materials; functional fluids; brake wear debris studies; brake interace reactions; new friction materials; tribology; light weight brakes for automotive. **Mailing Address:** 23721 Merrill Ave, Southfield, MI 48075.

JACKOBS, JOHN JOSEPH, PHYSICAL CHEMISTRY, X-RAY CRYSTALLOGRAPHY. **Personal Data:** b Hibbing, Minn, March 25, 1939; m 1965, c 3. **Education:** Wis State Univ, Superior, BA, 1961; Iowa State Univ, MS, 1964; Ariz State Univ, PhD (phys chem), 1967. **Professional Experience:** RETIRED; Jenzabar Inc, as of 2002; sr proj mgr, Cars Info Systs Corp, beginning 1988; programmer & analyst, Info Systs Inc, 1987-1988; registr & dir, Comput Ctr, Coe Col, 1975-1987; asst prof physics, Heidelberg Col, 1969-1975; res asst chem, Case Western Res Univ, 1967-1969. **Memberships:** AAAS; Am Crystallog Asn; Sigma Xi. **Research Statement & Publications:** X-ray diffraction studies of organic and small biological molecules. **Mailing Address:** Jenzabar Inc, 5 Cambridge Ctr Ste 11, Cambridge, MA 02142. **Fax:** 617-492-9081. **E-Mail:** john.jackobs@jenzabar.net

JACKOBS, JOSEPH ALDEN, AGRONOMY & INTERNATIONAL AGRICULTURE, SOY BEAN. **Personal Data:** b Shell Lake, Wis, October 23, 1917; m 1940, Marian; c 3. **Education:** Univ Wis, BS, 1940, MS, 1943, PhD (agron), 1947. **Professional Experience:** RETIRED; crop prod agronomist, Int Soybean Agronomist, 1979-1986; crop prod agronomist, US AID, Indonesia, 1973-1975; crop prod agronomist, US AID, India, 1967-1969; grass & fodder specialist, Int Coop Admin, India, 1958-1960; prof crop prod, assoc prof agron, Univ Ill, Urbana, 1951-1955; asst agronomist, Irrig Exp Sta, State Col Wash, 1946-1951. **Memberships:** Fel AAAS; fel Am Soc Agron; Sigma Xi. **Research Statement & Publications:** Alfalfa management, cutting treatments; legume, grass and fertility interactions; seed rotting in sweetclover caused by Pythium; genetic shifts in forage species when grown outside region of adaptation; establishment of forage species; soybean production in the tropics; grassland ecology. **Mailing Address:** 101 W Windsor Rd, Urbana, IL 61802.

JACKOVITZ, JOHN FRANKLIN, PHYSICAL INORGANIC CHEMISTRY. **Personal Data:** b Greensburg, Pa, November 9, 1939; m 1964, Maryanne; c Jan, Julie & Joyce. **Education:** St Vincent Col, BSc, 1961; Univ Notre Dame, PhD (chem), 1965. **Professional Experience:** RES FACULTY, UNIV PITTSBURGH, 2001-; adv scientist, Westinghouse Res & Develop Labs, 1976-2001; sr res scientist, Westinghouse Res & Develop Labs, 1973-1976; sr scientist, Westinghouse Res & Develop Labs, 1967-1973; res assoc, Univ Pittsburgh, 1967-1973; NSF vis scholar chem, Northwestern Univ, 1966-1967. **Memberships:** Soc Appl Spectros (pres, 1981); Am Chem Soc; Electrochem Soc; Coblentz Soc; Sigma Xi; Soc Electroanal Chem. **Research Statement & Publications:** Chelate chemistry, infrared and Raman spectra and force fields of inorganic molecules; uranium chemistry; electrod rxns. **Mailing Address:** Dept Chem, Univ Pittsburg, 314 Chevron Sci Ctr, Pittsburg, PA 15260. **Fax:** 412-624-8611. **E-Mail:** jackovitz@pitteon.org

JACKS, SID, ENGINEERING SCIENCE. **Personal Data:** b St Louis, Mo, August 20, 1924; m 1952, Maxine J; c Andrew & Louis. **Education:** Purdue Univ, BS, 1947; St Louis Univ, MS, 1971. **Honors & Awards:** 1st Prize, Dean Potter Award, Purdue Univ, 1947. **Professional Experience:** Supervised Demolition, Univ Ill, Sidney Jacks Assocs, 1970-1978; prof, indust eng, Wash Univ, 1965-1971. **Research Statement & Publications:** Water management in public housing; use of chemicals to treat potable water supply within US surgeon general guidelines. **Mailing Address:** 368 N Hanley Rd, St Louis, MO 63130.

JACKS, THOMAS JEROME, biochemistry, plant physiology; deceased, see previous edition for last biography

JACKS, THOMAS MAURO, MEDICAL MICROBIOLOGY. **Personal Data:** b Harrisburg, Pa, March 13, 1941; m 1969, Lynne; c 2. **Education:** Duquesne Univ, BS, 1964; Pa State Univ, MS, 1966, PhD (microbiol), 1968. **Professional Experience:** Mem, NJ State Bd Vet Med Examrs, 1984-; SR RES FEL, MERCK RES LABS, RAHWAY, NJ, 1976-; sr res microbiologist, Vet Microbiol Sect, Norwich Pharmacol Co, 1969-1976; instr, State Univ NY Agr & Tech Col Morrisville, 1969-1970 & 1974-1975; asst prof biol, State Univ NY Col New Paltz, 1968-1969. **Memberships:** NY Acad Sci; Am Soc Microbiol; Infectious Dis Soc Am. **Research Statement & Publications:** Escherichia coli pathogenicity in man and animals; bovine antibodies against Escherichia coli; salmonellosis in cattle and swine; swine dysentery; pneumonic pasteurellosis in cattle and swine; endocrinology-tropic hormone secretion. **Mailing Address:** Merck Res Labs, NJ 07065. **Fax:** 732-594-1298. **E-Mail:** tom_jacks@merck.com

JACKSON, ALBERT A, IV, PHYSICS, ASTRONOMY. **Professional Experience:** CHMN, ASTRODYN TECH COMT, AM INST AERONAUT & ASTRNAUT, as of 2003; vis scientist, Lunar & Planetary Inst, Houston, as of 2001. **Mailing Address:** Am Inst Aeronaut & Astronaut, Houston, TX 77258.

JACKSON, ALBERT S(MITH), COMPUTER SCIENCE, CONTROL SYSTEMS. **Personal Data:** b Sylvia, Kans, February 2, 1927; m 1978, Elaine S Spontak; c Linda, Jill, Terri, Steve & Craig. **Education:** Calif Inst Technol, BS, 1951, MS, 1952; Cornell Univ, PhD (elec eng), 1956. **Professional Experience:** Chmn prof group Human Factors Electronics, educ coordr Region 6 & corresp mem Educ Activ Bd, 1984-1985; lectr, Univ Calif, Irving, 1965- & Univ Calif, Los Angeles, 1978-1980; APPLN ENG MGR, MOTOROLA, INC,

1975-; pres, Opto Logic Corp, 1970-1975; chief scientist, Milgo Electronics Corp, 1965-1970; chmn prof group Human Factors Electronics, Inst Elec & Electronics Engrs, 1963-1964; pres, Control Technol, Inc, 1961-1965; mgr, Data Processing & Controls Dept, Thompson-Ramo-Wooldridge Prod Co, 1959-1961; Gen Dynamics/Convair, 1956-1958 & Naval Res Lab, 1957-1959; asst prof, Cornell Univ, 1956-1959; Consult, Gen Elec Co, 1953-1959; instr, Cornell Univ, 1952-1955; Engr, Bell Tel Labs, 1952. **Memberships:** Inst Elec & Electronics Engrs. **Research Statement & Publications:** Analog and digital computers; feedback control system theory; application of computers to control systems; human factors research; concurrent computer architecture; computer simulation, microprocessor-based system design. **Mailing Address:** Motorola Semiconductor, 101 Pacific 300, Irvine, CA 92718.

JACKSON, ANDREW, TRIBOLOGY. **Personal Data:** b Preston, Eng, December 5, 1948; m Lillian A. Rankel. **Education:** Imperial Col, London Univ, BSc, 1970, PhD (mech eng), 1974. **Honors & Awards:** Hunt Award, Am Soc Lubrication Engrs, 1977, Hodson Award, 1982, Bisson Award, 1993. **Professional Experience:** SECTION HEAD, EXXON MOBIL CORP, ANNANDALE, NJ, 1999-; SCIENTIST, PAULSBORO RES LAB, MOBIL RES & DEVELOP CORP, PAULSBORO, NJ, 1993-; sr res assoc, Cent Res Lab, Princeton, NJ, 1988-1993; Dir, Soc Tribologists & Lubrication Engrs, 1987 -2000; res assoc, Mobil Res & Develop Corp, 1984-1988; assoc, Mobil Res & Develop Corp, 1980-1984; sr res engr, Mobil Res & Develop Corp, 1976-1980; Res engr, Mobil Res & Develop Corp, 1974-1976. **Memberships:** Fel Soc Tribologists & Lubrication Engrs (treas 1992 secy 1993 vpres 1994 pres 1995); fel Am Soc Mech Engrs; Inst Mech Engrs. **Research Statement & Publications:** Lubrication science (tribology); elastohydrodynamic lubrication; traction; rolling contact fatigue; internal combustion engine lubrication; synthetic lubricants. **Mailing Address:** ExxonMobil Res & Engrs, 1545 Route 22 East, Annandale, NJ 08801. **Fax:** 908-730-3031. **E-Mail:** andrew.jackson@exxonmobil.com

JACKSON, ANDREW C, BIOMEDICAL ENGINEERING. **Personal Data:** b Loma Linda, Calif, August 10, 1940. **Education:** Univ Nev, Reno, BS, 1963, MS, 1966; Univ Miss, PhD (mech eng), 1972. **Professional Experience:** PROF BIOMED ENG, COL ENG, BOSTON UNIV, 1991-; vis prof, Lab Del Genie Med, Inst Physique Appl, Lausanne, Switz, 1991; chmn ad interim, Col Eng, Boston Univ, 1989-1992; vis prof, Univ Cape Town, Africa, 1989; assoc prof, Col Eng, Boston Univ, 1983-1991; from asst prof to assoc prof, Calif Primate Res Ctr, Sch Vet Med & Sch Med, Univ Calif, Davis, 1979-1983; asst prof pediat, Harvard Med Sch & Children's Hosp, 1976-1979; res assoc physiol, Harvard Sch Pub Health, 1972-1976. **Memberships:** Am Physiol Soc; Bio Med Eng Soc. **Mailing Address:** Dept Biomed Eng, Boston Univ, 44 Cummington St, Boston, MA 02215. **Fax:** 617-353-6766. **E-Mail:** ajax@bu.edu

JACKSON, ANDREW D, THEORETICAL NUCLEAR PHYSICS. **Personal Data:** b Orange, NJ, December 20, 1941; m 1966. **Education:** Princeton Univ, AB, 1963, MA, 1965, PhD (physics), 1967. **Professional Experience:** CHMN, BD NIELS BOHR ARCHIVES, as of 2004; PROF, NIELS BOHR INST, 1996-; Zernike Prof Physics, Univ Groningen, 1981-1982; vis prof, Univ Col London, 1982; prof, NORDITA, 1976-1977, 1986-1987; prof Physics, State Univ NY, Stony Brook, 1975-1996; vis prof, Niels Bohr Inst, 1971-1972; Alfred P Sloan Found fel, 1971-1972; from asst prof to assoc prof, State Univ NY Stony Brook, 1968-1975; NATO res fel, Univ Sussex, 1967-1968; res assoc physics, Princeton Univ, 1967. **Memberships:** Am Phys Soc. **Research Statement & Publications:** Nucleon-nucleon interaction and nuclear structure calculations. **Mailing Address:** Niels Bohr Inst, Blegdamsvej 17, DK-2100 Copenhagen, DK-2100, Denmark. **E-Mail:** jackson@nbi.dk

JACKSON, ANDREW OTIS, PLANT VIROLOGY. **Personal Data:** b Enterprise, Ala, April 14, 1941. **Education:** Okla State Univ, BS, 1964, MS, 1967; Univ Man, PhD (plant path), 1970. **Professional Experience:** PROF PLANT PATH, UNIV CALIF, BERKELEY as of 2002; assoc prof plant virol, Purdue Univ, beginning 1977; asst prof plant virol, Purdue Univ, 1973-1977; fel plant virol, Dept Agr Biochem, Univ Ariz & Dept Plant Path, Univ Nebr, 1970-1973. **Memberships:** Am Phytopathological Soc; AAAS; Sigma Xi; Soc Gen Microbiol. **Mailing Address:** Plant & Microbial Biol, Univ Calif, 111 Kashland Hall, Berkeley, CA 94720-3102. **Fax:** 510-642-9017. **E-Mail:** andyoj@uclink.berkeley.edu

JACKSON, ANNE LOUISE, IMMUNOLOGY. **Personal Data:** b Watertown, NY. **Education:** Cornell Univ, BS, 1956; Univ Mich, MS, 1957, PhD (microbiol), 1963. **Professional Experience:** RETIRED; mgr tech serv, Becton Dickinson Monoclonal Ctr, beginning 1980; mem staff, Dept Microbiol, Univ BC, 1977-1980; asst guest prof, Univ BC, beginning 1975; dir res immunol, Kent Labs, 1974-1977; dir tech serv, Meloy Labs, 1968-1974; asst prof microbiol, Sch Med & Dent, Georgetown Univ, 1963-1968; guest worker, Lab Immunol, Nat Inst Allergy & Infectious Dis, NIH, 1963-1965; res assoc biochem, Univ Mich, 1961-1963. **Memberships:** Am Asn Immunol; Fedn Am Socs Exp Biol; Can Asn Immunol; Am Fedn Clin Res. **Research Statement & Publications:** Production and development of immunologic tests for in vitro diagnostics. **Mailing Address:** 3613 NW 199th St, Ridgefield, WA 98642.

JACKSON, BENITA MARIE, PREVENTIVE MEDICINE, EPIDEMIOLOGY. **Personal Data:** b Englewood, NJ, August 14, 1956; m 1993, Lewis R Smoot Jr; c Lewis R Smoot III. **Education:** Mt Holyoke Col, AB, 1978; Howard Univ, MD, 1982; Emory Univ, MPH, 1989. **Professional Experience:** CLIN ASST PROF EPIDEMIOL, SCH PUB HEALTH, 1995-; Med dir epidemiol, Med Ctr, Ohio State Univ, 1995-1997; asst prof, Sch Pub Health, 1993-1995; clin asst prof, Sch Pub Health, 1992-1993; Epidemic intel officer, Ctrs Dis Control, 1990-1992. **Memberships:** Nat Med Asn; AMERICIAN PUBLIC HEALTH ASSOC, ASSOC OF TEACH OF PREVENTIVE MEDICINE, AM COLLEGE OF PREVENTIVE MEDICINE. **Research Statement & Publications:** Applied epidemiology; Injury Epidemiology health care policy. **Mailing Address:** Ohio State Univ School, 320 W 10th Ave, Columbus, OH 43210.

JACKSON, BENJAMIN A, TOXICOLOGY. **Personal Data:** b Hillburn, NY, July 8, 1929; m 1955, Gloria; c Benita M, Jolie A, Pamela S & Benjamin A Jr. **Education:** NY State Col Teachers, Albany, BA, 1950; Rensselaer Polytech Inst, MS, 1951; NY Univ, PhD (biol), 1957; Fairleigh Dickinson Univ, MBA, 1978, Acad Toxicol Sci, dipl, 1984, cert gen toxicol. **Professional Experience:** PVT CONSULT, 1992-; sr sci adv, Environ Corp, 1990-1992; prog mgr, Risk Assessment Res & Policy Develop, 1987-1990; dir path, Ctr Food Safety & Appl Nutrit, 1985-1990; chief, Color & Cosmetic Eval Br, Bur Foods, 1980-1985; adj asst prof pharmacol & toxicol, Howard Univ, 1980-1985; supvr petitions reviewers, Ctr Food Safety & Appl Nutrit Food & Drug Admin, 1978-1980; mgr teratology & mutagenicity, Toxicol Sect, 1975-1978; sr res toxicologist, Reproductive Safety Eval Group Toxicol Res, Lederle Labs, Am Cyanamid Co, 1969-1975; electron microscopist, Toxicol Dept, Sterling-Winthrop Res Inst, 1967-1969; res assoc, Cornell Med Col, 1964-1965; res biologist, Am Cyanamid Co, 1951-1967. **Memberships:** Soc Toxicol; fel Acad Toxicol Sci. **Research Statement & Publications:** Experimental liver tumors; short term effects of drugs; mitotic activity; drug toxicity; quantitation of morphological changes; electron microscopy; teratology; mutagenicity; correlation between mutagenicity and carcinogenic potential of drugs; regulatory toxicology; color additive toxicology; cosmetic ingredients safety evaluation; mutagenicity testing, submitting pathology data; risk assessment. **Mailing Address:** 3116 Birchtree Lane, Silver Spring, MD 20906. **Fax:** 301-871-6821.

JACKSON, BENJAMIN T, SURGERY, FETAL PHYSIOLOGY. **Personal Data:** b Jacksonville, Fla, April 28, 1929; wid Jean (Deceased); c Benjamin Jr, Leigh, Kimberly & Jillian. **Education:** Duke Univ, MD, 1954. **Professional Experience:** RES PROF SURG, BROWN UNIV, as of 2005; PROF EMER SURG, SCH MED, BROWN UNIV, 1998-; prof surg, Sch Med, Brown Univ, 1980-1998; chief surg serv, Providence Vet Admin Med Ctr, 1980-1998; asst chief surg serv, Boston Vet Admin Hosp, 1974-1980; from asst prof to prof surg, Sch Med, Boston Univ, 1964-1980; estab investr, Am Heart Asn, 1963-1968; instr, Med Col Va, 1963-1964; advan res fel, Am Heart Asn, 1961-1963; resident, Med Col Va, 1958-1962; USPHS res fel, Med Col Va, 1958-1962; asst resident surg, Univ Minn Hosps, 1957-1958; intern med, Duke Univ Hosp, 1954-1955. **Memberships:** Soc Gynec Invest; Am Fedn Clin Res; Am Soc Exp Path; Soc Univ Surg; Am Col Surg; Am Physiol Soc. **Research Statement & Publications:** Fetal cardiovascular and endocrine physiology; pathophysiology of congenital cardiovascular anomalies; fetal hormonal responses in diabetic pregnancy. **Mailing Address:** 11 October Lane, Weston, MA 02193. **E-Mail:** benjamin_jackson@brown.edu

JACKSON, BERNARD VERNON, SOLAR PHYSICS, INTERPLANETARY MEDIUM PHYSICS. **Personal Data:** b Peoria, Ill, November 7, 1942; m 1990, c 2. **Education:** Univ Ill, Urbana, BS, 1964; Ind Univ, Bloomington, MS, 1967, PhD (astrophys), 1970. **Honors & Awards:** Glacier named in honor, Jackson Glacier. **Professional Experience:** CO-INVESTIGATOR, SOLAR MASS EJECTION IMAGER, as of today; RES PHYSICIST, DEPT ELEC ENG & COMPUT SCI, UNIV CALIF, SAN DIEGO, 1993-; vis prof, Nagoya Univ, Japan, 1995 & Max Planck Inst Astron, Ger, 1996; assoc res physicist astrophys, Dept Elec Eng & Comput Sci, Univ Calif, San Diego, 1988-1993; asst res physicist, Dept Elec Eng & Comput Sci, Univ Calif, San Diego, 1979-1987; res assoc astrophys, Commonwealth Sci & Indust Res Orgn, Sydney, Australia, 1977-1979; res fel skylab, High Altitude Observ, Nat Ctr Atmospheric Res, Boulder, Colo, 1975-1977; sci programmer astrophys, Arecibo Observ, Cornell Univ, 1973-1975; geophysicist, Univ Calif, Los Angeles, 1970-1973; res asst, Ind Univ, Bloomington, 1964-1970. **Memberships:** Am Astron Soc; Am Geophys Union; Int Astron Union. **Research Statement & Publications:** Solar and interplanetary physics; solar wind and its interaction with other material as this plasma flows outward from the sun. **Mailing Address:** Sci & Eng Res Fac, Univ Calif San Diego, Rm 303 9500 Gilman Dr, La Jolla, CA 92093-0424. **Fax:** 858-534-0177. **E-Mail:** bvjackson@ucsd.edu

JACKSON, BILL GRINNELL, BETA-LACTAM ANTIBIOTICS, BIOCATALYTIC ORGANIC CHEMISTRY. **Personal Data:** b 1931; m 1954, Beverly Dunnette; c William B & Brenda J. **Education:** Iowa State Univ, BS, 1953, PhD (org chem), 1957. **Professional Experience:** PRES, BETA-EVAR INC, 1993-; res adv, Eli Lilly & Co, 1988-1993; sr res scientist, Eli Lilly & Co, 1970-1988; res scientist, Eli Lilly & Co, 1964-1970; Adj fac chem, Ind Purdue Univ, 1960-1991; Sr org chemist, Eli Lilly & Co, 1959-1964. **Memberships:** Am Chem Soc; Am Soc Microbiol. **Research Statement & Publications:** Methods for synthesis of beta lactam antibiotics with emphasis on biocatalytic processes and processes which provide single enantiomers as product. **Mailing Address:** 4230 Lincoln Rd, Indianapolis, IN 46228. **Fax:** 317-328-9692. **E-Mail:** bjackbeuar@worldnet.att.net

JACKSON, BRADLEY W, MATHEMATICS. **Professional Experience:** PROF MATH, DEPT MATH & COMPUT SCI, SAN JOSE STATE UNIV, as of 2004. **Mailing Address:** Dept Math & Comput Sci, San Jose State Univ, San Jose, CA 95192-0103. **Fax:** 408-924-5080. **E-Mail:** jackson@math.sjsu.edu

JACKSON, CARL WAYNE, EXPERIMENTAL HEMATOLOGY, RADIATION BIOLOGY. **Personal Data:** b Carbondale, Ill, November 27, 1942; m 1963, Ernestine. **Education:** Southern Ill Univ, BA, 1963; Univ Tenn, Knoxville, PhD (radiation biol), 1971. **Professional Experience:** ASSOC DIR ACAD PROGS, ST JUDE CHILDREN'S RES HOSP, as of 2006; MEM FAC, ST JUDE CHILDREN'S RES HOSP, 1987-; from asst mem to assoc mem, St Jude Children's Hosp, 1976-1987; from fel hemat to res assoc, St Jude Children's Hosp, 1971-1975; biol lab specialist physiol, Oak Ridge Nat Lab, 1963-1971. **Memberships:** Am Soc Hemat; Int Soc Exp Hemat; Int Soc Thrombosis & Haemostasis. **Research Statement & Publications:** Hemopoiesis; thrombopoiesis; cell kinetics; cell regulation and differentiation; radiation hematology; megakaryocyte differentiation; megakaryocytopoieses; animal models of defective platelet production; identification of megakaryocyte precursors. **Mailing Address:** St Jude Children's Res Hosp, 332 N Lauderdale PO Box 318, Memphis, TN 38101. **Fax:** 901-495-2176. **E-Mail:** carl.jackson@stjude.org

JACKSON, CARLTON DARNELL, BIOCHEMISTRY, ONCOLOGY. **Personal Data:** b Wiggins, Miss, December 1, 1938; div, c Martin & Janet. **Education:** Miss Col, BS, 1961; Univ Tenn, MS, 1963, PhD (biochem), 1967. **Professional Experience:** Pharmacologist, Div Nutrit Toxicol, 1988-; pharmacologist, Div Comp Toxicol, 1984-1988; pharmacologist, Off Sci Intel, Nat Ctr Toxicol Res, Food & Drug Admin, Div Molecular Biol, 1981-1984; chief, Div Carcinogenic Res, 1976-1979; ASSOC PROF BIOCHEM & INTERDISCIPLINARY TOXICOL, MED SCH, UNIV ARK, LITTLE ROCK, 1972-; res chemist carcinogenesis, Nat Ctr Toxicol Res, Food & Drug Admin, 1972-1975; asst prof biochem, Univ Tenn, 1969-1972; res biochemist carcinogenesis, Vet Admin Hosp, Memphis, 1969-1972; USPHS fel, Univ Miami, 1967-1969; res trainee biochem, St Jude Children's Res Hosp, 1964-1967. **Memberships:** Am Asn Cancer Res; Sigma Xi. **Research Statement & Publications:** Mechanisms of chemical carcinogenesis; molecular mechanism of hormone action; protein and nucleic acid synthesis; molecular biology of cell division and differentiation; nutrition and cancer. **Mailing Address:** Nat Ctr Toxicol Res, Food & Drug Admin, Jefferson, AR 72079.

JACKSON, C(HARLES) IAN, SCIENCE POLICY, SCIENCE HISTORY. **Personal Data:** b Keighley, Eng, February 11, 1935; Canadian & British citizen; div, c Janet Clare Louise. **Education:** Univ London, BA, 1956; McGill Univ, MSc, 1959, PhD (geog), 1961. **Honors & Awards:** Darton Prize, Royal Meteorol Soc, 1962; Evan Durbin Prize, Inst Econ Affairs, 1966. **Professional Experience:** ASSOC FEL, TIMOTHY DWIGHT COL, YALE UNIV, 1994-; dir, Chreod Ltd, Ottawa, 1993-1998; Dir, Chreod Ltd, (Ottawa, Can), 1991-1998; exec dir, Sigma Xi, 1981-1987; sr econ affairs officer, UN Econ Comn Europe, 1978-1981; tech officer, Can Habitat & Energy Secretariat, 1975-1978; exec dir, Can Habitat & Energy Secretariat, 1975; dir priorities & planning, Can Ministry State Urban Affairs, 1971-1975; head, Econ Geog Sect, Can Dept Energy, Mines & Resources, 1969-1971; Lectr geog, London Sch Econ & Polit Sci, 1959-1969. **Memberships:** Hakluyt Soc; Champlain Soc. **Research Statement & Publications:** Environmental protection; history of discovery; global warming; editor of volumes of original sci records for Champlain Soc (2000) and Hakluyt Soc (in progress). **Mailing Address:** 29 N Lake Dr, Hamden, CT 06517.

JACKSON, CRAIG MERTON, BIOCHEMISTRY, MEDICAL DEVICES & DIAGNOSTICS. **Personal Data:** b Staples, Minn, December 2, 1941; m 1995, Beth; c Brian A. **Education:** Wash State Univ, BS, 1963; Univ Wash, PhD (biochem), 1967. **Professional Experience:** PRES & PRIN SCIENTIST, HEMOSAGA DIAG CORP, as of 2004; independent consult, beginning 1996; pres, Reagents Appls Inc, San Diego, 1993-1995; chmn, Div Blood Dis & Resources, Nat Heart, Lung & Blood Inst, 1989-1990; mem adv comt, Div Blood Dis & Resources, Nat Heart, Lung & Blood Inst, 1987-1989; adj prof biochem, Sch Med, Wayne State Univ, beginning 1984; Am Red Cross estab investr, 1983-1992; sci dir, Southeast Mich Region, Am Red Cross, 1983-1992; chmn, Int Comt Thrombosis, 1982-1984; vis prof, Kyushi Univ, Japan, 1982; estab investr, Nat Heart, Lung & Blood Inst, res reviewer, Am Heart Asn, 1974-1979; mem coun thrombosis, Am Heart Asn, beginning 1971; res grants, Nat Heart, Lung & Blood Inst, res reviewer, Am Heart Asn, 1971-1974; from asst prof to prof chem, Sch Med, Wash Univ, 1969-1983; Am Cancer Soc fel chem physics, Unilever Res Lab, Port Sunlight, Eng, 1967-1969; res assoc, Col Med, Univ Ariz, 1967. **Memberships:** Fel Nat Acad Clin Biochem; fel AAAS; Int Soc Thrombosis & Hemostasis; Am Asn Clin Chem; Am Chem Soc; Am Heart Asn; Sigma Xi; Am Soc Qual Control. **Research Statement & Publications:** Protein chemistry and enzymology of blood coagulation, lipid-protein interactions in blood coagulation; physical chemistry of lipids; plasma proteins; invitro diagnostics. **Mailing Address:** Hemosaga Diag Corp, 7703 Convoy Ct, San Diego, CA 92111-1105. **Fax:** 858-505-9915. **E-Mail:** cjackso2@san.rr.com

JACKSON, CRAWFORD GARDNER, vertebrate biology, paleontology; deceased, see previous edition for last biography

JACKSON, CURTIS M(AITLAND), SHAPE-MEMORY ALLOYS, ALLOY DEVELOPMENT & PRODUCTION. **Personal Data:** b New York, NY, April 20, 1933; m 1957, c David C & Carol (Adams). **Education:** NY Univ, BMetE, 1954; Ohio State Univ, MS, 1959, PhD (metall), 1966. **Honors & Awards:** IR-100 Award, Indust Res Mag, 1976; Mordica Mem Award, Wire Asn Int, 1977, J Edward Donnellan Award, 1978; Meritous Technical Paper Award, 1981. **Professional Experience:** AT, C & M JACKSON ASSOCS INC, as of 2004; assoc mgr, Columbus Labs, Battelle Mem Inst, beginning 1977; dir, Wire Found, 1974-1986; dir, Wire J, 1973-1978; assoc chief, Specialty Alloys Div, 1967-1977; chmn, N Cent US region, Am Inst Mining, Metall & Petrol Engrs, 1965-1966; proj leader, Specialty Alloys Div, 1961-1967; prin metallurgist, Alloy Develop Div, Battelle Mem Inst, 1954-1961. **Memberships:** Am Inst Mining Metall & Petrol Engrs; Am Soc Metals; Am Vacuum Soc; Wire Asn Int (second vpres, 1973-1974, first vpres, 1974-1976, pres, 1976-1977); Sigma Xi. **Research Statement & Publications:** Physical metallurgy; alloy development; nucleation and growth of thin films; technical economics; shape-memory alloys; metal failure analysis; electrical and electronic alloys; melting, casting and mechanical working of metals; wire technology. **Mailing Address:** C & M Jackson Trucking, 5370 Carter Rd, Lake Mary, Fl 32746. **Fax:** 407-333-2209.

JACKSON, CURTIS RUKES, RESEARCH MANAGEMENT, FOREIGN AGRICULTURAL DEVELOPMENT. **Personal Data:** b Kansas City, Mo, July 25, 1927; m 1951, Sarah; c 6. **Education:** Univ Miami, BS, 1949; Fla State Univ, MS, 1951; Univ Fla, PhD (plant path), 1958. **Honors & Awards:** Res Award, Nat Peanut Coun. **Professional Experience:** RETIRED; dir, Off Res & Univ Rels Aid, Wash, 1986-1992; dir, Int Coop, Icrisat, India & Niger, 1983-1986; assoc dir, Agr Exp Sta, Univ Ga, 1973-1983; consult foreign agr develop proj, Indust & Govt, beginning 1970. **Research Statement & Publications:** Diseases of peanuts; vegetables and ornamental plants; soil microbiology; tropical agricultural development. **Mailing Address:** Rte One Box 1189, Clayton, GA 30525.

JACKSON, CYNTHIA L, PATHOLOGY. **Education:** Univ Ill, PhD, 1983. **Professional Experience:** ASSOC PROF PATHOBIOLOGY, BROWN UNIV, as of 2005. **Mailing Address:** Dept Path RI Hosp Univ Brown, APC Bldg Rm 12-121, Providence, RI 02903. **E-Mail:** cynthia_jackson@brown.edu

JACKSON, D MICHAEL, ENTOMOLOGY. **Education:** Mich State Univ, BS, 1971; Wash State Univ, MS, 1975 & Phd, 1978. **Professional Experience:** ADJ PROF, DEPT ENTOMOL, NC STATE UNIV, as of 2006. **Research Statement & Publications:** Develop improved insect control techniques and management strategies that reduce pesticide use while maintaining yield and quality of vegetable crops; investigates the interactions between insects, plants, and the environment in vegetable production systems. **Mailing Address:** Dept Entomol, NC State Univ, 2875 Savannah Hwy, Charleston, NC 29414. **Fax:** 843-763-7013. **E-Mail:** mjackson@awod.com

JACKSON, DALE LATHAM, zoology; deceased, see previous edition for last biography

JACKSON, DANIEL FRANCIS, LIMNOLOGY. **Personal Data:** b Pittsburgh, Pa, June 11, 1925; m 1951, Bettina Bush. **Education:** Univ Pittsburgh, BS, 1949, MS, 1950; State Univ NY, PhD (water resources), 1957. **Professional Experience:** Dir & prof, Inst Environ Studies, La State Univ, Baton Rouge, 1982-1986; MEM STAFF, JACKSON & JACKSON ASSOC, 1978-; dir, Drinking Water Qual Res Ctr, Fla Int Univ, 1976-1978; dir & prof environ & urban systs, Sch Technol, Fla Int Univ, 1973-1978; prof limnol, Syracuse Univ, 1963-1973; from asst prof to assoc prof, Univ Louisville, 1959-1963; asst prof, Western Mich Univ, 1955-1959; Dir, C C Adams Ctr, 1955-1959; asst col forestry, State Univ NY, 1953-1955; hydrologist, US Army Corps Engrs, Pa, 1952-1953; asst prof, Col Steubenville, 1951-1952; Lectr biol, Univ Pittsburgh, 1949-1951. **Memberships:** Am Soc Limnol & Oceanog; Ecol Soc Am; Am Micros Soc; Am Fisheries Soc; Int Asn Theoret & Appl Limnol; Soc Nat Sci. **Research Statement & Publications:** Limnology, primary productivity; environmental planning, plankton; pollution, environmental toxicology; biotechnology. **Mailing Address:** 3323 Guilford Court, Naples, FL 34112.

JACKSON, DARRYL DEAN, CHEMICAL INSTRUMENTATION. **Personal Data:** b Lexington, Okla, 1932; m 1959, c 2. **Education:** Univ Okla, BS, 1955, MS, 1956; Univ NMex, PhD (radiochem), 1968. **Professional Experience:** STAFF MEM, LOS ALAMOS NAT LAB, 1956-. **Memberships:** AAAS; Am Inst Chemists; Am Chem Soc; Sigma Xi. **Research Statement & Publications:** Structure of optically active inorganic complexes; chemistry of solutions of carrier-free iodine-131; radiochemistry of transuranium elements and fission products; development of automated instruments for chemical analysis. **Mailing Address:** Los Alamos Nat Lab, PO Box 1663, Los Alamos, NM 87545. **Fax:** 505-665-4737. **E-Mail:** djackson@lanl.gov

JACKSON, DAVID ARCHER, MOLECULAR BIOLOGY, VIROLOGY. **Personal Data:** b New York, NY, April 29, 1942; m 1966, c 1. **Education:** Harvard Univ, AB, 1964; Stanford Univ, PhD (molecular biol), 1969. **Professional Experience:** VPRES, DUPONT MERCK PHARMACEUT CO, as of 1994; DIR VIROL RES, DUPONT MERCK PHARMACEUT CO, 1991-; dir virol res, Biotechnol Res, E I duPont, 1989-1990; mem, bd dir, Indust Biotechnol Assoc, 1986-1989; dir, Biotechnol Res, E I duPont, 1986-1989; dir, Genex Corp, Rockville, Md, 1985; sr vpres, Genex Corp, Rockville, Md, 1983-1985; consult, President's Comn for Study Ethical Probs Med, Biomed & Behav Res 1981-; adj prof appl molecular biol, Univ Md Baltimore County, 1981-1986; mem, Adv Panel Comp Assessment Develop Biotechnol, Off Technol Assessment, 1981-1983; mem, AdHoc Comt on Nat Issues Genetic Eng, NSF, 1981-1982; vpres & sci dir, Genex Corp, Rockville, Md, 1980-1982; chmn sci adv bd, Genex Corp, Rockville, Md, 1977-1985; assoc prof, Univ Mich, Ann Arbor, 1977-1981; asst prof microbiol, Univ Mich, Ann Arbor, 1972-1976; USPHS fel, Nat Cystic Fibrosis Res Found basic sci fel, 1970-1972; USPHS fel, Med Sch, Stanford Univ, 1969-1970; fel, prof Paul Berg, Stanford. **Memberships:** Am Soc Microbiol; Genetic Soc Am. **Research Statement & Publications:** Molecular biology; enzymes acting on nucleic acids; mammalian viruses. **Mailing Address:** DuPont Merck Pharmaceut Co, PO Box 80400, Wilmington, DE 19880-0328.

JACKSON, DAVID DIETHER, GEOPHYSICS. **Personal Data:** b San Francisco, Calif, September 18, 1943; m 1968, Kathleen; c 2. **Education:** Calif Inst Technol, BS, 1965; Mass Inst Technol, PhD (geophys), 1969. **Professional Experience:** SCI DIR, SOUTHERN CALIF EARTHQUAKE CTR, as of 1999; pres-elect, Seismol Sect, Am Geophys Union, 1993-1994; secy, Seismol Sect, Am Geophys Union, 1992-1993; mem, Calif Earthquake Prediction Eval Coun, 1984-; sr resident res associateship, Nat Acad Sci/Nat Res Coun, 1981; PROF GEOPHYS, UNIV CALIF, LOS ANGELES, 1980-; mem, US Nat Comt Seismol, Panel Crustal Movement Measurements & Comt Geodesy/Seismol, 1978-1981; assoc prof, Univ Calif, Los Angeles, 1969-1980. **Memberships:** AAAS; fel Am Geophys Union; Seismol Soc Am; Seismol Soc Japan. **Research Statement & Publications:** Seismology; solid earth geophysics; geophysical inverse problems; applications of solid state physics to geophysics; earthquake prediction and control. **Mailing Address:** Dept Earth & Space sci, Univ Calif, Los Angeles, 595 Hilgard Ave, Los Angeles, CA 90095-1567. **Fax:** 310-825-2779. **E-Mail:** djackson@ess.ucla.edu

JACKSON, DAVID PHILLIP, FUSION, NUCLEAR FUEL CYCLE. **Personal Data:** b Toronto, Ont, October 2, 1940; m 1975, Susan; c Scott P & Timothy D. **Education:** Univ Toronto, BSc, 1962, MA, 1964, MASc, 1966, PhD (eng physics), 1968; Univ Ottawa, dipl, 1985, M. Eng. 1991. **Honors & Awards:** President, Canadian Nuclear Society, 2001-2002. **Professional Experience:** DIR, MCMASTER INSTITUTE FOR ENERGY STUDIES, 2006-, Adj Prof, DEPT ENG PHYSICS, McMASTER UNIV, as of 2006; Chmn, Int Atomic Energy Agency, Int Fusion Res Coun, 1993-1998; mem, Int Energy Agency, Fusion Power Coord Comt, 1986-; dir, Nat Fusion Prog, Atomic Energy of Can Ltd, 1986-1998; mgr fusion progs, Atomic Energy Can Ltd, 1985-1986; prof, Inst Energy Studies, 1981-; vis prof, Bell Labs, Murray Hill, 1981-1987; sr res officer, Atomic Energy Can Ltd, 1980-; mem staff, Inst Mat Res, 1979-1982; assoc prof eng physics, McMaster Univ, 1978-1981; Vis scientist, Max-Planck Inst Plasma Physics, 1975-1976; assoc, Atomic Energy Can Ltd, 1970-1980; asst res officer, Atomic Energy Can Ltd, 1968-1970; res asst, Inst Aerospace Studies, Toronto, 1965-1968; Mathematician, IBM, Toronto, 1962-1963. **Memberships:** Chem Inst Can. **Research Statement & Publications:** SUSTAINABILITY, NUCLEAR ENERGY, NUCLEAR FUEL CYCLE. **Mailing Address:** Dept Eng Physics, McMaster Univ, Hamilton, ON L8S 4L7, Can. **Fax:** 905-529-1975. **E-Mail:** jacksond@mcmaster.ca

JACKSON, DONALD CARGILL, PHYSIOLOGY. **Personal Data:** b Philadelphia, Pa, May 4, 1937; m 1966, c 2. **Education:** Geneva Col, BS, 1959; Univ Pa, PhD (physiol), 1963. **Professional Experience:** PROF PHYSIOL, BROWN UNIV, 1979-; assoc prof, Brown Univ, 1973-1979; asst prof, Sch Med, Univ Pa, 1968-1973; Pa Plan scholar, 1968-1971; res fel physiol, Sch Med, Univ Pa, 1965-1968; res asst, Duke Univ, 1963-1965; Res asst physiol, John B Pierce Lab, Conn, 1961-1963. **Memberships:** AAAS; Am Soc Zool; Am Physiol Soc. **Research Statement & Publications:** Acid-base physiology in reptiles. **Mailing Address:** Div Biomed Sci, Brown Univ, Box G, Providence, RI 02912-0001.

JACKSON, EARL GRAVES, PHYSICAL CHEMISTRY. **Personal Data:** b Springfield, Mass, March 27, 1920; m 1943, c 3. **Education:** Am Int Col, BS, 1942; Clark Univ, AM, 1943; Rutgers Univ, PhD (chem), 1951. **Professional Experience:** RETIRED; mgr admin, Kendall Co, 1980-1983; head adhesives sect, Lexington Res Lab, 1973-1979; dir chem physics lab, Res Div, USM Corp, Mass, 1969-1973; sr phys chemist, Nat Res Corp, Cambridge, 1960-1962 & United Shoe Mach Corp, 1962-1969; mem subcomt lubrication & wear, Nat Adv Comt Aeronaut, 1956-1958; supvr bearings, lubrication & seals develop, 1955-1960; lubricants specialist, Gen Elec Co, 1951-1955; chemist, Merck & Co, 1946-1948. **Research Statement & Publications:** Physical chemistry of polymeric soaps; properties and mechanisms of lubricating greases; high temperature lubrication and fatigue; structural sealants; shoe technology; pressure sensitive adhesives and tapes. **Mailing Address:** 201 Willow Oak Lane, Hendersonville, NC 28791.

JACKSON, EARL ROGERS, FOOD CHEMISTRY. **Personal Data:** b Madison, Ind, August 6, 1930; m 1951, c Deborah. **Education:** Hanover Col, AB, 1952. **Professional Experience:** SR VPRES RES, HEEKIN CAN, INC, 1990-; DIR RES, HEEKIN CAN, INC, 1978-; vpres res, Heekin Can Co, 1978-1990; asst res dir, Heekin Can Co, 1964-1977; chemist, Heekin Can Co, 1958-1964; Chemist, Am Can Co, 1952-1957. **Memberships:** Inst Food Technologists; Soc Soft Drink Technologists; Am Soc Testing & Mat. **Mailing Address:** 6220 Neuvelle Lane, Cincinnati, OH 45243.

JACKSON, EDGAR B, COMMUNITY MEDICINE & HEALTH. **Personal Data:** b Rison, Ark, May 30, 1935; m 1957, Thelma; c Gary, David, Michael & Laura. **Education:** Western Res Univ, BA, 1962, MD, 1966. **Professional Experience:** CLIN PROF MED, CASE WESTERN RES UNIV, 1986-; from asst clin prof to assoc clin prof, Case Western Res Univ, 1977-1986; commmunity health, Case Western Res Univ, 1977-1988; asst prof community med, Case Western Res Univ, 1974-1979; asst prof, Case Western Res Univ, 1971-1977; asst dean, Case Western Res Univ, 1971-1974; Carnegie Common Wealth Clin scholar, 1970-1972; sr instr med, Case Western Res Univ, 1970-1971; from intern to Chief resident med, Cleveland Metrop Gen Hosp, 1966-1970; US Army, 1959-1961. **Memberships:** Inst Med-Nat Acad Sci; Am Sickle Cell Anemia Asn Inc; Am Pub Health Asn. **Mailing Address:** Univ Hosp Cleveland, 11100 Euclid Ave, Cleveland, OH 44106.

JACKSON, EDWIN ATLEE, PHYSICS. **Personal Data:** b Lyons, NY, April 18, 1931; m 1954, c 2. **Education:** Syracuse Univ, BS, 1953, MS, 1955, PhD (physics), 1958. **Professional Experience:** Vis prof, Chalmers Univ, Sweden, 1984; JIFT vis prof, Nagoya Univ, Japan, 1984; mem adv bd, Physica D: Nonlinear Phenomena, 1980-; PROF PHYSICS, UNIV ILL, URBANA, 1977-; vis mem staff, Los Alamos Sci Lab, 1971; vis sr physicist, Found Fundamental Res Matter, Inst Plasma-Physics, Netherlands, 1967-1968; assoc prof physics & mech eng, Univ Ill, Urbana, 1963-1977; asst prof, Univ Ill, Urbana, 1961-1963; staff mem, Proj Matterhorn, Princeton Univ, 1959-1961; Nat Acad Sci res assoc, Air Res & Develop Command, Air Force Cambridge Res Ctr, Mass, 1958-1959; asst & instr, Brandeis Univ, 1957-1958; asst, Syracuse Univ, 1954-1957. **Memberships:** Am Phys Soc. **Research Statement & Publications:** Nonlinear dynamics; plasma physics; kinetic theory of gases. **Mailing Address:** Dept Physics Loomis Lab, Univ Ill 1110 W Green St, Urbana, IL 61801.

JACKSON, EDWIN KERRY, CARDIOVASCULAR & RENAL. **Personal Data:** b October 21, 1952; m 1973, Donna; c Ethan & Travis. **Education:** Univ Tex, Austin, BS, 1976; Univ

Tex, Dallas, PhD (pharmacol), 1979. **Honors & Awards:** Glaxo Cardiovasc Discovery Award. **Professional Experience:** PROF PHARMACOL, SCH MED, UNIV PITTSBURGH, 1991-; from assoc prof to prof pharmacol, Sch Med, Vanderbilt Univ, 1979-1991. **Memberships:** Am Soc Hypertension; Am Fedn Clin Res; Fedn Am Soc Exp Biol; Am Heart Asn. **Research Statement & Publications:** Cardiovascular pharmacology. **Mailing Address:** Ctr Clin Pharmacol, Univ Pittsburgh, 623 Scaife Hall, Pittsburgh, PA 15261. **Fax:** 412-648-7107. **E-Mail:** edj+@pitt.edu

JACKSON, EDWIN L, ELECTRICAL ENGINEERING. **Personal Data:** b Albany, Tex, January 21, 1930; m 1953, Ruby; c Elisabeth, Elaine & Gene. **Education:** Univ Okla, BSEE, 1952. **Professional Experience:** RETIRED; vpres & gen mgr, Div Elec Systs, beginning 1989; sr vpres & gen mgr, Dallas Corp, 1983-1988; vpres, Forney Eng Co, 1972-1983; prog mgr, E Syst, 1963-1968; staff, Div Static Power, Varo Inc, 1962-1963 & 1968-1972; sr design engr, Gen Dynamics, 1956-1962. **Research Statement & Publications:** Engineering; electronic systems. **Mailing Address:** 6010 Troon Circle, Garland, TX 75044.

JACKSON, ERNEST BAKER, agronomy, botany; deceased, see previous edition for last biography

JACKSON, ETHEL NOLAND, MOLECULAR BIOLOGY, RECOMBINANT DNA METHODOLOGY. **Personal Data:** b Geneva, NY, April 27, 1944; m 1966, David; c Holly (Bunting). **Education:** Harvard Univ, BA, 1966; Stanford Univ, PhD (biol sci), 1973. **Professional Experience:** RES MGR, CENT RES & DEVELOP DEPT, E I DU PONT DEL NEMOURS & CO, 1990-; res supvr life sci, Cent Res & Develop Dept, E I Du Pont Del Nemours & CO, 1987-1990; exec dir res opers, Molecular Genetics Dept, Genex Co, 1985; res dir, Molecular Genetics Dept, Genex Co, 1981-1985; asst prof microbiol, Dept Human Genetics, Sch Med, Univ Mich, 1974-1981; Am Cancer Soc fel, 1974; fel biochem genetics, Dept Human Genetics, Sch Med, Univ Mich, 1972-1974. **Memberships:** Am Soc Microbiol; Genetics Soc Am; AAAS; Am Women Sci. **Research Statement & Publications:** Biological regulatory mechanisms and biochemical genetics of bacterial viruses; chromosome structure of viruses; viral DNA packaging; vector systems for gene cloning in gram-positive bacteria; protein secretion by prokaryotes; protein expression systems; plant molecular biology. **Mailing Address:** Central Res & Develop, El DuPont Nemours & Co, E328/B43 PO Box 80328, Wilmington, DE 19880-0328. **E-Mail:** ethel.n.jackson@usa.dupont.com

JACKSON, FRANCIS J, PHYSICS, UNDERWATER ACOUSTICS. **Personal Data:** b Providence, RI, May 23, 1932; m 1983, Nancy; c 3. **Education:** Providence Col, BS, 1954; Brown Univ, MS, 1957, PhD (physics), 1960. **Professional Experience:** DIR PHYSICAL SCI, MISSION & FOCUS RES, BOLT BERANEK & NEWMAN INC, as of 2004; SR VPRES, BOLT BERANEK & NEWMAN INC, 1988-; sr vpres, BBN Labs, Inc, 1984-1988; corp vpres, Underwater Technol Div, 1977-1984; vpres, Underwater Technol Div, 1975-1977; vpres, Phys Sci Div, 1970-1975; adj prof, Cath Univ Am, 1968-1974; sr scientist, Bolt Beranek & Newman, Inc, 1960-1970; res assoc physics, Brown Univ, 1959-1960. **Memberships:** Acoust Soc Am; Inst Elec & Electronics Engrs. **Research Statement & Publications:** Nonlinear acoustics; underwater acoustics and sonar; underwater sound propagation; array theory and design. **Mailing Address:** Bolt Beranek & Newman Inc, Ten Moulton St, Cambridge, MA 02138.

JACKSON, FRANK M, AERONAUTICS. **Education:** Univ Tenn Space Inst, Phd. **Professional Experience:** CHIEF ENGR, INTEGERATED TEST & EVAL DEPT, AEDC, as of 2005. **Mailing Address:** Calspan Corp, AEDC Div M/S 430, Arnold AFB, TN 37389. **Fax:** 931-454-7741. **E-Mail:** frank.jackson@arnold.af.mil

JACKSON, GARY LESLIE, PLASMA PHYSICS, ELECTROMAGNETICS. **Personal Data:** b Minneapolis, Minn, January 5, 1945; m 1970, Melissa; c Shannon, Jeff & Courtney. **Education:** Univ Idaho, BS, 1967; Calif State Univ, Northridge, MS, 1972; Univ Ariz, PhD (elec eng), 1977. **Professional Experience:** VPRES RES, AM ELEC AUTOMOBILE CO INC 1999-; dir, Am Elec Automobile Co Inc, 1996-1999; prin scientist, Gen Atomics Co, beginning 1977. **Memberships:** Am Phys Soc; Am Vacuum Soc; Elec Automobile Asn. **Research Statement & Publications:** Fusion plasmas; plasma/wall interactions; electric vehicle. **Mailing Address:** Am Elec Automobile Co Inc, San Diego, CA 92111. **E-Mail:** jackson@gav.gat.com

JACKSON, GARY LOUCKS, NEUROENDOCRINOLOGY, REPRODUCTIVE PHYSIOLOGY. **Personal Data:** b Skidmore, Mo, November 4, 1938; m 1970, Dixie; c Andrea. **Education:** Univ Mo, BS, 1960, AM, 1963; Univ Ill, Urbana, PhD (animal sci), 1967. **Professional Experience:** RETIRED; prof endocrinol, Univ Ill, Urbana, 2002; panel mgr, animal reproduction panel, USDA, 1993; mem, Animal Reproduction Panel, USDA, 1989-1991; vis prof, Univ Bristol, 1985; NIH reprod biol study sect, 1983-1987; prof endocrinol, Univ Ill, Urbana, beginning 1977; assoc prof, Univ Ill, Urbana, 1968-1977; NIH fel, Univ Ill, Urbana, 1967-1968. **Memberships:** Soc Study Reproduction; Endocrine Soc; Brit Soc Study Fertil; Neuroscience Soc. **Research Statement & Publications:** Hypothalamic control of gonadotropin and prolactin secretion; biosynthesis of luteinizing hormone; biological rhythms. **Mailing Address:** 3516 Vet Med Basic Sci Bldg(MC-002), 2001 S Lincoln Ave, Urbana, IL 61802. **Fax:** 217-333-4628. **E-Mail:** gjackson@cvm.uiuc.edu

JACKSON, GEORGE C, AERONAUTICS. **Professional Experience:** STAFF, MARTING MARIETTA CORP, VA, as of 2005. **Memberships:** Am Inst Aeronaut & Astronauts. **Mailing Address:** Martin Marietta Corp, 11107 Sunset Hills Rd, Reston, VA 22090-5309. **Fax:** 703-707-6888.

JACKSON, GEORGE FREDERICK, III, PHYSICAL CHEMISTRY, ANALYTICAL CHEMISTRY. **Personal Data:** b Brooklyn, NY, May 16, 1943; m 1966, c 2. **Education:** MacMurray Col, BA, 1965; Northwestern Univ, PhD (chem), 1969. **Professional Experience:** DIV CHMN, UNIV TAMPA, 1982-; PROF CHEM, UNIV TAMPA, 1980-; assoc prof, Univ Tampa, 1973-1980; asst prof chem, Lake Forest Col, 1969-1973. **Memberships:** AAAS; Am Chem Soc. **Research Statement & Publications:** Studies of atomic inversion; involving arsenic and phosphorus atoms; properties of the allenic bond; use of NMR shift reagents for determination of molecular structures. **Mailing Address:** Div Sci & Math, Univ Tampa, 401 W Kennedy Blvd, Tampa, FL 33606.

JACKSON, GEORGE G, INTERNAL MEDICINE, MICROBIOLOGY. **Personal Data:** b Provo, Utah, October 5, 1920; m 1943, c 5. **Education:** Brigham Young Univ, AB, 1942; Univ Utah, MD, 1945. **Honors & Awards:** Maxwell Finland Award, Infectious Dis Soc Am, 1977; Alexander von Humboldt US Sr Scientist Award, 1978; Ernst Jung Prize Med, 1984. **Professional Experience:** PROF EMER, UNIV ILL, CHICAGO, 1987-; Keeton prof med, Univ Ill, 1979-1987; ed, J Infectious Dis, 1979-1984; vis prof, London Hosp Med Col, 1977-1978 & Max von Pettenkofer Inst, Univ Munich, Ger, 1978-1979; spec fel, Virus Res Dept, Trop Inst, Hamburg, Ger, 1968-1969; chief sect infectious dis, Univ Ill, 1959-1987; attend physician, Univ Ill, 1951-1987; from asst prof to prof, Univ Ill, 1951-1979; Milton fel, Med Sch, 1950-1951; asst med, Hosp & res fel, Thorndike Mem Lab, 1949-1951; res fel, Med Sch, 1949-1950; asst resident med, Hosp & teaching fel, Med Sch, 1948-1949; intern, II & IV Med Serv, Boston City Hosp, Harvard Univ, 1945-1946; consult, West Side Vet Admin Hosp, Chicago. **Memberships:** Asn Am Physicians; Am Col Physicians; emer mem Am Epidemiol Soc; Infectious Dis Soc Am (secy-treas, 1967-1972, pres 1974); Am Soc Clin Invest. **Research Statement & Publications:** Infectious diseases; antibiotics; virology and microbiology. **Mailing Address:** Col Med, Univ Ill 840 S Wood St, Chicago, IL 60612.

JACKSON, GEORGE JOHN, FOOD MICROBIOLOGY, PARASITOLOGY. **Personal Data:** b Vienna, Austria, December 10, 1931; American citizen. **Education:** Univ Chicago, AB, 1951, MS, 1954, PhD, 1958. **Professional Experience:** DEAN, STAFF COL, CFSAN/FDA, 2000-; actg dir, Off Spec Res Skills, Ctr Food Safety & Appl Nutrit, US Food & Drug Admin, 1994-2000; sect ed, J Asn Off Anal Chem Int, 1993-1995; spec asst to dir, Off Spec Res Skills, 1992-1994; chief, Food Microbiol Methods Develop Br, 1980-1992; FDA Food Microbiol Liaison with Int Orgn, 1987-; mem, microbiol adv comt, Calif State Univ, Riverside, 1985-1993; US deleg, Food Hyg Comt of Codex Alimentarius Comn of WHO/Food & Agr Orgn of UN, 1980-1988; ed, Exp Parasitol, 1976-1987; head lab parasitol, US Food & Drug Admin, 1972-1980; adj prof, Rockefeller Univ & Lehigh Univ, 1972-1976; fac mem, Rockefeller Univ, 1963-1972; guest researcher, Amazon Res Inst, Manaus, Brazil, 1963; USPHS res fel & guest investr, Rockefeller Inst, 1959-1963; res assoc & instr, Univ Chicago, 1958-1959; consult, Pathway Labs, 1958-1959; Fel, La State Univ, 1958. **Memberships:** Am Soc Parasitologists; Soc Protozoologists; Am Soc Trop Med & Hyg; Asn Off Anal Chem; Helminthol Soc. **Research Statement & Publications:** Immunity; invertebrate physiology; axenic culture; food borne parasites; anisakiasis; cyclospora epidemiology. **Mailing Address:** FDA, 5100 Paint Branch Pkwy, College Park, MD 20740-3835. **Fax:** 301-436-2643. **E-Mail:** george.jackson@cfsan.fda.gov

JACKSON, GEORGE RICHARD, CHEMISTRY. **Personal Data:** b Chagrin Falls, Ohio, September 27, 1920; m 1943, c 3. **Education:** Baldwin-Wallace Col, BS, 1942; Johns Hopkins Univ, MA, 1943, PhD (org chem), 1948. **Professional Experience:** CONSULT, 1978-; pres, Southern Shortenings, 1969-1977; Top-Scor Prod Inc, 1957-1961 & SuCrest Corp, 1961-1969; pres, Cliffdale Prod Corp, 1955-1957; dir res, H C Fisher Co, 1953-1955; From instr to asst prof chem, Western Reserve Univ, 1947-1953. **Memberships:** Am Chem Soc; Am Oil Chem Soc; Am Asn Cereal Chem; Inst Food Technol. **Research Statement & Publications:** Food chemistry; fats and oils; analytical chemistry. **Mailing Address:** 2828 N Atlantic Ave, Daytona Beach, FL 32118.

JACKSON, GILCHRIST LEWIS, SURGICAL ONCOLOGY, HEAD & NECK SURGERY. **Personal Data:** b Dayton, Ohio, September 30, 1948. **Education:** Vanderbilt Univ, BA, 1970; Univ Louisville, Sch Med, MD, 1974 Sugery Residency Ut Southwestern 1974-1979; Fellowship UT MDAnderson Surgical Oncology 1979-1980. **Honors & Awards:** Sword of Hope Award, Am Cancer Soc, 1983-1985, 1987; Chmn Cancer Committee, Kelsey-Seybold Clinc, 1998-Present; A J Miller Award, 1974. **Professional Experience:** CHIEF, DEPT SURG, KELSEY-SEYBOLD CLIN, as of 2003; cancer prog liason, Cancer Res Comt, 1992-; cancer prog liason, Cancer Prev Comt, 1992-; cancer prog liason, Physician/Am Col Surgeons Comn Cancer, St Luke's Episcopal Hosp, 1989-; MED DIR, KELSEY-SEYBOLD FOUND CANCER PREV CTR, 1988-; med dir, Kelsey-Seybold Cancer Prog, 1986-1993; clin asst prof surg, Baylor Col Med, 1985-; adj asst surgeon, M D Anderson Cancer Ctr, Univ Tex, 1985-; clin asst surgeon, Univ Tex Med Sch, 1984-; med dir, Joe & Jessie Crump Ctr Clin Cancer Res & Educ, Kelsey Seybold Found, 1983-; HEAD, NECK SURGEON & SURG ONCOLOGIST, KELSEY-SEYBOLD MED GROUP, 1981-; surgeon, St Luke's Episcopal Hosp, Houston, Tex Childrens Hosp, Houston, Vet Admin Hosp, Houston & Ben Taub Hosp, Harris Co Hosp Dist, 1981-; fel, Surg Oncol, Med Dept Anderson Hosp, 1979-1980; residency, Gen Surg, Univ Tex, 1975-1979; Internship, Parkland Mem Hosp, 1974-1975; Texal So Chair; Cancer Liaison Prog. **Memberships:** Am Col Surgeons; Soc Surg Oncol; Soc Head & Neck Surgeons; Int Soc Surg; Am Soc Head & Neck Surg. **Research Statement & Publications:** Cancer prevention-control; chemotherapy, chemoprevention trials; comparison ofdiagnostic-survival outcomes; breast cancer; diagnostic accuracy, needle biopsy-thyroid; localizing scans-parathyroid. **Mailing Address:** Kelsey Seybold Clin, 2727 W Holcombe Blvd, Houston, TX 77025. **Fax:** 713-442-0363. **E-Mail:** gijackson@kelsey-seyhold.com

JACKSON, GRANT D, SOIL & SOIL SCIENCE, AGRONOMY. **Personal Data:** b Perryton, Tex, April 3, 1945; m 1965, c 2. **Education:** Okla Panhandle State Col, BS, 1968; Mont State Univ, MS, 1970, PhD (crop & soil sci), 1974. **Professional Experience:** PROF AGRON, WESERN TRIANGLE AGR RES CTR, MONT STATE UNIV, as of 2005; AGRONOMIST CROP, MONT STATE UNIV, 1984-; agronomist crop & soil sci, Univ Wyo, 1977-1984; extern specialist cropping systs, Mont State Univ, 1977-1979; soil scientist, US Dept Agr, 1974-1977. **Memberships:** Am Soc Agron; Soil Sci Soc Am. **Research Statement & Publications:** Development of zero-till technology for dry land and irrigating cropping system; nutrient management for irrigated and dry land cropping systems. **Mailing Address:** Mont Res Ctr, Mont State Univ, PO Box 974, Conrad, MT 59425. **Fax:** 406-278-7797. **E-Mail:** gjackson@montana.edu

JACKSON, HAROLD, FOOD SCIENCE. **Personal Data:** b Preston, Lancashire, Eng, August 10, 1937; m 1961, c 3. **Education:** Univ Nottingham, BSc, 1959, MSc, 1961; Univ Alta, PhD (dairy sci), 1963. **Professional Experience:** RETIRED; prof food sci, Univ Alta, 1982-1997; prof food sci & chmn dept, Univ Alta, 1974-1982; assoc prof food sci, Univ Alta, 1969-1974; asst prof dairy & food microbiol, Univ Alta, 1963-1969. **Memberships:** Am Soc Microbiol; Inst Food Technologists; Can Inst Food Sci & Technol; Brit Soc Appl Bact; Int Asn Milk Food & Environ Sanitarians. **Research Statement & Publications:** Food microbiology; effects of environmental stress on microbial growth and activity; food-borne pathogens. **Mailing Address:** Dept Food Sci, Univ Alta, Edmonton, AB T6G 2P5, Can.

JACKSON, HAROLD LEONARD, POLYMER CHEMISTRY, FLUORINE CHEMISTRY, ORGANIC SOLVENTS. **Personal Data:** b Wichita, Kans, March 13, 1923; m 1952, Shirley Alvarado; c Sara, Ann, David & Thomas. **Education:** Munic Univ Wichita, AB, 1943, MS, 1946; Univ Ill, PhD (chem), 1949. **Professional Experience:** CONSULT CHEMIST, 1993-; consult chemist, DuPont Chem, 1993-2000; res fel, DuPont Chem, 1990-1992; res assoc, Petrochem Dept, 1978-1990; res assoc, Org Chem Dept, 1966-1977; Vis prof, Univ Kans, 1962-1963; Res chemist, Org Chem Dept, 1959-1965; Res chemist, Cent Res Dept, E I DuPont Del Nemours & Co, 1949-1959. **Memberships:** AAAS; Am Chem Soc; Fedn Socs Coating Technol; Sigma Xi. **Research Statement & Publications:** Organic solvents; polymer solvency; polymer characterization; fluorocarbon solvents and polymers; organic synthesis; paint removers; cleaning solvents. **Mailing Address:** Canterbury Hills, 102 Stratton Dr, Hockessin, DE 19707.

JACKSON, HAROLD WOODWORTH, ANALYTICAL CHEMISTRY. **Personal Data:** b Lawrence, Mass, March 14, 1928; m 1950, c 4. **Education:** Univ NH, BS, 1949; Univ

Conn, MS, 1951, PhD (biochem, dairy technol), 1955. **Professional Experience:** SR GROUP LEADER, BASIC FLAVOR CHEM RES & DEVELOP DIV, KRAFT, INC, 1978-; sr group leader, Kraftco Corp, 1975-1978; group leader chromatog & instrumental anal, Basic Flavor Chem Res & Develop Div, Kraft, Inc, 1969-1975; group leader chromatog & infrared spectros, Res & Develop Div, Fundamental Chem Sect, Nat Dairy Prod Corp, 1960-1969; group leader chromatog, Kraft Foods Res Lab, 1959-1960; res chemist, Kraft Foods Res Lab, 1955-1959; prod leader cheese, Kraft Foods Res Lab, 1954-1955; Instr dairy technol, Univ Conn, 1952-1953. **Memberships:** Am Oil Chemist's Soc; Am Chem Soc. **Research Statement & Publications:** Isolation and identification of natural flavor compounds; analytical methodology on fatty acid derivatives; gas chromatography; nuclear magnetic resonance; basic flavor chemistry; mass spectrometry. **Mailing Address:** 56 Sunny Shore Dr, Ormond Beach, FL 32176-3716.

JACKSON, HERBERT LEWIS, nuclear physics; deceased, see previous edition for last biography

JACKSON, HUNTER, NEUROSCIENCES. **Education:** Yale Univ, PhD (psychobiology). **Professional Experience:** CHM, PRES & CHIEF EXEC OFFICER, NPS PHARMACEUT, as of 2002. **Mailing Address:** NPS Pharmaceut Inc, 420 Chipeta Way, Salt Lake City, UT 84108.

JACKSON, IVOR MICHAEL DAVID, NEUROENDOCRINOLOGY, COMPARATIVE ENDOCRINOLOGY. **Personal Data:** b Glasgow, Scotland, April 17, 1936; American citizen; m 1972, Barbara; c Heather Rochelle & Amanda Ruth. **Education:** Univ Glasgow Med Sch, MB, ChB, 1960; FACP; FRCP, 1996. **Honorary Degrees:** MA, Brown Univ, 1985. **Honors & Awards:** Spinoza Prof, Univ Amsterdam, Neth, 1996. **Professional Experience:** PROF EMER MED, BROWN UNIV, 2004-; spinoza prof, Univ Amsterdam, Neth, 1996; Venezuelan Soc Endocrinol, Univ Caracas, 1988; Int Conf, NY Acad Sci, Md, 1987; vis prof med, Univ Ottowa, 1986; prof med, Brown Univ, beginning 1984; DIR, DIV ENDOCRINOL, RI HOSP, 1984-; vis prof med, Univ Toronto, Can, 1984; Salk Inst Biol Studies, La Jolla, 1984; Workshop Hormone Stand, NIH, 1982; mem, Spec Rev Comt, NIH, 1981; co-organizer & co-chmn, Fedn Am Soc Exp Biol, 1980; prin investr, Diabetes, Digestive & Kidney Dis, Nat Inst Arthritis, 1978-1981 & 1981-; from asst prof med to prof, Sch Med, 1973-1984; res fel endocrinol, Tufts Univ, 1972-1973; res fel neuroendocrinol, Univ Conn, 1971-1972. **Memberships:** Endocrine Soc; fel Am Col Physicians; Am Thyroid Asn; Soc Neuroscience; Am Soc Clin Invest; Asn Am Physicians; hon mem Endocrin Soc China. **Research Statement & Publications:** To determine the physiologic, cellular and molecular mechanisms regulating the biosynthesis and post-translational processing of proTRH, a 255 amino acid polyprotein which contains 5 copies of a thyrotrophin releasing hormone (TRH) progenitor sequence flanked by paired basic residues and the secretion of TRH in the various regions of the neuroendocrine system where TRH and its prohormone occur. **Mailing Address:** Dept Med, Brown Univ, Providence, RI 02912. **Fax:** 401-444-4921. **E-Mail:** ivor_jackson@brown.edu

JACKSON, J DAVID, HIGH ENERGY PHYSICS. **Education:** Msss Inst Technol, Cambridge, PhD (Physics), 1949. **Professional Experience:** PROF EMER PHYSICS, UNIV CALIF, BERKELEY, as of 2005. **Mailing Address:** Univ Calif Berkeley, 366 Le-Conte, Berkeley, CA 94720-7300. **Fax:** 510-486-6808. **E-Mail:** JDJackson@lbl.gov

JACKSON, JAMES EDWARD, PHYSICAL ORGANIC CHEMISTRY. **Personal Data:** b Boston, Mass, June 14, 1955; m 1987, Evelyn; c Kelvin C Parker. **Education:** Princeton Univ, PhD (chem), 1987. **Professional Experience:** Dir, MSU cen for fundamental mat res 2002-; ASSOC PROF CHEM, MICH STATE UNIV, 1994-; asst prof, Mich State Univ, 1988-1994; fel, Ohio State Univ, 1986-1988. **Memberships:** Am Chem Soc; AAAS; InterAm Photochem Soc; Mat Res Soc; Sigma Xi. **Research Statement & Publications:** Organic reactive intermediates and reaction mechanisms, design of organic-based magnetic materials; crystal engineering via dihydrogen bonding, mechanism-based discovery of new green catalytic processes. **Mailing Address:** Dept Chem, Mich State Univ, East Lansing, MI 48824. **Fax:** 517-353-1793. **E-Mail:** jackson@cem.msu.edu

JACKSON, JAMES EDWARD, MULTIVARIATE ANALYSIS, QUALITY CONTROL. **Personal Data:** b Rochester, NY, January 12, 1925; m 1947, Suzanne Montgomery; c James, Janice & Judith. **Education:** Univ Rochester, AB, 1947; Univ NC, MA, 1949; Va Polytech Inst, PhD, 1960. **Honors & Awards:** Brumbaugh Award, Am Soc Qual Control, 1978. **Professional Experience:** PVT CONSULT, 1985-; statistician, Kodak Park, Eastman Kodak Co, 1959-1985; asst prof, Va Polytech Inst, 1958-1959; asst process engr, Hercules Powder Co, 1957-1958; Statistician, Eastman Kodak Co, 1948-1957. **Memberships:** Psychomet Soc; fel Am Soc Qual Control; fel Am Statist Asn. **Research Statement & Publications:** Development of statistical methods, particularly multivariate analysis; quality control. **Mailing Address:** 16 Kettering Dr, Rochester, NY 14612.

JACKSON, JAMES FREDRICK, NUCLEAR ANALYSIS, NUCLEAR REACTOR SAFETY. **Personal Data:** b August 15, 1939; m 1960, Joan; c James D, Bret A, Tracy L & Wendy L. **Education:** Univ Utah, BS, 1961; Mass Inst Technol, MS, 1962; Univ Calif, Los Angeles, PhD (eng), 1969. **Honors & Awards:** EO Lawrence Award, Dept Energy, 1983. **Professional Experience:** CONSULT, NAT ACAD ENGRS, 1991-; DEP DIR, LOS ALAMOS NAT LAB, 1986-; assoc dir eng sci, Los Alamos Nat Lab, 1984-1986; energy div leader, Los Alamos Nat Lab, 1980-1984; reactor safety group leader, Los Alamos Nat Lab, 1976-1980; assoc prof eng, Brigham Young Univ, 1974-1976; res engr, Argonne Nat Lab, 1969-1974; res engr, Atomics Int, 1962-1966. **Memberships:** Nat Acad Eng; Am Nuclear Soc. **Research Statement & Publications:** Developed and applied advanced computer codes for nuclear reactor safety analysis; performed analysis and evaluation of advanced nuclear reactor systems. **Mailing Address:** Los Alamos Nat Lab, MS A101, Los Alamos, NM 87545.

JACKSON, JAMES OLIVER, MEDICAL MICROBIOLOGY, IMMUNOLOGY & APPLIED MICROBIOLOGY. **Personal Data:** b New Iberia, La, July 16, 1939; m 1964, Geraldine; c Jamie R. **Education:** Univ Southwestern La, BS, 1966, MS, 1967; Univ Kans, PhD (microbiol), 1970. **Professional Experience:** Coordr microbiol sect, Biol Sci Dept, 1984-1992; PROF MICROBIOL, CALIF STATE POLYTECH UNIV, POMONA, 1980-; from asst prof to assoc prof, Calif State Polytech Univ, Pomona, 1972-1980; ad hoc consult, NIH, 1970-1995; asst prof microbiol, Southern Univ, 1970-1972. **Memberships:** Am Soc Microbiol; Sigma Xi. **Research Statement & Publications:** Metabolic changes in experimental Listeria monocytogenes infections; extracellular proteins produced by Listeria monocytogenes; pathogenic mechanisms of Chromobacterium violecium; microorganisms associated with sea mammals. **Mailing Address:** Dept Biol Sci, Calif State Polytech Univ, Pomona, CA 91768. **Fax:** 909-869-4078. **E-Mail:** jojackson@csupomona.edu

JACKSON, JASPER ANDREW, EXPERIMENTAL PHYSICS, NMR. **Personal Data:** b Washington, DC, January 26, 1923; m 1961, Betty; c Paul S. **Education:** Univ Okla, BS, 1948, MS, 1950, PhD (physics), 1955. **Professional Experience:** RETIRED; mem staff, Los Alamos Nat Lab, 1956-1986; sr nuclear engr, Convair Div, Gen Dynamics Corp, 1955; mem staff, Los Alamos Sci Lab, 1951-1952; asst, Univ Okla, 1949-1951. **Memberships:** Fel AAAS; Soc Prof Well Log Analysts; Soc Magnetics Resonance Med. **Research Statement & Publications:** Nuclear magnetic resonance; infrared and Raman spectroscopy; dynamic nuclear polarization; mass spectrometry; nuclear magnetic resonance well logging. **Mailing Address:** 1600 Conestoga Dr SE, Albuquerque, NM 87123. **E-Mail:** jajbsj@attbi.com

JACKSON, JEREMY BRADFORD COOK, MARINE ECOLOGY, PALEOBIOLOGY. **Personal Data:** b Louisville, Ky, November 13, 1942. **Education:** George Wash Univ, AB, 1965, MA, 1967; Yale Univ, MPhil, 1970, PhD (geol), 1971. **Professional Experience:** PROF OCEANOG & DIR GEOSCIENCES DIV, SCRIPPS INST OCEANOG, UNIV CALIF, SAN DIEGO, as of 2001; SCIENTIST & DIR, NAOS ISLAND LAB, SMITHSONIAN TROP RES INST, PANAMA, 1994-; Marine Biol Lab, Woods Hole, 1979-; from assoc prof to prof marine ecol, Johns Hopkins Univ, 1977-1985; res assoc, Smithsonian Inst, 1976-; vis prof, Discovery Bay Marine Lab, Univ West Indies, 1976 & 1978; mem biol oceanog panel, NSF, 1975 & 1976; prin investr, NSF grants, 1971-; asst prof, Johns Hopkins Univ, 1971-1977. **Memberships:** Am Soc Limnol & Oceanog; Brit Ecol Soc; Ecol Soc Am; Int Bryozoology Asn; Int Soc Reef Studies; Sigma Xi. **Research Statement & Publications:** Population biology and evolution of marine clonal invertebrates; adaptive significance of form in sessile organisms; competitive theory; over 100 books published. **Mailing Address:** Smithsonian Trop Res Inst, Naos Island Lab Unit 948, APO AA, AA 34002-0948.

JACKSON, JEROME ALAN, ORNITHOLOGY, ECOLOGY. **Personal Data:** b Ft Benning, Ga, February 4, 1943; m 1984, Bette; c Jerome A Jr, Paul C, Ann C, Peter M, S Brent & Matthew C. **Education:** Iowa State Univ, BS, 1965; Univ Kans, PhD (zoology), 1970. **Honors & Awards:** Recognition for Contributions to Bird Conserv, Prov Assembly Popular Power, Havana, Cuba, 1987. **Professional Experience:** PROF, COL ARTS & SCI, FLA GULF COAST UNIV, 1999-; PROG DIR & WHITAKER EMINENT SCHOLAR, WHITAKER CTR SCI, MATH & TECHNOL EDUC, FLA GULF COAST UNIV, 1999-; J Field Ornithol, 1980-1985 & N Am Bird Bander, 1981-1983; prof biol sci, Miss State Univ, 1979-1999; pres, Eco-Inventory Studies Inc, 1978-; regional ed, Am Birds, 1978-1990; Ed, Inland Bird Banding, 1978-1981; ed, Mississippi Kite, 1976-; leader endangered species recovery team, US Fish & Wildlife Serv, 1975-1982; Ed, Wilson Bull, 1974-1978; from asst prof to assoc prof, Miss State Univ, 1970-1979; biologist, Kans Biol Sur, 1968-1970; teaching Asst, Dept Zoology, 1966-1968; instr biol, W High Sch, Bakersfield, Calif, 1965-1966. **Memberships:** Fel Am Ornith Union; Wilson Ornith Soc (treas, 1973-1974, vpres, 1979-, pres, 1983-1985); Sigma Xi; fel AAAS; Am Soc Mammalogists; Herpetologists League; Asn Field Ornithologists; fel Explorer's Club. **Research Statement & Publications:** Population dynamics and adaptation in hole-nesting birds; biology and ecology of endangered species; behavior of rat snakes, Elaphe. **Mailing Address:** Col Arts & Sci, Fla Gulf Coast Univ, 10501 FGCU Blvd S, Ft Myers, FL 33965-6565.

JACKSON, JO-ANNE ALICE, PHYSICAL CHEMISTRY. **Personal Data:** b Washington, DC, July 30, 1951. **Education:** Am Univ, BS, 1973, PhD (phys chem), 1977. **Professional Experience:** SR VPRES & TREASURER, RUTGERS UNIV, as of 2001; PHYS SCI FOREIGN TECH ANALYST, BUR EXPORT ADMIN, US DEPT COM, Wash, DC, 1986-; specialist, chem & mat export licensing, Int Trade Admin, 1981-1986; chemist, Nat Bur Stand, 1974-1981; teaching asst gen, quant anal & phys chem, Lab Nursing Gen Chem, Am Univ, 1973-1975. **Memberships:** Am Chem Soc; Soc Appl Spectros; Fedn Orgs Prof Women. **Mailing Address:** State Univ NJ, 83 Somerset St, New Brunswick, NJ 08901-1281.

JACKSON, JOHN DAVID, THEORETICAL PHYSICS. **Personal Data:** b London, Ont, January 19, 1925; American citizen; m Barbara; c Ian, Nan, Maureen & Mark. **Education:** Univ Western Ont, BSc, Honors Physics & Math, 1946; Mass Inst Technol, PhD (physics), 1949. **Honorary Degrees:** DSc, Univ Western Ont, 1989. **Professional Experience:** PROF EMER PHYSICS, UNIV CALIF, BERKELEY, as of 2004; participating retiree, physics div, Lawrence Berkeley National lab, 1993-; mem, Prog Adv Comt, SSC Lab, 1990-1992; sr vis res fel, Jesus Col, Oxford, 1988-1989; dep dir, SSC Cent Design Group, 1985-1987; assoc dir & head physics div, Lawrence Berkeley Lab, 1982-1984; chmn, Vis Comt for Fermilab, Univs Res Asn, 1980-1982; chmn Physics dept, Univ Calif, Berkeley, 1978-1981; ed, Annual Rev Nuclear & Particle Sci, 1977-1993; sci assoc, Europ Orgn Nuclear Res, 1976-1977; group leader theoret physics, Berkeley Lab, Univ Calif, Berkeley, 1974-1978; mem vis comt, Dept Physics, Mass Inst Technol, 1973-1976; head, Theoret Sect, Fermi Nat Accelerator Lab, 1972-1973; consult, Stanford Linear Accelerator Ctr, 1971-1973 & Nat Accelerator Lab, 1971-1975; vis fel, Clare Hall, Cambridge Univ, 1970; assoc ed, Rev Modern Physics, 1968-1972; Prof physics, Univ Calif, Berkeley, 1967-1992; Ford Found fel, Europ Orgn Nuclear Res, 1963-1964; consult, Argonne Nat Lab, 1962-1965, 1975-1978; from assoc prof to prof physics, Univ Ill, 1957-1967; Guggenheim fel, Princeton Univ, 1956-1957; from asst prof to assoc prof math, McGill Univ, 1950-1956; Res assoc physics, Mass Inst Technol, 1949. **Memberships:** Nat Acad Sci; fel AAAS; Fel Am Phys Soc; Am Acad Arts & Sci. **Research Statement & Publications:** Theoretical physics of fundamental particles; Classical electrodynamics. **Mailing Address:** Dept Physics, Univ Calif, 366 LeConte, CA 94720-7300. **Fax:** 510-486-6808. **E-Mail:** jdjackson@lbl.gov

JACKSON, JOHN ELWIN, FLUID-STRUCTURE INTERACTION, ANALYSIS OF METAL FLOW DURING FORMING. **Personal Data:** b Tuscaloosa, Ala, October 11, 1948; m 1971, c 3. **Education:** Univ Ala, BS, 1971, MS, 1973, PhD (eng mech), 1977. **Professional Experience:** PROF, AEROSPACE ENG, UNIV ALA, TUSCALOOSA, as of 2004; DIR, AEROSPACE ENG, UNIV ALA, TUSCALOOSA, 1998-; Dir, Aerospace & Defense Div, Univ Ala Eng res lab, 1997-1998; prof & head, Dept Aerospace Eng & Mech, Univ Ala, Tuscaloosa, 1996-1998; Campus rep, Ala Space Grant Consortium, 1996-1998; prof, eng mech & mech eng, Univ Clemson, SC, 1990; Dean's Adv Coun, Col Eng, 1990-1998; prof & head, Dept Aerospace Eng, Univ Ala, Tuscaloosa, 1990-1996; coordr, Eng mech program, Univ Clemson, SC, 1989-1990; coordr, Eng mech prog, Univ Clemson, SC, 1986-1988; temp asst prof, eng sci & mech, Univ Tenn, 1978; from asst prof to assoc prof eng mech, Clemson Univ, 1978-1990; temp Instr, Eng mech, Univ Ala, 1976; Mech eng, Tenn Valley Authority, 1976-1978; from res asst eng to res assoc eng, Univ Ala, 1970-1975; consult, finite element anal. **Memberships:** Am Soc Mech Engrs; Am Acad Mech; Sigma Xi; Am Soc Metals. **Research Statement & Publications:** Fluid-structure interaction including fluids in reactor containment vessels and underwater explosions on structures; improved design for nuclear power plant cable-tray hangers; finite element analysis of railroad track-structures; finite element analysis of nonlinear systems; finite element analysis of metal forming process; Published over 6 articles. **Mailing Address:** Dept Aerospace & Defence Div, Univ Ala, PO Box 870200, 122 Bevill Bdlg, Rm 122, Tuscaloosa, AL 35405. **Fax:** 205-348-9455. **E-Mail:** johnjackson@coe.eng.ua.edu

JACKSON, JOHN ERIC, CHEMICAL ENGINEERING. **Personal Data:** b Cincinnati, Ohio, July 25, 1937; m 1960, c 1. **Education:** Purdue Univ, BS, 1958; Univ Mich, MSE, 1959. **Professional Experience:** RETIRED; dir technol, Union Carbide Coating Serv

Corp, 1968-1993; supvr, Speedway Labs, Union Carbide Corp, 1966-1968; group leader welding & lasers, Speedway Labs, Union Carbide Corp, 1963-1966; res engr, Speedway Labs, Union Carbide Corp, 1959-1963. **Memberships:** Am Inst Chem Engrs; Am Welding Soc. **Research Statement & Publications:** Directing development of high performance materials for aircraft, nuclear, petroleum and related energy industries; wear and corrosion prevention; thermal barriers; composites; fossil fuel production and utilization; oil and gas extraction. **Mailing Address:** 60 Carnaby Dr, Brownsburg, IN 46112.

JACKSON, JOHN FENWICK, INTERNAL MEDICINE, GENETICS. **Personal Data:** b Kosciusko, Miss, November 19, 1928; m 1954, c 3. **Education:** Univ Miss, BA, 1950; Tulane Univ, MD, 1953; Am Bd Internal Med, dipl, 1965; Am Bd Med Genetics, Clin Genetics, Clin Cytogenetics, dipl, 1982. **Professional Experience:** PROF EMER INTERNAL MED & PREV MED, SCH MED, UNIV MISS, 1992-; chmn, Univ Miss, 1981; prof internal med, Univ Miss, 1980; vis investr, Pop Genetics Lab, Univ Hawaii, 1970-1971; consult, Vet Admin Hosp, Jackson, 1964-; attend physician, Univ Miss Hosp, Jackson, 1964-; from asst prof to assoc prof internal med & from assoc prof to prof prev med, Univ Miss, 1964-1992; vis physician, Charity Hosp La, New Orleans, 1963-1964; trainee, Inst Med Genetics, Univ Uppsala, 1962-1963; from instr to asst prof internal med, Tulane Univ, 1961-1964; res fel cancer, Univ Miss, 1960-1961; chief resident physician, Med Ctr, Univ Miss, 1960; resident res physician internal med, Med Ctr, Univ Miss, 1958-1960; gen pract, Minter City, Miss, 1954-1956; Intern, Philadelphia Gen Hosp, 1953-1954. **Memberships:** Am Fedn Clin; Sigma Xi; Am Soc Hemat; Soc Human Genetics. **Research Statement & Publications:** Hematology; medical genetics; cytogenetic investigations in human disease; human linkage studies. **Mailing Address:** Sch Med, Univ Miss, 2500 N State St, Jackson, MS 39216-4505.

JACKSON, KENNETH ARTHUR, CRYSTAL GROWTH THIN FILMS & PHASE TRANSFORMATIONS, MICRO ELECTRONIC PACKAGING MATERIALS, SEMICONDUCTOR PROCESSING. **Personal Data:** b Connaught, Ont, October 23, 1930; American citizen; c Stacy (Pendell) & Meredith. **Education:** Univ Toronto, BS, 1952, MS, 1953; Harvard Univ, PhD (appl physics), 1956. **Honors & Awards:** Matthewson Gold Metal, Minerals, Metals & Mat Soc, Am Inst Mining, Metall & Petrol Engrs, 1966; Crystal Growth Award, Am Asn Crystal Growth, 1993; Frank Prize, Intl Organ for Crystal Growth, 1999. **Professional Experience:** PROF EMER MAT SCI & ENG, UNIV ARIZ, as of 2005; ed-in-chief, Journ Optical Materials, 1999-; prof mat sci & eng, Univ Ariz, beginning 1989; lectr & consult, Chinese Univ Develop Prog, Nat Acad Sci, 1985; consult, Panel Mat Processing in Space, NASA, 1974 & 1982; dept head, AT&T Bell Labs, 1967-1989; mem tech staff, AT&T Bell Labs, 1962-1966; asst prof appl physics, Harvard Univ, 1958-1962. **Memberships:** Mat Res Soc (vpres, 1976-1977, pres, 1978); Am Asn Crystal Growth (pres, 1970-1976); fel Metall Soc; fel Phys Soc; fel AAAS. **Research Statement & Publications:** Crystal growth phenomena, surface and interface structures, modelling of kinetic processes of phase transformations, interface instabilities, computer modelling of crystal growth and thin film deposition process, optical materials, integrated surface waveguide structures, microelectric packaging materials. **Mailing Address:** Univ Ariz, 4715 E Ft Lowell Rd, Tucson, AZ 85712. **E-Mail:** kaj1@email.arizona.edu

JACKSON, KENNETH LEE, PHYSIOLOGY. **Personal Data:** b Berkeley, Calif, January 6, 1926; m 1948, c 4. **Education:** Univ Calif, Berkeley, BA, 1949, PhD (physiol), 1954. **Professional Experience:** PROF EMER, ENVIRON HEALTH, UNIV WASH, 1991-; consult, DOE Pac Northwest Lab, 1985-1987; consult, Fred Hutchinson Cancer Res Ctr, 1980-; vis scientist, Inst Exp Geront, TNO, Rijswijk, Netherlands, 1977; head div, Univ Wash, 1976-1991; chmn, Radiol Sci Group, Univ Wash, beginning 1967; from asst prof to prof environ health, Univ Wash, 1963-1991; head radiobiol group, Bioastronaut Sect, Boeing Co, 1960-1963; sr investr, Biochem Br, US Naval Radiol Defense Lab, 1954-1960; res physiologist, Off Naval Res Unit One, 1951-1953; res asst physiol, Donner Lab, Univ Calif, Berkeley, 1949-1951. **Memberships:** AAAS; Am Physiol Soc; Radiation Res Soc; Health Physics Soc; Sigma Xi. **Research Statement & Publications:** Biochemical and physiological mechanisms in mammalian radiation biology; cell and intestinal physiology. **Mailing Address:** Dept Environ Health, Univ Wash, 201 Health Sci Bldg, Seattle, MS 98195-4400. **Fax:** 206-543-3351.

JACKSON, KENNETH RONALD, NUMERICAL ANALYSIS & SCIENTIFIC COMPUTING, ORDINARY DIFFERENTIAL EDUCATION & LINEAR ALGEBRA. **Personal Data:** b Montreal, Que, March 3, 1951; m 1983, Ivana; c G Frederick & Katherine Alexandra. **Education:** Univ Toronto, BS, 1973, MS, 1974, PhD (comput sci), 1978. **Professional Experience:** Assoc chair, Univ Toronto, 2002-2005; PROF COMPUT SCI, UNIV TORONTO, 1992-; chmn, Comt Human Rights, Soc Indust & Appl Math, 1985-1994; 1999-; from asst prof to assoc prof, Univ Toronto, 1981-1992; Gibbs instr comput sci, Yale Univ, 1978-1981. **Memberships:** Soc Indust & Appl Math; Can Appl Math Soc (SIAM); can Appl Math Soc (CAMS). **Research Statement & Publications:** Numerical analysis; mathematical software; scientific computing; numerical solution of ordinary differentialequations and numerical linear algebra; computational finance. **Mailing Address:** Comput Sci Dept, Univ Toronto, Toronto, ON M5S 3G4, Can. **Fax:** 416-978-1931. **E-Mail:** krj@cs.toronto.edu

JACKSON, KENNETH WILLIAM, ANALYTICAL ATOMIC SPECTROMETRY. **Personal Data:** b Shipley, Yorkshire, Eng, February 11, 1944; m 1971, Pauline; c Paul J. **Education:** Royal Soc Chem, UK, GRSC, 1968; Univ London, MSc & DIC, 1970, PhD (anal chem), 1972. **Professional Experience:** RES SCIENTIST, WADSWORTH CTR, NY STATE DEPT. HEALTH, ALBANY, 1987-; PROF ENVIRON & ANAL CHEM, STATE UNIV NY, ALBANY, 1987-; CHAIR, DEPT ENVIRON HEALTH & TOX., STATE UNIV NY, ALBANY, 1987-1990; prof, Univ Sask, 1984-1987; from lectr to sr lectr anal chem, Sheffield City Polytech, UK, 1977-1984; res scientist, State Univ NY, Albany, 1972-1977. **Memberships:** Fel Royal Soc Chem UK. **Research Statement & Publications:** Electrothermal atomic absorption spectrometry with emphasis on mechanisms of atomization from slurry samples; chemistry and physics of the action of modifiers. **Mailing Address:** Dept Environ Sci, Univ Albany; & NY State Dept Health, Wadsworth Center, PO Box 509, Albany, NY 12201-0509. **Fax:** 518-485-5568. **E-Mail:** jackson@wadsworth.org

JACKSON, KERN CHANDLER, GEOLOGY. **Personal Data:** b Kansas City, Mo, October 13, 1920; m 1970, c 4. **Education:** Mich Technol Univ, BS, 1947, MS, 1950; Univ Wis, PhD (geol), 1951. **Professional Experience:** PROF EMER GEOL, UNIV ARK, 1984-; chmn dept, Univ Ark, 1955-1959; from asst prof to prof geol, Univ Ark, 1952-1984; From instr to asst prof geol, Univ Maine, 1950-1952. **Memberships:** AAAS; Am Mineral Soc; Geol Soc Am. **Research Statement & Publications:** Petrology and petrography; petrography of Arkansas syenites and lamprophyres. **Mailing Address:** 235 Baxter Lane, Fayetteville, AR 72701.

JACKSON, LAIRD GRAY, MEDICAL GENETICS. **Personal Data:** b Seattle, Wash, October 10, 1930; m 1997, Marie; c 3. **Education:** Pomona Col, BA, 1951; Univ Cincinnati, MD, 1955. **Professional Experience:** PROF OB-GYN IN GENETICS, DREXEL UNIV COLL OF MED, 2001-; PROF MEDICINE, PEDIATRICS, OBSTET & GYNEC, JEFFERSON MED COL, 1978-2001; DIR DIV MED GENETICS, PEDIAT, OBSTET & GYNEC, JEFFERSON MED COL, 1969-2001; assoc prof, Jefferson Med Col, 1969-1978; Leukemia Soc scholar, 1965-; from asst prof to assoc prof med, Jefferson Med Col, 1964-1969; Nat Cancer Inst res grants, 1964-1966 & 1965-1968; Nat Found res grant, 1964-1966; Leukemia Soc fel, 1963-1965; instr med, Jefferson Med Col, 1962-1964; NIH fel, 1961-1962; Capt USAF, Sch Aviation Med, Gunter AFB, Ala, 1956-1969. **Memberships:** Am Soc Human Genetics; Am Col Med Genetics; Intnl Soc Prenatal Diagnosis. **Research Statement & Publications:** Efficacy and safety of prenatal diagnostic methods. **Mailing Address:** Dept OB-Gyn, Drexel Univ Coll Med, 245 N 15th St MS 495, Philadelphia, PA 19102-1192. **Fax:** 215-762-1689. **E-Mail:** ljackson@drexelmed.edu

JACKSON, LARRY LAVERN, VETERINARY ANESTHESIOLOGY. **Personal Data:** b Charlotte, Mich, June 2, 1942; m 1982, Valerie; c George, Scott & Micah. **Education:** Mich State Univ, BS, 1964, DVM, 1966; Iowa State Univ, MS, 1971. **Professional Experience:** PROF VET MED, IOWA STATE UNIV, 1971-; assoc prof, Iowa State Univ, beginning 1971; instr, Iowa State Univ, 1968-1971; vet, Miller Animal Clin, Lansing, Mich, 1966-1968. **Memberships:** Am Vet Med Asn; Am Soc Vet Anesthesiol. **Research Statement & Publications:** Cardio-pulmonary function of the equine and bovine species while under the influence of various anesthetic agents. **Mailing Address:** Col Vet Med, Iowa State Univ, 1825D, Ames, IA 50011-1250. **Fax:** 515-294-9281. **E-Mail:** ljackson@iastate.edu

JACKSON, LARRY LEE, BIOCHEMISTRY. **Personal Data:** b Livingston, Mont, October 8, 1940; m 1962, c 4. **Education:** Mont State Univ, BS, 1962; NDak State Univ, PhD (biochem), 1965. **Professional Experience:** PROF EMER CHEM & BIOCHEM, MONT STATE UNIV, as of 2004; prof chem, Mont State Univ, beginning 1975; from asst prof to assoc prof, Mont State Univ, 1965-1975. **Memberships:** Int Soc Chem Ecol. **Research Statement & Publications:** Lipid chemistry and biochemistry; surface lipids of insects and plants; hydrocarbon biosynthesis; microbial cell wall chemistry; insect pheromone biochemistry; insect sterols. **Mailing Address:** Dept Chem & Biochem, Mont State Univ, 310 Culbertson Hall, Bozeman, MT 59717-0001. **E-Mail:** ljackson@montana.edu

JACKSON, LELAND BROOKS, DIGITAL SIGNAL PROCESSING, DIGITAL FILTERS. **Personal Data:** b Atlanta, Ga, July 23, 1940; m 1968, Diana; c Anita N. **Education:** Mass Inst Technol, SB & SM, 1963; Stevens Inst Technol, ScD, 1970. **Honors & Awards:** Tech Achievement Award, Acoust Speech & Signal Processing Soc. **Professional Experience:** NSF, 1983-1988; PROF ELEC ENG, UNIV RI, 1979-; Off Naval Res, 1977; res grants, NSF & Air Force Off Sci Res, 1976; assoc prof, Univ RI, 1974-1979; vpres eng, Rockland Systs Corp, 1970-1974; mem tech staff digital filters, Bell Tel Labs, 1966-1970; res eng radar, Sylvania Electronic Systs, 1964-1966. **Memberships:** Fel Inst Elec & Electronics Engrs. **Research Statement & Publications:** Optimum synthesis of digital filter structures; estimation of signal parameters and its application to speech analysis instrumentation and bioengineering. **Mailing Address:** Dept Elec Eng, Univ RI, Kelley Hall Rm A121, Kingston, RI 02881. **E-Mail:** jackson@ele.uri.edu

JACKSON, LIONEL ERIC, QUATERNARY GEOLOGY, ENVIRONMENTAL GEOLOGY. **Personal Data:** b San Mateo, Calif, January 20, 1947; Canadian citizen; m 1969, Carol; c Lisa C. **Education:** San Francisco State Univ, AB, 1968; Stanford Univ, MS, 1973; Univ Calgary, PhD (geol), 1977. **Honors & Awards:** Serv Award, Can Asn Petrol Geologists; Thomas Roy Award, Can Geotech Soc. **Professional Experience:** RES SCIENTIST, TERRAIN SCI DIV, GEOL SURV CAN, as of 2005; dir Inst Quart Res, 1989, 1991-1993; adj prof, Simon Fraser Univ, beginning 1986; instr, Univ Calgary, 1981; consult, Calif Dept Transp, 1979; geologist, Geol Surv Can, beginning 1977; hydrologist, US Geol Surv, 1971-1973; geologist, Hudson Bay Oil & Gas Ltd, 1969-1970. **Memberships:** Fel Geol Asn Can; Am Quaternary Asn; Can Soc Petrol Geologists. **Research Statement & Publications:** Quaternary geology and paleo-ecology of western interior plains and Rocky Mountain Foothills; natural hazards in northern Montana regions; quaternary geology of Yukon Territory. **Mailing Address:** Geol Surv Can, 101 Robson St, Vancouver, BC V6B 5J3, Can. **Fax:** 604-666-1124.

JACKSON, LLOYD K, MATHEMATICS. **Personal Data:** b Fairbury, Nebr, August 25, 1922; m 1943, c 1. **Education:** Univ Nebr, AB, 1943, MA, 1948; Univ Calif, Los Angeles, PhD, 1950. **Professional Experience:** RETIRED; prof, Univ Nebr, ending 1984; asst prof, Univ Nebr, Lincoln, beginning 1950. **Memberships:** Am Math Soc; Math Asn Am; Sigma Xi. **Research Statement & Publications:** Partial differential equations; function theory. **Mailing Address:** 810 Oldfather Hall, PO Box 880323, Lincoln, NE 68588-0323.

JACKSON, MARION T, PLANT ECOLOGY. **Personal Data:** b Versailles, Ind, August 19, 1933; m 1985, Jaleh; c Arshia & Grousha. **Education:** Purdue Univ, BS, 1961, PhD (plant ecol), 1964. **Honors & Awards:** Oak Leaf Award, The Nature Conservancy; James Mason Environ Serv Award, Audubon Soc. **Professional Experience:** PROF LIFE SCI, IND STATE UNIV, TERRE HAUTE, as of 2006; pres, Wabash Valley Audubon Soc, 1996-1997; pres, Nature Conservancy, Ind Chap, 1976-1982; prof life sci, Ind State Univ, Terre Haute, beginning 1971; from asst prof to assoc prof, Ind State Univ, Terre Haute, 1964-1971. **Memberships:** AAAS; Sigma Xi; Ecol Soc Am; Natural Areas Asn. **Research Statement & Publications:** Forest ecology of Midwest; flowering phenology; biotic inventories of natural areas and national parks; ecological life histories; regional plant geography; long-term ecological research of old-growth forests. **Mailing Address:** Dept Life Sci, Ind State Univ, Terre Haute, IN 47809. **Fax:** 812-237-4480.

JACKSON, MARTIN A, MATHEMATICS. **Education:** Univ Puget Sound, BS, 1984; Univ Ore, MS, 1985, PhD (physics), 1990. **Professional Experience:** PROF, DEPT MATH & COMPUT SCI, UNIV PUGET SOUND, 2002-. **Mailing Address:** Dept Math, Univ Puget Sound, 1500 N Warner, Tacoma, WA 98416. **Fax:** 206-685-0380.

JACKSON, MARTIN PATRICK ARDEN, SEDIMENTARY TECTONICS, TECTONIC MODELING. **Personal Data:** b Salisbury, Rhodesia, May 14, 1947; British citizen; m 1969, Josephine; c Britt & Kirsty. **Education:** Univ London, BSc, 1968, BSc, 1969; Univ Cape Town, PhD (geol), 1976. **Honors & Awards:** Robert H Dott Sr, Mem Award, Am Asn Petrol Geol, 1998; George C Matson Award, Am Asn Petrol Geol, 1990; JC Sproule Mem Award, Am Asn Petrol Geol, 1985. **Professional Experience:** Vchmn, Strategeic Planning Coun, John A & Katherine G Jackson Sch Geosci, Univ Tex, Austin, 2005; mem, Implementation Comt, Jackson Sch Geosci, Univ Tex, Austin, 2004; mem, Steering Comt, John A & Katherine G Jackson Sch Geosci, Univ Tex, Austin, 2003; Session Chmn & Co-chmn, Am Asn Petrol Geol, 1997; Co-convenor, Hedberg Int Res Conf, 1993; guest ed, Marine Petrol Geol, 1992; distinguished lectr, Am Asn Petrol Geol, 1991-1992; assoc ed, Am Asn Petrol Geolog Bull, 1985-1990 & Geol Soc Am Bull, 1989-; DIR, APPL GEODYNAMICS LAB, 1988-; mem, Int Union Geol Sci Comn Tectonics, 1987-; SR RES SCIENTIST, BUR ECON GEOL, UNIV TEX, AUSTIN, 1987-; vis scientist, Univ Uppsala, Sweden, 1984; lectr, Am Asn Petrol Geol Sch Struct Geol, 1984-1985; res scientist, Bur econ geol, Univ Tex, 1981-1987; Prin investr, Dept Energy, Tex Bur Econ Geol, 1980-1984; res sci assoc, Bur econ geol, Univ Tex, 1980-1981; lectr, Geol Dept, Univ Natal, SAfrica, 1976-1979; res assoc, Precambrian Res Unit, Univ Cape Town, 1972-1976; Proj geol, Cominco, SAfrica, 1970-1972; external PhD exam, Univ Uppsala. **Memberships:** Fel Geol Soc Am; Am Asn Petrol Geol; Am Geophys union; Houston Geol Soc. **Research Statement & Publications:** Diapirism and halokinesis; geodynamic modeling; petroleum structural traps; syndepositional deformation; geology of central Iran; structural analysis of Precambrian genesises and greenstone belts; metamorphic petrology and geochemistry; crustal evolution of Southern Africa; tectonic evolution of sedimentary basins; Phanerozoic tectonics of West Africa; tectonics of Triton; strain analysis; published over 30 articles. **Mailing Address:** Bur Econ Geol, Univ Tex Austin Univ Station Box X, Austin, TX 78713-7508. **Fax:** 512-471-0140. **E-Mail:** jacksona@begv.beg.utexas.edu

JACKSON, MATTHEW PAUL, BACTERIAL PATHOGENESIS, MICROBIAL TOXINS. **Personal Data:** b Kansas City, Mo, July 17, 1959. **Education:** Univ Mo, BS, 1980, MS, 1982; Kans State Univ, PhD (microbiol), 1985. **Professional Experience:** ASSOC PROF IMMUNOL & MICROBIOL, SCH MED, WAYNE STATE UNIV, as of 2005; asst prof microbiol, Sch Med, Wayne State Univ, beginning 1989; fel microbiol, Uniformed Serv Univ Health Sci, 1985-1989. **Memberships:** Am Soc Microbiol; AAAS. **Research Statement & Publications:** Genetic regulation and structure-function analyses of bacterial toxins; pathogenic mechanisms of diarrheagenic Escherichia coli with emphasis on the Shiga toxin family of cytotoxins. **Mailing Address:** Dept Immunol & Microbiol, Med Sch Wayne State Univ, 540 E Canfield St, Detroit, MI 48201-1928. **E-Mail:** mpjacks@med.wayne.edu

JACKSON, MEL CLINTON, PROTEIN PURIFICATION, ENZYMOLOGY. **Personal Data:** b Rochdale, Eng, November 3, 1962; m 1987, c 2. **Education:** Univ Keele, Staffordshire, Eng, BSc, 1984, DPhil, 1988. **Professional Experience:** ASST RES, DEPT PHARMACOL, UNIV HAWAII, 1993-; res fel biochem, Univ Hawaii, 1988-1993. **Memberships:** Soc Neurosci; MRNA and DNA sequencing. **Research Statement & Publications:** Enzymology research on mammalian small intestinal peptidases and a human plasma dipeptidase; enzyme purification; structural and kinetic characterization; substrate specificity studies; immunology; immunohistochemical localization; molecular cloning; electron microscopy; neurobiology. **Mailing Address:** Dept Pharmacol John A Burns Sch Med, Univ Hawaii Leahi Hosp 3675 Kilauea Ave, Honolulu, HI 96816. **Fax:** 808-732-8468.

JACKSON, M(ELBOURNE) L(ESLIE), ENVIRONMENTAL ENGINEERING. **Personal Data:** b Wisdom, Mont, September 27, 1915; m 1944, c 4. **Education:** Mont State Col, BS, 1941; Univ Minn, PhD (chem eng), 1948. **Honorary Degrees:** Dr, Montana State Univ, 1980. **Professional Experience:** RES PROF & DEAN EMER, UNIV IDAHO, 1980-; dean eng, Univ Idaho, 1973, 1978-1980, 1983; res prof chem eng, Grad Sch, 1971-1980; dean, Grad Sch, 1965-1970; E L Phillips intern, univ admin, Pa State Univ, 1963-1964; consult, indust firms, beginning 1953; prof chem eng & head dept, Univ Idaho, 1953-1965; head process develop br, US Naval Ord Test Sta, Calif, 1950-1953; asst prof, Univ Colo, 1948-1950; instr chem eng, Mont State Col, 1942-1944 & Univ Minn, 1944-1948. **Memberships:** fel Am Inst Chem Engrs; Am Chem Soc. **Research Statement & Publications:** Bioreactors for fermentation and waste water treatment. **Mailing Address:** Dept Chem Eng, Univ Idaho, Moscow, ID 83843. **E-Mail:** mlj@uidaho.edu

JACKSON, MELVIN ROBERT, METALLURGY, MATERIALS SCIENCE. **Personal Data:** b Norwood, Pa, November 21, 1943; m 1968, c 1. **Education:** Lehigh Univ, BS, 1965, MS, 1967, PhD (metall & mat sci), 1971. **Professional Experience:** METALLURGIST, CORP RES & DEVELOP, GEN ELEC CO, 1972-; metallurgist, Paul D Merios Res Labs, Int Nickel, 1971-1972. **Memberships:** Am Inst Mining Metall & Petrol Engrs; Sigma Xi. **Research Statement & Publications:** Phase equilibria of high temperature metal and metal-ceramic systems, metallurgical coatings, tool materials. **Mailing Address:** Gen Elec Global Res Ctr, PO Box 8, Schenectady, NY 12301. **Fax:** 518-387-7495. **E-Mail:** jacksmr@crd.ge.com

JACKSON, MEYER B, Synaptic transmission, Neural circuit function. **Personal Data:** b Iowa City, Iowa, March 24, 1951; m 1979, c 2. **Education:** Brandeis Univ, BA, 1973; Yale Univ, PhD (molecular biophysics & biochemistry), 1977. **Professional Experience:** PROF PHYSIOL & NEUROSCIENCE, MED SCH, UNIV WIS, 1990-; assoc prof biol, Univ Calif, Los Angeles, 1987-1990; asst prof, Univ Calif, Los Angeles, 1981-1987; NIH fel, 1978-1981. **Memberships:** Biophys Soc; Soc Neuroscience. **Research Statement & Publications:** Biophysical studies of electrical signaling in the nervous system. **Mailing Address:** Dept Physiology, Univ Wis, 1300 Univ Ave, Madison, WI 53706-1532. **Fax:** 608-265-5512. **E-Mail:** mjackson@physiology.wisc.edu

JACKSON, MICHAEL J, EPITHELIAL PHYSIOLOGY, MEMBRANE TRANSPORT. **Personal Data:** b Walton, Eng, April 12, 1938; m 1960, Beryl. **Education:** Univ London, BSc, 1963; Univ Sheffield, PhD (physiol), 1966. **Professional Experience:** EXEC DIR, FEDN AM SOC EXP BIOL, 1990-1999; dean res, Med Ctr, 1989-1990; assoc dean Res & Sponsor Prog, Med Ctr, 1985-1989; assoc ed, Am J Physiol, Gastrointestinal & Liver Physics, 1979-1985; consult, Vet Admin Merit Rev Bd Basic Sci, 1978-1980; guest worker, Sect Gastroenterol, Nat Inst Arthritis, Metab & Digestive Dis, 1975-1976; USPHS Res Career Develop Award, 1972-1977; from asst prof to prof physiol, George Wash Univ, 1967-1990; from asst lectr to lectr, Univ Sheffield, 1965-1967; res asst physiol, Univ Sheffield, 1963-1965; asst exp officer biochem, Vet Lab, Ministry Agr, Eng, 1957-1963. **Memberships:** Brit Physiol Soc; Coun Eng Sci Soc Execs; Am Physiol Soc. **Mailing Address:** Fedn Am Soc Exp Biol, 9650 Rockville Pike, Bethesda, MD 20814-3998. **Fax:** 301-634-7001. **E-Mail:** mjackson@execofc.faseb.org

JACKSON, NOEL, PLANT PATHOLOGY. **Personal Data:** b Northallerton, Eng, December 25, 1931; m 1956, c 2. **Education:** Univ Durham, BSc, 1953, Hons, 1954, PhD, 1960. **Honors & Awards:** USGA Green Sect Award, 1999. **Professional Experience:** PROF EMER, DEPT PLANT SCI & ENTOM, UNIV RI, as of 2003; prof entom, Univ RI, beginning 1977; prof plant path, Univ RI, beginning 1975; from asst prof to assoc prof, Univ Ri, 1965-1975; biologist, Sports Turf Res Inst, Eng, 1958-1965. **Memberships:** Brit Asn Appl Biol; Am Phytopath Soc; Trans Brit Mycol Soc; Brit Soc Plant Path; Int Turfgrass Soc. **Research Statement & Publications:** Diseases of turf grasses and ornamentals. **Mailing Address:** Dept Plant Sci & Entom, Univ RI, 234 Woodward Hall, Kingston, RI 02881. **E-Mail:** noeljack@uri.edu

JACKSON, PETER E, MATHEMATICS. **Education:** Univ Aston, Birmingham, 1979; Univ Leeds, PhD (artifical intelligence), 1982. **Professional Experience:** CHIEF RES SCIENTIST & VPRES, THOMSON CORP, 2005-. **Mailing Address:** Thomson Corp, 200 First Stamford Pl Fourth Fl, Stamford, CT 06902. **Fax:** 203-328-8301.

JACKSON, PETER RICHARD, PARASITOLOGY. **Personal Data:** b New York, NY, December 9, 1948; m 1976. **Education:** Seton Hall Univ, BA, 1970; Univ Tex, Austin, MA, 1973; Rice Univ, PhD (biol), 1976. **Professional Experience:** CHIEF, AIDS CLINICAL & EPIDEMIOL RES REV BRANCH, NAT INST ALLERGY & INFECTIOUS DIS, NIH, as of 2003; sci rev off, Nat Inst Allergy & Infectious Dis, NIH, beginning 1990; res mgr, Am Inst Biol Sci, Wash, DC, 1987-1990; Nat Res Coun assoc immunol, Walter Reed Army Inst Res, 1978-1987; NIH assoc parasitol dept biol, Rice Univ, 1976 & dept zoology, Univ Mass, 1976-1978. **Memberships:** Am Soc Parasitologists; Soc Protozoologists; AAAS; Am Inst Biol Sci; Am Soc Zoologist; Sigma Xi. **Research Statement & Publications:** Immunology of parasitic infections; biochemistry and physiology of parasites, especially parasitic protozoa. **Mailing Address:** AIDS Clinical & Epidemiol Res Rev Branch, Nat Inst Allergy & Infectious Dis, NIH, Rm 3140, 6700-B Rockledge, MCS-7616, Bethesda, MD 20892-7616. **Fax:** 301-402-2638. **E-Mail:** pjackson@niaid.nih.gov

JACKSON, PRINCE A, PHYSICS, MATHEMATICS. **Personal Data:** b Savannah, Ga, March 17, 1925; m 1950, c 4. **Education:** Savannah State Col, BS, 1949; NY Univ, MS, 1950; Boston Col, PhD (sci, ed), 1966. **Professional Experience:** RETIRED; prof math & physics, Savannah State Col, 1971-1980; pres, Savannah State Col, 1971-1980; chmn div natural sci, Savannah State Col, 1969-1971; assoc prof phys sci, Savannah State Col, 1966-1969; asst prof math & physics, Savannah State Col, 1961-1964; instr physics, Savannah State Col, 1955-1961; instr high sch, Ga, 1950-1955. **Memberships:** AAAS; Nat Sci Teachers Asn; Nat Inst Sci. **Research Statement & Publications:** Improvement of science and mathematics education at all levels of instruction; differential equations of mathematical physics; pedagogical interrelationship between science and mathematics; philosophy of science. **Mailing Address:** Dept Math & Physics, Savannah State Col, PO Box 20345, Savannah, GA 31404.

JACKSON, RAY DEAN, SOIL PHYSICS. **Personal Data:** b Shoshone, Idaho, September 28, 1929; m 1968, c 7. **Education:** Utah State Univ, BS, 1956; Iowa State Univ, MS, 1957; Colo State Univ, PhD (soil sci), 1960. **Honors & Awards:** Superior Serv Unit Award, USDA, 1963. **Professional Experience:** RETIRED; Orgn Econ Coop & Develop Sci fel, Eng, 1964; physicist, US Water Conserv Lab, 1962-1992; soil scientist, US Water Conserv Lab, 1960-1962; soil scientist soil physics, Soil & Water Conserv Res Div, Agr Res Serv, USDA, 1957-1960; adj prof soil & water sci, Univ Ariz, Tuscon. **Memberships:** Fel AAAS; fel Soil Sci Soc Am; fel Am Soc Agron; Am Geophys Union. **Research Statement & Publications:** Heat, water and water vapor transfer in soils; remote sensing of soil water and crop stress; agricultural remote sensing. **Mailing Address:** 710 E La Jolla Dr, Tempe, AZ 85282-5355. **E-Mail:** raydjackson@att.net

JACKSON, RAY WELDON, PHYSICS, SCIENCE POLICY. **Personal Data:** b Toronto, Ont, November 11, 1921; m 1951, Ruth; c Suzanne, Martha, Kathren & Fraser. **Education:** Univ Toronto, BASc, 1944; McGill Univ, PhD (physics), 1950. **Professional Experience:** RETIRED; vis prof, Carleton Univ, 1978-1980 & McMaster Univ, 1964-1965; sci adv, Sci Coun Can, 1969-1986; sci adv to sci secretariat, Privy Coun Off, Ottawa, 1966-1969; assoc labs dir, RCA Victor Co, Ltd, 1956-1965; sr engr physics res, Sprague Elec Co, 1954-1956; asst, Yale Univ, 1952-1954; Am Coun Learned Soc fel, Yale Univ, 1951-1952; res asst physics, McGill Univ, 1950-1951. **Memberships:** Sr mem Inst Elec & Electronics Engrs; Can Asn Physicists. **Research Statement & Publications:** Semiconductor physics; electronic circuitry; nuclear detectors; philosophy of science and technology; appropriate technology for development. **Mailing Address:** 208 Clemow, Ottawa, ON K1S 2B4, Can.

JACKSON, RAYMOND CARL, CYTOGENETICS. **Personal Data:** b Medora, Ind, May 7, 1928; m 1947, June; c Jeffrey W & Rebecca J. **Education:** Ind Univ, AB, 1952, AM, 1953; Purdue Univ, PhD, 1955. **Honors & Awards:** Cert Merit for Res, Am Bot Soc. **Professional Experience:** HORN PROF EMER BIOL, TEX TECH UNIV, as of 2003; paul whitfield horn prof biol, Tex Tech Univ, 1990-1997; prof, Tex Tech Univ, 1971-1990; from asst prof to prof bot, Univ Kans, 1958-1971; from instr to asst prof biol, Univ NMex, 1955-1958; asst, Purdue Univ, 1953-1955. **Memberships:** AAAS; Bot Soc Am; Am Soc Plant Taxon; Genetics Soc Am; Genetics Soc Can. **Research Statement & Publications:** Evolutionary mechanisms in haplopappus and machaeranthera; cytogenetics of haplopappus gracilis; genetics and cytogenetics of diploid species of triticum; evolution and genetics of polyploids. **Mailing Address:** Dept Biol Sci, Tex Tech Univ, Lubbock, TX 79409. **Fax:** 806-742-2963.

JACKSON, RICHARD H F, PRECISION ENGINEERING & MECHANICAL METROLOGY, MATHEMATICS & ENGINEERING & CONSTRUCTION ENGINEERING. **Personal Data:** b January 29, 1947; American citizen; m 1981, c 2. **Education:** Johns Hopkins Univ, BA, 1969; Southern Methodist Univ, MS, 1970; George Wash Univ, DSc(opers res), 1983. **Honors & Awards:** Engineering News Records Top 25 Newsmakers for 2004. **Professional Experience:** DIR, FIATECH, as of 2000; Dir, Mfg Eng Lab, Nat Inst Standards & Technol, beginning 1995; Dept Dir, Mfg Eng lab, beginning 1989; prog mgr, Mfg Technol Ctr Prog, 1988-1989; prog analyst, Nat Eng Lab, 1986-1987 & Off Dir, 1987-1988; proj leader & sr mathematician, Ctr Appl Mat, Gaithersburg, 1978-1986; math consult, Boulder, Colo, 1975-1978; opers res analyst, Appl Math Div, Nat Bur Standards, Wash, DC, 1971-1975; Res asst, Computer Sci & Opers Res Ctr, Southern Methodist Univ, 1969-1970; Assoc prof, Opers Res Dept, George Wash Univ, Wash, DC; mem & chmn, numerous comts, Opers Res Soc Am, Math Prog Soc & Soc Indust & Appl Math. **Memberships:** Opers Res Soc Am; Math Prog Soc; Soc Indust & Appl Math. **Mailing Address:** FIATECH, 3925 W Braker Lane, R4500, Austin, TX 78759-5316. **Fax:** 512-232-9677. **E-Mail:** rjackson@fiatech.org

JACKSON, RICHARD J, PUBLIC HEALTH & EPIDEMIOLOGY. **Personal Data:** b Newark, NJ, October 23, 1945; m 1975, Joan; c Brendan, Galen & Devin. **Education:** Univ Calif, San Francisco, MD; Univ Calif, Berkeley, MPH. **Professional Experience:** DIR, NAT CTR ENVIRON HEALTH, as of 2005; Sr Adv CDC Dir; mem, Comt Environ Hazards, Nat Acad Sci; chmn, Comt Environ Hazards, Am Acad Pediat. **Research Statement & Publications:** Acute and chronic health effects of environmental and infectious exposures. **Mailing Address:** Ctr Dis Control & Prev, 1600 Clifton Rd NE Mailstop D14, Atlanta, GA 30333. **Fax:** 404-639-7111. **E-Mail:** rxj4@cdc.gov

JACKSON, RICHARD LEE, BIOCHEMISTRY, PROTEIN CHEMISTRY. **Personal Data:** b Springfield, Ill, December 30, 1939. **Education:** Univ Ill, BS, 1963, PhD (microbiol), 1967. **Professional Experience:** PRES, RICHARD JACKSON ASSOCS, LLC, as of 2003; DIR, BIOMIRA INC, 2003-; vpres discovery res, Wyeth-Ayerst Res, Princeton, Nj, beginning 1993; vpres res sci, biochem sci, 1992; managing dir res sci & actg dir metab & inflammatory dis, biochem sci, 1990-1991; dir res sci & actg dir cell biol, biochem sci, 1990; assoc ed, J Lipid Res, 1988-1992; dir, biochem sci, 1986-1990; dir macromolecular biochem, Merrell Dow Res Inst, Cincinnati, Ohio, 1985-1990; Rockefeller Univ, NY, 1985; nat Cardiovasc Ctr Res Inst, Japan, 1984; prof pharmacol & cell biophys, head Div Lipoprotein Res, 1980-1986; chiba Univ, Japan, 1980 & 1982; vis prof, Biochem Lab, State Univ, Utrecht Neth, 1978, 1980-1981, 1983-1986; prof pharmacol & cell biophys, Univ Cincinnati Col Med, 1977-1992; vis prof, Hadassah Univ Hosp, Jerusalem, Israel, 1974; assoc prof exp med & cell biol, Baylor Col Med, 1973-1977; estab investr, Am Heart Asn, 1972-1977; asst prof exp med, Baylor Col Med, 1971-1973; nat Inst Arthritis & Metab Dis sr staff fel, 1970-1971; nat Heart & Lung Inst jr staff fel, 1969-1970; res assoc protein chem, Biol Dept, Brookhaven Nat Lab, 1967-1969; mem, Coun Arteriosclerosis. **Memberships:** AAAS; Am Soc Biochem & Molecular Biol; Am Fedn Clin Res; Am Heart Asn; Am Soc

Pharmacol & Exp Therapeut. **Research Statement & Publications:** Structure and metabolism of plasma lipoproteins and apolipoproteins; protein-glycosaminoglycan-lipid interaction; structure, mechamism of action and regulation of expression of lipoprotein lipase and hepatic triglyceride lipase; diet, high density lipoproteins and lipid metabolism; cellular mechanisms of atherosclerosis, ischemic heart disease and diabetes; oxygen radicals and disease; regulation of IL-1 expression; drugs affecting lipid metabolism, ischemic heart disease and diabetes. **Mailing Address:** Biomira Inc, 2011-94 St, Edmonton, AB T6N 1H1, Can. **Fax:** 780-450-4772.

JACKSON, RICHARD THOMAS, PHYSIOLOGY. **Personal Data:** b Detroit, Mich, January 19, 1930; m 1955, c 2. **Education:** Univ Detroit, BS, 1952, MS, 1954; Fla State Univ, PhD (physiol), 1960. **Honors & Awards:** Hon Award, Am Acad Otolaryngol. **Professional Experience:** RETIRED; consult, Va Med Ctr, equilibrium tests, beginning 1988; vis prof, Kagoshima Sch Med, Japan, 1985; consult, Yerkes Regional Primate Ctr, 1982-; PROF SURG, EMORY UNIV, 1976-; assoc prof, Emory Univ, 1971-1976; dir, Otolaryngol Lab, beginning 1967; instr ophthal & physiol, Emory Univ, 1963-1971; res assoc, Lab Ophthal Res, 1963-1967; from asst prof to assoc prof, Loyola Univ, La, 1959-1963; instr, Fla State Univ, 1957-1959; asst physiol, Fla State Univ, 1954-1957; consult, Comt Drugs, Am Acad Otolaryngol. **Memberships:** Asn Res Otolaryngol; Am Acad Otolaryngol. **Research Statement & Publications:** Nasal and eustachian tube physiology; control of blood flow to the nose and ear; clinical and animal testing of drugs that effect blood flow; equilibrium testing, antivertigo drugs. **Mailing Address:** Dept Surg 441 WMB, Emory Univ 1440 Clifton Rd NE, Atlanta, GA 30307-1053.

JACKSON, RICHARD W, AMINO ACIDS, PROTEINS. **Education:** Univ Ill, PhD (biochem), 1925. **Professional Experience:** RETIRED; chief fermentation div, US Dept Agr, Northern Regional Res Lab, 1947-1966. **Mailing Address:** 1319 N Inst Pl, Peoria, IL 61606-1024.

JACKSON, ROBERT W, MICROBIOLOGY, IMMUNOLOGY. **Education:** Purdue Univ, PhD (immunol), 1963. **Professional Experience:** PROF EMER, SOUTHERN ILL UNIV, as of 2005; exec assoc dean, Sch Med, Southern Ill Univ, beginning 1974. **Mailing Address:** Microbiol & Immunol Dept, Southern Ill Univ Med, PO Box 19230, Springfield, IL 62794-9230.

JACKSON, RONALD SPENCER, VITICULTURE, ENOLOGY. **Personal Data:** b Oshawa, Ontario, December 15, 1940; m 1975, Suzanne. **Education:** Queens Univ, BSc, 1964, MSc, 1967; Univ Toronto, PhD (plant path), 1970. **Professional Experience:** ADJ PROF COOL CLIMATE OENOLOGY AND VITICULTURE INST, BROCK UNIV, as of 1998; vis prof, Cornell Univ, 1979-1980; PROF BOT & MICROBIOL, BRANDON UNIV, 1972-1998; postdoctorate, Queen's Univ, 1970-1972; Teacher, RH King High Sch, 1964-1965. **Memberships:** Am Soc Enol & Viticult; Aust. Soc. Enol & Viticult; SA Soc. Enol and Viticult. **Research Statement & Publications:** Author of university texts "Wine Science" and "Wine Tasting" covering the theory and practice of commercial grape growing, wine production, wine sensory evaluation. **Mailing Address:** Cool Climate Oenology & Viticulture Inst, Brock Univ, 500 Glenridge Ave, St Catharines, ON L2S 3A1, Can. **Fax:** 418-736-5576. **E-Mail:** r.s.jackson@globetrotter.net

JACKSON, ROSCOE GEORGE, II, SEDIMENTOLOGY, FLUID DYNAMICS. **Personal Data:** b Eureka, Kans, May 14, 1948. **Education:** Univ Kans, BS, 1970; Univ Ill, Urbana-Champaign, MS, 1973, PhD (geol), 1975. **Professional Experience:** GEOLOGIST & PROJ COORDR, JACKSON BROS CO, 1981-; mem fac, Dept Geol Sci, Univ Mich, Ann Arbor, 1980-1981; asst prof geol, Northwestern Univ, Evanston, 1975-1980; Instr, Northwestern Univ, Evanston, 1974-1975. **Memberships:** Geol Soc Am; Int Asn Sedimentologists; Soc Econ Paleontologists & Mineralogists. **Research Statement & Publications:** Ancient and modern alluvial sediments; mathematical models and mechanics of bedforms, sediment transport and fluid flow in modern sedimentary environments; flow structures of geophysical turbulent boundary layers; petroleum geology. **Mailing Address:** 603 N Elm St, Eureka, KS 67045.

JACKSON, ROY, TWO-PHASE FLOW. **Personal Data:** b Manchester, Eng, October 6, 1931; m 1957, Susan Birch; c Fiona & Andrew. **Education:** Cambridge Univ, BA, 1954, MA, 1958; Univ Edinburgh, DSc(chem eng), 1968. **Honors & Awards:** Alpha Chi Sigma Award, Am Inst Chem Engr, 1980, Thomas Baron Award, 1993. **Professional Experience:** PROF EMER CHEM ENG, PRINCETON UNIV, as of 2003; prof chem eng, Princeton Univ, begining 1982; prof, Univ Houston, 1977-1982; consult, Shell Oil Co, beginning 1969; prof, Rice Univ, 1968-1977; reader, Univ Edinburgh, 1964-1968; lectr chem eng, Univ Edinburgh, 1961-1964; tech officer, Imp Chem Industs Ltd, 1955-1961; assoc ed, J Fluid Mech. **Memberships:** Am Inst Chem Engrs. **Research Statement & Publications:** Chemical reaction engineering; fluid-particle systems; granular materials. **Mailing Address:** Dept Chem Eng, Princeton Univ, Princeton, NJ 08544. **Fax:** 609-258-0211. **E-Mail:** rjackson@princeton.edu

JACKSON, ROY JOSEPH, PHOTOCHEMISTRY. **Personal Data:** b Cotton Port, La, February 8, 1944. **Education:** Southern Univ, Baton Rouge, BS, 1965, MS, 1969; Univ Calif, San Diego, PhD (chem), 1975. **Professional Experience:** RES CHEMIST, SHELL DEVELOP CO, 1975-; instr chem, Southern Univ, Baton Rouge, 1969-1970. **Memberships:** Am Chem Soc. **Research Statement & Publications:** Norish type II photoelimination, photocyclization reactions, especially new aryl-alkyl systems; photocure of resins; development of new photocure systems. **Mailing Address:** 12707 Havant Circle, Houston, TX 77077.

JACKSON, SHARON WESLEY, GENETICS, ENVIRONMENTAL SCIENCES. **Personal Data:** b Topeka, Kans, June 15, 1936; m 1957, c 3. **Education:** Kans Wesleyan Univ, BA, 1958; Univ Kans, MA, 1960; NC State Univ, PhD (genetics), 1967. **Professional Experience:** PRES, LAND INST, 1989-; co-dir, Land Inst, 1976-1989; dir, Environ Studies Ctr, 1974-1976; prof environ studies & chmn dept, Sacramento State Col, 1971; from asst prof to assoc prof, Kans Wesleyan Univ, 1967-1971; instr biol, Kans Wesleyan Univ, 1962-1964; teacher High Sch, Kans, 1960-1962. **Memberships:** AAAS; Int Asn Plant Taxon; Sigma Xi. **Research Statement & Publications:** Development of perennial grain crops. **Mailing Address:** Land Inst, 2440 E Waterwell Rd, Salina, KS 67401. **Fax:** 913-823-8728.

JACKSON, SHIRLEY ANN, THEORETICAL SOLID STATE PHYSICS. **Personal Data:** b Washington, DC, August 5, 1946; m Morris; c Alan. **Education:** Mass Inst Technol, SB, 1968, PhD (physics), 1973. **Honors & Awards:** NJ Governor's Award in Sci. **Professional Experience:** PRES, RENSSELAER POLYTECH INST, as of 1999; CHMN, NUCLEAR REGULATORY COMN, beginning 1995; prof physics, Rutgers Univ, 1991-1995; mem, Comt Educ & Employ Women Sci & Eng, Nat Acad Sci, 1981-1982; Lincoln Univ, 1980-; Lincoln Univ, 1980-; mem tech staff, Bell Tel Labs, 1976-1991; mem bd trustees, MIT Corp, 1975-1985; res assoc theoret physics, Fermi Nat Accelerator Lab, 1975-1976; vis sci assoc, Europ Orgn Nuclear Res, 1974-1975; grant, Ford Found, 1974-1975; res assoc theoret physics, Fermi Nat Accelerator Lab, 1973-1974; fel, Martin Marietta Corp, 1972-1973; adv study fel, Ford Found, 1971-1973. **Memberships:** Am Phys Soc; AAAS; NY Acad Sci; Sigma Xi; Nat Inst Sci; fel Am Acad Arts & Sci. **Research Statement & Publications:** Landau theories of charge density waves in one and two dimensions; transport properties of random systems; correlation effects in electron-hole plasmas; channeling in metals and semiconductors. theory; two dimensional yang-mills gauge theories; neutrino reactions. **Mailing Address:** Rensselaer Polytechnic Inst, 110 8th St, Troy, NY 12180.

JACKSON, STEPHEN THOMAS, PLANT ECOLOGY, PALEOECOLOGY. **Personal Data:** b East St Louis, Ill, May 28, 1955; m 1987, Anne. **Education:** Southern Ill Univ, Carbondale, BA, 1977, MS, 1978; Ind Univ, Bloomington, PhD (ecol & evolutionary biol), 1983. **Professional Experience:** Chair, Paleoecol Sect, Ecol Soc Am, 1992-1993; asst prof biol, northern ariz univ, 1990-1995; res assoc geol sci, Brown Univ, 1988-1990; NSF fel environ biol, Brown Univ, 1986-1988; vis asst prof biol, Ind Univ, 1983-1984 & Idaho State Univ, 1984-1985. **Memberships:** Ecol Soc Am; Am Quaternary Asn; AAAS; Soc Wetland Scientists; Sigma Xi. **Research Statement & Publications:** Vegetation-sensing properties of paleoecological data (pollen and plant macrofossils), and applying paleoecological data toward understanding ecological and climatic dynamics. **Mailing Address:** Dept Bot, Univ Wyo, Aven Nelson B3, Laramine, WY 82071. **E-Mail:** jackson@uwyo.edu

JACKSON, THOMAS A J, ENVIRONMENTAL SAMPLE CONTROL. **Personal Data:** b Sumter, SC, December 26, 1942. **Education:** Seton Hall Univ, BS, 1972; Fairleigh Dickinson Univ, MS, 1977. **Professional Experience:** SR RES SCIENTIST, NJ DEPT ENVIRON PROTECTION, 1984-; mgr anal chem, Boyle Midway Inc, 1979-1984; chemist, Sherwin Williams Co, 1973-1975; chemist, Ethican Inc, 1975-1979. **Memberships:** Fel Am Inst Chemists; Am Chem Soc. **Research Statement & Publications:** Gel chromatography and high performance liquid chromatography methods development for environmental samples; environmental sample clean up and computer applications in gel chromatography and high performance liquid chromatography. **Mailing Address:** 11 Anita Dr, Piscataway, NJ 08854-2430.

JACKSON, THOMAS EDWIN, MEDICINAL CHEMISTRY, PATENT LAW. **Personal Data:** b Amarillo, Tex, May 7, 1944; m 1969. **Education:** Rice Univ, BA, 1966; Mass Inst Technol, PhD (org chem), 1971; Widener Law Sch, JD, 1990. **Professional Experience:** PATENT, AGENT & ATTY, ELI LILLY & CO, as of 2001; PATENT LIAISON, AGENT & ATTY, ICI AMERICAS/ZENECA INC, 1985-; res chemist med chem, Biomed Res, ICI-Americas Inc, 1975-1985; sr scientist med chem, Sandoz Inc, 1973-1975; fel org chem, Univ SC, 1971-1973. **Memberships:** Am Chem Soc; Sigma Xi. **Research Statement & Publications:** Biochemical consideration in drug design; selectivity in organic synthesis; heterocyclic chemistry. **Mailing Address:** Eli Lilly & Co, Lilly Corp Ctr, Indianapolis, IN 46285. **Fax:** 317-277-1917.

JACKSON, THOMAS GERALD, ORGANIC CHEMISTRY. **Personal Data:** b Mt Sterling, Ala, December 26, 1936; m 1967. **Education:** Univ Southern Miss, BS, 1959, MS, 1961; Univ Tenn, Knoxville, PhD (org chem), 1965. **Professional Experience:** Consult, Res Prod Inc, Ala, beginning 1971; PROF CHEM, UNIV S ALA, 1965-; asst org chem, Univ Southern Miss, 1959-1961. **Memberships:** Am Chem Soc; Sigma Xi; Royal Soc Chem; Nat Asn Prev Health Prog Advisors. **Research Statement & Publications:** Synthesis of organic compounds ofpotential medicinal interest; metalation studies of nitrogen containing heterocycles; investigations of compounds containing the nitrogen-silicon bond. **Mailing Address:** Dept Chem, Univ S Ala, Rm 223, Mobile, AL 36688.

JACKSON, TOGWELL ALEXANDER, BIOGEOCHEMISTRY OF AQUATIC ENVIRONMENTS, LIMNOLOGY. **Personal Data:** b New York, NY, November 1, 1939; Canadian & American citizen; m 1967, Chung; c Bertrand & Alexander. **Education:** Columbia Univ, BA, 1961; Univ Wis-Madison, MSc, 1963; Univ Mo, Columbia, PhD (geol), 1969. **Professional Experience:** RES SCIENTIST, NAT WATER RES INST, as of 2003; Nat Water Res Inst, beginning 1990; Nat Hydrol Res Inst, 1986-1990; external examiner, PhD student, Univ Sask, 1984; conducted grad-level reading course, Univ Man, 1981-1982; adj prof soil sci, Univ Man, 1977-1980; res scientist biogeochem, Freshwater Inst, Winnipeg, 1972-1986; res assoc org geochem, Univ Calif, Santa Barbara, Dept Geol Sci, 1970-1972; res assoc soil microbiol, Yale Univ Sch Forestry, 1969-1970; fel org geochem, Woods Hole Oceanog Inst, Dept Chem, NSF, 1968-1969; A P Green fel clay mineral, Univ Mo, 1966-1968. **Memberships:** Sigma Xi; Rawson Acad Aquatic Sci. **Research Statement & Publications:** Humic matter in recent lakes and streams, and its ecological role; paleobiological significance of organic matter in ancient, especially pre-Cambrian, sediments; biogeochemistry of various toxic heavy metals, especially mercury, including methyl mercury in freshwater environments; forms speciation and bio-availability of metals; biochemical weathering of rocks; clay-organic interactions; freshwater environments polluted with various heavy metas from mines and smelters or with mercury; microbial ecology and biogeochemistry in sediments; biogeochemistry and related aspects of ecology; microbial transformations of metals; microbial ecology, effects of metal species, clay humic matter. **Mailing Address:** Dept Environ, Nat Water Res Inst, PO Box 5050, Burlington, ON L7R 4A6, Can. **Fax:** 905-336-6430. **E-Mail:** t.a.jackson@cciw.ca

JACKSON, WARREN, ELECTRICAL ENGINEERING. **Personal Data:** b Oak Park, Ill, May 8, 1922; m 1947, Sarah; c John B & Peter G. **Education:** Purdue Univ, BS, 1947; Case Inst Technol, MS, 1954. **Professional Experience:** RETIRED; sr res specialist, Alaska Iceberg Studies, res lab, 1982-1985; sr process control specialist, res & develop lab, 1974-1982; instrumentation supvr, res & develop, 1970-1974; sr proj leader, Mgt Sci Unit, 1961-1970; sr tech specialist, Process Eng Div, 1954-1961; elec engr, Chem & Physics Res Div, Standard Oil Co, Ohio, 1947-1954; radio engr, Purdue Univ, 1946-1947; radio engr, Police Dept, River Forest, Ill, 1941-1942. **Memberships:** Inst Elec & Electronics Engrs; hon memSoc Comput Simulation. **Research Statement & Publications:** On line digital computer process control; electronic instrumentation for petroleum research; electronic computers; analog computer simulation of physical and business systems; iceberg drift in Alaskan waters. **Mailing Address:** 4871 Westbourne Rd, Cleveland, OH 44124-2361.

JACKSON, WILLIAM ADDISON, PLANT NUTRITION, SOIL FERTILITY. **Personal Data:** b Castile, NY, April 24, 1926; m 1964, Barbara. **Education:** Cornell Univ, BS, 1950; Purdue Univ, MS, 1952; NC State Univ, PhD (soil sci), 1957. **Honors & Awards:** Co-recipient, Campbell Award, Am Inst Biol Sci, 1964. **Professional Experience:** EMER PROF SOIL SCI, NC STATE UNIV, 1993-; alumni distinguished grad prof, NC State Univ, 1984-1993; William Neal Reynolds prof soil sci, NC State Univ, 1972-1993; vis prof, Univ Ill, Urbana, 1970-1971; Mem comt post-doctoral fel eval, Div Biol & Agr, Nat Acad Sci-Nat Res Coun, 1965-1968; from asst prof to prof, NC State Univ, 1958-1972; Ford Found fel plant nutrit, Univ Mich, 1957-1958; Res instr soil sci, NC State Univ, 1952-1957. **Memberships:** Soil Sci Soc Am; Crop Sci Soc Am; Am Soc Agron; Am Soc Plant Pathologists; Japan Soc Soil Sci & Plant Nutrit; fel Australian Inst Biol Sci; fel Royal Irish Acad. **Research Statement &**

Publications: Absorption, assimilation and distribution of nitrogen by higher plants; effects of nitrogen assimilation on photosynthesis, respiration and mineral accumulation. **Mailing Address:** 3611 Swann Dr, Raleigh, NC 27612.

JACKSON, WILLIAM BRUCE, ANIMAL ECOLOGY. **Personal Data:** b Milwaukee, Wis, September 10, 1926; m 1952, Shirley; c Beth, Mark & Craig. **Education:** Univ Wis, BA, 1948, MA, 1949; Johns Hopkins Univ, ScD(hyg & vert ecol), 1952. **Honors & Awards:** Envioron Qual Award, US Environ Protection Agency, Region V, 1975. **Professional Experience:** Consult, 1985-; pres, Bio Cenotics Inc, 1985-; EMER PROF, BOWLING GREEN STATE UNIV, 1985-; distinguished univ prof, Environ Studies Ctr, 1981-1984; dir, Ctr Environ Res & Serv, 1980-1984; consult, WHO & Food & Agr Orgn, UN, 1969-; Ford Found, 1975; adj prof, community med, Med Col Ohio, Toledo, 1974-1980; consult ed, J Environ Educ, 1973-1977; chmn, Exec Comt, Ohio Biol Surv, 1970-1984; dir, Environ Studies Ctr, 1970-1980; asst dean grad sch, Col Lib Arts, 1969-1970; Collabr, US Fish & Wildlife Serv & Nat Pest Control Asn, 1964-; prof biol, Environ Studies Ctr, 1964-1981; asst dean, Col Lib Arts, 1964-1969; asst prof, Bowling Green State Univ, 1957-1964; biologist, Pac Sci Bd, 1955-1957; sr asst scientist ecol, USPHS, 1952-1955; res assoc animal behv, Am Mus Natural Hist, 1952; asst vert ecol, Johns Hopkins Univ, 1949-1952; Asst zool, Univ Wis, 1947-1949; chmn, subcomt E 35.17 vert pesticides, Am Soc Testing & Mgt. **Memberships:** Fel AAAS; Animal Behav Soc; Am Inst Biol Sci; Am Ornithologists' Union; Ecol Soc Am; Sigma Xi; Am Soc Mammal. **Research Statement & Publications:** Effects of insecticides on vertebrate populations; microclimatic factors in army ant behavior; ecology of small mammals and of arthropod disease vectors; economic and environmental biology; rodent and bird control methods; studies of anticoagulant resistance; environmental assessment. **Mailing Address:** Dept Biol Sci, Bowling Green State Univ, Bowling Green, OH 43403-0001. **Fax:** 419-372-2024. **E-Mail:** wbjackson@msn.com

JACKSON, WILLIAM DAVID, ELECTRICAL POWER SYSTEMS, MAGNETOHYDRODYNAMICS. **Personal Data:** b Edinburgh, Scotland, May 20, 1927; div, c 2. **Education:** Glasgow Univ, BSc, 1947, PhD (elec eng), 1960. **Honors & Awards:** Energy Res & Develop Admin Spec Achievement Award, 1976; SERI Award, 1978. **Professional Experience:** GEN CHMN, HMJ CORP, as of 2005; VPRES, CLEAN ENERGY COMBUSTION SYSTEMS INC, as of 2003; adj prof, George Wash Univ, 1992-; prog chmn, Intersoc Energy Conversion Eng Conf, 1989-; chmn & pres, Energy Develop Sub Comt, Inst Elec & Electronic Engrs, 1988-; prof, George Wash Univ, 1987-1992; pres, Power Generation Comt, 1986-; vis prof, George Wash Univ, 1986-1987; secy, Int Liaison Group Magnetohydrodynamics, 1984-; PRES, HMJ CORP, 1982-; mem, Energy Resources Operating Bd, Am Soc Mech Engrs, 1981-1983; prof lectr, George Wash Univ, 1979-1986; pres, Energy Consult Inc, 1979-1984; dir, Div Tech Anal & Spec Projs, Dept Energy, Wash, DC, 1977-1979; dir, Magnetohydrodynamics Div, 1975-1977 mgr, Magnethydrodynamics Prog, Off Coal Res & Energy Res & Develop Admin, Wash, DC, 1974-1975; chmn, Steering Comt, US-USSR Coop Prog Magnetohydrodynamics Power Generation, 1973-1979; mgr, Thermal-Mech Energy Conversion & Storage, Elec Power Res Inst, Palo Alto, 1973-1974; mem, Task Force Tech Aspects, Comt Conserv Energy, Nat Power Surv, Fed Power Comn, 1973; pres, Energy Develop Sub Comt, Inst Elec & Electronic Engrs, 1972-; prof elec eng, Univ Tenn Space Inst, 1972-1973; secy, US Steering Comt Eng Aspects Magnetohydrodynamics, 1971-; mem, US-Ger Natural Resources Panel Magnetohydrodynamics Power, 1970-1972; chmn, US Steering Comt Eng Aspects Magnetohydrodynamics, 1969-1970; chmn, Int Liaison Group Magnetohydrodynamics, 1968-1973; lectr, Mass Inst Technol, 1968-1972; prog chmn, US Steering Comt Eng Aspects Magnetohydrodynamics, 1968-1969; mem, US Steering Comt Eng Aspects Magnetohydrodynamics, 1967-; prin res scientist, Avco-Everett Res Lab, 1967-1972; mem, Int Liaison Group Magnetohydrodynamics, 1966-; prof, Univ Ill, Chicago Circle, 1966-1967; vis prof, Tech Univ Berlin, 1966; consult, Var Industs & Labs, UK, 1960-; from asst prof to assoc prof, Mass Inst Technol, 1958-1966; vis lectr, Mass Inst Technol, 1955-1957; fulbright travel scholar, UK, 1955-1957; lectr, Col Sci & Technol, Univ Manchester Inst Sci & Technol, 1954-1958; asst lectr elec eng, Col Sci & Technol, Univ Manchester Inst Sci & Technol, 1951-1954; asst, Royal Col Sci & Technol, Glasgow Univ, 1947-1951. **Memberships:** Fel Inst Elec & Electronics Engrs; Am Phys Soc; assoc fel Am Inst Aeronaut & Astronaut; fel Brit Inst Elec Engrs; fel Am Soc Mech Engrs. **Research Statement & Publications:** Electrical power systems; magnetohydrodynamic power generation; analysis of energy systems, especially electrical aspects; development of technology base and engineering design data for first of a kind technologies; engineering of magnetohydrodynamic power systems; power electronics. **Mailing Address:** HMJ Corp, 10400 Connecticut Ave Suite 404 PO Box 470, Kensington, MD 20895-0470. **Fax:** 301-946-4374. **E-Mail:** wdjacksonhmjcorp@aol.com

JACKSON, WILLIAM F, VASCULAR SMOOTH MUSCLE, LOCAL CONTROL OF BLOOD FLOW. **Personal Data:** b Detroit, Mich, November 18, 1952; m 1976, c 3. **Education:** Mich State Univ, PhD (physiol), 1979. **Professional Experience:** PROF, WESTERN MICH UNIV, 1994-; assoc prof, Western Mich Univ, 1989-1994; from asst prof to assoc prof physiol, Med Col Ga, 1983-1989. **Memberships:** Am Physiol Soc; Microcirculatory Soc Inc; Am Soc Zoologists; AAAS; Am Heart Asn. **Research Statement & Publications:** Regulation of blood flow in the microcirculation; cardiovascular physiology. **Mailing Address:** Dept Biol Sci, Western Mich Univ, 3169 Wood Hall 1903 W Mich Ave, Kalamazoo, MI 49008-5410. **Fax:** 269-387-2849. **E-Mail:** jackson@wmich.edu

JACKSON, WILLIAM G(ORDON), CHEMISTRY. **Personal Data:** b Iron Mountain, Mich, April 22, 1919. **Education:** Univ Mich, BS, 1942; Univ Ill, MS, 1943, PhD (org chem), 1945. **Professional Experience:** RETIRED; consult, Burdick & Jackson Labs, 1978-1984; pres, Burdick & Jackson Labs, 1959-1977; res chemist, Upjohn Co, 1946-1959; spec asst, Nat Defense Res Comt Proj, 1943-1945; asst chem, Univ Ill, 1942-1943. **Memberships:** Am Chem Soc; Sigma Xi. **Research Statement & Publications:** Antibiotics, vitamin; natural product fractionation and structure; chromatography; countercurrent distribution; organic synthesis; laboratory automation apparatus; high-purity solvents. **Mailing Address:** 3840 Mariner Way No 515, Cortez, FL 34215.

JACKSON, WILLIAM JAMES, NEUROPSYCHOLOGY. **Personal Data:** b Houston, Tex, August 1, 1940. **Education:** Univ Tex, El Paso, BA, 1962; Tex Tech Col, PhD (psychol), 1966. **Professional Experience:** ASSOC PROF EMER PHYSIOL, MED COL GA, as of 2005; ASSOC PROF EMER GRAD STUDIES, MED COL GA, as of 2005; assoc prof Physiol, Med Col GA, beginning 1977; asst prof, Med Col GA, 1971-1977; res asst prof, Univ S Fla, 1969-1971; res asst prof, Univ Houston, 1968-1969; Nat Acad Sci-Nat Res Coun fel psychol, Aeromed Res Lab, Holloman AFB, NMex, 1966-1968. **Memberships:** Soc Neuroscience. **Research Statement & Publications:** Neural substrate of learning and motivation; neuropsycho-pharmacology. **Mailing Address:** Dept Physiol & Endocrinol, Med Col Ga, 1120 15th St, Augusta, GA 30912. **E-Mail:** WMJACK@MCG.EDU

JACKSON, WILLIAM MORGAN, PHOTOCHEMISTRY, CHEMICAL PHYSICS. **Personal Data:** b Birmingham, Ala, September 24, 1936; m 1959, c Eric & Cheryl. **Education:** Morehouse Col, BS, 1956; Cath Univ Am, PhD (phys chem), 1961. **Honors & Awards:** Guggenheim Fel, 1989; Miller Fel, 1988. **Professional Experience:** Assoc dean, Col Lett & Sci, 1990-1993; PROF CHEM, UNIV CALIF, DAVIS, 1985-; Mem, US comt, Int Comn Optics, 1975-1977; prof, Howard Univ, 1974-1985; sr chemist, Goddard Space Flight Ctr, NASA, 1970-1974; vis assoc prof physics, Univ Pittsburgh, 1969-1970; sr chemist, Goddard Space Flight Ctr, NASA, 1967-1969; asst, Goddard Space Flight Ctr, NASA, 1964-1967; assoc, Nat Bur Stand, 1963-1964; res scientist, Martin-Marietta Corp, 1961-1963; Chemist res, Nat Bur Stand, 1960-196; Int Astron Union Comn on Comets. **Memberships:** AAAS; Am Chem Soc; Am Phys Soc; Int Astron Union; Optical Soc Am; Sigma Xi. **Research Statement & Publications:** Chemical kinetics; photochemistry; molecular beams; astrochemistry; mass spectroscopy; application of tunable lasers to problems in photochemistry and chemical kinetics; photochemistry of comets. **Mailing Address:** Dept Chem Rm 214, Univ Calif, Davis, CA 95616-5224. **Fax:** 530-752-8995. **E-Mail:** wmjackson@ucdavis.edu

JACKSON, WILLIAM MORRISON, INORGANIC CHEMISTRY, PHYSICAL CHEMISTRY. **Personal Data:** b Colbert Co, Ala, August 2, 1926; m 1954, Frances; c Gresory & Melissa. **Education:** Univ Ala, BS, 1950; Univ Tenn, MS, 1952 & 1960, PhD (chem), 1953; Am Bd Health Physics, cert, 1980. **Professional Experience:** RETIRED; tech consult, Biztek Consult Inc, beginning 1991; sr proj mgr, Inst Nuclear Powers Opers, 1983-1989; environ & health physics coordr, ALA Power Co, 1974-1983; syst chemist, ALA Power Co, 1970-1974; tech mgr, Am Nuclear Corp, 1968-1970; sr scientist, Oak Ridge Assoc Univs, Tenn, 1966-1968; group leader, Diamond Alkali Co, Ohio, 1961-1966; chemist, Union Carbide Corp, Oak Ridge Nat Lab, 1955-1961; chemist, Goodyear Atomic Corp, 1953-1955. **Memberships:** Am Chem Soc; Health Physics Soc, Am Asn Physics in Med. **Research Statement & Publications:** Radiochemistry; health physics. **Mailing Address:** 459 Bonner Rd, Carrollton, GA 30117.

JACKSON, WILLIAM ROY, NUCLEAR PHYSICS. **Personal Data:** b Port Lavaca, Tex, November 26, 1936. **Education:** Columbia Univ, BA, 1959; Rice Univ, MA, 1965, PhD (physics), 1967. **Professional Experience:** Assoc prof physics, Southwest Tex State Univ, 1971-2000; asst prof, Southwest Tex State Univ, 1967-1971. **Memberships:** Am Phys Soc. **Research Statement & Publications:** Low energy experimental nuclear physics; reaction mechanisms. **Mailing Address:** Dept Physics & Astron, Southwest Tex State Univ, San Marcos, TX 78666-4602.

JACKSON, WILLIAM THOMAS, PLANT PHYSIOLOGY. **Personal Data:** b Stockdale, Ohio, May 10, 1923; m 1949, c 3. **Education:** Ohio State Univ, BS, 1947; Duke Univ, PhD (bot), 1953. **Professional Experience:** CONSULT, 1990-; mem fel panel, NIH, 1963-1966; from asst prof to prof biol, Dartmouth, 1959-1990; from instr to asst prof bot, Yale Univ, 1953-1959; asst bot & plant physiol, Duke Univ, 1950-1953; instr biol, WVa Univ, 1949-1950. **Memberships:** Am Soc Plant Physiol; Bot Soc Am. **Research Statement & Publications:** Mitosis and other events of cell cycle. **Mailing Address:** 8335 SW 72nd Ave, Miami, FL 33143.

JACKSON, WINSTON JEROME, POLYMER CHEMISTRY. **Personal Data:** b Asheville, NC, February 4, 1926; m 1952, Louisa; c Ann & Blane. **Education:** Va Polytech Inst, BS, 1949; Duke Univ, PhD (org chem), 1952. **Professional Experience:** RETIRED; res fel, Eastman Chemicals Div, 1980-1991; sr res assoc, Eastman Kodak Co, 1973-1980; res assoc, Eastman Kodak Co, 1958-1972; from res chemist to sr res chemist, Eastman Kodak Co, 1952-1957. **Memberships:** Am Chem Soc. **Research Statement & Publications:** Organic synthesis; preparation, characterization and evaluation of new polymers and discovery of polymer-forming reactions; liquid crystalline polymers. **Mailing Address:** 4408 Greenspring Circle, Kingsport, TN 37664.

JACKSON-COOK, COLLEEN, GENETICS. **Education:** Univ Charleston, BS, 1978; W Va Univ, MS, 1980; Va Commonwealth Univ, PhD (human genetics), 1985. **Professional Experience:** ASSOC PROF, DEPT HUMAN GENETICS, VA COMMONWEALTH UNIV SCH MED, 2000-. **Mailing Address:** Dept Human Genetics Med Col Va, Sta Box 33 PO Box 980033, Richmond, VA 23298. **Fax:** 804-828-3760. **E-Mail:** jacksonc@hsc.vcu.edu

JACO, CHARLES M, INDUSTRIAL & MANUFACTURING ENGINEERING, PRODUCT RESEARCH & DEVELOPMENT. **Personal Data:** b Montgomery Co, Miss, January 28, 1924; m 1946, Jennie; c Charles E. **Education:** US Mil Acad, BS, 1946; Univ Del, MChE, 1957. **Professional Experience:** RETIRED; managing partner, JCI Consults, beginning 1985; partner, JCI Consults, beginning 1976; pres & chief oper officer, Midrex Corp, 1974-1976; pres, chief exec officer & gen mgr, Georgetown Ferreduction, 1972-1974; plant mgr, Midland Ross Corp, 1971-1972; mgr corp develop, Res & Develop Div, Dravo Corp, 1966-1971; mil attache & tech ad, US Embassy, Switz, 1963-1966; mil attache, US Embassy, Switz, 1962-1965; adj prof, Ballistic Res Lab Br, Univ Md, 1960; mem staff, Ord Off JTF Seven, Marshall Islands, 1954-1956; proj & contract officer, Redstone Arsenal, 1950-1954. **Memberships:** Am Mgt Asn; Inst Mgt Consults; Am Inst Chem Eng; Asn Iron & Steel Engrs; Defense Preparedness Asn. **Research Statement & Publications:** Management of corporate organizations, including role of research, development and engineering; role of research, development and engineering to corporate growth and development; systems and multi-discipline engineering; co-author of two textbooks; process engineering; general management consultant to over 600 companies including research, development and organizations. **Mailing Address:** 122 Pine Grove Circle, Clover, SC 29710.

JACO, WILLIAM HOWARD, TOPOLOGY. **Personal Data:** b Grafton, WVa, July 14, 1940; m 1978, Linda; c William, Brent, John & Andrew. **Education:** Fairmont State Univ, BA, 1962; Pa State Univ, MA, 1964; Univ Wis, PhD (math), 1968. **Professional Experience:** DIR GRAD STUDIES, OKLA STATE UNIV, 2000-; GRACE B KERR PROF MATH, OKLA STATE UNIV, 1993-; exec dir, Am Math Soc, 1988-1995; NSF fel math, Math Sci Res Inst, 1984-1985; prof, Okla State Univ, 1982-1993; head dept, Okla State Univ, 1982-1987; NSF fel math, Inst Advan Study, 1971-1972, 1978-1979; from asst prof to prof math, Rice Univ, 1970-1982; instr math, Univ Mich, 1968-1970; proj mathematician underwater activities, Ord Res Lab, 1961-1964. **Memberships:** Am Math Soc; hon mem Math Asn Am; Nat Coun Teachers Math; AAAS. **Research Statement & Publications:** Geometric topology with particular interest in classical three-manifold topology; classification problems for three-manifolds and geometric structures, algorithms and decision problems. **Mailing Address:** Dept Math, Okla State Univ, MSCS401 MS 502B 401 Math Sci Bldg, Stillwater, OK 74078. **Fax:** 405-744-8275. **E-Mail:** jaco@math.okstate.edu

JACOB, CHAIM OSCAR, IMMUNOGENETICS. **Personal Data:** b Carei, Romania, September 24, 1951; Israeli & American citizen. **Education:** Sackler Sch Med, Univ Tel-Aviv, Israel, MD, 1976; Weizmann Inst Sci, Rehovot, Israel, PhD (molecular immunol), 1985. **Honors & Awards:** J F Kennedy Mem Prize, Pvt Int Orgn, 1985; Res Presidential Award, Reticulo Endothelial Soc, 1987. **Professional Experience:** ASSOC PROF MED & MOLECULAR MICROBIOL & IMMUNOL, UNIV SOUTHERN CALIF, LOS ANGELES, 1994-; res fel immunogenetics, Stanford Univ Sch Med, 1985-1990. **Memberships:** Am Asn Immunologists; Am Asn human Genetics. **Research Statement & Publications:** Immunogenetic sbasis of autoimmune diseases; genetic basis of lymphokine production and the interactions between cytokines and major histocompatibility complex genes; author of 80 publications. **Mailing Address:** Sch Med, Univ Southern Calif, HMR 705 Mail Code 9094 HSC, Los Angeles, CA 90089. **Fax:** 323-442-2874. **E-Mail:** jacob@usc.edu

JACOB, DANIEL JAMES, ATMOSPHERIC CHEMISTRY, ENVIRONMENTAL ENGINEERING. **Personal Data:** b East Patchogue, NY, June 14, 1958; m 1990, Janice; c Eric Oscar & Richard Alex. **Education:** Advan Sch Physics & Indust Chem, Paris, chem eng, 1980; Calif Inst Technol, MS, 1982, PhD, 1985. **Honors & Awards:** Presidential Young Investr Award, NSF, 1987; James B Macelwane Young Investr Medal, Am Geophys Union, 1994. **Professional Experience:** VASCO MCCOY FAMILY PROF, ATMOSPHERIC/ENVIRON ENG, HARVARD UNIV, 2004-; Gordon McKay Prof, Atmospheric/Environ Eng, Harvard Univ, 1994-2004; assoc ed, Atmospheric Environ, 1992-; assoc prof, Harvard Univ, 1991-1994; Sci & eng fel, Packard Found, 1989; asst prof, Harvard Univ, 1987-1991; Res fel, Harvard Univ, 1985-1987. **Memberships:** Fel Am Geophys Union. **Mailing Address:** Harvard Univ, Pierce Hall 29 Oxford St, Cambridge, MA 02138. **Fax:** 617-495-4551. **E-Mail:** djacob@fas.harvard.edu

JACOB, FIELDEN EMMITT, ANALYTICAL CHEMISTRY, PHYSICAL CHEMISTRY. **Personal Data:** b Columbia, Mo, July 20, 1910; m 1937, c 3. **Education:** Univ Mo, AB, 1932, BS & MA, 1935, PhD (chem), 1939. **Professional Experience:** EMER PROF CHEM, DRAKE UNIV, 1980-; prof, Drake Univ, 1975-1980; assoc prof, Drake Univ, 1947-1975; assoc prof, Kans State Teachers Col, Emporia, 1945-1947; asst prof, Mont Sch Mines, 1942-1945; Instr chem, Univ Mo, 1939-1942. **Memberships:** Am Asn Univ Profs; Am Chem Soc. **Research Statement & Publications:** Colorimetric analysis; carotinoid pigments of egg yolks from hens on various diets; spectrophotometry; stability constants. **Mailing Address:** 1520 48th St, Des Moines, IA 50311.

JACOB, FRANCOIS, CELLULAR GENETICS. **Personal Data:** b Nancy, France, June 17, 1920; wid, c Pierre, Laurent, Odile & Henri. **Education:** Fac Med, Paris, MD, 1947; Fac Sci, Paris, DSc, 1954. **Honorary Degrees:** DSc, Univ Chicago, 1965. **Honors & Awards:** Nobel Prize in Physiol & Med, 1965; Charles Leopold Mayer Prize, 1962. **Professional Experience:** EMER PROF, PASTEUR INST, 1992-; EMER PROF CELLULAR GENETICS, COL FRANCE, 1992-; pres, Dept Cellular Genetics, 1982-1988; prof cellular genetics, Col France, 1964-1992; head, Dept Cellular Genetics, 1960-1992; Asst, Col France, 1950-1956. **Memberships:** Nat Acad Sci; foreign mem Royal Danish Acad Sci & Lett; Am Acad Arts & Sci; Am Philos Soc; Royal Acad Med Belg; Acad Sci Hungary. **Research Statement & Publications:** Genetics of bacterial cells and viruses; mechanisms of information transfer (messenger RNA) and genetic basis of regulatory circuits; early stages of the mouse embryo. **Mailing Address:** Pasteur Inst, 25 Rue du Dr Roux, Paris Cedex 15 75724, France.

JACOB, GARY STEVEN, SOLID STATE NUCLEAR MAGNETIC RESONANCE, GLYCOBIOLOGY. **Personal Data:** b St Louis, Mo, March 18, 1947; m 1975, c 2. **Education:** Univ Mo-St Louis, BS, 1969; Univ Wis-Madison, PhD (biochem), 1976. **Professional Experience:** CHIEF EXEC OFFICER & CHIEF SCI OFFICER, CALLISTO PHARMACEUT, as of 2004; Monsanto fel 1990-1998; head, Glycosci, Monsanto Co, 1990-1997; res mgr, Oxford Proj, GD Searle, 1986-1990; res specialist, Monsanto Co, St Louis, 1979-1986; Fel biophysics, Thomas J Watson Res Ctr, IBM Corp, 1976-1979. **Memberships:** AAAS; Am Chem Soc; Sigma Xi; Am Soc Biochem & Molecular Biol. **Research Statement & Publications:** Solid-state N-15 and C-13 nuclear magnetic resonance studies of bacterial metabolism, with emphasis on bacteria capable of degrading herbicides; cell-wall crosslinking in bacteria and nitrogen fixation; glycobiology; antivirals. **Mailing Address:** Callisto Pharmaceut, 420 Lexington Ave Ste 2500, New York, NY 10170. **Fax:** 212-297-0020. **E-Mail:** gsjacob318@aol.com

JACOB, GEORGE KORATHU, PARALLEL CIRCUIT SIMULATION, PARALLEL COMPILERS. **Personal Data:** b Calcutta, India, August 19, 1959; m 1989, c 1. **Education:** Indian Inst Technol, Kharagpur, BTech, 1981; Pa State Univ, MS, 1983; Univ Calif, Berkeley, PhD (elec eng & computer sci), 1987. **Professional Experience:** SOFTWARE ENG MGR, FRANZ, INC, COLUMBUS, OHIO, 1992-; software develop, Columbus, Ohio, Berkeley, Calif, 1989-1992; Software develop, Columbus, Ohio, Berkeley, Calif, 1987-1989. **Research Statement & Publications:** Parallel processing applications, especially circuit simulation; compilers and programming environments for parallel processes. **Mailing Address:** Franz Inc, 1995 University Ave, Berkeley, CA 94704.

JACOB, HARRY S, INTERNAL MEDICINE, HEMATOLOGY. **Personal Data:** b San Francisco, Calif, April 6, 1933; m 1954, c 3. **Education:** Reed Col, BA, 1954; Harvard Univ, MD, 1958. **Honors & Awards:** Conrad Elvehjem Mem Award, 1971; Hickam lectr, 1993. **Professional Experience:** FRANCIS WELD PEABODY SOC DISTINGUISHED VIS PROF, HARVARD UNIV, 1995-; CLARK RES PROF MED, MED SCH, UNIV MINN, 1992-; Ed- in-chief, Journal Lab & Clin Med, 1991-; VICE CHMN DEPT MED, MED SCH, UNIV MINN, MINNEAPOLIS, 1987-; PROF LAB MED & PATH, MED SCH, UNIV MINN, 1987-; PROF PATHBIOL, MED SCH, UNIV MINN, 1987-; prof, Med Sch, Univ Chicago, 1971; prof med, Univ Man, 1971; prof med & chief sect hemat, med sch, Univ Minn, Minneapolis, 1968-1997; assoc prof, Med Sch, Univ Minn, Minneapolis, 1968-1970; prof, Royal Postgrad Med Sch London, 1966; NIH res grants, 1965-; asst prof med, Sch Med, Tufts Univ, 1965-1968; tutor med sci, Harvard Med Sch, 1963-1965; NIH fels hemat, Thorndike Mem Lab, Harvard Univ, 1960-1963; resident, Boston City Hosp, 1959-1960; Intern med, Boston City Hosp, 1958-1959. **Memberships:** Am Soc Clin Invest; Am Fedn Clin Res; Am Soc Hemat (pres elect, 1997); Int Soc Hemat; Asn Am Physicians; fel AAAS. **Research Statement & Publications:** Red cell metabolism; hemoglobin function-structure relationships; granulocyte function; reticuloendothelial physiology; endothelial physiology. **Mailing Address:** Med Sch, Univ Minn, Box 480 Mayo, 420 Del St, SE, Minneapolis, MN 55455-0374. **Fax:** 612-625-6919. **E-Mail:** jacob002@tc.umn.edu

JACOB, HENRY GEORGE, JR, mathematics; deceased, see previous edition for last biography

JACOB, JANE M, NEUROSCIENCE. **Education:** Ohio Wesleyan Univ, BA, 1982; Case Western Res Univ, PhD, 1987. **Professional Experience:** ASST PROF, DEPT CELL BIOL, UNIV OKLA HEALTH SCI CTR, 1992-; res assoc, Dept Neurosciences, Case Western Res Univ, 1990-1992. **Mailing Address:** Dept Anat Sci, Univ Okla Health Sci Ctr, PO Box 26901BMSB 553, Okla, OK 73190. **E-Mail:** jane-jacob@uokhsc.edu

JACOB, JONAH HYE, LASER PHYSICS, PLASMA PHYSICS. **Personal Data:** b Calcutta, India, May 15, 1943; American citizen; m 1977, c 2. **Education:** London Univ, BSc, 1964; Yale Univ, PhD (plasma physics), 1970. **Professional Experience:** PRES, SCI RES LAB, 1983-; prin res scientist laser & plasma physics, Avco-Everett Res Lab, 1971-1982; res assoc plasma physics, Yale Univ, 1970-1971. **Memberships:** Am Phys Soc; AAAS. **Research Statement & Publications:** High power lasers; discharge physics; atomic physics; environmental physics. **Mailing Address:** Sci Res Lab Inc, 15 Ward St, Somerville, MA 02143-4241. **Fax:** 617-547-4104.

JACOB, KLAUS H, SEISMOLOGY, TECTONICS. **Personal Data:** b Stuttgart, Ger, August 20, 1936. **Education:** Univ Darmstadt, BS, 1960; Univ MainzUniv, MS, 1963; Frankfurt, PhD (goephys), 1968. **Professional Experience:** ASSOC ED, EARTHQUAKE SPECTRA, EERI, 1998-; chmn, NY State Emergency Management Office, 1989-1992; SR RES SCIENTIST SEISMOL & TECTONICS, LAMONT-DOHERTY GEOL OBSERV, COLUMBIA UNIV, 1983-; assoc ed, Geophys Res Lett, Am Geophys Union, 1983-; res assoc, Lamont-doherty Geol Observ, Columbia Univ, 1968-1983. **Memberships:** Am Geophys Union; Seismol Soc Am; Am Geol Inst; Ger Geophys Soc. **Research Statement & Publications:** Geophysics of active plate margins (subduction and continental collision zones) based on earthquake information; seismic and volcanic hazards; microearthquake studies in Alaska, Himalaya and Central America; earthquake prediction; earthquake engineering; published over 20 articles. **Mailing Address:** Lamont-Doherty Earth Observ, Columbia Univ, Rm 225, Seismol Bldg, 61 Rte 9W, Palisades, NY 10964-8000. **Fax:** 845-365-8150. **E-Mail:** jacob@ldeo.columbia.edu

JACOB, LEONARD STEVEN, CLINICAL INVESTIGATION. **Personal Data:** b Philadelphia, Pa, March 18, 1949; m 1969, c 2. **Education:** Philadelphia Col Pharm & Sci, BS, 1970; Temple Univ, PhD (pharmacol), 1975; Med Col Pa, MD, 1978. **Professional Experience:** CHMN & CHIEF EXEC OFFICER, INKINE PHARMACEUT CO, as of 2004; BD DIR, MED COL PA & HAHNEMANN UNIV, as of 2004; exec vpres & chief Oper Officer, Magainin Pharmaceut Inc, beginning 1992; exec vpres res & develop, Pharmaceut Div, 1991-1992; exec vpres, Pharmaceut Div, 1989-1991; vpres clin res & develop worldwide, Smith Kline & French, Labs, 1986-1988; group dir clin invest, vpres clin res & develop N Am, 1984-1986; group dir clin invest, Smith-Kline Beckman, 1983-1984; house staff anesthesiol, Hosp Univ Pa, 1978-; fel, Temple Univ Sch Med, 1973-1975; fel, Dept Pharmacol, Hahnemann Med Col, 1970-1971. **Memberships:** AMA; AAAS; Sigma Xi; fel Am Col Clin Pharmacol; Pharmaceut Mfrs Asn. **Research Statement & Publications:** Linking molecular biology to clinical trial design; pharmaceutical agents. **Mailing Address:** Inkine Pharmaceut Co Inc, 1787 Sentry Pkwy W Bldg 18, Blue Bell, PA 19422. **Fax:** 215-283-4602.

JACOB, MARY, NUTRITIONAL STATUS ASSESSMENT OF ELDERLY, NUTRIENT REQUIREMENT OF ELDERLY. **Personal Data:** b Kerala, India, May 28, 1933; American citizen. **Education:** Univ Madras, India, BS, 1953, MS, 1958; Univ London, MS, 1963; Univ Ill, Urbana, PhD (nutrit biochem), 1969. **Professional Experience:** PROF HUMAN NUTRIT, CALIF STATE UNIV, LONG BEACH, 1980-; vis res fel, Dept Pediat, Med Col Va, Richmond, 1979-1990; asst prof, Ariz State Univ, Tempe, 1977-1980; vis asst prof, Ariz State Univ, Tempe, 1977-1978; lectr nutrit, Western Australia Inst Technol, Perth, 1976-1977; asst res nutritionist, Univ Calif, Los Angeles, 1969-1976; res asst, Univ Bombay, India, 1958-1961. **Memberships:** Am Soc Nutrit Sci; Sigma Xi; Geront Soc Am; Am Col Nutrit; Inst Food Technol; NY Acad Sci. **Research Statement & Publications:** Calcium, zinc metabolism and interdependence of these on vitamin D status; changes in body composition with age with main focus on elderly; effect of calorie restriction on lean body mass. **Mailing Address:** Dept Family & Consumer Sci, Calif State Univ, 1250 Bellflower Blvd, Bldg FCS, Rm 125, Long Beach, CA 90840-0501. **Fax:** 562-985-4414. **E-Mail:** marjacob@csulb.edu

JACOB, PAUL B(ERNARD), ELECTRICAL ENGINEERING. **Personal Data:** b Columbus, Miss, June 9, 1922; m 1946, c 2. **Education:** Miss State Col, BS, 1944; Northwestern Univ, MS, 1948. **Professional Experience:** PROF EMER, MISS STATE UNIV, as of 2004; assoc head dept, Miss State Univ, 1961-1988; from instr to prof elec eng prof, Miss State Univ, 1946-1988; jr engr, Tenn Eastman Corp, 1944-1946. **Memberships:** Am Soc Eng Educ; Inst Elec & Electronics Engrs; Power Eng Soc. **Research Statement & Publications:** High voltage engineering; electric power system analysis. **Mailing Address:** Dept Elec Eng, Miss State Univ, PO Drawer Ee, Mississippi State, MS 39762.

JACOB, PEYTON III, DRUG METABOLISM, ORGANIC SYNTHESIS. **Personal Data:** b Ann Arbor, Mich, September 23, 1947. **Education:** Univ Calif, BS, 1969; Purdue Univ, PhD (chem), 1975. **Professional Experience:** RES CHEMIST, DIV MED & PSYCHIAT, CANCER CTR, UNIV CALIF, SAN FRANCISCO, as of 2004; ASSOC MEM, CANCER CTR, UNIV CALIF, SAN FRANCISCO, as of 2004; asst res chemist, Div Clin Pharmacol, Sch Med, Univ Calif, San Francisco & San Francisco Gen Hosp Med Ctr, beginning 1978; NIH fel, 1975-1978. **Memberships:** Am Chem Soc; Sigma Xi. **Research Statement & Publications:** Tobacco alkaloid metabolites; development of new analytical methodology for drugs and their metabolites in biologic fluids. **Mailing Address:** Cancer Ctr, Univ Calif, PO Box 0482, San Francisco, CA 94143-0482. **Fax:** 415-206-5080. **E-Mail:** peyton@itsa.ucsf.edu

JACOB, RICHARD JOHN, THEORETICAL PHYSICS. **Personal Data:** b Salt Lake City, Utah, October 9, 1937; m 1959, c 4. **Education:** Univ Utah, BS, 1958, PhD (physics), 1963. **Professional Experience:** PROF EMER PHYSICS, ARIZ STATE UNIV; as of 2005; DEAN, EMER COL, ARIZ STATE UNIV, 2004-; chmn dept, Ariz State Univ, 1985-1990; prof physics, Ariz State Univ, beginning 1978; vis prof, Univ Kaiserlautern, 1973, 1978-1979; vis prof, Univ Karlsruhe, 1970-1971; from asst prof to assoc prof, Ariz State Univ, 1963-1978. **Memberships:** Am Phys Soc; Am Asn Physics Teachers; Sigma Xi. **Research Statement & Publications:** Theoretical elementary particle physics. **Mailing Address:** Dept Physics & Astron, Ariz State, Tempe, AZ 85283. **Fax:** 480-965-7954. **E-Mail:** richard.jacob@asu.edu

JACOB, RICHARD L, THEORETICAL PHYSICS, QUANTUM THEORY. **Personal Data:** b Ripon, Wis, July 6, 1932; m 1967, Donna; c Martha. **Education:** Stanford Univ, BS, 1955; Univ Wis, MS, 1956, PhD (physics), 1959. **Professional Experience:** PROF EMER PHYS, CORNELL COL, 2001-; prof physics, Cornell Col, 1996-2001; prof physics & comput sci, 1982-1996; acad comp coordr, Cornell Col, 1972-1990; assoc prof, Cornell Col, 1968-1982; assoc prof, Claremont Men's Col, 1965-1968; asst prof physics, Tufts Univ, 1960-1965; res assoc, Univ Wis, 1959-1960. **Memberships:** Am Phys Soc; Am Asn Physics Teachers. **Research Statement & Publications:** Elementary particle physics; relativistic quantum mechanics; philosophy of physics. **Mailing Address:** Dept Physics, Cornell Col, 600 First St W, Mt Vernon, IA 52314. **Fax:** 319-895-5764. **E-Mail:** jacob@cornellcollege.edu

JACOB, ROBERT ALLEN, ANALYTICAL CHEMISTRY, CLINICAL CHEMISTRY. **Personal Data:** b Chicago, Ill, December 16, 1942; m 1971. **Education:** Ill Col, BA, 1965; Southern Ill Univ, MA, 1967, PhD (chem), 1970. **Professional Experience:** RES CHEMIST, GRAND FORKS, WESTERN HUMAN NUTRIT RES CTR, USDA, GRAND FORKS, as of 2001; res chemist, Boston, At Nutrit Res Ctr, USDA, San francisco, beginning 1981; sr chemist, Midwest Res Inst, Kemo, 1979-1981; res chemist, Human Nutrit Lab, 1975-1979. **Memberships:** Am Chem Soc; Am Asn Clin Chem; Sigma Xi. **Research Statement & Publications:** Trace metal analysis and metabolism; analytical chemistry of nutrients; clinical lab methods for assessing nutritional status; clinical chemistry; published over 110 related articles in scientific journals and textbooks. **Mailing Address:** Human Nutrit Res Ctr, USDA, PO Box 9034, Grand Forks, ND 58202. **Fax:** 701-795-8230. **E-Mail:** rjacob@gfhnrc.ars.usda.gov

JACOB, ROBERT J(OSEPH) K(ASSEL), HUMAN-COMPUTER INTERACTION. **Personal Data:** b Brooklyn, NY, November 11, 1950; m 1973, Kathryn; c Charlotte & Anne. **Education:** Johns Hopkins Univ, BA, 1972, MS, 1974, PhD (elec eng), 1976. **Professional Experience:** Vice chmn, Spec Interest Group Human-Comput Interaction, 2001-; VICE CHMN, ACM SIGCHI, 2001-; ASSOC PROF ELEC ENG & COMPUT SCI, TUFTS UNIV, 1994-; group leader, George Wash Univ/NSF Workshop, 1991; vice chmn, Spec Interest Group Human-Comput Interaction, 1990-1993; mem, Var Prog Comts, Asn Comput Mach, 1987-; prof lectr, George Wash Univ, 1978-1994; comput scientist, Human Comput Interaction Lab, Naval Res Lab, Wash, DC, 1977-1994; res asst & instr, Johns Hopkins Univ, 1972-1976. **Memberships:** Sigma Xi; Asn Comput Mach; Inst Elec & Electronics Engrs; Human Factors Soc; Am Asn Artificial Intel; AAAS. **Research Statement & Publications:** Human-computer interaction; eye movement-based interaction; tangible interfaces; formal specification of user-computer interfaces; visualization of multi-dimensional data; author of numerous publications on human-computer interaction; user interface software, non-wimp interfaces, virtual environments. **Mailing Address:** Dept Comput Sci Tufts Univ, 161 Col Ave Halligan Hall, Medford, MA 02155. **Fax:** 617-627-3220. **E-Mail:** jacob@cs.tufts.edu

JACOB, SAMSON T, RIBONUCLEIC ACID ENZYMOLOGY, GENE TRANSCRIPTION. **Education:** Agra Univ, India, PhD (biochem), 1964. **Professional Experience:** CHMN, DEPT PHARMACOL & MOLECULAR BIOL, CHICAGO MED SCH, 2000-; PROF, DEPT PHARMACOL & MOLECULAR BIOL, CHICAGO MED SCH, 1989-; chmn, dept pharmacol & molecular biol, chicago med sch, beginning 1989; prof pharmacol, Col Med, Pa State Univ, 1972-1989. **Research Statement & Publications:** Gene expression. **Mailing Address:** Dept Pharmacol & Molecular Biol, Chicago Med Sch, Off 333C Hamilton, 3333 Green Bay Rd, North Chicago, IL 60064. **Fax:** 614-688-5600. **E-Mail:** jacob.42@osu.edu

JACOB, STANLEY W, MEDICINE, SURGERY. **Personal Data:** b Philadelphia, Pa, January 7, 1924; m 1964, c 2. **Education:** Ohio State Univ, BA, 1945, MD, 1948. **Professional Experience:** GERLINGER DISTINGUISHED PROF, DEPT SURG, MED SCH, ORE HEALTH & SCI UNIV, 2002-; Gerlinger prof, Med Sch, Ore Health & Sci Univ, beginning 1981; assoc prof surg, Med Sch, Univ Ore, 1965-1981; asst prof, Med Sch, Univ Ore, 1959-1965; Instr surg, Harvard Med Sch, 1957-1959. **Memberships:** Am Col Surg; Soc Univ Surg; NY Acad Sci. **Research Statement & Publications:** Preservation and transplantation of tissues; biologic applications of dimethyl sulfoxide. **Mailing Address:** Ore Health & Sci Univ, 3181 S W Sam Jackson Park Rd, Portland, OR 97239.

JACOB, THEODORE AUGUST, ORGANIC CHEMISTRY, BIOCHEMISTRY. **Personal Data:** b Braddock, Pa, August 22, 1919; m D Eileen; c Gary, Robert & Lynn. **Education:** Col Wooster, BA, 1941; Rensselaer Polytech Inst, MS, 1943; Purdue Univ, PhD (org chem), 1949. **Professional Experience:** DIR ANIMAL DRUG METAB & RADIOCHEM, MERCK, SHARP & DOHME RES LABS, 1980-; sect dir, Merck, Sharp & Dohme Res Labs, 1976-1980; mgr animal drug metab, Merck, Sharp & Dohme Res Labs, 1969-1976; group leader natural prod develop, Merck, Sharp & Dohme Res Labs, 1957-1969; sr chemist, Merck, Sharp & Dohme Res Labs, 1949-1957; asst, Purdue Univ, 1946-1948; org chemist, Standard Oil Co, NJ, 1943-1946; Asst org chem, Rensselaer Polytech Inst, 1941-1943. **Memberships:** Am Chem Soc. **Research Statement & Publications:** Isolation, purification and identification of biologically active products from plant, animal and fermentation sources; preparation and isolation of synthetic peptides, steroids and nucleotides; isolation and identification of drug metabolites. **Mailing Address:** 828 St Marks Ave, Westfield, NJ 07090-2025.

JACOB, WILLIS HARVEY, INSTRUCTIONAL TECHNOLOGY, ACADEMIC ADVISEMENT. **Personal Data:** b Lake Charles, La, June 6, 1943. **Education:** Southern Univ, BS, 1965; Univ Kans, PhD (biochem & physiol), 1971. **Professional Experience:** ASSOC PROF BIOL & ANAT, SOUTHERN UNIV & A&M COL, 1991-; chief, Anat & Physiol Br, Acad Health Sci, 1988-1991; staff physiologist, Pharmaceut Syst, US Army Med Develop Activ, 1985-1988; prod mgr, Directorate Prod Mgt, US Army Med Res & Develop Command, 1983-1985; chief physiol serv, Madigan Army Med Ctr, 1981-1983; physiologist clin invest, Madigan Army Med Ctr, 1978-1981; assoc prof, Baylor Univ, 1976-1977; asst prof health sci, Baylor Univ, 1975-1976; chief, Basic Sci Br, Med & Surg Div, US Army Acad Health Sci, 1971-1977; asst prof biol, Southern Univ & A&M Col, 1970-1971. **Memberships:** Sigma Xi; Nat Inst Sci. **Research Statement & Publications:** Development of multimedia-based instructional materials in anatomy, physiology and general biology. **Mailing Address:** Dept Biol Sci, Southern Univ, Baton Rouge, LA 70813. **E-Mail:** wjacob@subrum.subr.edu

JACOBER, WILLIAM JOHN, chemistry, physics; deceased, see previous edition for last biography

JACOBI, ANTHONY MARK, THERMAL FLUID SCIENCES, HEAT TRANSFER. **Personal Data:** b Louisville, Ky, January 12, 1960; m 1981, Cindy; c Benjamin, Christopher & Mary. **Education:** Purdue Univ, BS, 1984, PhD (mech eng), 1989; Univ Cent Fla, MS, 1986. **Honors & Awards:** Exemplary Service, Journal Heat Transfer, Am So Mech Eng, 1994; Eng Counc Adv Outstanding Advising, UIUC, 1996; Stanley H Pierce Fac Award, Col Eng, UIUC, 1996; Effective Teacher Award, Mech & Ind Eng Alumni Assoc, UIUC, 1997. **Professional Experience:** PROF MECH ENG, UNIV ILL, URBANA, as of 2006; CO -DIR, ACRC NSF INDUST UNIV COOP RES CTR, as of 2006; asst prof mech eng, Univ Ill, Urbana, beginning 1992; asst prof mech eng, Johns Hopkins Univ, 1989-1992; res asst, Purdue Univ, 1986-1989; sr engr, Harris Corp, 1984-1986. **Memberships:** Am Soc Mech Engrs; Am Soc Heating Refrig & Air Conditioning Engrs; Am Soc Elec Eng. **Research Statement & Publications:** Experimental heat and mass transfer with an emphasis on phase change; connection in complex flows and thermal system modeling; applications in heat exchangers, HVAC/R, petro-chemical processing, alternative refrigerants and computer modeling. **Mailing Address:** Dept Mech & Indust Eng, Univ Ill, 140 Mech Eng Bldg, MC-244, Urbana, IL 61801. **Fax:** 217-244-6534. **E-Mail:** a-jacobi@uiuc.edu

JACOBI, GEORGE (THOMAS), ELECTRONICS ENGINEERING. **Personal Data:** b Mannheim, Ger, May 19, 1922; American citizen; m 1955, c 1. **Education:** Ohio State Univ, BEE, 1947, MSc, 1948. **Honors & Awards:** Wiener Medal, Am Soc Cybernetics, 1968. **Professional Experience:** CONSULT, 1990-; vpres technol, Johnson Controls, Inc, 1984-1990; dir bldg automotive syst, Johnson Controls, Inc, 1977-1984; dir comput & mgt sci res, ITT Res Inst, 1959-1977; mgr spec comput eng, Comput Dept, Calif, 1957-1959; electronic recording mach acct systs lab, Comput Dept, Calif, 1956-1957; mgr analog comput eng, Gen Eng Lab, 1950-1955; engr, Res Lab, Gen Elec Co, NY, 1948-1950; Asst, Betatron Lab, Ohio State Univ, 1948. **Memberships:** Sr mem Inst Elec & Electronics Engrs; Asn Comput Mach; NY Acad Sci; Sigma Xi. **Research Statement & Publications:** Computer logic and storage devices; system theory; electronic component technology; engineering management. **Mailing Address:** 2375 N Wahl Ave, Milwaukee, WI 53211-4513.

JACOBI, PETER ALAN, SYNTHETIC ORGANIC CHEMISTRY. **Personal Data:** b Abington, Pa, September 14, 1945; m 1975. **Education:** Univ NH, BS, 1967; Princeton Univ, MS, 1970, PhD (chem), 1973. **Professional Experience:** PROF CHEM, DARTMOUTH COL, 1997-; John Wesley Beach Prof Chem, 1993; consult, Anderson Oil Co, 1976-; asst prof chem, Wesleyan Univ, beginning 1975; corp appointee, Harvard Univ, 1973-1975. **Memberships:** Am Chem Soc; Royal Soc Chem; Sigma Xi. **Research Statement & Publications:** Mechanistic organic chemistry; chemistry of natural products. **Mailing Address:** Dept Chem, Dartmouth Col, Hanover, NH 03755. **E-Mail:** Peter.Jacobi@dartmouth.edu

JACOBI, W(ILLIAM) M(ALLETT), TECHNICAL MANAGEMENT. **Personal Data:** b Elizabeth, NJ, April 27, 1930; m 1962, c 4. **Education:** Syracuse Univ, BChE, 1951; Univ Del, MChE, 1953, PhD (chem eng), 1955. **Professional Experience:** CONSULT, 1991-; vpres, Westinghouse Govt Opers, 1989-1991; pres, Westinghouse Hanford Co, 1987-1988; vpres, Westinghouse Adv Power Systs, 1984-1986; gen mgr, Westinghouse Nuclear Fuel Div, 1981-1984; gen mgr, Westinghouse Nuclear Technol Div, 1979-1980; proj mgr, Clinch River Breeder Reactor Plant, systs eng mgr, Westinghouse Pressurized Water Reactor Systs Div, 1978-1979; eng mgr, Fast Flux Test Facil, Westinghouse Advan Reactors Div, 1970-1973; mgr mark 48 design eng, Weapons Dept, 1968-1970; mgr design & anal, systs & tech eng, 1966-1968; mgr adv reactor design, Westinghouse Astronuclear Lab, 1963-1966; consult, Nuclear Utilities Serv, Inc, 1961-1963; Supvry engr nuclear design, Bettis Atomic Power Div, Westinghouse Elec Corp, 1955-1961. **Memberships:** Am Nuclear Soc. **Research Statement & Publications:** Reactor physics; fluid flow and mechanical design. **Mailing Address:** 119 Mount Vernon Dr, Monroeville, PA 15146. **Fax:** 412-856-4655. **E-Mail:** jacobib@wcsmail.com

JACOBOWITZ, DAVID, PHARMACOLOGY, BIOCHEMISTRY. **Personal Data:** b Brooklyn, NY, July 15, 1931; m 1957, c 2. **Education:** City Col NY, BS, 1953; Ohio State Univ, MS, 1958, PhD (pharmacol), 1962. **Honors & Awards:** USPHS career develop award, 1966. **Professional Experience:** PROF ANAT, PHYSIOL & GENETICS, LAB CLIN SCI, NAT INST MENT HEALTH, as of 2003; lady davis vis prof, Hebrew Univ Jerusalem, Israel, 1981; HEAD, HISTOPHARMACOL SECT, LAB CLIN SCI, NIH, 1971-; from asst prof to assoc prof, Sch Med, Univ Pa, 1967-1971; assoc, Sch Med, Univ Pa, 1965-1967; instr, Sch Med, Univ Pa, 1963-1965; Pa Plan scholar, Sch Med, Univ Pa, 1963-1965; NIH fel pharmacol, Sch Med, Univ Pa, 1962-1963. **Memberships:** Neurochem Soc; Am Soc Pharmacol & Exp Therapeut; Neuroscience Soc; Am Col Neuropsychopharmacol & Psychoneuroendocrinol; Am Asn Anat. **Research Statement & Publications:** Endocrine pharmacology; effect of stress on pituitary and hypothalamic metabolism and adrenocorticotropic hormone synthesis; cellular pharmacology; localization and mechanism of action of the autonomic neurotransmitters; histochemistry of catecholamines and acetylcholinesterase; immunohistochemistry of peptides; localization of neuromodulatory and neurotransmitter pathways in the brain; two-dimensional electrophoresis of brain proteins; insituhybridization histochemistry; calcium binding proteins, fetal brain development. **Mailing Address:** Dept Anat, Physiol & Genetics, Lab Clin Sci, NIH, 4301 Jones bridge Rd, Bethesda, MD 20814. **Fax:** 301-295-3566. **E-Mail:** dwj@helix.nih.gov

JACOBOWITZ, ELLEN SUE, MUSEUM & TEMPLE ADMINISTRATION. **Personal Data:** b Detroit, Mich, February 21, 1948. **Education:** Univ Mich, BA, 1969, MA, 1970. **Professional Experience:** ADMINR, TEMPLE EMANU-EL, 1995-; adminr, Cranbrook Inst Sci, 1991-1994; Cur, Philadelphia Mus Art, 1972-1990. **Mailing Address:** Temple Emanuel, 14450 W 10 Mile Rd, Oak Park, MI 48237.

JACOBOWITZ, RONALD, ALGEBRAIC NUMBER THEORY, BIOSTATISTICS EDUCATION. **Personal Data:** b New York, NY, October 18, 1934; m 1960, c 3. **Education:** City Col New York, BA, 1955; Univ Chicago, SM, 1956; Princeton Univ, PhD (math), 1960. **Professional Experience:** PROF EMER MATH, ARIZ STATE UNIV, as of 2004; Vis statistician, NIH, 1979-1980; prof math, Ariz State Univ, beginning 1970; assoc prof, Univ Kans, 1966-1970; asst prof, Univ Ariz, 1962-1966; Instr math, Mass Inst Technol, 1960-1962. **Memberships:** Math Asn Am; Am Statist Asn. **Research Statement & Publications:** Algebra; biomedical statistics; theory of quadratic forms. **Mailing Address:** Dept Math, Ariz State Univ, Tempe, AZ 85287-0002.

JACOBS, ABIGAIL CONWAY, TOXICOLOGY, PHARMACOLOGY. **Personal Data:** b St Louis, Mo, November 11, 1942; m 1969, Verne; c 2. **Education:** Univ Mich, Ann Arbor, BS in CHEM, 1964; Univ Calif, Berkeley, PhD (biochem), 1968. **Professional Experience:** Assoc Dir Pharmacology/Toxicology, Office of New Drugs, Center for Drug Evaluation and Research, US Food and Drug Admin (USFDA) 2003-; Supervisory Pharmacol/Toxicol, Div Derm and Dental Drugs, USFDA, 1995-2003; Toxicologist, Div Antiviral Drug Prods, USFDA, 1991-1995; sr biochemist, Technical Resources, Inc, 1989-1991; assoc proj mgr & sr scientist, Carltech Assocs, 1982-1989; sr tech writer & researcher chem carcinogenesis, Tracor Jitco, 1979-1982; Res assoc, Nuffield Found, 1971-1972; Queen's Univ, Belfast, 1971-1972; res assoc biochem, Weizmann Inst Sci & Rehovot, Israel, 1970-1971; Fel immunochem, Am Cancer Soc, 1968-1970. **Memberships:** Soc Toxicol; Am Soc Photobiol; Eur Soc Photobiol; Am Coll Toxicol; Environ Mutag Soc; Am Chem Soc; AAAS; Sigma Xi. **Research Statement & Publications:** Carcinogenicity and phototoxicology of drugs; alternative toxicology methods. **Mailing Address:** 9621 McAlpine Rd, Silver Spring, MD 20901. **Fax:** 301-796-9855. **E-Mail:** abigail.jacobs@.fda.hhs.gov

JACOBS, ALAN M(ARTIN), RADIATION ENGINEERING, STATISTICAL MECHANICS. **Personal Data:** b New York, NY, November 14, 1932; m 1978, Sharon; c Fred, Heidi (Gearhart), Aaron & Seth. **Education:** Cornell Univ, BEngPhys, 1955; Pa State Univ, MS, 1958, PhD (physics), 1963. **Professional Experience:** PROG COORDR ENG PHYSICS, UNIV FLA, as of 2003; PROF NUCLEAR & RADIOL ENG, UNIV FLA, 1983-; prof & chmn nuclear eng sci, Univ Fla, 1980-1982; combustion Eng Inc, 1975- & Future-Tech Corp, 1986-; prof, Pa State Univ, Univ Park, 1968-1980; Millitron, Inc & HRB-Singer, Inc, 1963-; assoc prof nuclear eng, Pa State Univ, Univ Park, 1963-1968; consult, Westinghouse Astronuclear Lab, 1961-1962; res assoc, Pa State Univ, Univ Park, 1956-1963; consult, Allis-Chalmers Mfg Co, 1956-1959. **Memberships:** Sigma Xi; Am Soc Nondestructive Testing. **Research Statement & Publications:** Many body problems, especially radiation transport and plasma physics; radiography; image analysis and enhancement. **Mailing Address:** Dept Nuclear & Radiol Eng Univ Fla, 202 Nuclear Sci Bldg, Gainesville, FL 32611-8300. **Fax:** 352-392-3380. **E-Mail:** jacobs@ufl.edu

JACOBS, ALAN MARTIN, GEOLOGY. **Personal Data:** b New York, NY, February 17, 1942; m 1968, c 2. **Education:** City Col NY, BS, 1963; Ind Univ, MA, 1965, PhD (geol), 1967. **Honors & Awards:** Cert Merit, Am Inst Prof Geologists, 1984. **Professional Experience:** ASSOC PROF GEOL & ENVIRON SCI, YOUNGSTOWN STATE UNIV, YOUNGSTOWN, as of 2003; DIR, CTR ENVIRON STUDIES, YOUNGSTOWN STATE

UNIV, as of 2000; Geoscience mgr, IT Corp, 1988-; lectr, civil eng dept, carnegie-mellon univ, beginning 1987; pres, geoprobe, Alan M Jacobs Inc, 1981-; mfr rep, Westinghouse Elec Corp, 1981-1988; from asst proj geologist to sr proj geologist, STSD'Appolonia Ltd, 1974-1985; asst geologist, Ill State Geol Surv, 1967-1974; teaching assoc, Ind Univ, 1964; teaching asst, Ind Univ, 1963-1964. **Memberships:** Geol Soc Am; Am Inst Prof Geologists. **Research Statement & Publications:** Engineering geology; glacial and quaternary geology; geomorphology; geologic factors in site selection; seismicity; age-dating; environmental geology; borehole camera surveys; hazardous waste chemicals management. **Mailing Address:** Dept Geol & Environ Sci, Youngstown State Univ, One Univ Plaza, Youngstown, OH 44555. **Fax:** 330-742-1754. **E-Mail:** amjacobs@cc.ysu.edu

JACOBS, ALLAN EDWARD, THEORETICAL SOLID STATE PHYSICS. **Personal Data:** b Toronto, Ont, August 7, 1938; m 1962. **Education:** Univ Toronto, BASc, 1960; Univ Waterloo, MSc, 1962; Univ Ill, Urbana, PhD (physics), 1968. **Professional Experience:** PROF PHYSICS, UNIV TORONTO, 1983-; Nat Res Coun Can res grants, 1969-; from asst prof to assoc prof, Univ Toronto, 1969-1983; Nat Res Coun Can fel, Univ Hamburg, 1968-1969; res asst phys metall, Univ Toronto, 1960-1961. **Memberships:** Am Phys Soc; Can Asn Physicists. **Research Statement & Publications:** Theory of inhomogeneous superconductors; superfluid helium; incommensurate systems; spin glasses; disordered. **Mailing Address:** Dept Physics, Univ Toronto, 60 St George St, Toronto, ON M5S 1A7, Can. **Fax:** 416-978-2537. **E-Mail:** jacobs@physics.utoronto.ca

JACOBS, ALLEN LEON, PHARMACEUTICAL CHEMISTRY. **Personal Data:** b New York, NY, May 22, 1931; m 1954, c 3. **Education:** Columbia Univ, BS, 1952, MS, 1954, PhD (pharmaceut chem), 1962. **Professional Experience:** RETIRED; mgr analytical res, Sandoz Pharmaceut Inc, 1963-1994; res analystchemist, Sandoz Pharmaceut Inc, 1962-1963; instr chem, Col Pharmacol, Columbia Univ, 1960-1962. **Memberships:** Am Chem Soc; Am Pharmaceut Asn; Sigma Xi. **Research Statement & Publications:** Plant biochemistry; analytical chemistry. **Mailing Address:** 5 Alcor Rd, Randolph, NJ 07869.

JACOBS, BARRY LEONARD, NEUROSCIENCE, NEUROPHYSIOLOGY. **Education:** Univ Calif, Los Angeles, PhD (psychol & neurosci), 1971. **Professional Experience:** PROF Neuroscience, DEPT PSYCHOL, PRINCETON UNIV, 1972-. **Mailing Address:** Green Hall, Princeton Univ Green Hall, Princeton, NJ 08544-1099. **Fax:** 609-258-1113. **E-Mail:** barryj@princeton.edu

JACOBS, CARL HENRY, ORTHOPEDICS, BIOMATERIALS. **Personal Data:** b Lewisburg, Pa, January 29, 1948; m 1970, Anita; c Eliezer & Abraham. **Education:** Univ Vt, BS, 1970, MS, 1973, PhD (mech eng), 1974. **Professional Experience:** MANAGING DIR & SR SCI ADV, GENAISSANCE HEALTH CARE PARTNERS, AS OF 2004; dir mfg eng opers, Collagen Prod Div, Datascope Corp, beginning 1993; dir qual assurance, Osteonics Div, Stryker Corp, 1991-1993; vpres mfg, Orthomet Corp, 1989-1991; dir res labs & qual assurance, Zimmer Orthop Implant Div, Bristol-Myers Inc, 1983-1989; group leader, Res & Develop, Howmedica Corp, Pfizer Inc, 1979-1983; clin asst prof, Dept Clin Rehab Med, Emory Univ, 1977-1979; asst prof, Sch Mech Eng, Ga Inst Technol, 1974-1979. **Memberships:** Sigma Xi; Am Soc Mech Engrs; Soc Mfg Engrs; Orthop Res Soc; NY Acad Sci; Soc Biomat. **Research Statement & Publications:** Development and design of orthopedic implants; arterial implants; owner of several patents for novel medical devices. **Mailing Address:** Genaissance Health Care Partners, 500 S Clinton Ste 803, Chicago, IL 60607. **E-Mail:** cjacobs@genaissancehealthcare.com

JACOBS, CHARLES WARREN, CELL DIVISION, CYTOSKELETON. **Personal Data:** b Gainesville, Fla, November 2, 1954; m 1977, c 2. **Education:** Univ Miami, Fla, BS, 1976; Univ Tex, Austin, PhD (microbiol), 1983. **Professional Experience:** ASSOC DEAN, SCI DIV, HENRY FORD COMMUNITY COL, as of 2003; PROF BIOL, HENRY FORD COMMUNITY COL, 1994-; asst prof biol, Albion Col, 1989-1994; Instr phys sci, Eastern Mich Univ, 1989; fel cell biol Ohio State Univ, 1987-1989; fel cell biol, Univ Mich, 1983-1987. **Research Statement & Publications:** Regulation of microtubules during the cell cycle; analyzing mutants of and molecular cloning the beta-tubulin gene of ustilago maydis. **Mailing Address:** Sci Div, Henry Ford Community Ctr, 5101 Evergreen Rd, Dearborn, MI 48201. **E-Mail:** cjacobs@hfcc.edu

JACOBS, DAVID, EVOLUTION, PALEOBIOLOGY & MARINE SPECIATION. **Education:** Cornell Univ, BA, 1980; Univ Chicago, MS, 1985; Va Polytech Inst & State Univ, PhD (Geol Sci), 1990. **Professional Experience:** ASSOC PROF, DEPT ECOL & EVOLUTIONARY BIOL, UNIV CALIF, LOS ANGELES, as of 2004. **Mailing Address:** Dept Ecol & Evolutionary Biol, Univ Calif Los Angeles 5127B LS, Los Angles, CA 90024-1606. **E-Mail:** djacobs@ucla.edu

JACOBS, DAVID, PALEONTOLOGY. **Education:** Cornell Univ, BA, 1980; Univ Chicago, MS, 1985; Va Polytech Inst & State Univ, PhD, 1990. **Professional Experience:** ASSOC PROF DEPT ECOL & EVOLUTIONARY BIOL, UNIV CALIF, LOS ANGELES, as of 2006. **Mailing Address:** Dept Ecol & Evolutionary Biol, Univ Calif, Rm 5127B, Los Angeles, CA 90095. **E-Mail:** djacobs@ucla.edu

JACOBS, DAVID R, CARDIOVASCULAR EPIDEMIOLOGY, BIOSTATISTICS. **Personal Data:** b Brooklyn, NY, April 16, 1945; m 1993, Susan; c Stephen, Theodore, Adam J, Jennifer, Christopher & Patrick. **Education:** Hofstra Univ, BS, 1966; Johns Hopkins Univ, PhD (math statist), 1971. **Professional Experience:** PROF, DIV EPIDEMIOL, SCH PUB HEALTH, UNIV MINN, MINNEAPOLIS, 1988-; from asst to assoc prof, Sch Pub Health, Univ Minn, Minneapolis, 1977-1988; prin investr, Res Career Develop Award, 1977-1982; vis prof, Univ Oslo, Inst Nutri Res, Oslo, 1977; fel, Coun Epidemiol, Am Heart Asn, 1976; from asst prof to assoc prof biostatistic, Lab Physiol Hyg, Sch Pub Health, Univ Minn, Minneapolis, 1974-1981; dir, data processing ctr lab physiol hyg, Univ Minn, 1974-1983; asst prof biostatist, Dept Social & Prev Med, Univ Md, 1971-1974; asst prof, Towson State Col, 1970-1971; consult epidemiol & biostatist. **Memberships:** Am Statist Asn; Soc Epidemiol Res; Am Heart Asn; Am Epidemiol Soc. **Research Statement & Publications:** Cardiovascular epidemiology, including intervention methodologies for lowering the risk factors and relevant statistical techniques; evolution of cardiovascular risk in young adults; relationship of cholesterol to noncardiovascular diseases. **Mailing Address:** Div Epidemiol & Community Health, Sch Pub Health, Univ Minn, 1300 S Second St Ste 300, Minneapolis, MN 55454. **Fax:** 612-624-0315. **E-Mail:** jacobs@epi.umn.edu

JACOBS, DIANE MARGARET, IMMUNOLOGY. **Personal Data:** b Port-of-Spain, Trinidad, March 24, 1940; American citizen; m 1985, Michael; c Karen Brotherhood, Stephen Shelley & David Shelley. **Education:** Radcliffe Col, AB, 1961; Harvard Univ, PhD (bact), 1967. **Professional Experience:** CHMN, HLTH PROF, UNIV CENT FLA, as of 2001; PROF MICROBIOL 1994-; vpres res & grad studies, Univ Cent Fla, 1994-1998; assoc vchancellor res & dean Grad Sch, E Carolina Univ, 1989-1994; mem, Spec Sci RevComt, NIH, 1987; from assoc prof to prof microbiol, State Univ NY, Buffalo, 1980-1989; mem-cause & prev sci rev comt, Nat Cancer Inst, 1977-1981; Prin investr on res grants from NIH, 1974-1986 & Am Cancer Inst, 1977-1980; consult, Hoffman-LaRoche, 1975-1976 & 1978-1979; srres assoc, Salk Inst Biol Sci, 1974-1976; instr biol, Dept Biol, Univ Calif, San Diego, 1973-1974; New York Cancer Res Inst fel, Dept Biol, Univ Calif, San Diego, 1971-1973; lectr, HadassahMed Sch, Hebrew Univ, Jerusalem, 1968-1971; Instr immunol, Hadassah Med Sch, Hebrew Univ, Jerusalem, 1967-1968. **Memberships:** AAAS; NY Acad Sci; Am Asn Immunologists; Int EndotoxinSoc; Asn Women Sci. **Research Statement & Publications:** Immunomodulatory agents of bacterial origin, particularly lipopolysaccharide; mechanism of triggering lymphocytes; nature of interaction with lymphocytes; lymphocyte membrane determinants interacting with lipopolysaccharide; structural requirements for lipopolysaccharide biological activity. **Mailing Address:** Univ Cent Fla, HPA II - 210C, 4000 Cent Fla Blvd, Orlando, FL 32816-2205. **Fax:** 407-823-6138. **E-Mail:** jacobs@mail.ucf.edu

JACOBS, DONALD THOMAS, PHASE TRANSITIONS, CRITICAL PHENOMENA. **Personal Data:** m, c 2. **Education:** Univ S Fla, BA, 1971, MA, 1972; Univ Colo, PhD (physics), 1976. **Honors & Awards:** Am Phys Soc Prize Fac Mem Res Undergrad Inst, Fel Am Phys Soc. **Professional Experience:** PROF PHYSICS, COL WOOSTER, 1987-. **Memberships:** Am Phys Soc; Sigma Xi. **Research Statement & Publications:** Experimental investigations of critical phenomena in binary fluid mixtures; coexistence curves, heat capacity, turbidity, dielectric constant, and density. **Mailing Address:** Physics Dept, Col Wooster, Wooster, OH 44691. **Fax:** 330-263-2516. **E-Mail:** djacobs@wooster.edu

JACOBS, ELLIOTT WARREN, APPLIED MATHEMATICS. **Personal Data:** b Brooklyn, NY, February 10, 1950; m 1971. **Education:** State Univ NY, Stony Brook, BS, 1971; Adelphi Univ, MS, 1973, PhD (math), 1976. **Professional Experience:** ASSOC PROF MATH, EMBRY-RIDDLE AERONAUT UNIV, as of 2005; asst prof math, Embry-Riddle Aeronaut Univ, beginning 1978; asst prof math, Mt Union Col, 1977-1978; asst prof math, Muskingum Col, 1976-1977. **Memberships:** Am Math Soc; Math Asn Am. **Research Statement & Publications:** Differential equations; nonstandard analysis. **Mailing Address:** Dept Math, Embry-Riddle Aeronaut Univ, 600 S Clyde Morris Blvd Rm 118, Daytona Beach, FL 32114-3900. **E-Mail:** e.jacobs@141.com

JACOBS, EMMETT S, AIR POLLUTION. **Personal Data:** b Selma, NC, March 17, 1926; m 1952, c 2. **Education:** Univ NC, BS, 1950; Lehigh Univ, MS, 1955, PhD (anal chem), 1958. **Professional Experience:** RETIRED; div head, petrol additives & environ & mgr antiknocks tech serv, Petrol Lab, Petrochem Dept, 1978-1985; div head, Emissions & Eng Test Div, Petrol Lab, 1974-1978; supvr anal & environ studies, petrol Lab, 1971-1974; supvr automotive emission studies, petrol Lab, 1969-1971; res supvr anal res, Jackson Lab, Petrochem Dept, E I du Pont de Nemours & Co, Inc, 1966-1969; res chemist anal, Jackson Lab, Petrochem Dept, E I du Pont de Nemours & Co, Inc, 1958-1966; instr anal chem, Lehigh Univ, 1952-1955; chemist, Nitrogen Div, Allied Chem Corp, 1950-1952. **Memberships:** Am Chem Soc; Am Soc Testing & Mat. **Research Statement & Publications:** Analytical chemistry, especially gas chromatography, electrochemistry, x-ray and infrared spectroscopy; atmospheric chemistry and analysis of automotive emissions; gasoline quality and volume demand; gasoline blinding; lead in gasoline environmental issues. **Mailing Address:** 33 Paxon Dr, Wilmington, DE 19803.

JACOBS, FRANCIS ALBIN, BIOCHEMISTRY, NUTRITION. **Personal Data:** b Minneapolis, Minn, February 23, 1918; m 1953, c 5. **Education:** Regis Col, BS, 1939; St Louis Univ, PhD (biochem), 1949. **Professional Experience:** PROF EMER BIOCHEM, SCH MED, UNIV NDAK, 1987-; mem rev & evalcomt, NSF, 1960-1980; mem adv comt sci & math, Dept Pub Instr, NDak, 1959-1980; dir resparticipation for teacher training prog, Univ NDak, 1959-1963; from asst prof to prof, Sch Med, Univ NDak, 1954-1987; from instr to asst prof biochem, Sch Med, Univ Pittsburgh, 1951-1954; Nat Cancer Inst fel chemotherapeut, 1949 & 1950; biochemist, Off Sci Res & Develop, 1942-1945; chemist, Shattuck Chem Co, 1941; Asst chem, Univ Denver, 1939-1941. **Memberships:** Fel AAAS; Am Soc Biochem & Molecular Biol; Am Chem Soc; Soc Exp Biol &Med; Am Inst Nutrit; Sigma Xi. **Research Statement & Publications:** Antibiotics and antitumor agents from microorganisms; gastroenterology, intestinal transport of amino acids and lipids; audiovisual aids for teaching biochemisty and nutrition; trace metal nutrition and bioavailability of zinc and copper. **Mailing Address:** Dept Biochem & Molecular Biol, NDak Univ, 1525 Robertson Ct, Grand Forks, ND 58201.

JACOBS, GARY K, GEOCHEMISTRY. **Education:** Univ Vt, BA, 1976; Pa State Univ, PhD (Geochem), 1981. **Professional Experience:** DIV DIR, ENVIRON SCI DIV, OAK RIDGE NAT LAB, 1983-; Basalt Waste Isolation Proj, Rockwell Hanford Opers, Richland, 1981-1983; Grand Valley Univ Dept Geol, Allendale, 1980-1981. **Research Statement & Publications:** Problem solving; research; and management in the earth sciences; atmospheric science; ecology; microbiology; and societal-technology interactions. **Mailing Address:** Environ Sci Div, Oak Ridge Nat Lab, Oak Ridge, TN 37831-6037. **E-Mail:** jacobsgk@ornl.gov

JACOBS, GERALD DANIEL, PHYSICAL CHEMISTRY, SPECTROSCOPY. **Personal Data:** b Perrysburg, Ohio, January 19, 1935; m 1958, c 2. **Education:** Bowling Green State Univ, BA, 1957; Mich State Univ, PhD (microwave spectros), 1961. **Professional Experience:** PROF EMER CHEM, NORTHERN MICH UNIV, as of 2004; prof chem, Northern Mich Univ, beginning 1970; head dept, Northern MichUniv, 1970-1989; assoc prof, Northern Mich Univ, 1964-1970; res chemist, chem div, UnionCarbide Corp, 1963-1964. **Memberships:** Am Chem Soc. **Research Statement & Publications:** Microwave spectroscopy as applied to molecular structure determinations; determination of crystal structure by x-ray diffraction; physical chemistry of clathrates. **Mailing Address:** Dept Chem, Northern Mich Univ, 1401 Presque Isle Ave, Marquette, MI 49855-5301.

JACOBS, GERALD H, MEDICAL RESEARCH. **Education:** Univ Vt, BA; Ind Univ, PhD. **Professional Experience:** PROF, NEUROSCIENCE RES INST & DEPT PSYCHOL, UNIV CALIF, as of 2002. **Memberships:** Optical Soc Am; AAAS. **Mailing Address:** Dept Psychol Univ Calif, Bio Two Rm 6157, Santa Barbara, CA 93106. **E-Mail:** jacobs@psych.ucsb.edu

JACOBS, H KURT, CORONARY BLOOD FLOW, POSITIVE END EXPIRATORY PRESSURE. **Personal Data:** b September 8, 1943; c 2. **Education:** St Norbert Col, BS, 1965; Univ Mich, MS, 1968; Univ Mo, PhD (physiol), 1973. **Professional Experience:** PROF SURG & PHYSIOL, LOYOLA UNIV MED CTR, 1973-; res physiologist & dir, Hines Vet Admin Hosp. **Memberships:** Am Physiol Soc; Am Asn Lab Animal Sci. **Research Statement & Publications:** Cardiopulmonary interactions. **Mailing Address:** Dept Surg & Physiol, Loyola Univ Med Ctr, 2160 S First Ave, Maywood, IL 60153. **Fax:** 708-216-2319.

JACOBS, HAROLD ROBERT, MECHANICAL ENGINEERING, THERMAL SCIENCES. **Personal Data:** b Portland, Ore, November 19, 1936; m 1961, c 3. **Education:** Univ Portland, BS, 1958; Wash State Univ, MSME, 1961; Ohio State Univ, PhD (mech eng), 1965. **Professional Experience:** PROF EMER MECH ENG, COL ENG, as of 2003; DEPT HEAD MECH ENG, PA STATE, 1984-; assoc dean res, col eng, beginning 1981;

chmn dept civil eng, Col Eng, 1978-1979; prof mech eng, Univ Utah, beginning 1974; from asst prof to assoc prof mech eng, Col Eng, 1967-1974; mem tech staff, Aerospace Corp, 1965-1968; res & develop engr, Boeing Co, 1961-1962; res & develop engr, Gen ElecCo, 1958-1959. **Memberships:** Assoc fel Am Inst Aeronaut & Astronaut; Am Soc Mech Engrs; Sigma Xi. **Research Statement & Publications:** Heat transfer; fluid mechanics; geothermal energy; oil shale processing; direct contact processing; condensers; thermal stresses; fracture. **Mailing Address:** Col Eng, Pa State Univ, East Stroudsburg, PA 18301-9988.

JACOBS, HARRY LEWIS, PSYCHOPHYSIOLOGY, NUTRITION. **Personal Data:** b Philadelphia, Pa, April 10, 1925; m 1950, c 4. **Education:** Univ Del, BA, 1950, MA, 1951; Cornell Univ, PhD, 1955. **Professional Experience:** RETIRED; affil scientist, Worcester Found Exp Biol, beginning 1971; prof, Clark Univ, 1970-1976; assoc prof physiol, Clark Univ, 1966-1969; assoc dir behav sci div, US Army NatickLabs, 1966-1968; vis lectr nutrit & food sci, Mass Inst Technol, 1966-1967; assoc prof psychol, Univ Ill, 1961-1967; NIMH spec res fel physiol, Sch Med, Univ Rochester, 1959-1961; asst prof psychol, Bucknell Univ, 1954-1960. **Memberships:** AAAS; fel Am Psychol Asn; Am Physiol Soc; Am Inst Nutrit; Am Inst Biol Sci. **Research Statement & Publications:** Appetite, hunger and food habits. **Mailing Address:** 63 Moore Rd, Behav Sci Div Natick Labs, Wayland, MA 01778-1430.

JACOBS, HARVEY, PHYSICAL CHEMISTRY, ORGANIC CHEMISTRY. **Personal Data:** b Cleveland, Ohio, August 10, 1928; m 1953, c 3. **Education:** Ohio State Univ, BS, 1950; Temple Univ, MA, 1954, PhD (chem), 1956. **Professional Experience:** ANALYTICAL CHEMIST, GLIDDEN CO, 1972-; toxicologist, Philadelphia Med Exam Off, 1971-1972; Res chemist, Anal Lab, Rohm & Haas Co, 1956-1971. **Memberships:** Am Chem Soc; Soc Appl Spectros. **Research Statement & Publications:** Gas chromatography; nuclear magnetic resonance; mass spectrometry. **Mailing Address:** 1481 Blackmore Rd, Cleveland Heights, OH 44118-1314.

JACOBS, HYDE SPENCER, AGRONOMY. **Personal Data:** b Declo, Idaho, May 15, 1926; m 1950, c 5. **Education:** Univ Idaho, BS, 1952, MS, 1954; Mich State Univ, PhD (soil chem), 1957. **Professional Experience:** PROF EMER, KANS STATE UNIV, 1995-; dir, Kans Water Resource ResInst, 1988-1995; asst to dean agr, Kans Evapotranspiration Lab, 1987-1995; asst dir exten &dir agr progs, Kans Evapotranspiration Lab, 1981-1987; head dept agron, KansEvapotranspiration Lab, 1971-1980; assoc ed, J Agron Educ, 1970-1974; dir, KansEvapotranspiration Lab, 1968-1979; NSF fel, Utah State Univ, 1968-1969; prof soils, Kans WaterResources Res Inst, 1966-1980; dir, Kans Water Resources Res Inst, 1964-1974; consult, EarthSci Curric Proj, Am Geol Inst, 1964-1965; from asst prof to assoc prof, Kans State Univ, 1957-1966; instr soils, Mich State Univ, 1953-1957. **Memberships:** Fel Am Soc Agron; Soil Sci Soc Am. **Research Statement & Publications:** Agronomy, soils; irrigation; water resources. **Mailing Address:** 1520 Nichols Hall, Manhattan, KS 66503.

JACOBS, IRA, TELECOMMUNICATIONS, FIBER OPTICS. **Personal Data:** b Brooklyn, NY, January 3, 1931; m, c 3. **Education:** City Col NY, BS, 1950; Purdue Univ, MS, 1952, PhD (physics), 1955. **Honors & Awards:** Inst Elec & Electronics Engrs 3rd Millenium Serv Medal, 2000. **Professional Experience:** PROF ELEC ENG, VA TECH, 1987-; Bell Labs Director 1967-1987, Dept Head 1962-1967, Supervisor 1960-1962, MTS 1955-1960; Summer physicist, Signal Corps Eng Labs, 1952. **Memberships:** Life Fel Inst Elec & Electronics Engrs; Optical Soc Am, SPIE. **Research Statement & Publications:** Study of radar and military communications systems; analysis of transmission systems performance; development and evaluation of pulse code modulation transmission systems; research and development of fiber optic communication technology and systems. **Mailing Address:** Dept Elec & Comp Eng, Va Tech, 302 Whittemore (0111), Blacksburg, VA 24061. **Fax:** 540-231-3362. **E-Mail:** ijacobs@vt.edu

JACOBS, IRWIN MARK, COMMUNICATION THEORY, COMPUTER SCIENCES. **Personal Data:** b New Bedford, Mass, October 18, 1933; m 1954, c 4. **Education:** Cornell Univ, BEE, 1956; Mass Inst Technol, MS, 1957, ScD(elec eng), 1959. **Honors & Awards:** Biann Award Outstanding Contrib Aerospace Commun, Inst Aeronaut & Astronaut, 1980; First Ann Excellence Award, Am Electronics Asn, 1989; Nat Medal Technol, 1994. **Professional Experience:** CHMN & CHIEF EXEC OFFICER, QUALCOMM INC, as of 2006; pres, Qualcomm Inc, 1985-1991; FOUNDER, QUALCOMM INC, 1985-; pres, Linkabit Corp, 1968-1985; from assoc prof to prof info & comput sci, Univ Calif, San Diego, 1966-1972; Indust Teaching, Minneapolis-Honeywell, Inc, 1963 & Bolt Beranek & Newman, Inc, 1965; NASA resident res fel, Jet Propulsion Lab, 1964-1965; Lincoln Lab, Mass Inst Technol, 1961-1962; Consult, Appl Res Lab, Sylvania Elec Prod, Inc, 1959-; from asst prof to assoc prof, Mass Inst Technol, 1959-1966; res asst elec eng, Mass Inst Technol, 1958-1959; mem gov bd, Inst Elec & Electronics Engrs Commun Soc; chmn, Sci Adv Group, Defense Commun Agency & Eng Adv Coun, Univ Calif. **Memberships:** Nat Acad Eng; fel Inst Elec & Electronics Engrs; Asn Comput Mach; Sigma Xi. **Research Statement & Publications:** Information theory, coding theory and applications to digital communications; satellite multiple access, microprogrammed communications systems and packet switching; author of numerous technical publications. **Mailing Address:** Qualcomm Inc, 6455 Lusk Blvd, San Diego, CA 92121. **Fax:** 619-658-2500. **E-Mail:** ijacobs@qualcomm.com

JACOBS, ISRAEL S(AMSON), SOLID STATE PHYSICS. **Personal Data:** b Buffalo, NY, July 20, 1925; American citizen; m 1950, Judith; c 2. **Education:** Univ Mich, BS, 1947; Univ Chicago, SM, 1951, PhD (physics), 1953. **Professional Experience:** CONSULT, GEN ELEC GLOBAL RES, 1994-; res, Solid State Chem Lab, Univ Bordeaux, 1989; res, Mass Inst Technol, 1983-1984; Coolidge fel, Gen Elec, 1982; consult, Nat Res Coun, 1978, 1984 & 1986; consult, US Energy Res & Develop Admin, 1977; steering comt, Conf Magnetism & Magnetic Mat, 1968-1971; exec chmn, Int Cong Magnetism, 1966-1967; res, High Magnetic Field Lab, UnivGrenoble, 1965-1966; mem organizing comt, Int Cong Magnetism, 1962-1967 & 1979-1985; pub chmn, Conf Magnetism & Magnetic Mat, 1962-1964; prog chmn, Conf Magnetism & MagneticMat, 1961; Mem adv comt, Conf Magnetism & Magnetic Mat, 1959-1994; physicist, Gen ElecRes & Develop Ctr, 1954-1994; asst physics, Univ Chicago, 1949-1950. **Memberships:** fel Am Phys Soc; fel Inst Elec & Electronics Engrs; Magnetics Soc; fel AAAS. **Research Statement & Publications:** Magnetism and magnetic materials; high magnetic field phenomena; antiferromagnetism; low-dimensional magnetic model systems; industrial applications of magnetics research; microwave properties of composites; nanoparticle magnetics. **Mailing Address:** Gen Elec Global Res (KWB 1305), 1 Res Circle, Niskayuna, NY 12309-1027. **Fax:** 518-387-5299. **E-Mail:** jacobs@research.ge.com

JACOBS, JACK H, STRUCTURAL ENGINEERING. **Education:** Va Polytech Inst, PhD (Aerospace Eng), 1982. **Professional Experience:** MGR TECHNOL, DEFENSE & SPACE ELECTRONICS DIV, HONEYWELL INC, 1997-. **Mailing Address:** McDonnell Douglas Aerospace, PO Box 516 Mail Code 1021310, St Louis, MO 63166-0516. **Fax:** 314-849-6759.

JACOBS, JACQUELINE E, ENVIRONMENTAL BIOLOGY. **Personal Data:** b Wilkinsburg, Pa, June 17, 1923; m 1947, Harold W; c Patricia (Lipe), Janet (Bex) & James C. **Education:** Coker Col, AB, 1944; Univ SC, MS, 1961, PhD (biol), 1968. **Honorary Degrees:** LHD, Coker Col, 1986. **Honors & Awards:** SC Conserv Educ of Year Award, SC Wildlife Fedn; Conserv Award of Year, SC, Woodmen of the World, 1975; F Bartow Culp Award Distinguished Serv, SC Wildlife Fedn, 1975; Distinguished Serv Award, Nat Wildlife Fedn, 1982; Meritorious Service Award, SC Wildlife & Marine Resources Dept, 1983; Order of the Palmetto, Gov Richard Riley, 1983. **Professional Experience:** CONSULT, 1983-; mem, Harry Hampton Mem Wildlife Fund bd dir, 1983-1988; mem, Wildlife Adv Comt, Col Agr Sci, Clemson Univ, 1976-1982; exec dir, SC Wildlife Fedn, 1974-1983; mem bd trustees, Coker Col, SC, 1971-1977; Bd trustees, Coker Col, 1971-1977; instr, Spring Valley High Sch, 1971-1973; instr specialist, Instr TV, SC State Dept Educ, 1968-1971; grant, Belle W Baruch Found, Univ SC, 1967-1968; asst, Univ SC, 1964-1968; fel botany, W Gordon Belser, Univ SC, 1964-1965; teacher, Dreher High Sch, Columbia, 1958-1964; Teacher, Moultrie High, Mt Pleasant, SC, 1957-1958; life mem, bd, SC Wildlife Fedn. **Memberships:** The Wildlife Soc; Sigma Xi; Bot Soc Am. **Research Statement & Publications:** (Taxonomic Survey) Freshwater algae of South Carolina; a curriculum guide for life science on educational TV. **Mailing Address:** Five Northlake Rd, Columbia, SC 29223.

JACOBS, J(AMES) H(ARRISON), METALLURGICAL ENGINEERING. **Personal Data:** b St Charles, Mo, April 13, 1916; m 1942, c 2. **Education:** Pa State Univ, BS, 1936; Univ Mo, BS, 1939, MS, 1940. **Professional Experience:** TECH MGR CARBON/ZINC BATTERIES, BATTERY PROD DIV, UNIONCARBIDE CORP, 1972-; tech mgr nickel-cadmium battery develop, Consumer Prod Div, 1963-1972; mgr chem eng develop, Tech Dept, Union Carbide Metals Co Div, 1951-1963; metallurgist, US Bur Mines, 1941-1951; Chemist, Western Elec Co, Ill, 1936-1939. **Memberships:** Electrochem Soc; Am Inst Mining Metall & Petrol Engrs. **Research Statement & Publications:** Hydrometallurgy and electrometallurgy of non-ferrous metals. **Mailing Address:** Math Scis Dept, Cas-154, Bay Village, OH 44140.

JACOBS, JEROME BARRY, CANCER BIOLOGY, DIAGNOSTIC ELECTRON MICROSCOPY. **Personal Data:** b Worcester, Mass, December 15, 1942; c 3. **Education:** Univ Vt, BS, 1965, MS, 1967; Clark Univ, PhD (cell biol), 1971. **Professional Experience:** ASST CHIEF, DEPT LAB MED, ST VINCENT HOSP, 1971-; assoc prof path, Univ Mass Med Sch; prof life sci, Worcester Polytech Ins; prof cell biol, Clark Univ. **Memberships:** Int Acad Path; Am Asn Pathologists; Am Soc Clin Pathologists; Am Soc Cell Biol; AAAS; Am Asn Cancer Res; Sigma Xi. **Research Statement & Publications:** Renal diseases; bladder cancer. **Mailing Address:** 48 Stark Rd, Worcester, MA 01602.

JACOBS, JOHN EDWARD, BIOMEDICAL ENGINEERING, ELECTRICAL ENGINEERING. **Personal Data:** b Kansas City, Mo, June 15, 1920. **Education:** Northwestern Univ, BS, 1947, MS, 1948, PhD (elec eng), 1950. **Honorary Degrees:** ScD, Univ Strathclyde, 1971. **Honors & Awards:** Coffin Award, Gen Elec Co, 1953; Silver Medal, Am Soc Nondestructive Testing, 1968. **Professional Experience:** PROF EMER ELEC ENG SCI, NORTHWESTERN UNIV, 1990-; consult, Fed Coun Sci & Technol, 1971-1977; chmn, Manpower Comt, President's Adv Coun Mgt Improv, 1971-1973; mem, Automated Clin Lab Comt, Nat Inst Gen Med Sci, NIH, 1970-1974; exec dir, Biomed Eng Ctr, Walter P Murphy prof, 1969-1990; pres, Biomed Eng Resource Corp, 1969-1971; prof elec eng, Northwestern Univ, 1960-1969; elec engr, Res Lab, 1959-1960; adj prof, Rensselaer Polytech Inst, 1959-1960; McKay vis prof, Univ Calif, 1957-1958; mgr, Adv Develop Lab, 1953-1959; Lectr grad sch, Northwestern Univ, 1952-1958; Supvry res engr, X-Ray Dept, Gen Elec Co, 1950-1953; mem, Biomed Training Comt Consult Radiol Sect, Army Res Off. **Memberships:** Nat Acad Eng; Biomed Eng Soc (treas 1968-1972); Instrument Soc Am. **Research Statement & Publications:** Photoconduction electron optics; biomedicine; transducers. **Mailing Address:** dept elec & comput eng, Northwestern Univ, Evanston, IL 60201. **E-Mail:** jacobs@ece.northwestern.edu

JACOBS, JOSEPH DONOVAN, CIVIL ENGINEERING. **Personal Data:** b Motley, Minn, December 24, 1908; m 1937, c 1. **Education:** Univ Minn, BSCE, 1934. **Professional Experience:** RETIRED; chmn, US Nat Comt Tunneling Technol, Nat Acad Sci, 1977; sr officer, Jacobs Assocs, 1955-1978; chief engr, Kaiser-Walsh-Perini-Raymond, Australia, 1954-1955; civil engr & construct supvr, Walsh Construct Co, New York & San Francisco, 1934-1954. **Memberships:** Nat Acad Eng; fel Am Soc Civil Engrs; Am Inst Mining, Metal & Petrol Engrs; Nat Soc Prof Engrs. **Mailing Address:** 35 Bevmar Lane, Alamo, CA 94507.

JACOBS, JOSEPH JOHN, chemical engineering; deceased, see previous edition for last biography

JACOBS, JUDITH E, MATH EDUCATION. **Personal Data:** b Newark, NJ, June 16, 1943. **Education:** City Univ New York, BA, 1963, MA, 1967; NY Univ, PhD (math), 1973. **Honors & Awards:** Dora Helen Skipek Award, Int Women Math Educ, 1984. **Professional Experience:** ASSOC DIR, CTR EDUC & EQUITY MATH, SCI & TECHNOL, CALIF STATE POLYTECH UNIV, POMONA, as of 2002. **Memberships:** AAAS; Math Asn Am; Nat Coun Teachers Math. **Research Statement & Publications:** Math Education. **Mailing Address:** Ctr Educ & Equity Math, Sci & Technol, Calif State Polytech Univ, 3801 W Temple Ave, Pomona, CA 91768. **Fax:** 909-869-4616. **E-Mail:** jejacobs@csupomona.edu

JACOBS, KENNETH CHARLES, PHYSICS & ASTRONOMY, PHILOSOPHY OF SCIENCE. **Personal Data:** b McAllen, Tex, September 17, 1942; m 1968, Frances. **Education:** Mass Inst Technol, BS, 1964; Calif Inst Technol, PhD (physics), 1969. **Professional Experience:** PROF & CHAIR, PHYSICS DEPT, HOLLINS COL, ROANOKE, VA, 1994-; sabbatical researcher, Physics Dept, 1990-1991; assoc prof & chair, Physics Dept, 1984-1994; oper anal, AT&T Bell Labs, Whippany, NJ, 1979-1984; mem tech staff econ, Bell Tel Labs, Murray Hill, NJ, 1977-1979; vis researcher astrophysics, Max Planck Inst, Munich, WGer, 1977; Kapteyn Lab, Univ Groningen, Neth, 1975; Inst Astron, Cambridge Univ, Eng, 1974-1975; visprof, Max Planck Inst, Munich, WGer, 1972; asst prof astron, Astron Dept, Univ Va, Charlottesville, 1970-1976; Postdoctoral fel cosmology res, Physics Dept, Univ Md, CollegePark, 1968-1970; Res aide, Lampf Accelerator, Los Alamos, NMex, 1965. **Memberships:** Am Astron Soc; Int Astron Union; Sigma Xi; fel Royal Astron Soc. **Research Statement & Publications:** Cosmological models; quantum cosmology; relativistic astrophysics; radio galaxies/quasars; tachyon theory; solar neutrino problem; celestial mechanics of Jovian Galilean moons; philosophy of science (mathematics); author of three textbooks. **Mailing Address:** Dept Physics, Hollins Col Box 9661, Roanoke, VA 24020.

JACOBS, LAURENCE ALAN, THEORETICAL PHYSICS, ELEMENTARY PARTICLE PHYSICS. **Personal Data:** b Mexico City, Mex, December 17, 1949; div, c 2. **Education:** Nat Univ Mex, BS, 1972; Mass Inst Technol, PhD (physics), 1976. **Honors & Awards:** Gunnar Kallen Award, 1975. **Professional Experience:** MEM STAFF, THINKING MACH, 1990-; MEM STAFF, MASS INST TECHNOL, 1985-; mem staff, Bell Labs, 1983-1985;

asst prof, Inst Theoret Physics, Univ Calif, Santa Barbara, 1981-1983; asst prof physics, Nat UnivMex, 1979-1981; res assoc, Brookhaven Nat Lab, 1977-1979; res assoc physics, Mass InstTechnol, 1976-1977; sci adv physics, Nat Sci &Technol, Mex. **Memberships:** Am Phys Soc; Soc Mex Physics; Acad Invert Sci; NY Acad Sci. **Research Statement & Publications:** Theoretical physics, field theory; mathematical physics; statistical mechanics; condensed-matter physics. **Mailing Address:** Ctr Theo Phys, Mass Inst Technol, 77 Mass Ave, Cambridge, MA 02139.

JACOBS, LAURENCE STANTON, GENERAL ENDOCRINOLOGY, NEUROENDOCRINOLOGY. **Personal Data:** b Boston, Mass, March 24, 1940; m 1963, c 2. **Education:** Harvard Univ, AB, 1960; Univ Rochester, MD, 1965. **Professional Experience:** PROF EMER MED, UNIV ROCHESTER SCH MED & DENT, as of 2004; assoc dean stud affairs, Univ Rochester Sch Med &Dent, beginning 1990; mem, Biomed Sci Study Sect, NIH, 1987-1991; pres, Asn Clin Res Ctr Prog Dirs, 1987-1989; actg head gastroenterol, Clin Res Ctr, 1983-1988; chmn, Merit Rev Bd Endocrinol, Vet Admin, 1983-1986; sr physician, Strong Mem Hosp, Rochester, NY, 1982-; prof med, Univ Rochester Med Ctr, beginning 1982; dir, Clin Res Ctr, 1977-1991; sr assoc physician, Strong Mem Hosp, Rochester, NY, 1977-1982; assoc prof, Univ Rochester Med Ctr, 1977-1982; from asst prof to instr med, 1971-1977; asst physician & consult clin chem, Barnes Hosp, St Louis, 1971-1977; lt comdr & med officer lab med, Ctrs Dis Control, USPHS, 1968-1970; fel endocrinol, Barnes Hosp, 1970-1972; fel endocrinol, Wash Univ, 1967-1968; intern & resident internal med, Wash Univ & Barnes Hosp, 1965-1967; res asst, Res Inst Med & Chem, 1960-1961. **Memberships:** AAAS; Am Soc Clin Invest; Endocrine Soc; Am Soc Biol Chemists; Int Soc Neuroendocrinol; Am Diabetes Asn; Am Fed Clin Res; Central Soc Clin Res. **Research Statement & Publications:** Hypothalamic control and molecular mechanisms of secretion of growth hormone and prolactin; structure, composition and enzymatic activities of isolated adenohypophysial secretory granules. **Mailing Address:** Dept Med Endocrinol, Univ Rochester Sch Med & Dent, 601 Elmwood Ave Box 693, Rochester, NY 14642-8693. **Fax:** 585-256-2789.

JACOBS, LOIS JEAN, MEDICINE, GENETICS. **Personal Data:** b Portage, Wis, March 10, 1947. **Education:** Univ Wis-Madison, BS, 1969, PhD (genetics), 1977, MD, 1987. **Professional Experience:** PVT PRACT, 1990-; second yr resident, Bay State Med Ctr, affil Tufts UnivMed Sch, 1988-1990; first yr resident, Med Sch, Wis-Madison, 1987-1988; asst scientist, DeptMed Genetics, 1981-1983; res assoc genetics, Inst Med Res, 1977-1980. **Memberships:** Environ Mutagen Soc; AMA. **Research Statement & Publications:** Somatic cell genetics, specifically mutagenesis and carcinogenesis in diploid human cells.

JACOBS, LOUIS JOHN, FLUID MIXING TECHNOLOGY, PHASE SEPARATION TECHNOLOGY. **Personal Data:** b Chicago, Ill, March 27, 1943; m 1965, Phyllis Clark; c Julie A & Matthew L. **Education:** Univ Wis-Madison, BS, 1965; Washington Univ, St Louis, Mo, MS, 1969. **Professional Experience:** DIR PROCESS MFG, KOCH MTLS CO, 2001-; dir technol & eng, KOCH IND INC, 1991-; dir eng develop, Res & Develop Div, 1989-1991; vpres starch opers, Corp Eng Div, A E Staley Mfg Co, 1988-1989; dir, Corp Eng Div, A E Staley Mfg Co, 1982-1988; mgr technol risk anal, Monsanto Co, 1980-1982; bus develop mgr, Monsanto Co, 1979-1980; affil prof, Wash Univ, St Louis, 1978-1979; eng supt, Monsanto Co, 1977-1979; Chmn, St Louis Sect, 1977; Chmn, Mixing Comt, Am Inst Chem Engrs, 1975-1976; Engr, Monsanto Co, 1965-1977. **Memberships:** Am Inst Chem Engrs. **Research Statement & Publications:** Author of various publications. **Mailing Address:** 8955 Boxthorn Ct, Wichita, KS 67226.

JACOBS, LOYD DONALD, ACOUSTICS. **Personal Data:** b Wolcott, Ind, November 22, 1932; m 1956, c Paul, John (deceased) & Ann. **Education:** Emporia State Univ, BA, 1954; Univ Nebr, MS, 1958. **Professional Experience:** RETIRED; sr prin engr, Seattle, Wash, 1990-1994; prin engr, Seattle, Wash, 1982-1989; group engr, Seattle, Wash, 1974-1982; sr engr, Seattle, Wash, 1962-1973; engr, Boeing Co, Wichita, Kans, 1957-1962. **Memberships:** Acoust Soc Am; Sigma Xi. **Research Statement & Publications:** Control and reduction of aircraft noise; response of aircraft structure to noise; noise radiation from surfaces immersed in airflow. **Mailing Address:** 2004 128th Ave SE, Bellevue, WA 98005.

JACOBS, MARC QUILLEN, MATHEMATICS. **Personal Data:** b Chandler, Okla, June 28, 1938. **Education:** Univ Okla, BS, 1960, MA, 1963, PhD (math), 1966. **Professional Experience:** RES SCIENTIST, DIRECTORATE MATH & GEOSCIENCES, as of 2005; PROF MATH, UNIV MO-COLUMBIA, 1974-; assoc prof, Univ Mo-Columbia, 1971-1974; asst prof math, Rice Univ, 1967-1968; asst prof math, appl math, Brown Univ, 1968-1971; res asst prof appl math, Brown Univ, 1966-1967; instr math, Univ Okla, 1965-1966; jr mathematician, Int Bus Mach Corp, 1960-1961. **Memberships:** Am Math Soc; Math Asn Am; Soc Indust & Appl Math; Sigma Xi. **Research Statement & Publications:** Optimal control theory. **Mailing Address:** Air Force Off Sci Res, 4015 Wilson Blvd Rm 713, Arlington, VA 22203-1954.

JACOBS, MARK, PLANT DEVELOPMENT, CELL RECEPTOR PROTEINS. **Personal Data:** b Princeton, NJ, May 19, 1950; m 2000, Ellen; c Jeffrey, Robinson, Patrick & Madeleine. **Education:** Harvard Univ, BA, 1971; Stanford Univ, PhD (biol), 1976. **Professional Experience:** DEAN, BARRETT HONORS COL, ARIZ STATE UNIV as of 2005; assoc provost, Swarthmore Col, 1993-1996; NAm ed, Plant Physiol & Biochem, 1990-2001; CENTENNIAL PROF BIOL PLANT PHYSIOL & DEVELOP, SWARTHMORE COL, 1989-; chmn, Swarthmore Col, 1987-1988, 1988-1990, & 1999-2001; Guggenheim fel, Cambridge Univ, Eng, 1986-1987; NATO fel, Freiburg Univ, Ger, 1976-1977; from asst prof to assoc prof, Swarthmore Col, 1975-1989. **Memberships:** Am Soc Plant Physiol (treas, 1991-1997); Sigma Xi. **Research Statement & Publications:** Biochemical mode of action of the plant growth regulators; hormonal control of plant development. **Mailing Address:** Dept Biol, Swarthmore Col, Swarthmore, PA 19081. **Fax:** 610-328-8663. **E-Mail:** mjacobs1@cc.swarthmore.edu

JACOBS, MARTIN JOHN, MEDICINAL CHEMISTRY, PHARMACEUTICAL & ORGANIC CHEMISTRY. **Personal Data:** b Chicago, Ill, June 28, 1944; m 1966, Gail; c 5. **Education:** Ill Inst Technol, BS, 1969; Colo State Univ, PhD (org chem), 1975. **Professional Experience:** VIS PROF CHEM, INT MINERALS & CHEM CORP, 1994-; chmn, Wabash Valley Sect, Am Chem Soc, 1993; mgr, Int Minerals& Chem Corp, 1992-1993; sr res scientist, Int Minerals & Chem Corp, 1982-1992; res chemist, Int Minerals & Chem Corp, 1975-1982; bd dirs, Ind State Univ Chapter Sigma Xi. **Memberships:** Am Chem Soc; Sigma Xi; Am Asn Pharm Soc; AAAS. **Research Statement & Publications:** Synthesis of compounds as products for use in pharmaceutical application; industrial intermediates and processchemistry; preformulation of new pharmaceutical agents. **Mailing Address:** Dept Chem, Lifesci Rose Hulman Inst Technol, 5500 E Wabash Ave, Terre Haute, IN 47803. **E-Mail:** martin.jacobs@rose-hulman.edu

JACOBS, MARY ELIZABETH, LIFE SCIENCES. **Personal Data:** b Chicago, Ill, August 2, 1942. **Education:** Trinity Col, BA, 1964; Univ Ill, Urbana, MS, 1966, PhD (biophysics), 1969. **Professional Experience:** ASSOCIATE DIR, CBER, OFF BLOOD RES & REV, FOOD & DRUG ADMIN, as of 1998; DIR, DIV LIFE SCI, CTR DEVICES & RADIOL HEALTH, FOOD & DRUG ADMIN, 1989-; staff, Div Life Sci and of Ophthalmic Devices, Ctr Devices & Radiol Health, Food & Drug Admin, 1978-1989; res asst prof, George Wash Univ Med Sch, 1974-1977; Grass fel, Marine BiolLab, Woods Hole, 1972; Postdoctoral fel, Univ Iowa, 1969 & Ind Univ, 1970-1974. **Memberships:** AAAS; Asn Res Vision & Opthal; Biophys Soc; Asn Women Sci. **Research Statement & Publications:** Risk assessment; ocular properties. **Mailing Address:** Off Blood Res & Rev, Food & Drug Admin, HFM-300, Rockville, MD 20852. **Fax:** 301-827-3533. **E-Mail:** mary.jacobs@fda.hhs.gov

JACOBS, MARYCE MERCEDES, TOXICOLOGY, CARCINOGENESIS. **Personal Data:** b El Paso, Tex, June 15, 1944. **Education:** NMex State Univ, BS, 1966; Univ Calif, Los Angeles, PhD (biochem), 1970. **Professional Experience:** PRES, HEALTH SCI INST INC, as of 2006; vpres res, Am Inst Cancer Res, beginning 1988; biochem toxicologist, MetrekDiv, Mitre Corp, 1983-1988; opponent, Univ Oulu, Finland, 1980; indust contract coordr, EppleyInst Res Cancer, Univ Nebr, 1979-1983; consult, Nat Large Bowel Cancer Cadre, Nat CancerInst, 1978-1982; from asst prof to assoc prof, Eppley Inst Res Cancer, Univ Nebr, 1977-1983; co-chmn biochem, Grad Sch Biomed Sci, Houston, 1973-1975; asst prof & asst biochemist, M DAnderson Hosp & Tumor Inst, Univ Tex, 1972-1977; res assoc, M D Anderson Hosp & TumorInst, Univ Tex, 1971-1972; res assoc, Univ Colo Med Ctr, 1970-1971. **Memberships:** Am Asn Cancer Res; NY Acad Sci; Sigma Xi; Soc Toxicol; Am Acad Clin Toxicol. **Research Statement & Publications:** Inhibition of chemical carcinogenesis; dietary selenium inhibition of tumor induction by 1, 2-Dimethylhydrazine and other carcinogens in animals; determination of the mechanisms of inhibition in in-vivo and in-vitro systems. **Mailing Address:** Health Sci Inst, Inc, 1350 Beverly Rd Ste 115-206, Mclean, VA 22101-3924. **Fax:** 410-326-7049.

JACOBS, MERLE EMMOR, ZOOLOGY, INSECT BIOCHEMISTRY. **Personal Data:** b Hollsopple, Pa, November 30, m Elizabeth. **Education:** Goshen Col, AB, 1949; Univ Ind, PhD (zoology), 1953. **Honors & Awards:** Lalor Award, Sigma Xi. **Professional Experience:** RES PROF EMER, ZOOL, GOSHEN COL, as of 2004; res prof zool, Goshen Col, beginning 1964; prof biol, EM Col, Va, 1962-1964; grant, NIH, 1959-1985; asst prof biol, Bethany Col, WVa, 1957-1962; Instr zool, Goshen Col, 1953-1954 & Duke Univ, 1954-1957; Eigenmann fel, Ind Univ. **Memberships:** Sigma Xi; Am Men Sci; AAAS. **Research Statement & Publications:** Behavior and biochemical genetics; melanistic polymorphism, Darwinian sexual selection revision; Drosophila genetics. **Mailing Address:** Dept Biol, Goshen Col, Goshen, IN 46526. **E-Mail:** merleej@goshen.edu

JACOBS, MICHAEL MOISES, INFARED PHYSICS, ELECTRO-OPTIC SPACE SYSTEMS & SPACE SYSTEMS ENGINEERING. **Personal Data:** b Miami, Fla, June 21, 1950; m 1980, Gloria; c Nicole, Amber & Michael. **Education:** Univ Miami, BS, 1972, MS, 1973, PhD (physics), 1975. **Honors & Awards:** 1992 Aerospace Corp Group Achievement Award 2003, 04, 05 Aerospace Corp Performance Recognition Award. **Professional Experience:** PRINCIPAL ENGINEER, SPACE BASED, SURVEILLANCE SYSTS ENG, AEROSPACE CORP, EL SEGUNDO, CALIF, 1980-; physicist & mem tech staff electro-optics, Satellite Systs Div, Rockwell Int, Seal Beach, Calif, 1977-1980; Instr physics, Orange Coast Col, 1976-1979; Res physicist laser optics, Sci Applns Inc, Atlanta, Ga, 1976; Physicist, Space Systs Analyst. **Memberships:** Am Inst Physics affil; Sigma Pi Sigma Soc of Physics Students. **Research Statement & Publications:** Electro-optic infrared and laser physics; acousto-optics; radiative transfer; atmospheric and oceanic optics; systems engineering; infrared focal plane device physics; space sensor mission planning/requirements; surveillance systems; simulations and modeling. **Mailing Address:** Aerospace Corp, 2350 E El Segundo Blvd, El Segundo, CA 90245-4691. **Fax:** 310-336-6611. **E-Mail:** michael.m.jacobs@aero.org

JACOBS, MORTON HOWARD, ANALYTICAL CHEMISTRY, TECHNICAL MANAGEMENT. **Personal Data:** b Newark, NJ, June 28, 1924; m 1970, Helen; c Paul. **Education:** Univ Pa, BA, 1946. **Professional Experience:** RETIRED; sr proj chemist, Spec Projs, beginning 1990; sr proj chemist, Chromatography & Spectros Res Dept, beginning 1978; proj leader spectroscopy, Instrumentation & Anal Res Dept, beginning 1960; chemist, Res Dept, 1958-1960; chemist, Control Lab, Int Flavors & Fragrances Inc, 1953-1958; biochemist, Univ Hosp, Univ Mich, 1950-1952. **Memberships:** Am Chem Soc; Int Soc Magnetic Resonance; Soc Appl Spectros. **Research Statement & Publications:** Application of chromatographic and spectroscopic techniques; magnetic resonance to structure elucidation of flavor and aroma chemicals, both natural and synthetic. **Mailing Address:** 97 Cotswold Circle, Ocean, NJ 07712.

JACOBS, MYRON SAMUEL, PATHOLOGY, ANATOMY. **Personal Data:** b Jersey City, NJ, May 17, 1922; m 1959, Miriam Klebaner; c Louise S & Suzanne S. **Education:** Univ Pa, BA, 1945; NY Univ, MS, 1951, PhD, 1955. **Professional Experience:** PROF EMER PATH, COL DENT, NY UNIV, 1987-; vis prof histol & Neuroscience, embryol & neuroanat, NY Med Col, 1981-1985; from assoc prof to prof path, Col Dent, NY Univ, 1973-1987; adj assoc prof, Neural Sci & Gross Anat, Cornell Univ Med Col, 1967-1973; res assoc comp path, Osborn Lab Marine Sci, NY Aquarium, 1966-1972; dir cetaceanbrain lab, embryol & neuroanat, NY Med Col, 1962-1965; from asst prof to assoc prof anat, embryol & neuroanat, NY Med Col, 1957-1965; instr histol, embryol & neuro anat, NY Med Col, 1956-1957; lectr histol & embryol, Queen's Univ, Ont, 1954-1956; asst anat, Col Dent, NY Univ, 1951-1954. **Memberships:** Am Asn Anat; Soc Neuroscience; NY Acad Sci; Sigma Xi. **Research Statement & Publications:** Skin grafts and thermal changes in transplantation, rat; alloxan diabetes, hamster; cetacean nervous system. **Mailing Address:** Dept Path, NY Univ, New York, NY 10011.

JACOBS, NICHOLAS JOSEPH, BACTERIOLOGY. **Personal Data:** b Oakland, Calif, March 29, 1933; m 1959, c 1. **Education:** Univ Ill, BS, 1955; Cornell Univ, PhD, 1960. **Honorary Degrees:** MA, Dartmouth Col, 1985. **Professional Experience:** PROF MICROBIOL & IMMUNOL, DARTMOUTH MED SCH, 1980-; from instr to assocprof, Dartmouth Med Sch, 1964-1980; from asst bacteriologist to assoc bacteriologist, Am MeatInst Found, 1961-1964; Res assoc, Univ Ill, 1959-1961. **Memberships:** AAAS; Am Soc Microbiol; Sigma Xi. **Research Statement & Publications:** Bacterial physiology; pathogenic bacteriology; heme synthesis in bacteria, plants, and animals. **Mailing Address:** Dept Microbiol & Immunol, Dartmouth Med Sch, HB 7550, Hanover, NH 03755-3842.

JACOBS, PATRICIA ANN, GENETICS. **Personal Data:** b London, Eng, October 8, 1934. **Education:** Univ St Andrews, BSc, 1956, DSc(cytogenetics), 1966. **Professional Experience:** DIR GENETICS LAB, SALISBURY HOSP, WESSEX, as of 1997; PROF ANAT, SCH MED, UNIV HAWAII, 1973-; Scientist, Med Res Coun, 1957-1972. **Memberships:** Genetics Soc Gt Brit; Am Soc Human Genetics. **Research Statement & Publications:** Human cytogenetics. **Mailing Address:** Wessex Regional Genetics Lab, Gen Hosp, Fisherton St, Salisbury, UK.

JACOBS, PATRICIA ANNE, OPERATIONS RESEARCH. **Education:** Northwestern Univ, BS, 1969, MS, 1971, PhD (appl math), 1973. **Honors & Awards:** Elected Fellow of the

Royal Statistical Society 1980; Elected ordinary member of the International Statistical Institute 1991. **Professional Experience:** PROF OPERS RES, NAVAL POSTGRAD SCH, 1986-; Assoc ed, Mgt Sci, 1981- 1998& Naval Res Logistics, 1982-1992; assoc prof, Naval Postgrad Sch, 1978-1986; Asst prof opers res, Stanford Univ, 1972-1978. **Memberships:** Inst Math Statist; AAAS; Institute for Oper. Res. and the Management Sciences. **Research Statement & Publications:** Stochastic modeling and statistical analysis in operations research and related fields. **Mailing Address:** Opers Res Dept, Naval Postgrad Sch, Glasgow Hall 246, Monterey, CA 93943. **Fax:** 831-656-2595. **E-Mail:** pajacobs@nps.edu

JACOBS, PATRICK W M, SOLID STATE CHEMISTRY & CHEMICAL PHYSICS, COMPUTER SIMULATION. **Personal Data:** b Durban, SAfrica, September 15, 1923; m 1981, c Richard, Laura & Robert. **Education:** Univ Natal, BSc, 1941, MSc, 1943; Univ London, PhD (phys chem), 1951, DSc(physChem), 1963. **Honors & Awards:** Solid State Chem Medal, Royal Soc Chem, 1983. **Professional Experience:** PROF EMER PHYS CHEM, UNIV WESTERN ONT, 1989-; vis fel, WolfsonCol, Oxford, Eng, 1982; Overseas fel, Churchill Col, Cambridge, Eng, 1973-1974; sr prof, UnivWestern Ont, 1965-1989; reader, Univ Western Ont, 1964-1965; from asst lectr to sr lectr physchem, Univ Western Ont, 1950-1964; Beit fel, Imp Col, London, 1948-1950; lectr chem, RhodesUniv, SAfrica, 1946-1948. **Memberships:** fel Royal Soc Chem; Can Inst Chem; Can Asn Physicists. **Research Statement & Publications:** Decomposition of solids; optical and electrical properties of solids; computer simulation of condensed matter. **Mailing Address:** Dept Chem, Univ Western Ont, Off: Rm 126, Lab Rm 26, Chem Bldg, London, ON N6A 5B7, Can. **Fax:** 519-661-3022. **E-Mail:** pjacobs@uwo.ca

JACOBS, PETER MARTIN, QCD, HADRONIC PHYSICS. **Personal Data:** b Hamilton, Ont, November 7, 1957; m 1991, Karen; c Eliana S. **Education:** Univ Toronto, BS, 1979; Yale Univ, MPhil, 1982; Weizmann Inst Sci, PhD (physics), 1987. **Honors & Awards:** Alexander von Humboldt Soc Fel, 1994-1995; CERN Sci Assoc, 2004-2005; Am Phys Soc Fellow, 2005. **Professional Experience:** SR SCIENTIST, LAWRENCE BERKELEY NAT LAB, 1997-; div fel, Nuclear Sci Div, Lawrence Berkeley Nat Lab, 1992-1997; staff scientist, Nuclear Sci Div, Lawrence Berkeley Lab, 1990-1992; researcher, Nuclear Sci Div, Lawrence Berkeley Lab, 1988-1990; Researcher, Univ Calif, San Francisco, 1987-1988. **Memberships:** Am Phys Soc. **Research Statement & Publications:** Quantum Chromodynamics; Phase transitions and properties of strongly interacting matter. **Mailing Address:** Lawrence berkeley nat lab, 1 Cyclotron Rd, MS 70-319, Berkeley, CA 94720. **Fax:** 510-486-4818. **E-Mail:** pmjacobs@lbl.gov

JACOBS, RALPH R, QUANTUM ELECTRONICS, ENGINEERING PHYSICS. **Personal Data:** b Niagara Falls, NY, December 31, 1942; div, c Aleda A & Liana L. **Education:** NY Univ, BS, 1964; Yale Univ, MS, 1965, PhM, 1967, PhD (physics), 1969. **Professional Experience:** ASSOC DIR, INDUST EDUC PROG, as of 2002; dir, New Technol Initiatives, Lawrence Livermore Nat Lab, beginning 1990; dir, Corp Tech Develop, 1989-1990; eng mgr, Spectra-Physics, 1985-1989; mgr res & advan develop, Spectra-Physics, 1980-1985; sr physicist & proj mgr, laser-prog, Lawrence Livermore Lab, Univ Calif, 1972-1980; mem tech staff, GTE Labs Inc, Bayside, NY, 1969-1972; lab instr physics, Yale Univ, 1967-1969; mem bd govs, Lasers & Electro-optics Soc, Inst Elec & Electronics Engrs. **Memberships:** Sigma Xi; fel Am Phys Soc; fel Optical Soc Am; fel Inst Elec & Electronics Engrs Lasers & Electro-Optic Soc. **Research Statement & Publications:** Basic and applied aspects of atomic, molecular and laser physics in gaseous, liquid and solid state media; quantum electronics; laser spectroscopy-linear and nonlinear (ultraviolet, visible, infrared); low and high pressure gas discharges; high resolution microwave spectroscopy; rotational, vibrational, and electronic relaxation in molecules; new laser research and development various laser applications including areas of laser medicine, laser materials processing, laser metrology; heightened skills in management of technologists and strategic planning that emphasizes optimization of research and development, engineering, marketing, and manufacturing considerations for major program and commercial success. **Mailing Address:** Ctr Biophotonics Sci & Technol, Univ Calif, Davis, 4800 2nd Ave, Sacramento, CA 95817. **Fax:** 916-452-2034.

JACOBS, RICHARD L, ORTHOPEDIC SURGERY, BIOCHEMISTRY. **Personal Data:** b Elsberry, Mo, December 29, 1930; m 1954, c 3. **Education:** State Univ Iowa, BA, 1952, MD, 1956, MS, 1961. **Professional Experience:** US VET ADMIN HOSPS, 1968-; Prof orthop surg & head div, Albany Med Ctr, 1974-1996; Dixon State Sch, 1966-1974; from asst prof to prof orthop, Univ Ill Med Ctr, 1966-1974; consult, Ill Div Serv Crippled Children, 1965-1974; resident orthop surg, State Univ Iowa, 1962-1965; Orthop Res & Educ Found res fel orthop, Mass Gen Hosp-Harvard Univ, 1961-1962; Arthritis & Rheumatism Found fel, State Univ Iowa, 1959-1962. **Memberships:** AAAS; AMA; Am Chem Soc; Am Inst Chem; Am Acad Orthop Surg; Sigma Xi; Am Orthop Asn. **Research Statement & Publications:** Vitamin metabolism; collagen chemistry; immunology. **Mailing Address:** Albany Med Col, 47 New Scotland Ave, Albany, NY 12208-3412.

JACOBS, RICHARD LEE, ORGANIC CHEMISTRY. **Personal Data:** b Perrysburg, Ohio, August 4, 1931; m 1956, c 4. **Education:** Bowling Green State Univ, BA, 1953; Mich State Univ, MS, 1955, PhD (org chem), 1959. **Professional Experience:** RETIRED; assoc chair, Chem Dept, Bowling Green State Univ, 1988-1995; tech& legal mgr, Prin Bus Enterprises, 1982-1988; dir lab, Sherwin Williams Chems, 1966-1982; sr chemist, Maumee Chem Co, 1962-1966; res chemist, Koppers Co, Inc, Pa, 1959-1962; asst, Mich State Univ, 1953-1959. **Memberships:** Am Chem Soc; Soc Heterocyclic Chemists; Sigma Xi; fel Am Inst Chemists. **Research Statement & Publications:** Organic sulfur compounds, especially thiacyclopropanes and thiophene; nitriles preparation and reactions; alkylation and reaction mechanisms of aromatics; nitrogen heterocycles. **Mailing Address:** 558 Clover Lane, Perrysburg, OH 43551.

JACOBS, RICHARD M, ORTHODONTICS, ANATOMY. **Personal Data:** b Wloclawek, Poland, October 31, 1924; American citizen; m 1950, Federbusch; c Steven K. **Education:** Maximilian Univ, Dr med dent, 1948; NY Univ, DDS, 1952; Univ Calif, Berkeley, MPH, 1961; Med Col Va, PhD (anat), 1964; Univ Ill, MS (orthod), 1965. **Professional Experience:** PROF EMER ORTHOD, COL DENT, UNIV IOWA, as of 2000; chmn, Grad Educ Sect, Am Asn Dent Schs, 1973-1976; assoc dean col, Univ Iowa, 1967-1971; prof orthod, Col Dent, Univ Iowa, beginning 1966; actg head dept oral biol& curric coordr, Univ Iowa, 1966-1971; asst dean col dent, Univ Iowa, 1966-1967; assoc proforthod & head dept, Fac Dent, Univ BC, 1965-1966; Nat Inst Dent Res fel, Med Col Va, 1961-1963& Univ Ill, 1963-1965; dentist, Nev State Dept Pub Health, 1959-1960; resident dent, NY StateDept Ment Hyg, 1952-1953. **Memberships:** Fel Am Pub Health Asn; Am Asn Anat; Am Asn Orthod; fel Sigma Xi; Am EducRes Asn; Asn Study Higher Educ. **Research Statement & Publications:** Effects of spontaneous muscular activity on fetal development; relation between knowledge and diagnostic reasoning; cost effectiveness of professional education; organizational behavior and control in formal organizations; profiling providers of orthodontic services in general practice. **Mailing Address:** Col Dent, Univ Iowa, Iowa City, IA 52242.

JACOBS, ROBERT SAUL, MARINE PHARMACOLOGY, NEUROPHARMACOLOGY. **Education:** Northwestern Univ, PhB, 1964; Loyola Univ, PhD (pharmacol), 1971. **Professional Experience:** PROF PHARMACOL, DEPT ECOL, UNIV CALIF, SANTA BARBARA, 1995-; asst prof to assoc prof to prof, Dept Biol Sci, Univ Calif, Santa Barbara, 1974-1995. **Mailing Address:** Dept Biol Sci, Univ Calif, Off Bio 2 Rm 1115, Santa Barbara, CA 93106-0001. **Fax:** 805-893-4724. **E-Mail:** rsjacobs@chem.ucsb.edu

JACOBS, ROSS D, biochemistry; deceased, see previous edition for last biography

JACOBS, S LAWRENCE, CLINICAL CHEMISTRY, ANALYTICAL TOXICOLOGY. **Personal Data:** b New York, NY, November 27, 1929; m 1953, Charlotte; c 3. **Education:** Rensselaer Polytech Inst, BS, 1951; Univ Ill, MS, 1952, PhD (chem), 1955. **Professional Experience:** RETIRED; dir, Pacific Toxicol Labs, 1985-1986; dir, Dept Clin & Indust Toxicol, 1981-1984; dir, Dept Clin & Indust Toxicol, 1978-1981; mgr prof rels & corp accounts, Los Angeles Br Lab, Bio Sci Labs, 1976-1977; asst to dir, Los Angeles Br Lab, Bio Sci Labs, 1971-1975; qual assurance officer, Los Angeles Br Lab, Bio Sci Labs, 1968-1971; dir dept chem, Los Angeles Br Lab, Bio Sci Labs, 1966-1967; chief spec projs div, Los Angeles Br Lab, Bio Sci Labs, 1956-1965; res chemist, Northern Regional Lab, USDA, 1955; asst chem, Univ Ill, 1952-1955. **Memberships:** Am Chem Soc; Am Asn Clin Chem; Sigma Xi. **Research Statement & Publications:** Clinical chemistry; adrenal hormones; bile pigments; enzymes; lipids; quality assurance; analytical toxicology. **Mailing Address:** 16055 Miami Way, Pacific Palisades, CA 90272-4232.

JACOBS, SHEILA J, IMMUNOCHEMISTRY. **Personal Data:** b New York, NY, October 10, 1939; m 1985, Robert Carey; c Marcy (Little) & Sharon. **Education:** Carnegie Inst Technol, BS, 1961; Long Island Univ, MS, 1964; Columbia Univ, PhD (microbiol), 1968. **Professional Experience:** SECT LEADER, SCHERING-PLOUGH RES INST, 1985-; prin scientist, Schering-plough Res Inst, 1984-1985; sr scientist, Schering-plough Res Inst, 1982-1984; assoc prof microbiol, Wagner Col, 1981-1982; Adj prof microbiol, Rutgers Univ, 1981; res assoc prof med microbiol, NY Med Col, 1976-1981; Instr microbiol & immunol, Downstate Med Ctr, State Univ NY, 1968-1971. **Memberships:** Sigma Xi; AAAS; Am Chem Soc; Int Soc Interferon & Cytokine Res; Intl Cytokine Soc. **Research Statement & Publications:** Developing immunoassays for and investigating the structure and immunogenicity of biotechnol products such as cytokines and interferon alfa, interleukin-4, interleukin-10, as well as humanized monoclonal antibodies interleukin-5 antibody and an adenovirus vector containing P53; gene therapy vectors. **Mailing Address:** Schering-Plough Res Inst, 1011 Morris Avenue, Union, NJ 07083. **E-Mail:** sheila.jacobs@spcorp.com

JACOBS, SIGMUND JAMES, PHYSICS, FLUID DYNAMICS. **Personal Data:** b Minneapolis, Minn, March 25, 1912; m 1944. **Education:** Univ Minn, BChE, 1933, MS, 1952; Univ Amsterdam, PhD (physics), 1953. **Honors & Awards:** Meritorious Civilian Serv Award, US Navy, 1951, 1960; DuPont Medal, SocMotion Picture & TV Eng, 1964. **Professional Experience:** CONSULT DETONATION PHYSICS, NAVAL SURFACE WEAPONSCTR, WHITE OAK LAB, 1980-; sr scientist Explosives Div, Naval Surface Weapons Ctr, WhiteOak Lab, 1975-1980; sr scientist explosives res dept, Naval Ord Lab, 1957-1975; chief detonationdiv, Naval Ord Lab, 1950-1957; res physicist, Naval Ord Lab, 1946-1950; res assoc physics, Woods Hole Oceanog Inst, 1946; Res assoc, Carnegie Inst Technol, 1942-1945. **Memberships:** Am Phys Soc; Am Chem Soc; Soc Motion Picture & TV Eng; Combustion Inst. **Research Statement & Publications:** Deflagration of propellants and explosives; detonation of solid explosives; high pressure instrumentation; rapid expansion of gases; shock wave phenomena; electronic and photographic instrumentation; equation of fluid and solid states at high pressure. **Mailing Address:** 1208 Ruppert Rd, Silver Spring, MD 20903-1023.

JACOBS, STANLEY J, GEOPHYSICS, FLUID MECHANICS. **Personal Data:** b Milwaukee, Wis, February 11, 1936; m 1965, c 2. **Education:** Northwestern Univ, BS, 1959; Harvard Univ, AM, 1960, PhD (appl math), 1963. **Professional Experience:** PROF EMER OCEANOG, UNIV MICH, ANN ARBOR, as of 2004; prof oceanog, Univ Mich, Ann Arbor, beginning 1974; from asst prof toassoc prof, Univ Mich, Ann Arbor, 1964-1974; res fel atmospheric sci, Harvard Univ, 1963-1964. **Memberships:** Am Meteorol Soc. **Research Statement & Publications:** Geophysical fluid mechanics. **Mailing Address:** 2350 Haywart St, 1538 Space Res Bldg, Ann Arbor, MI 48109. **Fax:** 734-764-5137. **E-Mail:** sjj@umich.edu

JACOBS, STANLEY S, ANTARCTIC OCEANOGRAPHY. **Personal Data:** b Rochester, NH, USA, April 19, 1940; m 1979, Dee; c Robert C & Lara M. **Education:** Mass Inst Technol, BS, 1962. **Professional Experience:** SENIOR RES SCI, Lamont-Doherty Earth Observatory, Columbia Univ, 2000-; ed, J Geophys Res, 1999-2000; res scientist, Lamont-Doherty Earth Observ, Columbia Univ, 1994-1999; prin investr, NSF, NASA, NOAA & DOE, 1974-; sr staff assoc phys oceanog, Columbia Univ, 1974-1994; res staff assoc, Columbia Univ, 1972-1973; mem, Antarct Res Vessel Oversight Comt, 1998-2001; Comt Polar Res & Panel Antartic Oceanog, Nat Acad Sci-Nat Res Coun, 1971 & 1984; Chief scientist oceanog res, NSF, Columbia Univ & US Coast Guard ships, 1964-2004; Editor Board Ant Sci 1989-1996; 2001-; Antarc res ser, 1992-1998; from grad res asst to sr res asst, Columbia Univ, 1962-1972; ed vols 43 & 75, Antarc Res Series, Am Geophys Un, 1985, 1998; Res asst marine geophysics, Woods Hole Oceanog Inst, 1961-1962. **Memberships:** Am Geophys Union. **Research Statement & Publications:** Interactions between Southern Ocean and Antarctic ice shelves; Ocean data acquisition and reduction, studies of sea ice, ecosys and ocean variability, ocean circulation, icebergs, ice sheet mass balance, climate change. **Mailing Address:** Lamont-Doherty Earth Observ, Columbia Univ, Palisades, NY 10964. **Fax:** 914-365-8157. **E-Mail:** sjacobs@ldeo.columbia.edu

JACOBS, STEPHEN FRANK, OPTICS. **Personal Data:** b New York, NY, October 1, 1928; m 1963, Kathleen; c Henry, Tom & Jane. **Education:** Antioch Col, BS, 1951; Johns Hopkins Univ, PhD (physics), 1956. **Professional Experience:** PROF EMER OPTICAL SCI, UNIV ARIZ, 1965-; sr physicist, TRG, Inc, 1960-1965; engr, Perkin-Elmer Corp, 1956-1960. **Memberships:** Optical Soc Am; Am Phys Soc. **Research Statement & Publications:** Dimensional stability of materials. **Mailing Address:** Optical Sci Ctr Univ Ariz, Meinel Bldg 1630 E Univ Blvd, Tucson, AZ 85721. **Fax:** 520-621-4558. **E-Mail:** stephen.jacobs@optics.arizona.edu

JACOBS, VERNE LOUIS, ATOMIC PHYSICS. **Personal Data:** b Los Angeles, Calif, August 30, 1941; m 1969, Abigail; c Naomi S & Aviva R. **Education:** Mass Inst Technol, BS, 1964; Univ Calif, Berkeley, PhD (physics), 1968. **Professional Experience:** CTR CONSULT, MAT SCI & TECHNOL DIV, NAVAL RES LAB, 2000-; res physicist, Condensed Matter & Radiation Sci Div, Naval Res Lab, 1988-2000; res physicist, E O Hulburt Ctr Space Res, 1985-1988; fel, Am Phys Soc, 1985; res physicist, Plasma Physics Div, 1977-1985; scientist plasma physics, Sci Applns Inc, 1974-1977; Nat Res Coun assoc space physics, Goddard Space Flight Ctr, NASA, 1972-1974; res fel atomic physics, Queen's Univ, Belfast, 1971-1972; res fel appl math, Weizmann Inst Sci, Israel, 1968-1971.

Memberships: Fel Am Phys Soc. **Research Statement & Publications:** Atomic radiation processes in plasmas; about 60 publications on atomic physics. **Mailing Address:** Ctr Computational Mat Sci, Naval Res Lab, Code 6300, Washington, DC 20375. **Fax:** 202-404-7546. **E-Mail:** jacob@dave.nrl.navy.mil

JACOBS, WILLIAM PAUL, PLANT DEVELOPMENT. **Personal Data:** b Boston, Mass, May 25, 1919; m 1949, Jane Shaw; c Mark, Anne. **Education:** Harvard Univ, AB, 1942, MA, 1945, PhD (biol), 1946. **Honors & Awards:** Morrison Award, NY Acad Sci, 1951; Dimond Prize, Bot Soc Am, 1975; Barnes Awd for Life-time Acheiv, Am Soc Plant Physiol, 1998. **Professional Experience:** PROF EMER BIOL, PRINCETON UNIV, 1989-; vis profchem Univ Bristol, 1980; plant biol space, NASA, 1976-1978 & US-Soviet space flights, 1978; zool Univ Colo, 1972; Guggenheim fel, Univ Lausanne, 1967; sci fac fel, NSF, at Agiv, 1962; zool Sta, Univ Oxford, 1962; mem comt innovation lab instr, Biol Sci Curriculum Study, Am Inst Biol Sci, 1959-1964; sr fel NSF, Zool Sta, Napoli, 1957; 1956-1957; mem adv panel, develop biol, NSF, 1956; vis prof, Univ Calif, Berkeley, 1952; Lalor fel, marine biol, Woods Hole, 1950-1951; mem fac, Princeton Univ, 1948-1989; mem, Soc Fels, Harvard Univ, 1947-1948; fel histogenesis vascular plants, Harvard Univ, 1946-1947; Sheldon traveling fel, to Cal Tech. **Memberships:** Soc Develop Biol (secy 1958-1960 pres 1960-1961); Am Soc Plant Physiol; Bot Soc Am; Int Soc Plant Morphologists; Int Plant Growth Substances Asn; Int Phycol Soc. **Research Statement & Publications:** Internal factors controlling cell and organ differentiation and longevity; hormone transport and polarity; gravitational effects on giant coenocytes. **Mailing Address:** Dept Biol, Princeton Univ, Wash Rd, Princeton, NJ 08544-1003. **Fax:** 609-258-3980. **E-Mail:** wpjacobs@princeton.edu

JACOBS, WILLIAM WESCOTT, INTERMEDIATE ENERGY NUCLEAR PHYSICS. **Personal Data:** b Madison, Wis, September 8, 1943; m 1977, c 2. **Education:** Reed Col, Portland, BA, 1965; Univ Wash, MS, 1967, PhD (physics), 1974. **Professional Experience:** RES FAC & DIV HEAD NUCLEAR SCI, CYCLOTRON FACIL, IND UNIV, as of 2005; assoc res scientist intermediate energy nuclearphysics, Cyclotron Facil, Ind Univ, beginning 1979; res assoc, Cyclotron Facil, Ind Univ, 1976-1979; res assoc nuclear & atomic physics, Univ NC, Chapel Hill, 1974-1976. **Memberships:** Am Phys Soc; AAAS; Am Fedn Scientists. **Research Statement & Publications:** Intermediate-energy nuclear physics; polarization effects in nuclear reactions and scattering; nuclear astrophysics; heavy-ion x-ray production; tests of fundamental symmetries. **Mailing Address:** Ind Univ Cyclotron Facil Ind Univ, 2401 Milo B Sampson Lane, Bloomington, IN 47408. **Fax:** 812-855-6645. **E-Mail:** jacobs@iucf.indiana.edu

JACOBS, WILLIAM WOOD, ANIMAL BEHAVIOR, ETHOLOGY. **Personal Data:** b Harrisburg, Pa, May 23, 1947; m 1969, c 3. **Education:** Pa State Univ, BS, 1969; Univ Chicago, MS, 1971, PhD (biopsychology), 1973. **Professional Experience:** BIOLOGIST RODENTICIDES, US ENVIRON PROTECTION AGENCY, 1978-; fel olfaction & taste, Monell Chem Senses Ctr, 1975-1978; fel, US Nat Inst Neurol Dis & Stroke, 1975-1978; biologist rodenticides, US Environ Protection Agency, 1974-1975. **Research Statement & Publications:** Investigations of taste, food selection, social and individual behavior of small mammals; use of containers in closed system transfer of pesticides; development of protective bait stations for rodenticides; vertebrate pesticides. **Mailing Address:** US Environ Protection Agency, Insecticide-Rodenticide Br, 7505C Regist Div, 401 M St SW, Washington, DC 20460.

JACOBSEN, BARRY JAMES, PLANT PATHOLOGY, ADMINISTRATION. **Personal Data:** b Racine, Wis, August 6, 1947; m 1969, c 2. **Education:** Univ Wis-Madison, BS, 1969, MSc, 1971; Univ Minn, PhD (plant path), 1973. **Honors & Awards:** Campbell Award, Am Phytopath Soc, 1980; Merck Found Res Award. **Professional Experience:** SPECIALIST PLANT PATH, MONT STATE UNIV as of 2005; DEAN, COL AGR, MONT STATE UNIV & DIR MONT AGR EXP STA, 1992-; PROF & HEAD DEPT, AUBURN UNIV, 1987-; vis prof, Friedrich Wilhelms Univ, WGer, 1984-; proj leader, Univ Ill, Urbana-Champaign, 1979-1987; from asst prof to prof plant path, Univ Ill, Urbana-Champaign, 1973-1987. **Memberships:** Sigma Xi; Am Phytopathological Soc; Soc Nematologists; Organization Trop Am Nematologists; Potato Asn Am; Soc Sugarbeet Technologists. **Research Statement & Publications:** Studies on generalized disease resistance in wheat and tomatoes; effects of pesticides on non-target plant pathogens and interactions of plant parasitic nematodes and fungi in plant diseases; chemical control of plant diseases; grain storage; development of disease management strategies. **Mailing Address:** Dept Plant Path, Mont State Univ, PO Box 173150 509 Leon Johnson Hall, Bozeman, MT 59717-3140. **Fax:** 406-994-6042, 406-994-7600. **E-Mail:** uplbj@montana.edu

JACOBSEN, CHRIS J, X-RAY OPTICS. **Personal Data:** b Redwing, Minn, October 3, 1960; m 1982, c 2. **Education:** St Olaf Col, BA, 1983; State Univ NY, Stony Brook, PhD (physics), 1988. **Professional Experience:** PROF PHYSICS, STATE UNIV NY, STONY BROOK, as of 1997; mem, Biophys Prog, State Univ NY, Stony Brook, 1991-; assoc prof physics, State Univ Ny, Stony Brook, beginning 1991; researcher, State Univ NY, Stony-Brook, 1989-1991; Postdoctoral physics, Ctr X-Ray Optics, Lawrence Berkeley Lab, 1988-1989. **Memberships:** Optical Soc Am; Am Phys Soc. **Research Statement & Publications:** X-ray microscopy using holography and zone plates; biological applications of x-ray microscopy; image processing; x-ray lithography; coherent x-ray sources. **Mailing Address:** Dept Physics, State Univ NY, Stony Brook, NY 11794-3800. **Fax:** 516-632-8101. **E-Mail:** chris.jacobsen@sunysb.edu

JACOBSEN, DONALD WELDON, BIOCHEMISTRY, CHEMISTRY. **Personal Data:** b Portland, Ore, April 26, 1939; m 1962, Margaret; c Mark W & Gregg T. **Education:** Univ Pa, BA, 1961; Ore State Univ, MS, 1964, PhD (biochem, cell biol), 1967. **Professional Experience:** STAFF MEM DEPT CARDIOVAS MED, LERNER RES INST, as of 2005; adj prof Chem, Cleveland State Univ, 1997; dir, Lab Hampshire Res, 1997; chmn, Cleveland Sect, Am Chem Soc, 1992; chmn-elect, Cleveland Sect, Am Chem Soc, 1991; adj prof Biol, Cleveland State Univ, 1988-; dir, Biochem Core Lab, Cleveland Clin, 1987-1992; mem, Ad Hoc Adv Comt Food Hypersensitivity, Food & Drug Admin, 1985-1987; PROF STAFF, CLEVELAND CLIN FOUND, 1984-; Dernham fel, Am Cancer Soc, Calif, 1972; assoc biochem, Scripps Clin & Res Found, 1971-1984; NIH fel biochem, 1967-1971. **Memberships:** AAAS; Am Chem Soc; Biophys Soc; Am Soc Biochem & Molecular Biol; Am Soc Hemat; fel coun arteriosclerosis & hemostasis; fel Am Heart Assoc. **Research Statement & Publications:** Vasular biochemistry and metabolism of homocystein; Molecular targeting of Homocysteine and mechanisms of vascular damage; Homocysteine as a risk factor in cardiovascular and Alzheimer's disease. Vascular biochemistry of vitimin B12: Transcoblalmin receptor mediated uptake, cobalamin processing and conversion to coenzyme forms. **Mailing Address:** Dept Cell Biol, Lerner Res Inst FF4, Cleveland Clin Found, 9500 Euclid Ave, Cleveland, OH 44195-5139. **Fax:** 216-445-5480. **E-Mail:** jacobsd@ccf.org

JACOBSEN, EDWARD HASTINGS, PHYSICS, ELECTRON OPTICS. **Personal Data:** b Elizabeth, NJ, January 2, 1926; wid. **Education:** Mass Inst Technol, BS, 1950, PhD (physics), 1954. **Professional Experience:** PROF EMER PHYSICS, UNIV ROCHESTER, as of 2004; NIH, career develop fel, Biol Dept, Columbia Univ, 1979; vis scientist, Res LabElectronics, 1970-1972; vis prof, Mass Inst Technol, 1967-1968; Vis scientist, Molecular BiolLab, Harvard Med Sch, 1965; prof physics, Univ Rochester, beginning 1962; Brit Dept Sci &Indust Res fel, Nottingham, 1961; res physicist, Res Lab, Gen Elec Co, 1955-1961; Fulbright fel, Col France, 1954-1955. **Memberships:** Am Phys Soc; Sigma Xi. **Research Statement & Publications:** Magnetic resonance; x-ray and neutron diffraction; microwave ultrasonics; statistical mechanics; semiconductors; plasma physics; biophysics; machine computation. **Mailing Address:** Univ Rochester, Dept Physics, Rochester, NY 14627.

JACOBSEN, ERIC N, CHEMISTRY. **Personal Data:** b February 22, 1960. **Education:** NY Univ, BS, 1982. **Honors & Awards:** Arthur C Cope Award, Am Chem Soc, 1994. **Professional Experience:** SHELDON EMERY PROF, CHEM, HARVARD UNIV, 2001-; prof, Chem, Harvard Univ, 1993-2001; assoc Prof, Chem, Univ ill, Urbana-Champaign, 1991-1993; asst prof, Chem, Univ ill, Urbana-Champaign, 1988-1991. **Mailing Address:** Dept Chem, Harvard Univ, 12 Oxford St, Cambridge, MA 02138. **Fax:** 617-496-1880. **E-Mail:** jacobsen@chemistry.harvard.edu

JACOBSEN, FRED MARIUS, computer science, applied statistics; deceased, see previous edition for last biography

JACOBSEN, FREDERICK MARIUS, PSYCHOPHARMACOLOGY, BIOLOGICAL PSYCHIATRY. **Personal Data:** b Ames, Iowa, January 19, 1954; m 1983, Lillian. **Education:** Cornell Univ, BA, 1976; Univ Ill, MPH, 1978, MD, 1980. **Professional Experience:** CLIN PROF PSYCHIAT & BEHAV SCI, GEORGE WASH UNIV MED CTR, as of 2005; assoc clin prof psychiat & behav sci, George Wash Univ Med Ctr, beginning 1991; guest researcher, Lab Clin Sci, NIMH, beginning 1988; med adv, Depressive & Manic Depressive Asn, 1987-; consult, VOCA Corp, 1987-; med officer, NIMH, 1987-1988; med dir, Transcult Mental Health Inst, beginning 1986; asst clin prof psychiat, Georgetown Univ Sch Med, 1985-1991; clin assoc, NIMH, 1984-1987; fel, Yale Univ Sch Med, 1980-1984; chief resident psychiat, Yale Univ Sch Med, 1973-1984. **Memberships:** Soc Biol Sci; AAAS; Math Asn Am; Am Psychiat Asn; AMA; NY Acad Sci; Soc Biol Psychiat; Am Sleep Dis Asn; Am Soc Clin Psychopharmacol; Am Bd Psychiat & Neurol. **Research Statement & Publications:** Biological psychiatry; physiological bases of depression and manic-depressive illness; neuropsychiatric diagnosis; public health; manifestations of illness from a cultural perspective; psychopharmacology of mood and sleep disorders. **Mailing Address:** Dept Psychiat & Behav Sci, George Wash Univ Med Ctr, 2150 Pa Ave NW Eight Floor, Washington, DC 20037.

JACOBSEN, JEFFREY SCOTT, AGRONOMY. **Education:** Calif Polytech State Univ, BS, 1979; Oklahoma State Univ, PhD, 1985; Colorado State Univ, MS, 1982. **Honors & Awards:** Ciba-Geigy Agron, Am Soc Agron, 1994. **Professional Experience:** INTERIM DEAN, COL AGR, MONT STATE UNIV, as of 2004; INTERIM DIR, MONTANA AGR EXP STA, as of 2004. **Mailing Address:** Dept Land Resources & Environ Sci, Mont State Univ, PO Box 173120, Leon Johnson Hall, Bozeman, MT 59717-3120. **Fax:** 406-994-3933. **E-Mail:** jefj@montana.edu

JACOBSEN, NADINE KLECHA, PHYSIOLOGICAL ECOLOGY. **Personal Data:** b Milwaukee, Wis, December 13, 1941; m 1967. **Education:** Drake Univ, BA, 1964; Ore State Univ, MS, 1966; Cornell Univ, PhD (wildlife ecol), 1974. **Professional Experience:** ASSOC PROF EMER, DEPT WILDLIFE, FISH & CONSERV BIOL, UINV CALIF, DAVIS, as of 2004; assoc prof wildlife biol, Univ Calif, Davis, beginning 1974; fel, Dept Natural Resources, 1973-1974; res assoc, Dept Radiation Biol, Cornell Univ, 1968-1969; instr biol, Blue Mountain Community Col, 1966-1967. **Memberships:** Sigma Xi; Am Soc Mammal; Wildlife Soc; Am Soc Animal Scientists; Ecol Soc Am. **Research Statement & Publications:** Ecological energetics of wildlife, particularly deer, over the annual cycle and between birth and weaning of young; how energy and nutrient metabolism are affected by environmental, behavioral and physiological states. **Mailing Address:** Dept Wildlife, Fish & Conserv Biol, Univ Calif, One Shields Ave, Davis, CA 95616-8751. **E-Mail:** nkjacobsen@ucdavsis.edu

JACOBSEN, NEIL SOREN, ACADEMIC ADMINISTRATION. **Personal Data:** b Waterloo, Iowa, June 13, 1930; m 1954, Ruth; c Teresa, Dennis & Linda. **Education:** Univ Iowa, BA, 1952; Univ Denver, MS, 1956; Okla State Univ, PhD (physiol), 1965. **Professional Experience:** PROF EMER, NDAK STATE UNIV, as of 2006; assoc vpres acad affairs, NDak State Univ, 1981-1986; actg vpres acad affairs, NDak State Univ, 1979-1980; dean Univ studies, NDak State Univ, 1972-1986; assoc prof zool, NDak State Univ, 1971-1986; dir student acad affairs, NDak State Univ, 1969-1972; asst prof, NDak State Univ, 1966-1971; NIH fel, Univ Mass, 1964-1966; teacher high schs, Calif, 1957-1962. **Research Statement & Publications:** Lipid metabolism of intestinal parasites; effect of pesticides on the cardiovascular system. **Mailing Address:** 5283 A Beach Dr Sothwest, St Petersburg, FL 33705.

JACOBSEN, RICHARD T, MECHANICAL ENGINEERING, THERMODYNAMICS. **Personal Data:** b Pocatello, Idaho, November 12, 1941; m 1973, Bonnie; c Richard T, Eric E, Jay M, Erik D Lustig & Pamela S (Moats). **Education:** Univ Idaho, BS, 1963, MS, 1965; Wash State Univ, PhD (eng sci), 1972. **Professional Experience:** ASSOC LAB DIR & CHIEF SCIENTIST, IDAHO NATIONAL ENGR AND ENVIRONMENTAL LAB, 2001-; Dep Dir & Chief Scientist, Idaho Nat Eng & Environ Lab, 1999-2001; dean eng, Ctr Appl Thermodyn Studies, Univ Idaho, 1990-1999; dir, Ctr Appl Thermodyn Studies, Univ Idaho, 1986-1999; assoc dean eng, Ctr Appl Thermodyn Studies, prof mech eng & chmn dept, 1985-1990; assoc dir, Ctr Appl Thermodyn Studies, prof mech eng & chmn dept, 1980-1985; guest worker, Thermophysics Div, Nat Bur Stand, 1979, 1986-1999; mem correlating functions working panel, Int Union Pure & Appl Chem, 1973-1986; from instr to prof eng, Univ Idaho, 1964-1980. **Memberships:** Sigma Xi; fel Am Soc Mech Engrs (Vpres for Prof Practice, 1998-2001); Corp mem Soc Automotive Engrs; Corp mem Am Soc Heating Refrig & Air Conditioning Engrs; Corp mem Nat Soc Prof Engrs; Corp mem Am Soc Eng Educ. **Research Statement & Publications:** Thermodynamics; thermodynamic properties of fluids and fluid mixtures; thermodynamic system analysis; development of computer programs, tables and charts for engineering applications including envirnmentally-safe alternative refrigerants. **Mailing Address:** Idaho Nat Eng & Environ Lab, PO Box 1425, Idaho Falls, ID 83415-3810. **Fax:** 208-526-4236. **E-Mail:** jacor@inel.gov

JACOBSEN, STEIN BJORNAR, GEOCHEMISTRY. **Personal Data:** b Baerum, Norway, February 12, 1950. **Education:** Univ Oslo, Norway, BS, 1974, MS, 1975; Calif Inst Technol, PhD (geochem), 1980. **Professional Experience:** PROF GEOCHEM, HARVARD UNIV, as of 2002; assoc prof, Harvard Univ, beginning 1984; asst prof, Harvard Univ, 1981-1983; fel geochem, Calif Inst Technol, 1980-1981. **Memberships:** Am Geophys Union; Geol Soc Am; Am Chem Soc; Meteoritical Soc. **Research Statement & Publications:** Neodymium, strontium and lead isotope studies of mantle structure and differentiation, crustal evolution and chronology; petrological and geochemical studies of granulite and eclogite facies rocks, ophiolites, orogenic peridotites and chondritic meteorites. **Mail-**

ing Address: Dept Earth & Planetary Sci, Harvard Univ, 20 Oxford St, Cambridge, MA 02138. **Fax:** 617-495-8839. **E-Mail:** jacobsen@neodymium.harvard.edu

JACOBSEN, STEPHEN C, ENGINEERING. **Education:** Univ Utah, BS, 1967, MS, 1970; Mass Inst Technol, PhD (mech eng), 1973. **Honors & Awards:** Lawrence Poole Prize Fac Med, Univ Edinburgh, Scotland, 1982; BectonDickinson Award, Asn Advan Med Instrumentation, 1985; Leonardo da Vinci Design Award, AmSoc Mech Eng, 1987. **Professional Experience:** Chmn bd dir, Sarcos Orgn, 1983-; DISTINGUISHED PROF, DEPT MECH ENG, UNIV UTAH, 1981-; mem, bd dir, IOMED Inc, 1973-; RES PROF, DEPT BIOENG, 1973-; RES PROF, DEPT SURG, 1973-; DIR, CTR ENG DESIGN, 1973-; adj prof, Dept Comput Sci, Univ Utah, 1973-. **Memberships:** Nat Acad Eng; Inst Med-Nat Acad Sci; Am Inst Med & Biol Eng. **Mailing Address:** Dept Mech, Univ Utah, 350 Wakara Way, Salt Lake City, UT 84112. **Fax:** 801-581-8623. **E-Mail:** jacobsen@ced.utah.edu

JACOBSEN, TERRY DALE, PLANT SYSTEMATICS. **Personal Data:** b Nampa, Idaho, August 17, 1950; m 1979. **Education:** Col Idaho, BS, 1972; Wash State Univ, MS, 1975, PhD (bot), 1978. **Professional Experience:** PROF BIOL, CARNEGIE-MELLON UNIV, 2006; PRIN RES SCIENTIST, CARNEGIE-MELLON UNIV, 1993-2002; adj assoc prof biol, Carnegie-Mellon Univ, 1984-1993; ed, Bull HuntInst Bot Doc, 1981; asst dir & sr res scientist, Hunt Inst Bot Doc, 1981-1993; adj res scientist, Carnegie Mus Natural Hist, 1979; asst to dir & res scientist, Carnegie Mellon Univ, 1979-1981; instr bot, Biol Prog, Wash State Univ, 1978-1979; lectr, Biol Prog, Wash State Univ, 1977-1978. **Research Statement & Publications:** Cytotaxonomy, anatomy and numerical analysis of the genus Allium L in North America. **Mailing Address:** Hunt Inst Bot Doc, Carnegie-Mellon Univ 5000 Forbes Ave, Pittsburgh, PA 15213. **E-Mail:** tj50@andrew.cmu.edu

JACOBS-LORENA, MARCELO, MOLECULAR BIOLOGY, EMBRYOLOGY. **Personal Data:** b Sao Paulo, Brazil, May 5, 1942; m 1970, c 1. **Education:** Sao Paulo Univ, BS, 1964; Osaka Univ, MS, 1967; Mass Inst Technol, PhD (biol), 1972. **Professional Experience:** PROF MOLECULAR MICROBIOL & IMMUNOL, JOHN HOPKINS SCH PUB HEALTH, as of 2005; PROF DEVELOP GENETICS, CASE WESTERN RESERVE UNIV, as of 2004; assoc prof develop genetics, Case Western Reserve Univ, beginning 1983; asst prof, 1985-1990 & NSF, 1983-1986; asst prof, NIH, 1978-1983; asst prof, Case Western Res Univ, 1977-1983; asst prof, Am Cancer Soc Inst grant, 1977-1978; fel biol, Univ Geneva, 1972-1977; fel, Europ Molecular Biol Orgn, 1972-1974. **Memberships:** Soc Develop Biol; Soc Cell Biol. **Research Statement & Publications:** Drosophilia oogenesis and embryogenesis, Drosophila development and control of gene expression. **Mailing Address:** Dept Molecular Microbiol & Immunol, Johns Hopkins Bloomberg Sch Pub Health, 615 N Wolfe St Ste E5132, Baltimore, MD 21205. **Fax:** 410-955-0105. **E-Mail:** mlorena@jhsph.edu

JACOBSOHN, GERT MAX, BIOCHEMISTRY. **Personal Data:** b Berlin, Ger, August 1, 1929; American citizen; m 1959, Myra; c Hannah G, Jamie A, Diane R & Alice P. **Education:** Ill Col, AB, 1952; Purdue Univ, MS, 1955, PhD (biochem), 1957. **Professional Experience:** PROF BIOL CHEM, ALLEGHENY UNIV, 1977-; from asst prof to assoc prof, Allegheny Univ, 1962-1977; asst mem endocrinol, Albert Einstein Med Ctr, 1960-1961; fel, Col Physicians & Surgeons, Columbia Univ, 1957-1960; coun mem, Pan Am SocPigment Cell Res. **Memberships:** AAAS; fel Am Cancer Soc; Endocrine Soc; Am Soc Biochem & Molecular Biol. **Research Statement & Publications:** Metabolic control of blood enzymes; membrane transfer phenomena; steroid interconversion and function in plants; regulation of steroid, methods of steroid assay and instrumentation; metabolism of catechol estrogens; melanin formation; tyrosinase. **Mailing Address:** Dept Biochem, Allegheny Univ, Philadelphia, PA 19102. **E-Mail:** jacobsohng@allegheny.edu

JACOBSOHN, MYRA K, MEMBRANE BIOCHEMISTRY, BIOCHEMISTRY OF MELANIN. **Personal Data:** b New York, NY, February 13, 1939; c 4. **Education:** Columbia Univ, BA, 1960; Univ Pa, MS, 1962; Bryn Mawr Col, PhD (biol), 1975. **Honors & Awards:** Lindback Award, 1982. **Professional Experience:** PROF BIOL, BEAVER COL, 1990-; RES ASSOC, ALLGHENY COL, 1985-; from asst prof to assoc prof, Beaver Col, 1976-1990; lectr, Beaver Col, 1974-1976; fel biochem, Hahnemann Med Col, 1974-1976; res assoc, Hahnemann Med Col, 1971-1974. **Memberships:** AAAS; Pan-Am Soc Pigment Cell Res; Am Soc Biochem & Molecular Biol. **Research Statement & Publications:** Enzymes; membrane structure; melanin synthesis; lipid-enzyme interactions. **Mailing Address:** Dept Biol, Beaver Col, Glenside, PA 19038. **Fax:** 215-572-0240.

JACOBSON, ABRAM ROBERT, PHYSICS. **Honors & Awards:** Kapp Mem Lect, Am Soc Civil Engrs, 1974 & 1982; Crom Lectr, Univ Fla, 1978; Haley Mem Lect, Soc Civil Engrs, 1985. **Professional Experience:** AT SPACE & ATMOSPHERIC SCI, LOS ALAMOS NAT LAB, as of 2000; PARTNER, MUESER RUTLEDGE CONSULT ENGRS, 1973-; assoc, Mueser Rutledge Consult Engrs, 1955; in chargegeotech studies, Reconstruct E Front, US Capitol Bldg, 1955-1960, US Navy Dry Dock 6, 1956-1960, landslide study, Pac Palisades, Los Angeles, 1958-1960, underpinning, House RepWing, 1962-1964, NY Waterfront Redevelop, 195-1968 & Wash Metro Subway, staff mem, Mueser Rutledge Consult Engrs, 1953; staff mem, Earth Dams Sect, US Bur Reclamation, 1950-1953; eng asst, Harvard Univ, 1948-1949; US Army Corps Engrs, 1944-1945. **Memberships:** Am Soc Civil Engrs. **Research Statement & Publications:** Author of 30 publications. **Mailing Address:** Space & Atmospheric Sci Group, Los Alamos Nat Lab, MS D466, Los Alamos, NM 87545. **Fax:** 505-665-7395. **E-Mail:** ajacobson@lanl.gov

JACOBSON, ADA LEAH, PHYSICAL CHEMISTRY, BIOCHEMISTRY. **Personal Data:** b Boston, Mass, October 8, 1933; m 1958. **Education:** Mass Inst Technol, BS, 1954; Yale Univ, PhD (chem), 1957. **Professional Experience:** ASSOC PROF BIOCHEM, UNIV CALGARY, 1986-; sr fel, Can HeartFound, 1965-; from instr to assoc prof chem, Univ Calgary, 1960-1986; instr biochem, DartmouthMed Sch, 1959-1960; instr phys chem, Albertus Magnus Col, 1958-1959; Fel phys org chem, Yale Univ, 1958-1959; Chemist, Shell Develop Co, Calif, 1957-1958. **Memberships:** Am Chem Soc; Can Biochem Soc; Sigma Xi; Biophys Soc. **Research Statement & Publications:** Physical chemistry of proteins, solutions and polymers. **Mailing Address:** 312 Superior Ave SW, Calgary, AB T3C 2J2, Can.

JACOBSON, ALEXANDER DONALD, ARTIFICIAL INTELLIGENCE TECHNOLOGY, ELECTRICAL ENGINEERING. **Personal Data:** b New York, NY, December 1, 1933; m 1971, Rebecca; c Juliet A & David C. **Education:** Univ Calif, Los Angeles, BS, 1955, MS, 1958; Calif Inst Technol, PhD (electro-magnetic theory), 1964. **Honors & Awards:** Rank Prize, 1986. **Professional Experience:** PRES & CHIEF EXEC OFFICER, TRIVIDA, 1996-; pres & chief exec officer, Limbex Corp, 1995-1996; co-founder, chmn & chief exec officer, Inference Corp, 1979-1995; consult, 1977-1979; prog mgr liquid crystal displays progs, Indust Prod Div, 1976-1977; assocmgr, Explor Studies Dept, 1972-1976; head, Unconventional Imaging Sect, 1968-1972; memtech staff optics res, Hughes Res Labs Div, Hughes Aircraft Co, 1955-1968. **Research Statement & Publications:** Laser technology; electromagnetic theory; x-ray diffraction studies of crystals; display technology; computer systems; telecommunications; artificial intelligence computer software products; applications of artificial intelligence technology to the development of expert systems for industrial, commercial and military applications; development of computer software products that contain artificial intelligence technology for such purposes; electro-optic device technology. **Mailing Address:** Trivida, 3524 Hayden Ave, Culver City, CA 90232.

JACOBSON, ALLAN JOSEPH, INTERCALATION CHEMISTRY, SOLID STATE CHEMISTRY. **Personal Data:** b Newcastle, Eng, May 28, 1944; m 1968, c 1. **Education:** Oxford Univ, BA, 1966 MA, 1969, DPhil, 1969. **Professional Experience:** ROBERT A WELCH PROF, DEPT CHEM, UNIV HOUSTON, as of 2006; res assoc, Exxon Res & Eng Co, Exxon Corp, 1980-1991; sr staff chemist, Exxon Res & Eng Co, Exxon Corp, 1976-1980; lectr chem, Oxford Univ, 1970-1976. **Memberships:** Chem Soc; Am Chem Soc; Electrochem Soc; Mat Res Soc. **Research Statement & Publications:** Synthetic and structural solid state inorganic chemistry; neutron x-ray and electron diffraction; intercalation chemistry. **Mailing Address:** Dept Chem, Univ Houston, 136 Fleming Bldg 4800 Calhoun, Houston, TX 77204-5641. **Fax:** 713-743-2787. **E-Mail:** ajjacob@uh.edu

JACOBSON, ALLAN STANLEY (BUD), COMPUTER GRAPHICS, GAMMA RAY ASTRONOMY. **Personal Data:** b Chattanooga, Tenn, June 18, 1932; m 1986. **Education:** Univ Calif Los Angeles, AB, 1962; Univ Calif San Diego, MS, 1964 & PhD (physics), 1968. **Honors & Awards:** Bruno Rossi Prize, Am Astron Soc, 1986. **Professional Experience:** PRIN INVESTR, PLANET EARTH EOSDIS PROG, NASA, 1994-; PRIN INVESTR, APPL INFO SYS RES PROG, NASA, 1989-; asst sect mgr sci visualization & comput graphics, Jet Propulsion Lab, 1988-1990; consult, Ashton-Tate, 1985-1989; SR RES SCIENTIST, JET PROPULSION LAB, CALIF INST TECHNOL, 1981-; guest lectr, Calif Inst Technol, 1980-1982; tech group supvr, Jet Propulsion Lab, 1973-1986; prin investr, NASA, beginning 1970; memtech staff, Jet Propulsion Lab, 1969-1973; asst res physicist, Univ Calif San Diego, 1968-1969; res asst, Univ Calif San Diego, 1962-1968; mem, Comput Soc, Inst Elec & Electronic Engrs. **Memberships:** Fel Am Phys Soc; Am Astron Soc; Asn Comput Mach; Inst Elec & ElectronicsEngrs; Inst Elec & Electronics Engrs Computer Sci. **Research Statement & Publications:** Gamma-ray astronomy; computer-aided science visualization; visual science data analysis. **Mailing Address:** Jet Propulsion Lab, Calif Inst Technol, M/S 183-501, 4800 Oak Grove Dr, Pasadena, CA 91109. **Fax:** 818-354-0966. **E-Mail:** budj@apex.jpl.nasa.gov

JACOBSON, ALLEN F, MANUFACTURING ADMINISTRATION. **Personal Data:** b Omaha, Nebr, October 7, 1926. **Education:** Iowa State Univ, Ames, BS, 1947. **Honors & Awards:** Mgr Of The Yr, AMA, 1994. **Professional Experience:** RETIRED; emer chmn be & emer chief exec officer, 3M, 1991; chmn bd &chief exec officer, 3M, 1986-1991; exec vpres, Indust & Consumer Sector, pres, US Opers, 3M, 1984-1986; vpres, Tape & Allied Prod Group, 3M, 1975-1981; vpres, Europ Opers, 3M, 1975; exec vpres & gen mgr, 3M Can Ltd, 1973-1975; div vpres, 3M, 1970-1972; gen mgr, Indust TapeDiv, 3M, 1968-1970; mfg mgr, 3M, 1963-1968; tape prod mgr, Tape & Allied Prod Group, 3M, 1963; combined Tape & AC&S Opers, 3M, Bristol, 1961-1963; plant mgr, StPaul Tape Prod, 3M, 1959-1961; tape prod supt, 3M, Bristol, 1955- 1959; tech asst to plant mgr, 3M, Bristol, 1953-1955; tech asst to plant mgr, 3M, Hutchinson, 1950-1953; prod engr, Tape Lab, 3M, 1947-1950; mem, Bus Can, Washington, DC, Bus Roundtable, US-USSR Trade & Econ Coun, Inc & Bus Coun Sustainable Develop; chmn, US Coun Int Bus, Emergency Comt Am Trade; mem bd dirs, Am Qual Found, Chamber Com US & Nat Legal Ctr Pub Interest; dir, Mobil Corp, NY, Northern States Power Co, Minneapolis, Minn, US West, Inc, Englewood, Colo, ValmontIndusts, Inc, Valley, Nebr, Potlatch Corp, San Francisco, Calif, Sara Lee Corp, Chicago, Ill, MinnBus Partnership, Minneapolis. **Memberships:** Nat Acad Eng; hon mem Soc Mfg Engrs. **Mailing Address:** 3050 Minneapolis World Trade Ctr, 30 E Seventh St, St Paul, MN 55101-4901. **Fax:** 612-223-5107.

JACOBSON, ANN BEATRICE, MOLECULAR BIOLOGY. **Personal Data:** b New York, NY, July 24, 1938. **Education:** Univ Chicago, BS, 1958, PhD (bot), 1962; Purdue Univ, MS, 1961. **Professional Experience:** RES ASSOC PROF, DEPT MICROBIOL, STATE UNIV NY, STONYBROOK, 1986-; res asst prof, Dept Microbiol, State Univ NY, Stony Brook, 1980-1986; lectr, Dept Microbiol, State Univ NY, Stony Brook, 1976-1980; Europ Molecular Biol Orgn Fel, Dept Molecular Biol, Univ Geneva, Switz, 1975-1976; vis scientist, Max Planck Inst Biochem, Munich, 1971-1975; biologist, Biol Div, Oak Ridge Nat Lab, 1967-1971; res assoc plant biochem, Univ Chicago, 1963-1967. **Memberships:** AAAS; Am Soc Biochem & Molecular Biol. **Research Statement & Publications:** RNA folding, computer modeling and electron microscopy. **Mailing Address:** Dept Microbiol, Sch Med, State Univ NY, Stony Brook, NY 11794-5222. **Fax:** 516-632-8891. **E-Mail:** jacobson@abj.b10.sunsb.edu

JACOBSON, ANTONE GARDNER, DEVELOPMENTAL BIOLOGY. **Personal Data:** b Salt Lake City, Utah, May 22, 1929; m 1963, Jacqueline; c Lauren & Eric. **Education:** Harvard Univ, BA, 1951; Stanford Univ, PhD (exp embryol, biol), 1955. **Professional Experience:** PROF EMER, UNIV TEX, AUSTIN as of 2006; prof zool, Univ Tex, Austin, beginning 1968; from instr to assoc prof, Univ Tex, 1957-1968. **Memberships:** Am Asn Anatomists; Am Soc Zool; Soc Develop Biol; Int Soc Develop Biol. **Research Statement & Publications:** Embryonic induction, morphogenesis and development of the nervous system in embryos; segmentation of the mesoderm; pattern formation. **Mailing Address:** Sch Biol Sci, Univ Tex, One Univ Sta C0930, Austin, TX 78712. **Fax:** 512-471-9651. **E-Mail:** antone@mail.utexas.edu

JACOBSON, ARNOLD P, RADIATION BIOLOGY. **Personal Data:** b Rawlins, Wyo, July 21, 1932; m 1965. **Education:** Univ Wyo, BS, 1958, MS, 1960; Univ Mich, MPH, 1962, PhD (radiation biol), 1966. **Honors & Awards:** Marie Curie Gold Medal Award, Health Physics Soc. **Professional Experience:** PROF EMER DEPT ENVIRON HEALTH SCI, SCH PUB HEALTH, UNIV MICH, ANN ARBOR, as of 2003; prof environ & indust health, Sch Pub Health, Univ Mich, Ann Arbor, beginning 1979; assoc res scientist, Inst Environ & Indust Health, 1974-1980; assoc prof, Sch Pub Health, Univ Mich, Ann Arbor, 1971-1979; asst prof environ health, Sch Pub Health, Univ Mich, Ann Arbor, 1965-1979. **Memberships:** Am Radon Asn; Health Physics Soc. **Research Statement & Publications:** Indoor radon risk, mitigation and measurement; low dose effects of radiations. **Mailing Address:** Univ Mich, Sch Public Health, 109 Observatory St 3537 SPH I, Ann Arbor, MI 48109-2029. **Fax:** 734-763-5455.

JACOBSON, ARTHUR E, MEDICINAL CHEMISTRY. **Personal Data:** b New York, NY, May 2, 1928; m 1964, Linda; c Jay & Laura. **Education:** Fordham Univ, BS, 1949; Rutgers Univ, MS (pharm chem), 1952, MS (chem), 1954, PhD (org & phys chem), 1960. **Honors & Awards:** J Michael Morrison Award, 1990. **Professional Experience:** SR SCIENTIST, NIDDK, NIH, as of 2004; biol coordr, Drug Eval Comt, 1991-; chief, NIDDK, NIH, beginning 1991; adj prof pharmacol & toxicol, Med Col Va, VaCommonwealth Univ, 1984-1993; chmn, drug testing prog, 1977-1990; mem, Col Probs DrugDependence, 1974-1981; mem, Comt Probs DrugDependence, 1974-1981; instr spectros, Found Adv Ed Sci, Inc, 1964-1988; RES CHEMIST, NAT INST ARTHRITIS, METAB & DIGESTIVE-DIS, NIH, 1962-; Nat Insts Health, US Pub Health Serv fel & org chemist, Albert Einstein

ColMed, 1959-1962. **Memberships:** AAAS; Am Chem Soc. **Research Statement & Publications:** Synthesis of alkaloids and heterocycles; computer-assisted molecular modelling; spectroscopy; synthesis of affinity ligands for, and characterization of, opioid and phencyclidine receptors. **Mailing Address:** NIDDK, NIH, Bldg 8 Rm B1-22, Bethesda, MD 20892-0815. **E-Mail:** aej@helix.nih.gov

JACOBSON, BARUCH S, BIOPHYSICS. **Personal Data:** b New York, NY, November 23, 1925; m 1951, c 4. **Education:** Columbia Univ, AB, 1951; Univ Calif, PhD (biophys), 1956. **Professional Experience:** RETIRED; fac res fels, Battelle Pac Northwest Labs, Richland, Wash, 1985, 1986 & 1987; res fel, Battelle Pac Northwest Labs, Richland, Wash, 1982-1983; vis res prof, Inst Ecol, Univ Calif, Davis, 1975; assoc prof physics, Cent Mich Univ, 1968-1987; asst prof radiol, Univ Minn, Minneapolis, 1961-1968; from instr to asst prof zool, Univ Tex, 1958-1961; biophysicist, Donner Lab, Univ Calif, 1958; fel, Donner Lab, Univ Calif, 1956-1958. **Memberships:** AAAS; Biophys Soc; Radiation Res Soc; Sigma Xi. **Research Statement & Publications:** Cellular radiobiology; effects of ionizing radiation on cell reproduction; metabolic reversal of radiation damage; ultraviolet photobiology; environmental systems analysis. **Mailing Address:** Dept Pharm, Wash State Univ, 100 Sprout Rd, Richmond, WA 99352.

JACOBSON, BERNARD, MATHEMATICS. **Personal Data:** b Cleveland, Ohio, April 7, 1928; m 1956, c 2. **Education:** Western Reserve Univ, BS, 1951; Mich State Univ, MS, 1952, PhD (math), 1956. **Professional Experience:** PROF EMER MATH, FRANKLIN & MARSHALL COL, 1995-; prof Math, Franklin & Marshall Col, 1969-1994; assoc prof, Franklin & Marshall Col, 1963-1969; assoc dir comt on undergrad prog math, Math Asn Am, 1962-1963; from asst prof to assoc prof math, Franklin & Marshall Col, 1956-1961. **Memberships:** Am Math Soc; Math Asn Am. **Research Statement & Publications:** Number theory. **Mailing Address:** Dept Math, Franklin & Marshall Col, PO Box 3003, Lancaster, PA 17604.

JACOBSON, BERTIL, HUMAN IMPRINTING. **Personal Data:** b Stockholm, Sweden, January 21, 1923; div, c Cecilia & Magnus. **Education:** Karolinska Inst, MD, 1950. **Professional Experience:** RETIRED; prof med eng, Karolinska Inst, 1960-1989; Asst prof med electronics, Karolinska Inst, 1957-1960. **Research Statement & Publications:** Human imprinting; perinatal origin of self-destructive adult behavior. **Mailing Address:** Vastra Myrskaren 41, S-74691 Balsta, Sweden. **Fax:** 461-715-1212.

JACOBSON, BRUCE SHELL, BIOLOGICAL CHEMISTRY. **Personal Data:** b Los Angeles, Calif, January 11, 1940. **Education:** Calif State Col, Los Angeles, BA, 1962, MA, 1964; Univ Calif, Los Angeles, PhD (plant biochem), 1970. **Professional Experience:** PROF BIOCHEM, UNIV MASS, AMHERST, beginning 1986; from asst prof to assoc prof biochem, Univ Mass, 1977-1986; resassoc, Harvard Univ, 1973-1977; res biochemist, Univ Calif, Davis, 1971-1973; res biologist, Univ Calif, Riverside, 1970-1971; fel Maria Moor Cabot, Harvard Univ; NIH postdoctoral fel, Harvard Univ; NIH predoctoral fel, Univ Calif, Los Angeles; estab investr, Am Heart Asn. **Memberships:** Am Soc Biol Chem; Am Soc Cell Biologists. **Research Statement & Publications:** Molecular and cellular biology of biological membranes; interaction of plasma membrane receptors with the extracellular matrix and the cytoskeleton; transcellular polarity of the plasma membrane in vascular endothelial cells; protein targetting the apical and basolateral plasmamembrane domains during endo-lexocytosis, transcytosis, membrane protein synthesis and cell movement. **Mailing Address:** Dept Biochem & Molecular Biol, Univ Mass, Amherst, MA 01003. **E-Mail:** jacobson@biochem.umass.edu

JACOBSON, DAVID J, BOTANY. **Education:** Calif Polytech Univ, BS, 1981; Univ Calif, Berkeley, MS, 1985, PhD (plant path), 1989. **Professional Experience:** SPECIALIST BIOLL RES, DEPT PLANT & MICROBIAL BIOL, UNIV CALIF, 2000-; SR RES SCIENTIST, DEPT BIOL SCI, STANFORD UNIV, 1996-. **Mailing Address:** Dept Biol Sci Stanford Univ, 371 Serra Mall, Stanford, CA 94305-5020. **Fax:** 650-723-6132. **E-Mail:** djjacob@leland.stanford.edu

JACOBSON, ELAINE LOUISE, BIOCHEMISTRY & NUTRITION. **Personal Data:** b Miller, Kans, March 29, 1945; m 1967. **Education:** Kans State Univ, BS, 1967, PhD (biochem), 1970. **Professional Experience:** PROF, PHARMACOL & TOXICOL, ARIZ CANCER CTR, UNIV ARIZ; PROF, DEPT CLIN SCI & MARKEY CANCER CTR, UNIV KY, 1992-; prof, Univ NTex Health Sci Ctr, Ft Worth, 1991-1992; assoc prof med & biochem, Univ NTex Health Sci Ctr, Ft Worth, 1985-1991; assoc prof, Tex Woman's Univ, 1981-1985; NIH fel, Extramanal Assoc, 1979-1980; asst prof biol, Tex Woman's Univ, 1977-1981; res assoc biochem, Dept Chem, NTex State Univ, 1974-1977; res fel biochem, Mayo Clin, Found & Grad Sch Med, 1972-1973; NIH fel, Mayo Clin, Found & Grad Sch Med, 1972-1973. **Memberships:** Am Soc Biochem & Molecular Biol; Am Asn Cancer Res; Am Soc Nutrit Sci; Am Col Nutrit; Int Soc Cancer Prev; Women Cancer Res; Sigma Xi; Am Acad Dermatol. **Research Statement & Publications:** Regulation of poly (adenosine diphosphate ribose) synthesis with a particular interest in events following DNA damage by carcinogens; niacin status and cancer prevention; poly (adenosine disphosphate ribose) metabolism as a target for design of anti-cancer therapies. **Mailing Address:** Ariz Cancer Ctr, POB 245024, Univ Ariz, Rm 3985C Salmon Bldg, Tucson, AZ 85724. **Fax:** 520-626-8567. **E-Mail:** jacobse@pharmacy.arizona.edu

JACOBSON, ELIZABETH D, HEALTH SCIENCES. **Education:** State Univ NY, Binghamton, BA, 1970; Georgetown Univ, PhD (biol), 1975. **Honors & Awards:** Arthur S Flemming Award, 1984. **Professional Experience:** DEP DIR SCI, CTR DEVICES & RADIOL HEALTH, FOOD & DRUGADMIN, 1990-; dir, Off Sci & Technol, Ctr Devices & Radiol Health, Food & Drug Admin, 1985-1990; chief, Optical Radiation Br, Ctr Devices & Radiol Health, Food & Drug Admin, 1982-1985; res geneticist, Ctr Devices & Radiol Health, Food & Drug Admin, 1975-1982. **Memberships:** Am Soc Photobiol; Environ Mutagen Soc; AAAS. **Research Statement & Publications:** Development of programs to assure the safety and effectiveness of medical devices; reduce population exposure to radiation emitted from medical and consumer products. **Mailing Address:** Ctr Devices & Radiol Health, Food & Drug Admin, 9200 Corporate Blvd, Rockville, MD 20850. **E-Mail:** edj@cdrh.fda.gov

JACOBSON, EUGENE DONALD, PHYSIOLOGY. **Personal Data:** b Bridgeport, Conn, February 19, 1930; m 1973, Laura; c Laura E, Susan R, Morrid D, Daniel F & Miriam L. **Education:** Wesleyan Univ, BA, 1951; Univ Vt, MD, 1955; State Univ NY, MS, 1960; FACP. **Honorary Degrees:** Dr, Jagellonian Univ, 1996. **Professional Experience:** ACTG HEAD GASTROENTEROL, SCH MED, UNIV COLO, 1994-; PROFMED & PHYSIOL, WEBB-WARIN INST BIOMEDICAL RES SCH MED, UNIV COLO, 1990-; dean, Sch Med, Univ Colo, 1988-1990; dean, Sch Med, Univ Kans, 1985-1988; mem, Nat Digestive Dis Adv Bd, NIH, 1985-1987; vdean, Col Med, Univ Cincinnati, 1977-1985; chmn, Nat Comn Digestive Dis, 1977-1979; prof physiol, Baylor Col Med, 1972-1977; prof physiol & chmn dept, Univ Tex MedSch, Houston, 1971-1977; Vet Admin, 1969-1971 & Upjohn Co, Mich, 1970-1988; consult, Gen MedStudy Sect, NIH, 1968-1972; prof & chmn dept, Sch Med, Univ Okla, 1966-1971; NIH spec fel, NIH res career develop award, 1966; assoc prof physiol, Sch Med, Univ Calif, Los Angeles, 1964-1966; NIH spec fel, Univ Calif, Los Angeles, 1964-1966; resident internal med, State UnivNY, 1957-1960; Intern, State Univ NY, 1955-1956. **Memberships:** Am Physiol Soc; AMA; Am Soc Clin Invest; fel Am Col Physicians; AmGastroenterol Asn (pres, 1989-1990); Asn Am Physicians. **Research Statement & Publications:** Splanchnic circulation; gastrointestinal physiology. **Mailing Address:** Colo Health Sci Ctr, PO Box C321, 4200 E Ninth Ave, Denver, CO 80262.

JACOBSON, FRANK HENRY, physiology; deceased, see previous edition for last biography

JACOBSON, GAIL M, BIOCHEMISTRY. **Personal Data:** b Bartlesville, Okla, February 6, 1938; m 1963, c 3. **Education:** Mt Holyoke Col, BA, 1960, MA, 1962; Cornell Univ, PhD (biochem), 1966. **Professional Experience:** RETIRED; lectr, Dept Chem, Calif Polytech State Univ, 1976-1995; asst mem, Okla Med Res Found, 1968-1976; vis asst prof nutrit, Univ Okla, 1968-1975; res fel biochem, Calif Inst Technol, 1966-1968. **Memberships:** Sigma Xi. **Research Statement & Publications:** Enzymology; enzyme kinetics; coenzyme B12; enzymes; methylation of ribosomal RNA. **Mailing Address:** 156 Broad St, San Luis Obispo, CA 93405.

JACOBSON, GUNNARD KENNETH, FERMENTATION. **Personal Data:** b Phoenix, Ariz, February 19, 1947; m 1971, Claudia. **Education:** Univ Ariz, BS, 1969; Ore State Univ, PhD (microbiol), 1973. **Professional Experience:** AT LESAFFRE YEAST CORP, as of 2002; MGR, UNIVERSAL FOODS CORP, 1991-; proj scientist, molecular biol, 1988-1991; sr scientist, molecular biol, 1982-1988; scientist, Universal Foods Corp, 1977-1982; res assoc, Argonne Nat Lab, 1975-1977; fel, Univ Chicago, 1972-1975. **Memberships:** Am Soc Microbiol; AAAS; Genetics Soc Am; Sigma Xi. **Research Statement & Publications:** Genetics and molecular biology of industrial microorganisms-new strain construction and improvement by classical genetics and recombinant DNA technology. **Mailing Address:** Lesaffre Yeast Corp, 2702 W Greves, Milwaukee, WI 53208. **Fax:** 414-615-5525. **E-Mail:** gunnard.jacobson@lesaffreyeastcorp.com

JACOBSON, HARRY C, PHYSICS. **Personal Data:** b Bozeman, Mont, July 13, 1931; m 1964, Marilyn; c Kara C (Dallmam), Stephen C, Paula C & Aubrie C. **Education:** Col Holy Cross, BS, 1953; Yale Univ, MS, 1961; PhD (physics), 1965. **Professional Experience:** PROF EMER, DEPT PHYSICS & ASTRON, UNIV TENN, KNOXVILLE, as of 2004; prof, Dept Physics & Astron, Univ Tenn, Knoxville, beginning 1982; prof, Dept Physics & Astron, Univ Tenn, Knoxville, beginning 1964; physicist, Nuclear Div, Combustion Eng Inc, 1956-1960. **Memberships:** Am Phys Soc. **Research Statement & Publications:** Theory of atomic and molecular structure; theory of spectral line shapes. **Mailing Address:** Dept Physics & Astron, Univ Tenn, 401 Nielsen Physics, 1408 Circle Dr, Knoxville, TN 37996. **E-Mail:** hcj@utk.edu

JACOBSON, HARRY R, MEDICINE. **Personal Data:** b June 21, 1947; American citizen. **Education:** Univ Ill, Champaign, BS, 1969; Univ Ill, Chicago, MD, 1972; Am Bd Internal Med, cert, 1975. **Professional Experience:** VICE CHANCELLOR HEALTH AFFIARS, VANDERBILT UNIV, NASHVILLE, TENN, as of 2003; Mem, Nat Kidney & Urol Dis Adv Bd, NIH, 1990-; assoc ed, News Physiol Sci, 1988- & Kidney Int, 1990-; PROF MED & DIR, DIV NEPHROLOGY, DEPT MED, MEDCTR, VANDERBILT UNIV, NASHVILLE, TENN, 1985-; STAFFPHYSICIAN/NEPHROLOGIST, VET ADMIN HOSP, NASHVILLE, 1985-; from asst prof toassoc prof internal med, Univ Tex Health Sci Ctr, Dallas, 1978-1985; NIH res career developaward, 1978-1983; chief, Renal Sect, US Army Surg Res Ctr, Brooke Army Med Ctr, SanAntonio, Tex, 1976-1978; nephrology fel, Univ Tex Health Sci Ctr, Dallas, 1974-1976; medresidency, Johns Hopkins Hosp, Baltimore, Md, 1973-1974; internship med, Johns Hopkins Hosp, Baltimore, Md, 1972-1973. **Memberships:** Am Fedn Clin Res; Am Soc Nephrology; Int Soc Nephrology; Am Physiol Soc; Am Soc Clin Invest; Asn Am Physicians. **Research Statement & Publications:** Author of numerous publications. **Mailing Address:** Renal Div, Vanderbilt Univ Sch Med, Nashville, TN 37232-0001.

JACOBSON, HERBERT (IRVING), REPRODUCTIVE ENDOCRINOLOGY, BIOCHEMISTRY. **Personal Data:** b Chicago, Ill, March 17, 1923; m 1953, c 3. **Education:** Univ Chicago, SB, 1948, SM, 1949, PhD (chem), 1957. **Honors & Awards:** Res Career Develop Award, Nat Inst Arthritis & Metabolic Dis, 1966-1970; US Sr Scientist Award, Fed Repub Ger & Alexander Von Humboldt Found, 1975. **Professional Experience:** RES PROF BIOCHEM, DEPT OBSTET & GYNEC, ALBANY MED COL, 1975-; vis prof, Max Planck Inst Cell Biol, 1975-1976; CHIEF SECT REPRODSTUDIES, DEPT OBSTET & GYNEC, ALBANY MED COL, 1973-; assoc prof obstet & gynec, Dept Obstet &Gynec, Albany Med Col, 1964-1973; USPHS spec fel, Max Planck Inst Biochem, Munich, 1962-1963; res partic, Chem Div, Oak Ridge Nat Lab, 1961; asst prof, Ben May Lab Cancer Res, 1959-1964; res assoc & asst prof, Univ Chicago, 1957-1959; res assoc & instr, Univ Chicago, 1952-1957. **Memberships:** Endocrine Soc; Soc Exp Biol & Med; NY Acad Sci; Soc Study Reprod. **Research Statement & Publications:** Steroid biochemistry; mechanism of hormone action; regulation of hormone receptor synthesis; control processes in mammalian reproduction; response mechanisms in hormone-dependent cancer. **Mailing Address:** Dept Obstet & Gynec, Albany Med Col, 43 New Scotland Ave, Albany, NY 12208.

JACOBSON, HOMER, INFORMATION & BIOPOLYMER THEORY. **Personal Data:** b Cleveland, Ohio, November 27, 1922; m Bong Xi; c William, Guy, Ethan & Lisbeth. **Education:** Calif Inst Technol, BS, 1941; Columbia Univ, AM, 1942, PhD (chem), 1948. **Honors & Awards:** Guggenheim fel, Calif Inst Technol, 1959-1960. **Professional Experience:** EMER PROF CHEM, BROOKLYN COL, 1986-; NIH spec fel, 1960-1961; from instr to prof, Brooklyn Col, 1950-1986; instr chem, Hunter Col, 1949-1950; assoc chemist, Brookhaven Nat Lab, 1947-1949; Res scientist, Manhattan Proj, NY, 1944-1946. **Research Statement & Publications:** Chemical mutagenesis Physical models of self reproduction in bacterial viruses; virus growth in continuous culture; steady-state kinetics; information theory in biological systems; configurational entropy of superhelices and catenanes. **Mailing Address:** 140 Carrollwood Dr, Tarrytown, NY 10591. **Fax:** 914-332-7627.

JACOBSON, HOWARD NEWMAN, PHYSIOLOGY. **Personal Data:** b St Paul, Minn, August 13, 1923; m 1961. **Education:** Northwestern Univ, BS, 1947, BM, 1950, MD, 1951. **Professional Experience:** DIR, INST NUTRIT, UNIV S FLA, CHAPEL HILL, 1979-; prof communitymed, Rutgers Med Sch, Col Med & Dent NJ, 1974-1979; chmn, comt maternal nutrit, NatAcad Sci-Nat Res Coun, 1971-; mem food & nutrit bd, Nat Res Coun, 1970-; assoc prof obstet &gynec, Boston Hosp for Women & dir Macy prog, Harvard Med Sch, 1969-1974; assoc coordallied health professions, Sch Med & lectr pub health, Sch Pub Health, Univ Calif, San Francisco, 1967-1969; actg assoc prof obstet & gynec, Sch Med & lectr pub health, Sch Pub Health, UnivCalif, San Francisco, 1965-1967; mem adv panel maternal & child health, Children's Bur, 1964-; NIH res career develop award, 1964-1965; assoc, Harvard Med Sch, 1964-1965; instr, HarvardMed Sch, 1961-1964; asst obstet & gynec, Harvard Med Sch, 1960-1961; obstetrician-physiologist, PR Proj, Nat Inst Neurol Dis & Blindness, 1958-1960; resident, BostonLying-in-Hosp & Free Hosp for

Women, 1955-1957; Asn Aid Crippled Children fel, 1952-1955; res fel physiol, Harvard Med Sch, 1952-1954; resident obstet & gynec, Presby Hosp, Chicago, 1951-1952; intern med, Presby Hosp, Chicago, 1950-1951. **Memberships:** Am Soc Clin Nutrit; assoc Am Physiol Soc. **Research Statement & Publications:** Fetal physiology and responses of fetuses to asphyxia and hypoxia; autonomic nervous system in reproduction; maternity services, with emphasis on maternal nutrition; health manpower needs, nutrition monitoring. **Mailing Address:** Dept Community & Family Health Univ SFla, 13201 Bruce B Downs Blvd, Tampa, FL 33612. **E-Mail:** hjacobso@hsc.usf.edu

JACOBSON, HOWARD W, RESEARCH CHEMISTRY. **Honors & Awards:** Creative Invention Award, Am Chem Soc, 1994. **Professional Experience:** RES SCIENTIST, DUPONT CO INC. **Mailing Address:** DuPont, 211 Jackson Lab-Chamber Works, Deepwater, NJ 08023.

JACOBSON, IRA DAVID, FLIGHT MECHANICS, FLUID MECHANICS. **Personal Data:** b New York, NY, May 28, 1942; m 1964, Judy; c 2. **Education:** NY Univ, BS, 1963; Univ VA, MS, 1967, PhD (aerospace eng), 1970. **Honors & Awards:** Atwood Award, Am Inst Aeronaut & Astronaut, Am Soc Eng Educr. **Professional Experience:** EXEC VPRES ACAD, EMBRY RIDDLE AERO UNIV, as of 2001; vpres Acad, Embry Riddle Aero Univ, beginning 1993; dir comput & commun, Ctr Comput Aided Eng, 1991-1992; dir, Ctr Comput Aided Eng, 1983-1992; from asst prof to prof aerospace eng, Univ Va, 1973-1992; res scientist & lectr, Univ Va, 1970-1973; aerospace engr, NASA, 1963-1967; dir, Inst Comput Aided Eng, Ctr Innovative Technol. **Memberships:** Am Inst Aeronaut & Astronaut; Am Soc Eng Educr; Sigma Xi; Soc Mfg Engrs. **Research Statement & Publications:** Flight mechanics, especially stability and control; fluid mechanics, especially the magnus effect; vehicle systems, especially vehicle ride quality; computer aided design and manufacturing. **Mailing Address:** Embry Riddle Aero Univ, Spruance Hall Rm 22 6005 Clyde Morris Blvd, Daytona Beach, FL 32114-3966. **Fax:** 904-226-6299. **E-Mail:** idj@db.erau.edu

JACOBSON, IRVEN ALLAN, PHYSICAL CHEMISTRY, CHEMICAL KINETICS. **Personal Data:** b Denver, Colo, April 19, 1928; m 1964, c 1. **Education:** Univ Colo, BA, 1950. **Professional Experience:** RETIRED; chemical engr, Laramie Energy Res Ctr, Bur Mines, US DeptInterior, 1978-1983; res chemist & proj leader, Laramie Energy Technol Ctr, US Dept Energy, 1975-1978; res chemist, Laramie Energy Res Ctr, Bur Mines, US Dept Interior, 1960-1975; chemist, Laramie Energy Res Ctr, Bur Mines, US Dept Interior, 1950-1960. **Memberships:** Fel AAAS; Am Chem Soc; Sigma Xi. **Research Statement & Publications:** Directing research on the kinetics of oil shale thermal gasification and low temperature oxidation. **Mailing Address:** 2626 Park Ave, Laramie, WY 82070.

JACOBSON, JAMES W, BIOLOGY. **Education:** Wash Univ, PhD, 1986. **Professional Experience:** VPRES, RES & DEVELOP, LUMINEX CORP, as of 2003. **Mailing Address:** Luminex Corp, 12212 Technol Blvd, Austin, TX 78727. **E-Mail:** jwjacobs@luminexcorp.com

JACOBSON, JAY STANLEY, PLANT PHYSIOLOGY, AIR POLLUTION. **Personal Data:** b New York, NY, October 5, 1934; m 2004, Pamela; c Frank & John Jacobson. **Education:** Cornell Univ, BS, 1955; Columbia Univ, MA, 1957, PhD (plant biochem), 1960. **Professional Experience:** RETIRED; Plant Physiologist, Boyce Thompson Inst, 1970-1996; Assoc Plant Biochemist, Boyce Thompson Inst, 1960-1970; Adj Prof, Dept Natural Resources, Cornell Univ; Consult, USDA & Environ Protection Agency. **Research Statement & Publications:** Effects of air pollutants and acid rain on growth, development, yield and quality of agricultural crops and forest trees; chemical analysis of fluorine in vegetation. **Mailing Address:** 924 Hannah Branch Rd, Burnsville, NC 28714. **E-Mail:** jayjacobson@fastmail.fm

JACOBSON, JERRY I, JACOBSON RESONANCE, BIOELECTROMAGNETICS. **Personal Data:** b Brooklyn, NY, January 25, 1946; m 1975, Debra; c Solomon, Jacqueline & Faith. **Education:** Brooklyn Col, BA, 1966; Temple Univ, DDS-DMD, 1970; City Univ NY, PhD (physics), 1983; Bundelkhand Univ, PhD (Biophys), 2002. **Professional Experience:** CHIEF EXEC OFF & CHIEF SCI & TECHNOL OFFICER, JACOBSON RESONANCE ENTERPRISES INC, 2002-; chmn & pres, Jacobson Resonance Enterprises Inc, beginning 1996; FOUND, JACOBSON RESONANCE ENTERPRISES INC, as of 2001; lectr, Int Confs, beginning 1986; pres, Inst Theoret Physics, Alzheimersres Found, beginning 1985; pres, Perspectivism Found, beginning 1980. **Memberships:** Bioelectromagnetics Soc; Am Phys Soc; Europ Bioelectromagnetics Soc. **Research Statement & Publications:** Discovered a physico-mathematical apparatus called Jacobson Resonance which enables the scientist to establish magnetic field parameters by which to mechanically vibrate masses in a biological system to therein recrystallize critical molecules; reorder structures of ions in the plasma of a fusion test reactor. **Mailing Address:** Jaconson Resonance Enterprises Inc, 8200 Jog Rd, Suit 100, Boynton Beach, FL 33437. **Fax:** 561-752-3939.

JACOBSON, JIMMY JOE, GEOPHYSICS, EARTH SCIENCES. **Personal Data:** b Lonepine, Wyo, February 11, 1937; m 1973, c 3. **Education:** Univ Wyo, BS, 1959; Colo Sch Mines, MSc, 1964, DSc(geophys), 1969. **Professional Experience:** CONSULT GEOPHYS, 1983-; MCR Geothermal, Denver, 1980-1983; sr resscientist geophys, Pac Northwest Div, Battelle Mem Inst, 1977-1980; mgr field opers, Geonomics, Inc, 1974-1977; asst prof physics & geophys, Mont Col Mineral Sci & Technol, 1970-1974; geophysicist, Group Seven, Inc, 1969-1973; sr geophysicist, Westinghouse GeoresLabs, 1965-1967; from jr to sr geophysicist, Deco Electronics, 1960-1965. **Memberships:** Sigma Xi. **Research Statement & Publications:** Exploration of the earth and earth materials utilizing electrical and other geophysical tools. **Mailing Address:** 11009 W 65th Way, Arvada, CO 80004.

JACOBSON, JOAN, AUDIOLOGY, SPEECH PATHOLOGY. **Personal Data:** b Hull, Iowa, April 26, 1924; div. **Education:** Morningside Col, BA, 1944; Syracuse Univ, MA, 1948, PhD (speech corrections), 1958. **Professional Experience:** RETIRED; mem, ModelPresch Ctr Hearing-Impaired Children & Families, 1969-1972; mem, Gov Adv Comt Serv Hearing Impaired, 1964-1966; mem prof adv comt, Minn SocCrippled Children & Adults, beginning 1963; from assoc prof to prof speechsci, path & audiol, St Cloud State Univ, 1962-1993; asst prof speech path & audiol & audiologist, Eastern Ill Univ, 1958-1962; res asst speech path, Syracuse Univ, 1957-1958; therapist, BrooklinePub Schs, Mass, 1951-1957; therapist, Mass Gen Hosp, Boston, 1951-1957; instr speech path, Syracuse Univ, 1946-1951. **Memberships:** Am Speech Lang Hearing Asn; Am Cleft Palate Asn; Am Acad Rehab Audiol. **Research Statement & Publications:** Lip reading; cleft palate. **Mailing Address:** 915 Nineth St S, St Cloud, MN 56301.

JACOBSON, JOHN OBERT, MECHANICAL ENGINEERING. **Personal Data:** b Alexandria, Minn, October 23, 1939; c 1. **Education:** Wash State Univ, BS, 1962; Univ Wash, MS, 1965, PhD (bioeng), 1972. **Professional Experience:** Rev comt mem, NIH, 1986-; assoc prof mech eng, Seattle Univ, 1983-1985; comt mem, Nat Asn Fire Protection, 1981-; asst prof, Cogswell Col, 1979-1982; CONSULTENGR, JACOBSON ENGRS, 1978-; consult engr, Westinghouse Hausford, Olympic Engr, 1976-1978; res scientist, Va Mason Med Ctr, 1971-1974 & Flow Res Inc, 1974-1975; res consult, Appl Physics Lab, 1974; Consult engr, Engineered Indust Systs, Inc, 1966-1986; eng supvr, Lockheed Shipbuilding Co, 1965-1966; Safety engr, Boeing Co, 1962-1963. **Memberships:** Am Soc Mech Engrs; Human Factors Soc. **Research Statement & Publications:** Ultrasonic imaging for medical diagnostics; laser development for military applications; material development for ultra high pressure applications; design and development of ultra high gravity centrifuge. **Mailing Address:** 5220 Roosevelt Way NE, Seattle, WA 98105.

JACOBSON, KARL BRUCE, DNA DIAGNOSTICS. **Personal Data:** b Manning, Iowa, March 5, 1928; m 1951, Phyllis; c Deborah, Paul, Steven & Dan. **Education:** St Bonaventure Col, BS, 1948; Johns Hopkins Univ, PhD (biol), 1956. **Professional Experience:** RETIRED; adj prof biomed sci, Univ Tenn, as of 2003; biochemist Biol Div, Health Sci Res Div, Oakridge Nat Lab, Univ Tenn, 1958-1993; Am Cancer Soc fel chem, Calif Inst Technol, 1956-1958; prof biomed sci, Health Sci Res Div, Oakridge Nat Lab, Univ Tenn. **Memberships:** AAAS; Am Soc Biol Chem; Am Chem Soc; Human Genome Orgn. **Research Statement & Publications:** New technologies for DNA sequencing; development and differentiation in terms of biochemical changes; relationship of structure of transfer RNA to its function; biochemical genetics in Drosophila; mechanism of toxicity of cadmium and other metals. **Mailing Address:** 940 W Outer Dr, Oak Ridge, TN 37830. **Fax:** 615-574-1274. **E-Mail:** bru@ornl.gov

JACOBSON, KENNETH ALAN, RECEPTOR PHARMACOLOGY, MEDICINAL CHEMISTRY. **Personal Data:** b Euclid, Ohio, July 18, 1953; m 1978, Arlette; c Gabriel, Dorit & Mihal. **Education:** Reed Col, BA, 1976; Univ Calif, San Diego, MS, 1978, PhD (chem), 1981. **Honors & Awards:** Giuliana Fassina Award, Purine Club, 1996; ISI Highly Cited Researcher in Pharmacology. **Professional Experience:** Adj prof, Dept Anat, Physiol & Genetics, Uniformed Servs Univ Health Sci, Bethesda, MD, as of 2005; DIR, CHEM BIOL CORE FACIL, NIH, 2003-; DIR, CHEM BIOL CORE FACIL, Nat INST DIABETES, DIGESTIVE & KIDNEY DIS, 2003-; CHIEF, MOLECULAR RECOGNITION SECT, NIH, 1993-; scientific adv bd, Res Biochem, Inc, Natick, Mass, 1990-1991; res chemist, Nat Inst Diabetes, Digestive & Kidney Dis, NIH, Bethesda, MD, beginning 1988; instr, Found Advan Educ Sci, Bethesda, Md, 1984-1985; sr staff fel, 1983-1988; Bantrell res fel, Dept Org Chem, Weizmann Inst Sci, Rehovot, Israel, 1981-1983. **Memberships:** Am Chem Soc; Soc Neuroscience; Am Soc Pharmaceut & Exp Therapeut. **Research Statement & Publications:** Developing novel ligands for neurotransmitter receptors; chemistry and pharmacology of purines; muscarinic acetylcholine receptors; neurochemistry and imaging. **Mailing Address:** NIH, Bldg 8A Rm B1A 19, Bethesda, MD 20892-0810. **Fax:** 301-402-0008. **E-Mail:** kajacobs@helix.nih.gov

JACOBSON, KENNETH ALLAN, MEMBRANE BIOPHYSICS, CELL MOTILITY. **Personal Data:** b Milwaukee, Wis, October 29, 1941. **Education:** Univ Wis-Madison, BS, 1964, MS, 1966; State Univ NY, Buffalo, PhD (biophys), 1972; Univ Linkoping, Linkoping, Sweden, MD, 1993. **Professional Experience:** ASSOC DIR, DEPT CELL BIOL & ANAT CELL & MOLECULAR IMAGING FACILITY, UNIV NC, as of 2004; guest prof, Dept Physics, Tech Univ, Munich, Ger, beginning 1993; PROF CELL & DEVELOPMENTAL BIOL, UNIV NC, CHAPEL HILL, 1987-; ed, Comments Molecular & Cell Biophys, 1986-; prin investr grants, NIH, 1974-; prin investr, Am Cancer Soc, 1983-; pres, Fluorescence Unltd Consults, 1983-1990; assoc prof anat & core mem, Cancer Res Ctr, 1980-1987; ed, Cell Physiol Sect, Am J Physiol, 1980-1984; estab investr, Am Heart Asn, 1977-1982; chmn, Grad Group Biomembranes, 1977-1980; asst prof biophys, Ctr Theoret Biol, State Univ NY, Buffalo, 1976-1980; mem, Ctr Theoret Biol, State Univ NY, Buffalo, 1972-1980; sr cancer res scientist, Roswell Park Mem Inst, 1972-1980; physicist, Dow Corning Corp, 1966-1969. **Memberships:** Am Soc Cell Biol; Biophys Soc; AAAS. **Research Statement & Publications:** Development of fluorescence microscopy; use of digital image processing to measure the distribution of single classes of molecules in single, living cells; lateral diffusion in membranes; cell locomotion; nanovid microscopy and single particle tracking. **Mailing Address:** Dept Cell Biol & Anat, Univ NC, CB Ste 7090 120 Taylor Hall, Chapel Hill, NC 27599-9090. **Fax:** 919-966-1856. **E-Mail:** frap@med.unc.edu

JACOBSON, LARRY A, NUCLEAR PHYSICS, GEOPHYSICS. **Personal Data:** b Madison, Wis, October 29, 1940; m 1965, Adrienne. **Education:** Univ Wis-Madison, BS, 1963, MS, 1964, PhD (physics), 1969. **Professional Experience:** CHIEF SCIENTIST, HALLIBURTON ENERGY SERV INC, 2000-; mgr res, Halliburton Energy Serv Inc, 1996-2000; mgr nuclear res sect, Halliburton Energy Serv Inc, 1988-1995; mgr nuclear res group, Austin Res Ctr, Gearhart Industs Inc, 1984-1988; mgr nuclear logging, Schlumberger Well Serv Co, 1981-1984; mgr sensor physics, Pulsed Neutron Sect, 1980-1981; Distinguished vis prof, Elec Eng Dept, Univ Houston, 1980; dept mgr elec eng, Pulsed Neutron Sect, 1976-1979; sect mgr, Pulsed Neutron Sect, 1974-1976; develop proj physicist, Schlumberger Ltd, 1969-1974. **Memberships:** AAAS; Am Phys Soc; Soc Prof Well Log Analysts; Soc Petrol Eng; Sigma Xi. **Research Statement & Publications:** Negative ion source development; heavy ion nuclear elastic scattering; nuclear techniques in mineral and petroleum exploration and evaluation; data processing of nuclear data; computer simulations of nuclear processes; awarded 8 US patents. **Mailing Address:** Halliburton Energy Serv, PO Box 60078, Houston, TX 77204. **Fax:** 281-871-7211. **E-Mail:** larry.jacobson@halliburton.com

JACOBSON, LEWIS A, CELLBIOLOGY, BIOCHEMISTRY. **Personal Data:** b Brooklyn, NY, October 10, 1942; m 1967, c 2. **Education:** Amherst Col, AB, 1963; Univ Ill, MS, 1965, PhD (biochem), 1967. **Honors & Awards:** Fel of the AAAS, 2001. **Professional Experience:** ASSOC PROF BIOL SCI, UNIV PITTSBURGH, 1976-; From asst prof biophys to assoc prof biophys & microbiol, Univ Pittsburgh, 1967-1976; Vpres, Tutorials Group Inc. **Memberships:** AAAS; Am Soc Microbiol; Am Soc Biochem & Molecular Biol; Am Soc Cell Biol. **Research Statement & Publications:** Signal transduction; regulation of proteolysis in muscle; biochemistry and genetics of lysosomal proteases; neural control of muscle proteolysis. **Mailing Address:** Dept Biol Sci, 304 Langley Hall Univ Pittsburgh, Pittsburgh, PA 15260. **Fax:** 412-624-4759. **E-Mail:** ljac@pitt.edu

JACOBSON, LINDA JEN, BIOLOGY. **Education:** Harvard Univ, BA, 1962; Univ Ill, MS, 1965, PhD, 1967. **Professional Experience:** PROF, DEPT BIOL SCI, UNIV PITTSBURGH, as of 2006. **Mailing Address:** Dept Biol Sci, Univ Pittsburgh, 320 Clapp Hall, Pittsburgh, PA 15260. **E-Mail:** ljen@pitt.edu

JACOBSON, LOUIS, PLANT PHYSIOLOGY. **Personal Data:** b Chicago, Ill, November 21, 1915; m 1938, c 3. **Education:** Univ Calif, PhD (plant physiol), 1943; Univ Calif, Los Angeles, AB, 1936. **Professional Experience:** PROF PLANT NUTRIT & PLANT PHYSIOLOGIST EXP STA, DEPTSOILS & PLANT NUTRIT, UNIV CALIF, BERKELEY, 1958-; from asst prof & asst plantbiochemist to assoc prof nutrit & assoc plant biochemist, Radiation Lab, 1945-1958; radiochemist, Radiation Lab, 1942-1946; Analyst, Div Plant Nutrit, 1938-1942. **Memberships:** Am Chem Soc; Am Soc Plant Physiol; Bot Soc Am. **Research Statement & Publications:** Absorption and accumulation of ions by plants; inorganic nutrition of plants; plant physiology. **Mailing Address:** 150 Poplar St, Berkeley, CA 94708-1326.

JACOBSON, MARCUS, ENGINEERING MECHANICS. **Personal Data:** b Houston, Tex, May 2, 1930; m 1965. **Education:** Rice Univ, BA, 1951, BSME, 1952, MSME, 1954; Univ Calif, Los Angeles, PhD (eng), 1965. **Professional Experience:** RETIRED; eng specialist struct dynamics, Aircraft Div, Northrop Corp, 1964-1995; sr dynamics engr, Lockheed-Calif Co, 1963-1964; design engr, Douglas Aircraft Co, 1962; asst prof mech eng, Rice Univ, 1952-1962. **Memberships:** Am Inst Aeronaut & Astronaut. **Research Statement & Publications:** Structural dynamics. **Mailing Address:** 5337 S Holt Ave, Los Angeles, CA 90056.

JACOBSON, MARTIN, phytochemistry, pesticides; deceased, see previous edition for last biography

JACOBSON, MARTIN MICHAEL, BIOCHEMICAL PHARMACOLOGY. **Personal Data:** b New York, NY, November 24, 1934; m 1965. **Education:** City Col New York, BS, 1957; Long Island Univ, MS, 1968. **Professional Experience:** DIR RES PLANNING, SCI & FINANCIAL ADMIN, HOFFMANN-LAROCHE INC, 1985-; asst dir res qual assurance, Hoffmann- Laroche Inc, 1984-1985; asst dir pharm res & develop, Hoffmann- Laroche Inc, 1983-1984; asst dir resplanning & develop, Hoffmann- Laroche Inc, 1981-1983; asst dir exp therapeut, Hoffmann-Laroche Inc, 1980-1981; res planning mgr exp therapeut, Hoffmann- Laroche Inc, 1978-1980; coordr exp therapeut, Hoffmann- Laroche Inc, 1974-1978; sr scientist, Hoffmann- Laroche Inc, 1974; biochemist, Hoffmann- Laroche Inc, 1970-1973; res biochemist, Wellcome Res Labs, Burroughs Wellcome & Co, 1959-1970; Res technician, Rockefeller Inst Med Res, 1957-1958. **Memberships:** Am Soc Pharmacol & Exp Therapeut; NY Acad Sci; AAAS; Am Pharmaceut Asn; Acad Pharmaceut Sci; Sigma Xi; Drug Info Asn. **Research Statement & Publications:** Biochemical, pharmacologic and toxicologic effects and metabolism of drugs, carcinogens and steroids; involvement of the various disciplines in drug development. **Mailing Address:** Preclin Res & Develop, Hoffmann LaRoche Inc Bldg 76 5th Floor 340 Kingsland St, Nutley, NJ 07110-1199. **Fax:** 973-235-6253.

JACOBSON, MELVIN JOSEPH, APPLIED MATHEMATICS, WAVE PROPAGATION. **Personal Data:** b Providence, RI, November 25, 1928; m 2002, Gerzrude; c Deborah L (Karczewski) & Donald B. **Education:** Brown Univ, AB, 1950; Carnegie Inst Technol, MS, 1952, PhD (appl math), 1954. **Professional Experience:** EMER PROF MATH, RENSSELAER POLYTECH INST, 1991-; res consult, Rensselaer Polytech Inst, 1991-1995; adj prof, Inst Marine Sci, Univ Miami, 1969-1972; consult indust, 1965-; vis prof, Inst Marine Sci, Univ Miami, 1963-1964; Prin investr, US Navy, Army, NASA & Indust, 1957-1990; from asst prof to prof, Rensselaer Polytech Inst, 1956-1990; mem tech staff, Bell Tel Labs, Inc, 1954-1956; instr math, Carnegie Inst Technol, 1953-1954; res assoc, Carnegie Inst Technol, 1952-1953; Res mathematician, United Aircraft Corp, 1952. **Memberships:** Fel Acoust Soc Am; Soc Indust & Appl Math; Am Asn Univ Profs; Sigma Xi. **Research Statement & Publications:** Theories of underwater acoustics, including ocean environmental effects; mathematical studies of electromagnetic wave propagation in the atmosphere; low frequency atmospheric acoustics. **Mailing Address:** 4705 Chandlers Forde, Sarasota, FL 34235. **E-Mail:** melgeez@aol.com

JACOBSON, MICHAEL F, SCIENCE POLICY, MOLECULAR BIOLOGY. **Personal Data:** b Chicago, Ill, July 29, 1943; m 1989, c Sonya. **Education:** Univ Chicago, BA, 1965; Mass Inst Technol, PhD (microbiol), 1969. **Honors & Awards:** Harvey W Wiley Medal & Comnr's Spec Citation, US Food & Drug Admin. **Professional Experience:** Co-founder, Ctr Study Commercialism, 1990-1995; dir, Nat Coalition Dis Prev & Environ Health, 1979-1982; EXEC DIR, CTR SCI PUBLIC INTEREST, 1971-; Tech consult, Ctr Study Responsive Law, 1970-1971; Res assoc, Salk Inst Biol Studies, 1970-1971. **Research Statement & Publications:** Impact of dietary and environmental factors on human health. **Mailing Address:** Ctr Sci Pub Interest, 1875 Connecticut Ave NW Suite 300, Washington, DC 20009-5728.

JACOBSON, MICHAEL RAY, OPTICAL MEASUREMENTS, THIN FILM DEPOSITION. **Personal Data:** b Pittsburgh, Pa, January 11, 1950; m 1973, Simone; c Tivon, Shira & Natan. **Education:** Harvard Col, AB, 1971; Cornell Univ, MS, 1975, PhD (astron), 1977. **Professional Experience:** ASSOC, OPTICAL DATA ASSOCS, 1991-; consult, Sci Applns Int Corp, 1991-; visfac, Battelle Northwest Pac Lab, 1990-; ADJ ASSOC RES PROF OPTICAL SCI, OPTICAL SCI & MAT SCI & ENG DEPT, UNIV ARIZ, 1990-; assoc res scientist, Univ Ariz, 1986-1990; instr short course, Int SocOptical Eng, 1984-; consult, Energy Conversion Devices, 1980-1981& Dow Chem, 1989-; res specialist, Univ Ariz, 1977-1986. **Memberships:** Optical Soc Am; Am Vacuum Soc; Int Soc Optical Eng; Am Meteorol Soc. **Research Statement & Publications:** Optical materials, their deposition, characterization, and availability in thin film form; solar energy conversion materials; space applications; polymer films. **Mailing Address:** Optical Data Asn, 5237 E Seventh St, Tucson, AZ 85711.

JACOBSON, MURRAY M, CHEMICAL ENGINEERING, MATERIALS ENGINEERING. **Personal Data:** b Boston, Mass, January 2, 1915; m 1962, Madelyn Marder; c Marc, Paul & Richard. **Education:** Tufts Univ, BS, 1935. **Professional Experience:** PRES, JACON INDUSTS, 1975-; chief mat test div, Army Mat & Mech ResCtr, 1969-1974; liaison mem subpanel on chromium, Panel on Refractory Metals, Mat Adv Bd, 1949 & Comt Coatings, 1968-1969; chief prototypes lab, Army Mat & Mech Res Ctr, 1966-1969; dep chief, Mat Eng Div, Army Mat Res Agency, 1964-1966; Chem Metall Lab, 1956-1959 & Mat SciLab, 1959-1964; chief, Phys Chem Br, 1954-1956; chief, Surface Chem Sect, 1949-1954; chemengr, Watertown Arsenal Labs, 1946-1949; Army liaison mem, Subgroup on Greases, Coord ResCoun, War Adv Comt & Adv Comt on Corrosion, Ord Dept, 1942-1945; chief corrosion &lubrication sect, Watertown Arsenal Labs, 1940-1946; Chemist, Whiting Labs, Mass, 1936-1939. **Memberships:** Am Chem Soc; Nat Asn Corrosion Engrs; Am Soc Metals. **Research Statement & Publications:** Research management; corrosion; erosion; oxidation; wear; lubrication; protective coatings and treatments; antigalling coatings; titanium surface metallurgy. **Mailing Address:** Jacon Industs, PO Box 231, Boston, MA 02146-0002.

JACOBSON, MYRON J, TRAUMA SURGERY, THORACIC SURGERY. **Personal Data:** b New York, NY, June 19, 1932; c Barry, Michael & Daniel. **Education:** McGill Univ, BS, 1954; Univ Chicago, MD, 1958. **Professional Experience:** Police surgeon, NY Police dept, 1993-; vis prof surg, Ben Gerner Gurion Univ, 1984; CLIN ASSOC PROF, STATE UNIV NY, STONY BROOK, 1974-; CHIEF THORACIC SURG, NPORT VET ADMIN MED CTR, 1974-; assoc prof, Chicago Med Sch, 1966-1970; instr surg, Univ Chicago, 1964-1966. **Memberships:** Am Col Surgeons; Am Col Chest Physicians; Soc Thoracic Surgeons; Sigma Xi. **Research Statement & Publications:** Risk factors in patients undergoing lung resection; lung cancer; Risk factors in general surgery. **Mailing Address:** 653 Howard Ave, West Hempstead, NY 11552.

JACOBSON, MYRON KENNETH, BIOCHEMISTRY. **Personal Data:** b Richland Center, Wis, September 20, 1943; m 1967. **Education:** Univ Wis-Platteville, BS, 1965; Kans State Univ, PhD (biochem), 1970. **Professional Experience:** CHIEF SCI OFFICER, NIADYNE INC, as of 2005; PROF MED CHEM PHARMACOL & TOXICOL, UNIV ARIZ, as of 2003; assoc prof chem & basic health sci, NTEX State Univ, beginning 1980; asst prof, NTex State Univ, 1974-1980; from res asst to res assoc biochem, Mayo Clin & Found, 1973-1974; NIH fel biochem, Univ Utah, 1970-1972; FAC MEM, COL PHARM, UNIV KY. **Memberships:** AAAS; Am Soc Biol Chemists. **Research Statement & Publications:** Nicotinamide nucleotide metabolism, chemical carcinogenesis and DNA repair mechanisms. **Mailing Address:** Dept Pharmacol & Toxicol, Col Pharmacy, Ariz Cancer Ctr, Univ Ariz, 1515 N Campbell Ave Rm 3985B, Tucson, AZ 85724. **Fax:** 520-626-5990, 520-626-8567. **E-Mail:** jacobsm@pharmacy.arizona.edu

JACOBSON, NORMAN LEONARD, ANIMAL NUTRITION. **Personal Data:** b Eau Claire, Wis, September 11, 1918; m 1943, Gertrude; c Gary & Judy. **Education:** Univ Wis, BS, 1940; Iowa State Univ, MS, 1941, PhD (nutrit), 1947. **Honors & Awards:** award of honor, 1978; distinguished service award, am dairy assoc, 1989; Am Feed Mfgrs Award, 1955; Borden Award, 1960; Morrison Award, Am Soc Animal Sci, 1970. **Professional Experience:** L DISTINGUISHED PROF EMER, IOWA STATE UNIV, as of 2002; interim chair, Dept Food Sci & Human Nutrit, 1990-1992; dean grad col, Grad Col, 1988-1989; assoc provost res, Grad Col, 1988-1989; assoc vpres res, Grad Col, 1979-1988; assoc dean, Grad Col, 1973-1988; Moorman travel fel nutrit, 1966; distinguished prof agr, Iowa State Univ, beginning 1963; from asst prof to prof animal & dairy sci, Iowa State Univ, 1947-1953. **Memberships:** Fel AAAS; Am Dairy Sci Asn (vpres, 1971, pres, 1972); fel Am Inst Nutrit; fel Am Soc Animal Sci; Sigma Xi. **Research Statement & Publications:** Animal nutrition, particularly nutrition and physiology of the ruminant; relation of diet to coronary heart disease and artherosclerosis. **Mailing Address:** Dept Food Sci & Human Nutrit, Iowa State Univ, 313 Kildee Hall, Ames, IA 50011-3150.

JACOBSON, RALPH ALLEN, MOLECULAR BIOLOGY, BIOCHEMISTRY. **Personal Data:** b Jersey City, NJ, June 3, 1940; m 1963, Gail; c 3. **Education:** Montclair State Col, BA, 1962; Cornell Univ, PhD (biochem), 1966. **Professional Experience:** PROF EMER BIOCHEM, CALIF POLYTECH STATE UNIV, SAN LUIS OBISPO, 2005-; vis scientist, Molecular Biotechnol, Univ Wash, Seattle, 1994; prof biochem, Calif Polytech State Univ, San Luis Obispo, beginning 1983; vis scientist, W Alton Jones Cell Sci Ctr, NY, 1983-1984; from asst prof to assoc prof, Calif Polytech State Univ, 1975-1983; asst prof biochem, Univ Okla, 1968-1975; NIH res fel biol, Calif Inst Technol, 1966-1968. **Memberships:** AAAS; Sigma Xi; Am Chem Soc. **Research Statement & Publications:** Molecular biology and biotechnology recombinant DNA. **Mailing Address:** Dept Biochem, Coll Sci & Math, Calif Polytech State Univ, San Luis Obispo, CA 93407-0001. **Fax:** 805-756-5500. **E-Mail:** rjacobso@calpoly.edu

JACOBSON, RALPH H, AERONAUTICS. **Education:** US Naval Acad, BS, 1956; Airforce Inst Tech, MS, 1962. **Professional Experience:** RETIRED; pres & ceo, Draper Labs, ending 2005. **Mailing Address:** Charles S Draper Lab CSDL MS-1, 2200 Space Park Dr Suite 210, Houston, TX 77058. **Fax:** 281-333-5276.

JACOBSON, RAYMOND E, ELECTRONICS, COMPUTER SCIENCE. **Personal Data:** b St Paul, Minn, May 25, 1922; c Michael D, Karl R & Christopher E. **Education:** Yale Univ, BE, 1944; Harvard Univ, MBA, 1948; Oxford Univ, BA, 1950, MA, 1954. **Honors & Awards:** Prize for Excellence in mech Engineering, Yale Univ, 1943. **Professional Experience:** RETIRED; chmn cxr corp, 1988-1993; chmn, Anderson Jacobson, Ger, 1978-1983; chmn, UK, 1975-1985; chmn, Can, 1975-1985; chmn, France, 1974-1988; chmn & pres, Anderson Jacobson Inc, 1967-1988; dir, Micro-Radionics Inc, 1965-1967; mgmt consult, 1964-1967; pres, Maxson Electronics, 1963-1964; chmn, Whitehall Electronics Inc, 1961-1963; Staco Inc & Gen Electronic Controls, 1960-1963; vpres opers, Electro-Sci Investors Inc, 1960-1963; dir, Tamar Electronics Inc & Rawco Instruments Inc, 1960-1963; from div sales mgr to dir mkt, TRW Comput Co, 1957-1960; prod sales mgr, Curtiss Wright Corp, 1955-1957; asst to gen mgr, PRD Electronics Inc, 1950-1955. **Memberships:** Am Electronics Asn; Asn Am Rhodes Scholars; Sigma Xi Tau Beta Pi. **Research Statement & Publications:** Acoustic data couplers; specialized feature modems; high speed modems; dot matrix thermal printers; dot matrix needle printers; ink jet printers; cathode ray tube terminals. **Mailing Address:** 1247 Montcourse Lane, San Jose, CA 95131-2420.

JACOBSON, RICHARD MARTIN, SYNTHETIC ORGANIC CHEMISTRY. **Personal Data:** b New York, NY, December 23, 1947; m 1975. **Education:** Case Western Res Univ, BS, 1969; Columbia Univ, PhD (org chem), 1973. **Professional Experience:** RES FEL, ROHM & HAAS RES LAB, 1984-; sr res chemist, Rohm & Haas Res Lab, 1980-1984; asst prof chem, Ind Univ, Bloomington, 1975-1980. **Memberships:** Am Chem Soc. **Research Statement & Publications:** Design and synthesis of agricultural chemicals. **Mailing Address:** Rohm & Haas Chem LLC, 727 Norristown Rd PO Box 904, Spring House, PA 19477. **Fax:** 215-641-7857.

JACOBSON, ROBERT A, AERONAUTICS. **Professional Experience:** SCIENTIST, JET PROP LAB, NASA, as of 2002. **Memberships:** Am Inst Aeronaut & Astronaut. **Mailing Address:** Jet Propulsion Lab, 4800 Oak Grove Dr M/S 301-150, Pasadena, CA 91109-8001. **Fax:** 818-393-6388. **E-Mail:** Robert.A.Jacobson@jpl.nasa.gov

JACOBSON, ROBERT ANDREW, PHYSICAL CHEMISTRY, CRYSTALLOGRAPHY. **Personal Data:** b Waterbury, Conn, February 16, 1932; m 1962, Margaret; c Robert & Cheryl. **Education:** Univ Conn, BA, 1954; Univ Minn, PhD (phys chem), 1959. **Professional Experience:** PROF, IOWA STATE UNIV, 1999-; sr chemist, Ames Lab, 1969-1999; prof chem, Iowa State Univ, 1969-1999; assoc prof, Iowa State Univ, 1964-1969; chemist, Ames Lab, 1964-1969; from instr to asst prof chem, Princeton Univ, 1959-1964. **Memberships:** Am Crystallog Asn. **Research Statement & Publications:** Molecular structure of solids; x-ray and neutron diffraction. **Mailing Address:** Dept Chem, Iowa State Univ, Ames, IA 50011. **Fax:** 515-294-5233. **E-Mail:** raj@ameslab.gov

JACOBSON, ROBERT LEROY, CHEMICAL ENGINEERING. **Personal Data:** b Miles City, Mont, March 11, 1932; m 1953, Marie; c Robert Richard (deceased), Kim (Allen), Charles Leroy & Art Eric. **Education:** Mont State Univ, BS, 1954, PhD (chem eng), 1958. **Professional Experience:** REFORMING PROCESS CONSULT, 1989-; group leader process res explor, Chevron Res Co, Stand Oil Co, Calif, 1984-1989; group leader process develop, Chevron ResCo, 1977-1984; sr eng assoc, Chevron Res Co, 1972-1977; res engr petrol process develop, Chevron Res Co, 1958-1972. **Memberships:** Am Inst Chem Engrs; Am Chem Soc; Catalysis Soc. **Research Statement & Publications:** Petroleum process research and development; exploratory research. **Mailing Address:** Valley Springs, CA 95252.

JACOBSON, SHELDON H, AVIATION SECURITY, HEALTH CARE. **Personal Data:** b Montreal, Que. **Education:** McGill Univ, BS & MS; Cornell Univ, MS & PhD (opers res & indust eng). **Honors & Awards:** Appln Award, Opers Res Div, Inst Indust Engrs, 1998; Aviation Security Res Award, Aviation Security Int, 2002. **Professional Experience:** John Simon Guggenheim Mem Found fel, 2003-2004; PROF, DEPT MECH & INDUST ENG, UNIV ILL, URBANA-CHAMPAIGN, 2002-; assoc, Ctr Advan Study, Univ Ill, Urbana-

Champaign, 2002-2003; Willett fac scholar, Col Eng, Univ Ill, Urbana-Champaign, 2002-2005; assoc prof, Dept Mech & Indust Eng, Univ Ill, Urbana-Champaign, 1999-2002; assoc prof & dir Simulation & Optimization Lab, Dept Indust & Systs Eng, Va Tech Univ, 1993-1999; fac mem, Dept Opers Res, Weatherhead Sch Mgt, Case Western Res Univ, 1988-1993. **Memberships:** Inst Opers Res & Mgt Sci; Inst Indust Engrs; Am Soc Eng Educ; Soc Indust & Appl Math. **Research Statement & Publications:** Theory and applications of operations research. **Mailing Address:** Simulation & Optimization Lab, 1206 W Green St, MC-244, Urbana, IL 61801. **Fax:** 217-244-6534. **E-Mail:** shj@uiuc.edu

JACOBSON, STANLEY, NEUROANATOMY. **Personal Data:** b Chicago, Ill, August 24, 1937; m 1960, c 1. **Education:** Univ Ill, BS, 1959; Northwestern Univ, MS, 1961, PhD (anat), 1963. **Professional Experience:** PROF ANAT, SCH MED, TUFTS UNIV, 1980-; assoc prof, Sch Med, TuftsUniv, 1970-1980; asst prof, Sch Med, Tufts Univ, 1967-1970; biologist, Vet Admin Res Hosp, Chicago, 1965-1967; assoc, Med Sch, Northwestern Univ, 1965-1967; lectr, Sch Med, George Wash Univ, 1964-1965; Biologist, NIH, 1963-1965. **Memberships:** AAAS; Am Asn Anatomists. **Research Statement & Publications:** Structure of central nervous system in normal and diseased animals; connections between cerebral cortex and thalamus; degeneration of nerve fibers. **Mailing Address:** Dept Anat & Cellular Bio, Sackler Sch Grad Biomed Sci, Tufts Univ, 136 Harrison Ave Fifth Floor, Boston, MA 02111-1800. **E-Mail:** stan.jacobson@tufts.edu

JACOBSON, STEPHEN ERNEST, ORGANIC FLUORINE CHEMISTRY, CATALYSIS OF ORGANIC REACTIONS. **Personal Data:** b State Center, Iowa, April 6, 1945; m 1975, Lydia. **Education:** Iowa State Univ, BS, 1967; Ohio State Univ, MS, 1970, PhD (inorg chem), 1972. **Professional Experience:** SR RES ASSOC, E I DU PONT DE NEMOURS & CO, 1994-; res assoc, E I Du Pont DE Nemours & CO, 1987-1993; res assoc, Halcon Res, 1980-1986; res chemist inorg & catalysis, Allied-Signal Corp, 1975-1980; fel, Univ Ala, 1974-1975; fel, Univ Waterloo, 1972-1974. **Memberships:** Am Chem Soc; NAm Catalysis Soc; organic reactions Catalysis Soc. **Research Statement & Publications:** Process chemical research and development; new product research; organic synthesis; catalysis research; polymer synthesis; Fluorocarbon surface Chemistry. **Mailing Address:** DuPont Specialty Chem, Jackson Lab Chambers Works, Deepwater, NJ 08023. **Fax:** 609-540-4471. **E-Mail:** stephen.e.jacobson@usa.dupont.com

JACOBSON, STEPHEN RICHARD, GEOLOGY, PALEONTOLOGY. **Personal Data:** b New York, NY, September 25, 1944; m 1981, Rosemary; c 1. **Education:** Dickinson Col, BS, 1969; Harvard Univ, MA, 1972; Ohio State Univ, PhD (geol), 1978. **Professional Experience:** Group leader organic geochemistry, appln, Chevron USA Inc, 1986-; GROUP LEADER ORG CHEM, RESERVOIR ARCHIT, 1986-; biostratigraphic supvr & geo chem coord, Reservoir Archit, 1982-1986; GEOLOGIST, CHEVRON USA INC, 1978-; geologist, US Geol Surv, Coal Geol Lab, 1975-1976; lectr geol, Hunter Col, 1972-1973; instr geol, Lehman Col, 1971-1972; lectr geol, Calif State Univ Long Beach. **Memberships:** Paleont Soc; Am Asn Stratig Palynologists; Palaeont Asn; Am Asn Petrol Geologists. **Research Statement & Publications:** Stratigraphy; organic geochemistry; ordovician biostratigraphy, Cretaceous-Tertiary palynology, palynological techniques; petroleum source rock geochemistry; Ordovician and Permian acritarchs. **Mailing Address:** Chevron Oil Field Res Co, PO Box 446, La Habra, CA 90631.

JACOBSON, STUART LEE, CARDIAC PHYSIOLOGY, CARDIAC CELL CULTURE. **Personal Data:** b Chicago, Ill, April 29, 1934; m 1959, c 2. **Education:** Cornell Univ, BCE, 1957; Univ Minn, Minneapolis, MS, 1963, PhD (biophys), 1968. **Professional Experience:** RETIRED; from asst prof to assoc prof biol, Carleton Univ, 1968-1997; proj engr, Aeromed Lab, Wright Air Develop Ctr, USAF, 1957-1959. **Memberships:** Int Soc Heart Res; Biophys Soc; Soc Gen Physiologists. **Research Statement & Publications:** Engineering of systems for maintaining life in sealed environments; instrumentation for ecological studies; sensory physiology; electrophysiology, culture and electrophysiology of myocardial cells. **Mailing Address:** Dept Biol, Carleton Univ, Ottawa, ON K1S 5B6, Can.

JACOBSON-KRAM, DAVID, TOXICOLOGY. **Education:** Univ Conn, BA, 1971, PhD (develop biol), 1976. **Professional Experience:** AT BIORELIANCE CORP, as of 2004; vis assoc prof, Johns Hopkins Univ, Oncol Ctr, beginning 1990; vpres Toxicolgroup, Microbol Assocs Inc, beginning 1990; vpres, Genetic Toxicol Div, 1988-1990; actg brchief, Genetic & Molecular Toxicol Assessment Br, 1988; ed, Cell Biol & Toxicol, 1986-1988; assoc prof oncol, Dept Radiobiol, Johns Hopkins Univ, Oncol Ctr, 1984-1990; geneticist, Reproductive Effects Assessment Group, Off Health & Environ Assessment, Off Res & Develop, 1983-1988; from res asst prof to res assoc prof, Dept Radiol, George Wash Univ, SchMed, 1979-1984; biologist, Toxic Effects Br, Off Toxic Substances, US Environ Protection-Agency, 1979-1983; sr staff fel, Nat Inst Aging, NIH, 1979; staff fel, Nat Inst Aging, NIH, 1976-1979. **Memberships:** AAAS; Am Col Toxicol; Radiation Res Soc; Teratology Soc; Genetic Toxicol Asn; Environ Mutagen Soc; Soc Toxicol. **Research Statement & Publications:** Cell biology; toxicology. **Mailing Address:** Bioreliance Corp, 14920 Broschart Rd, Rockville, MD 20850. **Fax:** 301738-1036.

JACOBUS, DAVID PENMAN, MEDICINE, RADIOBIOLOGY. **Personal Data:** b Boston, Mass, February 26, 1927; m 1956, c 5. **Education:** Harvard Univ, BA, 1949; Univ Pa, MD, 1953. **Professional Experience:** RES MEM, AM COL RHEUMATOLOGY, as of 2004; OWNER, JACOBUS PHARMACEUT CO, INC, 1978-; chmn, Nat CancerInst Comt on Info Handling, 1978-; vpres basic res, Merck Sharp & Dohme Res Labs, vpres, 1974-1978; consult, St Luke's Hosp Ctr, New York, beginning 1971; trustee, Cold Spring Harbor Lab, beginning 1970; mem revision comt, US Pharmacopeia, beginning 1970; dir, Div Med Chem, 1965-1969; chief deptmed chem, Div Nuclear Med, Walter Reed Army Inst Res, 1963-1965; chief dept radiobiol, DivNuclear Med, Walter Reed Army Inst Res, 1959-1963; Resident & Researcher, Hosp Univ Pa, 1953-1957. **Memberships:** Am Chem Soc; Am Soc Info Sci; Asn Comput Mach; NY Acad Sci. **Research Statement & Publications:** Information handling. **Mailing Address:** Jacobus Pharmaceut Co, Inc, 37 Cleveland Lane, PO Box 5290, Princeton, NJ 08540. **Fax:** 609-799-1176.

JACOBUS, OTHA JOHN, ORGANIC CHEMISTRY. **Personal Data:** b Phoenix, Ariz, December 23, 1939; m 1962, c 2. **Education:** Southwestern at Memphis, BS, 1962; Univ Tenn, Knoxville, PhD (org chem), 1965. **Professional Experience:** VPRES, C H & A CORP, 1989-; chmn dept, Tulane Univ, 1980-1989; prof orgchem, Tulane Univ, 1978-1989; from asst prof to prof org chem, Clemson Univ, 1974-1976; instr, Princeton Univ, 1967-1969; NIH fel org chem, Princeton Univ, 1966-1967. **Memberships:** Am Chem Soc. **Research Statement & Publications:** Stereochemistry; NMR spectroscopy; reaction mechanisms. **Mailing Address:** Ch & A Corp, 2218 Northpark Dr, Humble, TX 77339. **Fax:** 281-358-2517.

JACOBUS, WILLIAM EDWARD, BIOCHEMISTRY. **Personal Data:** b Cleveland, Ohio, November 30, 1942; m 1966. **Education:** Ohio Wesleyan Univ, BA, 1964; Ohio State Univ, PhD (biochem), 1969. **Professional Experience:** PROF ANAT & NEUROBIOLOGY, MED COL OHIO, as of 2001; assoc prof med, biol & chem, Johns hopkins Sch Med, beginning 1982; asst prof med & physiol chem, Biol & Chem, Johns Hopkins Sch Med, 1977-1982; Nat Heart &Lung Inst res grant, 1974-1977; asst prof zoology, Univ Calif, Davis, 1973-1977; Heart Asn Md res fel & NIH res grant, Myocardial Infarction Res Unit, 1971-1973; fel biochem, Sch Med, Johns Hopkins Univ, 1970-1973. **Memberships:** AAAS; Am Chem Soc; Am Physiol Soc; Sigma Xi; Biophys Soc; Am Soc Biol Chem; Soc Magnetic Res Med; Int Soc Heart Res. **Research Statement & Publications:** Mitochondrial oxidative phosphorylation and ion transport; mitochondrial compartmentation and enzymology; metabolic regulation; cardiac bioenergetics; tissue nuclear magnetic resonance. **Mailing Address:** Med Univ Ohio, 3000 Arlington Ave, Toledo, OH 43614.

JACOBY, ALEXANDER ROBB, MATHEMATICS. **Personal Data:** b St Louis, Mo, October 8, 1922; m 1945. **Education:** Univ Chicago, SB, 1941, SM, 1942, PhD (math), 1946. **Professional Experience:** PROF MATH, UNIV NH, 1961-; Gen Elec Corp, 1957-1961; asst prof, Rutgers Univ, 1949-1957; asst prof, Univ Miami, 1947-1949; instr, Univ Chicago, 1945-1947; asst math, Univ Chicago, 1943-1945. **Research Statement & Publications:** Topology and algebra. **Mailing Address:** Dept Math, Univ NH, Durham, NH 03824.

JACOBY, HENRY I, GASTROINTESTINAL PHARMACOLOGY, RENAL PHARMACOLOGY. **Personal Data:** b Scranton, Pa, August 26, 1936; m 1967, c 2. **Education:** Philadelphia Col Pharm & Sci, BSc, 1958; Univ Mich, PhD (pharmacol), 1962. **Professional Experience:** DIR PHARM SERV, PROD SAFETY LABS, as of 2004; res fel gen pharm, Rw Johnson Pharmaceut Res Inst, beginning 1988; res fel gen pharmacol, McNeil Labs Pharmaceut, 1979-1987; prin scientist, McNeil Labs Pharmaceut, 1978-1979; group leader, McNeil Labs Pharmaceut, 1972-1977; res pharmacologist, Res Lab, Merck Sharpe & Dohme, 1963-1972. **Memberships:** Am Gastroent Asn; Am Soc Pharmacol & Exp Therapeut. **Research Statement & Publications:** Neurokinin and opioid receptors; gastrointestinal pharmacology especially drug effecting motility; intestinal secretion. **Mailing Address:** Prod Safety Labs, 2394 Hwy 130, Dayton, NJ 08810. **Fax:** 732-355-3275.

JACOBY, JAY, anesthesiology; deceased, see previous edition for last biography

JACOBY, JEAN, PHYSIOLOGY OF THE EYE MUSCLE. **Personal Data:** b New York, NY, March 8, 1951. **Education:** Univ Chicago, BS, 1972; Univ Ore, PhD (neurosci), 1979. **Professional Experience:** ASST PROF OPHTHAL, NY UNIV, 1988-; ASST PROF NEUROSCI, NY UNIV, 1988-; res scientist, Med Ctr, 1985-1988. **Memberships:** AAAS; Biophys Soc; Soc Neuroscience; Asn Res Vision & Ophthal. **Research Statement & Publications:** published over 25 articles. **Mailing Address:** Dept Physiol & Neurosci, NY Univ Med Ctr, 550 First Ave, New York, NY 10016-6402. **Fax:** 212-263-7602.

JACOBY, LAWRENCE JOHN, ORGANIC CHEMISTRY, ANALYTICAL CHEMISTRY. **Personal Data:** b Portland, Ore, May 19, 1943; m 1984, c 2. **Education:** Ore State Univ, BS, 1965; Colo State Univ, PhD (org chem), 1969. **Professional Experience:** QUAL ASSURANCE COORDR, COLUMBIA ANALYTIC SERV INC, KELSO, WASH, 1990-; client serv mgr, CH2M Hill, Redding, Calif, 1988-1990; lab mgr, CH2MHill, Corvallis, Ore, 1986-1988; anal chemist, Teledyne Wah Chang, Albany, 1976-1986; asst profchem, Chemeketa Community Col, 1971-1976; Asst prof org chem, Portland State Univ, 1969-1971. **Memberships:** Am Chem Soc; Asn Official Anal Chemists. **Research Statement & Publications:** Valence tautomerism induced by electron transfer. **Mailing Address:** 104 Hackett Rd, Longview, WA 98632-9611.

JACOBY, ROBERT OTTINGER, COMPARATIVE PATHOLOGY. **Personal Data:** b New York, NY, June 20, 1939. **Education:** Cornell Univ, DVM, 1963; Ohio State Univ, MSc, 1968, PhD (path), 1969. **Honors & Awards:** Res Award, Am Asn Lab Animal Sci, 1987; Griffin Award, Am Asn Lab Animal Sci, 1993. **Professional Experience:** Chmn Comparative Med, Yale Sch Med, as of 2005; DIR, ANIMAL RESOURCES CTR, as of 2002; PROF COMPARATIVE MED, YALE SCH MED, 1987-; chmn, Sect Comparative Med & Dir, Div Animal Care, Yale Sch Med, beginning 1978; from asst prof to assoc prof, Yale Sch Med, 1971-1987; NIH fel, Univ Chicago, 1969-1971; asst prof path, Ohio State Univ, 1969. **Memberships:** AAAS; Am Col Vet Pathologists; Am Vet Med Asn; Sigma Xi; Am Soc Investigative Pathologists; Am Soc Virol. **Research Statement & Publications:** Pathogenesis of infectious diseases; diseases of laboratory animals; animal models of human disease. **Mailing Address:** Dept Comparative Med, Sch Med, Yale Univ, PO Box 208016, New Haven, CT 06520-8016. **Fax:** 203-785-7499. **E-Mail:** robert.jacoby@yale.edu

JACOBY, RONALD LEE, MEDICINAL CHEMISTRY, COMPUTER-ASSISTED INSTRUCTION. **Personal Data:** b Muskegon, Mich, January 30, 1943; m 1966, c 3. **Education:** Ferris State Col, BSPharm, 1966; Univ Conn, PhD (med chem), 1971. **Professional Experience:** PROF MED CHEM, FERRIS STATE COL, 1980-; from asst prof to assocprof, Ferris State Univ, 1970-1980. **Research Statement & Publications:** Computer-assisted instruction. **Mailing Address:** Sch Pharm, Ferris State Univ, 901 S State St, Big Rapids, MI 49307-2251.

JACOBY, RUSSELL STEPHEN, METAMORPHIC PETROLOGY, URANIUM GEOLOGY. **Personal Data:** b Lehighton, Pa, June 23, 1939; m 1959, c 3. **Education:** Syracuse Univ, BS, 1961, MS, 1964; Queen's Univ, PhD (geol), 1968. **Professional Experience:** ASSOC PROF GEOL, ST LAWRENCE UNIV, 1973-; asst prof, St LawrenceUniv, 1971-1973; Asst prof geol, Cent Mo State Univ, 1968-1971. **Memberships:** Geol Soc Am; Geol Asn Can; Sigma Xi. **Research Statement & Publications:** Structural geology and metamorphic petrology of precambrian metamorphic shield areas; uranium exploration. **Mailing Address:** 67 State St, Canton, NY 13617.

JACOT, A DEAN, SMART STRUCTURES, POINTING CONTROL. **Personal Data:** b Tacoma, Wash, April 7, 1936; m Amie; c Christine, Bruce & Colleen. **Education:** Univ Wash, BSME, 1968, MSME, 1970. **Honors & Awards:** Eng Tech Achievement Award, Am Inst Aeronaut & Astronaut, 1997. **Professional Experience:** TECH FEL, BOEING CORP, 1992-. **Memberships:** Assoc fel Am Inst Aeronaut & Astronaut; Int Soc Optical Eng. **Research Statement & Publications:** Applying smart structures to spacecraft and aircraft; applying vibration isolation to spacecraft. **Mailing Address:** Boeing Defense & Space, PO Box 3999 MS 82-24, Seattle, WA 98124-2499. **E-Mail:** dean.jacot@boeing.com

JACOVIDES, LINOS J, ELECTRICAL ENGINEERING. **Personal Data:** b Paphos, Cyprus, May 10, 1940; American citizen; m Kathleen; c James, Michael, Christina & Julia. **Education:** Glasgow Univ, BSc, 1961, MSc, 1963; Univ London, PhD, 1965. **Professional Experience:** HEAD, ELEC & ELECTRONIC, GEN MOTORS, RES &DEVELOP CTR, 1988-; prin res engr, Elec Eng Dept, 1987-1988; dept res engr & asst dept head, Elec Eng Dept, 1985-1987; sr res engr, Res Labs, Warren, Mich, 1967-1975; sr res engr, Defense Res Labs, Gen Motors Corp, 1965-1967. **Memberships:** Fel Inst Elec & Electronics Engrs; Brit Inst Elec Engrs; Soc Automotive Engrs. **Research Statement & Publications:** Electromagnetics and electromagnetic energy conversion; high performance electric drive systems; automotive electrical systems; electric vehicles and locomotive electric drives; electromechanical devices; automotive powertrain and chassis control systems. **Mailing Address:** Dept Elec & Electronic, Res & Develop Ctr, Gen Motors, 30500 Mound Rd PO Box 9055, Warren, MI 48090-9055. **Fax:** 810-986-0886.

JACOX, ADA K, MEDICINE. **Education:** Columbia Univ, BS; Wayne State Univ, MS; Case Western Reserve Univ, PhD. **Honors & Awards:** Shirley Titus Award, Am Nurses Asn, 1988. **Professional Experience:** PROF EMER, COL NURSING, WAYNE STATE UNIV, as of 2003; CHMN, SICKLE CELL PAIN GUIDELINE PANEL, as of 1999; ASSOC DEAN RES, COL NURSING, WAYNE STATE UNIV, beginning 1996; prof independence found chmn & health policy, Sch Nursing, Johns Hopkins Univ, 1990-1995; profnursing, Sch Nursing, Univ Md, 1980-1990; dir, Ctr Nursing & Health Serv Res, 1980-1990; assoc dean res & doctoral prog & prof nursing, Sch Nursing, Univ Colo, 1976-1979; vet admin hosp, Iowa City, 1974-1976; clin cr, NIH, 1975-1979; actg dean advan studies, Grad Col, UnivIowa, 1975-1976; prin investr, HEW, 1972-1979; Iowa Vet Home, Marshalltown, 1972-1976; Carver fel, Univ Iowa, 1972; res consult, Ment Health Inst, Mt Pleasant, Iowa, 1970-1971; fromassoc prof to prof, Col Nursing, Univ Iowa, 1969-1976; psychiat nurse, Johnson County MentalHealth Ctr, Kans City, 1968-1969; asst prof, Dept Nursing Educ, Univ Kans, 1968-1969; dirnursing, Plymouth State Home & Training Sch, Northville, Mich, 1962-1964; assoc dir nursing &dir nursing educ, Plymouth State Home & Training Sch, Northville, Mich, 1961-1962; staff nurseacute & chronic pediat, Children's Hosp Mich, Detroit, 1959-1960; pvt duty nurse pediat &neurol, Columbia-Presby Hosp, NY, 1958-1959; staff nurse, Kalamazoo State Hosp, Mich, 1956-1957. **Memberships:** Inst Med-Nat Acad Sci; fel Am Acad Nurses; Am Nurses Asn; Am Nurses Found(pres, 1982-1985). **Research Statement & Publications:** Author of 6 books and over 20 journal articles. **Mailing Address:** Col Nursing, Wayne State Univ, 5557 Cass Ave, Detroit, MI 48202.

JACOX, MARILYN ESTHER, MOLECULAR SPECTROSCOPY, PHOTOCHEMISTRY. **Personal Data:** b Utica, NY, April 26, 1929. **Education:** Syracuse Univ, BA, 1951; Cornell Univ, PhD, 1956. **Honorary Degrees:** ScD, Syracuse Univ, 1993. **Honors & Awards:** Outstanding Alumnus Award, Utica Col, 1963; Award Phys Sci, Washington Acad Sci, 1968; Gold Medal Award for Distinguished Serv, US Dept Com, 1970; Federal Woman's Award, Fed Woman's Award Bd of Trustees, 1973; Samuel Wesley Stratton Award, Nat Bur Stand, 1973; Ellis R Lippincott Award, Coblentz Soc, 1989; Hilebrand Prize, Chem Soc Wash, 1990; WISE Lifetime Achievement Award, Interagency Comt Women Sci & Eng, 1991; E Bright Wilson Award in Spectroscopy, Am Chem Soc, 2003; George C Pimentel Award for Advances in Matrix Isolation Spectroscopy, Organizing Comt for 15th International Symposium on Matrix Isolation Spectroscopy, 2005. **Professional Experience:** EMER SCIENTIST, NAT INST STANDARDS & TECHNOL, 1996-; chief, Environ Chem Processes Sect, 1974-1978; Chief, Photochem Sect, Nat Bur Stand, 1973-1974; phys chemist, Nat Inst Standards & Technol, 1962-1995; fel spectros of solids, Mellon Inst Sci Res, 1958-1962; Res assoc phys chem, Univ NC, 1956-1958. **Memberships:** Fel Am Phys Soc; Am Chem Soc; Int-Am Photochem Soc; fel AAAS; Sigma Xi. **Research Statement & Publications:** Chemistry of free radicals and molecular ions; molecular spectroscopy. **Mailing Address:** Nat Inst Stand & Technol, Gaithersburg, MD 20899-8441. **Fax:** 301-869-5700. **E-Mail:** marilyn.jacox@nist.gov

JACQUET, HERVE, NUMBER THEORY. **Personal Data:** b France, August 4, 1939; wid, c 1. **Education:** Univ Paris, Licence, 1961, PhD (math), 1967. **Honors & Awards:** Prix Petit d'Ormoy, Acad Sci, Paris, 1979. **Professional Experience:** PROF MATH, COLUMBIA UNIV, 1974-; prof math, Grad Sch City UnivNew York, 1970-1974; assoc prof math, Univ Md, 1969-1970; mem, Inst Advan Studies, 1967-1969; researcher, Nat Ctr Sci Res, France, 1963-1965. **Memberships:** Am Math Soc. **Research Statement & Publications:** Automorphic L-functions. **Mailing Address:** Dept Math, Columbia Univ, 509 Math Bldg, 2990 Broadway, New York, NY 10027. **Fax:** 212-8548962. **E-Mail:** hj@math.columbia.edu

JACQUET, YASUKO F, BEHAVIORAL NEUROPHARMACOLOGY, OPIATE NEUROPHARMACOLOGY. **Personal Data:** b San Francisco, Calif, c 1. **Education:** Tsuda Col, Tokyo, Japan, dipl, 1951; State Univ Iowa, Iowa City, BA, 1953; IndUniv, Bloomington, PhD (exp psychol), 1962. **Professional Experience:** RETIRED; Mass Gen Hosp, Boston, 1982 & Columbia Univ Med Ctr, NewYork, 1983-1985; Uppsala Univ, Sweden, 1979; vis scientist, Nat Inst Med Res, London, UK, 1977; res scientist, NY State Dept Ment Hyg, NY, 1966-1993; staff fel, NIMH, Bethesda, Md, 1964-1965; Postdoctoral fel, Sch Med, Yale Univ, 1962-1964. **Memberships:** Am Soc Pharmacol & Exp Therapeut; Soc Neurosci; Europ Behav Pharmacol Soc; Am Pain Soc; Int Narcotics Res Conf; Asn Res Nervous & Ment Dis. **Research Statement & Publications:** Central nervous system sites involved in opiate effects; physiological actions of endogenous opiate peptides; neurotransmitters mediating opiate effects. **Mailing Address:** 200 California Rd No 22, Bronxville, NY 10708-4427.

JACQUIN, ARNAUD ERIC, IMAGE & VIDEO CODING, FRACTAL CODING. **Personal Data:** b Reims, France, February 18, 1964. **Education:** Higher sch Electricity, ESE, 1986; Ga Inst Tech, MS, 1987, PhD (math), 1989. **Honors & Awards:** Sr Award, Signal Processing Soc, Inst Elec & Electronics Engrs, 1993. **Professional Experience:** STAFF, BELL LABS, LUCENT TECHNOLOGIES, as of 2005; staff, Multimedia Commun Res Lab, as of 1999; mem staff signal processing res, Signal Processing dept, At&T Bell Labs, Murray Hill, Nj, beginning 1990. **Memberships:** Inst Elec & Electronics Engrs. **Research Statement & Publications:** Image processing; image and video coding. **Mailing Address:** Bell Labs, Lucent Technologies, 600 Mountain Ave, Murray Hill, NJ 07974. **Fax:** 908-582-5022. **E-Mail:** arnaud@lucent.com

JACQUOT, RAYMOND G, MECHANICAL ENGINEERING, ELECTRICAL ENGINEERING. **Personal Data:** b Casper, Wyo, November 16, 1938; div, c 1. **Education:** Univ Wyo, BS, 1960, MS, 1962; Purdue Univ, PhD (mech eng), 1969. **Professional Experience:** PROF EMER ELEC ENG & COMPUT ENG, UNIV WYO, as of 2002; vis prof elec & comput eng, Univ Calif, Davis, 1984; prof elec eng, Univ Wyo, beginning 1977; from asst prof to assoc prof, Univ Wyo, 1969-1977; instr, Purdue Univ, 1964-1965; instr, Univ Wyo, 1962-1964; supply instr mech eng, Univ Wyo, 1960-1962. **Memberships:** Am Soc Mech Engrs; Am Soc Eng Educ; Inst Elec & Electronics Engrs. **Research Statement & Publications:** Vibration of elastic systems; simulation of large scale systems by digital computer; digital control and signal processing; nonlinear system analysis; digital filtering. **Mailing Address:** Dept Elec & Comput Eng, Univ Wyo, 1000 E Univ Ave Rm 5055 Engr Bldg, Laramie, WY 82071. **Fax:** 307-766-2248. **E-Mail:** quot@uwyo.edu

JADHAV, A L, PHARMACOLOGY. **Professional Experience:** PROF ASST DEAN RES & GRAD EDUC, TEX SOUTHERN UNIV, 1991-. **Memberships:** Fedn Am Socs Exp Biol. **Research Statement & Publications:** Pharmacology. **Mailing Address:** Col Pharm & Health Sci, Tex Southern Univ, 3100 Cleburne, Houston, TX 77004-4598. **Fax:** 713-639-1889. **E-Mail:** pharaljadhav@tsu.edu

JADUS, MARTIN ROBERT, CYTOKINES, HEMATOLOGY. **Personal Data:** b Girardville, Pa, January 10, 1953; m Yolanda. **Education:** Univ Del, BA (biol), 1975, BA (chem), 1976; Fla Inst Technol, MS, 1978; Univ Fla, PhD (med sci), 1983. **Professional Experience:** Adj prof chem & biochem, Calif State Univ, Long Beach, 1996-; asst res, UnivCalif, Irvine, 1990-; HEALTH RES SPECIALIST, VET AFFAIRS MED CTR, 1990-; sr scientist, Marrow Tech Inc, 1988-1990; res scientist, Bio Therapeut Inc, 1986-1988; vis asst prof, UnivSFla, 1985-1986; res scholar, Univ Southern Calif, 1983-1985; lectr chem, Fla Inst Tech, 1977-1978. **Memberships:** AAAS; Am Asn Immunol; Soc Biol Ther; Am Asn Hematologists; Soc LeukocyteBiol; Int Soc Hemat. **Research Statement & Publications:** Immune regulation by cytokines and possible roles in the disease process; molecular biology of macrophage colony stimulating factor stimulating natural suppressor cells; Rosai-Dorfman disease and psoriasis. **Mailing Address:** Vet Affairs Med Ctr, 5901 E 7th St, Long Beach, CA 90822. **E-Mail:** martin.jadus@med.va.gov

JADUSZLIWER, BERNARDO, ELECTRON SCATTERING, ATOMIC FREQUENCY STANDARDS. **Personal Data:** b Buenos Aires, Arg, October 17, 1943; m 1968, c 1. **Education:** Univ Buenos Aires, Lic en physics, 1968; Univ Toronto, MSc, 1970, PhD (physics), 1973. **Professional Experience:** PRIN DIR, ELECTRONICS & PHYSICS LAB, 1999-; dir, Lasers & Optical Physics Dept, 1996-1999; mgr, Atomic Clocks Sect, 1993-1996; res scientist, Lasers & Optical Physics Dept, Aerospace Corp, 1987-1993; adj assoc prof, Univ Southern Calif, 1985-; mem tech staff, Lasers & Optical Physics Dept, Aerospace Corp, 1985-1987; Tech adv, Physics Today Buyers Guide, 1983-1993; from asst res prof to assoc res prof physics, NY Univ, 1981-1985; assoc res scientist, NY Univ, 1974-1978; Fel physics, Univ Toronto, 1973-1974. **Memberships:** Am Phys Soc; Inst Elec & Electronics Engrs. **Research Statement & Publications:** Low energy electron positron scattering on ground and excited state atoms and molecules; measurement of atomic and molecular polarizabilities; atom photon interaction; atomic frequency standards; fiber optic sensor systems. **Mailing Address:** Aerospace Corp M2- 238, PO Box 92957, Los Angeles, CA 90009. **E-Mail:** jaduszliwer@aero.org

JADVAR, HOSSEIN, BIOMEDICAL ENGINEERING, ONCOLOGY. **Personal Data:** b Tehran, Iran, April 6, 1961. **Education:** Iowa State Univ, BS, 1982; Univ Wis, MS, 1984; Univ Mich, Ann Arbor, MS, 1986, PhD, 1988; Univ Chicago, MD, 1993. **Professional Experience:** Interim dir, Nuclear Med Residency Prog, Univ Southern Calif, 2003-2004; ASST PROF BIOMED ENG, UNIV SOUTHERN CALIF, 2001-; FAC MEM, PROG BIOMED & BIOL SCI, UNIV SOUTHERN CALIF, 2001-; VIS ASSOC BIOENGINEERING, CALIF INST TECHNOL, 2001-; ASST PROF RADIOL, KECK SCH MED, UNIV SOUTHERN CALIF, 1999-; resident, Univ Calif, San Francisco, 1993-1994; sr res assoc, Pritzker Inst, Ill Inst Technol, 1989-1992; Sr res engr, Arzco Med Electronics Inc, 1988-1989. **Memberships:** AMA; Inst Elec & Electronics Engrs; Asn Advan Med Instrumentation; Biomed Eng Soc; Sigma Xi. **Research Statement & Publications:** Esophageal catheters; method and apparatus for detection of posterior ischemia; granted several patents. **Mailing Address:** Dept Radiol, Keck Sch Med, Univ Southern Calif, GNH 5250, 1200 N State St, Los Angeles, CA 90033. **Fax:** 323-226-5984. **E-Mail:** jadvar@usc.edu

JAECKER, JOHN ALVIN, CATALYSIS. **Personal Data:** b Troy, NY, February 21, 1945; m 1968, c 2. **Education:** Hope Col, BA, 1968; Purdue Univ, MA & PhD (inorg chem), 1973. **Professional Experience:** RES ADV, ATLANTIC RICHFIELD CO, 1984-; sr chemist, Atlantic Richfield Co, 1973-1984; purchasing agent. **Memberships:** Am Chem Soc; Catalysis Soc; Am Soc Testing & Math. **Research Statement & Publications:** Analytical chemistry of petroleum catalysts and products; studies of catalysts. **Mailing Address:** 1248 N Valle Vista Dr, Fullerton, CA 92631-1942.

JAECKS, DUANE H, ATOMIC PHYSICS, TIME RESOLVED SPECTROSCOPY. **Personal Data:** b Wausau, Wis, September 24, 1935; m 1959, c 3. **Education:** Univ Wis, BS, 1958; Miami Univ, MA, 1960; Univ Wash, Seattle, PhD (physics), 1964. **Professional Experience:** PROF EMER PHYSICS, UNIV NEBR, LINCOLN, as of 2003; assoc prof, Univ Nebr, Lincoln, ending 1974; prof Physics, Univ Nebr-Lincoln, beginning 1974; asst prof, Univ Nebr, Lincoln, beginning 1966. **Memberships:** Fel Am Phys Soc. **Research Statement & Publications:** Basic atomic collisions research. **Mailing Address:** Dept Physics, Univ Nebr, 116 Brace Lab, Lincoln, NE 68588-0111. **Fax:** 402-472-2879. **E-Mail:** djaecks@unl.edu

JAEGER, CHARLES WAYNE, DYES & INKS FOR COLOR PRINTERS. **Personal Data:** b Kissimmee, Fla, September 8, 1943; m 1965, Carol; c Jennifer & Sara. **Education:** Fla State Univ, BS, 1966; Purdue Univ, PhD (org chem), 1971. **Professional Experience:** GEN CHAIPERSON, TEKTRONIX INC as of 2004; mem bd dirs, Soc Imaging Sci & Technol, 1994-; gen chmn, Soc Photog Scientists & Engrs Fifth Int Cong Adv Non-Impact Printing Technol; bus develop & spec projmgr, Color Printing & Imaging Div, Tektronix Inc, 1985-1986; mgr, Ink Jet Technol Group, Tektronix Inc, 1984-1985; PRIN SCIENTIST, COLOR PRINTING & IMAGING DIV, TEKTRONIX INC, 1983-; sr res scientist IV, Tektronix Inc, 1981-1983; chemist III, Tektronix Inc, 1980-1981; res chemist, Dyes & Chem Div, Crompton & Knowles Corp, 1973-1980; res fel org chem, Ga Inst Technol, 1971-1973. **Memberships:** Am Chem Soc; Am Asn Textile Chem & Colorists; Soc Info Display; fel Soc Imaging Sci & Technol. **Research Statement & Publications:** Research, development and manufacture of specialty phase change and aqueous inks for color ink-jet printers; evaluation of dyes for special color applications; computer simulation and evaluation of experimental dyes. **Mailing Address:** Tektronix Inc, Xerox Corp, 26600 SW Pkwy, Wilsonville, OR 97070. **Fax:** 503-682-1183. **E-Mail:** wayne.jaeger@tek.com

JAEGER, DAVID ALLEN, ORGANIC CHEMISTRY. **Personal Data:** b San Diego, Calif, June 3, 1944; m 1968, c 1. **Education:** Stanford Univ, BS, 1965; Univ Calif, Los Angeles, PhD (org chem), 1970. **Professional Experience:** PROF CHEM, UNIV WYO, 1982-; from asst prof to assoc prof, Univ Wyo, 1971-1982; NSF fel chem, Stanford Univ, 1970-1971. **Memberships:** Am Chem Soc. **Research Statement & Publications:** Chemistry; micellar catalysis; surfactant chemistry. **Mailing Address:** Dept Chem, Univ Wyo, Physical Sci Bldg, Rm 423, Laramie, WY 82071-3838. **E-Mail:** daj@uwyo.edu

JAEGER, HEINRICH MARTIN, PHYSICS. **Personal Data:** b Flensburg, Ger, May 15, 1957. **Education:** Univ Minn, MS, 1982, PhD (physics), 1987. **Professional Experience:** DIR, MAT RES CTR, UNIV CHICAGO, 2001-; PROF PHYSICS, UNIV CHICAGO, 2000-; cottrell scholar, ResCorp, 1994; alfred P Sloan fel, 1992; from asst to assoc prof, Univ Chicago, 1991-2000; david & LucilePackard fel, 1991; sr researcher, Ctr Submicrotech, Neth, 1989-1991. **Memberships:** Am Phys Soc; Mat Res Soc. **Research Statement & Publications:** Experimental condensed matter physics; superconductivity; mesoscopic structures; granular materials. **Mailing Address:** James Frank Inst, Univ Chicago, 5640 S Ellis Ave, Chicago, IL 60637. **Fax:** 773834-0471. **E-Mail:** h-jaeger@uchicago.edu

JAEGER, HERBERT KARL, ORGANIC CHEMISTRY. **Personal Data:** b Harpolingen-Saeckingen, Ger, June 29, 1931; m 1959, c 1. **Education:** Univ Basel, PhD (org chem), 1958. **Professional Experience:** RETIRED; dir, fine chem prod, 1985-1990; group mgr, Upjohn Co, 1978-1985; res mgr org chem, Upjohn Co, 1970-1978; sect head, Upjohn Co, 1965-1970; resassoc, Upjohn Co, 1961-1965; res fel, Univ Calif, Los Angeles, 1960-1961; res fel chem, Univ Basel, 1958-1959. **Memberships:** Am Chem Soc. **Research Statement & Publications:** Isolation and chemistry of cardiac glycosides; microbial production and chemistry of carotenoids; process research and development of steroidal and other chemical products. **Mailing Address:** 4901 Gulf Shore Blvd N, Naples, FL 34103.

JAEGER, JAMES J, CARDIOVASCULAR PHYSIOLOGY, PULMONARY PHYSIOLOGY. **Education:** Rutgers Univ, PhD (physiol), 1973; Johns Hopkins Univ, BA. **Professional Experience:** DIR, ENVIRON HEALTH & SAFETY, UNIV MD, BALTIMORE, as of 2005; chief physiol br, Us Army Med Res Inst Chem Defense, beginning 1985; proj mgr, Walter Reed Army Inst Res, 1973-1985. **Mailing Address:** Univ Md, 714 W Lombard St, Baltimore, MD 21201-1010. **Fax:** 410-706-8212. **E-Mail:** jjaeger@ehs.umaryland.edu

JAEGER, KLAUS BRUNO, TECHNICAL MANAGEMENT. **Personal Data:** b Lubeck, Ger, May 8, 1938; American citizen; m 1969, c 1. **Education:** Syracuse Univ, BS, 1965, MS, 1968, PhD (physics), 1970. **Professional Experience:** PHYSICIST & METROLOGIST, JAEGER ENTERPRISES, as of 2003; mgr, Lockheed CO, 1985; PHYSICIST, LOCKHEED CO, 1982-; metrologist, Bubble Chamber, Argonne Nat Lab, 1982-1985; physicist, Brookhaven Nat Lab, 1980-1981; dep group leader measuring & testing superconducting magnets, Bubble Chamber, Argonne Nat Lab, 1980-1981; proj mgr 12ft solenoid magnet, Bubble Chamber, Argonne Nat Lab, 1977-1980; physicist, Argonne Nat Lab, 1975-1980; assoc group leader, Bubble Chamber, Argonne Nat Lab, 1971-1977; asst physicist, Argonne Nat Lab, 1971-1975; fel exp high energy physics, ArgonneNat Lab, 1970-1971. **Memberships:** Am Phys Soc; Am Inst Physics. **Research Statement & Publications:** Design and implementation of new particle detection techniques such as solenoidal magnets with shower counters; inclusive hadron physics at high and medium energies; colliding electron positron beams; design and implementation of measuring techniques for superconducting dipole and quadrapole magnets; primary standards development. **Mailing Address:** Jaeger Enterprises, 13685 Calle Tacuba, PO Box 2557, Saratoga, CA 95070-4918. **Fax:** 408-867-3705. **E-Mail:** jaegerenterprises@comcast.net

JAEGER, LESLIE GORDON, CIVIL ENGINEERING. **Personal Data:** b Southport, Eng, January 28, 1926; m 1981, Kathleen Grant; c Valerie Ann & Hilary Frances. **Education:** Cambridge Univ, BA, 1946, MA, 1950; London Univ, PhD, 1955, DSc, 1986. **Honors & Awards:** A B Sanderson Award, Can Soc Civil Eng, 1983; Gzowski Medal, Eng InstCan, 1985. **Professional Experience:** RES PROF EMER, CIVIL ENG & ENG MATH, DALHOUSIE UNIV, as of 2003; vpres, Tech Univ, NS, beginning 1986; spec asst to pres, Tech Univ, Ns, 1980-1985; acad vpres, Acadia Univ, 1975-1980; actg vpres, Col Eng, Univ NB, 1972-1973; dean, Col Eng, Univ NB, 1970-1975; Regius prof eng, Univ Edinburgh, 1964-1966; Nat ResCoun Can res grantee, 1962-; prof civil eng & appl mech, McGill Univ, 1962-1964 & 1966-1970; univ lectr, Cambridge Univ, 1956-1962; mem fac, Univ Col Khartoum, 1952-1956. **Memberships:** Fel Eng Soc Can; fel Can Soc Civil Eng. **Research Statement & Publications:** Author of numerous publications and research papers. **Mailing Address:** Dept Civil Eng & Eng Math, Dalhousie Univ, Sexton Campus, 1360 Barrington St, Rm 215 Bldg D, Halifax, NS B3J 1Z1, Can. **E-Mail:** leslie.jaeger@ns.sympatico.ca

JAEGER, MARC JULES, RESPIRATORY PHYSIOLOGY, SEPARATION OF GASES. **Personal Data:** b Berne, Switz, April 4, 1929; American citizen; m 1973, Ina; c David Forbes, Tammie & Olivia. **Education:** Univ Berne, Baccalaureat, 1948, MD, 1954. **Professional Experience:** PROF EMER, DEPT PHYSIOL & FUNCTIONAL GENOMICS, UNIV FLA, as of 1998; Dept Med, McGill Univ, Montreal, 1980-1981; prof physiol & dent, Col Med, Univ Fla, beginning 1970; vis prof, Yale Univ, 1968; asst prof physiol, Univ Fribourg, 1965-1970; res asst med, Univ Berne, 1963-1965; res assoc physiol, Col Med, Univ Fla, 1961-1963; res assoc med, Univ Berne, 1957-1961; fogarty fel. **Memberships:** Swiss Med Asn; Swiss Asn Physiol & Pharmacol; Swiss Soc Advan Sci; Int Union Physiol Sci; Sigma Xi. **Research Statement & Publications:** Mechanics of breathing; fluid dynamics; mechanical and analog computer modelling; environmental physiology, especially diving, smoking and air pollution; diffusion of gases; separation of gases and isotopes; granted 5 US patents. **Mailing Address:** Dept Physiol & Functional Genomics Univ Fla, M-544, Gainesville, FL 32610. **Fax:** 352-846-0270. **E-Mail:** mjaeger@phys.med.ufl.edu

JAEGER, RALPH R, INORGANIC CHEMISTRY. **Personal Data:** b Cincinnati, Ohio, January 30, 1940. **Education:** Univ Cincinnati, BS, 1962; Purdue Univ, PhD (inorg chem), 1967. **Professional Experience:** SR RES CHEMIST, MOUND LAB, MONSANTO RES CORP, 1967-. **Memberships:** Am Chem Soc; Am Inst Chemists. **Research Statement & Publications:** Chemical vapor deposition of refractory metals; high temperature chemistry of plutonium; fuel forms containing plutonium. **Mailing Address:** 5092 Benner Rd, Miamisburg, OH 45342-4202.

JAEGER, RICHARD CHARLES, MICROELECTRONICS, INTEGRATED CIRCUIT DESIGN. **Personal Data:** b New York, NY, September 2, 1944; m 1964, Joan; c Peter & Stephanie. **Education:** Univ Fla, BS, 1966, ME, 1966, PhD (elec eng), 1969. **Honors & Awards:** Outstanding Contrib Award, Computer Soc, Inst Elec & Electronics Engrs, Golden Core, IEEE Millenium Med. **Professional Experience:** COORDR, WIRELESS ENG, AUBURN UNIV, as of 2005; Ed, Solid-State Circuits, Inst Elec & Electronics Engrs, 1995-; chair, Int Solid-State Circuits conf, 1993; DISTINGUISHED UNIV PROF, AUBURN UNIV, 1990-; pres, Solid State Circuits Coun, 1990-1991; vpres, Solid State Circuits Coun, 1987-1989; secy, Solid State Circuits Coun, 1985-1987; mem, gov bd, comput soc, Inst Elec & Electronics Engrs, 1985-1986; dir, Ala Microelectronics Sci & Technol Ctr, 1984-; alumni prof, Auburn Univ, 1983-1988; assoc prof, Auburn Univ, 1979-1982; prog comt mem, Int Solid-State Circuits conf, 1978-1992; adv eng, IBM Corp, 1976-1979; res staff mem, IBM Corp, 1974-1976; adv eng, IBM Corp, 1972-1974; Staff eng, IBM Corp, 1969-1972. **Memberships:** Fel Inst Elec & Electronics Engrs. **Research Statement & Publications:** Microelectronic circuit, device and process design; electronic packaging and cooling; low temperature semiconductor electronics; Calibration considerations for piezoresistive-based stress sensors; Structural analysis of electronic packages using test chips with integral piezoresistive stress sensors; author of various articles. **Mailing Address:** Elect Eng Dept, Auburn Univ, 414 Broun Hall, Auburn, AL 36849. **Fax:** 334-844-1888. **E-Mail:** jaeger@eng.auburn.edu

JAEGER, ROBERT GORDON, BEHAVIORAL ECOLOGY. **Personal Data:** b Baltimore, Md, December 16, 1937. **Education:** Univ Md, BS, 1960, PhD (ecol), 1969; Univ Calif, Berkeley, MA, 1963. **Honors & Awards:** Stoye Award, Am Soc Ichthyol & Herpet, 1969. **Professional Experience:** PROF BIOL, UNIV LA, 1986-; Ed, J Herpetologica, 1982-2002; from asst prof to assoc prof, Univ LA, 1981-1986; adj asst prof, State Univ NY, Albany, 1980-1981; asst prof zool, State Univ NY, Albany, 1974-1980; res assoc zool, Univ Wis, Madison, 1971-1974; instr zool, Univ Md, 1970-1971; fac res asst ecol, Univ Md, 1969-1970. **Memberships:** Ecol Soc Am; Animal Behav Soc; Soc Study Evolution; Am Inst Biol Sci; Am Soc Ichthyol & Herpet; Sigma Xi. **Research Statement & Publications:** Competitive exclusion and environmental pressures in the distributions of salamander species; comparative phototactic responses of anuran species in relation to their natural habitats. **Mailing Address:** Dept Biol, Univ La, Lafayette, LA 70504-2451. **Fax:** 337-482-5834. **E-Mail:** biology@louisiana.edu

JAEGER, RUDOLPH JOHN, BIOCHEMISTRY. **Personal Data:** b Weehawken, NJ, January 17, 1944; m 1987, c 3. **Education:** Renesselaer Polytech Inst, BS, 1966; Johns Hopkins Univ, PhD (biochem toxicol), 1971. **Honors & Awards:** Leslie Silverman Award, Am Indust Hyg Asn, 1980. **Professional Experience:** Mem, Toxicol Info Prog Comt, NAS, 1990-; Womble, Sidley & Austin, 1989-; Womble, Polymerics Inc, 1989-; Womble, Carlyle, Sandridge & Rice, 1988-1990; hazardcommun training progs, Bell Commun Res, 1988-1989; Goodwin, Proctor & Hoar, 1987-; Womble, Lockheed Aeronaut Systs, 1987-1989; Toxicol consult, Esselte Letraset Mfg, 1985-; RES PROF ENVIRON MED, SCH MED, NY UNIV, 1985-; Toxicol consult, Southern Calif Edison, 1984-1987; tech support & prod eval, AT&T Bell Labs, 1983-1985; assoc prof, SchMed, NY Univ, 1979-1983; assoc prof, Harvard Sch Pub Health, 1978-1979; Toxicol consult, Polaroid Corp, 1977-; asst prof, Harvard Sch Pub Health, 1973-1978; res assoc toxicol, Harvard Sch Pub Health, 1971-1973. **Memberships:** Soc Toxicol; AAAS; NY Acad Sci; Am Indust Hygiene Asn; Sigma Xi; Am SocTesting Mat; Am Chem Soc; Am Col Toxicol; Am Asn Path; Am Acad Clin Toxicol. **Research Statement & Publications:** Inhalation toxicology of plastics monomers, pulmonary toxicology of combustion products. **Mailing Address:** Environ Med, NY Univ Med Ctr, 263 Ctr Ave, Westwood, NJ 07675-1701. **Fax:** 201-666-8119. **E-Mail:** jaegerr@env.med.nyu.edu

JAEGER, WOLFGANG, SPECTROSCOPY & CHEMISTRY, VAN DER WAALS COMPLEXES. **Personal Data:** b Husum, Ger, December 23, 1957. **Education:** Christian Albrecuts Univ, dipl, 1985, PhD (chem), 1989. **Honors & Awards:** Steacie fel, NSERC, 2002. **Professional Experience:** ASSOC PROF, DEPT CHEM, UNIV ALTA, as of 2004; asst prof, Dept Chem, Univ Alta, 1995-2001; postdoctoral fel & res assoc, Univ BC, 1989-1995. **Memberships:** Am Chem Soc. **Research Statement & Publications:** Molecular beam techniques and pulsed excitation; emission spectroscopic methods for study of weak intermolecular interactions; many-body non-additive interactions. **Mailing Address:** Dept Chem, Univ Alta, Edmonton, AB T6G 2G2, Can.

JAEHNING, JUDITH A, BIOCHEMISTRY. **Personal Data:** b Yakima, Wash, October 14, 1950. **Education:** Univ Wash, Seattle, BS, 1972; Wash Univ, St Louis, PhD (biol chem), 1977. **Professional Experience:** PROF, DEPT BIOCHEM & MOLECULAR GENETICS, UNIV COLO HEALTH SCI CTR, 1993-; from asst prof to assoc prof, Dept Biol, Ind Univ, 1985-1993; asst prof, Dept Biochem, Univ Ill, 1981-1985; asst prof, Ind Univ, 1985-1988; asst prof biochem, Univ Ill, Urbana, 1981-1985; fel biochem, Stanford Univ, 1978-1980; fel biochem, Univ Calif, Berkeley, 1977-1978. **Memberships:** Am Soc Microbio lo gists; Am Soc Biochem & Molecular Biol; Genetics Soc Am. **Research Statement & Publications:** Regulation and mechanisms of eukaryotic transcription; nuclear and mitochondrial RNA polymerase; saccharomyces cerevisiae. **Mailing Address:** Dept Biochem & Molecular Genetics, Univ Colo Health Sci Ctr, 4200 E Ninth Ave B121, Denver, CO 80262. **Fax:** 303-315-3326. **E-Mail:** Judith.Jaehning@uchsc.edu

JAENISCH, RUDOLF, RETROVIRUSES, MAMMALIAN DEVELOPMENT. **Personal Data:** German citizen. **Education:** Univ Munich, MD, 1967. **Honors & Awards:** Boehringer Mannheim Molecular Bioanalytics Prize, 1996; Peter Gruber Found Award, 2001; Robert Koch Prize, 2002; Charles Rodolphe Brupbacher Prize, 2003. **Professional Experience:** PROF BIOL, MASS INST TECHNOL, 1984-; MEM, WHITEHEAD INST, MASS INST TECHNOL, 1984-; prof, Henrich-Pette Inst, Hamburg, Ger, 1977-1984; asst prof, Salk Inst, San Diego, 1973-1977; postdoc fel, Princeton Univ, 1970-1972; postdoc fel, Max-Planck Inst, 1967-1969. **Memberships:** Nat Acad Sci; fel Am Acad Art & Sci; Am Acad Microbiol; AAAS. **Research Statement & Publications:** Control of mammalian development using retroviruses and transgenic technology; generation of insertional mutations which affect mouse development; interaction of retroviruses with embryos. **Mailing Address:** Dept Biol, Mass Inst Technol, Cambridge, MA 02142-1479. **Fax:** 617-258-6505. **E-Mail:** kemske@wi.mit.edu

JAFEK, BRUCE WILLIAM, NASAL & SINUS DISEASES, DISORDERS OF TASTE & SMELL. **Personal Data:** b Chicago, Ill, March 4, 1941; m Mary; c Lynette, Robert, Timothy, Britta, Kayla & Kristen. **Education:** Coe Col, Iowa, BS, 1962; Univ Calif, Los Angeles, MD, 1966; Oxford Univ, 2003, 2004. **Honors & Awards:** Fowler Award, Triologic Soc, 1983 Am Cancer Soc Champion of Hope-SVCA REHAB Volunteer Award, 1985 & 1986; Cottle Award, Am Rhinologic Soc, 1991; Honor Award, AAO-HNS, 1979; Physician's Recognition Award, AMA, 2005-2008. **Professional Experience:** PROF, OTOLARYNGOL & CHMN NECK-HEAD SURG (1976-1998), UNIV COLO, 1976-1998; asst prof otolaryngol, Univ Pa, 1973-1976; instr otolaryngol, Johns Hopkins Univ, 1971-1973; res otolaryngol, head & neck surg, 1968-1971; resident gen surg, Univ Calif, Los Angeles, 1967-1968; Intern gen surg, New Haven Hosp, 1966-1967. **Memberships:** Am Acad Facial Plastic Surg; Am Acad Otolaryngol-Head & Neck Surg, VP, 1985; Am Col Surgeons; Soc Univ Otolaryngologists; Triological Society, Western VP 1998-1999. **Research Statement & Publications:** Study of disorders of chemosensation of the head and neck region. **Mailing Address:** Dept Otolaryngol Box B-205, UCHSC, 4200 E Nintha Ave, Denver, CO 80262. **Fax:** 303-315-8787. **E-Mail:** bruce.jafek@uchsc.edu

JAFFA, ROBERT E, MATHEMATICS. **Personal Data:** b Berkeley, Calif, November 11, 1935. **Education:** Univ Calif, AB, 1957, MA, 1960, PhD (math), 1964. **Professional Experience:** PROF MATH, CALIF STATE UNIV, SACRAMENTO, as of 2004; prof math, Sacramento State Univ, beginning 1976; from asst prof to assoc prof math, Sacramento State Univ, 1965-1976; resmathematician, Univ Calif, 1964-1965. **Memberships:** Am Math Soc. **Research Statement & Publications:** Abstract algebra; functional analysis. **Mailing Address:** Dept Math, Calif State Univ, 6000 J St, Sacramento, CA 95819.

JAFFE, ANNETTE BRONKESH, PHYSICAL ORGANIC CHEMISTRY, PHYSICAL CHEMISTRY. **Personal Data:** b Munich, Ger, July 25, 1946; American citizen; m 1970, c Matthew & Elizabeth. **Education:** Douglass Col, Rutgers Univ, BA, 1968; Yale Univ, MPhil, 1970, PhD (phy chem), 1972. **Professional Experience:** CONSULT, ANNETTE JAFFE CONSULT, as of 2005; CONSULT DIGITAL COLOR IMAGING, as of 2003; prin scientist, imaging prods, Apple Comput Inc, santaclara, beginning 1990; mem res staff, Res Labs, IBM Corp, 1974-1990. **Memberships:** Am Chem Soc; sr mem Soc Photog Scientists & Engrs; Soc Imaging Sci &Technol. **Research Statement & Publications:** Solid state chemistry; electro-organic chemistry in aprotic solvents; reaction mechanisms; ink chemistry; electrophotography; contact electrification; color science; non-impact printing. **Mailing Address:** 328 S 17th St, San Jose, CA 95112. **E-Mail:** annette_jaffe@earthlink.net

JAFFE, ARTHUR MICHAEL, MATHEMATICAL PHYSICS. **Personal Data:** b NewYork, NY, December 22, 1937; m 1992, Sarah; c Margaret. **Education:** Princeton Univ, BA, 1959, PhD (physics), 1966; Cambridge Univ, BA, 1961. **Honorary Degrees:** MA, Harvard Univ, 1970. **Honors & Awards:** NY Acad Sci award, 1979; Dannie Heineman Prize, Am Inst Physics & Phys Soc, 1980. **Professional Experience:** LANDON T CLAY PROF MATH & THEORET SCI, HARVARD UNIV, 1985-; ed, Selecta Mathematica Sovietica, 1981-; ed, Progress Physics, 1980-1983; chief ed, Comn Math Physics, 1979-; John S

Guggenheim Found fel, 1977 & 1992; ed, Comn Math Physics, 1975-1979; Alfred P Sloan Found fel, 1968-1970; from asst prof to prof math physics, Harvard Univ, 1967-1985; visitor natural sci, Inst Advan Study, 1967; res assoc, Stanford Linear Accelerator Ctr, 1966-1967; actg asst prof math, Stanford Univ, 1966-1967; Nat Acad Sci-Nat Res Coun, Air Force Off Sci Res fel, 1965-1967; res assoc physics, Princeton Univ, 1965-1966. **Memberships:** Am Math Soc (pres, 1997-1998); fel Am Phys Soc; NY Acad Sci; AAAS; fel Am Acad Arts Sci; Int Asn Math Physics (pres, 1991-1996); fel AAAS; Nat Acad Sci; Asn Women Math; Soc Indus & Appl Math. **Research Statement & Publications:** Mathematics and theoretical physics; author or co-author of 4 books and more than 150 articles. **Mailing Address:** Dept Math & Theoret Sci, Harvard Univ, Lyman 338, 17 Oxford St, Cambridge, MA 02138-2901. **Fax:** 617-495-2895. **E-Mail:** jaffe@physics.harvard.edu

JAFFE, DONALD, MATERIALS SCIENCE, ELECTRONICS ENGINEERING. **Personal Data:** b New York, NY, May 17, 1931; m 1953, c 5. **Education:** Mass Inst Technol, BS, 1952, MS, 1953; Carnegie-Mellon Univ, PhD (metall eng), 1963. **Professional Experience:** DEPT DIR, MICROELECTRONICS PACKAGING, LEHIGH UNIV, 1990-; head, Analytical Technol Dept, AT&T Bell Labs, 1987-1989; head, Film Technol Dept, 1981-1984 & Film Circuits Design & Technol Dept, AT&TBell Labs, 1984-1987; supvr integrated circuit technol, AT&T Bell Labs, 1977-1981; supvrencapsulation mat, AT&T Bell Labs, 1972-1977; supvr thin film mat, AT&T Bell Labs, 1968-1972; mem tech staff magnetic mat, AT&T Bell Labs, 1965-1968; engr, Westinghouse ElecCo, 1958-1965; engr, Gen Elec Co, 1953-1958; instr eve sch, Carnegie-Mellon Univ. **Memberships:** Inst Elec & Electronics Engrs; Int Soc Hybrid Microelectronics; Am Vacuum Soc. **Research Statement & Publications:** Technical management involving structure, properties, design and assembly techniques relative to materials and components used for microelectronics applications. **Mailing Address:** 962 Donald Dr, Emmaus, PA 18049.

JAFFE, EDWARD E, ORGANIC CHEMISTRY. **Personal Data:** b Poland, September 22, 1928; American citizen; m 1954, Ann Swirski; c Rebecca, Linda & David. **Education:** City Col NY, BS, 1952; NY Univ, MS, 1954, PhD (org chem), 1957. **Honors & Awards:** NY Univ Founders Day Award; Armin J Bruning Award, Fedn Socs Coatings Technol; ACS Delaware sec award for conspicuous sci achiev in the area of chem. **Professional Experience:** CONSULT, CIBA-GEIGY CORP, 1995-; vpres res, Ciba-Geigy Corp, 1988-1995; dir res, Ciba-Geigy Corp, 1987-1988; distinguished res fel, Ciba-Geigy Corp, 1984-1987; res fel, E I du Pont de Nemours & Co, 1980-1984; res mgr, E I du Pont de Nemours & Co, 1978-1980; tech supt, E I du Pont de Nemours & Co, 1975-1978; res supvr, E I du Pont de Nemours & Co, 1973-1975; res assoc, E I du Pont de Nemours & Co, 1965-1973; from res chemist to sr res chemist, E I du Pont de Nemours & Co, 1957-1965; Tech asst res, Mt Sinai Hosp, NY, 1951-1954. **Memberships:** Am Chem Soc; Sigma Xi. **Research Statement & Publications:** Heterocyclic chemistry and the characterization of colored organic compounds; varied organic syntheses in the fields of organophosphorus chemistry, pigments, polymers; organic microchemistry; holder of over 300 United States and International patents. **Mailing Address:** 6 Penny Lane Ct, Wilmington, DE 19803-4022. **E-Mail:** eejaff@aol.com

JAFFE, EILEEN KAREN, PROTEIN STRUCTURE & FUNCTION, BIOINORGANIC BIOCHEMISTRY. **Personal Data:** b New York, NY, May 7, 1954; m 1983, George; c Elizabeth H Markham. **Education:** State Univ NY Col Cortland, BS, 1975; Univ Pa, PhD (biochem), 1979. **Honors & Awards:** EMPIRE WHO'S WHO OF EXECUTIVES AND PROFESSIONALS 2004. **Professional Experience:** SENIOR MEMBER, FOX CHASE CANCER CENTER 2003 -; ADJUNCT PROFESSOR, SCH. DENT. MED. 1998 -; MEMBER, INST CANCER RES, FOX CHASE CANCER CTR, 1991-2003; ADJASSOC PROF, SCH DENT MED, UNIV PA, 1991-1998; res assoc prof, Sch Dent Med, Univ Pa, 1990-1991; res asst prof biochem, Sch Dent Med, Univ Pa, 1984-1990; res asst prof biochem, Jefferson Med Col, Thomas Jefferson Univ, 1983-1984; NIH prin investr, Haverford Col, Jefferson Med Col, Univ Pa & Inst Cancer Res, 1981-; asst prof, Haverford Col, 1981-1983; NIHres fel chem, Harvard Univ, 1979-1981. **Memberships:** Am Chem Soc; AAAS; Sigma Xi; Am Asn Women Sci; Am Soc Biochem &Molecular Biol. **Research Statement & Publications:** Working of enzymes; enzyme reaction mechanisms, quaternary structure isoforms, morpheeins, metal ions in catalysis, metal ATP complexes, thiophosphates; porphobilinogen synthase; protein structure. **Mailing Address:** Fox Chase Cancer Center, 333 Cottman Ave, Philadelphia, PA 19111. **Fax:** 215728-2412. **E-Mail:** eileen.jaffe@fccc.edu

JAFFE, ELAINE SARKIN, HEMATOPATHOLOGY, IMMUNOPATHOLOGY. **Personal Data:** b Brooklyn, NY, August 27, 1943; m 1967, Michael; c Gregory & Caleb. **Education:** Cornell Univ, AB, 1965; Univ Pa, MD, 1969; Am Bd Path, cert, 1974. **Honors & Awards:** Pritzker Mem lectr, Acad Med, Toronto, Can, 1989; W M Barriss McAllisterMem lectr, Yale Univ, 1993. **Professional Experience:** ATG LAB CHIEF, LAB PATH, as of 2005; HEAD, HEMATOPATH SECT, NIH, as of 2005; PRIN INVESR PATH, NAT CANCER INST, as of 2004; clin prof path, sch med health sci, George Wash Univ, beginning 1985; dep chief, Hematopath Sect, NIH, 1982-; chief, Path Anat Br, Lab Path, Nat Cancer Inst, NIH, 1982-; chief, Hematopath Sect, NIH, 1980-; sr investr, NIH, 1974-1980; fel hematopath, NIH, 1972-1974; resident, Lab Path, Nat CancerInst, NIH, Bethesda, Md, 1970-1972; co-chair, Expert Panel Cytochem, ICSH. **Memberships:** Am Soc Hemat (vpres 1992-1994 pres 1994-1996); US-Can Int Acad Path (vpres 1996-1997 pres elect 1997-); Am Asn Pathologists; Soc Hematopath (pres 1994-1996); HistiocyteSoc; fel AAAS; Int Retrovirus Asn. **Research Statement & Publications:** Analysis of human malignant lymphomas and leukemia to determine relationship to normal immune system and their role as models of the normal immune system; immunologic characterization of lymphomas with delineation of new clinicopathologic entities. **Mailing Address:** Lab Path Nat Cancer Inst NIH, Bldg 10 Rm 2N202, Bethesda, MD 20892. **Fax:** 301-402-2415. **E-Mail:** ejaffe@mail.nih.gov

JAFFE, ERIC ALLEN, HEMATOLOGY, ONCOLOGY. **Personal Data:** b New York, NY, April 7, 1942; m 1971, c 2. **Education:** Downstate Med Ctr, State Univ NY, MD, 1966. **Honors & Awards:** Passano Found Young Scientist Award, 1977. **Professional Experience:** CHMN, DEPT MED, INTERFAITH MED CTR, as of 2003; PROF MED, CORNELL UNIV MED COL, 1982-; assoc prof, Cornell Univ Med Col, 1977-1982; Irma T Hirschl Career Scientist Award, 1976-1981 & NIH Res Career DevelopAward, 1976-1981; res fel, Nat Hemophilia Found, 1974-1976; career scientist, Health Res Coun City New York, 1974-1975; from instr to asst prof, Cornell Univ Med Col, 1971-1977; fel hemat, New York Hosp, 1970-1972; sr resident, New York Hosp, 1970; guest investr, Rockefeller Univ, 1969; resident, New York Hosp, 1968-1969; resident, Kings County Hosp, Brooklyn, 1967-1968; intern internal med, Kings County Hosp, Brooklyn, 1966-1967. **Memberships:** Asn Am Physicians; Am Soc Clin Invest; Am Soc Cell Biol; Am Soc Hematology; Am Asn Pathologists. **Research Statement & Publications:** Role of endothelial cells in coagulation and the relationship of enothelial cells to platelets, white cells, and atherosclerosis. **Mailing Address:** Dept Med, Interfaith Med Ctr, 1545 Atlantic Ave, Brooklyn, NY 11213. **Fax:** 718-613-4893. **E-Mail:** ejaffe@interfaithmedical.com

JAFFE, ERNST RICHARD, MEDICINE, HEMATOLOGY. **Personal Data:** b Chicago, Ill, January 4, 1925; m Anne; c Stephanie A (Green) & Richard S. **Education:** Univ Chicago, BS Anat, 1945, MD & MS Path, 1948; Am Bd Internal Med, Dipl & Cert Hemat. **Honorary Degrees:** LHD, Yeshiva Univ, 1987. **Honors & Awards:** Charles R Drew Award, Am Red Cross, 1990 Outstanding Serv Award, Am Soc of Hematology, 1998; Phi Beta Kappa 1944; Alpha Omega Alpha Honor Medical Society, 1947. **Professional Experience:** EMER DISTINGUISHED UNIV PROF MED, ALBERT EINSTEIN COL MED, 1992-; pres, Henry M & Lillian Stratton Found, 1992-1996; EMER SR ASSOC DEAN, ALBERT EINSTEIN COL MED, 1991-; chmn, Blood Serv Comt, 1988-1990; Nat Bd Govs, Am Red Cross, 1984-1990; adv coun Nat Diabetes, Digestive Kidney dir, NIH, 1984-1987; chmn, NIH Hemat, 1979-1981; assoc dean fac, Div Hemat, 1976-1983; sr assoc dean, 1974-1991; actg dean, 1972-1974 & 1983-1984; study sect, NIH Hemat, 1972-1979; head, Div Hemat, 1970-1982; co-ed, Sem in Hemat, 1968- 2000; attend physician, Med Serv, Bronx Munic Hosp Ctr, 1963- 1992; assoc vis physician, Lincoln Hosp, NY, 1963 -1973; career scientist, Health Res Coun, NY, 1961-1971; from instr to prof med, Albert Einstein Col Med, 1956-1984; from asst vis physician to assoc vis physician, Med Serv, Bronx Munic Hosp Ctr, 1955-1963; post dr res fel, Enstein Col Med Nat Found Infantile Paralysis fel, 1955-1957; clin asst vis physician, Med Serv, Bronx Munic Hosp Ctr, 1955-1956; asst resident, Med Serv, Presby Hosp, NY, 1949-1951 & 1953-1955; intern, Med Serv, Presby Hosp, NY, 1948-1949; asst physiol, Univ Chicago, 1947; Asst path, Univ Chicago, 1946 & 1947-1948; Emeritus Member, Association of American Medical Colleges 2000-. **Memberships:** Am Soc Hemat (pres, 1983); Am Fedn Clin Res emer mem; Am Physiol Soc; Asn Am Physicians; Soc Exp Biol & Med (pres, 1993-1995); Am Soc Clin Invest. **Research Statement & Publications:** Internal medicine and hematology; metabolism of the mammalian erythrocyte and hereditary enzyme deficiencies with hemolysis or methemoglobinemia. **Mailing Address:** 100 Harbor View Dr, Apt 201, Port Washington, NY 11050-4714. **Fax:** N/A. **E-Mail:** ejaffe@pol.net

JAFFE, FRED, ORGANIC CHEMISTRY, ORGANOPHOSPHORUS CHEMISTRY. **Personal Data:** b Cleveland, Ohio, April 5, 1930; m 1960, Barbara Mae Meyerson; c Beth, Lynn & David. **Education:** Western Reserve Univ, BS, 1952; Cornell Univ, PhD, 1957. **Professional Experience:** SCIENTIST, AKZO NOBEL CENTRAL RES, 1997-; sect head, Akzo NobelCentral Res, 1989-1996; res assoc, Eastern Res Ctr, Stauffer Chem Co, 1975-1988; sr reschemist, Eastern Res Ctr, Stauffer Chem Co, 1968-1975; res chemist, Miami Valley Labs, Procter& Gamble Co, 1965-1968; coordr oxidation chem, W R Grace & Co, Md, 1964-1965; sr reschemist, W R Grace & Co, Md, 1963-1965; res chemist, Wash Res Ctr, W R Grace & Co, Md, 1958-1963; Sloan fel, Cornell Univ, 1957-1958; mem, Global MatSafety Data Sheets Comm & New Idea Generation & Improvement Comt. **Memberships:** AAAS; Am Chem Soc; Royal Soc Chem; Soc Plastics Engrs; NY Acad Sci. **Research Statement & Publications:** Synthesis, stabilization and modification of formaldehyde polymers and copolymers; synthesis of para-bridged benzenes, liquid phase autoxidation, oxidation of decalin; hydroperoxides; carbanion oxidations; organometallic alkali chemistry; phosphorus and silicon; lubricant and hydraulic fluid base stocks and additives; flame retardants; plasticigers polymer additives, process development, organs phosphorus chemistry; granted 8 US patents. **Mailing Address:** Akzo Nobel Cent Res, 2 Livingstone Ave, Dobbs Ferry, NY 10522-3401.

JAFFE, HAROLD, NUCLEAR SCIENCE. **Personal Data:** b Chicago, Ill, May 8, 1930; m 1951, c 3. **Education:** Univ Ill, BS, 1951, PhD (nuclear chem), 1954. **Professional Experience:** SPEC ASST INT PROG, OFF HIGH ENERGY & NUCLEAR PHYSICS, DEPT ENERGY, 1994-; dir, Off Int Res & Develop Policy, 1981-1994; dep dir, Off Int Tech Coop, 1976-1981; tech asst toasst admin nuclear energy, Energy Res & Develop Agency, 1975-1976; chief isotope power systsproj br, mgr Isotope Flight Systs, 1972-1975; chief isotope power systs proj br, Space NuclearSysts Div, US Atomic Energy Comn, 1970-1972; mgr, San Ramon Plant & asst to pres, 1969-1970; mem bd dirs, Idaho Nuclear Corp, 1968-1970; asst prof, John F Kennedy Univ, 1966-1970; asst to vpres, Nuclear Div, 1966-1969; mgr appl sci div, Aerojet-Gen Nucleonics Div, Aerojet-Gen Corp, 1964-1966; asst mgr nuclear tech div, Aerojet-Gen Nucleonics Div, Aerojet-Gen Corp, 1962-1964; mgr fuel develop dept, Aerojet-Gen Nucleonics Div, Aerojet-GenCorp, 1960-1962; prog mgr gas-cooled reactor exp, Aerojet-Gen Nucleonics Div, Aerojet-GenCorp, 1957-1959; prin nuclear chemist, Aerojet-Gen Nucleonics Div, Aerojet-Gen Corp, 1956-1957; sr chemist, Tracerlab, Inc, 1955-1956; asst res chemist, Union Oil Co, 1954-1955. **Memberships:** AAAS; Am Nuclear Soc; Am Chem Soc; fel Am Inst Chemists. **Mailing Address:** Int Prog off High Energy & Nuclear Physics, Dept Energy, 1000 Independence Ave SW, Washington, DC 20585.

JAFFE, ISRAELI AARON, INTERNAL MEDICINE. **Personal Data:** b New York, NY, December 21, 1927; m 1952, Judith; c Naomi, Audrey & Caroline. **Education:** NY Univ, BS, 1946; Columbia Univ, MD, 1950; Am Bd Internal Med, dipl. **Professional Experience:** PROF CLIN MED, COL PHYSICIANS & SURGEONS, COLUMBIA UNIV, 1981-; ATTEND PHYSICIAN NY PRESBY HOSP, NY, 1981-; assoc dir rheumatic dis dept, hosp joint dis- orthop inst, NY, 1980-1981; prof clin med, mt sinai Col med, 1980-1981; prof clin med, Col Physicians & Surgeons, Columbia Univ, attend physician, presby hosp, NY, 1978-1980; CONSULT RHEUMAT, USPHS HOSP, NY, 1969-; prof med, NY Med Col, 1968-1978; from asst to assoc prof to prof med, NY Med Col, 1960-1968; dir rheumatic dis serv, ny med Col metrop hosp ctr, 1960-1978; CLIN ASSOC INSTR MED, COLUMBIA UNIV, 1957-; clin assoc, NIH, 1953-1955. **Memberships:** Am Col Physicians; AMA; Am Col Rheumat; NY Rheumat Asn. **Research Statement & Publications:** Rheumatic diseases and penicillamine treatment of rheumatoid arthritis. **Mailing Address:** Dept Med, Col Physicians & Surgeons, 16 E 60th St, New York, NY 10032. **Fax:** 212-342-6835. **E-Mail:** iaj1@columbia.edu

JAFFE, JAMES MARK, PHARMACEUTICS. **Personal Data:** b New York, NY, April 11, 1943; m 1964, c 2. **Education:** Univ Pittsburgh, BS, 1968, BA, 1969, MS, 1970, PhD (pharmaceut), 1972. **Professional Experience:** EXEC DIR PHARM DEPT, SANDOZ, 1993-; assoc prof, Sch Pharm, Univ Pittsburgh, 1975-1980; reviewer, J Pharmaceut Sci, 1974-; from instr to asst prof pharmaceut, Sch Pharm, Univ Pittsburgh, 1970-1975; asst pharmaceut, Sch Pharm, Univ Pittsburgh, 1968-1970; reviewer, Am J Hosp Pharm. **Memberships:** Am Pharmaceut Asn; Acad Pharmaceut Sci; Sigma Xi. **Research Statement & Publications:** Physiological and formulation factors that influence the absorption and excretion of drugs. **Mailing Address:** 66 W Main St, Mendham, NJ 07945.

JAFFE, JEROME HERBERT, PSYCHOPHARMACOLOGY, ADDICTION. **Personal Data:** b Philadelphia, Pa, July 6, 1933; m 1958, c 3. **Education:** Temple Univ, AB, 1954, MA, 1956, MD, 1958. **Professional Experience:** CLIN PROF PSYCHIAT, UNIV MD, 2003-; dir eval sci analysis & synthesis, Ctr Substanceabuse Treatment, Substance Abuse & Ment Health Serv Admin, beginning 1992; prof psychiat, Col Physicians & Surgeons, Columbia Univ, 1973-1992; consult, WHO, 1971-; consult to Pres for narcotics & dangerous drugs, 1971-1973; dir, Spec Action Off Drug AbusePrev, 1971-1973; from asst prof to assoc prof psychiat, Univ Chicago, 1968-1973; dir, Ill DrugAbuse Progs, 1967-1971; consult, NIMH, NY State Narcotics Control Comn & Ill Narcotics AdvCoun, beginning 1966; NIH grant, 1965-1971; NIMH res career develop award, 1964-1971; instr psychiat, Albert Einstein Col Med, 1964-1966; asst prof, Albert Einstein Col Med, 1964-1966; felpharmacol, Albert Einstein Col Med, 1961-1964. **Memberships:** AAAS; fel Am Col Neuropsychopharmacol; AMA; Am Psychiat Asn. **Research Statement & Publications:** Compulsive drug use; mechanisms of tolerance and physical dependence to narcotics and other drugs; treatment of drug dependence; social aspects of drug abuse. **Mailing Address:** Off Sci Anal & Eval Treat, 5600 Fishers Lane, Rockville, MD 20857.

JAFFE, JONAH, PHARMACY, TECHNICAL MANAGEMENT. **Personal Data:** b New York, NY, October 5, 1929; m 1951, c 2. **Education:** Columbia Univ, BS, 1953; Univ Md, MS, 1955, PhD (pharmaceut chem), 1956. **Professional Experience:** RETIRED; vpres, Res & Develop Labs, McNeil Consumer Prod Co, beginning1988; vpres sci affairs, Johnson & Johnson, 1985-1988; vpres res & develop, Johnson & Johnson, 1976-1985; asst vpres, Whitehall Labs Div, Am Home Prod, 1970-1976; tech dir, Whitehall LabsDiv, Am Home Prod, 1965-1970; dir, res, develop & prod, 1963-1965; dir, res & develop, Organon, US, 1962-1963; sr res chemist, E R Squibb, 1956-1962. **Memberships:** Am Pharmaceut Asn; Sigma Xi; AAAS; NY Acad Sci. **Research Statement & Publications:** Management of research and development; quality control; medical research and regulatory affairs; manufacture of proprietary and ethical drugs and toiletries. **Mailing Address:** 4 Partridge Ct, Cherry Hill, NJ 08003.

JAFFE, JULIAN JOSEPH, PHARMACOLOGY. **Personal Data:** b New York, NY, February 17, 1926; m 1953, Joy; c Douglas Grant, Kenneth Michael, Nina Beth & Paul David. **Education:** Univ Conn, BA, 1949; Harvard Univ, MA, 1951, PhD (biol), 1955. **Professional Experience:** PROF EMER, UNIV VT, as of 2006; mem, Panel Parasitic Dis, US-Japan Coop Med Sci Prog, 1971-1976 & Trop Med Parasitol Study Sect, 1977-1981; mem spec working group filariasis, WHO, 1977, 1980, 1983 & 1985; guest worker, Nuffield Inst Comp Med, 1967-1968; Wellcome res travel grants, Oxford Univ, 1958 & Nuffield Inst Comp Med, London, 1967; from assoc prof to prof pharmacol, Col Med, Univ Vt, 1961-1989; from instr to asst prof pharmacol, Sch Med, Yale Univ, 1956-1961; asst, Harvard Univ, 1956-1961; instr biol, USPHS fel, 1955-1956; Instr biol, Brown Univ, 1954-1955. **Memberships:** Am Soc Pharmacol & Exp Therapeut; Am Soc Parasitol; Am Soc Trop Med & Hyg; AAAS; Am Asn Univ Prof. **Research Statement & Publications:** Biochemical pharmacology; biochemistry of parasites. **Mailing Address:** 21 Ivy Lane, Burlington, VT 05401. **E-Mail:** profnjoy@msn.com

JAFFE, LAURINDA A, PHYSIOLOGY OF FERTILIZATION. **Personal Data:** b Pasadena, Calif, January 9, 1952. **Education:** Purdue Univ, BS, 1973; Univ Calif, Los Angeles, PhD (biol), 1977. **Professional Experience:** PROF & VICE CHAIR CELL BIOL, UNIV CONN, as of 2003; assoc prof physiol, Univ Conn, beginning 1986; assoc ed, Develop Biol, 1985-; vis fac, Univ Wash, 1985 & 1988; instr embryol, Marine Biol Lab, Woods Hole, 1983-1987; asst prof, Univ Conn, 1981-1986; NSF fel electrophysiol fertil, Univ Calif, San Diego, 1979-1981; NIH fel electrophysiol fertil, Marine Biol Lab, Woods Hole, Mass, 1978-1979. **Memberships:** Am Soc Cell Biol; Biophys Soc; Soc Develop Biol. **Research Statement & Publications:** Physiology of fertilization. **Mailing Address:** Dept Cell Biol, Univ Conn Health Ctr, 263 Farmington Ave, Farmington, CT 06032. **Fax:** 860-679-1269. **E-Mail:** ljaffe@neuron.uchc.edu

JAFFE, LEONARD, NUCLEAR SAFETY. **Personal Data:** b February 1, 1926; m 1949, Elaine; c Ronald H & Norman D. **Honors & Awards:** Inst Elec & ELectronics Engrs Award, 1967; Am Inst Aeronaut & Astronaut, 1978; William Pecora Award, DeptComn & NASA, 1981; Lloyd V Berkener Space Ulitization Award, Am Acad Sci. **Professional Experience:** RETIRED; pres, Earth Satellite, 1995-2000; chmn, NASA Space Appln Adv Comt, beginning 1986; vpres, Systs Group, Prog Mgt & Prod Assurance, 1984-1995; pres, Systs Div, 1982-1984; vpres systs group, prog mgt & prod assurance, Comput Sci Corp, 1981-1982; head, Tech Assessment Task Force, President's Comn Accident, Three Mile Island, 1979; specialist to chiefeng, Admin Space& Terrestrial Appln, Hq, 1978-1981; dep assoc, Admin Space& Terrestrial Appln, Hq, 1977-1978; dep assoc, Space Appln, 1971-1977; dep assoc, Admin Space & Sci Appln, 1969-1971; dir, Space Appln Prog, 1966-1969; dir, Commun & Navigation Prog, 1963-1966; dir, Comm Systs, 1961-1963; chief, Commun Satellite Prog, Hq, NASA, 1959-1961; chief, Data Systs Br, 1957-1959; aeronaut res scientist, Instruments Res Div, 1951-1957; aeronaut res scientist, Lewis Res Lab, Nat Adv Comt Aeronaut, 1948-1951. **Memberships:** Fel Inst Elec & Electronics Engrs; fel Am Inst Aeronaut & Astronaut; fel AmAstronaut Soc; Int Acad Astronaut; Int Astronaut Fedn (pres, 1974-1976). **Research Statement & Publications:** Development of communications satellite systems. **Mailing Address:** 418 Sisson Ct, Silver Spring, MD 20902.

JAFFE, LIONEL F, DEVELOPMENTAL PHYSIOLOGY, BIOPHYSICS. **Personal Data:** b New York, NY, December 28, 1927; m 1949, Miriam; c Laurinda, Amanda & David. **Education:** Harvard Univ, SB, 1948; Calif Inst Technol, PhD (embryol), 1954. **Honors & Awards:** Blinks Mem Lect, Hopkins Marine Station, 2003; Jenkinson Mem Lect, Oxford Univ, 1982; Tyler Mem Lect, Cal Tech, 1978. **Professional Experience:** SR SCIENTIST, MARINE BIOL LAB, WOODS HOLE, MASS, 1982-; dir, Nat Vibrating Probe Facil, 1982-1994; prof biol, Purdue Univ, 1967-1984; from asst prof to assoc prof, Univ Pa, 1960-1967; asst prof biol, Brandeis Univ, 1956-1960; fel marine biol, Scripps Inst, Calif, 1955-1956; fel, NSF, 1954-1956; Fel, Nat Res Coun, Hopkins Marine Sta, Stanford Univ, 1953-1955. **Memberships:** Am Asn Cancer Res; Am Physiol Soc, Soc Study Reproduction; Am Soc Cell Biol; Dev Biol Soc; Soc Gen Physiol. **Research Statement & Publications:** Development and nature of morphogenetic polarity; cellular tropisms; bioelectric and ionic aspects of development; calcium waves and gradients; carcinogenesis. **Mailing Address:** Marine Biol Lab, 7 MBL St, Falmouth, MA 02543. **Fax:** 508-540-6902. **E-Mail:** ljaffe@mbl.edu

JAFFE, MARVIN RICHARD, TEACHING CHEMISTRY FOR HEALTH SCIENCES, CONSUMER SCIENCES. **Personal Data:** b New York, NY, May 23, 1938. **Education:** Brooklyn Col, BS, 1960, MA, 1965; Fordham Univ, PhD (anal chem), 1970. **Professional Experience:** DEPUTY CHAIRPERSON, DEPT SCI, MANHATTAN COMMUNITY COL, as of 2004; PROF, DEPT SCI, MANHATTAN COMMUNITY COL, 1985-; from asst prof to assoc prof, Sci Dept, Manhattan Community Col, 1971-1984; guest jr res assoc, Brookhaven Nat Lab, 1969-1970; res asst, Fordham Univ, 1968-1970; instr chem, Bronx Community Col, 1965-1968; supvr prod develop, Schrafft's, NY, 1963-1965; prod develop chemist, Schrafft's, NY, 1962-1963; qual control chemist, Schrafft's, NY, 1960-1962. **Memberships:** Nat Sci Teachers Asn; Am Chem Soc; Sigma Xi. **Research Statement & Publications:** Consumer science; science education of non-scientists; kinetics and mechanisms of beta-diketones. **Mailing Address:** Dept Sci, Manhattan Community Col, 199 Chambers St, New York, NY 10007. **Fax:** 212-748-7471.

JAFFE, MICHAEL, POLYMER PHYSICS, PHYSICAL CHEMISTRY. **Personal Data:** b New York, NY, May 10, 1942; c 2. **Education:** Cornell Univ, BA, 1963; Rensselaer Polytech Inst, PhD (chem), 1967. **Professional Experience:** DIR, MED DEVICE CONCEPT LAB, UNIV NJ, as of 2006; CHIEF SCIENTIST, INDUST PROG, NJ CTR BIOMATERIALS, as of 2006; RES PROF BIOMED ENGR, NJ CTR BIOMATERIALS, NJ INST TECHNOL, 1998-. **Memberships:** Am Chem Soc; Am Phys Soc; fel NAm Thermal Anal Soc; fel AAAS; Nat Materials Adv Bd; fel Int Union Pure & Appl Chem; fel Polymeric Mat Sci & Eng. **Research Statement & Publications:** Morphology of crystalline high polymers; transition behavior of polymers; structure-property relationships of polymers and related materials; application of biology pardigms to material sciences. **Mailing Address:** Med Device Concept Lab, NJ Inst Technol, Univ Heights Sci Park, Coun Higher Educ Newark Rm 202 111 Lock St, Newark, NJ 07103. **E-Mail:** jaffe@adm.njit.edu

JAFFE, MIRIAM WALTHER, ASTRONOMY. **Personal Data:** b Clinton, Ind, February 6, 1922; m 1949, Lionel; c Laurinda A, Amanda J & David B. **Education:** Ind Univ, AB, 1943; Univ Va, MA, 1945; Radcliffe Col & Harvard Univ, PhD (astron), 1948. **Professional Experience:** RETIRED; asst prof astron, Purdue Univ, 1968-1985; asst prof astron, Haverford Col, 1965-1966; instr astron, Univ Southern Calif, 1949-1951 & Wellesley Col, 1948-1949. **Memberships:** Am Astron Soc. **Research Statement & Publications:** Photographic photometry; classification of stellar spectra. **Mailing Address:** 59 Cumloden Dr, Falmouth, MA 02540-1609.

JAFFE, MORDECAI J, PLANT PHYSIOLOGY. **Personal Data:** b New York, NY, July 7, 1933; m 1961, Amy C Cooke; c Jennie (Lane), Ben & Sam. **Education:** City Col New York, BS, 1958; Cornell Univ, PhD (veg physiol), 1964. **Professional Experience:** Permanent vis prof, Hebrew Univ, Jerusalem, 1984-; vis prof, Lady Davis visprof, 1984; BABCOCK PROF BOTANY, WAKE FOREST UNIV, 1980-; Bard res grant, 1980-1983; vis scientist, Boyce Thompson Inst Cornell Univ, 1980; NASA res grant, 1977-1984; vis prof, Hebrew Univ, Jerusalem, 1975; NSF res grant, 1967-1974 & 1975-1986; from asst profto prof, plant physiol, Ohio Univ, 1967-1980; Lectr & res assoc biol, Yale Univ, 1964-1967. **Memberships:** AAAS; Am Soc Plant Physiologists; Soc Develop Biol; Phytochem Soc NAm; Japanese Soc Plant Physiol. **Research Statement & Publications:** Sensory physiology and biochemistry; rapid movements in plants; biochemistry of touch mediated processes in plants; physiology of stress in plants; flowering mechanisms in plants. **Mailing Address:** Dept Biol, Wake Forest Univ, Winston-Salem, NC 27109. **Fax:** 910-759-6008. **E-Mail:** jaffemj@wfu.edu

JAFFE, MORRY, EXPERIMENTAL PHYSICS, APPLICATION DEVELOPMENT. **Personal Data:** b New York, NY, October 10, 1940; m 1990, Lou. **Education:** City Col NY, BS, 1962; Boston Univ, MA, 1964; City Univ NY, PhD (physics), 1971. **Honors & Awards:** Cert Appreciation, US Environ Protection Agency, 1978. **Professional Experience:** ASST COMNR, NY CITY DEPT RECORDS & INFO SERVS, 1994-; CONSULT, AGS, 1990-; data processing consult, Group 1988; data processing consult, New York, 1984-1990; lab asst, New York Dept Air Resources, 1973-1978; res asst, City Col New York, 1965-1969 & 1970-1971; lectr, 1964-1965; asst, Boston Univ, 1962-1964. **Research Statement & Publications:** Database administration. **Mailing Address:** Dept Records & Info Serv, 31 Chambers St, New York, NY 10007.

JAFFE, PHILIP MONLANE, INORGANIC CHEMISTRY. **Personal Data:** b Bronx, NY, August 14, 1927; m 1950, Mary; c 3. **Education:** City Col NY, BS, 1948; Polytech Inst Brooklyn, MS, 1953, PhD, 1962. **Professional Experience:** Dean, Div Sci Allied Health, 1985-1991; PROF CHEM, OAKTON COMMUNITY COL, 1970-; sr res chemist, Zenith Radio Corp, 1966-1972; sr staff scientist, Aerospace Res Ctr, Gen Precision Inc, 1963-1966; res chemist, Westinghouse Elec Co, 1953-1963; chemist, City Chem Corp, NY, 1948-1951. **Memberships:** fel AAAS; Am Chem Soc; fel Am Inst Chem; fel Sigma Xi. **Research Statement & Publications:** Inorganic phosphors and preparations; semiconductors; photoconductors; technical and educational writing. **Mailing Address:** 50 Willow Pkwy, Buffalo Grove, IL 60089.

JAFFE, RANDAL CRAIG, ENDOCRINOLOGY, BIOCHEMISTRY. **Personal Data:** b St Louis, Mo, December 18, 1947; m 1970, Rose-Lynn; c Tod, Aron & Tracy. **Education:** Univ Southern Calif, BS, 1968; Univ Calif, Davis, PhD (biochem), 1972. **Professional Experience:** PROF PHYSIOL & BIOPHYS, MED CTR, UNIV ILL, 1992-; vis fel med, Mass Gen Hosp, 1985-1986; vis assoc prof med & physiol, Harvard Univ, 1985-1986; from asst prof to assoc prof, Med Ctr, Univ Ill, 1975-1992; NIH fel, 1974-1975; fel cell biol, Baylor Col Med, 1973-1975; fel endocrinol, Sch Med, Vanderbilt Univ, 1972-1973. **Memberships:** AAAS; Endocrine Soc; Am Soc Biol Chem; Soc Study Reproduction. **Research Statement & Publications:** Mechanism of hormone action; comparative endocrinology; hormonal control of development. **Mailing Address:** Dept Physiol & Biophys, MC 901, Univ Ill, 901 S Wolcott, Chicago, IL 60612-7342. **Fax:** 312-996-1414. **E-Mail:** rcjaffe@uic.edu

JAFFE, ROBERT B, ENDOCRINOLOGY, OBSTETRICS & GYNECOLOGY. **Personal Data:** b Detroit, Mich, February 18, 1933; m 1954, c 2. **Education:** Univ Mich, MD, 1957; Univ Colo, MS, 1966; Am Bd Obstet & Gynec, dipl, 1967 & reproductive endocrin cert. **Professional Experience:** FRED GELLERT ENDOWED CHAIR, REPRODUCTIVE MED & BIOL, as of 2004; dir, Reprodctive Endocrinol Ctr, Univ Calif, San Francisco, 1973-2000; chmn dept, Univ Calif, San Francisco, 1973-1996; PROF OBSTET, GYNEC & REPRODUCTIVE SCI, UNIV CALIF, SAN FRANCISCO, 1973-; Josiah Macy, Jr Found fac fel, 1966-1969 & 1980-1981; from asst prof to prof obstet & gynec, Med Ctr, Univ Mich, Ann Arbor, 1964-1973; NIH fel reprod endocrinol, Hormone Lab, Karolinska Sjukhuset, Sweden, 1963-1964; resident obstet & gynec, Univ Colo, 1959-1963; USPHS fel endocrinol, Dept Internal Med, Med Ctr, Univ Colo, 1958-1959; rotating intern, Univ Colo, 1957-1958; lab asst biochem, Univ Mich, 1953-1954; vis prof, Univ Mich, Univ Mo, Cornell Univ, Univ Wash, Univ Ore, Yale Univ, Univ Wis, Univ Va & Wash Univ; mem, Human Embryol & Develop Study Sect, NIH, Sci Adv Bd, Nat Inst Child Health & Human Develop Coun, Reproductive Biol Study Sect, NIH, Med Adv Bd, Nat Pituitary Agency, Steering Comt, Perinatal Res Soc, Sci Adv Bd, Prog Appl Res Fertil Regulation & Biomed Comt; chmn, Div Endocrinol & Fertil, Am Col Obstetricians Gynecologists. **Memberships:** Inst Med-Nat Acad Sci; Endocrine Soc; Am Fedn Clin Res; Soc Gynec Invest (pres); fel Am Col Obstet & Gynec; Am Gynec Soc; Asn Am Physicians; Sigma Xi. **Research Statement & Publications:** Endocrinology; gynecology; author of numerous technical publications. **Mailing Address:** Univ Calif San Francisco, PO Box 0556, San Francisco, CA 94143. **Fax:** 415-502-7866. **E-Mail:** jaffer@obgyn.ucsf.edu

JAFFE, ROBERT LOREN, QUANTUM CHROMODYNAMICS, THEORY OF PARTICLES & FIELDS. **Personal Data:** b Bath, Maine, May 23, 1946; m 1977, Diana; c Rebecca Caroline & Samuel Pryor. **Education:** Princeton Univ, AB, 1968; Stanford Univ, MS, 1971, PhD (physics), 1972. **Professional Experience:** Morningstar Prof Physics 1999-; Dir Ctr for Theoretical Physics, Mass Inst Technol, 1998-2005; PROF & CHMN FAC, MASS INST TECHNOL, 1993-1995; Mass Inst Technol, MacVicar Faculty Fellow 1998-; consult, Los Alamos Nat Lab, 1985-1990, Brookhaven Nat Lab, 1985-; Brookhaven Sci Assoc, Sci & Tech Steering Comm, 1998-, chmn 2004-; PROF PHYSICS, MASS INST TECHNOL, 1983-; Sloan fel, 1975-1977; from asst prof to assoc prof, Mass Inst Technol, 1974-1983; Res assoc, Mass Inst Technol, 1972-1974. **Memberships:** Fel Am Phys Soc; fel AAAS. **Mailing Address:** Ctr for Theoretical Physics, Mass Inst Technol 77 Mass Ave, Cambridge, MA 02139. **Fax:** 617-253-8674. **E-Mail:** jaffe@mit.edu

JAFFE, RUSSELL M, IMMUNOLOGY. **Personal Data:** b Albany, NY, January 1, 1947. **Education:** Boston Univ, BA, MD & PhD (biochem & med sci), 1972. **Honors & Awards:** J D Lang Jr Investr Award, USPHS, 1975; Norman E Clarke Sr lectr, Am ColAdvan Med, 1992. **Professional Experience:** DIR, SERAMMUNE PHYS LAB, 1983-; LAB DIR & CHIEF EXEC OFFICER, ELISA as of 2006; dir, Princeton Bio Ctr, 1983-1992; fel, Health Studies Col, beginning 1979; collab investr, Nat Heart Lung & Blood Inst & LEA, 1976-1979; sr staff physician, Clin Ctr, NIH, 1975-1979; resident, Clin Ctr, NIH, 1973-1975; srassoc ed, New Physician, 1972-1973; intern, Univ Hosp, Boston Univ Med Col, 1972-1973; assoc ed, New Physician, 1971-1972. **Memberships:** AAAS; NY Acad Sci; Am Asn Clin Chemists; fel Am Col Nutrit; fel Am In-VitroAllergy/Immunol Soc; Am Prev Med Asn; Am Pub Health Asn; fel Am Soc Clin Pathologists; AmSoc Microbiol; Int Col Appl Nutrit; Royal Soc Med. **Research Statement & Publications:** Connective tissue; biology of mental function; coagulation; atherosclerosis; clinical biochemistry; biochemical immunology. **Mailing Address:** ELISA Biotechnologies, 14 Pidgeon Hill Dr, Ste 300, Sterling, VA 20165. **Fax:** 703-450-2981.

JAFFE, SIGMUND, physical chemistry, chemical kinetics of stratosphere; deceased, see previous edition for last biography

JAFFE, WERNER G, NUTRITION, BIOCHEMISTRY. **Personal Data:** b Frankfurt, Ger, October 27, 1914; m 1946, c 6. **Education:** Univ Zurich, PhD (chem), 1939; Cent Univ Venezuela, DrSc (biochem), 1950. **Honorary Degrees:** Hon Prof, Cent Univ & Univ Simon Bolivar. **Honors & Awards:** Nat Sci Award, Ministry of Educ, 1958; Gold Medal Sci Res, Cent UnivVenezuela, 1960; Nat Sci Award of Venezuela, 1978. **Professional Experience:** DIR POSTGRAD COURSE NUTRIT PLANNING, UNIV VENEZUELA, 1974-; PROF BIOCHEM, SCH SCI CENT, UNIV VENEZUELA, 1958-; ed, ArchLatinoamerican Nutrit; res assoc, Nat Nutrit Inst, 1950-; assoc prof biochem, Sch Sci, UnivVenezuela, 1950-1958; asst prof org chem, Sch Pharm, Univ Venezuela, 1947-1950. **Memberships:** AAAS; Venezuelan Asn Advan Sci (pres, 1956); Venezuelan Chem Soc (pres, 1953); cor mem Peruvian Chem Soc; cor mem Mex Chem Soc; Am Chem Soc. **Research Statement & Publications:** Enzymology; toxicology; lectins, enzyme inhibition; toxic food constituents. **Mailing Address:** 5TA Avenida No 211-1811, Los Palos Grandes, Caracas 1062, Venezuela.

JAFFEE, OSCAR CHARLES, experimental embryology; deceased, see previous edition for last biography

JAFVERT, CHAD TIMOTHY, Environmental Chemistry & Mass Transfer in Environmental Systems, Environmental Photochemistry. **Personal Data:** b Nevada, Iowa, December 2, 1956; m 1981, Mary; c Benjamin Aaron & Paul David. **Education:** Iowa State Univ, BS (Biochemistry), 1979; Univ Iowa, MS, 1982, PhD (Civil & Environmental Engineering), 1985. **Professional Experience:** Professor, Civil Eng, Purdue University, 1999-; Assoc Prof, 1995-1999; Area Head, Environ & Hydraulic Eng, 1994-2000; Assist Prof, 1991-1995; Research Environ Engineer, U.S. Environ Protection Agency, Athens, Ga, 1986-1991; Research Associate, National Research Council, 1985-1986. **Memberships:** Am Chem Soc; Soc Environ Toxicol & Chem; Sigma Xi; Asn Environ Eng Profs; Am Soc of Civil Engineers. **Research Statement & Publications:** Phase distribution, mass transfer, and reactivity of organic chemicals in the environment; remediation of contaminated soils and sediments. **Mailing Address:** Sch Civil Eng, Purdue Univ, West Lafayette, IN 47907-1284. **E-Mail:** jafvert@ecn.purdue.edu

JAGADEESH, GOWRA G, AUTONOMIC CARDIOVASCULAR, DRUG RECEPTOR-EFFECTOR COUPLING. **Personal Data:** b Karnataka, India, September 18, 1949; m 1978, Jayashree; c Shilpa & Neetal. **Education:** Bangalore Univ, India, BPharm, 1970; All-India Inst Med Sci, New Delhi, India, MS, 1971; Banaras Hindu Univ, India, PhD (pharmacol), 1980. **Professional Experience:** ADJ SCIENTIST, NAT INST CHILD HEALTH HUMAN DEVELOP, NIH, BETHESDA, MD, 1993-; EXPERT PHARMACOLOGIST, CARDIO-RENAL DIV, FOOD & DRUG ADMN, ROCKVILLE, MD 1990-; staff sci, Northeastern Univ Col Pharm, Boston, 1989-1990; vis res assoc, Northeastern Univ Col Pharm, Boston, 1986-1989; dept physiol, Univ Sask, Can, 1982-1985; from asst prof to assoc prof pharmacol, Banaras Hindu Univ, IT, Varanasi, India, 1975-1986; res officer, Inst Hist Med & Med Res, NDelhi, India, 1975. **Memberships:** Soc Exp Biol & Med. **Research Statement & Publications:** G-protein-coupled adrenergic and muscarinic receptors in liver, vascular and cardiac tissues; modulation by protein kinase c; signal transduction; structure-function study of angiotensin at-1 receptor in cos cells; regulatory review of new drug applications. **Mailing Address:** Food & Drug Admin, Rockville, MD 20850. **E-Mail:** jagadeeshg@cder.fda.gov

JAGANNATHAN, KANNAN, THEORETICAL HIGH ENERGY PHYSICS. **Personal Data:** b Madras, India, November 4, 1954. **Education:** Univ Madras, India, BS, 1973; Indian Inst Technol, Madras, MS, 1975; Univ Rochester, PhD (physics), 1980. **Professional Experience:** PROF PHYSICS, AMHREST COL, as of 2005; assoc prof physics, Amhrest Col, beginning 1987; asst prof, Amherst Col, 1981-1987; res assoc physics, Univ Rochester, 1980-1981. **Memberships:** Am Phys Soc; Am Asn Physics Teachers; Am Math Asn. **Research Statement & Publications:** Theoretical high energy physics; elementary particle physics; foundations of quantum mechanics. **Mailing Address:** Dept Physics Amherst Col, Amherst, MA 01002. **E-Mail:** kjagannathan@amherst.edu

JAGANNATHAN, SINGANALLUR N, NUTRITIONAL BIOCHEMISTRY, BIOCHEMICAL PATHOLOGY. **Personal Data:** b Coonoor, India, March 10, 1934; m 1968, c 2. **Education:** Univ Bombay, BSc, 1954, MSc, 1959, PhD (biochem), 1962. **Professional Experience:** PROF EMER PATH, SCH MED, WVA UNIV, as of 2005; assoc prof nutrit, Sch Dent, WVa Univ, beginning 1979; assoc prof path & biochem, dept path, sch med, WVa Univ, Mmorgantown, beginning 1977; asst prof path & biochem, Sch Dent, 1974-1977; fel, Coun Arteriosclerosis, Am Heart Asn, 1972; res scientist, lipid, lipoprotein & biochem, Col Med, Univ Iowa, 1970-1974; Brit Coun fel, 1964; Nat Res Coun Can fel nutrit biochem, Queen's Univ, Kingston, Ont, 1962-1964; res asst to sr resofficer, Indian Coun Med Res, Nat Inst Nutrit, 1956-1970. **Memberships:** Am Inst Nutrit; Am Soc Clin Nutrit; fel Am Heart Asn. **Research Statement & Publications:** Lipid and proteoglycans in relation to human atherosclerosis; platelet function; human nutrition; iron metabolism. **Mailing Address:** Dept Path, Robert C Byrd Health Sci Ctr, WVa Univ, Morgantown, WV 26506-9203. **Fax:** 304-293-1627. **E-Mail:** snjagannathan@hsc.wvu.edu

JAGEL, KENNETH I(RWIN), JR, CHEMICAL ENGINEERING. **Personal Data:** b Jamaica, NY, February 2, 1927; m 1951, c 2. **Education:** Columbia Univ, BSc, 1951, MSc, 1953, DEngSc, 1961. **Professional Experience:** PRES, TRAILTREE ASSOCS, 1989-; exec engr, Engelhard Corp, 1985-1989; dir prod develop, Engelhard Corp, 1982-1985; dir qual & mfg serv, Engelhard Corp, 1981-1982; dir prod assurance, Engelhard Minerals & Chem Corp, 1973-1981; mgr process eng & develop, Engelhard Minerals & Chem Corp, 1972-1973; mgr mfg, Engelhard Minerals & Chem Corp, 1971-1972; eng assoc, Mobil Res & Develop Corp, 1968-1971; group leader, Mobil Res & Develop Corp, 1965-1968; sr res engr, Socony Mobil Oil Co, Inc, 1959-1965; res engr, Socony Mobil Oil Co, Inc, 1957-1959; res asst, Columbia Univ, 1955-1957; Asst chem eng, Columbia Univ, 1951-1953. **Memberships:** AAAS; fel Am Inst Chem; Am Chem Soc; Am Inst Chem Engrs; Am Soc Testing & Mat. **Research Statement & Publications:** Catalyst manufacture; auto-exhaust emission control catalysts; cracking catalysts; oil shale retorting processes; distillation equipment. **Mailing Address:** Trailtree Assoc, Box 112, Stanton, NJ 08885.

JAGENDORF, ANDRE TRIDON, PLANT PHYSIOLOGY, BIOCHEMISTRY. **Personal Data:** b New York, NY, October 21, 1926; m 1952, Jean; c Suzanne, Judith & Daniel. **Education:** Cornell Univ, AB, 1948; Yale Univ, PhD (plant sci), 1951. **Honors & Awards:** Kettering Res Award, Am Soc Plant Physiologists, 1963, Kettering Award Photosyn, 1978; Charles Reid Barnes Award, 1989-. **Professional Experience:** LIBERTY HYDE BAILEY EMER PROF, CORNELL UNIV, 1997-; Liberty Hyde Bailey prof, Cornell Univ, 1981-1996; prof plant physiol, Cornell Univ, 1966-1996; Weizmann fel, 1962; from asst prof to prof biol, with McCollum-Pratt Inst, 1953-1966; from asst prof to prof biol, Johns Hopkins Univ, 1953-1966; Merck fel, 1951-1953; res assoc bot, Univ Calif, Los Angeles, 1951-1953. **Memberships:** Nat Acad Sci; Am Soc Photobiol; Am Soc Cell Biol; Am Soc Plant Physiol (pres, 1967-1968); fel AAAS; Am Acad Arts & Sci. **Research Statement & Publications:** Photosynthetic phosphorylation; biochemistry; chloroplast biogenesis; chloroplast DNA repair and recombination enzymes; plant salt stress. **Mailing Address:** Plant Biol Sect Cornell Univ, 261 Plant Sci Bldg, Ithaca, NY 14853. **Fax:** 607-255-5407. **E-Mail:** atj1@cornell.edu

JAGERMAN, DAVID LEWIS, MATHEMATICS, ELECTRICAL ENGINEERING. **Personal Data:** b August 27, 1923; m 1951, c 3. **Education:** Cooper Union Univ, BEE, 1949; NY Univ, MS, 1954, PhD (math), 1962. **Professional Experience:** CONSULT MATH, C & C REASEARCH LAB, NEC LABS, 1989-; distinguished mem tech staff, AT&TBell Labs, 1986-1989; prof, Stevens Inst Technol, 1967-1972; mem tech staff, AT&T Bell Labs, 1963-1986; Assoc prof math, Fairleigh Dickinson Univ, 1959-1966; staff mem math control systs, Syst Develop Corp, NJ, 1959-1964; design specialist trajectories, Gen Dynamics/Convair, Calif, 1957; staff scientist math guided missiles, Stavid Eng, NJ, 1955-1957 & 1957-1959; Sr engranalog comput, Reeves Instrument Corp, NY, 1951-1955. **Memberships:** Am Math Soc; sr mem Inst Elec & Electronics Engrs. **Research Statement & Publications:** Diophantine analysis and numerical quadrature theory with application to the mathematical properties of pseudo-random numbers; information theory; telephone traffic theory. **Mailing Address:** C & C Res Lab, NEC Labs, 4 Independence Way, Princeton, NJ 08540.

JAGGARD, DWIGHT LINCOLN, ELECTROMAGNETISM, OPTICS. **Personal Data:** b Oceanside, NY, April 14, 1948; m 1968, c 2. **Education:** Univ Wis-Madison, BSEE, 1971, MSEE, 1972; Calif Inst Technol, PhD (elec eng &appl physics), 1976. **Honorary Degrees:** MA, Univ Pa, 1982. **Professional Experience:** Dir, Ethicon Inc, 1992; assoc dean grad educ & res, Sch Eng & Appl Sci, Univ PA, 1992-1999; dir, Rohm & Haas, 1991; ed, J Electromagnetic Wave Applns, 1991-1995; dir, R&B Enterprises, 1991-1995; consult, Johns Hopkins Appl Physics Lab, 1991; consult, IDA, 1989; co-founder & pres, Main Line Waves Inc, 1988-; PROF ELEC & SYSTS ENG, MOORE SCHELEC ENG, UNIV PA, 1988-; dir, ExMSE Grad Prog, Technol & Leadership, Univ PA, 1988-1990; consult, Sohio, 1985; forensic consult, 1983-; consult, Naval Res Lab, 1982-1985; from asst prof to assoc prof, Dept Elec Eng, 1980-1988; consult, Environ Studies Lab, 1978-1981; asst prof optics & electromagnetics, Dept Elec Eng, Univ Utah, 1978-1980; res fel, Jet Propulsion Lab, Calif Inst Technol, 1976-1978; consult, Jet PropulsionLab, 1976-1978; engr imaging radar & DFB lasers, Jet Propulsion Lab, Calif Inst Technol, 1973-1976; res asst geophys & elec eng, Univ Wis-Madison, 1968-1972. **Memberships:** Fel Inst Elec & Electronics Engrs; Int Union Radio Sci; fel Optics Soc Am; SigmaXi; Electromagnetics Soc (vpres, 1985-1986, pres, 1986-1989). **Research Statement & Publications:** Electromagnetic chirality, fractal electrodynamics; inverse scattering and remote sensing; imaging and classification; light scattering from aerosols; wave interactions with knots and knotted media; chaos and fractals; imaging. **Mailing Address:** Complex Media Lab, Moore Sch Elec Eng, Univ Pa, 308 Moore Bdg 200 S 33rd St, Philadelphia, PA 19104-6390. **Fax:** 215-573-2068. **E-Mail:** jaggard@seas.upenn.edu

JAGGER, JOHN, RADIATION BIOLOGY, PHOTOBIOLOGY. **Personal Data:** b New Haven, Conn, February 22, 1924; m 1956, Mary; c Thomas & Yvonne. **Education:** Yale Univ, BS, 1949, MS, 1953, PhD (biophys), 1954. **Honors & Awards:** Lifetime Achievement Award, Am Soc Photobiol, 1991. **Professional Experience:** RETIRED; consult, Pure Pulse Technol, beginning 1993; sr lectr biol, Univ Tex, Dallas, 1991-1994; prof gen studies & biol, Univ Tex, Dallas, 1981-1986; vis prof, Univ Kyoto, Japan, 1979 & Pa State Univ, 1963; pres, US Nat Comt Photobiol, Nat Res Coun, 1978-1980; mem, US Nat Comt Photobiol, Nat Res Coun, 1975-1980; ed, Photochem & Photobiol, 1973-1975; consult, Aerojet Med & Biol Systs, 1971-1973; prof biol, Univ Tex, Dallas, 1969-1981; from assoc prof to prof biol, Southwest Ctr Advan Studies, 1965-1969; lectr, Univ Tenn, 1961-1965; biophysicist, Biol Div, Oak Ridge Nat Lab, 1956-1965; Nat Found Infantile Paralysis fel, Radium Inst, France, 1954-1956; asst, Yale Univ, 1953-1954 & Mem Hosp, NY, 1950-1951. **Memberships:** Fel AAAS; Health Physics Soc; Am Soc Photobiol(pres, 1983-1984). **Research Statement & Publications:** Effects of radiations on large molecules and cells; effects of ultraviolet on bacteria; photoprotection; effects of near ultraviolet on cell growth and membrane function; social impact of science. **Mailing Address:** 7532 Mason Dells Dr, Dallas, TX 75230-3246.

JAGIELLO, GEORGIANA MARY, GENETICS. **Personal Data:** b Boston, Mass, August 2, 1927; m 1957, Robert. **Education:** Boston Univ, AB, 1949; Tufts Univ, MD, 1955. **Honorary Degrees:** DS, Boston Univ, 1979. **Honors & Awards:** Distinguished Alumna Award, Boston Univ, 1974; Distinguished Service Award, College of Physicians & Surgeons, Columbia Univ, 1995; Sloan Hospital Award, 1997. **Professional Experience:** DAMON PROF EMER & SPEC LECTR OBSTET, GYNEC & HUMAN GENETICS, COL PHYSICIANS & SURGEONS, COLUMBIA UNIV, as of 1997; prof obstet, gynec & human genetics, Col Physicians & Surgeons, Columbia Univ, beginning 1970; res prof pediat, Sch Med, Univ Ill, Chicago Circle, 1969-1970; sr lectr cytogenetics, Guy's Hosp, London, 1966-1969; consult, Guy's Hosp, London, 1966-1969; NIH career develop award, 1965; mem, inst Advan Study, Univ Ill, 1964; asst prof, Sch Med, Univ Ill, Chicago Circle, 1961-1966; USPHS res fel cytogenetics, Guy's Hosp, London, 1960-1961; res fel, New Eng Med Ctr, Boston, 1958-1960; res fel endocrinol, Scripps Clin, La Jolla, 1957-1958; resident, New Eng Med Ctr, Boston, 1956-1957; intern med, res & Educ Hosps, Univ Ill, 1955-1956; exchange fel surg, St Bartholomew's Hosp, London, 1954. **Memberships:** Endocrine Soc; Teratology Soc; Environ Mutagen Soc; Am Soc Cell Biol; Soc Study Reproduction. **Research Statement & Publications:** Mammalian meiosis; reproductive endocrinology. **Mailing Address:** Dept Genetics, Col Physicians & Surgeons, Univ Columbia, 630 W 168th St, New York, NY 10032-8702. **Fax:** 212-923-2090.

JAGLAN, PREM S, HIGH-PERFORMANCE LIQUID CHROMATOGRAPHY, GAS-LIQUID CHROMATOGRAPHY. **Personal Data:** b India, September 17, 1929; American citizen; m 1951, Mohinder; c Vikramjit S, Samarjit S & Amarjit S. **Education:** Univ Calif, Riverside,

PhD (toxicol), 1969. **Professional Experience:** SR RES SCIENTIST IV BIOCHEM, UPJOHN CO, 1969-. **Memberships:** Am Chem Soc; Int Soc Study Xenobiotics. **Research Statement & Publications:** Separation science and identification of metabolites using chemical and instrumental methods. **Mailing Address:** 2713 Texel Dr, Kalamazoo, MI 49001. **Fax:** 269-385-7721.

JAGOE, CHARLES HENRY, ENVIRONMENTAL TOXICOLOGY, AQUATIC TOXICOLOGY. **Personal Data:** b Bethpage, NY, September 7, 1956; m 1986, Rosemary Herer; c Rebekah & William. **Education:** Clarkson Univ, BS, 1978; Univ Maine, MS, 1983, PhD (zool), 1988. **Professional Experience:** ASSOC RES ECOLOGIST, SAVANNAH RIVER ECOL LAB, UNIVGA, as of 2004; Adj asst prof, Inst Ecol, 1993-; Adj asst prof, Dept Pharmacol & Toxicol, ColPharm, Univ Ga, 1992-; asst res ecologist, Savannah River Ecol Lab, Univ Ga, beginning 1990; assoc, Div Pinelands Res, Ctr Coastal & Environ Studies, Rutgers Univ, 1988-1990; res asst, Dept Zool, 1986-1988; res assoc, Dept Zool, 1983-1986; biol technician fisheries, NatFisheries Contaminant Res Ctr, US Fish & Wildlife Serv, Field Sta Orono, 1980-1982; Teachingasst biol, Univ Maine, 1978-1980. **Memberships:** Am Fisheries Soc; Soc Environ Toxicol & Chem. **Research Statement & Publications:** Effects of pollutants, especially metals and radioactive substances on organisms; aquatic toxicology, physiological, morphological and behavioral responses of fish and amphibians to pollutants; genetic toxicology; biogeochemistry of mercury and radio-nuclides. **Mailing Address:** Savannah River Ecol Lab, PO Drawer E, Aiken, SC 29802. **Fax:** 803-725-3309. **E-Mail:** jagoe@srel.edu

JAGWANI, UTTAM, CHEMISTRY. **Education:** Maharaja Sayjirao Univ, Barada, India, MS, 1960 & PhD (Org Chem), 1969. **Professional Experience:** PROF, DEPT CHEM & PHYSICS, UNIV ARK, PINE BLUFF, as of 2005; vis assoc prof, Univ Ark med Sch, Little Rock, 1985-1986; vis assoc scientist, Brookhaven Nat lab, 1981-1983; fel, NCA & T State Univ, Greensboro, 1973-1974. **Research Statement & Publications:** Studies in flavanoid derivatives; ferrocene and bridged ferrocene derivatives and tetraphenyl porphyrin derivatives. **Mailing Address:** Dept Chem, Univ Ark, 1200 N Univ Dr, Pine Bluff, AR 71601. **E-Mail:** jagwani_u@uapb.edu

JAHANMIR, SAID, TRIBOLOGY, CERAMIC MACHINING. **Personal Data:** b Tehran, Iran, March 18, 1950; American citizen; m Feri; c Sam & Farid. **Education:** Univ Wash, BS, 1971; Mass Inst Technol, SM, 1973, PhD (mech eng), 1977. **Honors & Awards:** Dedicated Serv Award, Am Soc Mech Engrs, 1995; Int Award, SocTribologists & Lubrication Engrs, 1997. **Professional Experience:** VCHMN, CERAMIC MFG PROG, NIST, as of 2000; ed, Mach Sci & Technol J, 1997-; chmn, Versailles Proj Advan Mat & Stands, 1990-1993, Int Wear Stand Comn; group leader & div scientist, Ceramics Div, Nat Inst Stand & Technol, beginning 1987; adj prof, Dept Mech Eng, Univ Med, 1987-1997; prog dir, NSF, 1985-1987; sr staff engr, Exxon Res & Eng Co, 1980-1985; asst prof, dept mech eng, Cornell Univ, 1978-1980; lectr, Dept Mech Eng, Univ Calif, Berkeley, 1977-1978. **Memberships:** Fel Am Soc Mech Eng; fel Soc Tribologists & Lubrication Engrs. **Research Statement & Publications:** Machining, tribology and mechanical behavior of advanced materials; machinery of ceramics, mechanics of interfaces, mechanisms of wear, boundary lubrication and mechanical property testing. **Mailing Address:** Nat Inst Stand & Technol, A329 Materials Bldg, Gaithersburg, MD 20899. **Fax:** 301-9908-729. **E-Mail:** said.jahanmir@nist.gov

JAHAN-PARWAR, BEHRUS, NEUROBIOLOGY. **Personal Data:** b Ghoochan, Iran, May 26, 1938; American citizen; m 1966, c 2. **Education:** Univ Gottingen, MD, 1964, DMSc (physiol), 1965. **Professional Experience:** NSF grant, 1978-1982; Grass Found grant, 1975-1978; SR SCIENTIST NEUROBIOLOGY, WORCESTER FOUND EXP BIOL, 1973-; NIH res career develop award, 1970-1973; prin investr, NIH grants, 1969-1973, 1974-1977, 1975-1983 & 1978-1981; from asst prof to assoc prof physiol, Dept Biol, Clark Univ, 1968-1973; asst res neurophysiologist, Ment Health Res Inst, Univ Mich, 1966-1968; res assoc neurophysiol, Dept Physiol, Univ Gottingen, 1964-1966; ADJ PROF, ALBANY MED CTR. **Memberships:** Soc Neuroscience; Am Physiol Soc; Am Soc Zoologist; Europ Chemoreception Res Orgn. **Research Statement & Publications:** The elucidation of the principles of neuronal organization underlying processing of sensory information and generation and modification of behavior; neural mechanisms of chemoreception, learning and rhythmic behaviors such as feeding and locomotion. **Mailing Address:** 43 Carstead Dr, Slingerlands, NY 12159.

JAHIEL, RENE, HEALTH SERVICES RESEARCH, MICROBIOLOGY. **Personal Data:** b France, March 29, 1928; American citizen; m 1955, c 3. **Education:** NY Univ, BA, 1946; State Univ NY, MD, 1950; Columbia Univ, PhD (microbiol), 1957. **Professional Experience:** CONSULT, HEALTH SERV RES, 1989-; physician, Asn Children RetardedMental Develop, 1988-; res prof med, NY Univ, 1976-1988; prin investr, USPHS grants onseveral health res serv, 1968-1982; from res assoc prof prev med to res prof prev med, NY Univ, 1967-1976; career scientist, Health Res Coun NY, 1962-1966; asst prof pub health, Med Col, Cornell Univ, 1961-1967; asst prof path, Columbia Univ, 1959-1961; asst attend pathologist, MtSinai Hosp, NY, 1959-1961; asst prof microbiol, Sch Med, Univ Colo, 1957-1959; Expimmunologist, Nat Jewish Hosp, Denver, Colo, 1957-1959; fel, Mt Sinai Hosp, 1952-1955; res, Mt Sinai Hosp, 1951-1952; Intern, Montefiore Hosp, NY, 1950-1951. **Memberships:** NY Acad Sci; Soc Social Study Sci; Tissue Cult Asn; Am Pub Health Asn; AsnHealth Serv Res. **Research Statement & Publications:** Immunopathology; autoantibodies; tissue culture virology; tissue culture; interferon; community medicine; sociology of knowledge; health service research. **Mailing Address:** 60 E Eighth St 19 F, New York, NY 10003.

JAHN, CAROLYN L, BIOLOGY. **Education:** Cornell Univ, Graduate School of Medical Sciences, PhD (Genetics). **Professional Experience:** ASSOC PROF, CELL & MOLECULAR BIOL, NORTHWESTERN UNIV MED SCH, as of 2005. **Mailing Address:** Dept Cell & Molecular Biol Sci Northwestern Univ, 303 E Chicago Ave, Chicago, IL 60208. **E-Mail:** c-jahn@northwestern.edu

JAHN, ERNESTO, ANIMAL SCIENCE, RUMINANT NUTRITION. **Personal Data:** b Yumbel, Chile, March 29, 1942; m 1972. **Education:** Univ Concepcion, MgAgr, 1965; Va Polytech Inst & State Univ, MS, 1969, PhD (ruminant nutrit), 1974. **Professional Experience:** SR RES BIOLOGIST ANIMAL SCI, RES LABS, MERCK & CO, INC, 1974-; res asst animal sci, Va Polytech Inst & State Univ, 1972-1974; Agr engr ruminants, Inst Land & Cattle Invests, Chile, 1965-1972; RESEARCHER, INIA. **Memberships:** Latin Am Soc Animal Prod; Agron Soc Chile. **Mailing Address:** Casilla 426, Chillian, Chile.

JAHN, J RUSSELL, ANIMAL SCIENCE. **Personal Data:** b Spirit Lake, Iowa, December 2, 1926; m 1950, c 3. **Education:** SDak State Univ, BS, 1959, MS, 1960, PhD (animal sci), 1963. **Professional Experience:** RETIRED; prof animal sci & head, Dept Agr Sci, 1966-1988; assoc prof, UnivWis-Platteville, 1962-1966. **Memberships:** Am Soc Animal Sci. **Research Statement & Publications:** Artificial insemination of beef cattle. **Mailing Address:** 16864 255th Ave, Spirit Lake, IA 51360.

JAHN, LAURENCE R, migratory birds, aquatic areas; deceased, see previous edition for last biography

JAHN, LAWRENCE A, AQUATIC BIOLOGY, FISHERIES MANAGEMENT. **Personal Data:** b Cudahy, Wis, December 2, 1941; m 1966, Mary; c Nicholas & Christopher. **Education:** Univ Wis, BS, 1963; Mont State Univ, MS, 1966, PhD (zoology), 1968. **Professional Experience:** PROF EMER BIOL SCI, WESTERN ILL UNIV, as of 2004; dir, Inst Environ Mgt, 1988-; prof biol sci, Western Ill Univ, beginning 1981; from asst prof to assoc prof, Western Ill Univ, 1968-1981. **Memberships:** Am Fisheries Soc; Am Soc Ichthyol & Herpet. **Research Statement & Publications:** Fish management, ecology and life histories; aquarium management. **Mailing Address:** Dept Biol Sci, Col Arts & Sci, Western Ill Univ, 372 Waggoner Hall, Macomb, IL 61455. **Fax:** 309-298-2270. **E-Mail:** la-jahn@wiu.edu

JAHN, REINHARD, MECHANISMS OF NEURO-TRANSMITTER RELEASE. **Personal Data:** b Leverkusen, Ger. **Education:** Univ Gottingen, Ger, PhD, 1981. **Honors & Awards:** Max-Planck Res Prize, Max-Plank Inst, 1990. **Professional Experience:** ADJ PROF PHARMACOL, SCH MED, YALE UNIV, beginning 1997; DIR, MAX PLANCK INST BIOPHYS CHEM, GERMAN, beginning 1997; assoc prof pharmacol & cell biol, Yale Univ, 1991-1997; ASSOC INVESTR, HOWARD HUGHES MED INST, beginning 1991; group leader, Max-Planck Inst Psychol, 1986-1991; asst prof microbiol, Rockefeller Univ, 1985-1986; fel, Rockefeller Univ, 1983-1985; fel, Univ Gottingen, Ger, 1981-1983. **Memberships:** Am Soc Cell Biol; Am Soc Neuro Sci; Am Soc Biochem & Molecular Biol. **Mailing Address:** Dept Pharmacol, Sch Med, Yale Univ, PO Box 9812, New Haven, CT 06520. **Fax:** 207-737-1763. **E-Mail:** reinhard.jahn@yale.edu

JAHN, ROBERT G(EORGE), ENGINEERING PHYSICS, HUMAN/MACHINE ANOMALIES. **Personal Data:** b Kearny, NJ, April 1, 1930; m Catherine; c Eric G, Jill E, Nina M & Dawn A. **Education:** Princeton Univ, BS, 1951, MA, 1953, PhD (physics), 1955. **Honorary Degrees:** DSc, Andhra Univ, Vishakhapatnam, India, 1986. **Honors & Awards:** Curtis W McGraw Res Award, Am Soc Eng Educ, 1969 Medal for Outstanding Achievement in Electric Propulsion, 2005. **Professional Experience:** PROF & DEAN EMER AEROSPACE SCI, PRINCETON UNIV, as of 2006; mem bd dirs, Roy F Weston Inc, 1988- 1998; technol comt, Hercules Inc, 1987- 2001; strategic comt, Hercules Inc, 1987- 2001; compensation comt, Hercules Inc, 1987- 1989; mem bd dir, Hercules Inc, 1985-2001; mem bd dirs, Hercules Inc, 1985- 2001; vpres & counr, Soc Sci Explor, 1984-; mem, Soc Sci Explor, 1983- 1994; mem bd dirs, John E Fetzer Inst, 1983-1994; vchmn, John E Fetzer Inst, 1983; mem nat adv coun space systs & technol adv comt, NASA, 1978-; mem nominating comt, Assoc Univs Inc, Wash, DC, 1978-1979; chmn bd, Assoc Univs Inc, Wash, DC, 1977-1979; mem res & technol adv coun comt space propulsion & power, NASA, 1976-1977; trustee rep, Assoc Univs Inc, Wash, DC, 1974-1986; dean, Sch Eng & Appl, 1971-1986; mem res & technol adv comt space propulsion & power, NASA, 1971-1972; mem res & technol adv subcomt electrophys, NASA, 1968-1971; prof aerospace sci, Princeton Univ, beginning 1967; from asst prof to assoc prof, Princeton Univ, 1962-1967; asst prof jet propulsion, Calif Inst Technol, 1958-1961; asst prof physics, Lehigh Univ, 1955-1958. **Memberships:** fel Am Inst Aeronaut & Astronaut; fel Am Phys Soc; Am Inst Phys; vpres Soc Sci Expl; Am Soc Psych ical Res. **Research Statement & Publications:** Plasma propulsion; high temperature gasdynamics and fluid mechanics; shock tubes; plasmajets; ionization phenomena; electromagnetic wave propagation in ionized gases; engineering anomalies and human/machine interactions. **Mailing Address:** Dept Mech & Aerospace Eng, Princeton Univ, D-334 EQ SEAS, Princeton, NJ 08544-5263. **Fax:** 609-258-1993. **E-Mail:** rgjahn@princeton.edu

JAHNCKE, CATHERINE LEE, PHYSICS. **Personal Data:** b New Orleans, La, November 3, 1964. **Education:** Auburn Univ, BS, 1988; NC State Univ, PhD (physics), 1996. **Honors & Awards:** Assoc Res Corp Coltrell College Sci Award, 2001. **Professional Experience:** PROF PHYSICS, ST LAWRENCE UNIV, 1995-. **Memberships:** Am Phys Soc Sigma Xi, Am Asn Physics Teachers. **Research Statement & Publications:** Optical investigation of materials with sub wavelength resolution using near-field optical microscopy/spectroscopy. **Mailing Address:** Dept Physics, St Lawrence Univ, Canton, NY 13617. **Fax:** 315-229-7421.

JAHNGEN, EDWIN GEORG EMIL, ORGANIC CHEMISTRY, BIORGANIC CHEMISTRY. **Personal Data:** b Pittsburgh, Pa, January 8, 1946. **Education:** Bates Col, BSc, 1968; Univ Vt, PhD (org chem), 1974. **Professional Experience:** PROF, DEPT CHEM, UNIV MASS, LOWELL, as of 2005; consult, Med Sch, Univ Conn, 1978-; asst prof org chem, Wilkes Col, 1978-; group leader, New Eng Nuclear Corp, 1976-1978; res assoc nat prod, Univ BC, 1974-1976; NIH fel, Nat Res Coun, Univ BC, 1974-1976; chemist org synthesis, Polaroid Corp, 1968-1970; chemist, Water Improv Comn, Maine, 1967-1968. **Memberships:** Am Chem Soc; Sigma Xi. **Research Statement & Publications:** Studies of bioorganic systems; synthesis and modification of exogenous; endogenous drugs and hormones. **Mailing Address:** Dept Chem, Univ Mass, Lowell, 265 Riverside St, Lowell, MA 01854-2882. **Fax:** 978-934-4078. **E-Mail:** edwin_jahngen@uml.edu

JAHNS, HANS O(TTO), PETROLEUM ENGINEERING, ARCTIC ENGINEERING. **Personal Data:** b Kamen, Ger, September 4, 1931; m 1959, c 5. **Education:** Clausthal Tech Univ, dipl, 1955, dipl, 1956, Dr(Ing), 1961. **Professional Experience:** RES MGR, EXXON PROD RES CO, as of 2005; mem, Polar Adv Comt, NSF, 1985-1987; sr res scientist, Exxon Prod Res Co, beginning 1982; res scientist, Jersey Prod Res Co, Stand Oil Co NJ, Okla, 1980-1982; mem adv bd, Geophys Inst, Univ Alaska, 1978-1987; sr res adv, Jersey Prod Res Co, Stand Oil Co NJ, Okla, 1977-1980; mem, Polar Res Bd, 1976-1984; mem, Permafrost Comt, Nat Res Coun, 1975-1980; res adv, Jersey Prod Res Co, Stand Oil Co NJ, Okla, 1973-1977; res assoc, Jersey Prod Res Co, Stand Oil Co NJ, Okla, 1968-1973; res engr, Jersey Prod Res Co, Stand Oil Co NJ, Okla, 1965-1968; res engr prod res, Jersey Prod Res Co, Stand Oil Co NJ, Okla, 1962-1965; reservoir engr, Reservoir Lab, Wintershall AG, Ger, 1959-1962; res asst petrol eng, Inst Drilling& Petrol Prod, Clausthal Tech Univ, 1956-1959. **Memberships:** Soc Petrol Engrs; AAAS; Am Petrol Inst. **Research Statement & Publications:** Petroleum reservoir description; oceanography; arctic research; arctic engineering; sea ice mechanics; expert system, production geophysics; oil spill cleanup technology. **Mailing Address:** 8840 Larston St, Houston, TX 77055.

JAHNS, MONROE FRANK, PHYSICS. **Personal Data:** b Seguin, Tex, May 16, 1928; m 1954, c 2. **Education:** Tex A & M Univ, BS, 1949; Univ Tex, Austin, MA, 1964, PhD (physics), 1966. **Professional Experience:** RETIRED; assoc physicist & assoc prof biophysics, Univ Tex Anderson Hosp & Tumor Inst, Houston, 1968-1988; advan sr fel med physics, Univ Tex Anderson Hosp & Tumor Inst, Houston, 1967-1968; asst prof, Sam Houston State Col, 1966-1967; instr physics, Univ Tex, Austin, 1965-1966. **Memberships:** Am Phys Soc; Soc Nuclear Med; Am Asn Physicists Med. **Mailing Address:** 6319 Vanderbilt St, Houston, TX 77005.

JAHODA, FRANZ C, PLASMA DIAGNOSTICS, FIBER OPTIC SENSORS. **Personal Data:** b Vienna, Austria, September 16, 1930; American citizen; m 1955, c 2. **Education:**

Swarthmore Col, BA, 1951; Cornell Univ, PhD, 1957. **Professional Experience:** RETIRED; group leader, Los Alamos Nat Lab, 1974-1991; mem staff, Inst Voor Plasmafysica, Jutphaas, Neth, 1972-1973; mem staff, Culham Lab, Abingdon, Eng, 1964-1965; mem staff, Los Alamos Nat Lab, 1957-1991. **Memberships:** Optical Soc Am; Inst Elec & Electronics Engrs. **Research Statement & Publications:** Plasma physics; spectroscopy; lasers; optical diagnostics. **Mailing Address:** 819 Bishops Lodge Rd, Santa Fe, NM 87501.

JAHODA, GERALD, information science; deceased, see previous edition for last biography

JAHODA, JOHN C, ECOLOGY, MAMMALOGY. **Personal Data:** b Dalhart, Tex, February 9, 1944. **Education:** Univ Conn, BA, 1966; Okla State Univ, PhD (zoology), 1969. **Professional Experience:** PROF BIOL, DEPT BIOL SCI, BRIDGEWATER STATE COL, 1981-; consult, Raytheon Serv Co, 1970-; from asst prof to assoc prof, Bridgewater StateCol, 1970-1981; asst prof biol, State Univ NY Col Geneseo, 1969-1970; mem, Corp Bermuda Biosta Res. **Memberships:** Am Soc Mammalogists; Ecol Soc Am; Sigma Xi; Soc Marine Mammal. **Research Statement & Publications:** Ecology and ethology of mammals; salt marsh ecology; pollution of salt marshes. **Mailing Address:** Dept Biol Sci, Bridgewater Moakley Ctr, Bridgewater State Col, Bridgewater, MA 02325. **Fax:** 508-531-4635. **E-Mail:** jjahoda@bridgew.edu

JAICKS, FREDERICK G, ENGINEERING. **Professional Experience:** RETIRED; chmn, Inland Steel, Chicago. **Memberships:** Nat Acad Eng. **Mailing Address:** Meadow Lane, Lakeside, MI 49116.

JAIN, AHAMINDRA, PHYSICAL ORGANIC CHEMISTRY. **Education:** Harvard Univ, PhD (Organic Chem). **Professional Experience:** LECTR, DEPT CHEM, UNIV CALIF, BERKELEY, as of 2005. **Research Statement & Publications:** Organic chemistry. **Mailing Address:** Dept Chem, Univ Calif, Berkeley, 325 Latimer Hall, Berkeley, CA 94720-1460. **Fax:** 510-642-9675. **E-Mail:** ahamindra@cchem.berkeley.edu

JAIN, ANANT VIR, TOXICOLOGY. **Personal Data:** b Sardhana, India, March 15, 1940; American citizen; m 1971, c 2. **Education:** Meerut Univ, India, BS, 1959, MS, 1962; Purdue Univ, PhD (chem), 1972. **Professional Experience:** SR PUB SERV ASSOC, ATHENS DIAG LAB, UNIV GA, as of 2004; HEAD, TOXICOL SECT, ATHENS DIAG LAB, UNIV GA, 1997-; mem, Comt Prof Develop, 1996-; sr anal toxicologist, Univ Ga, 1990-1991; pres, Southeast Regional Sect Assoc, Off Analytical Chemists, 1986-1987; mem, AOAC Comt, Regional Sect, 1985-1990; assoc anal toxicologist, Univ Ga, 1981-1990; anal chemist, Univ Ga, 1974-1981; res assoc, Purdue Univ, 1972-1974; chem analyst, Purdue Univ, 1966-1972; res asst, Purdue Univ, 1964-1966; lectr chem, DAV Col, India, 1962-1964. **Memberships:** Am Chem Soc; Am Asn Vet Lab Diagnosticians; Am Acad Vet & Comp Toxicol; Asn Off Anal Chem Int. **Research Statement & Publications:** Analytical methods for the detection of poisons, drugs, and metals from biological and agricultural materials; analytical chemistry and toxicology of poisons; mycotoxin decontamination; diagnostic laboratory service; methods validation. **Mailing Address:** Athens Diag Lab Col Vet Med Univ Ga, 110 E Clayton St Ste 725, Athens, GA 30602. **Fax:** 706-542-5977. **E-Mail:** jain.a@adl300.vet.uga.edu

JAIN, ANIL KUMAR, ELECTRICAL ENGINEERING. **Personal Data:** b India, January 21, 1946. **Education:** Indian Inst Technol, Kharagpur, BTech, 1967; Univ Rochester, MS, 1969, PhD (elec eng), 1971. **Honors & Awards:** Image Coding Achievement Award, Int Picture Coding Symp, Tokyo, 1977; Donald G Fink Prize Award, Inst Elec & Electronics Engrs, 1983. **Professional Experience:** DEPT COMPUT SCI ENG, MICH STATE UNIV, as of 2004; proj dir, Univ Micro Projs, 1982-1986; proj dir, Off Naval Res, 1982-1984; PROF ELEC ENG, UNIV CALIF, DAVIS, 1979-; proj dir, ArmyRes Off, 1978-1985; actg assoc prof, Univ Calif, Davis, 1978-1979; proj dir, Naval Ocean Syst Ctr grant, San Diego, 1978-1979; proj dir, Army Res Off grant, 1976-1978; proj dir, Naval Undersea Ctr, San Diego, 1976-1977; proj dir, NASA res grant, 1975-1976; assoc prof elec eng, State Univ NY, Buffalo, 1974-1978; asst prof, Univ Southern Calif, 1971-1974; fel, Univ Southern Calif, 1970-1971; Topical ed, J Optical Soc Am. **Memberships:** Sr mem Inst Elec & Electronics Engrs; Optical Soc Am. **Research Statement & Publications:** Digital image processing; signal processing; pattern recognition; communication theory; systems theory; computer applications; real time systems. **Mailing Address:** Dept Comput Sci, Mich State Univ, 3115 Eng Bldg, East Lansing, MI 48824. **Fax:** 517-432-1061.

JAIN, ANRUDH KUMAR, POPULATION STUDIES, PUBLIC HEALTH & EPIDEMIOLOGY. **Personal Data:** b India, October 23, 1941; m 1971, Usha; c Anupma & Aparna. **Education:** Agra Univ, BSc, 1958; Delhi Univ, MA, 1960; Univ Mich, Ann Arbor, MA, 1965, PhD (sociol), 1968. **Professional Experience:** VPRES & DIR, INT PROG DIV, POP COUN as of 2005; sr dir, Policy & Regional Progs, Int Progs Div, Pop Coun, as of 2004; DIR PROG, DEMOGRAPHIC IMPACTS DEVELOP PROG, POP COUN, 1994-; dep dir, Progs Div, 1981-1994; SR ASSOC, DEMOGRAPHIC IMPACTS DEVELOPPROG, POP COUN, 1980-; vis scholar, Univ Mich, 1979-1980; assoc, Int Prog Div, Pop Coun, 1976-1979; asst dir biostatist, Pop Coun, Ny, 1973-1976; staff assoc, Pop Coun, India, 1971-1973; prog assoc family planning, Ford Found, India, 1970-1971; res assoc pop studies & asst prof sociol, Univ Mich, Ann Arbor, 1968-1970. **Memberships:** Int Union Sci Study Pop; Pop Asn Am; Indian Asn Study Pop. **Research Statement & Publications:** Consequences of population growth and determinants of fertility, fecundability, lactation and postpartum amenorrhea; assessing quality of family planning and health services; has edited, authored, or co-authored five books and approximately 70 research papers. **Mailing Address:** Pop Coun, One Dag Hammarskjold Plaza, New York, NY 10017. **Fax:** 212-755-6052. **E-Mail:** ajain@popcouncil.org

JAIN, ARIDAMAN KUMAR, APPLIED STATISTICS. **Personal Data:** b Delhi, India, April 14, 1938; m 1963, Nirmal; c Anjali & Arvind. **Education:** Delhi Univ, BSc, 1957; Purdue Univ, PhD (statist & indust eng), 1968. **Professional Experience:** Spec lectr, NJ Inst Technol, as of 2006; CONSULT, as of 2003; adj prof, Monmouth Col, 1993-; adj prof, NJ Inst Technol, 1993; DISTINGUISHED MEM TECH STAFF, BELL LAB INNOVATIONS, LUCENT TECHNOLOGIES, 1992-; dist mgr, Bell Labs, 1987-1991; distinguished mem tech staff, Bell Labs, 1984-1986; mem tech staff, Bell Labs, 1967-1983; statistician, Tata Oil Mills, Bombay, 1961-1963; Statistician, SQC Units Indian Statist Inst, Baroda & Bombay, 1960-1961. **Memberships:** Am Statist Asn; Oper Res Soc Am; Am Soc Qual Control; Inst Elec & Electronics Engrs. **Research Statement & Publications:** Data analysis; design of experiments; statistical modelling; monte-carlo simulation; survey sampling; quality assurance. **Mailing Address:** Bell Labs Innovations, Lucent Technologies, 600 Mountain Ave, Murray Hill, NJ 07974-0636. **E-Mail:** jain@adm.njit.edu

JAIN, ATUL, COMMUNICATIONS, SATELLITE SYSTEMS. **Personal Data:** b Dehradun, India, March 26, 1950. **Education:** Calif Inst Technol, BS & MS, 1970, PhD (elec eng/ physics), 1974. **Professional Experience:** TECHNICAL Fel BOEING, 1981-; mem tech staff, Jet Propulsion Lab, 1975-1981; res fel, Calif Inst Technol, 1973-1975; consult, Jet Propulsion Lab, 1973-1974. **Research Statement & Publications:** Pioneering undersanding of coherent speckle noise; invention and development of the inverse synthetic aperture radar and associated super-resolution imaging techniques; theoretical understanding of imaging of ocean waves with the synthetic aperture radar; airport surveillance radar systems; low observable systems; antennas, RCS and antenna pattern measurements; optics. **Mailing Address:** PO Box 45863, Los Angeles, CA 90045-0863. **E-Mail:** atul.jain@boeing.com

JAIN, DULI CHANDRA, MOLECULAR SPECTROSCOPY, DATABASE SYSTEMS. **Personal Data:** b Mungaoli, India, February 11, 1929; m 1951, Sunita; c Avanindra & Ahamindra. **Education:** Banaras Hindu Univ, BS, 1949; Univ Calcutta, MS, 1951, DPhil(sci), 1963; City Univ NY, MS, 1974. **Professional Experience:** PROF PHYSICS, YORK COL, CITY UNIV NY, 1986-; vis prof admin comput systs, Hofstra Univ, Hempstead, NY, 1980-1981; Adj assoc prof comput sci, Queens Col, 1978-; from asst prof to assoc prof, York Col, NY, 1971-1985; lectr, York Col, NY, 1968-1970; asst res scientist chem, NY Univ, 1964-1968; res fel, Saha Inst Nuclear Physics, India, 1962-1964; asst prof, Holkar Sci Col, India, 1960-1962; lectr physics, Holkar Sci Col, India, 1954-1960. **Memberships:** Am Phys Soc; Sigma Xi. **Research Statement & Publications:** Intensity distribution in molecular band systems; potential energy curves and vibrational wave functions of diatomic molecules; programming systems for computers; quantum chemical study of molecular complexes. **Mailing Address:** Dept Physics, York Col City Univ NY, 2F09a, Acad Core Bldg, Jamaica, NY 11451. **E-Mail:** dcj@york.cuny.edu

JAIN, FAQUIR C, CONDENSED MATTER PHYSICS. **Personal Data:** b India, March 23, 1946. **Education:** Agra Univ, BS, 1962, MS, 1963; Roorkee Univ, BSEE, 1965; Indian Inst Technol, MSEE, 1968; Univ Conn, PhD, 1973. **Professional Experience:** Prog dir, Univ Conn, beginning 1993; res scientist, NSF, 1989-1992; PROF ELEC & COMPUT ENG, UNIV CONN, 1987-; dept head, Elec & Systs Eng, 1986-1990; from asst prof to assoc prof, Univ Conn, 1973-1987. **Memberships:** Am Phys Soc; sr mem Inst Elec & Electronics Engrs; Sigma Xi; Optical Soc Am; Nat Asn Corrosion Engrs; Int Soc Hybrid Microelectonics; Int Soc Optical Eng. **Research Statement & Publications:** Electrical and optical processes in semi-conductors and their device applications. **Mailing Address:** Dept Elec & Comput Eng, Univ Conn, U-1157 ITE Bldg 465 371 Fairfield Rd, Storrs, CT 06269-1157. **Fax:** 860-486-2447. **E-Mail:** fcj@engr.uconn.edu

JAIN, HIMANSHU, ELECTRONIC & PHOTONIC MATERIALS, INORGANIC GLASSES. **Personal Data:** b Mainpuri, India, January 20, 1955; American citizen; m 1990, Sweety; c Isha H & Raina H. **Education:** Kanpur Univ, BS, 1970; Banaras Univ, MS, 1972; Indian Inst Technol, Kanpur, MTech, 1974; Columbia Univ, Eng, ScD(metall & mat sci), 1979. **Honors & Awards:** Fulbright Lecturer-Scholar Award for UK, 1997; Diamond chair Professorship, 1997, Lehigh Univ; Zachariasen Award, 1997, by J Non-crystalline solids, a biennial international prize for outstanding. **Professional Experience:** DIAMOND CHMN & PROF MAT SCI & ENG, LEHIGH UNIV, 1993-; vis prof, Univ Dortmund, Ger & Nat Hellenic Res Ctr, Athens, Greece, 1991-1992; Humboldt fel, Ger, 1991; asst prof to assoc prof ceramics, Lehigh Univ, 1985-1993; guest lectr, Krumb Sch Mines, Columbia Univ, 1985; consult, Mass Inst Technol Sch Chem Eng Pract, Brookhaven Nat Lab, Upton, NY, 1985; vis scientist, Inst Physics, Univ Dortmund, Ger, 1984 & Advan Ctr Mat Sci, Indian Inst Technol, 1985; assoc metallurgist nuclear waste, Brookhaven Nat Lab, Upton, NY, 1982-1985; postdotoral appointee, Argonne Nat Lab, Ill, 1980-1982. **Memberships:** fel Am Ceramic Soc; Ceramic Educ Coun Materials Research Soc (TMS). **Research Statement & Publications:** Electrical relaxation, photonic response, conductivity and dielectric properties of amorphous and crystalline ceramics; surface conduction and diffusion; effect of radiation on transport properties; diffusion and nuclear spin relaxation in glasses; corrosion of glass; sintering of ceramics; physical and chemical structure of glasses; author of various articles. **Mailing Address:** Dept Mat Sci & Eng, Whitaker Lab, Lehigh Univ, 5 E Packer Ave, Bethlehem, PA 18015. **Fax:** 610-758-4244. **E-Mail:** hj00@lehigh.edu

JAIN, KAILASH CHANDRA, FABRICATION METHODS, MICROSTRUCTURES. **Personal Data:** b Indore, January 1, 1943; American citizen; m 1969, c 3. **Education:** Banaras Hindu Univ, India, BEng, 1964; State Univ NY, Stony Brook, MS, 1969, PhD (mat sci), 1972; Hofstra Univ, NY, MBA, 1978. **Professional Experience:** Recruiter, Electronics Dept, Gen Motors Res Lab, 1980-1986; STAFF RESENGR ELECTRONICS, GEN MOTORS RES LABS, WARREN, MICH, 1979-; device engrintegrated circuits mfg, RCA Corp, West Palm Beach, Fla, 1977-1979; sr process engr integratedcircuits mfg, Gen Instrument Corp, NY, 1973-1976; res, Dept Earth & Space Sci, State Univ NY, Stony Brook, 1972-1973; consult, 1970-1976; teaching asst & lab instr variety, Dept Mat Sci, State Univ NY, Stony Brook, 1966-1972; sci officer, Alloy Dept, AEC India, 1964-1966. **Memberships:** Sr mem Inst Elec & Electronics Engrs. **Research Statement & Publications:** Develop new materials and processes to realize novel sensors, power devices, and integrated circuits; propose improved fabrication methods and device structures; develop processes to improve current product; net shape metal parts; granted seven patents. **Mailing Address:** 1939 Spiceway Dr, Troy, MI 48098.

JAIN, MAHAVIR, EXPERIMENTAL NUCLEAR PHYSICS. **Personal Data:** b Barther, India, January 1, 1941; American citizen; m 1966. **Education:** Agra Univ, BSc, 1957; Univ Delhi, MSc, 1959; Univ Md, Col Park, PhD (physics), 1969. **Honors & Awards:** Res Publ Award, Naval Res Lab, 1975. **Professional Experience:** MEM STAFF, LOS ALAMOS NAT LAB, 1978-; guest scientist, Los Alamos Sci Lab, 1974-1978; res assoc nuclear physics, Tex A&M Univ, 1971-1978; fel nuclear physics, Univ Man, 1969-1971. **Memberships:** Am Phys Soc. **Research Statement & Publications:** Direct interactions, especially quasi-free scattering from nucleons and clusters; excited states, breakup and polarization in three nucleon systems, neutron-proton scattering; polarization and pion production at LAMPF energies and transport calculations; diagnostics and simulations. **Mailing Address:** Los Alamos Nat Lab, PO Box 1663, Los Alamos, NM 87545. **Fax:** 505-665-4251. **E-Mail:** mvj@lanl.gov

JAIN, MAHENDRA KUMAR, BIOPHYSICS, NEUROSCIENCES. **Personal Data:** b Ujjain, India, October 12, 1938; m 1974, c 1. **Education:** Holker Col, India, Bsc, 1957; Vikram Univ, India, MSc, 1959; Weizmann Inst Sci, PhD (chem), 1967. **Professional Experience:** Vis prof chem, Indian Inst Sci, 1993-1994; PROF BIOCHEM, UNIV DEL, 1981-; from asst prof to assoc prof, Univ Del, 1973-1981; res assoc biochem, Ind Univ, Bloomington, 1967-1973; lectr chem, Educ Dept, Govt Madhya Pradesh, India, 1959-1964 & Punjab Univ, 1964-1965. **Memberships:** Biophys Soc; Fed Am Soc Exp Biol. **Research Statement & Publications:** Membrane structure and function; mode of action of phospholipases on bilayers; reconstitution; effect of drugs on the phase properties of membrane; inhibitors of phospholipase. **Mailing Address:** Dept Chem & Biochem, Univ Del, Newark, DE 19716-0001. **Fax:** 302-831-6335. **E-Mail:** mkjain@udel.edu

JAIN, MAHENDRA KUMAR, MATHEMATICAL ANALYSIS. **Personal Data:** b Muzaffarnagar, India, January 4, 1929; m 1949, Chandra; c Sushil, Anil, Dave & Parker. **Education:** Univ Lucknow, BS, 1948, MS, 1951, PhD (math), 1955. **Professional Experience:**

PROF MATH, UNIV TENN, MARTIN, 1983-; assoc prof, Univ Tenn, Martin, 1975-1983; asst prof, Wva Univ, 1969-1970; res instr, Wva Univ, 1967-1969; Agency IntDevelop fel, Univ Wis, 1963-1964; asst prof, Bihar Inst Technol, Sindri, 1959-1972; H D JainCol, Magadh Univ, 1955-1959; Vidyant Col, Univ Lucknow, 1952-1955; lectr math, M J InterCol Asara, 1951-1952. **Memberships:** Am Math Soc. **Research Statement & Publications:** Complex variables; integral transforms. **Mailing Address:** 2101 Meadowbrook Dr, Martin, TN 38237.

JAIN, NARESH C, TOXICOLOGY, ANALYTICAL CHEMISTRY. **Personal Data:** b Meerut, India, December 30, 1932; m 1987, Plomp. **Education:** Univ Lucknow, BS, 1951, MS, 1954; Univ Calif, Berkeley, PhD (criminol/toxicol), 1965. **Professional Experience:** PROF EMER PHARMACOL & TOXICOL, SCH MED, UNIV SOUTHERN CALIF, as of 2005; DIR TOXICOL, NAT TOXICOL LABS, as of 2005; consult, USAF, 1985-; consult, USN, 1983-; prof pharmacol & toxicol & prof community med & pub health, Sch Med, Univ Southern Calif, beginning 1978; mem clin toxicol devices panel, Food & Drug Admin, 1975-; assoc prof community med & pub health, Nat Toxicol Labs, 1972-1978; assoc prof pharmacol & toxicol, Nat Toxicol Labs, 1971-1978; assoc dir toxicol, SchMed, Ind Univ, 1966-1971; res toxicologist, Univ Calif, Berkeley, 1963-1966; sci officer toxicol, Govt Brit Guiana, 1959-1962. **Memberships:** Soc Toxicol; Am Acad Forensic Sci; Int Asn Toxicol; Soc Forensic Toxicologists. **Research Statement & Publications:** Toxicology both clinical and forensic; application of instrumentation in the detection of drugs from biological fluids; drug metabolism; interaction of drugs, marijuana and alcohol; laboratory services to drug abuse and overdose patients; environmental monitoring of toxic wastes, herbicides, and pesticides; expert witness in toxicology; interpretation of alcohol and drug levels for impairment; environmental toxicology. **Mailing Address:** Nat Toxicol Labs, 5451 Rockledge Dr, Buena Park, CA 90621. **Fax:** 714-521-3896. **E-Mail:** ncjain@pacbell.net

JAIN, NEMICHAND B, INDUSTRIAL PHARMACY, PHYSICAL PHARMACY. **Personal Data:** b Akola, India, July 1, 1951; m 1978, c 2. **Education:** Nagpur Univ, India, BSc, 1971; Univ Bombay, India, Bsc, 1974; Univ Kans, MS, 1976, PhD (pharmaceut), 1978. **Professional Experience:** DIR, PHARMACEUT RES & DEVELOP, BRISTOL-MYERS SQUIBB, as of 2004; res group leader & sect head, Bristol-Myers Squibb Co, beginning 1985; lab supvr, E R Squibb & Sons, 1982-1985; res investr, E R Squibb & Sons, 1980-1982; res pharmacist, Wyeth Labs, subsid Am Home Prod Corp, 1978-1980; res asst, Univ Kans, 1974-1978. **Memberships:** Am Pharmaceut Asn; Acad Pharmaceut Sci; Controlled Release Soc; AAAS. **Research Statement & Publications:** Development of pharmaceutical dosage forms; controlled drug delivery; in-vitro-in-vivo evaluation of dosage forms; drug stability degradation mechanisms; physio-chemical evaluation of drug entities. **Mailing Address:** Pharmaceut R&D, Bristol Myers Squibb, One Squibb Dr, New Brunswick, NJ 08903. **E-Mail:** jainn@bms.com

JAIN, PIYARE LAL, PHYSICS, RELATIVISTIC HEAVY ION INTERACTION. **Personal Data:** b Punjab, India, December 11, 1921; American citizen; m 1966, Sulakshna; c Navin K & Atul. **Education:** Punjab Univ, India, BA, 1944, MA, 1948; Mich State Univ, PhD (physics), 1954. **Professional Experience:** RETIRED; prof physics, State Univ NY Buffalo, 1967-; sci adv, Am Embassy AID, New Delhi, India, 1966; Fulbright vis prof, Rajasthan Univ, India, 1965-1966; vis prof, Bristol Univ, 1961-1962; mem staff, Lawrence Radiation Lab, Univ Calif, 1961-1962; res assoc, Univ Chicago, 1959-1960; from instr to assoc prof, State Univ NY Buffalo, 1954-1967; res assoc chem, Univ Minn, 1953-1954; asst physics, Mich State Univ, 1951-1953. **Memberships:** Fel Am Phys Soc. **Research Statement & Publications:** Solid state, electron and nuclear magnetic resonance; nuclear physics; cosmic radiation and high energy physics; radiation physics; heavy ion physics. **Mailing Address:** Dept Physics, State Univ NY, Buffalo, NY 14260. **Fax:** 716-645-2507. **E-Mail:** phyjain@buffalo.edu

JAIN, RAKESH KUMAR, TUMOR PHYSIOLOGY, MICROCIRCULATION. **Personal Data:** b Lalitpur, India, December 18, 1950. **Education:** Indian Inst Technol, Kanpur, BTech, 1972; Univ Del, Newark, MChE, 1974, PhD (chem eng), 1976. **Honors & Awards:** George Tallmann Ladd Award, Carnegie Mellon Univ, 1979; Abbott Microcirculation Award, European Soc Microcirculation, 1990; Instrumentation Physiol & Med Award, Am Microcirculation Soc; 1993, 1994; Eugene M Landis Award, Microcirculatory Soc, 1996; Gerritsen Award, Microcirculatory Soc, 2002. **Professional Experience:** DIR, EDWIN L STEELE LAB TUMOR BIO, MASS GEN HOSP, 1991-; PROF, DIVHEALTH SCI & TECHNOL, MASS INST TECHNOL, 1991-; ANDREW WORK COOK PROF TUMORBIOL, HARVARD MED SCH, 1991-; AFFIL FAC, DIV HEALTH SCI & TECHNOL, MASS INST TECHNOL, 1991-; mem bd dirs, Int Inst Microcirculation, 1987-; consult, Hybritech, 1987-; mem, Pittsburg Cancer Inst, 1986-; mem comt, Am Microcirculation Soc, 1986-1988 & meeting prog comt, Biomed Eng Soc, 1986-1989; assoc mem, Ctr Fluorescence Res Biol, 1985-; dept bioengineering, Univ Calif, San Diego & dept radiol, Stanford Univ Med Sch, 1984-; John Simon Guggenheim Mem Found fel, 1983-1984; vis prof, dept chem eng, Mass Inst Technol, 1983; chmn, Nat Prog Comt Life Sci, Am Inst Chem Engrs, 1981-1984; NIH res career develop award, 1980-1985; co-chmn, Conf Thermal Characteristics Tumors, NY Acad Sci, 1979-; from asst profto prof chem & biomed eng, Carnegie Mellon Univ, 1978-1991; adj prof neurosurg, UnivPittsburgh Sch Med, 1978-1980; consult, Pathophysiol Lab, Nat Cancer Inst, 1976-1984; asstprof chem & biomed engr, Columbia Univ, 1976-1978. **Memberships:** Am Asn Cancer Res; AAAS; Am Inst Chem Engrs; Am Microcirculation Soc; Biomed Eng Soc; Int Inst Microcirculation; NY Acad Sci. **Research Statement & Publications:** Develop a quantitative understanding of physiological events in the tumor microcirculation to improve cancer detection and treatment; transport of molecules in tumors; blood flow and microcirculatory hemodynamics in tumors; physiological studies in tissues isolated tumors; heat transfer and temperature distribution in tumors; rheology of malignant and non-malignant cells; interaction of cells with vasculature; author of various articles. **Mailing Address:** Steel Lab, Depart Radiation Oncol, Mass Gen Hosp, Cox 7, Boston, MA 02114. **Fax:** 617-724-1819. **E-Mail:** jain@steele.mgh.harvard.edu

JAIN, RAKESH KUMAR, SYNTHETIC ANTIGENS, SYNTHETIC ACCEPTORS FOR GLYCOSYLTRANSFERASES. **Personal Data:** b Ajmer, Rajasthan, December 12, 1956; m Rama; c Rohit & Rohini. **Education:** Rajasthan Univ, Jaipur, India, BS, 1976, MS, 1978; Kanpur Univ, PhD (chem), 1983. **Professional Experience:** CANCER RES SCIENTIST, ROSWELL PARK CANCER INST, 1990-; sr res officer, Nat Inst Immunol, 1987-1989; res affil, Roswell Park Cancer Inst, 1984-1987; res assoc, Coun Sci Indust Res, India, beginning 1983. **Memberships:** Soc Complex Carbohydrate. **Research Statement & Publications:** Synthesis of hydrophobic glycopeptides, glycolipids and peptidylglycolipids as potential immunostimulants; synthesis of tumor associated antigens and synthesis of sulfated and sialic acid oligosaccharide as acceptors for different glycosyltransferases. **Mailing Address:** Dept Gynec Oncol Res, Roswell Park Cancer Inst, Buffalo, NY 14263. **Fax:** 716-845-3545.

JAIN, RAVINDER KUMAR, ENVIRONMENTAL ENGINEERING, INTELLIGENT SYSTEMS. **Personal Data:** b Punjab, India, October 12, 1935; American citizen. **Education:** Calif State Univ, Sacramento, BS, 1961, MS, 1968; Tex Tech Univ, PhD (civil eng), 1971; Harvard Univ, MPA, 1980. **Honors & Awards:** Sustained Super Performance Awards, US Army Corps Engr, 1972, 1973 & 1974; Res & Develop Award, US Army, 1976, Commendations for Exemplary Performance & Except Mgt Res Prog, 1982-1990; Federal Engr of the Year & Recipient Founders Gold Medal, 1989. **Professional Experience:** DEAN, SCH ENG & COMP SCI, UNIV PACIFIC, as of 2002; dir, Army Environ Policy Inst, 1990-; Churchill Col fel, Cambridge Univ, Eng, 1986; res affil, Mass Inst Technol, 1984-; exec & prof develop fel, Harvard Univ, 1979-1980; adj prof, Univ Ill, Urbana-Champaign, 1975-; chief Environ Div Environ Res, US Army Corps Engrs, Construct Eng Res Lab, 1971-1989; civil engr, Develop & Resources Corp, 1968-1969; assoc engr water resources, Calif Dept Water Resources, 1964-1968; civil engr design, Spink Eng Corp, 1961-1964; UNIV CINCINNATI, ASSOC DEAN RES. **Memberships:** Fel Am Soc Civil Engrs; NY Acad Sci; AAAS. **Research Statement & Publications:** Environmental impact analysis, environmental quality management related to solid waste, air, water, noise pollution and hazardous waste; management of research and development organizations; environmental policy development; computer systems and artificial intelligence; author or co-author of twelve books. **Mailing Address:** Sch Eng & Comput Sci, Univ Pacific, 3601 Pacific Ave, Stockton, CA 95211. **E-Mail:** rjain@uop.edu

JAIN, SUBHASH C, FLUID MECHANICS. **Education:** Univ Iowa, PhD (Mech Hydraulics). **Professional Experience:** PROF EMER CIVIL & ENVIRON ENG RES ENG, as of 2005. **Mailing Address:** Univ Iowa, Inst Hyd Res, Iowa City, IA 53242. **Fax:** 319-335-5238. **E-Mail:** subhash-jain@uiowa.edu

JAIN, SUBODH K, POPULATION BIOLOGY, ECONOMIC BOTANY. **Personal Data:** b Nanauta, India, December 11, 1934; m 1957, Saroj Singhal; c Sudhanshu, Vinoo & Sarita. **Education:** Univ Delhi, BSc, 1954; Indian Agr Res Inst, New Delhi, IARI, 1956; Univ Calif, Davis, PhD (genetics), 1960. **Honors & Awards:** Central govt India Prize, 1954. **Professional Experience:** RETIRED; SLOAN grant, 1987; consult & vis prof, Plant Breeding Inst, Wageningen, 1984 & Turkey, 1993; consult & vis prof, Piracicaba, Brazil, 1983; mem, Nat AcadSci Panel Amaranth, 1982-1985; consult & vis prof, Mendoza, Argentina, 1982; SOHIO grant, 1981-1985; assoc ed, Evolution, 1981-1983; consult & vis prof, Hyderabad, India, 1979, 1982; Fulbright fel, 1978 & 1995; Indo-US fel, 1978-1979; mem, Orgn Int Symp in pop biol, 1978, 1983, 1986-1988; prof biol, Univ Calif, Davis, 1972-1994; Guggenheim Found fel & sr fel, CounSci & Indust Res Orgn, Australia, 1971-1972; NSF res grant, 1969-1971, 1976-1978, 1979-1982; assoc biologist, Univ Calif, Davis, 1967-1972; asst res geneticists, Univ Calif, Davis, 1963-1967; pool off genetics, Coun Sci & Indust Res, New Delhi, 1961-1963. **Memberships:** Soc Study Evolution; Am Soc Naturalists; Bot Soc Am; Am Inst Biol Sci. **Research Statement & Publications:** Population genetics; plant breeding; plant evolution; dynamics of grassland communities; genetics and ecology of avena, bromus, trifolium species; analysis of life histories and relative fitnesses; genetic resources in crop breeding; development of new crops; conservation of rare and endangered plants. **Mailing Address:** Dept of Agronomy & Range Sci, Univ of Calif, Davis, CA 95616.

JAIN, SURENDER K, RING THEORY, LINEAR ALGEBRA. **Personal Data:** b Amritsar, India, November 16, 1938; m 1963, c 2. **Education:** Panjab Univ, India, BA Hons, 1957, MA, 1959; Univ Delhi, India, PhD (ring theory), 1963. **Professional Experience:** DIR CTR RING THEORY & APPLN, OHIO UNIV, as of 2004; PROF MATH, OHIO UNIV, 1969-; reader math, Univ Delhi, India, 1965-1969; vis prof, Univ Frankfurt, Univ Chicago, McMaster Univ, Can, Kuwait Univ, RiyadUniv, Saudi Arabia, Ohio State Univ, NC State Univ & Univ Calif, Santa Barbara, 1963-1990; resmathematician & lectr, Univ Calif, Riverside, 1963-1965. **Memberships:** Am Math Soc; Math Asn Am; Soc Indust & Appl Math. **Research Statement & Publications:** Noncommutative ring theory and applied linear algebra; author of 60 research publications and 6 books. **Mailing Address:** Dept Math, Ohio Univ, Rm 315A, Morton 321, Athens, OH 45701-2979. **Fax:** 740-593-9805. **E-Mail:** jain@ohio.edu

JAIN, SUSHIL C, PRODUCTIVITY IMPROVEMENT, QUALITY CONTROL. **Personal Data:** b Lucknow, India, June 14, 1939; American citizen; m 1969, Usha; c Rachna & Mohit. **Education:** St John's Col, Agra, India, BS, 1957; Indian Inst Technol, Kharagpur, BS, 1961; Purdue Univ, Ind, MS, 1964. **Professional Experience:** MGR, QUAL ASSURANCE, AM FUJI SEAL, 1996-; dir qual, Mebane Packaging Group, 1995-1996; dir, qual assurance, Tekkote Corp, 1993-1994; process engr, Sealed Air Corp, 1990-1992; pres, Jain Consult, 1989; dir indust eng, Universal Folding Box Inc, 1981-1989; mgr indust eng, Unified Data Prod, 1979-1981; staff engr, Alco Gravure, Inc, 1973-1978; sr indust engr, Edwards Bros, Inc, 1971-1973; engr, Safran Printing Co, 1966-1968; indust engr, Ford Motor Co, 1964-1965, elec engr, Gwalior Rayons, India, 1961-1963. **Memberships:** Sr mem Inst Indust Engrs; sr mem Am Soc Qual Control. **Mailing Address:** 60 Winthrop Rd, Hillsdale, NJ 07642.

JAIN, SUSHIL KUMAR, DIABETES, NUTRITION. **Personal Data:** b Nabha, Punjab, India, March 31, 1950; m 1980, c 2. **Education:** Punjab Univ, Chandigarh, BS, 1970; Postgrad Inst Med Educ & Res, Chandigarh, MS, 1972, PhD (biochem), 1976. **Honors & Awards:** Founder's Award & Ross Award, Southern Soc Pediat Res; Beecham Award, Am Diabetes Asn. **Professional Experience:** Prin investr, Nat Am Diabetes Asn, 1987-; PROF PEDIAT, BIOCHEM & PHYSIOL, LA STATE UNIV MED CTR, SHREVEPORT, 1987-; CHIEF, SECT PEDIAT RES, 1987-; prin investr, NIH res grant, 1985-1988; from instr to asst prof, 1981-1991; fel hemat, Sch Med, Univ Calif, San Francisco, 1979-1981; fel pharmacol & nutrit, Univ Southern Calif, Los Angeles, 1977-1979; tutor biochem, Postgrad Inst Med & Res, 1976-1977. **Memberships:** Am Diabetes Asn; NY Acad Sci; Am Soc Biol Chemists; Am Soc Hemat; Soc Pediat Res; Am Inst Nutrit; Am Fed Clin Res. **Research Statement & Publications:** Diabetes complications, ntrition, mechanisms of cellular damage in diabetes, oxidative stress; hyperlipidemia; Glycation vascular inflammation, chromium, vitamin E, curcumin. **Mailing Address:** Dept Pediat, La State Univ Med Ctr, 1501 Kings Hwy, Shreveport, LA 71130. **Fax:** 318-675-5180. **E-Mail:** sjain@lsuhsc.edu

JAIN, VIJAY KUMAR, ELECTRICAL ENGINEERING. **Personal Data:** b Gwalior, India, November 15, 1937; m 1957, c 3. **Education:** Univ Rajasthan, BE, 1956; Univ Roorkee, ME dipl, 1957; Mich State Univ, PhD (elec eng), 1964. **Professional Experience:** DIR, CTR COMMUN & SIGNAL PROCESSING, UNIV S FLA, as of 2003; ACTG DIR CTR DIGITAL & COMPUTATIONAL VIDEO as of 2003; DISTINGUISHED PROF, DEPT ELEC ENG, UNIV S FLA, as of 2002; prof, Bell Lab, 1982-1984; prof elec eng, Univ S Fla, beginning 1980; prof, Ga Inst Technol, 1979-1980; prof, Univ S Fla, 1974-1979; assoc prof, Univ SFla, 1968-1974; assoc prof, Birla Inst Technol & Sci, India, 1966-1968; asst prof, Birla Inst Technol & Sci, India, 1965-1966; asst prof, Mich State Univ, 1964; asst prof elec eng, Birla Eng Col, India, 1957-1961; consult, Honeywell, Sperry, Vet Admin Hosp A Cnielsen. **Memberships:** Inst Elec & Electronics Engrs. **Research Statement & Publications:** Communication electronics; computer networking; digital signal-processing; pattern recognition; speech signals analysis; very-large-scale integration and microprocessors;

system identification. **Mailing Address:** Ctr Commun & Signal Processing, 4202 E Fowler Ave ENB 118, Tampa, FL 33620. **Fax:** 813-974-5250. **E-Mail:** jain@eng.usf.edu

JAIN, VINOD KUMAR, POLYMER TRIBOLOGY, MACHINE DESIGN. **Personal Data:** American citizen; m 1967, c 2. **Education:** Univ Roorkee, India, BE, 1964, ME, 1970; Iowa State Univ, PhD (mech eng), 1980. **Professional Experience:** PROF MECH & AEROSPACE ENG, UNIV DAYTON, 1989-; from instr to assoc prof, Univ Dayton, 1979-1989; lectr mech eng, Univ Roorkee, India, 1964-1975. **Memberships:** Am Soc Mech Engrs. **Research Statement & Publications:** Friction and wear of polymers; characterization of surface topography; fatigue of polymeric composites; lubrication technology; metal processing sciences; forging. **Mailing Address:** Dept Mech & Aerospace Eng, Univ Dayton, Off KL-106E, 300 Col Park, Dayton, OH 45469-0210. **Fax:** 937-229-4766. **E-Mail:** vinod.jain@notes.udayton.edu

JAINCHILL, JEROME, ENVIRONMENT, PHARMOCOKINETICS. **Personal Data:** b New York, NY, January 27, 1932; m 1964, Robert a Cohen; c Charles, Melissa & Susan. **Education:** NY Univ, BA, 1953, MS, 1960, PhD (genetics), 1963. **Professional Experience:** Mem, Long Island Environ Comt, Am Chem Soc; SCI EDUC, NEW YORK BD EDUC, 1981-; Cornell Univ, 1977-1980 & North Star Res, 1980-1981; res biochemist, Endo Labs, 1967-1977; res assoc biochem carcinogens, Dept Environ Med, NY Univ Med Ctr, 1965-1967; res assoc radiobiol, Sloan-Kettering Inst, NY, 1963-1965. **Memberships:** AAAS; NY Acad Sci. **Research Statement & Publications:** Biochemistry of carcinogenic agents on DNA; drug metabolism; pharmacokinetics; retrovirus; murine leukemia. **Mailing Address:** 957A Heritage Hls, Somers, NY 10589-1913.

JAISINGHANI, RAJAN A, RESEARCH & DEVELOPMENT FOR PRODUCT & BUSINESS DEVELOPMENT. **Personal Data:** b Karachi, Pakistan, January 21, 1945; c 2. **Education:** Banaras Hindu Univ, India, BS, 1969; Univ Wis, MS, 1973. **Professional Experience:** TECHNOVATION SYSTS INC, as of 2004; PRES, PROD DEVELOP ASSISTANCE INC, 1990-; mgr res & develop, Am Filtrona Corp, 1982-1990; mgr res, Nelson Indust, 1974-1982; res asst, Univ Wis, 1971-1973; engr, Fiebing Chem Co, 1971-1973. **Memberships:** Am Inst Chem Eng; Soc Automotive Eng; Am Asn Aerosol Res; Int Asn Colloid Scientists; Am Chem Soc; Am Inst Chem Engrs; Filtration Soc; Int Asn Colloid Scientists. **Research Statement & Publications:** Air and liquid filtration; colloid and aerosols; electrically simulated filtration; capillarity and other surface phenomena; fluid flow coalescence; research management and planning. **Mailing Address:** Technovation Systs Inc, 13511 E Boundary Rd Suites D & E, Midlothian, VA 23112. **Fax:** 804-744-0677. **E-Mail:** raj@technovation.org

JAKAB, GEORGE JOSEPH, PULMONARY IMMUNOLOGY, DISEASES & TOXICOLOGY. **Personal Data:** b Budapest, Hungary, April 7, 1939; m 1963, c 2. **Education:** Univ Wis-Madison, BS, 1965, MS, 1967, PhD (med microbiol), 1970. **Honors & Awards:** res career develop award, Nat Heart, Lung & Blood Inst, 1977. **Professional Experience:** ASSOC DEPT CHMN, SCH HYG & PUB HEALTH, UNIV JOHNS HOPKINS, 1990-; PROF, SCH HYG & PUB HEALTH, UNIV JOHNS HOPKINS, 1986-; assoc prof, Sch Hyg & Pub Health, Univ Johns Hopkins, 1977-1986; res assoc, Univ Vt, 1972-1977; fel, Univ Vt, 1970-1972; mem, Delta Omega Soc. **Memberships:** Infectious Dis Soc Am; Am Thoracic Soc; Reticuloendothelial Soc; Am Soc Microbiol; Soc Toxicol. **Research Statement & Publications:** Pulmonary defense mechanisms against infectious agents; interaction of infectious agents and environmental contaminants in the genesis and exacerbation of acute and chronic lung disease. **Mailing Address:** Sch Pub Health, Johns Hopkins Univ, E7034, Baltimore, MD 21205-2179. **Fax:** 410-955-0617. **E-Mail:** gjakab@jhsph.edu

JAKACKY, JOHN M, ATOM MOLECULE COLLISION, ACOUSTIC. **Personal Data:** b Hartford, Conn, July 22, 1956; m 1989, Mary. **Education:** Univ Conn, BS, 1978, MS, 1979, PhD (physics), 1984. **Professional Experience:** SR ANALYST, SONALYSTS INC, 1987-, analyst, 1984-1987. **Memberships:** Am Phys Soc. **Mailing Address:** 185 Pruitt Pl, Oakdale, CT 06353.

JAKEN, SUSAN, BIOLOGICAL CHEMISTRY. **Personal Data:** b Painesville, Ohio, October 23, 1950. **Education:** Bowling Green Univ, BS, 1972; Univ Mich, MS, 1974, PhD (biochem), 1977. **Professional Experience:** SR SCIENTIST, W ALTON JONES CELL SCI CTR INC, LAKE PLACID, NY, 1986-; sr staff fel, Div Virol, Ctr Drugs & Biol, Food & Drug Admin, 1985-1986; cancerexpert, Lab Cellular Carcinogenesis & Tumor Promotion, Nat Cancer Inst, 1983-1985; instr, Johns Hopkins Univ, 1981-1985; interdisciplinary prog health, Harvard Sch Pub Health, 1979-1981; prin investr, NIH, 1979; res fel med, Mass Gen Hosp & Harvard Med Sch, 1977-1979. **Memberships:** Am Soc Cell Biol; Am Asn Cancer Res. **Research Statement & Publications:** Biological Chemistry; author of 68 publications. **Mailing Address:** W Alton Jones Cell Sci Ctr, 10 Old Barn Rd, Lake Placid, NY 12946. **Fax:** 518-522-1849.

JAKES, KAREN SORKIN, MOLECULAR BIOLOGY. **Personal Data:** b Washington, DC, June 18, 1947; m 1970, c 2. **Education:** Brown Univ, BSc, 1969; Yale Univ, PhD (molecular biophys & biochem), 1974. **Professional Experience:** SR ASSOC, DEPT PHYSIOL & BIOPHYS, YESHIVA UNIV, as of 2005; res assoc genetics, beginning 1976; asst res genetics, Rockefeller Univ, 1971-1975. **Memberships:** AAAS. **Research Statement & Publications:** Mechanism of action and synthesis of colicin E3 and its immunity protein; export of colicins E1, E2 and E3; replication of bacteriophage fluid. **Mailing Address:** Dept Physiol & Biophys, Albert Einstein Col Med, Yeshiva Univ, 1300 Morris Park Ave, Bronx, NY 10461. **Fax:** 718-430-8819. **E-Mail:** jakes@aecom.yu.edu

JAKES, WILLIAM CHESTER, ELECTRICAL ENGINEERING. **Personal Data:** b Milwaukee, Wis, May 15, 1922; m 1948, Mary; c Robert & Elizabeth. **Education:** Northwestern Univ, BS, 1944, MS, 1947, PhD (elec eng), 1949. **Honorary Degrees:** PhD, Iowa Wesleyan Univ, 1961. **Honors & Awards:** Co-winner, Alexander Graham Bell Medal, Inst Elec & Electronics Engrs, 1987. **Professional Experience:** RETIRED; mem tech staff, dir Transmission Terminals & Radio Lab, 1984-1987; dir radio transmission lab, Bell Tel Labs, 1971-1984; head mobile radio res, Bell Tel Labs, 1962-1971; mem sci adv bd, Voice of Am, 1960-1962; mem tech staff, Bell Tel Labs, 1949-1962. **Memberships:** Fel Inst Elec & Electronics Engrs. **Research Statement & Publications:** Microwave propagation and antennas; satellite communication; microwave transmission systems development; cellular telephone research. **Mailing Address:** 58 Wildrose Dr, Andover, MA 01810.

JAKLEVIC, JOSEPH MICHAEL, PHYSICS, ENVIRONMENTAL SCIENCES. **Personal Data:** b Kansas City, Kans, January 16, 1941; m 1966, c 2. **Education:** Rockhurst Col, AB, 1962; Univ Notre Dame, PhD (physics), 1966. **Professional Experience:** SR STAFF SCIENTIST, DEPT INST SCI, LAWRENCE BERKELEY LAB, 1978-; staff scientist eng, Dept Inst Sci, Lawrence Berkeley Lab, 1969-1978; fel, Dept Inst Sci, Lawrence Berkeley Lab, 1967-1969; fel nuclear physics, Univ Notre Dame, 1966-1967. **Memberships:** Am Phys Soc; Mat Res Soc; Air Pollution Control Asn. **Research Statement & Publications:** Application of nuclear and atomic physics principles and techniques to problems of environmental sampling and analysis; x-ray and atomic physics techniques. **Mailing Address:** Lawrence Berkeley Lab, Cyclotron Rd No 1, Berkeley, CA 94720. **Fax:** 510-486-6816. **E-Mail:** jmjaklevic@lbl.gov

JAKLEVIC, ROBERT C, EXPERIMENTAL PHYSICS, CONDENSED MATTER. **Personal Data:** b Kansas City, Kans, July 27, 1934; m 1962, c 2. **Education:** Rockhurst Col, BS, 1956; Univ Notre Dame, PhD (physics), 1960. **Honors & Awards:** Tech Achievement Award, Ford Motor Co, 1990. **Professional Experience:** PRIN SCIENTIST, FORD SCI LABS, 1980-; staff scientist solid state physics, Ford Sci Labs, 1962-1980; Fel, Univ Notre Dame, 1961-1962. **Memberships:** Fel Am Phys Soc; Sigma Xi; Am Chem Soc. **Research Statement & Publications:** Superconductivity; Josephson tunneling; normal metal tunneling; photoelectric effect in metals; thin film technology; tunneling in semiconductors; organic conductors; surface science; scanning tunneling spectroscopy; nanoscale devices. **Mailing Address:** 28988 Augusta, Farmington, MI 48331-4812.

JAKOB, FREDI, ANALYTICAL CHEMISTRY. **Personal Data:** b Horstein, Ger, January 11, 1934; American citizen; m 1957, c 4. **Education:** City Col NY, BS, 1955; Rutgers Univ, PhD (anal chem), 1961. **Professional Experience:** PROF EMER CHEM, CALIF STATE UNIV, SACRAMENTO, 1996-; DIR, WEIDMANN-ACTI INC, 1995-; Univ Wollongong, Australia, 1982; vis prof, Victoria Univ, Wellington, NZ, 1971; prof chem, calif state univ, sacramento, 1969-1996; vis assoc prof, Univ Wis, Madison, 1968-1969; chmn dept, Calif State Univ, Sacramento, 1965-1968; consult, St Bd Equalization, 1962-1978; NSF grants, beginnning 1961; from asst prof to assocprof, Calif State Univ, Sacramento, 1961-1969; instr chem, Rutgers Univ, 1960-1961; consult chemist, Anal Assocs Inc. **Memberships:** Am Chem Soc. **Research Statement & Publications:** Theory and application of separation methods and chemical instrumentation; laboratory applications of computers. **Mailing Address:** Weidmann-Acti Inc, 4011 Power Inn Rd Ste G, Sacramento, CA 95826. **Fax:** 916-455-0191. **E-Mail:** fjakob@weidmann-acti.com

JAKOB, KARL MICHAEL, NUCLEIC ACIDS BIOLOGY, CELL BIOLOGY. **Personal Data:** b Berlin, Ger, November 5, 1921; American citizen; m 1954, c 2. **Education:** Univ Ill, BS, 1943, MS, 1948; Univ Calif, PhD (cytogenetics, bot), 1952. **Professional Experience:** ASSOC PROF, WEIZMANN INST SCI, ISRAEL, 1979-; sr scientist, Weizmann Inst Sci, Israel, 1969-1978; vis investr, Biol Div, Oak Ridge Nat Lab, 1963-1964; Vissr lectr, Univ Bar Ilan, Israel, 1962-1972; res assoc plant genetics, Weizmann Inst Sci, Israel, 1953-1968; asst bot & cytol, Univ Ill & Univ Calif, 1947-1951; Plant breeder, Marshall FarmServ, Ill, 1943-1945. **Memberships:** Int Soc Plant & Molecular Biol. **Research Statement & Publications:** Biochemistry of the cell division cycle of eukaryotes; plant RNA metabolism; use of antisense RNA probes to locate transcriptional activity by insitu hybridization; molecular biology of chromatin during DNA replication in vivo. **Mailing Address:** Dept Plant Genetics, Weizmann Inst Sci, Rehovot 76100, Israel.

JAKOBIEC, FREDERICK ALBERT, OPHTHALMOLOGY, PATHOLOGY. **Education:** Harvard Univ, MD. **Professional Experience:** CHIEF OPHTHAL, MASS EYE & EAR INFIRMARY, as of 2001; CHMN, MANHATTAN EYE, EAR, & THROAT HOSP, 1980-. **Research Statement & Publications:** Tumor surgery. **Mailing Address:** Mass Eye & Ear Infirmary, 243 Charles St, Boston, MA 02114-3004. **Fax:** 617-523-5498.

JAKOBSON, MARK JOHN, NUCLEAR PHYSICS. **Personal Data:** b Carlyle, Mont, May 4, 1923; m 1945, c 2. **Education:** Univ Mont, AB, 1944, MA, 1947; Univ Calif, PhD (physics), 1951. **Professional Experience:** PROF EMER, DEPT PHYSICS & ASTRON, UNIV MONT, as of 2003; chmn dept astron & physics, Univ Mont, 1968-1973; prof physics, Univ Mont, beginning 1958; from asst prof to assoc prof, Univ Mont, 1953-1958; instr physics, Univ Wash, 1952-1953; physicist, Radiation Lab, 1950-1952; asst physics, Univ Calif, 1947-1949. **Memberships:** Fel Am Phys Soc. **Research Statement & Publications:** Photonuclear reactions; accelerator design; pion interactions. **Mailing Address:** Dept Physics & Astron, Univ Mont, #1080, 32 Campus Dr, Missoula, MT 59812. **Fax:** 406-243-2085.

JAKOBSSON, ERIC GUNNAR, BIOPHYSICS, PHYSIOLOGY. **Personal Data:** b New York, NY, November 18, 1938; m 1963, Naomi; c 6. **Education:** Columbia Univ, BA, 1959, BS, 1960; Dartmouth Col, PhD (physics), 1969. **Professional Experience:** SR RES SCIENTIST, NAT CTR SUPERCOMPUTING APPLN, as of 2004; PROF DEPT MOLECULAR & INTEGRATIVE PHYSIOL, UNIV ILL, URBANA, as of 2004; sr res scientist, Nat Ctr Supercomputing Applns, beginning 1991; prof physiol, Biophys, Bioengineering, beginning 1991; assoc prof Bioengineering, Univ Ill, Urbana, beginning 1981; vis assoc prof physiol, Duke Univ, 1979; assoc prof physiol & biophys, Univ Ill, Urbana, beginning 1978; asst prof, Nat Ctr Supercomputing Applns, 1972-1978; res assoc, Nat Ctr Supercomputing Applns, 1971-1972; fel, NSF, 1970-1971; fel, Case Western Res Univ, 1969-1971; develop engr, Malaker Corp, 1962-1965; process engr cryog, Air Prod & Chem, 1960-1962. **Memberships:** Biophys Soc; AAAS; fel Am Phys Soc. **Research Statement & Publications:** Osmoregulation of animal cells; rhythmic and repetitive electrical activity in nerve physics of biological membranes; epithelial transport. **Mailing Address:** Nat Ctr Supercomputing Applns, Univ Ill, 4039 Beckman, Urbana, IL 61801. **Fax:** 217-244-2909. **E-Mail:** jake@ncsa.uiuc.edu

JAKOBY, WILLIAM BERNARD, BIOCHEMISTRY, ENZYMOLOGY. **Personal Data:** b Breslau, Ger, November 17, 1928; American citizen; c Michael & Robert. **Education:** Brooklyn Col, BS, 1950; Yale Univ, PhD (microbiol), 1954. **Professional Experience:** BD DIRS, FOUND ADV EDUC SCI INC, as of 2005; SCIENTIST EMER, NAT INST DIABETES & DIGESTIVE & KIDNEY DIS, as of 2003; assoc ed Hepatol, 1980-1985 & Protein Expression & Purification, 1990-1992; ed inchief, Anal Biochem, 1986-; CHIEF, LAB BIOCHEM & METAB, 1984-; mem, Comn BiochemNomenclature, 1974-1980; consult, Molecular Biol Panel, NSF, 1970-1973 & 1976; mem, Enzyme Comn, Int Union Biochem, 1969-1971; chief sect enzymes & intermediarymetab, Nat Inst Diabetes & Digestive & Kidney Dis, beginning 1968; Mem bd dirs, FoundAdvan Educ Sci, 1968-1987; sr investr, Nat Inst Arthritis, Metab & Digestive Dis, 1955-1968; fel biochem, NY Univ-Bellevue Med Ctr, 1954-1955; fel pharmacol, NY Univ-Bellevue Med Ctr, 1953-1954. **Memberships:** Am Soc Biol Chemists. **Research Statement & Publications:** Enzymology; detoxication. **Mailing Address:** Nat Inst Diabetes & Digestive & Kidney Dis, Nat Inst Health, NIH Bldg 10, Rm 9N119, Bethesda, MD 20892. **E-Mail:** wbjakoby@helix.nih.gov

JAKOI, EMMA RAFF, CELL BIOLOGY, MOLECULAR BIOLOGY. **Personal Data:** b Cornwall, Ont, May 10, 1946; American citizen; m 1971. **Education:** Wash State Univ, BS, 1968; Duke Univ, PhD (physiol, pharmacol), 1973. **Professional Experience:** ASSOC PROF, DEPT NEUROL, MED COL VA, 1989-; asst prof anat, Med Ctr, Duke Univ, 1977-1989; USPHS fel, 1975-1977; USPHS instnl res fel, 1974-1975; res assoc anat, Med Ctr, Duke Univ, 1973-1974. **Memberships:** Am Soc Cell Biol; Biophys Soc; Sigma Xi. **Research Statement & Publications:** Biochemical and morphological studies of ligatin, a membrane bound baseplate for cell surface proteins involved in intercellular adhesion during development of embryonic chick neural retina and in degradation of glycoproteins and glycolipids in suckling rat ileal epithelial cells. **Mailing Address:** Med Col VA, VA Commonwealth Univ, Box 599 MCV Sta, Richmond, VA 23298-0001. **Fax:** 804-371-6373.

JAKOWSKA, SOPHIE, PATHOBIOLOGY, ENVIRONMENTAL ETHICS & ECO-SPIRITUALITY. **Personal Data:** b Warsaw, Poland, February 12, 1922; American citizen; m 1941, Constantine L Jeannopoulos; c Peter, John & Marie-Helene. **Education:** Lycee Warsaw, Poland, cert, 1939; Univ Rome, cert, 1942; Fordham Univ, MS, 1945, PhD (biol), 1947. **Honors & Awards:** Tree Learning Award, Int Union Conserv of Nature & Natural Resources, 1988; Liga Ochrony Przyrody gold medal, League Protection Nature, 1989. **Professional Experience:** RETIRED; mem, Patronato Parque Nac Mirador Norte, 1996-; sr adv bd mem, Global Harmony Found, 1989-; liaison, World Coun Churches, 1988; mem, Int Union ConservNature & Natural Resources Working Group on Ehtics, 1984-; sci consult, 1977-; reviewerproposals & projs, Comn Educ, Int Union Conserv Nature; prof biol sci, Col Staten Island, CityUniv NY, 1970-1978; biologist, Food & Drug Admin, 1969-1971; res coordr & hon prof fac sci, Inst Marine Biol, Santo Domingo Univ, 1968-; consult, Span Dept, Grolier, Inc, NY, 1968-1975; spec proj dir, Nat Cystic Fibrosis Res Found, 1968-1969; tech adv & res coordr biol, SantoDomingo Univ, 1967-1968; pvt consult, 1966-; consult, Animal Med Ctr, 1964-1968; head, DeptPath, Food & Drug Res Labs, Inc, 1964-1967; consult, Inst Marine Biol, Santo Domingo Univ, 1963-; NSF biol teacher inst lectr, Iona Col, 1963-; asst to vpres med affairs, Nat Cystic FibrosisRes Found, 1961-1962; res assoc, Dept Labs, Beth Israel Hosp, 1959- & Inst Crippled &Disabled, 1962; res assoc exp biol, Dept Marine Biochem & Ecol, 1959-1962; vis prof, Grad Sch, St Louis Univ, 1957; collabr, Brookhaven Nat Lab, 1952-1962; collabr, NY Aquarium, NY ZoolSoc, 1948-1959; from asst prof to assoc prof, Col Mt St Vincent, 1948-1958; asst, ChemotherDiv, Sloan-Kettering Inst Cancer Res, 1947-1948; instr bact, Col Mt St Vincent, 1946. **Memberships:** Fel AAAS; Am Micros Soc; Soc Protozool; Am Soc Ichthyologists &Herpetologists; Am Inst Biol Sci; fel NY Acad Sci; Sigma Xi. **Research Statement & Publications:** Plant and animal cytology; comparative pathology and hematology; experimental biology; parasitology; radiobiology; biochemical ecology; mucous secretions; conservation and religious environmental education; writing books for children and new readers in Spanish on conservation and environmental education, e.g., on crocodiles, parrots, etc; author of numerous scientific papers and books; continuing work and education of environmental conservation with religious motivation. **Mailing Address:** Arz Merino 154 Z-1, Santo Domingo, Dominican Republic. **Fax:** 809-687-3948.

JAKUBIEC, ROBERT JOSEPH, ANALYTICAL CHEMISTRY. **Personal Data:** b Detroit, Mich, June 19, 1941; m 1964, c 2. **Education:** Univ Detroit, BS, 1963; Wayne State Univ, PhD (anal chem), 1968. **Professional Experience:** Adj fac chem, Roosevelt Univ, Chicago, as of 2004; PROF, ROOSEVELT UNIV, CHICAGO, 1995-; CONSULT, 1991-; vpres & lab dir, Enviro-Test, Perry Chicago Dairy Labs Inc, 1976-1991; instr, Chicago Gas Chromatog Sch, 1973-; guest lectr, Northwestern Univ, Roosevelt Univ, 1971-; sect mgr anal chem, Armak Co, Div Akzona, 1970-1976; sr chemist, Armak Co, Div Akzona, 1969-1970; sr chemist, Corn Prod Co, 1968-1969; Chemist, US Food & Drug Admin, 1963-1965; vis prof, Northeastern Univ, Chicago. **Memberships:** Am Chem Soc; Am Oil Chem Soc; Am Soc Testing & Mat; Water PollutionControl Fedn; Am Asn Cereal Chemists; Asn Off Anal Chemists. **Research Statement & Publications:** General analytical methods development; gas chromatography; thin layer chromatography; atomic absorption spectroscopy; ultraviolet and visible spectroscopy; residue analysis; general instrumentation; high pressure liquid chromatography; ion chromatography. **Mailing Address:** Dept Chem, Roosevelt Univ, 430 S Mich Ave, Chicago, IL 60605. **Fax:** 312-861-9184.

JAKUBOWSKI, ELIZABETH H, MATHEMATICS. **Education:** Univ S Fla, MS, 1982; Univ Ga, EdD, 1988. **Professional Experience:** ASSOC PROF, DEPT CURRIC & INSTR, FLA STATE UNIV, as of 2006. **Mailing Address:** Dept Curric & Instr, Fla State Univ, 209 Carothers Hall, Tallhassee, FL 32303-3420. **Fax:** 850-644-1880. **E-Mail:** ejakubow@coe.fsu.edu

JAKUBOWSKI, GERALD S, ENGINEERING EDUCATION ADMINISTRATION, LASER DOPPLER VELOCIMETRY. **Personal Data:** b Toledo, Ohio, November 22, 1949; m 1972, c 2. **Education:** Univ Toledo, BSME, 1974, MSME, 1976, PhD (eng sci), 1978. **Honors & Awards:** Ralph R Teetor Award, Soc Automotive Engrs, 1985. **Professional Experience:** VPRES & PROVOST, POLYTECH CAMPUS, ARIZ STATE UNIV, 2005; eng educ bd, Student Activ Comt, Soc Automotive Engrs, beginning 1990; dean, Col sci & Eng, Loyola Marymount Univ, beginning 1990; prof mech eng, Loyola Marymount Univ, beginning 1990; interim dean, Memphis State Univ, 1989-1990; assoc dean eng, Memphis State Univ, 1988-1989; mem, Student Activ Comt, Soc Automotive Engrs, 1986-; asst dean eng, Col Eng, Univ Toledo, 1986-1988; chair, New Eng Educ Comt, Am Soc Eng Educ, 1985-1986; fel, NASA-Lewis Res Ctr, 1984-1985; from asst prof to assoc prof mech eng, Col Eng, Univ Toledo, 1978-1986; grad & admin asst, Col Eng, Univ Toledo, 1974-1978. **Memberships:** Am Soc Eng Educ; Soc Automotive Engrs; Am Soc Mech Engrs; Am InstAeronaut & Astronaut. **Research Statement & Publications:** Thermodynamics; fluid mechanics; heat transfer and energy; pump cavitation; ice melting; laser Doppler velocimetry. **Mailing Address:** Polytech campus, Ariz Stat Univ, 7001 EWilliams Field Rd, Mesa, AZ 85212. **E-Mail:** gerald.jakubowski@asu.edu

JAKUBOWSKI, HIERONIM, ACCURACY OF PROTEIN SYNTHESIS, MECHANISMS OF HOMOCYSTEINE TOXICITY. **Personal Data:** b Szczecinek, Poland, September 30, 1946; American citizen; m 1969, Alina; c Mariusz & Marcin. **Education:** Poznan Univ, MSc, phys chem 1969; Agr Univ, Poznan, PhD, biochem, 1974; Inst Biochem & Biophysics, Warsaw, DrHabil, biochem 1978, Cold Spring Harbor Lab, NY, yeast genet mol biol 1987. **Honors & Awards:** J Parnas Award, Polish Biochem Soc, 1984. **Professional Experience:** ASSOC PROF MICROBIOL & MOLECULAR GENETICS, NJ MED SCH, NEWARK, 1999-; adj assoc prof 1991-1999, adj asst prof 1984-1991, NJ Med Sch, Newark; FEBS Fellow, Hanover Med Sch, Ger, 1982; dep chmn, Agr Univ, Poznan, 1981; EMBO Fellow, Imp Col, London, 1980; adj habil, Agr Univ, Poznan, 1979-1987; adj, Agr Univ, Poznan, 1975-1978; Postdoc, Univ NMex, Albuquerque, 1975-1976; sr res asst, Agr Univ, Poznan, 1973-1975; res asst, Agr Univ, Poznan, 1969-1973. **Research Statement & Publications:** Quality control and editing mechanisms in selection of amino acids for protein synthesis; molecular mechanisms of cellular defenses against homocysteine toxicity; the role of homocysteine in cardiovascular disease. **Mailing Address:** 9 Galloway Ct, West Orange, NJ 07052. **Fax:** 973-972-8982. **E-Mail:** jakubows@umdnj.edu

JAKUS, KARL, MECHANICAL ENGINEERING, CERAMICS ENGINEERING. **Personal Data:** b Gyor, Hungary, March 21, 1938; American citizen; c 2. **Education:** Univ Wis-Madison, BME, 1963; Univ Calif, Berkeley, MS, 1965, PhD (aeroscience), 1968. **Honors & Awards:** F H Norton Award, Am Ceramic Soc, 1993. **Professional Experience:** PROF MECH ENG, UNIV MASS, AMHERST, 1984-; from asst prof to assoc prof, Univ Mass, Amherst, 1970-1983; asst prof mech eng, Johns Hopkins Univ, 1968-1970; assoc ed, J Am Ceramic Soc; consult govt labs & indust. **Memberships:** Am Ceramics Soc. **Research Statement & Publications:** Mechanical behavior of ceramics. **Mailing Address:** Dept Mech & Indust Eng, Univ Mass, Rm 322 Eng Shop, Amherst, MA 01003-2210. **Fax:** 413-545-1027. **E-Mail:** jakus@zonker.ecs.umass.edu

JAKWAY, JACQUELINE SINKS, ANATOMY. **Personal Data:** b San Juan, PR, December 13, 1928; div. **Education:** Park Col, AB, 1950; Univ Kans, PhD (anat), 1958. **Professional Experience:** ASSOC PROF, DEPT ANAT & CELL BIOL, DOWNSTATE MED CTR, STATE UNIV NY, as of 2004; asst prof anat, State Univ NY, Downstate med ctr, beginning 1967; from instr to asst prof anat, Sch Dent, Univ Southern Calif, 1961-1967; Nat Cancer Inst fel, 1959-1961; res assoc animal path & hyg, Col Agr, Univ Nebr, 1959-1961; res assoc animal husb, Col Agr, Univ Nebr, 1959; asst animal path & hyg, Col Agr, Univ Nebr, 1958; asst anat, Univ, 1952-1957; asst histochem, Sch Med, Univ Kans, 1950-1952. **Memberships:** Fel AAAS; NY Acad Sci; Soc Neuroscience. **Research Statement & Publications:** Comparative neuroanatomy; animal behavior. **Mailing Address:** Dept Anat & Cell Biol, Downstate Med Ctr, State Univ NY, Brooklyn, NY 11226-2157. **E-Mail:** jjakway@downstate.edu

JALAL, SYED M, CLINICAL CYTOGENETICS. **Personal Data:** b Ranchi, India, December 2, 1938; American citizen; m 1966, Nikhat; c Shadeen. **Education:** Univ Bihar, BSc, 1959; Univ Wis, MS, 1962, PhD (cytogenetics), 1965; Am Bd Med Genetics, dipl, 1985. **Professional Experience:** PROF LAB MED, COL MED, MAYO CLIN, as of 2005; lab dir, NY Dept Health, 1991; assoc prof lab med, Col Med, Mayo Clin, beginning 1990; adj prof biol, Univ NTex, 1988-1990; dir, Cytogenetics Lab, Genetic Screening & Coun Serv, Tex, 1987-1990; human cytogenetics consult, 1980-1988; prof biol, Univ NDak, 1977-1988; vis prof, Univ Tex Cancer Ctr, Houston, 1974, 1979; from asst prof to assoc prof, Univ NDak, 1964-1977; CO-DIR, CYTOGENETICS LAB; CONSULT, MED GENETICS DEPT, DEPT LAB MED & PATH. **Memberships:** AMA; fel Am Col Med Genetics; Am Soc Human Genetics; Sigma Xi. **Research Statement & Publications:** Neonatal human cytogenetics; high resolution banded chromosome analysis; utility of fluorescent DNA probes for congential and hematologic disorders. **Mailing Address:** Dept Lab Med, Col Med, Mayo Clin, 4500 San Pablo Rd, Jacksonville, FL 32224.

JALBERT, JEFFREY SCOTT, NUCLEAR PHYSICS. **Personal Data:** b Bridgeport, Conn, January 9, 1940; m 1966, c 2. **Education:** Fairfield Univ, BS, 1961; Va Polytech Inst, PhD (physics), 1967. **Professional Experience:** PRES, JCC CONSULT INC, 1984-; dir, Comput Ctr, 1976-1984; prof physics, Comput Ctr, 1975-1986; assoc prof, Denison, 1967-1975; asst prof physics, Hollins Col, 1966-1967. **Memberships:** Am Phys Soc; Am Math Soc; Sigma Xi. **Research Statement & Publications:** Siting of power plants. **Mailing Address:** JCC Consult Inc, 600 Newark Rd PO Box 381, Granville, OH 43023. **Fax:** 740-587-0163. **E-Mail:** jeff@jcc.com

JALIFE, JOSE, CARDIAC ELECTROPHYSIOLOGY, ARRHYTHMIAS. **Personal Data:** b Mex City, Mex, March 7, 1947; m 1971. **Education:** Nat Univ Mex, BA, 1965, MD, 1972. **Honorary Degrees:** Dr, Univ Buenos Aires, Arg, 1985. **Honors & Awards:** Young Investr Award, Am Col Cardiol, 1979; Dr Harold Lamport Award, Am Physiol Soc, 1980; Develop Achievement Award, Am Heart Asn. **Professional Experience:** PROF BIOMED SCI PROG & MED, STATE UNIV NY, UPSTATE MED UNIV, as of 2003; DIR, INST CARDIOVASC RES, as of 2003; pres, res award, Health Sci Ctr, State Univ NY, 1990; PROF & CHMN PHARMACOL, HEALTH SCI CTR, STATE UNIV NY, SYRACUSE, 1988-; Fac exchange scholar, State Univ NY, 1987-; fel, Cardiovasc Sect, Am Physiol Soc, 1985; estab investr, AmHeart Asn, 1982-1987; from asst prof to prof, Health Sci Ctr, State Univ NY, Syracuse, 1980-1981; res scientist cardiac elec, Masonic Med Res Lab, Utica, NY, 1977-1981; cardiac elec, Masonic Med Res Lab, Utica, 1975-1977; fel pharmacol, Upstate Med Ctr, State Univ NY, Syracuse, 1973-1975; instr, Univ Mex, 1972-1973; fel pharmacol, Inst Cardiol, Mex, 1968-1970. **Memberships:** Am Physiol Soc; Cardiovasc Sec Am Physiol Soc; NY Acad Sci; AAAS; Electrophysiol Soc; Am Heart Asn; Biophys Soc; hon mem Arg Soc Cardiol. **Research Statement & Publications:** Theoretical and experimental work related to three major areas of experimental cardiology; cellular mechanism of cardiac arrhythmias; mechanism of pacemaker synchronization in heart cells; nervous control of heart rate and atrioventricular conduction. **Mailing Address:** Inst Cardiovasc Res, State Univ NY, Upstate Med Univ, 3139 Weiskotten Hall, Syracuse, NY 13210. **Fax:** 315-464-8000. **E-Mail:** jalifej@upstate.edu

JALIL, MAZHAR, ACAROLOGY, BACTERIOLOGY. **Personal Data:** b India, November 2, 1938; American citizen; m 1970, Betty; c Tariq, Khalid & Aisha. **Education:** Univ Agra, BS, 1952, MS, 1954; Univ Nottingham, MS, 1963; Univ Waterloo, PhD (biol), 1967; Am Registry Prof Entomologist cert, 1971. **Professional Experience:** SCIENTIST HEALTH, OHIO DEPT HEALTH, as of 1998; chmn, Sci Adv Comt, City Hall, Columbus, Ohio, 1990-1991; bd trustees, Islamic Ctr, Columbus, Ohio, 1988-1993; mem, Columbus Comn Ethics & Values, 1988-1991; consult, UN Develop Prog, NIH, Govt Pakistan, 1980-1981; ENTOMOLOGIST & MICROBIOLOGIST, OHIO DEPT HEALTH, 1969-; res assoc acarology, Univ Ky, 1967-1969; Ont Grad fel, 1965-1967; teaching fel, 1964-1967; instr biol, Univ Waterloo, 1964-1967; instr zoology, Univ Nottingham, 1962-1964; Lord Belper fel, 1962-1963; teacher & lectr agr, Govt Col, Sehore, 1956-1960; farm supt, R A K Agr Inst, Sehore, India, 1955-1956. **Memberships:** Acarological Soc Am; Entom Soc Am; Royal Agr Soc Eng. **Research Statement & Publications:** Bionomics and ecology of oribatid mites; genetic control of mites and insects; biology, ecology and reproductive physiology of mosquitoes; diagnosis of streptococcal infection; proficiency testing program for clinical labs. **Mailing Address:** Ohio Dept Health, PO Box 2568, Columbus, OH 43216-2568. **Fax:** 614-752-9863.

JALLOUL, LOUAY M A, ELECTRICAL ENGINEERING. **Personal Data:** b Beirut, Lebanon, October 24, 1964. **Education:** Okla Univ, BS, 1985; Ohio State Univ, MS, 1988; Rutgers Univ, PhD (elec eng), 1993. **Professional Experience:** ASSOC PROF, ELEC & COMPUTE ENG, AM UNIV BEIRUT, as of 2006; DIR, MORPHICS TECHNOL INC, CALIF, as of 2003; staff engr, Motorola Inc, beginning 1996; sr engr, Motorola Inc, 1994-1996; Wireless Info Network Lab, Rutgers, Univ, 1989-1993; res assoc, Electro SciLab, Ohio StateUniv, 1986-1988; Teaching assoc elec eng, Okla Univ, 1985-1986. **Memberships:** Inst Elec & Electronics Engrs. **Research Statement & Publications:** Wireless communications with emphasis on modulation and coding; spread spectrum systems and fading channel characterization; invented and applied new methods of demodulation for multi-user code division multiple access systems; designed new modems for high speed data over wireless links. **Mailing Address:** Morphics Technol Inc, 675 Campbell Technol Pkwy, Campbell, CA 95008-5059. **Fax:** 408-369-7210. **E-Mail:** lj07@aub.edu.lb

JALUFKA, NELSON WAYNE, ATOMIC PHYSICS, PLASMA PHYSICS. **Personal Data:** b Austwell, Tex, December 2, 1932; m 1962, c 2. **Education:** Lamar Univ, BS, 1962; Col William & Mary, MA, 1967; Univ Colo, Boulder, PhD (physics), 1972. **Professional Experience:** RES SCIENTIST ATOMIC & PLASMA PHYSICS, LANGLEY RES CTR, NASA, 1962-. **Memberships:** Am Phys Soc. **Research Statement & Publications:** Nuclear pumped lasers, experimental; solar pumped lasers, experimental; basic atomic processes in plasmas. **Mailing Address:** 505 Brokenbridge Rd, Yorktown, VA 23692.

JALURIA, YOGESH, NATURAL CONNECTION FLOWS & HEAT TRANSFER MATERIAL PROCESSING. **Personal Data:** b Nabha, Punjab, India, September 8, 1949; American citizen; m 1975, Anuradha; c Pratik, Aseem & Ankur. **Education:** Indian Inst Technol, Delhi, BS, 1970; Cornell Univ, MS, 1972, PhD (mech eng), 1974. **Honors & Awards:** Distinguished Alumni Award Ind Tech, Delhi, India, 1992; Young Scientist Medal, Indian Nat Sci Acad, 1979; Cert Recognition, Nat Inst Stand & Technol, 1982; Heat transfer memorial Award, Am Soc mech engr, 1995; Worcestr reed warner medal, Am Soc mech engr, 1999; Freeman scholar Award, Am Soc mech engr, 2000-. **Professional Experience:** BD OF GOVERNORS, RUTGERS UNIV, 2001-; prof II mech eng, rutgers univ, 1992-2001; prof mech eng, Rutgers Univ, 1985-1992; prin investr, NSF, 1982-; Dept Com, NSF, 1983-2000; CONSULT, SRI INT & OTHER CO, 1982-; from asst prof to assoc prof, Rutgers Univ, 1980-1985; consult, Steel Authority India, Ltd, 1979-1980; asst prof mech eng, Indian Inst Technol, Kanpur, 1976-1980; mem res staff thermal eng, Bell Tel Syst, Princeton, NJ, 1974-1976; asst & fel, Cornell Univ, 1970-1974; treas, heat transfer div, Am Soc Mech Engrs, 1998-2000; Vice chmn, heat transfer div, Am Soc Mech Engrs, 2001-2002; Chmn, heat transfer div, Am Soc Mech Engrs, 2002-2003. **Memberships:** Am Soc Mech Engrs; Combustion Inst; Am Phys Soc. **Research Statement & Publications:** Natural convection flows, cooling of electronic equipment, enclosure fires, environmental heat transfer, solar ponds, and numerical simulation of manufacturing processes; computational heat transfer and thermal stratification; heat transfer; fire; computer methods; manufacturing processes; combustion and fire modeling; author of over 350 technical publications. **Mailing Address:** Depart Mech & Aerospace Eng, Sch Eng, Rutgers State Univ NJ, 98 Brett Rd, Piscataway, NJ 08816. **Fax:** 732-445-3124. **E-Mail:** jaluria@jove.rutgers.edu

JAMASBI, ROUDABEH J, CLINICAL MICROBIOLOGY, CANCER IMMUNOLOGY. **Personal Data:** American citizen. **Education:** Univ Tehran, BS, 1966; Antaeus Res Inst, MT, 1969; Univ Ark, MS, 1970, PhD (microbiol & immunol), 1974. **Professional Experience:** PROF IMMUNOL, BOWLING GREEN STATE UNIV, as of 2004; assoc prof clin microbiol & tumor immunol, Bowling Green State Univ, beginning 1984; vis investr, Oak Ridge Nat Lab, 1982-; assoc mem, Antaeus ResInst, 1981-; asst prof microbiol & immunol, Bowling Green State Univ, 1981-1983; prog dirimmunol, Antaeus Res Inst, 1980-1981; cancer immunologist, Oak Ridge Nat Lab, 1978-1980; investr, Oak Ridge Nat Lab. **Memberships:** Am Asn Cancer Res; Am Soc Microbiol; Am Acad Microbiol; Am AsnImmunologists; Am Soc Clin Pathologists; Am Asn Blood Bank. **Research Statement & Publications:** Immunological characterization of respiratory and digestive tract carcinomas; production of monoclonal antibodies; demonstration of cellular heterogeneity; isolation and characterization of radiation and drug resistance phenotypes. **Mailing Address:** Dept Biol Sci, Bowling Green Univ, 516 LSC, Bowling Green, OH 43402. **E-Mail:** rjamasb@bgnet.bgsu.edu

JAMBHEKAR, SUNIL S, MEDICAL SCIENCES. **Education:** L M Col Pharm, Gujarat Univ, BS; Univ Nebr, MS, PhD. **Professional Experience:** PROF, DEPT PHARMACEUT SCI, SOUTHERN UNIV, as of 2006. **Mailing Address:** Dept Pharmaceut, Southern Univ, 709 Mall Blvd, Savannah, GA 31406-4805. **Fax:** 912-201-8070.

JAMBOR, PAUL EMIL, RINGS & MODULES. **Personal Data:** b Olomouc, Czech, March 29, 1937; American citizen; m Virginia. **Education:** Inst Advan Technol, Prague, Dipl Ing, 1962; Columbia Univ, MA, 1970; Charles Univ, Prague, PhD (math), 1973. **Professional Experience:** PROF MATH, UNIV NC, 1988-; assoc prof, Univ NC, 1981-1987; lectr, Univ Mich, 1977-1980; Assoc ed, Math Rev, 1977-1980; vis position, Math Inst, Tubingen, 1976-1977; Assoc prof math, Charles Univ, Prague, 1971-1976. **Memberships:** Am Math Soc; Math Asn Am. **Research Statement & Publications:** Homological properties and structure theory of associative unitary rings; rings with no superdecomposable modules. **Mailing Address:** 407 Wexford Pl, New Bern, NC 28562. **E-Mail:** pej@coastatuct.com

JAMDAR, SUBHASH C, LIPID BIOCHEMISTRY. **Personal Data:** b Nagpur, India, April 11, 1937. **Education:** Govt Col Sci, India, BS, 1958; Nagpur Univ, India, MS, 1960, PhD (biochem), 1966. **Professional Experience:** RES SCIENTIST & DIR ANAL LAB, DEPT ANESTHESIA, COLUMBIA-PRESBY MED CTR, 1988-; res assoc prof, Med Res Inst, Fla Inst Technol, 1979-1988; res asst prof, Dept Biochem & Anesthesiol, Med Col Va, 1974-1979; res assoc, Dept Med, Univ NC, Chapel Hill, 1971-1974. **Memberships:** Am Soc Biochem; Biol & Molecular Biol Soc. **Mailing Address:** Dept Anesthesiol, Columbia-Presby Med Ctr, P&S Box 46, New York, NY 10032. **Fax:** 212-305-6991.

JAMERSON, FRANK E, PHYSICS. **Education:** Mass Inst Technol, BS; Univ Notre Dame, PhD. **Honors & Awards:** Electric Cycle Asn. **Professional Experience:** FOUNDING MEM, ELECTRIC CYCLE ASN, as of 2000. **Mailing Address:** Electric Cycle Asn, 5915 Cincinnati Pt Trl, Petoskey, MI 49770. **Fax:** 231-347-0159.

JAMERSON, FRANK EDWARD, PHYSICS. **Personal Data:** b Lowell, Mass, November 5, 1927; m 1950, Joy Campbell; c Bruce, John, William, James & Sally Jamerson (Howlett). **Education:** Mass Inst Technol, BS, 1948; Univ Notre Dame, PhD (physics), 1952. **Professional Experience:** CONSULT, as of 1998; pres, RBC Technol, 1997-2000, consult 2001-; PRES, JAMERSON & ASSOC, 1993-; PRES, ELEC BATTERY BICYCLE CO, 1993-; asst prof mgr, US Advan Battery Consorium, Elec Vehicle Platform, Gen Motors Eng Staff, 1991-1993; mgr, div & staff contracts, 1987-1993; chmn comt pub policy, Am Inst Physics, 1985-1988; head, Electrochem Dept, 1985-1987; mem, comt educ, Am Phys Soc, 1983-1985 & Nat Mat Adv Bd, 1989-1992; chmn comt corp assoc, Am Inst Physics, 1979-1981; mem Nat Acad Sci-Nat Bur Standards eval panel, Inst Mat Res, 1974-1978 & panel Nat Measurement Lab, 1978-1980; chmn, Off Air & Water Measurement, 1973-1977; mem Nat Acad Sci-Nat Bur Standards eval panel, Off Air & Water Measurement, 1971-1972; head, Physics Dept, 1969-1985; supvry res physicist & supv phys electronics group, Physics Dept, 1963-1969; sr res physicist, Nuclear Power Eng Dept, Gen Motors Corp, 1957-1961 & Physics Dept, 1961-1963; head neutron physics sect reactors br, US Naval Res Lab, Wash, DC, 1954-1957; sr scientist atomic power div, Westinghouse Elec Corp, 1953; physicist atomics br, US Naval Res Lab, Wash, DC, 1951-1952. **Memberships:** AAAS; fel Am Phys Soc; Soc Automotive Engrs; Sigma Xi. **Research Statement & Publications:** Plasma physics; nuclear reactor physics; energy conversion; research management solid state physics; surface physics; chemical physics; electro optical physics; metal physics; electrochemistry; electric propusion advanced batteries. **Mailing Address:** Jamerson & Assoc, 6590 Ridgewood Dr, Naples, FL 33963-8252. **Fax:** 239 -566-2106.

JAMES, ALTON EVERETTE, JR, RADIOLOGY, NUCLEAR MEDICINE. **Personal Data:** b Oxford, NC, August 22, 1938; m 1998, Nancy Jane Farmer; c Everette III, Jeanette(Whitson) & Elizabeth. **Education:** Univ NC, AB, 1959; Duke Univ, MD, 1963; Johns Hopkins Univ, MS, 1971; Am Bd Radiol, dipl, 1969; Am Bd Nuclear Med, cert, 1972, Vanderbilt Law Sch, 1977-1979, Harvard Bus Sch, 1979. **Honors & Awards:** Hon fel cannadian radiological soc(1971) Army Commanation Medal(1966); Gold Medal, Soc Nuclear Med; Silver Medal, Am Roentgen Ray Soc; Bronze Medal, Soc Nuclear Med; Distinguished graduate Duke med sch(1994) Riddick soc, N Cardinal State, NCSU(2002) Carraway Award, State of NC(1994); Leonidas Polk soc NCSU(1999), Humanitarian Award, Duke med sch(2002). **Professional Experience:** LECT, JOHNS HOPKINS UNIV, 1994-; SR PROF, INST MED, NAT ACAD SCI, 1993-; prof biomed eng, Inst Pub Policy, 1981-1993; sr res assoc, Inst Pub Policy, 1980-1993; prof med admin & lectr legal med, radiol & radiol sci, Vanderbilt Univ, 1979-1993; prof & chmn dept, radiol & radiol sci, Vanderbilt Univ, 1975-1993; hon res fel, Univ Col, London, 1974; Nat Naval Med Ctr, 1974-1975 & Nuffield Inst Comp Zool, London, 1974; consult, Armed Forces Radiobiol Res Inst, 1973-; Nat Zool Park, Smithsonian Inst, 1973-; dir res radiol, Med Sch, Johns Hopkins Univ, 1973-1975; consult, Walter Reed Army Hosp, 1973-1975; from asst prof to assoc prof radiol sci, Med Sch, Johns Hopkins Univ, 1969-1975; Nat Acad Sci-Nat Res Coun James Picker fel, Sch Hyg & Pub Health, Johns Hopkins Univ, 1969-1971; chief res & fel, Harvard Med Sch, 1968-1969; resident radiol, Mass Gen Hosp, 1966-1968; Cap US Army SVN 1965-1966(Radiology) Intern med, Univ Fla, 1963-1964. **Memberships:** Emer mem, fel AAAS; Am Soc Clin Invest; Radiol Soc NAm: assoc univ rad(past pres) Soc Chmn Acad Radiol Depts, past pres; Am Roentgen Ray Soc, past pres; Am Inst Ultrasound Med (treas, 1978-1981); Sigma Xi; fel Royal Soc Med, pres. **Research Statement & Publications:** Cerebrospinal fluid physiology; avian respiration; computerized axial tomography; ultrasonography; medical jurisprudence; paleoradiology; nuclear magnetic resonance MRI; positron emission tomography; evaluation of authenticity of paintings; xerography; author or coauthor of 27 texts over 6 00 publications. **Mailing Address:** St James Pl Box 789, Robersonville, NC 27871. **Fax:** 919-942-0437. **E-Mail:** ejames@intrex.net

JAMES, BARRY R, MATHEMATICS. **Education:** Univ Calif, PhD (statist), 1972. **Professional Experience:** PROF, DEPT APPL COMPUTATIONAL MATH, UNIV MINN-DULUTH, as of 2006. **Mailing Address:** Dept Math, Univ Minn-Duluth, Solon Campus Ctr 140 1117 Univ Dr, Duluth, MN 55812. **Fax:** 218-726-8399. **E-Mail:** bjames@d.umn.edu

JAMES, BELA MICHAEL, BIOLOGICAL OCEANOGRAPHY, FATE & EFFECTS OF OIL SPILLS. **Personal Data:** b Wichita Falls, Tex, January 20, 1940; m 1968, c 2. **Education:** Tarleton State Col, BS, 1963; Tex A&M Univ, MS, 1966, PhD (biol oceanog), 1972. **Professional Experience:** STAFF ENVIRON SPECIALIST, OIL SPILLS, SHELL OIL CO, 1991-; sr scientist & off mgr, Continental Shelf Assocs, 1983-1991; exec vpres & chief researcher, Tereco Corp, 1973-1983; res scientist, Tex A&M Univ, 1970-1973; res asst oceanog, Tex A&M Univ, 1968-1970. **Research Statement & Publications:** Marine ecology; taxonomy and ecology of euphausiacean crustaceans and palaeotaxodont mollusks; deep-sea oceanography; water quality and pollution control; oil spill contigency planning; fate and effect of oil. **Mailing Address:** Shell Oil Co, One Shell Plaza PO Box 4320, Houston, TX 77210-4320. **E-Mail:** bjames@houston.rr.com

JAMES, BRENT, SURGERY. **Education:** Univ Utah, BS, MS, MD. **Professional Experience:** VPRES, MED RES, INTERMOUNTAIN HEALTH CARE, as of 2005; EXEC DIR, INST HEALTH CARE DELIVERY RES, INTERMOUNTAIN HEALTH CARE, as of 2005. **Mailing Address:** Intermountain Health Care, 36 S State St Suite 2200, Salt Lake City, UT 84111.

JAMES, BRIAN ROBERT, HOMOGENEOUS CATALYSIS, BIOINORGANIC CHEMISTRY. **Personal Data:** b Birmingham, Eng, April 21, 1936; m 1962, Jane; c Jennifer, Peter, Sarah & Andrew. **Education:** Oxford Univ, BA, 1957, MA, 1960, DPhil (chem), 1960. **Honors & Awards:** Noranda Award, Chem Inst Can, 1975, Can Catal Award, 1990, EWR Steacie Award, 1997; Award in Chem of Noble Metals & Compounds, Royal Soc Chem 1996. **Professional Experience:** PROF EMER INORG CHEM, UNIV BC, as of 2004; Killam fel, Can Coun, 1993; vis prof, Australian Nat Univ, 1991; vis prof, Univ Amsterdam, 1990; vis prof, Univ Venice, 1983; Guggenheim Fel, 1983; vis prof, Univ Pisa, 1979; ed, Catalysis Metal Complexes, 1975- & Can J Chem, 1978-1988; prof inorg chem, Univ BC, beginning 1974; mem, Nat Res Coun Chem Grants Selection Comt, 1974-1977; from asst prof to assoc prof, Univ BC, 1964-1974; sr sci officer, UK Atomic Energy Auth, 1962-1964; fel inorg reaction mechanisms, Univ BC, 1960-1962; bd dirs, Org Reaction Catalysis Soc. **Memberships:** Fel Chem Soc; fel Chem Inst Can; NY Acad Sci; Am Chem Soc; fel Japan SocProm Sci; fel Royal Soc Can; fel Royal Soc Chem. **Research Statement & Publications:** Synthesis, homogeneous catalytic properties of, and mechanistic studies on, coordination compounds, organometallics, and bioinorganic model systems; author of one book, several book chapters and 275 publications in journals. **Mailing Address:** Dept Chem, Univ BC, Vancouver, BC V6T 1Z1, Can. **Fax:** 604-822-2847. **E-Mail:** brj@chem.ubc.ca

JAMES, BRUCE R, SOIL CHEMISTRY. **Education:** Williams Col, MA, BS; Univ Vt, Burlington, MS & PhD. **Professional Experience:** DIR, ENVIRON SCI & POLICY PROG, UNIV MD, as of 2006; PROF SOIL CHEM, UNIV MD, as of 2006. **Mailing Address:** Dept Agronomy, Univ Md, 0102 Symons Hall, College Park, MD 20742-5565. **Fax:** 301-405-8570. **E-Mail:** bj5@umail.umd.edu

JAMES, CHARLES FRANKLIN, JR, INDUSTRIAL ENGINEERING. **Personal Data:** b Des Arc, Mo, July 16, 1931; m 1974, Mollie Keeler; c Thomas E & Matthew J. **Education:** Purdue Univ, BSc, 1958, MSc, 1960, PhD (indust eng), 1963. **Honors & Awards:** Silver Medal, Tech Univ Budapest. **Professional Experience:** RETIRED; mem, accreditation processes comt, Am Soc Eng Educ, 1986; Dean, Col Eng & Appl Sci, Univ Wis Milwaukee, 1984-; C Paul Stocker distinguished vis prof eng, Ohio Univ, 1982-1983; vis fac mem, Massey Univ, NZ, 1979; US Dept Transp res grant, 1972-1982; prof indust eng & chmn dept, Univ RI, 1967-1983; assoc prof, Univ Mass, 1966-1967; indust consult, US & foreign indust & govt agencies, 1965-1990; asst prof indust eng, Univ RI, 1963-1966; sr indust engr, McDonnell Aircraft Co, 1963. **Memberships:** Am Inst Indust Engrs; Am Soc Mech Engrs; Soc Mfg Engrs; Am Foundrymen's Soc; Am Soc Eng Educ; Am Arbit Soc; Nat Soc Prof Engrs; Sigma Xi. **Research Statement & Publications:** Materials processing; robotics; highway safety. **Mailing Address:** 26024 Ridge Rd, Excelsior Springs, MO 64024. **E-Mail:** cfjames@skylinkisp.com

JAMES, CHARLES WILLIAM, SYSTEMATIC BOTANY. **Personal Data:** b Dade City, Fla, August 13, 1929; m 1960, c 3. **Education:** Univ Fla, BS, 1950, MS, 1952; Duke Univ, PhD (bot), 1955. **Professional Experience:** PROF BOT & ASSOC DEAN COL ARTS & SCI, UNIV GA, 1970-; asst dean, Univ Ga, 1963-1970; from asst prof to assoc prof bot, Univ Ga, 1957-1970; res botanist herbarium, Harvard Univ, 1956-1957; instr bot, Univ Tenn, 1955-1956. **Memberships:** Am Soc Plant Taxon; Int Asn Plant Taxon. **Research Statement & Publications:** Taxonomy of seed plants primarily of the southeastern United States. **Mailing Address:** 1175 Whit Davis Rd, Athens, GA 30605.

JAMES, CHRISTOPHER ROBERT, PLASMA PHYSICS, ELECTROMAGNETICS. **Personal Data:** b Vancouver, BC, November 15, 1935; m 1956, c 5. **Education:** Univ BC, BASc, 1960, MASc, 1961, PhD (elec Eng), 1964. **Professional Experience:** RETIRED; vpres res, Univ Alta, 1987-1996; mem, Dept External Affairs Negotiating Team, beginning 1978; bd examiners, Asn Prof Engrs, Geologists & Geophysicists Alta, beginning 1974; chmn dept, Univ Alta, 1974-1987; dir negotiated develop grant, Nat Res Coun, 1971-

1975; fromasst prof to prof plasmas, Univ Alta, 1965-1996; grant, Nat Res Coun, 1965-1981; fel, Nat Res Coun-NATO, Oxford Univ, 1964-1965. **Memberships:** Can Asn Physicists; Eng Inst Can; Am Phys Soc; AAAS. **Research Statement & Publications:** Nonlinear laser heating of plasmas; laser-plasma interaction studies. **Mailing Address:** Univ Alta, 238 Civil Elec Bldg, Edmonton, AB T6G 2J9, Can.

JAMES, DAVID EUGENE, ORGANIC CHEMISTRY. **Personal Data:** b Washington, Iowa, June 19, 1945; div, c Carly, David. **Education:** Cornell Col, BA, 1967; Univ Iowa, PhD (org chem), 1975. **Professional Experience:** SR RES ASSOC, BP CHEM CO, 1975-; instr chem, Linn Mar Community Sch Dist, 1967-1971; pres, bd dirs, Sci & Technol Interactive Ctr. **Memberships:** Sigma Xi; Am Chem Soc; AAAS. **Research Statement & Publications:** Liquid chromatographic separations of industrially important compounds; homogeneous catalysis using transition metals; oxidation of aromatic hydrocarbons; condensation polymerization. **Mailing Address:** 1133 Woodland Hills Rd, Batavia, IL 60510. **Fax:** 630-961-6223. **E-Mail:** jamesde@bp.com

JAMES, DAVID EVAN, SEISMOLOGY. **Personal Data:** b Bellingham, Wash, December 14, 1939; m 1977, Jeri; c Kaitlin & Kristen. **Education:** Stanford Univ, BS, 1962, MS, 1963, PhD (geophysics), 1967. **Honors & Awards:** IRIS/SSA Distinguished Lecturer, 2004. **Professional Experience:** STAFF MEM GEOPHYS, DEPT TERRESTRIAL MAGNETISM, CARNEGIE INST, 1970-; assoc staff mem, Dept Terrestrial Magnetism, Carnegie Inst, 1968-1970; fel. geophys, Dept Terrestrial Magnetism, Carnegie Inst, 1966-1968. **Memberships:** Am Geophys Union (fel); Soc Explor Geophys (mem); Royal Astron Soc (fel). **Research Statement & Publications:** Seismic studies of continental lithosphere and subduction zones; evolution of central Andes; isotope and trace element geochemistry of volcanic arcs; paleomagnetism; formation and evolution of continents. **Mailing Address:** Carnegie Institution/Dept Terrestrial Magnetism, 5241 Broad Branch Rd NW, Washington, DC 20015-1305. **Fax:** 202-478-8821. **E-Mail:** james@dtm.ciw.edu

JAMES, DAVID F, FLUID MECHANICS, BIOMEDICAL ENGINEERING. **Personal Data:** b Belleville, Ont, July 9, 1939. **Education:** Queen's Univ, Ont, BSc, 1962; Calif Inst Technol, MS, 1963, PhD (mech eng), 1967; Univ Cambridge, MA, 1974. **Professional Experience:** PROF MECH ENG & INDUST ENG, UNIV TORONTO, 1979-; assoc prof, Univ Toronto, 1971-1979; asst prof, Univ Toronto, 1967-1971; vis prof, Caltech; vis prof, Univ Melbourne. **Research Statement & Publications:** Flow of dilute polymer solutions; rheology of non-Newtonian fluids; fluid mechanics of physiological systems. **Mailing Address:** Dept Mech & Indust Eng, Univ Toronto, 5 Kings Col Rd, Toronto, ON M5J 3G8, Can. **E-Mail:** james@mie.utoronto.ca

JAMES, DAVID RANDOLPH, BIOLOGICAL & RADIATION PHYSICS. **Personal Data:** b Atlanta, Ga, June 13, 1948. **Education:** Ga Inst Technol, BS, 1970, MS, 1971, PhD (physics), 1975. **Professional Experience:** RES STAFF MEM, HEALTH & SAFETY RES DIV, OAK RIDGE NATLAB, 1976-; res fel, Univ Tenn, Knoxville, 1975-1976; Res asst, Ga Inst Technol, 1970-1975. **Memberships:** Am Phys Soc; Sigma Xi. **Research Statement & Publications:** Approximately 34 open literature publications. **Mailing Address:** Oak Ridge Nat Lab, PO Box 30098, Knoxville, TN 37930.

JAMES, DAVID WINSTON, agronomy; deceased, see previous edition for last biography

JAMES, DEAN B, PHYSICAL INORGANIC & NUCLEAR POWER CHEMISTRY. **Personal Data:** b Ames, Iowa, June 14, 1934; m 1960, Ethel; c Katherine & Karen. **Education:** Iowa State Univ, BS, 1956, PhD, 1960. **Professional Experience:** SR CHEMIST, ULTRAPURE WATER TECH, 1988-; sr chemist, Advan Process Tech, Inc, 1985-1988; advan tech, Safeguards Audits, 1985-1988; mgr, Safeguards Audits, 1975-1985; prin engr, Nuclear Energy Group, Gen Elec Co, 1972-1975; fel scientist res & develop, Nuclear Mat & Equip Corp, Atlantic Richfield Co, Apollo, 1968-1971; group leader rare-earth res, Mich Chem Corp, 1966-1968; staff mem, Los Alamos Sci Lab, 1960-1966; res asst, Ames Lab, Atomic Energy Comn, 1952-1960. **Research Statement & Publications:** Ion exchange; waste treatment; process development; technical management; nuclear materials safeguards systems; nuclear power chemistry. **Mailing Address:** 20518 Deerpark Ct, Saratoga, CA 95070.

JAMES, DONALD GORDON, MATHEMATICS. **Personal Data:** b Auckland, NZ, March 18, 1938; m 1967, Ingrid; c Michael A. **Education:** New Zealand Univ, BSc, 1959, MSc, 1960; Mass Inst Technol, PhD (math), 1963. **Professional Experience:** RETIRED; prof emer math, Eberly Col Sci, Pa State Univ, ending 2004; prof math, Pa State Univ, Eberly Col Sci, beginning 1976; fel Alexander von Humboldt Stiftung, Ger, 1969-1970; from asst prof to assoc prof, Eberly Col Sci, PA State Univ, 1966-1976; lectr math, Univ Auckland, 1964-1965. **Memberships:** Am Math Soc. **Research Statement & Publications:** Algebra and number theory, particularly quadratic and hermitian forms, orthogonal and unitary groups. **Mailing Address:** 854 Bayberry Dr, State College, PA 16801. **E-Mail:** james@math.psu.edu

JAMES, DOUGLAS A, ORNITHOLOGY. **Education:** Univ Ill, PhD, 1957. **Professional Experience:** UA DISTINGUISHED PROF ZOOLOGY, UNIV ARK, as of 2002. **Mailing Address:** Dept Biol Sci Univ Ark, Fayetteville, AR 72701. **Fax:** 479-575-4010. **E-Mail:** djames@comp.uark.edu

JAMES, DOUGLAS GARFIELD LIMBREY, CHEMISTRY. **Personal Data:** b London, Eng, October 31, 1924; m 1959, c 3. **Education:** Cambridge Univ, BA, 1948, MA & PhD (chem), 1955. **Professional Experience:** RETIRED; from asst prof to prof chem, Univ BC, 1968-1990; vis fel chem, Aberdeen Univ, 1965-1966; lectr chem, Univ St Andrews, 1954-1959; consult. **Memberships:** Fel Chem Inst Can; fel Royal Soc Chem. **Research Statement & Publications:** Chemical kinetics; addition of free radicals to unsaturated molecules. **Mailing Address:** 391 Roland Rd, Salt Spring Island, BC V8K 1V1, Can.

JAMES, EDWARD JR, PHYSICAL CHEMISTRY, EXPLOSIVES. **Personal Data:** b El Paso, Tex, July 14, 1917; m 1940, c 1. **Education:** Univ Mich, BS, 1937. **Professional Experience:** Mem, Sci Adv Bd, USAF, 1985; CONSULT, 1980-; asst div leader, Lawrence-Livermore Nat Lab, Univ Calif, 1963-1980; sect leader, Lawrence Livermore Nat Lab, Univ Calif, 1960-1963; sect leader, Los Alamos Sci Labs, 1949-1960; chemist, Los Alamos Sci Labs, 1946-1949; chemist, Sherwin Williams Co, 1937-1946. **Memberships:** Am Chem Soc; AAAS. **Research Statement & Publications:** Resin bonded pigments for textiles; emulsion paints; polyester resins; plastic bonded explosives; explosives, polymer synthesis and manufacture; detonation hydrodynamics. **Mailing Address:** 1085 Peary Ct, Livermore, CA 94550-5611.

JAMES, ERIC R, BIOLOGY. **Education:** London, PhD, 1974. **Professional Experience:** ASSOC PROF OPHTHALMOLOGY, STORM EYE INST, as of 2005. **Mailing Address:** Storm Eye Inst, SEI 530, Charleston, SC 29425-2236. **Fax:** 803-792-1723. **E-Mail:** jameser@musc.edu

JAMES, FRANCES CREWS, ECOLOGY. **Personal Data:** b Philadelphia, Pa, September 29, 1930; c 3. **Education:** Mt Holyoke Col, AB, 1952; La State Univ, MS, 1956; Univ Ark, PhD (zoology), 1970. **Honors & Awards:** E P Edwards Prize, Wilson Ornith Soc. **Professional Experience:** FAC MEM EMER, DEPT BIOL SCI, FLA STATE UNIV, TALLAHASSEE, as of 2003; prof, Dept Biol Sci, Fla State Univ, Tallahassee, beginning 1984; assoc prof, Dept Biol Sci, Fla State Univ, Tallahassee, 1977-1984; assoc prog dir, Ecol Prog, NSF, 1976-1977; res assoc, Smithsonian Inst, beginning 1975; asst prog dir, Ecol Prog, NSF, 1973-1976; resassoc, Mus, 1971-1973; instr zool & bot, Univ Ark, 1960-1970. **Memberships:** Ecol Soc Am; Am Ornithologists Union (pres, 1984-1986); Soc Syst Zool; AAAS; Cooper Ornith Soc. **Research Statement & Publications:** Geographic variation in vertebrates; analysis of avian communities; habitat selection in birds; thermal behavioral ecology of lizards; avian systematics; allometry. **Mailing Address:** Dept Biol Sci, Fla State Univ, Tallahassee, FL 32306-2043. **Fax:** 850-644-9829. **E-Mail:** james@bio.fsu.edu

JAMES, FRANKLIN WARD, ANALYTICAL CHEMISTRY CHROMATOGRAPHY. **Personal Data:** b Montrose, Miss, September 2, 1922; m 1958, Jewell Slocum; c Craig & Nancy. **Education:** Miss Col, BS, 1947; Univ NC, PhD (chem), 1952. **Professional Experience:** EMER CALLAWAY PROF CHEM, MERCER UNIV, 1988-; Fuller E Callaway prof, Mercer Univ, 1970-1988; chmn dept, Mercer Univ, 1961-1980; prof chem, Mercer Univ, 1961-1970; sr chemist, Res & Tech Dept, Texaco, Inc, 1958-1961; From assoc prof to prof chem, Millsaps Col, 1951-1958. **Memberships:** Am Chem Soc. **Research Statement & Publications:** Standard electrode potentials of electrodes in aqueous glycerol solutions. **Mailing Address:** 4179 Vallie Dr, Macon, GA 31204-4758. **E-Mail:** fwjames2000@yahoo.com

JAMES, GARTH A, ENDODONTICS. **Personal Data:** b Malad City, Idaho, August 1, 1926; m 1947, c 7. **Education:** Utah State Univ, BS, 1948, MS, 1951; Univ Nebr, DDS, 1960. **Professional Experience:** RETIRED; chmn dept, Col Dent, Univ Nebr-Lincoln, 1970-1988; from assoc prof to prof endodontics, Col Dent, Univ Nebr-Lincoln, 1960-1988; res assoc bact, Col Dent, Univ Nebr-Lincoln, 1956-1960; dir bact, St Elizabeth Hosp, 1956-1960; instr bact & pub health, Utah State Agr Col & bacteriologist, Exp Sta, 1952-1956; res technician, Naval Biol Lab, UnivCalif, 1952; teacher pub sch, Idaho, 1947-1949. **Memberships:** Am Dent Asn; Am Asn Endodont; Am Soc Microbiol; fel Am Col Dentists; fel Int Col Dentists. **Mailing Address:** 1150 Mountain Ridge Rd, Provo, UT 84604.

JAMES, GEORGE ELLERT, ELECTRONICS ENGINEERING. **Personal Data:** b Douglas, Alaska, April 26, 1917; m 1953, Joan. **Education:** Univ Wash, BS, 1940; George Wash Univ, MS, 1962, DSc (eng sci), 1969. **Professional Experience:** RETIRED; vpres, Adcole Corp, 1972-1990; consult scientist, Missile Systs Div, Bedford Lab, Raytheon Co, 1971-1972; vpres, Adcole Corp, 1970-1971; tech staff mem, Inst Defense Anal, 1958-1970; dir, Boston Div, Ramo-Wooldridge Corp, 1956-1957; chief engr, Lab Electronics Inc, 1948-1956; asst proj engr, Hughes Aircraft Co, 1947-1948; chief engr, Gen Commun Co, 1946-1947; electronic develop engr, Gen Elec Co, 1940-1945. **Memberships:** Inst Elec & Electronics Engrs. **Research Statement & Publications:** Electromagnetic field theory; electronic circuit design; radar and control systems; applied mathematics; operations analysis; computer software development. **Mailing Address:** 14 Temple St Apt 3B, Framingham, MA 01701.

JAMES, GEORGE WATSON, III, MEDICINE. **Personal Data:** b Richmond, Va, July 3, 1918; m 1943, c 3. **Education:** Wash & Lee Univ, AB, 1940; Med Col Va, MD, 1943. **Professional Experience:** PROF MED, MED COL VA, 1965-; chmn, Div Hemat, Med Col Va, 1957-1983; consult, Keecoughtan Vet Hosp, 1952-1980; from asst prof to assoc prof, Med ColVa, 1949-1965; Markle scholar, Med Col Va, 1949-1954; consult, McGurie Vet Admin Hosp, 1948-; USPHS fel, 1948-1949. **Memberships:** AAAS; Am Soc Clin Invest; Am Fedn Clin Res; Am Clin & Climat Asn; Am SocClin Nutrit. **Research Statement & Publications:** Clinical investigations; bile pigment metabolism; red cell survival with N-15 label; leukemia and lymphoma chemotherapy; hematology. **Mailing Address:** Dept Med, Va Commonwealth Univ, Richmond, VA 23298. **Fax:** 804-371-8079.

JAMES, GORDON THOMAS, PROTEIN CHEMISTRY, CELL CULTURE. **Personal Data:** b Ft Scott, Kans, March 7, 1940. **Education:** Univ Calif, Riverside, PhD (biochem), 1971. **Professional Experience:** ANALYTICAL CHEMIST, NAT JEWISH HOSP, DENVER, 1989-; srbiochemist, Electropore Co, Boulder Co, 1986-1989; asst prof biochem, Dept Surg, Health Sci Ctr, Univ Colo, 1976-1986. **Memberships:** Am Soc Biochem & Molecular Biol. **Research Statement & Publications:** Protein chemistry; pharmacokinetics of tuberculosis drugs. **Mailing Address:** Nat Jewish Med & Res Ctr, 1400 Jackson St, Denver, CO 80206.

JAMES, HAROLD LEE, MOLECULAR BIOLOGY & BIOCHEMISTRY, GENERAL PHYSIOLOGY. **Personal Data:** b Taylorsville, NC, October 31, 1939; m 1965, c 1. **Education:** ETenn State Univ, BS, 1962; Univ Tenn, Memphis, PhD (biochem), 1968. **Professional Experience:** ASSOC PROF BIOCHEM, HEALTH CTR, UNIV TEX-TYLER, 1983-; resassoc prof med, Sch Med, Pulmonary Div, 1980-1983; res asst prof med, Sch Med, PulmonaryDiv, Temple Univ, 1976-1980; asst prof biochem, Univ Tenn Ctr for Health Sci, 1972-1975; res assoc, Lab Hemat, St Jude Children's Res Hosp, 1972-1975; res scientist, Blood Res Lab, AmNat Red Cross, 1970-1972; res instr med & biochem, Sch Med, Temple Univ, 1968-1970; resinstr biochem, Med Units, Univ Tenn, 1968; res technician, Med Units, Univ Tenn, 1962-1963. **Memberships:** Sigma Xi; Am Physiol Soc; Int Soc Thrombosis & Haemostasis; Am Heart Asn. **Research Statement & Publications:** Biochemistry and physiology of plasma and platelet fibrinogens; mechanism of interaction of alpha-1-antitrypsin with elastase; lung physiology of alpha-1-antitrypsin; animal models of emphysema; molecular biology of genetic variants of factors VIII and X; structure-function conclates of factors VIII and X; molecular. **Mailing Address:** Dept Biochem, Tex Health Sci Ctr PO Box 2003, Tyler, TX 75710-2003. **Fax:** 908-877-7558.

JAMES, HELEN JANE, ANALYTICAL CHEMISTRY. **Personal Data:** b Nebraska City, Nebr, June 15, 1943. **Education:** Univ Nebr, BS, 1965, PhD (anal chem), 1970. **Professional Experience:** PROF EMER CHEM DEPT & CHAIR, as of 2006; prof chem, Weber State Univl, 1980-2001; assoc prof chem, Weber State Univ, 1975-1980; asst prof, Weber State Univ, 1971-1975; fel, Univ Ariz, 1970-1971. **Memberships:** Sigma Xi; Am Chem Soc. **Research Statement & Publications:** Development and application of ion selective electrodes; the use of coated wire electrodes containing liquid membranes. **Mailing Address:** Dept Chem, Weber State Univ, 2503 Univ Circle, Ogden, UT 84408-2503.

JAMES, HERBERT I, PHYSICAL CHEMISTRY. **Personal Data:** b St Thomas, VI, March 30, 1933; American citizen; m 1962, c 2. **Education:** Hampton Inst, BS, 1955; Clark Univ, MA, 1958, PhD (chem), 1965. **Professional Experience:** REAL ESTATE AGENT; scientist, US, 1976-1984; teacher, Elec Storage BatteryCo, 1965-1976; scientist, Xerox Res Ctr, mgr affirmative action, Webster Res Ctr, Xerox, mgr personnel. **Memberships:** Electrochem Soc. **Research Statement & Publications:** Diffusion and sedimentation studies of macromolecules; nuclear and radiochemistry; bioelectrochemistry. **Mailing Address:** 49 Cumberland Dr, Mississauga, ON L5G 3N1, Can.

JAMES, HUGO A, PARASITOLOGY, HELMINTHOLOGY. **Personal Data:** b Bridgeport, Conn, May 24, 1930. **Education:** Univ Bridgeport, BA, 1957, MS, 1958; Univ Va, MA, 1961; Iowa State Univ, PhD (parasitol), 1968. **Professional Experience:** CONSULT, 1990-; chmn biol & dir, Div Biol & Health Technol, Univ Va, 1985-1990; prof biol, Univ Bridgeport, 1973-1985; NSF res grant, Univ Va, 1969; from instr toassoc prof, Univ Bridgeport, 1958-1973. **Memberships:** Am Soc Parasitol; Am Micros Soc (treas, 1979-1981). **Research Statement & Publications:** Host-parasite interrelationships of helminths, specifically the Cestoda; zoonotic associations, particularly aspects of taxonomy, morphology, pathology and evolution. **Mailing Address:** 7 Franklin St, Trumbull, CT 06611.

JAMES, JACK N, MISSILE & SPACE PROJECT ENGINEERING. **Personal Data:** b Dallas, Tex, November 22, 1920; m 1944, Ruth; c Jeffrey D, Jeremy R, Jack F & Susan E. **Education:** Southern Methodist Univ, BS, 1942; Union Col, MS, 1949. **Honors & Awards:** Hill Award, Am Inst Aeronaut & Astronaut, 1963; Except Sci Achievement Medal, 1965; Stuart Ballantine Medal, Franklin Inst, 1967. **Professional Experience:** RETIRED; Calif Inst Technol, Set Propulsion Orgn; asst lab dir, Defense & Civil Progs, Jet Propulsion Lab; asst lab dir, Tech & Space Prog Develop, Jet Propulsion Lab, 1976-1980; asst lab dir, Tech Divs, Jet Propulsion Lab, 1967-1976; dep asst lab dir, Lunar & Planetary Projs, Jet Propulsion Lab, 1965-1967; proj mgr, Jet Propulsion Lab, 1961-1965; dep prog mgr, Jet Propulsion Lab, 1960-1961; div mgr, Jet Propulsion Lab, 1958-1960; sect mgr, JetPropulsion Lab, 1956-1958; eng group supvr, Jet Propulsion Lab, 1954-1956; res engr, JetPropulsion Lab, 1950-1954; res engr, Radio Corp Am, 1949-1950; test engr, Gen Elec Co, 1942-1943, 1946-1949. **Memberships:** assoc fel Am Inst Aeronaut & Astronaut; fel Inst Elec & Electronics Engrs. **Research Statement & Publications:** Management of Mariner II to Venus and Mariner IV to Mars projects; guidance systems for Corporal and Sergeant missiles. **Mailing Address:** 1345 El Vago St, LaCanada Flintridge, CA 91011.

JAMES, JEFFREY, ANALYTICAL CHEMISTRY, INORGANIC CHEMISTRY. **Personal Data:** b Savannah, Ga, August 27, 1944. **Education:** Savannah State Col, BS, 1966; Tuskegee Inst, MS, 1970; Howard Univ, PhD (inorgchem), 1973. **Professional Experience:** PROF CHEM, SAVANNAH STATE COL, 1984-; res chemist, Lawrence LivermoreLab, 1978; res chemist, Savannah River Lab, 1975 & 1980; from asst prof to assoc prof, Savannah State Col, 1972-1984; res chemist, Eli Lily & Co, 1969; res chemist, Argonne Nat Lab, 1965, 1969, 1983. **Memberships:** Am Chem Soc; AAAS. **Research Statement & Publications:** Kinetic study of metalloporphyrins and oxidation of dithionite by manganese; hematoporphyrins in basic solution; characterization of mercury; electrodes; solubility products and thermodynamic functions for the Lanthanon fluridewater system. **Mailing Address:** Dept Chem, Savannah State Col, Drew-Griffith 205, Savannah, GA 31404. **Fax:** 912-691-6839. **E-Mail:** jamesj@savstate.edu

JAMES, JESSE, BIOCHEMISTRY. **Personal Data:** b Haynesville, La, January 26, 1937; m 1959, c 5. **Education:** Tex Southern Univ, BSc, 1961, MSc, 1962; Univ Tex, PhD (biochem), 1965. **Professional Experience:** PROF CHEM, KNOXVILLE COL, 1973-; chmn dept, Knoxville Col, 1973-1976; res chemist, Nat Bur Stand, 1970-; consult, Union Carbide Corp, Tenn, 1966-1970; assoc prof, Knoxville Col, 1965-1973. **Research Statement & Publications:** Kinetics and mechanisms of enzyme-catalyzed reactions; standardization of reference materials for clinical chemistry. **Mailing Address:** Dept Math & Sci, Knoxville Col, Rm 206 Sci Bldg 901 Col St, Knoxville, TN 37921-4724. **Fax:** 865-524-6603.

JAMES, JOHN CARY, ORGANIC CHEMISTRY. **Personal Data:** b Ceredo, WVa, May 8, 1926; m 1958, Geraldine; c Lisa. **Education:** WVa Wesleyan Col, BS, 1949; Univ Del, PhD (org chem), 1960. **Professional Experience:** DEPT DIR, DIV EXTRAMURAL OUTREACH & INFO RESOURCES, NIH, 1996-; asst dir spec projs, Div Res Grants, 1984-1995; chief, Res Anal & Eval Br, 1971-1984; chief, Sci Eval Sect, Res Anal & Eval Br, 1970-1971; exec secy, Med Chem Fel Rev Comt, DivRes Grants, NIH, 1967-1970; sr chemist, Northrop Carolina, Inc, 1966-1967; sr res chemist, Boston Labs, Monsanto Res Corp, 1959-1966; teacher, Callao High Sch, Peru, 1950-1953. **Memberships:** AAAS. **Research Statement & Publications:** Synthesis of anti-oxidants; research on jet fuels; antiradiation drug research; high temperature explosives; health sciences administration; research analysis and information science; electronic communications; peer review appeals. **Mailing Address:** Off Extramural Outreach & Info Resources, Nat Inst Health, Rm 6206, MSC 7910, 6701 Rockledge Dr, Bethesda, MD 20892-7910. **E-Mail:** jqj@odrockm1.od.nih.gov

JAMES, KAREN K(ANKE), IMMUNOLOGY. **Personal Data:** b Vinton, Iowa, June 2, 1944; m 1964, c 3. **Education:** Ohio State Univ, BS, 1967, MS, 1972; Rush Med Univ, PhD (immunol), 1980. **Professional Experience:** CONSULT IMMUNOL, 1993-; chmn, lab mgt comt, Bd Registry, 1986-; assoc prof path, Loyola Univ Med Ctr, Chicago, 1986-; actg ed, Lab Med, 1985-1986; consult, SmithKline Biosciences Labs, 1984-1986; assoc dir labs, Cent Dupage Hosp, 1982-1993; asst prof immunol, Rush Univ, 1980-1987; dir immunol, Rush Presby St Luke's Med Ctr, 1980-1982; clin asst prof, Med Lab Sci, Univ Ill, Chicago, 1977-1987; chmn, Immunol Comt, Bd Registry, 1977-1985; instr, Rush Presby St Luke's Med Ctr, 1976-1980; clin instr, Allied Med Professions, Ohio State Univ, 1973-1977; supv clin immunol, Ohio State Univ Hosp, 1973-1976; med technologist, Riverside Methodist Hosp, 1967-1971. **Memberships:** Am Soc Clin Path; Am Asn Immunol. **Research Statement & Publications:** Biologic response modifying properties of C reactive protein; natural killer cells; cellular immunology. **Mailing Address:** 1584 Hattie Hill Rd, Vilas, NC 28692.

JAMES, KRISTIN BOWMAN, INORGANIC CHEMISTRY. **Personal Data:** b Philadelphia, Pa, June 4, 1946; m 1976. **Education:** Univ Temple, BA, 1968, PhD (chem), 1974. **Honors & Awards:** Am Chem Soc Midwest Award, 2003. **Professional Experience:** Chair, Dept Chem, Univ Kans, 1995-2001; PROF SUPRAMOLECULAR & BIOMIMETIC CHEM, UNIV KANS, 1987-; from asst prof to assoc prof, Univ Kans, 1975-1987; fel res, Univ Ohio state, 1974-1975. **Memberships:** Am Chem Soc; Am Crystallographer's Asn. **Research Statement & Publications:** Structure reactivity aspects of transition metal complexes particularly with macrocyclic ligand systems; Published over 70 articles. **Mailing Address:** Dept Chem, Univ Kans, 1017 Malott Hall, Lawrence, KS 66045-0501. **Fax:** 785-864-5396. **E-Mail:** kbowman-james@ku.edu

JAMES, L DOUGLAS, GEOSCIENCES. **Education:** Stanford Univ, BS, MS, PhD, 1965. **Professional Experience:** PROG DIR, DIV EARTH SCI, NSF, VA, as of 2006. **Mailing Address:** NSF Geosciences, Rm 602, 4201 Wilson Blvd Rm 785, Arlington, Va 22230. **Fax:** 703-292-9025. **E-Mail:** ldjames@nsf.gov

JAMES, LARRY GEORGE, AGRICULTURAL ENGINEERING, IRRIGATION ENGINEERING. **Personal Data:** b Bellingham, Wash, May 1, 1947; m 1968, Elaine; c Gregory A, Jeffrey L, Elizabeth I & Carolyn N. **Education:** Wash State Univ, BS, 1970; Univ Minn, PhD (agr eng), 1975. **Professional Experience:** ASSOC EXEC V PRES, WASH STATE UNIV, 2005-; chancellor, Wash State Univ Tri-Cities, 1998-2005; interim dean College of Agriculture and Home Economics, Wash State Univ, 1995; assoc dean & dir acad progs, College of Ag and Home Economics, Wash State Univ, 1993-1994, 1995-1998; interim assoc dean & dir coop Exten, College of Ag and Home Economics, Wash State Univ, 1991-1993; prof & chair, Agr Eng, Wash State Univ, 1988-1991; from asst prof to assoc prof, Agr Eng, Wash State Univ, 1977-1988; Asst prof agr eng, Cornell Univ, 1975-1977. **Research Statement & Publications:** Plant water requirements; energy requirements for irrigation; sprinkler irrigation; infiltration; water resources management. **Mailing Address:** Office the Provost, Pullman, WA 99164-1046. **Fax:** 509-335-0103. **E-Mail:** jameslg@wsu.edu

JAMES, L(AURENCE) ALLAN, FLUVIAL GEOMORPHOLOGY & QUATERNARY SCIENCE, WATER RESOURCES & SEDIMENTATION IN WATERSHEDS & GLACIAL GEOMORPHOLOGY. **Education:** Univ Calif, Berkeley, BA, 1978; Univ Wis-Madison, MS, 1981, MS, 1983, PhD (geog& geol), 1988. **Professional Experience:** Instr, Dept Geol, Univ Calif, 1996; chair, Geomorphol Spec Group, Assn, Am Geographers, 1995-1996; ASSOC PROF, DEPT GEOG, UNIV SC, 1994-; nat Res Coun Com Am River, 1994-1996; pi & panelist, NSF (several times), asst prof, Geog Dept, Univ SC, 1988-1994; asst prof, Dept Geog, Univ S Carolina, 1988-1993; lectr physgeog, Univ Ga, 1987-1988; lectr phys geog, Univ Oregon, 1987; lectr phys geog, Geog Dept, Univ Wis-Madison, 1986. **Memberships:** Asn Am Geogr; Geol Soc Am; Am Geophys Union; Am Water Resources Asn; Am Quaternary Asn; Int Asn Geomorphologists; Int Asn Hydrologic Sci. **Research Statement & Publications:** Water and sediment yields from fluvial systems; historical anthropogenic sedimentation; monitoring long-term changes to anthropogenic sediment; using LIDAR to map gullies under forest canopy; Quaternary glacial mapping in Sierra Nevada, Calif. **Mailing Address:** Dept Geog, Univ SC, Callcott Bldg, Rm 206, Columbia, SC 29208. **Fax:** 803-777-4972. **E-Mail:** ajames@sc.edu

JAMES, LAYLIN KNOX, SURFACE CHEMISTRY. **Personal Data:** b Pittsburgh, Pa, September 17, 1927; m 1952, c 4. **Education:** Univ Mich, BS, 1950, MS, 1952; Univ Ill, PhD (chem), 1958. **Professional Experience:** EMER PROF CHEM, LAFAYETTE COL, 1990-; guest prof, Hohenheim Univ, Stuttgart, WGer, 1982; dept head, Lafayette Col, 1979-1985; prof chem, Lafayette Col, 1977-1990; actg dept head, Lafayette Col, 1970-1971; chemist, US Naval Res Lab, 1963; from asst prof to assoc prof, Lafayette Col, 1959-1977; res chemist, Procter & Gamble Co, 1958-1959; asst, Univ Ill, 1954-1956 & Wash State Univ, 1957-1958; chemist, Shell Chem Co, div Shell Oil Co, 1952-1954. **Memberships:** AAAS; Am Chem Soc. **Research Statement & Publications:** Surface chemistry of proteins and lipoproteins. **Mailing Address:** 18 E Santa Belia, Green Valley, AZ 85614-1537.

JAMES, LEE MORTON, FORESTRY. **Personal Data:** b New York, NY, December 14, 1916; m 1946. **Education:** Pa State Col, BS, 1937; Univ Mich, MF, 1943, PhD (forest econ), 1945. **Professional Experience:** EMER PROF, MICH STATE UNIV, as of 2004; chmn dept, Mich State Univ, 1966-1978; prof forestry, Mich State Univ, beginning 1958; assoc prof, Mich State Univ, 1951-1958; forest economist charge unitresource analysis, Div Forest Econ, Southern Forest Exp Sta, 1946-1951; forester, AppalachianForest Exp Sta, 1940-1941 & 1943-1946; unit supvr, New Eng Forest Emergency Proj, USForest Serv, 1938-1940; instr forestry, Pa State Col, 1937-1938; consult, Resources for Future, Inc, Forest Indust Coun, US Dept Interior, US Dept Com, Pub Land Law Rev Comt & President'sCoun Environ Qual. **Memberships:** Soc Am Foresters. **Research Statement & Publications:** Forest resource and forest industry analysis; timber products marketing; forest policy. **Mailing Address:** Dept Forestry, Mich State Univ, 126 Natural Resources Bldg, East Lansing, MI 48824.

JAMES, MARGARET OLIVE, BIOCHEMISTRY, TOXICOLOGY. **Personal Data:** b Haverfordwest, UK, July 9, 1948; m David; c Nathaniel & Kathleen. **Education:** Univ London, BS, 1969, PhD (org chem), 1972, DSc, 1993. **Professional Experience:** PROF MEDICINAL CHEMISTRY, COL PHARM, UNIV FLA, as of 2005; SCIENTIFIC ADV BD, ECOARRAY, LLC, as of 2004; Toxics Adv Comt, Coastal Ocean Prog, NOAA, 1992-; CHMN, DEPT MED CHEM, COL PHARM, UNIV FLA, 1991-; mem, Nat Environ Health Sci Rev Coomt, 1991-1995; PROF MED CHEM, COL PHARM, UNIV FLA, 1980-; sr staff fel, Nat Inst Environ Health Sci, 1978-1980; res assoc, Nat Inst Environ Health Sci, 1975-1978; Fel, Nat Inst Environ Health Sci, 1972-1975; prog dir, Superfund Basic Res Prog. **Memberships:** Int Soc Study Xenobiotics; Am Soc Pharmacol & Exp Ther; Am Chem Soc; Soc Toxicol; Am Asn Pharmaceut Sci; AAAS. **Research Statement & Publications:** In vivo and in vitro studies of xenobiotic metabolism in aquatic and mammalian species; enzymes which alter the toxicity of a xenobiotic. **Mailing Address:** Dept Med Chem, Col Pharm, Univ Fla, Rm P6-20, 1600 SW Archer Rd, PO Box 100485, Gainesville, FL 32610-0485. **Fax:** 352-846-1972. **E-Mail:** mojames@ufl.edu

JAMES, MARK, IMMUNOLOGY. **Professional Experience:** ASSOC PROF TROPICAL MED, TULANE UNIV, as of 2000. **Mailing Address:** Dept Tropical Med, Tulane Univ, Sch Public Health & Tropical Med, 1501 Canal St, New Orleans, LA 70112-2699. **E-Mail:** mjames@mailhost.tcs.tulane.edu

JAMES, MARLYNN REES, PHYSICAL CHEMISTRY. **Personal Data:** b Spanish Fork, Utah, November 20, 1933; m 1961, Jane; c Leslie J, Richard, Bruce, Mark, Karen & Jackie. **Education:** Brigham Young Univ, BS, 1958, MS, 1961; Univ Utah, PhD (theoret gaschromatography), 1965. **Professional Experience:** PROF EMER CHEM, UNIV NORTHERN COLO, as of 2004; prof Chem, Univ Northern Colo, beginning 1966; Res asst chem, PurdueUniv, 1964-1966. **Memberships:** Am Chem Soc; Nat Sci Supvrs Asn; Nat Sci Teachers Asn; Nat Asn Res SciTeaching. **Research Statement & Publications:** Chemical education and curriculum development involving computers. **Mailing Address:** Dept Chem, Univ Northern Colo, Greeley, CO 80639. **E-Mail:** mljames@bentley.unco.edu

JAMES, MICHAEL G, BIOCHEMISTRY, CRYSTALLOGRAPHY. **Personal Data:** b Vancouver, BC, May 16, 1940. **Education:** Univ Man, BC, 1962, MS, 1963; Oxford Univ, PhD (chem crystallog), 1966. **Honors & Awards:** Ayerst Award, Can Biochem Soc, 1979; G Malcolm Brown Award, 1992; Joseph F Foster lectr, Purdue Univ, 1994. **Professional Experience:** PROF, DEPT BIOCHEM, UNIV ALTA, as of 2006; lectr, Biochem Sem, Purdue Univ, 1980; Pfizer travelling fel, ClinRes Inst Montreal, 1977; sr res fel, Weizmann Inst Sci, Israel, 1975-1976; mem, MRC groupprotein struct & function, Dept Biochem, Univ Alta, 1974-; from asst prof to assoc prof, DeptBiochem, Univ Alta, 1968-1978; fel, Dept Biochem, Univ Alta, 1967-1968; fel, Dept Chem, Crystallog, Oxford Univ, 1966-1967. **Memberships:** Can Biochem Soc; Am Chem Soc; Fedn Am Soc Exp Biol; Am Crystallog Asn; fel Royal Soc Can. **Mailing Address:** Dept Biochem, Univ Alta, 431A Med Sci, Edmonton, AB T6G 2H7, Can. **Fax:** 780-492-0886. **E-Mail:** michael.james@ualberta.ca

JAMES, MICHAEL ROYSTON, MATERIALS SCIENCE. **Personal Data:** b London, Eng, September 11, 1950; American citizen; m 1972, Rita; c LeAnn, Ryan & Jeremy. **Education:** Tulane Univ, BS, 1972; Northwestern Univ, PhD (mat Sci), 1977. **Professional Experience:** EXEC DIR MAT SCI, ROCKWELL INST SCI CTR, as of 2003; dir mat sci, Rockwell Int Sci Ctr, beginning 1994; mgr tech staff, RockwellInt Sci Ctr, 1986-1994; mem tech staff, Rockwell Int Sci Ctr, 1978-1986; consult, Am Anal Corp, 1978; fel, Lab Metal Physics, State Univ Groningen, Neth, 1977-1978. **Memberships:** Soc Exp Mech; Metall Soc; Am Soc Metals. **Research Statement & Publications:** Nondestructive testing and component life prediction especially with residual stress measurement and its influence on metal fatigue; microstructural phenomena influencing microcrack initiation; mechanics of microelectronic packaging. **Mailing Address:** Rockwell Sci Ctr, 1049 Camino Dos Rios, Thousand Oaks, CA 91360. **Fax:** 805-373-4775. **E-Mail:** mrjames@scimail.risc.rockwell.com

JAMES, NOEL PATTISON, GEOLOGY. **Education:** FRSC. **Professional Experience:** RES CHAIR, DEPT GEOL SCI & GEOL ENG, QUEENS UNIV, CAN, as of 2005. **Mailing Address:** Dept Geol Sci, Queen's Univ, Kingston, ON K7L 3N6, Can.

JAMES, ODETTE BRICMONT, LUNAR PETROLOGY, IGNEOUS PETROLOGY. **Personal Data:** b San Jose, Calif, February 7, 1942; m 1980, David; c Jeffrey B Stewart. **Education:** Stanford Univ, BS, 1963, PhD (geol), 1967. **Professional Experience:** SCIENTIST EMER, EASTERN EARTH SURFACE PROCESSES TEAM, US GEOL SURV, as of 2004; mem, Lunar Planet Geoscience Review Panel, 1985-1987; chmn, Lunar Sample Anal Planning Team, NASA, 1981-1982; prin investr, Lunar Sample Anal, NASA, beginning 1975; mem, Lunar Sample Anal Planning Team, NASA, 1972-1974, 1980-1982; geologist, US Geol Surv, beginning 1967. **Memberships:** Fel Mineral Soc Am (treas 1981-1984); fel Geol Soc Am (Planet Geol Div vchmn 1993-1994, chmn 1995); mem Am Geophys Union; mem Meteoritical Soc. **Research Statement & Publications:** Petrology and chemistry of lunar highland rocks and mare basalts; igneous petrology; shock metamorphism. **Mailing Address:** Eastern Earth Process Team, US Geol Surv, Nat Ctr, MS 926A, 12201 Sunrise Valley Dr, Reston, VA 20192. **Fax:** 703-648-6032. **E-Mail:** ojames@usgs.gov

JAMES, PHILIP BENJAMIN, PLANETARY ATMOSPHERES. **Personal Data:** b Kansas City, Mo, March 18, 1940; m 1965, Sharon; c Eric, Kevin & Kirsten. **Education:** Carnegie-Mellon Univ, BS, 1961; Univ Wis-Madison, MS, 1963, PhD (physics), 1966. **Professional Experience:** Mem, Mars Observer Camera Team, 1992-; Dist Univ prof, Univ Toledo; CHMN DEPT PHYSICS & ASTRON, UNIV TOLEDO, 1990-; adj scientist, Lowell Observ, 1984-; ed, Am J Physics, 1982-1983; mem, Viking Mars Proj, 1977-1978; Nat Res Coun assoc, Jet Propulsion Lab, Calif Inst Technol, 1977-1978; from asst prof to prof physics, Univ Mo, St Louis, 1968-1990; Off Naval Res res assoc physics, Univ Ill, Urbana, 1966-1968; prin investr, Hubble Space Telescope Observing Prog; partic scientist, Mars Global Surv; co-investr, MARCI camera Mars Reconnaissance. **Memberships:** Am Geophys Union; Am Astron Soc; fel Am Phys Soc. **Research Statement & Publications:** Studies relevant to meteorology of and condensate cycles on Mars, includes analyses of spacecraft data, astronomical observations, and modeling. **Mailing Address:** Dept Physics & Astron, Univ Toledo, Toledo, OH 43606. **Fax:** 419-530-2723. **E-Mail:** pbj@physics.utoledo.edu

JAMES, PHILIP NICKERSON, DATA PROCESSING. **Personal Data:** b Boston, Mass, August 16, 1932; m 1954, c 2. **Education:** Mass Inst Technol, SB, 1954; Univ Ill, PhD (org chem), 1957. **Professional Experience:** PRES, STRATEGIC MGT SERV, 1988-; FAC MEM, COL BUS ADMIN, CALIF STATE UNIV, LONG BEACH, 1988-; chief, Strategic Info Systs Planning Div, DataProcessing Dept, Los Angeles Co, 1985-1988; dir, Info Inst & vpres, Int Acad, 1984-1985; dirstrategy planning data processing, Electronics Div, Northrop Corp, 1980-1984; sr res engr, Electronics Div, Northrop Corp, 1979-1980; dir mgt systs, Teledyne Systs Co, 1978-1979; diradmin & planning, Deluxe Gen Inc, 20th Century-Fox, 1977-1978; dir, Univ Southern Calif, Idyllwild Campus, 1974-1977; exec asst to chancellor, Univ Calif, San Diego, 1969-1974; asstvchancellor grad studies & res, Univ Calif, San Diego, 1966-1969; staff asst to dir, Systs Res Div, Technicolor Corp, 1964-1966; sr res chemist, Systs Res Div, Technicolor Corp, 1963-1966; projleader, Systs Res Div, Technicolor Corp, 1963; photog chemist, Systs Res Div, Technicolor Corp, 1962-1963; col rels rep, Lederle Labs, Am Cyanamid Co, 1960-1962; res chemist, Lederle Labs, Am Cyanamid Co, 1959-1960; asst prof, Univ Calif, Berkeley, 1958-1959; Instr chem, Univ Calif, Berkeley, 1957-1958. **Memberships:** Am Chem Soc; Fedn Am Scientists; AAAS; Sigma Xi; Asn Comput Mach; SocInfo Mgt. **Research Statement & Publications:** Biologically interesting compounds; structure; synthesis; chemical mechanisms; photographic chemistry; computer assisted solutions to synthetic problems; higher education; information management; information technology and society. **Mailing Address:** 11400 Edenberg Ave, Northridge, CA 91326-2110.

JAMES, RALPH BOYD, CONDENSED MATTER PHYSICS. **Personal Data:** b Nashville, Tenn, November 1, 1953; c 1. **Education:** Univ Tenn, BS, 1976; Ga Inst Technol, MS, 1977; Calif Inst Technol, MS, 1978, PhD (appl physics), 1980. **Professional Experience:** ASSOC LAB DIR, BROOKHAVEN NAT LAB, EENS, 2002-; CHAIR, BROOKHAVEN COUNTER TERRORISM, as of 2002; chmn, Soc Phot-Optical Instr Engrs Working Group Penetrating Radiation, 1996-; distinguished researcher & mgr, Sandia Nat Labs, 1984-2000; sr mem techstaff, Sandia Nat Labs, 1984-1995; Eugene P Wigner fel, Oak Ridge Nat Lab, 1981-1984; res fel, Calif Inst Technol, 1980-1981. **Memberships:** Fel Am Phys Soc; fel Inst Elec & Electronics Engrs; Sigma Xi; Mat Res Soc; Am Vacuum Soc; Soc Photo-Optical Instrumentation Engrs; fel Int Soc Optical Eng. **Research Statement & Publications:** Semiconductor physics and non-linear optics. **Mailing Address:** Brookhaven Nat Lab, PO Box 5000 Bldg 460, Upton, NY 11973-5000. **E-Mail:** rbjames@bnl.gov

JAMES, RALPH L, MATHEMATICS, NUMERICAL ANALYSIS. **Personal Data:** b Portland, Ore, April 12, 1941; m 1969, c 2. **Education:** Univ Wash, BS, 1963; Ore State Univ, MS, 1965, PhD, 1970. **Professional Experience:** PROF EMER, CALIF STATE COL, STANISLAUS, as of 2005; prof math, Calif State Col, Stanislaus, as of 2004; assoc prof math, Calif State Col, Stanislaus, beginning 1974; asst prof, Calif State Col, Stanislaus, 1970-1974; vis asst prof math, Col Idaho, 1965-1968. **Memberships:** Am Math Soc. **Research Statement & Publications:** Functional analysis; ordered topological vector spaces; positive operators; approximation theory. **Mailing Address:** Dept Math, Calif Univ Stanislaus, 264 Demergasso-Bava Hall Bldg, Turlock, CA 95382. **Fax:** 209-667-3848.

JAMES, RICHARD STEPHEN, GEOCHEMISTRY, PETROLOGY. **Personal Data:** b Hamilton, Ont, February 20, 1940; m 1964, c 2. **Education:** McMaster Univ, BSc, 1962, MSc, 1964; Univ Manchester, UK, PhD (geol), 1967. **Professional Experience:** PROF EMER, DEPT EARTH SCI, LAURENTIAL UNIV, as of 2005; prof & chmn, Dept Earth Sci, Laurential Univ, as of 2001; ASSOC PROF GEOL, 1980-; asst prof geol, 1970-1980; lectr geol, Univ Toronto, 1969-1970; fel, Univ Toronto, 1967-1969. **Memberships:** Mineral Soc Am; Mineral Asn Can; Mineral Soc Gt Brit & Ireland. **Research Statement & Publications:** Igneous and metamorphic petrology, application of experimental phase equilibria data to natural systems. **Mailing Address:** Dept Earth Sci, Laurentian Univ, Ramsey Lake Rd, Sudbury, ON P3E 2C6, Can. **Fax:** 705-673-6508. **E-Mail:** rjames@nickel.laurentian.ca

JAMES, ROBERT CLARKE, MATHEMATICAL ANALYSIS. **Personal Data:** b Bloomington, Ind, July 30, 1918; wid Edith M Peterson (deceased); c Judith M (Grounds), Linda (Anooshian), David V & Robert G. **Education:** Univ Calif, Los Angeles, BA, 1940; Calif Inst Technol, PhD (math), 1947. **Honorary Degrees:** DSc, Kent State Univ, 1987. **Professional Experience:** EMER PROF MATH, CLAREMONT GRAD SCH, 1981-; Jerusalem, 1976-1977 & Mittag-Leffler Inst, Sweden, 1978-1979; prof, Claremont Grad Sch, 1968-1981; prof, State Univ NY Albany, 1967-1968; Mem, Inst Advan Study, Princeton Univ, 1962-1963; prof & chmn dept, Harvey Mudd Col, 1957-1967; assoc prof, Haverford Col, 1951-1957; from instr to asst prof, Univ Calif, 1947-1951; Benjamin Pierce instr math, Harvard Univ, 1946-1947. **Memberships:** Am Math Soc; Math Asn Am; AAAS; Fedn Am Scientists. **Research Statement & Publications:** Normed vector spaces. **Mailing Address:** 14385 Clear Creek Pl, Grass Valley, CA 95949-8765.

JAMES, RODERICK VIVIAN, INFORMATION SCIENCE & SYSTEMS PROJECT MANAGEMENT. **Personal Data:** b Port of Spain, Trinidad, October 17, 1946; American citizen; m 1971, Marcia G McConney; c Rhoda M. **Education:** Univ Mo, Columbia, PhD (elec eng), 1975. **Professional Experience:** RES CONSULT, TEXACO EPTD, 1994-; asst to gen mgr, Texaco Angola, 1992-1994; chief, Moscow Comput Ctr, Texaco Europe Res Inc., 1990-1992; Mgr software develop proj, Texaco EPTD, 1985-1990; cert PMP, project management institute(PMI). **Memberships:** Inst Elec & Electronics Engrs; PMI, houston chapter & nat org. **Research Statement & Publications:** Protection of intellectual property. **Mailing Address:** 11234 Sharpcrest, Houston, TX 77072.

JAMES, RONALD VALDEMAR, SOIL CHEMISTRY. **Personal Data:** b Oakland, Calif, April 27, 1943; m 1964, c 2. **Education:** Univ Calif, Davis, BS, 1964; Univ Colo, Boulder, MS, 1967, PhD (inorg chem), 1969. **Professional Experience:** RES CHEMIST, US GEOL SURV, 1968-. **Memberships:** Am Chem Soc; AAAS; Am Geophys Union. **Research Statement & Publications:** Chemistry and transport of solutes in the unsaturated zone and ground water; mathematical modeling; fate of pollutants in environmental waters; kinetics and mechanisms of inorganic reactions; ion exchange. **Mailing Address:** 595 Morey Dr, Menlo Park, CA 94025.

JAMES, SHERMAN ATHONIA, BEHAVIORAL STRESS, PSYCHOPHYSIOLOGY. **Personal Data:** b Hartsville, SC, October 25, 1943; m 1990, Vera; c Alex & Scott. **Education:** Talladega Col, AB, 1964; Wash Univ, St Louis, PhD (psychol), 1973. **Professional Experience:** PROF PUB POLICY STUDIES TERRY SANFORD INST PUB POLICY, DUKE UNIV, as of 2005; Dir, Ctr Res On Ethinicitty, Culture & Health, as of 2004; Acad dean, Sch Pub Health, Univ Mich, 1993-1997; prof epidemiol, Univ Mich Ann Arbor, 1989-2003; vis prof, Dept Prev Med, Fed Univ Bahia, Salvador, Brazil, 1986-; consult, NIMH, 1979-1983 & NIH, 1985-; from asstprof to prof epidemiol, Univ NC, Chapel Hill, 1973-1989; fel coun epidemiol, Am Heart Asn. **Memberships:** Fel Acad Behav Med Res; fel Am Epidemiol Soc; Am Heart Asn; Soc Behav Med; Am Col Epidemiol; Am Pub Health Asn. **Research Statement & Publications:** Psychosocial factors and cardiovascular disease risk in Black populations. **Mailing Address:** Dept Epidemiol Sch Pub Health, Univ Mich, Ann Arbor, MI 48109. **E-Mail:** sjames@umich.edu

JAMES, STANLEY D, ELECTROCHEMISTRY. **Personal Data:** b Cardiff, UK, August 25, 1932; m 1961, c 2. **Education:** Univ Wales, BSc, 1953, PhD (phys chem), 1959. **Professional Experience:** CHEMIST, DEPT NAVY; chemist, Electrochem Br, US Naval Surface Weapons Ctr, 1967-; assoc chemist, Brookhaven Nat Lab, 1965-1967; asst chemist electrochem, Brookhaven Nat Lab, 1963-1965; res fel phys & inorg chem, Univ Melbourne, 1961-1963; Vis scientist phys chem, NIH, 1959-1960. **Memberships:** Electrochem Soc; Inst Elec & Electronics Engrs. **Research Statement & Publications:** Ion exchange membranes; electrokinetics; electrode kinetics; fused salt electrochemistry. **Mailing Address:** Carderock Div Naval Surface Warfare Ctr, 9500 MacArthur Blvd, West Bethesda, MD 20817-5700.

JAMES, STEPHANIE LYNN, IMMUNOPARASITOLOGY. **Personal Data:** b Little Rock, Ark, m 1982, c 2. **Education:** Hendrix Col, BA, 1972; Vanderbilt Univ, PhD (microbiol), 1976. **Professional Experience:** DEP DIR, ELLISON MED FOUND, 2001-; chief, parasitol & trop dis br, Nat Inst Allergy &Infectious Dis, Nih, beginning 1991; sr investr, Biomed Res Inst, 1988; parasitol prog officer, Parasitol & Trop Dis Br, Nat Inst Allergy & Infectious Dis, NIH, 1987-1990; assoc ed, JImmunol, 1985-1988; from asst res prof to assoc res prof med & microbiol, George Wash Univ, 1983-1987; vis lectr, Univ Del Sao Paulo, Brazil, 1982; prin investr, NIH, NSF, WHO &Clark Found grants, 1981-1988; travel award, Am Asn Immunologists, 1980 & 1983; res fel, LabParasitic Dis, NIH, Nat Inst Allergy & Infectious Dis, 1979-1983; res fel, dept med, Harvard MedSch, 1977-1979. **Memberships:** Am Soc Trop Med Hyg; Am Asn Immunologists. **Research Statement & Publications:** Parasite immunology, particularly in schistosomiasis, concentrating on the areas of immunopathology and vaccine production; elucidation of the roles of eosinophils and macrophages as effector cells of protective immunity which led to development of experimental vaccine based on cell-mediated immune mechanisms. **Mailing Address:** Ellison Med Found, Ste 204, 4710 Bethesda Ave, Bethesda, MD 20814-5226. **Fax:** 301-657-1828.

JAMES, STEPHEN P, EXPERIMENTAL BIOLOGY. **Personal Data:** b Columbus, Ohio, May 25, 1947; c 2. **Education:** Cornell Univ, BA, 1969; Johns Hopkins Univ, MD, 1973; Am Bd Internal Med, dipl, 1976, dipl gastroenterol, 1979. **Professional Experience:** DIR, DIV DIGESTIVE DIS & NUTRITION NAT INST, DIABETES & DIGESTIVE & KIDNEY DIS, NIH, as of 2005; prof med, Univ Md, as of 2001; head, Div Gastroenterol, Univ Md, 1991-2001; mem grants rev comt, Crohn's & Colitis Found Am, 1988-; assoc ed, J Immunol, 1988-; chmn clin res comt, Nat InstAllergy & Infectious Dis, 1988-1989; sr clin investr, Mucosal Immunity Sect, Lab Clin Invest, NatInst Allergy & Infectious Dis, 1982-1991; expert, Immunophysiol Sect, Metabol Br, Div CancerBiol & Diag, Nat Cancer Inst, 1980-1982; clin assoc, Liver Dis Sect, Nat Inst Arthritis, Diabetes, Digestive & Kidney Dis, NIH, Bethesda, 1977-1980; fel, Gastroenterol Div, Univ Md, Baltimore, 1976-1977; resident, Dept Med, Johns Hopkins Hosp, Baltimore, Md, 1975-1976; asst resident, Dept Med, Johns Hopkins Hosp, Baltimore, Md, 1974-1975; intern, Dept Med, Johns HopkinsHosp, Baltimore, Md, 1973-1974. **Memberships:** Am Col Physicians; Am Fedn Clin Res; Am Asn Study Liver Dis; Am AsnImmunologists; Am Gastroenterol Asn; Soc Mucosal Immunol; AAAS; Int Asn Study Liver. **Research Statement & Publications:** Regulatory functions of CD4 T cells; role of T cells in host defense and disease at mucosal surfaces; inflammatory bowel disease; gastrointestinal disease in immunodeficient patients; immune mechanisms in chronic liver disease; primary biliary cirrhosis. **Mailing Address:** NIH, Nat Inst Diabetes & Digestive & Kidney Dis, Bethesda, MD 21201. **Fax:** 410-328-8315.

JAMES, THARAPPEL C, MOLECULAR BIOLOGY. **Education:** Banaras Hindu Univ, PhD. **Professional Experience:** STAFF, MICROBIOL DEPT, TRINITY COL, UNIV DUBLIN, as of. **Mailing Address:** Dept Microbiol Trinity Col Univ Dublin, Dublin, Ireland.

JAMES, THOMAS LARRY, BIOPHYSICAL CHEMISTRY. **Personal Data:** b North Platte, Nebr, September 8, 1944; m 1991, Olga; c Marcus & Tristan. **Education:** Univ NMex, BS,

1965; Univ Wis-Madison, PhD (anal chem), 1969. **Professional Experience:** PROF, CHEM, PHARMACEUT CHEM & RADIOL, UNIV CALIF, SAN FRANCISCO, 1983-; Chair, Dept Pharmaceut Chem, 1995-; asst prof & assoc prof Chem, Pharm Chem, Radiol, Univ Calif, San Francisco, 1973-1983; NIH fellow, biophys, Johnson Res Found, Univ Pa, 1971-1973; res chemist, Tech Ctr, Celanese Chem Co, 1969-1971; NIH fellow, 1966-1969; NIH trainee biochem, Univ Wis-Madison, 1965-1966. **Memberships:** Am Chem Soc; Int Soc Magnetic Resonance; Soc Magnetic Resonance Med; AmBiophys Soc. **Research Statement & Publications:** Nuclear magnetic resonance applications to biochemical and biological systems; nucleic acids; proteins; drug discovery. **Mailing Address:** Dept Pharmaceut Chem, Sch Pharm, Univ Calif, Rm S-512D Genentech Hall, San Francisco, CA 94143-2280. **E-Mail:** james@picasso.ucsf.edu

JAMES, THOMAS NAUM, CARDIOVASCULAR DISEASES. **Personal Data:** b Amory, Miss, October 24, 1925; m 1948, c 3. **Education:** Tulane Univ, BS, 1946, MD, 1949; Am Bd Internal Med, dipl, 1957, cert cardiovascdis, 1960; Am Col Chest Physicians, dipl. **Professional Experience:** PROF CARDIOL, UNIV TEX MED BR, as of 2002; staff, Univ Tex Med Br, Univ Tex, Galveston, beginning 1988; chmn, Mary Gertrude Waters prof cardiol, 1977-1988; chmn, Dept Med, 1973-1988; dir cardiovasc res & training ctr, Cardiovasc Res & Training Ctr, 1970-1977; prof med, Med Ctr, Univ Ala, Birmingham, 1968-1988; prof path, Cardiovasc Res & Training Ctr, 1968-1973; sr scientist & dir res, Cardiovasc Res & Training Ctr, 1968-1970; pres, Cardiac Electrophysiol Group, 1965-1966; secy, Cardiac Electrophysiol Group, 1964-1965; chmn sect cardiovasc res, Henry Ford Hosp, 1959-1968; vis physician, Charity Hosp, New Orleans, 1955-1959; cardiologist, Ochsner Clin, New Orleans, La, 1955-1959; from instr to asst prof, Tulane Univ, 1955-1959; intern & resident med & cardiol, Henry Ford Hosp, 1949-1953. **Memberships:** Am Heart Asn; fel Am Col Physicians; fel Am Col Cardiol (vpres, 1970-1971); fel Am Col Chest Physicians; Soc Exp Biol & Med; Sigma Xi. **Research Statement & Publications:** Anatomy, pathology, physiology and pharmacology of the heart, particularly coronary arteries and conduction system. **Mailing Address:** Div Cardiol, Univ Tex Med Br, 301 Univ Blvd, Galveston, TX 77555-0553. **Fax:** 409-747-9680. **E-Mail:** tnjames@utmb.edu

JAMES, THOMAS RAY, MATHEMATICS. **Personal Data:** b Dayton, Ohio, March 23, 1946; m 1968, c 1. **Education:** Otterbein Col, BA, 1968; Ohio Univ, MS, 1971, PhD (math), 1974. **Professional Experience:** PROF MATH, OTTERBEIN COL, as of 2005; asst prof math, Otterbein Col, beginning 1979; asst prof math, Lake Erie Col, 1975-1979; instr math & physics, Sewickley Acad, 1974-1975; teaching asst, Ohio Univ, 1970-1974. **Memberships:** Am Math Soc; Asn Comput Mach; Math Asn Am; Inst Elec & Electronics Engrs. **Research Statement & Publications:** Point set topology. **Mailing Address:** Dept Math & Comput Sci, Otterbein Col, 135 Towers Hall, Westerville, OH 43081-2006. **Fax:** 614-823-3201. **E-Mail:** tjames@otterbein.edu

JAMES, VIRGIL EUGENE, CHEMICAL ENGINEERING. **Personal Data:** b Braxton Co, WVa, May 6, 1929; m 1955, Patricia; c Cynthia L. **Education:** WVa Univ, BS, 1951, MS, 1956, PhD (chem eng), 1958. **Professional Experience:** RETIRED; sr supvr, Textile Fibers Dept, 1967-1983; process supvr, Film Dept, Yerkes Res Lab, E I du Pont de Nemours & Co Inc, 1965-1967; res supvr, Film Dept, YerkesRes Lab, E I du Pont de Nemours & Co Inc, 1961-1965; res engr, Film Dept, Yerkes Res Lab, El du Pont de Nemours & Co Inc, 1958-1961; chem engr, Bur Mines, US Dept Interior, WVa, 1954-1958; chem engr, Nitrogen Div, Allied Chem & Dye Corp, Va, 1953-1954. **Memberships:** AAAS; Am Inst Chem Engrs. **Research Statement & Publications:** Film forming and polymer research; coal gasification research; synthetic fibers. **Mailing Address:** 214 Masters Ct, Chattanooga, TN 37343.

JAMES, WILLIAM JOSEPH, SOLID STATE CHEMISTRY & ELECTROCHEMISTRY, CRYSTALLOGRAPHY. **Personal Data:** b Providence, RI, September 17, 1922; m 1942, Arlene R Carll; c Varie L (Lynch) & Candice L (Metcalf). **Education:** Tufts Univ, BS, 1949; Iowa State Univ, MS, 1952, PhD (chem), 1953. **Honors & Awards:** Thomas Jefferson Award, UM Board Curators, 1986; Most Distinguished Scientist, Mo Acad Sci, 1996; UMR Chancellors Medal, 1996; UMR Acad Chem Engrs, 2003. **Professional Experience:** Pres, Mead Environ Assocs, 1994-; dir, Ctr Environ Sci & Technol, 1993-1997; bd dir, APR Inc, Redwood, Calif, 1987-1990; PROF EMER CHEM, UNIV MO, ROLLA, 1984-; pres, Incubator Technol Inc, Rolla, Mo, 1984-1986; vpres & bd dir, Filterteck Inc, 1982-; dir, GCMR, 1982-1983; bd dir, and VP Brewer Sci., 1981-; pres & founder, Mead Technol Inc, Rolla, Mo, 1976-; assoc dir, GCMR, Univ Mo, Rolla, 1975-1976; sr investr, Grad Ctr Mat Res, Univ Mo, Rolla, 1964-; dir, Grad Ctr Mat Res, Univ Mo, Rolla, 1964-1975; Fulbright res fel, Neel LabMagnetism, Grenoble, France, 1961-1962; from assoc prof to prof, Univ Mo, Rolla, 1953-1984; grad asst physics, Pa State Univ, 1952-1953. **Memberships:** Electrochem Soc; fel Am Inst Chemists; Am Chem Soc; Am Crystallog Asn; MatRes Soc. **Research Statement & Publications:** Lattice imperfections; magnetic and crystal structure determinations by x-ray and neutron diffraction; electrochemical kinetics and corrosion science; plasma-enhanced chemical vapor deposition of thin films. **Mailing Address:** Grad Ctr Mat Res, Univ Mo, Rolla, MO 65409. **Fax:** 573-341-2071. **E-Mail:** wjames@umr.edu

JAMESON, A KEITH, PHYSICAL CHEMISTRY. **Personal Data:** b Provo, Utah, June 11, 1933; m 1963, c 2. **Education:** Brigham Young Univ, BS, 1956, BSE & MS, 1957; Univ Ill, Urbana, PhD (physchem), 1963. **Professional Experience:** PROF CHEM, LOYOLA UNIV CHICAGO, 1980-; assoc prof chem, LoyolaUniv Chicago, 1973-1980; asst prof, Loyola Univ Chicago, 1968-1973; vis asst prof, Univ Ill, Urbana, 1967-1968; vis assoc prof chem, Ateneo Del Manila Univ, 1965-1967; Res chemist, EssoRes & Eng Co, 1962-1965. **Memberships:** Am Chem Soc; Am Phys Soc. **Research Statement & Publications:** Nuclear magnetic resonance; intermolecular interactions and spectroscopic observables; energy and environmental chemistry. **Mailing Address:** Dept of Chem, Loyola Univ, Chicago, IL 60626.

JAMESON, ANTONY, AEROSPACE ENGINEERING. **Personal Data:** b Gillingham, Eng, 1934. **Education:** Cambridge Univ, BA & MA, 1958, PhD, 1963. **Honors & Awards:** Except Sci Achievement Medal, NASA, 1980; Gold Medal, Brit RoyalAerospace Soc, 1988; W R Sears Distinguished Lectr, Cornell Univ, 1992; Fluid DynamicsAward, Am Inst Aeronaut & Astronaut, 1993; Spirit St Louis Medal, Am Soc Mech Engrs, 1995; Docteur Honoris Causa, Uppsala Univ, 2002. **Professional Experience:** THOMAS V JONES PROF ENG, DEPT AERONAUT & ASTRONAUT, STANFORD UNIV, 1997-; dir prog appl & computational math, Princeton Univ, 1986-1988; hon prof, N western Polytech Univ, Xian, China, 1986; prof aerospace eng, James S McDonnell Distinguished Univ, Princeton Univ, 1982-1997; prof mech & aerospace eng, Princeton Univ, 1980-1982; prof comput sci, courant inst math sci, NY Univ, 1974-1980; sr ressci, courant inst math sci, NY Univ, 1972-1974; staff engr, grumman aerospace corp, 1966-1972; chief mathematician, missile div, hawker siddeley dynamics, 1965-1966; economist, trades union cong, London, 1964-1965; res fel, trinity hall, Cambridge, 1960-1963. **Memberships:** Nat Acad Eng; fel Am Inst Aeronaut & Astronaut. **Research Statement & Publications:** Published numerous articles. **Mailing Address:** Dept Aeronaut & Astronaut, Stanford Univ, Rm 381, Durand Bldg, Stanford, CA 94305. **Fax:** 650-723-1685. **E-Mail:** jameson@baboon.stanford.edu

JAMESON, CHARLES WILLIAM, ORGANIC CHEMISTRY, CHEMICAL CARCINOGENESIS. **Personal Data:** b LaPlata, Md, February 3, 1948; m 1969, c 1. **Education:** Mt St Mary's Col, BS, 1970; Univ Md, PhD (org chem), 1975. **Professional Experience:** STAFF MEM, ENVIRON TOXICOL PROG, NAT INST ENVIRON HEALTH SCI, as of 2004; SR RES CHEMIST, OFF DIR, NAT INST ENVIRON HEALTH SCI, 1990-; prog leader chem, Nat Toxicol Prog, Nat Inst Environ Health Sci, 1980-1990; expert chem, Off Dir, Nat Inst Environ Health Sci, 1979-1980; sr chemist, Tracor Jitco Inc, Tracor Inc, 1978-1979; sr chemist Bioassay Prog & consult, Chem Selection Group, Nat Cancer Inst, 1976-1980; chemist bioassay, Tracor Jitco Inc, Tracor Inc, 1976-1978; fac grad asst, Univ Md, 1975-1976; mem, WHO task group Environ Health Criteria Partially Halogenated Chlorofluorocarbons. **Research Statement & Publications:** Structure activity relationships; toxicokinetics; leukemia. **Mailing Address:** Nat Inst Environ Health Sci, PO Box 12233, 79 Alexander Dr, Research Triangle Park, NC 27709-2233. **E-Mail:** jameson@niehs.nih.gov

JAMESON, DAVID LEE, EVOLUTION. **Personal Data:** b Ranger, Tex, June 3, 1927; m Marianne; c Roy A, David L, Robert C & Carol L. **Education:** Southern Methodist Univ, BS, 1948; Univ Tex, MA, 1949, PhD (zoology), 1952. **Professional Experience:** PROF EMER BIOL, UNIV HOUSTON, 1989-date Nat Acad Sci Exchange scholar, Bulgarian Acad Sci, 1977 & USSR Acad Sci, 1978; dir coastal ctr, Univ Houston, 1972-1976; dean, Univ Houston, 1972-1974; assoc dean grad sch, Univ Houston, 1971-1972; prof biol, Univ Houston, 1967-1990; from asst prof to prof zool, San Diego State Col, 1957-1967; from instr to asst prof, Univ Ore, 1953-1957; Asst prof biol, Pacific Univ, 1952-1953; Managing ed, Copeia, Am Soc Ichthyologists & Herpetologists. **Memberships:** Am Soc Mammal; Ecol Soc Am; Soc Study Evolution (secy 1968-1973); Am Soc Ichthyologists & Herpetologists; Am Inst Biol Sci; Genetics Soc Am. **Research Statement & Publications:** Genetics; amphibians; population genetics; mitochondrial DNA evolution. **Mailing Address:** Osher Lab Molecular Syst, Cal Acad Sci, 875 Howard St, San Francisco, CA 94103-3009. **E-Mail:** djameson@calacademy.org

JAMESON, DAVID M, BIOPHYSICS. **Personal Data:** b Cleveland, Ohio, April 5, 1948. **Education:** Ohio State Univ, BS, 1971; UIUC, MS, 1974, PhD (biochem), 1978. **Honors & Awards:** 2004 Gregorio Weber Award for Excellence in Fluorescence Theory and Application. **Professional Experience:** PROF BIOCHEM & BIOPHYS, UNIV HAWAII, MANOA, 1993-; assoc prof, UnivHawaii, 1989-1993; Asst prof biochem & biophys, Univ Tex, Dallas, 1983-1989. **Memberships:** Biophysical Society. **Research Statement & Publications:** Protein-Protein and Protein-Ligand Interactions; Fluorescence Spectroscopy of Biomolecules; Dynamin; Ribosomal Proteins. **Mailing Address:** Dept Cell & Mol Biol; Univ Hawaii, 2538 The Mall, Snyder 401, Honolulu, HI 96822-2233. **E-Mail:** djameson@hawaii.edu

JAMESON, EVERETT WILLIAMS, VERTEBRATE ZOOLOGY, MEDICAL ENTOMOLOGY. **Personal Data:** b Buffalo, NY, May 2, 1921; m 1969, Sumiko; c 5. **Education:** Cornell Univ, BS, 1943, PhD (vert zool), 1948; Univ Kans, MA, 1946. **Professional Experience:** EMER PROF ZOOL, UNIV CALIF, DAVIS, 1988-; vchmn dept, Exp Sta, 1969-1974; Guggenheim fel, 1958-1959; from asst zoologist to assoc zoologist, Exp Sta, 1948-1965; lab asst zool, Cornell Univ, 1946-1948; lab asst zool, Univ Kans, 1945-1946; from instr to prof zool, Univ Calif, 1944-1988; field observer, Hastings Reservation, Calif, 1942. **Memberships:** Am Soc Mammalogists; assoc Am Soc Ichthyologists & Herpetologists. **Research Statement & Publications:** Population investigations of small mammals; food habits of vertebrates; fat and reproductive cycles of reptiles; oxygen consumption of reptiles; ecological, zoogeographic and taxonomic investigations of fleas and mites in North America and the Far East. **Mailing Address:** Dept Evolution & Ecol, Univ Calif, Davis, CA 95616.

JAMESON, JAMES LARRY, GLYCOPROTEIN HORMONES, ENDOCRINOLOGY. **Personal Data:** b Ft Benning, Ga, June 21, 1954; m 1984. **Education:** Univ NC, BS, 1976, MD, 1981, PhD (biochem), 1981. **Professional Experience:** IRVING S CUTTER PROF MED, FEINBERG SCH MED, NWESTERN UNIV, as of 2004; CHMN, DEPT MED, FEINBERG SCH MED, NWESTERN UNIV, as of 2004; INSTR MED, LAB MOLECULAR ENDOCRINOL, MASS GEN HOSP, HARVARD MED SCH, 1985-; fel endocrinol, Mass Gen Hosp, Harvard Med Sch, 1983-1985; resident internal med, Mass Gen Hosp, Harvard Med Sch, 1981-1983. **Memberships:** AMA; AAAS. **Research Statement & Publications:** Regulation of glycoprotein hormone gene expression in eukaryotic cell line sand pituitary tumors; Aromatase-independent testosterone conversion into estrogenic steroids is inhibited by a 5th reductase inhibitor; ERE-independent ERalpha target genes differentially expressed in human breast tumors; author of various articles. **Mailing Address:** Feinberg Sch Med, Nwestern Univ, 251 E Huron St Galter Pavilion Ste 3-150, Chicago, IL 60611. **Fax:** 617-726-5072. **E-Mail:** ljameson@northwestern.edu

JAMESON, PATRICIA MADOLINE, MICROBIOLOGY, VIROLOGY. **Personal Data:** b Rhinelander, Wis, March 17, 1939. **Education:** Carroll Col, Wis, BS, 1961; Ind Univ, MS, 1963, PhD (microbiol), 1965; Univ Wis, Milwaukee, MLIS, 1988. **Professional Experience:** REF LIBRN, APPL SCI & TECHNOL, UNIV WIS, MILWAUKEE, 1991-; asst prof, Booth Libr, Eastern Ill Univ, 1989-1991; from instr to assoc prof microbiol, Med ColWis, 1969-1989; Microbiologist viruses, US Army Biol Labs, Ft Detrick, 1965-1969. **Memberships:** AAAS; Sigma Xi. **Research Statement & Publications:** Arboviruses; comparison of neuraminidases of neurotropic and nonneurotropic influenza virus strains, especially with respect to substrate specificity; interferon, especially standards, assay and inducers; feline leukemia virus. **Mailing Address:** 4075 Glenway St, Milwaukee, WI 53222-1150. **Fax:** 414-229-6791. **E-Mail:** pjameson@csd4.csd.uwm.edu

JAMESON, ROBERT A, PARTICLE ACCELERATOR PHYSICS & ENGINEERING. **Personal Data:** b Schenectady, NY, May 3, 1937; m 1959, c 2. **Education:** Univ Nebr, BS, 1958; Univ Colo, MS, 1962, PhD (elec eng), 1965; Univ NMex, MMgt, 1977. **Professional Experience:** STAFF MEM, ACCELERATOR TECHNOL DIV, LOS ALAMOS NAT LAB, 1988-; vis prof, Ministry Educ, Japan, 1988-1989; from dep div leader to div leader, Accelerator Technol Div, 1978-1987; group leader, Accelerator Systs, Group MP-9, MP-Div, Lampf, 1972-1980; from asst group leader to assoc group leader, Los Alamos Nat Lab, 1963-1971. **Memberships:** Fel Am Phys Soc. **Research Statement & Publications:** Application of automatic control theory to high power microwave systems; systems analysis and development of particle accelerator control and rf-accelerator systems; particle accelerator beam dynamics; electrical engineering. **Mailing Address:** Accelerator Technol Div, Los Alamos Nat Lab, PO Box 1663, Los Alamos, NM 87545. **Fax:** 505-665-2904. **E-Mail:** rjameson@lanl.gov

JAMESON, WILLIAM J, JR, NUMERICAL MATHEMATICS, SYSTEMS ANALYSIS. **Personal Data:** b Billings, Mont, June 8, 1930; m 1953, c 2. **Education:** Univ Mont, BA,

1952; Univ Tex, MA, 1954; Iowa State Univ, PhD (math), 1962. **Professional Experience:** ASSOC PROF, DEPT ELEC ENG, MONT STATE UNIV, 1987-; mem, Comt on Commun &Info Policy, Inst Elec & Electronics Engrs, 1985-1988; dir telecommunications, State Mich, 1985-1987; vpres, Collins Radio Co, Spectra Assocs, Inc, 1972-1985; chmn, Math Sect, Res Div, Am Defense Preparedness Asn, 1969-1978; mem, Pub Info Comt, Fedn Info Processing Socs, 1969-1972; assoc prof, Iowa State Univ, 1968-1972, 1980-1981; mem, Comn Nat Info SystMath, 1968-1970; corresp consult, Nat Acad Sci-Nat Acad Eng Comt Sci & Tech Commun, 1967-1969; mathematician, Collins Radio Co, Spectra Assocs, Inc, 1962-1972; part-time asst profmath, Iowa State Univ, 1962-1967; fel & teaching asst appl math, Iowa State Univ, 1959-1962; physicist, Lockheed Missiles & Space Co, 1958-1959. **Memberships:** Soc Indust & Appl Math (secy 1964-1969 vpres 1969-1974); Inst Elec & ElectronicsEngrs. **Research Statement & Publications:** Numerical analysis and computation telecommunications; systems analysis. **Mailing Address:** 1404 S Bozeman Ave, Bozeman, MT 59715-5646.

JAMIESON, ALEXANDER MACRAE, CHEMICAL PHYSICS, POLYMER SCIENCE. **Personal Data:** b Glasgow, Scotland, September 19, 1944; m 1971, c 3. **Education:** Univ Glasgow, BS, 1966; Oxford Univ, PhD (chem physics), 1969. **Professional Experience:** PROF & CHMN, DEPT MACROMOLECULAR SCI & ENG, CASE WESTERN RESERVE UNIV, as of 1995; prof macromolecular sci, dept macromolecular sci, Case Western Reserve Univ, beginning 1982; from asst prof to assoc prof, Case Western Reserve Univ, 1974-1982; from res assoc to sr res assoc, Case Western Reserve Univ, 1972-1974. **Memberships:** Am Phys Soc; Am Chem Soc; Soc Rheology. **Research Statement & Publications:** Physical characterization of polymer materials; hydrodynamic properties of macromolecules; rheological properties of polymer solutions; structure and function of polysaccharides and proteoglycans; dynamic light scattering. **Mailing Address:** Dept Macromolecular Sci & Eng, Case Western Reserve Univ, 314 Kent Smith Bldg, Cleveland, OH 44106. **Fax:** 216-368-4202. **E-Mail:** amj@case.edu

JAMIESON, DEREK MAITLAND, OPERATIONS RESEARCH, STATISTICS. **Personal Data:** b Dundee, Scotland, November 27, 1930; Canadian citizen; m 1983, Janet Morris. **Education:** St Andrews Univ, BSc, 1951, Hons, 1953. **Professional Experience:** RETIRED; Res dir, Comn Future Develop Univs Ont, 1984; adj prof math, InstAnal & Planning, Univ Guelph, 1982-; dir, Inst Anal & Planning, Univ Guelph, 1968-; planningexec, Simpac Div, Treas Bd, 1966-1968; chief, Indust Models Div, Nat Energy Bd, 1965-1966; mem tech staff, Mitre Corp, 1960-1965; sci off math & statist, Defence Res Bd Can, 1957-1960; Statistician, Can Industs, Ltd, 1953-1957. **Memberships:** Fel AAAS; Inst Mgt Sci; Can Opers Res Soc; fel Royal Statist Soc; Opers Res SocAm. **Research Statement & Publications:** Computer aided analysis and study of large systems. **Mailing Address:** RR2, Puslinch, ON N0B 2J0, Can. **Fax:** 519-767-1693. **E-Mail:** jamieson@exec.admin.uoguelph.ca

JAMIESON, GLEN STEWART, FISHERIES MANAGEMENT, INVERTEBRATE ECOLOGY. **Personal Data:** b Montreal, Que. **Education:** McGill Univ, BSc, 1967; Univ BC, MSc, 1970, PhD (zool), 1973. **Professional Experience:** RES SCIENTIST, FISHERIES RES BR, FISHERIES & OCEANS, NANAIMO, CAN, 1982-; head herring, Fisheries Res Br, Nanaimo, 1982-1984; resscientist, Fisheries Res Br, Halifax, 1981-1982; head shellfish, Fisheries Res Br, Fisheries & Oceans, Nanaimo, Can, 1981-1993; res scientist, Fisheries Res Br, Halifax, 1977-1981; sr marine biologist, Appl Marine Res Ltd, Halifax, 1975-1977; fcl, Dalhousie Univ, 1974-1975. **Research Statement & Publications:** Fisheries management, emphasizing invertebrates; spatial and temporal distributions; stock assessment methodology; predator-prey interactions. **Mailing Address:** Pac Biol Sta Fisheries & Oceans Can, Hammond Bay Rd, Nanaimo, BC V9T 6 N7, Can. **Fax:** 250-756-7138. **E-Mail:** jamiesong@pac.dfo-mpo.gc.ca

JAMIESON, GRAHAM ARCHIBALD, BIOCHEMISTRY, THROMBOSIS. **Personal Data:** b Wellington, NZ, August 14, 1929; m 1960, Barbara; c Brian. **Education:** Univ Otago, NZ, MSc, 1951; Univ London, PhD (org chem), 1954, DSc(biochem), 1972. **Honors & Awards:** Winzler Mem Lectr, Univ Fla, 1975; Shirley Johnson Lectr, Int Soc ThrombosisHaemostasis, 1997. **Professional Experience:** Vis prof, Imov, Barcelona, Spain, 1993; vis prof, Univ Sao Paulo, Brazil, 1992; SR SCIENTIST, AM NAT RED CROSS, 1984-; adj prof, Sch Med & Dent, Georgetown Univ, beginning 1974; res dir, Am Nat Red Cross, 1969-1984; asst dir res, Am Nat Red Cross, 1965-1969; res biochemist, Am Nat Red Cross, 1961-1964; vis scientist, NIH, 1957-1961; res assoc org chem, Royal Inst Technol, Sweden, 1955-1956 & Med Col, Cornell Univ, 1956-1957; john edmond fel, Univ Otago, NZ, 1951; sir george grey scholar, Univ Otago, NZ, 1950; ed, Thrombosis & Haemostasis Int J Haematol, Am Soc Biol Chemists; mem adv comt, Res Blood Prod & Preserv, Letterman Army Inst Res; mem, Blood Res Study Sect, NIH; mem exec comt, Thrombosis Coun, Am Heart Asn. **Memberships:** AAAS; Am Soc Biol Chem; Int Soc Thrombosis & Haemostasis; Am Chem Soc. **Research Statement & Publications:** Platelet receptor function and membrane biochemistry. **Mailing Address:** Am Nat Red Cross, Rockville, MD 20855. **Fax:** 301-738-0794. **E-Mail:** jamieson@usa.redcross.org

JAMIESON, JAMES C, GLYCOPROTEIN BIOSYNTHESIS. **Personal Data:** b Aberdeen, Scotland, May 15, 1939. **Education:** Aberdeen Univ, Scotland, PhD (biochem), 1967. **Professional Experience:** DEAN SCI, UNIV MAN, 1994-; PROF CHEM, UNIV MAN, 1978-. **Memberships:** Am Asn Biol Syst; Can Biochem Soc; Chem Inst Can; Royal Inst Chem; Soc Complex Carbohydrates. **Research Statement & Publications:** Studies on structure and biosynthesis of mammalian glycoproteins; morphological study coupled with cytochemistry and immunocytochemistry and published over 10 books. **Mailing Address:** Dept Chem, Univ Man, Rm 530 Parker Bldg, Winnipeg, MB R3T 2N2, Can. **Fax:** 204-474-7608. **E-Mail:** jamies@ms.umanitoba.ca

JAMIESON, JAMES DOUGLAS, CELL BIOLOGY. **Personal Data:** b Armstrong, BC, January 22, 1934; m 1964, c 2. **Education:** Univ BC, MD, 1960; Rockefeller Univ, PhD (cell biol), 1966. **Professional Experience:** DIR, MED STUDIES, SCH MED, YALE UNIV, as of 2005; chmn, Dept Cell Biol, Sch Med, Yale Univ, 1983-1992; PROF CELL BIOL, SCH MED, YALE UNIV, beginning 1975; assoc prof, Sch Med, Yale Univ, 1973-1975; from asst prof to assoc prof, Rockefeller Univ, 1967-1973; res assoc cell biol, Rockefeller Univ, 1966-1967. **Memberships:** Am Soc Cell Biol; Am Soc Biol Chemists. **Research Statement & Publications:** Intracellular transport of secretory proteins; membrane formation and function; cell-hormone interactions; immunocytochemistry; pathophysiology of vascular smooth muscle; cytodifferentiation of glandular epithelia. **Mailing Address:** Dept Cell Biol, Sch Med, Yale Univ, 333 Cedar St, New Haven, CT 06510. **Fax:** 203-785-6936. **E-Mail:** james.jamieson@yale.edu

JAMIESON, LEAH H, PARALLEL PROCESSING, SPEECH PROCESSING. **Personal Data:** b Trenton, NJ, August 27, 1949. **Education:** Mass Inst Technol, BS, 1972; Univ Princeton, MA & MSE, 1974, PhD (elec eng & comput sci), 1977. **Honors & Awards:** Bernard M Gordon Prize, US Nat Acad Eng, 2005; Inst Elec & Electronics Engr, Third Millennium Medal, 2000; Chester F Carlson Award, Am Soc Eng Educ, 1997. **Professional Experience:** ASSOC DEAN, COL ENG, UNIV PURDUE, 2004-; DIR, ENG PROJ COMMUNITY SERV, UNIV PURDUE, 2003-; RANSBURG PROF, ELECT & COMPUT ENG, UNIV PURDUE, 2002-; CO-DIR, NAT CTR ENG PROJ COMMUNITY SERV PROG, 1999-; Co-Dir, Ctr Eng Proj Community Serv, Sch Elect Eng, Univ Purdue, Ind, 1996-2002; Dir, grad admis, Sch elect & compt eng, Univ Purdue, 1994-1996; Grad Coordr, Sch Elect Eng, Univ Purdue, 1990-1994; Prof Elec Eng, Univ Purdue, 1986-2002; vis scientist, SRI Int, Menlo Park, Calif, 1986; vis scientist, SRI Int, Menlo Park, Calif, 1985; Assoc ed, J Parallel & Distrib Comput, 1985-1992; From asst prof to assoc prof, Univ Purdue, 1976-1986. **Memberships:** Fel Inst Elec & Electronics Engrs; Asn Comput Mach. **Research Statement & Publications:** Computer analysis and recognition of speech; design of parallel processing algorithms for digital speech, signal and image processing; software tools for parallel signal processing applications; Published over 100 articles. **Mailing Address:** Sch Elec Eng Purdue Univ, 465 Northwestern AvE, West Lafayette, IN 47907-2035. **Fax:** 765-494-3371. **E-Mail:** lhj@purdue.edu

JAMIESON, NORMAN CLARK, ORGANIC CHEMISTRY. **Personal Data:** b Edinburgh, Scotland, November 21, 1935; American citizen; m 1964, Wilma; c Anne. **Education:** Univ Edinburgh, BSc, 1958; Univ Alta, MSc, 1961; Univ Adelaide, PhD (org chem), 1966. **Professional Experience:** ASSOC DIR RES & DEVELOP SERV, MALLINCKRODT INC, 1992-; asst dir corp analyst res, Sci Prod Div, 1986-1992; dir res & develop, Sci Prod Div, 1980-1986; res assoc, Mallinckrodt, Inc, 1977-1980; sr chemist, Mallinckrodt, Inc, 1970-1977; sr res scientist, Merck & Co, Inc, 1967-1970; fel org chem, Rensselaer Polytech Inst, 1966-1967. **Memberships:** Am Chem Soc. **Research Statement & Publications:** Photochemistry; carbohydrates; analytical chemistry. **Mailing Address:** 14 Webster Acres, St Louis, MO 63119.

JAMIESON, WILLIAM DAVID, ANALYTICAL MASS SPECTROMETRY, QUALITY ASSURANCE. **Personal Data:** b Toronto, Ont, August 6, 1929; m 1951, c 1. **Education:** Dalhousie Univ, BSc & dipl chem eng, 1950, MSc, 1951; Cambridge Univ, PhD (physchem), 1954. **Honors & Awards:** Caledon Award, 1991. **Professional Experience:** PRIN ASSOC, SCOTIA CHEM TECHNOL ASSOCS, as of 2003; sr scientist, Fenwick Labs Ltd, beginning 1990; Stand Comt, Can AsnEnviron Anal Chem, beginning 1989; chair, Group Experts Stand & Ref Mat, Int Oceanog Comn, beginning 1987; mgr, Marine Anal Chem Stand Prog, 1979-1990; head marine anal chem, Atlantic Res Lab, Nat Res Coun Can, 1975-1990; head clean-up technol coord, Oper Oil, 1970; asst to dir, Atlantic ResLab, Nat Res Coun Can, 1964-1975; coordr, Atlantic Prov Interuniv Comt Sci, 1963-1965; prin res officer, Atlantic Res Lab, Nat Res Coun Can, 1954-1990. **Memberships:** Fel Chem Inst Can; Am Soc Mass Spectrometry; Spectros Soc Can; MarineTechnol Soc; Can Soc Mass Spectrometry. **Research Statement & Publications:** Mass spectrometry; instrumentation development; analytical chemistry; kinetics of gas phase ion reactions; oil pollution clean-up technology; marine analytical chemistry; development of analytical chemistry reference materials and standards; quality assurance in analytical chemistry. **Mailing Address:** 30 Colindale, Halifax, NS B3P 2A4, Can. **Fax:** 902-477-3720. **E-Mail:** wjamieso@fox.nstn.ca

JAMISON, DEAN T, ECONOMICS OF EDUCATION, INTERNATIONAL HEALTH ECONOMICS & POLICY. **Personal Data:** b October 10, 1943; m 1977, Kin; c Julian C, Eliot A & Leslie S. **Education:** Stanford Univ, AB, 1966, MS, 1967; Harvard Univ, PhD (econ), 1970. **Professional Experience:** Econ adv, Human Develop Dept, World Bank, beginning 1995; Dir, Ctr Pac Rim Studies, beginning 1993; dir, World Bank, 1992-1993; prof, Sch Pub Health & Grad Sch Educ, Univ Calif, Los Angeles, 1988-2005; economist & div chief, World Bank, 1976-1988; Asst prof, Stanford Univ, 1969-1973. **Memberships:** Inst Med-Nat Acad Sci. **Research Statement & Publications:** Theory and applications of cost-benefit and cost-effectiveness analysis in health and education. **Mailing Address:** Ctr Pac RIM Studies Univ Calif, 11292 Bunche Hall 405 Hilgard Ave, Los Angeles, CA 90095-1487. **Fax:** 301-206-4018. **E-Mail:** djamieson@isop.ucla.edu

JAMISON, DONALD K, CIVIL ENGINEERING. **Education:** Va Mil Acad, BS; Univ Calif, MS; Univ Wis, PhD. **Professional Experience:** COL EMER PROF DEPT CIVIL & ENVIRON ENG & ACAD ADV, INTER COL AHELETICS, as of 2000. **Mailing Address:** Dept Civil & Environ Eng, Va Mil Inst, 609 Nichols Eng Hall, Lexington, VA 24450-0304. **Fax:** 540-464-7618.

JAMISON, HOMER CLAUDE, EPIDEMIOLOGY, DENTISTRY. **Personal Data:** b Marion, NC, April 14, 1921; c 3. **Education:** Western Carolina Teachers Col, AB, 1942; Emory Univ, DDS, 1950; Univ Mich, MPH, 1957, DrPH(epidemiol), 1961; Am Bd Dent Pub Health, dipl. **Professional Experience:** RETIRED; emer prof, Sch Dent, Univ Ala, Birmingham, 1986; prof, Sch Dent, Univ Ala, Birmingham, 1972-1986; prof dent, Sch Dent, Univ Mo-Kansas City, 1968-1972; membd dirs, Jefferson Co Anti-Tuberc Asn, 1964-1968; Consult, Div Radiol Health, USPHS, 1964-1966; dir comput res lab, Med Ctr, Univ Ala, Birmingham, 1963-1964; dir grad prog, MedCtr, Univ Ala, Birmingham, 1962-1963; from asst prof to prof dent, Med Ctr, Univ Ala, Birmingham, 1960-1968; pub health dentist, Mich Dept Health, 1957-1958; dent officer, Mecklenburg Health Dept, 1954-1956; Pub health dentist, NC State Bd Health, 1951-1954. **Memberships:** Fel Am Pub Health Asn; Am Dent Asn; Biomet Soc; Am Statist Asn. **Research Statement & Publications:** Clinical studies of potential prophylactic and therapeutic agents; applications and uses of computers in health research; patterns and trends in oral health and diseases. **Mailing Address:** 3586 Rockhill Rd, Birmingham, AL 35223-1402.

JAMISON, JOEL DEXTER, ORGANIC CHEMISTRY. **Personal Data:** b Roanoke, Va, November 22, 1932; m 1959, c 3. **Education:** Col William & Mary, BS, 1955; Northwestern Univ, PhD (org chem), 1960. **Professional Experience:** RETIRED; mgr, Tech Div, 1979-1994; res scientist, Hurcules Inc, 1972-1979; res chemist, Hurcules Inc, 1960-1972. **Memberships:** Am Chem Soc. **Research Statement & Publications:** Molecular structure elucidation; synthesis and investigation of condensation reactions in strong acid; synthesis of biologically active organic compounds for screening as pesticides; synthesis of lubrication base stocks. **Mailing Address:** PO Box 1655, Hockessin, DE 19707-5655.

JAMISON, KING W, JR, MATHEMATICS. **Personal Data:** b Meridian, Miss, August 8, 1931; m 1953, c 4. **Education:** Union Univ, Tenn, BS, 1952; George Peabody Col, MA, 1953, PhD (math educ), 1962. **Professional Experience:** RETIRED; prof math, Middle Tenn State Univ, beginning 1972; from asst profto assocprof, Middle Tenn State Univ, 1962-1972; Lectr math, Vanderbilt Univ, 1961-1962. **Research Statement & Publications:** Mathematics education, especially the relationship of mathematical symbols to English words; variable base abacus as a visual aid. **Mailing Address:** Dept Math, Middle Tenn State Univ, Box 163, Murfreesboro, TN 37132. **E-Mail:** kjamieson@mtsu.edu

JAMISON, RICHARD MELVIN, CLINICAL VIROLOGY. **Personal Data:** b Rayne, La, October 28, 1938; div. **Education:** Univ Southwestern La, BS, 1958; Baylor Univ, MS, 1962, PhD (virol), 1966; Am Bd Med Microbiol, dipl, 1976. **Honors & Awards:** Fellow Am Academy of Microbiology. **Professional Experience:** PROF PEDIAT, LA STATE UNIV, SHREVEPORT, 1987-; trustee, Am Bd Med Microbiol, 1986-1989, 1991-1997; vis prof microbiol, Fac Med, Ala Fetah Univ, Tripoli, Libya, 1981-1982; dir, Diag Virol Lab, 1979-1985; PROF MICROBIOL & IMMUNOL, LA STATE UNIV, SHREVEPORT, 1978-; assoc prof, LA State Univ, Shreveport, 1970-1978; asst prof path, Univ Colo, Denver, 1967-1970; res assoc biol div, Oak Ridge Nat Lab, 1965-1967. **Memberships:** Am Soc Microbiol; Pam Am Soc Clin Virology. **Research Statement & Publications:** Replication of picornaviruses; rapid diagnosis of viral infections. **Mailing Address:** Dept Pediat La State Univ Sch Med, 1501 Kings Hwy, Shreveport, LA 71130.

JAMISON, ROBERT EDWARD, COMBINATORIAL GEOMETRY, GRAPH ALGORITHMS. **Personal Data:** b Tampa, Fla, December 21, 1948; m 1978, c Elizabeth N & Margaret I Jamison. **Education:** Clemson Univ, BS, 1970; Univ Wash, MS, 1973, PhD (math), 1974. **Professional Experience:** Vis prof, Univ Berne, 1986; vis prof, Cornell Univ, 1993-1994; Humboldt fel, Univ Freiburg, 1984; PROF MATH SCI, CLEMSON UNIV, 1983-; assoc prof, Clemson Univ, 1979-1983; vis prof, Tech Univ Darmstadt, 1979; Alexander von Humboldt fel, Univ Erlangen, 1976-1977; vis asst, Inst Appl Math, Univ Bonn, 1975-1976; asst prof, La State Univ, 1974-1979. **Research Statement & Publications:** Combinatorial problems of a geometric nature, especially those arising from ordered sets, graphs, and free structures. **Mailing Address:** Math Sci Dept, Clemson Univ, Clemson, SC 29634-1907. **E-Mail:** rejam@clemson.edu

JAMISON, RONALD D, MATHEMATICS. **Personal Data:** b 1931. **Education:** Univ Utah, PhD (math), 1965. **Professional Experience:** PROF EMER MATH, BRIGHAM YOUNG UNIV, as of 2002; prof math, brigham young univ, beginning 1963. **Memberships:** Am Math Soc. **Research Statement & Publications:** Differential equations & applied math. **Mailing Address:** Bringham Young Univ, 290 Talmage Math Bldg, Provo, UT 84602-1044. **Fax:** 801-422-0504.

JAMISON, WILLIAM H, MATHEMATICS. **Personal Data:** b Burlington, Iowa, May 4, 1932; m 1962. **Education:** Mont State Col, BS, 1959, MS, 1961. **Professional Experience:** PROF MATH, ROCKY MOUNTAIN COL, 1968-; chmn div natural sci & math, Rocky Mountain Col, beginning 1968; assoc prof, Rocky Mountain Col, 1962-1968; instr math, Mont StateCol, 1959-1962. **Memberships:** Math Asn Am; Am Math Soc; Am Asn Physics Teachers. **Research Statement & Publications:** Boolean algebra; logic; fossil fuel utilization. **Mailing Address:** Dept Phys & Math, Rocky Mountain Col, 1511 Poly Dr, Billings, MT 59101. **E-Mail:** jamisonb@rocky.edu

JAMMALAMADAKA, SREENIVASA RAO, DIRECTIONAL DATA ANALYSIS. **Personal Data:** b Munipalle, India, December 7, 1943; American citizen; m 1972, Vijaya; c Arvind & Aruna. **Education:** Indian Statist Inst, Calcutta, BS, 1964, MS, 1965, PhD (statist), 1969. **Professional Experience:** Member, Outreach Comt, Inter Indian Statist Asn, 2001-; chair, Dept Statist Appl Probability, Univ Calif, 1989-1993; chair, Southern Calif Chapter, Am Statist Asn, 1984-1990; PROF PROBABILITY & STATIST, UNIV CALIF, SANTA BARBARA, 1983-; dir, Statist Consult Ctr, Univ Calif, Santa Barbara, 1980-; from asst prof to assoc prof, Univ Calif, Santa Barbara, 1976-1983; vis prof, Univ Wis-Madison, 1975-1976 & Univ Leeds, 1976; asst prof, Ind Univ, 1970-1975; vis asst prof probability & statist, Ind Univ, 1969-1976; res scholar statist, Indian Statist Inst, 1965-1969. **Memberships:** Fel Am Statist Asn; fel Inst Math Statist; Royal Statist Soc; fel Int Statist Inst; fel Inst Combinatorics & Applications. **Research Statement & Publications:** Nonparametric statistical methods; inference based on sample spacings; large sample theory; efficiencies of test procedures; statistics of directional data; published over 100 articles. **Mailing Address:** Dept Statist & Appl Probability, Univ Calif, Santa Barbara, CA 93106-3110. **Fax:** 805-893-2334. **E-Mail:** rao@pstat.ucsb.edu

JAMMU, K S, PHYSICS. **Personal Data:** b India, January 1, 1935; m 1959, c 2. **Education:** Aligarh Muslim Univ, India, MSc, 1957; Univ Toronto, MA, 1960, PhD (physics), 1965. **Professional Experience:** PROF PHYSICS, UNIV PEI, 1982-; assoc prof, Univ PEI, 1969-1980; from asst prof to assoc prof, St Dunstan's Univ, 1967-1969; asst prof, Mem Univ, 1965-1967; Lectrphysics, Khalsa Col, Amritsar, India, 1957-1959. **Memberships:** Am Asn Physics Teachers; Can Asn Physicists. **Research Statement & Publications:** Molecular physics; spectroscopy. **Mailing Address:** Dept Physics, Univ PEI, Charlottetown, PE C1A 4P3, Can.

JAMNBACK, HUGO ANDREW, MEDICAL ENTOMOLOGY. **Personal Data:** b Fitchburg, Mass, September 18, 1926; m 1953, c 3. **Education:** Boston Univ, BA, 1948; Univ Mass, MS, 1951, PhD, 1953; London Sch Hyg & TropMed, Dipl, 1966. **Professional Experience:** RETIRED; sr res assoc, Col Environ Sci & Forestry, Syracuse Univ, beginning 1973; dir, NY State Sci Serv, 1971-1981; consult, WHO, beginning 1967; assoc scientist, NY State Mus & Sci Serv, 1967-1971; sr scientist, NY State Mus & Sci Serv, 1959-1967; scientist entom, NY State Mus & Sci Serv, 1953-1959. **Memberships:** Entom Soc Am; Am Mosquito Control Asn. **Research Statement & Publications:** Taxonomy, biology and control of biting flies. **Mailing Address:** 103 Heritage Rd Apt Eight, Guilderland, NY 12084-9658.

JAMPEL, ROBERT STEVEN, OPHTHALMOLOGY. **Personal Data:** b New York, NY, November 3, 1926; m 1952, c 4. **Education:** Columbia Univ, AB, 1947, MD, 1950; Univ Mich, MS, 1957, PhD (anat), 58. **Professional Experience:** CHMN EMER, KRESGE EYE INST, WAYNE STATE UNIV, as of 2003; chief, Dept Ophthal, Hutzel Hosp & Detroit Med Ctr, 1988; PROF OPHTHAL, KRESGE EYE INST, WAYNE STATE UNIV, beginning 1970; chmn, kresge Eye Inst, Wayne State Univ, beginning 1970; DIR, KRESGE EYE INST, WAYNE STATE UNIV, beginning 1970; assoc ophthal, Columbia Univ, 1962-1970; asst prof, State Univ NY, Downstate Med Ctr, 1958-1962; instrneurol, Univ Mich, 1957-1958; Clin instr ophthal, Univ Mich, 1956-1957. **Memberships:** Asn Res Vision & Ophthal; Am Acad Ophthal & Otolaryngol; Am Acad Neurol. **Research Statement & Publications:** Physiology of the ocular muscles. **Mailing Address:** Dept Opthal, Wayne State univ, 4717 St Antoine, Detroit, MI 48201. **Fax:** 313-577-5482. **E-Mail:** rjampel@med.wayne.edu

JAMPOLSKY, ARTHUR, OPHTHALMOLOGY, STRABISMUS & BINOCULAR VISION. **Personal Data:** b Bismarck, NDak, April 24, 1919; m 1957, c 3. **Education:** Univ Calif, AB, 1940; Stanford Univ, MD, 1944; Am Bd Ophthal, dipl, 1950. **Honors & Awards:** Mildred Weisenfeld Award, Asn Res Vision & Ophthal. **Professional Experience:** CO EXEC DIR, SMITH-KETTLEWELL EYE RES INST, as of 2004; chmn study sect, NIH, 1970-1971; vis sci study sect, NIH, 1967-1971; dir, Smith-Kettlewell Eye Res Inst, Calif Pac Med Ctr, beginning 1960; exec coun, comt onvision, Armed Forces-Nat Res Coun, 1960-1964; mem comt on vision, Armed Forces-Nat ResCoun, beginning 1958; chief strabismus clin, Smith-Kettlewell Eye Res Inst, Calif Pac Med Ctr, 1950-1960; spec consult, Nat Inst Neurol Dis & Blindness; regional consult ophthal, OakKnoll Naval Hosp, Oakland & Travis AFB; consult, Letterman Gen Hosp, San Francisco & CalifState Bd Health. **Memberships:** Am Optom Asn; Am Acad Ophthal; Am Ophthal Soc; Am Asn Ophthal; fel AmCol Surg. **Research Statement & Publications:** Binocular vision; strabismus; physiological optics. **Mailing Address:** Smith-Kettlewell Eye Res Inst, 2318 Fillmore St, San Francisco, CA 94115. **Fax:** 415-345-8455.

JAMRICH, JOHN XAVIER, ACADEMIC ADMINISTRATION, STATISTICS. **Personal Data:** b Muskegon Heights, Mich, June 12, 1920. **Education:** Univ Chicago, BS, 1943; Marquette Univ, MS, 1948; Northwestern Univ, PhD (admin), 1951. **Honorary Degrees:** LLD, Northern Mich Univ, 1968, Grand Valley State Col, 1985. **Professional Experience:** CONSULT, 1983-; pres, Northern Mich Univ, 1968-1983; consult, Study Capital Outlay Needs, Va State Comn Higher Educ, 1965 & Facil Study, SC Comn Hihgher Educ, 1966; consult, State Bd Regents Ohio, 1965; consult, Ford Found, Univ Nigeria, 1964; assoc dean, Col Educ, 1963-1968; accreditation examr & consult, NCent Asn Cols & Sec Schs, 1962-; Saginaw Valley, 1962 & Study Capital Outlay Needs, Ohio's State Insts Higher Educ, 1962-1963; dir, Surv Higher Educ Grand Rapids, 1959; prof & dir, Ctr Study Higher Educ, Mich State Univ, 1957-1963; From asst dir to assoc dir, Legis Surv Higher Educ, Mich, 1957-1961; dean fac, Doane Col, 1955-1957; dean students, Coe Col, 1951-1955; asst dean men, Northwestern Univ, 1949-1951; asst inst, Univ Wis, 1948-1949; Instr math, Marquette Univ, 1946-1948. **Memberships:** AAAS; Am Math Soc; Am Educ Res Asn. **Research Statement & Publications:** Educational statistics in connection with administration of the university; meteorology. **Mailing Address:** 523 Governors Green Dr, Venice, FL 34293.

JAMSHIDI, MOHAMMAD MO, ROBOTICS, COMPUTER-AIDED DESIGN. **Personal Data:** b Shiraz, Iran, May 10, 1944; American citizen; m 1974, c 2. **Education:** Ore State Univ, BS, 1967; Univ Ill, Urbana-Champaign, MS, 1969, PhD (eleceng), 1971. **Honorary Degrees:** Dr, Azerbaijan Nat Univ, 1999; Dr Engr, Univ Waterloo, Can, 2004, Tech Univ Crete, 2004. **Honors & Awards:** Centennial Medal, Inst Elec & Electronics Engrs. **Professional Experience:** SR RES SCIENTIST, US AIR FORCE RES LAB, 2006-; REGENT PROF ELEC & COMPUT ENG, UNIV NMEX, 2000-; FOUND DIR, ACE, 1995-; Oak Ridge Nat Lab, 1988- & Los Alamos Nat Lab, 1990-; Am Soc Mech Engrs Ser Robotics & Mfg, 1986- & Int J Computers & Elec Eng, 1989-; AT&T PROF MFG ENG, COMPUTER AIDED DESIGN LAB, 1989-; vis prof, George Wash Univ & Nat InstStandards & Technol, 1987-1988 & Univ Va, 1988; hon prof, Nanjing Aeronaut Inst, People's Repub China, 1986; consult, USAF Phillips Lab, 1984-; DIR, COMPUTER AIDED DESIGN LAB, 1984-; adv engr, Info Prod Div, Int Bus Mach, 1982-1983; PROF ELEC ENG, UNIV NMEX, 1980-; Ed, Inst Elec & Electronics Engrs Control Systs Mag, 1980-1984; prof, Dept Elec Eng, Pahlavi Univ, Iran, 1977-1979; scientist, Int Bus Mach Res Ctr, Yorktown Heights, 1975-1977; from asst prof to assoc prof, Dept Elec Eng, Pahlavi Univ, Iran, 1971-1975; res assoc, Univ Ill, 1970-1971. **Memberships:** Fel Inst Elec & Electronics Engrs; Inst Elec & Electronics Engrs Control SystsSoc; Soc Photo-Optical Instrumentation Engrs; Am Soc Mech Engrs. **Research Statement & Publications:** Intelligent control systems including fuzzy logic, neural network, and expert systems; robotics control; adaptive control of nuclear reactors; computer-aided design of control systems. **Mailing Address:** Dept Elec & Comput Eng, Sch Eng Univ NMex, Albuquerque, NM 87131. **E-Mail:** jamshidi@unm.edu

JAN, GEORGE C, OPTICS, MEDICAL LASERS. **Personal Data:** b Canton, China, August 20, 1934; m 1963, May; c Brend. **Education:** Taiwan Normal Univ, BA, 1959; Govt Ind Univ, MA, 1964; Georgetown Univ, PhD (phys), 1974. **Professional Experience:** RETIRED; scientist, Food & Drug Admin, beginning 1998; br chief, Gen Surg Devices Br, Food & Drug Admin, beginning 1991; sr reviewer, Div Ophthal, 1984-1991; chief, VV Radiation Sect, 1981-1984; regulatory officer, Regulation & Stand, Food Drug Admin, 1979-1981; regulation officer, Regulation & Stand, Food Drug Admin, 1974-1979. **Mailing Address:** 9404 Woodington Dr, Potomac, MD 20854. **E-Mail:** gcj@cdrh.fda.gov

JAN, KUNG-MING, CARDIOLOGY, CARDIOVASCULAR PHYSIOLOGY. **Personal Data:** b January 14, 1943; m 1975, Connie; c Rex, Stephen & Thomas. **Education:** Nat Taiwan Univ, Taipei, MD, 1967; Columbia Univ, PhD (physiol), 1971. **Professional Experience:** ASSOC ATTEND PHYSICIAN, PRESBY HOSP, 1978-; ASSOC PROF PHYSIOL & MED, COL PHYSICIANS & SURGEONS, COLUMBIA UNIV, 1968-. **Memberships:** Am Col Cardiol. **Research Statement & Publications:** Blood rheology; cardiovascular physiology; cell interaction; endothelial cell physiology. **Mailing Address:** Div Cardiol, Dept Med, Columbia Univ, 161 Ft Wash Ave, New York, NY 10032. **Fax:** 212-305-1061. **E-Mail:** kj3@columbia.edu

JAN, KWAN-HWA, IMAGING PROCESSING, SPEECH & DIGITAL SIGNAL PROCESSING. **Personal Data:** b Yung Ching, Chung Hua, Taiwan, January 23, 1956; American citizen; m Lih-Jih; c Oliver C. **Education:** Nat Cheng Kung Univ, Taiwan, Bachelor Sci, 1978; Northwestern Univ, MS, 1983, PhD (elec eng), 1991. **Professional Experience:** RES SCIENTIST, NORTHWESTERN UNIV, BIRL INDUST RES LAB, 1992-; consult, Dept Elec Eng & Comput Sci, 1991-1992; sr syst programmer, Dept Elec Eng &Comput Sci, 1984-1991; res engr, Sampo Electronic Co, Taipei, Taiwan, 1980-1981; Electronicsprogrammer, Hq Chinese Marine Corps, Taiwan, China, 1979-1980. **Memberships:** Inst Elec & Electronics Engrs; Acoustics Speech & Signals Processing Soc. **Research Statement & Publications:** Applying image processing, digital signal processing and pattern recognition techniques to solve industrial inspection and automation problems. **Mailing Address:** BIRL Indust Res Lab, Northwestern Univ, Chicago, IL 60611. **Fax:** 847-491-7105. **E-Mail:** k-jan@nwu.edu

JAN, LILY YEH, PHYSIOLOGY, BIOCHEMISTRY. **Personal Data:** b China, January 20, 1947; American citizen; m Yuh. **Education:** Nat Taiwan Univ, 1968; Calif Inst Technol, MSc, 1970, PhD (biophysics & physics), 1974. **Honors & Awards:** W Alden Spencer Award & Lectr, Columbia Univ, 1988; Javits neuroscience investr award, NatInst Neurol & Commun Dis & Stroke, 1988-. **Professional Experience:** Fac lectr, Univ Calif, San Francisco, 1995; DELORIS LANGE PROF PHYSIOL & BIOCHEM, UNIV CALIF, SAN FRANCISCO, 1985-; INVESTR, HOWARD HUGHES MED INST, 1984-; Klingensteinfel, 1983-1986; assoc prof, Howard Hughes Med Inst, 1983-1985; asst prof physiol, Howard Hughes Med Inst, 1979-1983; Alfred P Sloan res fel, 1977-1979; res fel, Dept Neurobiology, Harvard Med Sch, 1977-1979; res fel, Calif Inst Technol, 1974-1977. **Memberships:** Nat Acad Sci. **Mailing Address:** Dept Physiol & Biophys, Univ Calif, PO Box 0725, San Francisco, CA 94143-0725. **Fax:** 415-476-5774. **E-Mail:** gkw@itsa.ucsf.edu

JAN, YUH NUNG, BIOCHEMISTRY, PHYSIOLOGY. **Personal Data:** b Shanghai, China, December 20, 1946; m 1971, Lily. **Education:** Nat Taiwan Univ, BS, 1967; Calif Inst Technol, MS, 1970, PhD (biophys & physics), 1974. **Honors & Awards:** W Alden Spencer Lectr, Columbia Univ, 1988. **Professional Experience:** PROF PHYSIOL & BIOCHEM, UNIV CALIF, SAN FRANCISCO, 1985-; INVESTR, HOWARD HUGHES MED INST, 1984-; from asst prof to assoc prof, Howard Hughes Med Inst, 1979-1985; mcknight scholar, 1978; res fel, Dept Neurobiology, Harvard Med Sch, 1977-1979; res fel, Calif Inst Technol, 1974-1977; fel, ScottishRite Schizophrenia Res Prog, 1974-1976 & Muscular Dystrophy Asn, 1976-1978. **Memberships:** Nat Acad Sci; Genetics Soc Am; Soc Chinese Bioscientists Am; Am Soc Cell Biol; Soc Neuroscience; Soc Develop Biol 6. **Research Statement & Publications:** Function and development of thenervous system; cell fate specification; ion channels; neuronal morphogenesis. **Mailing Address:** Genetics, Univ Calif, 1550 4th St PO Box 2811, San Francisco, CA 94143. **E-Mail:** ynjan@itsa.ucsf.edu

JANABI-SHARIFI, FARROKH, MECHATRONICS, ROBOTICS & MANUFACTURING AUTOMATION. **Personal Data:** b Tabriz, Iran, February 6, 1960; Canadian citizen. **Education:** Middle E Techl Univ, BASc, 1987; Univ Toronto, MASc, 1990; Univ Waterloo, PhD, 1995. **Professional Experience:** ADJ PROF ELEC & COMPUT ENG, UNIV WESTERN ONT, as of 2006; ADJ PROF ELEC & COMPUT ENG, UNIV WATERLOO, as of 2006; ADJ PROF ELEC & COMPUT ENG, MCGILL UNIV, 1997-; ASSOC PROF MECH ENG, RYERSON UNIV, 1997-; lectr artificial intel, McGill Univ, 1996-1997; Nat sci & eng res coun postdoctoral fel, McGill Univ, 1995-1997. **Memberships:** Sr mem SME; Robotics Int Assoc; Sr mem Inst Elec & Electronics Engrs Robotics & Automation Soc; sr mem Inst Elec & Electronics Engrs Control Systs Soc. **Research Statement & Publications:** Development of an intelligent supervisory control system for visual-serving robotic manipulators, automatic grasp, path and visual feature planners have been designed and integrated; initiation and development of an adaptive velocity estimator for discrete-time position information to be used in haptic interfaces; development of smart vibration generator for fixtureless assembly and experimentation; author of numerous publications. **Mailing Address:** Dept Mech Eng, Ryerson Univ, Toronto, ON M5B 2K3, Can. **Fax:** 416-979-5265. **E-Mail:** fsharifi@ryerson.ca

JANAK, JAMES FRANCIS, ELECTRICAL ENGINEERING, PHYSICS. **Personal Data:** b Yonkers, NY, December 5, 1938; m 1965, c 2. **Education:** Mass Inst Technol, SB, 1960, SM, 1962, ScD (elec eng), 1964. **Professional Experience:** ADJ PROF PHYSICS, PACE UNIV, 1983-; adj assoc prof math, Pace Univ, 1978-1983; mem res staff theoret physics, Thomas J Watson res ctr, IBM Corp beginning 1965; Ford Found fel, 1964-1965; asst prof, Mass Inst Technol, 1964-1965; instr elec eng, Mass Inst Technol, 1962-1964. **Memberships:** Am Phys Soc; AAAS. **Research Statement & Publications:** Solid state physics. **Mailing Address:** Dept Chem, Pace Univ, One Pace Plaza 551 5th Ave, NY 10038.

JANAKIDEVI, K, GROWTH CONTROL MECHANISMS, GENE REGULATION. **Education:** Ofmania Univ, India, PhD (protozool), 1957. **Professional Experience:** ASSOC PROF MOLECULAR PATH, ALBANY MED SCH, 1970-. **Mailing Address:** 40 Marion Ave, Albany, NY 12203.

JANATA, JIRI, ELECTROANALYTICAL, SOLID STATE DEVICES. **Personal Data:** b Podebrady, Czech, July 12, 1939; British citizen; m 1962, c 2. **Education:** Univ Charles, Pargue, MSc, 1961, PhD (anal chem), 1965. **Professional Experience:** FAC, GA INST TECHNOL, SCH CHEM & BIOCHEM, as of 2003; assoc dir, Pacific Northwest Nat Lab, Wash, 1992-1997; prof, dept mat sci & eng, 1987-1981; vis Scientist, UK atomic energy authority, Eng, 1986-1987; vis fel, Wolfson col, Univ Oxford, 1986-1987; Prof & Chmn, Dept Bioengineering, 1983-1985; adj prof, dept chem, Univ Utah, beginning 1980; consult, Johnson & Johnson, beginning 1979; prin investr, NSF, NIH & Dept Defense, beginning 1976; prof Bioengineering, Univ Utah, 1976-1983; sr chemist, Imperial Chem Indust, 1968-1976; Res fel, Univ Mich, 1966-1968; asst lectr, Univ Charles, 1962-1966. **Memberships:** Royal Soc Chem; Electrochem Soc; Am Chem Soc; AAAS; Nat res counc. **Research Statement & Publications:** Electroanalytical chemistry: solid state chemically inactive devices and in flow through electrochemical detectors; Published over 15 articles. **Mailing Address:** Sch Chem & biochem, Ga Inst Technol, 1-24 Boggs Bldg, Atlanta, GA 30332-0400. **Fax:** 404-894-7452. **E-Mail:** jiri.janata@chemistry.gatech.edu

JANATOVA, JARMILA, BIOCHEMISTRY. **Personal Data:** b Pisek, Czech, January 9, 1939; American citizen; m 1962, c 2. **Education:** Charles Univ, MSc, 1961; Czech Acad Sci, PhD (biochem), 1965. **Professional Experience:** ASSOC PROF, DEPT BIOENGINEERING, UNIV UTAH, as of 2004; adj assoc prof, dept Bioengineering, Univ Utah, beginning 1989; acad mem, Ctr Biopolymers, Univ Utah, 1986-; sr acad vis, MRC Immunochem Unit, Dept Biochem, Univ Oxford, 1986-1987; RES ASSOC PROF, DEPT PATH, UNIV UTAH, 1985-; res asst prof, Univ Utah, 1981-1985; res instr, Univ Utah, 1979-1981; post doctoral res assoc, Dept Pathol, Univ Utah, 1977-1979; post doctoral res assoc, Dept Mat Sci & Eng, Univ Utah, 1976-1977; sr expo fficer, Dept Biochem, Univ Liverpool, Eng, 1975-1976; postdoctoral res assoc, Dept Biol, Univ Utah, 1973-1975; post doctoral res assoc, Univ Mich, 1966-1967; post doctoral res assoc, Biophysics Div, Inst Sci & Technol, Univ Mich, 1966-1967; sr lectr, Dept Phys Chem, Charles Univ, Prague, Czech, 1965-1966; sr lectr, Charles Univ, 1965-1966; res scientist, Inst Org Chem& Biochem, Czech Acad Sci, 1965. **Memberships:** Sigma Xi; AAAS; Am Chem Soc; Am Soc Biochem & Molecular Biol; Am AsnImmunol; NY Acad Sci. **Research Statement & Publications:** Biochemistry of complement proteins; protein chemistry structure or function of proteins from the complement system; isolation and characterization of proteins; biocompatibility of biomedical polymers. **Mailing Address:** Dept Bioeng, Univ Utah, 108 E Biomed Polymers Res Bldg, Salt Lake City, UT 84112. **Fax:** 801-585-5151. **E-Mail:** jarmila.janatova@m.cc.utah.edu

JANAUER, GILBERT E, PHYSICAL ANALYTICAL CHEMISTRY. **Personal Data:** b Vienna, Austria, February 26, 1931; m 1958, c 1. **Education:** Univ Vienna, PhD (chem), 1962. **Professional Experience:** PROF EMER, DEPT CHEM, STATE UNIV NY, BINGHAMTON, as of 2004; prof chem, State Univ NY, Binghanton, beginning 1981; vchmn, GordonRes Conf Ion Exchange, 1979; NSF fac adv, 1973 & 1976; vis prof, Graz Inst Technol, Austria, 1971-1972; speaker, Gordon Res Conf Ion Exchange, 1969, 1975, 1977; from asst prof to assocprof, State Univ NY, Binghamton, 1964-1980; res assoc chem, Clarkson Tech, 1963-1964; instranal chem, Anal Inst, Univ Vienna, 1961-1962; res asst, Anal Inst, Univ Vienna, 1960-1961; jrchemist, Oemvag, Austria, 1958-1960. **Memberships:** AAAS; Am Chem Soc; Sigma Xi. **Research Statement & Publications:** Ion exhange equilibria and kinetics in aqueous and aqueous-organic solvents; separation methods; trace preconcentration and analysis; reactive ion exchange; chemical disinfection. **Mailing Address:** Dept Chem, State Univ NY, PO Box 6000, Binghamton, NY 13902.

JANCA, FRANK CHARLES, GENETICS, DROSOPHILA MUTAGENESIS. **Personal Data:** b Chicago, Ill, October 27, 1946. **Education:** Western Mich Univ, BA, 1968; MA, 1972; La State Univ, PhD (zoology), 1978. **Professional Experience:** PROF SCI, GLEN OAKS COMMUN COL, as of 2004; adj asst prof, Western Mich Univ, 1990-; vis res scientist, Western Mich Univ, 1988-1990; res assoc reproductive toxicol, SDak State Univ, 1983-1986; fel genetics, Univ Alta, 1978-1981. **Memberships:** Genetics Soc Am; Environ Mutagen Soc; Sigma Xi. **Research Statement & Publications:** Mutagen testing and mutagenesis; bacteria; maize; Drosophila and mammalian systems; reproductive toxicology using mouse and rat testes as test system and flow cytometry as research tool. **Mailing Address:** Dept Sci, Glen Oaks Community Col, Off D251 6224 Shimmel Rd, Centreville, MI 49032. **E-Mail:** fjanca@glenoaks.cc.mi.us

JANCARIK, JIRI, PLASMA PHYSICS & DIAGNOSTICS. **Personal Data:** b Brno, Czech, October 9, 1941; American citizen; m 1963, Jarmila; c Alesh & John Peter. **Education:** Charles Univ, Prague, RNDr(exp physics), 1963; Czech Acad Sci, CSc(plasma physics), 1968. **Professional Experience:** PHYSICIST, LAWRENCE LIVERMORE NAT LAB, UNIV CALIF, LIVERMORE, 1981-; res scientist, Fusion Res Ctr, Univ Tex, Austin, 1972-1981; res assoc, Eng Dept, Univ Oxford, 1969-1972; res officer, Culham Lab, UK Atomic Energy Authority, 1968-1972; post drc, Inst Plasma Physics, Czech Acad Sci, 1963-1968. **Memberships:** Am Phys Soc. **Research Statement & Publications:** Plasma heating and containment for thermonuclear applications; study of plasma waves; turbulence using x-ray, magnetic and electromagnetic diagnostics; computer simulation of relativistic beams, plasma turbulence; collective ion accelerators; laser isotope separation. **Mailing Address:** 1954 Woodbury Ct, Walnut Creek, CA 94596. **Fax:** 925-423-8086. **E-Mail:** jancarik1@llnl.gov

JANDA, JOHN MICHAEL, INFECTIOUS DISEASES & MICROBIOL PATHOGENICITY & VIRULENCE, TAXONOMY & LAB DIAGNOSTICS. **Personal Data:** b Burbank, Calif, November 4, 1949; m 1979, Claudia; c Michael Jr, Matthew & Jennifer. **Education:** Loyola Univ, BS, 1971; Calif State Univ, Los Angeles, MS, 1975; Univ Calif, LosAngeles, PhD (microbiol & immunol), 1979. **Honors & Awards:** Aeromonas jandaei named in honor, 1991; Distinguished Alumni Award, CSULA, 1994, Foundation for Microbiology Lecturer, ASM, 1994 - 1996; 2003 Public Health Recognition Award, CDHS. **Professional Experience:** CHIEF, MICROBIAL DIS LAB, as of 2005; RES SCIENTIST, MICROBIAL DIS LAB, 1990-1998; Mem, subcomt Facultatively Anaerobic Gram-Negative Rods, Am Soc Microbiol, 1987-1990; Res Microbiologist, Microbiol Dis Lab, 1986-1990; Assoc Dir/Prof, Dept Microbiol, Mt Sinai Hosp, 1984-1986; asstdir/prof, Dept Microbiol, Mt Sinai Hosp, 1981-1984; Fel, Dept Microbiol, Mt Sinai Hosp, 1979-1981; Editorial Boards: J Clin Microbiol, Curr Microbiol, Infection, Eur J Clin Microbiol Infect Dis, Man Clin Microbiol; Mem ICSP (Enterobacteriaceae, Vibrionaceae). **Memberships:** Am Soc Microbiol; Phi Kapppa Phi; Soc Gen Microbiol; Assoc Mem APHL; Am Assoc Bioanalysts. **Research Statement & Publications:** Microbiol pathogenesis; clinical microbiology; diagnostic microbiology; Aeromonas pathogenesis and taxonomy; cellular replication and invasion by enteric bacteria; Vibrio infections; toxigenic bacteria. **Mailing Address:** 841 Meadow View Dr, Richmond, CA 94806. **Fax:** 510-412-3722. **E-Mail:** jjanda@dhs.ca.gov

JANDA, KENNETH CARL, MOLECULAR SPECTROSCOPY, SURFACE CHEMISTRY. **Personal Data:** b Denver, Colo, November 28, 1950; m 1971, c 2. **Education:** Hope Col, AB, 1973; Harvard Univ, AM, 1975, PhD (phys chem), 1977. **Professional Experience:** PROF, DEPT CHEM, UNIV CALIF, IRVINE, 1992-; prof, Dept Chem, Univ Pittsburgh, 1986-1992; fulbright fel, 1985; dreyfus fel, 1983-1985; A P Sloan fel, 1981-1984; asst prof, Calif Inst Technol, 1980-1985; res instr physics, A A Noyes, 1978-1980; fel, Univ Chicago, 1977-1978. **Memberships:** Am Chem Soc; Am Phys Soc; fel fulbright; fel Alfred P Sloan; fel NSF. **Research Statement & Publications:** Spectroscopy of weakly bound molecules in molecular beams and on solid surfaces; dynamics of energy transfer from strong to weak bonds; dynamics of molecular processes on surfaces, applications of lasers in physical chemistry. **Mailing Address:** Dept Chem, Univ Calif, 317C Rowland Hall, Irvine, CA 92697-2025. **Fax:** 949-824-8571. **E-Mail:** kcjanda@uci.edu

JANDA, KIM D, CHEMISTRY. **Personal Data:** b Cleveland, Ohio, August 23, 1958; c Nikole. **Education:** Univ SFla, BS, 1980; Univ Ariz, MS, 1983, PhD, 1984. **Professional Experience:** ELY R CALLAWAY JR CHMN CHEM, SCRIPPS RES INST, SKAGG INST CHEM BIOL, as of 2004; Alfred P Sloan fel, 1993-1995; ASSOC MEM, SCRIPPS RES INST, 1991-; First Award, NIH, 1990-1995; PROF CHEM, SCRIPPS RES INST, SKAGG INST CHEM BIOL, 1989-; asst mem, prof, Scripps Res Inst, 1989-1990; adj asst mem, Scripps Res Inst, 1987-1988; fel, Dept Molecular Biol, Scripps Res Inst, 1985-1986. **Memberships:** Am Chem Soc; fel Am Inst Chemists. **Research Statement & Publications:** Design of antigenic structures to be used for the induction of catalytic antibodies; design of novel transition state-multisubstrate analogues for enzyme inhibitor studies; synthesis of these complex molecules; kinetic studies on these catalytic antibodies and enzymes; matrix immobilized catalytic antibodies in organic synthesis; catalytic antibodies in nonaqueous solvents; probing the evolution of catalytic antibodies via site directed mutagenesis; antibodies-catalytic antibodies as biosensors; immunopharmacotherapy for the treatment of cocaine abuse; novel synthetic methodologies for obtaining encoded combinatorial peptide-peptidomimic libraries. **Mailing Address:** Dept Chem, Scripps Res Inst, Skaggs Inst Chem Biol, Rm BCC108 10550 N Torrey Pines Rd, La Jolla, CA 92037. **Fax:** 858-784-2595. **E-Mail:** kdjanda@scripps.edu

JANDACEK, RONALD JAMES, LIPID NUTRITION, FAT DIGESTION & ABSORPTION. **Personal Data:** b Chattanooga, Tenn, December 26, 1942. **Education:** Rice Univ, BA, 1964; Univ Tex, PhD (chem), 1968. **Professional Experience:** Adj prof, Col Med, Univ Cincinnati, as of 2005; OVER COUNTER HEALTH CARE TECHNOL DIV, HEALTH CARE RES CTR, PROCTER & GAMBLE, as of 2000; RES CHEMIST, MIAMI VALLEY LABS, PROCTER & GAMBLE CO, CINCINNATI, OHIO, 1968, 1970-. **Memberships:** Am Chem Soc; Am Oil Chemists Soc; Am Inst Nutrit. **Research Statement & Publications:** Physical and biological properties of lipids, including phase behavior, digestion and intestinal absorption; author of 40 publications and 3 book chapters. **Mailing Address:** Over-The-Counter Health Care Technol Div, Health Care Res Ctr, Procter & Gamble, Mason, OH 45040. **Fax:** 513-622-1955.

JANDHYALA, BHAGAVAN S, PHARMACOLOGY. **Education:** Univ Pittsburgh, MS, 1963, PhD, 1966. **Professional Experience:** DIR HEART & KIDNEY INST, DEPT PHARAMACOL & PHARMACEUT SCI, UNIV HOUSTON, as of 2004; PROF PHARMACOL, UNIV HOUSTON, 1973-. **Memberships:** Fedn Am Socs Exp Biol. **Research Statement & Publications:** Pharmacoloogy. **Mailing Address:** Dept Pharmacol & Pharmaceut Sci, Univ Houston, 460 Sci & Res Bldg 2, Houston, TX 77204-5515. **Fax:** 713-743-1232. **E-Mail:** jandhyala@uh.edu

JANDL, JAMES HARRIMAN, MEDICINE. **Personal Data:** b Racine, Wis, October 30, 1925; m 1950, Nancy Perrin Jandl; c Christine, Robert, Elizabeth, Susan & Charles. **Education:** Franklin & Marshall Col, BS, 1945; Harvard Med Sch, MD, 1949. **Professional Experience:** Ret, 2000; HEAD, DEPT HEMAT, HARVARD MED SCH, 1973-; GEORGE RICHARDS MINOT PROF MED, HARVARD MED SCH, BOSTON CITY HOSP, 1968-; dir, Harvard Med Unit, 1968-1970; from asst prof to assoc prof, Harvard Med Sch, 1959-1968; assoc, Harvard Med Sch, 1957-1959; instr med, Harvard Med Sch, 1955-1957; Res fel med, Harvard Med Sch, 1952-1955. **Memberships:** Am Soc Clin Invest; Am Fedn Clin Res; Asn Am Physicians; Am Clin & Climat Asn; Am Soc Hemat. **Research Statement & Publications:** Hematology; mechanisms of the anemias, especially the hemolytic anemias; immune hematology; functions of the reticuloendothelial system. **Mailing Address:** Harvard Med Sch, 25 Shattuck St, Boston, MA 02115-6027. **Fax:** 978-371-7244. **E-Mail:** mjandl@world.std.com

JANDORF, BERNARD JOSEPH, biochemistry, toxicology; deceased, see previous edition for last biography

JANE, JOHN ANTHONY, NEUROSURGERY. **Personal Data:** b Chicago, Ill, September 21, 1931; m 1960, c 4. **Education:** Univ Chicago, BA, 1951, MD, 1956, PhD (biol, psychol), 1967. **Honors & Awards:** Herbert Olivecrona Lectr. **Professional Experience:**

Assoc prof neurosurg, Sch Med, Case Western Res, ending 1996; CHMN DEPT NEUROLOGICAL SURG, SCH MED, UNIV VA, 1980-; PROF NEUROLOGICAL SURG, UNIV VA HEALTH SYST, 1969-; instr neurosurg, Sch Med, Case Western Res, beginning 1965. **Memberships:** Am Asn Anat; Am Physiol Soc. **Research Statement & Publications:** Head injury; neuroplasticity; craniofacial surgery. **Mailing Address:** Dept Neurological Surg, Sch Med, Univ Va, PO Box 800212, Charlottesville, VA 22908-0001. **Fax:** 434-924-9656. **E-Mail:** jaj6r@virginia.edu

JANECKE, JOACHIM WILHELM, NUCLEAR PHYSICS, NUCLEAR STRUCTURE. **Personal Data:** b Heidelberg, Ger, February 5, 1929; American citizen; m 1954, Christa; c Susanne & Roger. **Education:** Univ Heidelberg, Dipl Physics, 1952, Dr rer nat(physics), 1955. **Professional Experience:** PROF EMER PHYSICS, UNIV MICH, ANN ARBOR, 1998-; prof, Univ Mich, Ann Arbor, 1969-1998; assoc prof, Univ Mich, Ann Arbor, 1965-1969; res physicist, res ctr, Karlsruhe, Ger, 1962-1965; res assoc, Univ Mich, 1960-1962; res asst, Max-Planck-Inst, Heidelberg, Ger, 1955-1960; vis prof, Cntr Excellence, Osaka Univ, 1998; vis prof, Osaka Univ, 1994, 1995, 1997; fel, jap soc prom sci, 1993; vis prof, MPI, Heidelberg, Kvi Groningen, Tel Aviv Univ, 1972, 1979-1980, 1986, 1988, 1989, 1991. **Memberships:** Fel Am Phys Soc; Sigma Xi. **Research Statement & Publications:** Nuclear physics; nuclear astrophysics; nuclear reactions; accelerators; nuclear structure and masses; cosmo-chronology. **Mailing Address:** Univ Mich, Dept Physics, 2245 Randall Lab, Ann Arbor, MI 48109-1120. **Fax:** 734-764-6843. **E-Mail:** janecke@umich.edu

JANERO, DAVID R, MEDICAL RESEARCH. **Education:** Yale Univ Sch Med, PhD. **Professional Experience:** STAFF SCIENTIST, PHARMACEUT DIV, CIBA-GEIGY CORP, MD, as of 2006. **Mailing Address:** Ciba-Geigy Corp Res Dept, Pharmaceut Div 556 Morris Ave, Summit, NJ 07901-1398.

JANES, DONALD LUCIAN, SOLID STATE CHEMISTRY. **Personal Data:** b Fresno, Calif, July 1, 1939. **Education:** Grinnell Col, AB, 1961; Purdue Univ, PhD (inorg chem), 1966. **Professional Experience:** DIR, CORP ANAL LAB, 3M CO, 1990-; lab mgr, Appl Res Lab, 1985-1990; mgr, Info Storage Lab, 1981-1985; mgr, Magnetic Audio-Video Prod Div, 1979-1981; supvr, Magnetic Audio-Video Prod Div, 1973-1979; res specialist, Cent Res Lab, 3M Co, 1971-1973; sr chemist, Cent Res Lab, 3M Co, 1965-1971. **Memberships:** Am Chem Soc. **Research Statement & Publications:** Preparation and properties of magnetic materials. **Mailing Address:** 7337 Pinehurst Rd, St Paul, MN 55115.

JANES, DONALD WALLACE, BACTERIOLOGY, BIOLOGY. **Personal Data:** b Kansas City, Mo, June 12, 1929; m 1953, Janina; c Todd A, Jeffrey W, Scott Lee D & Nancy M. **Education:** Baker Univ, AB, 1951; Univ Kans, MA, 1956; Kans State Univ, PhD (zoology), 1962. **Professional Experience:** PROF EMER BIOL, COLO STATE UNIV, as of 2005; consult & examr, N Cent Asn Cols & Sec Schs, 1972-1993; assoc vpres acad affairs & dean grad sch, Colo State Univ, 1968-1978; intern Acad Admin, Am Coun Educ, 1968; from asst prof to prof biol, Colo State Univ, 1962-1993; asst prof, Parsons Col, 1961-1962; instr biol, Washburn Univ, 1957-1960; Fulbright fel, 1956-1957. **Memberships:** AAAS; Am Soc Zoologists; Am Soc Microbiol; Am Soc Mammal; Sigma Xi. **Research Statement & Publications:** Problems of vertebrate distribution and ecology; reproduction; vertebrate fauna of Colorado; chemistry and biosynthesis of bacterial pigments, particularly pigments of Serratia marcescens. **Mailing Address:** Dept Biol, Colo State Univ, 2200 Bonforte Blvd, Pueblo, CO 81001-4901. **E-Mail:** donaldjanes@msn.com

JANEWAY, RICHARD, MEDICINE, NEUROLOGY. **Personal Data:** b Los Angeles, Calif, February 12, 1933; m 1955, Katherine E Pillsbury; c Susan, David & Elizabeth. **Education:** Colgate Univ, AB, 1954; Univ Pa, MD, 1958. **Honors & Awards:** John and Mary R Markle Scholar, 1968-1973. **Professional Experience:** EXEC VICE PRES EMER & UNIV PROF, WAKE FOREST UNIV, SCH OF MED, 1997-; CEO, med sch, 1983-1997; mem, Nat Adv Coun Regional Med Prog, HEW; consult, US-Egypt Collab Prog Stroke; exec vpres health affairs, Bowman Gray Sch Med, Wake Forestt Univ, 1990-1997; exec dean, 1985-1994; Chmn of the Asn, Asn of Am Med Col, 1984-1985; vpres health affairs, Bowman Gray sch med, 1983-1990; chmn, Coun Deans, As Am Med Col, 1982-1985; mem Exec Comt, As Am Med Col, 1982-1986; Consult, US Saudi Arabia Joint Econ Develop Comn, Off of the Asst Secy of the Treas for Int Affairs, 1980; Consult, US Egypt Collaborative Prog on Stroke, 1977-1981; mem, Admin Board, As Am Med Col, 1977-1984; mem, Exec Coun, 1977-1986; mem, Nat advisory Coun on Regional Med Prog of the Health Res Admin, Dept of Health, Educ, & Welfare, 1974-1981; mem, Coun Deans, As Am Med Col, 1971-; prof neurol, Bowman Gray Sch Med, Wake Forest Univ, 1971-; dean, Bowman Gray sch med, 1971-1985; mem, Spec Procedures & Equip Study Group, Joint Comt Stroke Facil, 1970-1973; Consult, Task Force on Arteriosclerosis, Nat Heart & Lung Inst, 1970; mem, Ad Hoc Comt for "A Study of New Methods to Measure Cerebral Circulation, " Fed of Am Soc for Exp Biol, 1970; mem, Special Procedures & Equip Study Group of the Joint Comt for Stroke Facil (NINDS-NHLI), 1970-1973; prog dir, Cerebral Vascular Res Ctr, 1969-1971; actg chmn, Dept Neurol, 1969-1970; coun cerebrovascular dis, Am Heart Asn, 1969; mem spec task force, Joint Coun (NINDS-NHLI) Subcomt, Cerebrovascular Dis, 1968; from instr to assoc prof neurol, Bowman Gray Sch Med, Wake Forest Univ, 1966-1971; Inst to Assoc Prof of Neurol, 1966-1970; Prog admin, Cerebral Vascular Res Ctr, 1966-1969; resident neurol, NC Baptist Hosp, 1963-1966; US Air Force, Private to Cap, 1959-1963; Intern, Hosp Univ PA, 1958-1959. **Memberships:** Inst Med-Nat Acad Sci; fel Am Heart Asn; fel Am Col Physicians; Soc Med Adminr; Am Neurol Asn; AAAS; Sigma Xi; Am Med Asn; Am Clin & Climat Asn. **Research Statement & Publications:** Neurology; cerebrovascular disease; health care economics; health care organization. **Mailing Address:** School of Medicine, Medical Center Blvd, Wake Forest Univ, Winston-Salem, NC 27157.

JANG, RUEY-JEN, MATHEMATICS. **Education:** Tex Tech Univ, PhD, 1990. **Professional Experience:** STAFF, UNIV LA, as of 2005. **Mailing Address:** Univ La, Lafayette, LA 70504-1010. **Fax:** 337-482-5346.

JANG, SEI JOO, RELAXOR MATERIALS, OPTICS. **Personal Data:** b Andong, Korea, December 30, 1947; m 1983, c 2. **Education:** Sogang Univ, BS, 1973; Boston Col, MS, 1976; Pa State Univ, PhD (solid state sci), 1979. **Professional Experience:** SR RES ASSOC, MAT RES LAB, PA STATE UNIV, 1987-; ASSOC PROF SOLIDSTATE SCI, PA STATE UNIV, 1987-; pres, Matronix Inc, 1985-; secy, JBS Consult Inc, 1984-; res assoc, elec mat, Mat Res Labs, 1983-1987; sr res staff optics, AT&T Eng Res Ctr, 1979-1983; res asst mat, Pa State Univ, 1976-1979; teaching asst physics, Boston Col, 1974-1976; serv engrmed equip, Siemens Elec Eng Co, 1973-1974. **Memberships:** Am Ceramic Soc; Nat Inst Ceramic Engrs; Optical Soc Am. **Research Statement & Publications:** Relaxor materials; microwave measurements and materials; optics and electro-optics materials; electrostrictive abd piezoelectric materials for actuator, transducers and motors. **Mailing Address:** 220 Camelot Lane, State College, PA 16803.

JANGAARD, NORMAN OLAF, BIOCHEMISTRY. **Personal Data:** b Seattle, Wash, October 11, 1941; m 1963, c 2. **Education:** San Diego State Univ, BS, 1962; UnivCalif, Los Angeles, PhD (biochem), 1966; Univ Denver, JD, 1976. **Professional Experience:**
VPRES RES & DEVELOP, NUTRA SWEET KELCO CO, SAN DIEGO, 1992-; pres, Coors Biotech Inc, 1985-1992; vpres prod, regulatory affairs res & develop, 1983-1984; vpres qual assurance, regulatory affairs res & develop, 1981-1983; vpres eng & res & develop, Adolph Coors Co, 1980-1981; vpres qual assurance & res & develop, Adolph Coors Co, 1978-1980; dir qual assurance, Adolph Coors Co, 1974-1978; dir res, Adolph Coors Co, 1972-1974; Shell Develop Co, 1968-1972; biochemist, Pfizer Inc, 1966-1968; lab technician, Scripps Inst Oceanog, Univ Calif, San Diego. **Memberships:** Am Soc Brewing Chemists; Am Chem Soc; Inst Food Technologists; Am Asn Cereal Chemists; Master Brewer's Asn Am. **Research Statement & Publications:** Fermentation and yeast physiology; microbiological control; brewing and malting technology; packaging materials; breeding and growing of hops, barley and rice; waste treatment technology; vitamin production; food ingredient technology. **Mailing Address:** Nutra Sweet Kelco Co, 200 World Trade Ctr, Chicago, IL 60654.

JANGHORBANI, MORTEZA, STABLE ISOTOPES, NEUTRON ACTIVATION. **Personal Data:** b Isfahan, Iran, September 29, 1943; American citizen; m 1969, c 1. **Education:** Am Univ Beirut, Lebanon, BS, 1966; Oregon State Univ, MS, 1968, PhD (chem), 1972. **Professional Experience:** ADJ PROF NUTRIT MED, UNIV ILL, CHICAGO, as of 2004; prin res scientist, Mass Inst Technol, 1977-; group leader, Environ Trace Substances Res Ctr, Univ Mo, 1975-1977; res chemist, Univ Marburg, Ger, 1973-1975; assoc vis asst prof chem, UnivKy, 1972-1973; ASSOC PROF PATH, MALLORY INST PATH, BOSTON UNIV SCH MED. **Memberships:** Am Chem Soc; AAAS. **Research Statement & Publications:** Trace element research in relation to biology and human nutrition; analytical chemistry of trace elements. **Mailing Address:** Bio Chem Anal Corp Univ Ill, 2201 W Campbell Park Dr, Chicago, IL 60612-3501. **Fax:** 312-243-7283. **E-Mail:** mjanghor@uic.edu

JANICK, JULES, PLANT BREEDING, TISSUE CULTURE. **Personal Data:** b New York, NY, March 16, 1931; m 1952, c Peter J & Robin (Weinherger). **Education:** Cornell Univ, BS, 1951; Purdue Univ, MS, 1952, PhD (plant genetics & breeding), 1954. **Honorary Degrees:** DS, Univ Bologna, Italy, Tech Univ Lisbon. **Honors & Awards:** Shepard Award 1960 & 1970; Meadows Award 1971; Stark Award 1978 & 1982; Popenoe Award 1980; Post Award 1981; Childers Award 1982; James Troop Distinguished Prof 1988; Am Pomol Soc; Wilder Medal 1996; Am Hort Soc; Hort Writing Award 2001; ASHS; Outstanding Int Horticulturist 2003; Fulbright Distinguished Lecturere 2004. **Professional Experience:** DIR, CTR NEW CROPS & PLANT PROD, PURDUE UNIV, 1990-; consult, Equador, 1990; consult, Italy, 1989 & 1990; DISTINGUISHED PROF HORT, PURDUE UNIV, 1988-; consult, Morocco, 1988; consult, China, 1988; Hon res assoc bot, Univ Pisa, 1985; consult, Portugal, 1983, 1986, 1987, 1996; consult, World Bank, Indonesia, 1973; vis colleague, Univ Hawaii, 1969; Hon res assoc bot, Univ Col, Univ London, 1963 & 1985; horticulturist, AgrUniv Minas Gerais, 1963-1965; rom instr to prof, Purdue Univ, 1954-1988. **Memberships:** Am Pomol Soc; fel Am Soc Hort Sci (pres, 1986-1987); fel Portuguese Hort Asn; fel AAAS; Int Soc Hort Sci. **Research Statement & Publications:** Genetics and breeding of horticultural crops; new crops. **Mailing Address:** Dept Hort, Purdue Univ, West Lafayette, IN 47907-2010. **Fax:** 765-494-0391. **E-Mail:** janick@purdue.edu

JANICK-BUCKNER, DIANE, BIOLOGY. **Education:** Gettysburg Col, BA; Univ Vt, PhD. **Professional Experience:** PROF BIOL, DIV SCI, TRUMAN STATE UNIV, as of 2005. **Mailing Address:** Div Sci Truman State Univ, Off MG3066, Kirksville, MO 63501. **Fax:** 660-785-4045. **E-Mail:** djb@truman.edu

JANICKI, BERNARD WILLIAM, IMMUNOLOGY, MICROBIOLOGY. **Personal Data:** b Wilmington, Del, October 14, 1931; m 1954, c 5. **Education:** Univ Del, BA, 1953, MA, 1955; George Wash Univ, PhD (microbiol), 1960. **Professional Experience:** CONSULT, as of 2003; asst, pres office, Dana-Farber Cancer Inst, 1991-2001; dep dir, immunol, Allergic & Immunol Dis Prog, 1987-1998; Immunol & Biochem Br, Immunol Br, 1978-1983; health sci adminr, Nat Installergy & Infectious Dis, 1974-1987; spec lectr med, George Wash Univ, 1974-1979; chief, Immunol Br, 1974-1977; chief pulmonary immunol res lab, Tuberc Res Lab, Vet AdminHosp, DC, 1972-1974; lectr microbiol, Univ Md, 1969-1979; mem US tuberc panel, US-JapanCoop Med Sci Prog, 1969-1975; consult, Nat Inst Allergy & Infectious Dis, 1969-1975; chief microbiol res lab, Tuberc Res Lab, Vet Admin Hosp, DC, 1963-1972; chief, Tuberc Res Lab, VetAdmin Hosp, DC, 1960-1963; Microbiologist, Tuberc Res Lab, Vet Admin Hosp, DC, 1955-1960. **Memberships:** Am Soc Microbiol; Soc Exp Biol & Med; NY Acad Sci; Am Asn Immunol; AmThoracic Soc. **Research Statement & Publications:** Immunity and hypersensitivity in infectious diseases. **Mailing Address:** Dana-Farber Cancer Inst, 44 Binney St, Boston, MA 02115. **Fax:** 617-632-4452.

JANICKI, CASIMIR A, ANALYTICAL CHEMISTRY, COMPUTER VALIDATION. **Personal Data:** b Milwaukee, Wis, September 20, 1934; m 1959, Toni; c 2. **Education:** LaSalle Col, BA, 1956; Marquette Univ, MS, 1958; Loyola Univ, PhD (anal chem), 1964. **Professional Experience:** PHARMACEUT CONSULT, 1993-; tech dir anal qual control, McNeil Labs, Ft Wash, 1982-1993; sect head, McNeil Labs, Ft Wash, 1974-1981; sect head, McNeil Labs, Ft Wash, 1974-1980; group leader, McNeil Pharmaceut, Spring House, Pa, 1966-1974; sr anal chemist, McNeil Pharmaceut, Spring House, Pa, 1963-1966; anal chemist, Smith, Kline & Fr Labs, 1957-1960. **Memberships:** Am Asn Pharm Sci. **Research Statement & Publications:** Pharmaceutical analytical chemistry, including thin layer, chromatography, ultra violet visible and infrared spectrometry, separation techniques including high performance liquid and gas liquid chromatography; kinetics and drug stability; robotics in pharmaceutical analysis, laboratory computers, validation of computer systems in GMP area; FTIR in QC analysis. **Mailing Address:** 2888 Hickory Hill Rd, Norristown, PA 19403.

JANICKI, JOSEPH S, CARDIOLOGY. **Education:** PhD. **Professional Experience:** PROF & CHMN, CELL & DEVELOP BIOL & ANAT, UNIV SC, as of 2006. **Memberships:** Am Heart Asn. **Mailing Address:** Univ SC Sch Med, Columbia, SC 29208. **Fax:** 803-733-1533. **E-Mail:** jjanicki@gw.med.sc.edu

JANICZEK, PAUL MICHAEL, ASTRONOMY, NAVIGATION. **Personal Data:** b Hazleton, Pa, October 5, 1937. **Education:** King's Col, BA, 1960; Georgetown Univ, MA, 1965, PhD (astron), 1970. **Professional Experience:** DIV ASTRON APPLNS DEPT, US NAVAL OBSERV, 1990-1997; chiefephemerides div, Navig, 1984-1990; instr, Maryland Col Art & Design, 1981-1983; ed, Navig, 1978-1985; astronr, US Naval Observ, 1967-1984; programmer analyst sci satellites, Fed Syst Div, IBM Corp, 1961-1966; supvr qual control, Lansdale Div, Philco Corp, 1960-1961. **Memberships:** Am Astron Soc; AAAS; Inst Navigation; Sigma Xi; Int Astron Union. **Research Statement & Publications:** Dynamical astronomy; celestial navigation. **Mailing Address:** US Naval Observ, 3450 Mass Ave NW, Washington, DC 20392-5420.

JANIK, BOREK, CLINICAL CHEMISTRY, FILTRATION. **Personal Data:** b Brno, Czech, October 29, 1933; m 1965, Alice; c Peter & Dasha. **Education:** Purkyne Univ, Brno, MS, 1956; Czech Acad Sci, Brno, PhD (chem, biophys), 1964; Purkyne Univ, RNDr, 1966. **Professional Experience:** MGR, ASIA PAC AREA, CELMAN SCI, 1992-; OWNER,

MOREX, CHELSEA, MICH, 1991-; dir tech affairs, Biopore, Caan, France, 1990-1991; dir lab technol, Gelman Sci, 1985-1990; dir lab prod develop, Gelman Sci, 1982-1985; dir clin res & develop, Gelman Sci, 1979-1982; mgr res & develop, Ames Div, 1978-1979; mem staff & mgr res &develop, Res Prod Div, 1975-1978; sr res scientist phys biochem, Molecular Biol, Miles Lab, Inc, 1969-1974; res assoc electrochem, Univ Mich, Ann Arbor, 1968-1969; res scientist electrochem & biophys, Inst Biophys, Czech Acad Sci, Brno, 1967-1968; fel chem, Univ Mich, AnnArbor, 1966-1967; res scientist electrochem & biophys, Inst Biophys, Czech Acad Sci, Brno, 1964-1966; fel, Inst Biophys, Czech Acad Sci, Brno, 1960-1964; res assoc orgchem, Lachema, Pure Chem Corp, Czech, 1956-1960. **Memberships:** Electrophoresic Soc; Am Asn Clin Chem. **Research Statement & Publications:** Test and instrument programs in clinical chemistry and biotechnology (proteins, nucleic acids, immunochemistry, enzymology and hematology) utilizing separation technologies; binding and transfer of nucleic acids and proteins to binding membranes; author of over 70 technical publications; interdisciplinary applications of micro-filtration. **Mailing Address:** 13805 Waterloo Rd, Chelsea, MI 48118. **Fax:** 313-474-2441.

JANIK, GERALD S, ENVIRONMENTAL SCIENCES, ANALYTICAL CHEMISTRY. **Personal Data:** b Niagara Falls, NY, July 2, 1940; m 1967, c 3. **Education:** Niagara Univ, BS, 1961; Purdue Univ, MS, 1964; Tex A&M Univ, PhD (phy chem), 1966. **Professional Experience:** Div comt, Elec Power Res Inst, 1991-1994; task force, Elec Power Res Inst, 1986-1988; reviewer, NY State Energy Res & Develop Authority, 1981-; RES DIR, NY STATEELEC & GAS CORP, 1981-; Fossil Fuel Comn, Empire State Elec Energy Res Corp, 1976-; resengr, NY State Elec & Gas Corp, 1976-1981; engr, NY State Elec & Gas Corp, 1973-1976; srengr, Bell Aerospace Co, 1966-1972. **Research Statement & Publications:** Energy production and pollution control measures. **Mailing Address:** 817 Catalina Blvd, Endicott, NY 13760.

JANIK, TADEUSZ J, MATHEMATICS. **Education:** Tech Univ, MSc, PhD. **Professional Experience:** PROF, DEPT MATH SCI, UNIV ALA, as of 2006. **Mailing Address:** Dept Math Sci, Univ Ala - Huntsville, Huntsville, AL 35899. **Fax:** 256-824-7306. **E-Mail:** janik@math.uah.edu

JANINI, GEORGE M, PHYSICAL CHEMISTRY. **Education:** Georgetown Univ, PhD (phys chem), 1973. **Professional Experience:** SR SCIENTIST, NAT CANCER INST, FREDERICK, as of 2003. **Mailing Address:** SAIC Frederick Inc, Nat Cancer Inst, PO Box B, Frederick, MD 21702. **Fax:** 301-846-6037. **E-Mail:** janini@ncifcrf.gov

JANIS, ALLEN I(RA), GENERAL RELATIVITY. **Personal Data:** b Chicago, Ill, September 11, 1930; m Phyllis; c Stuart & Wynne. **Education:** Northwestern Univ, BS, 1951; Syracuse Univ, PhD (physics), 1957. **Professional Experience:** EMER PROF PHYSICS, UNIV PITTSBURGH, 1993-; EMER FEL, PHILOS SCI CTR, 1993-; assoc dir, Philos Sci Ctr, 1975-1992; Sr res assoc, Philos Sci Ctr, Univ Pittsburgh, 1967-1975; From instr to prof, Phy, 1957-1992. **Memberships:** AAAS; fel Am Phys Soc; Am Asn Physics Teachers; Philos Sci Asn. **Research Statement & Publications:** Gravitational theory; philosophy of physics. **Mailing Address:** Dept Physics & Astron, Univ Pittsburgh, Pittsburgh, PA 15260. **E-Mail:** aij@pitt.edu

JANIS, CHRISTINE MARIE, MAMMALIAN PALEOBIOLOGY & SYSTEMATICS. **Personal Data:** b London, Eng, October 18, 1950; American citizen; wid John. **Education:** Univ Cambridge, UK, BA, 1973; Harvard Univ, PhD (biol), 1979. **Honors & Awards:** G G Simpson Prize Paleont, 1985. **Professional Experience:** Benjamin Meaker Fel, Univ Bristol, UK, 2001; PROF BIOL, BROWN UNIV, 1999-; RES ASSOC GEOL, FIELD MUS, CHICAGO, 1994-; vis prof geophys sci, Univ Chicago, 1994-1995; RES ASSOC, HARVARD UNIV, 1984-; from asst prof to assoc prof biol, Div Biol & Med, Brown Univ, 1983-1999; res fel, Newnham Col, Univ Cambridge, UK, 1979-1983. **Memberships:** Soc Vert Paleont; Paleont Soc; Am Soc Mammalogists; Am Soc Zoologists; Int Soc Cryptozool. **Research Statement & Publications:** Paleoecology and patterns of evolutionary diversification in ungulates, hoofed mammals, in relation to environmental change; combining data from living and fossil taxa. **Mailing Address:** Dept Ecol & Evolutionary Biol, Brown Univ, Providence, RI 02912. **Fax:** 401-863-7544. **E-Mail:** christine_janis@brown.edu

JANIS, F TIMOTHY, TECHNOLOGY TRANSFER, THEORETICAL CHEMISTRY. **Personal Data:** b Chicago, Ill, April 11, 1940; m 1962, Kathryn; c Mark, Paul & Melissa. **Education:** Wichita State Univ, BS, 1962, MS, 1963; Ill Inst Technol, PhD (chem), 1968. **Professional Experience:** Pres, arac, inc, 1993-2006; dir, Arac, Inc, 1991-1993; founder & pres, J-Tech& Assocs, 1990-1993; technol transfer, Bus Develop Div, 1984-1990; dir prog develop, BusDevelop Div, 1983-1984; dir, Bus Develop Div, 1980-1983; actg dir, Indust Liaison Off, 1978-1980; admin mgr, Indianapolis Ctr Advan Res, 1977-1978; assoc prof & asst acaddean/registr, Franklin Col, 1974-1977; from asst prof to assoc prof chem, Ill Benedictine Col, 1969-1974; consult, Argonne Nat Lab, 1968-; instr chem & data processing, Col DuPage, 1968-1969; fel, Argonne Nat Lab, 1968; Res assoc chem, Argonne Nat Lab, 1966-1968. **Memberships:** Am Chem Soc; Technol Transfer Soc. **Research Statement & Publications:** Technology transfer methodology, systems, policy and brokering; ab-initio caculations on molecules. **Mailing Address:** ARAC Inc, 23 N Main St Ste C, Franklin, IN 46131. **Fax:** 317-262-5044.

JANIS, RONALD ALLEN, NEW DRUG DISCOVERY & DEVELOPMENT, CALCIUM CHANNEL MODULATORS. **Personal Data:** b Sask, October 11, 1943; m 1968, c Mary A & Joseph W. **Education:** Univ BC, BS, 1966, MS, 1968; State Univ NY Buffalo, PhD (biochem pharmacol), 1972. **Professional Experience:** Assoc clin prof, Univ Conn Health Ctr, 1989-1991; PRIN STAFF SCIENTIST, BAYER CORP, 1984-; prin res scientist, Miles Inst Preclin Pharmacol, 1984; assoc prof med, Univ Conn Health Ctr, 1981-1989; prin staff scientist, Miles Inst Preclin Pharmacol, 1980-1992; assoc prof, Univ Northwestern, 1980; asst prof physiol, Univ Northwestern, 1974-1980; Fel, pharmacol, Univ Alta, 1972-1974. **Memberships:** Am Soc Pharmacol & Exp Therapeut; Biophys Soc; Soc Neuroscience. **Research Statement & Publications:** Drug discovery and development; mechanisms of action of drugs acting on calcium and potassium channels and development of such drugs; ligand binding studies. **Mailing Address:** Bayer Corp, 400 Morgan Lane, W Haven, CT 06516-4175. **Fax:** 203-937-5467.

JANISCHEWSKYJ, WASYL, ELECTRICAL ENGINEERING. **Personal Data:** b Prague, Czech, January 21, 1925; Canadian citizen; m 1951, Emilia; c Roxoilana & Marko. **Education:** Univ Toronto, BASc, 1952, MASc, 1954. **Professional Experience:** PROF EMER ELEC ENG, UNIV TORONTO, 1990-; assoc dean fac, Appl Sci& Eng, 1978-1982; prof, Appl Sci & Eng, 1970-1990; consult, Elec Eng Consociates, 1968-; asst head, Elec Eng Dept, Univ Toronto, 1965-1970; Nat Res Coun Can res grant, 1961-; from lectr elec eng to assoc prof, Univ Toronto, 1959-1970; elecengr, Aluminum Labs, Ltd, 1955-1959; instr, Univ Toronto, 1954-1955; demonstr elec eng, UnivToronto, 1952-1954. **Memberships:** Fel Inst Elec & Electronics Engrs; Can Elec Asn. **Research Statement & Publications:** Distribution of mechanical stress in composite transmission-line conductors; extra high voltage transmission of electric power; radio interference caused by high voltage corona; fault behavior of complex electric power systems; methods of testing underground cable; lightning studies; microgap discharges; television interference. **Mailing Address:** Dept Elec & Comput Eng, Univ Toronto, Toronto, ON M5S 1A1, Can. **Fax:** 416-971-2325. **E-Mail:** janisch@ecf.utoronto.ca

JANKE, MARY KIRK, DRIVER ASSESSMENT OF AGE-RELATED FRAILTY. **Education:** Univ Chicago, BS; Calif State Univ, Sacramento, MA; Univ Calif, Berkeley, PhD (exppsychol). **Professional Experience:** RES SCIENTIST III, DEPT MOTOR VEHICLES, 1993-; res mgr II, DeptMotor Vehicles, 1989-1993; res prog specialist II, Dept Motor Vehicles, 1985-1989; opers resspecialist II, Dept Motor Vehicles, 1981-1985; res analyst I/II, Dept Motor Vehicles, 1976-1981; psychologist, Stockton State Hosp, 1969-1974; Asst prof psychol, Calif State Univ, Sacramento, 1968. **Research Statement & Publications:** Assessment system for drivers with dementia or age-related frailty; author of several publications in professional journals. **Mailing Address:** Res & Develop Br, Calif Dept Motor Vehicles, PO Box 932382 F-126, Sacramento, CA 94232-3820.

JANKE, NORMAN CHARLES, ENGINEERING GEOLOGY, MINING-PETROGRAPHY. **Personal Data:** b Milwaukee, Wis, September 5, 1923; m 1952, Mary Kirk; c Garth. **Education:** Univ Chicago, MS, 1952; Univ Calif, Los Angeles, PhD (geol), 1963. **Professional Experience:** EMER PROF GEOL, CALIF STATE UNIV, SACRAMENTO, 1983-; CONSULT GEOLOGIST, NORMAN JANKE ASSOC; consult mining, eng & forensic geol, fault & seismic risk, petrography; head dept, Calif State Univ, 1968-1974; trustee bd mem, Moss Landing Marine Lab, 1967-1971; from asst prof to prof, Calif State Univ, 1960-1983; instr geol & math, Calif State Univ, 1956-1960; instr geol, Fresno State Col, 1955; consult geologist, Geo-Sci Inc, Tex, 1953; since 1983, Consult Engr Geol, Forensic Geol. **Memberships:** NY Acad Sci; Sigma Xi; Asn Eng Geologists; Soc Econ Paleont & Mineral; Am Mil Eng; Am Soc Testing Mat; Soc Explosive Engrs; Soc Mining Engrs Scientists & Engrs sr mem (in all). **Research Statement & Publications:** Slumping and land sliding mechanisms; effects of shape upon settling velocity and sieving; photogrammetric uses of ordinary camera equipment; particle size and shape analysis, sieving and settling methods; swelling clays genesis and effects. **Mailing Address:** 2670 Fair Oaks Blvd, Sacramento, CA 95864. **E-Mail:** sac69915@saclink.csus.edu

JANKE, RHONDA RAE, AGRONOMY. **Personal Data:** b Junction City, Kans, April 20, 1958. **Education:** Kans State Univ, BS, 1980; Cornell Univ, MS, 1984, PhD (agron), 1987. **Professional Experience:** RES DIR, RODALE INST, 1992-; adj asst prof, Pa State Univ, Univ Park, beginning 1988; agron coordr, Rodale Inst, 1986-1992; regional rep, New World Agr Group. **Memberships:** Am Soc Agron; Weed Sci Soc Am; Brit Ecol Soc; Inst Alernative Agr; Sigma Xi. **Research Statement & Publications:** Agronomy. **Mailing Address:** Crystal Ridge Rd, Kutztown, PA 19530-9749.

JANKE, ROBERT A, PLANT ECOLOGY, PHYS ECOL. **Personal Data:** b Detroit, Mich, August 19, 1922; m 1944, Nadine Key; c David, Daniel, Steven & Janet. **Education:** Univ Mich, AB, 1944, MS, 1952; Mich Technol Univ, BS, 1948; Univ Colo, PhD (ecol), 1968. **Professional Experience:** EMER PROF BIOL, MICH TECHNOL UNIV, 1984-2002; NSF sci fac fel, U South Colorado, 1963-1965; assoc prof biol, Mich Technol Univ, 1962-1984; from instr to assoc prof physics, Mich Technol Univ, 1944-1962; Teacher math pub sch, 1944. **Memberships:** Ecol Soc Am; George Wright Soc. **Research Statement & Publications:** Fire ecology; boreal forest ecology; vascular flora inventory of Isle Royale National Park; physical ecology. **Mailing Address:** Dept Biol, Mich Technol Univ, Houghton, MI 49931.

JANKE, WILFRED EDWIN, SOIL SCIENCE. **Personal Data:** b Morris, Man, December 24, 1932; m 1958, c 4. **Education:** Univ Man, BSA, 1955, MSc, 1957; Univ Wis-Madison, PhD (soils, geol), 1962. **Professional Experience:** RES SPECIALIST, CAMPOTEX, 1991-; agronomist, CIDA Agr Can, 1988-1991; res & develop specialist, BASF Can, Inc, 1983-1988; mkt res sr analyst, Potash Corp, Saskatoon, 1981-1983; fertilize prod mgr, Federated Cooperatives Ltd, 1978-1981; resagronomist & mkt coordr, fertilizer mkt div, Sherritt Gordon Mines Ltd, 1966-1978; dir, SoilTesting Lab, Univ Man, 1963-1966; res scientist, Res Sta, 1962-1963; Pedologist, Soil Surv Div, Can Dept Agr, 1957-1959. **Memberships:** Am Soc Agron; Can Soc Soil Sci; Agr Inst Can; Int Soc Soil Sci. **Research Statement & Publications:** Soil fertility, nutrient requirements of various crops under various soil and climatic conditions; fertilizer research, development of new fertilizer products, determining agronomic uses and effectiveness; evaluation of pesticide products. **Mailing Address:** 14 DeGeer Crescent, Saskatoon, SK S7H 4P7, Can.

JANKOVIC, DRAGAN S, MATHEMATICS. **Professional Experience:** PROF, E CENTRAL UNIV, as of 2006. **Memberships:** Am Math Soc. **Mailing Address:** Math Dept, E Central Univ, Ada, OK 74820. **Fax:** 580-332-1623.

JANKOVIC, MIODRAG (MIKE) S, AEROSPACE ENGINEERING, EIGENVALUE ANALYSIS, ENHANCED OIL RECOVERY. **Personal Data:** b Belgrade, Yugoslavia, July 7, 1948; Canadian citizen. **Education:** Univ Belgrade, BASc, 1972; Univ Toronto, MASc, 1976, PhD (Aerospace Eng), 1979. **Professional Experience:** Pres, Universe Enterprises Ltd, 1989-; res scientist, Imp Oil Ltd, 1985-1989; enhanced oil recovery supvr, Dome Petrol, 1982-1985; design eng, Ont Hydro, 1979-1982. **Memberships:** sr mem Amer Inst Aeronaut & Astronautics; Amer Math Asn; Asn Prof Engrs Geologists & Geophysicists Alta. **Research Statement & Publications:** dynamics of flexible satellitles, linear and nonlinear EigenValue problems, enhanced oil recovery. **Mailing Address:** 3416 23 St NW, Calgary, AB T2L 0T9, Can. **E-Mail:** msjankovic@hotmail.com

JANKOWSKI, CECELIA, AERONAUTICS. **Education:** State Univ NY, BS; Polytech Univ, MS; Rutgers Univ, MBA. **Professional Experience:** MD, INST ELEC & ELECTRONICS ENGRS REGIONAL ACTIV, PISCATAWAY, NJ, as of 2006; STAFF, NORTHROP GRUMMAN CORP, as of 2006. **Memberships:** Inst Elec & Electronics Engrs. **Mailing Address:** Inst Elec & Electronics Engrs, Piscataway, NJ 11714. **Fax:** 732-463-3657. **E-Mail:** c.jankowski@ieee.org

JANKOWSKI, CHRISTOPHER K, ORGANIC CHEMISTRY. **Personal Data:** b Warsaw, Poland, July 31, 1940; m 1965, Iwona; c Agnes. **Education:** Univ Warsaw, MSc, 1963; Univ Montreal, PhD (chem), 1968; Univ Paris, DoctEtat(phys), 1985. **Professional Experience:** ADJ PROF, DEPT CHEM, UNIV MONCTON, 2005-; Univ NB, Can, 1990-1995; Univ Del Paris VI, France, 1989-; adj prof, UnivNacional Autonome, Mex, 1988-; dean, Fac Res & Grad Students, 1988-1995; PROF ORGCHEM, UNIV MONCTON, 1978-2005; res fel, Nuclear Res Ctr, Saclay, France, 1975-1979; res felchem, Syntex, SA, Mex, 1975; from asst prof to assoc prof, Univ Moncton, 1969-1978; asst prof, Univ Montreal, 1968-1969; fel, Univ Montreal, 1967-1968; asst org chem, Univ Warsaw, 1963-1964. **Memberships:** Fel Chem Inst Can; Fr-Can Asn Advan Sci. **Research Statement & Publications:** Synthesis of organic compounds with physiological activity; organic application of mass spectrometry and nuclear magnetic resonance; natural products; alkaloids, carbohydrates. **Mailing Address:** Dept Chem, Univ Moncton, A014, Moncton, NB E1A 3E9, Can. **Fax:** 506-858-4541. **E-Mail:** jankowc@umoncton.ca

JANKOWSKI, CONRAD M, ENVIRONMENTAL CHEMISTRY, ANAL CHEM. **Personal Data:** b Chicago, Ill, February 25, 1928; m 1953, Harris. **Education:** Mich State Univ, BS, 1951, MS, 1953; State Univ Iowa, PhD (anal chem), 1960. **Professional Experience:** EMER PROF ANALYTICAL CHEM & CHEM OCEANOG, NORTHEASTERN UNIV, 1991-; assoc prof anal chem & chem oceanog, Northeastern Univ, 1963-1991; asst prof anal chem, Northeastern Univ, 1960-1963; group leader instrumentation res, Cent Sci Co, 1955-1958; Chief anal chemist, Rayovac Corp, 1953-1955; vis prof, Trent Polytechnic Nottingham, Eng; Indust consult. **Memberships:** AAAS; Am Chem Soc; fel Royal Soc Chem; fel Am Inst Chemists. **Research Statement & Publications:** Electroanalytical chemistry; high temperature reactions; chemical instrumentation; air and water pollution measurements. **Mailing Address:** PO Box 305, West Hyannisport, MA 02672.

JANKOWSKI, FRANCIS JAMES, design engineering, nuclear engineering; deceased, see previous edition for last biography

JANKOWSKI, STANLEY JOHN, ANALYTICAL CHEMISTRY. **Personal Data:** b Detroit, Mich, December 19, 1928; m 1954, c 4. **Education:** Washington & Jefferson Col, BA, 1953; Univ Pittsburgh, PhD (anal chem), 1960. **Professional Experience:** RES SPECIALIST, ICI AMERICAS INC, 1981-; res supvr, Atlas Chem IndustInc, 1970-1981; sr res chemist, Atlas Chem Indust Inc, 1966-1970; sr anal chemist, CelaneseCorp Am, 1962-1966; anal chemist, Celanese Corp Am, 1960-1962; Supvr, Neville Chem Co, 1958-1960. **Memberships:** Am Chem Soc; Am Indust Hyg Asn. **Research Statement & Publications:** Instrumental methods of analysis; chromatographic methods of analysis; drugs; organic chemicals; industrial hygiene analysis. **Mailing Address:** 28 Amarante St, Laguna Niguel, CA 92677-8929.

JANNA, WILLIAM SIED, SPRAY RESEARCH. **Personal Data:** b Toledo, Ohio, March 23, 1949; m 1975, c 1. **Education:** Univ Toledo, BSME, 1971, MSME, 1973, PhD (transport phenomena), 1976. **Professional Experience:** Assoc dean, Grad studies res, Memphis State Univ, 1999-2003; PROF, DEPT MECH ENG, MEMPHIS STATE UNIV, 1987-; chmn, Dept Mech Eng, Memphis State Univ, 1987-1991; chmn dept, Univ New Orleans, 1978-1983; from asst prof to assoc prof mech eng, Univ New Orleans, 1976-1987. **Memberships:** Am Soc Mech Engrs; Am Soc Eng Educ. **Research Statement & Publications:** Windmill economics; droplet sizes of airless sprays; heat transfer from high pressure sprays; heat transfer from fluid flow in a tube to a cooled isothermal wall; economics of pipeline sizing. **Mailing Address:** Dept Mech Eng, Univ Memphis, Herff Col Eng Bldg Rm EN310E, Memphis, TN 38152. **Fax:** 901-678-5459. **E-Mail:** wsjanna@memphis.edu

JANNETT, FREDERICK JOSEPH, MAMMALOGY. **Personal Data:** b Newark, NJ, March 6, 1946; m 1972. **Education:** Cornell Univ, BS, 1967, PhD (ecol & evolutionary biol), 1977; Tulane Univ, MS, 1969. **Honors & Awards:** A B Howell Award, Am Soc Mammalogists, 1977. **Professional Experience:** ADJ ASST PROF CONSERVATION BIOL AND FISHERIES, CONSERV BIOL, UNIV MINN, ST PAUL, 1995-; RES ASSOC, SCI MUSEUM, 1997-; vis scientist, Acad Sci, USSR, 1988; assoc, Bell Mus Natural Hist, Univ Minn, Minneapolis, 1985-1993; Exchange scientist, Acad Sci, USSR, 1984; head & cur, Dept Biol, Sci Mus Minn, St Paul, 1982-1997; lectr mammal, Cornell Univ, 1981; fel, Cornell Univ, 1978-1981; vis fel, Cornell Univ, 1977-1978. **Memberships:** Am Soc Mammalogists; Ecolog Soc Am; Soc for Conserv Biol; Soc Pres Nat Hist collections; Am Assoc Museums; AAAS. **Research Statement & Publications:** Variation, social dynamics and demography of microtine rodents; strategies for inventorying and monitoring small mammals; effects of prairie management and clearcutting on mammals; mammals and diseases. **Mailing Address:** Univ Minn, 200 Hodson Hall, St Paul, MN 55108. **E-Mail:** jamme002@tc.umn.edu

JANNETTA, PETER JOSEPH, SURGERY. **Personal Data:** b Philadelphia, Pa, April 5, 1932; m 1954, c 6. **Education:** Univ Pa, AB, 1953, MD, 1957; Am Bd Surg, dipl, 1964; Am Bd Neurol Surg, dipl, 1969. **Professional Experience:** PROF, NEUROSURG DEPT, ALLEGHENY GEN HOSP, 1997-; chmn, neurosurg dept, sch med, Univ Pittsburgh, 1971-1997; chmn emer, Neurosurg Dept, Sch Med, Univ Pittsburgh, 1971-1997; prof Neurosurg, Sch Med, Univ Pittsburgh, 1971-1997; develop training grant, 1968-1971; res grants, Med Ctr, La State Univ, 1967-1970; assoc prof surg & chmn div neurosurg, Med Ctr, La State Univ, 1966-1971; assoc surg & neurosurg, Univ Calif, Los Angeles, 1963-1966; instr surg, Sch Med, Univ Pa, ending 1963; NIHtraining grant, Univ Pa, 1960-1963; asst instr, Sch Med, Univ Pa, beginning 1958. **Memberships:** Fel Am Col Surg; Soc Neurol Surgeons; Am Asn Neurol Surgeons; Cong NeurolSurgeons; Neurosurg Soc Am. **Research Statement & Publications:** Pheochromocytoma; catechol amine determinations; single unit recording in the vestibular system; mesoscopic central nervous system anatomy and pathology; trigeminal nerve function; trigeminal neuralgia; cranial nerve dysfunction syndromes-etiology and treatment; spinal cord injury. **Mailing Address:** Dept NeuroSurg, Allegheny Gen Hosp, 320 E N Ave, Pittsburgh, PA 15212.

JANNEY, DONALD HERBERT, PHYSICS. **Personal Data:** b Kansas City, Mo, November 26, 1931. **Education:** Univ Ill, BS, 1952; Stanford Univ, MS, 1953, PhD (appl physics), 1957. **Professional Experience:** RETIRED; staff mem, Los Alamos Nat Lab, 1981-1994; group leader, Los Alamos Nat Lab, 1974-1981; alt group leader, Los Alamos Nat Lab, 1965-1974; staff mem, Los Alamos Nat Lab, 1956-1965; asst, Microwave Lab, Stanford Univ, 1953-1956; asst, Los Alamos Sci Lab, 1952. **Memberships:** AAAS; Am Phys Soc; Inst Elec & Electronics Engrs; Sigma Xi. **Research Statement & Publications:** Gamma ray measurements; flash radiography; image processing; image analysis; non-destructive evaluation; intelligence analyst. **Mailing Address:** 323 Potrillo Dr, Los Alamos, NM 87544-2409. **E-Mail:** janney@rmi.net

JANNEY, GARETH MAYNARD, OPTICS. **Personal Data:** b Toledo, Ohio, February 19, 1934; m 1960, Carol; c 1. **Education:** Columbia Univ, AB, 1955; Georgetown Univ, MS, 1962, PhD (physics), 1965. **Professional Experience:** RETIRED; chief Scientist, Space & Strategic Eng Div, 1984-1989; proj mgr, Space Sensors Div, 1979-1984; asst dept mgr lasers, Hughes Res Labs, 1975-1979; from mem tech staff lasers to sr staff physicist, Hughes Aircraft Co, 1969-1975; physicist, US Army Night Vision Lab, US Army Electronics Command, 1965-1969. **Memberships:** Am Optical Soc; Inst Elec & Electronics Engrs. **Research Statement & Publications:** Diatomic molecular spectroscopy, gas laser research, laser mode control and diffractionoptics for high energy lasers, tunable electro-optical infrared filters. **Mailing Address:** 1446 NW First St, Bend, OR 97701.

JANOS, DAVID PAUL, TROPICAL PLANT ECOLOGY, MYCORRHIZAE. **Personal Data:** b Chicago, Ill, November 24, 1947. **Education:** Carleton Col, BA, 1969; Univ Mich, Ann Arbor, MS, 1971, PhD (bot), 1975. **Professional Experience:** Counr, Asn Trop Biol, 1992-1993; ASSOC PROF BIOL, UNIV MIAMI, 1984-; mem, Nat Acad Sci-Nat Res Coun Comt Selected Biol Probs Humid Trop, 1980-1981; asst prof, Univ Miami, 1979-1984; fel, Smithsonian Trop Res Inst, 1976-1979; Field sta mgr, Orgn Trop Studies, Inc, 1975; Herbarium asst trop bot, Field Mus Natural Hist, 1970; Bullard fel, Forest Res, Harvard Univ, 1994-1995; Managing Ed, Mycorrhiza, Springer Verlag, 1996-2001. **Memberships:** Mycol Soc Am; Asn Trop Biol; Sigma Xi; Ecol Soc Am; Orgn Trop Studies (secy, 1982-1983); Int Soc Trop Foresters. **Research Statement & Publications:** Evolutionary ecology of mutualistic associations, and the influences of mutualistic root associations on plant community composition and dynamics, especially those of vesicular-arbuscular mycorrhizae in the tropics. **Mailing Address:** Dept Biol, Univ Miami PO Box 249118, Miami, FL 33124-0421. **Fax:** 305-284-3039. **E-Mail:** djanos@umiami.ir.miami.edu

JANOS, LUDVIK, MATHEMATICS. **Personal Data:** b Brno, Czech, October 3, 1922; American citizen. **Education:** Charles Univ, Prague, Dr rer nat(math), 1950. **Professional Experience:** PROF MATH, DEPT MATH SCI, KENT STATE UNIV, KENT, OHIO, as of 1999; assoc prof math, Calif State Univ, Long Beach, 1986-; res prof, Univ Md, 1980-1986; assoc ed, Math Rev, Univ Mich, 1977-1980; assoc prof math, Wash State Univ, 1975-1977; vis prof, Univ Mont, Missoula, 1974-1975; assoc prof, Univ Fla, 1969-1974; vis assoc prof, Univ Fla, 1966-1969; assoc prof, Dalhousie Univ, 1965-1966; vis assoc prof math, George Wash Univ, 1963-1965; mathematician, Res Inst, Prague, 1950-1963. **Memberships:** Am Math Soc. **Research Statement & Publications:** Functional analysis applied to the theory of differential equations; theory of fixed points; general topology; mathematical statistics; algebraic topology applied to digital geometry and pattern recognition; mathematical logic; algebraic topology applied to dynamical systems; Ergodic theory; dimension theory; geom theory of Banach spaces. **Mailing Address:** Dept Math, Kent State Univ, Kent, OH 44242-0001. **Fax:** 330-672-7824. **E-Mail:** janos@mcs.kent.edu

JANOS, WILLIAM AUGUSTUS, PHYSICS, INFORMATION SCIENCE, ELECTROMAGNETIC MATERIALS. **Personal Data:** b Easton, Pa, November 9, 1926; m 1959, Charlene. **Education:** Rutgers Univ, BS, 1951; Univ Calif, Berkeley, MA, 1954, PhD (physics), 1958. **Professional Experience:** CONSULT, ELECTROMAGNETIC MAT, 1992-; staff consult, Aerojet Gen Corp, 1984-; staff specialist, Rockwell Int, 1984-1992; prin electronics engr, Interstate Electronics Corp, 1978-1984; sr staff engr, McDonnell Douglas Astronautics Co, 1974-1978; sr scientist, Technol Serv Corp, 1967-1974; sr staff physicist, Missile Syst Div Labs, Raytheon Co, 1967; prin scientist, Philco-Ford Aeronutronic Appl Res Lab, 1966-1967; US del, Plasma Physics Symp, Int Union Pure & Appl Chem, USSR, 1965; sr tech specialist, NAm Space& Info Systs Div, 1963-1966; USAEC del, Int ConfControlled Thermonuclear Fusion, 1961; staffphysicist, Res Div & Advan Develop Lab, Raytheon Co, 1960-1963; Res physicist, ConvairAstronaut Div, Gen Dynamics Corp, 1951-1960. **Memberships:** Sigma Xi; Am Phys Soc; Inst Elec & Electronics Engrs; Am Asn Advan Sci. **Research Statement & Publications:** Statistical physics and electromagnetics of Boltzmann and Fokker-Planck equations; Wiener-Hopf integral equations of statistical communications and information theory; systems analysis; phenomenology hydrodynamics; analytical modeling of physical systems, sensors and signal processing; mathematical physics; statistical optics. **Mailing Address:** 8381 Snowbird Dr, Huntington Beach, CA 92646.

JANOVY, JOHN, ZOOLOGY. **Personal Data:** b Houma, La, December 27, 1937; m 1961, c 3. **Education:** Univ Okla, BS, 1959, MS, 1962, PhD (zoology), 1965. **Professional Experience:** PAULA & D B VARNER PROF BIOL SCI, UNIV NEBR, LINCOLN, as of 2000; prof zoology, Dept Life Sci, Univ Nebr, Lincoln, 1974-; ASST DEAN ARTS & SCI, DEPT LIFE SCI, UNIV NEBR, LINCOLN, 1966-; assoc prof, Dept Life Sci, Univ Nebr, Lincoln, 1966-1974; trainee, Rutgers Univ, 1965-1966. **Memberships:** Am Soc Trop Med & Hyg; Am Soc Parasitol. **Research Statement & Publications:** Epidemiology of parasitic protozoa; comparative metabolism and evolution and of parasitic flagellates. **Mailing Address:** Sch Biol Sci, Univ Nebr, 424 Manter Hall, Lincoln, NE 68588-0118. **Fax:** 402-472-9642. **E-Mail:** jjanovy1@unl.edu

JANOWITZ, GERALD S(AUL), FLUID MECHANICS. **Personal Data:** b Bronx, NY, April 5, 1943; m 1968, Barbara; c David. **Education:** Polytech Inst Brooklyn, BS, 1963; Johns Hopkins Univ, MS, 1965, PhD (mech), 1967. **Professional Experience:** PROF MARINE EARTH & ATMOSPHERIC SCI, NC STATE UNIV, 1981-; prof marine sci eng, Nc State Univ, 1980-1981; assoc prof oceanog, NC State Univ, 1975-1980; asst prof fluid mech, Thermal & Aerospace Sci Case Western Res Univ, 1968-1975; fell mech, Johns Hopkins Univ, 1967-1968; res asst, Johns Hopkins Univ, 1966-1967; NASA grad fel, Johns Hopkins Univ, 1963-1966. **Memberships:** Am Geophys Union. **Research Statement & Publications:** Geophysical fluid mechanics; motion of bodies through stratified fluids; flows in lakes, ocean basins, and the coastal boundary layers. **Mailing Address:** Dept Marine Earth & Atmospheric Sci, Nc State Univ, Raleigh, NC 27695-8208. **Fax:** 919-515-7802. **E-Mail:** janowitz@ncsu.edu

JANOWITZ, HENRY DAVID, GASTROENTEROLOGY. **Personal Data:** b Paterson, NJ, March 23, 1915; m 1942, c Anna & Mary. **Education:** Columbia Univ, AB, 1935, MD, 1939, Univ Ill, MS, 1949. **Honors & Awards:** Friedenwald Metal, Am Gastroenterol Asn, 1984, Master Gastroenterol, 1994; Lifetime Clin Achievement Award, Am Col Gastroenterol, 1994. **Professional Experience:** PROF EMER, MT SINAI SCH MED, 1983-; chmn, Nat Inst Arthritis &Metab Dis, 1970; clin prof, Mt Sinai Sch Med, 1966-1985; mem, Am Bd Gastroenterol, 1965; mem prog proj comt, Nat Inst Arthritis & Metab Dis, 1965; ed sect alimentary canal, HandbookPhysiol, 1965; chmn gastroenterol res group steering comt, Am Bd Gastroenterol, 1965; ComfortMem lectr, Mayo Found, 1965; asst clin prof med, Columbia Univ, 1962-1966; dir NIH TrainingProg Gastroenterol, Mt Sinai Sch Med, 1959-1975; head, Div Gastroenterol, 1956-1983; ed, AmJ Digestive Dis, 1956-1965; chief Gastro-Intestinal Clin, Mt Sinai Sch Med, 1956-1962; McArthur lectr, Univ Edinburgh, 1956; hon lectr, Guy's Hosp, London, Eng, 1956; asstgastroenterol, Mt Sinai Sch Med, 1950-1954; asst physiol, Univ Ill, 1948-1949; resident med, MtSinai Hosp, 1947-1948; fel path, Mt Sinai Hosp, 1946; intern, Mt Sinai Hosp, 1939-1941; Pvt pract; consult, Bronx Vet Admin Hosp, Horton Hosp, Middletown, NY &Englewood Hosp, NJ. **Memberships:** Am Physiol Soc; Soc Exp Biol & Med; Am Soc Clin Investrs; Am GastroenterolAsn (pres 1972); Asn Am Physicians; hon mem Brit Gastroenterol Soc; hon fel Royal Soc Med. **Research Statement & Publications:** Clinical investigation in gastroenterology, especially of the natural history and therapy of inflammatory bowel disease. **Mailing Address:** Div Gastroenterol, Mt Sinai Sch Med, 11 E 100th St, New York, NY 10029.

JANOWITZ, MELVIN FIVA, ALGEBRA, CLUSTER ANALYSIS. **Personal Data:** b Minneapolis, Minn, May 8, 1929; c 3. **Education:** Univ Minn, BA, 1950; Wayne State Univ, PhD (math), 1963. **Professional Experience:** PROF EMER MATH, UNIV MASS, AMHERST, as of 2004; asst dean, Natural Sci & Math, 1979-1983; prof math, Univ Mass, Amherst, beginning 1970; assoc prof, Univ Mass, Amherst, 1967-1970; assoc prof, Western Mich Univ, 1966-1967; asst prof math, Univ NMex, 1963-1966. **Memberships:** Am Math Soc; Math Asn Am; Classification Soc. **Research Statement & Publications:** Lattice theory; mathematical models for ordinal cluster analysis; ordinal models for semiorders, internal orders and social choice functions; connections between percentile based cluster techniques and probabilistic metric spheres. **Mailing Address:** Dept Math & Statist, Univ Mass Leder le Grand Res Ctr PO Box 34515, Amherst, MA 01003-0113. **Fax:** 413-545-1801. **E-Mail:** melj@math.umass.edu

JANOWSKI, GREGG MICHAEL, MATERIALS CHARACTERIZATION, COMPOSITE MATERIALS. **Personal Data:** b Bay City, Mich, January 23, 1961; m 1988, Karen. **Education:** Mich Technol Univ, BS, 1983, MS, 1985, PhD (metall eng), 1988. **Professional Experience:** Associate Professor, Materials Science and Engineering, University of Alabama at Birmingham, 1996-Date Associate Chair, Materials Science and Engineering, University of Alabama at Birmingham, 1997-2001, Director, Tri-Campus Materials Science Program, University of Alabama System, 1995-1998 Assistant Professor, Materials Science and Engineering, University of Alabama at Birmingham, 1990-1996 Metallurgist, Metallurgy Division, National Institute of Standards and Technology, 1988-1990 Associate Metallurgist, Saginaw Division, General Motors Corporation, 1983. **Memberships:** ASM International, TMS, Am Soc for Engineering Education. **Research Statement & Publications:** Processing/Microstructure/Mechanical Property relationships, Electron Microscopy (SEM and TEM), X Ray Diffraction, Superalloys, Powder Metallurgy, Composite Materials, Intermetallic Compounds, Metallurgy of Iron and Aluminum Alloys. **Mailing Address:** Dept Materials Sci & Eng, Univ Ala at Birmingham, Birmingham, AL 35294-4461. **Fax:** 205-934-8485. **E-Mail:** janowski@uab.edu

JANOWSKY, DAVID STEFFAN, PSYCHOPHARMACOLOGY. **Personal Data:** b San Diego, Calif, June 24, 1939; m 1962, c 4. **Education:** Univ Calif, San Francisco, BS, 1961, MD, 1964. **Professional Experience:** PROF, DEPT PSYCHIAT, SCH MED, UNIV NC, CHAPEL HILL, 1986-; prof & chair, Dept Psychiat, Univ NC Chapel Hill, 1986-1994; prof, Dept Psychiat, Sch Med, Univ Calif, San Diego, beginning 1976; chief psychiat serv, Univ Hosp, Univ Calif, San Diego, 1974-1978; assoc prof, Univ Calif, San Diego, 1973-1976; chief, Vet Admin Liaison Serv, Univ Calif, San Diego, 1973-1974; assoc prof, Sch Med, Vanderbilt Univ, 1972-1973; asst prof pharmacol, Sch Med, Vanderbilt Univ, 1970-1973; asst prof psychiat, Sch Med, Vanderbilt Univ, 1970-1972; head physician, Crisis Clin, Psychiat Emergency Serv, Dept Psychiat, Harbor Gen Hosp, Calif, 1969-1970; Asst prof, Dept Psychiat, Sch Med, Univ Calif, Los Angeles, 1969-1970; prin investr, Ment Health Clin Res Ctr, NIMH, Univ Calif, SanDiego. **Memberships:** Am Col Neuropsycho pharmacol; Am Psychiat Asn; Psychiat Res Soc; Soc Neuroscience; Col Int Neuropsychopharmacol. **Research Statement & Publications:** Effects of adrenergic-cholinergic balance in the affective disorders, using cholinesterase inhibitors and psychostimulant challenges as investigative probes, and correlating these results with pre-clinical animal models. **Mailing Address:** Dept Psychiat, Med Sch, Univ NC, CB # 7160, Chapel Hill, NC 27599-7160. **Fax:** 919-966-0259. **E-Mail:** david_janowsky@med.unc.edu

JANS, JAMES PATRICK, mathematics; deceased, see previous edition for last biography

JANSEN, BERNARD JOSEPH, MATHEMATICS, SOFTWARE. **Personal Data:** b Rockville, Minn, August 10, 1927; m 1955, Kathryn; c Kathryn, Bernard Jr, Stephen & David. **Education:** St John's Univ, Minn, BA, 1950; St Louis Univ, MA, 1952. **Professional Experience:** RETIRED; instr math, Univ Wis, River Falls, 1990; mgr syst scheduling & planning, Comput Systs Div, Unisys Defense Systs, 1985-1988; underseas proj mgr, control & change proposals, Int Telecommun Div, 1982-1985; planning, control & change proposals, Int Telecommun Div, 1977-1982; systs & software, Int Systs Div, 1976-1977; avionics software, Unisys, 1969-1975; mem adv panel, Spaceborne Digital Comput Systs, NASA, 1968-1980; comput analyst prog, mgr Titan III software, 1966-1969; comput analyst prog, Unisys, 1955-1966; instr math, St John's Univ, Minn, 1954-1956. **Memberships:** Math Asn Am; Sigma Xi. **Research Statement & Publications:** Technical management of and application of computers to systems and software in the underseas, avionics, aerospace, command and control and telecommunications fields. **Mailing Address:** 848 Ivy Lane, Eagan, MN 55123-2425.

JANSEN, FRANK, THIN FILM TECHNOLOGY, ELECTRONIC FABRICATION PROCESSES. **Personal Data:** b Emmeloord, Neth, February 9, 1946; m 1973, c 3. **Education:** Tech Univ Delft, ingenieur, 1973; Case Western Res Univ, PhD (physics), 1977. **Professional Experience:** VPRES ENG & TECHNOL, BOC COATING TECHNOL, as of 2003; DIR TECHNOL, BOC COATING TECHNOL, 1994-; mgr, Tech Found Group, 1992-1994; mgr, Thin Film Technologies, BOC Group, 1990-1992; prog chmn, Thin Film Div, Am Vacuum Soc, 1990; chmn, Thin Film Div, Am Vacuum Soc, 1989; lectr, Am Vacuum-Soc, 1988-; prin scientist, Webster Res Ctr, Xerox Corp, 1986-1990; proj mgr & mem res staff, Webster Res Ctr, Xerox Corp, 1980-1986; tech specialist, Webster Res Ctr, Xerox Corp, 1977-1980. **Memberships:** Am Vacuum Soc. **Research Statement & Publications:** Management of thin film and vacuum technology; development of industrial coating processes for glass and plastic. **Mailing Address:** BOC Coating Technol, 4020 Pike Lane, Concord, CA 94524. **Fax:** 510-674-9419. **E-Mail:** frank.jansen@us.bocct.boc.com

JANSEN, GEORGE, CHEMICAL ENGINEERING. **Personal Data:** b Aloha, Ore, November 15, 1934; m 1956, c 4. **Education:** Ore State Univ, BS & BA, 1955; Mass Inst Technol, SM, 1957, ScD(chem eng), 1959. **Professional Experience:** RETIRED; proj engr, Jacobs Eng Group Inc, 1998-1999; prin mgr, Lockheed Martin Hanford Co, 1996-1997; at, WSU/Tri-Cities, 1989-1997; prin engr, Westinghouse Hanford Com, 1988-1996; sr engr, Golder Assoc Inc, 1987-1988; analysis engr, Battelle Mem Inst, 1981-1987; sr engr, Exxon NuclearCo, Inc, 1975-1981; res assoc, Battelle-Northwest, 1968-1975; sr develop engr, Battelle-Northwest, 1965-1968; sr engr, Hanford Labs, Gen Elec Co, Wash, 1962-1965; chemengr, Hanford Labs, Gen Elec Co, Wash, 1959-1962. **Memberships:** AAAS; Am Chem Soc; Am Inst Chem Engrs; Am Nuclear Soc. **Research Statement & Publications:** Ion exchange; heat transfer; process development in nuclear fuel processing; solvent extraction; radioactive waste disposal; risk analysis; centrifuge enrichment. **Mailing Address:** 126 Orchard Court, Richland WA, WA 99352-9645. **E-Mail:** gjansen@3-cities.com

JANSEN, GEORGE JAMES, MINERALOGY. **Personal Data:** b Canton, Ohio, April 22, 1925; m 1971, Marjorie Molloy; c George & Kenneth. **Education:** Univ Notre Dame, BS, 1951; Bryn Mawr Col, MA, 1952. **Professional Experience:** PRIN, ROCKY MOUNTAIN CONSULT PETROG, 1978-; mineralogist, Com Test & Eng Co, 1976-1978; mineralogist, Climax Molybdenum Lab, 1969-1976; supvr mineral & metallog, Res Ctr, Repub Steel Corp, Ohio, 1957-1969; prin geologist, Battelle Mem Inst, 1957; geologist, US Geol Surv, 1952-1957; Hydrol field asst, US Geol Surv, 1951. **Memberships:** Soc Econ Geologists fel. **Research Statement & Publications:** Mineralogy of base metals; quantitative metallography; reflected light optics; coal petrography. **Mailing Address:** 12870 W 15th Dr, Golden, CO 80401-3502. **E-Mail:** margieandjimjansen@junu.com

JANSEN, GUSTAV RICHARD, NUTRITION. **Personal Data:** b Staten Island, NY, May 19, 1930; m 1953, Coerene; c Norman, Barbara, Kathryn, Ellen. **Education:** Cornell Univ, BA, 1950, PhD (biochem), 1958. **Honors & Awards:** Cert of Merit, USDA, 1983; Babcock-Hart Award, Inst Food Technologists, 1985; Fel IFT; Fel ASNS. **Professional Experience:** PROF & DEPT HEAD EMER FOOD SCI & NUTRIT, COLO STATE UNIV, 1990-; mem, exec comt, Inst Food Technol, 1989-1991; Human Nutrit Bd Sci Counselors, USDA, 1986-1992; Prog mgr, USDA, competition grants prog human nutrit, 1981-1982; prof & dept head, Colo State Univ, 1969-1990; res fel, Merck Inst Therapeut Res, 1962-1969; res chemist, E I du Pont Del Nemours & Co, 1958-1962; asst biochem, Cornell Univ, 1954-1958; Jr & assoc chemist, Am Cyanamid Co, 1953-1954; comt mil nutrit res, Inst Med, Nat Acad Sci. **Memberships:** Am Soc Biochem & Molecular Biol; AAAS; fel Inst Food Technologists; Sigma Xi; Am Soc Nutr Sci. **Research Statement & Publications:** Control of cholesterol metabolism. **Mailing Address:** Dept Food Sci & Human Nutrit, Colorado State Univ, Ft Collins, CO 80523.

JANSEN, HENRICUS CORNELIS, RANGE MANAGEMENT. **Personal Data:** b Bergen op Zoom, Holland, August 3, 1942; American citizen; m 1977. **Education:** Univ Calif, Berkeley, BS, 1969, PhD (natural res sci & range mgt), 1974. **Professional Experience:** PROF EMER, COL AGR, CALIF STATE UNIV, CHICO, as of 2003; prof range mgt, calif state univ, chico, beginning 1986; range mgtexpert, UN Food & Agr Orgn, 1984-1985; Consult range conservationist, Soil Conserv Serv, 1979 & Bur Land Mgt, 1981; botanist, Fish & Wildlife Serv, 1980; from asst prof to assoc prof, CalifState Univ, Chico, 1976-1986; res forester range mgt, Pac Southwest Forest & Range Exp Sta, US Forest Serv, 1972-1976. **Memberships:** Soc Range Mgt; AAAS. **Research Statement & Publications:** Computerized planning method including documentation for the management of federal grazing lands; grazing management of arid lands in North Africa. **Mailing Address:** Dept Agr, Calif State Univ, First & Normal Sts, Chico, CA 95929.

JANSEN, MICHAEL, QUANTUM ELECTRONICS, SEMICONDUCTOR LASERS. **Personal Data:** b Bucharest, Romania, January 27, 1956; m 1984, c 2. **Education:** Univ Calif Los Angeles, BS, 1978, MS, 1979, PhD (quantum electronics), 1984. **Professional Experience:** VPRES RES & DEVELOP, APT, 1995-; lectr, Elec Eng Dept, Univ Calif LosAngeles, 1985-1986; sr scientist, Space & Technol Group, Advan Technol Div, Res Ctr, TRW, 1984-; res assoc, quantum electronics & electronics, UCLA, 1983-1984; Teaching asst & assocoptics, quantum electronics & electronics, UCLA, 1980-1983; Consult, Monosolar Industs, 1980-1981. **Memberships:** Inst Elec & Electronics Engrs. **Research Statement & Publications:** Design, development, and characterization of diode lasers and integrated optics; development of monolithic two-dimensional, coherent and incoherent surface-emitting arrays; monolithic components for optical integration; large optical cavity and evanescently-coupled and diffraction-coupled laser arrays; unstable resonators, amplifiers, and LEDs. **Mailing Address:** Coherent Inc, 5100 Patrick Henry Dr, Santa Clara, CA 95054.

JANSEN, ROBERT BRUCE, CIVIL ENGINEERING, ENGINEERING OF DAMS. **Personal Data:** b Spokane, Wash, December 14, 1922; m 1943, Barbara M Courtney. **Education:** Univ Denver, BSCE, 1949; Univ SCalif, MSCE, 1955. **Professional Experience:** Mem Water Sci & Technol Bd, Nat Acad Eng, 1982-1984; chmn, Nat Comt Safety Dams, Nat Res Coun, 1981-1983; CONSULT CIVIL ENG, 1980-; mem, US Comt Large Dams, chmn, 1979-1981; asst comnr, US Bus Reclamation, 1977-1980; chief design & cons, Calif Dept Water Resources, 1975-1977; dept dir, Calif Dept Water Resources, 1971-1975; chief oper, Calif Dept Water Resources, 1968-1971; Chief, Calif Div Dam Safety, 1965-1968. **Memberships:** Nat Acad Eng; Am Soc Civil Engrs. **Research Statement & Publications:** Response of dams to earthquake, flood and leakage; methods of dam rehabilitation. **Mailing Address:** 509 Briar Rd, Bellingham, WA 98225.

JANSEN, ROBERT WERNER, RADAR SCATTERING, OCEAN PHYSICS. **Education:** Mankato State Univ, BS, 1981; Ariz State Univ, PhD (theoret solid state physics), 1987. **Professional Experience:** US NAVAL RES LAB, as of 2003; RES PHYSICIST, NAVAL RES LAB, 1991-; res scientist, Dynamics Technol Inc, 1989-1991; res assoc, Nat Res Coun, 1987-1989. **Memberships:** Sigma Xi; Am Phys Soc. **Research Statement & Publications:** Predictions of defect formation, migration and energetics in semiconductors; wave propagation in the ocean and radar scattering from the ocean waves. **Mailing Address:** Naval Res Lab, 4555 Overlook Ave SW, Washington, DC 20375.

JANSING, JO ANN, ANALYTICAL CHEMISTRY. **Personal Data:** b Louisville, Ky, March 23, 1938. **Education:** Ursuline Col, Ky, BA, 1965; Fordham Univ, MS, 1967, PhD (anal & phys chem), 1970. **Professional Experience:** EMER PROF CHEM, IND UNIV SOUTHEAST, 2001-; prof chem, Ind Univ Southeast, 1981-2001; chair, Div Natural Sci, Ind Univ Southeast, 1979-1986; coordr Chem, Ind Univ Southeast, 1976-1979, beginning 1989; from asst prof to assoc prof, Ind Univ Southeast, 1970-1981; instr chem, Mt St Agnes Col, 1969-1970; teacher high sch, Ky, 1962-1965. **Memberships:** Am Chem Soc; Sigma Xi. **Research Statement & Publications:** X-ray crystallographic structure studies of organic molecules. **Mailing Address:** Dept Chem, Ind Univ SE, 4201 Grantline Rd, New Albany, IN 47150. **E-Mail:** jjansing@ius.edu

JANSKI, ALVIN MICHAEL, BIOCHEMISTRY. **Personal Data:** b Braham, Minn, May 27, 1949; m 1971, c 2. **Education:** St Cloud State Univ, Minn, BA, 1971; NDak State Univ, PhD (biochem), 1975. **Professional Experience:** DIR LIFE SCI, PITMAN-MOORE INC, 1986-; Prin investr, Int Minerals &Chem Corp, Northbrook, Ill, 1981-; mgr, Biochem Res Sect, Int Minerals & Chem Corp, 1981-1986; sr staff fel, Lab Metab, Nat Inst Alcohol Abuse & Alcoholism, 1978-1981; Res assoc, NIH fel, 1978; Res assoc, Dept Biochem & Biophys, Iowa State Univ, 1975-1978. **Memberships:** Am Soc Biol Chemists; NY Acad Sci; Am Chem Soc; AAAS; Endocrine Soc. **Research Statement & Publications:** Protein vaccines by recombinant DNA technology; metabolic pathways through intracellular compartmentation of metabolites and enzymes and hormone-depedent phosphorylation of enzymes; in vitro study of growth. **Mailing Address:** 14473 Brittanius Dr, 675 McDonnell Blvd, Chesterfield, MO 63017-8035.

JANSON, BLAIR F, PLANT PATHOLOGY. **Personal Data:** b East Trumbull, Ohio, January 6, 1918; m 1944, c 3. **Education:** Ohio State Univ, BS, 1940, MS, 1947, PhD, 1950. **Professional Experience:** EMER PROF PLANT PATH, OHIO STATE UNIV, 1980-; prof plant path, Ohio State Univ, 1962-1980; exten plant pathologist, Ohio State Univ, 1950-1980; asst instr bot, Ohio State Univ, 1947-1950; Asst exten plant pathologist, Ohio State Univ, 1946. **Memberships:** Am Phytopath Soc. **Research Statement & Publications:** Ornamental, fruit, cereal and forage crop diseases. **Mailing Address:** 266 Canyon Dr, Columbus, OH 43214.

JANSONS, VILMA KARINA, MICROBIOLOGY. **Personal Data:** b Riga, Latvia, American citizen. **Education:** Brooklyn Col, BA, 1961; Rutgers Univ, New Brunswick, PhD (microbiol), 1967. **Professional Experience:** ASSOC PROF MICROBIOL, NJ MED SCH, UNIV MED & DENT NJ, 1977-; asst prof microbiol, NJ Med Sch, Univ Med & Dent NJ, 1972-1977; mem res staffbiochem sci, Princeton Univ, 1970-1972; Lectr biol, Princeton Univ, 1968-1970. **Memberships:** AAAS; Am Soc Microbiol; Am Soc Cell Biol. **Research Statement & Publications:** Surface properties of normal and malignant cells; biochemistry of morphogenesis. **Mailing Address:** Dept Microbiol & Molecular Genetics, NJ Med Sch 185 S Orange Ave, Newark, NJ 07103-2714.

JANSSEN, FRANK WALTER, DRUG METABOLISM. **Personal Data:** b St Paul, Minn, September 10, 1926; m 1952, c 2. **Education:** Col St Thomas, BS, 1950; Iowa State Univ, MS, 1952. **Professional Experience:** RETIRED; mgr, Drug Disposition Sect, 1985-

1996; supvr, PharmacokineticEval Unit, 1978-1985; sr res scientist & group leader drug metab, Wyeth Labs, Inc, 1966-1978; res scientist protein chem, Wyeth Labs, Inc, 1961-1966; asst scientist biochem, Hormel Inst, Univ Minn, 1952-1961. **Memberships:** Sigma Xi. **Research Statement & Publications:** Drug disposition; biotransformation and pharmacokinetics of drugs. **Mailing Address:** 309 Westbrook Dr, Westchester, PA 19382.

JANSSEN, JERRY FREDERICK, ORGANIC CHEMISTRY. **Personal Data:** b Mason City, Iowa, March 22, 1936; m 1984, Carol; c Susan E & Eric P. **Education:** Iowa State Teachers Col, BA, 1957, MA, 1959; Mich State Univ, PhD (chem), 1967; JD, Suffolk Univ, 1983. **Professional Experience:** SR PATENT ATTY, ABBOTT LABS, 1989-; sr patent atty, BASF, 1988-1989; inst chem, Washtenaw Comm Col, 1985-1987; sr patentatty, Parke-Davis/Warner-Lambert, 1983-1988; chem patent agent, GTE Serv Corp, 1977-1983; sr environ engr, GTE Sylvania, Inc, Seneca Falls, NY, 1974-1977; from asst prof to assoc prof, Eisenhower Col, 1969-1974; consult, Sylvania Elec Prod, Inc, NY, 1969-1970; consult, VernayLabs, Ohio, 1968-1969; asst prof chem, Antioch Col, 1966-1969; asst instr, Mich State Univ, 1961-1963; instr sci & math, Mason City Jr Col, Iowa, 1959-1961; PATENT COUN, ELI LILLY & CO. **Memberships:** Am Chem Soc; fel Am Inst Chem; Am Bar Asn; Am Intellectual Property Law Asn. **Research Statement & Publications:** Organic reaction mechanisms; molecular photochemistry; rearrangement reactions of aromatic compounds. **Mailing Address:** Eli Lilly & Co, DC1111 Lilly Corp Ctr, Indianapolis, IN 46285.

JANSSEN, MICHAEL ALLEN, RADIO ASTRONOMY, PLANETARY SCIENCES. **Personal Data:** b Boise, Idaho, September 30, 1937; m 1979, Saundra; c 2. **Education:** Univ Calif, AB, 1963, PhD (atmospheric & space sci), 1972. **Honors & Awards:** NASA Except Sci Achievement Medal for Contrib to Cosmic Bakground Explorer, 1992. **Professional Experience:** PRIN SCIENTIST, JET PROPULSION LAB, CALIF INST TECH, NASA, as of 2005; ASST DIV MGR-DIV 32, JET PROPULSION LAB, CALIF INSTTECHNOL, 1997-2002; mem tech staff, Jet Propulsion lab, Calif Inst Technol, beginning 1976; sr scientist, Jet Propulsion Lab, Calif Inst Technol, 1974-1976; Nat Res Coun resident res assoc planetary radio astron, Jet Propulsion Lab, Calif InstTechnol, 1972-1974; physicist, Lawrence Radiation Lab, 1963-1967; particscientist, cosmic background explorer (COBE), Rosetta, Cassini; prin investr, Microwave Radiometer, Juno mission to Jupiter. **Memberships:** Int Union Radio Sci; Am Astron Soc; Am Geophys Union; Int Astron Union. **Research Statement & Publications:** Development of spaceborne microwave instrumentation; investigation of the atmospheres of Venus and the outer planets by microwave techniques; spacecraft microwave radiometry; cosmic microwave background; microwave remote sensing. **Mailing Address:** Jet Propulsion Lab, Calif Inst Technol, MC 169-506, 4800 Oak Grove Dr, Pasadena, CA 91109-8001. **Fax:** 818-354-8895. **E-Mail:** michael.a.janssen@jpl.nasa.gov

JANSSEN, ROBERT (JAMES) J, VIROLOGY, IMMUNOLOGY. **Personal Data:** b Geneva, Ill, February 28, 1931; m 1957, c 2. **Education:** Cornell Col, BA, 1953; State Univ Iowa, MS, 1955, PhD (bact), 1957. **Professional Experience:** ASSOC PROF EMER MICROBIOL & MED TECHNOL, UNIV ARIZ, 1992-; from asst prof to assoc prof microbiol & med technol, Univ Ariz, 1961-1992; med bacteriologist virol, Biol Labs, US Army Chem Corps, Md, 1957-1961. **Memberships:** Sigma Xi; Am Soc Microbiol. **Research Statement & Publications:** Smallpox, influenza, enteroviruses, arborviruses; combined infections with two or more microbial agents; aerobiology studies with viral agents; serological techniques; effects of certain drugs on viral infections. **Mailing Address:** Dept Microbiol Immunol, Univ Ariz, Tucson, AZ 85721.

JANSSENS, ROBERT V F, PHYSICS. **Education:** Catholic Univ Louvain, Belgium, BSc, 1973, PhD (Nuclear Physics), 1978. **Professional Experience:** SR SCIENTIST, PHYSICS DIV, ARGONNE NAT LAB, beginning 1993; adj prof, Univ Notre Dame, beginning 2004. **Mailing Address:** Dept Physics, Argonne Nat Lab, 9700 S Cass Ave, Argonne, IL 60439. **Fax:** 630-252-6210. **E-Mail:** janssens@anl.gov

JANSSENS, THOMAS J, TEACHING MATHEMATICS & ASTRONOMY. **Personal Data:** b Los Angeles, Calif, October 23, 1931; m 1985, Sadie; c Denise, Andrea, David & Karen. **Education:** Calif Inst Technol, BS, 1953; Stanford Univ, MS, 1961, PhD (physics), 1964. **Professional Experience:** ASST PROF MATH & ASTRON, CALIF LUTHERAN UNIV, 1989-; spec lectr, Soc Photo-optic Instrument Engrs, 1988-1989; lectr physics, Calif State Univ, Long Beach, 1968-1989; prin investr, Proj Sunwatch, 1967; mem tech staff, Aerospace Corp, 1965-1989; asst prof physics, Loyola Col, Montreal, Can, 1964-1965. **Memberships:** fel NSF; Astron Soc Pac. **Research Statement & Publications:** Optical and radio emissions from solar flares; track initiation of space objects from angles-only data from 2 or 3 optical sensors. **Mailing Address:** Calif Luthern Univ, 60 W Olsan Rd, MC 3750, Thousand Oaks, CA 91360.

JANSSON, CARL RICHARD ERLAND, PROCESS DEVELOPMENT WATER & WASTEWATER, HAZARDOUS WASTES. **Personal Data:** b Canwood, Sask, April 17, 1935; m Erline. **Education:** Univ Sask, BE, 1960; Univ Waterloo, MASc, 1970; Univ Wash, PhD (environ eng & sci), 89. **Professional Experience:** PRES & SR ENVIRON SCIENTIST, JANSSON CONSULT SERV INC, 1983-; sr environ engr, Keith Consult Engrs, 1973-1982; waste treat engr, Assoc Eng, 1972-1973; environ engr, Environ Can, 1970-1972; environ engr, H A Simons, Int, Ltd, 1970; instr technol, Sask Tech Inst, 1965-1969; engr, Edinburgh, Scotland Trade & Com, Can, 1964-1965; field rep, MacMilan Bloedel Ltd, 1961-1963; agr engr, Alta Agr, 1960-1961. **Memberships:** Am Waterworks Asn; Water Environ Fedn; Am Chem Soc. **Research Statement & Publications:** Utilization of persistant chlorine residuals to inactivate giardia lamblia consitive agent of giardiasis; development of advanced oxidation processes for destruction of taste and odor compounds in water and destruction of inorganic, organic toxic and hazardous materials in aqueous solutions. **Mailing Address:** Jansson Consult Serv, 2323 Lorne St, Regina, SK S4P 2N1, Can.

JANSSON, PETER ALLAN, OPTICAL PHYSICS, DIGITAL IMAGE PROCESSING. **Personal Data:** b Teaneck, NJ, May 20, 1942; m 1994, Lihong; c Karen, Jonathan & Eric. **Education:** Stevens Inst Technol, BS, 1964; Fla State Univ, PhD (physics), 1968. **Professional Experience:** ADJ RES PROF, OPTICAL SCI CTR, UNIV ARIZ 2000-; res fel, Digital Image Processing Group, Exp Sta, E I DuPont de Nemours & Co Inc, 1990-2001; sr res assoc, E I DuPont de Nemours & Co Inc, 1980-1990; res assoc, E I DuPont de Nemours & Co Inc, 1976-1980; sr res physicist, E I DuPont de Nemours & Co Inc, 1971-1976; res physicist, E I DuPont de Nemours & Co Inc, 1968-1971; instr & res asst, Iinfrared Physics, Fla State Univ, 1967-1968. **Memberships:** Inst Elect & Electronic eng; fel Optical Soc Am; Int Soc Optical Eng; Sigma Xi. **Research Statement & Publications:** Optics; digital image processing and analysis; optical information processing; physical optics; molecular spectroscopy; super resolving method of deconvolution; artificial neural networks; color science and engineering. **Mailing Address:** Col Optical Sci, Univ Ariz, 1630 E Univ Blvd, Tucson, AZ 85721-0094. **E-Mail:** pjansson@optics.arizona.edu

JANSSON, RICHARD KEITH, INTEGRATED PEST MANAGEMENT & BIORATIONAL PEST CONTROL, DISCOVERY OF NOVEL BIORATIONAL PESTICIDES. **Personal Data:** b New York, NY, July 8, 1957; m 1979, Carolyn; c Keith H, Kari L & Kate E. **Education:** Moravian Col, BS, 1980; Pa State Univ, MS, 1982, PhD (entom), 1985. **Professional Experience:** DIR & PROJ LEADER, CENTOCOR INC, JOHNSON & JOHNSON, as of 2006; adj assoc prof, Rutgers Univ, 1994-; sr res fel, Merck & Co, beginning 1993; assoc prof, Univ Fla, 1991-1993; adj assoc prof, Univ PR, 1991-1993; asst prof entom, Univ Fla, 1986-1991; res fel, Rutgers Univ, 1985-1986; grad res & teaching asst, Pa State Univ, 1981-1985. **Memberships:** Entom Soc Am. **Research Statement & Publications:** Discovery of novel biorational compounds for use in agricultural crop protection and development of resistance monitoring and management programs; development of biorational methods for managing temperate and tropical insect pests on vegetable crops. **Mailing Address:** Centocor, Inc, 200 Great Valley Pkwy, Malvern, PA 19355. **Fax:** 610-651-6100.

JANTZ, O K, ENTOMOLOGY, CROP PROTECTION. **Personal Data:** b Newton, Kans, June 16, 1934; m 1957, C June Whitney; c Tamara, Jodi & Preston. **Education:** Kans State Univ, BS, 1957, MS, 1962; Ore State Univ, PhD (entom), 1965. **Professional Experience:** RETIRED; ESA Foundation duties, 1996; Global Prod Develop Engr Insecticides, Dow Elanco, 1992-; global dir res & develop opers, NAm Agr Prod, Dow Chem USA, 1989-1991; dir res & develop, NAm Agr Prod, Dow Chem USA, 1985-1989; bus mgr agr herbicide, Tech Serv & Develop Plant Prod, Agr Prod Dept, 1977-1981 dir, agr prod develop & regist, 1984; mgr, Tech Serv & Develop Plant Prod, Agr Prod Dept, 1977-1981 dir, agr prod develop & regist, 1977-1984; mgr res & develop agr & spec prods, Dow Chem Pac Ltd, Hong Kong, 1973-1977; develop specialist, Field Res Sta, Miss, 1971-1973; mgr, Field Res Sta, Miss, 1968-1971; regional tech specialist, Dow Chem, Mich, 1967-1968; entomologist, Agr Res Serv, USDA, Mich, 1965-1967; res asst, Ore State Univ, 1963-1965; res asst entom, Kans State Univ, 1960-1963; entomologist, Agr Mkt Serv, USDA, Kans, 1957; biol aide, Agr Mkt Serv, USDA, Kans, 1955-1957; field aide, Agr Mkt Serv, USDA, Kans, 1953-1955; Lab asst entom, Kans State Univ, 1952-1953. **Memberships:** Entom Soc Am; Sigma Xi emer mem. **Research Statement & Publications:** Field development of agricultural chemicals; forest insects; stored grain pests; field crop insects. **Mailing Address:** 230 Crestwood E, Prescott, AZ 86303-5355. **E-Mail:** orlojune@cableone.net

JANTZEN, JENS CARSTEN, MATHEMATICS. **Professional Experience:** PROF, DEPT MATH, AARHUS UNIV, as of 2004. **Mailing Address:** Dept Math, Aarhus Univ, Aarhus, Denmark. **E-Mail:** jantzen@imf.au.dk

JANUS, ALAN ROBERT, SOLID STATE SCIENCE. **Personal Data:** b Utica, NY, December 27, 1937; m 1970. **Education:** Utica Col, BA, 1959; Syracuse Univ, PhD (inorg chem), 1964. **Professional Experience:** PROJ MGR, NORTHROP, 1984-; proj mgr, TRW, 1980-1984; dir res, Bourne, 1977-1980; Nat Micrometrics, 1974- & Optifilm, 1975-; sr scientist, Hughes Aircraft, Calif 1974-1980; Electron Tube Div, Bell & Howell, 1973-1974; dir eng, Electronic Mat Div, Bell & Howell Res Labs, 1971-1974; mgr thin film eng, Electronic Mat Div, Bell & Howell Res Labs, 1970-1971; consult, Am Safety Razor Div, Philip Morris Co, 1968-1970; asst prof, Roanoke Col, 1968-1970; Electron Tube Div, Int Tel & Tel, 1968-1970; assoc prog mgr ceramic develop, Sprague Elec Co, Mass, 1966-1968; sr chemist thin films, Sprague Elec Co, Mass, 1963-1966; res chemist organometallic, Solvay Process Div, Allied Chem Corp, 1960; Res technician, Metals Div, Kelsey Hayes Co, 1958-1959; Lab technician qual control, Utica Drop Forge & Tool Co, 1956-1959. **Memberships:** Am Vacuum Soc. **Research Statement & Publications:** Thin film preparation and evaluation; magnetic susceptibilities; organometallic compound preparation and evaluation; coordination chemistry; chrome photoplates; III-IV compounds; ferrites; microanalytical services; surface acoustic wave device development; microwave hybrid device development. **Mailing Address:** 3625 W Hidden Lane, Palos Verdes Peninsula, CA 90274.

JANUSEK, LINDA WITEK, NEONATAL SEPSIS, IMMUNE-ENDOCRINE INTERACTIONS. **Personal Data:** b La Salle, Ill, January 11, 1952; m 1975, Alan; c Alex, Marissa & Michael. **Education:** Bradley Univ, BS, 1974; Univ Ill, PhD (physiol), 1978. **Honors & Awards:** Young Investr Award, Circulatory Shock Soc, 1980. **Professional Experience:** PROF, MARCHELLA NIEHOFF SCH NURSING, LOYOLA UNIV MED CTR, as of 2006; PROF ACUTE, CHRONIC & LONG-TERM CARE NURSING, LOYOLA UNIV MED CTR, as of 2004; assoc prof maternal child health nursing, Loyola Univ, beginning 1984; assoc prof physiol & nursing, Loyola Univ, 1984-1993; asst prof, Loyola Univ, 1978-1984. **Memberships:** Am Physiol Soc; Circulatory Shock Soc; Fedn Am Soc Exp Biol. **Research Statement & Publications:** Metabolic and hormonal responses of the neonate to a septic insult; endocrine-immune interactions in the neonate-human. **Mailing Address:** Marcella Niehoff Sch Nursing, Loyola Univ Med Ctr, 2160 S First Ave Bldg 105 Rm 2911, Chicago, IL 60153. **Fax:** 708-216-9555. **E-Mail:** ljanuse@luc.edu

JANUSZ, GERALD JOSEPH, MATHEMATICS. **Personal Data:** b August 20, 1940; American citizen; m 1961, c 2. **Education:** Marquette Univ, BS, 1962; Univ Wis, MS, 1963; Univ Ore, PhD (math), 1965. **Professional Experience:** PROF MATH, UNIV ILL, URBANA, as of 2004; exec ed, J Math Rev, 1990-1992; from asst prof to assoc prof, Univ Ill, Urbana, 1968-1973; instr math, Univ Chicago, 1966-1968; mem, Inst Advan Study, 1965-1966. **Memberships:** Am Math Soc; Math Asn Am. **Research Statement & Publications:** Representations of finite groups; finite dimensional algebras. **Mailing Address:** Dept Math, Univ Ill, 375 Altgeld Hall 1409 W Green St, Urbana, IL 61801-2975. **Fax:** 217-333-9576. **E-Mail:** janusz@math.uiuc.edu

JANUSZ, MICHAEL JOHN, INFLAMMATION IMMUNOBIOLOGY. **Personal Data:** b Pawtucket, RI, February 18, 1954; m 1985. **Education:** RI Col, BA, 1976; Smith Col, AM, 1979; Univ NC, PhD (microbiol & immunol), 1985. **Professional Experience:** SR RES IMMUNOBIOLOGIST, MARION MERRELL DOW RES INST, 1989-; instr & res immunobiologist, Brigham & Women's Hosp & Harvard Med Sch, 1988-1989; fel immunol, Brigham & Women's Hosp & Harvard Med Sch, 1985-1988. **Memberships:** Am Asn Immunologists. **Research Statement & Publications:** Role of proteinases in connective tissue matrix turnover; immunobiology of inflammatory diseases. **Mailing Address:** Marion Merrell Dow Res Inst, 2110 E Galbraith Rd, Cincinnati, OH 45215.

JANUTOLO, DELANO BLAKE, PLANT PATHOLOGY, MYCOLOGY. **Personal Data:** b Bluefield, WVa, July 7, 1952; c 2. **Education:** WVa Univ, BS, 1973; Va Polytech Inst & State Univ, PhD (plant path), 1977. **Professional Experience:** PROF BIOL & DEAN, SCH SCI & HUMANITIES, ANDERSON UNIV, 1977-. **Memberships:** Am Phytopath Soc; Sigma Xi. **Research Statement & Publications:** Evaluation and testing of fungicides; systemic fungicides. **Mailing Address:** Dept Biol, Anderson Univ, 1100 E Fifth St, Anderson, IN 46012. **Fax:** 765-641-3851. **E-Mail:** janutolo@anderson.edu

JANZ, GEORGE JOHN, physical chemistry; deceased, see previous edition for last biography

JANZEN, ALEXANDER FRANK, INORGANIC CHEMISTRY, ORGANOMETALLIC CHEMISTRY. **Personal Data:** b Einlage, Ukraine, April 19, 1940; American citizen; m 1967, Frieda; c Mark, Sonya & Michael. **Education:** McMaster Univ, BSc, 1963; Western Ont Univ, PhD (chem), 1966. **Professional Experience:** Vis Sci, Brook Univ, 1999; PROF CHEM, UNIV MAN, 1978-; vis scientist, Max Planck Inst Exp Med, Ger, 1973; from asst prof to assoc prof, Univ Man, 1967-1978. **Memberships:** Am Chem Soc. **Research Statement & Publications:** Synthesis of inorganic fluorine compounds and study of dynamic properties and reaction mechanisms. **Mailing Address:** Dept Chem, Univ Man, 426 Parker Bldg, Winnipeg, MB R3T 2N2, Can. **Fax:** 204-474-7608. **E-Mail:** ajanzen@cc.umanitoba.ca

JANZEN, DANIEL HUNT, ECOLOGY, EVOLUTION. **Personal Data:** b Milwaukee, Wis, January 18, 1939; c 2. **Education:** Univ Calif, Berkeley, PhD (entom), 1965. **Honors & Awards:** Gleason Award, Am Bot Soc, 1975; Crawford Prize, Royal Swed Acad Sci, 1984. **Professional Experience:** THOMAS G & LOUISE E DIMAURA TERM CHAIR, DEPT BIOL, UNIV PA, as of 2004; PROF BIOL, UNIV PA, 1976-; from assoc prof to prof, Univ Mich, 1972-1976; from asst prof to assoc prof, Univ Chicago, 1968-1972; asst prof biol, Univ Kans, 1965-1968; adv, Orgn Trop Studies, Costa Rica & Costa Rican Nat Park Serv. **Memberships:** Nat Acad Sci; Ecol Soc Am; Am Soc Naturalists; Brit Ecol Soc; Asn Trop Biol; Soc Study Evolution. **Research Statement & Publications:** Interactions of plants and animals, with emphasis on tropical field systems. **Mailing Address:** Dept Biol, Univ Pa, 301 Leidy Lab, Philadelphia, PA 19104. **Fax:** 215-898-8780. **E-Mail:** edjanzen@sas.upenn.edu

JANZEN, EDWARD GEORGE, PHYSICAL ORGANIC CHEMISTRY. **Personal Data:** b Man, May 23, 1932; m 1952, Helen; c Charles G & Beth E. **Education:** Univ Man, BSc, 1957, MSc, 1960; Iowa State Univ, PhD (org chem), 1963. **Honors & Awards:** Fulmer Award, Iowa State Univ; Syntex Award, Can Soc Chem-Chem Inst Can. **Professional Experience:** PROF, UNIV GUELPH, 1986-; DIR MAGNETIC RESONANCE IMAGIN, 1986-; Vis prof & scientist, Okla Med Res Found, 1981 & IBM Instruments, Inc, San Jose, 1982; prof & chmn, Dept Chem, 1976-1986; from asst prof to prof spectros, Univ Ga, 1964-1975; Fel, Dept Chem, Iowa State Univ, 1963-1964. **Memberships:** Fel Can Inst Chem; Electron Paramagnetic Resonance Soc; Soc Free Radical Res; Sigma Xi; Am Chem Soc; Oxygen Soc; Am Soc Mass Spectros; Am Soc Biochem & MolecularBiol. **Research Statement & Publications:** Physical organic, biochemical and biomedical topics in electron spin resonance spectroscopy; spin trapping techniques, development and practice; magnetic resonance imaging and in vivo magnetic resonance spectroscopy. **Mailing Address:** Dept Clin Studies & Biomed Sci-Ont Vet Col, Univ Guelph, Guelph, ON N1G 2W1, Can.

JANZEN, HELMUT HENRY, SOILS & SOILS SCIENCE, ENVIRONMENTAL SCIENCES. **Personal Data:** b 1956; m 1978, Sandra; c Kristina, David & Robert. **Education:** Univ Sask, BSc, 1980, PhD (soil sci), 1984. **Honors & Awards:** b Coaldale, Alta, Aug 4, 1956. **Professional Experience:** RES SCIENTIST SOIL BIOCHEM, AGR & AGRI-FOOD CAN, AS OF 2006; mem sci steering comt, Greenhouse Gas Prog Agr Can, 1992. **Memberships:** Soil Sci Soc Am. **Research Statement & Publications:** Investigation of nutrient cycling (carbon, nitrogen and sulfur) in prairie agroecosystems; greenhouse gas emissions; organic matter dynamics; nitrogen volatilization; litter decomposition; elemental sulfur oxidation. **Mailing Address:** Agr & Agri-Food Can, PO Box 3000, Lethbridge, AB T1J 4B1, Can. **Fax:** 403-382-3156. **E-Mail:** janzen@abrsle.agr.ca

JANZEN, JAY, PHYSICAL CHEMISTRY. **Personal Data:** b Chickasha, Okla, March 24, 1940; m 1986, Charlene; c Paul C & Carla M. **Education:** Univ Kans, BS, 1962; Iowa State Univ, PhD (phys chem), 1968. **Professional Experience:** RES PROF, CHEM ENG DEPT, COLO SCH MINES, CO, 2001-; res assoc, Phillips Res Ctr, Phillips Petrol Co, 1986-; sr res chemist, Phillips Petrol Co, 1968-1986. **Memberships:** Am Chem Soc; Sigma Xi; Soc Rheology. **Research Statement & Publications:** Reinforcement of elastopolymers; polyolefin rheology and property-performance relationships; statistical morphology of particulate materials and composite media; random geometry. **Mailing Address:** Chem Eng Dept, Colo Sch Mines, Golden, CO 80401. **Fax:** 303-273-3730. **E-Mail:** jjanzen@mines.edu

JANZOW, EDWARD F(RANK), NUCLEAR ENGINEERING, MECHANICAL ENGINEERING. **Personal Data:** b St Louis, Mo, March 19, 1941; m 1967, Treva; c Lee A. **Education:** Wash Univ, BS, 1963; Univ Mo, MS, 1964; Univ Ill, Urbana, PhD (nucleareng), 1970; Univ Dayton, MBA, 1981. **Professional Experience:** CHIEF EXEC OFFICER, FRONTIER TECHNOL CORP, 1985-; mgr opers, Monsanto ResCorp, 1981-1984; mgr eng & qual assurance, Monsanto Res Corp, 1979-1981; mgr eng design &develop, Monsanto Res Corp, 1976-1979; supvr design & develop eng, Monsanto Res Corp, 1975-1976; mem comt, Sealed Radioactive Sources, Am Nat Standard Inst, 1974-; engr groupleader, Monsanto Res Corp, 1972-1975; sr res engr, Monsanto Res Corp, 1971-1972; nuclear engprog, Off Water Resources, 1969-1970; asst, Off Water Resources, 1968-1969; NSF traineeship, Univ Ill, Urbana, 1964-1968; NASA traineeship, Univ Mo, Columbia, 1963-1964. **Memberships:** Am Nuclear Soc; Am Soc Testing & Math. **Research Statement & Publications:** Nuclear radiation sources especially Cf-252 neutron sources; research, development and design of such sources and techniques, apparatus and facilities for fabrication; development and design of radioisotope shipping containers and shielding. **Mailing Address:** 1641 Burnett Dr, Xenia, OH 45434. **Fax:** 937-376-5692.

JAOUNI, KATHERINE COOK, MICROBIOLOGY. **Personal Data:** b Alexandria, Va, November 8, 1929; m 1964, Taysir; c Taysir M Jr. **Education:** Col William & Mary, BS, 1949; George Wash Univ, MS, 1952, PhD (microbiol), 1957. **Professional Experience:** RETIRED; pres, Grad Women Sci Inc, 1981-1982; res microbiologist, Infectious Dis Lab, 1978-1994; researcher, Max Planck Inst, Tuebingen, Ger, 1961-1962; researcher, Pasteur Inst & St Vincent de Paul Hosp, France, 1959-1961; virologist, Infectious Dis Lab, 1957-1978; parasitologist, Trop Dis Lab, Nat Inst Allergy & Infectious Dis, 1952-1957; bacteriologist, Alexandria Health Dept, 1949-1952. **Memberships:** Am Soc Trop Med & Hyg; Am Soc Microbiol; Sigma Xi; AAAS; Grad Women Sci. **Research Statement & Publications:** Tissue culture of protozoa and mode of action of drugs against toxoplasma; characterization and antigenic analysis of respiratory viruses; oncogenic virology; viruses of protozoa; mode of action of drugs against protozoa and viruses; science administration. **Mailing Address:** 515 Bradford Dr, Rockville, MD 20850.

JAOUNI, TAYSIR M, ORGANIC CHEMISTRY. **Personal Data:** b Jerusalem, Palestine, August 29, 1924; American citizen; m 1964, c 1. **Education:** Univ Calif, Berkeley, BA, 1950, MA, 1951, BSc, 1960; Univ Colo, MSc, 1963. **Professional Experience:** RES CHEMIST, LAB CHEM, NAT HEART & LUNG INST, NIH, 1963-; Asst chem, Univ Colo, 1960-1963. **Research Statement & Publications:** Synthesis of diribonucleoside phosphates; RNA codewords and protein synthesis; GC/MS. **Mailing Address:** 515 Bradford Dr, Rockville, MD 20850.

JAPAR, STEVEN MARTIN, ATMOSPHERIC CHEMISTRY & PHYSICS. **Personal Data:** b New York, NY, November 11, 1944; m 1984, Teresa Martusiewicz; c 2. **Education:** City Col New York, BS, 1965; Case Inst Technol, PhD (phys chem), 1969. **Honors & Awards:** Arch T Colwell Award, Soc of Automotive Engrs, 1981. **Professional Experience:** STAFF SCIENTIST & SUPVR ATMOSPHERIC CHEM GROUP, FORD MOTOR CO, 1991-; prin res scientist assoc, Res Lab, Ford Motor Co, 1981-1990; instr, NaturalSci Dept, Univ Mich, Dearborn, 1975-1976; sr res scientist, Ford Motor Co, 1973-1980; instr, Chem Dept, Drexel Univ, 1972-1973; fel, Chem Dept, Univ Calif, Riverside, 1971-1972; fel, Div Physics, Nat Res Coun Can, 1969-1971. **Memberships:** Am Chem Soc; Air & Waste Mgt Asn; Sigma Xi. **Research Statement & Publications:** Photochemistry, spectroscopy and chemical kinetics of species important in atmospheric chemistry; Chemistry and physics of gas phase aerosols generated from combustion sources. **Mailing Address:** Ford Motor Co, PO Box 6248, Dearborn, MI 48126. **Fax:** 313-594-2923.

JAPIKSE, DAVID, MECHANICAL ENGINEERING, MANUFACTURING. **Education:** Case Inst Technol, BS, 1965; Purdue Univ, MSc, 1968, PhD (eng sci), 1969. **Honors & Awards:** James Harry Potter Gold Medal, Am Soc Mech Engrs, 1992. **Professional Experience:** CHMN, CONCEPTS NREC BD DIR, as of 2006; FOUNDER, CHMN & CHIEF EXEC OFFICER, CONCEPTS ETI INC, as of 2002; pres, Concepts Eti Inc, 1980-2000; mem, Turbomach Comt, Div Fluids Eng, Am Soc Mech Engrs, 1973-; staff mem, Pratt & Whitney, Creare, Inc; lectr numerous foreigncountries. **Memberships:** Am Inst Aeronaut & Astronaut; Am Soc Mech Engrs; Soc Automotive Engrs; Sigma Xi. **Research Statement & Publications:** Fundamental modeling of turbomachinery processes, especially meanline performance codes; derivation and publishing of two-zone modeling equations suitable for any developing flow; introduction of the TEIS model to describe the thermodynamic state change typical of any bladed row. **Mailing Address:** Concepts ETI Inc, 4 Billings Farm Rd White River Jct, Norwich, VT 05001. **Fax:** 802-296-2325. **E-Mail:** eolson@conceptseti.com

JAQUES, ROBERT PAUL, INSECT PATHOLOGY. **Personal Data:** b Caledonia, Ont, January 1, 1931; m 1954, c 3. **Education:** Univ Toronto, BSA, 1952, MSA, 1954; Cornell Univ, PhD (insect ecol), 1960. **Professional Experience:** RETIRED; assoc fac, Univ Guelph, 1976-1984; res scientist insect path, Res Sta, Harrow, ON, 1967-1991; assoc prof, Acadia Univ, 1965-1967; res assoc biol, Acadia Univ, 1962-1965; res scientist, Can Dept Agr, Kentville, NS, 1954-1967; RES EMER SCIENTIST. **Memberships:** Entom Soc Can; Soc Invert Path; Entom Soc Am. **Research Statement & Publications:** Factors affecting development of disease in populations of insects; persistence of insect viruses in the environment; microbial control of insects. **Mailing Address:** 166 Augustine Dr, Kingsville, ON N9Y 1C5, Can.

JAQUITH, RICHARD HERBERT, INORGANIC CHEMISTRY. **Personal Data:** b Newton, Mass, March 31, 1919; m 1942, c 5. **Education:** Univ Mass BS, 1940, MS, 1942; Mich State Univ, PhD (inorg chem), 1955. **Professional Experience:** ASST VICE PRES, ACAD AFFAIRS, UNIV MD, as of 2003; PROF EMER CHEM, UNIV MD, COLLEGE PARK, as of 2000; ASST VCHANCELLOR ACAD AFFAIRS, UNIV MD, COLLEGE PARK, 1973-; prof chem, Univ MD, College Park, 1965-; from asst prof to assoc prof, UnivMD, College Park, 1954-1965; asst prof, Colby Col, 1947-1954; Instr chem, Univ Conn, 1942-1944 & 1946-1947. **Memberships:** Sigma Xi. **Research Statement & Publications:** Nonaqueous inorganic solvents; rare earth compounds. **Mailing Address:** 5807 Cherrywood Terr No 201, Greenbelt, MD 20770.

JARAMILLO, JORGE, PHARMACOLOGY. **Personal Data:** b Chinchina, Colombia, January 7, 1934; m 1961, c 4. **Education:** Univ Caldas, MD, 1958; Tulane Univ, MS, 1962, PhD (pharmacol), 1966. **Professional Experience:** DIR PHARMACOL, BIO-MEGA INC, 1988-; coordr pharmacol, Bio-MegaInc, 1984-1988; sr res assoc, Ayerst Res Labs, 1977-1984; res assoc pharmacol, Ayerst Res Labs, 1970-1977; sr pharmacologist, Ayerst Res Labs, 1968-1970; asst prof, Univ Conn, 1967-1968; instr, Tulane Univ, 1966-1967. **Memberships:** Pharmacol Soc Can; Soc Toxicol Can; Am Soc Pharmacol Exp Therapeut. **Research Statement & Publications:** Cardiovascular. **Mailing Address:** Dept Pharmacol Bio-Mega Inc, 2100 Cunard St Laval, Montreal, PQ H7S 2G5, Can. **Fax:** 514-682-8434.

JARBOE, CHARLES HARRY, TOXICOKINETICS. **Personal Data:** b Louisville, Ky, October 3, 1928; div, c Jamisene L, Charles H, Richard J, Herman H, Nancy H & Elizabeth A. **Education:** Univ Louisville, BSc, 1951, PhD (chem), 1956. **Professional Experience:** PROF EMER, DEPT PHARMACOL, SCH MED, UNIV LOUISVILLE, 1989-; King Faisal Univ Col Med, Saudi Arabia, 1982-1984 & US Naval Regional Med Ctr, Portsmouth, Va, 1982; vis prof, Univ Utah, 1980; vis prof, Med Sch, Auckland Univ, 1979; Ky Med Asst Prog Formulary Subcomt & Pest Control Adv Bd, Ky Environ Qual Comn, 1978-; vis prof, Med Col Va, Va Commonwealth Univ, 1974; consult, Am Horse Shows Asn, 1973; prof pharmacol & dir, Therapeut & Toxicol Lab, 1972-1989; vis scientist, Sci Div, Abbott Labs, 1970-1971; actg chmn dept pharmacol, Univ Louisville, 1968; asst dean planning & proj coordr, Univ Louisville, 1965-1967; assoc prof, Health Sci Ctr, 1962-1972; consult, Brown & Williamson Tobacco Corp, 1962-1964; spec fel, Nat Heart Inst, 1961-1962; res assoc pharmacol, Sch Med, 1958-1962; chief scientist, Brown & Williamson Tobacco Corp, 1958-1961; Consult, Brown & Williamson Tobacco Corp, 1957-1958; res asst prof org chem, AEC, Univ Louisville, 1956-1958; asst, AEC, Univ Louisville, 1956; Chemist, E I du Pont Del Nemours & Co, 1951-1953. **Memberships:** Am Chem Soc; The Chem Soc; Am Acad Clin Toxicol; Am Soc Pharmacol & Exp Therapeut; NY Acad Sci; Am Col Clin Pharmacol. **Research Statement & Publications:** Kinetic aspects of drug action; human pharmacokinetics; human toxicokinetics. **Mailing Address:** Dept Pharmacol & Toxicol Sch Med, Univ Louisville, Louisville, KY 40292. **Fax:** 502-852-7868.

JARBOE, JERRY K(ENT), ANALYTICAL METHODOLOGY, FOOD ANALYSIS. **Personal Data:** b Indianapolis, Ind, September 28, 1940; m 1977, Sharon; c Linda & Sean. **Education:** Marion Col, BS, 1962; Northeastern Univ, MS, 1970. **Professional Experience:** RETIRED; chief, Advan Foods Br, US Army Natick Res Develop & Eng Ctr, beginning 1993; br chief biohazards assessment & control br, US Army Natick Res Develop & Eng Ctr, 1991-1993; sect chief anal chem & biochem, US Army Natick Res Develop & Eng Ctr, 1988-1991; group leader anal chem, US Army Natick Res Develop & Eng Ctr, 1978-1988; res chemist food sci, US Army Natick Res Develop & Eng Ctr, 1962-1978. **Memberships:** Am Chem Soc; Inst Food Technologists; Sigma Xi. **Research Statement & Publications:** Separation and analysis of foods; food preservation technologies; methodologies for measuring protection against chemical warfare agents. **Mailing Address:** 9 Simpson Dr, Framingham, MA 01701.

JARBOE, THOMAS RICHARD, PLASMA PHYSICS. **Personal Data:** b Paxton, Ill, August 23, 1945; m 1970, c 5. **Education:** Univ Ill, BS, 1967; Univ Calif, Berkeley, PhD (plasma physics), 1974. **Professional Experience:** Adj prof physics, Univ Wash, as of 2002; PROF NUCLEAR ENG, UNIV WASH, 1989-; group leader, Los Alamos Nat Lab, 1983-1989; physicist fusion res, Los Alamos Nat Lab, 1974-1980; Pysicist optics, Naval

Weapons Ctr, China Lake, Calif, 1968. **Memberships:** Fel Am Phys Soc. **Research Statement & Publications:** Relaxation processes during the interaction of plasma and magnetic field in toroidal geometry; goal is to understand helicity conservation during plasma relaxation processes to understand relaxation in general. **Mailing Address:** Dept Aeronaut & Astronaut, Col Eng, Univ Wash, AERB 438 Box 352400, Seattle, WA 98195-2400. **Fax:** 206-543-4719. **E-Mail:** jarboe@aa.washington.edu

JARDETZKY, OLEG, MOLECULAR BIOLOGY, PHARMACOLOGY. **Personal Data:** b Belgrade, Yugoslavia, February 11, 1929; American citizen; m 1965, Erika; c Alexander, Theodore & Paul. **Education:** Macalester Col, BA, 1950; Univ Minn, MD, 1954, PhD (chem physiol), 1956. **Honorary Degrees:** DSc, Macalester Col, 1974; LLD, Calif Western Univ, 1978; MD, Karl-Franzens Univ, 1994. **Honors & Awards:** Irvine McQuarrie scholar award, 1954; Henry T Kaiser Award, 1973; Alexander von Humboldt Award, 1977; Merian lectr, Mich State Univ, 1984; LinusPauling lectr, 1984. **Professional Experience:** DIR EMER, MAGNETIC RESONANCE LAB, SCH MED, STANFORD UNIV, 1997-; co-dir, Int Sch Struct Biol & Magnetic Resonance, 1993-1997; lectr, 58th Ann Meeting Japanese Biochem Soc, 1985; vis lectr, Weismann Inst, Israel, 1984; vis prof, USSR Acad Sci, 1984; chmn, Nat Comn, 10th Int Conf Magnetic Resonance Biol Syst, Stanford Univ, 1982; vis prof, Univ Calif, Riverside, 1982; lectr, FrMinistry foreign affairs, 1979; vis prof, MPI, Heidelberg, 1977; vis fel, Merton Col, Oxford, 1976; dir, magnetic resonance lab, Sch Med, Stanford Univ, 1975-1997; actg chmn pharmacol, Sch Med, Stanford Univ, 1973-1974; USSR Acad Sci lectr, 1970; vis prof, Albany, 1970; PROF MOLECULAR PHARMACOL, SCH MED, STANFORD UNIV, 1969-; exec dir basic med sci, Merck Inst Therapeut Res, 1968-1969; basic sci lectr, Med Ctr, Univ Calif, San Francisco, 1968; dir, Dept Biophys & Pharmacol, Merck Sharp & Dohme Res Labs, NJ, 1966-1968; chem Students Asnlectr, Univ Amsterdam, 1966; vis scientist, Cambridge Univ, 1965-1966; Japan Chem Soc lectr, Univ Tokyo, 1965; consult coun drugs, AMA, 1964; vis prof, State Univ NY, Buffalo, 1963; consult, Mass Gen Hosp, 1961-1967; asst prof, Harvard Med Sch, 1959-1966; assoc pharmacol, Harvard Med Sch, 1957-1959; Nat Res Coun fel chem, Calif InstTechnol, 1956-1957; res asst physiol, Univ Minn, 1950-1954; Am Heart Asn fel, Univ Minn. **Memberships:** fel AAAS; Am Chem Soc; Sigma Xi; Biophys Soc; Int Soc Magnetic Resonance; Soc Magnetic Resonance Med; Am Soc Biochem & Molecular Biol; Protein Soc. **Research Statement & Publications:** Molecular mechanisms of protein function; biological applications of nuclear magnetic resonance. **Mailing Address:** Dept Molecular Pharmacol, Stanford Univ Sch Med, Stanford, CA 94305-5337. **Fax:** 650-723-2253. **E-Mail:** jardetzky@stanford.edu

JARDIN, STEPHEN CHARLES, PLASMA PHYSICS. **Personal Data:** b Oakland, Calif, August 28, 1947; m 1929, Marilyn; c Michael & Emily. **Education:** Univ Calif, Berkeley, BS, 1970; Mass Inst Technol, MS (nuclear eng) & MS (physics), 1973; Princeton Univ, PhD (astrophys), 1976. **Professional Experience:** DEP HEAD, PRINCETON PLASMA PHYSICS LAB, 1991-; PROF, DEPT ASTROPHYS SCI, PRINCETON UNIV, 1986-; PRIN RES PHYSICIST, PRINCETON PLASMA PHYSICS LAB, 1986-; Assoc prof, Dept Astrophys Sci, Princeton Univ, 1984-1986; res physicist, Princeton Plasma Physics Lab, 1981-1986; res staff, Princeton Plasma Physics Lab, 1978-1981; fel, Princeton Plasma Physics Lab, 1976-1978; physicist, Physics Int Co, 1970-1972; Sci comput programmer, Sandia Corp, 1967-1969; consult, EGG Idaho. **Memberships:** Fel Am Phys Soc. **Research Statement & Publications:** Theoretical and computational research of magnetohydrodynamics equilibrium, stability and transport of Tokamaks and other magnetically confined plasma configurations; granted four US patents. **Mailing Address:** Plasma Physics Lab, Princeton Univ PO Box 451, Princeton, NJ 08543.

JARDINE, D(ONALD) A(NDREW), COMPUTER SCIENCE. **Personal Data:** b Kingston, Ont, July 23, 1930; div, c 2. **Education:** Queen's Univ Ont, BSc, 1952, MSc, 1954; Univ Del, PhD, 1957. **Professional Experience:** PROF EMER COMPUT, QUEENS UNIV, as of 2005; prof, Queens Univ Ont, beginning 1973; head dept, Queens Univ Ont, 1973-1978; assoc prof comput sci, Queens Univ Ont, 1970-1973; res assoc, Du Pont Can Ltd, 1968-1970; pres, Common Comput Users Group, 1966-1968; res engr, Du Pont Can Ltd, 1956-1968. **Memberships:** Asn Comput Mach. **Research Statement & Publications:** Data base management systems; data description languages. **Mailing Address:** Dept Comput Sci, Queens Univ, Kingston, ON K7L 3N6, Can.

JARDINE, IAN, MASS SPECTROMETRY. **Personal Data:** b Glasgow, Scotland, September 17, 1948. **Education:** Univ Glasgow, BSc, 1970, PhD (chem), 1973. **Professional Experience:** DIR MKT, FINNEGAN MAT, 1992-; dir anal biochem, Finnegan Mat, 1988-1991; from assoc prof to prof pharmacol, Mayo Med Sch, 1979-1988; consult pharmacol, Mayo Clin, 1979-1988; asst prof med chem & pharmacog, Sch Pharm & Pharmacol Sci, PurdueUniv, West Lafayette, 1976-1979; fel pharmacol, Med Sch, Johns Hopkins Univ, 1973-1976. **Memberships:** Am Chem Soc; Am Soc Mass Spectrometry; AAAS. **Research Statement & Publications:** Development of mass spectrometric methods for biochemical and pharmacological analysis. **Mailing Address:** Finnegan Mat, 355 River Oaks Pkwy, San Jose, CA 95134. **Fax:** 408-435-1481. **E-Mail:** ijardine@finnigan.com

JARDINE, JOHN MCNAIR, ATOMIC ENERGY, MATHEMATICAL STATISTICS. **Personal Data:** b Moncton, NB, June 25, 1919; m 1945, c 2. **Education:** Mt Allison Univ, BSc, 1940; McGill Univ, MSc, 1948. **Professional Experience:** RETIRED; scientific adv mining, Atomic Energy Control Bd, Can, 1972-1981; res supt, Eldorado Nuclear Ltd, 1969-1972; supt, Metall Lab, Res & Develop Div, 1962-1969; chief chemist, Refining Div, Eldorado Mining & Refining Ltd, 1953-1962; chief analyst, Refining Div, Eldorado Mining & Refining Ltd, 1951-1953; res chemist, Refining Div, Eldorado Mining & Refining Ltd, 1948-1951. **Memberships:** Fel Chem Inst Can; Can Soc Chem Eng. **Research Statement & Publications:** Analytical chemistry in the Canadian uranium industry; solvent extraction of uranium and thorium; separation of copper, cobalt and nickel by solvent extraction; development of process for production of hafnium free zirconium metal from zircon sands; transportation of radioactive materials; uranium mining and milling. **Mailing Address:** 467 Broadview Ave, Ottawa, ON K2A 2L2, Can.

JARDINE, PHILIP M, SOIL CHEMISTRY. **Personal Data:** b November 13, 1959; m, c 2. **Education:** Univ Delaware, BS, 1981 & MS, 1983; Va Polytech Inat State Univ, PhD (Soil Chem/Physics), 1985. **Professional Experience:** RES STAFF SCIENTIST, ENVIRON SCI DIV, OAK RIDGE NAT LAB, 1986-; res assoc, Dept Agronomy, Va Polytech Inst & state Univ, 1985-1986; grad res asst, Dept Agronomy, Va Polytech Inst & state Univ, 1983-1985; grad res asst, Dept Plant & Soil Sci, Univ Delaware, 1981-1983; independent undergrad res, Dept Plant & Soil Sci, Univ Delaware, 1980-1981; independent undergrad res, Dept Chem, Univ Delaware, 1979-1980. **Mailing Address:** Environ Sci Div, Oak Ridge Nat Lab, POBox 2008 Bethel Valley Rd, Oak Ridge, TN 37831-6036. **Fax:** 865-576-8646. **E-Mail:** jardinepm@ornl.gov

JARED, ALVA HARDEN, WOOD TECHNOLOGY, DRAFTING & DESIGN. **Personal Data:** b Roseville, Ill, January 15, 1934; m 1955, c 2. **Education:** Western Ill State Col, BS, 1955; Ball State Teachers Col, MAE, 1956; Ariz State Univ, EdD (indust educ), 1968. **Professional Experience:** RETIRED; res asst, Ariz State Univ, 1965-1966; prof indust educ, Univ Wis-Platteville, beginning 1956; consult energy mgt & construct. **Memberships:** Int Technol Educ Asn; Nat Asn Indust Technol; Int Coun Indust Teacher Educators. **Research Statement & Publications:** Technology management; supervision and training of workers; construction management; energy management; technology education; author of several publications. **Mailing Address:** 945 St James Circle, Platteville, WI 53818.

JAREM, JOHN, ELECTRICAL ENGINEERING. **Personal Data:** b Jarembina, Czech, July 4, 1921; American citizen; c 4. **Education:** Polytech Inst Brooklyn, BEE, 1947, MEE, 1950; Univ Pa, MS, 1957, PhD (plasmaphysics), 1960. **Professional Experience:** RETIRED; Inst Defense Analysis, 1964- & Aero Chem, 1966-; prof, Dept ElecEng, Drexel Univ, 1964-1990; head, Dept Elec Eng, Drexel Univ, 1964-1968; Consult, RadioCorp Am, 1964-1965; staff engr dir & systs engr, Radio Corp Am, 1963-1964; sr staff mem, InstDefense Anal, 1962-1963; engr, Radio Corp Am, NJ, 1959-1962; mem systs eng tech staff, RadioCorp Am, NJ, 1954-1959; math specialist, Lockheed Aircraft Corp, Calif, 1951-1954; asst profelec eng & math, US Naval Postgrad Sch, 1948-1951; Electronic res engr, Tele-Register Corp, NY, 1947. **Memberships:** Sr mem Inst Elec & Electronics Engrs; Am Phys Soc. **Research Statement & Publications:** Systems engineering; applied mathematics; plasma physics. **Mailing Address:** Univ Ala, 4701 University Dr, Huntsville, AL 35899. **Fax:** 256-824-6463. **E-Mail:** jarem@ecu.uah.edu

JARETT, LEONARD, CLINICAL PATHOLOGY, BIOCHEMISTRY. **Personal Data:** b Lubbock, Tex, August 25, 1936; m 1962, c 3. **Education:** Rice Univ, BA, 1958; Univ Pa, MA, 1982; Wash Univ, MD, 1962. **Honors & Awards:** David Rumbough Award, Juv Diabetes Found, 1980; Cotlove Award, Acad Clin Lab Physicians & Scientists, 1985. **Professional Experience:** DISTINGUISHED PROF DEPT PATH & LAB MED, SCH MED, UNIV PA, as of 1999; mem sci adv bd, metab study sect, 1983-1987; mem adv bd, Juv Diabetes Found, 1981-1984; mem sci adv bd, St Jude Children's Res Hosp, 1980-1983; prof & chmn dept path & lab med, Sch Med, Univ Pa, beginning 1980; prof path & med, Sch Med, 1975-1980; dir labs & head div lab med, Barnes Hosp, 1969-1980; head div lab med, Wash Univ, 1969-1975; from instr path to assoc prof path & med, Wash Univ, 1966-1975; res assoc, sect cellular physiol, lab biochem, Nat Heart Inst, 1964-1966; resident, Barnes Hosp, St Louis, Mo, 1963-1964; intern path, Barnes Hosp, St Louis, Mo, 1962-1963. **Memberships:** Endocrine Soc; Acad Clin Lab Physicians & Scientists; Am Soc Biol Chemists; Am Fedn Clin Res; fel Am Soc Clin Path; Am Asn Physicians; Am Soc Clin Invest. **Research Statement & Publications:** Biochemical and ultrastructural techniques in the study of signal transduction by insulin. **Mailing Address:** Dept Path & Lab Med, Univ Pa, 217A John Morgan Bldg 6085, Philadelphia, PA 19104-4283. **Fax:** 215-573-2350. **E-Mail:** jarett@mail.med.upenn.edu

JARGIELLO, PATRICIA, MOLECULAR GENETICS. **Personal Data:** b Erie, Pa, July 9, 1944. **Education:** Mercyhurst Col, BA, 1966; Univ Pittsburgh, PhD (microbiol), 1973. **Professional Experience:** ASST RES PROF MICROBIOL, MED SCH, UNIV PITTSBURGH, 1977-; instr, Med Sch, Univ Pittsburgh, 1974-1976; vis fel cytogenetics, Southbury Training Sch Hosp, 1974; fel pediat, Med Sch, Univ Pittsburgh, 1973-1976; instr, Univ Parana, Brazil, 1972-1973; teaching asst biol, Univ Pittsburgh, 1967-1968; lab asst, Fed Bur Invest, 1966-1967. **Memberships:** Am Soc Human Genetics; Genetics Soc Am; Tissue Cult Asn; Am Soc Microbiol; AAAS. **Research Statement & Publications:** Regulation of genes coding for enzymes involved in deoxynucleoside catabolism and deoxyribose utilization in salmonella; regulation of globin chain synthesis and hemoglobin formation in human fibroblast-rabbit erythroblast heterokaryons; ribose metabolism in hepatoma; metaphase chromosome isolation. **Mailing Address:** Med Ctr, Univ Pittsburgh, Coraopolis, PA 15108.

JARGON, JERRY ROBERT, PETROLEUM ENGINEERING, CHEMICAL ENGINEERING. **Personal Data:** b Beckemeyer, Ill, August 2, 1939; m Jeannette. **Education:** Univ Ill, BS, 1963; Univ Denver, MS, 1967. **Professional Experience:** INDUST ADV, RESERVIOR ENG, IRESERVOIR.COM, as of 2003; consult, JRJ Consult, 2002-; eng adv bd, Univ Denver, 1989-1999; mgr, Dept Reservoir Mgt, Marathon Oil Co, 1988-1999; sr tech consult, Marathon Oil Co, 1987-1988; ed, Gaswell Testing, 1985-; sr staff engr, Marathon Oil Co, 1985-1987; tech ed, J Petrol Tech, 1985-1986; adv sr engr, Marathon Oil Co, 1980-1985; sr engr petrol technol, Marathon Oil Co, 1977-1980; mem, Monogr Rev Comt Gas Well Performance, 1977-1980; formation evalu comt, Nat Meeting, 1975; prog comt, Rocky Mt Region, 1974-1975; lectr continuing educ courses, Soc Petrol Engrs, 1973-1974; adv engr prod res, Marathon Oil Co, 1972-1977; engr, Marathon Oil Co, 1966-1972; assoc engr, Marathon Oil Co, 1963-1966; assoc engr res, Chicago Bridge & Iron Co, 1962. **Memberships:** Soc Petrol Engrs; assoc Inst Mech Engrs; Opers Res Soc Am. **Research Statement & Publications:** Reservoir modeling and engineering; pressure transient testing in wells; multiphase flow in wells and pipelines. **Mailing Address:** iReservoir Com, Ste 2000, 1490 W Canal Court, Littleton, CO 80120. **Fax:** 303-713-1112.

JARIWALA, SHARAD LALLUBHAI, FERMENTATION, BIOTECHNOLOGY. **Personal Data:** b Bombay, India, October 15, 1940; m 1969, c 2. **Education:** Univ Bombay, BSChE, 1962; Johns Hopkins Univ, PhD (chem eng), 1966. **Professional Experience:** VPRES FERMENTATION OPER, UPJOHN CO, 1984-; dir, FermentationRes & Develop, 1983-1984; group mgr, Fermentation Res & Develop, 1980-1983; mgr, Fermentation Res & Develop, 1977-1979; head fermentation prod prod, Fermentation Res &Develop, 1975-1976; sr scientist, Fermentation Res & Develop, 1970-1975; Res engr, TennecoChem, Inc, 1966-1970. **Memberships:** Am Inst Chem Engrs; Am Chem Soc. **Research Statement & Publications:** Developing new technology for the separation and recovery of antibiotics from fermentation broths; separations technology; reaction engineering in fixed and fluidized beds; liquid phase oxidations. **Mailing Address:** BIO Pharmic Int Inc, 512 Barberry, Portage, MI 49002.

JARIWALLA, RAXIT JAYANTILAL, VIROLOGY, INTEGRATIVE MEDICINE. **Personal Data:** b Bombay, India, November 18, 1949; American citizen; m 1990, Sonal; c Neil R & Nisha R. **Education:** Bombay Univ, BS, 1971; Med Col Wis, MS, 1974, PhD (microbiol), 1976. **Professional Experience:** STUDY DIR, CALIF INST MED RES, as of 2006; instr, bio informatics cert prog, UCSC Extension, 2000-; tech coordr, James Flood Sci & Technol Sch, 1996-1997; prin res investr, Calif Inst Med Res, beginning 1996; consult, Div AIDS Treatment Res Initiative, 1994-1996; head, Virol Prog, 1992-1996; co-organizer, XVI Int Herpesvirus Workshop, Asilomar, Calif, 1991; prin investr, NCI sponsored res grant, Linus Pauling Inst Sci Med, 1986-; head, Viral Carcinogenesis & Immunol Prog, 1986-1992; Guest lectr, virol course, Dept Med Microbiol, Stanford Univ, 1985-1986; sr scientist, Linus Pauling Inst Sci Med, 1984-1996; res scientist, Linus Pauling Inst Sci Med, 1982-1984; instr, Div Biophys, 1979-1982; fel, Div Biophys, Sch Hyg & Pub Health, Johns Hopkins Univ, 1976-1979. **Memberships:** AAAS. **Research Statement & Publications:** HIV suppression and immunomodulation by micronutrients; control of tumor growth and apoptosis by biological/dietary antioxidants. **Mailing Address:** Calif Inst Med Res, 2260 Clove Dr, San Jose, CA 95128. **E-Mail:** ganesh5@ix.netcom.com

JARKE, FRANK HENRY, PHYSICAL CHEMISTRY, ANALYTICAL CHEMISTRY. **Personal Data:** b Bloomington, Ill, March 28, 1946; m 1971, Lynn. **Education:** Southern Ill Univ, BA, 1969; Ill Inst Technol, MS, 1974. **Professional Experience:** SAFETY DIR, GE ENERGY, 2001-; dir, Support Serv, Mostardi-Platt Assoc Inc, 1995-2001; lab dir, Support Serv, Mostardi-Platt Assoc Inc, 1993-1995; mgr, Qual Prog, Geneva, 1987-1993; asst mgr, Environ Waste Mgt, EML Waste Mgt, Oak Brook, Ill, 1983-1987; mgr anal serv, chem waste mgt, Riverdale, Ill, 1981-1983; res chemist odor sci, IIT Res Inst, 1978-1981; asst chemist to assoc chemist, IIT Res Inst, 1969-1978. **Memberships:** Am Chem Soc; Am Soc Heating Refrig & Air-Conditioning Engrs. **Research Statement & Publications:** Fundamental and applied research of odors and air pollution; development and use of both subjective and objective methods using humans as detectors. **Mailing Address:** GE Energy Emissions, St Paul, MN 55102. **Fax:** 630-530-6630.

JARMAKANI, JAY M, PEDIATRIC CARDIOLOGY. **Personal Data:** American citizen. **Education:** Damascus Univ, BCP, 1956, MD, 1962. **Professional Experience:** DIR CARDIOPULMONARY LAB &, MED CTR, UNIV CALIF, LOS ANGELES, 1978-; PROF PEDIAT, UNIV CALIF, LOS ANGELES, 1978-; assoc prof, Med Ctr, Univ Calif, Los Angeles, 1973-1978; asst prof pediat, Med Ctr, Duke Univ, 1968-1973; fel, Med Ctr, Duke Univ, 1966-1968; fel pediatcardiol, Children's Hosp Pittsburgh, 1965-1966; pediat resident, Buffalo Children's Hosp & Children's Hosp Philadelphia, 1963-1965. **Memberships:** Soc Pediat Res; fel Am Col Cardiol; Am Heart Asn; Am Physiol Soc; Int Soc Heart Res. **Research Statement & Publications:** Developmental myocardial function with emphasis on congenital heart disease and the effect of hypoxia on cardiac cell function. **Mailing Address:** Dept Pediat, Univ Calif Med Ctr, Rm B2-441 10833 Le Conte Ave, Los Angeles, CA 90095-1398. **Fax:** 310-825-9524.

JARMIE, NELSON, nuclear physics, taxanomic mycology; deceased, see previous edition for last biography

JARNAGIN, KURT, STRUCTURE FUNCTION STUDIES ON G-PROTEIN COUPLED RECEPTORS, MECHANISM OF RECEPTOR SIGNAL TRANSDUCTION. **Personal Data:** b New Haven, Conn, March 9, 1956; m 1978, Alisha; c Karen & Helen. **Education:** NC State Univ, BS, 1978; Univ Wis-Madison, PhD (biochem), 1984. **Honors & Awards:** E K Frey-E Werle Prom Prize, 1993. **Professional Experience:** VPRES, DEPT BIOL SCI & CHEM GENOMICS, ICONIX PHARMACEUT INC, as of 2004; dept head, Syntex Discovery Res, beginning 1995; res sect leader, Syntex Discovery Res, 1990-1995; staff researcher II, Syntex Discovery Res, 1988-1990; staff researcher I, Syntex Discovery Res, 1986-1988; fel, Nat Juv Diabetes Found, 1985-1986; res assoc, Univ Calif, San Francisco, 1984-1986. **Memberships:** Protein Soc; Am Chem Soc. **Research Statement & Publications:** Mediators and mechanisms by which inflammation and pain begins and perpetuates; acute inflammation and pain, such as that occurring post injury and chronic inflammatory disease, such as arthritis and asthma; molecular biology of inflammatory receptors and intra cellular signal transduction molecules. **Mailing Address:** Iconix Pharmaceut, Inc, 325 E Middlefield R, Mtain View, CA 94043. **Fax:** 650-567-5545.

JARNAGIN, RICHARD CALVIN, PHYSICAL CHEMISTRY. **Personal Data:** b Dallas, Tex, August 26, 1930; m 1952, c 2. **Education:** Southern Methodist Univ, BS, 1952; Yale Univ, PhD, 1958. **Professional Experience:** PROF EMER, UNIV NC, CHAPEL HILL, as of 2004; Guggenheim fel, 1967-1968 & NSF fel, Sandia Nat Labs, 1978-1979; prof chem, Univ Nc, Chapel Hill, beginning 1968; from instr to assoc prof, Univ NC, Chapel Hill, 1958-1968; Res chemist, Wright Air Develop Ctr, US Air Force, 1953-1955. **Memberships:** Am Chem Soc; fel Am Phys Soc. **Research Statement & Publications:** Electrical and optical properties of molecular systems; photo conduction in organic solids and liquids; kinetics of excited molecular states; catalytic properties of solid oxides and stabilization of oxide films. **Mailing Address:** Dept Chem CB 3290, Univ NC, Chapel Hill, NC 27599.

JAROLMEN, HOWARD, MEDICAL MICROBIOLOGY, GENETICS. **Personal Data:** b New York, NY, October 19, 1937; c David & Amy. **Education:** Alfred Univ, BA, 1958; Hahnemann Med Col, MS, 1960, PhD (microbiol), 1964. **Professional Experience:** Prin res microbiologist, Fermentation Process Res & Develop Dept, Lederle Labs Div, 1980-1996; group leader, Dept Microbiol & Chemother, 1976-1980; head, Dept Microbiol & Chemother, 1974-1976; group leader bact chemother, Am Cyanamid Co, 1970-1974; res bacteriologist, Am Cyanamid Co, 1967-1970; NIH fel genetics, Cornell Univ, 1964-1967. **Memberships:** Am Soc Microbiol; Soc Indust Microbiol. **Research Statement & Publications:** In vitro and vivo studies of transferable resistance amongst the Enterobacteriaceae; veterinary microbiology; prophylaxis and therapy of experimental infections; bacterial mutagenicity testing; antibiotic discoveries, discovery of antimycobacterials and antiparasitics; strain and media improvement for antibiotic-producing cultures. **Mailing Address:** 41 Pleasant Ave, Saddle River, NJ 07458. **E-Mail:** jarolmem@cs.com

JARON, DOV, BIOMEDICAL ENGINEERING. **Personal Data:** b Tel Aviv, Israel, October 29, 1935; American citizen; m 1978, Brooke; c Shulamit & Tamara. **Education:** Univ Denver, BS, 1961; Univ Pa, PhD (biomed eng), 1967. **Professional Experience:** CALHOUN DISTINGUISHED PROF MED, SCH BIOMED ENG, SCI & HEALTH SYST, DREXEL UNIV, as of 2003; prof & dir biomed eng & sci inst, Drexel Univ, 1980-1996; chmn, Sixth Ann New Eng Bioengineering Conf, 1978; consult circulatory syst devices panel, Food & DrugAdmin, 1976-1979; from assoc prof toprof biomed eng, Univ RI, 1973-1980; dir surg res lab, Sinai Hosp, Detroit, 1970-1973; Sr res assoc, Maimonides Med Ctr, 1967-1970. **Memberships:** Biomed Eng Soc; AAAS; NY Acad Sci; fel Inst Elec & Electronics Engrs; Am SocArtificial Internal Organs; Eng Med & Biol Soc (vpres 1984-1985 pres 1986-1987); Int Soc ArtificialOrgans. **Research Statement & Publications:** Development, physiologic evaluation, control, and optimization of mechanical cardiac assist devices; Cardiovascular dynamics and assessment of cardiovascular function; Microcirculation dynamics; Cardiovascular function under stress; Modeling of biological systems; Biomedical instrumentation; Engineering aspects of health care; Mechanisms of nitric oxide in the microcirculation. **Mailing Address:** Sch Biomed Eng, Sci & Health Systs, Drexel Univ, Commonwealth 7-725, Philadelphia, PA 19104-0001. **Fax:** 215-895-4983. **E-Mail:** dov.jaron@drexel.edu

JAROS, JOHN A, PHYSICS. **Education:** Univ Calif, Berkeley, Phd (Physics), 1975. **Professional Experience:** CHAIR, SLAC HEP FACULTY, 2001-. **Mailing Address:** SLAC, 2575 Sand Hill Rd, Menlo Park, CA 94025. **Fax:** 650- 926-3826. **E-Mail:** john@slac.stanford.edu

JAROWSKI, CHARLES I, PHARMACEUTICAL CHEMISTRY. **Personal Data:** b Baltimore, Md, July 29, 1917; m 1945, c 3. **Education:** Univ Md, BS, 1938, PhD (pharmaceut chem), 1943. **Professional Experience:** RETIRED; chmn, Dept Allied Health & Indust Sci, 1978-1988; from assoc prof to prof pharmaceut, St Johns Univ, 1969-1988; dir, Chas Pfizer & Co, Inc, 1960-1969; mgr pharmaceut res & develop, Chas Pfizer & Co, Inc, 1950-1960; res chemist, Chas Pfizer & Co, Inc, 1948-1950; chief chemist, Vick Chem Co, NY, 1946-1948; res chemist, Wyeth Inc, Pa, 1944-1946; fel, Univ Ill, 1942-1944. **Memberships:** Am Pharmaceut Asn. **Research Statement & Publications:** Synthesis of antibacterial agents, antioxidants, and medicinals; antioxidant for food and drug industry; germicidal steam aerosolic compounds; antibiotic derivatives; drug detoxification; scientific nutrition; drug delivery systems. **Mailing Address:** 67 Harbor Lane, Massapequa Park, NY 11762.

JARRELL, JOSEPH ANDY, INSTRUMENTATION, BIOPHYSICS. **Personal Data:** b Bad Kissengr, Ger, March 5, 1950. **Education:** Mass Inst Technol, BS, 1971, PhD (physics), 1979. **Professional Experience:** SCIENTIST, WATERS CO, as of 2004; DIR, WATERS CHROMATOGRAPHY, DIV MILLTORE, 1986-; res assoc, Mass Inst Technol, 1978-1985. **Memberships:** Am Phys Soc; Am Vacuum Soc. **Mailing Address:** 11 Hyde Ave, Newton Highlands, MA 02161.

JARRELL, WESLEY MICHAEL, PLANT-SOIL RELATIONSHIPS, ECOSYSTEM SCIENCE. **Personal Data:** b Forest Grove, Ore, May 23, 1948; m 1972, Linda; c Benjamin & Emily. **Education:** Stanford Univ, BA, 1970; Ore State Univ, MS, 1974, PhD (soil sci), 1977. **Honors & Awards:** Alex B Laurie Award, Am Soc Hort Sci, 1979. **Professional Experience:** PROF & HEAD, DEPT NATURAL RESOURCES & ENVIRON SCI, UNIV ILL, URBANA-CHAMPAIGN, 2003-; sr scientist, Discovery Farms Prog, Univ Wis-Madison, 2001-2002; PRES, DYNAMBIO LLC, MADISON, 1999-; head environ sci & eng, Ore Grad Inst Sci & Technol, 1992-1998; prof environ sci & eng, Ore Grad Inst, 1991-1999; assoc prof, Ore Grad Inst Sci &Technol, 1988-1991; Benchmark, 1984 & Jardinier, 1987-; dir, Dry Lands Res Inst, 1985-1988; consult, Allergan Pharmaceut, 1980-1985; from asst prof to assoc prof soil & plant relationships, Univ Calif, Riverside, 1976-1988. **Memberships:** Soil Sci Soc Am; Am Soc Agron; Am Soc Hort Sci; Ecol Soc Am; AAAS. **Research Statement & Publications:** Relationships between soil conditions and plant growth, water quality and air quality; restoration of disturbed landscapes to stable ecosystems; nutrient and hydrologic cycles, particularly the interactions between hydrology and elemental transport. **Mailing Address:** Dept Natural Resources & Environ Sci Univ Ill, W-503 Turner Hall 1102 S Goodwin Ave, Urbana, IL 61801. **Fax:** 217-244-3219. **E-Mail:** wjarrell@uiuc.edu

JARRET, RONALD MARCEL, PHYSICAL ORGANIC. **Personal Data:** b Woonsocket, RI, December 22, 1960; m 1982, Elizabeth; c 3. **Education:** RI Col, BA, 1982, BS, 1982; Yale Univ, PhD (chem), 1987. **Professional Experience:** CHAIR & PROF CHEM, COL HOLY CROSS, as of 2004; assoc prof org chem, Col Holy Cross, beginning 1992; prin investr, NSFgrants, 1988-1994; asst prof, Col Holy Cross, 1986-1992. **Memberships:** Am Chem Soc. **Research Statement & Publications:** Generate novel carbocations and use spectroscopic methods for structure identification. **Mailing Address:** Dept Chem, Holy Cross Col, Haberlin 309, Worcester, MA 01610. **Fax:** 508-793-3530. **E-Mail:** rjarret@holycross.edu

JARRETT, ELZBIETA, MATHEMATICS. **Education:** Wroclaw Univ, Poland, MS; Western Mich Univ, PhD, 1981. **Professional Experience:** FAC, ACAD SENATE MODESTO JR COL, as of 2005. **Mailing Address:** Modesto Jr Col, 435 Col Ave, Modesto, CA 95350. **Fax:** 209-575-6859.

JARRETT, HARRY WELLINGTON, III, HPLC PROTEIN CHEMISTRY. **Personal Data:** b Charleston, SC, June 19, 1950; div, c Harry IV, Alexander & Patience. **Education:** Univ SC, BS, 1972; Univ NC, PhD (biochem), 1976. **Honors & Awards:** Lutcher Brown Distinguished PROF BIOCHEM, UTSA, 2006-present; NIH Grant Awards 1988-present; MDA Grant Awards 1992-present; SGAEC Excellence in Teaching Award, UTHSC, 1992; NIH Individual Postdoctoral Fellowship Award, 1977-1980. **Professional Experience:** PROF BIOCHEM, UNIV TX SAN ANTONIO, 2006-; PROF BIOCHEM, UNIV TENN, MEMPHIS, 1994-2005; assoc prof biochem, Univ Tenn, Memphis, 1989-1994; from asst prof to assoc prof biol, Ind Univ-Purdue Univ, Indianapolis, 1982-1989; asst biochemist biochem, Univ Ga, 1980-1982; fel chem, Univ Calif, San Diego, 1977-1980; fel biochem, Mayo Clin, 1976-1977. **Memberships:** Am Soc Biochem & Molecular Biol; Am Chem Soc. **Research Statement & Publications:** The signaling role of the membrane protein complex responsible for many muscular dystrophies is a main area; development of new supports for affinity, ion exchange, gel filtration and DNA high pressure liquid chromatography. **Mailing Address:** Dept Chem, 6900 N Loop 1604 W, San Antonio, TX 78249. **Fax:** 210-458-7428. **E-Mail:** harry.jarrett@utsa.edu

JARRETT, HOWARD STARKE, JR, solid state physics; deceased, see previous edition for last biography

JARRETT, JEFFREY E, MANAGEMENT SCIENCE. **Personal Data:** b Bronx, NY, December 13, 1940; m 1964, Ruth; c Michael, Debra & Daniel. **Education:** Univ Mich, BA, 1962; NY Univ, MBA, 1963, PhD (statist/opers res), 1967. **Professional Experience:** Outstanding res scholar, URICBA, 1991-1992; mem, Prog Community Pharm Mgt, W M S Apple Found, 1991; consult, RI Pub Utilities Comn, 1984; chmn, Dept Mgt Sci, 1983-1989; consult, RI Dept Health, 1983; prof, Ohio Savings & Loan Acad, 1981-1991; consult, Abt Assocs, 1979; Overseas Progs, Boston Univ, 1977-1978; res analyst, Social Security Admin, 1974-1975; Sears Found fed fac fel, Div Health Ins, Social Sec Admin, 1974-1975; PROF MGT SCI, UNIV RI, 1971-; prof statist/qual control, Wayne State Univ, 1966-1971; instr statist/opers res, Univ Scranton, 1965-1966; statistician, Columbia Rec Div, Cent Bur Statist, 1962-1963. **Memberships:** Am Statist Asn; Decision Sci Inst; Am Asn Univ Prof. **Research Statement & Publications:** Applying statistics to business decision making, forecasting, quality control, and other managerial problems. **Mailing Address:** Dept Mgt Sci Univ RI, Seven Lippitt Rd, Kingstown, RI 02881. **Fax:** 401-874-4312. **E-Mail:** jejarrett@mail.uri.edu

JARRETT, NOEL, METALLURGICAL PROCESS ENGINEERING. **Personal Data:** b Long Eaton, Eng, November 17, 1921; American citizen; m 1949, Violet; c Robert, Kenneth, James & Thomas. **Education:** Univ Pittsburgh, BS, 1948; Univ Mich, MS, 1951. **Professional Experience:** RETIRED; consult, Noel Jarrett Assoc, beginning 1987; lectr, Am Inst Mining, Metall & Petrol Engrs, beginning 1987; mem, numerous Nat Res Coun & Nat Mat Adv Bd comts, 1981-1990; tech dir chem engr res & develop, Alcoa Labs, 1981-1987; dir smelting res & develop, Aluminum Co Am, 1973-1981; mgr, Aluminum Co Am, 1969-1973; asst chief process metall div, Aluminum Co Am, 1960-1969; sect head chem eng, Aluminum Co Am, 1955-1959; res engr smelting, Aluminum Co Am, 1951-1955; sales engr indust oil sales, Freedom-Valvoline Oil Co, 1949-1950. **Memberships:** Nat Acad Eng; Am Inst Chem Engrs; Mat Soc; fel Am Soc Metals. **Research Statement & Publications:** Electrochemical cell development; optimization of Hall-Heroult Process; coker reactor and cell development of Alcoa Smelting Process; pollution control by scrubbing of chlorine from furnace effluent; high purity Al via crystallization; materials science engineering. **Mailing Address:** 149 Jefferson Ave, Lower Burrell, PA 15068-3127. **E-Mail:** noel.jarrett@att.net

JARRETT, STEVEN MICHAEL, PHYSICS. **Personal Data:** b New York, NY, March 17, 1936; m 1961, c 4. **Education:** City Col New York, BS, 1956; Univ Mich, MS, 1958, PhD (physics), 1963. **Professional Experience:** ENG PROJ MGR, SPECTRA PHYSICS, 1975-; pres, Quantum Systs Corp, 1971-1975; sr res, Coherent Radiation Labs, Calif, 1966-1971; sr scientist, TRG, Inc, ControlData Corp, NY, 1963-1966; Res assoc physics, Univ Mich, 1962-1963. **Memberships:** Am Phys Soc; Optical Soc Am. **Research Statement & Publications:** Lasers, especially gas, solid state and dye lasers; optics; spectroscopy. **Mailing Address:** 474 Los Ninos Way, Los Altos, CA 94022.

JARROLD, MARTIN F, CHEMISTRY. **Education:** Univ Warwick, BS, 1977, PhD, 1980. **Professional Experience:** PROF & ROBERT & MARJORIE MANN CHAIR, CHEM DEPT, IND UNIV, as of 2006; prof, Dept Chem, Northwestern Univ, as of 2002. **Mailing Address:** Dept Chem, Ind Univ, Rm C309A 800 E Kirkwood Ave, Bloomington, IN 47405-7102. **E-Mail:** mfj@indiana.edu

JARROLL, EDWARD LEE, BIOLOGY, PARASITOLOGY. **Personal Data:** b Huntington, WVa, January 4, 1948; div, c Christopher David. **Education:** WVa Univ, AB, 1969, MS, 1971, PhD (biol), 1977. **Professional Experience:** PROF PARASITOL, NORTHEASTERN UNIV, as of 2002; ASSOC DEAN, COL A & S, as of 2002; CHMN, NORTHEASTERN UNIV, 1996-; chmn, Cleveland State Univ, 1992-1996; from asst prof to prof, Cleveland State Univ, 1985-1996; asst prof biol, West Chester Univ, 1984; sr res assoc, Cornell Univ, 1980-1982; fel microbiol, Health Sci Ctr, Univ Oregon, 1977-1980; microbiologist, WVa dept health, 1977; from instr to asst prof biol, Salem Col, 1973-1977. **Memberships:** Am Soc Trop Med & Hyg; Am Soc Parasitologists; AAAS; Sigma Xi; Am SocCell Biol; Am Soc Microbiol; Soc Protozoologists. **Research Statement & Publications:** Giardia and Trichomonas culture; Acanthamoeba physiology, immunology, and epidemiology; efficacy of disinfectants on Giardia cyst viability; encystment pathways forming novel enzymes and a polysacharide. **Mailing Address:** Dept Biology, Northeastern Univ, 100 Meserve Hall, 360 Huntington Ave, Boston, MA 02115. **Fax:** 617-373-2942. **E-Mail:** e.jarroll@neu.edu

JARUZELSKI, JOHN JANUSZ, INDUSTRIAL ORGANIC CHEMISTRY & MANUFACTURING LUBRICATING OILS COMPONENTS. **Personal Data:** b Poland, October 4, 1926; American citizen; wid, c 2. **Education:** Alliance Col, BS, 1951; Pa State Univ, PhD (chem), 1954. **Professional Experience:** RETIRED; sr staff chemist & res assoc paramins, Technol Div, Exxon ChemCo, 1974-1993; sr chemist, Esso Res & Eng Co, 1960-1974; res chemist prod develop div, USSteel Corp, 1959-1960; fel, Mellon Inst, 1956-1959; res chemist, Pittsburgh Plate Glass Co, 1954-1956. **Memberships:** Am Chem Soc. **Research Statement & Publications:** Substitution reactions of aromatic hydrocarbons, especially chloroalkylations; esterification and polyesterification of alcohols and phenols; epoxydation and epoxy resins; thermosetting resins and reinforced plastics; chemistry of lubricating oils additives and antiwear chemicals; antioxidants. **Mailing Address:** 475 Channing Ave, Westfield, NJ 07090.

JARVI, ESA TERO, PHARMACEUTICAL CHEMISTRY, ORGANIC CHEMISTRY. **Personal Data:** b Turku, Finland, May 12, 1954; American citizen; m 1983, Edith; c 1. **Education:** Ohio State Univ, BS, 1975; Univ Wis-Madison, PhD (org chem), 1980. **Professional Experience:** SR RES CHEMIST, MALLINCKRODT INC, as of 2003; SR RES CHEMIST, MERRELL-DOW PHARMACEUT, 1982-. **Memberships:** Am Chem Soc. **Research Statement & Publications:** Synthesis of new potential drugs; enzyme inhibitors. **Mailing Address:** Mallinckrodt Chem Inc, PO Box 5439, St Louis, MO 63147. **Fax:** 314-654-5381. **E-Mail:** esa.jarvis@tycohealthcare.com

JARVIK, JONATHAN WALLACE, ORGANELLE MORPHOGENESIS. **Personal Data:** b Charleston, SC, March 18, 1945; c 3. **Education:** Columbia Col, BA, 1967; Mass Inst Technol, PhD (biol), 1975. **Professional Experience:** ASSOC PROF BIOL SCI, CARNEGIE-MELLON UNIV, 1984-; asst prof, Carnegie-mellon Univ, 1978-1983; Helen Hay Whitney fel, Yale Univ, 1975-1978. **Memberships:** Genetics Soc Am; Am Soc Microbiol; Am Soc Cell Biol; Soc Protozoologists. **Research Statement & Publications:** Genetic biochemical and ultrastructural analysisof eucaryotic flagellar morphogenesis. **Mailing Address:** Dept Biol Sci, Carnegie-Mellon Univ, 4400 Fifth Ave, Pittsburgh, PA 15213-2683. **Fax:** 412-268-7129. **E-Mail:** jarvik@cmu.edu

JARVIK, LISSY F, HUMAN GENETICS, GERIATRIC PSYCHIATRY. **Personal Data:** b The Hague, Neth, 1924; nat American citizen; m 1954, c 2. **Education:** Hunter Col, AB, 1946; Columbia Univ, MA, 1947, PhD (phychol), 1950; Western ResUniv, MD, 1954; Am Bd Pediat, dipl. **Honors & Awards:** Jack Weinberg Award Geriat Psychiat, Am Psychiat Asn, 1986; Robert Wkleemeier Award Outstanding Res Aging, Geront Soc Am, 1986; Edward B Allen Award, Am Geriat Soc, 1986; Irving S Wright Award Distinction, Am Fedn Aging Res, 1988; Founder's Award, Am Asn Geriat Psychiat, 1990. **Professional Experience:** EMER PROF, PSYCHIAT, UNIV CALIF, LOS ANGELES, as of 2005; bd mem, Am Aging Asn, 1991-; found fel, Ctr Advan Study Behav Sci, Stanford, 1988-1989; distinguished physician, Vet Admin, 1987-; Brookdale Nat Fel, med adv bd, 1987-; selection comt, Merck fel clin geriat pharmacol, Am Fed Aging Res, 1987-1989; co-ed, Alzheimer Dis & Assoc Disorders, Int J, 1987; Nat Inst Mental Health, Dept Health & Human-SErv coun, Alzheimer's Dis, Workshop, epidemiol, 1987; Nat Sci Adv Coun, Am Fed Aging Res, 1986-; action comt, White House conf aging, 1986; mem, Nat Adv Mental Health Coun, 1984-1987; CHIEF SECT NEUROPSYCHOGERIAT, UNIV CALIF, LOS ANGELES, 1983-; vis lectr geriat & geront, Am Asn Med Col, 1983-1984; testimony, Joint House Subcom hearings, alzheimer's Dis, 1983; vis McCleod prof, Univ Adelaide, SAustralia, 1981; bd dir & med & sciadv coun, Alzheimer's Dis & Rel Disords Asn, 1980-; prof psychiat, Univ Calif, Los Angeles, beginning 1972; tech comt res & develop, White House Conf Aging, 1971-1973; chiefpsychogenetics unit, Vet Admin Hosp Brentwood, Los Angeles, 1970-; mem jointpsychotomimetic adv comt, Nat Inst Ment Health-Food & Drug Admin, 1970-1972; vis assocprof, Univ Calif, Los Angeles, 1970-1971; res psychiatrist, NY State Psychiat Inst, 1969-1972; assoc res scientist & assoc attend psychiatrist, Radiation Safety Officer, NY State Psychiat Inst, 1963-1972; from asst clin prof to assoc clin prof psychiat, Columbia Univ, 1962-1972; fel, Vanderbilt Clin, 1957-1958; NSF traveling fel, Int Cong Human Genetics, Denmark, 1956; sr resscientist med genetics, Radiation Safety Officer, NY State Psychiat Inst, 1955-1962; Residentpediat, Columbia-Presby Med Ctr, 1955-1956; intern, Mt Sinai Hosp, New York, 1954-1955; asst, Western Res Univ, Sch Med, 1953; res assoc, Columbia Univ, 1948-1950; asst psychiat, Columbia Univ, 1946-1948. **Memberships:** Fel Am Psychol Asn; Am Soc Human Genetics; Soc Study Social Biol; AmPsychopath Asn; Am Psychiat Asn; Am Asn Geriat Psychiat; Am Geriat Soc; Geront Soc Am; Behav Genetics Asn; Int Asn Geront; World Psychiat Asn. **Research Statement & Publications:** Normal pathological mental changes with aging, particularly dementia of the Alzheimer type and depression; geriatric psychopathology; drug treatment and psychotherapy; basic biological mechanisms in Alzheimer's disease, especially microtubules; family studies. **Mailing Address:** 760 Westwood Plaza, BOX 951759 37-359 NPI, Los Angeles, CA 90024-1759. **Fax:** 310-268-4843. **E-Mail:** ljarvik@ucla.edu

JARVIK, MURRAY ELIAS, PHARMACOLOGY. **Personal Data:** b New York, NY, June 1, 1923; m 1954, c 2. **Education:** City Col NY, BS, 1944; Univ Calif, Los Angeles, MA, 1945; Univ Calif, Berkeley, MD, 1951, PhD, 1952. **Honors & Awards:** Career Develop Scientist Award, NIMH, 1971. **Professional Experience:** EMER PROF PSYCHIAT & PHARMACOL, UNIV CALIF, LOS ANGELES, as of 2004; chief, Psychopharmacol Unit, Vet Admin Hosp, West Los Angeles, beginning 1972; prof psychiat & pharmacol, Univ Calif, Los Angeles, beginning 1972; investr, VA MedRes, 1971; prof psychiat, Albert Einstein Col Med, 1969-1972; adv comt abuse stimulant &depressant drugs, Bur Drug Abuse Control, Food & Drug Admin, 1966-1968; mempsychopharmacology study sect, NIMH, 1965-1970; managing ed, Psychopharmacologia, 1965; adj asst prof physiol psychol, Grad Div, NY Univ, 1957; from asst prof to prof pharmacol, AlbertEinstein Col Med, 1956-1972; res assoc psychopharmacol, Long Island Biol Asn, NY, 1955-1956; vis asst prof, Univ Calif, 1955; lectr physiol psychol, Columbia Univ, 1953-1955; res assoc, Mt Sinai Hosp, NY, 1953-1955; res assoc comp physiol psychol, Yerkes Labs, Fla, 1951-1953; asst exp psychol, Univ Calif, Los Angeles, 1944-1945; res technician phys chem, Rockefeller Inst, 1943-1944. **Memberships:** Am Soc Pharmacol & Exp Therapeut; fel Am Psychol Asn; fel NY Acad Sci; AmCol Neuropsychopharmacol; Int Brain Res Orgn; fel CASBS Ctr Advon Study Behav Sci. **Research Statement & Publications:** Effects of drugs upon learning and retention; neurophysiological basis of learning; localization of drug effects in the central nervous system; psychopharmacology; primate behavior; techniques for chronic implantation of arterial catheters; smoking behavior nicotine addiction. **Mailing Address:** Vet Admin Hosp Brentwood 691-B151D, Willshire & Sawtelle Blvds, Los Angeles, CA 90073. **Fax:** 310-268-4498. **E-Mail:** mjarvik@ucla.edu

JARVINEN, RICHARD DALVIN, MATHEMATICS. **Personal Data:** b Virginia, Minn, December 5, 1938; m 1961, c 2. **Education:** St John's Univ, Minn, BA, 1960; Vanderbilt Univ, MAT, 1961; Syracuse Univ, PhD (math), 1971. **Professional Experience:** PROF MATH & STATIST, WINONA STATE UNIV, as of 2006; res math& statist, St Mary's Col, 1975-; from assoc prof to prof math & statist, St Mary's Col, 1972-1990; asst prof math, Carleton Col, 1967-1972; analyst missile simulations, Remington Rand Univac, 1961-1962. **Memberships:** Math Asn Am; Sigma Xi. **Research Statement & Publications:** Bases in topological linear spaces; applications of undergraduate mathematics; computer generated movies and slides for learning mathematics. **Mailing Address:** Dept Math & Statistics, 308 Gildemeister Hall, Winona, MN 55987. **Fax:** 507-457-5376. **E-Mail:** rdjarvinen@vax2.winona.msus.edu

JARVIS, BRUCE B, ORGANIC CHEMISTRY. **Personal Data:** b Van Wert, Ohio, September 30, 1942; m 1963, Nancy; c David, Laura & Jeffrey. **Education:** Ohio Wesleyan Univ, BA, 1963; Univ Colo, PhD (chem), 1966. **Honors & Awards:** AAAS Fellow, 1989. **Professional Experience:** PROF. Emeritus 2004. Chmn, Dept Chem & Biochem, Univ Md, 1993-1998; PROF CHEM & BIOCHEM, UNIV MD, COLLEGE PARK, 1979-; assoc prof, Dept Chem & Biochem, ending 1979; asst prof, Dept Chem & Biochem, beginning 1967; instr chem, Northwestern Univ, 1966-1967. **Memberships:** AAAS; Am Chem Soc; Sigma Xi; Am Soc Pharmacog; Int Soc Toxinology. **Research Statement & Publications:** Natural products chemistry; nucleophilic displacements; sulfur chemistry and molecular rearrangements; mycotoxins; indoor mold toxins. **Mailing Address:** Dept Chem & Biochem, Univ Md, Rm 2129, Chem Bldg 091, College Park, MD 20742-2021. **Fax:** 301-314-9121. **E-Mail:** bjarvis@umd.edu

JARVIS, CHRISTINE WOODRUFF, TEXTILE SCIENCE, PHYSICAL CHEMISTRY. **Personal Data:** b Raleigh, NC, June 19, 1949; m 1971, c 1. **Education:** Univ NC, Chapel Hill, 1971; Mass Inst Technol, PhD (phys chem), 1975. **Professional Experience:** DIR, CLEMSON APPAREL RES, as of 2004; J E SIRRINE PROF TEXTILES, CLEMSON UNIV, 1989-; res assoc, Nat Bur Stand, 1985; from asst prof to prof textiles, Clemson Univ, 1978-1989; instr chem, Clemson Univ, 1976-1978; res assoc textiles, Clemson Univ, 1976. **Memberships:** Am Chem Soc; Am Asn Textile Technologists; Sigma Xi; Am Asn TextileChemists & Colorists; Tech Asn Pulp & Paper Indust. **Research Statement & Publications:** Fiber physics; nonwovens; chemical kinetics of polymer flammability; cotton dust analysis; apparel manufacturing. **Mailing Address:** Dept Textiles, Sch Mat & Sci Eng, Clemson Univ, Clemson, SC 29634. **Fax:** 864656-1453.

JARVIS, ERIC, MOLECULAR BIOLOGY. **Education:** Univ Ore, PhD (Molecular Biol), 1989. **Professional Experience:** SR RES ASSOC, NAT RENEWABLE ENERGY LAB, 2000-; fel, Nat Renewable Energy, 1989-199. **Research Statement & Publications:** Gene cloning and manipulation; cell transformation; and control of gene regulation. **Mailing Address:** Nat Renewable Energy Lab, 1617 Cole Blvd, Golden, CO 80401.

JARVIS, FLOYD ELDRIDGE, GENETICS. **Personal Data:** b Richmond, Va, August 15, 1921; m 1953, c 1. **Education:** Univ Richmond, AB, 1947; Va Polytech Inst, PhD (biol), 1956. **Professional Experience:** RETIRED; from assoc prof to prof biol, Radford Univ, 1955-1987. **Memberships:** Entom Soc Am. **Research Statement & Publications:** Inheritance of insecticidal resistance; residual effectiveness of insecticide formulations. **Mailing Address:** 103 Dogwood Lane, Radford, VA 24141.

JARVIS, JACK REYNOLDS, MEDICINE. **Personal Data:** b Menomonie, Wis, October 31, 1915; m 1945, c 2. **Education:** Birmingham-South Col, BS, 1934; Vanderbilt Univ, MD, 1938; Am Bd Psychiat &Neurol, dipl, 1945. **Professional Experience:** Staff physician, Vet Admin Hosp, 1966-; staff physician, Regional Off, VetAdmin, 1965-; ASST PROF PSYCHIAT, SCH MED, EMORY UNIV, 1961-; area chiefpsychiat, Vet Admin Ga, 1961-1965; Chief psychiat serv, Vet Admin Hosp, Birmingham, Ala, 1955-1961; Assoc prof psychiat, Med Col Ala, 1948-1961. **Memberships:** Am Psychiat Asn. **Research Statement & Publications:** Psychiatry. **Mailing Address:** Vet Admin Hosp, Clairmont Rd, Decatur, GA 30033.

JARVIS, JAMES GORDON, ELECTROPHOTOGRAPHY. **Personal Data:** b Aultsville, Ont, July 13, 1924; American citizen; m 1947, Helen; c 2. **Education:** Queen's Univ, Can, BSc, 1945; Univ Rochester, MS, 1954. **Professional Experience:** RETIRED; sr lab head, Res Labs, 1969-1984; res assoc, Photomat Div, Eastman Kodak Co, 1946-1969; instr, Queen's Univ, Can, 1945-1946. **Memberships:** Optical Soc Am; Soc Photog Sci & Eng. **Research Statement & Publications:** Colorimetry; physiological optics; solid state physics; electrophotography. **Mailing Address:** 846 Dewitt Rd, Webster, NY 14580.

JARVIS, JAMES P, MATHEMATICS. **Education:** Mass Inst Technol, PhD (Opers Res), 1975. **Professional Experience:** PROF, MATH SCI & COORDR INSTR CLEMSON UNIV, as of 2005. **Mailing Address:** Dept Math Sci, Clemson Univ, Clemson, SC 29634-0975. **Fax:** 864-656-5230. **E-Mail:** jpjrv@clemson.edu

JARVIS, JOHN FREDERICK, PHYSICS. **Personal Data:** b Montreal, Que, June 22, 1941; American citizen; m 1963, c 5. **Education:** Univ Fla, BS, 1962; Duke Univ, PhD (physics), 1967. **Professional Experience:** RETIRED; assoc prof math & comput sci, Univ SC, Aiken, 1991-2001; adj prof, Elec Eng, Stevens Inst Technol, 1991; head, Robotics Systs Res Dept, 1982-1990; vis astronr, Kitt Peak Nat Observ, 1979-1981; vis lectr, Princeton Univ, 1978; mem tech staff systs res, AT&T Bell Labs, 1968-1982; instr & res assoc physics, Duke Univ, 1967-1968. **Memberships:** Inst Elec & Electronics Engrs;

AAAS; Am Astron Soc; Am Asn Physics Teachers. **Research Statement & Publications:** Computer graphics, computer vision, automated inspection, pattern recognition; robotics; astronomy. **Mailing Address:** 533 Regent Rd, Augusta, GA 30909. **E-Mail:** johnfjarvis@knology.net

JARVIS, JOHN J, TRANSPORTATION & DISTRIBUTION, LOGISTICS. **Personal Data:** b Donnelson, Tenn, August 7, 1941; m 1963. **Education:** Univ Ala, BSIE, 1963, MSIE, 1965; Johns Hopkins Univ, PhD (opers res), 1968. **Professional Experience:** PROF EMER, SCH INDUST & SYST ENG, GA INST TECHNOL, as of 2003; DIR, SCH INDUST & SYSTS ENG, GA INST TECHNOL, 1991-; CocaCola, 1984-1985 & Sears, 1984-1985; comput Aided Planning & Scheduling, Sohio, 1982; computAided Planning & Scheduling, Inc, 1978-; comput Aided Planning & Scheduling, EnvironProtection Agency, 1978-; consult, Southern Rwy Syst, 1969-1975; from assoc prof to profindust & systs eng, Sch Indust & Systs Eng, GA Inst Technol, 1968-1991; res assoc, JohnsHopkins Univ, 1965-1968; res asst, Univ Ala, 1963-1965; Numerical analyst, NASA, 1963. **Memberships:** Opers Res Soc Am; Inst Mgt Sci; Soc Indust & Appl Math; Am Inst Indust Engrs. **Research Statement & Publications:** Modeling and methodology in operations research and network theory-analysis; transportation, distribution and logistics systems analysis. **Mailing Address:** Sch Indust & Systs Eng, Ga Inst Technol, 765 Ferst Dr NW, Atlanta, GA 30332-0205. **Fax:** 404-894-2301. **E-Mail:** john.jarvis@isye.gatech.edu

JARVIS, LACTANCE AUBREY, organic polymer chemistry; deceased, see previous edition for last biography

JARVIS, NELDON LYNN, SURFACE & COLLOID CHEMISTRY, CHEMICAL MICROSENSOR TECHNOL. **Personal Data:** b Salt Lake City, Utah, November 16, 1935; m 1957, Magdalena; c Hilary, Lori, Neldon L, Suzanne, Mary L, Virginia & Owen C. **Education:** Brigham Young Univ, BS, 1952; Kans State Univ, PhD (agron), 1958. **Professional Experience:** VPRES, MICROSENSOR SYSTS INC, 1988-; head, Chem Div, 1986-1988; chief scientist, Res Directorate, US Army Chem Res Develop & Eng Ctr, 1984-1986; head, Surface Chem Br, Chem Div, 1969-1984; lectr, Am Univ, 1964 & 1969-; phys chemist, USNaval Res Lab, 1959-1969; Nat Acad Sci-Nat Res Coun res assoc, US Naval Res Lab, 1957-1959. **Memberships:** Sigma Xi; Am Chem Soc; Soc Lubrication Engrs. **Research Statement & Publications:** Adsorption-desorption phenomena at solid-liquid and liquid-air interfaces; wetting and spreading phenomena; tribology; lubricant development, analysis and condition monitoring; surface analysis; chemical microsensor development. **Mailing Address:** 120 S Union Ave, Havre de Grace, MD 21078-3112.

JARVIS, RICHARD S, HYDROLOGY. **Personal Data:** b Nottingham, Eng, February 13, 1949. **Education:** Cambridge Univ, BA, 1970, PhD (geog), 1975. **Professional Experience:** CHANCELLOR, ORE UNIV SYST, 2002-; prof & vpres geo sci, State Univ NY, Fredonia, beginning 1987; assoc prof geo sci, State Univ NY, Buffalo, beginning 1974; lectr geog, Durham Univ, 1973-1974. **Memberships:** Am Geophys Union; Asn Am Geographers; Inst Brit Geographers. **Research Statement & Publications:** Network analysis of hydrologic systems; fluvial geomorphology; digitized data systems in hydrology and geomorphology; computer applications in geography; biogeography. **Mailing Address:** Ore Univ Syst, PO Box 751, Portland, OR 97207. **Fax:** 503-725-5709.

JARVIS, ROGER GEORGE, ENVIRONMENTAL SCIENCES. **Personal Data:** b Hugglescote, Eng, April 26, 1928; Canadian citizen; m 1954, Ruth; c Alan R & Hugh W. **Education:** Oxford Univ, BA, 1949, MA & DPhil (physics), 1953. **Professional Experience:** RETIRED; sr res off, waste mgt technol, Atomic Energy Can, Ltd, 1956-1989; mem, Atomic Power Div, Gen Elec Co, Eng, 1956; res fel, Imp Chem Indust, Univ Liverpool, 1955; fel nuclear physics, Nat Res Coun, Chalk River, 1953-1954. **Memberships:** Can Appl Math Soc; Math Asn Am. **Research Statement & Publications:** Operations research, mainly in nuclear energy; risk analysis; mathematical modeling. **Mailing Address:** 38 Park Dale Box 1570, Deep River, ON K0J 1P0, Can.

JARVIS, SIMON MICHAEL, MEMBRANE TRANSPORT. **Personal Data:** b London, Eng, m 1980, Barbara Coubon; c Amanda & Mark. **Education:** Univ Nottingham, UK, BSc, 1977; Cambridge Univ, UK, PhD (physiol), 1981. **Professional Experience:** SR LECTR BIOCHEM, DEPT BIOSCI, UNIV KENT, CANTERBURY, 1992-; lectr, Dept Biosci, Univ Kent, Canterbury, 1986-1992; from asst prof to assoc profphysiol, Univ Alta, Edmonton, Can, 1982-1986; res fel cancer res, Cancer Res Unit, Univ Alta, Edmonton, Can, 1980-1982. **Memberships:** Am Physiol Soc; Biochem Soc; Physiol Soc; Brit Soc Parasitol. **Research Statement & Publications:** Nucleoside and nucleobase transport in mammalian cells and parasitic protozoa; facilitated-diffusion and sodium-dependent systems; comparison of sugar and nucleoside carriers; dopamine uptake by the central nervous system; physiological actions of adenosine. **Mailing Address:** Dept Biosci, Univ Kent Canterbury, Kent CT2 7NJ, UK. **E-Mail:** s.m.jarvis@ukc.ac.uk

JARVIS, WILLIAM R, EPIDEMIOLOGY, PEDIATRIC INFECTIOUS DISEASE. **Personal Data:** b Oakland, Calif, June 2, 1948; m 1982, Janine; c Ashley A & Danielle K. **Education:** Univ Calif, Davis, BS, 1970; Univ Tex, Houston, MD, 1974. **Honors & Awards:** Charles C Shepard Award, 1993; Alexander Langmour Award 2002; Philip Brachman Award, 2001. **Professional Experience:** ASSOC DIR PROF DEV, DHQP, 2000-; actg dir, Invest & Prevent Br, Hosp Infections Prog, Ctr Dis Control, 1996-1998; chief, Invest & Prevent Br, Hosp Infections Prog, Ctr Dis Control, 1987-2000; US PUB HEALTH SERV, US GOVT, 1980-; asst chief, Nat Nosocomial Infections Study, 1981-1986. **Memberships:** Infectious Dis Soc; Soc Hosp Epidemol Am; Am Soc Microbiol; Am Acad Pediat; Soc Pediat Res; Pres Shea 2001; Post Pres Shea 2002. **Research Statement & Publications:** Hospital epidemiology. **Mailing Address:** 827 W Ponce de Leon Ave, Decatur, GA 30030.

JARVIS, WILLIAM ROBERT, PLANT PATHOLOGY, MYCOLOGY. **Personal Data:** b Olney, Eng, November 15, 1927; m 1952, Josephine; c Sarah. **Education:** Univ Sheffield, BSc, 1951; Univ London, PhD (plant Path), 1953, DIC, 1953, cBiol, 1985. **Honors & Awards:** Bailey Award, Can Phytopath Soc, 1985. **Professional Experience:** PHYTOPATHOLOGIST EMER, CAN DEPT AGR, 1994-; srphytopathologist, Can Dept Agr, 1992-1994; chmn, Biol Control Comt chmn Publ Comt & Can Pythopath Soc, 1985-; head, Plant Path Sect, Can Dept Agr, 1974-1992; scientist, Dept Sci & Indust Res, New Zealand, 1969-1970; asst specialist, Univ Calif, 1963-1964; prin sci officer, Scottish Hort Res Inst, 1953-1974; ed, Hort Res; assoc ed, Can J Plant Path, sr ed, Plant Dis. **Memberships:** Am Phytopath Soc; Brit Fedn Plant Pathologists; Brit Mycol Soc; Can Phytopathol Soc. **Research Statement & Publications:** Biology of botrytis species; powdery mildews; biological control; diseases of field and greenhouse vegetables, small berry fruits and ornamental bulb crops; intelligent systems; managing diseases in greenhouse crops. **Mailing Address:** Agr Can Res Sta, Harrow, ON N0R 1G0, Can. **Fax:** 519-738-2929.

JARVIS, WILLIAM TYLER, PUBLIC HEALTH. **Personal Data:** b Takoma Park, Md, October 19, 1935; m 1962, Ada; c 2. **Education:** Univ Minn, Duluth, BS, 1961; Kent State Univ, Ohio, MA, 1968; Univ Ore, PhD (health educ), 1973. **Professional Experience:** PROF PUB HEALTH & PREV MED, LOMA LINDA UNIV, 1994-; PROF HEALTH PROM, LOMA LINDA UNIV, 1994-; prof pub health & prev med, Loma Linda Univ, 1989-1992; mem nat comt unproven methods cancer mgt, Am Cancer Soc, beginning 1986; assoc prof prev med, Loma Linda Univ, 1986-1988; prof pub health sci & chmn dept, Loma Linda Univ, 1982-1986; mem bd sci adv, Am Coun Sci & Health, beginning 1978; ed newslett, Nat Coun AgainstHealth Fraud, beginning 1978; from asst prof to prof prev & community dent, Loma Linda Univ, 1973-1982; fel health educ, Univ Ore, 1971-1973; asst prof health & phys educ, Loma LindaUniv, Calif, 1968-1971; Mt Vernon Acad, Ohio, 1962-1968; instr, Parkersburg Jr Acad, WVa, 1961-1962. **Memberships:** Nat Coun Against Health Fraud (pres, 1977-); Am Pub Health Asn; Am AsnHealth Phys Educ & Recreation; Am Cancer Soc. **Research Statement & Publications:** Consumer health education; health fraud, misinformation and quackery. **Mailing Address:** Dept Health Prom, Loma Linda Univ, PO Box 1276, Loma Linda, CA 92354. **E-Mail:** wjarvis_at_llchp@ccmail.llu.edu

JARZEN, DAVID MACARTHUR, ANGIOSERM EVOLUTION, ECOLOGY. **Personal Data:** b Cleveland, Ohio, October 19, 1941; m 1962, Susan; c Thomas & Robert J. **Education:** Kent State Univ, BS, 1967, MA, 1969; Univ Toronto, PhD (geol), 1973. **Professional Experience:** RES ASSOC, PALEOBOT, PALYNOLOGY, UNIV FLA, FLA MUS NATURAL HIST, GAINESVILLE, FLA, 2003-; dir educ, Marie Selby Bot Gardens 2002-2003; sr biol scientist, Collections Mgr, Fla Mus Nat History, 1997-2002; res scientist, Can Mus Nature, 1989-1997; vis scholar, Univ Queensland, Brisbane, Australia, 1987-1988; palynologist & cur fossil plants, Nat Mus Can, 1973-1989. **Memberships:** Can Asn Palynologists (pres, 1980); Am Asn Stratig Palynologists; Org Trop Studies; Int Fedn Palynology Soc (secy-treas, 1984-1988, vpres, 1992-1996); Fla Acad Sci Ohio Acad Sci, Asn Trop Biol; Bot Soc Am; Geol Asn Can; Int Asn Angiosperm Paleobot. **Research Statement & Publications:** Palynological investigations of terminal Cretaceous and lower Tertiary floras, to discover the paleoenvironmental setting based on the botanical affinities of the fossil pollen and spores; C retaceous spore pollen floras from Australasian (Gondwanan) sediments with an emphasis on evolutionary trends. **Mailing Address:** Div Paleobot & Palynology, Fla Mus Natural Hist, Univ Fla, Dickinson Hall PO Box 117800, Gainesville, FL 32611-7800. **Fax:** 352-846-0287. **E-Mail:** dmj@flmnh.ufl.edu

JARZYNSKI, JACEK, PHYSICS. **Personal Data:** b Warsaw, Poland, March 28, 1935; American citizen. **Education:** Imp Col, Univ London, BS, 1957, PhD (physics), 1961. **Professional Experience:** PROF, GA INST TECHNOL, as of 2004; res physicist, Naval Res Lab, beginning 1971; Consult, Naval Ord Lab, 1967-1970; assoc prof physics, Am Univ, 1963-1971; tech officer optics, Imp Chem Industs, Ltd, Gt Brit, 1963; Fel phys acoustics, Cath Univ Am, 1961-1962. **Memberships:** Acoust Soc Am; Am Phys Soc; Sigma Xi. **Research Statement & Publications:** Parametricunderwater acoustic arrays and sound propagation; development of ultrasonic methods for study of materials; measurement of thermodynamic properties of metals and alloys and comparison with pseudopotential theory. **Mailing Address:** Sch Mech Eng, Ga Inst Technol, 801 Ferst Dr N W, Atlanta, GA 30332-0405. **Fax:** 404-894-8336. **E-Mail:** jacek.jarznski@me.gatech.edu

JASANOFF, SHEILA SEN, LAW & SCIENCE, ENVIRONMENTAL POLICY. **Personal Data:** b Calcutta, India, February 15, 1944; American citizen; m 1968, Jay; c Alan & Maya. **Education:** Harvard Col, BA, 1964, PhD (ling), 1973, JD, 1976; Univ Bonn, W Ger, MA, 1966. **Honors & Awards:** Distinguished Achievement Award, Soc Risk Anal, 1992; JD Bernal Awrad, Soc Social Studies Sci, 2004. **Professional Experience:** PFORZHEIMER PROF SCI & TECHNOL STUDIES, 2002-; fel, Inst Advan Study, Berlin, Ger, 2001-2002; vis Prof, Kyoto Univ, 1999; vis scholar, Wolfson Col, Oxford, 1996; adj prof, Boston Univ Sch Law, 1993; chair, Dept Sci & Technol studies, 1991-1998; prof sci policy & law, prog sci, technol & soc, Cornell Univ, beginning 1990; vis prof, Yale Univ, 1990-1991; dir, Prog Sci, Technol & Soc, Cornell Univ, 1988-1991; contrib ed, Sci, Technol & Human Values, 1988-1991; mem, Nat Conf Lawyers &Scientists, 1985-1991; assoc prof, Prog Sci, Technol & Soc, Cornell Univ, 1984-1989; consult, Orgn Econ Coop & Develop, 1980-1989 & Off Technol Assessment, 1983-1987; sr res assoc sci policy & law, Prog Sci, Technol & Soc, Cornell Univ, 1978-1984; assoc, Bracken, Selig & Baram, 1976-1978. **Memberships:** Soc Social Studies Sci (pres, 1999-2001); Sigma Xi; Am Political Sci Assoc; fel AAAS; Am Bar Asn. **Research Statement & Publications:** Comparative studies of US and European health, safety and environmental regulation; US science policy; Law, science and technology; Chemicals, biotechnology, and global environmental policy. **Mailing Address:** Harvard Univ, L-354 79 John F Kennedy St, Cambridge, MA 02138. **Fax:** 617-496-5960. **E-Mail:** sheila_jasanoff@harvard.edu

JASELSKIS, BRUNO, ANALYTICAL CHEMISTRY, INORGANIC CHEMISTRY. **Personal Data:** b Suraitciai, Lithuania, March 9, 1924; American citizen; m 1955, c 6. **Education:** Union Univ, NY, BS, 1952; Iowa State Univ, MS, 1954, PhD, 1955. **Professional Experience:** PROF EMER CHEM, LOYOLA UNIV CHICAGO, as of 2003; prof chem, Loyols Univ Chicago, beginning 1969; from asst prof to assocprof, Loyola Univ Chicago, 1962-1969; asst prof, Univ Mich, 1959-1962; Instr chem, Univ Mich, 1956-1959. **Memberships:** Am Chem Soc; AAAS; Sigma Xi. **Research Statement & Publications:** Complex ions and their application to analytical problems; solution chemistry of Xenon compounds: determination of micro amounts of various substances. **Mailing Address:** Dept Chem, Loyola Univ, Chicago, IL 60626.

JASHNANI, INDRU, CHEMICAL ENGINEERING. **Personal Data:** b Ghotki, Pakistan, November 2, 1944. **Education:** Indian Inst Technol, Bombay, BTech, 1967; Univ Cincinnati, PhD (chem eng), 1971. **Professional Experience:** PRES & CEO, EASTERN RESIDENTIAL MORTGAGE INC, as of 1999; PRES, ENG & COMPUTER SERV INC, 1990-; SR STAFF ENGR, MARTIN MARIETTA CORP, 1977-; staff mem, Arthur D Little, Inc, 1974-1977; sr engr, APT, Inc, 1972-1974; fel chem & nuclear eng, Univ Cincinnati, 1971-1972. **Memberships:** Am Inst Chem Engrs; Am Chem Soc; Air Pollution Control Asn. **Research Statement & Publications:** Environmental control, air, water and solid, for process industries and utility boilers. **Mailing Address:** Eastern Residential Mortgage Inc, 5575 Sterrett Pl, Ste 250, Columbia, MD 21044.

JASIN, HUGO E, INTERNAL MEDICINE, IMMUNOLOGY. **Personal Data:** b Buenos Aires, Arg, January 22, 1933; American citizen; m 1966, c 3. **Education:** Univ Buenos Aires, MD, 1956. **Honors & Awards:** Master, Am College Rhematology, 1999. **Professional Experience:** PROF INTERNAL MED & DIR DIV RHEUMATOLOGY CLIN IMMUNOL, UNIV ARK MED SCI, 1991-; prof internal med, Univ Tex Southwestern Med Sch, 1978-1991; mem, Gen Med Study Sect, USPHS, 1974-1978; USPHS career develop award, 1973-1977; Arthritis Found fel, 1970-1972; from instr to assoc prof, Univ Tex Southwestern Med Sch, 1965-1978; Nuffield fel, Med Res Coun Rheumatism Res Unit, Eng, 1962-1964; fel internal med, Univ Tex Southwestern Med Sch, 1959-1962 & 1964-1965. **Memberships:** fel Am Col Physicians; Am Asn Immunologists; Am Rheumatism Asn; Am Soc Clin Invest; Am Asn Physicians. **Research Statement & Publications:** Immunological mechanisms in rheumatic diseases and chronic inflammation. **Mailing Address:** Univ Ark, 4301 W Markham, Little Rock, AR 72205. **Fax:** 501-603-1380. **E-Mail:** jasinhugoe@exchange.uams.edu

JASINSKI, DONALD ROBERT, CLINICAL PHARMACOLOGY. **Personal Data:** b Chicago, Ill, August 27, 1938; m 1964, c 4. **Education:** Loyola Univ, Ill, 1956-1959; Univ Ill, MD, 1963. **Professional Experience:** PROF MED, JOHNS HOPKINS BAYVIEW MED CTR, as of 2003; DIR, CTR CHEM DEPENDENCE, JOHNS HOPKINS BAYVIEW MED CTR, as of 2003; DIR, ADDICTION RES CTR, NAT INST DRUG ABUSE, 1977-; chief clin pharmacol sect, Addiction Res Ctr, Nat Inst Drug Abuse, 1969-1977; chief opiate unit, Addiction Res Ctr, Nat Inst Drug Abuse, 1967-1968; staff physician, Addiction Res Ctr, Nat Inst Drug Abuse, 1965-1967; fel neuropharmacol, Res & Educ Hosps, Univ Ill, Chicago, 1964-1965; intern, Res & Educ Hosps, Univ Ill, Chicago, 1963-1964; clin prof pharmacol & toxicol & mem grad fac, Univ Louisville, Ky; clin asst prof pharmacol, Univ Ill; assoc mem grad fac, Dept Pharmacol, Col Med, Univ Ky. **Memberships:** AAAS; Am Soc Clin Pharmacol & Therapeut; Am Soc Pharmacol & Exp Therapeut; Soc Neuroscience; Int Brain Res Orgn; Sigma Xi. **Research Statement & Publications:** Neuropharmacology; Psychopharmacology. **Mailing Address:** Ctr Chem Dependence, Johns Hopkins Bayview Med Ctr, 4940 Eastern Ave MFL Bldg, Baltimore, MD 21224-2780. **Fax:** 410-550-1912. **E-Mail:** djasinsk@mail.jhmi.edu

JASINSKI, JERRY PETER, X-RAY CRYSTALLOGRAPHY, SPECTROSCOPY, SOLID STATE MATERIALS. **Personal Data:** b Newport, NH, July 28, 1940; m 1966, Jacquelin; c Jana L, John M & Jennifer A. **Education:** Univ NH, BA, 1964, MST, 1968; Worcester Polytech Inst, MNS, 1968; Univ Wyo, PhD (chem), 1974. **Professional Experience:** DIR, Central New England Molecular Structure Center, 1990-; PROF CHEM, KEENE STATE COL, NH, 1989-; Chair of Chemistry 1999-; Chair of Physics, 2004-; consult, US Army Mat & Mech Res Ctr, Watertown, Mass, 1983-1996; coordr phys sci, 1981-1983; from asst prof to assoc. prof, New Eng Molecular Struct Ctr, 1978-1989; res assoc, Univ Va, 1974-1975; assoc Western Univs fel, Los Alamos Sci Lab, 1973-1974; teaching & res assoc chem, Univ Wyo, 1970-1973; Teacher, high schs, NY, NH & Vt, 1964-1970 & 1975-1978. **Memberships:** Am Chem Soc; New Eng Inst of Chemists, New Eng Chem Teachers Asn, Am Crystallog Asn. **Research Statement & Publications:** Experimental and theoretical molecular electronic spectroscopy; solid state and coordination chemistry; x-ray crystallography; bioinorganic chemistry; chemical design and molecular mechanics modelling; luminescence and laser spectroscopy. **Mailing Address:** Dept Chem, Keene State Col, 229 Main St, Keene, NH 03435-2001. **E-Mail:** jjasinski@keene.edu

JASINSKI, JOSEPH M, PHYSICS. **Education:** Dartmouth Col, AB, 1976; Stanford Univ, PhD (Chem), 1980. **Professional Experience:** PROG DIR, HEALTHCARE & LIFE SCI RES AT IBM THOMAS J.WATSON RES CTR, as of 2006. **Memberships:** Fellow Am Phys Soc. **Mailing Address:** IBM T J Watson Res Ctr, PO Box 218, Hawthorne, NY 10598. **Fax:** 914-945-2141. **E-Mail:** JMJASIN@US.IBM.COM

JASKOLL, TINA, DEVELOPMENTAL GENETICS, SIGNAL TRANSDUCTION OF DEVELOPING ORGANS. **Personal Data:** b New York, NY, January 24, 1950. **Education:** Yeshiva Univ, BA, 1971; City Univ NY, (develop biol), PhD, 1978. **Honors & Awards:** Prof Achievement Award, Yeshiva Univ, 1995. **Professional Experience:** PROF, UNIV SOUTHERN CALIF DENTAL SCH, 1999-; assoc prof, Yeshiva Univ, 1997-1998; DIR, LAB DEVELOP GENETICS, UNIV SOUTHERN CALIF, 1993-; from asst to assoc prof, Univ Southern Calif Dental School, 1991-1999. **Memberships:** affil, Endocrine Soc; affil, Am Asn Cell Biol; affil, Soc Develop Biol; affil, AAAS. **Research Statement & Publications:** Research focus on delineation of key signal transduction pathways during embryonic development; using the embryonic salivary gland as a model system to investigate the functional genomics of growth factor-mediated pathways which have been shown to be critical for salivary gland development; identification of the functional relationship between key signaling and transcriptional regulatory pathways; developing new drugs designed to functionally restore damaged, diseased, and aging salivary glands. **Mailing Address:** 925 W 34th St, DEN 4264 MC 0641, Los Angeles, CA 90089-0641. **Fax:** 213-740-7560. **E-Mail:** tjaskoll@usc.edu

JASKOSKI, BENEDICT JACOB, parasitology; deceased, see previous edition for last biography

JASMIN, GAETAN, PATHOLOGY. **Personal Data:** b Montreal, Que, November 24, 1924; m 1952, c 3. **Education:** St Laurent Col, BA, 1945; Univ Montreal, MD, 1951, PhD (exp med), 1956; CSPQ, 1968; FRCP (C), 1978. **Professional Experience:** Chmn dept path, Univ Montreal, 1970-1982; PROF PATH, UNIV MONTREAL, 1967-; ed, Methods & Achievements Exp Path, 1966-; ed, Revue Canadienne deBiologie, 1960-1970; med res assoc, Nat Res Coun Can, 1958-1970; from asst prof exp path toassoc prof path, Univ Montreal, 1956-1967. **Memberships:** Soc Exp Biol & Med; Am Physiol Soc; Histochem Soc; Can Soc Clin Invest; IntAcad Path. **Research Statement & Publications:** Endocrinology; muscle diseases and cancer. **Mailing Address:** Dept Path, Fac Med Univ Montreal CP 6128 Sta A, Montreal, PQ H3C 3J7, Can. **Fax:** 514-343-5755.

JASNOW, DAVID MICHAEL, CONDENSED MATTER THEORY. **Personal Data:** b New York, NY, April 27, 1943; m Çarol; c 2. **Education:** Cornell Univ, BA, 1964; Univ Ill Urbana-Champaign, MS, 1965, PhD (physics), 1969. **Professional Experience:** Div assoc ed, Phys Rev Lett, 1988-1994; ed bd, J Statist Physics 1995-1997; DEPT CHAIR & PROF PHYSICS, UNIV PITTSBURGH, 1982-; from asst prof to assoc prof, Univ Pittsburgh, 1971-1982; prin investr, NSF, NASA, DOE. **Memberships:** Fel Am Phys Soc. **Research Statement & Publications:** Theoretical research in statistical physics; phase transitions and critical phenomena; kinetics of phase transitions; equilibruim and non-equilibrium properties of interfaces; polymer statistical mechanics; biological physics. **Mailing Address:** Dept Physics & Astron, Univ Pittsburgh, 311 Allen Hall, Pittsburgh, PA 15260. **Fax:** 412-624-9163. **E-Mail:** jasnow@pitt.edu

JASNY, BARBARA R, GENETICS. **Education:** NY Univ, BA; Rockefeller Univ, PhD. **Professional Experience:** SUPVRY SR ED, SCIENCE, as of 2005. **Mailing Address:** AAAS, 1333 H St NW, Washington, DC 20005-4707. **E-Mail:** bjasny@aaas.org

JASNY, GEORGE R, chemical & nuclear chemical engineering; deceased, see previous edition for last biography

JASON, ANDREW JOHN, MOLECULAR PHYSICS, SURFACE PHYSICS. **Personal Data:** b Detroit, Mich, January 27, 1938; m 1962, c 1. **Education:** Mass Inst Technol, SB, 1959; Univ Chicago, MS, 1960, PhD (physics), 1967. **Professional Experience:** ASSOC PROF PHYSICS, UNIV ALA, 1973-; asst prof, Univ Ala, 1968-1973; Res assoc physics, Univ Chicago, 1967-1968. **Memberships:** AAAS; Am Phys Soc. **Research Statement & Publications:** Field ionization; atomic physics; high field studies of atoms and molecules; kinetics of evaporation; ion optics; mass spectrometry; optical properties of surfaces.

JASON, MARK EDWARD, PHYSICAL ORGANIC, REACTION MECHANISMS. **Personal Data:** b Grand Rapids, Mich, October 18, 1949; m 1973, Janet; c Elisabeth M & Amanda M. **Education:** Univ Mich, BS, 1971; Yale Univ, PhD (chem), 1976. **Professional Experience:** ASSOC FEL, MONSANTO, 1983-; vis prof, Cornell Univ, 1981; asst prof orgchem, Amherst Col, 1977-1983; assoc, NSF assoc, 1976-1977; assoc, Nwestern Univ, 1976. **Memberships:** Am Chem Soc. **Research Statement & Publications:** Physical organic chemistry; chemistry of small ring compounds; chelation chemistry. **Mailing Address:** Monsanto, 800 N Lindbergh Blvd T3W, St Louis, MO 63167-0002. **Fax:** 314-694-4575. **E-Mail:** mejaso@ccmail.monsanto.com

JASPER, DONALD EDWARD, VETERINARY MEDICINE, CLINICAL PATHOLOGY. **Personal Data:** b La Grande, Ore, December 30, 1918; m 1943, Elizabeth; c Donald R & Jean E (Edwards). **Education:** State Col Wash, BS, 1940; Iowa State Col, MS, 1944; Univ Minn, PhD (vet med), 1947. **Honors & Awards:** Borden Award, 1967. **Professional Experience:** RETIRED; distinguished prof, NZ, 1978; sr resscholar, Fulbright Hays, 1975; sr fel, 1968; prof clin path, Sch Vet Med, Univ Calif, Davis, 1954-1989; dean sch vet med & asst dir exp sta, Univ Calif, Davis, 1954-1962; from asst prof to assoc prof, UnivCalif, Davis, 1947-1954; asst clinician, Iowa State Col, 1942-1944. **Memberships:** US Animal Health Asn; Am Vet Med Asn; Am Soc Microbiol. **Research Statement & Publications:** Bovine mastitis; mycoplasma infections; discovered and named Mycoplasma californicum. **Mailing Address:** 7146 County Rd 25, Orland, CA 95963.

JASPER, DONALD K, BIOLOGY. **Personal Data:** b Miami, Fla. **Education:** Howard Univ, BS, 1952; Univ York, PhD (cell ultrastruct & physiol), 1969. **Professional Experience:** PROF EMER RES, ILL INST TECHNOL, 1996-; res prof, Ill Inst Technol, 1995-1996; assoc dean grad studies, Ill Inst Technol, 1986-1988; Fac res fel, Argonne Nat Lab, 1981-1986; assoc prof cell biol, Ill Inst Technol, 1975-1995; asst prof, Ill Inst Technol, 1969-1975; res fel cell biol, Univ York, 1966-1969; res asst cytol, Columbia Univ, 1960-1966; Electron microscopist, Rockefeller Inst Med Res, 1956-1960. **Memberships:** AAAS; Am Soc Cell Biol; Am Inst Biol Sci; Electron Micros Soc Am; Fedn AmSoc Exp Biol. **Research Statement & Publications:** Cellular ultrastructure as related to function, especially as mucosal epithelial and muscle cell structure and function. **Mailing Address:** Dept Biol, Ill Inst Technol, Chicago, IL 60616.

JASPER, HERBERT HENRY, NEUROPHYSIOLOGY. **Personal Data:** b La Grande, Ore, July 27, 1906; Canadian citizen; m 1983, Mary L McDougall; c Stephen & Joan. **Education:** Reed Col, BA, 1927; Univ Ore, MA, 1929; Univ Iowa, PhD (psychol), 1931; Univ-Paris, Dr es Sc(physiol), 1935; McGill Univ, MDCM, 1943. **Honorary Degrees:** Dr, Univ Bordeaux, 1949, Univ Aix-Marseille, 1960, McGill Univ, 1971, UnivWestern Ont, 1977 & Queens Univ, 1979 & Mem Univ, 1983. **Honors & Awards:** Officer Order Can, 1972; Ralph Gerard Prize, Soc Neurosci, 1981; Karl LashleyPrize, Am Philos Soc, 1982; McLaughlin Medal, Royal Soc Can, 1985; Milken Family MedFound Prize, Am Epilepsy Soc, 1993; Albert Einstein Prize, World Cult Coun, 1995. **Professional Experience:** EMER PROF NEUROPHYSIOL, UNIV MONTREAL, 1976-; hon consultneurosci, Univ Montreal & McGill Univ, 1975-; dir med res coun group neurol sci, Dept Physiol, Univ Montreal, 1967-1976; res prof neurophysiol, Labs Neurol Sci, Univ Montreal, 1965-1976; founding ed-in-chief & publ, Int J EEG & ClinNeurophysiol, 1949-1962; first pres, Int Fedn Socs EEG & Clin Neurophysiol, 1947-1949; profexp neurol & dir, Neurophysiol & EEG Labs, Montreal Neurol Inst, 1946-1964; asst prof neurol& neurosurg, McGill Univ, 1938-1946; asst prof, Brown Univ, 1933-1938; instr, Univ Iowa, 1929-1931; instr psychol, Univ Ore, 1927-1929; founding hon exec secy, Int Brain Res Orgn. **Memberships:** Am Physiol Soc; Am Neurol Asn; Am EEG Soc (pres 1946-1948); fel Royal SocCan; Int Brain Res Orgn (exec secy 1961-1963 hon exec secy 1971-1972). **Research Statement & Publications:** Brain research; behavioral sciences; neurology; electrical activity of the brain in man and experimental animals in relation to neuro chemistry; states of consciousness; epilepsy; sensori-motor functions and mechanisms of learning and memory; neuroscience. **Mailing Address:** 4501 Sherbrooke W No 1F, WestMt, PQ H3Z 1E7, Can.

JASPER, MARTIN THEOPHILUS, MECHANICAL & CHEMICAL ENGINEERING. **Personal Data:** b Hazlehurst, Miss, March 19, 1934; m 1963, c 5. **Education:** Miss State Univ, BS, 1955, MS, 1962; Univ Ala, PhD (mech eng), 1967. **Professional Experience:** PROF MECH ENG, MISS STATE UNIV, 1975-; from instr to assoc prof, Miss State Univ, 1960-1975; design engr, Missile Div, Chrysler Corp, 1959-1960; plant metallurgist, Vickers, Inc, 1957-1959; engr, Am Cast Iron Pipe Co, 1955-1956. **Memberships:** Am Soc Eng Educ; Am Soc Mech Engrs; Soc Mfg Engrs; NY Acad Sci. **Research Statement & Publications:** Parametric analysis, modeling and optimization of thermal and hydrodynamic systems. **Mailing Address:** 116 Mc Cain Eng Bldg, PO Box 9542, Mississippi State, MS 39762. **Fax:** 601-325-7618. **E-Mail:** jasper@engr.msstate.edu

JASPER, SAMUEL JACOB, MATHEMATICS. **Personal Data:** b Lancaster, Ohio, November 1, 1921; m 1944, c 3. **Education:** Univ Ohio, AB, 1943; Ohio State Univ, MA, 1946; Univ Ky, PhD (math), 1948. **Professional Experience:** PROF MATH, OHIO UNIV, 1967-; chmn, Dept Math, 1967-1968; dir hon col, Ohio Univ, 1963-1966; Asst dean col arts & sci, Ohio Univ, 1958-1963; from asst prof to assocprof, Ohio Univ, 1954-1967; asst prof, Kent State Univ, 1948-1951 & ETenn State Col, 1951-1954; Instr math, Univ Ohio, 1943-1944. **Memberships:** Math Asn Am. **Research Statement & Publications:** Differential geometry; homogeneous functions; calculus of variations. **Mailing Address:** 7399 Village Dr, Mason, OH 45040.

JASPERSE, CRAIG PETER, ORGANOLANTHANIDES, RADICALS. **Personal Data:** b Sheboygan, Wis, February 2, 1960; m 1991. **Education:** Calvin Col, BS, 1982; Univ Wis-Madison, PhD (org chem), 1987. **Professional Experience:** PROF, MINN STATE UNIV, as of 2006; asst prof org chem, Univ NDak, beginning 1989; fel, Univ Pittsburgh, 1987-1989. **Memberships:** Am Chem Soc. **Research Statement & Publications:** Organic chemistry, synthesis; ketyl radical anions, preparation and rearrangements; mechanism and application of SMI2 as a one-electron reducing agent; preparation and rearrangements of alkoxy radicals. **Mailing Address:** Dept chem, Minn State Univ, 411I Hagen Hall Sci Lab 003, Moorhead, MN 56563. **Fax:** 218-477-2137. **E-Mail:** jasperse@mnstate.edu

JASPERSE, JOHN R, PLASMA PHYSICS, SPACE PHYSICS. **Personal Data:** b Seattle, Wash, May 8, 1935; m 1958, c 2. **Education:** Harvard Univ, BA, 1957; Northeastern Univ, MS, 1963, PhD (physics), 1966. **Honors & Awards:** Marcus D O'Day Mem Award; Guenter Loeser Mem Award. **Professional Experience:** AT, AIR FORCE RES LAB, as of 2003; Vis scientist, Mass Inst Technol, 1979-; lectr, Northeastern Univ, 1968-1971; RES PHYSICIST, AIR FORCE GEOPHYS LAB, 1965-; res physicist, Arthur D Little, Inc, 1959-1965. **Memberships:** Am Geophys Union; Sigma Xi; Am Phys Soc. **Research Statement & Publications:** Quantum theory of atoms and molecules; scattering theory; three-body problem; electromagnetic theory; plasma theory; space physics. **Mailing Address:** 198 Conant Rd, Weston, MA 02193.

JASPERSON, STEPHEN NEWELL, SOLID STATE PHYSICS. **Personal Data:** b Wisconsin Rapids, Wis, May 10, 1941; m 1965, c 2. **Education:** Univ Wis, BS, 1963; Princeton Univ, MA, 1965, PhD (physics), 1968. **Professional Experience:** PROF PHYSICS, WORCESTER POLYTECH INST, as of 2004; DEPT HEAD, WORCESTER POLYTECH INST, 1984-; vis scientist, Nat Magnet Lab, Mass Inst Technol, 1982-1986; assoc prof physics, Worcester Polytech Inst, beginning 1974; res scientist, Physics Br, Naval

Weapons Ctr, 1971-1978; asst prof, Worcester Polytech Inst, 1970-1974; res assoc physics, Univ Ill, 1968-1970; res assoc physics, Princeton Univ, 1967-1968. **Memberships:** AAAS; Am Phys Soc. **Research Statement & Publications:** Optical properties of metals and semiconductors; modulation spectroscopy techniques such as electroreflectance, polarization modulation and magnetoreflectance. **Mailing Address:** Dept Physics, Worcester Polytech Inst, Olin Hall 215, Worcester, MA 01609. **Fax:** 508-831-5886. **E-Mail:** snj@wpi.edu

JASS, HERMAN EARL, BIOCHEMISTRY, PHARMACOLOGY. **Personal Data:** b Chicago, Ill, March 30, 1918; m 1947, Alaine Pabich; c Daniel K & Diane C. **Education:** Univ Ill, BS, 1939; Northwestern Univ, MS, 1950, PhD (chem), 1953. **Honors & Awards:** Cibs Sci Award, Cosmetic Toiletry & Fragrance Asn, 1978. **Professional Experience:** TECH MGT CONSULT, 1976-; vpres res, Carter Prod Div, Carter-Wallace, Inc, 1964-1976; Guest lectr, Columbia Col Pharm, 1964 & 1965; assoc res dir, Revlon, Inc, 1955-1964; group leader biochem, Armour & Co, 1953-1955; chief biochemist, Helene Curtis Indust, Inc, 1942-1951; Org chemist, Gas Res Dept, People's Gas Co, Ill, 1940-1941. **Memberships:** AAAS; Am Chem Soc; Soc Cosmetic Chem; Dermal Clin Eval Soc; Am Soc Consult Pharmacists. **Research Statement & Publications:** Proprietary drugs and toiletries; biochemistry and physiology of the skin; regulation and safety of cosmetics & drugs. **Mailing Address:** 29 Platz Dr, Skillman, NJ 08558.

JASSBY, DANIEL LEWIS, CONTROLLED NUCLEAR FUSION. **Personal Data:** b Montreal, Que, January 27, 1942; American citizen. **Education:** McGill Univ, BSc, 1962; Univ BC, MS, 1964; Princeton Univ, PhD (plasma physics), 1970. **Professional Experience:** RETIRED; prin res physicist, Princeton Plasma Physics Lab, 1980-1999; res physicist, Princeton Plasma Physics Lab, 1976-1980; res staff, Princeton Plasma Physics Lab, 1973-1976; Asst prof elec sci, Univ Calif, Los Angeles, 1970-1973. **Memberships:** Fel Am Phys Soc; Inst Elec & Electronics Engrs. **Research Statement & Publications:** Production, measurement and application of fusion neutrons; heating of toroidal plasmas; design of magnetic confinement fusion devices. **Mailing Address:** 348 Sayre Dr, Princeton, NJ 08540.

JASTAK, J THEODORE, ORAL & MAXILLOFACIAL SURGERY, DENTAL ANESTHESIOLOGY. **Personal Data:** b Astoria, NY, December 1, 1936; m 1962, c 3. **Education:** Seton Hall Univ, DDS, 1962; Univ Rochester, PhD (path), 1967. **Professional Experience:** PROF ORAL SURG, SCH DENT, ORE HEALTH SCI UNIV, 1980-2003; PROF & CHMN, DEPT HOSP DENT, SCH DENT, ORE HEALTH SCI UNIV, 1980-2003; assoc prof, Sch Dent, Ore HealthSci Univ, 1969-1980; vis asst prof, Dent Sch, Univ Detroit, 1968-1969; resident oralmaxillofacial surg, Henry Ford Hosp, Detroit, 1967-1969. **Memberships:** AAAS; Am Col Oral Maxillofacial Surg; Am Dent Soc Anesthesiol; Int Asn Dent Res. **Research Statement & Publications:** Anesthesia and pain control for dental outpatients. **Mailing Address:** Dept Hosp Dent, Ore Health Sci Univ, 3181 SW Sam Jackson, Portland, OR 97201-3011.

JASTROW, ROBERT, ASTRONOMY & PLANETARY SCIENCE. **Personal Data:** b New York, NY, September 7, 1925. **Education:** Columbia Univ, BA, 1944, MA, 1945, PhD (physics), 1948. **Honorary Degrees:** DSc, Manhattan Col, 1980. **Honors & Awards:** Arthur S Fleming Award, 1965; Medal for Excellence, Columbia Univ 1965. **Professional Experience:** RETIRED; dir, Mt Wilson Inst, 1992-2002; adj prof, Columbia Univ, beginning 1961 & Dartmouth Col, 1974-; prof physics & earth sci, Dartmouth Col, 1974-1992; ed, J Atmospheric Sci, Am Meteorol Soc, 1962-1974; dir, Inst Space Studies, 1961-1981; mem comt, Lunar Explor Comt, NASA, 1960-1962; chmn, Lunar Explor Comt, NASA, 1959-1960; head, Theoret Div, Goddard Space Flight Ctr, NASA, 1958-1961; consult nuclear physics, US Naval Res Lab, 1954-1958; asst prof physics, Yale Univ, 1953-1954; mem fac, Univ Calif, Berkeley, 1950-1953; mem, Inst Advan Study, Princeton Univ, 1949-1950, 1953; fel, Univ Leiden, 1948-1949. **Memberships:** Fel AAAS; fel Am Geophys Union; fel Am Phys Soc; Am Astron Soc; Am Meteorol Soc. **Research Statement & Publications:** Physics of atmosphere, the moon and terrestrial planets. **Mailing Address:** Mount Wilson Inst, 740 Holladay Rd, Pasadena, CA 91106. **Fax:** 310-470-8046. **E-Mail:** jastrow@mtwilson.edu

JASWAL, SITARAM SINGH, PHYSICS. **Personal Data:** b Bham, India, September 15, 1937; American citizen. **Education:** Univ Panjab, India, BSc, 1958, MSc, 1959; Mich State Univ, PhD (physics), 1964. **Professional Experience:** PROF PHYSICS, UNIV NEBR, LINCOLN, as of 2006; Fulbright fel, Tech Univ Vienna, Austria, 1986-1987; prof physics, Univ Nebr, Lincoln, beginning 1974; vis scientist, Max Planck Inst Solid State Res, 1974-1975; from asst prof to assoc prof, Univ Nebr, Lincoln, 1966-1974; fel, Univ Pa, 1964-1966; asst physics, Mich State Univ, 1961-1964; asst physics, Univ Alta, 1960-1961; asst geophys, Oil & Natural Gas Comn, India, 1959-1960. **Memberships:** Fel Am Phys Soc. **Research Statement & Publications:** Electronic structure and properties of metallic glasses and magnetic materials. **Mailing Address:** Dept Physics & Astron, Univ Nebr, 213AA Ferguson Hall, Lincoln, NE 68588. **E-Mail:** sjaswal1@unl.edu

JASZBERENYI, JOSEPH C, CHEMISTRY OF ANTIBIOTICS, HETEROCYCLIC CHEMISTRY. **Personal Data:** b Budafok, Hungary, August 19, 1948. **Education:** Kossuth L Univ, Debrecen, Hungary, dipl chem, 1972, Dr rer nat, 1975. **Professional Experience:** DIR RES, DEPT CHEM, TEX A&M UNIV, 1990-; vis assoc prof org chem, Dept Chem, Tex A&M Univ, 1988-; reader, Kossuth L Univ, Debrecen, Hungary, 1986; sr res felantibiotics, res group antibiotics, Debrecen, 1984-; postdoctoral org chem, Univ New CastleUpon Tyne, 1979-1980; res fel, Debrecen, 1977-1983; lectr, Kossuth L Univ Debrecen, 1976-1977; postdoctoral, Oxford Univ, Eng, 1975-1976; asst lectr chem, Kossuth L Univ Debrecen, 1972-1975. **Research Statement & Publications:** Development of new reagents for radical chemistry; new reactions applicablo to thc synthetic transformations of organic molecules; natural products. **Mailing Address:** Dept Chem, Tex A&M Univ, College Station, TX 77843.

JASZCZAK, RONALD JACK, MEDICAL PHYSICS, IMAGE PROCESSING PHYSICS. **Personal Data:** b Chicago Heights, Ill, August 23, 1942; m 1967, c 2. **Education:** Univ Fla, BS, 1964, PhD (physics), 1968. **Honors & Awards:** Paul C AEBERSOLD AWARD, Soc Nuclear Med, 2000. **Professional Experience:** Assoc prof biomed eng, Duke Univ, 1992; PROF, DEPT RADIOL, DUKE UNIV, 1989-; prin investr, Dept Energy, 1989-; assoc ed, Inst Elec & Electronics Engrs Trans Med Imaging, 1986-1992 & J Nuclear Med Technol, 1988-1995; prin investr, Nat Cancer Inst, 1983-; NIH res fel, 1980-1982; assoc prof, Dept Radiol, Duke Univ, 1979-1989; assoc prof dept biomed eng, Duke Univ, 1986-1991; res prof, Inst Statist & Decision Sci, 1991-1993; chief scientist, Nuclear Chicago Corp, Searle Diagnostics Inc, 1977-1979; res group leader, Nuclear Chicago Corp, Searle Diagnostics Inc, 1973-1977; sr prin res scientist, Nuclear Chicago Corp, Searle Diagnostics Inc, 1973; prin res scientist, Nuclear Chicago Corp, Searle Diagnostics Inc, 1971-1973; staff physicist, US AEC, Oak Ridge Nat Lab, 1969-1971; postdoctoral fel, US AEC, Oak Ridge Nat Lab, 1968-1969. **Memberships:** AAAS; Am Phys Soc; fel Inst Elec & Electronics Engrs; Am Asn Physicists Med; asoc Nuclear med. **Research Statement & Publications:** Nuclear medicine instrumentation; imaging systems for single photon emission computed tomography; nuclear radiation detectors; image reconstruction and restoration; Monte Carlo modeling; quantitative application of medical imaging. **Mailing Address:** Duke Univ Med Ctr, PO Box 3949, Durham, NC 27710. **Fax:** 919-684-7122. **E-Mail:** rjj@dec3.mc.duke.edu

JATLOW, JACOB LAWRENCE, ELECTRONICS, COMMUNICATIONS ENGINEERING. **Personal Data:** b Poland, April 7, 1903; American citizen; m 1951, c 1. **Education:** Rensselaer Polytech Inst, EE, 1924. **Honors & Awards:** Region 1 Award, Inst Elec & Electronics Engrs, 1983. **Professional Experience:** RETIRED; consult, ITT, 1977-1985; tech dir commun div, Systs Eng Lab, 1964-1977; dir, Systs Eng Lab, 1960-1964; assoc dir, Radio Transmission Lab, 1954-1960; chief engr, Wire Transmission Div, Defense Commun Div, Int Tel & Tel Inc, 1942-1954; chief engrphotochem res, Repub Eng Prod Inc, 1940-1942; develop engr, Photo Positive Corp, 1935-1940; asst chief engr, F A D Andrea Radio Corp, 1932-1935; develop engr, Conner Crouse Corp, 1924-1932. **Memberships:** Fel Inst Elec & Electronics Engrs; fel AAAS; NY Acad Sci. **Research Statement & Publications:** Communications systems engineering; wire and radio transmission; switching systems; command and control systems; communication and electronic equipment; development of alternating current operated radio sets and power supplies; development of photographic emulsions and photoprocesses. **Mailing Address:** 166 E 61st St Apt 12-J, New York, NY 10021.

JAUCHEM, JAMES ROBERT, CARDIOVASCULAR PHYSIOLOGY, RADIOFREQUENCY RADIATION BIOEFFECTS. **Personal Data:** b Washington, DC, March 22, 1951; m 1990, Wendy Friedman. **Education:** Heidelberg Col, BS, 1973; Baylor Col Med, PhD (physiol), 1978. **Honors & Awards:** Award Excellence, Soc Tech Commun, 1986; Scientist of the Year, Air Force Asn, 1998; First Place, Prof Category, Excellence in Govt Awards, 2000. **Professional Experience:** RES PHYSIOLOGIST, RADIOFREQUENCY RADIATION BR, DIRECTED ENERGY DIV USAF, 1987-; prin sci ed, Dept Info & Defense Progs, Tracor Inc, 1986-1987; Consult, Northrop Corp, 1986; res physiologist, Crew Tech Div, Sch Aerospace Med, USAF, 1985-1986; Nat Res Coun, sr res assoc, Med Sci Div, Johnson Space Ctr, NASA, 1984-1985; res scientist, Life Sci Div, Technol Inc, 1981-1984; fel, Dept Path, Health Sci Ctr, Univ Tex, San Antonio, 1980-1981; Res assoc, Microcirculatory Systs Res Group, Univ Missouri, 1977-1979. **Memberships:** Am Physiol Soc; Soc Exp Biol & Med; Aerospace Med Asn; Bioelectromagnetics Soc. **Research Statement & Publications:** Physiological effects of radiofrequency radiation; thermoregulation; cardiovascular pharmacology; circulatory shock; electromagnetic field bioeffects. **Mailing Address:** USAF Res Lab, Bldg 1162, 8308 Hawks Rd, Brooks AFB, TX 78235. **E-Mail:** jamesjauchem@brooks.af.mil

JAUHAR, PREM P, GENETICS, PLANT BREEDING. **Personal Data:** b India, September 15, 1937. **Education:** Agra Univ, India, BS, 1957, MS, 1959; Indian Agr Res Inst, New Delhi, PhD, 1963. **Professional Experience:** RES GENETICIST, USDA, NDAK, 1991-; res Geneticist, USDA, Utah State Univ, Logan, Utah, 1987-1991; res Geneticist, Dept Agron & Range Sci, Univ Calif, Davis, 1986-1987; res Geneticist, USDA, Berkeley, Calif, 1985-1986; res Geneticist & res dir, Res & Develop Corp, Riverside, Calif, 1982-1984; res assoc, City Hope Nat Res Inst, Duarte, Calif, 1981; asst res geneticist, Univ Calif, Riverside, 1978-1981; res assoc, Univ Ky, 1976-1978; assoc prof Genetics, Indian Agr Res Inst, New Delhi, 1975-1976; sr res scientist, Univ Wales, UK, 1972-1975; asst cytogeneticist & assoc prof genetics, Indian Agr Res Inst, 1963-1972; post grad fac, Indian Agr Res Inst, New Delhi, 1960-1970. **Memberships:** Genetics Soc Can; Crop Sci Soc Am; Am Genetic Asn; Indian Soc Genetics & Plant Breeding; Sigma Xi; Tissue Cult Asn Am. **Research Statement & Publications:** Regulatory mechanism that controls chromosome pairing in the polyploid species of Festuca; breeding work on Panicum and Pennisetum; tropical and temperature herbage crops; polyploidy and mutation breeding techniques. **Mailing Address:** Northern Crop Sci Lab, State Univ Sta, 1307 N 18 St PO Box 5677, Fargo, ND 58105-5677. **Fax:** 701-239-1369. **E-Mail:** jauharp@fargo.ars.usda.gov

JAUMARD, BRIGITTE, COMBINATORIAL OPTIMIZATION, MATHMATICAL PROGRAMMING. **Personal Data:** b Lyon, France, April 4, 1959; c 2. **Education:** Univ Paris VI, France, DEA, 1984, THab, 1990; Int Paris, France, PhD (comput sci), 1986. **Professional Experience:** PROF ELEC & COMPUT ENG, POLYTECH SCH MONTREAL, 2001-; RES CHAIR CAN, UNIV MONTREAL, 2001-; Fribourg Univ, Switz, 1995-1996; PROF OPERS RES, POLYTECH SCH MONTREAL, 1990-; vis prof, Princeton Univ, 1990-1991; women prof sci, NSF, 1990-1991; researcher, Polytech Inst Montreal, 1987-1990; researcher & postdoctoral, Rutgers Univ, 1985-1987; res engr, CNET, France, 1983-1985. **Memberships:** Inst Oper Res & Mgt Sci; Soc Indust & Appl Math. **Research Statement & Publications:** Operations research; theoretical work and practical work; frequency assignment in cellular network. **Mailing Address:** Dept Data Processing & Opers Res, Univ Montreal, CP 6128, Succ Downtown area, Montreal, PQ H3C 3J7, Can. **Fax:** 514-343-5834. **E-Mail:** jaumard@iro.umontreal.ca

JAUMOT, FRANK EDWARD, JR, SOLID STATE PHYSICS. **Personal Data:** b Charleston, WVa, August 3, 1923; m 1947, Jean Hite; c Cherie J (Kizer) & Frank E III. **Education:** Western Md Col, BS, 1947, DSc, 1966; Univ Pa, PhD (physics), 1951. **Honorary Degrees:** DSc, Western Md Col, 1966. **Professional Experience:** PRES, JAUMOT CONSULT, INC, 1984-; dir, Automotive Elec Bus Unit, 1983-1984; dir advan eng, Delco Electronics Div, 1979-1983; dir res & eng, Delco Radio Div, Gen Motors Corp, 1970-1979; dir res & eng semiconductors, Delco Radio Div, Gen Motors Corp, 1956-1970; vis asst prof, Univ Pa, 1954-1956; chief physics, Metals Sect, Labs Res & Develop, Franklin Inst, 1952-1956; Instr asst, Univ Pa, 1952-1954; Instr physics, Univ Pa, 1951-1952. **Memberships:** Am Phys Soc; Am Inst Aeronaut & Astronaut; Inst Elec & Electronics Engrs; Soc Auto Engrs; Am Asn Physics Teachers; Sigma Xi. **Research Statement & Publications:** Order-disorder phenomena and other cooperative phenomena; diffusion in metals; thermoelectricity; semiconductors. **Mailing Address:** 7549 Mahalo Hui Dr, Diamond Head, MS 39525-3836.

JAUSSI, AUGUST WILHELM, PHYSIOLOGY. **Personal Data:** b Paris, Idaho, August 26, 1925; m 1955, c 6. **Education:** Univ Idaho, BS, 1953; Brigham Young Univ, MS, 1955; Okla State Univ, PhD, 1960. **Professional Experience:** PROF EMER, BRIGHAM YOUNG UNIV, as of 2006; prof zoology, Brigham Young Univ, 1977-1990; prof physiol, Brigham Young Univ, 1972-1977; from asst prof to assoc prof, Brigham Young Univ, 1962-1972; from instr to asst prof physiol, Okla State Univ, 1956-1962. **Research Statement & Publications:** Environmental effects on physiological activity. **Mailing Address:** Dept Biol, Brigham Young Univ, Provo, UT 84602.

JAVAID, JAVAID IQBAL, BIOCHEMISTRY, PSYCHOPHARMACOLOGY. **Personal Data:** b Lahore, Pakistan, October 1, 1942. **Education:** Univ Panjab, W Pakistan, BS, Hons, 1964, MS, 1965; State Univ NY, Buffalo, PhD (biochem), 1972. **Professional Experience:** Adj prof, dept pharmaceut & pharmacodynamics, Col Pharm, Univ Ill Chicago, as of 2004; prof, dept pharmaceut & pharmacodynamics, Col Pharm, Univ Ill Chicago, beginning 1991; admin res scientist & assoc dir biol res, Ill State Psychiat Inst, 1989-1984; ASSOC PROF BIOCHEM, DEPT PSYCHIAT, UNIV ILL CHICAGO, 1988-; asst prof, dept psychiat, col med, Univ Ill Chicago, 1985-1988; res scientist 4, Ill State Psychiat Inst, 1978-1989; res scientist 3, Ill State Psychiat Inst, 1974-1978; res fel, Ill State Psychiat Inst, 1972-1974; res asst, W Regional Labs, Lahore, 1965-1967. **Memberships:** AAAS. **Mailing Address:** Dept Psychiat, Univ Ill Chicago, 912 S Wood St, Chicago, IL 60612. **Fax:** 312-413-4544. **E-Mail:** jij@psych.uic.edu

JAVAN, ALI, PHYSICS. **Personal Data:** b Tehran, Iran, December 27, 1926; American citizen; m 1962, c 2. **Education:** Columbia Univ, PhD (physics), 1954. **Honors & Awards:** Stuart Ballentine Medal, 1962; Hertz Found Award, 1966; Sepas Medal, GovtIran, 1971; Frederic Ives Medal, Optical Soc Am, 1975; Sr US Scientist Award, Humboldt Found, 1980. **Professional Experience:** PROF EMER PHYSICS, MASS INST TECHNOL, 1996-; FOUNDER & CHIEF SCIENTIST, LASER SCI INC, 1981-; Francis Wright prof, Laser Sci, Inc, 1978-1996; from assoc prof to prof, Laser Sci, Inc, 1962-1978; mem tech staff, Bell Tel Labs, Inc, 1959-1962; res assoc physics, Columbia Univ, 1954-1959. **Memberships:** fel Nat Acad Sci; fel Am Phys Soc; fel Optical Soc Am; Sigma Xi; fel Am Acad Arts & Sci; Soc Found Third World Acad Sci. **Research Statement & Publications:** Atomic spectroscopy and physics of quantum electronics. **Mailing Address:** Dept Physics, Mass Inst Technol, Rm 6-104 77 Mass Ave, Cambridge, MA 02139. **Fax:** 617-253-8554. **E-Mail:** ajavan@mit.edu

JAVEL, ERIC, NEUROPHYSIOLOGY. **Personal Data:** b Elizabeth, NJ, March 2, 1947; m 1968, c 3. **Education:** Johns Hopkins Univ, BA, 1968; Univ Pittsburgh, PhD (bioacoustics), 1972. **Professional Experience:** ASSOC PROF OTOLARYNGOL & NEUROBIOLOGY, UNIV MINN, as of 2004; res prof Otolaryngol & neurobiology, Dukr Univ Med Ctr, beginning 1989; vis res fel, Univ Melbourne, Australia, 1984-1985; dir, Ctr Hearing Res, Boys Town Nat Inst Commun Dis C, 1976-1989; NIH fel, Dept Neurophysiol, Med Sch, Univ Wis, 1973-1975; prof otolaryngol & physiol, Sch Med, Creighton Univ; mem comt hearing & bioacoustics, Nat Acad Sci; assoc prof psychol, Univ Neb. **Memberships:** Acoust Soc Am; Soc Neuroscience; Asn Res Otolaryngol; Sigma Xi. **Research Statement & Publications:** Stimulus coding in auditory nuclei; computer applications in physiology; developmental neurophysiology; neurosensory prostheses. **Mailing Address:** Dept otolaryngol, Univ Minn, 225 Lions Res Bldg 2001 Sixth St SE, Minneapolis, MN 55455. **Fax:** 612-626-9871. **E-Mail:** javel001@tc.umn.edu

JAVICK, RICHARD ANTHONY, ANALYTICAL CHEMISTRY, ENVIRONMENTAL CHEMISTRY. **Personal Data:** b Plains, Pa, August 29, 1932; m 1961, Betty; c Lawrence, Berhadette, Theresa, Ruth, Lorraine, Margaret, Mark, Matthew, Patrick & Eileen. **Education:** King's Col, Pa, BS, 1954; Pa State Univ, PhD (chem), 1958. **Professional Experience:** SR RES ASSOC, CHEM RES & DEVELOP CTR, FMC CORP, 1992-; from sr res chemist to sr res asst, Chem Res & Develop Ctr, Fmc Corp, 1980-1992; Chmn dept chem, King's Col, Pa, 1967-1969; asst prof chem, King's Col, Pa, 1959-1961 & State assoc prof, 1962-1969; res assoc, Pa Univ, 1961-1962; Res chemist, E I du Pont de Nemours & Co, Del, 1958-1959; Retired, fmc corp, 2/1/97. **Memberships:** Am Chem Soc; Chem Mfg Asn; Int Org Legal Metrol. **Research Statement & Publications:** Application of instrumental methods to analytical investigations; electrochemical kinetics; polymer chemistry, synthesis and applications thereof; applications of analytical methods to wastewater analysis; air and water monitoring for pesticides and pesticide/herbicide residue analysis. **Mailing Address:** 10 Wycombe Way, Princeton Junction, NJ 08550.

JAVID, MANUCHER J, NEUROSURGERY. **Personal Data:** b Tehran, Iran, January 11, 1922; American citizen; m 1951, Lida; c Roxane (Pfeiffer), Daria D, Jeffrey J & Claudia M. **Education:** Univ Ill, MD, 1946; Am Bd Neurol Surg, dipl, 1955. **Professional Experience:** PROF EMER, DEPT NEUROL SUR, UNIV WIS, MADISON, as of 2006; chmn dept, Sch Med, Univ Wis-Madison, 1963-1995; prof neurol surg, Sch Med, Univ Wis, Madison, beginning 1962; from instr to assoc prof, Sch Med, Univ Wis-Madison, 1953-1962; teaching fel, Harvard Med Sch, 1952; resident, Mass Gen Hosp, 1951-1953 & New Eng Ctr Hosp, 1950; res fel, Mass Gen Hosp, 1950; fel neuropath, Ill Neuropsychiat Inst, 1949; fel neurosurg, Lahey Clin, Mass, 1949; resident neurosurg, Augustana Hosp, Ill, 1948-1949; resident gen surg, Augustana Hosp, Ill, 1947-1948; intern, Augustana Hosp, Ill, 1946-1947. **Memberships:** AAAS; AMA; fel Am Col Surg; Am Asn Neurol Surg; Soc Neurol Surgeons; Int Intradiscal Ther Soc (pres, 1991-1992). **Research Statement & Publications:** Intracranial pressure, cerebrovascular diseases, intracranial neoplasms and chemonucleolysis; introduced the use of osmotic agent, urea for the reduction of intracranial and intraocular pressure, cerebrovascular diseases, intracranial neoplasms and chemonucleolysis. **Mailing Address:** Dept Neurosurg, Med Sch, Univ Wis, H4/346 Clin Sci Ctr H4 600 Highland Ave, Madison, WI 53792. **Fax:** 608-263-1728.

JAVIDI, BAHRAM, OPTICAL COMPUTING & PROCESSING, SIGNAL & IMAGE PROCESSING. **Personal Data:** b Tehran, Iran, February 14, 1959; American citizen; m Bethany. **Education:** George Wash Univ, BS, 1980; Pa State Univ, MS, 1982, PhD (elec eng), 1986. **Professional Experience:** Conf chmn, Prog Nonlinear Optical Processing, Inst Elec & Electronics Engrs, Lasers & Electro-optics Soc, 1991; consult, US Army & USAF, 1990-; prin investr, NSF presidential young investr, 1990-1995; reviewer & panelist, Nat Res Coun, 1990; pres young investr, NSF, 1990; guest ed, spec issue J Optical Eng, 1989 & 1992; prin investr, USAF & USArmy, 1989-1991; PROF ELEC & COMPUT ENG, UNIV CONN, 1988-; prin investr, USAF, 1988-1989; ed, spec issue J Optical Eng, 1988; prin investr, Inst Elec & Electronics Engrs & Eng Found, 1987-1988; prof elec eng, Mich State Univ, 1986-1988. **Memberships:** Optical Soc Am; Optical Eng Soc; Inst Elec & Electronics Engrs; fel Int SocOptical Eng. **Research Statement & Publications:** optical image processing; pattern recognition; neural networks; associative processing; nonlinear signal processing; holography; applications of spatial light modulators to information processing; communication systems. **Mailing Address:** Elec & Systs Eng Dept U-157, Univ Conn, 260 Glenbrook Rd, Storrs, CT 06269-2157. **Fax:** 860-486-2447. **E-Mail:** bahram@engr.uconn.edu

JAVITT, NORMAN B, MEDICINE, PHYSIOLOGY. **Personal Data:** b New York, NY, March 9, 1928; m 1955, Suzanne; c Jonathan, Daniel, Joel & Gail. **Education:** Syracuse Univ, AB, 1947; Univ NC, PhD (physiol), 1951; Duke Univ, MD, 1954; Am Bd Internal Med, dipl, 1962. **Professional Experience:** PROF MED & PEDIAT & DIR DIV HEPATIC DIS, NY UNIV MED CTR, 1983-; chief, Div Hepatic Dis, 1979-1983; assoc prof, Med Col, 1973-1983; chief, Div Gastroenterol, NY Hosp Med Ctr, 1973-1979; prof med, Cornell Univ, 1972-1984; assoc prof, Cornell Univ, 1968-1972; from instr to asst prof, Sch Med, NY Univ, 1962-1968; career investr, Health Res Coun City NY, 1962-1968; res assoc, Mt Sinai Hosp, 1961-1962; USPHS spec fel, Mt Sinai Hosp, 1961-1962; chief resident med, Mt Sinai Hosp, 1960; Am Heart Asn adv fel, Col Physicians & Surgeons, Columbia Univ, 1958-1959; asst resident, Mt Sinai Hosp, New York, 1957-1958; intern med, Mt Sinai Hosp, New York, 1954-1955. **Memberships:** Am Fedn Clin Res; fel Am Col Physicians; Am Soc Clin Invest; Am Gastroenterol Asn; Am Asn Study Liver Dis; Am Pediat Soc. **Research Statement & Publications:** Biochemical and physiological investigations related to human liver disease; development of the intrahepatic and extrahepatic pathways of bile acid synthesis. **Mailing Address:** Dept Med, NY Univ Med Ctr, 550 First Ave, New York, NY 10016. **Fax:** 212-263-8282. **E-Mail:** javitt@is.nyu.edu

JAWA, MANJIT S, APPLIED MATHEMATICS, CONTINUUM MECHANICS. **Personal Data:** b Patiala, India, August 5, 1934; m 1964, c 2. **Education:** Indian Inst Technol, PhD (appl math), 1967. **Professional Experience:** RETIRED; prof math, Fayetteville State Univ, beginning 1971; assoc prof, Hartwick Col, 1970-1971; asst prof appl math & eng mech, Univ Mo-Rolla, 1967-1970; lectr math, Punjab Univ Cols, India, 1958-1963 & Indian Inst Technol, 1966-1967; res asst statist, Punjab Govt, India, 1956-1958. **Research Statement & Publications:** Exact numerical analysis of fluid dynamics, heat transfer and magnetohydrodynamics problems on digital computers. **Mailing Address:** Dept Math, Fayetteville State Univ, Fayetteville, NC 28301. **E-Mail:** mjawa@uncfsu.edu

JAWAD, MAAN HAMID, STRUCTURAL ENGINEERING, ENGINEERING MECHANICS. **Personal Data:** b Baghdad, Iraq, December 2, 1943; American citizen; m 1968, c 2. **Education:** Al-Hikma Univ, BS, 1964; Univ Kans, MS, 1965; Iowa State Univ, PhD (struct eng), 1968. **Professional Experience:** PRES, GLOBAL ENG & TECHNOL, as of 2003; asst chief eng, Nooter Corp, beginning 1987; mgr eng design, Nooter Corp, 1977-1987; staff consult, Nooter Corp, 1970-1977; design engr, Nooter Corp, 1968-1970; bridge engr, Iowa State Hwy Comn, 1967-1968. **Memberships:** Am Soc Civil Engrs; Am Soc Mech Engrs. **Research Statement & Publications:** Pressure vessels area, mainly layered vessels, expansion joints, and high pressure gaskets. **Mailing Address:** 3007 Crossview Est, St Louis, MO 63129. **E-Mail:** maanjawad@aol.com

JAWED, INAM, PHYSICAL & CEMENT CHEMISTRY, MATERIALS SCIENCE. **Personal Data:** b Sagar, India, September 27, 1947; American citizen; m 1982, Nafeesa; c Aysha & Sarah. **Education:** Karachi Univ, BS, 1966, MS, 1968; Oxford Univ, PhD (chem), 1971, Tokyo Inst Technol, dipl. **Professional Experience:** PROJ MGR, NAT COOP HWY RES PROG, TRANSP RES BD, NAT RES COUN, NAT ACAD SCI, as of 2004; PROG MGR, STRATEGIC HWY RES PROG, NAT RES COUN, 1987-; mgr, res & eng, Martin Marietta Labs, 1983-1987; head, Anal Chem Dept, Martin Marietta Labs, 1980-1983; sr scientist, Martin Marietta Labs, 1978-1980; res scientist, Martin Marietta Labs, 1976-1978; vis prof inorg chem, Tokyo Inst Technol, 1974-1976; UNESCO fel, 1974; asst prof phys chem, Peshawar Univ, 1972-1974; Brit Coun fel, 1968. **Memberships:** Am Chem Soc; fel Am Ceramic Soc; Am Concrete Inst; Am Soc Testing & Mat. **Research Statement & Publications:** Materials science of cements, concrete, ceramics, and composite materials; technical management; kinetics of formation and hydration of silicates, aluminates, and ferrites; processing and properties of structural and electronic ceramics and composite materials. **Mailing Address:** Transp Res Bd, Nat Res Council, Nat Acad Sci, 2101 Constitution Ave N W, Washington, DC 20418. **Fax:** 202-334-2003. **E-Mail:** ijawed@nas.edu

JAWEED, MAZHER, EXERCISE, NERVE REGENERATION. **Education:** Osmania Univ, BS, 1962; WVa Univ, MS, 1966; Thomas Jefferson Univ, PhD (pharmacol), 1988. **Professional Experience:** DIR RES TRAINING & DEVELOP, PHYSICIAN RES NETWORK INC, as of 2003; clin assoc prof, Baylor Col, beginning 1993; prin investr, Nat Inst Disability & Rehab, beginning 1988; ed, J Archives Phys Med & Rehab, beginning 1988; res assoc prof rehab med, Thomas Jefferson Univ, 1982-1993; res asst prof pharmacol, ThomasJefferson Univ, 1979-1993; res asst, Thomas Jefferson Univ, 1978-1982; res assoc, Thomas Jefferson Univ, 1972-1978; biochemist rehab med, Thomas Jefferson Univ, 1970-1972; mem, Am Cong Rehab Med. **Memberships:** AAAS; NY Acad Sci; Sigma Xi. **Research Statement & Publications:** Nerve and muscle interactions as affected by drugs; evaluations of effects by electrophysiological, histochemical and immunological procedures. **Mailing Address:** Physician Res Network Inc, 2000 Crowford St, Ste 777, Houston, TX 77002. **Fax:** 713-773-2099. **E-Mail:** mjaweed@hclink.com

JAWOROWSKI, ANDRZEJ EDWARD, SOLID STATE PHYSICS. **Personal Data:** b Lublin, Poland, December 28, 1942; m 1965, Bozena Natecz; c Peter A. **Education:** Univ Warsaw, MSc, 1966, PhD (physics), 1974. **Honors & Awards:** Prize of Ministry Sci, Schs Acad Rank & Technol, Warsaw, Poland, 1975. **Professional Experience:** PRES, MICRONETICS, DAYTON, 1990-; rev, NSF, 1987-; Univ EnergySysts, Dayton, 1985-1988; assoc prof physics, semiconductor group leader, Wright State Univ, Dayton, Ohio, 1983-1989; consult, Mobil Solar Energy Co, Waltham, 1980-1985; sr res assoc, State Univ NY-Albany, 1978-1983; prog head, Inst Physics, Polish Acad Sci, Warsaw, 1976-1977; asst prof physics, Univ Warsaw, 1974-1978; lectr physics, Univ Warsaw, 1968-1974; res assoc, Radiation Physics Lab, Solid State Div, Inst Nuclear Res, Swierk, 1967-1974; Instr-physics, Univ Warsaw, 1966-1968. **Memberships:** Europ Phys Soc; Am Phys Soc; Polish Phys Soc; Electrochem Soc; Mat Res Soc. **Research Statement & Publications:** Physics of electronic materials; defects in semiconductors; radiation effects and damage; deep levels spectroscopy; hydrogen in solids; real-time measurements; chaos and complexity. **Mailing Address:** Micronetics, PO Box 31467, Dayton, OH 45437.

JAWOROWSKI, JAN W, TOPOLOGY. **Personal Data:** b Augustow, Poland, March 2, 1928; American citizen; m 1954, Wanda; c Eva. **Education:** Univ Warsaw, Magister, 1952; Polish Acad Sci, PhD (math), 1955. **Professional Experience:** PROF MATH, IND UNIV, 1965-; assoc prof, Cornell Univ, 1964-1965; extraordinary prof, Math Inst, Polish Acad Sci, 1963-1964; NSF grant, Inst Advan Study, 1960-1961; fel, Polish Acad Sci, 1957-1958; from adj to docent, Univ Warsaw, 1952-1963; asst math, Univ Warsaw, 1950-1952. **Memberships:** Am Math Soc; Polish Math Soc. **Research Statement & Publications:** Algebraic and geometric topology. **Mailing Address:** Ind Univ, Bloomington, IN 47405-5701.

JAWORSKI, DEBORAH C, ENTOMOLOGY. **Education:** Ohio State Univ, PhD, 1991. **Professional Experience:** ASST RESEARCHER, DEPT MOLECULAR BIOL & BIOCHEM, UNIV CALIF-IRVINE, as of 2005. **Mailing Address:** Dept Molecular Biol & Biochem, Univ Calif-Irvine, 2315 McGaugh Hall, Irvine, CA 92697-3900. **Fax:** 949-824-8551. **E-Mail:** djaworsk@uci.edu

JAWORSKI, ERNEST GEORGE, BIOLOGICAL CHEMISTRY, MOLECULAR BIOLOGY. **Personal Data:** b Minneapolis, Minn, January 10, 1926; m 1950, c 3. **Education:** Univ Minn, BChem, 1948; Ore State Col, MS, 1950, PhD (biochem), 1952. **Honors & Awards:** David Rivette Mem Lectr, Commonwealth Sci & Indust Res, Australia. **Professional Experience:** CONSULT, JAWORSKI CONSULT, as of 2000; Nat Res Coun, 1985-; chmn bd trustees, Gordon Res Conf Inc, 1978-1979; mem panel, Int Cell Res Orgn UNESCO, 1977-; trustee, Gordon Res Conf, Inc, 1975-1981; memed bd, J Am Soc Plant Physiologists, 1973-1983; chmn, Gordon Conf Plant Cell & TissueCulture, 1973-1975; distinguished sci fel, Monsanto Co, beginning 1970; mem, Frasch FoundAwards Comt, Am Chem Soc, 1969-; sr scientist, Monsanto Co, 1962-1970; scientist, MonsantoCo, 1960-1962; res group leader, Monsanto Co, 1954-1960; res biochemist, Monsanto Co, 1952-1954; asst biochem, Ore State Col, 1949-1952; asst chem, Ore State Col, 1948-1949. **Memberships:** Fel AAAS; Am Chem Soc; Sigma Xi; Am Soc Plant Physiologists;

Weed Sci SocAm. **Research Statement & Publications:** Plant growth regulation, hormones and metabolism; plant chemotherapeutic investigations; mechanism of action of herbicides; radioisotope techniques; biosynthesis of chitin; plant cell and tissue culture; plant organogenesis; cell biology; molecular biology; genetic engineering, biotechnology. **Mailing Address:** 11 Clerbrook Lane, St Louis, MO 63124-1202.

JAWORSKI, JAN GUY, BIOCHEMISTRY. **Personal Data:** b Woonsocket, RI, December 7, 1946; m 1969, c 2. **Education:** Col the Holy Cross, BA, 1968; Purdue Univ, PhD (biochem), 1972. **Professional Experience:** PRIN INVESTR, DONALD DANFORTH PLANT SCI CTR, ST LOUIS, MO, 2002-; prof, Dept Chem & Biochem, Miami Univ, as of 1974-2001; vis scientist, Plant Biol Dept, Carnegie Inst, 1995-1996; Japan Soc Prom Sci fel, Nat Inst Basic Biol, Okazaki, Japan, 1989; vis assoc prof, Dept Bot & Plant Pathol, Mich State Univ, 1988; asst prof chem, Miami Univ, beginning 1974; res biochemist, Dept Biochem & Biophys, Univ Calif, Davis, 1972-1974. **Memberships:** AAAS; Sigma Xi. **Research Statement & Publications:** Metabolism of prostaglandins, long chain fatty acids and lipids. **Mailing Address:** Donald Danforth Plant Sci Ctr, 975 N Warson Rd, St Louis, MO 63132. **Fax:** 314-587-1988. **E-Mail:** jjaworski@danforthcenter.org

JAWORSKI, NORBERT A, ENVIRONMENTAL PROTECTION. **Professional Experience:** RETIRED; dir, Nat Environ Res Ctr, beginning 1970. **Mailing Address:** Environ Protection Agency, Environ Res Lab, 27 Tarzwell Dr, Narragansett, RI 02882-1198.

JAY, JAMES MONROE, BACTERIOLOGY, MICROBIAL ECOLOGY. **Personal Data:** b Ben Hill Co, Ga, September 12, 1927. **Education:** Paine Col, AB, 1950; Ohio State Univ, MSc, 1953, PhD (bact), 1956. **Honors & Awards:** Probus Award, 1969. **Professional Experience:** PROF EMER, BIOL SCI, WAYNE STATE UNIV, as of 2005; adj prof biol sci, Univ Nev, Las Vegas, 1994; mem expert panel, Food Microbiol Div, Am Soc Microbiologists, Food Microbiol Div, Inst Food Technologists, beginning 1991; chmn, Food Microbiol Div, Am Soc Microbiologists, Food Microbiol Div, Inst Food Technologists, 1990-1991; Nat Adv Comt Microbiol Criteriia Foods, US Dept Agr, 1987-1991; distinguished fac fel, 1987; coun, Int Exchange of Scholars (Fulbright Prog), 1985-1988; mem, Govt Univ Indust Res Round Table, Nat Acad Sci, 1984-1987; from asst prof to prof biol sci, Wayne State Univ, 1961-1994; from asst prof to prof bact, Southern Univ, 1957-1961; res assoc, Ohio State Univ, 1956-1957; asst, Agr Exp Sta, 1955-1956; asst, Ohio State Univ, 1953-1955. **Memberships:** AAAS; Am Soc Microbiol; Inst Food Technologists; Sigma Xi; Int Asn Milk, Food & Environ Sanitarians Protection. **Research Statement & Publications:** Biochemistry and rapid techniques for measuring meat spoilage; rapid determination of microorganisms in foods; microbial ecology; limulus lysate test; lipopolysaccharides in foods; selective culture media for listeria; periplasmic binding proteins. **Mailing Address:** Dept Biol Sci, Wayne State Univ, 5047 Gullen Mall, Detroit, MS 48202. **Fax:** 313-577-6981. **E-Mail:** Jays@UNLV.edu

JAYACHANDRAN, TOKE, STATISTICS, MATHEMATICS. **Personal Data:** b Madras, India, American citizen. **Education:** V R Col, Nellore, India, BA, 1951; Univ Wyo, MS, 1962; Case Inst Technol, PhD (math statist), 1967. **Professional Experience:** BDM Corp, 1972-1975; Sci Appln Inc, Monterey, beginning 1978; opers analyst, Off NavalRes, Arlington, 1975-1977; assoc prof math, Naval Postgrad sch, beginning 1970; consult, Litton Sci Support Labs, Ft Ord, 1968-1972; PROF EMER MATH, NAVAL POSTGRAD SCH, 1967-; asst prof math, Naval Postgrad Sch, 1967-1970; grad asst math, Case Inst Technol, 1962-1967; res asst statist, Univ Wyo, 1961-1962. **Memberships:** Sigma Xi; Am Statist Asn; Am Math Soc. **Research Statement & Publications:** Design of experiments, prediction intervals, reliability and life testing. **Mailing Address:** Naval PostGrad Sch, 334 Glasgow Hall, Salinas, CA 93908. **Fax:** 831-656-2355. **E-Mail:** toke@math.nps.navy.mil

JAYADEV, T S, ELECTRICAL ENGINEERING, PHYSICS. **Personal Data:** b Bangalore, India, American citizen. **Education:** Univ Mysore, BSE, 1958; Ill Inst Technol, MS, 1962; Univ Notre Dame, PhD (elec eng), 1968. **Professional Experience:** PRES, SIERRA RES, 1992-; sr scientist, Lockheed Palo Alto Res Lab, 1982-1992; mgr, Thermoelec, Energy Conversion Devices, 1980-1982; sr to prin scientist, Solar Energy Res Inst, 1978-; prof elec eng, Univ Wis-Milwaukee, 1976-1978; mem, lab surface studies, Univ Wis-Milwaukee, 1968-1978; from asst prof to assoc prof, Univ Wis-Milwaukee, 1968-1976; prof, Karnatak Univ, India, 1964-1965; asst prof elec eng, Karnatak Univ, India, 1962-1964. **Memberships:** Inst Elec & Electronics Engrs; Am Phys Soc; Am Vacuum Soc; Int Solar Energy Soc. **Research Statement & Publications:** Infrared and visible sensors; sensor signal processing; solar, wind, geothermal energy conversion systems; solid state energy conversion; electromechanical conversion systems; electrical properties of thin films; thin film devices; device physics; surface physics. **Mailing Address:** Lockheed Palo Alto Res Lab, 3251 Hanover St, Palo Alto, CA 94304.

JAYAKUMAR, RAJGOPALAN, COMPUTER SCIENCE. **Education:** Univ Madras, BE, 1977; Indian Inst Technol, 1980; Concordia Univ, PhD (Computer Sci), 1984. **Professional Experience:** DIR & ASSOC PROF, DEPT COMPUT SCI, CONCORDIA UNIV, CAN, as of 2005. **Memberships:** Assoc Comput Mach. **Mailing Address:** Dept Comput Sci Concordia Univ, 1455 de Maisonneuve Blvd W, Montreal, PQ H3G 1M8, Can. **E-Mail:** jayakumar@cs.concordia.ca

JAYANT, NIKIL, ELECTRICAL COMMUNICATIONS ENGINEERING. **Education:** Indian Inst Sci, PhD (elec communeng), 1970. **Honors & Awards:** Browder J Thompson Mem Prize Award, Inst Elec & Electronics Engrs, 1974. **Professional Experience:** JOHN PIPPIN CHMN & PROF, SCH ELEC & COMP ENG, GEORGIA INST TECH, as of 2003; dir Multimedia Comm Res Lab, Lucent Technol, Bell Labs Innovations; mgr, SignalProcessing Res Dept & Adv Audio Technol Dept, Bell Labs Innovations. **Memberships:** Nat Acad Eng; fel Int Elec & Electronics Engrs. **Research Statement & Publications:** Creation and commercialization of technologies for audiovisual communication and multimedia information systems; published over 100 articles; granted 20 US patents. **Mailing Address:** Sch Elec & Comput eng, Georgia Inst Tech, 700 Mountain Ave Rm 20-540, Atlanta, GA 30332-0250. **Fax:** 404-894-5692. **E-Mail:** nikil.jayant@ece.gatech.edu

JAYANT, NUGGEHALLY S, COMMUNICATIONS SCIENCE, SPEECH PROCESSING. **Personal Data:** b Bangalore, India, January 9, 1946. **Education:** Univ Mysore, BSc, 1962; Indian Inst Sci, Bangalore, BE, 1965, PhD (elec commun), 1970. **Professional Experience:** HEAD, SIGNAL PROCESSING RES DEPT, BELL TEL LABS, 1986-; vis prof, Univ Calif, 1983; vis scientist, Indian Inst Sci, Bangalore, 1972, 1975; mem tech staff speech & acoust res, Signal Processing Res Dept, Bell Tel Labs, 1968-1986; res assoc commun, Stanford Univ, 1967-1968; fel Coun Sci & Indust Res, India, 1966-1967. **Memberships:** Fel Inst Elec & Electronics Engrs. **Research Statement & Publications:** Speech communication and information systems; image processing. **Mailing Address:** 135 Preston Dr, Gillette, NJ 07933.

JAYANTY, R K M, ANALYTICAL METHODS DEVELOPMENT & EVALUATION, ATMOSPHERIC CHEMISTRY. **Personal Data:** b June 29, 1946; m 1978, Lakshmi; c Nagendra & Phanindra. **Education:** Andhra Univ, BS, 1964, MS, 1966; Pa State Univ, MEng, 1975; Univ Bradford, PhD (chem), 1972. **Honors & Awards:** Frank A Chambers Award, Air & Waste Mgt Asn, 1991. **Professional Experience:** Mem, Sci Adv Bd, State NC, 1990-1992; UN vis fel, Coun Sci & Indust Res, India, 1990; adj prof, NC State Univ, beginning 1986; MGR, RES TRIANGLE INST, 1986-; chmn, Ambient Measurement Comt, Air & Waste Mgt Asn, beginning 1983; sr chemist, Res Triangle Inst, 1978-1986; sr scientist, TRC Res Corp New Eng, 1976-1978; res assoc, Pa State Univ, 1973-1976; scientist, Regional Res Lab, 1966-1969. **Memberships:** Am Chem Soc; fel Air & Waste Mgt Asn; fel Am Inst Chemists. **Research Statement & Publications:** Develop and evaluate sampling and analytical methods for toxic pollutant emissions from ambient, source and hazardous waste atmospheres. **Mailing Address:** Triangle Res Inst, PO Box 12194, Research Triangle Park, NC 27709. **Fax:** 919-541-7215. **E-Mail:** rkmj@rti.org

JAYAPRAKASH, CIRIYAM, PHYSICS. **Education:** Univ Ill Urbana, PhD, 1978. **Professional Experience:** PROF, OHIO STATE UNIV, as of 2003. **Mailing Address:** Dept Phys, Ohio State Univ, 191 W Woodruff Ave, Columbus, OH 43210-1117. **Fax:** 614-292-2911. **E-Mail:** jay@mps.ohio-state.edu

JAYARAM, BEBY, PURIFICATION CHARACTERIZATION OF PROTEINS, IDENTIFICATION OF NUCLEOTIDE BINDING DOMAIN PEPTIDES. **Education:** Mysore Univ, India, BS, 1974, MS, 1976; Bangalore Univ, India, PhD (chem), 1984. **Professional Experience:** RES ASSOC, UNIV KY, 1992-; scholar, Univ KY, 1989-1992; Robert Welchfel, Baylor Univ, 1988-1989. **Research Statement & Publications:** Purification and characterization of several enzymes/proteins from different brain tissues and blood serum samples; use of HPLC, FPLC, ion-exchange, affinity, gelfiltration etc chromatographic techniques for protein and nucleotide purification; use of prep cell, 2D, IEF-gel electrophoresis, Western blot analysis etc for protein purification and characterization; study of various aspects of protein-nucleotide interactions which regulate enzyme activity; synthesis and use of highly radioactive and non-radioactive nucleotide based antiviral agents; validation of these nucleotide analogs as active site directed reagents for various proteins/enzymes; identification and isolation of specific nucleotide binding domain peptides of different proteins/enzymes; use of high field NMR, IR, UV-Vis and various TLC techniques; use of 2D peptide mapping and phosphoamino acid analysis technique to study the difference between peptide generated from normal (non-demented) and Alzheimer's diseased brain proteins/enzymes. **Mailing Address:** Markey Cancer Ctr No 58, Univ Ky, Lexington, KY 40536. **Fax:** 606-323-2074.

JAYARAM, HIREMAGALUR N, EXPERIMENTAL ONCOLOGY. **Personal Data:** b India. **Education:** LM Col Pharm, India, BS, 1962; Andhra Univ, Wallier, India, MS, 1964; Indian Inst Sci, Bangalore, India, PhD (biochem/pharmacol), 1970. **Professional Experience:** PROF BIOCHEM & MOLECULAR BIOL & EXP ONCOL, IND UNIV SCHMED, 1985-; sr investr pharmacol, Nat Cancer Inst, 1975-1985; Fogarty int fel, Nat Cancer Inst, 1972-1974. **Memberships:** Am Soc Biochem & Molecular Biol; Soc Toxicol; Sigma Xi; Am Soc Cancer Res. **Mailing Address:** Dept Biochem & Molecular Biol, Ind Univ Sch Med, Vet Admin Med Ctr-151, Rm D3033, 1481 W 10th St, Indianapolis, IN 46202-5122. **Fax:** 317-554-0092. **E-Mail:** hjayaram@jupui.edu

JAYARAM, S, ELECTRICAL ENGINEERING. **Education:** Univ Eng Col, Bangalore, India, BE; Indian Inst Sci, Bangalore, India, MSc; Univ Waterloo, PhD. **Professional Experience:** PROF, ELEC & COMPUT ENG, UNIV WATERLOO, as of 2005. **Mailing Address:** Dept Elec & Comput Eng, Univ Waterloo, EIT 3105 200 Univ Ave W, Waterloo, ON N2L 3G1, Can. **Fax:** 519-746-3077. **E-Mail:** jayaram@ecemail.uwaterloo.ca

JAYARAMAN, AIYASAMI, HIGH PRESSURE PHYSICS. **Personal Data:** b Madras, India, December 5, 1926; m 1945, Kamala; c Geetha M & Chiltra N. **Education:** Univ Madras, BSc, 1946, MSc, 1954, PhD (solid state physics), 1960. **Honors & Awards:** Krishan Gold Medal, Int Geog Union, 1969; Alexander von Humboldt US Sr Scientist Award, 1979; Raman Centenary Medal, 1988. **Professional Experience:** RETIRED; vis res scientist, Geophys Lab Carnegie Inst Washington, 1998-2001; sr res scientist, Univ Hawaii, Hawaii Inst Geophys, Honolulu, 1992-1997; vis prof, JNC Indian Inst Sci, 1991-1992; distinguished mem tech staff, AT&T Bell Labs, 1983-1990; vis prof, Max Planck Inst, 1979-1980; Guggenheim fel, 1970-1971; vis scientist, Nat Aeronaut Lab, India, 1970-1971; vis prof, Indian Inst Sci, Bangalore, 1970-1971; mem tech staff, Bell Labs, NJ, 1963-1983; asst res geophysicist, Inst Geophys, Univ Calif, Los Angeles, 1960-1963; asst prof, Raman Res Inst, India, 1954-1960; res asst physics, Raman Res Inst, India, 1949-1954. **Memberships:** Fel Am Phys Soc; fel Indian Acad Sci (treas, 1956-1960); Sigma Xi; hon fel Mat Res Soc India. **Research Statement & Publications:** Optical, x-ray crystallography and luminescence; phase transitions in solids at high pressures; transport properties in semiconductors, magnetic and superconducting properties of metals and alloys. **Mailing Address:** 15906 Lahinch Cir, Odessa, FL 33556. **E-Mail:** aiyasami@hotmail.com

JAYARAMAN, GOPAL, BIOMECHANICS. **Education:** Univ Iowa, PhD. **Professional Experience:** PROF, DEPT ENG MECH, MICH TECH MECH ENG, MICH, as of 2006. **Mailing Address:** ME-EM Dept, Mich Technol Univ, Houghton, MI 49931. **E-Mail:** gjayar@mtu.edu

JAYARAMAN, H, ORGANIC CHEMISTRY. **Personal Data:** b Gudiattam, India, December 21, 1936; American citizen; m 1969, Padma; c Mythri. **Education:** Univ Madras, BSc, 1956, MA, 1958, PhD (chem), 1963. **Professional Experience:** Chmn, Petrol Abstr Indus Adv Coun, 1992-; TECH MGR RES & DEVELOP, PHILLIPS PETROL CO, OKLA, 1991-; supvr, Tech Planning & Intelligence Div, Res & Develop, 1986-1991; sr info scientist, Phillips Petrol Co, 1980-1986; info scientist, Phillips Petrol Co, 1973-1980; res assoc, Univ Pa, 1972-1973; res assoc, Univ Kans, 1970-1972; pool off, Madras Christian Col, India, 1969-1970; res assoc, Pa State Univ, 1966-1968; Fulbright fel, 1965-1968; Fulbright-Hays res fel, Univ Kans, 1965-1966; lectr, Madras Christian Col, India, 1957-1965. **Memberships:** Am Chem Soc. **Research Statement & Publications:** Computerized retrieval and dissemination of technical information; writing on topics of value to technology planning and administrative divisions of corporations. **Mailing Address:** Phillips Research ctr, 134 PLB, Bartlesville, OK 74004. **Fax:** 918-662-2171. **E-Mail:** amj@ppco.com

JAYARAMAN, NARAYANAN, CREEP-FATIGUE-ENVIRONMENT. **Personal Data:** b Tamilnadu, India, June 30, 1948; m 1977. **Education:** Indian Inst Sci, Bangalore, India, BE, 1970, ME, 1972, PhD (metal), 1979. **Professional Experience:** HEAD, DEPT MAT SCI ENG, UNIV CINCINNATI, as of 2001; ASSOC PROF METAL, UNIV CINCINNATI, 1985-; asst prof, UnivCincinnati, 1981-1985; vis asst prof, Univ Cincinnati, 1980-1981; fel, Univ Cincinnati, 1979-1980; scientist, Nat Aeronaut Lab, India, 1977-1979; res fel metal, Indian Inst Sci, 1972-1977. **Memberships:** Am Soc Metals; Metal Soc; AAAS; Sigma Xi. **Research Statement & Publications:** Fracture and fatigue behavior of ni-base superalloys in relationship with their microstructures; stress generation due to oxidation of metals and alloys; life prediction models for high temperature materials. **Mailing Address:** Dept Mat Sci & Metall Eng, Univ Cincinnati, Rm 489 PO Box 21002, Cincinnati, OH 45221-0012. **E-Mail:** narayanan.jayaraman@uc.edu

JAYAS, DIGVIR SINGH, GRAIN DRYING & STORAGE, MODELING OF BIOLOGICAL SYSTEMS. **Personal Data:** b Mant, Uttar Pradesh, India, January 10, 1958; Canadian citizen; m 1982, Manju; c Rajat, Ravi & Rahul. **Education:** G B Pant Univ, Pantnagar, BTech, 1980; Univ Man, Winnipeg, MSc, 1982; UnivSask, Saskatoon, PhD (agr eng), 1987. **Honors & Awards:** Fellow Am Soc Agr & Bio Eng, 2005; Fellow Can Soc Bioeng, 2005; Young Scientist Award, Appl Zoologists Res Asn, 1992; Eng Young Researcher Award, Am Soc Agr Engrs, 1994; Young Agr Engr, Can Soc Agr Eng, 1995. **Professional Experience:** Actg vpres & can res chair stored grain ecosyst, Univ Man, Winnipeg, 2003; ASSOC VPRES & CAN RES CHAIR STORED GRAIN ECOSYST, UNIV MAN, WINNIPEG, 2002-; prof & assoc vpres, Univ Man, Winnipeg, 2001-2002; prof & assoc dean, Agr & Food Sci, Univ Man, Winnipeg, 1999-2001; prof & head, Dept Biosyst Eng, Univ man, Winnipeg, 1997-1999; prof biosysts eng, Univ Man, 1995-1997; prof, Dept Agr Eng, Univ Man, Winnipeg, 1993-1995; from asst prof to assoc prof, Univ Man, 1985-1993; grad res assoc, Univ Sask, 1982-1985; pool scientist agr eng, G B Pant Univ, 1982; grad res assoc, Dept Agr Eng, Univ man, Winnipeg, 1982-1985; res assoc, Agr Eng Dept, Univ G.B. Pant, Pantnagar, 1980; grad res asst, Dept Agr Eng, Univ man, Winnipeg, 1980-1981; assoc ed, Can Agr Eng, ApplEng Agr & Trans Am Soc Agr Engrs. **Memberships:** Am Soc Agr & Bio Engrs; Can Soc Agr Eng; Can Inst Food Sci & Technol; Asian Asn Agr Engrs; Asn Prof Engrs; Agr Inst Can; Man Inst Agrologists. **Research Statement & Publications:** Physical and thermal properties of agricultural products; mathematical modelling of biological systems in relation to biotic and abiotic variables; controlled-atmosphere storage of agricultural products; instrumentation; sterilization of canned foods; digital image processing; food preservation; thermal processing. **Mailing Address:** Dept Biosyst eng, Univ Man, 207 Admin Bldg, Winnipeg, MB R3T 2N2, Can. **Fax:** 204-474-7568. **E-Mail:** digvir_jayas@umanitoba.ca

JAYASURIYA, KUMARA, MATHEMATICS. **Education:** Univ Wis, PhD. **Professional Experience:** ASSOC PROF, NAT SCI & MATH DEPT, IND UNIV E, as of 2005. **Mailing Address:** Dept Math, Ind Univ E, 2325 Chester Blvd, Richmond, IN 47374-1220. **Fax:** 765-973-8288. **E-Mail:** pjayasur@indiana.edu

JAYASURIYA, SUHADA, MATHEMATICS. **Education:** Wayne State Univ, PhD (Mech Eng), 1982. **Professional Experience:** DIR, SYS ENG PROG DEVELOP, COL ENG, TEX A&M UNIV, as of 2006. **Mailing Address:** Tex A&M Univ, 122 Eng/Physics Bldg Off Wing, College Station, TX 77845. **Fax:** 979-845-3081. **E-Mail:** sjayasuriya@tamu.edu

JAYASURIYA, SUHADA, ROBUST CONTROL & ACTIVE CONTROL OF VIBRATIONS, DYNAMICS. **Personal Data:** b Colombo, Sri Lanka, December 20, 1953; American citizen; m 1979, c Ruvin, Nilan & Sashinie. **Education:** Univ Sri Lanka, BSc, 1977; Wayne State Univ, MS, 1980, PhD (mech eng), 1982. **Honors & Awards:** Gustus E Larson Mem Award, 1997. **Professional Experience:** Distinguished fac fel, USN, 1996 & 1997; fac fel, NASA, 1995; MEINHARD H KOTZEBUE PROF & HEAD DEPT MECH ENG, TEX A&M UNIV, 1994-; vis prof mech eng, Univ Calif, Berkeley, 1991-1992; from assocprof to prof, Tex A&M Univ, 1987-1994; asst prof, Mich State Univ, 1983-1987; asst lectr mech eng, Univ Sri Lanka, 1978-1979. **Memberships:** fel Am Soc Mech Engrs; Inst Elec & Electronics Engrs; Soc Indust & Appl Math; NY Acad Sci; Am Soc Eng Educ. **Research Statement & Publications:** Robust control; control of uncertain nonlinear systems; mode localization; vibrations; dynamics; electro-magnetic actuators; frequency domain design; active noise control; smart structures; reconfigurable controls. **Mailing Address:** Dept Mech Eng, Tex A&M Univ, College Station, TX 77843-3123. **Fax:** 979-845-3081. **E-Mail:** sjayasuriya@mengr.tamu.edu

JAYASWAL, RADHESHYAM K, MOLECULAR BIOLOGY, MICROBIOLOGY. **Personal Data:** b Ramganj, India, July 6, 1949; American citizen; m 1977, Lara R; c Vikas & Kavita. **Education:** Bombay Univ, India, BSc, 1973, MSc, 1980; Purdue Univ, PhD (molecular genetics), 1985; Bhabha Inst, India, dipl anal methods, 1974. **Honors & Awards:** Recepient of Univ - Outstanding Researcher 2000. **Professional Experience:** DIR BIOTECH PGM, ILL STATE UNIV, as of 2004; Am Heart Asn Award, Am Heart Asn-Iowa, 1991-2002; NIH award, 1990- 2002; PROF MICROBIOL GENETICS, DEPT BIOL SCI, ILL STATE UNIV, NORMAL, 1988-; res assoc, Dept Biol, 1985-1988; res asst molecular biol, Dept Hort, Purdue Univ, 1980-1985; Sci asst molecular biol, Tata Inst Fundamental Res, Bombay, 1974-1980. **Memberships:** Am Soc Microbiol; Am Phytopath Soc; Am Heart Asn. **Research Statement & Publications:** Currently we are investigating three major projects in our lab: 1) identification and molecular characterization of staphylococcal genes involved in the pathogenicity, 2) genes involved in the acquisition of essential trace elements, and 3) drug resistance mechanism in S aureus. **Mailing Address:** Dept Biol Sci, Ill State Univ, Slb 341, Normal, IL 61790-0001. **Fax:** 309-438-3722. **E-Mail:** drjay@ilstu.edu

JAYAWEERA, KOLF, CLOUD PHYSICS. **Personal Data:** b Kalutara, Ceylon, December 2, 1938; m 1965, c 3. **Education:** Univ Ceylon, BS, 1960; Univ London, PhD (physics), 1965, Imp Col, Univ London, DIC(cloud physics), 1965. **Professional Experience:** PROF EMER PHYSICS, UNIV ALASKA FAIRBANKS, 1992-; DEAN, SCH NATURAL SCI & MATH, CALIF STATE UNIV, 1990-; dean, Col Natural Sci, 1985-1990; prog assoc meteorol, Air Force Off Sci Res, 1979-1984; prog assoc meteorol, NSF, 1978-1979; Nat Oceanog & Atmospheric Admin, 1973-1975 & Off Naval Res, 1972-1975; res grants, NSF, Geophys Inst, Univ Alaska, 1971-1984; from asst prof to prof geophys, Univ Alaska, 1970-1990; scientist, Commonwealth Sci & Indust Res Orgn res fel, Sydney, 1967-1970; lectr, Univ Ceylon, 1965-1967; asst lectr physics, Univ Ceylon, 1960-1962. **Memberships:** AAAS; fel Royal Meteorol Soc; Am Meteorol Soc; Am Geophys Union. **Research Statement & Publications:** Nucleation, growth and aerodynamics of ice crystals in clouds; weather modification; satellite meteorology and sea ice; atmosphere turbulence. **Mailing Address:** Sch Natural Sci & Math, Calif State Univ, PO Box 6850, Fullerton, CA 92834-6850. **Fax:** 714-278-5390. **E-Mail:** kjayaweera@fullerton.edu

JAYE, MURRAY JOSEPH, FOOD SCIENCE, MICROBIOLOGY. **Personal Data:** b New York, NY, August 17, 1937; m 1960, c 2. **Education:** Univ Ga, BS, 1959; Univ Ill, Urbana, MS, 1961, PhD (food sci), 1964. **Professional Experience:** TECH DIR, FAIRMONT FOODS CO, 1980-; mgr new food prod, Clorox Co, 1975-; mgr corp develop, Frito-Lay Inc, 1974-1975; prin scientist, Frito-Lay Inc, 1971-1973; sect mgr, Frito-Lay Inc, 1969-1970; sr scientist, Frito-Lay Inc, 1967-1968; res scientist, Hercules Inc, 1964-1967. **Memberships:** Am Chem Soc; Inst Food Technologists; Am Mgt Asn. **Research Statement & Publications:** New food products research; flavor chemistry and utilization; starch and hydrocolloid chemistry and utilization; food systems development; research administration. **Mailing Address:** 2517 Via Verde, Walnut Creek, CA 94598-3443.

JAYME, DAVID WOODWARD, BIOTECHNOLOGY, BIOMEDICAL APPLICATIONS. **Personal Data:** b Paterson, NJ, December 30, 1950; m 1973, Donna; c Lara, Stephen, Kent, Adam, Bethany & Nathan. **Education:** Univ Brigham Young, BS, 1974, MS, 1975; Univ Mich, PhD (biol chem), 1979. **Professional Experience:** SR DIR, CELL CULTURE RES & DEVELOP, GIBCO, INVITROGEN, 2000-; sci dir, Indust Cell Culture Appl, 1995-2000; tech dir, cell cult res & develop, Life Technologies Inc, 1992-1995; dir, Life Technologies Inc, 1988-1992; mgr, Life Technologies Inc, 1983-1988; res asst prof, pharmacol, Med Col Va, Va Commonwealth Univ, 1981-1983; fel, human genetics, Sch Med, Univ Yale, 1979-1981. **Memberships:** NY Acad Sci; Am Soc Cell Biol; Tissue Cult Asn; Am Chem Soc; AAAS. **Research Statement & Publications:** Serum-free nutrient optimization for research and biotechnology applications of cultured mammalian and invertebrate cells; cultivation of human and other mammalian cells for in vitro toxicology, cellular therapy, and other biomedical applications. **Mailing Address:** 3175 Staley Rd, Grand Island, NY 14072. **Fax:** 716-774-6996. **E-Mail:** david.jayme@invitrogen.com

JAYNE, JACK EDGAR, CHEMISTRY. **Personal Data:** b Spokane, Wash, December 18, 1925; m 1947, Doris; c Nancy, Thomas, Brian & Claudia. **Education:** Univ Wis, BS, 1947, MS, 1948; Lawrence Univ, MS, 1950, PhD, 1953. **Professional Experience:** RETIRED; corp environ dir, Green Bay Packaging, Inc, 1974-1988; sr res scientist, Kimberly-Clark Corp, 1952-1974. **Memberships:** Tech Asn Pulp & Paper Indust. **Research Statement & Publications:** Environmental research on effluents and emissions from pulp and paper manufacture. **Mailing Address:** N4218 Gonnering Ct, Kaukauna, WI 54130-7258. **E-Mail:** jayne@athenet.net

JAYNE, JERROLD CLARENCE, ANALYTICAL CHEMISTRY, INORGANIC CHEMISTRY. **Personal Data:** b Stevens Point, Wis, February 8, 1931; m 1960, c 2. **Education:** Univ Wis, BS, 1952, PhD (analytical chem), 1963. **Professional Experience:** PROF EMER CHEM, SAN FRANCISCO STATE UNIV, 1992-; prof chem, San Francisco State Univ, beginning 1975; partic, Water ChemProg, Univ Wis, 1970-1972; from asst prof to assoc prof, San Francisco State Univ, 1963-1974. **Memberships:** Am Chem Soc; Sigma Xi. **Research Statement & Publications:** Coordination chemistry; water chemistry. **Mailing Address:** Dept Chem & Biochem, San Francisco State Univ, 1600 Holloway Ave, San Francisco, CA 94132-4163. **Fax:** 415-338-2384.

JAYNES, HUGH OLIVER, FOOD SCIENCE. **Personal Data:** b Greeneville, Tenn, August 14, 1931; m 1953, c 2. **Education:** Univ Tenn, BS, 1953, MS, 1954; Univ Ill, PhD (food sci), 1970. **Professional Experience:** DEPT HEAD, UNIV TENN, KNOXVILLE, 1985-; coordr, Int Agr Progs, 1982-1985; Vis prof, Univ Alexandria, Egypt, 1980; PROF FOOD TECHNOL & SCI, UNIVTENN, KNOXVILLE, 1979-; assoc prof, Univ Tenn, Knoxville, 1970-1979; res fel food sci, Univ Ill, 1967-1970; sect leader chem, Res & Develop Ctr, Pet, Inc, 1963-1967; Bacteriologist, Res & Develop Ctr, Pet, Inc, 1956-1963. **Memberships:** Inst Food Technologists; Am Dairy Sci Asn; Sigma Xi. **Research Statement & Publications:** Applied research in food color, food chemistry and food product development. **Mailing Address:** 8221 Corteland Dr, Knoxville, TN 37909.

JAYNES, JOHN ALVA, FOOD SCIENCE. **Personal Data:** b Bonham, Tex, September 27, 1929; m 1955, c 2. **Education:** Sam Houston State Teachers Col, BS, 1951; Tex Tech Col, BS, 1956, MS, 1957; Mich State Univ, PhD (dairy), 1960. **Professional Experience:** VPRES OPERS GROCERY PROD, BORDEN INC, 1981-; vpres, CannedMilk Prod, 1980-1981; pres refrigerated prod, Canned Milk Prod, 1977-1979; vpres foods div, Canned Milk Prod, 1975-1976; pres beverage prod, Canned Milk Prod, 1973-1975; prod mgr, Canned Milk Prod, 1967-1973; assoc dir res, Borden Inc, 1963-1967; Proj leader food res, Borden Inc, 1960-1963. **Memberships:** Am Dairy Sci Asn. **Research Statement & Publications:** Canned sterile milk and milk based drinks. **Mailing Address:** 2776 W Dublin Grandville Rd, Columbus, OH 43235.

JAYNES, RICHARD ANDRUS, PLANT BREEDING. **Personal Data:** b New Iberia, La, May 27, 1935; m 1959, Sarah; c Burton, Linda & B Scott. **Education:** Wesleyan Univ, BA, 1957; Yale Univ, MS, 1959, PhD (bot), 1961. **Honors & Awards:** Edgar T Wherry Award, Am Rock Garden Soc, 1991; Gold medal, Am Rhododendron soc, 1999. **Professional Experience:** CONSULT, 1984-, horticulturist, Conn Agr Exp Sta, 1980-1984; from asst geneticist to geneticist, Conn Agr Exp Sta, 1961-1980; owner, Broken Arrow Nursery. **Memberships:** Am Soc Hort Sci; fel Int Plant Propagators Soc. **Research Statement & Publications:** Development of hybrid chestnut trees resistant to the chestnut blight fungus; biological control of the chestnut blight fungus; breeding improved woody ornamentals, especially laurel (Kalmia); vegetative propagation of woody plants. **Mailing Address:** 13 Broken Arrow Rd, Hamden, CT 06518. **Fax:** 203-287-1035.

JAZWINSKI, S MICHAL, GENETICS OF AGING, CELL CYCLE CONTROL. **Personal Data:** b Detroit, Mich, June 8, 1947; m 1970, Barbara; c Michal M & Peter M. **Education:** Warsaw Univ, Poland, MS, 1970; Stanford Univ, Calif, PhD (biochem), 1975. **Professional Experience:** Chair-elect, Eukaryotic Biol Div, Am Soc Microbiol, 1997; vpres, KROLFound, 1995-; CO-DIR, CTR ON AGING, 1992-; mem, Molecular Cytology Study Sect, NIH, 1991-1995; PROF BIOCHEM & MOLECULAR BIOL, LA STATE UNIV MED CTR, 1990-; assoc prof, Ctr On Aging, 1984-1990; asst prof, Rockfeller Univ, 1977-1984; Helen Hay Whitneyfel, Rockfeller Univ, 1975-1978. **Memberships:** Am Soc Biochem & Molecular Biol; Am Soc Microbiol; Genetics Soc Am; HarveySoc; Sigma Xi; fel Geront Soc Am. **Research Statement & Publications:** Genetics of aging; cloned a set of genes that are differentially expressed during the yeast life span; identified eight longevity assurance genes in this organism. **Mailing Address:** Dept Biochem & Molecular Biol, La State Univ Med Ctr 1901 Perdido St, New Orleans, LA 70112-1393.

JEAN, GEORGE NOEL, organic chemistry; deceased, see previous edition for last biography

JEAN, YANCHING JERRY, PHYSICS. **Education:** Marquette Univ, Ph.D. **Professional Experience:** CUR PROF, CHEM PHYSICS, UNIV MO, as of 2003. **Mailing Address:** Dept Chem, Univ Mo-Kansas City, Kansas City, MO 64110. **Fax:** 816-235-5502. **E-Mail:** JeanY@umkc.edu

JEAN-BAPTISTE, EMILE, MEDICINE, PHYSIOLOGY. **Personal Data:** b Port-au-Prince, Haiti, March 15, 1947; m 1968, c 2. **Education:** Fordham Univ, BS, 1971, MS, 1972, PhD (physiol), 1976; Med Col, Cornell Univ, MD, 1983. **Professional Experience:** MEM, ARTHUR ASHE INST URBAN HEALTH, as of 2003; EXEC DIR MED AFFAIRS, EUROPE, 1994-; DIR CLIN RES, DIRECT ACCESS DIAG, JOHNSON & JOHNSON, 1994-; assoc med dir, AIDS Inst, NY State Health Dept, 1993-1994; Brooklyn Borough Commnr, NY City Health Dept, 1990-1993; LAB BACT & IMMUNOL, LAB CELL BIOCHEM & PHARMACOL, ROCKEFELLER UNIV, 1989-; medepidemiologist, New York City Health Dept, 1989-1993; prof, Hofstra Univ, 1989-1992; prof, City Univ NY, 1987-; pres & founder, Haitian Biomed Found, 1986-; adj fac, Lab Cell Biochem & Pharmacol, Rockefeller Univ, 1985-; intern/resident internal med, Lab Cell Biochem & Pharmacol, 1983-1984; asst prof, Lab Cell Biochem & Pharmacol, 1980-1985; fel, NIH, 1978-1980; consult-tranlr, Fr ed, Med Lett, 1977-1987; fel, Rockefeller Univ, 1976-1980; res assoc metab & endocrinol, Europe, 1976-1980; asst prof, City Univ NY, 1975-1980; adj asst prof, Col New Rochelle, 1975-1976. **Memberships:** Am Soc Zoologists; Sigma Xi; AAAS; NY Acad Sci; Am Soc Pharmacol & Exp Therapeut; AMA; Am Acad Pain Mgt; Nat Coun Int Health. **Research Statement & Publications:** Hormonal regulation of lipolysis in adipose tissue; steroidogenesis in adrenal cortex; magnesium flux in plasma membranes; ACTH and glucagon analogs, endorphins, enkephelins, naloxone, luteinizing-hormone releasing hormone and their mechanism of action through the cyclic adenosine monophosphate system; endocrine pharmacology; biochemistry; public health; endocrinology; pharmacology. **Mailing Address:** Arthur Ashe Inst Urban Health, 450 Clarkson Ave, Brooklyn, NY 11203.

JEANLOZ, RAYMOND, MINERAL & MATERIALS PHYSICS, PLANETARY INTERIORS & HIGH PRESSURE RESEARCH. **Personal Data:** b Winchester, Mass, August 18, 1952. **Education:** Amherst Col, BA, 1975; Calif Inst Technol, PhD (geol & geophys), 1979. **Honors & Awards:** J B Macelwane Award, Am Geophys Union, 1984, First Birch Lectr, 1988; Presidential Young Investr Award, 1984; Mineral Soc Am Award, 1988; MacArthur Found Award, 1988; Eyring Lectr, Ariz State Univ, 1989; Hudnall Lectr, UnivChicago, 1990; Abelson Lectr, Carnegie Inst, Wash, 1994; Segre Lectr, Tel Aviv Univ, 1995; National Associate, National Academies, 2001; Highly Cited Researcher, Inst Scientific Information, 2002; J Tuzo Wilson Lecture, Univ Toronto, 2002; ZhongGuanCun Forum, Chinese Acad Sci, 2005; William Smith Lecture, The Geological Society (London), 2005. **Professional Experience:** Miller res prof, Berkeley, Calif, 1992; Fairchild scholar, Calif Inst Technol, 1988; PROF EARTH & PLANET SCI, UNIV CALIF, BERKELEY, 1985-; from asst prof to assoc prof, Univ Calif, Berkeley, 1982-1985; A P Sloan Found fel, 1981-1985; Mem, Mat Res Lab, Harvard Univ, 1979-1981; Asst prof, Harvard Univ, 1979-1981. **Memberships:** Fel AAAS; fel Am Geophys Union; Geol Soc Am; Mineral Soc Am; Mat Res Soc; fel Am Acad Arts & Sci; National Academy of Sciences. **Research Statement & Publications:** Experimental and theoretical study of minerals and other materials at high pressures, with particular application to the state of planetary interiors. **Mailing Address:** Dept Earth & Planetary Sci, Univ Calif, Berkeley, CA 94720-4767. **Fax:** 510-643-9980. **E-Mail:** jeanloz@uclink.berkeley.edu

JEANLOZ, ROGER WILLIAM, BIOCHEMISTRY, SYNTHETIC ORGANIC & NATURAL PRODUCTS. **Personal Data:** b Berne, Switz, November 3, 1917; American citizen; m 1945, Dorothea; c Patrick M (deceased), Claude A, Raymond F, Danielle R & Sylvie A. **Education:** Univ Geneva, BS, 1941, PhD (org chem), 1943. **Honorary Degrees:** MA, Harvard Univ, 1961; DSc, Univ Paris, 1980. **Honors & Awards:** Fr Soc Biol Chem Medal, 1960; Liege Univ Medal, 1964; Hudson Prize, Am Chem Soc, 1973; Alexander von Humboldt Sr Scientist Award, 1983. **Professional Experience:** HON BIOCHEMIST, SHRIVER CTR, 1992-; guest prof, Univ Kiel, 1984; guest prof, Univ Saar, 1983; Guggenheim Found fel, 1976-1977; guest prof, Univ Geneva, 1976; guest prof, Univ Tokyo & Univ Kyoto, 1975; lectr, Grenoble, 1972 & Lille, 1973; mem physiolchem B res study comn, Am Heart Asn, 1972-1975; Nat Acad Sci & Acad Sci USSR exchangefel, 1970; PROF EMER BIOL CHEM, HARVARD MED SCH, 1969-; mem, Study Sect PhysiolChem, NIH, 1964-1968 & 1969-1970; BIOCHEMIST, MASS GEN HOSP, 1961-; tutor, Harvard Univ, 1961; from asst prof to assoc prof, Dept Med, Harvard Med Sch, 1960-1969; guest prof, Univ Freiburg, 1960; NSF sr fel, 1959-1960; guest prof, Univ Cologne, 1959-1960; assoc org chem, Dept Med, Harvard Med Sch, 1957-1960; lectr, Swiss-Am Found Sci Exchange, 1953-1954; assoc biochemist, Mass Gen Hosp, 1951-1961; res assoc, Harvard Med Sch, 1951-1957; sr mem & head, Biochem Lab, Worcester Found Exp Biol, 1949-1951; NIH sr res fel, 1948; assoc, Univ Montreal, 1947; Swiss Found fel, Univ Basel, 1943-1945; instr chem, UnivGeneva, 1941-1944. **Memberships:** Am Chem Soc; Am Soc Biol Chemists; Royal Soc Chem; Swiss Chem Soc; Biochem Soc; fel AAAS. **Research Statement & Publications:** Chemistry of carbohydrates; amino sugars; mucopolysaccharides; glycolipids; glycoproteins; bacterial cell walls; deoxysugars; ribose derivatives; glycogen; steroids; metabolism of corticosteroids. **Mailing Address:** Dept Biol Chem, Eunice Kennedy Shriver Ctr, 200 Trapelo Rd, Waltham, MA 02454. **Fax:** 617-893-4018.

JEANMAIRE, ROBERT L, SCIENCE EDUCATION. **Personal Data:** b Rockford, Ill, February 28, 1920; m 1947, c 3. **Education:** Univ Ill, BS, 1950, MS, 1952; Rensselaer Polytech Inst, MS, 1965. **Professional Experience:** PROF EMER PHYSICS, CARTHAGE COL, as of 2006; from assoc prof to prof physics, Carthage Col, 1965-1992; instr physics & math, San Joaquin Delta Col, 1964-1965; Auburn High Sch, 1960-1964 & W Sr High Sch, 1952-1960; writer & teacher oper jet engine control, Woodward Governor Co, 1957-1958; teacher, Melvin Sibley High Sch, 1950-1952. **Research Statement & Publications:** Teaching general physics using a computer. **Mailing Address:** Dept Physics, Carthage Col, 2001 Alford Park Dr, Kenosha, WI 53140-1994.

JEANNE, ROBERT LAWRENCE, BEHAVIOR OF SOCIAL INSECTS. **Personal Data:** b New York, NY, January 14, 1942; m 1976, Louise; c Thomas L & James M. **Education:** Denison Univ, BS, 1964; Harvard Univ, MA, 1968, PhD (biol), 1971. **Honors & Awards:** Fellow, American Association for the Advancement of Science, 2004. **Professional Experience:** Assoc ed, Insectes Sociaux, 1986-2002; John Simon Guggenheim Mem fel, 1986-1987; PROF ENTOM, UNIV WIS, 1976-; asst prof biol, Boston Univ, 1971-1976; instrbiol, Univ Va, 1970-1971. **Memberships:** Am Assoc Advancement Sci; Animal Behav Soc; Entom Soc Am; Int Union Study Soc Insects; Assoc Tropi Biol. **Research Statement & Publications:** Behavior and evolution of tropical and temperate social wasps like Vespidae, with emphasis on communication, defense, nest architecture, colony size and cycle, and the rules governing colony integration and specialization. **Mailing Address:** Dept Entom, Univ Wis, 546 Russell Labs, 1630 Linden Dr, Madison, WI 53706. **Fax:** 608-262-3322. **E-Mail:** jeanne@entomology.wisc.edu

JEARLD, AMBROSE, FISHERIES BIOLOGY, FISHERIES RESEARCH. **Personal Data:** b Annapolis, Md, March 6, 1944; m 1976, c 1. **Education:** Univ Md, Eastern Shore, BS, 1965; Okla State Univ, MS, 1970, PhD (zoology), 1975. **Professional Experience:** CHIEF RES PLANNING & COORD, NORTHEAST FISHERIES CTR, WOODS HOLE LAB, as of 2003; supvry res fishery biologist, NorthEast Fisheries Ctr, Woods Hole Lab, US dept Com, beginning 1978; mem, Annapolis Environ Comn, 1977-1978; fac mem, Sandy Hook Lab, Dept Com, 1977-1978; asst prof animal behav & ecol, Howard Univ, 1977-1978; asst prof biol & anat, Lincoln Univ, 1975-1977; fel, Nat Sci, Okla State Univ, 1973; biol asst med res, US Army Edgewood Arsenal, 1969-1971; chemist, Publickers Indust Inc, 1965-1967. **Memberships:** Sigma Xi; Animal Behav Soc; Am Fisheries Soc; Int Asn Fish Ethologists. **Research Statement & Publications:** Animal behavior with emphasis on behavioral ecology in an aquatic environment; aging and growth problems and their influence on conservation and management of fishery resources in the northeast Atlantic. **Mailing Address:** Northeast Fisheries Sci Ctr /NMFS/NOAA, 166 Water St, Woods Hole, MA 02536. **Fax:** 508-495-2258. **E-Mail:** ambrose.jearld@noaa.gov

JEBSEN, ROBERT H, PHYSICAL MEDICINE & REHABILITATION. **Personal Data:** b New York, NY, September 5, 1931; m 1951, c 3. **Education:** Brooklyn Col, BA, 1953; State Univ NY, Downstate Med Ctr, MD, 1956; Ohio StateUniv, MMS, 1960. **Professional Experience:** CLIN PROF PHYS MED & REHAB, UNIV CINCINNATI, 1974-; prof physmed & rehab & dir, Univ Cincinnati, 1968-1974; from asst prof to assoc prof phys med & rehab, Univ Wash, 1963-1968; dir, Rehab Ctr & Muscular Dystrophy Clin, St Luke's Hosp, CedarRapids, Iowa, 1962-1963; consult, Knoxville Vet Admin Hosp, Iowa, 1962-1963; attendphysician, Iowa City Vet Admin Hosp, 1962-1963; chief phys med & rehab serv, Carswell AFBHosp, Fort Worth, Tex, 1960-1962; resident phys & rehab med, Ohio State Univ, Hosp, 1957-1960; intern, Harrisburg Hosp, Pa, 1956-1957. **Memberships:** Am Acad Phys Med & Rehab; Am Asn Electromyog & Electrodiag (pres 1974-1975); Am Cong Rehab Med; Asn Acad Physiatrists. **Research Statement & Publications:** Neuromuscular electrodiagnosis; orthotics; objective measurements of physical function. **Mailing Address:** Dept Phys Med & Rehb, 480 W 9th Ave, Columbus, OH 43210. **Fax:** 614-293-3809.

JECH, THOMAS J, LOGIC, TOPOLOGY. **Personal Data:** b Prague, Czech, January 29, 1944; American citizen; m 1965, Paula; c Pavel & Susanna. **Education:** Charles Univ, Prague, PhD (math), 1966. **Professional Experience:** STAFF, MATH INST ACAD SCI & CTR THEORET STUDY, CZECH REPUBLIC, 2000-; Fulbright prof, Hebrew Univ, 1989; guest prof, Beijing Normal Univ, 1985-; Univ Hawaii, 1984 & Calif Inst Technol, 1991; Univ Calif, Los Angeles, 1981; ed, Proceedings Am Math Soc, 1980-; prof math, Pa State Univ, 1974-2000; vis prof, Stanford Univ, 1974; Vis assoc prof, Univ Calif, Los Angeles, 1970-1971 & Princeton Univ, 1972; assoc prof math, State Univ NY, Buffalo, 1969-1974; Jr fel math, Univ Bristol, 1968-1969. **Memberships:** Inst Advan Study; Am Math Soc; Asn Symbolic Logic. **Research Statement & Publications:** Set theory. **Mailing Address:** Acad Sci, Math Inst, Zitna 25, Praha 1, Czech Republ. **E-Mail:** jech@math.cas.cz

JECK, RICHARD KAHR, CLOUD PHYSICS, AVIATION METEOROLOGY. **Personal Data:** b Iola, Kans, October 6, 1938; m 1963, c 2. **Education:** Rockhurst Col, Kansas City, BA, 1960; St Louis Univ, MS, 1963, PhD (physics), 1968. **Professional Experience:** RES METEROLOGIST/ PHYSICIST, FED AVIATION ADMIN TECH CTR, 1990-; res assoc prof, US Naval Acad, 1980-1981; res physicist, US Naval Res Lab, 1973-1990; staff scientist, Smithsonian Radiation Biol Lab, 1971-1973; res & develop physicist, Bruker Physik, Ger, 1970-1971; fel, Nat Acad Sci, Nat Res Coun, US Naval Res Lab, 1968-1970. **Memberships:** Am Meteorol Soc; Am Inst Aeronaut & Astronaut. **Research Statement & Publications:** Winter cloud characteristics and precipitation related to aircraft icing; Cloud physics instrumentation; Airborne measurements. **Mailing Address:** Fed Aviation Admin, Technical Center, Atlantic City Int'l Airport, NJ 08405. **E-Mail:** richard.jeck@faa.gov

JEDRZEJEK, CZESLAW, PHYSICS. **Education:** Jagiellonian Univ, MSc, PhD (physics). **Professional Experience:** RES ASSOC PROF, DEPT PHYSICS, TEX A & M UNIV, as of 2005. **Memberships:** Am Phys Soc. **Mailing Address:** Physics Bldg, Texas A&M Univ, College Station, TX 77843-4242.

JEDYNAK, LEO, ELECTRICAL ENGINEERING, MANAGEMENT. **Personal Data:** b Flint, Mich, September 15, 1928; m 1954, Mary; c Elizabeth, Thomas, Carol, Andrew & David. **Education:** Mich State Univ, BSc, 1954; Mass Inst Technol, MSc, 1956, ScD (elec eng), 1962. **Professional Experience:** RETIRED; consult, 1982-2002; vpres opers res & develop, Cue Paging Corp, 1988-1991; sr vpres corp res & develop, Oak Indust Inc, 1980-1988; prof elec eng, Univ Wis, Madison, 1976-1980; sci & eng consult, Oak Electronetics Corp, beginning 1971; mem bd dirs, Oak Industs Inc, beginning 1970; dir corp res, Oak Electronetics Corp, 1969-1971; from asst prof to assoc prof, Univ Wis, Madison, 1962-1976; instr, Mass Inst Technol, 1958-1962; teaching asst, Mass Inst Technol, 1957-1958; instr, Mich State Univ, 1956-1957; res asst elec eng, Mass Inst Technol, 1954-1956; prog engr, Gen Elec Co, 1954. **Memberships:** Sigma Xi. **Research Statement & Publications:** Insulation of high voltages in high vacuum; electric switches, contacts and relays; real time applications of microcomputer systems. **Mailing Address:** 28062 Via Cernuda, Mission Viejo, CA 92692. **Fax:** 949-951-8440. **E-Mail:** jedynak@prodigy.net

JEE, J RODNEY, MATHEMATICS. **Education:** Rice Univ, PhD, 1976. **Professional Experience:** STAFF, FAIR, ISAAC & CO, as of 2000. **Memberships:** Am Statist Asn. **Mailing Address:** Fair, Isaac & Co, 110 Theory, Irvine, CA 91791-1131. **Fax:** 703-684-2037. **E-Mail:** RodneyJee@FairIsaac.com

JEE, WEBSTER SHEW SHUN, ANATOMY. **Personal Data:** b Oakland, Calif, June 25, 1925; wid, c Kenneth W. **Education:** Univ Calif, BA, 1949, MA, 1951; Univ Utah, PhD (Anat), 1959. **Honors & Awards:** Highest Achievement Award, Int Cong Bone Morphometry, 1992; Honorary prof Guangdong Medical college, 1993; University of Utah Alumni Association Merit of Honor Award, 2003; Co-President First International Conference on Osteoporosis and Bone Research, Beijing, China, 2003, Outstanding Contribution Award; American Society of Bone Mineral Research, Excelllence in Mentorship Award, 2003; Jarabak Scholar in Orthodontics, Professor in Residence at Indiana University, 2004; International Chinese Hard Tissue Society (ICHTS) Award, 1998; ICHTS Ten Year Service Award, 2004; International Society Musculoskeletal and Neuronal Interactions and Journal, Outstanding Service Award, 2004; Co-President Second International Conference on Osteoporosis and Bone Research, Chengdu, China, 2005; Festschrift of a Continuing 54 Year Trip, Oakland, CA, USA, 2005. **Professional Experience:** Co-ed-in-chief, J Musculoskeletal & Neuronal Interactions, 2000; Hon Prof, Guangdong Med Col Zangjiang China, 1993; Spec consult, Eli Lilly, 1984-1986; Spec consult, Monsanto, 1983-1990; Spec consult, Colgate-Palmolive, 1979-1981; mem peer revcomt musculoskeletal physiol, Am Inst Biol Sci & NASA, 1978-1989; Spec consult, Upjohn Co, 1978-1987; mem, Comt Animal Models for Res on Aging, Nat Res Coun, 1978-1981; assoc ed, Calcified Tissue Res, 1977-1978; Spec consult, Proctor & Gamble, 1975-1978; actg dir Div Radiobiol, Radiol Div, 1973-1979; actg chmn anat, Radiol Div, 1973-1977; consult ed var jour, 1970-; assoc ed, Anat Rec, 1969-; mem sci comt 33, Nat Coun Radiation Protection & Measurements, 1969-1986; chmn, Nat Inst Dent Res, 1968-1970; PROF ANAT, COL MED, UNIV UTAH, 1967-; mem training comt, Nat Inst Dent Res, 1966-1970: Founder & Organizer International Sun Valley Hard Tissue Workshops, Sun Valley, Idaho, USA 1965-2003; dir training Prog Mineralized Tissues, Radiol Div, 1964-1974; mem staff, Radiol Health Res Activ, 1963-; assoc prof, Radiol Div, 1963-1967; Spec consult, Int Atomic Energy Agency, 1960 & 1964; asst res prof, Radiol Div, 1960-1961; instr, Radiol Div, 1959-1960; BONE GROUP LEADER RADIOBIOL DIV, Radiol Div, 1958-; actg bone group leader, Radiol Div, 1956-1958; asst anat, Univ Utah, 1952-1958; Asst zool, Univ Calif, 1949-1951; consult, Schering Plough Inc; Sch Dent, China Med Col, Taichung, Repub of China. **Memberships:** Radiation Res Soc; Am Asn Anat; Int Asn Dent Res; Geront Soc; Am Soc Bone & Mineral Res; Am Soc Gravitational & Space Biol; Int Chinese Hard Tissue Soc (pres, 1997), Chairman of the Board 1998-) International Soc of Musculoskeletal & Neuronal Interactions (Board Mem, 2000;). **Research Statement & Publications:** Physiology and metabolism of bone and teeth; radiation biology; hard tissue biology; osteoporosis and osteoarthritis research in animal models. **Mailing Address:** Div Radiobiol 729 Arapeen Dr, Ste 2338, Univ Utah Sch Med, Salt Lake City, UT 84108-1218. **Fax:** 801-581-7008. **E-Mail:** webster.jee@hsc.utah.edu

JEEJEEBHOY, KHURSHEED NOWROJEE, GASTROENTEROLOGY, EXERCISE PHYSIOLOGY. **Personal Data:** b Rangoon, Burma, August 26, 1935; Canadian citizen; m 1961, c 3. **Education:** Madras, India, MB & BS, 1959; FRCP, 1961; London Univ, PhD (clin gastrointestinalres) 1963; FRCP (E), 1966; FRCP (C), 1969; FRCP, 1975. **Professional Experience:** PROF, DEPT MED, UNIV TORONTO, as of 2006; vis prof, Santa Clara Valley Med Ctr, Stanford Univ, 1991; PROF, DEPT PHYSIOL, UNIV TORONTO,

1984-; PROF, DEPT NUTRIT SCI, 1981-; prof, Dept Nutrit & Food Sci, Univ Toronto, 1979-1981; hon lectr, Dept Nutrit & Food Sci, 1976-1979; PROF GASTROENTEROL, UNIV TORONTO, 1975-; spec lectr, Dept Nutrit, Univ Toronto, 1974-1976; Prin investr, three grants, Med Res Coun Can, 1968-; from asst prof to assoc prof, Univ Toronto, 1968-1975; head radiation, Radiation Med Ctr, Bombay, 1965-1967; in-chg, Bhabbha Atomic Res Ctr, Bombay, 1963-1965; staff radiation, Bhabbha Atomic Res Ctr, Bombay, 1963; Tutor gastroenterol, Postgrad Med SchLondon, 1961-1963. **Memberships:** Am Soc Clin Invest; Am Soc Clin Nutrit; Am Gastroenterol Asn; Can AsnGastroenterol; Can Soc Clin Invest; Nutrit Soc Can; Am Asn Physicians. **Research Statement & Publications:** Nutritional support of patientswith gastrointestinal disease; effect of nutrition on muscle performance; interaction of nutrition and sepsis; long term support of patients with a short bowel. **Mailing Address:** St Michaels Hosp Rm 372, 30 Bond St, Toronto, ON M5B 1W8, Can. **Fax:** 416-864-5882. **E-Mail:** kush.jeejeebhoy@utoronto.ca

JEEVANANDAM, MALAYAPPA, SURGICAL NUTRITION. **Personal Data:** b Tirumangalam, India, June 14, 1931; m 1959, Chellam; c 2. **Education:** Columbia Univ, PhD (chem), 1965. **Professional Experience:** DIR RES, TRAUMA CTR, ST JOSEPH'S HOSP, PHOENIX, Ariz, 1986-; assoc lab mem, Sloan-Kettering Cancer Ctr, 1981-1986; res assoc, Col Physicians & Surgeons, Columbia Univ, 1971-1981. **Memberships:** Inst Nutrit; Am Soc Clin Nutritionists; NY Acad Sci; AAAS. **Research Statement & Publications:** Nutrition of cancer; metabolism and nutrition of trauma victims. **Mailing Address:** Dir Res Trauma Ctr, St Josephs Hosp & Med Ctr, 350 W Thomas Rd, Phoenix, AZ 85013.

JEFCOATE, COLIN R, PHARMACOLOGY. **Personal Data:** b Chesham, Bucks, Eng, September 28, 1942. **Education:** Oxford Univ, Eng, BS, 1963, PhD (chem), 1966. **Professional Experience:** Dir, Environ Toxicol Ctr, 1983-2002; PROF PHARMACOL, UNIV WIS, MADISON, 1982-; mem, four study sects, NIH, 1976-; from asst prof to assoc prof, Dept Pharmacol, Med Sch, 1973-1982; res assoc, Dept Biochem, 1972-1973; Mem, NATOSci Comt Conf on Catalysis, Italy, 1972; MRC fel, Edinburgh Univ, Scotland, 1969-1972; NIH &NATO fel, Cornell Univ, Ithaca, 1967-1969; NATO fel, Basel Univ, Switz, 1966-1967. **Research Statement & Publications:** Author of numerous publications. **Mailing Address:** Dept Pharmacol, Univ Wis, B157 Steenbock Libr 550 Babcock Dr, Madison, WI 53705. **Fax:** 608-262-5245. **E-Mail:** jefcoate@wisc.edu

JEFFAY, HENRY, BIOCHEMISTRY. **Personal Data:** b Brooklyn, NY, February 9, 1927; m 1957, Ana; c Susan, Randall, Kevin, Jason & Stefanie. **Education:** Univ Wis, BS, 1948, MS, 1949, PhD (biochem), 1953. **Professional Experience:** PROF EMER, UNIV ILL, CHICAGO, as of 2005; dean, Univ Ill, 1976-1979; actg dean basic sci, Rockford Sch Med, Univ Ill, 1976-1979; dir basic sci, Rockford Sch Med, Univ Ill, 1974-1976; assoc dean basic sci, Univ Ill, 1972-1974; asst dean fac affairs, Univ Ill, 1970-1972; prof biochem, Univ Ill, 1968-1996; from asst prof to assoc prof, Univ Ill, 1956-1968; res assoc, Univ Ill, 1955-1956; instr biochem, Sch Med, Univ PR, 1953-1955; consult, Roosevelt Mem Hosp, dir med educ; consult, Vet Admin Hosp, Chicago & Norwegian Am Hosp. **Memberships:** AAAS; Am Chem Soc; Am Soc Biol Chemists; Int Asn Dent Res. **Research Statement & Publications:** Protein metabolism; metabolism of oral tissue; obesity. **Mailing Address:** Dept Biochem & Molecular Genetics, Univ Ill, Chicago, IL 60607. **E-Mail:** hjeffay@msn.com

JEFFCOAT, MARJORIE K, PERIODONTOLOGY, RADIOLOGY. **Personal Data:** b Boston, Mass, June 14, 1951; m 1973. **Education:** Mass Inst Technol, BS, 1972; Harvard Sch Dent Med, DMD, 1976, cert periodont, 1978. **Honors & Awards:** Young Investr Award, Int Asn Dent Res, 1986; Clin Res Award, Am Acad Periodont, 1992. **Professional Experience:** PROF PERIODONT, SCH DENT MED, UNIV PA, as of 2004; DEAN, SCH DENT MED, UNIV PA, 2003-; Rosen prof, Dept Periodont, Univ Ala, Birmingham, beginning 1991; chmn, Dept Periodont, Univ Ala, Birmingham, beginning 1988; prof, Dept Periodont, UnivAla, Birmingham, 1988-1991; consult, Children's Hosp Med Ctr, 1981 & Birmingham Vet AdminHosp; from instr to assoc prof, Harvard Sch Dent Med, 1978-1988; res fel periodont, HarvardSch Dent Med, 1975-1978. **Memberships:** Am Dent Asn; Am Acad Periodont; Int Asn Dent Res; Inst Elec & ElectronicsEngrs; Eng Med Biol Soc; Am Asn Dent Res. **Research Statement & Publications:** Bone resorption and diagnosis periodontal disease utilizing the following approaches, digital radiography, bone scanning, radiolabeled microsphere measurements of blood flow, studies of chemotherapeutic agents for treatment of periodontal disease, studies of the effects of local factors on periodontal disease. **Mailing Address:** Sch Dent Med, Univ PA, 3451 Walnut St, Philadelphia, PA 19104. **E-Mail:** jeffcoat@dental.upenn.edu

JEFFERIES, JOHN TREVOR, ASTROPHYSICS. **Personal Data:** b Kellerberrin, Western Australia, April 2, 1925; American citizen; m 1949, Charmian Candy; c Stephen R, Helen C & Trevor R. **Education:** Western Australia Univ, BSc, 1946, DSc(physics), 1961; Cambridge Univ, MA, 1949. **Professional Experience:** EMER ASTRONR, NAT OPTICAL ASTRON OBSERV, 1992-; astronr, Nat Optical Astron Observ, 1987-1992; dir, Nat Optical Astron Observ, 1983-1987; prof, Col France, 1970 & 1977; Guggenheim fel, 1970-1971; dir, Inst Astron, 1967-1983; prof astrophys, Univ Hawaii, 1964-1983; fel, Joint Inst Lab Astrophys, 1962-1964; res assoc, High Altitude Observ, 1961-1964; Adj prof, Univ Colo, 1961-1964; consult to dir, Nat Bur Stand, Colo, 1960-1962; prin res off astrophys, Commonwealth Sci & Indust Res Orgn, NSW, 1959-1960; res staff, High Altitude Observ, Colo, 1957-1958 & Sacramento Peak Observ, 1958-1959; res assoc, Harvard Col Observ, 1956-1957; Res off solar physics, Commonwealth Sci & Indust Res Orgn, NSW, 1949-1956. **Memberships:** Am Astron Soc. **Research Statement & Publications:** Solar physics; radiative transfer; spectral line information; analysis of stellar spectra. **Mailing Address:** 1652 E Camino Cielo, Tucson, AZ 85718. **Fax:** 520-797-8166. **E-Mail:** jtjeff@concentric.net

JEFFERIES, MICHAEL JOHN, TECHNICAL MANAGEMENT. **Personal Data:** b London, Eng, February 2, 1941; m 1969, Mary; c Kevin & Carlyn. **Education:** Univ Nottingham, BSc, 1963, PhD (elec eng), 1967. **Professional Experience:** RETIRED; vpres corp technol & mfg, Carrier Corp, 1993-1995; mem fac, Purdue Univ, 1990-1993; gen mgr technol, Gen Elec Motor Bus, 1987-1990; res & develop mgr, Eng Physics Labs, Corp Res & Develop, 1980-1987; managerial res & develop positions, Gen Elec Co, 1976-1980; elec engr, Gen Elec Co, 1967-1976. **Memberships:** Fel Inst Elec & Electronics Engrs; Brit Inst Elec Engrs; Inst Elec Engrs UK. **Research Statement & Publications:** Power systems: computer-aided design/computer-aided manufacturing, computers, controls, engineering analysis. **Mailing Address:** 4315 Hepatica Hill Rd, Manlius, NY 13104.

JEFFERIES, STEVEN R, SYNTHETIC BIOPOLYMERS. **Personal Data:** b Abington, Pa, September 27, 1951; m 1973. **Education:** Johns Hopkins Univ, BA, 1973; Rutgers, MS, 1977, Univ Md Dent Sch, DDS(dent), 1980. **Professional Experience:** VPRES PROD DEVELOP, DENTSPLY INT INC, as of 2003; dir clin res, ld culk div, Dentsply Int Inc, Milford, Del, beginning 1990; ed, Caulk Dent Educ Bull, 1986-; consult, Stacogen Corp, 1986-; clin res dentist, DentsplyInt Inc, 1986-1989; gen dent, Steven R Jefferies, DDS, Pa, 1983-1986; staff dentist, MunicipalHealth Servs Prog, Albert Witzke Med Ctr, 1981-1983; resident gen dent, USPHS Hosp, NewOrleans, 1980-1981; consult, Johns Hopkins Sch Med, 1977-1978; res intern, chem biochem eng, Dept Chem & Biochem Eng, Rutgers Univ, 1975-1977; res asst, environ health, Dept EnvironHealth, Johns Hopkins Sch Hygiene & Health, 1973-1975. **Memberships:** Am Asn Dent Res; Int Asn Dent Res; AAAS; Am Dent Asn. **Research Statement & Publications:** Naturaland synthetic biopolmers, controlled drug release technology, applied connective tissue research, clinical applications of collagen-based biomaterials, wound healing. **Mailing Address:** Dentsply Int Susquehanna Com Ctr, 221 W Philadelphia St PO Box 872, York, PA 17405-0872. **Fax:** 717-849-4762. **E-Mail:** sjefferies@dentsply.com

JEFFERS, THOMAS KIRK, PARASITOLOGY, POULTRY SCIENCE. **Personal Data:** b Syracuse, NY, April 30, 1941; m 1969, c 2. **Education:** Cornell Univ, BS, 1963; Univ Wis, PhD (zoology & poultry sci), 1969. **Honors & Awards:** P P Levine Award, Am Asn Avian Pathologists, 1974. **Professional Experience:** RETIRED; res dir animal sci discovery & develop res, Elanco Animal Health, Eli Lilly & Co, beginning 1986; head, Lilly Res Labs, 1983-1986; sr parasitologist, Lilly Res Labs, 1974-1983; dept head parasitol, Hess & Clark Div, Rhodia Inc, 1969-1974; geneticist, Animal Res Inst, Can Dept Agr, 1968-1969. **Memberships:** Am Soc Parasitologists; Soc Protozoologists; Sigma Xi; Am Asn Avian Pathologists; Poultry Sci Asn; World's Poultry Sci Asn. **Research Statement & Publications:** Avian coccidiosis; anticoccidial chemotherapy; intraspecific variation in the coccidia; anticoccidial drug resistance; host response to coccidia. **Mailing Address:** Lilly Corp Ctr, Eli Lilly & Co, Indianapolis, IN 46285.

JEFFERS, WILLIAM ALLEN, LOW TEMPERATURE PHYSICS. **Personal Data:** b Philadelphia, Pa, May 4, 1936; m 1958, c 3. **Education:** Amherst Col, AB, 1957; Mass Inst Technol, PhD (physics), 1962. **Professional Experience:** PROF EMER PHYSICS, LAFAYETTE COL, as of 2003; dean col, Lafayette Col, 1978-1987; assoc prof physics, Lafayette Col, beginning 1976; dean studies, Lafayette Col, 1972-1975; asst prof, Lafayette Col, 1966-1976; sr physicist, Battelle Mem Inst, 1962-1966. **Memberships:** Am Phys Soc; Am Asn Physics Teachers; Sigma Xi. **Research Statement & Publications:** Ultrasonic absorption in liquid helium; superconductivity; transport properties in metals. **Mailing Address:** Dept Physics, Lafayette Col, 124 Hugel Sci Ctr, Easton, PA 18042-1782. **Fax:** 610-330-5714.

JEFFERSON, CAROL ANNETTE, PLANT ECOLOGY. **Personal Data:** b Minneapolis, Minn, July 4, 1948; m 1975, c 2. **Education:** St Olaf Col, BA, 1970; Ore State Univ, PhD (bot), 1974. **Professional Experience:** PROF BIOL, WINONA STATE UNIV, 1976-; assoc prof biol, Winona State Univ, beginning 1981; asst prof, Winona State Univ, 1976-1981; asst prof biol, Eckerd Col, 1974-1976. **Memberships:** AAAS; Ecol Soc Am. **Research Statement & Publications:** Great Lakes sand vegetation; driftless area-relict communities; flood plain vegetation; wetland ecotones. **Mailing Address:** Biol Dept, Winona State Univ, Rm 215 Pasteur Hall, Winona, MN 55987. **E-Mail:** cjefferson@winona.edu

JEFFERSON, DAVID KENOSS, COMPUTER SCIENCE. **Personal Data:** b Pasadena, Calif, December 21, 1938; m 1967, c 2. **Education:** Calif Inst Technol, BS, 1960; Columbia Univ, AM, 1962; Univ Mich, PhD (comput sci), 1969. **Professional Experience:** CHIEF INFO SYSTS ENG DIV, NAT INST STAND & TECHNOL, 1987-; mgr, Database Archit Group, Nat Bur Stand, 1982-1987; lectr, Univ Md, 1977-1982; proj leader info syst design, David W Taylor Naval Ship Res & Develop Ctr, 1975-1982; res mathematician, Naval Weapons Lab, 1973-1975; vis prof comput sci, Naval Postgrad Sch, 1972-1973; mathematician, Naval Weapons Lab, 1960-1972. **Memberships:** Sigma Xi; Asn Comput Mach; Inst Elec & Electronics Engrs; Sr Exec Serv. **Research Statement & Publications:** Standards and guides for data dictionary systems, database languages, data interchange, graphics, data administration, database design, hypertext, object-oriented databases and knowledge-based systems; development and administration of conformance tests and procedures. **Mailing Address:** 8121 Langport Terr, Gaithersburg, MD 20877-1135.

JEFFERSON, DONALD EARL, SCIENCE POLICY, PHYSICAL OCEANOGRAPHY. **Personal Data:** b Homeland, Fla, September 27, 1927; m 1951, c 2. **Education:** Morehouse Col, BS, 1948; Howard Univ, MS, 1950. **Professional Experience:** RETIRED; sci adv to commander second fleet, Naval Surface Weapon Ctr, 1983-1985; sci adv to commander second fleet, Naval Assistance Prog, 1981-1982; elec engr, Naval Surface Weapon Ctr, 1972-1981; vpres eng, Copycomposer Corp, 1969-1971; elec engr, US Naval Ord Lab, 1954-1972; physicist, US Naval Ord Lab, 1951-1952; instr physics, Va Union Univ, 1949-1951. **Memberships:** Am Defense Preparedness Asn. **Research Statement & Publications:** Review of naval operational systems for modification or replacement as needed; design and modification of instrumentation for measuring ocean currents; statistical analysis and prediction of system and environment interactions; underwater acoustics. **Mailing Address:** 13321 Bea Kay Dr, Silver Spring, MD 20904.

JEFFERSON, EDWARD G, research administration; deceased, see previous edition for last biography

JEFFERSON, JAMES WALTER, PSYCHOPHARMACOLOGY, ANXIETY DISORDERS. **Personal Data:** b Mineola, NY, August 14, 1937; m 1965, Susan; c 3. **Education:** Univ Bucknell, BS, 1958; Univ Wis, MD, 1964. **Professional Experience:** DISTINGUISHED SR SCIENTIST, MADISON INST MED, 1998-; CLIN PROF PSYCHIAT, UNIV WIS MADISON, 1992-; dean found, Univ Wis Madison, 1992-1998; dir, Ctr Affective Dis, Madison, 1983-1992; prof, Univ Wis Madison, 1981-1992; co-dir, Lithium Info Ctr, Madison, 1974-; from asst prof to assoc prof, Univ Wis Madison, 1974-1981; staff psychiatrist, Vet Admin Hosp, Wis, 1974-1981; resident psychiat, Univ Wis Madison, 1971-1974; fel, Univ Chicago, 1967-1968; resident internal med, Univ Wis, 1965-1967; intern, St Lukes Hosp, NY, 1964-1965. **Memberships:** Am Psychiat Asn; Am Psychopath Asn; Int Neuropsychopharmacologium Soc; Am Soc Clin Psychoparmacol. **Research Statement & Publications:** Clinical psychopharmacology; compliation and dissertation of information through interactive computer programs in psychiatry; neuropsychiatric aspects of medical disorders; Published over 20 articles. **Mailing Address:** Madison Inst Med, 2711 Allen Blvd, Middleton, WI 53562. **Fax:** 608-827-2444.

JEFFERSON, LEONARD SHELTON, PHYSIOLOGY. **Personal Data:** b Maysville, Ky, January 14, 1939. **Education:** Eastern Ky Univ, BS, 1961; Vanderbilt Univ, PhD (physiol), 1966. **Honors & Awards:** Lilly Award, Am Diabetes Asn, 1979. **Professional Experience:** EVAN PUGH PROF & CHAIR CELLULAR & MOLECULAR PHYSIOL, COL MED, PA STATE UNIV, 1996-; assoc dean res & grad studies, col med, Pa State Univ, beginning 1991; prof & chmn, Col Med, PA State Univ, 1988-1996; prof physiol, Col Med, Pa State Univ, beginning 1975; assoc prof, Col Med, Pa State Univ, ending 1975; instr, Col Med, PA State Univ, beginning 1967; res assoc physiol, Col Med, Vanderbilt Univ, 1967; USPHS fel, 1966-1967; vis scientist, Cambridge Univ, 1966-1967. **Memberships:** Am Soc Biol Chemists; Biochem Soc; Am Physiol Soc; Am Diabetes Asn. **Research Statement & Publications:** Regulation of skeletal muscle and hepatic carbohydrate and protein metabolism by hormones and other factors, especially mechanism of action of insulin and growth hormone. **Mailing Address:** Dept Cellular & Molecular Physiol, Col Med, Pa State Univ, PO Box 850, Hershey, PA 17033. **Fax:** 717-531-7667. **E-Mail:** jjefferson@psu.edu

JEFFERSON, MARGARET CORREAN, GENETICS. **Personal Data:** b Eau Claire, Wis, August 22, 1947. **Education:** Univ Dubuque, BS, 1969; Univ Colo, MA, 1971; Univ Ariz, PhD (genetics), 1977. **Professional Experience:** PROF BIOL, CALIF STATE UNIV, LOS ANGELES, 1985-; assoc prof biol, Calif State Univ, Los Angeles, 1981-1985; prin invester biomed res support grants, NIH, 1977- &res apprenticeships minority high sch students, NSF, 1981-1982; consult, Compton Sickle CellEduc & Detection Ctr, beginning 1977; asst prof, Calif State Univ, Los Angeles, 1977-1981. **Memberships:** AAAS; Am Genetics Asn; Genetics Soc Am; Soc Study Evolution. **Research Statement & Publications:** Ecological and behavioral genetics of desert-adapted Drosophila; specifically, pheromonal regulation of reproductive strategies in desert-adapted Drosophila; genetics of learning behavior; cytogenetics of Cycads; eye pigmentation systems. **Mailing Address:** Dept Biol Calif State Univ, 5151 State Univ Dr, Los Angeles, CA 90032-8201. **Fax:** 323-343-6451. **E-Mail:** mjeffer@calstatela.edu

JEFFERSON, THOMAS BRADLEY, MECHANICAL ENGINEERING. **Personal Data:** b Urich, Mo, November 25, 1924; m 1946, c 3. **Education:** Kans State Col, BS, 1949; Univ Nebr, MS, 1950; PurdueUniv, PhD, 1955. **Professional Experience:** RETIRED; prof mech eng, Southern Ill Univ, beginning 1978; dean, Sch Eng & Technol, 1969-1978; assoc dean eng, Univ Ark, Fayetteville, 1968-1969; prof & head dept, Univ Ark, Fayetteville, 1958-1968; Martin Marietta Aerospace, Denver, 1958-1968; consult, Allison Div, Gen Motors Corp, 1956-1957; from instr to asst prof, Purdue Univ, 1952-1958; instr mech eng, Univ Nebr, 1949-1952. **Memberships:** Am Soc Mech Engrs; Am Soc Eng Educ. **Research Statement & Publications:** Heat transfer. **Mailing Address:** 901 S Glenview, Carbondale, IL 62901.

JEFFERSON, THOMAS HUTTON, MASS STORAGE, OPERATING SYSTEMS. **Personal Data:** b Mineola, NY, June 6, 1941. **Education:** Rensselaer Polytech Inst, BS, 1963; NC State Univ, MAM, 1965; Univ Colo, Boulder, PhD (appl math), 1969. **Professional Experience:** DISTINGUISHED MEM TECH STAFF, SANDIA LABS, LIVERMORE, 1969-. **Research Statement & Publications:** Computer software libraries; computer mass storage; nonlinear parameter determination. **Mailing Address:** Sandia Nat Lab, Livermore, CA 94551-0969.

JEFFERTS, KEITH BARTLETT, ATOMIC PHYSICS, FISHERIES MANAGEMENT. **Personal Data:** b Raymond, Wash, May 10, 1931; m 1953, c 4. **Education:** Univ Wash, PhD (physics), 1962. **Professional Experience:** PRES, NORTHWEST MARINE TECHNOL, 1972-; Mem tech staff physics, Bell Tel Labs, 1963-1975. **Memberships:** Am Phys Soc. **Research Statement & Publications:** Structure of simple molecules; molecular astrophysics; application of physical techniques to problems of fishery management. **Mailing Address:** Northwest Marine Technol, PO Box 427, Ben Nevis Loop Rd, Shaw Island, WA 98286. **Fax:** 360-468-3844. **E-Mail:** keith.jefferts@nmt.us

JEFFERY, DUANE ELDRO, GENETICS. **Personal Data:** b Delta, Utah, September 28, 1937; m 1961, c 3. **Education:** Utah State Univ, BS, 1962, MS, 1963; Univ Calif, Berkeley, MA, 1966, PhD (zoology, genetics), 1972. **Professional Experience:** PROF BIOLOGY, BRIGHAM YOUNG UNIV, as of 2004; assoc prof zoology, Brigham Young Univ, beginning 1977-; vis col genetics, Univ Hawaii, 1974-1975; asst prof, Brigham Young Univ, 1969-1977. **Memberships:** Soc Study Evolution; Genetics Soc Am; Am Soc Human Genetics; AAAS. **Research Statement & Publications:** Developmental and evolutionary genetics in Drosophila populations; human transmission genetics; cytogenetics. **Mailing Address:** Dept Zoology, Col Bio & Agr, Brigham Young Univ, 575 Widb, Provo, UT 84602-1049. **E-Mail:** duane_jeffery@byu.edu

JEFFERY, GEOFFREY MARRON, MALARIOLOGY. **Personal Data:** b Dundee, NY, May 13, 1919; m 1941, c 4. **Education:** Hobart Col, BA, 1940; Syracuse Univ, MA, 1942; Johns Hopkins Univ, ScD (parasitol), 1944; Yale Univ, MPH, 1961. **Honors & Awards:** Ashford Medal, Am Soc Trop Med & Hyg, 1959. **Professional Experience:** RETIRED; asst dir, Div Parasitic Dis, Bur Trop Dis, 1981-1985; dir, Vector Biol & Control Div, Bur Trop Dis, 1975-1981; asst dir, Cent Am Res Sta, Ctrs Dis Control, 1974-1975; Latin Am Cong Parasitol, 1973; chief, Cent Am Res Sta, Ctr Dis Control, 1969-1974; mem, Armed Forces Epidemiol Bd, 1969-1973; deleg, Teheran, 1968; chief, Lab Parasite Chemother, Nat Inst Allergy & Infectious Dis, 1967-1968; scientific group chemother malaria, Geneva, 1967; actg chief, Lab Parasite Chemother, Nat Inst Allergy & Infectious Dis, 1966; assoc mem, Comn Malaria, Armed Forces Epidemiol Bd, 1965-1969; parasitol malaria, Teheran, 1968; Cent Am Malaria Assessment Mission, AID, 1964; Int Cong Parasitol, Rome, 1964; mem expert panel malaria, WHO, beginning 1963; asst chief, Lab Parasite Chemother, Nat Inst Allergy & Infectious Dis, 1963-1966; deleg, Rio de Janeiro, 1963; sci dir, SC, 1960-1963; deleg, Int Cong Trop Med & Malaria, Lisbon, 1958; from scientist to sr scientist, SC, 1954-1960; from sr asst scientist to scientist, Malaria Res Lab, Lab Trop Dis, NIH, Ga, 1948-1954; asst prof, Univ Bridgeport, 1947-1948; from asst sanitarian to sr asst scientist, SchTrop Med, PR, 1946-1947; asst sanitarian, Commun Dis Ctr, Ga, 1945-1946; asst sanitarian, USPHS, 1944-1945; biol aide, Tenn Valley Authority, Wilson Dam, Alta, 1944. **Memberships:** AAAS; Am Soc Parasitol; Am Soc Trop Med & Hyg (secy treas, 1961-1967, vpres, 1971 & pres, 1975); Am Mosquito Control Asn; Royal Soc Trop Med & Hyg. **Research Statement & Publications:** Malarias of man and lower animals; chemotherapy of malaria and parasitic infections; epidemiology of malaria and intestinal parasites; biology of human malarias; immunology and pathology of malaria; diagnosis of parasitic infections; drug resistant strains of malaria parasites; methodology of malaria eradication and control. **Mailing Address:** 1093 Blackshear Dr, Decatur, GA 30033.

JEFFERY, LARRY S, WEED SCIENCE, WEED BIOLOGY. **Personal Data:** b Delta, Utah, June 21, 1936; m 1959, c Johan, Allen, Steve, R Dale, Iina, Paula & Katri. **Education:** Utah State Univ, BS, 1962; NDak State Univ, PhD (plant sci), 1966. **Professional Experience:** PROF AGRON & HORT, BRIGHAM YOUNG UNIV, 1984-. **Memberships:** Weed Sci Soc Am; Int Weed Sci Soc. **Research Statement & Publications:** Weed control in economic crops; development of weed control systems in corn, soybeans, grain sorghum, tobacco, alfalfa, small grains and pastures. **Mailing Address:** Dept Agron & Hort, Brigham Young Univ, 269 Widb, Provo, UT 84602-2760.

JEFFERY, LAWRENCE R, SYSTEMS DESIGN, SYSTEMS SCIENCE. **Personal Data:** b Memphis, Tenn, June 30, 1927; m 1948, c 5. **Education:** Univ Chicago, MS, 1953. **Professional Experience:** RETIRED; tech dir commun, Mitre Corp, Mass, 1973-1986; assoc tech dir, Mitre Corp, Mass, 1963-1973; dept head, Mitre Corp, Mass, 1961-1963; assoc dept head, MitreCorp, Mass, 1959-1961; sect leader, Lincoln Lab, Mass Inst Technol, 1958; staff mem command & control systs, Lincoln Lab, Mass Inst Technol, 1954-1958; engr, Raytheon Mfg Co, Mass, 1953-1954; instr electronic eng & math, Am TV Inst, Ill, 1946-1951. **Memberships:** Sr mem Inst Elec & Electronics Engrs. **Research Statement & Publications:** Design and evaluation of computer-based command; control and communication systems; military operations research; digital computer engineering. **Mailing Address:** 16 Sherwood Dr, Hollis, NH 03049.

JEFFERY, RONDO NELDEN, SOLID STATE PHYSICS, ELECTRONICS PHYSICS. **Personal Data:** b Provo, Utah, April 16, 1940. **Education:** Brigham Young Univ, BS, 1963, MS, 1965; Univ Ill-Urbana, PhD (physics), 1970. **Professional Experience:** PROF EMER PHYSICS, WEBER STATE UNIV, as of 2003; CSIP grant, 1987-1989; prof physics, Weber State Univ, 1986-2002; mem tech staff, TRW, 1986-2001; assoc prof, Weber State Col, 1983-1986; vis assoc prof, Weber State Col, 1980-1983; NSF res grant, 1978-1981; asst prof, Cottrell res grant, Res Corp, 1975-1978; asst prof, Wayne State Univ, 1973-1980; res assoc physics, Rensselaer Polytech Inst, 1970-1973. **Memberships:** Am Asn Physics Teachers. **Research Statement & Publications:** High pressure effects in solids; properties of point defects under high pressure, high temperature conditions using diffusion and positron annihilation techniques; developing microcomputer based physics laboratory experiment and electronics; physics education. **Mailing Address:** Dept Physics, Weber State Univ, Ogden, UT 84408-2508. **Fax:** 801-626-7445. **E-Mail:** rjeffery@weber.edu

JEFFERY, WILLIAM RICHARD, DEVELOPMENTAL BIOLOGY, CELL BIOLOGY. **Personal Data:** b Chicago, Ill, June 9, 1944. **Education:** Univ Ill, BS, 1967; Univ Iowa, PhD (zoology), 1971. **Professional Experience:** PROF & CHAIR BIOL, UNIV MD, as of 2004; prof zoology, Univ Calif, Davis, beginning 1990; dir embryol, Woods Hole, 1983-; instr, Woods Hole, 1980-1982; from asst prof to prof zoology, Univ Tex, 1977-1990; corp mem, Marine Biol Lab, Woods Hole, 1975-; asst prof biophys, Univ Houston, 1974-1977; res assoc biochem, Sch Med, Tufts Univ, 1972-1974; Am Cancer Soc fel oncol, Univ Wis, 1971-1972; NIH fel zoology, Univ Iowa, 1967-1971; res asst biol, Univ Ill, 1965-1966. **Memberships:** AAAS; Am Soc Cell Biol; Asn Develop Biol. **Research Statement & Publications:** Molecular and cellular mechanisms of cell development and differentiation. **Mailing Address:** Dept Biol, Univ MD, College Park, MD 20742-4415. **Fax:** 310-314-9358. **E-Mail:** wj33@umail.umd.edu

JEFFERYS, WILLIAM H, III, ASTRONOMY. **Personal Data:** b New Bedford, Mass, July 8, 1940. **Education:** Wesleyan Univ, BA, 1962; Yale Univ, MS, 1964, PhD (astron), 1965. **Professional Experience:** HARLAN J SMITH CENTENNIAL PROF EMER ASTRON, UNIV TEX, AUSTIN, as of 2005; adj prof, Univ Vt, as of 2005; Harlan J Smith Centennial Prof Astron, Univ Tex, Austin, beginning 1985; prof astron, Univ Tex, Austin, beginning 1979; from asst prof to assoc prof, Univ Tex, Austin, 1965-1979; Alfred P Sloan fel, 1965-1967; instr astron, Wesleyan Univ, 1964-1965. **Memberships:** AAAS; Am Astron Soc; Royal Astron Soc; Int Astron Union. **Research Statement & Publications:** Astrometry; celestial mechanics; dynamical astronomy; statistics. **Mailing Address:** Dept Astron, Univ Tex, Austin, TX 78712. **Fax:** 512-471-6016. **E-Mail:** bill@astro.as.utexas.edu

JEFFREDO, JOHN V, ROCKET SCIENCE, ANCIENT AMERICAN HUMANS. **Personal Data:** b Los Angeles, Calif, November 5, 1927; m 1981, Gerda; c Joyce J (Ryder), John V Jr, Michael J & Louise V (Warden). **Education:** Northrop Univ, BS, 1949; La Jolla Univ, MBA, 1981, PhD (psychol), 1984. **Professional Experience:** Chmn bd, Maritime Shoshone Inc, 1999-2002; mgr, Hughes Aircraft, 1985-1989; mgr eng, Control Data Corp, 1980-1984; mgr eng, Northrop Aircraft, 1954-1969; design engr, Douglas Aircraft Inc, 1954-1969; 2nd lieutenant, US Army Ordnance, 1950-1953. **Memberships:** Mem Planetary Soc; Nature Conservancy; Smithsonian Inst; Catalina Island Conservancy; Nat Geog Soc. **Research Statement & Publications:** Migration from northern Scandinavia and Northern Russia of maritime shoshone people on California's southern channel islands, 15, 000 years ago. **Mailing Address:** PO Box 387, 1629 Via Monserate, Fallbrook, CA 92003.

JEFFREY, KENNETH ROBERT, NUCLEAR MAGNETIC RESONANCE, X-RAY & NEUTRON DIFFRACTION. **Personal Data:** b Toronto, Ont, May 7, 1941; m 1967, Francis; c 2. **Education:** Univ Toronto, BSc, 1964, MA, 1966, PhD (physics), 1969. **Professional Experience:** PROF EMER PHYSICS, UNIV GUELPH, as of 2006; CHMN PHYSICS, UNIV GUELPH, 1993-; prof physics, Univ Guelph, beginning 1981; from asst prof to assoc prof, Univ Guelph 1969-1981. **Memberships:** Can Asn Physicists; Biophys Soc. **Research Statement & Publications:** Nuclear magnetic resonance studies of translational and reorientational motion and phase transitions in solids; biophysical techniques (nuclear magnetic resonance, x-ray and neutron diffraction, calorimetry), applied to model and biological membranes. **Mailing Address:** Dept Physics, Univ Guelph, MacN 433D MacNaughton Bldg Gordon St, Guelph, ON N1G 2W1, Can. **Fax:** 519-836-9967. **E-Mail:** krj@physics.uoguelph.ca

JEFFRIES, CHARLES DEAN, MICROBIOLOGY, MEDICAL MYCOLOGY. **Personal Data:** b Rome, Ga, April 9, 1929; m 1953, Virginia M Alford. **Education:** NGa Col, BS, 1950; Univ Tenn, MS, 1955, PhD (bact), 1958. **Professional Experience:** INTERIM DEAN BASIC SCI, SCH MED, ROSS UNIV, 1997-; PROF &DEPT CHAIR MICROBIOL & IMMUNOL, SCH MED, ROSS UNIV, 1996-; EMER PROF, COL SCI, 1996-; PROF BIOL SCI, COL SCI, 1990-; microbiologist consult, Vet Admin MedCtr, Allen Park, Mich, 1989-1992; guest res, Mycol Div, Ctrs Dis Control, US Pub Health Serv, Atlanta, Ga, 1980-1981; asst dean curric affairs & dir grad progs, Wayne State Univ, 1975-1980; vpres, State Mich, 1971-1972; prof immunol & microbiol, Wayne State Univ, 1970-1996; fromactg dep chmn to assoc chmn dept, Wayne State Univ, 1970-1975; ASSOC DERMAT, SCHMED, WAYNE STATE UNIV, 1968-; mem bd exam basic sci, State Mich, 1967-1972; Fulbrightlectr, Cairo Univ, 1965-1966; from instr to assoc prof, Wayne State Univ, 1958-1970; Med ServCorps, US Army, 1951-1953; Technician, Div Labs, State Dept Pub Health, Ga, 1950-1951. **Memberships:** Fel Am Acad Microbiol; Am Soc Microbiol; Soc Exp Biol & Med; Int Soc Human& Animal Mycol. **Research Statement & Publications:** Bacterial identification; medical mycology. **Mailing Address:** Ross Univ Sch Med, Box 266, Roseau, Dominica. **Fax:** 767-445-5383. **E-Mail:** cjeffries@webdom.rossmed.edu.dm

JEFFRIES, GRAHAM HARRY, INTERNAL MEDICINE, GASTROENTEROLOGY. **Personal Data:** b Barmera, South Australia, May 31, 1929; m 1955, c 4. **Education:** Univ NZ, BMedSc, 1949, MB, ChB, 1953; Oxford Univ, DPhil(physiol), 1955. **Professional Experience:** PROF EMER MED, COL MED, MILTON S HERSHEY MED CTR, PA STATE UNIV, as of 2006; prof med & chmn dept, col med, milton s hershey med ctr, Pa State Univ, beginning 1969; assoc prof med, Med Col, Cornell Univ, 1964-1969. **Memberships:** Am Fedn Clin Res; Am Gastroenterol Asn; Am Soc Clin Invest; fel Am ColPhysicians. **Research Statement & Publications:** Gastric secretion; vitamin B-12 metabolism; intestinal absorption; liver disease. **Mailing Address:** Penn State Milton S Hershey Med Ctr, Pa State Univ, 500 Univ Dr, Hershey, PA 17033. **Fax:** 717-531-4598. **E-Mail:** gjeffries@psu.edu

JEFFRIES, HARRY PERRY, ZOOLOGY. **Personal Data:** b Newark, NJ, April 15, 1929; m 1951, c 5. **Education:** Univ RI, BS, 1951, MS, 1955; Rutgers Univ, PhD (zool), 1959. **Professional Experience:** PROF EMER OCEANOG, UNIV RI, as of 2003; prof biol oceanog, Univ RI, beginning 1973; pres, Estuarine Res Fedn, 1973-1975; from asst prof toassoc prof, Univ RI, 1959-1973; asst, Rutgers Univ, 1956-1959; pharmacologist, CibaPharmaceut Prod, Inc, NJ, 1955-1956; asst biol oceanog, Univ RI, 1951-1955; pres, Nat Sci Found; pres, OffNaval Res; grants, Dept Energy, Nat Oceanog &Atmospheric Admin, Environ Protection Agency Sea Grant, Am Petroleum Inst. **Memberships:** Fel AAAS; Am Soc Limnol & Oceanog; Sigma Xi. **Research Statement & Publications:** Comparative ecology of estuarine habitats; biological fertility of inshore marine areas and characterization of community structure; chemical homeostasis of marine organisms in relation to environmental stress; biochemical systematics. **Mailing Address:** Dept Oceanog, Univ RI, Kingston, RI 02881.

JEFFRIES, JAY B, MOLECULAR PHYSICS. **Personal Data:** b June 3, 1947; American citizen. **Education:** Univ Iowa, BA, 1969; Univ Colo, PhD (physics), 1980. **Professional Experience:** PRIN INVESTR, MOLECULAR PHYSICS LAB, SRI INT, as of 1998; CHEM PHYSICIST, SRI INT, 1983-; assoc prof res, Univ Pittsburgh, 1980-1983; topical ed, J Appl Optics. **Memberships:** Am Phys Soc; Am Chem Soc; Combustion Inst; Mat Res Soc; fel Optical Soc Am. **Research Statement & Publications:** Laser-based diagnostic measurements of reacting flows and plasmas with ultimate goal of understanding the fundamental chemical mechanism of the process. **Mailing Address:** Molecular Physics Lab, SRI Int, 333 Ravenswood Ave Mail Code PS063, Menlo Park, CA 94025-3453. **Fax:** 650-859-6196. **E-Mail:** Jeffries@crvax.SRI.com

JEFFRIES, JOHN S, MATHEMATICS. **Professional Experience:** PROF MATH, NMEX HIGHLANDS UNIV, as of 2006. **Memberships:** Am Math Soc. **Mailing Address:** NMex Highlands Univ, 494 Christine Dr, Las Vegas, NM 87701-4675. **Fax:** 505-454-3558. **E-Mail:** jjeffries@cs.nmhu.edu

JEFFRIES, NEAL POWELL, MECHANICAL ENGINEERING. **Personal Data:** b Indianapolis, Ind, August 25, 1935; m 1958, c 2. **Education:** Purdue Univ, BS, 1957; Mass Inst Technol, MS, 1958; Univ Cincinnati, PhD (mecheng), 1969. **Professional Experience:** CO-FOUNDER, CTR MFG TECH, as of 2001; PRES, CTR MFG TECH, 1985-; exec dir, Ctr Mfg Tech, 1978-1985; mgrEduc Mech Eng Dept, Struct Dynamic Res Corp, 1974-1978; consult, & Avco Electronics, 1971-; consult, Vortex Corp, 1970-; US Navy grant, 1970-1971; asst prof, Univ Cincinnati, 1969-1974; consult, Honeywell Res Lab & Am Laundry Mfg, 1969-1970; consult, StructDynamics Res Corp, 1968-1974; res assoc mech eng, Univ Cincinnati, 1967-1969; proj mgr heattransfer, Gen Elec Co, Ohio, 1965-1967; lectr, Gen Elec Co, 1963-1974; engr, Gen Elec Co, Ohio, 1963-1965; res asst heat transfer, Stanford Univ, 1961-1963. **Memberships:** Am Soc Mech Engrs; Soc Mfg Engrs; Am Soc Eng Educ; Robotics Int; Comput &Automated Syst Asn. **Research Statement & Publications:** Heat transfer; fluid flow; thermodynamics; boiling phenomena; heat pipe; manufacturing engineering. **Mailing Address:** Ctr Mfg Tech, 9376 Hunters Creek Dr, Cincinnati, OH 45242.

JEFFRIES, QUENTIN RAY, CHEMICAL ENGINEERING. **Personal Data:** b Terre Haute, Ind, February 28, 1920; m 1951, c 2. **Education:** Rose Polytech Inst, BS, 1941; Univ Mich, MS, 1947; Univ Ill, PhD (chem eng), 1953. **Professional Experience:** CHEM ENGR RES, DEPT ENG, INTMINERALS CORP, 1965-; tech develop engr, Eng Dept, Int Minerals Corp, 1959-1965; princhem engr, Eng Dept, Int Minerals Corp, 1956-1959; prin chem engr, Battelle Mem Inst, 1953-1956; shift supvr, Penicillin Plant, Commercial Solvents Corp, 1949-1951; asst chem engr, Commercial Solvents Corp, 1948-1949; AT, CORN SOLVENTS CORP. **Memberships:** Am Chem Soc; Sigma Xi. **Research Statement & Publications:** Gaseous diffusion. **Mailing Address:** 11 Allendale, Terre Haute, IN 47802.

JEFFRIES, ROBERT ALAN, OPTICAL PHYSICS. **Personal Data:** b Indianapolis, Ind, November 11, 1933; m 1954, c 2. **Education:** Univ Okla, BS, 1954, MS, 1961, PhD (ionization kinetics), 1965. **Professional Experience:** CONSULT, 1989-; delegation, Nuclear Testing Talks, Geneva, 1986-1990; from staff mem to off dir, Los Alamos Nat Lab, 1957-1989; proj engr, Pontiac Motor Div, Gen Motors Corp, 1954-1955; mem, US-Soviet Bilateral Consultative Comn. **Memberships:** Am Phys Soc; Sigma Xi. **Research Statement & Publications:** Ionization kinetics; shock hydrodynamics; laser produced plasmas; electro optical instrumentation; arms control and verification technology. **Mailing Address:** 801 Calle Vado, Santa Fe, NM 87507.

JEFFRIES, THOMAS WILLIAM, BIOCHEMISTRY, METABOLIC ENGINEERING. **Personal Data:** b New Orleans, La, October 31, 1947; m Giovanna. **Education:** Calif State Univ, Long Beach, BS, 1969, MS, 1972; Rutgers Univ, PhD (microbiol), 1975. **Professional Experience:** DIR, INST MICROBIAL & BIOCHEM TECHNOL, USDA, 1999-; PROF, DEPT BACT, UNIV WIS, MADISON, 1993-; USDA career develop award, 1987; from microbiologist GS-12 to supvry microbiologist GS-15, Forest Prod Lab, USDA, 1979-1999; res assoc chem eng, Columbia Univ, 1977-1979; staff mem microbiol, Lawrence Livermore Lab, Univ Calif, 1975-1977; res intern, Rutgers Univ, 1972-1975; asst microbiol, Calif State Univ, Long Beach, 1969-1971. **Memberships:** Am Soc Microbiol; Soc Indust Microbiol; AAAS; Am Chem Soc; Tech Pulp & Paper Indust; fel Int Acad of Wood Sci; Sigma Xi. **Research Statement & Publications:** Metabolic engineering; genetic engineering; biochemical engineering; biochemistry; biotechnology; enzymology; microbial photosynthesis; biofuels; environmental toxicology; lignin biodegradation; pentose fermentation; yeasts; fermentation, metabolic regulation. **Mailing Address:** Inst Microbial & Biochem Technol, USDA, One Gifford Pinchot Dr, Madison, WI 53706. **Fax:** 608-231-9262. **E-Mail:** twjeffri@facstaff.wise.edu

JEFFRIES, WILLIAM BOWMAN, INVERTEBRATE ZOOLOGY. **Personal Data:** b Chicago, Ill, March 5, 1926; m 1988, Joanne; c Robert B, Linda C & Arthur C. **Education:** Univ Pittsburgh, BS, 1949; Univ NC, MA, 1952, PhD (zoology), 1955. **Professional Experience:** PROF EMER, DICKINSON COL, 1994-; chmn, Dept Biol, Dickinson Col, 1989-1990, 1983-1986; Charles A Dana prof biol, Dickinson Col, 1981-1994; res assoc, Dept Zool, Field Mus Natural Hist, beginning 1977; res assoc biochem, Sch Med, Univ Miami, 1968-1969; NIH spec res fel, Vet Admin Hosp, Miami, 1968-1969; chmn dept, Dickinson Col, 1965-1968; from asst prof to prof, Dickinson Col, 1959-1994; from instr to asst prof micro anat, Med Col Ga, 1956-1959; Nat Cancer Inst fel, Ind Univ, 1955-1956. **Memberships:** Soc Integrative & Comp Biol; Soc Protozool; Sigma Xi; Crustacean Soc. **Research Statement & Publications:** Physiology; parasitology; protozoology; biology of the barnacle genus Octolasmis. **Mailing Address:** Dept Biol, Dickinson Col, PO Box 1773, Carlisle, PA 17013.

JEFFS, GEORGE W, SPACE & COMMUNICATION TECHNOLOGY. **Personal Data:** b Stockton, Calif, March 9, 1925; m 1950, c Georgia M, James A & William P. **Education:** Univ Wash, BSAE & MSAE. **Honorary Degrees:** Alumnus Summa Laude Dignatus, Univ Wash, 1985; DEE, W Coast Univ, 1984. **Honors & Awards:** Distinguished Pub Serv Medal, NASA, 1973, 1982; Centennial Award, Univ WA; Presidential Medal Freedom, 1970; Golden Knight Mgt Award, Nat Mgt Asn, 1980; Astronaut Engr Award, Nat Space Club, 1982; Von Karman Lectr, Am Inst Aeronaut & Astronaut, 1983, Elmer Sperry Award, 1986. **Professional Experience:** RETIRED; sr consult, beginning 1991; Jimmy Doolittle educ fel, 1989; dir & vpres strategic defense & technol, Strategic Defense Ctr, 1988-1991; pres & ctr dir, Strategic Defense Ctr, 1986-1991; US deleg, Prog Indust & Tech Coop Aerospace, China, 1984; pres, N Am Aerospace Opers, 1978-1986; corp officer, Rockwell Int, 1976-1978; pres, Space Div, 1974-1976; vpres & prog mgr, Apollo CSM Progs, 1969-1973; asst prog mgr & chief prog engr, Apollo Command & Serv Modules Progs, 1966-1969; mem, Aerophys Lab, 1947-1966; sect chief advan eng & sect chief systs eng, Rockwell Int, 1947-1966; mgr corp tech develop & planning, Rockwell Int, 1947-1966; vpres & prog mgr, Paraglider Prog, Rockwell Int, 1947-1966; corp exec dir eng, Rockwell Int, 1947-1966; mem, Adv Panel Ballistic Missile Defense, Cong Off Technol Assessment. **Memberships:** Nat Acad Eng; fel Am Inst Aeronaut & Astronaut; fel Am Astronaut Soc; fel Inst Advan Eng. **Research Statement & Publications:** Advanced space engines; major launch vehicle propulsion engines; solid rockets; Many papers and presentations on Apollo Command and Serv Modules and shuttle orbiter through the years. **Mailing Address:** 1126 Corsica Dr, Pacific Palisades, CA 90272.

JEFFS, PETER W, ORGANIC CHEMISTRY. **Personal Data:** b Luton, Eng, January 9, 1933; m 1957, c 3. **Education:** Univ Natal, PhD (chem), 1961. **Professional Experience:** PROF ORG CHEM, DUKE UNIV, as of 2002; Prof Org Chem, Duke Univ, beginning 1971; from asst prof to assoc prof, DukeUniv, 1964-1971; lectr org chem, Univ Natal, 1960-1962; Res asst, Akers Res Labs, Imp ChemIndust, Eng, 1950-1957. **Memberships:** Am Chem Soc; fel The Chem Soc; assoc Royal Inst Chem. **Research Statement & Publications:** Chemistry of alkaloids, terpenes and mould metabolites; alkaloid biosynthesis; application of nuclear magnetic resonance to structure determination. **Mailing Address:** Glaxo Inc, Five Moore Dr, Research Triangle Park, NC 27701-4613.

JEFIMENKO, OLEG D, ELECTROMAGNETIC THEORY, GRAVITATION. **Personal Data:** b USSR, October 14, m Valentina. **Education:** Univ G^o06ttingen, Ger, Vordiplom, 1949; Lewis & Clark Col, BA, 1952; Univ Ore, MA, 1954, PhD (physics), 1956. **Honors & Awards:** Sigma Xi Prize, 1956. **Professional Experience:** PROF EMER PHYSICS, WVA UNIV, as of 2003; prof physics, Wva Univ, begining 1967; from asst prof to assoc prof, Wva Univ, 1956-1967; asst physics, Univ Ore, 1952-1955. **Memberships:** Am Phys Soc; Am Asn Physics Teachers; Electrostatic Soc Am. **Research Statement & Publications:** Electromagnetic theory; Special theory of relativity, gravitation, electrostatics; electrets; atomic physics. **Mailing Address:** Dept Physics, W Va Univ, 225 Lakeview Manor Dr, Morgantown, WV 26508. **Fax:** 304-594-1639. **E-Mail:** oleg.jefimenko@mail.wvu.edu

JEGLA, DOROTHY ELDREDGE, DEVELOPMENTAL BIOLOGY, PLANT BIOLOGY. **Personal Data:** b Brooklyn, NY, September 19, 1939; m 1965, c 2. **Education:** Mt Holyoke Col, AB, 1961; Yale Univ, MS, 1964, PhD (biol), 1985. **Professional Experience:** PROF EMER BIOL, KENYON COL, as of 2003; vis assoc prof biol, Rennsalaer Polytech Inst, 1988; assoc prof Biol, Kenyon Col, beginning 1987; plant tissue cult facil, Comprehensive Sch Improv Proj, NSF, 1987; Asst prof, Kenyon Col, 1972-1987. **Memberships:** AAAS; Bot Soc Am; Int Soc Plant Molecular Biologists. **Research Statement & Publications:** Organization and regulation of apical meristem development in the sunflower, Helianthus annus, by clonal analysis, grafting and sterile culture techniques. **Mailing Address:** Dept Biol, Kenyon Col, Higley Hall, Gambier, OH 43022-9623. **E-Mail:** jeglad@kenyon.edu

JEGLA, THOMAS CYRIL, MOLECULAR ENDOCRINOLOGY, INVERTEBRATE PHYSIOLOGY. **Personal Data:** b St Johns, Mich, July 5, 1935; m 1965, c John & Tim. **Education:** Mich State Univ, BS, 1958; Univ Ill, MS, 1960, PhD (zool), 1964. **Honorary Degrees:** DSc, Kenyon Col, 1997. **Honors & Awards:** Tomsich Res Award. **Professional Experience:** EMER PROF, KENYON COL, 1997-; vis res prof, Univ Iowa, 1994-1995; visres prof, Univ WFla, 1988; prof, Kenyon Col, 1985-1997; NIH res grant, 1985; vis assoc prof, Yale Univ, 1981-1983; vis prof, Univ Bonn, 1981, 1983, 1984; chmn dept, Kenyon Col, 1976-1979 & 1984-1987; NSF res grants, 1970, 1973, 1985-; from asst prof to assoc prof, Kenyon Col, 1966-1985; asst prof biol, Univ Minn, 1963-1964 & Yale Univ, 1964-1966. **Memberships:** AAAS; Am Soc Zool. **Research Statement & Publications:** Molting physiology of arthropods; invertebrate biology; comparative endocrinology; biochemistry of steroid and peptide hormones. **Mailing Address:** Dept Biol, Kenyon Col, Gambier, OH 43022. **E-Mail:** jegla@kenyon.edu

JEGLUM, JOHN KARL, FOREST ECOLOGY, SILVICULTURE. **Personal Data:** b Medford, Wis, December 9, 1938; m 1964, Susan Rogers; c Karl & John. **Education:** Univ Wis, BS, 1960, MS, 1962; Univ Sask, PhD (plant ecol), 1968. **Professional Experience:** PROF FOREST PEATLAND SCI, DEPT FOREST ECOL, SWEDISH UNIVAGR SCI, 1994-; Vis researcher, Dept Peatland Forestry, Univ Helsinki, 1984-1985; res scientistforestry ecol, Can Forestry Serv, 1968-1994; Asst prof bot, Eastern Ill Univ, 1965-1966. **Memberships:** Int Peat Soc UK. **Research Statement & Publications:** Wetland classification and ecology; boreal vegetational ecology; autecology of black spruce; regeneration silviculture; strip cutting in black spruce; environmental impacts of harvesting; peatland forestry. **Mailing Address:** Dept Forest Ecol, Swedish Univ Agr Sci, S-90183 Uppsala, Sweden. **Fax:** 469-078-67750. **E-Mail:** john.jeglum@sek.slu.se

JEKEL, EUGENE CARL, INORGANIC CHEMISTRY. **Personal Data:** b Holland, Mich, December 19, 1930; m 1960, Elaine; c 2. **Education:** Hope Col, AB, 1952; Purdue Univ, MS, 1955, PhD (inorg chem), 1964. **Honors & Awards:** Nat Award for Excellence in Coll Chem Teaching, Chemical Manufacturers Association, 1985. **Professional Experience:** EDWARD A & ELIZABETH HOFMA PROF EMER, DEPT CHEM, HOPE COL, as of 2005; chief health professions adv, Hope Col, 1977-1993; chmn dept, Hope Col, 1973-1976; vis prof, Univ Calif, Berkeley, 1970-1971; prof chem, Hope Col, beginning 1969; chmn dept, Hope Col, 1967-1970; from instr to assoc prof Hope Col, Hope Col, 1955-1969. **Memberships:** Asn Am Med Cols; Nat Sci Teachers Asn; Am Chem Soc; Sigma Xi. **Research Statement & Publications:** Thermodynamics of aqueous solutions at high temperature. **Mailing Address:** Dept Chem, Peale Sci Ctr, Hope Col, 35 E 12th St, Holland, MI 49422-9000. **Fax:** 616-395-7118. **E-Mail:** ramon@hope.edu

JEKEL, JAMES FRANKLIN, EPIDEMIOLOGY, PUBLIC HEALTH. **Personal Data:** b St Louis, Mo, October 14, 1934; m 1958, Janice; c Clifford, Mark, Linda & Timothy. **Education:** Wesleyan Univ, AB, 1956; Wash Univ, MD, 1960; Yale Univ, MPH, 1965. **Professional Experience:** PROF EMER, YALE UNIV, 1997-; Fulbright fel, 1985-1986; CEA Winslow Prof Public Health, Yale Univ, 1982-1997; prof epidemiol & pub health, Yale Univ, 1980-1997; assoc prof pub health, Yale Univ, 1971-1980; asst prof, Yale Univ, 1967-1971; epidemiologist, Ctrs Dis Control, 1962-1967; res asst pub health, St Louis Co Health Dept, 1958. **Memberships:** Am Pub Health Asn; fel Am Col Prev Med; fel Am Sci Affil. **Research Statement & Publications:** Program evaluation, especially health programs for teenage mothers; cocaine abuse; perinatal epidemiology; clinical epidemiology; public health planning and evaluation. **Mailing Address:** Dept Epidemiol & Pub Health, 60 Col St, New Haven, CT 06510-3210. **Fax:** 203-732-7185.

JEKELI, CHRISTOPHER, GEODESY, GLOBAL POSITIONING SYSTEMS. **Personal Data:** b Marburg, Ger, December 21, 1953; m 1984. **Education:** Univ McGill, BA, 1976; Univ Ohio State, MS, 1978, PhD (geod), 1981. **Honors & Awards:** Weikko A Herskanen

Award, Univ Ohio State, 1980. **Professional Experience:** PROF CIVIL & ENVIRON ENG & GEODETIC SCI, UNIV OHIO STATE, as of 2004; assoc prof geodesist Sci & Surv, Univ Ohio State, beginning 1993; geodesist, Air Force Geophys Lab, 1981-1993; Res assoc geod, Ohio State Univ, 1977-1981. **Memberships:** Am Geophys Union. **Research Statement & Publications:** Physical geodesy: methods to analyze and improve knowledge of the earth's external gravity field and application of these methods to gravimetric data. **Mailing Address:** Civil & Environ Eng & Geodetic Sci, Off 218B Bolz Hall, 470 Hitchcock Hall, 2070 Neil Ave, Columbus, OH 43210. **Fax:** 614-292-2957. **E-Mail:** jekeli.1@osu.edu

JELACHICH, MARY LOU, CELLULAR IMMUNOLOGY. **Personal Data:** b Munich, Ger. **Education:** DePauw Univ, BS, 1970; Northeastern Univ, MS, 1980; Northwestern Univ, PhD (immunol), 1985. **Professional Experience:** DIR IMMUNOL RES, EVANSTON HOSP, 1993-; dir immunol, Dept Surg, 1991-1993; Mult Sclerosis grant, Mult Sclerosis Soc, 1991; Res assoc, Dept Med, 1988-1991. **Memberships:** Am Asn Immunol. **Mailing Address:** Dir Immunobiol Res Dept WCH, Evanston Hosp 2650 N Ridge Ave, Evanston, IL 60201-1797. **Fax:** 847-570-1568.

JELEN, FREDERIC CHARLES, chemical engineering; deceased, see previous edition for last biography

JELEN, JAROSLAW ANDRZEJ, DOMAIN DECOMPOSITION & PARALLEL COMPUTING, COMPUTATIONAL FLUID DYNAMICS. **Personal Data:** b Nowy Targ, Poland, September 14, 1943; Canadian citizen; m 1971, Alicja; c Marek. **Education:** Univ Wroclaw, MSc, 1969; Acad Mining & Metall, Krakow, PhD (appl math), 1977. **Honors & Awards:** Prize, Polish Ministry Sci, 1978. **Professional Experience:** SR RES SCIENTIST, NOVA RES & TECHNOL CO, CALARY, 1985-; asst prof numerical anal, Univ Cracow, 1979-1984. **Memberships:** Am Metall Soc; Soc Indust & Appl Math. **Research Statement & Publications:** Numerical modelling of fluid flows; development of novel domain decomposition methods and finite difference schemes for solving partial differential equations. **Mailing Address:** 35 Sanderling Hill NW, Calgary, AB T3K 3B6, Can. **E-Mail:** jelenj@novachem.com

JELICKS, LINDA ANN, PHYSIOLOGY. **Education:** City Col NY, PhD, 1988. **Professional Experience:** ASSOC PROF, DEPT PHYSIOL & BIOPHYS, ALBERT EINSTEIN COL MED, as of 2005. **Mailing Address:** Albert Einstein Col Med, Rm U-323, Bronx, NY 10461.

JELINEK, ARTHUR GILBERT, SYNTHETIC ORGANIC CHEMISTRY. **Personal Data:** b Milwaukee, Wis, May 6, 1917; m 1945, c 3. **Education:** Univ Wis, BS, 1940, PhD (org chem), 1944. **Professional Experience:** RETIRED; sr res chemist, Biochem Dept, E I du Pont de Nemours & Co Inc, 1955-1979; res chemist, Grasselli Chem Dept, 1944-1955; asst org chem, Univ Wis, 1941-1944; res & control chemist, Fox River Paper Corp, Wis, 1940-1941. **Memberships:** Am Chem Soc. **Research Statement & Publications:** Agricultural chemicals. **Mailing Address:** 56 Kathy Lane, Wilmington, DE 19808.

JELINEK, CHARLES FRANK, ORGANIC CHEMISTRY. **Personal Data:** b Miles City, Mont, February 6, 1917; m 1944, c 2. **Education:** Mont State Col, BS, 1938; Oxford Univ, BSc, 1941; Univ Ill, PhD (org chem), 1944. **Professional Experience:** CONSULT, 1986-; dept dir phys sci, Bur Foods, Food & Drug Admin, 1979-1986; dept assoc dir technol, Bur Foods, Food & Drug Admin, 1975-1979; dir div chemtechnol, Bur Foods, Food & Drug Admin, 1972-1975, 1979-1986; coordr tech opportunities div, Dart Industs, Inc, 1971-1972; coordr new ventures, Enjay, 1966-1971; sr staff adv, Chem Staff, Esso Res & Eng Co, 1963-1966; dir dyestuff & chem div, Cent Res Lab, 1959-1963; mgr processres & develop dept, Gen Aniline & Film Corp, 1955-1959; mgr surfactants res, Gen Aniline &Film Corp, 1952-1955; sect leader appln res, Gen Aniline & Film Corp, 1950-1952; sales engr &asst dir cent sales develop dept, Gen Aniline & Film Corp, 1949-1950; asst to dir res, Gen Aniline& Film Corp, 1947-1949; res chemist, Gen Aniline & Film Corp, 1946-1947. **Memberships:** Am Chem Soc; Asn Off Anal Chemists; Am Inst Chemists; Com Develop Asn. **Research Statement & Publications:** Derivatives of acetylene; dyes; pigments; surfactants; polymers; solvents; coatings; chemical contaminants in foods. **Mailing Address:** Falls Church, VA 22041.

JELINEK, FREDERICK, ELECTRONICS ENGINEERING. **Personal Data:** b Prague, Czech, November 18, 1932; American citizen; m Milena; c Hannah (Sarbin) & William. **Education:** Mass Inst Technol, SB, 1956, SM, 1958, PhD (elec eng), 1962. **Honorary Degrees:** Dr (hon), Acad Senate Charles Univ Prague. **Honors & Awards:** 1999 - ESCA Medal for Outstanding Scientific Achievement in the Field of Speech Communication, by the European Speech Communication Association 2000 - The IEEE Third Millennium Medal in recognition and appreciation of valued services and outstanding contributions, by the Institute of Electrical and Electronics Engineers, Inc 2004 - Antonio Zampolli Prize for "Outstanding Contributions to the Advancement of Language Resources and Language Technology Evaluation within Human Language Technologies" presented by The European Language Resources Association (ELRA) 2005 - IEEE James L Flanagan Speech and Audio Processing Award for outstanding contributions to the advancement of speech processing presented at ICASSP 2005. **Professional Experience:** JULIAN SINCLAIR SMITH PROF ELEC & COMPUT ENG, JOHNS HOPKINS UNIV, 1993-; DIR, CTR LANG SPEECH PROCESSING, JOHNS HOPKINS UNIV, 1993-; sr mgr continous speech recognition, T J Watson Res Ctr, IBM Corp, beginning 1972; vis scientist, IBM T J Watson Res Ctr, 1968-1969; NASA contracts, 1966-1972; NSF grant, 1964-1966; from asst prof to prof, Cornell Univ, 1962-1974; vis lectr, Harvard Univ, 1962; instr elec eng, Mass Inst Technol, 1959-1962. **Memberships:** Fel Inst Elec & Electronics Engrs. **Research Statement & Publications:** Transmission of information; coding; data compression; speech recognition; information theory. **Mailing Address:** Ctr Lang & Speech Processing, John Hopkins Univ, 320 Barton Hall, 3400 N Charles St, Baltimore, MD 21218. **Fax:** 410-516-5050. **E-Mail:** jelinek@jhu.edu

JELINEK, ROBERT VINCENT, CHEMICAL ENGINEERING. **Personal Data:** b New York, NY, March 5, 1926; m 1955, c 3. **Education:** Columbia Univ, BS, 1945, MS, 1947, PhD (chem eng), 1953. **Professional Experience:** RETIRED; prof, Dept Paper Sci & Eng, Col Environ Sci & Forestry, 1980-1993; prof & dean, Sch Environ & Resource Eng, State Univ NY, 1972-1980; prog dir engchem, NSF, 1971-1972; dir summer res prog high sch teachers, Syracuse Univ, 1964-1969; chmn eng fac, Syracuse Univ, 1964-1965; fac secy, Syracuse Univ, 1962-1964; NSF res grant, 1959-1961; assoc, Danforth Found, 1956-1960; asst to dean eng, Syracuse Univ, 1955-1960; from asst prof to prof, Syracuse Univ, 1954-1972; asst prof chem eng, Columbia Univ, 1953-1954; chem engr, Develop Div, Standard Oil Develop Co, 1951-1953; instr chem eng, Columbia Univ, 1949-1951; asst drafting, Columbia Univ, 1943-1945. **Memberships:** Am Chem Soc; Electrochem Soc; Nat Asn Corrosion Engrs; Am Inst Chem Engrs. **Research Statement & Publications:** Reaction kinetics; corrosion; electrochemistry; adsorption; process design and computer simulation. **Mailing Address:** 6332 Ledgewood Dr, Jamesville, NY 13078-9512.

JELINSKI, LYNN W, PROTEIN FOLDING, BIOLOGICAL RECOGNITION. **Personal Data:** b Arlington, Va, January 19, 1949. **Education:** Duke Univ, BS, 1971; Univ Hawaii, PhD (chem), 1976. **Honors & Awards:** Order Hippocrates, Duke Univ; Krug Lect, Univ Il; Gamma Sigma Delta. **Professional Experience:** V CHAN RES & GRAD STUDIES, LA STATE UNIV, as of 2002; DIR, CTRADVAN TECHNOL, CORNELL UNIV, 1991-; head biophys, AT&T Bell Lab, 1985-1991; head polymer chem, AT&T Bell Lab, 1984-1985; mem tech staff chem, AT&T BellLab, 1980-1984; staff fel, biophysics, 1978-1980; fel, NIH, 1977-1978; fel chem, Johns Hopkins Univ, 1976-1977. **Memberships:** ACS; CIAR. **Research Statement & Publications:** Nuclear magnetic resonances and imaging; protein folding, biological recognition; author of various articles. **Mailing Address:** La State Univ, 240 Thomas Boyd Hall, Baton Rouge, LA 70803. **E-Mail:** jelinski@lsu.edu

JELLARD, CHARLES H, MEDICAL BACTERIOLOGY, PUBLIC HEALTH. **Personal Data:** b Abergavenny, Wales, December 25, 1916; m 1950, c 4. **Education:** Oxford Univ, BA & BM, BCh, 1942; Univ London, dipl bact, 1951; FRCPath, 1965; Oxford Univ, DM, 1975. **Honorary Degrees:** MA, Cambridge Univ, 1948. **Professional Experience:** RETIRED; assoc prof bacj & dep dir, Prov Lab Pub Health, Univ Alta, 1968-1982; Hon consult bacteriologist, Plymouth Hosps, UK, 1953-1968; Dir, Pub Health LabServ, Plymouth, UK, 1953-1968. **Memberships:** Path Soc Gt Brit & Ireland; Brit Soc Gen Microbiol. **Research Statement & Publications:** Diagnostic medical bacteriology; epidemiology. **Mailing Address:** 12504 Lansdone Dr, Edmonton, AB T6H 4L5, Can.

JELLIFFE, ROGER WOODHAM, CARDIOLOGY, CLINICAL PHARMACOLOGY. **Personal Data:** b Cleveland, Ohio, February 18, 1929; m 1954, Joyce Miller; c Susan, Amy, Elizabeth & Peter. **Education:** Harvard Col, AB, 1950; Columbia Univ, MD, 1954; Am Bd Internal Med, dipl, 1962; Am Bd Cardiovasc Dis, dipl, 1965. **Honors & Awards:** AAPS Res Achievement Award Clin Sci, 1997. **Professional Experience:** Chmn, Pharmaceut Sect, Am Soc Clin Pharmacol & Therapeut, 1995-1998; PROF MED, SCH MED, UNIV SOUTHERN CALIF, 1976-; NIH res grants digitalis & appl pharmacokinetics, 1964-; from instr to assoc prof, Sch Med, Univ Southern Calif, 1961-1976; Los Angeles Co Heart Asn res fel, Sch Med, Univ SouthernCalif, 1961-1963; resident med, Vet Admin Hosp, Cleveland, 1960-1961; staff physician, VetAdmin Hosp, Cleveland, 1958-1960; Nat Found Infantile Paralysis fel exp med, Sch Med, Western Res Univ, 1956-1958; asst resident, Univ Hosps, Cleveland, Ohio, 1955-1956; internmed, Univ Hosps, Cleveland, Ohio, 1954-1955; fel coun clin cardiol, Am HeartAsn. **Memberships:** Fel Am Col Physicians; fel Am Heart Asn; Am Soc Clin Pharmacol & Therapeut; fel Am Col Med Informatics. **Research Statement & Publications:** Cardiovascular pharmacology; chemical measurements of digitalis glycosides and mathematical descriptions of the kinetics of digitalis, kanamycin, gentamicin, streptomycin, procainamide, lidocaine and other drugs in man; computer assistance for planning, monitoring and adjusting dosage regimens of the above drugs; methods for optimal study and control of pharmacokinetic systems; population pharmacokinetic modeling; Multiple Model Bayesian adaptive control of drug dosage regimens. **Mailing Address:** Keck Sch Med, Univ Southern Calif, CSC 134B 2250 Alcazar St, Los Angeles, CA 90033. **Fax:** 323-442-1302. **E-Mail:** jelliffe@usc.edu

JELLINCK, PETER HARRY, BIOCHEMISTRY, ENDOCRINOLOGY. **Personal Data:** b Paris, France, February 20, 1928; m 1954, Mary Topham; c Susan, Caroline & Rosemary. **Education:** Cambridge Univ, BA, 1948; Univ London, BSc, 1950, MSc, 1952, PhD (biochem), 1954. **Professional Experience:** PROF EMER BIOCHEM, QUEEN'SUNIV, ONT, as of 2003; vis prof, Rockefeller Univ, 1978-1979, 1982-; prof biochem, Queen's Univ, ONT, begining 1967; head dept, Queen's Univ, Ont, 1967-1978; from asst prof to prof, Univ BC, 1960-1967; Nat Cancer Inst Can-Med Res Coun Can res grant, 1959-; lectr biochem, Middlesex Hosp Med Sch, 1958-1959; lectr biochem, St Bartholomew's Hosp Med Col, London, 1957-1958; lectr chem, Norwood Tech Col, Eng, 1956-1957; Can Nat Res Coun fel biochem, McGill Univ, 1955-1956. **Memberships:** Am Asn Cancer Res; Brit Biochem Soc; Can Biochem Soc; Endocrine Soc. **Research Statement & Publications:** Estrogen metabolism and action; hormonal carcinogenesis; Listed in over 100 publications in major journals. **Mailing Address:** Dept Biochem, Queen's Univ, Rm 254, Botterell Hall, Kingston, ON K7L 3N6, Can. **Fax:** 613-545-2497. **E-Mail:** phj1@post.queensu.ca

JELLINEK, MAX, ORGAN TRANSPLANTATION, SHOCK. **Personal Data:** b 1929; m 1965, c 3. **Education:** St Louis Univ, PhD (biochem), 1961. **Professional Experience:** RES FAC SURG, HANLON SURG SOCIETY, ST LOUIS UNIV, as of 2004; from asst to assoc prof Biochem, St Louis Univ, 1962-1996. **Memberships:** Am Physiol Soc; Am Chem Soc. **Research Statement & Publications:** Metabolism of ischimic hypoxic; organs and shock. **Mailing Address:** Dept Surg, Sch Med St Louis Univ, 1402 S Grand Blvd, St Louis, MO 63104. **Fax:** 573-771-1945.

JELLINEK, MICHAEL STEVEN, PSYCHIATRY, PEDIATRICS. **Personal Data:** b New York, NY, September 30, 1948; m 1970, Barbara; c David M, Abraham R, Isaiah T & Hanna R. **Education:** Columbia Col, BA, 1970; Albert Einstein Col Med, MD, 1973; Am Bd Pediat, dipl psychiat & child psychiat. **Honors & Awards:** Simon Wile Award, Am Acad Child Psychiat, 1993. **Professional Experience:** PROF PEDIAT PSYCHIAT, HARVARD UNIV, as of 2003; sr vpres admin, Ambulatory Servs, 1995-; sr vpres, Ambulatory Servs, 1994-; asst gen dir, Ambulatory Servs, 1992-; assoc prof pediat psychiat, Harvard Univ, beginning 1987; psychiatrist, Mass Gen Hosp, 1986-; pediatrician, Mass Gen Hosp, 1986-; dir outpatient psychiat, Mass Gen Hosp, 1984-1993; assoc pediatrician & psychiatrist, Mass Gen Hosp, 1984-1986; asst pediatrician, Mass Gen Hosp, 1981-1983; consult, Shriner Burns Inst, Boston, 1979-; CHIEF, CHILD PEDIAT SERVS, MASS GEN HOSP, 1979-; asst pediat, Mass Gen Hosp, 1979-1981; instr pediat, Montefiore Hosp & Med Ctr, New York, 1976-1979; asst instr, Columbia Univ, 1970. **Memberships:** fel Am Acad Pediat; fel Am Acad Child Psychiat (treas, 1991-1993); Soc Prof ChildPsychiat. **Mailing Address:** Children's Hosp, 300 Longwood Ave, Boston, MA 02115. **Fax:** 617-726-8479.

JELLING, MURRAY, INVENTION, PATENTS. **Personal Data:** b Brooklyn, NY, January 7, 1918. **Education:** Brooklyn Col, BS, 1937; Polytech Univ, Brooklyn, MS, 1941, PhD (chem), 1945. **Professional Experience:** AT, JELLING & ASSOC, as of 2000; pres, Jonelle Indust Prod, 1967-1972; CONSULT CHEMIST, 1957-; pres, Cidex Corp, 1948-1957; res dir org chem, Maguire Industs, Inc, 1945-1947; res assoc, polymer, Polytech Univ, 1943-1945; res chemist, Nopco Chem Co, Inc, 1941-1943; res chemist, Autoxygen, Inc, 1938-1941. **Memberships:** Am Chem Soc; Sigma Xi; Soc Asphalt Technologists; Asn Asphalt Paving Technologists; Asn Consult Chemists & Chem Engrs; Transp Res Bd. **Research Statement & Publications:** Industrial organic chemistry; polymers; textile maintenance (dry-cleaning and laundry) products; bituminous products; granted 30 patents; licensing. **Mailing Address:** 19375 Cypress Ridge, Terr 507, Lansdowne, VA 20176. **Fax:** 703-726-9989.

JELLINGER, THOMAS CHRISTIAN, CONSTRUCTION ENGINEERING. **Personal Data:** b Seaton, Ill, September 17, 1923; m 1946, c 3. **Education:** Univ Ill, Urbana, Champaign,

BS, 1949; Iowa State Univ, MS, 1963. **Professional Experience:** PROF EMER CIVIL CONSTRUCT & ENVIRON ENG, as of 2005; dir & vpres, Assoc Gen Contractor Educ & Res Found, 1970; prof in-chg construct eng, Iowa State Univ, beginning 1960; proprietor eng & architect, Thomas C Jellinger, 1957-1960; engr, Wagner Inc, 1952-1957; engr, various consult firms, Cincinnati, 1949-1952; founding dir, Am Inst Constructors. **Memberships:** Nat Soc Prof Engrs; Am Soc Eng Educ. **Research Statement & Publications:** Construction management, techniques, and advanced methods of construction scheduling. **Mailing Address:** Dept Civil Construct & Environ Eng, Iowa State Univ, 1350 Beardshear Hall, Ames, IA 50011.

JELLISON, GERALD EARLE, OPTICS, ELLIPSOMETRY. **Personal Data:** b Bangor, Maine, March 27, 1946; m 1970, Mary; c Lisa & Katie. **Education:** Bowdoin Col, BA, 1968; Univ Brown, MS, 1973, PhD (physics), 1977. **Professional Experience:** SR STAFF SCIENTIST, OAK RIDGE NAT LAB, 1978-; Nat Res Coun fel, Naval Res Lab, 1976-1978. **Memberships:** Am Phys Soc; Am Optical Soc; SPIE. **Research Statement & Publications:** Physics of semiconductors; measurement of optical properties of materials as a function of doping and temperature; spectroscopic ellipsometry and thin film diagnostics. **Mailing Address:** Condensed Matter Sci Div Bldg 3025, Oak Ridge Nat Lab, Oak Ridge, TN 37831-6030. **E-Mail:** jellisongejr@ornl.gov

JELLUM, MILTON DELBERT, AGRONOMY, PLANT BREEDING. **Personal Data:** b Starbuck, Minn, October 26, 1934; m 1957, c 2. **Education:** Univ Minn, BS, 1956; Univ Ill, MS, 1958, PhD (agron), 1961. **Professional Experience:** RETIRED; from assoc prof to prof agron, Ga Exp Sta, Univ Ga, 1967-1985; asst agronomist, Ga Exp Sta, Univ Ga, 1960-1967. **Memberships:** AAAS; Am Soc Agron; Crop Sci Soc Am; Am Oil Chem Soc; Am Asn Cereal Chem. **Research Statement & Publications:** Environmental and genetic study of oil content and fatty acid composition of corn grain oil; study of yield components of corn and corn breeding. **Mailing Address:** 920 Buck Creek Rd, Griffin, GA 30224.

JEMAL, MOHAMMED, PHARMACOKINETICS, DRUG METABOLISM. **Personal Data:** b 1947; Ethiopian citizen; c 1. **Education:** Haile Sellassie Univ, BS, 1970; Purdue Univ, PhD (pharm analyst), 1976. **Honors & Awards:** Haile Sellassie Medal Award. **Professional Experience:** SR RES FEL, DRUG DISPOSITION & BIOANAL SCI, BRISTOL-MYERS SUIBB PHARMACEUT CO, as of 2004; GROUP LEADER BIOANAL RES, BRISTOL-MYERS SQUIBB, 1982-; resinvestr anal res & develop, Squibb Inst med Res, 1978-1982; Post doctoral res, Purdue Univ, 1976-1977. **Memberships:** Am Chem Soc; Am Asn Pharmaceut Scientists. **Research Statement & Publications:** Quantification of drugs and metabolites in body fluids for assessment of pharmacokinetics and safety. **Mailing Address:** Bristol-Myers Squibb, PO Box 4500, Princeton, NJ 08543-4500.

JEMIAN, WARTAN A(RMIN), PHYSICAL METALLURGY. **Personal Data:** b Lynn, Mass, December 31, 1925; m 1951, c 4. **Education:** Univ Md, BS, 1950; Rensselaer Polytech Inst, MS, 1953, PhD (metall eng), 1956. **Professional Experience:** PROF EMER MECH ENG, AUBURN UNIV, 1994-; prof mat eng, Mat Eng Curric Comt, 1975-1993; chmn, Mat Eng Curric Comt, 1963-1982; from assoc prof to prof mecheng, Auburn Univ, 1962-1975; dir res & develop, Rectifier-Capacitor Div, Fansteel Metall Corp, 1962; sr fel & head power rectifiers fel, Mellon Inst, 1957-1962; lectr & adj prof, UnivPittsburgh, 1956-1962; engr, Semiconductor Dept, Westinghouse Elec Corp, 1955-1957. **Memberships:** Am Inst Mining Metall & Petrol Engrs; Am Soc Metals; Am Soc Eng Educ; Biomat Res Soc; Int Asn Math & Comput Simulation; Sigma Xi. **Research Statement & Publications:** Education; structure and properties of composite materials; computer analysis of materials; education in materials science and engineering. **Mailing Address:** Dept Mech Eng, Auburn Univ, Auburn, AL 36849-3501. **Fax:** 334-887-5705. **E-Mail:** jemian@aub.mindspring.com

JEMMERSON, RONALD RENOMER WEAVER, IMMUNOLOGY, BIOCHEMISTRY. **Personal Data:** b Baltimore, Md, March 7, 1951. **Education:** Western Md Col, BA, 1973; Northwestern Univ, PhD (biochem), 1978. **Professional Experience:** PROF, DEPT MICROBIOL, UNIV MINN, as of 2005; assoc prof, Dept Microbiol, Univ Minn, beginning 1991; asst prof, Dept Microbiol, Univ Minn, 1985-1991; res assoc, Scripps Clin & Res Found, 1984-1985; res assoc, La Jolla Cancer Res Found, 1981-1984; Damon Runyon-Walter Winchell fel, 1979-1980; res fel, Scripps Clin & Res Found, 1978-1981. **Memberships:** AAAS; Am Asn Immunologists; Protein Soc. **Research Statement & Publications:** Protein antigenicity; memory B lymphocytes; antibody and B cell repertoires; Cytochrome c release from CNS mitochondria and potential for clinical intervention in apoptosis-mediated CNS diseases; Activation of calcium-independent phospholipase A2 (iPLA2) in brain mitochondria and release of apoptogenic factors by BAX and truncated BID; Two pathways for tBID-induced cytochrome c release from rat brain mitochondria: BAK- versus BAX-dependence; author of various articles. **Mailing Address:** Dept Microbiol, Univ Minn Med Sch, 420 Del St SE, Minneapolis, MN 55455. **Fax:** 612-626-0623. **E-Mail:** jemme001@umn.edu

JEMSKI, JOSEPH VICTOR, MEDICAL MICROBIOLOGY. **Personal Data:** b Blackstone, Mass, March 19, 1920. **Education:** Fordham Univ, BS, 1942; Univ Pa, PhD (med microbiol), 1952. **Honors & Awards:** Barnett L Cohen Award, Am Soc Microbiol. **Professional Experience:** RETIRED; sr investr, US Army Res Inst Infectious Dis, 1972-1983; chmn Biol Safety Comt, Asn Lab Anal Sci, 1965-1971; comn Rickettsial Dis, Armed Forces Epidemiol Bd, 1965-1971; chief test sphere br, US Army Biol Defense Res Labs, 1959-1972; chief animal path sect, Chem Corps, 1955-1959; chief animal path unit, Ralph M Parsons Co, 1952-1955; head bact dept, Maltine Co, 1946-1949. **Memberships:** Am Soc Microbiol; Am Asn Lab Animal Sci; fel Am Acad Microbiol; Maryland Br ASM (Pres, 1974). **Research Statement & Publications:** Experimental aerosol induced diseases in laboratory animals; aerobiology; biological safety; immunogenesis and immunoprophylaxis of respiratory diseases. **Mailing Address:** 7922 Long Meadow Dr, Frederick, MD 21701.

JEN, CHIH KUNG, MICROWAVE PHYSICS. **Personal Data:** b Chin Yuan, Shansi, China, August 15, 1906; American citizen; m 1937, c 4. **Education:** Mass Inst Technol, SB, 1928; Univ Pa, SM, 1929; Harvard Univ, PhD (physics), 1931. **Professional Experience:** RETIRED; consult, Appl Physics Lab, 1978-1987; hon prof, Tsinghua Univ, Beijing & Univ Sci & Technol, Hefei, People's Repub China, 1978; vice chmn, William S Parsons visprof chem physics, 1966-1967; vice chmn, Res Ctr, Johns Hopkins Univ, 1958-1974; physicist & prin staff mem, Appl Physics Lab, 1950-1976; res lectr physics, Harvard Univ, 1946-1950; dir, RadioRes Int, 1937-1945; prof, Tsing Hua Univ, Peking, China, 1934-1937; prof, Shuntung Univ, China, 1933-1934; instr, Harvard Univ, 1932-1933; fel, China Found, 1931-1932; Asst physics, Harvard Univ, 1930-1932. **Memberships:** Fel Am Phys Soc; Acad Sinica, Taiwan. **Research Statement & Publications:** Ionosphere; quantum mechanics; electron tube phenomena; microwave spectroscopy. **Mailing Address:** 10203 Lariston Ln, Silver Spring, MD 20903.

JEN, JOSEPH JWU-SHAN, FOOD BIOCHEMISTRY, ACADEMIC ADMINISTRATION. **Personal Data:** b Sichuan, China, May 8, 1939; American citizen; m 1965, Salina; c Joanne P & Jeffrey J. **Education:** Nat Taiwan Univ, BS, 1960; Wash State Univ, MS, 1964; Univ Calif, Berkeley, PhD (comp biochem), 1969; Southern Ill Univ, MBA, 1986. **Professional Experience:** DEAN, COL AGR, CALIF POLYTECH STATE UNIV, 1992-; chmn fruit &vegetables prod, Inst Food Technol, 1988-1989; chmn, Div Food Sci & Technol, Univ Ga, 1986-1992; dir, biochem, Campbell Inst Res & Tech, 1985-1986; mgr, food enzyme, CampbellInst Res & Tech, Camden, NJ, mgr, vegetable biochem, 1983-1985; assoc prof, Mich State Univ, East Lansing, 1979-1980; vis prof, Nat Taiwan Univ, 1976; res food technologist, USDA, 1975; from asst prof to prof food biochem, Clemson Univ, SC, 1969-1979. **Memberships:** Inst Food Technol; Am Chem Soc; Chinese Am Foods Soc (pres 1977-1978). **Research Statement & Publications:** Food enzymology; vegetable texture; pectin chemistry and function; fruit and vegetable shelf-life extension and quality measurements; value added product development; food biotechnology; agriculture. **Mailing Address:** Col Agr, Calif PolytechState Univ, San Luis Obispo, CA 93407. **E-Mail:** jjen@calpoly.edu

JEN, JUN, ORGANIC CHEMISTRY. **Personal Data:** b China, October 5, 1927; American citizen; m 1951, c 2. **Education:** Shanghai Univ, BS, 1948; Carnegie Inst Technol, MS, 1949. **Professional Experience:** PRES, J J CHEM, INC, 1977-; mem staff, Chem Div, Union Camp Corp, 1975-1977; dir res & develop, Tenneco Chem Co, 1963-1975; res engr, Gen Elec Co, 1960-1963; mgr eng, Anaheim Plant, Oronite Chem Co Div, Calif Chem Co, Standard Oil Co, Calif, 1956-1960; res chemist, Am Cyanamid Co, 1951-1956. **Memberships:** Am Chem Soc. **Research Statement & Publications:** Polymers; water soluble resins; alkyds; acrylics; polyesters; pulp and paper; naval stores products; ore benefication. **Mailing Address:** 16 Gale Break Circle, Savannah, GA 31406-5205.

JEN, KAI-LIN CATHERINE, OBESITY, TYPE II DIABETES. **Personal Data:** b Taiwan, China, July 18, 1949; American citizen; m 1978, Paul; c Elizabeth & John. **Education:** Wayne State Univ, PhD (nutrit), 1977. **Professional Experience:** PROF & INTERIM CHAIR, DEPT NUTRIT & FOOD SCI, WAYNE STATE UNIV, 1992-; from asst prof to assoc prof, Wayne State Univ, 1984-1992; asst res scientist, Univ Mich, 1978-1983. **Memberships:** Am Inst Nutrit; Am Physiol Soc; N Am Asn Study Obesity; AAAS. **Research Statement & Publications:** Regulation of appetite and body weight; animal model of human gestational diabetes; exercise and obesity; lipid metabolism in obesity; type two diabetes and nutrition. **Mailing Address:** Dept Nutrit & Food Sci, Col Sci, Wayne State Univ, 3009 Sci Hall, Detroit, MI 48202. **Fax:** 313-577-8616. **E-Mail:** ac1578@wayne.edu

JEN, KEI-PENG, MECHANICAL ENGINEERING. **Education:** Feng-Chia Univ, Taiwan, BS, 1975; Tenn Technol Univ, MS, 1979, PhD (eng), 1983. **Professional Experience:** ASSOC PROF MECH ENG, COL ENG, VILLANOVA UNIV, as of 2004. **Mailing Address:** Dept Mech Eng, Villanova Univ, Tolentine 126 E 800 Lamcaster Ave, Villanova, PA 19085-1681. **Fax:** 610-519-4941. **E-Mail:** kei-peng.jen@villanova.edu

JEN, PHILIP HUNGSUN, AUDITORY PHYSIOLOGY, NEUROETHOLOGY. **Personal Data:** b Hunan, China, January 11, 1944; American citizen; m 1971, Betty. **Education:** Tunghai Univ BS, 1967; Wash Univ, MA, 1971, PhD (biol), 1974. **Professional Experience:** PROF NERVOUS SYST, UNIV MO, COLUMBIA, 1984-; prin investr, NIH, 1980-; prin investr, NSF, 1978-; guest lectr, Inst Acoust, Chinese Acad Sci, 1980; vis prof, J W Goethe Univ, Frankfurt, 1979; from asst prof to assoc prof, Univ Mo, Columbia, 1975-1984; res assoc, Wash Univ, 1974-1975. **Memberships:** Am Soc Zoologists; Acoust Soc Am; Soc Neuroscience; AAAS; NY Acad Sci. **Research Statement & Publications:** Neuroethological investigation of acoustic signal encoding, processing and control in the auditory system of echo-locating bats. **Mailing Address:** Dept Biol Sci, Univ Mo, Columbia, MO 65203. **Fax:** 573-882-5020. **E-Mail:** jenp@missouri.edu

JEN, SHEN, APPLIED PHYSICS. **Personal Data:** b Shanghai, China, December 8, 1947; m 1975. **Education:** Nat Taiwan Univ, BS, 1968; Harvard Univ, MS, 1970, PhD (appl physics), 1975. **Professional Experience:** SR MEM TECH STAFF, TEX INSTRUMENTS, 1988-; mem tech staff, Tex Instruments, 1984-1987; mem res staff, IBM, 1982-1984; mem res staff, Xerox Corp, 1979-1982; proj mgr, Xerox Corp, 1977-1978; res assoc light scattering spectros, Dept Chem, State Univ NY Stony Brook, 1975-1976. **Memberships:** Soc Photog Scientists & Engrs; Inst Elec & Electronics Engrs. **Research Statement & Publications:** Light scaterring spectroscopy; physics of liquid ceystals; electrophotography; magnetic storage technology; acoustic surface wave devices; microwave signal processing. **Mailing Address:** 1200 Stratford Dr, Richardson, TX 75080.

JENA, PURUSOTTAM, ATOMIC CLUSTERS & METAL DEFECTS, HYDROGEN STORAGE & NANOSTRUCTURES. **Personal Data:** b Orissa, India, February 5, 1943; m 1969, Tripti; c Anupam. **Education:** Utkal Univ, India, BSc, 1964, MSc, 1966; Univ Calif, Riverside, PhD (physics), 1970. **Honors & Awards:** FELLOW, AMERICAN PHYSICAL SOCIETY, 2000; OUTSTANDING FACULTY AWARD, STATE COUNCIL OF HIGHER EDUCATION, VA 2001, UNIVERSITY AWARD OF EXCELLENCE, VA COMMONWEALTH UNIV, 1993; OUTSTANDING SCHOLAR AWARD, VA COMMONWEALTH UNIV, 1987. **Professional Experience:** Prin investr, Dept Energy, beginning 1987; consult, BDM Corp, 1986-; prog dir, DivMat Res, NSF, 1986-1987; prin investr, Army Res Office, 1985-; prin investr, NSF, 1984-; DISTINGUISHED PROF PHYS, VA COMMONWEALTH UNIV, 2005-; PROF PHYSICS, VA COMMONWEALTH UNIV, 1980-; assoc prof physics, Mich Inst Technol Univ, 1978-1980; vis scientist, Argonne Nat Lab, 1977-1978; vis asst prof physics, Northwestern Univ, 1975-1977; res assoc physics, Univ BC, Vancouver, 1973-1975; fel, Dalhousie Univ, 1971-1973; lectr physics, State Univ NY, Albany, 1970-1971. **Memberships:** Am Phys Soc; Indian Phys Soc; Mat Res Soc. **Research Statement & Publications:** Theoretical condensed matter physics; defects in metals; small atomic clusters; Cluster assembled materials, hydrogen storage, spintronics, electronic structure and properties. **Mailing Address:** Physics Dept, Va Commonwealth Univ PO Box 842000, Richmond, VA 23284-2000. **Fax:** 804-828-7073. **E-Mail:** pjena@vcu.edu

JENCKS, WILLIAM PLATT, BIOCHEMISTRY, ORGANIC CHEMISTRY. **Personal Data:** b Bar Harbor, Maine, August 15, 1927; m 1950, c 2. **Education:** Harvard Univ, MD, 1951. **Honors & Awards:** Eli Lilly Co Award, Am Chem Soc, 1962; Merck Award, Am Soc Biol Chemists, 1993. **Professional Experience:** PROF EMER BIOCHEM, BRANDEIS UNIV, as of 2005; from asst prof to prof biochem, Brandeis Univ, 1957-1995; res fel, Harvard Univ, 1956-1957; res fel biochem, Res Lab, Mass Gen Hosp, 1955-1956; chief, DeptPharm, 1954-1955; res fel pharmacol, Army Med Serv Grad Sch, Walter Reed Army Med Ctr, 1953-1955; res fel biochem, Res Lab, Mass Gen Hosp, 1952-1953; intern, Peter Bent BrighamHosp, 1951-1952. **Memberships:** Nat Acad Sci; AAAS; Am Soc Biol Chem; Am Chem Soc; Am Acad Arts & Sci; fel Royal Soc. **Research Statement & Publications:** Mechanism and catalysis of carbonyl, acyl, phosphate transfer and other reactions; mechanism of enzyme action; intermolecular forces in aqueous solution; mechanism of coupled vectorial processes. **Mailing Address:** Dept Biochem, Brandeis Univ, 415 S St, Waltham, MA 02454-9110. **E-Mail:** jencks@brandeis.edu

JENDEN, DONALD JAMES, PHARMACOLOGY, ANALYTICAL CHEMISTRY. **Personal Data:** b Horsham, Eng, September 1, 1926; American citizen; m 1950, c 3. **Education:**

Univ London, BSc, 1947, MB, BS, 1950. **Honorary Degrees:** Dr, Univ Uppsala, Sweden, 1980. **Professional Experience:** EMER PROF PHARMACOL & BIOMATH, UNIV CALIF, LOS ANGELES, as of 2004; Wellcome vis prof, Univ Ala, Birmingham, 1984-; prof & chmn, deptpharmacol, 1968-1989; prof pharmacol & biomath, Univ Calif, Los Angeles, beginning 1967; Mem, Brain Res Inst, Univ Calif, Los Angeles, 1961-; NSF sr fel, hon res assoc, Univ ColUniv Col, Univ London, 1961-1962; actg chmn, Univ Calif, Los Angeles, 1956-1957; from asst prof to assoc prof, Univ Calif, Los Angeles, 1952-1967; lectr pharmacol, Univ Calif, 1950-1951; demonstr pharmacol, Univ London, 1948-1949. **Memberships:** Soc Neuroscience; Am Soc Pharmacol & Exp Therapeut; Am Physiol Soc; Am Soc Med Sch Pharmacol; fel Am Col Neuropsychopharmacol; AAAS; Am Chem Soc div Med Chem; Am Soc Neurochem; NY Acad Sci; Physiol Soc London; Int Union Pharmacol. **Research Statement & Publications:** Chemical and biochemical pharmacology; applications of mass spectrometry and stable isotopes in pharmacology and toxicology; cholinergic mechanisms; mathematical biology. **Mailing Address:** Dept Pharmacol Sch Med, Health Sci Univ Calif, 10833 Le Conte Ave, Los Angeles, CA 90024-1735. **Fax:** 310-825-6267. **E-Mail:** jenden@ucla.edu

JENDREK, EUGENE FRANCIS, X-RAY POWDER DIFFRACTION. **Personal Data:** b Baltimore, Md, June 11, 1949; m 1973, c 2. **Education:** Loyola Col, Baltimore, Md, BS, 1971; Univ Conn, Storrs, MS, 1973; Univ Md, Col Park, PhD (chem), 1979. **Professional Experience:** ANAL SPECIALIST, EG&G MOUND, 1989-; res specialist, Monsanto Res Group, 1979-1989; sr analyst, Davison Chem Div, W R Grace & Co, 1974-1975. **Memberships:** Am Chem Soc; Am Crystallog Soc. **Research Statement & Publications:** Powder X-ray diffraction computation; laboratory computer automation and data management. **Mailing Address:** EG&G Mound Appl Technol, PO Box 3000, Miamisburg, OH 45343-0987.

JENDRESEN, MALCOLM DAN, BIOMATERIALS. **Personal Data:** b Janesville, Wis, June 6, 1933; m 1954, c 1. **Education:** Marquette Univ, DDS, 1961; Univ Lund, Sweden, PhD (surface sci), 1980. **Professional Experience:** PROF EMER, SCH DENT, UNIV CALIF, SAN FRANCISCO, 1993-; consult, Surg Gen, US Army, 1979; consult, Nordisk Inst Odontologisk Mat, 1978-; vis prof, Univ Lund, Sweden, 1978-1979; consult, WHO, 1972-; asst dent res, Sch Dent, Univ Calif, San Francisco, 1972-1993; consult, Vet Admin Hosp, San Francisco, 1968-; prof biomat sci, Sch Dent, Univ Calif, San Francisco, 1968-1993; consult, USAF Sch Aerospace Med, 1968-1972; chief restoration dent, USAF Sch Aerospace Med, 1964-1968; instr & res assoc dent mat, Marquette Univ, Wis, 1961-1964; consult, NIH; consult, Nat Inst Dent Res; consult, Dept Health & Human Serv; consult, Pub Health Serv. **Memberships:** Fel Int Asn Dent Res; fel Am Col Dentists; fel Int Col Dentists; fel AAAS; felSigma Xi. **Research Statement & Publications:** General materials with emphasis on adhesion in biological environments; characterization of biofilm and the clinical adhesiveness of intact biological surfaces and subsequent adhesive events. **Mailing Address:** Dept Prev & Restorative Dent Sci, Sch Dent, Univ Calif, DDS 61 Marquette U, San Francisco, CA 94143-0758. **Fax:** 415-476-4226. **E-Mail:** mjend@itsa.ucsf.edu

JENEKHE, SAMSON A, SYNTHESIS & PROCESSING OF POLYMERS, PHOTOPHYSICS OF POLYMERS. **Personal Data:** b Okpella, Bendel State, Nigeria, March 3, 1951; American citizen. **Education:** Mich Technol Univ, BS, 1977; Univ Minn, MS, 1980, MA, 1981, PhD (chem eng), 1985. **Professional Experience:** PROF MAT SCI & CHEM, UNIV ROCHESTER, as of 2004; PROF CHEM ENG, UNIV ROCHESTER, 1994-; consult, McDonnellDouglas Corp, 1990-1992; from asst prof to assoc prof, Univ Rochester, 1988-1994; proj leaderelectronic polymers, Honeywell Inc, 1985-1987; prin res scientist, Honeywell Inc, 1984-1987; sr res scientist, Honeywell Inc, 1981-1984. **Memberships:** Am Inst Chem Engrs; Am Chem Soc; Mat Res Soc; Am Phys Soc; AAAS. **Research Statement & Publications:** Synthesis and processing of electronic, optoelectronic, and photonic polymers; optoelectronic and photonic properties of polymers; photoinduced charge transfer in polymers; photophysics in polymers and macromolecular assemblies; polymer nanocomposites; polymer complexes; polymer-based devices. **Mailing Address:** Dept Chem Eng, Univ Rochester, Rochester, NY 14627-0166. **Fax:** 585-442-6686. **E-Mail:** jenekhe@che.rochester.edu

JENERICK, HOWARD PETER, PHYSIOLOGY. **Personal Data:** b Cicero, Ill, May 20, 1923; m 1947, c 3. **Education:** Univ Chicago, PhB, 1946, SB, 1948, PhD (physiol), 1951. **Professional Experience:** RETIRED; dir, Extramural Inventions Off, 1990-1993; chief off prog anal, Nat Inst Gen Med Sci, NIH, 1976-1990; spec asst to the dir, Res Grants Br, 1972-1976; prog dir biophys sci, Res Grants Br, 1967-1972; chief, Res Grants Br, 1965-1967; chief, Spec Res Resources Br, Div Res Facil & Resources, NIH, 1964-1965; assoc prof physiol, Emory Univ, 1960-1964; exec secy, Res Training Br, Div Gen Med Sci, NIH, 1958-1960; from instr biol to asst prof gen physiol, Mass Inst Technol, 1951-1958. **Memberships:** Biophys Soc; Am Physiol Soc. **Research Statement & Publications:** Electrophysiology; scientific administration. **Mailing Address:** 5515 Huntington Pkwy, Bethesda, MD 20814.

JENG, DUEN-REN, FLUID MECHANICS, BIOENGINEERING. **Personal Data:** b Taipei, Taiwan, March 1, 1932; American citizen; m 1966, Susan F S Jeng; c Michael, Leslie & Robert. **Education:** Nat Univ Taiwan, BS, 1955; Univ Ill, MS, 1960, PhD (mech eng), 1965. **Professional Experience:** PROF MECH ENG, UNIV TOLEDO, 1977-; from asst prof to assoc prof, Univ Toledo, 1965-1977; asst prof, Univ Ala, 1965-1967; Asst mech eng, Nat Univ Taiwan, 1956-1969 & Univ Ill, 1960-1964. **Memberships:** Am Soc Mech Engrs; Sigma Xi; Am Inst Aeronaut & Astronaut. **Research Statement & Publications:** Metal cutting; thermal contact resistance and transient heat transfer in laminar boundary layer; wind energy; non-newtonian flow; radiation; Gas Mixing in Human Lungs. **E-Mail:** djeng@eng.utoledo.edu

JENG, RAYMOND ING-SONG, HYDROLOGY, HYDRAULICS. **Personal Data:** b Taipei, Taiwan, January 1, 1940; m 1971. **Education:** Nat Taiwan Univ, BS, 1962; Colo State Univ, MS, 1965, PhD (civil eng), 1968. **Professional Experience:** Chmn dept, Calif State Univ, Los Angeles, beginning 1985; vis prof, Nat Taiwan Univ, 1980-1983; PROF CIVIL ENG, CALIF STATE UNIV, LOS ANGELES, 1979-; consult, Los Angeles Co Flood Control Dist, 1971-1978; consult, Boise Cascade Property Inc, 1970; from asst prof to assoc prof, Calif State Univ, Los Angeles, 1968-1979; res asst hydrol invest, Colo State Univ, 1964-1967. **Memberships:** Am Soc Civil Engrs; Am Geophys Union; Am Water Works Asn. **Research Statement & Publications:** Hydrologic system analysis; statistical and stochastic hydrology. **Mailing Address:** Dept Eng & Technol, 5151 State Univ Dr Rm C-157A, Los Angeles, CA 90032-8151. **Fax:** 323-343-4555. **E-Mail:** rjeng@calstatela.edu

JENICEK, JOHN ANDREW, ANESTHESIOLOGY. **Personal Data:** b Chicago, Ill, 1922; m 1947, Alice; c 1. **Education:** Univ Ill, MD, 1946; Am Bd Anesthesiol, cert, 1957. **Professional Experience:** RETIRED; from assoc prof to prof anesthesiol, Univ Tex Med Br, Galveston, 1967-1992; chief anesthesiol & oper serv, Walter Reed Army Hosp, 1962-1967; consult anesthesiol, Surgeon Gen, US Army, 1962-1967; chief anesthesiol & oper serv, Brooke Army Hosp, 1957-1961; asst chief anesthesiol & oper serv, Walter Reed Army Hosp, 1955-1957; asst chief, Tripler Army Hosp, 1954-1955; chief anesthesiol & oper serv, Tripler Army Hosp, 1952-1954; resident anesthesiol, Brooke Army Hosp, 1949-1951; intern, St Mary Nazareth Hosp, Chicago, 1946-1947. **Memberships:** AMA; Am Soc Anesthesiol; fel Am Col Anesthesiol. **Mailing Address:** 2802 Beluche Dr, Galveston, TX 77551.

JENIKE, ANDREW W(ITOLD), MECHANICAL ENGINEERING. **Personal Data:** b Warsaw, Poland, April 16, 1914; American citizen; m 1943, c 2. **Education:** Warsaw Tech Univ, Dipl, 1939; Univ London, PhD (struct eng), 1948. **Honorary Degrees:** DTech, Univ Bradford, Eng, 1972. **Professional Experience:** RETIRED; consult engr, 1980-1985; Alexander von Humboldt Found sr scientist award, WGer, 1976; pres, Jenike & Johanson Inc, 1966-1979; consult engr, 1962-1966; res prof mech & mining eng & dir bulk solids flow proj, Eng Exp Sta, Univ Utah, 1956-1962; design & develop engr, 1939, 1948-1951. **Memberships:** Am Soc Mech Engrs; Am Inst Mining; Metall & Petrol Engrs; Am Inst Mech Engrs. **Research Statement & Publications:** Storage and flow of solids; flowability testing equipment. **Mailing Address:** Three Newcastle Dr No Two, Nashua, NH 03060.

JEN-JACOBSON, LINDA, BIOCHEMISTRY, BIOPHYSICS. **Personal Data:** b Kunming, China, October 29, 1941; American citizen; m 1967, c 2. **Education:** Radcliffe Col, AB, 1962; Univ Ill, MS, 1965, PhD (biochem), 1967. **Professional Experience:** PROF BIOL SCI, UNIV PITTSBURGH, as of 2004; grad fac, Univ Pittsburgh, 1984; res asst prof biol sci, Univ Pittsburgh, beginning 1981; res assoc biophys, Univ Pittsburgh, 1970-1980; lectr, Univ Pittsburgh, 1969-1970; res assoc biol sci, Univ Pittsburgh, 1967-1969. **Research Statement & Publications:** Physicochemical determinants of protein conformation; structure-function relationships in proteins; mechanisms of protein-nucleic acid interactions. **Mailing Address:** Dept Biol Sci, Univ Pittsburgh, 320 Clapp Hall 4249 Fifth Ave, Pittsburgh, PA 15260. **Fax:** 412-624-4759. **E-Mail:** ljen+@pitt.edu

JENKIN, HOWARD M, MICROBIOLOGY, LIPID BIOCHEMISTRY. **Personal Data:** b New York, NY, May 1, 1925; div, c Keith & Donna. **Education:** Univ Wis, BS, 1949; Univ Chicago, PhD (microbiol), 1960. **Professional Experience:** RETIRED; head microbiol sect, Hormel Inst, Grad Sch, 1966-1984; from assocprof to prof, Hormel Inst, Grad Sch, 1966-1984; from assoc prof to prof microbiol, Med Sch, Univ Minn, Minneapolis, 1966-1984; Head virol-tissue cult dept, US Naval Med Res Unit 2, Taiwan, 1963-1966; res asst prof prev med, Sch Med, Univ Wash, 1962-1966; mem staff, Immunol Br, 1961-1962; Nat Res Coun fel microbiol, Virus-Rickettsiae Div, Biol Labs, FtDetrick, Md, 1960-1961. **Memberships:** Am Soc Microbiol; Soc Trop Med & Hyg; Tissue Cult Asn. **Research Statement & Publications:** Comparative lipid biochemistry; biology and serology of members of Chlamydia; herpes virus; leptospires; treponema arbovirus rickettsial groups of microorganisms; tumor-lipid membrane studies; schemiar tissue cultures studies; deep sea diving-human, rat lipid studies; immunology testing-protection studies. **Mailing Address:** 520 Palm Springs Blvd Apt 407, Indian Harbor Beach, FL 32937.

JENKINS, ALVIN WILKINS, JR, PLASMA PHYSICS, ASTROPHYSICS. **Personal Data:** b Raleigh, NC, December 30, 1928; m 1951, c 2. **Education:** NC State Col, BEE, 1951, MS, 1955; Univ Va, PhD, 1958. **Professional Experience:** PROF EMER PHYSICS, NC STATE UNIV, as of 2004; assoc prof, beginning 1976; Actg Chmn Dept, 1966-1970; head dept, beginning 1976; actg chmn dept, beginning 1975; prof physics, Nc State Univ, beginning 1970; assoc prof physics, WichitaState Univ, 1961-1966; res physicist, Univ Res Inst, Denver, 1959-1961; sr physicist theoretphysics, Ord Res Lab, Univ Va, 1958-1959. **Memberships:** Am Phys Soc; Am Geophys Union; Am Astron Soc. **Research Statement & Publications:** Atmospheric and magnetospheric physics; plasma physics. **Mailing Address:** Dept Physics, NC State Univ, PO Box 8202, 2700 Stinson Dr, Raleigh, NC 27695.

JENKINS, CHARLES ROBERT, SANITARY ENGINEERING, AQUATIC BIOLOGY. **Personal Data:** b Newton, Ill, August 17, 1930; m 1953, c 4. **Education:** Eastern Ill State Col, BS, 1952; Univ Ill, MS, 1959; Okla State Univ, PhD (zool), 1964. **Professional Experience:** PROF EMER CIVIL ENG, WVA UNIV, as of 2004; prof civil Eng, Wva Univ, beginning 1980; prof environ eng, WVa Univ, 1977-1980; from asst prof to assoc prof sanit eng, WVa Univ, 1961-1977. **Memberships:** Am Soc Limnol & Oceanog; Water Pollution Control Fedn; Am Water Works Asn; Sigma Xi. **Research Statement & Publications:** Water pollution control; waste treatment. **Mailing Address:** Dept Civil Eng, WVa Univ, ESB B07, Morgantown, WV 26506. **Fax:** 304-293-7109.

JENKINS, DALE WILSON, ECOLOGY, ENVIRONMENTAL SCIENCES. **Personal Data:** b Wapakoneta, Ohio, June 17, 1918; m 1942, c 5. **Education:** Ohio State Univ, BSc, 1938, MA, 1939, PhD, 1947. **Honors & Awards:** Distinguished Serv Award, Ohio State Univ. **Professional Experience:** RES ASSOC, MARIE SELBY BOT GARDENS, as of 2003; ECOL & ENVIRON CONSULT, WHO, USAID, WORLDBANK, UN DEVELOP PROG, INTER-AM DEVELOP BANK, 1978-; dep dir, CtrHuman Ecol & Health, Pan Am Health Orgn, 1975-1978; dir ecol prog, Smithsonian Inst, 1970-1973; asst dir Bioscience progs, NASA Hq, 1966-1970; chief environ biol prog, NASA Hq, 1962-1966; planning conf partic, Life Sci Prog, NASA, 1960 & WHO, Bangkok, 1960; consult, USAF, 1959-; mem, Armed Forces Pest Control Bd, 1955-1964 & Interdept Pest Control Comt, 1958-1964; chmn bd gov, adv to UNESCO, 1957-; Nat Acad Sci-Nat Res Coun deleg, Int CongEntom, Montreal, 1956; chmn bd gov, Inst Lab Animal Resources, Nat Res Coun, 1955-1960; US Dept State deleg, Int Conf Peaceful Uses Atomic Energy, Geneva, 1955; dep chief allied scidiv, Army Med Labs, Md, 1954-1956; chief entom div, Army Med Labs, Md, 1953-1962; Lectr, Sch Pub Health & Hyg, Johns Hopkins Univ, 1950-; consult, Northern Insect Surv, Defence ResBd Can, 1949-1950; consult, USPHS, 1948; consult, USDA, Alaska, 1947; entomologist & chiefanimal ecol br, Army Med Labs, Md, 1946-1952; agr specialist, Foreign Econ Admin, Wash, DC, 1942-1943; instr, Univ Minn, 1941-1942; instr, Univ Ill, 1940-1941; instr, UnivChicago, 1939-1940; instr, Ohio State Univ, 1938-1939; ecologist, Soil Conserv Serv, 1935. **Memberships:** Fel AAAS; Ecol Soc Am; Lepidopterists Soc. **Research Statement & Publications:** Ecology of plants and animals; radioisotope tracers; laboratory animals; epidemiology; environmental impacts. **Mailing Address:** Marie Selby Bot Gardens, 811 S Palm Ave, Sarasota, FL 34236. **Fax:** 941-366-9807.

JENKINS, DAVID A, INTERMEDIATE ENERGY PHYSICS. **Personal Data:** b Seattle, Wash, December 28, 1937. **Education:** Yale Univ, BE, 1959; Univ Calif, Berkeley, MS, 1961, PhD (physics), 1964. **Professional Experience:** PROF PHYSICS, VA TECH, 1974-; dir, NSF, 1973-1974; assoc prof, VA Tech, 1967-1973; Res asst, Lawrence Berkeley Lab, 1967. **Memberships:** Sigma Xi; Am Phys Soc. **Research Statement & Publications:** Intermediate energy physics; mesonic atoms; pion-nucleon scattering; pion production; photodisintegration of light nuclei; meson photoproduction. **Mailing Address:** Physics Dept, Va Tech, Blacksburg, VA 24061. **E-Mail:** jenkins@vt.edu

JENKINS, DAVID GLENN, BIOLOGY. **Education:** Prudue Univ, BS, 1980; Va Polytech Inst & state Univ, Va, 1986 & PhD (Ecol), 1990. **Professional Experience:** ASSOC PROF & JAMES & ANNIE YING EMINENT SCHOLAR BIOL, UNIV CENT FLA, 2003-; vis scientist, Discovery Bay Marine Lab, Univ W Indies, 2001-2003; summer fac fel, NASA, Cape Canaveral, 1996-1997; from asst to assoc prof, Biol Dept, Univ Ill, 1993-2003; asst prof, dept biol sci, Salisbury State Univ, 1990-1993; teaching assoc, Va Polytech Inst & state Univ, 1989; scientist, Life Systs Inc, 1980-1983. **Research Statement & Publications:** Ecological processes affecting structure and function of aquatic ecological communities; especially the relative importance of spatial (metapopulation and metacommunity dynamics); local (predation; competition; resource availability); landscapes (habitat loss; climate change) processed; preservation of wetlands; biological indicators of exposure and hazard of toxic substances in aquatic ecosystems. **Mailing Address:** Univ Central Fla, Dept Biology, 4000 Central Fla Blvd, Orlando, FL 32816-2368. **E-Mail:** dgjenkin@mail.ucf.edu

JENKINS, DAVID I, SANITARY ENGINEERING. **Personal Data:** b Shropshire, Eng, October 4, 1935; m 1960, c 2. **Education:** Univ Birmingham, BSc, 1957; Univ Durham, PhD (sanit eng), 1960. **Professional Experience:** PROF GRAD SCH, DEPT CIVIL & ENVIRON ENG, UNIV CALF, as of 2004; sabbatical leave, Dept Eng & Appl Physics, Harvard Univ, 1969-1970; from asst prof to assoc prof, Sanit Eng Res Lab, 1963-1974; DIR, SANIT ENG RES LAB, 1961-; res chemist, Sanit Eng Res Lab, 1960-1961. **Memberships:** Am Chem Soc; Water Pollution Control Fedn; Asn Environ Eng Prof; fel Royal Inst Chem; Brit Inst Water Pollution Control. **Research Statement & Publications:** Chemistry and biochemistry of processes and phenomena associated with the control of environment, especially the upgrading of water quality; biological waste treatment processes; activated sludge operation. **Mailing Address:** Dept Civil & Environ Eng, Univ Calif, 655 Davis Hall, Berkeley, CA 94720-1710. **Fax:** 510-642-7483. **E-Mail:** jenkins@ce.berkeley.edu

JENKINS, DAVID JOHN ANTHONY, DIABETES, HYPERLIPIDEMIA. **Personal Data:** c 1. **Education:** Oxford Univ, Eng, PhD (clin nutrit), 1971, MD, 1976, DSc, 1986. **Honors & Awards:** Borden Award, Can, 1983; Goldsmith Award, Am Col Nutrit, 1985. **Professional Experience:** CHMN, CAN RES NUTRIT & METAB, UNIV TORONTO, as of 2003; PROF, DEPT NUTRIT SCI, UNIV TORONTO, 1980-. **Memberships:** Am Inst Nutrit; Am Soc Clin Nutrit. **Mailing Address:** Dept Nutrit Sci, Univ Toronto, FitzGerald Bldg, Rm 340, 150 Col St, Toronto, ON M5S 3E2, Can. **Fax:** 416-978-5310. **E-Mail:** cyril.kendall@utoronto.ca

JENKINS, DAVID R(ICHARD), STRUCTURAL MECHANICS, COMPOSITE MATERIALS. **Personal Data:** b Lima, Ohio, October 24, 1924; m 1947, Patricia; c 3. **Education:** Case Inst Technol, BSc, 1948; Ohio State Univ, MSc, 1954; Univ Mich, PhD (eng mech), 1962. **Professional Experience:** PROF EMER ENG, UNIV CENT FLA, as of 2000; chmn civil eng & environ sci, Univ Cent Fla, 1984-1990; actg chmn mech eng & aerospace sci, Univ Cent Fla, 1981-1982; prof eng, Univ Cent Fla, 1976-1993; prof civil eng & environ sci & actg chmn, Univ Cent Fla, 1975-1976; from asst prof to prof & chmn engr mech & mat sci, Univ Cent Fla, 1969-1975; sr res fel, Tech Ctr, Owens Corning Fiberglas Corp, 1965-1969; fac res grant, Univ Mich, 1965; asst prof, Univ Mich, 1962-1965; instr eng mech, Univ Mich, 1958-1962; proj leader, Battelle Mem Inst, 1955-1958; prin mech engr, Battelle Mem Inst, 1950-1955; tech asst, Battelle Mem Inst, 1948-1950; stress analyst, Airplane Div, Curtiss Wright Corp, 1948. **Memberships:** Am Soc Civil Engrs; Soc Exp Mech; Am Soc Metals; Soc Eng Sci; Am Soc Mech Engrs. **Research Statement & Publications:** Structural testing, composite materials; high temperature structural behavior; crack propagation in steel shells; aircraft structural investigations; yielding and strain hardening in metallic materials; composite materials. **Mailing Address:** Dept Civil & Environ Eng, Univ Cent Fla, 4000 Central Fla Blvd, Orlando, FL 32816.

JENKINS, DAVID T, BOTANY. **Education:** Univ Tenn, PhD (Botany), 1974. **Professional Experience:** ASSOC PROF, UNIV ALA, BIRMINGHAM, 1980-. **Mailing Address:** Univ Ala, Univ Station, Birmingham, AL 35294. **Fax:** 205-975-6097. **E-Mail:** biojenks@uab.edu

JENKINS, EDGAR WILLIAM, HIGH ENERGY PHYSICS. **Personal Data:** b Columbus, Ohio, April 29, 1933; m 1959, c 3. **Education:** Harvard Univ, AB, 1955; Columbia Univ, PhD (physics), 1962. **Professional Experience:** PROF EMER, UNIV ARIZ, as of 2002; prof physics, Univ Ariz, 1971; from asst prof to assoc prof, Univ Ariz, 1964-1971; from asst physicist to assoc physicist, Brookhaven Nat Lab, 1960-1964. **Memberships:** Am Phys Soc; Am Asn Physics Teachers. **Research Statement & Publications:** Interactions, properties and decays of elementary particles. **Mailing Address:** 4938 E Glenn St, Tucson, AZ 85712.

JENKINS, EDWARD BEYNON, ASTROPHYSICS. **Personal Data:** b San Francisco, Calif, March 20, 1939; m 1963, Myrna D Stewart; c Brian F & Eric D. **Education:** Univ Calif, Davis, BA, 1962; Cornell Univ, PhD (physics), 1966. **Honors & Awards:** Humboldt Sr US Scientist Res Award, 1992. **Professional Experience:** Mem, Astrophsics Subcomt, NASA, 1992-1993; mem, Sci Definition Teams, Space Telescope Imaging Spectrog & Far Ultraviolet Spectros Explorer, 1987-; mem, Comt Space Astron & Astrophys, 1986-1988; Prin investr of a sounding rocket & orbitial res prog, 1980-2002; SR RES ASTRONOMER, PRINCETON UNIV OBSERV, 1979-; res astronr, Princeton Univ Observ, 1973-1979; res staff mem, Princeton Univ Observ, 1967-1973; Res assoc astrophys, Princeton Univ Observ, 1966-1967. **Memberships:** Am Astron Soc (vpres, 1996-1999); Int Astron Union (Pres, comn 44, 1988-1991). **Research Statement & Publications:** Rocket and satellite ultraviolet astronomy; interstellarmedium; image sensor development. **Mailing Address:** Princeton Univ Observ, Princeton, NJ 08544-1001. **E-Mail:** ebj@astro.princeton.edu

JENKINS, ELIZABETH ELLEN, PARTICLE THEORY. **Personal Data:** b Tucson, Ariz, November 19, 1964; c Nathan & Peter. **Education:** Harvard Univ, AB, 1985, PhD (physics), 1989. **Professional Experience:** PROF PHYSICS, UNIV CALIF, SAN DIEGO, 2003-; vis, Univ Valencia, Spain, 1996; Alfred P Sloan res fel, Sloan Found, 1995-1997; Nat Young Investr Award, NSF, 1994- 1999; vis fel, Princeton Univ, 1994; assoc prof, Univ Calif, San Diego, 1997-2003; asst prof, Univ Calif, San Diego, 1992-1997; Sci assoc, Europ Orgn Nuclear Res, 1992-1993; Postdoctoral researcher, Univ Calif, San Diego, 1989-1992. **Memberships:** Am Phys Soc Phi Beta Kappa. **Research Statement & Publications:** Study of interactions and symmetries of elementary particles. **Mailing Address:** Physics Dept 0319, Univ Calif San Diego, La Jolla, CA 92093-0319. **E-Mail:** ejenkins@ucsd.edu

JENKINS, FARISH ALSTON, VERTEBRATE PALEONTOLOGY, ANATOMY. **Personal Data:** b New York, May 19, 1940; m 1963, c 2. **Education:** Princeton Univ, AB, 1961; Yale Univ, MSc, 1966, PhD (geol), 1968; Harvard Univ, MA, 1974. **Professional Experience:** ALEXANDER AGASSIZ PROF ZOOLOGY, HARVARD INST TECHNOL, DIV HEALTH SCI & TECHNOL, HARVARD UNIV, 1989-; PROF ANAT, HARVARD INST TECHNOL, DIV HEALTH SCI & TECHNOL, HARVARD UNIV, 1982-; PROF BIOL, DEPT ORGANISMIC & EVOLUTIONARY BIOL & CUR VERTPALEONT, MUS COMP ZOOLOGY, HARVARD UNIV, 1974-; assoc prof biol & assoc cur vertpaleont, Harvard-mass Inst Technol Div Health Sci & Technol, Harvard Med Sch, 1971-1974; from instr to asst prof anat, Col Physicians & Surgeons, Columbia Univ, 1968-1971. **Research Statement & Publications:** Vertebrate anatomy and evolution, especially reptiles and mammals; biomechanics of musculoskeletal system. **Mailing Address:** Dept Biol, Harvard Univ, 42 Church St, Cambridge, MA 02138. **Fax:** 617-384-8006. **E-Mail:** fjenkins@oeb.harvard.edu

JENKINS, HOWARD BRYNER, MATHEMATICS. **Personal Data:** b Arimo, Idaho, January 30, 1928; m 1951, c 3. **Education:** Mass Inst Technol, BS, 1950; Univ Southern Calif, PhD (math), 1958. **Professional Experience:** RETIRED; assoc head, Sch Math, 1971-; Vis assoc prof, Stanford Univ, 1966-1967; assoc prof, Univ Minn, Minneapolis, 1965-; asst prof, Univ Minn, Minneapolis, 1961-1965; vis asst prof, Stanford Univ, 1960-1961; res assoc, Inst Math Sci, NY Univ, 1959-1960; temp mem, Inst Math Sci, NY Univ, 1958-1959; instr, Calif Inst Technol, 1957-1958; Lectr math, Univ Southern Calif, 1954-1957. **Memberships:** Am Math Soc. **Research Statement & Publications:** Partial differential equations; variational problems; minimal surfaces. **Mailing Address:** Sch Math 127 Vincent Hall, Univ Minn 206 Church St SE, Minneapolis, MN 55455.

JENKINS, HOWARD JONES, pharmacology; deceased, see previous edition for last biography

JENKINS, HUGHES BRANTLEY, THEORETICAL PHYSICS. **Personal Data:** b Jacksonville, Fla, October 17, 1927. **Education:** Univ Ga, AB, 1948, MS, 1955; Univ Ky, PhD (physics), 1963. **Professional Experience:** RETIRED; assoc prof physics & astron, Valdosta State Col, 1968-1983; assoc prof, Ga State Col, 1962-1968; intsr physics, Univ Ky, 1958-1962; asst mathematician, Oak RidgeNat Lab, Union Carbide Corp, Tenn, 1957-1958; asst physicist, Oak Ridge Nat Lab, Union Carbide Corp, Tenn, 1955-1957; instr math & physics, Univ Ga, 1952-1955. **Research Statement & Publications:** Statistical mechanics and mathematical physics. **Mailing Address:** 810 Millpond Rd, Valdosta, GA 31602.

JENKINS, J STEVEN. **Personal Data:** b Memphis, Tenn, March 22, 1956. **Education:** Millsaps Col, BS, 1977; Southern Methodist Univ, MS, 1980; Univ Calif, LosAngeles, PhD (elec eng), 1987. **Professional Experience:** PRIN ENGR, JET PROPULSION LAB, CALIF INST TECHNOL, as of 2004; SOFTWARE ENGR, JET PROPULSION LAB INC, 1989-; Res fel, Dept Anesthesiol, Univ Calif, Los Angeles, 1987-1989. **Memberships:** Inst Elec & Electronics Engrs. **Mailing Address:** Jet Propulsion Lab, 4800 Oak Grove Dr, Pasadena, CA 91109-8099. **E-Mail:** steven.jenkins@jpl.nasa.gov

JENKINS, JAMES ALLISTER, MATHEMATICS, GEOMETRIC THEORY OF FUNCTIONS. **Personal Data:** b Toronto, Ont, September 23, 1923; American citizen. **Education:** Toronto, BA, 1944, MA, 1945; Harvard Univ, PhD (math), 1948. **Professional Experience:** Fulbright vis prof, Imp Col, Univ London, 1962; PROF EMER MATH, WASH UNIV, beginning 1959; mem, Inst Advan Study, 1957-1959, 1961-1962; from assoc prof to prof, Univ Notre Dame, 1954-1959; asst prof math, Johns Hopkins Univ, 1950-1954; Jewett fel, Harvard Univ, 1948-1949 & Inst Advan Study & Princeton Univ, 1949-1950. **Memberships:** Am Math Soc; Math Soc France; Ger Math Asn. **Research Statement & Publications:** Geometrical and analytical function theories; topological theory functions. **Mailing Address:** Dept Math, Wash Univ, St Louis, MO 63130.

JENKINS, JAMES THOMAS, MECHANICS OF GRANULAR MATERIALS. **Personal Data:** b Chicago, Ill, June 30, 1942; m 1983, Katharine; c Thomas Nelson & Peter Kelly. **Education:** Northwestern Univ, BS (ME), 1964; Johns Hopkins Univ, PhD (Mech), 1969. **Honorary Degrees:** Dr Honoris Causa, Univ de Rennes, 2001. **Professional Experience:** WS CARPENTER JR PROF, CORNELL UNIV, 2001-; prof theoretical mech, Cornell Univ, 1983-2001; from asst prof to assoc prof, Cornell Univ, 1971-1983; vis lectr, Strathclyde Univ, 1970-1971; postdoctoral assoc, Univ Paris, 1969-1970. **Research Statement & Publications:** Formulation of continuum theory for the deformation and flow of granular materials. **Mailing Address:** Dept Theoret & Appl Mech, Cornell Univ, 221 Kimball Hall, Ithaca, NY 14853. **Fax:** 607-255-2011. **E-Mail:** jtj2@cornell.edu

JENKINS, JAMES WILLIAM, ORGANIC CHEMISTRY. **Personal Data:** b Jamestown, NY, May 5, 1921; c 3. **Education:** Allegheny Col, BS, 1944; Univ Buffalo, MS, 1948, PhD (chem), 1950. **Professional Experience:** RETIRED; vpres res & Develop, consumer prod Div, 1969-1983; dir, Pfizer Inc, 1965-1969; res mgr, Colgate Palmolive Co, 1963-1964; sect head, Colgate Palmolive Co, 1960-1963; sr group leader, Colgate Palmolive Co, 1959-1960; group leader anal sect, Colgate Palmolive Co, 1954-1958; res anal chemist, Colgate Palmolive Co, 1952-1954; res anal chemist, Gen Aniline & Film Corp, 1951-1952; asst prof chem, Lafayette Col, 1949-1951. **Memberships:** Am Chem Soc; Sigma Xi. **Research Statement & Publications:** Product development; proprietary pharmaceuticals; toiletries and cosmetics; hair and skin research. **Mailing Address:** 135 Cheeskogili Way, Loudon, TN 37774-2524.

JENKINS, JEFF HARLIN, PLANT PATHOLOGY. **Personal Data:** b Gamaliel, Ky, March 8, 1937; m 1959, c 2. **Education:** Western Ky Col, BS, 1959; La State Univ, MS, 1961, PhD (plant path), 1963. **Professional Experience:** RETIRED; prof biol, Western Ky Univ, beginning 1974; from asst prof to assoc prof bot, Western Ky Univ, 1963-1974. **Memberships:** Am Phytopath Soc. **Research Statement & Publications:** Taxonomic mycology; fusarium wilt of alfalfa; bacterial leaf spot of bell pepper. **Mailing Address:** Dept Biol, Western Ky Univ, One Big Red Way St, Bowling Green, KY 42101-3576.

JENKINS, JIMMY RAYMOND, BIOLOGICAL STRUCTURE. **Personal Data:** b Selma, NC, March 18, 1943; m 1965, c 2. **Education:** Elizabeth City State Univ, BS, 1965; Purdue Univ, MS, 1970, PhD (biol educ), 1972. **Professional Experience:** PRES, EDWARD WATERS COL, FLA, 1997-; vice chancellor acad affairs, Elizabeth City State Univ, 1977-1997; instrnl consult, Halifax Co Schs, NC, 1975-1976; individualized instr, Region 15, Northeastern NC, 1975; adv coun mem, Albemarle Regional Planning & Develop Comn, 1974-; proposal reviewer, NSF, 1974; assoc prof biol & dean, Elizabeth City State Univ, 1973-1997; asst prof biol & asst acad dean, Elizabeth City State Univ, 1972-1974; teaching fel & res asst instrnl develop, Purdue Univ, 1970-1972; fel biol, Purdue Univ, 1969-1970; teacher high schs, Md, 1965-1969; mem, Health Manpower Develop Corp. **Memberships:** Nat Asn Res Sci Teaching. **Research Statement & Publications:** Instructional development and design geared to biology and the facilitation of biological concepts. **Mailing Address:** Edward Waters Col, 1658 Kings Rd, Jacksonville, FL 32209-6167. **Fax:** 904-366-2544.

JENKINS, JOE WILEY, NON-ABELIAN HARMONIC ANALYSIS. **Personal Data:** b Bronaugh, Mo, October 17, 1941; m 1975, c 5. **Education:** Univ Ill, Urbana, PhD (math), 1968. **Professional Experience:** PROF EMER, DEPT MATH, UNIV ALBANY, STATE UNIV NY, as of 2006; prof math, State Univ NY, Albany, beginning 1980; vis prof, Univ Wurzburg, 1978-1979; mem, Inst Advan Study, 1971-1972; asst prof to assoc prof, State Univ NY Albany, 1968-1980. **Memberships:** Am Math Soc. **Research Statement & Publications:** Analysis on lie groups; representation theory of nilpotent lie groups. **Mailing Address:** Dept Math, Univ Albany, State Univ NY, 1400 Wash Ave, Albany, NY 12222. **Fax:** 703-292-9032.

JENKINS, JOHN BRUNER, GENETICS. **Personal Data:** b Springfield, Mass, July 20, 1941; m 1963. **Education:** Utah State Univ, BS, 1964, MS, 1965; Univ Calif, Los Angeles, PhD (zoology), 1968. **Professional Experience:** Chmn biol, Swarthmore Col, beginning 1980; PROF BIOL, SWARTHMORE COL, 1980-; assoc prof, Swarthmore Col, 1974-1980; asst prof, Swarthmore Col, 1968-1974. **Memberships:** AAAS; Genetics Soc Am; Am Genetic Asn. **Research Statement & Publications:** Chemical mutagenesis in Drosophila and its relation to genetic fine structure. **Mailing Address:** Dept Biol, Swarthmore Col, 500 Col Ave, Swarthmore, PA 19081-1397. **Fax:** 610-328-8663. **E-Mail:** jjenkin1@swarthmore.edu

JENKINS, JOHNIE NORTON, PLANT GENETICS, AGRONOMY. **Personal Data:** b Barton, Ark, November 3, 1934; m 1959, c 2. **Education:** Univ Ark, BSA, 1956; Purdue Univ, MS, 1958, PhD (genetics), 1960. **Honors & Awards:** Mobay Cotton Res Recognition Award. **Professional Experience:** RES LEADER, GENETICS & PRECISION AGR, as of 2004; LOCATION COODR, MISS STATE LOCATION, as of 2004; DIR CROP SCI RES LAB, AGR RES SERV, USDA, 1980-; prof crop sci & mem grad fac, Miss State Univ, beginning 1964; res geneticist, Agr Res Serv, USDA, 1961-1980; res assoc agron, Univ Ill, 1960-1961. **Memberships:** Am Soc Agron; Crop Sci Soc Am; Entom Soc Am; AAAS. **Research Statement & Publications:** Host plant resistance to cotton insects and nematodes; investigations of basic causes of insect and nematode resistance in cotton plants and development of factors which will confer resistance. **Mailing Address:** Agr Res Serv, US Dept Agr, PO Box 5367, Miss State, MS 39762-5367. **Fax:** 662-320-7528. **E-Mail:** jnjenkins@msa-msstate.ars.usda.gov

JENKINS, KENNETH DUNNING, DEVELOPMENTAL BIOLOGY. **Personal Data:** b New York, NY, April 8, 1944; c 3. **Education:** Calif State Univ, Northridge, BA, 1966; Univ Calif, Los Angleles, PhD (develop biol), 1970. **Professional Experience:** PROF EMER BIOL, CALIF STATE UNIV, LONG BEACH, as of 2005; sci adv bd, US Environ Protection Agency, beginning 1982; dir inst, Molecular Ecol Inst, beginning 1982; mem panel on fate & effects drilling fluids marine environ, Nat Acad Sci, 1982-1983; prof biol, calif state univ, Long Beach, 1980-1997; dep assoc vpres acad affairs, Molecular Ecol Inst, 1978-1980; from asst prof to assoc prof biol, Calif State Univ, Long Beach, 1970-1980. **Memberships:** AAAS; Soc Develop Biol. **Research Statement & Publications:** Molecular ecology; aquatic toxicology. **Mailing Address:** Dept Biol, Calif State Univ, 3702 Csulb, Long Beach, CA 90840-0004.

JENKINS, KENNETH JAMES WILLIAM, BIOCHEMISTRY, NUTRITION. **Personal Data:** b Montreal, Que, October 1, 1929; m 1969, Betty; c Victoria. **Education:** McGill Univ, BSc, 1951; Univ Sask, MSc, 1953; Univ Wis, PhD (biochem), 1958. **Honors & Awards:** Borden Award, 1974; Medal Excellence Nutrit, Can Packers, 1984; Merit Award, Can Soc Animal. **Professional Experience:** RETIRED; prin scientist, Animal Res Ctr, Cent Exp Farm, beginning 1980; head, Trace Mineral Nutrit Sect, Trace Minerals & Pesticide Div, 1973-1980; res officer, Can Dept Agr, 1965-1973; asst prof biochem & nutrit, Ont Agr Col, Guelph, 1958-1965; asst biochem, UnivWis, 1954-1958; head res & develop emergency rations, Defense Res Med Labs, Dept Nat Defense, Can, 1953-1954. **Memberships:** Can Nutrit Soc; Can Biochem Soc; Can Soc Animal Sci; Am Dairy Sci Asn. **Research Statement & Publications:** Nutritional requirements of animals; biochemical role of mineral elements; tocopherol and selenium metabolism; neonatal nutrition and metabolism. **Mailing Address:** 63 Larkin Dr, Nepean, ON K2J 1B3, Can. **Fax:** 613-943-2353.

JENKINS, LESLIE HUGH, surface physics; deceased, see previous edition for last biography

JENKINS, MAMIE LEAH YOUNG, NUTRITION, BIOCHEMISTRY. **Personal Data:** b Washington, DC, July 10, 1940; m 1973. **Education:** Howard Univ, BS, 1962, MS, 1965, PhD (nutrit), 1980. **Professional Experience:** RES CHEMIST, DIV NUTRIT, FOOD & DRUG ADMIN, BUR FOODS, 1967-; chemist, Agr Res Serv, US Dept Agr, 1964-1967. **Memberships:** Animal Nutrit Res Coun; Am Chem Soc; Am Inst Nutrit. **Research Statement & Publications:** Protein quality, amino acid fortification, amino acid derivatives and vitamins; emphasis on the metabolic role of lecithin as a dietary choline source, and its interrelationships with other nutrients. **Mailing Address:** Food & Drug Admin, Laurel, MD 20708. **Fax:** 301-594-0517.

JENKINS, MELVIN EARL, METABOLISM. **Personal Data:** b Kansas City, Mo, June 24, 1922; m 1975, Maria Parker; c Janis, Carol, Lore & ingrid. **Education:** Univ Kans, AB, 1944, MD, 1946. **Honors & Awards:** Melvin E Jenkins MD Lectureship Pediat, Howard Univ, 1995 distinguished scholar - teacher award, Howard University, 1984; Leadership in Medicine, univ of Kansas, 1984. **Professional Experience:** EMER PROF PEDIAT, COL MED, HOWARD UNIV, 1986-; prof chmn dept pediat & child health, Col Med, Howard Univ, 1973-1986; prof, Col Med, Univ Nebr Med Ctr, Omaha, 1969-1973; From instr to assoc prof pediat, Col Med, Howard Univ, 1950-1969. **Memberships:** Am Acad Pediat; Sigma Xi; Am Pediat Soc; Soc for Pediat Res; Endocrin Soc. **Research Statement & Publications:** Gonadal function; human growth and development; sickle cell hemoglobin; fetal and newborn physiology; steroid metabolism. **Mailing Address:** 10401 Grosvenor Pl Apt 504, Rockville, MD 20852. **E-Mail:** mpark@aol.com

JENKINS, NANCY A, GENETICS. **Education:** Indiana Univ, PhD (Molecular and Cellular Biology). **Professional Experience:** CO-HEAD, MOUSE CANCER GENETICS PROGRAMME, NAT CANCER INST, as of 2005; GENETICISTS, NAT CANCER INST, as of 2005. **Mailing Address:** Nat Cancer Inst, PO Box 539 Bldg 539, Frederick, MD 21702-1201. **Fax:** 301-846-6666. **E-Mail:** jenkins@ncifcrf.gov

JENKINS, REESE V, HISTORY. **Education:** Cambridge Univ, PhD. **Professional Experience:** PROF HIST, RUTGERS STATE UNIV, NJ, as of 2005. **Mailing Address:** Hist Dept, Rutgers State Univ, VD 220, New Brunswick, NJ 08903. **Fax:** 732-227-0608. **E-Mail:** reese638@aol.com

JENKINS, ROBERT BRIAN, CYTOGENETICS. **Personal Data:** b October 23, 1955; c 2. **Education:** Northwestern Univ, BA, 1977; Univ Chicago, PhD (develop biol), 1981, MD, 1983. **Professional Experience:** PROF LAB MED, MAYO MED SCH, as of 2003; assoc mem, Biochem & Molecular Biol Dept, Mayo Grad Sch, 1990-; consult, Dept Lab Med & Path, Mayo Clin & Found, 1990-; asst prof lab med, Mayomed Sch, beginning 1989; assoc dir, Cytogenetics Lab, Mayo Clin, beginning 1987; sr assocconsult, Dept Lab Med & Path, Mayo Clin & Found, 1987-1990; instr, Lab Med, Mayo Med Sch, 1987-1989; fel hematopath & cytogenetics, Mayo Grad Sch Med, 1987; resident clin path, Mayo Grad Sch Med, 1986. **Memberships:** AAAS; AMA; Am Soc Clin Pathologists; Col Am Pathologists; Am Soc HumanGenetics; Am Asn Pathologists; Int Acad Path; Sigma Xi. **Mailing Address:** Dept Lab Med, Mayo Clin Col Med, 970 Hilton Bldg 200 First St SW, Rochester, MN 55905-0001. **Fax:** 507-284-0043. **E-Mail:** rjenkins@mayo.edu

JENKINS, ROBERT EDWARD, ANALOG SUBTHRESHOLD VERY LARGE SCALE INTEGRATION CIRCUIT DESIGN, NEURAL NETWORKS. **Personal Data:** b Baltimore, Md, June 2, 1938; m 1970, c 2. **Education:** Univ Md, BS, 1960, MS, 1966. **Professional Experience:** SR LECTR, DEPT ELEC & COMPUT ENG, JOHNS HOPKINS UNIV, as of 2002; prog coordr, Sch Continuing Prof Studies, 1986-1991; lectr elec eng, JohnsHopkins Univ, 1984-1991; vis prof, Johns Hopkins Univ, 1984-1985; vis scientist, Defense Mapping Agency, Wash, DC, 1978-1979; prin engr, Johns Hopkins Appl Physicslab, beginning 1961. **Memberships:** Inst Elec & Electronics Engrs. **Research Statement & Publications:** Implementation of advanced sensors and neural networks using analog very large scale integration circuits silicon methods for innovative information processing. **Mailing Address:** Dept Elec & Comput Eng Johns Hopkins Univ, 206 Barton Hall, Laurel, MD 20723-6399. **E-Mail:** robert.jenkins@jhu.edu

JENKINS, ROBERT ELLSWORTH, ECOLOGICAL CONSERVATION. **Personal Data:** b Lewistown, Pa, September 30, 1942; m 1964, c 2. **Education:** Rutgers Univ, AB, 1964; Harvard Univ, PhD (biol), 1970. **Honors & Awards:** Am Motors Prof Conserv Award, 1978. **Professional Experience:** MEM BD, SOC CONS BIOL, 1988-; SCI ADV, WNET NATURE SER, 1986-; counr, Xerces Soc, 1985-; mem adv coun, Inst Conserv Biol, 1984-; mem adv coun, Ctr Plant Conserv, 1984-; coun, Am Inst Biol Sci, 1984-1989; mem, US Man & Biosphere Directorate, Proj 8, 1978-; founder & nat dir, State Natural Heritage Progs, 1975-; mem, US Nat Comn, UNESCO, 1974-1976; mem bd, Rare Animal Relief Effort, 1974-1976; mem US comt, AAAS, 1972-1973; mem US comt, Rep biol sect comt, 1971-1974; assoc dir, Ctr Appl Res & Environ Sci, 1971-1973; res assoc, Smithsonian Inst, 1971-1972; mem, Fed Comt Res Natural Areas, 1970-; vpres sci progs, Nature Conserv, 1970-1999; mem bd gov, Am Inst Biol Sci, 1970-1984; mem US comt, Conserv Ecosysts Sect, Int Biol Prog, 1970-1975. **Memberships:** Fel AAAS; Am Inst Biol Sci; Ecol Soc Am; Soc Study Evolution; Wildlife Soc. **Research Statement & Publications:** Animal and plant ecology and evolution; human population and environment; applied research in land management, ecosystem preservation and restoration; ecological inventory and data banking. **Mailing Address:** The Nature Conservancy, 4245 N Fairfax Dr, St 100, Arlington, VA 22203-1606.

JENKINS, ROBERT GEORGE, COAL CONVERSION FUNDAMENTALS, MATERIALS CHARACTERIZATION. **Personal Data:** b Gwent, Wales, September 29, 1944; m 1969, Susan; c Sara & George. **Education:** Univ Leeds, Eng, BSc, 1967, PhD (fuel sci), 1970. **Professional Experience:** PROF & DEAN, DEPT ENG & ENG MATH, UNIV VT, 1999; assoc dean res, Col Eng, Univ Cincinnati, 1988-1991; prof chem eng, Col Eng, Univ Cincinnati, beginning 1988; from asst prof to prof fuel sci, Dept Mat Sci & Eng, Pa State Univ, 1978-1988; sr res assoc, Dept Mat Sci & Eng, Pa State Univ, 1975-1978; res felchem, Imp Col Sci & Technol, Eng, 1973-1975; res assoc, Dept Mat Sci, Pa State Univ, 1970-1973. **Memberships:** Fel Inst Energy; Sigma Xi; Am Chem Soc; Combustion Inst; Am Inst Chem Engrs. **Research Statement & Publications:** Coal conversion chemistry; modification and characterization of carbons and zeolites as molecular sciences and absorbants; carbons from waste materials, coal characterization. **Mailing Address:** Dept Mech Eng, Univ Vt, 201 Votey Bldg 202 Perkins, Burlington, VT 05405. **Fax:** 802-656-1929. **E-Mail:** robert.jenkins@uvm.edu

JENKINS, RONALD LEE, COMPARATIVE ANIMAL PHYSIOLOGIST, CELLULAR BIOLOGY-ENZYMOLOGY. **Personal Data:** b Atlanta, Ga, October 24, 1952; m 1978, c 2. **Education:** Carson-Newman Col, BS, 1974; Auburn Univ, MS, 1976, PhD (anat-physiol), 1980. **Professional Experience:** PROF BIOL, SAMFORD UNIV, BIRMINGHAM, as of 2006; chmn, curric renewal, Samford Univ, 1990-1991; CHAIR, DEPT BIOL, SAMFORD UNIV, BIRMINGHAM, 1988-; assoc prof biol, Dept Biol, Samford Univ, Birmingham, beginning 1988; lectr, Ala Gov Sch, beginning 1986; asst prof endocrinol, Univ Ala, Birmingham, 1985-1988; prin investr, res grants Am Diabetes Asn, 1985-1988; res chemist diabetes, Vet Admin Med Ctr, 1981-1988; asst prof biol, La Col, 1979-1981. **Memberships:** Am Physiol Soc; Am Diabetes Asn. **Research Statement & Publications:** Metabolic dysfunction of the heart of diabetic animals and humans; changes in isoenzymes and substrate specificities for the enzymes of nuclectide catabolism. **Mailing Address:** Dept Biol, Samford Univ, 800 Lakeshore Dr, Birmingham, AL 35229.

JENKINS, TERRY LLOYD, MATHEMATICS. **Personal Data:** b Beresford, SDak, November 7, 1935; m 1957, c 6. **Education:** Univ SDak, BA, 1957; Univ Iowa, MS, 1959; Univ Nebr, PhD (math), 1966. **Professional Experience:** PROF EMER MATH, UNIV WYO, as of 2006; prof math, Univ Wyo, beginning 1974; from asst prof to assoc prof, Univ Wyo, 1966-1974; from instr to asst prof, Univ Nebr, 1961-1966; instr math, Univ SDak, 1959-1960. **Memberships:** Am Math Soc; Math Asn Am. **Research Statement & Publications:** Ring theory; radicals of rings. **Mailing Address:** Dept Math, Univ Wyo, Ross Hall 220, Laramie, WY 82071. **Fax:** 307-766-6838. **E-Mail:** tjenkins@uwyo.edu

JENKINS, THOMAS GORDON, SYSTEMS ANALYSIS. **Personal Data:** b Ft Lewis, Wash, January 28, 1947; m 1968, c 2. **Education:** Univ Ark, BS, 1972, MS, 1974; Tex A&M Univ, PhD (animal breeding), 1977. **Professional Experience:** STAFF MEM, US MEAT & ANIMAL RES CTR, AGR RES SERV, USDA, as of 2000; RES ANIMAL SCIENTIST, US MEAT & ANIMAL RES CTR, AGR RES SERV, USDA, 1978-; res assoc, Tex A&M Univ, 1977-1978; consult, Wintock Int Livestock Res & Training Ctr, 1976. **Memberships:** Am Soc Animal Sci. **Research Statement & Publications:** Development and validation of the impact of innovative technologies on the efficiency of production of beef cattle and sheep production systems. **Mailing Address:** Roman L Hruska Meat Animal Res Ctr, Agr Res Serv, USDA, State Spur 18D, PO Box 166, Clay Center, NE 68933. **Fax:** 402-762-4148. **E-Mail:** jenkins@email.marc.usda.gov

JENKINS, THOMAS LLEWELLYN, ASTROPHYSICS. **Personal Data:** b Cambridge, Mass, July 16, 1927; m 1951, c 4. **Education:** Pomona Col, BA, 1950; Cornell Univ, PhD (physics), 1956. **Professional Experience:** PROF EMER PHYSICS, CASE WESTERN RESERVE UNIV, 1995-; sci & eng res coun fel, Southampton Univ, UK, 1983; prof physics, Case Western Reserve Univ, 1968-1995; from asst prof to assoc prof, Case Western Reserve Univ, 1960-1968; physicist, Lawrence Radiation Lab, Univ Calif, 1955-1960. **Memberships:** AAAS; Am Phys Soc. **Research Statement & Publications:** Neutrino induced reactions; low level counting; electron pair production; photoproduction of mesons; shock hydrodynamics; experimental elementary particle physics; gamma ray astronomy. **Mailing Address:** Dept Physics, Case Western Reserve Univ, Cleveland, OH 44106. **E-Mail:** tlj@case.edu

JENKINS, THOMAS WILLIAM, ANATOMY, NEUROPATHOLOGY. **Personal Data:** b Adrian, Mich, January 25, 1922; m 1948, Helen; c Jennifer, T Mark & Lori. **Education:** Kent State Univ, BS, 1947; Mich State Col, MS, 1950, PhD (zoology, anat), 1954. **Professional Experience:** RETIRED; NIH spec fel, Sch Med, Temple Univ, 1962-1963; from instr to prof anat & path, Mich State Univ, 1951-1988; asst zoology, Mich State Univ, 1948-1952; asst biol, Kent State Univ, 1941-1943, 1946-1947. **Memberships:** Am Asn Anat; Am Asn Vet Anat; Am Acad Neurol; Soc Neuroscience; Sigma Xi. **Research Statement & Publications:** Functional anatomy of the nervous system. **Mailing Address:** 3307 NE Stonebrook Loop, Bend, OR 97701-8231.

JENKINS, VERNON KELLY, RADIOLOGICAL HEALTH & RADIOBIOLOGY, EXPERIMENTAL HEMATOLOGY. **Personal Data:** b Chattanooga, Tenn, December 29, 1932; m 1954, Barbara Mae Caylor; c 2. **Education:** Carson-Newman Col, BS, 1954; Univ Tenn, Knoxville, MS, 1965, PhD (zool), 1967. **Professional Experience:** CONSULT, 1992-; from asst prof to prof, Univ Tex Med Br, Galveston, 1970-1992; asst prof, Baylor Col Med, 1969-1970; NIH fel exp biol, Baylor Col Med, 1968-1969; res scientist, Biol Div, Oak Ridge Nat Lab, 1967-1968; res assoc, Biol Div, OakRidge Nat Lab, 1959-1965. **Memberships:** Radiation Res Soc; Am Soc Exp Path; Soc Exp Hemat; Reticuloendothelial Soc; NY Acad Sci. **Research Statement & Publications:** Effects of radiation and drugs on hemopoiesis in mammals, including effects on the immune mechanism; studies of the interrelationships among radiation, drugs, immunity, hemopoiesis and the carcinogenic process. **Mailing Address:** 15938 La Avenida Ave, Houston, TX 77062.

JENKINS, WILLIAM KENNETH, ELECTRICAL ENGINEERING. **Personal Data:** b Pittsburgh, Pa, April 12, 1947; m 1970, Suzann. **Education:** Lehigh Univ, BSEE, 1969; Purdue Univ, MSEE, 1971, PhD (elec eng), 1974. **Honors & Awards:** Circuits & Systs Soc Distinguished Serv Award, Inst Elec & Electronics Engrs, 1990. **Professional Experience:** PROF & HEAD, DEPT ELEC ENG, PA STATE UNIV, as of 2006; Siliconix, Air Force Studies Bd, 1989-1990; dir, Coord Sci Lab, beginning 1986; prof elec eng, Univ Ill, Urbana-Champaign, beginning 1983; Siliconix, Lockheed Missiles & Space Co, 1983-1985; Siliconix, AT&T Bell Labs, 1983-1984; Siliconix Inc, 1978-1980; consult, Ill State Water, 1978; from asst prof to assoc prof, Coord Sci Lab, 1977-1983; res scientist assoc elec eng, Lockheed Missiles & Space Co Inc, 1974-1977. **Memberships:** Fel Inst Elec & Electronics Engrs (secy & treas, 1982-1984, pres, 1985); Am Soc Eng Educ. **Research Statement & Publications:** Circuit and system theory; digital signal processing: digital filters, algorithms and structures; adaptive signal processing; computed imaging. **Mailing Address:** Dept Elec Eng, Col Eng, Pa State Univ, 129 Elec Eng E, Univ Park, PA 16802. **Fax:** 814-865-7065. **E-Mail:** jenkins@engr.psu.edu

JENKINS, WILLIAM L, VETERINARY PHARMACOLOGY, VETERINARY PHYSIOLOGY. **Personal Data:** b Johannesburg, SAfrica, January 29, 1937; m 1961, c 4. **Education:** Univ Pretoria, BVSc, 1958, M Med Vet, 1968; Univ Mo, PhD (pharmacol), 1970. **Professional Experience:** PRES, LA STATE UNIV SYSTS, BATON ROUGE, 1999-; chancellor, La State Univ Systs, Baton Rouge, beginning 1996; vice chancellor, La State Univ Systs, Baton Rouge, 1993-1996; dean, Sch Vet Med, La State Univ, beginning 1988; USP Convention Comt, Vet Med, beginning 1987; mem, FDA/CVM Adv Comt, 1985-1988; prof vet physiol & pharmacol, Tex A&M Univ, 1978-1988; prof & head vet physiol & pharmacol, Univ Pretoria, 1976-1978; mem, Subcomt Radiation Appln, Agr S African Atomic Energy Bd, 1975-1978; vis prof physiol & pharmacol, Tex A&M Univ, 1975-1976; prof & head physiol & pharmacol, Univ Pretoria, 1971-1975; sr lectr, Univ Pretoria, 1969-1971; res assoc pharmacol, Univ Mo, 1966-1969; lectr vet med, Univ Pretoria, 1962-1966; asst pvt pract, 1959-1962. **Memberships:** Am Acad Vet Pharmacol & Therapeut; Am Col Vet Toxicologists; Am Soc Vet Physiologists & Pharmacologists; Am Vet Med Assoc. **Research Statement & Publications:** Veterinary pharmacology and therapeutics including comparative pharmacokinetics; pathophysiology of stress in cattle and sheep; ruminant physiology and pharmacology. **Mailing Address:** Pres Off, La State Univ Systs, 107 System Bldg, Baton Rouge, LA 70803-0001. **E-Mail:** wljenk@lsu.edu

JENKINS, WILLIAM ROBERT, NEMATOLOGY. **Personal Data:** b Hertford, NC, September 12, 1927; m 1951, c 3. **Education:** Col William & Mary, BS, 1950; Univ Va, MS, 1952; Univ Md, PhD (hort, plant path), 1954. **Professional Experience:** NORTHEAST ADMIN, DEPT BIOL, LIVINGSTONE COL, RUTGERS UNIV, as of 2004; dean, col, beginning 1977; assoc dean, col, 1974-1977; prof biol & chmn dept, livingston col, Rutgers Univ, beginning 1969; res prof, Col, 1965-1969; res specialist, Col, 1963-1965; assoc res specialist, Col, 1960-1963; from instr to asst prof, Univ Md, 1954-1960; asst plant path, Univ Md, 1951-1954; asst biol, Univ Va, 1950-1951. **Memberships:** Soc Nematologists. **Research Statement & Publications:** Nematodes in relation to water pollution; transmission of human pathogens in nematodes borne by domestic water supplies; nematodes in soil. **Mailing Address:** Livingstone Col, Rutgers Univ, Nelson Biol Labs, Rm A19 Bush Campus, Piscataway, NJ 08854-1059. **Fax:** 732-445-5870. **E-Mail:** jenkins@biology.rutgers.edu

JENKINS, WINBORNE TERRY, BIOLOGICAL CHEMISTRY, ENZYMOLOGY. **Personal Data:** b Waupun, Wis, March 23, 1932; div, c Christopher, Mary & Mark. **Education:** Cambridge Univ, BA, 1953; Mass Inst Technol, PhD (biol), 1957. **Professional Experience:** Career develop award, NIH, 1969-1974; PROF CHEM, IND UNIV, BLOOMINGTON, 1968-; assoc prof, Ind Univ, Bloomington, 1966-1968; spec res fel, NIH, 1961-1962; asst prof, Univ Calif, Berkeley, 1960-1966; instr, Mass Inst Technol, 1957-1958. **Memberships:** Am Soc Biochem & Molecular Biol; Protein Soc. **Research Statement & Publications:** Intermediary metabolism of amino acids, especially the purification, characterization and general enzymological properties of transaminases; enzymology of calcium and magnesium; F1-ATPases. **Mailing Address:** Dept Chem, Ind Univ, Bloomington, IN 47405. **Fax:** 812-855-8300. **E-Mail:** jenkinsw@indiana.edu

JENKINSON, STEPHEN G, PULMONARY DISEASE. **Personal Data:** b Shreveport, La, December 9, 1947. **Education:** La State Univ, Shreveport, MD, 1973. **Professional Experience:** Dir, Pulmonary Dis & Critical Care Med, Univ Tex Health Sci Ctr, as of 2004; PROF, DEPT MED, UNIV TEX HEALTH SCI CTR, as of 2006; CHIEF, PULMONARY DIS, AUDIE MURPHY VET ADMIN HOSP, 1982-. **Research Statement & Publications:** Glutathione, antioxidants, oxidant stress. **Mailing Address:** S Tex Vets Health Care Syst, Univ Tex Health Sci Ctr, 7400 Merton Minter Blvd, San Antonio, TX 78284-0001. **Fax:** 210-567-6677.

JENKS, JOHN B, PLASTICS. **Honors & Awards:** Bacon Person of Yr Award, Soc Plastics Indust, 1994. **Professional Experience:** CHMN, STYRENE INFO RES CTR, as of 1996. **Mailing Address:** Owens Corning, Fiberglass Tower, Toledo, OH 43659.

JENKS, RICHARD D, mathematics, computer algebra system language; deceased, see previous edition for last biography

JENKS, WILLIAM FURNESS, economic geology; deceased, see previous edition for last biography

JENKS, WILLIAM S, PHOTOCHEMISTRY. **Personal Data:** b Portland, Ore, July 30, 1964. **Education:** Univ Calif, Los Angeles, BS, 1986; Columbia Univ, PhD (chem), 1991. **Honors & Awards:** Career Award, NSF, 1995. **Professional Experience:** ASST PROF CHEM, UNIV IOWA, as of 1999; Cottrell scholar award, Res Corp, 1995; asst prof chem, Univ Iowa, beginning 1992; fel, Columbia Univ, 1991-1992. **Mailing Address:** 1605 Gilman Hall, Dept Chem, Univ Iowa, Ames, IA 50011. **Fax:** 515-294-0105. **E-Mail:** wsjenks@iastate.edu

JENNE, EVERETT A, GEOCHEMICAL MODELING, METAL BIOAVAILABILITY. **Personal Data:** b Beattie, Kans, March 2, 1930; m 1985, c 3. **Education:** Univ Nebr, BS, 1952, MS, 1953; Ore State Univ, PhD, 1960. **Professional Experience:** Geochem Environ Rel Health & Dis Comt, Nat Acad Sci, 1981-1983; RES SCIENTIST ENVIRON GEOCHEM, BATTELLE PAC Northwest LAB, RICHLAND, 1980-; memsubcomt, Geochem Environ Rel Health & Dis Comt, Nat Acad Sci, 1976-1981; mem ad hoc comttrace elements & uralithiasis incidence, Nat Acad Sci, 1975-1976; soil scientist, Calif, 1968-1979; soil scientist, US Geol Surv, Colo, 1962-1968; res fel rheology, Univ Calif, Berkeley, 1960-1962; res fel soil chem & clay mineral, Ore State Soil Dept, 1956-1960. **Memberships:** Soil Sci Soc Am; Soc Environ Geochem & Health; Am Geophys Union; AAAS; Am Chem Soc; Mineral Soc Am. **Research Statement & Publications:** Trace element geochemistry; trace element analyses and partitioning processesamong solute, sediment and biota; adsorption phenomenon; colloid chemistry of metal oxides; mineral-water reactions of fossil and nuclear fuel wastes; bioavailability of trace elements; metal adsorption by oxides and sediments; watershed acidification modeling; water-sediment reactions twenty five to one hundred twenty degrees celsius; aquifer thermal energy storage. **Mailing Address:** 4203 W Kennewick Ave No 34, Kennewick, WA 99336-2868.

JENNEMANN, VINCENT FRANCIS, COMPUTER SCIENCE, EXPLORATION GEOPHYSICS. **Personal Data:** b St Louis, Mo, November 27, 1921; m 1946, Frances; c Frances (Bohon), Catherine (Audley), Martha, Charles, Mark, Joseph & Mary (Broussard). **Education:** St Louis Univ, BS, 1947, MS, 1949; Univ Tulsa, PhD (earth sci), 1972. **Professional Experience:** RETIRED; staff comput analyst, Amoco Prod Co, Amoco Corp, 1974-1984; comput analyst, Amoco Prod Co, Amoco Corp, 1966-1974; sr res scientist, Amoco Prod Co, Amoco Corp, 1964-1966; sr res engr, Amoco Prod Co, Amoco Corp, 1958-1964; res engr, Amoco Prod Co, Amoco Corp, 1954-1958; asst, Lamont GeolObserv, Columbia Univ, 1951-1954; instr math, Lamar Col, 1949-1951; res comput, Seismog Dept, Sun Oil Co, 1948-1951; instr math, St Louis Univ, 1946-1948. **Memberships:** Seismol Soc Am; Soc Explor Geophys; Am Geophys Union; Sigma Xi. **Research Statement & Publications:** Various aspects of the metric system (SI). **Mailing Address:** 203 Sunset Dr, Tulsa, OK 74114-1239. **Fax:** 918-585-9962.

JENNER, DAVID CHARLES, ASTRONOMY, COMPUTER SCIENCE. **Personal Data:** b Seattle, Wash, October 21, 1943; m 1969, c 2. **Education:** Univ Wash, BS (physics) & BS (math), 1966; Univ Wis-Madison, PhD (astron), 1970. **Professional Experience:** CONSULT, 1989-; res assoc, Dept Astron & dir, Manastash Ridge Observ, Univ Wash, 1978-1989; adj asst prof astron, Univ Calif, Los Angeles, 1972-1978; asst prof astron, NMex State Univ, Las Cruces, 1970-1972. **Memberships:** Am Astron Soc; Int Astron Union. **Research Statement & Publications:** Masses of galaxies; stellar populations in galaxies; the nuclei of active galaxies; planetary nebulae; instrumentation and observational techniques; software systems; hardware systems; laboratory data acquisition and instrument control. **Mailing Address:** 3153 NE 84th St, Seattle, WA 98115-4717. **Fax:** 206-527-2019. **E-Mail:** djenner@halcyon.com

JENNER, EDWARD L, FREE RADICAL CHEMISTRY, HOMOGENOUS CATALYSIS BY TRANSITON METALS. **Personal Data:** b Pontiac, Mich, March 27, 1918; m 1942, Dorothy; c Charles A, Edward W & Margaret A. **Education:** Lake Forest Col, AB, 1939; Univ Mich, MS, 1940, PhD (chem), 1942. **Professional Experience:** RETIRED; res assoc cell physiol, Univ Calif, 1962-1963; res chemist, Exp Sta, E I DuPont de Nemours & Co Inc, 1945-1982; res chemist, Univ Mich, 1941-1945. **Memberships:** Emer mem Am Chem Soc; Sigma Xi; fel AAAS. **Research Statement & Publications:** Synthesis of nitramines; acid-catalyzed telomerizations; reactions of hydroxyl and amino radicals, halogen atoms and aliphatic free radicals; catalysis by soluble derivatives of transition metals; oxidative and photosynthetic phosphorylation; biochemistry of phytochrome; ozone damage to vegetation. **Mailing Address:** 726 Loveville Rd, Cottage 11, Hockessin, DE 19707-1504.

JENNESS, STUART EDWARD, GEOLOGY. **Personal Data:** b Ottawa, Ont, August 22, 1925; m 1980, Jean M Morgan; c John D & Mary G (Montgomery). **Education:** Queens Univ, Ont, BSc, 1948; Univ Minn, MS, 1950; Yale Univ, PhD (geol), 1955. **Professional Experience:** ED CONSULT GEOL, CAN JOUR RES, NAT RES COUN CAN, 1985-; publsupvr, Can Jour Res, Nat Res Coun Can, 1967-1985; geologist, Nfld Geol Surv, 1952-1953 & GeolSurv Can, 1954-1967; Instr geol, Muhlenberg Col, 1949-1951. **Memberships:** Fel Geol Soc Am; Geol Asn Can; Arctic Inst NAm; hon mem Asn Earth Sci Ed. **Mailing Address:** 9 2051 Jasmine Crescent, Gloucester, ON K1J 7W2, Can.

JENNETT, JOSEPH CHARLES, CIVIL & ENVIRONMENTAL ENGINEERING. **Personal Data:** b Dallas, Tex, June 11, 1940; m 1963, c 2. **Education:** Southern Methodist Univ, BSCE, 1963, MSCE, 1966; Univ NMex, PhD (sanit eng), 1969; Am Acad Environ Engrs, Dipl, 1978. **Professional Experience:** Provost & vpres acad affairs, Clemson Univ, 1992-1995; ACAD DEAN ENG & PROF ENVIRON SYST ENG, CLEMSON UNIV, 1981-; mem, Environ Eng Div, Res Coun, beginning 1978; ed, E N Am Minerals Environ J, 1978; mem, Prof Coord Comt, beginning 1977; vis res, Appl Geochem Res Group, Imp Col, UK, 1977; chmn, Comt Water Treatment & Water Resources Mgt, 1976; chmn, Task Force Toxic Trace Substances Water, 1975; prof civil eng & chmn dept, Syracuse Univ, 1975-1981; from asst prof to assoc prof civil eng, Univ Mo-Rolla, 1969-1975; consult engr, Pitotmeter Assocs, 1965-1966 & 1969; construct engr, Calif State Dept Water Resources, Orville, 1963-1964; engr, Southwestern Design Br, US Corp Engrs, 1962-1963. **Memberships:** Am Soc Civil Engrs; Am Acad Environ Engrs; Am Soc Eng Educ; Water Pollution Control Fedn; Nat Soc Prof Engrs; Am Asn Environ Eng Prof. **Research Statement & Publications:** Urban and rural runoff pollutants; drying of digested sludge; industrial waste treatment techniques; effects of heavy metals on aquatic ecosystems and treatment devices; biological operations on domestic and industrial wastes; analysis and treatment of toxic metals and trace organics; urban and rural run-off quality. **Mailing Address:** Tex A&M Univ, 5201 Univ Blvd, Loredo, TX 78041.

JENNEY, ELIZABETH HOLDEN, PHARMACOLOGY. **Personal Data:** b Bennington, Vt, November 4, 1912. **Education:** Mt Holyoke Col, AB, 1934; Univ Ill, MS, 1947. **Professional Experience:** PHARMACOLOGIST, BRAIN BIO CTR, 1973-; res scientist, SectPharmacol, Bur Res, NJ Neuropsychiat Inst, 1960-1973; instr, Sch Med, Emory Univ, 1954-1960; res assoc, Univ Ill Col Med, 1948-1954; med technologist, Cooly Dickinson Hosp, Northampton, Mass, 1941-1943; med technologist, Rutland Hosp, Vt, 1937-1941; Asstpharmacol, Sch Med, Boston Univ, 1935-1936. **Memberships:** Sigma Xi; Am Soc Pharmacol & Exp Therapeut. **Research Statement & Publications:** Neuropharmacology; psychopharmacology; schizophrenia. **Mailing Address:** Pennswood Village J-212, Newtown, PA 18940.

JENNI, DONALD ALISON, ETHOLOGY. **Personal Data:** b Pueblo, Colo, June 20, 1932; m 1985, Catherine; c Robert, William, Karen, Thomas, Jeffrey, Elizabeth & Benjamin. **Education:** Ore State Univ, BS, 1953; Utah State Univ, MS, 1956; Univ Fla, PhD (zool), 1961. **Professional Experience:** Prin investr, NSF, 1991-1993; assoc dean biol sci, Col

Arts & Sci, 1988-1991; prin investr, NSF, 1985; vis prof, Univ Melbourne & James Cooke Univ, 1985; prin investr, Campfire, 1983; vis prof, Univ Wash, 1979-1980; prin investr, BLM, 1977-1980; vis prof, Cornell Univ, 1975; chmn dept, Univ Mont, 1972-1975 & 1985-1988; PROF ZOOL, UNIV MONT, 1971-; prin investr, NSF, 1970-1976; assoc prof zool, Univ Mont, 1966-1971; NIH fel & res biologist, Univ Leiden, 1964-1966; Asst prof zool, Univ Fla, 1961-1962 & Eastern Ill Univ, 1962-1966. **Research Statement & Publications:** Ethology and behavioral ecology, especially behavioral approach to classic ecological problems; adaptation and evolution of behavioral patterns including social organization in response to ecological pressures; evolution of mateship systems, especially non-monogamous systems; behavioral problems of territoriality. **Mailing Address:** 17 Greenbrier Dr, Missoula, MT 59802. **Fax:** 406-243-4184.

JENNINGS, ALFRED ROY, HYDRAULIC FRACTURING, FORMATION DAMAGE. **Personal Data:** b Duncan, Okla, September 27, 1945; m 1967, c 3. **Education:** Okla Univ, BS, 1967, MS, 1972. **Professional Experience:** CONSULT, ENHANCED WELL STIMULATION INC, 1995; res assoc, Mobil Res & Develop Corp, beginning 1982; chmn, work group, 1981-; sect supvr, Halliburton Serv, 1979-1982; mem comts, Am Petrol Inst, 1977-1983; groupleader, Halliburton Serv, 1977-1979; dev engr, Halliburton Serv, 1974-1977; sr engr, HalliburtonServ, 1972-1974; chemist, Halliburton Serv, 1967-1972. **Memberships:** Soc Petrol Engrs; Asn Inst Mech Engrs. **Research Statement & Publications:** Formation fines and damage control; well stimulation; authored 95 US patents pertaining to applications and techniques for well stimulation. **Mailing Address:** Enhanced Well Stimulation, Inc, 2802 CR 4825, Athens, TX 75752. **E-Mail:** ewstim@flash.net

JENNINGS, ALFRED S(TONEBRAKER), CHEMICAL ENGINEERING. **Personal Data:** b St Louis, Mo, September 30, 1925; m 1949, c 4. **Education:** Wash Univ, St Louis, BS, 1948, MS, 1949, DSc (chem eng), 1951. **Professional Experience:** RETIRED; sr res assoc, Separations Eng Div, 1980-1985; res mgr, Separations Eng Div, 1968-1980; res supvr, Savannah River Lab, E I du Pont de Nemours & Co Inc, 1957-1968; chem engr, Savannah River Lab, E I du Pont de Nemours & Co Inc, 1951-1957. **Memberships:** Am Chem Soc; Am Inst Chem Engrs. **Research Statement & Publications:** Radiochemical separations and solvent extraction process development; isotope separation processes; high-level waste immobilization. **Mailing Address:** 1469 Canterbury Ct SE, Aiken, SC 29801.

JENNINGS, ALLEN LEE, PESTICIDES, TOXIC CHEMICALS. **Personal Data:** b Quincy, Ill, July 5, 1943; m 1967, c 3. **Education:** Western Ill Univ, BS, 1965; Univ Ark, PhD (chem), 1970. **Professional Experience:** DIR, OFF PEST MGT POLICY, USDA, as of 2006; DIR, BIOL & ECON ANAL DIV, 1987-; dir, Chem & Statist Policy Div, 1985-1987; RES ASSOC BIOCHEM, US ENVIRON PROTECTION AGENCY, 1971-; res assoc biochem, Iowa State Univ, 1970-1971. **Memberships:** AAAS; Am Chem Soc. **Mailing Address:** USDA, Off Pest Mgmt Policy, 1400 Independence Ave, SW Rm 3871 S Bldg Mail Stop 0315, Washington, DC 20250-0315. **Fax:** 202-690-3662. **E-Mail:** allen.jennings@usda.gov

JENNINGS, BOJAN HAMLIN, ORGANIC CHEMISTRY. **Personal Data:** b Waukegan, Ill, April 4, 1920; m 1942, c 3. **Education:** Bryn Mawr Col, AB, 1942; Radcliffe Col, MA, 1943, PhD (chem), 1955. **Professional Experience:** PROF EMER CHEM, WHEATONCOL, MASS, as of 2002; chmn dept, Wheaton Col, Mass, beginning 1968; prof chem, Wheatoncol, Mass, beginning 1962; from instr to assoc prof, Wheaton Col, Mass, 1943-1962; res chemist, Dewey & Almy Chem Co, 1942-1943. **Memberships:** Am Chem Soc; NY Acad Sci; Asn Women Sci. **Research Statement & Publications:** Steroid chemistry; cancer research; physical organic chemistry; photochemistry. **Mailing Address:** 25 Priscilla Rd, White Horse Beach, MA 02381.

JENNINGS, BYRON KENT, THEORETICAL PHYSICS. **Personal Data:** b Musquodoboit, NS, March 29, 1951. **Education:** Mt Allison Univ, BSc, 1972; McMaster Univ, MSc, 1973, PhD (physics), 1976. **Professional Experience:** Adj prof, Simon Fruser Univ, 1987-; vis prof, Univ Toronto, 1986; assoc ed, Can J Physics, 1983-1989; RES SCIENTIST, TRIUMF, 1982-; res fel physics, McGill Univ, 1980-1982; lectr physics, Univ Regensburg, 1980; fel physics, State Univ NY, Stony Brook, 1976-1980. **Research Statement & Publications:** Study of nucleon structure as it impacts on nuclear properties. **Mailing Address:** TRIUMF, 4004 Wesbrook Mall, Vancouver, BC V6T 2A3, Can. **Fax:** 604-222-1074. **E-Mail:** jennings@triumf.ca

JENNINGS, CARL ANTHONY, ORGANIC CHEMISTRY, CHEMICAL MANUFACTURING MANAGEMENT. **Personal Data:** b Harrisburg, Ill, December 28, 1944; m 1965, c 2. **Education:** Southern Ill Univ, BS, 1967, PhD (org chem), 1971. **Professional Experience:** EXEC VPRES, BASF CORP, 1992-; PRES, CHEM DIV, BASF CORP, 1992-; dir mfg & technol, Basf Wyandotte Corp, beginning 1985; mgr agr chem mfg, Ind Chem, 1980-1985; mgr develop chem, Ind Chem, 1978-1980; from asst to vpres, Ind Chem, 1977-1978; from res chemist to mgr, Photog Emulsion Mfg, GAF Corp, 1972-1977; res assoc org chem, Univ Ill, 1971-1972. **Memberships:** Am Chem Soc; Am Inst Chem Engrs; Soc Chem Indust. **Research Statement & Publications:** Agricultural chemicals; chemical manufacturing management; polyoxyalkylenes and organic oxide chemicals; urethanes; organic synthesis; photographic emulsion theory; organometallics. **Mailing Address:** Basf Corp, 3000 Continental Dr N, Mt Olive, NJ 07828-1234. **Fax:** 973-426-3213.

JENNINGS, CHARLES DAVID, OCEANOGRAPHY. **Personal Data:** b Newtonia, Mo, May 21, 1939; c 2. **Education:** Northwest Nazarene Col, BA, 1961; Ore State Univ, MS, 1966, PhD (oceanog), 1968. **Professional Experience:** PROF PHYSICS, WESTERN ORE STATE COL, 1978-; assoc prof physics, Ore Col Educ, 1974-1978; asst prof oceanog, Ore Col Educ, 1970-1974; oceanogr, US Bur Com Fisheries, 1968-1970; asst prof, World Campus Afloat, 1968; instr oceanog, World Campus Afloat, 1966; instr physics, Ore Col Educ, 1962-1963. **Memberships:** AAAS; Am Soc Limnol & Oceanog. **Research Statement & Publications:** Radioactivity and trace elements in the marine environment; circulation of estuaries; marine radioecology. **Mailing Address:** 7762 Sportsman Club Rd NE, Bainbridge Island, WA 98110.

JENNINGS, CHARLES WARREN, ELECTROCHEMISTRY. **Personal Data:** b Toledo, Ohio, December 3, 1918; m 1949, Donna; c Charles J, Mary M (Hoskins) & Anabelle (Muchmone). **Education:** Univ Toledo, BEng, 1940; Univ Calif, MS, 1943; Duke Univ, PhD (chem), 1951. **Professional Experience:** RETIRED; mem staff, Sandia Corp, 1957-1988; assoc prof chem, NC State Col, 1950-1957; res assoc, Res Proj, Duke Univ, 1948-1950; res assoc, Nat Bur Stand, 1947-1948; chemist, Nat Bur Stand, 1946-1947; res chemist, Dow Chem Co, Calif, 1942-1943. **Research Statement & Publications:** Physical properties of electrodeposited metals; electrochemistry of batteries and fused salt systems; chlorination of hydrocarbons; thermal batteries; printed circuit boards; adhesives. **Mailing Address:** 1209 Mesilla NE, Albuquerque, NM 87110.

JENNINGS, DANIEL THOMAS, FOREST ENTOMOLOGY, ARACHNOLOGY. **Personal Data:** b Fulton, Ky, July 4, 1935; m 1955, c 2. **Education:** Colo State Univ, BS, 1960; Univ NMex, MS, 1967, PhD (biol), 1972. **Professional Experience:** Fac assoc, Univ Maine, 1976-1991; prin res entomologist, Northeastern Forest Exp Sta, 1976-1991; adj asst prof biol, Univ NMex, 1974-1977; COLLABR, ENVIRON QUAL INST, BIOL ACTIVE NATURAL PROD LAB, AGR RES SERV, BELTSVILLE, MD, 1973-; res entomologist, Rocky Mountain Forest & Range Exp Sta, 1968-1976; res entomologist, NC Forest Exp Sta, 1965-1968; entomologist, Forest Serv, USDA, 1962-1965. **Memberships:** Charter Am Arachnological Soc; Brit Arachnological Soc; Int Arachnological Soc; Sigma Xi. **Research Statement & Publications:** Life histories and habits of forest insects, their biological control by natural enemies and pheromones; the arachnid fauna associated with forest trees; checklist of Maine spiders. **Mailing Address:** PO Box 130, Garland, ME 04939-0130.

JENNINGS, DAVID PHIPPS, MEDICAL INFORMATICS, VETERINARY MEDICINE. **Personal Data:** b Columbia, Mo, August 3, 1941; m 1964, c 2. **Education:** Univ Mo, BS, 1963, DVM, 1965; Okla State Univ, PhD (physiol), 1969. **Professional Experience:** PROF EMER VET PHYSIOL, MISS STATE UNIV, as of 2005; clin neurol trainee, Univ Ga, 1978; prof physiol, Miss State Univ, beginning 1977; NIH spec fel anat, Sch Med, Univ Calif, Los Angeles, 1971-1972; from asst prof to assoc prof physiol, Okla State Univ, 1968-1977; fel, NIH, 1966-1968; NIH trainee, 1965-1966. **Memberships:** AAAS; Am Vet Med Asn; Am Asn Vet Anatomists; Am Asn Vet Cols; Am Soc Vet Physiol & Pharmacol. **Research Statement & Publications:** Central nervous system mechanisms for control of physiologic systems; medical informatics and computerized medical records. **Mailing Address:** Col Vet Med, Miss State Univ, Box 9825, Mississippi State, MS 39762.

JENNINGS, DONALD B, MEDICINE, PHYSIOLOGY. **Personal Data:** b Windsor, Ont, July 20, 1932; m 1957, Gail; c Robert D, Elizabeth A, Lisa E & Hugh D. **Education:** Queen's Univ, Ont, MD, CM, 1957, MSc, 1960, PhD (physiol), 1962. **Professional Experience:** PROF EMER PHYSIOL, QUEEN'S UNIV, ONT, as of 2006; vis prof, Univ Calif, San Francisco, 1990; vis prof, Med Sch, Dartmouth Col, 1981; fel, Max Planck Inst Exp Med, 1981; assoc ed, Can J Physiol Pharmacol, 1978; prof Physiol, Queen's Univ, Ont, beginning 1974; from asst prof to assoc prof, Queen's Univ, Ont, 1964-1974; Can Heart Found sr res fel physiol, 1964-1969; res fel med & physiol, Cardiovasc ResInst, Med Ctr, Univ Calif, San Francisco, 1962-1964; George Christian Hoffman fel path, 1962-1963; jr asst res med, Montreal Gen Hosp, 1958-1959; jr intern, Montreal Gen Hosp, 1957-1958. **Memberships:** Can Physiol Soc (secy, 1975-1978); Am Physiol Soc; Can Soc Clin Invest. **Research Statement & Publications:** Humoral and nervous regulation of cardiovascular, respiratory, metabolic and erythropoietic adjustments to high carbon dioxide and low oxygen environments and anaemic anoxia; interaction of temperature regulation with the cardio-respiratory admustment to acute and chronic hypercapnia and hypoxia; role of unin-angioleases system and vasopression in the central regulation of ventilation; application of the physicochemistry of H plus homeostasis to respiratory control. **Mailing Address:** Dept Physiol, Queen's Univ, Kingston, ON K7L 3N6, Can. **Fax:** 613-533-6880. **E-Mail:** jennings@post.queensu.ca

JENNINGS, DONALD EDWARD, MOLECULAR SPECTROSCOPY. **Personal Data:** b New Rochelle, NY, May 30, 1948; m 1970. **Education:** Northern Ariz Univ, BS, 1970; Univ Tenn, PhD (physics), 1974. **Professional Experience:** ASTROPHYSICIST, NASA GODDARD SPACE FLIGHT CTR, LAB EXTRATERRESTRIAL PHYSICS, PLANETARY SYSTS BR, 1977-; Nat Acad Sci-Nat Res Coun resident res assoc, Goddard Space Flight Ctr, NASA, 1976-1977; res assoc physics, Univ Tenn, Knoxville, 1974-1975. **Research Statement & Publications:** Molecular spectroscopy; fourier transform, tuneable diode laser, and grating spectroscopy; planetary infrared astronomy; radio astronomy of interstellar molecules. **Mailing Address:** Goddard Space Flight Ctr, NASA, Code 693, Greenbelt, MD 20771. **Fax:** 301-286-1683. **E-Mail:** donald.e.jennings@nasa.gov

JENNINGS, LAURENCE DUANE, SOLID STATE PHYSICS. **Personal Data:** b New Haven, Conn, November 14, 1929; m 1951, c 3. **Education:** Mass Inst Technol, SB, 1950, PhD (physics), 1955. **Professional Experience:** RETIRED; solid state physicist, US Army Mat Tech Lab, 1959-1988; asst profchem, Iowa State Univ, 1955-1959. **Memberships:** Am Phys Soc; Am Crystallog Asn; Inst Elec & Electronics Engrs. **Research Statement & Publications:** Diffraction; equilibrium properties of solids. **Mailing Address:** 128 Gibbs St, Newton, MA 02159-1928.

JENNINGS, LISA HELEN KYLE, EXPERIMENTAL HEMATOLOGY, PLATELET MEMBRANE BIOCHEMISTRY. **Personal Data:** b Kingsport, Tenn, April 1, 1955; m 1976, David; c 1. **Education:** Univ Tenn, BA, 1976; Memphis State Univ, MS, 1978; Univ Tenn, PhD (biochem), 1983. **Professional Experience:** PROF, DEPT SURG, UNIV TENN, 2002-; DIR, vascular Biol Ctr Excellence, UNIV TENN, 2001-; dir, Vascular Biolo Prog, Univ Tenn Health Sci Ctr, 1999-2001; prof, Dept Molecular Sci Univ Tenn, 1999-; prof tenure, Dept Med, div Hematology Oncol Univ Tenn, 1998-; dir, invest res, hemat & oncol div, Univ Tenn, Memphis, 1995-2001; adjun prof, Joint Prog Biomed Eng, Univ Memphis, 1990-; adjun prof, Joint Prog Biomed Eng, Univ Tenn, 1990-; estab investr, Am Heart Asn, 1991-1996; assoc prof, dept med & biochem, Univ Tenn, Memphis, beginning 1985; Young investr, Am Heart Asn, 1985-1987; res fel, Leon Journey fel, 1984-1985; res fel, dept biochem, St Jude Children's Res Hosp, Memphis, Tenn, 1983-1984. **Memberships:** AAAS; Soc Anal Cytol; Am Soc Hemat; Int Soc Thromb & Haem. **Research Statement & Publications:** Structure and function of platelet membrane surface proteins and their role in thrombosis and hemostasis, particularly the mechanism by which plateletsurface proteins mediate platelet aggregation and integrin signaling; author of various articles. **Mailing Address:** Dept Med Div Hemat Oncol, Univ Tenn, 956 Ct Ave Rm H300, Memphis, TN 38163. **Fax:** 901-448-7181. **E-Mail:** ljennings@utmem.edu

JENNINGS, MICHAEL LEON, TRANSPORT PHYSIOLOGY, MEMBRANE BIOCHEMISTRY. **Personal Data:** b Cleveland, Ohio, June 10, 1948; m 1976, Paula. **Education:** Mass Inst Technol, SB, 1970; Harvard Univ, PhD (biophysics), 1976. **Professional Experience:** PROF & CHAIR, DEPT PHYSIOL & BIOPHYS, UNIV ARK MED SCI, 1995-; prof, Dept Physiol & Biophys, Univ Tex Med Br, Galveston, 1987-1995; asst prof physiol, Col Med, Univ Iowa, 1978-1987; fel, Max Planck Inst Biophysics, 1977-1978. **Memberships:** Biophys Soc; Am Physiol Soc; Sigma Xi; ASBMB; Soc Gen Physiol; Soc Gen Physiol (pres, 1997-1998). **Research Statement & Publications:** Structure and function of biological ion transport proteins, Regulation of intracellular ions. **Mailing Address:** Dept Physiol & Biophys, Univ Ark Med Sci, Little Rock, AR 72205. **Fax:** 501-686-8167. **E-Mail:** jenningsmichaell@uams.edu

JENNINGS, PAUL C(HRISTIAN), EARTHQUAKE ENGINEERING, APPLIED MECHANICS. **Personal Data:** b Brigham City, Utah, May 21, 1936; m 1981, Millicent; c Kathryn & Margaret. **Education:** Colo State Univ, BS, 1958; Calif Inst Technol, MS, 1960, PhD (civil eng), 1963. **Honors & Awards:** Walter Huber Res Prize, Am Soc Civil Engrs, 1976, Nathan M Newmark Medal. **Professional Experience:** Actg vpres bus & finance, Div Eng

& Appl Sci, 1995-1996; vpres & provost, Div Eng & Appl Sci, 1989-1995; chmn, Div Eng & Appl Sci, 1985-1989; exec officer appl mech & eng, Calif Inst Technol, 1975-1979; PROF CIVIL ENG & APPL MECH, CALIF INST TECHNOL, 1972-; Erskine fel, Univ Canterbury, 1970, 1985; from asst prof to prof appl mech, Calif Inst Technol, 1966-1975; mem, eng panel, Nat Acad Sci Comt Alaskan Earthquake, 1965-; from instr to assoc prof mech, USAF Acad, 1963-1966; consult, Exxon Corp, Ertec Western Inc, AC Martin & Assocs & Stand Oil, Calif. **Memberships:** Nat Acad Eng; Am Soc Civil Engrs; Seismol Soc Am (pres, 1980); Earthquake Eng Res Inst (pres, 1981-1983); Am Soc Eng Educ; Am Geophys Union; fel AAAS; fel Am Acad Arts & Sci. **Research Statement & Publications:** Structural dynamics and engineering seismology, especially response of structures to earthquake motion; earthquake engineering. **Mailing Address:** Mail Code 104-44, Calif Inst Technol, Pasadena, CA 91125-0001.

JENNINGS, PAUL W, ORGANOMETALLIC CHEMISTRY, COMPLEX MATERIALS. **Personal Data:** b Denver, Colo, September 24, 1936; m 1961, c 2. **Education:** Univ Colo, BA, 1958, MS, 1961; Univ Utah, PhD (org chem), 1965. **Professional Experience:** PROG DIR, GRAD RES TRAINEESHIPS, DIV GRAD EDUC, NSF, as of 2004; prof chem, Mont State Univ, 1975-1994; from asst prof to assoc prof, Mont State Univ, 1966-1975; res fel chem, Calif Inst Technol, 1964-1966. **Memberships:** Am Chem Soc; Sigma Xi. **Research Statement & Publications:** Organometallic chemistry; photochemical energy transfer; chemistry of bituminous materials. **Mailing Address:** Div Grad Educ, Nat Sci Found, 4201 Wilson Blvd, Arlington, VA 22230. **Fax:** 703-292-9048. **E-Mail:** pjenning@nsf.gov

JENNINGS, RICHARD LOUIS, CIVIL ENGINEERING, APPLIED MECHANICS. **Personal Data:** b Newark, NJ, July 28, 1933; m 1956, c 2. **Education:** Univ Ohio, BS (math), 1956, BS (civil eng), 1957; Univ Ill, MS, 1958, PhD (civil eng), 1964. **Professional Experience:** PROF EMER CIVIL ENG, UNIV VA, as of 2004; assoc prof civil eng, Univ Va, beginning 1967; asst prof, Univ VA, 1963-1967; consult, Babcock & WilcoxCorp, Va. **Memberships:** Am Soc Civil Engrs. **Research Statement & Publications:** Earthquake and nuclear blast resistant design structures; mechanical vibrations of thin shells; structural design of large steerable radio telescopes; rehabilitation engineering; highway pavement analysis. **Mailing Address:** Dept Civil Eng, Univ Va, 351 McCormick Rd PO Box 400742, Charlottesville, VA 22904-4742. **Fax:** 434-982-2951. **E-Mail:** rlj@virginia.edu

JENNINGS, ROBERT BURGESS, PATHOLOGY, EXPERIMENTAL PATHOLOGY. **Personal Data:** b Baltimore, Md, December 14, 1926; m 1952, Linda; c Carol L, Mary G, John B, Anne E & James R. **Education:** Northwestern Univ, BS, 1947, MS, 1949, MD, 1950; Am Bd Path, dipl AP, 1954, EP, 1955. **Honors & Awards:** Peter Harris Award, Int Soc Heart Res, 1992. **Professional Experience:** JAMES B DUKE PROF PATH, MED SCH, DUKE UNIV, 1980-; mem, Cardiol Adv Comt, Nat Heart, Lung & Blood Inst, NIH, 1978-1982; chmn dept, Med Sch, Duke Univ, 1975-1989; prof, Med Sch, Duke Univ, 1975-1980; attend staff, Northwestern Mem Hosp, 1972-1975; from instr to prof, Magerstadt prof path & chmn dept, 1969-1975; consult physician, Vet Admin Res Hosp, Chicago, Ill, 1969-1975; attend physician & chief labs, Passavant Mem Hosp, 1969-1972; vis scientist, Middlesex Hosp Med Sch, London, 1961-1962; mem path A study sect, USPHS, 1960-1965; Markle scholar, 1958-1963; pathologist, Community Hosp, Evanston, Ill, 1957-1967; attend physician, Vet Admin Res Hosp, Chicago, Ill, 1955-1969; from instr to prof, Med Sch, Northwestern Univ, Ill, 1953-1969; lab officer, US Navy, 1951-1953; resident path, Passavant Mem Hosp, Chicago, Ill, 1950-1951; intern, Passavant Mem Hosp, Chicago, Ill, 1949-1950. **Memberships:** Am Asn Pathologists; Soc Exp Biol & Med; Int Soc Heart Res (pres, 1978-1980); Am Soc Cell Biol; Am Heart Asn; Am Soc Nephrol. **Research Statement & Publications:** Cardiovascular and renal disease; cell physiology; cell injury; electron microscopy; biology of experimental myocardial infarction; molecular mechanisms which cause the death of ischemic myocytes. **Mailing Address:** Dept Path, Duke Univ, Med Ctr Box 3712, Durham, NC 27710. **Fax:** 919-684-4352.

JENNINGS, VIVAN M, AGRICULTURAL RESEARCH. **Personal Data:** b Columbus Junction, Iowa, May 2, 1936. **Education:** Iowa State Univ, BS, MS, PhD (agron). **Professional Experience:** Interim sr exten adv, Polish Ministry Agr & Food Econ, 1990; interim assoc admin, Exten Serv, USDA, 1989; DEP ADMIN AGR, EXTEN SERV, USDA, 1985-; assoc dean & assoc dir, Iowa Exten Serv; prof plant path, seed& weed sci & exten specialist, Integrated Pest Mgt, Weed Control & Agron, Iowa State Univ. **Memberships:** Am Soc Agron; Crop Sci Soc Am. **Research Statement & Publications:** Integrated pest management; pesticide impact assessment; pesticide applicator training; urban gardening; farm safety and farmers with disabilities along with more traditional programs of farm management, marketing, crop and livestock production systems and agricultural engineering. **Mailing Address:** USDA, SW Ste 3252 Waterfront Ctr, Washington, DC 20024. **Fax:** 202-720-4924. **E-Mail:** vjennings@esusda.gov

JENNINGS, WALTER GOODRICH, GAS CHROMATOGRAPHY. **Personal Data:** b Sioux, Iowa, March 2, 1922; m 1947, c 3. **Education:** Univ Calif, BS, 1950, MS, 1952, PhD (agr chem), 1954. **Honors & Awards:** Medal, Univ Bologna, 1967; Medal, Fr Asn Agr Chemists, 1971; BeckmanAward in Gas Chromatog, 1990; MJE Golay Award in Capillary Chromatography, 1996. **Professional Experience:** CONSULT, J & W SCI, 1975-; spec award srAm scientist, Alexander von Humboldt Found, 1973; NIH sr scientist award, Vienna, Austria, 1967-1968; prof food sci & chem exp sta, Univ Calif, Davis, 1965-1989; from asst prof to assocprof food sci, Univ Calif, Davis, 1959-1965; from jr chemist to assoc chemist, Univ Calif, Davis, 1954-1965; instr dairy indust, Univ Calif, Davis, 1954-1959; founder J & W Sci, Inc, Rancho Cordova, Calif; ed, J High Resolution Chromatography & Chromotography Commun, J Food Chem &Chemi, Mikrobiologie, Technologie der Lebensmittel; consult, several indust firms. **Memberships:** Am Chem Soc; hon mem Soc Flavor Chemists. **Research Statement & Publications:** Isolation and characterization of trace volatiles; flavor chemistry; glass capillary gas chromatography; author of over 300 publications. **Mailing Address:** 23104 Park Sorrento, Calabasas, CA 91302. **Fax:** 916-985-1101.

JENNINGS, WILLIAM HARNEY, BIOPHYSICS. **Personal Data:** b Ames, Iowa, December 6, 1931; m 1957, c 2. **Education:** Duke Univ, BS, 1954; George Wash Univ, MS, 1959. **Professional Experience:** RETIRED; res physicist, Nat Inst Arthritis, Metab & Digestive Dis, 1961-1988; physicist, Naval Med Res Inst, 1954-1958. **Memberships:** AAAS; Chem Soc. **Research Statement & Publications:** Laboratory computers, dedicated, multi-user and networks. **Mailing Address:** 5442 Cassons Neck Rd, Cambridge, MA 21613.

JENNISON, DWIGHT RICHARD, SURFACE SCIENCE, ELECTRONIC STRUCTURE. **Personal Data:** b Teaneck, NJ, June 11, 1943; m 1968, Mary; c Amy, David & Matthew. **Education:** Rensselaer Polytech Inst, BS, 1965, MS, 1973, PhD (physics), 1974. **Professional Experience:** PRIN MEM TECH STAFF, SANDIA NAT LAB, ALBUQUERQUE, 1992-; vis scientist, Tech Univ Munich, Ger, 1985; vis scientist, Univ Liverpool, UK, 1983, 1991, 1992; supvr, condensed matter theory div, Sandia Nat lab, 1980-1992; mem tech staff, Solid State Theory Div, Sandia Nat Lab, 1977-1980; res asst prof physics, Dept Physics & Mat Res Lab, Univ Ill, Urbana, 1976-1977; assoc, Dept Physics & Mat ResLab, Univ Ill, Urbana, 1974-1976; res assoc, Dept Physics & Mat Res Lab, Univ Ill, Urbana, 1974-1975; NIH trainee, Rensselaer Polytech Inst, 1971-1974; teaching asst, Rensselaer Polytech Inst, 1971; res asst physics, Univ NDak, 1969-1970. **Memberships:** Am Phys Soc; Am Vacuum Soc. **Research Statement & Publications:** Electronic structure of solids, surfaces, clusters and molecules; theory of surface spectroscopies and electronically stimulated desorption; theory of high-temperature superconducting compounds. **Mailing Address:** Dept Surface & Interface Sci, Sandia Nat Lab, MS 1421, Albuquerque, NM 87185-1415. **Fax:** 505-844-4045. **E-Mail:** drjenni@sandia.gov

JENNRICH, ELLEN COUTLEE, ANIMAL BEHAVIOR, ECOLOGY. **Personal Data:** b Kankakee, Ill, December 16, 1939; m 1971, Robert; c Alison & Tamara. **Education:** Wayne State Univ, BA, 1960, MS, 1962; Univ Calif, Los Angeles, PhD (zoology), 1966; Pac Lutheran Theol Sem, MDiv, 1996. **Professional Experience:** Substitute teacher sci & biol, Westlake Sch, Los Angeles, 1985-1990; lectr zoology, Univ Calif, Los Angeles, 1968-1972; lectr, Univ Calif, Riverside, 1966-1968; lectr biol, Mt St Mary's Col, 1963-1964. **Research Statement & Publications:** Population biology of starlings; comparative breeding behavior of goldfinches, fluctuations in population size, avian communication, maintenance and agonistic behavior. **Mailing Address:** 3400 Purdue Ave, Los Angeles, CA 90066.

JENNRICH, ROBERT I, STATISTICS. **Personal Data:** b Milwaukee, Wis, February 11, 1932; m 1971, c 2. **Education:** Univ Wis, BS, 1954, MS, 1956; Univ Calif, Los Angeles, PhD (math), 1960. **Professional Experience:** EMER PROF MATH & BIOMATH, UNIV CALIF, LOS ANGELES, as of 2004; prof math & biomath, Univ Calif, Los Angeles, beginning 1974; assocprof math & biomath, Univ Calif, Los Angeles, 1970-1974; asst prof math & asst res statistician, Univ Calif, Los Angeles, 1962-1970; Asst prof math, Univ Wis, 1960-1962. **Memberships:** Am Statist Asn; Inst Math Statist. **Research Statement & Publications:** Computer algorithms for data analysis; non-linear least squares, methods and statistical properties; factor analysis, rotation and maximum likelihood algorithms; analysis of variance, properties of the mixed model; time series analysis. **Mailing Address:** UCLA Dept Math, box, 951555 405 Hilgard Ave, Los Angeles, CA 90024-1554. **E-Mail:** rij@math.ucla.edu

JENNY, HANS K, ELECTRONIC & ELECTRICAL ENGINEERING. **Personal Data:** b Glarus, Switz, September 14, 1919; American citizen; m 1949, Hanny; c Haus-Dieter, Christopher & Susanne. **Education:** Swiss Fed Inst Technol, MSEE, 1943. **Honors & Awards:** Fellow Award, Institute of Electrical & Electronic Engineers. **Professional Experience:** RETIRED; asst prof & res engr, Swiss Fed Inst Technol, 1943-1946. **Memberships:** Fel Inst Elec & Electronics Engrs. **Research Statement & Publications:** Parametric amplifiers; variable capacitance and tunnel amplifiers; phase shifters; microwave laser modulators and detectors; microwave devices and systems; engineering organizations; technical information, including communications, publications and information systems. **Mailing Address:** 210 Riveredge Dr RD 1, Leola, PA 17540.

JENNY, NEIL ALLAN, PESTICIDE CHEMISTRY. **Personal Data:** b Milwaukee, Wis, September 6, 1936; m 1960, c 5. **Education:** Univ Wis, BS, 1958; Univ Kans, PhD (med chem), 1963. **Professional Experience:** GROUP LEADER PAPER CHEM, WITCO CORP, 1993-; prod develop mgr, Berlin, 1990-1992; sr res chemist, Berlin, 1986-1990; contract mfg coordr, Div Schering Ag, 1977-1979; supvr anal res, Nor-Am Agr Prod, 1969-1985; res chemist, Org Div, 1966-1969; res chemist, Polymer Div, Morton Chem Co, Ill, Sherex, 1963-1966. **Memberships:** Am Chem Soc; Am Pharmaceut Asn; Tech Asn Pulp & Paper Indust. **Research Statement & Publications:** Resistance factors of crops; pesticide residue analytical methods; pesticide metabolism; effect of pesticide residues on environment; retail pharmacy; pesticide formulation; quality control; production and contract manufacturing; residue chemistry; paper chemistry; surfactant chemistry. **Mailing Address:** 2001 Afton Rd PO Box 1018, Janesville, WI 53545.

JENS, WAYNE H(ENRY), MECHANICAL ENGINEERING & NUCLEAR ENGINEERING. **Personal Data:** b Manitowoc, Wis, December 20, 1921; m 1946, c 4. **Education:** Univ Wis, BS, 1943; Purdue Univ, MS, 1948, PhD (mech eng), 1949. **Honors & Awards:** Gold Award, Eng Soc Detroit, 1978. **Professional Experience:** PRES, JENS & JENS INC, 1988-; mem, Nuclear Training Accrediting Bd, InstNuclear Power Opers, 1985-1988; vpres nuclear oper, Detroit Edison Co, 1980-1986; mem, Nuclear power div comn, Elec Power Res Inst, beginning 1978; asst vpres eng & construct, Detroit EdisonCo, 1978-1980; mem bd trustees, Argonne Univ Asn, beginning 1977; mgr eng & construct, Detroit-Edison Co, 1976-1978; gen mgr, Atomic Power Develop Assocs Inc, 1957-1971; proj leader &mgr, Nuclear Develop Corp Am, 1953-1957; head eng anal group, Argonne Nat Lab, 1949-1953; eng asst heat transfer, Purdue Univ, 1946-1949; eng designer, NAm Aviation, Inc, 1943-1944. **Memberships:** Fel Am Nuclear Soc; Am Soc Mech Engrs. **Research Statement & Publications:** Boiling heat transfer; nuclear fuel irradiation stability; reactor design; nuclear operations and training. **Mailing Address:** 1220 Wild Azalea Pt, Seneca, SC 29678. **E-Mail:** wjens@ibm.net

JENSEN, ALBERT CHRISTIAN, ECOLOGY, MARINE ENVIRONMENTAL SCIENCE. **Personal Data:** b New York, NY, January 26, 1924; c 4. **Education:** State Univ NY Syracuse, BS, 1951, MS, 1954. **Honors & Awards:** George Wash Hon Medal, Freedoms Found, 1973; Spec Sci Book Award, NY Acad Sci, 1979. **Professional Experience:** Prof, Cent Fla Community Col, 1978-; CONSULT, COASTAL ENVIRON, ENVIRON ASSOCS, 1977-; asst prof, Grad Dept Marine Sci, C W Post Col, 1975-1977; adv, Atlantic States Marine Fisheries Comn, Wash, DC, 1967-1980; US deleg, Int Comn N W Atlantic Fisheries, 1972-1975; asst dir coastal environ, NY State Dept Environ Conserv, 1967-1977; managing ed marine sci, Marine Lab, Univ Miami, 1965-1967; res biologistmarine fisheries, US Fish & Wildlife Serv, Woods Hole, Mass, 1954-1965. **Memberships:** Nat Marine Educrs Asn; Am Inst Fishery Res Biologists; Fla Acad Sci. **Research Statement & Publications:** Marine science education; coastal zone management; fisheries management. **Mailing Address:** Gladys St, Inglis, FL 34449.

JENSEN, ARNOLD WILLIAM, ORGANIC CHEMISTRY, POLYMER CHEMISTRY. **Personal Data:** b Racine, Wis, April 30, 1928; m 1960, Marianne; c Mary K. **Education:** Dana Col, Nebr, BA, 1950; Okla State Col, PhD (chem), 1958. **Professional Experience:** RETIRED; res assoc, Textile Fibers Dept, E I Du Pont de Nemours & Co, Inc, 1958-1992; res chemist, Dow Chem Co, Tex, 1952-1953. **Memberships:** AAAS; Am Chem Soc; Sigma Xi. **Research Statement & Publications:** Nuclear magnetic resonance; infrared; synthetic fibers. **Mailing Address:** 213 Camellia Dr, Charlottesville, VA 22903-4208.

JENSEN, ARTHUR SEIGFRIED, ELECTRONIC PHYSICS. **Personal Data:** b Trenton, NJ, December 24, 1917; m 1941, Lillian; c Deane Ellsworth, Alan F & Nancy L. **Education:** Univ Pa, BS, 1938, MS, 1939, PhD (physics), 1941; Westinghouse Sch Appl Eng Sci, dipl(advan eng technol) 1972, dipl (comput sci), 1977. **Professional Experience:** RETIRED; consult physicist, Electronic Systs, 1991-1994; vchmn, Md State Bd Prof Engrs, 1979-1986; regist prof eng, Md, 1966; sr adv physicist, Defense & Electronics Ctr,

1965-1991; mgr spec electron devices, Electronic Tube Div, Appl Res Dept, Westinghouse Elec Corp, 1957-1965; res physicist, RCA Labs, 1945-1957; res physicist, Naval Res Lab, Wash, DC, 1941; instr physics, US Naval Acad, 1941-1946; lab asst physics, Univ Pa, 1938-1939. **Memberships:** AAAS; Am Phys Soc; Am Asn Physics Teachers; fel Inst Elec & Electronics Engrs; Nat Coun Eng Examrs; Sigma Xi; Soc Photo Optical Instrumentation Engrs. **Research Statement & Publications:** Solid state electro-optical imaging systems; imaging techniques and sensing devices; image quality and information theory; noise and image sensor detection limitations; electron optics and integrated circuits; infrared image sensors and systems; modeling solid state devices and systems; granted 25 US patents. **Mailing Address:** 8820 Walther Blvd, Parkville, MD 21234.

JENSEN, BETTY KLAINMINC, ENVIRONMENTAL POLICY, RISK COMMUNICATION. **Personal Data:** b Poland, June 20, 1949; American citizen; m 1971, c 4. **Education:** Brooklyn Col, BS, 1970; Columbia Univ, NY, MS, 1973, MPhil, 1974, PhD (physics), 1976; St Johns Univ, NY, MBA, 1981. **Professional Experience:** PRIN ENGR, PUB SERV ELEC & GAS CO, as of 2004; NJ Inst Technol, 1989-; Off Technol Assessment, 1982-1984; FUELS & ENVIRON SCI MGR, PUB SERV ELEC & GAS CO, 1988-; Nuclear & Environ Prog mgr, Pub Serv Elec & Gas Co, 1984-1988; adv, Gas Cooled Res Assocs, 1979-1988; prin physicist, PubServ Elec & Gas Co, 1979-1984; adv, Mass Inst Technol, 1978-1989; adv, Elec Power Res Inst & Princeton Plasma Physics Lab, 1977-; sr physicist, Pub Serv Elec & Gas Co, 1976-1979; Instrphysics, City Univ NY, 1973-1976. **Memberships:** Air & Waste Mgt Asn; AAAS; Inst Elec & Electronics Engrs; Am Phys Soc; Bioelectromagnetics Soc; Sigma Xi. **Research Statement & Publications:** Environmental impact of electric power generation, transmission and distribution; risk communication; commercialization of new technologies. **Mailing Address:** Pub Serv Elec & Gas Co, PO Box 570 80 Park Plaza 18 A, Newark, NJ 07102. **Fax:** 973-242-6074. **E-Mail:** betty.jensen@pseg.com

JENSEN, BRUCE A, MATHEMATICS. **Personal Data:** b Spencer, Iowa, August 6, 1930; m 1951, c 2. **Education:** Dana Col, BA, 1952; Univ Wis-Madison, MS, 1955; Univ Nebr-Lincoln, PhD (math), 1966. **Professional Experience:** DEPT CHMN, PORTLAND STATE UNIV, 1986-; PROF MATH, PORTLAND STATE UNIV, 1973-; assoc prof, Portland State Univ, 1966-1973; from asst profto assoc prof, Nebr Wesleyan Univ, 1959-1966; asst prof math, Dana Col, 1958-1959; instr math& physics, Dana Col, 1955-1958. **Memberships:** Am Math Soc; Math Asn Am. **Research Statement & Publications:** Algebraic semigroups; finiteness conditions on infinite semigroups; extensions of semigroups; decompositions of semigroups. **Mailing Address:** 59715 Kimberly Ct, Bend, OR 97702.

JENSEN, BRUCE DAVID, PHARMACEUTICAL RESEARCH & DEVELOPMENT, CLINICAL DIAGNOSTIC RESEARCH & DEVELOPMENT. **Personal Data:** b Chicago, Ill, March 22, 1954; m 1987, Colleen P Gabryelski; c Sean M. **Education:** Univ Calif, Berkeley, AB, 1977; Univ Rochester, MS, 1980, PhD (biophys), 1984. **Professional Experience:** DIR, ZYNAXIS, INC, 1993-; res group leader, Zynaxis Cell Sci, Inc, 1988-1993; assoc sr investr, Smith Kline & French Labs, 1987-1988; Res assoc, Smith Kline &French Labs, 1983-1987. **Memberships:** Biophys Soc; NY Acad Sci; Am Soc Cell Biol; Soc Anal Cytol. **Research Statement & Publications:** Production of novel clinical diagnostic assays; novel drug delivery systems. **Mailing Address:** Dept In Vitro Diags, Zynaxis Inc 371 Phoenixville Pike, Malvern, PA 19355-9603.

JENSEN, BRUCE L, ORGANIC CHEMISTRY. **Personal Data:** b Three Rivers, Mich, August 6, 1944; m 1965, c 2. **Education:** Western Mich Univ, BS, 1966, PhD (org chem), 1975. **Professional Experience:** Sabbatical leave, Univ Southern Calif, 1983-1984; ASSOC PROF CHEM, UNIV MAINE, ORONO, 1978-; asst prof, Univ Maine, Orono, 1973-1978; instr chem, Univ Maine, Orono, 1972-1973; Nat Cancer Inst fel, Univ Mich, Ann Arbor, 1970-1972. **Memberships:** Am Chem Soc. **Research Statement & Publications:** Organic synthesis; infrared, nuclear magnetic resonance and mass spectroscopy; heterocycles; natural products; medicinal chemistry; halonium ion chemistry; steroids; antineoplastic drugs; antiarrhythmic drugs. **Mailing Address:** Dept Chem, Univ Maine, Orono, ME 04469. **E-Mail:** bjensen@maine.edu

JENSEN, CRAIG LEEBENS, METALLURGY. **Personal Data:** b Rochester, Minn, December 8, 1950. **Education:** Univ Minn, BS, 1973; Iowa State Univ, PhD (metall), 1977. **Professional Experience:** DIR, MAT & MECH, PACKER ENG INC, as of 2004; sr sci assoc, Alcoa Tech Co, beginning 1981; asst prof mat sci, Univ Minn, 1977-1981. **Memberships:** Am Soc Metals Int; Am Inst Mining Metall & Petrol Engrs; Sigma Xi; Minerals Metals & Mats Soc. **Research Statement & Publications:** Transport properties of hydrogen in transition metals. **Mailing Address:** Dept Mat & Mech, Packer Eng Inc, 1950 N Wash St, Naperville, IL 60563. **Fax:** 630-505-1986.

JENSEN, CREIGHTON RANDALL, SOIL PHYSICS. **Personal Data:** b Harlan, Iowa, December 27, 1929; div. **Education:** Calif State Polytech Col, BS, 1956; Iowa State Univ, MS, 1959, PhD (agron), 1961. **Professional Experience:** DIR, JENSEN INSTRUMENTS, 1968-; soil physicist, Univ Calif, Riverside, 1962-1967; res asst soil physics, Iowa State Univ, 1956-1961. **Memberships:** Int Soc Soil Sci; Am Soc Agron; Soil Sci Soc Am. **Research Statement & Publications:** Soil aeration. **Mailing Address:** 2021 S Seventh St, Tacoma, WA 98405-3014.

JENSEN, CYNTHIA G, CELL BIOLOGY. **Personal Data:** b Wheeling, WVa, November 7, 1938; m 1960, Lawrence C Winston; c Ellen & Kristen. **Education:** Brown Univ, AB, 1960; Univ Minn, PhD (zool), 1966. **Professional Experience:** ASSOC PROF ANAT, SCH MED, UNIV AUCKLAND, 1988-; Vis scientist, NY State Dept Health, Albany, 1984-1985 & 1993; sr lectr anat, Sch Med, Univ Auckland, 1972-1987; asst prof path, Univ Utah, 1968-1971; Res assoc biol, Univ Ore, 1966-1968. **Memberships:** NZ Soc Electron Micros (vpres, 1983-1985, pres, 1985-1987); Am Soc Cell Biol; Australia & NZ Soc Cell Biol (NZ secy/treas, 1986-, vpres, 1990-); Anat Soc Australia N; AsiaPac Orgn Cell Biol (vpres, 1994-). **Research Statement & Publications:** Ultrastructural studies of cell division; microtubule structure and organization; cells exposed to anti-tumor drugs; neural cytoskeleton; asbestos in living cells. **Mailing Address:** Dept Anat Sch Med, Univ Auckland, Auckland, New Zealand. **Fax:** 649-373-7484. **E-Mail:** c.jensen@auckland.ac.nz

JENSEN, DAVID JAMES, ANALYTICAL CHEMISTRY. **Personal Data:** b Racine, Wis, May 10, 1935; m 1956, c 5. **Education:** Univ Wis-Milwaukee, BS, 1958; Purdue Univ, MS, 1965, PhD (biochem), 1967. **Professional Experience:** RETIRED; assoc prof, Suginaw Valley State Univ, 1994-1995; adj prof, Suginaw Valley State Univ, 1993-1996; sr lab supvr, Dow Chem USA, 1984-1993; res chemist, Dow Chem USA, 1967-1984; instr anal chem, Purdue Univ, 1961-1967; staff chemist, Ind, 1961-1967; instr chem, Univ Wis-Milwaukee, 1957-1961. **Memberships:** Am Chem Soc; Sigma Xi. **Research Statement & Publications:** Studies on pesticide residues; analysis of pesticide formulations and associated analytical methods development; priority pollutants analysis by, product analysis, and industrial quality assurance. **Mailing Address:** 5904 Partridge Lane, Midland, MI 48640-3218.

JENSEN, DONALD RAY, MATHEMATICAL STATISTICS. **Personal Data:** b Nashville, Tenn, April 25, 1932; m 1964, c 4. **Education:** Univ Tenn, BS, 1955; Iowa State Univ, MS, 1957, PhD (statist, soils), 1962. **Professional Experience:** PROF EMER STATIST, VA POLYTECH INST & STATE UNIV, as of 2005; prof statist, VA Polytech Inst & State Univ, beginning 1973; NIH careerdevelop award, 1967-1972; from asst prof to assoc prof, Va Polytech Inst & State Univ, 1965-1973; asst prof statist, Ore State Univ, 1962-1965. **Memberships:** Biomet Soc; Am Statist Asn; Am Inst Math Statist; Soc Indust Appl Math. **Research Statement & Publications:** Probability inequalities; multivariate statistical analysis; multivariate distributions; simultaneous statistical inference; large-sample theory. **Mailing Address:** Dept Statist, Va Polytech Inst & State Univ, 412 Hutcheson Hall, Blacksburg, VA 24061-0439. **Fax:** 540-231-3863. **E-Mail:** djensen@vt.edu

JENSEN, DONALD REED, MAMMALIAN PHYSIOLOGY, HISTOLOGY. **Personal Data:** b Pocatello, Idaho, May 4, 1931; m 1956, Brigitte; c Linda, Donna & David. **Education:** Idaho State Univ, BS, 1953; Univ Wash, BA, 1954; Utah State Univ, MS, 1961, PhD (physiol), 1964. **Professional Experience:** RETIRED; prof physiol, Dept Biol Sci, 1969-1994; asst chmn, Dept Biol Sci, 1968-1978; asst prof, Ill State Univ, 1966-1969; NIH fel, Inst Physiol Chem, Univ Cologne, 1964-1966. **Memberships:** Fel AAAS. **Research Statement & Publications:** Toxic effect of gossypol on physiological processes. **Mailing Address:** 1303 S Linden St, Normal, IL 61761.

JENSEN, DOUGLAS ANDREW, ELEMENTARY PARTICLE PHYSICS. **Personal Data:** b Muskegon, Mich, October 18, 1940; m 1965, c 2. **Education:** Kalamazoo Col, AB, 1963; Univ Chicago, MS, 1965, PhD (physics), 1970. **Professional Experience:** TENURED STAFF, FERMI NAT ACCELERATION LAB, as of 2004; scientist, Fermi Nat Acceleration Lab, beginning 1990; assoc prof physics, Univ Mass, Amherst, 1977-1990; asst prof physics, Joseph Henry Labs, Princeton Univ, 1971-1977; NSF fel, Joseph Henry Labs, Princeton Univ, 1970-1971. **Memberships:** Am Asn Physics Teachers; Am Phys Soc. **Research Statement & Publications:** Elementary particle physics; weak interaction and symmetries; hadron production of strange and charmed particles. **Mailing Address:** Fermi Nat Acceleration Lab, PO Box 500, Batavia, IL 60510. **E-Mail:** djensen@fnal.gov

JENSEN, EDWIN HARRY, forage alfalfa; deceased, see previous edition for last biography

JENSEN, ELWOOD VERNON, ENDOCRINOLOGY. **Personal Data:** b Fargo, NDak, January 13, 1920; m 1983, Hiltrud Herberg; c Karen C & Thomas E. **Education:** Wittenberg Col, AB, 1940; Univ Chicago, PhD (org chem), 1944. **Honorary Degrees:** DSc, Wittenberg Univ, 1963, Acadia Univ, 1976, Med Col Ohio, 1991, MD, UnivHamburg, 1994. **Honors & Awards:** D R Edwards Medal, 1970; La Madonnina Prize, 1973; GHA Clowes Award, 1975; Papanicolaou Award, 1975; Prix Roussel, 1976; Nat Award, Am Cancer Soc, 1976; AmoryPrize, 1977; Gregory Pincus Mem Award, 1978; Gairdner Award, 1979; C F Kettering Prize, 1980; Lucy Wortham James Award, 1980; Nat Acad Clin Biochem Award, 1981; PharmaciaAward, 1982; Rolf Luft Medal, 1983; Hubert Humphrey Award, 1983, Renzo Grattavola Medal, 1984, Fred Conrad Kuch Award, 1984, Axel Munthe Award, 1985, von Humboldt Sr Res Prize, 1992, Joseph Bolivar DeLee Award, 1995. **Professional Experience:** PROF, INST HORMONE & FERTIL RES, UNIV HAMBURG, 1992-; EMERPROF BIOL, UNIV CHICAGO, 1990-; scholar-in-residence, Fogarty Int Ctr, NIH, 1988 & MedCol, Cornell Univ, 1990-1991; res dir, Ludwig Inst Cancer Res, Zurich, Switz, 1983-1987; profbiochem & Chas B Huggins distinguished serv prof biol sci, Univ Chicago, 1980-1990; profphysiol, Univ Chicago, 1977-1982; prof biophys, Univ Chicago, 1973-1982; dir, Lab, UnivChicago, 1969-1982; vis prof, Max Planck Inst, Munich, Ger, 1958 & Kyoto Univ, 1965; AmCancer Soc-Charles Hayden Found res prof, Dept Physiol & Ben May Lab Cancer Res, 1963-1969; USPHS spec fel, 1958; from asst prof to prof, Ben May Lab Cancer Res, 1951-1963; from asst prof to assoc prof, Dept Biochem, 1951-1960; asst prof, Dept Surg, Univ Chicago, 1947-1951; Guggenheim fel, Swiss Fed Inst Technol, 1946-1947. **Memberships:** Nat Acad Sci; Am Acad Arts & Sci; Am Chem Soc; Am Soc Biol Chemists; Endocrine Soc (pres, 1980-1981); Am Asn Cancer Res; AAAS. **Research Statement & Publications:** Steroid hormone receptors; breast cancer; proteins; organophosphorus chemistry; antihormone action. **Mailing Address:** Inst Hormone & Fertil Res, Grandweg 64, 22529 Hamburg, Ger. **Fax:** 494-256-190864.

JENSEN, EMRON ALFRED, PARASITOLOGY, PROTOZOOLOGY. **Personal Data:** b Richfield, Utah, January 5, 1925; m 1949, c 8. **Education:** Utah State Univ, BS, 1950, MS, 1961, PhD (zoology), 1963. **Professional Experience:** PROF EMER ZOOL, WEBER STATE COL, as of 2003; chmn dept, Weber State Col, 1970-1983; from asst prof to prof, Weber State Col, 1963-1983; lab instr zool, Utah State Univ, 1959-1963; teacher elem sch, Utah, 1954-1959; technician, Am Cyanamid Co, 1952-1953; teacher high sch, Idaho, 1950-1952. **Research Statement & Publications:** Parasite protozoa, particularly trichomonads. **Mailing Address:** 897 E 1700 N, Ogden, UT 84414-3117.

JENSEN, ERIK HUGO, PHARMACEUTICAL QUALITY CONTROL. **Personal Data:** b Fredericia, Denmark, June 27, 1924; American citizen; m 1949, Alice Olesen; c Jan, Lisa & Linda. **Education:** Royal Danish Sch Pharm, BSc, 1945, MS, 1948, PhD, 1954. **Honors & Awards:** W E Upjohn Award, 1962. **Professional Experience:** PRES, JENSEN ENTERPRISES, 1986-; exec dir control develop & admin, Upjohn Co, 1985-1986; dir, Upjohn Co, 1981-1985; asst dir qual control, Upjohn Co, 1966-1981; mgr, Upjohn Co, 1963-1966; sect head qual control, Upjohn Co, 1962-1963; resassoc pharm, Upjohn Co, 1957-1962; head pharmaceut res & develop dept, Ferrosan Inc, Malmo, Sweden, 1956-1957; Res assoc, Upjohn Co, 1950-1956. **Memberships:** Am Chem Soc; Am Asn Pharmaceut Scientists. **Research Statement & Publications:** Controlled release of pharmaceuticals; stability of pharmaceuticals; assays of pharmaceuticals; analytical applications of sodium borohydride; analytical chemistry; quality control procedures. **Mailing Address:** 2125 Crosswind, Kalamazoo, MI 49008-1734.

JENSEN, FARRELL E, MANAGEMENT SCIENCE. **Personal Data:** b April 9, 1965. **Education:** Utah State Univ, BS, 1964; Kans State Univ, MS, 1966, PhD (econs), 1972. **Professional Experience:** SR RES ASSOC/RES COORD, BRINGHAM YOUNG UNIV, as of 2005. **Mailing Address:** Bringham Young Univ, 130 FOB, Provo, UT 84602. **Fax:** 801-422-0194. **E-Mail:** farrell_jensen@byu.edu

JENSEN, GARY RICHARD, DIFFERENTIAL GEOMETRY. **Personal Data:** b Miles City, Mont, March 19, 1941; m 1965, Jen; c Ragna A, Niels G & Leah. **Education:** Mass Inst Technol, BS, 1963; Univ Calif, Berkeley, PhD (math), 1968. **Professional Experience:** Vis prof, Math Res Inst, Berkeley, 1993; chmn dept, Wash Univ, StLouis, 1990-1995; PROF MATH, WASH UNIV, ST LOUIS, 1983-; vis assoc profmath, Univ Calif, Berkeley, 1976-1977 & Univ Nancy, France, 1982-1983; from asst prof to assocprof, Wash Univ, St Louis, 1970-1982; fel, Wash Univ, St Louis, 1969-1970; Asstprof math, Carnegie-Mellon Univ, 1968-1969. **Memberships:** Am Math Soc. **Research Statement & Publications:** Differential geometry, especially of submanifolds of homogeneous spaces. **Mailing Address:** Dept Math, Wash Univ, PO Box 1146, One Brookings Dr, St Louis, MO 63130. **E-Mail:** gary@math.wustl.edu

JENSEN, GORDON D, PEDIATRICS, PSYCHIATRY. **Personal Data:** b Seattle, Wash, January 28, 1926; m 1957, c 3. **Education:** Yale Univ, MD, 1949. **Professional Experience:** PROF EMER PSYCHIAT & PEDIAT, SCH MED, UNIV CALIF, DAVIS, as of 2001; prof psychiat & pediat, Sch Med, Univ Calif, Davis, beginning 1969; srconsult child psychiat, Sacramento Med Ctr, 1969-1974; mem core staff, Regional Primate ResCtr, Univ Wash, 1967-1969; from asst prof to assoc prof, 1965-1969; asst psychiat, 1962-1965; res asst prof psychiat, 1961-1962; asst prof pediat, Sch Med, Univ Wash, 1957-1960. **Memberships:** Soc Biol Psychiat; Animal Behav Soc; Am Acad Pediat; Am Col Psychiat; PsychiatRes Soc. **Research Statement & Publications:** Primate behavior; sexuality; aging. **Mailing Address:** 221 Monterey Ave, Capitola, CA 95010-3357. **E-Mail:** gdjensen@ucdavis.edu

JENSEN, GORDON L, CLINICAL NUTRITION, INTERNAL MEDICINE. **Personal Data:** b Columbia, Mo, May 29, 1953. **Education:** Pa State Univ, BS, 1975; Univ NH, MS, 1977; Cornell Univ, MD, 1984, PhD (nutrit& biochem), 1981. **Professional Experience:** ASSOC PROF MED, DIV GASTROENTEROL, VANDERBILT MED CTR, as of 2003; DIR, CTR HUMAN NUTRIT, VANDERBILT MED CTR, as of 2003; adj assoc prof nutrit, Pa State Univ, beginning 1990; res assoc critical caremed, Dept Gastroenterol & Nutrit, beginning 1990; clin asst prof med, Jefferson Med Col, beginning 1989; dir, Sect Nutrit Support, Geisinger Med Ctr, beginning 1988; assoc, Dept Gastroenterol & Nutrit, beginning 1988. **Memberships:** Am Soc Clin Nutrit; Am Inst Nutrit; Am Soc Parenteral & Internal Nutrit; Am ColPhysicians; Am Geriat Soc; AMA. **Mailing Address:** Med Ctr, Vanderbilt Univ, C-2104 MCN, Nashville, TN 37232-2279. **Fax:** 615-343-1587. **E-Mail:** gordon.jensen@vanderbilt.edu

JENSEN, HANNE MARGRETE, PRECANCER. **Personal Data:** b Copenhagen, Denmark, December 9, 1935; div. **Education:** Univ Wash, MD, 1961; Am Bd Path, cert anatomic & clin path, 1968, cert blood banking, 1979. **Professional Experience:** MED DIR, DEPT PATH, SCH MED, UNIV CALIF, DAVIS, as of 2004; PROF PATH, DEPT PATH, SCH MED, UNIV CALIF, DAVIS, 1979-; prin investr, Contract Breast Cancer Task Force, 1978-1981; mem Treatment Comt, Breast Cancer Task Force, Nat Cancer Inst, 1977-1981; asst prof, Dept Path, Sch Med, Univ Calif, Davis, 1969-1979; fel exp path, Dept Path, Sch Med, Univ Wash, 1965-1967. **Memberships:** AAAS; Am Asn Blood Banks; Am Soc Clin Pathologists; Int Acad Path. **Research Statement & Publications:** Assessment of precancer of breast parenchyma, using assays for angiogenesis factor; assays of breast fluids for angiogenesis factor; prediction of high cancer risk; morphologic studies of precancer of the prostate gland. **Mailing Address:** Dept Path Sch Med, Univ Calif, 3440 Tupper Hall, Davis, CA 95616. **Fax:** 530-752-4548. **E-Mail:** hmjensen@ucdavis.edu

JENSEN, HARBO PETER, POLYMER CHEMISTRY. **Personal Data:** b Boston, Mass, March 27, 1948; m 1982, Tyna; c Sarah Elizabeth. **Education:** Northeastern Univ, BA, 1971; Mass Inst Technol, PhD (org chem), 1974. **Professional Experience:** VPRES INT TECH SERVS, CHEVRON CORP, 1994-; mgr, Chevron Inst Oil Co, Calif, 1990-1993; pres & chmn, Cal Bionics, 1981-; foreign staff adv, Chevron USA, 1981-1990; govt affairs coordr, Chevron USA, 1980-1981; proj supvr, Huntington Beach Co, 1978-1980; pres, Timoc, 1975-1980; Chevron Res Co, Standard Oil Co Calif, 1974-1978; Polaroid Corp, 1967-1970. **Memberships:** AAAS; Am Chem Soc; Sigma Xi; Contact Lens Mfrs Asn. **Research Statement & Publications:** Petroleum science and synthetic fuels; polymer science, especially hydrophilic polymers for soft contact lenses. **Mailing Address:** Chevron Corp, 6001 Bollinger Canyon Rd, San Ramon, CA 94583.

JENSEN, HAROLD JAMES, NEMATOLOGY. **Personal Data:** b Sunnyside, Wash, September 16, 1921; m 1946, c 3. **Education:** Univ Calif, BS, 1947, PhD (nematol), 1950. **Professional Experience:** RETIRED; consult, Hawaiian Sugar Planters Asn, 1958; from asst prof to prof bot & nematologist, Ore State Univ; from asst nematologist to nematologist, Ore State Univ, 1951-1984; instr & asst, Ore State Univ, 1950-1951. **Memberships:** Am Phytopath Soc; Soc Nematol (vpres, 1970-1971, pres, 1971-1972). **Research Statement & Publications:** Identification, symptomatology and pathology of plant diseases caused by nematodes; nematological control techniques, taxonomy, and teaching; relationships of nematodes with other plant pathogens. **Mailing Address:** 23619 Harris Rd, Philomath, OR 97370.

JENSEN, JAMES LE ROY, nutrition; deceased, see previous edition for last biography

JENSEN, JAMES N, ENVIRONMENTAL ENGINEERING. **Education:** Calif Inst Technol, BS, 1980; Univ NC, Chapel Hill, MSPH, 1983, PhD, 1988. **Professional Experience:** ASSOC PROF, DEPT CIVIL, STRUCT & ENVIRON ENG, STATE UNIV NEW YORK, as of 2006. **Mailing Address:** Dept Civil Eng, SUNY, Buffalo, NY 14260. **E-Mail:** jjensen@acsu.buffalo.edu

JENSEN, JOHN HENRY, CHEMICAL ENGINEERING. **Personal Data:** b Aurora, Ill, June 17, 1916; m 1948, Isabel. **Education:** SDak Sch Mines & Tech, BS, 1939; Iowa State Univ, MS, 1942, PhD (chem eng), 1948. **Professional Experience:** RETIRED; sr chem engr, Tenn Eastman Co, 1948-1981; instr, Iowa State Univ, 1940-1948. **Memberships:** Instrument Soc Am. **Research Statement & Publications:** Production of acetic anhydride; application of a digital computer to a chemical manufacturing process; process control by analog instruments or by digital computer; analog computing; interactive computer graphics system. **Mailing Address:** 4560 Old Stage Rd, Kingsport, TN 37664.

JENSEN, JOHN R, REMOTE SENSING. **Education:** Calif State Univ, BA, 1971; Brigham Young Univ, MA, 1972; Univ Calif, Los Angeles, PhD, 1976. **Professional Experience:** DISTINGUISHED PROF, DEPT GEOG, UNIV SC, COLUMBIA, as of 2006. **Mailing Address:** Dept Geog Rm 327, Univ SC Callcott, Columbia, SC 29208. **Fax:** 803-777-4972. **E-Mail:** jrjensen@sc.edu

JENSEN, KEITH FRANK, FORESTRY. **Personal Data:** b Fontanelle, Iowa, April 9, 1938; m 1960, c 3. **Education:** Iowa State Univ, BS, 1960, PhD (plant physio physiol, silvicult), 1963. **Professional Experience:** ASST DIR, FOREST SERV, USDA, 1992-; res fel, Univ Wis, 1973-1974; plant physiologist, Dis Div, US Forest Serv, 1963-1992. **Memberships:** Bot Soc Am; Air Pollution Control Asn; Sigma Xi. **Research Statement & Publications:** Effect of air pollution and environmental stresses on growth and development of forest trees. **Mailing Address:** USDA Forest Serv, 5 Radnor Corp Ctr Ste 200, Radnor, PA 19087-4585. **E-Mail:** kfjen@aol.com

JENSEN, KEVIN B, GENETICS. **Education:** Tex A & M Univ, PhD. **Professional Experience:** RES GENETICIST, FORAGE & RANGE RES LAB, UTAH STATE UNIV, as of 2006. **Mailing Address:** Forage & Range Res Lab, Utah State Univ, Logan, UT 84322-6300. **Fax:** 435-797-3075. **E-Mail:** kevin@cc.usu.edu

JENSEN, KLAVS FLEMMING, SYNTHESIS & PROCESSING OF ADVANCED INORGANIC MATERIALS MATHEMATICAL MODELLING OF MATERIALS PROCESSING SYSTEMS. **Personal Data:** b Cambridge, Eng, August 5, 1952; American citizen. **Education:** Tech Univ Denmark, MSc, 1976; Univ Wis-Madison, PhD (chem eng), 1980. **Honors & Awards:** Presidential Young Investers Award, NSF, 1984; Allan P Colburn Award, AmInst Chem Engrs, 1987, CMA Stine Award. **Professional Experience:** LAMMOT DU PONT PROF CHEM ENG & PROF MAT SCI & ENG, MASS INST TECHNOL, as of 2004; prof chem eng & mat sci, Mass Inst Technol, beginning 1989; John Simon Guggenheim fel, 1987; fel, Minn Supercomput Inst, 1986-1989; from asst prof to prof chem eng, Univ Minn, Twin Cities, 1980-1989. **Memberships:** Am Inst Chem Engr; Am Chem Soc; Mat Res Soc; Electrochem Soc; AAAS. **Research Statement & Publications:** Processing and characterization of advanced inorganic materials, including chemical vapor deposition of semiconductors and metals, laser assisted processing and fabrication of inorganic composites; synthesis and characterization, as well as mathematical models. **Mailing Address:** Mass Inst Technol, Dept Mat Sci & Eng, Rm 66-566 77 Mass Ave, Cambridge, MA 02139. **E-Mail:** kfjensen@mit.edu

JENSEN, LEO STANLEY, ANIMAL NUTRITION. **Personal Data:** b Bellingham, Wash, February 28, 1925; m 1954, Sylvia; c Peter, Eric, Carol & Kristin. **Education:** Wash State Univ, BS, 1949; Cornell Univ, PhD (animal nutrit), 1954. **Honors & Awards:** AFMA Award, Poultry Sci Asn, 1966; Merck Award, Poultry Sci Asn, 1979. **Professional Experience:** D W BROOKS DISTINGUISHED PROF EMER, UNIV GA, 1991-; D W Brooks distinguished prof, Univ GA, 1984-1991; prof poultry sci, Univ GA, 1973-1984; chmn grad prog nutrit, Wash State Univ, 1970-1973; Oak Ridge Inst Nuclear Studies res partic, AEC, Univ Tenn, 1964-1965; from asst prof to prof poultry sci, Wash State Univ, 1954-1973; jr poultry scientist, Wash State Univ, 1949-1951. **Memberships:** Poultry Sci Asn; Am Inst Nutrit; Soc Exp Biol & Med. **Research Statement & Publications:** Vitamins, minerals, fatty acids and unidentified factors in poultry nutrition; nutritional factors affecting abdominal fat accumulation; amino acid requirements and interactions. **Mailing Address:** Dept Poultry Sci, Univ Ga, Athens, GA 30602. **Fax:** 706-542-1827.

JENSEN, LYLE HOWARD, BIOPHYSICAL CHEMISTRY. **Personal Data:** b East Stanwood, Wash, November 24, 1915; m 1940, c 3. **Education:** Walla Walla Col, BA, 1939; Univ Wash, PhD (phys chem), 1943. **Professional Experience:** PROF EMERITUS BIOL STRUCT & BIOCHEM, UNIV WASH, as of 2005; prof anat, Univ Wash, beginning 1961; from instr to assoc prof anat, Univ Wash, 1949-1961; Anderson fel x-ray diffraction, Univ Wash, 1948-1949; actg asst prof, Univ Wash, 1947-1948; res assoc, Ohio State Univ, 1946-1947; assoc prof chem, Emmanuel Missionary Col, 1944-1946; res assoc, Univ Chicago, 1943-1944. **Memberships:** AAAS; Am Chem Soc; Am Crystallog Asn; Am Asn Anat; Sigma Xi. **Research Statement & Publications:** Chemistry of heavy metals; low temperature thermodynamics of gases; molecular structure; x-ray diffraction studies of biologically important molecules. **Mailing Address:** Dept Biol Struct & Biochem, Univ Wash, SM-20, Seattle, WA 98195-0001. **Fax:** 206-543-1524.

JENSEN, MARCUS MARTIN, MEDICAL MICROBIOLOGY. **Personal Data:** b Mantua, Utah, May 26, 1929; m 1990, Mary Davis; c Joni, Mark & Bruce. **Education:** Utah State Univ, BS, 1952, MS, 1954; Univ Calif, Los Angeles, PhD (med microbiol), 1961. **Honorary Degrees:** Dr, Utah State Univ, 1991. **Honors & Awards:** George N Raines Award, Am Psychiat Asn, 1962. **Professional Experience:** EMER PROF MICROBIOL, BRIGHAM YOUNG UNIV, 1994-; pres, Robbins Aseptic Air Systs Inc, Calif, 1968-1969 & Jensen Res Labs, Utah, 1969-; from assoc prof to prof, Brigham Young Univ, 1969-1994; Assoc mem, Brain Res Inst, Med Sch, Univ Calif, Los Angeles, 1968-1969; asst prof med microbiol, Sch Med, Univ Calif, Los Angeles, 1963-1969; Res virologist, Res Serv, Vet Admin Ctr, 1961-1963. **Memberships:** Am Soc Microbiol; Am Asn Avian Pathologists. **Research Statement & Publications:** Natural resistance to infectious diseases, influence of emotional stress on suscepsusceptibility to viral infections; role of viruses in kidney diseases; methods of controlling the airborne spread of microorganisms in hospitals; development of vaccines for turkey diseases. **Mailing Address:** Dept Microbiol, Brigham Young Univ, Provo, UT 84604.

JENSEN, MARVIN E(LI), AGRICULTURAL ENGINEERING HYDROLOGY. **Personal Data:** b Clay Co, Minn, December 23, 1926; m 1947, Doris; c Connie, Jeffrey & Eric. **Education:** N Dak State Univ, BS, 1951, MS, 1952; Colo State Univ, PhD, 1965. **Honorary Degrees:** DSc, NDak State Univ, 1988. **Honors & Awards:** Huber Res Prize, Am Soc Civil Engrs, 1968; Hancor Soil & Water Eng Award, Am Soc Agr Engrs, 1974; R J Tipton Award, 1982; John Deere Medal Award, 1982; Arid Lands Hydraul Eng Award, Am Soc Civil Engrs, 1990. **Professional Experience:** RETIRED; consult, as of 1997; dir, Colo Inst Irrig Mgt, Colo State Univ, 1987-1992; pres, Int Comn Irrig & Drainage, 1984-1987; nat prog leader, Water Mgt, 1979-1987; dir, Snake River Conserv Res Ctr, Sci & Educ Admin, 1969-1979; invests leader water mgt, Northwest Br, 1961-1969; invests leader irrig, drainage & water storage facil, 1959-1961; agr eng, Agr Res Serv, USDA, 1955-1959; asst prof agr eng & asst agr engr, NDak State Univ, 1954-1955; instr & asst agr engr, N Dak State Univ, 1952-1954; asst, N Dak State Univ, 1951-1952. **Memberships:** Nat Acad Eng; Am Soc Civil Engrs; Am Soc Agron; Am Soc Agr Engrs (vpres, 1983-1986). **Research Statement & Publications:** Irrigation engineering research; crop water requirement and irrigation scheduling; irrigation management. **Mailing Address:** 1207 Springwood Dr, Ft Collins, CO 80525.

JENSEN, NORMAN P, MEDICINAL CHEMISTRY. **Personal Data:** b Pontiac, Mich, December 12, 1938; m 1965, Sara; c Marshall, Mitchell & Christine. **Education:** Univ Mich, BS, 1961; Mass Inst Technol, PhD (org chem), 1965. **Professional Experience:** Vpres chem, Jacobus Pharmaceut, 1996-2002; EXEC COMT, ORGANIC DIV, AM CHEM SOC, 1995-; asst vpres, Wyeth-Ayerst, 1983-1995; dir, Merck & Co, 1966-1983; NIH fel org chem, Stanford Univ, 1965-1966; res chemist, Socony Mobil, 1961. **Memberships:** Am Chem Soc (exec comt, organic div, 1996-1999); AAAS; Inflamation Res Asn. **Research Statement & Publications:** Search for new drugs in the fields of cardiovascular, anti-inflammatory, antimalarials metabolic and central nervous system diseases. **Mailing Address:** 54 Lochinvar Rd, San Rafael, NJ 94901.

JENSEN, OLIVIA G, GEOPHYSICS. **Personal Data:** b Alberta, Canada, January 22, 1943; div, c Anders & Annelise. **Education:** Univ BC, BSc, 1964, MSc, 1966, PhD (geophys), 1971. **Professional Experience:** PROF GEOPHYS, DEPT EARTH & PLANETARY SCI, MCGILL UNIV, 1986-; assoc prof geophys, Dept Geol Sci, McGill Univ, 1984-1986; asst & assoc prof appl geophys, Dept Mining & Metall Eng, McGill Univ, 1973-1984. **Mailing Address:** Dept Earth & Planetary Sci McGill Univ, 3450 Univ St, Montreal, PQ H3A 2A7, Can. **Fax:** 514-398-4680. **E-Mail:** olivia@transsexy.geophys.mcgill.ca

JENSEN, PAUL ALLEN, OPERATIONS RESEARCH, ELECTRICAL ENGINEERING. **Personal Data:** b Chicago, Ill, August 27, 1936; m 1963, c 4. **Education:** Univ Ill, BS, 1959; Univ Pittsburgh, MS, 1963; Johns Hopkins Univ, PhD (opers res), 1967. **Professional Experience:** PROF MECH ENG, UNIV TEX, AUSTIN, as of 2006; from asst prof to assocprof, Univ Tex, Austin, 1967-1973; Engr, Surface Div, Westinghouse Elec Corp, 1959-1963. **Memberships:** Opers Res Soc Am; Inst Mgt Sci; Inst Indust Eng. **Research**

Statement & Publications: Mathematical optimization theory and application; network flow techniques used for optimization; reliability engineering; transportation systems; water resources. **Mailing Address:** Dept Mech Eng, Univ Tex, I Univ Sta C2200, Austin, TX 78712-0292. **Fax:** 512-232-1494. **E-Mail:** pjensen@mail.utexas.edu

JENSEN, PAUL EDWARD T, SYSTEMS ANALYSIS, OPERATIONS RESEARCH. **Personal Data:** b New Orleans, La, April 27, 1926; m 1953, c 3. **Education:** Tulane Univ, BS, 1947, BBA, 1949; Golden Gate Univ, MBA, 1976. **Professional Experience:** PROF & DEAN, DEPT BUS ADMIN & MGT, SCH BUS & INFO TECHNOL, NORTHWESTERN POLYTECH UNIV, as of 2006; lectr, Northwestern Polytech Univ, Fremont, beginning 1988; SR STAFF ENG SYSTEM, ESL INC, 1982-; at, GTE ProdCorp, 1980-1982; lectr, Cogswell Col, San Francisco, 1979-; at, Stanford Univ, 1977-1979; sr eng specialist, Electronic Defense Labs, GTE Prod Corp, 1976-1982; consult, Asn Continuing Educ, Stanford, Calif, 1974-1982; eng specialist, ElectronicDefense Labs, GTE Prod Corp, 1964-1976; mgr tech pub, Electronic Defense Labs, GTE ProdCorp, 1963-1964; supvr tech pub, Electronic Defense Labs, GTE Prod Corp, 1960-1963; developengr, Electronic Defense Labs, GTE Prod Corp, 1959-1960; sr engr, Electronic Defense Labs, GTE Prod Corp, 1955-1959; asst mgr, Atlantic Gulf Sugar Co, Cuba, 1952-1955. **Memberships:** Am Phys Soc; Inst Elec & Electronics Engrs; assoc fel Soc Tech Comm. **Research Statement & Publications:** Systems analysis of tactical and strategic communications and electronics systems; electronic warfare vulnerability analysis. **Mailing Address:** Dept Bus Admin & Mgt, Sch Bus & Info Technol, Northwestern Polytech Univ, 117 Fourier Ave, Fremont, CA 94539. **Fax:** 510-657-8975. **E-Mail:** jpauljensen@cs.com

JENSEN, PETER S, CHILD PSYCHIATRY. **Personal Data:** b Logan, Utah, November 14, 1949; m 1973, Susie. **Education:** Brigham Young Univ, BS, 1974; George Wash Univ, MD, 1978. **Honors & Awards:** Joyce Res Award, 1982; Reiger McGavin Award, Am Psychiat Asn, 1996; Agnes Purcell. **Professional Experience:** RUANE PROF PSYCHIAT, COLUMBIA UNIV, 2000-; DIR, CTR ADVAN C MENTAL HEALTH, 2000-; assoc dir c res, child adolescent dis res br, div clin & treat res, NIMH, NIH, 1997-1999; chief, child adolescent dis res br, div clin & treat res, NIMH, NIH, 1989-1997; res psychiatrist, Med Ctr, WalterReed Army inst res, 1988-1989; chair, Task Force PrevSubstance Abuse, 1987-1988; dir fel training, Eisenhower Army Med Ctr, 1986-1988; chief, Child Adolescent & Family Psychiat Serv, Eisenhower Army Med Ctr, 1985-1988; asst chief, ChildAdolescent & Family Psychiat Serv, Eisenhower Army Med Ctr, 1983-1986; mem, Coun res, Am Psychiat Asn. **Memberships:** Am Pediat Asn; Am Acad Child & Adolescent Psychiat (secy); Soc Biol Psychiat; Int Soc Res Child & Adolescent Psychopath; Sigma Xi; AAAS. **Research Statement & Publications:** Child and adolescent clinical trials for psychiatric disorders; attention deficit hyperativity disorder; psychiatric epidemiology; diagnosis and classification. **Mailing Address:** Ctr Advan C Mental Health, 1051 Riverside Dr, New York, NY 10032. **Fax:** 212-543-5260. **E-Mail:** pj131@columbia.edu

JENSEN, REED JERRY, PHYSICAL CHEMISTRY. **Personal Data:** b December 16, 1936; m 1960, Nancy; c Grace, Julie, Ellen, Stuart, Grant & Ann. **Education:** Brigham Young Univ, BA, 1960, PhD (phys chem), 1965. **Professional Experience:** PRES, RENEWABLE ENERGY CORP, as of 2000; DIR, SOLAR ENERGY LTD, as of 2000; mem staff, Los Alamos Nat Lab, beginning 1993; dep assoc dir, Chem & Mat, 1989-1993; alt div leader laser chem, Los Alamos Nat Lab, 1976-1989; group leader chem lasers, Los Alamos Nat Lab, 1972-1976; staff mem phys chem, Los Alamos Nat Lab, 1969-1972; asst prof, Brigham Young Univ, 1967-1969; staff mem, Los Alamos Sci Lab, 1966-1967; fel physchem, Univ Calif, Berkeley, 1965-1966. **Memberships:** Am Chem Soc. **Research Statement & Publications:** Research in lasers and applications to chemistry; chemical separations with lasers and modern methods; chemical process development for nuclear systems and transmutation processes. **Mailing Address:** Solar Energy Ltd, 112C Longview Dr, Los Alamos, NM 87544-3728. **Fax:** 505-672-0209.

JENSEN, RICHARD A, MATHEMATICS. **Education:** Princeton Univ, BA; Univ Wisc, Madison, MA, PhD. **Professional Experience:** FAC, DEPT MATH & COMPUT SCI, NORMANDALE COMMUNITY COL, as of 2006. **Mailing Address:** Dept Math & Comput Sci, Normandale Community Col, 9700 France Ave S, Bloomington, MN 55431. **Fax:** 952-487-8265. **E-Mail:** richard.jensen@normandale.edu

JENSEN, RICHARD ALAN, MACHINE DESIGN, MATERIALS TESTING. **Personal Data:** m 1971, Betty; c David J, Sandra R, Andrew M & Penelope J. **Education:** Cooper Union, BE, 1966; Columbia Univ, MS, 1967, Eng, 1975; St Johns Univ, MBA, 1983. **Professional Experience:** PROF MECH ENG, HOFSTRA UNIV, as of 2004; ASSOC PROF ENG, HOFSTRA UNIV, 1989-; prin engr, Burns & Roe, 1979-1989; Mech engr, Burns & Roe, 1973-1979. **Memberships:** Am Soc Mech Engrs; Am Phys Soc; AAAS; Am Vacuum Soc; NY Acad Sci; Sigma Xi. **Research Statement & Publications:** Nondestructive testing of polyethylene gas piping and in the end use of natural gas. **Mailing Address:** Dept Mech Eng, Hofstra Univ, 0201C Weed Hall, Hempstead, NY 11549-1000. **Fax:** 516-463-4939. **E-Mail:** richard.a.jensen@hofstra.edu

JENSEN, RICHARD ARTHUR, PHARMACOLOGY. **Personal Data:** b Ogden, Utah, October 24, 1936. **Education:** Univ Ore, BS, 1960; Univ Wash, MS, 1963, PhD (pharmacol), 1966. **Professional Experience:** DIR CARDIOVASC PHARMACOL PROG, STANFORD RES INST, 1978-; sr pharmacologist, Stanford Res Inst, 1974-1978; asst prof pharmacol, Univ Calif, San Francisco, 1969-1974; fel, Univ Calif, San Francisco, 1966-1968. **Memberships:** Am Soc Pharmacol & Exp Therapeut. **Research Statement & Publications:** Evaluation of the effects of drugs and other chemicals on cardiac electrical and mechanical activity; antiarrhythmic drug action, the electrophysiological action of drugs that induce cardiac arrhythmias; drug induced cardiac muscle dis; hemodynamic studies in conscious dogs using biotelemetry. **Mailing Address:** Stanford Res Inst, Menlo Park, CA 94025.

JENSEN, RICHARD DONALD, VETERINARY PATHOLOGY. **Personal Data:** b Hartington, Nebr, October 6, 1936; m 1957, c 4. **Education:** Iowa State Univ, DVM, 1964; Univ Minn, St Paul, PhD (vet path), 1970. **Professional Experience:** DIR TOXICOL & PATH, MERCK INST THERAPEUT RES, MERCK & CO INC, 1977-; res fel path, Merck & Co Inc, 1970-1976. **Memberships:** Am Col Vet Path; Int Acad Path; Am Vet Med Asn. **Research Statement & Publications:** Avian mycoplasma infection; toxicologic and pathologic evaluation of potential therapeutic agents. **Mailing Address:** 463 Ferry Rd, Doylestown, PA 18901.

JENSEN, RICHARD ERLING, ANALYTICAL CHEMISTRY, TOXICOLOGY. **Personal Data:** b Des Moines, Iowa, April 3, 1938; m 1960, c 2. **Education:** Iowa State Univ, BS, 1960; Univ Iowa, MS, 1964, PhD (anal chem), 1965. **Professional Experience:** DIR ALCOHOL TOXICOL, MEDTOX LABS, as of 2004; PRES & DIR, FORENSIC ASSOCS, 1984-; asst dir, Alcohol Sect, Forensic Sci Lab, State Minn, 1980-1984; supvr, Alcohol Sect, Forensic Sci Lab, State Minn, 1979-1980; from asst prof to assoc prof, Gustavus dolphus Col, 1966-1979; asst prof anal chem, Mankato State Col, 1965-1966. **Memberships:** Am Chem Soc; Am Acad Sci; Sigma Xi. **Research Statement & Publications:** Alcohol and drug analysis for evidential purposes; trace analysis of metals using spectrophotometry, fluorescence and atomic absorption. **Mailing Address:** Forensic Assocs, 4690 Ids Ctr 80 S Eighth St, Minneapolis, MN 55402-2207. **Fax:** 612-349-677.

JENSEN, RICHARD EUGENE, physics; deceased, see previous edition for last biography

JENSEN, RICHARD GRANT, BIOCHEMISTRY, METABOLISM IN PLANTS. **Personal Data:** b Los Angeles, Calif, April 16, 1936; m 1961, Annette; c Karl, Jennifer, Byron & Bruce. **Education:** Brigham Young Univ, BA, 1961, PhD (biochem), 1965. **Professional Experience:** PROF EMER, DEPT BIOCHEM & PLANT SCI, UNIV ARIZ, as of 2004; prog dir, Photosynthesis Prog, Competitive Res Grants Off, Sci & Educ Admin, USDA, 1981; prof biochem & plant sci, Univ Ariz, 1979-1997; assoc prof plant sci, Univ Ariz, 1976-1979; consult, Agr Div, Monsanto Co, 1976; vis prof, Bot Inst, Univ Bern, Switz, 1975; vis prof, Chem Inst Tech Univ Munich, Freising-Weihens Tephan, W Ger, 1974-1975; from asst prof to assoc prof biochem, Univ Ariz, 1967-1979; NIH fel, Lawrence Radiation Lab, Univ Calif, 1965-1967; Chas F Kettering res fel biochem, Chas F Kettering Res Lab, Ohio, 1963-1965. **Memberships:** Am Soc Biol Chemists; Am Soc Plant Physiol; fel AAAS. **Research Statement & Publications:** Cell biology and metabolism; photosynthesis; metabolic regulation in plant cells; carbon dioxide fixation; metabolism of plants during salt and water stress, plant cyclitols and polyols. **Mailing Address:** Dept Biochem & Molecular Biophys, Univ Ariz, 1041 E Lowell St BioScis W 531, Tucson, AZ 85721-0088. **Fax:** 520-621-9288. **E-Mail:** Jensenr@u.arizona.edu

JENSEN, RICHARD HARVEY, ANATOMY, IMMUNOLOGY. **Personal Data:** b Estherville, Iowa, June 14, 1941; m, c 2. **Education:** Univ Northern Iowa, BA, 1963; Univ Iowa, MA, 1969, PhD (anat), 1973. **Professional Experience:** DIR, DEPT PHYS THER, MARQUETTE UNIV, as of 2005; MEM STAFF PROG PHYS THER, MARQUETTE UNIV, 1977-; asst prof gross anat, Univ Nebr Med Ctr, Omaha, 1973-1977; grant seed res, Univ Nebr Med Ctr, Omaha, 1973-1975; consult design & orgn gross anat prog phys ther, Fla Int Univ, 1973; vis instr gross anat, Univ Miami, 1972; from teaching asst to instr gross anat, Univ Iowa, 1969-1973; clin phys therapist, Univ Iowa, 1967-1968; instr math & sci, Charles City High Sch, Iowa, 1963-1966. **Memberships:** Am Phys Ther Asn; Am Asn Anatomists; Am Col Sports Med. **Research Statement & Publications:** Hematology, especially stimulation of bone marrow; biomechanics, with emphasis on kinetic and kinematic analysis of extremities. **Mailing Address:** Dept Phys Ther, Marquette Univ, Walter Schroeder Complex, Milwaukee, WI 53233.

JENSEN, RICHARD JORG, SYSTEMATIC BOTANY. **Personal Data:** b Erie Co, Ohio, January 17, 1947; m 1970. **Education:** Austin Peay State Univ, BS, 1970, MS, 1972; Miami Univ, PhD (bot), 1975. **Professional Experience:** Lilly Found grant, 1990; dir, Greene-Nieuwland Herbarium, 1989-; sr res fel, Austin Peay State Univ Ctr Field Biol, 1986-1987; elected fel, Ind Acad Sci, 1986; res corp grant, 1984; guest assoc prof biol, Univ Notre Dame, beginning 1981-; PROF BIOL, ST MARYS COL, 1979-; asst prof biol, Wright State Univ, 1975-1979; Sigma Xi grant aid res, 1974; res grant, NSF, 1973, 1978, 1984 & 1987. **Memberships:** Torrey Bot Club; Int Asn Plant Taxon; Bot Soc Am; Sigma Xi; Am Soc Plant Taxonomists (pres, 2005-2006); Soc Syst Zoology. **Research Statement & Publications:** Systematic and taxonomic studies of Quercus, the oaks, emphasizing numerical taxonomic and morphometric approaches. **Mailing Address:** Dept Biol, St Marys Col, Notre Dame, IN 46556. **Fax:** 574-284-4875. **E-Mail:** rjensen@saintmarys.edu

JENSEN, ROBERT ALAN, NEUROBIOLOGY, PSYCHOBIOLOGY. **Personal Data:** b Bainbridge, NY, September 25, 1940; m 1985, Melissa. **Education:** Col Wooster, Ohio, BA, 1965; Kent State Univ, MA, 1970; Northern Ill Univ, PhD (biopsychol), 1976. **Professional Experience:** PROF EMER PROF, DEPT PSYCHOL, SOUTHERN ILL UNIV, CARBONDALE, as of 2006; actg dean, Col Liberal Arts, 1996-1999; PROF, SCH MED, 1989-; assoc dean, Col Liberal Arts, beginning 1988; assoc prof, Dept Psychol, Southern Ill Univ, Carbondale, beginning 1983; consult, G D Searle Co, Skokie, Ill, 1983-1985; asst prof, Sch Med, 1981-1983; managing ed, Behav & Neural Biol, 1978-1981; asst res psychobiologist, Univ Calif, Irvine, 1976-1981; fel, Univ Calif, Irvine, 1975-1978; instr psychol, Kent State Univ, 1968-1971; prin investr res grant, Natural Sci R J Reynolds Tobacco Co, Off Naval Res. **Memberships:** AAAS; Soc Neuroscience; Sigma Xi. **Research Statement & Publications:** Neurobiological aspects of memory modulation; role of catecholamine and opioid systems in the modulation of learning and memory; electrophysical correlates of neural plasticity; neurobiological basis of smoking behavior and alcohol consumption; recovery of function following brain damage. **Mailing Address:** Dept Psychol, Southern Ill Univ, Mailcode 6519, Carbondale, IL 62901-6502. **Fax:** 618-453-3563. **E-Mail:** rajensen@siu.edu

JENSEN, ROBERT GORDON, MILK LIPIDS, LIPASES. **Personal Data:** b Carthage, Mo, January 2, 1926; m 1947, Helene C Wickstrom; c Gordon L & Jeffrey A. **Education:** Univ Mo, BS, 1950, MS, 1951, PhD (dairy bact), 1954. **Honors & Awards:** Macy-Gyorgy Award, Int Soc Res Human Milk Lactation Supelco Nicholas Pelicb, Am oil cham sec award. **Professional Experience:** EMER PROF, UNIV CONN, 1991-; prof nutrit sci, Univ Conn, 1970-1990; from asst prof to prof dairy mfg, Univ Conn, 1956-1970; from instr to asst prof dairy bact, Univ Mo, 1954-1956. **Memberships:** Hon fel Int Soc Res Human Milk & Lactation; Am Oil Chem Soc; Am Dairy Sci Asn; Am Inst Nutrit. **Research Statement & Publications:** Human milk lipids; bovine milk lipids; lipases. **Mailing Address:** Univ Conn Dept Nutrit Sci, 186 Chafferville Rd, Storrs, CT 06268-2637. **Fax:** 860-423-5361.

JENSEN, ROBERT J, MATHEMATICS. **Education:** Univ Rochester, BS; Fla Int Univ, MS; Univ Ga, EdD. **Professional Experience:** ASSOC PROF MATH EDUC & DIR GRAD STUDIES, EMORY UNIV, as of 2006. **Mailing Address:** Div Educ Studies, Emory Univ, 1784 N Decatur Rd Suite 240, Atlanta, GA 30322. **Fax:** 404-727-2799. **E-Mail:** rjensen@emory.edu

JENSEN, RONALD HARRY, BIOPHYSICAL CHEMISTRY, CYTOCHEMISTRY. **Personal Data:** b Chicago, Ill, November 25, 1938; m 1958, Judith; c 3. **Education:** Lawrence Col, BS, 1960; Calif Inst Technol, PhD (chem), 1964. **Professional Experience:** FAC SUPVR, CANCER CTR GENOME ANAL CORE FACIL, UNIV CALIF SAN FRANCISCO, 1996-; ASSOC FAC, LAWRENCE BERKELEY LAB, BERKELEY, 1994-; PROF LAB MED, UNIV CALIF, SAN FRANCISCO, 1991-; sect leader cytochem, Lawrence Livermore Nat Lab, 1980-1991; life scientist biol & med, Lawrence Livermore Nat Lab, 1975-1991; sr investr microbiol, Smith Kline & French Labs, 1970-1975; res scientist molecular biol, Int Minerals & Chem Corp, IL, 1967-1969; res fel biol, Calif Inst Technol, 1964-1967. **Memberships:** Am Soc Mass Spectrometry. **Research Statement & Publications:** Molecular genetics of prostate cancer; molecular cytometry; molecular genetics cancer microarray analysis. **Mailing Address:** Dept Lab Med, Univ Calif San Francisco, PO Box 0808, San Francisco, CA 94143-0808. **Fax:** 415-476-8218. **E-Mail:** rjensen@cc.ucsf.edu

JENSEN, ROY A, MICROBIOLOGY, BIOCHEMISTRY. **Personal Data:** b Racine, Wis, April 8, 1936; m 1956, c 5. **Education:** Ripon Col, BA, 1958; Univ Tex M D Anderson

Hosp & Tumor Inst, PhD (biochem, genetics), 1963. **Professional Experience:** PROF MICROBIOL & CELL SCI, UNIV FLA, 1986-; prof biol & dir Ctr Somatic-Cell Genetics & Biochem, 1978-1986; prof biol, State Univ NY, Binghamton, 1976-1986; prof biol, Univ Tex M D Anderson Hosp & Tumor Inst Houston, 1973-1976; assoc prof microbiol, Baylor Col Med, 1968-1973; asst prof biol, State Univ NY, Buffalo, 1966-1968; Res instr, Sch Med, Univ Wash, 1965; USPHS fel microbiol, Sch Med, Univ Wash, 1964-1966. **Memberships:** Am Soc Microbiol; Tissue Cult Asn. **Research Statement & Publications:** Biochemical genetics; gene-enzyme relationships; regulation of gene and enzyme activities; metabolic interlock; plant tissue culture. **Mailing Address:** Dept Microbiol & Cell Sci, Univ Fla, Gainesville, FL 32611. **Fax:** 352-475-3849. **E-Mail:** rjensen@ufl.edu

JENSEN, SUSAN ELAINE, ANTIBIOTICS, STREPTOMYCES. **Personal Data:** b Edmonton, Alta, January 30, 1950; m 1971. **Education:** Univ Alta, BSc, 1970, PhD (microbiol), 1975. **Professional Experience:** PROF BIOL SCI, UNIV ALTA, as of 2003; ALTA HERITAGE FOUND MED RES SCHOLAR MICROBIOL, UNIV ALTA, 1981-; sessional lectr & res assoc, Univ Alta, 1977-1981; teaching fel, Univ BC, 1974-1976. **Memberships:** Am Soc Microbiol; Can Soc Microbiologists. **Research Statement & Publications:** Biosynthesis of beta-lactam antibiotics by Streptomyces; cell-free enzymatic synthesis of unnatural beta-lactam antobiotics; isolation of genes coding for enzymes involved in antibiotic biosynthesis; published over 10 articles. **Mailing Address:** Dept Biol Sci, Univ Alta, Rm M 450, Biol Sci Bldg, Edmonton, AB T6G 2E9, Can. **Fax:** 780-492-9234. **E-Mail:** susan.jensen@ualberta.ca

JENSEN, THOMAS E, CELL BIOLOGY. **Personal Data:** b Waverly, Iowa, September 21, 1932; m 1956, c 2. **Education:** Wartburg Col, BA, 1958; SDak State Univ, MA, 1962; Iowa State Univ, PhD (cytol), 1965. **Professional Experience:** CHMN BIOL, LEHMAN COL, CITY UNIV NY, as of 2003; PROF BIOL, LEHMAN COL, CITY UNIV NY, 1973-; assoc prof, Lehman Col, 1970-1972; asst prof biol, Wayne State Univ, 1965-1970; res assoc, Iowa State Univ, 1964-1965. **Memberships:** AAAS; Electron Micros Soc Am; Am Soc Cell Biol; Bot Soc Am; Sigma Xi. **Research Statement & Publications:** Ultrastructure of cells. **Mailing Address:** Dept Biol Sci, Lehman Col, 250 Bedford Park Blvd W, Bronx, NY 10468-1589.

JENSEN, THORKIL, MICROBIOLOGY. **Personal Data:** b Vejle, Denmark, January 23, 1919; American citizen; m 1943, c 1. **Education:** Gustavus Adolphus Col, BA, 1941; Univ Minn, MS, 1949, PhD (zoology), 1952. **Professional Experience:** PROF EMER, DEPT MICROBIOL, as of 2005; consult, Baptist Mem Hosp, Kansas City, beginning 1965; prof, Sch Med, Univ Kans, beginning 1963; consult, Midwest Res Inst, 1961-1963; China Med Bd fel, 1955; consult, Vet Admin Hosp, Mo, 1954-1961; consult, St Mary's Hosp, Kansas City, 1953-1958; from asst prof to assoc prof microbiol, Sch Med, Univ Kans, 1952-1963; instr embryol & histol, Vet Sch, Univ Minn, 1951-1952. **Memberships:** Am Soc Parasitol; Am Trop Med & Hyg; Sigma Xi. **Research Statement & Publications:** In vitro culture of some parasitic protozoa and helminths; possible host-parasite relationships between viruses and protozoa and helminths; biochemistry of excystation in acanthamoeba. **Mailing Address:** Univ Kans Sch Med, Dept Microbiol, Kansas City, KS 66160. **Fax:** 913-588-7295.

JENSEN, TIMOTHY B(ERG), CHEMICAL ENGINEERING, PRESSURE SENSITIVE TAPE. **Personal Data:** b Willmar, Minn, October 25, 1939; m 1991, Susan; c 2. **Education:** Univ Minn, Minneapolis, BS, 1961; Princeton Univ, PhD (chem eng), 1965. **Professional Experience:** CONSULT, JENSEN & ASSOC, 2001-; sr tech mgr, 3M Co, 1997-2001; tech serv mgr, 3M Co, 1989-1997; res mgr, 3M Co, 1984-1989; tech mgr, 3M Co, 1973-1984; res supv, 3M Co, 1968-1973; sr chem engr, 3M Co, 1964-1968. **Memberships:** Am Soc Testing & Mat; Am Inst Chem Engrs; Pressure Sensitive Tape Coun. **Research Statement & Publications:** Pressure sensitive adhesives; chemical reactor design; PSA tape formulation; oriented films; packaging products; environmental concerns/regulations; technical service. **Mailing Address:** 2221 Newton Ave S, Minneapolis, MN 55405. **E-Mail:** tbjensen@alumni.princeton.edu

JENSEN, TOMMY GERT, PHYSICAL OCEANOGRAPHY, COMPUTATIONAL FLUID DYNAMICS. **Personal Data:** b Copenhagen, Denmark, March 4, 1954; m 1989, Louise; c Gianna Majbritt Mattacchione. **Education:** Univ Aarhus, BS, 1978; Univ Copenhagen, MS, 1981, PhD (phys oceanog), 1986; Fla Stae Univ, PhD (geophys fluid dynamics), 1989. **Professional Experience:** ED, J CLIMATE, 2003-; res affil, Dept Oceanog, Univ Hawaii, 2001-; assoc ed, J Climate, 2001-2003; ASSOC RES, UNIV HAWAII, 1998-; res scientist/lectr, Colo State Univ, 1996-1998; vis sr scientist, Int Res Ctr Comput Hydrodyn, Danish Hydraulic Inst, Denmark, 1994-1996; prin investr, US Dept Energy, 1992-2000; lectr, phys oceanog, air-sea interaction, Colo State Univ, 1990-1998; Lectr equatorialdynamics, Univ Sau Paulo, Brazil, 1990; Res Assoc, Colo State Univ, 1989-1996; lectr phys oceanog, Univ Copenhagen, 1985; grad fel researcher, Univ Copenhagen, 1983-1985; Asst teacher oceanog, Univ Copenhagen, 1979-1984. **Memberships:** Am Met Soc; Am Geophys Union; Oceanog Soc; PACON Int; Sigma Xi; Phi Kappa Phi. **Research Statement & Publications:** Numerical modelling of the ocean, primarily with respect to climate change; computational fluid dynamics; interaction between the ocean and atmosphere and coastal processes; Indian Ocean dynamics. **Mailing Address:** Int Pac Res Ctr, Sch Ocean & Earth Sci, Univ Hawaii, Honolulu, HI 96822. **Fax:** 808-956-9425. **E-Mail:** tjensen@hawaii.edu

JENSEN, TORKIL HESSELBERG, plasma physics; deceased, see previous edition for last biography

JENSEN, WILLIAM AUGUST, BOTANY. **Personal Data:** b Chicago, Ill, August 22, 1927; m 1987. **Education:** Univ Chicago, PhB, 1949, MS, 1950, PhD (bot), 1953. **Honors & Awards:** NY Bot Garden Award, Bot Res, 1960. **Professional Experience:** PROF, COL BIOL SCI, OHIO STATE UNIV, 1984-; dean, Col Biol Sci, Ohio State Univ, 1984-1989; Prog dir develop biol, NSF, 1973-1974; chmn dept, Univ Calif, Berkeley, 1971-1984; from asst prof to prof, Univ Calif, Berkeley, 1957-1984; asst prof biol, Univ Va, 1956-1957; NSF fel, Univ Brussels, 1955-1956; USPHS fel, Calif Inst Technol, 1953-1955. **Memberships:** Bot Soc Am (vpres 1975-1976 pres 1977-1978); Soc Develop Biol (secy 1962-1964). **Research Statement & Publications:** Botanical histochemistry; botanical cytology; plant embryology. **Mailing Address:** 576 Aronoff Bldg, 318 12th Ave, Columbus, OH 43210. **Fax:** 614-292-8345.

JENSEN, WILLIAM PHELPS, CHEMISTRY. **Personal Data:** b Minneapolis, Minn, May 22, 1937; m 1962, c 3. **Education:** Univ Minn, BS, 1959; Univ Iowa, MS, 1962, PhD (inorg chem), 1964. **Professional Experience:** PROF CHEM, SDAK STATE UNIV, 1977-2004; assoc prof, Sdak State Univ, 1967-1977; vis asst prof, La State Univ, 1966-1967; res chemist, Pittsburgh Plate Glass Co, 1963-1966. **Memberships:** Am Chem Soc. **Research Statement & Publications:** Chemistry of lanthanide and actinide elements; structure determination of complex compounds by x-ray diffraction. **Mailing Address:** Dept Chem, SDak State Univ, Brookings, SD 57007.

JENSH, RONALD PAUL, RADIATION EMBRYOLOGY, BEHAVIORAL TERATOLOGY. **Personal Data:** b New York, NY, June 14, 1938; m 1962, Ruth; c Victoria & Elizabeth. **Education:** Bucknell Univ, BA, 1960, MA, 1962; Jefferson Med Col, PhD (anat), 1966. **Professional Experience:** PROF EMER PATH ANAT & CELL BIOL, THOMAS JEFFERSON UNIV, as of 2005; prof path, Anat & Cellular Biol, 1994-; Neurochem Int, 1990 & Lea & Febiger Co, 1992; Battelle, Neurotoxicol & Teratology, 1990, 1993 & 1994; SECT CHIEF MICROS ANAT, THOMAS JEFFERSON UNIV, 1988-; Battelle, Growth Develop & Aging, 1988 & 1990; Am Cyanamid Co, Mobil Oil Corp, 1987-1988; Sci, Radiation Res, 1985 & 1986; Battelle, Pac NW Labs, 1985; vice chmn anat, Thomas Jefferson Univ, 1984-1994; Sci, Lab Animal Sci, 1984 & 1985; Sci, Int J Radiation Biol, 1984-1985, 1987, 1990 & 1993-1994; sci, AAAS, 1984-1985; Embryol & Human Develop Study Sect, NIH, 1983; reviewer, Bioelectromagnetics, 1982-1984 & 1986; reviewer, J Am Toxicol, 1982-1983; Food, Argus Res Labs Inc, 1979-; Food, Drug & Chem Audits Inc, 1979-1985; Food, Bio Search Inc, 1979-1985; reviewer, J Abnormal Develop, 1977-; consult, Ortho Res Found, 1971-1985; from asst prof to prof anat, Thomas Jefferson Univ, 1968-1994; from asst to assoc prof radiol, Thomas Jefferson Univ, 1968-1991; investr, NIH grants, Dept Anat & Pediat, Jefferson Med Col, 1966-; instr anat & res assoc radiol, Thomas Jefferson Univ, 1966-1968. **Memberships:** Am Asn Anatomists; Teratology Soc (treas, 1989-1992); Neurobehav Teratology Soc (pres, 1985-1986); Sigma Xi; Soc Exp Biol & Med; Am Asn Univ Professors; Int Asn Human Biologists; Radiation Res Soc. **Research Statement & Publications:** Teratology; embryology, statistical applications; behavioral toxicology; reproductive biology, developmental biology and radiobiology; author of numerous publications. **Mailing Address:** Dept Path Anat Cell Biol, Thomas Jefferson Univ, 562 Jefferson Alumni Hall 1020 Locust St, Philadelphia, PA 19107-6799. **Fax:** 215-923-3808. **E-Mail:** ronald.jensh@mail.tju.edu

JENSKI, LAURA JEAN, MHC RESTRICTION, CYTOXIC T-LYMPHOCYTE. **Personal Data:** b Chicago, Ill, February 23, 1952. **Education:** Northern Ill Univ, BS, 1973, MS, 1975; Univ NC, PhD (oncol), 1979. **Professional Experience:** PROF BIOL, IND UNIV-PURDUE UNIV, INDIANAPOLIS, as of 2004; assoc Prof Biol, Ind Univ-Purdue Univ, Indianapolis, 1991-; asst prof, Ind Univ-purdue Univ, Indianapolis, 1987-1991; grants, Var Corp & Inst, 1986-1992; res assoc, Childrens Hosp Res Found, 1983-1986. **Memberships:** Am Asn Immunologists; Am Soc Cell Biol; AAAS; Asn Women Sci. **Research Statement & Publications:** T-lymphocyte activity and regulation; immunological effects of long chain omega three fatty acids. **Mailing Address:** Dept Biol, Ind Univ-Purdue Univ, Indianapolis, IN 46202-5132. **E-Mail:** ljenski@indyvax.iupui.edu

JENSON, A BENNETT, IMMUNOPATHOLOGY, IMMUNOVIROLOGY. **Education:** Baylor Col Med, MD, 1966. **Professional Experience:** PROF PATH, GEARGETOWN STATE UNIV, as of 2000; ACTG CHMN, DEPT DENT, MED & GRAD PATH, GEORGETOWNUNIV, 1980-. **Mailing Address:** Dept Path, Med Ctr, Georgetown Univ, 3900 Reservoir Rd NW, Washington, DC 20007-2197. **Fax:** 202-687-8935.

JENSSEN, THOMAS ALAN, ANIMAL BEHAVIOR, ECOLOGY. **Personal Data:** b South Bend, Ind, March 18, 1939; m 1962, c 3. **Education:** Univ Redlands, BS, 1962; Southern Ill Univ, MA, 1964; Univ Okla, PhD (zoology), 1969. **Professional Experience:** ASSOC PROF BIOL, VA POLYTECH INST & STATE UNIV, 1977-; asst prof, biol, VA polytech inst & state univ, 1971-1977; nat inst ment health assoc herpet, Harvard Univ, 1969-1971; res asst, Med Ctr, Univ Okla, 1969-1970. **Memberships:** Am Soc Ichthyol & Herpet; Animal Behav Soc; Int Soc Behav Ecol; Soc StudyAmphibians & Reptiles; Sigma Xi. **Research Statement & Publications:** Behavior and ecology of various species of anurans and lizards, especially communicative value of anoline lizard displays. **Mailing Address:** Dept Biol, Va Polytech Inst & State Univ, 4104 Derring Hall, Blacksburg, VA 24061-0406. **Fax:** 540-231-9307. **E-Mail:** tjenssen@vt.edu

JENTOFT, JOYCE EILEEN, STRUCTURE-FUNCTION RELATIONSHIPS, PHYSICAL BIOCHEMISTRY. **Personal Data:** b Canton, Ohio, March 10, 1945; m 1926, Neil. **Education:** Univ Capital, BS, 1966; Univ Minn, PhD (inorg chem), 1971. **Professional Experience:** PROF, DEPT BIOCHEM, SCH MED, UNIV CASE WESTERN RES, as of 2000; VICE PROVOST & DEAN, SCH GRAD STUDIES, UNIV CASE WESTERN RES, 1996-; asst provost, Dept Pediat, 1994-1996; assoc prof, Dept Biochem, Sch Med, Univ Case Western res, beginning 1989; asst prof, Dept Pediat, 1981-1989; sr res assoc phys biochem, Dept Pediat, 1979-1981; instr biochem, Univ Case Western Res, 1979-1981; immunol, Univ Case Western Res, 1978; fel phys biochem, Univ Case Western Res, 1977; Fel phys biochem, Univ Minn, 1972. **Memberships:** Am Chem Soc; Biophys Soc; Am Soc Biochem & Molecular Biol. **Research Statement & Publications:** Structure-function relationships in proteins and enzymes; protein-nucleic acid interactions; molecular virology (retroviruses); biological spectroscopy (fluorescence, CD, NMR); Published over 10 articles. **Mailing Address:** Dept Biochem, Case Western Res Univ, 10900 Euclid Ave, Cleveland, OH 44106-7004. **Fax:** 216-368-3419. **E-Mail:** jej@po.cwru.edu

JENTOFT, RALPH EUGENE, PHYSICAL CHEMISTRY, ANALYTICAL CHEMISTRY. **Personal Data:** b Tacoma, Wash, November 30, 1918; m 1954, Betty; c Elisabeth (Norosky) & Rolf E. **Education:** Univ Wash, BS, 1941, PhD (chem), 1952. **Professional Experience:** CONSULT, 1980-; sr res assoc phys & anal chem, Chevron Res Co, Stand Oil Co, Calif, 1964-1979; sr res chemist, Chevron Res Co, Stand Oil Co, Calif, 1960-1964; res chemist, Chevron Res Co, Stand Oil Co, Calif, 1952-1960; chemist, Oceanog Surv Philippines, US Fish & Wildlife Serv, 1947-1948. **Memberships:** AAAS; Am Chem Soc. **Research Statement & Publications:** Phase studies and thermodynamic measurements in field of petroleum chemistry; separation and purification; trace analysis for hydrocarbons and petrochemicals; analytical separations; liquid chromatography and supercritical fluid chromatography; quantum chemistry. **Mailing Address:** 11601 Occidental Rd, Sebastopol, CA 95472.

JEON, KWANG WU, CELL BIOLOGY, MOLECULAR BIOLOGY. **Personal Data:** b Korea, November 10, 1934; m Myong; c 2. **Education:** Seoul Nat Univ, BS, 1957, MS, 1959; Univ London, PhD (cell physiol), 1964. **Professional Experience:** PROF CELLULAR BIOL, UNIV TENN, KNOXVILLE, 1976-; assoc prof, Univ Tenn, Knoxville, 1970-1975; Ed, Int Rev Cytol, 1967-; res asst prof cell physiol, State UnivNY, Buffalo, 1965-1969; Res fel electron micros, Middlesex Hosp, Univ London, 1964-1965. **Memberships:** Am Soc Cell Biol; Soc Protozoologists (pres 1992-1993); fel AAAS; Int Soc Endocytobiol (pres 1989-1995). **Research Statement & Publications:** Cell growth and division; nucleocytoplasmic interactions; cell organelle structure and function; symbiosis. **Mailing Address:** Dept Biochem, Univ Tenn, Knoxville, TN 37996-0840. **Fax:** 865-974-6306. **E-Mail:** jeon@utk.edu

JEONG, DAVID Y, MATHEMATICS. **Education:** Tufts Univ, BS & MS; Lehigh Univ, PhD (Appl Mech). **Professional Experience:** MECH ENG, VEHICLE CRASHWORTHINESS DIV, US DEPT TRANSP, as of 2006. **Mailing Address:** Mail Code DTS 76, 55 Broadway, Cambridge, MA 02142-1093. **Fax:** 617-494-3616. **E-Mail:** Jeong@volpe.dot.gov

JEONG, TUNG HON, HOLOGRAPHY. **Personal Data:** b Kwangtung, China, December 19, 1931; American citizen; m 1963, Anna; c Allan, Alec & Alicia. **Education:** Yale Univ, BS, 1957; Univ Minn, PhD (physics), 1962. **Honors & Awards:** Robert Millik Medal, Am Asn Physics Teachers, 1976; Progress Medal (1999); Photog Soc of Am SAXBY Medal (2002); Royal photog Soc of Great Britain Life tine Achivement Award (2001); inter Holographic manufacturers assoc. **Professional Experience:** Prof emer PHYSICS, LAKE FOREST COL, 1978-; from asst prof to assoc prof, Lake Forest Col, emeritus 1963-1978; res assoc physics, Univ Minn, 1962-1963; tech consult; DIR, CTR PHOTONICS STUDIES; PRES, INTEGRAF. **Memberships:** Am Asn Physics Teachers; Soc Photo-Optical Instrumentation Engrs; fel Optical Soc Am. **Research Statement & Publications:** Precision proton-nuclear elastic scattering; linear proton accelerator injector; H-source for pre-injectors; optics; physics education; lasers and holography; non-destructive testing; laser applications and holography. **Mailing Address:** Dept Physics, Lake Fores Col 555 N Sheridan Rd, Lake Forest, IL 60045. **Fax:** 847-615-0835. **E-Mail:** jeong@lfc.edu

JEPPESEN, RANDOLPH H, PHYSICS & ASTRONOMY. **Education:** Univ Mont, BA, 1958; Univ Ill, MS, 1960; NMex State Univ, PhD (physics), 1980. **Professional Experience:** PROF EMER PHYSICS & ASTRON, UNIV MONT, as of 2004; Collabr, exps 665 & 770, Los Alamos Nat Lab, 1987; prof physics &astron, Univ Mont, beginning 1981; AWA fac partic grants, Los Alamos Nat Lab, 1981-1986; chmndept, Univ Mont, 1973-1981; coprin investr, AEC grant, Dept Energy, 1972-1980; from instr toassoc prof, Univ Mont, 1961-1981; IBM res staff mem, Thomas J Watson Res Ctr, 1960-1961. **Memberships:** Am Phys Soc. **Mailing Address:** Dept Phys & Astron, Univ Montana, 32 Campus Dr, 1080, Missoula, MT 59812. **Fax:** 406-243-2085. **E-Mail:** pc_rhj@selway.umt.edu

JEPPSON, ROLAND W, CIVIL ENGINEERING, FLUID MECHANICS & HYDRAULICS, POROUS MEDIA. **Personal Data:** b Brigham City, Utah, August 30, 1933; m 1959, Mary; c Lori (Anderson), David, Gordon, Brian, Camille (Strigam Theron), Kevin & Chad. **Education:** Utah State Univ, BS, 1958, MS, 1960; Stanford Univ, PhD (civil eng), 1967. **Honors & Awards:** J C Stevens Award, Am Soc Civil Engrs, 1968; Horton Award, Am Geophys Union, 1976. **Professional Experience:** PROF, DEPT CIVIL & ENVIRON ENG, UTAH STATE UNIV, 1994-; head, Dept Civil & Environ Eng, 1973-1977; prof, Dept Civil & Environ Eng, 1971-1994; assoc prof civil eng, Dept Civil & Environ Eng, 1966-1971; res engr, summers, Utah State Univ, 1961-1964; asst prof civil eng, Humboldt State Col, 1960-1964; res engr, Utah State Univ, 1958-1960. **Memberships:** Am Soc Civil Engrs; Am Soc Eng Educ; Am Geophys Union. **Research Statement & Publications:** Numerical solutions to free surface fluid and porous media flow problems; water resource planning and design; pipeline hydraulics; open channel hydraulics. **Mailing Address:** Dept Civil & Environ Eng, Utah State Univ, 4110 Old Main Hill, Logan, UT 84321-4110. **Fax:** 435-797-1185. **E-Mail:** jeppson@lab.cee.usu.edu

JEPPSON, RONALD, MATHEMATICS. **Education:** Univ Utah, BS; Mont State Univ, MS, PhD. **Professional Experience:** DEAN, COL SOCIAL & NAT SCI, MINN STATE UNIV, 1997-. **Mailing Address:** Dept Math, Minn State Univ, Moorhead, MN 56563. **Fax:** 218-477-4372. **E-Mail:** jeppson@mnstate.edu

JEPSEN, DONALD WILLIAM, SURFACE PHYSICS, STATISTICAL MECHANICS & SCIENTIFIC COMPUTER PROGRAMMING. **Personal Data:** b Lincoln, Nebr, January 14, 1932; m 1975, Judith Hajos; c Stephanie H. **Education:** Univ Rochester, BS, 1953; Univ Wis, MS, 1956, PhD (theoret chem), 1959. **Honors & Awards:** Surface Struct Prize, 7th Int Conf, Struct Surfaces 21-26, Newcastle City Hall, Newcastle, NSW, Australia, 2002. **Professional Experience:** RETIRED; staff mem, IBM Corp Res Ctr, 1960-1995; Gen Motors fel, Inst Fluid Dynamics & Appl Math, Univ Md, 1959-1960. **Memberships:** Am Phys Soc; Am Chem Soc; Sigma Xi; Asn Comput Mach. **Research Statement & Publications:** Theoretical chemical physics; nonequilibrium properties of large systems; properties of solid surfaces and low energy electron diffraction. **Mailing Address:** 507 Woodland Hills Rd, White Plains, NY 10603. **E-Mail:** jepsen1@cyburban.com

JEREMIAH, LESTER EARL, MEAT SCIENCES. **Personal Data:** b Walla Walla, Wash, December 9, 1941; m 1993, Suzette; c William E, Johanna S & John D. **Education:** Wash State Univ, BS, 1965; Univ Mo, MS, 1967; Tex A&M Univ, PhD (meat sci), 1971. **Professional Experience:** RES SCIENTIST MEAT SCI, CAN DEPT AGR, 1975-; tech writer humannutrit, Agriserv Found, 1974-1975; co exten dir, Colo State Univ, 1973-1974; salesman real estate, David A Gamache Real Este Co, 1972-1973; grad asst meat sci, Tex A&M Univ, 1969-1971; exten agent, Wash State Univ, 1967-1969; res asst, Univ Mo, 1965-1967; Meat lab technician, Wash State Univ, 1965. **Memberships:** Am Soc Animal Sci; Inst Food Technologists; Am Meat Sci Asn; Can Meat SciAsn. **Research Statement & Publications:** Beef and pork tenderness, quality, preservation, retail case-life, and meat handling systems; frozen storage and display of meat; sensory evaluation and consumer acceptance. **Mailing Address:** Agr & Agr Food, Can Res Ctr, 6000 C & E Trail, Lacombe, AB T4L 1W1, Can. **Fax:** 403-782-6120. **E-Mail:** jeremiahl@em.agr.ca

JEREMIAS, CHARLES GEORGE, ORGANIC CHEMISTRY, INORGANIC CHEMISTRY. **Personal Data:** b Marlborough, Mass, July 8, 1920; m 1980, c 2. **Education:** Univ Ga, BS, 1942; Tulane Univ, PhD (chem), 1949. **Professional Experience:** Consult, Delta 2 Finishing Plant, J P Stevens Co, 1965-1970 & James Flett Orgn, Inc, 1977-1979; PROF CHEM & HEAD DEPT, NEWBERRY COL, 1964-; assoc prof & actghead dept, Newberry Col, 1962-1964; group leader res, Southern Dyestuff Co, Martin-MariettaCo, 1960-1962; res chemist, Tenn Eastman Co, 1948-1960; Chemist, US Rubber Co, 1942-1945. **Memberships:** Am Chem Soc; Am Inst Chemists. **Research Statement & Publications:** Organic intermediates for synthetic fibers, dyes and insecticides; sulfur dyes and intermediates. **Mailing Address:** 2103 Johnstone St, Newberry, SC 29108.

JERGER, E(DWARD) W, MECHANICAL ENGINEERING. **Personal Data:** b Milwaukee, Wis, March 13, 1922; m 1982, Elizabeth; c Betty A (Murphy) & Barbara L (Smyth). **Education:** Marquette Univ, BS, 1946; Univ Wis, MS, 1947; Iowa State Univ, PhD (theoret &appl mech), 1951. **Professional Experience:** PROF EMER MECH ENG, UNIV NOTRE DAME, 1987-; prof, Univ NotreDame, 1982-1987; assoc dean eng, Univ Notre Dame, 1968-1982; educ consult, DominicanRepub, 1965-1967; prof & head dept, Univ Notre Dame, 1961-1968; consult engr, 1960-; assoc prof, Univ Notre Dame, 1955-1961; asst prof mech eng, Iowa State Col, 1948-1955; dir processing, Wis Malting Co, 1946-1948. **Memberships:** Am Soc Mech Engrs; Am Soc Eng Educ; Nat Fire Protection Asn; Int Asn ArsonInvestr. **Research Statement & Publications:** Thermal systems; fire protection engineering; protective construction; product liability. **Mailing Address:** Dept Mech Eng, Col Eng, Univ Notre Dame, 365 Fitzpatrick Hall, Notre Dame, IN 46556-5637. **Fax:** 574-631-8341. **E-Mail:** edward.w.jerger.3@nd.edu

JERINA, DONALD M, ORGANIC CHEMISTRY, BIOCHEMISTRY. **Personal Data:** b Chicago, Ill, January 17, 1940; m 1964, Colleen; c Derek & Julianne. **Education:** Knox Col, Ill, BA, 1962; Northwestern Univ, PhD (org chem), 1966. **Honors & Awards:** Hillebrand Prize, Am Chem Soc, 1979; Brodie Award, Am Soc Pharmacol & Exp Therapeut, 1982. **Professional Experience:** CHIEF, OXIDATION MECHANISMS SECT, NAT INST DIABETES, DIGESTIVE & KIDNEY DIS, NIH, 1973-; res chemist, Nat Inst Arthrities, Diabetes, Digestive & Kidney Dis, 1970-1973; sr fel, Nat Inst Arthrities, Diabetes, Digestive & Kidney Dis, 1969-1970; fel org chem & biochem, Nat Inst Arthrities, Diabetes, Digestive & Kidney Dis, 1966-1968. **Memberships:** AAAS; Am Chem Soc; Am Cancer Soc; Fedn Am Socs Exp Biol; Am Soc Biochem & Molecular Biol. **Research Statement & Publications:** Synthesis of peptides and oligonucleotides on polymer supports; enzymes drug metabolism; microsomal hydroxylation; biochemical mechanisms; migration of ring substituents during aryl hydroxylation, particularly the NIH shift; chemistry and biochemistry of arene oxides; chemical carcinogenesis; mutagenesis; DNA adducts. **Mailing Address:** Nat Inst Diabetes & Digestive & Kidney Dis, NIH, Lab Bioorganic Chem, Bldg 8 Rm 1A01, Bethesda, MD 20892-0820. **Fax:** 301-402-0008. **E-Mail:** donaldj@bdg8.niddk.nih.gov

JERIS, JOHN S(TRATIS), ENVIRONMENTAL ENGINEERING, SCIENCE. **Personal Data:** b Boston, Mass, June 6, 1930; m 1958, c Joanne & Paul. **Education:** Mass Inst Technol, BS, 1953, MS, 1954, ScD(sanit eng), 1962. **Honors & Awards:** Kenneth Allen Mem Award, NY Water Pollution Control Asn, 1975; Thomas R Camp Medal, Water Pollution Control Fedn, 1979, DeLa Salle Medal, 1985. **Professional Experience:** PROF EMER CIVIL ENG, MANHATTAN COL, as of 2004; prof civilL eng, Manhattan Col, beginning 1971; vpresres & develop, Ecolotrol Inc, 1970-; dir environ eng & sci grad prog, Manhattan Col, 1966-1978& 1986-1994; from asst prof to assoc prof, Manhattan Col, 1962-1971; res asst, Mass InstTechnol, 1959-1962; proj engr, Stearns & Wheler, NY, 1956-1959; consult, Environ Eng. **Memberships:** Sigma Xi; Am Water Works Asn; Water Pollution Control Fedn; Am Soc CivilEngrs; Asn Environ Eng prof. **Research Statement & Publications:** Biological waste treatment; use of biological fluid beds, degradation of hazardous chemicals; anaerobic and aerobic stabilization of sludges. **Mailing Address:** Dept Environ Eng, Manhattan Col, Leo Eng Bldg, 3825 Corlear Ave, Bronx, NY 10463-2348. **Fax:** 718-862-8035. **E-Mail:** jsjscd@aol.com

JERISON, HARRY JACOB, NEUROBIOLOGY. **Personal Data:** b Bialystok, Poland, October 13, 1925; American citizen; m 1950, Irene Landkof; c Jon, Andy & Elizabeth. **Education:** Univ Chicago, BS, 1947, PhD (psychol), 1954. **Honors & Awards:** James Arthur lectr, Am Mus Nat Hist, 1989. **Professional Experience:** EMER PROF BIOBEHAV SCI, DEPT PSYCHIAT, SCH MED & PROF, DEPT PSYCHOL, UNIV CALIF, LOS ANGELES, 1992-; fel, Hanse Wissenschaftskolleg, Delmenhorst, German, 1998-1999; vis prof neurobiol, Max-Plank Inst Biol Cybernetics, Tuebingen, Ger, 1989; vis prof psychol, Univ Hawaii, 1987; vis prof anthrop, Univ Florence, Italy, 1986-1987; acad vis, Oxford Univ, 1986; vis scholar, Rockefeller Found Bellagio Ctr, 1983; vis scientist, Med Res Coun, Appl Psychol Unit, Cambridge, Eng, 1978-1979; hon res assoc, Dept Vert Paleont, Los Angeles County Mus, 1970-; prof, Univ Calif, Los Angeles, 1969-1992; prof biol, Behav Res Lab, 1968-1969; fel, Ctr Advan Study Behav Sci, 1967-1968; prof psychol, Behav Res Lab, 1964-1968; dir, Behav Res Lab, 1957-1969; assoc prof psychol, Antioch Col, 1957-1964; res psychologist, AeroMed Lab, USAF, 1949-1957. **Memberships:** Am Psychol Asn; Soc Vert Paleont. **Research Statement & Publications:** Paleoneurology; evolutionary biopsychology; evolution of specialized and generalized behavioral and cognitive capacities in vertebrates, and its relation to allometry and encephalization (brain/body relations) among living and fossil animals; quantitative neuroanatomy. **Mailing Address:** 503 W Rustic Rd, Santa Monica, CA 90402. **Fax:** 310-454-3325. **E-Mail:** hjerison@ucla.edu

JERKOFSKY, MARYANN, VIROLOGY, CELL CULTURE. **Personal Data:** b Alameda, Calif, February 18, 1943. **Education:** Univ Tex, BA, 1965; Baylor Col Med, PhD (virol), 1969. **Professional Experience:** ASSOC PROF EMER MICROBIOL, UNIV MAINE, ORONO, as of 2005; Tokyo Univ Fisheries, Japan, 1992; Am Univ Les Cayes, Haiti, 1988; vis prof, Univ Amsterdam, Neth, 1983; assoc prof microbiol, Univ Maine, Orono, 1981-1995; asst prof, Univ Maine, Orono, 1976-1981; res asst prof, Sch Med, Univ Miami, 1974-1975; instr, Col Med, Pa State Univ, 1973-1974; res assoc, Col Med, Pa State Univ, 1972-1973; fel microbiol, Col Med, Pa State Univ, 1969-1972. **Memberships:** Am Soc Microbiol; Sigma Xi; Am Soc Virol; AAAS. **Research Statement & Publications:** Herpes viruses in vitro model for Reye's Syndrome; lipid metabolism modifications produced by herpes viruses; interaction between unrelated animal viruses; characterization of tumors produced in fish by herpes viruses. **Mailing Address:** Dept Biochem Microbiol & Molecular Biol, Univ Maine, 5735 Hitchner Hall, Orono, ME 04469-5735. **Fax:** 207-581-2801.

JERMANN, WILLIAM HOWARD, ELECTRICAL ENGINEERING. **Personal Data:** b Cleveland, Ohio, June 29, 1935; m 1963, c 3. **Education:** Univ Detroit, BEE, 1958, MA, 1962; Univ Conn, PhD (elec eng), 1967. **Professional Experience:** PROF, DEPT ELEC & COMPUT ENG, MEMPHIS STATE UNIV, 1977-; NSF res grant, 1969-1970; from asst prof to assoc prof, Dept Elec Eng, Memphis State Univ, 1967-1977; asstprof, USCG Acaad, 1962-1967; instr elec eng, Univ Detroit, 1961-1962; jr engr, Toledo EdisonCo, Ohio, 1958. **Memberships:** Am Soc Eng Educ; Simulation Coun. **Research Statement & Publications:** Hybrid Monte-Carlo solutions to partial differential equations; development of engineering concepts curriculum project. **Mailing Address:** Univ Memphis, Eng Bldg Rm 204B, Memphis, TN 38117. **E-Mail:** wjermann@memphis.edu

JERNER, R CRAIG, METALLURGICAL ENGINEERING, MATERIALS SCIENCE. **Personal Data:** b St Louis, Mo, October 12, 1938; m 1992, Jann; c Michael, Elisabeth, Stephen & Elizabeth A. **Education:** Wash Univ, St Louis, BS, 1961, MS, 1962; Univ Denver, PhD (metall), 1965. **Professional Experience:** PRES, J E I METALL INC, DALLAS, TEX, 1990-; pres, Jerner Eng Inc, Okla, 1988-1995; adj prof, Col Eng, Univ Kan, 1987-1991; sr prof staff mem, Eng & Mat Tech Corp/ EMTEC Corp, Okla, 1987; pres & sr prof staff mem, Eng & Mat Technol Corp/EMTEC Corp, Okla, 1979-1987; assoc staff mem & modal instr, US Dept Transp, Transp Safety Inst, Okla, 1973-1978; S W Metall Consult Inc, 1973-1979; asst dean, Grad Col, Univ Okla, 1971-1972; adj prof Chem Eng & Mat Sci, 1976-1978; from asst prof to assoc prof metall eng, Univ Okla, 1965-1976. **Memberships:** Am Soc metals/mats; Am Soc Testing Mat; Sigma Xi; Soc Mfg Engrs; Nat Asn Corrosion Engrs; Am Welding Soc; Okla Soc Prof Engrs; Tex Soc Prof Engrs. **Research Statement & Publications:** Application of scanning electron microscopy and energy dispersive x-ray spectroscopy to the analysis of metallic and non-metallic product failures. **Mailing Address:** 7703 Queens Ferry Lane, Dallas, TX 75248-1720. **Fax:** 972-233-5909. **E-Mail:** r.c.jerner@metallurgist.com

JERNIGAN, HOWARD MAXWELL, BIOCHEMISTRY. **Personal Data:** b Winston-Salem, NC, April 13, 1943; m 1968, Diane; c 1. **Education:** WVa Univ, BS, 1965; Univ NC, Chapel Hill, PhD (biochem), 1970. **Professional Experience:** PROF OPHTHAL, UNIV TENN, 1996-; PROF BIOCHEM, UNIV TENN, MEMPHIS, 1990-; res assoc, Lab Vision Res, Nat Eye Inst, NIH, 1978-1980; from asst prof to assoc prof, Ophthal, 1973-1990; fel, Dept Biochem, Univ Fla, 1970-1973. **Memberships:** Am Soc Biochem & Molecular Biol; Am Chem Soc; Sigma Xi; Asn Res Vision & Ophthal; Sigma Xi; Int Soc Eye Res. **Research Statement & Publications:** Biochemistry of the eye; lens metabolism; cataract; oxidative damages to tissues; membrane transport; amino acids; lipid metabolism. **Mailing Address:** Hamilton Eye Inst, 930 Madison Ave Ste 100, Memphis, TN 38163. **E-Mail:** hjernigan@utmem.edu

JERNIGAN, ROBERT LEE, BIOINFORMATICS, BIOMOLECULAR SIMULATIONS. **Personal Data:** b Portales, NMex, May 4, 1941; div, c Alexander L. **Education:** Calif Inst Technol, BS, 1963; Stanford Univ, PhD (phys chem), 1967. **Professional Experience:** DIR, LAURENCE H BAKER CTR BIOINFORMATICS & BIOL STATIST, IOWA STATE UNIV, 2002-; PROF, DEPT BIOCHEM, BIOPHYS & MOLECULAR BIOL, IOWA STATE UNIV, 2002-; publ comn, Biophys Soc, 2001-; fel, Inst Adv Studies, Hebrew Univ, 1999; NATO Collab Res Grant, 1996-1997; Merit Award, NIH, 1995; Resource Adv Comt, Parallel Processing Resource, Cornell Univ, 1993-2001; head, Sect Molecular Struct, NIH, 1992-2002; US Israel Binat Found Grants, 1992-2000; dep lab chief, NIH, 1989-2002; theoret chemist, NIH, 1975-2002; sr staff fel chem, Lab Theoret Biol, NIH, 1970-1975; NIH fel, Univ Calif, San Diego, 1968-1970. **Memberships:** AAAS; Am Chem Soc; Biophys Soc; Protein Soc. **Research Statement & Publications:** Protein, polypeptide and NA conformations; dimensional, electrical and optical properties; conformations of biopolymers; biophysics; residue-residue interactions in proteins; DNA flexibility; protein folding; RNA folding; drug design; protein engineering. **Mailing Address:** Dept Biochem Biophys & Molecular Biol, Iowa State Univ, 112 Off & Lab Bldg, Ames, IA 50011. **Fax:** 515-294-5256. **E-Mail:** jernigan@iastate.edu

JERNIGAN, ROBERT WAYNE, Computational Statistics, Data Analysis. **Personal Data:** b Jacksonville, Fla, February 4, 1951; m 1973, Rose; c Nicholas & Laura. **Education:** Univ S Fla, BA, 1973, MA, 1975, PhD (math), 1978. **Honors & Awards:** Scholor -Teacher of the Year 1997, Amer Univ. **Professional Experience:** Researcher, Lab Molecular Systematics, Smithsonian Inst, 1992, 2000; Dept Chair of Math & Statist, Am Univ, 1990-1993, 1995-1998; Prof Statistics, Am Univ, 1986-; Sr statistician, Statistical Policy Br, US Environmental Protection Agency, 1984-1990; Asst Prof, Assoc Prof, Am Univ, 1978-1986. **Memberships:** Am Statist Asn; Inst Math Statist; AAAS; Math Asn Am; Soc Study Evolution. **Research Statement & Publications:** Development and application of probability and statistical theory and computational statistical methods to the study of ecological systems and evolutionary biology. **Mailing Address:** Dept Math/Stat, Am Univ, 4400 Mass Ave, NW, Washington, DC 20016. **E-Mail:** jernigan@american.edu

JERNOW, JANE L, ORGANIC CHEMISTRY. **Personal Data:** b Shanghai, China, American citizen; m 1965, c 1. **Education:** Univ Ill, Urbana, BS, 1958, MS, 1961; Pa State Univ, PhD (org chem), 1963. **Professional Experience:** CONSULT, 1989-; prog dir, Nat Acad Sci, Wash, DC, 1986-1989; group leader, Hoffmann-La Roche Inc, 1971-1986; res assoc, State Univ NY Albany, 1969-1990; reschemist, Sterling Winthrop Res Inst, 1968-1969; NIH fel chem, Cornell Univ, 1964-1965. **Memberships:** Am Chem Soc; Sigma Xi; Asn Women Sci. **Research Statement & Publications:** Mechanism study in organic chemistry; synthetic and medicinal chemistry. **Mailing Address:** 343 Hartford Rd, South Orange, NJ 07079-2432.

JEROME, JOSEPH WALTER, SEMICONDUCTOR MODELING, NONLINEAR SYSTEMS. **Personal Data:** b Philadelphia, Pa, June 7, 1939; div. **Education:** St Joseph's Col, Pa, BS, 1961; Purdue Univ, MS, 1963, PhD (math), 1966. **Professional Experience:** Adj vis prof, Rush Med Col, 1994-1997; vis scholar, Univ Chicago, 1985; vis mem tech staff, Bell Labs, NJ, 1981, 1982-1983; vis prof, Univ Tex, 1978-1979; PROF MATH, NORTHWESTERN UNIV, 1976-; sr fel, British Sci Coun, 1974-1975; vis sr fel, Oxford Univ, 1974-1975; from asst prof to assoc prof, Northwestern Univ, 1970-1976; asst prof, Case Western Res Univ, 1968-1970; asst prof math, Math Res Ctr, Univ Wis-Madison, 1966-1968; NSF grad fel, 1961-1965. **Memberships:** Am Math Soc; Soc Indust Appl Math. **Research Statement & Publications:** Approximation of nonlinear partial differential equation models; ionic channels; free boundary problems. **Mailing Address:** Dept Math, Northwestern Univ, 2033 Sheridan Rd Lunt 213, Evanston, IL 60208-2730. **Fax:** 847-491-8906. **E-Mail:** jwj@math.northwestern.edu

JEROME, NORGE WINIFRED, PUBLIC HEALTH, NUTRITIONAL ANTHROPOLOGY. **Personal Data:** b Grenada, WI, November 3, 1930; American citizen. **Education:** Howard Univ, BS, 1960; Univ Wis-Madison, MS, 1962, PhD (nutrit, anthrop), 1966. **Honors & Awards:** Spotlight Award, US Dept Labor; Higuchi Res Achievement Award. **Professional Experience:** PROF EMER PREV MED & PUB HEALTH, UNIV KANS MED CTR, KANSAS CITY, 1996-; ASSOC DEAN MINORITY AFFAIRS, UNIV KANS MED CTR, KANSAS CITY, 1996-; cancer prev & control study sect, 1994-; dir, Dept Prev Med, Community Nutrit Div, 1981-1995; man-food systs interaction comt, Nat Res Coun, 1980-1982; prof, Dept Community Health, Sch Med, 1978-1995; mem, Lipid Metab Adv Comt, Nat Heart, Lung & Blood Inst, NIH, 1978-1982; mem, Nat Adv Coun, 1977-; mem study panel 12, World Food & Nutrit Study, Nat Acad Sci, 1976; Cancer & Nutrit Sci Review Comt, Diet, Nutrit & Cancer Prog, Nat Cancer Inst, NIH, 1976-1978; mem, Food & Nutrit Coun, Am Pub Health Asn, 1975-1978; mem nat adv panel, Childrens Advert Rev Unit, 1974-; chairperson comt nutrit anthrop, 1974-1977; dir, Educ Resources Ctr, Div Learning Resources, 1974-1977; mem nat adv coun, Childrens TVWorkshop, 1974-1975; assoc prof human ecol & community health, Col Health Sci, 1972-1978; assoc ed, J Nutrit Educ, 1971-1977; asst prof human ecol, Univ Kans Med Ctr, Kansas City, 1970-1972; asst prof nutrit, Univ Kans Med Ctr, Kansas City, 1969-1970; mem awards bd, Am Dietetic Asn, 1968-1971; res assoc nutrit & anthrop, Univ Wis-Madison, 1966-1967; mem, Inst Res Poverty, Univ Wis-Madison, 1966-1967; Instr foods & nutrit, Howard Univ, 1962-1963. **Memberships:** Fel Am Anthrop Asn; Am Dietetic Asn; Am Pub Health Asn; Soc Med Anthrop; Am Inst Nutrit; Inst Food Technologists. **Research Statement & Publications:** Dietary patterns of population groups; modernization, diet and health; compliance to medical regimen; consumer response to nutritional and health prescriptions; dietary interventions to reduce chronic diseases. **Mailing Address:** Dept Prev Med & Pub Health, Univ Kans Med Ctr, 3901 Rainbow Blvd, MS 1008, Kansas City, KS 66160. **Fax:** 913-588-2780. **E-Mail:** njerome@kumc.edu

JERRARD, RICHARD PATTERSON, FIXED POINTS, MULTIPLE-VALUED FUNCTIONS. **Personal Data:** b Evanston, Ill, July 23, 1925; m 1951, Margot; c Laura, Leigh & Robert. **Education:** Univ Wis, BS, 1949, MS, 1950; Univ Mich, PhD (math), 1958. **Professional Experience:** PROF EMER MATH, UNIV ILL, URBANA, 1995-; dir grad studies, Univ Ill, Urbana-champaign, 1991-1995; vis fel, Cambridge Univ, 1972-1973; Vis fel, Univ Warwick, 1965-1966, 1977, 1985 & 1990; from asst prof to prof, Univ Ill, Urbana-champaign, 1958-1969; mathematician, Bell Labs, 1957-1958; instr math, Univ Mich, 1956-1957; E\\engr, Gen Elec Co, 1950-1954. **Memberships:** Am Math Soc; Math Asn Am; Sigma Xi. **Mailing Address:** Univ Ill, 1409 W Green, Urbana, IL 61801. **E-Mail:** jerrard@uiuc.edu

JERRARD, ROBERT J, MATHEMATICS. **Professional Experience:** PROF MATH, CONCORDIA UNIV COL, ALBERTA, as of 2006. **Memberships:** Am Math Soc. **Mailing Address:** Math Dept, Concordia Col, 7128 Ada Blvd, Edmonton, AB T5B 4E4, Can. **Fax:** 780-474-1933. **E-Mail:** rjerrard@math.concordia.ab.ca

JERRELLS, THOMAS RAY, TUMOR IMMUNOLOGY, CELLULAR IMMUNOLOGY. **Personal Data:** b Wickenburg, Ariz, February 28, 1944; m 1965, c 2. **Education:** Univ Ariz, BS, 1972; Wash State Univ, MS, 1974, PhD (microbiol), 1976. **Professional Experience:** PROF PATHOL & MICROBIOL, MED CTR, UNIV NEBR, as of 2004; prof cell biol, La State Univ Med Ctr, beginning 1991; assoc prof path, Univ Tex, 1987-1991; mem staff, Dept Rickettsial Dis, Walter Reed Army Inst Res, 1980-1987; head, Immunoregulation Sect, 1978-1980; tumor immunologist, Litton Bionetics Inc, 1976-1978. **Memberships:** Am Soc Microbiol; Am Med Technologists. **Research Statement & Publications:** Defining immunoregulatory cells involved in cell-mediated immune responses and role in the immunodepression associated with tumor burden. **Mailing Address:** Dept Pathol & Microbiol, Med Ctr, Univ Nebr, Omaha, NE 68198-7460. **E-Mail:** tjerrell@unmc.edu

JERRI, ABDUL J, APPLIED MATHEMATICS. **Personal Data:** b Amarah, Iraq, July 20, 1932; c 3. **Education:** Univ Baghdad, BSc, 1955; Ill Inst Technol, MSc, 1960; Ore State Univ, PhD (math), 1967. **Professional Experience:** PROF EMER MATH, CLARKSON UNIV, as of 2005; prof math, Clarkson Univ, ending 2004; vis assoc prof, Am Univ Cairo, 1986-1988; assoc prof, Kuwait Univ, 1978-1979, 1989-1990; vis assoc prof, Am Univ Cairo, 1973-1974; head dept, Am Univ Cairo, 1972-1973; assoc prof math, clarkson Univ, beginning 1970; asst prof, Clarkson Univ, 1967-1970; asst physicist, IIT Res Inst, 1959-1962; instr physics, Baquba Teacher Col, Iraq, 1956-1958. **Memberships:** Am Math Soc; Soc Indust & Appl Math; Pattern Recognition Soc. **Research Statement & Publications:** Sampling expansion; integral and discrete transforms; numerical method. **Mailing Address:** Dept Math, Clarkson Univ, Box 5815, Potsdam, NY 13699. **Fax:** 315-268-2371. **E-Mail:** jerria@clarkson.edu

JERRY, L MARTIN, CANCER IMMUNOLOGY. **Personal Data:** b Toronto, Ont, January 2, 1937. **Education:** Univ Toronto, MD, 1961, PhD (immunol), 1971. **Professional Experience:** HON CLIN PROF, DEPT ONCOL, UNIV CALGARY, as of 2006; DIR WHO, COLLAB CTR CANCERCONTROL, TOM BAKER CANCER CTR, 1993-; dir cancer serv, Tom Baker Cancer Ctr, 1977-1992. **Memberships:** Am Asn Cancer Res; Am Asn Immunol; Am Col Physicians; Can Soc Immunol; Can Oncol Soc. **Research Statement & Publications:** Cancer Immunology. **Mailing Address:** WHO Collaborating Ctr Cancer Control, 189 Carey Dr, Calgary, AB T1W 2R7, Can. **Fax:** 403-678-9750. **E-Mail:** mjerry@cb.monarch.net

JERSEY, GEORGE CARL, VETERINARY PATHOLOGY. **Personal Data:** b Highland Park, Mich, August 20, 1940; m 1958, c 2. **Education:** Eastern Mich Univ, BA, 1964; Mich State Univ, BS, 1965, DVM, 1967, MS, 1969, PhD (vet path), 1973. **Professional Experience:** CONSULT, 1980-; res specialist path, Toxicol Res Lab, Dow Chem Co, 1972-1980; instr clin path, Dept Path, Mich State Univ, 1970-1972; instr, Dept Path, Mich State Univ, 1968-1970; Upjohn fel, Dept Path, Mich State Univ, 1967-1968. **Memberships:** Am Vet Med Asn. **Research Statement & Publications:** Pathological and toxicological evaluation of industrial, agricultural and consumer chemicals; chemical products in laboratory animals to help establish safe production, handling, transportation and use of these materials. **Mailing Address:** 6401 Gillard Rd, Spruce, MI 48762.

JERSILD, RALPH ALVIN, MICROSCOPIC ANATOMY, CELL BIOLOGY. **Personal Data:** b Janesville, Wis, September 29, 1931; m 1953, c 2. **Education:** St Olaf Col, BA, 1953; Univ Ill, MS, 1957, PhD (zoology), 1961. **Professional Experience:** PROF EMER ANAT, IND UNIV, AS OF 2006; prof anat, Sch Med, Ind Univ, Indianapolis, beginning 1971; from instr to assoc prof, Ind Univ, 1961-1971. **Memberships:** Am Asn Anat; Electron Micros Soc Am; Am Soc Cell Biol. **Research Statement & Publications:** Electron microscopy; intestinal lipid absorption and transport; glycoprotein synthesis and transport; golgi apparatus; cell surface. **Mailing Address:** Ind Univ Sch Med, 635 Barnhill Dr, Indianapolis, IN 46223.

JERUCHIM, MICHEL CLAUDE, COMPUTER SIMULATION OF COMMUNICATION SYSTEMS, INTERFERENCE ANALYSIS OF COMMUNICATIONS SYSTEMS. **Personal Data:** b Paris, France, April 4, 1937; American citizen; m 1969, c 2. **Education:** City Col NY, BEE, 1961; Univ Pa, MSEE, 1963, PhD (elec eng/commun), 1967. **Professional Experience:** CONSULT, as of 2005; vice chmn, Subcomt Comput-Aided Modeling, Anal & Design Commun Systs, Inst Elec & Electronics Engrs Commun Soc, 1986-; sr staff consult commun sci, Geaerospace/Lockheed Martin, beginning 1984; secy, Subcomt Comput-Aided Modeling, Anal & Design Commun Systs, Inst Elec & Electronics Engrs Commun Soc, 1984-1986; sr commun engr, Space Systs Div, Gen Elec Co, 1971-1984; commun engr, Space Systs Div, Gen Elec Co, 1961-1971. **Memberships:** Fel Inst Elec & Electronics Engrs. **Research Statement & Publications:** Analysis and design of communications systems, especially satellite-based systems; developing computer-aided tools such as simulation, for doing the analysis and design. **Mailing Address:** 88 Birch Lane, Paoli, PA 19301.

JERUSSI, THOMAS P, CENTRAL NERVOUS SYSTEM. **Personal Data:** b New York, NY, March 24, 1940. **Education:** City Col NY, BS, 1962; Hunter Col, MS, 1972; Mt Sinai Med Sch, PhD (pharmacol), 1974. **Professional Experience:** DEPT PHARAMCOL, SEPRACOR INC, as of 2001; sect mgr, Cent Nerv Syst, Ohmeda PPD, beginning 1988; group leader centnerv syst, Ohmeda PPD, 1987-1988; sr researcher, Ohmeda PPD, 1985-1987; researcher pharmacol, Ohmeda PPD, 1984-1985. **Memberships:** AAAS; Soc Neuroscience; Am Soc Pharmacol & Exp Therapeut. **Mailing Address:** Dept Pharmacol, Sepracor Inc, 84 Waterford Dr, Marlborough, MA 01752. **Fax:** 508-357-7493. **E-Mail:** tjerussi@sepracor.com

JERVIS, HERBERT HUNTER, MOLECULAR GENETICS. **Personal Data:** b Wilmington, Del, June 25, 1942; m 1974, Mary. **Education:** Springfield Col, BS, 1964, MEd, 1966; Fla State Univ, MS, 1971, PhD (genetics), 1973; St John's Univ, JD, 1987. **Professional Experience:** ATTY, PIONEER HI-BRED INT, as of 2004; ATTY, SMITHKLINE BEECHAM CORP, as of 2004; ASST PATENT COUN, SMITHKLINE BEECHAM, 1993-; patent atty, Smithkline Beecham, 1990-1993; patent atty, Fitzpatrick, Cella, Haper & Scinto, 1987-1989; from asst prof to assoc prof biol, Adelphi Univ, 1981-1987; res assoc biochem, VA Polytech Inst & State Univ, 1973-1975. **Memberships:** Patent & Trademark Off Soc; Sigma Xi; Am Biol Asn; AAAS; Am Intellectual Property Law Asn. **Research Statement & Publications:** Role of transfer RNAs in the development and differentiation of fungi, especially Neurospora and Allomyces. **Mailing Address:** Pioneer Hi-Bred Int, 7100 NW 62nd Ave PO Box 1000, Johnston, IA 50131.

JERVIS, ROBERT ALFRED, BOTANY, ECOLOGY & ORNITHOLOGY. **Personal Data:** b Wilmington, Del, May 15, 1938; m 1981, Linda; c Michael & Rebecca. **Education:** Dartmouth Col, BA, 1960; Rutgers Univ, MS, 1962, PhD (ecol), 1964. **Professional Experience:** INSTR, JOHNSON STATE COL, as of 2006; adj fac natural sci, Johnson State Col, beginning 1983; instr, Harwood Union High Sch, Moretown, 1981-1993; prof, Community-Col Vt, 1981-1984; dir, Goddard Col non-resident ecol study projs, Southeast & Southwest US, 1971-1972 & Northwest & Alaska, 1976 &Bahamas, 1978; prof, Goddard Col, 1968-1981; from asst prof to assoc prof biol, Emory & Henry Col, 1964-1968; adj fac biol, Community Col, Vt; dir, Goddard Col, Raptor Rehab Ctr & Summer Prog Outdoor Col. **Memberships:** Ecol Soc Am; Am Nature Study Soc; Am Littoral Soc. **Research Statement & Publications:** Freshwater marsh vegetation and productivity; vegetation patterns in the south Appalachians; New England ecology; ornithology; travel study programs in ecology. **Mailing Address:** 719 Ctr Rd, Middlesex, VT 05602. **E-Mail:** rjerv@aol.com

JERVIS, ROBERT E, RADIOCHEMISTRY, APPLICATIONS. **Personal Data:** b Toronto, Ont, May 21, 1927; m 1950, Frances; c Ann K & Peter R. **Education:** Univ Toronto, BA, 1949, MA, 1950, PhD (phys chem), 1952. **Honors & Awards:** Lewis Medal, Can Nuclear Soc; Ressovsky Medal, Russ Acad Sci; Hevesy Medal. **Professional Experience:** PROF EMER, DEPT CHEM ENG, UNIV TORONTO, 1992-; vchmn, NuclearSafety Comt, Atomic Energy Control Bd, Can Fed Govt, chmn, 1988-1995; res chmn, UnivToronto, 1981-1985; Energy Res Group, Cambridge Univ, 1978; Energy Res Group, Nat Univ Malaysia, 1979; assocdean res eng, Univ Toronto, 1974-1978; prof appl chem, dept chem eng, univtoronto, beginning 1966; vis prof, Fac Sci, Univ Tokyo, 1965-1966; vchmn, Can Sci Fairs Coun, 1963-1965; assoc prof, Univ Toronto, 1958-1967; assoc res officer, Atomic Energy Can, Ltd, Ont, 1952-1958. **Memberships:** Can Soc Forensic Sci; fel Chem Inst Can; fel Can Nuclear Soc; fel Indian AcadForensic Sci; fel Royal Soc Can. **Research Statement & Publications:** Radioactivation research, especially application of nuclear detection methods to crime detection and to environmental pollution problems from heavy metals, mercury, arsenic, cadmium and lead; radiochemical studies of nuclear power reactor safety. **Mailing Address:** Dept Chem Eng, Univ Toronto, Toronto, ON M5S 3E5, Can. **Fax:** 416-978-8605.

JESAITIS, ALGIRDAS JOSEPH, CELL BIOLOGY, IMMUNOLOGY. **Personal Data:** b Ger, August 21, 1945; American citizen; m 1979, c 3. **Education:** Sch Eng & Sci, NY Univ, BS, 1967; Calif Inst Technol, PhD (biophys), 1973. **Professional Experience:** Head, Dept Microbiol, Mont State Univ, beginning 1992; PROF, DEPT MICROBIOL, MONT STATE UNIV, 1992-; res prof, Dept Chem & Biochem, 1989-1992; asst mem, Scripps Clin & Res Found, 1985-1989; fel, Scripps Clin & Res Found, 1979-1985; fel, Univ Calif, San Diego, 1975-1979; Fel, Univ Freiburg, WGer, 1973-1975. **Memberships:** Biophys Soc; AAAS; Am Soc Cell Biol; Protein Soc; Soc Leukocyte Biol; AmHeart Asn. **Research Statement & Publications:** Biophysics and cell biology of sensory transduction mechanisms; role of cell membrane processes in inflammation, chemotaxis and mechanisms of host defense; structure of neutrophil cytochrome b and chemotactic receptor. **Mailing Address:** Dept Microbiol, Mont State Univ, 114 Lewis Hall, Bozeman, MT 59717-3520. **Fax:** 406-994-4926. **E-Mail:** umbaj@montana.edu

JESAITIS, RAYMOND G, PHYSICAL ORGANIC CHEMISTRY. **Personal Data:** b Vilnius, Lithuania, January 20, 1943. **Education:** Cooper Union, BChE, 1963; Cornell Univ, PhD (org chem), 1967. **Professional Experience:** INTERIM DEAN COMPUT SCI, STATE UNIV NY COL TECHNOL, UTICA, 2005-; PROF COMPUT SCI, STATE UNIV NY COL TECHNOL, UTICA, 1984-; from assoc prof to prof chem, State Univ NY Col Technol, Utica, 1974-1984; asst prof, State Univ NY, Stony Brook, 1968-1974; res fel chem, Univ Calif, Berkeley, 1967-1968. **Memberships:** Am Chem Soc; Royal Soc Chem. **Research Statement & Publications:** Physical and theoretical organic chemistry, including molecular structure; molecular interactions; ecological systematics. **Mailing Address:** Dept Comput Sci, State Univ NY Col Technol, Utica, NY 13504-3050. **E-Mail:** ray@sunyit.edu

JESCHOFNIG, PETER, CHEMISTRY. **Personal Data:** b November 6, 1943; m 1978, Linda Pope; c Autumn. **Education:** WTex State Univ, BSc, 1970; Southern Methodist Univ, MH, 1973; Western State Col, MA, 1988; Colo State Univ, PhD (environ educ), 1992. **Honors & Awards:** Colorado Distance Educator of the Year, Telecommunication cooperative for Colorado, 2000. **Professional Experience:** Fulbright prof, Dept Geol & Geophysics, Addis Ababa Univ, Ethiopia, 1995-1996; NSF grantee, State Univ NY, 1995; PROF, DEPT ENVIRON STUDIES, COLO MOUNTAIN COL, 1993-; NSF grantee, Nat Training Ctr, US Geol Surv, 1993; assoc prof environ studies & chem, Dept Environ Studies, Colo Mountain Col, 1988-1993; anthrop & sci instr, Dept Environ Studies, Colo Mountain Col, 1987-1988; independent geol consult, Salida, Colo, 1986-1988; chief geologist, Madagascar, 1985-1986; sr int staff geologist, Occidental Explor & Prod, Calif, 1983-1985; chief geologist, Occidental, Tunisia, 1981-1983; int staff geologist, Occidental Explor & Prod, Calif, 1979-1981; lead offshore geologist, Enserch Explor Inc, Tex, 1975-1978 & Santa Fe Energy Co, 1978-1979; instr anthrop, Eastfield Col, 1975-1976; Res asst, Karisoke Res Ctr, Rwanda, 1975; well site geologist, Oil Serv Co Iran, 1974-1975; Grad asst, Southern Methodist Univ, 1970-1973. **Memberships:** Am Assoc for the adavancement of sci Am assoc of phy teach; Nat Sci teach asn; Colorado Alliance for sci Higher edu council; Nat Sci Teachers Asn Partnership for Environmental Technol education, Board Mem, 2000-2002. **Research Statement & Publications:** Effects of acid-mine drainage on aquatic populations; developing science labs for distance education. **Mailing Address:** Dept Sci Colo Mountain Col, 3000 County Rd 114, Glenwood Springs, CO 81601. **E-Mail:** pjeschofnig@coloradomtn.edu

JESKEY, HAROLD ALFRED, IMMUNOPARASITOLOGY. **Personal Data:** b St Louis, Mo, August 6, 1923; m 1950, Elizabeth E Ahlgren; c 4. **Education:** St Louis Col Pharm, BS, 1933; Wash Univ, BA, 1937; Univ Wis, PhD (org chem), 1942. **Professional Experience:** EMER PROF VET PATH, RES INST, IOWA STATE UNIV, 1989-; chmn, Dept Immunobiol, 1975-1980; from asst prof to prof vet path & vet med, Res Inst, Iowa StateUniv, 1967-1989; res asst prof parasitol, Sch Vet Med, 1967; fel, Univ Pa, 1965-1967; Chief-parasitologist, Pa Dept Health, 1955-1963. **Memberships:** Emer mem Am Asn Immunologists. **Research Statement & Publications:** Characterization of parasitic nematode antigens involved in white cell reactions of vertebrate hosts; macrophage as effector mechanisms of resistance to infection. **Mailing Address:** 501 Theo Wirth Pkwy, Golden Valley, MN 55422-5340.

JESKEY, HAROLD ALFRED, ORGANIC CHEMISTRY. **Personal Data:** b St Louis, Mo, August 18, 1912; m 1939, Margaret; c Janet S & Judith J (Watson). **Education:** St Louis Col Pharm, BS, 1933; Wash Univ, BA, 1937; Univ Wis, PhD (org chem), 1942. **Professional Experience:** EMER PROF CHEM, SOUTHERN METHODIST UNIV, 1979-; prof biochem, Southwestern Med Sch, Univ Tex, 1980-1987; chmn dept, Southern Methodist Univ, 1962-1974; prof, Southern Methodist Univ, 1957-1979; from asst prof to assoc prof, Southern Methodist Univ, 1945-1957; from instr to asst prof, Univ Tenn, 1941-1944; asst, Univ Wis, 1938-1941; instr chem, St Louis Col Pharm, 1935-1938; asst chemist, James F Ballard Inc, 1933-1935. **Memberships:** Am Chem Soc. **Research Statement & Publications:** Organic synthesis; carbonation of phenols. **Mailing Address:** 2929 Fondren Dr, Dallas, TX 75205.

JESMOK, GARY J, INFLAMMATION & IMMUNOPHARMACOLOGY, IMMUNOPATHOLOGY. **Personal Data:** b Milwaukee, Wis, December 13, 1947; m Diane; c Garrett & Desiree. **Education:** Med Col Wis, PhD (pharmacol), 1976. **Professional Experience:** SR STAFF SCIENTIST, INST INFLAMMATION & EXP MED, MILES INC; assoc dir, Dept Pharmacol, Cetus Corp, Emeryville, Calif. **Memberships:** Am Soc Pharmacol & Exp Therapeut; Am Heart Asn; AAAS; Soc Exp Biol & Med. **Research Statement & Publications:** Biopharmaceutical research and development; immunopharmacology and immunopathology; granted 3 patents. **Mailing Address:** Inst Inflammation & Exp Med, Miles Inc 400 Morgan Lane, West Haven, CT 06516. **Fax:** 203-937-2526.

JESPERSEN, DENNIS C, MATHEMATICS. **Education:** PhD. **Professional Experience:** SCIENTIST, AMES RES CTR, NASA, as of 2006. **Memberships:** Am Astron Soc. **Mailing Address:** Ames Res Ctr, NASA, MS T27B-1, Moffett Field, CA 94035-1000. **Fax:** 650-604-4377. **E-Mail:** jesperse@nas.nasa.gov

JESPERSEN, JAMES, RADIOPHYSICS, COMMUNICATION THEORY. **Personal Data:** b Weldona, Colo, November 17, 1934; c 3. **Education:** Colo Univ, BA, 1956, MS, 1961. **Honors & Awards:** Bronze Plaque, Korean Stand Res Inst, 1978. **Professional Experience:** Consult, UN Develop Plan, 1978-1979; consult, Korean Stand Res Inst, 1977-1978; CONSULT THEORET RADIO PROPAGATION STUDIES, NAT BUR STAND, 1974-; consult, Inst-Range Instrumentation Group, 1973-1979; Dept Comm Sci fel & consulttelecommun, 1972-1973; chief time & frequency, Dissemination Res Group, Exp & Theoret-Studies Time Dissemination, Nat Bur Stand, 1969-1972; consult time broadcast studies, Nat BurStand, 1967-1968; group leader satellite ionospheric scintillation studies, Cent Radio PropagationLab, 1964-1966; exchange scientist theory VLF radio propagation, Radio Res Lab, Slough, Eng, 1962-1963; proj leader radio astron, Cent Radio Propagation Lab, 1956-1961. **Memberships:** Sr mem Inst Elec & Electronics Engrs; Sigma Xi; Inst Navig. **Research Statement & Publications:** Radio astronomy; ionospheric physics; radio propagation; communication and information theory; time dissemination and navigation systems; communication aids for the deaf. **Mailing Address:** 87 Camino Bosque, Boulder, CO 80302.

JESPERSEN, NEIL DAVID, ANALYTICAL CHEMISTRY. **Personal Data:** b Brooklyn, NY, March 5, 1946; m 1970, c 2. **Education:** Wash & Lee Univ, BS, 1967; Pa State Univ, PhD (chem), 1971. **Professional Experience:** PROF CHEM, ST JOHN'S UNIV, as of 2005; CHMN, GRAD DIV ARTS & SCI, ST JOHN'S UNIV, as of 2004; assoc prof chem, St John's Univ, Ny, beginning 1980; asst prof, St John's Univ, NY, 1977-1980; asst prof chem, Univ Tex, Austin, 1971-1977. **Memberships:** Am Chem Soc; AAAS; Sigma Xi. **Research Statement & Publications:** Thermometric titrimetry; clinical analysis; environmental mutagens. **Mailing Address:** Dept Chem, St John's Univ, 323 St Albert Hall 8000 Utopia Pkwy, Jamaica, NY 11439-0001. **Fax:** 718-990-1876. **E-Mail:** jespersn@stjohns.edu

JESSE, KENNETH EDWARD, SOLID STATE PHYSICS. **Personal Data:** b Chicago, Ill, January 3, 1933; m 1959, Sandra Helen; c 3. **Education:** U of Illiuois, BS, eng physics 1961; U of wyoming MS, 1962; Arizona state u, PhD, 1967. **Professional Experience:** RADIATION SAFETY OFFICER, ILL STATE UNIV, 1971-; PROF prof, emer physics PHYSICS, ILL STATE UNIV, 1967-1994; Res physicist, Aerospace Res Lab, Wright-Patterson AFB, 1966-1967. **Memberships:** Am Asn Physics Teachers; Sigma Xi secy, treas of sigma Xi since 1971. **Research Statement & Publications:** Thermoelectrical and electrical properties of nonmetallic materials; 4 texts on general physics. **Mailing Address:** 8 Knollcrest Ct, Ill State Univ, Normal, IL 61761. **E-Mail:** kejesse@ilstu.edu

JESSEN, CARL ROGER, RADIOLOGY, GENETICS. **Personal Data:** b Fairmont, Minn, January 12, 1933; m 1955, c 3. **Education:** Univ Minn, BS, 1954, DVM, 1956, PhD (genetics), 1969. **Professional Experience:** ASSOC DEAN VET MED SERV, DEPT CLIN SCI, COL VET MED, UNIVMINN, ST PAUL, 1978-; PROF VET CLIN SCI, DEPT CLIN SCI, COL VET MED, UNIVMINN, ST PAUL, 1977-; assoc prof vet clin sci, Dept Clin Sci, Col Vet Med, Univ Minn, StPaul, 1974-1977; RADIOLOGIST, DEPT CLIN SCI, COL VET MED, UNIV MINN, STPAUL, 1969-; pvt pract, 1956-1964. **Memberships:** Am Vet Med Asn; Am Vet Radiol Soc; Genetics Soc Am. **Research Statement & Publications:** Canine hip dysplasia; bone dysplasias in general. **Mailing Address:** Dept Clin Sci, Univ Minn, St Paul, MN 55108. **Fax:** 612-624-8753. **E-Mail:** c-jessen@maroon.tc.umn.edu

JESSEN, NICHOLAS C, NUCLEAR ENGINEERING. **Personal Data:** b Ger, February 13, 1913. **Professional Experience:** RETIRED; dir technol, Babcock & Wilcox Co, 1930-1978; instr metall, Univ Akron, 1938-1942. **Memberships:** Fel Am Soc Metals Int; Am Welding Soc. **Research Statement & Publications:** Development of welding processes for heavy pressure vessels and tubular products for low and high alloy steels; developed original guidelines for welding of stainless steel. **Mailing Address:** 4307 Village Oaks Lane, Atlanta, GA 30338.

JESSEN, NICHOLAS C, METALLURGICAL ENGINEERING. **Personal Data:** b Barberton, Ohio, March 29, 1944. **Education:** Univ Tenn, BS, 1967, MS, 1972. **Professional Experience:** SUPT, MARTIN MARIETTA CORP, 1986-. **Memberships:** Fel Am Soc Metals; Nat Mgt Asn. **Mailing Address:** 12123 N Fox Den Dr, Knoxville, TN 37922.

JESSER, WILLIAM AUGUSTUS, METAL PHYSICS, MATERIALS SCIENCE. **Personal Data:** b Waynesboro, Va, December 20, 1939; m 1962, Barbara; c William A & Nicole E. **Education:** Univ Va, BA, 1962, MS, 1964, PhD (physics), 1966. **Honors & Awards:** Alan Talbott Gwathmey Award, 1967. **Professional Experience:** Bd adv, US-Israel Binational Sci Found, 2000-2001; DEPT CHMN, UNIV VA, 1992-2003; vis prof physics, Huna Univ, Changsha, 1990; THOMAS GOODWIN DIGGES PROF, UNIV VA, 1989-; co-ed, Low Energy Dislocation Struct, 1986, 1989 & 1995; vis prof, Univ Witwatersrand, 1983; vis prof, Univ Pretoria, 1982, 1987; vis prof, Nagoya Univ, Japan, 1978; fel, Japan Soc Prom Sci, 1978; from asst prof to prof mat sci, Univ Va, 1968-1989; mem, Ctr Advan Studies, Univ Va, NSF, 1968-1970; lectr physics, Univ Witwatersrand, 1966-1967. **Memberships:** Am Soc Metals; Minerals Metals & Mat Soc; Mat Res Soc; fel Am Soc Metals Int. **Research Statement & Publications:** Growth and properties of thin films; transmission electron microscopy and diffraction; surface and interface properties; radiation damage; electronic materials. **Mailing Address:** Dept Mat Sci & Eng, Univ Va 116 Engineer's Way, PO Box 400745, Charlottesville, VA 22904-4745. **Fax:** 434-982-5660. **E-Mail:** waj@virginia.edu

JESSOP, ALAN MICHAEL, GEOTHERMICS, GEOTHERMAL ENERGY. **Personal Data:** b Wellingborough, UK, February 4, 1934; British & Canadian citizen; m 1959, c 3. **Education:** Univ Nottingham, BSc, 1955, PhD (mining), 1958. **Professional Experience:** RETIRED; res scientist, Geol Surv Can, Calgary, 1986-1993; secy, Int Heat Flow Comn, 1971-1975; res scientist, Earth Phys Br, 1965-1986; mem, Int Heat Flow Comn, 1963-1975; sci officer, Dominion Observ, Dept Energy Mines & Resources, Ottawa, 1962-1965; Nat Res Coun Can fel geophysics, Univ Western Ont, 1960-1962; res officer, Brit Cotton Indust Res Asn, 1958-1960. **Memberships:** Am Geophys Union. **Research Statement & Publications:** Thermal state, thermal history, and hydrodynamics of sedimentary basins; energy content of deep groundwater; applications to formation and migration of hydrocarbons. **Mailing Address:** 333 Silver Ridge Crescent NW, Calgary, AB T3B 3T6, Can.

JESSOP, PHILIP GREGORY, HOMOGENEOUS CATALYSIS, GREEN CHEMISTRY. **Personal Data:** b Ottawa, Ont, June 26, 1963; British & Canadian citizen; m 1986, Lorena; c David & Michael. **Education:** Univ Waterloo, BS, 1986; Univ BC, PhD (inorg chem), 1991. **Honors & Awards:** Canada Research Chair, 2003 Canadian Catalysis Lectureship Award, 2004. **Professional Experience:** ASSOC PROF INORG CHEM, QUEEN'S UNIV, 2003-; Asst Prof Inorg Chem, Univ Calif Davis, 1996-2003; researcher, Erato Molecular Catalyst Proj, Res Develop Corp Japan, 1993-1996; Postdoctoral fel chem, Univ Toronto, 1991-1992. **Memberships:** Am Chem Soc; Chem Inst Can. **Research Statement & Publications:** Environmentally friendly solvents for homogeneous catalysis and synthesis of chiral products; conversion of waste CO2 to useful products. **Mailing Address:** Dept Chem, Queen's Univ, Kingston, ON K7L 3N6, Can. **Fax:** 613-533-6669. **E-Mail:** jessop@chem.queensu.ca

JESTER, GUY EARLSCORT, STRUCTURAL DYNAMICS, SOIL MECHANICS. **Personal Data:** b Dyersburg, Tenn, October 20, 1929; m 1993, Babette Sale; c Mark A, Robin A (Harrington), Margarete E (Carey) & Guy L. **Education:** US Mil Acad, BS, 1951; Univ Ill, MS, 1958, PhD (civil eng), 1969. **Honors & Awards:** Pres Citation, Am Soc Civil Engrs, 1979, Award Merit, 1983. **Professional Experience:** SR CONSULT, BOOKER ASSOCS, 1995-; pres, Int Constructors Ltd, 1991-1996; vpres & dir, Int Waste Energy Systs; pres, Asn Improvement Miss River, 1974-1978; vpres corp planning & mkt & vpres & dir, J S Albericiconstruct Co Inc, 1973-1994; dist engr, Corp Engrs, St Louis Dist, 1971-1973; asst to chief res & develop & chief of info systs, VietNam, 1968-1971; div engr, Viet Nam, 1968-1969; dep dir & actg dir, Dept Res & Mgt, Waterways Exp Sta, 1965-1967; asst prof civil eng, US Mil Acad, 1962-1965; chief, Eng Br, Corps Engrs, Europ, US Army, 1959-1961. **Memberships:** Am Soc Civil Engrs; fel Soc Am Mil Engrs; Sigma Xi. **Research Statement & Publications:** Soil-structure interaction; soils; structural design under dynamic loading conditions. **Mailing Address:** 2 Daryl Lane, St Louis, MO 63124-1241.

JESTER, JAMES VINCENT, EXPERIMENTAL PATHOLOGY, OPHTHALMOLOGY. **Personal Data:** b Riverside, Calif, September 7, 1950; m 1977. **Education:** Univ Southern Calif, BS, 1972, PhD (exp path), 1978. **Professional Experience:** PROF OPTHAL, UNIV TEX, SOUTHWESTERN MED CTR DALLAS, as of 2001; INSTR, DEPT OPHTHAL & PATH & VIS PROF, DEPT BIOL, UNIV SOUTHERN CALIF, 1981-; Prin investr, 1981-1982; fel ophthalpath, Estelle Doheny Eye Found, 1978; fel pathology, Univ Southern Calif, 1974-1978. **Memberships:** Asn Res Vision & Ophthal; AAAS. **Research Statement & Publications:** Ophthalmic experimental pathology with specific emphasis on elucidating the pathogenetic mechanism involved in corneal and lid margin disease using morphologic and biochemical techniques; Published over 100 artilces. **Mailing Address:** Dept Ophthal, Univ Tex Southwestern Med Sch, 5323, Harry Hines Blvd, Dallas, TX 75235-7200.

JESWIET, JACOB, MANUFACTURING AUTOMATION. **Personal Data:** b Neth, February 24, 1946; Canadian citizen; m 1975, c 3. **Education:** Queens Univ, BS, 1970, MS, 1974, PhD (mech eng), 1981. **Professional Experience:** PROF MECH & MAT ENG, QUEEN'S UNIV, as of 2003; assoc prof mech eng, Queens Univ, 1986-; asst prof, Queens Univ, 1982-1986; asst prof eng, Univ NB, 1979-1982; design & maintenance engr, Celanese, 1971-1973; design engr, DuPont Can, 1970-1971. **Memberships:** Sr mem Soc Mfg Engrs; NAm Mfg Res Inst; Am Soc Mech Engrs. **Research Statement & Publications:** Friction and temperature at metal forming inter-faces; manufacturing automation, fns and fnc with emphasis upon diagnostic and robotic use. **Mailing Address:** Dept Mech & Mat Eng Queens Univ, McLaughlin Hall, Kingston, ON K7L 3N6, Can. **Fax:** 613-533-6489. **E-Mail:** jeswiet@me.queensu.ca

JETER, DAVID YANDELL, CHEMISTRY OF COPPER II. **Personal Data:** b Cooper, Tex, December 19, 1946; m 1968, Brenda; c Andrew. **Education:** East Texas State Univ, BS (Chem), 1968; Univ North Carolina, Chapel Hill, PhD (Inorg Chem), 1971. **Professional Experience:** Prof Chem, Rhodes College, 1993-; Chair Chem, Rhodes College, 1988-2004; Assoc Prof Chem, Rhodes College 1977-1993; Asst Prof Chem, Rhodes College, 1973-1977. **Memberships:** Am Chem Soc, 1973-. **Research Statement & Publications:** Structure and characterization of five coordinate complexes of copper II. **Mailing Address:** Rhodes Col, 2000 N Parkway, Memphis, TN 38112. **E-Mail:** jeter@rhodes.edu

JETER, HEWITT WEBB, ENVIRONMENTAL RADIOCHEMISTRY, GEOPHYSICS. **Personal Data:** b Cincinnati, Ohio, September 9, 1941; m 1966, Gerrie; c Mark & Paul. **Education:** Yale Univ, BE, 1963; Ore State Univ, PhD (oceanog), 1972. **Professional Experience:** SR SCIENTIST GEOPHYS, TELEDYNE ISOTOPES, 1978-; LAB MGR RADIOCHEM, TELEDYNE ISOTOPES, 1974-; scientist oceanog, Teledyne, 1972-1974. **Research Statement & Publications:** Mathematical modeling geophysics and oceanography; development of radiochemical procedures. **Mailing Address:** Teledyne Brown Eng Environ Servs, 50 Van Buren Ave, Westwood, NJ 07675. **Fax:** 201-664-5586.

JETER, JAMES ROLATER, CELL DIFFERENTIATION, CELL PROLIFERATION. **Personal Data:** b Ennis, Tex, September 4, 1940; m 1963, c 1. **Education:** Tex Tech Col, BS, 1965; Univ Tex, San Antonio, PhD (anat), 1973. **Professional Experience:** PROF ANAT, TULANE UNIV, as of 2004; CO-DIR, GRAD PROG STRUCT & CELLULAR BIOL, TULANE UNIV, as of 2004; pres elect, Int Cell Cycle Soc, 1990-1992; ed adv bd, Cell Biol, A Series Monographs, 1985-1990; secy & treas, Int Cell Cycle Soc, 1984-1990; assoc prof anat, Neuroscience, Cell Biol & Histol, Tulane Univ, beginning 1978; asst prof anat, Neuroscience, Cell Biol & Histol, Tulane Univ, 1975-1978; consult, NIH. **Memberships:** AAAS; Am Asn Anatomists; Am Asn Cancer Res; Am Heart Asn; Am Soc Cell Biol; Int Cell Cycle Soc; Sigma Xi. **Research Statement & Publications:** Role of nuclear proteins and protein phonylation in controlling cell proliferation and differentiation. **Mailing Address:** Dept Anat, Med Sch Tulane Univ, 1430 Tulane Ave Box SL 49, New Orleans, LA 70112-2669. **Fax:** 504-584-1687. **E-Mail:** jjeter@tulane.edu

JETER, RANDALL MARK, MICROBIAL GENETICS. **Personal Data:** b Iowa City, Iowa, August 4, 1952. **Education:** Univ Ariz, BS, 1974; Univ Okla, MS, 1976; Univ Calif, Davis, PhD (microbiol), 1982. **Professional Experience:** ASSOC PROF BIOL SCI, TEX TECH UNIV, 1991-; Asst Prof, Tex Tech Univ, 1985-1991; Postdoc Fel & Res Assoc, Univ Utah, 1982-1985. **Memberships:** Am Soc Microbiol; fel AAAS; Genetics Soc Am; Sigma Xi. **Research Statement & Publications:** Regulation of gene expression in microorganisms, including vitamin B12 biosynthesis and oxyanion reduction; gene transfer among bacteria in natural environments. **Mailing Address:** Dept Biol Sci, Tex Tech Univ, Lubbock, TX 79409-3131. **Fax:** 806-742-2963. **E-Mail:** randall.jeter@ttu.edu

JETER, SHELDON M, SOLAR ENGINEERING. **Education:** Clemson Univ, BS, 1968; Univ Fla, MS, 1972; Ga Inst Technol, PhD, 1979. **Professional Experience:** ASSOC PROF, GA INST TECHNOL, as of 2006. **Mailing Address:** Sch Mech Eng, Ga Inst Technol, Atlanta, GA 30332. **Fax:** 404-894-3733. **E-Mail:** sheldon.jeter@me.gatech.edu

JETER, WAYBURN STEWART, MEDICAL MICROBIOLOGY, IMMUNOLOGY. **Personal Data:** b Cooper, Tex, February 16, 1926; m 1947, Margaret McDonald; c Randall, Monette & Marcus. **Education:** Univ Okla, BS, 1948, MS, 1949; Univ Wis, PhD (med microbiol), 1950; Am Bd Med Microbiol, dipl. **Professional Experience:** EMER PROF PHARMACOL, TOXICOL, MICROBIOL & IMMUNOL, UNIV ARIZ, 1992-; PRES, SCI RELS SERV, 1988-; prof pharmacol & toxicol, Lab Cellular Immunol, 1984-1992; dir, Lab Cellular Immunol, 1976-1992; dir, Med Technol Prog, Univ Ariz, 1975-1977; head, dept microbiol, 1968-1983; prof microbiol, dept microbiol, 1963-1992; from asst prof to assoc prof, Col Med, Univ Iowa, 1952-1963; assoc, Col Med, Univ Iowa, 1951-1952; instr bact, Col Med, Univ Iowa, 1950-1951; asst med microbiol, Univ Wis, 1948-1950; Instr plant sci, Univ Okla, 1948. **Memberships:** AAAS; Am Soc Microbiol; Soc Exp Biol & Med; Am Asn Immunol; Sigma Xi; Am Acad Microbiol; emer mem. **Research Statement & Publications:** Hypersensitivity; complement; transfer factor; tissue transplantation; pathogenic bacteria. **Mailing Address:** 5140 N Via Sempreverde, Tucson, AZ 85750-5966. **E-Mail:** wayjeter@aol.com

JETT, JAMES HUBERT, FLOW CYTOMETRY. **Personal Data:** b Washington, DC, November 27, 1938; m 1962, Evangeline; c Stephen D & Kathleen M. **Education:** Univ NMex, BS, (Physics, Math, Honors in Math), 1960, MS (Physics), 1961; Univ Colo, PhD (nuclear physics), 1969. **Professional Experience:** Lab Fel, beginning 1997; dir, Nat Flow Cytometry Resource, 1992-2001; DEP GROUP LEADER, CELL BIOL GROUP, LIFE SCI DIV, LOS ALAMOS NAT LAB, 1986-; adj prof, Dept Cell Biol, Univ NMex, Albuquerque, beginning 1985; mem staff, Exp Pathol Group, 1971-1986; fel, Physics Div, 1969-1971. **Memberships:** Am Phys Soc; AAAS; Soc Anal Cytology (secy-treas, 1985-1990). **Research Statement & Publications:** Biomedical instrumentation, development, application and data interpretation; interpretation of biological experiments and computer applications. **Mailing Address:** 545 Navajo, Los Alamos, NM 87544-2625. **E-Mail:** jett@lanl.gov

JETT, MARTI, HOST RESPONSES TO PATHOGENIC AGENTS & BIOINFORMATICS, MODELING OF GENE PROFILES FROM EXPOSURES TO PATHOGENS & SIGNAL TRANSDUCTION. **Personal Data:** b Springfield, Ohio, July 22, 1941; m 1971, George; c Claire & Nicholas. **Education:** Ind Wesleyan Univ, BA, 1962; Georgetown Univ, PhD (biochem), 1973. **Professional Experience:** CHIEF, MOLECULAR PATH, WALTER REED ARMY INST RES, (1995-); Co-Director, Sci & Eng Apprentice Prog (1990-) STAFF SCIENTIST, WALTER REED ARMY INST RES, (1982-1995); Sr Fel, Nat Res-Coun, Walter Reed Army Inst Res, 1981-1982; adj prof, Georgetown Univ & Univ Md, 1990-; Res scientist, Blood Res Lab, Am Red Cross, 1975-1980; fel biochem, Blood Res Lab, Am RedCross, 1973-1975. **Memberships:** Am Soc Biochemistry and Molecular Biol; Am Chem Soc; AAAS; Am Soc for Cancer Res; Asn; Am Women Sci; Am Soc Microbiol. **Research Statement & Publications:** Correlation of host gene responses to pathogens with systems biology; regulatory mechanisms involved in the generation of bioactive lipids; mechanism for stimulation of cellular growth or cascades of inflammatory mediators by bioactive lipids; involvement of fatty acid binding proteins in regulation of bioactive lipid functions. **Mailing Address:** Chief, Dept Molecular Pathology, Walter Reed Army Inst Res, 503 Robert Grant Rd, Silver Spring, MD 20910. **Fax:** 202-319-9699. **E-Mail:** marti.jett@us.army.mil

JETTE, ARCHELLE NORMAN, PHYSICS SURFACES, STRUCTURE DEFECT CENTERS. **Personal Data:** b Portland, Ore, May 15, 1934; m 1972, Jamie Drago; c Andrea N. **Education:** Univ Calif, Riverside, AB, 1961, MA, 1963, PhD (physics), 1965. **Professional Experience:** Instr, Whiting Sch Eng, 1983-1990; vis scientist, Ctr Interdisciplinary Res, UnivBielefeld, WGer, 1980; Vis prof solid state physics, Cath Univ, Rio Del Janeiro, Brazil, 1972; RESPHYSICIST, APPL PHYSICS LAB, JOHNS HOPKINS UNIV, 1965-; Res assoc fel physics, Columbia Univ, 1965. **Memberships:** Am Phys Soc; Am Vacuum Soc. **Research Statement & Publications:** Surface structure; defect centers in ionic crystals; atomic and molecular physics. **Mailing Address:** 4021 Arjay Circle, Ellicott City, MD 21042. **Fax:** 301-953-6904. **E-Mail:** anj@aplcomm.jhvapl.edu

JETTE, DAVID, MATHEMATICS. **Professional Experience:** EXEC DIR, LAWRENCE H LANZL INST, as of 2005. **Memberships:** Am Asn Physicists Med. **Mailing Address:** Lawrence H Lanzl Inst, 3600 15th Ave W Suite 205, Seattle, WA 98119-1330. **Fax:** 206-789-4668. **E-Mail:** dave@lanzl.com

JETTEN, ANTON MARINUS, DIFFERENTIATION, RETINOIDS. **Personal Data:** b June 26, 1946; c 2. **Education:** Univ Nijmegen, Neth, PhD (biochem), 1973. **Professional Experience:** HEAD, CELL BIOL GROUP & LAB PULMONARY PATH, NAT INST ENVIRON HEALTH SCI, NIH, 1982-. **Memberships:** Am Asn Cancer Res; Am Soc Cell Biol. **Research Statement & Publications:** Understanding the molecular mechanisms that regulate the proliferation and differentiation of tracheo bronchial epidermal cells. **Mailing Address:** Nat Inst Environ Health Sci, NIH, PO Box 12233, MD D2-01, Res Triangle Park, NC 27709-2233. **Fax:** 919-541-4133. **E-Mail:** jetten@niehs.nih.gov

JEUTTER, DEAN CURTIS, ELECTRONICS & RADIO FREQUENCY ENGINEERING. **Personal Data:** b Bradford, Pa, December 27, 1944; m 1967, c 1. **Education:** Drexel Univ, BS, 1967, MS, 1969, PhD (biomed eng), 1974. **Honors & Awards:** Earl W Hatz Mem Award, 1984. **Professional Experience:** PROF BIOMED ENG, MARQUETTE UNIV, as of 2002; consult, Symbion Inc, 1985-1988; ASSOC PROF ELEC & COMPUT, MARQUETTE, 1983-; asst clin prof neurosurg, Med Col Wis, 1978-; adj asst prof physiol, Dept Physiol, Med Col Wis, 1977-; adj asst prof physiol, Dept Biol, Drexel Univ, 1975-1976; asst prof biomed eng, Comput & Biomed Eng, Marquette, 1976-1983; fel reprod biol, Dept Obstet & Gynec, Univ Pa, 1974-1976; res assoc biotelemetry, Dept Biomed Eng, Drexel Univ, 1970-1974; chief engr, Electronics Div, Ventron Corp, 1969-1970. **Memberships:** Sr mem Inst Elec & Electronics Engrs; Sigma Xi; sr mem Biomed Eng Soc. **Research Statement & Publications:** Transcutaneous data and powering; cochlear prostheses; totally implanted artificial heart; sensors; signal processing; regenerative electrical stimulation. **Mailing Address:** Haggerty Eng, Col Eng, Marquette Univ, Rm 351 PO Box 1881, Milwaukee, WI 53201-1881. **E-Mail:** jeutterd@marquette.edu

JEVNING, RON, BIOPHYSICS. **Personal Data:** b Winnemucca, Nev, October 20, 1942. **Education:** Stanford Univ, PhD, 1971. **Professional Experience:** SR RES FEL BIOL SCI, CALIF STATE UNIV, LONG BEACH, 1988-; Asst prof, Dept Med, Med Ctr, Univ Calif, Irvine, 1972-1988. **Memberships:** Am Physiol Soc; Am Soc Psychophysiol Res; Soc Neuroscience; Soc Behav Med; AmAsn Scientists Practicing TM Tech. **Research Statement & Publications:** Subjective foundations of science - in particular, as expressed in theory of measurement and theory of probability. **Mailing Address:** 210 W S St, Rialto, CA 92376.

JEWELL, FREDERICK FORBES, SR, HISTOPATHOLOGY, PATHOLOGICAL ANATOMY OF CONIFERS & HARDWOODS. **Personal Data:** b Oil City, Pa, June 4, 1928; m 1978, Daphne Cooper; c Fred Jr, Kimberly, Robert, Michael, Heather & Jessica. **Education:** Mich State Col, BS, 1951, MS, 1952; Univ WVa, PhD, 1955. **Professional Experience:** PROF, LA TECH UNIV, as of 2004; PROF FOREST PROTECTION, LA TECH UNIV, 1969-; assoc prof, LATech Univ, 1967-1969; prin plant pathologist forest tree dis, Southern

Inst Forest Genetics, 1955-1967; Asst plant path, Univ WVa, 1952-1955. **Memberships:** Am Phytopath Soc; Soc Am Foresters. **Research Statement & Publications:** Disease resistance in forest trees; rust-resistance in Southern pines; pathological anatomy; needle cast diseases. **Mailing Address:** La Tech Univ Sch Forestry, PO Box 3178, Ruston, LA 71272.

JEWELL, JACK LEE, DIODE LASERS, MICRO-OPTICS. **Personal Data:** b Jacksonville, Fla, January 7, 1954; m 1983, c 1. **Education:** Univ Fla, BS, 1975; Fla Inst Technol, MS, 1977; Univ Ariz, MS, 1981, PhD (opticalsci), 1984. **Professional Experience:** CHIEF TECHNOL OFFICER, PICOLIGHT INC, as of 1999; COFOUNDER & VPRES, PHOTONICS RES INC, 1991-; distinguished lectr, Inst Elec & Electronics Engrs Lasers & Electro-Optics Soc, 1991-1992; mem tech staff, AT&T Bell Labs, 1984-1991. **Memberships:** Optical Soc Am; Am Phys Soc; Soc Photo-Optical Instrumentation Engrs; Inst Elec & Electronics Engrs. **Research Statement & Publications:** Vertical-cavity surface-emitting microlasers; decreasing electrical resistance; extending wavelength range; opto-electronic integration with transistors; micro-optic integration. **Mailing Address:** Picolight Inc, 4665 Nautilus Ct S, Boulder, CO 80301. **Fax:** 303-530-4897.

JEWELL, NICHOLAS PATRICK, BIOSTATISTICS & TIME SERIES, EPIDEMIOLOGY & BIOINFORMATICS. **Personal Data:** b Paisley, Scotland, September 3, 1952; American & British citizen; m 1980, Debra; c Britta Lisa. **Education:** Univ Edinburgh, BS, 1973, PhD (math), 1976. **Professional Experience:** Interim Vice Chancellor, Capital Projects, Univ Calif, Berkeley, 1997-1998; vice provost, Univ Calif, Berkeley, 1994-2000; PROF BIOSTATISTICS and STATIST, UNIV CALIF, BERKELEY, 1987-; from asst prof to assoc prof, Univ Calif, Berkeley, 1981-1987; asst prof statist, Princeton Univ, 1979-1981; res fel, Univ Edinburgh, UK, 1978-1979; Harkness fel, Commonwealth Fund, NY, 1976-1978. **Memberships:** Am Statist Asn; Inst Math Statist (treas, 1985-); Biomet Soc. **Research Statement & Publications:** Biostatistics; mathematical statistics; functional analysis; Epidemiology. **Mailing Address:** Div Biostatistics, Sch Pub Health, Univ Calif, Berkeley, CA 94720. **Fax:** 510-643-5163. **E-Mail:** jewell@berkeley.edu

JEWELL, PAUL WILLIAM, SURFACE WATER HYDRODYNAMICS, BIOGEOCHEMICAL CYCLES. **Personal Data:** b Ogden, Utah, December 15, 1952; m 1982, Teresa; c Scott. **Education:** Beloit Col, BS, 1978; Univ Utah, MS, 1984; Princeton Univ, PhD (geol), 1989. **Professional Experience:** Prin investr, Petrol Res Fund, beginning 1990; ASSOC PROF GEOL & GEOPHYS, UNIV UTAH, 1989-; geol consult, Biomyne, Inc, beginning 1987; assoc geologist, Univ Utah Res Inst, 1980-1981; geol asst, Newmont Mining Co, 1979. **Memberships:** Geol Soc Am; Geochem Soc; Am Geophys Union; Asn Eng Geologists. **Research Statement & Publications:** Surface water hydrodynamics and the role that it plays in the cycles of carbon, nutrients and oxygen in the natural environment. **Mailing Address:** Dept Geol, Univ Utah, 135 S 1460 E Rm 719, Salt Lake City, UT 84112-0111. **Fax:** 801-581-7065. **E-Mail:** pwjewell@mines.utah.edu

JEWELL, THOMAS K, FLUID MECHANICS. **Education:** Univ Mass, PhD, 1980. **Professional Experience:** PROF & CHAIR CIVIL ENG, DIR INT PROG ENG COMUT SCI, UNION COL, as of 2005. **Mailing Address:** Civil Eng, Union Col, Schenectady, NY 12308. **Fax:** 518-388-6778. **E-Mail:** jewellt@union.edu

JEWELL, WILLIAM R, SURGERY. **Personal Data:** b Evanston, Ill, October 7, 1935; m 1960, c 4. **Education:** Blackburn Col, BA, 1957; Univ Ill, BS, 1959, MD, 1961. **Honors & Awards:** Meade Johnson Sr Res Award Surg, 1966, Health Sci Achievement Award, 1971. **Professional Experience:** ADJ FAC, GRAND VALLEY STATE UNIV, as of 2003; prof med & chief gen surg, Univ Kans Med Ctr, beginning 1978; assocprof med, Univ Kans Med Ctr, 1971-1978; Consult, US Vet Admin Hosp, Lexington, Ky, 1968-; Asst prof surg, Med Ctr, Univ Ky, 1968-1971. **Research Statement & Publications:** Carcinogenesis; protein metabolism in cancer bearing hosts; oncologic immunology; wound healing. **Mailing Address:** Sch Pub & Nonprofit Admin, Grand Valley State univ, 401 W Fulton Street, Grand Rapids, MI 49504.

JEWETT, DON L, EVOKED POTENTIAL A-WAVES, Q-SEQUENCE DECONVOLUTION. **Personal Data:** b Eureka, Calif, January 28, 1931; m, c 2. **Education:** San Francisco State Col, AB, Univ Calif, Berkeley, 1954-1956; Univ Calif, SanFrancisco, MD, 1960; Oxford Univ, DPhil(physiol), 1963. **Professional Experience:** PROF EMER, UNIV CALIF, SAN FRANCISCO, 1991-; DIR RES, ABRATECH CORP, 1991-; prof, Dept Orthop Surg, 1989-1991; assoc prof, Dept Orthop Surg, 1975-1989; clin instr, Dept Orthop Surg, 1972-1975; asst prof, DeptNeurosurg, 1966-1972; asst prof, Dept Physiol, Univ Calif, San Francisco, 1964-1972; NIH fel, Yale Univ, 1963-1964. **Memberships:** Sigma Xi. **Research Statement & Publications:** Neuroscience for detection of clinical conditions using scalp far field potentials, including ABR and A-waves by QSD; Advanced source localization using EF-plane analysis of FEA head conductivity-models. **Mailing Address:** Abratech Corp, 475 Gate S Rd, Ste 213, Sausalito, CA 94965. **E-Mail:** jewett@abratech.com

JEWETT, JOHN GIBSON, PHYSICAL ORGANIC CHEMISTRY. **Personal Data:** b Birmingham, Ala, January 21, 1937; m 1962, Susan; c Elizabeth & Jennifer. **Education:** Harvard Univ, AB, 1958; Mass Inst Technol, PhD (org chem), 1962. **Professional Experience:** PROF CHEM, UNIV VT, 1977-; dean Col Arts & Sci, Univ VT, 1977-1989; from asst prof to prof chem, Ohio Univ, 1964-1977; res assoc org chem, Ind Univ, 1962-1964. **Memberships:** AAAS; Am Chem Soc; Sigma Xi. **Research Statement & Publications:** Reaction mechanisms; isotope effects; simple displacement reactions; carbonyl addition reactions. **Mailing Address:** Chem Dept, Univ Vt, Sci Bldg, Burlington, VT 05405-0125. **Fax:** 802-656-8705. **E-Mail:** jjewett@moose.uvm.edu

JEWETT, SANDRA LYNNE, BIOCHEMISTRY, BIO-ORGANIC CHEMISTRY. **Personal Data:** b Lone Pine, Calif, November 13, 1945. **Education:** Univ Calif, Santa Barbara, BA, 1967, PhD (chem), 1971. **Professional Experience:** Jerome Richfield scholar, 1993; prof chem, calif state univ, northridge, 1988-2003; from asst prof to assoc prof, Calif State Univ, Northridge, 1977-1988; asst prof chem, Williams Col, 1975-1977; res fel enzyme immunoassays, Syva Co, Palo Alto, Calif, 1974-1975; NIH fel, 1972-1973; res fel biochem, Stanford Univ, 1971-1973. **Memberships:** AAAS; Am Chem Soc; Sigma Xi. **Research Statement & Publications:** Studies of erythrocyte superoxide dismutase; chemical studies of active site and intersubunit interactions; formation of and properties of metal deficient enzymes; reaction of copper-zinc dismutase with hydrogen peroxide; iron-catecholamine complexes. **Mailing Address:** Dept Chem, Calif State Univ, Northridge, CA 91330-8262. **Fax:** 818-677-4068. **E-Mail:** sandra.jewett@csun.edu

JEWETT, STEPHEN C, FISH & WILDLIFE SCIENCES. **Education:** John Brown Univ, BA, 1971; Univ Alaska MS, 1977, PhD, 1997. **Professional Experience:** RES PROF MARINE SCI, UNIV ALASKA, as of 2006. **Mailing Address:** Inst Marine Sci, Univ Alaska, Fairbanks, AK 99775.

JEYAPALAN, KANDIAH, PHOTOGRAMMETRY. **Personal Data:** b Sri Lanka, June 24, 1938; m 1964, Nalini; c Suriya & Manjula. **Education:** Univ Ceylon, BSc, 1960; Univ London, MSc, 1967, PhD (photogram), 1972. **Professional Experience:** Vis prof, Naval Postgrad Sch, Montrey, Calif, 1987; UN fel, 1986; PROF SURV, GEOD & PHOTOGRAM, IOWA STATE UNIV, 1979-; prof, geod & photogram, CalifState Univ, Fresno, 1978-1979; res civil engr, US Geol Surv, 1977; assoc prof, geod &photogram, Calif State Univ, Fresno, 1974-1978; sr lectr, Univ Dar-es-Salaam, Tanzania, 1973 &1974; asst prof surv, geod & photogram, Calif State Univ, Fresno, 1972-1974; admin asst, Highway Dept, Columbus, Ohio, 1972; res assoc, Dept Geodetic Sci, Ohio State Univ, 1969-1972; lectr, Dept Geod Sci, Ohio State Univ, 1969-1972; chief photogrammetrist, SurvDept, Sri Lanka, 1967-1969; UN fel, UN Educ & Sci Orgn, 1966; scholar, Ceylon Govt, 1963; asst supt, Surv Dept, Sri Lanka, 1961-1967. **Memberships:** Am Soc Photogram; Am Congress Surv & Mapping; Sigma Xi. **Research Statement & Publications:** Photogrammetry: development of analytical plotter, calibration of cameras, analytical triangulation, shortrange photogrammetry and digital terrain model; geodesy: electronic surveying, Doppler surveying and geoposition system; numerical cadastral survey; global positioning system; surveying, land surveying, geographic information system. **Mailing Address:** Dept Civil Construct & Environ Eng, Iowa State Univ, 428 Town Eng Bldg, Ames, IA 50011. **Fax:** 515-294-8216. **E-Mail:** kjp@iastate.edu

JEZAK, EDWARD V, PHYSICS. **Personal Data:** b Czestochowa, Poland, March 29, 1934; American citizen; m 1962, c 2. **Education:** Harvard Univ, AB, 1957; Univ Minn, PhD (physics), 1962. **Professional Experience:** ASSOC PROF MATH, DEPT MATH & COMPUT SCI, ROYAL MIL COL, 1968-; Asst prof physics, Boston Col, 1962-1968. **Memberships:** Am Phys Soc. **Research Statement & Publications:** Nuclear theoretical physics; three body problem; molecular dynamics. **Mailing Address:** Dept Math & Comput Sci, Royal Mil Col, PO Box 17000, Station Forces, Kingston, ON K7K 7B4, Can. **Fax:** 613-541-6584. **E-Mail:** jezak-e@rmc.ca

JEZEK, KENNETH CHARLES, GEOPHYSICS. **Personal Data:** b Chicago, Ill, May 17, 1951; m 1984, Rosanne M Graziano. **Education:** Univ Ill, BSc, 1973; Univ Wis, MSc, 1977, PhD (geophys), 1980. **Professional Experience:** Grant, ONR, 1992; mem, Environ Task Force, 1992; coordr, Sea IceElectromagnetic Accelerated Res Initiative, Off Naval Res, 1992; assoc ed, J Geophys Res, 1991-; prin investr, Greenland Ice Sheet, 1991-1992; ASSOC PROF GEOL & DIR, BYRDPOLAR RES CTR, OHIO STATE UNIV, 1989-; prin investr, Greenland Sea, 1988; res asst prof, Thayer Sch Eng, Dartmouth Col, 1987-1989; grant, NASA, 1985-1993; mgr, Polar Oceans & IceSheets Prog, NASA, Wash, 1985-1987; grant, CRREL, 1985-1986; grant, Off naval Res, 1984-1989; geophysicist, Cold Regions Res & Eng Lab, US Army, Hanover, NH, 1983-1985, 1987-1989; cons, Polar Ice Coring Off, Greenland, 1983; prin investr, Greenland, 1982 & 1985; grant, NSF, 1982-1984; geophysicist, East Antarctica, 1981-1982; geophysicist, Southern Greenland Ice Sheet, 1981; proj assoc, Geophys & Polar Res Ctr, Univ Wis, 1981-1983; fel, Inst Polar Studies, Ohio State Univ, Columbus, 1980-1981; field leader, Dome C East Antarctica, 1978-1979; geophysicist, Camp Century Greenland, 1977; field leader, Ross Ice Shelf, 1976-1977; geophysicist, Devon Island Ice Cap, 1975; geophysicist, Ross Ice Shelf, Antarctica, 1974-1975; observer, Bartol Res Found Cosmic Ray Lab, McMurdo Sta, Antarctica, 1973-1974. **Memberships:** Am Geophus Union; Soc Exploration Geophysicists; Int Glaciological Soc; SigmaXi. **Mailing Address:** Byrd Polar Res Center Ohio State Univ, 1090 Carmack Rd, Columbus, OH 43210. **E-Mail:** jezej.1@osu.edu

JEZL, JAMES LOUIS, ORGANIC CHEMISTRY, RESEARCH ADMINISTRATION. **Personal Data:** b Tobias, Nebr, December 12, 1918; m 1964. **Education:** Univ Nebr, AB, 1941; Pa State Col, MS, 1942; Univ Del, PhD (org chem), 1949. **Professional Experience:** Pub & Auth, Kane Trail Pub, 1998-; RETIRED; mgr explor res, Res & Develop Dept, 1976-1986; divdir, Naperville Tech Ctr, Amoco Chem Corp, 1970-1976; dir res, Avisun Corp, 1968-1970; mgr res div, Avisun Corp, 1960-1968; sect chief, Pa, 1958-1960; res group leader, Pa, 1954-1958; res chemist, Pa, 1949-1954; develop chemist, Pa, 1947-1949; sr anal chemist, Sun Oil Co, Ohio, 1945-1947; jr anal chemist, Sun Oil Co, Ohio, 1943-1945; Supvry chemist, US Rubber Co, 1942-1943. **Memberships:** AAAS; Am Chem Soc. **Research Statement & Publications:** Diabetic Nutrition. **Mailing Address:** 35 W 094 Army Trail, St Charles, IL 60174. **Fax:** 630-587-8350. **E-Mail:** JLJEZL@ATTGLOBAL.NET

JEZOREK, JOHN ROBERT, ANALYTICAL CHEMISTRY, INORGANIC CHEMISTRY. **Personal Data:** b Baltimore, Md, June 12, 1942; m 1967, c 4. **Education:** Loyola Col, Md, BS, 1964; Univ Del, PhD (analytical chem), 1970. **Professional Experience:** PROF EMER CHEM & BIOCHEM, UNIV NC, 2004-; prof analytical chem, Univ Nc, Greensboro, 1982-2004; res assoc, Univ Ariz, 1977-1978; from asst prof to assoc prof, Univ NC, Greensboro, 1970-1981; res assoc, Univ Mich, 1969-1970. **Memberships:** Am Chem Soc; Sigma Xi. **Research Statement & Publications:** Liquid chromatography; design of novel LC stationary phases; surface modification chemistry. **Mailing Address:** Dept Chem, Univ NC, 228 Petty Bldg, Greensboro, NC 27412. **Fax:** 910-334-5402. **E-Mail:** jezorekj@iris.uncg.edu

JEZYK, PETER FRANKLIN, VETERINARY MEDICINE. **Personal Data:** b Ware, Mass, November 7, 1939; c 2. **Education:** Univ Mass, BS, 1961, PhD (zoology), 1966; Univ Pa, VMD, 1975. **Professional Experience:** PROF EMER, DEPT VET MED, UNIV PA, as of 2005; adj assoc prof med genetics, Sch Vet Med, Univ Pa, beginning 1981; dir, Metab Screening Lab, Children's Hosp Philadelphia, 1976-; asst prof, Sch Vet Med, Univ PA, 1975-1981; asst prof biochem, Med Col Va, 1967-1971; NIH fel biol chem & res assoc, Univ Mich, 1966-1967. **Memberships:** AAAS; Am Vet Med Asn. **Research Statement & Publications:** Metabolic aspects of inherited disease in companion animals. **Mailing Address:** Sch Vet Med, Univ Pa, 3800 Spruce St, Philadelphia, PA 19104.

JHA, KRISHNA K, MICROBIOLOGY. **Professional Experience:** ADJ ASSOC PROF, DEPT MICROBIOL & MOLECULAR GENETICS, UNIV MED & DENT NJ, as of 2005. **Memberships:** Exec Mem eHealth-Care Project. **Mailing Address:** Dept Microbiol & Molecular Genetics Univ Med & Dent NJ, 185 S Orange Ave, Newark, NJ 07103-2714.

JHA, MAHESH CHANDRA, COAL CONVERSION TECHNOLOGY, PROCESS DEVELOPMENT. **Personal Data:** b Bihar, India, March 13, 1945; American citizen; m 1964, c 2. **Education:** Bihar Inst Technol, India, BScEng, 1965; Mich Tech Univ, MS, 1970; Iowa StateUniv, Ames, PhD (metall & chem eng), 1974. **Honors & Awards:** Extractive Metall Technol Award, Metall Soc, 1986. **Professional Experience:** MGR ENERGY RES & DEVELOP, AMAX RES & DEVELOP CTR, 1987-; mgr contract res & develop, Amax Res & Develop Ctr, 1985-1986; sect supvr, Amax Res &Develop Ctr, 1978-1984; group leader, Amax Res & Develop Ctr, 1975-1978; res metallurgist, Amax Res & Develop Ctr, 1973-1975; grad res asst, Inst Mineral Res, Mich Tech Univ, 1969-1970 &Ames Lab, Iowa State Univ, 1970-1973; Lectr extractive metall, Bihar Inst Technol, India, 1965-1966& Univ Roorkee, India, 1966-1969. **Memberships:** Am Inst Mining Metall & Petrol Engrs; Am Inst Chem Engrs. **Research Statement & Publications:** Improving the processes for extraction of non-ferrous metals such as nickel, cobalt, molybdenum, tungsten, gold, silver from low-grade ores; waste streams; coal conversion and utilization tehnology. **Mailing Address:** Amax Res & Develop Ctr, Golden, CO 80403-7499.

JHA, SHACHEENATHA, EXPERIMENTAL NUCLEAR PHYSICS. **Personal Data:** b Darbhanga, Bihar, India, November 15, 1918; m 1955, c 4. **Education:** Patna Univ, BS, 1939, MS, 1941; Univ Edinburgh, PhD (nuclear physics), 1950. **Professional Experience:** PROF EMER PHYSICS, UNIV CINCINNATI, as of 2003; prof physics, Univ Cincinnati, beginning 1969; assoc prof, Case Western Reserve Univ, 1966-1969; asst prof, Carnegie Inst Technol, 1961-1966; fel, Tata InstFundamental Res, India, 1956-1961; res fel physics, Tata Inst Fundamental Res, India, 1951-1956; asst prof, Patna Sci Col, 1951; govt bihar scholar nuclear physics, Univ Edinburgh, 1946-1951; lectr, Patna Sci Col, 1944-1946; res scholar physics, Patna Sci Col, 1941-1944. **Memberships:** fel Am Phys Soc; Am Asn Physics Teachers. **Research Statement & Publications:** Nuclear spectroscopy and reaction; Mossbauer effect; molecular spectroscopy. **Mailing Address:** Dept Physics, Univ Cincinnati, 145 McMicken Hall, PO Box 210037, Cincinnati, OH 45221-0037. **Fax:** 513-556-0142. **E-Mail:** shacheenatha.jha@uc.edu

JHAMANDAS, KHEM, PHARMACOLOGY. **Personal Data:** b East Africa, May 11, 1939; m 1971. **Education:** Univ London, BSc, 1964; Univ Alta, MSc, 1966, PhD (pharmacol), 1969. **Professional Experience:** Vis scientist, Univ Melbourne, 1987; vis scientist, Kyoto Univ, 1986; vis scientist, Mayo Clinic & Killam res fel, 1980-1981; PROF PHARMACOL & TOXICOL, FAC MED, QUEEN'S UNIV, ONT, 1975-; asst prof, Fac Med, Queen's Univ, Ont, 1970-1975; med Res Coun Can fel pharmacol & therapeut, Univ Man, 1969-1970. **Memberships:** Pharmacol Soc Can; Am Soc Pharmacol & Exp Therapeut; Soc Neuroscience. **Research Statement & Publications:** Neuropharmacology; action of drugs on transmitter substances in the central nervous system; mechanisms underlying drug dependence on opioids; neuropharmacology of enkephalins, endorphins and neuropeptides; excitotoxins. **Mailing Address:** Dept Pharmacol & Toxicol, Queen's Univ, 563 Botterell Hall, Kingston, ON K7L 3N6, Can. **Fax:** 613-545-6412. **E-Mail:** jhamanda@post.queensu.ca

JHANWAR, SURESH CHANDRA, CYTOGENETICS. **Education:** Univ Delhi, India, PhD (genetics), 1976. **Professional Experience:** DIR, CYTOGENETICS LAB, SLOAN-KETTERING CANCER CTR as of 2004; ASST PROF GENETICS & ASST ATTEND GENETICIST, SLOAN-KETTERING CANCER CTR, 1976-. **Mailing Address:** Sloan-Kettering Cancer Ctr, Box 147 1275 York Ave, New York, NY 10021-6094. **Fax:** 212-794-5830.

JHIRAD, DAVID JOHN, PHYSICS, SCIENCE POLICY. **Personal Data:** b India, May 29, 1939; American citizen; m Anna; c Dylan, Nicholas & Alexander. **Education:** Delhi Univ, BSc, 1958; Cambridge Univ, BA, 1961, MA, 1964; Harvard Univ, PhD (appl physics), 1972. **Professional Experience:** EXEC VPRES & SECY, GEMSATR GROUP INC, as of today; CONSULT, 1984-; sr adv, multilateral bilateral affairs, dept energy, 2000-2001; dep asst secy, dept energy, 1995-2000; dir, energy efficiency renewable energy prog, US Agency for Int Develop, 1988-1995; sr energy adv, US Agency for Int Develop, 1984-1988; dir, Int Energy Prog, Brookhaven Nat Lab, 1980-1984; sr res scientist energy, Jet Propulsion Lab, Calif Inst Technol, 1979-1980; sr staff scientist & dir, Union Concerned Scientists, 1975-1979; asst prof physics, Univ Mass, 1970-1975; asst prof physics, Boston Univ, 1970-1974; chmn, dept nat sci, Boston Univ, 1970-1971. **Memberships:** Am Phys Soc; AAAS; Int Solar Energy Soc; Scientists Inst Pub Info; AMWS. **Research Statement & Publications:** New power technology, energy technology assessment and policy analysis; energy and global climate change; international power project financing; thermodynamics and statistical mechanics. **Mailing Address:** 3009 Daniel Ln NW, Washington, DC 20015. **Fax:** 202-687-5528. **E-Mail:** davidjhirad@starband.net

JHON, MYUNG S, POLYMER ENGINEERING, TRIBOLOGY. **Personal Data:** b Korea, American citizen. **Education:** Seoul Nat Univ, Seoul, Korea, BS, 1967; Univ Chicago, PhD (physics), 1974. **Professional Experience:** Vis prof, Magnetics Recording Inst, Int Bus Mach, 1985 & Univ Calif, Berkeley, 1989; PROF CHEM ENG, CARNEGIE MELLON UNIV, 1988-; vis scientist, Int Bus Mach ResDiv, Almaden Res Ctr, 1988; sr vis prof, Naval Res Lab, Wash, DC, 1986; consult, UNIndust Develop Orgn, 1986; from asst prof to assoc prof, Carnegie Mellon Univ, 1980-1988; resspecialist chem, Univ Minn, 1976-1980; postdoctoral fel physics, Univ Toronto, 1974-1976; res asst physics, James Franck Inst, Univ Chicago, 1970-1974. **Memberships:** Am Inst Chem Engrs; Am Phys Soc; Am Chem Soc; Sigma Xi; NY Acad Sci. **Research Statement & Publications:** Magnetic and magneto-optical recording; polymer and suspension rheology; interfacial dynamics; membrane science and technology; equilibrium and nonequilibrium statistical mechanics; chemical kinetics; fluid mechanics; turbulent drag reduction. **Mailing Address:** Carnegie-Mellon Univ, Doherty Hall 1100, Pittsburgh, PA 15217. **Fax:** 412-268-7139. **E-Mail:** mj3a+@andrew.cmu.edu

JI, CHUENG RYONG, PARTICLE & NUCLEAR THEORY. **Personal Data:** b Seoul, Korea, January 7, 1954; m 1983, Mikyoung; c Stephen, Lisa & David. **Education:** Seoul Nat Univ, BS, 1976; Korea Advan Inst Sci & Technol, MS, 1978, PhD, 1982. **Honors & Awards:** Dirac scholarship award, the third international conference on the intersections between practicle and nuclear physics, 1988; Korea Sci and engr foundation fellowship, 1982. **Professional Experience:** Prof phys, NC state univ, 1997-; vis prof, Seoul Nat Univ, 1993; ASSOC PROF PHYSICS, NC STATE UNIV, 1992-; prin investr, Dept Energy, 1990-; theory consult, Continuous Electron Beam Accelerator Facil, 1990; asst prof nuclear physics, NC State Univ, 1987-1992; res assoc, Brooklyn Col, City Univ New York, 1986-1987; Particle & nuclear physics, Stanford Univ, 1984-1986; Vis scholar elem particle physics, Stanford Linear Accelerator Ctr, 1982-1986. **Memberships:** Am Phys Soc; Sigma Xi; Phi Kappa Phi. **Research Statement & Publications:** Quantum chromodynamics, self-organizing relativistic quantum field theory, Quark and gluon structures of hadron theory of strong interaction based on the light cone formulation; theory of strong interaction, quantum chromodynamics, based on the light cone formulation; form factors of meson, nucleon and deuteron, non-topological soliton physics. **Mailing Address:** Dept Physics, NC State Univ, Raleigh, NC 27695-8202. **Fax:** 919-515-2471. **E-Mail:** ji@ncsu.edu

JI, GUANGDA WINSTON, III-V SEMICONDUCTOR DEVICES RESEARCH & DEVELOPMENT, REACTIVE ION ETCHING AND PLASMA ENHANCED CHEMICAL VAPOR DEPOSITION SPECIALIST. **Personal Data:** b Tianjin, China, c 1. **Education:** Univ Ill Urbana, MS, 1981, PhD (physics), 1986. **Honors & Awards:** Chinese Award in Sci & Technol, 1982. **Professional Experience:** RES SCIENTIST, SUNNYBROOK HEALTH SCI CTR, TORONTO, 1993-; Res assoc elec eng, Ont Laser & Lightwave Res Ctr, 1988-1991; Res assoc elec eng, Coord SciLab, Univ Ill, Urbana, 1986-1988. **Memberships:** Am Phys Soc. **Research Statement & Publications:** Semiconductor laser; optoelectronic devices; high-speed semiconductor electronic devices; device modeling and optical measurements for superlattice and heterojunction devices in III-V semiconductors; reactive ion etching and plasma enhanced chemical vapor deposition techniques and diagnosis; author of one publication; x-ray medical image processing. **Mailing Address:** 145 St George St Apt 301, Toronto, ON M5R 2M1, Can. **E-Mail:** chi@srcl.sunnybrook.utoronto.ca

JI, INHAE, HORMONES, RECEPTORS. **Personal Data:** b Seoul, Korea, May 17, 1938; m 1965, c 2. **Education:** Seoul Nat Univ, BS, 1961, MS, 1963; Univ Wyo, PhD (biochem), 1977. **Professional Experience:** RES PROF MOLECULAR BIOL, UNIV KY, 1991-; res asst biochem, UnivWyo, 1978-1991; postdoctoral biochem, Harvard Med Sch, 1977-1978. **Memberships:** Endocrine Soc; Am Soc Cell Biologists. **Mailing Address:** Dep Chem Univ Ky, 249C Chem Physics Bldg, Lexington, KY 40506-0055. **Fax:** 606-257-3229. **E-Mail:** inhaeji@pop.uky.edu

JI, SUNGCHUL, BIOPHYSICS, CELL PHYSIOLOGY. **Personal Data:** b Sheenweejoo, Korea, December 17, 1937; m 1967, c 1. **Education:** Univ Minn, Duluth, BA, 1965; State Univ NY Albany, PhD (org chem), 1970. **Professional Experience:** ASSOC PROF, DEPT PHARAMACOL & TOXICOL, RUTGERS UNIV, as of 2004; FAC, ENVIRON & OCCUP HEALTH SCI INST, as of 2004; res asst prof, dept pharmacol, Univ NC, 1979-; res scientist, Max Planck Inst Systs Physiol, 1976-; res assoc, Johnson Res Found, Univ Pa, 1974-1976; NIH trainee & res asst prof, Inst Enzyme Res, UnivWis-Madison, 1970-1974; asst prof chem, Mankato State Col, 1968-1970; GRAD PROG TOXICOL, RUTGERS UNIV. **Memberships:** Am Chem Soc; AAAS; Sigma Xi. **Research Statement & Publications:** Anion radical chemistry; electron transfer reactions in organic solvents; energy-coupling mechanism in mitochondria; nicotinamide-adenine dinucleotide fluorescence photography; micro-light guide tissue photometry; flow-metabolism coupling in the liver; alcohol-induced liver injury; lobular oxygen gradient in the liver. **Mailing Address:** Dept Pharmacol & Toxicol, Rutgers, State Univ NJ, 170 Frelinghuysen Rd, Piscataway, NJ 08854. **Fax:** 732-445-0119. **E-Mail:** sji@eohsi.rutgers.edu

JI, TAE H(WA), BIOCHEMISTRY, MOLECULAR BIOLOGY. **Personal Data:** b Seoul, Korea, April 7, 1941; American citizen; m 1961, c 2. **Education:** Seoul Nat Univ, BS, 1964; Univ Calif, San Diego, PhD (biol), 1968. **Honors & Awards:** Burlington Northern Award, 1989. **Professional Experience:** PROF CHEM, UNIV KY, 1999-; PROF EMER, UNIV WYO, 1999-; consult, Pioneer Hybrid Inc, 1996; mem, Physiol Chem Study Sect, NIH, 1990-1994; sr fac res award, Am Cancer Soc, 1983-1988; prof biochem, Univ Wyo, 1984-1999; vis prof, Harvard Univ, 1977-1978; scholar award cancer res, Univ Calif, 1977; from asst prof to assoc prof, Univ Wyo, 1970-1984; fel, Univ Minn, 1969-1970; inst Biomed Res fel, Am Med Asn, 1968-1969; regent fel, Univ Calif, 1964. **Memberships:** Am Soc Biochem & Molecular Biol; Endocrine Soc; Soc Study Reproduction; Protein Soc; Am Soc Microbiol. **Research Statement & Publications:** Structure function and gene expression of gonadotropin receptors; photoaffinity labeling. **Mailing Address:** Dep Chem, Univ Ky, Lexington, KY 40506-0055. **Fax:** 859-257-3229. **E-Mail:** tji@pop.uky.edu

JIA, QUANXI, ELECTRONIC MATERIALS, THIN FILMS, SEMICONDUCTOR & SUPERCONDUCTOR DEVICES. **Personal Data:** b Hunan Prov, China, September 3, 1957; m 1985, c Shawn & Richard. **Education:** Jiaotong Univ, Xian, China, BS, 1982, MS, 1985; State Univ NY, Buffalo, PhD (elec & comput eng), 1991. **Honors & Awards:** Asian-American Engineer of the Year award, 2005; Laboratory Fellow at Los Alamos National Laboratory, 2003; R & D 100 Awards for Underground Radio in 1998 and Flexible Superconducting Tape in 2003 (the R & D 100 Awards Program honors the 100 most technolgically significant new products, materials, process, software or sys with commercial promise of the yr by R & D Magazine). **Professional Experience:** TECHNICAL STAFF MEM, LOS ALAMOS NAT LAB, 1993-; Lab Fellow, 2003-; Vis assoc prof, Kumamato Univ, Japan, 1993; res assoc, State Univ NY Buffalo, 1991-1993; asst prof, Jiaotong Univ, 1987-1988; res assoc, Jiaotong Univ, 1985-1987. **Memberships:** Mat Res Soc; Am Ceramic Soc. **Research Statement & Publications:** Synthesis and structure-property relationships of nanostructured materials, multifunctional materials, thin films and multilayer systems; development and fabrication of high-temperature superconducting films; research on advanced semiconductor devices and materials; thin film growth and device development; more than 250 peer-reviewed journal articles and 9 book chapters patentee in field; 25 US patents issued and 12 filed in the fields of electronic materials and devices. **Mailing Address:** Los Alamos Nat Lab, MS K763, Los Alamos, NM 87545. **Fax:** 505-665-3164. **E-Mail:** qxjia@lanl.gov

JIANG, JACK BAU-CHIEN, ORGANIC CHEMISTRY, MEDICINAL CHEMISTRY. **Personal Data:** b Sze-chuan, China, November 15, 1947; m 1973, Lily; c Melody & Hanson. **Education:** Nat Cheng Kung Univ, BS, 1970; Mich State Univ, PhD (org chem), 1975. **Professional Experience:** VPRES CHEM RES, PRO-NEURON INC, 1996-; vpres chem, Phytera, 1993-1995; adj asst prof, Col Pharm, Univ NC, Chapel Hill, 1991-; vpres chem res, Sphinx Pharmaceut Corp, 1991-1993; dir med chem, Sphinx Pharmaceut Corp, 1989-1991; group leader, Du Pont Pharmaceut, 1987-1989; scientist, DuPont Pharmaceuts, 1984-1987; sr scientist, OrthoPharm Corp, 1981-1984; scientist, Ortho Pharm Corp, 1979-1981; res chemist drug synthesis, Am Cyanamid Co, 1977-1979; res specialist, Univ Minn, 1975-1977. **Memberships:** Am Chem Soc; Am Asn Cancer Res. **Research Statement & Publications:** Design and synthesis of medicinal agents; anticancer chemotherapy discovery and development; natural products. **Mailing Address:** 62 Kato Dr, Sudbury, MA 01776-2448. **Fax:** 978-443-0040.

JIANG, NAI-SIANG, BIOCHEMISTRY. **Personal Data:** b Nanking, China, June 6, 1931; m 1958, c 2. **Education:** Nat Taiwan Univ, BS, 1955; Emory Univ, MS, 1959, PhD (biochem), 1962. **Professional Experience:** HEAD SECT CLIN CHEM, MAYO MED SCH, UNIV MINN, 1984-; PROF LAB MED, MAYO MED SCH, UNIV MINN, 1980-; assoc prof biochem & lab med, MayoGrad Sch Med, 1975-1980; Dir & consult, Endocrine Lab, Dept Lab Med, Mayo Clin & Found, 1971-; asst prof biochem, Mayo Grad Sch Med, 1967-1975; consult, Dept Endoctrine Res, 1967-1970; res assoc, Mayo Found, Mayo Clinic, 1966-1967; Instr biochem, Emory Univ, 1962-1966. **Memberships:** AAAS; Am Chem Soc; Sigma Xi. **Research Statement & Publications:** Measurement of hormones in body fluid. **Mailing Address:** Dept Lab Med, Mayo Clin & Found, Rochester, MN 55905.

JIANG, SHAOYI, THERMODYNAMICS & STATISTICAL MECHANICS, COMPUTATIONAL MATERIALS SCIENCE. **Personal Data:** b August 17, 1964; m Qiuming; c Allen J. **Education:** Hua Qiao Univ, China, BS, 1985; Nanjing Univ Chem Technol, China, MS, 1988; Cornell Univ, PhD (chem eng), 1993. **Professional Experience:** ASSOC PROF CHEM ENG, UNIV WASH, as of 2003; INVESTR, NESAC-BIO, as of 2003; asst prof chem eng, Kans State Univ beginning 1997; res fel chem, CalifInst Technol, 1994-1996; vis scientist, Lawrence Berkeley Lab, 1993-1994; postdoctoral fel, Univ Calif, Berkeley, 1993-1994. **Memberships:** Am Inst Chem Engrs; Am Chem Soc; AAAS; Mat Res Soc. **Research Statement & Publications:** Thermodynamics. statistical mechanics, molecular simulation, abinitio quantum chemistry, parallel computing and experiment (surface proximal probes, absorption and thermophysical properties of fluids) with applications to interfacial phenomena, molecular tribology and advanced materials. **Mailing Address:** Dept Chem Eng, Univ Wash, PO Box 351750, Seattle, WA 98195-1750. **Fax:** 206-685-3451. **E-Mail:** sjiang@u.washington.edu

JIBSON, RANDALL W, GEOLOGIC HAZARDS RES, EARTHQUAKE-TRIGERED LANDSLIDES. **Personal Data:** b San Jose, Calif, April 17, 1956; m 1982, Linda; c Matthew, Daniel & Karen. **Education:** San Diego State Univ, BS, 1980; Stanford Univ, MS, 1983, PhD (geol), 1985. **Professional Experience:** RES GEOLOGIST, US GEOL SURV, 1994-; supvry geologist & geomech res coordr, US Geol Surv, 1988-1994; mem, Landslide Comt, Asn Eng Geologists, 1987-1998; res fel, Japan Pub Works Res Inst, 1987; geologist, US Geol Surv, 1983-1988. **Memberships:** Geol Soc Am mem. **Research Statement & Publications:** Basic and applied research in the field of geologic hazards, specifically in earthquake effects, ground-failure processes and coastal erosion. **Mailing Address:** US Geol Surv MS 966 Denver Fed Ctr, Box 25046, Denver, CO 80225. **E-Mail:** jibson@usgs.gov

JICHA, HENRY LOUIS, ECONOMIC GEOLOGY, EARTH SCIENCE. **Personal Data:** b New York, NY, June 25, 1925; m 1951, Jeanette; c 3. **Education:** Columbia Univ, BA, 1948, MA, 1951, PhD (econ geol), 1952. **Professional Experience:** RETIRED; dir res, Wood Gundy Corp, NY, 1983-1989; vpres & sr analyst, Prudential Bache Securities Inc, New York, 1974-1983; mgr res, Jesup & Lamont, 1971-1973; sr analyst, Newberger, Loeb & Co, 1970-1971; mgr, New York Res, Courts & Co, 1962-1970; ed-analyst, Value Line Invest Surv, Metals, Oils, Brewing, 1961-1962; analyst mining & metal stocks, Baker, Weeks & Co, 1958-1961; consult, Baumgartner Oil Co, Colo, 1957-1958; asst prof geol, Colo Sch Mines, 1956-1958; econ geologist, NMex Bur Mines & Mineral Resources, 1951-1956; field asst, NMex Bur Mines & Mineral Resources, 1950-1951; geologist, Mineral Deposits Br, US Geol Surv, Colo, 1948-1949 & Fla, 1949. **Memberships:** Sigma Xi. **Research Statement & Publications:** Uranium deposits in Colorado, phosphate deposits in Florida; lead-zinc deposits in Europe; tertiary volcanics, lead-zinc-silver deposits, Mesa del Oro Quadrangle and manganese deposits in New Mexico. **Mailing Address:** 12 Western Dr, Ardsley, NY 10502.

JILES, CHARLES WILLIAM, electrical engineering; deceased, see previous edition for last biography

JILKA, ROBERT LAURENCE, MOLECULAR ENDOCRINOLOGY, BONE METABOLISM. **Personal Data:** b Salina, Kans, November 26, 1948. **Education:** Univ Kans State, BS, 1970, MS, 1972; Univ St Louis, PhD (biochem), 1975. **Professional Experience:** PROF INTERNAL MED, UNIV ARK MED SCI, as of 2004; RES SCIENTIST, CENT ARK VET HEALTHCARE SYST, UNIV ARK MED SCI, as of 2004; adj asst prof, Dept Biochem, Univ Kans Med Ctr, 1979-; staff scientist, Calcium Res Lab, Vet Admin Med Ctr, Kans, 1978-; fel, Roche Inst Molecular Biol, 1975-1978; VET ADMIN MED CTR, IND POLIS; AT DEPT INT MED, UNIV ARK. **Memberships:** Am Soc Bone & Mineral Res. **Research Statement & Publications:** Biochemical changes caused by parathormone, vitamin D and calcitonin on bone in organ culture and partially purified bone cells in tissue culture; both normal and genetically defined osteopetrotic bone is studied; Published over 6 articles. **Mailing Address:** Div Endocrinol, Univ Ark Med Sci, 4301 W Markham Slot 587, Little Rock, AR 72205. **Fax:** 501-686-8954. **E-Mail:** rljilka@life.uams.edu

JIM, KAM FOOK, CARDIOVASCULAR PHARMACOLOGY, BIOCHEMICAL PHARMACOLOGY. **Personal Data:** b Po On, China, November 13, 1953. **Education:** NY Univ, BA, 1976; State Univ NY, Buffalo, PhD (pharmacol), 1981. **Professional Experience:** SR MGR, SANDOFI-SYNTHELABO RES, 2002-; sr med writer, OTSUKA Md Res Inst, 1998-2002; prin sci writer clin commun, Wyeth-Ayerst Res, 1988-1998; consult, Med Col Pa, 1986-1988; postdoctoral scientist pharmacol, SmithKline & French Lab, SmithKline Beecham Co, 1983-1986; res assoc, Cornell Univ Med Col, 1981-1983; postdoctoral fel biochem, Case Western Res Univ, 1980-1981. **Memberships:** Fel Am Col Clin Pharmacol; Am Soc Pharmacol & Exp Therapeut; AAAS. **Research Statement & Publications:** Writing responsibilities include clinical trials reports and global regulatory submission documents for cardiovascular and metabolic drugs including angiotensin II antagonists, lipid-lowering agents, and antiarrhythmic and antianginal compounds. **Mailing Address:** 2402 Cobblestone Way, Frederick, MD 21702. **Fax:** 610-889-6908. **E-Mail:** kam.jim@sanofi-synthelabo.com

JIMBOW, KOWICHI, DERMATOLOGY, PATHOLOGY. **Personal Data:** b Nagoya City, Japan, June 4, 1941; c 5. **Education:** Sapporo Med Col, MD, 1966, PhD (med sci), 1974. **Honors & Awards:** Alfred-Marchionini Prize, Int Asn Dermat, 1982; Seiji Mem Prize, Japanese SocDermat, 1984. **Professional Experience:** CHMN COMT, SAPPORO MED UNIV, as of 2005; DEAN, SAPPORO MED UNIV, as of 2004; chmn & organizer, Third Meeting Pan Am Soc Pigment Cell Res, 1990-; PROF PATH, UNIV ALTA, EDMONTON, 1988-; PROF & DIR DERMAT & CUTANEOUS SCI, UNIV ALTA, EDMONTON, 1987-; mem organizing comt, Second Int Melanoma Conf, 1986-; counr, Int Soc Pigment Cell Res, 1984-1987; from asst prof to assoc prof, Sapporo Med Col, Japan, 1975-1987; vis assoc prof dematopath, Dept Path, Univ Ark, 1975-1978; instr dermat, Mass Gen Hosp, Boston, 1974-1975. **Memberships:** Am Soc Cancer Res; Am Soc Photobiol; Can Dermat Asn; fel Am Acad Dermat. **Mailing Address:** Univ Alta, 260G Heritage Med Res Ctr, Edmonton, AB T6G 2S2, Can.

JIMENEZ, AGNES E, NEUROENDOCRINOLOGY. **Personal Data:** b Farrell, Pa, October 21, 1943. **Education:** Univ Louisville, PhD (physiol), 1976. **Professional Experience:** ASSOC PROF PHYSIOL, SCH MED, UNIV LOUISVILLE, 1985-; asst prof, Univ Louisville, 1977-1985. **Memberships:** Soc Neuroscience; Am Physiol Soc; Sigma Xi. **Mailing Address:** Dept Physiol & Biophysics Sch Med, Univ Louisville 2301 S Third St, Louisville, KY 40292-0001.

JIMENEZ, SERGIO A, BIOCHEMISTRY, MOLECULAR BIOL. **Personal Data:** b Cuzco, Peru, February 21, 1942. **Education:** Univ San Marcos, Lima, Peru, Bs, 1958, MD, 1964. **Honorary Degrees:** MS, Univ Pa. **Honors & Awards:** Joseph Lee Hollander award, 2000. **Professional Experience:** PROF MED, BIOCHEM & MOLECULAR BIOL, THOMAS JEFFERSON UNIV, as of 2002; prof, Sch Med, Univ Pa, 1985-1987; assoc prof med & rheumatology, Sch Med, Univ Pa, 1980-1985; dir, Collagen Res, Dept Med, Univ Pa, 1973-1987; NIH Gen Med Study Sect, Arthritis Found Res Comt. **Memberships:** Am Col Rheumatology; Osteoarthritis Res Soc Int; Orthop Res Soc; Am Soc Biochem Molecular Biol; Am Col Physicians. **Research Statement & Publications:** Biochemistry and molecular biology of inherited and acquired connective tissue diseases. **Mailing Address:** Biochem & Molecular Biol, Thomas Jefferson Univ, Blue Life Sci Bldg Rm 509 233 S Tenth St, Philadelphia, PA 19107-5541. **Fax:** 215-923-4649.

JIMERSON, GEORGE DAVID, inorganic chemistry, analytical chemistry; deceased, see previous edition for last biography

JIMESON, ROBERT M(ACKAY), JR, FUEL TECHNOLOGY & PETROLEUM ENGINEERING, RESOURCE MANAGEMENT. **Personal Data:** b Charleroi, Pa, January 29, 1921; m 1946, Rosemarie Wolny; c Robyn, Shelley, Robert III & Jeffery. **Education:** Pa State Univ, BS, 1942; George Wash Univ, MS, 1965. **Honors & Awards:** Sen Jennings Randolph Award, 1996. **Professional Experience:** CONSULT, ENERGY FUELS, ENVIRON MGT, INT ACTIV & CHEM ENG, 1978-; Lectr, George Washington Univ Grad Sch Eng, 1977-1979; mgr, Fossil Technol Overview, Dept Energy, 1976-1978; staff, Off Technol Assessment, US Cong, 1974-1976; asst adv environ qual, Fed Power Comn, 1970-1974; phys sci adminstr, USPH Serv, HEW, 1964-1970; phys sci adminstr, US Bur Mines, US Dept Interior, 1959-1964; Lectr, McKeesport Ctr, Pa State Univ, 1957-1959 chem engr, US Bur Mines, US Dept Interior, 1949-1959; res assoc, Sales Admin, Union Carbide Corp, 1947-1949; res assoc org synthesis, Mellon Inst Indust Res, 1945-1947; Engr, Glenn L Martin Co, 1942-1945; consult, RMJ Assoc. **Memberships:** Am Chem Soc; fel Am Inst Chem Engrs (treas, 1964-1965, pres, 1974-1975); Nat Soc Prof Engrs. **Research Statement & Publications:** Engineering administration; processes for production of natural fuels, synthetic fuels and chemicals; formulation of plans and policies affecting federal programs in fuels, energy prevention and control of air pollution. **Mailing Address:** 1501 Gingerwood Ct, Vienna, VA 22182-1437. **Fax:** 703-759-7751.

JIN, DOO JUNG, SEISMOLOGY, GROUND WATER. **Personal Data:** b Hadong, Korea, August 6, 1942; m 1973, Bong Ja; c Sungsoo, Sue Young & Hye won. **Education:** Inha Inst Technol, BS, 1963; Stanford Univ, MS, 1971; Southern Methodist Univ, PhD (geophys), 1979. **Professional Experience:** PROF ENVIRON TECHNOL/MATH, COLUMBIA BASIN COL, 1992-; consult geoscientist, Geoenviron Consult, 1991-1992; Lectr, Univ Md, 1988; sr staff scientist, Rust Grotech Inc, 1987-1991; consult geophysicist, Geoeng Consult, 1985-1987; sr geohysicist, Texaco Houston Res Ctr, 1979-1985; mem tech staff, Tex Instruments Inc, 1974-1976; KoreanGroundwater Develop Corp, 1969 & Advance Oil & Gas Co, 1973-1974; teaching fel, SouthernMethodist Univ, 1971-1973; Geophysicist, Geol Surv Korea, 1968. **Memberships:** Soc Explor Geophysicists; Am Geophys Union; Nat Groundwater Asn; Korean-Am Scientist & Engrs Asn Am. **Research Statement & Publications:** Magnetic induced polarization applied to environmental problems; complex seismic signatures; seismic surface wave phase velocity partial derivatives; hormorphic deconvolution; tru temperature determination of geothermal reservoirs; discriminant function for the determination of productive groundwater well sites. **Mailing Address:** 2223 Camas Ave, Richland, WA 99352. **Fax:** 509-546-0401. **E-Mail:** djin@ctc.ctc.edu

JIN, RONG-SHENG, PLANETARY MAGNETISM. **Personal Data:** b Foochow, Fukien, China, December 4, 1933; m 1962, Shirley; c Craig, Deborah & Laural. **Education:** Denison Univ, BS, 1957; Ohio State Univ, PhD (physics), 1965. **Professional Experience:** ASSOC PROF SPACE SCI & PHYSICS, FLA INST TECHNOL, 1969-; assoc scientist, Lockheed Missiles & Space Co, Calif, 1967-1969; asst prof, Loyola Univ, Calif, 1965-1967; instr physics, Denison Univ, 1959-1960. **Memberships:** Sigma Xi; Am Geophys Soc. **Research Statement & Publications:** Nuclear and space physics; planetary magnetism; secular variations of the geomagnetic field and the magnetic field reversals. **Mailing Address:** Dept Physics & Space Sci, Fla Inst Technol, Melbourne, FL 32901. **Fax:** 321-674-7482. **E-Mail:** rsjin@winnie.fit.edu

JIN, SUNGHO, MATERIALS SCIENCE ENGINEERING. **Personal Data:** b Daejon, Korea, November 6, 1945; American citizen; m 1972, c 2. **Education:** Seoul Nat Univ, BS, 1969; Univ Calif, Berkeley, MS, 1972, PhD (phys metall), 1974. **Professional Experience:** PROF MAT SCI & ENDOWED CHAIR, DEPT MECH & AEROSPACE ENG, UNIV CALIF, SAN DIEGO, 2002-; tech mgr, AT&T Bell Labs, Murray Hill, 1981-2002; mem tech staff, AT&T Bell Labs, Murray Hill, 1976-1981; res staff, Univ Calif, Berkeley, 1974-1976. **Memberships:** Am Soc Metals; Am Inst Mining Metall & Petroleum Engrs Metall Soc; Mat Res Soc. **Research Statement & Publications:** New alloys and thin films with unique magnetic, mechanical, electrical or thermal properties useful for applications in electronics or telecommunications industry. **Mailing Address:** Dept Mech & Aerospace Eng, Univ Calif, San Diego, 9500 Gilman Dr, La Jolla, CA 92093-0403. **Fax:** 858-534-5698. **E-Mail:** jin@ucsd.edu

JINDRAK, KAREL, pathology; deceased, see previous edition for last biography

JINKS-ROBERTSON, SUE, GENETICS, MOLECULAR BIOLOGY. **Personal Data:** b Panama City, Fla, January 22, 1955; m John; c 3. **Education:** Agnes Scott Col, BA, 1977; Univ Wis-Madison, PhD (genetics), 1983. **Professional Experience:** PROF BIOL, EMORY UNIV, as of 2006; assoc ed, Genetics, beginning 1993; assoc prof Biol, Emory Univ, beginning 1993; asst prof, Emory Univ, 1987-1993; fel, Univ Chicago, 1983-1986. **Memberships:** AAAS; Am Soc Microbiol; Genetics Soc Am; Sigma Xi. **Research Statement & Publications:** Recombination and mutation in yeast. **Mailing Address:** Dept Biol, Emory Univ, Atlanta, GA 30322. **Fax:** 404-727-2880. **E-Mail:** jinks@biology.emory.edu

JIRGENSONS, ARNOLD, polymer chemistry; deceased, see previous edition for last biography

JIRKA, GERHARD HERMANN, ENVIRONMENTAL FLUID MECHANICS, WATER POLLUTION CONTROL. **Personal Data:** b Kasten, Austria, September 14, 1944; m 1968, Sonia Kull; c Astrid, Andres & Stefan. **Education:** Univ Bodenkultur, Vienna, Austria, 1969, Mass Inst Technol, MS, 1971, PhD (civileng) 1973. **Honors & Awards:** Freeman Hydraul Prize, Am Soc Civil Engrs, 1981, Huber Res Prize, 1983; A TIppen Award, Int Asn Hydrol Res, 1989. **Professional Experience:** Vis Prof, Univ Canterbury, NZ, & Mass Inst-Tech, USA, 1999-2000; PROF & DIR, INSTHYDROMECHANIK, UNIV KALSRUHE, 1995-; Vis prof, Inst Hydraul & Hydrol Tech Univ Vienna, 1991-1992; chmn, Fluid Mech Sect, Int Asn Hydraul Res, 1990-; chmn, HydraulDiv, Am Soc Civil Eng, 1989-1990; PROF CIVIL & ENVIRON ENG, CORNELL UNIV, 1987-; DIR, DEFREES HYDRAUL LAB, CORNELL UNIV, 1984-; vis prof, Inst HydromechZurich, 1983-1984; from asst prof to assoc prof, Cornell Univ, 1977-1987; lectr & res engr, Energy Lab Mass Inst Technol, 1973-1977; FulbrightScholar, US Info Agency. **Memberships:** Fel Am Soc Civil Eng; Int Asn Hydraul Res; Am Geophys Union. **Research Statement & Publications:** Environmental fluid mechanics, transport phenomena, hydraulic engineering, water quality prediction, waste heat disposal, turbulent mixing. **Mailing Address:** Inst Hydromechanics, Univ Karlsruhe, Kaiserstr,. **Fax:** 721-661-686. **E-Mail:** jirka@uka.de

JIRKOVSKY, IVO, MEDICINAL CHEMISTRY, RESEARCH ADMINISTRATION. **Personal Data:** b Prague, Czech, June 26, 1935; Canadian citizen; m 1965. **Education:** Chem Univ, Prague Dipl chem eng, 1958; Czech Acad Sci, PhD (org chem), 1963. **Professional Experience:** DIR CHEM, WYETH-AYERST RES, 1989-; assoc dir, Wyeth-Ayerst ResLabs, 1984-1989; sr res assoc, Wyeth-Ayerst Res Labs, 1977-1984; sect head med chem, Wyeth-Ayerst Res Labs, 1973-1977; sr res chemist, Wyeth-Ayerst Res Labs, 1968-1973; Fel, Univ NB, 1966-1967; assoc res chemist, Res Inst Pharm & Biochem, Prague, 1963-1968; asst res chemist, Res Inst Pharm & Biochem, Prague, 1958-1960. **Memberships:** Am Chem Soc; fel Chem Inst Can; AAAS. **Research Statement & Publications:**

Organic syntheses; alkaloids; heterocycles; physical organic chemistry; biochemistry; structure-activity relationships; antihypertensives; psychotherapeutics and cognition enhancers; hypoglycemic drugs; enzyme inhibitors; antiobesity and hypolipidemic agents; immunoregulation; atherosclerosis; bone metabolism; steroidal research. **Mailing Address:** Wyeth-Ayerst Res, Bldg 222/2126, Pearl River, NY 10965.

JIRMANUS, MUNIR N, CRYOGENICS. **Personal Data:** b Jerusalem, April 23, 1944; American citizen; m 1968, c 2. **Education:** Am Univ, BSc, 1964; Tufts Univ, MSc, 1966, PhD (physics), 1973. **Professional Experience:** TECH DIR, JANIS RES CO, 1989-; sr appl engr cryogenics, Janis Res CO, 1978-1988; asst prof, Am Univ, Lebanon, 1975-1977; Lectr physics, Tufts Univ, 1974-1975. **Memberships:** Am Phys Soc; Mat Res Soc; Am Chem Soc. **Research Statement & Publications:** Design and testing of cryogenic equipment for low temperature physics research. **Mailing Address:** Janis Res Co Inc, 2 Jewel Dr, PO Box 696, Wilmington, MA 01887-0696. **Fax:** 978-658-0349. **E-Mail:** mjirmanus@janis.com

JIRSA, JAMES O, STRUCTURAL ENGINEERING, EARTHQUAKE ENGINEERING. **Personal Data:** b Lincoln, Nebr, July 30, 1938; m 1965, Marion; c David & Stephen. **Education:** Univ Nebr, BS, 1960; Univ Ill, MS, 1962, PhD (civil eng), 1963. **Honors & Awards:** Raymond C Reese Award, Am Soc Civil Engr, 1970 & 1991, Walter L HuberRes Prize, 1978; Wason Medal, Am Concrete Inst, 1977, Raymond C Reese Struct Award, 1977& 1979, Alfred E Lindau Award, 1986 & 1992, Delmar E Bloem Award, 1990; A J BoaseAward, Reinforced Concrete Res Coun, 1993; Hocott Award for Research, University of Texas, College of Engineering, 1994; Joe W Kelley Award, American Concrete Institute, 1997; George Winter Lecture, American Concrete Institute, 2000; Joe J King Professional Achievement Award, University of Texas, College of Engineering, 2001. **Professional Experience:** JANET S COCKRELL CENTENNIAL CHAIR ENG, UNIV TEX, AUSTIN, 1988-; CHMN, DEPT CIVIL ENG, UNIV TEX, AUSTIN, 1996-2001; Erskine fel, Canterbury Univ, NZ, 1991; bd dir, Am Concrete Inst, 1987-1990; dirFerguson Struct Eng Lab, Univ Tex, Austin, 1985-1988; Phil M Ferguson prof, Univ Tex, Austin, 1984-1988; Stanley P Finch prof eng, Univ Tex, Austin, 1982-1984; Fulbright scholar, H JDegenkolb Assocs, 1980; from assoc prof to prof, Univ Tex, Austin, 1972-1982; from asst profto assoc prof, Rice Univ, 1965-1971; Fulbright scholar, Portland Cement Asn, 1965; asst profcivil eng, Univ Nebr, 1964-1965; Fulbright scholar, Inst Appl Res Reinforced Concrete, France, 1963-1964; bd dir, Earthquake Eng Res Inst. **Memberships:** Nat Acad Eng; Am Soc Civil Engrs; fel Am Concrete Inst; Earthquake Eng ResInst; Int Asn Bridge & Struct Engrs. **Research Statement & Publications:** Reinforced concrete behavior and design of reinforced concrete structures; earthquake engineering; repair and strengthening of structures. **Mailing Address:** Dept Civil, Architectural, & Environmental Eng, Univ Tex, Austin, TX 78712. **Fax:** 512-471-1944. **E-Mail:** jirsa@uts.cc.utexas.edu

JIRTLE, RANDY L, PATHOLOGY. **Personal Data:** b Kewaunee, Wis, November 9, 1947. **Education:** Univ Wis-Madison, BS, 1970, MS, 1973, PhD (radiation biol), 1976. **Professional Experience:** MEM INTEGRATED TOXICOL PROG, BASIC RES LIVER SURG PROG, 1992-; DIR, BASIC RES LIVER SURG PROG, 1992-; DIR, DIV RADIATION & MOLECULAR ONCOL RES, 1991-; PROF RADIOL & PATH, DUKE UNIV, 1990-; PROF RADIATION ONCOL & PATH, DUKE UNIV, 1990-; vis res scientist, Ctr Nuclear Study, Rome, 1982; vis asst prof human oncol, Univ Wis-Madison, 1981; from asst prof to assoc profradiol & path, Duke Univ, 1980-1990; asst prof radiol, Duke Univ, 1979-1980; assoc radiol, Duke Univ, 1977-1979; fel physiol, Univ Wis-Madison, 1976-1977. **Memberships:** Am Asn Cancer Res; Radiation Res; Am Asn Pathologists; Soc Toxicol; Fedn AmSoc Exp Biol; AAAS. **Research Statement & Publications:** Promotion of hepatocellular tumor formation; breast cancer chemo prevention; radiation response of the liver. **Mailing Address:** Dept Radiol Oncol, Duke Univ, Med Ctr Box 3433, Durham, NC 27710-0001. **Fax:** 919-684-5584. **E-Mail:** jirtle@radonc.duke.edu

JISCHKE, MARTIN C(HARLES), FLUID MECHANICS. **Personal Data:** b Chicago, Ill, August 7, 1941; m 1970, Patricia; c Charles & Marian. **Education:** Ill Inst Technol, BS, 1963; Mass Inst Technol, MS, 1964, PhD (aeronaut &astronaut), 1968. **Honors & Awards:** Ralph R Teetor Award, Soc Automotive Engrs, 1970; Centennial Medallion, Am Soc Eng Educ, 1993. **Professional Experience:** PRES, PURDUE UNIV, 2000-; pres, Comn Twenty-First Century State & Land-Grand Univ, 1995; dir, Bankers Trust Co, 1995; dir, Kerr-McGee Corp, 1993; pres, Iowa State Univ, Ames, 1991-2000; chancellor, Univ Mo, Rolla, 1986-1991; interim pres, Univ Okla, 1985; dean eng, Univ Okla, 1981-1986; prin investr, USAF, 1977-; prin investr, US Nuclear Regulatory Comn, beginning 1977; on leave, WhiteHouse fel, US Dept Transp, 1975-1976; from asst prof to prof aerospace & mech eng, Univ Okla, 1968-1981; asst aeronaut & astronaut, Mass Inst Technol, 1966-1968. **Memberships:** Fel Am Inst Aeronaut & Astronaut; Am Phys Soc; Soc Automotive Engrs; SigmaXi; fel AAAS; fel Am Soc Mech Engrs; Nat Soc Prof Engrs. **Research Statement & Publications:** Viscous flows; aerodynamics; geophysical; fluid dynamics; heat transfer. **Mailing Address:** Purdue Univ, West Lafayette, IN 47907.

JIVIDEN, GAY MELTON, MANAGEMENT OF MOLECULAR BIOLOGY & GENETIC ENGINEERING, MANAGEMENT OF PLANT BREEDING PROJECTS. **Personal Data:** b Charleston, WVa, November 18, 1935; m Loretta Harper; c Jon D & Ann M. **Education:** WVa State Univ, BS, 1962; NC State Univ, PhD (plant physiol), 1972. **Professional Experience:** SR DIR, AGR RES DIV, COTTON INC, as of 1999; dir agr res, Cotton Inc, beginning 1988; assoc dir, Cotton Inc, 1983-1988; adj fac, NC State Univ, beginning 1974; mgr, Cotton Inc, 1973-1983; asst to dir, Southeastern Plant EnvironLab, NC State Univ, 1967-1973; res technician, Union Carbide Corp, 1962-1965; math & sciteacher, Kanawha Co Schs, Charleston, WVa, 1959-1961; Qual control analyst, Nat Lead Corp, 1956-1958. **Memberships:** Am Soc Plant Physiol; Am Soc Agron & Crop Sci; Am Oil Chemists; Sigma Xi. **Research Statement & Publications:** Determine the direction, scope and funding levels of cotton research for a coordinated national effort in the fields of plant physiology, genetics and molecular biology. **Mailing Address:** Agr Res Div, Cotton Inc, 6399 Weston Pkwy, Cary, NC 27513. **Fax:** 919-881-9874.

JIZBA, ZDENEK VACLAV, EXPLORATION GEOLOGY. **Personal Data:** b Prague, Czech, February 25, 1927; American citizen; m 1960, c 3. **Education:** State Col Wash, BS, 1949, MS, 1950; Univ Wis, PhD, 1953. **Professional Experience:** RETIRED; sr res assoc, Chevron Oil Field Res Co, Standard Oil Co, Calif, 1967-1986; sr res geologist, Chevron Res Co, 1962-1967; Res geologist, Chevron Res Co, 1955-1962. **Research Statement & Publications:** Mathematical geology; man-machine interaction to solve complex geological problems; computer applications in geology. **Mailing Address:** 1341 Rebecca Dr, La Habra, CA 90631-2614.

JOANNOPOULOS, JOHN DIMITRIS, PHOTONIC BAND GAP MATERIALS, AB-INITIO CALCULATIONS. **Personal Data:** b New York, NY, April 26, 1947; m 1993, Kyriaki. **Education:** Univ Calif, Berkeley, BA, 1968, PhD (physics), 1974; Univ Calif, Davis, MA, 1970. **Honors & Awards:** David Adler prize, 1997. **Professional Experience:** FRANCIS WRIGHT DAVIS PROF PHYSICS, MASS INST TECHNOL, 1996-; prof physics, Mass Inst Technol, 1983-1995; fel, John Simon Guggenheim Found, 1981-1982; fel, Alfred P Sloan Found, 1976-1980; from asst prof to assoc prof, Mass Inst Technol, 1974-1983. **Memberships:** Am Phys Soc; Am Vacuum Soc Mat Res Soc, Opt Soc Am. **Research Statement & Publications:** Theoretical condensed matter physics: including properties of crystalline solids, surfaces of solids, defects and amorphous solids; photonic crystals. **Mailing Address:** Dept Physics, Mass Inst Technol, Rm 12-116 77 Mass Ave, Cambridge, MA 02139. **Fax:** 617-258-2562. **E-Mail:** joannop@mit.edu

JOB, ROBERT CHARLES, INORGANIC CHEMISTRY. **Personal Data:** b Honolulu, Hawaii, May 19, 1943. **Education:** Univ Calif, Berkeley, BS, 1967; Univ Mich, PhD (inorg chem), 1971. **Professional Experience:** RES CHEMIST, UNION CARBIDE CHEM, as of 2005; ASST PROF CHEM, COLO STATE UNIV, 1975-; res chemist, Univ Calif, Santa Barbara, 1974-1975; assoc chem, Univ Calif, Santa Barbara, 1971-1974. **Memberships:** Sigma Xi. **Research Statement & Publications:** Inorganic analogs of biological systems; organometallic chemistry of transition metals with Group IV-a prosthetics; asymmetric induction involving optically active transition metal systems; coordination chemistry. **Mailing Address:** Union Carbide Chem, PO Box 1967, Midland, MI 48674.

JOBE, ALAN, PULMONARY SURFACTANT. **Education:** Univ Calif, San Diego, MS & PhD, 1973. **Honors & Awards:** E Mead Johnson Res Award, Am Acad Pediat, 1986. **Professional Experience:** PROF PEDIAT, CINCINNATI CHILDREN'S HOSP MED CTR, as of 2006. **Memberships:** Am Pediat Soc (secy-treas, 2003-2009). **Mailing Address:** Cincinnati Children's Hosp Med Ctr, 3333 Burnet Ave, Cincinnati, OH 45229-3039. **Fax:** 513-636-8691. **E-Mail:** alan.jobe@cchmc.org

JOBE, JOHN M, TOPOLOGY. **Personal Data:** b Ponca City, Okla, June 9, 1933; m 1954, c 5. **Education:** Univ Tulsa, BS, 1955; Okla State Univ, MS, 1963, PhD (math), 1966. **Professional Experience:** PROF EMER MATH, OKLA STATE UNIV, as of 1998; prof math, Okla State Univ, beginning 1977; from asst prof to assoc prof, Okla State Univ, 1974-1977; Teacher high sch, Okla, 1955-1962. **Memberships:** Math Asn Am; Am Math Soc. **Research Statement & Publications:** Point set topology. **Mailing Address:** Dept Math, Okla State Univ, Stillwater, OK 74078.

JOBE, LOWELL ARTHUR, CHEMICAL ENGINEERING, SYSTEMS ENGINEERING. **Personal Data:** b Lead, SDak, August 28, 1914; m 1985, Lorraine; c Donna (Oltmanns) & David. **Education:** SDak Sch Mines & Technol, BS, 1938; Univ Iowa, MS, 1939. **Professional Experience:** RETIRED; instr process technol, Eastern Idaho Voc Tech Sch, 1980-1985; mem staff, Exxon Nuclear, 1977-1980; sr process control engr, Idaho Chem Prog, Allied Chem Corp, 1971-1977; sr process control engr, Idaho Nuclear Corp, 1966-1971; process control engr, Atomic Energy Div, Phillips Petrol Co, 1960-1966; from asst prof to assoc prof chem eng, Univ Idaho, 1947-1960; chief chemist & chem engr, Graver Tank & Mfg Co Inc, 1939-1947; asst metall, Univ Iowa, 1938-1939. **Memberships:** Instrument Soc Am; Am Inst Chem Engrs. **Research Statement & Publications:** Automatic process control; industrial water and waste treatment; nuclear engineering. **Mailing Address:** 14469 N 55th E, Idaho Falls, ID 83401.

JOBE, PHILLIP CARL, NEUROPHARMACOLOGY. **Personal Data:** b Carlsbad, NMex, January 9, 1940; m 1959, c 2. **Education:** Univ NMex, BS, 1963; Univ Ariz, PhD (pharmacol), 1970. **Professional Experience:** PROF PHARMACOL, DEPT BIOMED & THERAPEUT SCI, UNIV ILL COL MED, PEORIA, as of 2002; chair, Dept Biomed & Therapeutic Sci, Univ Ill Col Med, Peoria, 1985-2001; prof pharmacol, therapeut & psychiat, Sch Med, La State Univ, Shreveport, beginning 1980; assoc prof, La State Univ, 1975-1980; consult neuropharmacol & clin pharmacologist, Vet Admin Hosp, 1974-; asst prof, La State Univ, 1974-1975; dir, Drug Abuse Ctr, 1971-1974; asst prof, Northeast La Univ, 1970-1974; asst prof pharmacol, Univ Nebr, 1969-1970; assoc, Univ Ariz, 1963-1967; teaching asst, Univ Ariz, 1960-1963. **Memberships:** Soc Neuroscience; Sigma Xi. **Research Statement & Publications:** Role of central nervous system neurotransmitters in the regulation of seizure intensity and susceptibility with special emphasis on the relative importance of discrete catecholaminergic neuron systems. **Mailing Address:** Dept Biomed & Therapeut Sci, Col Med, Univ Ill, One Illini Dr PO Box 1649, Peoria, IL 61656-1649. **Fax:** 309-693-8927. **E-Mail:** pcj@uic.edu

JOBES, FORREST CROSSETT, JR, PHYSICS. **Personal Data:** b Trenton, NJ, November 26, 1935; m 1958, c 1. **Education:** Oberlin Col, AB, 1957; Yale Univ, MS, 1958, PhD (physics), 1962. **Professional Experience:** MEM RES STAFF, PLASMA PHYSICS, PHYSICS LAB, PRINCETONUNIV, 1971-; sr res physicist, Mobil Oil Corp, 1965-1971; res physicist cent res div lab, MobilOil Co, 1962-1965; Asst physics, Yale Univ, 1957-1962. **Memberships:** Am Phys Soc; Sigma Xi. **Research Statement & Publications:** Plasma and nuclear physics. **Mailing Address:** PPPL Princeton Univ, PO Box 451, Princeton, NJ 08543.

JOBS, STEVEN PAUL, ELECTRONICS. **Personal Data:** b Los Altos, Calif, February 24, 1955. **Honors & Awards:** Nat Technol Medal, Pres Reagan, 1985; Jefferson Award, 1987. **Professional Experience:** DIR, APPLE COMPUT INC, 1997-; CHIEF EXEC OFF, APPLE COMPUT INC, 1996-; pres, Pixar Animation Studios, beginning 1995; CHMN, PIXAR ANIMATION STUDIOS, 1991-; CHIEF EXEC OFFICER, PIXAR ANIMATION STUDIOS, 1986-; pres & chmn, Next Comput, Inc, 1985-1997; co-founder, Apple Comput, 1976; bd dirs, Pixar; chmn, exec vpres & genmgr, Macintosh Div. **Memberships:** Nat Acad Sci; Nat Acad Eng. **Research Statement & Publications:** Co-designed Apple II; implementation of PostScript and LaserWriting which helped create the desktop publishing industry. **Mailing Address:** Apple Comput Inc, One Infinite Loop, Cupertino, CA 95014.

JOBSIS, FRANS FREDERIK, PHYSIOLOGY. **Personal Data:** b Batavia, Indonesia, April 1, 1929; American citizen; m 1951, Joan; c Catherine T, Gerrit J, William T, Maria M & Paul D. **Education:** Univ Md, BS, 1951; Univ Mich, MS, 1953, PhD (zoology), 1958. **Professional Experience:** PROF EMER CELL BIOL, DUKE UNIV, as of 2004; Guggenheim fel, 1971-1972; prof physiol, Duke Univ, beginning 1969; from asst prof to assoc prof, Duke Univ, 1964-1969; asst prof biophys & physiol, Univ, 1962-1964; res assoc, Johnson Found, Univ Pa, 1961-1962; fel, Nobel Inst Neurophysiol, Sweden, 1960-1961; fel biochem, Univ Amsterdam, 1959-1960; res fel biophys, Johnson Found, Univ Pa, 1958-1959; Hon prof physiol, Semmelweis Med Univ, Budapest, Hungary. **Memberships:** Fel AAAS; Am Physiol Soc; Int Soc Transport Oxygen to Tissues. **Research Statement & Publications:** Physiology, biochemistry and biophysics of muscle and nervous tissue; comparative physiology; physiology of behavior; near infrared spectroscopy of organs and tissues; non-invasive monitoring of physiologic and pathophysiologic activities in viro; oxygen delivery and utilization in sitis. **Mailing Address:** Dept Cell Biol, Duke Univ, PO Box 3011 Med Ctr Durham, Durham, NC 27710. **Fax:** 919-684-3687. **E-Mail:** frans.jobsis@duke.edu

JOBST, JOEL EDWARD, NUCLEAR PHYSICS. **Personal Data:** b South Milwaukee, Wis, May 13, 1936; m 2000, Priscilla; c Brian, Kevin & Erin. **Education:** Marquette Univ,

BS, 1959; Univ Wis, MS, 1961, PhD (physics), 1966. **Professional Experience:** CONSULT, 1995-; sci specialist, Remote Sensing Lab, EG&G, 1966-1995; owner, Solar Energy Co. **Memberships:** Health Physics Soc; Am Nuclear Soc; Solar Energy Soc. **Research Statement & Publications:** Nuclear research; detector technology; operation and development of particle accelerators and neutron generators; airborne remote sensing, including infrared scanner; preparation of terrestrial radiation maps from gamma data recorded on an aerial survey platform; solar energy systems. **Mailing Address:** 3013 Bryant Ave, Las Vegas, NV 89102.

JOCHLE, WOLFGANG, THERIOGENOLOGY, CLINICAL PHARMACOLOGY. **Personal Data:** b Munich, Ger, October 5, 1927; m 1964, Maria Frank. **Education:** Univ Munich DrVet Med, 1952, DrMedVet, 1953; Am Col Theriogenologists, dipl, 1975. **Professional Experience:** Hon prof, Sch Vet Med, Hannover, Ger, 1987; PRES, WOLFGANG JOCHLE ASSOCS, INC, 1975-; Consult, 1975-; int vetsect, Syntex Corp, Mex, 1973-1975; dir vet syntex res, Palo Alto, Calif, 1968-1973; Dir vet syntexres, Syntex Corp, Mex, 1966-1968; res dir vet med, Fecunda AG, Switz, 1964-1965; vet resscientist, Schering AG, 1959-1963; asst animal husb, Vet Fac, Free Univ Berlin, 1956-1959; vetres scientist, Hormon-Chemie, 1954-1956; Ger Res Asn fel endocrinol, Vet Fac, UnivMunich, 1953-1954. **Memberships:** Am Vet Med Asn; Soc Study Reproduction; Am Soc Animal Sci; Soc Theriogenol; NY Acad Sci; Royal Soc Med UK. **Research Statement & Publications:** Interaction between environment and reproductive functions in animals; use of hormones as therapeutic and managerial tools in veterinary medicine and animal industry; comparative reproductive neuroendocrinology; endocrinology of parturition; new drug development in the animal health field; animal models for clinical conditions. **Mailing Address:** Wolfgang Jochle Assocs, Inc, 10 Old Boonton Rd, Denville Township, NJ 07834-2920. **Fax:** 973-627-6345. **E-Mail:** jochle@infi.net

JOCHMAN, RICHARD LEE, MEDICINAL CHEMISTRY, ORGANIC CHEMISTRY. **Personal Data:** b Appleton, Wis, January 10, 1948; m 1969, c 1. **Education:** St Norbert Col, BS, 1970; Univ Kans, MS, 1974, PhD (med chem), 1978. **Professional Experience:** RETIRED; assoc prof chem, Col St Benedict, St John's Univ, beginning 1985; from instr to asst prof, Col St Benedict, 1977-1985. **Memberships:** AAAS; Am Chem Soc. **Research Statement & Publications:** Synthesis of metabolically stable analogs of neuropeptides. **Mailing Address:** Dept Chem, Col St Benedict, St Joseph, MN 56374.

JOCHSBERGER, THEODORE, PHYSICAL ORGANIC CHEMISTRY. **Personal Data:** b New York, NY, March 6, 1940; m 1984, c 2. **Education:** Hunter Col, AB, 1961, MA, 1963; City Univ NY, PhD (phys chem), 1969; Brooklyn Col Pharm, BS, 1977. **Professional Experience:** PROF PHARMACEUT, ARNOLD & MARIE SCHWARTZ COL PHARM & HEALTH SCI, LONG ISLAND UNIV, 1968-. **Memberships:** NY Acad Sci; Am Chem Soc. **Research Statement & Publications:** Kinetics and mechanisms of free radical reactions; polymers and polymerization mechanisms; metal-peroxide catalyzed reactions; biopharmaceutics. **Mailing Address:** Dept Pharmaceut, Arnold & Marie Schwartz Col Pharm & Health Sci, Long Island Univ, 75 DeKalb Ave, Brooklyn, NY 11201-5497.

JOCKUSCH, CARL GROOS, COMPUTABILITY THEORY. **Personal Data:** b San Antonio, Tex, July 13, 1941; m Elizabeth; c William, Elizabeth & Rebecca. **Education:** Swarthmore Col, BA, 1963; Mass Inst Technol, PhD (math), 1966. **Professional Experience:** PROF EMER, UNIV ILL, URBANA-CHAMPAIGN, as of 2004; prof math, Univ Ill, Urbana-Champaign, 1975-2004; ed, Proceedings Am Math Sci 1997-; ed, J Symbolic Logic, 1974-1975; from asst prof to assoc prof, Univ Ill, Urbana-champaign, 1967-1975; Instr math, Northeastern Univ, 1966-1967. **Memberships:** Am Math Soc; Math Asn Am; Asn Symbolic Logic. **Research Statement & Publications:** Computability theory and its connections with other areas of mathematics. **Mailing Address:** Dept Math, Univ Ill Urbana-Champaign, 301 Altgeld Hall, Urbana, IL 61801. **Fax:** 217-333-9576. **E-Mail:** jockusch@math.uiuc.edu

JOCOY, EDWARD HENRY, ELECTRICAL ENGINEERING. **Personal Data:** b Buffalo, NY, October 24, 1933; m 1968, c 1. **Education:** Rensselaer Polytech Inst, BEE, 1955; Univ Buffalo, MS, 1959; Cornell Univ, PhD (elec eng), 1969. **Professional Experience:** CONSULT, as of 2002; PRIN ENGR, CALSPAN CORP, 1974-; head radar & electronics sect, CalspanCorp, 1964-1965, 1971-1974; electronics engr, Calspan Corp, 1955-1964. **Memberships:** Inst Elec & Electronics Engrs; Sigma Xi. **Research Statement & Publications:** Radar and communications; analytical and experimental research of radar and communications systems; mathematical modeling; signal processing. **Mailing Address:** 100 Wiltshire Rd, Williamsville, NY 14221-4943.

JODEIT, MAX A, MATHEMATICS HARMONICANALSIS. **Personal Data:** b Tulsa, Okla, April 14, 1937; div, c Neal, Ann & Lynn. **Education:** Rice Univ, BA, 1962, MA, 1965, PhD (math), 1967. **Professional Experience:** PROF MATH, UNIV MINN, 1992-; assoc prof math, Univ Minn, Minneapolis, 1973-1992; vis asst prof, Univ Chicago, 1969-1970; instr math, Univ Chicago, 1967-1969. **Memberships:** Am Math Soc. **Research Statement & Publications:** Mathematical analysis; singular integrals harmonic analysis. **Mailing Address:** Sch Math, Univ Minn, 206 Church St SE Ste Vin H 127, Minneapolis, MN 55455-0488. **E-Mail:** jodeit@math.umn.edu

JODRY, RICHARD L, EXPLORATION GEOLOGY. **Personal Data:** b Toledo, Ohio, May 17, 1922; m 1945, Betty McElraevy; c Ann, Mary, Louis F, Richard M, Patricia, Michael & Thomas. **Education:** Mich State Univ, BS, 1945, MS, 1954. **Professional Experience:** PRES, ENERGY & NATURAL RESOURCE CONSULTS, INC, 1977-; mem, Bd Mineral Resources, Nat Res Coun, Nat Acad Sci, 1975-1978; chief geologist geothermalenergy, Billings Res Group, Sun Oil Co, 1970-1977; distinguished lectr, Am Asn Geologists, 1970-1972; from res geologist & group supvr to sr res geologist, Billings Res Group, Sun Oil Co, 1955-1970; chief geologist, Rex Oil & Gas Co, 1950-1955; Geologist, Magnolia Petrol Co, 1945-1947& Ohio Oil Co, 1947-1950. **Memberships:** Am Asn Petrol Geologists; Geol Soc Am; Soc Econ Paleontologists &Mineralogists; Soc Explor Geophys; Geothermal Resources Coun (vpres 1974-1975). **Research Statement & Publications:** Deposition of carbonate sediments; formation of carbonate rocks and their petrographic and petrophysical characteristics; unexplored basin evaluation; world hydrocarbon resource evaluation; coal and geothermal exploration and development. **Mailing Address:** 641 Strings Dr, San Antonio, TX 78216.

JOE, HARRY, MATHEMATICS. **Education:** Univ Victoria, BSc, 1978; Univ BC, MSc, 1979; Fla State Univ, PhD, 1982. **Professional Experience:** PROF, DEPT STATIST, UNIV BC, as of 2006. **Research Statement & Publications:** Multivariate models and dependence; inference methods for multivariate models; non-normal time series; extreme value inference. **Mailing Address:** Dept Statist, Univ BC, 333 6356 Agr Rd, Vancouver, BC V6T 1Z2, Can. **Fax:** 604-822-6960. **E-Mail:** harry@stat.ubc.ca

JOEBSTL, JOHANN ANTON, ENERGY CONVERSION. **Personal Data:** b Graz, Austria, July 17, 1927; American citizen; m 1957, Erika; c Barbara. **Education:** Tech Univ, Graz, Austria, dipl eng, 1954, DrTechSci, 1956. **Professional Experience:** RETIRED; tech adv, Belvoir Res & Develop Ctr, 1985-1988; div chief, Electrochem Div, Mobility Equip Res & Develop Command, 1981-1985; br chief, Eng Res & Develop Lab, US Army, 1976-1981; res chemist, Mobility Equip Res & Develop Ctr, 1968-1976; res chemist, Eng Res & Develop Lab, US Army, 1958-1968; asst, Tech Univ, 1955-1975. **Memberships:** Am Chem Soc. **Research Statement & Publications:** Electrocatalysis; novel electrolytes; advanced fuel conditioning techniques; fundamental investigations in electrochemistry; fuel cells. **Mailing Address:** 6641 Wakefield Dr, Alexandria, VA 22307.

JOEDICKE, INGO BERND, INORGANIC CHEMISTRY. **Personal Data:** b Grossfurra, Ger, May 17, 1948; American citizen; m 1968, c 2. **Education:** Univ Wash, BS, 1970; Ore State Univ, PhD (inorg chem), 1976. **Professional Experience:** CHIEF SCIENTIST, ISP MINERAL PROD INC, as of 2005; SR INORG CHEMIST, GAF CORP, 1976-; res asst inorg chem, Ore State Univ, 1971-1976. **Memberships:** Am Chem Soc; Sigma Xi. **Research Statement & Publications:** Homogeneous catalysis of coordinated phosphorus ester autooxidation; high temperature chemistry of silicates and clays; silicate films and coatings. **Mailing Address:** ISP Mineral Prod Inc, 34 Charles St, Hagerstown, MD 21740-3899. **Fax:** 301-733-4003. **E-Mail:** ijoedicke@ispcorp.com

JOEL, AMOS EDWARD, ELECTRICAL ENGINEERING. **Personal Data:** b Philadelphia, Pa, March 12, 1918; c 3. **Education:** Mass Inst Technol, BS, 1940, MS, 1942. **Honors & Awards:** Outstanding Patent Award, NJ Coun Res & Develop, 1972; Alexander Graham-BellMedal, Inst Elec & Electronics Engrs, 1976; Columbian Award, City of Genoa, 1984; ITUAward, ITU Geneva Switz, 1983; Kyoto Prize, 1989; Nat Medal Technol, 1993. **Professional Experience:** RETIRED; switching consult, LocalSwitching Lab, 1967-1983; dir, Local Switching Lab, 1962-1967; switching consult, Switching Systs Develop Lab, 1961-1962; dir, Switching Systs Develop Lab, 1961-1962; head, Electronic Switching Planning Dept, 1960-1961; switching systs develop engr, Bell Tel Labs Inc, 1952-1961. **Memberships:** Nat Acad Eng; Asn Comput Mach; fel Inst Elec & Electronics Engrs; AAAS; felAm Acad Arts & Sci; Sigma Xi. **Research Statement & Publications:** Design of automatic telephone switching systems; communication privacy systems; design of research computer systems; relay and transistor switching circuits; design of automatic accounting systems; teaching telephone switching circuit design and system principles; electronic information processing systems. **Mailing Address:** Bell Tel Labs, Holmdel, NJ 07733.

JOEL, CLIFFE DAVID, NERUOSCIENCE. **Personal Data:** b Saskatoon, Sask, August 10, 1932; American citizen; m 1994, Emma; c Lisa, Eric & Sara. **Education:** Pomona Col, AB, 1953; Harvard Univ, MA, 1955, PhD (biochem), 1959. **Professional Experience:** PROF EMER CHEM, LAWRENCE UNIV, as of 2003; vis prof psychol, Colo Col, 1991, 1993, 1992; fel ophthal, Baylor Col Med, 1982-1984; vis scientist, Inst Animal Psychol, Cambridge, Eng, 1974-1975; chmn dept, LawrenceUniv, 1971-1973, 1984-1987; prof chem, Lawrence Univ, 1968-1997; career develop award, Nat Inst Neurol Dis & Stroke, 1968; biochemist, Mass Ment Health Ctr, 1963-1968; from instr to asst prof, Harvard Med Sch, 1960-1968; NIH res fel, 1959-1960; res fel biol chem, Harvard MedSch, 1959-1960. **Memberships:** Am Soc Neurochem. **Research Statement & Publications:** Chemistry and metabolism of lipids, especially polyunsaturated fatty acids; neurochemistry; chemistry of the eye; chemical education. **Mailing Address:** Dept Chem, Lawrence Univ, PO Box 599, Appleton, WI 54912.

JOEL, DARREL DEAN, EXPERIMENTAL PATHOLOGY, IMMUNOLOGY. **Personal Data:** b Woodlake, Minn, April 26, 1933; m 1965, Gretchen Lawrence. **Education:** Univ Minn, BS, 1956, DVM, 1958, PhD (vet path), 1964. **Professional Experience:** Chmn, Med Dept, 1991-1996; res prof, State Univ NY Stony Brook, 1985-; SR SCIENTIST, BROOKHAVEN NAT LAB, 1979-; Assoc prof, State Univ NY Stony Brook, 1972-1985; from asst scientist to scientist, Brookhaven Nat Lab, 1964-1979; res fel exp path, Univ Minn, 1960-1964; Instr vet path, Univ Minn, 1958-1960. **Memberships:** AAAS; Am Physiol Soc. **Research Statement & Publications:** Lymphocyte kinetics and immune responses; experimental pathology; radiation biology and experimental therapy. **Mailing Address:** Med Res Ctr, Brookhaven Nat Lab, Upton, NY 11973.

JOERN, ANTHONY, POPULATION BIOLOGY, INSECT ECOLOGY. **Personal Data:** b Omaha, Nebr, September 6, 1948; m 1979. **Education:** Univ Wis, BS, 1970; Univ Tex, PhD (pop biol), 1977. **Professional Experience:** PROF ECOL, UNIV NEBR, 1978-. **Memberships:** Ecol Soc Am; Soc Study Evolution; Entom Soc Am; Orthopterists Soc; Sigma Xi; Asn Study Animal Behav; Brit Ecol Soc. **Research Statement & Publications:** Factors responsible for resource use by assemblages of grasshoppers; factors influencing the population dynamics of grasshoppers; the evolution of diet by herbivores. **Mailing Address:** Sch Biol Sci, Univ Nebr, PO Box 880118, Lincoln, NE 68588-0118. **Fax:** 402-472-2083. **E-Mail:** jjoern1@unl.edu

JOESTEN, MELVIN D, INORGANIC CHEMISTRY, SCIENCE EDUCATION. **Personal Data:** b Rochelle, Ill, October 27, 1932; m 1953, Maribel Hicks; c Jo Ellen & Charles. **Education:** Northern Ill Univ, BS, 1954; Univ Ill, MS, 1959, PhD (inorg chem), 1962. **Honors & Awards:** Fulbright Lectr, Trinity Col, Dublin, Ireland, 1972-1973. **Professional Experience:** Emer prof of Chem, Vanderbilt Univ, 1998-; Vis prof, Univ NC, 1982-1983; chmn dept, Vanderbilt Univ, 1976-1982; PROF CHEM, VANDERBILT UNIV, 1975-; assoc prof, Vanderbilt Univ, 1966-1975; asst prof chem, Southern Ill Univ, 1962-1966; Teacher, Ill High Sch, 1956-1958. **Memberships:** Am Chem Soc; Sigma Xi; Nat Sci Teachers Asn. **Research Statement & Publications:** Hydrogen bonding; bioinorganic and coordination chemistry; science education; chemistry education. **Mailing Address:** Dept Chem, Vanderbilt Univ, Nashville, TN 37235. **E-Mail:** joesten@ctrvax.vanderbilt.edu

JOESTEN, RAYMOND, METAMORPHIC PETROLOGY. **Personal Data:** b San Francisco, Calif, September 12, 1944; m 1967, c 2. **Education:** San Jose State Col, BS, 1966; Calif Inst Technol, PhD, 1974. **Professional Experience:** DEPT HEAD GEOL & GEOPHYS, UNIV CONN, as of 2004; PROF GEOL & GEOPHYS, UNIV CONN, 1988-; vis assoc prof, dept Earth & Planetary Sci, Univ Johns Hopkins, 1987; head dept, Geol & Geophys, Univ Conn, 1983-1988; vis scholar, Dept Mineral & Petrol, Univ Cambridge, 1979; from instr to assoc prof, Geol & Geophys, Univ Conn, 1971-1983. **Memberships:** fel Geol Soc Am; Mineral Soc Am; Am Geophys Union; Geochem Soc. **Research Statement & Publications:** Analysis of mass transport in metamorphic rocks through study of natural systems and modelling using methods of non-equilibrium thermodynamics. **Mailing Address:** Dept Geol & Geophys, Univ Conn, Bldg Beach Hall 207, Storrs, CT 06269-2045. **E-Mail:** raymond.joesten@uconn.edu

JOFFE, ANATOLE, MATHEMATICS. **Personal Data:** b Belg, September 1, 1932; c 2. **Education:** Univ Brussels, Lic Sc & advan teaching degree agr, 1954, Lic Sc, 1955; Cornell Univ, PhD (sci math), 1959. **Professional Experience:** PROFESSEUR TITULAIRE, UNIV MONTREAL, as of 2005; mem, Comt Basic Sci Coun Univ, 1974-; mem, Comt Aid Nat Res Coun, 1974-1977; PROF MATH, MATH RES CTR, UNIV MONTREAL, 1973-; DIR, MATH RES CTR, UNIV MONTREAL, 1973-; from asst prof to assoc prof, Math Res Ctr, Univ Montreal, 1961-1973; asst prof math, McGill Univ, 1960-1961. **Memberships:** Am Math Soc; Inst Math Statist; Math Soc Can. **Research Statement & Publications:**

Theory of pure and applied probability; Galton-Watson process; some of independent random variables index by a tree and applications to biology. **Mailing Address:** Math Res Ctr, Univ Montreal, PO Box 6128, Montreal, PQ H3C 3J7, Can. **Fax:** 514-343-5700. **E-Mail:** joff@dms.umontreal.ca

JOFFE, FREDERICK M, BIOCHEMISTRY, FOOD & PAPER TECHNOLOGY. **Personal Data:** b Chicago, Ill, October 26, 1936; m 1959, Ruth; c 4. **Education:** Mich State Univ, BS, 1958, MS, 1959; Rutgers Univ, PhD (food sci), 1961. **Professional Experience:** DIR PAPER PROD DEVELOP, PROCTER & GAMBLE INT, 1995-; assoc dir, Procter & Gamble, 1977-1995; assoc dir toilet goods prod develop, Procter & Gamble, 1972-1976; head shampoo prod develop, Procter & Gamble, 1970-1972; head prod res & prof serv, Folger Coffee Co, 1968-1970; prod res group leader, Folger Coffee Co, 1964-1968; process develop group leader, Folger Coffee Co, 1963-1964; Basic develop scientist, Foods Div, Procter & Gamble Co, 1962-1963. **Research Statement & Publications:** Kinetics of enzyme activity; autooxidation of lipids; instant coffee processes; extraction; spray and freeze drying; sensory perception effects on food acceptability; products research; process development and packaging management. **Mailing Address:** 368 Oliver Rd, Cincinnati, OH 45215. **E-Mail:** joffefm@pg.com

JOFFE, STEPHEN N, LASER SURGERY, GASTROENTEROLOGY. **Personal Data:** b Springs, SAfrica, January 11, 1943; c 2. **Education:** Univ Witwatersrand, SAfrica, MD, 1967. **Professional Experience:** CHMN BD & CHIEF EXEC OFFICER, LASER CTR AM VISIONS INC, CINCINNATI, as of 2004; ESTEEMED QUONDAM PROF SURG, UNIV CINCINNATI, as of 2004; prof surg, Univ Cincinnati, beginning 1980; healthcare consult, Lasers Med & Surg. **Research Statement & Publications:** Laser surgery and general surgery; gastroenteroloy. **Mailing Address:** Laser Ctr Am, 7840 Montgomery Rd, Cincinnati, OH 45236. **Fax:** 513-792-5620.

JOFFEE, IRVING BRIAN, ORGANIC CHEMISTRY, SURFACE CHEMISTRY. **Personal Data:** b Rochester, NY, September 9, 1946; m 1968, Elga; c Atara, Micha & Danielle. **Education:** Mass Inst Technol, SB, 1968; Brandeis Univ, MA, 1971, PhD (org chem), 1973. **Professional Experience:** ASSOC DIR, RES & DEVELOP, PALL CORP, 1987-; mgr anal res, Res & Develop, Pall Corp, 1983-1987; res chemist, Res & Develop, Pall Corp, 1975-1983; sr chemistres & develop, Dead Sea Bromine Co Ltd, Israel, 1974-1975; fel, Hebrew Univ, Israel, 1973. **Memberships:** Am Chem Soc; Parenteral Drug Asn. **Research Statement & Publications:** Polymer modification; membrane technology; filtration technology; filing and prosecution of patents; product development. **Mailing Address:** 19 Clearview St, Huntington, NY 11743.

JOFRIET, JAN CORNELIUS, STRUCTURAL ANALYSIS, BULK SOLIDS FLOW. **Personal Data:** m 1957, Marlene; c Peter & Eric. **Education:** Tech Col Amsterdam, dipl, 1950; Univ Waterloo, MASc, 1969, PhD (civil eng), 1972. **Honors & Awards:** Award for Excellence, Can Soc Agr Eng, 1985, Maple Leaf Award, 1995. **Professional Experience:** PROF EMER, UNIV GUELPH, 1995-; dir, Univ Guelph, 1993-1995; profsolid mech & eng design, Univ Guelph, 1973-1995; grad res asst, Dept Civil Eng, Univ Waterloo, 1968-1973; prin struct engr, James F MacLaren Ltd, Consult Eng, Toronto, 1960-1968; BCPower Comn, 1957-1959 & Sir William Halcrow & Partners, Eng, 1959-1960; struct engr, Gore &Storrie Ltd, Toronto, 1955-1957; struct designer, Norman Wagner & Assocs, Hamilton, 1953-1955; royal engrs, Royal Dutch Army, 1950-1953. **Memberships:** fel Can Soc Civil Engrs; fel Can Soc Agr Engrs; Am Soc Agr Engrs. **Research Statement & Publications:** Advanced structural analysis; behavior of plant materials; numerical methods of analysis; reinforced concrete use in agricultural structures and corrosion; published numerous papers, technical reports, articles and publications. **Mailing Address:** Dept Civil eng, Sch Eng, Univ Guelph, Thornbrough Bldg, Rm 222, Guelph, ON N1G 2W1, Can. **Fax:** 519-836-0227. **E-Mail:** jofriet@uoguelph.ca

JOH, TONG HYUB, BIOCHEMISTRY, MOLECULAR BIOLOGY. **Education:** NY Univ, PhD (biochem), 1971; Univ Mo, MS, 1965. **Professional Experience:** DIR, MOLECULAR BIOL LAB, BURKE REHAB HOSP, as of 2004; PROF NEUROBIOLOGY, CORNELL UNIV MED COL, 1972-. **Mailing Address:** Burke Rehab Hosp, 785 Mamaroneck Ave, White Plains, NY 10605. **Fax:** 914-948-9541.

JOHAL, GURMUKH S, GENETICS. **Education:** Punjab Agr Univ, MS; Simon Fraser Univ, PhD (biol scis). **Professional Experience:** ASSOC PROF PLANT PATH, PURDUE UNIV, 2004-. **Mailing Address:** Dept Bot & Plant Path Purdue Univ, 915 W State St, West Lafayette, IN 47907-2054. **Fax:** 765-494-0363.

JOHAL, SARJIT S, BIOCHEMISTRY. **Personal Data:** b Punjab, India, February 15, 1951. **Education:** Univ Calif, Los Angeles, BS, 1974, MS, 1976; Univ Ariz, PhD (biochem), 1980. **Professional Experience:** AT GRAIN PROCESSING CORP, as of 2004; mgr process develop, Ecosci Corp, beginning 1992; group leader biochem, Enichem, 1990-1992; sr proj leader, Brit Petrol, 1985-1990; proj leader, Brit Petrol, 1983-1985; res fel biochem, Univ Nebr, 1980-1983. **Memberships:** Am Chem Soc; Am Soc Biochem & Molecular Biol. **Research Statement & Publications:** Biochemistry. **Mailing Address:** Grain Processing Corp, 1600, Ore St, Muscatine, IA 52761. **Fax:** 563-264-4289.

JOHANNES, ROBERT, PHYSICS OPTOELECTRON MATH STATISTICS, PRECISION GUIDED MILLSES & LOS & PN COMPUTER SIMULATED TRAJECTORICS AS A FUNCTION OF ATMOSPHERIC CONDITIONS IN A DESERT ENVIRON. **Personal Data:** b Philadelphia, Pa, January 16, 1927; m 1961, Nicia; c Stephanie, William & Douglas. **Education:** Dickinson Col, BS, 1950; Lehigh Univ, MS, 1952, PhD (physics), 1961. **Professional Experience:** RETIRED; prin scientist, Calspan Corp, 1973-1993; res physicist, Calspan Corp, 1972-1977; sr scientist, Superior Electronics Res Lab, Que, 1970-1972; sr scientist, Westinghouse Res Lab, 1966-1970; res specialist, Appl Res Lab, 1964-1966; proj scientist res lab, Philco Corp, Ford Motor Co, 1960-1964; res asst, Lehigh Univ, 1958-1960; asst physics, Lehigh Univ, 1952-1958. **Memberships:** Am Phys Soc. **Research Statement & Publications:** Most unclassified public relate to applied optics, ferroelectrics, and optical data processing about 19 publications or presentation prior to 1972 are unclassified Electro-optics; ferroelectrics; infrared spectroscopy; optical data processing; optical properties; transition metal oxides; lasers; optics; system analysis; All publications that are classified (after 1972) relate to lasers and CM/CCM analyses for the DOD (dept of defense) I had about 100 publications as prin author or co authors author of the Lexion published by the precision guided weapon CM test and evaluation directorate at white sands M Range. **Mailing Address:** 1217 Edgewood Ave, Las Cruces, NM 88005.

JOHANNES, ROBERT EARL, MARINE ECOLOGY. **Personal Data:** b North Battleford, Sask, September 26, 1936; m 1959, Christa E Pfeiff; c Gregory. **Education:** Univ BC, BSc, 1958, MSc, 1959; Univ Hawaii, PhD (zool), 1963. **Professional Experience:** PRIV CONSULT, 1994-; Pew Scholars Prog Conserv & Environ fel, 1993-; srprin res scientist, Commonwealth Sci & Indust Res Orgn Dept, Fisheries Div, 1979-1993; visassoc researcher, Hawaii Inst Marine Biol, 1977-1979; Guggenheim fel, 1974-1975; from asst-prof to assoc prof, Dept Zool, 1966-1977; res assoc, Dept Zool, 1965-1966; res assoc, MarineInst, Univ Ga, 1963-1965; res asst, Univ Hawaii, 1960-1963; res asst, Univ BC, 1958-1959. **Research Statement & Publications:** Marine resource management and ethnobiology in tropical marine communities; marine environmental impacts pulp milk; biology of krill. **Mailing Address:** 24 Darling Parade, Mt Stuart Tas 7000, Australia. **Fax:** 612283235. **E-Mail:** bobjoh@netspace.au

JOHANNES, VIRGILIVANCICH, DIGITAL TELECOMMUNICATIONS SYSTEMS & HARDWARE, HIGH-SPEED DIGITAL CIRCUITS. **Personal Data:** b Omaha, Nebr, February 7, 1930; m 1962, Rachelma; c Laura. **Education:** City Col NY, BS, 1953; Columbia Univ, MS, 1954, ScD(eng), 1961. **Professional Experience:** PRES, VIRGIL I JOHANNES INC, 1989-; vchmn, Study Group XVIII, IntConsultative Comt Tel & Tel, 1978-1993; adj assoc prof, Columbia Univ, 1964-1968; dept head, AT&T Bell Labs, 1963-1989; prof & chmn, Elec Eng Dept, Fairleigh Dickinson Univ, 1962-1963; lectr elec eng, City Col New York, 1953-1958. **Memberships:** Fel Inst Elec & Electronics Engrs. **Research Statement & Publications:** High speed digital transmission systems on copper, optical fiber and satellite media (system concepts and detailed implementation); international standards for digital telecommunications. **Mailing Address:** 230 Balfoor Dr, Winter Park, FL 32792. **Fax:** 407-679-0845. **E-Mail:** v.johannes@ieee.org

JOHANNESSEN, CARL L, BIOGEOGRAPHY, CULTURAL GEOGRAPHY & HORTICULTURE. **Personal Data:** b Santa Ana, Calif, July 28, 1924; m Doris; c Bruce E. **Education:** Univ Calif, Berkeley, BA, 1950, MA, 1953, PhD (geog), 1959. **Professional Experience:** PROF EMER, DEPT GEOG, UNIV ORE, as of 1997; mem, ConfLatin Am Geogr, chair, 1984-1986; Agr Develop Coun grant, Brazil, 1979; pres, Neopropagations, Inc, 1969-1978; Agr Develop Coun grant, Guggenheim Found fel, 1965-1966; Agr Develop Coun grant, Costa Rica, 1965; prof, Univ Ore, beginning 1959; instr geog, UnivCalif, Davis, 1959; grantee, NSF, Univ Ore Found. **Memberships:** AAAS; Asn Am Geogr; Am Geog Soc; Soc Econ Bot; Sigma Xi; Soc Ethnobiol. **Research Statement & Publications:** Ways in which humans have modified plants and animals in the domestication process and the distributions of domestic and wild biota; Latin America, Himalayas and India and China in pre-Columbian times. **Mailing Address:** Dept Geog, Univ Ore, 102 Condon Hall, Eugene, OR 97403-1251. **Fax:** 541-346-2067. **E-Mail:** carljohann@oregon.uoregon.edu

JOHANNESSEN, GEORGE ANDREW, HORTICULTURE, PLANT BREEDING. **Personal Data:** b Seattle, Wash, January 10, 1919; m 1949, Patricia; c Neil, Ann, Sue & Kirsten. **Education:** Rutgers Univ, BS, 1941; Purdue Univ, MS, 1948; Cornell Univ, PhD (veg crops, plant breeding, physiol), 1950. **Professional Experience:** AGR CONSULT, as of 2004; DIR EMER, CALIF TOMATO RES INST, 1990-; consult, Food & Agr Orgn, UN, Ivory Coast, Africa, 1980; dir, Calif Tomato Res Inst, 1978-1990; mgr, Calif Processing Tomato Adv Bd, 1972-1978; mem gov bd, Agr Res Inst, Wash, DC, 1971-1973; dir, Calif Tomato Res Inst, 1968-1972; consult tomato & pineapple prod, Agency Int Develop, Africa, 1968; dir raw prod res, Calif Canners & Growers, 1964-1967; vis assoc prof, Cornell Univ, 1963-1964; head plant breeding dept, Pineapple Res Inst Hawaii, 1960-1964; Affil mem grad fac, Univ Hawaii, 1960-1964; western area agronomist, Am Can Co, 1953-1960; assoc prof veg crops & pomol, Cornell Univ, 1950-1953; asst hort, NY Exp Sta, Cornell Univ, Geneva, 1948-1950; asst hort, Purdue Univ, 1946-1948; Asst soil technologist, Va Truck Exp Sta, 1946. **Memberships:** Fel Am Soc Hort Sci; Am Path Soc; Sigma Xi; Inst Food Technologists. **Research Statement & Publications:** Vegetable crops; physiology; tomato fruit cracking; histology of tomato fruit skin; fruit and vegetable crop production; post-harvest handling and storage of fruit and vegetable crops; tomato and pineapple breeding; research administration. **Mailing Address:** 333 Hartford Rd, Danville, CA 94525.

JOHANNESSEN, PAUL ROMBERG, SOLID STATE ELECTRONICS. **Personal Data:** b Oslo, Norway, August 12, 1926; American citizen; m 1950, c 2. **Education:** Mass Inst Technol, SB & SM, 1953, ScD, 1958. **Professional Experience:** CHIEF EXEC OFFICER, MEGAPULSE INC, as of 2004; CHMN, MEGAPULSE INC, 1993-; PRES, MEGAPULSE INC, 1970-; vpres, Symbionics, 1969-1970; sr scientist, Sylvania Elec Prod Inc, 1959-1969; asst prof, Electronic Systs Lab, Mass Inst Technol, 1958-1959; res asst & instr, Electronic Systs Lab, MassInst Technol, 1956-1958; res engr, Electronic Systs Lab, Mass Inst Technol, 1953-1956. **Memberships:** Sr mem Inst Elec & Electronics Engrs; Sigma Xi. **Research Statement & Publications:** Solid state power sources; automatic controls; nonlinear circuits; electronics. **Mailing Address:** Megapulse Inc, Four Billerica Bus Ctr 101 Billerica Ave, North Billerica, MA 01862. **Fax:** 978-670-3776.

JOHANNINGSMEIER, ARTHUR GEORGE, ECOLOGY. **Personal Data:** b Lafayette, Ind, November 5, 1930; m 1956, c Edward & Charles. **Education:** Purdue Univ, BS, 1956, MS, 1962, PhD, 1966. **Professional Experience:** Consult water qual, New Eng Interstate Water Pollution Control Comn, Boston, 1975-1978; CHMN SCI DEPT, CUSHING ACAD, 1972-; NSF fac fel, Grasslands IBP, Colo State Univ, 1971-1972; asst prof biol, Boston Univ, 1964-1971; teaching asst biol & zool, bot & zool, Purdue Univ, 1962-1964; instr biol, bot & zool, Purdue Univ, 1958-1962; teacher, high sch, Mich, 1956-1958. **Memberships:** Ecol Soc Am; Am Inst Biol Scientists; Sigma Xi; Am Soc Mammal. **Research Statement & Publications:** Food and energy relationships of small mammals in natural communities; development of field methods for the study of small mammal movements and physiology; water quality assessment. **Mailing Address:** Dept Sci, Cushing Acad, Sci Bldg, Ashburnham, MA 01430. **Fax:** 508-827-6927. **E-Mail:** ajoh97@aol.com

JOHANNSEN, CHRISTIAN JAKOB, SOILS & SOIL SCIENCE, REMOTE SENSING. **Personal Data:** b Randolph, Nebr, July 24, 1937; m Joanne; c Eric C & Peter J. **Education:** Univ Nebr, Lincoln, BS, 1959, MS, 1961; Purdue Univ, PhD (soil physics, agron), 1969. **Honors & Awards:** Technol Innovation Award, NASA, 1979; Outstanding Serv Award, Am SocPhotogram & Remote Sensing, 1992; Ag Alumni Award, Uni of Nebraska (1995); Cert of Acheievement (1996), International Service Award (1987, 2000), Global Facilitator Award (2004) Epsilon Sigma Phi; Career Award, Purdue Uni Coop Ext Spec Assoc (2003); Medal of Achievement (2005), Katholieke Universiteit Leuven, Belgium; Hugh Hammond Bennett Award (2005), Soil & Water Cons Soc; Cert of Achievement (2006), Purdue Ag Alumni Assoc. **Professional Experience:** DIR EMER & PROF EMER, APPLNS REMOTE SENSING LAB, PURDUE UNIV, as of 2003; Adjunct Professor, 2000-2004, Katholieke Universiteit Leuven, Belgiumvis chief scientist, Space Imaging Inc, 1996-1997; dir, Environ Sci & Eng Inst, 1994-1996; dir, Natural Resources Res Inst, 1987-1993; dir, Applns Remote Sensing Lab, Purdue Univ, beginning 1986; agr data network, Lab Appln Remote Sensing, 1985-1986; exten agronomist, Univ Mo, Columbia, 1972-1985; prog leader, Lab Appln Remote Sensing, 1969-1972; res agronomist, Lab Appln Remote Sensing, 1966-1969; res asst soil physics, PurdueUniv, 1965-1966; exten agronomist, Purdue Univ, 1963-1965; Area agronomist, Chevron ChemCo, 1961-1962. **Memberships:** Fel Am Soc Agron; fel Soil Sci Soc Am; fel Soil & Water Conserv Soc (pres, 1982-1983); fel Am Soc Photogram; fel Indiana Acad Sci; Int Soil Sci Soc; Sigma Xi, Gamma Sigma Delta, Sigma Epsilon Philos. **Research Statement & Publications:** Developing natural resources data and information; emphasis on remote sensing, geographic information systems and global positioning systems for use in land degradation and global change application. **Mailing Address:** Dept Agron, Purdue Univ, 915 W State St, Lilly Hall Life Sci, West Lafayette, IN 47907-2054. **Fax:** 765-496-2926. **E-Mail:** johan@purdue.edu

JOHANNSEN, FREDERICK RICHARD, RISK ASSESSMENT. **Personal Data:** b St Louis, Mo, February 17, 1946; c 2. **Education:** William Jewell Col, AB, 1968; Univ Mo, MS, 1970, PhD (toxicol), 1973; Am Bd Toxicol, dipl, 1981. **Professional Experience:** SR CONSULT TOXICOL & TEAM LEADER, MONSANTO CO, 1994-; adj assoc prof toxicol, Sch Pub Health, St Louis Univ, 1992-; worldwide dir copr toxicol, EnvironHealth Lab, 1992-1994; dir toxicol, Environ Health Lab, 1986-1992; dir, Toxicol LabAccreditation BRD Inc, 1982-1988; Lectr, Am Indust Hyg Asn, 1979-; toxicol mgr, EnvironHealth Lab, 1979-1986; group leader, Environ Health Lab, 1979-1980; toxicologist specialist, Monsanto Co, 1978-1979; sr toxicologist, Monsanto Co, 1973-1978; res assoc, Toxicol Lab, Univ Mo, 1972-1973; Grad res asst toxicol, Toxicol Lab, Univ Mo, 1968-1972. **Memberships:** Soc Toxicol; Am Chem Soc; fel Acad Toxicol Sci. **Research Statement & Publications:** Toxicology and risk assessment for use in support of environmental and occupational safety. **Mailing Address:** Monsanto Co, 800 N Lindbergh Blvd, St Louis, MO 63167. **E-Mail:** frjoha@ccmail.monsanto.com

JOHANSEN, ELMER L, ELECTRICAL ENGINEERING. **Personal Data:** b Lake Forest, Ill, June 28, 1930; m 1958, c 4. **Education:** Harvard Univ, BA, 1952; Univ Mich, Ann Arbor, MSEE, 1954, PhD (elec eng), 1964. **Honors & Awards:** Barry Carleton Award, Inst Elec & Electronics Engrs Group on Aerospace &Electronic Systs, 1973. **Professional Experience:** RES ENGR, ENVIRON RES INST, MICH, 1973-; lectr elec eng, Univ Mich, Ann Arbor, 1966-1970; res engr, Univ Mich, Ann Arbor, 1965-1977; assoc res engr, Univ Mich, Ann Arbor, 1963-1965; res assoc, Univ Mich, Ann Arbor, 1960-1963; res asst radar systs, UnivMich, Ann Arbor, 1958-1960; Sr engr, Cook Res Labs, 1956-1958. **Memberships:** Inst Elec & Electronics Engrs; Sigma Xi. **Research Statement & Publications:** Radar systems; electromagnetic scattering properties of radar targets; radar systems engineering; synthetic aperture radar; radar cross-section measurements; radar propagation; radar data analysis; millimeter-wave radar. **Mailing Address:** 2630 Manchester Rd, Ann Arbor, MI 48104-6500.

JOHANSEN, ERLING, DENTISTRY, ORAL PATHOLOGY. **Personal Data:** b Overhalla, Norway, April 8, 1923; American citizen; m 1952, c 3. **Education:** Tufts Col, DMD, 1949; Univ Rochester, PhD, 1955. **Honorary Degrees:** PhD, Univ Athens, 1981. **Professional Experience:** Chmn, Coun Dent Res, Am Dent Asn, 1986-1987; mem, Coun Dent Res, AmDent Asn, 1983-1987; PROF & DEAN DENT SCI, SCH DENT MED, TUFTS UNIV, 1980-; merit award, Rochester Acad Med, 1980; prof clin dent, Sch Med & Dent, Univ Rochester, 1974-1980; consult, King Abdulaziz Univ, Sch Dent, Jeddah, Saudi Arabia; USPHS grants; ed, JDent Educ; int lectr, Venezuela, 1974; hon prof, Yonsei Univ Col Dent, Seoul, Korea, PeruvianUniv, Lima, Peru, 1973; int lectr & adv, Pan-Am Health Orgn, WHO, Colombia, Peru & Chile, 1973; travelling scholar, Int Col Dentists, Asian Pac Countries, 1970; hon guest prof, KanagawaDent Sch, Japan, 1969; spec consult, Comt Asn Role & Function, mem comt advan educ, TaskForce on Advan Educ & Exec Comt, chmn sect advan educ & vpres, Advan Educ Prog, Am AsnDent Schs; lectr, XIVth World Dent Cong, Paris, France, First Pan-Pac Cong Dent Res, Tokyo, Japan & Asian Pac Regional Orgn Cong, Bangkok, Thailand; consult, Bur Environ Health, memclin fel rev panel & anat & path fel comt, USPHS; consult, Nat Inst Dent Res; Margaret & CyWelcher prof, Univ Rochester, 1966-1980; chmn dept, Sch Med & Dent, Univ Rochester, 1955-1980; from asst prof to prof dent res, Sch Med & Dent, Univ Rochester, 1955-1966; instrhistol, Eastman Sch Dent Hyg, 1952-1964; asst, Dent Sch, Tufts Col, 1946-1949. **Memberships:** Fel AAAS; Am Dent Asn; Norweg Dent Asn; Int Asn Dent Res; Sigma Xi; AmAsn Dent Schs; fel Am Col Dentists; fel Int Col Dentists; hon mem Korean Dent Asn; hon memPedodontic Soc Peru; hon mem Am Acad Dent Sci. **Research Statement & Publications:** Experimental dental caries; electron microscopy; mineralized tissues; graduate education. **Mailing Address:** 69 Windsor Rd, Needham, MA 02192-1440.

JOHANSEN, HANS WILLIAM, MARINE PHYCOLOGY. **Personal Data:** b Worcester, Mass, June 11, 1932; m 1982, Frances; c Eric J. **Education:** San Jose State Col, BA, 1955; San Francisco State Col, MA, 1961; Univ Calif, Berkeley, PhD (phycol), 1966. **Professional Experience:** PROF EMER BIOL, DEPT BIOL, CLARK UNIV, as of 2003; prof biol, Dept Biol, Clark Univ, beginning 1981; assoc prof, Dept Biol, Clark Univ, 1972-1981; asst prof bot, Dept Biol, Clark Univ, 1968-1972; USPHS fel, 1966-1968; teacher, San Mateo High Sch, 1956-1960. **Memberships:** Phycol Soc Am; Int Phycol Soc; Sigma Xi. **Research Statement & Publications:** Systematics, structure, reproduction and morphogenesis of Corallinaceae; ecology of marine benthic algae. **Mailing Address:** Dept Biol, Clark Univ, 950 Main St, Worcester, MA 01610. **E-Mail:** hjohansen@clarku.edu

JOHANSEN, JACK T, ENGINEERING. **Personal Data:** b 1943. **Professional Experience:** PRES & FOUND, BOSTON PROBES, INC, as of 2004; sr vpres sci & Technol, Millipore Corp, beginning 1987; from sr mgt topres, Carlbiotech, Copenhagen. **Mailing Address:** Boston Probes, Inc, 75 E Wiggins Ave, Bedford, MA 01730.

JOHANSEN, NILS IVAR, GEOTECHNICAL ENGINEERING, PERMAFROST ENGINEERING. **Personal Data:** b Oslo, Norway, December 25, 1941. **Education:** Purdue Univ, BS, 1966, MS, 1967, PhD (civil eng & eng geol), 1971. **Professional Experience:** Secy, Ind Acad Sci, 2001-2004; prof geol eng, Univ Southern Ind, beginning 1996; UNIV DIV ADV, UNIV SOUTHERN IND, 1996-; chmn, Eng Sect, Ind Acad Sci, 1991 & 1994; head, Mining Technol, 1990-1995; vis assoc prof & acad skills coordr, Univ Southern Ind, 1988-1989; vis prof, Univ Mo, Rolla, 1981-1982; consult, Geotech Eng, 1973-; from asst prof to prof eng, Univ Alaska, 1971-1996; hwy engr, Ind Dept Highways, 1967-1971. **Memberships:** fel Am Soc Civil Engrs; Soc Mining Engrs; Sigma Xi; Nat Asn Develop Educ. **Research Statement & Publications:** Geotechnical engineering and permafrost engineering; resource development in arctic and subarctic regions; infrastructure related to resource development; engineering education. **Mailing Address:** Univ Southern Ind, 8600 Univ Blvd, Evansville, IN 47712-3596. **Fax:** 812-421-9880. **E-Mail:** johansen@usi.edu

JOHANSON, CHRIS ELLYN, PSYCHOPHARMACOLOGY. **Personal Data:** b Tacoma, Wash, June 18, 1945; m 1972. **Education:** Univ Ill, Chicago, BS, 1968; Univ Chicago, PhD (psychol), 1972. **Professional Experience:** Merrell-Nat Labs, 1974-1976; Schering Labs, 1972-1976; RES ASSOC, DEPT PSYCHIAT, UNIV CHICAGO, 1972-; consult behav res, Behav Res & Action Social Sci, 1972-1974; USPHS trainee psychol, Dept Psychiat, Univ Chicago, 1968-1972. **Memberships:** Am Psychol Asn; Behav Pharmacol Soc; Int Asn Study Drug Dependence. **Research Statement & Publications:** The effects in the rhesus monkey of a variety of environmental and pharmacological variables on drug self-administration and effect of chronic drug administration on behavior. **Mailing Address:** 5353 Strathmore Ave, Kensington, MD 20895-1160.

JOHANSON, CONRAD EARL, PHYSIOLOGY & BIOLOGY OF CHOROID PLEXUS. **Personal Data:** b Brockton, Mass, August 6, 1942. **Education:** Eastern Nazarene Col, BA, 1965; Univ Kans, PhD (physiol), 1970. **Professional Experience:** PROF CLIN NEUROSCIENCE & DIR NEUROSURG RES, BROWN UNIV, 1986-; NIH res careerachievement award, 1977; from asst prof to assoc prof pharmacol, Univ Utah, 1974-1986. **Memberships:** Soc Neuroscience; Pharmacol Soc; Am Physiol Soc. **Research Statement & Publications:** Physiology and biology of choroid plexus; published over 10 articles. **Mailing Address:** Dept Clin NeuroSci, Brown Univ, 593 Eddy St, Aldrich Bldg 401, Providence, RI 02903. **Fax:** 401-444-8727. **E-Mail:** conrad_johanson@brown.edu

JOHANSON, DONALD CARL, PHYSICAL ANTHROPOLOGY. **Personal Data:** b Chicago, Ill, June 28, 1943; m 1988, Lenora. **Education:** Univ Ill, BA, 1966; Univ Chicago, MA, 1970, PhD, 1974. **Honorary Degrees:** DSc, John Carroll Univ, 1979, Col Wooster, 1985. **Honors & Awards:** Jared Potter Kirtland Award, Outstanding Sci Achievement, Cleveland MusNatural His, 1979; Prof Achievement Award, Univ Chicago, 1980; San Francisco ExplorationAward, 1986; Int Premio Fregene Award, 1987. **Professional Experience:** PROF ANTHROP, ARIZ STATE UNIV, 1997-; DIR, INST HUMAN ORIGINS, ARIZ STATE UNIV, 1997-; prof anthrop, Stanford Univ, 1983-1989; PRES, FOUNDER, PALEOANTHROPOLOGIST, INST HUMAN ORIGINS, BERKELEY, CALIF, 1981-; adj prof, CaseWestern Reserve Univ & Kent State Univ, 1978-1981; cur, Dept Phys Anthrop, Cleveland Mus Natural Hist, 1974-1981; mem, Dept Phys Anthrop, Cleveland Mus Natural Hist, 1972-1981; grant, Wenner-Gren Found, NSF, NatGeog Soc, LSB Leakey Found, Cleveland Found, George Gund Cound, Roush Found. **Memberships:** Fel AAAS; fel Royal Geog Soc; Am Asn Phys Anthropologists; Int Asn Dent Res; Int Asn Human Biologists; Am Asn Africanist Archaeologissts; Soc Vert Paleont; Soc StudyHuman Biol; Founders Coun; Asn Int Study Human Paleont; Explorers Club; Nat Ctr Sci Educ. **Research Statement & Publications:** Field and laboratory research into human crisis; field work in Ethiopia and Tanzania, searching for fossilized remains of our ancestors. **Mailing Address:** Inst Human Origins, Ariz State Univ, PO Box 874101, Tempe, AZ 85287-4101. **Fax:** 480-727-6570.

JOHANSON, LAMAR, PLANT PHYSIOLOGY. **Personal Data:** b Kyle, Tex, October 31, 1935; m 1960. **Education:** Southwest Tex State Col, BS, 1957, MA, 1958; Tex A&M Univ, PhD (plant physiol), 1967. **Professional Experience:** RETIRED; dean, Col Arts & Sci, Tarleton State Univ, 1988-2001; prof biol & head, Dept Biol Sci, Tarleton State Univ, 1971-2001; assoc prof, Tarleton State Univ, 1967-1971; asst plant physiol, Tex A & M Univ, 1963-1965; instr, Tarleton State Univ, 1961-1963; asst biol, Southwest Tex State Col, 1956-1958. **Memberships:** AAAS; Am Soc Plant Physiologists; Scandinavian Soc Plant Physiologists; Am Inst Biol Sci; Am Oil Chemists' Soc; Sigma Xi. **Research Statement & Publications:** Nutrition of excised plant tissues and algae, especially calcium and sodium requirements; lateral root formation; biochemistry and physiology of the peanut; mineral nutrition, oil quality and response to irrigation. **Mailing Address:** Col Arts & Sci, Tarleton State Univ, Stephenville, TX 76402-0001.

JOHANSON, L(ENNART) N(OBLE), CHEMICAL ENGINEERING. **Personal Data:** b Salt Lake City, Utah, May 3, 1921; m 1948, c 3. **Education:** Univ Utah, BS, 1942; Univ Wis, MS, 1943, PhD (chem eng), 1948. **Professional Experience:** PROF EMER, DEPT CHEM ENG, UNIV WASH, as of 2005; prof chem eng, Univ Wash, beginning 1961; from asst prof to assocprof, Univ Wash, 1951-1961; process engr, Richfield Oil Corp, Calif, 1948-1951; instr chem eng, Univ Wis, 1947-1948; assoc process engr, Richfield Oil Corp, Calif, 1944-1945; chem engr, US Bur Mines, Utah, 1942; consult. **Memberships:** Am Chem Soc; Am Soc Eng Educ; Am Inst Chem Engrs; Tech Asn Pulp & Paper Indust; Sigma Xi. **Research Statement & Publications:** Pulp, paper technology; chemical engineering kinetics; reactor design; fluidization; high temperature technology. **Mailing Address:** Dept Chem Eng, Univ Wash, PO Box 351750, Seattle, WA 98195-1750.

JOHANSON, ROBERT GAIL, THIN FILM DEPOSITION. **Personal Data:** b San Francisco, Calif, August 26, 1936; m 1964, Joan; c 5. **Education:** Reed Col, AB, 1960; Univ Vt, PhD (org chem), 1969. **Professional Experience:** SR STAFF ENGR, SEAGATE RECORDING MEDIA GROUP, 1992-; dir mfg eng, KMI Magnetics Inc, 1990-1992; mgr thin film eng, Akashic Memories Corp, 1988-1990; mgr, appln lab, CPA Inc, 1984-1988; consult, Disk Consults, 1983-1984; mgr head & disk develop, Datapoint Corp, 1981-1983; sr mem staff, Signetics Corp, 1976-1981; staff mem, Raychem Corp, 1970-1976; fel org chem, Case Western Res Univ, 1969-1970; chemist, Aerojet-Gen Corp, 1961-1966. **Memberships:** Am Chem Soc; Sigma Xi; Inst Elec & Electronics Engrs; Am Vacuum Soc. **Research Statement & Publications:** Thin film deposition and analysis. **Mailing Address:** 517 Kenilworth Ct, Sunnyvale, CA 94087.

JOHANSON, WALDEMAR GUSTAVE, INTERNAL MEDICINE, PULMONARY DISEASES. **Personal Data:** b St Paul, Minn, September 9, 1937; m 1960, c 3. **Education:** Gustavus Adolphus Col, BS, 1959; Univ Minn, Minneapolis, MD, 1962. **Professional Experience:** PROF & CHAIR, DEPT MED, NJ MED SCH, as of 1999; CHIEF, PULMONARY DIS SECT, 1974-; assoc prof, Pulmonary Dis Sect, 1974-1978; from instr to assoc prof med, Univ Tex Health Sci Ctr, Dallas, 1969-1974; Nat Inst Arthritis & Infectious Dis fel, Univ Tex Health Sci Ctr, Dallas, 1968-1971; resident, Minneapolis Vet Admin Hosp & St Paul Ramsey Hosp, 1965-1967; intern med, Med Ctr, Univ Calif, Los Angeles, 1962-1963. **Memberships:** Am Thoracic Soc; Am Fedn Clin Res. **Research Statement & Publications:** Pulmonary disease models; infectious disease of the lungs. **Mailing Address:** Dept Med, NJ Med Sch, 185 S Orange Ave, Newark, NJ 07103.

JOHANSON, WILLIAM RICHARD, RARE-EARTH MAGNETISM, SPECIFIC HEAT MEASUREMENTS. **Personal Data:** b Oakland, Calif, August 8, 1948. **Education:** Univ Hawaii, Manoa, BS, 1972; Univ Calif, Riverside, MS, 1974, PhD (physics), 1978. **Professional Experience:** ASSOC PROF PHYSICS & DEPT CHMN, SANTA CLARA UNIV, 1989-; res assoc, Argonne Nat Lab, 1984; res assoc, Univ Calif, Riverside, 1983-1989; asst prof physics, Pomona Col, 1983-1989; instr, Univ NMex, Los Alamos, 1983; res fel, Argonne Nat Lab, 1978-1981; res fel, Los Alamos Nat Lab, 1981-1983. **Memberships:** Am Asn Physics Teachers; Am Phys Soc; Sigma Xi. **Research Statement & Publications:** Low temperature solid state physics; specific heat; magnetic materials. **Mailing Address:** Dept Physics, Santa Clara Univ, Santa Clara, CA 95053.

JOHANSSON, KARL RICHARD, MICROBIAL ECOLOGY, MEDICAL MICROBIOLOGY. **Personal Data:** b Bay City, Mich, June 28, 1920; m 1943, Dorothy Heilig; c Sandra, Peter & Steven. **Education:** Univ Wis, BS, 1942, MS, 1946, PhD (bact), 1948. **Professional Experience:** RETIRED; vis scholar, Calif Space Inst, Univ Calif, San Diego, 1986-; fac fel, NASA, 1983 & 1984; prof biol sci, NTex State Univ, 1973-1986; Consult, Tex Col Osteop Med, 1973-1986; chmn dept, NTex State Univ, 1973-1979; dep dir sci affairs, Wistar Inst, 1970-1973; prof microbiol, Univ Tex Med Sch San Antonio, 1969-1970; exec secy virol study sect, Div Res Grants, 1965-1969; chief res grants br, Nat Inst Neurol Dis & Blindness, NIH, 1963-1965; assoc prof environ health eng, Calif Inst Technol, 1961-1963; exec secy, Virol & Rickettsiol Study Sect, Div Res Grants, NIH, 1959-1961; Consult, Minneapolis-Honeywell, 1958-1959; Consult, Gen Mills, Inc, 1953; from asst prof to assoc prof bact & immunol, Univ Minn, 1949-1959; instr dairy bact, Univ Calif, Davis, 1948-

1949; asst bact, Univ Wis, 1946-1948; asst vet sci, Univ Wis, 1946; asst bact, Univ Wis, 1942-1943; Anal chemist, Swift & Co, 1942. **Memberships:** AAAS; Am Soc Microbiol; Am Acad Microbiol. **Research Statement & Publications:** Pathogenesis, including role of surface proteins, in legionella pneumophila; survival of legionellae in the natural environment; biotransformation and cometabolism of humic compounds; space biology; exobiology. **Mailing Address:** 825 Santa Regina, Solana Beach, CA 92075. **E-Mail:** krjohansson@earthlink.net

JOHANSSON, SONNY L, GENITAL CANCER, UROLOGICAL DISEASES. **Personal Data:** b Falkoping, Sweden, October 27, 1942. **Education:** Univ Goteborg, BS, 1965, MD, 1972, PhD (path), 1976. **Professional Experience:** PROF & DIR PATH, UNIV NEBR MED CTR, 1985-; assoc prof path, Univ Goteborg, 1976-1985. **Memberships:** Am Asn Cancer Res; AMA; Am Asn Path. **Mailing Address:** Dept Path & Microbiol, Univ Nebr Med Ctr, 983135 Nebr Med Ctr, Omaha, NE 68198-3135. **Fax:** 402-559-6018. **E-Mail:** sjohanss@unmc.edu

JOHANSSON, SUNE, FIRE RETARDANT COATINGS & TREATMENTS, HIGH TEMPERATURE COATINGS. **Personal Data:** b Falkenberg, Sweden, April 8, 1928; Canadian citizen; m 1953, Anna; c Rolf. **Education:** Hogre Tekniska Laroverket, BE, 1949. **Professional Experience:** RETIRED, tech expert, Teltech Resource Network Corp, beginning 1989; RETIRED, tech dir, Flame Control Coatings, beginning 1982; tech dir, Wood-Tech, 1978-1982; tech dir, Ocean Chem, 1962-1978; chief chemist, Ocean Chemicals, 1961-1962; chief chemist, Acme Paint & Varnish, 1955-1961; chemist, Acme Paint & Varnish, 1951-1955. **Memberships:** Am Chem Soc. **Research Statement & Publications:** Fire retardant coatings and treatments; high temperature coatings; general chemical coatings. **Mailing Address:** Flame Control Coatings, 4120 Hyde Park Blvd, Niagara Falls, NY 14305. **Fax:** 716-285-6303.

JOHAR, J(OGINDAR) S(INGH), ENVIRONMENTAL CHEMISTRY, FLUORINE CHEMISTRY. **Personal Data:** b Rawalpindi, Pakistan, January 1, 1935; m 1960, Manjit; c Ravijot, Jasjot & Navjot. **Education:** Panjab Univ, India, BSc, 1957, MSc, 1959; Univ Fla, PhD (chem), 1966. **Professional Experience:** PROF CHEM, WAYNE STATE COL, 1968-; chmn sci & math div, ClevelandState Community Col, 1967-1968; Fel, Univ Idaho, 1966-1967; Lectr chem, Govt Col, Ludhiana, India, 1959-1962. **Memberships:** AAAS; Am Chem Soc; Nat Educ Asn. **Research Statement & Publications:** Synthesis and study of fluorine compounds containing nitrogen sulfur and phosphorus; volatile products and use of non-aqueous solvents. **Mailing Address:** Head Math-Sci Div, Wayne State Col, 1111 Main St, Wayne, NE 68787-1119. **Fax:** 402-375-7204.

JOHARI, OM, ELECTRON MICROSCOPY, METALLURGY. **Personal Data:** b Jodhpur, India, August 13, 1940; m 1967, c 2. **Education:** Indian Inst Technol, Kharagpur, BTech, 1962; Univ Calif, Berkeley, MS, 1963, PhD (metall), 1965. **Honors & Awards:** Grossman Award, Am Soc Metals, 1966. **Professional Experience:** Ed & managing ed, Cell & Mat, 1991-; ed & managing ed, Food Microstruct & Food Struct, 1981-; pres, Johari Assocs Inc, 1978-1988; SECY & TREAS, SCANNING MICROS INT INC, 1977-; ed & managing ed, Scanning Electron Micros & Scanning Micros, 1968-; mgr metal physics, IIT Res Inst, 1968-1977; res metallurgist, IIT Res Inst, 1966-1968; asst prof, Drexel Inst Technol, 1965-1966; consult, Lockheed-Ga Co, 1965-1966; res fel & lectr, Univ Calif, Berkeley, 1965; res asst metall, Univ Calif, Berkeley, 1962-1965. **Research Statement & Publications:** Relationship between structure and properties of materials; applications of scanning and transmission electron microscopy in material sciences and other branches of science and technology; failure analysis of metallic materials. **Mailing Address:** Scanning Micros Int, PO Box 66507, Chicago, IL 60666-0507. **Fax:** 847-985-6698. **E-Mail:** 73211.647@compuserve.com

JOHN, DAVID THOMAS, MEDICAL PARASITOLOGY. **Personal Data:** b Kano, Nigeria, April 25, 1941; American citizen; m 1984, Rebecca; c David Andrew & Sarah Katherine. **Education:** Asbury Col, AB, 1963; Univ NC, Chapel Hill, MSPH, 1966, PhD (parasitol), 1970. **Honors & Awards:** Mem Am Trop med Delegation to PR China 1978. **Professional Experience:** ASSOC DEAN BASIC SCI, GRAD STUDIES, CTR HLTH SCI COL OSTEOPATH MED, OKLA STATE UNIV, 1997-; PROF MICROBIOL PARASITOL & ASSOC DEAN BASIC SCI, GRAD STUDIES, CTR HLTH SCI COL OSTEOPATH MED, OKLA STATE UNIV, 1990-; chair, Sch Med, Oral Roberts Univ, 1983-1990; from assoc prof to prof, Sch Med, Oral Roberts Univ, 1980-1990; from asst prof to assoc prof microbiol, Med Col, Va Commonwealth Univ, 1972-1980; NIH malariology training res assoc, Univ Ga, 1970-1972. **Memberships:** Am Soc Parasitologists; Am Soc Trop Med & Hyg; Soc Protozool; Sigma Xi; fel Am Acad Microbiol; fel Royal Soc Trop Med & Hyg, London; Int Soc Protistologists. **Research Statement & Publications:** Opportunistic amebae; environmental isolation and characterization; factors affecting resistance and virulence. **Mailing Address:** Ctr Health Sci, Okla State Univ, 1111 W 17th St Main Campus Rm A-342, Tulsa, OK 74107. **Fax:** 918-561-8414. **E-Mail:** chs@okstate.edu

JOHN, E ROY, NEUROPHYSIOLOGY & PSYCHOPHYSIOLOGY. **Personal Data:** b Brownsville, Pa, August 14, 1924; m, c 6. **Education:** Univ Chicago, BS, 1948, PhD (physiol psychol), 1954. **Professional Experience:** Res scientist, Nathan S Kline Inst, beginning 1987; prof physiol, New York Med Col, 1972-1977; City New York Health Res Coun career scientist awards, 1964-1975; PROF PSYCHIAT & DIR, BRAIN RES LABS, NY UNIV, 1963-; prof psychol & dir, Ctr Brain Res, Univ Rochester, 1960-1963; assoc prof psychol, Univ Rochester, 1959-1960; assoc res physiologist, Univ Calif, Los Angeles, 1957-1958; assoc res anatomist, Univ Calif, Los Angeles, 1956-1957; res assoc, Comn Behav Sci, 1954-1956; res consult chem, C FPease Co, Chicago, 1952-1955; res asst psychol, Univ Chicago, 1951-1954; sr res technician radiochem, Argonne Nat Labs, AEC, 1946-1951; ed, Brain & Behav Res; assoc ed, Behav Biol; mem, Nat Adv Coun Brain Res. **Memberships:** Am Physiol Soc; Am Psychopath Soc; Int Brain Res Orgn; Soc Neuroscience; Am EEG Soc. **Research Statement & Publications:** Mechanisms of learning and memory; automatic computer evaluation of brain activity; assessment of minimal brain dysfunction in children; cognitive deficit in aging. **Mailing Address:** Brain Res Lab NY Univ Med Ctr, Belleview Eighth Fl 27th St & First Ave, New York, NY 10016. **Fax:** 212263-6457.

JOHN, GEORGE, NUCLEAR ENGINEERING, NUCLEAR RADIATION DETECTION. **Personal Data:** b November 24, 1921; m Anne Homer; c Mark & Craig. **Education:** Ohio State Univ, PhD (nuclear chem), 1952. **Professional Experience:** PROF EMER NUCLEAR ENG, AIR FORCE INST TECHNOL, AIR UNIV, 1992-; prof, Nucleonics Br Mat Lab, 1980-1992; assoc profnuclear eng & physics, Nucleonics Br Mat Lab, 1956-1980; Group leader, Nucleonics Br MatLab, 1953-1956. **Memberships:** Am Chem Soc; Am Asn Physics Teachers; Health Physics Soc; AAAS. **Research Statement & Publications:** Nuclear radiation detection; Mossbauer spectrometry applied to materials science. **Mailing Address:** Eng Physics, Air Force Inst Technol, Air Univ, Rm 66, Bldg 640, 2950 P St, Wright-Patterson AFB, OH 45433-7765. **Fax:** 937-255-2921. **E-Mail:** george.john@afit.edu

JOHN, HUGO HERMAN, EDUCATION & RESEARCH ADMINISTRATION, NATURAL RESOURCE POLICY & DEVELOPMENT. **Personal Data:** b Natoma, Kans, February 13, 1929; m 1950, Prudence P Shuck; c 3. **Education:** Univ Minn, BS, 1959, MS, 1961, PhD (forestry & statist), 1964. **Professional Experience:** PROF EMER NATURAL RESOURCES, UNIV CONN, 1994-; sr consult, UNDP, NY, 1988-; prof, Col Agr & Natural Resources, Univ Conn, dir admin, Agr Exp Sta &Coop Exten Serv, 1988-1994; dean admin, Col Agr & Natural Resources, Univ Conn, dir admin, Agr Exp Sta & Coop Exten Serv, 1984-1987; chmn, nat prog comm, Soc Am Foresters, 1979; dir, Water Resources Res Ctr, 1975-1977; dean & prof admin & res, Sch Natural Resources, Univ Vt, 1973-1983; assoc dean & prof admin & res, Col Forestry & Wildlife, Univ Idaho, 1972-1973; expert, & Columbia, 1969-1971; dir & sta statistician, Agr Exp Sta, 1967-1969; fromasst prof to prof res, Col Forestry, Univ Minn, 1965-1972; expert, Food & Agr Orgn, UN, Nicaragua, 1964-1965; instr forestry, Col Forestry, Univ Minn, 1962-1964. **Memberships:** Soc Am Foresters. **Research Statement & Publications:** Development of natural resource and agricultural information and the organizational structures and constraints to their development, management and conservation; land use planning and development; agriculture and natural resource development and allocation policy tropical; tropical deforestation causes and affects; agriculture and natural resource development in Third World; environmental evaluation and policy. **Mailing Address:** 501 SE Fourth Ave, PO Box 732, Mapleton, MN 56065. **Fax:** 860-486-5408. **E-Mail:** h.john@canr1.cag.uconn.edu

JOHN, JAMES EDWARD ALBERT, MECHANICAL ENGINEERING. **Personal Data:** b Montreal, Que, November 6, 1933; American citizen; m 1958, c 4. **Education:** Princeton Univ, BSE, 1955, MSE, 1957; Univ Md, PhD (mech eng), 1963. **Professional Experience:** PRES, KETTERING UNIV, 1991-; dean, Col Eng, Univ Mass, Amherst, 1983-1991; prof & chmn dept mech eng, Ohio State Univ, 1977-1983; chmn dept, UnivToledo, 1971-1977; exec dir, Nat Acad Sci comt motor vehicle emissions, 1971-1972; consult, Goddard Space Flight Ctr, NASA, 1963-1968; from instr to prof mech eng, Univ Md, 1959-1971; res engr metall div, Air Reduction Co, Inc, NJ, 1956-1959. **Memberships:** Am Soc Mech Engrs; Am Soc Eng Educ; Soc Automotive Engr. **Research Statement & Publications:** Space simulation; vacuum; cryogenics; automotive emissions; thermal pollution; fluid dynamics. **Mailing Address:** Pres Off, Kettering Univ, 1700 W Third Ave, Flint, MI 48504. **Fax:** 810-762-9755. **E-Mail:** jjohn@kettering.edu

JOHN, JOSEPH, NUCLEAR SCIENCE, INSTRUMENTATION. **Personal Data:** b Madura, India, March 14, 1938; m 1967. **Education:** Madras Christian Col, India, BSc, 1958; Univ Madras, MA, 1960; Fla State Univ, PhD (nuclear physics), 1968. **Professional Experience:** PRES, JOSUMA CORP, as of 2005; mgr, Nuclear Systs Div, 1978-1984; vpres, Nuclear Systs Div, 1977-1984; mgr, NDI Systs Div, 1976-1978; mgr, NDI Systs Dept, 1975-1976; mgr, NDT Technol Dept, Intelcom Rad Tech, IRT Corp, 1973-1975; mgr, Californium-252 Demonstration Ctr, San Diego, 1972-1978; prog mgr technol appl, Gulf Radiation Tech, San Diego, 1972-1973; staff scientist, Gulf Gen Atomic, San Diego, 1971-1972; sr scientist, Gulf Gen Atomic, San Diego, 1968-1970; jr res officer, Bhabha Atomic Res Ctr, Govt India, 1963-1964; sci officer nuclear physics, Bhabha Atomic Res Ctr, Govt India, 1959-1962; Indian AEC fel, Bhabha Atomic Res Ctr, Govt India, 1958-1959. **Memberships:** Am Phys Soc; Am Nuclear Soc; Am Soc Nondestructive Test; Am Mgt Asn; Am Soc Test & Mat. **Research Statement & Publications:** Applied nuclear physics; applications of nuclear techniques for nondestructive evaluation; neutron radiography, radiation gauging, mineral exploration technology, nuclear materials measurement, automation and computer control of nondestructive inspection systems. **Mailing Address:** Josuma Corp, PO Box 1115, Menlo Park, CA 94026-1115.

JOHN, KAVANAKUVHIY V, VITAMIN A GLYCOLIPIDS, TUMOR ANTIGENS. **Education:** Indian Inst Sci, PhD (biochem), 1969. **Professional Experience:** DIR RES & DEVELOP, ST JOSEPH'S HOSP, MILWAUKEE, 1978-. **Research Statement & Publications:** DNA probes; flourescent immunoassays; protein electrophoresis; biochemistry of the retinoids. **Mailing Address:** 1075 Vista View Dr, Brookfield, WI 53005.

JOHN, KURUVILLA, NEUROSCIENCE. **Professional Experience:** PROF NEUROL, SECT CHIEF, WVA UNIV, as of 2005. **Memberships:** Am Public Health Asn. **Mailing Address:** Dept Neurol, WVa Univ Health Sci Ctr, 3110 MacCorkle Ave Southeast, Charleston, WV 25304. **Fax:** 304-388-1586. **E-Mail:** kjohn@hsc.wvu.edu

JOHN, MALIYAKAL EAPPEN, GENETIC ENGINEERING. **Personal Data:** b March 29, 1949; m 1975, Manorama; c Benjamin J. **Education:** Poona Univ, India, PhD, 1975. **Professional Experience:** GEN MGR, WIS TECHNOL FOUND, as of 2005; INTELLECTUAL PROPERTY MGR, WIS ALUMNI RES FOUND, as of 2004; DIR FIBER TECH, AGRACETUS, 1993-; scientist, Agracetus Inc, 1986-1992. **Memberships:** Am Soc Biol Chemist. **Research Statement & Publications:** Plant gene expression; identification and characterization of agriculturally useful genes; integration and expression in crop plants; plant transformation. **Mailing Address:** Wis Alumni Res Found, 614 Walnut St, Madison, WI 53726. **Fax:** 608-263-1064. **E-Mail:** maliyakal@warf.org

JOHN, PETER WILLIAM MEREDITH, MATHEMATICAL STATISTICS. **Personal Data:** b Porthcawl, Wales, August 20, 1923; American citizen; m 1954, c 2. **Education:** Oxford Univ, BA, 1944, MA, 1948, dipl, 1949; Univ Okla, PhD (math), 1955. **Professional Experience:** Vis prof, Univ Ky, 1970-1971; PROF MATH, UNIV TEX, AUSTIN, 1967-; from assoc prof to prof, Univ Calif, Davis, 1961-1967; res statistician, Chevron Res Corp, Stand Oil Calif, 1958-1961; vis prof, Univ Calif, Berkeley, 1958-1961; assoc res statistician, Chevron Res Corp, Stand Oil Calif, 1957-1958; asst prof, Univ NMex, 1955-1957; math master, Casady Sch, Okla, 1952-1953; instr math, Univ Okla, 1949-1952 & 1953-1955. **Memberships:** Am Statist Asn; Inst Math Statist; Royal Statist Soc; Int Statist Inst. **Research Statement & Publications:** Design of experiments; engineering applications of mathematical statistics; quality assurance. **Mailing Address:** Dept Math, Univ Tex, One Univ Sta C1200, Austin, TX 78712-0257. **Fax:** 512-471-9038. **E-Mail:** pwmj@math.utexas.edu

JOHN, WALTER, ENVIRONMENTAL PHYSICS. **Personal Data:** b Oklahoma City, Okla, February 16, 1924; m 1954, Carol Salin; c Kenneth, Laura, Claudia, & Leslie. **Education:** Calif Inst Technol, BS, 1950; Univ Calif, PhD, 1955. **Honors & Awards:** Fellow, American Physical Soc, 1965. **Professional Experience:** Vis scholar, Univ Calif, Berkeley, 1993-1996; Pres, Particle Sci, Calif Dept Health, 1974-1992; prof physics & phys sci & chmn dept, Stanislaus State Col, 1971-1974; physicist, Lawrence Radiation Lab, Univ Calif, 1958-1971; Instr physics, Univ Ill, 1955-1958. **Memberships:** Fel Am Phys Soc; Am Asn Aerosol Res; Am Asn Physics Teachers; Sigma Xi; Am Conf Govt Indust Hygienists. **Research Statement & Publications:** Experimental nuclear physics, especially nuclear reactions, fission and bent-crystal gamma ray spectroscopy; photonuclear reactions; x-rays; air pollution; aerosol physics; particulate matter in the atmosphere.

JOHNK, CARL THEODORE ADOLF, ELECTROMAGNETICS, ANTENNA THEORY & DESIGN. **Personal Data:** b Lutterbeck, Ger, October 22, 1919; American citizen; m Jeanette; c William, James, Robert & Richard. **Education:** Shurtleff Col, BS, 1941; Mo

Sch Mines, BS, 1942; Univ Ill, MS, 1948, PhD (elec eng), 1954. **Professional Experience:** PROF EMER ELEC ENG, UNIV COLO, BOULDER, as of 2004; prof elec eng, Univ Colo, Denver, beginning 1965; consult, Ramo-Woolridge Corp, 1960-1961; consult, Denver Res Inst, 1959-1962; assoc prof, Univ Colo, Boulder, 1954-1965; res assoc, Univ Ill, 1949-1954; from instr to asst prof, Univ Mo, Rolla, 1946-1949; instr elec eng, Univ Mo, Rolla, 1942-1944; elec engr, Radio Corp Am, NJ, 1942. **Memberships:** Inst Elec & Electronics Engrs; fel Am Soc Eng Educ. **Research Statement & Publications:** Antenna and array theory; modeling of antennas above lossy surfaces; modeling of very low frequency propagation in earthionosphere waveguide; electromagnetic fields; passive and active network theory. **Mailing Address:** Campus Box 110, P O Box 173364, Dept elec eng, Univ colo, Denver, CO 80217-3364. **Fax:** 303-556-2383. **E-Mail:** carl.johnk@colorado.edu

JOHNS, DAVID GARRETT, PHARMACOLOGY, BIOCHEMISTRY. **Personal Data:** b Prince Rupert, BC, October 18, 1929; m 1962, c Gerald & Audrey. **Education:** McGill Univ, BSc, 1954, MD, 1958, PhD (biochem), 1963. **Professional Experience:** EMER SCIENTIST, NAT CANCER INST, 1993-; chief lab med chem & biol, Lab Chem Pharmacol, 1978-1993; actg chief lab med chem & biol, Lab Chem Pharmacol, 1975-1978; head drug metab sect, Lab Chem Pharmacol, 1970-1975; from asst prof to assocprof, Sch Med, Yale Univ, 1965-1970; vis fel pharmacol, Sch Med, Yale Univ, 1963-1965; Asst prof med, McGill Univ, 1962-1963. **Memberships:** Am Soc Clin Invest; Asn Cancer Res; Am Soc Pharmacol & Exp Therapeut; IntSoc Antiviral Res. **Research Statement & Publications:** Mode of action and metabolism of antiviral and cancer chemotherapeutic agents. **Mailing Address:** Nat Cancer Inst, Bldg 37, Rm 5B22, 37 Convent Dr, MSC 4255, Bethesda, MD 20892-4255. **Fax:** 301-496-5839. **E-Mail:** johnsd@dc37a.nci.nih.gov

JOHNS, DENNIS MICHAEL, PROCESS RESEARCH & DEVELOPMENT, PILOT PLANT SCALE-UP. **Personal Data:** b Toledo, Ohio, April 7, 1948; m 1972, Martha; c Daniel & Matthew. **Education:** Univ Detroit, BS & MS, 1971; Purdue Univ, PhD (chem eng), 1976. **Professional Experience:** ENG SPECIALIST, AVCA CORP, 1997-; sr scientist, Dow Elanco, 1989-1996; res leader, Dow Chem, 1985-1989; proj leader, Dow Chem, 1981-1985; sr res engr, Dow Chem, 1976-1981; Teaching asst, Purdue Univ, 1972-1974. **Memberships:** Am Chem Soc; Am Inst Chem Engrs. **Research Statement & Publications:** Granulation and other solids processing systems. **Mailing Address:** AVCA Corp, 1684 Woodlands Dr, Maumee, OH 43537.

JOHNS, KENNETH CHARLES, STABILITY, TIMBER ENGINEERING & ENGINEERING EDUCATION. **Personal Data:** b Montreal, Que, June 26, 1944; m 1998, c 3. **Education:** McGill Univ, BS, 1966; Univ Col London, Eng, PhD (civil eng), 1970. **Professional Experience:** Vis prof, Canterbury Univ, Christchurch, 2004; PROF STRUCT ENG, DEPT CIVIL ENG, UNIV SHERBROOKE, 1993-; vice-rector admin, Univ Sherbrooke, 1991-1993; vis prof civil eng, Univ BC, Vancouver 1987, proj dir int develop, Univ Sherbrooke, 1986-1992; consult struct engr, Can Int Develop Agency, Africa, 1984-1986; dean fac appl sci, Univ Sherbrooke, 1981-1985; vis prof civil eng, Univ BC, Vancouver 1980; sr vis fel, Cranfield Inst Technol, UK, 1973. **Memberships:** Order Engrs Que; Can Soc Civil Eng. **Research Statement & Publications:** Stability and dynamics of civil engineering structures; timber structures, fracture and buckling of commercial lumber; engineering education reform; Third World technical and engineering education. **Mailing Address:** Dept Civil Eng, Univ Sherbrooke, 2500 Univ Blvd, Sherbrooke, PQ J1K 2R1, Can. **Fax:** 819-821-7974. **E-Mail:** kenneth.johns@usherbrooke.ca

JOHNS, LEWIS E(DWARD), CHEMICAL ENGINEERING. **Personal Data:** b Pittsburgh, Pa, December 13, 1935; m 1957, c 3. **Education:** Carnegie Mellon Univ, BS, 1957, PhD (chem eng), 1964. **Professional Experience:** PROF CHEM ENG, UNIV FLA, 1980-; assoc prof, Univ Fla, 1976-1980; asst prof, Univ Fla, 1967-1976; instr, Saginaw Valley Col, 1964; chem engr, Dow Chem Co, 1962-1967. **Memberships:** Am Inst Chem Engrs; Sigma Xi. **Research Statement & Publications:** Fluid mechanics; diffusion. **Mailing Address:** Dept Chem Eng Univ Fla, PO Box 116005, Gainesville, FL 32611-6005. **E-Mail:** johns@che.ufl.edu

JOHNS, MARTIN WESLEY, NUCLEAR PHYSICS. **Personal Data:** b Chengtu, China, March 23, 1913; Canadian citizen; m 1981, Elsie; c Robert (deceased), Elizabeth, Kenneth & Kathryn. **Education:** McMaster Univ, BA, 1932, MA, 1934; Univ Toronto, PhD, 1938. **Honorary Degrees:** DSc, Brandon Univ, 1975. **Professional Experience:** RETIRED; vis scientist, Atomic Energy Can, 1967-1968; chmn dept, McMaster Univ, 1961-1967, 1970-1977; travel grant, Nuffield, Oxford Univ, 1959-1960; from asst prof to prof physics, McMaster Univ, 1947-1981; assoc res physicist, Nat Res Coun Can, 1946-1947; prof physics, Brandon Col, 1937-1946. **Memberships:** Am Phys Soc; Am Asn Physics Teachers; fel Royal Soc Can; Can Asn Physicists. **Research Statement & Publications:** Atomic spectroscopy; neutron physics; nuclear decay schemes; angular correlation of gamma rays; nuclear structure spectroscopy. **Mailing Address:** 115 Dalewood Cres, Hamilton, ON L8S 4B8, Can.

JOHNS, MICHAEL MARIEB EDWARD, OTOLARYNGOLOGY. **Personal Data:** b Detroit, Mich, January 27, 1942; c Christina & Michael. **Education:** Wayne State Univ, BS, 1964; Univ Mich, MD, 1969; Am Bd Otolaryngol, dipl. **Professional Experience:** CHIEF EXEC OFFICER, ROBERT W WOODRUFF HEALTH SCI CTR, as of 2004; PROF, DEPT SURG, SCH MED, 1996-; EXEC VPRES HEALTH AFFAIRS, DEPT SURG, SCH MED, EMORY UNIV, 1996-; CHMN BD, EMORY HEALTH CARE, EMORY UNIV, 1996-; prin investr, Robert Wood Johnson Found, 1992; mem, Greater Baltimore Com, 1991-; dean med fac & vpres med, Sch Med, Johns Hopkins Univ, 1990-1996; prof, Sch Med, Johns Hopkins Univ, 1984-1996; prof, Univ Va Med Ctr, 1982-1984; from asst prof to assoc prof, Univ Va Med Ctr, 1977-1982; resident otolaryngol, Univ Hosp, AnnArbor, 1971-1975; resident gen surg, St Josephs Mercy Hosp, Ann Arbor, 1970-1971; intern, Univ Hosp, Ann Arbor, 1969-1970. **Research Statement & Publications:** Otolaryngology; co-author of one publication. **Mailing Address:** Emory Univ, 1440 Clifton Rd Ste 400, Atlanta, GA 30322. **Fax:** 404-778-3100. **E-Mail:** mmejohns@emory.edu

JOHNS, MILTON VERNON, MATHEMATICAL STATISTICS. **Personal Data:** b Berkeley, Calif, September 27, 1925; m 1954, c 2. **Education:** Stanford Univ, BA, 1949; Columbia Univ, PhD (math & statist), 1956. **Professional Experience:** PROF STATIST, STANFORD UNIV, 1966-; from asst prof to assoc prof, Stanford Univ, 1957-1966; res assoc, Stanford Univ, 1956-1957. **Memberships:** AAAS; Am Math Soc; Math Asn Am; Inst Math Statist; Am Statist Asn; Sigma Xi. **Research Statement & Publications:** Statistical decision theory. **Mailing Address:** Sequoia Hall, Stanford, CA 94305.

JOHNS, PHILIP TIMOTHY, ORGANIC CHEMISTRY. **Personal Data:** b Bismarck, NDak, July 17, 1943; m 1973, c 3. **Education:** Gustavus Adolphus Col, BA, 1965; Univ NDak, PhD (biochem), 1970. **Professional Experience:** CHAIR, DEPT CHEM, UNIV WIS, WHITEWATER, as of 2004; asst prof chem, Univ Wis, Whitewater, beginning 1976; asst prof chem, Va Union Univ, 1972-1976; fel biochem, Fla Heart Asn, Col Med, Univ Fla, 1970-1972. **Memberships:** Am Chem Soc; AAAS. **Research Statement & Publications:** Metabolic control; biosynthesis of plasma lipoproteins; enzymology and control of carbohydrate metabolism. **Mailing Address:** Dept Chem, Univ Wis, 1101 Univ Ave, Whitewater, WI 53706-1396. **Fax:** 608-262-0381. **E-Mail:** johnsp@uww.edu

JOHNS, RICHARD JAMES, MEDICINE. **Personal Data:** b Pendleton, Ore, August 19, 1925; wid Carol; c 3. **Education:** Univ Ore, BS, 1947; Johns Hopkins Univ, MD, 1948; Am Bd Internal Med, dipl. **Honors & Awards:** Centennial Med, Inst Elec & Electronics Engrs, 1984, Career AchievementAward, 1990. **Professional Experience:** University Distinguished Professor, Emeritus, JOHNS HOPKINS UNIV, as of 2005; Prof Biomed Eng, Prof Medicine Appl Physics Lab, Johns Hopkins Univ, beginning of, 1991; Massey prof biomed eng, Sub-Dept Biomed Eng, 1966-1970 & Dept Biomed Eng, 1980-1991; dir, Sub-Dept Biomed Eng, 1966-1970 & Dept Biomed Eng, 1970-1991; Prin Prof Staff, Applphysics Lab Johns Hopkins Univ, beginning of, 1967; Prof MedJohns Hopkins Univ, beginning of, 1966; asst dean admis, JohnsHopkins Univ, 1962-1966; physician, Johns Hopkins Hosp, 1956-; from instr to assoc prof, JohnsHopkins Univ, 1955-1966; resident physician, Johns Hopkins Hosp, 1955-1956; fel, JohnsHopkins Univ, 1953-1955; asst, Johns Hopkins Univ, 1951-1953; Asst resident physician, JohnsHopkins Hosp, 1951-1953; Intern med, Johns Hopkins Hosp, 1948-1949. **Memberships:** Inst Med-Nat Acad Sci; Am Soc Clin Invest; Am Clin & Climatol Asn; BiomedEng Soc; fel Am Col Physicians; Asn Am Physicians; fel AAAS; fel Royal Soc Med; Sigma Xi. **Research Statement & Publications:** Biomedical engineering; chemical sensors. **Mailing Address:** Johns Hopkins Univ Sch Med, 1830 E Monument St, Ste 501, Baltimore, MD 21287. **E-Mail:** rjohns@jhmi.edu

JOHNS, VARNER JAY, JR, internal medicine, cardiology; deceased, see previous edition for last biography

JOHNS, WILLIAM DAVIS, GEOCHEMISTRY. **Personal Data:** b Waynesburg, Pa, November 2, 1925; wid Carla Waal; c Sydney, Susan, David & Amy Sydney(Receased). **Education:** Col Wooster, AB, 1947; Univ Ill, MS, 1951, PhD (geol), 1952. **Honors & Awards:** Alexander von Humboldt US Sr Scientist Award, 1977. **Professional Experience:** PROF EMER, UNIV MO-COLUMBIA, 1998-; Fulbright scholar, Univ Vienna, 1983-1984 & Univ Pittsburgh, 1990-1991; vis prof, Univ Vienna, 1983-1984 & 1995-1996; prof geol, Univ Mo-Columbia, beginning in 1970; Fulbright scholar, Univ Heidelberg, 1968-1969; chmn, Dept Earth Sci, 1962-1969; Fulbright scholar, Univ Gottingen, 1959-1960; from asst prof to prof, Wash Univ, 1955-1970; asst geol, Eng Exp Sta, Univ Ill, 1952-1955; spec asst petrol, Eng Exp Sta, Univ Ill, 1949-1952. **Memberships:** Fel Geol Soc Am; Am Mineral Soc; Mineral Soc Gt Brit & Ireland; Geochem Soc; Clay Minerals Soc. **Research Statement & Publications:** Mineralogy of clays; recent sediments; diagenesis; organic geochemistry; burial diagenesis of pelitic sediments and dispersed organic matter; role played by clay mineral matrix in catalyzing organic reactions involved in transformation of dispersed organic matter in shale source rocks into petroleum hydrocarbons. **Mailing Address:** Dept Geol, Univ Mo, Columbia, MO 65211. **E-Mail:** johnsu@missouri.edu

JOHNS, WILLIAM E, COMPUTATIONAL ADHESION SCIENCE. **Personal Data:** b Detroit, Mich. **Education:** Mich Tech Univ, BS, 1966; Univ Mich, MS, 1968; Univ Minn, PhD (wood & matsci), 1972. **Professional Experience:** Alcoa Res Found researcher, 1990; vis scientist, Swed Forest Prod Lab, 1985-1986; vis scientist, Food & Agr Orgn, UN, 1983; ASSOC PROF MAT SCI, SCH MECH & MAT ENG, WASH STATE UNIV, 1978-; asst wood researcher, Forest Prod Lab, Univ Calif, Berkeley, 1974-1978; res technologist, Am Plywood Asn, Tacoma, 1972-1974. **Memberships:** Adhesion Soc; Am Chem Soc. **Research Statement & Publications:** Adhesion; wood science. **Mailing Address:** Sch Mech & Mat Eng, Wash State Univ, Pullman, WA 99164-2920. **E-Mail:** w_johns@mme.wsu.edu

JOHNS, WILLIAM FRANCIS, ORGANIC CHEMISTRY, MEDICINAL CHEMISTRY. **Personal Data:** b Chicago, Ill, August 31, 1930; m 1950, c 3. **Education:** Univ Chicago, PhB, 1948, MS, 1951; Univ Wis, PhD (org chem), 1955. **Professional Experience:** RETIRED; sr dir med chem, Sterling Winthrop Res Inst, 1982-1993; dir chem res, Searle Labs, G D Searle & Co, 1973-1982; asst dir chem res, G D Searle & Co, 1971-1973; res fel, G D Searle & Co, 1965-1971; sr res chemist pharmaceut, G D Searle & Co, 1955-1965; jr res chemist org synthesis, Merck & Co, 1951-1953. **Memberships:** Am Chem Soc; AAAS; NY Acad Sci. **Research Statement & Publications:** Organic synthesis, especially steroids, antialdosterone agents. **Mailing Address:** 12787 Hunters Ridge Dr, Bonita Springs, FL 34135.

JOHNSEN, EUGENE CARLYLE, MATHEMATICAL SOCIOLOGY, SOCIAL NETWORKS. **Personal Data:** b Minneapolis, Minn, January 27, 1932; m 1957, Marjorie. **Education:** Univ Minn, BChem, 1954; Ohio State Univ, PhD (math), 1961. **Professional Experience:** Chair, Math Sociol Sect, Am Sociol Asn, 1995-1997; EMER PROF MATH, UNIV CALIF, SANTA BARBARA, 1994-; vis scholar, Harvard Univ, 1984-1985; guest ed, Social Networks, 1983; NSF res grants, 1977-1978; Fulbright Hays res grant, Univ Tubingen, 1969; vis lectr, Univ Mich, 1968-1969; from asst prof to prof, Univ Calif, Santa Barbara, 1964-1994; Air Force Off Sci res grants, 1964-1973; lectr, Univ Calif, Santa Barbara, 1963-1964; Nat Acad Sci-Nat Res Coun res assoc, Nat Bur Stand, 1962-1963; instr math, Ohio State Univ, 1962; instr chem & math, Univ Minn, 1956-1957; gen ed, Discovery, Univ Calif, Santa Barbara, J Undergrad Res. **Memberships:** AAAS; Am Math Soc; Math Asn Am; Soc Indust & Appl Math; Int Network Soc Network Anal; Am Sociol Asn; Am Statist Asn. **Research Statement & Publications:** Mathematical models in the social sciences; social network theory; matrix theory; combinatorial designs and matrices; combinatorial algebraic structures. **Mailing Address:** Dept Math, Univ Calif, Santa Barbara, CA 93106. **Fax:** 805-893-2385. **E-Mail:** johnsen@math.ucsb.edu

JOHNSEN, KJELL, PHYSICS, ELECTRICAL ENGINEERING. **Personal Data:** b Meland, Norway, June 11, 1921; m 1945, Aase B Jordal; c Arnlaug, Georg K & Ottar. **Education:** Tech Univ Norway, BSEE, 1948, DTech, 1954. **Honors & Awards:** Norsk Data Physics Prize, Norweg Phys Soc, 1981; Robert R Wilson Prize, AmPhys Soc, 1990. **Professional Experience:** RETIRED; chmn, HERA mach eval comt, Deutsches Elekronen-Synchrotron, Hamburg, Ger, 1984-1991; tech dir, ISA proj, Brookhaven Nat Lab, NY, 1979-1982; profphysics, Univ Bergen, Norway, 1972-1986; proj dir, CERN, Switz, 1966-1974; sr scientist-CERN, Switz, 1959-1986; prof elec eng, Tech Univ, Norway, 1957-1959; physicist, CERN, Switz, 1952-1957; res asst, Chr Michelsen Inst, Norway, 1948-1952. **Research Statement & Publications:** Author of numerous articles. **Mailing Address:** Chemin du Molard, La Rippe CH-1278, Switzerland.

JOHNSEN, KURT H, PHYSIOLOGICAL GENETICS. **Personal Data:** b Huntington, NY, September 4, 1959; m Lisa; c Soven & Jenny R. **Education:** Univ Vt, BS, 1985; Va Tech, MS, 1987; Univ Ga, PhD (forest genetics & treephysiol), 1990. **Professional Experience:** STAFF MEM, USDA FOREST SERV, as of 2005; PROJ LEADER, CAN FOREST SERV, 1990-; res scientist, Forestry Can, 1990-1992. **Memberships:** Am Inst Biol Sci; Ecol Soc Am. **Research Statement & Publications:** Designed to quantity and partition genetic variation in black spruce morphological and physiological responses to environmental change (elevated carbon dioxide, drought, temperature extremes). **Mailing Address:** Dept Forestry, Va Polytech Inst & State Univ, Blacksburg, VA 24061. **Fax:** 613-589-2275. **E-Mail:** kjohnsen/srs_rtp@fs.fed.us

JOHNSEN, PETER BERGHSEY, RESEARCH MANAGEMENT, SENSORY PHYSIOLOGY, FLAVOR CHEMISTRY. **Personal Data:** b Madison, Wis, May 23, 1950; m 1974, Paula Stewart Johnsen; c 2. **Education:** Univ Wis-Madison, BS, 1974, MS, 1976, PhD (zool), 1978. **Honors & Awards:** Outstanding Researcher, Catfish Farmers Am; Royal Swedish acad of agr & forestry, 2000; pres meritorious exec, Sr Exec Service, 1999. **Professional Experience:** DIR USDA-NAT CTR AGR UTIL RES, 1994-; affil prof, Grad Fac, La State Univ, 1988-1994; res leader, USDA Agr Res Serv, 1988-1994; res physiologist, USDA Agr Res Serv, 1986-1988; instr, Col Vet Med, Univ Pa, 1980-1983 & Dept Biol, 1984-1986; Olin fel, Olin Found, Oslo, Norway, 1983; from asst mem to assoc mem, Monell Chem Senses Ctr, 1980-1986; postdoctoral fel, Univ Pa, 1978-1980. **Memberships:** Inst Food Scientists; Sigma Xi. **Research Statement & Publications:** Biochemical process for food flavor formation; chemical identification of flavor compounds and relationship to human perception of taste and smell; technology transfer and research management. **Mailing Address:** USDA-ARS Nat Ctr Agr Util Res, 1815 N Univ St, Peoria, IL 61604. **Fax:** 309-681-6682. **E-Mail:** pjohnsen@ncaur.usda.gov

JOHNSEN, RAINER, PHYSICS. **Personal Data:** b Kiel, Ger, January 23, 1940; m 1965, c 2. **Education:** Univ Kiel, Ger, dipl physics, 1965, Dr rer nat, 1966. **Professional Experience:** PROF, DEPT PHYSICS & ASTRON, UNIV PITTSBURGH, as of 2004; assoc prof physics, Univ Pittsburgh, beginning 1971; res asst prof, Univ Pittsburgh, 1968-1971; res assoc physics, Univ Pittsburgh, 1966-1968. **Memberships:** Am Phys Soc; AAAS. **Research Statement & Publications:** Atomic physics; atomic collisions; physics of upper atmosphere; mass spectroscopy; laser plasma research. **Mailing Address:** Dept Physics & Astron, Univ Pittsburgh, 310 SRCC, Pittsburgh, PA 15260. **Fax:** 412-624-9163. **E-Mail:** rj@pitt.edu

JOHNSEN, RICHARD EMANUEL, INSECTICIDE TOXICOLOGY. **Personal Data:** b Brooklyn, NY, February 8, 1936; m 1957, Esther; c Kathryn, Rebecca & Christopher. **Education:** St Olaf Col, BA, 1957; Iowa State Univ, MS, 1959, PhD (entom), 1962. **Professional Experience:** FAC EMER BIO AGR SCI & PEST MGT, COLO STATE UNIV, as of 2004; sabbatical & fel, Dept Pharmacol & Toxicol, Vet Col Norway, Oslo, 1976-1977; assoc prof entom, Colo State Univ, beginning 1970; asst prof, Colo State Univ, x1965-1970; asst entom, Iowa State Univ, 1962. **Memberships:** AAAS; Am Chem Soc; Entom Soc Am; NY Acad Sci; Sigma Xi. **Research Statement & Publications:** Pesticides and related environmental pollutants, their metabolism, distribution and persistance in plants, soils and the physical environment; microbial degradation; analytical methodology for pollutant studies. **Mailing Address:** Dept Bio Agr Sci & Pest Mgt, Colo State Univ, 129 plant Sci, Ft Collins, CO 80523-1170. **Fax:** 970-491-0564. **E-Mail:** rjohnsen@shep.agsci.colostate.edu

JOHNSEN, ROGER CRAIG, genetics; deceased, see previous edition for last biography

JOHNSEN, RUSSELL HAROLD, RADIATION CHEMISTRY, ACADEMIC ADMINISTRATION. **Personal Data:** b Chicago, Ill, August 5, m Dorothy; c Peter B & Margaret A. **Education:** Univ Chicago, BS, 1947; Univ Wis, PhD (chem), 1951. **Honors & Awards:** fell AAAS 1955. **Professional Experience:** EMER PROF CHEM & DEAN, FLA STATE UNIV, 1993-; dean, Grad Studies, 1986-1993; assoc dean grad studies, Col Arts & Sci, Fla State Univ, 1977-1986; Assoc provost, Col Arts & Sci, Fla State Univ, 1974-1977; from asst prof to prof, Fla State Univ, 1951-1993; Res chemist, Ninol Lab, 1946-1947. **Memberships:** Fel AAAS; Am Chem Soc. **Research Statement & Publications:** Kinetics of reactive intermediates, mechanistic studies; free radical reactions in the atmosphere; electron spin resonance studies. **Mailing Address:** 1329 Hollow Oak Circle, Tallahassee, FL 32308. **Fax:** 850-644-8281. **E-Mail:** johnsen@chem.fsu.edu

JOHNSEN, THOMAS NORMAN, SOIL-PLANT NUTRIENT CYCLING, PLANT SUCCESSION. **Personal Data:** b Chicago, Ill, July 3, 1929; m 1956, Ardith; c Paul T & Suzanne L. **Education:** Univ Ariz, BS, 1950, MS, 1954; Duke Univ, PhD (bot), 1960. **Honors & Awards:** W R Chapling Res Award, Soc Range Mgt, 1988. **Professional Experience:** Fac assoc, Range Plants & Habitats, Ariz State Univ, 1991-1992; COLLABRATOR STAFF BIOL SCI, AGR RES SERV, USDA, 1990-; res scientist range ecol, USDA, 1978-1990; res leader, USDA, 1972-1978; adj prof forestry, NAriz Univ, 1958-1978; res scientist range weed control, USDA, 1956-1972. **Memberships:** Soil Sci Soc Am; Ecol Soc Am; Weed Sci Soc Am; Soc Range Mgt; Am Soc Agron; Sigma Xi. **Research Statement & Publications:** Evaluation and development of methods to revegete semiarid grazing land; fate of herbicides in plant, soils and water; plant life history; plant population changes and trends; plant competition; development of crimson poppy as a crop. **Mailing Address:** Biolcl Sci Collab, Agr Res Serv, 2000 E Allen Rd, Tucson, AZ 85719. **Fax:** 520-670-5550.

JOHNSGARD, PAUL AUSTIN, ZOOLOGY. **Personal Data:** b Fargo, NDak, June 28, 1931; m 1956, Lois; c Jay, Scott, Ann & Karin. **Education:** NDak State Univ, BS, 1953; Wash State Univ, MS, 1955; Cornell Univ, PhD (vertzool), 1959. **Honors & Awards:** Mari Sandoz Award, 1984; Loren Eiseley Award, 1987. **Professional Experience:** FOUND PROF EMER, UNIV NEBR, LINCOLN, as of 2003; Found Prof, Univ Nebr-Lincoln, beginning 1980; mem bd dirs, Int WildWaterfowl Asn, 1972-1976; Guggenheim Found fel, 1971; NSF res grants, 1968-1971 & 1963-1967; from instr to prof, Univ Nebr-Lincoln, 1961-1980; NSF fel zool, USPHS fel, 1960-1961; NSF fel zool, Bristol Univ, 1959-1960. **Memberships:** Am Ornith Union; Wilson Ornith Soc; Cooper Ornith Soc. **Research Statement & Publications:** Systematics of birds, especially the family Anatidae; comparative behavior of birds; ecology of vertebrates; speciation and isolating mechanisms; sympatry and hybridization in birds. **Mailing Address:** Dept Biol, Univ Nebr, 348 Manter Hall, Lincoln, NE 68588-0118. **Fax:** 402-472-2083.

JOHNSON, A WILLIAM, ORGANIC CHEMISTRY. **Personal Data:** b Calgary, Alta, December 16, 1933; American citizen; m 1956, Joan; c Patricia, Nancy, Robert & Katherine. **Education:** Univ Alta, BSc, 1954; Cornell Univ, PhD (chem), 1957. **Professional Experience:** RETIRED; vis prof, US Mil Acad, West Point, beginning 1994; vis prof, Univ Mass, Amherst, 1989; dir, N Dak Regional Environ Assessment Prog, 1975-1977; prof, Univ NDak, 1967-1994; dean grad sch, Univ N Dak, 1967-1988; dir res & develop, Univ N Dak, 1967-1975; assoc prof & chmn dept, Univ Sask, Regina, 1965-1967; from asst prof to assoc prof, Univ N Dak, 1960-1965; fel org chem, Mellon Inst, 1957-1960; asst chem, Cornell Univ, 1955. **Memberships:** Fel AAAS; Am Chem Soc; Sigma Xi; fel Chem Inst Can. **Research Statement & Publications:** Chemistry of ylids; d orbital interactions; synthetic organic chemistry; environmental assessment. **Mailing Address:** Nine Tanyard Lane, Bella Vista, AR 72714. **E-Mail:** awjohnson@ipa.net

JOHNSON, ADRIAN EARL, JR, CHEMICAL ENGINEERING, MATHEMATICS. **Personal Data:** b Port Arthur, Tex, December 17, 1928; m 1949, c 3. **Education:** La State Univ, BS, 1948; Mass Inst Technol, SM, 1949; Univ Fla, PhD (chem eng), 1958. **Professional Experience:** PROF CHEM ENG, LA STATE UNIV, BATON ROUGE, 1968-; staff consult, Real Time Systs, Inc, 1967-1968; consult & mgr, Mgt Serv Dept, Union Carbide Corp, NY, 1962-1967; asst dir, Comput Res Ctr & Eng Res Ctr, La State Univ, 1960-1962; appl scientist, Int Bus Mach Corp, La, 1957-1960; instr, Univ Fla, 1954-1957; asst prof chem eng, Lamar State Univ, 1953-1954; Process engr, Mobil Oil Co, Tex, 1949-1953. **Memberships:** Am Inst Chem Engrs. **Research Statement & Publications:** Computer control of petrochemical processes; optimization and control of distillation columns and methanol plants. **Mailing Address:** 9126 Pine Moss Dr, Baton Rouge, LA 70817-6931.

JOHNSON, ALAN ARTHUR, MATERIALS SCIENCE & ENGINEERING, FAILURE ANALYSIS & ACCIDENT RECONSTRUCTION. **Personal Data:** b Beckenham, Eng, August 18, 1930; m 1990, Barbara Davidson; c Stephen G, Michael A, David N, Brian P & Susan C, Elizabeth A Banks. **Education:** Univ Reading, BSc, 1952; Univ Toronto, MA, 1954; Univ London Imp Col, dipl & PhD (metal physics), 1960. **Professional Experience:** PRES, METALS RES INC, LOUISVILLE, KY 40202, 1998-; prof mat sci, Univ Louisville, 1975- 2002; dean grad sch, Univ Louisville, 1975-1976; prof mat sci & chmn dept mat sci & eng, Wash State Univ, 1971-1975; head dept phys & eng metall, Polytech Inst Brooklyn, 1967-1971; prof phys metall, Polytech Inst Brooklyn, 1965-1971; dir res, Mat Res Corp, NY, 1963-1965; lectr, Imp Col, Univ London, 1960-1962; res fel, Imp Col, Univ London, 1957-1960; res asst metall, Imp Col, Univ London, 1956-1957; sci officer, Royal Naval Sci Serv, 1954-1956; Demonstr physics, Univ Toronto, 1952-1954; Indust consult & expert witness, prod liability personal injury litigations. **Memberships:** Fel Inst Physics; fel Am Soc Metals; Sigma Xi; fel Inst Mat; fel AAAS. **Research Statement & Publications:** Materials science especially physical metallurgy; Dislocations, power defects, phase transformations, failure analysis; accident reconstruction; approximately 1 2 0 articles in journals and conference proceedings. **Mailing Address:** 1861 Woodfiel Way, Louisville, KY 40205.

JOHNSON, ALAN KIM, BEHAVIORAL BIOLOGY. **Personal Data:** b Altoona, Pa, August 15, 1942; m 1965, c 1. **Education:** Pa State Univ, BS, 1964; Temple Univ, MA, 1966; Univ Pittsburgh, PhD (psychobiol), 1970. **Honors & Awards:** Res Scientist Develop Award, NIMH, 1975. **Professional Experience:** PROF PHARAMACOL, UNIV IOWA, 1983-; PROF PSYCHOL, UNIV IOWA, 1982-; vis prof, Dept Pharmacol, Univ Heidelberg, 1977; res fel, Alexander von Humboldt Found, GFR, 1977-1978; vis scientist, Univ Wash, 1978-1979; assoc prof psychol, Univ Iowa, 1978-1982; asst prof, Univ Iowa, 1973-1978; fel psychobiol, Inst Neurol Sci, Univ Pa, 1970-1973; NIH fel, 1970. **Memberships:** Sigma Xi; AAAS; Soc Neuroscience; Am Physiol Soc; Am Heart Asn; NY Acad Sci. **Research Statement & Publications:** Neurobiology and endocrinology of feeding and drinking; physiological bases of motivation and reinforcement. **Mailing Address:** Dept Psychol & Pharmaceut, Univ Iowa, E 20 Seashore Hall, Iowa City, IA 52242-1407. **Fax:** 319-335-0191. **E-Mail:** alan-johnson@uiowa.edu

JOHNSON, ALAN L, OVARIAN FOLLICULAR DIFFERENTIATION & ATRESIA, OVARIAN CANCER. **Personal Data:** b Quincy, Mass, September 8, 1950; m 1985, Joanne; c Jennifer A & Kari L. **Education:** Univ Vt, BA, 1972, MS, 1975; Cornell Univ, PhD (physiol), 1979. **Professional Experience:** PROF PHYSIOL, UNIV NOTRE DAME, 1993-; prof physiol, Rutgers Univ, 1981-1993; Res assoc, Cornell Univ, 1979-1981. **Memberships:** Endocrine Soc; Soc for the Study of Reproduction. **Research Statement & Publications:** Vertebrate ovarian follicular differentiation and atresia via the actions of gonadotropins, growth factors and protooncogenes; apoptosis in ovarian follicle. **Mailing Address:** Dept Biological Scis, Univ Notre Dame, Notre Dame, IN 46556. **Fax:** 574-631-7413. **E-Mail:** johnson.128@nd.edu

JOHNSON, ALAN T, ENGINEERING. **Professional Experience:** ASST PROF, ENG DEPT, UNIV PA, as of 2002; packard fel, David & Lucille Packard Found, 1994. **Mailing Address:** Dept Eng, Univ Pa, Philadelphia, PA 19104-6316.

JOHNSON, ALBERT LLEWELLYN, II, RESEARCH ADMINISTRATION, INFORMATION SCIENCE & SYSTEMS. **Personal Data:** b Pittsburgh, Pa, August 29, 1960. **Education:** Carnegie-Mellon Univ, BS, 1983, MS, 1989. **Professional Experience:** SR ANALYST SCI & TECHNOL, CORNING INC, 1995-; sr analyst info technol, Corning Inc, 1991-1995; m em tech staff, Software Eng Inst, 1985-1991. **Research Statement & Publications:** Strategy and economics of industrial research and development; administration and planning. **Mailing Address:** Corning Inc, Sullivan Pk SP-FR-02, Corning, NY 14831. **E-Mail:** johnsonal@corning.com

JOHNSON, ALBERT SYDNEY, III, HABITAT ECOLOGY & MANAGEMENT. **Personal Data:** b Clarkston, Ga, December 27, 1933; m 1959, Nedra; c Dorothy (Callaway), Linda (Fleming), Brian T (deceased) & Merry (Maxey). **Education:** Univ Ga, BS, 1959; Auburn Univ, MS, 1962, PhD (zoology), 1969. **Honors & Awards:** C W Watson Award, SE Sect, Asn Fish & Wildlife Agencies, SE Sect, Wildlife Soc & S Div Am Fisheries Soc. **Professional Experience:** PROF EMER FOREST RESOURCES, UNIV GA, 1995-; assoc dir, Inst Natural Resources & prof, 1968-1995; instr wildlife biol & zool, Auburn Univ, 1963-1968; wildlife biologist, Ala State Dept Conserv, 1962-1963; res asst wildlife biol, Auburn Univ, 1959-1962; fire control aide, US Forest Serv, 1958. **Memberships:** Wildlife Soc; Am Soc Mammalogists. **Research Statement & Publications:** Wildlife habitat biology and management; wildlife foods and habitat relationships; responses to management. **Mailing Address:** D B Warnell Sch Forest Resources, Univ Ga, Athens, GA 30602.

JOHNSON, ALBERT W, PLANT ECOLOGY. **Personal Data:** b Belvidere, Ill, July 29, 1926; m 1970, c 5. **Education:** Colo Agr & Mech Col, BS, 1949; Univ Colo, MS, 1951, PhD (bot), 1956. **Professional Experience:** PRES, SAN DIEGO STATE UNIV LIB, as of 2003; PROF EMER BIOL, SAN DIEGO STATE UNIV, 1991-; vpres, acad affairs, 1978-1991; actg vpres, acad affairs, 1977-1978; prof biol, San Diego State Univ, 1969-1991; dean, Col Sci, 1969-1977; from asst prof to assoc prof, San Diego State Univ, 1964-1969; jr res botanist, Univ Calif, Los Angeles, 1962-1964; from instr to assoc prof bot, NSF fac sci fel, 1960-1961; from instr to assoc prof bot, Univ Alaska, 1956-1962; instr biol, Univ Colo, 1954-1955. **Memberships:** AAAS; Sigma Xi. **Research Statement & Publications:** Arctic and alpine plant ecology and taxonomy; cytogenetics. **Mailing Address:** Lib & Info Access, San Diego State Univ, 5500 Campanile Dr, San Diego, CA 92182-8050. **Fax:** 619-287-6756. **E-Mail:** awj@rohan.sdsu.edu

JOHNSON, ALBERT WAYNE, ENTOMOLOGY. **Personal Data:** b Mullins, SC, July 19, 1944; m 1965, c 3. **Education:** Clemson Univ, BS, 1966, MS, 1968; Auburn Univ, PhD (entom), 1971. **Professional Experience:** PROF ENTOM, PEE DEE RES & EDUC CTR, CLEMSON UNIV, 1980-; assoc prof entom, 1976-1980; asst prof entom, 1970-1976. **Memberships:** Entom Soc Am; crop Sci. **Research Statement & Publications:** Insecticide screening, economic thresholds, scouting techniques, insect surveys of pests and beneficials, cultural control practices, biological control, host-plant resistance studies and development of insect-resistant varieties. **Mailing Address:** Pee Dee Res & Educ Ctr, Clemson Univ, 2200 Pocket Rd, Florence, SC 29506-9706. **Fax:** 843-661-5676. **E-Mail:** ajhnsn@clemson.edu

JOHNSON, ALEXANDER LAWRENCE, ORGANIC CHEMISTRY. **Personal Data:** b Gisborne, NZ, October 13, 1931; American citizen; m 1961, c 3. **Education:** Victoria Univ, Wellington, BSc, 1954, MSc, 1955; Univ Rochester, PhD (org chem), 1964. **Honors & Awards:** Eastman Kodak Prize, Univ Rochester, 1962. **Professional Experience:** RES MGR, MED PROD DEPT, E I DUPONT DEL NEMOURS & CO, INC, 1990-; RES MGR, DUPONT MERCK PHARMACEUTICAL CO, 1990-; sr res supvr, Biochem Dept, 1987-1989; res supvr, Biochem Dept, 1982-1987; res assoc, Biochem Dept, 1981-1982; res chemist, Cent Res Dept, 1963-1981; s ec sch teacher chem, Rongotai Col, NZ, 1955-1960. **Memberships:** Am Chem Soc; NZ Inst Chem. **Research Statement & Publications:** Elucidation of the structures of natural products; synthetic organic chemistry relating to these and to heterocyclic systems; application of physical methods to the solution of organic chemical problems; medicinal chemistry. **Mailing Address:** 1372 John Adams Dr, Lancaster, PA 17601.

JOHNSON, A(LFRED) BURTRON, CORROSION, NUCLEAR MATERIALS. **Personal Data:** b Salt Lake City, Utah, April 8, 1929; m 1954, Joann; c Melinda, Sherry, Laurie & Julie. **Education:** Univ Utah, BS, 1954, PhD (fuel technol) minor, nuclear physics, 1958. **Honors & Awards:** Mishima Award, Am Nuclear Soc. **Professional Experience:** RETIRED; sr staff scientist, Pac Northwest Div, 1981-1992; lectr, Richland Grad Ctr, 1974-; mem staff, Univ Wis, 1973; staff scientist, Battelle Mem Inst, 1965-1981; mem staff, Hanford Labs, Gen Elec Co, 1961-1965; lectr, Univ Dayton, 1960-1961; US deleg, Int Atomic Energy Agency Comt, Vienna, Austria; US coord, US/FRG nuclear fuel info exchange. **Memberships:** Am Nuclear Soc; Nat Asn Corrosion Engrs. **Research Statement & Publications:** Corrosion in fission and fusion reactors; nuclear plant life extension; corrosion of ancient metals; spent nuclear fuel storage; author or coauthor of over 300 publications and author of one book. **Mailing Address:** Pac Northwest National Lab, Battelle Mem Inst, Richland, WA 99352. **Fax:** 509-372-6421. **E-Mail:** aburt.johnson@pnl.gov

JOHNSON, ALFRED C, MOLECULAR BIOLOGY. **Personal Data:** b Marion Junction, Ala, August 17, 1957. **Education:** Albany State Col, BS, 1979; Univ Tenn, PhD (biomed sci), 1985. **Honors & Awards:** Director's Award, NIH, 1993. **Professional Experience:** INVESTR MOLECULAR BIOL, NIH, 1994-; res expert molecular biol, NIH, 1992-1994; sr staff fel, NIH, 1990-1992; fel, NIH, 1987-1990; Am Cancer Soc fel molecular biol, NIH, 1985-1987. **Memberships:** AAAS; Am Soc Biochem & Molecular Biol; Am Asn Cancer Res. **Mailing Address:** Lab Molecular Biol, Nat Cancer Inst, NIH, Bldg 37 Rm 2D18 37 Convent Dr MSC 4255, Bethesda, MD 20892-4255. **Fax:** 301-496-2212. **E-Mail:** ajohnson@helix.nih.gov

JOHNSON, ALFRED THEODORE, ELECTRICAL ENGINEERING. **Personal Data:** b Philadelphia, Pa, June 24, 1941; m 1983. **Education:** Drexel Univ, BS, 1963; Univ Pa, PhD (elec eng), 1969. **Professional Experience:** PROF EMER ELEC ENG, WIDENER UNIV, as of 2005; prof elec eng, Widener Univ, beginning 1990; chmn, dept elec eng, Widener Univ, beginning 1990; from asst prof to assoc prof elec eng, Widener Univ, 1974-1989. **Memberships:** Inst Elec & Electronics Engrs. **Research Statement & Publications:** Approximation problem using analog and digital filters; analog fault analysis; circuit theory. **Mailing Address:** Dept Elec Eng, Widener Univ, One Univ Pl, Chester, PA 19013. **E-Mail:** alfred.t.johnson.jr@widener.edu

JOHNSON, ALICE RUFFIN, PHARMACOLOGY, IMMUNOLOGY. **Personal Data:** b Charlottesville, Va, September 22, 1936; div, c 2. **Education:** Univ Va, BS, 1958; Emory Univ, MS, 1960, PhD (pharmacol), 1968. **Professional Experience:** RETIRED; assoc prof pharmacol, Southwestern Med Sch, Univ Tex Health Sci Ctr, Dallas, as of 2003; Nat Heart Lung & Blood Inst res grant, 1975-; asst prof pharmacol, Southwestern Med Sch, Univ Tex Health Sci Ctr, Dallas, beginning 1974; vis scientist, Scripps Clin & Res Found, 1972-1974; NIH spec fel, Scripps Clin & Res Found, 1972-1974; Nat Inst Allergy & Infectious Dis res grant, 1969-1972; from instr to asst prof pharmacol, Sch Med, Emory Univ, 1968-1972. **Memberships:** AAAS; Am Soc Pharmacol & Exp Therapeut. **Research Statement & Publications:** Release of pharmacologically active substances; mast cells; endothelial cells; peptides; allergy. **Mailing Address:** Dept Biochem, Univ Tex Health Sci Ctr, PO Box 2003, Tyler, TX 75710.

JOHNSON, ALLAN ALEXANDER, OVERWEIGHT/OBESITY, Health Disparities. **Personal Data:** b Georgetown, Guyana, September 18, 1946; m 1972, Lily; c Liliahn & Alexis. **Education:** McGill Univ, BS, 1972; Cornell Univ, MNS, 1974, PhD (int nutrit), 1978. **Honors & Awards:** Res Award, Nat Soc Allied Health; Johnetta M Davis Service Award. **Professional Experience:** Chairman, PROF NUTRIT SCI, HOWARD UNIV, 1999-; assoc prof, Howard Univ, 1982-1999; asst prof, Howard Univ, 1978-1982; biochem, Cornell Univ, 1974-1975; nutrit sci, Cornell Univ, 1974; res asst, Cornell Univ, 1972-1978. **Memberships:** Ame Soc Nutrit Sci; American Public Health Association. **Research Statement & Publications:** Barriers, motivators and facilitators of prenatal care utilization; Factors influencing overweight and obesity; Prevention of overweight and obesity; factors related to disparities in nutrition-related diseases. **Mailing Address:** Dept Nutrit Sci, Howard Univ, 2400 Sixth St, NW, Washington, DC 20059-0009. **Fax:** 202-806-9233. **E-Mail:** ajohnson@howard.edu

JOHNSON, ALLEN NEILL, PATHOLOGY. **Personal Data:** b Colfax, Wash, December 29, 1944; m 1971, Julia; c Beverly & Cameron. **Education:** Wash State Univ, DVM, 1969; Univ Wis, PhD (vet sci), 1977; Am Col Vet Pathologists, dipl, 1978. **Professional Experience:** RETIRED; dir, R W Johnson Pharmaceut Res Inst, beginning 1991; asst dir, R W Johnson Pharmaceut Res Inst, 1989-1991; asst dir, Ortho Pharmaceut Corp, 1987-1989; res mgr, Ortho Pharmaceut Corp, 1983-1987; group leader path, Ortho Pharmaceut Corp, 1978-1983; pathologist, Lederle Labs, 1976-1978; asst prof, vet path, Univ Ga Vet Med Col, 1974-1976; res asst, Univ Wis-Madison, 1971-1974. **Memberships:** emer Am Col Vet Pathologists; Am Vet Med Asn. **Research Statement & Publications:** Evaluation of tissues from laboratory animals and farm species to determine and resolve pathologic lesions associated with dosing of experimental drugs. **Mailing Address:** 341 Mine Brook Rd, Bernardsville, NJ 07924-2111.

JOHNSON, ALVA WILLIAM, NEMATOLOGY, PLANT PATHOLOGY. **Personal Data:** b Tifton, Ga, November 8, 1936; m 1960, Barbara; c Janet Paige. **Education:** Univ Ga, BSA, 1963, MS, 1964; NC State Univ, PhD (plant path), 1967. **Honors & Awards:** Distinguished Res Award, Sigma Xi, Tifton, 1995. **Professional Experience:** RES LEADER NEMATOLOGIST, AGR RES SERV, USDA, as of 1997; supvry res nematologist, Coastal Plain Exp Sta, Sci & Educ Admin, Us Dept Agr, beginning 1967. **Memberships:** Fel Soc Nematologists; Am Phytopath Soc; Orgn Trop Am Nematologists; Sigma Xi. **Research Statement & Publications:** Nematode control; population dynamics; nematode-fungus interactions; multiple plant-pest control; nematode resistance in plants; development of integrated pest management systems to manage nematode populations that are effective, economical and environmentally sound. **Mailing Address:** Nematodes, Weeds & Crops Unit, USDA, PO Box 748, Tifton, GA 31793. **Fax:** 912-386-3437. **E-Mail:** nemweeds@tifton.cpes.peachnet.edu

JOHNSON, ANNE BRADSTREET, NEUROPATHOLOGY, NEUROSCIENCES. **Personal Data:** b Boston, Mass, March 5, 1927; m 1948, Jack; c Ellen & Paul. **Education:** Cornell Univ, BA, 1948, MD, 1951. **Honors & Awards:** Moore Awards, Am Asn Neuropathologists. **Professional Experience:** ASSOC PROF EMER PATH & NEUROSCIENCE, ALBERT EINSTEIN COL MED, as of 2003; assoc prof path & Neuroscience, Albert Einstein Col Med, beginning 1977; asst prof, Albert Einstein Col Med, 1970-1977; prin investr, NIH grants, other grants, 1968-; pvt pract internal med, self-employed, Cleveland, 1955-1957. **Memberships:** Am Asn Neuropathologists; Soc Neuroscience; Histochem Soc; Am Soc Cell Biol; Int Acad Path; AAAS; NY Acad Sci. **Research Statement & Publications:** Abnormal nervous systems including; Alzheimer's disease; multiple schlerosis; genetic leukodystrophies and work identifying genetic basis of Alexander disease; enzyme histochemistry; immunocytochemistry; using tissue and tissue culture, light and electron microscope approaches; medical sciences. **Mailing Address:** Dept Path, Albert Einstein Col Med, Rm 604 Rose F Kennedy Ctr 1410 Pelham Pkwy S, Bronx, NY 10461. **E-Mail:** abminkoff@worldnet.att.net

JOHNSON, ARLO F, MECHANICAL ENGINEERING. **Personal Data:** b Franklin, Idaho, December 2, 1915; m 1947, c 4. **Education:** Calif Inst Technol, BS & MS, 1942; Stanford Univ, PhD, 1952. **Professional Experience:** RETIRED; prof, Bandung Technol Inst, 1961-1963; mem staff, Sandia Corp, 1959; aeronaut res engr, Ames Lab, NASA, 1957; head dept, Univ Utah, 1955-1957; from assoc prof to prof mech eng, Univ Utah, 1951-1963; asst, Stanford Univ, 1948-1951; instr, Univ Utah, 1947-1948; asst prof aeronaut eng, Univ Ill, 1946-1947; aerodynamicist, Douglas Aircraft Corp, 1942-1945. **Research Statement & Publications:** Boundary layer theory; gas dynamics; applied mechanics. **Mailing Address:** 2070 E 3620 S, Salt Lake City, UT 84109.

JOHNSON, ARMEAD H, IMMUNOGENETICS, HISTOCOMPATIBILITY. **Personal Data:** b Waco, Tex, December 16, 1942. **Education:** Univ Tex, BS, 1964; Baylor Col Med, MS, 1970, PhD (microbiol & immunol), 1971. **Professional Experience:** DIR IMMUNOGENETICS, DEPT PEDIAT, GEORGETOWN UNIV, as of 2004; PROF DEPT BIOL, SCH MED, GEORGETOWN UNIV, as of 2004; DIR, TISSUE TYPING LAB, 1985-; asst prof pediat & microbiol, Sch Med, Georgetown Univ, beginning 1980; consult, 1980-1985; consult, Blood Bank, Charity Hosp La, New Orleans, beginning 1975; asst prof, Med Ctr, Duke Univ, 1975-1980; assoc, Med Ctr, Duke Univ, 1974-1975. **Memberships:** Transplantation Soc; Am Asn Immunologists; Am Soc Histocompatibilty & Immunogenetics; Sigma Xi. **Research Statement & Publications:** Serological identification, characterization and genetics of antigens within the human major histocompatibility complex and investigation of their role in the immune response. **Mailing Address:** Dept Pediat, Georgetown Univ Sch Med, LD8D Preclinical Sci Bldg & 334 Reiss Hall, Washington, DC 20057. **Fax:** 202-687-7161. **E-Mail:** johnsoa2@georgetown.edu

JOHNSON, ARNOLD, VASCULAR INFLAMATION. **Education:** Albany Med Col, PhD (physiol), 1981. **Professional Experience:** SR RES SCIENTIST, VA MED CTR, as of 2002; ASSOC PROF RES PULMONARY PHYSIOL, ALBANY MED COL, 1984-; asst prof res pulmonary physiol, Albany Med Col, beginning 1984. **Research Statement & Publications:** Published more than 25 articles. **Mailing Address:** Albany Med Col, 43 New Scotland Ave, Albany, NY 12208-3479. **E-Mail:** jmurd@msn.com

JOHNSON, ARTHUR ALBIN, PARASITOLOGY. **Personal Data:** b Chicago, Ill, February 24, 1925. **Education:** Univ Minn, AB, 1950; Univ Ill, MS, 1952, PhD (zoology), 1955. **Professional Experience:** DISTINGUISHED PROF EMER BIOL, HENDRIX COL, 1990-; Harold & Lucy Cabe distinguished prof, Hendrix Col, 1955-1990; mem, NSF Radiation Biol Inst, Argonne Nat Lab, 1965; vis lectr, Univ Ill, 1963 & 1964; from asst prof to prof biol, Hendrix Col, 1955-1990. **Memberships:** Fel AAAS; Am Micros Soc; Am Soc Parasitol; Am Inst Biol Sci; Sigma Xi. **Research Statement & Publications:** Mermithidae; parasites of grackles. **Mailing Address:** Dept Biol, Hendrix Col, 1600 Wash Ave, Conway, AR 72032. **E-Mail:** amjohnson@alltel.net

JOHNSON, ARTHUR EDWARD, PHYSICAL BIOCHEMISTRY & PROTEIN STRUCTURE, FUNCTION & TRAFFICKING AT MEMBRANES. **Personal Data:** b Graceville, Minn, July 4, 1942; m 1965, Linda; c Christine, Robert & Edward. **Education:** Calif Inst Technol, BS, 1964; Univ Ore, PhD (biochem), 1973. **Honors & Awards:** Fellow of American Association for the Advancement of Science, 2004; Prof of year Okla, Council advan and support educ, Wash DC, 1990. **Professional Experience:** DISTINGUISHED PROF CHEM, TEX A&M UNIV, 2002-; WEHNER-WELCH CHAIR & DISTINGUISHED PROF, DEPT MED BIOCHEM & GENETICS, TEX A&M UNIV SYST HLTH SCI CTR, 1994-; PROF, DEPTS CHEM & BIOCHEM & BIOPHYSICS, TEX A&M UNIV, 1994-; Director, Molecualr Biophsyics, Tex A&M Univ, 2000-2005; Grayce B Kerr Prof, Chem & Biochem Dept, Univ Okla, 1992-1994; consult, Promega Corp, 1991-1997; adj prof, Dept Biochem & Molecular Biol, Univ Okla Health Sci Ctr, 1987-1994; mem, NSF Biochem Grant Proposal Adv Panel, 1985-1987; mem, spec study sects NIH, 1984 & 1991; vis prof, Dept Biochem & Biophys, Univ Calif, San Francisco, 1984-1985; adj asst prof, Dept Biochem & Molecular Biol, Univ Okla Health Sci Ctr, 1983-1987; prin investr, NIH, Am Heart Asn, Am Chem Soc & Res Corp grants, 1979-; from asst prof to prof, Chem & Biochem Dept, Univ Okla, 1977-1992; Helen Hay Whitney res assoc, Chem Dept, Columbia Univ, 1974-1977; instr sci, Milton Acad, Mass, 1964-1969. **Memberships:** Am Soc Biochem & Molecular Biol; Am Chem Soc; Am Soc Cell Biol; biophys soc; Am asn adv sci. **Research Statement & Publications:** Molecular mechanisms of: protein translocation, retro-translocation, and integration at mitochondrial, bacterial, and endoplasmic reticulum membranes; cell lysis by bacterial toxins; protein folding; blood coagulation; protein synthesis. Aminoacyl-tRNA analogues; fluorescence; FRET. **Mailing Address:** Arthur E Johnson Col Med, Tex A&M Univ Syst Health Sci Ctr, 116 Reynolds Med Bldg, 1114 TAMU, College Station, TX 77843-1114. **Fax:** 979-862-3339. **E-Mail:** ajohnson@medicine.tamhsc.edu

JOHNSON, ARTHUR FRANKLIN, PHYSICS. **Personal Data:** b Can, October 8, 1917; American citizen; m 1943, Audrey; c William F, Paul E, David J & Blake C. **Education:** Univ Alta, BSc, 1938; Univ Toronto, MA, 1947, PhD (physics), 1949. **Professional Experience:** RETIRED; asst Dean, Sch of Eng & Appl Sci, Wash Univ, 1978-1984; prof physics & chmn dept, Monmouth Col, Ill, 1966-1978; prof physics, Gustavus Adolphus Col, 1964-1966; res supvr, Minn Mining & Mfg Co, 1955-1964; res physicist tire eng res, Honeywell Res Ctr, Minneapolis-Honeywell Regulator Co, 1952-1955; res physicist tire eng res, US Rubber Co, 1949-1952. **Memberships:** Am Asn Physics Teachers. **Research Statement & Publications:** Magnetism; photoconductivity and electrical properties of solids. **Mailing Address:** N 8151 Island Lake Rd, Spooner, WI 54801.

JOHNSON, ARTHUR GILBERT, MICROBIOLOGY. **Personal Data:** b Eveleth, Minn, February 1, 1926; m 1951, c 4. **Education:** Univ Minn, BA, 1950, MSc, 1951; Univ Md, PhD (bact), 1955. **Professional Experience:** PROF EMER MED MICROBIOL & IMMUNOL, SCH MED, UNIV MINN, DULUTH, as of 2003; chmn, bact & mycol study sect, NIH, 1985-1987; mem, bact & mycol study sect, NIH, 1983-1987; mem, Nat Bd Med Examrs, 1980-1984; prof & head, Dept Med Microbiol & Immunol, Sch Med, Univ Minn, Duluth, beginning 1978; ed, Infection & Immunity, 1977-1987; Mem, Nat Inst Dent Res Coun, 1972-1975; prof bact & immunol, Med Sch, Univ Mich, Ann Arbor, 1966-1978; from instr to assoc prof, Med Sch, Univ Mich, Ann Arbor, 1955-1966; biochemist, Immunol Div, Walter Reed Army Inst Res, DC, 1952-1955. **Memberships:** Am Soc Microbiol; Am Asn Immunologists; Int Soc Immunopharmacol; Reticuloendothelial Soc; Am Acad Microbiol; Infectious Dis Soc; Immunocompromised Host Soc; Soc Biol Therapy. **Research Statement & Publications:** Antibody formation; mode of action of bacterial endotoxins; host resistance factors; immunological aspects of aging. **Mailing Address:** Dept Med Microbiol & Immunol, Sch Med, Univ Minn, Ten Univ Dr, Duluth, MN 55812-2487. **Fax:** 218-726-6235. **E-Mail:** ajohnso1@umn.edu

JOHNSON, ARTHUR R, MATHEMATICS. **Education:** Boston Univ, PhD (appl maths), 1981. **Professional Experience:** MECH ENG, ARMY RES LAB, NASA LANGLEY RES CTR, as of 2005. **Memberships:** Am Chem Soc. **Mailing Address:** NASA, Langley Res Ctr, Hampton, VA 23665. **Fax:** 757-864-8912. **E-Mail:** arthur.r.johnson@nasa.gov

JOHNSON, ARTHUR THOMAS, BIOENGINEERING, BIOLOGICAL ENGINEERING. **Personal Data:** b East Meadow, NY, February 21, 1941; m 1963, c 4. **Education:** Cornell Univ, BAE, 1964, MS, 1967, PhD (bio eng), 1969. **Professional Experience:** Chmn, Northeast Agr/Biol Eng Conf, 1997-1998; dir, Am Soc Agr Engrs, 1995-1997; chmn, Am Soc Eng Educ, Biol Agr Eng Div, 1987-1988; PROF BIOL RESOURCES ENG, UNIV MD, 1986-; pres, Alliance Eng in Med & Biol, 1984-1988; consult, Nat Bur Stand Energy Related Devices Prog, 1978-; from asst prof to assoc prof agr eng & assoc prof phys educ, Univ MD, 1978-1986; grant, Nat Inst Occup Safety & Health, HEW, 1978-1981; res bio engr, US Army, Edgewood Arsenal, Md, 1971-1975; dir, Am Inst Med & Biol Engrs. **Memberships:** Fel Am Soc Agr Engrs; sr mem Inst Elec & Electronics Engrs; Am Indust Hyg Asn; Am Conf Govt Indust Hygienists; fel Am Soc Eng Educ; fel Am Inst Med & Biol Engrs; sr mem Biomed Eng Soc; Inst Biol Engrs (pres, 1998); Int Soc Respiratory Protection. **Research Statement & Publications:** Instrumentation and control; biological process engineering; respiratory stress and modelling; exercise physiology and physiological modelling. **Mailing Address:** Dept Biol Resources Eng, Univ Md, 1429 Animal Sci-Agr Eng Bldg 142, College Park, MD 20742-2315. **Fax:** 301-314-9023. **E-Mail:** aj16@umail.umd.edu

JOHNSON, B CONNOR, biochemistry, nutrition; deceased, see previous edition for last biography

JOHNSON, B LAMAR, INTERNAL MEDICINE, INFECTIOUS DISEASES. **Personal Data:** b Minneapolis, Minn, May 31, 1930; m 1954, c 4. **Education:** Denison Univ, BA, 1951; Univ Calif, Los Angeles, MD, 1955. **Professional Experience:** PROF MED, UNIV CALIF, SCH MED, LOS ANGELES, 1969-; Attend med, Wadsworth Vet Admin Hosp, beginning 1963; asst dean, Univ Calif, Sch Med, Los Angeles, 1963-1965; asst prof, Univ Calif, Sch Med, Los Angeles, 1962-1969. **Research Statement & Publications:** Drug induced nephropathy; endocarditis. **Mailing Address:** Univ Calif, Los Angeles, CA 90024.

JOHNSON, BARRY LEE, RESEARCH ADMINISTRATION, BIOMEDICAL ENGINEERING. **Personal Data:** b Sanders, Ky, October 24, 1938; m 1960, c 5. **Education:** Univ Ky, BS, 1960; Iowa State Univ, MS, 1962, PhD (elec eng), 1967. **Professional Experience:** ADJ PROF, DEPT ENVIRON & OCCUP HEALTH, EMORY UNIV, as of 2006; asst adminr, Agency Toxic Substances & Dis Registry, beginning 1986; res adminr, Nat Inst Occup Safety & Health, 1978-1986; biomed engr, Nat Inst Occup Safety & Health, 1974-1978; lectr, Univ Cincinnati, 1968-1969; biomed engr, USPHS, 1962-1964, 1967-1974; mem, Permanent Comn Occup Health; mem, Am Conf Govt Indust Hygientists; consult ed, Arch Environ Health, Neurotoxicol, J Indust Health & Toxicol, J Clean Technol & Environ Sci. **Memberships:** Sigma Xi; Am Pub Health Asn; Am Col Toxicol. **Research Statement & Publications:** Behavioral toxicology; sensory evoked potentials; electroencephalography; mathematical modelling of physiological systems; occupational safety and health; neurotoxicology. **Mailing Address:** Dept Environ & Occup Health, Rollins Sch Pub Health, Emory Univ, Grace Crum Rollins Bldg 1518 Clifton Rd, Atlanta, GA 30322. **E-Mail:** bljadm@aol.com

JOHNSON, BARRY W, ELECTRICAL ENGINEERING. **Education:** Univ Va, BS, 1979, ME, 1980, PhD (elec eng), 1983. **Honors & Awards:** Frederick Emmons Terman Award, Am Soc Eng Educ, 1991. **Professional Experience:** CO-FOUNDER, CHMN, PRES & CHIEF EXEC OFFICER, PRIVARIS INC, as of 2004; DIR, CTR SEMICUSTOM INTEGRATED SYSTS, UNIV VA, as of 2002; co-dir, Ctr Semicustom Integrated Systs, Univ Va, beginning 1998; PROF, DEPT ELEC ENG, UNIV VA, 1994-; assoc prof, Dept Elec Eng, Univ Va, 1989-1994; asst prof, Dept Elec Eng, Univ Va, 1984-1989; assoc prin engr, Harris Corp, 1982-1984; staff, Harris Corp, Melbourne, Fla; chair, Opers Comt, Inst Elec & Electronics Engrs. **Memberships:** fel Inst Elec & Electronics Engrs Comput Soc (pres, 1997); Sigma Xi. **Research Statement & Publications:** Fault-tolerant computing; safety-critical systems; dependability modeling; microprocessor-based systems. **Mailing Address:** Dept Elec Eng, Univ Va, Thornton Hall E213, Charlottesville, VA 22903. **Fax:** 434-924-8818. **E-Mail:** bwj@virginia.edu

JOHNSON, BECKY BEARD, PHYSIOLOGY. **Personal Data:** b Denver, Colo, May 4, 1942; m 1962. **Education:** Okla State Univ, BS, 1964; Univ Ill, Urbana, MS, 1966, PhD (physiol), 1968. **Professional Experience:** PROF & HEAD BOT, OKLA STATE UNIV, as of 2003; assoc prof bot, Okla State Univ, beginning 1980; asst prof biol, Okla State Univ, 1974-1980; NIH fel, 1969-1970. **Memberships:** Am Soc Plant Physiologists; Am Tissue Cult Asn; Sigma Xi. **Research Statement & Publications:** Plant tissue culture and protoplast fusion for use in plant breeding and genetics. **Mailing Address:** Dept Bot, Okla State Univ, 318 Life Sci E, Stillwater, OK 74078-0001. **Fax:** 405-744-0355. **E-Mail:** bjohnso@okstate.edu

JOHNSON, BEN BUTLER, INTERNAL MEDICINE. **Personal Data:** b Brooklyn, NY, May 23, 1920; m 1962, Barbara A Maltby; c Louis, Charles, Michael, Mary & Margaret. **Education:** Harvard Univ, AB, 1942; Harvard Med Sch, MD, 1944; Am Bd Internal Med, dipl & cert nephrology. **Professional Experience:** CLIN ASSOC PROF MED, SCH MED, UNIV MISS, 1990-; head, Div Renal Dis, 1959-1990; from asst prof to assoc prof med, Sch Med, Univ Miss, 1959-1990; head diabetes clin, Univ Hosps, Stanford Univ, 1956-1959; from instr to asst prof med, Stanford Univ, 1955-1959; dir, Grad Training Prog Metab Dis, Univ, 1955-1959; Sch Med, Stanford Univ, 1950-1953; Res fel, Bassett Hosp, Cooperstown, NY, 1949-1950; asst resident med, NY Univ Div, Bellevue Hosp, 1947-1949; asst, Med Col, Cornell Univ, 1946-1947; intern path, NY Hosp, 1944-1945. **Memberships:** Int Soc Nephrology; Am Soc Nephrology; fel Am Col Physicians; Endocrine Soc; AMA; Sigma Xi. **Research Statement & Publications:** Renal disease; aldosterone and edema; metabolic diseases. **Mailing Address:** Dept Med, Univ Miss Med Ctr, 2500 N State Street, Jackson, MS 39216-4505.

JOHNSON, B(ENJAMIN) M(ARTINEAU), CHEMICAL ENGINEERING, MECHANICAL ENGINEERING. **Personal Data:** b Chiralla, South India, October 28, 1930; American citizen; m 1954, Mary; c Daniel & Judith. **Education:** Cornell Univ, BChE, 1952; Univ Wis, MS, 1953, PhD (chem eng), 1956. **Professional Experience:** MGR, TANK WASTE REMEDIATION TECHNOL DEVELOP, PAC NW LABS, 1991-; mgr, Energy Sci Dept, 1986-1991; mem, Coord Comt, US/USSR Coop Prog in Thermal Power Plant Heat Rejection Systs, 1975-1980; affil prof, Univ Wash & Wash State Univ, beginning 1974; sr engr prog mgr, Fluid & Energy Systs, 1974-1986; mgr, Fluid & Energy Systs, 1969-1974; mgr, Sodium Fluid Syst Sect, Fast Flux Text Facil, 1967-1969; coordr chem eng joint ctr grad study, Univ Wash & Wash State Univ, 1965-1976; affil assoc prof, Univ Wash & Wash State Univ, 1965-1974; mgr, Eng Anal Unit, Pac NW Labs, 1965-1967; sr engr, Chem Res & Develop, Hanford Labs, Gen Elec Co, 1956-1964. **Memberships:** Fel Am Inst Chem Engrs; Sigma Xi; Am Nuclear Soc; fel Am Inst Chemists. **Research Statement & Publications:** Heat and mass transfer; fluid mechanics; economic analysis; nuclear reactor technology; project (development, design, construction) management. **Mailing Address:** 2336 Davison Ave, Richland, WA 99352-1921.

JOHNSON, BERTRAND H, OPTICAL ENGINEERING. **Education:** Rutgers Univ, BSc. **Honors & Awards:** Eng Excellence Award, Optical Soc Am, 1992. **Professional Experience:** DISTINGUISHED MEM TECH STAFF, AT&T BELL LAB, as of 2002. **Mailing Address:** AT&T Bell Res Lab, 600 Mountain Ave, Murray Hill, NJ 07974-2008.

JOHNSON, BOB DUELL, CYTOLOGY, TOXINOLOGY. **Personal Data:** b Pocahontas, Ark, June 24, 1936; c 2. **Education:** Ark State Univ, BS, 1958; Ariz State Univ, MS, 1964, PhD (zoology), 1967. **Professional Experience:** PROF EMER ZOOLOGY, ARK STATE UNIV, beginning 1990; prof zoology, Ark State Univ, beginning 1980; assoc prof, Ark State Univ, 1974-1980; asst prof, Ark State Univ, 1967-1974; res assoc, Acad Year Inst, Ariz State Univ, 1966-1967; res asst toxinol, Acad Year Inst, Ariz State Univ, 1963-1966; partic zoology, Acad Year Inst, Ariz State Univ, 1962-1963; teacher, Northeast Independent Sch Dist, Tex, 1958-1962. **Memberships:** Int Soc Toxinol; Sigma Xi. **Research Statement & Publications:** Effects of toxins on enzyme systems and morphology of cells. **Mailing Address:** Ark State Univ, State Univ, AR 72467-0599. **Fax:** 870-972-3962.

JOHNSON, BOBBY RAY, LIPID SCIENCE, FLAVOR CHEMISTRY. **Personal Data:** b Oakwood, Okla, October 30, 1941; m 1962, c 2. **Education:** Okla State Univ, BS, 1963, MS, 1966, PhD (biochem), 1970. **Professional Experience:** ASST MGR, CAMPBELL INST RES TECHNOL, CAMPBELL SOUP CO, 1976-; asst prof food sci, NC State Univ, 1970-1976; USPHS fel, Univ Calif, Davis, 1969-1970; instr biochem, Okla State Univ, 1967-1968; instr chem, Okla Christian Col, 1966-1967. **Memberships:** Am Oil Chemists Soc; Inst Food Technol; Am Dairy Sci Asn. **Research Statement & Publications:** Fats and oil chemistry; natural antioxidants; dairy science. **Mailing Address:** 129 Kipling Rd, Cherry Hill, NJ 08003.

JOHNSON, BRANN, STRUCTURAL GEOLOGY. **Personal Data:** b Annapolis, Md, December 4, 1946; m 1988, c 2. **Education:** Univ Calif, Berkeley, BA, 1968; Pa State Univ, MEng, 1973, PhD (geol), 1975. **Professional Experience:** DIR, CTR TECTONOPHYSICS, TEX A&M UNIV, as of 2004; ASSOC PROF GEOL & GEOPHYSICS, DEPT GEOL & GEOPHYSICS, TEX A&M UNIV, 1980-; Los Alamos Sci Lab, 1976-1978; Div Basic Energy Res, Dept Energy, beginning 1979; subpanel mem, Nat Res Coun, 1979-1980; civil eng, 1976-1979; geophysics, 1979-1980; vis staff scientist, Los Alamos Sci Lab, 1976-1981; res assoc, Ctr Tectonophysics, Tex A&M Univ, beginning 1975; asst prof geol, Dept Geol & Geophysics, Tex A&M Univ, 1975-1980; prin investr, Cambridge Labs, US Air Force, 1975-1977; instr geol, Div Geol & Planetary Sci, Calif Tech, 1974-1975; asst geol, Dept Geol & Geophysics, Pa State Univ, 1968-1971; geologist, Marine Geol & Hydrol Div, US Geol Surv, 1968. **Memberships:** Int Glaciol Soc; Am Geophys Union. **Research Statement & Publications:** Crustal geologic processes; development of mathematical models; glacial abrasion cracks; landslide mechanics; thermal cracking of rock; fracture permeability; water and rock interaction; mechanics of geologic discontinuities. **Mailing Address:** Dept Geol & Geophys, Tex A&M Univ, Rm 363, MT Halbouty Bldg, College Station, TX 77843-3115. **Fax:** 979-845-6162. **E-Mail:** johnson@geo.tamu.edu

JOHNSON, BRANT MONTGOMERY, RELATIVISTIC HEAVY-ION & SPIN PHYSICS, ION-SOURCE DEVELOPMENT. **Personal Data:** b Houston, Tex, August 25, 1949; m 1973, Marcia; c Anna & Austin. **Education:** Univ Tex, Austin, BS, 1971, MA, 1974, PhD (physics), 1975. **Professional Experience:** PHYSICIST, PHYSICS DEPARTMENT, BROOKHAVEN NAT LAB, 1999-; RHIC DEPARTMENT, RHIC Liaison for PHENIX, 1993-1999; Dept Appl Sci, 1984-1999; Sci Secy PHENIX, 1994-, Mgr PHENIX Office, 1997-, Chair, RHIC & AGS Users' Exec. Comm., 2005-2006, member, 2001-; NSLS subgroup rep for atom & molecular sci, 1991-1993; prin investr, Atomic Phys Res, Dept Energy, 1990-1993 and Nucl Sci Teach Learn Sci, Dept Energy, 1997-, assoc ed, Phys Rev Lett, 1988-; PRE, 1993-; PRST-AB, 1998-; PRA, 1990-1994; vis prof, Latin Am Sch Physics, 1989; Ger Acad Exchange Serv study visit, 1984; lectr, Brookhaven Semester Prog, Brookhaven Nat Lab, 1981; vis scientist, Lawrence Berkeley Lab & Oak Ridge Nat Lab, 1977 & Triumf Lab, BC, 1980; Brookhaven Nat Lab, assoc physicist, 1979-1980; asst physicist, 1977-1979; res assoc, 1975-1977; Univ Tex Austin, res sci assoc II, Welch Found Fel, 1973-1975; res sci assoc II, 1971-1973. **Memberships:** Am Phys Soc, Divs nucl, particles & fields, atomic, beam, plasma physics. **Research Statement & Publications:** Nuclear, elementary particle, atomic, beam, and plasma physics; relativistic heavy-ion collisions; proton spin physics; atomic collisions; atomic processes in high termperature plasmas; atomic physics with synchroton radiation. **Mailing Address:** Box 5000, Bldg 51OC, Brookhaven National Lab, Upton, NY 11973-5000. **Fax:** 631-344-3253. **E-Mail:** brant@bnl.gov

JOHNSON, BRIAN JAMES, ANALYTICAL METHODS DEVELOPMENT FOR ATMOSPHERIC SPECIES, BIOGEOCHEMICAL CYCLES. **Personal Data:** b Caldwell, Idaho, August 6, 1961; m 1992, Linda. **Education:** Col Idaho, BS, 1982; Univ Ariz, PhD (chem), 1988. **Professional Experience:** ASSOC PROF CHEM, UNIV, NEV, LAS VEGAS, 1994-; res chemist, Environ Protection Agency, 1990; asst prof, Univ, Nev, Las Vegas, 1988-1994; res assoc, Univ Ariz, 1988. **Memberships:** Am Chem Soc; Am Geophys Union. **Research Statement & Publications:** Atmospheric chemistry; development and evaluation of new analytical methods and biogeochemical cycles; analytical chemistry, especially ion chromatography. **Mailing Address:** Dept Chem, Univ Nev, PO Box 4003 4505 Md Pkwy, Las Vegas, NV 89154-4003. **Fax:** 702-895-4072. **E-Mail:** bjj@nevada.edu

JOHNSON, BRIAN JOHN, BIOCHEMISTRY, EDUCATIONAL ADMINISTRATION. **Personal Data:** b Reading, Eng, October 28, 1938; m 1968. **Education:** Univ Leeds, BSc, 1960; Univ London, PhD (org chem) & Imp Col, dipl, 1963; Univ London, DSc, 1977; Inst Educ Mgt, Harvard Univ, 1981. **Professional Experience:** CO-DIR GRAD PROG, MED SCH, UNIV ALA, BIRMINGHAM, 1978-; ASSOC PROF MICROBIOL, MED SCH, UNIV ALA, BIRMINGHAM, 1971-; asst prof chem, Tufts Univ, 1966-1971; res assoc, Mass Inst Technol, 1965-1966; res assoc, St John's Univ, 1964-1965; res assoc org chem, State Univ NY Buffalo, 1963-1964. **Memberships:** Am Chem Soc. **Research Statement & Publications:** Synthesis, structure and biological properties of peptides and proteins;

biochemistry of lipid-protein interactions; immunopharmacology; complement; allergy. **Mailing Address:** 3724 Woodvale Rd, Birmingham, AL 35223-1444.

JOHNSON, BRUCE, CHEMISTRY. **Education:** Univ Minn, BA, 1975; Univ Wis, PhD (chem), 1981. **Professional Experience:** EXEC DIR, RICE QUANTUM INST, as of 2005. **Mailing Address:** Rice Quantum Inst, Space Science 102, Athens, GA 30608. **Fax:** 713-348-5010. **E-Mail:** johnson@rice.edu

JOHNSON, BRUCE, NAVAL ARCHITECTURE, OCEAN ENGINEERING. **Personal Data:** b Hawarden, Iowa, September 4, 1932; m 1955, c 2. **Education:** Iowa State Univ, BSME, 1955; Purdue Univ, MSME, 1962, PhD (mech eng), 1965. **Professional Experience:** DEPT NAVAL ARCHIT & OCEAN ENG, US NAVAL ENG, as of 2005; chmn, Symbols & Truminology Group, 1985-; chmn, 18th Am Towing Tank Conf, 1977; dir, Hydromech Lab, 1976-1987; dir, Hydromech Lab, US Naval Acad, 1976-1987; US Rep Info Comt Int Towing Tank Conf, 1975-1984; command prof Hydromech, Naval Sea Systs, 1975-1986; Western Elec Fund award eng teaching, 1971; assoc prof, US Naval Acad, 1964-1970; instr mech eng, Purdue Univ, 1959-1964; Instr marine eng, US Naval Acad, 1957-1959; co-auth, Introd to Naval Archit. **Memberships:** Am Soc Mech Engrs; Am Soc Eng Educ; Soc Naval Architects & Marine Engrs; Am Soc Naval Engrs. **Research Statement & Publications:** Hydrodynamics, ship model testing and brain wave analysis. **Mailing Address:** Dept Naval Archit & Ocean Eng, US Naval Acad, Mail Stop 11d 590 Holloway Rd, Annapolis, MD 21402-5042. **Fax:** 410-293-2219. **E-Mail:** johnson@usna.edu

JOHNSON, BRUCE FLETCHER, ORGANIC CHEMICALS, NEW CHELATORS. **Personal Data:** b Brooklyn, NY, April 5, 1956; m 1984, c 1. **Education:** Mass Inst Technol, BS, 1978; Harvard Univ, MS, 1980, PhD (chem), 1984. **Professional Experience:** STATE MEM, CORP RES & DEVELOP, GEN ELEC CO, 1986-; fel, Dept Chem, Columbia Univ, 1984-1986. **Research Statement & Publications:** Development of efficient synthetic routes leading to organic chemicals; investigation of novel monomers and polymers; synthesis and study of new chelators and binding materials. **Mailing Address:** Bldg K1 Rm 3C27, GE Corp Res & Develop PO Box Eight, Schenectady, NY 12301-0008.

JOHNSON, BRUCE MCDOUGALL, ANALYTICAL CHEMISTRY. **Personal Data:** b Ottawa, Ill, September 24, 1943; m 1963, c 3. **Education:** Univ Wis-Madison, BS, 1966, MS, 1967, PhD (chem), 1972. **Professional Experience:** SR DIR, ATHEROGENICS, 1999-; sect head, Analysis Res Dept, Pfizer Inc, beginning 1985-; sr res investr, Analysis Res Dept, Pfizer Inc, 1983-1985; from res scientist to sr res scientist, Analysis Res Dept, Pfizer Inc, 1977-1983; asst prof human oncol, Ctr Health Sci, Univ Wis-Madison, 1975-1977; asst prof clin oncol, Ctr Health Sci, Univ Wis-Madison, 1972-1975. **Memberships:** AAAS; Am Chem Soc; Am Soc Mass Spectrometry. **Research Statement & Publications:** Metabolism of antineoplastic drugs and carcinogens; analysis of pharmaceuticals; application of gas chromatography and mass spectrometry to biomedical and biological problems. **Mailing Address:** AtheroGenics Inc, 8995 Westside Pkwy, Alpharetta, GA 30004. **Fax:** 678-336-2501.

JOHNSON, BRUCE PAUL, HIGH FREQUENCY ELECTRONICS, COMPUTER AIDED DESIGN. **Personal Data:** b Lewiston, Maine, August 8, 1938; m 1961, Marcia Ann Duarte; c Michael, Robyn, Samuel & Rebecca. **Education:** Bates Col, BS, 1960; Univ NH, MS, 1963; Univ Mo, Columbia, PhD (physics), 1967. **Honors & Awards:** IEEE third Millennium medal, 2000. **Professional Experience:** Vpres, res & develop, Caddo Enterprises Inc, 1990-1992; PROF ELEC ENG, UNIV NV, RENO, 1978-; chmn elec eng, Univ NV, Reno, 1978-1983 & 1991-1994; presidential appointment, US Metric Bd, 1978-1980 & 1980-1982; assoc prof elec eng, Univ NV, RENO, 1974-1978; supvr, Solid State Lamp Proj, 1970-1974; advan physicist, Gen Elec Co, 1967-1970; instr physics, Hobart & William Smith Cols, 1962-1964. **Memberships:** Inst Elec & Electronics Engrs; Am Soc Eng Educ; Sigma Xi. **Research Statement & Publications:** Biomedical Instrumentation; solid state electronic materials and devices; electronic computer aided design and manufacturing; high frequency electronic design. **Mailing Address:** 3190 W Seventh, Reno, NV 89503. **Fax:** 702-784-6627. **E-Mail:** johnson@ee.unr.edu

JOHNSON, BRUCE R, MATHEMATICS. **Education:** Ore State Univ, MA; Univ Ore, PhD, (appl math). **Professional Experience:** ASSOC PROF EMER, UNIV VICTORIA, as of 2006. **Memberships:** Math Asn Am. **Mailing Address:** Dept Math & Statist, Univ Victoria, Victoria, BC V8W 3P4, Can. **Fax:** 250-721-8962. **E-Mail:** johnsonb@uvic.ca

JOHNSON, BRUCE VIRGIL, PHYSICS. **Personal Data:** b November 24, 1935; m 1959, Peggy K Gaalaas; c Karen E, Paul L & Eric V. **Education:** Univ Minn, BS, 1958, MS, 1960; Univ Conn, MS, 1966, PhD (fluid dynamics), 1972. **Honors & Awards:** Gas Turbine Award, Am Soc Mech Engrs, 1991. **Professional Experience:** GROUP LEADER HEAT TRANSFER, ABB SWISS RES CTR, 1994-; supvr heat & mass transfer technol, United Technol Res Ctr, beginning 1968; res engr, United Technol Res Ctr, 1966-1968; assoc res engr, United Technol Res Ctr, 1963-1966; asst res engr, United Technol Res Ctr, 1960-1963. **Memberships:** Am Soc Mech Engrs; sr mem Am Inst Aeronaut & Astronaut. **Research Statement & Publications:** Experimental and analytical studies influid mechanics and heat transfer studies relating to gas turbines and convection in rotation turbine blade coolant passages and rotating disc-cavity configurations. **Mailing Address:** ABB Swiss Ltd Corp Res, Segelhof 1, CH-5405, Baden-Daettwil, Switzerland.

JOHNSON, BRYAN HUGH, ENDOCRINE PHYSIOLOGY. **Personal Data:** b Hammond, La, August 15, 1940; m 1962, c 2. **Education:** Southeastern La Univ, BS, 1963; La State Univ, MS, 1966; Okla State Univ, PhD (reproduction), 1969. **Professional Experience:** PROF, DEPT ANIMAL SCI, KLEBERG CTR, TEX, as of 2006; Biomed res grant, NDak State Univ, 1976, 1978; ASSOC PROF ENDOCRINE PHYSIOL, NC STATE UNIV, 1971-; NIH res fel, Okla State Univ, 1960-1971. **Memberships:** Soc Study Reproduction; Am Soc Animal Sci; Sigma Xi. **Research Statement & Publications:** Testicular steroidogenesis; adrenal-testicular interrelationship. **Mailing Address:** Dept Animal Sci, Tex A&M Univ, Kleberg Ctr, College Station, TX 77843-2471. **Fax:** 979-845-6970. **E-Mail:** bh-johnson@tamu.edu

JOHNSON, BRYCE VINCENT, INORGANIC CHEMISTRY, ORGANOMETALLIC CHEMISTRY. **Personal Data:** b Minneapolis, Minn, October 24, 1949; m 1971. **Education:** St Olaf Col, BA, 1971; Yale Univ, MS & MPhil, 1972, PhD (chem), 1975; Univ Chicago, MBA, 1986. **Professional Experience:** PRES & CHIEF EXEC OFFICER, PEPTIDES INT, 2005-; vpres, Fluoro Thermal Plastics, Dyneon Llc, beginning 1996; bus develop mgr, 3M Corp, 1991-1996; tech mgr, 3M Corp, 1989-1990; prod develop specialist, 3M Corp, 1986-1989; sr chemist, Amoco Res Ctr, Amoco Chem Corp, 1979-1986; asst prof chem, Univ Louisville, 1975-1979. **Memberships:** Am Chem Soc; Sigma Xi; Soc Plastics Engrs. **Research Statement & Publications:** Organometallic synthesis; transition metal isocyanide complexes; homogeneous catalysis; fluxional systems; polyolefin additives; fluoroplastics and elastomers. **Mailing Address:** Peptides Int Inc, 11621 Electron Dr, Louisville, KY 40299. **Fax:** 502-267-1329.

JOHNSON, BYRON F, CELL BIOLOGY, MICROBIAL PHYSIOLOGY. **Personal Data:** b St Mary's, Pa., USA, July 25, 1928; Canadian citizen; m 1967, Hazel; c 4. **Education:** Pa State Univ, BS, 1950; Univ Calif, Los Angeles, MA, 1958, PhD (zoology), 1960. **Professional Experience:** ADJ FAC MEM BIOL, CARLETON UNIV, as of 2004; adj res prof biol, Carleton Univ, beginning 1990; adv bd, CRC Crit Rev Biotechnol, 1981-2005; mem, Int Comn Yeasts, 1980-2005; vis scientist, Nat Inst Med Res, London, Eng, 1968-1969; res officer, Div Biol Sci, Nat Res Coun Can, 1962-1990; Nat Cancer Inst fel zool, Univ Edinburgh, 1960-1962. **Memberships:** Am Soc Cell Biol; Am Soc Microbiol; Can Soc Cell Biol; Can Soc Microbiologists. **Research Statement & Publications:** Cell cycle; cellular growth and division; growth of cell organelles; biosynthesis of wall polysaccharides; regulation of cell size; temperature effects in biological systems; cytoplasmic genetics; chemostat culture; flocculation; microbial physiology; cytology of Eimeria. **Mailing Address:** Dept Biol, Carleton Univ, 220 Nesbitt Bldg, 1125 Colonel By Dr, Ottawa, ON K1S 5B6, Can. **Fax:** 613-520-3539. **E-Mail:** bjohnson@ccs.carleton.ca

JOHNSON, C D, CONTROL SYSTEMS. **Education:** Univ Tn, Knoxville, MS, 1958; Purdue Univ, PhD, 1963. **Professional Experience:** DISTINGUISHED PROF, DEPT ELEC & COMPUT ENG, UNIV ALA, HUNTSVILLE, as of 2005. **Research Statement & Publications:** Control of dynamical systems in the face of uncertain disturbances and parameter variations. **Mailing Address:** Dept Elec & Comput Eng, Univ Ala-Huntsville, 301 Sparkman Dr, Huntsville, AL 35899. **Fax:** 256-824-6803. **E-Mail:** johnson@ece.uah.edu

JOHNSON, C RICHARD, JR, ELECTRICAL ENGINEERING. **Education:** Ga Inst Technol, BE, 1973; Stanford Univ, MS, 1975, PhD, 1977. **Professional Experience:** PROF, DEPT ELEC & COMPUT ENG, SCH ELEC & COMPUT ENG, CORNELL UNIV, as of 2006. **Mailing Address:** Dept Elec & Comput Eng, Sch Elec & Comput Eng, Cornell Univ, 224 Phillips Hall, Ithaca, NY 22202. **Fax:** 607-254-9072. **E-Mail:** johnson@ece.cornell.edu

JOHNSON, C SCOTT, PHYSICS, BIOPHYSICS. **Personal Data:** b Sullivan, Mo, February 4, 1932. **Education:** Univ Mo-Rolla, BS, 1954; Wash Univ, PhD (physics), 1959. **Professional Experience:** H EAD, MARINE BIOSCIENCE DIV, NAVAL UNDERSEA CTR, 1969-; sr res scientist, Naval Undersea Ctr, 1967-1969; physicist, Naval Ord Test Sta, 1963-1967; Res assoc physics, Fermi Inst Nuclear Studies, Univ Chicago, 1959-1963. **Memberships:** Am Phys Soc; Acoust Soc Am; Sigma Xi. **Research Statement & Publications:** Marine mammal bioacoustics; shark behavioral studies; nuclear physics. **Mailing Address:** 1876 Sefton Pl, San Diego, CA 92107.

JOHNSON, C WALTER, METALLURGICAL ENGINEERING. **Personal Data:** b Warren, Pa, April 19, 1910. **Professional Experience:** RETIRED; consult, Autoclave Eng, McInnes Steel Co, 1966-1983; dir metall, Nat Forge, 1960-1966; mem staff, Nat Forge, 1929-1966. **Memberships:** Fel Am Soc Metals. **Mailing Address:** Five E Third Ave, Warren, PA 16365.

JOHNSON, CAGE SAUL, INTERNAL MEDICINE, HEMATOLOGY. **Personal Data:** b New Orleans, La, March 31, 1941; m 1968, Shirley; c Stephanie & Michelle. **Education:** Creighton Univ, MD, 1965. **Professional Experience:** PROF HEMAT, UNIV SOUTHERN CALIF, 1988-; bd dirs, Sickle Cell Self Help Asn, Los Angeles, 1982-1986; active, Nat Med Fel Inc, Chicago, 1979-; DIR, HEMOGLOBINOPATHY LAB, LOS ANGELES, 1976-; from asst prof to assoc prof, Univ Southern Calif, 1974-1988; instr, Univ Southern Calif, 1971-1974; resident, Univ Southern Calif, 1969-1971; resident, Univ Cincinnati, 1966-1967; intern, Univ Cincinnati, 1965-1966; mem bd dirs, Sickle Cell Dis Res Found & dir, Comprehensive Sickle Cell Ctr. **Memberships:** Fel NY Acad Sci; Am Col Angiol; Am Soc Hemat; Am Fedn Clin Res; Int Soc Biocheology. **Research Statement & Publications:** Hemoglobinopathies: structure and function. **Mailing Address:** Univ Southern Calif, Norris Cancer Hosp 304, 1441 Eastlake Ave, Los Angeles, CA 90033. **Fax:** 323-442-1255. **E-Mail:** cagejohn@usc.edu

JOHNSON, CALVIN KEITH, RESINS & POLYMERS, NEW PRODUCT DEVELOPMENT. **Personal Data:** b Litchfield, Minn, December 15, 1937; m 1960, c 3. **Education:** Olivet Nazarene Univ, AB, 1959; Mich State Univ, PhD (org chem), 1963. **Honors & Awards:** Award of Sci Merit, Am Foundrymens Soc, 1996. **Professional Experience:** PRES, C JOHNSON & ASSOC, LLC, 1998-; vpres & tech dir, Borden Chem Inc, 1995-1998; tech dir foundry & indust resins, Borden Chem Inc, 1993-1994; sr vpres & tech dir, Acme Resin Corp, 1985-1993; vpres res & develop, Acme Resin Corp, 1977-1985; tech dir res, Acme Resin Corp, 1969-1977; group leader polymer res, CPC Int, 1967-1969; res chemist, Minn Mining & Mfg Co, 1964-1967; res chemist, 3M Co, 1964-1967; NIH fel org chem, Columbia Univ, 1963-1964. **Memberships:** Am Chem Soc; Soc Petrol Eng; Am Foundrymens Soc; Asn Consult Chem & Chem Eng. **Research Statement & Publications:** synthesis and reactions of small ring compounds; mechanisms of polymer decomposition; latent curing resin systems; phenolic, thermosetting and foundry resins; polymers; molding compounds; urethane polymers; metal casting processes; orthopedic bandages. **Mailing Address:** C Johnson & Assoc LLC, 15055 W 139th St, Homer Glen, IL 60441. **Fax:** 708-301-0428. **E-Mail:** cjohnson@cjohnson-associates.com

JOHNSON, CANDACE SUE, LEUKEMIA RESEARCH. **Personal Data:** b Columbus, Ohio, April 10, 1949. **Education:** Ohio State Univ, PhD (microbiol), 1977. **Professional Experience:** SR VPRES TRANSL RES, ROSEWELL PK CANCER INST, as of 2004; SR MEM, DEPT PHARMCOL & THERAPEUTICS, ROSEWELL PK CANCER INST, as of 2004; prof pharmacol, Univ Pittsburgh Sch Med, beginning 1989; assoc prof otolaryngol & path, Sch Med, Univ Pittsburgh, beginning 1989; lab chief exp hemat, AMC Cancer Res Ctr, Lakewood, Colo, 1988-1989; sr scientist, AMC Cancer Res Ctr, Lakewood, Colo, 1981-1989. **Research Statement & Publications:** T-cells; monoclonal antibodies. **Mailing Address:** Roswell Park Cancer Inst, Elm & Carlton St, Buffalo, NY 14263. **Fax:** 716-845-5865. **E-Mail:** candace.johnson@roswellpark.org

JOHNSON, CARL, BIOLOGY. **Education:** PhD, Biological Sci, Vanderbilt Univ. **Professional Experience:** INSTR, DEPT BIOL SCI, VANDERBILT UNIV, as of 2001. **Mailing Address:** Dept Biol Sci, Vanderbilt Univ, POBox 351634 Sta B, Nashville, TN 37235-1634. **Fax:** 615-343-6707.

JOHNSON, CARL ARNOLD, ORGANIC CHEMISTRY. **Personal Data:** b Bend, Ore, March 5, 1925; m 1949, c 2. **Education:** Reed Col, BA, 1950; State Col Wash, MS, 1952, PhD (chem), 1956. **Professional Experience:** RETIRED; bd dirs, Toastmasters Int, 1978-1980; res assoc chem support, textile opers, Tech Ctr, Owens Corning Fiberglas Co, 1975-1986; sr scientist chem support, Owens-Ill Co, 1974-1975; proj mgr glass fiber reinforcements technol & chem develop, Owens-Ill Co, 1969-1974; consult coatings & optical mat, Owens-Ill Co, 1968-1969; mgr appln res, Owens-Ill Co, 1964-1968; chief org chem res, Owens-Ill Co, 1960-1964; chief forest prod res, Owens-Ill Co, 1959-1960; fel org synthesis, Mellon Inst, 1956-1959. **Memberships:** Am Chem Soc; Sigma Xi; AAAS. **Research Statement & Publications:** Development of new glass fiber size systems. **Mailing Address:** 51 Meredith St, Port Ludlow, WA 98365.

JOHNSON, CARL BOONE, TOXICOLOGY, ENVIRONMENTAL HEALTH. **Personal Data:** b Jacksonville, Fla, March 11, 1938; m 1964, c 1. **Education:** Fla State Univ, Tallahassee, BS, 1959; Am Univ, MS, 1967; Georgetown Univ, PhD (biochem), 1974. **Professional Experience:** TOXICOLOGIST, CFSAN, FOOD & DRUG ADMIN, 1981-; sci adminr, Cfsan, Food & Drug Admin, 1976-1981; res scientist, Microbiol Assocs, 1974-1976; Res chemist, Nat Naval Med Ctr, 1963-1972. **Memberships:** AAAS. **Research Statement & Publications:** Solubilized and partially purified a glucagon-binding protein from rat liver plasma membranes; uptake of drugs by rat kidney lysosomes. **Mailing Address:** 12800 Teaberry Rd, Silver Spring, MD 20906.

JOHNSON, CARL E, JR, AERONAUTICS. **Education:** Oberlin Col, AB, 1964; Duke Univ, JD, 1968. **Professional Experience:** STAFF, ROBINSON, BRADSHAW & HINSON PA, as of 2005. **Mailing Address:** Structural Dyn & Loads Lambert Field, 101 N Tryon St., Ste 1900, Charlotte, NC 28246. **Fax:** 704-373-3927. **E-Mail:** cjohnson@rbh.com

JOHNSON, CARL EDWARD, SEISMICITY, SEISMIC NETWORKS. **Personal Data:** b Marshalltown, Iowa, November 27, 1946; m 1973, c 2. **Education:** Mass Inst Technol, BS & MS, 1972; Calif Inst Technol, PhD (geophysics), 1979. **Professional Experience:** ASSOC PROF, DEPT GEOL, UNIV HAWAII, as of 2006; vis res assoc, Seismol Lab, Calif Inst Technol, beginning 1979; geophysicist, Off Earthquake Studies, US Geol Surv, 1979-1988. **Memberships:** Seismol Soc; Am Geophys Union. **Research Statement & Publications:** Seismicity studies related to earthquake prediction research including the development of real-time data acquisition and earthquake data base systems. **Mailing Address:** Dept Geol, Univ Hawaii, 200 W Kawili St, Hilo, HI 96720-4091. **Fax:** 808-974-7677. **E-Mail:** carlj@hawaii.edu

JOHNSON, CARL EDWIN, ORGANIC CHEMISTRY. **Personal Data:** b Jamestown, Kans, June 24, 1917; m 1946, c 2. **Education:** Bethany Col, Kans, BS, 1938; Univ Kans, MA, 1941, PhD (chem), 1943. **Professional Experience:** RETIRED; vpres res & develop, Amoco Chem Corp, 1969-1980; gen mgr, Amoco Chem Corp, 1967-1969; coordr res & develop, Standard Oil Co Ind, 1965-1967; dir org chem res, Amoco Chem Corp, 1961-1965; dir new chem res, Standard Oil Co, Ind, 1959-1961; sect leader, Standard Oil Co, Ind, 1947-1959; dir res, Mich Chem Corp, 1946-1947; c hemist, Standard Oil Co Ind, 1943-1946. **Memberships:** Am Chem Soc; Am Inst Chem Engrs; Am Inst Chemists; Sigma Xi. **Research Statement & Publications:** Chemicals; polymers; hydrocarbon separations; conversions. **Mailing Address:** 1217 Somerset Lane, Elk Grove Village, IL 60007.

JOHNSON, CARL ERICK, ORGANIC CHEMISTRY. **Personal Data:** b Chicago, Ill, February 17, 1914; m 1941, c 2. **Education:** Univ Chicago, BS, 1938, MS, 1949. **Professional Experience:** RETIRED; consult, beginning 1976; res mgr, Brookhaven Res Lab, 1974-1976; res mgr, res assoc Miss, 1971-1974; res assoc, Metal Indust Div, 1968-1971; res mgr, Metal Indust Div, 1960-1968; sect head, Cent Res, Nalco Chem Co, 1959-1960; sr technol adv, Nat Aluminate Corp, 1956-1959; dir inorg res, Nat Aluminate Corp, 1952-1956; chief org chemist, Nat Aluminate Corp, 1945-1952; chemist, Western Shade Cloth Co, Ill, 1938-1945. **Memberships:** AAAS; Am Chem Soc; Nat Asn Corrosion Engrs. **Research Statement & Publications:** Water and textile treatment; flotation of minerals; synthesis of organic compounds; measurement of the film pressure of insoluble films; organic chemistry of boiler water treatment; aqueous corrosion; ion exchange; industrial lubrication, especially metal rolling and emulsion technology. **Mailing Address:** 401 McNair St, Brookhaven, MS 39601-3744.

JOHNSON, CARL LYNN, PHARMACOLOGY, BIOCHEMISTRY. **Personal Data:** b Beaumont, Tex, August 22, 1941. **Education:** Rice Univ, BA, 1964; Univ Houston, MS, 1968; Baylor Col Med, PhD (pharmacol), 1971. **Professional Experience:** ASSOC PROF PHARMACOL, COL MED, UNIV CINCINNATI, 1977-; asst prof pharmacol, Mt Sinai Sch Med, 1973-1977; assoc, Mt Sinai Sch Med, 1972-1973; instr, Mt Sinai Sch Med, 1971-1972. **Research Statement & Publications:** Hormone receptors and adenylate cyclase; molecular pharmacology. **Mailing Address:** Dept Pharmacol & Cell Biophys, Univ Cincinnati Col Med, 231 Bethesda Ave, Cincinnati, OH 45267-0575. **Fax:** 513-558-2349.

JOHNSON, CARL RANDOLPH, ORGANIC CHEMISTRY. **Personal Data:** b Charlottesville, Va, April 28, 1937; m 1966, Mary; c Gregory. **Education:** Med Col Va, BS, 1958; Univ Ill, PhD (chem), 1962. **Honors & Awards:** A C cope sr scholar, Am chem soc, 2002. **Professional Experience:** DISTINGUISHED PROF EMER, 2002-; chair, Chem 1997-2001; Humboldt sr scientist, 1991; distinguished prof chem, Wayne State Univ, 1990-2001; assoc ed, J Am Chem Soc, 1984-1989; BD DIRS, ORGANIC SYNTHESES INC, 1981-; adv bd, J of Org Chem, 1976-1981; Alfred P Sloan fel, 1965-1968; from asst prof to prof, Wayne State Univ, 1962-1990; NSF res fel chem, Harvard Univ, 1962. **Memberships:** Am Chem Soc. **Research Statement & Publications:** Organic sulfur chemistry, especially sulfoxides and sulfoximines; exploratory synthetic chemistry; synthesis of compounds of potential medicinal activity; organometallic chemistry; synthesis of natural products; enzymes in synthesis. **Mailing Address:** Dept Chem, Wayne State Univ, 221 Chem Bldg, Detroit, MI 48202-3489. **Fax:** 313-577-3585. **E-Mail:** crj@chem.wayne.edu

JOHNSON, CARL WILLIAM, PLANT BREEDING. **Personal Data:** b Mound Valley, Kans, February 11, 1942; m 1968, c 2. **Education:** Kans State Univ, BS, 1965; NDak State Univ, MS, 1967; Univ Nebr, PhD (agron), 1974. **Honors & Awards:** Distinguished Rice Res & Educ Award; First McCaughey Mem Inst Vis Scientists Award, Australia. **Professional Experience:** PLANT BREEDER, CALIF COOP RICE RES FOUND, 1974-. **Memberships:** Crop Sci Soc Am; Am Soc Agronomy; Coun Agr Sci & Technol; Sigma Xi. **Research Statement & Publications:** Development of rice varieties for the California rice industry. **Mailing Address:** Ca Coop Rice Res Found, Rice Exp Sta, 955 Butte City Hwy, Biggs, CA 95917. **E-Mail:** cwjohnson@crrf.org

JOHNSON, CARLTON ROBERT, PETROLEUM GEOLOGY, GROUNDWATER GEOLOGY. **Personal Data:** b Chicago, Ill, September 19, 1926; m 1951, c 2. **Education:** Monmouth Col, Ill, BA, 1949; Univ Iowa, MS, 1954, PhD, 1956. **Professional Experience:** 3D MODELING PETROL RESERVOIR DESCRIPTION RES, EXXON PROD RES CO, 1991-; res adv, Exxon Prod Res Co, 1979-1991; sr res assoc, Exxon Prod Res Co, 1972-1979; res assoc, Exxon Prod Res Co, 1969-1972; sr res geologist, Esso Prod Res Co, 1965-1969; res geologist, Jersey Prod Res Co, 1956-1965; Geologist, US Geol Surv, 1950-1956. **Memberships:** Soc Petrol Engrs. **Research Statement & Publications:** Computer mapping and modeling programs; geology and performance of oil, gas and water reservoirs; well testing procedures and instrumentation. **Mailing Address:** 620 Fulton Ave N 406, Rockport, TX 78382-5722.

JOHNSON, CARROLL KENNETH, CRYSTALLOGRAPHY, APPLIED MATHEMATICS. **Personal Data:** b Greeley, Colo, September 18, 1929; m Carol; c Cindy, Valerie, Greg, Gary & Amy. **Education:** Colo State Univ, BS, 1955; Mass Inst Technol, PhD (biophys), 1959. **Honors & Awards:** Buerger Award, Am Crystallog Asn, 1997. **Professional Experience:** Consult; RETIRED; Vis scientist, Naval Res Lab, 1981; v is scientist, Stanford Comput Dept, 1975-1976; sr scientist comput chem, Chem Sci Div, Oak Ridge Nat Lab, 1962-1996; Am Cancer Soc res fel x-ray crystallog, Inst Cancer Res, Pa, 1959-1962; asst biophys, Mass Inst Technol, 1956-1959; a sst biol, Mass Inst Technol, 1955-1956. **Memberships:** Am Crystallog Asn (pres, 1977). **Research Statement & Publications:** Crystallographic topology; neutron diffraction; crystallography; automated graphics for illustrating crystal structures; crystallographic thermal-motion analysis; combinatorial chemistry; expert systems; machine vision engineering. **Mailing Address:** 212 Orchard Knob Rd, Clinton, TN 37716. **E-Mail:** johnsonckj@ornl.gov

JOHNSON, CECIL GRAY, INDUSTRIAL & SYSTEMS ENGINEERING. **Personal Data:** b Nanafalia, Ala, February 26, 1922; m 1948, Mary; c Gray W, Mark C & Celia (McDaniel). **Education:** Ga Inst Technol, BS, 1948 & 1949, MS, 1957. **Honors & Awards:** Distinguished Serv Award, Am Inst Indust Engrs. **Professional Experience:** PROF EMER, GA INST TECHNOL, as of 2005; prof indust & systs eng, Ga Inst Technol, as of 2004; chmn, 11E Heritage Task Force, 1987-1993; mem, 11E Heritage Task Force, 1986-1987; mem, 11E Fel Scholar Comt, 1985-1987; prin, Systs Study Rehab Serv Blind, State Ga, 1980-1983; prin, Prime DOC Commun Syst, Fulton County, Ga, 1980; prin, Atlanta Assessment Proj, Atlanta Pub Schs, HEW, 1976; partic, Stanford-Ames NASA-ASEE Educ Res Study, 1974; HEW, Univ Ga, 1969, Days Inns Am, Burch-Lowe, Crown-Zellerbach, Gulf States; consult, Delta Air Lines, 1960-; res assoc, Off Naval Res, Univ Calif, Los Angeles, 1959; Mgt & systs eng consult, 1955-; prof, GA Inst Technol, 1955-1991; ed-in-chief, J Am Inst Indust Engrs, 1955-1965; indust engr, Gen Shoe Corp, 1949-1950 & Am Art Metals Co, 1950-1955. **Memberships:** Fel Am Inst Indust Engrs (vpres 1965-1967); Nat Soc Prof Engrs. **Research Statement & Publications:** Human performance and organizational theory; educational systems, especially American universities; analysis and design methodology for complex systems; improving productivity from mental and physical activity, especially among university educated individuals. **Mailing Address:** 3211 Argonne Dr NW, Atlanta, GA 30305.

JOHNSON, CHARLES ANDREW, MATHEMATICS. **Personal Data:** b Chicago, Ill, May 8, 1915; m 1940, c 2. **Education:** Northern Ill Univ, BEd, 1937; Northwestern Univ, MA, 1940; Univ Kans, PhD (math), 1950. **Professional Experience:** PROF EMER, UNIV MO-ROLLA, as of 2005; res assoc, Argonne Nat Lab, 1962; instr, Univ Kans, 1948-1950; prof math, Univ Mo-Rolla, 1946-; teacher, Ill, 1940-1943; teacher & prin pub schs, Ill, 1938-1940. **Memberships:** Am Soc Eng Educ; Am Math Asn; Sigma Xi. **Research Statement & Publications:** Mathematical education. **Mailing Address:** Dept Math, Univ Mo, 326 Math Comp Sci Bldg, Rolla, MO 65409-0020.

JOHNSON, CHARLES B, FLUID MECHANICS. **Education:** NMex State Univ, BS, 1961; Wash Univ, MS, 1963. **Honorary Degrees:** DSc, Wash Univ, 1971. **Professional Experience:** PROF CHEM ENG, NMEX STATE UNIV, as of 2006. **Memberships:** Am Inst Aeronaut & Astronaut; Inst Elec Electronics Engrs. **Mailing Address:** NMEX State Univ, MSC 3805, Las Cruces, NM 88003. **E-Mail:** cjohnson@nmsu.edu

JOHNSON, C(HARLES) BRUCE, PHOTOELECTRONICS, DETECTORS & IMAGERS. **Personal Data:** b Sioux City, Iowa, August 5, 1935; m June; c Kimberly J & Kirsten J. **Education:** Iowa State Univ, BS, 1957; Univ Minn, Minneapolis, MSEE, 1963, PhD (elec eng), 1967. **Honors & Awards:** Fellow of the Institute of Electrical and Electronics Engineers in 1991 for contributions to both the theory and application of photoelectronics, image conversion and electron multiplication; Certificates of Recognition from NASA for "A Magnetically Focused Image Tube Employing an Opaque Photocathode, " 1974, "X-Ray Sensitive Oblique Imaging Device, " 1976, "Image Tube, " 1980; State of Indiana, Governor's Certificate of Appreciation Award, Indiana Corporation for Science and Technology, 1987"; "Laser Focus World, Commercial Technology Achievement Award, JAN94"; "Litton Industries Advanced Technology Achievement Award, 26MAY94" He received the "IEEE Third Millennium Medal in 2000 for Outstanding Achievements and Contributions". **Professional Experience:** Pres, Johnson Sci Group Inc, Phoenix Ariz, Consult, 1996-; tech dir, new prod develop, litton electron devices, Tempe, Ariz, 1991-1996; tech dir, Electro-Optical Prods Div, 1978-1991 & sr tech staff eng, Aerospace Div, 1991; prin engr, Int Tel & Telegraph Corp, Ft Wayne, 1974-1977; sr staff engr, Bendix Res Labs, 1970-1974; engr, RCA Electronics Components, 1967-1970; res fel, Univ Minn, 1963-1967; res asst gaseous electronics, Univ Minn, 1961-1963; Assoc scientist, Electronics Group, Gen Mills, Inc, 1958-1961. **Memberships:** Am Phys Soc; fel Inst Elec & Electronics Engrs; Optical Soc Am; Soc Photo-Optical Instrumentation; Am Astron Soc. **Research Statement & Publications:** Space-charge-effects in vacuum and gases; charged particle optics; electro-optical image transfer characteristics, especially modulation transfer function studies; high resolution image-intensifier and camera-tube development; charged particle transport in gases; high altitude instrumentation; infrared studies; electrical-optical sensor analysis; photon-counting imaging. **Mailing Address:** 15204 S 21st St, Phoenix, AZ 85048-9544. **Fax:** 480-759-7871. **E-Mail:** cbj@johnsonscientificgroup.com

JOHNSON, CHARLES C, JR, environmental engineering; deceased, see previous edition for last biography

JOHNSON, CHARLES EDWARD, ATOMIC PHYSICS. **Personal Data:** b Pennington Gap, Va, November 19, 1940; m 1970, c 2. **Education:** Yale Univ, BS, 1962, MS, 1965, PhD (physics), 1967. **Professional Experience:** PROF PHYSICS, NC STATE UNIV, 1983-; from asst prof to assoc prof, NC State Univ, 1973-1983; res physicist, Lawrence Radiation Lab, Univ Calif, Berkeley, 1967-1972. **Memberships:** Am Phys Soc. **Research Statement & Publications:** Measurement of the fundamental properties of free atoms and molecules using the techniques of optical pumping and atomic beam magnetic resonance. **Mailing Address:** Dept Physics, NC State Univ, Box 8202, Raleigh, NC 27695-8202. **Fax:** 919-515-7331. **E-Mail:** charles_johnson@ncsu.edu

JOHNSON, CHARLES F, MEDICINE, ELECTRON MICROSCOPY. **Personal Data:** b Chicago, Ill, September 15, 1927; m 1961, c 1. **Education:** Univ Chicago, PhB, 1949, MD, 1954; Am Bd Internal Med, dipl, 1962. **Professional Experience:** Head, Vet Admin Hosp, Indianapolis, 1971-; ASSOC PROF MED, IND UNIV-PURDUE UNIV, INDIANAPOLIS, 1967-; a sst head gastroenterol, Vet Admin Hosp, Indianapolis, 1967-1971; f rom instr to asst prof, Sch Med, Univ Chicago, 1958-1967; head sect gastroenterol, St Vincent's Hosp, Indianapolis, consult, Vet Admin Hosp, Indianapolis. **Memberships:** AAAS; Am Soc Cell Biologists; Electron Micros Soc Am. **Research Statement & Publications:** Electron microscopy of lipid absorption and various human gastrointestinal diseases. **Mailing Address:** 5654 N Pennsylvania St, Indianapolis, IN 46220.

JOHNSON, CHARLES HENRY, MATHEMATICAL STATISTICS. **Personal Data:** b Chicago, Ill, June 12, 1925; m 1948, c 3. **Education:** Bradley Univ, BA, 1949, MS, 1950; Okla State Univ, PhD (math), 1963. **Professional Experience:** PROF MATH & CHMN DEPT, UNIV WIS-STEVENS POINT, 1967-; from asst prof to assoc prof math & astron, DePauw Univ, 1955-1967; sect chief, Continental Casualty Co, 1952-1955; a sst math,

Univ Pittsburgh, 1950-1952. **Research Statement & Publications:** Astronomy. **Mailing Address:** 2755 S County Rd P, Stevens Point, WI 54481.

JOHNSON, CHARLES LESLIE, AEROSPACE. **Personal Data:** b Ashland, Ky, March 1, 1962; m 1988, Carol; c Carl Stuart & Leslie Arlene. **Education:** Transylvania Univ, BA, 1984; Vanderbilt Univ, MS, 1986. **Professional Experience:** AEROSPACE PHYSICIST, NASA-MARSHALL SPACE FLIGHT CTR, HUNTSVILLE, 1990-; consult, Gen Res Corp, 1990-1991; res physicist, Gen Res Corp, 1986-1990. **Memberships:** Am Inst Aeronaut & Astronaut; Nat Space Soc; World Future Soc; Am GeophysUnion. **Research Statement & Publications:** Contributed many articles to professional journals. **Mailing Address:** NASA Prog Develop PSOZ, Marshall Space Flight Ctr, Huntsville, AL 35812.

JOHNSON, CHARLES MINOR, PHYSICS, SYSTEM ANALYSIS. **Personal Data:** b Nashville, Tenn, May 31, 1925; m Anne; c Jane Clarke & Steve Aubrey. **Education:** Vanderbilt Univ, BE, 1944; Duke Univ, PhD (physics), 1951. **Honors & Awards:** Dept Army Medal Exceptional Civilian Serv, 1973. **Professional Experience:** SR PRIN ENGR, MITRE CORP, 1988-; prin scientist, Anser, 1986-1988; external adv, Ga Tech Res Inst, 1980-1985; consult, Develop & Readiness Command, US Army, 1976; dep dir, World Wide Mil Command & Control Syst Archit Develop, 1973-1986; sci adv, Joint Strategic Target Planning Staff, 1972-1981; dep safeguard syst mgr, Sci & Technol, Dept Army, 1967-1973; res mgr, IBM Corp, 1961-1967; res dir, Emerson Res Lab, 1960-1961; res mgr, Electronic Commun, Inc, 1956-1961; consult, Sperry-Rand Corp, 1955 & Eng Res & Develop Lab, US Army, 1959-; res scientist, Radiation Lab, Johns Hopkins Univ, 1953-1956; res assoc, Radiation Lab, Johns Hopkins Univ, 1951-1953. **Memberships:** Am Phys Soc; sr mem & life mem Inst Elec & Electronics Engrs. **Research Statement & Publications:** Microwave physics, ferrite devices, phased array radars, millimeter wave techniques, microwave spectroscopy; radiation scattering, lasers and optics; semiconductor devices; ballistic missile defense; command and control systems. **Mailing Address:** 3152 Gracefield Rd, Apt 516, Silver Spring, MD 20904. **E-Mail:** charlesj@mitre.org

JOHNSON, CHARLES NELSON, APPLIED PHYSICS. **Personal Data:** b Mt Hope, Kans, June 17, 1915; m 1967, Ruth; c Janet A (LaMotte), Diana G (Lee) & Charles B Jr. **Education:** Friends Univ, AB, 1938. **Professional Experience:** CONSULT PHYSICIST, ENVIRON RES INST MICH, SEARLE CONSORTIUM, 1974-; chief phys sci group, Countermine-Counter Intrusion Dept, 1971-1973; chief detection br, Intrusion, Detection & Sensor Lab, 1967-1971; supvry res physicist, US Army Engr Res & Develop Ctr, 1955-1967; sr physicist, Ballistic Instrumentation Dept, Naval Proving Ground, 1951-1955; sr physicist, Aviation Ord Dept, 1946-1951; physicist, Norfolk Navy Yard, Va, 1942-1946; physicist, Bur Ord, US Dept Navy, Wash, DC & Naval Operating Base, Norfolk, Va, 1941-1942; j r instr eng physics, Johns Hopkins Univ, 1938-1941. **Memberships:** Fel AAAS; Am Phys Soc; Sigma Xi. **Research Statement & Publications:** Interior and exterior ballistic measurements; weapons systems evaluation and counter-measures; barrier and intrusion detection systems; remote multiband sensor systems; land mines, concealed explosives, letter bombs and booby trap detectors. **Mailing Address:** 3100 N Oxford St, Arlington, VA 22207.

JOHNSON, CHARLES ROBERT, ORNAMENTAL HORTICULTURE. **Personal Data:** b Ft Collins, Colo, June 8, 1941; m 1964, c 2. **Education:** Colo State Univ, BS, 1964; Ore State Univ, PhD (hort physiol), 1970. **Honors & Awards:** Porter Henegar Res Award, Nurserymen's Asn, 1980. **Professional Experience:** RETIRED; prof horticulture, Wash State Univ, Vancouver Res & Extn Unit, beginning 1998; prof & chair, Dept Hort & Landscape Archit, Wash State Univ, 1990-1997; prof & head dept, Dept Hort, Univ Ga, 1985-1990; assoc prof, Univ Fla, 1980-1984; bd dir, Int Plant Propagators Soc, 1980-1982; res & teaching ornamental hort, Univ Fla, 1973-1980; res & teaching, Dept Hort, Clemson Univ, 1970-1973; res floricult, K Stormly Hansen Greenhouses, Copenhagen, Denmark, 1964-1965. **Memberships:** Am Soc Hort Sci; Int Plant Propagators Soc. **Research Statement & Publications:** Physiological aspects of plant-soil microbial symbiosis, growth and develpoment, stress physiology and urban horticulture. **Mailing Address:** Vancouver Res & Extn Unit, Wash State Univ, 1919 NE 78th St, Vancouver, WA 98665. **Fax:** 360-576-6032.

JOHNSON, CHARLES ROYAL, ALGEBRA, APPLIED MATHEMATICS. **Personal Data:** b Elkhart, Ind, January 28, 1948. **Education:** Northwestern Univ, BA, 1969; Calif Inst Technol, PhD (math, econ), 1972. **Honors & Awards:** Award Outstanding Sci Achievement Math Sci, Wash Acad Sci, 1976; Va Outstanding Fac Award, State Coun Higher Educ Virginial, 2001. **Professional Experience:** PROF MATH, COL WILLIAM & MARY, 1987-; prof math sci, Clemson Univ, 1985-1987; consult, Icase, 1982-; vis staff mem, Los Alamos Sci Lab, 1974-; res prof appl math & econ, Inst Phys Sci & Technol, Univ Md, College Park, 1974-1984; consult, Appl Math Div, Nat Bur Stand, 1974-1982; res assoc fel math, Appl Math Div, Nat Bur Standards, 1972-1974. **Memberships:** Am Math Soc; Soc Indust & Appl Math; Math Asn Am; Int Linear Algebra Soc. **Research Statement & Publications:** Matrix analysis and applications; combinatorics; mathematical economics; combinatorial matrix analysis, eigenvalues, inequalities and norms. **Mailing Address:** Dept Math, Col William & Mary, Jones Hall 102C PO Box 8795, Williamsburg, VA 23187-8795. **Fax:** 757-221-7400. **E-Mail:** crjohnso@math.wm.edu

JOHNSON, CHARLES SIDNEY, PHYSICAL CHEMISTRY. **Personal Data:** b Albany, Ga, March 7, 1936; m 1958, Ellen; c David M & Daniel C. **Education:** Ga Inst Technol, BS, 1958; Mass Inst Technol, PhD (phys chem), 1961. **Professional Experience:** M A SMITH, PROF CHEM, UNIV NC, CHAPEL HILL, 1988-; dir Grad Studies Chem, Univ NC, 1975-1980; John Simon Guggenheim Found fel, 1972-1973; ed bd, J Magnetic Resonance, 1971-; prof Chem, Univ NC, Chapel Hill, 1967-1988; Alfred P Sloan Found res fel, 1966-1972; from asst prof to assoc prof phys chem, Yale Univ, 1962-1967; instr Phy Chem, 1962; Nat Acad Sci-Nat Res Coun fel, 1961-1962. **Memberships:** Fel AAAS; fel Am Phys Soc; Am Chem Soc. **Research Statement & Publications:** Nuclear magnetic resonance; spin relaxation; chemical rate processes; laser light scattering; electrophoretic nuclear magnetic resonance; diffusion ordered nuclear magnetic resonance. **Mailing Address:** Dept Chem, Univ NC, Kenan Labs, Chapel Hill, NC 27599-3290. **Fax:** 919-962-2388. **E-Mail:** charles_johnson@unc.edu

JOHNSON, CHRIS ALAN, PSYCHOPHYSICS, PHYSIOLOGICAL OPTICS. **Personal Data:** b Roseburg, Ore, October 1, 1949; m 1971, Debra; c Kristin & Matthew. **Education:** Univ Ore, BA, 1970; Pa State Univ, MSc, 1972, PhD (psychol), 1974. **Honors & Awards:** Distinguished Serv Award, 1987, Honor Award, Am Acad Ophthal, 1988. **Professional Experience:** RES CHAIR, ORE LIONS ANDERSON, 1999-; DIR, DIAG RES & SR SCIENTIST, DEVERS EYE INST, 1997-; prof ophthal, Univ Calif, Davis, 1989-1997; NIH fels, 1978; res fel, Univ Calif, Davis, 1977-1978; res fel ophthal, Univ Fla, 1975-1977; Nat Eye Inst, NIH fels, 1975 & 1977; res asst psychol, Univ Ore & Pa State Univ, 1970-1975. **Memberships:** Asn Res Vision & Ophthal; Optical Soc Am; Int Perimetric Soc; Am Acad Ophthal; Am Acad Optometry; Optical Soc Am. **Research Statement & Publications:** Visual psychophysics, analysis of the accommodation mechanism, examination of peripheral visual functions and development and adaptation of psychophysical tests to quantitative perimetry and visual field testing; night vision; vision and driving. **Mailing Address:** OR Lions Anderson-Chenoweth-Ross Vision Res, 1225 NE 2nd Ave, Portland, OR 97232. **Fax:** 503-413-5179. **E-Mail:** pobox@discoveriesinsight.org

JOHNSON, CHRIS E, MATHEMATICS. **Education:** Univ Pa, BSE, 1983, MA, 1988, PhD (geol), 1989. **Professional Experience:** ASSOC PROF, DEPT CIVIL & ENVIRON ENG, SYRACUSE UNIV, as of 2006. **Memberships:** Soil Sci Soc Am; Brit Soc Soil Sci; Am Geophys Union. **Mailing Address:** Dept Civil & Environ Eng, Syracuse Univ, Syracuse, NY 13244. **Fax:** 315-443-1243. **E-Mail:** cejohns@mailbox.syr.edu

JOHNSON, CHRISTOPHER R, SCIENTIFIC COMPUTING, SCIENTIFIC VISUALIZATION. **Personal Data:** b Kansas City, Kans, January 17, 1960; m Katherine. **Education:** Wright State Univ, BS, 1982; Univ Utah, MS, 1984, PhD (biophys), 1989. **Honors & Awards:** Whitaker Award, 1991; First Award, NIH, 1992; A C Suhren Jr Lectr, Tulane Univ, 1993; Dept Energy Computational Sci Award, 1997; Par Excellence Award, Univ Utah Alumni Asn, 1997; Presidential Teaching Scholar Award, Univ Utah, 1997; Governor's Medal for Sci & Technol, Gov Michael Leavitt of Utah. **Professional Experience:** CO-DIR, CTR INTEGRATIVE BIOMED COMPUT, as of 2005; FAC MEM, COMPUT ENG & SCi PROG, as of 2005; FAC MEM, BRAIN INST, as of 2005; CO-FOUNDER, VISUAL INFLUENCE INC, as of 2005; CO-ED, VISUALIZATION HANDBOOK, as of 2005; DISTINGUISHED PROF COMPUT SCI, UNIV UTAH, 2003-; ADJ PROF PHYSICS, UNIV UTAH, 2002-; RES PROF BIOENG, UNIV UTAH, 2002-; prof Comput Sci, Univ Utah, 2001-2003; DIR, SCI COMPUT & IMAGING INST, UNIV UTAH, 2000-; DIR, NIH CTR BIOELECTRIC FIELD MODELING, STIMULATION, & VISUALIZATION, 2000-; assoc prof comput sci, Univ Utah, 1996-2001; assoc chm comput sci, Univ Utah, 1996-1997; res consult, Smith & Nephew Res Ctr, 1995-1996; pres fac fel, NSF, 1995; Nat Young Investr Award, NSF, 1994; res asst prof physics, Univ Utah, 1993-1996; asst prof, Univ Utah, 1993-1996; adj asst prof bioeng, Univ Utah, 1992-1996; res asst prof comput sci, Univ Utah, 1992-1993; patent consult, Vanderbilt Univ, 1992-1993; adj asst prof math, Univ Utah, 1991-1996; res asst prof, Univ Utah, 1990-1992; res assoc internal med, Univ Utah, 1989-1990; asst prof physics, Westminster Col, 1985-1989; eng physicist, Advan Technol Div, 1984-1985. **Memberships:** Asn Comput Mach; Inst Elec & Electronics Engrs Comput Soc; Soc Math Biol; Soc Indust & Appl Math; Biomed Eng Soc; Am Inst Physics. **Research Statement & Publications:** Scientific computing; computational steering, inverse and imaging problems; adaptive methods for partial differential equations; automatic mesh generation, numerical analysis, large scale computational problems in medicine and scientific visualization. **Mailing Address:** Univ Utah, 3490 Merrill Eng Bldg, Salt Lake City, UT 84112-1107. **Fax:** 801-585-6513. **E-Mail:** crj@sci.utah.edu

JOHNSON, CLARENCE DANIEL, systematic entomology, ecology; deceased, see previous edition for last biography

JOHNSON, CLARENCE EUGENE, ENGINEERING, AGRICULTURE. **Personal Data:** b Elk City, Okla, November 1, 1941. **Education:** Okla State Univ, BS, 1963; Iowa State Univ, MS, 1968, PhD (agr eng), 1969. **Professional Experience:** PROF EMER, BIOSYSTEMS ENG, COL AGR, AUBURN UNIV, as of 2001; prof agr eng, Auburn Univ, beginning 1979; agr engr, Columbia Plateum Conserv Res Ctr, USDA Agr Res Serv, Ore, 1977-1979; assoc prof, SDak State Univ, 1970-1977; instr agr eng, Iowa State Univ, 1964-1969. **Memberships:** Am Soc Agr Engrs; Nat Soc Prof Engrs; Sigma Xi; Int Soil Tillage Res Orgn. **Research Statement & Publications:** Soil dynamics; tillage and traction; harvesting systems; machinery system simulation; similitude. **Mailing Address:** Dept Agr Eng, Auburn Univ, Auburn, AL 36849-5417. **Fax:** 334-844-3530. **E-Mail:** cej@eng.auburn.edu

JOHNSON, CLARK E, JR, MAGNETIC RECORDING. **Personal Data:** b Minneapolis, Minn, August 3, 1930; div, c 6. **Education:** Univ Minn, Minneapolis, BS, 1950, MS, 1961. **Professional Experience:** ASSOC DIR, RES PROGS, MASS INST TECHNOL, as of 2002; DIR, MASTER COMMUN GROUP, 1996-; PRES, TECHNOLOGIES, 1995-; pres, USA-Nat Host, 1994-1998; pres, Card Systs Testing Labs, 1990-1996; chmn bd dirs, Appl Info Systs, 1989-1994 & Rastech, Inc, 1989-1994; cong sci fel, 1988; dir, Magnum Technol, & Megabyte Storage Systs, 1987-1990; CONSULT, 1985-; pres, Magnetics Soc, 1983-1984; pres & chmn, Vertmag Systs Corp, 1981-1985; vpres, Magnetics Soc, 1981-1982; dir, Sciencare Corp, 1977-1984; dir, res & develop, Buckeye Int, Inc, 1977-1980; finance comt chmn, Magnetics Soc, 1975-1980; pres, Micro-Commun Corp, 1972-1977; consult physicist, Graham Magnetics Inc, 1968-1974; vpres eng, Vibrac Corp Div, USM Corp, 1967-1972; vpres, Minnetech Labs, 1963-1966; pres, Telostat Corp, 1961-1963; pres res & develop, Leyghton-Paige Corp, 1959-1961; sr physicist, Cent Res Labs, Minn Mining & Mfg Co, 1950-1959; dir & tech adv, Trans Data Syst. **Memberships:** fel Inst Elec & Electronics Engrs, Pres Magnetics Soc, 1983-1984; Treas, 1973-1982. **Research Statement & Publications:** Magnetic theory; magnetic recording and recording materials; fine particle magnetic theory; electromagnetic transducers and devices; electro-optic transducers and devices; new techniques for recording information using magnetic properties of materials; perpendicular magnetic recording. **Mailing Address:** PO Box 50116, Minneapolis, MN 55405. **Fax:** 612-922-8820. **E-Mail:** clark@fcomm.net

JOHNSON, CLELAND HOWARD, nuclear physics; deceased, see previous edition for last biography

JOHNSON, CLIFFORD VICTOR, STRING THEORY. **Personal Data:** b London, Eng, March 1968. **Education:** Univ London, BSc, 1989; Univ Southampton, PhD (physics), 1992. **Honors & Awards:** Maxwell Prize and Medal, Institute of Physics (UK), 2005. **Professional Experience:** PROF, DEPT PHYS & ASTRON, UNIV SOUTHERN CALIF, as of 2003; Prof, dept math sciences, Univ Durham (UK), 2002-2003; Sen. lect & reader., dept math sciences, Univ Durham (UK), 2000-2002; asst prof, dept phys & astron, Univ KY, 1997-1999; Res assoc, Inst Theoret Physics, Univ Calif, Santa Barbara, 1995-1997; lectr phys, Princeton Univ, 1995; Res assoc, Inst Advan Study, Princeton, 1992-1994. **Research Statement & Publications:** Origins and mechanisms underlying matter and fundamental interactions at the most basic level; particle physics and quantum gravity; black holes and cosmology; string theory. **Mailing Address:** Dept Phys & Astron, Univ Southern Calif, Los Angeles, CA 90089-0484. **Fax:** 213-740-6653. **E-Mail:** johnson1@usc.edu

JOHNSON, CONOR DEANE, ACTIVE & PASSIVE VIBRATION SUPPRESSION. **Personal Data:** b Charlottesville, Va, April 20, 1943; m 1966, Laura; c William & Catherine. **Education:** Va Polytech Inst, BS, 1965; Univ Clemson, MS, 1967, PhD (eng mech), 1969. **Honors & Awards:** Struct & Mat Award, Am Soc Mech Engrs, 1981. **Professional Experience:** PRES, CSA ENG INC, 1982-; vpres, San Carlos, Calif, 1981-1982; prog mgr, Aerospace Struct Info & Anal Ctr, 1975-1982; prin engr, San Carlos, Calif, 1975-1981; sr struct analyst, Anamet Labs, Dayton, Ohio, 1973-1975; fel, NDEA, 1967-1968. **Memberships:** Am Inst Aeronaut & Astronaut; Am Soc Mech Engrs; Sigma Xi. **Research Statement & Publications:** Modal strain energy method for damping analysis using finite element techniques; combined system analysis techniques (integration of finite element techniques, damping analysis, component mode synthesis, other engineer disciplines, experimental data); Published Over 30 articles and granted several patents. **Mailing Address:** 2565 Leghorn St, Mtain View, CA 94043-1613. **Fax:** 650-210-9001. **E-Mail:** conor.johnson@csaEng.com

JOHNSON, CORINNE LESSIG, DEVELOPMENT INFORMATION SYSTEMS, SCIENCE EDUCATION SOFTWARE. **Personal Data:** b Wilmington, Del, October 29, 1938. **Education:** Wellesley Col, AB, 1960; Univ Rochester, MS, 1964, PhD (biol), 1969. **Professional Experience:** Mgr, admin serv, Develop Comput Serv, 1991-1996; prog chair, New Eng Chap, Asn Women Sci, 1990-1991; training coordr, educ technol database, Harvard Univ, 1986-1991; temp proj dir, educ technol database, Harvard Univ, 1985-1986; software specialist, Gibco Labs, 1984-1985; biol ed & gen mgr, Edutech Inc, 1981-1983; treas, Alliance Independent Scholars, 1980-1985; res assoc microbiol, Sch Med, Boston Univ, 1978-1979; asst prof biol, Carleton Col, 1977-1978; vis asst prof biol, Vassar Col, 1975-1977; asst prof microbiol, Dent Ctr, NY Univ, 1975; assoc res scientist & instr biochem, Dent Ctr, NY Univ, 1972-1974; fel, Albert Einstein Col Med, 1970-1972; Sci Res Coun res asst & fel biochem, Univ Leicester, 1969-1970. **Memberships:** AAAS; Am Soc Microbiol; Asn Women Sci; Asn Comput. **Mailing Address:** 36 Highland Ave No 48, Cambridge, MA 02139.

JOHNSON, CRAIG M, MATHEMATICS. **Education:** Purdue Univ, PhD. **Professional Experience:** PROF, DEPT MATHS, MARYWOOD UNIV, as of 2005. **Mailing Address:** Marywood Univ, 2300 Adams Ave, Scranton, PA 18509. **Fax:** 717-348-6020. **E-Mail:** johnsonc@marywood.edu

JOHNSON, CURTIS ALAN, MATERIAL SCIENCE, CERAMIC SCIENCE. **Personal Data:** b Johnstown, Pa, January 22, 1948; m 1969, Michele; c Gregory M & Eric D. **Education:** Pa State Univ, BS, 1969, PhD (metall), 1974. **Professional Experience:** STAFF SCIENTIST CERAMICS, GEN ELEC CORP RES & DEVELOP CTR, 1973-. **Memberships:** Am Ceramics Soc; Am Soc Testing & Mats. **Research Statement & Publications:** Mechanical and physical properties of metals and ceramics, in particular high temperature structural ceramics; fabrication methods; densification processes and phase transformations of ceramics. **Mailing Address:** Gen Elec Corp Res & Develop Bldg, 1 Res Ctr K1 Mb 187, Schenectady, NY 12309.

JOHNSON, CURTIS ALLEN, AGRICULTURAL ENGINEERING. **Personal Data:** b Mead, Nebr, April 3, 1917; m 1954, c 2. **Education:** Univ Nebr, BSc, 1940; Iowa State Univ, MS, 1955. **Professional Experience:** EMER PROF AGR ENG, UNIV MASS, AMHERST, 1979-; assoc prof, Univ Mass, Amherst, 1957-1979; agr workshop adv, US State Dept, Int Coop Admin, Pakistan, 1955-1957; instr agr eng, Iowa State Univ, 1950-1955; prin, Friendsville Acad, Tenn, 1949-1950; asst prof agr eng, Univ Del, 1946-1948; test engr, Tractor Testing Lab, Int Harvester Co, 1940-1941. **Memberships:** Am Soc Agr Engrs. **Research Statement & Publications:** Relationship of milking machines to mastitis; liquid handling of agricultural wastes; world-wide water resources planning; farm homes and buildings; design of economical houses for minimal waste of structural materials and fossil fuel energy inputs and storage of summer time heat for use in winter, with concurrent storage of cold (as ice) for use to air condition homes developed. **Mailing Address:** 51 Brainerd St, Mt Holly, NJ 08060.

JOHNSON, DALE A, PHYSICAL CHEMISTRY, INORGANIC CHEMISTRY. **Personal Data:** b Chicago, Ill, November 18, 1937; m 1960, Evelyn; c Keith & Scott. **Education:** Univ Ill, BS, 1959; Northwestern Univ, PhD (chem), 1964. **Professional Experience:** PROF CHEM, UNIV ARK, FAYETTEVILLE, 1973-; from asst prof to assocprof, Univ Ark, Fayetteville, 1963-1973. **Memberships:** Am Chem Soc. **Research Statement & Publications:** Thermal and photochemical reactions of transition metal complexes; reactions of coordinated molecules; spectroscopy of inorganic compounds. **Mailing Address:** Dept Chem, Univ Ark, Fayetteville, AR 72701-1202.

JOHNSON, DALE E, TAXONOMY & EVOLUTION OF PLANTS, BIBLIOGRAPHY & HISTORY OF BOTANY. **Personal Data:** b Griffith, Ind, January 26, 1949; m 1991, Marie. **Education:** Grinnell Col, BA, 1971; Univ Calif, Berkeley, PhD (bot), 1978. **Professional Experience:** BOT ED, TIMBER PRESS INC, as of 2006; RESIDENT SCIENTIST, TIMBER PRESS INC, as of 2006; ed dir, Timber Press Inc, beginning 1991; cur bot lit, Mo Bot Garden, 1985-1991; ed supvr & actg prod mgr, Academic Press Inc, 1982-1985; Hunt fel, Hunt Inst Bot Doc, Carnegie Mellon Univ, 1978-1979; co-ed, Index to Plant Chromosome Numbers, Mo Bot Garden. **Memberships:** Am Soc Plant Taxonomists; Int Asn Plant Taxon; Soc Hist Nat Hist; Bot Soc Am. **Research Statement & Publications:** History and bibliography of botany; taxonomy and floristics of plants, especially Compositae. **Mailing Address:** Timber Press Inc, Haseltine Bldg, 133 SW Second Ave Ste 450, Portland, OR 97204. **Fax:** 503-227-3070. **E-Mail:** dale@timberpress.com

JOHNSON, DALE HOWARD, CONSUMER PRODUCT DEVELOPMENT, COSMETIC CHEMISTRY. **Personal Data:** b Los Angeles, Calif, February 23, 1945; m 1977, c 3. **Education:** Univ Redlands, BS, 1966; Northwestern Univ, PhD (org chem), 1971. **Professional Experience:** RETIRED; mgr prod develop, Hair Care, Helen Curtis Inc, 1990-1997; sr group leader, Toiletries, Amway Corp, 1988-1990; bus tech mgr, James River Corp, 1985-1987; sect head oral hyg, Vicks Div Res, Richardson-Vicks Inc, 1981-1984; mgr prod develop, Helene Curtis Indust Inc, 1977-1981; sect head, Appln Lab, Armak Indust Chem, Div Akzona Inc, 1973-1977; res chemist toiletries, Alberto-Culver Co, 1971-1973. **Memberships:** Am Chem Soc; Soc Cosmetic Chemists; Sigma Xi. **Research Statement & Publications:** Development of personal care products including hair, skin, oral hygiene, cleansers, fine fragrances and treatment products; cosmetic, toiletries and over the counter topical drug type product development. **Mailing Address:** 1505 Lark Lane, Naperville, IL 60565-1342. **E-Mail:** daledoc@eart.link.net

JOHNSON, DANIEL LLOYD, BIOGEOGRAPHY, INSECT ECOLOGY. **Personal Data:** b Yankton, SDak, September 30, 1953; m Pamela; c Sam, Eric & Margaret & Lucy. **Education:** Univ Sask, BSc, 1978; Univ BC, MSc, 1980, PhD (plant sci, ecology), 1983. **Honors & Awards:** C Gordon Hewitt Award in Can Entom, Entom Soc Can, 1992; Issac Walton Killam Scholar. **Professional Experience:** RES SCIENTIST, AGR CAN RES STA, ALTA, as of 2002; proj monitor, Can Int Develop Agency; proj mgr, Alta Res Coun; adj assoc prof biogeog, Dept Geog, Univ Lethbridge, Alta. **Memberships:** Entomol Soc Can; Soc Environ Toxical Chem; Am Inst Biol Sci (exec). **Research Statement & Publications:** Environmental health and ecology of grassland agroecosystems; grassland insect ecology and control. **Mailing Address:** Agr Can Res Ctr, PO Box 3000, Lethbridge, AB T1J 4B1, Can. **Fax:** 403-382-3156. **E-Mail:** johnsondl@em.agr.ca

JOHNSON, DANIEL P, MATHEMATICS. **Education:** Univ Wis, PhD, 1983. **Professional Experience:** ASST PROF, ROCHESTER INST TECHNOL, as of 2005. **Mailing Address:** Rochester Inst Technol, Golisano Bldg, Rochester, NY 14623-5608. **Fax:** 585-475-4935. **E-Mail:** dlgipk@rit.edu

JOHNSON, DARELL JAMES, STATISTICAL MECHANICS, FLUIDS. **Personal Data:** b Brooklyn, NY, December 22, 1949; m 1973, c 3. **Education:** Univ Calif, Riverside, BS, 1971, MS, 1972, PhD (math), 1973; Mass Inst Technol, PhD (physics), 1986. **Professional Experience:** ASST PROF PHYSICS, MO WESTERN STATE COL, 1990-; asst prof math, Tex Tech Univ, 1986-1990; asst prof, NMex State Univ, 1975-1979; instr math, Mass Inst Technol, 1973-1975. **Memberships:** Am Phys Soc; Am Math Soc; Soc Indust Appl Math; Am Astron Soc; AAAS. **Research Statement & Publications:** Theoretical investigation of a strongly interacting many body model system using predominately numerical simulation experimental techniques. **Mailing Address:** Dept Physics, MO Western State Col, 4525 Downs Dr Rm 113B Sci & Math Bldg, St Joseph, MO 64507. **E-Mail:** johnd@mwsc.edu

JOHNSON, DAVID, HIGH ENERGY PHYSICS. **Personal Data:** b Newark, NJ, September 3, 1944. **Education:** Univ Calif, Berkeley, AB, 1966; Iowa State Univ, PhD (high energy physics), 1972. **Professional Experience:** PHYSICIST & UNIV RES ASSOC, FERMI NAT ACCELERATOR LAB, 1973-; assoc & instr physics, Iowa State Univ, Ames Lab, US-AEC, 1972-1973; res assoc & instr physics, Iowa State Univ, Ames Lab, USAEC, 1967-1972. **Memberships:** AAAS; Sigma Xi; Am Phys Soc. **Research Statement & Publications:** High energy accelarator design and research; high energy experimental research. **Mailing Address:** Acceleration Div, Fermi Nat Accelerator Lab, PO Box 500, Batavia, IL 60510.

JOHNSON, DAVID ALFRED, PHYSICAL CHEMISTRY OF SOLUTIONS, EXPERIMENTAL & THEORETICAL STUDIES OF SOLIDS. **Personal Data:** b Muskegon, Mich, March 13, 1938; m 1960, c 3. **Education:** Greenville Col, AB, 1960; La State Univ, PhD (chem), 1966. **Professional Experience:** Fac fel, Argonne Nat Lab, 1990; Am Chem Soc-PFR fel, 1985 & 1986; NASA fel & Nat Aerospace Serv Asn fel, 1980-1982; fel, Dept Chem, La State Univ, 1970-1971; PROF CHEM, SPRING ARBOR COL, 1966-; instr, La State Univ, 1964-1965; asst prof chem, Greenville Col, 1962-1964; chemist, Pet Milk Res Labs, 1960. **Memberships:** Am Chem Soc; Sigma Xi. **Research Statement & Publications:** Physical chemistry of electrolytes; five coordinate complexes of transition metals; thermodynamics of solid state. **Mailing Address:** Dept Chem, Spring Arbor Col, St 14, Spring Arbor, MI 49283. **Fax:** 517-750-2108. **E-Mail:** djohnson@admin.arbor.edu

JOHNSON, DAVID ANDREW, BIOCHEMISTRY, PROTEOLYTIC ENZYMES & THEIR INHIBITORS. **Personal Data:** b Memphis, Tenn, 1944; m 1967, Judith; c 3. **Education:** Univ Memphis, BS, 1967, PhD (chem), 1973; Univ Ga (post-doc), 1973-1976. **Honors & Awards:** ETSU Foundation Research Award 1987 Visiting Professor, Strangeways Laboratory, Cambridge; Oxford University, Southampton University. **Professional Experience:** PROF BIOCHEM, E TENN STATE UNIV, QUILLEN COL MED, 1990-; from asst prof to assoc prof, James H Quillen Col Med, 1978-1990; asst biochemist, Univ Ga, 1976-1978; Indust consult. **Memberships:** AAAS; Am Soc Biochem & Molecular Biol; Sigma Xi; Protein Soc. **Research Statement & Publications:** Biochemistry; proteolytic enzymes and their inhibitors; mast cell proteases; human blood proteins. **Mailing Address:** Dept Biochem & Molecular Biol, E TENN STATE UNIV, Quillen Col Med, Johnson City, TN 37614. **Fax:** 423-439-2030. **E-Mail:** davidj@etsu.edu

JOHNSON, DAVID B, DYNAMICS & CONTROL, FLUID FLOW SIMULATION. **Personal Data:** b Big Spring, Tex, January 11, 1940; m Sara; c Jennifer L, William P & Molly K. **Education:** Univ Tex, Austin, BSME, 1963, MSME, 1964; Stanford Univ, PhD (eng mech), 1968. **Professional Experience:** PROF MECH ENG, SOUTHERN METHODIST UNIV, 1983-; exec vpres, J Y Taylor Mfg, 1981-1982; assoc prof eng sci & mech, Iowa State Univ, 1975-1981; a ssoc prof mech eng, Southern Methodist Univ, 1968-1973. **Memberships:** Am Soc Mech Engrs; Am Soc Eng Educ; Soc Mfg Engrs. **Research Statement & Publications:** Dynamics; vibrations; vehicle dynamics; free surface fluid flow simulation. **Mailing Address:** Dept Mech Eng, Southern Methodist Univ, Dallas, TX 75275-0337. **E-Mail:** dbj@engr.smu.edu

JOHNSON, DAVID BARTON, BIO-ORGANIC CHEMISTRY, BIO-ANALYTICAL CHEMISTRY. **Personal Data:** b Providence, RI, June 5, 1946; m 1970, c 3. **Education:** Univ RI, BS, 1969; Duke Univ, PhD (org chem), 1975. **Professional Experience:** RES SCIENTIST II, UPJOHN CO, 1980-; sr chemist bio-org chem, Midwest Res Inst, 1976-1980; NIH fel biochem pharmacol, Med Sch, Duke Univ, 1974-1976. **Memberships:** Am Chem Soc; Sigma Xi. **Research Statement & Publications:** Bio-organic chemistry dealing in the synthesis, biosynthesis, analysis, and structural elucidation of xenobiotic metabolites; analysis of metabolites in biological samples; in vitro studies of xenobiotic metabolizing enzymes; radiochemical synthesis. **Mailing Address:** 3099 Maine Ave, Perry, OH 44081-9566.

JOHNSON, DAVID EDSEL, ELECTRICAL ENGINEERING, APPLIED MATHEMATICS. **Personal Data:** b Chatham, La, August 16, 1927; m 1959, Frances; c Stephen, Nancy, Sandra & Katherine. **Education:** La Tech Univ, BS & BA, 1949; Auburn Univ, MS, 1952, PhD (math), 1958. **Professional Experience:** PROF EMER MATH, BIRMINGHAM-SOUTHERN COL, as of 2004; prof math, Birmingham-Southern Col, 1983-1994; prof elec eng, LaState Univ, 1962-1983; NSF fac fel, Stanford Univ, 1961-1962; assoc prof math, La State Univ, 1954-1962; mathematician, Nat Bur Stand, 1952; draftsman, La Power & Light Co, 1949-1950. **Memberships:** Sigma Xi. **Research Statement & Publications:** Electric circuits and systems. **Mailing Address:** Div Sci & Math, Birmingham-Southern Col, Birmingham, AL 35254.

JOHNSON, DAVID GREGORY, ENDOCRINOLOGY, CLINICAL PHARMACOLOGY. **Personal Data:** b Belvidere, Ill, July 11, 1940; m 1965, Inger; c Elisabeth, Lars &Leif. **Education:** Yale Univ, BA, 1962; Dartmouth Med Sch, BMed Sci, 1964; Harvard Univ, MD, 1967. **Professional Experience:** PROF MED & PROF PHARMACOL, HEALTH SCI CTR, UNIV ARIZ, as of 1999; ASSOC ED, LIFE SCI, 1981-; assoc prof, Dept Internal Med, Health Sci Ctr, Univ Ariz, 1978-1982; from asst prof to assoc prof, Univ Wash, 1973-1978; fel, Univ Wash, 1971-1973; res assoc, NIH, 1969-1971; resident, Univ Calif, San Francisco, 1967-1969. **Memberships:** Am Diabetes Asn; Am Soc Pharmacol & Exp Therapeut; Endocrine Soc; Am Fedn Clin Res. **Research Statement & Publications:** Experimental and clinical research regarding diabetes, pancreatic endocrine secretion, gastro intestinal hormones and catecholamine physiology; development and testing of drugs, particularly for the treatment of diabetes. **Mailing Address:** Dept Pharm, Univ Ariz, PO Box 389, Tucson, AZ 85721. **Fax:** 512-237-2437. **E-Mail:** djohnson@sprd1.mdacc.tmc.edu

JOHNSON, DAVID HARLEY, HEAT TRANSFER, FLUID MECHANICS. **Personal Data:** b Brooklyn, NY, May 31, 1941; m 1961, c 2. **Education:** Purdue Univ, BS, 1963, MS, 1964; Cornell Univ, PhD (appl physics), 1975. **Professional Experience:** Flow Industs Inc, 1981-; GROUP MGR, SOLAR ENERGY RES INST, 1980-; Consult, Appl Physics Lab, Johns Hopkins Univ, 1979-1980; PRIN ENGR, SOLAR ENERGY RES INST, 1979-; asst group leader, Appl Physics Lab, Johns Hopkins Univ, 1978-1979; sr staff physicist, Appl Physics Lab, Johns Hopkins Univ, 1973-1979; teaching asst statist thermodyn, Cornell

Univ, 1970-1972; adj instr hydraul, Tompkins-Cortland Community Col, 1969-1970; s taff mem, Sandia Corp, 1964-1967. **Memberships:** Am Soc Mech Engrs; Sigma Xi. **Research Statement & Publications:** Dynamics of stratified fluids in the ocean and in solar ponds; direct contact heat transfer phenomena important to the design of open-cycle thermal energy conversion power plants and other heat exchangers. **Mailing Address:** 9658 Masterworks Dr, Vienna, VA 22181-6131.

JOHNSON, DAVID LEE, SOFTWARE SYSTEMS. **Personal Data:** b Benson, Minn, April 28, 1946; m 1976, c 1. **Education:** Univ Minn, BS, 1964; Syracuse Univ, MS, 1971; Univ Minn, PhD (math), 1976. **Professional Experience:** VPRES & GEN MGR, GEN DYNAMICS CORP, as of 2001; DIR, ELEC SYST, GEN DYNAMICS CORP, 1997-; prog mgr, Gte Govt Systs, beginning1993; dept prog mgr, Gte Govt Systs, 1990-1993; eng orgn mgr, Gte Govt Systs, 1988-1990; dept mgr, Nat Ctr Systs Directorate, 1987-1988; dept software eng mgr, Rockville, 1986-1987; dept mgr, Hughes Aircraft Co, 1985-1986; asst dept mgr, Radar Systs Group, 1984-1985; sr mem tech staff, El Sequndo, 1981-1984; mem tech staff, Logicon Inc, 1980-1981; asst prof math, Univ Southern Calif, 1978-1980; asst prof math, Univ Ark, 1980-1981; John Wesley Young res instr, Dartmouth Col, 1976-1978. **Memberships:** Am Math Soc; Math Asn Am; Inst Elec & Electronics Engrs. **Research Statement & Publications:** Functional analysis dealing with distribution theory; continuous group representations on general locally compact groups. **Mailing Address:** Gen Dynamics Corp, 2941 Fairview Park Dr Ste 100, Falls Church, VA 22042. **Fax:** 703-876-3125.

JOHNSON, DAVID LINTON, THEORETICAL SOLID STATE PHYSICS. **Personal Data:** b Chicago, Ill, July 9, 1945; div, c Kelsey & Sean. **Education:** Univ Notre Dame, BS, 1967; Univ Chicago, MS, 1969, PhD (physics), 1974. **Professional Experience:** PROG MGR, SCHLUMBERGER-DOLL RES CTR, 2001-; SCI ADV, SCHLUMBERGER DOLL RES CTR, 1988-; res physicist, Schlumberger Doll Res Ctr, 1979-1988; consult, GTE Labs, 1979; asst prof physics, Northeastern Univ, 1976-1979; fel, Ames Lab, Iowa State Univ, 1974-1976; fel physics, Michelson Lab, Naval Weapons Ctr, 1972-1974. **Memberships:** fel Am Phys Soc; Acoust Soc Am; Soc Exp Geol; Am Geophys Union. **Mailing Address:** Schlumberger Doll Res Ctr, Old Quarry Rd, Ridgefield, CT 06877-4108. **E-Mail:** djohnson@ridgefield.sdr.slb.co

JOHNSON, D(AVID) LYNN, SINTERING, PROCESSING. **Personal Data:** b Provo, Utah, April 2, 1934; m 1959, c 5. **Education:** Univ Utah, BS, 1956, PhD (ceramic eng), 1962. **Honors & Awards:** Technol Inst Teaching Award, 1982; fel AAAS, 1997; Outstanding Educr Award, Am Ceramic Soc, 2001. **Professional Experience:** WALTER P MURPHY PROF EMER MAT SCI & ENG, NORTHWESTERN UNIV, as of 2006; Walter P Murphy Prof Mat Sci & Eng, Northwestern Univ, beginning 1971; from asst prof to assoc prof, Northwestern Univ, 1962-1971; mining engr trainee, US Smelting, Ref & Mining Co, 1956. **Memberships:** fel Am Ceramic Soc; Am Inst Mining Metall & Petrol Engrs; Mat Res Soc; Am Powder Metall Inst. **Research Statement & Publications:** Mechanisms of material transport in the sintering of oxides and metals; impurity effects in sintering; grain boundary diffusion in sintering; plasma and microwave processing of ceramics and ceramic composites; processing of high temperature superconductors. **Mailing Address:** 1231 Gregory Ave, Wilmette, IL 60091-3340.

JOHNSON, DAVID M, BOTANY. **Personal Data:** b Conway, Ark, December 3, 1955; American & Egyptian citizen. **Education:** Hendricks Col, BA, 1978; Univ Mich, MS, 1981, PhD (bot), 1985. **Professional Experience:** PROF BOT & MICROBIOL, OHIO WESLEYAN UNIV, as of 2002; Prof Botany/Microbiol, Ohio Wesleyan Univ, Fulbright scholar, Univ Dares Salaam, Tanzinia, 1996; assoc prof bot & microbiol, Ohio Weleyan Univ, beginning 1994; asst prof, Ohio Weleyan Univ, 1989-1994; res asst, NY Bot Garden, 1986-1989. **Memberships:** Am Soc Plant Taxonomists (secy 1993); Int Asn Plant Taxonomists; Am Fern Soc. **Mailing Address:** Dept Bot & Microbiol, Ohio Wesleyan Univ, Rm 204, Bigelow, Rice Hall, Delaware, OH 43015. **Fax:** 614-368-3999. **E-Mail:** dmjohnso@owu.edu

JOHNSON, DAVID RUSSELL, PHYSICAL CHEMISTRY. **Personal Data:** b Manaus, Brazil, October 23, 1945; m 1967, c 2. **Education:** Austin Col, BA, 1967; Tex Christian Univ, PhD (chem), 1970. **Professional Experience:** SR RES ASSOC, DU PONT CHEM, FREON RES & DEVELOP, E I DU PONT DEL NEMOURS & CO INC, WILMINGTON, DEL, 1988-; proj liaison leader, Petrochemicals-AED, 1985-1988; tech supt pretrochemicals, Cape Fear Plant, 1984-1985; chief supvr tritium technol, 1982-1984; res supvr hydrogen technol, Savannah River Lab, 1981-1982; res supvr anal chem, 1979-1981; staff chemist, 1978-1979; res chemist separations chem, 1975-1978; res chemist textile fibers, E I du Pont Del Nemours & Co Inc, Waynesboro, Va, 1973-1975; fel, Univ Fla, 1972-1973; fel radiation chem, Baylor Univ, 1970-1972. **Memberships:** Am Chem Soc. **Research Statement & Publications:** Plutonium soil migration studies; environmental dose-to-man modelling methods; uranium fuel fabrication methods; chemical separations processes for nuclear fuel recycle and waste management programs; process development for CFC alternatives. **Mailing Address:** 1803 Streamside Dr, Friendswood, TX 77546.

JOHNSON, DAVID S, MATHEMATICS. **Education:** Amherst Col, BA, 1967; Mass Inst Technol, SM, 1968, PHD, 1973. **Professional Experience:** HEAD, ALGORITHM & OPTIMIZATION DEPT, AT&T LABS, 1996-. **Mailing Address:** AT&T Labs - Res, Florham Park, NJ 07932-0971. **Fax:** 973-360-8178. **E-Mail:** dsj@research.att.com

JOHNSON, DAVID SIMONDS, meteorology; deceased, see previous edition for last biography

JOHNSON, DAVID STIFLER, COMPUTER SCIENCE, MATHEMATICS. **Personal Data:** b Washington, DC, December 9, 1945; m 1982, Dorothy; c Jack Carlos. **Education:** Amherst Col, BA, 1967; Mass Inst Technol, SM, 1968, PhD (math), 1973. **Honors & Awards:** Lanchester Prize, Inst Opers Res & Mgt Sci, 1979 ACM Fellow, 1994 AT&T Fellow, 2005. **Professional Experience:** HEAD, ALGORITHMS AND OPTIMIZATION DEPT, AT&T Labs - Research, 1995-; head, Math Found Comput Dept, AT&T Bell Labs 1988-1995; Vis prof, Comput Sci Dept, Univ Wis, 1980-1981; mem tech staff, AT&T Bell Labs, 1973-1988. **Memberships:** Asn Comput Mach (Council mem, 1996-2004); Soc Indust & Appl Math, Informs, Math prog soc, ACM special interest group on algorithms & computation theory (chair, 1987-1991). **Research Statement & Publications:** Design and analysis of algorithms; Computational complexity theory; experimental analysis at algorithms. **Mailing Address:** AT&T Labs - Research, 180 Park Ave Rm C239, Florham Park, NJ 07932-0971. **Fax:** 973-360-8178. **E-Mail:** dsj@research.att.com

JOHNSON, DAVID W, CERAMIC PROCESSING, ELECTRONIC CERAMICS. **Personal Data:** b Windber, Pa, September 23, 1942; m 1964, c Analee J & Bradley D. **Education:** Pa State Univ, BS, 1964, PhD (ceramic sci), 1968. **Honors & Awards:** Ross Coffin Purdy Award, Am Ceramic Soc, 1981, Fulroth Award, 1984; Taylor lectr, Pa State Univ, 1987, Nat Acad Eng, 1993. **Professional Experience:** Dept head, Bell Labs, 1988-; supvr, Bell Labs, 1984-1988; ADJ PROF MAT SCI, STEVENS INST TECHNOL, 1982-; mem tech staff, Bell Tel Labs, 1968-1983. **Memberships:** Nat Acad Eng; Am Ceramic Soc (vpres, 1990-1992, treas, 1992-1993, pres elect, 1993-1994); AAAS; Am Soc Metals; Mat Res Soc; Metall Soc. **Research Statement & Publications:** Dielectric relaxation in doped strontium titanate; characterization of fine oxide particles; magnetic ceramics; ionic conductors; sol gel glasses; oxide superconductors. **Mailing Address:** 5 Oakura Lane, Bedminster, NJ 07921. **E-Mail:** dwj@bell-labs.com

JOHNSON, DAVID WILLIS, FOOD PRODUCTS. **Personal Data:** b Tumut, Australia, August 7, 1932; m 1966, Sylvia Raymonde Wells; c David Ashley Lawrence, Justin ChristopherKendall & Harley Alista Kent. **Education:** Univ Sydney, B econs, 1954, dipl educ, 1955; Univ Chicago, MBA, 1958. **Professional Experience:** Chmn bd, Campbell Soup Co, 1993; PRES, CHIEF EXEC OFFICER & DIR, CAMPBELL SOUP CO, 1990-; chmn & chief exec officer, pres & chief exec officer, Gerber Prod Co, 1989-1990; chmn, pres & chief exec officer, Gerber Prod Co, 1987-1989; pres & chief exec officer, Entenmann's Inc & Gen Foods Corp, 1982-1987; pres & chief exec officer, Entenmann's Div, Warner-Lambert Co, Bayshore, NY, 1982; vpres, Am Chicle Div, 1980-1982; pres specialty foods group, Am Chicle Div, 1980-1981; exec vpres & gen mgr, Entenmann's Div, Warner-Lambert Co, Bayshore, NY, 1979; pres, Am Chicle Div, 1978; pres, Personal Prod Div, Warner Lambert Co, Morris Plains, NJ, 1977; pres, Warner-Lambert/Parke Davis Asia, 1973-1976; chmn & managing dir, Colgate-Palmolive, Sydney, 1967-1972; asst gen mgr & mktg dir, Colgate-Palmolive, Sydney, 1966; gen prod mgr, Colgate-Palmolive, Sydney, 1964-1965; brands mgr, Colgate-Palmolive, Sydney, 1963; asst to managing dir, Colgate-Palmolive, Sydney, 1962; prod mgr, Colgate-Palmolive, Sydney, 1961; mgt trainee, Colgate-Palmolive, Sydney, 1959-1960; adv coun, Univ Notre Dame Col Bus Admin; Mem bd dirs, Colgate-Palmolive Co; Exec trainee, Ford Motor Co, Australia. **Memberships:** Am Bakers Asn; Grocery Mfrs Am. **Mailing Address:** Campbell Soup Co, World Hq Campbell Pl, Camden, NJ 08103-1799.

JOHNSON, DEBORAH G, ETHICS IN COMPUTER SCIENCE. **Professional Experience:** ANNE SHIRLEY CARTER OLSSON PROF APPL ETHICS, UNIV VA, 2001-. **Mailing Address:** Sch Eng & Appl Sci, Univ Va, 351 McCormick Rd PO Box 400744, Charlottesville, VA 22904-4744. **E-Mail:** dgj7p@virginia.edu

JOHNSON, DENNIS A, AERONAUTICS. **Professional Experience:** ADV, NASA AMES RES CTR, CA, as of 2004. **Memberships:** Am Inst Aeronaut & Astronauts. **Mailing Address:** NASA Ames Res Ctr, Aerodynamics Branch M/S 229-1, Moffett Field, CA 94035. **Fax:** 650-604-3068.

JOHNSON, DENNIS DUANE, NEUROSCIENCES. **Personal Data:** b Can, March 11, 1938; c 4. **Education:** Univ Sask, BSP, 1960, MSc, 1962; Univ Wash, PhD (pharmacol), 1965. **Professional Experience:** BD DIR, SHERBROOKE FOUND, INC, as of 2004; HEAD, SYNCHROTRON INST, as of 2002; ASSOC VPRES RES, COL MED, 1992-; bd dirs, VIDO, 1992; bd dirs, Sask Res Coun, 1992; bd dirs, Royal Soc Eval Unit, 1992; bd dirs, Nat Res Coun Plant Biotechnology Inst, 1992; bd dirs, Ag-West Biotechnology, 1992; Univ Sask Technol, Inc, 1992; mem adv comt, Pharmaceut Mfrs Asn Can, 1988-; counr, Med Res Coun Can, 1987-; bd dirs, Med Res Coun Can, 1987-1992; head, Dept Pharmacol, 1986-1992; ASST DEAN, COL MED, 1981-; PROF PHARMACOL, UNIV SASK, 1975-; f rom asst prof to assoc prof, Col Med, 1966-1975; l ectr pharmacol, Univ Sask, 1965-1966. **Memberships:** Nat Cancer Inst Can; Am Soc Neurosci; Am Soc Pharmacol & Exp Therapeut; Pharmacol Soc Can. **Research Statement & Publications:** Pharamcology and biochemistry of epilepsy; neurochemistry ofneuropharmacology. **Mailing Address:** Univ Sask, Kirk Hall Rm 217 117 Science Pl, Saskatoon, SK S7N 5C8, Can.

JOHNSON, DEWEY, BIOCHEMISTRY, NUTRITION. **Personal Data:** b Sapulpa, Okla, September 23, 1926; m 1953, Patricia; c Joseph, Paul, Mary Anne (Crane) & Richard E. **Education:** Colo State Univ, BS, 1950; Univ Conn, MS, 1955; Rutgers Univ, PhD, 1958; Nat Registry Clin Chemists. **Professional Experience:** RETIRED; underwriter, Metrop Life Ins Co, NY, 1989-1992; supv anal chemist, Metrop Life Ins Co, NY, 1981-1989; dir clin lab, Equitable Live Assurance Soc US, New York, 1968-1979; biochemist, Equitable Live Assurance Soc US, New York, 1963-1968; nutritionist, Food & Drug Res Lab, 1962-1963; assoc animal nutrit, Lime Crest Res Lab, Limestone Prod Corp Am, NJ, 1958-1962; asst poultry nutrit, Rutgers Univ, 1955-1958; chemist, Environ Protection Agency. **Memberships:** Am Soc Animal Sci; Am Dairy Sci Asn; Poultry Sci Asn. **Research Statement & Publications:** Metabolism of amino acids; metabolism of drugs; biochemical changes in alcoholism; automated clinical chemistry techniques; folic acid and vitamin B12 metabolism; extraction and detection of pesticides. **Mailing Address:** 12 Barbara Pl, Edison, NJ 08817.

JOHNSON, DIANE L, MATHEMATICS. **Education:** Univ Ore, PhD, 1983. **Professional Experience:** PROF, DEPT MATH, HUMBOLDT STATE UNIV, as of 2006. **Mailing Address:** Math Dept, Humboldt State Univ, Arcata, CA 95521. **Fax:** 707-826-3140. **E-Mail:** dlj1@axe.humboldt.edu

JOHNSON, DIANNA AMMONS, NEUROBIOLOGY, OPTHAMOLOGY. **Personal Data:** b Many, La, October 21, 1943; m 1965, c 1. **Education:** Centenary Col, BS, 1964; Univ Kans, PhD (neurobiol), 1972. **Honorary Degrees:** DSc, Centenary Col, 1996. **Honors & Awards:** Distinguished Prof Women's Award, Univ Tex, Houston, 1996, 1983 Houston fedn Prof Women, Outstanding Woman in Sci Award, 1977-1981 NIH ResCareer Development Award. **Professional Experience:** HIATT PROF & DIR RES, DEPT OPHTHAL & DEPT ANAT & NEUROBIOLOGY, UNIV TENN, MEMPHIS, 1996-; 1994-1996 Jules& Doris Stein Res to Prevent Blindness Professorship; asst dean res training, Med Sch, Univ Tex, Houston, 1988-1996; from asst prof to prof Neurobiology, Med Sch, Univ Tex, Houston, 1974-1996; Fel psychobiol, Univ Calif, Irvine, 1972-1974, 1964-1965 NSF Predoctural Fel; 1972-1974 NIH Postdoctural Fel. **Memberships:** Asn Res Vision Opthal; Soc Neuroscience; Neurochem Soc; Soc Cell Biol; Am Soc Biol Chem; Asn Women in Sci; fel AAAS; Int Soc Develop Neuroscience; Am Soc for Neurochemistry. **Research Statement & Publications:** The nature of chemical transmission in neuronal tissue; mechanisms of neurotransmitter release, identification of functional neurotransmitters, modulation of chemical transmission by intrinsic and extrinsic factors; development of in vitro techniques for biochemical analysis of neurotransmitter systems; neurochemistry of the retina, effects of GABA, glutamate, nitric oxide and polyamines on neuronal development prior to and during synapse formation, and the identification of what receptors and signal transduction pathways might be involved in neuronal development, Initiation of signaling molecules and transduction pathways due to glaucoma, inherited retinal diseases, ischemia, and retinal trauma. **Mailing Address:** Univ Tenn Dept Ophthal, 855 Monroe Ave, Memphis, TN 38163. **E-Mail:** dijohnson@utmem.edu

JOHNSON, DON H, MATHEMATICS. **Education:** Mass Inst Technol, SB, 1970, SM, 1971, EE, 1971, PhD, 1974. **Professional Experience:** JS ABERCROMBIE PROF, RICE UNIV, as of 2005. **Mailing Address:** Dept Elec & Comput Eng, Rice Univ PO Box 1892, Houston, TX 77251-1892. **Fax:** 713-348-5686. **E-Mail:** dhj@rice.edu

JOHNSON, DON H, ACOUSTICAL ENGINEERING. **Education:** Mass Inst Technol, BS, 1970, MS, 1971, PhD, 1974. **Professional Experience:** JS ABERCROMBLE PROF, RICE UNIV, as of 2006. **Mailing Address:** Rice Univ, 6100 Main St, Houston, TX 77005. **Fax:** 713-348-5686. **E-Mail:** dhj@rice.edu

JOHNSON, DONALD B, AERONAUTICS. **Professional Experience:** STAFF, MCDONNELL DOUGLAS CORP, beginning 2000. **Memberships:** Am Inst Aeronaut & Astronauts. **Mailing Address:** McDonnell Douglas Corp, PO Box 516 D341 MS 1064950, St Louis, MO 63166. **Fax:** 314-234-3826.

JOHNSON, DONALD CHARLES, ENDOCRINOLOGY. **Personal Data:** b Black River Falls, Wis, January 30, 1927; m 1952, Eleanore J Latuvnik; c 1. **Education:** Univ Wis, BS, 1949; Univ Iowa, MS, 1950, PhD (zool), 1956. **Professional Experience:** PROF EMER OBSTET, GYNEC & PHYSIOL, SCH MED, UNIV KANS, 1996-; res prof human reproduction, Gynec & Physiol, Sch Med, Univ Kans, 1978-1996; from asst prof to prof, Gynec & Physiol, Sch Med, Univ Kans, 1963-1996; res asst prof, Univ Iowa, 1959-1963; res assoc, Univ Iowa, 1956-1958; a sst zool, Univ Iowa, 1953-1956. **Memberships:** AAAS; Endocrine Soc; Am Physiol Soc; Soc Gynec Invest; Soc Study Reprod; Sigma Xi. **Research Statement & Publications:** Reproductive physiology and endocrinology; comparative physiology of gonadotrophins; control gonadal steroidogenic enzymes; reproductive toxicology. **Mailing Address:** Dept Obstet & Gynec, Univ Kans, Med Ctr, Kansas City, KS 66160. **Fax:** 913-588-5677. **E-Mail:** djohnsol@kumc.edu

JOHNSON, DONALD CURTIS, ORGANIC CHEMISTRY. **Personal Data:** b Minneapolis, Minn, March 21, 1935; m 1956, c 3. **Education:** Hamline Univ, BS, 1957; Univ Minn, PhD (org chem), 1962. **Professional Experience:** SR SCI ADV, WEYERHAEUSER CO, 1990-; sci adv, Weyerhaeuser CO, 1982-1990; co-ed, J Wood Chem & Technol, 1981; scientific specialist fiber chem, Weyerhaeuser CO, 1977-1982; c hmn, Gordon Res Conf Chem & Physics Paper, 1972-1974; prof org chem, Inst Paper Chem, 1970-1977; res assoc & chmn dept chem, Inst Paper Chem, 1967-1977; res aide org chem, Inst Paper Chem, 1961-1967. **Memberships:** Am Chem Soc; Tech Asn Pulp & Paper Indust. **Research Statement & Publications:** Cellulose chemistry, including reactions in solution and mechanisms of chain degradation; lignin chemistry, particularly delignification processes with selective oxidants; bacterial cellulose production and applications. **Mailing Address:** 33936 134th Ave SE, Auburn, WA 98092.

JOHNSON, DONALD ELWOOD, COMPUTER SCIENCE, SOFTWARE SYSTEMS. **Personal Data:** b Joliet, Ill, July 23, 1935; m 1956, c 2. **Education:** NCent Col, BA, 1957; Univ Wis-Madison, MS, 1959; Ill Inst Technol, PhD (math), 1973. **Professional Experience:** PROF EMER MATH & COMPUT SCI, NCENT COL, 1997-; prof math & comput sci, NCentral Col, 1994-1997; prof comput sci, Div Natural Sci & Math, 1982-1994; prof & chairperson comput sci, Div Natural Sci & Math, 1982-1988; chairperson, Div Natural Sci & Math, 1978-1983; prof math, NCent Col, 1978-1982; chairperson math, NCent Col, 1969-1973 & 1975-1978; from instr to assoc prof, NCent Col, 1961-1978; a sst mathematician, Argonne Nat Lab, 1959-1961. **Memberships:** Math Asn Am; Inst Elec & Electronics Engrs Comput Soc; Am Asn Univ Prof. **Mailing Address:** Dept Math & Comput Sci, N Cent Col, 30 N Brainard St, Naperville, IL 60540-4690. **E-Mail:** dej@nccseq.noctrl.edu

JOHNSON, DONALD EUGENE, ANIMAL NUTRITION. **Personal Data:** b Sykeston, NDak, November 17, 1938; m 1961, c 3. **Education:** NDak State Univ, BS, 1960, MS, 1963; Colo State Univ, PhD (animal nutrit), 1966. **Professional Experience:** PROF ANIMAL SCI & NUTRIT & DIR METAB LAB, COLO STATE UNIV, FOOTHILLS CAMPUS, 1980-; assoc prof, Colo State Univ, Foothills Campus, 1972-1980; asst prof ruminant nutrit, Univ Ill, Urbana, 1968-1972; res assoc, Cornell Univ, 1966-1968; res asst animal nutrit, Colo State Univ, 1963-1966; res asst animal nutrit, NDak State Univ, 1961-1963; Brody Mem Lectr; Blankenbaker Lectr. **Memberships:** AAAS; Am Soc Animal Sci. **Research Statement & Publications:** Animal energy metabolism; metabolic rat variation; rumen function; body composition; methane emissions. **Mailing Address:** Dept Animal Sci, Colo State Univ, Ft Collins, CO 80523-1171. **Fax:** 770-491-5326. **E-Mail:** don.johnson@colostate.edu

JOHNSON, DONALD GLEN, MATHEMATICS EDUCATION. **Personal Data:** b Detroit, Mich, January 29, 1931; American citizen; m 1975, Patricia; c Randall C, Edyth L & Claudia C Lavoie. **Education:** Albion Col, AB, 1953; Mich State Univ, MS, 1957; Purdue Univ, PhD (math), 1959. **Professional Experience:** PROF EMER MATH, NMEX STATE UNIV, 1988-; from assoc prof to prof, Nmex State Univ, 1965-1988; From asst prof to assoc prof math, Pa State Univ, 1959-1965. **Memberships:** Am Math Soc; Math Asn Am; Nat Coun Teachers Math. **Research Statement & Publications:** Lattice ordered rings; rings of continuous functions. **Mailing Address:** 5 W Oak St, Ramsey, NJ 07446. **E-Mail:** dgjohnson@member.ams.org

JOHNSON, DONALD L(EE), METALLURGICAL ENGINEERING. **Personal Data:** b Denver, Colo, February 19, 1927; m 1947, c 4. **Education:** Colo Sch Mines, MetE, 1950, MS, 1956; Univ Nebr, Lincoln, PhD (chem eng), 1968. **Professional Experience:** PROF EMER MECH ENG, METALL PROG, UNIV NEBR, LINCOLN, as of 2001; prof mech eng, metall prog, Univ Nebr, Lincoln, beginning 1975; Univ Nebr Res Coun-NASA-Ames Res Ctr fel, Univ Nebr, Lincoln, 1971-1972; co nsult, Brunswick Corp, 1969-; assoc prof metall, Metall Prog, Univ Nebr, Lincoln, 1963-1975; sr metallurgist, NAm Rockwell Corp, 1960-1963; asst prof metall eng, Wash State Univ, 1956-1959; metall engr, Mine & Smelter Supply Co, 1953-1956; t rainee, Allis Chalmers Mfg Co, 1950-1951. **Memberships:** Am Soc Metals; Nat Asn Corrosion Engrs. **Research Statement & Publications:** Gas-metal equilibria; hydrogen transport in metallic alloys; polarization analysis of corrosion in aqueous systems; leaching kinetics. **Mailing Address:** Dept Mech Eng, Univ Nebr, Lincoln, IA 68502.

JOHNSON, DONALD LEE, CHEMICAL ENGINEERING, POLYMER & CARBOHYDRATE CHEMISTRY. **Personal Data:** b Aurora, Ill, March 9, 1935; m 1960, Virginia A Wesoloski; c 4. **Education:** Univ Ill, Urbana, BS, 1962; Wash Univ, DSc(chem eng), 1966. **Professional Experience:** DIR, RES & DEVELOP, GRAIN PROCESSING CORP, as of 2000; VPRES DISCOVERY RES, GRAIN PROCESSING CORP, 1996-; vpres res & develop, Grain Processing Corp, 1989-1996; dir chem renewable resources, Indust Prod Res & Develop Dept, 1980-1987; dir, Indust Prod Res & Develop Dept, 1975-1980; group leader, Indust Prod Dept, 1970-1975; group leader, Spec Prod Develop Dept, 1967-1970; res engr, Eng Res Dept, A E Staley Mfg Co, 1965-1967. **Memberships:** Nat Acad Eng; Am Inst Chem Engrs; Tech Asn Pulp & Paper Industs; Am Asn Cereal Chemists; Sigma Xi; Am Chem Soc; Inst Food Technologists. **Research Statement & Publications:** Physical chemistry of surfaces; polymer engineering as applied to paper, film and foil converting; biochemical engineering; biomass utilization; business assessment of biomass utilization plan, organize and directproduct development; commercialize products, and develop strategies for biomass utilization in agriculture, chemical, and industrial commerce. **Mailing Address:** Grain Processing Corp, 1600 Oregon St, Muscatine, IA 52761-1494. **Fax:** 563-264-4289.

JOHNSON, DONALD R, AERONAUTICS. **Honors & Awards:** Aerodyn Decelerator Syst Award, Am Inst Aeronaut & Astronaut, 1991. **Professional Experience:** PROF EMER, SPACE SCI ENG, UNIV WIS-MADISON, as of 2006; prof, Space Sci Eng, Univ Wis-Madison, as of 2004. **Mailing Address:** Space Sci & Eng, Univ Wis-Madison, 1225 W Dayton St, Madison, WI 53706. **Fax:** 608-262-5974. **E-Mail:** donj@ssec.wisc.edu

JOHNSON, DONALD R, METEOROLOGY. **Personal Data:** b McPherson, Kans, April 1, 1930; m 1953, c 3. **Education:** Bethany Col, BS, 1952; Univ Wash, BS, 1953; Univ Wis, MS, 1960, PhD (meteorol), 1965. **Professional Experience:** PROF EMER ATMOSPHERIC & OCEANIC SCI, UNIV WIS, MADISON, as of 2002; assoc dir, Space Sci & Eng Ctr, beginning 1977; chief ed, Monthly Weather Review, 1977-1980; chmn dept, Univ Wis-Madison, 1973-1976; prof atmospheric & oceanic sci, Univ Wis-Madison, beginning 1970; vis assoc prof, Pa State Univ, 1968-1969; from asst prof to assoc prof, Univ Wis-Madison, 1964-1966; from proj asst to proj assoc, Univ Wis-Madison, 1959-1964. **Memberships:** Nat Weather Asn; Am Meteorol Soc; Am Geophys Union. **Research Statement & Publications:** Dynamic climatology and meteorology; secondary and general circulation studies. **Mailing Address:** Dept Atmospheric Oceanic Sci, Univ Wis, 1225 W Dayton St, Madison, WI 53706. **Fax:** 608-262-0166. **E-Mail:** donj@ssec.wisc.edu

JOHNSON, DONALD RALPH, VERTEBRATE ECOLOGY. **Personal Data:** b Newport, Wash, August 18, 1931; m 1955, c 3. **Education:** Univ Idaho, BS, 1953, MS, 1958; Colo State Univ, PhD (wildlife ecol), 1962. **Professional Experience:** PROF EMER ZOOL, UNIV IDAHO, 1995-; prof biol, Univ Idaho, 1975-1995; assoc prof, Univ Idaho, 1968-1975; assoc prof, Minot State Col, 1965-1968; from asst prof to assoc prof biol, Ft Lewis Col, 1961-1965. **Memberships:** Am Soc Mammal; Sigma Xi. **Research Statement & Publications:** Small mammal ecology; effects of 2, 4-D on rodent food habits; energy relations of pikas; diets of sympatric lizards; osprey ecology. **Mailing Address:** Dept Biol Sci, Univ Idaho, 375 S Line St, Moscow, ID 83843-4140.

JOHNSON, DONALD REX, MOLECULAR SPECTROSCOPY, RADIO ASTRONOMY. **Personal Data:** b Tacoma, Wash, July 19, 1938; m 1959, c 2. **Education:** Univ Puget Sound, BS, 1960, Univ Idaho, MS, 1962; Univ Okla, PhD (physics), 1967. **Professional Experience:** DIR, NAT TECH INFO SERV, as of 2002; dir, Nat Measurement Lab & Technol Serv, Nat Inst Stand & Technol, beginning 1990; actg dir, Nat Measurements Lab, 1982-1990; dep dir resources & opers, Nat Bur Stand, 1980-1982; dep dir progs, Nat Bur Stand, 1978-1980; prog analyst, Nat Bur Stand, 1976-1978; physicist, Nat Bur Stand, 1967-1976; technol mgt, Technol Transfer, State & Local Econ Develop. **Memberships:** Am Phys Soc; Am Astron Soc; AAAS; Am Soc Testing & Mat; Int Astron Union. **Research Statement & Publications:** Molecular radio astronomy; microwave spectroscopy of free radicals and transient chemical species in the gas phase. **Mailing Address:** Nat Tech Info Serv, Forbes Bldg No 200, Springfield, VA 22161.

JOHNSON, DONALD ROSS, URBAN ENTOMOLOGY, MOSQUITO CONTROL. **Personal Data:** b Chicago, Ill, February 9, 1920; m 1947, Beryl; c Gary R, Lynn K (Larson), Lee R & Laura K (Conway). **Education:** Univ Ill, BSc, 1943; Univ Minn, MSc, 1950. **Professional Experience:** RETIRED; vis consult & lectr, Int Ctr Pub Health Res, Univ SC, beginning 1982; entomologist & consult, dis, vectors & pest control, beginning 1974; malaria res advisor, USAID, Indonesia, 1974; capt, USPHS, Foreign Quarantine Prog, US Army, Vietnam, 1969-1970; dir sanit, Malaria Eradification Prog, Ctrs Dis Control, 1966-1973; chief spec servs, Aedes Egypti Eradication, Communicable Dis Ctr, USPHS, 1964-1966; dep chief malaria eradication, USAID, 1957-1964; med entomologist, Pub Health Admin, Div Int Health, USPHS, 1953-1957; malaria advisor, malaria control, US Econ Coop Admin, US Dept State, Indonesia, 1951-1953; asst state entomologist insect surv & control, Minn Dept Agr, 1948-1951; asst, insecticide res, Dept Entom, Univ Minn, 1946-1948; lieutenant malaria control, US Navy, 1943-1946; adv, H D Hudson Mfg Co, Chicago. **Memberships:** Am Mosquito Control Asn; Entom Soc Am. **Research Statement & Publications:** Mosquitoes, malaria and control of arthropods of public health importance, domestic and international vector control. **Mailing Address:** 80 Walnut St SW, Atlanta, GA 30306.

JOHNSON, DONALD W, VETERINARY MEDICINE. **Personal Data:** b Worthington, Minn, May 4, 1929; m 1950, c 2. **Education:** Univ Minn, BS, 1951, DVM, 1953, PhD (microbiol), 1963. **Professional Experience:** DIR GRAD STUDY, UNIV MINN, ST PAUL, 1980-; PROF VET MED, UNIV MINN, ST PAUL, 1969-; prof vet med, Univ Mo-Columbia, 1967-1969; From instr to assoc prof vet med & clins, Col Vet Med, Univ Minn, 1955-1967. **Research Statement & Publications:** Viral and bacterial respiratory diseases of cattle and horses; host response to infectious diseases; cell mediated immune response of the bovine. **Mailing Address:** Institut Agronomique, ET Veterinaire Hassan II, BT 6202 Rabat, Morocco.

JOHNSON, DONOVAN EARL, MICROBIOLOGY, BIOCHEMISTRY. **Personal Data:** b Holdrege, Nebr, June 26, 1942; m 1965, c 2. **Education:** Univ Nebr, BS, 1964, MS, 1966; Univ Wis-Madison, PhD (microbiol), 1972. **Professional Experience:** RETIRED; res microbiologist, Us Grain Mkt Res Lab, Agr Res Serv, USDA, beginning 1981; proj leader microbiol, Northern Regional Res Lab, 1974-1981; adj prof chem, Bradley Univ, 1974; from res asst to res assoc microbiol, US Grain Mkt Res Lab, Agr Res Serv, USDA, 1966-1974. **Memberships:** Sigma Xi; Am Soc Microbiol; Soc Invert Path. **Research Statement & Publications:** Biological insecticides; microbiology of insect pathogens; physiology of bacterial sporulation. **Mailing Address:** 1515 Col Ave, Manhattan, KS 66502. **Fax:** 785-537-5584. **E-Mail:** johnson@usgmrl.ksu.edu

JOHNSON, DOUGLAS ALLAN, PLANT PHYSIOLOGY, RANGE ECOLOGY. **Personal Data:** b Montevideo, Minn, December 6, 1949; m 1972, c 3. **Education:** Augustana Col, SDak, BA, 1971; Utah State Univ, MS, 1973, PhD (range ecol), 1975. **Honors & Awards:** Outstanding Achievement Award, Soc Range Mgr, 1996. **Professional Experience:** Grant, USDA-OICD, 1991 & 1993; USDA-Coop State Res Serv grant, 1985-1988, 1987-1989 & 1992-1995; grant, Western Regional IPM, 1985-1988; US-Spain grant, 1984-1988; Commonwealth Sci & Indust Res Orgn Australia vis scientist award, 1981-1982; USDA grant, 1979-1981; RES PLANT PHYSIOLOGIST RANGE PLANT IMPROV, FORAGE & RANGE RES LAB, AGR RES SERV, USDA, 1976-; res assoc, Dept Biol, Augustana Col, 1975-; NSF grant, 1975-1976; res asst tundra plant water rel, Dept Range Sci, Utah State Univ, 1971-1975; Nat Defense Educ Act fel, 1971-1973; ADJ PROF, PLANT ECOPHYSIOLOGY, UTAH STATE UNIV. **Memberships:** Crop Sci Soc Am; fel Am Soc Agron; Soc Range Mgt. **Research Statement & Publications:** Development of superior forage plants for the Intermountain West of US; defining physiological basis of range legumes resistance to drought stress; nitrogen fixation in range legumes. **Mailing Address:** USDA-Agr Res Serv, Forage & Range Res Lab, Utah State Univ, 690 N 1100 E Rm 309, Logan, UT 84322-6300. **Fax:** 435-797-3075. **E-Mail:** daj@cc.usu.edu

JOHNSON, DOUGLAS H, MATHEMATICS. **Education:** Univ Minn, BA; Univ Wis, MS; NDak State Univ, PhD (zoology). **Professional Experience:** RES STATIST & SR SCI, NORTHERN PRAIRIE WILDLIFE RES CTR, US GEOL SOC, as of 2006. **Memberships:**

Am Asn Advan Sci. **Mailing Address:** Northern Prairie Wildlife Res Ctr, US Geol Soc, 8711 37th St SE, Jamestown, ND 58401. **Fax:** 701-253-5553. **E-Mail:** Douglas_h_Johngon@usgs.gov

JOHNSON, DOUGLAS I, MICROBIOL. **Education:** Prude Univ, PhD, 1983. **Professional Experience:** PROF MICROBIOL & MOLECULAR GENETICS, VT CANCER CTR, UNIV VT, as of 2005. **Mailing Address:** Dept Microbiol & Molecular Genetics Univ Vt, A-191 Given Bldg 202B Stafford Hall, Burlington, VT 05405-0001. **Fax:** 802-656-8749. **E-Mail:** douglas.johnson@uvm.edu

JOHNSON, DOUGLAS L, BIOLOGY. **Education:** Ohio Univ, BS; Univ Minn, PhD. **Professional Experience:** PROF BIOL, UNIV WIS, as of 2005; ASST DEAN, COL ARTS & SCI, UNIV WIS, as of 2005. **Mailing Address:** Dept Biol Univ Wis, 400 Ag Sci Bldg, River Falls, WI 54022. **Fax:** 715-425-3785. **E-Mail:** douglas.l.johnson@uwrf.edu

JOHNSON, DOUGLAS WILLIAM, REMOTE SENSING, ATMOSPHERIC SPECTROSCOPY. **Personal Data:** b Marion, Ind, September 15, 1953; m 1975, c 2. **Education:** Rensselaer Polytech Inst, BS, 1975; Univ Fla, PhD (astron), 1980. **Professional Experience:** MGR, STAND STRATEGY, DEPT CORP STAND, SUN MICROSYSTEMS INC, as of 2004; sr staff scientist, Sun Microsystems, beginning 1996; sr staff scientist, AER Inc, 1989-1996; prin res scientist, Battelle Mem Inst, 1987-1989; sr res scientist, Battelle Mem Inst, 1984-1987; res scientist, Battelle Mem Inst, 1983-1984; teaching res assoc, Battelle NW, 1980-1982; teaching asst physics, Univ Fla, 1975-1980. **Memberships:** Am Astron Soc; AAAS; Am Geog Union; Sigma Xi; NY Acad Sci; Am Soc Photogammetry & Remote Sensing. **Research Statement & Publications:** Integration of remotely sensod imaging data of diverse types using imaging sattuore to aid in interpretation and understanding. **Mailing Address:** Sun Microsysts Inc, 4150 Network Circle, Santa Clara, CA 95054. **E-Mail:** douglas.johnson@east.sun.com

JOHNSON, DUDLEY PAUL, MATHEMATICS, MATHEMATICAL STATISTICS. **Personal Data:** b Burbank, Calif, September 22, 1940; m 1964, Ann; c Eric A & Amanda G. **Education:** Yale Univ, BSc, 1962; Mass Inst Technol, PhD (math), 1966. **Professional Experience:** PROF MATH, UNIV CALGARY, 1990-; from asst prof to assoc prof, Univ Calgary, 1971-1990; asst prof math, Univ Calif, 1966-1971. **Research Statement & Publications:** Stochastic processes. **Mailing Address:** Dept Math & Statist, Univ Calgary, 2500 Univ Dr NW, Calgary, AB T2N 1N4, Can. **Fax:** 403-282-5150. **E-Mail:** johnson@math.ucalgary.ca

JOHNSON, EARNEST J, OPTICS. **Personal Data:** b Philipsburg, Pa, February 23, 1931; m 1956, c 8. **Education:** Pa State Univ, BS, 1953; Purdue Univ, MS, 1954, PhD (physics), 1964. **Professional Experience:** Mem staff, GTE Lab, Waltham, Mass, 1974-; mem resstaff, Lincoln Lab, Mass Inst Technol, 1964-1974; staff mem, NAm Aviation, Inc, 1955-1956 &Hughes Aircraft Co, 1956-1958; AT MOTOROLA INC. **Memberships:** Optical Soc Am; Am Phys Soc. **Research Statement & Publications:** Study of band structure of solids by observation of optical absorption and luminescence and effects of doping, magnetic fields and strains; laser materials; quantum electronics; fiber optic subsystems. **Mailing Address:** EL508 2100 E Elliot Rd, Motorola Inc, Tempe, AZ 85284.

JOHNSON, EDGAR MCCARTHY, RESEARCH PSYCHOLOGY. **Personal Data:** b Jacksonville, Fla, October 29, 1941; m 1967, Fatima; c Victoria C & David M. **Education:** Ga Inst Technol, BS, 1964; Tufts Univ, MS, 1967, PhD (exp psychol), 1969. **Honors & Awards:** Franklin V Taylor Award, Inst Elec & Electronics Engrs, 1984. **Professional Experience:** RETIRED; dir, US Army Res Inst, beginning 1993; chief psychologist, US Army Res Inst, beginning 1982; tech dir, Systs Res Lab, 1982-1993; dir, Systs Res Lab, 1980-1982; chief, Human Factors Sect, 1978-1980; res psychologist, US Army Res Inst, 1970-1978. **Memberships:** Fel Am Psychol Asn; fel Am Psychol Soc; fel Human Factors & Ergonomics Soc; Inst Elec & Electronics Engrs; Ergonomics Soc; Sigma Xi. **Mailing Address:** 5315 Renaissance Ct, Burke, VA 22015-2194.

JOHNSON, EDWARD A, BIOLOGY. **Education:** Univ Wis, BSc, 1967; Univ NH, MSc, 1972; Univ Sask, PhD, 1977. **Professional Experience:** PROF, DEPT BIOL SCI, UNIV CALGARY, as of 2005; DIR, KANANASKIS FIELD STA, as of 2005. **Mailing Address:** Dept Biol Univ Calgary, 2500 Univ Dr NW, Calgary, AB T2N 1N4, Can. **Fax:** 403-289-9311. **E-Mail:** johnsone@ucalgary.ca

JOHNSON, EDWARD A, PHYSIOLOGY. **Education:** Univ Sheffield, MD, 1953. **Professional Experience:** PROF EMER PHYSIOL, DUKE UNIV, as of 2004; James B Duke Prof & Chmn, Dept Physiol, Duke Univ Sch Med, as of 2002. **Mailing Address:** Dept Physiol, Duke Univ Sch Med, PO Box 3005, Durham, NC 27710. **Fax:** 919-383-1649.

JOHNSON, EDWARD ARNOLD, VEGETATION SCIENCES. **Personal Data:** b Long Branch, NJ, August 24, 1943; m 1994, Kiyoko; c Joanne Sonia. **Education:** Univ Wis, BSc, 1967; Univ NH, MSc, 1972; Univ Sask, PhD, 1977. **Honors & Awards:** William S Cooper Award, Ecol Soc Am, 1986. **Professional Experience:** PROF BIOL SCI, UNIV CALGARY, 1993-; dir, Kananaskis Field Stas, 1992-; assoc ed, Can J Forest Res, 1992-; assoc ed, Vegetation Sci, 1990-1997; from asst prof to assoc prof, Univ Calgary, 1979-1993. **Memberships:** Int Asn Veg Sci; Ecol Soc Am; Sigma Xi; Am Soc Naturalists. **Research Statement & Publications:** Plant population dynamics; forest fire behavior and ecological effects; ecological mechanics, aerodynamics and small particle dispersal models; ecological effects of natural disturbances; contributed many articles to professional journals. **Mailing Address:** Dept Biol Sci, Univ Calgary, 2500 Univ Dr NW, BI 338, Calgary, AB T2N 1N4, Can. **Fax:** 403-289-9311. **E-Mail:** johnsone@ucalgary.ca

JOHNSON, EDWARD MICHAEL, INITIATION OF DNA REPLICATION, CHROMOSOME STRUCTURE. **Personal Data:** b Kenosha, Wis, April 9, 1945; m Elizabeth; c Nathaniel L. **Education:** Pomona Col, BA, 1967; Yale Univ, PhD (pharmacol), 1971. **Honors & Awards:** Fac Res Award, Am Cancer Soc, 1982-1987. **Professional Experience:** PROF, DERALD H RUTTENBERG CANCER CTR, as of 2003; PROF, DEPT PATH, MT SINAI SCH MED, 2000-; vchmn res, Mt Sinai Sch Med, beginning 2000; PROF MOLECULAR BIOL, MT SINAI SCH MED, 1985-; adj prof genetics, Rockefeller Univ, 1985-1992; adj prof genetics, Cornell Grad Sch Med Sci, 1979-1985; from asst prof to assoc prof cell biol, Rockefeller Univ, 1975-1985; res assoc, Sloan-Kettering Cancer Ctr, 1973-1975; spec fel, Leukemia Soc Am, 1973-1975; fel, Rockefeller Univ, 1971-1973. **Memberships:** Am Asn Cancer Res; Am Soc Inest Path; Am Soc Cell Biol; Am Soc Pharmacol & Exp Therapeut; NY Acad Sci; Am Soc Biochem & Molecular Biol. **Research Statement & Publications:** Control of DNA replication in mammalian cells; structure and chromosomal organization of individual genes, including ways in which hormones and other developmental signals regulate gene activity during development; regulation of gene expression in higher organisms. **Mailing Address:** Dept Path, Mt Sinai Sch Med, Annenberg Bldg 15th Floor, New York, NY 10029. **Fax:** 212-534-7491. **E-Mail:** edward.johnson@mssm.edu

JOHNSON, EDWIN C, NEUROPHYSIOLOGY, SINGLE ION CHANNEL RECORDING. **Personal Data:** b Morristown, NJ, November 4, 1958. **Education:** Purdue Univ, BS, 1979, PhD (electrophysiol), 1984. **Professional Experience:** HEAD, ELECTROPHYSIOL DEPT, SALK INST, 1992-; assoc prof med physiol, Marshall Univ Sch Med, 1987-1992; res fel phototransduction, Brandeis Univ, 1984-1987. **Memberships:** Soc Neuroscience; Biophys Soc; Soc Gen Physiologists. **Research Statement & Publications:** Neurophysiology; single ion channel recording. **Mailing Address:** Neuro Sci Inc, 505 Coast Blvd S, La Jolla, CA 92037-4641. **Fax:** 619-452-9279.

JOHNSON, EDWIN WALLACE, PHYSICAL CHEMISTRY. **Personal Data:** b New Ulm, Minn, May 2, 1923; m 1955, c 2. **Education:** Harvard Univ, BS, 1944, MA, 1948, PhD (phys chem), 1950. **Professional Experience:** ADV ENG, METALL DEPT, WESTINGHOUSE ELEC CORP, 1974-; adv phys chemist, 1955-1974; Res phys chemist, 1949-1955. **Memberships:** Am Chem Soc; Electrochem Soc; Am Inst Mining Metall & Petrol Eng. **Research Statement & Publications:** Molecular state of carboxylic acid vapors; solubility and diffusivity of hydrogen in metals; hydrogen embrittlement of steels; process metallurgy of titanium base alloys; vacuum arc melting; low pressure arc phenomena; properties of thermoelectric materials; measurement of thermal conductivity of liquid semiconductors at high temperatures; coated-electrode welding of austenitic high temperature alloys. **Mailing Address:** 3388 MacArthur Rd, Murrysville, PA 15668.

JOHNSON, EINER WESLEY, JR, ORTHOPEDIC SURGERY. **Personal Data:** b Bemidji, Minn, July 5, 1919; m 1951, c 4. **Education:** Univ Minn, BA, 1941, BS, 1942, BM, 1944, MD, 1945, MA, 1950. **Professional Experience:** PROF ORTHOP SURG, MAYO GRAD, UNIV MINN, SCH MED, 1971-; f rom instr to assoc prof, Mayo Grad, Univ Minn, Sch Med, 1952-1971; Consult, Mayo Clin, Rochester Methodist Hosp & Rochester-St Mary's Hosp. **Memberships:** Am Acad Orthop Surgeons; Clin Orthop Soc; Am Orthop Asn; Mid-Am Orthop Asn. **Mailing Address:** 201 First Ave SW No 411, Rochester, MN 55902-3155.

JOHNSON, ELIJAH, PHYSICAL CHEMISTRY. **Personal Data:** b Eutawville, SC, January 1, 1948. **Education:** Penn State Univ, BS, 1969; Univ Ill, PhD (chem), 1976. **Professional Experience:** ASSOC PROF, ENVIRON SCI INST, FLA A&M UNIV, as of 2005; asst prof, Fla A&M Univ, beginning 1999; E P Wigner fel, Oak Ridge Nat Lab, 1977-; chemist, Oak Ridge Nat Lab, 1976-1998. **Memberships:** Am Chem Soc; Am Phys Soc. **Research Statement & Publications:** Theoretical studies of liquids and proteins and x-ray and neutron scattering. **Mailing Address:** Environ Sci Inst, Sci Res Ctr, Fla A&M Univ, 1520 S Bronough St Rm 306 F FSH, Tallahassee, FL 32307. **Fax:** 850-561-2248. **E-Mail:** elijah.johnson@famu.edu

JOHNSON, ELLIS LANE, Operations Research, Optimization. **Personal Data:** b Athens, Ga, July 26, 1938; m, c Michael, Catherine Robison & Frederick. **Education:** Ga Inst Technol, BA, 1960; Univ Calif, Berkeley, MA, 1962, PhD (eng sci), 1965. **Honors & Awards:** Von Neumann Prize, Fellow of INFORMS, Lanchester Prize, Dantzig Prize. **Professional Experience:** COCA-COLA CHAIR PROF, SCH INDUST & SYST ENG, GA INST TECHNOL, as of 2004; SCHOOL OF INDUST & SYSTS ENG, GA INST TECHNOL, 1990-; vis engr sci develop, IBM, France, 1973-1974; adj prof, Univ Waterloo, 1972-1978; mem res staff math sci, Thomas J Watson Res Ctr, IBM Corp, 1968-1993; a sst prof admin sci, Yale Univ, 1964-1968; v is assoc prof, Univ Waterloo, 1960-1961. **Memberships:** Nat Acad Eng; INFORMS, AGIFORS. **Research Statement & Publications:** Theory and algorithms for integer programming; study of combinatorial polyhedra and mathematical programming; airline planning and scheduling. **Mailing Address:** Sys Indust & Syst Eng, Ga Inst Technol, Groseclose 0205, Rm 415, Atlanta, GA 30332-0205. **Fax:** 404-894-2301. **E-Mail:** ellis.johnson@isye.gatech.edu

JOHNSON, ELMER MARSHALL, EMBRYOLOGY & TOXICOLOGY, ENVIRONMENAL HEALTH. **Personal Data:** b Midlothian, Ill, June 16, 1930; m 1976, Sharon; c Mark, Kim, Erik & Lora. **Education:** Agr & Mech Col Tex, BS, 1954, MS, 1955; Univ Calif, Berkeley, PhD (anat), 1959. **Professional Experience:** PROF EMER ANAT, JEFFERSON MED COL, THOMAS JEFFERSON UNIV, as of 2003; prof anat & chmn, Jefferson Med Col, Thomas Jefferson Univ, beginning 1972; DIR, DANIEL BAUGH INST ANAT, 1972-; prof human morphol & chmn dept, Col Med, Univ Calif, Irvine, 1971-1972; prof anat sci, Univ Fla, 1968-1971; assoc prof anat, Univ Fla, 1960-1968; instr anat & physiol, Contra Costa Col, 1958-1959; asst gross anat & histol, Univ Calif, 1955-1958; asst researcher histochem, Surg Gen, US Army, 1954; asst zool, microtech & bot, Agr & Mech Col Tex, 1953-1955; dir, March Dimes & NIH grant's & NIEHS pre & postdoctoral training prog. **Memberships:** AAAS; Teratology Soc (pres, 1974-1975); Am Asn Anatomists; Soc Toxicol; Am Chem Soc; Europ Teratology Soc; Am Col Toxicol. **Research Statement & Publications:** Experimental teratology and nutrition; reproductive physiology; molecular biology; electron microscopy; histochemistry; developmental toxicity risk estimation; safety evaluation; in vitro toxicology. **Mailing Address:** Dept Anat & Develop Biol, Jefferson Med Col, Thomas Jefferson Univ, 1020 Locust St, Philadelphia, PA 19107-5587.

JOHNSON, EMMETT JOHN, MICROBIOLOGY. **Personal Data:** b New Orleans, La, April 17, 1929; m 1955, c 2. **Education:** Loyola Univ the South, BS, 1952; La State Univ, MS, 1954, PhD (bact), 1957. **Professional Experience:** PROF EMER BACT GENETICS, TULANE UNIV SCH MED, as of 2006; res assoc molecular biol, Pasteur Inst, Paris, France, 1974-1975; prof microbiol & immunol, Med Sch, Tulane univ, beginning 1970; assoc prof, Med Sch, Tulane Univ, 1967-1970; lectr, 1966-1967; res assoc, Bruce Lyon Mem Res Inst, Oakland, Calif, 1966-1967; teaching assoc, 1965-1966; res scientist, Exobiol Div, Ames Res Ctr, NASA, 1965-1966; res consult, Oak Ridge Nat Lab, 1963-1964; lederle Med Fac award, 1962-1965; from asst prof to assoc prof microbiol, Med Sch, Univ Miss, 1958-1965; res assoc microbiol, Stanford Med Sch, 1957-1968; Nat Res Coun fel, Sch Med, Stanford Univ, 1957-1958. **Memberships:** AAAS; fel Am Acad Microbiol; Am Soc Microbiol; Am Soc Biol Chemists; Am Chem Soc. **Research Statement & Publications:** Molecular mechanisms of genetic and biochemical regulation; biochemical basis of chemolithotrophic autotrophy; genetic and biochemical characterization of common enterobacterial antigens. **Mailing Address:** Dept Microbiol & Immunol, Tulane Univ, 1430 Tulane Ave, New Orleans, LA 70112. **Fax:** 504-588-5144.

JOHNSON, ERIC F, BIOCHEMISTRY. **Personal Data:** b Cedar Rapids, Iowa, May 3, 1946. **Education:** Univ Tex, Austin, BS, 1964; Univ Ill, PhD (chem), 1972. **Professional Experience:** ACTG HEAD, DIV BIOCHEM, SCRIPPS RES INST, as of 2005; PROF BIOCHEM, SCRIPPS RES INST, as of 2003; fel, Scripps Res Inst, beginning 1990; assoc mem, Scripps Res Inst, 1983-1990; asst mem, Scripps Res Inst, 1977-1982. **Memberships:** Am Soc Pharmacol & Exp Therapeut; AAAS; Am Chem Soc; Am Soc Biochem & Molecular Biol. **Mailing Address:** Dept Molecular & Exp Med, Scripps Res Inst, 10550 N Torrey Pines Rd, La Jolla, CA 93037-9701. **Fax:** 858-784-7978. **E-Mail:** johnson@scripps.edu

JOHNSON, ERIC G, LASERS. **Personal Data:** b Klamath Falls, Ore, June 17, 1936; div, c 2. **Education:** Mass Inst Technol, BS, 1957; Harvard Univ, MA, 1960, PhD (physics), 1963. **Professional Experience:** PRIN INVESTR, ADVAN DESIGN CONSULT INC, as of 2003; gen physicist, Boulder Labs, Nat Bur Stand, beginning 1962. **Memberships:** Sigma

Xi; Laser Inst Am. **Research Statement & Publications:** Measurement theory; unitary matrix field theory; laser properties measurements. **Mailing Address:** Advan Design Consult Inc, 126 Ridge Rd PO Box 187, Lansing, NY 14882-0187. **Fax:** 607-533-3618.

JOHNSON, ERIC RICHARD, PROTEIN CHEMISTRY & ENZYMOLOGY, CHEMISTRY EDUCATION. **Personal Data:** b Elkhart, Ind, March 11, 1947; m 1990, c 3. **Education:** Rose-Hulman Inst Technol, BS, 1969; Univ Minn, PhD (biochem), 1974. **Professional Experience:** PROF CHEM, BALL STATE UNIV, 1988-; res fel, USAF, 1988; vis assoc prof biol chem, Univ Calif, Los Angeles, 1984-1985; from asst prof to assoc prof, Ball State Univ, 1976-1988; fel, Nat Inst Environ Health Sci, Duke Univ Med Ctr, 1975-1976; res assoc biochem, Duke Univ Med Ctr, 1974-1976; USPHS fel biochem, Univ Minn, 1969-1974; asst chemist, Uniroyal Inc, 1968. **Memberships:** Sigma Xi. **Research Statement & Publications:** Protein and peptide chemistry; high pressure liquid chromatography of protein and peptides; protease enzymology. **Mailing Address:** Dept Chem, Ball State Univ, CP 305L, Muncie, IN 47306-0445. **E-Mail:** ejohnson@bsu.edu

JOHNSON, ERIC VAN, ORNITHOLOGY. **Personal Data:** b Medford, Mass, March 11, 1943; div, c Kristina M & Eric L. **Education:** Brown Univ, BA, 1964; Cornell Univ, PhD (wildlife sci), 1969. **Professional Experience:** PROF EMER BIOL SCI, CALIF POLYTECH STATE UNIV, SAN LUIS OBISPO, 1998-; prof biol, Calif Polytech State Univ, San Luis Obispo, 1979-1998; from asst prof to assoc prof, Calif Polytech State Univ, 1969-1979. **Memberships:** Cooper Ornith Soc; Am Ornith Union; Wilson Ornith Soc. **Research Statement & Publications:** Avian taxonomy, behavior and population ecology; endangered species biology. **Mailing Address:** Dept Biol Sci, Calif Polytech State Univ, San Luis Obispo, CA 93407.

JOHNSON, ERNEST F(REDERICK), CHEMICAL ENGINEERING. **Personal Data:** b Jamestown, NY, April 4, 1918; m 1944, M Ruth McMullin; c David (deceased), Carolyn (Walton), Arthur & Melissa (Bonner). **Education:** Lehigh Univ, BS, 1940; Univ Pa, PhD (chem eng), 1949. **Honors & Awards:** Jubilee Medal, Am Inst Chem Engrs, 83. **Professional Experience:** Sr adv pres, Princeton univ, 1988-1991; EMER PROF CHEM ENG, PRINCETON UNIV, 1986-; clerk fac, Princeton univ, 1983-1986; chmn dept, Dept Chem Eng, 1977-1978; dir grad studies, Dept Chem Eng, 1969-1974; dir, Autodynamics, Inc, 1967-1985; chmn, Assoc Univs, Inc, 1965-1967; trustee, Assoc Univs, Inc, 1962-1968; assoc dean fac, Princeton Univ, 1962-1966; assoc, Plasma Physics Lab, 1955-1988; Consult chem engr, 1950-; from asst prof to prof, Princeton Univ, 1948-1986; From res & develop engr to tech supvr synthetic org chem mfg, Barrett Div, Allied Chem & Dye Corp, 1940-1946. **Memberships:** Fel AAAS emer mem; Am Chem Soc emer mem; fel Am Inst Chem Engrs; fel Am Inst Chemists. **Research Statement & Publications:** Thermodynamic and transport properties of fluids; automatic process control; industrial wastes management; technological aspects of controlled thermonuclear fusion. **Mailing Address:** Dept Chem Eng, Princeton Univ Eng Quadrangle, Princeton, NJ 08544.

JOHNSON, ERNEST WALTER, SPONSORED RESEARCH PROGRAM DEVELOPMENT. **Personal Data:** b Paterson, NJ, December 15, 1943; m 1977, Janet; c Rebecca, Jeffrey, Jennifer & Thomas. **Education:** Muhlenberg Col, BS, 1965; Univ Vt, PhD (physiol, biophys), 1970. **Professional Experience:** PROF CELLULAR & MOLECULAR PHYSIOL, PENN STATE UNIV COL MED, HERSHEY MED CTR, as of 2004; DIR, RES AFFAIRS, PENN STATE UNIV COL MED, HERSHEY MED CTR, 1994-; dir, Ctr Grants & Contacts, Pa State Univ, 1991-1994; dir, Div Diabetes, Endocrinol & Metab Dis, Nat Inst Diabetes, Digestive & Kidney Dis, 1984-1991; br chief diabetes, Nat Inst Arthritis, Metab & Digestive Dis, 1979-1984; sect chief diabetes, NIH, 1977-1979; grants assoc, NIH, 1976-1977; AAAS fel & legis asst health sci, US Senate, 1975-1976; asst prof physiol, med Ctr, Univ Colo, 1972-1975; res assoc physiol, Med Ctr, Univ Colo, 1970-1972; NIH fel, Med Ctr, Univ Colo, 1970-1972. **Memberships:** AAAS; Nat Counc Univ Res adminr; Soc Res adminr. **Research Statement & Publications:** Provides leadership for sponsored programs including basic biomedical research, clinical research, clinical trials, epidemiology, health service research, training and career development, research centres and institutes, education, community service, and patient care. **Mailing Address:** Milton S Hershey Med Ctr, Pa State Univ, 500 Univ Dr PO Box 850, Hershey, PA 17033-0850. **Fax:** 717-531-5352. **E-Mail:** ejohnson@psu.edu

JOHNSON, ERWIN H, AERONAUTICS. **Education:** Stanford Univ, PhD. **Professional Experience:** STAFF, MACNEAL SCHWENDLER CO, as of 2000. **Memberships:** Am Inst Aeronaut & Astronaut. **Mailing Address:** MacNeal Schwendler Co, 815 Colorado Blvd, Los Angeles, CA 90041-1720. **Fax:** 213-259-4959.

JOHNSON, EUGENE A, BIOSTATISTICS. **Personal Data:** b Crosby, Minn, February 24, 1925; m 1947, c 4. **Education:** Univ Minn, BA, 1949, MA, 1950, PhD (biostatist), 1956. **Professional Experience:** DIR GRAD STUDY, COL MED SCI, UNIV MINN, MINNEAPOLIS, 1980-; PROF BIOMET, COL MED SCI, UNIV MINN, MINNEAPOLIS, 1969-; assoc prof & dir biomed data processing unit, Col Med Sci, Univ Minn, Minneapolis, 1964-1969; prof math & head dept, Gustavus Adolphus Col, 1962-1964; assoc prof indust eng, Univ Minn, Minneapolis, 1960-1962; f rom asst prof to assoc prof biostatist, Univ Minn, Minneapolis, 1956-1960. **Memberships:** Am Statist Asn; Biomet Soc; Inst Math Statist; Sigma Xi. **Research Statement & Publications:** Biomedical computing; computing in biology; mathematics; operations research. **Mailing Address:** 1580 Fulham St, Falcon Heights, MN 55108-1312.

JOHNSON, EUGENE MALCOLM, PHARMACOLOGY. **Personal Data:** b Baltimore, Md, October 20, 1943; m 1965, c 2. **Education:** Univ Md, BS, 1966, PhD (med chem), 1970. **Professional Experience:** CO-DIR, ALZHEIMER'S DIS RES CTR, 1994-; NORMAN J STUPP PROF, DEPT NEUROL, 1994-; PROF, DEPT MOLECULAR BIOL & PHARMACOL, SCH MED, WASH UNIV, ST LOUIS, 1983-; assoc prof pharmacol, sch med, wash Univ, St Louis, 1978-1983; asst prof, Sch Med, Wash Univ, 1976-1978; asst prof, Med Col Pa, 1973-1976; fel pharmacol, Sch Med, Wash Univ, 1970-1973; instr med Chem, Dept Med Chem, Univ Md, 1968-1969. **Research Statement & Publications:** Autonomic pharmacology; role of sympathetic nervous system in hypertension; effect of drugs on development of the sympathetic nervous system. **Mailing Address:** Dept Pharmacol, Wash Univ Sch Med, 660 S Euclid Ave PO Box 8103, St Louis, MO 63110. **Fax:** 314-362-7058. **E-Mail:** emjohnson@msnotes.wustl.edu

JOHNSON, EUGENE W, ALGEBRA. **Personal Data:** b El Paso, Tex, May 25, 1939; m 1959, c 1. **Education:** Univ Calif, Riverside, BA, 1963, MA, 1964, PhD (algebra), 1966. **Professional Experience:** PROF EMER MATH, UNIV IOWA, as of 2005; prof math, Univ Iowa, beginning 1975; from asst prof to assoc prof, Univ Iowa, 1966-1975; asst prof math, Eastern NMex Univ, 1966. **Memberships:** Am Math Soc; Math Asn Am. **Research Statement & Publications:** Noetherian rings and abstract ideal theory. **Mailing Address:** Dept Math, Col Lib Arts & Sci, Univ Iowa, 14 MLH, Iowa City, IA 52242. **Fax:** 319-335-0627. **E-Mail:** eugene-johnson@uiowa.edu

JOHNSON, EVERT WILLIAM, FORESTRY, PHOTOGRAMMETRY. **Personal Data:** b Astoria, NY, April 6, 1921; m 1950, c 3. **Education:** Univ NH, BS, 1943; Yale Univ, MF, 1947; Syracuse Univ, PhD, 1957. **Professional Experience:** PROF EMER FORESTRY, AUBURN UNIV, 1986-; prof, Auburn Univ, 1980-1986; asst forester, Auburn Univ, 1953-1957; from instr to assoc prof forestry, Auburn Univ, 1950-1967; asst, Auburn Univ, 1950-1953; forester chg aerial surv, Sable Mt Corp, Vt, 1947-1950; fel, Soc Am Foresters. **Memberships:** Soc Am Foresters; Am Soc Photogram; Sigma Xi. **Research Statement & Publications:** Applications of photogrammetry, statistics and computer science to forest measurements. **Mailing Address:** Dept Forestry, Auburn Univ, Auburn, AL 36849.

JOHNSON, E(WELL) CALVIN, ELECTRICAL ENGINEERING. **Personal Data:** b Tampa, Fla, April 18, 1926; div, c Cynthia. **Education:** Ga Inst Technol, BEE, 1947; Mass Inst Technol, SM, 1949, EE, 1950, ScD(elec eng), 1951. **Professional Experience:** CORP STAFF, UBC INC, 1989-; dir res & develop, Aerosonic Corp, 1988-1989; consult, Vincent Corp, 1985-1987; pres, Vincent Corp, 1980-1985; consult, 1975-1980; vpres res & develop, Gould, Inc, 1973-1975; vpres eng & res, Res Labs Div, Bendix Corp, 1969-1973; vpres res & dir labs div, Res Labs Div, Bendix Corp, 1967-1969; asst gen mgr, Res Labs Div, Bendix Corp, 1965-1967; mgr info & control systs lab, Res Labs Div, Bendix Corp, 1962-1965; head comput dept, Res Labs Div, Bendix Corp, 1958-1962; supvry engr, Res Labs Div, Bendix Corp, 1956-1958; proj engr, Res Labs Div, Bendix Corp, 1954-1956; sr engr, Res Labs Div, Bendix Corp, 1951-1954; res asst, Mass Inst Technol, 1947-1951. **Memberships:** Fel Inst Elec & Electronics Engrs. **Research Statement & Publications:** Feedback control systems; analog and digital computers; machine-tool control; photogrammetric instruments; aerospace information and control systems; automotive electronics; industrial automation systems. **Mailing Address:** UBC Inc, PO Box 18751, Tampa, FL 33679.

JOHNSON, F BRENT, VIROLOGY. **Personal Data:** b Monroe, Utah, March 31, 1942; m 1965, Paula; c Brian, Matthew, Christopher, Wesley & Stephanie. **Education:** Brigham Young Univ, BS, 1966, MS, 1967, PhD (microbiol), 1970. **Professional Experience:** LAB DIR, MICROVIR LABS, 1989-; res grants, Thrasher Fund, 1987-1990; LAB DIR, RICHARDS LABS, 1986-; PROF MICROBIOL, BRIGHAM YOUNG UNIV, 1980-; res grants, Air Force Off Sci Res, 1977-1978, 1979-1982; NIH res grants, 1973 & 1976; from asst prof to assoc prof, Richards Labs, beginning 1986; Microvir Labs, 1972-1980; fel virol, NIH, 1970-1972. **Memberships:** Am Soc Microbiol; AAAS; Sigma Xi; Am Soc Virol; Am Asn Lab Animal Sci. **Research Statement & Publications:** Viral replication; structure of viruses and biology of virus infections; diagnostic virology. **Mailing Address:** Dept Microbiol & Molecular Biol, Brigham Young Univ, 887 Widtsoe Bldg, Provo, UT 84602. **E-Mail:** brent_johnson@byu.edu

JOHNSON, F CLIFFORD, GENETICS, ECOLOGY. **Personal Data:** b Ft Worth, Tex, November 4, 1932; m 1958, c 3. **Education:** Univ Tex, BA, 1955, MA, 1960, PhD (zoology), 1961. **Professional Experience:** PROF ZOOL, UNIV FLA, 1970-; assoc prof, NMex Inst Mining & Technol, 1967-1970; asst prof biol & chmn dept, NMex Inst Mining & Technol, 1962-1966; asst prof genetics, Va Polytech Inst, 1961-1962; instr zool, Duke Univ, 1960-1961. **Research Statement & Publications:** Genetics of polymorphic variation. **Mailing Address:** Dept Zool Univ Fla, 223 Bartram Hall, Gainesville, FL 32611-2009.

JOHNSON, FATIMA NUNES, DEVELOPMENT OF SPECIFICATIONS FOR FOOD CHEMICALS & DRUGS. **Personal Data:** b Rizal, Philippines, January 1, 1939; American citizen; m 1967, Edgar; c Victoria C & David M. **Education:** Adamson Univ, Manila, BS, 1959; Boston Col, MS, 1961, PhD (org chem), 1964. **Professional Experience:** DIR, FOOD CHEM CODEX, NAT ACAD SCI, as of 2004; STUDY DIR, INST MED, NAT ACAD SCI, WASH, DC, 1992-; chemist, Drug Enforcement Admin, Wash, DC, 1991-1992; sr staff officer, Inst Med, Nat Acad Sci, Wash, DC, 1990-1991; scientist drug stand, US Pharmacopeia, Rockville, Md, 1971-1990; res chemist, Org Chem Labs, Edgewood Arsenal, Md, 1969-1970; proj leader org med chem, Arthur D Little Inc, Mass, 1964-1969. **Memberships:** Am Chem Soc; Asn Off Anal Chemists Int. **Research Statement & Publications:** Organo-fluorine compounds; organometallics; molecular rearrangements; nitrogen heterocyclics. **Mailing Address:** Food Chem Codex, Nat Acad Sci, 2101 Const Ave N W, Washington, DC 20418. **Fax:** 202-334-2316. **E-Mail:** fjohnson@nas.edu

JOHNSON, FLOYD HOWARD, INTERNET TECHNOLOGIES, ISSUES RAISED BY THE COMPUTING SCIENCES. **Personal Data:** b San Fernando, Calif, November 24, 1950; m 1974, Sandra; c 3. **Education:** Univ Evansville, MS, 1986; Univ Nebr, MSEd, 1994. **Professional Experience:** ASST PROF, DEPT COMPUT SCI, ROBERTS WESLEYAN COL, as of 2005; asst prof, dept comput sci, Northwestern Col, beginning 1992; asst prof comput sci & info technol, Univ Nebr, 1987-1992; Prof comput info systs, Bartlesville Wesleyan Col, 1983-1987. **Memberships:** Asn Comp Mach; Asn Christians Math Sci; Inst Elec & Electronics Engrs Comput Soc. **Research Statement & Publications:** Internet, both as a technology and as its impact on society. **Mailing Address:** Dept Compu Sci, Roberts Wesleyan Col, 2301 Westside Dr, Rochester, NY 14624-1997. **E-Mail:** floydj@netins.net

JOHNSON, FRANCIS, PHARMACOLOGY. **Personal Data:** b Bristol, Eng, March 12, 1930; m 1955, c 3. **Education:** Glasgow Univ, BSc, 1951, PhD (org chem), 1954. **Professional Experience:** Consult res dir, Ganes Chemicals Inc, NJ, 1990-; consult, Qm res Corps, US Army, 1956-1958 & Dow Chem Co, 1974-; PROF PHARMACOL & CHEM, STATE UNIV NY STONY BROOK, 1974-; res scientist, Eastern res lab, Dow Chem Co, 1969-1974; vis scientist, Oxford Univ, 1966-1967; from res chemist to assoc scientist, Eastern res lab, Dow Chem Co, 1957-1969; eve lectr, Boston Univ, 1956-1970; fel org chem, Boston Univ, 1954-1957. **Memberships:** Am Chem Soc; Royal Soc Chem; assoc Royal Inst Chem; fel Royal Soc Arts; NY Acad Sci. **Research Statement & Publications:** Synthetic organic chemistry, especially natural product and aliphatic areas; medicinal chemistry. **Mailing Address:** Dept Chem, State Univ NY, Grand Chem Bldg Rm 607, Stony Brook, NY 11794-3400. **E-Mail:** francis.johnson@sunysb.edu

JOHNSON, FRANCIS SEVERIN, SPACE PHYSICS, METEOROLOGY. **Personal Data:** b Omak, Wash, July 20, 1918; m 1943, Maurine; c Sharan (Fry). **Education:** Univ Alta, BSc, 1940; Univ Calif, Los Angeles, MA, 1942, PhD (meteorol), 1958. **Honors & Awards:** Space Sci Award, Am Inst Aeronaut & Astronaut, 1966; Henryk Arctowski Medal, Nat Acad Sci, 1972; Except Sci Achievement Medal, NASA, 1973; John A Fleming Award, Am Geophys Union, 1977 Distinguished Tex Scientist Award, Tex Acad Sci, 1984. **Professional Experience:** EMER PROF, UNIV TEX, DALLAS, 1990-; mem comt solar physics, Nat Acad Sci, 1986-1988; mem Aerocibo Adv bd, Nat Astron & Ionospher Ctr, 1985-1988; mem nat acad sci bd Atmospheric Sci & Climate, 1984-1987; asst dir Astron, Atmospheric, Earth Ocean Sci, NSF, Wash, DC, 1979-1983; mem, Climate Res Bd, Nat Acad Sci, 1977-1979; vpres, Comt Space Res, Int Coun Sci Unions, 1975-1980; chmn, US Nat Comt, 1973-1976; mem, climatic impact comt, Nat Acad Sci, 1972-1976; mem geophys res bd, nat acad Sci 1977-1978; Panel Adv Cent Radio Propagation Lab, Nat Bur Stand, 1971-1975; prof & dir, Ctr Advan Studies, 1971-1974; chmn, Panel Adv Cent Radio

Propagation Lab, Nat Bur Stand, 1971-1974; mem, Nat Adv Comt Oceans & Atmosphere, 1971-1973; mem nat acad sci comt adv to Nat Oceanic & Atmospheric Admin, 1971-1972; vice chmn, US Nat Comt, 1970-1973; actg pres, Univ Tex, Dallas, 1969-1971; mem Nat Acad Sci space sci bd, 1969-1981; mem, Air Force Sci Adv Bd, 1968-1979; secy, US Nat Comt, 1967-1970; Panel Adv Cent Radio Propagation Lab, Nat Bur Stand, 1966-1979; mem comt adv to Environ Sci Serv Admin, 1966-1971; mem, mem adv comt to Air Force Systs Command panel on re-entry physics, 1965-1968; mem panel on weather & climate modification, Panel Adv Cent Radio Propagation Lab, Nat Bur Stand, 1964-1970; chmn, US Comn IV, Int Union Radio Sci, 1964-1967; prof & dir, Earth & Planetary Sci Lab, Southwest Ctr Advan Studies, 1962-1969; mem adv panel atmospheric sci, NSF, 1962-1966; mem, Panel Adv Cent Radio Propagation Lab, Nat Bur Stand, 1962-1965; Consult, NASA, 1960-1979; space physicist, Lockheed Missiles & Space Co, 1955-1962; physicist, US Naval Res Lab, 1946-1955. **Memberships:** Am Meteorol Soc; Am Geophys Union; Am Inst Aeronaut & Astronaut; Inst Elec & Electronics Engrs; Sigma Xi. **Research Statement & Publications:** Upper atmospheric and magnetospheric physics; space science; planetary atmospheres; upper atmosphere and space physics; planetary science; solar radiation; synoptic and physical meteorology. **Mailing Address:** 13619 Sprucewood Dr, Dallas, TX 75240.

JOHNSON, FRANK BACCHUS, PATHOLOGY. **Personal Data:** b Washington, DC, February 1, 1919; m 1947, c 2. **Education:** Univ Mich, BS, 1940; Howard Univ, MD, 1944. **Honors & Awards:** Citation Admin & Tech Proficiency, Vet Admin, 1958; Commendation Outstanding Contributions Histochem, 1964. **Professional Experience:** CHIEF, DEPT CHEM PATH, ARMED FORCES INST PATH, as of 2004; chmn, dept chem path, Armed Forces Inst Path, beginning 1974; chief, Histochem Br, 1972-1974; chief basic sci div, Armed Forces Inst Path, 1960-1972; pathologist, Armed Forces Inst Path, 1952-1960; res assoc, Univ Chicago, 1950-1952; AEC fel med sci, Univ Chicago, 1948-1950; dir clin labs, Howard Univ, 1946-1948; from intern to resident path, Med Ctr, Jersey City, 1944-1946; Dipl Am Bd Path Path Anat. **Memberships:** Am Crystallog Soc; Am Chem Soc. **Research Statement & Publications:** Histochemistry in pathology. **Mailing Address:** Dept path, Armed Forces Inst Path, Rm G-071 Bldg Ste 54 6825 16th St NW, Washington, DC 20306-6000. **Fax:** 800-441-0094. **E-Mail:** johnson@afip.osd.mil

JOHNSON, FRANK JUNIOR, ANALYTICAL CHEMISTRY. **Personal Data:** b Rosendale, Mo, August 24, 1930; m 1951, c 3. **Education:** Northwest Mo State Col, BS, 1952; Univ Mo, MSc, 1961. **Professional Experience:** RETIRED; chief, PE Serv Br, Tenn Authority, 1986; head serv, Tenn Authority, 1969-1986; anal chemist, head serv, Tenn Authority, 1962-1969; instr agr chem, Univ Mo, 1955-1962. **Memberships:** Asn Off Anal Chemists (pres-elect, 1985-1986 & pres, 1986-1987); Am Chem Soc; Fertilizer Soc. **Research Statement & Publications:** Fertilizer chemistry; investigation of new or improved analytical methods pertaining to fertilizer and related materials. **Mailing Address:** 205 Westmeade Ct, Florence, AL 35630.

JOHNSON, FRANKLIN M, GENETICS. **Personal Data:** b Cloquet, Minn, November 1, 1940; m 1981, Dorothy; c Erik, David & Olen. **Education:** Univ Minn, Duluth, BA, 1962; Univ Hawaii, MS, 1964; Univ Tex, Austin, PhD (zoology), 1966. **Professional Experience:** DIV INTRAMURAL RES, NAT INST ENVIRON HEALTH SCI, as of 1997; RES GENETICIST, NAT INST ENVIRON HEALTH SCI, 1977-; sr geneticist, Res Triangle Inst, 1974-1977; asst prof genetics, NC State Univ, 1968-1974; res scientist, Univ Tex, Austin, 1967-1968; NIH fel, 1966-1967. **Memberships:** AAAS; Genetics Soc Am; Soc Environ Toxicol Chem; Am Soc Human Genetics. **Research Statement & Publications:** Genetic variability in natural populations; genotype-environment relationships; developmental variation in the skeleton; mutagenesis; genetic risk; carcinogenesis. **Mailing Address:** Div Intramural Res, Nat Inst Environ Health Sci, Research Triangle Park, NC 27709. **Fax:** 919-541-1460.

JOHNSON, FRED LOWERY, INDUSTRIAL ORGANIC CHEMISTRY. **Personal Data:** b San Angelo, Tex, October 24, 1927; m 1949, Dorothy; c Ellen, Mary & Fred. **Education:** Univ Tex, BS, 1951, PhD (chem), 1959. **Professional Experience:** RETIRED; sr proj chemist, Texaco Chem Co, 1976-1987; proj chemist, Jefferson Chem Co Inc, 1968-1976; sr res chemist, Jefferson Chem Co Inc, 1964-1968; res chemist, Jefferson Chem Co Inc, 1962-1964; s r process chemist, Am Cyanamid Co, La, 1959-1962. **Memberships:** Am Chem Soc; Sigma Xi. **Research Statement & Publications:** Catalytic research and process development for petrochemicals. **Mailing Address:** 3002 Yellowpine Terr, Austin, TX 78757-1629.

JOHNSON, FRED M, LASER PHYSICS. **Education:** City Col NY, BS, 1949; Columbia Univ, MA, 1951; PhD (physics), 1958. **Professional Experience:** PROF EMER PHYSICS, CALIF STATE UNIV, as of 2003; prof, Dept Physics & Astron, Calif State Univ, beginning 1971. **Memberships:** Am Phys Soc; Int Astron Union. **Mailing Address:** Dept Physics, Calif State Univ, PO Box 6866, Fullerton, CA 92834-6866. **Fax:** 714-278-5810.

JOHNSON, FREDERIC ALLAN, INORGANIC CHEMISTRY, PHYSICAL CHEMISTRY. **Personal Data:** b Concord, NH, March 6, 1932; m 1956, c 3. **Education:** Univ NH, BS, 1954, MS, 1955; Univ Wis, PhD (chem), 1958. **Professional Experience:** RETIRED; assoc prof chem, Auburn Univ, 1970-1992; group leader anal chem, Redstone Arsenal Res Div, Rohm & Haas Co, 1962-1970; chemist, Redstone Arsenal Res Div, Rohm & Haas Co, 1958-1962; lab instr, Univ NH, 1954. **Memberships:** Am Chem Soc. **Research Statement & Publications:** Fluorine and metal coordination chemistry; nuclear magnetic resonance; kinetics. **Mailing Address:** 821 Heard Ct, Auburn, AL 36830-6243.

JOHNSON, FREDERIC DUANE, FOREST ECOLOGY, DENDROOGY. **Personal Data:** b Chicago, Ill, October 24, 1925; m 1948, Virginia; c Paul D, Jacqveline S, Laure M, Judith M & Mark F. **Education:** Ore State Col, BS, 1950; Univ Idaho, MS, 1952. **Professional Experience:** PROF EMER FOREST ECOL, UNIV IDAHO, 1972-; assoc prof forest ecol, Univ Idaho, 1967-1972; from instr to asst prof forest mgt, Univ Idaho, 1956-1967; Radioisotopes technologist, Univ Idaho, 1952-1956; emer prof 1990; adj prof, Inst Agron Vet, Morocco. **Memberships:** Ecol Soc Am; fel Soc Am Foresters. **Research Statement & Publications:** Forest ecology-temperate and tropical, ecologic accessment; temperate and tropical dendrology. **Mailing Address:** Col Natural Resources, Univ Idaho, Moscow, ID 83843-4199.

JOHNSON, FREDERICK ALLAN, NUCLEAR PHYSICS. **Personal Data:** b Winnipeg, Man, November 7, 1923. **Education:** Univ Man, BSc, 1945; McGill Univ, PhD (nuclear physics), 1952. **Professional Experience:** DEFENCE SCI SERV OFFICER NUCLEAR PHYSICS, DEFENCE RES BD, DEFENCE RES ESTAB, 1971-; Defence Sci Serv Officer Chem, Biol & Radiation Labs, 1959-1971; Defence Sci Serv officer nuclear physics, Suffield Exp Sta, 1955-1959; sr engr, Can Aviation Electronics Co, 1953-1955; res assoc nuclear physics, Radiation Lab, McGill Univ, 1952-1953. **Memberships:** Am Phys Soc; Can Asn Physicists. **Research Statement & Publications:** Spectroscopy of nuclear radiations from cyclotron-produced cadmium and silver isotopes; auger transitions in silver; industrial design of radiation detectors; nanosecond pulse electronics; neutron time-of-flight spectroscopy; beam pulsing and deflection; pulse-shape discrimination circuits for neutron identification; neutron activation; radiological protection and health physics. **Mailing Address:** Six Esquimalt Ave, Nepean, ON K2H 6Z3, Can.

JOHNSON, FREDERICK CARROLL, APPLIED MATHEMATICS, RESOURCE MANAGEMENT. **Personal Data:** b Sheridan, Wyo, October 23, 1940; m 1964, c 1. **Education:** Univ NDak, BS, 1962; Univ Wash, MS & PhD (appl math), 1966. **Honors & Awards:** Silver Medal, Dept Commerce, 1978. **Professional Experience:** SR TECH MGR COMPUT SCI, MATH, INFO & COMPUTATIONAL SCI DIV, 1999-; coordr, comput, Nat Inst Stand & Technol, as of 1995; assoc dir Comput, Nat Inst Stand & Technol, beginning 1987; chief, Math Anal Div, 1984-1987; partner, Nat Res consult, 1982-1984; chief, Math Anal Div, 1977-1982; mathematician, Nat Bur Stand, 1973-1977; res scientist appl math, Boeing Sci Res Labs, 1968-1973; res analyst real-time data processing, DBA Systs Inc, 1966-1968. **Memberships:** Soc Indust & Appl Math; Inst Elec & Electronics Engrs; Asn Comput Mach; Am Fisheries Soc; Sigma Xi. **Research Statement & Publications:** Applications of mathematical modeling to physical systems; high performance computing; scientific visualization for mathematical modeling. **Mailing Address:** Math, Info & Computational Sci, 19901 Germantown Rd, Germantown, MD 20874. **Fax:** 301-903-7774. **E-Mail:** fjohnson@cam.nist.gov

JOHNSON, G ALLAN, MEDICAL IMAGING. **Personal Data:** b Champaigne, Ill, January 17, 1947; m 1969, c 2. **Education:** St Olaf Col, BA, 1969; Duke Univ, PhD (physics), 1974. **Professional Experience:** DIR, CTR IN VIVO MICROSCOPY, DUKE UNIV MED CTR, as of 2005; CHARLES E PUTMAN UNIV PROF PHYSICS, RADIOL, BIOMED ENG, DUKE UNIV MED CTR, 2002-; PROF, DEPT PHYSICS, DUKE UNIV MED CTR, 1998; PROF, DEPT RADIOL, DUKE UNIV MED CTR, 1998; PROF BIOMED ENG, DUKE UNIV MED CTR, 1994-; from asst prof to assoc prof, Dept Radiol, Duke Univ Med Ctr, 1978-1983; dir diag physics, Dept Radiol, Duke Univ Med Ctr, 1979-; assoc physics, Dept Radiol, Duke Univ Med Ctr, 1978. **Memberships:** Sigma Xi; Am Phys Soc; Am Asn Physicists Med; Soc Magnetic Resonance Med; Am Inst Med & Biol Eng. **Research Statement & Publications:** Implementation and enhancement of new imaging technologies in medicine; magnetic resonance microscopy and its extension to basic sciences; author of various articles. **Mailing Address:** Ctr In Vivo Microscopy, Duke Univ Med Ctr, PO Box 3302 Rm 141, Durham, NC 27710. **Fax:** 919-684-7158. **E-Mail:** gaj@orion.duhs.duke.edu

JOHNSON, GARLAND A, BIOCHEMISTRY, PHARMACOLOGY. **Personal Data:** b Laona, Wis, July 16, 1936; m 1958, c 4. **Education:** Carroll Col, Wis, BS, 1958; Ohio State Univ, MSc, 1960, PhD (physiol chem), 1963. **Professional Experience:** RES ASSOC, UPJOHN CO, 1964-; staff fel, Nat Inst Neurol Dis & Blindness, 1963-1964; res assoc biochem, Res Found, Ohio State Univ, 1963. **Memberships:** AAAS; Am Soc Pharmacol & Exp Therapeut. **Research Statement & Publications:** Metabolism of catecholamines and serotonin; effect of drugs on biogenic amines. **Mailing Address:** 2566 Villa Lane, Cincinnati, OH 45208-1121.

JOHNSON, GARY DEAN, GEOLOGY. **Personal Data:** b Sioux City, Iowa, December 2, 1942; m 1965, c 1. **Education:** Iowa State Univ, BS, 1964, MS, 1967, PhD (geol), 1971. **Professional Experience:** PROF GEOL, DEPT EARTH SCI, DARTMOUTH COL, 1987-; chmn dept, Dartmouth Col, 1980-1983; from asst prof to assoc prof, Dartmouth Col, 1971-1986; res assoc, Iowa State Univ, 1971-1972; instr geol, Iowa State Univ, 1969-1971. **Memberships:** Geol Soc Am; Soc Econ Paleont & Mineral; Int Asn Sedimentologists. **Research Statement & Publications:** Stratigraphy and sedimentology; Cenozoic terrestrial deposits of Asia and Africa; geology of the Himalayas; paleopedology; geochronology. **Mailing Address:** Dept Earth Sci, Dartmouth Col, 6105 Fairchild Hall 408 Fairchild, Hanover, NH 03755. **Fax:** 603-646-3922. **E-Mail:** gary.johnson@dartmouth.edu

JOHNSON, GARY L, MOLECULAR BIOLOGY, CELL GROWTH & DIFFERENTIATION. **Personal Data:** b Oxford, Nebr, September 18, 1949. **Education:** Calif State Univ, Northridge, BS, 1971; Univ Colo, PhD (pharmacol), 1976. **Professional Experience:** PROF & CHMN, DEPT PHARMACOL, UNIV NC, CHAPEL HILL, 2003-; MEM, LINEBERGER COMPREHENSIVE CANCER CTR & CO-DIR, PROG MOLECULAR THERAPEUT, 2003-; vice chair, Health Sci Ctr, Univ Colo, 2002-2003; MEM, SCI ADV & PHARMACOL REV BD, ATHEROGENICS INC, 2001-; assoc dir basic res, Comprehensive Cancer Ctr, Univ Colo, 1999-2003; dir cell biol, Cadus Pharmaceut, 1994-1999; prof pharmacol, Health Sci Ctr, Univ Colo, 1988-2003; sr scientist, Nat Jewish Med & Res Ctr, 1988-2000; prof, Med Ctr, Dept Biochem, 1987-1988; assoc prof, dept biochem & molecular biol, Sch Med, Univ Mass, 1981-1988; asst prof, Univ Mass, 1979-1987; fel, Univ Calif, San Francisco, 1976-1979. **Memberships:** Am Soc Microbiol; Am Soc Biochem & Molecular Biol. **Mailing Address:** Dept Pharmacol, Univ NC, 1108 Mary Ellen Jones Bldg, PO Box 7365, Chapel Hill, NC 27599. **Fax:** 919-966-5640. **E-Mail:** gary_johnson@med.unc.edu

JOHNSON, GARY LEE, ELECTRICAL ENGINEERING. **Personal Data:** b Osage City, Kans, November 20, 1938; m 1960, Jolene; c Kirk & Janel. **Education:** Kans State Univ, BS, 1961, MS, 1963; Okla State Univ, PhD, 1966. **Professional Experience:** PROF EMER ELEC ENG, KANS STATE UNIV, 1994-; consult, Kansas City Power & Light Co, 1971-1972; from asst prof to prof, Kans State Univ, 1966-1994. **Memberships:** Inst Elec & Electronics Engrs; Am Wind Energy Asn; Int Tesla Soc. **Research Statement & Publications:** Power systems; wind electric systems. **Mailing Address:** Dept Elect & Comput Engr, Kans State Univ, 261 Durland Hall, Manhattan, KS 66506. **E-Mail:** gjohnson@ksu.edu

JOHNSON, GEAROLD ROBERT, ENGINEERING DESIGN, ENGINEERING COMPUTER GRAPHICS. **Personal Data:** b Des Moines, Iowa, January 11, 1940; m 1962, c 2. **Education:** Purdue Univ, BS, 1962, MS, 1968, PhD (mech eng), 1972. **Professional Experience:** ACAD VPRES, NAT TECHNOL UNIV, as of 2001; dir, NTU-Eurosud Found, Paris, 1992-1993; vis scientist, Shape Data Ltd, Cambridge, UK, 1985-1986; G T ABELL CHMN, COLO STATE UNIV, 1984-; vis prof, Calif Inst Technol, 1984; vis prof, Univ Kent, Canterbury, UK, 1978-1979; from asst prof to prof, Colo State Univ, 1973-1984; NATO fel fluid mech, von Karman Inst, 1970-1971; engr, aerospace, Boeing Co, 1962-1966. **Memberships:** Inst Elec & Electronics Engrs; Inst Elec & Electronics Engrs Comput Soc; Math Asn Am; Am Soc Eng Educ. **Research Statement & Publications:** Application of computers to engineering problems such as solar energy, fluid mechanics, solid modeling, etc; uses of computer technology to support engineering education in design. **Mailing Address:** Nat Tech Univ, 700 Ctr Ave, Ft Collins, CO 80526-1842. **Fax:** 970-498-0601. **E-Mail:** gerry@ntu.edu

JOHNSON, GEORGE, MEDICINE, SURGERY. **Personal Data:** b Wilmington, NC, April 6, 1926; m 1950, c 4. **Education:** Univ NC, BS, 1949; Cornell Univ, MD, 1952; Am Bd Surg, dipl, 1960; Am Bd Thoracic Surg, dipl, 1963. **Professional Experience:** ROSCOE B G COWPER DISTINGUISHED PROF EMER SURG, SCH MED, UNIV NC, CHAPEL HILL, as of 2004; vchmn, Dept Surg, Univ Nc, Chapel Hill, beginning 1977; Roscoe B G

Cowper prof surg, Div Gen Surg, Sch Med, Univ Nc, Chapel Hill, beginning 1973; prof, Dept Surg, ending 1973; chief, Div Gen Surg, Sch Med, Univ Nc, Chapel Hill, beginning 1969; asst prof, Dept Surg, beginning 1961; instr surg, Cornell Univ, 1958-1959. **Memberships:** Am Col Surgeons; Soc Univ Surgeons; Soc Vascular Surgeons; Am Asn Surg of Trauma; Asn Acad Surgeons. **Research Statement & Publications:** Vascular and thoracic surgery; hemodynamics associated with cirrhosis of the liver; local and systematic hemodynamics of an arteriovenous fistula; gall bladder surgery. **Mailing Address:** Dept Surg, Sch Med, Univ NC, CB No 7210, Chapel Hill, NC 27599-7210.

JOHNSON, GEORGE FREDERICK, organic chemistry; deceased, see previous edition for last biography

JOHNSON, GEORGE LEONARD, GEOLOGICAL OCEANOGRAPHY. **Personal Data:** b Englewood, NJ, May 18, 1931; m 1989, c 3. **Education:** Williams Col, BA, 1953; NY Univ, MS, 1965; Univ Copenhagen, PhD (marine geol), 1975. **Professional Experience:** SR SCIENTIST, UNIV ALASKA, FAIRBANKS, 1994-; dir geophys sci, Phys Sci Admin, 1985-1994; dir arctic progs, Phys Sci Admin, 1980-1985; Panel Polar Eng, Nat Res Coun, 1977- & Comn Tectonic Chart World, 1977-; sci consult, Intergovt Oceanog Comn, Int Hydrographic Off, 1975-; c onsult, Polar Res Bd, Natural Acad Sci, 1975-; sci adminr arctic prog, Off Naval Res, 1975-1980; oceanogr, US Naval Oceanog Off, Md, 1965-1975; res asst marine geol, Lamont-Doherty Geol Observ, 1957-1965; chmn, Arctic Geol-Geophys Comt, Arctic Geol Comt, Lithosphere Comn, secy, US-USSR Ocean Bilateral, Int Arctic Sci Comt, W G Arctic Marine Geol, Nansen Arctic Drilling Prog. **Memberships:** Am Geophys Union; Arctic Inst NAm; Polar Soc. **Research Statement & Publications:** Geophysics with specialization in marine geomorphology and physiography of the world's oceans; arctic and antarctic marine geology; naval arctic research; polar regions. **Mailing Address:** 7708 Lake Glen Dr, Glendale, MD 20769.

JOHNSON, GEORGE PATRICK, TECHNOLOGY ASSESSMENT, CIVIL ENGINEERING. **Personal Data:** b Pine Bluff, Ark, June 16, 1932; m 1967, Jean M Lennon; c Heather, Patrick & Margaret. **Education:** Univ Miss, BSCE, 1954; Stanford Univ, MS, 1967, Engr, 1969, PhD (civil eng), 1971. **Honors & Awards:** Chapter Honor Mem BER Sigma-Xi. **Professional Experience:** PROG MGR SBIR, NSF, 1995-; sr policy analyst, Off Europe, 1990-1995; head, Off Europe, 1988-1990; sr policy analyst, NSF, 1984-1988; prog mgr tech assessment, NSF, 1974-1984; water resource engr, US Army Eng Inst Water Resources, 1971-1974; Consult, Rand Corp, 1970-1971; res engr water resources, INTASA, Inc, 1969-1971; oper analyst housing res, Stanford Res Inst, 1967-1969; Res civil engr int develop, C S McCandless & Co, 1965-1967. **Memberships:** AAAS; Sigma Xi. **Research Statement & Publications:** Technology assessment methods and utilization; policy research and analysis; water resources planning; technological forecasting; futures research; structural modeling; decision analysis for public policy. **Mailing Address:** SBIR Prog NSF, 4201 Wilson Blvd, Arlington, VA 22230. **Fax:** 703-292-8057. **E-Mail:** gpjohnson@nsf.gov

JOHNSON, GEORGE PHILIP, MATHEMATICAL ANALYSIS. **Personal Data:** b Minneapolis, Minn, November 13, 1926; m 1985, Marvel; c 4. **Education:** Univ Minn, BS, 1948, MA, 1949, PhD (math), 1956. **Professional Experience:** RETIRED; consult-evaluator, NCent Asn Cols & Schs, 1972-1991; dean, Grad Sch, 1969-1981; prof, Oakland Univ, 1965-1994; chmn dept, Oakland Univ, 1965-1970; assoc prof, Wesleyan Univ, 1960-1964 & Univ South, 1964-1965; Off Naval Res assoc, 1963-1964; sr mathematician, Stand Oil Co Calif, 1956-1960; instr math, Univ Minn, 1955-1956; mathematician, Nat Security Agency, 1951-1954; asst math & statist, Univ Minn, 1948-1951. **Memberships:** Am Math Soc; Math Asn Am. **Research Statement & Publications:** Abstract harmonic analysis; numerical analysis and computing. **Mailing Address:** 654 W Buell Rd, Rochester, MI 48309. **E-Mail:** gpjohnso@oakland.edu

JOHNSON, GEORGE ROBERT, ANIMAL HUSBANDRY. **Personal Data:** b Caledonia, NY, August 2, 1917; m 1942, c 4. **Education:** Cornell Univ, BS, 1939; Mich State Univ, MS, 1947, PhD, 1954. **Professional Experience:** RETIRED; from assoc prof animal sci to prof animal sci & chmn dept, Ohio State Univ, 1955-1983; from instr to assoc prof animal husb, Cornell Univ, 1943-1955; asst county agt agr, Canton, NY, 1942-1943; pub sch teacher, NY, 1939-1942. **Memberships:** Am Soc Animal Sci. **Research Statement & Publications:** Administration in animal science, especially teaching, research and extension; sheep production and management. **Mailing Address:** 251 Fairlawn Dr, Columbus, OH 43214.

JOHNSON, GEORGE S, CELL BIOLOGY, MOLECULAR BIOLOGY. **Personal Data:** b Cokato, Minn, August 25, 1943. **Education:** Mich State Univ, PhD (biochem), 1969. **Professional Experience:** DEVELOP THERAPEUT PROG, DIV CANCER TREAT & DIAG, as of 2003; RES CHEMIST, NAT CANCER INST, NIH, 1974-. **Memberships:** Am Soc Biol Chem; Am Soc Microbiologists. **Research Statement & Publications:** Oncology. **Mailing Address:** Nat Cancer Inst, 6130 Executive Blvd Rm 8152, Bethesda, MD 20892-7456. **Fax:** 301-402-5200. **E-Mail:** johnsong@exchange.nih.gov

JOHNSON, GERALD III, CARDIOVASCULAR PHYSIOLOGY, NUCLEAR CARDIOLOGY. **Personal Data:** b Liberty, Tex, August 16, 1945; m 1985, Delynda. **Education:** Park Col, BS, 1968; Univ Okla, MA, 1971, PhD (autonomic physiol), 1980. **Professional Experience:** Sci consult, Cis Bio Int Adv Panel, 1995; sci consult, Bracco Diags Adv Panel, 1995; lab dir, W K Warren Med Res Inst, beginning 1990; ASSOC PROF, DEPT MED, UNIV OKLA HEALTH SCI CTR, 1990-; sci consult, Bristol-Myers Squibb Pharmaceut Res Inst, 1990; consult, McGee Rehab Inst, 1990; sr res fel, Ischemia-Shock Res Inst, Jefferson Med Col, 1988-1990; asst prof, Dept Physiol, Oral Roberts Univ Sch Med, 1984-1988; res assoc, Dept Physiol, Oral Roberts Univ Sch Med, 1982-1984; consult, City Faith Hosp, 1982; consult, Oral Roberts Univ Sch Med, 1981-1982; clin & res electrophysiologist, Children's Med Ctr, 1980-1982; fel, Circ Coun, Am Heart Asn. **Memberships:** Am Heart Asn; Am Soc Nuclear Cardiol; Int Soc Heart Res; Sigma Xi; NY Acad Sci; Soc Nuclear Med; Am Physiol Soc. **Research Statement & Publications:** Improvement of diagnostic imaging in normal and cardiovascular disease states; clearance kinetics of novel radiopharmaceuticals are studied with regard to their efficacy in providing diagnostic information about myocardial perfusion, function and viability. **Mailing Address:** 6465 S Yale Ave Ste 1010, William K Warren Medical Res Inst, Tulsa, OK 74136. **Fax:** 918-481-7957.

JOHNSON, GERALD GLENN, MATERIALS SCIENCE. **Personal Data:** b Renovo, Pa, November 10, 1939; m 1963, c 2. **Education:** John Carroll Univ, BS, 1962; Pa State Univ, PhD (solid state sci), 1965. **Professional Experience:** ASSOC PROF EMER, COMPUT SCI & ENG, PA STATE UNIV, as of 2005; CHAIR ZEOPAK CONSORTIUM, as of 2005; assoc prof, Comput Sci, Pa State Univ, 1971-; asst prof solid state sci, PA State Univ, 1965-1971; j r physicist, Erie Registor Corp, 1960-1962; mem, Nat Res Coun. **Memberships:** AAAS; Am Phys Soc; Am Crystallog Asn; Am Soc Testing & Mat; Sigma Xi. **Research Statement & Publications:** Information retrieval as applied to x-ray powder diffraction identification systems; high resolution powder diffraction techniques using Guinier Cameras and automatic microdensitometers. **Mailing Address:** Dept Comput Sci & Eng, Pa State Univ, 123 Transp Res Bdg, Univ Park, PA 16802. **E-Mail:** GGJ@psu.edu

JOHNSON, GERALD WINFORD, CIVIL ENGINEERING. **Personal Data:** b Minneapolis, Minn, October 31, 1932; m 1958, c 3. **Education:** Purdue Univ, BS, 1955; Ohio State Univ, MS, 1960; Univ Wis-Madison, PhD (civil eng), 1969. **Professional Experience:** ASSOC PROF CIVIL, UNIV MINN, MINNEAPOLIS, 1980-; asst prof civil eng, Univ Minn, Minneapolis, beginning 1969; programmer analyst, Syst Develop Corp, Calif, 1961-1965; field serv engr, Boeing Co, Wash, 1960-1961. **Memberships:** Am Soc Civil Engrs; Am Cong Surv & Mapping; Am Soc Photogram; Arctic Inst N Am; Am Inst Navig. **Research Statement & Publications:** Reliability of atmospheric refraction in polar astronavigation; cartography and map rectification in north Greenland; application of computers to survey net adjustments. **Mailing Address:** Dept Civil Eng, Univ Minn, 500 Pillsbury Dr SE, Minneapolis, MN 55455. **Fax:** 612-626-7750. **E-Mail:** johns018@umn.edu

JOHNSON, GLEN ERIC, OPTIMAL MECHANICAL DESIGN. **Personal Data:** b Rochester, NY, May 29, 1951; m 1975, Kathryne DeLoach; c Edward & Eric. **Education:** Worcester Polytech Inst, BS, 1973; Ga Inst Technol, MSME, 1974; Vanderbilt Univ, PhD (mech eng), 1978. **Honors & Awards:** Ralph Teetor Award, Soc Automotive Engrs, 1984. **Professional Experience:** DEAN, COL ENG, TENN TECH UNIV, 1999-; prof & chair, Dept Mech & Aerospace Eng, Univ Dayton, 1993-1999; chair, Design Div, Am Soc Mech Engrs, 1993-1994; dir, Design Lab, 1991-1993; assoc prof, Univ Mich, 1989-1993; assoc ed, J Mech Trans Automation Design, 1982-1983; assoc prof, Vanderbilt Univ, 1981-1989; assoc ed, J Mech Design, Am Soc Mech Engrs, 1981-1982; PRIN INVESTR, NSF, 1980-; co-prin investr, US Dept Transp, 1980-1981; asst prof, mech eng, Vanderbilt Univ, 1978-1979 & Univ Va, 1979-1981; mech eng, Machine Design, Tenn Eastman Co, 1974-1976. **Memberships:** Am Soc Mech Engrs; Am Soc Eng Educ. **Research Statement & Publications:** Development of algorithmic and ad hoc optimization strategies; application of optimization theory to the design of mechanical systems and machines; machine design; system modeling and analysis; noise and vibration control. **Mailing Address:** N Peachtree Avenue, Cookeville, TN 38505-0001. **E-Mail:** gohnson@tntech.edu

JOHNSON, GLENN M, ENGINEERING. **Personal Data:** American citizen. **Education:** Pa State Univ, BS, 1964; Northwestern Univ, MS, 1965; Am Acad Environ Engrs, dipl. **Professional Experience:** VPRES, ROY F WESTON INC, as of 2001; GROUP MGR, ROY WESTON INC, 1972-; proj engr, Roy Weston Inc, 1965-1968; asst proj engr, Nat Forge Co, 1962-1963; designer & draftsman, Chicago Bridge & Iron Co, 1961-1962; Surveyor, US Forest Serv, 1960. **Memberships:** Am Soc Civil Engrs; Am Water Resources Asn. **Research Statement & Publications:** Water resources engineering; resource economics; wastewater management systems design. **Mailing Address:** Roy Weston Inc, 1400 Weston Way, West Chester, PA 19380. **E-Mail:** johnsog@mail.rfweston.com

JOHNSON, GLENN RICHARD, PLANT BREEDING. **Personal Data:** b Geneseo, Ill, February 19, 1938. **Education:** Iowa State Univ, BS, 1960, PhD (plant breeding), 1965. **Professional Experience:** PRIN RES DIR, DEKALB GENETICS CORP, 1989-; plant breeder maize & area res dir, 1965-1989. **Memberships:** AAAS; Sigma Xi; Am Soc Agron; Am Genetic Asn; NY Acad Sci. **Research Statement & Publications:** Plant breeding, including applied statistical techniques in relation to plant breeding problem. **Mailing Address:** DeKalb Genetics Corp, 101 Tomaras Ave, Savoy, IL 81674. **Fax:** 217-356-7863. **E-Mail:** djohnson@dekalb.com

JOHNSON, GORDON CARLTON, PHYSICAL CHEMISTRY, SURFACTANTS. **Personal Data:** b Newport, RI, February 9, 1929; m 1956, c 3. **Education:** City Col New York, BChE, 1952; Pace Univ, MBA, 1983. **Professional Experience:** CONSULT, SURFACTANTS, 1984-; technol mgr, Silicones Div, Union Carbide Corp, 1977-1984; group leader, Silicones Div, Union Carbide Corp, 1966-1977; proj leader silicone prod develop & tech serv, Silicones Div, Union Carbide Corp, 1962-1966; d evelop engr, Silicones Div, Union Carbide Corp, 1952-1962; Consult, Paper Recycling. **Memberships:** Am Chem Soc; Am Oil Chemists' Soc. **Research Statement & Publications:** Silicone chemistry; polymer synthesis and characterization; emulsification; resin catalysis and cure; rheology; textile applications; paper release coating; fiber lubricant; surfactants; fiber intermediates; ethylene oxide derivates; paper deinking. **Mailing Address:** 50 Cedar Hollow Rd, Wakefield, RI 02879-1435.

JOHNSON, GORDON E, PHARMACOLOGY. **Personal Data:** b Welland, Ont, September 21, 1934; m 1958, c 6. **Education:** Univ Toronto, BScPhm, 1957, MA, 1959, PhD (pharmacol), 1961. **Professional Experience:** PROF EMER PHARMACOL, UNIV SASK, 1995-; DIR SASK DRUG RES INST, SASKATOON, 1995-; prof pharmacol, Univ Sask, 1986-1995; prof & head dept, Univ Sask, 1973-1986; from asst prof to prof pharmacol, Univ Toronto, 1963-1973; med Res Coun Can fel physiol, Karolinska Inst, Sweden, 1962-1963. **Memberships:** Am Soc Pharmacol & Exp Therapeut; Pharmacol Soc Can; Am Soc Clin Pharmacol; Can Soc Clin Pharmacol; Can Hypertension Soc. **Research Statement & Publications:** Catecholamines; thermoregulation and influence of environmental temperature on drug action; drug metabolism. **Mailing Address:** Dept Pharmacol, Univ Sask, Saskatoon, SK S7N 0W0, Can.

JOHNSON, GORDON GUSTAV, MATHEMATICS. **Personal Data:** b Chicago, Ill, June 23, 1936; m 1957, Nancy; c Cathy L, Kim M, Carl G & David H. **Education:** Ill Inst Technol, BS, 1958; Univ Tenn, PhD (math), 1964. **Honors & Awards:** NASA space act award 1999. **Professional Experience:** Vis prof, Univ Tex, 2001; dir, R L Moore Legacy, Edu Advancement Found, 2000; security agency, 2000; res mem, IDA 1990-1992; vis prof, IDA, 1990-1992; vis prof, Emory Univ, 1983-1984; sr res assoc, nat res council, Johnson Space Ctr, NASA, 1978-1980 & NASA Hq, 1980-1981; sr resident res, Nat Res Coun, 1978-1979; ed, Houston J Math, 1974-1979, 1984-1989; PROF MATH, UNIV HOUSTON, 1974-; managing ed, Houston J Math, 1974-1979 & 1984-1989; assoc prof, Univ Houston, 1971-1974; assoc prof, Va Polytech Inst, 1969-1971; asst prof math, Univ Ga, 1964-1969; fel, Oak Ridge Inst Nuclear Studies, 1963-1964. **Memberships:** Swedish Math Soc; Sigma Xi; Am Math Soc; Math Asn Am. **Research Statement & Publications:** Analysis; granted one patent. **Mailing Address:** 2010 Fairwind Rd, Houston, TX 77062. **E-Mail:** Gordon.Johnson@mail.uh.edu

JOHNSON, GORDON LEE, GENERAL CHEMISTRY. **Personal Data:** b Newark, Ohio, December 21, 1932; m 1954, Laurel; c Cheryl Arndt Johnson & Cynthia Stair Calley. **Education:** Ohio Univ, BA, 1954; Univ Ill, PhD (inorg chem), 1958. **Honorary Degrees:** Dsc, Kenyon Col, 1996. **Professional Experience:** PROF EMER, DEPT CHEM, KENYON COL, as of 2001; chmn dept, Kenyon Col, 1986-1992; proj dir, NSF, 1985-1987; vis prof, Ohio State Univ, 1983-1984; vis scientist, Oak Ridge Nat Lab, 1975-1976; vis prof, Iowa State Univ, 1969-1970; fac fel, NSF, Iowa State Univ Sci & Technol, 1969-1970; chmn, Chem Dept, Kenyon Col, 1968-1969, 1970-1975; prof chem, Kenyon Col, 1962-1996. **Memberships:** Am Chem Soc. **Research Statement & Publications:** Metal-ion hydrolysis of esters-bioinorganic chemistry; titanium in molten salt systems; synthetic heme type compounds bioinorganic chemistry; author of 13 articles and books. **Mailing Address:** Dept Chem, Kenyon Col, Gambier, OH 43022. **E-Mail:** johnsong@kenyon.edu

JOHNSON, GORDON OLIVER, SOLID STATE PHYSICS. **Personal Data:** b Portland, Ore, June 2, 1944; m 1971, c 3. **Education:** Walla Walla Col, BS, 1966; Calif Inst Technol, MS, 1967, PhD (elec eng), 1972. **Professional Experience:** PROF PHYSICS, WALLA WALLA COL, 1980-; assoc prof, Walla Walla Col, 1977-1980; asst prof, Walla Walla Col, 1974-1977; res assoc elec eng, Purdue Univ, 1972-1974. **Memberships:** Inst Elec & Electronics Engrs; Am Asn Physics Teachers. **Research Statement & Publications:** Magnetic materials; processes of magnetization; magneto resistance phenomena. **Mailing Address:** Dept Physics, Walla Walla Col, 204 S Col Ave, College Pl, WA 99324. **E-Mail:** johngo@wwc.edu

JOHNSON, GORDON V, SOIL FERTILITY. **Personal Data:** b Harvey, NDak, January 9, 1940; m 1962, c 2. **Education:** NDak State Univ, BS, 1963; Univ Nev, MS, 1966; Univ Nebr, PhD (agron), 1969. **Professional Experience:** REGENTS PROF SOIL SCI, EXTEN SOIL SPECIALIST, OKLA STATE UNIV, 1998-; interim dir, Soil, Water & Forages Anal Labs, 1995-1996; prof soil sci, exten soil specialist, Okla State Univ, 1983-1998; dir agron serv, Okla State Univ, 1977-1990; from assoc prof to prof agron, Okla State Univ, 1977-1983; from asst prof to assoc prof agr chem & soils, Univ Ariz, 1969-1977; instr, Univ Nebr, 1968-1969; res fel Soil Chem, Univ Nebr, 1966-1969; res asst, Univ Nevada, 1964-1966. **Memberships:** Int Turfgrass Soc; Crop Sci Soc Am; Am Soc Agron; fel Soil Sci Soc Am; Okla Plant Food Educ Soc; Sigma Xi. **Research Statement & Publications:** Evaluation of micro-nutrient supplying status of soils; evaluation of interferences in the spectrophotometric determination of iron with ethylenediamine Di (o-hydroxyphenylacetic acid); turfgrass management and nutrition; subirrigation of turfgrass; soil-turfgrass systems for tertiary sewage effluent treatment; effects of temperature and nitrogen on turfgrass root decline; soil fertility and soil salinity. **Mailing Address:** Dept Plant & Soil Sci, Okla State Univ, 269 N Agr Hall, Stillwater, OK 74078-6028. **Fax:** 405-744-5269. **E-Mail:** gvj@mail.pss.okstate.edu

JOHNSON, GORDON VERLE, PLANT PHYSIOLOGY. **Personal Data:** b Long Beach, Calif, September 5, 1933; m 1960, c 4. **Education:** Univ Calif, Berkeley, BS, 1955, MS, 1959; Univ Ariz, PhD (agr chem, soils), 1965. **Professional Experience:** REGENTS PROF SOIL SCI, OKLAHOMA STATE UNIV, as of 2004; assoc prof Biol, Univ Nmex, beginning 1970; asst prof, Univ Nmex, 1965-1970; asst prof, Ore State Univ, 1964-1965; resassoc bot, Ore State Univ, 1963-1964; Regents Prof Soil Sci. **Memberships:** AAAS; Am Soc Plant Physiol; Sigma Xi. **Research Statement & Publications:** Absorption and metabolism of iron by plants; physiological effects of stress on plants; algal nutrition; biological nitrogen fixation; plant tissue and cell culture. **Mailing Address:** Dep Plant & Soil Sci, 269 N Ag Hall, OSU, Stillwater, OK 74078. **Fax:** 405-744-5269. **E-Mail:** gvj@mail.pss.okstate.edu

JOHNSON, GROVER LEON, PHYSICAL CHEMISTRY. **Personal Data:** b Bunn, Ark, January 9, 1931; m 1962, c 3. **Education:** Rice Inst, BA, 1953; Univ Tex, PhD (phys chem), 1960. **Professional Experience:** CONSULT, 1990-; consult, Socony Mobil Oil Co, beginning 1964; asst prof chem, Univ Tex, Arlington, 1964-1990; sr res chemist corrosion, Socony Mobil Oil Co, 1960-1964. **Memberships:** Am Chem Soc. **Research Statement & Publications:** Electrochemistry; corrosion. **Mailing Address:** 1716 Cheryl Lane, Arlington, TX 76013.

JOHNSON, GUY, MATHEMATICAL ANALYSIS. **Personal Data:** b Dallas, Tex, March 11, 1922; m 1942, Jean; c Guy III, Kenneth & Bonnie. **Education:** Agr & Mech Col Tex, BS, 1943, MS, 1952; Harvard Univ, MBA, 1947; Rice Inst, PhD, 1955. **Professional Experience:** PROF EMER MATH, SYRACUSE UNIV, 1987-; prof math, Syracuse Univ, 1969-1987; assoc prof, Syracuse Univ, 1966-1969; vis prof, Syracuse Univ, 1964-1966; from instr to assoc prof math, Rice Univ, 1954-1966; a sst eng, Tex Eng Exp Sta, 1948-1950. **Memberships:** Am Math Soc; Math Asn Am. **Research Statement & Publications:** Potential theory. **Mailing Address:** Dept Math, Syracuse Univ, Syracuse, NY 13244.

JOHNSON, GUY HENRY, NUTRITION, FOOD SCIENCES. **Personal Data:** b Chicago, Ill, October 24, 1949; m 1977, Jean G Graham; c Adel M & Tess H. **Education:** Univ Ill, Urbana-Champaign, BS, 1971, PhD (nutrit sci), 1976. **Professional Experience:** DIR, NUTRIT, GRAND METROP FOOD SECTOR, 1989-; dir, Infant Nutrit, 1985-1989; nutrit specialist, Gerber Prods Co, 1979-1985; Res assoc, Ky State Univ, 1976-1979. **Memberships:** Am Oil Chemists Soc; Inst Food Technologists; fel Am Col Nutrit; Am Inst Nutrit; Am Soc Clin Nutrit; Sigma Xi. **Research Statement & Publications:** Use current information in nutrition to develop and market nutritionally improved food products and provide effective nutrition educational materials. **Mailing Address:** Pillsbury Co, 330 Univ Ave SE, Minneapolis, MN 55414-2130. **Fax:** 612-330-1851. **E-Mail:** guy_h_johnson@pbtc.com

JOHNSON, HAL G(USTAV), ORGANIC CHEMISTRY, MARKETING. **Personal Data:** b Saginaw, Mich, April 30, 1915; m 1940, Elizabeth Schreiner; c Judith L, David & John B. **Education:** Beloit Col, BS, 1936, MS, 1938; Univ Wis, PhD (org chem), 1941. **Professional Experience:** Mem, bd dir, Marsh Prod, Batavia, Ill, 1984-; PROF EMER MKT, NORTHERN ILL UNIV, 1984-; guest prof int & indust mkt, Linkoping Univ, Sweden, 1977-1978; from assoc prof to prof, Northern Ill Univ, 1971-1984; dir chem develop, Chem Plastics Group, Develop Div, Borg Warner Corp, 1969-1971; mgt consult, Hal Johnson Assocs & Barnes Res Assocs, 1966-1969; vpres mkt & sales, Southwest Potash Div, Am Metal Climax, Inc, 1962-1966; chem & mgt consult, 1959-1962; vpres, Vick Chem Co, 1957-1959; dir chem & rubber div, Bus & Defense Serv Admin, US Dept Com, Wash, DC, 1957-1958; dir develop dept, Res & Eng Div, 1954-1957; dir res & develop, Western Div, Calif, 1952-1954; asst dir, Gen Develop Dept, 1949-1952; mgr org intermediate & pharmaceuts, Org Develop Dept, Monsanto Chem Co, 1946-1949; asst gen mgr, Dykem Co, St Louis, Mo, 1945-1946; org chemist, Com Solvents Corp, Ind, 1941-1945; asst, Univ Wis, 1938-1941; i nstr chem, Beloit Col, 1935-1938; Educ & mgt consult; chmn, bd dir, Ill Bus Hall Fame, Macomb. **Memberships:** AAAS; Am Chem Soc; Com Develop Asn. **Mailing Address:** 1060 S Adams St, Lancaster, WI 53813.

JOHNSON, HARLAN BRUCE, PHYSICAL CHEMISTRY. **Personal Data:** b Indianapolis, Ind, July 3, 1922; m 1944, c 4. **Education:** Purdue Univ, BS, 1943; Iowa State Col, MS, 1948; Kans State Col, PhD (chem), 1952. **Professional Experience:** RETIRED; mem staff, PPG Industs Inc, 1970-1993; dir res, Columbia Nitrogen Corp, 1967-1970; asst dir res, Petro-Tex Chem Corp, 1966-1967; res supvr, Petro-Tex Chem Corp, 1957-1967; chmn sci div, Washburn Univ, 1956-1957; prof & head dept, Washburn Univ, 1952-1957; from instr to asst prof chem, Ft Hays Kans State Col, 1948-1952; asst, Atomic Res Inst, 1946-1948; prod supvr, Tenn Eastman Corp, 1944-1946; org res chemist, Eastman Kodak Co, 1943-1944. **Memberships:** Am Chem Soc; Am Inst Chem Engrs; Sigma Xi. **Research Statement & Publications:** Electrolytic solutions; thermodynamics; petrochemicals; electrochemistry. **Mailing Address:** 1038 N Jefferson No 9, Medina, OH 44256-1203.

JOHNSON, HARLAN PAUL, MARINE GEOLOGY, GEOPHYSICS. **Personal Data:** b Chicago, Ill, December 18, 1939; m 1972, c 2. **Education:** Univ Ill, BS, 1963; Southern Ill Univ, MS, 1966; Univ Wash, PhD (geophysics), 1972. **Professional Experience:** AFFIL PROF, DEPT GEOL SCI, 1994-; PROF GEOL & GEOPHYS, SCH OCEANOG, UNIV WASH, 1990-; vis prof, Inst Geol, Univ Rennes, France, 1981; res assoc prof, Dept Geol Sci, 1980-1990. **Memberships:** Am Geophys Union; fel Geol Soc Am. **Research Statement & Publications:** Origin and evolution of oceanic crust; rock magnetism; source of marine magnetic anomalies. **Mailing Address:** Sch Oceanog, Univ Wash, PO Box 357940, Seattle, WA 98195-7940. **E-Mail:** johnson@ocean.washington.edu

JOHNSON, HAROLD DAVID, PHYSIOLOGY. **Personal Data:** b Verona, Mo, February 28, 1924; m 1949, Lonetta; c Michael, Tina, Deborrah, Leah. **Education:** Drury Col, BS, 1949; Univ Mo, MA, 1952, PhD (dairy husb), 1956. **Honors & Awards:** Animal Biometeorol Award, Am Meteorol Soc, 1972; Peterson Award, Int Soc Biometeorol, 1972; Gamma Sigma Delta Fac Res Award, 1975. **Professional Experience:** PROF ENVIRON PHYSIOL, UNIV MO-COLUMBIA, 1977-; from asst to prof dairy husb, Univ Mo-columbia, 1952-1977; asst zool, Univ Mo-columbia, 1951-1952; drug rep, Kendall Co, Ind, 1949-1950; Asst biol, Drury Col, 1948-1949; Mem comt bioclimatol & meteorol, Agr Bd, Nat Acad Sci. **Memberships:** AAAS; Am Soc Animal Sci; Am Physiol Soc; Am Dairy Sci Asn; Int Soc Biometeorol. **Research Statement & Publications:** Environmental physiology; investigations on effects of climate and environment on growth and production; related biochemical and physiological reactions of cattle and smaller laboratory mammals. **Mailing Address:** Dept Animal Sci Col Agr, Univ Mo 114 Animal Sci Res Ctr, Columbia, MO 65211. **Fax:** 573-882-6827. **E-Mail:** johnsonh@missouri.edu

JOHNSON, HAROLD HUNT, MATHEMATICS. **Personal Data:** b Gary, Ind, September 20, 1929; m 1958, Betsy; c Ruth, David, Paul & Marty. **Education:** San Jose State Col, BA, 1951; Univ Calif, MA, 1956, PhD (math), 1957. **Professional Experience:** RETIRED; prof math, Trinity Col, 1977-1992; vis assoc prof math, George Wash Univ, 1974-1976; assoc prof, Univ Wash, 1961-1974; instr math, Princeton Univ, 1958-1961; instr math, Stanford Univ, 1957-1958. **Memberships:** Am Math Soc; Math Asn Am. **Research Statement & Publications:** Differential geometry; systems of exterior differential forms; infinite pseudo-groups. **Mailing Address:** 222 Harbour Dr No 311, Naples, FL 33940. **E-Mail:** harold29@naplesnet.com

JOHNSON, HARRY MCCLURE, METEOROLOGY, OCEANOGRAPHY. **Personal Data:** b Chicago, Ill, May 15, 1925; m 1948, c 4. **Education:** Mass Inst Technol, BS, 1946; Cornell Univ, MS & PhD (environ ecol, physics), 1954. **Professional Experience:** RES METEOROLOGIST, NAT OCEANIC & ATMOSPHERIC ADMIN, NAT ENVIRON SCI SERV, MD, 1974-; res meteorologist, Nat Environ Satellite Ctr, 1961-1968 & Nat Hurricane Ctr, Fla, 1968-1974; assoc meteorologist & oceanogr, Meteorol Div, Inst Geophys, Univ Hawaii, 1960-1961; asst prof meteorol & chg div meteorol, 1948-1950 & zool, 1954-1959; math, 1948-1950 & zool, 1950-1952; asst physics & math, Cornell Univ, 1947-1948; Officer-in-chg, Navy Weather Unit, Alaska, 1946. **Memberships:** AAAS; Ecol Soc Am; Wilderness Soc; Cooper Ornith Soc. **Research Statement & Publications:** Satellite meteorology; arctic, subarctic, subtropical and tropical meteorology; oceanography; micrometeorology and ocean-atmosphere interactions; environmental ecology and physiology; wilderness and habitat preservation. **Mailing Address:** 13310 Warburton Dr, Ft Washington, MD 20744.

JOHNSON, HARRY WILLIAM, JR, ORGANIC CHEMISTRY. **Personal Data:** b Waverly, Fla, January 2, 1927; m 1957, Margaret Ann Dahlgren; c Anne E (Johnston), Jill A & Gail L (Macmillan). **Education:** Mass Inst Technol, SB, 1951; Univ Ill, PhD (chem), 1954. **Professional Experience:** EMER PROF CHEM, UNIV CALIF, RIVERSIDE, 1988-; assoc dean, Grad Div, 1982-1990; dean, Grad Div, 1974-1980; prof, Univ Calif, 1967-1988; From instr to assoc prof & chmn dept, Univ Calif, 1954-1967. **Memberships:** AAAS; Am Chem Soc; Royal Soc Chem. **Research Statement & Publications:** Organic reaction mechanisms; reactions of heterocycles; isocyanate and isocyanide chemistry. **Mailing Address:** 2555 Flanders Rd, Riverside, CA 92507. **E-Mail:** huckj27@earthlink.net

JOHNSON, HERBERT GARDNER, ASTHMA, CHRONIC AIRWAYS DISEASES. **Personal Data:** b Wessington, SDak, March 22, 1933; m 1953, c 3. **Education:** Univ Ill, Urbana, BS, 1958, MS, 1959; Univ Mich, Ann Arbor, PhD (immunol), 1969. **Professional Experience:** RETIRED; sr scientist, Upjohn Co, Kalamazoo, Mich, 1984-1995; v is scholar pharmacol, Univ Calif, San Francisco, 1980-1981; sr res scientist, Upjohn Co, Kalamazoo, Mich, 1978-1984; res scientist, Upjohn Co, Kalamazoo, Mich, 1975-1978; res assoc immunol, Upjohn Co, Kalamazoo, Mich, 1969-1975; res asst biochem, Upjohn Co, Kalamazoo, Mich, 1959-1966. **Memberships:** Am Asn Immunologists; Am Asn Physiologists; Am Soc Microbiol. **Research Statement & Publications:** Role of lipoxygenase metabolites of arachidonic acid in chronic airways diseases; immunopharmacology of lipid mediators and their pharmacologic control as related to airways, smooth muscle and glands. **Mailing Address:** 829 Berkshire Dr, Kalamazoo, MI 49001.

JOHNSON, HERBERT GORDON, PLANT PATHOLOGY. **Personal Data:** b Granite Falls, Minn, April 11, 1916; m 1941, Jean; c Newton H & Barbara J (Pozner). **Education:** Univ Minn, BS, 1939, PhD, 1953. **Professional Experience:** RETIRED; prof, Univ Minn, St Paul, 1964-1980; exten plant pathologist, Univ Minn, St Paul, 1956-1980; assoc prof plant path, Univ Minn, St Paul, 1956-1964; plant pathologist, Green Giant Co, 1953-1956; asst plant path, Univ Minn, 1948-1953; plant pathologist & horticulturist, Yoder Bros, Inc, 1940-1942 & 1945-1948; agt barberry eradication, USDA, 1939-1940. **Memberships:** Am Phytopath Soc. **Research Statement & Publications:** Applied plant pathology. **Mailing Address:** 2175 Rosewood Lane S, St Paul, MN 55113.

JOHNSON, HERBERT WINDAL, GENETICS, PLANT BREEDING. **Personal Data:** b Tenn, July 3, 1920; m 1948, c 3. **Education:** Univ Tenn, BSc, 1943; Univ Nebr, MSc, 1948, PhD (agron), 1950. **Professional Experience:** PROF EMER AGRON & PLANT GENETICS, INST AGR, UNIV MINN, ST PAUL, as of 1999; prof agron & plant genetics, Inst Agr, Univ Minn, St Paul, beginning 1964; res agronomist, Crops Res Div, Agr Res Serv, 1953-1964; agronomist plant breeding, USDA, NC, 1948-1953; Instr genetics, Univ Nebr, 1947-1948. **Memberships:** Fel Am Soc Agron. **Research Statement & Publications:** Quantitative genetics; plant breeding procedures. **Mailing Address:** Dept Agr & Plant Genetics, Univ Minn, St Paul, MN 55741.

JOHNSON, HERMAN LEONALL, HUMAN NUTRITIONAL STATUS. **Personal Data:** b Whitehall, Wis, April 1, 1935; m 1976, Barbara A Badger. **Education:** N Cent Col, Ill, BA, 1959; Va Polytech Inst & State Univ, Blacksburg, MS, 1961, PhD (biochem-nutrit), 1963. **Professional Experience:** RES PHYSIOLOGIST HUMAN RES, WESTERN HUMAN NUTRIT RES CTR, USDA, PRESIDIO SAN FRANCISCO, 1980-; nutrit chemist human res, US Army Med Res & Nutrit Lab, Denver, 1965-1974 & US Army Western Inst Res Ctr, Presidio, San Francisco, 1974-1980; res biochemist, S R Noble Res Fedn, Ardmore, Okla, 1963-1965. **Memberships:** Am Inst Nutrit; Am Col Nutrit; Am Col Sports Med; Am Soc Clin Nutrit; AAAS; NY Acad Sci. **Research Statement & Publications:** New and improved methods for determining human body composition and energy metabolism-expenditure; effects of nutritional status on body composition and energy metabolism in humans especially during weight loss. **Mailing Address:** 256 Alden Ave, Rohnert Park, CA 94928-3704. **Fax:** 415-556-1432.

JOHNSON, HILDING REYNOLD, ANALYTICAL CHEMISTRY. **Personal Data:** b Sweden, February 14, 1920; American citizen; m 1947. **Education:** Clarkson Col Technol, BS, 1942. **Professional Experience:** RETIRED; mgr anal serv, Tenneco Chem Inc, 1975-1981; supvr, Tenneco Chem Inc, 1970-1975; group leader anal chem, Heyden Newport Chem Corp, 1948-1970; chemist, Heyden Chem Corp, 1942-1948. **Memberships:** Am Chem Soc. **Mailing Address:** 19 Lois Ct, Wayne, NJ 07470.

JOHNSON, HOLLIS RALPH, ASTRONOMY, SPECTROSCOPY & SPECTROMETRY. **Personal Data:** b Tremonton, Utah, December 2, 1928; m 1954, Grete; c Carol A (Harrison), Wayne L, Lyle D, Charlotte (Willian), Lise M (Tyner) & Richard L. **Education:** Brigham Young Univ, BA, 1955, MA, 1957; Univ Colo, PhD (astrogeophysics), 1960. **Professional Experience:** EMER PROF ASTRON, IND UNIV, BLOOMINGTON, 1994-; vis prof, Niels Bohr Inst, Univ Copenhagen, 1990 & 1994-1997; F C Donders vis prof, Univ Utrecht, Netherland, 1989; sr fel, Nat Res Coun, NASA Ames Res Ctr, Moffett Field, Calif, 1982-1983; chmn dept, Ind Univ, Bloomington, 1978-1982 & 1990-1993; vis scientist, High Altitude Observ, Nat Ctr Atmospheric Res, 1971-1972; prof, Ind Univ, Bloomington, 1969-1994; assoc prof, Ind Univ, Bloomington, 1963-1969; res assoc astron, Yale Univ, 1961-1963; NSF fel, Paris, France, 1960-1961. **Memberships:** Int Astron Union; Sigma Xi; Am Astron Soc; AAAS; Am Asn Univ Prof. **Research Statement & Publications:** Stellar atmospheres and chemical composition; ultraviolet spectroscopy of stars; molecular opacities; radiative transfer and spectal line formation; orbit of the moon. **Mailing Address:** Dept Astron, Ind Univ, Swain Hall W 319, Bloomington, IN 47405.

JOHNSON, HOLLISTER, CHEMISTRY. **Personal Data:** b Watertown, NY, January 14, 1929; m 1997, Shirely; c William & Katherine J (Kristansen). **Education:** Univ Rochester, BS, 1959. **Professional Experience:** RETIRED; consult, Eastman Kodak Res Labs, 1986-1989; res assoc, Eastman Kodak Res Labs, 1953-1986. **Memberships:** Am Chem Soc. **Research Statement & Publications:** Solution formulation and coating technology. **Mailing Address:** 302 Killarney Dr, Rochester, NY 14616.

JOHNSON, HORACE RICHARD, PHYSICS, ELECTRICAL ENGINEERING. **Personal Data:** b Jersey City, NJ, April 26, 1926; m 1950, c 5. **Education:** Cornell Univ, BEE, 1946; Mass Inst Technol, PhD (physics), 1952. **Professional Experience:** CHMN BD, WATKINS-JOHNSON CO, 1988-; ASSOC, DEPT ELEC ENG, 1968-; pres, Watkins-Johnson Co, 1968-1987; lectr, Stanford Univ, 1958-1968; exec vpres, Watkins- J ohnson C o, 1958-1968; lectr, Univ Calif, Los Angeles, 1956-1957; head, Microwave Tube Dept, Res Lab, Hughes Aircraft Co, 1952-1957; Asst physics, Cornell Univ, 1946-1947.; Mem bd dirs, Nat Asn Mfrs; asst, Mass Inst Technol. **Memberships:** Nat Acad Eng; Am Phys Soc; Sigma Xi; fel Inst Elec & Electronics Engrs; Res Soc Am. **Research Statement & Publications:** Microwave spectroscopy; electron devices; microwave systems; author of 21 technical publications; granted 3 patents. **Mailing Address:** Watkins-Johnson Co, 3333 Hillview Ave, Palo Alto, CA 94304-1223.

JOHNSON, HORTON ANTON, MEDICINE, PATHOLOGY. **Personal Data:** b Cheyenne, Wyo, November 12, 1926. **Education:** Colo Col, AB, 1949; Columbia Univ, MD, 1953; Am Bd Path, dipl, 1958. **Honors & Awards:** Lederle Med Fac Award. **Professional Experience:** RETIRED; prof path, Columbia Univ, 1984-1991; dir path, St Lukes-Roosevelt Hosp Ctr, 1984-1991; prof path & chmn dept, Sch Med, Tulane Univ, 1975-1984; prof, Sch Med, Ind Univ, Indianapolis, 1972-1975; prof path, State Univ NY, Stony Brook, 1970-1972; scientist & attend pathologist, Brookhaven Nat Lab, 1963-1970; asst prof, Univ Utah, 1960-1963; res assoc, Brookhaven Nat Lab, 1958-1960; resident, Pondville Hosp, Walpole, Mass, 1957-1958; resident path, Univ Mich, 1954-1957; intern, Univ Mich, 1953-1954. **Memberships:** Radiation Res Soc; Am Asn Path; Biophys Soc; ColAm Path; Int Acad Path. **Research Statement & Publications:** Radiation pathology; kinetics of cell proliferation; thermal injury; information theory. **Mailing Address:** 3 Lincoln Ctr Plaza 28G, New York, NY 10023.

JOHNSON, HOWARD B(EATTIE), REFRACTORIES, HEAT TRANSFER. **Personal Data:** b Willits, Calif, April 27, 1936; m 1962, Kathryn; c Mark, Christine, Terrance & David. **Education:** Univ Pac, BS (chem), 1958; Univ Minn, MS, 1966; Univ Utah, PhD (ceramic eng), 1966. **Professional Experience:** Vpres & tech dir, CCPI Inc, 1988-2002; tech dir, CCPI Inc, 1982-1988; dir res, Vesuvius Crucible Co, 1977-1982; dir process develop, Pittsburgh Corning Corp, 1969-1977; sr ceramist, Pittsburgh Corning Corp, 1966-1969; res chemist, PPG Indust Inc, 1960-1963. **Memberships:** Fel Am Ceramic Soc; Am Chem Soc; Sigma Xi. **Research Statement & Publications:** Develop monolithic refractories, inorganic thermal insulation materials and refractory raw materials, disposable refractories for steel and aluminum casting; kinetics and thermodynamics of gas-solid reactions; thermal and electrical properties of ceramic materials. **Mailing Address:** 11627 Currier Lane, Cincinnati, OH 45249. **E-Mail:** orhbj@prodigy.net

JOHNSON, HOWARD C, MATHEMATICS. **Education:** Chicago State Univ, BS; Univ Ill, MS; Northwestern Univ, PhD. **Professional Experience:** DEAN, UNIV GRAD SCH, SYRACUSE UNIV, as of 2001. **Mailing Address:** Math Dept, Syracuse Univ, 304 Tolley Admin Bldg Acad Affairs, Syracuse, NY 13210-1100. **Fax:** 315-443-2583. **E-Mail:** hojohnso@syr.edu

JOHNSON, HOWARD ERNEST, FRESH WATER ECOLOGY, TOXICOLOGY. **Personal Data:** b Livingston, Mont, September 21, 1935; m 1959, c 3. **Education:** Mont State Univ, BS, 1959, MS, 1961; Univ Wash, PhD (fisheries), 1967. **Professional Experience:** RETIRED; chief, Bur Fish Mgt, Mont Fish Wildlife & Parks, 1989-1995; coordr, Clark Fork River Proj, Off Gov, Mont, 1984-1989; res assoc, Mont Environ Qual Coun, 1981-1984; coordr toxic substances, Mich Serv & Educ Admin Grant Prog, beginning 1978; dir, Inst Water Res, 1978-1981; coordr environ contamination, Pesiticide Res Ctr, 1978-1981; prof fisheries, Mich State Univ, 1975-1981; Panel mem, Comt Water Qual Criteria, Nat Acad Sci, 1971-1972; from asst prof to assoc prof, Mich State Univ, 1967-1975. **Memberships:** Am Fisheries Soc; Am Inst Fisheries Res Biologists. **Research Statement & Publications:** Toxicity tests with aquatic organisms; production and culture of fish. **Mailing Address:** 4136 Fox Ridge Dr, Helena, MT 59602.

JOHNSON, HOWARD LAURENCE, MEDICINAL CHEMISTRY, PHARMACOLOGY. **Personal Data:** b San Leandro, Calif, January 4, 1933; m 1956, c 4. **Education:** Univ Calif, BS, 1956, PhD, 1963. **Professional Experience:** LICENSED PRIVATE PILOT, FED AVIATION ADMIN, 1981-; MGR BIOPHYS CHEMOTRICS, LIFE SCI RES, STANFORD RES INST, 1978-; RES ASSOC, UNIV CALIF, MED CTR, 1972-; sr pharmacol chemist, Life Sci Res, Stanford Res Inst, 1972-1978; chemist pharmaceut chem, Life Sci Res, Stanford Res Inst, 1965-1971; fel chem pharmacol, Nat Heart Inst, 1963-1965; Pharmaceut educ fel, 1959-1961; clin lab officer, US Air Force, 1957-1959. **Memberships:** AAAS; Am Chem Soc; Am Pharmaceut Asn; Acad Pharmaceut Sci; Am Soc Pharmacol & Exp Therapeut. **Research Statement & Publications:** Chemistry, pharmacology of autonomic agents; extrapyramidal central nervous system pharmacology; drug distribution, metabolism and mechanisms of action; structure activity relationships; biochemical pharmacology of biogenic amines; histamine; drug-receptor interaction. **Mailing Address:** 612 Princeton Dr, Sunnyvale, CA 94087.

JOHNSON, HOWARD MARCELLUS, LYMPHOCYTE FUNCTION, SOLUBLE MEDIATORS. **Education:** Ohio State Univ, PhD (immunol), 1962. **Professional Experience:** GRAD RES PROF, UNIV FLA, as of 2003; PROF COMP EXP PATH, UNIV FLA, 1983-. **Research Statement & Publications:** published numerous articles. **Mailing Address:** Dept Microbiol & Cell Sci, Univ Fla, PO Box 110700, Gainesville, FL 32611-0700. **Fax:** 352-392-5922. **E-Mail:** johnsonh@ufl.edu

JOHNSON, HOWARD P, HYDROLOGY & WATER RESOURCES. **Personal Data:** b Odebolt, Iowa, January 27, 1923; m 1952, c 3. **Education:** Iowa State Univ, BS, 1949, MS, 1950, PhD (agr & civil eng), 1959; Univ Iowa, MS, 1954. **Honors & Awards:** Hancor Soil & Water Eng Award, Am Soc Agr Engrs, 1978. **Professional Experience:** ANSON MARSTON DISTINGUISHED PROF EMER, IOWA STATE UNIV, 1988-; head agr eng, Iowa State Univ, 1980-1988; dir, Am Soc Agr Engrs, 1976; vis prof, Univ Mo, Columbia, 1966-1967; from asst prof to prof, Iowa State Univ, 1959-1980. **Memberships:** Fel AAAS; fel Am Soc Agr Engrs; Soil Conserv Soc Am; Am Soc Eng Educ. **Research Statement & Publications:** Hydrology, water quality and soil mechanics problems related to irrigation, drainage, erosion control and small watersheds. **Mailing Address:** Dept Agr & Biosystems Eng, Iowa State Univ, Ames, IA 50011-2021.

JOHNSON, HUGH MITCHELL, X-RAY, ASTRONOMY. **Personal Data:** b Des Moines, Iowa, March 4, 1923. **Education:** Univ Chicago, AB, 1948, SB, 1949, PhD (astron), 1953. **Professional Experience:** RETIRED; lectr, Stanford Univ, 1971-1975 & 1980-1982; staff scientist & mem res lab, Lockheed Missiles & Space Co, 1963-1986; assoc scientist, Nat Radio Astron Observ, 1962-1963; assoc prof & assoc astronr, Univ Ariz, 1960-1962; vis fel, Australian Nat Univ, 1958-1959; asst prof, Univ Iowa, 1954-1959; res assoc, Yerkes Observ, Univ Chicago, 1953-1960; asst astron, Yerkes Observ, Univ Chicago, 1950-1953. **Memberships:** Emer mem Astron Soc; emer mem Int Astron Union. **Research Statement & Publications:** Nebulae; galaxies; x-ray astronomy; x-ray, uv, photographic, ir and microwave. **Mailing Address:** 1017 Newell Rd, Palo Alto, CA 94303.

JOHNSON, I BIRGER, ENGINEERING. **Personal Data:** b Brooklyn, NY, September 29, 1913; m 1942, Johanna Mortensen; c Bruce E & Richar B. **Education:** Polytech Univ, BEE, 1937, MEE, 1939. **Honors & Awards:** William MartinHabirshaw Award, Inst Elec & Electronics Engrs, 1966, Centennial Award, 1984 & Lamme Medal, 1986. **Professional Experience:** RETIRED; consult, 1978-1988; mgr & instr elec eng, Gen Elec, 1939-1978; g rad prof & res asst elec eng, Polytech Univ, 1937-1939. **Memberships:** Nat Acad Eng; Inst Elec & Electronics Engrs; Int Conf Large High Voltage Elec Syst. **Research Statement & Publications:** Contributions to the reliability and economy of extra high voltage electric power systems in the analysis of lightning and switching surge phenomena and in the protection and coordination of insulation systems. **Mailing Address:** The Commons, 1786 Union St No 210, Niskayuna, NY 12309-4120.

JOHNSON, IRVING STANLEY, ONCOLOGY, ENDOTHELIAL CELL BIOLOGY. **Personal Data:** b Grand Junction, Colo, June 30, 1925; m 1949, Alwyn; c Rebecca L, Bryan G, Kirsten S & Kevin B. **Education:** Washburn Univ, MS, 1948; Univ Kans, PhD (develop biol), 1953. **Honors & Awards:** Cain Award Preclin res, Am Asn Cancer res; First Annual Corp Award Leadership Biomed res, US Cong. **Professional Experience:** BIOMED RES CONSULT, 1988-; mem develop therapeut comt, Nat Cancer Inst, 1978-; assoc ed, Cancer Res, 1974-; vpres res, Biol res Div, 1973-1988; exec dir, Biol Res Div, 1972-1973; ed adv bd, Cancer Res, 1971-1973; mem consult panel, Nat Cancer Prog, 1971; ed bd, Chemico-Biol Interactions, 1968-1973; dir, Biol res Div, 1968-1972; asst dir, Biol-Pharmacol res Div, Eli Lilly Res Labs, 1953-1968; asst zoology, embryol & zoology, Univ Kans, 1950-1953; asst instr parasitol, embryol & zoology, Univ Kans, 1948-1950; asst instr anat, Washburn Univ, 1947-1948. **Memberships:** Fel AAAS; Am Asn Cancer Res; Am Soc Cell Biologists; Immunol Soc; NY Acad Sci. **Research Statement & Publications:** Anti-tumor chemotherapy; antiviral chemotherapy; tissue culture techniques; experimental embryology; oncogenic viruses; maintenance of biological function in tissue culture; recombinant DNA and public policy. **Mailing Address:** Indian Pt Rd, Stonington, ME 04681. **Fax:** 941-472-4782.

JOHNSON, IVAN M, ZOOLOGY, PHYSIOLOGY. **Personal Data:** b Mansfield, Wash, May 30, 1940; m 1962, c 2. **Education:** Whitworth Col, Wash, BS, 1962; Univ Mont, PhD (zoology), 1969. **Professional Experience:** NERE SUNDET PROF BIOL, CONCORDIA COL, as of 2004; assoc prof biol, Concordia Col, beginning 1978; asst prof, Concordia Col, 1971-1978; Nat Inst Gen Med Sci fel biol, Yale Univ, 1969-1971; asst zoology, Univ Mont, 1963-1969. **Memberships:** Sigma Xi; Raptor Res Found. **Research Statement & Publications:** Osmoregulation of vertebrates. **Mailing Address:** Dept Biol, Concordia Col, 130 Sci Ctr S 901 S Eighth St, Moorhead, MN 56562. **Fax:** 218-299-3804. **E-Mail:** ijohnson@gloria.cord.edu

JOHNSON, J A, III, PHYSICS. **Education:** Yale Univ, PhD (physics), 1965. **Professional Experience:** PROF SCI ENG, FLA A&M UNIV, as of 2002. **Memberships:** Adv Coun Math Phys Sci Directorate Nat Sci Found. **Mailing Address:** Fla A&M Uni, 1800-3 E Paul Dirac Dr, Tallahassee, FL 32310. **Fax:** 904-561-2474. **E-Mail:** johnsonj@lmfp.nhmfl.gov johnsonj@lmfp.nhmfl.gov

JOHNSON, J DAVID, MUSCLE BIOCHEMISTRY, CALCIUM BINDING PROTEINS. **Education:** Mich State Univ, PhD (biophysics), 1977. **Professional Experience:** PROF BIOPHYS, OHIO STATE UNIV, 1983-. **Memberships:** Am Soc Biochem & Molecular Biol; Biophys Soc. **Research Statement & Publications:** Role of calcium binding proteins in health and disease; cardiovascular drugs. **Mailing Address:** Dept Med Biochem, Ohio State Univ, 484 W 12th Ave, Columbus, OH 43210-1292. **Fax:** 614-292-4118. **E-Mail:** johnson.52@osu.edu

JOHNSON, JACK DONALD, RESEARCH ADMINISTRATION, ENVIRONMENTAL SCIENCE. **Personal Data:** b Huntington, Ore, August 23, 1931; m 1958, c 4. **Education:** San Diego State Col, BA, 1959; Univ Minn, MS, 1967, PhD (environ health), 1971. **Professional Experience:** PROF EMER ARID LANDS, UNIV ARIZ, as of 2005; COORDR SPEC PROJ, UNIV ARIZ, as of 2002; prof Aird Lands, Univ Ariz, as of 1999; ASSOC DEAN FACIL & RES, UNIV ARIZ, as of 1999; pres, Ariz Technol Develop Corp, beginning 1987; dir off technol trans, Interdisciplinary Progs, Univ Ariz, beginning 1985; assoc dean, Col Agr, 1981-1984; DIR, AID NATURAL RESOURCES PROG, 1974-; desertification consult, AID, 1974; asst coordr, Interdisciplinary Progs, Univ Ariz, beginning 1971; dir, Off Arid Lands Studies, Univ Ariz, beginning 1971; res fel, Univ Minn, 1967-1970; syst engr, Jet Propulsion Labs, Calif Inst Technol, 1963-1966; sect chief aerospace,

Martin-Marietta Corp, 1960-1963; proj engr, Humphrey, Inc, 1956-1960; dir, Slandrau Sci Ctr. **Memberships:** AAAS; Am Water Resources Asn; Am Geophys Union; Inst Environ Sci; Inst Int Develop; Sigma Xi. **Research Statement & Publications:** Desertification; less developed country development; utilization of arid land resources; hydrology; natural resources mangement; biomass and bioenergy development. **Mailing Address:** Div Facil & Res, Univ Ariz, Tucson, AZ 85721-0066. **E-Mail:** jack@email.arizona.edu

JOHNSON, JACK (LAMAR), ANALYTICAL CHEMISTRY. **Personal Data:** b Elkhart, Ind, March 30, 1930; m 1956, c 2. **Education:** Western Mich Univ, BS, 1952; Wayne State Univ, MS, 1954, PhD (anal chem), 1959. **Professional Experience:** SR RES CHEMIST, RES LABS, GEN MOTORS CORP, 1959-; a nal chemist, Ethyl Corp, Mich, 1954. **Memberships:** AAAS; Am Chem Soc. **Research Statement & Publications:** Chemical microscopy; microchemical techniques of analysis; development of instrumental methods for microanalysis and characterization of micro samples; x-ray diffraction analysis of materials. **Mailing Address:** 26026 Newport Ave, Warren, MI 48089-1327.

JOHNSON, JACK WAYNE, SOLID STATE CHEMISTRY, CATALYSIS. **Personal Data:** b Cannon Falls, Minn, July 8, 1950; m 1973, c 3. **Education:** Carleton Col, BA, 1972; Univ Wis-Madison, MS, 1974, PhD (inorg chem), 1976. **Professional Experience:** SR STAFF CHEMIST, INORG CHEM, CORP RES LABS, EXXON RES & ENG, 1983-; staff chemist, Exxon Res & Eng, 1981-1983; sr chemist, Exxon Res & Eng, 1979-1981; res chemist, Exxon Res & Eng, 1977-1979; NSF fel inorg chem, Cornell Univ, 1976-1977. **Memberships:** Am Chem Soc; Sigma Xi; Clay Minerals Soc. **Research Statement & Publications:** Intercalation chemistry and layered solids; solid state chemistry; pillared clays; catalysis in petroleum refining. **Mailing Address:** Exxon Res & Eng Co, Clinton Rte 22E, Clinton, NJ 08801. **E-Mail:** jackwjohnson@exxonmobil.com

JOHNSON, JAMES ALLEN, HEALTH POLICY & APPLIED SOCIAL SCIENCES. **Personal Data:** b Selma, Ala, November 13, 1954; m 1980, Peggy; c Allen, Adam & Elizabeth. **Education:** Univ SAla, BA, 1978, MS, 1980; Auburn Univ, MPA, 1982; Fla State Univ, PhD, 1987. **Honors & Awards:** Res & Mgt Award, Asn Mgt, 1988. **Professional Experience:** CHMN, DHA ADV COUN, CENT MICH UNIV, as of 2005; PROF, HEALTH SCI & ADMIN, CENT MICH UNIV, as of 2005; prof & chmn, Health Admin, Med Univ SC, beginning 1989; health ed, J Health & Human Resources, 1988-; ed, J Mgt Pract, 1988-1990; consult, Upjohn Healthcare Serv, 1987-1990; instr, Tusculum Col, 1987-1989; bd mem, Alliance for Blind, 1987-1989; instr, Fla State Univ, 1983-1986; asst prof health admin, Memphis State Univ, 1986-1989; sr assoc pub admin, Fla Ctr Productivity, 1983-1986; resident, Vet Admin Hosp, 1982-1983. **Memberships:** Acad Mgt; Am Pub Health Asn; Am Col Healthcare Execs; Nat Social Sci Asn; Am Soc Pub Admin. **Research Statement & Publications:** Health policy and delivery systems; applied behavioral science research in health delivery; risk behavior, and acquired immunodeficiency syndrome policy and prevention. **Mailing Address:** Dept Health Admin Prog Cent Mich Univ, 802 Indust Dr, Mt Pleasent, MI 48858.

JOHNSON, JAMES BLAKESLEE, BIOLOGICAL CONTROL, SYSTEMATICS. **Personal Data:** b January 25, 1951; m 1993, Linda; c Shannon & Heather. **Education:** Univ Mich, BS, 1973; Univ Calif, Berkeley, PhD (entom), 1982. **Professional Experience:** PROF ENTOM, DEPT PLANT, SOIL & ENTOM SCI, UNIV IDAHO, 1981-. **Memberships:** Entom Soc Am; Coleopterist's Soc; Hymenopterist's Soc; Am Inst Biol Sci; Int Orgn Biol Control; AAAS. **Research Statement & Publications:** Biological control of arthropod pests using predators and parasites; Russian wheat aphid; biosystematics of green lacewings. **Mailing Address:** Div Entom, Univ Idaho, Moscow, ID 83844.

JOHNSON, JAMES DANIEL, Theoretical Physics, Statistical Mechanics. **Personal Data:** b Toledo, Ohio, March 21, 1944; m 1966, Suzanne; c Ian Johnson. **Education:** Case Inst Technol, BS, 1966; State Univ NY, Stony Brook, MA, 1968, PhD (physics), 1972. **Professional Experience:** Staff mem physics, Los Alamos Nat Lab, 2001-2005; dep group leader, physics, Los Alamos Nat Lab, 1991-2001; actg group leader, Los Alamos Nat Lab, 1990-1991; dep group leader, Los Alamos Nat Lab, 1989-1990; mem US Deleg, Nuclear Testing Talks, 1988; proj leader, Los Alamos Nat Lab, 1985-1989; prin investr, Los Alamos Nat Lab, 1981; staff mem physics, Los Alamos Nat Lab, 1976-1989; fel, Los Alamos Nat Lab, 1974-1976; Res assoc physics, Rockefeller Univ, 1972-1974. **Memberships:** Am Phys Soc; AAAS. **Research Statement & Publications:** Exact models and rigorous results in statistical mechanics; equation of state studies for materials of interest to energy development programs and to detonation physics. **Mailing Address:** T-1 MS-B221, Los Alamos Nat Lab, Los Alamos, NM 87545. **Fax:** 505-665-5757. **E-Mail:** jdt1@lanl.gov

JOHNSON, J(AMES) DONALD, ENVIRONMENTAL CHEMISTRY, ANALYTICAL CHEMISTRY. **Personal Data:** b Inglewood, Calif, August 1, 1935; m Joanne; c Katherine (Bumgardner) & Christopher. **Education:** Univ Calif, Los Angeles, BS, 1957; Univ NC, PhD (anal chem), 1962. **Honors & Awards:** Tanner Award WaterRes, US Environ Protection Agency Sci Adv Bd. **Professional Experience:** EMER PROF ENVIRON CHEM, SCH PUB HEALTH, RETIRED UNIV NC, CHAPEL HILL, 1990-; chmn, Environ Chem Div, Am Chem Soc, 1987-1988; visiting sci EAWAG, Switzerland, 1981-1982; environ fel, Gothenburg Univ, Sweden, 1970-1971 & Nobel symp, 1971; Vis lectr, NC Wesleyan Col, 1963-1964; From asst prof to prof water chem, Sch Pub Health, Univ NC, Chapel Hill, 1961-1990. **Memberships:** Am Chem Soc. **Research Statement & Publications:** Chemistry of natural aqueous solutions; analysis and kinetics of chlorine and bromine; drinking, cooling, and waste-water disinfection chemistry. **Mailing Address:** 100 Highland Trail, Chapel Hill, NC 27516. **E-Mail:** donjoannej@hotmail.com

JOHNSON, JAMES EDWARD, radiation biophysics; deceased, see previous edition for last biography

JOHNSON, JAMES EDWIN, PHYSICAL CHEMISTRY. **Personal Data:** b Berwind, WVa, June 5, 1917; m 1955, c 2. **Education:** Emory & Henry Col, BS, 1942; Va Polytech Inst, MS, 1949, PhD, 1952. **Professional Experience:** RETIRED; from assoc prof to prof chem, Appalachian State Univ, 1961-1983; res chemist, Chemstrand Corp, 1952-1962; instr chem, Emory & Henry Col, 1946-1948. **Memberships:** Am Chem Soc. **Research Statement & Publications:** Solid State physics; physical chemistry of high polymers. **Mailing Address:** 160 Blanwood Dr, Boone, NC 28607.

JOHNSON, JAMES HARMON, CLINICAL CHILD PSYCHOLOGY, CHILDHOOD PSYCHOPATHOLOGY. **Personal Data:** b Martin, Tenn, March 30, 1943; m 1967, c 2. **Education:** Murray State Univ, BS, 1966, MS, 1968; Northern Ill Univ, PhD (psychol), 1976. **Professional Experience:** Conf coordr, Fla Conf Child Health Psychol, 1988-; PROF PSYCHOL, UNIV FLA, 1987-; pres, Sect Clin Child Psychol, Am Psychol Asn, 1987; mem, planning comt, Nat Conf Training Clin Child Psychologists, 1983-1985; mem, Sect Clin Child Psychol, Am Psychol Asn, 1982-1987; assoc ed, J Clin Child Psychol, 1982-1986; assoc prof clin psychol, Univ Fla, 1979-1987; asst prof psychol, Univ Wash, Seattle, 1975-1979; Instr child psychol, Univ Tex Med Br, 1972-1975. **Memberships:** Am Psychol Asn; Soc Pediat Psychol. **Research Statement & Publications:** Linking stress to problems of both physical health and psychological adjustment; assessment of stress; variables that mediate the impact of stress on individuals; the relationship between stress and fluctuations in health status of those with chronic illness; child psychopathology; effects of stress on children. **Mailing Address:** Dept Clin & Health Psychol, Univ Fla, PO Box 100165, Gainesville, FL 32610-0165. **Fax:** 352-265-0294. **E-Mail:** jhj@ufl.edu

JOHNSON, JAMES LESLIE, CHEMISTRY. **Personal Data:** b Kipling, NC, February 13, 1921; m 1945, Agatha; c James B & Gilbert C Johnson. **Education:** Univ NC, BS, 1943; Univ Ill, PhD (chem), 1949. **Professional Experience:** RETIRED; from div dir to vpres, Upjohn Co, 1962-1983, chemist, 1949-1962; chemist, Stamford Res Labs, Am Cyanamid Co, 1943-1946. **Memberships:** AAAS; Am Chem Soc; Sigma Xi. **Research Statement & Publications:** Natural products; spectroscopy; quality control; clinical chemistry. **Mailing Address:** 5400 Glen Harbor Dr, Kalamazoo, MI 49009-9535.

JOHNSON, JAMES M(ELTON), CHEMICAL ENGINEERING. **Personal Data:** b Pittsboro, NC, December 29, 1915; m 1954. **Education:** NC State Col, BS, 1937. **Professional Experience:** SR PROCESS ENGR CATALYST & SULFUR MFG, MOBIL OIL CO, INC, 1962-; asst chief chemist, Refinery Labs, 1949-1962; chief chemist, Bead Catalyst Plant Lab, 1944-1949; c hem engr, Res & Develop Dept, Socony Vacuum Labs, Socony Mobil Oil Co, Inc, 1937-1944. **Memberships:** Am Chem Soc; Am Inst Chem Engrs. **Research Statement & Publications:** Bead catalyst; petroleum refinery control; Claus sulfur plant and tail gas unit design and operation. **Mailing Address:** 645 Washington Ave, Haddonfield, NJ 08033.

JOHNSON, JAMES NORMAN, SOLID MECHANICS. **Personal Data:** b Tacoma, Wash, September 6, 1939; m 1959, Carol; c Kevin R, Kerry J & Timothy J. **Education:** Univ Puget Sound, BS, 1961; Wash State Univ, PhD (physics), 1966. **Professional Experience:** NATO sr scientist, Cavendish Lab, Cambridge, UK, 1985-1986; CONSULT TECH STAFF, LOS ALAMOS NAT LAB, 1976-; staff consult, Terra Tek Inc, 1973-1976; mem tech staff, Sandia Labs, 1967-1973; res fel physics, Wash State Univ, 1966-1967. **Memberships:** Am Geophys Union; Sigma Xi; Am Phys Soc. **Research Statement & Publications:** Theory of wave propagation and dynamic failure in solids including geophysical materials; constitutive relations for solids; initiation of solid explosives. **Mailing Address:** Los Alamos Nat Lab, PO Box 1663, Los Alamos, NM 87545. **Fax:** 505-665-4055. **E-Mail:** jnj@lanl.gov

JOHNSON, JAMES S, MATHEMATICS. **Education:** Cloud State Univ, BA, 1962; Louisiana State Univ, MA, 1967; Univ Northern Colo, PhD, 1973. **Professional Experience:** ASST PROF MATH, SAINT JOHN'S UNIV, as of 2005. **Mailing Address:** Dept Math St John's Univ, PO Box 2000, Collegeville, MN 56321. **Fax:** 320-363-5179. **E-Mail:** jjohnson@csbsju.edu

JOHNSON, JAMES T, AERONAUTICS. **Education:** Iowa State Univ, BS, 1964, MS, 1965. **Professional Experience:** RETIRED; pres & chief operating officer, Gulfstream Aerospace Corp, beginning 1997. **Memberships:** Am Inst Aeronaut & Astronaut. **Mailing Address:** Gulfstream Aerospace Corp., 500 Gulfstream Rd, Savannah, GA 06118-1873. **Fax:** 912-965-3084.

JOHNSON, JAMES W, AERONAUTICS. **Professional Experience:** CHMN, CANAVERAL COUN TECH SOCS, FLA SPACE RES INST, as of 2004. **Memberships:** Am Inst Aeronautics & Astronaut. **Mailing Address:** Fla Space Res Inst, Bldg M6-306 Rm 9030, Orlando, FL 32899. **Fax:** 713-244-7929.

JOHNSON, JANICE KAY, PHYSICAL SCIENCE, SCIENCE EDUCATION. **Personal Data:** b Burke, SDak, April 12, 1946; m 1968. **Education:** Dakota State Col, BS, 1968; Southern Ill Univ, MS, 1969; Syracuse Univ, PhD (sci educ), 1976. **Professional Experience:** SUPT, GUNNISON WATERSHED SCH DIST, 1991-; mem gov bd, Wash Elementary Sch Dist, 1985-; sci coordr, Glendale Union High Sch Dist, 1982-1991; coordr info systs, Ariz State Univ, 1979-1982; NSF grant proposal reviewer, 1978-1981; prog developer, Rio Salado Col, 1978-1979; consult, Ariz State Dept Educ, Energy Res, 1978; instr phys sci, Mesa Community Col, 1977-1979; grad intern sci educ, Syracuse Univ, 1974-1976; teacher sci, Pine Grove Middle Sch, NY, 1969-1974; grad intern educ, Southern Ill Univ, 1968-1969. **Memberships:** Nat Sci Teachers Asn; Nat Asn Res Sci Teaching. **Research Statement & Publications:** Cognitive development and its relation to science education; business-industry partnerships in education; mastery learning; strategic planning; grant proposal writing. **Mailing Address:** 190 Park Dr, Gunnison, CO 81230.

JOHNSON, JAY ALLAN, WOOD SCIENCE, ENGINEERING MECHANICS. **Personal Data:** b Two Harbors, Minn, July 15, 1941; m 1971. **Education:** Univ Minn, BS, 1964; Col Environ Sci & Forestry, Syracuse Univ, MS, 1971; Univ Wash, PhD (wood sci), 1973. **Professional Experience:** PROF, WOOD SCI, COL FOREST RESOURCES, UNIV WASH, as of 2005; SCI SPECIALIST WOOD COMPOSITE MAT, WEYERHAEUSER CO, 1977-; asst prof wood physics, Va Polytech Inst & State Univ, 1973-1977. **Memberships:** AAAS; Soc Wood Sci & Technol; Forest Prods Res Soc; Am Soc Testing & Mat. **Research Statement & Publications:** Development of wood particulate materials; modeling stress development in wood during drying; evaluation of fracture mechanics for testing procedures for wood and wood based materials. **Mailing Address:** Col Forest Resources, Univ Wash, Box 352100, Seattle, WA 98195-2100. **Fax:** 206-685-3091. **E-Mail:** jjohnson@u.washington.edu

JOHNSON, JEAN ELAINE, PSYCHOLOGY, STRESS & COPING. **Personal Data:** b Wilsey, Kans, March 11, 1925. **Education:** Kans State Univ, BS, 1948; Yale Univ, MS, 1965; Univ Wis-Madison, MS, 1969, PhD (social psychol), 1971. **Honors & Awards:** Distinguished Contrib Nursing Sci, Am Nurses Found & Am Nurses Asn, 1983; First Distinguished Researcher Award, Oncol Nursing Soc, 1992; Outstanding Contrib Nursing & Health Psychol, Am Psychol Asn, 1993. **Professional Experience:** RETIRED; vis prof, Col Nursing, Univ Utah, 1996-1997; mem, Breast Cancer Prog Integration Panel, US Army Med Res & Develop Command, 1993-1996; site dir, Robert Wood Johnson Clin Nurse Scholars Prog, 1984-1991; mem, Behav Med Study Sect, NIH, 1982-1986; prof nursing, Univ Rochester, 1979-1995; a ssoc dir nursing oncol & clin nursing chief oncol, Strong Mem Hosp, 1979-1993; from assoc prof to prof res & nursing & dir, Ctr Health Res, Col Nursing, Wayne State Univ, 1971-1979; res asst nursing res, Sch Nursing, Yale Univ, 1965-1967; in-serv coordr nursing, Gen Rose Hosp, Denver, Colo, 1960-1963; i nstr nursing, var nursing schs, 1948-1960. **Memberships:** Inst Med-Nat Acad Sci; AAAS; Sigma Xi; Am Nurses' Asn; Oncol Nursing Soc; Acad Behav Med Res; Am Psychol Asn. **Research Statement & Publications:** Development of psychological theories about reactions to threatening events, and clinical tests of the effects on patient welfare of care activities deduced from such theories. **Mailing Address:** Sch Nursing, Univ Rochester Med Ctr, Rochester, NY 14642. **Fax:** 585-473-1059.

JOHNSON, JEAN LOUISE, MOLYBDENUM ENZYMES. **Personal Data:** b Memphis, Tenn, June 17, 1947; m 1969, c 2. **Education:** Cornell Col, BA, 1969; Duke Univ, PhD (biochem), 1974. **Professional Experience:** RES ASST PROF, DEPT BIOCHEM, DUKE UNIV MED CTR, 1986-; res assoc, 1974-1986. **Memberships:** Am Soc Biol Chemists. **Research Statement & Publications:** Structure and role of molybdenum cofactor in molybdoenzymes; molybdenum cofactor biosynthesis; molybdenum cofactor deficiency disease. **Mailing Address:** Dept Biochem, Duke Univ Med Ctr, Durham, NC 27710-0001. **Fax:** 919-684-8919. **E-Mail:** jean_johnson@biochem.duke.edu

JOHNSON, JEFFERY LEE, NEUROPHYSIOLOGY. **Personal Data:** b Milwaukee, Wis, March 6, 1941; m 1968, c 1. **Education:** Lakeland Col, BS, 1964; Ind Univ, Indianapolis, PhD (physiol), 1968. **Professional Experience:** ASSOC PROF PHYSIOL & PHARMACOL, SCH MED, UNIV SDAK, 1976-; asst prof, Sch Med, Univ Sdak, 1970-1976; NIH grants, Inst Psychiat Res, Med Ctr, Ind Univ, Indianapolis, 1968-1970. **Memberships:** AAAS; Soc Neuroscience. **Research Statement & Publications:** Axoplasmic flow; regeneration; transmitter systems; topographic distribution of amino acids and enzymes in nervous system; electrophysiological analysis of nervous system activity. **Mailing Address:** Dept Physiol & Pharmacol, Sch Med, Univ SDak, Lee Med 257 1400 W 22d St, Sioux Falls, SD 57105. **Fax:** 605-357-1311. **E-Mail:** jjohns06@usd.edu

JOHNSON, JEROME H, ELECTRICAL ENGINEERING. **Personal Data:** b Moscow, Idaho, November 22, 1918; m 1943, c 3. **Education:** Univ Idaho, BS, 1942; Ore State Univ, MS, 1947, PhD (elec eng), 1953. **Professional Experience:** PROF EMER ENG, UNIV REDLANDS, 1977-; prof & coordr eng sci, Univ Redlands, 1958-1977; staff mem res, Sandia Corp, 1953-1958; asst prof elec eng, Univ Wyo, 1946-1947 & Wash State Univ, 1947-1953. **Memberships:** Inst Elec & Electronics Engrs; Sigma Xi. **Research Statement & Publications:** High energy shock excited pulse generators; solid state lasers; digital-analog computer elements. **Mailing Address:** 1718 Rossmont Dr, Redlands, CA 92373.

JOHNSON, JERRY A, MATHEMATICS. **Education:** Okla State Univ, BS, 1964; Univ Ill, MS, 1966, PhD, 1969. **Professional Experience:** PROF MATH, UNIV NEV, 1993-. **Mailing Address:** Dept Math Univ Nevada, Reno, NV 89557. **Fax:** 775-784-6378. **E-Mail:** jerryj@unr.edu

JOHNSON, JERRY WAYNE, AGRONOMY. **Personal Data:** b Perry, Ga, July 22, 1948; m 1968. **Education:** Univ Ga, BSA, 1970; Purdue Univ, MS, 1972, PhD (agron), 1974. **Professional Experience:** PROF CROP & SOIL SCI, UNIV GA, 1986-; from asst prof to assoc prof, Univ GA, 1977-1986; asst prof plant breeding & genetics, Univ Md, 1974-1977; res asst hybrid wheat, Purdue Univ, 1970-1974. **Memberships:** Am Soc Agron; Crop Sci Soc Agron. **Research Statement & Publications:** Development of barley and wheat varieties that are early and have disease resistance and milling and baking quality; a better feed barley being developed with a higher protein content. **Mailing Address:** Dept Crop & Soil Sci, Univ Ga, 1109 Exp St, Griffin, GA 30223-1797. **Fax:** 770-229-3215. **E-Mail:** jjohnso@gaes.griffin.peachnet.edu

JOHNSON, JOE W, hydraulic engineering; deceased, see previous edition for last biography

JOHNSON, JOHN ALAN, PROCESS CONTROL. **Personal Data:** b Gary, Ind, January 30, 1943; m 1965, c 2. **Education:** Grinnell Col, BA, 1965; Carnegie-Mellon Univ, MS, 1967, PhD (physics), 1970. **Professional Experience:** RETIRED; prin scientist, Idaho Nat Eng Lab, 1979-2001; asst prof physics, Wittenberg Univ, 1976-1979; asst prof physics, Kenyon Col, 1969-1976. **Memberships:** Acoust Soc Am; Am Welding Soc; Int Neural Network Soc; Am Soc Metall Int. **Research Statement & Publications:** Nondestructive evaluation; ultrasonics; microcomputers; process sensing and control. **Mailing Address:** Idaho Nat Eng Lab, Mailstop 7129, Idaho Falls, ID 83415-2209. **Fax:** 208-533-4531.

JOHNSON, JOHN CHRISTOPHER, ECOLOGY, ORNITHOLOGY. **Personal Data:** b Gunnison, Colo, November 28, 1924; m 1948, c 3. **Education:** Ohio State Univ, BS, 1947; Univ Okla, MS, 1952, PhD (zoology), 1957. **Professional Experience:** PROF EMER BIOL, PITTSBURG STATE UNIV, 1987-; registr, Rocky Mountain Biol Lab, Colo, beginning 1972; dir, Rocky Mountain Biol Lab, Colo, 1968-1977; trustee, Rocky Mountain Biol Lab, Colo, beginning 1964; prof, Pittsburgh State Univ, 1962-1987; actg chmn dept biol, Pittsburgh State Univ, 1960-1962; from asst prof to assoc prof zoology, Pittsburgh State Univ, 1956-1962; actg dir, Rocky Mountain Biol Lab, Colo, 1954; instr, Univ Okla, 1950-1956; teacher, Sch Dependents, Ramey, PR, 1948-1949; pub sch teacher, Ohio, 1948. **Memberships:** Am Ornithologists Union; Soc Syst Zoology; Am Inst Biol Sci. **Research Statement & Publications:** Vertebrate zoology; bioecology; ornithology. **Mailing Address:** Dept Biol, Pittsburg State Univ, Pittsburg, KS 66762.

JOHNSON, JOHN E, ELECTRON MICROSCOPY. **Personal Data:** b Ft Worth, Tex, August 21, 1945. **Education:** Tulane Univ, PhD (neurosci), 1973. **Professional Experience:** ASST PROF NEUROSCIENCE, TULANE UNIV, 1979-. **Mailing Address:** 2340 Mistletoe Ave, Ft Worth, TX 76110-1147.

JOHNSON, JOHN E(DWIN), CIVIL & STRUCTURAL ENGINEERING. **Personal Data:** b Detroit, Mich, January 18, 1931; m 1983, c 6. **Education:** Gonzaga Univ, BSCE, 1956; Stanford Univ, MSCE, 1957; Purdue Univ, PhD, 1963. **Honors & Awards:** Z W Craine Award; NSF Award. **Professional Experience:** PROF EMER CIVIL & ENVIRON ENG, UNIV WIS, MADISON, as of 2006; PRES ENG FORENSICS & TESTING, UNIV WIS-MADISON, 1972-; prof civil & environ eng, Univ Wis-Madison, beginning 1972; consult to over 100 Co, 1965-; from asst prof to assoc prof civil eng, Univ Wis- Madison, 1965-1972; res engr, Dow Chem Co, 1962-1965; instr, Purdue Univ, 1960-1962; design engr, Detroit Edison Co, 1958-1960; various fels. **Memberships:** Am Soc Civil Engrs; Am Soc Eng Educ; Am Concrete Inst; Nat Soc Prof Engrs; Am Soc Testing & Mat; Sigma Xi; Am Inst St Construct. **Research Statement & Publications:** Composite behavior; use of plastics as structural materials; analysis and testing of the physical behavior of engineering materials; large number of papers, articles, design manuals and one textbook. **Mailing Address:** Dept Civil Eng, Univ Wis, 1415 Eng Dr, Madison, WI 53706-1691. **Fax:** 608-262-5199.

JOHNSON, JOHN HAL, ORGANIC & FOOD CHEMISTRY. **Personal Data:** b Benjamin, Utah, July 1, 1930; m 1958, c 4. **Education:** Brigham Young Univ, BS, 1955, MS, 1957; Ohio State Univ, PhD (food sci), 1963. **Honors & Awards:** Virginia F Cutler Lectr, 1978. **Professional Experience:** PROF EMER FOOD SCI & NUTRIT, BRIGHAM YOUNG UNIV, as of 1997; prof food sci & nutrit, Brigham Young Univ, beginning 1969; asst biochemist food sci, Agr Exp Sta, Univ Fla, 1963-1968; res asst food chem, Agr Exp Sta, Ohio State Univ, 1960-1963; l ab instr chem, Brigham Young Univ, 1959-1960. **Memberships:** Inst Food Technologists; Sigma Xi. **Research Statement & Publications:** Chemical reactions occurring in foods during processing and storage; effects on functional qualities of cooker extruded soy enriched cereal flours; development of cereal-based complemented foods. **Mailing Address:** Dept Food Sci & Nutrit, Brigham Young Univ, Provo, UT 84602.

JOHNSON, JOHN HAROLD, LIQUID CHROMATOGRAPHY, SPECTROSCOPY. **Personal Data:** b Chicago, Ill. **Education:** Monmouth Col, Ill, BA, 1968; Univ Ark, PhD (organ chem), 1974. **Professional Experience:** SR RES INVESTR, ANALYTIC DEVELOP, KRAFT GEN FOODS, 1988-; group leader, Anal Develop, Dupont Critical Care, 1980-1988; supvr chem anal, G D Searle Co, 1978-1980; res investr, Nalco Environ & Chem Sci Corp, 1977-1978; l ectr, Fac Inst, Argonne Nat Lab, 1976-1979 & Am Chem Soc Speakers Tour, 1977; s r scientist, US Environ Protection Agency, 1973-1977. **Memberships:** Acad Pharmaceut Sci; Am Chem Soc; Am Inst Chemists; Asn Off Anal Chemists. **Research Statement & Publications:** Separation techniques as applied to food componets water soluble polymers; basic studies into new chromatographic separation, spectroscopic and laboratory automation techniques as applied to food analyis and structure identification. **Mailing Address:** 320 Juniper Pkwy, Libertyville, IL 60048-3527.

JOHNSON, JOHN HARRIS, MODELING OF DIESEL ENGINES. **Personal Data:** b Fond du Lac, Wis, February 10, 1937; m EleanorHousding. **Education:** Univ Wis-Madison, BS, 1959, MS, 1960, PhD (mech eng), 1964. **Honors & Awards:** Arch T Colwell Merit Award, Soc Automotive Engrs, 1983 & 1996, Horning Mem Award, 1992; Soc Automotive Engrs Myers Award, 1998. **Professional Experience:** RES PROF EMER, MICH TECHNOL UNIV, as of 2006; Fuel Ecom Comt, 2001; Stanford Res Inst, 1981-1982 & Fleetguard Inc, 1988-; dir, Eng, Exten Col Eng, 1993-1999; dept labor, 1988 & Nat Acad Sci Fuel Econ Comt, 1991-1992; chmn dept, Eng, Exten Col Eng, 1986-1993; mem, Nat Res Coun, 1986-1989; mem bd dir, Soc Automotive Engrs, 1982-1985; distinguished presidential prof, Mich Technol Univ, beginning 1981; Off Tech Assess, A D Little, 1980-1981; mem, Mine Health Res Adv Comt, Dept Health, Educ & Welfare, 1979-1981; consult, Nat Acad Sci, 1979-1981; Off Tech Assess, US Cong, 1979; consult, NASA, 1978-1981; consult, US Bur Mines, 1977-1979; consult, US Environ Protection Agency, 1971-1977; from asst prof to prof, Eng, Exten Col Eng, 1970-1980; coordr, Res Coun Air Pollution Res Comt, 1968-1987; chief engr appl eng res, Int Harvester Co, Ill, 1966-1970; proj engr, US Army Tank-Automotive Ctr, 1964-1966; res asst mech eng, Univ Wis-Madison, 1959-1964. **Memberships:** Fel Soc Automotive Engrs; Combustion Inst; Am Soc Mech Engrs; Air Pollution Control Asn; Am Soc Eng Educ; Am Conf Govt Indust Hygienists. **Research Statement & Publications:** Experimental combustion studies; computer calculations of single fuel drop motion and vaporization; computer cycle analysis; hybrid engine research; emissions and air pollution; instantaneous temperature measurements in internal combustion engines; tribology; diesel particulate emissions measurement and control; wear particle measurement; pollutants in underground mining; cooling system modeling. **Mailing Address:** Dept Mech Eng & Eng Mech, Mich Technol Univ, Rm 1015 1400 Townsend Dr, Houghton, MI 49931-1295. **Fax:** 906-487-2822. **E-Mail:** jjohnson@mtu.edu

JOHNSON, JOHN IRWIN, ZOOLOGY. **Personal Data:** b Salt Lake City, Utah, August 18, 1931. **Education:** Univ Notre Dame, AB, 1952; Purdue Univ, MS, 1955, PhD (psychol), 1957. **Honors & Awards:** NIH career develop award, 1965-1972. **Professional Experience:** PROF ANAT, MICH STATE UNIV, 1981-; from assoc prof to prof biophys, psychol & zool, 1965-1981; Fulbright res scholar physiol, Univ Sydney, 1964-1965; USPHS spec res fel lab neurophysiol, Univ Wis, 1960-1963; from instr to asst prof, Marquette Univ, 1957-1960; instr psychol, Purdue Univ, 1956-1957. **Memberships:** AAAS; Am Soc Zool; Soc Neuroscience; Am Asn Anat; Am Soc Mammalogists; hon mem Anat Asn Australia & New Zealand. **Research Statement & Publications:** Brain function; neuroanatomy; animal behavior. **Mailing Address:** Dept Anat, Mich State Univ, A515 E Fee Hall, East Lansing, MI 48824-1316. **Fax:** 517-336-2443. **E-Mail:** johnso48@pilot.msu.edu

JOHNSON, JOHN LOWELL, PLASMA PHYSICS. **Personal Data:** b Butte, Mont, March 18, 1926. **Education:** Mont State Univ, BS, 1949; Yale Univ, MS, 1950, PhD (physics), 1954. **Professional Experience:** RETIRED; prin res scientist, Plasma Physics Lab, Princeton Univ, 1985-1996; consult scientist, Res & Develop Ctr, 1979-1985; vis sr res physicist, Plasma Physics Lab, Princeton Univ, 1971-1985; adv scientist, Res Labs, 1968-1979; vis res physicist, Plasma Physics Lab, Princeton Univ, 1968-1971; fel physicist, Res Labs, 1964-1968; vis mem res staff, Plasma Physics Lab, Princeton Univ, 1955-1968; sr scientist, Atomic Power Dept, Westinghouse Elec Corp, 1954-1964. **Memberships:** Am Phys Soc. **Research Statement & Publications:** Theoretical plasma physics associated with the controlled thermonuclear research program with principal emphasis directed towards investigation of the magnetohydrodynamic properties of toroidal confinement configurations. **Mailing Address:** 540 Ewing St, Princeton, NJ 08540. **E-Mail:** jlj@pppl.gov

JOHNSON, JOHN MARSHALL, CARDIOVASCULAR PHYSIOLOGY. **Personal Data:** b McCamey, Tex, August 10, 1944; m 1970, Cheryl; c Julia & Sarah. **Education:** Rice Univ, BA, 1966; Univ Tex Southwestern Med Sch, PhD (physiol), 1972. **Professional Experience:** DEPUTY CHMN, DEPT PHYSIOL, 2005-; PROF PHYSIOL, UNIV TEX HEALTH SCI CTR, SAN ANTONIO, 1989-; from asst prof to prof, Univ Tex Health Sci Ctr, San Antonio, 1975-1989; res assoc physiol, Sch Med, Univ Wash, 1974-1975; s r fel, Sch Med, Univ Wash, 1972-1974. **Memberships:** Am Heart Asn; fel Am Physiol Soc; Am Col Sports Med. **Research Statement & Publications:** Reflex control of the circulatory system; cardiovascular physiology regulation of cutaneous blood flow. **Mailing Address:** Dept Physiol, Univ Tex Health Sci Ctr, 7703 Floyd Curl Dr, San Antonio, TX 78229-3900. **Fax:** 210-567-4410. **E-Mail:** johnson@uthscsa.edu

JOHNSON, JOHN MORRIS, BOTANY & CYTOLOGY, PLANT TAXONOMY. **Personal Data:** b Boise, Idaho, March 16, 1937; m 1959, c 2. **Education:** Col Idaho, BS, 1959; Ore State Univ, MS, 1961, PhD (bot, tissue cult), 1964. **Professional Experience:** Chmn, Natural Sci & Math Div, 1985-1993; PROF BIOL, WESTERN ORE STATE COL, 1974-; assoc prof, Western Ore State Col, 1969-1974; USPHS fel, Univ Chicago, 1965-1966; f rom asst prof to assoc prof biol, Cent Col Iowa, 1964-1969. **Memberships:** AAAS; Bot Soc Am; Am Soc Cell Biologists. **Research Statement & Publications:** Plant tissue culture; behavior and function of nucleus and nucleolar vacuoles; plant taxonomy of Oregon plants; ecology of wet-land species especially Juncus. **Mailing Address:** Dept Biol, Western Ore State Col, Monmouth, OR 97361.

JOHNSON, JOHN RICHARD, BIOPHYSICS, HEALTH PHYSICS. **Personal Data:** b Edmonton, Alta, July 6, 1942; m 1967, Carell; c Richard A & Lisa S. **Education:** Univ BC, BS, 1967, MS, 1970, PhD (physics), 1973. **Honors & Awards:** Distinguished Achievement Award, Can Radiation Protection Asn, 1987; Outstanding Serv Award, Int Radiation Protection Asn, 1992. **Professional Experience:** CONSULT SCIENTIST, TRI UNIV MESON FACIL, UNIV BC, 1999-; PRES, INT DOSEMETRY INSTRUMENTS & SERVS INC, 1996-; EMER SCIENTIST, LIFE SCI CTR, PAC NORTHWEST LAB, 1996-; chief scientist, Health Protection Dept, 1993-1996; adj prof, McMaster Univ, 1984-1990 & Wash

State Univ, 1991-; mgr, Health Physics Dept, Life Sci Ctr, 1988-1993; head, Dosimetric Res Br, Health Sci Div, 1984-1988; dir, Can Radiation Protection Asn, 1982-1983; head, Biomed Res Br, 1981-1984; res officer, Chalk River Nuclear Lab, 1973-1981; mem, Nat Coun Radiation Protection & Measurements. **Memberships:** Radiation Res Soc; Health Physics Soc; Can Radiation Protection Asn (pres, 1984-1985); Soc Radiation Protection; Soc Risk Anal. **Research Statement & Publications:** Dosimetric and metabolic models for internal dosimetry including radon daughters; improvement of instrumentation for measuring internal contamination in humans; instrumentation for internal dosimetry and exposure monitoring; internal contamination control and risk assessment for toxic materials. **Mailing Address:** Tri Univ Meson Facil, Univ BC, 4004 Wesbrook Mall, Vancouver, BC V6T 2A3, Can. **Fax:** 604-222-1074. **E-Mail:** jrjcan@acj-associates.com

JOHNSON, JOHNNY ALBERT, LATTICES, RINGS. **Personal Data:** b El Paso, Tex, March 6, 1938; m Betty; c Johnny A & Brenda L. **Education:** Univ Calif, Riverside, BA, 1965, MA, 1966, PhD (math), 1968. **Professional Experience:** Ed, Houston J Math, 1984-; Univ Houston, leave grant, 1980; PROF MATH, UNIV HOUSTON, 1978-; Univ Houston res grant, 1978; assoc managing ed, Houston J Math, 1974-1984; sr engr, Jet Propulsion Lab, Calif Inst Technol, 1969-1971; Univ Houston res initiation grant, 1969; from asst prof to assoc prof, Univ Houston, 1968-1978; NSF fel, Univ Calif, Riverside, 1965-1968. **Memberships:** Math Asn Am; Am Math Soc. **Research Statement & Publications:** Commutative algebra. **Mailing Address:** Dept Math, Univ Houston, Houston, TX 77204-3008. **E-Mail:** JJohnson@uh.edu

JOHNSON, JOHNNY R(AY), APPLIED MATHEMATICS, ELECTRICAL ENGINEERING. **Personal Data:** b Chatham, La, December 19, 1929; m 1990, Barbara; c Todd Michael, John Fitzgerald & Shauna Renee. **Education:** La Tech Univ, EE, 1951; Auburn Univ, MS, 1953, PhD (math), 1959. **Honors & Awards:** Centennial Medal, Inst Elec & Electronics Engrs. **Professional Experience:** RETIRED; prof emer, Dept Elec & Comput Eng, Auburn Univ, as of 2001; prof math, Univ NAla, 1984-1995; eng specialist, Gen Dynamics, 1983-1984; from assoc prof to prof elec eng, La State Univ, Baton Rouge, 1970-1983; assoc prof, Appalachian State Univ, 1962-1963; asst prof math, La Tech Univ, 1958-1962; Electronic engr, Pitman-Dunn Lab, Frankford Arsenal, 1953-1954. **Memberships:** Sigma Xi. **Research Statement & Publications:** Special functions; boundary value problems; analog and digital filters. **Mailing Address:** 222 Meadowcrest Dr, Florence, AL 35630.

JOHNSON, J(OSEPH) ALAN, ENDOCRINOLOGY. **Personal Data:** b West Palm Beach, Fla, February 1, 1933; m 1956, Janice Van de Water; c Robert A & Gary F. **Education:** Butler Univ, BA, 1963; Ind Univ Med Ctr, PhD (physiol), 1968. **Professional Experience:** PROF PHYSIOL, UNIV MO-COLUMBIA, 1985-; RES PHYSIOLOGIST, VET ADMIN HOSP, 1974-; from asst prof to assoc prof, Univ Mo-Columbia, 1971-1985; USPHS fel, 1969-1971. **Memberships:** Am Physiol Soc; Endocrine Soc; Am Soc Nephrol; Soc Exp Biol & Med; Am Heart Asn. **Research Statement & Publications:** Cardiovascular and endocrine physiology; mechanisms in the production of hypertension in animal models. **Mailing Address:** Res Serv 151, Truman Mem Vet Admin Hosp, Columbia, MO 65201-5297. **Fax:** 573-884-4276.

JOHNSON, JOSEPH ANDREW, III, TURBULENCE, NONEQUILIBRIUM FLOW. **Personal Data:** b Nashville, Tenn, May 26, 1940; m 1961, Lynette; c Christopher E, Bradley R, Kyla G & Tayari J. **Education:** Fisk Univ, BA, 1960; Yale Univ, MS, 1961, PhD (physics), 1965. **Honorary Degrees:** DSc, Fisk Univ, 1991. **Honors & Awards:** Bouchet Award, Am Phys Soc, 1995. **Professional Experience:** DIR, LAB MOD FLUID PHYSICS, FLA A & M UNIV, as of 2002; DIR, CTR NONLINEAR & NONEQUILIBRIUM AEROSCI, 1992-; DISTINGUISHED PROF SCI & ENG, PROF PHYSICS & AFFL PROF MECH ENG, FLA A&M UNIV, 1991-; prof physics, Kayser prof sci & eng, 1991-1993; prof physics, City Col NY, 1981-1993; Res & Develop Ctr, Gen Elec Corp, 1978-1980 & Grambling State Univ, 1980-1983; consult, Bell Labs, 1975-1976; assoc prof physics, Rutgers Univ, 1973-1981; consult, Yale Univ, 1973-1975; consult, Fermi Nat Lab, 1973; consult, Von Karman Gas Dynamic Facil, 1969-1977; chmn & prof physics, Southern Univ, Baton Rouge, La, 1969-1972; vis asst prof eng & appl sci, Yale Univ, 1968-1969; c onsult, Gen Appl Sci Lab, 1968-1969; mem tech staff, Bell Labs, Whippany, NJ, 1965-1968; consult, Sikorsky Aircraft Corp, 1962-1965. **Memberships:** Assoc fel Am Inst Aeronaut & Astronaut; fel Am Phys Soc; Third World Acad Sci. **Research Statement & Publications:** Experimental and theoretical studies of turbulence in fluids and plasmas, nonequilibrium processes, and fundamental interactions. **Mailing Address:** Ctr Nonlinear & Nonequilibrium Aerosci, Fla A&M Univ, 1800-3 E Paul Dirac Dr, Tallahassee, FL 32310. **Fax:** 904-561-2474. **E-Mail:** johnsonj@cennas.nhmfl.gov

JOHNSON, JOSEPH EGGLESTON, III, INTERNAL MEDICINE, INFECTIOUS DISEASE. **Personal Data:** b Elberton, Ga, September 17, 1930; m 1956, c Joseph IV, Judith A & Julie M. **Education:** Vanderbilt Univ, BA, 1951, MD, 1954. **Professional Experience:** Pres, Int Soc Internal Med, as of 2004; adj prof med, Univ Pa, 1994-; interim exec vpres, Univ PA, 1994-1995; SR VPRES, AM COL PHYSICIANS, 1993-; PROF INTERNAL MED, DIV INFECTIOUS DIS, UNIV MICH, ANN ARBOR, 1990-; dean & prof internal med, Med Sch, Univ Mich, 1985-1990; chmn, Federated Coun Internal Med, 1982-1983; mem, Federated Coun Internal Med, 1978-; chmn bd gov, Am Bd Int Med, 1977-1983; prof med & chmn dept, Bowman Gray Sch Med, 1972-1985; assoc dean, Infectious Dis Div, 1970-1972; sabbatical, Royal Soc Med traveling fel, 1970-1971; sabbatical, London Clin Res Ctr, 1970-1971; chief, Infectious Dis Div, 1968-1972; dir, Nat Insts Allergy & Infectious Dis training grant & contract Food & Drug Admin, 1967-1972; from assoc prof to prof, Col Med, Univ Fla, 1966-1972; prin investr, Off Surgeon Gen, US Dept Army res grant, 1966-1971; consult, US Army Biol Lab, Ft Detrick, Md, 1966-1971; prog dir, USPHS Med Student Res Training Grant, 1963-1966; asst dean student affairs, Sch Med, Johns Hopkins Univ, 1963-1966; John & Mary R Markle scholar acad med, 1962-1967; from instr to asst prof, Sch Med, Johns Hopkins Univ, 1961-1966; Am Col Physicians Mead Johnson scholar, 1960-1961; res physician, Osler Med Serv, Johns Hopkins Hosp, 1960-1961; fel med, Osler Med Serv, Johns Hopkins Hosp, 1958-1959; asst resident, Osler Med Serv, Johns Hopkins Hosp, 1957-1958 & 1959-1960; Intern, Osler Med Serv, Johns Hopkins Hosp, 1954-1955. **Memberships:** Am Asn Immunologists; Am Soc Microbiol; Soc Exp Biol & Med; fel Royal Soc Med; Am Clin & Climat Asn; Asn Am Physicians; Int Dis Soc Am; Am Col Physicians (pres, 1982-1983); Asn Prof Med (pres, 1982-1983). **Research Statement & Publications:** Pathogenesis of staphylococcal infection; role of bacterial hypersensitivity and immunity in infection; epidemiology of hospital and laboratory acquired infection; pulmonary host defense mechanisms; adverse drug reactions; epidemiology and mechanisms. **Mailing Address:** Independence Mall West, Sixth St Race, Philadelphia, PA 19106-1572. **Fax:** 215-351-2759. **E-Mail:** jjohnson@acponline.org

JOHNSON, JOYCE M, PSYCHIATRY. **Personal Data:** b Baton Rouge, La, January 30, 1952. **Education:** Luther Col, BA, 1972; Univ Iowa, MA, 1976; Mich State Univ, DO, 1980. **Professional Experience:** DIR, DIV NAT TREAT DEMONSTRATIONS, CTR SUBSTANCE ABUSE TREAT, as of 2003; DIR, OFF PHARMACOL & ALTERNATIVE THER, USPHS, 1996-; asst surgeon gen, 1994-1995; dept chief med officer, 1994. **Mailing Address:** Substance Abuse & Mental Health Serv Admin, Rm 12-105 Parklawn Bldg 5600 Fishers Lane, Rockville, MD 20857. **Fax:** 301-480-3045. **E-Mail:** jjohnson@samhsa.gov

JOHNSON, JUDI MATHIS, MATHEMATICS. **Professional Experience:** ASST PROF, LESLEY UNIV, as on 2006. **Memberships:** Int Soc Technol Educ. **Mailing Address:** Lesley Univ, 29 Everett St, Cambridge, MA 02138. **Fax:** 617-349-8599. **E-Mail:** jjohnso1@lesley.edu

JOHNSON, KAREN ELISE, PHYSICS, HISTORY OF PHYSICS. **Personal Data:** b Ballston Spa, NY, October 3, 1950. **Education:** Grinnell Col, BA, 1972; Univ Minn, MS, 1976, PhD (hist sci), 1986. **Professional Experience:** HENRY PRIEST CHMN PHYSICS, ST LAWRENCE UNIV, 1995-; ASSOC PROF PHYSICS, ST LAWRENCE UNIV, 1992-; asst prof, St Lawrence Univ, 1988-1992; vis asst prof, Cath Univ, 1987; asst prof physics, Bates Col, 1986-1988. **Memberships:** Am Asn Physics Teachers; Hist Sci Soc; Sigma Xi. **Research Statement & Publications:** History of 20th century physics; nuclear and chemical physics; history of women in science. **Mailing Address:** Dept Physics, St Lawrence Univ, Bewkes Hall 219, Canton, NY 13617. **Fax:** 315-229-7421. **E-Mail:** kjohnson@stlawu.edu

JOHNSON, KAREN LOUISE, BOTANY, PLANT ECOLOGY. **Personal Data:** b Flint, Mich, February 4, 1941. **Education:** Swarthmore Col, BA, 1963; Univ Ill, Urbana, MS, 1965, PhD (bot), 1970. **Professional Experience:** RETIRED; chief cur, Natural Hist, Man Mus Man & Nature, beginning 1991; cur bot, Natural Hist, Man Mus Man & Nature, 1972-1991; fel bot, Univ Man, 1969-1972; instr biol, Colby Col, 1966-1968. **Memberships:** Ecol Soc Am. **Research Statement & Publications:** Alpine plant communities and soils; vegetation mapping and description; establishment of ecological reserves and natural areas; boreal forest plant geography. **Mailing Address:** Man Mus Man & Nature, 190 Rupert Ave, Winnipeg, MB R3B 0N2, Can. **Fax:** 204-942-3679. **E-Mail:** kjohnson@mbnet.mb.ca

JOHNSON, KEITH E, STATISTICAL PROCESS CONTROL. **Personal Data:** m 1990, Martha; c Kristin & Kathryn. **Education:** Univ Wis-Stevens Point, BS, 1965; Univ Wis-Madison, MS, 1967; Univ Ga, PhD (math & topology), 1971. **Professional Experience:** STATISTICIAN, BELL SOUTH TELECOMMUN, 1984-; math analyst, SCent Bell, 1974-1984; asst prof math, Univ Southern Ala, 1971-1973. **Mailing Address:** 3535 Colonnade Pkwy Rm S9C1, Birmingham, AL 35243. **E-Mail:** keith.e.johnson@bridge.bellsouth.com

JOHNSON, KEITH EDWARD, ANALYTICAL CHEMISTRY, physical chemistry. **Personal Data:** b Feltham, Eng, January 4, 1935; American citizen; m Hilary; c 2. **Education:** Univ London, BSc & ARCS, 1956; Univ London, DIC & PhD (phys chem), 1959, DSc(chem), 1974. **Professional Experience:** Sask Power Corp, 1979-1980 & Oak Ridge Nat Lab, Oak Ridge, Tenn, 1987-1988; emeritus/adjunct PROF, 2000- PROF INORG & ANAL CHEM, UNIV REGINA, 1972-; Vis prof, Univ Calif, Riverside, 1972-1973; from asst prof to assoc prof, Univ Regina, 1966-1972; lectr, Sir John Cass Col, Eng, 1963-1966; asst lectr phys chem, Sir John Cass Col, Eng, 1962-1963; Res assoc anal chem, Univ Ill, 1959-1962. **Memberships:** Electrochem Soc; fel Chem Inst Can; Am Chem Soc. **Research Statement & Publications:** Molten salt electrochemistry; acids and bases in ionic liquids; industrial applications of ionic liquids; coordination of transition metal ions in melts; structural studies of inorganic complexes; azolium ion chemistry; superacidic melts. **Mailing Address:** Dept Chem, Univ Regina, Regina, SK S4S 0A2, Can. **Fax:** 306-337-2476. **E-Mail:** keith.johnson@uregina.ca

JOHNSON, KENNETH ALLEN, CELL MOTILITY, ENZYME MECHANISMS. **Personal Data:** b Davenport, Iowa, March 10, 1949; m 1970, c 2. **Education:** Univ Iowa, BS, 1971; Univ Wis, PhD (molecular biol), 1975. **Professional Experience:** ROGER WILLIAMS CENTENNIAL PROF, DEPT CHEM & BIOCHEM, INST CELLULAR & MOLECULAR BIOL, UNIV TEX, AUSTIN, 1998-; paul berg prof, Biochem, Pa State Univ, 1987-1998; guest scientist, Brookhaven Nat Lab, 1981-; asst prof, biochem, PA State Univ, 1979-1984; fel biophys, Univ Chicago, 1975-1979. **Memberships:** Biophys Soc; Am Soc Cell Biol. **Research Statement & Publications:** Cell motility, especially structure, mechanism and regulation of the dynein adenosine tryphosphatase in cilia and flagella; microtubule assembly pathway; rapid transient kinetic analysis of enzyme reaction pathways; DNA polymerization mechanism; Published over 5 articles. **Mailing Address:** Inst Cell & Molecular Biol, Univ Tex, 2500 Speedway MBB 3 122 A4800, Austin, TX 78735. **Fax:** 512-471-0435. **E-Mail:** kajohnson@mail.utexas.edu

JOHNSON, KENNETH DUANE, PLANT PHYSIOLOGY. **Personal Data:** b Los Angeles, Calif, January 18, 1944; m 1966, c 2. **Education:** Univ Calif, Santa Barbara, BA, 1966, PhD (biol), 1969. **Professional Experience:** PROF BIOL, SAN DIEGO STATE UNIV, 1980-; from asst prof to assoc prof, San Diego State Univ, 1972-1980. **Memberships:** Am Soc Plant Physiol; Sigma Xi. **Research Statement & Publications:** Plant cell biology; biochemistry of growth and development; glycoprotein processing. **Mailing Address:** Dept Biol, San Diego State Univ, San Diego, CA 92182-0001. **E-Mail:** kjohnson@sunstroke.sdsu.edu

JOHNSON, KENNETH GEORGE, GEOMORPHOLOGY, SEDIMENTATION. **Personal Data:** b Oneonta, NY, February 22, 1930; m 1953, Nancy; c Lisa F, Craig A & Ilse D. **Education:** Union Col, NY, BS, 1952; Mich State Univ, MS, 1957; Rensselaer Polytech Inst, PhD (geol), 1968. **Honors & Awards:** Skidmore Fac Res lectr, 1981. **Professional Experience:** PROF EMER GEOL, SKIDMORE COL, as of 2003; treas, Eastern Sect, Am Asn Petrol Geologists, 1993-1994; dir, Environ Studies Prog, Skidmore Col, beginning 1992; prof geol, Skidmore Col, beginning 1978; chmn dept, Environ Studies Prog, 1966-1993; from asst prof to assoc prof, Environ Studies Prog, 1966-1978; geologist, Western Hemisphere Explor div, Gulf Oil Corp, 1958-1961 & Bolivian Gulf Oil Co, 1961-1964. **Memberships:** Soc Econ Paleontologists & Mineralogists; Nat Asn Geol Teachers; Geol Soc Am; Am Quaternary Asn. **Research Statement & Publications:** Applications of geomorphology to military geology and petroleum exploration; photogeology in petroleum exploration; coastal depositional systems and nearshore marine processes. **Mailing Address:** Dept Geol, Skidmore Col, N Broadway, Saratoga Springs, NY 12866-1632. **Fax:** 518-584-3023. **E-Mail:** kjohnson@skidmore.edu

JOHNSON, KENNETH GERALD, INTERNAL MEDICINE. **Personal Data:** b New York, NY, February 12, 1925; m 1950. **Education:** Manhattan Col, BS, 1944; State Univ NY, MD, 1950; Dartmouth Col, MA, 1974. **Professional Experience:** ADJ PROF COMMUNITY MED, MT SINAI SCH MED, as of 2006; Greenwall Found, 1983- & Commonwealth Fund, 1985-; consult, Surgeon Army, 1977-; Dean, State Univ NY, Binghamton clin campus, 1977-; Dean, NY State dept Health, 1977-; consult, Am Col Obstet & gynec, 1976-; sr prog consult, Robert Wood Johnson Found, 1975-; chmn, NY State Comn Formulate Plan for Pub Med Schs, 1975-1976; prof community med, mt sinai sch med, beginning 1974; prof community med, chmn dept & assoc dean, Dartmouth Med Sch, 1971-1974; assoc attend physician, New York Hosp, 1967-; prof community med & dir, div

Epidemiol res, Cornell Univ, Med Col, 1967-1971; vis lectr, Hiroshima Univ, Col Med, 1964-1967; chief med, Atomic Bomb Casualty Comn, Japan, 1964-1967; consult cardiologist, Yale-New Haven Med Ctr & Hosp St Raphael, New Haven, Conn, 1955-1965; from instr to assoc prof, Yale Univ, Sch Med, 1954-1964; Nat Heart trainee, 1953-1954; James Hudson Brown fel med physics, 1951-1952; from intern to chief resident internal med, Yale-New Haven Med Ctr, 1950-1954. **Memberships:** Fel Am Col Cariol; Am Soc Aging; fel Am Col Prev Med; Am Pub Health Asn. **Research Statement & Publications:** Research and development of health services. **Mailing Address:** Health Serv Res Ctr, PO Box 2230, Kingston, NY 12401-0227.

JOHNSON, KENNETH HARVEY, VETERINARY PATHOLOGY. **Personal Data:** b Hallock, Minn, February 17, 1936; m 1960, c Jeffrey, Gregory & Sandra. **Education:** Univ Minn, BS, 1958, DVM, 1960, PhD (vet path), 1965. **Honors & Awards:** Norden Award, 1970; Beecham Award for Res Excellence, 1989; Ralston Purina Small Animal Res Award, 1990. **Professional Experience:** RETIRED; chmn dept vet Pathobiology, Univ Minn, 1977-1983; actg chmn dept vet Pathobiology, Univ Minn, 1976-1977; head sect path, Univ Minn, 1974-1976; prof vet path, Col Vet Med, Univ Minn, St Paul, beginning 1973; path consult, Medtronic Inc, 1972-1980; path consult, Minn Mining & Mfg Co, 1966-1971; USPHS biomed sci support grant, 1968-1993; from asst prof to assoc prof, Univ Minn, 1965-1973; NIH training fel, Univ Minn, 1960-1965; consult, Natural-Y Surg Specialties Inc, Los Angeles. **Memberships:** Am Asn Investigative Path; Int Soc Amyloidosis; Fedn Am Soc Exp Biol; hon mem Am Col Vet Path. **Research Statement & Publications:** Amyloidosis; feline diseases; ultrastructural studies; polymer tumorigenesis in mice; diabetes mellitus in cats. **Mailing Address:** Dept Vet Pathobiology, Univ Minn Col Vet Med, St Paul, MN 55108. **Fax:** 612-624-8707. **E-Mail:** johns049@umn.edu

JOHNSON, KENNETH LANGSTRETH, MECHANICAL ENGINEERING. **Personal Data:** b Barrow in Furness, UK, March 19, 1925; m 1954, Dorothy Rosemary; c Marian R, Hilary C & Andrew R. **Education:** Manchester Univ, UK, BS, 1944, MS, 1949, PhD, 1955. **Honors & Awards:** Mayo D Hersey Award, Am Soc Mech Engrs, 1991. **Professional Experience:** RETIRED; from lectr to prof, Cambridge Univ, 1954-1992; asst lectr, Manchester Univ, 1949-1954; t ech asst, Rotol Ltd, 1944-1949. **Memberships:** Fel Inst Mech Engrs; fel Royal Acad Eng; hon fel Am Soc Tribology & Lubrication Engrs. **Research Statement & Publications:** Contributed articles to journals. **Mailing Address:** 1 New Sq, Cambridge CB1 1EY, UK. **E-Mail:** kln1000@eng.com.ac.uk

JOHNSON, KENNETH MAURICE, NEUROPHARMACOLOGY. **Personal Data:** b Houston, Tex, December 7, 1944; m 1968, c 2. **Education:** Stephen F Austin State Univ, BS, 1967; Univ Houston, PhD (biophys sci), 1974. **Professional Experience:** Pharmacol review subcomt, Nat Inst Drug Abuse, 1988-1992; PROF PHARMACOL, UNIV TEX MED BR, 1987-; prin investr, Nat Inst Drug Abuse, 1979-; from asst prof to assoc prof, Univ Tex Med Br, 1977-1987; fel, Nat Inst Drug Abuse, 1976-1977; fel pharmacol, Med Col Va, 1975-1977; instr physics, Houston Independent Sch Dist, 1967-1969. **Memberships:** AAAS; Am Soc Pharmacol & Exp Therapeut; Soc Neuroscience; Sigma Xi. **Research Statement & Publications:** Neurochemical and behavioral pharmacology of cannabinoids, opiates, hallucinogens, dissociative anesthetics and psychomotor stimulants; biochemistry of excitatory amino acid receptors, regulation of neurotransmitter synthesis, release and receptor; neuroendocrine effects of psychoactive drugs. **Mailing Address:** Dept Pharmacol & Toxicol, Univ Tex Med Br, Tenth Mkt St, Galveston, TX 77550-1031. **Fax:** 409-772-9642. **E-Mail:** kmjohnso@utmb.edu

JOHNSON, KENNETH OLAFUR, NEUROPHYSIOLOGY, BIOMEDICAL ENGINEERING. **Personal Data:** American citizen. **Education:** Univ Wash, BS, 1961; Syracuse Univ, MS, 1965; Johns Hopkins Univ, PhD (biomed eng), 1970. **Professional Experience:** PROF Neuroscience & BIOMED ENG, JOHNS HOPKINS UNIV, 1987-; assoc prof Neuroscience, Johns Hopkins Univ, 1981-1987; staff mem, Univ Melbourne, 1972-1980; asst prof physiol & biomed eng, Johns Hopkins Univ, 1971-1972. **Memberships:** AAAS; Soc Neuroscience. **Research Statement & Publications:** Neural mechanisms in sensation and perception. **Mailing Address:** Mind-Brain Inst, Johns Hopkins Univ Med Sch, 720 Rutland Ave, Baltimore, MD 21205-2109. **Fax:** 410-516-8648. **E-Mail:** kenneth.johnson@jhu.edu

JOHNSON, KENNETH OSCAR, PETROLEUM. **Personal Data:** b Center City, Minn, April 11, 1920; m 1945, Margery; c Eric W. **Education:** Univ Minn, BS, 1942. **Professional Experience:** SR VPRES, COASTAL CORP, 1988-; chmn & chief exec officer, Belcher Oil Co, 1974-1988; wholesale fuels sales mgr, Mkt Dept, 1972-1974; heavyfuels mgr, Supply Dept, 1968-1972; engr, Exxon Corp, 1942-1974; bd dirs, Coastal Corp & Petrol Indust Found. **Research Statement & Publications:** Granted patents in petroleum engineering. **Mailing Address:** 2655 Northbrooke Dr, Naples, FL 34119.

JOHNSON, KENNETH PETER, NEUROLOGY. **Personal Data:** b Jamestown, NY, March 12, 1932; m Jacquelyn; c Peter, Thomas, Diane & Douglas. **Education:** Upsala Col, BA, 1955; Jefferson Med Col, MD, 1959; Am Bd Psychiat & Neurol, dipl. **Honors & Awards:** Weil Award, Am Asn Neuropath, 1967; Zimmerman Lectr, Stanford Univ, 1981; John J Dystel Award, National MS Society and American Academy of Neurology 2000. **Professional Experience:** PROF DIR, MD CTR MULTIPLE SCLEROSIS, UNIV MD, 1981-; chief neurol, Vet Admin Hosp, Baltimore, 1981-1983; prof, Univ Calif, San Francisco, 1974-1981; assoc prof, Case Western Res Univ, 1971-1974; res career develop award, NIH, 1968-1973; asst prof neurol, Case Western Res Univ, 1968-1971; resident, Hosp Cleveland, 1963-1965; intern, Buffalo Gen Hosp, 1959-1960. **Memberships:** Fel Am Neurol Asn; Am Acad Neurol; Am Soc Virol; Am Clin & Climat Asn; Am Cong Rehab Med; Am Soc Neurorehab; Teratology Soc; Soc Exp Neuropath; Int Soc Neuroimmunol. **Research Statement & Publications:** Neurology; Multiple sclerosis therapy. **Mailing Address:** Univ Md Sch Med, 11 S Paca St, Ste 300A, Baltimore, MD 21201. **Fax:** 410-328-5425. **E-Mail:** kjohnson@som.umaryland.edu

JOHNSON, KENNETH SUTHERLAND, HYDROGEOLOGY, ECONOMIC & ENVIRONMENTAL GEOLOGY. **Personal Data:** b Brooklyn, NY, September 16, 1934; m 1959, Dorothea; c Lisa, David & Mark. **Education:** Univ Okla, BS, 1959 & 1961, MS, 1962; Univ Ill, Urbana, PhD (geol), 1967. **Honors & Awards:** Sr Fel, Geol Soc Am; Hon Life Mem, Okla City Geol Soc. **Professional Experience:** GEOLOGIST EMER, OKLA GEOL SURV, 2000-; mem, Environ Adv Bd US Army CEng, 1992-1996; chmn, Okla Hazardous Waste Mgt Coun, 1981-1993; assoc dir, Okla Geol Surv, 1978-2000; dir, Okla Mining & Mineral Resources Res Inst, 1978-1980; vis prof geol & geol eng, Univ Okla, 1973-2000; CONSULT GEOLOGIST, 1968-; teaching asst, Univ Ill, Urbana, 1965-1967; geologist, Okla Geol Surv, 1962-2000; teaching asst, Univ Okla, 1958-1961. **Memberships:** Geol Soc Am; Am Asn Petrol Geologists; Am Inst Prof Geologists; Asn Eng Geologists; Int Asn Hydrogeologists. **Research Statement & Publications:** Economic geology; stratigraphy; field mapping of geologic structures and mineral resources; photogeology; environmental geology; earth-science education; geology of evaporites and redbeds; disposal of radioactive and industrial wastes; hydrogeology; Karst in evaporite rocks (salt and gypsum). **Mailing Address:** 1321 Greenbriar Dr, Norman, OK 73072. **Fax:** 405-325-7069. **E-Mail:** ksjohnson@ou.edu

JOHNSON, KENT J, IMMUNOPATHOLOGY. **Personal Data:** b Minot, NDak, November 4, 1946. **Education:** Univ Ndak, BS, 1968; Univ Conn, MD, 1976. **Professional Experience:** PROF PATH, SCH MED, UNIV MICH, as of 2004; assoc prof path, Sch Med, Univ Mich, beginning 1983; asst prof, sch Med, Univ Mich, 1980-1983. **Memberships:** Am Asn Immunologists; Am Asn Pathologists. **Mailing Address:** Dept Path, Univ Mich Sch Med, 7520 MSRBI 1301 E Catherine Rd, Ann Arbor, MI 48109-0602. **E-Mail:** kjjkjj@umich.edu

JOHNSON, KIRK R, EARTH SCIENCE. **Education:** Yale Univ, PhD (geol & paleobot). **Professional Experience:** VPRES, RES & COLLECTIONS, DENVER MUSEUM NATURAL HIST, CO, as of 2006; CHIEF CUR, DEPT EARTH SCI, DENVER MUSEUM NATURAL HIST, CO, 2004-; chair, Dept Earth Sci, Denver Museum Natural Hist, CO, 2001-2004; cur paleont, Dept Earth Sci, Denver Museum Natural Hist, CO, 1991-2001. **Mailing Address:** Dept Earth Sci, Denver Mus Natural Hist, 2001 Colorado Blvd, Denver, CO 80205. **Fax:** 303-331-6492. **E-Mail:** kjohnson@dmns.org

JOHNSON, KRISTINA MARY, ELECTRICAL ENGINEERING. **Education:** Stanford Univ, BS, MS, PhD. **Honors & Awards:** Int Denis Gabor Medal, 1993. **Professional Experience:** BD DIRS, DYCOM INDUS, INC, MINERALS TECHNOL, INC & GUIDANT CORP, as of 2004; DEAN, PRATT SCH ENG, DUKE UNIV, 1999-; co-founder & dir, NSF Eng Res Ctr, Optoelectronic Comput Systs Ctr, 1993-1997; prof elec & comput eng, Univ Colo, 1985-1999. **Memberships:** Fel Inst Elec & Electronics Engrs; Optical Soc Am; Int Soc Optical Eng; Sigma Xi; Am Soc Eng Educ. **Mailing Address:** Pratt Sch Eng Duke Univ, 305 Teer Bldg Box 90271, Durham, NC 27708-0271. **Fax:** 919-684-4860. **E-Mail:** kristina.johnson@duke.edu

JOHNSON, KURT EDWARD, DEVELOPMENTAL BIOLOGY. **Personal Data:** b Needham, Mass, July 6, 1943; m 1982, Julie; c Melissa, Abraham, Justine & Alexander. **Education:** Johns Hopkins Univ, BS, 1965; Yale Univ, MPhil, 1969, PhD (develop biol), 1970. **Professional Experience:** PROF ANAT, MED CTR, GEORGE WASH UNIV, 1982-; assoc prof, Med Ctr, George Wash Univ, 1977-1982; asst prof anat, Med Ctr, Duke Univ, 1971-1977; fel develop biol, Yale Univ, 1970-1971. **Memberships:** AAAS; Sigma Xi; Am Soc Cell Biologists; Soc Develop Biologists. **Research Statement & Publications:** Experimental morphogenesis; experimental analysis of amphibian gastrulation. **Mailing Address:** Dept Anat, George Wash Univ Med Sch, 2300 I St NW, Washington, DC 20037-2337. **Fax:** 202-994-8885. **E-Mail:** annkej@gwomc.edu

JOHNSON, KURT P, MECHANICAL ENGINEERING. **Personal Data:** b Chicago, Ill, October 6, 1938; m 1961, c 1. **Education:** Northwestern Univ, BS, 1960, PhD (mech eng), 1963. **Professional Experience:** VPRES ENG, B F GOODRICH AERO MOTION DIV, 1992-; group vpres eng, Farrel Corp, 1990-1992; dir laser commun systs, McDonnell Douglas Corp, 1989-1990; dir eng & opers, McDonnell Douglas Corp, 1984-1989; dir corp diversification technol, McDonnell Douglas Corp, 1976-1984; sr staff engr, McDonnell Douglas Astronaut Co, 1963-1975; NSF fel. **Memberships:** Soc Mfg Engrs. **Research Statement & Publications:** Energy systems; transportation systems technology. **Mailing Address:** B F Goodrich Aerospace, Motion Controls, 197 Ridgedale Ave, Cedar Knolls, NJ 07927. **Fax:** 201-267-8114.

JOHNSON, LADON JEROME, ANIMAL HUSBANDRY. **Personal Data:** b Gardner, NDak, September 11, 1934. **Education:** NDak State Univ, BS, 1956, MS, 1957; Ohio State Univ, PhD (animal sci), 1965. **Professional Experience:** PROF EMER, DEPT ANIMAL & RANGE SCI, NDAK STATE UNIV, 1994-; Prof animal husb, Coop Exten Ser, NDak State Univ, 1974-1993; from asst exten animal husbandman to exten animal husbandman, Coop Exten Ser, NDak State Univ, 1966-1974; tech aide, Ohio Agr Res & Develop Ctr, 1964-1965; res asst animal sci, Ohio Agr Res & Develop Ctr, 1961-1964; asst county agent com agr, NDak Coop Exten Serv, 1959-1961; res asst animal sci, Ohio State Univ, 1956-1957. **Memberships:** AAAS; Am Soc Animal Sci. **Research Statement & Publications:** Physiological differences associated with different gaining ability of beef cattle; effect of stage of maturity on yield and nutritive value of corn silage; improvement of corn silage by chemical additives. **Mailing Address:** NDak State Univ, 1301 12th Avenue N, Fargo, ND 58105.

JOHNSON, LANE R, GEOPHYSICS. **Education:** Univ Minn, BS, 1960 & MS, 1962; Cal Tech PhD, 1966. **Professional Experience:** EMER PROF GEOPHYS, DEPT EARTH & PLANETARY SCI, UNIV CALIF-BERKELEY, as of 2005. **Research Statement & Publications:** Earth & planetary science; geophysical methods of studying structure & processes within the earth; seismic sources; monitoring of nuclear test ban treaties; theoretical & computational methods of treating wave propagation in realistic earth models. **Mailing Address:** Dept Geol & Geophys, Univ Calif-Berkeley, 479 McCone Hall, Berkeley, CA 94720. **Fax:** 510-643-9980. **E-Mail:** lane@seismo.berkeley.edu

JOHNSON, LARRY, MATHEMATICS. **Education:** Western State Col, BS; Univ Wyo, MS, Ph.D. **Professional Experience:** PROF MATH, METROPOLITAN STATE COL DENVER, as of 2005; DIR, CTR MATH, SCI & ENVIRON EDUC, as of 2005. **Mailing Address:** Metro State Math& Comput Sci Admin Bldg - Rm 127A, PO Box 173362 Campus Box 38, Denver, CO 80217. **Fax:** 303-556-5107. **E-Mail:** johnsonl@mscd.edu

JOHNSON, LARRY CLAUD, PHYSICS. **Personal Data:** b Roby, Tex, August 24, 1936; m 1956, c 2. **Education:** Tex Christian Univ, BA, 1958; Mass Inst Technol, SM, 1960; Princeton Univ, PhD (astrophys), 1966. **Professional Experience:** MEM JOIN CTR TEAM, INTER JOINT WORKS SITE, 1995-; mem res staff, Plasma Physics Lab, Princeton Univ, 1969-1995; res assoc, Plasma Physics Lab, Princeton Univ, 1966-1969. **Memberships:** AAAS; Am Phys Soc. **Research Statement & Publications:** Plasma physics; plasma spectroscopy and laser scattering; atomic collision cross sections. **Mailing Address:** ITER Joint Works Site, 11025 N Torey Pines Rd, La Jolla, CA 92037. **Fax:** 619-546-8602.

JOHNSON, LARRY DON, PHYSICS. **Personal Data:** b Winnfield, La, November 20, 1940; m 1962. **Education:** La Polytech Inst, BS, 1962; Univ Tenn, MS, 1964, PhD (physics), 1967. **Professional Experience:** ASSOC PROF PHYSICS, NORTHEAST LA UNIV, 1967-. **Memberships:** Am Asn Physics Teachers; Am Phys Soc; AAAS; Sigma Xi. **Research Statement & Publications:** Statistical mechanics and phase transitions; human biomechanics. **Mailing Address:** Dept Physics, Northeast La Univ, 700 Univ Ave, Monroe, LA 71209.

JOHNSON, LARRY RAY, INDUSTRIAL ENGINEERING. **Personal Data:** b Atlanta, Ga, December 18, 1935; m 1958, c 3. **Education:** Ga Inst Technol, BCerE, 1958, BIE, 1960, MSIE, 1962; Okla State Univ, PhD (indust eng), 1969. **Professional Experience:** PROF INDUST ENG, MISS STATE UNIV, 1976-; from asst prof to assoc prof indust eng, Miss State Univ, 1963-1976; a ssoc mfg res engr, Lockheed-Ga Co, 1961-1963. **Memberships:** Am Inst Indust Engrs. **Research Statement & Publications:** Hospital systems; occupational safety and health; energy conservation; work methods. **Mailing Address:** Dept Indust Eng, Miss State Univ, Mississippi State, MS 39762.

JOHNSON, LARRY REIDAR, PULMONARY EPIDEMIOLOGY. **Personal Data:** b Seattle, Wash, January 5, 1945; m 1968, Elaine; c Carolyn & Daniel. **Education:** Univ Wash, Seattle, BS, 1966; State Univ NY, Buffalo, PhD (physiol), 1973. **Professional Experience:** MED CONSULT, ORE HEALTH SCI UNIV KAISER CTR HEALTH RES, 2000-; Proj coordr, Ore Health Sci Univ Lung Health Study, 1986-2000; SR RES ASSOC, ORE HEALTH SCI UNIV, 1982-2000; asst prof physiol, Ore Health Sci Univ, 1976-1982; res assoc, Harvard Sch Pub Health, Boston, Mass, 1972-1976. **Research Statement & Publications:** Epidemiology of pulmonary function, quality control of spirometry; pulmonary software maintenance and development. **Mailing Address:** Ore Health Sci Univ Lung Res Lab, CR115 3181 SW Sam Jackson Park Rd, Portland, OR 97201-3098. **Fax:** 503-494-5407. **E-Mail:** johnsnla@ohsu.edu

JOHNSON, LAVELL R, BIOCHEMISTRY, ORGANIC CHEMISTRY. **Personal Data:** b Salt Lake City, Utah, January 16, 1935; m 1958, c 6. **Education:** Univ Utah, BS, 1959; Brigham Young Univ, PhD (biochem), 1965. **Professional Experience:** PRES, JOHNSON RES, 1971-; assoc res dir dept med, Latter-Day Saints Hosp, 1968-1971; sr scientist biochem, Ames Co Div, Miles Labs, 1964-1968. **Memberships:** AAAS; Am Chem Soc. **Research Statement & Publications:** Mechanism of action of adrenocorticotropic hormone; pregnenolone synthesis by adrenal preparations; analysis of growth hormone, testosterone, metanephrine, insulin and adrenocorticotropic hormone. **Mailing Address:** Johnson Res, 3201 Teton Dr, Salt Lake City, UT 84109.

JOHNSON, LAWRENCE ALAN, PROCESSING OF CROPS. **Personal Data:** b Columbus, Ohio, April 30, 1947; m 1969, Bernice; c Bradley & David. **Education:** Ohio State Univ, BS, 1969; NC State Univ, MS, 1971; Kans State Univ, PhD (food sci), 1978. **Honors & Awards:** ADM Award, Am Oil Chemists Soc, 1987; Utilization Res Award, United Soybean Bd, 1993. **Professional Experience:** DIR, CTR CROPS UTILIZATION RES, IOWA STATE UNIV, as of 2006; PROF AGR & BIOSYSTEMS ENG, IOWA STATE UNIV, 1997-; PROF FOOD TECHNOL, CTR CROPS UTILIZATION RES, IOWA STATE UNIV, 1988-; PROF FOOD SCI & HUMAN NUTRIT, IOWA STATE UNIV, 1988-; assoc prof, Ctr Crops Utilization Res, Iowa State Univ, 1985-1988; assoc res chemist, Food Protein Res & Develop Ctr, Tex A&M Univ, 1983-1985; asst res chemist, Food Protein Res & Develop Ctr, Tex A&M Univ, 1978-1983; res asst grain sci, Food Sci, Kans State Univ, 1975-1978; res chemist food prod develop, Dwight P Joyce Res Ctr, Durkee Foods, 1973-1975; food adv, US Army QM Corp, 1971-1973; res asst food sci, NC State Univ, 1969-1971. **Memberships:** Am Asn Cereal Chemists; Inst Food Technologists; Am Oil Chemists Soc; Am Soc Agr Engrs. **Research Statement & Publications:** Developing new product or processing technologies to utilize agricultural products; product applications include both food and non-food industrial products; processes include new techniques in crop separations, ingredient conversions, and food refabrication; oil extraction. **Mailing Address:** Dept Agr & Biosystems Eng, Iowa State Univ, 1041 Food Sci Bldg, Ames, IA 50011-1061. **Fax:** 515-294-6193. **E-Mail:** ljohnson@iastate.edu

JOHNSON, LAWRENCE ARTHUR, REPRODUCTIVE PHYSIOLOGY. **Personal Data:** b Luck, Wis, July 9, 1936; m 1959, c 3. **Education:** Univ Wis, River Falls, BS, 1961; Univ Minn, St Paul, MS, 1963; Univ Md, PhD (animal physiol & biochem), 1968. **Honors & Awards:** Outstanding Res Award Physiol & Endocrinol, Am Soc Animal Sci, 1991. **Professional Experience:** CONSULT, GAMETE PHYSIOLOGY, as of 2004; res leader, germplasma & gamete physiol lab, Agr Res Serv, USDA, 1990-2000; vis Scientist, Res Inst Animal Production, Zeist, 1977-1978; res physiologist animal sci, Agr Res Serv, USDA, 1972-1990; res chemist, Agr Res Serv, USDA, 1966-1972; chemist, Agr Res Serv, USDA, 1964-1966. **Memberships:** Soc Study Reproduction; fel Am Soc Animal Sci; Soc Anal Cytol; Int Embryo Transfer Soc. **Research Statement & Publications:** Reproductive physiology and biochemistry of mammalian semen and fertilization processes; artificial insemination; frozen semen; sex pre-selection. **Mailing Address:** 1420 Maple Ave, Essex, MD 21221.

JOHNSON, LAWRENCE LLOYD, IMMUNOLOGY INFECTIOUS DISEASES. **Personal Data:** b Bangor, Maine, December 30, 1941; m 1976, c 1. **Education:** Univ Maine, BA, 1964, MA, 1973, PhD (zoology), 1980. **Professional Experience:** MEM, TRUDEAU INST, 2000-; adj assoc prof, dept Microbiol & Immunol, Albany Med Ctr, 1998-; assoc mem, Saranac Lake, NY, 1990-2000; asst mem, Saranac Lake, NY, 1984-1989; lectr, lab Genetics, 1983-1984; fel, McArdle lab, Univ Wis-Madison, 1980-1983. **Research Statement & Publications:** Immunity to infection. Resistance to Toxoplasma gondii. **Mailing Address:** Trudeau Inst, Inc, 154 Algonquin Ave, Saranac Lake, NY 12983. **Fax:** 518891-5126. **E-Mail:** ljohnson@trudeauinstitute.org

JOHNSON, LAWRENCE ROBERT, ANALYTICAL CHEMISTRY, PHYSICAL CHEMISTRY. **Personal Data:** b Gyor, Hungary, February 14, 1931; American citizen. **Education:** Eotvos Lorand Univ, Budapest, dipl, 1953; Columbia Univ, PhD (chem), 1961. **Professional Experience:** CONSULT, 1994-; chemist water treat, City Utilities Co, Corbin, Ky, 1981-1993; consult, 1978-1981; actg head dept, Union Col, Ky, 1969-1973; assoc prof anal & phys chem, Union Col, Ky, 1965-1978; asst prof instrumental, anal & phys chem, Lafayette Col, 1962-1965; group leader polymer res radioisotopes, Rohm & Haas Co, Pa, 1960-1962; AEC res asst, Columbia Univ, 1957-1959; Res chemist, Lever Bros Res Ctr, NJ, 1956-1957. **Research Statement & Publications:** Kinetics of polymer adsorption, flocculation and deflocculation; radioisotopes; instrumental analysis; electrochemistry and electroanalysis; atomic absorption spectrophotometry. **Mailing Address:** 701 Rose Lane, Corbin, KY 40701.

JOHNSON, LAYNE MARK, INFORMATION SCIENCE & SYSTEMS. **Personal Data:** b Northfield, Minn, June 4, 1953; m 1978. **Education:** Dana Col, BA, 1975; Iowa State Univ, MS, 1978, PhD (microbiol), 1980. **Professional Experience:** SR DIR, GLOBAL INFO NETWORKS, PHARMACIA CORP, as of 2004; Mgr Tech Info, Am Cyanamid Co, Pearl River, Ny, beginning 1991; sr info scientist, Am Cyanamid CO, Pearl River, NY, 1987-1991; microbial ecologist, Am Cyanamid CO, Pearl River, NY, 1984-1987; sr res microbiologist, Cytox Corp, Allentown, Pa, 1982-1984; p ostdoctoral fel, Univ Okla, Norman, 1980-1982. **Memberships:** Soc Indust Microbiol; Pharmaceut Mfg Asn. **Research Statement & Publications:** Management of published information, including scientific literature and patents pertaining to drug development processes within the pharmaceutical industry; manage state-of-the-art end user search program. **Mailing Address:** Pharmacia Corp, 7000 Portage Rd, Kalamazoo, MI 49001. **Fax:** 269-833-8603. **E-Mail:** layne.m.johnson@pharmacia.com

JOHNSON, LEANDER FLOYD, SOIL-BORNE PLANT DISEASES. **Personal Data:** b Lecompte, La, August 3, 1926; m 1948, c 2. **Education:** Southwestern La Inst, BS, 1948; La State Univ, MS, 1951, PhD (plant path), 1953. **Professional Experience:** RETIRED; from asst prof to prof plant path, Univ Tenn, Knoxville, 1954-1990; instr bot, Univ Tenn, Knoxville, 1953-1954. **Memberships:** Am Phytopath Soc; Sigma Xi. **Research Statement & Publications:** Biological control of plant diseases; methods of approach and basic concepts of soil microbiology. **Mailing Address:** 2004 Plumb Ridge Rd, Knoxville, TN 37932.

JOHNSON, L(EE) ENSIGN, ELECTRICAL ENGINEERING, BIOENGINEERING. **Personal Data:** b New River, Tenn, May 26, 1931; m 1955, c 4. **Education:** Vanderbilt Univ, BE, 1953, BD, 1959; Case Western Reserve Univ, MS, 1963, PhD, 1964. **Professional Experience:** PROF EMER ELEC ENG, VANDERBILT UNIV, as of 2004; prof elec eng, vanderbilt univ, beginning 1972; assoc provost, Vanderbilt Univ, 1970-1975; from instr to assoc prof, Vanderbilt Univ, 1959-1972; prod line mgr, Aladdin Electronics, Div Aladdin Indust, 1955-1959. **Memberships:** Inst Elec & Electronics Engrs. **Research Statement & Publications:** Physiological control systems; iron kinetics in humans; reliability modeling and engineering. **Mailing Address:** Dept Elec Engg, Sch Eng, Vanderbilt Univ, 334 Featheringill Hall, Sta B 351722, Nashville, TN 37235-1722. **Fax:** 615-343-6702. **E-Mail:** johnsole@vuse.vanderbilt.edu

JOHNSON, LEE FREDERICK, MOLECULAR BIOLOGY, MOLECULAR GENETICS. **Personal Data:** b Philadelphia, Pa, January 10, 1946; m 1967, Ann; c Adam & Karl. **Education:** Muhlenberg Col, BS, 1967; Yale Univ, MPhil, 1969, PhD (molecular biophysics & biochemistry), 1972. **Honors & Awards:** Faculty Research Award, American Cancer Society, 1980-1985. **Professional Experience:** PROFESSOR EMERITUS, MOLECULAR GENETICS, OHIO STATE UNIV, 2005; CHMN MOLECULAR GENETICS, OHIO STATE UNIV, 1990-2005; PROF MOLECULAR GENETICS, OHIO STATE UNIV, 1987-2005; PROF BIOCHEM, OHIO STATE UNIV, 1985-2000; molecular biol panel, NSF, 1980-1984; mem, Molecular, Cellular & Develop Biol Progs, Ohio State Univ, 1976-; from asst prof to assoc prof, Ohio State Univ, 1975-1985; Fel, Am Cancer Soc, 1972-1974; Fel cell biol, Mass Inst Technol, 1971-1975. **Memberships:** Am Soc Cell Biol; Am Soc Biochem & Molecular Biol; Am Soc Microbiol. **Research Statement & Publications:** Regulation of growth, RNA metabolism and gene expression in cultured mammalian cells; genetic engineering. **Mailing Address:** Dept Molecular Genetics, The Ohio State Univ, Columbus, OH 43210. **Fax:** 614-292-4466. **E-Mail:** johnson.6@osu.edu

JOHNSON, LEE MURPHY, MATHEMATICS. **Personal Data:** b Lufkin, Tex, September 11, 1934; m 1957, c 1. **Education:** Univ Tex, Austin, BSChE, 1957, MA, 1965, PhD (math), 1968. **Professional Experience:** PROF MATH, NORTHERN ARIZ UNIV, 1983-; assoc prof, asst prof, Northern Ariz Univ, 1967-1983; res chem engr, Humble Oil & Refining Co, 1957-1962. **Memberships:** Am Math Soc; Math Asn Am. **Research Statement & Publications:** General measure theory. **Mailing Address:** 5717 N Aztec St, Flagstaff, AZ 86011-0001.

JOHNSON, LEE W, MATHEMATICS. **Personal Data:** b Appleton, Minn, October 25, 1938; m 1963. **Education:** La State Univ, BS, 1963, MS, 1965; Mich State Univ, PhD (math), 1967. **Professional Experience:** PROF MATH, VA POLYTECH INST & STATE UNIV, as of 2003; assoc prof math, Va Polytech Inst & State Univ, beginning 1974; asst prof, Va Polytech Inst & State Univ, 1967-1974. **Memberships:** Am Math Soc; Soc Indust & Appl Math. **Research Statement & Publications:** Numerical analysis and approximation theory. **Mailing Address:** Dept Math, Va Polytech Inst & State Univ, 468 McBryde Hall, Blacksburg, VA 24061. **Fax:** 540-231-5960. **E-Mail:** johnsonl@vt.edu

JOHNSON, LELAND GILBERT, DEVELOPMENTAL PHYSIOLOGY, LARVAL ECOLOGY. **Personal Data:** b Roseau, Minn, October 16, 1937; m 1978, c 3. **Education:** Augustana Col, SDak, BA, 1959; Northwestern Univ, MS, 1961, PhD (biol sci), 1965. **Professional Experience:** Leigh Marine Lab, Univ Auckland, NZ, 1996; George C Marshall fel, Australian Inst Marine Sci, 1989, 1990, 1991, 1992 & 1995; George C Marshall fel, Fulbright scholar, 1983; George C Marshall fel, Biol Inst, Odense Univ, Denmark, 1977; PROF BIOL, AUGUSTANA COL, SDAK, 1973-; NSF sci fac fel, Queen Mary Col, 1970-1971; from asst prof to assoc prof, Augustana Col, Sdak, 1964-1973. **Memberships:** AAAS; Western Soc Naturalists; Soc Develop Biol; Asn Biol Lab Educ; Sigma Xi. **Research Statement & Publications:** Developmental physiology; effects of temperature on developmental processes; author of two general biology texts and a developmental biology laboratory manual; thyroxine affects on invertebrate development. **Mailing Address:** Dept Biol, Augustana Col, 2001 S Summit Ave, Sioux Falls, SD 57197. **Fax:** 605-274-4718. **E-Mail:** johnson@augie.edu

JOHNSON, LENNART INGEMAR, MATERIALS & PROCESS ENGINEERING, SPECIFICATIONS & STANDARDS. **Personal Data:** b Minneapolis, Minn, December 23, 1924; m 1961, Grant; c 1. **Education:** Univ Minn, BS, 1948. **Honors & Awards:** Leadership & Serv Award, Soc Automotive Engrs, Dedication & Distinction Award Prize Paper Award, Inst Elec Engrs. **Professional Experience:** CONSULT, SOC AUTOMOTIVE ENGRS, 1989-; staff eng, Defense Systs Div, 1987-1988; chmn composites comt, Soc Automotive Engrs, 1986-1988; supvr, Eng Plastics Lab, 1969-1987; prin engr, Ordinance Div, Honeywell, 1967-1969; Sr engr, Ordinance Div, Honeywell, 1949-1967. **Memberships:** Soc Automotive Engrs, chairman composites comm, 1988; fel emer, Am Inst Chemists. **Research Statement & Publications:** Development of casting resins involving urethane and epoxy polymers; development of stain-free injection molding of thermoplastic polymers; development of aerospace material specifications. **Mailing Address:** 14109 M Terr, Minnetonka, MN 55345.

JOHNSON, LEO FRANCIS, LASERS. **Personal Data:** b White Plains, NY, November 6, 1928; m 1962, Barbara; c David, Kathleen, Mark & Christopher. **Education:** Univ Vt, BA, 1951; Syracuse Univ, MS, 1955, PhD (physics), 1959. **Professional Experience:** RETIRED; res assoc, Ctr Res Electro-Optics & Lasers, Univ Cent Fla, 1990-1991; consult, Amoco Laser Co, 1987-1989; consult, Amoco Res Ctr, 1989-1994; mem tech staff physics, Bell Tel Labs, 1959-1986; res asst physics, Syracuse Univ, 1954-1959; tech engr, Gen Elec Co, 1951-1953. **Memberships:** Fel Am Phys Soc; Sigma Xi. **Research Statement & Publications:** Photoconductivity of semiconductors; optical spectroscopy of rare earth and transition metal ions in crystals; investigations of laser phenomena in crystals; interference diffraction gratings; sub-micron surface structures; distributed feedback lasers. **Mailing Address:** 150 Riverwood Ave, Bedminster, NJ 07921.

JOHNSON, LEON JOSEPH, SOIL MINERALOGY. **Personal Data:** b Detroit, Mich, January 17, 1929; m 1952, c 3. **Education:** Pa State Univ, BS, 1954, MS, 1955 PhD (agron), 1957. **Professional Experience:** PROF SOIL MINERAL, PA STATE UNIV, 1980-; assoc prof, PA State Univ, 1967-1980; asst prof soil technol, PA State Univ, 1959-1967; res geologist, Cities Serv Res & Develop Co, 1957-1959. **Memberships:** Am Soc Agron; Clay Minerals Soc. **Research Statement & Publications:** Weathering of soil minerals; formation of soil profiles; clay mineralogy. **Mailing Address:** Pa State Univ, 116 Agr Sci Bldg, University Park, PA 16802. **E-Mail:** ljj1@psu.edu

JOHNSON, LEONARD EVANS, GEOPHYSICS. **Personal Data:** b Ogden, Utah, November 13, 1940; m 1987, c 1. **Education:** Mass Inst Technol, BS, 1962; Univ Calif, San Diego, MS, 1967, PhD (geophys), 1971. **Professional Experience:** Assoc dir, Off Sci & Technol Centers Develop, NSF, 1988; prog dir, Continental Lithosphere, NSF, 1984-1989; prog dir seismol, Continental Lithosphere, NSF, 1982-1984; prog dir geophys, Continental Lithosphere, NSF, 1979-1982; prof lectr, George Wash Univ, 1977-1986; PROG DIR, CONTINENTAL DYNAMICS, NSF, 1974-; assoc prog dir, Continental Lithosphere, NSF, 1974-1979; vis prof, Univ Calif, Berkeley, 1973-1974; vis fel, Coop Inst Res Environ Sci, Univ Colo, 1971-1973; res assoc geophys, Boeing Sci Res Labs, 1962-1965; mem comt math geophys, Int Union Geod & Geophys. **Memberships:** Am Geophys Union; Seismol Soc Am; AAAS. **Research Statement & Publications:** Theoretical and observational seismology, inverse problems in geophysics. **Mailing Address:** Nat Sci Found, Rm 785 S 4201 Wilson Blvd, Arlington, VA 22230. **Fax:** 703-292-9025. **E-Mail:** lejohnso@nsf.gov

JOHNSON, LEONARD ROY, PHYSIOLOGY. **Personal Data:** b Chicago, Ill, January 31, 1942; c 3. **Education:** Wabash Col, AB, 1963; Univ Mich, Ann Arbor, PhD (physiol), 1967. **Honorary Degrees:** MD, Copernicus Med Sch, Cracow, 1990. **Honors & Awards:** Hoffmann-LaRoche Prize, Am Physiol Soc; Horace W Davenport Distinguished Lectr; RD McKenna Mem lectr, Can Asn Gastroenterol. **Professional Experience:** THOMAS A GERWIN PROF & ACTG VICE CHANCELLOR RES, DEPT PHYSIOL, HEALTH SCI CTR, UNIV TENN, MEMPHIS, 1990-; chmn, Physiol Test Comt, 1988-1991; mem, Vet Admin Merit Rev Bd, 1987-1991; nat bd med examiners, Physiol Test Comt, 1983-1991; NIH study sect gastroenterol clin nutrit, 1980-1982; ed, Am J Physiol, 1979-1985; prof physiol, Univ Tex Med Sch, Houston, 1972-1989; NIH res career develop award, 1972-1977, grant, 1973-; res grant, Univ Okla, 1970-1973; G A Manahan Trust grant, 1970-1972; from asst prof to assoc prof, Sch Med, Univ Okla, 1969-1972; NIH fel & instr physiol, Sch Med, Univ Calif, Los Angeles, 1967-1969. **Memberships:** Am Gastroenterol Asn; Am Physiol Soc; Endocrine Soc; Soc Exp Biol & Med; hon mem Polish Physiol Soc; Am Soc Cell Biol. **Research Statement & Publications:** Role of polyamines in mucosal growth and cell migration; regulation of growth of gastrointestinal mucosa and gastrin receptor binding. **Mailing Address:** Dept Physiol, Health Sci Ctr, Univ Tenn, Rm 426 Nash Bldg 894 Union Ave, Memphis, TN 38163. **Fax:** 901-448-7752. **E-Mail:** ljohn@physio1.utmem.edu

JOHNSON, LEROY FRANKLIN, NUCLEAR MAGNETIC RESONANCE. **Personal Data:** b Seattle, Wash, February 4, 1933; m 1956, Margaret Lindsley; c Noel L & Brett N. **Education:** Ore State Univ, BS, 1954, MS, 1956. **Honors & Awards:** Excep Achievement Award, Am Chem Soc, 1992. **Professional Experience:** CONSULT, NUCLEAR MAGNETIC RESONANCE INSTRUMENTS, 1994-; analytical nuclear magnetic resonance mgr, Broker Instruments Western Region, 1992-1994; mgr, Appln Labs, sr scientist & mgr, Analytical Nuclear Magnetic Resonance, Gen Elec Nuclear Magnetic Resonance Instruments, 1983-1992; chmn, Exp Nuclear Magnetic Resonance Conf, 1978; vpres, Nicolet Magnetics Corp, 1972-1983; TEACHER NMR SHORT COURSES, AM CHEM SOC, 1966-; dept mgr, Varian Assocs, 1957-1972. **Memberships:** Am Chem Soc; Soc Appl-Spectros; Int Soc Magnetic Resonance. **Research Statement & Publications:** Applications of nuclear magnetic resonance spectroscopy; development of nuclear magnetic resonance instrumentation; utilization of minicomputers with nuclear magnetic resonance instruments. **Mailing Address:** 10155 Western Dr, Cupertino, CA 95014. **E-Mail:** ffdr20a@prodigy.com

JOHNSON, LESLYE, ALLERGY RESEARCH. **Professional Experience:** CHIEF, ENTERIC DIS BR, NAT INST ALLERGY & INFECTIOUS DIS, NIH, 1989-. **Mailing Address:** Nat Inst Allergy & Infectious Dis, NIH, Rm 3A22 Solar Bldg 6003 Exec Blvd, Rockville, MD 20852. **E-Mail:** lj7m@nih.gov

JOHNSON, LOERING M, CONTROL SYSTEMS DESIGN & ANALYSIS, ENGINEERING QUALITY SYSTEMS DOCUMENTATION. **Personal Data:** b Dickinson, NDak, September 22, 1926; m Maral; c Mairi V, Maureen K, Marc D & Mara E. **Education:** Univ NDak, BS, 1952; Rennselaer Polytech Inst, MS, 1961. **Professional Experience:** CONSULT, LMJ ENTERPRISES, as of 2006; PRIN ENGR, LMJ ENTERPRISES, 1993-; assoc prof teaching, Univ Hartford, 1986-1993; mgr off automation, inst control & elect syst, 1982-1985; Dir, Nat Soc Prof Engrs, 1981-1984; mgr records control, inst control & elect syst, 1980-1982; mem, Stand Bd, Inst Elec & Electronics Engrs, 1978-1981; mgr stand, inst control & elect syst, 1970-1980; Secy, Nuclear Power Eng Comt, 1966-1978; mgr, Inst Control & Elect Syst, 1960-1970; supvr comput appl, elec syst design, Combustion Eng Inc, 1958-1960; eng, elec syst design, Combustion Eng Inc, 1955-1958; engr elec syst design, El DuPont Del Nemours Inc, 1952-1955. **Memberships:** Nat Soc Prof Engrs; fel Inst Elec & Electronics Engrs; Sigma Xi. **Research Statement & Publications:** Published numerous papers and book sections on instrumentation and control, standards, and technical writing; developing on-line courses for professional engineers. **Mailing Address:** LMJ Enterprises, PO Box 372, Tariffville, CT 06081-0372. **E-Mail:** bluejayl26@juno.com

JOHNSON, LOUISE H, MATHEMATICS EDUCATION. **Personal Data:** b Minneota, Minn, October 22, 1927. **Education:** Augsburg Col, BA, 1949; Univ Northern Colo, MA, 1961, DEduc, 1971; Univ Ill, MA, 1963. **Professional Experience:** RETIRED; dean sci & technol, St Cloud State Univ, 1984-1990; dean lib arts & sci, St Cloud State Univ, 1976-1990; assoc dean lib arts & sci, St Cloud State Univ, 1974-1976; prof math, St Cloud State Univ, 1963-1990; teacher high schs, Minn, 1949-1962. **Memberships:** Nat Coun Teachers Math. **Mailing Address:** 2030 Stockinger Dr, St Cloud, MN 56303.

JOHNSON, LOWELL BOYDEN, PLANT MOLECULAR BIOLOGY, PLANT TISSUE CULTURE. **Personal Data:** b Dwight, Ill, October 12, 1935; m 1956, Wanda M Thorndyke Johnson; c Linda R (Butler) & David E. **Education:** Univ Ill, BS, Agr Ed 1957; Purdue Univ, West Lafayette, MS, 1962, PhD (plant path), 1964. **Professional Experience:** Vis Scholar Dept Biol, Ind Univ, Bloomington, 1992; Vis scholar, Div Biol Sci, Univ Mich, Ann Arbor, 1985; PROF PLANT PATH, KANS STATE UNIV, 1982-; from asst prof to assoc prof, Kans State Univ, 1968-1982; Asst res plant pathologist, Univ Calif, Davis, 1964-1968. **Memberships:** AAAS; Am Phytopath Soc; Am Soc Plant Biologists Int Soc Plant Molecular Biol. **Research Statement & Publications:** Plant transformation; plant cell culture and regeneration; alfalfa molecular genetics; Xanthomonas oryzae rice interactions. **Mailing Address:** Dept Plant Path, Kans State Univ Throckmorton Hall, Manhattan, KS 66506-5502. **Fax:** 785-532-5692. **E-Mail:** ljohnson@plantpathksu.edu

JOHNSON, LOYD, SOIL & WATER MANAGEMENT, AGRICULTURAL EXPERIMENT STATION MANAGEMENT. **Personal Data:** b Somerville, Ala, March 18, 1927. **Education:** Ala Polytech Inst, BS, 1950, MS, 1955. **Honors & Awards:** Kishida Int Award, Am Soc Agr Engrs, 1995. **Professional Experience:** Develop & mgt, Pakistan, 1994; CONSULT, 1993-; develop & mgt, Ethiopian Exp Stas, 1993; remote sensing bananas, Honduras, 1992-1993; res sta develop specialist, Pakistan, 1990; res sta develop specialist, Burma, 1986-1989; small farm mach, Indonesia, 1985; agr exp sta develop & mgt specialist, Indonesia, 1984; agr engr, Winrock Int, 1982-1990; irrig specialist, Bangladesh, 1982-1983; vis scientist, Int Fertilizer Develop Ctr, 1981-1982; rice specialist, Ecuador Nat Inst for Land & Cattle Investigations, beginning 1977; Int Agr Develop Serv, 1978-1981; vis scientist, La State Univ, 1974-1975; int Ctr Trop Agr, Colombia, 1968-1977; agr engr, NC State Univ, 1967-1968; agr engr, Rockefeller Found, 1960-1982; agr engr, Int Rice Res Inst, 1960-1968; sr proj engr, Cia Agricola Guatemala, 1956-1960; asst engr, Gen Off, United Fruit Co, 1956-1957; asst agr eng, Ala Agr Exp Sta, Auburn, 1953-1954; asst dist supt farm develop, Tela RR Co, 1951-1952 & 1956. **Memberships:** Am Soc Agr Engrs. **Research Statement & Publications:** Rice specialist and development of irrigation, fertilizer, drainage, roads, bridges, sanitation, machine and processing systems for agricultural experiment stations and food production in the lowland tropics; machinery management. **Mailing Address:** 287 Herman Bailey Rd, Somerville, AL 35670.

JOHNSON, LYNWOOD ALBERT, INDUSTRIAL ENGINEERING, OPERATIONS RESEARCH. **Personal Data:** b Macon, Ga, October 4, 1933. **Education:** Ga Inst Technol, BIE, 1955, MS, 1959, PhD (indust eng), 1965. **Professional Experience:** PROF EMER INDUST ENG, SCH INDUST & SYST ENG, GA INST TECHNOL, 1994-; Vis Prof Dept Mech Eng, Univ Wash, 1985; Vis Prof Dept Systs & Indust Eng, Univ Ariz, 1981-1982; prof, GA Inst Technol, 1968-1993; Vis prof, Thayer Sch Eng, Dartmouth Col, 1967; assoc prof, GA Inst Technol, 1966-1968; supvr opers res, Kurt Salmon Assocs, Inc, 1964-1966; from instr to asst prof indust eng, Ga Inst Technol, 1958-1964; Indust engr, E I du Pont Del Nemours & Co, Inc, 1955-1957. **Memberships:** Inst Indust Engrs; Am Prod & Inventory Control Soc. **Research Statement & Publications:** Production systems analysis; inventory systems; optimization methods; decision theory. **Mailing Address:** Sch Indust & Syst Eng, Ga Inst Technol, 765 Ferst dr, NW, Atlanta, GA 30332-0205. **Fax:** 404-894-2301. **E-Mail:** lynwood.johnson@isye.gatech.edu

JOHNSON, MALCOLM PRATT, INORGANIC CHEMISTRY. **Personal Data:** b New Haven, Conn, August 9, 1941; m 1964, Patricia; c David & Christopher. **Education:** Amherst Col, BA, 1963; Northwestern Univ, PhD (inorg chem), 1967. **Professional Experience:** Vice President, Dixie Chemical MGR MKT, DIXIE CHEM CO, 1980-, VPRES INT MKT; mgr com develop, Southwest Specialty Chem Inc, 1977-1980; gen mgr, Gulf Coast Div, Humphrey Chem Co, 1971-1977; res chemist, Linde Div, Tarrytown, NY, 1969-1971; Res chemist, Chem Div, Union Carbide Corp, 1966-1969. **Memberships:** Am Chem Soc; NY Acad Sci. **Research Statement & Publications:** Oxygen and nitrogen complexes of transition metals; organometallic chemistry; homogeneous catalysis; Lewis basicity; polyethylenimine chemistry; infrared spectroscopy. **Mailing Address:** Dixie Chem Co, PO Box 130410, Houston, TX 77219. **Fax:** 713-863-8316. **E-Mail:** mjohnson@dixiechemical.com

JOHNSON, MARC A, AGRICULTURE. **Education:** Emporia State Univ, BA, 1970; Mich State Univ, MA, 1973, PhD, 1975. **Professional Experience:** DEAN EMER AGR & DIR, AGR EXP STA & COOP & PROF EMER, KANS STATE UNIV, as of 2006. **Mailing Address:** Kans Agr Exp Sta 114 Waters Hall, Kans State Univ, Manhattan, KS 66506-4008.

JOHNSON, MARIE-LOUISE T, DERMATOLOGY, MEDICAL EDUCATION. **Personal Data:** b New York, NY, July 26, 1927; m Kenneth. **Education:** Manhattanville Col, BA, 1948; Yale Univ, PhD (microbiol), 1954, MD, 1956. **Professional Experience:** PVT PRACT, SCH MED, YALE UNIV, 1993-; Eighth Cong, 1988 & Ninth Cong, Japan, 1989; Seventh Cong, Moscow, 1987; mem bd dirs, Am Dermat Asn, 1986-; mem, Task Force Manpower, 1986-1989; Third Cong, Neth, 1983; deleg, Cong Int Physicians Against Nuclear War, Cambridge, 1982; XVI Int Cong Dermat, Tokyo, 1982; CLIN PROF DERMAT, SCH MED, YALE UNIV, 1980-; dir med educ, Benedictine Hosp, Kingston, NY, 1980-1993; vpres med affairs, Benedictine Hosp, Kingston, NY, 1980-1982; Coun Educ Affairs, Am Acad Dermat, 1980-1982; chmn, Med & Sci Comt, Dermat Found, 1974-1975; vis lectr, 79th All-Japan Dermat Meeting, Hiroshima & Postgrad Course Venereal Dis, Yugoslavia, 1980; bd dirs, Eval Comt, Am Acad Dermat, 1977-1980; mem, Eval Comt, Am Acad Dermat, 1976-1982; from assoc prof to prof dermat, Sch Med, NY Univ, 1974-1980; chief, Dermat Serv, Bellevue Hosp, 1974-1980; head, Div Educ & Commun, Nat Prog Dermat, 1973-1975; chief, Ambulatory Serv, 1973-1974; chief, Dermat Serv, Vet Admin Hosp, White River Jet, Vt, 1971-1974; assoc prof internal med, Dartmouth Med Sch, 1971-1974; assoc prof clin dermat, Sch Med, NY Univ, 1969-1970; assoc prof, Sch Med, NY Univ, 1967-1969; chief dermat, Atomic Bomb Casualty Comn, Hiroshima & Nagasaki, 1964-1967; actg head, Div Dermat, 1961-1962; from instr to asst prof med, Sch Med, Yale Univ, 1958-1964; pres, Maternity & Early Childhood Found. **Memberships:** Inst Med-Nat Acad Sci; Am Dermat Asn (vpres, 1991-); Am Acad Dermat; Soc Invest Dermat; Int Physicians Prev Nuclear War; NY Acad Med; AMA; Soc Trop Dermat. **Research Statement & Publications:** Epidemiology studies of late radiation effects in Hiroshima and Nagasaki; population studies as with the Health and Nutrition Examination Survey; prevalence of Hansen's Disease in Pohnpei, Micronesia; author of 6 scientific publications. **Mailing Address:** Dept Dermat, Yale Sch Med, Kingston Med Arts Bldg 368 Broadway Ste 202, Kingston, NY 12401-5159. **Fax:** 845-338-0538.

JOHNSON, MARK ALAN, DYNAMICS & CONTROL, SOLID MECHANICS. **Education:** Univ Nebr, BS, 1989; MS, 1992; Cornell Univ, PhD (eng mech), 1996. **Professional Experience:** MECH ENGR, GEN ELEC CORP RES & DEVELOP, 1996-. **Memberships:** Am Soc Mech Engrs. **Mailing Address:** 1 Research Circle, Niskayuna, NY 12309.

JOHNSON, MARK EDWARD, STATISTICS, OPERATIONS RESEARCH. **Personal Data:** b Chicago, Ill, June 27, 1952; m 1976. **Education:** Univ Iowa, BA, 1973, MS, 1974, PhD (indust & mgt eng), 1976. **Professional Experience:** DIR, INST STATIST, UNIV CENT FLA, as of 1997; vis Scientist, Nat Hurricane Ctr, 1996; vis prof, Univ Toulouse, 1996; PROF, DEPT STATIST, UNIV CENT FLA, 1990-; chair, Univ Cent Fla, 1990-1996; prof indust eng, Ga Inst Tech, 1988-1990; staff mem statist, Los Alamos Nat Lab, 1976-1988. **Memberships:** Fel Am Statist Asn; Math Asn Am; Inst Math Statist. **Research Statement & Publications:** Applied statistics; random variate generation; Monte Carlo methods; probability distributions. **Mailing Address:** Dept Statist, Univ Cent Fla, Rm 214 Comput Ctr One, Orlando, FL 32816-2370. **E-Mail:** mejohnso@pegasus.cc.ucf.edu

JOHNSON, MARK SCOTT, PROGRAMMING LANGUAGES, COMPILER TECHNOLOGY. **Personal Data:** b Oakland, Calif, April 16, 1951. **Education:** Univ Calif, BS, 1973, MS, 1974; Univ BC, PhD (comput sci), 1978. **Professional Experience:** DIR ENG, SOFTWIRE CORP, 1997-; chief tech officer, Vivid Studios, 1995-1997; sr engr mgr, Sun Microsysts, 1993-1995; mgr prof serv, Microtec Res Inc, 1990-1993; mem coun, Sigplan, Asn Comput Mach, 1990-1992; vchair, chair Sig bd, 1990-1992; chair, Sigplan, Asn Comput Mach, 1987-1989; mgr lang prods, Sun Microsysts, 1986-1990; vchair, Sigplan, Asn Comput Mach, 1983-1987; mem tech staff, Hewlett-Packard Labs, 1980-1986; asst prof, San Francisco State Univ, 1978-1980; mem, Spec Interest Group Planning Languages & Spec Interest Group Software Eng. **Memberships:** Asn Comput Mach. **Research Statement & Publications:** Develop and teach course in software engineering, software development methods, and programming tools and environments, particulary software debugging. **Mailing Address:** Softwine Corp, 900 Larkspur Landing Circle No 270, Larkspur, CA 94939. **E-Mail:** msj@mri.com

JOHNSON, MARTIN R, CHEMISTRY. **Personal Data:** b Chicago, Ill, November 24, 1958. **Education:** Reed Col, BA, 1981; Univ Tex, PhD, 1989. **Professional Experience:** Asst prof org chem, George Wash Univ, 1992-1995; fel, Chem Dept, Northwestern Univ, 1989-1992; fel, Robert A Welch Found, 1985-1988; Reed Energy Assoc, 1983; Amgen, Inc, 1982. **Memberships:** Am Chem Soc; Sigma Xi; Am Soc Mech Engrs. **Mailing Address:** Dept Chem, George Wash Univ, 2035 H St NW, Washington, DC 20052-0001.

JOHNSON, MARVIN, MATHEMATICS. **Honors & Awards:** Meritorious Service Award. **Professional Experience:** ASSOC PROF MATH, KY STATE UNIV, 1966-1969; 1972-1977; 1978. **Mailing Address:** Dept Math, KY State Univ, 400 E Main St, FrankFt, KY 40601. **Fax:** 502-597-6239. **E-Mail:** marvin@kysu.edu

JOHNSON, MARVIN ELROY, PARTICLE PHYSICS. **Personal Data:** b Red Wing, Minn, November 3, 1945; m 1970, Anna; c David. **Education:** Univ Minn, BS, 1967; Yale Univ, MPhil, 1969, PhD (physics), 1973. **Professional Experience:** STAFF PHYSICIST, FERMI NAT ACCELERATOR LAB, 1973-. **Memberships:** Sigma Xi. **Research Statement & Publications:** Heavy quark physics with emphasis on CP violation. **Mailing Address:** Fermilab, PO Box 500 MS 352, Batavia, IL 60510-0500. **E-Mail:** mjohnson@fnal.gov

JOHNSON, MARVIN FRANCIS LINTON, PHYSICAL CHEMISTRY. **Personal Data:** b Chicago, Ill, June 6, 1920; m 1943, Jane Brown; c David L, Gail J (Davis) & Mark A. **Education:** Loyola Univ, Ill, BS, 1940, MS, 1942. **Professional Experience:** CONSULT, 1986-; sr res adv, Harvey Tech Ctr, Atlantic Richfield Co, 1984-1985; c hmn, subcomt Phys Chem Catalysts, Am Soc Testing & Mat, 1980-1985; sr res assoc, Harvey Tech Ctr, Atlantic Richfield Co, 1979-1984; res assoc, Harvey Tech Ctr, Atlantic Richfield Co, 1973-1979; sr res chemist, Harvey Tech Ctr, Atlantic Richfield Co, 1969-1973; res chemist, Sinclair Res Labs, 1950-1969; res chemist, Res & Develop Dept, Sinclair Refining Co, 1941-1950. **Memberships:** Catalysis Soc; Am Chem Soc. **Research Statement & Publications:** Heterogeneous catalysis; adsorption of gases by catalysts; pore structures of catalysts; physical-chemical characterizations of catalysts. **Mailing Address:** 1124 Elder Rd, Homewood, IL 60430.

JOHNSON, MARVIN M, KINETICS, CATALYSIS. **Personal Data:** b Salt Lake City, Utah, March 21, 1928; m 1951, c 4. **Education:** Univ Utah, BS, 1950, PhD (chem eng), 1956. **Honors & Awards:** Nat Medal Technol, 1986; Achievement Award, Indust Res Inst, 1993. **Professional Experience:** CORP RES FEL 1990-; RES & DEVELOP FEL, PHILLIPS RES CTR, 1989-; PROF CHEM ENG, OKLA STATE UNIV, 1989-; consult, Phillips Res Ctr, 1986-1989; vis prof, Colo Sch Mines, 1982; a dj prof chem eng, Univ Kans, 1981-1982; sr scientist catalysis, Phillips Res Ctr, 1978-1986; sr res assoc, Phillips Res Ctr, 1974-1978; res assoc, Phillips Res Ctr, 1968-1974; mgr hydrocarbon process, Phillips Res Ctr, 1965-1968; s r res engr, Phillips Res Ctr, 1956-1965. **Memberships:** Nat Acad Eng; Am Inst Chem Engrs; Sigma Xi; Nat Soc Prof Engrs; Am Chem Soc. **Research Statement & Publications:** New catalysts and processes related to production and refining of petroleum and petrochemicals. **Mailing Address:** Phillips Res Ctr, 354 PL, Bartlesville, OK 74004.

JOHNSON, MARY FRANCES, CLINICAL TRIALS, SURVIVAL ANALYSIS. **Personal Data:** b Milford, Conn, November 21, 1951; m 1978. **Education:** Tufts Univ, BS, 1973; Yale Univ, MPH, 1975, PhD (biostatist), 1978. **Professional Experience:** SR VPRES, PHARMANET, INC, as of 2004; VPRES, G H BESSELAAR ASSOC, 1986-; math statistician, Div Biomet, Bur Drugs, Food & Drug Admin, 1978-1986; student ed, Yale J Biol & Med, Yale Univ, 1975-1978; teaching asst, Div Biostatist, 1975-1977; res asst, Conn Cancer Epidemiol Unit, 1975-1976; consult, Waterford Conserv Comn, Conn, 1974-1975; Data analyst, Dept Epidemiol & Public Health, Yale Univ, 1973-1974. **Memberships:** Am Statist Asn; Biomet Soc. **Research Statement & Publications:** Design and statistical analysis of therapeutic drug trials and epidemiological studies; applications of parametric and non-parametric models for failure time data. **Mailing Address:** Pharmanet, Inc, 504 Carnegie Ctr, Princeton, NJ 08540. **Fax:** 609-951-6800.

JOHNSON, MARY FRANCES, INORGANIC CHEMISTRY. **Personal Data:** b Green Bay, Wis, November 17, 1940. **Education:** Marquette Univ, BS, 1963, MS, 1965; St Louis Univ, PhD (inorg chem), 1972. **Professional Experience:** PROF & CHMN CHEM, FONTBONNE COL, 1972-. **Memberships:** Am Chem Soc; Sigma Xi. **Research Statement & Publications:** Spectroscopy and synthesis of lanthanide chelates involving nitrogen donor ligands. **Mailing Address:** Dept Chem, Fontbonne Univ, 4334 Va Ave, St Louis, MO 63111-1150.

JOHNSON, MARY IDA, NEUROBIOLOGY, PEDIATRIC NEUROLOGY. **Personal Data:** b Harlingen, Tex, October 30, 1942; m 1975, c 3. **Education:** Wash State Univ, BS, 1964; Johns Hopkins Univ, MD, 1968. **Professional Experience:** PROF PEDIAT, HEALTH SCI CTR, UNIV NMEX, as of 2005; prof pediat, Health Sci Ctr, Univ Ariz, as of 2003; assoc prof pediat, anat & neurol, 1984-1989; res asst prof neurol, Wash Univ Sch Med, 1974-1984; fel neurol, Wash Univ Sch Med, 1971-1974; intern & resident, Johns Hopkins Hosp, 1968-1971. **Memberships:** Soc Neuroscience; Child Neurol Soc; Am Acad Neurol; Soc Pediat Res; Am Neurol Asn. **Research Statement & Publications:** Differentiation of neuronal form, growth cone function, dendritic development; development of neurotransmitter function in the autonomic nervous system. **Mailing Address:** Dept Neurol, Health Sci Ctr, Univ NMex, One Univ NMex, Albuquerque, NM 87131-0001. **Fax:** 505-272-6692.

JOHNSON, MARY KNETTLES, BACTERIOLOGY. **Personal Data:** b Detroit, Mich, September 2, 1929; m 1955, c 2. **Education:** La State Univ, BS, 1954, MS, 1955, PhD (bact), 1957. **Professional Experience:** PROF EMER MICROBIOL, SCH MED, TULANE UNIV, as of 2004; prof microbiol, Sch Med, Tulane Univ, LA, beginning 1980; assoc prof, Sch Med, Tulane Univ, LA, 1967-1980; asst prof microbiol, Sch Med, Univ Miss, 1958-1965; instr, Millsaps Col, 1958-1961; res assoc pharmacol, Stanford Univ, 1957-1958. **Memberships:** Fel Am Acad Microbiol; Am Soc Microbiol. **Research Statement & Publications:** Bacterial physiology; mechanisms of pathogenicity. **Mailing Address:** Dept Microbiol, Tulane Univ Sch Med, 1430 Tulane Ave, New Orleans, LA 70112-2699. **Fax:** 504-588-5144. **E-Mail:** mjohns03@tulane.edu

JOHNSON, MARY LYNN MILLER, FUEL SCIENCE, AIR POLLUTION. **Personal Data:** b Pampa, Tex, March 12, 1938. **Education:** Univ Tex, El Paso, BS, 1958; NMex State Univ, MS, 1961; Pa State Univ, PhD (fuel sci), 1970. **Professional Experience:** CONSULT CHEM, 1994-; instr chem, Highland Park High Sch, Dallas, 1986-1994; instr chem, Brookhaven Col, Dallas, 1980-1987 & 1991-1994; instr chem, Hockaday Sch, Dallas, 1975-1986; asst prof chem, Univ Tex, Arlington, 1968-1975; independent consult air pollution, 1964-1968; chemist, El Paso City-County Health Unit, Tex, 1959-1960 & 1961-1963 & Tex State Health Dept, 1963-1964; fel, Am Inst Chemists. **Memberships:** Combustion Inst; Am Chem Soc; AmInst Chemists. **Research Statement & Publications:** Investigation of odor counteractants; combustion reactions, especially in the afterburning region, oxides of carbon and sulfur; analytical methods for measurement of air pollutants; air pollution chemistry; flame chemistry; combustion, new energy sources and air pollution. **Mailing Address:** 3004 Croydon, Denton, TX 76201. **E-Mail:** jjj3004@verizon.net

JOHNSON, MARYL RAE, CARDIOLOGY, HEART FAILURE & TRANSPLANT CARDIOLOGY. **Personal Data:** b Ft Dodge, Iowa, April 15, 1951. **Education:** Iowa State Univ, BS, 1973; Univ Iowa, MD, 1977; Am Bd Internal Med, dipl Internal Medicine & Cardiovascular Diseases. **Honors & Awards:** Clin Investr Award, NIH, 1981; New Investr Res Award, 1986. **Professional Experience:** PROF & MED DIR, UNIV WIS, 2002-; Assoc ed, J Heart & Lung Transplantation, 1995-2000; ASSOC Prof Northwestern University Medical School 1998-2002; ASSOC PROF, RUSH UNIV, 1994-1997; assoc med dir, Rush Heart Failure & Cardiac Transplant Prog, 1994-1997; chairperson, NIH, 1992-1993; biomed res tech rev comt, NIH, 1990-1993; med director heart failure and transplantation Northwestern Memorial Hospital 1998-2002; assoc med dir heart failure and transplantation Rush Presbyterian St. Luke's Medical Center 1994-1997; assoc med dir cardiac transplantation, Loyola Univ, 1988-1994; prof med, Loyola Univ, 1988-1992; med dir cardiac transplantation, Univ Iowa Hosp, 1986-1988; asst prof med, Cardiovasc Div, 1986-1988; assoc cardiol, Univ Iowa Hosps & Clin, 1982-1986; Mem, Nat Heart Lung Blood Adv Coun, 1979-1983; from intern to resident, Univ Iowa Hosps, 1977-1981. **Memberships:** AMA; AAAS; Am Col Physicians; Int Soc Heart & Lung Transplantation; Am Heart Asn; Am Fedn Clin Res; Am Col Cardiol; Am Soc Transplantation. **Mailing Address:** Dept Med, Univ Wis, E5/582D CSC 600 Highland Ave, Madison, WI 53792. **Fax:** 608-265-1918. **E-Mail:** mrj@medicine.wisc.edu

JOHNSON, MELVIN ANDREW, MEDICAL PHYSIOLOGY. **Personal Data:** b Springfield, Ohio, September 4, 1929; m 1953, c 2. **Education:** Cent State Univ, BS, 1950; Miami Univ, MS, 1955; Jefferson Med Col, PhD (med physiol), 1969. **Professional Experience:** Prog dir, NIMH grant, NIH, 1990-; DEAN, COL ARTS & SCI, 1985-; ADJ PROF PHYSIOL, SCH MED, WRIGHT STATE UNIV, 1985-; res reviewer, Ohio Affiliate, Am Heart Asn, 1985-1987; prog dir, NASA grant, 1977-1979; item writer, Educ Testing Serv, 1975-1977; prof, Sch Med, Wright State Univ, 1974-1985; ad hoc consult, Div Res Resources, 1973-1980; PROF BIOL, CENT STATE UNIV, 1972-; prog dir minority biomed support grant, NIH, 1972-1988; prin investr, NIH, 1972-1977 & 1980-1988; Am Heart Asn res grant, 1970-1972; chmn dept, Cent State Univ, 1969-1985; from instr to assoc prof, Cent State Univ, 1961-1972; instr biol, Grambling Col, 1955-1959; grad asst zool, Miami Univ, 1954-1955; a sst anat, Western Reserve Univ, 1951-1953. **Memberships:** Nat Inst Sci (pres 1979-1981 treas 1984-); AAAS; Am Physiol Soc; Sigma Xi; Am Heart Asn; Fedn Am Socs Exp Biol & Med. **Research Statement & Publications:** Hemodynamic and metabolic responses to hemorrhagic stress following surgical alterations in liver and splenic tissue; effect of certain atmospheric pollutants on small mammals; effect of calcium channel-blockers on peripheral circulation. **Mailing Address:** Col Arts & Sci, 589 Wilson Dr, Xenia, OH 45385-1835.

JOHNSON, MELVIN CLARK, TOXICOLOGY, PHARMACOLOGY. **Personal Data:** b Newark, NJ, August 29, 1938; m 1975, Yvonne; c Marion, Denise & Eric. **Education:** Rutgers Univ, BS, 1962; McGill Univ, MS, 1968; Howard Univ, PhD (pharmacol), 1972; Am Bd Toxicol, dipl. **Professional Experience:** RETIRED; mgr health & safety affairs, Agr Div, Am Cyanamid Co, 1987-1994; dir toxicol, Am Cyanamid Co, 1977-1987; toxicologist med dept, Hercules, Inc, 1972-1976; from assoc scientist to scientist pharmacol, Warner-Lambert Res Inst, 1962-1970. **Memberships:** Am Inst Biol Sci; Am Acad Clin Toxicol; NY Acad Sci; Soc Toxicol. **Research Statement & Publications:** Toxicology and pharmacology; safety of food additives, pesticides, animal drugs, food packaging materials and other consumer products; evaluation of potential exposures. **Mailing Address:** 101 Highland Ridge Rd, Manalapan, NJ 07726. **Fax:** 732-275-3523. **E-Mail:** johnson@unidial.com

JOHNSON, MELVIN WALTER, JR, AGRONOMY, GENETICS. **Personal Data:** b Chicago, Ill, May 27, 1928; m 1954, c 2. **Education:** Univ Ill, BS, 1950; Univ Wis, MS, 1951, PhD (plant breeding), 1954. **Professional Experience:** ASSOC PROF EMER PLANT BREED, PA STATEUNIV, 1999-; assoc prof agron, Pa State Univ, University Park, 1965-1999; assoc prof & assoc agronomist, WVa Univ, 1960-1965; asst prof & asst agronomist, WVa Univ, 1956-1960; asst agron, Univ Wis, 1950-1954. **Memberships:** Am Soc Agron; AAAS. **Research Statement & Publications:** Plant breeding; plant genetics; corn breeding; basic and applied corn breeding and genetics research. **Mailing Address:** Col Agr Sci, Pa State Univ, 201 Agr Admin, Univ Park, PA 16802.

JOHNSON, MICHAEL D, HUMAN PHYSIOLOGY. **Personal Data:** b Chicago, Ill, December 29, 1948. **Education:** Wash State Univ, BS, 1970; Univ Mich, PhD (physiol), 1976. **Professional Experience:** PROF HUMAN PHYSIOL, WVA UNIV SCH MED, 1988-; from asst prof to assoc prof, WVA Univ Sch Med, 1979-1988; researcher renal hypertension, 1976-1979. **Memberships:** Am Physiol Soc. **Mailing Address:** Bus Off HSC, 3074 Health Scis, PO Box 9229, Morgantown, WV 26506-9229. **Fax:** 304-293-3850. **E-Mail:** mjohnson@hsc.wvu.edu

JOHNSON, MICHAEL EVART, BIOPHYSICS. **Personal Data:** b Cody, Wyo, September 4, 1945; c 1. **Education:** Univ Wyo, BS, 1968; Northwestern Univ, MS, 1970, PhD (biophys), 1973. **Professional Experience:** PROF & DIR CTR PHARMACEUT BIOTECH, UNIV ILL, CHICAGO, as of 2004; assoc dean, Univ Ill, Chicago, beginning 1986; prof med chem, Univ Ill, Chicago, beginning 1984; estab investr, Am Heart Asn, 1979-1984; from asst prof to assoc prof, Med Ctr, 1976-1984; guest scientist, Argonne Nat Lab, 1975-; res assoc & NIH fel biophys, Univ Pittsburgh, 1973-1975. **Memberships:** Biophys Soc; AAAS; Am Chem Soc; Sigma Xi. **Research Statement & Publications:** Sickling mechanism in sickle cell anemia; applications of magnetic resonance and computer aided molecular modeling in molecular structure analysis and design. **Mailing Address:** Ctr Pharmaceut BioTechnol, Univ Ill, Chicago, 900 S Ashland Ave Rm 3022, Chicago, IL 60607-7173. **Fax:** 312-413-9303. **E-Mail:** mjohnson@uic.edu

JOHNSON, MICHAEL J, MATHEMATICS. **Professional Experience:** PROF, DEPT MATH & COMPUT SCI, KUWAIT UNIV, as of 2005. **Memberships:** Am Math Soc. **Mailing Address:** Dept Math & Comput Sci, Kuwait Univ, PO Box 5969, Safat, 13060, Kuwait. **Fax:** 965-483-6127. **E-Mail:** johnson@mcc.sci.kuniv.edu.kw

JOHNSON, MICHAEL L, PROTEIN CHEMISTRY. **Personal Data:** b Myrtle Point, Ore, November 12, 1947. **Education:** Univ Conn, PhD (biophysics), 1974. **Professional Experience:** PROF PHARMACOL & INTERNAL MED, UNIV VA, as of 2004; DIR, CTR BIOMATHEMATICAL TECHNOL, UNIV VA, as of 2003; dir, biophysics prog & diabetes res & training ctr, beginning 1985; assoc prof phrmacol, Univ VA, beginning 1985; from res asst prof to asst prof, 1980-1985. **Memberships:** Biophys Soc; Calorimetry Soc; Am Soc Biol Chemists. **Research Statement & Publications:** Biochemical, physical chemical, and thermodynamic pathways by which one portion of a biological organism transfers information to other portions of the same organism. **Mailing Address:** Dept Pharmacol, Univ Va, 800735 UVA Health Sys, 1300 Jefferson Park Ave, Charlottesville, VA 22908-0001. **Fax:** 434-982-3878. **E-Mail:** mlj8e@virginia.edu

JOHNSON, MICHAEL PAUL, PLANT ECOLOGY. **Personal Data:** b Oakland, Calif, September 13, 1937; m 1971, c 3. **Education:** Univ Calif, Davis, BS, 1959; Univ Ore, PhD (biol), 1966. **Professional Experience:** MEM STAFF, SCI EDUC ADMIN, USDA, 1980-; assoc prof biol, Kans State Univ & assoc dir, Konza Prairie Res Natural Area, 1972-1980; asst prof biol sci, Fla State Univ, 1968-1972; asst prof ecol, Kent State Univ, 1965-1968; i nstr bot, San Francisco State Col, 1960-1961. **Memberships:** Soc Study Evolution; Ecol Soc Am; Brit Ecol Soc; Am Soc Naturalists; Sigma Xi. **Research State-**

ment & Publications: Population biology; ecological genetics; botany; ecology. **Mailing Address:** Dept Computer Sci, Ore State Univ, Corvallis, OR 97331.

JOHNSON, MICHAEL ROSS, ORGANIC & STRUCTURAL CHEMISTRY, SYNTHETIC & NATURAL PRODUCTS CHEMISTRY, MEDICAL CHMESITRY. **Personal Data:** b Detroit, Mich, October 27, 1944; m 1964, Charlotte; c Michael & Greg. **Education:** Univ Calif, Berkeley, BS, 1967; Univ Calif, Santa Barbara, PhD (org chem), 1970. **Professional Experience:** Pres & chief executive officer, G F pharmaceutials, 1999-; pres & chief executive officer, Trimeris, 1995-1999; PRES & CHIEF EXEC OFFICER, PARNASSUS PHARMACEUT INC, 1994-; distinguished res fel, NIH, 1989-1999; vpres, Div Chem, Glaxo, Inc, 1989-1994; asst dir med chem & dir chem, Cent Nerv Syst & Metab Dis Res, 1987-1989; mgr, Cent Nerv Syst & Metab Dis Res, 1981-1985; sr res investr & proj leader, Pfizer Inc, 1976-1980; sr res scientist, Pfizer Inc, 1973-1976; res chemist, Pfizer Inc, 1971-1973; NIH fel, Berkeley, 1970-1971; NDEA Title IV fel, Univ Calif, Santa Barbara, 1968-1970; NSF undergrad res fel, Calif State Col, Los Angeles, 1964. **Memberships:** Am Chem Soc; Sigma Xi; NY Acad Sci; AAAS; Am Soc Pharmacol & Exp Therapeut; Pharmaceut Mfrs Asn. **Research Statement & Publications:** Mechanism and stereochemistry of carbonium ion, carbanion, organometallic and hydride reduction reactions; synthesis of pharmacalogically active heterocycles and natural products; synthesis of cannabinoid derived therapeutants; rational d rug design. **Mailing Address:** 102 Hazlenut Ct, Chapel Hill, NC 27516. **E-Mail:** mrj102744@aol.com

JOHNSON, MIKKEL BORLAUG, THEORETICAL NUCLEAR, PARTICLE PHYSICS. **Personal Data:** b Waynesboro, Va, January 2, 1943; m 1965, c 2. **Education:** Va Polytech Inst, BS, 1966; Carnegie-Mellon Univ, MS, 1968, PhD (physics), 1971. **Honors & Awards:** Humboldt Award Sr US Scientists, 1986. **Professional Experience:** ACTG DEP GROUP LEADER, LOS ALAMOS NAT LAB, UNIV CALIF, as of 2003; consult, Oak Ridge Nat Lab, 1986; vis prof, Dept Physics, State Univ NY, Stony Brook, 1981-1982; assoc ed nuclear physics, North-Holland Publ Co, 1975-; STAFF MEM PHYSICS & LAB FEL, LOS ALAMOS NAT LAB, UNIV CALIF, 1972-; res assoc, Cornell Univ, 1970-1972; consult physics, Rand Corp, 1967 & 1968. **Memberships:** Fel Am Phys Soc. **Research Statement & Publications:** Effective interactions in nuclear physics; intermediate energy nuclear theory. **Mailing Address:** Los Alamos Nat Lab, Univ Calif, Mail Stop H846, Los Alamos, NM 87545. **Fax:** 505-665-7920. **E-Mail:** mbjohnson@lanl.gov

JOHNSON, MILES F, SYSTEMATIC BOTANY. **Personal Data:** b Frederic, Wis, March 9, 1936; m 1981. **Education:** Wis State Univ, River Falls, BS, 1958; Univ Wis-Madison, MS, 1962; Univ Minn, Minneapolis, PhD (bot), 1968. **Professional Experience:** PROF BIOL, VA COMMONWEALTH UNIV, 1980-; from asst prof to assoc prof, VA Commonwealth Univ, 1968-1980; instr, Univ Minn, Minneapolis, 1968; teaching asst bot, Univ Minn, Minneapolis, 1964-1967; instr bot & zoology, Univ Wis-Madison, 1962-1964; teaching asst bot, Univ Wis-Madison, 1960-1962; High Sch teacher, Wis, 1958-1960. **Memberships:** Bot Soc Am; Am Soc Plant Taxon; Int Soc Plant Taxon. **Research Statement & Publications:** Taxonomy and systematics of Compositae; genus Ageratum; flora of Virginia. **Mailing Address:** Dept Biol, Va Commonwealth Univ, Box 2012, Richmond, VA 23284-9004.

JOHNSON, MILLARD WALLACE, CONTINUUM MECHANICS, RHEOLOGY. **Personal Data:** b Racine, Wis, February 1, 1928; m 1953, Ruth; c Millard W III, Jeannette (Brooks), Charles G & Peter A. **Education:** Univ Wis, BS, 1952, MS, 1953; Mass Inst Technol, PhD (math), 1957. **Professional Experience:** EMER PROF ENG MECH & MATH, UNIV WIS-MADISON, 1994-; mem adv bd, Int Math & Statist Libr, 1971-1993; mem exec comt, Rheol Res Ctr, Univ Wis, 1969-; mem staff, Math Res Ctr, Univ Wis, 1958-; from asst prof to prof eng mech& math, Univ Wis-madison, 1958-1994; instr math, Mass Inst Technol, 1953-1958. **Memberships:** Soc Rheol; Soc Indust & Appl Math; fel Am Soc Mech Engrs; Brit Soc Rheol. **Research Statement & Publications:** Research papers in applied mathematics, rheology, elasticity and paper mechanics. **Mailing Address:** Dept Eng Physics, Univ Wis, 1415 Eng Dr, Madison, WI 53706. **Fax:** 608-238-0019. **E-Mail:** millard@engr.wisc.edu

JOHNSON, MILTON RAYMOND, ELECTRONICS ENGINEERING. **Personal Data:** b Shreveport, La, November 5, 1919; m 1942, c 3. **Education:** La Polytech Inst, BS, 1940; Okla State Univ, MS, 1951; Tex A&M Univ, PhD, 1963. **Professional Experience:** RETIRED; head dept, La Tech Univ, 1980-1985; NSF sci fac fel, 1960-1961; prof elec eng, La Tech Univ, 1954-1986; consult, Delta Res & Develop Corp, 1952-1960; from asst prof to assoc prof, La Tech Univ, 1947-1954; design engr, Gen Elec Co, 1941-1947. **Memberships:** Am Soc Eng Educ; Inst Elec & Electronics Engrs. **Research Statement & Publications:** Electromechanical energy converters; automatic control systems. **Mailing Address:** 6130 Kilbourn, Chicago, IL 60646-5020.

JOHNSON, MITCHELL E, CHEMISTRY. **Education:** Univ Mass, Amherst, PhD, 1993. **Professional Experience:** ASSOC PROF, BAYER SCH NATURAL & ENVIRON SCI, DUQUESNE UNIV, as of 2005. **Research Statement & Publications:** Trace analysis of molecular species, fluorescence spectroscopy, high-speed separations, biochemical analysis. **Mailing Address:** Duquesne Univ, Bayer Sch Natural & Environ Sci, 100 Mellon Hall, Pittsburgh, PA 15282. **E-Mail:** johnsonm@duq.edu

JOHNSON, MORRIS ALFRED, PLANT BIOCHEMISTRY, CANCER. **Personal Data:** b International Falls, Minn, August 3, 1937; m Catherine; c Raymond, Sigmond, Armond & Normond. **Education:** NDak State Univ, BS, 1960, MS, 1962; Ore State Univ, PhD (biochem), 1966. **Professional Experience:** SEMI-RETIRED, 1999-; sci instructor, Fox Valley Tech Col, 1989- 1999; res assoc, Inst Paper Chem, 1974-1989; assoc prof, Inst Paper Chem, 1973-1989; chmn dept, Inst Paper Chem, 1970-1979; Asst prof & res fel biochem, Inst Paper Chem, 1966-1973. **Memberships:** Emer mem Am Chem Soc; Phytochem Soc, NAm. **Research Statement & Publications:** Intermediary metabolism and oxidative phosphorylation in plants; natural plant growth and development regulators; biochemistry of tree callus and suspension cultures; cancer mechanism. **Mailing Address:** W 7805 Sch Rd, Greenville, WI 54942. **E-Mail:** cajmaj@juno.com

JOHNSON, MYRLE F, PHYSICAL CHEMISTRY. **Personal Data:** b Jerico Springs, Mo, December 12, 1918; m 1957, Beverly; c Robert A & Linda A. **Education:** Southwest Mo State Col, AB, 1941; Univ Wis, PhD (phys chem), 1950. **Professional Experience:** RETIRED; res assoc, Eastman Kodak Co, 1971-1983; from res chemist to sr res chemist, Eastman Kodak Co, 1953-1971; assoc prof chem, Southwest Mo State Col, 1950-1953. **Memberships:** Am Chem Soc. **Research Statement & Publications:** Rheology and colloid chemistry. **Mailing Address:** 29 Margate Dr, Rochester, NY 14616-5503.

JOHNSON, NANCY EBERSOLE, HUMAN & MINERAL NUTRITION. **Personal Data:** b Sioux Falls, NDak, December 12, 1925. **Education:** Iowa State Univ, BS, 1947, MS, 1949; Univ Wis, Madison, PhD (nutrit sci), 1969. **Professional Experience:** PROF EMER AGR & LIFE SCI & NUTRIT SCI, UNIV WIS, 2001-; chmn, dept food sci & human nutrit, Univ Hawaii, beginning 1986; from asst prof to prof nutrit, Col Agr & Life Sci, Univ Wis, 1969-1986. **Memberships:** Inst Food Technologists; Am Inst Nutrit; AAAS. **Research Statement & Publications:** Human and mineral nutrition. **Mailing Address:** Dept Agr & Life Sci & Nutrit Sci, Univ Wis, 1415 Linden Dr, Madison, WI 53706.

JOHNSON, NANCY J, MATHEMATICS. **Education:** Monmouth Col, BS, 1985. **Professional Experience:** STAFF, ZURICH LEGAL SERVICES, as of 2006. **Mailing Address:** Zurich N Am, 1400 Am Ln, Schaumburg, IL 60196. **Fax:** 877-962-2567. **E-Mail:** nancy.johnson@zurichna.com

JOHNSON, NEIL FRANCIS, PATHOLOGY, CYTOLOGY. **Personal Data:** b Heighington, Co Durham, UK, March 15, 1948; m 1970, c 3. **Education:** London Univ, BSc, 1969; City Univ, London, MSc, 1971; Glasgow Univ, PhD (exp path), 1976. **Professional Experience:** Clin assoc prof, Col Pharm, Univ NMex, 1991-; chmn, Task Group: Molecular Biol Carcinogenesis, Med Res Coun, 1989-1991; GROUP SUPVR EXP PATH, MOLECULAR & CELLULAR TOXICOL, INHALATION TOXICOL RES INST, 1986-; scientist Toxicol Univ, Med Res Coun, UK, 1986; vis scientist exp path, Los Alamos Nat Lab, 1984-1986; lectr gen path, Inst Sci & Technol, Univ Wales, 1980-1984; scientist exp path, Pneumoconiosis Unit, Penarth, Med Res Coun, UK, 1977-1984; res asst ocular path, Tennent Inst Ophthal, Glasgow Univ, 1971-1977. **Memberships:** Am Soc Testing & Mat; Soc Toxicol; Royal Col Pathologists. **Research Statement & Publications:** Determining the cells at risk from carcinogenesis from inhaled materials with particular emphasis on radon progeny and natural and manmade mineral fibers. **Mailing Address:** Inhalation Toxicol Res Inst, PO Box 5890, Albuquerque, NM 87185. **Fax:** 505-845-1198. **E-Mail:** njohnson@lucy.tli.org

JOHNSON, NICHOLAS L, AERONAUTICS. **Professional Experience:** CHIEF SCIENTIST, JOHNSON SPACE CTR, NASA, as of 2006. **Memberships:** Nat Acad Eng. **Mailing Address:** NASA Johnson Space Ctr, Houston, TX 77058. **Fax:** 281-483-5276. **E-Mail:** Nicholas.L.Johnson@nasa.gov

JOHNSON, NOAH R, PROPERTIES OF HIGHLY EXCITED NUCLEI. **Personal Data:** b Kingsport, Tenn, October 15, 1928; m 1950, Rosemary; c Kurt, Margaret Ann, Gregory & Gwendolyn. **Education:** E Tenn State Univ, BS, 1950; Fla State Univ, PhD, 1956. **Professional Experience:** RETIRED; res prof, Univ Tenn, 1995-1997; sr scientist, Oak Ridge Nat Lab, 1991-1994; group leader nuclear physics, Oak Ridge Nat Lab, 1980-1990; fulbright scholar & Guggenheim fel, Niels Bohr Inst, Copenhagen, 1962-1963; nuclear chemist, Oak Ridge Nat Lab, 1956-1980; pub sch teacher, Tenn, 1950-1952. **Memberships:** Fel Am Phys Soc; Sigma Xi; Am Chem Soc. **Research Statement & Publications:** Nuclear spectroscopy and reactions; coulomb excitation; Doppler-shift lifetime measurements; studies of high-angular momentum behavior in nuclei; development of complex gamma-ray detector systems; Author, 1 book and over 300 scientific papers; Editor; 4 books. **Mailing Address:** Oak Ridge Nat Lab, PO Box 2008, Oak Ridge, TN 37831-6371. **Fax:** 865-574-1268. **E-Mail:** johnson@mail.phy.ornl.gov

JOHNSON, NOBLE MARSHALL, ELECTRONIC DEFECTS IN CRYSTALLINE & AMORPHOUS SEMICONDUCTORS, HYDROGEN IN SEMICONDUCTORS & INGAALN MATERIALS FOR OPTOELECTRONIC DEVICES. **Personal Data:** b San Francisco, Calif, February 23, 1945. **Education:** Univ Calif, Davis, BS, 1967, MS, 1970; Princeton Univ, PhD (eng & appl sci), 1974. **Honors & Awards:** Distinguished Sr US Scientist Award, Alexander Von Humboldt Found, Ger, 1987. **Professional Experience:** Distinguished US sr scientist, Inst Appl Physics, Univ Erlangen-Nurnberg, Ger, 1988; PRIN SCIENTIST, ELECTRONIC MAT LAB, PALO ALTO CTR, XEROX CORP, 1987-; mem coun, Mat Res Soc, 1986-1988; vis lectr, Dept Elec Eng & Comput Sci, Sch Eng & Appl Sci, Princeton Univ, 1986; sr mem res staff, Electronic Mat Lab, Palo Alto Ctr, Xerox Corp, 1985-1987; mem res staff, Electronic Mat Lab, Palo Alto Ctr, Xerox Corp, 1976-1985; mgr, Optoelectronic Mat & Devices, Electronic Mat Lab, Palo Alto Res Ctr, Xerox Corp. **Memberships:** Fel Am Phys Soc; sr mem Inst Elec & Electronics Engrs; Mat Res Soc. **Research Statement & Publications:** Experimental reseach on semiconductor materials and devices. **Mailing Address:** Palo Alto Res Ctr, 3333 Coyote Hill Rd, Palo Alto, CA 94304. **E-Mail:** njohnson@parc.com

JOHNSON, NORMAN ELDEN, FOREST MANAGEMENT, SILVICULTURE. **Personal Data:** b Mesa, Ariz, April 26, 1933; m 1954, c 2. **Education:** Ore State Univ, BSF, 1955, MS, 1957; Univ Calif, PhD, 1961. **Professional Experience:** SR VPRES TECHNOL, CORP RES & DEVELOP, WEYERHAUSER CO, TACOMA, 1990-; Mem, Pres Reagan's Agr 7 Forestry Mission, Honduras, 1982-1983 & Zaire, 1985; NC region, New Bern, NC, 1980-1984; vpres, Far E region, Indonesia, 1978-1980; mgr, tropical forestry & res, 1975-1978; adj prof, Sch Forestry Resources, NC State Univ, 1972; forestry res mgr, Southern Forestry Res Ctr, Weyerhaeuser Co, Ark, 1969-1975; assoc prof dept entom, Cornell Univ, 1967-1969; forest bioprotection leader, Forestry Res Ctr, 1966-1969; forest entomologist, Forestry Res Ctr, 1956-1966; forest entom asst, Southwest Lumber Mills, 1955; forest engr, Southwest Lumber Mills, 1954-1955; forestry aide, US Forest Serv, 1951-1952; mem bd dir, Pacific Sci Ctr, Sci Adv Coun, NC State Univ & Ore State Univ; chmn, Coop Forestry Adv Comt, US Dept Agr, McIntire-Stennis Res Prog; assoc ed, J Appl Forestry; mem bd dir & Long Range Res Planning Comt, Wash Technol Ctr, US Nat Comt, Man & Biosphere Prog. **Memberships:** Soc Am Foresters. **Research Statement & Publications:** Forest plantation management. **Mailing Address:** 27229 Eighth Ave S, Des Moines, WA 98198.

JOHNSON, NORMAN L, GEOMETRY. **Personal Data:** b Tillamook, Ore, July 27, 1939; m 1964, c 3. **Education:** Portland State Univ, BA, 1964; Wash State Univ, MA, 1966, PhD (math), 1968. **Professional Experience:** Sci Res Coun researcher, Great Britain, 1978-; PROF, DEPT MATH, UNIV IOWA, 1978-; res fel, Univ Bergen, 1973-1974; researcher, NSF fel, 1971-1972; asst prof, Univ Iowa, 1969-1978; a sst prof math, Eastern Wash State Col, 1968-1969. **Research Statement & Publications:** Finite projective planes; classification of semitranslation planes and their construction; translation planes; collineation groups. **Mailing Address:** Dept Math, Univ Iowa, 14 MLH, Iowa City, IA 52242-0001. **Fax:** 319-335-0627. **E-Mail:** njohnson@math.uiowa.edu

JOHNSON, NORMAN LLOYD, STATISTICS. **Personal Data:** b Ilford, Eng, January 9, 1917; American citizen; m 1964, Regina. **Education:** Univ Col London, BSc, 1936 & 1937, MSc, 1938, PhD (statist), 1948, DSc, 1963. **Honors & Awards:** Shewhart Medal, Am Soc Qual Control, 1984; Wills Mem Medal, Am Statist Asn, 1992. **Professional Experience:** EMER PROF STATIST, UNIV NC, CHAPEL HILL, 1982-; co-ed in chief, Encycl Statist Sci (10 vols), 1982-1988; chmn dept, Univ NC, Chapel Hill, 1971-1976; Univ NSW, Australia, 1969; prof, Univ NC, Chapel Hill, 1962-1982; vis prof, Case Inst Technol, 1960-1961; reader, Univ Col London, 1956-1962; vacation consult, Road Res Lab, Eng, 1956-1959; Vis assoc prof, Univ NC, Chapel Hill, 1952-1953; lectr, Univ Col London, 1946-1956; asst lectr statist, Univ Col London, 1938-1939; 1945-1946. **Memberships:** sr mem Fel Inst Math Statist; fel Am Statist Asn; Am Soc Qual Control; fel Royal Statist Soc; Int Statist Inst. **Research Statement & Publications:** Systems of frequency distributions; checks on completeness of samples; reliability; process capability indices. **Mailing Address:** Dept Statist, Univ NC, Chapel Hill, NC 27599-3260. **Fax:** 919-962-1279. **E-Mail:** janice@email.unc.edu

JOHNSON, OLIN G, MATHEMATICS. **Education:** Southern Methodist Univ, BS, MS; Univ Calif, Berkeley, PhD. **Professional Experience:** PROF COMPUT SCI, UNIV HOUSTON, as of 2005. **Mailing Address:** Dept Comp Sci, Univ Houston, Houston, TX 77024-3475. **Fax:** 713-743 3335. **E-Mail:** johnson@cs.uh.edu

JOHNSON, OLIVER WILLIAM, VERTEBRATE ZOOLOGY, PHYSIOLOGY. **Personal Data:** b Maud, Okla, March 30, 1930; m 1958, c 1. **Education:** Fresno State Col, AB, 1955; Ore State Univ, MS, 1959, PhD (zoology), 1965. **Professional Experience:** PROF EMER, NORTHERN ARIZ UNIV, 1989-; from assoc prof to prof zool, Northern Ariz Univ, 1964-1989; res assoc entom, Ore State Univ, 1963-1964; asst prof zool, Ariz State Col, 1961-1963; instr ecol, Ore State Univ, 1959-1961. **Memberships:** AAAS; Am Soc Mammalogists; Am Soc Ichthyologists & Herpetologists; SigmaXi. **Research Statement & Publications:** Amphibian and reptilian temperature adaptation; biochemical taxonomy. **Mailing Address:** 63 Pine Ridge Dr, Flagstaff, AZ 86001.

JOHNSON, OSCAR WALTER, ORNITHOLOGY, ECOLOGY. **Personal Data:** b Chicago, Ill, March 28, 1935; m 1955, c 2. **Education:** Mich State Univ, BS, 1957; Wash State Univ, MS, 1959, PhD (zool), 1964. **Professional Experience:** 199, 1992 & 1996; ADJ PROF BIOL, MONT STATE UNIV, 1990-; AEC & Dept Energy, Nat Geog Soc, 1982, 1984, 1987, 1988, 1990; Med Sch, Univ Ariz, 1975; mem, Int Comn Avian Anatomical Nomenclature, 1973-; Med Sch, Res Corp, 1973; Grantee, Ariz State Univ, 1971-1972; AEC & Dept Energy, Univ Hawaii, 1970, 1973, 1978, 1979 & 1980; from asst prof to prof biol, Moorhead State Univ, 1965-1990; g rantee, NSF, 1965-1966 & 1967-1969; a sst prof biol, Western State Col Colo, 1963-1965. **Memberships:** Am Ornith Union; Cooper Ornith Soc; Wilson Ornith Soc; Asn Field Ornith. **Research Statement & Publications:** Ecology and behavior in shorebirds, particularly long-distance migrant species of the insular Pacific. **Mailing Address:** Dept Biol, Mont State Univ, Bozeman, MT 59717. **Fax:** 406-994-3190.

JOHNSON, OWEN W, SOLID STATE PHYSICS. **Personal Data:** b Provo, Utah, March 31, 1931; m 1957, c 3. **Education:** Univ Utah, BA, 1957, PhD (physics), 1962. **Professional Experience:** RETIRED; adj assoc prof mat sci, Univ Utah, 1968-1996; from asst prof to prof physics, Univ Utah, 1965-1996; asst prof ceramic eng, Univ Utah, 1964-1965; asst res prof physics, Univ Utah, 1962-1964. **Memberships:** Am Phys Soc. **Research Statement & Publications:** Electronic and optical properties of oxides and semiconductors; infrared spectroscopy; electronic properties of thin films. **Mailing Address:** 725 Tenth Ave, Salt Lake City, UT 84103.

JOHNSON, PATRICIA ANN J, CLINICAL NEUROPSYCHOLOGY, PSYCHOLOGY. **Personal Data:** b New York, NY, October 10, 1943; m 1964, Malcolm P; c David M & Christopher P. **Education:** Univ Houston, BS, MA, PhD (psychol), 1977. **Professional Experience:** Clin instr, Univ Tex, Houston, 1993-; clin asst prof psychol, Univ Houston, 1978-; PVT PRACT, 1977-; Found Land & Learning Opportunities, 1977-1980; Exec dir & clin neuropsychologist, 1977-1980; NIH fel, 1974-1977. **Memberships:** Nat Acad Neuropsychol; Int Neuropsychol Soc; Soc Personality Assessment; Am Psychol Asn; Biofeedback Soc Am. **Research Statement & Publications:** Etiology and neuropsychology of learning and language disorders in children. **Mailing Address:** Patricia J Johnson & Assoc PC, 3722 N Main St, Baytown, TX 77521-3304.

JOHNSON, PATRICIA R, CELL CULTURE, GENETIC OBESITY. **Personal Data:** b Waco, Tex, February 28, 1931; div, c 2. **Education:** Baylor Univ, AB, 1952, MA, 1958; Rutgers Univ, PhD (biochem), 1967. **Professional Experience:** WILLIAM R KEENAN CHAIR, DEPT BIOL, 1981-; PROF BIOL, VASSAR COL, 1975-; CHMN, DEPT BIOL, 1975-; adj prof, Rockefeller Univ, 1975-1980; adj assoc prof, Rockefeller Univ, 1971-1975; from instr to assoc prof biol, dept Biol, 1964-1975; res asst, Bur Biol res, Rutgers Univ, 1961-1964; instr biol & chem, Malone Col, 1960-1961; high sch teacher, Tex, 1956-1960; anal chemist, Va Carolina Chem Corp, Tex, 1953-1954; health physicist, Rocky Flats Plant, Dow Chem Corp, 1952-1953. **Memberships:** AAAS; NY Acad Sci; Am Inst Nutrit; Sigma Xi. **Research Statement & Publications:** Adipose tissue growth and development in genetically obese mice and rats: behavior; metabolism; cell culture of fetal hepatocytes and precursor adipocyres from the genetically obese zucker rat. **Mailing Address:** Dept Biol Vassar Col, PO Box 377, Poughkeepsie, NY 12601.

JOHNSON, PAUL CHRISTIAN, PHYSIOLOGY. **Personal Data:** b Ironwood, Mich, February 3, 1928; m 1955, Genevieve; c Ciri, Philip & Christopher. **Education:** Univ Mich, BS, 1951, MA, 1953, PhD (physiol), 1955. **Honorary Degrees:** MD, Univ Limburg, Maastricht, Neth. **Honors & Awards:** Eugene M Landis Res Award, Microcirc Soc, 1976; Carl J Wiggers Award, Am Physiol Soc, 1981. **Professional Experience:** PROF EMER PHYSIOL, COL MED, UNIV ARIZ, 1994-; chmn publs comt, circulation sect, Am Physiol Soc, 1985-1989; mem coun, circulation sect, Am Physiol Soc, 1978-1982; chmn, circulation sect, Am Physiol Soc, 1974; mem steering comt, circulation sect, Am Physiol Soc, 1971-1974; mem physiol study sect, NIH, 1968-1972; head dept, Col Med, Univ Ariz, 1967-1987; prof physiol, Col Med, Univ Ariz, 1967-1994; NIH fel, 1965-1966; from asst prof to assoc prof, Sch Med, Ind Univ, 1958-1967; instr, Western Res Univ, 1956-1958; instr physiol, Univ Mich, 1955-1956. **Memberships:** AAAS; Am Physiol Soc; Microcirc Soc (pres, 1967-1968). **Research Statement & Publications:** Local regulation of blood flow, microcirculation; capillary filtration and exchange. **Mailing Address:** Dept Physiol Univ Ariz, Health Sci Ctr, Tucson, AZ 85724-5051.

JOHNSON, PAUL HICKOK, BIOPHYSICS, GENETICS. **Personal Data:** b Syracuse, NY, March 3, 1943; m 1981, c 4. **Education:** State Univ NY Buffalo, BS, 1965, PhD (biochem), 1970. **Professional Experience:** SR VPRES RES & DEVELOP & CHIEF SCI OFFICER, NASTECH PHARMACEUT CO, 2003-; Vpres Res & Develop & Chief Sci Officer, Epigenx Pharmaceut, 2001-2003; dir, Dept Molecular Bio, Sri Int, beginning 1984; sr molecular biologist, Dept Molecular Biol, SRI Int, 1981-1984; NIH Genetics Study Sect, 1978-1982; assoc prof biochem, Wayne State Univ, 1978-1981; asst prof biochem & molecular biol, Wayne State Univ, 1974-1978; USPHS grant molecular biol, Wayne State Univ, 1974-1977; Am Cancer Soc fel, Calif Inst Technol, 1970-1974. **Memberships:** AAAS; Am Chem Soc; Am Asn Microbiol; Sigma Xi; Am Soc Biochem & Molecular Biol. **Research Statement & Publications:** Protein and nucleic acid biochemistry; genetic engineering; protein drug development; enzymology. **Mailing Address:** NASTECH Pharmaceut Co Inc, 3450 Monte Villa Pkwy, Bothell, WA 98021.

JOHNSON, PAUL H(ILTON), CHEMICAL ENGINEERING. **Personal Data:** b Nevis, Minn, May 2, 1916; div, c Robert P & Patricia J. **Education:** Univ Minn, BChE, 1938. **Professional Experience:** RETIRED; consult carbon black environ health, process & feed stock, 1981-1991; mgr, Carbon Black Br, Res Ctr, 1969-1981; mgr, Petrol Process Br, 1960-1969; sect chief, Res & Develop Dept, 1954-1960; res engr, Phillips Petrol Co, 1941-1954; process engr, Minn Gas Co, 1938-1941. **Memberships:** Am Chem Soc. **Research Statement & Publications:** Process development; petroleum refining; petrochemicals; carbon black environmental health; carbon black feed stock; characterization, evolution. **Mailing Address:** 1951 Southview, Bartlesville, OK 74003. **Fax:** 918-337-0769. **E-Mail:** hil38phs@aol.com

JOHNSON, PAUL LORENTZ, COMPUTER SOFTWARE. **Personal Data:** b Hawarden, Iowa, September 19, 1941; m 1971, c 3. **Education:** St Olaf Col, BA, 1963; Wash State Univ, PhD (phys chem), 1968. **Professional Experience:** RETIRED; chemist, Argonne Nat Lab, 1991-2003; comput scientist, Argonne Nat Lab, 1977-1991; res assoc, Argonne Nat Lab, 1975-1977; res assoc, Univ Ariz, 1973-1975; Royal Norwegian Coun Sci & Indust res fel, Univ Bergen, Norway, 1972-1973; instr, Lansing Community Col, 1972; res assoc, Univ Mich State, 1971-1972; res assoc, Univ Ariz, 1969-1971; Fel, Univ Ill, Urbana-Champaign, 1968-1969. **Memberships:** Asn Comput Mach; Am Crystallog Asn; Sigma Xi. **Research Statement & Publications:** Neutron and x-ray crystallographic experiments applied to structures of organic, biological and inorganic interest; one-dimensional conducting compounds; portability of computer software; scientific applications of computers; analytical chemistry. **Mailing Address:** 2 Oak Leaf Ct, Woodridge, IL 60517-4270. **E-Mail:** pj@anl.gov

JOHNSON, PAUL W, FORESTRY. **Education:** Univ Mich, BS & MS. **Professional Experience:** DIR, IOWA DEPT NATURAL RESOURCES, AGR RES SERV, USDA, as of as of 1998; CHIEF, NATURAL RESOURCES CONSERV SERV, USDA, 1994-. **Mailing Address:** Natural Resources Conserv Serv USDA, PO Box 2890, Washington, DC 20013-2890.

JOHNSON, PETER, CHEMISTRY. **Mailing Address:** 2451 Nott St E, Niskayuna, NY 12309.

JOHNSON, PETER DAVID, SURFACE STATES, THIN FILMS. **Personal Data:** b Wellingborough, Eng, January 30, 1952; m 1981, Lynn; c Robert & Catherine. **Education:** Imp Col London, BS, 1972; Warwick Univ, PhD (physics), 1977. **Professional Experience:** ACTG ASSOC CHAIR, BROOKHAVEN NAT LAB, as of 2003; Adj prof, Mat Sci Dept, Stony Brook, 1991-; PHYSICIST, PHYSICS DEPT, BROOKHAVEN NAT LAB, 1986-; assoc physicist, Physics Dept, Brookhaven Nat Lab, 1983-1986; fel, AT&T Bell Labs, 1981-1982; fel, Warwick Univ, 1976-1981. **Memberships:** Fel Am Phys Soc; Am Vacuum Soc; Mat Res Soc. **Research Statement & Publications:** Spin resolved electronic structure of surfaces, thin films and related multilayers. **Mailing Address:** Physics Dept, Brookhaven Nat Lab, Upton, NY 11973. **Fax:** 516-282-2739. **E-Mail:** pdj@bnl.gov

JOHNSON, PETER DEXTER, APPLIED PHYSICS. **Personal Data:** b Norwich, Conn, July 1, 1921; div, c 3. **Education:** Harvard Univ, SB, 1942; Univ NC, MA, 1948, PhD (phys chem), 1949. **Professional Experience:** RETIRED; patent agent, 1981-1993; vis assoc prof, Cornell Univ, 1958-1959; res assoc, Gen Elec Co, 1949-1984; supvr ballistic testing, Hercules Powder Co, Va, 1942-1943. **Memberships:** Fel AAAS; fel Am Inst Chemists; Am Chem Soc; fel Am Phys Soc; Optical Soc Am; Sigma Xi. **Research Statement & Publications:** Optical properties of phosphors and semiconductors; luminescence theory; optics and optical instrument design; optical properties of gas discharges. **Mailing Address:** 1100 Merlin Dr, Schenectady, NY 12309.

JOHNSON, PETER GRAHAM, GEOMORPHOLOGY. **Personal Data:** b St Helens, Eng, August 28, 1945; m 1967, c 2. **Education:** Univ Leeds, BSc, 1966, PhD (geog), 1969. **Professional Experience:** Pres, Asn Can Universities Northern Studies, 1997-2001; PROF GEOG, UNIV OTTAWA, 1985-; from asst prof to assoc prof, 1969-1985. **Memberships:** Geol Asn Can; Asn Am Geog; Arctic Inst NAm; Can Asn Geog. **Research Statement & Publications:** Alpine hydrology; rock glacier mechanics and drainage systems; ice cored landform formation and degradation; southwest Yukon Territory; glacier hydrology. **Mailing Address:** Dept Geog, Univ Ottawa, Simard Hall Rm SMD017 60 Univ, Ottawa, ON K1N 6N5, Can. **Fax:** 613-562-5145. **E-Mail:** peterj@uottawa.ca

JOHNSON, PETER YOUNG, ORGANIC CHEMISTRY. **Education:** Univ Ill, BS, 1965; Mass Inst Technol, PhD, 1968. **Professional Experience:** PROF CHEM, ILL INST TECHNOL, 1990-. **Mailing Address:** Illinois Inst Technol, 298 Life Sci Bldg, Chicago, IL 60616. **Fax:** 312-567-3210. **E-Mail:** johnson@charlie.iit.edu

JOHNSON, PHILIP L, ECOLOGY. **Personal Data:** b Oneonta, NY, May 26, 1931; m 1973, Judy. **Education:** Purdue Univ, BS, 1953, MS, 1955; Duke Univ, PhD (bot), 1961. **Honors & Awards:** Ecological soc of Am. **Professional Experience:** Exec dir, USC Artic Res Comm, Wash DC, 1988-1994; Gov's Task Force Advan Labor & Mgt Relations, 1984-1986 & exec dir, John E Gray Inst, Lamar Univ, 1981-1986; mem polar res bd, Nat Acad Sci, 1981-1985; mem, US Comn, UNESCO, 1978-1980; mem exec comt, East Tenn Cancer Res Ctr, Knoxville, 1975-1978; mem regional comt Southeastern Plant Environ Lab, 1975-1977; exec dir, Oak Ridge Assoc Univs, 1974-1981; mem fel adv panel environ affairs, Rockefeller Found, 1974-1976; mem US Comt Man & Biosphere Prog, 1973-1974; vchmn interagency comt ecol res, Fed Coun Sci & Technol-Coun Environ Qual, 1972; div dir environ systs & resources, NSF, 1970-1974; mem environ biol panel foreign currency prog, Smithsonian Inst, 1969-1970; deciduous forest biome coord comt, Int Biol Prog, 1968-1970; adv comt tundra biome, Int Biol Prog, 1968-1970; assoc prog dir, environ biol prog, NSF, 1968-1969; assoc prof forest resources, Univ Ga, 1967-1970; mem primary productivity comt, Int Biol Prog, 1967-1968; mem NH Pesticide Control Bd, 1965-1967; vis asst prof biol, Dartmouth Col, 1963 & 1965-; res collabr, Brookhaven Nat Lab, 1963-1965; res ecologist, Cold Regions Res & Eng Lab, NH, 1962-1967; res botanist, Range Res, US Forest Serv, Wyo, 1961-1962; instr bot, Univ Wyo, 1959-1961; ed bd ecol monographs, 1968-1970; ed bd J Remote Sensing Res, 1971-1973. **Research Statement & Publications:** Production and processes in arctic and alpine tundra; aerial sensing of ecological patterns; mineral cycling in ecosystems applications of environmental sciences; interdisciplinary research and training; regional economic development; Res policy. **Mailing Address:** 118 Maid Marion Pl, Williamsburg, VA 23185.

JOHNSON, PHILIP M, PHYSICAL CHEMISTRY, MOLECULAR SPECTROSCOPY. **Personal Data:** b Vancouver, Wash, October 22, 1940; m 1964, c 2. **Education:** Univ Wash, BS, 1962; Cornell Univ, PhD (phys chem), 1967. **Professional Experience:** Guggenheim fel, 1982-1983; PROF CHEM, STATE UNIV NY STONY BROOK, 1978-; fel, Joint Inst Lab Astrophys, Colo, 1975-1976; from asst prof to assoc prof, State Univ NY Stony Brook, 1968-1978; NIH fel, Univ Chicago, 1966-1968. **Memberships:** Am Phys Soc. **Research Statement & Publications:** Ultraviolet and vacuum ultraviolet spectroscopy; evolution of electronic energy in molecules; multiphoton ionization spectroscopy. **Mailing Address:** Dept Chem, State Univ NY, Stony Brook, NY 11794. **E-Mail:** philip.johnson@sunysb.edu

JOHNSON, PHILLIP EUGENE, MATHEMATICS. **Personal Data:** b Bostic, NC, February 25, 1937; m 1959, Carolyn; c Marc. **Education:** Appalachian State Teachers Col, BS, 1959; George Peabody Col, MA, 1963, PhD (math), 1968; Am Univ, MA, 1966. **Professional Experience:** ASSOC PROF MATH, UNIV NC, CHARLOTTE, 1976-; asst prof,

Univ NC, Charlotte, 1971-1976; vis asst prof, NC State Univ, 1971; from instr to asst prof, Vanderbilt Univ, 1966-1971; instr math, Univ Richmond, 1963-1965; High Sch teacher, Va, 1960-1963. **Memberships:** Math Asn Am; Nat Coun Teachers Math; Am Math Soc. **Research Statement & Publications:** Mathematics history and education. **Mailing Address:** Dept Math, Univ NC, Fretwell 390K, Charlotte, NC 28223-0001. **Fax:** 704-687-6415. **E-Mail:** pejohnso@email.uncc.edu

JOHNSON, PHYLLIS ELAINE, AGR RES ADMIN, TRACE METAL NUTRITION. **Personal Data:** b Grafton, NDak, February 19, 1949; wid Robert (Deceased); c Erik & Sara. **Education:** Univ NDak, BS, 1971, PhD (phys chem), 1976. **Honors & Awards:** Arthur S Flemming Award, 1989. **Professional Experience:** DIR, BELTSVILLE AREA, BELTSVILLE AGR RES CTR, 1997-; assoc dir, Beltsville Area, 1996-1997; assoc dir, Pac West Area, USDA, 1991-1996; res leader, Nutrit Biochem & Metab Unit, Human Nutrit Res Ctr, 1987-1991; clin instr, Sch Med, 1981-1991; chemist, Grand Forks Human Nutrit Res Ctr, USDA, Agr Res Serv, 1979-1986; chemist, Univ NDak, 1977-1979; fel, Univ NDak, 1975-1977; lab instr chem & biochem, Mary Col, NDak, 1971-1972. **Memberships:** Am Chem Soc; Am Soc Nutrit; Sigma Xi; Int Soc Trace Element Res Humans (Secy, 1992-1998); AAAS. **Research Statement & Publications:** Trace metal absorption; biological metal-ligand complexes; lactation and infant nutrition; absorption, metabolism and bioavailability of trace metals, especially iron, zinc, copper and manganese, are investigated in humans using stable and radioactive metal isotopes as tracers. **Mailing Address:** USDA-Agr Res Serv, Beltsville Agr Res Ctr, 10300 Baltimore Ave Bldg 003 Rm 223, Beltsville, MD 20705-2350. **Fax:** 301-504-5863. **E-Mail:** johnsonp@ba.ars.usda.gov

JOHNSON, PHYLLIS TRUTH, INVERTEBRATE PATHOLOGY. **Personal Data:** b Salem, Ore, August 8, 1926. **Education:** Univ Calif, PhD (parasitol), 1954. **Honors & Awards:** Bronze Medal, US Dept Com, 1981. **Professional Experience:** RETIRED; biologist, Nat Marine Fisheries Serv, 1972-1990; mem comt animal models & genetic stocks, Nat Res Coun, 1971-1975; consult, Off Environ Sci, Smithsonian Inst, 1971-1972; res fel, Calif Inst Technol, 1970-1971; from asst res pathobiologist to assoc res pathobiologist, Univ Calif, Irvine, 1964-1970; med entomologist, Gorgas Mem Lab, 1959-1963; res assoc, USDA, 1958-1963; c onsult, US Naval Med Res Unit 3, Cairo, Egypt, 1957-; entomologist, Entom Res Br, USDA, 1955-1958; entomologist, Dept Entom, Walter Reed Army Inst Res, Wash, DC, 1950-1955; p arasitologist med entom, Bur Vector Control, State Dept Health, Calif, 1948-1950. **Memberships:** Sigma Xi; fel AAAS; Soc Invert Path (vpres, 1978-1980 & pres, 1981-1982); Am Soc Trop Med & Hyg; Am Soc Parasitol. **Research Statement & Publications:** Leishmaniasis; taxonomy of Siphonaptera and Anoplura; pathological processes in invertebrates; viruses in crustaceans; histopathology of crustaceans. **Mailing Address:** 4721 E Harbor Dr, Friday Harbor, WA 98250-9349.

JOHNSON, PORTER W, MATHEMATICAL PHYSICS, SCIENCE EDUCATION. **Personal Data:** b Chattanooga, Tenn, September 4, 1942; m, c 2. **Education:** Case Inst Technol, BS, 1963; Princeton Univ, MA, 1965, PhD (physics), 1967. **Professional Experience:** Interim chmn, Dept Math & Sci Educ, 2000-2001; chmn, Physics Dept, Ill Inst Tech, 1984-1995; PROF PHYSICS, ILL INST TECHNOL, 1983-; asst chmn, Physics Dept, Ill Inst Tech, 1976-1981; from asst prof to assoc prof, Ill Inst Technol, 1969-1983; res assoc, Case Western Reserve Univ, 1967-1969; teaching asst & res asst, NSF fel & NASA Trainee, Princeton Univ, 1963-1967. **Memberships:** Am Phys Soc; Am Asn Physics Teachers. **Research Statement & Publications:** Study of nonlinear equations arising in elementary particle physics; dynamical symmetry breaking in quantum field theory; science education; webpage development. **Mailing Address:** Dept Physics, Ill Inst Technol, 296 Life Sci Bldg 3101 S Dearborn St, Chicago, IL 60616. **Fax:** 312-567-3494. **E-Mail:** johnsonpo@iit.edu

JOHNSON, PRESTON BENTON, ELECTRICAL ENGINEERING. **Personal Data:** b Benson, NC, March 7, 1932; m 1954, c 3. **Education:** NC State Univ, BSEE, 1958, MS, 1962; Va Polytech Inst, PhD (elec eng), 1966. **Professional Experience:** PRES, JOHNSON BRADLEY RES CORP, as of 1994; VPRES, SIGMA CONSULTS, INC, 1975-; chmn, Dept Elec Eng, Old Dominion Univ, 1974-1977; ASSOC PROF ELEC ENG, OLD DOMINION UNIV, 1966-; asst prof, Va Polytech Inst, 1962-1966; instr elec eng, NC State Univ, 1961-1962. **Memberships:** Inst Elec & Electronics Engrs; Am Soc Eng Educ; Instrument Soc Am. **Research Statement & Publications:** Negative-resistance electronic devices based on superconductive tunneling between thin films; oceanographic instrumentations. **Mailing Address:** 1005 Briarwood Pt, Virginia Beach, VA 23452.

JOHNSON, R BARRY, OPTICS. **Professional Experience:** PRES, OPTICAL ETC INC, as of 1987. **Memberships:** Int Soc Optical Engrs. **Mailing Address:** Optical ETC Inc, Huntsville, AL 35899. **Fax:** 205-880-9792. **E-Mail:** oetcbarryj@aol.com

JOHNSON, R R, NUCLEAR PHYSICS. **Personal Data:** b Cloquet, Minn, August 7, 1938. **Education:** Univ Minn, BSc, 1960, MS, 1962, PhD, 1965. **Professional Experience:** PROF EMER MED PHYSICS, UNIV BC, as of 2004; fac mem, Dept Physics, Univ BC, beginning 1968; res assoc, Univ Colo, 1965-1968; vis scientist, SIN, Switz, 1979-1980. **Memberships:** Am Phys Soc. **Research Statement & Publications:** published around 10 articles. **Mailing Address:** Dept Physics, Univ BC, 6224 Agr Rd, Vancouver, BC V6T 1Z1, Can. **Fax:** 604-822-5324. **E-Mail:** johnson@physics.ubc.ca

JOHNSON, RALEIGH FRANCIS, NUCLEAR MEDICINE, RADIOLOGICAL PHYSICS. **Personal Data:** b Hazard, Ky, January 24, 1941; m 1963, c 2. **Education:** Berea Col, BA, 1964; Univ Miami, MS, 1965; Purdue Univ, PhD (radiol physics), 1969. **Professional Experience:** DIR RADIOL SCI, UNIV TEX MED BR, as of 2005; ASSOC PROF RADIOL, UNIV TEX MED BR, GALVESTON, 1991-; asst prof radiol & magnetic resonance imaging & tech dir, Univ Tex Med Br, Galveston, 1984-1991; asst prof radiol & nuclear med & physicist, Univ Tex Med Br, Galveston, 1972-1984; consult, Scientists & Engrs for Appalachia, 1971-; assoc radiol & nuclear med & physicist, Duke Univ & Vet Admin Hosp, 1969-1972. **Memberships:** Health Physics Soc; Nuclear Med Soc; Sigma Xi; Creation Res Soc; Am Asn Physicists Med; Soc Magnetic Resonance Med; Soc Magnetic Resonance Imaging. **Research Statement & Publications:** Oblique imaging techniques in magnetic resonance imaging; quality control of magnetic resonance imaging systems; magnetic resonance imaging using contrast enhancement labeled agents; evaluation of high energy collimators for scintillation gamma cameras; evaluation of microprocession controlledautomatic well-type scintillation counting system; evaluation of multipeak scintillation imaging; caordiac magnetic resonance imaging; 3D MRI imaging and 3D video display techniques. **Mailing Address:** Dept Radiol, Univ Tex Med Br, 301 Univ Blvd, Galveston, TX 77555-0144. **Fax:** 409-772-6216. **E-Mail:** rjohnson@utmb.edu

JOHNSON, RALPH, ELECTRICAL ENGINEERING, SEMICONDUCTORS. **Professional Experience:** AT DIV MICRO SWITCH, HONEYWELL, INC, as of 1997. **Mailing Address:** Micro Switch Div, Honeywell, Inc, 830 E Arapaho Rd, Richardson, TX 75081.

JOHNSON, RALPH ALTON, GENERAL ATMOSPHERIC SCIENCES. **Personal Data:** b Alton, Ill, September 14, 1919; m 1954, c 1. **Education:** Hastings Col, BA, 1940; Univ Colo, MS, 1942; Univ Minn, PhD (chem), 1949. **Professional Experience:** ENVIRON ODOR CONSULT, 1983-; sr res chemist, Shell Develop Co, 1955-1983; from instr to asst prof anal chem, Univ Ill, 1948-1955; j r chemist, Manhattan Proj, Hanford Eng Works, E I du Pont Del Nemours & Co, 1944-1945. **Memberships:** Am Chem Soc; Air Pollution Control Asn; Am Soc Testing & Mat; Sigma Xi. **Research Statement & Publications:** Psychophysics, odor measurement; wastewater processing and analysis; precipitation studies; spectrophotometric and electron microscopic investigations; neutron activation analysis. **Mailing Address:** 13135 Bohme, Houston, TX 77079.

JOHNSON, RALPH M, NUTRITION. **Personal Data:** b Ririe, Idaho, April 19, 1918; m 1940, Gwen; c Karen (Babcock), Christian & Wilford. **Education:** Utah State Agr Col, BS, 1940; Univ Wis, MS, 1944, PhD (biochem), 1948. **Professional Experience:** RETIRED; dean, Col Sci & prof chem, Utah State Univ, 1968-1984; dean, Col Biol Sci, 1966-1968; dir, Inst Nutrit & Food Technol, 1963-1968; dir & res prof, Inst Nutrit & Food Technol, 1960-1968; from assoc prof to prof physiol chem, Ohio State Univ, 1959-1968; dir labs, Ohio State Univ, 1959-1963; res assoc prof, Ohio State Univ, 1959-1960; asst prof biochem, Col Med, Wayne State Univ, 1948-1959. **Memberships:** Am Soc Biochem & Molecular Biol; Am Inst Nutrit. **Research Statement & Publications:** Role of the essential unsaturated fatty acids; lipid metabolism; metabolism of phosphorous compounds; hormonal and hereditary factors in carcinogenesis; biochemical role of vitamin E. **Mailing Address:** 2044 N 13th E, Logan, UT 84321.

JOHNSON, RALPH STERLING, JR, MATERIALS SCIENCE, METALLURGICAL ENGINEERING & CORROSION ENGINEERING. **Personal Data:** b Shickshinny, Pa, April 2, 1926; m 1951, Margaret Master; c Ralph III (deceased). **Education:** Univ Akron, BS, 1957, MS, 1960; Univ Mich, Ann Arbor, PhD (mat sci & metall eng), 1970. **Honors & Awards:** Apollo Achievement Award, NASA, 1969. **Professional Experience:** MANAGING PARTNER, R S J ASSOCS CONSULT ENGRS, 1993-; mgr, Mat Eng, Mead Paper Co, 1986-1992; sr consult, Brit Petrol, Dallas, Tex, 1984-1986; mem, Sci Adv Comn, Alaska Found, Univ Alaska, 1983-1985; consult mat corrosion & mfg processes & mem, Corrosion Task Force, Sohio Alaska Petrol Co, Anchorage, 1981-1984; consult mat corrosion & mfg processes, Aramco, Dhahran, Saudi Arabia, 1979-1981; Mem water qual task force, Bechtel Power Corp, 1975-1979; consult mat corrosion & mfg processes, Res & Eng Dept, Bechtel Nat, Inc, San Francisco, 1973-1979; sr staff engr, Seismic Equip Dept, Bendix Aerospace Systems Div, Ann Arbor, 1962-1972; Sr res engr mat & mfg res, Res & Develop Dept, Goodyear Aerospace Corp, 1949-1961; consult, Arctic Res Comn. **Memberships:** Nat Asn Corrosion Engrs; Sigma Xi; Am Soc Metals; Tech Assoc Pulp & Paper Indust. **Research Statement & Publications:** Materials performance and corrosion of materials in flue gas desulfurization systems; feedwater and steam generating systems in steam electric plants; oil field production facilities materials of construction and corrosion control; corrosion control pulp & paper. **Mailing Address:** 26 Timberlane Dr, Chillicothe, OH 45601-1941. **Fax:** 740-775-0475.

JOHNSON, RALPH T, SOLID STATE PHYSICS, RESEARCH SUPERVISION. **Personal Data:** b Salina, Kans, April 29, 1935; m 1958, Ruth; c Barbara, Thomas, Gregory & Janet. **Education:** Kans State Univ, BS, 1957, MS, 1959, PhD (physics), 1964. **Professional Experience:** RETIRED; mem nat res coun bd, Assessment Nat Bur Stand, Panel Basic Stand, 1987-1990; mgr measurement stand, Sandia Nat Labs, 1985-1997; mem energy conversion panel, NMex Gov Energy Task Force, 1974; res supvr elec transport & electronic properties mat, Sandia Nat Labs, 1970-1985; staff mem solid state physics, Sandia Nat Labs, 1965-1970; proj officer, Air Force Weapons Lab, 1963-1965; asst physics, Kans State Univ, 1958-1963; physicist, Aircraft Nuclear Propulsion Dept, Gen Elec Co, 1957-1958. **Memberships:** Am Phys Soc; Sigma Xi. **Research Statement & Publications:** X-ray diffraction topography; dislocations and martensitic transformations; rocket-borne magnetometers and optical spectrometers; semiconductor radiation defects, ionization effects and neutron detectors; electrical properties of amorphous semiconductors; thermoelectrics; solid electrolytes; electronic properties of dielectric materials. **Mailing Address:** 6601 Arroyo del Oso NE, Albuquerque, NM 87109.

JOHNSON, RANDOLPH MELLUS, BIOCHEMICAL PHARMACOLOGY, NEUROPHARMACOLOGY. **Personal Data:** b Los Angeles, Calif, September 6, 1950; m 1980, Charlyn; c Maile, Lani & Peter. **Education:** Calif State Univ, Long Beach, BS, 1974, MA, 1978; Univ SC, PhD (pharmacol), 1984. **Professional Experience:** VPRES PRECLINICAL RES & DIR CENT NERVOUS SYST, DURECT CORP, 1998-; head, Dept Neurobiology, Roche Bioscience, beginning 1995; res sect & proj team leader, Syntex Discovery, 1992-1995; staff researcher II, Syntex Discovery, 1991-1992; consult, Quantex Corp, 1989-1991; scientist biomolecular pharmacol, Genentech, Inc, 1988-1991; res asst prof endocrine pharmacol, Sch Med, Univ Va, 1987-1988; res assoc endocrine pharmacol, Sch Med, Univ Va, 1984-1987. **Memberships:** Am Soc Pharmacol & Exp Therapeut; Am Soc Biochem & Molecular Biol; Endocrine Soc; AAAS; Soc Neuroscience; Western Pharmacol Soc (secy, 1996-). **Research Statement & Publications:** Biomolecular mechanisms of growth factors, neurotransmitters and novel experimental therapeutics as it relates to second messenger formation and protein phosphorylation events in cell activation. **Mailing Address:** DURECT Corp, 10260 Bubb Rd Bldg A, Cupertino, CA 95014-4166. **Fax:** 408-777-3577.

JOHNSON, RANDY ALLAN, HIGH ENERGY PHYSICS. **Personal Data:** b Minneapolis, Minn, February 9, 1947; m 1978. **Education:** Princeton Univ, AB, 1969; Univ Calif, Berkeley, PhD (physics), 1975. **Professional Experience:** PROF, DEPT PHYSICS, UNIV CINCINNATI, 1984; physicist, Brookhaven Nat Lab, 1976-1984; fel physics, Lawrence Berkeley Lab, 1975-1976. **Memberships:** Sigma Xi. **Research Statement & Publications:** Particle scattering at high energies. **Mailing Address:** Physics Dept, Univ Cincinnati, Rm 417 Geol/Physics Bldg PO Box 210011, Cincinnati, OH 45221-0011. **Fax:** 513-556-3425. **E-Mail:** randy.johnson@uc.edu

JOHNSON, RAY EDWIN, SOIL FERTILITY. **Personal Data:** b East View, Ky, August 9, 1936; m 1985, c 1. **Education:** Univ Ky, BS, 1957, MS, 1959; NC State Univ, PhD (mineral nutrit), 1962. **Professional Experience:** RETIRED; prof agron, soil fertil & soil chem, Western Ky Univ, beginning 1973; from asst prof to assoc prof agron, soil fertil & soil chem, 1967-1973; res plant physiologist, US Regional Soybean Lab, Crops Res Div, Agr Res Serv, Ill, 1963-1967; res assoc, Mineral Nutrit Pioneering Res Lab, USDA, 1962-1963. **Memberships:** Am Soc Agron; Sigma Xi. **Research Statement & Publications:** Mineral nutrition and interaction in plants; relationship of fertilizer response to soil test results. **Mailing Address:** Dept Agr, Western KY Univ, One Big Red Way St, Bowling Green, KY 42101-3576.

JOHNSON, RAY LELAND, PHYSICAL CHEMISTRY, ENVIRONMENTAL & ANALYTICAL CHEMISTRY. **Personal Data:** b LaGrange, Ohio, November 7, 1939; m 1962, Penelope; c Karen, Ray & Cheryl. **Education:** Kent State Univ, BS, 1961; Ohio Univ, PhD (phys chem), 1966. **Professional Experience:** PROF EMER CHEM, DIV NATURAL SCI, HILLSDALE COL, as of 2005; chair chem, Div Natural Sci, Hillsdale Col, 1992-2000; prof chem, Div Natural Sci, Hillsdale Col, beginning 1980; assoc prof & actg chmn, Div Natural Sci, Hillsdale Col, 1977-1979; W K Kellogg Found res grant water qual studies, 1971-1973; asst prof, Div Natural Sci, Hillsdale Col, 1969-1977; sr res chemist, PPG Industs Inc, 1966-1969. **Memberships:** AAAS; Am Chem Soc. **Research Statement & Publications:** Thermodynamics and kinetics; surface and colloid chemistry; solution chemistry; chemical investigations of water quality in lakes and streams; chemical methods of waste water treatment and analysis; development of multimedia and hypermedia materials for use in chemical education. **Mailing Address:** Dept Chem, Hillsdale Col, 33 E Col St, Hillsdale, MI 49242. **Fax:** 517-437-3923. **E-Mail:** rlj@hillsdale.edu

JOHNSON, RAY O, ELECTRO-OPTICS, OPTICAL SIGNAL PROCESSING. **Personal Data:** b Kansas City, Mo, May 25, 1955; m Joan; c Jennifer, Michael & Alexander. **Education:** Okla State Univ, BSEE, 1984; Air Force Inst Technol, MSEE, 1987, PhD (elec eng). **Professional Experience:** SR VPRES, SCI APPLN INT CORP, as of 2004; MEM, SCI ADV BD, USAF, as of 2004; BD DIRS, AGILUX CORP, as of 2004; CHIEF INFO OFFICER, ENTERGY SERV INC, 2000-; res engr, Wright Lab, USAF, beginning 1993; t elecommun engr, Hq Strategic Air Command, 1987-1990; t elecommun engr, Foreign Technol Div, USAF, 1984-1986. **Memberships:** Inst Elec & Electronics Engrs; Soc Photo-Optical Instrumentation Engrs. **Research Statement & Publications:** Infrared remote sensing and imaging; optical signal processing; laser radar. **Mailing Address:** Sci Appln Int Corp, 11251 Roger Bacon Dr PO Box 4875, Reston, VA 22090. **Fax:** 703-709-1042. **E-Mail:** johnsoro@wl.wpafb.af.mil

JOHNSON, RAYMOND C, ELECTRONICS. **Personal Data:** b Galveston, Tex, September 29, 1922; c 9. **Education:** Tex A&M Univ, BS, 1945; Univ Fla, MS, 1949. **Professional Experience:** RETIRED; dir, Electronic Commun Lab, beginning 1976; sect head, Electronic Res Sect, 1959-1990; from asst prof to prof elec eng, Univ Fla, 1946-1990. **Research Statement & Publications:** Electronics systems. **Mailing Address:** 204 NW 32nd St, Gainesville, FL 32607.

JOHNSON, RAYMOND EARL, ZOOLOGY. **Personal Data:** b Peru, Nebr, October 26, 1914; m 1941. **Education:** Doane Col, BA, 1936; Univ Nebr, MA, 1938; Univ Mich, PhD (zool), 1942. **Professional Experience:** CONSULT, NAT WILDLIFE FEDN, 1974-; dep div dir, NSF, 1972-1974; chief off environ qual, Bur Sport Fisheries & Wildlife, 1971-1972; asst dir, Bur Sport Fisheries & Wildlife, 1959-1971; chief br fed aid, Bur Sport Fisheries & Wildlife, 1958-1959; chief fish div, Bur Sport Fisheries & Wildlife, 1956-1958; asst fed aid supvr, Bur Sport Fisheries & Wildlife, 1951-1956; fisheries res supvr, US Fish & Wildlife Serv, Univ Minn, 1947-1951; a quatic biologist, US Fish & Wildlife Serv, Univ Minn, 1945-1946. **Memberships:** Am Soc Ichtyologists & Herpetologists; Am Fisheries Soc; Am Soc Limnol & Oceanog; Wildlife Soc; Sigma Xi. **Research Statement & Publications:** Taxonomy and distribution of freshwater fishes in North America; fisheries management; life history of freshwater fishes. **Mailing Address:** Jefferson No 1725, 900 N Taylor St, Arlington, VA 22203.

JOHNSON, RAYMOND LEWIS, MATHEMATICS. **Personal Data:** b Alice, Tex, June 25, 1943; wid, c Malcolm. **Education:** Univ Tex, Austin, BA, 1963; Rice Univ, PhD (math), 1969. **Professional Experience:** Chmn, Univ Md, 1991-1996; assoc chmn grad studies, Univ Md, 1987-1990; sabbatical leave, McMaster Univ, Hamilton, Can, 1983-1984; PROF MATH, UNIV MD, 1980-; sabbatical leave, Howard Univ, 1976-1978; sabbatical leave, Inst Mittag-Leffler, DJursholm, 1974-1975; From asst prof to assoc prof, Univ Md, 1968-1978; Gen Res Bd grant, 1968 & 1971. **Memberships:** Am Math Soc; Math Asn Am; Nat Asn Math Assoc. for Women in Math. **Research Statement & Publications:** Parabolic partial differential equations; representation theorems; spaces of functions defined by difference conditions; harmonic analysis. **Mailing Address:** Dept Math, Univ Md, College Park, MD 20742. **Fax:** 301-314-0827. **E-Mail:** rlj@math.umd.edu

JOHNSON, RAYMOND NILS, ANALYTICAL CHEMISTRY. **Personal Data:** b New York, NY, July 26, 1941; m 1965, Lola; c Jennifer & Sarah. **Education:** Franklin & Marshall Col, AB, 1963; Middlebury Col, MS, 1965; Clarkson Univ, PhD (chem), 1969. **Professional Experience:** ASST VPRES ANALYTICAL RES & DEVELOP, WYETH-AYERST RES INC, 1995-; sr dir, Wyeth-Ayerst res, Inc, 1988-1995; asst vpres, Wyeth-Ayerst res, Inc, 1985-1987; dir anal res & serv, Wyeth-Ayerst res, Inc, 1985; assoc dir, Wyeth-Ayerst res, Inc, 1983-1984; asst dir anal res & develop, Wyeth-Ayerst res, Inc, 1978-1983; sect head anal chem, Wyeth-Ayerst res, Inc, 1975-1978; from res assoc anal chem to group leader, Wyeth-Ayerst res, Inc, 1969-1975. **Memberships:** Am Chem Soc; Acad Pharmaceut Sci; Sigma Xi. **Research Statement & Publications:** Pharmaceutical analysis using liquid chromatography and mass spectrometry; emphasis placed on analysis of novel chemical derivatives and development of analytical methods that are precise, accurate and specific; automation; raw material characterization; stability of raw materials and dosage forms. **Mailing Address:** Anal Res & Div Wyeth-Ayerst Res Inc, 401 N Middletown Rd, Pearl River, NY 12979. **Fax:** 914-732-5189.

JOHNSON, RAYMOND ROY, SYSTEMATIC BOTANY, VERTEBRATE ZOOLOGY. **Personal Data:** b Phoenix, Ariz, June 19, 1932; m 1976, Lois T Haight; c Elaine, Donna, Wayne, Korin & Catherine. **Education:** Ariz State Univ, BS, 1955; Univ Ariz, MS, 1960; Univ Kans, PhD (bot), 1964. **Professional Experience:** Prof, Renewable Nat Res, Univ Ariz, 1980-1995; sr res scientist, Coop Nat Park Resources Study Unit, 1980-1992; sr res scientist, Grand Canyon, Nat Park Serv, Univ Ariz, 1976-1979; res scientist, Grand Canyon, Nat Park Serv, Univ Ariz, 1974-1975; from assoc prof to prof biol, Prescott Col, 1968-1974; assoc prof biol, Univ Tex, El Paso, 1965-1968; Asst prof biol, Western NMex Univ, 1964-1965. **Memberships:** Am Ornith Union; Am Soc Mammal SW assoc nat, AZ-NV acad sci. **Research Statement & Publications:** Plant taxonomy, conservation biology; animal distribution; riparian ecology; desertification and arid land ecology; avian ecology; biogeography of North American Southwest. **Mailing Address:** 3755 S Hunters Run, Tucson, AZ 85730. **Fax:** 520-298-8418. **E-Mail:** rjohnso@msn.com

JOHNSON, R(ICHARD) A(LLAN), ELECTRICAL ENGINEERING. **Personal Data:** b Winnipeg, Man, March 21, 1932; m 1957, c 3. **Education:** Univ Man, BSc, 1954, MSc, 1956. **Professional Experience:** RETIRED; provost progs, Elec Eng Dept, 1992-1997; assoc vpres, Elec Eng Dept, 1987-1992; assoc vpres planning & anal, Elec Eng Dept, 1982-1987; dir, Comt Accepting Eng Curric, Can Coun Prof Eng, 1980-1982; pres, APEM, 1979; provost, Elec Eng Dept, 1977-1982; head, Elec Eng Dept, 1973-1976; actg dir planning, Univ Man, 1969-1970; prof elec eng, Elec Eng Dept, 1966-1997; mem, Can Accreditation Bd, 1964-1967; prof eng, Can Coun, 1960-1962; from asst prof to assoc prof, Univ Man, 1955-1966; chmn, Comt Accepting Eng Curric. **Memberships:** Inst Elec & Electronics Engrs. **Research Statement & Publications:** Circuits and systems theory; nonlinear oscillations; chaos and catastrophe theory and applications. **Mailing Address:** Univ Man, 208 Admin Bldg, Winnipeg, MB R3T 2N2, Can.

JOHNSON, RICHARD ALLEN, PHYSICAL CHEMISTRY. **Personal Data:** b Panama City, Fla, August 13, 1945; m 1968, c 2. **Education:** Ill Inst Technol, BS, 1967; Mich State Univ, PhD (chem physics), 1971. **Professional Experience:** MGR PROD CONTROL, UPJOHN CO, 1976-; sr res scientist, Control Anal Res & Develop Unit, 1974-1976; res scientist, Control Anal Res & Develop Unit, 1973-1974; s cientist, Control Anal Res & Develop Unit, 1971-1973. **Memberships:** Am Chem Soc; Am Phys Soc. **Research Statement & Publications:** Molecular spectroscopy of solids; solid state chemistry; physical characterization of pharmaceutical solids; application of computers to online data acquisition from analytical laboratory instrumentation. **Mailing Address:** 7689 Fieldwood Point, Mattawan, MI 49071.

JOHNSON, RICHARD D, CHEMISTRY. **Personal Data:** b Zanesville, Ohio, October 28, 1934; m 1969, Catherina Collins; c 4. **Education:** Oberlin Col, BA, 1956; Carnegie Inst Technol, MS, 1961, PhD (chem), 1962; Mass Inst Tech, SM, 1982. **Honors & Awards:** Except Serv Medal, NASA, 1977. **Professional Experience:** Prin, SRI Int, 1990-1993; sr technol consult, SRI Int, 1985-1990; Sloan fel, 1981-1982; chief, Biosystems Div, 1976-1985; chief, Flight Exp Off, Life Sci, NASA, 1975-1976; l ectr, Stanford Univ, 1974-1986; res scientist, Ames Res Ctr, 1963-1985; sr scientist, Jet Propulsion Lab, Calif Inst Technol, 1962-1963; f el phys org chem, Univ Calif, Los Angeles, 1961-1962. **Memberships:** AAAS; Am Inst Aeronaut & Astronaut; Am Chem Soc; Inst Elec & Electronics Engrs. **Research Statement & Publications:** Exobiology and the detection of extraterrestrial life; Apollo lunar sample analysis; 1976 Viking Mars life detection experiment; space colonies; 1976 Stanford-Ames study on space settlements; space shuttle experiments; space biomedical experiments; space commercialization; aerospace technology; human factors; technology management. **Mailing Address:** 11564 Arroyo Oaks Dr, Los Altos, CA 94024.

JOHNSON, RICHARD DEAN, PHARMACEUTICAL LICENSING, TECHNOLOGY TRANSFER, INTELLECTUAL PROPERTY. **Personal Data:** b DeKalb, Ill, July 8, 1936; m 1969, Paula Marcellus; c Janet Bijur, Julie McVeigh, Richard Jr & Brodie. **Education:** Univ Calif Berkeley, BS, 1960, MS, 1962; Univ Calif, San Francisco, PhD (pharm chem), 1965; Rockhurst Col, Kans City, MBA, 1984. **Honors & Awards:** President's Award, Marion Labs, 1980, 1981. **Professional Experience:** Mem bd dir, Aus-Am Biotech Inc, 2001-2002; TRUSTEE, UNIV KANS CITY, 1996-; pres, Pharm Found, 1996-1998; mem bd dir, Microbiologix Biotech Inc, 1995-2001; adj grad prof, Sch Pharm, Univ Mo, Kans City, 1994-; trustee, Sch Pharm Found, Univ Mo Kans City, 1992-1996; mem bd dir, Immuno Pharmaceut Inc, 1991-1994; mem bd dir, US Pharmaceut Rev Comt, 1990-; adj prof, Sch Pharm, Univ Mo, Kans City, 1990-1994; mem bd dir, US Bioscience Inc, 1989-1990; Marion Merrell Dow Inc, 1989-1990; mem bd dir, Dey Labs, 1985-1989; mem bd dir, Tanabe-Marion Labs, 1984-1990; corp pres, Marion Labs Inc, 1984-1989; lectr, Bus Sch, Rockhurst Col, Kans City, 1983; vpres licensing, Marion Labs, Inc, 1980-1983; lectr, Bus Sch, Univ SC, 1975-1977; dir corp licensing, Marion Labs, Inc, 1973-1979; mem, Pres Comn Exec Interchange, White House, 1970-1971; dir regulatory affairs, Syntex Labs, Inc, 1968-1973; assoc dir med serv, Syntex Labs Inc, 1967-1968; res chemist & sect head, Allergan Pharmaceut Co, 1965-1967; fels, Am Found Pharmaceut Educ, 1963-1965; mem, Henry S Wellcome, 1963-1965; teaching asst, Univ Calif, San Francisco, 1962-1964; pharmacist, Alta Vista Drug Co, 1960-1961. **Memberships:** AAAS; Am Pharmaceut Asn; Am Chem Soc; Acad Pharmaceut Sci; Licensing Exec Soc; Am Asn Pharmaceut Sci. **Research Statement & Publications:** Thermal titration; thermal electric methods for studying physical and chemical properties of solutions of pharmaceutical. **Mailing Address:** 222 W Gregory Apt 235, Kansas City, MO 64114-1127. **Fax:** 816-363-1343. **E-Mail:** rdjohnson@webtv.net

JOHNSON, RICHARD EVAN, ORNITHOLOGY, ZOOGEOGRAPHY. **Personal Data:** b Pomona, Calif, November 9, 1936. **Education:** Univ Calif, Berkeley, BS, 1958; Univ Mont, MS, 1968; Univ Calif, Berkeley, PhD (zoology), 1972. **Professional Experience:** DIR, CONNER MUS, as of 2003; res dir, Conner Mus, beginning 1993; ASSOC PROF ZOOLOGY, WASH STATE UNIV, 1978-; ed, Murrelet, 1976-1980; dir, Charles R Conner Mus, 1972-1992; asst prof, Conner Mus, 1972-1978. **Memberships:** Am Ornithologists Union; Cooper Ornith Soc; Wilson Ornith Soc; Soc Study Evolution; Soc Syst Zoology; Am Soc Mammalogists. **Research Statement & Publications:** Zoogeography, ecology and speciation of birds; evolution of arctic and alpine ecosystems; mammals of the Northwest; biogeography of alpine plants. **Mailing Address:** Dept Zoology, Wash State Univ, Pullman, WA 99164-4236. **Fax:** 509-335-3184. **E-Mail:** johnsonre@wsu.edu

JOHNSON, RICHARD HARLAN, METEOROLOGY. **Personal Data:** b Portland, Ore, November 4, 1945; m 1965, LaVonne; c Chris & Brian. **Education:** Ore State Univ, BS, 1967; Univ Chicago, MS, 1969; Univ Wash, PhD (atmospheric sci), 1975. **Professional Experience:** PROF ATMOSPHERIC SCI, COLO STATE UNIV, 1986-; from asst prof to assoc prof, Colo State Univ, 1980-1986; asst prof atmospheric sci, Univ Wis-Milwaukee, 1977-1979; res meteorologist, Nat Hurricane Res Lab, 1976-1977; Bd trustees, Univ Corp Atmospheric Res. **Memberships:** Am Meteorol Soc; AAAS; Japan Meteorol Soc; Am Geophys Union. **Research Statement & Publications:** Atmospheric convection and the planetary boundary layer; mesoscale meteorology; synoptic meteorology; study of precipitating clouds and their interaction with the atmospheric circulation on various scales. **Mailing Address:** Dept Atmospheric Sci, Colo State Univ, 4216, Breakwater Ct, Ft Collins, CO 80525. **Fax:** 970-491-8449. **E-Mail:** johnson@atmos.colostate.edu

JOHNSON, RICHARD JOSEPH, PROTEIN CHEMISTRY, COMPLEMENT ACTIVATION & INFLAMMATION. **Personal Data:** b Pittsburgh, Pa, 1954; m 1982, Beverly; c Matthew, Timothy & Sara-Ann. **Education:** Pa State Univ, BA, 1976; Duquesne Univ, MS, 1978, PhD (biochem), 1982. **Professional Experience:** BAXTER RES SCIENTIST, BAXTER HEALTHCARE, 1993-; sr res scientist, Baxter Healthcare, 1990-1993; res scientist, Baxter Healthcare, 1987-1990; sr res assoc, Baxter Healthcare, 1986-1987; fel, Univ Calif, San Diego/Vet Admin Med Ctr, 1982-1986. **Memberships:** AAAS; Am Asn Immunologists. **Research Statement & Publications:** Role of complement and particularly C5A in mediating an inflammatory response, particularly in a biomaterials setting such as during hemodialysis and C5A-receptor interaction; areas of cell capture technology in the transplantation area, flow cytometry analysis of PBL and molecular biology. **Mailing Address:** 442 W Quigley, Mundelein, IL 60060.

JOHNSON, RICHARD LAWRENCE, ORGANIC CHEMISTRY. **Personal Data:** b Glendale, WVa, February 3, 1939; m 1960, c 2. **Education:** Washington & Jefferson Col, BA, 1960; Univ Ky, MS, 1962; Univ Iowa, PhD (org chem), 1966. **Professional Experience:** RES ASSOC, E I DUPONT DEL NEMOURS & CO INC, 1982-; sr res chemist, E I Dupont Del Nemours & CO Inc, 1973-1982; l ectr, Parkersburg Br, WVa Univ, 1970-1971 & Parkersburg Community Col, 1971-1973; chemist, E I Dupont Del Nemours & CO Inc, 1966-1973; chemist, Rayonier, Inc, 1965-1966. **Memberships:** Am Chem Soc; Sigma Xi. **Research Statement & Publications:** Fluorocarbon polymers and fluorocarbon synthesis; nylon polymerization and extrusion compounding; fluorocarbon dispersion applications; acrylic resins. **Mailing Address:** 565 Blennerhassett Heights Rd, Parkersburg, WV 26101.

JOHNSON, RICHARD LEON, SIGNAL PROCESSING, RADIO DIRECTION FINDING. **Personal Data:** b Enid, Okla, June 12, 1938; m 1962, Ethel; c Andrew & Blake. **Educa-**

tion: Univ Tex, Arlington, BSEE, 1963; Southern Methodist Univ, MSEE, 1966; Okla State Univ, PhD (elec eng), 1970. **Professional Experience:** RETIRED; mem, Wave Propagation Stands Comt Antennas & Propagation Soc, Inst Elec & Electronics Engrs, beginninig 1991; inst scientist electromagnetics, Southwest Res Inst, 1970-2000; res asst, Okla State Univ, 1966-1970; aerosyst engr electronics, Gen Dynamics Corp, Ft Worth, Tex, 1964-1966. **Memberships:** Int Union Radio Sci; fel Inst Elec & Electronics Engrs; Nat Soc Prof Engrs. **Research Statement & Publications:** Superresolution spectrum estimation; digital signal processing; antennas and radio wave propagation analysis. **Mailing Address:** 422 Rockhill, San Antonio, TX 78209.

JOHNSON, RICHARD NED, MANUFACTURING & PROCESSING, INFORMATION ANALYSIS. **Personal Data:** b Perry, Iowa, January 4, 1942; m 1986, Karen; c Jana, David & Rachel. **Education:** Univ Wis-Madison, BS, 1964, PhD (eng mech), 1972; Case Inst Technol, MS, 1968; Roosevelt Univ, MBA, 1978. **Professional Experience:** DIR MFG PROG DEVELOP, ILL INST TECHNOL RES INST, 1996-; assoc dir, Northwestern Univ, 1990-1996; vpres, Axionixx, 1989-1992; mgr indust eng, Packer Eng, 1989; mgr mat & mfg res, Borg Warner Res, 1982-1988; consult, Psych Systs, 1982-1984; mgr mat eng, GATX/GARD, 1971-1982; res assoc, Univ Wis-Madison, 1970-1971; researcher, Lewis Res Ctr, NASA, 1964-1970. **Memberships:** Soc Mfg Engrs. **Research Statement & Publications:** Gear and bearing manufacturing; manufacturing technology information analysis; advanced aerospace alloys materials characterization and testing; laser processing of materials; industry/public partnerships for manufacturing R&D. **Mailing Address:** 15W755 Shepard Lane, Burr Ridge, IL 60521. **Fax:** 312-567-4329. **E-Mail:** rjohnson@iitri.com

JOHNSON, RICHARD NORING, BIOMEDICAL ENGINEERING. **Personal Data:** b Wethersfield, Conn, April 12, 1934; m 1960, c 2. **Education:** Tri-State Col, BSc, 1961; Worcester Polytech Inst, MSc, 1965; Univ Va, DSc(biomed eng), 1969. **Professional Experience:** PROF EMER BIOMED ENG, UNIV NC, as of 2002; prof biomed eng & neurol, Sch Med, Univ NC, Chapel Hill, 1979-1981; assoc prof, Schs Eng & Med, Univ Va, 1977-1979; asst prof biomed eng & neurol, Schs Eng & Med, Univ Va, 1972-1977; Fel biomed eng, Johns Hopkins Univ, 1971-1972; instr, Schs Eng & Med, Univ Va, 1970-1971; res assoc neurol, Schs Eng & Med, Univ Va, 1969-1970; Instr elec technol, Hartford State Tech Col, 1961-1965. **Memberships:** AAAS; Am Soc Eng Educ; Soc Neurosci; Biomed Eng Soc; Am Epilepsy Soc. **Research Statement & Publications:** Neurophysiological control systems; neural models. **Mailing Address:** Dept Biomed Eng, Sch Med, Univ NC, 152 MacNider Hall, CB#7575, Chapel Hill, NC 27599-7575. **Fax:** 919-966-2963.

JOHNSON, RICHARD R, MECHANICAL ENGINEERING. **Education:** Univ, Cape Town, BS, MS; Univ Fla, PhD (eng). **Professional Experience:** ASSOC PROF MECH ENG, NC STATE UNIV, 1981-. **Mailing Address:** Dept Mech Eng, NC State Univ, Raleigh, NC 27695.

JOHNSON, RICHARD T, NEUROLOGY, VIROLOGY. **Personal Data:** b Grosse Pointe Farms, Mich, July 16, 1931; m 1954, Francis; c Carlton, Erica, Matthew & Nathan. **Education:** Univ Colo, AB, 1953, MD, 1956. **Honors & Awards:** Weil Award, Am Asn Neuropath, 1967; Sydney Farber Res Award, 1974 & 1976; Humboldt Prize, 1975; Weinstein-Goldson Award, 1979; Gordon Wilson Medal, 1980; Charcot Award, Int Fed MS Soc, 1985; Smadel Medal, 1986; MS Medal, Asn British Neurol, 1986; Outstanding Serv Award, Nat Mult Sclerosis Soc, 1989; Soriano Award, World Fed Neurol, 1993; Pioneer Awd, Intn'l Soc Novo, 1998. **Professional Experience:** ADD FAC MICROBIOL, SCH MED, JOHNS HOPKINS UNIV, as of 2004; prof & dir neurol, Sch Med, Johns Hopkins Univ, 1989-1998; neurologist chief, Johns Hopkins Hosp, 1989-1998; prof, Neuroscience, Johns Hopkins Hosp, 1989; jt appointment, Dept Molecular Microbiol & Immunol, Johns Hopkins Sch Hyg & Pub Health, 1984-; hon prof, Univ Peruana Cayetano Heredia, 1980; prof microbiol, Sch Med, Johns Hopkins Univ, beginning 1974; Dwight D Eisenhower-United Cerebal Palsy prof neurol, Johns Hopkins Hosp, 1969-1989; assoc prof microbiol, Johns Hopkins Hosp, 1969-1974; from asst prof to assoc prof neurol, Sch Med, Case Western Res Univ, 1964-1969; asst neurologist, Highland View Hosp, Cleveland, 1964-1969; assoc neurologist, Cleveland Metrop Gen Hosp, Ohio, 1964-1969; mem comn, Asn Res Nervous & Ment Dis, 1964, 1969-1977; fel microbiol, John Curtin Sch Med, Canberra, Australia, 1962-1964; first neurol asst, Univ Newcastle, Eng, 1961-1962; teaching fel neurol & neuropath, Harvard Med Sch, 1959-1961. **Memberships:** Inst Med-Nat Acad Sci; Am Soc Clin Invest; Am Asn Neuropath; Am Neurol Asn; Asn Am Physicians. **Research Statement & Publications:** Clinical neurology; pathogenesis of viral infections of the nervous system; neurologic complications of HIV infection. **Mailing Address:** Dept Neurol, Johns Hopkins Univ Med Sch, Baltimore, MD 21287. **E-Mail:** rtj@jhmi.edu

JOHNSON, RICHARD T(ERRELL), MECHANICAL ENGINEERING. **Personal Data:** b Shreveport, La, July 28, 1939; m 1988, Mary; c Deborah, Patricia, Jenifer & Rebecca. **Education:** Mo Sch Mines, BSME, 1962, MS, 1964; Univ Iowa, PhD (mech eng), 1967. **Honors & Awards:** Delos Lab Develop Award, Am Soc Eng Educ. **Professional Experience:** PROF OF MECH ENG & DEAN, COL ENG & TECHNOLOGY, BRADLEY UNIV, as of 1999; PROF MECH ENG & chmn mech eng, Wichita State Univ, 1989-1999; prof mech eng, Univ Mo-Rolla concluding 1999, dir, Inst Flexible Mfg & Indust Automation, 1984-1988; beginning 1967; instr mech eng, Univ Iowa, 1964-1966; instr eng mech, Univ Mo-Rolla, 1962-1964. **Memberships:** Am Soc Mech Engrs; Soc Automotive Engrs; Sigma Xi; Soc Mfg Engrs; Am Soc Eng Educ. **Research Statement & Publications:** Mechanical engineering design; control systems and instrumentation; alternate fuels for transportation engines; improved efficiency of combustion engines; manufacturing automation and systems integration; applications of artificial intelligence and expert systems to design and manufacturing. **Mailing Address:** Col Eng & Technol, Bradley Univ, Rm 124, Jobst Hall, 1501 W Bradley Ave, Peoria, IL 61625. **Fax:** 309-677-3670. **E-Mail:** rtj@bradley.edu

JOHNSON, RICHARD WILLIAM, BIO-ORGANIC CHEMISTRY, ELECTRO-ORGANIC CHEMISTRY. **Personal Data:** b Denver, Colo, July 11, 1950; m 1975, Katharine Kappaut; c Matthew, Kevin, David & Donald. **Education:** Northwestern Univ, BA & MS, 1972; Columbia Univ, MPhil, 1974, PhD (chem), 1976. **Professional Experience:** GLOBAL REGULATORY MGR, PLASTICS ADDITIVES BUS, ROHM & HAAS CO, as of 2004; SECT MGR, ROHM & HAAS CO, 1983-; a sst prof org chem, Harvard Univ, 1977-1983. **Memberships:** Am Chem Soc. **Research Statement & Publications:** New synthetic procedures based on organic electrochemical reactions; haptea-antibody interactions as model systems for enzymes; polymeric additives for PVC. **Mailing Address:** Rohm & Haas Co, 727 Norristown Rd, PO Box 904, Spring House, PA 19477-0904.

JOHNSON, ROBERT A, CIRCUIT THEORY, ACOUSTICS. **Personal Data:** b Chicago, Ill, September 27, 1932; m Lois O'Loughlin. **Education:** Univ Calif, Los Angeles, BS, 1955, MS, 1963. **Professional Experience:** CONSULT, ROCKWELL INT, 1996-; prin engr & sales mgr, Rockwell Int, 1984-1996; var positions, Rockwell Int, 1957-1984. **Memberships:** Fel Inst Elec Electronics Engrs. **Research Statement & Publications:** Electromechanical filters; awarded 14 US patents; author, co-author and series editor of numerous books. **Mailing Address:** Rockwell Int, Filter Prod 2990 Airway Ave, Costa Mesa, CA 92626.

JOHNSON, ROBERT ALAN, SOLID STATE PHYSICS, MATERIALS SCIENCE. **Personal Data:** b New York, NY, January 2, 1933; m 1954, Joyce; c 3. **Education:** Harvard Univ, BA, 1954; Rensselaer Polytech Inst, PhD (physics), 1962. **Professional Experience:** PROF EMER MAT SCI, UNIV VA, 2000-; prof mat sci, Univ Va, 1969-2000; scientist, Physics, Brookhaven Nat Lab, 1962-1969. **Memberships:** fel Am Phys Soc; Mat Res Soc; Sigma Xi. **Research Statement & Publications:** Theoretical study of interatomic forces, defects, surfaces and radiation damage in metals; Use is made of computer simulation techniques and computer solutions of kinetic equations. **Mailing Address:** Dept Mat Sci & Eng, Univ Va, Thornton Hall, Charlottesville, VA 22903. **Fax:** 434-982-5660. **E-Mail:** raj@virginia.edu

JOHNSON, ROBERT ANDREW, ANT ECOLOGY & BEHAVIOR, ENVIRONMENTAL ASSESSMENTS & THREATENED & ENDANGERED SPECIES. **Education:** Univ Ill, Champaign-Urbana, BS, 1978, MS, 1980; Ariz State Univ, Tempe, PhD (zoology), 1989. **Professional Experience:** Prin investr, Nat Geog Soc, 1993-1994; VOL, US FISH & WILDLIFE SERV, 1992-; ADJ FAC BOT, ARIZ STATE UNIV, 1991-; prin investr, Southwest Parks & Monument Asn, 1990-1991; CONTRACT ECOLOGIST, JOHNSON & ASSOCS, 1987-; contract ecologist, Mus Northern Ariz, 1980-1983. **Memberships:** Ecol Soc Am; Am Soc Naturalists; Soc Study Evolution; Asn Study Animal Behav. **Research Statement & Publications:** Community structure and distribution patterns of ants, especially as they relate to soil texture and interactions with other ants; ecology of rare cactus species. **Mailing Address:** Dept Plant Biol, Az State Univ Box 871601, Tempe, AZ 85287-1601. **E-Mail:** robert.johnson4@asu.edu

JOHNSON, ROBERT BRITTEN, GEOLOGY. **Personal Data:** b Cortland, NY, September 24, 1924; m 1947, Garnet Brown; c Robert Jr, Richard & Elizabeth. **Education:** Syracuse Univ, AB, 1949, MS, 1950; Univ Ill, PhD (geol), 1954. **Honors & Awards:** E B Burwell Jr Mem Award, Geol Soc Am, 1989; C B Holdredge Award, Asn Eng Geologists, 1990. **Professional Experience:** GEOLOGIST, ELDERHOSTEL FAC, 1991-; EMER PROF GEOL, COLO STATE UNIV, 1988-; head earth resources actg dept, Colo State Univ, 1979-1980; geologist, US Geol Surv, 1976-1988; mem comt A2L05, Transp Res Bd, 1975-1986; prof geol prog, Colo State Univ, 1973-1977; chmn dept geol, Colo State Univ, 1969-1973; prof geol, Colo State Univ, 1967-1988; prof geol & head dept geol & geog, DePauw Univ, 1966-1967; INDUST CONSULT, 1962-; from asst prof to prof geol, Purdue Univ, 1956-1966; sr geologist & geophysicist, C A Bays & Assocs, 1955-1956; lectr, Univ Ill, 1955-1956; asst prof geol & staff geologist, Syracuse Univ, 1954-1955; asst geologist, State Geol Surv, Ill, 1953-1954; asst, State Geol Surv, Ill, 1951-1953; asst, Syracuse Univ, 1947-1950; chmn comt A2L01, Transp Res Bd, 1976-1982; mem comt A2L01, Transp Res Bd. **Memberships:** Sr fel Geol Soc Am; Asn Eng Geologists; Int Asn Eng Geol. **Research Statement & Publications:** Engineering geology, especially landslides and geophysical and remote sensing applications. **Mailing Address:** Dept Earth Resources, Colo State Univ, Ft Collins, CO 80523. **Fax:** 970-491-6307. **E-Mail:** arby@picea.cnr.colostate.edu

JOHNSON, ROBERT CHANDLER, ANALYTICAL SCIENCE, GENERAL PHYSICS. **Personal Data:** b Detroit, Mich, October 19, 1930; m 1955, Mary J Wood; c Andrew, Douglas, Sarah & Michael. **Education:** Univ Mich, BS, 1952; State Univ Iowa, MA, 1957; Stanford Univ, PhD (physics), 1962. **Professional Experience:** LECTR, DEPT MATH, UNIV DURHAM, as of 2001; RES & DEVELOP MGR, CENT RES & DEVELOP DEPT, E I DU PONT Del NEMOURS & CO INC, 1993-; res supvr analytical sci, thermal analysis, 1978-1993; res physicist, thermal analysis, 1975-1978; res physicist, res & develop planning, 1973-1975; v is scientist, Am Inst Physics, 1972-1975; res physicist, E I du Pont Del Nemours & Co, Inc, 1962-1973. **Memberships:** Fel NAm Thermal Anal Soc (secy 1979-1981 & pres 1985-1986); Am Phys Soc; Am Chem Soc; Mat Res Soc. **Research Statement & Publications:** Magnetic field effects on triplet excitons; exciton physics of organic crystals; Kapitza resistance in liquid helium; low temperature physics; thermal analysis; x-ray synchrotron applications at Advanced Photon Source. **Mailing Address:** Dept Math Sci, Univ Durham, Sci Lab, S Rd, Durham, DH1 3LE, United Kingdom. **E-Mail:** bob.johnson@durham.ac.uk

JOHNSON, ROBERT E, PHYSICAL CHEMISTRY. **Personal Data:** b Los Angeles, Calif, March 23, 1945. **Education:** Johns Hopkins Univ, BS, 1967, MS, 1969, PhD (biochem), 1975. **Professional Experience:** RES SCIENTIST, G D SEARLE, 1988-; asst prof biochem, Chem Dept, Univ Ariz, 1980-1988; res chemist, Vet Hosp Kans City, 1977-1980; f el, Chem Dept, Univ Ariz, 1975-1977. **Memberships:** Am Chem Soc. **Mailing Address:** G D Searle & Co Rm P-320, 4901 Searle Pkwy, Skokie, IL 60077-1099.

JOHNSON, ROBERT ED, MEDICINAL CHEMISTRY. **Personal Data:** b Highland Park, Ill, November 14, 1942; m 1964, c 2. **Education:** Univ Wis, BS, 1964; Univ Minn, PhD (org chem), 1968. **Professional Experience:** RES CHEMIST, GROUP LEADER, SECT HEAD & ASSOC RES DIR MED CHEM, STERLING RES GROUP, 1968-. **Memberships:** Am Chem Soc; NY Acad Sci; AAAS. **Research Statement & Publications:** Synthesis of novel heterocyclic and aromatic compounds that may have useful medicinal properties. **Mailing Address:** Sterling Res Group, 270 Richard Way, Collegeville, PA 19426-0900.

JOHNSON, ROBERT EDWARD, PLANETARY SCIENCE. **Personal Data:** b Chicago, Ill, July 3, 1939; m 1970, c 2. **Education:** Colo Col, BA, 1961; Wesleyan Univ, MA, 1963; Univ Wis, Madison, PhD (physics), 1968. **Professional Experience:** JOHN LLOYD NEWCOMB PROF ENG PHYSICS & MAT SCI, 1991-; Bell Tel Lab, 1979-1989 & Uppsala Univ, 1985-1995; fac fel, Argonne Nat Lab, 1982; NSF & NASA grants prin investr, 1978-; vis scientist, Ctr Earth & Planetary Physics, Harvard Univ, 1977-1978; NATO fel, Univ Copenhagen, 1976; PROF ENG PHYSICS, UNIV VA, 1984-; from asst prof to assoc prof eng physics, Univ Va, 1971-1984; consult, Dept Physics, Denver Univ, 1970; asst prof physics, Southern Ill Univ, 1969-1971; res fel, Queen's Univ, Belfast, Ireland, 1968-1969. **Memberships:** Am Phys Soc; Am Geol Phys Union; Am Astron Soc. **Research Statement & Publications:** Atomic and molecular physics; problems of interest in the Jovian magnetosphere, and interaction of ionizing radiations with solids and surfaces. **Mailing Address:** Dept Mat Sci & Eng, Univ Va, PO Box 400745, Charlottesville, VA 22904-4745. **Fax:** 434-924-1353. **E-Mail:** rej@virginia.edu

JOHNSON, ROBERT F, TEXTILE ENGINEERING. **Personal Data:** b Crestwood, Ky, March 20, 1929; div, c 4. **Education:** Univ Ky, BS, 1951; Ga Inst Technol, MS, 1958; Swiss Fed Inst Technol, DSc(indust & eng chem), 1963. **Professional Experience:** RETIRED; prof textiles & clothing, dir Grad Studies, 1981-1985; prof textiles & clothing, Univ Minn, 1972-1992; consult, Phillips Petrol Co, 1969-1970; prof textile eng & dir, Chem Processes Lab, Textile Res Ctr, Tex Tech Univ, 1968-1972; res sect mgr, Phillips Petrol Co, 1966-1968; assoc prof textile eng, Ga Inst Technol, 1965-1966; res chemist, Dow Chem Co, 1958-1965. **Memberships:** Am Asn Textile Chem & Colorists; Am Chem Soc;

Brit Soc Dyers & Colourists; Am Coun Consumer Interests. **Research Statement & Publications:** Physical and chemical properties of textile materials; chemistry of dyes; characterization of fire hazards of clothing. **Mailing Address:** 1500 6 St S, Minneapolis, MN 55454.

JOHNSON, ROBERT GLENN, PALEOCLIMATOLOGY. **Personal Data:** b Green Mountain, Iowa, December 12, 1922; m 1949, Elizabeth; c 5. **Education:** Case Inst Technol, BS, 1947; Iowa State Col, PhD (physics), 1952. **Honors & Awards:** H W Sweatt Award, Honeywell Inc, 1968 & 1985. **Professional Experience:** RETIRED; staff scientist, Honeywell Sensors & Systs Develop Ctr, Bloomington, Minn, 1967-1990; sr res physicist, Honeywell Sensors & Systs Develop Ctr, Bloomington, Minn, 1955-1967; proj engr, Bendix Aviation Corp, 1952-1955; asst physics, Iowa State Univ, 1949-1952; adj prof, Dept Geol & Geophys, Univ Minn. **Memberships:** emer mem Inst Elec & Electronics Engrs; AAAS; Sigma Xi; Geol Soc Am, Am-Geophysical Union. **Research Statement & Publications:** paleoclimatology; gas discharge phenomena; ultraviolet light sensor technology; silicon microstructures. **Mailing Address:** 12814 March Circle, Minnetonka, MN 55305-2742.

JOHNSON, ROBERT GUDWIN, ORGANIC CHEMISTRY. **Personal Data:** b Milwaukee, Wis, November 23, 1927; m 1958, Virginia; c Greg, Mark, Ellen & Chris. **Education:** Marquette Univ, BS, 1949; Iowa State Col, PhD (chem), 1954. **Professional Experience:** RETIRED; chmn dept chem, Xavier Univ, Ohio, 1966-1975, 1984-1986; prof chem, Xavier Univ, Ohio, 1965-1993; vis prof, Purdue Univ, 1960, 1963; from inst to assoc prof, Xavier Univ, Ohio, 1954-1965; asst chem, Iowa State Col, 1949-1953. **Memberships:** Am Chem Soc. **Research Statement & Publications:** Hunsdiecker-Borodine reaction; oxygen-containing heterocycles; hypolipidemic agents; anti-cancer compounds; aromatic substitution. **Mailing Address:** 2106 Townhill Dr, Cincinnati, OH 45238-3219. **E-Mail:** rgudwinj@aol.com

JOHNSON, ROBERT H, DENTISTRY. **Personal Data:** b Montreal, Que, June 23, 1936; m 1970, Barbara. **Education:** McGill Univ, BS, 1958, DDS, 1962; Ind Univ, MSD, 1964; Univ Wash, cert periodontics, 1971; Am Bd Oral Med, dipl; FRCD(C). **Professional Experience:** DIR, UNDERGRAD PROG, UNIV WASH, as of 2003; vis prof, Oral Med, Univ Glasgow, 1991-1992; PROF PERIODONT, UNIV WASH SCH DENT, SEATTLE, 1981-; chmn div periodont, 1978-1981; from assoc prof to prof dent, Univ Western Ont, 1971-1980; asst prof dent & dir hosp dent serv, Med Ctr, Univ Ky, 1966-1969; chief oral diag clin, Montreal Gen Hosp, 1964-1966; asst prof dent, McGill Univ, 1964-1966. **Memberships:** Am Acad Periodont; fel Am Acad Oral Path. **Research Statement & Publications:** Chemotherapeutic plaque and inflammation control; maintenance dental implants; mechanical toothbrushes. **Mailing Address:** Health Sci Ctr, Univ Wash Sch Dent, PO Box 35744, Seattle, WA 98195-7444. **Fax:** 206-616-7478. **E-Mail:** rhjperio@u.washington.edu

JOHNSON, ROBERT L, ENGINEERING. **Personal Data:** b Winslow, Ariz, May 16, 1920. **Education:** Univ Calif, Berkeley, BS, 1941, MS, 1942. **Honors & Awards:** James H Wyld Mem Award, Am Rocket Soc. **Professional Experience:** RETIRED; corp vpres aerospace group exec, McDonnell Douglas Astronaut Co, 1980-1987; pres, McDonnell Douglas Astronaut Co, 1975-1980; corp vpres eng & res, McDonnell Douglas Corp, 1973-1975; asst secy army for res & develop, Dept Army, 1969-1973; from mem staff to vpres, Manned Orbiting Lab, Douglas Aircraft Co, 1946-1969; mem, Eng Adv Coun, Univ Calif. **Memberships:** Nat Acad Eng; fel Am Inst Aeronaut & Astronaut. **Mailing Address:** 30881 Greens E Dr, Laguna Niguel, CA 92677.

JOHNSON, ROBERT LEE, PHYSIOLOGY. **Personal Data:** b Dallas, Tex, April 28, 1926; m 1952, c 2. **Education:** Southern Methodist Univ, BS, 1947; Northwestern Univ, MD, 1951. **Honors & Awards:** Sci Accomplishment Award, Thoracic Soc, 1996. **Professional Experience:** Mem Heart Lung & Blood Inst Rev Comt, 1985-; prog chmn, Cardiopulmonary Coun, Am Heart Asn, 1979-1981 & chmn, 1985-1987; mem, Cardiovasc Develop Res Study Comt, 1981-1983; assoc ed, J Clin Invest, 1972-1977; PROF INTERNAL MED, SOUTHWESTERN MED CTR, UNIV TEX, DALLAS, 1969-; from instr to assoc prof, Southwestern Med Ctr, Univ Tex, Dallas, 1957-1969; res fel physiol, Grad Sch Med, Univ Pa, 1956-1957; res fel internal med, Southwestern Med Sch, Univ Tex, 1955-1956; intern, Cook Co Hosp, Chicago, 1951-1955. **Memberships:** Am Heart Asn; Am Asn Physicians; Am Fedn Clin Res; Am Thoracic Soc; Am Physiol Soc; Am Soc Clin Invest. **Research Statement & Publications:** Exercise physiology; adaptation to high altitude; control of capillary circulation and diffusing surface in the lung. **Mailing Address:** Univ Tex Southwestern Med Ctr, 5323 Harry Hines Blvd, Dallas, TX 75235-9034. **Fax:** 214-648-8027. **E-Mail:** rjohn2@mednet.swmed.edu

JOHNSON, ROBERT LEROY, MATHEMATICS. **Personal Data:** b Chicago, Ill, September 22, 1940; m 1963, c 2. **Education:** Augustana Col, Ill, AB, 1962; Univ Kans, MA, 1965, PhD (math), 1967. **Professional Experience:** PROF MATH, AUGUSTANA COL, ILL, 1980-; assoc prof, Augustana Col, Ill, 1972-1980; asst prof, Augustana Col, Ill, 1968-1972; Asst prof math, Iowa State Univ, 1967-1968. **Memberships:** Math Asn Am; Am Math Soc; Sigma Xi. **Research Statement & Publications:** Topological rings. **Mailing Address:** Dept Math, Augustana Col, Rock Island, IL 61201.

JOHNSON, ROBERT M, METALLURGICAL ENGINEERING. **Personal Data:** b Oklahoma City, Okla, March 28, 1939; m 1999, Gloria. **Education:** Univ Okla, BS, 1962, MMetEng, 1965, PhD (eng sci), 1967. **Professional Experience:** Assoc dean eng res, Grad Sch, 1995-1996; actg provost res & dean grad sch, Grad Sch, 1993-1994; assoc dean, Grad Sch, 1980-1993; PROF MECH ENG & MAT SCI, UNIV TEX, ARLINGTON, 1979-; sr scientist, Vought Corp Advan Technol Ctr, 1977-1978; assoc prof mat sci, Univ Tex, Arlington, 1971-1979; asst prof eng mech & mat sci, Univ Tex, Arlington, 1967-1971. **Memberships:** Am Soc Metals; Am Soc Eng Educ; Sigma Xi. **Research Statement & Publications:** Basic deformation processes in mechanical metallurgy; dislocation mechanisms; fracture mechanics; corrosion; superplasticity; granted one patent. **Mailing Address:** Mech Eng Dept, Univ Tex, 325 Woolf Hall Box 19031, Arlington, TX 76019. **Fax:** 817-272-2538. **E-Mail:** johnson@uta.edu

JOHNSON, ROBERT MICHAEL, BIOCHEMISTRY. **Personal Data:** b Brooklyn, NY, November 24, 1937; c 1. **Education:** Fordham Col, AB, 1961; Columbia Univ, PhD (biochem), 1970. **Professional Experience:** PROF BIOCHEM, MED SCH, WAYNE STATE UNIV, 1992-; vis prof, Int Cell Path, Bicetre, France, 1982; assoc prof, Med Sch, Wayne State Univ, 1979-1992; asst prof, Med Sch, Wayne State Univ, 1973-1979; instr, Med Sch, Wayne State Univ, 1972-1973; NIH fel, Cornell Univ, 1971-1972. **Memberships:** Sigma Xi; Am Heart Assoc; Am Soc Biol Chemists; Soc Rheology; AAAS; Am Soc Hemat. **Research Statement & Publications:** Biochemistry of biological membranes; protein structure, erythrocyte function. **Mailing Address:** Dept Biochem, Wayne State Univ Med Sch 540 E Canfield Rd, Detroit, MI 48201-1908. **Fax:** 313-577-2765.

JOHNSON, ROBERT OSCAR, APPLIED MATHEMATICS. **Personal Data:** b Detroit, Mich, May 7, 1926; m 1961, c 3. **Education:** Univ Mich, Ann Arbor, BS (eng) & BS (math), 1946, MS, 1949; Univ Ill, Urbana, MS, 1952; Ohio State Univ, PhD (math), 1975. **Professional Experience:** PROF COMPUT SCI, FROSTBURG STATE UNIV, 1990-; prof comput sci, Marshall Univ, 1986-1990; div chmn, Eng Technol, 1981-1985; prof engr, Data Control Ctr, Ohio State Hwy Dept, 1969-1975; prof math, Franklin Univ, 1968-1986; Teaching assoc, dept math, Ohio State Univ, 1964-1969; res specialist, Columbus Div, NAm Rockwell, Inc, 1964-1968; mgr advan design, Arde, Inc, 1962-1963; proposal mgr altitude control systs, Aerospace Div, Walter Kidde & Co, Inc, 1958-1962; admin engr, Teterboro Div, Bendix Corp, 1954-1958; procurement rep aircraft systs, Repub Aviation, Inc, 1952-1953; Sr engr, ITT Labs, 1950-1952. **Memberships:** Asn Comput Mach; Inst Elec & Electronics Engrs; Math Asn Am. **Research Statement & Publications:** Mathematical modeling. **Mailing Address:** PO Box 30011, Gahanna, OH 43230-0011. **E-Mail:** rjohnson@gcfn.org

JOHNSON, ROBERT R, COMPUTER SCIENCE. **Education:** Purdue Univ, PhD. **Professional Experience:** PROF RHETORIC, MICH TECH UNIV, as of 2006. **Mailing Address:** Mich Tech Univ, 1400 Townsend Dr, Houghton, MI 49931. **Fax:** 906-487-3213. **E-Mail:** rrjohnso@mtu.edu

JOHNSON, ROBERT REINER, ORGANIC CHEMISTRY. **Personal Data:** b Chicago, Ill, June 8, 1932; m 1967, c 1. **Education:** Brown Univ, ScB, 1954; Rice Univ, PhD (chem), 1958. **Professional Experience:** RETIRED; scientist, Brown & Williamson Tobacco Corp, 1967-1991; group leader, Brown & Williamson Tobacco Corp, 1959-1967; res assoc chem, Johns Hopkins Univ, 1958-1959. **Memberships:** Am Chem Soc. **Research Statement & Publications:** Physical organic chemistry and chemistry of natural products. **Mailing Address:** 503 Penwood Dr, Louisville, KY 40206-3031.

JOHNSON, ROBERT S, MATHEMATICS. **Personal Data:** b Pikeville, Ky, November 23, 1937. **Education:** Georgetown Col, BS, 1959; Univ NC, MA, 1962, PhD (ring theory), 1966. **Professional Experience:** CINCINNATI PROF MATH, WASH & LEE UNIV, as of 2005; prof math & head dept, Wash & Lee Univ, 1975-1983; from instr to assoc prof, 1965-1975. **Memberships:** Am Math Soc; Sigma Xi. **Research Statement & Publications:** Group theory and ring theory; conditions implying commutativity. **Mailing Address:** Dept Math, Wash & Lee Univ, Lexington, VA 24450. **Fax:** 540-458-8024.

JOHNSON, ROBERT SHEPARD, NUMERICAL ANALYSIS. **Personal Data:** b Wilkinsburg, Pa, November 24, 1928; m 1959, c 3. **Education:** Northwestern Univ, BS, 1950, MS, 1951; Univ Pa, PhD (math), 1959. **Professional Experience:** ENGR, RCA CORP, 1959-; res assoc, Inst Coop Res, Univ Pa, 1953-1959. **Memberships:** Am Math Soc; Soc Indust & Appl Math. **Research Statement & Publications:** Approximation theory; moments. **Mailing Address:** 2102 Brandeis Ave, Riverton, NJ 08077-3513.

JOHNSON, ROBERT WARD, MARINE SCIENCES, OPERATIONS RESEARCH. **Personal Data:** b Hampton, Va, December 19, 1929; m 1955, c 4. **Education:** Va Polytech Inst & State Univ, BS, 1950; Pa State Univ, MS, 1954; NC State Univ, PhD (marine sci), 1975. **Professional Experience:** RETIRED; res scientist marine sci, Langley Res Ctr, NASA, 1970-1990; res & develop engr, Langley Res Ctr, NASA, 1963-1970; design develop res engr, Carrier Corp, 1957-1963; E I du Pont de Nemours & Co, Inc, 1954-1957; develop engr, Philco Corp, 1952-1953. **Memberships:** Am Soc Photogram. **Research Statement & Publications:** Application of remote sensing (aircraft and satellite) techniques to monitor pollution sources and to study processes in marine ecosystems; atmospheric studies research. **Mailing Address:** 30 Orchard Ave, Hampton, VA 23661.

JOHNSON, ROBERT WILLIAM, JR, ORGANIC CHEMISTRY. **Personal Data:** b Jacksonville, Fla, October 9, 1927; m 1957, c 4. **Education:** Univ Fla, BS, 1953, PhD (org chem), 1959; Purdue Univ, MS, 1956. **Professional Experience:** CONSULT, 1993-; tech assoc, Process Chem Dept, 1986-1992; sr chemist, Process Chem Dept, 1973-1986; mgr, Chem Div, Prod Develop Dept, Union Camp Corp, 1967-1973; supt, Prod Develop Dept, 1965-1967; supt, Compound Develop Dept, Chem Div, Union Bag-Camp Paper Corp, 1962-1965; res chemist, Ethyl Corp, 1959-1962. **Memberships:** Am Chem Soc; Am Oil Chemists Soc; NY Acad Sci; fel Am Inst Chemists; Am Inst Chem Engrs. **Research Statement & Publications:** Tall oil; fatty acids; organic synthesis; organometallics; separation technology; instrumental methods of analysis; rosin and derivatives; hydrogenation. **Mailing Address:** 227 Groveland Circle, Savannah, GA 31405.

JOHNSON, RODNEY L, PEPTIDES, AMINO ACIDS. **Education:** Univ Kans, PhD (med chem), 1976. **Professional Experience:** Dir grad stud Med Chem, Univ Minn, Twin Cities, 1997-2002; PROF MED CHEM, UNIV MINN, TWIN CITIES, 1989-; assco prof med Chem, Univ Minn, 1981-1989. **Mailing Address:** Col Med Chem Res Pharm, Univ Minn, 308 Harvard St SE, Minneapolis, MN 55455. **Fax:** 612-624-0139. **E-Mail:** johns022@tc.umn.edu

JOHNSON, ROGER A, MECHANISMS OF HORMONE ACTION. **Personal Data:** b Geneva, Ill, February 4, 1943. **Education:** Iowa State Univ, BS, 1964; Univ Southern Calif, PhD (pharmacol), 1968. **Professional Experience:** PROF PHYSIOL & BIOPHYS, STATE UNIV NY, STONY BROOK, 1986-; VCHMN, DEPT PHYSIOL & BIOCHEM, STATE UNIV NY, STONY BROOK, 1986-; from instr to assoc prof physiol, Vanderbilt Univ Med Sch, 1970-1986; f el, Vanderbilt Univ Med Sch, 1968-1970. **Memberships:** Am Soc Biochem & Molecular Biol. **Mailing Address:** Dept Physiol & Biophys, Health Sci Ctr State Univ NY, Stony Brook, NY 11794-8661. **Fax:** 631-444-3432. **E-Mail:** rjohnson@ms.cc.sunysb.edu

JOHNSON, ROGER D, MATHEMATICS. **Personal Data:** b Richmond, Va, May 27, 1930; m 1955, c 3. **Education:** Dartmouth Col, BA, 1951; Univ Va, MA, 1953, PhD (math), 1956. **Professional Experience:** PROF EMER MATH, GA INST TECHNOL, as of 2005; assoc prof math, Ga Inst Technol, beginning 1961; asst prof, GA Inst Technol, 1956-1961; Instr math, Univ Va, 1955-1956. **Memberships:** Am Math Soc; Math Asn Am. **Research Statement & Publications:** Homology theory and its relationship to certain topics of general topology such as connectedness and dimension. **Mailing Address:** Dept Math, Ga Inst Technol, Atlanta, GA 30332-0001. **Fax:** 404-894-4409.

JOHNSON, ROGER W, MATHEMATICS. **Education:** Univ Calif, Phd, 1968. **Professional Experience:** CHAIR & ASSOC PROF, DEPT MATH & COMPUT SCI, SDAK SCH MINES & TECH, as of 2006. **Mailing Address:** Dept Math & Comput Sci SDak Sch Mines & Tech, 501 E St. Joseph St, Rapid City, SD 55057-4025. **Fax:** 605-394-6078. **E-Mail:** Roger.Johnson@sdsmt.edu

JOHNSON, ROGER W, VIROLOGY, CELL CULTURE. **Personal Data:** b Kalamazoo, Mich, May 4, 1929; m 1958, c Andrew & Paul. **Education:** Valparaiso Univ, BS, 1952; Univ Ky, MS, 1958, PhD (microbiol), 1963. **Professional Experience:** DIR OPERS, WHITTAKER BIOPROD, 1981-; head dept virus prod, Frederick Cancer Res Ctr, Nat Cancer Inst, 1972-1981; prin investr, Biol Defense Res Ctr, 1969-1972; Microbiologist,

Biol Labs, US Army, 1963-1969. **Memberships:** AAAS; Am Soc Microbiol; Sigma Xi. **Research Statement & Publications:** Parameters of seed stock development; scale up and production of oncogenic or suspected oncogenic viruses from tissue culture; large scale culture of mammalian cells. **Mailing Address:** 7003 Summerfield Dr Rte 7, Frederick, MD 21701.

JOHNSON, ROLLAND PAUL, Particle Accelerators, Experimental Particle Physics. **Personal Data:** b Stewartville, Minn, January 1, 1941; m 1990, Linda; c Jenifer & Russell. **Education:** Univ Calif, Berkeley, AB, 1964, PhD (physics), 1970. **Professional Experience:** Owner/scientist, Muons, Inc. 2002-; private consultant, 1997-2001; adv US Dept Energy, 1994-1996; sr staff scientist, Jefferson Lab, 1993-1996; sr accelerator physicist, Maxwell Labs, Brobeck Div, 1991-1992; adj prof, Ill Univ, 1990-1992; adj prof, Univ Houston, 1990-1991; mem, Univ Chicago Rev Comt, High Energy Physics Div, Argonne Nat Lab, 1984-1986; Europ Orgn Nuclear Res, Geneva, Switz, 1980-1981; physicist, Fermi Nat Accelerator Lab, 1974-1991; Vis scientist, Inst High Energy Physics, Serpukhov, USSR, 1972-1973; res assoc, Lawrence Berkeley Lab, Univ Calif, Berkeley, 1970-1974; Res asst physics, Lawrence Berkeley Lab, Univ Calif, Berkeley, 1967-1970. **Memberships:** Am Phys Soc. **Research Statement & Publications:** Particle accelerator design, construction, operation, and controls. Project Management. Experimental High Energy Physics Research. Teaching. **Mailing Address:** 45 Jonquil Lane, Newport News, VA 23606. **E-Mail:** roljohn@aol.com

JOHNSON, RONALD CARL, INORGANIC CHEMISTRY. **Personal Data:** b Milwaukee, Wis, September 5, 1935; m Susan; c Erica & Laura. **Education:** Lawrence Col, BS, 1957; Northwestern Univ, PhD (chem), 1961. **Professional Experience:** PROF EMER CHEM, EMORY UNIV, 2001-; assoc dean, Emory Univm, 1990-1992; prof chem, Emory Univ, 1973-2001; from asst prof to assoc prof, Emory Univ, 1961-1973. **Memberships:** AAAS; Am Chem Soc. **Research Statement & Publications:** Reactions of compounds of transition metals; mechanisms of reactions. **Mailing Address:** 702 Luckie Lane NE, Atlanta, GA 30329-4213. **E-Mail:** ronald.johnson@emory.edu

JOHNSON, RONALD ERNEST, PHYSICAL OCEANOGRAPHY. **Personal Data:** b Portland, Ore, October 14, 1939; m 1968, Roberta; c Robert R & Ronald R. **Education:** Ore State Univ, BS, 1962, MS, 1963, PhD (phys oceanog), 1972. **Professional Experience:** UNIV PROF OCEANOG, OLD DOMINION UNIV, as of 2004; ASSOC DIR GRAD STUDIES, OLD DOMINION UNIV, 1985-; assoc prof oceanog, Old Dominion Univ, beginning 1978; asst prof, Old Dominion Univ, 1968-1978; assoc sr engr, Lockheed-Calif Co, 1963-1964. **Memberships:** Sigma Xi; Am Geophys Union. **Research Statement & Publications:** Circulation and distribution of intermediate waters of the worlds oceans; waves and tides. **Mailing Address:** Dept Oceanog, Old Dominion Univ, Norfolk, VA 23529-0276. **Fax:** 757-683-5303. **E-Mail:** rejohnso@odu.edu

JOHNSON, RONALD GENE, RADIATION BIOPHYSICS, RADIOLOGICAL HEALTH. **Personal Data:** b Detroit, Mich, November 14, 1941; m 1964, c 2. **Education:** Eastern Mich Univ, AB, 1963; Univ Kans, MS, 1968, PhD (radiation biophys), 1970. **Professional Experience:** PRES, MALONE COL, as of 2002; exec vpres, Malone Col, beginning 1981; assoc prof clin radiation biophys radiol, Northeastern Ohio Univs Col Med, 1978-; prof Physics, Malone Col, beginning 1978; vis assoc prof radiation biophys, Univ Kans, 1976-1977; assoc prof, Malone Col, 1974-1978; consult, Med Physics Serv, Inc, 1973-; Radiation biologist, Aultman Hosp, 1973-; asst prof, Malone Col, 1970-1974; high sch teacher, Mich, 1964 & Ohio, 1964-1965. **Memberships:** Am Asn Physics Teachers; Sigma Xi. **Research Statement & Publications:** Effect of glucose on the sensitivity of Escherichia coli to Mitomycin C; radiation repair mechanisms; radiation-induced atrophy of bone; quality control in diagnostic radiology; effects of diagnostic x-rays during first trimester of pregnancy. **Mailing Address:** Malone Col, 515 NW 25th St, Canton, OH 44709.

JOHNSON, RONALD ROY, biochemistry, animal nutrition; deceased, see previous edition for last biography

JOHNSON, RONALD SANDERS, PHYSICAL BIOCHEMISTRY, INORGANIC BIOCHEMISTRY. **Personal Data:** b Chicago, Ill, March 9, 1952. **Education:** Northwestern Univ, BA, 1973, PhD (biochem & molecularbiol), 1978. **Professional Experience:** PROF BIOCHEM, SCH MED, E CAROLINA UNIV, 1994-; assoc prof biochem, Sch Med, E Carolina Univ, 1987-1994; asst prof biochem & phys biochem, Sch Med, E Carolina Univ, 1981-1987; fel, NIH & Miller Inst Basic Res Sci, Univ Calif, Berkeley, 1978-1981; instr biochem & res tech, Northwestern Univ, 1978. **Memberships:** Am Chem Soc; Sigma Xi; Am Soc Biol Chemists. **Research Statement & Publications:** Application of biophysical techniques to explore the mechanism of gene regulation in the bacterium E coli, encompassing protein-nucleic acid as well as protein-protein interactions. **Mailing Address:** Dept Biochem Sch Med, East Carolina Univ Rm 5W-37, Greenville, NC 27858. **E-Mail:** johnsonro@mail.ecu.edu

JOHNSON, ROSS BYRON, ENVIRONMENTAL GEOLOGY, FUELS GEOLOGY. **Personal Data:** b Ladd, Ill, June 4, 1919; m 1942. **Education:** Univ NMex, BS, 1946, MS, 1948. **Professional Experience:** CONSULT GEOLOGIST, 1974-; res geologist, US Geol Surv, 1962-1974; geologist, US Geol Surv, 1948-1962. **Memberships:** Fel Geol Soc Am; Sigma Xi. **Research Statement & Publications:** Formation of sand dunes, rock glaciers, joints, and faults and their effects on the environment and engineering structures; stratigraphic, structural, and igneous geology; geologic mapping and photo-geology; petroleum and coal resources of the Southern Rocky Mountains and adjacent high plains of Colorado and New Mexico. **Mailing Address:** 240 Quay St, Denver, CO 80226.

JOHNSON, ROSS GLENN, CELL BIOLOGY. **Personal Data:** b McKeesport, Pa, October 5, 1942; m 1964, c 2. **Education:** Augustana Col, Ill, BA, 1964; Iowa State Univ, MS, 1966, PhD (cell biol), 1968. **Professional Experience:** PROF GENETICS & CELL BIOL, UNIV MINN, ST PAUL, 1980-; assoc prof, Univ Minn-Minneapolis, 1976-1980; assoc prof zoology, Univ Minn, Minneapolis, 1973-1976; asst prof cytol & zoology, Univ Minn, St Paul, 1968-1973; NIH fel, Bush sabbatical fel. **Memberships:** AAAS; Am Soc Cell Biol. **Research Statement & Publications:** Involvement of cell junctions in cell communication; structure and function of cell organelles. **Mailing Address:** Dept Genetics, Cell Biol & Develop, Univ Minn, 321 Church St SE 6-160 Jackson Hall, Minneapolis, MN 55455. **Fax:** 612-624-0426. **E-Mail:** gaplab@tc.umn.edu

JOHNSON, ROY ALLEN, ORGANIC CHEMISTRY. **Personal Data:** b Bemidji, Minn, July 26, 1937; m 1963, c 2. **Education:** Univ Minn, BCh, 1959, PhD (org chem), 1965; Univ BC, MSc, 1961. **Professional Experience:** CONSULT, GEMIN X BIOTECHNOLOGIES INC, 1999-; chem forum lectr, 1990; vis scientist, Mass Inst Technol, 1982-1983; sr scientist, Upjohn Co, beginning 1965. **Memberships:** Am Chem Soc; AAAS; NY Acad Sci. **Research Statement & Publications:** Synthetic organic chemistry; prostaglandin chemistry; microbial oxidations; stereochemistry, phospholipid chemistry and superoxide chemistry. **Mailing Address:** Gemin X Biotechnologies Inc, 3576 Ave du Parc Ste 4310, Montreal, PQ H2X 2H7, Can. **Fax:** 514-281-1065.

JOHNSON, ROY ANDREW, MEASURE THEORY, REAL FUNCTIONS. **Personal Data:** b Oak Park, Ill, March 20, 1939; m 1967, Carole; c Jennifer & Mark. **Education:** St Olaf Col, BA, 1960; Univ Iowa, PhD (math), 1964. **Professional Experience:** PROF EMER MATH, WASH STATE UNIV, as of 2005; vis prof, Univ Lodz, Poland, 1985-1986; prof math, Wash State Univ, 1984-1998; from asst prof to assoc prof, Wash State Univ, 1966-1984; asst prof, Univ Col, Addis Ababa, 1965-1966; asst lectr math, Univ Lagos, 1964-1965. **Memberships:** Am Math Soc; Math Asn Am; Nat Coun Teachers Math. **Research Statement & Publications:** Products of Borel measures; extensions of the usual real topology. **Mailing Address:** Dept Math, Wash State Univ, PO Box 643113, Pullman, WA 99164-3113. **Fax:** 509-335-1188. **E-Mail:** johnson@math.wsu.edu

JOHNSON, ROY RAGNAR, PLASMA PHYSICS, SOLID STATE PHYSICS. **Personal Data:** b Chicago, Ill, January 23, 1932; m 1963, Martha; c Linnea M & Kaisa A. **Education:** Univ Minn, BSEE, 1954, MSEE, 1956, PhD (elec eng), 1959. **Honors & Awards:** Fellowship, American Physical Society, 1979. **Professional Experience:** CLASSIFICATION/RECORDS MGR, INERTIAL CONFINEMENT FUSION PROG, LAWRENCE LIVERMORE NAT LAB, 1994-; inertial confinement fusion prog ADC, Classification/records Mgr, Lawrence Livermore Nat Lab, 1992-1994; mem bd indust adv, Rose Hulman Inst Technol, 1982-; tech dir, KMS Fusion Inc, 1972-1991 & Innovation Assocs, 1991-1992; vis scientist, Royal Inst Technol, Sweden, 1963-1964; sr basic res scientist, Boeing Sci Res Lab, 1959-1972; lectr, Univ Wash, 1959-1960; asst solid state physics, Univ Minn, 1954-1956. **Memberships:** AAAS; fel Am Phys Soc; life Inst Elec & Electronics Engrs; NY Acad Sci; Plasma Sci Soc. **Research Statement & Publications:** Fluids physics; solids fluctuations; inertial confinement fusion. **Mailing Address:** Lawrence Livermore Nat Lab, 7000 E Ave, Livermore, CA 94550. **Fax:** 925-424-2495. **E-Mail:** johnson3@llnl.gov

JOHNSON, RUSSELL CLARENCE, MEDICAL MICROBIOLOGY. **Personal Data:** b Wausau, Wis, August 3, 1930; m 1955, Patricia; c 3. **Education:** Univ Wis, BS, 1957, MS, 1958, PhD (microbiol), 1960. **Honors & Awards:** Gold Medal Award, Slovak Med Soc, 1993. **Professional Experience:** PROF MICROBIOL, MED SCH, UNIV MINN, MINNEAPOLIS, 1974-; mem comn viral infections, Armed Forces Epidemiol Bd, 1970-1973; mem, Subcomt Taxon Leptospira & Subcomt Taxon Spirochaetales, Int Comt Syst Bact, 1969-1995; res grant, 1966-; USPHS spec fel, 1963-1965; from instr to assoc prof, Med Sch, Univ Minn, Minneapolis, 1962-1974; res microbiologist, Ft Detrick, Md, 1961-1962; Nat Acad Sci-Nat Res Coun res assoc, 1960-1961; res assoc microbiol, Univ Wis, 1960. **Memberships:** AAAS; Am Soc Microbiol; Soc Exp Biol & Med; Am Leptospirosis Res Conf; fel Am Acad Microbiol; fel Infectious Dis Soc Am. **Research Statement & Publications:** Biology of pathogenic spirochetes and ehrlichia. **Mailing Address:** Dept Microbiol, Univ Minn Med Sch, Minneapolis, MN 55455. **Fax:** 612-626-0623. **E-Mail:** johnson@lenti.med.umn.edu

JOHNSON, RUSSELL DEE, JR, OPERATIONS RESEARCH. **Personal Data:** b Granite City, Ill, December 10, 1928; m 1953, c 4. **Education:** Univ Rochester, BS, 1950; Univ Calif, PhD (phys chem), 1954. **Professional Experience:** SR SCIENTIST, OPERS RES, INC, 1962-; physicist, Opers Res, Inc, 1956-1962; c hemist, Dow Chem Co, Mich, 1953-1956. **Memberships:** Am Chem Soc; Sigma Xi. **Research Statement & Publications:** Weapons systems analysis; applied game theory. **Mailing Address:** 1902 Ventura Ave, Wheaton, MD 20902-2930.

JOHNSON, SAMUEL EDGAR, II, MARINE ECOLOGY. **Personal Data:** b San Jose, Calif, September 27, 1944; m 1970. **Education:** Stanford Univ, BS, 1966, PhD (biol), 1973. **Honors & Awards:** Arthur C Giese Award, Stanford Univ, 1973. **Professional Experience:** GRAD TEACHING ASST, COL HEALTH & HUMAN SCI, ORE STATE UNIV, as of 2003; dir planned giving, Ore Health Sci Univ Found, 1991-1993; dir spec projs, Ore Hist Soc, 1987-1989; exec dir, Nat Conservancy, 1981-1987; res assoc, New Eng Res Inc, beginning 1973-; asst prof zoolology, Clark Univ, 1973-1981; scholar biophys ecol, Dept Bot, Univ Mich, 1972-1973. **Memberships:** Am Soc Zoologists; Ecol Soc Am; Am Meteorol Soc; Sigma Xi; Int Biometeorol Soc. **Research Statement & Publications:** Biophysical ecology, microclimatology and biometeorology of the marine rocky intertidal region with emphasis on heat and mass transfer processes as they affect intertidal organisms, particularly amphipods and molluscs; estuarine ecology and coastal zone resource management. **Mailing Address:** Col Health & Human Sci, Ore State Univ, 024 Womens Bldg, Corvallis, OR 97331-6802. **Fax:** 541-737-6613. **E-Mail:** johnssam@onid.orst.edu

JOHNSON, SAMUEL Y, NEOTECHTRONICS. **Personal Data:** b San Diego, Calif, August 12, 1951. **Education:** Univ Calif, BS, 1976; Univ Wash, MS, 1978, PhD (geol sci), 1982. **Professional Experience:** CHIEF SCIENTIST, WESTERN REGION COASTAL & MARINE GEOL TEAM, US GEOL SURV, as of 2006; GEOLOGIST, CENT REGION, GEOL HAZARDS TEAM, US GEOL SURV, COLO, 1997-; asst prof, Wash State Univ, 1982-1984. **Memberships:** Geol Soc Am; Am Geophys Union; Soc Sedimentary Geol; Seismol Soc Am; Int Asn Sedimetologists; Am Asn Petrol Geologists. **Mailing Address:** Pacific Sci Ctr, US Geol Surv, 400 Natural Bridges Dr, Santa Cruz, CA 95060. **Fax:** 831-427-4709. **E-Mail:** sjohnson@usgs.gov

JOHNSON, SARAH DURSTON, COSMIC RAY PHYSICS, PROTON-ANTIPROTON COLLIDER PHYSICS. **Personal Data:** b Weymouth, Eng, October 21, 1964; American & British citizen; m 1993, Mark W; c Evan, Tristan. **Education:** State Univ NY, Albany, BS, 1986; Univ Rochester, MA, 1988, PhD (physics), 1993. **Professional Experience:** ASSOC PROF PHYSICS, UNIV LA VERNE, 1997-; asst prof physics, State Univ NY, Geneseo, 1995-1997; vis res assoc, Univ Rochester, 1994-1997; vis asst prof physics, Hobart & William Smith Col, 1994-1995; Postdoctoral res, Niels Bohr Inst, 1993-1994. **Memberships:** Am Asn Physics Teachers; Sigma Xi; Assoc Women Sci. **Research Statement & Publications:** Experimental particle physics. **Mailing Address:** Dept Math & Physics & Comput Sci, Univ La Verne, 1950 Third St, La Verne, CA 91750. **Fax:** 909-392-2709. **E-Mail:** johnsosa@ulv.edu

JOHNSON, SHIRLEY MAE, REPRODUCTIVE PHYSIOLOGY. **Personal Data:** b Ironwood, Mich, May 26, 1940; m 1975. **Education:** Northern Mich Col, BS, 1962; Mich State Univ, MS, 1965, PhD (physiol), 1970; Univ Mich, MPH, 1972. **Professional Experience:** Educ consult, Tri-County Family Planning Ctr, Lansing, Mich, beginning 1975-; PROF FAMILY & COMMUNITY MED, MICH STATE UNIV, 1972-; asst to vpres, Off Res Develop, 1971; res consult, Mich Cancer Found, 1970; lab technician, Endocrine Res Unit, 1965-1970; teacher pub sch, Grand Rapids, Mich, 1962-1963. **Memberships:** Am Pub Health Asn; Am Asn Sex Educr Counr & Therapists; Sigma Xi. **Research Statement & Publications:** Influence on health care of knowledge, attitudes, concerns and beliefs patients have toward reproductive physiology and family planning; contraceptive use and advertising. **Mailing Address:** Dept Family Med, Mich State Univ, B209 W Fee Hall, Lansing, MI 48824-1316. **Fax:** 517-353-6613. **E-Mail:** bordinat@msu.edu

JOHNSON, STANLEY HARRIS, AUTOMATIC CONTROL SYSTEMS. **Personal Data:** b Fresno, Calif, December 3, 1938; m 1965, c 1. **Education:** Univ Calif, Berkeley, BS,

1962, MS, 1967, PhD (mech eng), 1972. **Professional Experience:** PROF, DEPT MECH ENG & MECH, LEHIGH UNIV, 1979-; DuPont assoc prof, DuPont Univ Sci & Eng grant, 1978-1980; fac fel, Dryden Flight Res Ctr, 1974, 1975; from asst prof to assoc prof, Dept Mech Eng & Mech, Lehigh Univ, 1973-1979; sr engr comput control, Mobil Res & Develop Corp, 1967-1970; syst engr comput sales, Int Bus Mach Co, 1965-1967; design engr physics res, Lawrence Radiation Lab, 1961-1965. **Memberships:** Am Soc Mech Engrs; Am Asn Univ Prof. **Research Statement & Publications:** Numerical simulation of dynamical systems; development of the methodology of simulation; simulation validity and verification; numerical solution of partial differential equations; application of optimal control theory. **Mailing Address:** Dept Mech Eng & Mech, Lehigh Univ, Bethlehem, PA 18015. **Fax:** 610-758-6224. **E-Mail:** shj0@lehigh.edu

JOHNSON, STANLEY O(WEN), NUCLEAR ENGINEERING. **Personal Data:** b Bismarck, NDak, December 28, 1930; div, c 2. **Education:** Univ Colo, BS, 1953. **Professional Experience:** VPRES & DIR, ASPEN SECURITY ADV INC, 1985-; vpres, Rockwood Growth Fund Inc, 1985-1991; dir, ITI-Japan, Inc, 1981-1986; dir, Ene-Con, Inc, 1978-1981; pres, Intermountain Technol, Inc, 1973-1986; mgr, Aerojet Nuclear Co, 1971-1973; mgr, Idaho Nuclear Corp, 1969-1971; mgr, Spert Proj, 1968-1969; sect chief anal & data processing, Atomic Energy Div, Phillips Petrol Co, 1963-1968; group leader reactor safety & dynamics anal, Atomic Energy Div, Phillips Petrol Co, 1961-1963; supvr nuclear reactor kinetics, Bettis Atomic Power Lab, 1960-1961; scientist, Bettis Atomic Power Lab, 1954-1960; Student engr, Westinghouse Elec Corp, 1953-1954. **Memberships:** Fel Am Nuclear Soc; Nat Soc Prof Engrs. **Research Statement & Publications:** Nuclear reactor safety research; nuclear reactor dynamics; computer simulation of nuclear reactors. **Mailing Address:** 1312 Azalea Dr, Idaho Falls, ID 83404.

JOHNSON, STANLEY R, AGRICULTURAL ECONOMICS, ECONOMETRICS. **Personal Data:** b Burlington, Iowa, August 26, 1938; m 1993, Maureen; c Peter & Ben. **Education:** Western Ill Univ, BA, 1961; Tex Tech Univ, MS, 1962, Tex A&M Univ, PhD, 1966. **Honorary Degrees:** LHD, Western Ill Univ, 1988. **Honors & Awards:** Chancellor's Award, 1980; Int Hon Award, Off Int Coop & Develop, USDA, 1987; Wilton Park Int Serv Award, 1993. **Professional Experience:** VPROVOST UNIV EXTEN, IOWA STATE UNIV, 1996-; academician VI Lenin All-Union Acad Agr Sci, Ukraine, 1993; academician VI Lenin All-Union Acad Agr Sci, Moscow, Russ, 1991; chmn bd dirs, InstPolicy Reform, as of 1990; adminr, Iowa State Univ USSR All-Union Acad Agr Sci Exchange Agreement, 1988-1993; chmn bd, Midwest Agribus Trade Res & Info Ctr, 1987-; prof, Univ Mo, Columbia, 1985-; PROF ECON & DIR, CTR AGR & RURAL DEVELOP, IOWA STATE UNIV, AMES, 1985-; exec dir, Food & Agr Policy Res Inst, 1984-; vis prof econ, Univ Calif-Berkeley, 1981; vis prof econ, Univ Ga, 1975-1976; economist, Agr Can, Ottawa, 1975; chmn, Dept Econ, 1972-1974; vis assoc prof agr econ, Purdue Univ, 1971-1972; vis assoc prof agr econ, Univ Calif-Davis, 1970; from assoc prof to prof econ & agr econ, 1967-1985; assoc prof agr econ, Univ Conn, Storrs, 1966-1967; asst prof econ, 1964-1966. **Memberships:** Fel Am Agr Econ Asn. **Research Statement & Publications:** Policy issues in agriculture and rural development; published extensively in economic theory, econometrics, consumer demand, and agricultural price, trade, and policy analysis. **Mailing Address:** Iowa State Univ, 2150 Beardshear Hall, Ames, IA 50011-2046. **Fax:** 515-294-4715. **E-Mail:** srjohnso@iastate.edu

JOHNSON, STEPHEN ALLEN, COMBUSTION RESEARCH & DEVELOPMENT. **Personal Data:** b Worcester, Mass, April 26, 1948; m 1970, c 2. **Education:** Worcester Polytech Inst, BS, 1970. **Professional Experience:** VPRES, APPL COMBUSTION TECHNOLS, PHYS SCI INC, 1990-; area mgr, Appl Combustion Technols, Phys Sci Inc, 1983-1990; prog mgr, Sci Applns, Inc, 1981-1983; group supvr, Babcock & Wilcox Co, 1976-1981; sr res engr, Riley Stoker Corp, 1971-1976; res & develop, E F Laurence Mfg Co, 1970-1971. **Memberships:** Am Inst Chem Engrs; Combustion Inst. **Research Statement & Publications:** Developed advanced combustion processes to achieve 80 percent reduction; exploring mineral matter transformations in flames to predict and control ash deposition problems in large furnaces; developing processes to control emissions in coal-fueled diesel and gas turbine engines and waste incinerators; effects of fuels on equipment operation; development of technologies to control emission of nitrogen oxides; sulfur dioxide and airbone toxic. **Mailing Address:** 20 New EngBus Ctr, Andover, MA 01810.

JOHNSON, STEPHEN D, COMPUTER SCIENCE. **Education:** Ind Univ, PhD (Comput Sci), 1983. **Professional Experience:** PROF, COMPUT SCI DEPT, IND UNIV, as of 2004. **Mailing Address:** Ind Univ, 215 Lindley Hall, Bloomington, IN 47405-4101. **Fax:** 812-855-4829. **E-Mail:** sjohnson@cs.indiana.edu

JOHNSON, STEPHEN THOMAS, WEARABLE COMPUTING, MODEL BASED DEFINITION & ASSEMBLY. **Personal Data:** b Washington, DC, May 31, 1954; m 1983. **Education:** Northeastern Univ, BMET, 1978. **Professional Experience:** BOEING, Scientist/Engineer, 1992-; sr tool designer, Sikorsky Aircraft Co, United Technologies, 1981-1992; propulsion engr, 1981; tool designer, Boeing Aircraft Co. 1978-1981; tech aide, US Army Natick Res & Develop, 1975-1978; Draftsman, Hollingsworth & Vose, 1973-1974. **Research Statement & Publications:** Advanced Manufacturing Concepts for Aerospace Assembly. **Mailing Address:** 13713 SE 237th Pl, Kent, WA 98042. **E-Mail:** stephen.t.johnson@boeing.com

JOHNSON, SUSAN BISSEN, FATTY ACIDS. **Personal Data:** b Austin, Minn, July 20, 1951; m 1977. **Education:** Mankato State Univ, BS, 1973. **Professional Experience:** RES TECHNOLOGIST, MAYO CLIN, ROCHESTER, MINN, 1991-; scientist, Hormel Inst, Univ Minn, 1985-1991; consult, Travenol Lab, 1984-1985; from asst to assoc, Hormel Inst, Univ Minn, 1977-1985; jr scientist, Hormel Inst, Univ Minn, 1973-1977. **Memberships:** Am Soc Clin Pathologists. **Research Statement & Publications:** Study and measurement of electrophysiologic properties of the heart; metabolism of fatty acids in normal and disease conditions. **Mailing Address:** Mayo Clin, St Mary's Hosp, 1216 Second St SW Mary Brigh-2 Surgical Servs, Rochester, MN 55905.

JOHNSON, SUSAN E, CELL BIOLOGY, BONE BIOLOGY. **Personal Data:** b White Plains, NY, July 16, 1953. **Education:** State Univ NY, Albany, BS, 1978, MS, 1984, PhD (molecular biol), 1989. **Professional Experience:** ASSOC RES FEL, RHONE-POULENC RORER, 1995-; sr res scientist, Rhone-poulenc Rorer, 1992-1995; Am Heart & Lung fel, Wistar Inst, 1989-1992; NIH fel, State Univ NY, Albany, 1989. **Memberships:** AAAS; Am Soc Cell Biol; Sigma Xi; Am Soc Bone & Min Res; Fed Am Soc Exper Biol. **Research Statement & Publications:** Osteoblast differentiation. **Mailing Address:** Rhone-Poulenc Rorer Inc, N-W 15 500 Arcola Rd PO Box 1200, Collegeville, PA 19426-0107. **Fax:** 610-454-3340. **E-Mail:** johnsse@rpr.rpna.com

JOHNSON, SYLVIA MARIAN, SYNTHESIS & PROCESSING, CHARACTERIZATION. **Personal Data:** b Sydney, Australia, August 29, 1954; m 1985, c 2. **Education:** Univ New South Wales, BS Hons, 1977; Univ Calif, Berkeley, MS, 1979, PhD (Engineering & Materials Science), 1983. **Professional Experience:** Branch Chief, Thermal Protection Materials and Systems Branch, NASA Ames Research Center, 2000 to date; Program Manager, Ceramics, SRI Int, 1988-2000; Senior Materials Scientist, SRI Int, 1986-1988; Materials Scientist, SRI Int, 1982-1986. **Memberships:** Am Ceramic Society. **Research Statement & Publications:** Thermal Protection materials, Ultra High Temperature Ceramics; Synthesis of oxide and non-oxide ceramic powders; Processing of ceramics; Characterization and evaluation of structural ceramics; Joining of ceramics. **Mailing Address:** Thermal Protection Mat & Syst Br, M/S 234-1, Ames Res Ctr, NASA, Moffett Field, CA 94035. **E-Mail:** sylvia.m.johnson@nasa.gov

JOHNSON, TERRELL KENT, GENETICS, INSECT CELL CULTURE. **Personal Data:** b Inglewood, Calif, November 23, 1947; m 1980, Barbara; c Alexandra. **Education:** Univ Calif, San Diego, BA, 1970; Calif State Univ, Northridge, MS, 1972; Univ Tex, Austin, PhD (zoology), 1976. **Professional Experience:** SR CHEMIST, SIGMA CHEM CO, 1992-; chemist, Sigma Chem CO, 1989-1992; res assoc, Kans State Univ, 1979-1989; USPHS trainee, Kans State Univ, 1977-1979; res fel genetics, Calif Inst Technol, 1976-1977. **Memberships:** Genetics Soc Am; Soc Develop Biol; Sigma Xi; Tissue Cult Asn. **Research Statement & Publications:** Media development for insect cell; development of toxicology assays. **Mailing Address:** Tissue Cult, Sigma Chem Co, PO Box 14508, St Louis, MO 63178. **E-Mail:** tjohnson@sial.com

JOHNSON, TERRY R(OBERT), NUCLEAR FUEL CYCLE. **Personal Data:** b Chicago, Ill, November 16, 1932; m Janet; c Kenneth, Martin, Karen & Jennifer. **Education:** Rice Univ, BA, 1954, BS, 1955; Univ Mich, MS, 1956, PhD (chem eng), 1959. **Professional Experience:** RETIRED; sr engr, Argonne Nat Lab, 1985-1995; chem engr, Argonne Nat Lab, 1975-1985; sr process engr, Aglomet Inc, 1974-1975; vis prof, Iowa State Univ, 1970; assoc chem engr, Argonne Nat Lab, 1958-1974. **Memberships:** Am Inst Chem Engrs; Am Nuclear Soc; Sigma Xi. **Research Statement & Publications:** Radiation chemistry of aqueous systems; nuclear fuel recovery; chemistry of liquid metals and salts; nuclear wastes. **Mailing Address:** 1424 S Main St, Wheaton, IL 60187-6482. **E-Mail:** janetry@aol.com

JOHNSON, TERRY WALTER, JR, MYCOLOGY. **Personal Data:** b Waukegan, Ill, January 13, 1923; m 1948, c 3. **Education:** Univ Ill, BS, 1948; Univ Mich, MS, 1949, PhD (bot), 1951. **Professional Experience:** ED-IN-CHIEF, MYCOLOGIA, 1981-; chmn dept, Duke Univ, 1963-1971; mem systs panel, NSF, 1963-1966; Guggenheim fel, 1960-1961; from asst prof to prof bot, Duke Univ, 1954-1985; asst prof biol, Univ Miss, 1953-1954; mycologist, Chem Corps Biol Labs, Camp Detrick, 1951-1953; instr bot, Univ Mich, 1950-1951. **Memberships:** Bot Soc Am; Mycol Soc Am; Brit Mycol Soc. **Research Statement & Publications:** Aquatic phycomycetes; Mycetozoa; marine fungi. **Mailing Address:** 3505 Manford Dr, Durham, NC 27707.

JOHNSON, THEODORE REYNOLD, AGING, CANCER BIOLOGY. **Personal Data:** b Willmar, Minn, March 20, 1946; m 1970, Michelle Flaherty; c Carrie, Eric & Daniel. **Education:** Augsburg Col, BA, 1968; Univ Ill Med Ctr, MS, 1970, PhD (microbiol), 1973. **Professional Experience:** Mayo Clin, 1992; vis scientist Oak Ridge Nat Lab, 1991; vis scientist, Trudeau Inst, 1983-1984; CONSULT, DONALDSON CORP, 1980-; consult, St Joseph's Hosp, 1974-1977; PROF BIOL, ST OLAF COL, 1977-; asst prof biol, Mankato State Univ, 1972-1977; res asst microbiol, Rush-Presby St Lukes Hosp, 1968-1972. **Memberships:** Am Soc Microbiol; AAAS; Sigma Xi. **Research Statement & Publications:** Biodegradation of toxic wastes and in soil; cancer and immune systems of hibernating animals; aging and cancer immunity; soil microbiology; resistance to disinfectants. **Mailing Address:** Dept Biol, St Olaf Col, Northfield, MN 55057. **Fax:** 507-646-3104. **E-Mail:** johnsont@stolaf.edu

JOHNSON, THOMAS, QUALITY CONTROL, ECONOMETRICS. **Personal Data:** b Halletsville, Tex, February 12, 1936; m 1956, Cleta; c David, Michael & Mark. **Education:** Univ Tex, Austin, BA, 1957; Tex Christian Univ, MA, 1962; NC State Univ, MES, 1967, PhD (economet & statist), 1969. **Professional Experience:** PROF ECON & STATIST, NC STATE UNIV, 1978-; assoc prof, NC State Univ, 1974-1978; assoc prof, Southern Methodist Univ, Dallas, Tex, 1974; asst prof econ & statist, Southern Methodist Univ, Dallas, Tex, 1969-1974; oper analyst, Res Triangle Inst, 1964-1969; eng specialist, LTV-Vought Aeronaut Div, Dallas, Tex, 1961-1964; nuclear engr, Convair, Fortworth, Tex, 1957-1961. **Memberships:** Am Statist Asn; Am Soc Qual Control; Am Agr Econ Asn. **Research Statement & Publications:** Statistics and mathematics applications to management and economic issues; analysis of dynamics of social and biological systems; resource economics; data analysis. **Mailing Address:** Dept Agr & Resource Econ, NC State Univ Box 8109, Raleigh, NC 27695. **Fax:** 919-515-1824. **E-Mail:** tom_johnson@ncsu.edu

JOHNSON, THOMAS CHARLES, LIMNOLOGY, GEOLOGICAL PROCESSES IN LARGE LAKES. **Personal Data:** b Virginia, Minn, August 15, 1944; m 1990, Katherine Taylor Whittaker; c Heidi Lena & Ryan Kent. **Education:** Univ Wash, BS, 1967; Scripps Inst Oceanog, PhD (oceanog), 1975. **Professional Experience:** PROF GEOL SCI, UNIV MINN, as of 1998; PROF & DIR, LARGE LAKES OBSERV, UNIV MINN, 1994-; fulbright scholar, France, 1993-1994; from assoc prof to prof, Duke Univ, 1983-1994; dir, NC Oceanog Consortium, 1983-1994; from asst prof to assoc prof, Univ Minn, 1975-1983. **Memberships:** Fel Geol Soc Am; AAAS; Am Soc Limnol & Oceanog; Am Geophys Union; Soc Int Limnol. **Research Statement & Publications:** Paleoclimate and sedimentological research on large lakes of the world, including North America, East Africa, Central America, and Central Asia. **Mailing Address:** Large Lakes Observ, Univ Minn, 207, Res Lab Bldg, 2205 E 5th St, Duluth, MN 55812. **Fax:** 218-726-6979. **E-Mail:** tcj@d.umn.edu

JOHNSON, THOMAS EUGENE, GENETICS OF AGING, GENETICS OF ALCOHOL ABUSE. **Personal Data:** b Denver, Colo, June 19, 1948; m 1982, Victoria Simpson; c Katherine E, P Andrew & Ariel R. **Education:** Mass Inst Technol, BS, 1970; Univ Wash, PhD (genetics), 1975. **Honors & Awards:** Ewald Busse Award for Biomed Geront, 1993; Nathan Shock Award, 1995- 1998 Senior fel Ellison Biolmedical found. **Professional Experience:** PROF, UNIV COLO, BOULDER, 1996-; assoc prof, Inst Behav Genetics, 1988-1996; asst prof, Dept Molecular Biol & Biochem, Univ Calif, 1982-1988; fel molecular, cellular & develop biol, 1977-1982; Fel genetics, Cornell Univ, 1975-1977. **Memberships:** Genetics Soc Am; AAAS; fel Geront Soc Am; Am Aging Asn; Am Fedn Aging Res; Res Soc Alcoholism. **Research Statement & Publications:** Genetics of aging in the nematode; genetics of alcohol sensitivity in the mouse. **Mailing Address:** Lab Molecular Genetic Inst Behav Genetics, Box 447, Univ Colo, Boulder, CO 80309-0447. **Fax:** 303-492-8063. **E-Mail:** johnsont@ibg.colorado.edu

JOHNSON, THOMAS F, SPORTS MEDICINE. **Personal Data:** b Philadelphia, Pa, March 10, 1917. **Education:** Springfield Col, BS, 1940; NY Univ, MA, 1946; Univ Md, PhD (phys educ), 1967. **Professional Experience:** RETIRED; assoc Dean, Grad Sch, Howard Univ, 1974-1978. **Memberships:** Am Physiol Soc. **Mailing Address:** 130 Ingraham St NW, Washington, DC 20011-6618.

JOHNSON, THOMAS RAYMOND, CELL BIOLOGY. **Personal Data:** b Washington, DC, July 8, 1944; m 1973, Candice E Brown; c 2. **Education:** Harvard Univ, BA, 1966; Case

Western Reserve Univ, PhD (biol), 1971. **Professional Experience:** ADJ INSTR ANAT, CASE WESTERN RESERVE UNIV, as of 1993; SR RES ASSOC, CASE WESTERN RESERVE UNIV, 1973-; i nstr, Univ Ill, Chicago Med Ctr, 1971-1973. **Memberships:** AAAS. **Research Statement & Publications:** Expression of insulin gene family; relationship of insulin-like growth factors to cancer. **Mailing Address:** 3062 Huntington, Shaker Heights, OH 44120. **Fax:** 216-368-1357.

JOHNSON, THYS B(RENTWOOD), MINING ENGINEERING, OPERATIONS RESEARCH. **Personal Data:** b Duluth, Minn, March 20, 1934; m 1958, c 3. **Education:** Univ Minn-Minneapolis, BS, 1956, MS, 1958; Univ Calif, Berkeley, PhD (opers res), 1968. **Professional Experience:** PROF EMER, DEPT INDUST ENG, UNIV MINN, DULUTH, as of 2003; dir appl res, nat resources res inst & prof indust eng, Univ Minn, Duluth, beginning 1985; head dept, Colo Sch Mines, 1974-1985; prof mining eng, Colo Sch Mines, 1972-; supvry opers res analyst, US Bur Mines, 1969-1972; supvry mining engr, US Bur Mines, 1968-1969; mining engr, US Bur Mines, 1968; mining methods res engr, US Bur Mines, 1964-1968; mathematician, Minn Ore Opers, US Steel Corp, 1961-1964; m ining engr, Minn Ore Opers, US Steel Corp, 1958-1961. **Memberships:** Opers Res Soc Am; Am Inst Mining Metall & Petrol Engrs. **Research Statement & Publications:** Research and development of operations research techniques as applied to problems of the mineral industry; developed mathematical and dynamic programming techniques for open pit mine planning and production scheduling. **Mailing Address:** Dept Indust Eng, Univ MN, Voss-Kovach Hall, Rm 105, 10 Univ Dr, Duluth, MN 55811 -2496. **Fax:** 218-726-8596. **E-Mail:** ie@d.umn.edu

JOHNSON, TIMOTHY A, CARDIOLOGY. **Education:** ILL State Univ, BS; Chicago State Univ, MS; Univ NC, PhD (biomed eng). **Professional Experience:** PROF INTERNAL MED, DEPT BIOMED ENG, UNIV NC, as of 2006. **Mailing Address:** Univ NC, 151-B MacNider Hall, Chapel Hill, NC 27599-7075. **E-Mail:** tjohnson@bme.unc.edu

JOHNSON, TIMOTHY JAY, FOURIER TRANSFORM INFRARED SPECTROSCOPY. **Personal Data:** b Minneapolis, Minn, March 25, 1959; m 1997. **Education:** Carleton Col, BA, 1981; WashState Univ, PhD (chem physics), 1987. **Professional Experience:** SR RES & DEVELOP SCIENTIST, BRUKER OPTICS, 1996-; l ectr instrumental chem, York Univ, 1994-1996; sr res assoc, York Univ, Toronto, 1993-1996; applns scientist, Bruker Optics, 1992-1993; staff scientist, Max-Planck Inst, Ger, 1990-1992; Fel, Max-Planck Inst, Ger, 1988-1990. **Memberships:** Am Phys Soc; Am Geophys Union; Am Radio Relay League; Optical Soc Am; Am Inst Chemists. **Research Statement & Publications:** Fundamental physical properties of gas phase species, particularly those of atmospheric importance; more accurate and sensitive ways to measure such species. **Mailing Address:** Bruker Optics, 19 Fortune Dr, Billerica, MA 01821-3923.

JOHNSON, TIMOTHY JOHN ALBERT, MEMBRANE BIOCHEMISTRY. **Education:** Univ Wis, PhD (biochem), 1974. **Professional Experience:** OWNER, SCIENCE FOR KIDS, 1992-; a sst prof, Colo State Univ, 1979-1992. **Research Statement & Publications:** Gluteraldehyde fixations; collidal gold labbing of membrane proteins. **Mailing Address:** 1337 Stonehenge Dr, Ft Collins, CO 80525.

JOHNSON, TIMOTHY WALTER, PHYSICAL CHEMISTRY & POLYMER CHEMISTRY. **Personal Data:** b Hartford, Conn, September 17, 1941; m 1966, Linda; c Anne & Loretta. **Education:** Trinity Col, BS, 1963, MS, 1965; Purdue Univ, PhD, 1970. **Professional Experience:** SR SCIENTIST, AKRO FIREGUARD, 2000-as of today; res assoc, Phillips Petroleum Co, 1981-1999; res chemist, Phillips Petroleum Co, 1973-1981; res assoc, Northwestern Univ, 1969-1973. **Memberships:** AAAS; SAMPE; Am Chem Soc. **Research Statement & Publications:** Physical chemistry of polymer solutions; polymer rheology; electrical properties of polymers; electrically conductive polymers; polymer morphology; polymer properties; polymer composites; surface science; adhesion; size exclusion chromatography. **Mailing Address:** Akro Fireguard, 9001 Rosehill Rd, Lenexa, KS 66215. **Fax:** 913-888-7372. **E-Mail:** twjohns@ionet.net

JOHNSON, TOM MILROY, INTERNAL MEDICINE. **Personal Data:** b Northville, Mich, January 16, 1935; m 1959, c 2. **Education:** Col Wooster, BA, 1956; Northwestern Univ, Ill, MD, 1961. **Professional Experience:** RETIRED; prof emer internal med, Mich State Univ, 1998-1999; chief exec officer, Kalamazoo Ctr Med Studies, Mich, 1994-1998; prof med & assoc dean, Sch Med, Mich State Univ, 1988-1998; prof internal med & dean, Sch Med, Univ N Dak, 1977-1988; assoc prof med, Col Human Med, Mich State Univ, 1971-1977, asst dean, Grand Rapids Campus, Univ Mich, 1971-1977; asst prof med, Mich State Univ, 1968-1971; Am Thoracic Soc fel pulmonary dis, Med Ctr, Univ Mich, 1967-1968. **Memberships:** Am Thoracic Soc; fel Am Col Physicians; Am Col Chest Physicians. **Research Statement & Publications:** Relationship of community and university medical education; pulmonary disease. **Mailing Address:** 1804 Highland Nist Lane, San Antonio, TX 78251-3105.

JOHNSON, TORRENCE VAINO, PLANETARY SCIENCES, ASTRONOMY. **Personal Data:** b Rockville Centre, NY, December 1, 1944; m 1967, c 2. **Education:** Wash Univ, BS, 1966; Calif Inst Technol, PhD (planetary sci), 1970. **Honorary Degrees:** Dr, Univ Padua, Italy, 1997. **Honors & Awards:** Sci Achievement Medal, NASA, 1980 & 1981; fel, Am Geophys Union. **Professional Experience:** Pres, Planetology Sect, Am Geophys Union, 1990-1992; SR RES SCIENTIST, JET PROPULSION LAB, CALIF INST TECHNOL, 1981-; vis assoc prof planetary sci, Calif Inst Technol, 1981-1983; res scientist, Optical Astron Group, 1980-1981; MEM, VOYAGER IMAGING SCI TEAM, 1978-; SCIENTIST, PROJ GALILEO, NASA, 1977-; group supvr, Optical Astron Group, 1974-1985; mem, Outer Planets Probe Working Group, 1974-1976; mem, Uranus Sci Adv Comt, NASA, 1973-1975; sr scientist, Calif Inst Technol, 1973-1974; resident res assoc planetology, Nat Res Coun Calif Inst Technol, 1971-1973; mem res staff planetary astron, Planetary Astron Lab, Mass Inst Technol, 1969-1971. **Memberships:** Sigma Xi; AAAS; Am Astron Soc (secy-treas, 1977); Int Astron Union; Am Geophys Union. **Research Statement & Publications:** Telescopic observations of planetary surfaces and atmospheres; laboratory studies of silicates and ices; interpretation of planetary spacecraft data. **Mailing Address:** Jet Propulsion Lab, 4800 Oak Grove Dr 183-501, Pasadena, CA 91109. **Fax:** 818-354-6256. **E-Mail:** tjohnson@jpltvj.jpl.nasa.gov

JOHNSON, VERN RAY, EDUCATIONAL ADMINISTRATION, SOCIAL TECHNOLOGY. **Personal Data:** b Salt Lake City, Utah, February 25, 1937; m 1959, Gladys; c Bradley, Brenda June Ciminski, Steven & Sherrie June Suedberg. **Education:** Univ Utah, BS, 1960, PhD (elec eng, physics), 1965. **Honors & Awards:** Meritorius Service Award, Inst Elec & Electronics Engrs-EAB, 1991; Arizona Governor's Quality Award Excellence, 1994, 1995; Millennium Medal, Inst Elec & Electronics Engrs, 2000. **Professional Experience:** ASSOC DEAN, COL ENG & MINES, UNIV ARIZ, 1979-; assoc prof elec eng, Col Eng & Mines, Univ Ariz, 1967-1979; res engr, Microwave Electronics Div, Teledyne Inc, 1964-1967; res asst, Microwave Devices Lab, Utah, 1960-1964. **Memberships:** Inst Elec & Electronics Engrs; Am Soc Eng Educ. **Research Statement & Publications:** Microwave acoustic amplification; photoelastic interactions in solid materials; surface wave acoustics; engineering manpower system simulation and demand projections; communication; application of engineering techniques to social problems; total quality management; engineering design; educational assessment, learning. **Mailing Address:** Col Eng & Mines, Univ Ariz, 200 Eng Bldg, Tucson, AZ 85721. **Fax:** 520-621-9995. **E-Mail:** vjohnson@arizona.edu

JOHNSON, VERNER CARL, ENVIRONMENTAL GEOLOGY, EXPLORATION GEOPHYSICS. **Personal Data:** b Chicago, Ill, September 14, 1943; c Richard & Seyha. **Education:** Southern Ill Univ, BS, 1967, MS, 1970; Univ Tenn, PhD (geol), 1975. **Professional Experience:** PROF GEOL, MESA STATE COL, GRAND JCT, COLO, as of 2003; assoc prof, Mesa State Col, Grand Jct, Colo, beginning 1984; asst prof, Mesa State Col, Grand Jct, Colo, 1977-1984; geologist, Bendix Field Eng Corp, 1977-1983; asst prof, Mesa Col, 1976-1977; proj geophysicist, Gulf Res & Develop Corp, 1974-1976; instr, Calif State Univ, 1972-1974. **Memberships:** Am Asn Petrol Geologists; Am Geophys Union; Geol Soc Am; Soc Explor Geophysicists; Nat Ground Water Asn; Comput Oriented Geol Soc. **Research Statement & Publications:** Application of geophysical methods in ground water. **Mailing Address:** Dept Geol, Mesa State Col, Wubben 237 1100 N Ave, Grand Junction, CO 81501. **Fax:** 970-248-1131. **E-Mail:** vjohnson@mesastate.edu

JOHNSON, VINCENT ARNOLD, ZOOLOGY, PHYSIOLOGY. **Personal Data:** b York, Nebr, January 5, 1928; m 1953, Lucille; c Krista E, Cydna R & Curtis J. **Education:** Univ Nebr, BSc, 1952, MSc, 1955, PhD (zool, physiol), 1964. **Professional Experience:** PROF EMER BIOL, ST CLOUD STATE UNIV, as of 2002; prof biol, St Cloud State Univ, beginning 1972; from asst prof to assoc prof, St Cloud State Univ, 1967-1972; asst prof, Augustana Col, Ill, 1964-1967; spec instr biol, Univ Tex, 1957-1961. **Memberships:** Am Soc Zool; Soc Protozoologists; AAAS; Sigma Xi. **Research Statement & Publications:** Cellular growth and metabolism. **Mailing Address:** Dept Biol Sci, St Cloud State Univ, 720 Fourth Ave S, St Cloud, MN 56301-4498.

JOHNSON, VIRGIL ALLEN, agronomy; deceased, see previous edition for last biography

JOHNSON, W REED, NUCLEAR ENGINEERING. **Personal Data:** b Chattanooga, Tenn, September 3, 1931; m 1956, c 3. **Education:** Va Mil Inst, BS, 1953. **Honorary Degrees:** DSc (eng physics), Univ Va, 1962. **Professional Experience:** PROF EMER NUCLEAR ENG, UNIV VA, as of 2004; mem, Atomic Safety & Licensing Appeal Bd, beginning 1974; prof nuclear eng, Univ Va, beginning 1968; proj engr, Div Reactor Licensing, US Atomic Energy Comn, 1968-1969; asst dir reactor facil, Philippine Atomic Energy Comn Proj, 1966-1974; assoc prof, Philippine Atomic Energy Comn Proj, 1966-1968; res dir, Philippine Atomic Energy Comn Proj, 1964-1966; proj dir, Philippine Atomic Energy Comn Proj, 1962-1964; proj engr reactor facil, Univ Va, 1958-1962; nuclear engr, Alco Prod, Inc, 1955-1957; shielding engr, Elec Boat Div, Gen Dynamics Corp, 1954-1955. **Memberships:** fel Am Nuclear Soc; Am Soc Eng Educ. **Research Statement & Publications:** Radiation shielding; reactor safety; experimental engineering. **Mailing Address:** Dept Nuclear Eng, Univ Va, 115 Falcon Dr, Charlottesville, VA 22901-2035.

JOHNSON, W THOMAS, NUTRITIONAL BIOCHEMISTRY. **Personal Data:** b Butte, Mont, 1945; m 1987. **Education:** Mont State Univ, BS, 1968; Univ NDak, PhD (biochem), 1976. **Professional Experience:** RES CHEMIST, HUMAN NUTRIT RES CTR, USDA, 1987-; res prof biochem, 1985-1987; state employee, Grand Forks Human Nutrit Res Ctr, beginning 1979. **Memberships:** Am Inst Nutrit; Am Soc Biochem & Molecular Biol; AAAS. **Research Statement & Publications:** Effects of nutrients on biological membranes; roles of nutrients in transmembrane signalling. **Mailing Address:** Human Nutrit Res Ctr, USDA, 2420 Second Ave N, Grand Forks, ND 58202. **Fax:** 701-795-8220. **E-Mail:** tjohnson@gfhnrc.ars.usda.gov

JOHNSON, WALLACE DELMAR, ORGANIC CHEMISTRY. **Personal Data:** b Idaho Falls, Idaho, June 5, 1939; m 1958, c 6. **Education:** Brigham Young Univ, BS, 1961; Univ Utah, PhD (org chem), 1969. **Professional Experience:** LICENSING COORD, PHILLIPS PETROL CO, 1984-; patent liaison, 1972-1984; res chemist, 1961-1964 & 1968-1972. **Memberships:** Am Chem Soc; Sigma Xi; AAAS. **Research Statement & Publications:** Organophosphorus chemistry; synthesis of rubbers and plastics. **Mailing Address:** 3700 Redbud Lane, Bartlesville, OK 74006-4916.

JOHNSON, WALLACE W, PHARMACOLOGY, DENTISTRY. **Personal Data:** b LaMoure, NDak, November 23, 1926; m 1951, c 4. **Education:** NDak State Col, BS, 1950; Univ Iowa, DDS, 1957, MS, 1958. **Professional Experience:** Prof Oper Dent, Col Dent, Univ Iowa, beginning 1965; from instr to assoc prof oper dent, Col Dent, Univ Iowa, 1958-1965; Asst dent, Col Dent, Univ Iowa, 1957-1958; PROF EMER OPER DENT, COL DENT, UNIV IOWA. **Memberships:** Am Dent Asn; Am Col Dentists; Am Asn Dent Res; Am Asn Dent Schs. **Research Statement & Publications:** Drugs and their use in dentistry; educational research; dental materials research. **Mailing Address:** 720 Greenwood Dr, Iowa City, IA 52246.

JOHNSON, WALTER C(URTIS), ELECTRONIC MATERIALS & DEVICES. **Personal Data:** b Weikert, Pa, January 6, 1913; m 1934, Caroline Shirk; c Walter C Jr, William S & David E. **Education:** Pa State Col, BSE, 1934, EE, 1942. **Honors & Awards:** Western Elec Award for Excellence in Eng Educ, Am Soc Eng Educ, 1967. **Professional Experience:** EMER PROF ELEC ENG, PRINCETON UNIV, 1981-; Resident vis, Bell Labs, 1968, consult; Arthur LeGrand Prof Eng, Princeton Univ, 1963-1981; chmn dept, Princeton Univ, 1951-1965; from instr to prof, Princeton Univ, 1937-1981; s tud elec engr, Gen Elec Co, NY, 1934-1937. **Memberships:** Am Soc Eng Educ; Am Phys Soc; fel Inst Elec & Electronics Engrs. **Research Statement & Publications:** Semiconductor materials and devices; charge transport and trapping in insulators; insulator reliability; electronic properties of interfaces between semiconductors and insulators. **Mailing Address:** 20 McCosh Circle, Princeton, NJ 08540.

JOHNSON, WALTER CURTIS, BIOPHYSICAL CHEMISTRY. **Personal Data:** b Princeton, NJ, February 11, 1939; m 1960, Susan; c Walter C III & Heather L. **Education:** Yale Univ, BA, 1961; Univ Wash, PhD (phys chem), 1966. **Honors & Awards:** Milton Harris Award. **Professional Experience:** PROF EMER BIOPHYS & BIOCHEM, ORE STATE UNIV, as of 2004; mem BBCA panel, NIH, 1988-1991; mem panel biol instrumentation, NSF, 1980-1982; mem panel equip, NIH, 1979, 1983, & 1984; prof biophys, Ore State Univ, beginning 1978; USPHS grant, protein conformation & function, beginning 1974; assoc prof, Ore State Univ, 1972-1978; NSF grant circular dichroism & conformation biopolymers, beginning 1968; asst prof, Ore State Univ, 1968-1972; NSF fel, Univ Calif, Berkeley, 1966-1968; adv bd Biopolymers. **Memberships:** Biophys Soc. **Research Statement & Publications:** Spectroscopic properties of biopolymers, principally their circular dichroism, their conformation and resulting biological function. **Mailing Address:** Dept Biochem & Biophys, Ore State Univ, 2133 Agr Life Sci, Corvallis, OR 97331-7505. **Fax:** 541-737-0481. **E-Mail:** johnsowc@ucs.orst.edu

JOHNSON, WALTER HEINRICK, JR, PHYSICS, MASS SPECTROMETRY. **Personal Data:** b Minneapolis, Minn, September 20, 1928; m 1958, Harriet Willingham; c Bradford & Lee. **Education:** Univ Minn, BA, 1950, MA, 1952, PhD (physics), 1956. **Professional Experience:** EMER PROF PHYSICS, UNIV MINN, MINNEAPOLIS, 1993-; assoc dean, Dept Physics, 1991-1993; actg dean, Dept Physics, 1977-1979; Comn on Atomic Weights, 1971-1985 & secy, 1972-1975; assoc dean, Dept Physics, 1971-1977; actg chmn, Dept Physics, 1969-1970 & 1983; prof physics, Univ Minn, 1968-1993; Mem, Comn on Atomic Masses & Fundamental Constants, Int Union Pure & Appl Physics, 1966-1972; from asst prof to assoc prof, Univ Minn, 1958-1968; exp physicist, Knolls Atomic Power Lab, Gen Elec Co, 1957-1958; Res assoc, Univ Minn, 1956-1957. **Research Statement & Publications:** Mass spectroscopy; measurement of atomic masses; nuclear binding energy; neutron cross-section measurements. **Mailing Address:** Sch Physics & Astron, 116 Church St SE, Minneapolis, MN 55455. **E-Mail:** cork@tc.umn.edu

JOHNSON, WALTER HUDSON, NEURAL NETWORKS, ROBOTICS. **Personal Data:** b Fayetteville, NC, December 21, 1942; m 1977, Lea; c Erin & Adam. **Education:** Rice Univ, BA, 1965; Harvard Univ, MS, 1967, PhD (physics), 1973. **Professional Experience:** PROF PHYSICS & CHMN, DEPT PHYSICS, SUFFOLK UNIV, 1973-; researcher high energy physics, Harvard Univ, 1973-1979. **Memberships:** Int Neural Network Soc; Inst Elec & Electronics Engrs; Am Phys Soc. **Research Statement & Publications:** Neural networks, image processing, autoware media, robot control; ellipsometry, detection of environmental gases; high energy particle physics; high pressure liquids, propagation of ultrasonic waves. **Mailing Address:** Suffolk Univ, Dept Physics, Off Archer 304, Boston, MA 02108. **Fax:** 617-573-8513. **E-Mail:** wjohnson@suffolk.edu

JOHNSON, WALTER K, ENVIRONMENTAL & CIVIL ENGINEERING. **Personal Data:** b Minneapolis, Minn, August 28, 1923; m 1950, Geneva; c Kristine, Karen & Konstance. **Education:** Univ Minn, BCE, 1948, MSCE, 1951, PhD (sanit eng), 1963; Am Acad Environ Eng, dipl, 1965. **Honors & Awards:** Radebaugh Award, Cent States Water Pollution Control Asn, 1965. **Professional Experience:** PROF EMER, UNIV MINN, AS OF 2006; dir planning, Metro Waste Control Comn, St Paul, 1975-1989; Environ Protection Agency res fel, Brit Water Pollution Res Lab, Stevenage, Eng, 1970; from asst prof to prof, Univ Minn, Minneapolis, 1963-1975; lectr civil eng, Univ Minn, Minneapolis, 1955-1963; sanit engr, Toltz, King, Duvall & Anderson, Consult Engrs, Minn, 1952-1955; sanit engr, Infilco Inc, Ariz, 1951-1952; asst, Univ Minn, 1949-1951; civil engr, Greeley & Hansen, 1948-1949. **Memberships:** Am Soc Civil Engrs; Am Acad Environ Eng; Am Water Works Asn; Water Environ Asn. **Research Statement & Publications:** Biological treatment of waste waters and the removal of nitrogen and phosphorus from waste waters by biological and chemical means. **Mailing Address:** 5321 29th Ave S, Minneapolis, MN 55417.

JOHNSON, WALTER RICHARD, PHYSICS. **Personal Data:** b Richmond, Va, February 25, 1929; m 1952. **Education:** Univ Mich, BSE, 1952, MS, 1953, PhD (physics), 1958. **Professional Experience:** FRANK M FREIMANN CHAIR, DEPT PHYSICS, UNIV NOTRE DAME, 1992-; PROF PHYSICS, UNIV NOTRE DAME, 1967-; from asst prof to assoc prof, Univ Notre Dame, 1958-1967; Instr physics, Univ Mich, 1957-1958. **Memberships:** Am Physics Soc. **Research Statement & Publications:** Hydrodynamics; atomic physics; quantum electrodynamics. **Mailing Address:** Dept Physics, Univ Notre Dame, Nieuwland Sci Hall 334, Notre Dame, IN 46556-5670. **Fax:** 574-631-5952. **E-Mail:** johnson@nd.edu

JOHNSON, WALTER ROLAND, JET ENGINE TECHNOLOGIES, ELECTRONICS MANUFACTURING IN GENERAL. **Personal Data:** b Boston, Mass, February 10, 1927; m 1962, Janet; c Meryl A, Leah K & Christa H. **Education:** Mass Inst Technol, BS, 1958. **Professional Experience:** METALLURGIST & CONSULT, 1969-; metallurgist, Missile Systs Div, Raytheon Co, 1958-1969; chmn, QUBE Resources. **Memberships:** Am Soc Metals Life mem. **Research Statement & Publications:** Aerospace; electronics; metallurgy. **Mailing Address:** Metallurgist Consult, 35 Norseman Ave, Gloucester, MA 01930. **Fax:** 508-281-3195. **E-Mail:** wjohnson@user1.channel1.com

JOHNSON, WARREN VICTOR, BIOCHEMISTRY. **Personal Data:** b Duluth, Minn, September 26, 1951; m 1973, c 3. **Education:** Univ Minn, Duluth, BA, 1973; Univ Wis-Milwaukee, MS, 1978; Univ Iowa, PhD (biochem), 1984. **Professional Experience:** ASSOC PROF BIOCHEM & MOLECULAR BIOL, UNIV WIS, GREENBAY, 1992-; asst prof chem, molecular biol & biochem, 1987-1992; postdoctoral assoc biochem, Univ Minn, Duluth, 1986-1987; postdoctoral fel, Revlon Biotech Res Ctr, Rockville, Md, 1984-1986; res asst biochem, Univ Iowa, 1978-1984; teaching asst chem, Univ Wis-Milwaukee, 1976-1978; teacher sci & math, Strandquist High Sch, Minn, 1975-1976; teacher sci & math, St Michael's Sch, Duluth, Minn, 1974-1975. **Memberships:** Am Soc Biochem & Molecular Biol; Am Chem Soc. **Research Statement & Publications:** Structure, function and gene of the developmentally regulated glycoprotein fetuin; role of the carbohydrated moieties of glycoproteins; proteolytic processing; molecular diagnosis of phylogenetic relationships. **Mailing Address:** Dept Biochem, Univ Wis-Green Bay, LS 451 2420 Nicolet Dr, Green Bay, WI 54311-7001. **E-Mail:** johnsonw@uwgb.edu

JOHNSON, WAYNE A, PHYSIOLOGY. **Education:** Univ Wash, PhD, 1985. **Professional Experience:** PROF PHYSIOL & BIOPHYS, CARVER COL MED, UNIV IOWA, as of 2005. **Mailing Address:** Dept Physiol & Biophysics Univ Iowa, Bowen Sci Bldg 6-472, Iowa City, IA 52242. **Fax:** 319-335-7330. **E-Mail:** wayne-a-johnson@uiowa.edu

JOHNSON, WAYNE DOUGLAS, ELECTRON TRANSPORT. **Personal Data:** m 1972, c 3. **Education:** Lebanon Valley Col, BS, 1973; Univ Del, PhD (physics), 1978. **Professional Experience:** PROJ LEADER, DOW CHEM CO, 1979-; res fel, Univ Pa, 1978-1979. **Memberships:** Am Phys Soc. **Research Statement & Publications:** Electron transport. **Mailing Address:** New Ventures Dow N Am, 100 Larkin Ctr, Midland, MI 48674.

JOHNSON, WAYNE JON, AUTOMOTIVE ENGINEERING. **Personal Data:** b Elroy, Wis, May 14, 1939; m 1964, c 3. **Education:** Univ Wis, BS, 1961, MS, 1962, PhD (elec eng), 1968. **Professional Experience:** MGR, POWERTRAIN CONTROL SYST LAB, FORD RES LAB, FORD MOTOR CO, 1987-; prin staff engr, Electronic Syst Dept, 1982-1987; prin res, eng assoc, Dept Physics, 1973-1982; sr res engr, Ford Motor Co, 1969-1973; sr res engr, Lab di Cibernetica, Naples, Italy, 1968-1969; res engr, Res Dept, Collins Radio Co, Cedar Rapids, 1962-1964; engr, Res Dept, Collins Radio Co, Cedar Rapids, 1960 & 1961. **Memberships:** Inst Elec & Electronics Engrs; Soc Automotive Engrs; Eng Soc Detroit. **Research Statement & Publications:** Nonlinear wave propagation; superconducting devices; semiconductor device physics; combustion research on internal combustion engines; plasma probing techniques; electromagnetic interference phenomena; networking and distributed computing techniques applied to the automobile; dynamic control systems. **Mailing Address:** Powertrain Control Syst Lab, Ford Res Lab, Ford Motor Co, Mail Drop 1170 PO Box 2053, Dearborn, MI 48121.

JOHNSON, WAYNE ORRIN, AGRICULTURAL CHEMISTRY. **Personal Data:** b Valley City, NDak, May 26, 1942; m 1965, c 1. **Education:** Concordia Col, BA, 1964; Mich State Univ, MS, 1966; Univ Ore, PhD (org chem), 1969. **Professional Experience:** MGR, DEPT ANAL RES & PHYS MEASUREMENT SCI, ROHM & HAAS CO, as of 1999; res mgt biocides & spec polymers, Agr Prod Res, Agr Chem, Rohim & Haas Co, beginning 1985; pres, Rohm & Haas Seeds, 1983-1985; mgr hybrid crops, 1979-1983; mgr res farms & liaison activ, 1976-1979; goup leader, 1969-1976. **Memberships:** Am Chem Soc; Plant Growth Regulator Working Group; Am Seed Trade Asn. **Research Statement & Publications:** Synthetic structure-activity chemistry related to biological sciences, especially pesticidal research; microbiology; polymer chemistry. **Mailing Address:** Dept Anal Res & Phys Measurement Sci, Res Lab, Rohm & Haas Co, 727 Norristown Rd, Spring House, PA 19477-0904. **Fax:** 215-619-1607. **E-Mail:** rsrwoj@rohmhaas.com

JOHNSON, WENDEL J, ANIMAL ECOLOGY, ZOOGEOGRAPHY. **Personal Data:** b Oak Park, Ill, July 13, 1941; m 1982, c 3. **Education:** Mich State Univ, BS, 1963, MS, 1965; Purdue Univ, PhD (mammalian ecol), 1969. **Professional Experience:** PROF BIOL, UNIV WIS CTR-MARINETTE, beginning 1986; Wis Alumni Res Found fel, 1970; from asst prof to assoc prof, Univ Wis Ctr-marinette, 1969-1986; Sigma Xi grant-in-aid, 1964, 1970. **Memberships:** AAAS; Ecol Soc Am; Am Soc Mammal. **Research Statement & Publications:** Zoogeographical analysis of reptiles and amphibians in the Northern Peninsula of Michigan; population dynamics of small mammals in Isle Royale National Park; population regulation in small mammals; environmental problems from human numbers; Green Bay lampreys. **Mailing Address:** Dept Biol Sci, Univ Wis Ctr Syst, 750 W Bayshore, Marinette, WI 54143. **Fax:** 715-735-4307. **E-Mail:** wjohnson@uwc.edu

JOHNSON, WHITNEY LARSEN, STATISTICS, COMPUTER SCIENCE. **Personal Data:** b Brigham City, Utah, July 11, 1927; m 1954, c 11. **Education:** Utah State Univ, BS, 1954; Univ Minn, Minneapolis, MS, 1957. **Professional Experience:** PROF EMER DATA & TEL SYSTS, NORTHERN MICH UNIV, 1992-; dir, Northern Mich Univ, 1986-1992; dir mgt info serv, Northern Mich Univ, 1972-1986; adminr automated data processing systs, State Coun Higher Educ, Va, 1969-1972; c oordr comput ctr, Va Polytech Inst & State Univ, 1962-1964 & dir, 1964-1968; a ssoc prof statist, Va Polytech Inst & State Univ, 1962-1968. **Memberships:** Am Statist Asn; Asn Comput Mach; Int Asn Comput Educ. **Research Statement & Publications:** Moments of serial correlation coefficients and computing networks on regional and statewide basis; management information for education. **Mailing Address:** Northern Mich Univ, 1401 Presque Isle Ave, Marquette, MI 49855. **E-Mail:** wjohnson@nmu.edu

JOHNSON, WILEY CARROLL, PLANT BREEDING. **Personal Data:** b Asheville, NC, January 1, 1930; m 1951, c 2. **Education:** Wake Forest Col, BS, 1949; NC State Col, BS, 1951, MS, 1953; Cornell Univ, PhD (plant breeding), 1956. **Professional Experience:** RES AGRONOMIST, USDA, 1989-; prof plant breeding, Auburn Univ, beginning 1969; assoc prof, Auburn Univ, 1957-1969; res agronomist, Cornell Univ, 1956-1957. **Memberships:** Am Soc Agron; Crop Sci Soc Am; Am Genetics Asn. **Research Statement & Publications:** Genetics and breeding of clovers. **Mailing Address:** Coastal Plain Exp Sta, 108 Plant Sci Dr, Tifton, GA 31793-0748. **Fax:** 229-386-3437. **E-Mail:** cjohnson@tifton.usda.gov

JOHNSON, WILLIAM, MICROBIOLOGY. **Personal Data:** b Boston, Mass, October 6, 1941; m 1965, c 3. **Education:** Marietta Col, BS, 1963; Miami Univ, MS, 1965; Rutgers Univ, PhD (microbiol), 1968. **Professional Experience:** PROF & VICE CHMN MICROBIOL, COL MED, UNIV IOWA, 1980-; assoc prof, Col Med, Univ Iowa, 1974-1980; asst prof microbiol, Col Med, Univ Iowa, 1970-1974; Nat Acad Sci-Nat Res Coun fel, Army Biol Res Ctr, Ft Detrick, Md, 1968-1970. **Memberships:** AAAS; Am Soc Microbiol; NY Acad Sci; Am Acad Microbiol. **Research Statement & Publications:** Pathogenic microbiology; microbial toxins. **Mailing Address:** Dept Microbiol, Univ Iowa Col Med, 51 Newton Rd, 3403 Bowen Sci, Iowa City, IA 52242. **E-Mail:** william-johnson@uiowa.edu

JOHNSON, WILLIAM BOWIE, HALL EFFECT, ELECTRONIC BAND STRUCTURE. **Personal Data:** b Washington, DC, September 25, 1954; m 1987, c 1. **Education:** George Mason Univ, BS, 1976; Univ Md, MS, 1978, PhD (physics), 1982. **Professional Experience:** SR PHYSICIST PHYSICS, LAB PHYS SCI, 1982-. **Memberships:** Am Phys Soc; Inst Elec & Electronics Engrs. **Research Statement & Publications:** Characterization of the electrical properties of materials at low temperatures and high magnetic fields; materials under development include semimagnetic semiconductors, quasicrystals, silicon carbide, gallium arsenide and rare earth semiconductors. **Mailing Address:** 1730 Tarrytown Ave, Crofton, MD 21114.

JOHNSON, WILLIAM BUHMANN, MATHEMATICAL ANALYSIS. **Personal Data:** b Palo Alto, Calif, December 5, 1944. **Education:** Southern Methodist Univ, BA, 1966; Iowa State Univ, PhD (math), 1969. **Professional Experience:** Positivity, Trans Am Math Soc, 1996-; ed, Geometric & Functional Anal, 1991-; DISTINGUISHED PROF MATH, TEX A&M UNIV, 1989-; ed, Ill J Math, 1987-1993; A G & M E OWN CHAIR, TEX A&M UNIV, 1984-; prof, Tex A&M Univ, 1984-1989; ed, Trans Am Math Soc, 1982-1986; Vis prof math, Univ Tex, Austin, 1975 & Tex A&M Univ, College Station, 1981; fel, Inst Advan Studies, Hebrew Univ, Jerusalem, 1977-1978; from asst prof to prof, Ohio State Univ, 1971-1984; Asst prof math, Univ Houston, 1969-1971. **Memberships:** Am Math Soc; Math Asn Am. **Research Statement & Publications:** Functional analysis; isomorphic theory of Banach spaces; probability theory. **Mailing Address:** Dept Math, Tex A&M Univ, College Station, TX 77843. **E-Mail:** w-johnson@tamu.edu

JOHNSON, WILLIAM CONE, INTERNAL MEDICINE. **Personal Data:** b Eastland, Tex, November 20, 1926; m 1956, c 3. **Education:** NTex State Univ, BS, 1949; Univ Tex, MD, 1954; Am Bd Internal Med, dipl, 1963; Am Bd Pulmonary Dis, dipl, 1968. **Professional Experience:** Morris Mem Hosp, Coleman, Tex, 1980-; Shepperd Mem Hosp, Burnet, Tex, 1976-1980; clin assoc prof med, Tex Tech Univ, Sch Med, 1974-; Med Ctr Hosp, Big Spring, 1973-1974; Rolling Plains Mem Hosp, Sweetwater, 1970-; MED DIR RESPIRATORY THER SERV & PULMONARY FUNCTION LABS, WTEX MED CTR HOSP, ABILENE, 1970-; med dir, respiratory ther serv, Cox Mem Hosp, Abilene, 1970-1975; Root Mem Hosp, Colorado City, Tex, 1970; clin asst prof med, Univ Tex, Southwestern Med Sch Dallas, 1969-; clin asst prof med, Univ Tex Health Sci Ctr, Dallas, 1969-; med dir, Work Eval & Rehab Unit, Methodist Hosp Dallas, 1969-1970; mem bd dirs, WTex Med Ctr Res Found, 1969; Hendrick Mem Hosp, Abilene, 1968-1969 & 1970- & Shannon WTex Mem Hosp, San Angelo, 1969; consult, WTex Med Ctr Hosp, 1968-; dir respiratory ther serv & pulmonary physiol labs, Hendrick Mem Hosp, Abilene, 1968-1969; med examr, Fed Aviation Agency, 1966-; consult, Vet Admin Hosps, 1965-; inhalation ther serv, Scott & White Mem Hosp, 1965-1968; dir pulmonary physiol labs, Scott & White Mem Hosp, Temple, Tex, 1963-1968; c onsult, Sect Clin Physiol, Scott & White Clin, Temple, 1963-1968; med dir inhalation ther serv, Scott & White Mem Hosp, Temple, Tex, 1963-1965; chief pulmonary & infectious dis serv, Wilford Hall Hosp, Aerospace Med Div, Lackland AFB, Tex, 1961-1963; pulmonologist, Wilford Hall Hosp, Aerospace Med Div, Lackland AFB, Tex, 1960-1961; f rom intern to chief resident, John Sealy Hosp, Univ Tex Hosps, 1954-1958; chief med serv, 1604th USAF Hosp, 1958-1960. **Memberships:** AAAS; Am Asn Inhalation Therapists; fel Am Col Chest Physicians; fel Am Col Physicians; Am Fedn Clin Res. **Research Statement & Publications:** Pulmonary physiology. **Mailing Address:** 6250 Reg Plaza, Suite 1030, Abilene, TX 79606-5223.

JOHNSON, WILLIAM CRAIG, PHASE TRANSFORMATIONS, ELASTICITY. **Personal Data:** b Evergreen Park, Ill, November 4, 1954; m 1978, Lisa; c Hannah, Ian & Norah. **Education:** Mich Technol Univ, BS, 1976, MS, 1978, PhD (metall eng), 1980. **Honors & Awards:** Robert Lansing Hardy Gold Medal, TMS, Am Inst Mining Metall & Petrol Engrs, 1983; Bradley Stoughten Outstanding Young Teacher, ASM, 1988, (fel, 2000); Henry Marion Howe Award, 1988; Fellow ASM 2000; All-University Outstanding Teaching Award 1998-1999; VEF Distinguished Faculty Award 2005. **Professional Experience:** PROF MAT SCI, UNIV VA, 1993-; Guest prof metall physics, Tech Univ Berlin, 1990-1991; Prof mat sci, Carnegie Mellon Univ, 1982-1993; NRC Postdoc NBS 1980-1982. **Memberships:** ASM Int; TMS-AIME; AAAS. **Research Statement & Publications:** Influence of stress on phase transformations, diffusion and thermodynamics, especially in crystalline systems and thin films. **Mailing Address:** Dept Materials Sci & Eng, Univ Va, Charlottesville, VA 22904-4745. **Fax:** 434-982-5799. **E-Mail:** wcj2c@virginia.edu

JOHNSON, WILLIAM E, MEDICAL ENTOMOLOGY. **Personal Data:** b Plano, Tex, July 20, 1930; m 1953, c 3. **Education:** Huston-Tillotson Col, BS, 1951; Univ Okla, MS, 1953, PhD (zoology), 1961. **Professional Experience:** RETIRED; Dept Vet Sci, Tuskegee Inst, 1980-1993; dean grad studies, Ala State Univ, 1974-1980; prof biol, Ala State Univ, 1969-1980; asst vpres acad affairs, Ala State Univ, 1969-1974; chmn div sci & math, Albany State Col, 1960-1969; mus asst, Univ Okla, 1957-1960; instr biol, Tuskegee Inst, 1955-1957. **Memberships:** Am Mosquito Control Asn. **Research Statement & Publications:** Mosquito ecology. **Mailing Address:** 809 E Gardendale Dr, Montgomery, AL 36108.

JOHNSON, WILLIAM HILTON, QUATERNARY GEOLOGY. **Personal Data:** b Indianapolis, Ind, February 14, 1935; m 1956, c 3. **Education:** Earlham Col, AB, 1956; Univ Ill, MS, 1961, PhD (geol), 1962. **Professional Experience:** PROF EMER, UNIV ILL, URBANA, as of 2004; prof geol, Univ Ill, Urbana, beginning 1987; from instr to assoc prof, Univ Ill, Urbana, 1968-1987; partic, Ill State Geol Surv. **Memberships:** Geol Soc Am; Sigma Xi; Nat Asn Geol Teachers; Am Quaternary Asn. **Research Statement & Publications:** Sedimentology and stratigraphy of Pleistocene deposits and glacial geology; relict Pleistocene periglacial forms; geomorphology. **Mailing Address:** Dept Geol Univ Ill, 1301 W Green St, Urbana, IL 61801-2919. **E-Mail:** whjohnso@uiuc.edu

JOHNSON, WILLIAM HOWARD, AGRICULTURAL ENGINEERING. **Personal Data:** b Sidney, Ohio, September 3, 1922; m 1943, Wyoma; c Lawrence A, Cheri E (Graham) & Dana S (Heston). **Education:** Ohio State Univ, BS, 1948, MS, 1953; Mich State Univ, PhD (agr eng), 1960. **Professional Experience:** RETIRED; dir, Eng Exp Sta, 1981-1987; prof agr eng & head dept, Kans State Univ, 1970-1981; vis scientist & lectr, Tex A&M Univ, 1969-1970; actg chmn dept, Ohio Agr Res & Develop Ctr, assoc chmn dept, 1968-1969; agr eng consult, beginning 1957; from instr to prof agr eng, Ohio Agr Res & Develop Ctr, assoc chmn dept, 1953-1968. **Memberships:** Fel Am Soc Agr Engrs (pres, 1986-1987). **Research Statement & Publications:** Power and machinery area of agricultural engineering; determination of functional requirements and design; efficiency of harvesting and tillage machine components. **Mailing Address:** 2121 Meadowlark Rd, Manhattan, KS 66502.

JOHNSON, WILLIAM HUGH, CROP PROCESS ENGINEERING, SYSTEM DESIGN AND ANALYSIS. **Personal Data:** b Fayetteville, NC, September 14, 1932; m 1958, Glenda Noble; c William C & Richard C. **Education:** NC State Univ, BS, 1954, MS, 1956, PhD (agr eng), 1961. **Honors & Awards:** Philip Morris Distinguished Achievement Tobacco Sci, 1973; cert Merit Gamma sigma Delta, 1972. **Professional Experience:** PROF EMER, NC STATE UNIV, 1994-; asst dir, NC Agr Res Serv, NC State Univ, 1983-1994; Fifth Int Tobacco Sci Cong, Hamburg, 1970; consult, Indian Inst Technol, Ford Found Proj, Kharagpur, India, 1966; partic & spec reporter, Fourth Int Tobacco Sci Cong, Athens, 1966; from asst prof to prof agr eng, NC State Univ, 1961-1983; res instr, NC State Univ, 1956-1961. **Memberships:** Am Soc Agr Engrs; Sigma Xi. **Research Statement & Publications:** Bioengineering of plant materials; energy and mass transfer relations during processing; physical, chemical and enzymatic changes in response to dynamic process variables; health-related modifications of tobacco; systems engineering; biological engineering; solar and heat energy recovery systems engineering. **Mailing Address:** PO Box 7625, Raleigh, NC 27695-7625. **Fax:** 919-515-7760. **E-Mail:** wjohnson@unity.ncsu.edu

JOHNSON, WILLIAM JACOB, INORGANIC CHEMISTRY. **Personal Data:** b Gladwin, Mich, June 23, 1914; m 1944, c 2. **Education:** Univ Calif, Davis, BS, 1937; Kans State Univ, MS, 1948, PhD (plant biochem), 1962. **Professional Experience:** Vis sr lectr, Univ Zambia, 1970-1971; CHMN DIV NATURAL SCI & MATH, TABOR COL, 1963-; PROF CHEM, TABOR COL, 1962-; from asst prof to assoc prof, Tabor Col, 1952-1962; bus mgr, Tabor Col, 1950-1952; instr, Tabor Col, 1947-1950; sci teacher, Kans High Sch, 1944-1946. **Memberships:** Am Chem Soc. **Research Statement & Publications:** Nature of zinc and other micronutrients in plant extracts. **Mailing Address:** 212 S Madison, Hillsboro, KS 67063.

JOHNSON, WILLIAM JOSEPH, IMMUNOLOGY. **Personal Data:** b Junction City, Kans, February 20, 1954. **Education:** Mankato State Univ, BA, 1976; Univ Wis, MS, 1979, PhD (microbiol), 1980. **Honors & Awards:** Fel, Leukemia Soc, 1982. **Professional Experience:** SR DIR PROJ MGT, G D SEARLE, 1993-; dir proj acquisition planning & mgt, G D Searle, 1991-1993; dir res develop, G D Searle, 1988-1991; sr investr immunol, Smith Kline, 1987-1988; assoc sr investr immunol, Smith Kline, 1984-1987; asst med res prof, Duke Univ, 1982-1984; f el macroface cell biol, Duke Univ, 1980-1982. **Memberships:** Am Soc Immunologists. **Mailing Address:** G D Searle & Co, 4901 Searle Pkwy A2E, Skokie, IL 60077-2980. **Fax:** 847-982-4690.

JOHNSON, WILLIAM K, ORGANIC CHEMISTRY. **Personal Data:** b Kalamazoo, Mich, January 4, 1927; m 1952, c 1. **Education:** Univ Mich, BS, 1950, MS, 1951, PhD (pharm chem), 1954. **Professional Experience:** CONSULT, 1987-; dir petrochemicals, Catalytica Assocs, 1985-1987; mgr mkt res & planning, SRI Int, 1983-1985; mgr mkt res & planning, Monsanto Intermediates Co, 1979-1982; mgr markets & prod, Process Chem Group, Monsanto Indust Chem Co, 1976-1979; dir res & commercial develop, Process Chem Group, Monsanto Indust Chem Co, 1971-1976; mgr technol gen chem, Org Div, 1969-1971; mgr commercial develop plasticizers & gen chem, Org Div, 1967-1969; mgr mkt res, Org Div, 1965-1967; proj mgr, Org Develop Dept, 1960-1965; Chemist res & eng div, Monsanto Co, 1953-1960. **Memberships:** Am Chem Soc; Commercial Develop Asn; Ger Chem Soc; Chem Mkt Res Asn. **Research Statement & Publications:** Organometallics and organic synthesis; intermediates and fine chemicals. **Mailing Address:** 7356 Via Laguna, San Jose, CA 95135-1341.

JOHNSON, WILLIAM LAWRENCE, RUMINANT NUTRITION, FORAGE UTILIZATION. **Personal Data:** b Keene, NH, August 28, 1936; m 1984, Thais; c Maya (Bellomo), Laisa (Bellomo), Warren, Susan & Steven. **Education:** Univ NH, BS, 1958; Cornell Univ, MS, 1964, PhD (dairy cattle nutrit), 1966. **Professional Experience:** Campus coordr, Ctr World Environ & Syst Develop, Duke, NC State Univ & Univ NC, 1993-; vis scientist, Empresa Brasiliera Del Pesquisa Agropecuaria, Brazil, 1992; res & inst develop adv, Nat Inst for Agr Res, Lima, Peru, 1988-; PROF ANIMAL SCI, NC STATE UNIV, 1982-; prin investr small ruminants collab res, Indonesia, Morocco & Brazil, 1978-1988; co-leader forage & animal nutrit prog, Agr Mission to Peru, 1970-1973; f rom asst prof to assoc prof, NC State Univ, 1966-1982; Dairy husb res specialist, Nat Agrarian Univ, La Molina, Peru, 1966-1969. **Memberships:** Am Soc Animal Sci; Int Goat Asn. **Research Statement & Publications:** Factors influencing utilization of forages, and roughage by products, including tropical feedstuffs, by cattle, sheep and goats; sustainability of livestock-based agriculture in tropical ecosystems. **Mailing Address:** Dept Animal Sci, NC State Univ, Raleigh, NC 27695-7621. **Fax:** 919-515-7780.

JOHNSON, WILLIAM LEWIS, PHASE TRANSITIONS. **Personal Data:** b Bryan, Tex, July 6, 1940; m 1963, Patricia; c Paul. **Education:** Univ Southern Miss, BA, 1962; Naval Postgrad Sch, MS, 1966, PhD (physics), 1969. **Professional Experience:** PROF PHYSICS, WESTMINSTER COL, PA, 1971-; res assoc, Univ Ill, 1969-1971; Instr physics, Naval Postgrad Sch, 1963-1969. **Memberships:** Am Phys Soc; Am Asn Physics Teachers; Sigma Xi. **Research Statement & Publications:** Critical point phenomena; microgravity fluids. **Mailing Address:** Dept Physics, Westminster Col, New Wilmington, PA 16172. **E-Mail:** bjohnson@westminster.edu

JOHNSON, WILLIAM LEWIS, SOLID STATE PHYSICS, MATERIALS SCIENCE. **Personal Data:** b Bowling Green, Ohio, July 26, 1948; m 1984, c Jessica. **Education:** Hamilton Col, BA, 1970; Calif Inst Technol, PhD (appl physics), 1974. **Honors & Awards:** Hume Rothery Award, Am Metals Soc & Am Inst Mech Engrs, 1995; Gold Medal, Int Symp Mech Alloyed Nancrystalline & Amorphous Metals, 1995. **Professional Experience:** RUBEN & DONNA METTLER PROF ENG & APPL SCI, CALIF INST TECHNOL, 1989-; Alexander von Humbolt sr scientist award, 1988; consult, Hughes Res Labs, beginning 1984; consult, Lawrence Livermore Lab, 1984-1992; prof mat sci, Calif Inst Technol, 1984-1989; consult, Gen Motors, beginning 1983; consult, Jet Propulsion Lab, Calif Inst Technol, Pasadena, beginning 1980; from asst prof to prof mat sci, Calif Inst Technol, 1977-1988; fel, T J Watson Res Ctr, IBM Corp, 1975-1977; fel appl physics, Calif Inst Technol, 1974-1975. **Memberships:** Am Phys Soc; AAAS; Am Soc Metals; Mat Res Soc. **Research Statement & Publications:** Low temperature physics; superconductivity; amorphous materials; bulk metallic glasses; properties of metastable metallic materials. **Mailing Address:** Dept Mat Sci, Calif Inst Technol, Keck Lab Eng, Pasadena, CA 91125. **Fax:** 626-795-6132. **E-Mail:** wlj@yperfine.caltech.edu

JOHNSON, WILLIAM RANDOLPH, POLYMER CHEMISTRY, THEORETICAL CHEMISTRY. **Personal Data:** b Oxford, NC, July 25, 1930; m 1954, c 3. **Education:** NC Col Durham, BS, 1950; Univ Notre Dame, MS, 1952; Univ Pa, PhD (chem), 1958. **Professional Experience:** VIS PROF CHEM, HAMPDEN-SYDNEY COL, as of 2000; adj prof chem, Hampden-Sydney Col, beginning 1994; sr scientist, Chem Res Div, 1990-1994; mgr spec affairs, Chem Res Div, 1981-1990; exec residence, Va Union Univ, 1979-1981; mgr, Chem Res Div, 1975-1979; chemist, Philip Morris Ops Ctr, 1963-1975; adj prof chem, Va Union Univ, 1963-1973; chemist, W R Grace & Co, 1961-1963; prof, Fla A&M Univ, 1958-1961; instr, Prairie View A&M Col, 1952-1953. **Research Statement & Publications:** Polymer synthesis; smoke chemistry; smoke formation mechanisms; pyrolysis mechanisms. **Mailing Address:** Dept Chem, Hampden-Sydney Col, Hampden-Sydney, VA 23943. **E-Mail:** wjohn19@netscape.net

JOHNSON, WILLIAM ROBERT, MATERIALS SCIENCE. **Personal Data:** b Buffalo, Okla, September 24, 1939; m 1961, Lynn Charlene; c Chad Andrew & Heather Lynn (Dillon). **Education:** San Jose State Col, BS, 1964; Stanford Univ, MS, 1967, PhD (mat sci), 1969. **Professional Experience:** RETIRED; CONSULT SCIENTIST, 2001-; sr prin scientist, 1997-2001; sr staff scientist, Gen Atomics, 1990-1997; mgr mats eval, General Atomics, 1981-1990; staff engr, General Atomics, 1973-1981; sr engr, General Atomics, 1972-1973; staff assoc, General Atomics, 1971-1972; assoc scientist, General Atomics, 1970-1971; scientist & prod mgr vacuum metallization, St Clair-Field Inc, Mt View, Calif, 1969-1970. **Memberships:** Am Soc Metals; Am nuclear soc. **Research Statement & Publications:** Structure of materials; mechanical behavior of materials (fracture, creep and stress rupture); environmental effects (corrosion, irradiation, etc) on materials. **Mailing Address:** 12243 Riesling Ct, San Diego, CA 92131. **E-Mail:** wrbobj@juno.com

JOHNSON, WILLIAM S(TANLEY), MECHANICAL & ENVIRONMENTAL ENGINEERING. **Personal Data:** b Camden, Tenn, December 9, 1939; m 1967, Jacquelyn Smith; c Steve & Kathryn. **Education:** Univ Tenn, Knoxville, BS, 1961; Clemson Univ, MS, 1965, PhD (eng), 1967. **Professional Experience:** PROF MECH ENG, UNIV TENN, 1977-; from asst prof to assoc prof, Univ Tenn, 1967-1977; Asst design engr, Pratt & Whitney Aircraft Div, United Aircraft Corp, 1961-1962. **Memberships:** Am Soc Mech Engrs; Am Soc Heating Vent & Air Conditioning Engrs; Am Soc Eng Educ. **Research Statement & Publications:** Application of pulse-jet flow in low area ratio ejectors; determination of velocity characteristics of two-dimensional fluid jets; boundary layer control on submarine surfaces; energy conservation analysis in buildings; heat pump evaluations; Evaluation of geothermal heat pumps environmental chamber testing of various heating and cooling devices, Aerodynamics and hydrodynamics studies of aircraft, submarines and nuclear reactors. **Mailing Address:** Dept Mech & Aerospace Eng, Univ Tenn, Knoxville, TN 37996-2210. **Fax:** 865-974-5274. **E-Mail:** wsjohnson@utk.edu

JOHNSON, WILLIAM W, GEOPHYSICS. **Personal Data:** b Provo, Utah, July 11, 1934; m 1969, c 2. **Education:** Brigham Young Univ, BS, 1956; Univ Utah, MS, 1958; Univ Pittsburgh, PhD (geophys), 1965. **Professional Experience:** CONSULT, 1985-; prin res geophysicist, Atlantic Richfield Co, 1969-1985; Res assoc, Lamont-Doherty Geol Observ, Columbia Univ, 1966-1967; Sr res scientist, Sinclair Oil Corp, 1965-1969. **Memberships:** AAAS; Soc Explor Geophysicists. **Research Statement & Publications:** Propagation of elastic waves in anisotropic media; geological interpretation of gravity and magnetic data; seismic wave propagation. **Mailing Address:** 707 Parkview Circle, Richardson, TX 75080.

JOHNSON, WILLIAM WAYNE, GENETICS. **Personal Data:** b Minneapolis, Minn, October 12, 1934. **Education:** Univ Minn, BS, 1957, MS, 1959, PhD (zool), 1963. **Professional Experience:** ASSOC PROF BIOL, UNIV NMEX, 1968-; asst prof, Univ Nmex, 1963-1968; i nterim asst prof biol, Univ Fla, 1962-1963. **Memberships:** AAAS; Genetics Soc Am; Am Inst Biol Sci; Sigma Xi. **Research Statement & Publications:** Experimental population genetics of Drosophila. **Mailing Address:** Dept Biol, Univ NMex Main Campus 1 University Campus, Albuquerque, NM 87131-0001.

JOHNSON, WOODROW E, COMPUTER SCIENCE. **Personal Data:** b Chisolm, Minn, February 28, 1925; m 1946, c 5. **Education:** Univ Minn, BS, 1950. **Professional Experi-**

ence: CONSULT, COMPUT CODE CONSULTS, 1973-; Systs, Sci & Software, 19 1967-1971 & Sci Applns Inc, 1971-1973; prin res scientist, Honeywell Inc, 1965-1967; staff mem, Gen Atomic Div, Gen Dynamics Corp, 1960-1965; staff mem, Los Alamos Sci Lab, 1959-1960; staff mem, Gen Atomic Div, Gen Dynamics Corp, 1958-1959; staff mem, Los Alamos Sci Lab, 1953-1958; res engr, High Speed Flight Sta, Nat Adv Comt Aeronaut, 1951-1953. **Memberships:** Am Phys Soc; Am Sci Affiliation. **Research Statement & Publications:** Use of high speed computers for the numerical treatment of radiation flow, neutronics and hydrodynamics; one, two and three dimensional hydrodynamic, strength of materials and radiation codes to solve problems in high energy fluid dynamics. **Mailing Address:** 114 Brompton Rd, Garden City, NY 11530.

JOHNSON, WOODROW ELDRED, PHYSICS. **Personal Data:** b Forest Lake, Minn, October 22, 1917; m 1942, c 4. **Education:** Hamline Univ, BS, 1937; Brown Univ, MS, 1939, PhD (physics), 1942. **Honorary Degrees:** DS, Hamline Univ, 1961. **Professional Experience:** RETIRED; vpres & gen mgr, Transp Div, Westinghouse Elec Corp, 1971-1985; vpres & gen mgr, Astronuclear Underseas Div, Westinghouse Elec Corp, 1968-1971; corp vpres, Astronuclear Lab, Westinghouse Elec Corp, 1967-1985; gen mgr, Astronuclear Lab, Westinghouse Elec Corp, 1964-1968; gen mgr, Pa Adv Reactor Proj, Atomic Power Dept, 1961-1964; dir proj, Pa Adv Reactor Proj, Atomic Power Dept, 1959-1961; proj mgr, Pa Adv Reactor Proj, Atomic Power Dept, 1955-1959; corp mem, Indust Atomic Power Study Group, 1954-1955; corp tech consult, Matahorn Proj, Princeton Univ, 1954; asst dir develop, Prototype Reactor Facil, Idaho, 1953-1954; mgr tech opers, Prototype Reactor Facil, Idaho, 1951-1953; sect mgr, Bettis Atomic Power Lab, Westinghouse Corp, 1949-1951; sr physicist, Manhattan Proj, Oak Ridge Nat Lab, 1947-1949; sr physicist, Tenn Eastman Corp, 1944-1946; asst prof, Syracuse Univ, 1946-1947; from instr to asst prof physics, Syracuse Univ, 1941-1944; asst, Brown Univ, 1937-1940. **Memberships:** Nat Acad Eng; Inst Elec & Electronics Engrs; Am Nuclear Soc; Nat Asn Mfg; Am Phys Soc. **Research Statement & Publications:** Photoelectricity; electron diffraction; physics of thin metallic films; effect of radiation on solids. **Mailing Address:** 100 Hilton Ave, Garden City, NY 11530.

JOHNSON-LUSSENBURG, CHRISTINE MARGARET, VIROLOGY, MOLECULAR BIOLOGY. **Personal Data:** b Hawkesbury, Ont, January 29, 1931; m 1972, c 6. **Education:** McGill Univ, BSc, 1952, MSc, 1953; Univ Ottawa, PhD, 1967. **Professional Experience:** RETIRED; assoc prof, Univ Ottawa, 1978-1993; asst prof microbiol, Univ Ottawa, 1967-1978. **Memberships:** Can Soc Microbiologists; Am Soc Microbiol. **Research Statement & Publications:** Structural and antigenic studies of components involved in virus replication, including myxoviruses, herpesvirus and coronavirus. **Mailing Address:** 1928 Oakdean Crescent, Gloucester, ON K1J 6H3, Can.

JOHNSON-THOMPSON, MARIAN, BIOLOGY. **Education:** Howard Univ, BS, MS; Georgetown Univ, PhD (molecular virol). **Professional Experience:** DIR, OFF EDUC & BIOMED RES DEVELOP, NAT INST ENVIRON HEALTH SCI, as of 2003. **Mailing Address:** Off Educ & Biomed Res Develop, Nat Inst Environ Health Sci, Rm 216, Nottingham Bldg, Research Triangle Park, NC 27709-2233. **Fax:** 919-541-2583. **E-Mail:** johnso21@niehs.nih.gov

JOHNSON-WINEGAR, ANNA, MICROBIAL TOXINS. **Personal Data:** b Frederick, Md, May 27, 1945; m 1980. **Education:** Hood Col, BA, 1976; Catholic Univ Am, MS, 1979, PhD (microbiol), 1981. **Honors & Awards:** Meritorious Serv Award, US Dept Defense, 2003; Gold Medal, Nat Defense Indust Asn. **Professional Experience:** SR ADV, MCKENNA, LONG & ALDRIDGE, LLP, WASHINGTON, DC, 2003-; dep asst, Secy Defense Chem & Biol Defense, 1999-2003; sci adminr, US Army Med Mat Develop Activ, beginning 1990; microbiologist, US Army Med Mat Develop Activ, 1985-1990; mem, Comt on Status Women Microbiologists & Fed Orgn Prof Women, 1983-; reviewer, Appl Environ Microbiol, 1983-; microbiologist, US Army Med Res Inst Infectious Dis, 1976-1985; med technician res, US Army Med Res Inst Infectious Dis, 1966-1976; guest lectr var insts. **Memberships:** Fel Am Soc Microbiologists; AAAS; Int Soc Toxinol; NY Acad Sci; Sigma Xi; Am Cancer Soc. **Research Statement & Publications:** Purification and biochemical analysis of bacterial toxins; immunology of toxin-derived components; pathogenesis of toxins; fermentation techniques; animal models; genetic control of toxin production. **Mailing Address:** McKenna, Long & Aldridge, LLP, 1900 K Street NW, Washington, DC 20006-1108. **Fax:** 202-496-7756.

JOHNSON-WINT, BARBARA PAULE, MORPHOGENESIS, CELL INTERACTIONS. **Education:** Mich State Univ, PhD (zool), 1976; Reed Col, BA, 1969. **Professional Experience:** ASSOC PROF, DEPT BIOL SCI, NORTHERN ILL UNIV, DEKALB, ILL, as of 2004; asst prof, Sch Med, Harvard univ, 1984-1987; instr, Harvard Med Sch, 1979-1984; Post doctoral fel, Harvard Med Sch, 1976-1979. **Mailing Address:** Dept Biol Sci, Northern Illinois Univ, Rm 119 A, Montgomery Hall, DeKalb, IL 60115-2861. **E-Mail:** barbara-johnson-wint@niu.edu

JOHNSTON, A SIDNEY, NUCLEAR PHYSICS. **Personal Data:** b Hinton, WVa, April 4, 1937. **Education:** Va Polytech Inst, BS, 1959; Carnegie-Mellon Univ, MS, 1961, PhD (physics), 1965; Chicago Kent Col Law, JD, 1978. **Professional Experience:** SR PATENT ATTY, DIGITAL EQUIP CORP, 1978-; private law pract, 1978-; mem staff, Dept Nuclear Med, Michael Reese Hosp, 1974-1978; asst prof, Pratt Inst, 1968-1974; sr scientist physics, Westinghouse Astronuclear, 1965-1968. **Memberships:** AAAS; Am Phys Soc. **Research Statement & Publications:** Nuclear engineering; solid state physics; science and society. **Mailing Address:** 51 Quaboag Rd, Acton, MA 01720.

JOHNSTON, ALAN ROBERT, OPTICAL PHYSICS. **Personal Data:** b Long Beach, Calif, June 26, 1931; m 1956, c 3. **Education:** Calif Inst Technol, BS, 1952, PhD (physics), 1956. **Professional Experience:** MEM TECH STAFF, JET PROPULSION LAB, 1971-; res group supvr optical physics, 1962-1971; Res scientist, 1956-1962. **Memberships:** Optical Soc Am; Sigma Xi. **Research Statement & Publications:** Fiber optic systems; optoelectronic sensors. **Mailing Address:** Jet Propulsion Lab, 4800 Oak Grove Dr, Pasadena, CA 91109.

JOHNSTON, ANDREA, MATHEMATICS. **Personal Data:** b Minneapolis, Minn, March 13, 1921. **Education:** St Mary Col, Kans, BA, 1948; Cath Univ, MS, 1952, PhD (math), 1954. **Professional Experience:** RETIRED; Chmn, Dept Math, St Mary Col, Kans, 1954-1990. **Research Statement & Publications:** Mathematics. **Mailing Address:** Mother House, St Mary Col, Leavenworth, KS 66048-5082.

JOHNSTON, ARCHIBALD CURRIE, GEOPHYSICS. **Personal Data:** b Charlotte, NC, May 19, 1945; m 1992, Jill Diana Stevens. **Education:** Rhodes Col, BS, 1967; Dartmouth Col, 1967-1968; Univ Col PhD (geol sci & geophysics), 1979. **Professional Experience:** Mem, Nat Earthquake Prediction Evaluation Coun, 1990-; PROF GEOL SCI, UNIV MEMPHIS, 1988-; mem adv panel, Br Global Seismol & Geomagnetism, Nat Earthquake InfoCtr, 1988-1990; chmn panel regional seismic networks comt seismol, Nat Acad Sci, 1988-1990; dir, Ctr Excellence State Tenn, 1984-1992; dir, CtrEarthquake Res & Info, Memphis State Univ, 1979-1992; from asst prof to assoc prof, MemphisState Univ, 1979-1988; DIR RES, CTR EARTHQUAKE RES & INFO, UNIV MEMPHIS, 1978-; Capt, USAF, 1968-1973; consult, Lawrence Livermore Nat Lab, Berkeley, Electric Power Res Inst, Palo Alto, US ArmyCorps Engrs, Vicksburg, Miss, Tenn Tech Found, Knoxville, Geomatrix Consult Inc, SanFrancisco, Law Environ, Atlanta, Battelle Inst, Seattle, SKB-Swedish Nuclear Fuel; grants, NSF, US Nuclear Regulatory Comn, TVA, US Geol Survey, Electric Power Res Inst, Memphis Light, Gas & Water Utility. **Memberships:** AAAS; Am Geophys Union; Seismol Soc Am (vpres 1991-1992 pres 1992-1993). **Mailing Address:** Ctr Earthquake Res & Info, Univ Memphis, Memphis, TN 38152. **Fax:** 901-678-4734. **E-Mail:** johnston@ceri.memphis.edu

JOHNSTON, C EDWARD, AQUACULTURE. **Personal Data:** b Ont, m 1964, Marcia; c Heather, Andrew & Melanie. **Education:** Univ NB, BA, 1964, PhD (biol), 1968. **Professional Experience:** RETIRED; Mem Univ, Nfld, 1986-1987 & Univ Man, 1993-1994; Vis prof, BiolSta, NB, 1979-1980; from asst prof to prof biol, Univ Pei, 1969-1984; Asst prof, Prince WalesCol, 1968-1969. **Memberships:** Am Fisheries Soc; Can Aqua Soc; Fish & Wildlife Soc. **Research Statement & Publications:** Effect of low pH on parr-smolt transformation of Atlantic salmon; effect of temperature regimes on salmonid physiology; rapid and slow acclimation procedures on ionoregulatory mechanisms of rainbow trout; Atlantic salmon reproductive physiology and ichthyoplankton; Alosa aestivalis reproductive biology; thyroid physiology; blood chemistries; alkaline phosphatase. **Mailing Address:** Biol Dept, Univ PEI, Charlottetown, PQ C1A 4P3, Can.

JOHNSTON, CAROL A, NATURAL RESOURCES & WETLANDS, GEOGRAPHIC INFORMATION SYSTEMS. **Education:** Cornell Univ, BS, 1974; Univ Wis-Madison, MS, 1977, PhD (soil sci), 1982. **Professional Experience:** PROF, DEPT MICROBIOL & BIOL, S DAKOTA STATE UNIV, as of 2003; DIR, CTR BIOCOMPLEXITY STUDIES, S DAKOTA STATE UNIV, as of 2003; Prog dir, NSF, 2000-2002; res ecologist, US Environ Protection Agency, 1989-1990; sr res assoc, Univ Minn, 1986-2000; postdoctoral assoc, Univ Minn, 1985-1986; natural resources supvr, Wis Dept Natural Resources, 1978-1983. **Memberships:** Ecol Soc Am; Soc Wetland Scientists (pres vpres 1991-1993); Am Inst Biol Sci; Soil Sci Soc Am; Asn Women Soil Scientists; Am Soc Photogrammetry & Remote Sensing. **Research Statement & Publications:** Land/water interactions within landscapes, wetland ecosystems, wetland soils, and the application of Geographic Information Systems to ecological research. **Mailing Address:** Dept Biol & Microbiol, S Dakota State Univ, PO Box 2140, NPB 115, SDSU Brookings, SD 57007. **E-Mail:** carol.johnston@sdstate.edu

JOHNSTON, CLIFF T, SOIL SCIENCE. **Personal Data:** b Colorado Springs, Colo, October 3, 1955; m 1977, Gail; c Nathaniel C, Jessica H & Julie M. **Education:** Univ Calif, Riverside, BSc, 1979, PhD (soil & environ chem), 1983. **Professional Experience:** ASSOC ED, CLAY MINERAL SOC, as of 1993; ASSOC PROF AGRON, PURDUE UNIV, as of 1993; vis prof, Cath Univ, Leuven, Belg, 1992; from asst prof to assoc prof, Dept Soil Sci, Univ Fla, 1985-1993; fel, Los Alamos Nat Lab, 1983-1985. **Memberships:** Am Chem Soc; Clay Minerals Soc; Coblentz Soc; Soil Sci Soc Am. **Research Statement & Publications:** Agronomy. **Mailing Address:** Crop Soil & Environ Sci, Purdue Univ, West Lafayette, IN 47907-1968. **Fax:** 765-496-2926. **E-Mail:** clays@purdue.edu

JOHNSTON, COLIN DEANE, CIVIL ENGINEERING, MATERIALS SCIENCE. **Personal Data:** b Northern Ireland, April 28, 1940; m 1967, c 2. **Education:** Queen's Univ, Belfast, BSc, 1962, PhD (civil eng), 1967, DSc, 1996. **Honors & Awards:** Wason Medal, Am Concrete Inst, 1977. **Professional Experience:** PROF EMER CIVIL ENG, UNIV CALGARY, as of 2004; prof Civil Eng, Univ Calgary, beginning 1978; assoc prof, Univ Calgary, 1967-1978; tech mgr concrete prod, Pre-Mix Concrete Ltd, 1967; site engr, Govt Northern Ireland, 1966-1967. **Memberships:** Fel Am Concrete Inst; Am Soc Testing & Mat; Brit Concrete Soc; Transp Res Bd; Int Union Testing & Res Labs Mats & Structs. **Research Statement & Publications:** Concrete, fiber reinforced concrete, durability, deicing salts, fly ash, silica fume, and chemical admixtures in concrete, asphalt concrete; structural and paving applications. **Mailing Address:** Dept Civil Eng, Univ Calgary, 2500 Univ Dr N W, Calgary, AB T2N 1N4, Can. **Fax:** 403-282-7026.

JOHNSTON, CYRUS CONRAD, INTERNAL MEDICINE, ENDOCRINOLOGY. **Personal Data:** b Statesville, NC, July 16, 1929; m 1960, c 2. **Education:** Duke Univ, AB, 1951, MD, 1955; Am Bd Internal Med, dipl. **Honors & Awards:** Sandoz Award for Geront Res, 1993; Frederic C Bartter Award, Am Soc Bone & Mineral Res, 1996. **Professional Experience:** DISTINGUISHED PROF EMER MED, IND UNIV PURDUE UNIV, INDIANAPOLIS, as of 2004; distinguished prof med, Ind Univ, Indianapolis, beginning 1997; assoc ed, BONE, 1995-; vpres bd trustees, Nat Osteoporosis Found, 1992-; prof med, Med Ctr, 1969-1997; dir, Div Endocrinol & Metab, 1968-1994; dir, Gen Clin Res Ctr, 1967-1988; assoc dir, Gen Clin Res Ctr, 1962-1967; from instr to assoc prof med, Ind Univ, Indianapolis, 1961-1969; fel endocrinol & metab, Ind Univ, Indianapolis, 1959-1961; resident, Barnes Hosp, St Louis, 1956-1957; intern med, Duke Hosp, 1955-1956. **Memberships:** AAAS; Am Fedn Clin Res; Endocrine Soc; fel Am Col Physicians; Am Soc Bone & Mineral Res; Sigma Xi; Asn Osteobiol; Am Asn Cancer Educ; Am Col Clin Adminr; AMA; Cent Soc Clin Res. **Research Statement & Publications:** Metabolism of bone both in human subjects and in the experimental animal; osteoporosis. **Mailing Address:** Dept Med, Ind Univ Purdue Univ, 541 N Clinical Dr CL 459, Indianapolis, IN 46202-5111. **Fax:** 317-278-0658. **E-Mail:** cjohnsto@iupui.edu

JOHNSTON, DANIEL, CELLULAR MECHANISMS OF LEARNING & MEMORY. **Personal Data:** b Passaic, NJ, December 9, 1947. **Education:** Univ Va, BS, 1970; Duke Univ, PhD (biomed eng), 1974. **Professional Experience:** DIR, GRAD STUDIES, BAYLOR COL MED, as of 2002; PROF NEUROSCIENCE, BAYLOR COL MED, 1986-; from asst prof to assoc prof, Baylor Col Med, 1977-1986; res asst, Univ Minn, Minneapolis, 1974-1977. **Memberships:** Soc Neuroscience; Am Physiol Soc. **Research Statement & Publications:** Mechanisms of epilepsy. **Mailing Address:** Dept Neurosci Baylor Col Med, One Baylor Plaza, Houston, TX 77030-3498. **Fax:** 713-799-8544. **E-Mail:** dan@mossy.neusc.bcm.tmc.edu

JOHNSTON, DAVID CARL, SOLID STATE PHYSICS, STRONGLY CORRELATED ELECTRON SYSTEMS. **Personal Data:** b Flint, Mich, May 19, 1947. **Education:** Univ Calif, Santa Barbara, BA, 1969; Univ Calif, San Diego, PhD (physics), 1975. **Honors & Awards:** Fellow, American Physical Society, 1988; Chair, Gordon Conference on Superconductivity, 1993; Award for Outstanding Achievement in Research, Iowa State University, 1997; Distinguished Professor, Iowa State University, 2000. **Professional Experience:** Vis scientist, Nat Res Inst Metals, Tokyo, 1991; SR PHYSICIST, AMES LAB, USDOE, 1987-; PROF PHYSICS, IOWA STATE UNIV, 1987-; res staff, Exxon Res & Eng Co, 1978-1987; a sst res physicist, Univ Calif, San Diego, 1975-1978. **Memberships:** Fel Am Phys Soc; AAAS; Am Asn Univ Prof. **Research Statement & Publications:** Solid state physics and chemistry; synthesis and characterization of new materials; high temperature superconductivity in copper oxides and mechanism; magnetic, electronic transport, x-ray diffraction and thermal measurements. **Mailing Address:** Dept Physics & Astron, Iowa State Univ, A209 Physics, Ames, IA 50011. **Fax:** 515-294-0689. **E-Mail:** johnston@ameslab.gov

JOHNSTON, DAVID HERVEY, SEISMOLOGY, ROCK PHYSICS. **Personal Data:** b Syracuse, NY, August 25, 1951; m 1972, Linda; c Elizabeth. **Education:** Mass Inst Technol, SB, 1973, PhD (geophysics), 1979. **Honors & Awards:** Best Presentation SEG 1993. **Professional Experience:** Distinguished lectr, Soc Petrol Engrs, 1992-1993; SR RES SPECIALIST GEOPHYSICS, EXXON PROD RES CO, 1979-. **Memberships:** Am Geophys Union; Soc Explor Geophysicists (secy-treas, 1989-1990); Soc PetrolEngrs. **Research Statement & Publications:** Reflection seismology; seismic processing; velocity analysis and interpretation; applications of geophysics to oil reservoir development and production; rock physics; relationship of rock microstructure to acoustic, electrical and flow properties; extraction of rock properties from seismic data; structure and evolution of planetary interiors; reservoir geophysics. **Mailing Address:** Exxon Prod Res Co, 13501 Katy Freeway, Houston, TX 77079-1348. **Fax:** 281-870-6661.

JOHNSTON, DAVID OWEN, PHYSICAL CHEMISTRY. **Personal Data:** b Franklin, Tenn, July 27, 1930; wid, c Kathy, Susie, David E & Beth. **Education:** George Peabody Col, BS, 1951; Mid Tenn State Col, MA, 1958; Univ Miss, PhD (chem), 1963. **Professional Experience:** RETIRED; from asst prof to prof chem, 1986-1991; fel res, Vanderbilt Univ, 1965 1966, 1969; from asst prof to prof chem, David Lipcomb Col, 1963-1986; instr phys sci, Mid Tenn State Col, 1958-1960; teacher pub schs, Tenn, 1951-1953, 1954-1958. **Memberships:** Am Chem Soc. **Research Statement & Publications:** Transport properties of rare earth salts in nonaqueous solvents; kinetics of inorganic oxidation-reduction reactions. **Mailing Address:** 1492 Clairmont Pl, Nashville, TN 37215.

JOHNSTON, DAVID WARE, AVIAN PHYSIOLOGY, AVIAN ECOLOGY. **Personal Data:** b Miami, Fla, November 23, 1926; m 1948, c 3. **Education:** Univ Ga, BS, 1949, MS, 1950; Univ Calif, PhD, 1954. **Professional Experience:** RETIRED; biol dept, George Mason Univ, 1979-1988; prof zool, Univ Fla, 1974-1979; assoc prof biol sci & zool, Univ Fla, 1963-1974; assoc prof, Wake Forest Col, 1959-1963; assoc prof, Mercer Univ, 1954-1959. **Memberships:** Ecol Soc Am; Cooper Ornith Soc; Am Ornith Union; Nat Audubon Soc. **Research Statement & Publications:** Fat deposition in birds; pesticide levels in birds; ecology of insular avifaunas. **Mailing Address:** 5219 Concordia St, Fairfax, VA 22032.

JOHNSTON, DEAN, TUMOR IMMUNOLOGY. **Personal Data:** b South Bend, Ind, April 12, 1947. **Education:** Wayne State Univ, PhD (biochem), 1974. **Professional Experience:** RES ASST PROF DERMAT, NY UNIV MED CTR, 1982-. **Memberships:** Am Soc Biol Chemists; AAAS. **Mailing Address:** Dept Dermat, Sch Med, NY Univ, Tisch Hosp 3 357, New York, NY 10016. **Fax:** 212-263-8561. **E-Mail:** dean.johnston@med.nyu.edu

JOHNSTON, DENNIS ADDINGTON, BIOSTATISTICS. **Personal Data:** b Oak Ridge, Tenn, September 17, 1944; m 1966, c 2. **Education:** Arlington State Col, BS, 1965; Univ Tex, Austin, MS, 1966; Tex Tech Univ, PhD (math), 1971. **Professional Experience:** PROF BIOMATHEMATICS, UNIV TEX M D ANDERSON CANCER CTR, as of 2003; assoc prof biomathematics, Univ Tex M D Anderson Cancer Ctr, beginning 1978; mem fac, Grad Sch Biomathematics Sci, Univ Tex, Houston, 1973-; adj assoc prof, Dept Statist, Rice Univ, 1973-; asst prof biomathematician, Univ Tex M D Anderson Cancer Ctr, 1972-1978. **Memberships:** Am Statist Asn; Inst Elec & Electronics Engrs. **Research Statement & Publications:** Biomedical image processing; consultant in mathematical and statistical models; biostatistics; automated chromosome analysis. **Mailing Address:** Dept Biomath, Univ Tex M D Anderson Cancer Ctr, 1515 Holcombe Blvd PO Box 237, Smithville, TX 78957. **E-Mail:** daj@mdanderson.org

JOHNSTON, DON RICHARD, CHEMICAL PHYSICS. **Personal Data:** b Union City, Ind, August 10, 1937; c 2. **Education:** Earlham Col, BA, 1957; Brown Univ, PhD (chem), 1961. **Professional Experience:** SUBSECT MGR CHEM & ELEC INSULATION, GEN ELEC CO, 1970-; unit mgr phys chem, M&P Lab, 1968-1970; insulation engr, M&P Lab, 1960-1967. **Memberships:** Am Chem Soc; Inst Elec & Electronics Engrs; Metals Properties Coun. **Research Statement & Publications:** Mechanism of corona degradation of electrical insulation; electrical polarization currents for metallic corrosion. **Mailing Address:** 5140 Bliss Rd, Galway, NY 12074.

JOHNSTON, E(LWOOD) RUSSELL, CIVIL ENGINEERING. **Personal Data:** b Philadelphia, Pa, December 26, 1925; m 1951, c 2. **Education:** Univ Del, BCE, 1946; Mass Inst Technol, MS, 1947, ScD(civil eng), 1949. **Professional Experience:** Head dept, Univ Conn, 1972-1977; g uest prof, Swiss Fed Inst Technol, Zurich, 1970 & 1977; PROF CIVIL ENG, UNIV CONN, 1963-; prof, Worcester Polytech Inst, 1957-1963; from asst prof to prof, Lehigh Univ, 1949-1957; struct designer, Fay, Spofford & Thorndike, 1947-1949; asst civil eng, Mass Inst Technol, 1946-1947. **Memberships:** Am Soc Civil Engrs; Am Soc Eng Educ; Int Asn Bridge & Struct Engrs; Am Acad Mech. **Research Statement & Publications:** Structural engineering; applied mechanics; vibrations. **Mailing Address:** Dept Civil & Environmental Eng, Univ Conn, 261 Glenbrook Rd Unit 2037, Storrs, CT 06269-2037. **Fax:** 860-486-2298.

JOHNSTON, FRANCIS E, CHILD GROWTH DEVELOPMENT. **Personal Data:** b Paris, Ky, October 9, 1931; m 1955, Patricia; c 3. **Education:** Univ Ky, BA, 1959, MA, 1960; Univ Pa, PhD (anthrop), 1962. **Professional Experience:** PROF EMER ANTHROP, UNIV PA, as of 2004; by-fel, Churchill Col, Univ Cambridge, 2000-2001; managing ed, Am J Phys Anthrop, 1977-; prof Anthrop, Univ Pa, beginning 1973; prof anthrop, Temple Univ, 1971-1973; assoc prof anthrop, Univ Tex, Austin, 1968-1971; fel, Inst Cancer Res, 1967-1968 & 1975-; fel, Univ London Inst Child Health, 1966-1967; consult growth & develop, Nat Ctr Health Statist, 1963-; asst cur phys anthrop, Univ Mus, 1963-1966; from instr phys anthrop to asst prof anthrop, Univ Pa, 1960-1966. **Memberships:** Am Asn Phys Anthrop; Am Anthrop Asn; Brit Soc Study Human Biol; Human BiolCoun; fel Royal Soc Med; Am Inst Nutrit. **Research Statement & Publications:** Child growth and development; population biology; human genetics; ecology of nutrition in human populations. **Mailing Address:** Dept Anthrop, Univ Pa, Philadelphia, PA 19104-6398. **Fax:** 215-898-7462. **E-Mail:** fjohnsto@mail.sas.upenn.edu

JOHNSTON, FRANCIS J, CHEMICAL KINETICS, RADIATION CHEMISTRY. **Personal Data:** b Ferryville, Wis, September 20, 1924; m 1948, Joyce; c Michael F. **Education:** Univ Wis, BS, 1947, PhD (chem), 1952. **Professional Experience:** PROF EMER CHEM, UNIV GA, as of 2001; assoc prof chem, Univ GA, beginning 1960; from asst prof to assoc prof chem, Univ Louisville, 1954-1960; chemist, E I du Pont Del Nemours & Co, 1952-1954. **Memberships:** Am Chem Soc; Sigma Xi. **Research Statement & Publications:** Experimental studies of the effects of ionizing radiation in heterogeneous systems. **Mailing Address:** Dept Chem, Univ Ga, Athens, GA 30606-4818. **Fax:** 706-542-9454. **E-Mail:** johnston@chem.uga.edu

JOHNSTON, GEORGE I, ELECTRICAL ENGINEERING. **Personal Data:** b Bryn Mawr, Pa, May 29, 1929; m 1961, c 1. **Education:** Johns Hopkins Univ, BS, 1955. **Professional Experience:** ASSOC PROF & DIR, INSTRUMENT & SAFETY SERV, UNIV ORE, 1976-; dir res, Instrument Serv, Med Sch, 1958-1976; med electronics engr, NIH, 1955-1958; e lectronics technician, Sch Med, Johns Hopkins Univ, 1948-1955; Asst sanit engr, USPHS. **Memberships:** Inst Elec & Electronics Engrs; Sigma Xi. **Research Statement & Publications:** Biomedical engineering. **Mailing Address:** 5462 SW Dover Lane, Portland, OR 97225. **Fax:** 503-245-5603.

JOHNSTON, GEORGE LAWRENCE, PLASMA PHYSICS, THEORETICAL PHYSICS. **Personal Data:** b Los Angeles, Calif, November 11, 1932; m 1959, Patricia A. **Education:** Calif Inst Technol, BS, 1954; JD, Harvard Univ, 1957 Univ Calif, Los Angeles, MS, 1962, PhD (physics), 1967. **Honorary Degrees:** JD, Harvard Univ, 1957. **Professional Experience:** Co-P.I., NSF Wireless Field Tests, Old Colorado City Communications, 1995-1997; Special Consult, Edestron Corp, 1996- RES SCIENTIST, PLASMA FUSION CTR, MASS INST TECHNOL, 1980-1993; adv comnr, Calif Energy Comn, 1977-1978; Res assoc, Mass Inst Technol, 1975-1977; assoc prof, Sonoma State Univ, 1974-1980; asst prof physics, Sonoma State Univ, 1969-1974; asst res physicist, Univ Calif, Los Angeles, 1967-1969; Mem tech staff, Space Technol Labs, Inc, 1957-1960 & Aerospace Corp, 1960-1964. **Memberships:** Am Phys Soc; Sigma Xi. **Research Statement & Publications:** Plasma kinetic theory; nonlinear plasma theory; mathematical physics; free electron lasers; relativistic electron beams; dynamics of nonlinear oscillators with time-delay coupling. **Mailing Address:** 12 Billings St, Acton, MA 01720-2702.

JOHNSTON, GEORGE ROBERT, CYTOGENETICS. **Personal Data:** b Salt Lake City, Utah, July 4, 1934; m 1959, c 3. **Education:** Univ Utah, BS, 1959, MS, 1961, PhD (genetics), 1964. **Professional Experience:** PROF EMER BIOL, CALIF STATE UNIV, HAYWARD, 1997-; prof biol, calif state univ, hayward, 1977-1997; consult, Biomed Div, Lawrence Livermore Lab, beginning 1975; consult pediat, Kaiser Hosp, Oakland, Calif, beginning 1973; from asst prof to assoc prof, Calif State Univ, Hayward, 1967-1977; asst prof zool, Univ Wyo, 1965-1967; fel genetics, Univ Calif, Berkeley, 1964-1965. **Memberships:** Fel AAAS; Asn Cytogenetics Technologists. **Research Statement & Publications:** Human chromosome identification linked to clinical defects and the structure of mammalian chromosomes. **Mailing Address:** Dept Biol, Calif State Univ, 25800 Carlos Bee Blvd, N Sci 429, Hayward, CA 94542-3000.

JOHNSTON, GEORGE TAYLOR, OPTICAL PHYSICS, PROJECT MANAGEMENT. **Personal Data:** b Princeton, WVa, April 18, 1942; m 1966, Linda; c Chet & Jill. **Education:** Mich State Univ, BS, 1962, MS, 1965, PhD (physics), 1967; Univ Dayton, MS, 1974. **Honors & Awards:** Public Serv Medal, NASA, 2000. **Professional Experience:** PROG MGR, OPTICAL COATING LAB INC, 1982-; sr scientist, Rocketdyne, Div Rockwell Int, 1981-1982; res physicist, Univ Dayton, Res Inst, 1972-1981; asst prof, Univ Dayton, 1969-1972; res assoc physics, Brown Univ, 1967-1969. **Memberships:** Soc Photo-optical Instrumentation Engrs. **Research Statement & Publications:** Optical properties of materials; optical instrumentation and metrology; analysis, test and evalutation of high energy laser optical components and component materials, including optical thin films and laser damage mechanisms in coatings, mirrors and transparent materials. **Mailing Address:** 1829 Sherwood Ct, Santa Rosa, CA 95405. **Fax:** 707-547-6616. **E-Mail:** johjerry@msn.com

JOHNSTON, GEORGEANN V, MATHEMATICS. **Education:** Univ Tex, Phd, 1982. **Professional Experience:** Math Consult, Lutcher Stark High Sch, ending 1977. **Mailing Address:** 3717 Malone Dr, Austin, TX 78749. **Fax:** 409-883-3530. **E-Mail:** gevajo@juno.com

JOHNSTON, GERALD ANDREW, aeronautics, astronautics; deceased, see previous edition for last biography

JOHNSTON, GERALD C, MICROBIOLOGY. **Education:** York Univ, PhD. **Honors & Awards:** Queen's Golden Jubilee Medal, Max Forman Research Prize, Dalhousie Medical Res Found. **Professional Experience:** PROF & HEAD, DEPT MICROBIOL & IMMUNOL, DALHOUSIE UNIV, as of 2005; CHAIR, CANCER RES ADV COMT, DALHOUSIE UNIV, as of 2005. **Mailing Address:** Dept Microbiol Dalhousie Univ, Seven E Tupper Bldg, Halifax, NS B3H 4H7, Can. **E-Mail:** g.c.johnston@dal.ca

JOHNSTON, GERALD SAMUEL, NUCLEAR MEDICINE. **Personal Data:** b Johnstown, Pa, August 4, 1930; m 1956, Dorothy Jones; c Joy (Biciocchi), Jill (Verna), Jana (Moritzkat), Gerald Jr, Amy (Tapparo) & Douglas. **Education:** Univ Pittsburgh, BS, 1952, MD, 1956. **Professional Experience:** CHMN, DEPT NUCLEAR MED, WASH HOSP CTR, Wash, DC, 1993-; actg chmn diag radiol, radiol, oncol & chief nuclear med, Univ Md, Baltimore, 1989-1992; prof med, radiol, oncol & chief nuclear med, Univ Md, Baltimore, 1982-1993; prof radiol & nuclear med, Uniformed Serv, Univ Health Sci, Bethesda, Md, 1979-; c lin assoc prof med, Georgetown Univ, 1974-; dir nuclear med, NIH, 1971-1982; nuclear med, Letterman Gen Hosp, San Francisco, 1969-1971; chief nuclear medicine, Walter Reed Gen Hosp, 1963-1969; comdr, Mobile Army Surg Hosp, Korea, 1961-1962; resident internal med, Brooke Gen Hosp, San Antonio, 1957-1960; i ntern rotating, Walter Reed Gen Hosp, US Army, 1956-1957. **Memberships:** Soc Nuclear Med; Am Col Physicians; Am Med Asn; Am Col Radiol; Am Col Nuclear Med; Am Col Nuclear Med (pres 2000). **Research Statement & Publications:** Renal function; renal transplantation; nuclear medicine applications to renal function and cardiac function; nuclear medicine applications in oncology. **Mailing Address:** Dept Nuclear Med, Wash Hosp Ctr, 110 Irving St, NW, Washington, DC 20010.

JOHNSTON, GORDON ROBERT, ORGANIC CHEMISTRY. **Personal Data:** b Portland, Ore, July 13, 1928; m 2000, Irina; c Catherine, Therese, William & Dennis. **Education:** Univ Portland, BS, 1950, MS, 1952; Univ Ill, PhD (org chem), 1956. **Professional Experience:** CONSULT, REGULATORY COMPLIANCE & OCCUP SAFETY HEALTH ASN, 1991-; trainee, Mass Inst Technol, 1976-1977; asst prof chem, Pa State Univ, 1966-1991; asst prof org chem, Col Women, San Diego, 1964-1966; res fel, Calif Inst Technol, 1963-1964; res chemist, Aerojet-Gen Corp, 1962-1963; res chemist, Crown Zellerbach Corp, 1960-1962; res assoc org chem, Med Sch, Univ Ore, 1958-1960; res org chemist, Dow Chem Co, 1956-1958. **Memberships:** Am Chem Soc. **Mailing Address:** 541 Navato Pl Apt 2, Pittsburgh, PA 15228-1226. **Fax:** 412-531-6489. **E-Mail:** gxj2@psu.edu

JOHNSTON, G(ORDON) W(ILLIAM), ENGINEERING PHYSICS. **Personal Data:** b Toronto, Ont, December 10, 1926; m 1955, c 2. **Education:** Univ Toronto, BSc, 1948, MASc, 1950, PhD (aerophys), 1953. **Professional Experience:** PROF EMER, INST AEROSPACE STUDIES, UNIV TORONTO, as of 2004; prof, fluids & computational fluids, Inst Aerospace Studies, Univ Toronto, beginning 1970; aerodyn consult, Plasma Dynamics Dept, United Aircraft Res Labs, Conn, 1967-1970; head adv proj group, Del Haviland Aircraft Can, Ltd, 1963-1970; dir short take off & landing res proj, Del Haviland Aircraft Can, Ltd, 1960-1963; lectr, Inst Aerophys, Univ Toronto, 1957-1959; proj engr, Del Haviland Aircraft Can, Ltd, 1955-1963; head gas dynamics sect, Res Div, Ford Motor Co,

Mich, 1954-1955; res supvr sci lab, Res Div, Ford Motor Co, Mich, 1953-1954; asst, Defense Res Bd Can, 1952-1953; design engr, A V Roe, Co, Ltd, Can, 1949-1951; mem assoc comt aerodyn noise, Nat Res Coun Can. **Memberships:** Can Aeronaut Inst. **Research Statement & Publications:** Transonic and low-speed aerodynamics; boundary layer control; stability and control of fixed and rotating wing aircraft configurations; slipstream wing aerodynamics. **Mailing Address:** Inst Aerospace Studies, Univ Toronto, Toronto, ON M9A 4P5, Can. **E-Mail:** gwj@utias.utoronto.ca

JOHNSTON, HARLIN DEE, PETROLEUM CHEMISTRY, PILOT PLANT. **Personal Data:** b Ogden, Utah, March 16, 1942; m 1963, Ann; c Matthew, Jennifer, Kelly & Jason. **Education:** Brigham Young Univ, BA, 1965, PhD (inorg chem), 1968. **Professional Experience:** RES ASSOC PHILLIPS RES CTR, PHILLIPS PETROL CO, 1991- res associate; sect supvr, Phillips Petrol Co, 1983-1990; sr res chemist, Phillips Petrol Co, 1974-1982; res chemist, Phillips Petrol Co, 1968-1973. **Memberships:** Am Chem Soc; Sigma Xi. **Research Statement & Publications:** Sulfurremoval from petrolean fuels Pilot plant design, operation, and supervision; heterogenous catalysis of solid-gas and solid-liquid-gas systems; laboratory and pilot plant automation. **Mailing Address:** Phillips Res Ctr, Phillips Petrol Co, Bartlesville, OK 74004. **Fax:** 918-661-8761. **E-Mail:** hdjohns@ppco.com

JOHNSTON, HAROLD SLEDGE, PHYSICAL CHEMISTRY. **Personal Data:** b Woodstock, Ga, October 11, 1920; m 1948, Mary; c Shirley, Linda, David & Barbara (Dial). **Education:** Emory Univ, AB, 1941; Calif Inst Technol, PhD (chem), 1948. **Honorary Degrees:** DSc, Emory Univ, 1965. **Honors & Awards:** Gold Medal Award, Calif Sect, Am Chem Soc, 1956, Pollution Control Award, 1974, Award Chem Contemporay Technol Probs, 1985; Bourke Lectr, Faraday Soc, 1961; George B Kistiakowsky Lectr, Harvard Univ, 1973; G N Lewis Lectr, Univ Calif, 1975; Cassett Found Lectr, Temple Univ, 1978; Tyler Prize, 1983; Award Chem Serv to Soc, Nat Acad Sci, 1993; Nat Medal of Sci, 1997. **Professional Experience:** PROF EMER, UNIV CALIF, as of 2005; Acad Senate Fac res lectr, Univ Calif, Berkeley, 1988-1989; assoc ed, J Geophys Res, 1977-1981; nat lectr, Sigma Xi, 1973; Mat & Molecular Res Div, Lawrence Berkeley Lab, 1966- & others; dean, Col Chem, Univ Calif, Berkeley, 1966-1970; NATO vis prof, Univ Rome, Italy, 1964; res grants, USPHS, 1963-1970; Guggenheim fel, Belg, 1960-1961; res grants, NSF, 1959-1968 & 1975-1978; prof chem, Col Chem, Univ Calif, Berkeley, 1957-1991; assoc prof chem, Nat Defense Res Comt, Calif Inst Technol, 1956-1957; res grants, Stand Oil Calif, 1955-1957; res grants, M W Kellogg Co, 1951-1953; res grants, Off Naval Res, 1950-1956; from instr to assoc prof, Stanford Univ, 1947-1956; asst, Nat Defense Res Comt, Calif Inst Technol, 1942-1945. **Memberships:** Nat Acad Sci; fel AAAS; Am Chem Soc; fel Am Phys Soc; Am Acad Arts & Sci; fel Am Geophys Union; Sigma Xi. **Research Statement & Publications:** Fast gas phase reactions; kinetic isotope effects; photochemistry; unimolecular reactions; atmospheric chemistry; author of 2 books and numerous publications. **Mailing Address:** Dept Chem, Univ Calif, Berkeley, CA 94720. **Fax:** 510-643-2156.

JOHNSTON, HERBERT NORRIS, CHEMISTRY. **Personal Data:** b Cleveland, Ohio, August 9, 1928; m 1950, c 2. **Education:** Ohio Univ, BS, 1949. **Professional Experience:** MGR INDUST MKT OFF, COLUMBUS LABS, BATTELLE MEM INST, 1978-; mgr polymer & paper chem, Columbus Lab, 1972-1978; chief polymer & paper technol div, Columbus Lab, 1968-1972; assoc chief, Battelle Mem Inst, 1952-1968; res chemist coatings res, Glidden Co, 1949-1952. **Memberships:** Am Chem Soc; Sigma Xi; Tech Asn Pulp & Paper Indust; Am Mkt Asn; Am Mgt Asn. **Research Statement & Publications:** Coatings, polymers, adhesives and inks for paper, wood and metals; powdered polymers, service life of polymeric materials, processing of plastics. **Mailing Address:** 1883 Andover Rd, Columbus, OH 43212-1001.

JOHNSTON, HIRAM D, MATHEMATICS. **Professional Experience:** PROF MATH, GA STATE UNIV, as of 2006. **Memberships:** US Math Educ. **Mailing Address:** Dept Curr & Instr Ga State Univ, Univ Plaza, Atlanta, GA 30303. **Fax:** 404-651-2000. **E-Mail:** johnston@gsu.edu

JOHNSTON, IAN S, BIOLOGY. **Education:** Cambridge Univ, BA, 1970, MA, 1974; Univ Calif, Los Angeles, PhD, 1978. **Professional Experience:** ASSOC PROF BIOL, BETHEL UNIV, as of 2005. **Mailing Address:** Bethel Univ, St Paul, MN 55112. **Fax:** 612-638-6001. **E-Mail:** johian@homer.acs.bethel.edu

JOHNSTON, JAMES BAKER, SPATIAL ANALYSIS, SCIENCE EDUCATION, COASTAL ECOSYSTEMS. **Personal Data:** b Baton Rouge, La, September 10, 1946; m 1970, Sheri; c Jamey, Stefanie, Robyn & Chris. **Education:** La State Univ, Baton Rouge, BS, 1970, MEd, 1971; Univ Southern Miss, PhD (sci educ, biol), 1973. **Honors & Awards:** Edward H Hillard Award, Nat Wildlife Fedn, 1972. **Professional Experience:** CHIEF, U S ECOL SUR, NAT WETLANDS RES CTR, 1992-; adj prof, Univ Lafayette Sch Appl Sci, 1996-; SUPV ECOLOGIST, US FISH & WILDLIFE SERV, US DEPT INTERIOR, 1985-; consult, Environ Can, 1984-1986; ecologist, US Fish & Wildlife Serv, US Dept Interior, 1976-1985; oceanogr marine biol, Bur Land Mgt, New Orleans, 1974-1976; marine fisheries mgt consult, Miss Marine Res Coun, 1973-1974; marine res asst, Univ Southern Miss, Gulf Univs Res Consortium, 1972-1973; math instr & NSF consult, Prentiss Inst & Jr Col, 1972-1973. **Memberships:** Ecol Soc Am; Explorers Club; Estuarine Res Fedn; Coastal Soc; Wildlife Soc. **Research Statement & Publications:** Characterization and spatial analysis of coastal ecosystems; ecosystem characterization and system analysis for Louisiana coastal wetlands restoration development of coastal science education programs; studies on wetlands and coastal barriers. **Mailing Address:** Nat Wetlands Res Ctr, US Geol Surv, 700 Cajundome Blvd, Lafayette, LA 70506. **Fax:** 337-266-8616. **E-Mail:** jimmy_johnston@usgs.gov

JOHNSTON, JAMES BENNETT, APPLIED BIOCHEMISTRY, BIOCHEMICAL TECHNOLOGY. **Personal Data:** b San Diego, Calif, December 31, 1943; m 1969, Margaret; c Mary E & Amy R. **Education:** Univ Md, Col Park, BS, 1966; Univ Wis-Madison, PhD (biochem), 1970. **Professional Experience:** RES CHEMIST, BIOCOAT INC, as of 2006; prin investr, Beacon Res, Inc, beginning 1999; founder & exec vpres, JWT, Inc, 1995-1999; dir res, Enzymatics, Inc, 1989-1994; res fel, Enzymatics, Inc, 1987-1989; sr investr, Smith Kline & Fr, 1983-1987; Pan-Am Health Orgn, 1980- & Agrobiotics Corp, 1981-; prin investr, Var Grants, 1977-; asst prof, Univ Ill, Urbana, 1976-1983; consult, Ill Environ Protection Agency, 1976-1981; consult, Cetus Corp, 1976-1980; vis asst prof, Univ Ill, Urbana, 1974-1976; res fel, Univ Kent, Canterbury, UK, 1971-1974; fel, Inst Pasteur, Paris, 1970-1971. **Memberships:** Am Chem Soc; Am Soc Artificial Internal Organs. **Research Statement & Publications:** Recovery, detection and identification of environmental mutagens, especially in potable waters, and the genetics of hydrocarbon degradation by bacteria; manipulation of bacteria for production of specialty chemicals; invention and development of instrument-dependent, diagnostic devices; development of hyaluronan-based biocompatible coatings for medical devices. **Mailing Address:** Biocoat Inc, 211 Witmer Rd, Horsham, PA 19044. **Fax:** 215-734-0889.

JOHNSTON, JAMES P(AUL), MECHANICAL ENGINEERING, FLUID DYNAMICS. **Personal Data:** b Pittsburgh, Pa, May 11, 1931; m 1957, c 5. **Education:** Mass Inst Technol, BS & MS, 1954, ScD(mech eng), 1957. **Honors & Awards:** Robert T Knapp Award, Am Soc Mech Engrs, 1975. **Professional Experience:** PROF EMER MECH ENG, STANFORD UNIV, 1994-; chmn, Thermosciences Div, Standford Univ, 1985-1990; prof, Stanford Univ, beginning 1973; vis res scientist, Nat Phys Lab, Teddington, Eng, 1967-1968; Am Soc Mech Engrs-Freeman fel, 1967; from asst prof to assoc prof, Stanford Univ, 1961-1973; instr, Night Grad Sch Prog, Lehigh Univ, 1959-1960; res engr, Ingersoll-Rand Co, NJ, 1958-1961. **Memberships:** AAAS; Am Soc Mech Engrs; Am Inst Aeronaut & Astronaut. **Research Statement & Publications:** Fluid dynamics of real fluids, particularly two and three-dimensional turbulent boundary layers; effects of coordinate system rotation on the turbulent boundary layer; fluid flow in ducts, diffusers and tubomachinery. **Mailing Address:** Dept Mech Eng, Stanford Univ, Stanford, CA 94305. **Fax:** 650-723-4548. **E-Mail:** jpj@stanford.edu

JOHNSTON, JEAN VANCE, ORGANIC CHEMISTRY. **Personal Data:** b Shippensburg, Pa, February 17, 1912. **Education:** Smith Col, AB, 1934; Yale Univ, PhD (org chem), 1938. **Professional Experience:** Assoc prof, Shippensburg Univ, 1976 & 1977; ASSOC PROF EMER CHEM, CONN COL, 1974-; fel, Pa State Univ, 1969-1970; from instr to assoc prof chem, Conn Col, 1942-1974; asst prof chem, Furman Univ, 1940-1942; instr pvt sch, Conn, 1940; Asst chem, Smith Col, 1939. **Memberships:** Am Chem Soc; Sigma Xi. **Research Statement & Publications:** Synthesis of organic compounds of medicinal interest; amidines. **Mailing Address:** 505 W King St, Shippensburg, PA 17257.

JOHNSTON, JOHN, RUBBER CHEMISTRY. **Personal Data:** b Newcastle-on-Tyne, Eng, November 8, 1925; American citizen; m 1977, Naruse; c Ian, Trevor & Alan. **Education:** Hull Col Technol, BSc, 1958. **Professional Experience:** DIR APPLNS ENG, TESA TAPE INC, 1989-; dir res, Tuck Industs, 1977-1989; dir, Tech Serv, Johnson & Johnson, 1975-1977; chmn tech comt, Pressure Sensitive Tape Coun, & planning comt, 1974-1976; vpres res, Develop & Tech Opers, 1973-1975; dir res & develop, Arno Adhesive Tape Inc, 1971-1973; dir res, Arno Adhesive Tape Inc, 1968-1971; asst dir res pressure sensitive adhesives, Arno Adhesive Tape Inc, 1967; lectr, Purdue Univ, NRegional Campus, 1965-1971; res chemist, Arno Adhesive Tape Inc, 1959-1967; chemist, Stand Oil Co, Saltend, 1949-1950 & T J Smith & Nephew Ltd, Hull, 1950-1958; t eacher, Co Educ Authorities, Hull, Eng, 1948-1949; vchmn, Adhesive Tape Tech Comt, Nat Elec Mfr Asn. **Memberships:** Am Chem Soc; Am Soc Testing & Mat; Inst Elec & Electronics Engrs. **Research Statement & Publications:** Theory and practice of pressure sensitive adhesives. **Mailing Address:** Tesa Tape Inc, 5825 Carnegie Blvd, Charlotte, NC 28209. **Fax:** 704-553-5677.

JOHNSTON, JOHN B(EVERLEY), CONTOUR MODEL OF OPERATIONAL SEMANTICS, SYNTAX-DIRECTED COMPILING EDITORS. **Personal Data:** b Los Angeles, Calif, August 11, 1929; m 1966, Leatrice H Shaw; c Sharilee M. **Education:** Calif Inst Technol, BS, 1951, PhD (math), 1955. **Professional Experience:** PROF COMPUT SCI, NMEX STATE UNIV, 1971-; info scientist, Gen Elec Res & Develop Ctr, NY, 1969-1971; assoc prof comput sci, Ind Univ, Bloomington, 1968-1969; mathematician, Gen Elec Res & Develop Ctr, NY, 1964-1968; from asst prof to assoc prof, Univ Kans, 1958-1964; asst prof, Univ Kansas City, 1957-1958; i nstr math, Cornell Univ, 1955-1957. **Memberships:** Asn Comput Mach; Sigma Xi. **Research Statement & Publications:** Structure of computation; computer languages; structure of computer systems. **Mailing Address:** Dept Comput Sci, NMex State Univ, Las Cruces, NM 88001. **E-Mail:** jbj@nmsu.edu

JOHNSTON, JOHN ERIC, POLYMER & ANALYTICAL CHEMISTRY, LUBRICANTS & FUELS. **Personal Data:** b Detroit, Mich, February 5, 1948; m 1985, Cathleen. **Education:** Univ Notre Dame, BS, 1970; Univ Akron, PhD (polymer sci), 1975. **Professional Experience:** SR SCI ADV, ADVAN VEHICLES FUEL RES & DEVELOP, EXXONMOBIL RES & ENG CO, as of 2004; CHMN, NAT VIS COMT, as of 2004; SECT HEAD, ADVAN FUELS & LUBRICANTS, EXXON RES & ENG CO CORP RES, 1991-; component mgr viscosity modifiers, Polyalkene Tech, 1990-1991; LEADER, DISCHARGE ELIMINATION TASK FORCE, EXXON CHEM CO, 1989-; head, Polyalkene Tech, 1988-1989; head, Viscosity Index Modifier Res Group, Exxon Chem Co, 1981-1988; sr chemist polymer synthesis & characterization, Union Carbide Corp, 1976-1980; fel polymer sci, Ctr Macromolecular Res, 1975; vis comt mem, NSF Advan Technol Educ Prog. **Memberships:** Am Chem Soc; Soc Automotive Engrs; AAAS. **Research Statement & Publications:** Basic research related to fuel and lubricant additives, combustion characteristics, lube tribology and rheology, genetic algoritm application to molecular design. **Mailing Address:** Exxonmobil Res & Eng Co, 1545 US Route 22 E Rm LB226, Annandale, NJ 08801.

JOHNSTON, JOHN MARSHALL, BIOCHEMISTRY. **Personal Data:** b North Platte, Nebr, November 14, 1928; m 1953, c 3. **Education:** Hastings Col, BA, 1949; Univ Colo, PhD, 1953. **Professional Experience:** PROF OBSTET & GYNEC, UNIV TEX HEALTH SCI CTR, DALLAS, 1974-; PROF BIOCHEM, UNIV TEX HEALTH SCI CTR, DALLAS, 1966-; NSF sr res fel, Univ Lund, 1962-1963; from instr to assoc prof, Univ Tex Health Sci Ctr, Dallas, 1955-1966; resassoc, Walter Reed Inst Res, 1953-1955. **Memberships:** AAAS; Am Chem Soc; Am Soc Biol Chemists; Sigma Xi. **Research Statement & Publications:** Lipid metabolism in absorption; fetal lung maturation, partuition and membranes. **Mailing Address:** Dept Biochem, Southwest Med Sch, 5323 Harry Hines, C3-209, Dallas, TX 75235-9051. **Fax:** 214-648-8856. **E-Mail:** johnston@grnctr.swmed.edu

JOHNSTON, JOHN O'NEAL, BIOCHEMICAL ENDOCRINOLOGY, NEUROENDOCRINE PHARMACOLOGY. **Personal Data:** b Baltimore, Md, July 21, 1939; m 1977, Laura; c Stuart H Johnston & Shannon O Schroeder. **Education:** Univ Md, Col Park, BS, 1961, MS, 1965, PhD (reproductive physiol), 1970. **Professional Experience:** President, Endocrine Associates, LLC; 1995-; Sr Res Sci & group leader endocrinology, Marion Merrell Dow Res Inst, Marion Merrell Dow Inc, 1993-1995; sci adv bd, Cincinnati Zoo, 1985-1993; Sr Res Endocrinologist, ENDOCRINOL, MARION MERRELL DOW RES INST, MARION MERRELL DOW INC, 1981-; biol consult, Life Sci Div, Res Triangle Park, NC, 1975-1978; sect head endocrinol, Endocrinol, marion Merrell Dow Res Inst, Marion Merrell Dow Inc, 1973-1981; Consult vet pharmaceut, Jensen-Salsbery Labs, Kansas, Mo, 1972-1979; res endocrinologist, Endocrinol, marion Merrell Dow Res Inst, Marion Merrell Dow Inc, 1971-1973; res scientist fertil res, Upjohn Co, 1969-1971; res asst, Dept Animal Sci, Univ Md, 1965-1969; Res asst reproductive physiol, Agr Res Serv, USDA, 1961-1965. **Research Statement & Publications:** Development of therapeutic agents for control of male and female fertility; regulation of hormonal action via receptor mechanism in target tissues; animal growth stimulants; neuroendocrine pharmacology of animal behavior; development of enzyme inhibitors for regulation of endocrine dependent cancer, endocrine hypertension and reproductive processes. **Mailing Address:** Endocrine Assoc, 9 Crooked Creek, Milford, OH 45150. **Fax:** 513-831-1758. **E-Mail:** onealj1@aol.com

JOHNSTON, JOHN SPENCER, ENTOMOLOGY. **Personal Data:** b Phoenix, Ariz, May 27, 1944; m 1966, c 1. **Education:** Univ Wash, BS, 1966; Univ Ariz, PhD (genetics), 1972. **Professional Experience:** PROF ENTOMOL & GENETICS, TEX A&M UNIV, as of 2005; assoc prof genetics, Tex A&M Univ, 1979-; asst prof biol, Baylor Univ, Waco, 1975-1979; res grant, Energy Res Develop Asn & Univ Tex, Austin, 1973-; NIH fel, Univ Tex,

Austin, 1972-1975. **Memberships:** AAAS; Genetics Soc Am; Evolution Soc Am; Soc Am Naturalists. **Research Statement & Publications:** Ecological genetics of Drosophila species. **Mailing Address:** Entom Dept, Tex A&M Univ, College Station, TX 77843-0100. **Fax:** 979-845-6300. **E-Mail:** spencerj@tamu.edu

JOHNSTON, KATHARINE GENTRY, industrial organic chemistry; deceased, see previous edition for last biography

JOHNSTON, KENNETH JOHN, ASTRONOMY. **Personal Data:** b New York, NY, October 9, 1941; m 1966. **Education:** Manhattan Col, BEE, 1964; Georgetown Univ, PhD (astron), 1969. **Honors & Awards:** Sigma Xi; Alexander von Humboldt. **Professional Experience:** SCI DIR, US NAVAL OBSERV, 1993-; ASTRONR, US NAVAL OBSERV, 1993-; supt, Remote Sensing Div, NRL, 1991-1992; chief scientist & dir, Ctr Advan Space Sensing, NRL, beginning 1990; br head radio & IR astron, NRL, beginning 1980; astronr, Naval Res Lab, 1971-1993; res assoc astron, Nat Acad Sci-Nat Res Coun, 1969-1971. **Memberships:** Am Astron Soc; Int Astron Union. **Research Statement & Publications:** Radio astronomy; variable stars. **Mailing Address:** US Naval Observ, 3450 Mass Ave NW, Washington, DC 20392-5420.

JOHNSTON, LAURANCE S, SPINAL CORD RESEARCH. **Personal Data:** b St Paul, Minn, August 4, 1950; m 1975, Pauline. **Education:** Hamline Univ, BS, 1972; Northwestern Univ, Evanston, MS, 1973, PhD (biochem & molecular biol), 1977; George Mason Univ, MBA, 1985. **Professional Experience:** CONSULT 1997-; DIR, PARALYZED VET AM SPINAL CORD RES & EDUC FOUND, 1992-; dir, Div Sci Rev, 1986-1992; health scientist adminr & exec secy, Nat Inst Child Health & Human Develop, NIH, 1981-1986; Drug Admin, Wash, DC, 1978-1981; fel, Chicago Med Sch, 1977-1978; fel, Dept Biochem & Molecular Biol, Northwestern Univ, 1976-1977; dep dir, Div Sci Rev; consumer safety officer, Off Compliance, Bur Foods, Food. **Memberships:** Soc Res Adminr; Nat Coun Univ Res Adminr; Soc Neuroscience; Am Paraplegia Soc. **Research Statement & Publications:** Foundation funding source for spinal cord research and education grants. **Mailing Address:** Paralyzed Vet Am, 801 18th St NW, Washington, DC 20006. **Fax:** 202-416-7641.

JOHNSTON, LA VERNE ALBERT, BOTANY. **Personal Data:** b Hallettsville, Tex, March 7, 1930; m 1961, c 2. **Education:** Baylor Univ, AB, 1951, MA, 1957; Southwestern Baptist Theol Sem, MRE, 1954. **Professional Experience:** RETIRED; pres, Johnston Enterprises; tech writer, 1980-1983; res asst bot, Univ Tex, Austin, 1976-1980 & 1983-1990; instr & asst prof biol, Baylor Univ, 1954-1960; teacher, Gonzales Ind Sch Dist, 1951-1952. **Memberships:** Am Inst Biol Sci; Bot Soc Am. **Research Statement & Publications:** Phycology; angiosperm taxonomy. **Mailing Address:** 10412 Double Spur Loop, Austin, TX 78759.

JOHNSTON, LAWRENCE HARDING, OPTICAL PHYSICS. **Personal Data:** b Tse-Nan-Fu, China, February 11, 1918; American citizen; m 1942, Mildred Hillis; c Mary, Margaret, Daniel, Lois & Karen. **Education:** Univ Calif Berkeley, AB, 1940, PhD (physics), 1950. **Honors & Awards:** Significant Patents Ground Controlled Approach Radar blind landing sys, patent number 2, 555, 101 Electric Initiator with Exploding Bridgewire, patent number 3, 040, 660. **Professional Experience:** EMER PROF PHYSICS, UNIV IDAHO, 1988-; prof, Univ Idaho, 1967-1988; sr staff mem, Stanford Linear Accelerator Ctr, 1963-1967; sr scientist, Aerospace Corp, 1961-1963; from instr to assoc prof physics, Univ Minn, Minneapolis, 1950-1961; Staff mem, Los Alamos Nat lab, 1944-1945; Res assoc, Radiation Lab, Mass Inst Technol, 1940-1943. **Memberships:** Fel Am Phys Soc; fel Am Sci Affil; Phi Beta Kappa. **Research Statement & Publications:** Far infrared physics; molecular spectroscopy; microwave radar; atom bomb development; proton linear accelerator development; nuclear and high energy particle physics; proton-proton scattering; submillimeter wave laser stark spectroscopy. **Mailing Address:** 917 E Eighth St, Moscow, ID 83843. **E-Mail:** johnston@uidaho.edu

JOHNSTON, MALCOLM CAMPBELL, TERATOLOGY, DEVELOPMENTAL BIOLOGY. **Personal Data:** b Montague, PEI, February 13, 1931; m 1955. **Education:** Univ Toronto, DDS, 1954, MScD, 1956; Univ Rochester, PhD (anat), 1965. **Professional Experience:** PROF EMER ORTHOD & CELL BIOL & ANAT, SCH DENT, UNIV NC, as of 2003; sect ed, Cleft Palate J, 1981-; prof orthodont & anat, Sch Dent & Med, Univ NC, beginning 1976; vis scientist, NIH, Bethesda, Md, 1969-1976; asst & assoc prof hist, Sch Dent & Med, Univ Toronto, 1964-1969; res assoc clin res, Cleft Palate Res & Treat Ctr, Hosp Sick Children, Toronto, 1956-1960. **Memberships:** Sigma Xi; Am Cleft Palate Asn; Teratology Soc; Am Asn Anatomists. **Research Statement & Publications:** Normal and abnormal embryonic craniofacial development in mice, with limited studies on man. **Mailing Address:** Dept Orthod, Cell Biol & Anat, Sch Dent, Univ NC, Manning Dr & Columbia St CB # 7450, Chapel Hill, NC 27599-7450.

JOHNSTON, MANLEY RODERICK, ORGANIC POLYMER CHEMISTRY. **Personal Data:** b Edmonton, Alta, October 2, 1942; m 1967, c Cindy & Christine. **Education:** Univ Alta, BSc, 1964; Univ Ill, Urbana, MS, 1966 & PhD (org chem), 1969. **Professional Experience:** TECH DIR, 3M CO, EUROPE, 1989-; dir, Disposible Prod Div, 1986-1989; dir Life Sci Res Lab, Nonwovens Technol Ctr, 1983-1986; lab mgr, Nonwovens Technol Ctr, 1982-1983; tech mgr, Bldg Serv & Cleaning Prod Div, 1978-1982; supvr, 3M Co, 1973-1978; res specialist, 3M Co, 1972-1973; sr chemist, 3M Co, 1968-1972. **Memberships:** Am Chem Soc; Royal Soc Chem. **Research Statement & Publications:** Small ring compounds; organic coatings; metal finishing; adhesion; high temperature polymers; fibers; polymerization catalysts; fluorine chemistry. **Mailing Address:** 352 Quail Rd, St Paul, MN 55110.

JOHNSTON, MARGARET IRENE, IMMUNOLOGY. **Education:** Carnegie Mellon Univ, BS, 1972; Tufts Univ, PhD (biochem), 1977. **Professional Experience:** ASST DIR DIV AIDS, NAT INST ALLERGY & INFECTIOUS DIS, NIH, 1993-; assoc dir, Basic Res & Develop Prog, 1991-1993; chief, Develop Therapeut Br, 1990-1991; chief, Targeted Drug Discovery Sect, 1988-1989; adj assoc prof, Dept Biochem, Uniformed Serv Univ Health Sci, 1987-1993; prog officer, Develop Therapeut Br, NIH, 1987-1988; NSF, 1983-1986; NIH, 1984-1987; prin investr, Uniformed Serv Univ Health Sci, 1983-1986; asst prof, Dept Biochem, Uniformed Serv Univ Health Sci, 1982-1987; sr staff fel, Lab Chem, Nat Inst Diabetes, Digestive & Kidney Dis, NIH, 1980-1982; staff fel, Lab Chem, Nat Inst Diabetes, Digestive & Kidney Dis, NIH, 1978-1980; assoc, Rega Inst Med Res, Cath Univ Leuven, Belg, 1977-1978. **Memberships:** AAAS; Am Soc Biochem & Molecular Biol; Am Soc Microbiol; Asn Women Sci; Int Soc AIDS Res; Int Soc Antiviral Res. **Research Statement & Publications:** Human immunovirus/acquired immunodeficiency syndrome therapeutics and vaccine design, evaluation, development; human immunovirus/acquired immunodeficiency syndrome basic research and pathogenesis. **Mailing Address:** Nat Inst Allergy & Infectious Dis, NIH, 1400 I St NW Ste 1220, Washington, DC 20005. **Fax:** 202-408-1818.

JOHNSTON, MARILYN FRANCES MEYERS, BIOCHEMISTRY, IMMUNOLOGY. **Personal Data:** b Buffalo, NY, March 30, 1937. **Education:** Dameon Col (Rosary Hill Col), BS, 1966; St Louis Univ, PhD (biochem), 1970, MD, 1975. **Professional Experience:** PROF PATH, MED SCH, ST LOUIS UNIV, as of 2006; mem comt transfusion pract, Am Asn Blood Banks, 1984-1989; vchmn inspection & accreditation, Am Asn Blood Banks, 1983-; med dir, Mo-Ill Regional Red Cross, 1983-1988; from asst prof to assoc prof, Med Sch, St Louis Univ, 1980-1991; fel path & med, Med Sch, St Louis Univ, 1979-1980; resident path, Sch Med, Wash Univ, 1972-1975 & St John's Mercy Med Ctr, 1977-1979; AMA J Goldberger fel, St Louis Univ, 1974; instr biochem, Sch Med, St Louis Univ, 1972-1975; NIH fel, Wash Univ, 1970-1972; prin investr; med dir blood bank, Transfusion Serv, Apheris, St Louis Univ Hosp. **Memberships:** Am Asn Blood Banks; Col Am Pathologists; Am Asn Immunologists; Int Soc Blood Transfusion; Sigma Xi; Am Soc Clin Path. **Research Statement & Publications:** Transfusion medicine; red cell surface antigens; erythoporetin. **Mailing Address:** Sch Med, St Louis Univ Hosps, 11133 Dunn Rd, St Louis, MO 63136.

JOHNSTON, MARSHALL CONRING, SYSTEMATIC BOTANY. **Personal Data:** b San Antonio, Tex, May 10, 1930; m 1961, c 2. **Education:** Univ Tex, BS, 1951, MA, 1952, PhD (bot), 1955. **Professional Experience:** Dir, Rare Plant Study Ctr, 1972-; PROF BOT, UNIV TEX, AUSTIN, 1972-; sci asst, Univ Munich, 1968-1969; assoc prof, Univ Tex, Austin, 1961-1972; res scientist bot, Univ Tex, Austin, 1959-1961; asst prof biol, Sul Ross State Col, 1958-1959; fel, Rice Inst, 1955. **Memberships:** AAAS; Bot Soc Am; Am Soc Plant Taxon; Int Soc Plant Taxon; Am Inst Biol Sci; Sigma Xi. **Research Statement & Publications:** Distribution of vegetation types; systematics and historical biogeography of vascular plants of southwestern United States and northern Mexico; flora of Texas. **Mailing Address:** 10412 Double Spur Loop, Austin, TX 78759-6912. **Fax:** 512-471-3878.

JOHNSTON, MELVIN ROSCOE, food technology; deceased, see previous edition for last biography

JOHNSTON, MILES GREGORY, SHOCK, INFLAMMATION. **Education:** Univ Toronto, PhD (exp path), 1978. **Professional Experience:** PROF PATH, UNIV TORONTO, as of 2004; assoc prof path, Univ Toronto, beginning 1981. **Mailing Address:** Sunnybrook & Women's Col Health Sci CentreTrauma Res Prog, Rm S-111, 2075 Bayview Ave, Toronto, ON M4N 3M5, Can. **Fax:** 416-480-5737. **E-Mail:** miles.johnston@swchsc.on.ca

JOHNSTON, MILTON DWYNELL, PHYSICAL CHEMISTRY, MOLECULAR SPECTROSCOPY. **Personal Data:** b Hillsboro, Ore, November 4, 1943. **Education:** Portland State Univ, BA, 1965; Princeton Univ, AM, 1968, PhD (chem), 1969. **Professional Experience:** PROF CHEM, UNIV SFLA, 1994-; assoc prof chem, Univ SFla, 1980-1994; asst prof, Univ SFla, 1973-1980; res assoc, Tex A&M Univ, 1971-1973; res assoc nuclear magnetic resonance, Univ Ariz, 1970-1971. **Memberships:** Am Chem Soc; Royal Soc Chem; Sigma Xi; NY Acad Sci; Am Phys Soc. **Research Statement & Publications:** Nuclear magnetic resonance solvent effects; theory of nuclear magnetic resonance spectral parameters; theory of liquids and liquid solutions and of intermolecular forces. **Mailing Address:** Dept Chem, Univ SFla, 4202 E Fowler Ave CHE 114, Tampa, FL 33620-5250. **E-Mail:** johnston@chuma1.cas.usf.edu

JOHNSTON, NORMAN JOSEPH, ORGANIC POLYMER CHEMISTRY, POLYMER MATRIX COMPOSITES TECHNOLOGY. **Personal Data:** b Charles Town, WVa, December 15, 1934; m 1957, Joy; c Jennifer, Robin, Susan & Carol. **Education:** Shepherd Col, BS, 1956; Univ Va, PhD (org chem), 1963. **Honors & Awards:** NASA Except Serv Medal. **Professional Experience:** MGR, COMPOSITES TECHNOL, LANGLEY RES CTR, NASA, 1991-; chief scientist-Mat, NASA, 1988-1990; sr scientist, NASA, 1981-1988; head polymer sect, NASA, 1970-1980; aerospace technologist & chemist, NASA, 1967-1970; Nat Acad Sci-Nat ResCoun resident res fel, NASA, 1966-1967; asst prof chem, Va Polytech Inst & State Univ, 1963-1966; chemist insulating mat dept, Gen Elec Co, 1961-1963. **Memberships:** Am Chem Soc; Soc Aerospace Mat & Process Engrs; Am Soc Composites. **Research Statement & Publications:** Synthesis and characterization of high performance polymers and their evaluation as composite matrices; toughened high performance composites; resin property-composite property relationships; composite fabrication technology. **Mailing Address:** NASA Langley Res Ctr, Mail Stop 226, Hampton, VA 23681-0001. **Fax:** 757-864-8312. **E-Mail:** norm_johnston@qmgate.larc.nasa.gov

JOHNSTON, NORMAN PAUL, ANIMAL NUTRITION, REPRODUCTION BIOLOGY. **Personal Data:** b Salt Lake City, Utah, April 5, 1941; m 1966, c 5. **Education:** Brigham Young Univ, BA, 1966; Ore State Univ, MS, 1967, PhD (avian nutril), 1971; Univ Utah, MBA, 1969. **Professional Experience:** INT NNUTRITIONIST, BRIGHAM YOUNG UNIV, as of 2004; PROF ANIMAL SCI, BRIGHAM YOUNG UNIV, 1971-; Animal Nutritionist, Brookfield Prod Inc, 1969-1970. **Memberships:** Sigma Xi; Poultry Sci; Am Soc Animal Sci; World Poultry Sci. **Research Statement & Publications:** Poultry reproduction, in particular artificial insemination; animal nutrition - rabbits, goats, poultry; international agriculture. **Mailing Address:** Agron Dept, Brigham Young Univ, 275 Widb, Provo, UT 84602-1049. **E-Mail:** paul_johnston@byu.edu

JOHNSTON, NORMAN WILSON, POLYMER CHEMISTRY. **Personal Data:** b Pittsburgh, Pa, June 18, 1942; m 1965, c 3. **Education:** Clarion State Col, BS, 1964; Univ Akron, PhD (polymer sci), 1968. **Professional Experience:** PRES & CHEIF EXEC OFFICER, SOLVAY AUTOMOTIVE INC, as of 2005; vpres technol & eng, Libbey-Owens-Ford Co, as of 2002; mgr bus & tech planning, Owens-Corning Fiberglass Corp, beginning 1981; res dir, Owens-Corning Fiberglass Corp, 1978-1981; lab dir, Owens-Corning Fiberglass Corp, 1977-1979; assoc dir res & develop, Owens-Corning Fiberglass Corp, 1976-1977; group leader adhesives, coatings & moldings, 1972-1976; proj scientist, Union Carbide Corp, 1971-1972; sr chemist, Union Carbide Corp, 1968-1971; chemist polymer chem, Ethyl Corp, 1965. **Memberships:** Am Chem Soc. **Research Statement & Publications:** Polymer structure: property relationships, polymer synthesis, coatings, adhesives, fire retardance, molding and extrusion, composites, polymer blends, degradable plastics, cement, foams, insulation. **Mailing Address:** Solvay Automotive Inc, 2565 W Maple Rd, Troy, MI 48084.

JOHNSTON, PAUL BRUNS, MEDICAL MICROBIOLOGY. **Personal Data:** b Chicago, Ill, April 2, 1927; wid, c 3. **Education:** Northwestern Univ, BS, 1949; Loyola Univ, Ill, MS, 1951; Univ Chicago, PhD (microbiol), 1957. **Professional Experience:** ASSOC PROF MICROBIOL, SCH MED, UNIV LOUISVILLE, 1964-; asst prof microbiol, Jefferson Med Col, 1960-1964; v irologist, US Naval Med Res Unit 2, Taiwan, 1957-1960; Instr, Univ Chicago, 1957-1960. **Memberships:** Am Soc Microbiol; Soc Exp Biol & Med; Tissue Cult Asn; Am Asn Immunol. **Research Statement & Publications:** Nature of latent virus infections; simian foamy virus immunology; adenoviruses. **Mailing Address:** Dept Microbiol Sch Med, Univ Louisville, 2301 S Third St, Louisville, KY 40292-0001. **Fax:** 502-852-7531. **E-Mail:** john01@ulkyvm.louisville.edu

JOHNSTON, PAULINE KAY, SCIENCE POLICY, INFORMATION DISSEMMINATION. **Personal Data:** b Elgin, Ill, March 17, 1951. **Education:** Univ Ill Champaign, BS, 1973; Northwestern Univ, MS, 1974, PhD (biol sci), 1979. **Professional Experience:** SR CHEM-

IST, US ENVIRON PROTECTION AGENCY, 1987-1994 & 1996-; sr chemist, US Consumer Prod Safety Comn, 1985-1987; environ scientist, Sci Appln Int Corp, 1979-1985. **Research Statement & Publications:** Reviews scientific information related to indoor air quality issues and provides input to scientific policy decisions in this area. **Mailing Address:** US Environ Protection Agency, 1200 Pa Ave NW, Washington, DC 20460-0001. **Fax:** 202-565-2038. **E-Mail:** johnston.pauline@epa.gov

JOHNSTON, PERRY MAX, VERTEBRATE EMBRYOLOGY. **Personal Data:** b Edgewood, Tex, February 6, 1921; m 1943, c 4. **Education:** NTex State Col, BS, 1940, MS, 1942; Univ Mich, PhD (zoology), 1949. **Professional Experience:** PROF EMER ZOOL, UNIV ARK, FAYETTEVILLE, 1983-; prof zool, Univ Ark, Fayetteville, beginning 1983; chmn dept, Univ Ark, Fayetteville, beginning 1966; asst prof zool, Univ Ark, Fayetteville, ending 1954; res partic, Oak Ridge Inst Nuclear Studies, 1953-1954; asst prof zool, Univ Ark, Fayetteville, beginning 1949. **Memberships:** Am Soc Zool; Am Micros Soc; Sigma Xi. **Research Statement & Publications:** Vertebrate embryology; embryology of centrarchid fishes; utilization of radioisotopes by vertebrate embryos. **Mailing Address:** Dept Zool, Univ Ark, 800 Hotz Hall, Fayetteville, AR 72701. **E-Mail:** pjohn@uark.edu

JOHNSTON, PETER RAMSEY, FLUID FILTRATION. **Personal Data:** b Tampa, Fla, August 19, 1926; m 1949, Helen; c Frederick, Rebecca, Terrance & Christopher. **Education:** Miami Univ, Ohio, BA, 1948. **Professional Experience:** RETIRED; sr proj eng, Ametek, Inc, 1980-1992; prod develop filter media, Com Filters, Gelman Sci & Ametek, 1972-1992. **Memberships:** Am Chem Soc; Am Inst Chem Engrs; fel Am Soc Testing & Mat; Am Filtration Soc. **Research Statement & Publications:** Liquid filtration; electrochemistry; polymer chemistry; author of books, encyclopedia articles, and many papers on filtration. **Mailing Address:** 302 Morningside Dr, Carrboro, NC 27510-1249.

JOHNSTON, RAYMOND F, PHYSIOLOGY, PHARMACOLOGY. **Personal Data:** b Fenton, Mo, June 29, 1913; m 1935, c 1. **Education:** Univ Mo, BS, 1935; Mich State Univ, MS, 1948, DVM, 1949; Univ Minn, PhD, 1959. **Professional Experience:** Sr mem team vet to Indonesia, 1960-1962; PROF PHYSIOL, MICH STATE UNIV, 1949-; asst physiol, Mich State Univ, 1947-1949; asst path, Mich State Univ, 1945-1947; i nstr voc agr, Univ Mo, 1935-1945. **Memberships:** Fel Am Vet Med Asn. **Research Statement & Publications:** Toxicology; cardiovascular physiology; neurophysiology; biomedical communications. **Mailing Address:** 4583 Sequoia Terr, Okemos, MI 48864.

JOHNSTON, RICHARD BOLES, PEDIATRICS, IMMUNOLOGY. **Personal Data:** b Atlanta, Ga, August 23, 1935; m 1960, c 3. **Education:** Vanderbilt Univ, BA, 1957, MD, 1961. **Honorary Degrees:** MS, Univ Pa, 1986. **Professional Experience:** EXEC VPRES, ACAD AFFAIRS, NAT JEWISH MED & RES CTR, 2004-; ASSOC DEAN RES DEVELOP, UNIV COLO SCH MED, 2001-; consult dean, Univ ColoSch Med, 2000-2001; PROF, DEPT PEDIAT, UNIV SCH MED & NAT JEWISH MED & RES CTR, 1999-; pediat consult, March Dimes Birth Defects Found, 1999-2002; med dir, March Dimes Birth Defects Found, 1992-1998; chmn, William Bennett prof, 1986-1992; chmn, Dept Pediat, Univ Pa Sch Med, 1986-1990; chmn bd trustees, Int Pediat Res Found, 1983-1987 & 1995; vis prof, Rockefeller Univ, NY, 1983-1984; vchmn dept, Sch Med, Univ Colo, 1980-1986; prof pediat, Sch Med, Univ Colo, 1977-1986; dir dept pediat, Nat Jewish Hosp & Res Ctr, Denver, 1977-1986; Macy Found scholar, Rockefeller Univ, NY, 1976-1977; from asst prof to assoc prof pediat & microbiol, Univ Ala, Birmingham, 1970-1977; NIH spec fel, Harvard Med Sch, 1969-1970; USPHS training grant, Harvard Med Sch, 1968-1969; NIH fel, Harvard Med Sch, 1967-1968. **Memberships:** Inst Med-Nat Acad Sci; Am Asn Immunologists; Asn Am Physicians; Am Soc Clin Invest; Am Pediat Soc (pres, 1996-1997); Soc Pediat Res (pres, 1980-1981); fel AAAS. **Research Statement & Publications:** Mechanisms of resistance to infection; phagocyte function; complement; physiology and pathology of neutrophils and mononuclear phagocytes; immunodeficiency disease. **Mailing Address:** Dept Pediat, Univ Colo Sch Med, Office the Dean C 290, Denver, CO 80262. **Fax:** 303-315-8494. **E-Mail:** richard.johnston@uchsc.edu

JOHNSTON, RICHARD FOURNESS, SYSTEMATICS, ECOLOGY. **Personal Data:** b Oakland, Calif, July 27, 1925. **Education:** Univ Calif, BA, 1950, MA, 1953, PhD, 1955. **Honors & Awards:** Coues Award, Am Ornith Union, 1975. **Professional Experience:** PROF EMER ZOOL, UNIV KANS, 1992-; ed, Current Ornith, 1981-1986; chmn, Dept Zool, 1979-1982; ed, Annual Rev Ecol & Systematics, 1968-1992; prog dir syst biol, NSF, 1968-1969; cur birds, Mus Natural Hist, 1967-1992; Ed, Syst Zool, Soc Syst Zool, 1967-1970; from assoc cur to cur birds, Mus Natural Hist, 1963-1992; from asst prof to prof zool, Univ Kans, 1958-1992; Instr biol, NMex State Univ, 1956-1957. **Memberships:** Fel AAAS; Ecol Soc Am; fel Am Ornith Union; Soc Syst Zool (pres 1977-1979); Cooper Ornith Soc. **Research Statement & Publications:** Systematics; evolutionary biology; behavior and ecology of pigeons. **Mailing Address:** Dept Ecol & Evolutionary Biol, Univ Kans, 1200 Sunnyside Ave, Lawrence, KS 66045-7534. **Fax:** 785-864-5335. **E-Mail:** rjon@ku.edu

JOHNSTON, RICHARD H, HYDROGEOLOGY, IMPACT OF DEVELOPMENT ON LARGE AQUIFER SYSTEMS. **Personal Data:** b Philadelphia, Pa, April 7, 1929; m 1966, Mary; c Richard. **Education:** Pa State Univ, BS, 1957; Univ Wyoming, MA, 1959. **Professional Experience:** RETIRED; consult, US Geol Surg, 1984-1995; groundwater hydrologist, US Geol Surg, 1969-1984; geologist, US Geol Surg, 1959-1969. **Memberships:** Fel Geol Soc Am; Int Asn Hydro-geologists. **Research Statement & Publications:** Regional aquifer systems; Karst hydrogeology; ground-water budgets. **Mailing Address:** 108 Tolomato Trace, St Simons Island, GA 31522-1812.

JOHNSTON, ROBERT BENJAMIN, biochemistry; deceased, see previous edition for last biography

JOHNSTON, ROBERT E, BEHAVIOR, ETHOLOGY & PHEROMONES. **Personal Data:** b Philadelphia, Pa, April 16, 1942; m 1970, Joan; c Alexander E & Robert A. **Education:** Dartmouth Col, BA, 1964; Univ Rockefeller, PhD (behav & life sci), 1970. **Professional Experience:** USSR Acad Sci, A N Severtson Inst Evolutionary Animal Morphol & Ecol, 1991; PROF PSYCHOL & BIOL, UNIV CORNELL, 1987-; vis prof, Dept Zool, Univ Tex, 1980; f rom asst prof to assoc prof, Univ Cornell, 1970-1987; prin investr, numerous grants. **Memberships:** Animal Behav Soc; Sigma Xi; Am Soc Mammalogists; Soc Study Reproduction. **Research Statement & Publications:** Mechanisms and evolution of behavior, especially reproductive and aggressive behavior; communication, including olfactory (pheromones), auditory and visual signals; relationships between hormones and behavior; neural mechanisms of olfaction; human ethology; human evolution; animal cognition; Published over 20 articles. **Mailing Address:** Dept Psychol, Univ Cornell, 278 E Uris Hall, Ithaca, NY 14853-7601. **Fax:** 607-255-8433. **E-Mail:** rej1@cornell.edu

JOHNSTON, ROBERT EDWARD, VIROLOGY, VACCINES. **Personal Data:** b Houston, Tex, September 19, 1947; m 1976, Jane; c 4. **Education:** Rice Univ, BA, 1968; Univ Tex, Austin, PhD (microbiol), 1973. **Honors & Awards:** World Technology Network Award in Health & Medicine, 2001. **Professional Experience:** PROF MICROBIOL & IMMUNOL, VIROLOGY, UNIV NC, 1989-; assoc prof, NC State Univ, 1980-1989; NIH Young investr grant, NC State Univ, 1978-1981; asst prof microbiol, NC State Univ, 1976-1980; Med Res Coun fel microbiol, Queens Univ, 1973-1976. **Memberships:** Am Soc Microbiol; Am Soc Virol; AAAS. **Research Statement & Publications:** Host cell influence on virus replication; viral pathogenesis; design of viral vaccines and vaccine vectors. **Mailing Address:** Dept Microbiol & Immunol, Lineberger Comprehensive Cancer Ctr, Univ NC, Campus Box 7290 831 Mary Ellen Jones, Chapel Hill, NC 27599-7295. **Fax:** 919-843-6924. **E-Mail:** rjohnst@med.unc.edu

JOHNSTON, ROBERT WARD, PHYSICS, ACADEMIC ADMINISTRATION. **Personal Data:** b Buffalo, NY, May 27, 1925; m 1959, Catherine Pratt; c David R & Brian H. **Education:** Cornell Univ, BEE, 1946, PhD (physics), 1952. **Professional Experience:** RETIRED; dep dir admin, Nat Acad Sci-Nat Res Coun, 1985-1987; dir personnel & appts, Nat Acad Sci-Nat Res Coun, 1982-1985; assoc exec officer, Nat Acad Sci-Nat Res Coun, 1973-1982; vchancellor res, Wash Univ, 1969-1973; exec asst to dir, NSF, Washington, DC, 1965-1969; spec asst to assoc dir res, phys & eng sci div NSF, 1961-1965; NSF spec asst to asst dir math, phys & eng sci div, 1961; assoc prog dir, NSF, 1960-1961; NSF asst prog dir physics, NSF, 1959-1960; mgr sci & tech rels, Adv Res & Develop Div, Avco Corp, Mass, 1957-1959; physicist, Electronics Lab, Gen Elec Co, NY, 1951-1957; physicist, Cornell Aeronaut Lab, 1947-1948; asst physics, Cornell Univ, 1946-1951. **Memberships:** AAAS; Am Phys Soc. **Research Statement & Publications:** Soft x-ray spectroscopy; magnetic materials; solid state physics; research administration. **Mailing Address:** 12705 Huntsman Way, Potomac, MD 20854.

JOHNSTON, ROGER GLENN, PHYSICAL SECURITY, NUCLEAR SAFEGUARDS. **Personal Data:** b Lincoln, Nebr, February 15, 1954; m Janie. **Education:** Carleton Col, BA, 1977; Univ Colo, Boulder, MS, 1983, PhD (physics), 1983. **Honors & Awards:** LANL Fellows Prize for Outstanding Research (2004) ASIS "Excellence in Performance Measure" Award (2002) Distinguished Performance Award from a government agency (2002) Two R&D 100 Awards (1992 & 1994) "Best of What's New" Award from Popular Science magazine (1992). **Professional Experience:** Head, Vulnerability Assessment Team, Los Alamos Nat Lab 1993-; sect leader, Los Alamos Nat Lab, 1994-2004; consult, 1990-; STAFF MEM, CHEM DIV, LOS ALAMOS NAT LAB, 1990-; proj leader, Los Alamos Nat Lab, 1988-; prin investr, Los Alamos Nat Lab, 1986-; staff mem biophys, Chem Sci & Technol Div, Los Alamos Nat Lab, 1985-1990; fel flow cytometry, Chem Sci & Technol Div, Los Alamos Nat Lab, 1983-1985; g rad student chem physics, Univ Colo, 1977-1983. **Memberships:** Am Physics Society American Soc for Industrial Security (ASIS International). **Research Statement & Publications:** Novel approaches and technology for physical security, vulnerability assessments, cargo security, tamper/intrusion detection, and nuclear nonproliferation. Light scattering and interferometry. **Mailing Address:** Los Alamos Nat Lab, MS J565, PO Box 1663, Los Alamos, NM 87545. **Fax:** 505-665-4631. **E-Mail:** rogerj@lanl.gov

JOHNSTON, RONALD HARVEY, ELECTRONICS ENGINEERING. **Personal Data:** b Drumheller, Alta, May 11, 1939; m 1969. **Education:** Univ Alta, BSc, 1961; Univ London, DIC & PhD (elec eng), 1967. **Professional Experience:** PROF & HEAD, ELEC & COMPUT ENG, UNIV CALGARY, as of 2004; assoc prof Electronics, Univ Calgary, beginning 1977; asst prof, Univ Calgary, 1970-1977; mem scientific staff res & develop, Northern Elec Co Ltd, 1967-1969; res asst electronics, Queen's Univ, Belfast, 1964-1967; eng trainee, Can Gen Elec, 1961-1962. **Memberships:** Inst Elec & Electronics Engrs. **Research Statement & Publications:** Frequency multipliers; transistor amplifiers and multipliers; microwave measurements; semiconductor circuits. **Mailing Address:** Dept Elec & Comput Eng, Univ Calgary, 2500 Univ Dr NW, Calgary, AB T2N 1N4, Can. **Fax:** 403-282-6855. **E-Mail:** johnston@enel.ucalgary.ca

JOHNSTON, ROY G, STRUCTURAL ENGINEERING, EARTHQUAKE ENGINEERING. **Personal Data:** b Chicago, Ill, January 7, 1914. **Education:** Univ Southern Calif, BS, 1935. **Professional Experience:** RETIRED; mem, State Bldg Stand Comn, 1986-1994; dir, Earthquake Eng Res Inst, 1979-1981; FOUNDER, BRANDOW & JOHNSTON ASSOCS, 1945-; exec vpres & secy, Brandow & Johnston Assocs, beginning 1945; staff mem, Los Angeles Off, Lummus Co, 1941-1945; consult eng, Clyde Deuel, 1935-1941; s taff mem, Los Angeles Co Building Dept, 1935; mem earthquake Study, Vet Admin, Jet Propulsion Lab, Univ Southern Calif & Kaiser Hosps; consult earthquake studies. **Memberships:** Nat Acad Eng; fel Am Soc Civil Engrs; fel Am Concrete Inst; fel Earthquake Eng Res Inst (vpres, 1981). **Research Statement & Publications:** Structural design of over 10, 000 projects; earthquake engineering. **Mailing Address:** Brandow & Johnston Assocs, 1660 W Third St, Los Angeles, CA 90017.

JOHNSTON, RUSSELL SHAYNE, PLASMA PHYSICS, APPLIED MATHEMATICS. **Personal Data:** b Ft William, Ont, November 4, 1948; m 1976, c 3. **Education:** McGill Univ, BSc, 1970; Princeton Univ, PhD (plasma physics), 1975. **Professional Experience:** ASSOC PROF PHYSICS, JACKSON STATE UNIV, 1983-; asst prof appl physics, Columbia Univ, 1976-1983; res fel plasma physics, Lawrence Berkeley Lab, Univ Calif, 1974-1976; res asst plasma physics, Plasma Physics Lab, Princeton Univ, 1970-1974. **Memberships:** Am Phys Soc. **Research Statement & Publications:** Theoretical plasma physics, particularly nonlinear interactions among waves and particles. **Mailing Address:** Dept Physics & Atmospheric Sci, Jackson State Univ, Jackson, MS 39217.

JOHNSTON, STEPHEN A, GENETICS. **Education:** Univ Wisc-Madison, BS, 1975, PhD (genetics), 1981. **Professional Experience:** PROF MICROBIOL, UNIV TEX-SOUTHWESTERN MED CTR, 1999-; DIR, CTR BIOMED INVENTIONS, 1997-. **Mailing Address:** Dept Internal Med Univ Tex SW Med Ctr, 5323 Harry Hines Blvd, Dallas, TX 75235-9573. **Fax:** 214-648-1450. **E-Mail:** stephen.johnston@utsouthwestern.edu

JOHNSTON, STEPHEN A, GENETICS. **Education:** Phd, Univ Wis, 1981. **Professional Experience:** ASSOC PROF, SCH EARTH & OCEAN SCI, UNIV VICTORIA, as of 2005. **Mailing Address:** Univ Victoria, Petch Rm 188, Victoria, BC V8W 2Y2, Canada. **Fax:** 250-721-6200. **E-Mail:** stj@uvic.ca

JOHNSTON, STEPHEN CHARLES, HUMAN PERFORMANCE, EXERCISE IN HEALTH. **Personal Data:** b Vancouver, Wash, September 15, 1950. **Education:** Univ Utah, BS, 1974, PhD (physiol exercise), 1985. **Professional Experience:** DIR, SPORT SCI, US SKI TEAM, 1991-; assoc prof exercise & sport sci, Univ Utah, 1991; chair, Sports Med Comt, Southwest Alliance for Health, Phys Educ, Recreation & Dance, 1989-1991; DIR, HUMAN PERFORMANCE RES LAB, UNIV UTAH, 1987-; adj asst prof, Div Foods & Nutrit, Univ Utah, 1987-; asst prof, Univ Utah, 1987-1991; dir physiol, Sports Med Coun, US Ski Team, 1987-1991; exercise consult, Neuropsychol Dept, Vet Admin Hosp, Salt Lake City, Utah, 1985-; vis asst prof, Univ Utah, 1984-1987; exercise consult, Holy Cross Hosp, Salt Lake City, Utah, 1983-; adj assoc prof, Dept Bioeng & Div Foods & Nutrit, Univ Utah. **Memberships:** AAAS; Am Asn Univ Profs; Am Alliance Health Phys Educ Recreation & Dance; Am Col Sports Med. **Research Statement & Publications:** Effects of exercise and environment on the muscular, cardiovascular, respiratory, nervous and thermoregulatory systems of the human body; work with training response and optimization of training in elite athletes. **Mailing Address:** Dept Exercise & Sport Sci, Univ Utah, Salt Lake City, UT 84112.

JOHNSTON, TAYLOR JIMMIE, AGRONOMY, PLANT PHYSIOLOGY. **Personal Data:** b Newbern, Tenn, May 11, 1940; m 1966, Paulette; c Bryan & Blair. **Education:** Univ Tenn, Martin, BS, 1963; Univ Ill, MS, 1965, PhD (agron), 1968. **Professional Experience:** PROF CROP & SOIL SCI, MICH STATE UNIV, 1991-; from asst dean to assoc dean, Mich State Univ, 1981-1991; PROF CROP SCI, MICH STATE UNIV, 1976-; from asst prof to assoc prof, Mich State Univ, 1968-1976. **Memberships:** Am Soc Agron; Crop Sci Soc Am; Sigma Xi; Nat Asn Col & Teachers Agr; AAAS. **Research Statement & Publications:** Photosynthesis of soybeans and general crop physiology and ecology. **Mailing Address:** Col Agr & Natural Resources, Mich State Univ, 286 PSS Bldg, East Lansing, MI 48824-1325. **E-Mail:** johnsto4@msu.edu

JOHNSTON, TUDOR WYATT, PLASMA PHYSICS. **Personal Data:** b Montreal, Que, January 17, 1932; m 1958, c 3. **Education:** McGill Univ, BEng, 1953; Cambridge Univ, PhD (eng physics), 1958. **Professional Experience:** PROF, INRS-ENERGY & MAT, UNIV QUE, 1973-; vis prof, Univ Rochester, 1985; Laser Lab, Univ Rochester, 1981-; consult, KMS Fusion, 1980-1981; consult, Can Dept Commun, 1971; consult, RCA, 1970; assoc prof physics, Univ Houston, 1969-1973; sr res scientist, Plasma & Space Physics Lab, 1967-1969; vis prof, Tex A&M Univ, 1967; sr res scientist, Microwave & Plasma Physics Lab, RCA Victor Co, Ltd, 1958-1967. **Memberships:** Fel Am Phys Soc; Can Asn Physicists; sci comm ICPP-2000. **Research Statement & Publications:** Plasma theory; computer simulation; nonlinear wave-plasma; laser-plasma interaction. **Mailing Address:** Div INRS-Energy & Mat, Univ Que, 1650 boul Lionel-boulet C P 1020, Varennes, PQ J3X 1S2, Can. **Fax:** 450-929-8102. **E-Mail:** johnston@emt.inrs.ca

JOHNSTON, WALTER EDWARD, STATISTICS. **Personal Data:** b Clarksville, Ark, April 8, 1939; m 1960, c 3. **Education:** Tex A&M Univ, BS, 1960, MS, 1965, PhD (statist), 1970. **Professional Experience:** PROF EMER QUANT METHODS, SOUTHWEST TEXSTATE UNIV, SAN MARCOS, as of 2003; assoc prof, Southwest Texstate Univ, San Marcos, beginning 1980; from asst prof to prof exp statist, Clemson Univ, 1967-1978; teacher, Tex High Sch, 1960-1961; prof Quant Methods Tex A&M Univ. **Memberships:** Am Statist Asn. **Research Statement & Publications:** Application of statistical methods in agricultural and biological research. **Mailing Address:** Southwest Texstate Univ, 35 Derrick Hall, Buda, TX 78610. **Fax:** 512-245-1452. **E-Mail:** wj02@business.swt.edu

JOHNSTON, WARREN E, LAND ECONOMICS, COMMERCIAL AGRICULTURE. **Personal Data:** b Woodland, Calif, May 27, 1933; m, c 2. **Education:** Univ Calif, Davis, BS, 1959; NC State Col, MS, 1963; NC State Univ, PhD (agr econ & statist), 1964. **Honors & Awards:** Fellow - American Agricultural Economics Association, 1997 Distinguished Scholar - Western Agricultural Economics Association, 2004. **Professional Experience:** PROF EMER AGR ECON, UNIV CALIF, DAVIS, as of 2003; dir, Am Agr Econ Asn, 1985-1988 & Int AgribusMgt Asn, 1991-1994; Fulbright res scholar, NZ, 1976-1977; Alexander vonHumboldt res fel, WGer, 1969-1970; Prof Agr Econ, Univ Calif, Davis, Beginning 1963. **Memberships:** Am Agr Econ Asn (pres 1990-1991); Western Agricultural Economics Asn; Am Soc Farm Managers & Rural Appraisers (Academic Vice President, 1992-1995). **Research Statement & Publications:** Agricultural, natural resources and environmental economics and public policy; commercial and sustainable agriculture; land economics; land markets; adjustments to policy and economic changes. **Mailing Address:** Dept Agr Econ, Rm 2109 Social Sci & Humanities Bldg, Univ Calif, Davis, CA 95616. **Fax:** 530-752-5614. **E-Mail:** warren@primal.ucdavis.edu

JOHNSTON, WILBUR DEXTER, JR, PHYSICS, ELECTRICAL ENGINEERING. **Personal Data:** b New Haven, Conn, July 6, 1940; m 1963, Anne; c Elizabeth, Alicia. **Education:** Yale Univ, BS, 1961; Mass Inst Technol, PhD (physics), 1966. **Professional Experience:** Dir, laser products and manufacturing techolo, multiplex inc, 2001- TECH MGR, LIGHTWAVE DEVICE RES, LUCENT TECHNOL BELL LABS, 1996- 2001; supvr, Solid State Mat, 1980-1996; mem tech staff, AT&T Bell Labs, 1966-1979; Res asst electronics, Mass Inst Technol, 1961-1966. **Memberships:** Inst Elec & Electronics Engrs fel; pres 1996-1997 IEEE electron Devices soc. **Research Statement & Publications:** Optical communications; laser physics; non-linear optics; semiconductor lasers; solar cells; heterojunction and compound semiconductor device physics; vapor phase epitaxial growth of semiconductor materials; materials science. **Mailing Address:** 30 Oak Knoll Rd, Mendham, NJ 07945.

JOHNSTON, WILLIAM DWIGHT, INORGANIC CHEMISTRY. **Personal Data:** b Bellevue, Pa, January 17, 1928; m 1950, c 3. **Education:** Univ Pittsburgh, BS, 1949, MS, 1951, PhD (chem), 1953. **Professional Experience:** RETIRED; tech dir int opers, Pittsburgh Corning Corp, 1974-1989; dir res &develop, Pittsburgh Corning Corp, 1969-1974; asst dir res, Pittsburgh Corning Corp, 1965-1969; res chemist, Pittsburgh Corning Corp, 1962-1965; adv chemist, Res Labs, Westinghouse ElecCorp, 1957-1962; res engr, Res Labs, Westinghouse Elec Corp, 1953-1957. **Memberships:** Am Chem Soc; Am Ceramic Soc. **Research Statement & Publications:** Glass research; solid state chemistry; crystallography; semiconductors; magnetic materials; inorganic preparations; phase diagrams; thermodynamics; metal chelates. **Mailing Address:** 2416 Collins Rd, Pittsburgh, PA 15235.

JOHNSTON, WILLIAM V, PHYSICAL CHEMISTRY & METALLURGY. **Personal Data:** b Berkeley, Calif, May 6, 1927; m 1951, Marian; c David, Donald, Carol & Cynthia. **Education:** Col Wooster, BA, 1950; Univ Pittsburgh, PhD (phys chem), 1955. **Professional Experience:** RETIRED; dep dir div reactor safety, Regional, 1986-1990; chief, Eng Br, 1985-1986; chmn, Halden Reactor Proj, Orgn Econ Coop & Develop, 1981; asst dir div eng, chief, Core Performance Br US Nuclear Regulatory Comn, 1980-1985; chmn working group nuclear safety, Orgn Econ Coop & Develop/Int Energy Agency, 1975-1980; br, chief, Fuel Behav Res Br, US Nuclear Regulatory Comn, 1974-1980; nuclear engr, US AEC, 1972-1974; mem tech staff, Rocketdyne Div, 1969-1972; prin scientist, NAm Rockwell Corp, 1969; group leader phys metall, Sci Ctr, 1962-1969; res specialist, Atomics Int Div, NAm Aviation Corp, 1961-1962; res assoc, Knolls Atomic Power Lab, Gen Elec Co, 1955-1961; sr cryogenic operator, Ohio State Univ, 1952; asst, Univ Pittsburgh, 1950-1955. **Memberships:** Emer mem Am Chem Soc; Emer mem Am Inst Mining, Metall & Petrol Engrs; fel AAAS; Emer mem Am Nuclear Soc. **Research Statement & Publications:** Metal physics; calorimetry; nuclear fuels; solid electrolytes; solution thermodynamics; nuclear safety; nuclear materials. **Mailing Address:** 2 Ruth Lane, Downingtown, PA 19335.

JOHNSTON, WILLIAM WEBB, PATHOLOGY, CYTOLOGY. **Personal Data:** b Statesville, NC, August 26, 1933. **Education:** Davidson Col, BS, 1954; Duke Univ, MD, 1959; Am Bd Path, dipl. **Honors & Awards:** Ortho Award, Can Soc Cytol, 1972. **Professional Experience:** PROF EMER PATH, MED CTR, DUKE UNIV, 1997-; prof path, Med Ctr, Duke Univ, 1972-1997; FAC CLIN CANCER TRAINING PROG, MED CTR, DUKE UNIV, 1966-; DIR CYTOPATH, MED CTR, DUKE UNIV, 1966-; consult path, Durham Vet Admin Hosp, 1966-; from asst prof to assoc prof, Duke Univ, 1965-1972; assoc, Duke Univ, 1963-1965; res fel path, Duke Univ, 1961-1963; res training prog grant, Duke Univ, 1960-1961; mem bd dirs, Am Cancer Soc, Durham County. **Memberships:** Am Asn Path; Am Soc Cytol (pres, 1981-1982); fel Am Soc Clin Path; fel Int Acad Cytol. **Research Statement & Publications:** Basic diagnostic methods in cytopathology. **Mailing Address:** Dept Path, Duke Univ Med Ctr, Box 3322, Durham, NC 27710.

JOHNSTON, ZELPHA B, BIOSTATICS. **Education:** Univ Ark, BS, MA, MS, PhD. **Professional Experience:** ASSOC PROF, DEPT ANIMAL SCI, UNIV ARK, as of 2005. **Mailing Address:** Animal Sci, Univ Ark, Fayetteville, AR 72701. **E-Mail:** zelphaj@uark.edu

JOHNSTONE, C(HARLES) WILKIN, NUCLEAR PHYSICS, INSTRUMENTATION. **Personal Data:** b Alamosa, Colo, August 22, 1916; m 1947, c 2. **Education:** Colo Col, AB, 1938; Dartmouth Col, AM, 1940. **Professional Experience:** RETIRED; sr develop proj engr, Eng Physics Dept, 1966-1982; sect head nuclear physics, Schlumberger Well Serv, 1960-1968; develop proj engr, Schlumberger Well Serv, 1956-1960; mem staff electronics res, Los Alamos Sci Lab, Calif, 1947-1956; in-chg marine radar design & develop, NY, 1945-1947; Naval Res Lab, Wash, DC, 1944-1945; proj engr, Navy Dept Proj, Sperry Gyroscope Co, NY, 1941-1944; PaState Col, 1940-1941; Dartmouth Col, 1938-1940; asst physics, Colo Col, 1937-1938. **Memberships:** Inst Elec & Electronics Engrs. **Research Statement & Publications:** Specialized electronic circuits for, radar and nuclear research, and instrumentation; radioactivity techniques and apparatus for well logging. **Mailing Address:** 2055 Brentwood Dr, Houston, TX 77019.

JOHNSTONE, DONALD BOYES, MICROBIOLOGY. **Personal Data:** b Newport, RI, July 25, 1919; m 1949, c 3. **Education:** RI State Col, BS, 1942; Rutgers Univ, MS, 1943, PhD (microbiol), 1948. **Professional Experience:** EMER FAC, UNIV VT, 2003-; dean, Grad Col, Agr Exp Sta, 1969-1985; chmn, Dept Agr Biochem, Agr Exp Sta, 1959-1985; microbiologist, Agr Exp Sta, 1948-1985; from asst prof to prof microbiol, Univ Vt, 1948-1985; bacteriologist, Woods Hole Oceanog Inst, 1942-1943, 1946. **Memberships:** AAAS; Am Soc Microbiol; fel Am Acad Microbiol. **Research Statement & Publications:** Marine bacteriology; antibiotics from higher plants; isolation of streptomycin producing actinomycetes; vitamin B 12 sources; whey utilization; azotobacter metabolism; classification; fluorescent pigments; extra cellular polysaccharides; pesticide degradation. **Mailing Address:** Dept Microbiol & Biochem, Univ Vt, Burlington, VT 05405. **E-Mail:** donald.johnstone@uvm.edu

JOHNSTONE, DONALD LEE, BACTERIOLOGY, MICROBIOLOGY. **Personal Data:** b Bluefield, WVa, February 4, 1939; m 1962, c 1. **Education:** Eastern Wash State Univ, BA, 1964; Wash State Univ, MS, 1966, PhD (aquatic bact), 1970. **Professional Experience:** ASSOC PROF CIVIL & ENVIRON ENG, WASH STATE UNIV, 1976-; asst prof civil eng & asst sanit scientist, Res Div, Col Eng, Wash State Univ, 1969-1976; mem, Int Conf Dis Nature Commun Man, 1964; vis fac, Battelle, PNL. **Memberships:** Am Soc Microbiol; Air & Waste Mgt; Am Water Works Soc; Sigma Xi. **Research Statement & Publications:** Interaction of bacteria and soil; microbial degradation of contaminants in groundwater systems; survival of intestinal bacteria in the aquatic environment; effects of hydrocarbons on indicator bacteria in groundwater; ecology of fresh water bacteria. **Mailing Address:** Civil & Environ Eng, Wash State Univ, One SE Stadium Way, Pullman, WA 99164-0001. **E-Mail:** johnstne@wsu.edu

JOHNSTONE, JOHN WILLIAM, CHEMISTRY. **Personal Data:** b Brooklyn, NY, November 19, 1932; m 1956, Claire; c Thomas E, James R & Robert A. **Education:** Hartwick Col, BA, 1954. **Honorary Degrees:** DSc, Hartwick Col, 1990. **Professional Experience:** RETIRED; pres & chief exec officer & chmn, Olin Corp, 1988-1996; bd dirs, Am Brands, Phoenix Home Life Ins Co; chief operating officer, Olin Corp, 1986-1987; pres, OlinCorp, 1985-1987; corp vpres & pres chem group, Olin Corp, Stamford, Conn, 1980-1985; vpres& gen mgr indust prods, sr vpres chem group, Olin Corp, 1979-1980; pres, Airco Alloys, DivAirco Inc, 1976-1979; group vpres, Hooker Chem Corp, 1973-1975; staff mem, Hooker ChemCorp, 1954-1975. **Memberships:** Am Mgt Asn; Soc Chem Indust; Soap & Detergent Asn; Chem Mfrs Asn. **Research Statement & Publications:** Chemical products development. **Mailing Address:** 467 Carter St, New Canaan, CT 06840.

JOHNSTONE, ROSE M, BIOCHEMISTRY. **Personal Data:** b Lodz, Poland, May 14, 1928; Canadian citizen; wid Douglas (deceased); c Michael & Eric. **Education:** McGill Univ, BS, 1950, PhD (biochem), 1953. **Honors & Awards:** Queen's Jubilee Medal, 1977. **Professional Experience:** GILMAN CHENEY PROF EMER BIOCHEM, MCGILL UNIV, 1990-; NIH grantee 1988-1991; Gilman-Chney prof biochem, McGill Univ, 1985-1990; chmn, Dept Biochem, McGill Univ, 1980-1990; prof, McGill Univ, 1977-2001; res grant, Nat Cancer Inst Can, 1965-1970; Med Res Coun grant, 1965-2001; assoc prof, McGill Univ, 1965-1976; asst prof, McGill Univ & Montreal Gen Hosp Res Inst, 1961-1965; Nat Cancer Inst Can fel, 1954-1957; res assoc biochem, McGill Univ & Montreal Gen Hosp Res Inst, 1953-1965. **Memberships:** Can Fedn Biol Soc; Can Biochem Soc; Am Soc Biol Chemists; Royal Soc Can (treas, 1994-1998); Can Soc Cell Biol. **Research Statement & Publications:** Transport of organic substances into mammalian cells; development and cloning of transport systems; reconstitution of transport systems; membrane remodeling during development of red cells; targeting of proteins for externalization during red cell maturation; exosomes and their protein content. **Mailing Address:** Dept Biochem, McGill Univ, Rm 804, McIntyre Medical Bldg, Montreal, PQ H3G 1Y6, Can. **Fax:** 514-398-7384. **E-Mail:** rose.johnstone@mcgill.ca

JOINER, R(EGINALD) GRACEN, MIDDLE ATMOSPHERE RESEARCH, SPACE RADIATION EFFECTS. **Personal Data:** b Hawkinsville, Ga, February 10, 1933; m 1952, c 2. **Education:** Univ Ga, BS, 1958, MS, 1959. **Professional Experience:** PROG MGR SPACE PHYSICS, OFF NAVAL RES, 1982-; supvry phys sciadminr, Off Naval Res, 1980-1982; physicist, Off Naval Res, 1964-1980; Physicist, US NavalOrdnance Lab, 1959-1964. **Memberships:** Am Geophys Union. **Research Statement & Publications:** Extremely low frequency-very low frequency radio propagation; ionosphere; space. **Mailing Address:** Off Naval Res, 800 N Quincy St, Arlington, VA 22217.

JOINER, WILLIAM CORNELIUS HENRY, SOLID STATE PHYSICS. **Personal Data:** b Camden, NJ, June 8, 1936; m 1964. **Education:** Rutgers Univ, BA, 1957, PhD (physics), 1962. **Professional Experience:** PROF EMER PHYSICS, UNIV CINCINNATI, as of 2003; HEAD DEPT, UNIV CINCINNATI, 1974-; prof physics, Univ Cincinnati, beginning 1973; from asst prof to assoc prof, Univ Cincinnati, 1965-1973; fel physicist, Aerospace Div, Westinghouse Elec Co, 1965; sr physicist, Aerospace Div, Westinghouse Elec Co, 1961-1965. **Memberships:** Am Phys Soc; Sigma Xi. **Research Statement & Publications:** Superconductivity; low temperature physics. **Mailing Address:** Dept Physics, Univ Cincinnati, Off 448 PO Box 210011, Cincinnati, OH 45221. **Fax:** 513-556-3425. **E-Mail:** william.joiner@uc.edu

JOIST, HEINRICH J, HEMATOLOGY, COAGULATION DISORDERS. **Personal Data:** b Bergisch, Gladbach, Ger, January 9, 1935. **Education:** McMaster Univ, PhD (exp path), 1977; Univ Cologn, Ger, MD, 1962. **Professional Experience:** PROF MED & PATH, DIV BMT, ONCOL HEMAT, ST LOUIS MED CTR, 1983-; DIR HEMOSTASIS & THROMBOSIS LABS, DIV BMT, ONCOL HEMAT, ST LOUISMED CTR, 1983-; CO-DIR, REGIONAL HEMOPHILIA COMP DIAG & TREATMENT CTR, MO, ILL, 1977-. **Research Statement & Publications:** Hematology; coagulation disorders. **Mailing Address:** Dept Path, St Louis Health Sci Ctr, 1402 South Grand, St Louis, MO 63104. **Fax:** 314-268-5110. **E-Mail:** path@slu.edu

JOKELA, JALMER JOHN, FOREST GENETICS. **Personal Data:** b Ely, Minn, September 20, 1921; m 1953, c 3. **Education:** Univ Minn, BSF, 1947, MS, 1951; Univ Ill, PhD (agron), 1963. **Professional Experience:** RETIRED; from instr to assoc prof forest res, Univ Ill, Urbana, 1959-1986; res assoc, Univ Ill, Urbana, 1959-1969; asst, Univ Minn, 1949-1951; asst, Univ Ill, Urbana, 1947-1949 & 1951-1959; agr aide, Lake States Forest Exp Sta, 1946. **Memberships:** Soc Am Foresters; Sigma Xi. **Research Statement & Publications:** Genetics and breeding of cottonwoods; silviculture; mensuration. **Mailing Address:** 1661 Saari Rd, Ely, MN 55731-8238.

JOKERST, NAN MARIE, OPTICS, SOLID STATE PHYSICS. **Personal Data:** b St Louis, Mo, May 11, 1961; m 1988, Martrin; c Nathaniel & Joanna. **Education:** Creighton Univ, BS, 1982; Univ Southern Calif, MS, 1984, PhD (elec eng), 1989. **Professional Experience:** J A JONES DISTINGUISHED PROF, ELEC & COMPUT ENG, DUKE UNIV, as of 2005; Joseph M Petit prof, Ga Inst Technol, as of 2000; assoc prof, Sch Elec Comp Eng, Ga Inst Technol, beginning 1995-; consult, Foster-Miller, Inc, 1990-; NSF presidential young investr, 1990; asst prof elec eng, Ga Inst Technol, 1989-1995. **Memberships:** Sr mem CPMT Soc; Optical Soc Am; Inst Elec & Electronics Engrs; Am PhysSoc; Sigma Xi. **Research Statement & Publications:** Monolithic deposition of GaAs and InP onto host substrates such as silicon, glass, lithium niobate, polymers for optoelectronic integrated circuits; solar cells; semiconductor lasers; nonlinear optics in semiconductors. **Mailing Address:** Dept Elec & Comput Eng Duke Univ, PO Box 90291, Durham, NC 27708-0291. **Fax:** 919-613-9158. **E-Mail:** njokerst@ee.duke.edu

JOKIEL, PAUL L, MARINE SCIENCE. **Education:** Univ Hawaii, PhD, 1985. **Professional Experience:** RESEARCHER, HAWAII INST MARINE BIOL, as of 2005. **Mailing Address:** Hawaii Inst Marine Biol, PO Box 1364, Kaneohe, HI 96744-1364. **Fax:** 808-236-7443. **E-Mail:** jokiel@hawaii.edu

JOKINEN, EILEEN HOPE, INVERTEBRATE ZOOLOGY, PARASITOLOGY. **Personal Data:** b Detroit, Mich, July 22, 1943. **Education:** Wayne State Univ, BS, 1965, PhD (zool), 1971. **Professional Experience:** Adj curator Molluscs, NY State Mus; INTERIM DIR, CONN INST WATERRESOURCES, UNIV CONN, STORRS, 1993-; asst dir, Conn Inst Water Resources, Univ Conn, Storrs, 1987-1993; vis asst prof gen ecol & invert zool, Conn Inst Water Resources, Univ Conn, Storrs, 1980-1986; asst & assoc prof invert zool, ecol, parasitol, comp anat, embryol & introdzool, Suffolk Univ, Boston, Mass, 1972-1980; instr comp anat, Univ Mich, Dearborn, Mich, 1972; instr introd biol, Wayne Co Community Col, Detroit, Mich, 1971-1972. **Memberships:** Am Malacol Soc; Am Soc Zoologists; Am Inst Biol Sci. **Research Statement & Publications:** Freshwater malacology; community ecology of freshwater littoral zone benthos; biogeography of freshwater snails. **E-Mail:** jbarnes@museum.nysed.gov

JOKIPII, JACK RANDOLPH, THEORETICAL PHYSICS, ASTROPHYSICS. **Personal Data:** b Ironwood, Mich, September 10, 1939. **Education:** Univ Mich, BS, 1961; Calif Inst Technol, PhD (physics), 1965. **Professional Experience:** REGENTS PROF, THEORETICAL ASTROPHYSICS, SPACE PHYSICS, LUNAR & PLANETARY LAB, UNIV ARIZ, as of 2005; ASTRONR, STEWARD OBSERV, UNIV ARIZ, as of 1999; prof, Lunar & Planetary Lab, Univ Ariz, beginning 1999; prof astron & planetary sci, Univ Ariz, beginning 1974; assoc prof theoret physics, Downs Lab Physics, Calif Inst Technol, 1969-1973; Alfred P Sloan Found fel, 1969; asst prof, Inst & Univ, 1967-1969; res assoc physics, Enrico Fermi Inst Nuclear Studies, Univ Chicago, 1965-1967. **Memberships:** Am Phys Soc; Am Geophys Union; Int Astron Union. **Research Statement & Publications:** Theoretical space physics; cosmic ray acceleration and propagation; interpretation of space vehicle observations; solar physics; interstellar physics. **Mailing Address:** Dept Planetary Sci, Lunar & Planetary Lab, Univ Ariz, PO Box 210092, Tucson, AZ 85721. **Fax:** 520-621-8250. **E-Mail:** jokipii@lpl.arizona.edu

JOKLIK, G FRANK, RESEARCH ADMINISTRATION. **Personal Data:** b Vienna, Austria, May 30, 1928. **Education:** Univ Sydney, BSc, 1949, PhD (geol), 1953. **Professional Experience:** HONORARY CONSUL, UTAH CONSUL CORP, as of 2004; CHMN, MK GOLD INC, as of 2001; PRES & CHIEF OPERATING OFFICER, MK GOLD INC, 1995-; pres & chief exec officer, Salt Lake City, 1989-1993; pres & chief execofficer, B P Minerals Am, 1987-1989; sr vpres, Metals Mining Standard Oil Co, Ohio, 1982-1987; pres, Salt Lake City, 1980-1987; vpres, Kennecott Corp, NY, 1974-1979; corp vpres, Amax, Inc, 1972-1974; mgr, Amax, Inc, 1963-1972; explor geologist, Kennecott Corp, NY, 1954-1963; Fulbright scholar, Columbia Univ, 1953-1954; mem bd, Am Mining Cong, Am Inst Mining, Metall & Petrol Engrs & Australian Inst Mining & Metall; dir, First Security Corp. **Memberships:** Nat Acad Eng. **Mailing Address:** 60 E S Temple Ste 2100, Salt Lake City, UT 84111. **Fax:** 801-297-6940. **E-Mail:** ijourney@mkgold.com

JOKLIK, WOLFGANG KARL, MOLECULAR BIOLOGY, VIROLOGY. **Personal Data:** b Vienna, Austria, November 16, 1926; m 1977, Patricia; c Richard G & Vivien H. **Education:** Univ Sydney, BS, 1948, MS, 1949; Oxford Univ, DPhil(biochem), 1952. **Professional Experience:** CHMN EMER & JAMES B DUKE PROF EMER, DEPT MICROBIOL & IMMUNOL, MED CTR, DUKE UNIV, as of 1996; James B Duke prof microbiol, Duke Univ, beginning 1992; ed-in-chief, Microbiol Rev, 1990-1994; mem, RecDNA Adv Comt, 1982-1987; group counr, Group IV, Virol Div, Am Soc Microbiol, 1981-1983; mem, Coun Res & Clin Awards, Am Cancer Soc, 1980-1983 & 1988-1991; assoc ed, J BiolChem, 1978-1989; mem exec comt, Int Comn Taxon Viruses, 1978-1984; ed-in-chief, Virol, 1976-1993; chmn, Virol Study Sect, NIH, 1973-1975; James B Duke prof microbiol & immunol & chmn dept, Duke Univ, 1968-1992; pres, Virol Div, Am Soc Microbiol, 1968-1989; from assoc prof to prof cell biol, Albert Einstein Col Med, 1962-1968; USPHS traveling fel, 1959-1960; fel microbiol, Australian Nat Univ, 1952-1962. **Memberships:** Nat Acad Sci; Inst Med of Nat Acad Sci; Am Soc Microbiol; Am Med SchMicrobiol Chmns Asn (pres 1979); Am Soc Virol (pres 1982-1983); Am Soc Biochem &Molecular Biol. **Research Statement & Publications:** Biochemistry of virus multiplication, including the mechanisms of nucleic acid replication, transcription and translation of genetic information, regulation of gene expression and the mechanisms of protein synthesis; molecular virology; molecular genetics. **Mailing Address:** Dept Microbiol, Duke Univ Med Ctr, Box 3020, Durham, NC 27710. **Fax:** 919-684-8735. **E-Mail:** joklik@abacus.mc.duke.edu

JOLESZ, FERENC ANDRAS, RADIOLOGY, NEUROLOGY. **Personal Data:** b Budapest, Hungary, May 21, 1946; m Anna; c Marta & Klara. **Education:** Semmelweis Med Sch, MD, 1971. **Honorary Degrees:** Dr, Pannon Agr Univ, 1996. **Honors & Awards:** Visions in Med Award, Gen Elec Med Systs, 1991. **Professional Experience:** DIR, HARVARD IMAGING CTR, BOSTON, 2001-; vchmn magnetic resonance imaging, Brigham & Women's Hosp, Harvard Med Sch, beginning 2000; B LEONARD HOLMAN PROF RADIOL, BRIGHAM & WOMEN'S HOSP, HARVARD MED SCH, 1998-; PROF RADIOL, HARVARD MED SCH, BOSTON, MA, 1996-; assoc ed, J Acad Radio, 1994-; DIR, IMAGE GUIDED THER PROG, BRIGHAM & WOMEN'S HOSP, BOSTON, 1993-; Whitaker Found, 1992-1995 & Nat Cancer Inst, 1995-; grantee, Off Naval Res, 1992-1994; grantee, Nat Multiple Sclerosis Soc, 1991-1994; mem res comt, Harvard Laser Ctr, 1990-; mem res comt, Dept Radiol, 1990-; grantee, NIH, 1990-1994; DIR, DIV MAGNETIC RESONANCE IMAGING, BRIGHAM & WOMENS HOSP, 1988-; Children's Hosp Boston, 1986-; W Roxbury Vet Admin Hosp, 1987-; grantee, Milton Fund, 1987-1988; dir, Neuro Imaging Sect, 1987-1988; radiologist, Brigham & Women's Hosp, 1985-; consult, Dana Farber Cancer Inst, 1985-; Col Phys Educ, Brigham & Women's Hosp, 1985-; from asst prof to assoc prof, Harvard Med Sch, 1985-1996; Children's Med Hosp, Boston, 1985- & Wellesley Col, 1985-1986; Col Phys Educ, Harvard Med Sch, 1984-; resident radiol, Brigham & Women's Hosp, 1982-1985; clin fel radiol, Harvard Med Sch, 1982-1985; res assoc, Harvard Med Sch, 1981-1982; res fel, Harvard Med Sch, 1980-1982; Milton res fel physiol, Harvard Med Sch, 1980; res fel neurol, Mass Gen Hosp, 1979-1980; resident neurosurg, Inst Neurosurg, Hungary, 1975-1979; adj prof, Dept Physiol, Col Phys Educ, Hungary, 1974-1975; asst prof, Dept Physiol, Col Phys Educ, Hungary, 1973-1974; Col Phys Educ, Hungary, 1971-1975; instr, Dept Physiol, Col Phys Educ, Hungary, 1971-1973; intern, Semmelweis Med Sch, Hungary, 1970-1971; lectr, Semmelweis Med Sch, 1969-1971; ed, J Magnetic Resonance Imaging & Magnetic Resonance Med. **Memberships:** Inst Med-Nat Acad Sci; Soc Magnetic Resonance Med; sr mem Am Soc Neuroradiol; Asn Univ Radiologists; Soc Magnetic Resonance Imaging; Radiol Soc NAm; Am Bd Neuroradiol cert 1988; Am Bd Radiol cert 1987. **Research Statement & Publications:** Brain morphology; white matter function and pathology; magnetic resonance imaging methods; interventional/surgical applications of magnetic resonance imaging. **Mailing Address:** Harvard Med Sch, Brigham & Women's Hosp, Dept Radiol, 75 Francis St, Boston, MA 02115. **Fax:** 617-582-6033. **E-Mail:** jolesz@bwh.harvard.edu

JOLICOEUR, PAUL, MOLECULAR BIOLOGY. **Education:** MD, PhD. **Professional Experience:** DIR, MOLECULAR BIOL RES UNIT, INST RES CLIN MONTREAL, CAN, as of 2005. **Mailing Address:** Molecular Biol Lab, Clin Res Inst Montreal 110 ouest ave des Pins, Montreal, PQ H2W 1R7, Can. **Fax:** 514-987-5794. **E-Mail:** Paul.Jolicoeur@ircm.qc.ca

JOLICOEUR, PIERRE, BIOMATHEMATICS, BIOMETRICS. **Personal Data:** b Montreal, Que, April 5, 1934; m 1969, c Lucie, Francine & Andre'. **Education:** Univ Montreal, BA, 1953, BSc, 1956; Univ BC, MA, 1958; Univ Chicago, PhD (paleozool), 1963. **Professional Experience:** PROF PSYCHOL, UNIV WATERLOO, as of 2004; chmn, Dept Biol Sci, 1973-1977; PROF BIOL, UNIV MONTREAL, 1972-; vis assoc scientist, NIH, 1967; Vis assoc prof, Univ Kans, 1966; from asst prof to assoc prof biol, UnivMontreal, 1961-1972. **Memberships:** Fel AAAS; Biomet Soc. **Research Statement & Publications:** Biological applications of mathematics and statistics, multivariate analysis; allometry and nonlinear growth curves; vertebrate zoology; ecology of animal populations. **Mailing Address:** Dept Psychol, Univ Waterloo, 200 University Ave W, Waterloo, ON N2L 3G1, Can. **Fax:** 519-746-8631. **E-Mail:** pjolicoe@cgl.uwaterloo.ca

JOLIVETTE, PETER LAUSON, NUCLEAR STRUCTURES. **Personal Data:** b Madison, Wis, May 27, 1941; m 1967, c 2. **Education:** Univ Wis-Madison, BS, 1963, PhD (physics), 1971; Purdue Univ, MS, 1965. **Professional Experience:** RETIRED; prof physics, Hope Col, ending 2001; assoc prof physics, Hope Col, beginning 1983; asst prof, HopeCol, 1976-1983; vis asst prof physics, Univ Notre Dame, 1975; res assoc, Univ Notre Dame, 1970-1976. **Memberships:** Fel Am Physics Soc; Am Inst Physics; Am Asn Physics Teachers. **Research Statement & Publications:** Low and intermediate energy nuclear physics; isospin and charge symmetry effects. **Mailing Address:** Dept Physics, Hope Col, 54 W 8th St, Holland, MI 49423.

JOLLES, MITCHELL IRA, SOFTWARE SYST, SOLID MECHANICS. **Personal Data:** b Bronx, NY, February 10, 1953. **Education:** Polytech Inst, Brooklyn, BS & MS, 1973; Va Polytech Inst & State Univ, PhD (eng mech), 1976. **Honors & Awards:** Alan Berman res pub award, Naval res lab, 1989; Sigma Xi, 1975; R Teetor Award, Soc Automotive Engrs, 1979; Jimmie Hamilton Award, Am Soc Naval Engrs, 1989. **Professional Experience:** SR TECH CONSULT, HEWLETT-PACKARD, 2000-; sr syst dev, Towers-Perrin, 1997-2000; prof mech eng, Widener Univ, 1988-1997; chmn dept, Widener Univ, 1988-1991; head, Fracture Mech Sect, Naval Res Lab, 1982-1988; assoc prof mech & aero eng/nuclear eng, Univ Mo, 1979-1982; asst prof aerospace & mech eng, Univ Notre Dame, 1976-1979; Va Polytech Inst & State Univ, instr, 1973-1976. **Memberships:** Sigma Xi. **Research Statement & Publications:** constitutive theory and material damage models; structural integrity methodology; nonlinear systems; advanced quant technologies. **Mailing Address:** 1145 Putnam Blvd, Wallingford, PA 19086.

JOLLEY, DAVID KENT, SIGNAL PROCESSING ALGORITHMS, GEOLOCATION TECHNIQUES. **Personal Data:** b Park City, Utah, January 25, 1944; m 1970, c 4. **Education:** Univ Utah, BA, 1966, PhD (physics), 1973. **Professional Experience:** VPRES ENG, ASTECH, INC, 1988-; dept mgr, ESL Inc, 1984-1988; sr engr, Advent Inc, 1982-1984; Sr engr, ESL Inc, 1972-1982. **Research Statement & Publications:** Development of signal processing algorithms and signal processing systems for government agencies primarily in the areas of reconnaissance and surveillance. **Mailing Address:** Nichols Res Corp, 5272 S College Dr Suite 300, Murray, UT 84123.

JOLLEY, JOHN ERIC, MATERIALS SCIENCE. **Personal Data:** b Blackpool, Eng, June 26, 1929; American citizen; m 1955, Faith; c Susan, Linda & Melissa. **Education:** Univ Liverpool, BS, 1950, PhD (phys chem), 1953. **Professional Experience:** CONSULT, 1985-; res fel, photog & electronic prod dept, 1967-1985; techmgr develop dept, Exp Sta, 1964-1967; res supvr, Res Lab, E I du Pont Del Nemours & Co, Inc, 1960-1964; res chemist cent res dept, Res Lab, E I du Pont Del Nemours & Co, Inc, 1960; res chemist film dept, Res Lab, E I du Pont Del Nemours & Co, Inc, 1958-1960; fel, Univ Calif, Berkeley, 1955-1957; fel, Univ Rochester, 1953-1955. **Memberships:** Sigma Xi; Am Ceramic Soc; Int Soc Hybrid Microelectronics; Soc Info Display. **Research Statement & Publications:** Kinetics; radical reactions; solubility; polymer chemistry; electronic materials; magnetism; photographic science; glasses; ceramics; rheology. **Mailing Address:** 20 Boulder Brook Dr, Wilmington, DE 19803. **E-Mail:** ejolley@tower_hill.pvt.k12.de.us

JOLLEY, ROBERT LOUIS, ENVIRONMENTAL CHEMISTRY. **Personal Data:** b Little Rock, Ark, July 11, 1929; m 1950, c 2. **Education:** Friends Univ, BA, 1950; Univ Tenn, Knoxville, PhD (ecol), 1973. **Professional Experience:** CHEM ECOLOGIST, OAK RIDGE NAT LAB, 1973-; County comnr, Anderson County, Tenn, 1959-; chemist, Oak Ridge Nat Lab, 1956-1973; chemist, SouthwestGrease & Oil Co, 1951-1955; Asst chem, Friends

Univ, 1949-1950 & Univ Chicago, 1950-1951. **Memberships:** Am Chem Soc; AAAS; Sigma Xi. **Research Statement & Publications:** Measurement and identification of organic constituents in natural and polluted waters; determination of chlorination effects and analysis of chloro-organics in process effluents and condenser cooling waters for electric power plants; evaluation of treatment technologies for low-level radioactive waste and hazardous waste. **Mailing Address:** 120 N Seneca Rd, Oak Ridge, TN 37830-4898.

JOLLEY, WELDON BOSEN, PHYSIOLOGY. **Personal Data:** b Gunnison, Utah, September 8, 1926; m 1983, c 5. **Education:** Brigham Young Univ, AB, 1952; Univ Southern Calif, PhD (cell physiol), 1959. **Professional Experience:** PRES, GOLDEN OPPORTUNITIES, as of 2000; adv, Nucleic Acid Res Inst, beginning 1995; pres, Nucleic Acid Res Inst, beginning 1985; prof physiol, Jerry L Pettis Vet Admin Hosp, 1980-1995; prof physiol, biophys & surg & assoc dir, Surg Res Lab, Loma Linda Univ, 1971-1980; asst prof physiol & co-dir, Surg Res Lab, Univ Southern Calif, 1959-1971; instr, Univ Southern Calif, 1958-1959; instr, Compton Col, 1956; res assoc, Univ Southern Calif, 1953-1959; vpres & sr scientist, ICN Pharmaceut Inc; mem bd dirs, SPI Pharm Inc, sr vpres bd dirs, ICN Pharm Inc; mem bd, ICN Pharmaceut Inc; mem bd, Life Resources, Inc; dir, Bio Nuclear Corp. **Memberships:** AAAS; AMA; Am Fedn Clin Res; Am Physiol Soc; Transplantation Soc. **Research Statement & Publications:** Antiviral agents; immunologic modulators; cancer immunology; transplantation of skin, pancreas, heart, kidneys; endotoxic and hemorrhagic shock; biological effects of pulsed electromagnetic fields. **Mailing Address:** Golden Opportunities, PO Box 833, Batavia, IL 60510. **E-Mail:** wjolley@goldone.com

JOLLICK, JOSEPH DARRYL, MICROBIAL GENETICS, MEDICAL MICROBIOLOGY. **Personal Data:** b Denbo, Pa, May 15, 1941; m 1963, c 2. **Education:** Calif State Col, BS, 1963, Am Univ, MS, 1966; WVa Univ, PhD (microbiol), 1969. **Professional Experience:** PROF MICROBIOL, OHIO UNIV, 1984-; asst prof, Sch Med, 1978-1980; assoc prof microbiol, Col Osteop Med, Ohio Univ, 1976-1984; NIH grant, Wayne State Univ, 1974-; asst prof microbiol, Sch Med, Wayne State Univ, 1972-1977; instr, Sch Med, Wayne State Univ, 1970-1972; Nat Res Coun grant, Biol Sci Lab, Ft Detrick, 1969-1970; biologist, Nat Cancer Inst, 1963-1964. **Memberships:** AAAS; Am Soc Microbiol; Am Asn Univ Professors. **Research Statement & Publications:** Genetics of Caulobacter; mechanism and transfer of antibiotic resistance in Serratia and Pseudomonas. **Mailing Address:** Dept Biomed, Ohio univ, 408 Grosvenor, Athens, OH 45701. **Fax:** 740-593-1730. **E-Mail:** jollickj@ohiou.edu

JOLLIE, MALCOLM THOMAS, COMPARATIVE ANATOMY, ZOOLOGY. **Personal Data:** b Lakewood, Ohio, July 11, 1919; m 1950, c 2. **Education:** Western Reserve Univ, BS, 1941; Univ Colo, MS, 1943; Stanford Univ, PhD (comp anat), 1954. **Professional Experience:** RETIRED; prof biol, Northern Ill Univ, 1965-1988; asst & assoc prof zool, Univ Pittsburg, 1956-1965; asst & assoc prof zool, Univ Idaho, 1947-1956; instr sci, Western NMex Teachers Col, 1945-1947; mus technician birds & asst zool, Univ Calif, 1943-1945; asst biol, Univ Colo, 1941-1943. **Research Statement & Publications:** Comparative anatomy relating to origin and phylogeny of chordates and vertebrates; systematic ornithology and ichthyology. **Mailing Address:** 19074 N 91st St, Scottsdale, AZ 85255.

JOLLIE, WILLIAM PUCETTE, ANATOMY, CELL & DEVELOPMENTAL BIOLOGY. **Personal Data:** b Passaic, NJ, June 27, 1928; m 1950, Ludmila; c William P Jr & Michael Konstantin. **Education:** Lehigh Univ, BA, 1950, MS, 1952; Harvard Univ, PhD (biol), 1959. **Honors & Awards:** AJ Ladman/AAA/ Wiley Exemplary Service Award, 2000. **Professional Experience:** PROF EMER ANAT, MED COL, VA COMMONWEALTH UNIV, as of 2004; prof anat & chmn dept, Med Col Va, Va Commonwealth Univ, 1969-1995; from asst prof to prof anat, Sch Med, Tulane Univ, 1961-1969; lectr histol & embryol, Queen's Univ, Ont, 1959-1961. **Memberships:** Am Asn Anatomists; Am Soc Cell Biologists; Teratology Soc. **Research Statement & Publications:** Controlling mechanisms for placental transport; visualization of placental transport mechanisms; maternal accommodations to implantation and placental formation; effects of alcohol on acquisition of neonatal immunity. **Mailing Address:** Dept Anat, Col Med, Va Commonwealth Univ, MCV Sta 11th & Marshall St PO Box 980709, Richmond, VA 23298-0709. **Fax:** 804-828-9477. **E-Mail:** wjollie@hsc.vcu.edu

JOLLOW, DAVID J, TOXICOLOGY. **Personal Data:** b Sidney, Australia, May 5, 1936. **Education:** Monarch Univ, Australia, PhD (biochem), 1967. **Professional Experience:** PROF PHARMACOL & DIR ENVIRONHAZARDS ASSESSMENT RES, UNIV SC, 1992-; Fac Med U SC-Molecular toxicology. **Research Statement & Publications:** Toxicology. **Mailing Address:** Cell & Molecular Pharmacol, 173 Ashley Ave, BSB 303, PO Box 250505, Charleston, SC 29425. **Fax:** 843-792-2475. **E-Mail:** jollowd@musc.edu

JOLLS, CLAUDIA LEE, PLANT ECOLOGY, PLANT POPULATION BIOLOGY. **Personal Data:** b Detroit, Mich, May 20, 1953. **Education:** Univ Mich, Ann Arbor, BS, 1975; Univ Colo, Boulder, PhD (biol), 1980. **Professional Experience:** ASSOC PROF, BIOL DEPT, E CAROLINA UNIV, 1990-; Helms res award, Chap Sigma Xi, ECarolina Univ, 1990; res assoc, Univ Colo, 1988; res assoc & vis fac, Univ Mich, 1985-1993; asst prof, Biol Dept, ECarolina Univ, 1984-1989; residentterrestrial ecologist, Biol Sta, Univ Mich, 1981-1984; prog coordr, Naturalist-Ecologist TrainingProg, Biol Sta, Univ Mich, 1981-1984; fel, Kellogg Biostation, Mich State Univ, 1981; fel plantpop biol, Mich State Univ, 1980-1981; adv, Traineeship Prog, Mt Res Sta, Inst Arctic & AlpineRes, Univ Colo, NSF, 1977 & 1978; res asst plant ecol, Dept Environ, Pop & Organismic, UnivColo at Audubon-Whittel Res Ranch, Ariz, 1976; teaching asst ecol, bot & human physiol, DeptEnviron Pop & Organismic, Univ Colo, 1975-1980. **Memberships:** Assoc Southeastern Biologists; Natural Areas Assoc; S Appalachian Bot Soc; AmInst Biol Sci; Bot Soc Am; Ecol Soc Am; Sigma Xi. **Research Statement & Publications:** Plant ecology and population biology: conservation biology, population dynamics, breeding biology, forest succession; field-based studies in wetlands; northern hardwoods, alpine tundra, dunes. **Mailing Address:** Dept Biol, E Carolina Univ, Greenville, NC 27858-4353. **Fax:** 252-328-4178. **E-Mail:** jollsc@mail.ecu.edu

JOLLS, KENNETH ROBERT, PHASE BEHAVIOR, COMPUTER GRAPHICS. **Personal Data:** b Baltimore, Md, October 19, 1933; c 1. **Education:** Duke Univ, AB, 1958; NC State Univ, BSChE, 1961; Univ Ill, MS, 1963, PhD (chem eng), 1966. **Professional Experience:** PROF CHEM ENG, IOWA STATE UNIV, 1990-; Vis prof chem eng, Univ Calif, Berkeley, 1981-1983 & Cornell Univ, 1984; assoc prof chem eng, Iowa State Univ, 1970-1990; from asst prof to assoc prof, Polytech Inst Brooklyn, 1965-1970; Asst chem eng, Univ Ill, 1961-1965. **Memberships:** Am Inst Chem Engrs; Sigma Xi; Am Chem Soc; Asn Comput Mach. **Research Statement & Publications:** Fluid mechanics; thermodynamics; application of electronic instrumentation in chemical engineering; computer graphics; scientific visualization. **Mailing Address:** Dept Chem Eng, Iowa State Univ, 2155 Sweeney Hall, Ames, IA 50011-2230. **Fax:** 515-294-2689. **E-Mail:** jolls@eng.iastate.edu

JOLLY, ALISON BISHOP, PRIMATE BEHAVIOR. **Personal Data:** b Ithaca, NY, May 9, 1937; m 1963, c 4. **Education:** Cornell Univ, BA, 1958; Yale Univ, PhD (zool), 1962. **Professional Experience:** VIS SR RES FEL, UNIV SUSSEX, as of 2003; vis lectr, Princeton Univ, beginning 1987; guest investr, Rockefeller Univ, 1982-1987; res assoc, Sch Biol, Univ Sussex, 1968-1981; NSF res grant, 1962-1964; res assoczool, NY Zool Soc, 1962-1964. **Memberships:** Int Primatol Soc(former pres); Wildlife Preserv Trust Int; Animal Behav Asn; Sigma Xi; Am Primatology Asn; fel AAAS; fel Am Acad Arts & Sci. **Research Statement & Publications:** Conservation of natural ecosystems in Madagascar; primate behavior, particularly that of prosimians; evolution of human behavior. **Mailing Address:** Dept Biol, Univ Sussex, Sussex House, Falmer, UK. **E-Mail:** ajolly@central.susx.ac.uk

JOLLY, CLIFFORD J, PHYSICAL ANTHROPOLOGY, PRIMATOLOGY. **Personal Data:** b Southend, Eng, January 21, 1939; m 1961, c 2. **Education:** Univ London, BA, 1960, PhD (phys anthrop), 1965. **Professional Experience:** PROF PHYS ANTHROP, NY UNIV, 1975-; from asst prof to assoc prof, NY Univ, 1967-1975; asst lectr, Univ Col, London, 1965-1967; vis res fel, Makerere Univ Col, Uganda, 1965-1966; res asst phys anthrop, Univ Col, London, 1963-1965. **Memberships:** Am Asn Advan Sci; Am Asn Phys Anthropologists; Soc Study Human Biol; Zoology Soc London; Royal Anthrop Inst; Sigma Xi. **Research Statement & Publications:** Primate functional anatomy; serology and biology. **Mailing Address:** 60 Eighth St, Hoboken, NJ 07030-5057.

JOLLY, JANICE LAURENE WILLARD, ECONOMIC GEOLOGY, PETROLOGY. **Personal Data:** b Bakersfield, Calif, July 23, 1931; m 1956, c 3. **Education:** Univ Ore, BA, 1956, MS, 1957. **Professional Experience:** CHIEF STATISTICIAN, INT COPPER STUDY GROUP, LISBON, PORT, 1993-; sr commodity specialist, Copper, 1981-1993; chief, Off Geog Statist, 1981-1983; intern, Exec Managerial Develop Prog, Dept Interior, 1980-1981; mineral commodity area specialist, USBur Mines, 1973-1980; res geologist, RST Tech Serv Ltd, Zambia, 1967-1972; Geologist, USGeol Surv, 1958-1967. **Memberships:** Fel Geol Soc Am; AmInst Mining Metall & Petrol Engrs. **Research Statement & Publications:** Geology of the Monument Quadrangle, Oregon; petrography of the crystalline rocks, Potomac River gorge, Maryland-Virginia; ore deposit controls in Mississippi and Appalachian Valleys lead-zinc deposits; eastern United States heavy metal and massive sulfide deposits; geochemistry of copper deposits of Zambia; commodity surveys of copper and iron oxide pigments; international mineral industry studies in Africa and Middle East; supply and demand of strategic and critical minerals; mineral economics; world copper markets; industry and statistics. **Mailing Address:** Int Copper Study Group, Rua Almirante Barroso 38 6th Floor, Lisbon 1000, Portugal.

JOLLY, STUART MARTIN, SYSTEMS DESIGN. **Personal Data:** b London, Eng, August 29, 1946; American citizen. **Education:** Haverford Col, BA, 1968; Cornell Univ, MS, 1971. **Professional Experience:** ASSOC SECT LEADER, INFRASTRUCTURE & APPLN, MITRECORP, 2001-; ASSOC DEPT HEAD, MITRE CORP, 1985-; group leader, Mitre Corp, 1979-1985; mem tech staff, Mitre Corp, 1977-1979; vpres, res & develop, 1974-1977; mem staff, RobinsonAssocs Inc, 1972-1974. **Research Statement & Publications:** Analysis and design of communications systems, security systems and speech processing. **Mailing Address:** The MITRE Corp, 202 Burlington Rd MS M315, Burlington, MA 01730-1420. **Fax:** 781-271-2964. **E-Mail:** smjolly@mitre.org

JOLLY, WAYNE TRAVIS, PETROLOGY, VOLCANOLOGY. **Personal Data:** b Jacksonville, Tex, August 15, 1940. **Education:** Univ Tex, Austin, BS, 1963, MS, 1967; State Univ NY, Binghamton, PhD (geol), 1970. **Professional Experience:** UNDERGRAD PROG ADV, EARTH SCI, BROCK UNIV, as of 2005; prof earth sci, Brock Univ, as of 1997; assoc prof geol, Brock Univ, beginning 1975; asst prof, Brock Univ, 1971-1975; fel geol, Univ Sask, 1970-1971. **Memberships:** Geol Soc Am; Geol Asn Can; Mineral Asn Can. **Research Statement & Publications:** Geochemical petrology and metamorphic petrology of volcanic rocks with emphasis on prehnite-pumpellyite facies and origin of Archean volcanics. **Mailing Address:** Dept Earth Sci, Brock Univ, MC D425, St Catharines, ON L2S 3A1, Can.

JOLLY, WILLIAM LEE, INORGANIC CHEMISTRY. **Personal Data:** b Chicago, Ill, December 27, 1927; m 1995, Jane; c 3. **Education:** Univ Ill, BS, 1948, MS, 1949; Univ Calif, PhD (chem), 1952. **Professional Experience:** PROF EMER CHEM, UNIV CALIF, BERKELEY, 1991-; prof, Radiation Lab, 1962-1991; from asst prof to assoc prof, Radiation Lab, 1955-1962; chemist, Radiation Lab, 1953-1955; instr, Univ Calif, 1952-1953. **Memberships:** AAAS; Am Chem Soc; Royal Soc Chem. **Research Statement & Publications:** Liquid ammonia chemistry; chemistry of the volatile hydrides; studies of the bonding in transition metal complexes; x-ray photoelectron spectroscopy; chemistry of the photographic process. **Mailing Address:** Dept Chem, Univ Calif, 419 Latimer Hall, Berkeley, CA 94720-1460. **Fax:** 510-642-9675. **E-Mail:** wljolly@socrates.berkeley.edu

JOLLY-WOODRUFF, SUSAN, THEORETICAL CHEMISTRY. **Personal Data:** b Wakefield, RI, August 18, 1940; m 1963, c 2. **Education:** Oberlin Col, AB, 1962; Johns Hopkins Univ, MAT, 1963; Univ Calif, Irvine, PhD (chem), 1977. **Professional Experience:** CONSULT, DOTLESS BRAILL, AS OF 2004; Emem staff chem & fel, Los Alamos Sci Lab, 1977-1993. **Memberships:** Am Chem Soc. **Research Statement & Publications:** Chemical dynamics; chemical kinetics; classical trajectorymethodology; quantum chemistry; potential energy surfaces; surface chemistry; computer capabilities. **Mailing Address:** 120 Dos Brazos St, Los Alamos, NM 87544-2431. **E-Mail:** easjolly@ix.netcom.com

JOLY, HELEN A, CHEMISTRY. **Education:** Laurentian Univ, BSc & MSc; Queen's Univ, PhD. **Professional Experience:** PROF, DEPT CHEM & BIOCHEM, LAURENTIAN UNIV, as of 2005. **Research Statement & Publications:** Metal-Atom-Mediated Chemical Transformations; metal vapour synthesis; characterization and study of the reactivity of intermediates resulting from Al atom reactions of thiols and organosulfides; study of metal activation of C-halogen bonds; reduction of aromatic compounds by metal atoms; metal assisted coupling of alkenes and ketones; comparing the efficiency of the cryostat technique to conventional methods of producing metal atoms. **Mailing Address:** Dept Chem & Biochem, Laurentian Univ, S 421, Sudburg, ON P3E 2C6, Can. **Fax:** 705-675-4844. **E-Mail:** hjoly@laurentian.ca

JOLY, LOUIS PHILIPPE, PHARMACEUTICAL CHEMISTRY. **Personal Data:** b Montreal, Que, July 23, 1928; m 1954, c 3. **Education:** Laval Univ, BA, 1949, BSc, 1953; Univ Bordeaux, France, PhD, 1965. **Professional Experience:** RETIRED; prof med chem, Col Pharm, Univ Laval, 1971-1994; consult, Neuropsychopharmacol Res Univ, 1969-; assoc prof, Col Pharm, Univ Laval, 1958-1971; Chiefpharmacist, Robert Giffard Hosp Ctr, 1957-1969; Lectr, Col Pharm, Univ Laval, 1957-1958. **Memberships:** AAAS; NY Acad Sci; Am Pharmaceut Asn; Can Pharmaceut Asn. **Research Statement & Publications:** Synthesis and essay by cell culture methods of new alkylating agents as antineoplastics; biotransforms of long acting psychotrophic drugs. **Mailing Address:** 1324 Rue Marechal Foch, Quebec, PQ G1S 2C4, Can.

JONA, FRANCO PAUL, SURFACE PHYSICS, METASTABLE PHASES. **Personal Data:** b Pistoia, Italy, October 10, 1922; American citizen; m 1952, c FredErico & Franco. **Education:** Swiss Fed Inst Technol, dipl, 1945, PhD (physics), 1949. **Professional Experience:** PROF, STATE UNIV NY STONY BROOK as of 2006; leading prof, State Univ NY Stony Brook, beginning, 1969; staff physicist res lab, Int Bus Mach Corp, NY, 1959-1969; res physicist res labs, Westinghouse Elec Corp, 1957-1959; asst prof, Pa State Univ, 1954-1957; res assoc, Pa State Univ, 1952-1954; Instr physics, Univ Bern, 1945-1946 & Swiss Fed Inst Technol, 1946-1952. **Memberships:** Fel Am Phys Soc; Swiss Phys Soc; European phys Soc. **Research Statement & Publications:** Ferroelectricity; crystallography; elasticity; piezoelectricity; crystal growth; surface studies; epitaxy; ultrathin films; Metastable phases. **Mailing Address:** Col Eng, State Univ NY, Stony Brook, NY 2275. **Fax:** 516-632-8052. **E-Mail:** franco.jona@sunsb.edu

JONAH, CHARLES D, RADIATION CHEMISTRY. **Personal Data:** b Lafayette, Ind, March 19, 1943; m 1969, Margaret. **Education:** Oberlin Col, BA, 1965; Columbia Univ, PhD (chem), 1970. **Professional Experience:** SR CHEM, ARGONNE NAT LAB, 1997-; CHEMIST RADIATION CHEM, ARGONNE NAT LAB, 1977-; asst scientist, Argonne Nat Lab, 1974-1977; fel, Argonne Nat Lab, 1971-1974; fel phys chem, Columbia Univ, 1969-1971. **Memberships:** Am Phys Soc; Am Chem Soc. **Research Statement & Publications:** Mechanism of reactions; fast kinetic measurements; instrumentation; radiation chemistry of aqueous systems solvation of electrons. **Mailing Address:** Chem Div Argonne Nat Lab, 9700 S Cass Ave, Argonne, IL 60439. **Fax:** 630-252-4993. **E-Mail:** jonah@anlchm.chm.anl.gov

JONAH, MARGARET MARTIN, CELL SURFACE BIOLOGY. **Personal Data:** b Berkeley, Calif, October 25, 1942; m 1969, Charles. **Education:** Pomona Col, Calif, BA, 1964; Columbia Univ, PhD (chem biol), 1971. **Professional Experience:** PROF BIOL, ROSARY COL, DOMINICAN UNIV, as of 2004; prin investr, NIH area grantee, 1989-1993; prin investr, NSF, Inst Land Info grantee, 1988-1991; assoc prof Biol, Rosary Col, Dominican Univ, beginning 1984; RESIDENT ASSOC, ARGONNE NAT LAB, 1976-; asst prof, Argonne Nat Lab, 1976-1984; res assoc, Argonne Nat Lab, 1975-1976; appointee biol, Argonne Nat Lab, 1973-1975; res fel biochem, Northwestern Univ, Ill, 1971-1973. **Memberships:** AAAS; Am Inst Biol Sci; Am Chem Soc; Am Soc Microbiol; Int Radiation Res Soc; Sigma Xi; Am Asn Dent Res. **Research Statement & Publications:** Functions of lipids in membrane formation and surface specificity; metabolism of streptococcus mutans; interactions of biologically active molecules with lipids; cell surface receptors; role of heavy metals in cell metabolism; cadmium metabolism in mammals. **Mailing Address:** Dept Biol, Rosary Col, Dominican Univ, Sci 106, River Forest, IL 60305-1066. **E-Mail:** jonahmm@dom.edu

JONAK, ZDENKA L, CELLULAR & MOLECULAR BIOLOGY. **Personal Data:** b Iomouc, Czechoslavakia, March 9, 1946; American citizen; m 1969, Gerald; c Peter, Elizabeth & Thomas. **Education:** Charles Univ, Prague, Czechoslovakia, BS, 1968; Yale Univ, MS, 1971, PhD (biol-biochem), 1975. **Professional Experience:** ASSOC DIR CELLULAR BIOCHEM, SMITH KLINE BEECHAM PHARMACEUT, 1993-; asst dir cellular biochem & immunol, Smith Kline Beecham Pharmaceut, 1988-1993; sr investr cell biol, Smith Kline Beecham Pharmaceut, 1985-1988; sr investr immunol, Smith Kline Beecham Pharmaceut, 1984-1985; res assoc human genetics, Univ Pa, 1980-1984; res investr immunobiochem group, Wistar Inst Anat & Biol, 1978-1980; res fel immunol, Joseph Stokes Jr Res Inst, Children's Hosp, 1975-1978; fel, NSF, 1973-1974. **Memberships:** AAAS; Am Asn Immunol; Fed Am Soc Exp Biol; Sigma Xi. **Research Statement & Publications:** Humane immune system particularly cellular and molecular biology of B-cells and the consequences of alterations resulting in disease status; generation of fully human monoclonal antibodies to specific targets. **Mailing Address:** Smith Kline Beecham Dept Molecular Immunol, 709 Swedeland Rd PO Box 1539, King of Prussia, PA 19406. **Fax:** 610-270-4899.

JONAS, ALBERT MOSHE, PATHOLOGY, COMPARATIVE MEDICINE. **Personal Data:** b New Haven, Conn, October 3, 1931; m 1954, c 3. **Education:** Univ Toronto, DVM, 1955; Am Col Vet Path, dipl, 1963. **Honorary Degrees:** MA, Yale Univ, 1974. **Professional Experience:** CHMN, BD DIRS, VETCOR. 1997-; actg dir, Animal Resources Ctr, 1991-1995; actg chair comput med, Dept Path, Pritzker Sch Med, Univ Chicago, 1991-1995; visprof, Dept Path, Pritzker Sch Med, Univ Chicago, 1990-1995; PRES, RES ANIMAL-CONSULTS, INC, 1987-; chief, Sci Resources, Res Animal Consults, Inc, 1983-1986; vis prof, Univ Tokyo, 1983; fel, Japanese Soc Prom Sci, 1983; sr staff scientist & dir, Lab Animal Med &Comp Path, Jackson Lab, Res Animal Consults, Inc, 1982-1986; chmn comp med & lab animalsci, Vet Sch, 1981-1982; adv bd, Northeast Regional Primate Ctr, 1979-1982; comt vet med sci, Nat Acad Sci, 1979-1980; prof exp path, Med Sch, 1978-1982; first dean, Vet Sch Tufts Univ, 1978-1981; cause & prev sci rev comt, Nat Cancer Inst, 1978-1981; prof comp med & path &chmn sect comp med, Div Health Sci Res & Path & chief sect comp med, 1977-1978; mem techrev comt, Bioassay Prog, Nat Cancer Inst, 1977-1978; eval panel, Primate Res Ctrs Prog, NIH, 1977-1978; prof comp med, Div Health Sci Res & Path & chief sect comp med, 1974-1977; mem, Orgn Comt Symp on Lab Animal Housing, Nat Acad Sci, 1974-1975; mem adv comt comppath, Armed Forces Inst Path, 1973-1976; prof animal sci & path, Sch Med, Yale Univ, 1973-1974; chmn comt, Longterm Holding Lab Rodents, Inst Lab Animal Res, Nat Acad Sci, 1973-1976; mem animal res adv comt, Div Res Resources, NIH, 1972-1976; assoc prof path, SchMed, Yale Univ, 1971-1973; mem, Am Asn Accreditation Lab Animal Care, 1968-1975; assocprof animal sci & chief lab, Sch Med, Yale Univ, 1968-1973; mem coun, Inst Lab AnimalResources, Nat Acad Sci, 1965-1969; from instr to asst prof, Sch Med, Yale Univ, 1963-1968; dir animal care, Sch Med, Yale Univ, 1961-1978; res asst path, Sch Med, Yale Univ, 1961-1963; pvt pract, 1955-1961. **Memberships:** Am Asn Lab Animal Sci; Am Vet Med Asn; Int Acad Path; Am Col Vet Path; SocPharmacol & Environ Path. **Research Statement & Publications:** Naturally occurring diseases in laboratory animals with specific interests in animal model systems; pulmonary pathology including pulmonary hemodynamics and infectious diseases with emphasis in pathogenesis. **Mailing Address:** 17 Cumberland St, Boston, MA 02115.

JONAS, ANA, BIOCHEMISTRY. **Personal Data:** b Rokiskis, Lithuania, November 24, 1943; American citizen; m 1968, Jiri. **Education:** Univ Ill, Chicago, BS, 1966; Univ Ill, Urbana, PhD (biochem), 1970. **Honors & Awards:** Lyman Duff Lectr, Am Heart Asn, 1996. **Professional Experience:** Consult, Nat Res Coun, 1989-1992; consult, Am Heart Asn, 1985-2001; adv bd, J Lipid Res, 1984-2001; PROF BIOCHEM, UNIV ILL, URBANA, 1984-; Fogarty fel, Ctr Molecular Biophys, Nat Ctr Res Sci, Orleans, France, 1981; res grants, Am Heart Asn, 1980-1983; Coun Arteriosclerosis fel, Am Heart Asn, 1980-; consult, Nat Heart Lung & Blood Inst, 1978-1991; estab investigatorship, Am Heart Asn, 1974-1979; res grants, Nat Heart Lung & Blood Inst, 1973-2002; NATO fel, Max Planck Med Res Inst, Heidelberg, WGer, 1973; from asst prof to assoc prof, Univ Ill, Urbana, 1972-1984; NIH trainee, Univ Ill, Urbana, 1970-1972. **Memberships:** Am Heart Asn; Am Soc Biochem & Molecular Biol. **Research Statement & Publications:** Structure and function of high density serum lipoproteins; protein-lipid interactions; interfacial-lipolytic enzymes; protein folding and dynamics. **Mailing Address:** Dept Biochem, Col Med Urbana-Champaign, Univ Ill, 190 Med Sci Bldg 506 S Mathews, Urbana, IL 61801. **Fax:** 217-333-8868. **E-Mail:** a-jonas@uiuc.edu

JONAS, EDWARD CHARLES, CLAY MINERALOGY. **Personal Data:** b San Antonio, Tex, July 24, 1924; m 1949, c 3. **Education:** Rice Inst, BS, 1944; Univ Ill, MS, 1952, PhD (geol), 1954. **Professional Experience:** Fulbright sr res award, NZ, 1960-1961; from asst prof to prof, Univ Tex, Austin, beginning 1954; asst geologist, Ill StateGeol Surv, 1952-1954; EMER PROF GEOL, UNIV TEX, AUSTIN. **Memberships:** Fel AAAS; fel Geol Soc Am; fel Mineral Soc Am; Geochem Soc; Mineral Soc GtBrit & Ireland. **Research Statement & Publications:** Mineralogy of clays and uranium deposits in the Texas Gulf Tertiary. **Mailing Address:** Rte 1 Box 117, Marchaca, TX 78652.

JONAS, HERBERT, plant physiology; deceased, see previous edition for last biography

JONAS, JIRI, PHYSICAL CHEMISTRY, MOLECULAR SPECTROSCOPY. **Personal Data:** b Prague, Czech, April 1, 1932; American citizen. **Education:** Tech Univ Prague, BS, 1956; Czech Acad Sci, PhD (chem), 1960. **Honors & Awards:** Joel Henry Hildebrand Award, Theoret & Exp Chem of Liquids, Am Chem Soc, 1983; US Scientist Award, Alexander von Humboldt Found, WGer. **Professional Experience:** PROF EMER, UNIV ILL, URBANA, 2001-; prof, Ctr Advan Study, 1996-2001; dir, Beckman Inst Advan Sci & Technol, 1993-2001; dir, Sch Chem Sci, 1983-1993; assoc mem, Ctr Advan Study, Univ Ill, 1976-1977; prof chem, Univ Ill, Urbana, 1972-2001; fel, Alfred P Sloan Found, 1967-1969 & J S Guggenheim Found, 1972-1973; sr staff mem mat res, Univ Ill, Urbana, 1970-1992; from asst prof to assoc prof, Univ Ill, Urbana, 1966-1972; vis scientist, Univ Ill, Urbana, 1963-1965; res assoc chem, Czech Acad Sci, 1960-1963. **Memberships:** Nat Acad Sci; Am Chem Soc; fel Am Phys Soc; fel AAAS; fel Am Inst Chemists; fel Am Acad Arts & Sci. **Research Statement & Publications:** Nuclear magnetic resonance; raman spectroscopy; dynamic structure of liquids; glasses, molecular solids and biopolymers; high pressure research; behavior of materials under extreme conditions of pressure and temperature. **Mailing Address:** 166 Roger Adam Lab, 1209 W Calif, Urbana, IL 61801. **E-Mail:** j_jonas@uiuc.edu

JONAS, JOHN JOSEPH, ORGANIC CHEMISTRY. **Personal Data:** b Budapest, Hungary, December 9, 1914; American citizen; m 1941, c 3. **Education:** Pazmany Peter Univ, PhD (chem, physics. math), 1937. **Professional Experience:** SCI MGT CONSULT, RES & DEVELOP DIV, KRAFT, INC, 1977-; Consult, Protein Resources Study, NSF, 1975-1976; assoc mgr indust prod, Res & Develop Div, Kraft Inc, 1951-1977; asst div leader pharmaceut & nutrit res, Inst Heiligenberg, Ger, 1946-1951; chemist, Hungary Viscose Corp, 1943-1945; chemist, Darmol Pharmaceut Co, Budapest, 1939-1943; Asst & instr org & pharmaceut chem, Pazmany Peter Univ, 1936-1939. **Memberships:** Am Chem Soc; Inst Food Technol; Am Inst Chemists. **Research Statement & Publications:** Metabolic diseases of dairy cattle; seaweed hydrocolloids; food emulsifying systems; high protein foods; dairy analogues, vegetable proteins, synthetic nutrients. **Mailing Address:** Rte 2 Box 246, Meadows of Dan, VA 24120.

JONAS, JOHN JOSEPH, PHYSICAL METALLURGY, MECHANICAL METALLURGY. **Personal Data:** b Montreal, Que, December 8, 1932; m 1963, Holly; c Jennifer, Jeremy, Jonathan & Jodie. **Education:** McGill Univ, BEng, 1954; Cambridge Univ, PhD (mech sci), 1960. **Honors & Awards:** Frank Garofalo Mem Lectr, Northwestern Univ, 1980; Reaumur Silver Medal, Fr Metall Soc, 1980; Hatchett Medal & Award, Metals Soc UK, 1982; Dofasco Mat Eng Award, Can Inst Mining & Metal, 1982, Alcan Award, 1990; Gold Medal, Can Metal Physics Asn, 1983; Michael Tenenbaum Award, Iron & Steel Soc, Am Inst Mining Metall & Petrol Engrs, 1989 & 1996, Robert W Hunt Silver Medal, 1997; Gold Medal, French Soc Metall & Mat, 1991; Sawamura Award, Iron & Steel Inst Japan, 1992 & 1995; Officer Order of Can, 1993 fel, Candian acaademy of engr, fel, Candian instit fo mining and metallurgy 1994; prix du Quebec (Marie-Victorin) (Quebec 'Scientist of the year' award'), 1995; Asm international Cananda council lectu for 1996-1997; Alexander von humboldt res award of the German Avh found, visiting fell, Japan soc for the promotion fo sci, Charles S Barrett silver medal, ASM, 1998; Alpha sigma mu lecturer, and alpha sigma mu distinguished life mam (prof soc for materials sci and engr), Yukawa mem lectur and silver medallist, iron and steel insti of Japan, Killam Prize in engr, Chevalier, Order of Quebec, 2000; 14th Khwarizmi inter award, Iran, presented by the president of Iran, prix Urgel-Archambault (Physical Sci, math and engr), Assoc canadienne-francaise pour l'avancement des sci (ACFAS), 2001. **Professional Experience:** BIRKS PROF METALL, MCGILL UNIV, 1992-; Chmn res & develop, adv panel, Atomic Energy Can, 1992 & 1993; CSIRA prof steel processing, 1985-1996; assoc dean, Fac Grad Studies & Res, 1971-1975; From asst prof to prof phys metall, McGill Univ, 1960-1985; co-dir, McGill Metals Processing Ctr. **Memberships:** Fel Am Soc Metals; Am Inst Mining, Metall & Petrol Engrs; Honorary mem Iron & Steel Inst Japan; fel Can Inst Mining & Metall; fel Royal Soc Can; fel Can Acad Eng; Honorary mem, Indian Institute of metals. **Research Statement & Publications:** Mechanical metallurgy; elevated temperature deformation of metals and crystalline materials; microstructural changes and stress-strain rate-temperature relationships during hot working; plastic instability; thermal activation analysis, textures, yield surfaces and formabilty. **Mailing Address:** Dept Materials Eng McGill Univ, 3610 Univ St, Montreal, PQ H3A 2B2, Can. **Fax:** 514-398-4492. **E-Mail:** john.jonas@mcgill.ca

JONAS, LEONARD ABRAHAM, physical chemistry; deceased, see previous edition for last biography

JONAS, ROBERT JAMES, animal ecology, wildlifemanagement; deceased, see previous edition for last biography

JONCAS, JEAN HARRY, VIROLOGY, INFECTIOUS DISEASES. **Personal Data:** b Montreal, Que, June 27, 1930; m 1955, Anita; c Maryse, Genevieve, Francois, Nathalie & Simon. **Education:** Jean de Brebeuf Col, BA, 1948; Univ Montreal, MD, 1955, PhD (microbiol, immunol), 1967. **Professional Experience:** PROF MICROBIOL & IMMUNOL, SCH MED, UNIV MONTREAL, as of 1997; health & welfare contract, Epstein Barr Virus Nat Ctr, 1985-; HEAD VIROLRES LAB, STE JUSTINE HOSP, MONTREAL, 1985-; head, Dept Microbiol, 1977-1985; NatCancer Inst Can grant, 1975-1981; res assoc virol, Inst Microbiol & Hyg, 1971-1976; Fed Provpub health res grant, 1971-1975; demonstr, Dept Pediat, McGill Univ, 1970-; consult, MontrealChildren's Hosp, 1970-; Med Res Coun Can grant, 1970-1986; Nat Defence Res grant, 1970-1976; head, Infectious Dis Sect, Ste Justine Hosp, Montreal, 1970-1976; mem adv comt infection, Immunity& Ther, Defence Res Bd Can, 1970-1974; asst prof, Sch Med, Univ Montreal, 1967-1970; lectr, Sch Med, Univ Montreal, 1964-1967; res asst, Univ Montreal, 1960-1970; clin asst, MontrealChildren's Hosp, 1959-1970; fel, Sch Med, Wayne State Univ, 1956. **Memberships:** Am Soc Microbiol; Int Soc Antiviral Res; fel Infectious Dis Soc Am; CanInfectious Dis Soc. **Research Statement & Publications:** Etiology and epidemiology of infectious mononucleosis; the Epstein-Barr herpes virus; cell-virus relationship; Epstein-Barr virus and oncogenesis; diagnosis of viral infections by rapid immunological methods and molecular biology;

pediatric infectious diseases, epidemiology, diagnosis and treatment. **Mailing Address:** Dept Microbiol & Immunol, St Justine Hosp 3175 Ste-Catherine Rd, Montreal, PQ H3T 1C5, Can. **Fax:** 514-345-4801.

JONEJA, MADAN GOPAL, TERATOLOGY, ULTRASTRUCTURAL CELL BIOLOGY. **Personal Data:** b Lyallpur, India, December 25, 1936; Canadian citizen; m 1965, Asha; c Mala & Navin. **Education:** Panjab Univ, India, MSc, 1958; Queen's Univ, Ont, PhD (biol), 1965. **Professional Experience:** PROF EMER ANAT, QUEENS UNIV, ONT, as of 2004; head, Dept Anat, 1981-1996; prof anat, Queens Univ, Ont, beginning 1976; chmn grad studies anat, Queens Univ, 1970-1980; From lectr to assoc prof, Queens Univ, 1965-1976. **Memberships:** Teratology Soc; Am Asn Anatomists; Can Asn Anatomists (pres 1993-1995). **Research Statement & Publications:** Cytological mechanisms of teratogenesis; scan electron microscope and transmission electron microscope of in vitro differentiation of the neural tube and cytoskeleton. **Mailing Address:** Dept Anat & Cell Biol, Queen's Univ, Botterell Hall, Kingston, ON K7L 3N6, Can. **Fax:** 613-533-2566. **E-Mail:** jonejam@post.queensu.ca

JONER, BRUNO, ENGINEERING. **Professional Experience:** RETIRED; Staff, Boeing Co, ending 2002. **Memberships:** US Naval Inst. **Mailing Address:** Boeing Aerospace, PO Box 24002 M/S JR-41, Huntsville, AL 35824. **Fax:** 256-461-3412.

JONES, ALAN A, POLYMER CHEMISTRY. **Personal Data:** b Jamestown, NY, November 15, 1944; m 1972. **Education:** Colgate Univ, AB, 1966; Univ Wis, PhD (phys chem), 1972. **Professional Experience:** Actg provost, Clark Univ, 1987-1988; vis prof, Univ Wis, 1985; PROF CHEM, CLARK UNIV, 1981-; chmn dept, Clark Univ, 1981-1987; from asst prof to assoc prof, Clark Univ, 1974-1988; res instr polymer chem, Dartmouth Col, 1972-1974; adj prof physics, Clark Univ. **Memberships:** Am Chem Soc; Am Phys Soc. **Research Statement & Publications:** The dynamic properties of macromolecules in solution and in the bulk are probed by nuclear magnetic resonance spectroscopy or dielectric response and discussed in terms of models relating specific motions to the experimental observations. **Mailing Address:** Dept Chem, Clark Univ, Worcester, MA 01610-1473. **E-Mail:** ajones@clarku.edu

JONES, ALAN LEE, PLANT PATHOLOGY. **Personal Data:** b Albion, NY, June 23, 1939; m 1967, c 2. **Education:** Cornell Univ, BS, 1961, MS, 1963; NC State Univ, PhD (plant path), 1968. **Honors & Awards:** Nat Award in Agr, Am Phytopath Soc, 1978. **Professional Experience:** Sabbatical leave, Dept Plant Path, NY State Agr Exp Sta, Cornell Univ, Geneva, NY, 1989; sabbatical leave, Bayer Agr, Leverkusen, Fed Repub Ger, 1982; PROF PLANT PATH, MICH STATE UNIV, 1977-; sabbatical leave, Plant Protection Inst, Agr ResCtr, USDA, Beltsville, Md, 1974-1975; from asst prof to assoc prof, Mich State Univ, 1968-1977. **Memberships:** AAAS; Can Phytopath Soc; fel Am Phytopath Soc. **Research Statement & Publications:** Epidemiology and control of tree fruit diseases; phytobacteriology; fungicide and antibiotic resistance in tree fruit pathogens. **Mailing Address:** Dept Bot & Plant Path, Mich State Univ, East Lansing, MI 48824-1312. **Fax:** 517-353-5598. **E-Mail:** hahnp@pilot.msu.edu

JONES, ALAN RICHARD, PHYSICAL CHEMISTRY, CHEMICAL ENGINEERING. **Personal Data:** b Denver, Colo, December 25, 1939; m 1964, Susan; c Deborah A & Andrew T. **Education:** Univ Colo, BSChE, 1962; Lawrence Univ, MS, 1964, PhD, 1967. **Honors & Awards:** Hugh D Camp Award, Union Camp Corp, 1973. **Professional Experience:** ASST DIR APPLN ENG, UNION CAMP CORP, 1993-; div tech dir, Union Camp Corp, 1985-1993; tech dir, Union Camp Corp, 1983-1985; asst tech dir, Union CampCorp, 1978-1983; leader chem processes group, Union Camp Corp, 1974-1978; leader paper prod group, Union Camp Corp, 1969-1974; res scientist, Union Camp Corp, 1967-1969. **Memberships:** Am Inst Chem Engr; Tech Asn Pulp & Paper Indust; AAAS; Am Soc Testing & Mat. **Research Statement & Publications:** Mechanical and optical properties of paper, characterization of papermaking pulps, development and optimization of pulping, by-product chemical, and papermaking processes; environmental regulation; pollution prevention. **Mailing Address:** Union Camp Corp, PO Box 570, Savannah, GA 31402.

JONES, ALBERT CLEVELAND, FISHERY SCIENCE. **Personal Data:** b Coalinga, Calif, August 18, 1929; m 1955, Patricia Curry; c Thomas A, Michael R & Mark D. **Education:** Univ Wash, BS, 1951; Univ Calif, MA, 1954, PhD (zoology), 1959. **Professional Experience:** Fishery consult, 1998-; dir res mgt div, Southeast Fisheries Sci Ctr, Nat Marine Fisheries Serv, 1990-1998; dir econ & statist, Off in-chg, 1985-1990; dir Miami Lab, Off in-chg, 1984-1985; adj prof, Univ Miami, 1976-; asst dir fishery mgt, Off in-chg, 1976-1984; prog mgr, Off in-chg, 1972-1976; adj assoc prof, Univ Miami, 1968-1976; asst dir, Trop Atlantic Biol Lab, Nat Marine Fisheries Serv, 1965-1971; Ministry Agr, Fisheries & Food fel, Eng, 1964-1965; res asst prof fisheries, Univ Miami, 1959-1965; asst ichthyol, Calif Acad Sci, 1958-1959; asst zool, Univ, 1954-1958; asst, Sagehen Creek Wildlife Fisheries Sta, Univ Calif, 1953-1954; biologist, Fisheries Res Inst, Wash, 1952; biologist, Ore Fish Comn, 1951; asst, Ore Fish Comn, 1949-1950. **Memberships:** Am Fisheries Soc; Am Soc Ichthyol & Herpet; fel Am Inst Fishery Res Biologists. **Research Statement & Publications:** Population dynamics; biometrics; ecology; fishery science research; stock assessment; fishery biology and statistics; living mariine resource management. **Mailing Address:** 8950 SW 62 Ct, Miami, FL 33156. **E-Mail:** albertcljones@juno.com

JONES, ALFRED, PLANT GENETICS. **Personal Data:** b Richmond, Va, March 25, 1932; m 1962, c 2. **Education:** Va Polytech Inst, BS, 1953; NC State Col, MS, 1957, PhD (plant breeding & path), 1961. **Honors & Awards:** L M Ware Res Award, Am Soc Hort Sci, 1979. **Professional Experience:** RETIRED; res geneticist, Veg& Ornamentals Res Br, Plant Sci Res Div, US Veg Breeding Lab, USDA, 1962-1989; res asstcotton breeding, Field Crops Dept, NC State Col, 1961-1962. **Memberships:** Am Soc Hort Sci; Am Genetic Asn; Crop Sci Soc Am; Am Soc Agron; Sigma Xi. **Research Statement & Publications:** Cytogenetics of sweetpotato, especially nature of ploidy in Ipomoea and its relation to speciation, recombination and breeding systems; quantitative genetic techniques of breeding for disease and insect resistant types. **Mailing Address:** 2421 Pristine View Rd, Charleston, SC 29414.

JONES, ALICE J, SOIL & WATER CONSERVATION. **Personal Data:** b Michigan City, Ind, April 9, 1953; m 1988, Lloyd; c Janet & Steve. **Education:** Mich Tech Univ, BS, 1978; Mont State Univ, MS, 1978; Utah State Univ, PhD (soil physics), 1982. **Professional Experience:** PROF SOIL & WATER CONSERVE UNIV NEBR, LINCOLN, 1995-; dir sustainable agr res & educ, USDA, 1993-1995; from asst prof to assoc prof, Lincoln, 1985-1995; vis scientiist, Univ Alaska, 1984; asst prof, Mont State Univ, 1983-1985; asst prof, Mont Col Sci & Tech, 1981-1983; instr, Mont State Univ, 1980-1981. **Memberships:** Fel Soil & Water Soc (vpres, 1991-1992); Soil Sci Soc Am; Am Soc Am; Sigma Xi; Int Soil Tillage Res Orgn. **Research Statement & Publications:** Soil and water conservation in combination with an emphasis on sustainable agriculture, topics include soil erosion, soil-plant-water relations and compaction. **Mailing Address:** Dept Agronomy Univ Nebr, 254 Keim Hall E Campus, Lincoln, NE 68583-0915. **Fax:** 402-472-7904. **E-Mail:** ajones@unlinfo.unl.edu

JONES, ALISON M, FERMENTATION, MICROBIAL ECOLOGY. **Personal Data:** b Saskatoon, Sask, March 29, 1964. **Education:** Univ Sask, BSc, 1986; McGill Univ, PhD (microbiol), 1991. **Professional Experience:** SOLUTIONS DEVELOP MGR, CARGILL FEED APPLNS, CARGILL INC, 2001-: sr res scientist, Cargill Inc, 1995-2001; res assoc, Biotechnol Res Inst, Nat Res Coun Can, 1993-1995; postdoctoral fel, Dept Appl Microbiol & Food Sci, Univ Sask, 1992-1993; res assoc, Dept Biochem, Brandeis Univ, 1991-1992. **Memberships:** Am Soc Microbiol; Soc Indust Microbiol. **Research Statement & Publications:** Fermentation. **Mailing Address:** Cargill Feed Applns, 12900 Whitewater Dr, MS 75, Minnetonka, MN 55343.

JONES, ALISTER VALLANCE, AERONOMY, AURORA. **Personal Data:** b Christchurch, NZ, February 4, 1924; m 1951, Catherine Fergusson; c Elizabeth (Villeneuve), Catriana V (Gallant) & Alasdair F. **Education:** Univ NZ, BSc, 1945, MSc, 1946; Cambridge Univ, PhD (physics), 1950. **Honors & Awards:** Fellow, Royal Soc of Canada (1965;). **Professional Experience:** CONTRACTOR, CAN SPACE SCI PROG, 1997-; guest worker, solar terrestrial physics, Herzberg Inst Astrophys, 1989-1997; chmn, Div 2, Int Asn Geomag & Aeronomy, 1987-1991; prin investr, Canopus Proj, 1980-1989; assoc ed, Aeronomy & Space Physics, Can J Physics, 1979-; prin res officer, Planetary Sci Sect, 1976-1989; sr res officer, Upper Atmosphere Res Sect, Astrophys Br, Nat Res Coun Can, 1968-1976; Ed, Physics Can, Can Asn Physicists, 1963-1966; from asst prof to prof physics, Univ Sask, 1953-1968; Nat Res Coun Can fel, 1949-1951. **Memberships:** Can Asn Physicists; Royal Soc Can. **Research Statement & Publications:** Infrared, auroral and airglow spectroscopy and modelling, Far UV satellite imaging of aurora; Book 1974 Reidel. **Mailing Address:** 2145 Fillmore Cr, 100 Sussex Dr PO Box 7275, Ottawa, ON K1L 8E3, Can. **Fax:** 613-952-0974. **E-Mail:** jones@canott.dan.sp-agency.ca

JONES, ALLAN W, BIOLOGY, PHYSIOLOGY. **Personal Data:** b Scranton, Pa, June 3, 1937; m 1991, Elaine; c Christian, Heather, Nicol, Jay M, Rachel & Jill. **Education:** Princeton Univ, BSE, 1959; Univ Pa, PhD (physiol), 1965. **Honors & Awards:** Merit Award, NIH, 1986. **Professional Experience:** INTERIM CHAIR, DEPT MED PHARMACOL & PHYSIOL, 2002-; interim dir, Ctr Diabetes & Cardiovasc Health, 2002; chair, ECS Study Sect, NIH, 1989-1990; ASSOC DIR, DALTON CARDIOVASC RES CTR, UNIV MO, COLUMBIA, 1986-; chmn, Dept Physiol, Sch Med, Univ Mo, Columbia, 1983-2002; PROF PHYSIOL, SCH MED, UNIV MO, COLUMBIA, 1978-; estab investr, Am Heart Asn, 1974-1979; assoc prof, Dalton Cardiovasc Res Ctr, 1972-1978; assoc dir, Bockus Res Inst, Grad Hosp, 1970-1972; asst prof, Sch Med, Univ Pa, 1969-1972; assoc, Sch Med, Univ Pa, 1968-1969; fel, Oxford Univ, 1966-1968; trainee & instr physiol, Sch Med, Univ Pa, 1965-1966; James O Davis Prof Cardiovasc Res. **Memberships:** Am Pharmacol Soc; Am Physiol Soc; Coun High Blood Pressure Res; Int Soc Hypertension; Am Soc Hypertension. **Research Statement & Publications:** Hypertension; electrolyte metabolism of arteries; cardiovascular research; pharmaco-mechanical coupling in arteries; effects of ischamia and exercise on arteries. **Mailing Address:** Dept Physiol, Sch Med, Univ Mo, MA415 Med Sci Bldg, Columbia, MO 65212-0001. **Fax:** 573-884-4276. **E-Mail:** jonesa@health.missouri.edu

JONES, ALMUT GITTER, PLANT TAXONOMY. **Personal Data:** b Oldenburg, Nieders, Ger, September 8, 1923; American citizen; wid. **Education:** Univ Ill, Urbana, BS, 1958, MS, 1960, PhD (bot), 1973. **Professional Experience:** RETIRED; emer assoc prof; emer curator; assoc prof plant biol, Univ Ill, Urbana, 1989- 1993; Asst prof bot, 1974-1975 & 1979-1988; cur herbarium, Univ Ill, Urbana, 1973- 1993. **Memberships:** Emer mem, Am Soc Plant Taxonomists; emer mem, Am Bot Soc; emer mem, Int Asn Plant Taxon. **Research Statement & Publications:** Taxonomy, phytogeography and biosystematics of Aster, Compositae; flora of Illinois. **Mailing Address:** Dept Plant Biol, Univ Ill, 505 S Goodwin Ave, Urbana, IL 61802. **Fax:** 217-333-9758.

JONES, ALUN RICHARD, PHYSICS, RADIATION DOSIMETRY. **Personal Data:** b Ipoh, Malaya, May 6, 1928; Canadian citizen; m 1955, Betty; c 2. **Education:** Univ Bristol, BSc, 1952; McGill Univ, MSc, 1954. **Professional Experience:** RETIRED; consult to pres comn, Three Mile-Island, 1979; sr res officer, Biol& Health Div, Dosimetric Res Br, Atomic Energy Can Ltd, 1965-1990; exchange worker, Inst Cancer Res, UK, 1962-1963; mem, Biol & Health Div, Dosimetric Res Br, Atomic Energy Can Ltd, 1956-1990; mem, Physics Div, Electronics Br, Atomic Energy Can Ltd, 1954-1956. **Memberships:** Health Physics Soc. **Research Statement & Publications:** External dosimetry of gamma and beta rays; thermoluminescence dosimetry; monitoring of alpha, beta and gamma contamination; detectors of ionising radiation (Geiger Mueller counters and silicon junction detectors); radiation protection. **Mailing Address:** 683 Vera Cruz Ave, Los Altos, CA 94022.

JONES, AMELIA C, MATHEMATICS. **Education:** Univ Ore, PhD, 1993. **Professional Experience:** ASST PROF, DEPT MATH, VASSAR COL, as of 1999. **Mailing Address:** Dept Math, Vassar Col, 306 Rockefeller Hall, Poughkeepsie, NY 95616. **Fax:** 845-437-7654.

JONES, ANITA KATHERINE, COMPUTER SCIENCE. **Personal Data:** b Ft Worth, Tex, m William; c Karin & Ellen. **Education:** Rice Univ, BA, 1964; Univ Tex, MA, 1966; Carnegie-Mellon Univ, PhD (comput sci), 1973. **Honors & Awards:** US Air Force Meritorious Civilian Serv Award & Distinguished Pub Award. **Professional Experience:** LAWRENCE R QUARLES PROF COMPUT SCI, SCH ENG & APPLI SCI, UNIV VA, as of 2004; univ prof eng & appl sci, Univ Va, beginning 1997; dir, Defense Res & Eng, Dept Defense, 1994-1997; prof & dept chair, Comput Sci, Univ Va, 1988-1994; vpres & founder, Tartan Labs, Pittsburgh, Pa, 1981-1987; assoc prof computsci, Carnegie-Mellon Univ, 1978-1981; asst prof, Carnegie-Mellon Univ, 1973-1978; programmer, IBMCorp, 1966-1968; vice chmn, Nat Sci Bd; dir, Sci Appln Int Corp; trustee, Mitre Corp; consult, NSF, Defense Advan Res Proj Agency, Nat Res Coun & Indust. **Memberships:** Defense Sci Bd Charles Stark Draper Lab Corp Nat ResCoun Adv Coun Policy & Global Affairs; Nat Acad Eng; fel Inst Elec & Electronic Engrs; Sigma Xi; fel Asn Comput Mach. **Research Statement & Publications:** Design and implementation of programmed systems on computers, including enforcement of security policies on computers, operating systems and scientific data bases. **Mailing Address:** Dept Comput Sci, Sch Eng & Appl Sci, Univ VA, PO Box 400740, Charlottesville, VA 22903-2442. **Fax:** 434-982-2214. **E-Mail:** jones@cs.virginia.edu

JONES, BARBARA, INFRARED ASTRONOMICAL INSTRUMENTATION. **Personal Data:** b Ipswich, Eng, February 19, 1948. **Education:** Univ Col, London, PhD (physics), 1977. **Professional Experience:** PROF PHYSICS, UNIV CALIF, SAN DIEGO, 1983-; res physicist, Univ Calif, San Diego, 1980-1983; postdoctoral, Univ Minn, 1977-1980. **Memberships:** Fel Am Phys Soc; Am Astron Union; Am Asn Univ Women; Am Asn Physics Teachers; Int Astron Union. **Research Statement & Publications:** Study of luminous infrared galaxies and active galactic nuclei through observations with novel infrared instrumentation. **Mailing Address:** Univ Calif San Diego, CASS 0424 9500 Gilman Dr, La Jolla, CA 92093-0424. **E-Mail:** b2jones@ucsd.edu

JONES, BARBARA ELLEN, NEUROSCIENCE, NEUROANATOMY. **Personal Data:** b Philadelphia, Pa, December 19, 1944; m 1972, John; c James. **Education:** Univ Del, BA, 1966, PhD (psychol), 1971. **Professional Experience:** Vs scientist physiol, Ctr Med Univ, Geneva, Switz, 1991-1992; PROF NEUROL & COORD COMPLEX NEURAL SYS, MCGILL UNIV, 1989-; vis scientist human anat, Oxford Univ, UK, 1984-1985; scholar, Ctr Med Res, Que, 1983-1986; scholar, Med Res Coun Can, 1978-1983; from asst prof to assoc prof, McGill Univ, 1977-1989; res assoc & asst prof psychiat, Univ Chicago, 1975-1977; vis lectr med physiol, Univ Nairobi, 1974-1975; res assoc psychiat, Univ Chicago, 1972-1974; fel neurochem, Col France, Paris, 1970-1972. **Memberships:** Soc Neuroscience; Asn Psychophysiol Study Sleep. **Research Statement & Publications:** Neuroanatomical and neurochemical substrates of mechanisms of the sleep-waking cycle; neurophsiology. **Mailing Address:** Dept Neurol & Neurosurg, Montreal Neurol Inst, McGill Univ, 3801 Univ St, Montreal, PQ H3A 2B4, Can. **Fax:** 514-398-5871. **E-Mail:** barbara.jones@mcgill.ca

JONES, BARCLAY G(EORGE), NUCLEAR ENGINEERING, MECHANICAL ENGINEERING. **Personal Data:** b Lafleche, Sask, May 6, 1931; American citizen; m 1959, c 4. **Education:** Univ Sask, BE, 1954; Univ Ill, MS, 1960, PhD (nuclear eng), 1966. **Honors & Awards:** Power Eng Educ Award, Edison Elec Inst, 1991. **Professional Experience:** Head, Dept Nuclear Plasma & Radiol Eng, Univ Ill, Urbana, 1987-2000; actg head, Univ Ill, Urbana, 1986-1987; Helliburton educ award, 1983; assoc chmn nuclear eng, Univ Ill, Urbana, 1981-1986; consult, Fauske & Assocs, Burr Ridge, Ill, 1981-1985; consult, Argonne Nat Lab, 1976-; consult, Arnold Res Orgn, Inc, Tullahoma, Tenn, 1974-1980; PROF NUCLEAR & MECH ENG, UNIV ILL, URBANA, 1972-; consult, WVa Pulp & Paper Co, Va, 1968; from asst prof to assoc prof, Univ Ill, 1966-1972; instr nuclear eng, Univ Ill, 1963-1966; res asst, Univ Ill, 1958-1960; engr, Nuclear Div, Canadair Ltd, Montreal, Que, 1957-1958; Atomic Energy Res Estab, Harwell, 1955-1957; Athlone fel, Eng Elec Co, Rugby, Eng, 1954-1955. **Memberships:** Fel Athlone; Am Nuclear Soc; Can Soc Mech Engrs; Am Soc Mech Engrs; EngInst Can; Am Inst Aeronaut & Astronaut; Sigma Xi; Am Soc Eng Educ. **Research Statement & Publications:** Experimental fluid mechanics and heat transfer, reactor safety, two-phaseflow, turbulence, simulation and training. **Mailing Address:** Dept Nuclear Plasma & Radiol Eng Univ Ill, 214 Nuclear Eng Lab 103 S Goodwin Ave, Urbana, IL 61801-2984. **Fax:** 217-333-2906. **E-Mail:** bgjones@uiuc.edu

JONES, BARRY N, MOLECULAR BIOLOGY. **Personal Data:** b NC. **Professional Experience:** DIR MOLECULAR & CELLULAR BIOL, STERLING WINTHROP INC, 1989-. **Research Statement & Publications:** Molecular biology. **Mailing Address:** Sterling Winthrop Inc, 1250 S Colville Rd, Collegeville, PA 19426.

JONES, BENJAMIN A(NGUS), AGRICULTURAL ENGINEERING, AGRICULTURAL DRAINAGE, SURFACE WATER MANAGEMENT. **Personal Data:** b Mahomet, Ill, April 16, 1926; m 1949, Georgeann; c Nancy K (Kepple) & Ruth A (Sommers). **Education:** Univ Ill, BS, 1949; MS, 1950, PhD (civil eng), 1958. **Honors & Awards:** Hancor Award, Am Soc Agr Engrs, 1977. **Professional Experience:** RETIRED; emer prof agr eng, Ill Agr Exp Sta, Univ Ill, Urbana-Champign, 1992; emer assoc dir, Ill Agr Exp Sta, Univ Ill, Urbana-Champign, 1992; assoc dir, Ill Agr Exp Sta, Univ Ill, Urbana-Champign, 1973-1992; prof agr eng & head soil & water div, Ill Agr Exp Sta, Univ Ill, Urbana-Champign, 1964-1973; from instr to assoc prof, Ill Agr Exp Sta, Univ Ill, Urbana-Champign, 1952-1964; asst prof & asst agr engr, Agr Exten Serv, 1950-1952; actg chmn, Dept Agr Eng, Univ Vt, 1950-1951; asst agr eng, Univ Ill, 1949-1950; consult engr, Ill Drainage Dist. **Memberships:** fel, Am Soc Agr Engrs; Soil Conserv Soc Am; Sigma Xi; Coun Agr Sci & Technol; Alpha Epsilon Gamma Sigma Delta. **Research Statement & Publications:** Agricultural land drainage and irrigation; agricultural hydrology and the hydraulics of erosion control structures. **Mailing Address:** 2012 B Eagle Ridge Ct, Urbana, IL 61802-8617.

JONES, BENJAMIN FRANKLIN, MATHEMATICS. **Personal Data:** b Texas, April 15, 1936; American citizen; m Beverly; c Marianna, Elaine & David. **Education:** Rice Univ, BA, 1958, PhD (math), 1961. **Honors & Awards:** MAA Distinguished Teaching Award, 1995. **Professional Experience:** Res assoc, Williams College, 1994, vis mem, Math Inst, Oxford Univ, 1985-1986; NOAH HARDING PROF MATH, RICE UNIV, 1974-; vis prof, Univ Minn, 1969-1970; Mem, Inst Advan Study, 1965-1966; from asst prof to prof, Rice Univ, 1962-1974; temp mem, Courant Inst Math Sci, NY Univ, 1961-1962. **Memberships:** Am Math Soc; Math Asn Am. **Research Statement & Publications:** Partial differential equations; real analysis. **Mailing Address:** Dept Math, Rice Univ, MS 136, 6100 S Main St, Houston, TX 77005-1892. **Fax:** 713-348-5231. **E-Mail:** fjones@math.rice.edu

JONES, BENJAMIN LEWIS, BIOCHEMISTRY. **Personal Data:** b Muncy Valley Twp, Pa, August 19, 1952; m 1980, Betty R Mann; c 1. **Education:** Pa State Univ, BS, 1974; Univ Tenn, MS, 1978, PhD (biochem), 1980. **Professional Experience:** RES PROG LEADER, CAMPBELL INST RES TECHNOL, 1993-; sr resscientist, Campbell Inst Res Technol, 1990-1993; res scientist, Campbell Inst Res Technol, 1985-1990; sr res chemist, Campbell Inst Res Technol, 1984-1985; res chemist, Lipid Metab Lab, Vet Admin Hosp, 1982-1984; Res assoc, Kettering Res Lab, 1980-1982. **Memberships:** Am Soc Biochem & Molecular Biol; Am Chem Soc; Inst Food Technologists. **Research Statement & Publications:** Developing beef and chicken type reaction flavors using yeast extracts, meats, enzymes and natural chemicals; processing methods and conditions for production of reaction flavors; scale up of reaction flavors. **Mailing Address:** Campbell Res & Develop, Box 57X Campbell Pl, Camden, NJ 08103-1702. **Fax:** 609-342-4858.

JONES, BERNARD M, AGRICULTURE. **Education:** Murray State Univ, BS, 1956; Univ Ky, MS, 1960. **Professional Experience:** PROF, DEPT ANIMAL BIOTECHNOL, UNIV NEV, as of 2005. **Mailing Address:** Nev Agr Exp Sta Dir Off 222, Univ Nev, Reno, NV 89557-0004. **Fax:** 775-784-1375. **E-Mail:** bjones@cabnr.unr.edu

JONES, BERNE LEE, BIOCHEMISTRY & PROTEIN CHEMISTRY, ENZYMOLOGY. **Personal Data:** b Rochester, Ind, May 30, 1941. **Education:** Wabash Col, BA, 1963; Wash State Univ, PhD (chem), 1967. **Professional Experience:** SUPVRY RES CHEMIST BIOCHEM, USDA, 1989-; PROF AGRON, UNIV WIS, MADISON, 1989-; res chemist, biochem, 1977-1989; asst prof plant sci, Univ Man, 1972-1977; fel biochem, Univ Alta, 1969-1972; fel biochem, Univ Colo, 1967-1969. **Memberships:** Am Asn Brewing Chemists. **Research Statement & Publications:** Biochemistry of cereal proteins; enzymology of malting; endoproteinase biochemistry; plant endoproteinase inhibitors. **Mailing Address:** Dept Agron, Univ Wis, 1575 Linden Dr, Madison, WI 53706. **Fax:** 608-264-5528. **E-Mail:** bljones@facstaff.wisc.edu

JONES, BERWYN E, ANALYTICAL CHEMISTRY. **Personal Data:** b Scottsbluff, Nebr, March 11, 1937; m 1958, Janet; c Roderick H & Bruce G. **Education:** Nebr Wesleyan Univ, BA, 1958; Kans State Univ, PhD (anal chem), 1965. **Professional Experience:** CHOIR MGT, COLO WELSH SOC, as of 2002; nat qual mgt coordr, Nat Water Qual Lab, US Geol Surv, beginning 1990; qual control off, Nat Water Qual Lab, US Geol Surv, Denver, 1985-1990; asst lab dir, Nat Water Qual Lab, US Geol Surv, Atlanta, 1980-1985; res chemist, Nat Water Qual Lab, US Geol Surv, Atlanta, 1978-1980; assoc prof, Longwood Col, 1977-1978; prof, Upper Iowa Univ, Fayette, 1975-1977; res assoc, Argonne Nat Lab, 1970-1971; vis asst prof, Univ Ill, 1969-1970; from instr to assoc prof chem, Monmouth Col, Ill, 1963-1975. **Memberships:** Welsh Soc; AAAS; Am Chem Soc; Soc Appl Spectros; Sigma Xi; Am Soc Qual Control. **Research Statement & Publications:** Absorption and fluorescence spectroscopy; chromatography; atomic emission spectroscopy; molecular fluorescence spectroscopy; quality assurance of chemical analysis; total quality management. **Mailing Address:** Colo Welsh Soc, 30926 Shawnee Lane, Evergreen, CO 80439. **E-Mail:** berwynjones@worldnet.att.net

JONES, BLAIR FRANCIS, GEOLOGY. **Personal Data:** b April 14, 1934; m 1955, c 2. **Education:** Beloit Col, BA, 1955; Johns Hopkins Univ, PhD, 1963. **Honors & Awards:** Meritorious Serv Award, Dept Interior, 1981 & Distinguished Serv Award, 1986. **Professional Experience:** SR SCIENTIST, WATER RESOURCES DIV, US GEOL SURV, NAT CTR, 1983-; Reston, Wash, DC, 1981-1984; res adv geochem, Wash, DC, 1974-1977; guest investr, Rothamsted Exp Sta, Herpenden, Herts, UK, 1972; vis prof, State Univ NY-Binghamton, 1970; res geologist, Water Resources Div, 1958-1974; Deposits Br, US Geol Surv, 1956-1957; geologist, US Geol Surv, 1955; lab instr geol, Beloit Col, 1954-1955; instr, Rockford Col, 1954. **Memberships:** Fel Geol Soc Am; Geochem Soc; fel Mineral Soc Am; Am Geophys Union; ClayMinerals Soc; Sigma Xi; Mineral Soc UK. **Research Statement & Publications:** Hydrogeochemistry; sedimentary petrology; geochemistry of weathering; brines, lacustrine sediments and evaporites; solutes in natural water. **Mailing Address:** US Geol Surv, 432 Nat Center, Reston, VA 20192-0001. **E-Mail:** bfjones@usgs.gov

JONES, BRAD, ANALYTICAL CHEMISTRY. **Education:** Wake Forest Univ, BS, 1984; Univ Fla, PhD, 1988. **Professional Experience:** PROF & CHAIR, DEPT CHEM, WAKE FOREST UNIV, as of 2005; postdoctoral res assoc, Univ Fla, 1988-1989. **Mailing Address:** Dept Chem, Wake Forest Univ, Salem Hall Box 7486, Winston-Salem, NC 27109. **E-Mail:** jonesbt@wfu.edu

JONES, BRIAN HERBERT, MATERIALS SCIENCE, MECHANICAL ENGINEERING. **Personal Data:** b Chester, Eng, April 23, 1937; American citizen; m 1974. **Education:** Univ Liverpool, BEng, 1961, PhD (appl mech), 1965; Univ Calif, Los Angeles, cert bus admin, 1969. **Professional Experience:** PRES & CHIEF OPERATING OFFICER, COMPOSITEK CORP, SUBSIDSHELL OIL CO, 1975-; vpres eng, Goldsworthy Eng Inc, 1972-1975; consult, ARAP Inc, 1969-1972; group leader mat technol, Douglas Aircraft Co, 1966-1969; Clayton fel, Inst Mech Engrs, London, 1963-1965; Busk fel, Royal Aeronaut Soc, London, 1963-1964. **Memberships:** Am Inst Aeronaut & Astronaut; Am Soc Mech Engrs; Soc Plastics Indust; Soc Automotive Engrs. **Research Statement & Publications:** Composite materials product design and analysis; lightweight structures; plasticity of metals; process development; machine design. **Mailing Address:** 407 Country Club Dr, San Gabriel, CA 91775.

JONES, BURTON FREDRICK, ASTROMETRY. **Personal Data:** b Manistique, Mich, October 28, 1942; m 1982, Mary; c Kristine & Michelle. **Education:** Univ Chicago, BS, 1965, MS, 1968, PhD (astron), 1970. **Professional Experience:** ASTRONOMER & PROF, LICK OBSERV, UNIV CALIF SANTA CRUZ, 1987-; from asst res astronomer to asst astronomer & prof, Lick Observ, Univ Calif Santa Cruz, 1975-1987; res fel, Univ Tex, 1974-1975; sr res fel, Royal Greenwich Observ, 1972-1974; fel astron, Lick Observ, Univ Calif, 1970-1971. **Memberships:** Int Astron Union; Am Astron Soc; Astron Soc Pac. **Research Statement & Publications:** Stellar proper motions; cluster membership. **Mailing Address:** Lick Observ, Univ Calif, ISB 367, Santa Cruz, CA 95064. **E-Mail:** jones@ucolick.org

JONES, BYRON W, THERMODYNAMICS. **Education:** Kans State Univ, BS, 1971; Okla State Univ, MS, 1973, PhD, 1975. **Professional Experience:** ASSOC DEAN, KANS STATE UNIV, 1997-. **Mailing Address:** Kans State Univ, 148 Rathbone Hall, Manhattan, KS 66506. **Fax:** 785-532-7810. **E-Mail:** jones@ksu.edu

JONES, C ROBERT, CELL PHYSIOLOGY. **Personal Data:** b Scranton, Pa, May 8, 1933; m 1957, c 4. **Education:** Univ Scranton, BS, 1954; Fordham Univ, MS, 1956, PhD (physiol), 1962. **Professional Experience:** PROF EMER BIOL SCI, LEHMAN COL, as of 2000; chmn dept biol sci, Lehman Col, 1974-1984; prof cell biol, Lehman Col, beginning 1968; assoc prof cell biol, Lehman Col, 1968-1974; NSF res grant, Div Metab Biol, 1964-1966; from instr to asst prof physiol, Lehman Col, 1963-1968; fel, Fordham Univ, 1962-1963; lectr, Bronx Community Col, 1962-1963; res asst chemother, Sloan-Kettering Inst Cancer Res, 1958-1959. **Memberships:** AAAS; Entom Soc Am. **Research Statement & Publications:** Activity of respiratory enzymes during the metamorphosis of holometabolous insects; identification of Lysosomes in insect tissues; mammalian physiology. **Mailing Address:** Dept Biol Sci, Lehman Col, 250 Bedford Park Blvd, West Bronx, NY 10468-1589. **Fax:** 718-960-8236.

JONES, CARL E, PHYSIOLOGY, BIOPHYSICS. **Personal Data:** b Capman, Ala, February 9, 1942; div, c Jon R. **Education:** William Casey Col, BS, 1965; Univ Miss Sch Med, PhD (physiol & biophysics), 1968. **Professional Experience:** RETIRED; prin investr, Upjohn Pharmaceut, 1991-1994; assoc dean basic sci, Aerospace Med Inst, Tex Col Osteopath Med, 1986-1993; dir, Aerospace Med Inst, Tex Col Osteopath Med, 1986-1987; prin investr, NASA, 1986; prin investr, Am Heart Asn, 1985-1987 & 1988-1992; prin investr, Nat Osteopath Found, 1985-1986 & 1988-1990; prin investr, NIH, 1985-1989, 1985-1990, 1988-1993, 1990-1994, 1991-1994; vchmn, Dept Biomed Sci, 1984-1991; prof, Dept Physiol, 1982-1993; chmn, Dept Physiol, Tex Col Osteopath Med, 1982-1993; adj prof, Dept Biol Sci, Univ NTex, 1982-1993; Univ Tenn, Am Acad AnesthesiaAssoc, 1981; pres, Brazoz Div, Am Heart Asn, 1980-1981; Univ Tenn, Ctr Health Sci, 1979; prof, Dept Physiol, Tex A&M Univ, Col Med, 1978-1981; mem bd dir, Brazoz Div, Am HeartAsn, 1977-1981; invited lectr, Loyola Univ, 1977; assoc prof, Dept Physiol, Tex A&M Univ, ColMed, 1976-1978; invited lectr, Tex A&M, Col Med & Col Vet Med, 1975; from asst prof toassoc prof, Dept Physiol & Biophys, Univ Miss, Sch Med, 1968-1975; fel, NIH, 1965-1968. **Memberships:** Fel Am Heart Asn; fel Am Physiol Soc; Microcirculatory Soc; Int Soc Heart Res; NY Acad Sci; AAAS. **Research Statement & Publications:** Physiology; biophysics; author of 13 publications. **Mailing Address:** Dept Physiol, 3500 Camp Bowie Blvd, Ft Worth, TX 76107-2699.

JONES, CARL JOSEPH, BIOCONTROL, IMMUNOPARASITOLOGY. **Personal Data:** b Ithaca, NY, January 1, 1949; m 1982, Frances Woollard; c Heather M, Wendy A & Christopher M. **Education:** Cornell Univ, BS, 1970; Univ Wyo, MS, 1979, PhD (entom), 1982. **Professional Experience:** Adj prof vet PATHOBIOLOGY, Univ Ill, as of 2003; HEAD & PROF, DEPT ENTOM & PLANT PATH, UNIV TENN, 2000-; prof parasitol, Univ Ill, 1997-2000; assoc Prof, Univ Ill, 1993-1997; affil, IllNatural Hist Surv Ctr Econ Entom, 1991-; asst prof vet med entom, Univ Ill, 1989-1993; adj fac mem, Gulf Coast Community Col, 1989; biol adminr, Off Entom, State Fla, 1982-1989; postdoctoral res assoc, Dept Entom, Univ Fla, 1982; res specialist, Dept Entom, Cornell Univ, 1975-1977; experimentalist,

Dept Entom, Cornell Univ, 1970-1974. **Memberships:** Entom Soc Am; Sigma Xi. **Research Statement & Publications:** Biological control of arthopods, physiological interactions of vertebrates and their hematophagous arthropod parasites; behavior and ecosystem dynamics of ticks; population dynamics and physiology of anautogenous muscoid flies; genetics of dispersal in arthropods. **Mailing Address:** Dept Entom & Plant Path, Univ Tenn, 2018 Ellington Plant Sci Bldg, Knoxville, TN 37901-1071. **Fax:** 217-244-7421. **E-Mail:** cjones17@utk.edu

JONES, CAROL A, BIOPHYSICS. **Personal Data:** b Kremmling, Colo, September 10, 1936; m 1955, c 7. **Education:** Univ Surrey, UK, BSc, 1971, PhD, (biochem), 1974. **Professional Experience:** Vis prof chem, Cent Conn State Univ, as of 2004; SR FEL, ELEANOR ROOSEVELT INST CANCER RES, 1980-; ASSOC PROF BIOPHYS & GENETICS, UNIV COLO HEALTH SCI CTR, 1980-; asst prof, USPHS, 1974-1980; res assoc biophys & genetics, USPHS, 1971-1974; fel biophys, USPHS, 1969-1971. **Memberships:** AAAS; Am Soc Human Genetics; Am Asn Immunol. **Research Statement & Publications:** Cell biology; somatic cell genetics; cell surface molecules. **Mailing Address:** Dept Chem, Cen Conn State Univ, Maria Sanford 106, Connecticut, CT 06050. **Fax:** 860-832-2704. **E-Mail:** jonesca@ccsu.edu

JONES, CHARLES, ROTARY ENGINES, TECHNICAL MANAGEMENT. **Personal Data:** b New York, NY, February 27, 1926; m 1950, Gisele; c Corinne & Leslie. **Education:** Columbia Univ, BS, 1950, MS, 1953. **Honors & Awards:** Edward N Cole Award, Soc Automotive Engrs, 1987, Forest McFarlandAward, 1991. **Professional Experience:** CONSULT ENGR, 1991-; adj lectr, Stevens inst Technol, 1986-1987; chieftechnologist, John Deere Technologies Int, 1984-1991; dir res eng, Appl Mech, Curtiss-WrightCorp, 1969-1984; chief engr, Appl Mech, Curtiss-Wright Corp, 1968-1969; chief design engr, Appl Mech, Curtiss-Wright Corp, 1962-1968; sect head, Appl Mech, Curtiss-Wright Corp, 1955-1962. **Memberships:** Fel Soc Automotive Engrs. **Research Statement & Publications:** Rotary engines design and development; author of over 30 technical publications; awarded 76 patents. **Mailing Address:** 37 Harbor Cir, Centerport, NY 11721. **Fax:** 516-261-1002. **E-Mail:** cenptjones@aol.com

JONES, CHARLES E, MOLECULAR PHYSICS, ATOMIC PHYSICS. **Personal Data:** b Oklahoma City, Okla, June 10, 1928; m 1949, c 5. **Education:** Univ Ark, Fayetteville, BS, 1951, MS, 1955; Tex A&M Univ, PhD (physics), 1965. **Professional Experience:** RETIRED; prof physics & head dept, Etex State Univ, 1970-1991; consult, NSF-Agency Int Develop Summer Inst, 1969; asst & assoc prof, Univ Ark, 1961-1970; instr physics, Mo Sch Mines, 1955-1957; instr physics, Tex A&M Univ, 1957-1961; aerodyn engr, McDonnell Aircraft Co, 1952-1953; jr thermo engr, Convair Aircraft Co, 1951-1952. **Memberships:** Am Asn Physics Teachers; Am Phys Soc. **Research Statement & Publications:** Atoms and molecules in inert matrices at low temperatures by means of absorption and emission spectroscopy. **Mailing Address:** 18959 Shoreline Way, Fayetteville, AR 72703.

JONES, CHARLES MILLER, JR, PHYSICS. **Personal Data:** b Atlanta, Ga, February 25, 1935. **Education:** Ga Inst Technol, BS, 1957; Rice Univ, MA, 1959, PhD (physics), 1961. **Professional Experience:** CONSULT, 1995-; oper mgr, Physics Div, 1992-1994; tech dir, Holifield Heavy Ion Res Facil, 1983-1992; physicist, Oak Ridge Nat Lab, 1962-1994; Res assoc, Rice Univ, 1961-1962. **Memberships:** AAAS. **Research Statement & Publications:** Research facility Management. **Mailing Address:** 103 Burgess Lane, Oak Ridge, TN 37830. **Fax:** 423-483-8944.

JONES, CHRISTINE, HIGH ENERGY ASTROPHYSICS, COSMOLOGY. **Personal Data:** b Minneapolis, Minn, February 3, 1949; m 1973, William; c Julia, Miranda & Daniel. **Education:** Harvard Univ, BA, 1971; MA, 1972, PhD (astrophys), 1974. **Honors & Awards:** Bart J Bok Prize, Dept Astron, Harvard Univ, 1985; Bruno Rossi Prize, Am Astron Soc, 1985. **Professional Experience:** SR ASTROPHYSICIST, SMITHSONIAN ASTROPHYS OBSERV, 1978-; jr fel, Harvard Univ, 1975-1978; fel, Ctr Astrophys, 1974-1975; NASA Seas Adv Comt. **Memberships:** Am Astron Soc; fel AAAS. **Research Statement & Publications:** X-ray observatories to study the formation of large scale structure including the evolution of clusters and investigate the physics of the hot gas in galaxies and clusters. **Mailing Address:** Harvard-Smithsonian Ctr Astrophys, 60 Garden St, Cambridge, MA 02138. **Fax:** 617-495-7356. **E-Mail:** cjones@cfa.harvard.edu

JONES, CLARENCE S, physics, engineering; deceased, see previous edition for last biography

JONES, CLARIS EUGENE, POLLINATION BIOLOGY, BIOSYSTEMATICS. **Personal Data:** b Columba, Ohio, December 15, 1942; m 1966, Teresa; c Douglas E, Philip C & Elizabeth L. **Education:** Ohio Univ, BS, 1964; Ind Univ, PhD (bot), 1969. **Honors & Awards:** Golden key, nat honor Soc, Hon mem, 1999. **Professional Experience:** CHAIR, DEPT BOT, 1989-; PROF BOT, CALIF STATE UNIV, FULLERTON, 1977-; dir, Fullerton Arboretum, 1970-1980; dir, Faye A MacFadden Herbarium, Calif State Univ, 1969-; from asst prof to assoc prof, Dept Bot, 1969-1977. **Memberships:** AAAS; Am Soc Plant Taxonomists; Int Asn Plant Taxon; Ecol Soc Am; Soc Study Evolution; Bot Soc Am. **Research Statement & Publications:** Pollination ecology of rare or endangered plant species, especially with reference to their coevolution with specific pollinators, insular biogeography in the Hawaiian Islands, biosystematics studies in the family Cucurbitaceae, and the honeybee dance language. **Mailing Address:** Dept Biol Sci, Calif State Univ, Fullerton, CA 92834. **Fax:** 714-278-3426. **E-Mail:** cejones@fullerton.edu

JONES, CLAYTON M, AERONAUTICS. **Education:** Univ Tenn, BA; George Wash Univ, MBA. **Professional Experience:** CHMN, PRES & CHIEF EXEC OFF, ROCKWELL COLLINS, 2002-. **Memberships:** Nat Security Telecommunications Adv Comt. **Mailing Address:** Rockwell Intl Corp Aero Suite 1200, 1745 Jefferson Davis Hwy, Arlington, VA 22202-3402. **Fax:** 703 553-6890.

JONES, CLIFFORD KENNETH, STRATEGIC PLANNING, PROJECT MANAGEMENT. **Personal Data:** b London, Eng, December 29, 1932; American citizen; m 1957, c 2. **Education:** Univ London, BSc, 1957, PhD (physics), 1960. **Professional Experience:** RETIRED; asst prof physics, Univ Calif, Los Angeles; dir, Northropgrummon, 1997-1998; mgr spec projs, Westinghouse Res & Develop Ctr, 1988-1997; dir strategic planning, Westinghouse Res & Develop Ctr, 1980-1988; mgr spec projs, Westinghouse Res & Develop Ctr, 1975-1980; mgr cryogenics, Westinghouse Res & Develop Ctr, 1967-1975; mem staff superconductor develop prog, Westinghouse Res & Develop Ctr, 1962-1967. **Memberships:** Fel Am Phys Soc; Inst Elec & Electronics Engrs. **Research Statement & Publications:** Cryogenics and fusion power technology; co-authored more than 80 publications in physical acoustics, metal physics and superconducting technology. **Mailing Address:** Northrop Grummon, 1310 Beulah Rd, Pittsburgh, PA 15235.

JONES, CLIVE GARETH, ECOSYSTEM ENGINEERING BY SPECIES, ECOLOGICAL COMPLEXITY & THEORY. **Personal Data:** b Cirencester, England, March 3, 1951; American citizen; m 1992, Donna; c Gordon & Heather. **Education:** Univ Salford, England, BSc, 1974; Univ York, England, Dphil (biology), 1978. **Honors & Awards:** Laureat, Chaire Internationale de Recherche Blaise Pascal, Fondation Ecole Normale Superior, 2005; The Barnum Museum Lecturer, Tufts University, 1999; Simon Guggenheim Memorial Fellow, 1994; Fellow, American Association for the Advancement of Science, 1992; The Winston Churchill Traveling Fellowship, 1989; British Ecological Society Traveling Fellowship, 1986. **Professional Experience:** Senior Scientist, Institute of Ecosystem Studies, 2004 - Present; Scientist, Institute of Ecosystem Studies, 1993 - 2004; Associate Scientist, Institute of Ecosystem Studies, 1987 - 1992; Assistant Scientist, Institute of Ecosystem Studies, 1983 - 1986; Chemical Ecologist, Cary Arboretum, 1980 - 1983; Postdoctoral Fellow, University of Georgia, 1978 - 1980. **Memberships:** Fellow, Am Asn for the Advancement of Science; British Ecological Sciety; Ecological Soc of Am; Sigma Xi. **Research Statement & Publications:** Links between species and ecosystems focusing on ecosystem engineering by species (abiotic modification), ecological complexity and ecological theory. **Mailing Address:** Inst Ecosystem Studies, PO Box AB, Millbrook, NY 12545. **Fax:** 845-677-5976. **E-Mail:** jonesc@ecostudies.org

JONES, CLYDE J, MAMMALIAN ECOLOGY, TAXONOMY. **Personal Data:** b Scottsbluff, Nebr, March 3, 1935. **Education:** Hastings Col, BA, 1957; Univ NMex, MS, 1960, PhD (biol). 1964. **Professional Experience:** FROM PROF SCI TO HORN PROF & ASSOC CHMN BIOL SCI, TEX TECHUNIV, 1982-; dir, Denver Wildlife Res Ctr, 1979-1982; dir, Nat Fish & Wildlife Lab, 1973-1979; RES ASSOC, SMITHSONIAN INST, 1971-; BIOLOGIST, ANTARCTIC INSPECTION, OPER DEEPFREEZE, 1971-; zoologist, Bur SportFisheries & Wildlife, Nat Mus Natural Hist, 1970-1973; res assoc, DeltaRegional Primate Res Ctr, 1967-1970; res investr field studies, Rio Muni, WAfrica, Nat Geog Soc, 1966-1968; asst prof, Tulane Univ, 1965-1970; asst curbiol, Univ NMex, 1962-1965. **Memberships:** Am Soc Mammal; Soc Syst Zool; Ecol Soc Am. **Research Statement & Publications:** Systematics, taxonomy, biogeography, biodiversity and conservation mammals; conservation and management of specimens in museums. **Mailing Address:** Dept Biol Sci, Tex Tech Univ, Lubbock, TX 79409-0001. **E-Mail:** cjones@packrat.musu.ttu.edu

JONES, CURT A, MATHEMATICS. **Education:** Lock Haven, BS; Univ Iowa, MS; PA State Univ, PhD. **Professional Experience:** ASSOC PROF, BLOOMSBURG UNIV PA, as of 2005. **Mailing Address:** Math Dept, Bloomsburg Univ Pa, Bloomsburg, PA 17815. **Fax:** 570-389-4741.

JONES, CYNTHIA M, FISHERIES SCIENCE. **Education:** Boston Univ, BA, 1968; Univ RI, MS, 1973 & PhD (Oceanog), 1984. **Honors & Awards:** Phi Beta Kappa; Special Achievement Award, Nat Marine Fisheries Serv, 1981; Fulbright Sr Scholar Award, Australia, 1999. **Professional Experience:** PROF, DEPT OCEAN, EARTH & ATMOSPHERIC SCI, OLD DOM UNIV, 2004-; EMINENT SCHOLAR, OLD DOM UNIV, 2003-; prof, Dept Biol Sci, Old Dom Univ, 1998-2003; DIR, CTR QUANT FISHERIES ECOL, OLD DOM UNIV, 1998-; assoc dir, Appl Marine Res Lab, Old Dom Univ, 1988-2001; asst res prof, Dept Biol Sci, Old Dom Univ, 1988-2001; assoc prof, Dept Biol Sci, Old Dom Univ, 1993-1998; asst prof, Dept Oceanog, Old Dom Univ, 1986-1988; adj asst prof, Va Inst Marine sci, Col William & Mary, 1986-1988; assoc, Dept Natural Resources, Cornell Univ, 1984-1985; proj leader, NY Lake Ontario-Lake Erie Creel Surv, 1984-1985; co-prin investr, Larval Striped Bass Res Proj, Hudson River Found; Consult, Applied Sci Assocs, RI, 1982-1983; from grad res asst to grad res assoc, Univ RI, 1968-1973. **Research Statement & Publications:** Persistence of fish populations; the recruitment of young fish to adult populations underlies the regeneration of populations. **Mailing Address:** Dept Ocean, Earth & Atmospheric Sci, Old Dom Univ, 800 W 46th St, Norfolk, VA 23508. **Fax:** 757-683-5293. **E-Mail:** cjones@odu.edu

JONES, DALE ROBERT, PHYSICS. **Personal Data:** b Galesburg, Ill, June 17, 1924. **Education:** Univ Cincinnati, BSc, 1948; Wash Univ, PhD, 1953. **Professional Experience:** PROF EMER PHYSICS, UNIV CINCINNATI, as of 2003; prof physics, Univ Cincinnati, beginning 1962; from asst prof to assoc prof, Univ Cincinnati, 1953-1962. **Memberships:** Am Phys Soc; Sigma Xi. **Research Statement & Publications:** Cosmic rays; atomic physics. **Mailing Address:** Dept Physics, Univ Cincinnati, 145 McMicken Hall PO Box 210037, Cincinnati, OH 45221-0037. **Fax:** 513-556-0142. **E-Mail:** dale.jones@uc.edu

JONES, DALLAS WAYNE, PHYSICS. **Personal Data:** b Tiplersville, Miss, September 13, 1938. **Education:** Memphis State Univ, BS, 1960; Univ Va, MS, 1962, PhD (physics), 1966. **Professional Experience:** PRES, AM TECH INST, 1985-; dir, Ctr Nuclear Studies, 1973-1985; assoc prof physics, Memphis State Univ, 1969-1985; res physicist, US Naval Res Lab, 1965-1969; res asst, Univ Va, 1963-1965; teaching asst physics, Univ Va, 1960-1963. **Memberships:** Am Phys Soc. **Research Statement & Publications:** Quantum physics; nuclear spectroscopy; reactor technology. **Mailing Address:** 2773 Johnson Rd, Germantown, TN 38139.

JONES, DANE ROBERT, PHYSICAL CHEMISTRY. **Personal Data:** b Park City, Utah, November 27, 1947; m 1974. **Education:** Univ Utah, BA, 1969; Stanford Univ, PhD (phys chem), 1974. **Professional Experience:** CONSULT, POLYMER MFR, as of 2006; PROF CHEM, CALIF POLYTECH STATE UNIV, SAN LUIS OBISPO, 1985-; from asst prof to assoc prof, Calif Polytech State Univ, San Luis Obispo, 1976-1985; res assoc & instr phys chem, Univ Utah, 1975-1976; res assoc phys chem, Phys Chem Inst, Univ Uppsala, 1974-1975. **Memberships:** Am Chem Soc. **Research Statement & Publications:** Light scattering; surfaces and molecular complexes. **Mailing Address:** Dept Chem & Biochem, Coll Arts & sci, Calif Polytech State Univ, Fac Off E Bldg 25-122, San Luis Obispo, CA 93407. **Fax:** 805-756-5500. **E-Mail:** djones@calpoly.edu

JONES, DANIEL DAVID, RESEARCH & REGULATORY POLICY ON FOOD & AGRICULTURAL BIOTECHNOLOGY, AGRICULTURAL-HEALTH SCIENCES ADMINISTRATION. **Personal Data:** b Cedar Rapids, Iowa, January 9, 1943; m 1975, Mary. **Education:** Univ Iowa, BS, 1965; Univ Mich, PhD (biochem), 1970. **Professional Experience:** NAT PROG LEADER, BIOTECHNOL USDA COOP STATE RES, EDUC & EXTEN SERV, 1996-; competitive res grant admin team leader, construct site review, Ind Univ Inst Molecular Cell Biol, 1990; chmn biotech workshop, US Off Tech Assessment & Nat Agr Biotech Coun, 1990; biotechnologist & dep dir, Off Agr Biotechnol, 1987-1996; br chief & food technologist, USDA Food Safety & Inspection Serv Stand & Labeling Div Stand Br, 1980-1986; consumer safety officer, US Food & Drug Admin, Div Food & Color Additives, 1976-1980; staff assoc, Asn Am Med Col Div Biomed Res, 1975-1976; consult protein sequence & struct, Carnegie Mellon Univ, 1975-1976; biomed specialist, Info Syst Prog, Gen Elec Co, 1973-1975; res assoc, Brookhaven Nat Lab, 1973; res assoc, Chem Dept, Georgetown Univ, 1971-1972. **Memberships:** Am Chem Soc; Sigma Xi; NY Acad Sci. **Research Statement & Publications:** Development of government policy, guidelines, regulations, and research thrusts for the application of modern biotechnology to agricultural research and production, research biosafety, food processing and safety, health and the environment. **Mailing Address:** 4138 Orchard Dr, Fairfax, VA 22032. **Fax:** 202-401-1602. **E-Mail:** ddjones@reeusda.gov

JONES, DANIEL DAVID, PLANT PHYSIOLOGY, PHYCOLOGY. **Personal Data:** b Olney, Ill, February 23, 1943; m 1965, c Christine A & Keith A. **Education:** Purdue Univ, BS, 1965, MS, 1967; Mich State Univ, PhD (plant physiol), 1970. **Professional Experience:** PROF EMER BIOL, UNIV ALA, as of 2004; prof Biol, Univ Ala, Birmingham, beginning 1988; grad prog dir biol, Dept Biol, Univ Ala, Birmingham, 1981-; interim chair, Dept Biol, Univ Ala, Birmingham, 1974; from asst prof to assoc prof, Univ Ala, Birmingham, 1970-1988. **Memberships:** Am Soc Plant Physiol; Am Inst Biol Scientists; Am Soc Microbiol. **Research Statement & Publications:** Microbiology of Wastewater treatment and composting; gene-probe based detection of specific microbes. **Mailing Address:** Dept Biol, Univ Ala, 109CH, Birmingham, AL 35294-1170. **Fax:** 205-975-6097. **E-Mail:** ddjones@uab.edu

JONES, DANIEL ELVEN, PHYSICAL CHEMISTRY, COMPUTER SCIENCE. **Personal Data:** b New Orleans, La, September 9, 1943; m 1965, Diana; c Dana L & David M. **Education:** La State Univ, Baton Rouge, BS, chem 1965; Univ Calif, Berkeley, PhD (phys chem), 1970; Tulane Univ, New Orleans, MSE, 1996. **Professional Experience:** SR PROCESS CHEMIST, STOCKHAUSEN LA LLC, 1996-; prof engr chem eng, 1996; sr prod chemist, Nalco Chem Co, 1994-1996; res assoc, Tulane Univ, 1993-1994; sr res chemist, Freeport-McMoRan, 1979-1993; res chemist, Freeport-McMoRan, 1976-1978; res comput specialist, Am Cyanamid Co, 1971-1976; res chemist, Am Cyanamid Co, 1970-1971. **Memberships:** Am Chem Soc; Math Asn Am; Sigma Xi; Nat Soc Prof Engrs. **Research Statement & Publications:** Carbon-13 Fourier transform nuclear magnetic resonance; application of digital computers and computing techniques for improvement of analytical instrumentation; uranium recovery from phosphoric acid; anaerobic biodegradation kinetics; exact tank volumes. **Mailing Address:** 232 Stately Oaks Dr, BatonRouge, LA 70810. **Fax:** 985-535-6712. **E-Mail:** drdjones@compuserve.com

JONES, DANIEL PATRICK, HISTORY OF SCIENCE, HISTORY OF TECHNOLOGY. **Personal Data:** b Lima, Ohio, August 21, 1941; m 1964, Carol; c Colin A. **Education:** Univ Louisville, BS, 1963; Harvard Univ, AM, 1965; Univ Wis-Madison, PhD (hist sci), 1969. **Honors & Awards:** Fel AAAS; Hist Sci Soc; Am Chem Soc; Am Asn Hist Med; Soc Hist Technol. **Professional Experience:** SR PROG OFFICER, DIV RES PROG, NAT ENDOWMENT HUMANITIES, WASH, DC, 1984-; asst prof hist sci, Ctr Humanistic Studies, Med Ctr, Univ Ill, 1980-1984; vis prof, Ctr Humanistic Studies, Med Ctr, Univ Ill, 1978-1980; asst prof hist sci, Ore State Univ, 1970-1978; fel hist med & biol sci, Johns Hopkins Univ, 1969-1970. **Memberships:** AAAS; Hist Sci Soc; Am Chem Soc; Am Asn Hist Med; Soc Hist Technol. **Research Statement & Publications:** History of biochemistry and organic chemistry, 19th and early 20th century; relationships between science and society; history of public health. **Mailing Address:** Div Res & Educ, Nat Endowment Humanities, 1100 Pa Ave NW Rm 318, Washington, DC 20506. **Fax:** 202-606-8394. **E-Mail:** djones@neh.fed.us

JONES, DANIEL SILAS, PHYSICAL CHEMISTRY, X-RAY CRYSTALLOGRAPHY. **Personal Data:** b Charlotte, NC, November 16, 1943; m 1967, Linda; c Amanda. **Education:** Wake Forest Col, BS, 1965; Harvard Univ, AM, 1966, PhD, 1970. **Professional Experience:** ASSOC PROF CHEM, UNIV NC, CHARLOTTE, 1978-; asst prof, Univ NC, Charlotte, 1973-1978; Nat Acad Sci-Nat Res Coun resident res assoc, Lab Struct Matter, Naval Res Lab, Wash, DC, 1971-1973; teaching-res assoc, State Univ NY, Buffalo, 1970-1971. **Memberships:** Am Chem Soc; Am Crystallog Asn. **Research Statement & Publications:** Crystal and molecular structures by single crystal x-ray diffraction techniques; Chloro(1, 5-cyclooctadiene)(triphenylphosphine)rhodium(I); author of various articles. **Mailing Address:** Dept Chem, Univ NC, Charlotte, NC 28223-0001. **Fax:** 704-687-3151. **E-Mail:** djones@email.uncc.edu

JONES, DAVID A, JR, ORGANIC CHEMISTRY, PEPTIDE SYNTHESIS. **Personal Data:** b McCook, Nebr, February 9, 1937; m 1976, E Ann Hallinan; c Katherine, Sean, David & Christopher. **Education:** Tex A&M Univ, BS, 1958; NMex State Univ, MS, 1964; Purdue Univ, PhD (org chem), 1968. **Professional Experience:** PRES & CHIEF EXEC OFFICER, D J BIOTECH INC, 1995-; sr serv eng, Appl Biosysts Div, Perkin-Elmer Corp, 1986-1995; mem staff, res scientist II, 1977-1986; memstaff, Dept Med Chem, G D Searle & Co, 1968-1981. **Memberships:** AAAS; Am Chem Soc. **Research Statement & Publications:** Organometallic chemistry of silicon, magnesium, lithium; organic chemistry of phosphorus; amino acid and peptide chemistry; protein sequencing and instrumentation. **Mailing Address:** 135 Barton Ave, Evanston, IL 60202. **Fax:** 847-328-1565. **E-Mail:** biotech@mcs.net

JONES, DAVID ALWYN, ECOLOGICAL GENETICS OF CYANOGENESIS IN PLANTS, CHEMICAL ECOLOGY. **Personal Data:** b Colliers Wood, Eng, June 23, 1934; American citizen; m 1959, Hazel; c Catherine S (Thompson), Edmund M & Hugh F. **Education:** Univ Cambridge, UK, BA, 1957, MA, 1960; Univ Oxford, UK, DPhil(genetics), 1963. **Honors & Awards:** The int sco of chem ecology - award for distingushied service, 2001. **Professional Experience:** PROF, DEPT BOT, UNIV FLA, 1989-; head, Dept Plant Biol & Genetics, 1983-1989; prof, Univ Hull, UK, 1973-1989; lectr genetics, Univ Birmingham, UK, 1961-1973; res grants, Sci & Eng Coun, Natural Environ Res Coun, Royal Soc, Ministry Agr Fisheries & Food, USDA Forest Serv. **Memberships:** Brit Asn Advan Sci; fel Inst Biol; Int Soc Chem fem himn sr Ecol (pres, 1987-1988); Am Soc Naturalists; Soc Study Evolution; Genetical Soc UK; AAAS; Bot Soc Am. **Research Statement & Publications:** First clear demonstration of chemical defense (cyanogenesis) by plants against herbivores using genetic variation; established criteria by which chemical defense can be proved; ecological genetics, chemical ecology and plant breeding. **Mailing Address:** Dept Bot Univ Fla, PO Box 118526 220 Bartram Hall, Gainesville, FL 32611-8526. **Fax:** 352-392-3993. **E-Mail:** david_jones@his-locker.net

JONES, DAVID B, PATHOLOGY. **Personal Data:** b Canton, China, December 1, 1921; American citizen; m 1944, c 3. **Education:** Syracuse Univ, AB, 1943, MD, 1945; Am Bd Path, dipl. **Professional Experience:** PROF PATH, STATE UNIV NY UPSTATE MED CTR, 1962-; from asst prof to assoc prof, State Univ NY Upstate Med Ctr, 1950-1962. **Memberships:** Am Asn Pathologists & Bacteriologists; Am Soc Cytol; Sigma Xi. **Research Statement & Publications:** Electron microscopy. **Mailing Address:** 226 Lockwood Rd, Syracuse, NY 13214-2035.

JONES, DAVID HARTLEY, BIOCHEMISTRY. **Personal Data:** b Kansas City, Mo, February 10, 1939; m 1965, c 3. **Education:** Bethany Nazarene Col, BS, 1961; Univ Okla, MS, 1964; Cornell Univ, PhD (biochem), 1968. **Professional Experience:** CHMN, DEPT CHEM, GROVE CITY COL, as of 2004; PROF CHEM, GROVE CITY COL, as of 2004; assoc prof biochem, Oral Roberts Univ, 1978-1980; assoc prof, Albany Med Col, Union Univ, 1975-1978; asst prof, Albany Med Col, Union Univ, 1969-1975; USPHS fel biochem, Univ Calif, Los Angeles, 1967-1969. **Memberships:** AAAS. **Research Statement & Publications:** Oxidative phosphorylation in mitochondria; functional state transitions in the mammary gland; mitochondrial biogenesis during functional state transitions in the mammary gland. **Mailing Address:** Grove City Col, 100 Campus Dr Box 3105, Grove City, PA 16127. **E-Mail:** dhjones@gcc.edu

JONES, DAVID LAWRENCE, GEOLOGY, PALEONTOLOGY. **Personal Data:** b Chicago, Ill, November 12, 1930; m 1953, c 4. **Education:** Yale Univ, BS, 1952; Stanford Univ, MS, 1953, PhD, 1956. **Professional Experience:** PROF EMER GEOL & GEOPHYS, UNIV CALIF, BERKELEY, 1996-; prof geol, Dept Geol, Univ Calif, Berkeley, ending 1996; geologist, Western Region, Us Geol Surv, beginning 1955. **Memberships:** Geol Soc Am; Paleont Soc. **Research Statement & Publications:** Molluscan paleontology; Cretaceous of the Pacific coast region of North America; stratigraphy, structural, biostratigraphy and molluscan paleontology of upper Mesozoic rocks of the Pacific Coast of North America. **Mailing Address:** Dept Geol & Geophys, Univ Calif, 301 McCone Hall, Berkeley, CA 94720-4767. **Fax:** 510-643-9980.

JONES, DAVID ROBERT, PHYSIOLOGY OF DIVING ANIMALS, CARDIOVASCULAR DYNAMICS. **Personal Data:** b Bristol, Eng, January 28, 1941; Canadian citizen; m 1962, Valerie; c Melanie & Vivienne. **Education:** Southampton Univ, UK, BSc, 1962; Univ E Anglia, UK, PhD (biol), 1965. **Honors & Awards:** Fry Medal, Can Soc Zool, 1991; Killiam Res Prize, 1993. **Professional Experience:** PROF PHYSIOL, DEPT ZOOL, UNIV BC, as of 2002; mem, Grant Selection Comt, Nat Sci & Eng Res Coun Can, 1990-1994; vis prof, Univ Melbourne, Australia, 1988; comt mem, Can Soc Zoologists, 1985-1988; sr fel, Killiam Found, Can, 1973 & 1990; lectr zool, Univ Bristol, UK, 1966-1969; res fel biol, Univ E Anglia, UK, 1965-1966. **Memberships:** Am Soc Zoologists; Am Physiol Soc; Soc Exp Biol; Can Soc Zoologists; CanPhysiol Soc; Royal Soc Can. **Research Statement & Publications:** Control of cardiovascular and respiratory responses to diving, altitude and exercise in birds and mammals; cardiovascular dynamics of invertebrates and vertebrates. **Mailing Address:** Dept Zool, Univ BC, 6270 Univ Blvd, Vancouver, BC V6T 1Z4, Can. **Fax:** 604-822-2416. **E-Mail:** jones@zoology.ubc.ca

JONES, DEAN PAUL, Metabolomics, oxidative stress. **Personal Data:** b Hazard, Ky, September 13, 1949; m 1997, Paula; c Holly Nicole & Christopher Steven. **Education:** Ore Health Sci Univ, PhD (biochem), 1976. **Professional Experience:** Dir, Clinical Biomarkers Lab(s), Emory Univ, 2006; PROF MED, EMORY UNIV, 2006-; Dir, Nutrit Health Sci, Emory Univ, 1998; Prof Biochem, Emory Univ, 1991-2003; from asst prof to assoc prof, Emory Univ, 1979-1991. **Memberships:** Soc Free Radical Biol Med, Am Soc Biochem & Molecular Biol; Am Soc Cell Biol; Am Physiol Soc; Am ChemSoc; AAAS; Soc Toxicol. **Research Statement & Publications:** Use of metabolomics and proteomics in predictive health; Oxidative stress and redox signaling mechanisms; Oxygen metabolism in health and disease; diet and cancer; functions of glutathione in detoxification of carcinogens and other toxic compounds. **Mailing Address:** Dept Med/Pulmonary Whitehead Res Ctr Ste 205P, Emory Univ 625 Michael St, Atlanta, GA 30322-1100. **Fax:** 404-712-2974. **E-Mail:** dpjones@emory.edu

JONES, DEREK WILLIAM, DENTAL MATERIALS. **Personal Data:** b Birmingham, Eng, December 9, 1933; Canadian citizen; m 1957, c 4. **Education:** Univ Birmingham, BS, 1965, PhD (dent mat sci), 1970; Inst Ceramics, AICeram, 1970, FICeram, 1978; Brit Royal Soc Chem, CChem, FRSC, 1985; Inst Mat, FIM, 1993. **Honors & Awards:** Wilmer Souder Distinguished Scientist Award, Int Asn Dental Res, 1988; Award Merit, Can Stand Asn, 2002. **Professional Experience:** Hon fel, Int Col Dentists, 2005; PROF EMER BIOMAT SCI, DALHOUSIE UNIV, as of 2002; PRES, CAN DENT MAT GROUP, as of 2002; chair, restorative mat, Int Stand Org Comt, 1998-2005; chair, Can Dent Asn, Dent Mat & Devices Comt, 1993-1998; pres, Int Dent Mat Group, 1990-1991; mem, Nat Adv Panel Adv Indust Mat, Fed Govt Can, 1990-; prof, Fac Med & Heath Professions, Col Pharm, Dalhousie Univ, 1990-2000; adj prof, Dept Mech Eng, Tech Univ Nova Scotia, 1990-1995; vpres-pres, Can Asn Dent Res, 1990-1995; pres, Int Dent Mat Group, IADR, 1990-1991; Chmn, Dept Appl Oral Sci, Dalhousie Univ, 1988-1997; pres, Dent Mat Group Chap, CADR/IADR, 1988-1992; chmn, dent mat group prog, 1988; assist dean res, Dalhousie Univ, Fac Dent, 1987-1995; mem, Med Res Coun, Can Grants Comt, 1981; mem, Can Stand Steering Comt Health Care Technol, Can Stand Comt Implant Mat, 1979; chmn, Can Adv Comt, Int Stand Org, 1979-2005; secretariat, Int Stand Comt, 1979-2005; prof & actg chmn appl oral sci, beginning 1979; head div dent biomat sci, Dalhousie Univ, 1979-1997; chmn comt dent, Can Stand Asn, 1978-; comt mem coun dent mat & devices, Int Stand Orgn, 1977-; prof-in-chg dent biomat, Dept Appl Oral Sci & Head Div Dent Biomat Sci, Fac Dent, Dalhousie Univ, 1977-1979; brit expert rep, Can rep, beginning 1975; assoc prof dent biomat, Dept Appl Oral Sci & Head Div Dent Biomat Sci, Fac Dent, Dalhousie Univ, 1975-1977; Brit expert rep, Int Stand Orgn, 1973-1975; mem comt & consult, Brit Stand Comt Dent Mat, 1970-1975; examr, City & Guilds London Inst, 1966-1973; instr dent technol & mat, Univ Birmingham, 1965-1975; vis lectr, Mathew Boulton Tech Col, 1961-1968; asst dean res & prof, Col Pharm; chmn Can adv comt, tech comt 106; vis prof 9 dental schs, lectr 14 countries. **Memberships:** Can Asn Dent Res (pres, 1992-1995); Int Asn Dent Res; Soc Biomat; Inst Ceramics; Royal Soc Chem; hon mem Asn Prosthodontists Can. **Research Statement & Publications:** Conducted research on a wide range of biomaterials and material properties covering ceramics, refractories, hard and soft polymers, composites, dental cement, bone cement, mercury pollution, biocompatibility of materials and synthesis of glass and polymer materials and the release of drugs from biomaterials; authored or Co-authored over 290 papers and abstracts and contributed chapters and sections on ceramics and biomaterials in eight books; two patents on biomaterials. **Mailing Address:** Dept Biomat, Dalhousie Univ, 337 Arts & Admin Bldg 5981 Univ Ave, Halifax, NS B3H 3J5, Can. **Fax:** 902-494-1675. **E-Mail:** d.w.jones@dal.ca

JONES, DONALD AKERS, ACTUARIAL SCIENCE. **Personal Data:** b Topeka, Kans, December 27, 1930; m 1956, c 4. **Education:** Iowa State Univ, BS, 1952; Univ Iowa, MS, 1956, PhD (math), 1959. **Professional Experience:** ASSOC PROF EMER MATH, UNIV MICH, ANN ARBOR, 1991-; from asst prof to assoc prof, Univ Mich, Ann Arbor, 1959-1991. **Memberships:** Am Statist Asn; Soc Actuaries; Am Acad Actuaries. **Research Statement & Publications:** Acturial science. **Mailing Address:** Univ Mich, Dept Math, 4200 Angell, Ann Arbor, MI 48109-1003. **Fax:** 734-763-0937.

JONES, DONALD EUGENE, ANALYTICAL CHEMISTRY. **Personal Data:** b South Bend, Ind, August 1, 1934; m 1955, c 3. **Education:** Manchester Col, AB, 1957; Purdue Univ, PhD (anal chem), 1963. **Professional Experience:** PROF EMER CHEM, WESTERN MD COL, as of 2002; mem, field bus ctr, Lee Col, as of 2002; chem consult, USN, 1984-; prof chem, Western Md Col, 1976-1999; head dept, Western MD Col, 1976-1982; chem consult, Carroll County Gen Hosp, 1974-1979; vis assoc prof, Purdue Univ, 1971-1972; from asst prof to assoc prof, Western MD Col, 1963-1976; instr chem, Wabash Col, 1961-1963; res chemist, E I du Pont Del Nemours & Co, 1960; Chemist, Bendix Corp, Ind, 1957. **Memberships:** Am Chem Soc. **Research Statement & Publications:** Fluorescence of materials as applied to analytical procedures; trace analysis of materials; computer applications to chemical analysis; analytical chemistry as applied to clinical situations. **Mailing Address:** NSF Esie, Arlington, VA 22230.

JONES, DONALD R, MATHEMATICS. **Education:** Univ Tex, BA, MBA, PhD. **Professional Experience:** ASSOC PROF, TEX TECH UNIV, as of 2005. **Mailing Address:** Tex Tech Univ, Lubbock, TX 79409-2101. **Fax:** 806-742-3193. **E-Mail:** djones@ba.ttu.edu

JONES, DONLAN F(RANCIS), ELECTRICAL ENGINEERING, COMPUTER SCIENCES. **Personal Data:** b San Francisco, Calif, February 5, 1930; m 1957, Angela; c Kathleen A, Robert F, Michael P & Terese M (Kemble). **Education:** Univ Santa Clara, BEE, 1952; Univ Calif, Los Angeles, MS, 1954; Stanford Univ, Engr, 1972. **Professional Experience:** RETIRED; math teacher, Our Lady Lake Grammar Sch, beginning 1991; appln mkt mgr, Graphics Work Sta Div, 1985-1991; eng mgr, Data Commun, Info Display Div, 1981-1984; eng mgr, Mass Storage Syst, 1978-1981; eng mgr, Meg Systs, 1974-1978; eng mgr, Comput Terminal Prods, Tektronix Inc, 1969-1974; eng specialist, Sylvania Electronics Systs Div, Gen Tel & Electronics Corp, 1965-1969; adv develop engr, Sylvania Electronics Systs Div, Gen Tel & Electronics Corp, 1963-1965; consult, Sonoma State Hosp, Calif, 1962-1963; NSF sci fac fel, 1961-1962; adv develop engr, Sylvania Electronics Systs Div, Gen Tel & Electronics Corp, 1957-1963; asst prof elec eng, Univ Santa Clara, 1956-1963; res engr, Hughes Aircraft Co, 1952-1956; math instr, Clackamas Community Col; registered prof engr. **Memberships:** Sigma Xi; Tau Beta Pi. **Research Statement & Publications:** Application of computers to engineering and non-scientific problems; threshold logical design; graphic computer systems. **Mailing Address:** 427 Laurel St, Lake Oswego, OR 97034.

JONES, DOUGLAS EMRON, PHYSICS. **Personal Data:** b Long Beach, Calif, August 19, 1930; m 1955, c 5. **Education:** Brigham Young Univ, BS, 1957, MS, 1959, PhD (physics), 1964. **Honors & Awards:** Karl G Maeser Res Award. **Professional Experience:** EMER PROF PHYSICS, BRIGHAM YOUNG UNIV, as of 2004; prof, Brigham YoungUniv, beginning 1974; from asst prof to assoc prof, Brigham Young Univ, 1964-1974; spacescientist, Jet Propulsion Lab, Calif Inst Technol, 1959-1962; group supvr, Collins Radio Co, 1957; apprentice engr, Collins Radio Co, 1956; technician radio repair, Southern Calif Edison Co, 1954-1955. **Memberships:** Am Geophys Union; Am Phys Soc. **Research Statement & Publications:** Solar physics; interplanetary magnetic fields; planetary atmospheres; experimental space physics; measurement of microwave emission of planets; magnetic fields of comets and planets and in interplanetary space; space plasma simulations; soft x-ray studies of the sun. **Mailing Address:** Dept Physics & Astron, Brigham Young Univ, Provo, UT 84602. **E-Mail:** jonesd@xray.byu.edu

JONES, DOUGLAS EPPS, GEOLOGY, PALEONTOLOGY. **Personal Data:** b Tuscaloosa, Ala, May 28, 1930; m 1955, c 3. **Education:** Univ Ala, BS, 1952; La State Univ, PhD (geol), 1959. **Professional Experience:** PROF EMER GEOL, UNIV ALA, 2003-; CUR INVERT PALEONT, ALA MUS NATURAL HIST, as of 2003; actg acad vpres, Col Arts & Sci, Univ Ala, 1988-1990; dir, Ala Mus Natural Hist, beginning 1984; dean, Col Arts & Sci, Univ Ala, 1969-1984; prof geol, Univ Ala, beginning 1966; head, Dept Geol & Geog, Univ Ala, 1966-1969; from asst prof to prof geol, UnivAla, 1958-1966; res geologist, La Geol Surv, 1955-1958. **Memberships:** Geol Soc Am; Paleont Soc; Am Asn Petrol Geologists. **Research Statement & Publications:** Stratigraphy and paleontology of Gulf Coastal plain region of the United States. **Mailing Address:** Dept Geol Univ Ala, 166 Rose Admin Box 870144, Tuscaloosa, AL 35487-0144. **Fax:** 205-348-8320.

JONES, DOUGLAS L, CARDIOVASCULAR PHYSIOLOGY, REGULATORY & INTEGRATIVE PHYSIOLOGY. **Personal Data:** b Calgary, Alta, November 3, 1948; m 1971, c Cara M, Sean A & Brian M. **Education:** Univ Alta, BSc, 1972, MSc, 1974; Univ Calgary, PhD (med physiol), 1977. **Professional Experience:** SCIENTIST, LAWSON HEALTH RES INST, LONDON, 1991-as of today; prof physio & med, Univ Western Ont, 1991-; vis res fel, Univ Melbourne, Australia, 1993-1994; assoc scientist, J P Robarts Res Inst, London, 1986-1991; career scientist, Ont Ministry Health, 1986 & 1989; from asst prof to assoc prof physio & med, Univ Western Ont, 1981-1991; Med Res Coun fel, 1980-1985; L L scholar, 1980; Lady Davis scholar, 1975. **Memberships:** Fel Am Col Cardiol; Am Heart Asn; Am Phys Soc; Can Physiol Soc; AAAS; SocNeuroscience; Can Asn Neuroscience. **Research Statement & Publications:** Cardiovascular physiology; regulatory and integrative physiology; electrophysiology; neuroscience; electrocardiology. **Mailing Address:** Dept Physiol & Med, Univ Western Ont, Med Sci Bldg, London, ON N6A 5C1, Can. **Fax:** 519-661-3827. **E-Mail:** doug.jones@med.uwo.ca

JONES, DOUGLAS LINWOOD, FRACTURE MECHANICS, DESIGN OPTIMIZATION. **Personal Data:** b Limeton, Va, December 26, 1937; m 1975, Mary. **Education:** George Wash Univ, BME, 1963, MSE, 1965, DSc, 1970. **Professional Experience:** PROF EMER ENG, MECH & AEROSPACE ENG, GEORGE WASH UNIV, as of 2005; ASSOC DEAN MECH & AEROSPACE ENG, GEORGE WASH UNIV, as of 2003; NKF Eng, 1990 & US Dept Transp, 1990-; Intelsat Corp, 1986-1988; Alcoa, 1983; prof eng, George Wash Univ, 1982-; Du Pont Corp, 1982-1985; chmn mech engr curric, George Wash Univ, 1981-1985; Systs Technol Labs Inc, 1980-1982; assoc prof, George Wash Univ, 1977-1982; Ensco Inc, 1977-1978; consult, Eng Servs Co, 1976-1981; consult, Comsat Labs, 1974-1976; from asst res prof to assoc res prof, George Wash Univ, 1971-1977; consult, Seal & Co, 1970-1971; from instr to asst prof eng & appl sci, George Wash Univ, 1967-1971; Univ fel eng, George Wash Univ, 1966-1967; prin Ore co-prin investr res grants, NASA, Dept Defense, NSF. **Memberships:** Am Acad Mech; Am Soc Testing & Mat; Am Soc Mech Engrs; Am Soc Eng Educ; Soc Exp Mech; Sigma Xi. **Research Statement & Publications:** Fatigue, fracture and fracture mechanics of metals and composite materials; computer aided engineering, computer aided design and optimization; fractography and failure analysis; experimental stress analysis; evaluation and development of constitutive relations in continuum mechanics; analysis and testing of composite materials. **Mailing Address:** Acad Ctr, George Wash Univ, T723, Washington, DC 20052. **Fax:** 202-994-0238. **E-Mail:** jone@gwu.edu

JONES, DUVALL ALBERT, vertebrate zoology, herpetology; deceased, see previous edition for last biography

JONES, EARLE DOUGLAS, ELECTRONICS. **Personal Data:** b Birmingham, Ala, April 10, 1931; m 1961. **Education:** Ga Inst Technol, BS, 1956; Stanford Univ, MS, 1958. **Professional Experience:** REG MTG DIR, KOREA, 1988-; exec dir, SRI-ASIA, 1986-1988; Asst math, Ga Inst Technol, 1955-1956. **Memberships:** Inst Elec & Electronics Engrs; Sigma Xi. **Research Statement & Publications:** Space electronics; communication systems research in satellite meteorology; display devices and digital control research; bioengineering. **Mailing Address:** 380 Conil Way, Menlo Park, CA 94028.

JONES, EDWARD DAVID, PLANT ENTOMOLOGY. **Personal Data:** b Rockland, Wis, May 8, 1920; m 1947, c 4. **Education:** Univ Wis, BS, 1946, MS, 1947, PhD (plant path), 1953. **Professional Experience:** EMER PROF, DEPT PLANT PATH, CORNELL UNIV, 1988-; Henry & Mildred Uihlein prof plant path, Dept Plant Path, Cornell Univ, 1987-1988; Henry Uihlein II tissue cult facil at Uihlein Farm, Lake Placid, NY, 1977-; Uihlein Farm, Cornell Univ, 1961-; In-chg found & cert seed potato prog NY state, 1960-; from asst prof to prof, Dept Plant Path, Cornell Univ, 1958-1987; plant pathologist, Red Dot Foods, Inc, 1953-1958; Instr plant path, Univ Wis, 1948-1953. **Memberships:** Am Phytopath Soc; hon Potato Asn Am (vpres, 1981-1982, pres, 1984-1985); Sigma Xi. **Research Statement & Publications:** Production of disease-free nuclear seed stocks by tissue culture; disease problems relating to the production of seed potatoes. **Mailing Address:** PO Box 260, Big Hills Lake, Wild Rose, WI 54984.

JONES, EDWARD GEORGE, NEUROBIOLOGY. **Personal Data:** b Upper Hutt, NZ, March 26, 1939; m 1963, Elizabeth; c Christopher & Philippa. **Education:** Univ Otago, NZ, MB, ChB, 1962, MD, 1970; Oxford Univ, DPhil(anat), 1968. **Honorary Degrees:** Dr, Univ Salamanca, Spain, 1997. **Honors & Awards:** Symington Mem Prize, Anat Soc Gt Brit & Ireland, 1968; Rolleston Mem Prize, Oxford Univ, 1970; Cajal Prize, Am Asn Anatomists, 1989; Karl Spencer Lashley award, American Philosophical soc, 2001; Henry Gray Award, Am asson Anatomists, 2001; member National Academy of Sciences of the USA, 2004. **Professional Experience:** Distinguished prof, Univ Calif, Davis, 2002-; PROF PSYCHIAT, DIR CTR NEUROSCIENCE, UNIV CALIF, DAVIS, 1998-; Adjunct Prof, Dept Neuropharmacology, Scripps Rsrch Inst La Jolla Calif 1995-1998 dir, Neurol Systs Lab, Frontier Res Prog, Riken, Japan, 1988-1996; prof & chmn, Univ Calif Irvine, 1984-1995; assoc, Neuroscience Res Prog, 1984-1993; assoc ed, J Neuroscience, 1981-1988; prof neuroscience, SchMed, 1981-1984; dir, James O'Leary Div Exp Neurol & Neurol Surg, Wash Univ, George H &Ethel Ronzon scholar Neuroscience & sr scientist, McDonnell Ctr Study Higher Brain Function, 1981-1984; Macy Found sr fac scholar, Monash Univ, Australia, 1978-1979; Green vis prof, MedBr, Univ Tex, Galveston, 1978; prof anat & neurobiology, Sch Med, 1975-1984; assoc ed, J CompNeurol, 1975-1980; assoc prof anat, Wash Univ, 1972-1975; assoc prof, Univ Otago, NZ, 1971-1972; NZ Med Res Coun grant, Sch Med, Otago Univ, 1969-1971; lectr, Balliol Col, 1966-1968; from asst lectr to lectr, Univ Otago, NZ, 1965-1970; Nuffield Dom demonstr, OxfordUniv, 1965-1968; Demonstr anat, Univ Otago, NZ, 1964-1965. **Memberships:** Anat Soc Gt Brit & Ireland; Am Asn Anatomists; Soc Neuroscience (pres 1998); AAAS; Am College of Neuropsychopharmacology. **Research Statement & Publications:** Structure, function and development of sensory systems particularly in primates and with emphasis on cerebral cortex and thalamus. **Mailing Address:** Ctr NeuroSci, 203J 1544 Newton Ct, Davis, CA 95616. **E-Mail:** egjones@ucdavis.edu

JONES, EDWARD GRANT, CHEMICAL PHYSICS. **Personal Data:** b Toronto, Ont, February 16, 1942; m 1972, c 3. **Education:** Univ Toronto, BSc, 1965, MSc, 1967, PhD (phys chem), 1969. **Professional Experience:** Dir, Ctr Neuroscience, Univ Calif Davis, 1998-; RES ASSOC PROF CHEM, WRIGHT STATE UNIV, 1977-; consult, Systs Res Labs, 1975-; res asst prof chem, Wright State Univ, 1975-1977; sr res chemist & proj mgr, Systs Res Labs, 1972-1975; res assoc, Purdue Univ, 1971-1972; consult, Systs Res Labs, 1971-1972; vis res scientist, Ohio State Univ Res Found, 1969-1971. **Memberships:** Sr mem Am Chem Soc; sr mem Am Soc Mass Spectrometry. **Research Statement & Publications:** Gas phase kinetics; ion-neutral collision phenomena; unimolecular decomposition; chemiluminescence; thermal degradation of polymers; kinetics of polymerization. **Mailing Address:** Ctr NeuroSci, Univ Calif Davis, 1544 Newton Ct, Davis, CA 45373-9702. **Fax:** 530-757-8827. **E-Mail:** ejones@ucdavis.edu

JONES, E(DWARD) M(CCLUNG) T(HOMPSON), MICROWAVE ELECTRONICS. **Personal Data:** b Topeka, Kans, August 19, 1924; m 1949, c 3. **Education:** Swarthmore Col, BS, 1944; Stanford Univ, MS, 1948, PhD (elec eng), 1950. **Professional Experience:** CHMN BD, TCI, 1990-; vpres develop, TCI, 1982-1990; exec vpres, TCI, 1971-1982; vpres eng & technol, TCI, 1968-1971; eng mgr, Antennas & Transmission Lines Div, Granger Assocs, 1967-1968; dir eng, Menlo Park Div, TRG, Inc, Control Data Corp, 1961-1967; head microwave group, Stanford Res Inst, 1957-1961; sr res engr, Stanford Res Inst, 1950-1957; Res assoc elec eng, Stanford Univ, 1948-1950. **Memberships:** Inst Elec & Electronics Engrs; Sigma Xi. **Research Statement & Publications:** Microwave components and antennas; antennas. **Mailing Address:** 2161 Via Escalera, Los Altos, CA 94024.

JONES, EDWARD O(SCAR), mechanical engineering; deceased, see previous edition for last biography

JONES, EDWARD RAYMOND, AGRICULTURAL BUSINESS & MANAGEMENT, GENERAL AGRICULTURE. **Personal Data:** b Steubenville, Ohio, January 27, 1943; m 1964, Brenda; c Kelly. **Education:** Ohio State Univ, BS, 1965; Pa State Univ, MS, 1967, PhD (agron), 1969. **Honors & Awards:** Merit Award, Forage & Grassland Coun, 1988. **Professional Experience:** PROF AGRON, DEL STATE UNIV, 1977-; from asst prof to assoc prof, Del State Col, 1969-1977; adj prof plant sci, Univ Del, Newark. **Memberships:** Am Soc Agron; Am Forage & Grassland Coun. **Research Statement & Publications:** Forage crop management and utilization. **Mailing Address:** Dept Agr & Natural Resource, Del State Univ, 1200 N DuPont Hwy, Dover, DE 19901-2277. **Fax:** 302-739-4997.

JONES, EDWARD STEPHEN, ORGANIC CHEMISTRY, ORGANOFLUORINE CHEMISTRY. **Personal Data:** b Boston, Mass, April 17, 1931; m 1956, Mary; c Geraldine A, Stephen M & Lori E. **Education:** Northeastern Univ, BS, 1953; Purdue Univ, MS, 1956; Wayne State Univ, PhD (org chem), 1961. **Professional Experience:** RETIRED; sr res chemist, Halocarbon Prod Corp, 1980-1996; sr res chemist, Specialty Chem Div, Buffalo, 1969-1980; res chemist, Gen Chem Div, Allied Chem Corp, NJ, 1960-1969. **Memberships:** Am Chem Soc. **Research Statement & Publications:** Organic fluorine chemistry; applications, process research and development; basic research; product research and development. **Mailing Address:** 224 Oakhurst Dr, North Augusta, SC 29860.

JONES, EDWIN C, ELECTRICAL ENGINEERING, EDUCATION. **Personal Data:** b Parkersburg, WVa, June 27, 1934; m Ruth; c Charles, Cathleen & Helene. **Education:** WVa Univ, BS, 1955; Imp Col, Univ London, Dipl, 1956; Univ Ill, Urbana, PhD (elec eng), 1962. **Honors & Awards:** Centennial Medal, Inst Elec & Electronics Engrs, 1984, Accreditation Activ Award, 1986 Award, 1986, Linton E Grinter Distinguished Service Award, Accreditation Board of Engr and Technol (ABET), 2001 Fellow, IEEE, ASEE, AAAS, ABET. **Professional Experience:** UNIV PROF EMER ELEC AND COMPUTER ENG, IOWA STATE UNIV, 2001-; bd dirs, Accreditation Bd Eng & Technol, 1984-1987; ed, Inst Elec & Electronics Engrs Trans Educ, 1981-1984; mem, Eng Accreditation Comn, 1980-1984; pres, Inst Elec & Electronics Engrs Educ Soc, 1975-1976; vpres, Inst Elec & Electronics Engrs Educ Soc, 1973-1974; Univ Prof, Iowa State Univ 1995-2001 prof, Iowa State Univ, 1972-1995; vpres continuing educ, Nat Electronics Conf, 1971; secy, Inst Elec & Electronics Engrs Educ Soc, 1970-1978; awards chmn, Nat Electronics Conf, 1969-1970; secy, Nat Electronics Conf, 1969; prog chmn, Nat Electronics Conf, 1968; from asst prof to assoc prof, Iowa State Univ, 1966-1972; proc chmn, Nat Electronics Conf, 1965; from instr to asst prof elec eng, Univ Ill, 1960-1966; Engr, 1962 & Westinghouse Elec Co, 1959; Teaching asst elec eng, Univ Ill, 1958-1959; Engr, Gen Elec Co, 1955. **Memberships:** Fel Inst Elec & Electronics Engrs; fel Am Soc Eng Educ; fel AAAS; Soc Hist Technol; fel Accreditation Bd Eng & Technol. **Research Statement & Publications:** Circuit theory; experimental engineering techniques; educational methods; technology and social change. **Mailing Address:** Dept Elec & Comput Eng, Iowa State Univ, Ames, IA 50011. **E-Mail:** n2ecj@iastate.edu

JONES, EDWIN RUDOLPH, SOLID STATE PHYSICS, SCIENCE EDUCATION. **Personal Data:** b Lumberton, NC, August 3, 1938; m 1960, c Caroline, Edwin, Robert & Katherine. **Education:** Clemson Univ, BS, 1960; Univ Wis, MS, 1962, PhD (physics), 1965. **Professional Experience:** DISTINGUISHED PROF EMER PHYSICS, UNIV SC, as of 2005; Comt Physics, High Sci, 1997-2000; chair, Comt Undergrad Educ, Am Asn Physics Teachers, 1993-1994; mem, Comt Undergrad Educ, Am Asn Physics Teachers, 1991-1994; vis prof, Univ de El Salvador, 1978; prof physics, Univ Sc, beginning 1977; from asst prof to assoc prof, Univ SC, 1965-1977. **Memberships:** Am Phys Soc; Am Asn Physics Teachers; Southern Atlantic Coast Sect, Am Asn Physics Teachers (pres, 2000-2001); SC Acad Sci; SC Sci Coun. **Research Statement & Publications:** Three dimensional imaging for video and computer displays; development of instrument materials; author of two textbooks. **Mailing Address:** Dept Physics, Univ SC, 712 Main St, Columbia, SC 29208. **E-Mail:** rjones@sc.edu

JONES, ELEANOR GREEN DAWLEY, Abstract algebra. **Personal Data:** b Norfolk, Va, August 10, 1929; div, c Edward A Dawley, III & Everette B Jones Jr. **Education:** Howard Univ, BS, 1949, MS, 1950; Syracuse Univ, PhD (math), 1966. **Honors & Awards:** Distinguished Serv Award, Nat Asn Mathematicians, 1994; Lifetime Achievement Award, Nat Asn Mathematicians, 2001. **Professional Experience:** Bd dir, Asn Women Math, 1990-; reader, Col Bd Advan Placement Exam Math, 1989-1995; exec bd, Nat Asn Mathematicians, 1988-1995; bd gov, Math Asn Am, 1983-1986; prof math, Norfolk State Col, 1967-2001; assoc prof, Hampton Inst, 1966-1967; teaching asst, Syracuse Univ, 1964-1966; instr, Hampton Inst, 1955-1962. **Memberships:** Am Math Soc; Math Asn Am; Nat Asn Math (vpres, 1975-1980); Asn Women Math; Sigma Xi. **Research Statement & Publications:** Abelian groups and their endomorphism rings; direct decompositions and quasi-endomorphisms of torsion free abelian groups. **Mailing Address:** 6301 Bucknell Circle, Virginia Beach, VA 23464. **E-Mail:** eljones@acninc.net

JONES, ELIZABETH W, MOLECULAR GENETICS, CELL BIOLOGY. **Personal Data:** b Seattle, Wash, March 8, 1939. **Education:** Univ Wash, BS, 1960, PhD (genetics), 1964. **Honors & Awards:** USPHS res career develop award, 1971-1974 Fellow, Am Assoc Advancement Science 1980 Fellow, American Academy of Microbiology, 1998 Howard Hughes Medical Institute professor, 2002- President, Genetics Society of America, 1987. **Professional Experience:** Assoc ed, Ann Rev Genetics, 1990-; adj prof psychiat, Univ Pittsburgh, 1985-; assoc ed, Yeast, 1985-; FREDERICK A SCHWERTZ UNIV PROF BIOL SCI, CARNEGIE-MELLON UNIV, 1982-; HEAD BIOL SCI, CARNEGIE-MELLON UNIV, 2000-; assoc ed, Genetics, 1980-1996, Editor-in-Chief, Genetics, 1997-; ed board, Molecular Biology Cell, 1991-2000; ed comm Annual Rev Genetics 1984-1986, Assoc ed Annual Rev Genetics, 1990-; Genetics Study Sect, NIH, 1976-1980 & 1984-1986, chair, 1990-1993; assoc prof, Carnegie-Mellon Univ, 1974-1982; NIH Genetics Training Comt, 1972-1973; USPHS res grant, 1970-; asst prof biol & microbiol, Case Western Reserve Univ, 1969-1974; instr, Mass Inst Technol, 1967-1969; res assoc, Mass Inst Technol, 1964-1967; USPHS trainee, Univ Wash, 1960-1964. **Memberships:** Fel AAAS; Genetics Soc Am (vpres 1986 pres 1987); Am Soc Microbiol; AmSoc Cell Biol, Am. Soc. Human Genetics. **Research Statement & Publications:** Organization and expression of genetic material in yeast; protein targeting and organellar assembly. **Mailing Address:** Dept Biol Sci, Carnegie-Mellon Univ, Mellon Inst, 4400 Fifth Ave, Pittsburgh, PA 15213. **Fax:** 412-268-1811. **E-Mail:** ej09@andrew.cmu.edu

JONES, ELMER EVERETT, NATURE STUDY EDUCATION. **Personal Data:** b Hinsdale, Ill, September 2, 1926; m 1956, Alice; c Laura A. **Education:** Univ Chicago, PhB, 1948, BS, 1950; Wash Univ, PhD, 1957. **Professional Experience:** RETIRED; assoc prof chem, Northeastern Univ, 1962-1990; asst prof chem, Northeastern Univ, 1958-1962; res assoc, Tannhauser Lab, Boston Dispensary, 1956-1958; asst, Wash Univ, 1950-1955. **Memberships:** Am Chem Soc; Sigma Xi. **Mailing Address:** 67 Brook Rd, Weston, MA 02193-1766.

JONES, ERIC DANIEL, SOLID STATE PHYSIC, OPTICAL SPECTROSCOPY. **Personal Data:** b Oakland, Calif, January 6, 1936; m Mary; c Jennifer, Eric Jr, Kelly, Kim & Suzanne. **Education:** Ore State Univ, BS, 1957; Univ Wash, MS, 1959, PhD (physics), 1962. **Honors & Awards:** Directors Award, National High Magnetic Field Laboratory, Florida State University, 2002. **Professional Experience:** RETIRED; Senior Scientist Sandia Nat Labs, 1997-2002, Distinguished Mem Tech staff, Sandia Nat Labs, 1990-1997; Chmn, User's Comt, Nat High Magnetic Field Lab, 1993-1995; External AdvComt, Nat High Magnetic Field Lab, Fla State Univ, 1991-1994; Users' Comt for Francis Bitter Nat MagnetLab, Mass Inst Technol, 1990-1993; secy-treas, Instruments & Measurement Sci Top Group, AmPhys Soc, 1988-1990; bd ed, Rev Sci Instruments, 1986-1989; adj prof, Physics Dept, UnivNMex, Albuquerque, NMex, 1985-; mem tech staff Sandia Semiconductor Physics, Sandia Corp, Sandia Nat Labs, 1985-1990; mem staff laser res, Sandia Corp, Sandia Nat Labs, 1982-1985; mem, Adv Comt Grad Studies, Elec & Comput Eng, Univ NMex, 1976-1988; pres, AlbuquerqueChap Laser Inst Am, 1972-1976; mem, Adv Comt-Optics Prog, Idaho State Univ, 1970-1976; supvr laser effects res, Sandia Corp, Sandia Nat Labs, 1968-1982; mem staff solid state physicsres, Sandia Corp, Sandia Nat Labs, 1965-1968; mem tech staff, Bell Tel Labs, NJ, 1962-1965; Woodrow Wilson fel, 1960. **Memberships:** Fel Am Phys Soc; sr mem Inst Elec & Electronics Engrs. **Research Statement & Publications:** Study of ferromagnetism, antiferromagnetism, paramagnetism in insulators and metals by the use of nuclear magnetic resonance techniques; high power laser energy deposition in solids; ultrashort laser pulse generation and applications; magneto-optics of semiconductors, and pressure effects in semiconductors; semiconductor physics. **Mailing Address:** PO Box 2379, Edgewood, NM 87015. **E-Mail:** edjones@MailAPS.org

JONES, ERIC MANNING, HYDRODYNAMICS, ASTROPHYSICS. **Personal Data:** b Goldsboro, NC, March 25, 1944. **Education:** Calif Inst Technol, BS, 1966; Univ Wis-Madison, PhD (astron), 1969. **Professional Experience:** RETIRED; staff, Los Alamos Nat Lab, ending 1999; co-ed Ben R Finney, Interstellar Migration& Human Exp, Univ Calif Press, 1985; lab fel, Los Alamos Nat Lab, 1982-1999; group leader, Los Alamos Nat Lab, 1976-1981; staff mem hydrodyn, Los Alamos Nat Lab, 1969-1975; Nat Res Coun Comt on Nuclear Winter. **Memberships:** Am Astron Soc. **Research Statement & Publications:** Supernova remnants; interstellar medium; nuclear explosion phenomenology; numerical hydrodynamics; space development. **Mailing Address:** 820 47th St PO Box 301, Los Alamos, NM 87544. **E-Mail:** honais@austarnet.com.au

JONES, ERIC WYNN, VETERINARY MEDICINE. **Personal Data:** b St Martins, Eng, September 24, 1924; American citizen; m 1948, c 1. **Education:** MRCVS, 1946 London; Cornell Univ, PhD (vet surg), 1950; Am Col Vet Surg, dipl, 1971; Am Col Vet Anesthesiol, dipl, 1978. **Honorary Degrees:** FRCVS, London, 1987. **Professional Experience:** Prof emer vet med Miss State Univ, 1992-; PROF VET MED, MISS STATE UNIV, 1987-; prof, Col Vet Med, Miss State Univ, 1986-1987; from asst to vpres, Col Vet Med, Miss State Univ, 1984-1986; interim dean, Col Vet Med, Miss State Univ, 1983-1984; vdean, Col Vet Med, Miss State Univ, 1978-1983; Consult, Col Vet Med, Miss State Univ, 1974-1978; dir clin res, 1956-1977. **Memberships:** Am Vet Med Asn; Brit Vet Asn; Am Soc Anesthesiol; Am Soc Vet Anesthesiol; Am Acad Vet Pharmacol & Toxicol; Am Asn Equine Practrs. **Research Statement & Publications:** Drug and biologic and model development; program and facilities consulting national and international; spleen function in infectious anemia; enteritis; mechanical ventilators; malignant hyperthermia; drug testing. **Mailing Address:** Col Vet Med PO Drawer 9825, Miss State Univ, Mississippi State, MS 39762.

JONES, ERNEST ADDISON, PHYSICS. **Personal Data:** b Columbia, Ky, June 5, 1918; m 1943. **Education:** Western Ky State Teachers Col, BS, 1942; Vanderbilt Univ, MS, 1943; Ohio State Univ, PhD (phys chem), 1948. **Professional Experience:** PROF EMER PHYSICS, VANDERBILT UNIV, 1985-; from asst prof to prof physics, Vanderbilt Univ, 1950-1985; res chemist, Carbide & Carbon Chem Co, 1948-1950; res physicist, Manhattan Dist, Columbia Univ, 1943-1945. **Memberships:** Am Phys Soc; Optical Soc Am. **Research Statement & Publications:** Infrared and Raman spectroscopy. **Mailing Address:** Dept Physics & Astron, Vanderbilt Univ, 6301 Stevenson Ctr 37240, Nashville, TN 37201. **Fax:** 615-343-7263.

JONES, ERNEST AUSTIN, JR, PETROLEUM GEOLOGY. **Personal Data:** b Orange, NJ, March 24, 1960. **Education:** Princeton Univ, AB, 1983; Harvard Univ, AM, 1989, PhD (geol), 1989. **Professional Experience:** RES GEOLOGIST, MOBIL CORP, 1989-; Geologist, US Geol Surv, 1984-1987. **Memberships:** Am Asn Petrol Geologists. **Research Statement & Publications:** Development of diagenetic models to predict sandstone reservoir quality; clastic petrology and hydrogeology, Anadarko basin, Denver basin, Llamos basin & NW Shelf, Australia. **Mailing Address:** 4242 N Capistrano Dr, Dallas, TX 75287.

JONES, ERNEST OLIN, RADIOLOGICAL PHYSICS. **Personal Data:** b Atlanta, Ga, February 1, 1923; m 1946, c 2. **Education:** Emory Univ, AB, 1948, MS, 1949; US Naval Postgrad Sch, MS, 1959; NC State Univ, PhD (nuclear eng), 1964; Am Bd Radiol, dipl radiol physics, 1975. **Professional Experience:** Prof radiol, Col Med, 1972-; assoc prof radiol, Col Dent, 1969-; assoc prof radiol, Col Med, Univ Nebr, Omaha, 1968-1972; dir, Div Biometrics, 1967-1968; Dep dir nuclear med, Walter Reed Army Inst Res, 1964-1967; EMER PROF RADIOL, COL MED & DENT, UNIV NEBR, OMAHA. **Memberships:** Soc Nuclear Med; Am Asn Physicists Med; Asn Mil Surgeons US; Am Col Nuclear Physicians; Am Col Med Physics; fel Am Col Radiol. **Research Statement & Publications:** Radiation therapy dosimetry; diagnostic x-ray dosage reduction, medical computer applications. **Mailing Address:** Box 4334, Pagosa Springs, CO 81157.

JONES, EUGENE LAVERNE, geophysics, geochemistry; deceased, see previous edition for last biography

JONES, EVAN EARL, biochemistry; deceased, see previous edition for last biography

JONES, EVERETT, FLUID MECHANICS, HEAT TRANSFER. **Personal Data:** b Albany, NY, January 25, 1930; m 1957, Carolyn; c Karen Lee, Kalinock Kristine & Anne Kraus. **Education:** Rensselaer Polytech Inst, BAE, 1956, MAE, 1960; Stanford Univ, PhD (aeronaut & astronaut), 1968. **Professional Experience:** PROF EMER AEROSPACE ENG, UNIV MD, COLLEGE PARK, as of 2005; David W Taylor res prog, Naval Ship Res Ctr, 1985 & US Army fac res eng prof, 1983; engr, US Naval Surface Weapons Ctr, 1977-1983; fac res fel, NASA-ASER fac res prog, 1970; prof, Univ MD, College Park, 1969-1995; res assoc, Dept Aeronaut & Astronaut Sci, Stanford Univ, 1968-1969; lectr heat transfer, San Jose State Col, 1967-1968; res asst, Dept Aeronaut & Astronaut Sci, Stanford Univ, 1966-1968; res specialist, Lockheed Missiles & Space Co, 1964-1969; sr engr, Lockheed Missiles & Space Co, 1961-1964; sr thermodynamicist, Lockheed Missiles & Space Co, 1959-1961; res asst aeronaut eng, Rensselaer Polytech Inst, 1957-1959; advan study scientist, Lockheed Missiles & Space Co, 1956-1957. **Memberships:** Sr mem Am Inst Aeronaut & Astronaut. **Research Statement & Publications:** Fluid mechanics, heat transfer and aerodynamics; emphasis on applications for aerospace vehicles, computational fluid mechanics and blood flow. **Mailing Address:** Dept Aerospace Eng, Univ Md, College Park, MD 20742. **Fax:** 301-405-9001. **E-Mail:** everettjn@aol.com

JONES, EVERETT BRUCE, HYDROLOGY, WATER RESOURCES ENGINEERING. **Personal Data:** b Ft Collins, Colo, September 23, 1933; m 1956, Margie; c Elizabeth G & Janet L. **Education:** Univ Wyo, BS, 1955; Pa State Univ, MS, 1959; Colo State Univ, PhD (watershed mgt), 1964. **Professional Experience:** PROJ MGR ENG GROUP, JACOBS ENG GROUP, 1991-; dist mgr, Groundwater Tech Inc, Englewood, Colo, 1990-1991; assoc, Bishop-Brogden Assocs, Lakewood, Colo, 1988-1990; mgr, Water Resources Dept, Environ Sci & Eng Inc, 1987-1988; pres, Resource Consults, Inc, 1977-1987; pres, M W Bittinger & Assocs, Inc, 1977; vpres, M WBittinger & Assocs, Inc, 1970-1977; coordr water resources, Environ Serv Oper, EG&G, Inc, 1969; asst dir inst for res on land & water resources, in-chg water resources ctr & asst profmeteorol, Pa State Univ, 1965-1968; engr-hydrologist, Douglas W Barr, Consult Hydraul Engrs, Minn, 1964-1965; asst interstate streams comnr, State Wyo, 1961; chief waterdevelop, Wyo Natural Resources Bd, 1959-1961; vpres, Wyo Well. **Memberships:** Am Soc Civil Engrs; Am Meteorol Soc; Am Geophys Union. **Research Statement & Publications:** Groundwater hydrology; surface-water hydrology and hydrometeorology, especially water resources management aspects. **Mailing Address:** 495 Spring Creek Dr, Divide, CO 80814.

JONES, FABER BENJAMIN, POLYMER CHEMISTRY. **Personal Data:** b December 4, 1932; American citizen; m 1954, c 4. **Education:** Ohio State Univ, BSc, 1954. **Professional Experience:** VPRES RES & DEVELOP, PHILLIPS PETROL CO, 1990-; vpres, planning& budgeting, 1986-1990; div mgr polymer mat res, Polymer Appln Br, 1982-1986; dir polymermat res, Polymer Appln Br, 1980-1981; mgr, Polymer Appln Br, 1979; mgr, Chem Appln Br, Phillips Petrol Co, 1964-1979; tech dir adhesives res, Evans Adhesives Corp, 1963-1964; Asst divchief polymer res, Battelle Mem Inst, 1953-1963. **Memberships:** Am Chem Soc; Adhesion Soc; Soc Plastic Engrs. **Research Statement & Publications:** Polymer research and technology, especially on adhesives, coatings and reinforced plastic systems. **Mailing Address:** 2412 Kyles Court, Bartlesville, OK 74006-6339.

JONES, FLOYD BURTON, TOPOLOGY. **Personal Data:** b Cisco, Tex, November 22, 1910; div, c Phyllis, Marion, Clay & Lesley. **Education:** Univ Tex, BA, 1932, PhD (math), 1935. **Professional Experience:** Distinguished vis scientist, Auburn Univ, 1982; Mary Moody northern chair, VMI, 1979; PROF EMER, UNIV CALIF, RIVERSIDE, 1978-; vis fel, Univ Houston, 1977; Fulbright-Hays fel, NZ, 1975; vis fel, Inst Advan Study, Australian Nat Univ, 1968; prof math, Univ Calif, Riverside, 1962-1978; sr fel, NSF, 1957-1958; mem, Inst Advan Study, Australian Nat Univ, 1957-1958; prof math, Univ NC, 1950-1962; res assoc, Underwater SoundLab, Harvard Univ, 1942-1944; asst prof to assoc prof, Univ Tex, 1940-1950; instr pure math, Univ Tex, 1932-1940. **Memberships:** Am Math Soc; Math Asn Am. **Research Statement & Publications:** Pointset theoretic topology. **Mailing Address:** Univ Calif, 3775 Modoc Dr No 74, Santa Barbara, CA 93105-4474.

JONES, FRANCIS THOMAS, PHYSICAL CHEMISTRY. **Personal Data:** b Pottsville, Pa, October 19, 1933; m 1981, Nuran Kumbaraci; c Anne & Marian. **Education:** Pa State Univ, BS, 1955; Polytech Inst Brooklyn, PhD (phys chem), 1960. **Honorary Degrees:** MEng, Stevens Inst Technol, 1975. **Professional Experience:** Grad adv, chem prog, Stevens Inst, 1990-; head, Dept Chem & Chem Eng, 1979-1990; Adj assoc prof anesthesiol, NY Med Col, 1977-1989; PROF CHEM, STEVENSINST TECHNOL, 1971-; from asst prof to assoc prof chem, Stevens Inst Technol, 1964-1971; chemist, Union Carbide Corp, 1962-1964; Gen Elec Co Ltd fel radiation chem, Univ Leeds, 1960-1962. **Memberships:** Am Chem Soc. **Research Statement & Publications:** Radiation chemistry; photochemistry; catalysis; mass spectrometry; kinetics; instrumentation design. **Mailing Address:** 692 Stewart St, Ridgefield, NJ 07657. **Fax:** 201-216-8240. **E-Mail:** fjones@stevens_tech.edu

JONES, FRANCIS TUCKER, CHEMISTRY. **Personal Data:** b Rocklin, Calif, January 17, 1905; m 1942, c 3. **Education:** Pac Univ, Ore, AB, 1928; Univ Ore, AM, 1931; Cornell Univ, PhD (chem micros), 1934. **Professional Experience:** RETIRED; chemist, Mkt & Nutrit Div, Agr Res Serv, USDA, 1942-1974; prof, Pac Univ, Ore, 1934-1942; asst chem, Univ Ore, 1929-1931; Cornell Univ, 1932-1934; teacher pubsch, Ore, 1928-1929; asst chem, Pac Univ, Ore, 1926-1928. **Memberships:** Am Chem Soc; Sigma Xi. **Research Statement & Publications:** Physical and analytical chemistry; chemical microscopy applied to determination of optical and crystallographic properties and phase relations; scanning electron microscopy. **Mailing Address:** 912 Regal Rd, Berkeley, CA 94708-1428.

JONES, FRANK CULVER, COSMIC RAY PHYSICS, THEORETICAL ASTROPHYSICS. **Personal Data:** b Ft Worth, Tex, July 30, 1932; m 1955, Andythe; c Chery (Mattis) & Timothy. **Education:** Rice Inst, BA, 1954; Univ Chicago, MS, 1955, PhD (physics), 1961. **Professional Experience:** SR SCIENTIST, LAB HIGH ENERGYASTROPHYS, GODDARD SPACE FLIGHT CTR, NASA, 1995-; head, Theoret High Energy Astrophys Off, 1995; coun mem, Am PhysSoc, 1994-1997; secy, Astrophys Div, Am Phys Soc, 1988-1992; Ed & Publ, Cosnews, Newsletter Cosmic Ray Comn Int Union Pure & Appl Physics, 1987-; astrophysicist, Lab High Energy Astrophys, 1977-1993; Vis scientist, Max Planck Inst NuclearPhysics, 1977; physicist, Theoret Studies Group, 1965-1977; Nat Acad Sci-NatRes Coun resident res assoc, Theoret Studies Group, 1963-1965; instr, Princeton Univ, 1961-1963; res assoc, Princeton Univ, 1960-1961; Res assocphysics, Univ Chicago, 1960. **Memberships:** Sigma Xi; Fedn Am Scientists; Fel AAAS; fel Am Phys Soc; Am Astron Soc; AmGeophys Union. **Research Statement & Publications:** Physics of the origin of cosmic rays and related astrophysical problems; statistical physics of cosmic ray origin and propagation in the galaxy. **Mailing Address:** Lab High Energy Astrophys, Goddard Space Flight Ctr, NASA, Greenbelt, MD 20771. **Fax:** 301-286-1682. **E-Mail:** frank.c.jones@nasa.gov

JONES, FRANK NORTON, POLYMER SYNTHESIS, ORGANIC COATINGS. **Personal Data:** b Columbia, Mo, December 27, 1936; div, c David. **Education:** Oberlin Col, AB, 1958; Univ Duke, PhD (org chem), 1962. **Honors & Awards:** Roon Found Prizes, 1986, 1987, 1991; Matiello lectr, 1995; Roy W Tess award, 2001. **Professional Experience:** PROF & DIR, COATINGS RES CTR, NSF, 1990-; prof & chair, Dept Polymers & Coatings, NDak State Univ, 1983-1990; res & develop mgr, Cargill Inc, 1979-1983; tech mgr, Celanese Polymer Specialties Co, 1973-1979; res supvr, Cent Res Dept, E I Du Pont Co, 1970-1973; staff chemist, Cent Res Dept, E I Du Pont Co, 1968-1970; res chemist, Cent Res Dept, E I Du Pont Co, 1963-1968; fel, Mass Inst Technol, 1962-1963; instr, org chem, Univ Duke, 1961-1962. **Memberships:** Am Chem Soc; Fedn Soc Coatings Technol. **Research Statement & Publications:** Synthetic polymer chemistry; polymer structure/property relationships; polymeric materials; coatings; Published Over 130 articles. **Mailing Address:** Coatings Res Inst 430 W Forest Ave, Eastern Mich Univ, Ypsilanti, MI 48197. **Fax:** 313-483-0085. **E-Mail:** frank.jones@emich.edu

JONES, FRANKLIN DEL, COMBAT STRESS, PSYCHOPHARMACOLOGY. **Personal Data:** b Hereford, Tex, September 22, 1935; m 1957, June; c Gregory, Geoffrey, Gresham & Giselle. **Education:** Baylor Univ, BS, 1957; Univ Tex, Dallas, MD, 1961. **Professional Experience:** PROF, TEX SOUTHERN UNIV, as of 2003; secy treas, Neuropsychiat & Human Serv Found, 1995-; psychiat & neurol consult, Surgeon Gen Army, 1977-1981; psychiat & Neurol consult, Army Surgeon Gen, 1977-1981; CLIN PROF, UNIFORMED SERVS, UNIV HEALTH SCI, 1975-; clin consult psychiat, 1973-; clin prof, Georgetwon Univ Med Sch, 1973-1994; dir pyschiat educ, Walter Reed Army Med Ctr, 1971-1973 & forensic psychiat, 1973-1977 & 1985-1988; chief psychiat sev, Walter Reed Army Med Ctr, 1971-1973 & forensic psychiat, 1973-1977; dir res ward, Walter Reed Army Med Ctr, 1968-1973; resident psychiat, Walter Reed Army Med Ctr, 1961-1965; intern med & surg, Ireland Army Hosp, Ft Knox, Ky, 1961-1962. **Memberships:** World Psychiat Asn (pres 1977-1983 secy 1983-1989); fel Am Psychiat Asn. **Research Statement & Publications:** Studies of combat stress in Vietnam, Egypt and Israel; post-traumatic stress disorder in combat veterans and rape victims; psychopharmacology of eating disorders and performance; use of BEAM (brain electrical activity mapping) in ADHD; author of six books. **Mailing Address:** Sch Pub Affairs, Tex Southern Univ, Rockville, MD 20852-3733. **Fax:** 301-881-3732.

JONES, FRANKLIN M, SCIENCE EDUCATION. **Personal Data:** b Reidsville, NC, March 10, 1933; m 1963, c 2. **Education:** Appalachian State Teachers Col, BS, 1955, MA, 1960; Univ NC, MEd, 1960; Univ Ga, EdD(sci educ), 1966. **Honors & Awards:** Donald M. Dedmon Award Prof Excellence, 1995. **Professional Experience:** Prof emer, Radford Univ, 1996-; RETIRED; prof phys sci, RadfordUniv, 1968-1996; assoc prof, Radford Univ, 1966-1968; prof chem, Ferrum JrCol, 1960-1964; Teacher, High Sch, Va, 1955-1956 & NC, 1956-1958. **Mailing Address:** 28 Pine View Dr, Radford, VA 24141.

JONES, FREDERICK GOODWIN, permanent magnets, powder metallurgy; deceased, see previous edition for last biography

JONES, GALEN EVERTS, MARINE MICROBIOLOGY, MICROBIAL BIOGEOCHEMISTRY. **Personal Data:** b Milwaukee, Wis, September 9, 1928; m 1986, Eleonore Angell Jones; c Galen R, Swenith G & Christopher. **Education:** Dartmouth Col, AB, 1950; Williams Col, MA, 1952; Rutgers Univ, PhD (microbiol), 1956. **Professional Experience:** EMER PROF, UNIV NH, 1991-; UNIV NH, 1991-; Interim Sea Grant, 1986-1987; chmn dept, Microbiol, 1975-1980 & Marine Sci Labs, 1985-1987; vis prof, Scripps Inst Oceanog, Univ Calif, 1981; mem exec panel, Oceanog Div, NSF, 1979-1980; mem, Inst Ecol Adv Panel to Nat Comn Water Qual, Washington, DC, 1974-1976; mem adv panel biol oceanog, NSF, 1971-1972, 1974-1975; vis prof oceanog, Univ Liverpool, 1971-1973; lectr, Marine Biol Lab, Woods Hole, 1971-1972; Consult Arthur D Little Co, Mass, 1969-1970 & 1973-1974 & Normandeau Assocs, Inc, NH, 1970-1971; mem, Santa Barbara Oil Spill Panel, Exec Off of the Pres, 1969-1970; prof microbiol, Univ NH, 1966-1991; dir, Jackson Estuarine Lab, 1966-1972 & 1983-1987; dir, Jackson Estuarine Lab, Univ NH, 1966-1972; mem, Nat Sea-Grant Univ Comt, 1965-1967; nonresident assoc microbiol, Woods Hole Oceanog Inst, 1964-1972; Off Naval Res contract, 1963-1964 & 1966-1968; assoc prof biol, Boston Univ, 1963-1966; Bendix-Pac, Calif, 1960; Div Water Supply & Pollution Control, USPHS, 1959-1962, 1963-1966; consult, Eli Lilly & Co, Ind, 1958-1959; Res grants, Nat Inst Allergy & Infectious Dis, 1957-1959; from jr res microbiologist to asst res microbiologist, Div Marine Biol, Scripps Inst Oceanog, Univ Calif, 1955-1963; from jr res microbiologist to asst res microbiologist, Rockefeller fel, 1955-1957; res asst, Tex Gulf Sulfur, Rutgers Univ, 1952-1955; Asst, WilliamsCol, 1950-1952. **Memberships:** Fel AAAS; fel Am Acad Microbiol (pres, aquatic microbiol, 1969-1970); Sigma Xi; Am Soc Microbiol; Oceanog Soc. **Research Statement & Publications:** Biochemicals and trace elements in sea water; chemosynthesis; fractionation of stable isotopes of sulfur in microorganisms; biogeochemistry; elemental composition of bacteria. **Mailing Address:** 6684 Michaeljohn Dr, La Jolla, CA 92037. **Fax:** 858-459-6688.

JONES, GARTH, NUCLEAR PHYSICS. **Personal Data:** b Victoria, BC, March 27, 1932. **Education:** Univ BC, BA, 1953, MSc, 1955, PhD (physics), 1959. **Professional Experience:** PROF EMER PHYSICS, UNIV BC, as of 1997; prof physics, Univ BC, beginning 1969; Guggenheimfel, 1967-1968; from asst prof to assoc prof, Univ BC, 1961-1969; Rutherford Mem fel, Nat ResCoun Can overseas fel nuclear physics, 1960-1961; Rutherford Mem fel, Clarendon Lab, OxfordUniv, 1960; jr sci officer electronics, Atomic Energy Can, Ltd, 1955-1956. **Memberships:** Can Asn Physicists; Am Phys Soc. **Research Statement & Publications:** Nuclear reactions; positron annihilation; intermediate energy physics. **Mailing Address:** Dept Physics, Univ BC, Vancouver, BC V6T 1Z1, Can. **E-Mail:** jones@physics.ubc.ca

JONES, GARTH WICKS, MICROBIOLOGY. **Personal Data:** b Aberdare, Wales, September 23, 1940; m 1964, c 3. **Education:** Univ Reading, BSc, 1969, PhD (microbiol), 1972. **Professional Experience:** PROF EMER MICROBIOL & IMMUNOL, UNIV MICH, ANN ARBOR, as of 2005; from asst prof microbiol to prof microbiol & immunol, Univ Mich, Ann Arbor, beginning 1975; scholar, Univ Mich, Ann Arbor, 1974-1975; sr sci officer microbiol, Inst Res Animal Dis, Brit Agr Res Coun, 1972-1975. **Memberships:** Soc Gen Microbiol; Brit Soc Appl Bact; Am Soc Microbiol. **Research Statement & Publications:** Nature and function of the adhesive properties of bacteria, particularly enteric pathogens, and the composition of the eukaryotic cell components with which bacterial adhesive substances interact. **Mailing Address:** Dept Microbiol, Univ Mich Med Sch, 1301 Catherine Rd 6643 Med Sci Bldg 2, Ann Arbor, MI 48109-0608.

JONES, GARY EDWARD, GENETICS, CELL BIOLOGY. **Personal Data:** b Metropolis, Ill, June 2, 1940; m 1964, c 1. **Education:** Univ Ill, Urbana, BS, 1962, MS, 1964; Univ Calif, Berkeley, PhD (biophys), 1970. **Professional Experience:** ASSOC PROF GENETICS, UNIV CALIF, RIVERSIDE, 1979-; asst prof genetics, Univ Calif, Riverside, 1978-1979; asst prof biol, Univ Calif, Riverside, 1973-1978; staff geneticist, Hosp for Sick C, Toronto, Ont, 1971-1973; NIH fel biophys, Pa State Univ, 1970-1971. **Memberships:** Sigma Xi; AAAS; Genetic Soc Am; Am Soc Microbiol. **Research Statement & Publications:** Biochemical genetics of amino acid utilization in yeast; somatic cell genetics of cultured animal and plant cells. **Mailing Address:** Dept Bot & Plant Sci, Univ Calif, 900 Univ Ave, Riverside, CA 92521.

JONES, GEOFFREY MELVILL, NEUROSCIENCES, AEROSPACE MEDICINE. **Personal Data:** b Shelford, Eng, January 14, 1923; m 1953, Jenny; c Kathanne, Francis, Andrew & Dorothy. **Education:** Cambridge Univ, BA, 1944, MA, 1947, MB, BCh, 1949. **Honors & Awards:** Harry G Armstrong Award Res Aerospace Med, Aerospace Med Asn, 1968, Arnold D Tuttle Award, 1971; Skylab Achievement Award, NASA, 1974; Dohlman Medal, Dohlman Soc, 1987; Quinquennial Gold Medal, Barany Soc, 1988; Wilbur Franks Award, 1988; Stewart Mem LectrAward, Royal Aeronaut Soc London, 1989; Ashton Graybiel Lectr Award, US Naval Aerospace Med Res Lab, 1989; Buchanan-Barbour Award, 1990; McLaughlinMedal, Royal Soc Can, 1991. **Professional Experience:** ADJ PROF, DEPT CLIN NEUROSCIENCE, UNIV CALGARY, as of 2004; vis prof, clin neuroscience, Univ Calgary, beginning 1991; prof emer physiol, Mcgill Univ, Can, beginning 1991; vis prof, Univ Calgary, 1983; vis prof, Univ Tex, Galveston, 1982; adj prof, Col France, 1979 & 1995; vis prof, Col Del France, Paris, 1979; Hosmer res prof, McGillUniv, 1978-1991; vis prof, Stanford Univ, 1971-1972; sr res assoc, Nat Acad Sci, 1971-1972; prof physiol & dir, McGill Univ, 1968-1988; dir aviation med, Aerospace Med Res Unit, 1961-1988; assoc prof, McGill Univ, 1961-1968; sci officer, Med Res Coun, Gt Brit, 1955-1961; sci medofficer, RAF Inst Aviation Med, Eng, 1951-1955; surgeon, Ear, Nose & Throat, AddenbrookesHosp, Cambridge, 1950-1951; house surgeon, Middlesex Hosp, London, 1949-1950; assoc mem, Ctr Studies Age & Aging, McGill Univ & Dept Neurol & Neurosurg. **Memberships:** Can Physiol Soc; UK Physiol Soc; Am Soc Neuroscience; fel Can Aeronaut & SpaceInst; fel Royal Soc Can; fel Royal Soc London; fel Royal Aeronaut Soc London; fel AmAerospace Med Asn; Can Soc Aerospace Med Soc. **Research Statement & Publications:** Neurophysiology of postural control, vestibular and oculomotor systems; respiration at high altitude; long duration flying fatigue; high altitude bail out; pilot disorientation; adaptive plasticity in brainstem reflexes; cognitive management of subcortical reflexes; author of numerous publications. **Mailing Address:** Dept Physiol, Univ Calgary, Heritage Med Res Bldg, 3330 Hosp Dr N W, Calgary, AB T2N 4N1, Can. **Fax:** 403-283-8731. **E-Mail:** gmelvill@ucalgary.ca

JONES, GEORGE HENRY, BIOCHEMISTRY, MOLECULAR BIOLOGY. **Personal Data:** b Muskogee, Okla, February 21, 1942; m 1965. **Education:** Univ Fla, BS, 1980; Univ Calif, Berkeley, MS, 1985, PhD (mat sci eng), 1987. **Professional Experience:** Goodrich C White Prof Biol, Emory Univ, 1996-; prof biol, Emory Univ, 1995-1996; assoc vpres res & grad studies & dean grad scharts & sci, Emory Univ, 1989-1995; assoc prof biol sci & cell & molecular biol, Univ Mich, Ann Arbor, 1974-1990; asst prof zoology, Univ Mich, Ann Arbor, 1971-1974; fel, Univ Geneva, 1970-1971; Helen HayWhitney Found fels, NIH, 1968-1970. **Memberships:** Am Soc Biochem & Molecular Biol; Dir Coalition AdvanBlacks Biomedical Sci; NY Acad Sci; Am Soc Microbiol; AAAS. **Research Statement & Publications:** Mammalian protein biosynthesis, specifically initiation mechanisms; immunoglobulin biosynthesis; cellular regulatory mechanisms. **Mailing Address:** Grad Sch Arts & Sci Emory Univ, 202 Admin Bldg, Atlanta, GA 30322-2690. **Fax:** 404-727-4990. **E-Mail:** george.h.jones@emory.edu

JONES, GERALD MURRAY, DAIRY SCIENCE, ANIMAL PRODUCTION FOOD SAFETY. **Personal Data:** b Gouverneur, NY, April 17, 1941; m 1963, Joanne; c Jere, Tim & Michelle. **Education:** Cornell Univ. BS, 1962; Univ Maine, MS, 1964; Penn State Univ, PhD (dairy sci), 1968. **Honors & Awards:** West Agro Award Mastitis Res, Am Dairy Sci Asn. **Professional Experience:** RETIRED, PROF EMER, VA POLYTECH INST & STATE UNIV, as of 2002; prof & exten dairy scientist, Dairy Sci, Va Tech, 1997-2002; assoc dir, Agr & Natural Resources, Va Tech, 1995-1997; assoc dir progs & asst dir, ANR, Va Tech, 1994-1995; exten progs coordr & asst dir, ANR, Va Tech, 1992-1994; asst dir, Agr & Natural Resources, Va Tech, 1991-1992; prof & dairy exten proj leader, Dairy Sci, Va Tech, 1979-1991; EXTEN DAIRY SCIENTIST, VA POLYTECH INST & STATE UNIV, 1974-; assoc prof, VA PolytechInst & State Univ, 1974-1979; from asst prof to assoc prof animal sci, Macdonald Col, McGill Univ, 1968-1979; grad asst, Pa State Univ, 1964-1968; grad fel, Univ Maine, 1963-1964; grad asst, Univ Maine, 1962-1963. **Memberships:** Nat Mastitis

Coun; Am Dairy Sci Asn. **Research Statement & Publications:** Milking management, practices and systems; mastitis; calf nutrition and management; dairy cattle nutrition; dairy herd management. **Mailing Address:** 1010 Madison Lane, Blacksburg, VA 24060. **E-Mail:** gmjones@vt.edu

JONES, GERALD WALTER, PHOTOGRAPHIC CHEMISTRY, POLYMER APPLICATIONS. **Personal Data:** b Utica, NY, June 25, 1942; m 1977, Terry. **Education:** Hartwick Col, BA, 1964; Syracuse Univ, PhD (org chem), 1970. **Professional Experience:** SR ENGR, IBM CORP, 1981-; res chemist, GAF Corp, 1974-1981; fel, Ohio State Univ, 1970-1974; lab asst chem, Hartwick Col, 1964-1965. **Memberships:** Am Chem Soc. **Research Statement & Publications:** Photolysis of alpha, beta-unsaturated ketones and carbene chemistry; photographic science, resilient sheet vinyl flooring and photoresists; photoresists. **Mailing Address:** 1070 Forest Hill Rd, Apalachin, NY 13732.

JONES, GIFFIN DENISON, ORGANIC CHEMISTRY. **Personal Data:** b Fond du Lac, Wis, December 16, 1918; m 1939, c 4. **Education:** Univ Wis, BS, 1939; Univ Ill, PhD (org chem), 1942. **Professional Experience:** RES SCIENTIST, PHYS RES LAB, DOW CHEM CO, 1970-; dir, E C BrittonLab, Dow Chem Co, 1968-1970; dir, Phys Res Lab, Dow Chem Co, 1956-1968; res chemist, Phys Res Lab, Dow Chem Co, 1947-1956; res chemist, Cent Res Labs, Gen Aniline & Film Corp, Pa, 1944-1947; civilian with Off Sci Res & Develop, 1944; instr org chem, Univ Iowa, 1942-1944. **Memberships:** Am Chem Soc. **Research Statement & Publications:** Polymers; organic reaction mechanism. **Mailing Address:** 4002 Cambridge St, Midland, MI 48642-3694.

JONES, GLENN CLARK, ORGANIC & POLYMER CHEMISTRY, TECHNICAL MANAGEMENT. **Personal Data:** b Raleigh, NC, August 22, 1935; m 1965, c 2. **Education:** Wake Forest Col, BS, 1957; Duke Univ, PhD (chem), 1962. **Professional Experience:** RES ASSOC, TENN EASTMAN CO, 1984-; from res chemist to sr reschemist, Tenn Eastman CO, 1962-1984; Res assoc org chem, Duke Univ, 1961-1962. **Memberships:** Am Chem Soc; Sigma Xi. **Research Statement & Publications:** Base catalyzed rearrangements; polymer feasibility studies; free radical chemistry; organic electrochemistry; hydroquinone, solvent and powder coatings. **Mailing Address:** 3620 Hemlock Park Dr, Kingsport, TN 37663-2057.

JONES, GORDON ERVIN, PHYSICS. **Personal Data:** b Greenwood, Miss, July 23, 1936; m 1961, Linda; c Gordon S & Chad M. **Education:** Miss State Univ, BS, 1958; Duke Univ, PhD (physics), 1964. **Professional Experience:** DEAN EMER, SCH SCI & MATH, COL CHARLESTON, as of 2002; chancellor, Col Charleston, 1992-1993; PROF PHYSICS SCH SCI & MATH, COL CHARLESTON, 1991-; dean, Sch Sci & Math, Col Charleston, 1991-2001; prof, Miss State Univ, 1972-1991; from asst prof to assoc prof physics, MissState Univ, 1964-1972. **Memberships:** Am Phys Soc; Am Asn Physics Teachers; Am Asn Higher Educ. **Research Statement & Publications:** Microwave spectroscopy. **Mailing Address:** Dept Physics & Astron, Sch Sci & Math, Col Charleston, 402, Bell Bldg, Charleston, SC 29424. **Fax:** 843-953-4824. **E-Mail:** jonesg@cofc.edu

JONES, GORDON HENRY, ORGANIC CHEMISTRY. **Personal Data:** b Stockport, Eng, April 2, 1940; m 1963, c 2. **Education:** Cambridge Univ, BA, 1962, MA, 1966, PhD, 1965. **Professional Experience:** RES CHEMIST, SYNTEX INST ORG CHEM, 1966-; fel org chem, Syntex Inst Org Chem, 1965-1966. **Memberships:** Am Chem Soc; Royal Soc Chem. **Research Statement & Publications:** Application of new reactions in carbohydrate and nucleoside chemistry; peptide chemistry. **Mailing Address:** 2635 Park Blvd, Palo Alto, CA 94306.

JONES, GRAHAM ALFRED, AGRICULTURAL MICROBIOLOGY. **Personal Data:** b London, Eng, May 8, 1935; m 1963, Judy; c Alison M, Kevin G, Susan E & Jennifer D. **Education:** Univ Leeds, BSc, 1957; McGill Univ, MSc, 1958, PhD (agr bact), 1963. **Honors & Awards:** Queen's Jubilee Medal, 1977. **Professional Experience:** PROF EMER APPL MICROBIOL & FOOD SCI, UNIV SASK, as of 2003; ASSOC DEAN AGR, UNIV SASK, 1994-; vis scientist, Agr Can, 1992-1993; prof appl microbiol & food sci, Univ Sask, beginning 1982; head dept, Dept Microbiol, SchMed, 1981-1992; assoc, Dept Microbiol, Sch Med, 1979-1992; vis scientist, Agr Res Coun InstAnimal Physiol, Babraham, Eng, 1978-1979; lectr microbiol, Univ Sask, 1975-1979; vis prof, NatRes Coun Can, 1974; from assoc prof to prof dairy & food sci, Univ Sask, 1967-1982; asst profdairy sci, Univ Sask, 1963-1968; lectr agr bact, McGill Univ, 1958-1960. **Memberships:** Am Soc Microbiol; Can Soc Microbiol (secy-treas, 1970-1973, pres, 1982-1983); AgrInst Can; Can Soc Animal Sci. **Research Statement & Publications:** Rumen microbiology; agricultural fermentations. **Mailing Address:** Dept Appl Microbiol & Food Sci, Univ Sask, 6D60, Agr Bldg, Saskatoon, SK S7N 5A8, Can. **Fax:** 306-966-8894. **E-Mail:** jonesg@sask.usask.ca

JONES, GUILFORD II, PHYSICAL ORGANIC CHEMISTRY, PHOTOCHEMISTRY. **Personal Data:** b Jackson, Tenn, November 24, 1943; m 1966, c Jason G & David D. **Education:** Rhodes Col, BS, 1965; Univ Wis-Madison, PhD (chem), 1970. **Professional Experience:** PROF PHOTONICS RES, BOSTON UNIV, 1994-; PROF BIOPHYSICS, SCH MED, BOSTON UNIV, 1994-; dept chmn, Boston Univ, 1989-1993; PROF CHEM, BOSTON UNIV, 1982-; from asst prof to assoc prof, Boston Univ, 1971-1982; NIH fel, Yale Univ, 1969-1971. **Memberships:** Am Chem Soc; Sigma Xi; Interamerican Photochem Soc; AAAS. **Research Statement & Publications:** Photochemical conversion of energy; mechanisms and applications of photochemical reactions; dye photochemistry; photoeffects for polymer-bound chromophores; photoactive peptides. **Mailing Address:** Dept Chem, Boston Univ, 590 Commonwealth Ave, Boston, MA 02215. **Fax:** 617-353-6466. **E-Mail:** jones@chem.bu.edu

JONES, GUY LANGSTON, PLANT BREEDING. **Personal Data:** b Kinston, NC, June 7, 1923; m 1948, Margaret W; c Margaret (Harvey) & Guy L Jr. **Education:** NC State Col, BS, 1947, MS, 1950; Univ Minn, PhD, 1952. **Honors & Awards:** Agron Exten Educ Award, Am Soc Agron. **Professional Experience:** Inst Soil Sci, Mex, 1987-1991; Inst Soil Sci, Guatemala, 1987 & 1988; Inst Soil Sci, Dominican Repub, 1987 & 1988; PROF EMER CROP SCI, NC STATE UNIV, 1985-; Inst Soil Sci, Nanjing, China, 1985-1991; head crop sci exten, NC State Univ, 1975-1985; Agency Int Develop, Guatemala, 1964-1965 & Philippines, 1964-1965 & Food & Agr Orgn, Arg, 1974; TOBACCO PROD & AGRON EXTEN PROGS, NC STATE UNIV, 1971-; head agron exten, NC State Univ, 1965-1975; Inst Tobacco, Dominican Repub, 1963; prof crop sci, NC State Univ, 1961-1985; prof crop sci, NC State Univ, 1961-1965; Ministry Agr, Venezuela, 1959; assoc prof field crops, NC State Univ, 1958-1961; asst prof dept agron, NC State Univ, 1952-1958; asst dept agron & plant genetics, Univ Minn, 1950-1952; Supt br sta, NC Agr Exp Sta, 1947-1949; assoc ed, Agron J. **Memberships:** Fel Am Soc Agron; Sigma Xi; Crop Sci Soc Am. **Research Statement & Publications:** Tobacco genetics; tobacco variety evaluation; agronomy extension. **Mailing Address:** Dept Crop Sci, NC State Univ, 3435 Blue Ridge Rd, Raleigh, NC 27612-8014. **Fax:** 919-787-7542.

JONES, GWILYM STRONG, MAMMALOGY, VERTEBRATE ECOLOGY. **Personal Data:** b Cincinnati, Ohio, May 4, 1942; m 1967, c 3. **Education:** Hanover Col, BA, 1964; Purdue Univ, MS, 1967; Ind State Univ, PhD (mammal syst), 1981. **Professional Experience:** DIR, CTR VERT STUDIES, NORTHEASTERN UNIV, as of 2005; Nature Conservancy, 1984; US Fish Wildlife Serv, 1983; grants, NH Fish Game Dept, 1980-1986; Pub Archeol Lab, Brown Univ, 1980; grants, US Dept Health & Human Serv, 1978 & 1981; PROF BIOL, NORTHEASTERN UNIV, 1976-; grants, Theodore Roosevelt Mem Fund & Am Mus Natural Hist, 1974; mus specialist, Smithsonian Inst, 1970-1971; grants, Am Inst Biol Sci, 1970; Collabr mammal div, Smithsonian Inst, 1970; adv, Chinese Asn Conserv Nature & Natural Resources, 1969-1970; res investr, Naval Med Res Unit 2, Taiwan, 1967-1969. **Memberships:** Am Soc Mammalogists; Soc Syst Zoology; Sigma Xi; Soc Marine Mammalogy; Wildlife Soc. **Research Statement & Publications:** Mammalian systematics; vertebrate food habits; ectoparasites and demographics. **Mailing Address:** Dept Biol, Northeastern Univ, 360 Huntington Ave 134 Mugar Life Sci, Boston, MA 02115-5096. **Fax:** 617-373-3724. **E-Mail:** g.jones@nunet.neu.edu

JONES, HAROLD LESTER, ORGANIC CHEMISTRY. **Personal Data:** b Nampa, Idaho, June 19, 1943; m 1965, Pamela; c Rhiannon & Dorothy. **Education:** Ore State Univ, BS, 1965; Univ Colo, PhD (chem), 1969. **Professional Experience:** PROF CHEM, COLO COL, 1986-; dept chair, colo col, 1981-1995; assoc prof, Colo Col, 1976-1986; res assoc, Univ Colo, 1972; asst prof, Colo Col, 1969-1976; res asst, Univ Colo, 1965-1969. **Memberships:** Am Chem Soc. **Research Statement & Publications:** Nuclear magnetic resonance; small ring chemistry, bicyclic systems and cyclopropanols; free radical reactions in cyclopropanols; photochemistry of bicyclic-spiro-compounds; molecular modeling, computational chemistry. **Mailing Address:** Dept Chem, Colo Col, 14 E Cache La Poudre St, Colorado Springs, CO 80903-1989. **Fax:** 719-389-6182. **E-Mail:** hjones@ColoradoCollege.edu

JONES, HELENA L, ANATOMY, MEDICAL SCIENCES. **Personal Data:** b Columbus, Ohio, June 26, 1940; m 1965, c 2. **Education:** Ohio State Univ, BSc, 1962, PhD (anat) 1968. **Professional Experience:** Eau Claire Community cancer grant, 1980, 1981, 1982; fels biomed sci, Wash, DC, 1977 & 1978; consult, Adv Comt Estab Med HistolTechnicians Assoc Degree, 1976-; ASST PROF BIOL, UNIV WIS-EAU CLAIRE, 1975-; NIH staff fel, Nat Inst Environ Health Sci 1972-1975; instr anat, Med Ctr, Ind Univ, Indianapolis, 1968-1969; mem review panels, NSF. **Memberships:** Am Asn Anatomists; Sigma Xi; NY Acad Sci. **Research Statement & Publications:** Skin cancer; endocrinology; bone. **Mailing Address:** 5729 Elm Rd Rte 3, Eau Claire, WI 54701.

JONES, HOBART WAYNE, ANIMALBREEDING. **Personal Data:** b Logansport, Ind, April 15, 1921; m 1943, c 4. **Education:** Purdue Univ, BSA, 1943; Ohio State Univ, MSA, 1946, PhD (animal prod), 1960. **Professional Experience:** EMER PROF ANIMAL SCI, PURDUE UNIV, 1989-; from assoc prof to prof animal sci, Purdue Univ, 1950-1989. **Memberships:** Am Soc Animal Sci. **Research Statement & Publications:** Animal production; swine nutrition and environmental studies. **Mailing Address:** 104 N Sharon Chapel Rd, W Lafayette, IN 47906.

JONES, HOWARD ST CLAIRE, JR, electronics engineering, microwave physics; deceased, see previous edition for last biography

JONES, IRA, ZOOLOGY, PARASITOLOGY. **Personal Data:** b Bartow, Fla, January 22, 1934; m 1957, c 2. **Education:** Benedict Col, BS, 1955; Atlanta Univ, MS, 1957; Wayne State Univ, PhD (biol), 1966. **Professional Experience:** PROFBIOL, CALIF STATE UNIV, LONG BEACH, as of 1999; dir & consult parasitol, Jones Biomed & Lab, Long Beach, Calif, beginning 1977; from asst prof to assoc prof, Calif State Univ, Long Beach, 1969-1977; Calif State Univ Long Beach Found grant, 1969-1971; PR Nuclear Ctr grant, 1969; consult, Nat Commun Dis Ctr, 1969; Sigma Xi res grant, 1968-1969; grant, Caribbean Inst & Study Ctr for Latin Am, 1968-1969; assoc prof, Inter-Am Univ PR, 1966-1969; assoc prof, Fla Agr & Mech Univ, 1964-1966; USPHS fel, 1961; instr biol, SavannahState Col, 1957-1959. **Memberships:** Am Soc Parasitol; Am Inst Biol Sci; Soc Protozool. **Research Statement & Publications:** Research on the endosymbionts of Sipunculids, including, zoogeography of parasitism, host specificity, life cycles of parasites and the cytochemistry and ultra-structure of Sipunculids sporozoa. **Mailing Address:** Dept Biol, Calif State Univ 3702 Csulb, Long Beach, CA 90840-0004. **E-Mail:** irajones@csulb.edu

JONES, IRENE M, GENETICS. **Education:** Univ Rochester, BS, BA; Univ Ill, PhD (molecular biol). **Professional Experience:** SR STAFF SCIENTIST, LAWRENCE LIVERMORE NAT LAB, as of 2005. **Mailing Address:** Biomed Sci Div Lawrence Livermore Nat Lab, L-452 7000 E Ave PO Box 5507, Livermore, CA 94551-5507. **Fax:** 925-422-2282. **E-Mail:** jones20@llnl.gov

JONES, IRVING WENDELL, STRUCTURAL ENGINEERING & MECHANICS. **Personal Data:** b Washington, DC. **Education:** Howard Univ, BS, 1953; Columbia Univ, MS, 1957; Polytech Inst Brooklyn, PhD (appl mech), 1967. **Professional Experience:** PROF CIVIL ENG, SCH ENG, HOWARD UNIV, 1972-; assoc prof, Howard Univ, 1969-1972; lectr, Grad Sch, Stevens Inst Technol, 1968-1969; mem, Pressure Vessel Res Coun, Welding ResFound, 1964-1969; asst dir & partner, Appl Technol Assocs Inc, 1963-1969; asst aerospace &mech, Polytech Inst Brooklyn, 1962-1963; consult, Space Div, Fairchild-Hiller Corp, 1962-1964 & Dist Eng Serv Inc, beginning 1977; struct engr, Grumman Aerospace Corp, 1957-1962; asst civil eng, Columbia Univ, 1956-1957. **Memberships:** Am Soc Civil Engrs (pres, 1969); Am Soc Mech Engrs (pres, 1964); Am Soc Eng Educ (pres, 1969). **Research Statement & Publications:** Developed methods for computer-aided structural analysis including high temperature effects; helped develop shock-absorbing mounts and foundations for sensitive shipboard equipment; developed analysis methods for effects of high temperature on aerospace structures. **Mailing Address:** Dept Civil Eng, Sch Eng, Howard Univ, 2300 6th St NW, Washington, DC 20059. **E-Mail:** jones@cldc.howard.edu

JONES, IVAN DUNLAVY, FOOD SCIENCE. **Personal Data:** b Holdrege, Nebr, December 10, 1903; m 1996, Ruby; c Lucia & Ivan Jr. **Education:** Nebr Wesleyan Univ, AB, 1926; Univ Minn, PhD (agr biochem), 1931. **Professional Experience:** Vis prof, Middle East Tech Univ, Ankara, Turkey 1979-1980; consult food sci& technol, beginning 1970; PROF EMER FOOD SCI, NC STATE UNIV, 1970-; consult dir, Spec Fund, UN, Brazil & Dominican Repub, 1962; prof food sci, NC State Univ, 1961-1970; prof hort, NCState Univ, 1945-1961; assoc horticulturist, Exp Sta, NC State Univ, 1931-1945; instr agrbiochem, Univ Minn, 1929-1930. **Memberships:** Am Chem Soc; fel Inst Food Technol; fel Am Pub Health Asn; fel Am Inst Chem; Sigma Xi. **Research Statement & Publications:** Chemical composition of fruits and vegetables and their processing by freezing, canning, dehydration and brining; estimation of chlorophylls and their metal derivatives; influence preservation technique on chlorophyll. **Mailing Address:** Dept Food Sci, NC State Univ, 100 Schaub Food Sci Bldg, PO Box 7624, Raleigh, NC 27601. **Fax:** 919-515-4694.

JONES, J BENTON, SOIL FERTILITY, PLANT NUTRITION. **Personal Data:** b Tyrone, Pa, April 4, 1930; m 1955, c 3. **Education:** Univ Ill, BS, 1952; Pa State Univ, MS, 1956, PhD (agron), 1959. **Honorary Degrees:** Dr, Univ Hort, Budapest, Hungary, 1987. **Professional Experience:** PROF EMER HORT, UNIV GA, as of 2003; VPRES, MICRO-MACRO

INT INC, ATHENS, GA, 1990-; exec ed, J PlantNutrit, 1979-; prof hort, Univ Ga, 1979-1989; Agron Comt, Nat Fertilizer Solutions Asn, 1976-1980; mem, Inst Ecol, 1975-1989; div chmn, Dept Hort, Univ Ga, 1974-1979; bd mem, subcomt Environ Qual, 1974-1977; bd mem, Coun Agr Sci & Technol, 1973-1978; secy-treas, Soil Sci Soc Am, 1972-; exec ed, Commun Soil Sci & Plant Anal, 1969-; PRES, BENTON LABS INC, ATHENS, GA, 1969-; assoc referee, Plant Preparation, 1969-1989; assoc referee, Plant Anal Emission Spectros, Asn Off Anal Chemists, 1969-1983; Soil Testing & Plant AnalComt, Coun Soil Testing & Plant Anal, 1969-1972; prof agron, agr exten-agron, 1968-1979; consult, St Louis Testing Labs, 1967-1975; Soil Testing & Plant Anal Comt, Soil Sci Soc Am, 1967-1969; chmn, Micronutrient Comt, 1967-1969; from assoc prof to prof agron, Ohio AgrRes & Develop Ctr, 1959-1968. **Memberships:** Fel AAAS; fel Am Soc Agron; fel Soil Sci Soc Am; Int Soc Soil Sci; Am Soc HortSci; Asn Off Anal Chemists; Hydroponic Soc Am; Sigma Xi. **Research Statement & Publications:** Soil and plant chemistry, especially the micronutrients; soil fertility and plant nutrition related to crop production; soil testing and plant analysis; techniques of analysis by emission spectroscopy; techniques of giving plants in soilless media and hydroponically; author of numerous articles, books and book chapters and videos. **Mailing Address:** Dept Hort Univ Ga, PO Box 2007, Athens, GA 30612-2007. **Fax:** 706-548-4891.

JONES, J P, MATHEMATICS. **Personal Data:** b Los Angeles, Calif, September 9, 1941. **Education:** Univ Wash, BS, 1963, MS, 1966, PhD (math), 1968. **Honors & Awards:** Lester R Ford Award, Math Asn Am, 1977. **Professional Experience:** PROF EMER MATH, UNIV CALGARY, 1996-; fom asst prof to prof, Univ Calgary, 1968-1996. **Memberships:** Am Math Soc; Math Asn Am; Asn Symbolic Logic; Can Math Soc; Fibonacci Asn. **Research Statement & Publications:** Mathematical logic; number theory; recursive function theory; diophantine equations. **Mailing Address:** Dept Math & Statist, Univ Calgary, 2500 Univ Dr NW MS432, Calgary, AB T2N 1N4, Can. **Fax:** 403-282-5150. **E-Mail:** jpjones@math.ucalgary.ca

JONES, JACK EARL, AGRONOMY, PHYTOPATHOLOGY, PLANT BREEDING. **Personal Data:** b Elbert Co, Ga, July 30, 1925; m 1946, Henrietta; c Lynda J (Burdette). **Education:** Univ Ga, BS, 1948, MS, 1950; La State Univ, PhD, 1961. **Honors & Awards:** Gamma Sigma Delta Res Awards Merit 1978; First MS Award, Excellence in Ressearch 1978; Cotton Genetics Res Award, 1985; Doyle Chambers Res Award, 1988; Outstanding Alumni Award, LSU Ag Center 1999. **Professional Experience:** PROF EMER AGRON, LA STATE UNIV, BATON ROUGE, 1990-; from asst prof to prof, La State Univ, Baton Rouge, 1950-1990; consult. **Memberships:** Am Soc Agron; Crop Sci Soc Am; Sigma Xi LA Assoc Agron. **Research Statement & Publications:** Cotton breeding for superior fiber properties; resistance to diseases nematodis and insects; genetics of quantitative characters of cotton; cotton production practices. **Mailing Address:** Dept Agron, La State Univ, Baton Rouge, LA 70803-4001. **Fax:** 225-578-5855.

JONES, JACK EDENFIELD, POULTRY SCIENCE. **Personal Data:** b Jacksonville, Fla, October 24, 1929; m 1959, c 3. **Education:** Univ Fla, BS, 1951, MS, 1964, PhD (physiol), 1966. **Professional Experience:** RETIRED; prof, Clemson Univ, 1976-1989; from asst prof to assoc prof poultry, Clemson Univ, 1968-1976; asst dir res, Coop Mills, 1966-1968; sanitarian, St JohnsCounty Health Dept, 1958-1961; supvr farm mgt, Farmers Home Admin, 1956-1958. **Memberships:** Poultry Sci Asn. **Research Statement & Publications:** Nutrition; physiological-environmental relationships with turkeys and game birds. **Mailing Address:** 357 Mountain View Dr, Central, SC 29630.

JONES, JACK RAYMOND, RESERVOIR ENGINEERING, PRESSURE TRANSIENT ANALYSIS. **Personal Data:** b Tulsa, Okla, January 5, 1950; m 1970, Nora Metzger. **Education:** Univ Tulsa, BS, 1978, MS, 1982, PhD (petrol eng), 1985. **Professional Experience:** SR PETROL ENGR, BP TRINIDAD & TOBAGO, CAN, 2000-; Amoco Trinidad BU UNK, 1998; sr res engr, Amoco Prod Co, 1985-1997. **Memberships:** Soc Petrol Engrs; Sigma Xi. **Research Statement & Publications:** Identifying rock properties from pressure versus time responses of producing wells; effects of two-phase flow on such responses; methods for quantitative predicting rate and reserves from past well performance. **Mailing Address:** BP Can Energy Co, PO Box 200, 240 - 4th Ave SW, Calgary, AB T2P 2H8, Can.

JONES, J(AMES) B(EVERLY), MECHANICAL ENGINEERING. **Personal Data:** b Kansas City, Mo, August 21, 1923; m 1945, c 2. **Education:** Va Polytech Inst, BS, 1944; Purdue Univ, MS, 1947, PhD (mech eng), 1951. **Professional Experience:** PROF EMER MECH ENG, VA POLYTECH INST & STATE UNIV, 1988-; prof mech eng & head dept, Va Polytech Inst & State Univ, 1964-1988; NSF fac fel, Swiss FedInst Technol, 1961-1962; prof, Purdue Univ, 1957-1964; assoc prof mech eng, Purdue Univ, 1954-1957; sr proj engr, Allison Div, Gen Motors Corp, 1953; asst prof mech eng, Purdue Univ, 1951-1954; develop engr, Gen Elec Co, 1951-1952; serv engr, Babcock & Wilcox Co, 1948; instr, Purdue Univ, 1947-1951; asst instr mech eng, Purdue Univ, 1945-1947; asst mech engr, Eng Bd, US War Dept, Va, 1944-1945; CONSULT. **Memberships:** Am Soc Mech Engrs; Am Soc Eng Educ; Am Inst Aeronaut & Astronaut; SigmaXi. **Research Statement & Publications:** Fluid mechanics; thermodynamics. **Mailing Address:** Dept Mech Eng, VA Polytech Inst & State Univ, 100 Randolph Hall, Blacksburg, VA 24060.

JONES, JAMES DARREN, ACOUSTICS, VIBRATIONS. **Personal Data:** b Oak Ridge, Tenn, June 7, 1959; m 1982, c 2. **Education:** Tenn Technol Univ, BS, 1981; Va Polytech Inst & State Univ, MS, 1982, PhD (mech eng), 1987. **Honors & Awards:** Ruth & Joel Spira Award Excellence Teaching, Mec Eng Sch, Purdue Univ, 1997. **Professional Experience:** ASSOC HEAD, PURDUE UNIV, 1998-; ASSOC PROF, MECH ENG, PURDUE UNIV, 1991-; consult, Elgin Sweeper Co, 1989; NSF res grant active vibration control, 1988-1991; res grants, various agencies, 1988-1991; consult, Douglas Aircraft Co, McDonnell Douglas Corp, 1988; consult, Artesian Indust, 1988, 1990-; asst prof, Purdue Univ, 1987-1981; instr, Va Polytech Inst & State Univ, 1983-1987; res assoc, Acoust & Noise Reduction Div, NASA Langley Res Ctr, 1982-1983; res asst mech eng, Va Polytech Inst & State Univ, 1981-1982. **Memberships:** Acoust Soc Am; Am Inst Aeronaut & Astronaut; Am Soc Eng Educ; Am SocHeating Vent Air-conditioning & Refrig Engrs; Am Soc Mech Engrs; Inst Noise Control Eng. **Research Statement & Publications:** Acoustics, noise control, vibrations; active noise and vibration control; intelligent structures, distributed sensors and actuators; machinery noise, shell dynamics, structural/acoustics interactions; biomechanics, bionics, prosthetics; author of numerous publications on acoustics, noise control and vibrations. **Mailing Address:** Sch Mech Eng Purdue Univ, 1077 Ray W Herrick Labs, West Lafayette, IN 47907-1288. **Fax:** 765-494-0539. **E-Mail:** jonesjd@ecn.purdue.edu

JONES, JAMES DONALD, BIOCHEMISTRY. **Personal Data:** b Fond du Lac, Wis, October 5, 1930; m 1956, c 3. **Education:** Ripon Col, BA, 1952; Univ Wis, MS, 1956, PhD (biochem), 1958. **Professional Experience:** Mem, Am Bd Clin Chem, 1973; CONSULT, SECT CLIN CHEM, MAYO CLIN, 1961-; asst to staff sect biochem, Sect Clin Chem, Mayo Clin, 1960-1961; asst prof animal nutrit, Iowa State Univ, 1958-1960; prof lab med & assoc prof biochem, Mayo Med Sch. **Memberships:** Am Chem Soc; Am Inst Nutrit; Am Asn Clin Chem; fel Am Inst Chemists; fel NatAcad Clin Biochem. **Research Statement & Publications:** Nitrogen and electrolyte metabolism in animals; biochemistry of the young; metabolism of guanidines; inborn errors of metabolism. **Mailing Address:** Sect Clin Chem, Mayo Clin 200 First St SW, Rochester, MN 55905-0001.

JONES, JAMES HENRY, COMPARATIVE PHYSIOLOGY, RESPIRATORY-EXERCISE PHYSIOLOGY. **Personal Data:** b Phoenix, Ariz, October 23, 1952. **Education:** Univ Ariz, BS & BA, 1974, MS, 1976; Duke Univ, PhD (zoology), 1979; Colo State Univ, DVM, 1983. **Honors & Awards:** Scholander Award, Am Physiol Soc, 1986. **Professional Experience:** CHAIR, UNIV CALIF, DAVIS, as of 2005; PROF PHYSIOL, UNIV CALIF, DAVIS, 1996-; vis prof, Biosci Inst, Univ Sao Paulo, Brazil, 1990; from asst prof to assoc prof, Univ Calif, Davis, 1986-1996; vis prof, Anat Inst, Univ Berne, Switz, 1986; lectr biol, Harvard Univ, 1983-1986. **Memberships:** Am Physiol Soc; Am Soc Zoologists. **Research Statement & Publications:** Elucidate mechanisms limiting aerobic and anaerobic exercise performance in animals, especially birds and mammals; understand allometric (body-size) relationships between structure and function. **Mailing Address:** Dept Surg & Radiol Sci Univ Calif, 2112 Thurman Hall, Davis, CA 95616. **Fax:** 530-752-0414. **E-Mail:** jhjones@ucdavis.edu

JONES, JAMES HOLDEN, ORGANIC CHEMISTRY. **Personal Data:** b Parkersburg, WVa, February 2, 1928; m 1951, c 2. **Education:** WVa Univ, BS, 1950; Duke Univ, PhD (chem), 1958. **Professional Experience:** SR INVESTR, MERCK SHARP & DOHME RES LABS, 1984-; SR RESFEL, MERCK SHARP & DOHME RES LABS, 1980-; res fel, Merck & Co, Inc, 1964-1980; reschemist, Merck & Co, Inc, 1960-1964; Process chemist, Merck & Co, Inc, 1958-1960. **Memberships:** Am Chem Soc; Sigma Xi; AAAS. **Research Statement & Publications:** Diuretics; central nervous system. **Mailing Address:** 6036 Cannon Hill Rd, Ft Washington, PA 19034.

JONES, JAMES ROBERT, ANIMAL HUSBANDRY, NUTRITION. **Personal Data:** b Quicksand, Ky, December 8, 1931; m 1958, c 3. **Education:** Univ Ky, BS, 1953, MS, 1957; Cornell Univ, PhD (animal husb), 1961. **Professional Experience:** PROF EMER ANIMAL SCI (HUSB), NC STATE UNIV, as of 2003; HEAD, SWINE EXTEN, 1980-; exten specialist, Nc State Univ, beginning 1964; Experimentalist animal husb, Cornell Univ, 1961-1964. **Memberships:** Am Soc Animal Sci; Am Registry Prof Animal Scientists. **Research Statement & Publications:** Swine nutrition. **Mailing Address:** Dept Animal Sci, 201 Polk Hall, NC State Univ Box 7621, Raleigh, NC 27695-0001. **Fax:** 919-515-7780.

JONES, JANICE LORRAINE, BIOPHYSICS, CELL PHYSIOLOGY. **Personal Data:** b Takoma Park, Md, March 10, 1943; m 1967, Ronald; c Michael & Catherine. **Education:** St Bonaventure Univ, BS, 1965; Johns Hopkins Univ, PhD (biophys), 1970. **Professional Experience:** PROF PHYSIOL & BIOPHYS, GEORGETOWN UNIV, as of 2005; assoc prof physiol, Georgetown Univ, beginning 1987; prin investr, defibrillator induced dysfunction, 1981-1987; prin investr, NIH, defibrillator waveshape optimization, 1979-; from asst prof to assoc prof physiol, Sch Med, Case Western Res Univ, 1978-1987; res assoc, Dept Med, 1978; asst prof med technol, Univ Vt, 1970-1974; assoc ed, Biomed Electronics; consult, Physiocontrol Corp & Cardiac Pacemakers-NIH Study Sect. **Memberships:** Biophys Soc; Int Soc Heart Res; Am Physiol Soc; NAm Soc Pacing & Electrophysiol; fel Am Inst Med & Biol Eng. **Research Statement & Publications:** Cardiac physiology; physiology of cardiac cells in tissue culture; electrically induced myocardial damage. **Mailing Address:** Dept Physiol, Georgetown Univ, DVA Med Ctr 50 Irving St 247 Basic Sci, Washington, DC 20422. **E-Mail:** jjones04@georgetown.edu

JONES, JAY, BIOLOGY. **Education:** Southern Ill Univ, BA, BS, MS; Ind Univ, MA, PhD. **Professional Experience:** PROF BIOL & BIOCHEM, UNIV LA VERNE, as of 2005. **Mailing Address:** Dept Biol, Univ La Verne, 1950 Third St, La Verne, CA 91750. **E-Mail:** jonesj@ulv.edu

JONES, JEANETTE, MEDICAL MYCOLOGY, HISTOTECHNIQUES. **Personal Data:** b Ft Valley, Ga, September 19, 1950. **Education:** Ft Valley State Col, BSc, 1972; Ohio State Univ, MSc, 1973, PhD (bot, med mycol), 1976. **Honors & Awards:** Hons Award, NASA, 1985. **Professional Experience:** FAC SENATE PRES, ALA A&M UNIV, as of 2004; PROF, MED MYCOL, ALA A&M UNIV, 1986-; adj prof, Sch Pharm, Fla A&M Univ, 1985; Southern Asn Cols & Schs Reaffirmation Comt, 1982; prin investr, Biomed Res Training Prog, NIH, 1980; Nat Adv Coun, Sixteen Insts Health Sci Consortium, NC, 1979-1981; prin investr, Grad Traineeships, NSF, 1979; Northeast Ala State Jr Col, NSF, 1979-1980; Northeast Ala State Jr Col, NIH, 1978-1981, 1983; Northeast Ala State Jr Col, Riville, Ala, 1977; MEM GRAD FAC, ALA A&M UNIV, 1976-; consult, Ft Valley State Col, Ft Valley Ga, 1976; from asst prof to assoc prof, Ala A&M Univ, 1976-1985; grad teaching assoc, Ohio State Univ, 1973-1975; res apprenticeship org chem, Forestry Exp Lab, Macon, Ga, 1972; instr biol, Ft Valley State Col, 1972; Univ fel, Ohio State Univ, 1972-1973. **Memberships:** Med Mycol Soc Am; Sigma Xi; Int Soc Human & Animal Mycosis; Am Soc Microbiol; Am Soc Allied Health Professionals; Mycol Soc Am; AAAS; Med Mycologists Am. **Research Statement & Publications:** Isolation and control of growth of pathogenic fungi; nutrition, growth and morphogenesis of pathogenic fungi; Published over 5 articles. **Mailing Address:** Dept Biol, Ala A&M Univ, Rm 310-B Carter Hall 4900 Meridian St, Normal, AL 35762. **Fax:** 256-372-5905. **E-Mail:** aamjxj01@aamu.edu

JONES, JEFFREY B, PLANT PATHOLOGY. **Education:** PhD (plant pathol), Va Polytech Inst & State Univ, Blacksburg, 1980. **Professional Experience:** PROF PLANT PATHOL, UNIV FLA, 1998-. **Mailing Address:** Dept Plant Pathol, Univ Fla, PO Box 110680, Gainesville, FL 32611-0680. **Fax:** 352-392-6532. **E-Mail:** jbjones@ufl.edu

JONES, JEROLD W, THERMAL SYSTEMS, FLUID SYSTEMS. **Personal Data:** b Salt Lake City, Utah, July 6, 1937; m 1961, c 5. **Education:** Univ Utah, BS, 1962, PhD (mech eng), 1970; Stanford Univ, MS, 1965. **Professional Experience:** PROF EMER MECH ENG, UNIV TEX, AUSTIN, as of 2004; prof mech eng, Univ Tex, Austin, beginning 1983; mem, Steering Comt Energy Conserv Bldg, Nat Res Coun, 1979-1980; assoc prof mech eng, Univ Tex, Austin, 1976-1983; asst dir & prin investr, Ctr Energy Studies, Univ Tex, Austin, 1975-1984; asst prof arch eng, Univ Tex, Austin, 1973-1976; asst prof mech eng, Ohio State Univ, 1970-1973; fel, Ohio State Univ, 1969-1970; res scientist heat transfer, Ames Res Ctr, NASA, 1962-1966. **Memberships:** Am Soc Heating Refrig & Air-Conditioning Engrs; Am Soc Mech Engrs. **Research Statement & Publications:** Heat transfer and thermodynamics with particular applications in systems modeling; design and analysis for improving energy use efficiency of buildings and heating and air conditioning equipment. **Mailing Address:** Dept Mech Eng, Univ Tex, One Univ Sta C2200, Austin, TX 78712. **Fax:** 512-471-1045. **E-Mail:** jwjones@mail.utexas.edu

JONES, JERRY LATHAM, CHEMICAL PROCESS, PRODUCT DEVELOPMENT. **Personal Data:** b St Louis, Mo, October 20, 1946; m 1973, c 2. **Education:** Cornell Univ, BS, 1968, ME, 1969; Stanford Univ, MS, 1976. **Professional Experience:** DIR, CORP ENVI-

RON HEALTH & SAFETY, RAYCHEM CORP, as of 1999; DIR CHEM ENG, DEVELOP CTR, SRI INT, 1990-; dir chem eng lab, SRI Int, 1982-1989; dir environ & biochem eng, SRI Int, 1978-1982; mgr environ control group, SRI Int, 1976-1978; sr chem engr, SRI Int, 1975-1976; environ engr, SRI Int, 1973-1975; pilotplants supvr, Monsanto Biodize Systs, 1969-1971. **Memberships:** Am Inst Chem Engrs; Am Chem Soc; Water Pollution Control Fedn; Soc IndustMicrobiol; Parenteral Drug Asn. **Research Statement & Publications:** Manufacturing process development and evaluation; pharmaceuticals and specialty chemical product development; bioprocesses; pollution control technologies and thermal processes; separations technology. **Mailing Address:** Raychem Corp 106/8210, 300 Constitution Dr, Menlo Park, CA 94025-1164.

JONES, JESS HAROLD, VIBRATION, STATISTICAL ANALYSIS OF DYNAMIC DATA. **Personal Data:** b Melville, La, March 30, 1935; m 1958, Lessie; c Yvonne, Greg, Doug & Matt. **Education:** La State Univ, BS, 1958. **Professional Experience:** RETIRED; br chief, Induced Environ Br, George C Marshall Space Flight Ctr, NASA, 1992-1995; team leader, Environ Mental Anal Br, 1975-1987; team leader, Unsteady Flow Team, George C Marshall Space Flight Ctr, NASA, 1972-1975, 1987-1992; chief, Acoust Sect, George C Marshall Space Flight Ctr, NASA, 1966-1972; aerospace engr, George CMarshall Space Flight Ctr, NASA, 1964-1966; sr engr, Brown Eng Co, 1964; engr, Brown EngCo, 1961-1964. **Memberships:** Acoust Soc Am; Am Soc Mech Engrs. **Research Statement & Publications:** Theoretical and experimental investigations of the basic noise generation mechanisms of rocket exhaust flows and fluctuating pressure fields associated with space vehicles; analysis of random processes; fluid mechanics; wave propagation; sonic boom analysis; structural dynamics; rotating machinery; turbomachinery analysis; diagnostic analysis of dynamic data; fast fourier transforms analysis; ignition overpressure analysis and testing; acoustics. **Mailing Address:** 707 Fagan Springs Dr SE, Huntsville, AL 35801. **Fax:** 205-544-1215.

JONES, JESSE C, MECHANICAL ENGINEERING. **Professional Experience:** PRIN INVESTR, TEX TECH UNIV, as of 2003. **Memberships:** Tex Tech Univ. **Mailing Address:** Texas Tech Univ, Mech Eng Dept, Lubbock, TX 79409. **Fax:** 806-742-3540.

JONES, JESSE W, CHEMISTRY. **Personal Data:** b Troup, Tex, January 16, 1931; m 1955, c 5. **Education:** Tex Col, BS, 1954; NMex Highlands Univ, MS, 1956; Ariz State Univ, PhD (org chem), 1963. **Professional Experience:** PROF CHEM, BAYLOR UNIV, as of 2004; prof chem, Bishop Col, beginning 1967; head div natural sci, Tex Col, 1964-1967; prof, Tex Col, 1963-1967; Nat Inst Gen Med Sci & Welch Found grants, 1963-1965; head dept, Tex Col, 1963-1964; res assoc, Ariz State Univ, 1958-1963; asst prof chem, Tex Col, 1956-1958; asst biochem, Univ Utah, 1955-1956; asst chem, NMex Highlands Univ, 1954-1955. **Memberships:** AAAS; Am Chem Soc. **Research Statement & Publications:** Synthesis, mechanism of action and biochemical studies of certain nitrogen heterocycles. **Mailing Address:** Dept Chem & Biochem, Baylor Univ, PO Box 97348, Waco, TX 76798-7348. **E-Mail:** jesse_jones@baylor.edu

JONES, JIM N, MATHEMATICS. **Professional Experience:** PROF MATH, RICHLAND COMMUNITY COL, as of 2004. **Mailing Address:** Dept Math, Richland Community Col, One Col Park, Decatur, IL 62521. **E-Mail:** james@richland.cc.il.us

JONES, JOE MAXEY, IMMUNOPATHOLOGY. **Personal Data:** b Herpel, Ark, March 20, 1942; m Olcay; c Kristina, Regan, Shannon & John. **Education:** Univ Wichita State, BS, 1964, MS, 1966; Univ NC, Chapel Hill, PhD (immunol), 1970. **Professional Experience:** ASSOC PROF IMMUNOL, UNIV ARK MED SCI, 1983-; res, career develop award, Nat Cancer Inst, 1979-1984; head, immunol & immunochem, Nat Ctr Toxicol Res, 1977-1980; assoc, Scripps Clin Res Found, 1973-1977; fel, immunopathology, Scripps Clin Res Found, 1970-1973. **Memberships:** Am Asn Immunologists; AAAS; Res Soc Alcoholism. **Research Statement & Publications:** Tumor immunology; genetic control of immune responses. **Mailing Address:** Univ Ark Med Sci, 4301 W Markham Slot 517, Little Rock, AR 72205. **Fax:** 501-686-5874.

JONES, JOHN ACKLAND, ENTOMOLOGY. **Personal Data:** b Alexandria, Va, November 6, 1934; m 1960, Shirley; c Ackland. **Education:** Univ the South, BS, 1956; Univ Va, MS, 1963; Iowa State Univ, PhD (entom), 1973. **Professional Experience:** ASSOC PROF ENTOM, UNIV NEBR, LINCOLN, 1984-; asst prof, UnivNebr, Lincoln, 1978-1984; state entomologist regulatory, Nebr Dept Agr, 1973-1978; assoc prof zool & bot, Parsons Col, 1963-1966; med lab technician histol, US Army Med Serv Corps, 1958-1960; instr zool, bot & limnol, Univ South, 1957-1958. **Memberships:** Entom Soc Am; Sigma Xi. **Research Statement & Publications:** Insect morphology and development; insect pests of shelter belts; horticultural pests. **Mailing Address:** Dept Entom, Univ Nebr 202 Plant Indust Bldg, Lincoln, NE 68583-0816. **Fax:** 402-472-4687.

JONES, JOHN A(RTHUR), ENVIRONMENTAL SCIENCES, AQUATIC ECOLOGY. **Personal Data:** b Port Chester, NY, April 6, 1932; c 1. **Education:** Univ Ill, Urbana, BS, 1954; Tex A&M Univ, MS, 1960; Univ Miami, PhD (marine sci), 1968. **Professional Experience:** PROF ENVIRON TECHNOL & NATURAL SCI, MIAMI-DADE COMMUNITY COL, 1980-; consult, 1971-; assoc prof environ technol, Miami-Dade Community Col, 1970-1980; seminar assoc, Columbia Univ, 1968-; acting dir, Lake Erie Environ Studies &adj asst prof biol, State Univ NY Col, Fredonia, 1968-1970; Res assoc marine biol, Univ Miami, 1964-1967. **Memberships:** AAAS; Am Geophys Union; Am Soc Limnol & Oceanog. **Research Statement & Publications:** Environmental measurements; graphic and statistical analysis of enviromental data, especially in aquatic enviroments; comparative properties of environmental fluids. **Mailing Address:** Miami-Dade Community Col, 11011 SW 104th St, Miami, FL 33176.

JONES, JOHN BRYAN, ORGANIC CHEMISTRY, ORGANIC BIOCHEMISTRY. **Personal Data:** b Colwyn Bay, NWales, December 11, 1934; m 1962, c 2. **Education:** Univ Wales, BSc, 1955, PhD (chem), 1958; Oxford Univ, DPhil (chem), 1960. **Professional Experience:** PROF EMER BIOL & ORG CHEM, UNIV TORONTO, as of 2005; prof org chem, Univ Toronto, beginning 1974; from asst prof to assoc prof, Univ Toronto, 1963-1974; Imp Chem Indust fel, Oxford Univ, 1962-1963; NIH res fel, Calif Inst Technol, 1961-1962; Fel org chem, Mass Inst Technol, 1960-1961. **Memberships:** Fel Am Chem Soc; Chem Inst Can. **Research Statement & Publications:** Organic chemical applications of enzymes; immobilized enzymes. **Mailing Address:** Dept Chem, Lash Miller Chem Lab, Univ Toronto, 80 St George St, Toronto, ON M5S 3H6, Can. **Fax:** 416-978-1553. **E-Mail:** jbjones@chem.utoronto.ca

JONES, JOHN EVAN, INTERNAL MEDICINE, ENDOCRINOLOGY. **Personal Data:** b Mt Pleasant, Utah, October 29, 1930; m 1954, c 3. **Education:** Univ Utah, BS, 1952, MD, 1955; Am Bd Internal Med, dipl, cert endocrinol & metab, 1973. **Professional Experience:** DEAN SCH MED, SCH MED, WVA UNIV, 1974-; PROF MED &ENDOCRINOL, SCH MED, WVA UNIV, 1970-; chmn, Div Metab-Endocrinol, 1967-1974; from asst prof to assoc prof endocrinol, WVa Univ, 1963-1970; from instr to asst prof med, WVaUniv, 1961-1963; dir USPHS trainee, WVa Univ, 1960-1961; Dir USPHS trainee endocrinol, Univ Minn Hosps, 1959. **Memberships:** Fel Am Col Physicians; Endocrine Soc; Am Fedn Clin Res; Am Soc Clin Nutrit. **Research Statement & Publications:** Mineral metabolism; thyroid metabolism; adrenal hormone metabolism. **Mailing Address:** Health Sci, Med Col Va, PO Box MCV Stat 0549, Richmond, VA 23298-0549. **Fax:** 804-371-7737.

JONES, JOHN F(REDERICK), CHEMICAL ENGINEERING. **Personal Data:** b Scranton, Pa, August 19, 1932; m 1962, c 3. **Education:** Pa State Univ, BS, 1954; Univ Del, MS, 1956; Univ Colo, PhD (chem eng), 1960. **Professional Experience:** CONSULT 1987-; dir res & develop, Indust Chem Group, 1977-1987; busventure & tech mgr, Philadelphia, 1975-1977; dir, coal & coke technol, 1974-1975; mgr, ProjCOED, 1972-1974; asst mgr, Proj COED, 1968-1972; sr res chem engr, FMC Corp, 1963-1968; res chem engr, FMC Corp, 1960-1963; instr chem eng, Univ Colo, 1958-1960; chem engr, EssoRes & Eng Co, 1956-1958. **Memberships:** Am Chem Soc; Am Inst Chem Engrs; Indust Res Inst; AAAS; Sigma Xi. **Research Statement & Publications:** Petroleum refining; carbonization; gasification and liquefaction of coal; sewage and water treatment; industrial chemicals. **Mailing Address:** Maple St, PO Box 116, Stowe, VT 05672-0116.

JONES, JOHN LLOYD, ELECTRICAL ENGINEERING. **Personal Data:** b Henry, Ill, June 5, 1918; m 1943, Margaret; c Patricia (Crampton), Gary H & Elizabeth (Eller). **Education:** Univ Ill, BS, 1940, MS, 1941; Univ Md, MS, 1949, PhD, 1963. **Professional Experience:** EMER PROF, BRADLEY UNIV, AS OF 2006; assoc prof elec eng, Bradley Univ, 1963-1977; physicist, US NavalOrd Lab, 1942-1963. **Memberships:** Acoust Soc Am; Am Soc Eng Educ. **Research Statement & Publications:** Acoustics; circuit theory; electromagnetic theory; shock and vibration. **Mailing Address:** 1110 Warren St, Henry, IL 61537.

JONES, JOHN PAUL, PLANT PATHOLOGY. **Personal Data:** b Warren, Ohio, December 10, 1924; m 1950, Joyce; c 3. **Education:** Ohio Univ, BS, 1950; Univ Nebr, MA, 1953, PhD, 1956. **Professional Experience:** PROF EMER, UNIV ARKANSAS, as of 2002; Adj prof, univ Nebr MIAC proj, 1987-1990; Plant pathologist, Arab Repub Egypt, 1981-1985; prof plant path, Univ Ark, Fayetteville, 1960-1987; Plant pathologist, Delta Exp Sta, Agr Res Serv, USDA, 1955-1960. **Memberships:** Am Phytopath Soc. **Research Statement & Publications:** Phytopathology; diseases of field crops; etiology and control of cereal crops diseases. **Mailing Address:** 2147 Loren Circle, Fayetteville, AR 72701.

JONES, JOHN PAUL, VEGETABLE PLANT PATHOLOGY. **Personal Data:** b Stockdale, Ohio, February 24, 1932; m 1961, Peggy; c 3. **Education:** Ohio State Univ, BS, 1953, MS, 1955, PhD (plant path), 1958. **Honors & Awards:** Presidential Gold Medal, Fla State Hort Soc, Coun Award; Res Award, FlaFruit & Veg Asn. **Professional Experience:** Vis prof, Int Rice Res Inst, Philippines, 1980-1981; PROF PLANT PATH, GULF COAST RES & EDUC CTR, UNIV FLA, 1972-; from asst prof to assoc prof, Gulf CoastRes & Educ Ctr, Univ Fla, 1958-1969; plant path asst, Ohio Agr Exp Sta, 1954-1958. **Memberships:** Am Phytopath Soc; Sigma Xi. **Research Statement & Publications:** Nature and control of vegetable diseases; biology of plant pathogens. **Mailing Address:** Gulf Coast Res & Educ Ctr Univ Fla, 5007 60th St E, Bradenton, FL 34203.

JONES, JOHN PAUL, MATHEMATICS. **Personal Data:** b Takoma Park, Md, November 17, 1940; m 1966, c 1. **Education:** Alderson-Broaddus Col, BS, 1962; WVa Univ, MA, 1964; Pa State Univ, DEd (math), 1971. **Professional Experience:** PROF MATH, FROSTBURGSTATE UNIV, as of 1999; assoc prof math & dept head, Frostburg State Univ, beginning 1974; asst prof, Frostburg State Univ, 1971-1974; instr math, Allegheny Col, 1964-1967. **Memberships:** Am Math Soc; Math Asn Am. **Research Statement & Publications:** Algebra-groups and rings. **Mailing Address:** Dept Math, Frostburg State Univ, Dunkle Hall 201A, Frostburg, MD 21532. **E-Mail:** j_jones@frostburg.edu

JONES, JOHN RICHARD, LIMNOLOGY. **Personal Data:** b Bremerton, Wash, August 23, 1947; m 1969, c 1. **Education:** Western Wash State Col, BA, 1969; Iowa State Univ, MS, 1972, PhD (limnol), 1974. **Professional Experience:** J MICHAEL DUNMIRE PROF WATER QUAL & DEPT CHAIR LIMNOL, UNIV MO-COLUMBIA, as of 2005; assoc prof limnol, Univ Mo-Columbia, beginning 1980; asst prof, Univ Mo-columbia, 1975-1980; fel, Iowa State Univ, 1974-1975. **Memberships:** Am Soc Limnol & Oceanog; Ecol Soc Am; Am Fisheries Soc; Sigma Xi. **Research Statement & Publications:** Eutrophication process in lakes and reservoirs; attention to phosphorous and algal biomass. **Mailing Address:** Fisheries & Wildlife, Univ Mo-Columbia, Natural Resources Bldg 302 Anheuser-Busch, Columbia, MO 65211-7240. **Fax:** 573-884-5070. **E-Mail:** jonesj@missouri.edu

JONES, JOHN TAYLOR, CERAMICS ENGINEERING, METALLURGY. **Personal Data:** b Salt Lake City, Utah, January 4, 1932; m 1953, c 5. **Education:** Univ Utah, BS, 1957, PhD (ceramic eng, metall), 1965. **Professional Experience:** VPRES RES & DEVELOP, LENOX MFG DIV, LENOX, INC, NJ, 1980-; res & develop mgr, Lenox Mfg Div, Lenox, Inc, NJ, 1978-1980; res & develop mgr, Pfaltzgraff Co, Pa, 1974-1978; process develop mgr, Interspace Corp, Calif, 1974; assoc prof ceramic eng, Iowa State Univ, 1966-1974; asst dir res, Vesuvius Crucible Co, Pa, 1965-1966; develop engr, Coors Porcelain Co, Colo, 1961-1962; prod supt, Coors Porcelain Co, Colo, 1960-1961; res engr, Coors Porcelain Co, Colo, 1957-1960; ed, Ceramic Indus MAC. **Memberships:** Nat Inst Ceramic Engrs; fel Am Ceramic Soc; Ceramic Educ Coun; Am SocTesting & Mat. **Research Statement & Publications:** Ceramic whitewares; author of one publication. **Mailing Address:** Lenox Mfg Div Tech Ctr, 65 Fire Rd, Absecon, NJ 08201.

JONES, JOHN VERRIER, RHEUMATOLOGY, IMMUNOLOGY. **Personal Data:** b Shrewsbury, Eng, November 29, 1930. **Education:** Univ Oxford, MD, 1955. **Professional Experience:** MEM EMER, AM COL RHEUMATOLOGY, as of 2004; HEAD RHEUMATOLOGY, DALHOUSIE UNIV, 1982-. **Mailing Address:** Dept Rheumatology, Dalhousie Univ, 5938 Univ Ave, Halifax, NS B3H 1V9, Can.

JONES, JOHN W, NUTRITION. **Professional Experience:** ASSOC DIR, OFF CONSTITUENT OPER, CTR FOOD SAFTEY & APPL NUTRIT, as of 2004. **Mailing Address:** Off Constituent Oper, Ctr Food Safety & Appl Nutrit, 200 C St SW Rm 4803, Washington, DC 20204. **Fax:** 202-401-2893.

JONES, JOHNNYE M, ELECTRON MICROSCOPY, MYCOLOGY & PLANT PHYSIOLOGY. **Personal Data:** b Henderson, Tex, April 3, 1943; m. **Education:** Prairie View A&M Univ, BS, 1965; Atlanta Univ, MA, 1970, PhD (bot & mycol), 1979. **Honors & Awards:** Giant Sci Award, Qual Educ for Minorities, Wash, DC, 2002. **Professional Experience:** VPRES ACAD AFFAIRS, JARVIS CHRISTIAN COL, HAWKINS, TEX, 2000-; dean, Sch Sci, Hampton Univ, 1996-2000; from assoc prof biol to prof biol, Hampton Univ, 1979-2000; res assoc, Brookhaven Nat Lab, 1979-1981; instr biol & math, Mercer Univ, Atlanta, Ga, 1975-1979; fac fel, Nat Inst Gen Med Sci, NIH, 1974; instr biol & math, Morgan State Univ, Baltimore, Md, 1970-1974; instr biol & math, Chicago Pub Schs, 1967-1969; instr biol & math, Carthage Pub Schs, 1965-1967; post doctorate, Brookhaven Nat Labs, NY. **Memberships:** Mycol Soc Am; Electron Micros Soc Am; Nat Asn Minority Med Educr. **Research Statement & Publications:** Ultrastructural studies on certain species of fungi ascomycetes and oomycetes, especially developmental and physiological aspects; cytochemical localization of proteins. **Mailing Address:** Jarvis Christian Col, Hwy 80 E, PO Box 1470, Hawkins, TX 75765-1470. **Fax:** 903-769-5005. **E-Mail:** johnnye_jones@jarvis.edu

JONES, JOIE PIERCE, MEDICAL ULTRASONICS, ACOUSTICAL MICROSCOPY. **Personal Data:** b Brownwood, Tex, March 4, 1941; m 1965, Kay. **Education:** Univ Tex, Austin, BA, 1963, MS, 1965; Brown Univ, PhD (physics), 1971. **Professional Experience:** Vis prof, Univ Paris, 1996; vis prof, Kings Col, London, 1982, 1989, 1992; PROF RADIOL SCI, UNIV CALIF, IRVINE, 1977-; mem, President's Sci & Technol adv comt, 1976-1979; reviewer, Nat Sci Found & NIH, 1975-; assoc prof med physics, Case Western Reserve Univ, 1975-1977; consult, var pvt Co & govt agencies, 1971-; sr scientist, Bolt-Beranek & Newman, 1970-1975. **Memberships:** Acoust Soc Am; fel Am Inst Ultrasound Med; Am Asn Physicists Med; Inst Elec & Electronics Engrs. **Research Statement & Publications:** Medical ultrasonics; ultrasonic tissue characterization; medical imaging; acoustical microscopy. **Mailing Address:** Dept Radiol Sci Univ Calif, Irvine, CA 92697-5000. **Fax:** 949-824-6532. **E-Mail:** jpjones@uci.edu

JONES, JOYCE HOWELL, EMBRYOLOGY, ANIMAL SCIENCE & NUTRITION. **Personal Data:** b Roanoke, Va, May 4, 1944; m 1968. **Education:** Va Polytech Inst & State Univ, BS, 1966, MS, 1971, PhD (genetics), 1974. **Professional Experience:** RETIRED; exten specialist & asst prof poultry, Va Polytech Inst & State Univ, 1977-1985; asst prof biol, Ferrum Col, 1974-1977; jr high sch phys sci teacher, 1969-1970. **Memberships:** Poultry Sci Asn; Am Genetic Asn; AAAS; Sigma Xi. **Research Statement & Publications:** Genetical, physiological and behavioral relationships in avian and mammalian pre and postnatal development. **Mailing Address:** Happy Valley E, Abingdon, VA 24210.

JONES, KATHLEEN F, GEOPHYSICS. **Education:** Mass Inst Technol, BS; Univ Wash, MS, MSE. **Professional Experience:** RES PHYS SCIENTIST, USACE ENG RES & DEVELOP CTR, COLD REGIONS RES & ENG LAB, NH, as of 2006. **Mailing Address:** USACE Eng Res & Develop Ctr, Cold Regions Res & Eng Lab, 72 Lyme Rd, Hanover, NH 03755-1290. **Fax:** 603-646-4644. **E-Mail:** Kathleen.F.Jones@erdc.usace.army.mil

JONES, KAY H, ENVIRONMENTAL HEALTH, TOXICOLOGY. **Personal Data:** b Spokane, Wash, January 13, 1935; c 6. **Education:** Univ Washington, BS, 1956; Univ Calif, Berkeley, MS, 1961, PhD (sanit eng), 1968. **Honors & Awards:** State-of-the-Art Civil Eng Award, Am Soc Civil Engrs, 1975. **Professional Experience:** PRES ZEPHRY CONSULT, 1990-; vpres, Roy Weston Inc, 1981-1990; prof environ eng, Drexel Univ, Pa, 1979-1981; mem, Coun Environ Qual, Exec Off Pres, 1975-1979; consult, WHO, 1974-1975; mem, Off Air Prog, Environ Protection Agency, 1970-1974; Mem staff, Nat Air Pollution Control Admin, Dept Health, Educ & Welfare, 1967-1970. **Memberships:** Am Soc Civil Engrs; Air Pollution Central Asn. **Research Statement & Publications:** Ambient air quality data analysis; air pollution impact analysis; population exposure modeling; environmental epidemiology; environmental toxicology; industrial hygiene; air pollution central engineering; risk assessment. **Mailing Address:** Zephyr Consult, 2600 Fairview Ave, Seattle, WA 98102. **Fax:** 206-720-4992.

JONES, KEITH WARLOW, EXPERIMENTAL ATOMIC PHYSICS, APPLIED PHYSICS. **Personal Data:** b Lincoln, Nebr, August 30, 1928; m 1954, c 3. **Education:** Princeton Univ, AB, 1950; Univ Wis, MS, 1951, PhD (physics), 1955. **Professional Experience:** DIV HEAD, DEPT APPL SCI, 1984-; Group leader, dept Physics, Brookhaven Nat lab, 1976-1984; SR PHYSICIST, BROOKHAVEN NAT LAB, 1975-; fromassoc physicist to physicist, dept Appl Sci, 1963-1975; from asst prof to assoc prof, Ohio StateUniv, 1958-1963; res assoc, Columbia Univ, 1955-1958; asst prof physics, Univ NC, 1954-1955. **Memberships:** Fel Am Phys Soc. **Research Statement & Publications:** Beam foil spectroscopy; heavy ion-atom collisions; trace element and isotope identification techniques; micro-beam methods and applications; synchrotron radiation experiments. **Mailing Address:** Dept Appl Sci, Brookhaven Nat Lab, Bldg 815, Upton, NY 11973. **Fax:** 516-344-5271. **E-Mail:** kwj@bnl.gov

JONES, KENNETH CHARLES, ALGOLOGY, MOLECULAR GENETICS. **Personal Data:** b San Pedro, Calif, July 20, 1934; m 1956, c 2. **Education:** Univ Calif, Los Angeles, BA, 1957, MA, 1962, PhD (plant sci), 1965. **Professional Experience:** PROF EMER BIOL, CALIF STATE UNIV, as of 2005; dept chmn, Calif State Univ, Northridge, 1979-1980; actg dean grad studies &res, Calif State Univ, Northridge, 1977-1978; prof biol, Calif State Univ, Northridge, beginning 1971; from asst prof to assoc prof, Calif State Univ, Northridge, 1964-1971. **Memberships:** AAAS; Sigma Xi. **Research Statement & Publications:** Chemical regulation of plant growth; genetic control mechanisms; physiology of germination of Chara. **Mailing Address:** Dept Biol, Calif State Univ, 11000 Univ Pkwy, Northridge, CA 91330. **E-Mail:** kenneth.jones@csun.edu

JONES, KENNETH WAYNE, CLINICAL MICROBIOLOGY. **Personal Data:** b Decatur, Ill, December 22, 1946; m 1968, c 2. **Education:** Southern Conn State Col, BS, 1970; Univ NC, MPH, 1974, PhD (public health microbiol), 1976. **Professional Experience:** CHIEF MICROBIOLOGIST, SANITARY MICROBIOL LAB, RI DEPT HEALTH, 1976-; res asst, Centers Dis Control, 1975-1976; microbiologist, Conn Health Dept, Greenwich, 1971-1973; AT HEALTH LABS, PROVIDENCE, RI. **Memberships:** Sigma Xi; Am Soc Microbiol; Am Public Health Asn. **Research Statement & Publications:** Diagnostic procedures in clinical and public health microbiology; microbiological methods for monitoring environmental quality. **Mailing Address:** Dept Health Labs, 50 Orms St, Providence, RI 02904. **Fax:** 401-277-6984. **E-Mail:** kenj@doh.state.ri.us

JONES, KEVIN, PHYSICS. **Education:** Univ Witwatersrand, SAfrica, BS & BS; Rutgers Univ, PhD. **Professional Experience:** LEAD, DYNAMIC EXPERIMENTATION DIV, LOS ALAMOS NAT LAB, as of 2005. **Memberships:** Am Phys Soc. **Mailing Address:** Los Alamos Nat Lab, PO Box 1663 AOT-6 MS-H812, Los Alamos, NM 87545.

JONES, KEVIN F, BACTERIAL PATHOGENESIS & VACCINE RESEARCH. **Personal Data:** b East Stroudsburg, Pa, September 20, 1952. **Education:** Moravian Col, BS, 1974; Cornell Univ, MS, 1977, PhD (immunol), 1981. **Professional Experience:** DIR VACCINE RES, SIGA TECHNOLOGIES INC, NY, as of 2001; dir bact res, M-G Pharmaceut, 1992-1996; sr scientist, Lederle-Praxis Biol, 1990-1992; asst prof immunol, Rockefeller Univ, 1985-1990; res fel streptoccoial pathogenesis, Rockefeller Univ, 1981-1985. **Memberships:** Am Soc Microbiol; Am Asn Immunologists; Int Soc Vaccines. **Mailing Address:** SIGA Technol, Inc, Ste 601 420 Lexington Ave, New York, NY 10170. **Fax:** 212-697-3130.

JONES, KEVIN MCDILL, LASER COOLING OF ATOMS, PHOTOASSOCIATION SPECTROSCOPY. **Personal Data:** b Washington, DC, December 31, 1955; m 1983, Moira; c Sophie & Schuyler. **Education:** Williams Col, BA, 1977; Stanford Univ, PhD (physics), 1984. **Professional Experience:** William Edward McElfresh Professor of Physics, Williams College 2003- Physics Dept chair 1992-2003, 2005-2006; guest researcher NIST Gaithersburg 1992-; Prof of Physics Williams Col 1996-2003; Associate Prof. of Physics Williams Col 1991-1996; Consultant, Lawrence Livermore Nat Lab, 1987-1988; Asst Prof Williams Col 1984-1991; Postdoctoral fel, Hydrogen Maser Lab Williams College 1983-1984. **Memberships:** Am Phys Soc; Sigma Xi; Optical Soc Am; Coun Undergrad Res; Am Asn Physics Teachers. **Research Statement & Publications:** Laser spectroscopy of atoms and molecules; photoassociation of cold atoms for the study of long range molecules and atomic scattering. **Mailing Address:** Physics Dept, Williams Col, Williamstown, MA 01267. **E-Mail:** kevin.jones@williams.edu

JONES, KEVIN SCOTT, SEMICONDUCTOR RESEARCH, TRANSMISSION ELECTRON MICROSCOPY STUDIES. **Personal Data:** b Gainesville, Fla, February 20, 1958; m Debra. **Education:** Univ Fla, BS, 1980; Univ Calif, Berkeley, MS, 1985, PhD (mat sci eng), 1987. **Professional Experience:** PROF, DEPT MAT SCI & ENG, UNIV FLA, as of 2005; CHMN, MAT SCI ENG, UNIV FLA, as of 2004; organizer, IX Int Conf Ion Implantation Technol, 1992; NSF presidential young investr award, 1990-1995; co-organizer, Compound Semiconductor Growth, Processing & Devices 1990's, Japan/US Topical Conf, 1987; assoc prof, Dept Mat Sci & Eng, Univ Fla, beginning 1989; organizer, meeting session electronic mat, 1989; asst prof, Dept Mat Sci & Eng, Univ Fla, 1987-1989; researcher, Univ Calif, Berkeley, 1987; consult, TRW, Inc, 1985-1986; teaching & res asst, Univ Calif, Berkeley, 1982-1987; tech proc engr, E I DuPont & Co, Wash Works Plant, 1980-1982. **Memberships:** Am Soc Metals; Electron Micros Soc Am; Mat Res Soc; Metall Soc; Electrochem Soc. **Research Statement & Publications:** Processing and characterization of elemental and compound semiconductors; ion implantation; ion beam induced phase transformations; transmission electron microscopy. **Mailing Address:** Dept Mat Sci & Eng Univ Fla, 100-B RHN PO Box 116400, Gainesville, FL 32611-6400. **Fax:** 352-392-7219. **E-Mail:** kjones@eng.ufl.edu

JONES, LARRY HUDSON, GENETICS, MOLECULAR BIOLOGY. **Personal Data:** b Dillon, SC, July 3, 1948; m 1988, Leslie; c Houston H & Jonathan A. **Education:** Wofford Col, BS, 1970; Univ NC, Chapel Hill, PhD (bot), 1976. **Professional Experience:** ASSOC DEAN COL, UNIV S, SEWANEE, 1993-; PROF BIOL, UNIV S, SEWANEE, 1990-; vis assoc prof biol, Reed Col, Portland, Ore, 1989-1990; dept chair, Univ S, 1988-1993; vis res assoc, USDA Res Ctr, Florence, SC, 1984; from asst prof to assoc prof, Univ S, 1977-1990; vis asst prof biol, Swarthmore Col, 1976-1977; res assoc biochem & microbiol, Cook Col, Rutgers Univ, 1975-1976. **Memberships:** Am Soc Plant Biologists; Sigma Xi. **Research Statement & Publications:** Tissue culture; effects of methylation of RNA on biological systems; coordination of protein synthesis in chloroplasts and mitochondria; plant hormones; genetics. **Mailing Address:** Dept Biol, Univ S, 735 Univ Ave, Sewanee, TN 37383. **Fax:** 931-598-3229. **E-Mail:** ljones@sewanee.edu

JONES, LARRY PHILIP, VETERINARY PATHOLOGY. **Personal Data:** b Hamilton, Mont, December 11, 1934; m 1959, c 2. **Education:** Wash State Univ, BA, 1957, DVM, 1958; Am Col Vet Path, dipl, 1968. **Professional Experience:** PROF MICROBIOL, UNIV TEX, EL PASO, as of 2006; pathologist & head dept path, Tex Vet Med Diag Lab, 1969-; asst prof vet path, Inst Trop Vet Med, 1965-1969; res assoc path, Agr Res Lab, Univ Tenn, 1958-1960. **Memberships:** Am Vet Med Asn; Wildlife Dis Asn; Wildlife Soc; Sigma Xi. **Research Statement & Publications:** Infectious diseases of domestic and wild ruminants. **Mailing Address:** Dept Biol Sci, Univ Tex, El Paso, TX 79968-0001. **E-Mail:** larryj@utep.edu

JONES, LARRY WARNER, PLANT PHYSIOLOGY, ENVIRONMENTAL ENGINEERING. **Personal Data:** b Huntington Co, Ind, February 14, 1934; m 1957, Martha A Crawford; c 3. **Education:** Univ Ariz, BS, 1955, MS, 1959; Univ Tex, PhD (bot), 1964. **Professional Experience:** Assoc dir, Appl Sci Div, Hazardous Waste Res & Educ Inst, Univ Tenn, 1996-1997; dir Appl Sci Div, Hazardous Waste Res & Educ Inst, Univ Tenn, 1985-1996; consult, Waterways Exp Sta, US Army Corps Engrs, 1976-; visprof, Ore State Univ, 1974-1975; PROF BOT, PLANT PHYSIOL & GENETICS, UNIV TENN, KNOXVILLE, 1973-; from asst prof to assoc prof bot, Univ Tenn, 1965-1973; res scientist, Res Inst Adv Studies, Div Martin Co, 1964-1965; vpres, VeriTec Corp. **Memberships:** Am Soc Plant Physiol; Am Pollution Control Asn; Water Pollution Control Fedn. **Research Statement & Publications:** Immobilization and stabilization of hazardous wastes; environmental effects and monitoring; algal physiology; photosynthesis and hydrogen production. **Mailing Address:** Waste Mgt Inst, Univ Tenn, Knoxville, TN 37996-0710. **Fax:** 423-974-3892.

JONES, LAWRENCE WILLIAM, HIGH ENERGY PHYSICS, COSMIC RAY PHYSICS. **Personal Data:** b Evanston, Ill, November 16, 1925; m 1950, Ruth; c Douglas W Jones, Carol (Dwyer) & Ellen (Dillman). **Education:** Northwestern Univ, BS, 1948, MS, 1949; Univ Calif, PhD (physics), 1952. **Professional Experience:** PROF EMER PHYSICS, UNIV MICH, ANN ARBOR, 1998-; vis prof, Falkiner Dept, High Energy Physics, Univ Sidney, 1991; vis prof, Univ Auckland, 1991; distinguished vis scholar, Univ Adelaide, 1991; physicist, Signal Syst Corp Cent Design Group, Lawrence Berkeley Lab, 1987; trustee, Univ Res Asn, 1982-1987; chmn, Dept Physics, Univ Mich, 1982-1987; vis prof, Tata Inst, Bombay, 1979; vis prof & Sci Res Coun Fel, Westfield Col, London, 1977; vis physicist, Fermi Nat Accelerator Lab, Batavia, Ill, 1971-; Guggenheim Found fel, CERN, 1965; vis physicist, Brookhaven Nat Lab, Upton, NY, 1963-; prof physics, Univ Mich, Ann Arbor, 1963-1998; vis scientist & assoc, European Laboratory for Particle Physics (CERN), Geneva, Switz, beginning 1961; vis physicist, Lawrence Berkeley Radiation Lab, Univ Calif, 1959-1970; from instr to assoc prof, Univ Mich, Ann Arbor, 1952-1963; res asst, Radiation Lab, Univ Calif, 1950-1952; consult, Space Tech Labs Inc, Thompson-Ramo-Wooldridge Inc, NASA, Arnold & Porter; consult, Signal Syst Corp Cent Design Group, DOE, Inst Physics (Great Britain). **Memberships:** Fel Am Phys Soc; AAAS; Int Asn Hydrogen Energy. **Research Statement & Publications:** High energy strong interactions of elementary particles; High energy cosmic ray physics; hadron production of dilepions and prompt neutrinos; hydrogen energy systems; medical physics instrumentation; hadron production of charm mesons; electron positron interactions at high energies. **Mailing Address:** Univ Mich, Dept Physics, 353 W Hall, Ann Arbor, MI 48109-1120. **Fax:** 734-936-1817. **E-Mail:** lwjones@umich.edu

JONES, LEE BENNETT, ORGANIC CHEMISTRY. **Personal Data:** b Memphis, Tenn, March 14, 1938; m 1964, Vera; c David & Michael. **Education:** Wabash Col, BA, 1960; Mass Inst Technol, PhD (org chem), 1964. **Honorary Degrees:** DSc, Wabash Col, 1992. **Professional Experience:** EXEC VICE PRES & PROVOST EMER, UNIV NEBR, as of 2000; prof chem, Univ Nebr, beginning 1985; provost, Grad Col & Health Sci, 1980-1982; dean, Grad Col, Univ Ariz, 1977-1980; head dept, Univ Ariz, 1973-1977; prof chem, Univ Ariz, 1972-1985; asst head dept, Univ Ariz, 1971-1973; from asst prof to assoc prof, Univ Ariz, 1964-1972; NSF fel chem, Calif Inst Technol, 1964. **Memberships:** AAAS; Am Chem Soc; Royal Soc Chem. **Research Statement & Publications:** Photochemistry; carbonium ion reactions; nucleophilic substitutions; isotope effects. **Mailing Address:** Dept Chem, Univ Nebr, 106 Varner Hall, Lincoln, NE 68583. **Fax:** 402-472-4240. **E-Mail:** lbjones@uneb.edu

JONES, LEE K, MATHEMATICS. **Education:** Tufts Univ, BS, 1965; Stanford Univ, PhD, 1968. **Professional Experience:** PROF, DEPT MATH SCI, UNIV MASS, LOWELL, as of

2006. **Memberships:** Inst Elec & Electronics Engrs. **Mailing Address:** Dept Math Sci Univ Mass Lowell, One Univ Ave, Lowell, MA 01854-2881. **Fax:** 978-934-3022. **E-Mail:** Lee_Jones@uml.edu

JONES, LEE W, AERONAUTICS. **Professional Experience:** ASST DIR, PROPULSION LAB, MARSHALL SPACE FLIGHT CTR, NASA, as of 1996. **Memberships:** Am Inst Aeronaut & Astronaut. **Mailing Address:** Marshall Space Flight Ctr, Propulsion Lab M/C EP-21, Huntsville, AL 35812. **Fax:** 205-544-3960.

JONES, LEONIDAS JOHN, SOFTWARE SYSTEMS. **Personal Data:** b Warrenton, NC, May 17, 1937; m 1963, c 3. **Education:** Duke Univ, BS, 1958, MS, 1960, PhD (elec eng), 1966. **Professional Experience:** MGR, RES & DEVELOP CTR, GEN ELEC CO, 1979-; adminr, Res & Develop Ctr, Gen Elec CO, 1977-1979; Gen Elec rep, Conf Data Syst Lang, 1971-1977; scientist, Res & Develop Ctr, Gen Elec CO, 1966-1977. **Memberships:** Asn Comput Mach; Sigma Xi. **Research Statement & Publications:** Computer-aided design and database systems for industrial automation. **Mailing Address:** 534 Devils Ln, Ballston Spa, NY 12020.

JONES, LESTER TYLER, PHYSICAL CHEMISTRY, RESEARCH ADMINISTRATION. **Personal Data:** b Des Moines, Iowa, December 5, 1939; m 1962, Ardith; c Trent, Lance & Kevin. **Education:** Univ Iowa, BS, 1961; Wash State Univ, PhD (phys chem), 1966. **Professional Experience:** RETIRED; sr patent liaison specialist, 3M Co, 1994-1999; mgr, Technol Assessment & Univ Rels, Corp Res Labs, 1982-1994; mgr, Cent Res Labs, 3M Co, 1974-1982; supvr, Cent Res Labs, 3M Co, 1973-1974; res specialist, Cent Res Labs, 3M Co, 1972-1973; sr chemist, Cent Res Labs, 3M Co, 1965-1972. **Memberships:** Am Chem Soc. **Research Statement & Publications:** Corrosion of metals; nuclear quadruple resonance; charge transfer complexes; dye adsorption; controlled release; biomaterials; technology transfer; intellectual property. **Mailing Address:** 2215 S Shore Blvd, St Paul, MN 55110.

JONES, LEWIS HAMMOND, IV, SEMICONDUCTOR PHYSICS, FREQUENCY TIMING GENERATORS. **Personal Data:** b Cleveland, Ohio, February 26, 1941. **Education:** Ohio Wesleyan Univ, BA, 1963; Univ Ill, MS, 1965, PhD (physics), 1971. **Professional Experience:** SR PROD ENGR, INTEGRATED CIRCUIT SYST, 1994-; test engr, EG&G Reticon, Sunnyvale, Calif, 1992-1994; sr yield enhancement engr, Advan Micro Devices, Santa Clara, Calif, 1989-1992; sect head, Nat Semiconductor Corp, Santa Clara, Calif, 1988-1989; mem res staff, Fairchild Camera & Instrument Corp, Palo Alto, test eng staff, 1985-1987; asst res physicist, Univ Calif, Irvine, 1978-1979; res assoc physics, Univ Md, College Park, 1974-1977; Nat Lab, Frascati, Italy, 1972-1974; vis scientist physics, Ctr Nuclear Energy, Saclay, France, 1971-1972. **Memberships:** Inst Elec & Electronics Engrs. **Research Statement & Publications:** Frequency timing generators; semiconductor characterization; semiconductor product engineering. **Mailing Address:** Integrated Circuit Syst, 1271 Parkmoor Ave, San Jose, CA 95126-3448. **Fax:** 408-925-9460.

JONES, LILY ANN, MICROBIAL GENETICS, MOLECULAR BIOLOGY. **Personal Data:** b Montevideo, Minn, July 6, 1938; div, c 2. **Education:** Univ Minn, BA, 1960, MS, 1963, PhD (microbiol), 1964. **Professional Experience:** PROF IMMUNOL & MICROBIOL, WAYNE STATE UNIV, as of 2002; assoc prof immunol & microbiol, Wayne State Univ, beginning 1976; asst prof microbial genetics, Wayne State Univ, 1970-1976; instr, Wayne State Univ, 1964-1970. **Memberships:** AAAS; Am Soc Microbiol. **Research Statement & Publications:** Genetics of Streptomyces; phylogeny of actinomycetes; bacterial resistance to antibiotics; life-cycle and structure of actinophage; bacteriophage classification and taxonomy. **Mailing Address:** Dept Immunol & Microbiol, Wayne State Univ Med Sch, 540 E Canfield, Detroit, MI 48201-1928. **E-Mail:** ljones@med.wayne.edu

JONES, LINCOLN D, ELECTRICAL ENGINEERING. **Personal Data:** b Los Angeles, Calif, December 4, 1923; m 1944, c 3. **Education:** Univ Ariz, BS, 1951, MS, 1956; Stanford Univ, Engr, 1964. **Professional Experience:** RETIRED; emer prof, San Jose State Univ, 1994; from asst prof to prof eleceng, San Jose State Univ, 1956-1994; asst prof, Calif State Polytech Col, 1954-1956; instr eleceng, Univ Ariz, 1951-1954. **Memberships:** Inst Elec & Electronics Engrs; Am Soc Eng Educ; Soc Comput Simulation. **Research Statement & Publications:** Finding system models for second order nonlinear systems that exhibit jump resonance. **Mailing Address:** 1962 Schrader Dr, San Jose, CA 95124.

JONES, LLEWELLYN CLAIBORNE, ANALYTICAL CHEMISTRY. **Personal Data:** b Chester, Pa, November 4, 1919. **Education:** Harvard Univ, BS (Chem), 1943. **Professional Experience:** RETIRED; head, mgr loss Control-Logistics, 1976-1980; analytic mgr, Analytic Dept, Royal Dutch Shell Lab, Netherlands, 1972-1976; head, Analytic Dept, Royal Dutch Shell Lab, Netherlands, 1970-1972; head process develop dept, Res Ctr, Shell Berre, France, 1969-1970; head analytic dept, Emeryville Res Ctr, Shell Develop Co, 1965-1969; asst chief res physicist, Wood River Res Lab, 1957-1965; res chemist, Thorton Res Ctr, Shell Res Ltd Eng, 1956-1957; group leader, Houston Res Lab, Shell Oil Co, 1943-1944; Wood River Res Lab, 1946-1956; res chemist, Houston Res Lab, Shell Oil Co, 1943-1944; Wood River Res Lab, 1944-1946. **Research Statement & Publications:** Absorption spectroscopy; infrared and vacuum ultraviolet; ion exchange chromatography; instrumental methods of analysis. **Mailing Address:** 8203 E Del Caverna, Scottsdale, AZ 85258. **E-Mail:** lcj@aol.com

JONES, L(LEWELLYN) E(DWARD), HYDRAULIC ENGINEERING, NUMEROGRAPHICAL METHODS. **Personal Data:** b Montreal, Que, March 25, 1910; m 1938, Dorothy I Mudge; c James L & William R. **Education:** Univ Man, BScCE, 1931, Univ Toronto, MASc, 1933, PhD (hydraul), 1941. **Honors & Awards:** Sons of Martha Medal, 1965; Queen's Silver Jubilee Medal, 1977. **Professional Experience:** PROF EMER MECH ENG, UNIV TORONTO, 1975-; ASSOC, INSTENVIRON STUDIES, UNIV TORONTO, 1971-; ENG ARCHIVIST & CUR, UNIVTORONTO, 1970-; Ford Found res grant, 1963; gen consult, 1957-; from asst prof to prof mecheng, Univ Toronto, 1944-1975; hydraul engr, Hydro-Elec Power Comn Ont, 1941-1957; instr &lectr appl physics, Univ Toronto, 1936-1944; jr engr, Can Pac Rwy Co, 1929-1930 & Man ProvGovt, 1931-1933. **Memberships:** Am Soc Civil Eng; Am Soc Mech Engrs; Royal Can Inst; fel Brit Inst Mech Engrs; fel Eng Inst Can. **Research Statement & Publications:** Applied physics; optics; photography; metrology; fluid mechanics; water resources; applied mathematics; data processing and interpretation; computers and numerical methods; technical publication; engineering history; optimal interpretation of experimental data; memorial authorship and calligraphy. **Mailing Address:** 29 Prince George Dr, Islington, ON M9A 1X9, Can. **Fax:** 416-971-2291.

JONES, LLOYD GEORGE, horticulture; deceased, see previous edition for last biography

JONES, LOUISE HINRICHSEN, APPLIED MATHEMATICS, COMPUTER SCIENCE. **Personal Data:** b Ames, Iowa, December 24, 1930; m 1952. **Education:** Radcliffe Col, AB, 1952, MA, 1953; Univ Del, MA, 1968, PhD (appl math), 1970. **Professional Experience:** RETIRED; supvr, E I du Pont de Nemours & co, Inc, 1976-1985; mem staff, E I du Pont de Nemours & co, Inc, 1974-1976; asst prof appl math & comput sci, Univ Del, 1969-1974; res physicist, Textile Fibers Dept, E I du Pont de Nemours & Co, Inc, 1959-1966; physicist, Textile Fibers Dept, E I du Pont de Nemours & Co, Inc, 1953-1959. **Memberships:** Am Math Soc; Soc Indust & Appl Math; Asn Comput Mach. **Research Statement & Publications:** Nonlinear eigenvalue problems; numerical solution of integral equations; automata theory; microprogramming; optimization. **Mailing Address:** 233 Cheltenham Rd, Newark, DE 19711.

JONES, LYLE VINCENT, PSYCHOMETRICS. **Personal Data:** b Grandview, Wash, March 11, 1924; m 1949, c Christopher, Susan & Tad. **Education:** Univ Wash, BS, 1947, MS, 1948; Stanford Univ, PhD (psych), 1950. **Professional Experience:** PROF EMER, DEPT PSYCHOL, UNIV NC, CHAPEL HILL, as of 2003; res prof, Univ NC, Chapel Hill, beginning 1992; alumni distinguished prof psychol, Univ NC, Chapel Hill, 1969-1992; vchancellor & dean, Grad Sch, Univ NC, Chapel Hill, 1969-1979; fel, Ctr Advan Study Behav Sci, 1964-1965 & 1981-1982; dir, Thurstone Psychometric Lab, 1957-1974 & 1979-1992; from assoc prof to prof, Univ NC, Chapel Hill, 1957-1969; vis assoc prof psychol, Univ Tex, 1956-1957; asst prof psychol, Univ Chicago, 1951-1957; fel, Univ Chicago, 1950-1951; fel, Nat Res Coun, 1950-1951. **Memberships:** Inst Med Nat Acad Sci; fel Am Acad Arts & Sci; fel Am Psychol Asn (pres, 1963-1964); Psychometric Soc (pres, 1962-1963); fel Am Statist Asn; Am Educ Res Asn; fel AAAS. **Research Statement & Publications:** Psychological measurement; monitoring student achievement trends, especially in mathematics and science for minority students. **Mailing Address:** Dept Psychol CB 3270, Davie Hall Univ NC, Chapel Hill, NC 27599-3270. **Fax:** 919-962-2537. **E-Mail:** lvjones@email.unc.edu

JONES, MAITLAND, ORGANIC CHEMISTRY. **Personal Data:** b New York, NY, November 23, 1937; m 1960, Susan; c Maitland III, Hilary Lincoln & Stephanie Margaret. **Education:** Yale Univ, BS, 1959, MS, 1960, PhD (chem), 1963. **Professional Experience:** Freiwillige Akademische Gesellschaft Prof, Univ Basel, 2002; vis Prof, Fudan Univ, 1994; vis prof, Kiev Polytechnic, 1990; vis prof, Harvard Univ, 1986; DAVID B JONES PROF CHEM, PRINCETON UNIV, 1983-; master, Stevenson Hall, Princeton Univ, 1974-1981; prof chem, Princeton Univ, 1973-1983; vis prof, Free Univ, Amsterdam, 1973-1974 & 1978; vis asst prof, Columbia Univ, 1969-1970; Alfred P Sloan res fel, 1967-1969; from asst prof to assoc prof, Princeton Univ, 1966-1973; fel chem, Univ Wis, 1963-1964; fel, Yale Univ, 1963. **Memberships:** Am Chem Soc. **Research Statement & Publications:** Chemistry of reactive intermediates; carborange chemistry; more that 200 publications. **Mailing Address:** Dept Chem, Princeton Univ, Princeton, NJ 08544. **Fax:** 609-258-2383. **E-Mail:** mjjr@princeton.edu

JONES, MARGARET ZEE, NEUROPATHOLOGY, PATHOLOGY. **Personal Data:** b Swedesboro, NJ, June 24, 1936; m 1959, c 3. **Education:** Univ Pa, BA, 1957; Med Col Va, MD, 1961. **Professional Experience:** RETIRED; mem, Coun, 1989-; mem, Inst Lab Animal Resources, Nat Res Coun, Nat Acad Sci, 1985-1988; mem, Neurol Prog Comt, Nat Inst Neurol & Commun Disorders & Stroke, NIH, 1985-1988; hon consult, Western Gen Hosp & sr lectr, Univ Edinburgh, Edinburgh, Scotland, 1983-1984; fel biochem, NIH grant, 1980-1987; grant, Nat Inst Neurol Dis & Stroke, Mich State Univ, 1980-1983; prof path, Mich State Univ, 1978-2003; vis prof, Muscular Dystrophy Res Labs, Newcastle Gen Hosp, Engl, 1976-1977; grant, Nat Multiple Sclerosis Soc, 1971-1972; from asst prof to assoc prof path, Mich State Univ, 1970-1978; fel biochem, Nat Inst Neurol Dis & Stroke, Mich State Univ, 1970-1971; lectr, Sch Med, Yale Univ, 1969-; actg dir, Div Neuropath, 1968-1969; from instr to asst prof, Med Col Va, 1967-1969; resident neuropath, Med Col Va, 1966-1967; from intern to resident path & neuropath, Univ Wash, 1962-1965; clin asst, Sch Med, Univ Wash, 1962-1965; ed-in-chief, ILAR J. **Memberships:** Am Fedn Clin Res; Am Asn Neuropath; Soc Neuroscience; Am Asn Pathologists. **Research Statement & Publications:** Inherited metabolic diseases; developmental neurobiology; medical education; neuropathology, particularly developmental and neuromuscular disorders. **Mailing Address:** Dept Path, Mich State Univ, 618 E Fee Hall, East Lansing, MI 48824-0001. **Fax:** 517-336-1053.

JONES, MARJORIE ANN, FETAL-MATERNAL INTERACTIONS, PROSTAGLANDINS. **Personal Data:** b Flint, Mich, December 11, 1944; m 1966, c 1. **Education:** Cent Mich Univ, BS, 1970, MS, 1972; Univ Ill, MS, 1973; Univ Tex, PhD (biochem), 1982. **Professional Experience:** PROF BIOCHEM, ILL STATE UNIV, AS OF 2006; asst prof, Ill State Univ, 1985-1989; sr res assoc, Health Sci Ctr, Univ Tex, 1984-1985; Res assoc biochem, Health SciCtr, Univ Tex, 1982-1984. **Memberships:** Soc Study Reproduction; Int Embryo Transfer Soc; Am Fertility Soc; Soc StudyFertility; Am Chem Soc; NY Acad Sci. **Research Statement & Publications:** Role of lipids in biological processes, especially the regulation and initiation of events involved in reproduction; interaction between developing embryo and the maternal system, with emphasis on signals exchanged between the two separate systems. **Mailing Address:** Dept Biochem, Ill State Univ, 320 Sci Lab Bldg, Normal, IL 61790-4160. **Fax:** 309-438-5538. **E-Mail:** mjones@xenon.che.ilstu.edu

JONES, MARK MARTIN, INORGANIC CHEMISTRY. **Personal Data:** b Scranton, Pa, January 7, 1928; m 1951, Shirley; c Mark & Theodore. **Education:** Lehigh Univ, BS, 1948, MS, 1949; Univ Kans, PhD (chem), 1952. **Professional Experience:** PROF INORG CHEM, VANDERBILT UNIV, 1964-; from asst prof to assoc prof, Vanderbilt Univ, 1957-1964; chief develop unit, Explosives Res Sect, 1957; chemist, Picatinny Arsenal, 1955-1957; instr chem, Univ Ill, 1953-1955; fel hydrazine chem, Univ Ill, 1952-1953. **Memberships:** Fel AAAS; Emer mem Am Chem Soc; Emer mem Soc Toxicol. **Research Statement & Publications:** Therapeutic chelating agents for toxic heavy metals. **Mailing Address:** Dept Chem, 7330 Stevenson Ctr, Sta B 351822, Nashville, TN 37235. **Fax:** 615-343-1234. **E-Mail:** jonesmm0@ctrvax.vanderbilt.edu

JONES, MARK T, MATHEMATICS. **Education:** Duke Univ, PhD (comput sci), 1990. **Professional Experience:** ASST PROF, UNIV TENN KNOXVILLE, as of 2005. **Mailing Address:** Dept Comput Sci, Univ Tenn, Knoxville, TN 37996-1301. **Fax:** 865-974-6576. **E-Mail:** jones@cs.utk.edu

JONES, MARTHA OWNBEY, BIOLOGICAL CHEMISTRY, ORGANIC CHEMISTRY. **Personal Data:** b Colfax, Wash, December 10, 1940; m 1968, c 1. **Education:** Grinnell Col, BA, 1962; Purdue Univ, PhD (chem), 1975. **Professional Experience:** ASST PROF CHEM, UNION COL, 1982-; lectr org chem, Princeton Univ, 1978-1982; from instr to asst prof chem, Drew Univ, 1968-1978; instr, Purdue Univ, 1966-1967. **Memberships:** Am Chem Soc; AAAS; Sigma Xi; Am Asn Univ Profs. **Research Statement & Publications:** Protein chemistry and enzymology; protein folding and the relationship between structure and biological activity of proteolytic enzymes. **Mailing Address:** 123 Mountainside Dr, Randolph, NJ 07869-3316.

JONES, MARTIN L, PROBABILITY, MATHEMATICS. **Personal Data:** b Hazelton, Ga. **Education:** Warren Wilson Col, NC, BA, 1979; Univ SC, MS, 1983; Ga Inst Technol, PhD (math), 1989. **Professional Experience:** Univ Del Oriente, Venezuela, 1994 & Univ Costa Rica, 1997-1998; ASSOC PROF MATH, COL CHARLESTON, 1996-; vis prof, Univ

Del los Andes, Venezuela, 1994-1995; Fulbright lectr, Venezuela, 1994-1995; Grad prog dir, Master Sci Prog Math, 1992-1994; asstprof, Col Charleston, 1989-1996. **Research Statement & Publications:** Mathematical probability theory including optimal stopping theory, sequential decision theory and stochastic processes. **Mailing Address:** Dept Math, Col Charleston, 66 George St, Charleston, SC 29424-0001. **Fax:** 843-953-1410. **E-Mail:** jonesm@cofc.edu

JONES, MARVIN RICHARD, DEVELOPING PROCEDURES & EQUIPMENT FOR MAKING & TESTING PRODUCTS. **Personal Data:** b Bristow, Okla, November 3, 1914; m 1935, c 3. **Honors & Awards:** Oil Drop Award, Am Soc Mech Engrs, 1988, Silver Patent Award, 1989. **Professional Experience:** CONSULT ENGR, 1985-; vpres res & develop, Koomey Inc, 1981-1985; dirres & mgr eng serv, Cameron Iron Works, Inc, 1956-1979; pres, Petrol Mech Develop Co, 1949-1955; chief engr, Oil Ctr Tool Co, 1946-1949; prod develop engr, Cameron Iron Works, Inc, 1939-1943; prod designer, Hughes Tool Co, 1937-1939; prod draftsman, Am Iron & MachWorks, 1936-1937. **Memberships:** Fel Am Soc Mech Engrs; Soc Petrol Engrs. **Research Statement & Publications:** Developing high pressure equipment for drilling and producing oil wells; author of numerous publications; granted 66 US patents and 81 foreign patents. **Mailing Address:** 414 Flintdale Rd, Houston, TX 77024. **Fax:** 713-467-1860.

JONES, MAURICE HARRY, PHYSICAL CHEMISTRY, ORGANIC CHEMISTRY. **Personal Data:** b London, Eng, January 7, 1927; m 1952, Eleanor; c Derek R & Heather A. **Education:** Univ London, BSc, 1947, PhD (chem), 1950. **Professional Experience:** EXEC DIR, CAN RES MGT ASN, 1988-; consult, 1984-1988; vpres opers, Dept Res Coord & Planning, Ont Res Found, Can, 1983-1984; vpres interdept prog, Dept ResCoord & Planning, Ont Res Found, Can, 1977-1983; dir, Dept Res Coord & Planning, Ont ResFound, Can, 1972-1977; dir dept phys chem, Ont Res Found, Can, 1963-1972; asst dir deptchem, Ont Res Found, Can, 1954-1963; bakelite res fel polymerization, Univ Birmingham, 1952-1953; fel photochem, Nat Res Coun, Can, 1950-1952. **Memberships:** Am Chem Soc; fel Chem Inst Can; Can Res Mgt Asn. **Research Statement & Publications:** Polymerization; membranes; electroplating; pollution; research management. **Mailing Address:** 4642 Badminton Dr, Mississauga, ON L5M 2Y1, Can.

JONES, MELTON RODNEY, GENETICS, BIOLOGY. **Personal Data:** b Richmond, Va, January 13, 1945; m 1968, Energelia; c 2. **Education:** Am Univ, BS, 1966; Howard Univ, MS, 1968, PhD (zoology), 1972. **Professional Experience:** VPRES, ACAD & STUDENT SERV, JOHN TYLER COMMUNITY COL, as of 2004; DEAN ACAD & STUDENT SERV, JOHN TYLER COMMUNITY COL, 1986-; prof biol &chmn, Dept Sci, 1978-1986; asst to dean, Community Col, Baltimore, 1978-1986; asst to dean, Col Osteop med, Ohio Univ, 1978-1986; asst to assoc dean basic sci, Ohio Univ, 1977-1978; asst prof biol, Univ Colo, Boulder, 1975-1977; Div chmn, Natural Sci & Math, Shaw Univ, 1972-1975. **Memberships:** AAAS; Am Inst Biol Sci; Sigma Xi. **Research Statement & Publications:** Biochemical genetics with respect to enzyme activity and gene dosage. **Mailing Address:** Acad & Stud Serv, John Tyler Community Col, Moyar Hall, M101C, Chester, VA 23831-5399. **Fax:** 804-796-4362. **E-Mail:** mjones@jtcc.edu

JONES, MELVIN D, PROSTHODONTICS. **Personal Data:** b Hardisty, Alta, November 16, 1943; m 1983, c 5. **Education:** Univ Alta, DDS, 1966; Ind Univ, Indianapolis, MSD, 1969. **Professional Experience:** MEM STAFF, UNIV CALGARY, 1975-; supvr audiovisual sect, Fac Dent, Univ Alta, 1970-1971; assoc prof dent, UnivAlta, 1969-1975; mem, Am Asn Dent Schs, 1969-1970; instr, Ind Univ, Indianapolis, 1968-1969; Can Fund Dent Educ fel, 1967-1969; asst prof dent, Univ Alta, 1966-1967; mentor, Calgary & Dist Grathological Soc. **Memberships:** AAAS; Calgary & Dist Dent Soc; Can Dent Asn; Can Acad Restorative Dent; Am Acad Crown & Bridge Prosthodontics; Asn Prosthodontists Can. **Research Statement & Publications:** Phosphate-bonded investments for regular gold castings; three dimensional recordings of mandibular movement; interactive video uses in teaching; audiovisual education; failures of cast restorations long term clinical study; myofacial pain syndrome clinical study; differential diagnosis of temporomandibular joint pain. **Mailing Address:** 1321 Hillside Dr, Vestal, NY 13850-1211.

JONES, MERRELL ROBERT, COMPUTER SCIENCE, PHYSICS INSTRUCTION. **Personal Data:** b Salt Lake City, Utah, June 27, 1938; m 1959, Carol; c Ruth, Mark R, Daniel M, Stephen E, Rebecca & David P. **Education:** Univ Utah, BS, 1960, PhD (physics), 1970. **Professional Experience:** PROF COMPUT SCI, SOUTHERN UTAH STATE COL, as of 2005; prof comput sci, Southern Utah State Col, beginning 1983; dir, Comput Ctr, 1974-1982; chmn dept eng & phys sci, Southern Utah State Col, 1973-1976; from asst prof to prof physics, Southern Utah State Col, 1966-1983. **Memberships:** Asn Comput Mach; Digital Equip Corp Users Soc. **Research Statement & Publications:** Computer science; computers in undergraduate instruction; methods and curricula in astronomy physics and computer science in elementary and secondary schools; piezoelectricity; point defects in crystals. **Mailing Address:** Dept Math & Comput Sci, Southern Utah State Col, Cedar City, UT 84720. **Fax:** 435-865-8051. **E-Mail:** jones@suu.edu

JONES, MERRILL C(ALVIN), REAL TIME SOFTWARE, NERWORK-SYSTEM MANAGEMENT. **Personal Data:** b Salona, Pa, January 4, 1925; m 1950, c 4. **Education:** Univ NMex, BS, 1952, MA, 1970. **Professional Experience:** RETIRED; sr mem tech staff, Sandia Nat Labs, 1990-2002; mem tech staff, Sandia Nat Labs, 1985-1990; div supvr, Sandia Nat Labs, 1977-1985; mem tech staff, Sandia Nat Labs, 1965-1977; sect supvr & mem tech staff, Sandia Nat Labs, 1955-1965; sect supvr metrol, SandiaNat Labs, 1953-1955; measurement engr, Sandia Nat Labs, 1952-1953; electronics technician, Sandia Nat Labs, 1948-1952; eng technician, Indust Apparatus Div, Sylvania Elec Prod, Inc, 1944-1948. **Memberships:** Comput Soc; Inst Elec & Electronics Engrs; Asn Comput Mach. **Research Statement & Publications:** Measurement of electrical and physical quantities; application of computers to scientific and administrative disciplines; software design and maintenance; real time data collection and reduction; user-computer interface; computer languages/applications; network and system administration/management. **Mailing Address:** 1416 Ariz NE, Albuquerque, NM 87110.

JONES, MICHAEL E, NUCLEAR PHYSICS. **Personal Data:** b Mobile, Ala, September 3, 1952. **Education:** Univ NC, MS, 1974; Auburn Univ, BS, 1973, PhD (physics), 1978. **Professional Experience:** RES, DEPT ENERGYS, LOS ALAMOS NAT LAB, as of 2003; plasma physics appln group, Los Alamos Nat Lab, beginning 1978. **Memberships:** fel Am Phys Soc. **Mailing Address:** Los Alamos Nat Lab, B259, PO Box 1663, Los Alamos, NM 87545. **Fax:** 505-665-3389.

JONES, MICHAEL R, HUMAN NUTRITION. **Personal Data:** b Jacksonville, Tex, March 9, 1946. **Education:** Univ Calif, Los Angeles, PhD (org chem), 1983. **Professional Experience:** ASSOC DIR, CLIN AFFAIRS, DIV RENAL RES, BAXTER HEALTHCARE CORP, as of 1997; SR RES MGR NUTRIT, BAXTER HEALTH CARE CORP, 1993-. **Research Statement & Publications:** Human nutrition. **Mailing Address:** Div Renal Res, Baxter Health Care Corp, 1620 Waukegan Rd, McGaw Park, IL 60085. **Fax:** 847-473-6923.

JONES, MILLARD LAWRENCE, JR, CHEMICAL ENGINEERING. **Personal Data:** b August 14, 1933; m 1959, c 2. **Education:** Univ Utah, BS, 1955; Univ Mich, Ann Arbor, MS, 1958, PhD (chem eng), 1961. **Professional Experience:** PROF, DEPT CHEM & ENVIRON ENG, UNIV TOLEDO, 1990-; Consult, Owens-Ill Corp, 1967-1987; from asst prof to assoc prof chem eng, Univ Toledo, 1966-1990; Res engr, DowChem Corp, 1961-1966. **Memberships:** Am Inst Chem Engrs. **Research Statement & Publications:** Process dynamics and controls. **Mailing Address:** Dept Chem & Environ Eng, Univ Toledo, Toledo, OH 43606-3390. **Fax:** 419-530-8086. **E-Mail:** mjones@eng.utoledo.edu

JONES, MILTON BENNION, SOIL FERTILITY, RANGE SCIENCE & IMPROVEMENT. **Personal Data:** b Cedar City, Utah, January 15, 1926; m 1951, Grace G; c Milton Bennion Jr, Richard Wayne, Tammera, Jolayne, Sherilee & Karolyn. **Education:** Utah State Univ, BS, 1952; Ohio State Univ, PhD (soil fertil), 1955. **Professional Experience:** Dept Agr & Res, Basque Govt, 1987; lectr, Univ Evora, Portugal, 1984; res sulfur nutrit forage crops, CSIRO, Canberra, Australia, 1974; AGRONOMIST, HOPLAND FIELD STA & LECTR, UNIV CALIF, 1969-; teacher forage crops & range mgt, Univ Calif, Davis, 1967-; Res mineral nutrit of trop legumes, IRI Res Inst, Brazil, 1963-1965; Assoc agronomist, Sta, 1955-1969. **Memberships:** Fel Am Soc Agron, 1987; Am Soc Range Mgt; fel Soil Sci Soc Am. **Research Statement & Publications:** Range plant nutrition; range soils; range fertilization; range management, pasture management. **Mailing Address:** 3501 Leland Lane, Ukiah, CA 95482. **E-Mail:** mbjggj@juno.com

JONES, MORTON EDWARD, physical chemistry; deceased, see previous edition for last biography

JONES, NOEL DUANE, CRYSTALLOGRAPHY, DRUG DESIGN. **Personal Data:** b Omaha, Nebr, August 4, 1937; m 1963, Katharine; c Evan & Leonard. **Education:** Rensselaer Polytech Inst, BS, 1959; Calif Inst Technol, PhD (chem), 1964. **Professional Experience:** RETIRED; vpres drug design, Eli Lilly & Co, 1994-2000; vis res scientist, Yale Univ, 1984-1985; res adv, Eli Lilly & Co, 1967-1993; NIH fel, Univ Berne, 1964-1966. **Memberships:** Am Chem Soc; Am Crystallog Asn. **Research Statement & Publications:** Structure-based design of biologically active compounds. **Mailing Address:** 3 Flagstone Path, Woodlands, TX 77381-6621. **Fax:** 936-273-3854. **E-Mail:** ndj@lcc.net

JONES, NOLAN T(HOMAS), ELECTRICAL ENGINEERING. **Personal Data:** b Manhattan, Kans, May 5, 1927; m 1985, c 3. **Education:** Univ Nebr, BSc, 1951; Mass Inst Technol, SM, 1954. **Professional Experience:** PRES, MIDDLESEX CANAL ASN, as of 1999; proj leader, Mitre Corp, Bedford, 1964-1966; from tech staff to comput syst engr, Mitre Corp, Bedford, 1959-1992; sub-dept head, Mitre Corp, Bedford, 1959-1973; Res engr electronic eng, Lincoln Lab, Mass Inst Technol, 1951-1958. **Memberships:** Inst Elec & Electronics Engrs. **Research Statement & Publications:** Applications of digital computers for real-time automatic control. **Mailing Address:** Middlesex Canal Asn, PO Box 333, Billerica, MA 01821. **E-Mail:** ntjones@dragon.mv.com

JONES, NORRIS W, GEOLOGY. **Education:** Carleton Col, BS, 1959; Univ Min, MS, 1963; Va Tech, PhD, 1968. **Professional Experience:** EMER PROF GEOL, UNIV WIS, OSHKOSH, 2000-. **Mailing Address:** Univ Wis, Oshkosh, WI 54901. **Fax:** 920-424-0240. **E-Mail:** jonesnw@uwosh.edu

JONES, OLIVER WILLIAM, MEDICINE, BIOCHEMISTRY. **Personal Data:** b Ft Smith, Ark, February 7, 1932; m 1955, c 4. **Education:** Northeastern State Col, Okla, BS, 1954; Univ Okla, MD, 1957. **Professional Experience:** OBSTETRIX MED GROUP COLO, 2000-; Dept Obstet& Gynec, Sch Med, Univ Colo, 1991-2000; prof med & pediat, Sch Med, Univ Calif, San Diego, 1973-1981; NIH grants, 1969-1975; Am Cancer Soc res grant, 1969-1973; dir Div Med Genetics, Sch Med, Univ Calif, San Diego, 1968-1981; assoc prof, SchMed, Univ Calif, San Diego, 1968-1973; Damon Runyon Found res grant, 1968-1971; assoc prof med & biochem, Duke Univ, 1967-1968; co-dir, Res Training Prog, Med Ctr, Duke Univ, 1966-1968; asst prof biochem, Duke Univ, 1966-1967; Nat Inst Arthritis & Metab Dis res grant, 1965-1968; asst profmed, Duke Univ, 1965-1966; NIH career develop award, 1963-1968; fel biochem, Stanford Univ, 1963-1965; res assoc biochem genetics, Nat Heart Inst, 1961-1963; sr resident, Med Ctr, Duke Univ, 1960-1961; Arthritis & RheumatismAsn fel, Duke Univ, 1959-1960; from intern to jr resident med, Med Ctr, DukeUniv, 1957-1959. **Memberships:** AAAS; Am Soc Human Genetics; Am Soc Cell Biol; Am Soc Biol Chemists; SocPediat Res. **Research Statement & Publications:** Genetic counseling; regulation of pyrimidine biosynthesis; cytogenetics. **Mailing Address:** 1601 E 19th Ave, Ste 6500, Denver, CO 80218. **Fax:** 303-839-7761. **E-Mail:** bill.jones@childrenwithdiabetes.com

JONES, ORDIE R (REGGIE), CONSERVATION TILLAGE, WIND & WATER EROSION CONTROL. **Personal Data:** b Memphis, Tex, August 7, 1937; m 1957, c 3. **Education:** Tex Tech Univ, Lubbock, BS, 1959; WTex State Univ, Canyon, MS, 1971. **Professional Experience:** AGRIPARTNER COORDR, TEX AGR EXTENSION SERV, AMARILLO, 1998-; res soil scientist, Agr Res Serv, Bushland, Tex, Us Dept Agr, 1968-1997; coordr, AgriPartner Prog, Tex A&M; field agronomist. **Memberships:** Soil Sci Soc Am; Am Soc Agron; fel Soil & Water Conserv Soc; Int Soc Soil Sci. **Research Statement & Publications:** Developing soil and water conservation practices for use in dryland cropping in semi-arid areas; cropping and tillage practices that conserv water, reduce erosion and increase water use efficiency of crops. **Mailing Address:** Tex Agr Extension Serv, Panhandle Dist 1, Tex A&M Univ, 6500 Amarillo Blvd W, Amarillo, TX 79016. **Fax:** 806-358-9718. **E-Mail:** or-jones@tamu.edu

JONES, ORVAL ELMER, WEAPON SAFETY, APPLIED MECHANICS. **Personal Data:** b Ft Morgan, Colo, April 9, 1934; m 1954, Pauline; c Carol, Sharon & Lawrence. **Education:** Colo State Univ, BS, 1956; Calif Inst Technol, MS, 1957, PhD (mech eng), 1961. **Honors & Awards:** Amer Soc of Mech Engrs Ind Appreciation Award, 1989. **Professional Experience:** RETIRED; consult, Sandia Nat Labs, beginning 1993; distinguished assoc award, US Dept Energy, 1993; hon consult mech eng, UnivNMex, 1991-1992; exec vpres tech progrs, Sandia Corp, 1986-1993; vpres defenseprogs, Sandia Corp, 1983-1986; vpres tech support, Sandia Corp, 1982-1983; dir eng sci, Sandia Corp, 1978-1982; dir nuclear waste&environ progs, SandiaCorp, 1977-1978; dir nuclear security systs, Sandia Corp, 1974-1977; dir solidstate sci res, Sandia Corp, 1971-1974; mgr phys res dept, Sandia Corp, 1968-1971; vis lectr, Univ NMex, 1964 & 1968; div supvr dynamic stress res, Sandia Corp, 1964-1968; staff mem, Sandia Corp, 1961-1964; res engr, HydromechLab, Calif Inst Technol, 1960-1961; NSF fel, 1959-1960; tech staff mem, Res & Develop Labs, Hughes Aircraft Co, Calif, 1956-1957. **Memberships:** Fel Soc Mech Eng; Am Phys Soc; Sigma Xi. **Research Statement & Publications:** Response of piezoelectrics, ferroelectrics and semiconductor to shock loading; nuclear security safeguards and safety systems for transportation and storage of nuclear materials and weapons; underground repository and technology development for nuclear waste isolation; engineering applications of structural dynamics, transport phenomena, and rock mechanics. **Mailing Address:** 12321 Eastridge Dr NE, Albuquerque, NM 87112-4604. **E-Mail:** oejones@aol.com

JONES, OWEN C, FLUID MECHANICS. **Professional Experience:** PROF ENVIRON & ENERGY ENG, RENSSELAER POLYTECH INST, as of 1998. **Mailing Address:** Rensselaer Polytech Inst, 110 Eigth St, Troy, NY 12180-3590.

JONES, OWEN LLOYD, PHYSICAL CHEMISTRY, RADIOCHEMISTRY. **Personal Data:** b Hackensack, NJ, July 31, 1935; c 6. **Education:** Drew Univ, AB, 1957; WVa Univ, MS, 1960, PhD (phys chem), 1967. **Professional Experience:** ASSOC PROF CHEM, US NAVAL ACAD, 1973-; asst prof, US Naval Acad, 1965-1973; instr chem, WVa Univ, 1960-1965. **Memberships:** Am Chem Soc; Sigma Xi. **Research Statement & Publications:** Solution kinetics; exchange rate studies using isotopic tracer techniques. **Mailing Address:** Dept Chem, US Naval Acad, Annapolis, MD 21402-5088.

JONES, OWEN THOMAS, MOLECULAR NEUROBIOLOGY, ION CHANNELS. **Education:** Univ Newcastle, Eng, BSc (Hons), 1979; Univ London, Eng, MSc, 1980; Univ Southampton, Eng, PhD (biochem), 1984. **Professional Experience:** Proj supvr, Univ Manchester, UK; consultfluorescence spectros visible genetics, 1994; ASST PROF PHARMACOL & NEUROSCI, TORONTO WESTERN HOSP, 1991-; res instr, Dept Molecular Physiol, Baylor ColMed, 1987-1991; Molecular Neurobiol Univ, Med Res Coun, Univ Cambridge, UK, 1986-1987; fel, Dept Biochem, Univ Calif, Davis, 1984-1986. **Memberships:** Am Soc Cell Biol; Am Soc Neurosci. **Research Statement & Publications:** Studying the molecular basis for ion-channel trafficking in nerve cells using fluorescence microscopy molecular biology and biochemistry; epilepsy and other neurological disorders and neurobiology generally. **Mailing Address:** Univ Manchester, Div Neuroscience Sch Biol Sci, 1.124 Stopford Bldg Oxford Rd, Manchester, M13 9PT, UK. **Fax:** 011-44-161-275-5363. **E-Mail:** owen.t.jones@man.ac.uk

JONES, PATRICIA PEARCE, IMMUNOLOGY. **Personal Data:** b 1947; m Robert. **Education:** Oberlin Col, BA, 1969; Johns Hopkins Univ, PhD (biol), 1974. **Professional Experience:** PROF CELL & DEVELOP BIOL, GENETICS & MOLECULAR BIOL, STANFORD UNIV, 1990-; from asst prof to assoc prof, Stanford Univ, 1978-1990. **Memberships:** Am Asn Immunologists. **Research Statement & Publications:** Immunogenetics; genetics, structure, function and expression of histocompatibility proteins. **Mailing Address:** Dept Biol Sci, Stanford Univ, Gilbert Rm 326A, Stanford, CA 94305-5020. **Fax:** 650-725-5807. **E-Mail:** patjones@.stanford.edu

JONES, PATRICK RAY, PHYSICAL CHEMISTRY. **Personal Data:** b Austin, Tex, October 22, 1943; m 1968, c 2. **Education:** Univ Tex, Austin, BA & BS, 1966; Stanford Univ, PhD (chem), 1971. **Professional Experience:** PROF & CHMN, DEPT CHEM, UNIV PCA, as of 2004; vis scholar chem, Stanford Univ, 1979-1980; MEM FAC CHEM, UNIV PAC, beginning 1974-; res fel chem, Calif inst technol, 1973-1974; res fel chem, Nat Acad Sci, 1971-1973. **Memberships:** Am Chem Soc; Sigma XI. **Research Statement & Publications:** Matrix isolation studies of oxygen, fluorine and chlorine atom reactions; electron-impact excitation of gases; combined liquid chromatography and mass-spectrometry; physical chemistry of organometallics. **Mailing Address:** Chem Dept, Univ Pac, 3601 Pac Ave, Stockton, CA 95211-0197. **Fax:** 209-946-2607. **E-Mail:** pjones@pacific.edu

JONES, PAUL HASTINGS, GEOLOGY. **Personal Data:** b Fostoria, Mich, August 31, 1918; m 1941, Romaine Frances Grohman; c Susan F, Roger P, Jeffrey T& Alan G. **Education:** Mich State Col, BS, 1941; La State Univ, MS, 1951, PhD, 1968. **Honors & Awards:** Meritorious Serv Award, US Dept Interior, 1975. **Professional Experience:** CONSULT, 1977-; mem fac, dept geol, La State Univ, 1974-1977; mem NatAcad Sci adv team, India, 1971; consult, India, Nepal & Bangladesh, UN, 1970; consult, WorldBank, 1966 & 1983-1987; res hydrologist, Gulf Coastal Plain, US Geol Surv, 1965-1974; chiefradiohydrol sect, Water Resources Div, US Geol Surv, DC, 1962-1964; res proj chief, GroundWater Br, Nat Reactor Testing Sta, US Geol Surv, Idaho, 1959-1962; dist geologist, US GeolSurv, Tenn, 1958-1959; tech adv, Groundwater Geol Surv, Int Co-op Admin, US Geol Surv, India, 1955-1957; dist geologist charge, US Geol Surv, Pa, 1952-1955; from geologist togeologist charge groundwater invests, US Geol Surv, La, 1942-1952; geophysicist, HalliburtonOil Well Cementing Co, Tex, 1941-1942. **Memberships:** Soc Econ Geol; fel Geol Soc Am; Am Asn Petrol Geol; Soc Petrol Eng; Am SocTest & Mat. **Research Statement & Publications:** Quantitative interpretation of borehole geophysical logs; hydrogeology of deep sedimentary basins; role of geopressure in the fluid hydrocarbon regime; hydrology of waste disposal; enhanced production of petroleum and natural gas; geothermal resources of Northern Gulf of Mexico Basin. **Mailing Address:** 3256 McConnell Dr, Baton Rouge, LA 70809.

JONES, PAUL KENNETH, BIOMETRICS, BIOSTATISTICS. **Personal Data:** b Des Moines, Iowa, January 5, 1943; m 1971, Susan. **Education:** Grinnell Col, BA, 1964; Univ Iowa, MS, 1969, PhD (statist), 1972. **Professional Experience:** ASSOC PROF EPIDEMIOL & BIOSTATIST, CASE WESTERN RES UNIV, 1980-; asst prof, Case Western Res Univ, 1973-1980; sr instr, Case Western Res Univ, 1972-1973; res asst statist, Am Col Testing, 1968-1972. **Memberships:** Am Statist Asn; Biomet Soc; Soc Epidemiologic Res. **Research Statement & Publications:** Quantitative methods in health care/health services research; statistical methods; regression, logistic regression. **Mailing Address:** Dept Epidemiol & Biostatist, Sch Med, Case Western Res Univ, Wood Bldg WG-74, Cleveland, OH 44106-4945. **Fax:** 216-368-3970. **E-Mail:** pkj@hal.case.edu

JONES, PAUL RAYMOND, ORGANIC CHEMISTRY, HISTORY OF CHEMISTRY. **Personal Data:** b Chicago, Ill, July 19, 1930; m 1958, Meredyth Manns; c Paul G, Amy E & Sarah R. **Education:** Albion Col, BA, 1952; Univ Ill, PhD, 1956. **Professional Experience:** Fulbright Sr Res Fel, 1991-1992; vis prof, Deutsches Mus, Munich, Ger, 1982-1983; Fulbright res fel, Chem Inst, Univ Freiburg, Ger, 1973; PROF CHEM, UNIV NH, 1965-; NSF sci fac fel, Max-Planck Inst, Gottingen, 1964-1965; from asst prof to assoc prof, Univ NH, 1956-1965. **Memberships:** Am Chem Soc; Hist Sci Soc. **Research Statement & Publications:** Macrocycles; ring-chain tautomerism; anhrydro dimers; history of chemistry. **Mailing Address:** Dept Chem, Univ NH Parsons Hall, Durham, NH 03824-4724.

JONES, PAUL RONALD, ORGANOMETALLIC CHEMISTRY. **Personal Data:** b York, Pa, December 19, 1940; m 1967, Priscilla; c Kevin & Anne. **Education:** Pa State Univ, BS, 1962; Purdue Univ, PhD (chem), 1966. **Honors & Awards:** W T Doherty Award, Dallas-Ft Worth Sect, Am Chem Soc, 1985. **Professional Experience:** Consult, Korean Small Indust Prom Corp, Seoul, 1990; founder & dir, Ctr Organometallic Res & Educ, 1985-1991, 1994-1999; vis scientist, Korea Advan Inst Sci & Technol, 1984; PROF CHEM, UNIV NTEX, 1979-; assoc prof, Univ Ntex, 1973-1979; asst prof, Univ Ntex, 1968-1973; res assoc chem, Univ Wis-Madison, 1966-1967. **Memberships:** Am Chem Soc; Sigma Xi. **Research Statement & Publications:** Organometallic chemistry, especially involving synthesis structure and reactions of group IV compounds; bonding in organometallic compounds; stereochemistry and mechanism of the reactions of subvalent organosilicon intermediates; polysilyl polyacetylenes. **Mailing Address:** Dept Chem, Univ NTex, PO Box 305070, Denton, TX 76203. **E-Mail:** pjones@unt.edu

JONES, PETER D, LIPID METABOLISM, FATS IN NUTRITION. **Personal Data:** b Palmerston North, NZ, April 27, 1940; m 1967, c 3. **Education:** Victoria Univ Wellington, BS, 1961, MS, 1963; Duke Univ, PhD (biochem), 1968. **Professional Experience:** PROF BIOCHEM, UNIV TENN CTR HEALTH SCI, 1983-; asst dean, Acad Affairs, Col Med, 1979-1985; from asst prof to assoc prof biochem, Univ Tenn Ctr Health Sci, 1972-1983; lectr, Victoria Univ Wellington, 1969-1972; res assoc, Univ Ariz, 1968-1969. **Memberships:** Am Soc Biochem & Molecular Biol; Memphis Area Nutrit Coun; Tenn Nutrit Coun; AAAS; Sigma Xi; Nutrit Today Soc; Am Soc Biol Chemists. **Research Statement & Publications:** Oxidative desaturation of long chain fatty acids; structure and function of the electron transport chains of the endoplasmic reticulum; nutritional role of fatty acids and lipids. **Mailing Address:** Dept Biochem, Univ Tenn Col Med, 858 Madison Ave Rm 401D MSB, Memphis, TN 38163-0001. **Fax:** 901-448-8462. **E-Mail:** pdjones@utmem.edu

JONES, PETER FRANK, PHYSICAL CHEMISTRY, AEROSPACE ENGINEERING & SPACE TECHNOLOGY. **Personal Data:** b Brooklyn, NY, March 15, 1937; m 1978, Susan; c Lisa, Robin, Jennifer, Julieanne, William & Daniel. **Education:** Univ Kans, BA, 1960; Univ Chicago, MS, 1961; Univ Calif, Los Angeles, PhD (high pressure spectros), 1967. **Professional Experience:** SR RES ENGR, UNIV NMEX, 1996-; sr engr technol develop, Forensic Sci Sect, 1987-1996; consult forensic sci & gunshot residue, 1977; head, Anal Sci Dept, 1974-1987; head, Forensic Sci Sect, 1973-1974; mem tech staff, Aerospace Corp, 1966-1973. **Research Statement & Publications:** Coordinate with other government agencies the development of space technology at the Air Force Research Lab Space Technology Directorate. **Mailing Address:** Air Force Res Lab, 3550 Aberdeen Ave SE, Kirtland AFB, NM 87117-5776. **E-Mail:** peter.jones@kirtland.af.mil

JONES, PETER HADLEY, MEDICINAL CHEMISTRY, CARDIOVASCULAR DISEASES. **Personal Data:** b Cleveland, Ohio, August 14, 1934; m 1957, Joan; c Laura F (Nelson), Peter H Jr & David P. **Education:** Harvard Univ, AB, 1956; Univ Calif, Los Angeles, PhD (org chem), 1960. **Professional Experience:** PRES, MCD6 CONSULTS, 1992-; adj prof med chem, Univ Ill, Chicago, 1987-; sr dir, Gastrointestinal Dis Res, 1986-1992; dir med chem, Searle Labs, G D Searle & Co, 1985-1986; sect had gastrointestinal dis, Searle Labs, G D Searle & Co, 1980-1985; vpres & dirres, Interx Corp, 1979-1980; head cardiovasc res, Abbott Labs, 1975-1979; mgr med chem, Abbott Labs, 1971-1975; assoc res fel, Abbott Labs, 1970-1971; instr, Dept Biochem, Med Sch, Nwestern Univ, 1969-1973; sr res chemist, Abbott Labs, 1960-1970. **Memberships:** Am Chem Soc; AAAS; Sigma Xi; fel Am Inst Chemists; NY Acad Sci. **Research Statement & Publications:** Reactions of diphenylcarbenes; chemistry of macrolide antibiotics; chemistry of hypertensive agents; development of new drugs for hypertension angina; chemical drug delivery systems; gastrointestinal drugs and diseases; polymer delivery systems. **Mailing Address:** MCD6 Consults, 1112 S Fleming Rd, Woodstock, IL 60098.

JONES, PHILIP ARTHUR, ENTOMOLOGY. **Personal Data:** b Prince George, BC, March 1, 1924. **Education:** Univ BC, BSc, 1949; Univ Wis-Madison, MSc, 1956, PhD (entom), 1963. **Professional Experience:** RETIRED; environ scientist, Environ Can, 1977-1993; tech dir, Agr Chem Div, FMC of Can Ltd, 1974-1977; mem tech comt, Can Agr Chem Asn, 1974-1977; from asst prof to assoc prof entom, SDak State Univ, 1965-1974; from proj asst to proj assoc biol control, Univ Wis, 1960-1964; res officer, Forest Biol Div, Can Dept Agr, 1958-1960; res asst forest entom, Univ Wis, 1952-1958; asst forest biologist sci serv, Can Dept Agr, 1949-1952. **Research Statement & Publications:** Environmental assessment of toxic chemicals. **Mailing Address:** PO Box 1943, Vernon, BC V1T 8Z7, Can. **E-Mail:** philip_jones@telus.net

JONES, PHILLIP B C, MEDICAL RESEARCH. **Education:** Calif State Univ, BA, MA; Univ Calif, PhD (pharmacol / physiol); Univ Ky Col Law, JD. **Professional Experience:** FREELANCE WRITER & ED, 2002-. **Mailing Address:** Seattle, WA. **E-Mail:** PhillJones@nasw.org

JONES, PHILLIPS RUSSELL, PHYSICS. **Personal Data:** b Troy, NY, August 25, 1930; m 1952, Ereda; c Linda, Kevin & Sharon. **Education:** Univ Mass, BS, 1951; Univ Conn, MA, 1956, PhD (physics), 1959. **Professional Experience:** PROF EMER PHYSICS, UNIV MASS, AMHERST, 1993-; from asst prof to prof, Univ Mass, Amherst, 1958-1993; asst physics, Univ Conn, 1954-1958; teacher, Mass PubSch, 1952. **Memberships:** Am Phys Soc. **Research Statement & Publications:** Experimental atomic physics. **Mailing Address:** Dept Physics, Univ Mass, Amherst, MA 01003. **Fax:** 413-545-1691. **E-Mail:** prjones@physics.umass.edu

JONES, PHYLLIS EDITH, NURSING. **Personal Data:** b Barrie, Ont, September 16, 1924. **Education:** Univ Toronto, BScN, 1950, MSc, 1969. **Professional Experience:** EMER PROF NURSING, UNIV TORONTO, 1989-; hon mem, Finnish Soc Prof Nursing, 1987; dean nursing, Univ Toronto, 1979-1988; from asst prof to prof, Univ Toronto, 1963-1989; external examr, Univlbadan; consult, WHO; res referee, On Ministry Health, Nat Health Res & Develop Prog; membd, Von Metro Toronto. **Memberships:** Can Pub Health Asn; fel Am Pub Health Asn; NAm Nursing Diag Asn. **Research Statement & Publications:** Innovations in community health nursing, in collaboration with physician services; nursing diagnoses. **Mailing Address:** RR 2, Owensound, ON N4K 5N4, Can.

JONES, R E DOUGLAS, MATHEMATICS. **Personal Data:** b Kansas City, Mo, November 28, 1933; m 1954, c 4. **Education:** Univ Okla, BA, 1955, MA, 1957; Iowa State Univ, PhD (math), 1962. **Professional Experience:** PROF MATH, MCKENDREE COL, 1971-; assoc prof, Univ Mo-Rolla, 1965-1971; asst prof, Wichita State Univ, 1962-1965; consult, Boeing Co, Kans, 1962-1964; instr math, Iowa State Univ, 1958-1962; Aerophys engr, Convair-Ft Worth, 1956-1958. **Memberships:** Am Math Soc; Math Asn Am. **Research Statement & Publications:** Topologies generated by metric densities; opaque sets. **Mailing Address:** Div Sci & Math, McKendree Col, 701 College Rd, Lebanon, IL 62254. **Fax:** 618-537-6259.

JONES, R NORMAN, SPECTROCHEMISTRY. **Personal Data:** b Manchester, Eng, March 20, 1913; Canadian citizen; m 1939, Magda; c R Kemeny & David L. **Education:** Univ Manchester, BSc, 1933, MSc, 1934, PhD (chem), 1936, DSc, 1954. **Honorary Degrees:** DSc, Univ Poznan, 1972, Tokyo Inst Technol, 1982. **Honors & Awards:** Herzberg Award, Spec Soc Can; Fisher Award, Chem Soc Can. **Professional Experience:** OFFICER, ORDER CAN, GOV GEN CAN, 1999-; guest scientist, Univ Alta, 1992-1978; guest researcher, Tokyo Inst Technol, Japan, 1985-1986; adj prof, Queen's Univ, Kingston, Ont, 1984; distinguished visitor, Univ Alta, 1982-1983; guest worker, Nat Res Coun Can, beginning 1979-; guest prof, Tokyo Inst Technol, Japan, 1979-1982; PVT CONSULT CHEM SPECTROS, 1977-; mem adv comt, UNISIST-UNESCO, 1974-1977; mem bur, Comt Data Sci & Technol, Int Coun Sci Unions, 1970-1974; secy taskgroup comput use, Comt Data Sci & Technol, Int Coun Sci Unions, 1967-1975; chmn, Molecular Spectros comn, Int Union Pure & Appl Chem, 1967-1971; from assoc res officer toprin res officer, Nat Res Coun Can, 1946-1977; asst prof, Queen's Univ, Can, 1943-1946; lectr chem, Queen's Univ, Can, 1942-1943; tutor biochem, Harvard Univ, 1939-1941. **Memberships:** Am Chem Soc; Royal Soc Can; Chem Inst Can; Royal Soc Chem; Int Union Pure& Appl

Chem (vpres to pres Phys Chem Div 1971-1977 emer pres 1977-). **Research Statement & Publications:** Molecular spectroscopy; use of ultraviolet, infrared and Raman spectroscopy for the elucidation of molecular structure, with special reference to steroids and other natural products; use of computers for data logging and as aids in evaluation, storage and retrieval of spectral data; molecular structure determination and analysis by vibrational spectroscopy. **Mailing Address:** Gov Gen Can, Rideau Hall One Sussex Dr, Ottawa, ON K1A 0A1, Can. **Fax:** 613-998-1664.

JONES, REESE TASKER, PSYCHOPHARMACOLOGY, DRUG DEPENDENCE. **Personal Data:** b Philadelphia, Pa, June 7, 1932; m 1956, c 3. **Education:** Univ Mich, BS, 1954, MD, 1958. **Honors & Awards:** NIMH res career develop award, beginning 1967. **Professional Experience:** DIR, DRUG DEPENDENCE RES CTR & PROF PSYCHIAT, SCH MED, UNIV CALIF, SAN FRANCISCO, 1976-; STAFF PSYCHIATRIST, LANGLEY PORTER NEUROPSYCHIAT INST, 1967-; asst prof toassoc prof res, Med Ctr, Univ Calif, 1967-1976; res psychiat, Langley Porter NeuropsychiatInst, 1962-1967. **Memberships:** Am Psychiat Asn; Psychiat Res Soc; Am Col Neuropsychopharmacol; Soc BiolPsychiat. **Research Statement & Publications:** Objective indices of psychopathology; human neurophysiology; psychopharmacology; drug dependence. **Mailing Address:** Dept Psychiat, Sch Med, Univ Calif, 401 Parnassus Ave, San Francisco, CA 94143-9911. **E-Mail:** reese@itsa.ucsf.edu

JONES, RENA TALLEY, MICROBIOLOGY. **Personal Data:** b Chipley, Ga, August 3, 1937. **Education:** Morris Brown Col, BA, 1960; Atlanta Univ, MS, 1967; Wayne State Univ, PhD (microbiol), 1974. **Professional Experience:** PROF BIOL, SPELMAN COL, as of 2003; instr biol, Spelman Col, beginning 1973; NSF grant, Atlanta Univ, 1966; instr biol, Pub Schs, Ga, 1960-1966. **Memberships:** Am Soc Microbiol; AAAS; SigmaXi. **Research Statement & Publications:** Staphylococcal and slime molds; enzymes; immunochemistry. **Mailing Address:** Dept Biol, Spelman Col, 350 Spelman Lane SW Box 343, Atlanta, GA 30314-4399. **Fax:** 404-270-5725. **E-Mail:** rjones1@spelman.edu

JONES, RICHARD BRADLEY, NUCLEAR SCIENCE, APPLIED MATHEMATICS. **Personal Data:** b Norristown, Pa, June 21, 1947. **Education:** Va Polytech Inst & State Univ, BS, 1970, MS, 1971, PhD (nuclear eng), 1974. **Professional Experience:** VPRES, HARTFORD STEAM BOILER INSPECTION, 1992-; consult, 1981-1992; vis prof appl math, Univ Florence, Italy, 1981; asst prof comput sci, State Univ NY, Plattsburgh, 1978-1981; consult, W Alton Jones Cell Sci Ctr, 1978; consult, Chem-Nuclear SystInc, 1978; mem tech staff, nuclear risk anal, Sandia Lab, 1977-1978; fel appl math, Univ Ill, 1975-1977; lectr nuclear eng, Univ Calif, Santa Barbara, 1974-1975. **Memberships:** Am Nuclear Soc; Am Soc Eng Educ; Soc Indust & Appl Math; AAAS. **Research Statement & Publications:** Applied mathematics; mathematical modeling of cell regeneration; computer animation effects in education; systems design. **Mailing Address:** Hartford Steam Boiler Inspection & Ins Co, One State St, Hartford, CT 06102-5025. **Fax:** 860-7225530. **E-Mail:** Richard_Jones@hsb.com

JONES, RICHARD CONRAD, botany; deceased, see previous edition for last biography

JONES, RICHARD DELL, CARDIOVASCULAR PHYSIOLOGY, BIOMATERIALS. **Education:** Case Western Reserve Univ, PhD (physiol), 1962. **Professional Experience:** RETIRED; dir physiol, Div Surg Res, St Luke's Hosp, as of 1975. **Mailing Address:** Div Surg Res, St Luke's Hosp 3108 Lincoln Blvd, Cleveland Heights, OH 44118-2036. **Fax:** 216-368-8194.

JONES, RICHARD ELMORE, PHYSICAL PHARMACY. **Personal Data:** b Rochester, NY, July 16, 1944; m 1969, c 1. **Education:** Dartmouth Col, AB, 1965; Stanford Univ, PhD (phys chem), 1970. **Professional Experience:** VPRES, RES & DEVELOP, MATRIX PHARMACEUT INC, 1991-; vpres, Pharmaceut Develop, Pharmetrix Corp, 1989-1991; vpres develop, Liposome Technol Inc, 1988-1989; actg dir, Pharmaceut Mfg, 1985 & 1986; dir, pharmaceut res & develop, Genentech Inc, 1984-1988; dept head, Inst Pharmaceut Sci, Syntex Res, 1978-1984; sr staff researcher, Inst Pharmaceut Sci, Syntex Res, 1977-1978; adj prof, Univ Pac Sch Pharm, 1974-1975, 1980-1984; staff researcher, Inst Pharmaceut Sci, Syntex Res, 1971-1977; sr progammer & analyst, Syntex Corp, 1969-1971. **Memberships:** Am Chem Soc; AAAS; NY Acad Sci; Am Asn Pharmaceut Scientists. **Research Statement & Publications:** Percutaneous absorption; experimental design in formulation problems; pharmaceutical aerosols; protein drug delivery. **Mailing Address:** Matrix Pharmaceut Inc, 34700 Campus Dr, Fremont, CA 94555.

JONES, RICHARD EVAN, COMPARATIVE ENDOCRINOLOGY, REPRODUCTIVE BIOLOGY. **Personal Data:** b Sacramento, Calif, May 13, 1940; m 1980, c 4. **Education:** Univ Calif, Berkeley, BA, 1961, MA, 1964, PhD (zoology), 1968. **Professional Experience:** PROF EMER BIOL, UNIV COLO, BOULDER, as of 2005; prof biol, Univ Colo, Boulder, beginning 1980; res career develop award, NIH, 1974-1979; from asst prof to assoc prof, Univ Colo, Boulder, 1969-1980; asst prof behave sci, Hershey Med Ctr, Pa State Univ, 1968-1969. **Research Statement & Publications:** Control of ovarian follicular growth; reptilian reproduction; control of uterine contraction. **Mailing Address:** Dept EPO Biol, Univ Colo, Campus Box 334, Boulder, CO 80309. **Fax:** 303-492-8699. **E-Mail:** michael.breed@colorado.edu

JONES, RICHARD EVAN, PHYSICAL CHEMISTRY, INORGANIC CHEMISTRY. **Personal Data:** b Oak Park, Ill, August 3, 1940; m 1964, c 1. **Education:** Monmouth Col, BA, 1962; Univ Hawaii, PhD (chem), 1970. **Professional Experience:** PROF CHEM, LEWIS & CLARK COMMUNITY COL, 1980-; assoc prof, Lewis & Clark Community Col, 1970-1980; NDEA Title IV fel, 1967; lab mgr plastics, Gat Ke Corp, 1964-1966; res scientist, Continental Can Co, 1962-1964; lab asst qual control, RalphWells & Co, 1961-1962. **Memberships:** Am Chem Soc. **Research Statement & Publications:** Aqueous-nonaqueous solvent extraction of metals; better methods for presentation of chemistry in lower division courses. **Mailing Address:** Lewis & Clark Community Col, 5800 Godfrey Rd, Godfrey, IL 62035. **E-Mail:** richardj81@adl.com

JONES, RICHARD HUNN, BIOSTATISTICS, COMPUTER SCIENCE. **Personal Data:** b Ridley Township, Pa, October 31, 1934; m 1981, Julie; c 4. **Education:** Pa State Univ, BS, 1956, MS, 1957; Brown Univ, PhD (appl math), 1961. **Professional Experience:** PROF EMERITUS BIOMET, UNIV COLO SCH MED, DENVER, 2005-; prof biomet, Univ Colo sch med, Denver, 1975-2005; dir, Sci & Comput Ctr, 1975-1982; chmn dept, Univ Hawaii, 1970-1973; Consult, Tripler Army Hosp, Hawaii, 1969-1973; prof info & comput sci, Univ Hawaii, 1968-1975; from asst prof to assoc prof statist, Johns Hopkins Univ, 1962-1968; Consult, RCA Serv Co, Fla, 1962-1966; Consult, Swed Meteorol & Hydrol Inst, 1962; NSF fel, Univ Stockholm, 1961-1962. **Memberships:** Biomet Soc; fel Am Statist Asn. **Research Statement & Publications:** Time series analysis; stochastic processes; statistical data analysis. **Mailing Address:** Dept Prev Med & Biometrics, Sch Med Univ Colo PO Box B-119, Denver, CO 80262. **Fax:** 303-315-3183. **E-Mail:** richard.jones@uchsc.edu

JONES, RICHARD LAMAR, INSECT PHYSIOLOGY, INSECT BEHAVIOR. **Personal Data:** b Charleston, Miss, May 31, 1939; m 1964, c 2. **Education:** Miss State Univ, BS, 1963, MS, 1965; Univ Calif, Riverside, PhD (insect toxicol), 1968. **Professional Experience:** DEAN & DIR, UNIV FLA, as of 2001; prof & head, dept entom, Univ Minn, beginning 1984; Fulbright Scholar, Univ Leiden, Netherlands, 1980; assoc prof insect physiol, Dept Entom, Univ Minn, 1977-1984; res assoc, Univ Ga, 1969-1977; insect physiologist, Southern Grain Insect Res Lab, Agr ResServ, USDA, 1968-1977. **Memberships:** AAAS; Entom Soc Am; Am Chem Soc. **Research Statement & Publications:** Investigation of chemicals associated with insect behavior. **Mailing Address:** Inst Food & Agr Sci, Univ Fla, Gainesville, FL 32611.

JONES, RICHARD LEE, LUNG PHYSIOLOGY. **Personal Data:** b Mendota, Ill, June 27, 1944; m 1980, c 1. **Education:** St Thomas Col, BS, 1966; Univ Marquette, MS, 1969, PhD (physiol), 1970. **Professional Experience:** PROF MED, UNIV ALTA, 1986-; sci assoc, Royal Alexandria Hosp, beginning 1977; assoc prof physiol, Univ Alta, 1977-1986; dir, Pulmonary Lab, Univ Hosp, beginning 1973; asst prof, Univ Alta, 1973-1977; Lectr, Univ Alta, 1971-1973. **Memberships:** Sigma Xi; Am Physiol Soc; Am Col Chest Physicians; NY Acad Sci; Can Soc ClinInvest. **Research Statement & Publications:** High frequency ventilation; regional lung function; exercise training in patients with lung disease; Published over 10 articles. **Mailing Address:** Dept Med, Univ Alta, 2E4 42 Walter Mackenzie Ctr, Edmonton, AB T6G 2B7, Can. **E-Mail:** rjones@sol.uah.ualberta.ca

JONES, RICHARD S, BIOLOGY. **Education:** Univ Mo, AB, 1979; Wesleyan Univ, PhD, 1984. **Professional Experience:** PROF BIOL, SOUTHERN METHODIST UNIV, 2004-. **Mailing Address:** Dept Biol Sci Southern Methodist Univ, Fondren Sci Bldg 333 DLS, Dallas, TX 75275-0376. **Fax:** 214-768-3955. **E-Mail:** rjones@smu.edu

JONES, RICHARD THEODORE, MEDICINE, BIOCHEMISTRY. **Personal Data:** b Portland, Ore, November 9, 1929; m 1953, c 3. **Education:** Univ Ore, BS, 1953, MS & MD, 1956; Calif Inst Technol, PhD (chem), 1961. **Professional Experience:** PROF EMER BIOCHEM, MED SCH, UNIV ORE, as of 2004; spec consult to pres, Univ Ore Health Sci Ctr, 1978-1979; actg pres, Univ OreHealth Sci Ctr, 1977-1978; prof biochem & chmndept, med sch, Univ Ore, beginning 1966; assoc prof exp med & biochem, Med Sch, Univ Ore, ending 1966; asst prof exp med & biochem, Med Sch, Univ Ore, beginning 1961; intern med, Hosp Univ Pa, 1956-1957; mem, Biochem Training Comt, NIH, Med Scientist Training Comt, Sickle Cell Ctr Rev Comt & Blood Res Rev Group; med scientist, Training Comt, Nat Inst GenMed Serv; former mem biochem comt, Nat Bd Med Examrs. **Memberships:** Am Soc Hemat; Int Soc Hemat; Am Fedn Clin Res; Am Soc Biol Chemists. **Research Statement & Publications:** Medical and biochemical genetics, structure and function of normal and abnormal hemoglobins and other human proteins. **Mailing Address:** Dept Biochem, Sch Med, Ore Health Sci Univ, L224 3181, SW Sam Jackson Park Rd, Portland, OR 97201. **Fax:** 503-494-8393. **E-Mail:** brennanr@ohsu.edu

JONES, RICHARD VICTOR, SOLID STATE PHYSICS ELECTROMAGNETISM & SOLID STATE PHYSICS. **Personal Data:** b Oakland, Calif, June 8, 1929; m 1960, Bernice; c Jonathan, Daniel & Joshua. **Education:** Univ Calif, BA, 1951, PhD (physics), 1956. **Honorary Degrees:** MA, Harvard, 1961. **Professional Experience:** ROBERT L WALLACE RES PROF APPL PHYSICS, DIV ENG & APPL SCI, HARVARD UNIV, 2003-; Robert L Wallace prof appl physics, Harvard Univ, 1982-2003; prof appl physics, Harvard Univ, 1971-1982; dean grad sch arts & sci, Harvard Univ, 1971-1972; assoc dean div eng & appl physics, Harvard Univ, 1969-1971; vis MacKay Prof, Univ Calif, Berkeley, 1967-1968; Guggenheim fel, 1960-1961; from asst prof to assoc prof appl physics, Harvard Univ, 1957-1971; sr engr, Shockley Semiconductor Lab, Beckman Instruments, Inc, 1955-1957. **Research Statement & Publications:** Optical physics and electromagnetic phenomena; electronic and optical materials; ceramics; theory and application of magnetism and ferroelectricity. **Mailing Address:** Div Eng & Appl Sci, Harvard Univ, 29 Oxford St, Cambridge, MA 02138. **E-Mail:** jones@deas.harvard.edu

JONES, ROBERT CHARLES, DESIGN OF DISPLAYS, DESIGN OF ASPHERICAL ASYMMETRIC LENSES FOR COLOR TELEVISIONS. **Personal Data:** b Pottsville, Pa, December 11, 1938; div, c Eric C & Jared R. **Education:** Lehigh Univ, BS, 1961; Drexel Univ, MS, 1965. **Professional Experience:** ENGR, FIDELITY TECHNOL CORP, 1996-; PROG MGR, FIDELITYTECHNOL CORP, 1992-; consult, China, 1989-1991; syst engr, Valley Forge, Pa, 1987-1989; mgr optical design eng, Gen Elec Co, Syracuse, NY, 1972-1987; Syst design engr, Univac-SperryRand Corp, 1970-1972; Sr engr, Philco-Ford Corp, Philadelphia, 1961-1970. **Memberships:** Optical Soc Am. **Research Statement & Publications:** Front end design and process development of new state of the art color cathode ray tubes; directed technical personnel and initiated product research and development on a variety of consumer electronic products; fabrication of electron guns for CRTs. **Mailing Address:** 2501 Kutztown Rd, Reading, PA 19605-2961. **Fax:** 610-921-9446.

JONES, ROBERT CLARK, OPTICS. **Personal Data:** b Toledo, Ohio, June 30, 1916; m 1977. **Education:** Harvard Univ, AB, 1938, AM, 1939, PhD (physics), 1941. **Honors & Awards:** Lomb Medal, Optical Soc Am, 1944, Frederic Ives Medal, 1972; ThomasYoung Medal & Prize, Brit Inst Physics, 1977. **Professional Experience:** RETIRED; res fel physics, Polaroid Corp, 1967-1982; sr physicist, PolaroidCorp, 1944-1967; mem tech staff, Bell Tel Labs, 1941-1944. **Memberships:** Fel Optical Soc Am; fel Acoust Soc Am; fel Soc Photog Sci & Eng (vpres, 1959-1963); fel Am Acad Arts & Sci. **Research Statement & Publications:** Theoretical physics; theoretical optics; detectivity and detective quantum efficiency of radiation detectors; theoretical models of photographic films; theory of absorption of light by developed photographic films. **Mailing Address:** 1716 Cambridge St Apt 27, Cambridge, MA 02138.

JONES, ROBERT EDWARD, PHYSICS. **Personal Data:** b Yonkers, NY, January 14, 1923; m 1948, c 2. **Education:** Oberlin Col, BA, 1948; Univ Mich, MA, 1949; Pa State Univ, PhD (physics), 1953. **Professional Experience:** RETIRED; emer prof physics, Linfield Col, 1987; chmn, Div Natural Sci &Math, 1974-1979; actg dir, Linfield Res Inst, 1965-1968; prof, Div Natural Sci & Math, 1963-1987; physicist, Field Emission Corp, 1961-1963; physicist, Linfield Res Inst, beginning 1956; from actg head to head dept, Linfield Col, 1956-1974; assoc prof, Linfield Col, 1955-1963; assoc prof& actg dir, Ionosphere Res Lab, Pa State Univ, 1954-1955; instr physics, Ionosphere Res Lab, PaState Univ, 1953-1954; res asst eng res, Ionosphere Res Lab, Pa State Univ, 1952-1953. **Memberships:** AAAS; Am Asn Physics Teachers; Optical Soc Am. **Research Statement & Publications:** Physics of the upper atmosphere. **Mailing Address:** 708 NW Meadowood Circle, McMinnville, OR 97128.

JONES, ROBERT F, GENERAL SURGERY, SURGICAL ONCOLOGY. **Personal Data:** b Dallas, Tex, December 30, 1926; m 1953, Jerri; c 4. **Education:** Univ Tex, Dallas, MD, 1952; Am Bd Surg, cert, 1964. **Professional Experience:** RETIRED; from assoc prof to prof surg, Med Sch, Univ Wash, 1974-1992; NIH res fel, Rosnell Park Mem Inst, Buffalo, 1967-1968; from instr to assoc prof, Univ Tex Health Sci Ctr, Dallas, 1963-1974; Am Cancer Soc advan clin fel, 1963-1966; res fel surg, USPHS fel, 1962-1963; fel surg oncol,

MD Anderson Hosp, Houston, 1961-1962; res fel surg, Univ Tex Southwestern Med Sch, Dallas, 1955. **Memberships:** Am Col Surgeons; Am Soc Clin Oncol; Am Asn Cancer Educ; Am Cancer Soc; Soc Surg Oncol. **Research Statement & Publications:** Viral and surgical oncology; tumor immunology; clinical cancer. **Mailing Address:** 20105 SE 32nd St, Sammamish, WA 98075-7404. **Fax:** 425-391-1827.

JONES, ROBERT JAMES, CROP PHYSIOLOGY, AGRONOMY. **Personal Data:** b Dawson, Ga, June 10, 1951; m 1970, c 1. **Education:** Ft Valley State Col, BS, 1973; Univ Ga, MS, 1975; Univ Mo, PhD (crop physiol), 1978. **Professional Experience:** PROF & SR VICE PRES STUD DEVELOP, as of 2001; from assoc prof, fisheries & wild life, to vice provost fac & acad personnel, Univ Minn, beginning 1980; asst prof corn physiol, Fisheries & Wildlife, Univ Minn, 1978-1980; soil conservationist, Soil Conserv Serv, 1970-1973. **Memberships:** Crop Sci Soc Am; Am Soc Agron; Am Soc Plant Physiologists. **Research Statement & Publications:** Corn physiology; major interest in the relationship between photosynthesis and dark respiration during plant ontogeny and as affected by nutritional and environmental stress factors. **Mailing Address:** DeptAgron & Plant Genetics, Univ Minn, 100 Church St SE 236 Morrill Hall, Minneapolis, MN 55455. **Fax:** 612-625-1268. **E-Mail:** jones012@umn.edu

JONES, ROBERT L, SOIL MINERALOGY. **Personal Data:** b Wellston, Ohio, January 26, 1936; m, c 3. **Education:** Ohio State Univ, BSc, 1958, MSc, 1959; Univ Ill, PhD (soil mineral), 1962. **Professional Experience:** PROF SOIL MINERAL & ECOL, UNIV ILL, URBANA, as of 2004; from asst prof to assoc prof, 1964-1973; res assoc, 1962-1964. **Memberships:** Am Soc Agron; Mineral Soc Am; Soc Environ Geochem Health. **Research Statement & Publications:** Soil mineral analysis techniques; applied mineralogy in soil genesis studies; biogeochemistry. **Mailing Address:** Dept Nat Res Env Sci, Univ Ill, Urbana, IL 61801. **E-Mail:** rljones1@uiuc.edu

JONES, ROBERT MILLARD, SOLID MECHANICS. **Personal Data:** b Mattoon, Ill, August 8, 1939; m 1963, Donna; c Mark, Karen & Christopher. **Education:** Univ Ill, Urbana, BS, 1960, MS, 1961, PhD (theoret & appl mech), 1964. **Honors & Awards:** 2002 Am Soc Composites Composite Materials Award. **Professional Experience:** RETIRED; Heath Techn, 1987 & TRW, 1993; consult, Atlantic Res, 1986-1987; dir, Composite Mat & Struct Ctr, 1985-1987; consult, Bell Helicopter, 1985; EMERITUS PROF ENG SCI & MECH, VA POLYTECH INST & STATE UNIV, 1981-; consult, Boeing, 1980; consult, Lockheed Missile & Space Co, 1976 & 1979; prof, Inst Technol, Southern Methodist Univ, 1975-1981; consult, USAF Mat Lab, 1971-1979; assoc prof solid mech, Inst Technol, Southern Methodist Univ, 1970-1974; Mem Tech Staff, The Aerospace Corp, 1964-1970; Instr theoret & appl mech, Univ Ill, Urbana, 1963-1964. **Memberships:** Fel Am Inst Aeronaut & Astronaut; Am Acad Mech; Fellow Am Soc Mech Engrs; Fellow Am Soc Composites. **Research Statement & Publications:** Shell buckling; shell stress analysis; mechanics of composite materials; finite element; stress analysis of axisymmetric solids; plasticity. **Mailing Address:** Dept Eng Sci & Mech, Va Polytech Inst & State Univ, Norris Hall, Blacksburg, VA 24061. **Fax:** 540-231-4574. **E-Mail:** rmjones@vt.edu

JONES, ROBERT R, ENGINEERING. **Professional Experience:** SECY, MD TAXPAYERS ASN INC, as of 2000. **Mailing Address:** Md Taxpayers Asn, Inc, One Bay Tree Lane, Bethesda, MD 20816.

JONES, ROBERT SIDNEY, MARINE BIOLOGY, ICHTHYOLOGY. **Personal Data:** b Gatesville, Tex, December 17, 1936; c 2. **Education:** Univ Tex, BA, 1959, MA, 1963, PhD (zool), 1967. **Professional Experience:** DIR EDUC, BERMUDA BIOL STA RES, 1993-; dir, Marine Sci Inst, UnivTex, 1984-1993; managing dir found, Johnson Sci Lab, Harbor Br Found, Inc, 1982-1984; dir, Johnson Sci Lab, Harbor Br Found, Inc, 1976-1982; prog mgr admin, Univ Tex, 1976; fisheriesbiologist, Harbor Br Found Inc, 1974-1976; Dir & prof biol, Univ Guam Marine Lab, 1967-1974. **Memberships:** Am Soc Ichthyologists & Herpetologists; Sigma Xi. **Research Statement & Publications:** Ecology and behavior of marine fishes. **Mailing Address:** Bermuda Biol Sta Res Inc, 17 Biological Lane, Ferry Reach, St Georges, GE-01, Bermuda, Bermuda. **Fax:** 809-297-8143. **E-Mail:** bob@bbsr.edu

JONES, ROBERT WILLIAM, HIGH ENERGY LASERS, FREE ELECTRON LASERS. **Personal Data:** b Dyersburg, Tenn, September 7, 1944; m 1969, Glenda; c Thomas Edmund. **Education:** Univ Ala, BA, 1967, MS, 1972, PhD (physics), 1983. **Professional Experience:** RETIRED; chief radiation, Hardened Microelectronic Div, Missile Defense & Space Technol Center, US Army Space & Missile Defense Command, 1992-1999; chmn, Systs Eng & Tech Assistance Task Force, US Army Strategic Defense Command, 1990-1992; CHIEF, LASER SENSOR DIV, AOA PROJ OFF, US ARMY STRATEGIC DEFENSE COMMAND, 1988-; chief, Free Electron Laser Div, Ground Based Laser Proj, Off, 1986-1988; instr, Univ Ala, Huntsville, 1985-1986; proj engr, US Army Missile Command, 1983-1986; consult, Eng Math Co, 1979-1988; res physicist, US Army Missile Command, 1971-1983; teaching asst physics, Univ Ala, Huntsville, 1970-1971; physicist, Teledyne-Brown Eng, 1968-1970. **Memberships:** Emer mem Optical Soc Am; Sigma Xi. **Research Statement & Publications:** High energy repetitively pulsed and continuous wave lasers; resonator design and transverse mode formation; free electron laser; laser radarn; radictin Hardened ecectronics; granted eight patents. **Mailing Address:** 807 Argonne Terr SE, Huntsville, AL 35802-3650.

JONES, ROBERT WILLIAM, GEOLOGY. **Personal Data:** b Seattle, Wash, January 20, 1927; m 1953, c 3. **Education:** Univ Wash, Seattle, BS, 1950, MS, 1957, PhD (geol), 1959. **Professional Experience:** PROF EMER GEOL, UNIV IDAHO, 1990-; assoc prof geol, Univ Idaho, beginning 1966; from instr to asst prof, UnivIdaho, 1958-1966; ground water geologist, US Geol Surv, 1951-1955. **Memberships:** Geol Soc Am; Am Asn Petrol Geol; Nat Asn Geol Teachers; Int Asn Volcanology; Sigma Xi. **Research Statement & Publications:** Petrology and structure of igneous and metamorphic rocks. **Mailing Address:** Dept Geol, Univ Idaho, PO Box 443022, Moscow, ID 83844-3022. **Fax:** 208-885-5724.

JONES, ROBIN L(ESLIE), PHYSICAL METALLURGY, MATERIALS ENGINEERING. **Personal Data:** b Stanley, Eng, May 19, 1940; m 1965, c 1. **Education:** Cambridge Univ, BA, 1962, MA, 1966, PhD (metall), 1966. **Professional Experience:** VPRES, ENERGY CONVERSION, ELEC POWER RES INST, as of 2003; from vpres nuclear res to vpres, sci & technol develop, Elec Power Res Inst, beginning 1995; dir, Mat & Chem Dept, 1993-1995; sr prog mgr, Corrosion Control, 1985-1993; prog mgr nuclear systs & mat, Elec Power Res Inst, 1980-1985; proj mgr, Elec Power Res Inst, 1978-1980; mgr metall prog, SRI Int, 1972-1978; group leader, Metall Lab, 1971-1972; sr res metallurgist, Res Labs, Franklin Inst, 1966-1971. **Memberships:** Am Soc Mech Engrs; Nat Asn Corrosion Engrs; Am Inst Mining Metall & Petrol Engrs; Am Soc Testing & Mat. **Research Statement & Publications:** Physical and mechanical metallurgy, particularly the relations between mechanical properties and fine microstructure; fracture mechanics; ductile fracture of metallic materials; corrosion; environmentally assisted fracture of metals and ceramics; corrosion cracking damage in nuclear power plant materials. **Mailing Address:** Elec Power Res Inst, 3412 Hillview Ave, Palo Alto, CA 94304. **E-Mail:** askepri@epri.com

JONES, ROBIN RICHARD, PATHOLOGY, BIOCHEMISTRY. **Personal Data:** b Little Rock, Ark, October 18, 1937. **Education:** Univ Ark, BS, 1961, MD, 1962, MS, 1966, PhD (biochem), 1967. **Professional Experience:** PROF PATH, MED SCH, UNIV ARK, 1988-; asst prof med technol, UnivArk, 1974-1976; from asst prof to assoc prof path, Univ Ark, 1967-1988; spec instr, Univ Ark, 1965-1969. **Memberships:** Sigma Xi. **Research Statement & Publications:** Vitamin E deficiency; muscular dystrophy; interactive videodisc in pathology education. **Mailing Address:** Med Sch, Univ Ark, 4301 W Markham St Slot 517, Little Rock, AR 72205-7101.

JONES, ROGER, BOTANY. **Personal Data:** b Kimbolton, Herefordshire, Eng, March 19, 1940; m 1965, c 2. **Education:** Univ Wales, BSc, 1962, PhD (ecol), 1967; Kans State Univ, MSc, 1964. **Professional Experience:** PROF EMER BIOL, TRENT UNIV, 2000-; prof, Trent Univ, 1985-2000; from asst prof to assoc prof, Trent Univ, 1967-1985. **Memberships:** Brit Ecol Soc; Soc Int Limnol. **Research Statement & Publications:** Plant ecology; paleolimnology. **Mailing Address:** Dept Biol, Trent Univ, ESC Bldg 16 Westbank Dr, Peterborough, ON K9J 7B8, Can. **Fax:** 705-748-1205. **E-Mail:** rjones@trentu.ca

JONES, ROGER ALAN, NUCLEIC ACID CHEMISTRY. **Personal Data:** b York, Pa, March 25, 1947; div, c 1. **Education:** Univ Del, BS, 1969; Univ Alta, PhD (chem), 1974. **Honors & Awards:** Fac Res Award, Am Cancer Soc, 1986-1991. **Professional Experience:** CHAIR, DEPT CHEM CHEMICAL BIOL, 1996-; PROF CHEM, RUTGERS UNIV, 1988-; from asst prof to assoc prof, Rutgers Univ, 1977-1988; NIH fel, Dept Chem, Mass Inst Technol, 1975-1976. **Memberships:** Fel AAAS; Am Chem Soc. **Research Statement & Publications:** Synthesis and characterization of modified and/or isotopically labelled DNA and RNA oligonucleotides to study DNA polymorphism. **Mailing Address:** Dept Chem, Rutgers Univ, 610 Taylor Rd, Piscataway, NJ 08854. **Fax:** 732-445-5866. **E-Mail:** jones@rutchem.rutgers.edu

JONES, ROGER C(LYDE), ELECTRICAL ENGINEERING, PLASMA PHYSICS. **Personal Data:** b Lake Andes, SDak, August 17, 1919; m 1952, c 2. **Education:** Univ Nebr, BS, 1949; Univ Md, MS, 1953, PhD, 1963. **Professional Experience:** PROF EMER ELEC & COMPUT ENG & RADIATION ONCOL, UNIV ARIZ, 1989-; prof radiation-oncol, Appl Res Lab, UnivAriz, 1987-1989; guest prof, Kraeftforskningsinstituttet, Aarhus, Denmark, 1982-1983; adj profradiol, Appl Res Lab, Univ Ariz, 1978-1987; prof elec eng, Appl Res Lab, Univ Ariz, 1964-1989; actg dir, Appl Res Lab, Univ Ariz, 1964-1965; chief scientist physics, Electronics-Physics ResCtr, 1964; head physics sect, Phys Sci Lab, 1959-1964; consult proj engr, Antenna & RadiationSysts Lab, 1958-1959; sr staff engr, Melpar Inc, Westinghouse Air Brake Co, 1957-1958; electronic scientist, Naval Res Lab, 1950-1957; electronic engr, Naval Res Lab, 1949-1950. **Memberships:** Fel AAAS; Am Phys Soc; sr mem Inst Elec & Electronics Engrs; Optical Soc Am; Bioelectromagnetics Soc. **Research Statement & Publications:** General physical electronics; infrared engineering; gas and solid state lasers; hyperthermia; bioelectromagnetics. **Mailing Address:** Dept Elec & Comput Eng, Tucson, AZ 85711-1519.

JONES, ROGER FRANKLIN, REINFORCED THERMOPLASTICS, THERMOPLASTICS ALLOYS. **Personal Data:** b Philadelphia, Pa, October 31, 1930; m 1953, Caryl; c Ellen (Heckman), Evan R & Mitchell R. **Education:** Haverford Col, BS, 1952. **Professional Experience:** BD CHMN, PLASTICOMP INC, 2003-; PRES, FRANKLIN INT LLC, 2000-; pres, Franklin Polymers, Inc, 1989-2000; managing dir eng plastics, BASF Corp, 1984-1989; chmn & pres, InolexChem Co, 1981-1983; group mgr chem, Beatrice Foods Co, 1976-1981; pres & gen mgr, LNPCorp, 1967-1981; sr staff supvr polymer res, Avisun Corp, 1960-1967; develop engr, AtlanticRefining Co, 1958-1960; lieutenant, US Navy, 1955-1958; process eng, E I DuPont Del NemoursCo, Inc, 1952-1954. **Memberships:** Am Inst Chemists (vchmn 1980-1981 secy 1981-1984); Am Chem Soc; fel Soc Plastics Engrs; Sigma Xi. **Research Statement & Publications:** The development of novel reinforced and modified thermoplastic composites; surfactants and polymer intermediates. **Mailing Address:** Franklin Int, LLC, Four Kenny Circle, Broomall, PA 19008. **E-Mail:** jones@plasticomp.com

JONES, ROGER L, ERGODIC THEORY, MARTINGALES. **Personal Data:** b Holland Patent, NY, June 2, 1949; m 1974. **Education:** State Univ NY, Albany, BS, 1971; Rutgers Univ, PhD (math), 1974. **Professional Experience:** RETIRED, Prof maths, Depaul Univ, 1984-; from asst prof to assoc prof, DePaulUniv, 1974-1984. **Memberships:** Am Math Soc; Math Asn Am. **Research Statement & Publications:** Classical harmonic analysis and its application to problems in ergodic theory and probability; maximal inequalities. **Mailing Address:** 2119 Plum Creek Ave, St Germain, WI 54558. **Fax:** 773-325-7807. **E-Mail:** rjones@condor.depaul.edu

JONES, ROGER STANLEY, PHYSICS EDUCATION, PHILOSOPHY OF PHYSICS. **Personal Data:** b New York, NY, June 17, 1934; m 1956, c 2. **Education:** City Col New York, BS, 1955; Univ Ill, MS, 1957, PhD (physics), 1961. **Professional Experience:** PROF EMER PHYS, SCH PHYSICS & ASTRON, UNIV MINN, 1999-; Prof Phys, 1997-1999; assoc prof physics, Univ Minn, Minneapolis, 1967-1997; from asst physicist to assoc physicist, Brookhaven Nat Lab, 1964-1967; USAF Off Sci Res fel, Nat Comt Nuclear Energy Labs, Frascati, 1962-1963; Res assoc physics, Univ Ill, 1961-1962. **Memberships:** Am Phys Soc; Sigma Xi. **Research Statement & Publications:** High energy experimental physics and elementary particle physics; epistemology and symbolism of physics; physics education. **Mailing Address:** Sch Physics & Astron, Univ Minn, 116 Church St S E, Minneapolis, MN 55455. **E-Mail:** jones001@umn.edu

JONES, RONALD DALE, COMPUTER SCIENCE. **Personal Data:** b Stillwater, Okla, July 18, 1932; div, c 2. **Education:** Okla State Univ, BA, 1955; Univ Kans, MPA, 1960; Univ Southern Calif, DPA, 1964. **Professional Experience:** Lectr, Kansas City Art Inst, 1972-; PROF COMPUT SCI, SCH ADMIN, UNIV MO-KANSAS CITY, 1966-; engr, Rand Corp, 1963-1965; sr res engr, Los Angeles Div, NAm Aviation, Inc, 1961-1963; admin intern, City Beverly Hills, Calif, 1960-1961; Admin aidebudget & mgt, City Wichita, Kans, 1959-1960. **Memberships:** Asn Comput Mach. **Research Statement & Publications:** Simulation of social-psychological systems, particularly bureaucracies; security of computer systems. **Mailing Address:** Dept Comput Sci Univ Mo, 5100 Rockhill Rd, Kansas City, MO 64110-2446.

JONES, RONALD GOLDIN, ORGANIC CHEMISTRY. **Personal Data:** b Yorkville, Ga, November 29, 1933; m 1957, Sara E Sanford; c Laurilyn D. **Education:** Emory Univ, BA, 1955, MS, 1957; Ga Inst Technol, PhD (org chem), 1961. **Professional Experience:** PROF EMER ORG CHEM, GA STATE UNIV, as of 2004; prof org chem, Ga State Univ, beginning 1967; from asst prof to assoc prof, GA State Univ, 1961-1967; chem prod develop & qual control, Southern Latex Corp, Ga, 1951-1955. **Memberships:** Am Chem Soc; Sigma Xi. **Research Statement & Publications:** Applications of nuclear magnetic resonance spectroscopy in organic chemistry and polysaccharides of microbial origin; organic reaction mechanisms. **Mailing Address:** Dept Chem, Ga State Univ, 33 Gilmer St, Atlanta, GA 30303. **E-Mail:** ronjones@gsu.edu

JONES, RONALD MCCLUNG, PHYSIOLOGICAL ECOLOGY, RESPIRATORY PHYSIOLOGY. **Personal Data:** b Palo Alto, Calif, May 6, 1951; m 1974, c 1. **Education:** Swarthmore Col, BA, 1972; Univ Calif, Riverside, PhD (biol), 1978. **Professional Experience:** FEL PHYSIOL, DARTMOUTH MED SCH, HANOVER, 1978-. **Memberships:** AAAS; Am Inst Biol Sci; Am Soc Zoology; Sigma Xi. **Research Statement & Publications:** Physiological ecology of vertebrates. **Mailing Address:** 13175 Franklin Ave, Mtain View, CA 94040.

JONES, RONDALL E, MATHEMATHICS. **Education:** Univ NMex, PhD (Math). **Professional Experience:** TECH STAFF, SANDIA NAT LABS, as of 2005. **Memberships:** Asn Comput Mach. **Mailing Address:** Sandia Nat Labs, PO Box 5800, Albuquerque, NM 87115. **Fax:** 505-284-5437. **E-Mail:** rejones@sandia.gov

JONES, ROSEMARY C, PULMONARY DISEASE. **Personal Data:** b Caerleon, Wales, UK, December 26, 1941. **Education:** Univ London, PhD (exp path), 1980. **Honors & Awards:** Nat Res Serv Award, 1986-1988; Fogarty Int Res Collab Award, NIH, 1995-1998. **Professional Experience:** ASSOC PROF PATH, SCH MED, HARVARD UNIV, as of 1999. **Memberships:** Inst Med Lab Sci London UK; fel Inst Med Lab Sci London UK; assoc fel Inst Med Lab Sci London UK. **Mailing Address:** Dept Anaesthesia & Critical Care, Mass Gen Hosp, 55 Fruit St, Boston, MA 02114.

JONES, ROY CARL, MATHEMATICS. **Personal Data:** b New York, NY, August 3, 1939; m 1964, c 4. **Education:** Case Inst Technol, BS, 1962; Western Res Univ, MS, 1964, PhD (math), 1966. **Professional Experience:** Asst prof math, Fla Technol Univ, beginning 1969; asst prof, Univ Fla, 1966-1969. **Memberships:** Am Math Soc; Math Asn Am. **Research Statement & Publications:** Approximation theory, characterizing and finding best uniform or Tchebycheff approximations; numerical methods including developing algorithms or iterative procedures that converge to the best approximations. **Mailing Address:** Univ Cen Fla, PO Box 25000 MAP 231A, Orlando, FL 32816-0001. **Fax:** 407-823-6253. **E-Mail:** rcjones@pegasus.cc.ucf.edu

JONES, RUFUS SIDNEY, MEMBRANE SCIENCE & TECHNOLOGY, ELECTRO-OPTICALLY ACTIVE POLYMERS. **Personal Data:** b Warrenton, NC, May 9, 1940; m 1968, Martha; c Laura R. **Education:** Duke Univ, BS, 1962; Purdue Univ, PhD (org chem), 1968. **Professional Experience:** RETIRED; dir, Technol & Bus Develop, 1990-1997; prog mgr, Hoechst Celenese Corp, 1988-1989; proj leader/res supvr, Celanese Corp, 1983-1987; qual adminr, Celanese Corp, 1982-1983; res assoc, Celanese Corp, 1981-1982; sr res chemist, Celanese Corp, 1972-1980; Res chemist, Celanese Corp, 1968-1972. **Memberships:** Am Chem Soc; NAm Membrane Soc. **Research Statement & Publications:** Synthesis, characterization, and application of novel polymers for use in devices and systems which rely upon a unique functional polymer property rather than a structural property; materials for optical data storage; gas and liquid separations. **Mailing Address:** 123 Mountainside Dr, Randolph, NJ 07869. **Fax:** 704-588-7393.

JONES, RUSSEL C(AMERON), CIVIL ENGINEERING. **Personal Data:** b Tarentum, Pa, October 18, 1935; m 1958. **Education:** Carnegie Inst Technol, BS, 1957, MS, 1960, PhD (sci mat), 1964. **Honors & Awards:** Int Medal Distinguished Contributions Eng Educ, Australasian Asn Eng Educ, 1993. **Professional Experience:** UNIV RES PROF, UNIV DEL, 1987-; vpres acad affairs, Boston Univ, 1981-1987; dean, Sch Eng, Univ Mass, 1977-1981; prof & chmn dept, Ohio State Univ, 1971-1977; assoc prof, Mass Inst Technol, 1966-1971; asst prof civil eng, Mass Inst Technol, 1963-1966; assoc engr, Missiles & Space Systs Div, Douglas Aircraft Co, 1960; struct designer, hunting, larsen & dunnels engrs, Pa, 1957-1959. **Memberships:** AAAS; Am Soc Eng Educ; Nat Soc Prof Engrs; Metall Soc; Am Soc Testing &Mat. **Research Statement & Publications:** Science of materials; composite materials; building systems; housing; construction management; engineering education. **Mailing Address:** Univ Del, Col Eng, Dean's off, Newark, DE 19716. **Fax:** 302-831-8179.

JONES, RUSSELL HOWARD, MATERIALS SCIENCE, METALLURGY. **Personal Data:** b Oakland, Calif, July 7, 1944; m 1968, c 3. **Education:** Calif State Polytech Col, BS, 1967; Univ Calif, Berkeley, MS, 1968, PhD (metall), 1971. **Professional Experience:** SR STAFF SCI & TECH GROUP MGR PAC NORTHWEST LAB, BATTELLE MEM INST, as of 1997; mgr struct res sec scientist, Pac Northwest Lab, Battelle Mem Inst, beginning 1990; staff scientist metall, Pac Northwest Lab, Battelle Mem Inst, 1980-1990; sr res scientist, Pac Northwest Lab, Battelle Meml nst, 1973-1980; engr metall, Westinghouse Elec Corp, 1971-1973. **Memberships:** Am Soc Metals; Am Inst Mining Metall & Petrol Engrs; Mat Res Soc; Electrochem Soc. **Research Statement & Publications:** High temperature alloys; radiation damage and stress corrosion; ceramic and metal matrix composites. **Mailing Address:** Pac Northwest Lab, PO Box 999 MSIN P8-15, Richland, WA 99352. **Fax:** 509-376-0418. **E-Mail:** rj_jones@pnl.gov

JONES, RUSSELL K, veterinary public health; deceased, see previous edition for last biography

JONES, RUSSELL LEWIS, PLANT PHYSIOLOGY. **Personal Data:** b Dyserth, Wales, May 10, 1941; c 3. **Education:** Univ Col Wales, BSc, 1962, PhD (bot), 1965. **Honorary Degrees:** Dr Honoris Causa, Mendel Univ Agr, Brno, Czech Republic, 2002; Dr Honoris Causa, Univ Paul Sabatier, Toulouse, 2003. **Honors & Awards:** John Simon Guggenheim Fellow, 1972 Miller Research Professor, Univ California 1975 Alexander von Humboldt Senior Scientist, 1986 RIKEN Eminent Scientist Award, 1996 Corresponding Lifetime Member, Australian Soc Plant Physiology, 1997 Fellow, AAAS, 2001 Distinguished Research Award, IPGSA, 2001 Charles Reid Barnes Honorary Life Membership, American Soc Plant Biology, 2002. **Professional Experience:** PROF PLANT BIOL, UNIV CALIF, BERKELEY, as of 2004; mem, Life Sci Div Working Group, 1988-; mem, Life sci Peer Rev Panel, NASA, 1987-; prog mgr, Plant Growth & Develop Panel, USDA CRGO, 1987-1988; Alexander von Humbolt sr scientist, Univ Gottingen, Fed Repub Ger, 1986-1987; mem, Plant Growth & Develop Panel, USDA CRGO, 1984-1986; chmn, Col Letters & Sci Comt Res, 1983-1984; actg dir, Univ Calif Herbarium, 1982-1983; mem comt res, Miller Inst Basic Res, 1981-; chmn dept bot, Miller Inst Basic Res, 1981-1986; mem exec comt, Miller Inst Basic Res, 1977-1981; actg chmn, Dept Instruction Biol, 1977-1978; chmn, Col Letters & Sci Comt on Courses, 1976-1979; Miller res prof, Univ Calif, Berkeley, 1975-1976; assoc ed, Annual Rev Plant Physiol, 1972-; Guggenheim Mem Found fel, 1972-1973; Peer panel mem, adv, Panel Develop Biol, NSF, 1970-1973; from asst prof to assoc prof, Univ Calif, Berkeley, 1966-1974; AEC fel, Mich State Univ-AEC Plant Res Lab, 1965-1966. **Memberships:** Am Soc Plant Physiol; Int Plant Growth Substances Asn. **Research Statement & Publications:** Biochemistry and physiology of the action of gibberellic acid and calcium. **Mailing Address:** Dept Plant Biol, Univ Calif, 311A Koshland, Berkeley, CA 94720. **Fax:** 510-642-4995. **E-Mail:** rjones@nature.berkeley.edu

JONES, SAMUEL B, BOTANY, HORTICULTURE. **Personal Data:** b Roswell, Ga, December 18, 1933; m 1955, c 3. **Education:** Auburn Univ, BS, 1955, MS, 1961; Univ Ga, PhD (bot), 1964. **Honors & Awards:** Silver Shield Award, Nat Coun State Garden Clubs. **Professional Experience:** PROF EMER BOT, UNIV GA, 1991-; CO-OWNER, PICCADILLY FARM PERENNIAL NURSERY, 1991-; dir, Bot Garden, 1981-1984; from asst prof to prof bot, Univ Ga, 1967-1991; asst prof, Univ Southern Miss, 1964-1967; instr bot, Auburn Univ, 1959-1961; teacher, SCobb High Sch, 1958-1959; NSF res grants; Calloway Found res grant. **Memberships:** Garden Writers Asn Am; Am Soc Plant Taxonomists; Am Asn Nurserymen. **Research Statement & Publications:** Systematics of higher plants; landscaping with native plants; flora of southeastern United States; the genus Hosta (Liliacene); shade gardening; perennials. **Mailing Address:** Dept Plant Biol, Univ Ga, Athens, GA 30602.

JONES, SAMUEL STIMPSON, PHYSICAL CHEMISTRY. **Personal Data:** b Buckingham Co, Va, April 9, 1923. **Education:** Hampden-Sydney Col, BS, 1943; Cornell Univ, PhD (phys chem), 1950. **Professional Experience:** RETIRED; indust carbon consult, Allied Signal, 1984-1996; R&D Carbon, Switz, 1984-1996; indust carbon consult, Anaconda Aluminum Co & Arco Metals Co, 1983; mgrcarbon & mat res, Anaconda Aluminum Co & Arco Metals Co, 1981-1983; sr staff res scientist, Ctr Technol, Kaiser Aluminum & Chem Corp, 1970-1981; res assoc Pac Northwest Lab, Battelle Mem Inst, Wash, 1965-1970; tech specialist, Hanford Labs, 1963-1965; radiation effects specialist, Defense Syst Dept & Electronics Lab, 1961-1963; radiation chemist, Vallecitos Atomic Lab, 1957-1961; res assoc phys chem, Knolls Atomic Power Lab, Gen Elec Co, 1950-1957; chemist, Manhattan Proj, Monsanto Chem Co, 1944-1946. **Memberships:** AAAS; Am Chem Soc; NY Acad Sci; Am Carbon Soc. **Research Statement & Publications:** Radiochemistry; complex ions; radiation chemistry; radiation effects on electronic materials; graphite physics and chemistry; chemistry and physics of carbon. **Mailing Address:** PO Box 43698, Tucson, AZ 85733.

JONES, SANFORD L, REPRODUCTIVE ENDOCRINOLOGY. **Personal Data:** b Lost Creek, Ky, September 22, 1925. **Education:** Eastern Ky State Col, BS, 1950; Univ Ky, MS, 1956; Univ Tenn, PhD (physiol, biochem), 1960. **Professional Experience:** RETIRED; chmn dept, Eastern Ky Univ, 1979-1992; from asst prof to prof biol, Eastern Ky Univ, 1961-1992; res assoc physiol, Univ Tenn, 1960-1961; sec teacher, Perry Co Schs, Ky, 1950-1955. **Memberships:** Am Soc Zool; Sigma Xi. **Research Statement & Publications:** Effects of antithyroid compounds on metabolism of thyroxine; absorption of iodinated compounds in amphibians and reptiles; radioimmunoassay of luteinizing hormone. **Mailing Address:** 204 Bristol Dr, Richmond, KY 40475.

JONES, SHARON LYNN, NEUROPHARMACOLOGY, NEUROANATOMY. **Personal Data:** b Pasadena, Calif, December 19, 1960. **Education:** Univ NMex, BS, 1983; Univ Iowa, PhD (pharmacol), 1987. **Professional Experience:** Asst prof pharmacol, univ okla, 1990-2000. **Memberships:** Soc Neuroscience; Int Asn Study Pain; Am Pain Soc; Sigma Xi. **Research Statement & Publications:** Organization and function of endogenous pain suppression systems that modulate spinal nociceptive transmission by using anatomical, pharmacological and physiological techniques. **Mailing Address:** Dept Cell Biol, Univ Okla Col Med, PO Box 26901, Oklahoma City, OK 73190. **Fax:** 405-271-3548.

JONES, STANLEY B, MEDICAL ADMINISTRATION. **Personal Data:** b July 27, 1938. **Education:** Dartmouth Col, BA, 1960. **Professional Experience:** Dir, Health Ins Reform Proj, George Wash Univ, 1994-; CONSULT HEALTHPOLICY, 1989-; chmn, Panel Long Range Planning Dis Res, 1989; mem, Robert Wood Johnson Rev Comt Prog Promote Long-Term Care InsElderly, 1988; chmn, Ad Hoc Comt Educ Health Professionals & Invitational Workshop Utilization Mgt, Inst Med-Nat Acad Sci, 1987; pres, Consol Consult Group, 1986-1989; vpres, Consol Healthcare Inc, 1986-1989; mem, DC Gen Hosp Comn, 1985-1987; mem, Robert Wood Johnson Fel Bd & Bd Ment Health & Behav Med, Inst Med-NatAcad Sci, 1980-1986; vpres, Wash Representation, Blue Cross & Blue Shield Asn, 1980-1983; fel, Inst Soc, Ethics & Life Sci, Hastings Ctr, 1978-1989; founding partner, Fullerton, Jones &Wolkstein, Health Policy Alternatives, 1978-1980 & 1983-1986; prog develop officer, InstMed-Nat Acad Sci, 1977-1978; chief, Planning Systs Br & dir, Off Mgt Policy, Health Serv &Ment Health Admin, NIH, 1969-1971; from staff mem to assoc dir, Div Computer Res &Technol, HEW, NIH, 1964-1969. **Memberships:** Inst Med-Nat Acad Sci. **Research Statement & Publications:** Author of various publications on health care administration. **Mailing Address:** Washington, DC 20001.

JONES, STANLEY BENNETT, GEOPHYSICS. **Personal Data:** b San Francisco, Calif, January 14, 1922; wid Yvonne (deceased); c 2. **Education:** Univ Calif, PhD (physics), 1950. **Professional Experience:** RETIRED; assoc dir tech servs, Soc Explor Geophysicists, 1985-1989; mgr, Systs & Eng Serv Div, Chevron Oil Field Res Co, 1981-1985; geophys res consult, Chevron Oil Field Res Co, 1979-1980; mgr, Develop & Implementation Div, Chevron Geosci Co, 1977-1978; mgr, Geophys Div, Chevron Oil Field Res Co, 1968-1976; sect supvr, Geophys Sect, 1963-1968; sect supvr, Well Logging & Basic Prod Sect, 1958-1963; res physicist oil field res, Chevron Oil Field Res Co, 1950-1958; physicist, Radiation Lab, Univ Calif, 1948-1950. **Memberships:** Am Phys Soc; Am Geophys Union; Soc Explor Geophys; Europ Asn Explor Geophys; Soc Explor Geophysicists (vpres, 1984-1985). **Research Statement & Publications:** Cosmic rays; meson physics; oil well logging, oil producing and geophysics research. **Mailing Address:** 7823 Calif Ave, Whittier, CA 90602-2708.

JONES, STANLEY C(ULVER), CHEMICAL ENGINEERING, PERMEABILITY MEASUREMENT. **Personal Data:** b Spokane, Wash, August 31, 1933; m 1957, Barbara Larson; c 3. **Education:** Wash State Univ, BSE, 1956; Univ Mich, MSE, 1959, PhD (chem eng), 1962. **Honors & Awards:** Henry Mattson TechServ Award, Soc Petrol Engrs, 1989; Advan Technol Achievement Award, Litton Ind, 1992. **Professional Experience:** CONSULT, WESTERN ATLAS LOGGING SERV, 1994-; res & developdept, Core Labs, 1986-1994; res assoc, Denver Res Ctr, Marathon Oil Co, 1975-1986; sr resscientist, Denver Res Ctr, Marathon Oil Co, 1971-1975; adv res engr, Denver Res Ctr, MarathonOil Co, 1962-1971; Engr, Kaiser Aluminum & Chem Corp, 1956-1958. **Memberships:** Soc Petrol Engrs; Sigma Xi; Am Inst Chem Engrs; Soc Core Analysts. **Research Statement & Publications:** Anodizing processes for aluminum alloys; behavior of a pulsed extraction column; movement of water through aquifers in contact with natural gas; secondary and tertiary oil recovery processes; reservoir rock properties; petroleum production. **Mailing Address:** 875 Front Range Rd, Littleton, CO 80120.

JONES, STANLEY E, APPLIED MATHEMATICS, ENGINEERING MECHANICS. **Personal Data:** b Mt Vernon, NY, July 20, 1939; m 1994, Barbara; c Lara E & Robert T. **Education:** Univ Del, BA, 1963, MS, 1966, PhD (appl sci), 1967. **Honors & Awards:** Siam lectr, 1983. **Professional Experience:** Adj prof, Metall & Mat Eng, Univ Ala, as of 1999; lectr, Naval Surface Weapons Ctr, 1994; RES PROF, UNIV ALA, 1991-; distinguished vis prof, USAF Acad, 1989-1991; dept head Eng Mech, Univ Ala, 1987-1989; NSF 1983 & Nat Water Resources Inst, 1984; USAF, Eglin AFB, Fla, 1981-; vis prof, Ga Inst Tech, 1979-1980; vis prof, Univ Iowa, 1969; consult, Marshall Space Flight Ctr, NASA, 1970; prof eng mech, Univ Ky, 1967-1987. **Memberships:** Am Soc Mech Engrs; Am Soc Mech. **Research Statement & Publications:** Fluid transients, plasticity analysis and nonlinear mechanics;

co-author one book and author of approximately 100 research papers. **Mailing Address:** Dept Aerospace & Eng Mech, Univ Ala, PO Box 870280, Tuscaloosa, AL 35487-0280. **Fax:** 205-348-2094. **E-Mail:** sejones@coe.eng.ua.edu

JONES, STANLEY LESLIE, ANALYTICAL CHEMISTRY. **Personal Data:** b Waltham, Mass, March 22, 1919; m 1948, Anna; c Cheryl, Ronald, Marion, Arthur & Peter. **Education:** Tufts Col, BS, 1941, MS, 1947; Harvard Univ, AM, 1949, PhD (anal chem), 1951. **Professional Experience:** RETIRED; consult chemist, Knolls Atomic Power Lab, Gen Elec Co, 1960-1981; appl res chemist, Knolls Atomic Power Lab, Gen Elec Co, 1955-1960; res chemist, Merck & Co, Inc, 1950-1955; jr chemist chemanal, US Navy Yard, Mass, 1942-1944; res chemist drying oils, Bird & Son, Inc, 1941-1942. **Memberships:** Am Chem Soc; AAAS; Sigma Xi. **Research Statement & Publications:** Analytical research; colloid science. **Mailing Address:** 1413 Fox Hollow Rd, Schenectady, NY 12309-2509.

JONES, STANLEY TANNER, PHYSICS. **Personal Data:** b Palo Alto, Calif, March 10, 1945; m 1977, Charlotte; c Patrick, Tanner & Laurie (Norwierski). **Education:** Stanford Univ, BS, 1966; Univ Ill, Urbana, MS, 1968, PhD (physics), 1970. **Professional Experience:** Asst dean, Col Arts & Sci, Univ Ala, beginning 1989-; PROF & CHMN, DEPT PHYSICS, UNIV ALA, 983-; from asst prof to assoc prof, Univ Ala, 1970-1983. **Memberships:** Am Phys Soc. **Research Statement & Publications:** Elementary particle physics. **Mailing Address:** A&S Dean's Off, Univ AL, PO Box 870268, Tuscaloosa, AL 35487-0324. **Fax:** 205-348-9642. **E-Mail:** stjones@bama.ua.edu

JONES, STEPHEN BENDER, CIRCULATORY, MEDICAL EDUCATION. **Personal Data:** b Lansing, Mich, October 19, 1945; m 1970, c 3. **Education:** Cent Mich Univ, BS, 1967, MS, 1969; Univ Mo-Columbia, PhD (physiol), 1975. **Professional Experience:** PROF PHYSIOL & SURG, LOYOLA UNIV, CHICAGO, as of 2004; INVESTR, BURN & SHOCK TRAUMA INST, LOYOLA UNIV, CHICAGO, as of 2004; Dept Pharmacol, Univ Melbourne, Australia, 1987; assoc prof physiol, Stritch Sch Med, Loyola Univ, Chicago, beginning 1982; asst prof, Stritch Sch Med, Loyola Univ, Chicago, 1976-1982; res assoc physiol, Stritch Sch Med, Loyola Univ, Chicago, 1975-1976; Vis prof, Nat Res Coun, Ottawa, Can, 1971; instr, Cent Mich Univ, 1969-1971; asst instr, Cent Mich Univ, 1968-1969; teaching asst biol, Cent Mich Univ, 1967-1968. **Memberships:** Sigma Xi; Am Physiol Soc; Shock Soc. **Research Statement & Publications:** Neural control of circulation in developing control; control of peripheral neurotransmitter; plasma catacholamines. **Mailing Address:** Burn & Shock Trauma Inst, Med Ctr, Loyola Univ, 2160 S First Ave, Maywood, IL 60153. **Fax:** 708-327-2813. **E-Mail:** sjones@lumc.edu

JONES, STEPHEN S, GENETICS. **Education:** Calif State Univ, BS, 1980; Univ Calif, Davis, MS, 1986, PhD, 1991. **Professional Experience:** ASSOC PROF, WASH STATE UNIV, as of 2005; ASSOC AGRONOMIST, WASH STATE UNIV, as of 2005. **Mailing Address:** Wash State Univ, 383 Johnson Hall PO Box 646420, Pullman, WA 99164-6420. **E-Mail:** joness@wsu.edu

JONES, STEPHEN THOMAS, ORGANIC CHEMISTRY. **Personal Data:** b Washington, NC, February 12, 1942; m 1963, Wanda; c Scott R. **Education:** E Carolina Univ, AB, 1964; Emory Univ, PhD (org chem), 1968. **Professional Experience:** DIR PROD DEVELOP & MKT RES, LORILLARD INC, 1992-; opers & planning, 1983-1992; opers & planning, 1977-1983; dir mkt res, 1972-1977; mgr prod develop, 1972-1977; supvr prod develop, Lorillard Inc, 1970-1972; res chemist, Lorillard Inc, 1968-1970. **Memberships:** Am Chem Soc. **Research Statement & Publications:** Steroid synthesis; syntheses of hydroazulenes; syntheses of heterocyclic compounds; tobacco chemistry. **Mailing Address:** Lorillard Res Ctr, PO Box 21688, Greensboro, NC 27420.

JONES, STEPHEN WALLACE, NEUROSCIENCES. **Personal Data:** b Steubenville, Ohio, November 7, 1953. **Education:** Mich State Univ, BS, 1974; Cornell Univ, PhD (neurobiol), 1980. **Professional Experience:** ASSOC PROF, DEPT PHYSIOL & BIOPHYS, CASE WESTERN RES UNIV, CLEVELAND, OHIO, 1991-; asst prof physiol, dept physiol & biophys, Case Western Res Univ, Cleveland, Ohio, 1986-1991; res asst prof, Dept Neurobiology & Behav, State Univ NY, Stony Brook, 1984-1986; NIH teaching fel, Dept Neurobiology & Behav, State Univ NY, Stony Brook, 1982-1984; lectr neurobiology, Cornell Univ, 1981; assoc teaching fel muscular dystrophy, Dept Neurobiology & Behav, Cornell Univ, 1979-1982. **Memberships:** Biophys Soc; Soc Neuroscience; AAAS. **Research Statement & Publications:** Electrophysiology and pharmacology of vertebrate neurons, primarily in autonomic ganglia; voltage clamp analysis of voltage dependent currents and of the actions of neurotransmitters. **Mailing Address:** Dept Physiol & Biophys, Case Western Res Univ, Sch Med 10900 Euclid Ave Rm E535, Cleveland, OH 44106-4975. **Fax:** 216-368-4950. **E-Mail:** swj@po.cwru.edu

JONES, STEVEN WAYNE, MEMBRANE RECEPTOR BIOCHEMISTRY, SIGNAL TRANSDUCTION MECHANISMS. **Personal Data:** b Glenwood Springs, Colo, November 12, 1953; m 1979, Paula J Hoisington; c Harrison W & Benjamin J. **Education:** Western Ill Univ, BS, 1977; Univ Nebr, PhD (biochem), 1983. **Professional Experience:** DIR MOLECULAR BIOL, CORTECH, INC, 1988-; Harvard Univ, 1983-1988 &NIH, 1984-1987; Fel, Leopold Schepp Found, 1983-1984. **Memberships:** AAAS; fel Am Soc Microbiol; Protein Soc; fel Am Asn Biochem & MolecularBiol; fel Fedn Am Soc Exp Biol. **Research Statement & Publications:** G protein-linked membrane receptors that are implicatedin human diseases; signal transduction events associated with these receptors; discovery of novel, human therapeutics. **Mailing Address:** 4317 W 110th Pl, Westminster, CO 80030. **Fax:** 303-650-1217. **E-Mail:** sjones@.cortech.com

JONES, SUSAN MURIEL, EPITHELIAL TRANSPORT, RENAL HORMONES, FLUID & ELECTROLYTE BALANCE. **Personal Data:** b Providence, RI, April 12, 1952. **Education:** State Univ NY, PhD (pharmacol), 1978. **Professional Experience:** PROF PHARM, HIST ANAT & PHYSIOL, TOURO COL, NY, 1991-; CONSULT, PSIM COMMUNS, 1991-; asst prof, Med Col, Cornell Univ, 1987-1991. **Memberships:** Am Physiol Soc; NY Acad Sci; AMWA. **Research Statement & Publications:** Effect of hormones that act in the kidney to help regulate fluid and electrolye balance. **Mailing Address:** 57 Windmill Ct, Huntington Station, NY 11746. **Fax:** 631-271-6855.

JONES, T STEPHEN, SUBSTANCE ABUSE HIV PREVENTION. **Education:** MD, MPH. **Professional Experience:** RES FEL, CTRS DIS CONTROL & PREV, GA, as of 2006. **Mailing Address:** Ctrs Dis Control & Prev, Bldg One 1600 Clifton Rd NE, Atlanta, GA 30333.

JONES, TAPPEY HUGHES, CHEMICAL ECOLOGY, MICRO ANALYTICAL ORGANIC CHEMISTRY. **Personal Data:** b Norfolk, Va, June 6, 1948. **Education:** Va Mil Inst, BS, 1970; Univ NC, PhD (org chem), 1974. **Professional Experience:** PROF ORG CHEM, VA MIL INST, 1993-; staff fel res, Lab Biophys Chem, Nat Heart, Lung & Blood Inst, Bethesda, Md, 1987-1993; asst prof teaching & res, Chem Dept, Col William & Mary, 1985-1987; asst prof teaching& res, Chem Dept, US Naval Acad, 1981-1985; postdoctoral fel res, Entom Dept, Univ Ga, Athens, 1979-1981; asst prof teaching & res, Chem Dept, Furman Univ, 1977-1979; postdoctoral fel res, Chem Dept, Cornell Univ, 1975-1977; USDA Nat Prog Leader Biochem/Biotechnology/Crop Physiol. **Memberships:** Am Chem Soc. **Research Statement & Publications:** Over 64 publications, with more than 50 of them in the area of insect natural products; venom chemistry of myrmicine ants; developed a number of structure proof methods and syntheses for micro-scale organic analysis. **Mailing Address:** Dept Chem, Va Mil Inst, 403E Sci Bldg, Lexington, VA 24450-0304. **Fax:** 540-464-7261. **E-Mail:** jonesth@vmi.edu

JONES, THEODORE CHARLES, GENETICS, BIOCHEMISTRY. **Personal Data:** b Pittsburgh, Pa, November 9, 1939; m 1962, c 2. **Education:** Amherst Col, AB, 1961; Univ Wash, PhD (genetics), 1967. **Professional Experience:** Consult, Environ Protection Agency, 1979-; BIOLOGIST, ENVIRON PROTECTION AGENCY, 1979-; asst prof biol, Mt Holyoke Col, 1972-1979; asst prof biol, Amherst Col, 1969-1972; fel, Univ Wis, 1967-1969. **Memberships:** Genetics Soc Am; Am Soc Microbiol; Sigma Xi. **Research Statement & Publications:** Regulation of enzyme synthesis and enzyme localization in microorganisms. **Mailing Address:** 201 First St SW V234, Washington, DC 20024-4267.

JONES, THEODORE HAROLD DOUGLAS, BIOCHEMISTRY, MICROBIOLOGY. **Personal Data:** b Belfast, Northern Ireland, October 30, 1938; m 1976, Jeanie. **Education:** Univ Edinburgh, BSc, 1959; Mass Inst Technol, PhD (biochem), 1966. **Professional Experience:** PROF CHEM, UNIV SAN FRANCISCO, 1982-; from asst prof to assoc prof, Univ San Francisco, 1970-1982; NIH traineeship aging res, Retina Found, 1968-1970; Damon Runyon Fund Cancer Res fel, Harvard Med Sch, 1966-1968; res asst biochem, Detroit Inst Cancer Res, 1959-1961. **Memberships:** NY Acad Sci; AAAS. **Research Statement & Publications:** Biochemistry of differentiation, particularly events occurring during germination of spores of the cellular slime molds; biochemistry of membrane proteins and their changes during differentiation; clinical enzymology; peptide hormones in microorganisms; processing of peptide hormones. **Mailing Address:** Dept Chem, Harney Sci Ctr, Univ San Francisco, 2130 Fulton St, San Francisco, CA 94117-1080. **Fax:** 415-422-5157. **E-Mail:** jonest@usfca.edu

JONES, T(HOMAS) BENJAMIN, ELECTRICAL ENGINEERING. **Personal Data:** b Madison, Md, August 26, 1912; m 1947, c 2. **Education:** Johns Hopkins Univ, BE, 1933, Dr Eng, 1937. **Professional Experience:** RETIRED; sr assoc, Trident Eng Assocs, 1973-1988; dielectrics specialist, Bell Tel Labs, 1967-1973; tech supvr, Bell Tel Labs, 1958-1967; mem tech staff, Bell Tel Labs, 1956-1958; res contract dir, Army Ord Corps, 1954-1956; consult, E I du Pont de Nemours & Co Inc, 1954-1956; res contract dir, Off Naval Res, 1948-1954; from asst prof to assoc prof eleceng, Johns Hopkins Univ, 1946-1956; proj engr bur ships, US Navy, 1946-1950; commercial mgr, C & P Tel Co, Md, 1945-1946; personnel supvr, C & P Tel Co, Md, 1944-1945; foreign wire rels engr, C & P Tel Co, Md, 1941-1944; mem tech staff, Bell Tel Lab, NY, 1937-1941; asst instr elec eng, Johns Hopkins Univ, 1936-1937. **Memberships:** Inst Elec & Electronics Engrs. **Research Statement & Publications:** Dielectrics and insulation; electrical capacitors; electrical discharges, arcs and welding; electrical measurements; oxidation of impregnated paper insulation. **Mailing Address:** 5309 River Crescent Dr, Annapolis, MD 21401.

JONES, THOMAS CARLYLE, VETERINARY PATHOLOGY, COMPARATIVE PATHOLOGY. **Personal Data:** b Boise, Idaho, September 29, 1912; wid, c 3. **Education:** Wash State Univ, BS & DVM, 1935. **Honorary Degrees:** DSc, Ohio State Univ, 1970. **Professional Experience:** Mem vis comt sch vet med, Tufts Univ, 1983-1987; EMER PROF COMPPATH, HARVARD UNIV, 1982-; prof comp path, New Eng Regional Primate Res Ctr, HarvardMed Sch, 1971-1982; mem adv comt animal resources, NIH, 1965-1968; assoc clin prof path, Med Sch, Harvard Univ, 1963-1971; mem consult staff, Peter Bent Brigham Hosp, Boston, 1962-1978; mem comt animal health, Nat Acad Sci-Nat Res Coun, 1962-1965; mem comt path training, Nat Inst GenMed Sci, 1960-1963; consult, ArmedForces Inst Path, 1958- & Nat Cancer Inst, 1961-1962; res assoc path, Cancer Res Inst, New Eng Deaconess Hosp, 1957-1967; dirdept path, Angell Mem Animal Hosp, Boston, 1957-1967; clin assoc, Med Sch, Harvard Univ, 1957-1963; chief vet path sect, Armed Forces Inst Path, 1953-1957; chief vet dept, Army MedField Lab, Heidelberg, Ger, 1950-1953; Master res, Grad Coun, George Wash Univ, 1947-1951; chief vet path sect, Armed Forces Inst Path, Wash, DC, 1946-1950; Officer inchg, US Army Vet Res Lab, Front Royal Qm Depot, Va, 1939-1946. **Memberships:** Am Vet Med Asn; Am Col Vet Pathologists (secy-treas 1948-1950 & 1953-1960 pres 1962-1963); Am Asn Path; Int Acad Path (pres 1970-1971); Conf Res Workers Animal Dis. **Research Statement & Publications:** Genetics and cytogenetics applied to disease in animals. **Mailing Address:** 1301 Arenal Ct, Santa Fe, NM 87501.

JONES, THOMAS EVAN, ANALYTICAL CHEMISTRY, INORGANIC CHEMISTRY. **Personal Data:** b Basin, Miss, December 26, 1944; c 2. **Education:** Col Great Falls, BS, 1970; Wash State Univ, PhD (chem), 1974. **Professional Experience:** MGR, ENVIRON COMPLIANCE PROG, PAC NORTHWEST LAB, 1992-; sr res chemist, Environ Compliance Prog, Pac Northwest Lab, 1985-1992; staff chemist, Rockwell Hanford Opers, 1980-1985; asst prof chem, Univ NMex, 1975-1980; res assoc, Wayne State Univ, 1974-1975; teaching asst chem, Wash State Univ, 1970-1974. **Memberships:** Am Chem Soc; Sigma Xi. **Research Statement & Publications:** Provide programmatic guidance for technical support of Hanford Site environmental restoration activities; guided characterization of mixed hazardous/radioactive waste stored in Hanford Site single shell tanks. **Mailing Address:** Pac Northwest Labs, PO Box 999, Richland, WA 99352. **Fax:** 509-373-6603.

JONES, THOMAS HUBBARD, PHYSICAL CHEMISTRY, LIGHT-SENSITIVE MATERIALS. **Personal Data:** b Batavia, Ill, June 8, 1936; m 1958, c 2. **Education:** Augustana Col, Ill, BA, 1958; Univ Minn, Minneapolis, PhD (phys chem), 1963. **Professional Experience:** PROJ LEADER, ILL TOOL WORKS, ITW TECHNOL CTR, GLENVIEW, 1990-; sr chemist, London Chem Co, Bensenville, Ill, 1986-1990; sr chemist, Turtle Wax Inc, Chicago, 1984-1986; res assoc, Richardson Co, Melrose Park, 1980-1982; res supvr, Richardson Co, Melrose Park, 1978-1980; proj chemist, Richardson Co, Melrose Park, 1969-1978; res chemist, Photo Prod Res Lab, E I Du Pont Del Nemours & Co Inc, 1963-1969. **Memberships:** Am Chem Soc. **Research Statement & Publications:** Photopolymerization; applications of polymers and photopolymers in printed circuit resists. **Mailing Address:** 1032 Douglas Ave, Naperville, IL 60540-4320.

JONES, THOMAS S, GENERAL EARTH SCIENCES. **Personal Data:** b Oakland, Md, November 11, 1929; m 1955, Diane; c 3. **Education:** Univ Ill, BS, 1950, MS, 1951; Pa State Univ, PhD (metall), 1961. **Professional Experience:** PHYS SCIENTIST & COMMODITY SPECIALIST, US GEOL SURV, 1996-; phys scientist, US Bur Mines, 1974-1996; staff metallurgist, US Bur Mines, 1971-1974; sr resmetallurgist, Allegheny Ludlum Res Ctr, 1962-1970; res assoc, Pa State Univ, 1961-1962; resasst metall, Gen Elec Res Lab, 1951-1956. **Memberships:** Am Inst Mining Metall & Petrol Engrs. **Research Statement & Publications:** Phase equilibria in metal and oxide systems at high temperatures; kinetics of reduction in metallurgical systems; steelmaking. **Mailing Address:** US Geol Surv, 983 Nat Ctr, Reston, VA 20192. **Fax:** 703-648-7757. **E-Mail:** tjones@usgs.gov

JONES, THOMAS SCOTT, NONDESTRUCTIVE TESTING, NDT OF METALS & COMPOSITE MATERIALS. **Personal Data:** b Newport News, Va, May 30, 1953; m 1975, Diane; c Kristine M & Heather S. **Education:** Va Polytechnic Inst & State Univ, BS, 1975, MS, 1977. **Honors & Awards:** Charles W Briggs Award, Am Soc Testing Mat, 1997 Fellow, Am Soc Nondestructive Testing, 1991. **Professional Experience:** Director, ASTM International, 2005 - Quality Manager, Howmet Research Center, 2002 - Sr. Dev. Engr, Howmet Research Center 2001 - Chairman ASTM Committee E07 on Nondestructive Testing, 2002 - 2005; Vpres, Indust Qual Inc, 1992-2001; Chairman, ASTM E07.06 ULTRASONIC METHOD, 1992-1998; Chairman ASTM E07.02 Ref Radiol Images, 1990-1993; mgr res & eng, Indust Qual Inc, 1989-1992; Chmn, Aerospace Comn, Am Soc Nondestruct Testing, 1989-1991; sr nondestruct testing eng, Indust Qual Inc, 1987-1989; From engr to lead engr, McDonnell Aircraft Co, 1977-1987; secy, E-7 Nondestructive Testing, Am Soc Testing & Mat Comt. **Memberships:** Fel Am Soc Nondestructive Testing; Am Soc Testing & Mats' chmn, comt E07 on Nondestructive Testing, Am Soc Testing & Mat; Am Scientific Affiliation; Am Soc for Quality. **Research Statement & Publications:** Nondestructive testing technology; research and development of ultrasonic characterization of materials; digital x-ray imaging; simulation of radiographic imaging and infrared thermography applications. **Mailing Address:** Howmet Research Center, 1500 S Warner St, Whitehall, MI 49461-1895. **Fax:** 231-894-7293. **E-Mail:** tjones@howmet.com

JONES, THOMAS V, RESEARCH ADMINISTRATION. **Personal Data:** b Pomona, Calif, July 21, 1920. **Education:** Stanford Univ, BS, 1942. **Honorary Degrees:** LLD, George Wash, 1967. **Honors & Awards:** Reed Aeronaut Award, Am Inst Aeronaut & Astronaut, 1985; Wright BrosMem Trophy, Nat Aeronaut Asn, 1989. **Professional Experience:** RETIRED; mem, bd dirs, Northrop Corp, 1990-1991; chmn bd govs, Aerospace Indust Asn, 1985; chmn bd, Northrop Corp, 1963-1990; chief exec officer, NorthropCorp, 1960-1989; pres, Northrop Corp, 1959-1960; sr vpres develop planning, Northrop Corp, 1958-1959; mem bd dirs, MCA, Inc; asst to chief engr, Northrop Corp, 1953-1958; mem staff, Rand Corp, 1951-1953; prof & dept head, Aeronaut Inst Technol, Brazil, 1951-1953; tech adv, Brazilian Air Ministry, Rio de Janeiro, 1947-1951. **Memberships:** Nat Acad Eng; Aerospace Indust Asn; hon fel Am Inst Aeronaut & Astronaut. **Mailing Address:** 650 N Sepulveda Blvd, Los Angeles, CA 90049.

JONES, THOMAS W, PHYSIOLOGY. **Education:** Univ Md, PhD. **Professional Experience:** DEAN, HENSON SCH SCI & TECHNOL, SALISBURY UNIV, 1998-. **Mailing Address:** Salisbury State Univ, PO Box 775, Salisbury, MD 21801. **Fax:** 410-543-6184. **E-Mail:** twjones@salisbury.edu

JONES, THOMAS WALTER, THEORETICAL ASTROPHYSICS. **Personal Data:** b Odessa, Tex, June 22, 1945; m 2001, Lynne; c Walter B. **Education:** Univ Tex, Austin, BS, 1967; Univ Minn, MS, 1969, PhD (physics), 1972. **Professional Experience:** PROF ASTRON, UNIV MINN, 1984-; chmn, Dept Astron, 1981-1997; from asst prof to assoc prof, Univ Minn, 1978-1984; assoc scientist, Nat Radio Astron Observ, 1977; asst scientist, Nat Radio Astron Observ, 1975-1977; Asst res physicist, Univ Calif, San Diego, 1972-1975. **Memberships:** Am Astron Soc; Int Astron Union; Sigma Xi; Royal Astron Soc, Am Physical Society. **Research Statement & Publications:** Studies of physical processes in energetic environments; active galaxies and quasars; galaxy clusters; numerical hydrodynamics; supernova remnants; cosmic rays. **Mailing Address:** Dept Astron, Univ Minn, Minneapolis, MN 55455. **Fax:** 612-626-2029. **E-Mail:** twj@astro.umn.edu

JONES, TIMOTHY ARTHUR, NEUROPHYSIOLOGY. **Personal Data:** b Pomona, Calif, m 1992, Sherri; c Marnie & Catie. **Education:** Univ Calif, PhD (physiol), 1980. **Professional Experience:** PROF, DEPT MED PHARMACOL & PHYSIOL, UNIV MO, as of 2004; Prof, Sch Med, Univ MD, Columbia, 1998; assoc prof, Sch Med, Univ Mo, Columbia, 1994-1998; From asst prof to assoc prof physiol, Univ Nebr, Lincoln, 1982-1994; NASA res assoc award, Stanford Univ, 1080 & 1901. **Research Statement & Publications:** Ontogeny of sensory systems; gravitational physiology. **Mailing Address:** Dept Med Pharmacol &Physiol, Univ Mo Med Sch, MA415 Med Sci Bldg, Columbia, MO 65212. **Fax:** 573-884-4276. **E-Mail:** jonest@missouri.edu

JONES, TODD KEVIN, MEDICAL CHEMISTRY, SYNTHETIC METHODS IN ORGANIC CHEMISTRY. **Personal Data:** b Denver, Colo, m 1980. **Education:** Colo Sch Mines, Golden, BS, 1980; Univ Ill, Urbana, PhD (org chem), 1985. **Professional Experience:** DIR CHEM, ONTOGEN CORP, 1999-; asst dir med chem, Ligand pharaceut, 1992-1999; res fel, Merck Res Labs, 1991-1992; sr res chemist, Merck Res Labs, 1987-1991; NIH fel, Harvard Univ, 1985-1987. **Memberships:** Am Chem Soc; AAAS. **Research Statement & Publications:** Synthesizing small organic molecules that interact with intracellular receptors. **Mailing Address:** Ontogen Corp Corp Hq, 6451 El Camino Real, Carlsbad, CA 92009. **Fax:** 760-930-0200. **E-Mail:** ods@ontogen.com

JONES, TREVOR O, ENGINEERING. **Personal Data:** b Maidstone, Eng, m Jennie. **Honors & Awards:** Hooper Mem Prize, Brit Inst Elec Engrs, 1950; Arch T Colwell Award, Soc Automotive Engrs, 1974 & 1975, Vincent Bendix Automotive ELectronics Eng Award, 1976, Buckendale Lectr, 1986 & Edward N Cole Automotive Eng Award, 1988; Safety Award Eng Excellence, US Dept Transp, 1978; H H Bliss Award, 1991. **Professional Experience:** CHMN & FOUNDER, BIOMEC INC, 1998-; mem bd dirs, Libbey-Owens-Ford, 1994-1997; CHMN & CHIEF EXEC OFFICER, INT DEVELOP CORP, 1994-; pres & chief exec officer, Libbey-Owens-Ford, 1993-1994; chmn bd, Libbey-Owens-Ford, 1987-1994; group vpres sales & mkt, TRW Inc, 1985-1987; group vpres strategic progs, Automotive Worldwide Sector, TRW Inc, 1985; group vpres & gen mgr, Transp ElectronicsGroup, TRW Inc, 1979-1985; vpres eng, AutomotiveWorldwide Sector, TRW Inc, 1978-1979; chmn, Nat Hwy Safety Adv Comt, 1978; mem, Nat Hwy Safety Adv Comt, 1975-1978; Gen Motors Proving Ground, Gen Motors, 1974-1978; Advan Prod Eng, Gen Motors, 1972-1974; vchmn, Nat Motor Vehicle Safety Adv Coun, 1972; mem, Nat Motor Vehicle Safety Adv Coun, 1971-; Automotive Electronic Control Systs, Gen Motors, 1970-1972; dir, Delco Electronics Div, Gen Motors, 1959-1970; mem, Transp Res Bd Comt, Nat Res Coun; pres, Int Develop Corp; mem, Safety Res for a Changing Hwy Environ Comt, Nat Acad Eng, Nat Interests an Age Global Technol Comt. **Memberships:** Nat Acad Eng; fel Brit Soc Elec Engrs; fel Am Inst Elec & Electronics Engrs; fel Soc Automotive Engrs; Brit Inst Elec Engrs. **Research Statement & Publications:** Automotive safety and electronics; granted several patents. **Mailing Address:** Biomec, Inc, 1771 E 30th St, Cleveland, OH 44114. **Fax:** 216-937-2812. **E-Mail:** info@biomec.com

JONES, VAUGHAN F R, MATHEMATICS. **Personal Data:** b Gisborne, NZ, December 31, 1952; m 1979, Martha; c Bethany Martha, Ian Randal & Alice Collins. **Education:** Auckland Univ, BSc, 1972, MSc, 1973. **Professional Experience:** PROF MATH, UNIV CALIF BERKELEY, 1985-; assoc prof math, Univ Calif Berkeley, 1984-1985; asst prof math, Univ Calif Berkeley, 1981-1984. **Mailing Address:** Dept Math, Univ Calif, 925 Evans Hall, Berkeley, CA 94720-0001. **E-Mail:** vfr@math.berkeley.edu

JONES, VICTOR ALAN, FOOD ENGINEERING, FOOD SCIENCE. **Personal Data:** b Fremont, Mich, February 24, 1930; m 1954, c 4. **Education:** Mich State Univ, BS, 1952, MS, 1959, PhD (agr eng), 1962. **Professional Experience:** PROF EMER FOOD ENG, NC STATE UNIV, 1993-; vis prof, Ore StateUniv, 1971; from asst prof to prof, NC State Univ, 1962-1993. **Memberships:** Am Soc Agr Engrs; Inst Food Technologists; Am Dairy Sci Asn; Sigma Xi. **Research Statement & Publications:** Unit operations and control for ultrahigh temperature pasteurization or sterilization of foods; packaging materials and equipment. **Mailing Address:** Dept Food Sci, NC State Univ, Campus Box 7624, Raleigh, NC 27695-7624. **Fax:** 919-515-7124. **E-Mail:** victor_jones@ncsu.edu

JONES, VICTOR T, III, CHEMISTRY. **Professional Experience:** PRES, EXPLORATION TECHNOLOGIES INC, as of 2004. **Memberships:** Am Chem Soc. **Mailing Address:** Exploration Tech Inc, 3698 Westchase, Houston, TX 77042. **Fax:** 713-785-1550. **E-Mail:** etimail@eti-geochemistry.com

JONES, WALTER F, AERONAUTICS. **Education:** Clemson Univ, Clemson, SC, BS, 1978, MS, 1981, PhD (eng mech), 1982. **Professional Experience:** DIR, PLANS & PROGS, AIR FORCE RES LAB, WRIGHT-PATTERSON AFB, 2005-. **Mailing Address:** Air Force Office Sci Res, AFOSR/NA Bolling AFB, Washington, DC 20332. **Fax:** 202-767-0470. **E-Mail:** walter.jones@wpafb.af.mil

JONES, WALTER H(ARRISON), CHEMISTRY COMPUTATIONAL CHEMISTRY THERMODYNAMICS. **Personal Data:** b Griffin, Sask, September 21, 1922; American citizen; wid. **Education:** Univ Calif, Los Angeles, BS, 1944, PhD (phys org chem), 1948. **Professional Experience:** NSF Grantee, 2000-; VIS RES CHEMIST, UNIV CALIF, LOS ANGELES, 1994-; consult, Eng Soc Comn Energy, 1982-1983 & Naval Surface Weapons Ctr, 1982-; ENG SOC COMN ENERGY, 1982-1983 & NAVAL SURFACE WEAPONS CTR, 1982-; vis prof, Univ Toronto, 1978-1979 & 1994; prof chem, Univ WFla, 1975-1994; consult, Fla Energy Comt & Solar Energy Ctr, 1974-1979; from assoc prof to prof aeronaut syst, Univ WFla, 1969-1975; dir, Corpus Christi Ctr, 1969-1975; sr scientist & head adv tech, Hughes Aircraft Co, 1964-1968; head, Propulsion Dept, Aerospace Corp, 1963-1964; panel chmn, Inst Defense Anal, 1960-1963; Chmn, Thermochem Panel, Joint Army-Navy-Air Force-Adv Res Proj Agency, NASA, 1960-1962; mgr, Chem Dept, Aeronutronic Div, Ford Motor Co, 1956-1960; sr res engr, NAm Aviation, Inc, 1954-1956; chemist, Western Regional Res Lab, USDA, 1948-1951 & Los Alamos Sci Lab, 1951-1954; Res assoc, Univ Calif, Los Angeles, 1948; 1954 Research Corp Grantee, 1985-1986; vis-prof, Queensland Univ, 1998. **Memberships:** Am Chem Soc; fel Am Inst Chemists; NY Acad Sci; AAAS; Int Solar Energy Soc; World Asn Theoret Org Chemists. **Research Statement & Publications:** Chemical kinetics; polymer chemistry; thermodynamics; combustion; propulsion; missile and space systems analysis and engineering; energy systems analyses; quantum chemistry; chemistry at high pressures. **Mailing Address:** 355 Calle Loma Norte, Santa Fe, NM 87501. **Fax:** 505-983-8123.

JONES, WANDA K, HIV AIDS RESEARCH. **Education:** PhD. **Professional Experience:** ASST DEP SECY, US DEPT HEALTH & HUMAN SERV & DIR, OFF WOMENS HEALTH, GA, 1998-. **Memberships:** NIH. **Mailing Address:** Ctrs Dis Control & Prev, Bldg One 1600 Clifton Rd NE, Atlanta, GA 30333.

JONES, WAYNE E, PHOTOCHEMISTRY, PHOTOINDUCED ELECTRON TRANSFER. **Personal Data:** b Springfield, Mass, June 25, 1965; m 1988, Michele; c Meghan & Erin. **Education:** St Michael's Col, BS, 1987; Univ NC, Chapel Hill, PhD, 1991. **Professional Experience:** ASSOC PROF INORG & MAT CHEM, STATE UNIV NY, BINGHAMTON, as of 2004; asst prof inorg chem, State Univ Ny, Binghamton, beginning 1993; fel, Univ Tex, Austin, 1992-1993; res asst, Univ NC, Chapel Hill, 1988-1991; teaching asst, Univ NC, Chapel Hill, 1987-1988. **Memberships:** Am Chem Soc; AAAS; Sigma Xi. **Mailing Address:** Dept Chem, State Univ NY, Binghamton, NY 13902-6016. **Fax:** 607-777-4478. **E-Mail:** wjones@binghamton.edu

JONES, WILBER CLARK, INORGANIC CHEMISTRY. **Personal Data:** b Grove City, Pa, January 21, 1941; m 1962, Carolee; c Wendy & Tracy. **Education:** Westminster Col, Pa, BS, 1962; Univ Tenn, PhD (chem), 1966. **Professional Experience:** PROF EMER CHEM, CONCORD COL, as of 2005; prof chem, Concord Col, 1977-2004; chmn, dept physics sci, Concord Col, 1974-1994; from asst prof to assoc prof, Concord Col, 1966-1977. **Memberships:** Am Chem Soc. **Research Statement & Publications:** Synthesis and structural studies on coordination compounds. **Mailing Address:** Dept Phys Sci, Concord Col, Vermillion St, Athens, WV 24712-1000. **Fax:** 304-384-9044. **E-Mail:** jonesw@concord.edu

JONES, WILBUR DOUGLAS, BIOLOGY, CLASSIFICATION, IDENTIFICATION & GENETICS OF MYCOBACTERIA. **Personal Data:** b Augusta, Ga, July 3, 1927; m 1952, Buell; c Wilbur K & Robert W. **Education:** Emory Univ, AB, 1949; WVa Univ, MS, 1951; Med Col Ga, PhD (microbiol), 1968. **Professional Experience:** RETIRED; res microbiologist, Ctr Dis Control, USPHS, 1962-1990; chief bacteriologist, Training Lab, 1960-1962; bacteriologist, Ga State Health Dept, 1953-1960; instr sci, Truett-McConnell Jr Col, 1951-1953; asst, WVa Univ, 1951. **Memberships:** Am Soc Microbiol; fel Am Acad Microbiol. **Research Statement & Publications:** Genetics and phage typing of the mycobacteria; genetics and molecular biology of the mycobacteriophages. **Mailing Address:** 4182 Smithfield Dr, Tucker, GA 30084. **E-Mail:** wjones23@bellsouth.net

JONES, WILLIAM B, ASSISTIVE DEVICES FOR HANDICAPPED, POLYMER FRACTURE. **Personal Data:** b Littlefield, Tex, June 10, 1937; m 1956, c 6. **Education:** Tex Tech Univ, BS, 1959, MS, 1960; Univ Utah, PhD (mech eng), 1970. **Professional Experience:** CHIEF ENGR, B J ENTERPRISES, 1989-; assoc prof, Tex Tech Univ, 1982-1989; lectr, Kent State Univ, 1978-1982 & Univ Calif, Los Angeles, 1979-1985; Textron, BellHelicopter, 1974-1975 & Fredrick R Harris, 1978-1979; mat res engr, Wright AFB Aero Labs, 1975-1982; consult, Lockheed Propulsion Co, 1967-1969; Res asst mech eng, Univ Utah, 1966-1969; mem tech staff, Rocketdyne Div, Rockwell Int, 1960-1975; Teaching asst mech eng, Tex Tech Univ, 1959-1960. **Memberships:** Adhesion Soc; Soc Aerospace Mat & Process Engrs; Am Chem Soc; Am SolarEnergy Soc. **Research Statement & Publications:** Fracture mechanics of polymers and adhesive joints; materials and processes for adhesives and advanced composite materials. **Mailing Address:** 1200 W 14th St, Littlefield, TX 79339.

JONES, WILLIAM B, APPROXIMATION THEORY & NUMERICAL ANALYSIS. **Personal Data:** b Spring Hill, Tenn, September 24, 1931; m 1956, Martha; c 5. **Education:** Jacksonville State Col, BA, 1953; Vanderbilt Univ, MA, 1955, PhD (math), 1963. **Honors & Awards:** Gold Medal Award, US Dept Com, 1965. **Professional Experience:** RETIRED; vis Fulbright prof, Fulbright res scholar, 1991-1992; chmn dept, Univ Colo, 1987-1990; Fulbright res-scholar award, 1984-1985; vis Fulbright prof, Univ Trondeim, Norway, 1984-1985; award grant, Norwegian Marshall Fund, 1984-1985; vis prof, Univ Kent, Canterbury, UK, 1977; prof math, Univ Colo, Boulder, beginning 1973; assoc chmn dept, Univ Colo, 1972-1974; consult, Off Telecommun-Inst Telecommun Sci, 1970-1973;

mathematician, Off Telecommun-Inst Telecommun Sci, 1970-1971; assoc prof math, Univ Colo, 1968-1973; consult, Nat Bur Stand, 1964-1965 & Environ Sci Servs Admin, 1965-1970; asst prof appl math, Univ Colo, 1964-1968; actg asst prof math, Univ Colo, 1963-1964; mathematician, Nat Bur Stand, 1958-1963. **Memberships:** Am Math Soc; Math Asn Am; Soc Indust & Appl Math. **Research Statement & Publications:** Numerical analysis; approximation theory; continued fractions; Pade Approximants; moment theory. **Mailing Address:** Univ Colo, 395 Univ Colo Boulder, Boulder, CO 80309-0395. **Fax:** 303-492-7707. **E-Mail:** william.jones@colorado.edu

JONES, WILLIAM BARCLAY, PHYSICS. **Personal Data:** b San Francisco, Calif, August 18, 1919; wid, c Kathleen (Dale), William B & M David. **Education:** Univ Calif, AB, 1947, PhD (physics), 1964. **Professional Experience:** CONSULT 1985-; physicist, Brookhaven Nat Lab, 1975-1985; res assocphysics, Yale Univ, 1968-1975; nuclear physicist, Tech Measurement Corp, 1962-1967; accelerator supvr, Crocker Lab, Univ Calif, 1955-1962. **Memberships:** Am Phys Soc; AAAS. **Research Statement & Publications:** Low and intermediate energy; experimental nuclear physics. **Mailing Address:** 1036 Randall St, Eugene, OR 97401.

JONES, WILLIAM B(ENJAMIN), ELECTRICAL ENGINEERING. **Personal Data:** b Fairburn, Ga, September 17, 1924; m 1948, Mary; c William B III, Katherine P Boerstler & Joseph L. **Education:** Ga Inst Technol, BS, 1945, MS, 1948, PhD (elec eng), 1953. **Professional Experience:** RETIRED; vis prof, Univ Fla, 1984-1985; prof elec eng, Tex A&M Univ, 1967-1990; head dept, Tex A&M Univ, 1967-1984; prof elec eng, Ga Inst Technol, 1958-1967; res engr, Hughes Aircraft Co, 1954-1958; from instr to assoc prof elec eng & res assoc, Ga InstTechnol, 1948-1954; engr, radar develop, R I Sarbacher & Assoc, 1947-1948. **Memberships:** Sr mem Inst Elec & Electronics Engrs; Optical Soc Am; Am Soc Eng Educ. **Research Statement & Publications:** Communications theory and systems; optical communication systems. **Mailing Address:** 43 Hyalite Rd, Dahlonega, GA 30533-8831.

JONES, WILLIAM DAVIDSON, INORGANIC CHEMISTRY, ORGANIC CHEMISTRY. **Personal Data:** b Folsom, Pa, October 26, 1953; m 1977, c 3. **Education:** Mass Inst Technol, BS, 1975; Calif Tech, PhD (chem), 1979. **Professional Experience:** C F HOUGHTON PROF CHEM, UNIV ROCHESTER, as of 2003; Royal Soc fel, 1988-1989; Fulbright fel, 1988-1989; Guggenheim fel, John S Guggenheim, 1988; Camillle & Henry Dreyful fel, 1985-1988; Ap Sloan fel, Sloan Found, 1984; prof chem, Univ Rochester, beginning 1980; NSF postdoctoral, chem, Univ Wis, Madison, 1979-1980. **Memberships:** Am Chem Soc. **Research Statement & Publications:** Inorganic and organometallic chemistry; mechanism and thermodynamics of carbon-hydrogen bond activity by homogeneous transition metal complexes; published over 10 articles. **Mailing Address:** Univ Rochester, Box 270216, Rochester, NY 14627-0216. **Fax:** 585-473-6889. **E-Mail:** jones@chem.rochester.edu

JONES, WILLIAM E, MATHEMATICS. **Professional Experience:** EMER PROF PHYSICS, UNIV MONTEVALLO, as of 2006. **Memberships:** Int Stud Adv Comt. **Mailing Address:** Dept Math & Physics, Univ Montevallo Sta 6, Montevallo, AL 35115. **Fax:** 205-665-6000. **E-Mail:** wjones@montevallo.edu

JONES, WILLIAM ERNEST, PHYSICAL CHEMISTRY & SPECTROSCOPY, ATOMIC & MOLECULAR PHYSICS. **Personal Data:** b Sackville, NB, 1936; m 1958, Norma; c Mary E, Jennifer A, Sarah A & K Martha. **Education:** Mt Allison Univ, BSc, 1958, MSc, 1959; McGill Univ, PhD (phys chem), 1963. **Professional Experience:** Adj prof chem, Saint Mary's Univ, Halifax, as of 2005; ACTG DEAN FAC GRAD STUDIES & RES, SAINT MARY'S UNIV, HALIFAX, as of 2003; prof chem, Univ Windsor, 1991-2001; prof chem & dean sci, St Mary's Univ, 1989-1991; from asst prof to prof phys chem, chmn Dalhousie Senate, 1983-1989; chmn chem dept, Dalhousie Univ, 1974-1983; from asst prof to prof phys chem, Dalhousie Univ, 1962-1989; res assoc, Mt Allison Univ, 1959-1960. **Research Statement & Publications:** Kinetics; spectroscopy; surface chemistry; catalysis; gas phase kinetics of atoms and free radicals; atomic and molecular spectroscopy. **Mailing Address:** Dept Grad Studies & Res, St Mary's Univ Halifax NS, Halifax, NS B3H 3C3, Can. **Fax:** 902-420-5162. **E-Mail:** william.jones@smu.ca

JONES, WILLIAM HOWRY, RGANIC CHEMISTRY, CATALYSIS, HIGH PRESS, RES. **Personal Data:** b Lancaster, Pa, November 6, 1920; m 1949, c 4. **Education:** Juniata Col, BS, 1942; Columbia Univ, MA, 1944; Mass Inst Technol, PhD (org chem), 1947. **Professional Experience:** RETIRED; res assoc, Merck Sharp & Dohme Res Labs, 1959-1985; res chemist, Merck Inc, 1949-1959; instr chem, Univ Ill, 1948-1949; Du Pont fel nuclear alkylation, Univ Ill, 1947-1948; asst, Anti-Malarial Proj, Mass Inst Technol, 1945-1946; asst, Manhattan Proj, SAM Labs, 1944-1945; lectr, Columbia Univ, 1943; lab asst, Columbia Univ, 1942-1944; lab asst chem, Juniata Col, 1939-1942. **Memberships:** Am Chem Soc; fel NY Acad Sci; Sigma Xi. **Research Statement & Publications:** Synthesis of physiologically active compounds; reaction mechanisms; synthesis of substituted diamines and quinoline derivatives; catalytic hydrogenation; high pressure research. **Mailing Address:** 115 Hazelwood Ave, Metuchen, NJ 08840-2112. **E-Mail:** wilmarjones@att.net

JONES, WILLIAM J, ENGINEERING PHYSICS. **Personal Data:** b New York, NY, March 23, 1915; m 1942, Dorothy Powell; c Peter, Geoffrey & Marc. **Education:** Tufts Univ, BS, 1941; Newark Col Eng, MS, 1950. **Professional Experience:** SR STAFF RES ASSOC, ENERGY LAB, MASS INST TECHNOL, 1972-; lectr physics, Harvard Univ, 1963-1972. **Research Statement & Publications:** physics; energy technologies issues and policies; & Environmental Impacts. **Mailing Address:** 92 Bullough Park, Newton, MA 02160. **Fax:** 508-693-4249.

JONES, WILLIAM JONAS, ORGANIC CHEMISTRY, TEXTILE FIBERS. **Personal Data:** b Whaleyville, Va, November 18, 1941; m 1980, Annette. **Education:** Col William & Mary, BS, 1963; Duke Univ, PhD (org chem), 1966. **Professional Experience:** SR RES ASSOC, DACRON RES LAB, E I DU PONT DEL NEMOURS & CO INC, 1992-; res assoc, E I du Pont Del Nemours & Co Inc, 1985-1992; sr res chemist, E I du Pont Del Nemours & Co Inc, 1974-1985; res chemist, E I du Pont Del Nemours & Co Inc, 1966-1974. **Memberships:** Am Chem Soc. **Research Statement & Publications:** Heterocyclic organic compounds; polymers; chemistry of textile fibers; fiber engineering; polyester filling products. **Mailing Address:** 417 Falcon Circle, Greenville, NC 27834.

JONES, WILLIAM MAURICE, SYNTHETIC INORGANIC & ORGANOMETALLIC CHEMISTRY. **Personal Data:** b Campbellsville, Ky, January 12, 1930; m 1956, c 3. **Education:** Union Univ, Tenn, BS, 1951; Univ Ga, MS, 1953; Univ Southern Calif, PhD (org chem), 1955. **Professional Experience:** DISTINGUISHED SERV PROF EMER, UNIV FLA, as of 2000; distinguished serv prof, Univ Fla, beginning 1990; mem ed bd, Petrol ResFund Adv Bd, 1990-1993; mem ed bd, J Organic Chem, 1974-1979; mem ed bd, Chem Rev, 1971-1974; NATO sr sci fel, 1971; chmn dept, Univ Fla, 1968-1973; prof chem, Univ Fla, 1965-1990; sloan fel, 1963-1967; from asst prof to assoc prof, Univ Fla, 1956-1965; instr chem, Univ Southern Calif, 1955-1956. **Memberships:** Am Chem Soc. **Research Statement & Publications:** Mechanisms of organic reactions; strained allenes and their transition metal complexes; transition metal complexes of conjugated carbocyclic carbenes; transition metal organometallic rearrangements. **Mailing Address:** Dept Chem Univ Fla, PO Box 117200, Gainesville, FL 32611-7200. **Fax:** 352-392-8758. **E-Mail:** jones@chem.ufl.edu

JONES, WILLIAM PHILIP, EXPERIMENTAL NUCLEAR PHYSICS. **Personal Data:** b Chicago, Ill, October 2, 1942; m 1964, Mary; c Catherine M (Gottlieb) & Robert W. **Education:** Univ Notre Dame, BS, 1964; Univ Mich, MS, 1965, PhD (physics), 1969. **Professional Experience:** STAFF PHYSICIST, PROTON THER SYSTS DIV & BEAM DELIVERY SYSTS, IND UNIV, BLOOMINGTON, 1971-; res assoc, Ind Univ, Bloomington, 1969-1971. **Memberships:** Am Phys Soc; Sigma Xi; AAAS. **Research Statement & Publications:** Medium energy nuclear physics; charged-particle reactions; properties of nuclear energy levels; cyclotron orbit dynamics; charged particle beam optics. **Mailing Address:** Proton Ther Systs Div, Ind Univ Cyclotron Facil, 2401 Milo B Sampson Lane, Bloomington, IN 47408-1368. **Fax:** 812-855-6645. **E-Mail:** jones@iucf.indiana.edu

JONES, WILLIAM R, METALLURGY. **Education:** Pa State Univ. **Professional Experience:** CHIEF EXEC OFFICER, SOLAR ATMOSPHERE INC, PA, as of 2005. **Memberships:** Am Soc Metals. **Mailing Address:** Solar Atmosphere Inc, 1969 Clearview Rd, Souderton, PA 18964-0476.

JONES, WINTON D, JR, MEDICINAL CHEMISTRY, ORGANIC CHEMISTRY. **Personal Data:** b Terre Haute, Ind, June 23, 1941; m 1964, Sandra Myrdock; c 2. **Education:** Butler Univ, BS, 1963, MS, 1966; Univ Kans, PhD (med chem), 1970. **Professional Experience:** SCIENTIST, HOECHST MARION ROUSSEL, 1991-; Org chemist, Merrell-Dow Pharmaceut, Inc, Dow Chem Co, 1980-1991; Cong sci consult, 1979-1980. **Memberships:** Am Chem Soc. **Research Statement & Publications:** Medicinal chemistry, antiallergic agents; synthesis of central nervous system, cardiotonic agents, antihypertensives, antiviral and anti-cancer agents. **Mailing Address:** Hoechst Marion Roussel, 2110 Galbraith Rd, Cincinnati, OH 45215.

JONES-LEE, REBECCA ANNE, AQUATIC TOXICOLOGY, WATER QUALITY. **Personal Data:** b Menominee, Mich, January 23, 1951. **Education:** Southern Methodist Univ, BS, 1973; Univ Tex, Dallas, MS, 1975, PhD (environ sci), 1978. **Honors & Awards:** Charles B Dudley Award, Am Soc Testing & Mat, 1984. **Professional Experience:** VPRES, G FRED LEE & ASSOCS, 1989-; assoc prof environ eng, water qual & aquatic toxicol, NJ Inst Technol, 1984-1989; res assoc & lectr environ eng, Tex Tech Univ, Lubbock, 1982-1984; coordr aquatic biol, Fluor Engrs, Irvine, Calif, 1982; proj assoc, G Fred Lee & Assoc, 1978-; res asst prof civil eng, Colo State Univ, 1978-1981. **Research Statement & Publications:** Chemical and biological aspects of surface and groundwater supplies and quality; sources, significance and fate of chemical contaminants in the environment; chemical and biological aspects of water pollution control in surface and groundwaters, rivers, lakes, estuaries and the oceans. **Mailing Address:** G Fred Lee & Assocs, 27298 E El Macero Dr, El Macero, CA 95618-1005. **Fax:** 916-753-9956. **E-Mail:** gfredlee@aol.com

JONG, ING-CHANG, SOLID MECHANICS, Mechanics Education. **Personal Data:** b Yunlin, Taiwan, February 5, 1938; American citizen; m 1966, c David & Vida. **Education:** Nat Taiwan Univ, BS, 1961; SDak Sch Mines & Technol, MS, 1963; Northwestern Univ, Evanston, PhD (theoret & appl mech), 1965. **Honors & Awards:** Outstanding educator of Am, 1971; Halliburton Outstanding Teacher, 1994; Ark Academy of Mech Engineering, 2001; Best Paper Award, Mechanics Div, ASEE, 2002. **Professional Experience:** AT MECH ENG DEPT, UNIV ARK, prof, beginning 1974; assoc prof, 1969-1974; asst prof, 1965-1969; prin investr, eng mech res grant, NSF, 1969-1971; prin investr, eng res initiation grant, NSF, 1967-1969. **Memberships:** Am Soc Mech Engrs; Am Soc Eng Educ. **Research Statement & Publications:** Engg Mechanics; nonconservative stability of damped structures; vibrations and dynamic stability of structural systems exhibiting yielding and hysteresis; educational research in mechanics; senior author of three books. **Mailing Address:** Univ Ark, 2684 Stanton Ave, Fayetteville, AR 72703. **Fax:** 479-575-6982. **E-Mail:** icj@engr.uark.edu

JONG, SHUNG-CHANG, MYCOLOGY. **Personal Data:** b Taiwan, November 12, 1936; American citizen; m 1965, Chiu-Hwa; c Maria, Cynthia & Victoria. **Education:** Nat Taiwan Univ, BS, 1960; Western Ill Univ, MS, 1966; Wash State Univ, PhD (mycol), 1969. **Honors & Awards:** J Roger Porter Award, 1997; Agr Award, PR China, 1988; Agr Award Int Sci & Technol Co oper, Ministry. **Professional Experience:** HEAD, DEPT MYCOL & BOT, AM TYPE CULT COLLECTION, as of 2003; AFFIL PROF, GEORGE MASON UNIV, as of 2003; HON PROF, WUHAN UNIV, as of 2003; DIR & SR STAFF SCIENTIST, YEAST GENETIC STOCK CTR, AM TYPE CULT COLLECTION, 1997-; dir, Mycol& Protistol Prog, 1994-1996; Sci Found grants, beginning 1975; cur & head mycol & bot dept, Am TypeCult Collection, 1974-1994; cur fungi, Am Type Cult Collection, 1971-1973; sr mycologist, AmType Cult Collection, 1969-1971; asst instr mycol, Nat Taiwan Univ, 1963-1965; asst plantpathologist, Taiwan Agr Res Inst, 1961-1963. **Memberships:** Brit Mycological Soc; Chinese Med & Health Asn; Int Soc Human & AnimalMycol; Med Mycol Soc Am; Mycol Soc Am; Int Asn Plant Tissue Culture; Int Mushroom Soc forTropics; Int Soc Plant Molecular Biol; Japan Antibiotics Res Asn; Sigma Xi; Soc FermentationTechnol; US Fedn Culture Collections. **Research Statement & Publications:** Preservation and industrial applications of living fungi; biology of fungi in culture. **Mailing Address:** Dept Mycol & Bot, Am Type Cult Collection, 12301 Parklawn Dr, Rockville, MD 20852. **E-Mail:** sjong@atcc.org

JONGSMA, CALVIN, MATHEMATICS. **Education:** Univ Toronto, PhD, 1982. **Professional Experience:** PROF, DORDT COL, as of 2006. **Mailing Address:** Dordt Col, 498 4th Ave NE, Sioux Center, IA 51250. **Fax:** 712-722-1671. **E-Mail:** pkal@pkal.org

JONNARD, AIMISON, CHEMICAL ENGINEERING. **Personal Data:** b Sewanee, Tenn, August 3, 1916; m 1961, c 4. **Education:** Kans State Univ, BS, 1938; Columbia Univ, MS, 1939; Univ Pittsburgh, PhD (chem eng), 1949. **Professional Experience:** SR ANALYST, US INT TRADE COMN, as of 1997; chief, energy & chem div, US Int Tradecomn, beginning 1971; sr corp planner, Exxon Chem Co, 1963-1971; vpres, Celanese Chem Co, 1961-1963; mgr, mkt res & develop, US Indust Chem Co Div, Nat Distillers & Chem Co, 1959-1961; mgr & mkt anal, Shell Chem Co, 1954-1959; sr technologist, Shell Chem Co, 1949-1954; instr chem eng, Kans State Univ, 1941-1945; engr, Exp Sta, E I du Pont Del Nemours & Co, 1939-1941. **Memberships:** Am Chem Soc; Am Inst Chem Engrs. **Research Statement & Publications:** Chemical economics. **Mailing Address:** US Int Trade Comn, 500 E St SW, Washington, DC 20436.

JONSEN, ALBERT R, MEDICAL ETHICS, MEDICAL EDUCATION. **Personal Data:** b San Francisco, Calif, April 4, 1931; m 1976, Mary Elizabeth Carolan. **Education:** Gonzaza Univ, BA, 1955, MA, 1956; Univ Santa Clara, STM, 1963; Yale Univ, PhD, 1967. **Honors & Awards:** McGovern Award, Am Osler Soc; Annual Award, Soc Health & Human Value; Davies Award, Am Col Physicians; Convocation Medal, Am Col Cardiol GUGENHEIM FEL 1996-1997; LIFETIME ACHIEVEMENT AWARD, AM SOC OF BIOTECH AND HUMANITIES 1999. **Professional Experience:** Vis prof of bioethics, Stanford Univ Sch Med 2001; vis prof bioethics, Yals Univ 1999-2000; prof emer of ethics in med, Univ Wash Sch of Med 1999; chmn, Dept Med Hist & Ethics Univ Wash Sch Med 1987-1999; CHMN DEPT, DEPT MED HIST & ETHICS, UNIV WASH, SCH MED, 1989-; PROF, DEPT MED HIST & ETHICS, UNIV WASH, SCH MED, 1988-; CHMN, DEPT MED HIST & ETHICS UNIV CALIF SAN FRANCISCO 1972-1987 BD DIR, SIERRA FOUND, 1986-; mem, Nat Bd Med Examnrs, 1985-1987; Mem, pres Commission Study Ethical Problems in Med, 1979-1982; consult, Am Bd Internal Med, 1978-; Mem, Nat Commission Protection Human Subj Biomed Behavioral Res, 1974-1978; prof med ethics, Sch Med, Univ Calif, San Francisco, 1972-1988; pres, Univ San Francisco, 1969-1972; Assoc prof theol & philos, Univ San Francisco, 1967-1972. **Memberships:** Inst Med-Nat Acad Sci; fel Inst Soc Ethics & Life Sci; Soc Health Human Values (pres, 1986); Am Soc Law & Med. **Research Statement & Publications:** Ethics of care for dying; genetics; history of bioethics. **Mailing Address:** 1333 JONES ST, San Francisco, CA 94109. **E-Mail:** arjonsen@cs.com

JONSSON, BJARNI, UNIVERSAL ALGEBRA, LATTICE THEORY. **Personal Data:** b Draghals, Iceland, February 15, American citizen; m 1969, Harriet; c Eric, Meryl & Kristin. **Education:** Univ Calif, Berkeley, AB, 1943, PhD (math), 1946. **Honorary Degrees:** DSc, Univ Iceland, 1986. **Professional Experience:** DISTINGUISHED PROF EMER MATH, VANDERBILT UNIV, 1993-; distinguished prof math, Vanderbilt Univ, 1966-1993; vis prof & res mathematician, Univ Calif, Berkeley, 1962-1963; from assoc prof to prof, Univ Minn, 1956-1966; vis assoc prof, Univ Calif, Berkeley, 1955-1956; Vis prof, Univ Iceland, 1954-1955; From instr to asst prof, Brown Univ, 1946-1956. **Memberships:** Am Math Soc; Am Asn Univ Prof. **Research Statement & Publications:** Universal algebra; lattice theory. **Mailing Address:** Dept Math, Vanderbilt Univ, Stevenson Ctr 1324, Nashville, TN 37240. **E-Mail:** jonsson@math.vanderbilt.edu

JONSSON, COLLEEN, BIOCHEMISTRY. **Education:** Univ Mo-St Loius, BS (Chem & Biol); Prudue Univ, PhD (Chem). **Professional Experience:** DIR, EMERGING PATHOGENS RES DEPT, SOUTHERN RES INST, 2004-; ASSOC PROF, DEPT BIOCHEM & MOLECULAR GENETICS, as of 2004. **Mailing Address:** Southern Res Inst, 2000 Ninth Ave S POBox 55305, Birmingham, AL 35205-5305. **Fax:** 205-581-2000.

JONSSON, HALDOR TURNER, JR, BIOCHEMISTRY. **Personal Data:** b State College, Pa, January 5, 1929; m 1964, c 2. **Education:** Tex A&M Univ, BS, 1952, MS, 1961; Baylor Univ, PhD (biochem), 1965. **Professional Experience:** FROM ASSOC PROF BIOCHEM TO PROF EMER, MED UNIV SC, as of 2004; clin chem consult, Vet Admin Hosp, Charleston, 1966-; asst prof chem, Med Univ SC, 1966-1970; res assoc, Sch Med, Boston Univ, 1965-1966; res asst biochem, Tex A&M Univ, 1959-1961 & Col Med, Baylor Univ, 1961-1965; res asst plastics & resins, Shell Chem Corp, 1956-1959. **Memberships:** Am Chem Soc; Am Soc Biol Chem; Am Oil Chemists' Soc; NY Acad Sci. **Research Statement & Publications:** Gonadotropins and their influence on ovarian function; role of prostoglandins and essential fatty acids in wounds; gas-liquid chromatography; long term effects of pesticides on mammals. **Mailing Address:** Dept Biochem, Med Univ SC 171 Ashley Ave, Charleston, SC 29425-0001.

JONSSON, WILBUR JACOB, MATHEMATICS. **Personal Data:** b Winnipeg, Man, September 18, 1936. **Education:** Univ Man, BSc, 1958, MSc, 1959; Univ Tubingen, Dr rer nat(math), 1963. **Professional Experience:** PROF MATH, MCGILL UNIV, as of 2003; assoc prof math, Mcgill Univ, beginning 1966; lectr, Univ Birmingham, 1965-1966; asst prof, Univ Man, 1962-1965; lectr math, Univ Man, 1959-1960. **Research Statement & Publications:** Projective planes; group theory; combinatory mathematics; foundations of geometry. **Mailing Address:** Dept Math, McGill Univ, 805 Sherbrooke St W, Montreal, PQ H3A 2K6, Can. **E-Mail:** wilbur.jonsson@mcgill.ca

JONTE, JOHN HAWORTH, GEOCHEMISTRY, INORGANIC CHEMISTRY. **Personal Data:** b Moscow, Idaho, October 21, 1918; m 1942, Eloise; c Barbara, Sharon, Michael & Dorothy. **Education:** Univ the Pac, AB, 1940; Wash State Univ, MS, 1942; Univ Ark, PhD (chem), 1956. **Professional Experience:** RETIRED; consult, beginning 1985; prof emer chem, SDak Sch Mines & Technol, 1985-1995; prof chem & head dept, SDak Sch Mines & Technol, 1969-1985; assoc prof geochem & anal, SDak Sch Mines & Technol, 1966-1969; group leader geochem, Texaco Inc, Tex, 1961-1966; res chemist, Texaco Inc, Tex, 1955-1961; instr geol, Univ Ark, 1954-1955; instr chem, Iowa State Univ, 1946-1951; Jr chemist, US Bur Mines, Nev, 1942-1944 & Shell Develop Co, Calif, 1944-1946. **Memberships:** AAAS; Am Chem Soc; Geochem Soc; Am Inst Chem; Sigma Xi. **Research Statement & Publications:** Geochemistry of radio-elements fractionations in hydrothermal transport processes; studies of the origin of petroleum in sedimentary rocks; occurrence of radium and radon in hyrdothermal waters. **Mailing Address:** 2025 S San Vincent Dr, Green Valley, AZ 85614. **E-Mail:** hjonte@kachina.net

JONZON, ANDERS, NEONATOLOGY, PEDIATRIC CARDIOLOGY. **Personal Data:** b Stockholm, Sweden, May 6, 1948; m 1972, c 3. **Education:** Uppsala Univ, MedKand, 1970, MedDr(physiol), 1972, Lakarexamen, 1977. **Professional Experience:** CONSULT & LECTR PEDIAT CARDIOL & PEDIAT INTENSIVE CARE, DEPT PEDIAT, UNIVERSITY HOSP, UNIV UPPSALA, 1990-; CONSULT & LECTRNEONATOLOGY, DEPT PEDIAT, UNIVERSITY HOSP, UNIV UPPSALA, 1984-; JuliusComroe Jr fel, Cardiovasc Res Inst, Univ Calif, San Francisco, 1984-1986. **Memberships:** Europ SocPediat Res; Scand Physiol Soc; Am Physiol Soc. **Research Statement & Publications:** Positive pressure breathing; control of respiration; lung development. **Mailing Address:** Dept Pediat, Univ Hosp, Uppsala S-751 85, Sweden. **Fax:** 461-866-5583. **E-Mail:** anders.jonzon@ped.uas.lul.se

JOOS, BARBARA, ANIMAL PHYSIOLOGY. **Personal Data:** b South Amboy, NJ, November 2, 1957. **Education:** Rutgers Univ, BA, 1979; Univ Mich, MS, 1982, PhD (biol sci), 1986. **Professional Experience:** Vis researcher, Cook Col, Rutgers Univ, 1989-; ASST PROF BIOL, DEPT BIOL, MUHLENBERG COL, 1989-; fel, Dept Biol, 1988-1989; researcher, Cook Col, Rutgers Univ, 1986-1988; lectr physiol, Univ Mich, 1985. **Memberships:** AAAS; Am Soc Zoologists. **Research Statement & Publications:** Energetics of locomotion in insects and mechanics of terrestrial locomotion in larval insects; temperature effects and size effects on energetics and performance of ectothermic insects. **Mailing Address:** Dept Biol Muhlenberg Col, 2400 Chew St, Allentown, PA 18104.

JOOS, BELA, THEORETICAL SOLID STATE PHYSICS. **Personal Data:** b Montreal, Que, August 7, 1953; c Felix. **Education:** Loyola Montreal, BSc, 1974; McGill Univ, PhD (physics), 1979. **Professional Experience:** Vpres, Canadian Assoc Physics, 2001-2003; hon assoc ed, Physics Can, 1996-; chmn, Dept Physics, 1997-2000; PROF PHYSICS, UNIV OTTAWA, 1996-; honorary assoc ed, Physics Can, 1996-; from asst prof to assoc prof, Univ Ottawa, 1984-1996; assoc ed, Can J Physics, 1984-1993; asst prof, Simon Fraser Univ, 1982-1984; res assoc, Simon Fraser Univ, 1981-1982; res fel, Univ Calif, Berkeley, 1979-1981. **Memberships:** Can Asn Physicists; Am Phys Soc; AAAS Exec, Canadian Assoc Physics; Mats Res Soc. **Research Statement & Publications:** Theoretical solid state physics; structural properties of surfaces, interfaces and monolayers; properties of strained materials including soft materials rubber, membranes, etc; dislocation kinetics. **Mailing Address:** Dept Physics, Univ Ottawa, Ottawa, ON K1N 6N5, Can. **Fax:** 613-562-5190. **E-Mail:** bjoos@Sci.uottawa.ca

JOOS, RICHARD W, BIOCHEMISTRY. **Personal Data:** b Cologne, Minn, September 22, 1934; m 1960, c 4. **Education:** Col St Thomas, BS, 1958; Univ Minn, PhD (biochem), 1964. **Professional Experience:** AT MED SERV, VET ADMN HOSP, MINNEAPOLIS, MINN, as of 1996; Instr, Univ Minn Dent Sch, 1971-; RES SPECIALIST, 3M CTR, MINNMINING & MFG CO, 1967-; biochemist, Vet Admin Hosp, Minneapolis, 1966-1967; res assocmed, Univ Minn, 1962-1966; Teaching asst biochem, Univ Minn, 1958-1962. **Memberships:** Int Asn Dent Res. **Research Statement & Publications:** Ion binding to macromolecules; humoral factors against bacteria; preventive agents for dental disease; dental materials. **Mailing Address:** Med Serv, Vet Admn Hosp, Minneapolis, MN 55417.

JOP, KRZYSZTOF M, TOXICOLOGY IDENTIFICATION EVALUATION, HAZARDOUS WASTE SITE ECOLOGICAL RISK ASSESSMENT. **Personal Data:** b Krakow, Poland, August 15, 1950; m Susan. **Education:** Jagiellonian Univ, Doctorat (hydrobiol), 1980. **Professional Experience:** PROG MGR, SPRINGBORN LABS, 1986-; lab mgr, Battelle, 1986-1988; res scientist, N Tex State, 1982-1986. **Memberships:** Soc Environ Toxicol & Chem; NAm Benthol Soc. **Research Statement & Publications:** Provide technical expertise and management of industrial and municipal wastewater programs and hazardous site programs. **Mailing Address:** Springborn Lab Inc, 790 Main St, Wareham, MA 02571.

JOPLIN, KARL HENRY, MOLECULAR ASPECTS OF INSECT DEVELOPMENT, INVOLVEMENT OF HEAT SHOCK PROTEINS IN ENVIRONMENTAL STRESS. **Personal Data:** b Charleston, WVa, July 23, 1948; m 1969, Claire; c Amber R & Mikal L. **Education:** Univ Wash, BSc, 1973; Ohio State Univ, MSc, 1982, PhD (molecular cellular & develop biol), 1989. **Professional Experience:** ASSOC PROF, DEPT BOIL SCI, E TENN STATE UNIV, as of 2003; asst prof biol, E Tenn State Univ, beginning 1994; Res assoc, Dept Entom, Ohio State Univ, 1989-1994. **Memberships:** AAAS; Soc Develop Biol; Entom Soc Biol. **Research Statement & Publications:** Differential expression of diapause-specific genes in the brains of diapausing pupae. **Mailing Address:** Dept Biol Sci, E Tenn State Univ, Box 70, 703, Johnson City, TN 37614-0703. **Fax:** 423-439-5958. **E-Mail:** joplin@etsu.edu

JOPPA, LEONARD ROBERT, GENETICS, CYTOGENETICS. **Personal Data:** b Billings, Mont, September 29, 1930; m 1959, Catherine; c Teresa, William R, Barbara L & Margaret A. **Education:** Mont State Univ, BS, 1957, PhD (genetics), 1967; Ore State Univ, MS, 1962. **Honors & Awards:** Res Award, Sigma Xi, 1985. **Professional Experience:** RETIRED; res geneticist plants, Agr Res Serv, USDA, 1967-1998; res asst agron, Mont Agr Exp Sta, 1964-1967; asst agronomist, Mont Agr Exp Sta, 1962-1964; asst agron, Mont Agr Exp Sta, 1957-1962; adj prof agron, Dept Plant Sci NDak State Univ. **Memberships:** Fel AAAS; fel Am Soc Agron; fel Crops Sci Soc Am; Genetics Soc Am; Genetics Soc Can; Sigma Xi. **Research Statement & Publications:** Genetics and cytogenetics of wheat and its relatives. **Mailing Address:** 90 24th Ave N, Fargo, ND 58102.

JOPPA, RICHARD M, electrical engineering electronics, construction project management; deceased, see previous edition for last biography

JOPSON, HARRY GORGAS MICHENER, ZOOLOGY, HERPETOLOGY. **Personal Data:** b Philadelphia, Pa, June 23, 1911; wid Hope P Wilson (deceased); c Loliett (Bulfner) & Harriet J (Mercer). **Education:** Haverford Col, BS, 1932; Cornell Univ, MA, 1933, PhD (vert zool), 1936. **Honorary Degrees:** ScD, Bridgewater Col, 1977. **Professional Experience:** PROF EMER BIOL, BRIDGEWATER COL, 1981-; chmn, Rockingham Co Bd Educ, 1974-1976; trustee, Nat Parks & Conserv Asn, 1965-1980; trustee, Rockingham Co Bd Educ, 1957-1976; prof biol, Bridgewater Col, 1946-1981; Asst dir, Overseas Oper, United Seamen's Serv, 1943-1946; from asst prof to assoc prof, Bridgewater Col, 1936-1946; Instr biol, Iowa State Teachers Col, 1936. **Memberships:** Am Soc Ichthyol & Herpet; Am Soc Mammal; AmOrnith Union. **Research Statement & Publications:** Salamanders of southeastern United States; vertebrate natural history. **Mailing Address:** Dept Biol, Bridgewater Col, 402 E Col St, Bridgewater, VA 22812.

JORCH, HARALD HEINRICH, PHYSICS, SEMICONDUCTOR SURFACE. **Personal Data:** b WGer, February 17, 1951; Canadian citizen; m 1975, c 3. **Education:** Univ Waterloo, BSc, 1974, BSc, 1975; Univ Guelph, MSc, 1977, PhD (physics), 1982. **Professional Experience:** ASST PROF PHYSICS & COMPUT, WILFRID LAURIER UNIV, 1986-; asst prof physics, Royal Roads Mil Col, 1983-1986; Fel, Chalk River Nuclear Lab, AtomicEnergy Can Co, 1981-1983; Tech collabr, Brookhaven Nat Lab, 1979-1981. **Memberships:** Can Asn Physicists; Chem Inst Can; Soc Italiana Fisica; Europ Phys Soc. **Research Statement & Publications:** Properties of surfaces and interfaces using particle beams (ions and positrons). **Mailing Address:** Dept Physics & Comput, Wilfrid Laurier Univ, Waterloo, ON N2L 3C5, Can.

JORDAN, ALEXANDER WALKER, III, ENDOCRINOLOGY, REPRODUCTIVE PHYSIOLOGY. **Personal Data:** b Richmond, Va, April 12, 1945; m 1972. **Education:** Roanoke Col, BS, 1967; Univ Richmond, MA, 1969; Rutgers Univ, PhD (zoology), 1975. **Professional Experience:** PHARMACOLOGIST, CTR DRUG EVAL RES, FOOD & DRUG ADMIN, as of 2004; STAFF FEL ENDOCRINOL, FOOD & DRUG ADMIN, HEW, 1978-; fel endocrinol, Dept Physiol & Biophysics, Colo State Univ, 1975-1978; fel, Rockefeller Found, 1975-1977. **Memberships:** Sigma Xi; Soc Study Reproduction. **Research Statement & Publications:** Reproductive endocrinology; investigation into the mechanism of action of peptide hormones and prostaglandins on steroidogenesis. **Mailing Address:** Ctr Drug Eval Res, Food & Drug Admin, HFD-530, Rm N431, Rockville, MD 20850. **E-Mail:** alexander.jordan@fda.hhs.gov

JORDAN, ANDREW G, AGRICULTURAL RESEARCH. **Personal Data:** b Wrens, Ga, May 18, 1939; c 3. **Education:** Univ Ga, BS, 1962; Clemson Univ, MS, 1972, PhD (eng), 1977. **Honors & Awards:** Distinguished Serv Award, Cotton Foundation, 2000. **Professional Experience:** VPRES, TECH SERV, NAT COTTON COUN, as of 2004; EXEC DIR & SECY, RES SCREENING COMT, NAT COTTON COUN, as of 2004; dir tech serv, Nat Cotton Coun, beginning 1983; asst dir tech serv, Nat Cotton Coun, 1982-1983; mgr mkt & processing technol, Nat Cotton Coun, 1976-1981; res scientist & instr, Agr Eng, Clemson Univ, 1971-1976; supvr, Advan Technol Training, Lockheed-Ga Aircraft Corp, 1965-1970; systs engr, Western Elec Co, 1962-1965; joint cotton breeding policycomt; Cong task force rural transp. **Memberships:** Agr Res Inst; Am Soc Agr Engrs. **Research Statement & Publications:** Agricultural engineering. **Mailing Address:** Nat Cotton Coun, PO Box 820285, Memphis, TN 38182-0265. **Fax:** 901-725-0510.

JORDAN, ANGEL G, ELECTRICAL ENGINEERING, COMPUTER ENGINEERING. **Personal Data:** b Pamplona, Spain, September 19, 1930; American citizen; m 1956, c 3. **Education:** Univ Zaragoza, Spain, MS, 1952; Univ Madrid, Spain, PhD (physics), 1956; Carnegie Mellon Univ, MS, 1959, PhD (elec eng), 1959. **Honorary Degrees:** Dr, Polytech Univ Madrid. **Honors & Awards:** Premio Extaordinario, Univ Zaragoza, Spain; NATO SeniorScientist Award. **Professional Experience:** UNIV PROF EMER ELECT & COMPUT ENG & ROBOTICS, CARNEGIE-MELLON UNIV, 1999-; Joseph F Keithley & Nancy P Keithley ProfElec & Comput Eng, Carnegie Mellon Univ, 1997-1999; prof elec & comput eng, Mellon Col Sci, 1990-1997; actg dean, Mellon Col Sci, 1987-1988; actg dir, Software Eng Inst, 1986; provost, Carnegie Mellon Univ, 1983-1990; actg pres, Mellon Inst, 1983-1985; dean, Carnegie Inst Technol, 1979-1983; actg chmn, Biomed Eng Prog, 1976-1978; vis sr scientist, Health & Safety Exec, Sheffield, Eng, 1976; visprof, Indian Inst Technol, Kampur, India, 1971; head, Dept Elec & Comput Eng, 1969-1979; prof, Dept Elec Eng, 1966-1976; from asst prof to assoc prof, DeptElec Eng, 1959-1966; res fel, Mellon Inst Indust Res, 1958-1959; instr, DeptElec Eng, Carnegie Mellon Univ, 1956-1958; adj asst prof electronics, NavalOrd Sch, Madrid, Spain, 1953-1956. **Memberships:** Nat Acad Eng; Academia de Ingenieria Spain; fel Inst Elec & Electronics Eng; fel Am AssocAdvan Sci; Am Phys Soc; Sigma Xi. **Research Statement & Publications:** Solid state devices; integrated circuits; thin films; high definition television; flat panel displays; intelligent sensors; robotics; automation; knowledge engineering and software engineering focusing on technological change and technology transfer. **Mailing Address:** Carnegie Mellon Univ, Robotics Inst, 5000 Forbes Ave WEH 4618, Pittsburgh, PA 15213. **Fax:** 412-268-2338. **E-Mail:** ajordan@cs.cmu.edu

JORDAN, ARTHUR KENT, ELECTROMAGNETIC INVERSE SCATTERING, OPTICAL INTEGRATED CIRCUITS. **Personal Data:** b Philadelphia, Pa, December 28, 1932; m 1965, Mary; c Thomas B, Edward M & Elizabeth A. **Education:** Pa State Univ, BSc, 1957; Univ Pa, MSc, 1971, PhD (elec eng), 1972. **Professional Experience:** Vis scientist, Mass Inst Technol, beginning 1989; PROG MGR, OFF NAVAL RES, 1986-; mem, Advan Res Workshop Electromagnetic Imaging, NATO, Wger, 1983; ELECTRONICS ENGR, REMOTE SENSING DIV, OFF NAVAL RES, 1973-; res fel, Dept Elec Eng, Univ Pa, 1971-1973; res asst, Moore Sch Elec Eng, Univ Pa, 1969-1973; physicist, Aerospace Physics Lab, Gen Elec Co, 1964-1969; engr, Astro-Electronics Div, Radio Corp Am, 1962-1964; res engr, Res Div, Philco Corp, 1958-1961. **Memberships:** Fel Inst Elec & Electronics Engrs; Electromagnetics Acad; Sigma Xi; Am Phys Soc; fel Optical Soc Am; Soc Indust & Appl Math; Inst Elec & Electronics Engrs Antennas & Propagation Soc; Inst Elec & Electronics Engrs Lasers & Electro-Optics Soc; Int Union RadioSci; AAAS. **Research Statement & Publications:** Electromagnetic inverse scattering theory; electromagnetic field theory; quantum electronics; optical waveguides and devices; remote sensing theory; author of numerous publications; holder of two US patent. **Mailing Address:** Remote Sensing Div, Naval Res Lab, Code 7227, 4555 Overlook Ave SW, Washington, DC 20375-5351. **Fax:** 202-767-0005. **E-Mail:** jordan@ccf.nrl.navy.mil

JORDAN, BRIGITTE, MEDICAL ANTHROPOLOGY, CROSSCULTURAL OBSTETRICS. **Personal Data:** b Ger. **Education:** Calif State Univ, Sacramento, BA, 1969, MA, 1971; Univ Calif, Irvine, PhD (soc sci), 1975. **Honors & Awards:** Margaret Mead Award, Soc Appl Anthrop, 1980. **Professional Experience:** AT XEROX PARC, as of 2006; CONSULT CORP ANTHROPOLOGIST, as of 2004; sr res scientist, Palo Alto Res Ctr, Xerox Corp, beginning 1989; mem exec bd, Soc Med Anthrop, beginning 1985; assoc prof, Dept Anthrop& Pediat, 1980-1988; prin investr res grant, Crosscult Invest Childbirth Pract, Nat Inst ChildHealth & Human Develop, NIH, 1977-1979 & Cult Influences Response Physicians Diag, NSF, 1984-1986; asst prof, Dept Anthrop & Community Med, Mich State Univ, 1975-1980; res assoc, Feminist Women's Health Ctr, Santa Ana, Calif, 1972-1975; consult, WHO, Geneva, Switz. **Memberships:** fel Am Anthrop Asn; Soc Appl Anthrop; Soc Med Anthrop; Soc Visual Anthrop. **Research Statement & Publications:** Design of culturally appropriate maternal and child health care delivery systems; integration of traditional and western medicine in developing countries; methodology, including videographic methods for documentation and analysis; patient-practitioner relationship; alternate systems of health care delivery; symbolic language of advertising; status of women; Maya Indians of Yucatan, Mexico. **Mailing Address:** Xerox PARC, 3333 Coyote Hill Rd, Palo Alto, CA 94304. **Fax:** 650-812-4396. **E-Mail:** jordan@akamail.com

JORDAN, BYRON DALE, COMPUTER VISION, COLORIMETRY. **Personal Data:** b Akron, Ohio, January 24, 1947; Canadian citizen; m 1969, Kate; c Crispin & Alayne. **Education:** Hiram Col, BA, 1969; McMaster Univ, PhD (physics), 1975. **Honors & Awards:** Richard S Hunter Prize, Tech Asn Pulp & Paper Indust, 1993. **Professional Experience:** Auxiliary prof chem eng, McGill Univ, 1985-; PRIN SCIENTIST & HEAD, OPTICAL STAND, PULP & PAPER RES INST CAN, 1977-; physicist, Welwyn Res Ltd, 1975-1977. **Memberships:** Am Phys Soc; Pulp & Paper Tech Asn Can; Tech Asn Pulp & Paper Indust; Inter-Soc Color Coun; Am Soc Testing Mat; Soc Appl Spectros; Sigma Xi. **Research Statement & Publications:** Paper physics; optical properties of paper; application of image processing to study random textures and fiber morphology; colorimetry and optical methods of quality control. **Mailing Address:** Pulp & Paper Res Inst Can, 570 St John's Blvd, Pointe Claire, PQ H9R 3J9, Can. **Fax:** 514-630-4134. **E-Mail:** bjordan@paprican.ca

JORDAN, CARL FREDERICK, ECOLOGY. **Personal Data:** b New Brunswick, NJ, December 10, 1935; m 1967, c 2. **Education:** Univ Mich, BS, 1958; Rutgers Univ, MS, 1964, PhD (ecol), 1966. **Honors & Awards:** Mercer Award, Ecol Soc Am, 1973. **Professional Experience:** SR RES SCI, INST ECOL, UNIV GA, as of 2005; adj assoc prof, Univ GA, 1984-1989; SR RES ECOLOGIST, INST ECOL, UNIV GA, 1979-; vis scientist, Ecol Ctr, Venezuelan Inst Sci Invest, 1974-; RES ASSOC, INST ECOL, UNIV GA, 1974-; from asst ecologist to assoc ecologist, Radiol & Environ Res Div, Argonne Nat Lab, 1969-1974; assoc scientist, P R Nuclear Ctr, AEC, 1966-1969. **Memberships:** AAAS; Ecol Soc Am; Soil Sci Soc Am; Sigma Xi. **Research Statement & Publications:** Movement of chemical elements in soil; radiation recovery and mineral cycling in the tropical rain forest; application of systems analysis techniques to ecology; shifting agriculture in the Amazon Basin; laungya agriculture in Thailand. **Mailing Address:** Inst Ecol Univ Ga, 126 Ecol Bldg, Athens, GA 30602-2202. **Fax:** 706-542-4819. **E-Mail:** cfjordan@uga.edu

JORDAN, CHRIS SULLIVAN, BIOLOGY. **Personal Data:** b Yangchow, China, August 6, 1924; American citizen; m 1947, c 3. **Education:** Drake Univ, BA, 1948; Univ Iowa, MS, 1951, PhD (zoology), 1955. **Professional Experience:** RETIRED; chmn, Div Sci & Math, Dallas Baptist Col, 1967-1993; prof, Houston Baptist Col, 1963-1967; res grant, NIH, 1959-1962; prof biol, Howard Payne Col, 1956-1963; supvr bact & parasitol, Terrell's Labs, Tex, 1955-1956; clin lab technologist, VetAdmin Hosp, Iowa City, Iowa, 1952-1955. **Memberships:** Am Inst Biol Sci; AAAS; Am Soc Parasitol; Am Soc Microbiol; Sigma Xi. **Research Statement & Publications:** Parasitology and medical bacteriology. **Mailing Address:** 1214 Hilltop Run, Lindale, TX 75771.

JORDAN, CONSTANCE (LOUISE) BRINE, NUTRITION. **Personal Data:** b Newton, Mass, December 26, 1919. **Education:** Harvard Univ, MPH, 1948; Cornell Univ, PhD (food, nutrit), 1954. **Honorary Degrees:** DSc, Framingham State Col, 1987. **Professional Experience:** RETIRED; emer prof, Food & Nutrit, Framingham State Col, beginning 1984; dean grad studies, Framingham State Col, 1973-1978, prof 1978-1984; prof home econ & head dept, Framingham State Col, 1956-1973; consult, Arthur D Little, Inc & Mkt Res Corp Am, 1954-1958; Anna Cora Smith fel, Cornell Univ, 1953; assoc prof food & nutrit, Univ RI, 1948-1956; asst nutrit, Harvard Univ, 1946-1948; asst dir sch lunch, Pub Schs, Newton, 1945-1946; chief dietitian, Newton-Wellesley Hosp, 1943-1945. **Research Statement & Publications:** Absorption of calcium; institutional dietary studies; nutritional status; nontraditional education at graduate level. **Mailing Address:** Eight Beacon St, Natick, MA 01760. **E-Mail:** cbjordan@juno.com

JORDAN, CRAIG ALAN, GRANT ADMINISTRATION, COMMUNICATION SCIENCES. **Personal Data:** b Elyria, Ohio, 1955. **Education:** Ohio State Univ, BS, 1977; Univ Tex, Galveston, PhD (med microbiol), 1984. **Professional Experience:** DIR, DIV EXTRAMURAL ACTIV, NIDCD, NIH, 2003-; chief, Sci Review Br, NIDCD NIH, 1996-2003; HEALTH SCIENTIST ADMIN, NIDCD, NIH, 1990-. **Memberships:** Asn Res Otolaryngol. **Research Statement & Publications:** Scientific evaluation of applications dealing with communication sciences and disorders; voice, speech, language, taste, smell, balance and hearing; viral replication in the central nervous system and gene expression by oligodendrocytes and glial cells. **Mailing Address:** Nat Inst Deafness & Other Commun Disorders, EPS Rm 400C, Bethesda, MD 20892-7180. **Fax:** 301-402-6250. **E-Mail:** jordanc@nih.gov

JORDAN, DAVID CARLYLE, BACTERIOLOGY. **Personal Data:** b Brampton, Ont, July 11, 1926; m 1954, Marian; c Mark, Scott & Peter. **Education:** Univ Toronto, BSA, 1950, MSA, 1951; Mich State Univ, PhD, 1955, Can Col Microbiol, RM, 1979. **Professional Experience:** RETIRED; chmn dept, Ont Agr Col, Univ Guelph, 1971-1981; Nuffield traveling fel, 1959; from asst prof to prof microbiol, Ont Agr Col, Univ Guelph, 1956-1987; lectr bact, Ont Agr Col, Univ Guelph, 1952-1956; asst res, Ont Agr Col, Univ Guelph, 1950-1952. **Memberships:** Can Soc Microbiol. **Research Statement & Publications:** Bacterial physiology as related to Rhizobium species; Rhizobium taxonomy; antibiotic mode of action. **Mailing Address:** Eight Young St, Guelph, ON N1G 1M2, Can. **E-Mail:** djordan@uoguelph.ca

JORDAN, DAVID M, ORGANIC CHEMISTRY. **Personal Data:** b Ashtabula, Ohio, August 19, 1937; m 1961, c 2. **Education:** Col Wooster, BA, 1959; Ohio State Univ, PhD (chem), 1965. **Professional Experience:** EMER PROF CHEM, STATE UNIV NY COL POTSDAM, 1996-; from assocprof to prof, State Univ NY Col Potsdam, 1965-1996. **Memberships:** Am Chem Soc; Sigma Xi. **Research Statement & Publications:** Diazoacetophenone decompositions; reaction of ketenes; techniques for thin-layer chromatography on cylindrical surfaces; styryl azide decompositions. **Mailing Address:** 372 Outer Main St, Potsdam, NY 13676.

JORDAN, DIANE KATHLEEN, MEDICAL CYTOGENETICS. **Personal Data:** b Peoria, Ill, January 3, 1954; m 1976, John. **Education:** Bradley Univ, BS, 1976; Univ Iowa, PhD (genetics), 1987. **Professional Experience:** DIR CYTOGENETICS LAB, OSF ST FRANCIES MED CTR, PEORIA, ILL, beginning 2000; asst dir, Cytogenetics Lab, Univ Iowa, Iowa city, IA, 1991-2000; co-dir, Med Cytogenetics Prog, Univ Iowa, 1991-1994; res asst, Cytogenetics Lab, Univ Iowa, 1987-1991; supvr, Cytogenetics Lab, Wash Univ, St Louis, 1976-1979. **Memberships:** fel Am Col Med Genetics; Am Soc Human Genetics; Asn Cyto Genetic Technologists. **Research Statement & Publications:** Cancer cytogenetics; chromosomal abnormalities and fragile site formation in tumors; numerical chromosome changes in leukemia and prostate cancer patients. **Mailing Address:** Dir, Cytogenetics Lab, OSF Dt Francis Med Ctr, 530 NE Glen Oak Ave, Peoria, IL 61637.

JORDAN, DON, MATHEMATICS. **Education:** Univ SC, PhD. **Honors & Awards:** Helms Award, SC Sci Coun & SC Hall Sci & Technol, 1990. **Professional Experience:** PROF MATH, COL APPL PROF SCI, UNIV SC, as of 1998. **Mailing Address:** Univ SC, Col Appl & Prof Sci, Columbia, SC 29208. **Fax:** 803-777-4396. **E-Mail:** jordan@gwm.sc.edu

JORDAN, DONALD J, ENGINEERING. **Personal Data:** b New York, NY, 1916. **Education:** NY Univ, BS, 1938. **Professional Experience:** RETIRED; eng mgr, Power Systs Div, United Technologies, 1975-1978; eng mgr, Pratt & Whitney, 1971-1975; mem staff, Pratt & Whitney, 1948-1971; power plant staff engr, Chance Vought Aircraft, 1944-1948. **Memberships:** Nat Acad Sci; Nat Acad Eng. **Mailing Address:** 113 Evergreen Lane, Glastonbury, CT 06033.

JORDAN, DUANE PAUL, MECHANICAL ENGINEERING. **Personal Data:** b Glendale, Calif, July 17, 1935; c 2. **Education:** Stanford Univ, BS, 1957, MS, 1958, PhD (mech eng), 1961. **Honors & Awards:** Dedicated Serv Award, Am Soc Mech Engrs, 1988. **Professional Experience:** VICE CHAIR & MEM, OLD GUARD COMT, as of 2005; Fanning, Fanning, Agnes Consult Engrs, 1976-1978; assoc prof mech eng, Tex Tech Univ, beginning 1967; Profit Index Systs Inc, 1966-1984; asst prof mech eng, Tex Tech Univ, 1964-1967; consult, LawrenceRadiation Lab, 1963-1965; sr engr, integrated controls dept, Electronics Assocs, Inc, 1963-1964; mech engr, Lawrence Radiation Lab, Univ Calif, 1960-1963. **Memberships:** Am Soc Mech Engrs; Am Soc Eng Educ. **Research Statement & Publications:** Thermal, physical and social economic systems analysis and simulation using digital and analog computer techniques. **Mailing Address:** Dept Mech Eng, Tex Tech Univ, PO Box 41021, Lubbock, TX 79409-1021. **E-Mail:** djordan@coe.ttu.edu

JORDAN, EDWARD DANIEL, RELIABILITY ENGINEERING. **Personal Data:** b Bridgeport, Conn, March 14, 1931; m 1957, Margaret A.; c Christopher E., Kathleen M., Daniel E., David E., Mar garet J. **Education:** Fairfield Univ, BS, 1953; NY Univ, MS, 1955; Univ Md, PhD (nuclear eng), 1965. **Professional Experience:** PROF EMER MECH ENG, CATHOLIC UNIV AM, 1992-; prof, Catholic Univ Am, 1983-1992; dir info syst & planning off, Catholic Univ Am, 1968-1983; from assoc prof to prof nuclear eng, Catholic Univ Am, 1959-1968; US Atomic Energy Comn, 1957-1959; Reactor physicist nuclear eng, Foster Wheeler Corp, 1955-1957. **Memberships:** Sigma Xi. **Research Statement & Publications:** Computer modeling of complex engineering system reliability. **Mailing Address:** 13469 Brightview Way, Gainesville, VA 20155. **E-Mail:** ejordan@always-online.com

JORDAN, ELKE, MOLECULAR BIOLOGY, GENETICS. **Personal Data:** b Gottingen, Ger, April 8, 1937. **Education:** Goucher Col, BA, 1957; Johns Hopkins Univ, PhD (biochem), 1962. **Honorary Degrees:** DSc, Goucher Col, 1992. **Professional Experience:** RETIRED; Dep Dir, Nat Ctr Human Genome Res Inst, Nih, beginning 1989; dir, Off HumanGenome Res, NIH, 1988-1989; assoc dir prog activ, genetics prog, NIH, 1981-1988; dep dir, genetics prog, NIH, 1978-1981; prog admin, Nat Inst Gen Med Sci, NIH, 1976-1978; coordrcollab res, Nat Cancer Inst, NIH, 1973-1976; grants assoc, Nat Cancer Inst, NIH, 1972-1973; resassoc, Univ Wis-Madison, 1968-1969 & Univ Calif, Berkeley, 1969-1972; fel, Helen Hay WhitneyFound, 1965-1968; fel, Univ Cologne, 1964-1968; NIH fel, 1962-1965; fel, Harvard Univ, 1962-1964. **Memberships:** Genetics Soc Am; fel AAAS; Am Soc Microbiol; Am Soc Human Genetics. **Research Statement & Publications:**

Gene regulation in prokaryotes, genetic recombination. **Mailing Address:** Nat Human Genome Res Inst, Nat Inst Health, Bldg 31, Rm 4B09, Bethesda, MD 20892-2152. **Fax:** 301-402-0837. **E-Mail:** elkej@mail.nih.gov

JORDAN, FRANK, BIO-ORGANIC CHEMISTRY, BIOPHYSICAL CHEMISTRY. **Personal Data:** b Budapest, Hungary, January 28, 1941; American citizen; m 1965, Rosy; c Michael J & Lisa J. **Education:** Drexel Univ, BS, 1964; Univ Pa, PhD (chem), 1967. **Honors & Awards:** Recipient 1983 Rutgers Univ Board Trustees Award Excellence Res; Johnson & Johnson Res Discovery Fel 1998-1990; Am Inst Chemists, N Jersey Sect, 1995-; Elected Fel AAAS, 1995-; Rutgers Univ Board Gov prof chem 1997 spec prof title highest rank Rutgers; Excellence edu Award N Jersey Sect, Am Chemical Soc 1998; Ad hoc number Phy Biochem Study Sect Nat Inst Health, 1998-1999; Phy Biochem Study Sect Nat Inst Health 2000-2004. **Professional Experience:** NSF grants, 1982-1992; PROF CHEM, RUTGERS UNIV, NEWARK, 1979-; assoc prof, Rutgers Univ, Newark, 1975-1979; NIH grants, USPHS, 1974-1982 & 1984-; asst prof, Rutgers Univ, Newark, 1970-1975; NIH fel bio-org chem, Chem Dept, Harvard Univ, 1968-1970; NATO fel quantum chem, Univ Paris, France, 1967-1968. **Memberships:** Am Chem Soc; AAAS; Sigma Xi; Biophys Soc; Am Soc Biol Chem & Molecular Biol. **Research Statement & Publications:** Enzyme mechanism studies on enzymes sythesizing and utilizing thiamine diphosphate; purine nucleoside phosphorylase; glyoxalase I and serine proteases. **Mailing Address:** Dept Chem, Rutgers Univ Newark Col Arts, Rm 1010 73 Warren St, Newark, NJ 07102. **Fax:** 973-648-1264. **E-Mail:** frjordan@newark.rutgers.edu

JORDAN, FREDDIE LOUISE, BIOCHEMISTRY, NEUROSCIENCES. **Personal Data:** b Yazoo City, Miss, August 14, 1954; c 3. **Education:** Jackson State Univ, BS, 1978; Meharry Med Col, PhD (biochem), 1986. **Professional Experience:** DIR & ASST ADJ PROF DEPT ORAL BIOL, OHIO STATE UNIV, 1995-; vis scientist, Fedn Am Socs Exp Biol, Soc Cell Biol, 1990-; vis asst prof, Oral Biol Dept, Ohio State Univ, 1989-1995; res assoc, Ohio State Univ, 1988-1989; fel Neurobiology, Meharry Med Col, 1986-1988. **Memberships:** Int Asn Dent Res; Am Asn Dent Res; Soc Cell Biol; AAAS. **Research Statement & Publications:** Transmembrane signalling in the cerebral cortex. **Mailing Address:** Student Affairs, Col Dent, Ohio State Univ, 305 W 12th Ave, Columbus, OH 43210-1241. **E-Mail:** jordan.1@osu.edu

JORDAN, GARY BLAKE, ELECTRONICS PROGRAM MANAGEMENT, MARKETING. **Personal Data:** b Urbana, Ill, February 3, 1939; m 1968, Gloria J Heppler; c Gareth K & Glynis J. **Education:** Ohio Univ, BS, 1961; Pac Southern Univ, DEE, 1977; Sussex Col Technol, Eng, PhD (elec eng), 1977. **Honors & Awards:** Fellow: Lambda Xi Pi, Life member, Washington Academy of sciences. **Professional Experience:** SYSTEM COMM ENG, Northrop Grumman Areo Systems, 1997-present; ELECTRONIC ENGR, ANALYSIS & TECHNOL, INC, 1994-; DIR, JORDAN & ASSOCS, 1989-; prog mgr, Sci Atlanta, 1988-1989; prog mgr, Cubic Corp, 1987-1989; prog mgr, ESL Subsid TRW Inc, 1979-1987; dir, Nat Intel Agency, 1976-1979; Sr prog mgt engr, Ford Aerospace, 1975-1979; Exec vpres, EW Orgn, 1969-1975. **Memberships:** Fel Am Biog Inst; sr mem Soc Tech Commun; corp mem Radio Soc Gt Brit; Armed Forces Commun & Electronics Asn; AAAS; US Naval Inst; Am Radio Relay League; Inst Elec & Electronics Engrs. **Research Statement & Publications:** Electronic warfare as applied to electronics in the battlefield and on battlefield training ranges; spread spectrum, digital and advanced communications systems. **Mailing Address:** 13392 Fallen Leaf Rd, Poway, CA 92064. **E-Mail:** waltkt@aol.com

JORDAN, GEORGE SAMUEL, MATHEMATICS. **Personal Data:** b Dallas, Tex, April 11, 1944; m 1966. **Education:** Southern Methodist Univ, BA, 1966; Univ Wis-Madison, MS, 1969, PhD (math), 1971. **Professional Experience:** PROF MATH, UNIV TENN, KNOXVILLE, 1984-; ASSOC HEAD DEPT, UNIV TENN, KNOXVILLE, 1980-; from asst prof to assoc prof, Univ Tenn, Knoxville, 1971-1984. **Memberships:** Am Math Soc; Math Asn Am; Sigma Xi; Soc Ind & Appl Math. **Research Statement & Publications:** Integral and differential equations; Tauberian theory; functions of a complex variable. **Mailing Address:** Dept Math, Univ Tenn, 313 Ayres Hall, 1403 Circle Dr, Knoxville, TN 37916. **Fax:** 865-974-6576. **E-Mail:** jordan@math.utk.edu

JORDAN, HAROLD VERNON, MICROBIOLOGY. **Personal Data:** b Boston, Mass, August 18, 1924; m 1950, c 3. **Education:** Univ NH, BS, 1949; Univ Md, MS, 1952, PhD (microbiol), 1956. **Professional Experience:** RETIRED; res scientist oral microbiol, Forsyth Dent Ctr, 1969-1987; vis scientist, Royal Dent Sch, Malmo, Sweden, 1965-1966; res scientist oral microbiol, Nat Inst Dent Res, 1949-1969. **Memberships:** AAAS; fel Am Col Dent; Am Soc Microbiol; Int Asn Dent Res. **Research Statement & Publications:** Lactic acid bacteria, metabolism and taxonomy; microbiology of dental caries and periodontal disease; gnotobiotic techniques in dental research; oral microbiology. **Mailing Address:** Eight Anawan Ave, Saugus, MA 01906.

JORDAN, HELEN ELAINE, VETERINARY PARASITOLOGY. **Personal Data:** b Bridgewater, Va, July 19, 1926. **Education:** Bridgewater Col, BA, 1946; Va Polytech Inst, MS, 1955; Univ Ga, DVM, 1955, PhD (parasitol), 1962. **Professional Experience:** PROF EMER INFECTIOUS DIS & PHYSIOL, COL VET MED, OKLA STATE UNIV, 1993-; prof vet parasitol, Col Vet Med, Okla State Univ, 1969-1993; from asst prof toassoc prof vet parasitol, Univ Ga, 1955-1969. **Memberships:** Am Soc Parasitol; Am Vet Med Asn; Am Asn Vet Parasitol; World Asn VetParasitol. **Research Statement & Publications:** Life cycle study of flukes; surveillance and epidemiology parasites in wild and domestic animals; parasite-host interactions and parasite ecology. **Mailing Address:** Col Vet Med, Okla State Univ, 2923 Fox Ledge Dr, Stillwater, OK 74074. **E-Mail:** hjordan@ums.ucc.okstate.edu

JORDAN, HOWARD EMERSON, ELECTRICAL ENGINEERING. **Personal Data:** b State College, NMex, May 14, 1926; m 1949, c 2. **Education:** Univ Wis, BS, 1946; Case Inst Technol, MS, 1958, PhD (elec eng), 1962. **Honors & Awards:** Distinguished Serv Citation, Univ Wis-Madison, 1989. **Professional Experience:** RES SCIENTIST, CTR ELECTROMECHANICS, UNIV TEX, AUSTIN, as of 2002; dir corp res & develop, Ac Mach, 1991-1993; corp res & develop mgr, Ac Mach, beginning 1984; chief eng, Ac Mach, beginning 1983; mgr corp res & develop eng, Ac Mach, beginning 1981; sr engr advan systs develop, Reliance Elec & Eng Co, Cleveland, 1966-1971; sr develop engr, Reliance Elec & Eng Co, Cleveland, 1963-1966; develop engr, Reliance Elec & Eng Co, Cleveland, 1954-1963; appln engr, Ray-O-Vac Co, Wis, 1946-1952; consult. **Memberships:** fel Inst Elec & Electronics Engrs. **Research Statement & Publications:** Development and design of electrical rotating machinery and electromechanical devices; development of computer methods for design; technology management. **Mailing Address:** Ctr Electromechics, Univ Tex, Austin, TX 78712.

JORDAN, JAMES A, APPLIED MATHEMATICS. **Personal Data:** b Berkeley, Calif, December 28, 1936; m 1961, c 2. **Education:** Ohio State Univ, BSc, 1958; Univ Mich, MSc, 1959, PhD (physics), 1964. **Professional Experience:** CHIEF EXEC OFFICER, AS TECH CUPPERTINO, 1993-; mgr power systanalysis, IBM Palo Alto Sci Ctr, 1974-1993; mgr appl math, IBM Houston Sci Ctr, 1971-1974; sci staff mem, IBM Houston Sci Ctr, 1969-1971; asst prof atomic physics, Rice Univ, 1964-1970; asst res physicist, Univ Mich, 1960-1964; Physicist, USAF Aeronaut Res Lab, 1960. **Memberships:** Inst Elec & Electronics Engrs; Am Phys Soc; Optical Soc Am; Sigma Xi, Pi Mu Epsilon & Phi Beta Kappa. **Research Statement & Publications:** Optical data processing, computer holography; network analysis; atomic collisions; atomic spectroscopy; scientific computations; simulation and control of power systems; data management. **Mailing Address:** 21914 Granada Ave, Cupertino, CA 95014. **Fax:** 408-253-0134. **E-Mail:** jjordan@cup.portal.com

JORDAN, JAMES HENRY, MATHEMATICS. **Personal Data:** b Sacramento, Calif, October 16, 1931; m 1958, c 3. **Education:** Southern Ore Col, BS, 1953; Univ Ore, MA, 1958; Univ Colo, PhD (math), 1962. **Professional Experience:** CHMN, PROG SCI & MATH TEACHING, 1977-; PROF MATH, WASH STATE UNIV, beginning 1970; from asst prof to assoc prof, prog sci & math teaching, 1962-1970; teacher elem sch, Ore, 1953-1956. **Memberships:** Math Asn Am; Am Math Soc. **Research Statement & Publications:** Number theory in general, specifically Kth power reciprocity, consecutive residues, Gaussian integers and simple continued fractions. **Mailing Address:** Dept Pure & Appl Math, Wash Univ, Pullman, WA 99164-2930.

JORDAN, JOHN PATRICK, BIOCHEMISTRY, INTERMEDIARY METABOLISM, ENZYME CHEM. **Personal Data:** b Salt Lake City, Utah, April 23, 1934; wid Peggy (deceased); c Sharon, Dennis (deceased), Jeffrey, Kevin, Maureen, Shaun, Kelly & Clancy. **Education:** Univ Calif, Davis, BS, 1955, PhD (comp biochem), 1963. **Honorary Degrees:** Doctor of Humanities, Lincoln Univ, MO, 1990. **Honors & Awards:** Lab dir of year, Fed lab consortium, 2000; Distinguished serv award, New Orleans fed exec bd, 1997; Presidential rank award, White House, 1988; Distinguished serv award, USDA, 1986; Bond Award, Am Oil Chem Soc, 1967. **Professional Experience:** CTR DIR, SOUTHERN REGIONAL RESEARCH CTR, AGR RES SERV, USDA, NEW ORLEANS, LA, 1994-; adminr coop, State Res Serv, USDA, Washington, DC, 1983-1994; dir, Univ Exp Sta, 1972-1983; NSF curric res grant, 1971; prof biochem, Proj Biocotie, 1971-1983; gen chmn ann meeting, Am Inst Biol Sci, 1971; dir, Proj Biocotie, 1970-1983; Boettcher Found res grant, 1970-1971; NIH biomed sci support grant, 1969-; assoc dean, Col Natural Sci & dir biol core curric, 1968-1972; Prof biochem, Colo state univ, 1971-1985; assoc prof biochem, Colo State Univ, 1968-1971; consult space med, NASA, 1965-1970; NIH res grant, 1965-1968; Okla Heart Asn res grant, 1965-1966; prin investr, Frontiers Sci Found Okla, Inc res grant, 1964-1965; Grant dir, NASA res grant, 1963-; From asst prof to assoc prof chem, Okla City Univ, 1962-1968. **Memberships:** Fel AAAS; fel Am Inst Chem; Brit Biochem Soc; Am inst biolog sci (pres, 1989, pres elect, 1988); Soc Exp Biol & Med. **Research Statement & Publications:** Intermediary metabolism, particularly the effects of artificial atmospheres on metabolism; curricular development, especially in biology and chemistry; research administration; Author of Agr for Encyclopedia Britannica's Sci and the Future, 1976-2000. **Mailing Address:** Ctr Dir Southern Regional Research Ctr, USDA Agr Res Serv PO Box 19687, New Orleans, LA 70179. **Fax:** 504-286-4234. **E-Mail:** pjordan@srrc.ars.usda.gov

JORDAN, KENNETH A(LLAN), AGRICULTURAL ENGINEERING, BIOSYSTEMS ENGINEERING. **Personal Data:** b Plainfield, NJ, June 30, 1930. **Education:** Purdue Univ, BS, 1952, MS, 1956, PhD (agr eng), 1959. **Professional Experience:** PROF EMER, UNIV ARIZ, 2001-; prof, Univ Ariz, Tucson, 1986-2001; vis prof, Univ Tokyo, 1971; prof farm struct, Univ Minn, St Paul, 1967-1984; from asst prof to assoc prof farm struct, NC State Univ, 1958-1967; res instr, Purdue Univ, 1957-1958; dir, Microprocessor Instrumentation Lab Sensor Technol Develop. **Memberships:** Sigma Xi; Am Soc Agr Engrs; Inst Elec & Electronics Engrs; Japan Soc Biol Control; Am Soc Heating Refrig & Air-Conditioning Eng. **Research Statement & Publications:** Animal shelter and greenhouse simulation; weather pattern frequency; plant and animal modeling; machine vision; sensor technology development; transpiration; C3, C4, CAM plants; micropropagation. **Mailing Address:** Dept Agr & Res Ecos Univ Ariz, Shantz 403, Tucson, AZ 85721-0038. **Fax:** 520-621-3963. **E-Mail:** kajordan@ag.arizona.edu

JORDAN, KENNETH DAVID, PHYSICAL CHEMISTRY, THEORETICAL CHEMISTRY. **Personal Data:** b Norwood, Mass, February 25, 1948; m 1981, Sandra; c Erin & Kate. **Education:** Northeastern Univ, BA, 1970; Mass Inst Technol, PhD (chem), 1974. **Honors & Awards:** Chancellor's Distinguished Res Award, Univ Pittsburgh, 1995; Vis Scholar, Univ Nebraska, 1977. **Professional Experience:** CHMN, DEPT CHEM, UNIV PITTSBURGH, 2002-2005; Fel, Joint Inst Lab Astrophics, 1997; vis prof, Australian Nat Univ, 1991 & Univ Utah, 1994 & 1995; chmn, Theoret Chem Subdiv, Phys Chem Div, Am Chem Soc, 1990-1991; adj prof, Carnegie-Mellon Univ, 1988-; PROF CHEM, UNIV PITTSBURGH, 1985-; prog dir theoretical chem physics, NSF, 1984-1985; John Simon Guggenheim fel, 1981-1982; from asst prof to assoc prof, Univ Pittsburgh, 1978-1985; Camille& Henry Dreyfus Found teacher scholar, 1977-1982; Alfred P Sloan Found fel, 1977-1979; asst prof, Yale Univ, 1976-1978; vis asst prof, Univ Utah, 1976 &1977; J W Gibbs instr eng & appl sci, Yale Univ, 1974-1976. **Memberships:** Am Chem Soc; Sigma Xi; Keck Nanoscale Molecular Electronics Lab; AT Nanomaterials & Electronic Struct Algorithms Team NCSA Alliance; fel Am Phys Soc; fel John Simon Guggenheim; fel Alfred P Sloan Found. **Research Statement & Publications:** Theoretical studies of the electronic structure of molecules; properties of atomic and molecular clusters; hydrogen-bonding; charge localization in clusters; Monte Carlo optimization and simulation methods; published over 80 articles. **Mailing Address:** Dept Chem, Univ Pittsburgh, 219 Parkman Ave, Pittsburgh, PA 15260. **Fax:** 412-624-8611. **E-Mail:** jordan@a.psc.edu

JORDAN, KENNETH GARY, PHYSICAL CHEMISTRY, TECHNICAL FIBERS. **Personal Data:** b Anderson, SC, November 18, 1935; m 1957, Joyce Hackaby; c Kenneth G Jr & Christopher A (deceased). **Education:** Clemson Univ, BS, 1957, MS, 1961, PhD (phys chem), 1963. **Professional Experience:** EXEC ACCT MGR, E I DU PONT DEL NEMOURS & CO, INC, 1992-; fromaccount mgr to sr account mgr, Indust Fibers Div, 1982-1991; sr mkt rep, Wilmington, 1981; mktrep, Wilmington, 1978-1981; develop assoc, Wilmington, 1977-1978; textile fibers end use mktspecialist, Wilmington, 1975-1977; Dacron Textile Res Lab, Wilmington, 1970-1975; sr reschemist, Dacron Technol Div, NC, 1969-1970; res chemist, Dacron Technol Div, NC, 1963-1968; chemist, E I du Pont Del Nemours & Co, Inc, 1957. **Memberships:** Am Chem Soc. **Research Statement & Publications:** Semiconductor properties of polymers; polyester catalysis and kinetics; new polymer technology; synthetic fiber and fabric characterization and evaluation; industrial fiber sales and development. **Mailing Address:** 4502 Lanier Ave, Anderson, SC 29624.

JORDAN, KENNETH L(OUIS), ELECTRICAL ENGINEERING, COMMUNICATIONS. **Personal Data:** b Portland, Maine, May 10, 1933; m 1962, c 3. **Education:** Rensselaer Polytech Inst, BEE; Mass Inst Technol, MS, 1956, ScD(elec eng), 1961. **Professional Experience:** CONSULT, as of 2004; COOP VPRES, SCI APPLN INC, 1992-; TREAS & CHIEF SCIENTIST, SCI APPLN INC, 1979-; prin dep asst secy res & develop, Off Secy Air Force, Pentagon, 1976-1979; group leader, Lincoln Lab, Mass Inst Technol, 1968-1976; asst group leader, Lincoln Lab, MassInst Technol, 1967-1968; Staff mem commun,

Lincoln Lab, Mass Inst Technol, 1960-1967. **Memberships:** Fel Inst Elec & Electronics Engrs. **Research Statement & Publications:** Random processes; modulation and coding; satellite communications. **Mailing Address:** Sci Appln Int Corp, 1710 Goodridge Dr, McLean, VA 22102. **Fax:** 703-356-0959. **E-Mail:** jordank@saic.com

JORDAN, LARRY, MOTOR CONTROL PHYSIOLOGY. **Personal Data:** b Paris, Tex, March 18, 1944. **Education:** Univ Tex, BA, 1966; SW Med Sch, Dallas, PhD (physiol), 1971. **Professional Experience:** Chair Phyiol, Univ Man, 1993-2002; Distinguished lectr, Hollfelder Found, 1989; DIR, NEUROSCIENCE RES PROG, UNIV MAN, 1989-; CO-DIR, SPINAL CORD RES CTR, HEALTH SCI CTR & UNIV MAN, 1987-; PROF PHYSIOL, UNIV MAN, 1986-; from prof & dept head Neuroscience to head/prof physiol, Univ Man, beginning 1985; from asstprof to assoc prof, Univ Man, 1972-1985; researcher neuropharmacol, Univ Man, 1970-1972. **Memberships:** Can Asn Neurosci (treas 1983-1985); AAAS; Am Physiol Soc; Can Physiol Soc; SocNeurosci. **Mailing Address:** Dept Physiol, Fac Med, Univ Man, 425 Basic Sci Bldg, 433 - 730 William Ave, Bannatyne Campus, Winnipeg, MB R3E 3J7, Can. **Fax:** 204-789-3934. **E-Mail:** larry@scrc.umanitoba.ca

JORDAN, LAWRENCE M, COMPUTER SCIENCE. **Personal Data:** b Greensboro, NC, April 6, 1936. **Education:** Fisk Univ, BA, 1957; Princeton Univ, PhD (physics), 1964. **Honors & Awards:** Bronze Medal, US Dept Transp, 1979, Group Achievement Award, EmergencyTransp Proj, 1985. **Professional Experience:** Mem subcomt grad prog, Univ Tenn, 1993; prin investr, Nat Inst Arthritis &Musculoskeletal & Skin Dis, 1992-1994; ASSOC PROF BIOMED ENG, UNIV TENN, MEMPHIS, 1990-; Mgr neurosci, 3-D Micros Lab, 1989; assoc prof comput sci, Univ Tenn, Memphis, 1988-1989; oper res analyst, Transp Syst Ctr, Cambridge, Mass, 1976-1988; physicist, Electronics Res Ctr & Transp Syst, NASA, 1970-1976; staff scientist & sr scientist, Avco SpaceSyst Div, Lowell, Mass, 1966-1970; asst prof, Colgate Univ, Hamilton, NY, 1964-1966; Instrphysics, Colgate Univ, Hamilton, NY, 1962-1964. **Memberships:** Am Phys Soc. **Research Statement & Publications:** Novel densitometric techniques for osteoporosis; computer assisted ultrasound diagnosis of liver and kidney disease; a vector mode doppler ultrasound technique; author of 30 publications. **Mailing Address:** Biomed Eng Dept, Univ Tenn 899 Madison Ave Rm 801, Memphis, TN 38163.

JORDAN, LOWELL STEPHEN, PLANT PHYSIOLOGY. **Personal Data:** b Vale, Ore, April 23, 1930; m 1980, Catalina; c Gary S, Diane L (Hankla), Lauraly N (Ramos), James L & Sharon T (Luster). **Education:** Ore State Univ, BS, 1954; Univ Minn, PhD (agron, bot), 1957. **Professional Experience:** EMER PHYSIOLOGIST & PROF HORT SCI, UNIV CALIF, RIVERSIDE, AS OF 2000; physiologist & prof, Univ Calif, Riverside, 1970-1993; from asst to assoc plant physiologist, Univ Calif, Riverside, 1959-1970; asst prof plant industs, Southern Ill Univ, 1957-1959; asst agron, Univ Minn, 1954-1957. **Memberships:** Fel Weed Sci Soc Am; Am Soc Plant Physiol; Am Soc Hort Sci; Am Coun Sci & Health; Coun Agr Sci & Technol. **Research Statement & Publications:** Weed science; herbicide physiology, mechanism of action and metabolism in plants. **Mailing Address:** Dept Bot & Plant Sci, Univ Calif, Riverside, CA 92521.

JORDAN, MARILYN, ECOLOGY. **Education:** Rutgers State Univ, MS, PhD (plant ecol). **Professional Experience:** STEWARDSHIP ECOLOGIST, THE NATURE CONSERVANCY, as of 2006. **Mailing Address:** The Nature Conservancy, 250 Lawrence Farm Rd, Cold Spring Harbor, NY 11724. **E-Mail:** mjordan@tnc.org

JORDAN, MARK H(ENRY), CIVIL ENGINEERING, CONSTRUCTION MANAGEMENT. **Personal Data:** b Lawrence, Mass, April 10, 1915; m 1939, Louise; c Mary Elizabeth & Margaret Michaela. **Education:** US Naval Acad, BS, 1937; Rensselaer Polytech Inst, BCE, 1941, MCE, 1942, MS, 1965, PhD (mgt), 1968. **Professional Experience:** PRINC CONSULT ENGR, 1976-; arbitrator, Am Arbit Asn, 1970-; mem, Rensselaer County Charter Comn, 1969-1971; prof civil eng, Rensselaer Polytech inst, 1968-1977; dean continuing studies, Rensselaer Polytech inst, 1967-1972; assoc prof civil eng, construct & mgt, Univ Mo, 1966-1967; officer in charge, Naval Civil Engrs Corps Officers Sch, Pt Hueneme, Calif, 1960-1963; Eng adminr, US Navy, 1942-1960. **Memberships:** Fel Am Soc Civil Engrs; Am Soc Eng Educ; Nat Soc Prof Engrs; Soc Am Mil Engrs; Am Cons Engrs Coun; Am Arbit Asn. **Research Statement & Publications:** Industrial management, application of contemporary management concepts to engineering construction. **Mailing Address:** 46 E Rd, Troy, NY 12180. **E-Mail:** mjordan2@nycap.rr.com

JORDAN, MARY ANN, MICROTUBULES, CANCER CHEMOTHERAPEUTICS. **Personal Data:** b Minneapolis, Minn, July 31, 1940; m 1984, David; c Andrea (Lommen) & Kate (Lommen). **Education:** Univ Minn, BA, 1962; Univ Rochester, MS, 1964, PhD (biol), 1969. **Professional Experience:** Chair, Breast Cancer Res Prof Coun, 2000-2001; ADJ PROF, UNIV CALIF, SANTA BARBARA, 1996-; RES BIOLOGIST, UNIV CALIF, SANTA BARBARA, 1995-; assoc res biologist, Univ Calif, Santa Barbara, 1991-1975; asst res biologist, Univ Calif, Santa Barbara, 1982-1990; postdoctoral fel, Univ Calif, Santa Barbara, 1978-1982; researcher biol, Univ Mich, 1972; researcher biol, Utah State Univ, 1974-1977; asst prof, Univ Wyo, 1968-1969; vis prof, Univ Marseille, France. **Memberships:** AAAS; Am Soc Cell Biol; Am Asn Cancer Res. **Research Statement & Publications:** Microtubule structure and function; regulation by drug and physiological compounds; cell death and mechanism of action of anti-mitotic drugs, vinblastine and taxol. **Mailing Address:** Dept Molecular Cellular & Develop Biol, Univ Calif, Santa Barbara, CA 93106. **Fax:** 805-893-4724. **E-Mail:** jordan@lifesci.ucsb.edu

JORDAN, MARY LUCILLE, SCIENCE LAW. **Education:** St Bonaventure Univ, BA, 1971; Anitoch Sch Law, JD, 1976. **Professional Experience:** COMNR, FED MINE SAFETY & HEALTH REV COMN, 2003-; comnr, Fed Mine Safety & Health Rev Comn, 2001-2002; chmn, Fed Mine Safety & Health Rev Comn, 1994-2001; sr staff atty, United Mine Workers Am, 1977-1994; atty, Off Fed Regist, Nat Archives & Records Admin. **Memberships:** State NY Bar; DC Bar. **Mailing Address:** Fed Mine Safety & Health Rev Comn, 601 NJ Ave N W, Washington, DC 20001.

JORDAN, MICHAEL A, PHYSICS. **Education:** Univ Kans, BS, 1966; Univ Tex, MA, 1970, PhD, 1978. **Professional Experience:** ASSOC PROF, DEPT GEOLOGY, TEX A&M UNIV, as of 2005. **Mailing Address:** TEX A&M UNIV, 700 University Blvd, Kingsville, TX 78363-8202. **Fax:** 361-593-4026.

JORDAN, MICHAEL I, MATHEMATICS. **Education:** Ariz State Univ, MS; Univ Calif, San Diego, PhD. **Professional Experience:** PROF, DEPT ELEC ENG & COMPUT SCI & DEPT STATIST, UNIV CALIF, BERKELEY, as of 2005. **Mailing Address:** Dept Elec Eng & Comput Sci, Univ Calif, Berkeley, 731 Soda Hall Ste 1776, Berkeley, CA 02139. **Fax:** 510-642-5775. **E-Mail:** jordan@cs.berkeley.edu

JORDAN, NEAL F(RANCIS), ENGINEERING PHYSICS. **Personal Data:** b Franklinville, NY, July 8, 1932; m 1994, Vaida Mikits; c Kirk G & Sarah E (Towler). **Education:** Cornell Univ, BEngPhys, 1955; Purdue Univ, MS, 1959, PhD (eng sci), 1963. **Professional Experience:** Mgr subsurface imaging Exxon prod res, Tex, 1984-1997; res assoc, Tex, 1968-1984; sr res engr, Tex, 1965-1968; res engr, Jersey Prod Res Co, Okla, 1963-1965; Instr continuum mech, Purdue Univ, 1960-1963; Consult, Gen Tech Corp, Ind, 1959-1963. **Memberships:** Soc Eng Sci Charter, Secy; Soc Explor Geophys sr mem. **Research Statement & Publications:** Geophysics; nonlinear theories of continuous media; elastic wave propagation; exploration applications of potential fields. **Mailing Address:** 330 Knipp, Houston, TX 77024.

JORDAN, PAUL H, GASTROENTEROLOGY, SURGERY. **Personal Data:** b Bigelow, Ark, November 22, 1919; m 1944, c 3. **Education:** Univ Chicago, BS, 1941, MD, 1944; Univ Ill, MS, 1950. **Honors & Awards:** Distinguished Philanthropist Award, Am Col Surg. **Professional Experience:** RETIRED; prof surg, Baylor Col Med, beginning 1964; chief staff, Vet Admin Hosp, Houston, 1969-1970; chief surg, Vet Admin Hosp, Houston, 1964-1983; assoc prof, Sch Med, UnivFla, 1959-1964; fel, NIH, 1958-1959; asst prof surg, Sch Med, Univ Calif, Los Angeles, 1955-1958; fel, Am Col Surg. **Memberships:** Am Surg Asn; Soc Exp Biol & Med; Soc Univ Surg; AmGastroenterol Asn. **Research Statement & Publications:** Gastrointestinal physiology. **Mailing Address:** Dept Surg, Baylor Col Med, One Baylor Plaza, Houston, TX 77030. **Fax:** 713-798-8460.

JORDAN, PETER A, ECOLOGY, WILDLIFE MANAGEMENT. **Personal Data:** b Oakland, Calif, January 2, 1930; div, c Chris, Marcon & Bennett. **Education:** Univ Calif Berkeley, AB, 1955, PhD (zoology), 1967. **Honors & Awards:** Distinguished Moose Biologist, 1998; N Am Moose Biologist Group, 1999. **Professional Experience:** ASSOC PROF EMER, DEPT FISHERIES & WILDLIFE, UNIV MINN, as of 2004; assoc prof, dept fisheries & wildlife, Univ Minn, beginning 1974; asst prof wildlife ecol, Sch Forestry, Yale Univ, 1967-1974; res assoc ecol moose & wolves, Purdue Univ, 1963-1966; instr, Sch Forestry, Univ Calif Berkeley, 1962-1963; teaching asst zool, Sch Forestry, Univ Calif Berkeley, 1961-1962; asst specialist studies migratory deer, Sch Forestry, Univ Calif Berkeley, 1955-1961. **Memberships:** Wildlife Soc; Am Soc Mammal; Soc Conservation Biol. **Research Statement & Publications:** Behavior, population dynamics and food habits of wild ungulates and carnivores; impact of herbivorous mammals upon forest vegetation; sodium acquisition and aquatic feeding by forest herbivores; management of big game; ecosystem processes; integration of wildlife habitat with timber management. **Mailing Address:** Fisheries, Wildlife & Conserv Biol, Univ Minn, 1980 Folwell Ave, St Paul, MN 55108-1037. **Fax:** 612-625-5299. **E-Mail:** pajordan@umn.edu

JORDAN, PETER C H, THEORETICAL CHEMISTRY. **Personal Data:** b London, Eng, May 3, 1936; American citizen; m 1979, Barbara. **Education:** Calif Inst Technol, BS, 1957; Yale Univ, PhD (quantum mech), 1960. **Professional Experience:** Vis scientist, Univ Groningen, 1993-1994; vis scientist, Univ Houston, 1986-1987; PROF & CHMN CHEM, BRANDEIS UNIV, 1981-; Marion & Jaspar Whiting fel, 1978-1979; vis prof, Dept Biol, Konstanz Univ, 1978-1979; Guggenheim fel, 1971-1972; assoc prof, BrandeisUniv, 1970-1981; asst prof chem, Brandeis Univ, 1964-1970; asst res chemist, Univ Calif, SanDiego, 1962-1964; NSF fel, 1960-1962. **Memberships:** AAAS; Am Phys Soc; Biophys Soc; Am Chem Soc. **Research Statement & Publications:** Statistical mechanics; quantum chemistry; irreversible thermodynamics; membrane transport. **Mailing Address:** Dept Chem, Brandeis Univ, MS 015, 415 S St, Waltham, MA 02454. **Fax:** 781-736-2516. **E-Mail:** jordan@brandeis.edu

JORDAN, ROBERT KENNETH, ULTRA-FINE INORGANIC PARTICLES. **Personal Data:** b Clearfield, Pa, December 12, 1925; m 1948, c 3. **Education:** Tufts Col, BS, 1954. **Professional Experience:** DIR METALLIDING INST, 1983-; SCIENTIST, GANNON UNIV, as of 2004; DIR ENG RES & DEVELOP, ENG RES INST, GANNON UNIV, 1980-; indust consult, 1975-1982; expert deleg, NATO, Comm Challenges Modern Soc Conf, Steel Indust, 1975-1978; consult, energy-indust, Brookhaven Nat Lab, 1974-1980; proj mgr new prod, US Steel Corp, 1965-1973; mgr new prod, Gen Tire Chem-Plastics, 1960-1965; mgr, nuclear div & asst mgr chem, plastics &metals, res div, Curtiss-Wright Corp, 1956-1960; chemist, energy res & develop, Olin-MathiesonChem Co, 1954-1956. **Research Statement & Publications:** Metallurgical (Metalliding), ceramics, minerals extraction, metals processes, organic and inorganic fluorides, organic nitrogenous and inorganic phosphorous fertilizers research and development; crude oil conversion to petrochemicals, organic intermediates, polymers and plastics-elastomers; metals surface and subsurface alloying. **Mailing Address:** Eng Res Inst, Gannon Univ, Erie, PA 16541. **Fax:** 814-455-2631.

JORDAN, ROBERT LAWRENCE, ANATOMY, TERATOLOGY. **Personal Data:** b Miami, Fla, May 7, 1941; div, c 2. **Education:** Fla Southern Col, BS, 1965; Univ Fla, 1965-1966; Univ Cincinnati, PhD (anat), 1969. **Professional Experience:** Vis prof anat, St Georges Med Sch, Greneda, West Indies, 1979-; ASSOC PROF ANAT, MED COL VA, 1974-; Asst prof, Med Col VA, 1970-1974; USPHS fel teratology & toxicol, Kettering Lab, Univ Cincinnati, 1969-1970. **Memberships:** Teratology Soc; Am Asn Anat; Sigma Xi. **Mailing Address:** Dept Anat Sci, St Georges Univ PO Box 7, St Georges, Grenada. **Fax:** 473-444-2887.

JORDAN, ROBERT MANSEAU, animal science; deceased, see previous edition for last biography

JORDAN, ROBERT R, GEOLOGY. **Personal Data:** b New York, NY, June 5, 1937; m 1958, c 2. **Education:** Hunter Col, AB, 1958; Bryn Mawr Col, MA, 1962, PhD (geol), 1964. **Honors & Awards:** Pres Award Divi enviorn Geosci Am Asn Pit Geol 2001; Campbell Medal, Am Geol Inst 1996; Honorary mem 1996, Am Inst Prof Geol Coher Award, E S Am Assoc Pit Geol 1995; Galey Award, 1992 Autometric Award, Am Inst Prof Geologists, 1990; Cert Merit, Distinguished Serv Award, 1988; Am Asn Petrol Geologists, 1987, Presidential Cert Merit, Am Soc Photogrammetry, 1976. **Professional Experience:** RETIRED; Policy Comt, 1993-1994; mem, Comt Offshore Energy Technol & Alaska, 1992-1994; pres, Del Acad Sci, 1991; 2002 mem, US Nat Comt Geol, 1990-; house of delegates, Am Asn Petrol Geologists, 1990-; pres-elect, Del Acad Sci, 1990; Prof Geol, Univ Del, 1988-2003; gov rep, Outer Continental Shelf, Dept Interior, 1974-1977 & Policy Comt, 1985-; chmn, Nam Comn Stratig Nomenclature, 1982-1983 & 1990-1991; vchmnsecy, Nam Comn Stratig Nomenclature, 1978-1982 & 1989-1990; regional coordr, Asn Am Petrol Geologists, 1978-1984; mem, Nat Acad Sci-Nat Res Coun, 1978-1980; mem, Nam Comn Stratig Nomenclature, 1978; Chmn, Outer Continental Shelf, Dept Interior, 1974-1977; Chmn, Del State Boundary Comn, 1971-; State geologist & Dir, Del Geol Surv, 1969-2003; from instr to assoc prof geol, Univ Del, 1962-1988; From geologist to asst state geologist, Del Geol Surv, 1958-1969. **Memberships:** Asn Am State Geol (secytreas, 1977-1981, vpres, 1981-1982m, pres-elect, 1982-1983, pres, 1983-1984); Am Inst Prof Geol; Ed, Hon fel Geol Soc Am; Soc Econ Paleont & Mineral; hon Am Asn Petrol Geologists; Nat Asn Geol Teachers; Sigma Xi; Am Geol Inst (treas, 1992-1993). **Research Statement & Publications:** Sedimentary petrology; stratigraphy; geology of the Atlantic Coastal Plain; ground water supplies. **Mailing Address:** Del Geol Surv, Univ Del, Newark, DE 19717-0001. **E-Mail:** rrjorfdan@udel.edu

JORDAN, ROBIN G, PHYSICS. **Education:** Univ Sheffield, England, BS, 1963, PhD (physics), 1967. **Professional Experience:** PROF, DEPT PHYSICS, FLA ATLANTIC UNIV, as of 2006. **Mailing Address:** Physics Dept, Fla Atlantic Univ, Rm 106 Sci & Eng Bldg, Boca Raton, FL 33431. **Fax:** 561-297-2662. **E-Mail:** jordanrg@physics.fau.edu

JORDAN, RUSSELL THOMAS, VIROLOGY, IMMUNOCHEMISTRY. **Personal Data:** b Geneseo, NY, m 1946, c 6. **Education:** Univ Ark, BS, 1949, MS, 1951; Univ Mich, PhD (virol), 1953. **Professional Experience:** PRES, MED-X-CONSULT, FT COLLINS, 1977-; res dir, Chemex Corp, 1975-1977; pres & chmn bd, Vipont Chem & Res Ctr, 1973-1975; vpres sci & technol, C FKettering Found, dir, C F Kettering Lab & vpres, Kettering Sci Res, Inc, 1971-1973; chief spacebiomed res, Aerospace Group, Martin-Marietta Corp, Colo, 1966-1971; dir res & labs, BiomedRes Labs Div, Bio-Organic Chem Inc, 1963-1971; asst prof, Sch Med, Univ Colo, Denver, 1961-1971; chief, Dept Exp Immunol, Nat Jewish Hosp, Denver, 1960-1963; res fel immunol chem, Calif Inst Technol, 1958-1959; lectr, Univ Calif, Los Angeles, 1956-1959; chmn dept microbiol, City Hope Med Ctr, Calif, 1954-1960; clin asst prof infectious dis, Sch Med, Univ Calif, Los Angeles, 1954-1959; asst prof bact, Sch Med, Univ Mich, 1953-1954; Rackhamres fel, Sch Med, Univ Mich, 1953. **Memberships:** Am Asn Immunol; Soc Exp Biol & Med; Am Asn Cancer Res; Sigma Xi; NY AcadSci. **Research Statement & Publications:** Microbiology; interference phenomenon; infection and resistance; virus induced neoplasms; immunochemistry of cancer; immunochemical properties of tumor specific antigens and antibodies. **Mailing Address:** 1809 Indian Meadows Lane, Ft Collins, CO 80525.

JORDAN, SCOTT WILSON, PATHOLOGY. **Personal Data:** b Iola, Kans, August 22, 1934; m 1955, c 3. **Education:** Univ Kans, AB, 1956, MD, 1959. **Professional Experience:** From PROF to EMER PROF PATH, SCH MED, UNIV NMEX, beginning1982; consult, Midwest Res Inst, Mo, 1962-1963 & Nat Cancer Inst, 1974-1977; from asst prof toassoc prof, Sch Med, Univ NMex, 1965-1982; pathologist, Nat Acad Sci-Nat Res Coun AtomicBomb Casualty Comn, 1963-1965; USPHS fel, Med Ctr, Univ Kans, 1960-1963; from intern toresident path, Med Ctr, Univ Kans, 1959-1963. **Memberships:** Am Soc Cytol (past pres); Am Asn Path; Int Acad Path; fel Am Bd Path. **Research Statement & Publications:** Pathology of radiation injury; diagnostic cytology; digital image analysis. **Mailing Address:** Dept Path, Univ NMex Sch Med, Albuquerque, NM 87131-0001. **Fax:** 505-277-7224. **E-Mail:** sjordan@unm.edu

JORDAN, STANLEY CLARK, PEDIATRICS, PEDIATRIC NEPHROLOGY. **Personal Data:** b Elkin, NC, April 13, 1947; m 1976, c 1. **Education:** Univ NC, Chapel Hill, AB, 1969, MD, 1973. **Professional Experience:** DIR PEDIAT NEPHROL, CEDARS-SINAI MED CTR, as of 2004; DIR, TRANSPLANT IMMUNOL LAB & MED DIR, RENAL TRANSPLANT PROG, as of 2004; PROF PEDIAT, UNIV CALIF, SCH MED, LOS ANGELES, as of 2004; asst prof pediat, Univ Calif, Losangeles, beginning 1980; Prin investr, NIH clin investr award, 1980-1983; Asst clin prof pediat, Univ Southern Calif, 1979-1980; Pediatric Nephrology, & Med Dir kidney transplantation, Cedars-Sinai Med Center Los Angeles. **Memberships:** Am Soc Pediat Nephrol. **Research Statement & Publications:** Renal immmunopathology and transplantation immunology. **Mailing Address:** Cedars-Sinai Med Ctr, 8700 Beverly Blvd, Los Angeles, CA 90048-1804. **Fax:** 310-652-0681. **E-Mail:** sjordan@mailgatecsmc.edu

JORDAN, STEVEN LEE, COMPUTER GRAPHICS, MATHEMATICS EDUCATION. **Personal Data:** b Jersey City, NJ, February 17, 1943; m 1966, c 2. **Education:** Princeton Univ, AB, 1965; Univ Calif, Berkeley, MA, 1967, PhD (math), 1970. **Professional Experience:** RETIRED; prof math, Univ Ill, Chicago, beginning 1995; co-dir, Univ Ill Chicago/Chicago Cir Ctr, Partnership Prog, beginning 1987; assoc prof oral & maxillofacial surg, Univ Ill, Chicago, beginning 1987; Dept Educ grants, beginning1986; HEW res grant, 1985-1986; Carnegie Found res grant, 1975-1976; from asst prof to assoc prof math, Univ Ill, Chicago, 1970-1996; NSF res grant, 1970-1972; dir math comp educ, Univ Calif Berkeley; consult bds educ & biochem labs. **Memberships:** Am Math Soc; Math Asn Am; Sigma Xi; Nat Coun Teachers Math. **Research Statement & Publications:** Differential geometry and complex manifolds; all levels of mathematics teacher education; history of mathematics; applications of computer graphics, statistics, and modelling to radiology and oral surgery. **Mailing Address:** Math Dept, Univ Ill, M/C 249 851 S Morgan, Chicago, IL 60607. **E-Mail:** jordan@uic.edu

JORDAN, STUART DAVIS, SOLAR PHYSICS. **Personal Data:** b St Louis, Mo, July 25, 1936; m 1961, Elizabeth; c John S & James W. **Education:** Wash Univ, BS, 1958; Univ Colo, Boulder, PhD (physics, astrophys), 1968. **Professional Experience:** SR STAFF SCIENTIST, GODDARD SPACE FLIGHT CTR, NASA, 1989-; head, Solar Physics Br, 1984-1989; coordr, Nonthermal Stellar Atmospheres, NASA, 1978-1993; proj scientist, Solar Optical Telescope, 1976-1985; actg chief solar physics, NASA Hq, 1974; res scientist, Lab Astron & Solar Physics, 1968-1984; res asst, Joint Inst Lab Astrophys, 1963-1968; Res adminr plasma dynamics, Air Force Off Sci Res, 1959-1963. **Memberships:** Am Astron Soc; Int Astron Union; Sigma Xi; Am Astron Soc; Am Geophys Union; Tau Beta Pi. **Research Statement & Publications:** Spectral line formation in solar atmosphere; shock wave heating of solar atmosphere; energy balance and temperature structure of stellar atmospheres; solar tarrestrial infunces; published over 40 articles. **Mailing Address:** Lab Astron & Solar Physics, Code 682, Solar Physics Br, Goddard Space Flight Ctr, Greenbelt, MD 20771. **Fax:** 301-286-1617. **E-Mail:** Stuart.D.Jordan@nasa.gov

JORDAN, TERESA M, AERONAUTICS. **Honors & Awards:** Am Inst Aeronaut & Astronaut Sustained Serv Award, 2002. **Professional Experience:** STAFF, SANDIA NAT LAB, as of 2006. **Mailing Address:** Flight Dynamics, Dept Sandia Nat Lab, PO BOX 5800, Albuquerque, NM 87185. **Fax:** 505-844-6098.

JORDAN, THOMAS FREDRICK, THEORETICAL PHYSICS. **Personal Data:** b Duluth, Minn, June 4, 1936; div. **Education:** Univ Minn, Duluth, BA, 1958; Univ Rochester, PhD (physics), 1962. **Professional Experience:** PROF EMER, DEPT PHYSICS, UNIV MINN, DULUTH, 1970-; Sloan Found fel, 1965-1967; from asst prof to assoc prof, Univ Pittsburgh, 1964-1970; NSF fel, Berne, 1963-1964; instr, Univ Rochester, 1962-1963; Res assoc physics, Univ Rochester, 1961-1962. **Research Statement & Publications:** Mathematical physics; quantum mechanics; field theory; relativistic particle dynamics; scattering theory; elementary particle interactions; quantum theory of optical coherence; hydrodynamics of Great Lakes circulation; general relativity; Nonlinear quantum spin dynamics; Symmetries without conservation laws. **Mailing Address:** Dept Physics, 358 MWAH, Univ Minn, 10 Univ Dr, Duluth, MN 55812. **Fax:** 218-726-6942. **E-Mail:** tjordan@d.umn.edu

JORDAN, THOMAS HILLMAN, GEOPHYSICS. **Personal Data:** b Coco Solo, Canal Zone, October 8, 1948; m 1973, c 1. **Education:** Calif Inst Technol, BS, 1969, MS, 1970, PhD (geophys), 1972. **Honors & Awards:** James B Macelwane Award, Am Geophys Union, 1983; George P Woollard Award, Geol Soc Am, 1998. **Professional Experience:** DIR, SOUTHERN CALIF EARTHQUAKE CTR, 2002-; W M KECK PROF EARTH SCI, UNIV SOUTHERN CALIF, LA, 2000-; head, dept earth atmospheric & planetary sci, Mass Inst Technol, 1988-1998; alfred p sloan fel, physics, 1980-1982; assoc prof geophys, Scripps Inst Oceanog, Univ Calif, San Diego, 1975-1988; Asst prof geophys, Princeton Univ, 1972-1975. **Memberships:** Fel Am Geophys Union; Geol Soc Am; Nat Acad Sci. **Research Statement & Publications:** Structure of the earth's interior; earthquake processes; mantle dynamics; wave propagation; inverse theory. **Mailing Address:** Dept Earth Sci, Univ Southern Calif, 3651 Trousdale Pkwy, Los Angeles, CA 90089. **Fax:** 213-740-0011. **E-Mail:** tjordan@earth.usc.edu

JORDAN, THOMAS L, BACTERIOLOGY. **Personal Data:** b Yazoo City, Miss, April 27, 1943; m 1979, c 1. **Education:** Rockhurst Col, Kansas City, Mo, BA, 1964; Univ Wis-Madison, MS, 1968, PhD (bact), 1972. **Professional Experience:** ASSOC PROF BIOL, NC AGR & TECH STATE UNIV, as of 2004; asst res prof, Univ SC, Columbia, 1983-1984; fac biol, Nc Agr & Tech State Univ, beginning 1981; fel, Sch Med, Tulane Univ, 1980-1981; fel, Marine Biol Lab, 1979; Dillard Univ, New Orleans, 1978-1981; fac biol, Alcorn State Univ, Miss, 1976-1978; NIH fel bact, UnivWash, Seattle, 1972-1975. **Memberships:** Am Soc Microbiol. **Research Statement & Publications:** Relationship between energy metabolism and starvation induced arrest of the cell cycle in Caulobacter crescentus. **Mailing Address:** Dept Biol, Nc A&T State Univ, Rm 25 Barnes Hall, Greensboro, NC 27401-3209. **Fax:** 910-334-7105. **E-Mail:** jordant@aurora.ncat.edu

JORDAN, TRUMAN H, PHYSICAL CHEMISTRY. **Personal Data:** b Wayne, Mich, November 18, 1937; m 1961, Linda; c Jennifer, Jackie & Joy. **Education:** Albion Col, BA, 1959; Harvard Univ, MA, 1962, PhD (chem), 1964. **Professional Experience:** PROF EMER CHEM, CORNELL COL, as of 2004; vis prof, Univ Iowa, 1978-1979, 1986-1987; prof chem, Cornell Col, beginning 1977; NIH fel, Nat Bur Stand, 1972-1973; from asst prof to assoc prof, Cornell Col, 1966-1977; NASA fel & res assoc crystallog, Univ Pittsburgh, 1964-1966. **Memberships:** AAAS; Am Chem Soc; Am Crystallog Asn; Int Asn Dent Res. **Research Statement & Publications:** Molecular structure by means of x-ray crystallography; dental chemistry. **Mailing Address:** Dept Chem, Cornell Col, 600 First St W, Mt Vernon, IA 52314. **Fax:** 319-895-5764. **E-Mail:** tjordan@cornellcollege.edu

JORDAN, V CRAIG, ENDOCRINE PHARMACOLOGY. **Personal Data:** b New Braunfels, Tex, July 25, 1947; m 1993, Monica; c Helen & Alexandra. **Education:** Univ Leeds, Eng, BS (Hons), 1969, PhD (pharmacol), 1972, DSc, 1985. **Honors & Awards:** Bruce Cain Mem Award, Am Asn Cancer Res, 1989; Inaugural Brinker Int Breast Cancer Award, Susan G Komen Breast Cancer Found, 1992; Cameron Prize, Univ Edinburgh, Scotland, 1993; Sir John Gaddum Mem Award, Brit PharmacolSoc, 1993; Am Soc Pharmacol & Exp Therapeut Award, 1993; William L McGuire Mem Award, San Antonio, 1994; Ital-Am Award for Sci Excellence in Med, 1995; Sixth Cino Del Duca AwardOncol, Paris, 1997; Gaddum Mem Award. **Professional Experience:** VPRES & SCI DIR MED SCI DIV, FOX CHASE CANCER CTR, as of 2006; DIANA, PRINCESS WALES PROF CANCER RES, ROBERT H LURIE COMPREHENSIVE CANCER CTR, NORTHWESTERN UNIV, as of 2004; PROF MOLECULAR PHARMACOL & BIOL CHEM, FEINBERG SCH MED, NORTHWESTERN UNIV, as of 2004; DIR LYNN SAGE BREAST CANCER RES PROG, ROBERT B LURIE CANCER CTR, NORTHWESTERN UNIV, 1993-; prof human oncol & pharmacol, ClinCancer Ctr, Univ Wis, 1985-1993; from asst prof to prof human oncol, Clin Cancer Ctr, UnivWis, 1980-1985; head endocrinol unit, Ludwig Inst Cancer Res, Switz, 1979-1980; fac lectr pharmacol, Univ Leeds, 1974-1978; vis scientist, Worcester Found Exp Biol, 1972-1974. **Memberships:** Endocrine Soc; Soc Surg Oncol; fel Royal Soc Chem; Brit Pharm Soc; Am AsnCancer Res; Am Soc Pharmacol & Exp Therapeut. **Research Statement & Publications:** Development of taroxifer and understanding of the molecular mechanisms of estrogen and antiestrogen acid. **Mailing Address:** Fox chase Ctr, 8258 Olson 710 N Fairbanks Ct, Chicago, IL 60611. **Fax:** 312-908-1372. **E-Mail:** vcjordan@northwestern.edu

JORDAN, WADE H(AMPTON), ELECTROCHEMICAL KINETICS, BATTERIES. **Personal Data:** b Edenton, NC, June 1, 1932; m 1954, c 5. **Education:** ECarolina Univ, AB, 1954; Univ Tex, PhD (phys chem), 1964. **Professional Experience:** ENVIRON OFFICER, US ARMY, 1992-; proj mgt engr, US Army, 1990-1992; staff electrochemist, Eveready Battery Co, 1982-1990; sr develop engr, Imp CleviteCorp, 1980-1982; head dept, Col Albemarle, 1976-1979; assoc prof chem, Col Albemarle, 1970-1979; res chemist, E I du Pont Del Nemours & Co, Inc, 1963-1970; Sr chemist, Tracor, Inc, 1958-1962. **Memberships:** Electrochem Soc; Am Chem Soc; NY Acad Sci. **Research Statement & Publications:** Primary and secondary lithium battery systems; kinetic studies of metal deposition and dissolution; reclamation of battery materials. **Mailing Address:** One Mountain Top Rd, High Knob, Front Royal, VA 22630.

JORDAN, WAYNE ROBERT, PLANT PHYSIOLOGY, BIOCHEMISTRY. **Personal Data:** b Kankakee, Ill, January 7, 1940; m 1960, Dorothy; c 6. **Education:** Univ Ill, Urbana, BS, 1961, MS, 1962; Univ Calif, Davis, PhD (plant physiol), 1968. **Honors & Awards:** Dep Chancellor's Award Res, Tex A&M Univ, 1983. **Professional Experience:** DIR, TEX WATER RESOURCES INST, TEX A&M UNIV, 1984-; resident dir, Black Land Res Ctr, Tex Agr Exp Sta, 1980-1983; assoc ed, Agron J, 1978-1981; prof cropphysiol, Tex Agr Exp Sta, 1975-; from asst prof to prof, Tex Agr Exp Sta, 1968-1975. **Memberships:** Am Soc Plant Physiol; fel Crop Sci Soc Am; fel Am Soc Agron; Am Water Resources Asn; Am Water Works Asn. **Research Statement & Publications:** Plant water relations; drought resistance; root physiology; hormonal regulation of abscission; perception and transduction of environmental stimuli. **Mailing Address:** Tex Water Resources Inst, Tex A&M Univ, 301 Scoates Hall MS 2118, College Station, TX 77843-2118. **Fax:** 979-845-8554. **E-Mail:** wadoj@cox-internet.com

JORDAN, WILLARD CLAYTON, NUCLEAR PHYSICS. **Personal Data:** b Richmond, Ind, May 13, 1922; m 1946, c 2. **Education:** Miami Univ, BA, 1945; Univ Mich, MS, 1948, PhD, 1954. **Professional Experience:** SCIENTIST, LOCKHEED MISSILES & SPACE RES LABS, PALO ALTO, 1964-; vis physicist, Lawrence Radiation Lab, Univ Calif, 1958-1964; physicist, Res Labs, Bendix Corp, 1954-1964; asst physicist, Exp Nuclear Physics, 1953-1954; Res assoc, Argonne Nat Lab, 1951-1953; Asst, Univ Mich, 1948-1953. **Memberships:** Am Phys Soc; Am Nuclear Soc; Am Asn Physics Teachers; Sigma Xi. **Research Statement & Publications:** Radioactive decay; nuclear reactors; thermonuclear research; space physics. **Mailing Address:** 24 Oak St, Los Altos, CA 94022-2266.

JORDAN, WILLIAM DITMER, MECHANICAL ENGINEERING. **Personal Data:** b Selma, Ala, February 5, 1922; m 1947, Carolyn; c William Jr, Lucy & Rebecca. **Education:** Univ Ala, BS, 1942, MS, 1949; Univ Ill, PhD (theoret & appl mech), 1952. **Professional Experience:** PROF EMER ENG MECH, UNIV ALA, 1986-; distinguished eng fel, Univ Ala, 1988; from assoc prof eng mech to prof, head Dept Eng Mech, 1961-1986; from assoc prof eng mech to prof, head Dept Eng Mech, 1961-1986; from assoc prof eng mech to prof, Univ Ala, 1952-1986; from assoc prof eng mech toprof, Univ Ala, 1952-1986; asst theoret & appl mech, Univ Ill, 1950-1952; asst prof eng mech, Univ Ala, 1946-1950.

Memberships: Am Soc Eng Educ; fel Am Soc Mech Engrs; Am Soc Mech Engrs; Am AcadMech; Nat Soc Prof Engrs. **Research Statement & Publications:** Strength of materials; structures; stress analysis; thermalstresses; buckling. **Mailing Address:** Dept Eng Mech, PO Box 870278, Tuscaloosa, AL 35487.

JORDAN, WILLIAM MALCOLM, HISTORY OF GEOLOGY. **Personal Data:** b Brooklyn, NY, June 19, 1936; m 1963, c 2. **Education:** Columbia Univ, BA, 1957, MA, 1961; Univ Wis, Madison, PhD (geol), 1965. **Professional Experience:** PROF EMER GEOL, MILLERSVILLE UNIV, as of 1999; prof, Dept Earth Sci, Millersville Univ, beginning 1969; chmn geol, Millersville Univ, 1967-1972; assoc prof Geol, Millersville Univ, 1966-1969; Esso Prod Res Co, Tex, 1965-1966; res geologist, Jersey Prod Res Co, Okla, 1964-1965; secy & treas, Hist Geol Div, Geol Soc Am. **Memberships:** Am Asn Petrol Geologists; Geol Soc Am; Hist Sci Soc; Nat Asn Geol Teachers; Soc Econ Paleont & Mineral; Hist Earth Sci Soc. **Research Statement & Publications:** Mature clastic sediments; paleocurrents and paleoclimatology; sedimentary facies and petroleum accumulation; history of geology. **Mailing Address:** Dept Earth Sci Millersville Univ, PO Box 1002, Millersville, PA 17551-0302. **Fax:** 717-871-4725.

JORDAN, WILLIAM R, III, ECOLOGICAL RESTORATION, HISTORY OF IDEAS ABOUT RELATIONSHIP BETWEEN HUMANS & ENVIRONMENT. **Personal Data:** b Denver, Colo, April 30, 1944; m 1966, Barbara; c 1. **Education:** Marquette Univ, BS, 1966; Univ Wis-Madison, PhD (bot), 1971, MA, 1974. **Professional Experience:** OUT REACH PROG MGR EMER ARBORETUM, UNIV WIS-MADISON, 1999-; vis scholar, NSF, Univ NTex, 1993-1994; consult, Environ Adv Prog, QuestFound, 1991-; out reach prog mgr, Arboretum, Univ Wis-Madison, 1977-1999; newswriter, Publ & Outreach Prog, Am Chem Soc, 1975-1976. **Memberships:** Soc Ecol Restoration. **Research Statement & Publications:** Ecological restoration as a technique for research, a teaching technique and a performing art; history of ideas about the relationship between human being and the rest of nature, through intellectual history, anthropology, literature and the arts. **Mailing Address:** Dept Arboretum, Univ Wis, 1207 Seminole Hwy, Madison, WI 53711. **Fax:** 608-262-5209. **E-Mail:** newacademy@sbcglobal.net

JORDAN, WILLIAM STONE, PUBLIC HEALTH & EPIDEMIOLOGY. **Personal Data:** b Fayetteville, NC, September 28, 1917; m 1947, Marion; c William S III & Marion A. **Education:** Univ NC, AB, 1938; Harvard Univ, MD, 1942. **Professional Experience:** Consult, Nat Vaccine Prog Off, Pub Health Servs, 1991-; EMER DIR & VOL, MICROBIOL & INFECTIOUS DIS PROG, NAT INST ALLERGY & INFECTIOUS DIS, 1987-; dir, Microbiol & Infectious Dis Prog, Nat Inst Allergy & Infectious Dis, 1976-1987; mem, Panel Rev Viral & Rickettsial Vaccines, Food & Drug Admin, 1973-1976; prof med & community med, Univ Ky, 1967-1974; dean, Col Med, 1967-1974; mem infectious dis adv comt, Nat Inst Allergy & Infectious Dis, 1967-1971; mem, comn epidemiol & vet follow-up studies, Nat Acad Sci, 1965-1972; prof prev & internal med & chmn dept prev med, Sch Med, Univ Va, 1958-1967; from instr to asst prof med, Sch Med, Western Res Univ, 1948-1958; from instr to assoc prof prev med, Sch Med, Western Res Univ, 1948-1958; teaching fel prev med & med, Sch Med, Western Res Univ, 1947-1948; resident, 2nd Med Serv, Boston City Hosp, 1946-1947; from intern to asst resident, 2nd Med Serv, Boston City Hosp, 1942-1943; dir comn acute respiratory dis, Epidemiol Bd, US Armed Forces; consult, Surgeon Gen. **Memberships:** Am Epidemiol Soc (pres, 1972-1998); Am Soc Clin Invest; Am Asn Immunol; Asn Am Physicians; Am Soc Microbiol; Infectious Dis Soc Am. **Research Statement & Publications:** Etiology and epidemiology of acute respiratory disease; accelerated development of new vaccines. **Mailing Address:** NIH, 6700 Rackledge B Rm 3234 mse 7630, Bethesda, MD 20892. **Fax:** 301-571-7411.

JORDAN-MOLERO, JAIME E, PLANT PHYSIOLOGY, WEED CONTROL. **Personal Data:** b Utauado, PR, January 5, 1941; m 1972, c 3. **Education:** Univ PR, BS, 1963, MS, 1970; Univ Ill, Urbana Champaign, PhD (agron), 1977; Harvard Univ, IEM, 1984. **Professional Experience:** ASSOC PROF AGR RES, AGR EXP STA, UTUADO REGIONAL COL, UNIV PR, 1979-; asst dean & dir, Agr Exp Sta, Univ PR, 1979-1984; prof crop physiol, Mayaguez Campus, Univ PR, 1977-; asst dir, Agr Exp Sta, Univ PR, 1977-1979; asst agronomist agr res, Univ PR, 1969-1979; res asst agr, Univ PR, 1963-1969; prof tropical crops, LosAngeles Montana Regional Col-Utuado PR. **Memberships:** Am Soc Agr Sci; Weed Sci Soc Am. **Research Statement & Publications:** Crop nutrition; coffee genetics and selection; plant physiology; weed control physiology and ecology; citrus breeding. **Mailing Address:** Agr Exp Sta, Call Box 2500, Utuado, PR 00641. **Fax:** 787-894-2891.

JORDEN, JAMES ROY, FORMATION EVALUATION, WELL LOGGING. **Personal Data:** b Oklahoma City, Okla, April 16, 1934; m 1956, Shirley A Swan; c Philip T & David E. **Education:** Univ Tulsa, BS, 1957. **Honors & Awards:** Distinguished Serv Award, Soc Petrol Engrs, 1988, DeGolyer Distinguished Serv Medal, 1991. **Professional Experience:** Consult, Quicksilver Resources, Inc, 1998-; trostee, Amer Inst, Metal and Petrol Engr 2000-2002; pres, Soc Petrol Engrs Found, 1995-1997; sr vpres, Soc Petrol Engrs Found, 1993-1995; mgr CPI training, Head Off Explor & Prod, 1993-1995; treas, Soc Petrol Engrs Found, 1991-1992; mgr tech training, Shell Oil Co, 1988-1993; pres, Soc Petrol Engrs Serv Corp, 1986 & 1989-1990; mgr, Petrol Eng Res, Shell Develop Co, 1985-1988; bd chmn, Soc Petrol Engrs Serv Corp, 1985; sr tech specialist petrophys eng, Head Off Prod, 1981-1985; Dir, Soc Petrol Engrs, 1979-1982; Mem eng staff, Shell Oil Co, 1960-1981. **Memberships:** Hon mem Soc Petrol Engrs (pres, 1984). **Research Statement & Publications:** Co-author of a two -volume series on formation evaluation and well logging. **Mailing Address:** 10926 Piping Rock Lane, Houston, TX 77042-2728.

JORDEN, ROGER M, ENVIRONMENTAL ENGINEERING, WATER CHEMISTRY. **Personal Data:** b Carthage, Mo, November 15, 1935; m 1975, Joan; c Cherlynne. **Education:** Univ Tex, Austin, BS, 1959; Univ Ariz, MS, 1962; Univ Ill, Urbana, PhD (civil eng), 1968. **Honors & Awards:** Eddy Award, Water Pollution Control Fedn, 1976. **Professional Experience:** PRES, CLEAR CORP, 1987-; consult water mgt, 1982-1987; proj mgr watermgt, Colo Ute Elec Asn, Inc, 1979-1981; proj mgr, Elec Power Res Inst, Calif, 1976-1979; assoc prof, Univ Colo, Boulder, 1975-1976; asst prof environ eng, Univ Colo, Boulder, 1968-1975; resfel, Univ Ill, Urbana, 1967-1968; res assoc sanit eng, Univ Ill, Urbana, 1964-1967; res assoc, Travelers Res Inst, 1962-1964; res asst hydrol, Inst Water Utilization, Univ Ariz, 1959-1962. **Memberships:** AAAS; Am Water Works Asn; Water Pollution Control Fedn; Am Chem Soc. **Research Statement & Publications:** Coagulation-flocculation of dilute colloidal suspensions; physical-chemical removal of trace elements; environmental transport of trace elements; water pollution control in oil shale; side-stream lime softening; water management of zero discharge water systems in power plants. **Mailing Address:** Clear Corp, 1750 30th St 605, Boulder, CO 80301. **E-Mail:** clearcor@ecentral.com

JORDI, HOWARD, CHEMISTRY. **Education:** Northern Ill Univ, PhD. **Professional Experience:** CEO, JORDI FLP, as of 2005. **Mailing Address:** Jordi FLP, 4 Mill St, Bellingham, MA 02019-1542. **Fax:** 508-966-4063. **E-Mail:** hjordi@jordiflp.com

JORDON, ROBERT EARL, DERMATOLOGY, IMMUNOLOGY. **Personal Data:** b Buffalo, NY, May 7, 1938; m 1969, c 1. **Education:** Hamilton Col, BA, 1960; State Univ NY Buffalo, MD, 1965; Univ Minn, Minneapolis, MS, 1970. **Honors & Awards:** Discovery Award, Dermat Found, 2000. **Professional Experience:** PROF & CHMN DERMAT, UNIV TEX HOUSTON MED SCH, 1977-; Nat Inst Arthritis, Metab & Digestive Dis res fel, Univ Minn, 1972-1973; vis asst prof & assoc mem grad fac, Univ Minn, Minneapolis, 1971-; Asst prof dermat & immunol, Mayo Med Sch Med, Univ Minn, Rochester, 1971-1977; Training grant dermat, Mayo Clin, 1968-1969. **Memberships:** AAAS; Am Asn Immunol; Am Fedn Clin Res; Soc Invest Dermat; Sigma Xi; Lupus Erythematosus Soc; Harris County Med Soc; Chicago Dermat Soc; Wis Dermat Soc. **Research Statement & Publications:** Immunopathology of bullous skin diseases using immunofluorescence, and complement research technics. **Mailing Address:** Dept Dermat Univ Tex Med Sch, 6431 Fannin Ste One 204, Houston, TX 77030-1501. **Fax:** 713-500-7173. **E-Mail:** rjordon@uth.tmc.edu

JORDY, GEORGE Y, ENERGY. **Personal Data:** b Pittsburgh, Pa, May 2, 1932. **Education:** Carnegie Mellon Univ, BS, 1954; Univ Pennsylvania, MBA, 1955; Univ Maryland, PhD, (math education), 1976. **Professional Experience:** DIR PROF ANAL, OFF ENERGY RES, US DEPT ENERGY, as of 1991; MEM STAFF, ENERGY RES DEPT, OFF PROG ANALYSIS, DEPTENERGY, 1980-. **Mailing Address:** Off Energy Res, US Dept Energy, 1000 Independence Ave SW, Washington, DC 20585. **Fax:** 202-586-4403.

JORGENS, JOSEPH III, BIOMEDICAL ENGINEERING. **Education:** MD, PhD. **Professional Experience:** BIOMED ENGR, Ctr Devices & Radiol Health, Md, as of 1998. **Mailing Address:** Ctr Devices & Radiol Health HFK-147, FDA 5600 Fishers Lane, Rockville, MD 20857.

JORGENSEN, CLIVE D, ENTOMOLOGY. **Personal Data:** b Orem, Utah, July 14, 1931; m 1955, c 3. **Education:** Brigham Young Univ, BS, 1954, MS, 1957; Ore State Univ, PhD (entom), 1964. **Professional Experience:** PROF EMER ZOOL, BRIGHAMYOUNG UNIV, as of 2002; chmn dept, brigham young univ, beginning 1974; prof zool, brigham young univ, beginning 1973; coordr biol instr, Brigham Young Univ, 1972-1974; NSF grant, asst profzool, Iowa State Univ, 1971-1972; USDA res grant, 1965-1967; from instr to assoc prof zool &entom, Brigham Young Univ, 1963-1973; US Atomic Energy Comn res grant, 1963-1966; fielddir ecol res, Brigham Young Univ, 1960-1963. **Memberships:** AAAS; Entom Soc Am; Am Soc Mammal. **Research Statement & Publications:** Ecological research. **Mailing Address:** 1155 E 140 N, Orem, UT 84601.

JORGENSEN, ERIK, ENVIRONMENTAL MANAGEMENT, FORESTRY. **Personal Data:** b Denmark, October 28, 1921; Canadian citizen; m 1946, c 2. **Education:** Royal Vet & Agr Col, Denmark, MF, 1946. **Professional Experience:** CONSULT PROF FORESTER, 1987-; dir & prof environ biol, Univ Guelph Arboretum, 1978-1986; chief urban forestry prog, Forest Mgt Inst, Can Forestry Serv, DeptEnviron, 1973-1978; prof forestry, Shade Tree Res Lab, Univ Toronto, 1967-1973; in chg lab, Shade Tree Res Lab, Univ Toronto, 1963-1972; assoc prof, Shade Tree Res Lab, Univ Toronto, 1963-1967; agr prof forest path, Univ Toronto, 1959-1963; res officer chg plantation dis, CanDept Agr, 1955-1959; amanuensis, col & proj leader, Forest Exp Sta, Royal Vet & Agr Col, Denmark, 1953-1955; asst forest path, Royal Vet & Agr Col, Denmark, 1949-1953. **Memberships:** Can Phytopath Soc; Arboricult Res & Educ Acad (pres 1976-1978). **Research Statement & Publications:** Urban forestry management and planning; environmental impact on/and by trees; tree diseases, physiology and breeding; arboriculture. **Mailing Address:** 507-172 Metcalfe St, Guelph, ON N1E 6J5, Can.

JORGENSEN, GEORGE NORMAN, BIOCHEMISTRY, VIROLOGY. **Personal Data:** b Omaha, Nebr, February 22, 1936; m Geraldine; c Lee (Deceased) & Emily. **Education:** Univ Nebr, BS, 1957; Univ Ill, MS, 1968, PhD (biochem), 1972. **Professional Experience:** RETIRED; res assoc, Univ Tex Med Sch Houston, Obstet Gynec, 1979-1980; res assoc biol, Rice Univ, 1977-1978; res assoc biochem virol, Baylor Col Med, 1972-1976; res asst radiation biol, M D Anderson Hosp & Tumor Inst, 1959-1966; Lab technician, Shell Chem Co, 1957-1958. **Memberships:** Am Chem Soc; AAAS; Sigma Xi. **Research Statement & Publications:** Studies of enzymes of snail metabolism such as urease, super oxide desmutase and mannitol oxidase concerned with comparative aspects of nitrogen metabolism and energy sources of snails; isolation and studies of hormone relaxin. **Mailing Address:** 8302 Greenbush St, Houston, TX 77025.

JORGENSEN, HELMUTH ERIK MILO, PHYSICAL CHEMISTRY. **Personal Data:** b Odense, Denmark, June 19, 1927; American citizen; m 1953, c 3. **Education:** Polytech Inst Brooklyn, BS, 1950; Rutgers Univ, PhD (phys chem), 1959. **Professional Experience:** PROF EMER, HUDSON VALLEY COMMUNITY COL, 1990-; adj prof, Hudson Valley Comm Unity Col, 1986-1990; from assoc prof to prof, Hudson Valley Community Col, 1969-1984; assoc res chemist, Sterling-Winthrop Res Inst, NY, 1960-1969; res chemist, Distillation Prod Industs, Eastman Kodak Co, 1958-1960; asst, Rutgers Univ, 1954-1958; develop chemist, Am Cyanamid Co, 1953-1954; res chemist, Schering Corp, 1952-1953; Develop chemist, Sterling-Winthrop Res Inst, 1950-1951. **Memberships:** Am Chem Soc. **Research Statement & Publications:** Physical chemistry of polymers and colloids; new methods of teaching chemistry. **Mailing Address:** Hudson Valley Community Col, 80 Vandenburgh Ave, Troy, NY 12180.

JORGENSEN, JAMES D, SOLID STATE PHYSICS. **Personal Data:** b Salina, Utah, March 23, 1948; m 1970, Ramona; c 6. **Education:** Brigham Young Univ, BS, 1970, PhD (physics), 1975. **Honors & Awards:** Warren Diffraction Physics Award, 1991; Barrett Award Powder Diffraction, 1997. **Professional Experience:** SR PHYSICIST, ARGONNE NAT LAB, 1990-; asst physicist to physicist, Argonne Nat Lab, 1977-1990; fel, Argonne Nat Lab, 1975-1977; mem, US Nat Comt Crystallog, Neutron Scattering Comn. **Memberships:** Fel Am Phys Soc; Am Crystallog Asn; Int Union Crystallog. **Research Statement & Publications:** Powder neutron diffraction at pulsed neutron sources; ternary superconductors; neutron diffraction at high pressure; oxide superconductors; colossal magnetoresistive materials; battery and fuel cell materials. **Mailing Address:** Mat Sci Div Argonne Nat Lab, Bldg 223, Argonne, IL 60439. **Fax:** 630-252-7777. **E-Mail:** jjorgensen@anl.gov

JORGENSEN, JAMES H, PATHOLOGY, MICROBIOLOGY. **Personal Data:** b Dallas, Tex, July 11, 1946; m 1978, Jane. **Education:** NTex State Univ, BA, 1969, MS, 1970; Univ Tex, PhD, 1973. **Honors & Awards:** Becton-Dickinson & Co Award Clin Microbiol, 1992. **Professional Experience:** CROSS-APP PROF, MICROBIOL & CLIN LAB SCI, HEALTH SCI CTR, as of 2004; chmn, Nat Comt Clin Lab Stand Subcomt Antimicrobiol Susceptibility Testing, beginning 1991; prof path, med, microbiol & clin lab sci, Health Sci Ctr, beginning 1984; dir clin microbiol labs, Univ Hosp, Univ Tex, beginning 1975; consult microbiologist, Audie Murphy Vet Admin Hosp, San Antonio, beginning 1973; from instr to assoc prof path & microbiol, Health Sci Ctr, 1973-1984; assoc dir, Bexar Co Hosp, 1973-1975; James W McLaughlin pre-doctoral fel, Infection & Immunity, Med Branch Univ Tex, 1971-1973; res assoc, Shriners Hosp Crippled C, 1970-1973. **Memberships:** fel Infectious Diseases Soc Am; fel Am Acad Microbiol; Am Soc Microbiol. **Research Statement**

& Publications: Rapid microbiology testing methods; anti-microbial susceptibility testing; Streptococcus pneumoniae and Haemophilus influenzae. **Mailing Address:** Dept Path, Univ Tex Health Sci Ctr, 7703 Floyd Curl Dr, San Antonio, TX 78229-3900. **Fax:** 210-567-2367. **E-Mail:** jorgensen@uthscsa.edu

JORGENSEN, JENS ERIK, MECHANICAL ENGINEERING, SYSTEMS ANALYSIS. **Personal Data:** b Oslo, Norway, July 2, 1936; American citizen; m 1962, c 2. **Education:** Mass Inst Technol, SB, 1959, MS, 1963, PhD, 1968, ScD (mech eng), 1969. **Honors & Awards:** Ralph Teetor Award, Soc Automotive Engrs, 1971; Bernard M Gordon Prize, Nat Acad Eng, 2006. **Professional Experience:** PROF EMER, MECH ENG, UNIV WASH, as of 2005; BOEING PROF MFG, UNIV WASH, 1987-; consult, Metro, 1981-1983 & Boeing Com Airlines, 1983-1985; prof, Mech Eng, Univ Wash, 1979-2005; consult, Weyerhaeuser Co, 1979-1981; assoc prof, Univ Wash, 1973-1979; consult, Pac Northwest Forest & Range Exp Sta, US Forest Serv, 1971-1977; consult, Wash Iron Works, 1969-1970; NIH fel Bioengineering, 1969; asst prof, Univ Wash, 1968-1973; instr, Mass Inst Technol, 1965-1968; res asst mech eng, Mass Inst Technol, 1963-1965; res engr, MHD Inc, Calif, 1962; res engr, Cadilac Gage Co, Calif, 1959-1961. **Memberships:** Am Soc Mech Engrs; Soc Mfg Engrs; Sigma Xi. **Research Statement & Publications:** Fluid power systems analysis; design and analysis of fluidic devices; control systems analysis; instrumentation design and performance analysis; design and control of large scale off road equipment for logging in national forests; manufacturing systems analysis and automation of manufacturing processes. **Mailing Address:** Dept Mech Eng, Univ Wash, Box 35260, Seattle, WA 98195-2600. **Fax:** 206-685-8047. **E-Mail:** jorgen@u.washington.edu

JORGENSEN, NEAL A, AGRICULTURAL ADMINISTRATION, DAIRY SCIENCE. **Personal Data:** b Luck, Wis, February 3, 1935; m 1955, c 1. **Education:** Univ Wis-River Falls, BS, 1960; Univ Wis-Madison, MS, 1962, PhD (dairy sci), 1964. **Professional Experience:** FROM EXEC ASSOC DEAN & DIR TO EMER PROF DAIRY SCI, COL AGR & LIFE SCI, UNIV WIS-MADISON, 1991-; mem, Bd Agr, 1990-; exec dir, Col Agr & Life Sci, UnivWis-Madison, 1990-1991; chmn, animal systs subcomt, exp sta comt orgn & policy, beginning 1989; assoc dean, Col Agr & Life Sci, Univ Wis-Madison, 1984-1991; assoc dir, Col Agr & Life Sci, Univ Wis-Madison, 1984-1989; asst dir, Col Agr & Life Sci, Univ Wis-Madison, 1984; Mem, Comt Animal Nutrit, Nat Res Coun, 1981-1988; from asst prof to prof diary sci, Col Agr & LifeSci, Univ Wis-Madison, 1968-1984. **Memberships:** Am Dairy Sci Asn (pres 1990-1991); Am Soc Animal Sci. **Research Statement & Publications:** Agricultural administration; dairy cattle nutrition and management; preservation and utilization of forage crops; fiber requirements, amount, source, physical form; vitamin D and calcium metabolism. **Mailing Address:** Univ Wis Found, 1848 Univ Ave PO Box 8860, Madison, WI 53708-8860. **Fax:** 608-263-0781. **E-Mail:** nealj@uwfound.wisc.edu

JORGENSEN, PALLE E T, OPERATOR ALGEBRAS, MATHEMATICAL PHYSICS. **Personal Data:** b Copenhagen, Denmark, October 8, 1947; American citizen; m 1975, Soon; c Anton, Greta & Tina. **Education:** Univ Aarhus, Denmark, AB, 1968, MS, 1970, PhD (math), 1973. Postdocs & teaching positions at the Univ Pennsylvania, & at Stanford Univ. **Professional Experience:** Ed, Am Math Soc, 1988-; speaker, US-Japan Operator Algebra Conf, Philadelphia, 1988; PROF MATH, UNIV IOWA, 1983-; ed, D Reidel Publ Co, 1982-; vis assoc prof, Univ Pa, 1982-1984; assoc prof, Aarhus, 1979-1982; asst prof, Stanford Univ, 1977-1980; Res fel, Danish Res Coun, 1976-1977 & NSF, 1977-; Fel math, Univ Wash, 1973-1974 & Univ Pa, 1974-1977. Recent books: Wavelets through a looking glass (with Bratteli), Birkhauser (2002). And: Analysis and Probability: wavelets, signals, fractals; Springer, GTM vol 234 (2006). **Memberships:** Danish Acad Sci; Am Math Soc; Danish Math Soc; Soc Indust & Appl Math; fel Royal Swed Acad Sci; NY Acad Sci. **Research Statement & Publications:** My research is on the interface of applied harmonic analysis and signal processing: wavelets. **Mailing Address:** Dept Math, Univ Iowa, MacLean Hall, Iowa City, IA 52242. **Fax:** 319-335-0627. **E-Mail:** jorgen@math.uiowa.edu

JORGENSEN, PAUL J, MATERIALS SCIENCE, CHEMISTRY. **Personal Data:** b Midway, Utah, September 1, 1930; m 1959, Ardelle; c Paula, Mark, Janet, LaDell, Brett & Scott. **Education:** Brigham Young Univ, BS, 1954; Univ Utah, PhD (mat sci), 1960. **Honors & Awards:** I R 100 Award, 1967. **Professional Experience:** EXEC VPRES, SRI INT, 1994-; mem, Int Panel Adv Technol, Singapore Inst Stand & Indust Res, 1990-1994; mem, David Sarnoff Res Ctr, 1988-1994; exec vpres & chief operating officer, Mat Res Ctr, 1988-1994; mem, adv coun, Kansai Res Inst, 1987-1993; mem, Devco, 1987-1993; mem, Plant Cell Res Inst, 1987-1991; mem, SRI Int, 1986-; mem, bd dirs, Mirage Systs, 1984-; chmn, Adv Coun, Col Eng, Univ Utah, 1983-1984; mem, Comt High Temp Chem, Nat Res Coun-Nat Acad Sci, 1971-1974 & Nat Mat Adv Bd, 1981-1984; sr vpres sci group, Mat Res Ctr, 1980-1988; vpres phys & life sci, Mat Res Ctr, 1977-1980; exec dir phys sci, Mat Res Ctr, 1976-1977; dir, Mat Res Ctr, 1974-1976; consult, GTE Sylvania, Inc, 1971-; lectr, Univ Calif, Berkeley, 1969-1970; chmn, Ceramics Dept, Stanford Res Inst, 1968-1974; Ceramist, Gen Elec Res Lab, 1960-1968. **Memberships:** Fel Am Ceramic Soc; AAAS; Sigma Xi; Am Electronics Asn; Am Mgt Asn. **Research Statement & Publications:** Kinetics of transport processes in ceramics, including sintering, solute segregation, grain growth, diffusion, electrical conductivity, oxidation, corrosion and permeation. **Mailing Address:** SRI Int, 333 Ravenswood Ave, Menlo Park, CA 94025-3493. **Fax:** 650-326-5512.

JORGENSEN, T, MOLECULAR PHYSICS. **Personal Data:** b Long Ridge, Conn, November 13, 1905. **Education:** Univ Nebr, BS, 1929, MS, 1931; Harvard Univ, PhD (physics), 1935. **Professional Experience:** RETIRED; fac mem, Dept Physics, Univ Nebr, 1934-1975. **Memberships:** Am Phys Soc. **Mailing Address:** 4932 High St, Lincoln, NE 68506.

JORGENSEN, WILLIAM L, ORGANIC CHEMISTRY, THEORETICAL CHEMISTRY. **Personal Data:** b New York, NY, October 5, 1949. **Education:** Princeton Univ, AB, 1970; Harvard Univ, PhD (chem physics), 1975. **Honors & Awards:** Ann Medal, Int Acad Quantum Molecular Sci, 1986; Arthur C Cope Scholar Award 1990; Am Chem Soc Award Comput Chem & Pharmaceut Res, 1998. **Professional Experience:** C P WHITEHEAD PROF CHEM, YALE UNIV, 1990-; A C Cope scholar, 1990; H C Brown prof chem, Purdue Univ, 1985-1990; A P Sloan Found fel, 1979-1981; Dreyfusteacher-scholar, Camille & Henry Dreyfus Found Inc, 1978-1983; from asst prof to prof orgchem, Purdue Univ, 1975-1990. **Memberships:** Int Soc Quantum Biol & Pharmacol (vpres, 2000; pres, 2001); Conn Acad Arts &Sci; Am Chem Soc; AAAS. **Research Statement & Publications:** Theoretical organic chemistry; computer simulations of molecular liquids and solutions; computer assisted synthetic analysis. **Mailing Address:** Dept Chem, Yale Univ, PO Box 208107, New Haven, CT 06520-8118. **E-Mail:** william.jorgensen@yale.edu

JORGENSON, EDSEL CARPENTER, zoology, nematology; deceased, see previous edition for last biography

JORGENSON, GORDON VICTOR, THIN FILMS. **Personal Data:** b Sunburg, Minn, January 3, 1933; m 1957, c 2. **Education:** St Olaf Col, BA, 1954. **Professional Experience:** SECT CHIEF, HONEYWELL INC, 1991-; res staff scientist, Honeywell Inc, 1984-1990; sr prin res scientist, Honeywell Inc, 1980-1984; prin res scientist, Honeywell Inc, 1978-1979; sr physicist, Midwest Res Inst, 1975-1978; sr physicist, NStar Res & Develop Inst, 1966-1975; sr scientist, Appl Sci Div, Litton Indust, Inc, 1963-1966; sr scientist, Gen Mills, Inc, 1961-1963; assoc scientist, Gen Mills, Inc, 1957-1961; prin lab attendant, Univ Minn, 1956-1957; Physicist, Wright Air Develop Ctr, Wright-Patterson AFB, 1954-1955. **Memberships:** Soc Photo-Optical Instrumentation Engrs; Am Vacuum Soc. **Research Statement & Publications:** Surface physics research utilizing sputtering; effects of solar-wind bombardment of bodies in space; electrohydrodynamics; research in vacuum deposited thin films; optical coating technology. **Mailing Address:** 14609 Summit Oaks Dr, Burnsville, MN 55337.

JORGENSON, JAMES WALLACE, CHROMATOGRAPHY, ELECTROPHORESIS. **Personal Data:** b Kenosha, Wis, September 9, 1952; m 1978. **Education:** Northern Ill Univ, BS, 1974; Ind Univ, PhD (chem), 1979. **Professional Experience:** CHMN & W R KENAN JR PROF, DEPT CHEM, UNIV NC, as of 2004; from prof chem to dept chmn & fp venable prof chem, Univ Nc, chapel hill, beginning 1987; from asst prof to assoc prof, Univ NC, Chapel Hill, 1979-1987. **Memberships:** Am Chem Soc; AAAS. **Research Statement & Publications:** Chemical separations; fundamental studies of gas chromatography; liquid chromatography and electrophoresis. **Mailing Address:** Dept Chem, Univ NC, PO Box 3290, Venable & Kenan Lab, Chapel Hill, NC 27599-3290. **Fax:** 919-962-2388. **E-Mail:** jj@unc.edu

JORIZZO, JOSEPH L, IMMUNODERMATOLOGY, NEUTROPHILS & IMMUNE COMPLEX REACTIONS IN THE SKIN. **Personal Data:** b Rochester, NY, October 6, 1951; c 1. **Education:** Boston Univ, AB, 1972, MD, 1975; Am Bd Dermat, 1979. **Honors & Awards:** Royal Soc Med Trust Lectureship, UK, 1994. **Professional Experience:** DIR DERMAT RESIDENCY PROG, BOWMAN GRAY SCH MED, WAKE FOREST UNIV, WINSTON-SALEM, NC, 1987-; PROF & CHAIR, DEPT DERMAT, BOWMAN GRAY SCH MED, WAKE FOREST UNIV, WINSTON-SALEM, NC, 1986-; CONSULT, VET ADMIN CLIN, WINSTON -SALEM, NC, 1986-; from asst prof to assoc prof, Dept Dermat, Univ Tex Med Br, Galveston, 1980-1986; clin asst prof, Dept Dermat, Univ Tex Med Br, Galveston, 1979-1980; chief resident, NC Mem Hosp, 1978-1979; resident dermat, NC MemHosp, 1976-1978; Intern internal med, NC Mem Hosp, 1975-1976. **Memberships:** Soc Invest Dermat; Am Acad Dermat (vpres-elect 2002); Am Dermat Asn; fel AmColPhysicians; AMA; Int Soc Trop Dermat; Asn Profs Dermat. **Research Statement & Publications:** Histamine induced localized vasculitis in patients with reactive vascular dermatoses; circulating immune complex-mediated aspects of secondary syphilis; dermatologic aspects of circulating immune complexes; dermatologic aspects of rheumatoid arthritis; histamine related mediators of inflammation; immunologic investigations in Behcet's disease and bowel disease; immune enhancers, prostaglandin synthesis blockers; collagen vascular diseases-experimental therapies for cutaneous aspects. **Mailing Address:** Dept Dermat, Bowman Gray Sch Med, Wake forest Univ, Med Ctr Blvd, Winston-Salem, NC 27157-0001. **Fax:** 336-716-7732.

JORNE, JACOB, ELECTROCHEMISTRY, MICROELECTRONICS PROCESSING. **Personal Data:** b Tel Aviv, Israel, July 24, 1941; American citizen; m 1985, Judith; c Ariel, Eli & Alexander. **Education:** Technion Israel Inst Technol, BS, 1963, MS, 1967; Univ Calif, Berkeley, PhD (chem eng), 1972. **Honors & Awards:** Battery Res Award, Electrochem Soc, 1989, Carl Wagner Mem Award, 1993. **Professional Experience:** Adj prof, Wayne StateUniv, 1984-; PROF CHEM ENG, UNIV ROCHESTER, 1982-; CONSULT, 1972-; from asst prof to prof, Wayne State Univ, 1972-1982; res asst chem eng, Lawrence Berkeley Lab, 1967-1972; CEO, CUPRICON INC. **Memberships:** Electrochem Soc; Am Inst Chem Engrs. **Mailing Address:** Dept Chem Eng Univ Rochester, 206 Gavett Hall, Rochester, NY 14627-0166. **Fax:** 585-442-6686. **E-Mail:** jorne@che.rochester.edu

JORNS, MARILYN SCHUMAN, ENZYMOLOGY. **Personal Data:** b New York, NY, August 24, 1943; m 1971. **Education:** State Univ NY Binghamton, BA, 1965; Univ Mich, MS, 1967, PhD (biochem), 1970. **Honors & Awards:** Linus Pauling Award, 1987. **Professional Experience:** PROF BIOCHEM, DREXEL UNIV, 1998-; prof biochem, Allegheny Univ, 1993-1998; dir, Molecular Biol & Biotechnol Grad Prog, 1991-1995; prof biochem, Hahnemann Univ Sch Med, 1987-1993; assoc prof biochem, Hahnemann Univ Sch Med, 1982-1987; asst prof chem, Ohio State Univ, 1975-1982; res assoc biochem, Univ Tex Health SciCtr Dallas, 1972-1975; Am Cancer Soc fel chem, Univ Konstanz, 1970-1972. **Memberships:** AAAS; Am Soc Photobiol; Am Chem Soc; Am Soc Biol Chemists. **Research Statement & Publications:** Mechanism of catalysis by flavoproteins. **Mailing Address:** Dept Biochem, Drexel Univ, Philadelphia, PA 19102. **Fax:** 215-762-4452. **E-Mail:** marilyn.jorns@drexel.edu

JORSTAD, JOHN LEONARD, METALLURGY. **Personal Data:** b Richmond, Va, September 17, 1935; c 3. **Honors & Awards:** Achievement Award, NAm Die Casters Asn, 1987; Award of Sci Merit, Am Foundrymen's Soc, 1990; Nyselius Award NADCA, 2002. **Professional Experience:** PRES, JLJ TECHNOLOGIES INC, as of 2004; mem, Tech Coun, Nam Die Casters Asn, 1991-; chmn, Cast Metals Coun, SocMfg Engrs, 1978-1981 & Tech Coun, Am Foundrymen's Soc, 1990-1992; mgr ingot & foundry technol, Reynolds Metals Co, 1985-1993; dept mgr, Prod Develop Lab, 1981-1985; develop engr, Prod Develop Lab, 1968-1981; res scientist, Metall Lab, ReynoldsMetals Co, 1965-1968; technician, Metall Lab, Reynolds Metals Co, 1957-1965. **Memberships:** Fel Am Soc Metals Int; Am Foundrymen's Soc; NAm Die Casters Asn; Soc MfgEngrs; Soc Automotive Engrs; Am Soc Testing & Mat. **Research Statement & Publications:** Aluminum casting alloys; casting processes and processing parameters; casting applications for automotive use, especially engines. **Mailing Address:** JLJ Technologies Inc, Richmond, VA 23229. **E-Mail:** jjorstad@aol.com

JORTNER, JOSHUA, PHYSICAL CHEMISTRY. **Personal Data:** b Poland, March 14, 1933; m 1960, Ruth Sanger; c 2. **Education:** Hebrew Univ Jerusalem, PhD. **Honors & Awards:** Joseph O. Hirschfelder Prize Theoretical Chemistry, 1997; Dedication XVIISymposium Molecular Beams, Univ Paris, Orsay, France, 1997; August Wilhelm von HofmannMedal, 1995; Festschrift Journal Phys Chem, 1994; Hon J. Heyrovsky Medal, 1993; Commemorative Issue Israel Journal Chem The Wolf Prize, 1989; Wolf Prize in Chemistry, 1988; Israel Prize in Exact Sci, 1982; Kolthof Prize, 1976; Rothschild Prize, 1976; Weizmann Prize, 1973; InterNat Academy of Quantum Sci Award, 1972. **Professional Experience:** Vis prof chem, UnivCopenhagen, 1978; Univ Calif, Los Angeles & Berkeley, 1975; vis prof, H COrsted Inst, Univ Copenhagen, 1974; Heinemann Prof Chem, Tel Aviv Univ, beginning 1973; vpres, Inst Chem, Tel Aviv Univ, 1970-1972; from prof to PROF EMER, TEL AVIV UNIV, beginning 1966; head, Inst Chem, Tel Aviv Univ, 1966-1972; dep rector, Inst Chem, Tel AvivUniv, 1966-1969; assoc prof, Tel Aviv Univ, 1965-1966; sr lectr, Dept Phys Chem, Hebrew Univ Jerusalem, 1963-1965; res assoc, Univ Chicago, 1962-1964; instr, Dept Phys Chem, Hebrew Univ Jerusalem, 1961-1962. **Memberships:** Foreign mem Learned Soc Czech Republic; 1998 foreign memRoyal Netherlands Acad Arts & Sci; foreign assoc NatAcad Sci USA; DeutscheAkademie der Naturforscher Leopoldina; foreign fel Indian Nat SciAcademy; Russian Acad Sci; Academia Scientiarum et Artium

Europaea; hon mem RomanianAcademy of Sci; Polish Academy Sci; foreign hon mem Am Acad Arts & Sci; memRoyal Danish Academy of Sci and Letters; foreign mem of theAm Philosophical Soc; Inter AcadQuantum Molecular Sci; Israel Nat Acad Sci & Humanities. **Research Statement & Publications:** Intramolecular radiationless transitions. **Mailing Address:** Sch Chem, Tel Aviv Univ, Bldg Omstein, Tel Aviv, 69978, Israel. **Fax:** 972-364-15054. **E-Mail:** jortner@chemsg1.tau.ac.il

JORY, FARNHAM STEWART, physics; deceased, see previous edition for last biography

JORY, HOWARD ROBERTS, MICROWAVE ELECTRON TUBES, ELECTRON ACCELERATOR SYSTEMS FOR CANCER THERAPY. **Personal Data:** b Berkeley, Calif, December 8, 1931; m 1957, Carol; c Kevin, Craig & Thomas. **Education:** Univ Calif, Berkeley, BS, 1954, MS, 1955, PhD (elec eng), 1960. **Professional Experience:** STAFF SCIENTIST, COMMUNIUCATIONS & POWER INDUST, 1995-, chmn, Subcomt Electron Tubes, Inst Elec & Electronics Engrs, 1983; develop mgr, Varian Assocs, 1976-1995; Consult, High Power Microwave Study Panel, Naval Res Lab, 1976; eng mgr, Varian Assocs, 1972-1976; res & develop engr, Varian Assocs, 1962-1972; officer, US Army Electronics Res & Develop Lab, 1960-1962. **Memberships:** Fel Inst Elec & Electronics Engrs; Sigma Xi. **Research Statement & Publications:** Commercial gyrotrons; high power millimeter wave generators used in magnetic fusion laboratories. **Mailing Address:** Communication & Power Ind, M/S B-450, Po Box 50750, Palo Alto, CA 94303.

JOSE, JORGE V, PHYSICS. **Personal Data:** b Mexico City, Mex, September 13, 1949; c 3. **Education:** Nat Univ Mex, BS, 1971, MS, 1973, PhD (physics), 1976. **Honors & Awards:** Manuel Sandoval Vallarta Award, Univ Metropolitana Mexico, 2004. **Professional Experience:** Mem, eng dean eval comt, 2004; MATTHEWS DISTINGUISHED UNIV PROF, DEPT PHYSICS, NORTHEASTERN UNIV, as of 2003; Mem, sel comt, Am Phys soc, 2002-2004; mem provost search Comt, 2002; DIR, CTR INTERDISCIPLINARY RES COMPLEX SYSTS, NORTHEASTERN UNIV, 1995-; prof physics, Northeastern Univ, beginning 1988; vis scientist, Schlumberger, Dallas, 1984; vis scientist, Inst Physics, Mex, 1984; consult, Exxon ResEng, 1982; vis prof, Inst Physics, Mex, 1981 & 1985; from asst prof to assoc prof, NortheasternUniv, 1980-1988; asst prof res, Rutgers Univ, 1979-1980; guest scholar, Kyoto Univ, Japan, 1979; James Franck fel physics, Univ Chicago, 1977-1979; asst prof res, Brown Univ, 1976-1977; res assoc physics, Brown Univ, 1974-1976; res assoc physics, Nat univ, 1972-1974. **Memberships:** Am Phys Soc; AAAS; Mex Physics Soc. **Research Statement & Publications:** Theoretical condensed matter physics; Classical solutions of an electron in magnetized wedge billiards; Entrainment Arnold tongues and duality in a periodically driven integtate and fire model; published over 100 articles. **Mailing Address:** Dept Physics Northeastern Univ, Boston, MA 02115. **E-Mail:** jjv@neu.edu

JOSE, PEDRO A, PEDIATRIC NEPHROLOGY. **Personal Data:** b Dingras, Ilocos Norte, Philippines, December 6, 1942; American citizen; m 1969, Nora; c Kristina M & Maria E. **Education:** Univ Santo Tomas, MD, 1965; Georgetown Univ, PhD (physiol), 1976. **Honors & Awards:** William Peck Mem Award, Resin Kidney Dis, Interstate Postgrad Med Soc, 1972; Apolinario Mabinin Award, Asn Philippine Physicians Am, 1990. **Professional Experience:** ASSOC DIR & VCHMN PEDIAT, GEORGR TOWN UNIV, as of 2006; PROF PEDIAT, GEORGETOWN UNIV, 1983-. **Memberships:** Soc Pediat Res; Am Fedn Clin Res; Am Soc Nephrology; Am Soc Pediat Nephrology; Am Soc Pediatr nephrol, (pres, 1990-1991); fel Am Heart Asn. **Research Statement & Publications:** Role of dopamine and adrenergic receptors on sodium transport in specific nephron segments during development in normotensive and spontaneously hypertensive rat; and in human essential hypertension. **Mailing Address:** Pasquerilla Healthcare Ctr, Georgetown Univ Hosp, F2004, Washington, DC 20057-0001. **Fax:** 202-687-7161. **E-Mail:** pjose01@georgetown.edu

JOSEFSON, CLARENCE MARTIN, CHEMICAL EDUCATION, COMPUTATIONAL CHEMISTRY. **Personal Data:** b Chicago, Ill, April 11, 1943; m 1966, Carol; c Rebecca, James & Jennifer. **Education:** Univ Ill, Urbana, BS, 1965; Southern Ill Univ, Carbondale, PhD (phys chem), 1973. **Professional Experience:** CHMN, MILLIKIN UNIV, 1991-; vis res scientist pharmacol, Univ Gothenburg, Sweden, 1988; Vis asst prof, Inst Environ Studies, Univ Ill, 1980-1981; PROF CHEM, MILLIKIN UNIV, 1973-. **Memberships:** Am Chem Soc; AAAS. **Research Statement & Publications:** Developing project-based laboratories for undergraduate chemistry; computational chemistry of psycoactive drugs; adsorption of trace organic compounds onto polymers. **Mailing Address:** Dept Chem, Millikin Univ, Decatur, IL 62522. **Fax:** 217-424-3993. **E-Mail:** cjosefson@mail.millikin.edu

JOSELYN, JO ANN CRAM, SOLAR PHYSICS, SPACE PHYSICS. **Personal Data:** b St Francis, Kans, October 5, 1943. **Education:** Univ Colo, BS, 1965, MS, 1967, PhD (astrogeophys), 1978. **Professional Experience:** SECY, GEN INTL UNION GEODESY & GEOPHYS, 1999-; US deleg, Study Group Six, Consult Comt Ionospheric Radio, 1981 & 1983; Physicist, solar & Geomagnetic Forecasting, Space Environ Servs Ctr, Space Environ Lab, 1978-1999; physicist res solar wind, NatOceanic & Atmospheric Admin, 1976-1978; physicist res magnetospheric physics, Nat Oceanic & Atmospheric Admin, 1975-1976; physicist res ionospheric physics, Nat Oceanic & Atmospheric Admin, 1968-1975; Space Scientist, Nat Oceanic & Atmospheric Admin, 1967-1999. **Memberships:** Am Geophys Union; Union Radio Scientists Int; AAAS; Sigma Xi; Am Inst Aeronaut & Astronaut. **Research Statement & Publications:** Astro geophysics, especially solar physics and solar wind physics; also solar-terrestrial relationships, especially geomagnetism. **Mailing Address:** NOAA Space Environ Ctr, 325 Broadway, Boulder, CO 80303-3328. **Fax:** 303-497-3645. **E-Mail:** jjoselyn@sel.noaa.gov

JOSENHANS, JAMES GROSS, SOLID STATE ELECTRONICS. **Personal Data:** b Toledo, Ohio, December 19, 1932; m 1961, c 2. **Education:** Univ Toledo, BSc, 1956; Ohio State Univ, MSc, 1958, PhD (elec eng), 1962. **Professional Experience:** MEM TECH STAFF, BELL TEL LAB, 1963-; asst prof elec eng, ElectronDevice Lab, Ohio State Univ, 1962-1963; from res asst to res assoc, Electron Device Lab, OhioState Univ, 1957-1962; teaching asst physics, Univ Toledo, 1953-1956; Engr, StorerBroadcasting Co, Ohio, 1951-1953. **Memberships:** Am Phys Soc; Inst Elec & Electronics Engrs; Sigma Xi; Am Acoust Soc; AudioEngr Soc. **Research Statement & Publications:** Silicon integrated circuit development strategies to satisfy projected telephone systems needs. **Mailing Address:** 397 Diamond Hill Rd, Berkeley Heights, NJ 07922.

JOSEPH, ALFRED S, PHYSICS. **Personal Data:** b Cortland, NY, June 27, 1932; m 1956, c 2. **Education:** Union Col, NY, BS, 1956; Case Inst Technol, MS, 1960, PhD (physics), 1962. **Professional Experience:** RETIRED; sr eng exec technol appln, Autonetics, 1977-1980; sr tech adv, Autonetics, 1976-1977; dir solid state electronics, Sci Ctr, 1972-1976; group leader, Sci Ctr, 1968-1972; mem tech staff, Atomics Int Div, Corp Eng, Rockwell Int, 1962-1968; sr physicist, Atomics Int Div, Corp Eng, Rockwell Int, 1962; consult, Gen Elec Co, Ohio, 1959-1961; instr, Case Inst Technol, 1958-1962. **Memberships:** Am Phys Soc. **Research Statement & Publications:** Studies of the electronic properties of metals through the de Haas van Alphen effect; superconducting phenomena; semiconductors and semiconductor devices. **Mailing Address:** 688 Laguna Dr, Simi Valley, CA 93065.

JOSEPH, BERNARD WILLIAM, VEHICLE EMISSION. **Personal Data:** b Detroit, Mich, June 7, 1929. **Education:** Wayne State Univ, BA (Math), 1968. **Honors & Awards:** Arch T Colwell Award, Soc Automotive Engrs, 1974. **Professional Experience:** RETIRED; sr develop engr, eng staff, 1980-1986; assoc sr res physicist, Res Labs, Gen Motors Corp, 1951-1980. **Memberships:** corp mem, NY Acad Sci. **Research Statement & Publications:** Optical properties of materials, optical design, radiometry, photometry and photochemistry; exhaust emision measurement; optical engineering. **Mailing Address:** 37239 Glenbrook Dr, Clinton Township, MI 48036. **E-Mail:** kblix@arrl.net

JOSEPH, DANIEL D, MECHANICAL ENGINEERING, FLUID MECHANICS RHEOLOGY. **Personal Data:** b Chicago, Ill, March 26, 1929; m 1990, Kay Jaglo; c 3. **Education:** Univ Chicago, MA, 1950; Ill Inst Technol, BS, 1959, MS, 1960, PhD (mech eng), 1963. **Honors & Awards:** GI Taylor Medal, Soc Eng Sci, 1990; Bingham Medal, Soc Rheology, 1990; Timashenko Medal, Am Soc Mech Engrs, 1995; Thomas Baron Fluid Particle Syst Award, Am Inst Chem Engrs, 1996. **Professional Experience:** REGENTS' PROF, UNIV MINN, 1994-; Guggenheim fel, 1969 & 1970; PROF AEROSPACE ENG & MECH, UNIV MINN, 1968-; from asst prof to assoc prof fluid mech, Univ Minn, 1963-1968; asst prof, Univ Minn, 1962-1963; Asst mech eng, Ill Inst Technol, 1959-1962; assoc ed seven journals. **Memberships:** Nat Acad Sci; Nat Acad Eng; Soc Natural Philol; Am Soc Mech Engrs; Am Phys Soc; Am Acad Arts & Sci. **Research Statement & Publications:** Fluid mechanics, flow through porous media and hydrodynamic stability; applied mathematics; theory of hydrodynamic stability and bifurcation theory; rheology of viscoelastic fluids; multi-phase flow. **Mailing Address:** Dept Mech & Aerospace Eng, Univ Minn, Minneapolis, MN 55455. **Fax:** 612-626-1558. **E-Mail:** joseph@aem.umn.edu

JOSEPH, DAVID WINRAM, ELEMENTARY PARTICLE PHYSICS. **Personal Data:** b Evanston, Ill, June 28, 1930; m 1960, c 3. **Education:** Roosevelt Col, BS, 1952; Univ Chicago, MS, 1957, PhD (elem particle physics), 1959. **Professional Experience:** RETIRED; prof emer physics, Univ Nebr-Lincoln, beginning 1968; from asst prof to assoc prof, Univ Nebr-lincoln, 1963-1968; res assoc, US Naval Res Lab, Wash, DC, 1961-1963; res assoc physics, Purdue Univ, 1959-1961; physicist, Ballistic Res Labs, Aberdeen Proving Ground, Md, 1953-1955. **Memberships:** Fel Am Phys Soc. **Research Statement & Publications:** Group and algebraic methods. **Mailing Address:** Univ NE, 128 501 Bldg, Lincoln, NE 68588-0244. **Fax:** 402-472-6803. **E-Mail:** djoseph1@unl.edu

JOSEPH, DONALD J, OTOLARYNGOLOGY. **Personal Data:** b Summerfield, Ill, September 24, 1922; m 1945, Margaret; c Thomas D & Doris McGuire. **Education:** St Louis Univ, MD, 1946; Baylor Univ, MS, 1953. **Honors & Awards:** Bronze Star Medal, 1957; Legion of Merit, 1968. **Professional Experience:** Prof surg, Univ Mo, Sch Med, Columbia, 1971-1985; prof emer, 1985; CHIEF OTOLARYNGOL, UNIV MO, SCH MED, COLUMBIA, 1967-; Assoc prof, Univ MO, Sch Med, Columbia, 1967-1971; communicative sci study sect, NIH, 1962-1964; mem comt hearing & bioacoust, Nat Res Coun, 1961-1967; Consult, US Army Surgeon Gen, 1961-1964. **Memberships:** Fel Am Acad Ophthal & Otolaryngol; fel Am Col Surg; fel Am Laryngol, Rhinol & Otol Soc. **Research Statement & Publications:** Communicative sciences; audiology; speech pathology. **Mailing Address:** 1026 Merrill Dr Box 159, Lebanon, IL 62254-0159.

JOSEPH, EARL CLARK, II, STRATEGIC MANAGEMENT. **Personal Data:** b St Paul, Minn, March 2, 1956; m 1974, Holly. **Education:** Univ Minn, BS, 1978, PhD (strategic mgt), 1983. **Professional Experience:** RES VPRES, IDC, HIGH PERFORMANCE SYST, as of 2004; dir competitive anal & snz prod mgr, Cray Res, beginning 1995; dir strategic planning, Concurrent Comput Corp, 1992-1995; mkt req & res, Cray Res Inc, 1988-1992; prog mgt, Unisys, 1986-1988; financial planner, Sperry-Univac, 1984-1985; vis lectr, Metro Univ, Minn, 1983 & AT&T MgtTraining Ctr, Mankato Univ & St Thomas Col, 1985; systs planner, Sperry-Univac, 1983-1984. **Research Statement & Publications:** The development and application of strategic management tools for use in exploring the potential future of products proposed for research and currently being developed; future product planning for computer systems of all types. **Mailing Address:** Idc Res, 365 Summit Ave, St Paul, MN 55102. **E-Mail:** ejospeph@idc.com

JOSEPH, J WALTER, JR, MECHANICAL ENGINEERING. **Personal Data:** b Oak Park, Ill, October 8, 1928; m 1953, c 2. **Education:** NC State Col, BS, 1950; Pa State Univ, MS, 1954. **Professional Experience:** SAVANNAH RIVER PLANT, E I DU PONT DEL NEMOURS & CO, INC, 1985-; supt, Equip Engr Dept, supt, Site Quality Dept, 1983-1985; supt, LStartup Proj Team, 1980-1983; supt, Traffic & Transp Dept, 1978-1980; chief supvr, Reactor Tech Dept, 1976-1978; asst chief supvr, Reactor Tech Dept, 1971-1976; mech engr, Reactor Tech Dept, 1965-1971; mech engr, Savannah River Lab, E I Du Pont Del Nemours & Co Inc, 1954-1965; thermal res lab, Pa State Univ, 1953-1954; Asst eng res, Pa State Univ, 1950-1951. **Research Statement & Publications:** Participatve leadership nuclear reactor project management; mechanical and welding development supporting nuclear operations; remote equipment, nuclear waste management; isotopic heat sources; shipping containers; resistance welding; high pressure gas technology. **Mailing Address:** 340 Cherbourg Pl, Aiken, SC 29801.

JOSEPH, JAMES, MARINE BIOLOGY. **Personal Data:** b Los Angeles, Calif, October 28, 1930; m 1958, Patricia; c Michael & Jerry. **Education:** Humboldt State Col, BS, 1956, MS, 1958; Univ Wash, PhD, 1966. **Honorary Degrees:** Dr (Hon) Causa, Univ Bretagne Occidental, France. **Honors & Awards:** Nautilus Award, Marine Technol Soc; Dave Wallace Award, Nautilus Press; Roger Revelle Perpetual Award Marine Sci. **Professional Experience:** CONSULT, FOOD & AGRI ORGN UN, LA JOLLA, as of 2003; dir invest, Scripps Inst Oceanog, as of 1999; affil prof, Univ Wash, beginning 1969; res assoc, Inst Marine Res, Scripps Inst Oceanog, beginning 1969; res assoc, Inst Marine Ins, Scripps Inst Oceanog, beginning 1969; dir, Inter-Am Trop Tuna Comn, 1969; prin scientist, Inter-Am Trop Tuna Comn, 1964-1969; scientist, Inter-Am Trop Tuna Comn, 1958-1963. **Memberships:** Am Inst Fishery Res Biol; Sigma Xi. **Research Statement & Publications:** Dynamics of the stocks of marine fishes and mammals and effects of man's exploitation of them; development of international arrangements for the conservation of living marine resources. **Mailing Address:** IATTC, Scripps Inst Oceanog 8604 La Jolla Shores Dr, La Jolla, CA 92037-1508. **Fax:** 619-546-7133.

JOSEPH, JEYMOHAN, NEUROIMMUNOLOGY, ENDOTHELIAL CELL BIOLOGY. **Personal Data:** b Jodhpur, India, January 20, 1953; m 1987, c 1. **Education:** Univ Wis-Madison, PhD (immunol), 1983. **Professional Experience:** CHIEF, HIV NEUROVIROL, GENETICS & MOLECULAR THERAPEUT PROG, CTR MENT HEALTH RES AIDS, as of 2004; ASST PROF NEUROIMMUNOL, THOMAS JEFFERSON UNIV, 1989-; instr, Thomas Jefferson Univ, 1987-1989; res assoc neuroimmunol, Thomas Jefferson Univ, 1985-1987; res assoconcol, Wis Clin Cancer Ctr, 1983-1985. **Memberships:** Int Soc Neuroimmunol; Am Asn Immunologists; AAAS; NY Acad Sci. **Research Statement &

Publications: Role of endothelial cells in immune and inflammatory events following virus infection. **Mailing Address:** Ctr Ment Health Res, Nat Inst Ment Health, Rm 6202, MSC 9619, 6001 Exec Blvd, Bethesda, MD 20892-9619. **Fax:** 301-443-9719. **E-Mail:** jjeymoha@mail.nih.gov

JOSEPH, JOHN MUNDANCHERIL, CHROMATOGRAPHY, SPECTROSCOPY. **Personal Data:** b Kerala, India, February 21, 1947; American citizen; m 1981, c 3. **Education:** Kerala Univ, India, BS, 1968; Univ Jabalpur, India, MS, 1971; Drexel Univ, Philadelphia, MS & PhD (biochem), 1980. **Professional Experience:** GROUP LEADER ANALYTICAL CHEM & DOSAGE FORM ANALYSIS, BRISTOL-MYERS SQUIBB PHARMACEUT RES INST, 1981-; Fel biochem, Drexel Univ, Philadelphia, 1975-1981; teaching & res asst biochem, Drexel Univ, Philadelphia, 1975-1980; Midvale Heppenstal, Philadelphia, 1973-1975; chemist, McDowell Distillery, Kerala, 1971-1973; Lectr chem, Kerala Univ, India, 1968-1969. **Memberships:** Sigma Xi; Am Asn Pharmaceut Scientists; Am Chem Soc. **Research Statement & Publications:** Examination of the stereochemical requirements for the biological activity of cholesterol in terms of its metabolism to other functional sterols and its proper fit into biological membranes, investigated in both enzymatic and functional membranous systems; chemical synthesis of cholesterol analogues; conformational and configurational analysis of sterols by hydrogen and carbon 13-nuclear magnetic resonance; in-vitro dissolution testing; pharmaceutical testing and regulatory affairs. **Mailing Address:** Dept Anal Lab Bristol-Myers, 1 Squibb Dr PO Box 191, New Brunswick, NJ 08903.

JOSEPH, MARTHA R, CHEMISTRY. **Education:** PhD (chem), Univ KY. **Professional Experience:** ASSOC PROF & CHAIR DEPT CHEM, WESTMINSTER COL, as of 2006. **Mailing Address:** Dept Chem, Westminister Col, 363 Hoyt Science Ctr, New Wilmington, PA 16172. **Fax:** 724-946-6220. **E-Mail:** josephm@westminster.edu

JOSEPH, PETER D(ANIEL), ELECTRICAL ENGINEERING. **Personal Data:** b Brooklyn, NY, January 21, 1936; m 1957, c 1. **Education:** Mass Inst Technol, BS & MS, 1958; Purdue Univ, PhD (elec eng), 1961. **Professional Experience:** RETIRED; Lab mgr, TRW Systs & Energy Group, 1976-1991; mgr, Sensor Design & Anal Dept, 1970-1976; mgr, Syst Anal & Software Dept, 1966-1970; head, Guidance Sect, 1964-1966; mem tech staff, TRW Systs & Energy Group, 1961-1964; Instr elec eng, Purdue Univ, 1958-1961. **Memberships:** Inst Elec & Electronics Engrs; Am Inst Aeronaut & Astronaut. **Research Statement & Publications:** Guidance of missiles and space vehicles; optimal control theory; optimal filter theory; electro-optical sensors; Filtering of Stochastic Processes with Application to Guidance. **Mailing Address:** 2740 W 233 St, Torrance, CA 90505-3112. **E-Mail:** PDJoseph@compuserve.com

JOSEPH, PETER MARON, MEDICAL PHYSICS. **Personal Data:** b Ridley Park, Pa, January 26, 1939; m 1980, Susan. **Education:** Lafayette Col, BS, 1959; Harvard Univ, MA, 1961, PhD (physics), 1967. **Honorary Degrees:** MPh, Univ Pa, 1987. **Honors & Awards:** Sylvia Greenfield Prize, Am Asn Physicists Med. **Professional Experience:** PROF RADIOL PHYSICS, UNIV PA, PHILADELPHIA, 1991-; assoc prof, Univ PA, Philadelphia, 1983-1991; assoc prof diag images physics, Univ Md, Baltimore, 1980-1982; asst prof, Columbia-Presby Med Ctr, 1975-1980; instr radiol, Columbia-Presby Med Ctr, 1973-1975; NIH fel, Memorial-Sloan Kettering Cancer Ctr, 1972-1973; asst prof, Carnegie-Mellon Univ, 1970-1972; Instr physics, Cornell Univ, 1967-1970. **Memberships:** Am Phys Soc; Am Asn Physicists Med; fel Inst Elec & Electronics Engrs; Soc Magnetic Resonance Med; Radiol Soc Nam. **Research Statement & Publications:** High energy electromagnetic phenomena; experimental tests of quantum electrodynamics; photo production of vector mesons; energy range relations; x-ray spectra and attenuation curves; radiographic image quality; computerized axial tomography; magnetic resonance image; air pollution and asthma. **Mailing Address:** Radiology Dept Univ Pa, 3400 Spruce St, Philadelphia, PA 19104. **E-Mail:** joseph@rad.upenn.edu

JOSEPH, RAMON R, GASTROENTEROLOGY, ENDOSCOPY. **Personal Data:** b New York, NY, May 17, 1930; m Mary; c Ricardo G, Maria A (Thompson) & Lisa M (Benson). **Education:** Manhattan Col, BS, 1952; Cornell Univ, MD, 1956. **Professional Experience:** EMER PROF INTERNAL MED, UNIV MICH ANN ARBOR, 1998-; med dir, Henry Ford Med Ctr, 1987- 1995; chair, gastroenterol, St Mary Hosp, 1985-1990; prof internal med, Med Sch, 1975-1984; asst dean, Med Sch, 1973-1984; pres med staff, Wayne Co Gen Hosp, 1971-1972; St Mary Hosp, Mich Dept Educ, 1969-1973; assoc prof internal med, Univ Mich, Ann Arbor, 1968-1975; chmn res dept, Wayne Co Gen Hosp, 1964-1985; asst dir, Dept Med, Wayne Co Gen Hosp, 1964-1973; dir, Dept Med, 1973-1985; ST MARY HOSP, LIVONIA, 1962-; consult, Annapolis Hosp, Wayne, 1962-1988; dir, Gastroenterol Sect, Wayne Co Gen Hosp, Westland, 1962- 1985; from instr to prof internal med, Univ Mich, Ann Arbor, 1962-1975; staff physician, Wayne Co Gen Hosp, 1962-1964; Fel, Wayne Co Gen Hosp, 1961-1962; resident, Wayne Co Gen Hosp, 1959-1962; Intern med, Meadowbrook Hosp, Hempstead, 1956-1957. **Memberships:** AAAS; fel Am Col Physicians; NY Acad Sci; Asn Am Med Col; AMA; Am Gastroenterol Asn; Am Soc Internal Med; Am Soc Gastrointestinal Endoscopy; Am Med Asn. **Research Statement & Publications:** Origin and nature of human serum lactic dehydrogenase; multiple molecular forms of enzyme amylase; biochemical diagnosis in gastroenterology; endoscopic aspects of gastroenterology. **Mailing Address:** 13755 W Via Montoya, Sun City West, AZ 85375. **Fax:** 623-214-8326. **E-Mail:** rjoseph514@aol.com

JOSEPH, RICHARD ISAAC, SOLID STATE PHYSICS. **Personal Data:** b Brooklyn, NY, May 25, 1936; m 1961, c 3. **Education:** City Col NY, BS, 1957; Harvard Univ, PhD (physics), 1962. **Professional Experience:** JACOB SUTER JAMMER PROF ELEC ENG & COMPUT ENG, JOHNS HOPKINS UNIV as of 2003; prof Elec Eng & Comput Eng, beginning 1970; from asst prof to assoc prof, Johns Hopkins Univ, 1966-1970; sr res scientist solid state physics, Raytheon Co, 1961-1966. **Memberships:** AAAS; Am Phys Soc. **Research Statement & Publications:** Statistical mechanics; theory of magnetism and properties of magnetic materials; microwave physics; theory of solid state; exchange interactions in solids; critical phenomena; solitons; non-linear wave equations; Theory of Simulated Raman Scattering in Optical Fibers in the Pulse Walk-Off Regime. **Mailing Address:** 3400 N Charles St, 105 Barton Hall, Baltimore, MD 21218. **Fax:** 410-516-5566. **E-Mail:** rjoseph@jhu.edu

JOSEPH, ROSALINE RESNICK, MEDICINE, HEMATOLOGY. **Personal Data:** b New York, NY, August 21, 1929; m 1954, c 2. **Education:** Cornell Univ, AB, 1949; Women's Med Col Pa, MD, 1953; Temple Univ, MS, 1958. **Professional Experience:** PROF MED, MED COL PA, 1996-; Prof clin oncol, Am Cancer Soc, 1989-1994; prof med & chief Hematol & Oncol Dept, Med Col PA, 1977-1996; course coordrretinculo-endothelial, Syst Interdisciplinary Course Comt, 1968-1973; assoc prof med, Med Ctr, Temple Univ, 1963-1977; assoc med, Med Ctr, Temple Univ, 1960-1963; Instr hematol, MedCtr, Temple Univ, 1957-1960. **Memberships:** Am Fedn Clin Res; Am Soc Hematol; Fel Am Col Physicians; Am Asn CancerEduc; Am Soc Clin Oncol. **Research Statement & Publications:** New modalities in the treatment of cancer and hematologic disorders. **Mailing Address:** Med Col Pa, 3300 Henry Ave, Philadelphia, PA 19129.

JOSEPH, ROY D, APPLIED MATHEMATICS. **Personal Data:** b Fremont, Ohio, July 26, 1937; m 1969. **Education:** Fenn Col, BEE, 1960; Case Inst Technol, MSEE, 1962, PhD (eng), 1965. **Professional Experience:** ASSOC PROF ELEC & COMPUT ENG, SPACE INST, UNIV TENN, as of 2002; assoc prof elec eng, Space Inst, Univ Tenn, beginning 1980; asst prof, Space Inst, UnivTenn, 1973-1980; asst prof eng, State Univ NY, Stony Brook, 1966-1972; resassoc, Case Inst Technol, 1965-1966. **Memberships:** Inst Elec & ElectronicsEngrs; Soc Indust & Appl Math; Am Asn Univ Profs. **Research Statement & Publications:** Active network synthesis; optimal control signal processing; digital signal processing. **Mailing Address:** Elec Eng, Space Inst, Univ Tenn, Tullahoma, TN 37388-9700. **Fax:** 931-454-2271. **E-Mail:** rjoseph@utsi.edu

JOSEPH, SAMMY WILLIAM, MICROBIOLOGY, MEDICAL BACTERIOLOGY. **Personal Data:** b Jacksonville, Fla, October 10, 1934; m 1967, Marianne; c Jeffrey Keith & Jennifer Michelle. **Education:** Univ Fla, BSA, 1956; St John's Univ, NY, MS, 1964, PhD (microbiol), 1970. **Honors & Awards:** Fel, Am Asn Advan Sci. **Professional Experience:** Vis scientist, Naval Med Res Inst, Bethesda, Md, 1995; PROF, DEPT MICROBIOL, UNIV MD, 1981-; chmn dept, Dept Microbiol, Univ MD, 1981-1989; prog mgr infectious dis, Naval Med Res & Develop Command, Nat Naval Med Ctr, 1978-1981; vis scientist, Off Naval Res, London, 1977; dep chmn, Microbiol Dept, Naval Med Res Inst, 1975-1978; exec officer; comndg officer, Naval Unit, Ft Detrick, 1974-1975; microbiologist & asst OIC, Naval Med Res Unit 2, Jakarta Detachment, Indonesia, 1970-1973; Navy contract fel bact, St John's Univ, NY, 1967-1970; head, Bact & Mycol Br, 1963-1967; head, Bact, Serol & Mycol Br, US Naval Hosp, St Albans, NY, 1958-1963; asst head, Serol Br, US Naval Med Sch, Nat Naval Med Ctr, 1957-1958. **Memberships:** Am Soc Microbiol; fel Am Acad Microbiol; AAAS; NY Acad Sci; Am Soc Clin Path; Sigma Xi. **Research Statement & Publications:** Studies on bacteria of clinical significance, particularly those causing gastroenteritis; purification and characterization of bacterial toxins; role of antibiotics in treatment; bacterial adherence to surfaces; genetic basis of pathogenic mechanisms; bacterial taxonomy and systematic classification; studies of food-bourne disease caused by bacteria; antibiotic resistance of enterococci and salmonella from farms; survival mechanisms of bacteria; human pathogens in the environment. **Mailing Address:** Univ Md, Dept Cell Biol & Molecular Genetic, 2118 Microbiol, College Park, MD 20742. **Fax:** 301-345-9489. **E-Mail:** sj13@umail.umd.edu

JOSEPH, SOLOMON, industrial chemistry; deceased, see previous edition for last biography

JOSEPH, STANLEY ROBERT, MEDICAL ENTOMOLOGY, INSECT PEST MANAGEMENT. **Personal Data:** b Jacobus, Pa, May 21, 1930; m 1956, Minna; c Minna L (Leydorf), Jane C & John H. **Education:** Gettysburg Col, BA, 1952; Pa State Univ, MS, 1954; Univ Md, PhD (entom), 1968. **Professional Experience:** RETIRED; chief, Mosquito Control Sect, 1980-1992; entomologist, pest mgtsect, Md Dept Agr, 1973-1979; from asst entomologist to assoc entomologist, Md State Bd Agr, 1956-1973. **Memberships:** Sigma Xi; Am Mosquito Control Asn. **Research Statement & Publications:** Methods and insecticides for use in mosquito control in Maryland; ultra low volume insecticide applications with air and ground equipment; biology of Culiseta melanura in Maryland; insect physiology; toxicology of malathion to vertebrates. **Mailing Address:** 1631 Gen Hwy, Annapolis, MD 21401.

JOSEPH, STEPHEN C, HEALTH SCIENCES. **Personal Data:** b New York, NY, November 25, 1937. **Education:** Harvard Col, BA, 1959; Yale Univ, MD, 1963; Johns Hopkins Univ, MPH, 1968; Am Bd Pediat, dipl, 1968. **Honors & Awards:** Pub Serv for Med Award, Am Col Physicians, 1989. **Professional Experience:** RETIRED; pres & CEO, Nat Ctr Genome Resources, 1999-2001; asst secy defense health affairs, US Dept Defense, 1993-1997; dean, Sch Pub Health, Univ Minn, 1991-1993; Sol Fleischman vis prof med, Harvard Community Health Plan, 1990; mem, Nat Adv Comt HIV, Ctrs Dis Control, 1988-1991; mem bd trustees, US Conf Local Health Officers, 1987-1989; comnr health, New York City, 1986-1990; spec coordr child health & survival, UN Children's Fund, 1983-1986; chief pediat, Grenfell Regional Health Serv, St Anthony, Can, 1982-1983; consult & lectr, Int Develop Res Ctr, Can, 1981-1982; actg asst adminr, Bur Develop Support, Agency Int Develop, 1981; dep asst adminr, Human Resources Develop, Bur Develop Support, Agency Int Develop, 1978-1981; mem, Nat Coun Int Health, 1975-1978; lectr, Dept Maternal & Child Health, 1974-1978; asst med, Children's Hosp Med Ctr, 1974-1978; asst med, Children's Hosp Med Ctr, 1974-1978; dir, Off Int Health Progs, Harvard Sch Pub Health, 1974-1978; dir med educ & planning & consult to pres, Univ Wyo, 1973-1974; prof pediat & community health, Univ Ctr Health Sci, Yaounde, Cameroon, 1971-1973; fel, Comp Child Care Proj, Dept Pediat, Sch Med, Johns Hopkins Univ, 1967-1968; asst resident, Boston Children's Hosp, 1966-1967; intern pediat, Boston Children's Hosp, 1963-1964. **Memberships:** Inst Med-Nat Acad Sci; fel Am Pub Health Asn; fel Am Acad Pediat. **Research Statement & Publications:** Author of over 350 publications. **Mailing Address:** Dept Defense, Rm 3E-346, Washington, DC 70301. **Fax:** 703-614-3537.

JOSEPHS, JESS J, MUSICAL ACOUSTICS. **Personal Data:** b New York, NY, January 4, 1917; m 1962, c 2. **Education:** NY Univ, AB, 1938, MSc, 1940, PhD (phys chem), 1943. **Professional Experience:** PROF EMER PHYSICS, SMITH COL, 1987-; prof, Smith Col, 1956-1987; asst prof physics, Boston Univ, 1950-1956; asst prof phys sci, Univ Chicago, 1947-1950; instr phys chem, Northwestern Univ, 1946-1947; Res assoc, Northwestern Univ, 1945-1946. **Memberships:** Am Phys Soc; Am Asn Physics Teachers; Audio Eng Soc; Sigma Xi. **Research Statement & Publications:** Solid state physics, psychoacoustics; acoustical study of the violin; distortion in electronically reproduced music. **Mailing Address:** 3300 Darby Rd C1004, Haverford, PA 19041-1066.

JOSEPHS, MELVIN JAY, plant physiology, information science; deceased, see previous edition for last biography

JOSEPHS, ROBERT, BIOPHYSICS, STRUCTURAL BIOLOGY. **Personal Data:** b Philadelphia, Pa, June 29, 1937; m 1990. **Education:** Univ Ill, BS, 1959; Hebrew Univ, MSc, 1962; Johns Hopkins Univ, PhD (biol), 1966. **Honors & Awards:** Res Career Develop Award, NIH. **Professional Experience:** DIR, LAB ELECTRON MICROS & IMAGE ANAL, UNIV CHICAGO, as of 1999; PROF MOLECULAR GENETICS & CELL BIOL, UNIV CHICAGO, 1990-; res grants, NIH, beginning 1978; SR SCIENTIST & ASSOC, POLYMER DEPT, WEIZMAN INST, UNIV CHICAGO, 1977-; scientist, Weizman Inst, 1973-1977; fel struct biol, Weizman Inst, 1970-1973; fel, MRC Lab Molecular Biol, 1968-1969; res assoc muscle biol, Johns Hopkins Univ, 1966-1967. **Memberships:** Electron Micros Soc Am; Biophys Soc. **Research Statement & Publications:** Structural biology; sickle cell anemia; electron crystallography; cryoelectron microscopy; structure of erythrocyte spectrin in partially expanded skeletons. **Mailing Address:** Div Biol Sci Univ Chicago, Rm 145 CLSC, 920 E 58th, Chicago, IL 60637. **E-Mail:** bob@befvax.uchicago.edu

JOSEPHSON, ALAN S, medicine, immunology; deceased, see previous edition for last biography

JOSEPHSON, BRIAN DAVID, PHYSICS. **Personal Data:** b Cardiff, Eng, January 4, 1940. **Education:** Cambridge Univ, BA, 1960, MA, 1964, PhD (physics). **Honorary Degrees:** DSc, Univ Wales, 1974, Exeter Univ, 1983. **Honors & Awards:** Nobel Prize in Physics, 1973; Fitz London Award, 1972; Guthrie Medal, 1972; van der Pol Medal, 1972; Elliot Cresson Medal, 1972; Hughes Medal, 1972; Holweck Medal, 1973; Faradax Medal, 1982; Sir George Thompson Medal, 1984. **Professional Experience:** Univ Mo, Rolla, 1987; Indian Inst Sci, Bangalore, 1984; vis prof, Dept ComputSci, Wayne State Univ, 1983; co-ed, Consciousness & the Phys World, 1980; vis fac, MaharishiEurop Res Univ, 1975; FROM PROF PHYSICS TO DIR MIND-MATTER UNIFICATION PROJ THEORY-CONDENSED MATTER GROUP CAVENDISH LAB, CAMBRIDGE UNIV, beginning 1974; reader, Cambridge Univ, 1972-1974; Dir res, Cambridge Univ, 1967-1972; fel, Trinity Col, Cambridge, 1962-. **Memberships:** Hon foreign mem Am Acad Arts & Sci; hon mem Inst Elec & Electronics Engrs; fel Royal Soc. **Mailing Address:** Cavendish Lab Univ Cambridge, Madingley Rd, Cambridge CB3 0HE, UK. **E-Mail:** bdj10@cam.ac.uk

JOSEPHSON, DONALD A, MATHEMATICS. **Education:** Univ Okla, PhD, 1978. **Professional Experience:** ASSOC PROF MATH, WHEATON COL, 1982-. **Mailing Address:** Dept Math Wheaton Col, 501 Col Ave, Wheaton, IL 60187-4306. **Fax:** 630-752-5285. **E-Mail:** josephson@wheaton.edu

JOSEPHSON, ROBERT KARL, COMPARATIVE PHYSIOLOGY. **Personal Data:** b Somerville, Mass, July 12, 1934; m 1956, c 3. **Education:** Tufts Univ, BS, 1956; Univ Calif, Los Angeles, PhD (zoology), 1960. **Professional Experience:** Guggenheim fel, 1977-1978; PROF NEUROBIOLOGY & BEHAV, DEPT ECOL & EVOLUTIONARY BIOL, UNIV CALIF, IRVINE, 1971-; from assoc prof to prof biol, Case Western Reserve Univ, 1965-1971; from asst prof to assoc prof zool, Univ Minn, 1962-1965; NATO fel, Univ Tubingen, 1961; mem, Marine Biol Lab Corp. **Memberships:** AAAS; Am Soc Zoology; Brit Soc Exp Biol; Soc Gen Physiol; Soc Neuroscience; Sigma Xi; Soc Biophys; Am Physiol Soc. **Research Statement & Publications:** Mechanical power and efficiency of muscle. **Mailing Address:** Dept Ecol & Evolution, Univ Calif, 321 Steinhaus Hall, Irvine, CA 92697. **Fax:** 949-824-2447. **E-Mail:** rkjoseph@uci.edu

JOSEPHSON, RONALD VICTOR, FOOD SCIENCE, NUTRITION. **Personal Data:** b Bellefonte, Pa, May 19, 1942; m 1969, Judith; c Kirsten E & Erika L. **Education:** Pa State Univ, BS, 1964; Univ Minn, St Paul, MS, 1966, PhD (food sci), 1970. **Professional Experience:** Coordr, San Diego State Univ, 1992-1993; pres, San Diego Chap, Sigma Xi, 1986-1987; chmn, Basic Symp Comt, Inst Food Technol, 1985-1987; PRIN INVESTR GRANTS, NAT OCEANIC & ATMOSPHERIC ADMIN, US ARMY, NAT FISHERIES INST, 1977-; FROM ASSOC PROF & PROF FOODS & NUTRITION TO PROF EXERCISE & NUT SCI, SAN DIEGO STATE UNIV, 1975-; asst prof food sci & nutrit, Ohio State Univ, 1971-1975; Asst prof dairy technol, Ohio State Univ, 1970-1971. **Memberships:** Am Dairy Sci Asn; Inst Food Technol; Sigma Xi. **Research Statement & Publications:** Chemistry analysis and storage stability of foods; milk and dairy foods; fish and seafoods; medical foods; and human and cow's milk proteins. **Mailing Address:** Dept Exercise & Nutrit Sci San Diego State Univ, 5500 Campanile Dr, San Diego, CA 92182-7251. **Fax:** 619-594-6553.

JOSHI, ARAVIND KRISHNA, COMPUTER & INFORMATION SCIENCE. **Personal Data:** b Poona, India, August 5, 1929; m 1963, c 2. **Education:** Univ Poona, BE, 1951; Indian Inst Sci, Bangalore, dipl, 1952; Univ Pa, MS, 1958, PhD (elec eng), 1960. **Professional Experience:** CO-DIR, INST RES COGNITIVE SCI, UNIV PA, as of 2004; HENRY SALVATORI PROF COMPUT & COGNITIVE SCI, UNIV PA, 1972-; guggenheim fel, 1971-1972; mem, Inst Advan Study, 1971-1972; iing consult, Western Reserve, 1964-; consult info theory & ling, Philco Res Lab, Pa, 1962-1963; from asst prof to assoc profelec eng & ling, Univ PA, 1961-1972; assoc, transformations & discourse anal proj, NSF, 1958-; assoc ling anal, Univ PA, 1958-1961; prof engr, Radio Corp Am, NJ, 1954-1958; res asstelectronics, Indian Inst Sci, Bangalore, 1952-1953 & Tata Inst Fundamental Res, Bombay, 1953. **Memberships:** Asn Comput Mach; fel Inst Elec & Electronics Engrs; Am Math Soc; Sigma Xi. **Research Statement & Publications:** Information theory; structural analysis of natural languages and formal linguistics; natural language processing; artificial intelligence; mathematical linguistics. **Mailing Address:** Inst Res Cognitive Sci, Univ Pa, 3401 Walnut St, Ste 400A, Philadelphia, PA 19104-6228. **Fax:** 215-573-9247. **E-Mail:** joshi@cis.upenn.edu

JOSHI, BHAIRAV DATT, PHYSICAL CHEMISTRY, QUANTUM CHEMISTRY. **Personal Data:** b Dungrakot, Almora, India, March 5, 1939; American citizen; m 1967, Barbara. **Education:** Univ Delhi, BS, 1959, MS, 1961; Univ Chicago, MS, 1963, PhD (chem), 1964. **Professional Experience:** PROF CHEM, STATE UNIV NY COL GENESEO, 1985-2001; from asst prof to assoc prof, State Univ NY Col Geneseo, 1970-1984; res assoc, State Univ NY Stony Brook, 1969-1970; reader, Univ Delhi, 1967-1969; lectr, Indian Inst Technol, Kanpur, 1966-1967; fel chem, Dept Phys, Univ Chicago, 1965-1966. **Memberships:** Am Chem Soc; Sigma Xi. **Research Statement & Publications:** Quantum mechanical studies of the electronic structure of small atoms and molecules; use of computers in undergraduate education. **Mailing Address:** Dept Chem, State Univ NY, One Col Circle, Geneseo, NY 14454-9511. **Fax:** 585-245-5288. **E-Mail:** joshi@uno.cc.geneseo.edu

JOSHI, CHANDRASHEKHAR JANARDAN, PHYSICS OF BEAMS. **Personal Data:** b India, July 22, 1953. **Education:** London Univ, BS, 1974; Hall Univ, Eng, PhD (appl physics), 1978. **Honors & Awards:** Excellence Plasma Physics Res Award APS, 1996; USPAS Prize Achievement Accelerator Physics & Tech, 1997. **Professional Experience:** DIR, CTR HIGH FREQUENCY ELECTRONICS, UNIV CALIF, LOS ANGELES, as of 2005; PROF, DEPT ELEC ENG, UNIV CALIF, LOS ANGELES, 1988-; res physicist, Nat Res Coun, Ottawa, Can, 1978-1980. **Memberships:** Inst Physics (UK); Am Phys Soc; Inst Elec & Electronics Engrs. **Research Statement & Publications:** Physics of beams. **Mailing Address:** Dept Elec Eng, Univ Calif, 56-125B Eng IV Bldg PO Box 951594, Los Angeles, CA 90095-1594. **E-Mail:** joshi@ee.ucla.edu

JOSHI, JAY B, MOLECULAR NEUROBIOLOGY, NEUROPEPTIDE GENE EXPRESSION. **Personal Data:** b Bombay, India, December 22, 1949; m 1975, Bharati. **Education:** Univ India, Bombay, BS, 1972, MS, 1976, PhD (molecular biol), 1980. **Professional Experience:** ASSOC PROF MOLECULAR BIOL, MICROBIOL DEPT, GEORGEWASH UNIV SCH MED & PUB HEALTH, 1993-; CHIEF MOLECULAR BIOL, VET ADMIN MED CTR, 1992-; chief, Molecular Biol Unit, 1990-1992; sr staff fel, Lab Biochem Genetics, Nat Heart Lung & Blood Inst, 1985-1990; res assoc fel, Virol Lab, Univ Nebr, 1982-1984; rRes fel, Virol Lab, Univ Nebr, 1980-1982. **Memberships:** Am Soc Biochem & Molecular Biol; AAAS; Soc Neuroscience; Soc Exp Biol & Med. **Research Statement & Publications:** Molecular neurobiology; neuropeptide geneexpression; molecular neurovirology. **Mailing Address:** Molecular Biol Lab, Vet Admin Med Ctr, Res Bldg Rm 1F145 50 Irving St NW, Washington, DC 20422. **Fax:** 202-462-2006. **E-Mail:** jayjoshi@gwis2.circ.gwu.edu

JOSHI, JAYANT GOPAL, BIOCHEMISTRY. **Personal Data:** b Poona, India, July 22, 1932; m 1958, c 2. **Education:** Univ Poona, BSc, 1952, MSc, 1954, PhD (biochem), 1957. **Professional Experience:** PROF BIOCHEM, UNIV TENN, KNOXVILLE, 1979-; rev panel, Environ Protection Agency, 1989; vis scientist, Inst Clin Chem, Uppsala, Sweden, 1972 & 1973; assoc prof, Univ Tenn, Knoxville, 1970-1979; asst prof, DukeUniv, 1968-1970; assoc, Duke Univ, 1966-1968; sci pool officer, Nat Chem Labs, Poona, India, 1964-1966; res fel, Duke Univ, 1959-1964; jr sci officer, Cent Food Tech Res Inst, Mysore, 1958-1959; Indian Coun Med Res-Rockefeller Found fel biochem, Nutrit Res Labs, Coonoor, India, 1956-1958; consult, Biol Div, Oak Ridge NatLabs. **Memberships:** Am Soc Biol Chemists; Am Soc Microbiol. **Research Statement & Publications:** Comparative biochemistry; mechanism of enzyme action; pyridine nucleotide, metabolism, biosynthesis and regulation, biochemical change induced by ultraviolet light; metal toxicity. **Mailing Address:** Dept Biochem, Univ Tenn, Knoxville, TN 37996-0840. **Fax:** 615-974-6306.

JOSHI, MADHUSUDAN SHANKARRAO, REPRODUCTIVE PHYSIOLOGY, ENDOCRINOLOGY. **Personal Data:** b Jamkandi, India, October 21, 1928; m 1953, c 2. **Education:** Karnatak Univ, India, BSc, 1949; Univ Bombay, MSc, 1953; Weizmann Inst Sci, PhD (biol), 1970. **Honors & Awards:** Golden Apple Award, Am Med Students Asn, 1982 & 1989. **Professional Experience:** PROF EMER ANAT, UNIV NDAK, as of 2003; prof, Dept Anat, Univ Ndak, beginning 1985; assoc prof, Dept Anat, UnivNdak, 1980-1985; mem fac, Dept Anat, Univ Ndak, 1977-1980; asst prof anat, State Univ NYDownstate Med Ctr, 1970-1977; asst res officer physiol reprod, Cancer Res Ctr, Parel, Bombay, 1956-1966. **Memberships:** Soc Study Fertil UK; Soc Study Reproduction; Am Asn Anat; Am Physiol Soc. **Research Statement & Publications:** Mechanisms involved in fertilization and implantation; study of hormone dependent enzymes in uterus and in oviduct; proteins in cerebrospinal fluid; sperm maturation. **Mailing Address:** Dept Anat, Univ NDak Sch Med, 501 N Columbia Rd, Grand Forks, ND 58203-2817. **E-Mail:** mjoshi@chorus.net

JOSHI, MUKUND SHANKAR, PHARMACEUTICAL CHEMISTRY, ORGANIC CHEMISTRY. **Personal Data:** b India, June 11, 1947; m 1973, c 2. **Education:** VJ Tech Inst, Bombay, India, 1969; Univ Md, MS, 1973, PhD (chem engr), 1976. **Professional Experience:** SR DIR, PHARMACIA & UPJOHN CO, as of 2001; assoc dir, bioprocess res & develop, Pharmacia & Upjohn Co, beginning 1987; resscientist, Bioprocess Res & Develop, Upjohn CO, 1976-1987; Vis scientist, Danish Atomic Energy Comn, 1975-1976; prof radiol consult Tata MemorialHosp, Mumbai. **Memberships:** Am Inst Chem Engrs; Am Chem Soc. **Research Statement & Publications:** Chemical process research and development work to commercially manufacture pharmaceutical products; synthesis of steroids and prostaglandins; feasibility studies risk analysis, economic evaluation and supervision of laboratory; bioengineering and biomedical eng. **Mailing Address:** Pharmacia & Upjohn Co, 7000 Portage Rd, Kalamazoo, MI 49001-0102.

JOSHI, NAYAN H, SYNTHETIC INORGANIC & ORGANOMETALLIC CHEMISTRY, SYNTHETIC ORGANIC & NATURAL PRODUCTS CHEMISTRY. **Personal Data:** b Gondal, India, July 31, 1952; American citizen; m 1983, Pragna; c Devang & Jayraj. **Education:** Saurashta Univ, India, BS, 1973, MS, 1975; Gujarat Univ, India, PhD (elec chem), 1980. **Honors & Awards:** MASCOT Award, Electrochem Soc India, 1980. **Professional Experience:** SR RES CHEMIST, ATOTECH USA INC, AS OF 2006; production supvr, Fema Electronics, NJ, 1984-1988; sr chemist, Gujarat Steel Tubes, Ahmedabad, India, 1981-1984; chief chemist, SamratChem, Keshad, India, 1980-1981; jr lectr chem, UP Arts & Sci Col, Pilvai, India, 1975-1980; Anal chemist, Brooke Bond India Ltd, 1973-1975. **Memberships:** Am Electroplaters & Surface Finishers Soc. **Research Statement & Publications:** Improvement of metallization process for electronic applications as well as metallization of non-conductors for electromagnetic shielding and decorative applications; surface modification of polymers. **Mailing Address:** Atotech USA Inc, 1750 Overview Dr, Rock Hill, SC 29730. **Fax:** 803-817-3502. **E-Mail:** njoshi@atousa.com

JOSHI, RAMESH CHANDRA, MATERIAL SCIENCE, GEOTECHNICAL ENGINEERING. **Personal Data:** b May 6, 1932; Canadian citizen; m 1955, c 3. **Education:** Rajputana Univ, India, BE, 1956; Punjab Univ, India, MSc, 1966; Iowa State Univ, MSc, 1968, PhD (civil eng), 1970. **Professional Experience:** PROF EMER CIVIL ENG, UNIV CALGARY, as of 2004; vis fel, Japan Soc Promotion Sci, 1990-1991; prof civil eng, Univ Calga, beginning 1977; adj lectr, Univ Mo, 1976-1977; sr proj engr, Woodward Clyde Consuts, 1970-1977; res assoc, Eng Res Inst, Iowa State Univ, 1966-1970; exec engr, Rajasthan Pub Works Dept, India, 1956-1966. **Memberships:** Fel Am Soc Civil Eng; Can Geotech Soc; Int Soc Soil mech & Found Eng; EngInst Can. **Research Statement & Publications:** Coal ash, particularly fly ash, utilization; model testing of piles; leachgate migration control; properties of frozen soil; soft soil fabric and consolidation. **Mailing Address:** Dept Civil Eng, Univ Calgary, Calgary, AB T2N 1N4, Can. **Fax:** 403-282-7026. **E-Mail:** joshir@ucalgary.ca

JOSHI, RAVINDRA PRABHAKAR, MICRO & NANO ELECTRONICS & HIGH SPEED HIGH POWER SEMI-CONDUCTOR SWITCHES, BIO-ELECTRICS & BIO-PHYSICS. **Personal Data:** b Allahabad, India, September 23, 1960; American citizen; m 1993, Bela; c Sailee Alyssa & Rohan K. **Education:** Indian Inst Technol, BTech, 1983, MTech, 1985; Ariz State Univ, PhD (elec eng), 1988. **Professional Experience:** PROF, DEPT ELEC & COMPUT ENG, OLD DOM UNIV, 2001-; vis scientist, Motorola Corp., 1999; vis scientist, Oak Ridge Nat Lab, 1996; prin investr, NASA & Dept Energy, 1996; Assoc Prof, Old Dom Univ, 1995-2001; vis fac, Phillips Lab, 1995; Mission Res Corp, Calif, 1995; prin investr, Off Naval Res, beginning 1994; res consult, Tetra Corp, NMex, 1994; Prin investr, Dept Energy, 1992-1993; asst prof, Old Dom Univ, 1989-1995; fel, Ariz State Univ, 1988-1989; Res assoc, Ariz State Univ, 1985-1988. **Memberships:** Sr mem Inst Elec & Electronics Engrs; Am Phys Soc; Int Soc Opt Engrs. **Research Statement & Publications:** Semiconductor device simulation; physicsand modeling of sub-micron semiconductor devices; optical interactions in semiconductors; ultrafast processes in photo excited semiconductor plasmas; high field non-linear electron transport; gas discharge phenomena; Bio-electrics. **Mailing Address:** Dept Elec & Comput Eng, 1321 Old Dom Univ, 262 Kaufman Hall, Norfolk, VA 23529-0246. **Fax:** 757-683-3220. **E-Mail:** rjoshi@odu.edu

JOSHI, SADANAND D, HORIZONTAL DRILLING, RESERVOIR ENGINEERING. **Personal Data:** b Panwel, India, March 15, 1950; American citizen; m 1979, c 2. **Education:** WCE Col, India, BE, 1972; Indian Inst Technol, MTech, 1974; Iowa State Univ, Ames, PhD (mech eng), 1978. **Professional Experience:** Indust teacher, AmAsn Petrol Geologists & Soc Petrol Engrs, 1989-; PRES, JOSHI TECHNOLOGIES, INC, 1988-; Indust teacher, Univ Tulsa, 1988-; Res engr, PhillipsPetrol Co, 1980-1988. **Memberships:** Am Soc Mech Engrs; Soc Petrol Engrs, Canadian Institute of Mining; Am Asn of Petroleum Geologists. **Research Statement & Publications:** Drilling mechanism and petroleum production research using horizontal drilling; author of one book. **Mailing Address:** Joshi Technol Int Inc, 801 E 41st St, Ste 603, Tulsa, OK 74135. **Fax:** 918-665-0807. **E-Mail:** jti@joshitech.com

JOSHI, SHARAD GOPAL, REPRODUCTIVE ENDOCRINOLOGY & PHYSIOLOGY. **Personal Data:** b Nagpur, India. **Education:** Univ Nagpur, India, BS, 1952, MS, 1954; Univ Bombay, PhD (biochem), 1959. **Honors & Awards:** Edward Tyler Award, Int Soc Reproductive Med, 1981. **Professional Experience:** LAB DIR, LEADING INST FERTILITY ENHANCEMENT, as of 2004; DIR, FERTIL STUDIES LAB, ALBANY MEM HOSP, 1988-; prof obstet & gynec, gynec & biochem, Albany Med Col, 1982-1988; assoc prof obstet, gynec & biochem, Albany Med Col, 1973-1982; Southwest Fedn Res & Educ, 1966-1973; staff scientist endocrinol, Syntex Inst Hormone Biol, 1965-1966; assoc prof reproductive physiol, Inst Med Sci, India, 1963-1965; fel endocrinol, Worcester Fedn & Harvard Med Sch, 1959-1963. **Memberships:** Endocrine Soc; Soc Study Reproduction; Int Soc Reproductive Med; NY Acad Sci. **Research Statement & Publications:** Hormonal control and role of endometrium in human pregnancy; fertility control in human subjects; effects of toxic agents on human pregnancy; role of human endometrium and placenta in pregnancy; development of in vivo and in vitro models to study human placenta and endocrine-related tumors; monitoring human reproductive functions and tumor growth using biochemical markers. **Mailing Address:** Leading Inst Fertility Enhancement, 130 Everett Rd, NY 12205. **Fax:** 518-489-6210.

JOSHI, SHRINIVAS G, ACOUSTICAL ENGINEERING. **Education:** Univ Poona, India, BS, 1962; Indian Inst Sci, India, MS, 1963; Univ Calif, PhD, 1968. **Professional Experience:** PROF, DEPT ELEC & COMPUT ENG, MARQUETTE UNIV, as of 2005. **Mailing Address:** Marquette Univ, Olin 403, Milwaukee, WI 53233. **Fax:** 414-288-5579. **E-Mail:** shri.joshi@marquette.edu

JOSHI, SURESH MEGHASHYAM, CONTROL SYSTEMS RESEARCH, AEROSPACE SYSTEMS DYNAMICS & CONTROL RESEARCH. **Personal Data:** b Poona, India, American citizen. **Education:** Banaras Univ, India, BS, 1967; Indian Inst Technol, MS, 1969; Rensselaer Polytech Inst, PhD (elec eng), 1973. **Honors & Awards:** DuMont Prize, RPI, 1973; Inst Elec & Electronics Engrs Control System Technol Award, Inst Elec &Electronics Engrs, 1995; Inst Elec & Electronics Engrs Judith A Resnik Award, Inst Elec &Electronics Engrs, 2003. **Professional Experience:** Vis prof, Univ Va, 1992-1993; mem, bd govs, Inst Elec & Electronics Engrs, 1989-1994; mem, tech comt astrodyn, Am Inst Aeronauts & Astronauts, 1988-1990; chmn, aerospace syst & tech panel, Am Soc Mech Engrs, 1987-1991; Adj prof, George Wash Univ, 1986-2002; Adj prof, & Pa State Univ, 1986-1991; SR SCIENTIST, LANGLEY RES CTR, NASA, 1983-; assoc prof elec & mech eng, Old Dominion Univ Res Found, 1975-1983; post docres fel, Nat Res Coun, Langley Res Ctr, NASA, 1973-1975; Eng, Stone & Webster Corp, 1972-1973. **Memberships:** Fel Inst Elec & Electronics Engrs; Fel Am Soc Mech Engrs; Fel Am Inst Aeronauts &Astronauts. **Research Statement & Publications:** author of approximately 200 technical articles and three books; Research Interests: Multivariable robust and adaptive control theory and applications to advanced aerospace systems, aircraft, spacecraft; active noise control. **Mailing Address:** NASA Langley Res Ctr, Mail Stop 308, Hampton, VA 23681. **E-Mail:** suresh.m.joshi@nasa.gov

JOSHI, UMESHWAR PRASAD, HIGH SPEED DATA COMMUNICATIONS, COMPUTER ARCHITECTURES. **Personal Data:** b Kathmandu, Nepal, December 28, 1953. **Education:** Indian Inst Technol, Kanpur, MSc, 1976; Univ Calif, Santa Barbara, PhD (elem particle physics), 1984. **Professional Experience:** TENURED FAC, FERMI NAT ACCELERATOR LAB, as of 2004; APPL SCIENTIST, FERMI NAT ACCELERATOR LAB, 1994-; assoc scientist, Fermi Nat Accelerator Lab, 1989-1994; vis scientist, Fermi Nat Accelerator Lab, 1988-1989; res assoc, Rutgers Univ, 1984-1988. **Research Statement & Publications:** High-speed data communications with primary emphasis on data acquisition systems for high energy physics experiments. **Mailing Address:** Fermi Nat Accelerator Lab, Mail Station, 318 PO Box 500, Batavia, IL 60510. **E-Mail:** joshi@fnal.gov

JOSHI, VIJAY S, MATHEMATICS. **Personal Data:** b Pune, India, May 25, 1939; American citizen; m 1962, Rohini; c Swati & Madhavi. **Education:** Gujarat Univ, India, BS, 1959, MS, 1962, PhD (physics), 1969. **Professional Experience:** ASSOC PROF MATH, VA INTERMONT COL, 1992-; instr math, DurhamTech Community Col, 1981-1992; instr physics, Fayetteville Tech Community Col, 1973-1981; teacher math, JK High Sch, NC, 1971-1973. **Memberships:** Am Asn Physics Teachers; Math Asn Am; Nat Coun Teachers Math. **Mailing Address:** Va Intermont Col, 1013 Moore St, Bristol, VA 24201-4298. **Fax:** 276-669-5763. **E-Mail:** joshi@vic.edu

JOSHUA, HENRY, ORGANIC CHEMISTRY, SEPARATION SCIENCE. **Personal Data:** b Hamburg, Ger, December 8, 1934; m 1968, c 3. **Education:** Bar-Ilan Univ, Israel, BS, 1959; NY Univ, MS, 1962, PhD (chem), 1964. **Professional Experience:** VPRES, AURA INDUST INC, NY, as of 2004; RES & DEVELOP MGR, AURA INDUST INC, 1993-; sr res fel, Merck ResLabs, 1991-1993; res fel, Merck Res Labs, 1978-1991; sr res chemist, Merck Res Labs, 1965-1978; res fel chem, Princeton Univ, 1964-1965; res chemist, Res Div, Col Eng, NY Univ, 1960-1961. **Memberships:** Am Chem Soc; Asn Off Anal Chemists. **Research Statement & Publications:** Chromatographic methods development; development of instrumentation for liquid chromatography, laboratory automation and environmental analysis. **Mailing Address:** Aura Indust Inc, 5 W 545 8th Ave, New York, NY 10018. **Fax:** 212-290-9191.

JOSIAS, CONRAD S(EYMOUR), ELECTRICAL ENGINEERING. **Personal Data:** b New York, NY, June 12, 1930; m 1963, c 3. **Education:** NY Univ, BEE, 1951; Polytech Inst Brooklyn, MEE, 1955. **Honors & Awards:** Award, NASA Inventions & Contrib Bd, 1964. **Professional Experience:** PRES, JOSIAS ASSOCS, INC, 1979-; pres, Analog Technol Corp, Pasadena, 1965-1979; instr, Pasadena City Col, 1959-1961; from res engr, missile guid systs to eng groupsupvr, space electronics group, space sci div, Jet Propulsion Lab, Calif Inst Technol, 1956-1965; Engr electronic develop, Airborne Instruments Lab, Inc, NY, 1951-1956. **Memberships:** Sr mem Inst Elec & Electronics Engrs. **Research Statement & Publications:** Electronic devices and systems; scientific instruments for laboratory and space applications; analytical instruments for industrial laboratories. **Mailing Address:** 4733 Hillard Ave, La Canada Flintridge, CA 91011.

JOSIASSEN, RICHARD CARLTON, PSYCHOPATHOLOGY, NEUROPHYSIOLOGY. **Personal Data:** b Oroville, Calif, April 29, 1947. **Education:** Westmont Col, BA, 1969; Fuller Theol Sem, MA, 1975; Fuller Grad Sch Psychol, PhD (psychol), 1979. **Professional Experience:** EXEC DIR & CHIEF SCIENTIST, ARTHUR P NOYES RES FOUND, as of 2003; assoc prof Psychiat, Med Col Pa, beginning 1987; assoc secy gen, IV World Congress & Biol Psychiat, Philadelphia, 1985; vis asst prof, Dept Neurol, Hahnemann Univ, 1981-; from asst prof to assoc prof psychiat, Temple Univ Med Sch, 1980-1987; fel Neuroscience, NIMH, 1980-1982; consult, Dept Defense, 1969-1973. **Memberships:** Soc Biol Psychiat; Am Psychopathol Asn; Soc Res Psychopathol; NY Acad Sci. **Research Statement & Publications:** Neurophysiological mechanisms which underlie major mental illness. **Mailing Address:** Arthur P Noyes Res Found, 1001 Sterigere St, Norriston, PA 19401. **Fax:** 610-313-5753. **E-Mail:** richardjosiassen@noyesfoundation.net

JOSLIN, ROBERT SCOTT, PHARMACEUTICAL CHEMISTRY. **Personal Data:** b Indianapolis, Ind, May 28, 1929; m 1984, c 3. **Education:** Purdue Univ, BS, 1951, MS, 1955, PhD (phys pharm), 1959. **Honors & Awards:** Lunsford Richardson Award, 1957. **Professional Experience:** CONSULT, JOSLIN & ASSOC LTD, as of 2005; consult, beginning 1978; dir pharmaceut & anal res &develop, Baxter Labs, 1978; assoc dir pharmaceut & chem develop, G D Searle & Co, 1974-1978; dir depts pharmaceut sci & asst dir res, Res Div, William H Rorer, Inc, 1968-1974; dir prod improv, William H Rorer, Inc, 1965-1968; sr pharmaceut chemist, Eli Lilly & Co, 1958-1965; assoc pharmaceut chemist, Eli Lilly & Co, 1953-1954. **Memberships:** Fel Am Inst Chemists; Am Chem Soc; fel Acad Pharmaceut Sci; Int PharmaceutFedn; NY Acad Sci; fel Am Asn Pharmaceut Scientists. **Research Statement & Publications:** Pharmaceutical formulation; biopharmaceutics; process and product development. **Mailing Address:** Joslin & Assoc Ltd, 291 Deer Trail Ct Ste C, Barrington, IL 60010-1773.

JOSLYN, DENNIS JOSEPH, INSECT CYTOGENETICS, EVOLUTIONARY GENETICS OF INSECTS. **Personal Data:** b Chicago, Ill, April 29, 1947; m 1976, c 2. **Education:** St Procopius Col, BS, 1969; Univ Ill, Urbana, MS, 1973, PhD (zoology), 1978. **Professional Experience:** PROF ZOOL, RUTGERS UNIV, 1993-; assoc dean fac, Rutgers Univ, beginning 1993; from asst prof to assoc prof, Rutgers Univ, 1979-1993; res assoc, Insects Affecting Man & Animals Res Lab, USDA, 1976-1979; asst res scientist insect genetics, Univ Fla, 1976-1979. **Memberships:** Genetics Soc Am; Am Genetic Asn; Am Mosquito Control Asn. **Research Statement & Publications:** Evolutionary genetics and insect cytogenetics; genetics of insects of medical; veterinary and agricultural importance; biology of eukaryotic chromosomes; molecular carcinogenesis. **Mailing Address:** Dept Biol Rutgers Univ, 406 Penn St, Camden, NJ 08102-1400. **Fax:** 856-225-6498. **E-Mail:** joslyn@crab.rutgers.edu

JOSS, PAUL CHRISTOPHER, THEORETICAL ASTROPHYSICS, ATMOSPHERIC PHYSICS. **Personal Data:** b Brooklyn, NY, May 7, 1945; m 1992, Karen; c Susan E & Matthew A. **Education:** Cornell Univ, BA, 1966, PhD (astron, space sci), 1971. **Honors & Awards:** Helen B Warner Prize, Am Astron Soc, 1980. **Professional Experience:** Ed-in-chief, Astrophys J, 1997-; pres, Los Alamos Nat Lab, 1993-; PRES, JOSS CONSULT ASSOC, 1992-; vis scientist & inst, theoret physics, Univ Calif, Santa Barbara, 1992; mem, Sci Coun Astron & Space Physics, Univ Space Res Asn, 1988-1992; mem, High Energy Astrophys Mgt Opers Working Group, Nat Aeronaut & Space Admin, 1988-1990; mem, Adv Comt, Inst Geophys & Planetary Physics, Los Alamos Nat Lab, 1987-1992; PROF PHYSICS, MASS INST TECHNOL, 1983-; assoc head, Astrophys Div, Dept Physics, Mass Inst Technol, 1983-1988; spec asst, Los Alamos Nat Lab, 1980-1992; consult, Visidyne, Inc, 1979-1982, 1992-1993; vis staff mem, Los Alamos Nat Lab, 1979; vis scientist, Inst Astron, Univ Cambridge, 1977 & 1993; alfred p sloan res fel, 1976-1980; vis scientist, Dept Nuclear Physics, Weizmann Inst Sci, 1974-1975, 1978; mem, Ctr Theoret Physics, Mass Inst Technol, 1973-; from asst prof to assoc prof, Ctr Theoret Physics, Mass Inst Technol, 1973-1983; mem, Inst Advan Study, 1971-1973. **Memberships:** Am Astron Soc; Am Phys Soc; Int Astron Union. **Research Statement & Publications:** Theoretical and observational studies of compact x-ray sources; theoretical research on the structure and evolution of stars and binary stellar systems, supernovae, extragalactic astrophysics, the spectra of quasars, and the origin and orbital evolution of comets; theoretical and observational studies of atmospheric physics and global climatic change. **Mailing Address:** Dept Physics Mass Inst Technol, Rm 37-607 77 Mass Ave, Cambridge, MA 02139-4307. **Fax:** 617-253-8554. **E-Mail:** joss@space.mit.edu

JOSSEM, EDMUND LEONARD, PHYSICS. **Personal Data:** b Camden, NJ, May 19, 1919. **Education:** City Col NY, BS, 1938; Cornell Univ, MS, 1939, PhD (physics), 1950. **Honors & Awards:** Oersted Medal& Phillips Medal, Am Assoc Phys Teach, 1995; Distinguished Serv Award, Ohio State Univ, 2001. **Professional Experience:** PROF EMER, DEPT PHYSICS, OHIO STATE UNIV, as of 2004; Inv panelist, Redesign Sci Educ Conf, Ohio State Univ, 2000; mem comn physic educ, Int Union Pure & Applied Physics, 1981-; mem honbd, Int Conf X-ray & Atomic Inner Shell Physics, 1981-1982; mem physics surveycomt, panel on educ, Nat Acad Sci-Nat Res Coun, 1970-1972; chmn dept, OhioState Univ, 1967-1980; mem, Nat Adv Coun Educ Professions Develop, 1967-1970; mem bd dirs, Mich-Ohio Educ Lab, 1967-1969; chmn, Comn Col Physics, 1966-1971; exec secy, Comn Col Physics, 1964-1965; prof physics, ohio state univ, beginning 1964; Staff physicist, Comn Col Physics, 1963-1964; from asst prof to assoc prof, Ohio State Univ, 1956-1964; actg asst prof, Cornell Univ, 1955-1956; resassoc, Cornell Univ, 1950-1955; asst physics, Cornell Univ, 1946-1950; memstaff, Los Alamos Sci Lab, 1945-1946; instr, Cornell Univ, 1942-1945; asstphysics, Cornell Univ, 1940-1942. **Memberships:** IUPAP; Fel AAAS; Am Phys Soc; Am Asn Physics Teachers (vpres 1971-1972 pres 1973-1974); Sigma Xi (vpres 1978-1979 pres 1980-1981). **Research Statement & Publications:** Solid state physics; x-ray physics. **Mailing Address:** Dept Physics, Ohio State Univ, 4150 Smith Lab, Columbus, OH 43210. **Fax:** 614-292-7557. **E-Mail:** jossem@mps.ohio-state.edu

JOSSI, JACK WILLIAM, OCEANOGRAPHY, ECOLOGY. **Personal Data:** b Portland, Ore, April 4, 1937; m 1970, Gayle; c Neah Jossi, Maija Jossi & Taber Jossi Caton. **Education:** Pac Univ, BS, biology, 1959; Univ Wash, Seattle, BS, Physical ocednography, 1962; Univ Miami, MS, Marina sci, 1972. **Professional Experience:** SUPVRY OCEANOGR, NAT OCEANIC & ATMOSPHERIC ADMIN, US DEPT COM, 1991-; res oceanogr ocean climat, Atlantic Environ Group, 1978-1991; deputy chief, Field Group, US Dept Com, 1974-1978; chief, Continuous Plankton Recorder Surv, Field Group, US Dept Com, 1972-1974; mgr, Fishery Climat Prog, Southeast Fisheries Ctr, 1971-1972; consult, Smithsonian Inst, 1970; Fel, Univ Miami, 1967-1968; oceanogr, Trop Atlantic Biol Lab, 1965-1970; Phys oceanogr Wash Biol Lab, US Dept Interior, 1962-1965. **Memberships:** Marine Biol Asn UK. **Research Statement & Publications:** Ocean climatology; modeling and forecasting of distribution and abundance of living marine resources. **Mailing Address:** Nat Marine Fisheries Serv, 28 Tarzwell Dr, Narragansett, RI 02882. **Fax:** 401-782-3201. **E-Mail:** jack.jossi@noaa.gov

JOST, DANA NELSON, PHYCOLOGY, ENVIRONMENTAL BIOLOGY. **Personal Data:** b Arlington, Mass, May 11, 1925; m 1947, c 3. **Education:** Univ Mass, BS, 1949; Harvard Univ, PhD (biol), 1953. **Professional Experience:** PROF EMER, FRAMINGHAM STATE COL, AS OF 2006; chmn dept, Framingham State Col, 1964-1976; prof biol, Framingham State Col, 1959-1990; from asst prof to assoc prof, Framingham State Col, 1955-1959; instr, Framingham State Col, 1953-1955. **Memberships:** AAAS; Phycol Soc Am; Bot Soc Am; Int Phycol Soc; Mycol Soc Am; Am InstBiol Sci. **Research Statement & Publications:** Growth and reproduction of chlorophycean algae; evolution of microorganisms; environmental influences on algal growth; distribution and identification of freshwater periphyton. **Mailing Address:** Four William J Heights, Framingham, MA 01701-6134.

JOST, ERNEST M, PHYSICAL CHEMISTRY. **Personal Data:** b El Ferrol, Spain, September 6, 1928; American citizen; m 1955, c 4. **Education:** Univ Berne, license, 1955, PhD (phys chem), 1958. **Professional Experience:** PRES, CHEMET CORP, 1980-; dir prod res dept, Mat & Elec Prod Group, Tex Instruments Inc, Attleboro, 1974-1980; consult, Nat Acad Sci, 1971; dir res & develop, Mat & Elec Prod Group, Tex Instruments Inc, Attleboro, 1962-1974; mgr develop, Ciba A G, Switz, 1961-1962; mem tech staff, Metals & Controls Div, Tex Instruments Inc, 1958-1961. **Memberships:** Electrochem Soc; Royal Chem Soc. **Research Statement & Publications:** Metallurgy; electrochemistry; diffusion; solid state physics; semiconducting ceramics. **Mailing Address:** Nine Mirimichi St, Plainville, MA 02762. **Fax:** 508-695-4180.

JOST, HANS PETER, TRIBOLOGY, CENTRALIZED LUBRICATION SYSTEMS. **Personal Data:** b Berlin, Ger, January 25, 1921; British citizen; m 1948, Margaret Kadesh; c Jennifer Margot & Gillish Frances. **Education:** Univ Manchester Inst Sci & Technol, HNC, 1943. **Honorary Degrees:** DSc, Univ Salford, 1970, Univ Bath, 1990; DTech, Coun Nat Acad Awards, 1987; DrSc, Slovak Univ, Bratislava, 1987; DEng, Univ Leeds, 1989. **Honors & Awards:** Colclough Med & Prz, Inst of Mat, 1992; Comdr of the Order of the BritEmpire, HM the Queen, 1969; Georg Vogelpohl Insignia, Ger Tribology Soc, 1979; First NuffieldMedal, Inst Prod Engrs, 1981; Merit Medal, Hungarian Sci Soc Mech Engrs, 1983; Gold Insigniaof the Order of Merit, Supreme Coun of State of the Polish Repub, 1986. **Professional Experience:** Hon prof mech eng, Univ Wales, 1986; Found Sci & Technol, 1985 & Parliamentary Group Eng Develop, 1986; hon indust prof, Liverpool Polytechnic, 1983; ASSOCTECHNOL GROUP LTD & ENG & GEN EQUIP LTD, K S PAUL GROUP, 1977-; CHMN, KS PAUL GROUP, 1974-; chmn, Centralube Ltd, 1974-1977; Peppermill Brass Foundry Ltd, 1970-1976 & Indust Technol Mgt Bd, Dept Trade & Indust, 1972-1974; dir, Stothert & Pitt Plc, 1971-1985; mem, Comt Terotechnol, Dept Trade & Indust, 1971-1972; lubrication consult, Richard Thomas & Baldwins Ltd, 1969-1976; dir, Williams Hudson Ltd, 1967-1975; ComtTribology, Ministry, Technol, Dept Trade & Indust, 1966-1974; chmn, Lubrication Educ & ResWorking Group, Dept Educ & Sci, 1964-1965; managing dir, K S Paul Group, 1955-1989; Managing dir, Centralube Ltd, 1955-1977; gen mgr & dir, Trier Bros Ltd, 1949-1955; chiefplanning engr, Datim Mach Tool Co Ltd, 1946-1949; methods engr, K & L Steelfounders & EngrLtd, 1943. **Memberships:** Fel Am Soc Mech Engrs; fel Soc Mfg Engrs; fel Inst Metals; hon mem Inst Plant-Engrs; hon mem Chinese Mech Eng Soc; hon fel Inst Elec Engrs. **Research Statement & Publications:** Surface finish measurement; oil-free steam cylinder lubrication; solid lubricants and surface treatments; tribology. **Mailing Address:** K S Paul Prods Ltd, Angel Lodge Labs & Works Eley Estate, London N18 3DB, UK. **Fax:** 441-818-072023. **E-Mail:** hp.jost@t-online.de

JOST, JEAN-PIERRE, BIOCHEMISTRY CELL & MOLECULAR BIOLOGY. **Personal Data:** b Avenches, Switz, October 10, 1937; American citizen; m 1968, Tse Y Chim; c Isabelle King Yi & Alain King Ho. **Education:** Swiss Fed Inst Technol, MS, 1961, PhD (biol, biochem), 1964. **Professional Experience:** GROUP LEADER, FRIEDRICH MIESCHER INST, SWITZ, 1971-; NIH, Health, Educ & Welfare & NSF, 1970; res grants, Am Cancer Soc, 1969; molecular biologist, NatJewish Hosp & Res Ctr, Denver, 1968-1971; Asst prof, Dept Biophys & Genetics, Med Sch, Univ Colo, Denver, 1968-1971; fel, Lab Molecular Biol, 1967-1968; proj assoc, McArdle MemLab Cancer Res, Univ Wis-Madison, 1964-1966. **Research Statement & Publications:** Hormonal regulation of the expression of specific genes in eukaryotes, DNA methylation and genes expression and cell differentiation; transgenes inactivation in plants and animals linked to DNA methylation. **Mailing Address:** Friedrich Miescher Inst, Postfach 2543, CH-4002 Basel, Switzerland. **Fax:** 416-172-14091. **E-Mail:** jost@imi.ch; jean-pierre.jost@fmi.ch

JOST, PATRICIA COWAN, BIOPHYSICAL CHEMISTRY, MOLECULAR BIOLOGY. **Personal Data:** b St Louis, Mo. **Education:** Memphis State Univ, BS, 1952; Univ Ore, PhD (biol), 1966. **Honors & Awards:** CAS Alumni Fel, Univ Ore, 1989. **Professional Experience:** Co-dir, Biophys Prog, NSF, 1984-1986; SR RES ASSOC MOLECULARBIOL, INST MOLECULAR BIOL, UNIV ORE, 1968-; res assoc molecular genetics, InstMolecular Biol, Univ Ore, 1966-1968; NIH fel, Univ Ore, 1966-1968. **Memberships:** Biophys Soc. **Research Statement & Publications:** Membrane structure; reporter groups and magnetic resonance; membrane biology, lipid-lipid and lipid-protein interactions. **Mailing Address:** 750 E 27th St, Eugene, OR 97405.

JOSTLEIN, HANS, VACUUM ENGINEERING, EXPERIMENTAL PHYSICS. **Personal Data:** b Munich, WGer, December 27, 1940; American citizen; m 1967, Angela; c Christian, Thomas & Barbara. **Education:** Technische Hochschule M^unchen, Dipl Eng, 1965, Ludwigs Maximilian Univ, W Ger, PhD (physics), 1969. **Professional Experience:** FAC, STAFF, FERMILAB NAT ACCELERATOR LAB, as of 2006; PHYSICIST RES & ACCELERATION SUPPORT, FERMI NAT ACCELERATOR LAB, as of 2006; asst prof, State Univ NY, Stony Brook, 1973-1979; res asst, Univ Rochester, 1970-1973; fel high energy res, Univ Munich, 1969-1970. **Memberships:** APS. **Research Statement & Publications:** High energy particle physics, specifically muon; muon inelastic scattering; high mass pair production for leptons and hadrons to test quark theory; drell-yan processes and resonance production; very high lumosity pair production. **Mailing Address:** 122 Fermilab, PO Box 500 MS 208, Batavia, IL 60510. **E-Mail:** jostlein@fnal.gov

JOTHY, SERGE, MOLECULAR & CELL BIOLOGY. **Personal Data:** b Bordeaux, France, May 18, 1944; Canadian & French citizen; m Marie; c Vanessa & Antoine. **Education:** Univ Bordeaux, France, MD, 1968, MS, 1972; McGill Univ, PhD (exp med), 1976. **Professional Experience:** CHIEF, DEPT LAB MED & PATHOBIO, ST MICHAEL'S HOSP, 2002-; ASSOC MEM, DEPT ONCOL, MCGILL UNIV, 1992-; PROF DEPT PATH, MCGILL UNIV, 1991-; ASSOC MEM, CTR CLIN IMMUNOBIOL & TRANSPLANTATION, FACMED, MCGILL UNIV, 1989-; vis scientist, Pasteur Inst, Paris, France, 1986-1987; SR PATHOLOGIST, ROYALVICTORIA HOSP, MONTREAL, 1984-; from asst prof to assoc prof, Royal VictoriaHosp, Montreal, 1978-1990; asst pathologist, Royal Victoria Hosp, Montreal, 1978-1982; res asst, Dept Physiol, Univ Montreal, 1970-1971; asst profbiophys, Dept Med Biophys, Univ Bordeaux, France, 1968-1970. **Memberships:** Int Adv Board Advances in Clin & Exp Med Univ Med Sch Wroclaw; AAAS; Am Soc Cancer Rese; Am SocInvestigative Path; Int Acad Path; Int Soc Oncodevelopmental Biol & Med; WorldAsn Soc Path. **Research Statement & Publications:** Cellular and molecular biology of cell adhesion proteins; molecular biology of alterations of met oncogene; colon and breast cancer. **Mailing Address:** St Michael's hosp, 30 Bond St, Toronto, ON M5B 1W8, Can. **Fax:** 416-864-5648. **E-Mail:** jothys@smh.toronto.on.ca

JOUBERT, WAYNE DAVID, NUMERICAL ANALYSIS, NUMERICAL LINEAR ALGEBRA. **Personal Data:** b Opelousas, La, January 28, 1959; m 1996, Shirley Bleasdale. **Education:** Univ Southwestern La, BSc, 1981; Univ Tex, PhD (math), 1990. **Honors & Awards:** R & D 100 Award, 1997. **Professional Experience:** PRIN INVESTR, LOS ALAMOS NAT LAB, 1996-; TECH STAFF MEM, LOS ALAMOS NAT LAB, 1995-; postdoctoral fel, Los Alamos Nat Lab, 1992-1995; schlumberger Found fel, 1991; postdoctoral fel, Univ Tex, 1990-1992; Collabr, Advan ComputLab, Los Alamos Nat Lab, 1990-1991. **Memberships:** Soc Indust & Appl Math; Am Math Soc; Math Asn Am; Sigma Xi. **Research Statement & Publications:** Numerical analysis; numerical linear algebra; iterative linear system solvers; software development and parallel computing; oil reservoir simulation; ground water modeling; radiation diffusion modeling. **Mailing Address:** Los Alamos Nat Lab, Group CIC-19 MS B256, Los Alamos, NM 87545. **Fax:** 505-665-4972. **E-Mail:** wdj@lanl.gov

JOUBIN, FRANC RENAULT, CHEMISTRY. **Personal Data:** b San Francisco, Calif, November 15, 1911; Canadian citizen; m 1938, c 1. **Education:** Univ BC, BA, 1936, MA, 1941. **Honorary Degrees:** DSc, Univ BC, 1957. **Honors & Awards:** Can Mining Hall Fame; Leonard Gold Medal, Eng Inst Can, 1955; Blaylock Gold Medal, Can Inst Mining & Metall, 1957. **Professional Experience:** RETIRED; consult to adminr, UN Develop Prog, 1968-1977; pres, Bralorne Pioneer Mines, 1958-1960; dir, Guaranty Trust of Can, 1957-1960; geol consult, Rio Tinto Co, Eng, 1956-1958; dir, Rio Algom Mines, 1956-1958; Managing dir, Pronto, Pater, Rixahabasca, Rexspar, Lake Nordic, Spanish-Am & Panel Uranium Mines, 1953-1956; pres & managing dir, Algom Uranium Mines, 1953-1956; from mine geologist to explor geologist, Pioneer Gold Mines Co, 1938-1948. **Memberships:** Am InstMining, Metall & Petrol Eng; Can Inst Mining & Metall (vpres, 1957-1958); GeolAsn Can; Royal Can Inst. **Research Statement & Publications:** Geology; geophysics. **Mailing Address:** 581 Ave Rd, Toronto, ON M4V 2J6, Can.

JOULLIE, MADELEINE M, ORGANIC CHEMISTRY. **Personal Data:** b Paris, France, March 29, 1927; American citizen; m 1959, Richard. **Education:** Simmons Col, BS, 1949; Univ Pa, MS, 1950, PhD, 1953. **Honors & Awards:** ACS Henry Hill Award (1994) Lindback Award; Am Inst ChemAward; Garvan Medal. **Professional Experience:** PROF CHEM, UNIV PA, 1977-; from instr to assoc prof, Univ Pa, 1953-1977. **Memberships:** Fel NY Acad Sci; AAAS; Am Chem Soc; Sigma Xi. **Research Statement & Publications:** Mechanisms of organic reactions; heterocyclic chemistry; synthesis of potential antimetabolites; peptide synthesis; peptide mimetics. **Mailing Address:** Chem Dept, Univ Pa, 231 S 34th St, 455 N, Philadelphia, PA 19104-6323. **E-Mail:** mjoullie@sas.upenn.edu

JOUNG, JOHN JONGIN, CHEMICAL PROCESS ENGINEERING, BIOENGINEERING. **Personal Data:** b Korea, June 29, 1941; m 1968, c 2. **Education:** Seoul Nat Univ, BS, 1963, MS, 1967; Univ NMex, PhD (chem eng), 1970. **Professional Experience:** SR RES ENGR, AMOCO CORP, 1981-; sci adv, Am Hosp Supply Corp, 1978-1981; sr scientist, Colgate-Palmolive Co, 1976-1978; res supvr, Univ Chicago, 1971-1976; Res fel, Ames Lab, 1970-1971; assst investr, Korea Inst Sci & Technol, 1967-1968; vcmndgofficer, Chem Smoke Generator Co, Korea, 1963-1965. **Memberships:** Am Inst Chem Engrs; Am Chem Soc; Soc Plastics Engrs; Am Mgt Asn. **Research Statement & Publications:** Process and product research in the areas of chemical, polymer, energy and health care business; cancer and clinical pathology; process development for chemical and biological products, including recombinant DNA products; polymer applications for biomedical and personal care products; reaction engineering. **Mailing Address:** 6095 Millbridge Lane, Lisle, IL 60532.

JOURDIAN, GEORGE WILLIAM, BIOCHEMISTRY, MICROBIOLOGY. **Personal Data:** b Northampton, Mass, April 21, 1929; m 1954, c 2. **Education:** Amherst Col, BA, 1949; Univ Mass, MS, 1953; Purdue Univ, PhD (bact), 1958. **Professional Experience:** PROF EMER, DEPT BIOL CHEM, MED SCH, UNIV MICH, as of 2005; Fogarty sr int fel, 1978-1979; prof biol chem, Med Sch, Univ Mich, Ann Arbor, beginning 1965; res assoc internal med, Med Sch, Univ Mich, Ann Arbor, 1965-1974; from instr to assoc prof biol chem & biochem, MedSch, Univ Mich, Ann Arbor, 1961-1974; Arthritis Found fel, 1958-1961. **Memberships:** Am Soc Biol Chem; Am Chem Soc; Soc Complex Carbohydrates. **Research Statement & Publications:** Biochemistry of glycosaminoglycans and glycoproteins. **Mailing Address:** Dept Biol Chem, Med Sch, Univ Mich, 1301 E Catherine Box 0606 RM 5413 Med Sci I, Ann Arbor, MI 48109-0606. **E-Mail:** gjourdia@umich.edu

JOURNEAY, GLEN EUGENE, MEDICINE. **Personal Data:** b Orange, Tex, June 14, 1925; m 1948, Betty; c Carol A (Kaler), David G, Stephen D, Nancy C (Jackson) & Janet E (Slack). **Education:** Rice Univ, Houston, BA, 1945, BS, 1947; Univ Tex, Austin, PhD (org chem), 1952, Galveston, MD, 1960. **Honors & Awards:** M D Anderson Excellency in Oncol Award, 1985. **Professional Experience:** RETIRED; lectr, Univ Tex, Austin, beginning 1966; vis prof biomed eng, Univ Tex, Austin, 1964-1966; physician pvt pract, 1963-1993; physician, Beeler Manske Clin, Toxicity, 1961-1993; res chemist, Monsanto Chem, 1951-1956. **Memberships:** AMA; Am Acad Family Physicians; fel Am Chem Soc; fel Am Inst Chemists; Tx Med Assn; Acad Physicians. **Research Statement & Publications:** Cyanoethylation; hydrocyanic acid reactions; toxicity of acrylonitrile and acrylamide; neurotoxicity; environmental toxicology. **Mailing Address:** 3908 Sierra Dr, Austin, TX 78731-3912. **E-Mail:** journeay@mail.utexas.edu

JOURNET, ALAN, ECOLOGY. **Personal Data:** b London, Eng, m Kathy Conway. **Education:** Univ Wales, Glamorganshire, UK, Bsc, 1967; McGill Univ, Que, PhD, 1973. **Professional Experience:** FAC, DEPT BOIL, SOUTHEAST MO STATE UNIV, as of 2006. **Mailing Address:** Dept Biol, Southeast Mo State Univ, Rhodes 202, Cape Girardeau, MO 63701. **E-Mail:** ajournet@semo.edu

JOVANCICEVIC, VLADIMIR, ELECTROCHEMISTRY, CORROSION & PASSIVITY. **Personal Data:** b Belgrade, Yugoslavia, December 14, 1947; m 1969, c 1. **Education:** Univ Belgrad, BSc 1972, MSc 1976; Univ Paris VI, France, PhD (phys chem), 1980. **Honors & Awards:** W R Grace Res Award. **Professional Experience:** STAFF MEMBER, BAKER PETROLITE, as of 2000; SR RES CHEMIST, W R GRACE & CO, COLUMBIA, MD, 1989-; res chemist mat sci, W R Grace & CO, Columbia, MD, 1987-1989; sr res assocelectrochem, Tex A&M Univ, 1984-1987; sr scientist mat sci, Sasilor-Sollac, Thionville, France, 1982-1984; Nat Ctr Sci Res, Paris, 1981-1982; res assoc, Elec France, 1980-1981; res asstelectrochem, InstTech Sci, Belgrad, 1975-1978. **Memberships:** Electrochem Soc; Am Chem Soc; Nat Asn Chem Engrs. **Research Statement & Publications:** Investigation of the physico-chemical properties of metal-solution interfaces; spectroscopic characterization of the structure, composition and reactivity of the adsorbed and thin surface layers as related to the corrosion, passivation and electrodeposition; corrosion in cooling toxiers and boiler systems. **Mailing Address:** Baker Petrolite, 12645 Westairport Blvd, Sugarland, TX 77478. **Fax:** 281-275-7395. **E-Mail:** vladimir.jovancicevic@bakerpetrolite.com

JOVANOVIC, DRASKO D, HIGH ENERGY PHYSICS. **Personal Data:** b Belgrade, Yugoslavia, May 24, 1930. **Education:** Belgrade Univ, BS, 1953; Univ Chicago, MS, 1956, PhD (physics), 1959. **Professional Experience:** RETIRED; res scientist, fermi nat accelerator lab, beginning 1972. **Memberships:** Fel Am Phys Soc. **Mailing Address:** Fermi Nat Accelerator Lab, PO Box 500, Batavia, IL 60510. **E-Mail:** smphy@fnal.gov

JOVANOVICH, JOVAN VOJISLAV, HIGH ENERGY & NUCLEAR PHYSICS, NUCLEAR POWER. **Personal Data:** b Belgrade, Yugoslavia, July 30, 1928; m 1955, Anica; c Goran & Vera. **Education:** Univ Belgrade, BSc, 1950; Univ Man, MSc, 1956; Wash Univ, St Louis, PhD (physics), 1961. **Professional Experience:** SR SCHOLAR, UNIV MAN, as of

2005; PROF PHYSICS, UNIV MAN, 1979-; vis scientist, Orgn Europ Nuclear Res, 1971-1972 & 1978-1979; from asst prof to assoc prof, Univ Man, 1965-1979; develop officer, Oxford Univ, Nuclear Physics Lab, 1964-1965; res assoc, Brookhaven Nat Lab, 1961-1964; asst, Wash Univ, 1957-1961; Univ Belgrade, 1953-1955 & Univ Man, 1955-1957; asst physics, InstBrois Kidric, Belgrade, Yugoslavia, 1950-1954. **Memberships:** Am Phys Soc; Can Asn Physicists; Can Radiation Protect Asn; Can Nuclear Soc. **Research Statement & Publications:** Investigation of properties of neutral K mesons; elementary inelastic proton-proton interaction; search for quarks, pion properties; Chernobyl accident; sustainable development and nuclear power; raditation protection. **Mailing Address:** Physics Dept, Univ Man, Winnipeg, MB R3T 2N2, Can. **Fax:** 204-269-8489. **E-Mail:** jovan@physics.umanitoba.ca

JOVANOVICH, KIM DAYNE, FIBER OPTIC SENSOR RESEARCH & DEVELOPMENT, OPTICAL TELECOMMUNICATION SYSTEM DEVELOPMENT. **Personal Data:** b New Orleans, La, January 16, 1951; m 1974, Janet; c Brett, Eric & Mark. **Education:** Tulane Univ, BS, 1972; Univ Southern Miss, MS, 1978. **Professional Experience:** PRES, OMNI TECHNOL INC, 1994-; adj prof, Univ Col, Tulane, beginning 1993; tech dir, Omnicron Telecommun, beginning 1991; tech dir, Omnicron Telecommun, 1991-1994; staff electrooptics engr, Naval Res Lab, Stennis Space Ctr, NASA, 1990-1991; adj prof elec eng, UnivNew Orleans, beginning 1980; dir fiber optics res, Litton Data Systs Div, 1980-1991; sr commun engr, Comput Sci Corp, 1977-1980; capt, Sch Appl Aerospace Sci, USAF, 1972-1977. **Memberships:** Inst Elec & Electronics Engrs. **Research Statement & Publications:** Use of fiber optics to measure various physical phenomenon and environmental conditions; high speed laser and fiber optic telecommunicationand network design. **Mailing Address:** Omni Technols, Inc, 7412 Lakeshore Dr, New Orleans, LA 70124. **Fax:** 504-288-2899.

JOVANOVICH, MARINA, ENVIRONMENTAL CHEMISTRY. **Professional Experience:** AT LAWRENCE LIVERMORE NAT LAB, as of 1995. **Mailing Address:** Lawrence Livermore Nat Lab, Univ Calif, 7000 E Ave, Livermore, CA 94550-9234. **Fax:** 925-422-1370.

JOWETT, DAVID, STATISTICS, BOTANY. **Personal Data:** b Liverpool, Eng, October 14, 1934; m 1957, c 2. **Education:** Univ Wales, BSc, 1956, PhD (bot), 1959. **Professional Experience:** PROF EMER MATH, UNIV WIS-GREEN BAY, as of 2006; ACTG VICE CHANCELLOR ACAD AFFAIRS, UNIV WIS-GREEN BAY, as of 1986; intern, Acad Admin, Am Coun Educ, 1976-1977; prof math, Univ Wis-Green Bay, beginning 1972; assoc prof, Univ Wis-green Bay, 1970-1972; from asst prof to assocprof statist, Iowa State Univ, 1965-1970; Rockefeller Found fel, Iowa State Univ, 1962-1963; srsci officer, Plant Breeding, EAfrican Agr & Forestry Res Orgn, Uganda, 1959-1965; demonstragr bot, Univ Col NWales, 1956-1959. **Memberships:** AAAS; Brit Ecol Soc; Am Statist Asn; Inst Math Statist; Am Soc Nat; fel RoyalStatist Soc; Sigma Xi. **Research Statement & Publications:** Heavy metal resistance and tolerance of low nutrient levels in plants; improved varieties hybrids of sorghum for Africa; sorghum agronomy crown rust epiphytology; biostatistics; biomathematics; statistical computing. **Mailing Address:** Dept Math, Univ Wis, 2420 Nicolet Dr, Green Bay, WI 54311-7003.

JOY, DAVID CHARLES, ELECTRON MICROSCOPY, MATERIALS SCIENCE. **Personal Data:** b Colchester, Eng, November 15, 1943; American citizen; m 1979, Carolyn. **Education:** Cambridge Univ, BA, 1966; Oxford Univ, DPhil (metall), 1969. **Honors & Awards:** Burton Medal, Electron Micros Soc Am, 1978; Birks Award, Microbeam Anal Soc, 1985, Castaing Award, 1993. **Professional Experience:** DISTINGUISHED PROF, UNIV TENN, as of 2004; DISTINGUISHED SCIENTIST, OAK RIDGE NAT LAB, 1987-; prof, Univ Tenn, beginning 1987; gen ed, J Micros, 1981-1991; mem tech staff electron micros, Bell Tel Labs, 1974-1987; Warren res fel, Royal Soc London, 1972-1974; fac metall, Oxford Univ, 1969-1974; res fel, Imp Chem Industs, 1969-1971; res fel, Oxford Univ, 1969-1972. **Memberships:** Electron Micros Soc Am; Royal Micros Soc London. **Research Statement & Publications:** Electron microscopy and electron spectroscopy applied to microstructural and microchemical analysis; computer modeling of electron-solid interactions; electron holography; published over 350 articles. **Mailing Address:** Dept Biochem Cellular Molecular Biol, Univ Tenn, 232 Sci & Eng Res Facil, Knoxville, TN 37966-0810. **Fax:** 865-974-9449. **E-Mail:** djoy@utk.edu

JOY, EDWARD BENNETT, ANTENNA MEASUREMENTS, ANTENNA & RADOME DESIGN. **Personal Data:** b Troy, NY, November 15, 1941; m 1966, Patricia; c Frederick & Rebecca. **Education:** Ga Inst Technol, BEE, 1963, MS, 1967, PhD (elec eng), 1970. **Honors & Awards:** Young Scientist Year, URSI Comm A, 1972. **Professional Experience:** JOY ENG CO, GA INST TECHNOL, SCH ELEC ENG, 1981-; prof elec eng, Ga Inst Technol, Sch Elec Eng, 1980; PROF EMER ELEC ENG, GA INST TECHNOL, SCH ELEC ENG, 1980-; Prin investr, US Army, USAF, Elec Power Res Inst, NSF & Joint Ser Electronics Prog, 1970-; from asst prof to assoc prof, GA Inst Technol, Sch Elec Eng, 1970-1980; consult, Martin Marietta Aerospace, Sci Atlanta, Ford Aerospace, Harris Corp, Fed Aviation Admin, Westinghouse Elec, Sperry Corp, Gen Elec Corp & Alcoa, 1970-; lectr, US, Can, Europe, Mid East & Far East. **Memberships:** Fel Inst Elec & Electronics Engrs; Antenna Measurement Techniques Asn (vpres 1983-1084); Sigma Xi. **Research Statement & Publications:** Development of the theory, technique and application of far-field, anechoic chamber, compact and near-field antenna measurements; radome analysis, design and measurement; earth grounding of power delivery systems; holds three patents; over 120 publications. **Mailing Address:** Ga Inst Technol, 777 Atlantic Dr NW, Atlanta, GA 30332-0250.

JOY, GEORGE CECIL, III, INORGANIC CHEMISTRY. **Personal Data:** b Lincoln, Nebr, April 22, 1948; m 1970, c 1. **Education:** Grinnell Col, BA, 1970; Northwestern Univ, MS, 1971, PhD (inorg chem), 1975. **Professional Experience:** RES SCIENTIST, RES & TECH DIV, ALLIED-SIGNAL INC, 1990-, DIRRES & TECHNOL, EUROPE; dir, Tech Dept, Automotive Catalyst Div, 1987-1990; mgr applcatalysis res, Allied-Signal Inc, 1981-1986; group leader, Allied-Signal Inc, 1976-1981; reschemist, Allied-Signal Inc, 1974-1976. **Memberships:** Am Chem Soc; Nat Catalysis Soc; Soc Automotive Engrs; Inst Chem Engrs (UK). **Research Statement & Publications:** Studies in heterogeneous catalysis; inorganic aspects of preparation and characterization of catalysts. **Mailing Address:** 151 Mendham Rd, Bernardsville, NJ 07924.

JOY, JOSEPH WAYNE, PHYSICAL OCEANOGRAPHY. **Personal Data:** b Iowa City, Iowa, April 12, 1930; m 1958, c 3. **Education:** State Col Wash, BA, 1955; Univ Calif, San Diego, MS, 1958. **Professional Experience:** RETIRED; opers res analyst, US Navy Personnel Res & Develop Ctr, SanDiego, Calif, 1992-1994; comput spec, US Navy Personnel Res & Develop Ctr, San Diego, Calif, 1988-1992; comput spec, Nat Marine Fisheries Serv, Nat Oceanic & Atmospheric Admin, US Dept Com, 1984-1988; staff oceanogr, Intersea Res Corp, 1974-1984; specialist oceanog, Scripps Inst Oceanog, Univ Calif, San Diego, 1970-1974; sr scientist, Westinghouse Ocean Res Lab, Calif, 1967-1970; res oceanogr, Meteorol Res Inc, 1966-1967; oceanogr, Marine Adv, BendixCorp, 1961-1966; res oceanogr, Marine Phys Lab, Univ Calif, San Diego, 1956-1961. **Memberships:** AAAS; Am Geophys Union; Am Meteorol Soc. **Research Statement & Publications:** Surface waves and currents; radar oceanography; radar as oceanographic tool. **Mailing Address:** 1210 Agate St, San Diego, CA 92109.

JOY, KENNETH WILFRED, PLANT PHYSIOLOGY. **Personal Data:** b Sunderland, Eng, May 13, 1935; c 2. **Education:** Bristol Univ, BSc, 1956, PhD (plant physiol), 1959. **Professional Experience:** Killam prof, Can Coun, 1994-1996; PROF BIOL, CARLETON UNIV, 1968-; assoc prof bot, Univ Toronto, 1966-1968; Fulbright travel fel, 1964-1965; vis res assoc agron, Univ Ill, Urbana, 1964-1965; res assoc plant physiol, Imp Col, Univ London, 1959-1964. **Memberships:** Am Soc Plant Physiol; Can Soc Plant Physiol (secy 1968-1969). **Research Statement & Publications:** Nitrogen metabolism of plants, especially amino acid metabolism; synthesis and utilization of amides. **Mailing Address:** Dept Biol Carleton Univ, 1125 Colonel By Dr, Ottawa, ON K1S 5B6, Can.

JOY, MICHAEL LAWRENCE GRAHAME, BIOMEDICAL ENGINEERING. **Personal Data:** b Toronto, Ont, July 31, 1940; m 1967, Jane; c Robert, Gwendolyn & Eleanor. **Education:** Univ Toronto, BSc, 1963, MASc, 1968, PhD (elec eng), 1970. **Professional Experience:** ASSOC DIR GRAD STUDIES, INST BIOMAT & BIOMED ENG, UNIV TORONTO; PROF & CHMN, DEPT ELEC & COMPUT ENG, UNIV TORONTO, 2004, 2005; assoc chmn, elec & comput eng, Univ Toronto, beginning 1993; assoc prof biomed & elec eng, Univ Toronto, beginning 1976; asst prof elec eng, Univ Toronto, 1970-1976. **Memberships:** Can Med & Biol Eng Soc; Inst Elec & Electronics Engrs; Soc Magnetic Resonance. **Research Statement & Publications:** Electric current density and conductivity imaging by magnetic resonance. **Mailing Address:** Inst Biomat & Biomed Eng Univ Toronto, Rm 411 Rosebrugh Bldg 164 Col St, Toronto, ON M5S 3G9, Can. **Fax:** 416-978-4317. **E-Mail:** mike.joy@utoronto.ca

JOY, ROBERT JOHN THOMAS, INTERNAL MEDICINE, PHYSIOLOGY. **Personal Data:** b South Kingstown, RI, April 5, 1929; m 1985, Janet; c Robert L F & Lisa. **Education:** Univ RI, BS, 1950; Yale Univ, MD, 1954; Harvard Univ, MA, 1965. **Honors & Awards:** Osler Medal, Am Asn Hist Med, 1954; Hoff Mem Medal Mil Med, 1959; J S Billings Award, 1966; Clements Award, 1980; Davies Award, 2002. **Professional Experience:** PROF EMER MED HIST, UNIFORMED SERV UNIV HEALTH SCI, 1996-; ed, Jour Hist Med & Allied Sci, 1982-1987; prof, Uniformed Serv Univ Health Sci, 1981-1996; prof mil med & hist & chmn dept, Uniformed Serv Univ Health Sci, 1976-1981; dir & comdr, Walter Reed Army Inst Res, 1975-1976; dep dir, Directorate Defense Res & Eng, 1971-1975; dep biol & med res, Directorate Defense Res & Eng, 1969-1971; chief Med Res Div, US Army Med Res & Develop Command, Wash, DC, 1968-1969; dep dir, US Army Res Inst Environ Med, MA, 1966-1968; chief med res team, Walter Reed Army Inst Res, Vietnam, 1965-1966; comdr & mem res staff, Army Res Inst Environ Med, 1961-1963; chief, Bioastronaut Br, Army Med Res Lab, Ft Knox, KY, 1959-1961; resident, Walter Reed Gen Hosp, 1956-1958; med Corps, US Army, 1954-1981; intern, Walter Reed Gen Hosp, 1954-1955. **Memberships:** Am Asn Hist Med; fel AAAS; Am Physiol Soc; fel Am Col Physicians; Osler Soc. **Research Statement & Publications:** Environmental physiology and medicine; history of medicine; military medical history; research administration and management. **Mailing Address:** Uniformed Serv Univ Health Sci, 4301 Jones Bridge Rd, Bethesda, MD 20814-4799.

JOY, VINCENT ANTHONY, internal medicine; deceased, see previous edition for last biography

JOYCE, BLAINE R, PHYSICAL CHEMISTRY. **Personal Data:** b Jeannette, Pa, November 13, 1925; m 1955, c 3. **Education:** Univ Pittsburgh, BS, 1949; Univ Toledo, MS, 1965. **Professional Experience:** CONSULT & PRES, ACTIVATED TECH SERV CO, 1986-; tech dir activated carbon, Carbon Prod Div, 1980-1986; sr develop engr, Carbon Prod Div, 1968-1980; mgr activated carbon prod eng, Union Carbide Corp, 1965-1968; group leader activated carbon, Union Carbide Corp, 1960-1965; develop engr, Union Carbide Corp, 1953-1960; Res assoc activated carbon, Mellon Inst, 1949-1951. **Memberships:** Am Chem Soc. **Research Statement & Publications:** Production and applications of arc carbons for lighting and metal processing applications; development of activated carbon products and cost studies for business product planning. **Mailing Address:** 453 Cranston Dr, Berea, OH 44017.

JOYCE, EDWIN A, MARINE SCIENCE. **Personal Data:** b Hampton, Va, February 23, 1937; m 1978, Mary; c Chris, Kelly, Beth, Trip, Kathy, Carson & Kim. **Education:** Butler Univ, BA, 1959; Univ Fla, Gainesville, MS, 1961. **Professional Experience:** RETIRED; dir, Div Marine Resources, 1975-1988; chief, Bur Marine Sci & Technol, 1972-1975; supvr, Marine Res Lab, 1968-1972; sr fisheries biologist, Fla Dept Natural Resources, 1967-1968; marine biologist, Fla Bd Conserv, 1961-1967. **Memberships:** Am Fisheries Soc; fel Am Inst Fishery Res Biologists; Sigma Xi; Nat Shellfisheries Asn. **Research Statement & Publications:** Research and publications on shellfish issues and administrative activities in fishery management and research supervision. **Mailing Address:** 14130 N Meridian Rd, Tallahassee, FL 32312.

JOYCE, GERALD F, MOLECULAR EVOLUTION. **Personal Data:** b Manhattan, Kans, November 28, 1956. **Education:** Univ Chicago, BS, 1978; Univ Calif, San Diego, MD & PhD (nucleic acids), 1984. **Honors & Awards:** Molecular Biol Award, Nat Acad Sci, 1994. **Professional Experience:** INVESTR, SKAGGS INST CHEM BIOL, SCRIPPS RES INST, as of 2002; PROF, DEPT CHEM & MOLECULAR BIOL, SCRIPPS RES INST, 1996-; assoc prof, Dept Chem & Molecular Biol, Scripps Res Inst, 1992-1996; asst prof, Dept Chem & Molecular Biol, Scripps Res Inst, 1989-1992; Merck fel, Life Sci Res Found, 1985-1988. **Memberships:** Am Chem Soc; Int Soc Study Origins Life. **Research Statement & Publications:** Molecular biology; biochemistry. **Mailing Address:** Dept Molecular Biol, Scripps Res Inst, MB 4B 10550 N Torrey Pines Rd, La Jolla, CA 92037. **Fax:** 858-784-2943. **E-Mail:** gjoyce@scripps.edu

JOYCE, GLENN RUSSELL, PLASMA PHYSICS. **Personal Data:** b St Louis, Mo, June 24, 1939; m 1962, c 1. **Education:** Cent Methodist Col, BA, 1961; Univ Mo, MS, 1963, PhD (physics), 1966. **Professional Experience:** SR RES SCIENTIST, NAVAL RES LAB, 1981-; vis res scientist, Goddard Space Flight Ctr, NASA, 1975-1979; Vis assoc prof, Hunter Col, 1974; res scientist physics, Max Planck Inst Plasma Physics, 1969; from assoc prof to prof physics, Univ Iowa, 1968-1981; Res assoc, Univ Iowa, 1966-1968. **Memberships:** Am Phys Soc. **Research Statement & Publications:** Plasma theory; interaction of test particles with plasmas; particle simulation of plasmas; numerical simulation and kinetic theory of plasmas. **Mailing Address:** Plasma Physics Div, Naval Res Lab, Code 6794, Washington, DC 20375-5346. **Fax:** 202-767-0631. **E-Mail:** joyce@ppd.nrl.navy.mil

JOYCE, JAMES MARTIN, ATOMIC COLLISIONS, COMPUTER APPLICATIONS. **Personal Data:** b Bayonne, NJ, January 27, 1942; m 1965, c 2. **Education:** LaSalle Col, BA, 1963; Univ Pa, MS, 1964, PhD (physics), 1967. **Professional Experience:** DIR UNDER GRAD STUDIES, E CAROLINA UNIV, as of 2003; ASST CHMN, DEPT PHYSICS, E

CAROLINA UNIV, as of 2003; Prof Physics, E Carolina univ, 1979-; Dir Digital Syst, E Carolina univ, 1976-; from asst prof to assoc prof, E Carolina Univ, 1970-1979; dir accelerator lab, E carolina Univ, 1970-1976; Res assoc nuclear physics, Univ NC, Chapel Hill, 1967-1970. **Memberships:** Am Phys Soc; Sigma Xi. **Research Statement & Publications:** Experimental atomic physics and applied physics; computer systems and interface design; physics applied to medicine; Analyzing Gastric Electrical Control Activity; Continuum Electron Intramolecular Outscattering from Bare MeVin El and He Projectiles Traversing Hydrocarbon Oases. **Mailing Address:** Dept Physics E Carolina Univ, Greenville, NC 27858-4353. **Fax:** 252-328-6314. **E-Mail:** joycej@mail.ecu.edu

JOYCE, JOHN RANDAL, INSTRUMENT DESIGN & AUTOMATION. **Education:** Univ Tulsa, BS, 1977; Tex A&M Univ, PhD (anal chem), 1983. **Professional Experience:** CONTRIB ED, SCI COMPUT & AUTOMATION, GORDON PUBL, 1994-; LIMS MGR, DIVCONSOL LAB SERV, COMMONWEALTH VA, 1993-; proj leader, Instrument Develop &Automation Group, Dow Chem Co, 1983-1993. **Research Statement & Publications:** Internet and laboratory automation; coordinate LIMS development and instrument automation activities for state laboratory. **Mailing Address:** DGS Div Consol Lab Serv, 1 N 14th St, Richmond, VA 23219. **Fax:** 501-423-7555. **E-Mail:** jjoyce@dgs.state.va.us

JOYCE, NANCY C, CELL BIOLOGY, PHARMACOLOGY OF THE CORNEAL ENDOTHELIUM. **Personal Data:** b New Haven, Conn, August 28, 1945. **Education:** Alburtos Magnis Col, BA, 1967; Yale Univ, PhD (cellular biol), 1985. **Professional Experience:** ASSOC PROF OPHTHAL, MED SCH, HARVARD UNIV, as of 2003; SR SCIENTIST, MED SCH, HARVARD UNIV, as of 2003; asst prof res, Harvard Univ, beginning 1992; assoc scientist, Schepens Eye Res Inst, beginning 1992; asst scientist, Harvard, Univ, 1987-1992; res fel, YaleUniv, 1985-1987. **Memberships:** Asn Res Vision & Ophthal; Am Soc Cell Biol; AAAS. **Research Statement & Publications:** Cell biology; pharmacology of the corneal endothelium. **Mailing Address:** Schepens Eye Res Inst, 20 Staniford St, Boston, MA 02114. **Fax:** 617-912-0144. **E-Mail:** njoyce@vision.eri.harvard.edu

JOYCE, RICHARD ROSS, ASTRONOMY. **Personal Data:** b Wilmington, Del, June 28, 1944; m 1979, Sandra. **Education:** Williams Col, BA, 1965; Univ Calif, Berkeley, PhD (physics), 1970. **Professional Experience:** SUPPORT SCIENTIST ASTRON, KITT PEAK NAT OBSERV, 1973-; lectr, State Univ NY, Stony Brook, 1972-1973; fel astron, State Univ NY, Stony Brook, 1970-1972; Res asst physics, Lawrence Radiation Lab, Univ Calif, Berkeley, 1966-1970. **Memberships:** Am Phys Soc; Astron Soc Pac; Am Astron Soc. **Research Statement & Publications:** Infrared detector development; telescope optimization for infrared use; study of heavily obscured and/or cool sources in infrared; study of infrared emission line sources; infrared instrumentation for large telescopes. **Mailing Address:** National Optical Astron Observatory, PO Box 26732, Tucson, AZ 85726-6732. **E-Mail:** rjoyce@noao.edu

JOYCE, WILLIAM, CHEMISTRY. **Personal Data:** b Greensburg, Pa, December 15, 1935; m Kathleen; c William, Susan & Diana. **Education:** Pa State Univ, BS, 1957; NY Univ, MBA, 1971, PhD, 1974. **Honors & Awards:** Nat Medal Technol, Pres Clinton, NSF, 1993; Indust Achievement Award, Plastics Acad, 1994. **Professional Experience:** CHMN, UNION CARBIDE CORP, 1996-; PRES & CHIEF EXEC OFFICER, UNION CARBIDE CORP, 1993-; BD DIR, UNION CARBIDE CORP, 1992-; exec vpres opers, Union Carbide, 1992-1993; dir-at-large, chmn & immediate past chmn, bd dirs, Soc Plastics Indust, 1988-1991; pres, Polyolefins Div, Union Carbide, 1985-1992; pres, Silicones& Urethane Intermediates Div, Union Carbide, 1982-1985; vpres, licensing/technol, UnionCarbide, 1979; vpres, Marketing, Union Carbide, 1978-1979; dir, Polyolefins Opers, UnionCarbide, 1976-1978; opers mgr, Union Carbide, 1974-1976; prod mgr, Chem & Plastics Group, Union Carbide, 1971-1974; engr, Union Carbide, 1957-1968; bd trustees, Univ Res Asn, Inc; bd dirs, Chem Mfr Asn, Am PlasticsCoun, Melville Corp & Reynolds Metals Co. **Memberships:** Nat Acad Eng; Inst Elec & Electronics Engrs. **Mailing Address:** Union Carbide Corp, 39 Old Ridgebury Rd L4, Danbury, CT 06817-0001.

JOYCE, WILLIAM B, THEORETICAL PHYSICS. **Personal Data:** b Columbus, Ohio, October 17, 1932; m 1958, Alice Barker; c Ann, John, Wendy & William Chuck. **Education:** Cornell Univ, BEP, 1955; Ohio State Univ, PhD (physics), 1966. **Professional Experience:** CONSULT, LUCENT BELL LABS, 2004-; fel, Agere Sys, 2001-2003; fel Lucent, Bell Labs, 1988-2001; distinguished mem tech staff, AT&T Bell Labs, 1982-1988; mem tech staff, AT&T Bell Labs, 1966-1981; mgr advan technol, Accuray Corp, Ohio, 1963-1966. **Memberships:** Am Phys Soc. **Research Statement & Publications:** Applied theoretical physics. **E-Mail:** wbj@mailaps.org

JOYNER, CLAUDE REUBEN, MEDICINE. **Personal Data:** b Winston-Salem, NC, December 4, 1925; m 1950, c 2. **Education:** Univ NC, BS, 1947; Univ Pa, MD, 1949; Am Bd Internal Med, dipl, 1957; Am BdCardiovasc Dis, dipl, 1963. **Professional Experience:** PROF MED, MED COL PA, 1988-; DIR DEPT MED, ALLEGHENY GENHOSP, PITTSBURGH, 1972-; clin prof med, Univ Pittsburgh, 1972-1988; prof med, HahnemannMed Col, 1971-1972; attend cardiologist, Vet AdminHosp, Philadelphia, beginning 1963; from instr to assoc prof, Sch Med, Univ Pa, 1953-1971; Nat HeartInst trainee & asst instr, Sch Med, Univ Pa, 1952-1953; Resdient med, Bowman Gray Sch Med, 1950; mem coun arteriosclerosis, Am Heart Asn. **Memberships:** fel AAAS; Am Heart Asn; fel Am Col Physicians; Am Fedn Clin Res; fel Am ColCardiol. **Research Statement & Publications:** Academic medicine; cardiology; phonocardiography; ultrasound. **Mailing Address:** Allegheny Gen Hosp, 320 E North Ave, Pittsburgh, PA 15212-4772.

JOYNER, H(OWARD) SAJON, ENGINEERING. **Personal Data:** b Ft Worth, Tex, June 6, 1939; m 1969, Mary E Yankoff; c 3. **Education:** Univ Tex, Austin, BS, 1962, MA, 1964; Univ Mo, Rolla, MS, 1967, PhD, 1970. **Professional Experience:** PRES, KINETIC CORP, 1977-; dir planning, res& develop, Univ Kans Sch Med, Wichita, 1975-1977; asst prof mech eng, Wichita State Univ, 1969-1975; Nuclear engr, Gen Dynamics-Ft Worth, 1964; adj prof, Wichita State Univ. **Research Statement & Publications:** Thermal systems, especially anti-ice systems on aircraft wings and tails. **Mailing Address:** Kinetic Corp, PO Box 8161, Wichita, KS 67208.

JOYNER, JOHN T, III, INTERNAL MEDICINE. **Personal Data:** b Winston-Salem, NC, June 27, 1928; m 1950, c 3. **Education:** Wake Forest Col, BS, 1948, MD, 1952; Am Bd Internal Med, 1962. **Professional Experience:** Asst prof clin med, Duke Univ, 1977-1990; CHIEF MED SERV, VET ADMIN HOSP, ASHVILLE, 1975-; chief nuclear med, 1965-1975; chief gen med, Vet Admin Hosp, Ashville, 1961; staff physician, 1958-1961; Chief resident med, Hosp, Emory Univ, 1957-1958. **Memberships:** AMA; Am Col Physicians; Am Soc Nuclear Med. **Mailing Address:** Vet Admin Hosp, Asheville, NC 28805. **Fax:** 704-298-7911 Ext 5608.

JOYNER, POWELL AUSTIN, research management; deceased, see previous edition for last biography

JOYNER, RONALD WAYNE, CARDIAC ELECTROPHYSIOLOGY, NEUROPHYSIOLOGY. **Personal Data:** b Wake Forest, NC, March 21, 1947; m 1969, c 1. **Education:** Univ NC, BS, 1969; Duke Univ, MD, 1974, PhD (physiol), 1973. **Professional Experience:** PROF PEDIAT & PHYSIOL, EMORY UNIV, 1987-; asst prof physiol, UnivIowa, 1977-1987; asst prof physiol, Duke Univ, 1976-1977. **Memberships:** Biophys Soc. **Research Statement & Publications:** Mechanisms of propagation of cardiac action potentials related to cardiac arrythmias, by electrophysiological and numerical simulation techniques; synaptic transmission and motor control in squid. **Mailing Address:** Dept Pediat & Physiol, Emory Univ, 2040 Ridgewood Dr, Atlanta, GA 30322. **Fax:** 404-727-6024. **E-Mail:** rjoyner@cellbio.emory.edu

JOYNER, WEYLAND THOMAS, NUCLEAR PHYSICS, ELECTRONICS. **Personal Data:** b Suffolk, Va, August 8, 1929; m 1955, c 3. **Education:** Hampden-Sydney Col, BS, 1951; Duke Univ, MA, 1952, PhD (physics), 1955. **Professional Experience:** PROF EMER PHYSICS & ASTRON, HAMPDEN-SYDNEY COL, as of 2005; NASA sr fel, 1984 & 1985; vis prof, Dartmouth Col, 1981; chmn physics comt, Col Entrance Exam Bd, 1971-1972; chmn dept, Hampden-Sydney Col, beginning 1969; prof physics, Hampden-Sydney Col, beginning 1967; dir Col physics prog, Am Inst Physics, 1967-1968; staff physicist, Univ Mich, Ann Arbor, 1966-1967; vis prof, Pomona Col, 1965; respartic, Ames Lab, AEC, 1964, 1965; prof, Hampden-Sydney, Col, 1963-1966; consult, OakRidge Inst Nuclear Studies, 1960-1966; assoc prof, Hampden-Sydney, Col, 1959-1963; asst prof, Hampden-Sydney, Col, 1957-1959; physicist, dept defense, 1954-1957; fel, Duke Univ, 1953-1954; asst physics, Duke Univ, 1951-1953. **Memberships:** Am Phys Soc; Am Asn Physics Teachers; Inst Elec & Electronics Engrs; fel AAAS. **Research Statement & Publications:** Positron lifetimes; picosecond circuitry; x-ray fluorescence; silicon deep impurity devices; radon. **Mailing Address:** Dept Physics & Astron, Hampden-Sydney Col, Gilmer 009 PO Box 608, Hampden-Sydney, VA 23943. **E-Mail:** tomj@tiger.edu

JOYNER, WILLIAM HENRY, JR, COMPUTER SCIENCE. **Personal Data:** b Washington, DC, September 21, 1946; m 1968, c 2. **Education:** Univ Va, BS, 1968; Harvard Univ, SM, 1969, PhD (appl math), 1973. **Professional Experience:** ACCT EXEC, SEMICONDUCTOR RES CORP, as of 2004; RES STAFF MEM COMPUT SCI, IBM THOMASJ WATSON RES CTR, 1973-. **Memberships:** Asn Comput Mach. **Research Statement & Publications:** Computer program verification; automated theorem proving; machine description languages; VLSI design. **Mailing Address:** Semiconductor Res Corp, Suite 120, Brighton Hall, 1101 Slater Rd, Durham, NC 27703. **Fax:** 919-941-9450. **E-Mail:** joyner@src.org

JOYNER, WILLIAM LYMAN, PHYSIOLOGY. **Personal Data:** b Farmville, NC, June 10, 1939; m 1982, Chris; c William J, Candace D, Andrew W & Evan C. **Education:** Davidson Col, BS, 1965; Univ NC, MSPH, 1967, PhD (physiol), 1971. **Professional Experience:** DIR, CARDIOVASC RES INST, E TENN STATE UNIV, as of 2004; PROF PHYSIOL & CHMN, COL MED, E TENN STATE UNIV, 1989-; pres, Microcircular Soc Inc, 1987; prof, Col Med, Univ Nebr Med Ctr, 1983-1989; pharm travel grantee, Microcirculatory Soc, 1975; from asst prof to assoc prof physiol, Col Med, Univ Nebr Med Ctr, 1973-1983; trainee, Med Ctr, Duke Univ, 1971-1973; res assoc physiol, Univ NC, 1967-1969; res technician animal med, Univ NC, 1965-1967. **Memberships:** Am Physiol Soc; Microcurculatory Soc; AAAS; Soc Exp Biol & Med; Royal Soc Med; Europe Soc Microcirculation. **Research Statement & Publications:** Cardiovascular physiology particularly the microcirculation, molecular transport, vascular reactivity and controlling mechanisms; hypertension, diabetes and alterations in blood coagulation and hemostasis related to hemodynamic responses of the microcirculation in various tissues. **Mailing Address:** Dept Physiol James H Quillen Col Med E Tenn Univ, PO Box 70576, Johnson City, TN 37614. **Fax:** 423-439-2052. **E-Mail:** joynerw@xtn.net

JOYNSON, REUBEN EDWIN, PHYSICS. **Personal Data:** b Winfield, Kans, December 27, 1926. **Education:** Kans State Univ, BS, 1949, MS, 1950; Mass Inst Technol, PhD (physics), 1954. **Professional Experience:** RETIRED; physicist, Res & Develop Ctr, 1963-1987; consult physicist, Comput Lab, Gen Elec Co, 1960-1963; res physicist, Continental Oil Co, 1954-1960. **Memberships:** AAAS; Am Phys Soc; Sigma Xi. **Research Statement & Publications:** X-ray diffraction; digital computer design and programming; cryogenics; thin film devices; artificial intelligence; visual image processing. **Mailing Address:** 251 Alplaus Ave, PO Box 118, Alplaus, NY 12008.

JOYNT, ROBERT JAMES, NEUROLOGY. **Personal Data:** b LeMars, Iowa, December 22, 1925; m Margaret; c Robert, Patricia, Mary, Anne, Thomas & Kathleen. **Education:** Westmar Col, BA, 1949; Univ Iowa, MD, 1952, MS, PhD (anat), 1963; Am BdPsychiat & Neurol, dipl, 1959. **Honorary Degrees:** DSc, Westmar Col, 1964. **Honors & Awards:** Netter Award, Am Acad Neurol, 1988; George W Jacoby Award, Am NeurolAsn, 1992; Gold-Headed Cane Award, Univ of California 1986; Scripps Medal 1991; Yoder Award 1991; Distinguished Alumni Award, Univ of Iowa 1999. **Professional Experience:** Mem, Bd Regents, Nat Library Med, 1992-1996; vpres, health affairs, 1989-1994; dean, Sch Med & Dent, 1985-1990; vprovost, Sch Med & Dent, 1985-1989; ed, Arch Neurol, 1982-; bd adv, off biometry & epidemiol, NINCDS, 1976-1984; Mem res traininggrant comt, Nat Inst Neurol Dis & Blindness, 1963-1967 & neurol study sect, div res grants, NIH, 1967-1972; mem Inst of Med 1989; prof neurol & anat & chmn dept neurol, Med Ctr, Univ Rochester, 1966-1984; Distinguished University Professor 1996-; from asst prof to assoc prof, Univ Iowa, 1958-1966; Assoc neurol, Univ Iowa, 1957-1958. **Memberships:** Am Neurol Asn; Am Acad Neurol; Am Electroencephalog Soc; Am Med Asn; InstMed; fel AAAS. **Research Statement & Publications:** Investigation of fluid control by central nervous system; correlation of performance tests with lesions in brain damaged patients; Alzheimer's disease. **Mailing Address:** Sch Med & Dent, Univ Rochester, Rochester, NY 14642. **Fax:** 585-442-6480. **E-Mail:** robert_joynt@urmc.rochester.edu

JOYS, TERENCE MICHAEL, RECOMBINANT DNA, VACCINES. **Personal Data:** b Hull, Eng, January 19, 1935; m 1960, c 3. **Education:** Leeds Univ, Eng, BSc, 1957; London Univ, Eng, PhD (microbiol gen), 1961. **Professional Experience:** ASSOC PROF IMMUNOL, TEX TECH HEALTH SCI CTR, as of 2002; vis scientist, Max Planck Inst, Munich, Ger, 1990; assoc prof med microbiol, Pa State Univ, 1976; career develop award, US Pub Health Dept, 1969-1974; asst prof bact genetics, Univ Ore MedSch, 1965-1976; instr bact, Univ Minn, 1964-1965. **Memberships:** Am Soc Microbiol; Am Acad Microbiol; Southern Asn Agr Scientists. **Research Statement & Publications:** Structure of bacterial flagellan filament protein and its use in vaccine development. **Mailing Address:** Dept Microbiol, Tex Tech Univ Sch Med 3601 Fourth St, Lubbock, TX 79430-0002.

JOZEFOWICZ, RALPH F, NEUROLOGY. **Education:** Johns Hopkins Univ, BA, 1975; Columbia Univ, MD, 1979. **Professional Experience:** PROF NEUROL & MED & ASSOC CHAIR EDUC & NEUROL, UNIV ROCHESTER SCH MED & DENT, as of 2006. **Memberships:** Am Acad Neurol. **Mailing Address:** Dept Neurol, Univ Rochester, Rochester, NY 14642.

JU, FREDERICK D, THEORETICAL & APPLIED MECHANICS. **Personal Data:** b Shanghai, China, September 21, 1929; American citizen; m 1956, Ruby; c Wilfred, Manfred & Winifred. **Education:** Univ Houston, BS, 1953; Univ Ill, MS, 1956, PhD (theoret & appl mech), 1958. **Honors & Awards:** Soc Theoret & Appl Mech Award, 1986; Chinese Soc Mat Sci Award, 1986. **Professional Experience:** RETIRED; chmn dept, Halliburton prof mech eng, beginning 1992; chmn dept, 1973-1976 & 1989-1992 pres prof, 1985-1992; prin investr, Off Naval Res, beginning 1981; vis staff mem, Los Alamos Nat Lab, beginning 1972; nat vis prof, Nat Sci Coun, Repub of China, 1971-1972; Consult, Los Alamos NatLab, beginning 1962; prin investr, Air Force Off Sci Res, 1961-1972; from asst prof to prof, Univ NMex, 1958-1994. **Memberships:** Fel Am Soc Mech Engrs; Soc Eng Sci; Sigma Xi. **Research Statement & Publications:** Fracture diagnosis in structures; thermo-mechanical cracking from friction loading; structural safety of reactor; reliability of tribo-coatings. **Mailing Address:** Dept Mech Eng, Univ NMex, Albuquerque, NM 87131-1361.

JU, JIN SOON, PROTEIN NUTRITION, AGING & NUTRITION. **Personal Data:** b Hamhung, Ham-nam Prov, October 20, 1921; m 1948, c 2. **Education:** Seoul Nat Univ, MD, 1947, PhD (nutrit), 1959. **Honors & Awards:** Korea Nat Acad Sci Award, 1985. **Professional Experience:** DIR, KOREA GERONT CTR, HALLYM UNIV, SEOUL, 1990-; EMER-PROF BIOCHEM & NUTRIT, KOREA UNIV MED COL, SEOUL, KOREA, 1987-; DIR &PROF NUTRIT, KOREA NUTRIT INST, HALLYM UNIV, CHUN-CHON, KOREA, 1987-; prof, Korea Univ Med Col, 1953-1987; prof nutrit, Nat Fisheries Col, Pusan, Korea, 1950-1953; researcher nutrit, Nat Chem Lab, Korea, 1947-1950. **Memberships:** Am Inst Nutrit; Int Union Nutrit Sci; Pac Sci Asn; Korea Nat Acad Sci. **Research Statement & Publications:** Protein metabolism in human and animals, especially protein requirement of Korean. **Mailing Address:** 691-8 Jayang-dong, Hallym U Hanyang Villa No 203 Suengdong-ku, Seoul 133-192, South Korea. **Fax:** 822-633-0018.

JUANG, JER-NAN, TEST METHODS FOR SPACESTRUCTURES, LINEAR ALGEBRA. **Personal Data:** b Tou-Liu, Taiwan, July 21, 1945; American citizen; m 1977, Lily; c Philo & Derek. **Education:** Nat Cheng Kung Univ, Taiwan, BS, 1969; Tenn Technol Univ, MS, 1971; Va Polytech Inst, PhD (eng mech), 1974. **Honors & Awards:** Dirk BrouwerAward, Am Astronaut Soc, 1991; Mech & Control Award, Am Inst Aeronaut & Astronaut, 1993; Merit Awards, Am Soc Mech Engrs; Spec Achievment, NASA. **Professional Experience:** PROF LECTR ENG & PRIN SCIENTIST, LANGLEY RES CTR, NASA, as of 2003; J Guidance, J Vibration & Acoust, 1991-; adj prof, Univ Colo, Boulder, 1988-1991; J Guidance, Control & Dynamics, 1988-1991; mem, Tech Comt Composite LargeSpace Struct, 1987-; assoc ed, J Astronaut Sci, 1986-1989; mem, Tech Comt Composite Mat, Am Astronaut soc, 1982-; sr res scientist, Langley Res Ctr, Nasa, beginning 1982; sr staffengr, Martin Marietta Corp, 1981-1982; tech staff res, Jet Propulsion Lab, 1979-1981; staff engr, Martin Marietta Corp, 1977-1979; tech staff engr, Comput Sci Corp, 1975-1977; res assoc, Va Polytech Inst, 1974-1975. **Memberships:** Fel Am Astronaut Soc; fel Am Inst Aeronaut & Astronaut; Soc Indust & ApplMath. **Research Statement & Publications:** Active and passive control, tracking, modal parameter identification, system realization, and other dynamic problems for large space structures; nonlinear control problems and parameter estimation in distributed-parameter systems. **Mailing Address:** Langley Res Ctr, NASA, 227 Hunting Ave, MS 335, Hampton, VA 23681-2199. **Fax:** 757-864-5894.

JUANG, LING LING, NUMERICAL ANALYSIS. **Personal Data:** b Taipei, Taiwan, October 10, 1949; m 1973, c 1. **Education:** Nat Taiwan Univ, BS, 1972; State Univ NY Stony Brook, MS, 1973, PhD (appl math), 1976. **Professional Experience:** PROJ MGR, GEN ELEC CO, as of 2004; COMPUT PROCESS CONTROL SPECIALIST, GEN ELEC CO, 1980-; asst mathematician energy models, Brookhaven Nat Lab, 1976-1980; Syst analyst heat transfer prob, KLD Assoc, Inc, 1975-1976. **Memberships:** Am Commun Mach; Soc Mfg Eng. **Research Statement & Publications:** Economic-energy modeling of depletable resources; computer aided manufacturing system design. **Mailing Address:** 4293 Berryhill Lane, Cincinnati, OH 45242.

JUBB, GERALD LOMBARD, PEST MANAGEMENT. **Personal Data:** b Ayer, Mass, January 3, 1943; m 1967, Carole; c Thomas & Carrie. **Education:** NMex Highlands Univ, BA, 1965; Univ Ariz, MS, 1967, PhD (entom), 1970. **Professional Experience:** ASST DEAN, COL AGR & LIFE SCI, as of 2004; PROF ENTOM, AGR EXP STA, VA POLYTECH INST & STATE UNIV, 1989-; ASSOC DIR, VA AGR EXP STA, VA POLYTECH INST & STATE UNIV, 1989-; 1989 & gov bd, secy & treas, Eastern Br, 1985-1988; prof entom & ctr head, Western Md Res & Educ Ctr, Univ Md, 1984-1989; pres, secy & treas, Eastern Br, 1978-1981; Pres, Entom Soc Pa, 1972; from asst prof to prof entom, Erie Co Field Res Lab, PaState Univ, 1970-1984; NSF trainee entom, Univ Ariz, 1967-1970. **Memberships:** Entom Soc Am; NY Entom Soc; Acarological Soc Am; Sigma Xi. **Research Statement & Publications:** Insects and mites attacking grapes; economic injury levels; monitoring techniques; pesticide impact in vineyards; small fruit pest management. **Mailing Address:** Agr Exp Sta, Va Polytech Inst & State Univ, 104 Hutcheson Hall, Blacksburg, VA 24061-0402. **Fax:** 540-231-4163. **E-Mail:** jubbg@vt.edu

JUBERG, RICHARD KENT, MATHEMATICS. **Personal Data:** b Cooperstown, NDak, May 14, 1929; m 1989, Sandra; c Alison, Kevin, Hilary & Ian. **Education:** Univ Minn, BS, 1952, PhD (math), 1958. **Professional Experience:** PROF EMER MATH, UNIV CALIF, IRVINE, 1991-; math Inst Technol, Gothenburg, Sweden, 1981; vis prof, Univ Sussex, 1972-1973; NSF sci fac fel, Pisa, 1965-1966; from instr to prof, Univ Calif, Irvine, 1958-1991; temp mem, Courant Inst Math Sci, NY Univ, 1957-1958. **Memberships:** Am Math Soc. **Research Statement & Publications:** Problems in analysis and partial differential equations. **Mailing Address:** Dept Math, Univ Calif, Irvine, CA 92697-3875. **E-Mail:** rkjuberg@uci.edu

JUBERTS, MARIS, ELECTRO-MAGNETICS, ROBOTICS IN MILITARY & SPACE STATION APPLICATIONS. **Personal Data:** b February 5, 1941. **Education:** George Wash Univ, MS, 1969. **Professional Experience:** SUPVRY ELECTRONICS ENGR, INTELLIGENT SYSTS DIV, NAT INST STAND &TECHNOL, as of 2002; GROUP LEADER, INTELLIGENT SYSTS DIV, NAT INST STAND &TECHNOL, 1990-; group leader electromech, Goddard Space Flight Ctr, 1988-1990. **Memberships:** Am Welding Soc. **Mailing Address:** Intelligent Systs Div, Nat Inst Stand & Technol, 100 Bureau Dr, Gaithersburg, MD 20899-8230. **Fax:** 301-990-9688. **E-Mail:** maris.juberts@nist.gov

JUBY, PETER FREDERICK, MEDICINAL CHEMISTRY. **Personal Data:** b Great Yarmouth, Eng, October 27, 1935; American citizen; m 1970, c 2. **Education:** Univ Nottingham, BSc, 1957, PhD (org chem), 1961. **Professional Experience:** SCI EXPERIENCE COORDR, LE MOYNE COL, SYRACAUSE, NY, as of 2003; dir gastrointestinal chem, 1982-1987; dir, Cent Nervous Syst Therapeut Area Opers, 1987-1994; dir gastrointestinal chem, Bristol Myers Co, 1982-1987; prin investr, Bristol Labs Inc, 1976-1982; sr res scientist, Bristol Labs Inc, 1962-1976; Nat Res Coun Can fel, 1960-1962. **Memberships:** Am Chem Soc. **Research Statement & Publications:** Natural product chemistry; biosynthesis of alkaloids; synthesis of medicinal agents; arthritis; allergies; gastrointestinal diseases. **Mailing Address:** Off Career Serv, Le Moyne Col, 1419 Salt Springs Rd, Syracuse, NY 13214-1399. **E-Mail:** JubyPF@lemoyne.edu

JUCHAU, MONT RAWLINGS, PHARMACOLOGY, TOXICOLOTY & TERATOLOGY. **Personal Data:** b Virginia, Idaho, November 11, 1934; m 1960, Elizabeth; c Curtis M, Lauri, Christopher T, Michelle & Nanette. **Education:** Idaho State Univ, BS, 1960; Wash State Univ, MS, 1963; Univ Iowa, PhD (pharmacol), 1966. **Honors & Awards:** Delbert-Putnam Award, 1959; Rexall Award, 1960. **Professional Experience:** PROF EMER PHARMACOL, SCH MED, UNIV WASH, as of 2003; prof pharmacol, Sch Med, Univ Wash, beginning 1980; assoc prof, SchMed, Univ Wash, 1973-1980; asst prof, Sch Med, Univ Wash, 1969-1973; from instr to asst profbiochem pharmacol, State Univ NY, Buffalo, 1966-1969; pharmacist, Trolinger Pharm, TickKlock Drug, 1960-1963. **Memberships:** AAAS; Am Soc Pharmacol & Exp Therapeut; Int Soc Biochem Pharmacol; Soc Toxicol; Teratology Soc. **Research Statement & Publications:** Investigation of the biotransformation of drugs in the human foetoplacental unit. **Mailing Address:** Sch Med Univ Wash, Box 357280, Seattle, WA 98195-7280. **E-Mail:** jachau@u.washington.edu

JUD, HENRY G, ELECTRICAL ENGINEERING. **Personal Data:** b Rochester, NY, September 19, 1934; wid, c 4. **Education:** Valparaiso Univ, BS, 1956; Univ Pittsburgh, MS, 1959, PhD (elec eng), 1962. **Professional Experience:** RETIRED; dir systs technol, Unisys Corp, 1989-1994; sr staff systs eng, Unisys Corp, 1985-1989; develop engr, IBM Corp, Md, 1976-1985; develop engr, IBM Fed Systs Div, NY, 1971-1976; advan engr, IBM Fed Systs Div, NY, 1970-1971; staff engr, IBM Fed Systs Div, NY, 1968-1970; from asst prof to assoc prof elec eng, Valparaiso Univ, 1964-1968; specialistmissile systs, Autonetics Div, NAm Aviation Inc, 1962-1964; electronics technician, WesternElec Co, 1956-1957. **Memberships:** Inst Elec & Electronics Engrs. **Research Statement & Publications:** Missile system error analysis; automatic control; random input control systems; computer systems design. **Mailing Address:** 15327 Waterloo Rd, Amissville, VA 20106.

JUDAY, GLENN PATRICK, FOREST ECOLOGY, CONSERVATION. **Personal Data:** b Elwood, Ind, May 4, 1950; m 1971, c 4. **Education:** Purdue Univ, BS, 1972; Ore State Univ, PhD (plant ecol), 1976. **Professional Experience:** PROF FOREST ECOL, UNIV ALASKA, FAIRBANKS, as of 2004; asst prof forest ecol, Univ Alaska, Fairbanks, beginning 1987; pres, Natural Areas Asn, 1985-1987, 1987-1988; vis assoc prof, Agr & Forestry Exp Sta, Univ Alaska, 1981-1987; coordr ecol reserves, Inst Northern Forestry, Forest Serv, USDA, 1978-1981; coordrecol reserves, Arctic Environ Info & Data Ctr, Univ Alaska, 1978; coordr ecol reserves, JointFed-State Land Use Planning Comn, Alaska, 1977-1978; fel ecol & conserv, Ore State Univ, 1976-1977. **Memberships:** AAAS; Ecol Soc Am; Soc Am Foresters; Natural Areas Asn. **Research Statement & Publications:** Systematic plan for conserving ecological reserves using vegetation, wildlife, and geologic classifications; old-growth forest structure, including stocking, basal area, age height and spacing; post-glacial primary succession; fire effects research. **Mailing Address:** Dept Forest Sci Sch Natural Resources & Agr Sci Univ Alaska, 232 AHRB, Fairbanks, AK 99775. **Fax:** 907-474-7439. **E-Mail:** ffgpj@uaf.edu

JUDD, BRIAN RAYMOND, THEORETICAL PHYSICS, ATOMIC PHYSICS. **Personal Data:** b Chelmsford, Eng, February 13, 1931. **Education:** Oxford Univ, BA, 1952, MA & DPhil, 1955. **Honors & Awards:** Frank H Spedding Award, Rare Earth Res, 1988. **Professional Experience:** PROF EMER PHYSICS, JOHNS HOPKINS UNIV, 1997-; hon fel, Brasenose Col, Oxford, 1983-; chmn, Physics Dept, 1979-1984; consult, Argonne Nat Lab, 1977-1988; prof, Physics Dept, 1966-1996; staff mem nuclear chem, Lawrence Radiation Lab, Univ Calif, Berkeley, 1964-1966; assoc prof spectros, Univ Paris, 1962-1964; chemist, Lawrence Radiation Lab, Univ Calif, Berkeley, 1959-1962; instr physics, Univ Chicago, 1957-1958; fel, Magdalen Col, Oxford Univ, 1955-1962. **Memberships:** Fel Am Phys Soc. **Research Statement & Publications:** Theoretical studies of atoms, molecules and solid state physics, particularly application of group theory. **Mailing Address:** Dept Physics & Astron, Johns Hopkins Univ, Baltimore, MD 21218-2686. **Fax:** 410-516-7239. **E-Mail:** juddbr@pha.jhu.edu

JUDD, BURKE HAYCOCK, GENETICS. **Personal Data:** b Kanab, Utah, September 5, 1927; m 1953, Barbara; c Sean M, Evan P & Timothy B. **Education:** Univ Utah, BS, 1950, MS, 1951; Calif Inst Technol, PhD (genetics), 1954. **Professional Experience:** RETIRED; corresp ed, Molecular & Gen Genetics, 1986-1995; prog Genetics, Duke Univ, Durham, NC, 1980-2000; adj prof biol, Univ NC, Chapel Hill, 1979-1998; chief, Lab Genetics, Nat Inst Environ Health Sci, Res Triangle Park, NC, 1979-1995; dir, Genetics Inst, Univ Tex, Austin, 1977-1979; Gosney vis prof, Div Biol, Calif Inst Technol, 1975-1976; assoc ed, Genetics, 1973-1978; prof, Univ Tex, Austin, 1969-1979; mem panel genetic biol, NSF, 1969-1972; geneticist, AEC, Wash, DC, 1968-1969; from instr to assoc prof zool, Univ Tex, Austin, 1956-1969; Am Can Soc Fel, Univ Tex, Austin, 1954-1956. **Memberships:** Fel AAAS; Genetics Soc Am (vpres, 1979 & pres, 1980); Am Soc Nat (secy, 1968-1970). **Research Statement & Publications:** Chromosome organization; gene function and regulation; recombination mechanism; genetics of Drosophila. **Mailing Address:** 411 Clayton Rd, Chapel Hill, NC 27514. **Fax:** 919-942-7463. **E-Mail:** bhjudd@aol.com

JUDD, FLOYD L, HIGH ENERGY PHYSICS, OPTICS. **Personal Data:** b Janesville, Wis, January 25, 1934; m 1962, c 3. **Education:** Carroll Col, BS, 1956; Iowa State Univ, MS, 1960, PhD, 1966. **Professional Experience:** RETIRED; prof physics & chmn, Calif State Univ, Fresno, 1971-1977; assocprof physics, Fresno State Col, 1970-1971; asst prof, Fresno State Col, 1967-1970; asst prof, Northwestern State Col, La, 1959-1962, 1964-1967. **Mailing Address:** Dept Physics, Calif State Univ, 2345 E San Ramon, Fresno, CA 93740.

JUDD, FRANK WAYNE, POPULATION ECOLOGY, PHYSIOLOGICAL ECOLOGY. **Personal Data:** b Wichita Falls, Tex, August 23, 1939; m 1969, Jane; c Amy & Naomi. **Education:** Midwestern State Univ, BS, 1965; Tex Tech Univ, MS, 1968, PhD (zoology), 1973. **Professional Experience:** RES PROF, DEPT BIOL, UNIV TEX, 2003-; chmn, Dept Biol, Univ Tex, Pan Am, 1996-1999; vis prof, Dept Wildlife & Fisheries Sci, Tex A&M Univ, 1989-; prof biol & dir, Coastal Studies Lab, 1984-1996; dir, Coastal Studies Lab, 1984-1994; adj prof, Dept Biol Sci, Tex Tech Univ, 1983-1989; PROF, DEPT BIOL, UNIV TEX, 1982-; from asst prof to prof, Biol Dept, Pan Am Univ, 1972-1982; res asst & instr, Dept Biol, Tex Tech Univ, 1969-1971; instr, Biol Dept, Pan Am Univ, 1968-1969; Teaching asst biol, Dept Biol, Tex Tech Univ, 1965-1968. **Memberships:** Am Soc Ichthyologists & Herpetologists; Am Soc Mammalogists; Ecol Soc Am; Herpetologists' League. **Research Statement & Publications:** Ecology of the coastal zone of southern Texas and northern Mexico; barrier island ecology; black mangrove distribution; oyster reef distribution; tortoise demography. **Mailing Address:** Dept Biol Univ Tex, 1201 W Univ Dr, Edinburg, TX 78539-2999. **Fax:** 956-381-3657. **E-Mail:** fjudd@utpa.edu

JUDD, GARY, BIOMEDICAL ENGINEERING. **Personal Data:** b Humene, Czech, September 24, 1942. **Education:** Rensselaer Polytech Inst, BS, 1963, PhD (metall eng), 1967. **Honors & Awards:** Alfred Geisler Award, Eastern NY Chapter, Am Soc Metals.

Professional Experience: PROF MGT & MAT ENG, RENSSELAER POLYTECH INST, 1997-; DEAN FAC, GRAD SCH, RENSSELAER POLYTECH INST, 1993-; actg provost & vpres, Acad Affairs, 1982-1983, 1985-1986; dean grad sch, Rensselaer Polytech Inst, beginning 1979; vice provost, Acad Affairs, 1979-1993; metall eng consult ed, McGraw-Hill Sci & Technol Encycl, 1975-; vice provost, Plans & Resources, 1975-1978; actg chmn, Dept Mat Eng, 1974-1975; consult, Oak Ridge Nat Lab, 1968-1970; consult, Watervliet Arsenal, 1968-1978; from asst prof to prof, Rensselaer Polytech Inst, 1967-1976; res asst, Rensselaer Polytech Inst, 1966-1967. **Memberships:** Fel Am Soc Metals Int; Minerals Metals & Mat Soc; Sigma Xi; Microbeam Anal Soc; AAAS. **Research Statement & Publications:** Structure sensitive properties of materials, particularly strengthening mechanisms, precipitation kinetics, defect structures, biomaterials and corrosion; electron probe microanalysis; scanning electron microscopy; forensic science. **Mailing Address:** Rensselaer Polytech Inst, 2112 Pittsburgh Bldg 110 Eigth St, Troy, NY 12180. **Fax:** 518-276-8661. **E-Mail:** juddg@rpi.edu

JUDD, JOSEPH T, HUMAN NUTRITIONAL RESEARCH, LIPIDS. **Personal Data:** b Nashville, Tenn, April 22, 1935. **Education:** NC State Univ, PhD (nutrit), 1963. **Professional Experience:** ACTG DIR, BELTSVILLE HUMAN NUTRIT RES CTR, USDA, as of 2004; res leader, Diet & Human Performance Lab, Humannutrit Res Ctr, USDA, Beltsville, beginning 1977. **Research Statement & Publications:** Human nutrition; lipids. **Mailing Address:** Human Nutrit Res Ctr, USDA, Lipid Nutrit Lab Bldg 308-E Rm 126A, Beltsville, MD 20705. **Fax:** 301-504-9192. **E-Mail:** judd@bhnrc.arsusda.gov

JUDD, LEWIS LUND, PSYCHIATRY, CHILD PSYCHIATRY. **Personal Data:** b Los Angeles, Calif, February 10, 1930; m 1974, c 3. **Education:** Univ Utah, BS, 1954; George Wash Univ, 1954-1956; Univ Calif, Los Angeles, MD, 1958. **Honorary Degrees:** DSc, Med Col Ohio, Toledo. **Honors & Awards:** William C Menninger Award, Am Col Physicians, 1995. **Professional Experience:** PROF & CHMN, UNIV CALIF, SAN DIEGO, as of 2005; counr, Int Acad Biomed & Drugs Res, 1993-; MARY GILMAN MARSTON PROF PSYCHIAT, UNIV CALIF, SAN DIEGO, 1992-; counr, Am Asn, chmn Depts Psychiat, 1992-1994; dir, Nat Inst Mental Health, Dept Health & Human Serv, 1987-1990; pres med staff, Med Ctr, Univ Calif, San Diego, 1982-1984; chmn, Dept Radiol, Univ Calif, San Diego, 1978; chair, Dept Psychiat, Univ Calif, San Diego, 1977; co-chmn dept, Univ Calif, 1975-1977; vice chmn & dir clin progs, Dept Psychiat, Univ Calif, San Diego, 1975; actg chmn dept, Univ Calif, 1974-1975; prof psychiat, Univ Calif, San Diego, 1973-; psychiat consult, San Diego Co Dept Pub Health, 1972-; chief psychiat serv, Vet Admin Med Ctr, San Diego, 1972-1978; chmn, Social & Behav Sci Course, Sch Med, Univ Calif, San Diego, 1970-; dir, Univ Calif Drug Abuse Progs, 1970-1973; assoc prof, Univ Calif, 1970-1973; assoc prof, Ctr Health Sci, Univ Calif, Los Angeles, 1970; Scottish Rites Comt Res Schizophrenics, 1969; dir educ, Child & Adolescent Psychiat, Dept Psychiat, Marion Davies Pediat Clin, Ctr Health Sci, Univ Calif, Los Angeles, 1968-1970; psychiat consult, Dept Phys Med & Rehab, Marion Davies Pediat Clin, Ctr Health Sci, Univ Calif, Los Angeles, 1967-1970; NIMH fels, 1967-1969; State Calif Fel, 1966; fel, child psychiat, Ctr Health Sci, Univ Calif, Los Angeles, 1966; supvr psychiat, Adolescent Outpatient Unit, Marion Davies Pediat Clin, Ctr Health Sci, Univ Calif, Los Angeles, 1965-1970; supvr psychiat consult serv, Dept Pediat, Marion Davies Pediat Clin, Ctr Health Sci, Univ Calif, Los Angeles, 1965-1970; psychiat consult, Calif State Bd Rehab, Sacramento, 1965-1970; asst prof psychol & psychiat, Ctr Health Sci, Univ Calif, Los Angeles, 1965-1970; asst attend physician, Hosp, Marion Davies Pediat Clin, Ctr Health Sci, Univ Calif, Los Angeles, 1965-1970; fel, child psychiat, Ctr Health Sci, Univ Calif, Los Angeles, 1964-1965; resident psychiat, Ctr Health Sci, Univ Calif, Los Angeles, 1959-1960, 1962-1964; intern internal med, Ctr Health Sci, Univ Calif, Los Angeles, 1958-1959. **Memberships:** Fel Calif Coun Sci & Tech; Inst Med-Nat Acad Sci; Am Orthopsychiatric Asn; Soc Res Child Develop; Am Soc Adolescent Psychiat; Psychiat Res Soc; fel Am Psychiat Asn (vpres 1992-1994); fel Am Col Neuropsychopharmacology; fel Am Col Psychiatrists; Am Acad Child Psychiat; Asn Acad Psychiat; Soc Neuroscience; Adv Comt Eval Drug Abuse Progs Co, San Diego. **Research Statement & Publications:** Substance abuse in adolescents; developmental psychopathology; epidemiology of deviant populations; clinical psychopharmacology; author of numerous publications. **Mailing Address:** Dept Psychiat, Univ Calif San Diego, 9500 Gilman Dr Rm No 2072, La Jolla, CA 92093-0603. **Fax:** 619-534-7653. **E-Mail:** ljudd@ucsd.edu

JUDD, O'DEAN P, LASERS & OPTICS, ATOMIC & MOLECULAR PHYSICS. **Personal Data:** b Austin, Minn, May 26, 1937. **Education:** St Johns Univ, BS, 1959; Univ Calif, Los Angeles, MS, 1961, PhD (physics), 1968. **Honors & Awards:** Hughes Masters Fellow-1959 Hughes Doctoral Fellow-1963 Fellow-Los Alamos National Laboratory Fellow-Institute of Electrical and Electronic Engineers (IEEE) Fellow-American Association for the Advancement of Science (AAAS) "Distinguished Scientist of the Year" San Fernado Valley Engineers Council, 1990 Fellow- Institute of Advancement and Engineering Secretary of Defense Medal for Exceptional Meritorious Civilian Service-1990 Meritorious Civilian Service Award, Department of the Air Force, 2003. **Professional Experience:** PRIVATE TECH ADV & CONSULT, 1994-; Member of numerous govt. commissions related to science and technology, defense and national security; Mem. sci. adv. bd. USAF, 1999-2003. Nat Intel Officer Sci & Technol, Nat Intel Covn, Wash DC, 1993-1994; fel, Los Alamos Nat Lab, 1990-; chief scientist energy & environ, Los Alamos Nat Lab, 1990-1993; chief scientist, strategic defense initiative, Pentagon, Wash, DC, 1987-1990; chief scientist, Defense Res, 1982-1987; adj prof physics and astronomy, Univ NMex, 1981-; consult, 1980-; mem staff, Appl Photochem Div, 1977-1982; group leader advan laser res, Theoret Div, Los Alamos Nat Lab, Univ Calif, 1975-1977; assoc group leader, Theoret Div, Los Alamos Nat Lab, Univ Calif, 1972-1975; consult, 1972-1974; fel plasma physics, Univ Calif, Los Angeles, 1968-1969; Hughes fel, 1964; staff physicist, Hughes Res Lab, 1959-1967 & 1969-1972; Hughes masters fel, 1959. **Memberships:** Am Phys Soc; fel Inst Elec & Electronics Engrs; fel AAAS; fel Inst Advan Eng. **Research Statement & Publications:** Non-linear optics; laser physics, atomic and molecular physics; plasma physics; quantum electronics and laser chemistry, theoretical and experimental; 3 US patents and numerous publications on science research and technology, and national defense S&T and policy. **Mailing Address:** 101 Zuni, Los Alamos, NM 87544. **E-Mail:** ojudd@lanl.gov

JUDD, RALPH C, MICROBIOLOGY. **Education:** Univ Mont, MS, 1974, PhD, 1979. **Professional Experience:** PROF, DIV BIOL SCI, UNIV MONT, as of 2006. **Mailing Address:** Div Biol Sci, Univ Mont, Missoula, MT 59812. **Fax:** 406-243-2347. **E-Mail:** ralph.judd@mso.umt.edu

JUDD, ROBERT LEE, BIOCHEMICAL PHARMACOLOGY. **Personal Data:** b Kingsport, Tenn, August 23, 1964; m Holloy; c 3. **Education:** Hendrix Col, BA, 1986; Northeast La Univ, PhD (pharmacol & toxicol), 1990. **Professional Experience:** ASSOC PROF PHARMACOL, AUBURN UNIV, AS OF 2006; asst prof pharmacol, northeast la univ sch pharm, 1998; Researcher, Endocrine Res Unit, Mayo Clin, 1990-1993. **Memberships:** AAAS; Am Soc Pharmacol & Exp Therapeut; Am Diabetic Asn. **Research Statement & Publications:** Diabetes research; fatty acid transport. **Mailing Address:** Dept Anat, Physiol & Pharmacol, Coll Vet Med, Auburn Univ, AL 36849. **Fax:** 334-844-5388. **E-Mail:** juddrob@vetmed.auburn.edu

JUDD, ROSS LEONARD, HEAT TRANSFER, FLOW INDUCED VIBRATIONS. **Personal Data:** b London, Ont, June 3, 1936; m 1962, Joyce; c Mary Ellen & David. **Education:** Univ Western Ont, BESc, 1958; McMaster Univ, MEng, 1963; Univ Mich, PhD (heat transfer), 1968. **Honors & Awards:** Order Hon, Prof Eng Ont, 2002; R R Teetor Award, Soc Automotive Engrs; L Stuart Laughland Medal, Univ Western Ont. **Professional Experience:** PROF EMER MECH ENG, MCMASTER UNIV, as of 2004; prof Mech Eng, McMaster Univ, beginning 1980; from asst prof to assoc prof, Mcmaster Univ, 1967-1980; lectr, Mcmaster Univ, 1963-1967; develop engr, Civilian Atomic Power Dept, Can Gen Elec, 1958-1961. **Memberships:** Coun Prof Eng Ontario Am Soc Mech Engrs; Soc Automotive Engrs. **Research Statement & Publications:** Boiling heat transfer; two phase flow; flow induced vibrations; heat pipes. **Mailing Address:** Dept Mech Eng, McMaster Univ, 1280 Main St W JHE 308B, Hamilton, ON L8S 4L7, Can. **Fax:** 905-572-7944. **E-Mail:** juddr@mcmaster.ca

JUDD, STANLEY H, ENVIRONMENTAL HEALTH, COMPUTERIZED HEALTH & SAFETY INFORMATION MANAGEMENT SYSTEMS. **Personal Data:** b Denver, Colo, February 12, 1928; m 1977, Dorothy Newington; c Richard A & Nancy E. **Education:** Univ Calif, Los Angeles, BS, 1949; Univ Calif, Berkeley, MPH, 1956; Am Bd IndustHyg, cert, 1966. **Professional Experience:** RESOURCE CONSULT, HFP ACOUST CONSULTS, 1991-; INDUST HYGCONSULT, 1990-; lectr & nat secy, Am Indust Hyg Asn, 1990-1993; sr consult toxicol & health info res, Chevron Environ HealthCtr, Richmond, Calif, 1989-1990; mgr, Health Surveillance Serv, 1980-1988; staff industhygienist, Chevron Res Corp, Calif, 1978-1980; environ health & pollution engr, Chevron ResCorp, Calif, 1969-1978; sr indust hygienist, Chevron Res Corp, Calif, 1965-1969; industhygienist, Chevron Res Corp, Calif, 1958-1965; res chemist, Chevron Res Corp, Calif, 1956-1958; chemist, US Army Environ Health Lab, 1950-1952; chemist, State Calif Dept PubHealth, 1949-1950, 1953-1956; mem fac, Ctr Occup &Environ Health, Univ Calif, Berkeley; mem fac, Inst Noise Control Eng & Inst Safety & SystMgt, Univ Southern Calif Extension. **Memberships:** Am Indust Hyg Asn; Am Acad Indust Hyg; Am Chem Soc. **Research Statement & Publications:** Engineering noise control at the source to prevent hearing loss, interference with communications and annoyance; safe handling of pesticide and petrochemical products including facilities designs; occupational health information systems design; biomedical surveillance. **Mailing Address:** 220 Lombard St No 823, San Francisco, CA 94111-1113. **E-Mail:** 71520.3435@compuserve.com

JUDD, WALTER STEPHEN, PLANT SYSTEMATICS. **Personal Data:** b Fairbanks, Alaska, April 14, 1951; m 1972. **Education:** Mich State Univ, BS, 1973, MS, 1974; Harvard Univ, PhD (biol), 1979. **Professional Experience:** PROF, DEPT BOT, UNIV FLA, as of 2003; assoc prof bot, dept bot, Univ Fla, beginning 1978. **Memberships:** Am Soc Plant Taxonomists; Int Asn Plant Taxon; Am Bryological &Lichenological Soc; Bot Soc Am. **Research Statement & Publications:** Systematics and evolution of flowering plants with specific interest in the Ericaceae and Melastomataceae; floras of the West Indies and Florida. **Mailing Address:** Dept Bot Univ Fla, 378 Dickinson Hall, Gainesville, FL 32611-2009. **Fax:** 352-392-3993. **E-Mail:** wjudd@botany.ufl.edu

JUDD, WILLIAM ROBERT, ROCK MECHANICS, GEOTECHNICAL ENGINEERING. **Personal Data:** b Denver, Colo, August 16, 1917; m 1942, Rachel Douglas; c Judith (Soden), Jeanne (Wadley), Dayna (Grandmason), Pamela & Connie. **Education:** Univ Colo, AB, 1941. **Honors & Awards:** Spec Award Outstanding Contrib Rock Mech Res, US Nat Comt Rock Mech, 1982; Alex du Toit Mem Lectr, SAfrica & Rhodesia, 1967; Distinguished Pract Award, Geol Soc Am, 1989; Hans Cloos Medal, Int Asn Eng Geologists, 1994. **Professional Experience:** Honorary ed, Int J Eng Geol, 1996-; EMER PROF CIVIL ENG, PURDUE UNIV, 1988-; Nat Res Coun Comt Dam Safety, 1977-1978 & Comt Safety Existing Dams, 1982-1983; mem Adv Bd Applied Phys Math and Biol Sci, NSF, 1979-1981; mem, Exec Coun, US Comt Large Dams, 1977-1983; sr adv panel res, US Nat Comt Rock Mech, 1977-1981; mem, comt Earthquakes, 1976-1990; head geotech eng, Sch Civil Eng, 1976-1987; chmn panel awards, US Nat Comt Rock Mech, 1974-1978; ed-in-chief, Int J Eng Geol, 1972-1992; tech dir, Underground Explor & Rock Properties Info Ctr, 1972-1980; chmn, Panel Ocean Sci Comt Inst Coop, 1971-1985; reviewer, Appl Mech Reviews, 1968-1973; prof rock mech, Sch Civil Eng, 1966-1987; geo-sci ed, Am Elsevier Publ Co Inc, 1966-1971; mem panel geophys, USAF Sci Adv Bd, 1964-1968; founder & chmn, US Nat Comt Rock Mech, 1963-1969; head basing technol group, Rand Corp, Calif, 1960-1965; consult to various US & foreign govt agencies & comts & pvt industs, 1958-; mem adv bd, mountain & arctic warfare, US Army, 1956-1962; consult geologist & engr, 1950-; CONSULT ENG GEOLOGIST, 1950-; instr, Lowry AFB, 1946-1951; Eng geologist, US Bur Reclamation, head geol sect I, Off Chief Engr, 1944-1960; Eng geologist, Water Conserv Bd, Colo, 1941-1942 & Denver & Rio Grande West Rwy, 1942-1944. **Memberships:** Fel SAfrican Inst Mining & Metall; fel Am Soc Civil Engrs; fel Geol Soc Am; Int Soc Eng Geologists; Am Arbit Asn; hon mem India Soc Eng Geol; hon mem Asn Eng Geologists; Sigma Xi. **Research Statement & Publications:** Seismic effects on underground openings, dam safety; rock tunnels. **Mailing Address:** 10 Elder Ct, Lafayette, IN 47905.

JUDD, WILLIAM WALLACE, ENTOMOLOGY. **Personal Data:** b Windsor, NS, October 22, 1915; m 1946, c 4. **Education:** McMaster Univ, BA, 1938; Univ Western Ont, MA, 1940; Univ Toronto, PhD (zool), 1946. **Professional Experience:** PROF EMER ZOOL, UNIV WESTERN ONT, 1981-; prof, Univ Western Ont, 1965-1981; assoc prof, Univ Western Ont, 1952-1964; asst prof, Univ Western Ont, 1950-1951; asst prof, McMaster Univ, 1948-1950; lectr zool, McMaster Univ, 1946-1948; asst meteorol, Dept Transport, Ottawa, 1942-1945; Agr asst, Can Dept Agr, 1937-1942. **Research Statement & Publications:** Aquatic insects; insect morphology. **Mailing Address:** Dept Zool, Univ WesternOnt, London, ON N6A 5B7, Can.

JUDGE, DARRELL L, PHYSICS. **Personal Data:** b Albion, Ill, November 2, 1934; m 1959, c 3. **Education:** Eastern Ill State Col, BS, 1956; Univ Southern Calif, MS, 1963, PhD (physics), 1965. **Honors & Awards:** NASA Except Scientific Achievement Medal & NASA Pub Serv GroupAchievement Award to Pioneer 1910 Scientific Instrument Team, 1974. **Professional Experience:** PROF PHYSICS, UNIV SOUTHERN CALIF, 1975-; Douglas Aircraft Co, 1961 & Planetary Atmospheres Adv Subcomt, Space Sci & Applns Steering Comt, NASA, 1969-1970; from asst prof to assoc prof, Univ Southern Calif, 1966-1975; vis asst prof, Univ Southern Calif, 1965-1966; lectr math, Univ Southern Calif, 1961-1963; consult, Space Physics Dept, Thompson-Ramo-Wooldridge Corp, 1960-1971; mem tech staff, Thompson-Ramo-WooldridgeCorp, 1958-1959. **Memberships:** Am Geophys Union; Am Phys Soc. **Research Statement & Publications:** Space physics and spectroscopy. **Mailing Address:** Dept Physics Space Sci Ctr SHS 270, Univ Southern Calif Univ Park, Los Angeles, CA 90089. **Fax:** 213-740-6342. **E-Mail:** djudge@lism.usc.edu

JUDGE, JOSEPH MALACHI, POLYMER CHEMISTRY, INFORMATION RETRIEVAL. **Personal Data:** b Carbondale, Pa, June 10, 1930; m 1957, c 5. **Education:** Kings Col, Pa, BS, 1952; Univ Notre Dame, PhD (chem), 1958. **Professional Experience:** TECH-

NOL TRANSFER AGENT, NAT TECHNOL TRANSFER CTR, 1993-; mgr database construct, Comput Appl Serv, Inc, 1992; technol info consult, Lanxide Corp, 1989-1991; mgr, Tech Info Ser, 1980-1986 & Techol Transfer, 1986-1989; res chemist, Armstrong-World Indust, 1958-1980; Res chemist, Polychems Dept, E I du Pont Del Nemours & Co, 1955-1958. **Memberships:** AAAS; Am Soc Info Sci; Am Chem Soc. **Research Statement & Publications:** Vinyl polymerization; polymeric blends; polyvinyl chloride modifications; structure to dynamic properties relationships; elastomer synthesis; high energy radiation; information retrieval. **Mailing Address:** 436 Manor View Dr, Millersville, PA 17551.

JUDGE, LEO FRANCIS, microbiology; deceased, see previous edition for last biography

JUDGE, MAX DAVID, ANIMAL SCIENCE, FOOD SCIENCE. **Personal Data:** b Shirley, Ind, October 14, 1932; m 1953, c 3. **Education:** Purdue Univ, BS, 1954, PhD (animal physiol), 1962; Ohio State Univ, MSc, 1958. **Professional Experience:** RETIRED; from inst to prof animal sci, Purdue Univ, 1958-1995; res fel, Univ Wis, 1964-1965. **Memberships:** Am Meat Sci Asn; Am Soc Animal Sci; Inst Food Technol. **Research Statement & Publications:** Physiological and endocrine control of muscle properties and subsequent utilization of muscle as a food. **Mailing Address:** Seven Cougar Run, Hilton Head Island, SC 29926.

JUDGE, ROGER JOHN RICHARD, AERONAUTICAL ENGINEERING, ASTRONAUTICAL ENGINEERING. **Personal Data:** b London, Eng, November 22, 1938; American citizen; m 1974, c 2. **Education:** Univ Nottingham, BSc, 1960, PhD (physics), 1964. **Professional Experience:** STAFF SCIENTIST, IRT CORP, 1979-; prin engr, Orincon Corp, 1978-1979; Vis prof, Univ Ottawa, 1967-1969 & Univ Calif, San Diego, 1975-; res physicist, Univ Calif, SanDiego, 1969-1975; fel, Nat Res Coun Can, 1967-1969; Staff scientist, Bell Can Labs, 1963-1967. **Memberships:** Am Geophys Union. **Research Statement & Publications:** Upper atmosphere and space physics; spacecraft technology; nuclear survivability. **Mailing Address:** 1301 Virginia Way, La Jolla, CA 92037.

JUDISH, JOHN PAUL, CHEMICAL PHYSICS. **Personal Data:** b Canonsburg, Pa, May 23, 1926; m 1958, c 3. **Education:** Univ Pittsburgh, BS, 1950; Univ Tenn, PhD (physics), 1974. **Professional Experience:** RES STAFF MEM PHYSICS, OAK RIDGE NAT LAB, 1975-; engr, Van deGraaff Accelerator, Oak Ridge Nat Lab, 1951-1974. **Memberships:** Am Phys Soc; Inst Elec & Electronics Engrs. **Research Statement & Publications:** Atomic and molecular physics; visible and vuv spectroscopy; interaction of optical radiation with gases; lasers; excitation and ionization of gases by high energy ions; superconducting resistance at high frequencies. **Mailing Address:** 107 Wendover Circle, Oak Ridge, TN 37830.

JUDISH, ROBERT M, ELECTRICAL ENGINEERING. **Personal Data:** b December 8, 1952. **Education:** Colo State Univ, MA, 1978. **Honors & Awards:** Chmn, Conf Prec Electromagnetic Measurement, 1998. **Professional Experience:** Pres, Nat Inst Stand & Technol, 2001-2003; GROUP LEADER, NAT INST STAND & TECHNOL, 1993-; tech staff, Microwave Metrol Group, 1980-1993. **Memberships:** Am Soc Qual Control; Inst Elec Engrs. **Mailing Address:** Nat Inst Stand & Technol, 325 Broadway, Boulder, CO 80303. **Fax:** 303-497-3122. **E-Mail:** judish@boulder.nist.gov

JUDKINS, JOSEPH FAULCON, SANITARY ENGINEERING. **Personal Data:** b Richmond, Va, May 12, 1938; m 1961, c 3. **Education:** Va Polytech Inst, BS, 1961, MS, 1965, PhD (civil eng), 1967. **Professional Experience:** PROF EMER, AUBURN UNIV, as of 2003; DIR WATER RESOURCES RES INST, AUBURN UNIV, 1989-; pvt eng pract, 1981-1989; Gottlieb prof civil eng, Auburn Univ, 1977-1981; Gottlieb assoc prof, Auburn Univ, 1971-1977; asst prof civil eng, Auburn Univ, 1967-1971. **Memberships:** Am Soc Civil Engrs; Water Pollution Control Fedn; Am Water Works Asn. **Research Statement & Publications:** Industrial and domestic waste treatment; water supply engineering; Water Treatment Sludge Filtration Studies. **Mailing Address:** Auburn Univ Civil eng Dept, 238 Harbert Eng Ctr, Auburn, AL 36849-5337. **Fax:** 334-844-6290. **E-Mail:** jjudkins@eng.auburn.edu

JUDKINS, RODDIE REAGAN, COAL CONVERSION SYSTEMS. **Personal Data:** b Sunbright, Tenn, December 31, 1941; div, c 3. **Education:** Tenn Polytech Inst, BS, 1963, MS, 1965; Ga Inst Technol, PhD (phys chem), 1970. **Professional Experience:** DIR, MGR, FOSSIL ENERGY PROG, OAK RIDGE NAT LAB, 1988-; mgr, Fossil Energy Mat Prog, Oak Ridge Nat Lab, 1986-1988; task leader, Martin Marietta Energy Systs, 1984-1986; task leader, Union Carbide Corp, 1981-1984; develop engr, Union Carbide Corp, 1977-1981; tech assoc, E R Johnson Assocs, Inc, 1973-1977; plant mgr, Nuclear Chem & Metals Corp, 1970-1973; instr chem, Ga Inst Technol, 1965-1970; Eng assoc, Union Carbide Corp, 1964-1966. **Memberships:** Am Soc Metals Int; Sigma Xi; Am Soc Mech Engrs. **Research Statement & Publications:** Materials of construction for coal conversion and utilization systems; thorium metal process development and improvement; corrosion mechanisms in coal liquefaction processes; nuclear fuel fabrication technology and economics. **Mailing Address:** Oak Ridge Nat Lab, one Bethel Valley Rd, Oak Ridge, TN 37831-6036. **Fax:** 865-574-5812. **E-Mail:** judkinsrr@ornl.gov

JUDSON, CHARLES LEROY, INSECT PHYSIOLOGY. **Personal Data:** b Lodi, Calif, October 21, 1926; m 1950, c 3. **Education:** Univ Calif, BA, 1951, PhD (entom), 1956. **Professional Experience:** PROF EMER, EXP STA, UNIV CALIF, DAVIS, as of 2001; prof entom, Univ Calif, Davis, beginning 1977; assoc prof entom, UC Davis, 1970-1977; asst prof, UC Davis, 1962-1970; Vector Controlspecialist, Calif Dept Pub Health, beginning 1955; assoc, Exp Sta, Univ Calif, Davis, beginning 1955. **Memberships:** Entom Soc Am. **Research Statement & Publications:** Insect biochemistry; physiology of hatching; mosquito eggs. **Mailing Address:** Dept Entom, UC Davis, One Shields Ave, Davis, CA 95616. **Fax:** 530-752-1537.

JUDSON, CHARLES MORRILL, ANALYTICAL CHEMISTRY. **Personal Data:** b Washington, DC, July 2, 1919; m 1944, c Molly & Ellen. **Education:** Swarthmore Col, BA, 1940; Univ Pa, MS, 1942, PhD (phys chem), 1947. **Professional Experience:** RETIRED; dir, Mass Spectrometry Lab, Univ Kans, 1980-1989; res assoc, Univ Southern Calif, 1979-1980; chief scientist, Analog Technol Corp, 1976-1979; mgr, Microtrace Anal Serv, 1975-1977; scientist, Analog Technol Corp, 1973-1976; consult mass spectrometry, 1971-1973; res scientist, Granville Phillips Co, 1970-1971; dir eng, Anal & Control Div, Consol Electrodyn Corp, 1963-1970; chief anal develop sect, Anal & Control Div, ConsolElectrodyn Corp, 1962-1963; mgr chem physics sect, Am Cyanamid Co, 1957-1962; groupleader, Am Cyanamid Co, 1954-1957; res chemist, Am Cyanamid Co, 1947-1954; res chemist, Stand Oil Co, Ind, 1944-1945; res chemist, Columbia Univ, 1942-1944; asst instr chem, Univ Pa, 1940-1942. **Memberships:** Am Chem Soc; Am Phys Soc; Am Soc Mass Spectrometry; Soc Appl Spectros. **Research Statement & Publications:** Mass spectrometry; instruments; radio-tracers; electrolytes; surface agents. **Mailing Address:** 608 Seabrook Pl, Lawrence, KS 66046.

JUDSON, HORACE AUGUSTUS, ORGANIC CHEMISTRY. **Personal Data:** b Miami, Fla, August 7, 1941; m Gail; c 4. **Education:** Lincoln Univ, AB, 1963; Cornell Univ, PhD (org chem), 1970. **Professional Experience:** PRES, GRAMBLING STATE UNIV, 2004-; pres, State Univ NY Col Plattsburgh, NY, 1994-2003; provost & vpres acad affairs, Calif State Univ, Stanislaus, 1991-1994; chmn, dept chem, Morgan State Univ, 1982-1986; prof chem & vpres acad affairs, Morgan State Univ, 1974-1979; assoc dean col, Morgan State Univ, 1973-1974; Asst prof, Morgan State Univ, 1969-1974; Asst prof chem, Bethune-Cookman Col, 1969. **Memberships:** Am Chem Soc; Nat Inst Sci; Am Counil Edu; Sigma Xi; Am Asn Higher Educ; Intl Asn Univ Pres; Kappa Delta Pi; Phi Kappa Phi; Am Asn State Cols & Univs. **Research Statement & Publications:** Decomposition mechanisms of organic peroxides and peresters; synthesis of strained ring compounds via peresters. **Mailing Address:** Grambling State Univ, 100 Main St, Grambling, LA 71245. **Fax:** 318-274-3292. **E-Mail:** judsonha@gram.edu

JUDSON, PHOEBE T, MATHEMATICS. **Education:** Univ Tex, Austin, PhD, 1988. **Professional Experience:** PROF EMER, MATH DEPT, TRINITY UNIV, as of 2006. **Mailing Address:** Math Dept Trinity Univ, One Trinity Pl, San Antonio, TX 78212. **Fax:** 210-999-8264. **E-Mail:** math@trinity.edu

JUDSON, WALTER EMERY, MEDICINE. **Personal Data:** b Roxbury, Mass, June 5, 1916; m 1943, c 3. **Education:** Tufts Univ, BS, 1938; Johns Hopkins Univ, MD, 1942; Am Bd Internal Med, dipl, 1950; Am Bd Cardiovasc Dis, cert, 1950. **Professional Experience:** PROF EMER MED, SCH MED, UNIV IND, INDIANAPOLIS, as of 2003; prof med, Sch Med, Univ Ind, Indianapolis, beginning 1965; assoc prof, Sch Med, Univ Ind, Indianapolis, 1956-1965; from instr to asst prof, Sch Med, Boston Univ, 1950-1955; asst med, Sch Med, Boston Univ, 1948-1949. **Memberships:** Fel Am Col Physicians; AMA; Am Heart Asn; Am Fedn Clin Res; Sigma Xi. **Research Statement & Publications:** Cardiovascular research. **Mailing Address:** Dept Med, Sch Med, Indiana Univ, 1120 S Dr, Fesler Hall 302, Indianapolis, IN 46202-5114. **Fax:** 317-274-8439.

JUDZIEWICZ, EMMET JOSEPH, TAXONOMY & CONSERVATION OF VASCULAR PLANTS. **Personal Data:** b Milwaukee, Wis, December 8, 1953. **Education:** Univ Wis-Parkside, BA, 1979; Univ Wis-Madison, MS, 1985, PhD (bot), 1987. **Professional Experience:** ASST PROF BIOL, UNIV WIS, STEVENS POINT, as of 2003; CUR VASCULAR PLANTS & ROBERT W FRECKMANN HERBARIUM, UNIV WIS, STEVENS POINT, as of 2003; res assoc, Dept Bot, Milwaukee Pub Mus, beginning 1997; SR CONSERV BIOLOGIST, WIS DEPT NATURAL RESOURCES, 1995-; asst scientist, Dept Bot, UnivWis-Madison, 1991-1995; postdoctoral fel, Dept Bot, Smithsonian Inst, 1987-1991. **Memberships:** Am Soc Plant Taxonomists; Int Union Conserv Nature. **Research Statement & Publications:** Taxonomy, ecology and conservation of New World bamboos; inventory and conservation of vascular plants of the western Great Lakes region. **Mailing Address:** Dept Biol, Univ Wis, 301 CNR Bldg, Stevens Point, WI 54481. **E-Mail:** ejudziew@uwsp.edu

JUENGE, ERIC CARL, PHARMACEUTICAL & ORGANOMETALLIC CHEMISTRY. **Personal Data:** b Weehawken, NJ, January 12, 1927; m 1971, c 3. **Education:** NY Univ, BA, 1951, PhD (chem), 1957. **Professional Experience:** RETIRED; chemist, Div Drug Anal, Food & Drug Admin, 1978-1989; asst resprof chem, Coop State Res Serv, Ft Valley State Col, 1975-1978; res assoc, Coop State Res Serv, Ft Valley State Col, 1974-1975; from assoc prof to prof chem, Kans State Col, Pittsburg, 1961-1974; sr chemist agr chem, Spencer Chem Co, 1959-1961; res chemist organometallic field, Ethyl Corp, La, 1956-1959; asst, NY Univ, 1955-1956; jr chemist pharmaceut, Hoffmann-LaRoche Inc, 1951-1952. **Memberships:** Am Chem Soc. **Research Statement & Publications:** Organic chemistry; agricultural chemistry; chemical nitrogen fixation; methods research in pharmaceutical chemistry. **Mailing Address:** 1351 N Second St No 10, Belleville, IL 62226.

JUERGENS, JOHN LOUIS, INTERNAL MEDICINE. **Personal Data:** b Mankato, Minn, March 29, 1925; m 1948, c 4. **Education:** Univ Minn, Minneapolis, BS, 1946, MS, 1956; Harvard Univ, MD, 1949. **Professional Experience:** PROF MED, MAYO SCH MED, UNIV MINN, 1978-; assoc prof clin med, Mayo Sch Med, Univ Minn, 1967-1978; asst prof med, Mayo Sch Med, Univ Minn, 1962-1967; CONSULT CARDIOVASC DIS & INTERNAL MED, MAYO CLIN, 1956-; fel internal med, Mayo Grad Sch Med, Univ Minn, 1953-1956. **Memberships:** Fel Am Col Physicians. **Research Statement & Publications:** Peripheral vascular diseases. **Mailing Address:** Mayo Clin, Rochester, MN 55905-0002.

JUERGENSMEYER, ELIZABETH B, SPACE BIOLOGY. **Personal Data:** b Columbia, Mo, May 28, 1940; m 1963, John; c Margaret A & Frances E. **Education:** Ore State Univ, BS, 1962; Univ Ill, Urbana, MS, 1964, PhD (biol), 1967. **Professional Experience:** Chair div sci & math 1999-; PROF BIOL, JUDSON COL, ILL, 1980-; assoc prof, Judson Col, Ill, 1969-1980; asst prof, Harper Col, 1968-1969; asst, Univ Ill, Chicago Circle, 1965-1968. **Memberships:** AAAS; Am Inst Biol Sci; Am soc for gravitational & space biol; Am Soc Microbiol. **Research Statement & Publications:** Effects of space environment on microbial physiology. **Mailing Address:** Dept Biol, Judson Col 1151 N State St, Elgin, IL 60123. **Fax:** 847-695-2669. **E-Mail:** bjuergensmeyer@judson-il.edu

JUHASZ, STEPHEN, MECHANICS. **Personal Data:** b Budapest, Hungary, December 26, 1913; American citizen. **Education:** Royal Inst Technol, Budapest, dipl Ing, 1936; Royal Inst Technol, Sweden, MSc, 1949, Tekn Lic, 1951. **Professional Experience:** CONSULT, 1984-; ed, Appl Mech Rev, beginning 1960; dir, Southwest Res Inst, 1960-1984; exec ed, Appl Mech Rev, 1953-1960; res assoc, Fuels Res Lab, Mass Inst Technol, 1952-1953; mem staff, Univ Toronto, 1951-1952; mem staff, Royal Inst Technol, Stockholm, 1949-1951; mgr & engr, Oeconomia Ltd, Combustion & Salgotarjan Coal Mines, Hungary, 1936-1946. **Memberships:** Fel Am Soc Mech Engrs; Sigma Xi; Am Inst Aeronaut & Astronaut; fel Am AsnAdvan Sci. **Research Statement & Publications:** Heat transfer; boiler availability; information retrieval. **Mailing Address:** San Antonio, TX 78201.

JUHASZ, STEPHEN EUGENE, PSYCHIATRY. **Personal Data:** b Kecskemet, Hungary, September 20, 1923; Canadian citizen; m 1965. **Education:** Med Univ Budapest, MD, 1951; McGill Univ, PhD, 1962. **Professional Experience:** RETIRED; attend psychiatrist, Alexian Bros Med Ctr, 1975-1993; instr psychiat, Stritch Sch Med, Loyola Univ, 1975-1978; resident psychiat, Vet Admin Hosp, Hines, 1972-1975; prof, Stritch Sch Med, Loyola Univ, 1970-1972; res microbiologist, Vet Admin Hosp, Hines, 1967-1972; assoc prof microbiol, Stritch Sch Med, Loyola Univ, 1967-1970; asst prof microbiol, Univ BC, 1964-1966; staff researcher, Res Inst Exp Biol & Med, Borstel, W Ger, 1963-1964; guest researcher, Univ Lausanne, 1962-1963; res asst, McGill Univ, 1958-1962; res assoc, Royal Edward Laurentian Hosp, 1957; asst prof, Med Univ Budapest, 1956; lectr, MedUniv Budapest, 1954-1956; instr bact, Med Univ Budapest, 1951-1954. **Memberships:** Sigma Xi. **Research Statement & Publications:** Bacterial cytology; spheroplasts and L forms of Salmonella; morphogenetics of mycobacteria; phage typing and lysogeny in mycobacteria; transduction and transformation in mycobacteria. **Mailing Address:** 5415 N Sheridan Rd No 1001, Chicago, IL 60640.

JUHL, WILLIAM G, CHEMICAL ENGINEERING. **Personal Data:** b Luverne, Minn, June 30, 1924; m 1956, c 2. **Education:** Univ Minn, BChE, 1945; Iowa State Col, PhD (chem eng), 1953. **Professional Experience:** PROCESS TECHNOL DIR, MONSANTO CO, 1974-; process tech mgr, Monsanto CO, 1965-1974; group leader res, Monsanto CO, 1955-1964; Res engr, Lion Oil Co, 1953-1955. **Memberships:** Am Inst Chem Engrs; Am Chem Soc. **Research Statement & Publications:** Process development studies of hydrocarbons, conversion and petrochemical production. **Mailing Address:** 203 Millcreek Dr, El Dorado, AR 71730.

JUHOLA, CARL, ELECTRICAL ENGINEERING. **Personal Data:** b Bismarck, NDak, January 28, 1920; m 1944, Margaret; c Roger, David & Margaret J. **Education:** Univ Wash, Seattle, BSEE, 1943. **Professional Experience:** RETIRED; mgr, Ctr Technol Innovation, USM Corp, 1981-1984; mgr, Electronics Lab, USM Corp, 1973-1981; dir, Comput Control Lab, USM Corp, 1970-1973; dept mgr, indust & mach develop, United Shoe Mach Corp, 1961-1970; eng exec, electronic develop, United Shoe Mach Corp, 1946-1961; plant engr, Boeing Aircraft Co, Seattle, 1941-1943; surveyor, US Bur Reclamation, 1940-1941. **Memberships:** Sr mem Inst Elec & Electronics Engrs; Sigma Xi. **Research Statement & Publications:** Management; electronic controls; dielectric heating; fasteners; packaging adhesive systems; development of minicomputer and micro-computer control systems; robotics and computer-aided design; computer-aided manufacturing systems. **Mailing Address:** RR Two Box 399, E Lebanon, ME 04027.

JULES, LEONARD HERBERT, ORGANIC CHEMISTRY. **Personal Data:** b Cleveland, Ohio, October 5, 1922; m 1953, c 2. **Education:** Univ Southern Calif, AB, MS, 1949. **Professional Experience:** RETIRED; consult, beginning 1985; plant mgr, Philip A Hunt Chem Corp, 1969-1985; res chemist, Philip A Hunt Chem Corp, 1962-1969; res chemist, Nat Res & Chem Co, 1958-1962; res chemist, Purex Corp, 1955-1958; res chemist, Sahyun Labs, 1950-1955. **Memberships:** Am Chem Soc; Soc Photog Sci & Eng. **Research Statement & Publications:** Pharmaceuticals; organic intermediates; organic chlorine bleaches; surfactants; asphalt additives; corrosion inhibitors; photographic chemicals. **Mailing Address:** 6035 Wooster Ave, Los Angeles, CA 90056-1433.

JULIAN, DONALD BENJAMIN, PHOTOGRAPHIC CHEMISTRY, CHEMICAL MICROSCOPY. **Personal Data:** b Pelham, Mass, June 6, 1922; m 1945, Anna; c Helen J (Heffer), Margaret J (Leonard) & Donna L. **Education:** Univ Mass, BS, 1945. **Professional Experience:** RETIRED; sr res assoc, Eastman Kodak Res Labs, 1974-1980; res assoc chem, Eastman Kodak Res Labs, 1962-1974; from res chemist to sr res chemist, Eastman Kodak Res Labs, 1948-1962; jr chemist, Eastman Kodak Res Labs, 1945-1948. **Memberships:** Am Chem Soc; Soc Photog Scientists & Engrs. **Research Statement & Publications:** Determination of image structure of color photographic films and papers by optical microscope methods; dispersions of oil soluble couplers and other components in aqueous gelatin; chemistry and physics of color photography. **Mailing Address:** 1079 Shoemaker Rd, Webster, NY 14580-8764.

JULIAN, GLENN MARCENIA, SOLID STATE PHYSICS. **Personal Data:** b Knoxville, Tenn, October 1, 1939; m 1968, Elizabeth; c Daniel, Cynthia & Gerald. **Education:** Carnegie-Mellon Univ, BS, 1961, MS, 1963, PhD (physics), 1967. **Professional Experience:** PROF PHYSICS, MIAMI UNIV, 1980-; from asst prof to assoc prof, Miami Univ, 1968-1979. **Memberships:** Am Phys Soc; Am Geophys Union; Sigma Xi; Am Asn Physics Teachers. **Research Statement & Publications:** Studies of magnetic ordering by Moessbauer spectroscopy. **Mailing Address:** Dept Physics, Miami Univ, Oxford, OH 45056. **Fax:** 513-529-5629. **E-Mail:** juliangm@muohio.edu

JULIAN, GORDON RAY, CHEMISTRY. **Personal Data:** b Wenatchee, Wash, May 29, 1928; m 1952, c 2. **Education:** Univ Utah, BS, 1950; Univ Ore, MA, 1955, PhD (chem), 1960. **Professional Experience:** RETIRED; vis prof, Friedrich Miescher Inst, Basel, Switz, 1975-1976; foreign vis scientist, Szeged, Hungary, 1974-1975; NIH res grant, 1965-1968; from asst prof to prof chem, Mont State Univ, 1964-1986; res assoc, Harvard Med Sch, 1962-1964; res fel pharmacol, Harvard Med Sch, 1960-1962. **Memberships:** AAAS; Am Chem Soc. **Research Statement & Publications:** Biochemical processes at elevated temperature; in vitro protein synthesis; early biochemical events in plant development. **Mailing Address:** 3369 Bear Canyon Rd, Bozeman, MT 59715-6669.

JULIAN, MAUREEN M, PHYSICAL CHEMISTRY, CRYSTALLOGRAPHY. **Personal Data:** b New York, NY, July 3, 1939; m 1968, c 2. **Education:** Hunter Col, AB, 1961; Cornell Univ, PhD (phys chem), 1966. **Professional Experience:** ADJ FAC, DEPT GEOL SCI, VA POLYTECH & STATE UNIV, as of 2002; sr scientist, EnvironTesting Systs, Inc, Roanoke, Va, 1979-; vis asst prof, Va Polytech Inst, Blacksburg, 1978-; asstprof chem, Hollins Col, Va, 1978-1981; head dept sci, Wood Lawn Sch, 1974-; consult chem, Kirtland AFB, NMex, 1971-1973; sr chemist, Kirtland AFB, NMex, 1969-1970; chemist, UnivCol, Univ London, 1966-1968. **Memberships:** Am Chem Soc; Am Phys Soc; Am Crystallog Asn; AAAS; Royal Soc Chem. **Research Statement & Publications:** Zeolites, optical crystallography of anthracene; solid state reactions; photodimerization of anthracene; history of crystallography; teaching of crystallography to undergraduates; symmetry; thermodynamics; computers; software for environmental chemistry. **Mailing Address:** Dept Geo Sci, Virginia Poly Inst & State Univ, 4044 Derring Hall, Blacksburg, VA 24061. **E-Mail:** ireland@vtvm1.cc.vt.edu

JULIAN, WILLIAM H, MATHEMATICS. **Personal Data:** b Chicago, Ill, September 27, 1939. **Education:** Mass Inst Technol, BS, 1961, PhD (math), 1965. **Professional Experience:** PROF EMER, NMEX STATE UNIV, as of 2005; prof, Nmex State Univ, beginning 1986; from asst to assoc prof, NMex State Univ, 1969-1986; res fel astron, Calif Inst Technol, 1967-1969; instr appl math, Univ Chicago, 1965-1967. **Memberships:** Math Assoc Am; Am Astron Soc; AAAS; Am Math Soc; Sigma Xi. **Research Statement & Publications:** Research in mathematics as applied to astrophysics; rotation of Halley's Comet. **Mailing Address:** Math Dept, NMex State Univ, Hall Rm 230 PO Box 30001, Las Cruces, NM 88003. **Fax:** 505-646-1064. **E-Mail:** wjulian@nmsu.edu

JULIANELLE, TONY, MATHEMATICS. **Education:** Univ Mass, PhD. **Professional Experience:** LECTR, UNIV VT, 2005. **Mailing Address:** Univ Vt, 107 Mansfield, Burlington, VT 05405-0156. **Fax:** 802-656-2552. **E-Mail:** tjuliane@cem.uvm.edu

JULIANO, PETER C, POLYMER CHEMISTRY. **Personal Data:** b New Kensington, Pa, October 10, 1941; m 1965, c 3. **Education:** St Vincent Col, BS, 1963; WVa Univ, MS, 1965; Univ Akron, PhD (polymer sci), 1968. **Professional Experience:** Chmn, Gordon Conf Elastomers, 1981; MGR RES & DEVELOP, POLYMER PHYSICS & ENG BR, GEN ELEC CO, 1976-; tech coordr, Polymer Physics & Eng Br, Gen Elec Co, 1971-1972; Chemist, Polymer Physics & Eng Br, Gen Elec Co, 1968-1971. **Memberships:** Acct Control Syst; Soc Plastic Engrs. **Research Statement & Publications:** Synthesis and properties of block polymers; use of organometallic and organosiloxane intermediates for polymer forming reactions. **Mailing Address:** Chem Lab Gen Elec Co Res & Develop Ctr, One Res Circle KWD 275, Schenectady, NY 12301.

JULIANO, RUDOLPH LAWRENCE, CELL BIOLOGY & ADHESION MOLECULES, BIOPHYSICS. **Personal Data:** b NY, July 18, 1941; m 1963, c 2. **Education:** Cornell Univ, BS, 1963; Univ Rochester, PhD (biophys), 1970. **Professional Experience:** NC Biotechnol Ctr, 93-94. Prog Comt, Am Soc Pharmacol & Exp Therapeut, 1994-1997; prog Comt, Am Asn Cancer Res, 1991; assoc ed, molecular pharmacol, 1990-1995; ed, Advan Drug Delivery Revs, 1987-1992; chmn, NY Acad Sci Symp, 1987; chmn, Gordon Res Conf, 1987; CHMN PHARMACOL, UNIV CHAPEL HILL, 1986-; prof pharmacol, Univ Tex Med Sch, Houston, 1986; mem, Oversight Panel, NSF, 1985; assoc ed, Cancer Res, 1981-1989; assoc prof pharmacol, Univ Tex Med Sch, Houston, 1978-1982; asst prof, dept med biophys, Univ Toronto, beginning 1973; investr cell biol, res inst, Hosp Sick Children, Toronto, 1972-1980; cancer res scientist cell biol, Roswell Park Mem Inst, 1970-1972; sci teacher, US Peace Corps, Philippines, 1964-1966; engr, Radio Corp Am, 1963-1964. **Memberships:** AAAS; BiophysSoc; Can Biochem Soc; Am Asn Cancer Res; Am Soc Cell Biol; Am Soc Pharmacol & Exp Therapeut. **Research Statement & Publications:** Signal transduction processes mediated by cell adhesion receptors; drug delivery systems. **Mailing Address:** Dept Pharmacol, Univ NC Med Sch, 1017 Mary Ellen Jones Bldg, Chapel Hill, NC 27514. **E-Mail:** arjay@med.unc.edu

JULIEN, HIRAM PAUL, PHYSICAL CHEMISTRY. **Personal Data:** b Syracuse, NY, October 21, 1929; m 1983, c 4. **Education:** DePauw Univ, AB, 1951; Mass Inst Technol, PhD (phys chem), 1955. **Professional Experience:** RETIRED; mgr, Advn Technol & Testing Dept, Jim Walter Res Corp, 1967-1981; mgr, Ceramics & Metall Dept, Res & Develop Div, 1964-1967; mgr, Develop Dept, 1962-1964; mgr, Adv Studies Dept, Bonded Abrasives Div, Carborundum Co, 1959-1961; group head, Prod Res, Esso Res & Eng Co, 1958-1959; res chemist, Prod Res, Esso Res & Eng Co, 1955-1958; asst phys chem, Mass Inst Technol, 1951-1955. **Memberships:** Am Chem Soc. **Research Statement & Publications:** Thermodynamics; automotive and jet fuels; bonded abrasives; high temperature materials and composites; building materials; cellular plastics; mineral fibers; inorganic fillers. **Mailing Address:** 700 Starkey Rd No 822, Largo, FL 34641-2302.

JULIEN, HOWARD L, HEAT TRANSFER, FLUID MECHANICS. **Personal Data:** b Oak Park, Ill, December 13, 1942; m 1965, c 2. **Education:** Ill Inst Technol, BS, 1964, MS, 1967; Stanford Univ, PhD (heat & mass transfer), 1969. **Professional Experience:** SUPVR, ALLIEDSIGNAL-WSTF, DEPT PROJ SECT LAB, as of 1999; assoc prof mech eng, Univ NMex, 1989-; prin engr, Kaiser Engrs, Inc, 1977-1988; from assoc sr res engr to sr res engr, Gen Motors Res Labs, 1969-1977; CONSULT. **Memberships:** fel Am Soc Mech Eng 1998; Am Soc Mech Engrs; Sigma Xi; Soc AutomotiveEngrs; Am Nuclear Soc. **Research Statement & Publications:** Basic experimental/analytical convective heat transfer research; gas turbine heat transfer; experimental fluid mechanics; thermodynamic cycle analysis of alternative automotive power plants; heat transfer in nuclear waste processing and storage facilities; cooling of solid state lasers. **Mailing Address:** Met 1300-G, El Paseo No 278, Las Cruces, NM 88001.

JULIEN, JEAN-PIERRE, MOLECULAR NEUROBIOLOGY. **Personal Data:** b Montreal, Que, November 20, 1952. **Education:** Univ Que, BSc, 1976; McGill Univ, PhD (biochem), 1982. **Professional Experience:** RES PROF & ASSOC PROF NEUROL, MCGILL UNIV, 1989-; res assoc & asst prof biochem, Univ Montreal, 1985-1989; med Res Coun Can fel, Nat Inst Med Res, London, 1982-1985; dir, Transgenic Core Facil, Can Neuroscience Net. **Memberships:** Am Soc Cell Biol; AAAS. **Research Statement & Publications:** Transgenic mouse-models of neurofilament-induced pathology; neurofilament expression and function. **Mailing Address:** Dept Neurol, McGill Univ, Montreal Gen Hosp Res Inst, 1650 Cedar Ave, Montreal, PQ H3G 1A4, Can. **Fax:** 514-934-8265.

JULIEN, LARRY MARLIN, PHYSICAL CHEMISTRY. **Personal Data:** b Nora Springs, Iowa, August 16, 1937; m 1959, c 2. **Education:** Wis State Univ, River Falls, BS, 1962; Univ Iowa, MS, 1965, PhD (chem), 1966. **Professional Experience:** ASSOC PROF EMER, MICH TECHNOL UNIV, as of 2004; pres, Mich Technol Univ, 1975-1976; vpres, Mich Technol Univ, 1973-1975; asst prof, Mich Technol Univ, 1966-1973. **Memberships:** Am Chem Soc. **Research Statement & Publications:** Thermodynamics; molecular spectroscopy and wood-bark surface properties. **Mailing Address:** Dept Chem, Mich Technol Univ, 1400 Townsend Dr, Houghton, MI 49931. **E-Mail:** lmjulien@mtu.edu

JULIEN, ROBERT M, PHARMACOLOGY, ANESTHESIOLOGY. **Personal Data:** b Port Townsend, Wash, March 24, 1942. **Education:** Univ Wash, PhD (pharmacol), 1970; Univ Calif, MD, 1977. **Professional Experience:** COURSE INSTR, NORTHWEST PSYCHOPHARMACOLOGY SEMINARS, as of 2006; STAFF ANESTHESIOLOGIST, ST VINCENT HOSP & MED CTR, beginning 1983; Anesthesiologist, Ore Health Sci Univ, 1980-1983. **Research Statement & Publications:** A Primer of Drug Action. **Mailing Address:** Northwest Psychopharmacology Seminars, PO Box 80808, Portland, OR 97280-1808. **Fax:** 503-977-7880.

JULIENNE, PAUL SEBASTIAN, THEORETICAL SPECTROSCOPY, SCATTERING THEORY. **Personal Data:** b Spartanburg, SC, May 8, 1944; m 1968, Marietta; c Marianne & Alicia. **Education:** Wofford Col, BS, 1965; Univ NC, Chapel Hill, PhD (chem), 1969. **Honors & Awards:** Samuel Wesley Stratton Award, 1962. **Professional Experience:** FEL, NAT INST STANDARDS & TECHNOL, QUANTUM PROCESSES & METROL GROUP, 2004-; group leader, quantum processes & metrol group, 1995-2004; res chemist, Molecular Physics Div, 1976-1995; res chemist, Phys Chem Div, nat inst standards & technol, Nat Bur Standards, 1974-1976; res physicist, plasma physics div, naval res lab, Wash, DC, 1973-1974; res chemist, Phys Chem Div, Nat Bur Standards, 1971-1973; Nat Acad Sci-Nat Res Coun res assoc, Phys Chem Div, Nat Bur Standards, 1969-1971. **Memberships:** Fel, Am Phys Soc; fel, Physics Lab; Am Geophys Union. **Research Statement & Publications:** Molecular spectroscopy; photodissociation; line broadening theory; atomic collision theory; collisions of laser cooled atoms. **Mailing Address:** Nat Inst Stand & Technol, Rm B 160 Physics Bldg, 100 Bureau Dr, Gaithersburg, MD 20899. **Fax:** 301-990-1350. **E-Mail:** pjulienne@nist.gov

JULIUS, STEVO, MEDICINE. **Personal Data:** b Kovin, Yugoslavia, April 15, 1929; c 2. **Education:** Univ Zagreb, MD, 1953, DMSc, 1964. **Honorary Degrees:** MD, Univ Goteborg, Sweden, 1979. **Honors & Awards:** Astra Award, Int Soc Hypertension; Arthur C Corcoran Mem Lectr, Coun HighBlood Pressure, Am Heart Asn. **Professional Experience:** PROF EMER INTERNAL MED & MOLECULAR PHYSIOL, UNIV MICH, ANN ARBOR, as of 2005; prof physiol, Univ Mich, Ann Arbor, beginning 1980; prof internal med & dir, Hypertension Unit, Med Ctr, Univ Mich, Ann Arbor, beginning 1974; from instr to assoc prof, Hypertension Unit, Med Ctr, Univ Mich, Ann Arbor, 1965-1974; sr instr, Univ ZagrebHosp, 1962-1964; res asst med, Med Ctr, Univ Mich, Ann Arbor, 1961-1962; resident internalmed, Univ Zagreb Hosp, 1955-1960; intern, Univ Zagreb Hosp, 1953-1954; mem, Coun Epidemiol & med adv bd-coun, High Blood Pressure Res, Am Heart Asn. **Memberships:** Am Col Cardiol; Am Heart Asn; Am Fedn Clin Res; Int Soc Cardiol; Am PhysiolSoc; Int Soc Hypertension; Am Asn Physicians. **Research Statement & Publications:** Hemodynamics of borderline hypertensions; patho-physiology of hypertension; insulin resistance; pathophysiology of coronary risk in hypertension. **Mailing Address:** Univ Mich Hosp, Dept Internal Med, 3918 Taubman Ctr, Ann Arbor, MI 48109-0356. **Fax:** 734-936-8898. **E-Mail:** sjulius@umich.edu

JULIUSSEN, J EGIL, COMPUTER SCIENCE, INFORMATION SCIENCE. **Personal Data:** b Stavanger, Norway, May 4, 1943; American citizen; c 4. **Education:** Purdue Univ, BS, 1969, MS, 1970, PhD (elec eng), 1972. **Professional Experience:** PRES & FOUNDER, ETFORECASTS, 1999-; pres, Comput Indust Almanac Inc, 1986-1999; chmn, Future Comput Inc, 1981-1986; chmn, Store Bd Inc, 1986-1990; chmn, Workstation labs, 1986-1992; sr mem tech staff, Tex Instruments Corp Eng Ctr, 1977-1981; sr mem tech staff elec eng, Tex Instruments, Inc, 1973-1981; mem tech staff, Tex Instrument Corp, 1973-1977; Engr, Norden, Div United Technols, 1972-1973. **Memberships:** Inst Elec & Electronics Engrs; Asn Comput Mach. **Research Statement & Publications:** Computer technology trends; technology forecasting; computer market analysis, trends and projections. **Mailing Address:** eTForecasts, 304 W White Oak, Arlington Heights, IL 60005. **Fax:** 847-758-3686. **E-Mail:** ejuliussen@etforecasts.com

JULL, ANTHONY JOHN TIMOTHY, RADIOISOTOPE DATING, ACCELERATOR MASS SPECTROMETRY. **Personal Data:** b Leeds, Eng, December 18, 1951; Canadian citizen. **Education:** Univ BC, BSc, 1972; Univ Bristol, PhD (chem), 1976. **Professional Experience:** Ed, J Radiocarbon & Meteoritics Planetary Sci, as of 2006; SR RES SCIENTIST GEOSCIENCE, UNIV ARIZ, as of 2004; res scientist Geoscience, Univ Ariz, beginning 1981; res assoc, Dept Geoscience, Univ Ariz, 1981-1984; vis scientist geochem, Max Planck Inst Chem, Mainz, 1979-1981; res fel geochem, NATO fel, 1977-1979; res fel geochem, Dept mineral & petrol, Univ Cambridge, 1976-1979; teaching res asst geochem, Org Geochem Unit, Univ Bristol, 1975-1976. **Memberships:** Am Geophys Union; Meteoritical Soc; Royal Soc Chem; Geol Soc Am. **Research Statement & Publications:** Radiocarbon dating by accelerator mass spectrometry; studies of cosmogenic radionuclides in meteorites and terrestial samples; development of Carbon 14 sample preparation methods for accelerator dating; isotope and light element geochemistry; published over 10 articles. **Mailing Address:** Dept Geosci, Univ Ariz, Gould Simpson Bldg 77 1040 E Fourth St, Tucson, AZ 85712. **Fax:** 520-621-9619. **E-Mail:** jull@u.arizona.edu

JULL, EDWARD VINCENT, ELECTROMAGNETIC WAVE THEORY. **Personal Data:** b Calgary, Alta, August 8, 1934; m 1965, Anne; c Victoria, Charlotta, Walter & Philip. **Education:** Queen's Univ Ont, BS, 1956; Univ London, PhD (elec eng), 1960. **Honorary Degrees:** DSc (Eng), Univ London, 1979. **Honors & Awards:** J T Bolljahn Award, Inst Elec & Electronics Engrs, 1965. **Professional Experience:** PROF EMER, UNIV BC, 2000-; series ed, IEE Electomagnetic Waves, London, 1994-2003; guest prof, Elecromagnetic Theory, Royal Inst Technol, Stockholm, 1992-1993; prof elec eng, Univ BC, 1980-2000; assoc ed, Radio Sci, Int Union RadioSci, 1980-1983; vis res officer, Nat Res Coun Can, 1979-1980; chmn, Can comn VI, Int UnionRadio Sci, 1973-1976; assoc prof, Univ BC, 1972-1980; assoc res officer, Radio & Elec Eng Div, Nat Res Coun Can, 1967-1972; guest researcher, Microwave Dept, Royal Inst Technol, Sweden, 1965; guest researcher, LabElectromagnetic Theory, Tech Univ Denmark, 1963-1965; asst res officer, Radio & Elec EngDiv, Nat Res Coun Can, 1961-1972; asst prof elec eng, Univ Alta, 1960-1961; jr res officer, Radio & Elec Eng Div, Nat Res Coun Can, 1956-1957. **Memberships:** Life Fel Inst Elec & Electronics Engrs; Int Union Radio Sci (vpres, 1987-1990, pres, 1990-1993, past pres, 1993-1996); Electromagnetics Acad. **Research Statement & Publications:** Antennas; antenna far-field/near-field prediction; electromagnetic diffraction theory; geometrical theory of diffraction; electromagnetic diffraction gratings; Beam and beam array scattering and diffraction. **Mailing Address:** Dept Elec Eng, Univ BC, Vancouver, BC V6T 1Z4, Can. **Fax:** 604-822-5949. **E-Mail:** jull@ece.ubc.ca

JULL, GEORGE W(ALTER), ELECTRONICS ENGINEERING. **Personal Data:** b Calgary, Alta, June 22, 1929; m 1956, c 1. **Education:** Univ Alta, BS, 1951; Univ London, DIC & PhD (elec eng), 1955. **Professional Experience:** RETIRED; sr consult, Commun Res Directorate, 1975-1986; prog mgr, Info Directorate, 1971-1975; defense scientist, High Frequency Systs, Defense Res TelecommunEstab, 1955-1971. **Memberships:** Optical Soc Am; Inst Elec & Electronics Engrs. **Research Statement & Publications:** Advanced communications systems techniques; coherent optical systems; new voice, video and data systems analysis; telecommunications policy research. **Mailing Address:** 72 Stinson Ave, Nepean, ON K2H 6N4, Can.

JULLIEN, GRAHAM ARNOLD, SIGNAL PROCESSING, ELECTRONIC SYSTEMS. **Personal Data:** b Wolverhampton, Eng, June 16, 1943; m 1970, c 2. **Education:** Loughborough Univ Technol, BTech, 1965; Univ Birmingham, MS, 1967; UnivAston, PhD (elec eng), 1969. **Honors & Awards:** Chmn, NSERC Doctoral Prizes Comm, 1999-2001; Fel, Inst Elec & Electronics Engrs, 2003-. **Professional Experience:** ICORE RES CHR ADV TECH INFO PROC SYS, DEPT ELEC & COMP ENG, UNIV CALGARY, 2001-; adj prof, Univ Windsor Nat Sci & Eng Res Coun grant, Can, 1980-1986; prof elec eng, Univ Windsor, 1978-2000; sr res engr, Cent Res Labs, EMI Ltd, UK, 1975-1976; pres, Micrel Ltd, beginning 1974; res asst elec eng, Univ Aston, 1967-1969; Engr, English Elec Co, 1965-1966; dir, ATIPS Lab, Univ Calgary. **Memberships:** Inst Elec &Electronics Engrs; SPIE. **Research Statement & Publications:** Digital signal processing; image processing; high speed digital hardware; microprocessor systems; Computer Arithmetic, Integrated Circuits and System-on-Chip. **Mailing Address:** Dept Elec & Comp Eng, Univ Calgary, 2500 Univ Dr NW, Calgary, AB T2N 1N4, Can. **Fax:** 403-282-6855. **E-Mail:** jullien@atips.ca

JULYAN, FREDERICK JOHN, ANATOMY, HISTOLOGY. **Personal Data:** b Cleveland, Ohio, May 21, 1927; m 1960, Caroline; c Candice, David, Mark & Ernest. **Education:** Western Res Univ, AB, 1950; Ohio State Univ, PhD (zoology), 1962. **Professional Experience:** RETIRED; prof & chmn dept anat, Kirksville Col Osteop Med, Kirksville, MO, 1975-1992; prof anat, Chicago Col Osteop Med, 1974-1975; chmn dept, Chicago Col Osteop Med, 1973-1975; from asst prof to assoc prof, Chicago Col Osteop Med, 1967-1973; from instr to asst prof anat, Ohio State Univ, 1962-1966; instr zool, Capital Univ, 1960-1961. **Memberships:** AAAS. **Research Statement & Publications:** Teaching techniques. **Mailing Address:** RR One PO Box 320, Kirksville, MO 63501.

JUMARIE, GUY MICHAEL, INFORMATION THEORY & APPLICATIONS, INFORMATION SCIENCE & CONTROL SYSTEMS. **Personal Data:** b Dakar City, Senegal, March 18, 1939; French & Canadian citizen; m 1962, Nadia; c Catherine. **Education:** Univ Paris, BSc, 1960 & 1961, Dr Math, 1962; Univ Lille, D Univ, 1972, DSc(physics), 1981. **Honors & Awards:** Silver Medal, Soc Encouragement Invention Res, 1975. **Professional Experience:** Invited prof, Inst Theoret Physics, Univ Stuttgart, Ger, 1987; invited prof, FedUniv, Rio Del Janeiro, 1984; invited prof, Nat Automic Univ Mex, 1983; invited lectr, Int Ctr Theoret Physics, 1978, 1987, 1996; PROF APPL MATH & STATIST, UNIV QUE, MONTREAL, 1976-; invited prof, Nat Inst Statist, Morocco, 1974-1979; assoc prof appl math, Univ Que, Montreal, 1970-1976; group leader, syst eng comput, MATRA, Paris, 1968-1970; res engr aeronauts, SNIA, Paris, 1966-1968; lectr, Univ Paris, 1963-1966; engr missile guidance, SNIA, Paris, 1962-1966. **Memberships:** Int Asn Cybernetics; Austrian Soc Cybernetic Study. **Research Statement & Publications:** Application of theory of relative information and theory of information of deterministic functions to such questions as systems science, automatic control, approximate reasoning, robotics, computer vision and nonlinear physics. **Mailing Address:** Dept Math, Univ Que, Longueuil, PQ J4H 3X5, Can. **Fax:** 514-987-8935. **E-Mail:** jumarie.guy@uqam.ca

JUMARS, PETER ALFRED, BIOLOGICAL OCEANOGRAPHY. **Personal Data:** b Dinkelsbuhl, Ger, June 3, 1948; American citizen; m 1976, Mary; c Alyssa Perry Jumars. **Education:** Univ Del, BA, 1969; Univ Calif, San Diego, PhD (oceanogr), 1974. **Honors & Awards:** ASLO G Evelyn Hutchinson award, 1994. **Professional Experience:** PROF MARINE SCI & OCEANOG, UNIV MAINE, 1999-; AFFIL PROF, SCH OCEANOG, UNIV WASH, 1999-; ed, Limnol & Oceanog, 1986-1992; prof oceanog, Univ Wash, 1983-1999; Sci officer, Environ Sci div, Off Naval Res, 1980-1982; from asst prof to assoc prof, Univ Wash, 1975-1983; Res assoc oceanog, Allan Hancock Found, Univ Southern Calif, 1974-1975. **Memberships:** AAAS; Am Soc Limnol & Oceanog; fel, Am Geophys Union (pres, 2002 - 2004); fel British Ecol Soc; The Oceanographic Soc; Soc Integrative & Comparative Biol. **Research Statement & Publications:** Algal biophysics; Biological-physical interactions; deposit feeding; succession; spatial scales of community processes; biology of polychaetes; Clonal fitness of attached bacteria predicted by analog modeling. **Mailing Address:** Darling Marine Ctr 193 Clark's Cove Rd, Univ Maine, Walpole, ME 04573-3307. **Fax:** 207-563-3119. **E-Mail:** jumars@maine.edu

JUMP, J ROBERT, COMPUTER ARCHITECTURE. **Personal Data:** b Kansas City, Mo, February 15, 1937; m 1962, Gerry; c Stephen & Kathryn. **Education:** Univ Cincinnati, BS, 1960, MS, 1962; Univ Mich, MS, 1965, PhD (comput sci), 1968. **Professional Experience:** RETIRED; prof emer, elec eng, rice Univ, as of 1995; prog dir, NSF, 1993-; ed, Inst Elec & Electronics Engrs Trans Parallel & Distributed Systs, 1991-1993; master, Lovett Col, 1984-1989; prof elec eng, Rice Univ, beginning 1980; Assoc ed, Inst Elec & Electronics Engrs Trans Computs, 1979-1981; from asst prof to assoc prof, Rice Univ, 1968-1979; Elec engr, Avco Corp, 1960-1961 & IBM Corp, 1962-1964. **Memberships:** Inst Elec & Electronics Engrs; Asn Comput Mach. **Research Statement & Publications:** Digital systems design; parallel computing; simulation of computer systems. **Mailing Address:** Dept Elec Eng, Rice Univ, 3030 Duncan Hall PO Box 1892, Houston, TX 77251. **E-Mail:** jrj@rice.edu

JUMP, LORIN KEITH, GENETICS, PLANT BREEDING. **Personal Data:** b Bloomington, Ill, March 7, 1928; m 1951, c 4. **Education:** Univ Ill, BS & MS, 1951. **Professional Experience:** MGR PROD DEVELOP, FUNK SEEDS INT, 1983-; MGR SEED PROD RES & FOUND SEED, FUNK SEEDS INT, 1978-; assoc res dir, Funk Seed Int, 1975-1977; assoc dir co res, Funk Seed Int, 1970-1975; mgr hybrid corn res, Funk Seed Int, 1968-1970; asst mgr res opers, Funk Seed Int, 1963-1967; mgr res cent corn belt, Funk Seed Int, 1957-1962; corn breeder, Funk Seed Int, 1951-1956; mem comt intellectual property rights, Am Seed Trade Asn; Mem, Agr Res Inst, Nat Acad Sci-Nat Res Coun. **Memberships:** AAAS; Am Soc Agron; Sigma Xi. **Research Statement & Publications:** Development of commercial corn, sorghum and wheat varieties for the United States and the world. **Mailing Address:** 1301 W Washington St, Bloomington, IL 61701-4721.

JUMPER, CHARLES FREDERICK, PHYSICAL CHEMISTRY. **Personal Data:** b Prosperity, SC, November 4, 1934; m 1967, c 1. **Education:** Univ SC, BS, 1956, MS, 1957; Fla State Univ, PhD (phys chem), 1961. **Professional Experience:** RETIRED; head dept, The Citadel, beginning 1982; prof chem, The Citadel, beginning 1969; from asst prof to assoc prof, The Citadel, 1962-1969; res assoc, Bell Tel Labs NJ, 1961-1962; instr chem, Univ SC, 1960-1961. **Memberships:** Am Chem Soc; Sigma Xi. **Research Statement & Publications:** Hydrogen bonding; nuclear magnetic resonance; ion exchange; kinetics of very fast reactions; structure of liquids; vibrational spectroscopy. **Mailing Address:** 26 Meander Row, Charleston, SC 29412.

JUMPER, ERIC J, GAS DYNAMICS, LASER PHYSICS. **Personal Data:** b Washington, DC, August 18, 1946; m 1967, Marjorie; c Eric J Jr & Christine A. **Education:** Univ NMex, BS, 1968; Univ Wyo, MS, 1969; Air Force Inst Technol, PhD (mech eng, laser physics), 1975. **Professional Experience:** Vis prof, Dept Aeronautics, US Air Force Acad, CO, 2001-2002; PROF, DEPT AEROSPACE & MECH ENG, UNIV NOTRE DAME, 1989-; chief, Laser Devices Div, Air Force Weapons Lab, Kirtland AFB, NMex, 1987-1989; prof, Dept Aeronaut & Astronaut, Air Force Inst Technol, Wright-Patterson AFB, 1981-1987; assoc ed, Aeronaut Dig, USAF Acad, 1981-1983; consult heat transfer, Broadcast Prod Div, Harris Corp, 1979-1982; bd dir, Shroud of Turin Proj, 1978-1986; ed, Aeronaut Dig, USAF Acad, 1978-1981; consult laser probs, Air Force Weapons Lab, 1976-1985; assoc prof, Dept Aeronaut, USAF Acad, 1976-1981; Co-coodr, Shroud of Turin Proj, 1974-1984; aerodynamicist fluid dynamics & laser physics, Technol Div, Air Force Weapons Lab, 1974-1976; Aerospace Med Res Lab, Wright-Patterson AFB, Ohio, 1969-1972; lab mech engr, Human Eng Div, 1965-1970. **Memberships:** Assoc fel Am Inst Aeronaut & Astronaut; Am Soc Eng Educ. **Research Statement & Publications:** Supersonic drag predictions; physical chemistry of heterogeneous reactions; gas dynamics of lasers; laser-target interaction physics; unsteady aerodynamics; aero-optics; unsteady aerodynamics; laser-fluid interactions; Model for Oxygen Recombination on Reaction-Cured Glass. **Mailing Address:** Dept Aerospace & Mech Eng, Univ Notre Dame, Notre Dame, IN 46556. **Fax:** 219-631-8355. **E-Mail:** jumper.1@nd.edu

JUMPER, SIDNEY ROBERTS, RESOURCES, AGRICULTURAL MARKETING. **Personal Data:** b Gaston, SC, December 10, 1930; m 1954, Mary J Scarcela; c 1. **Education:** Univ SC, AB, 1951, MS, 1953; Univ Tenn, PhD (geog), 1960. **Honors & Awards:** Distinguished Geog Educ, Nat Geog Soc, 1989. **Professional Experience:** Chmn Bd, Tenn Geog Alliance, Inc, 1986-; head, Dept Geog, Univ Tenn, 1977-1995; ed, Southeastern Geogr, Asn Am Geographers, 1975-1979; PROFGEOG, UNIV TENN, 1972-; assoc prof, Univ Tenn, 1967-1972; head dept geog, philos &sociol, Tenn Technol Univ, 1962-1967; from asst prof to prof, Tenn Technol Univ, 1957-1967; instr, Univ Tenn, 1956-1957; instr geog, Univ SC, 1952-1953; Tenn State geogr. **Memberships:** Asn Am Geographers; Nat Geog Soc; Sigma Xi. **Research Statement & Publications:** Marketing of agricultural products, particularly fresh fruits and vegetables; economic geography; geography education. **Mailing Address:** Dept Geog, Univ Tenn, Knoxville, TN 37996-1420. **Fax:** 423-974-6025. **E-Mail:** sjumper@utk.edu

JUNCOSA, MARIO LEON, APPLIED MATHEMATICS, NUMERICAL ANALYSIS. **Personal Data:** b Lima, Peru, September 18, 1921; American citizen; m 1946, Vera; c Raymond, William, Adrian, Alexander & Sylvia. **Education:** Hofstra Col, BA, 1943; Cornell Univ, MS, 1945, PhD (appl math), 1948. **Professional Experience:** Fel, Grad Sch Bus, Calif State, Long Beach, 1996; vis lectr & vis assoc prof, lectr Col Eng, 1983-1985; vis lectr & vis assoc prof, Econ Dept, Univ Calif, Los Angeles, 1981-1989; lectr, Grad Sch Bus, Calif State, Long Beach, 1979-1981; consult, Div Comput Res, NSF, 1971-1975; SR MATHEMATICIAN, RAND CORP, 1970-; mem comput adv panel, NatCtr Atmospheric Res, 1968-1975; mem adv coun, Sw Regional Lab Educ Res & Develop, 1968-1972; chmn satellite tracking accuracy panel, Nat Acad Sci Adv Comt to Air Force SystsCommand, 1967-1969; consult math & comput sci adv group, AEC, 1963-1972; ed chief, AsnComput Mach J, 1959-1963; instr & lectr Univ Calif Exten, Los Angeles, 1956-1958; Instr, Univ Southern Calif Exten, 1954; mathematician, Rand Corp, 1953-1970; mathematician, ExteriorBallistics Lab & Comput Lab, Ballistics Res Labs, Aberdeen Proving Ground, Md, 1949-1953; math, Johns Hopkins Univ, 1948-1950; instr, Cornell Univ, 1947-1948; asst mech, Cornell Univ, 1945-1947; asst physics, Cornell Univ, 1943-1947. **Memberships:** Soc Indust & Appl Math. **Research Statement & Publications:** Applied math, probability, statistics, ordinary and partial differential equations and applications, general numerical and problem analysis, digital computation, mathematical programing and applications, privacy in computerized data banks, and mathematical applications in medicine; models; analyses of terrorism; chaos and aggregation in combat models. **Mailing Address:** 1122 El Medio Ave, Pacific Palisade, CA 90272-2421. **E-Mail:** marie_uncosa@rand.org

JUNEJA, VIJAY KUMAR, EFFECT OF MULTIPLE FOOD FORMULATIONS ON FATE OF BACTERIA IN FOODS, THERMAL INACTIVATION OF SPORE FORMING BACTERIA IN FOODS. **Personal Data:** b Jammu, India, July 1, 1956; American citizen; m 1985, Poonam; c Komal & Nikhil. **Education:** G B Pant Univ, BVSc & AH, 1978; Univ Tenn, Knoxville, MS, 1988, PhD (food technol & sci), 1991. **Honorary Degrees:** BVSC, GB Pant Univ, 1988; AH, GB Pant Univ, 1988. **Professional Experience:** SUPVRY MICROBIOLOGIST & LEAD SCIENTIST, AGR RES SERV, USDA, 1993-; microbiologist & actg lead scientist, Agr Res Serv, USDA, 1992-1993; microbiologist, Agr Res Serv, USDA, 1991-1992; grad asst, Dept Food Tech, Univ Tenn, 1988-1991; grad asst, Dept Animal Sci, Univ Tenn, 1986-1988; Vet surgeon animal husbandry, Punjab, India, 1978-1985. **Memberships:** Inst Food Technologists; Int Asn Milk Food & Environ Sanitarians. **Research Statement & Publications:** Effect of multiple food formulations on the growth of spoilage and pathogenic bacteria in foods; food fermentations; diagnostic microbiology techniques including immunological and molecular biology methods. **Mailing Address:** Eastern Regional Res Ctr, Agr Res Serv, USDA, 600 E Mermaid Lane, Wyndmoor, PA 19038. **Fax:** 215-233-6581. **E-Mail:** vjuneja@errc.ars.usda.gov

JUNG, CHAN YONG, TRANSMEMBRANE TRANSPORT, INSULIN ACTIONS. **Personal Data:** b Chungju, Korea, August 12, 1928; American citizen; m Sooja. **Education:** Univ Rochester, NY, PhD (biophys), 1964. **Professional Experience:** PROF BIOPHYS, RES PROF MED, 1983-; PROF BIOPHYS, STATE UNIV NY, BUFFALO, 1981-; assoc prof, State Univ NY, Buffalo, 1977-1981; CHIEF BIOPHYS RES, VET ADMIN MED CTR, BUFFALO, 1975-; res assoc prof, State Univ NY, Buffalo, 1974-1977; res asst prof biophys, State Univ NY, Buffalo, 1967-1974; res assox pharmacol, Univ Louisville, 1965-1967; res assoc radiation biol, Univ Rochester, 1964-1965. **Memberships:** Am Biophys Soc; Am Soc Biol Chem; Am Diabetes Asn; NY Acad Sci; AAAS; Red Cell Club. **Research Statement & Publications:** Molecular elucidation of membrane-related functions; transmembrane solute translocation; information transduction; receptor-ligand interactions; insulin-mediated stimulation of glucose transport function in peripheral tissues. **Mailing Address:** Vet Admin Med Ctr Bldg 20 Rm 215, 3495 Bailey Ave, Buffalo, NY 14215. **Fax:** 716-862-6526. **E-Mail:** cyjung@acsu.buffalo.edu

JUNG, DENNIS WILLIAM, ION TRANSPORT, MITOCHONDRIA. **Education:** Univ Ill, PhD (biol), 1974. **Professional Experience:** AT, MED BIOCHEM, OHIO STATE UNIV, as of 2001; RES SCIENTIST PHYSIOL, DEPT PHYSIOL CHEM, OHIO STATE UNIV, 1976-. **Research Statement & Publications:** Heart biochemistry. **Mailing Address:** Dept Med Biochem, Ohio State Univ, 484 W 12th Ave, Columbus, OH 43210-1292. **Fax:** 614-292-1538.

JUNG, DONALD T, PHARMACOKINETICS, BIOPHARMACEUTICS. **Personal Data:** b Los Angeles, Calif, April 10, 1953. **Education:** Univ Calif, Davis, BS, 1974; Univ Calif, San Francisco, MS, 1978; Univ Ariz, PhD (pharmaceut sci), 1980. **Professional Experience:** ASSOC DIR, CLIN PHARMACOL, ROCHE PALO ALTO, as of 1999; adj asst prof pharmacokinetics, Univ Ill, Chicago, 1987-; asst prof pharmacokinetics, Univ Ill, Chicago, 1981-1987. **Memberships:** Am Asn Pharmaceut Sci; Acad Pharmaceut Sci; Am Pharmaceut Asn; Drug Info Asn. **Research Statement & Publications:** Effect of disease states on pharmacokinetics, pharmacokinetic/pharmacodynamic modeling, drug metabolism drug interaction, bio equivalence, clinical trials. **Mailing Address:** 3431 Hillview Ave, A2-230, Palo Alto, CA 94304. **Fax:** 650-855-5560. **E-Mail:** donald.jung@roche.com

JUNG, FREDERIC THEODORE, physiology; deceased, see previous edition for last biography.

JUNG, GERALD ALVIN, AGRONOMY, PLANT ECOLOGY. **Personal Data:** b Milwaukee, Wis, July 16, 1930; m 1957. **Education:** Univ Wis, BS, 1952, MS, 1954, PhD, 1958. **Honors & Awards:** Res Award, Northeast Br, Am Soc Agron, 1984; Goddard Mem lectr, UnivTenn, 1988; John Peters Mem lectr, WVa Univ, 1990. **Professional Experience:** RETIRED; Pa Forage & Grassland Coun res award, 1987; mem, Presidium, 12th Int Grassland Cong, Moscow, USSR, 1974; adj prof agron, Pa State Univ; tech adv for soil-fertility &physiol & biochem technol, USDA, 1971-1981; res agronomist & res leader, US-Regional Pasture Res Lab, Agr Res Serv, 1970-1994; prof agron & genetics, WVa Univ, 1967-1970; assoc prof, WVa Univ, 1962-1967; asst prof agron, WVa Univ, 1958-1962; biologist, Chem Warfare Lab, Ft Detrick, Md, 1954-1956. **Memberships:** Fel Am Soc Agron; Am Forage & Grassland Coun; Soc Cryobiol; fel Crop Sci SocAm. **Research Statement & Publications:** Forage crop adaptation and production on marginal lands; nutritional value of forage crops as influenced by soils and fertilizers; physiology of cold tolerance of alfalfa. **Mailing Address:** 22 Oyster Bay Pl, Hilton Head, SC 29926.

JUNG, GLENN HAROLD, OCEANOGRAPHY, METEOROLOGY. **Personal Data:** b Lyons, Kans, October 11, wid Jean; c Lynn (Parsons), Lawrence E, Leslie M, Richard B & Dale. **Education:** Mass Inst Technol, SB, Meteorology 1949, SM, Meteorology 1952; Tex A&M Univ, PhD (phys oceanog), 1955. **Professional Experience:** Vis fac mem, Naval Postgrad Sch, 1987-1988 & 1990-1991; EMER PROF, NAVAL POSTGRAD SCH, 1983-; vis fac mem, Inst Phys Oceanog, Univ Copenhagen, 1971-1972; prof oceanog, Naval Postgrad Sch, 1965-1983; Consult, US Naval Oceanog Off, 1965 & 1966; assoc prof oceanog, Naval Postgrad Sch, 1958-1965; assoc oceanog & asst prof phys oceanog & phys meteorol, Tex A&M Univ, 1955-1957; asst oceanog, Tex A&M Univ, 1953-1954; Fulbright fel, Univ Oslo, Norway, 1954-1955 (Oceanography; mem staff, Div Indust Co-op, MIT, 1952; Asst meteorol, Mass Inst Technol, 1950-1951; Weather Officer, USAAF, 1944-1947. **Research Statement & Publications:** Energy transfer by sea and air, especially across air-sea boundary; oceanographic analysis and forecasting; For coastal Southern Africa; Phillipines and Caribbean Sea. **Mailing Address:** 24651 Cabrillo St, Carmel, CA 93923. **E-Mail:** ocjunger@aol.com

JUNG, HILDA ZIIFLE, PHYSICAL CHEMISTRY, PLASMA PHYSICS. **Personal Data:** b Gretna, La, September 7, 1922; m 1968, Julius. **Education:** Tulane Univ, BS, 1943. **Professional Experience:** RETIRED; res physicist, Southern Regional Res Ctr, USDA, 1944-1979; release clerk, Higgins Aircraft Co, 1943-1944. **Memberships:** Sigma Xi; Am Chem Soc; AAAS. **Research Statement & Publications:** Physical and physical chemical reactions and properties of natural polymers; kinetics of reactions; crystalline orientation; elasticity; low temperature plasma reactions; application of statistical techniques. **Mailing Address:** 109 Kennedy Dr, Gretna, LA 70053.

JUNG, JAMES MOSER, ORGANIC CHEMISTRY. **Personal Data:** b Kannapolis, NC, May 25, 1928; m Patty; c Anita, Dayna, Alisa, David & Krystal. **Education:** Davidson Col, BS, 1949; Univ NC Chapel Hill, PhD (org chem), 1962. **Professional Experience:** PROF CHEM & CHMN DEPT, CAMPBELL UNIV, 1962-. **Research Statement & Publications:** Preparation, properties and cyclization of azomethines. **Mailing Address:** Dept Chem, Campbell Univ, Buies Creek, NC 27506. **Fax:** 910-893-1887. **E-Mail:** jung@campbell.edu

JUNG, JOHN ANDREW, ORGANIC CHEMISTRY, CATALYSIS. **Personal Data:** b Jersey City, NJ, May 3, 1938. **Education:** St Peter's Col, BS, 1961; Univ Iowa, PhD (org chem), 1966. **Professional Experience:** STAFF CHEMIST, INTERMEDIATES DIV, EXXON CHEM, 1981-; sr reschemist, Chem Systs Inc, 1972-1981; res chemist, M W Kellogg Co, 1967-1971; res chemist, US Army Ballistic Res Labs, Md, 1966-1967. **Memberships:** Am Chem Soc; Catalysis Soc; Sigma Xi. **Research Statement & Publications:** Oxo process catalysis. **Mailing Address:** 6628 Milstone Dr, Baton Rouge, LA 70808.

JUNG, LAWRENCE KWOK LEUNG, IMMUNOLOGY, MEDICAL SCIENCE. **Personal Data:** b Canton, China, August 6, 1950; Canadian citizen; m 1977, c 2. **Education:** Univ Sask, BSc, 1971, MD, 1975; FRCP (C), 1980; Am Acad Pediat, dipl, 1980. **Professional Experience:** ASST PROF & CHIEF, CLIN IMMUNOL SERV, OKLA CHILDREN'S MEM HOSP, 1986-; ASST MEM, OKLA MED RES FOUND IMMUNOL PROG, 1986-; Prin investr, NIH grants, 1984-; sr clin scientist, Clin Immunol Serv, Okla Children's Mem Hosp, 1982-1986; res fel, dept pediat, Okla Children's Mem Hosp, 1982-1984; res fel, Sloan-Kettering Inst Cancer Res, 1980-1982; pediat immunol fel, McMaster Univ Med Ctr, Toronto, 1978-1980; sr resident pediatrician, McMaster Univ Med Ctr, Toronto, 1977-1978; sr resident pediatrician, Hosp Sick Children, Toronto, 1975-1977. **Memberships:** Am Asn Immunologists; Clin Immunol Soc; NY Acad Sci; AAAS; AMA. **Research Statement & Publications:** The role of human T cell differentiation antigens on T cell ontogeny, activation and differentiation in normal and immunodeficiency states. **Mailing Address:** Dept Pediat Immunol, 55 Lake Ave, Worcester, MA 01605-2377. **Fax:** 508-856-5500.

JUNG, MICHAEL ERNEST, SYNTHETIC ORGANIC CHEMISTRY, NATURAL PRODUCTS CHEMISTRY. **Personal Data:** b New Orleans, La, May 14, 1947; m 1969. **Education:** Rice Univ, BS, 1969; Columbia Univ, PhD (chem), 1973. **Professional Experience:** PROF CHEM, UNIV CALIF, LOS ANGELES, 1983-; Fulbright-Hays grant, US Res Scholar Award, 1980-1981; Alfred P Sloan Found res fel, 1979-1981; Camille & Henry Dreyfus Teacher-Scholar grant, 1978-1983; from asst prof to assoc prof, Univ Calif, Los Angeles, 1974-1983; NATO fel, Swiss Fed Inst Technol, 1973-1974; mem, Cancer Ctr, Univ Calif, Los Angeles. **Memberships:** Am Chem Soc; Royal Chem Soc; Sigma Xi. **Research Statement & Publications:** Organic synthesis, particularly of biologically interesting natural products; development of new synthetic methods; chemistry of organic compounds of group IVb metals, such as silicon and tin, and their use in organic synthesis. **Mailing Address:** Dept Chem & biochem, Univ Calif, 607 Charles E Young Dr E, Los Angeles, CA 90024-1569. **Fax:** 310-206-3722. **E-Mail:** jung@chem.ucla.edu

JUNG, RANU, BIOMEDICAL ENGINEERING. **Education:** Case Western Reserve Univ, PhD, 1991. **Professional Experience:** CO-DIR, BIODESIGN INST & ASSOC PROF BIOENGINEERING, ARIZ STATE UNIV, ARIZ, as of 2005. **Mailing Address:** Ariz State Univ, PO Box 879709 Dept Bioengineering, Tempe, AZ 85287-9709. **Fax:** 480-727-7624. **E-Mail:** jung@asu.edu

JUNG, RODNEY CLIFTON, TROPICAL MEDICINE, CLINICAL PARASITOLOGY. **Personal Data:** b New Orleans, La, October 9, 1920; m 1986. **Education:** Tulane Univ, BS, 1941, MD, 1945, MS, 1950, PhD (parasitol), 1953. **Honors & Awards:** Geiger Medal Pub Health. **Professional Experience:** PROF EMER TROP MED, TULANE UNIV, 1992-; clin prof med, Tulane Univ, 1974-1991; dir health, City New Orleans, 1963-1970 & 1979-; Markle scholar, 1953-1958; from instr to prof trop med, Tulane Univ, 1950-1974; asst parasitol, Tulane Univ, 1948-1950; asst zool, Tulane Univ, 1939-1942; sr vis physician, Charity Hosp, La; consult, US Quarantine Serv. **Memberships:** Am Soc Trop Med & Hyg; Am Soc Parasitologists; fel Am Col Physicians; Royal Soc Trop Med & Hyg; hon mem Brazilian Soc Trop Med. **Research Statement & Publications:** Clinical aspects of parasitic infections. **Mailing Address:** Dept Trop Med, Tulane Univ, 1430 Tulane Ave, New Orleans, LA 70112. **Fax:** 504-587-7313.

JUNGA, FRANK ARTHUR, SOLID STATE PHYSICS. **Personal Data:** b Patchogue, NY, May 15, 1934; m 1956. **Education:** Yale Univ, BS, 1956; Univ Calif, Berkeley, MA, 1959, PhD (physics), 1963. **Professional Experience:** RES SCIENTIST SOLID STATE PHYSICS, LOCKHEED RES LAB, 1963-; grad prog student, Lockheed Res Lab, 1956-1963. **Memberships:** Am Phys Soc. **Research Statement & Publications:** Basic mechanisms involved in optical and/or electrical phenomena in semiconductors; photoconductivity; photovoltaic effects; laser phenomena; radiation effects in semiconductors; research on surface phenomena in compound semiconductors. **Mailing Address:** Lockheed Res Lab Bldg 202 Dept H154, 3251 Hanover St, Palo Alto, CA 94304-1187.

JUNGALWALA, FIROZE BAMANSHAW, BIOCHEMISTRY, NEUROCHEMISTRY, NEUROSCIENCE. **Personal Data:** b India, August 28, 1936; American citizen; m 1968, Khorshed; c Ferzin & Jehangir. **Education:** Gujarat Univ, India, BS, 1956, MS, 1958; Indian Inst Sci, Bangalore, PhD (biochem), 1963. **Honors & Awards:** Career Develop Award, NIH. **Professional Experience:** PROF BIOCHEM & MOLECULAR PHARMCOL, UNIV MASS MED SCH, WORCESTER, 2000-; ed bd, Jour Neurochemistry, 1994-; chmn, Biomed Sci, Shriver Ctr Ment Retard, 1993-1997; assoc prof neuroscience, Dept Neurol, Harvard Med Sch, 1989-2000; assoc ed, Journal Lipid Res, 1980-1982; SR NEUROSCIENTIST, E K SHRIVER CTR MENT RETARDATION, WALTHAM, MA, 1971-. **Memberships:** Int Soc Neurochem; Am Soc Neurochem; Fedn Am Socs Exp Biol. **Research Statement & Publications:** Lipids; role of lipids in membrane formation and organization; cerebral membranes, systhesis function and breakdown of lipids in health and diseases. **Mailing Address:** Dept Biomed Sci, E K Shriver Ctr Ment Retardation, 200 Trapelo Rd, Waltham, MA 02254. **Fax:** 781-642-0116. **E-Mail:** firoze.jungalwala@umassmed.edu

JUNGAS, ROBERT LEANDO, ENERGY METABOLISM. **Personal Data:** b Mt Lake, Minn, September 25, 1934; m 1957, Lois. **Education:** St Olaf Col, BA, 1956; Harvard Univ, PhD (biochem), 1961. **Professional Experience:** Assoc dean preclin educ, Univ Conn Health Ctr, 1985-1990; CHAIR & PROF PHYSIOL, UNIV CONN HEALTH CTR, 1974-; assoc prof, biol chem, Harvard Med Sch, 1971-1974; asst prof, biol chem, Harvard Med Sch, 1968-1971; assoc, Harvard Med Sch, 1965-1968; instr biochem, Harvard Med Sch, 1963-1965; USPHS training grant biochem, Harvard Med Sch, 1960-1963. **Memberships:** Am Soc Biol Chemists; Biochem Soc. **Research Statement & Publications:** Action of hormones on adipose tissue metabolism. **Mailing Address:** Dept Physiol, Univ Conn Health Ctr, MC 3505 263 Farmington Ave, Farmington, CT 06030. **Fax:** 860-679-1269. **E-Mail:** yukonrlj@aol.com

JUNGBAUER, MARY ANN, INORGANIC CHEMISTRY. **Personal Data:** b Phoenix, Ariz, August 10, 1934; c 1. **Education:** Immaculate Heart Col, BA, 1957; Univ Notre Dame, MS, 1961, PhD (inorg chem), 1964. **Professional Experience:** PROF CHEM, DEPT PHYS SCI, BARRY UNIV, 1992-; CHMN, DEPT PHYS SCI, BARRY UNIV, 1980-; assoc prof, dept phys sci, Barry Univ, 1972-1992; adj assoc prof, dept phys sci, Barry Univ, 1969-1972; asst prof chem, Drew Univ, 1967-1969; instr chem, Immaculate Heart Col, 1963-1967; teacher, Pub Schs, 1956-1959. **Memberships:** Am Chem Soc; Sigma Xi. **Mailing Address:** 704 Jeronimo Dr, Coral Gables, FL 33146. **Fax:** 305-899-3439. **E-Mail:** jungbaver@buaxp1.barry.edu

JUNGCK, GERALD FREDERICK, TOPOLOGY, FIXED POINT THEORY. **Personal Data:** b Dubuque, Iowa, March 1, 1929; m, c 2. **Education:** Wartburg Col, BA, 1956; Univ Wis, MA, 1959; State Univ NY, Binghamton, PhD (math), 1978. **Honors & Awards:** Who's Who Among American Teachers, 2004-2005. **Professional Experience:** DEPT CHMN, BRADLEY UNIV, 1989-1995; PROF MATH, BRADLEY UNIV, 1982-; NSF fac fel, Rutgers Univ, 1968; from asst prof to assoc prof, Bradley Univ, 1961-1982; instr, Bradley Univ, 1959-1961. **Memberships:** Am. Math. Soc. **Research Statement & Publications:** Fixed point theorems for commuting and compatible mappings on metric spaces; local homeomorphisms. **Mailing Address:** Dept Math, Bradley Univ, BR 452, Peoria, IL 61625-0160. **E-Mail:** gfj@hilltop.bradley.edu

JUNGCK, JOHN RICHARD, MOLECULAR EVOLUTION. **Personal Data:** b Moorhead, Minn, August 17, 1944; m 1965, c Peder. **Education:** Univ Minn, BS, 1966, MS, 1968; Univ Miami, PhD (biol & chem), 1973. **Professional Experience:** ED, 1996-; ED, BIOQUEST LIBR, 1986-; ED BIOSCENE, ASN MIDWESTERN COL BIOL TEACHERS, 1988-; Fulbright Scholar, Chiang Mai Univ, Thailand, 1985-1986; ed, Am Biol Teacher, 1984-1985; assoc ed, Bulletin Math Biol, 1982-1986; PROF & MEAD CHAIR SCI, DEPT BIOL, BELOIT COL, 1979-; from asst prof to assoc prof, Clarkson Col, 1975-1979; asst prof, biol, Merrimack Col, 1971-1975; PRIN INVESTR, BEDROCK. **Memberships:** Soc Study Evolution; Int Soc Study Origins Life (chair, educ comt, 1995-); Soc Math Biol; Soc Systematic biol; fel AAAS; fel Nat Inst Sci Educ; Am Inst Biol Sci (educ comt, 1998-); Int Soc Molecular Evolution. **Research Statement & Publications:** Origins of and mathematical properties of the genetic code; computer analysis of nucleic acid and protein sequences; genetic language; algorithms for analyzing sequence data; philosophy of biology; computer assisted learning-strategic simulations; combinatorics and finite mathematics; published over 10 articles. **Mailing Address:** Biol Dept Beloit Col, 700 Col St, Beloit, WI 53511-5595. **E-Mail:** jungck@beloit.edu

JUNGCLAUS, GREGORY ALAN, ANALYTICAL CHEMISTRY, ENVIRONMENTAL CHEMISTRY. **Personal Data:** b Yankton, SDak, December 16, 1947; m 1966, c 2. **Education:** Univ SDak, BA, 1970, MA, 1972; Ariz State Univ, PhD (chem), 1975. **Professional Experience:** Sr chemist, Midwest Res Inst, beginning 1981; res chemist, Battelle Columbus Labs, 1978-1981; sr res scientist, Ford Motor Co, 1977-1978; res assoc chem, Mass Inst Technol, 1975-1977. **Memberships:** Am Chem Soc; Am Soc Mass Spectrom; Meteoritical Soc; Sigma Xi. **Research Statement & Publications:** Technical direction of projects concerning analytical method development and application; agent demilitarization and installation restoration; gas chromatographic mass spectrometry. **Mailing Address:** Midwest Res Inst, 425 Volker Blvd, Kansas City, MO 64110-2299. **Fax:** 816-753-8420.

JUNGE, DOUGLAS, BIOPHYSICS, APPLIED MATHEMATICS. **Personal Data:** b Milwaukee, Wis, January 16, 1938; m 1960, c 2. **Education:** Calif Inst Technol, BS, 1959; Univ Calif, Los Angeles, PhD (physiol), 1965. **Professional Experience:** Ed, J Theoret Neurobiology, 1981-; PROF ORAL BIOL, SCH DENT, UNIV CALIF, LOS ANGELES, 1979-; NSF grant, 1972-1974; contract, 1969-1971; NIH grant, 1968-1971; from asst prof to assoc prof, Sch Dent, Univ Calif, Los Angeles, 1967-1979; fel, Scripps Inst Oceanog, 1965-1967. **Memberships:** Am Physiol Soc; Biophys Soc; Soc Neuroscience, Am Asn Oral Biologists; Int Asn Dent Res. **Research Statement & Publications:** Electrophysiology of excitable membranes; ionic properties of nerve; computer analysis of BMG signals in painful or tender muscles; neurosciences. **Mailing Address:** Dept Oral Biol & Med, Univ Calif Los Angeles Sch Dent, 63-078 CHS 10833 Le Conte Ave, Los Angeles, CA 90095-1668. **E-Mail:** djunge@ucla.edu

JUNGER, MIGUEL C, ACOUSTICS, APPLIED MECHANICS. **Personal Data:** b Dresden, Ger, January 29, 1923. **Education:** Mass Inst Technol, BS, 1944, MS, 1946; Harvard Univ, ScD(appl mech), 1951. **Honors & Awards:** Raleigh lectr, Am Soc Mech Engr, 1987; Per Bruel Gold Medal, 1992; Trent-Crede Medal, Acoust Soc Am. **Professional Experience:** Chmn bd & prin scientist, Cambridge Acoust Assoc, 1990-1997; vis prof, Compiegne Technol Univ, France 1975 & 1977-1981; consult, Off Naval Res, London, 1975; sr vis lectr, Mass Inst Technol, 1968-1978; pres, Cambridge Acoust Assoc, 1959-1990; partner, Cambridge Acoust Assoc, 1955-1959; Res fel, Harvard Univ, 1951-1955. **Memberships:** Fel Acoust Soc Am; fel Am Soc Mech Engr. **Research Statement & Publications:** Physical acoustics, particularly underwater sound; dynamics of elastic systems in an acoustic medium; noise control; mechanical vibrations and shock. **Mailing Address:** 90 Fletcher Rd, Belmont, MA 02478-2017.

JUNGERMAN, JOHN (ALBERT), PHYSICS. **Personal Data:** b Modesto, Calif, December 28, 1921; m 1948, c 4. **Education:** Univ Calif, AB, 1943, PhD (physics), 1949. **Professional Experience:** PROF EMER PHYSICS, UNIV CALIF, DAVIS, as of 2001; chmn, Physics Dept, 1983-1987; consult, Int Atomic Energy Agency, UnivChile, 1982; assoc prof, Univ Grenoble, France, 1972; dir, Crocker Nuclear Lab, 1969-1980; prof physics, Univ Calif, Davis, beginning 1960; res physicist, Univ Calif, Davis, 1951-1969; resphysicist, Lawrence Berkeley Lab, Univ Calif, 1950-1951; AEC fel, Cornell Univ, 1949-1950; Los Alamos Sci Lab, 1945-1946 & Lawrence Berkeley Lab, 1946-1949; res physicist, Radiation Lab, 1944-1945; asst physics, Univ Calif, 1943-1944. **Memberships:** Fel Am Phys Soc; Sigma Xi. **Research Statement & Publications:** Charged particle induced fission; beta ray spectroscopy; sector-focused cyclotrons; particle scattering; medical physics; physics and society. **Mailing Address:** Dept Physics, Univ Calif, Davis, CA 95616. **E-Mail:** jajungerman@ucdavis.edu

JUNGERMANN, ERIC, SURFACE ACTIVE AGENTS, ANTIMICROBIAL AGENTS. **Personal Data:** b Mainz, Ger, September 8, 1923; American citizen; m 1951, Eva; c William C. **Education:** City Col NY, BS, 1949; Polytech Inst Brooklyn, MS, 1953, PhD (org chem), 1957. **Honors & Awards:** Award of Merit, Am Oil Chemists Soc, 1971; Soc Cosmetic Chemists Award, 1975. **Professional Experience:** Sr vpres technol, Neutrogena Corp, 1983-1992; mem bd dirs, Lee Pharmaceut Corp, 1979-1989; mem sci adv bd, Lowes Corp, 1979-1985; PRES, JUNGERMANN ASSOCS INC, 1978-; dir corp develop, Helene Curtis Indust, 1975-1978; vpres res & develop, Armour Dial Inc, 1971-1975; dir household res & develop, Armour & Co, 1965-1971; mgr res, Soap Div, 1959-1965; sect head chem synthesis, Armour Indust Chem Co, 1957-1959; res chemist, Colgate-Palmolive Co, 1946-1957; assoc ed, J Am Oil Chemists Soc. **Memberships:** Am Oil Chemists' Soc; Soc Cosmetic Chemists; Am Chem Soc. **Research Statement & Publications:** Soap, detergent and cosmetic technology, both from the fundamental and practical viewpoint; fat based surfactants; fatty acid derivatives; soaps; hair and skin care products; antimicrobials; organophosphorus compounds. **Mailing Address:** 2323 N Central Ave Ste 1001, Phoenix, AZ 85004. **E-Mail:** ejungermann@netzero.net

JUNGHANS, RICHARD PAUL, HEMATOLOGY, ONCOLOGY. **Personal Data:** b North Ft Atkinson, Wis, February 28, 1951. **Education:** Univ Calif, Berkeley, PhD (molecular biol & virol), 1975. **Professional Experience:** Assoc prof med, New Eng Deaconess Hosp, 1991-2004; Asst Prof Med, Harvard Med Sch, Dir, Biotherapeutics Dev Lab, Beth IsraelDeaconess Med Cen. **Research Statement & Publications:** Hematology; oncology; molecular biology; virology. **Mailing Address:** Biotherapy Develop Prog Harvard Med Sch Dept Med Div Hemat & Oncol, New England Deaconess Hosp 99 Brookline Ave Rm 301, Boston, MA 02215. **Fax:** 617-432-7007. **E-Mail:** junghans@hms.harvard.edu

JUNGKIND, DONALD LEE, MEDICAL MICROBIOLOGY, CLINICAL LABORATORY ADMINISTRATION. **Personal Data:** b Washington, DC, April 16, 1943; m 1965, c 4. **Education:** Lamar State Univ, BS, 1965; Univ Houston, MS, 1968; Univ Tex Med Br Galveston, PhD (microbiol), 1972. **Professional Experience:** PROF MICROBIOL & IMMUNOL, SCH MED, THOMAS JEFFERSON UNIV, 1988-; PROF PATH, ANAT & CELL BIOL, THOMAS JEFFERSON UNIV, 1988-; pres, Microbiol Consult Inc, beginning 1978; from asst prof to assoc prof, Clin Microbiol Lab, 1973-1988; HOSP MICROBIOLOGIST & DIR MICRO BIOL & SEROL LABS, THOMAS JEFFERSON UNIV, 1973-; fel clin microbiol, Sch Med, Temple Univ, 1972-1973. **Memberships:** Am Soc Microbiol; Am Soc Clin Path; Asn Clin Scientists. **Research Statement & Publications:** Diagnostic microbiology and immunology with emphasis on automation of procedures; microbial physiology and effects of antimicrobial agents on cells; sexually transmitted diseases. **Mailing Address:** Clin Microbiol Lab, Thomas Jefferson Med Col, Thomas Jefferson Univ, 207 Pavilion Bldg, Philadelphia, PA 19107-5001. **E-Mail:** Donald.Jungkind@jefferson.edu

JUNGMANN, RICHARD A, MOLECULAR BIOLOGY. **Personal Data:** b Volklingen, Switz, October 29, 1928; American citizen; m 1961, Suzanne. **Education:** Univ Saarland, 1950; Univ Basel, PhD, 1958. **Professional Experience:** PROF MOLECULAR BIOL, MED SCH, NORTHWESTERN UNIV, 1980-; PROF BIOCHEM, MED SCH, NORTHWESTERN UNIV, 1974-; from asst prof to assoc prof biochem, Med Sch, Northwestern Univ, 1968-1974; dept med, Med Sch, Northwestern Univ, 1965-; sr res investr biochem, Dept Res, Chicago Wesley Mem Hosp, 1963-1968; res assoc, Med Sch, Northwestern Univ, 1963-1968; consult, McGean Chem Co, 1963-1964; lectr, Cleveland State Univ, 1960-1963; dir org res, McGean Chem Co, Ohio, 1959-1963; res staff mem biochem, Worcester Found Exp Biol, Mass, 1958-1959. **Memberships:** AAAS; Am Chem Soc; fel Am Inst Chem; Swiss Chem Soc; Endocrine Soc; FASEB. **Research Statement & Publications:** Role of signal transduction in gene expression; effect of potein kinase on mRNA stabilization. **Mailing Address:** Northwestern Univ Med Sch, 303 E Chicago Ave, Chicago, IL 60611. **Fax:** 312-503-7107. **E-Mail:** rjungman@northwesternedu

JUNGST, RUDOLPH GEORGE, III, CHEMISTRY. **Education:** Luther Col, BA, 1968; PhD. **Professional Experience:** SANDIA NAT LABS, as of 2006. **Mailing Address:** Sandia Nat Labs, POBox 5800, Albuquerque, NM 87185. **Fax:** 505-844-6972. **E-Mail:** rgjungs@sandia.gov

JUNI, ELLIOT, BACTERIAL PHYSIOLOGY. **Personal Data:** b NY, August 6, 1921; m 1944, c 2. **Education:** City Col NY, BEE, 1944; Western Reserve Univ, PhD (microbiol), 1951. **Professional Experience:** PROF EMER MICROBIOL, MED SCH, UNIV MICH, ANN ARBOR, as of 2004; prof microbiol, Med Sch, Univ Mich, Ann Arbor, beginning 1966; fromassoc prof to prof, Sch Med, Emory Univ, 1956-1966; asst prof bact, Univ Ill, 1951-1956. **Memberships:** AAAS; Am Soc Microbiol; Am Soc Biol Chem. **Research Statement & Publications:** Bacterial metabolism; taxonomy. **Mailing Address:** Dept Microbiol, Univ Mich Med Sch Sci Bldg II, Ann Arbor, MI 48109-0001. **E-Mail:** juni@umich.edu

JUNK, WILLIAM A(RTHUR), JR, CHEMICAL ENGINEERING. **Personal Data:** b Uniontown, Pa, March 12, 1924; m 1956, c 2. **Education:** Pa State Col, BS, 1948; Univ Ill, MS, 1950, PhD (chem eng), 1952. **Professional Experience:** CHEM ENGR, STANDARD OIL CO, 1952-. **Memberships:** Am Chem Soc. **Research Statement & Publications:** Physical properties of hydrocarbons; separation processes. **Mailing Address:** 18344 Aberdeen Ave, Homewood, IL 60430.

JUNKER, BOBBY RAY, ELECTRONICS, RF SYSTEMS. **Personal Data:** b San Antonio, Tex, August 29, 1943; m 1996, Virginia; c Bryce Allyn, Combs Melissa Sheryl & Evan Ryan. **Education:** Univ Southwestern La, BS, 1965; Univ Tex, Austin, MA, 1967, PhD (chem), 1969. **Professional Experience:** HEAD, INFO ELECTRONICS & SURVILLANCE DEPT, ONR, 1995-; dir math, Phys Sci Directorate, Off Naval Res, 1986-1995; dir, Physic Div, 1983-1986; physicist, Phys Sci Directorate, Off Naval Res, 1977-1983; asst prof physics, Univ Ga, 1972-1976; res assoc physics, Univ Pittsburgh, 1970-1972; Instr chem, Univ Tex, Austin, 1969-1970. **Memberships:** Am Phys Soc; Sigma Xi; AAAS. **Research Statement & Publications:** Theoretical atomic physics, including electron-atom and ion-atom collisions. **Mailing Address:** Off Naval Res Code 31, 800 N Quincy St, Arlington, VA 22217-5660. **E-Mail:** junkerb@ont.navy.mil

JUNKER, BRIAN W, MATHEMATICS. **Education:** Univ Minn, BA, 1980; Univ Ill, MS, 1986, PhD (statist), 1988. **Professional Experience:** PROF STATIST, CARNEGIE MELLON UNIV, 2001-; from asst to assoc prof statist, Carnegie Mellon Univ, 1991-2001. **Mailing Address:** Dept Statist, Carnegie Mellon Univ, 5000 Forbes Ave, Pittsburgh, PA 15213-3890.

JUNKER, MICHAEL LEE, MODELING & SIMULATION, ON & IN-LINE PROCESS ANALYZERS. **Personal Data:** b St Louis, Mo, January 1, 1943; m 1964, Linda; c Penelope A (Piercy) & Mark Louis (deceased). **Education:** Ind Univ, AB, 1964; Purdue Univ, MS, 1967; Univ SC, PhD (phys chem), 1973; La State Univ, MSChE, 1977. **Professional Experience:** MGR, QUALITY SERV, DSM ELASTOMERS AMERICAS, 1999-; sr scientist, DSM Copolymer Inc, 1996-1999; tech mgr, DSM Copolymer Inc, 1993-1996; group leader, DSM Copolymer Inc, 1986-1993; res chemist, DSM Copolymer Inc, 1983-1986; instr comput prog, McNeese State Univ, 1982; sr staff engr high-density polyethylene, Cities Serv Corp, 1980-1983; develop engr OnLine Analyzers, Celanese Corp, 1977-1983; vis prof phys chem, Univ Nebr, 1974-1975; vis prof, Univ NC, 1973-1974; instr, Univ SC, 1972-1973; asst prof anal chem, Newberry Col, 1966-1972. **Memberships:** Am Chem Soc; Instrument Soc Am. **Research Statement & Publications:** Investigating new technologies and working to integrate them into the plants. **Mailing Address:** 1040 S Eugene St, Baton Rouge, LA 70806. **E-Mail:** mike.junker@dsm.com

JUNKHAN, GEORGE H, MECHANICAL ENGINEERING. **Personal Data:** b Peoria, Ill, January 30, 1929; m 1956, c 2. **Education:** Iowa State Univ, BS, 1955, MS, 1959, PhD (mech eng, appl mech), 1964. **Professional Experience:** PROF EMER MECH ENG, IOWA STATE UNIV, as of 2005; assoc prof mech eng, Iowa State Univ, beginning 1966; from instr to asst prof, Iowa State Univ, 1957-1966. **Memberships:** Am Soc Mech Engrs; Am Soc Eng Educ; Sigma Xi. **Research Statement & Publications:** Heat transfer and fluid mechanics, particularly testing of turbomachinery and experimental heat transfer. **Mailing Address:** Dept Mech Eng, Iowa State Univ, 2025 H M Black Eng Bldg, Ames, IA 50011-2161. **Fax:** 515-294-3261.

JUNKINS, JOHN LEE, AEROSPACE ENGINEERING, APPLIED MATHEMATICS. **Personal Data:** b Carters, Ga, May 23, 1943; m 1965, c 2. **Education:** Auburn Univ, BAE, 1965; Univ Calif, Los Angeles, MS, 1967, PhD (eng), 1969. **Honors & Awards:** Mech & Control of Flight Award, Am Inst Aeronaut & Astronaut, 1988, JohnLeland Atwood Award, 1988, Von Karman Lect, 1997. **Professional Experience:** DIR, CTR MECH & CONTROL, TEX A&M UNIV, as of 2004; GEORGE J EPPRIGHT ENDOWED CHMN PROF, TEX A&M UNIV, 1989-; DISTINGUISHED PROF AEROSPACE ENG, TEX A&M UNIV, 1998-; distinguished chmn holder, Tex A&M Univ, 1985-1989; consult, Univ Va, 1978-; prof eng mech, Va Polytech Inst, 1978-1985; assoced, J Astronaut Sci, 1977-; consult, US Engr Topog Lab, 1977-; consult, US Defense Mapping Agency, 1977-; consult, Univ Space Res Asn, 1975-1976; assoc prof, Univ Va, 1974-1978; prin investr, Apollo 15-17 Lunar Sci Team, 1974-1977; consult, US Army Topog Maps Command, 1971-1974; assist prof Univ Va, 1970-1974; consult, US Naval Surface Weapons Labs, 1970-1973; engr & scientist aerospaceeng, McDonnell Douglas Astronaut Co, 1966-1970; aerospace engr, NASA, 1965-1966. **Memberships:** Nat Acad Eng; Am Inst Aeronaut & Astronaut; Am Geophys Union; AmAstronaut Soc; Am Soc Photogram; Int Acad Astronaut. **Research Statement & Publications:** Satellite dynamics and control; mathematical modeling of dynamical systems; geophysics; remote sensing; published over 350 articles. **Mailing Address:** Dept Aerospace Eng, Tex A&M Univ, 722 H R Bright Bldg 3141 TAMU, College Station, TX 77843-3141. **Fax:** 979-845-6051. **E-Mail:** junkins@tamu.edu

JUO, PEI-SHOW, BIOCHEMISTRY, MOLECULAR BIOLOGY. **Personal Data:** b Shantung, China, February 6, 1930; m 1965. **Education:** Taiwan Prov Chung Hsing Univ, BS, 1957; Univ Toronto, MS, 1963; Univ NH, PhD (virol), 1966. **Professional Experience:** PROF EMER, DEPT BIOL, STATE UNIV NY COL, POTSDAM, as of 2004; prof biol, State Univ NY Col, Potsdam, beginning 1974; assoc prof, StateUniv NY Col, Potsdam, 1968-1974; res biochemist, Kitchawan Res Lab, 1966-1967 & Gulf SouthRes Inst, 1967-1968. **Memberships:** AAAS; Am Soc Microbiol. **Research Statement & Publications:** Purification and characterization of proteins and other macromolecules; immunological and electrophoretic analysis of protein antigens. **Mailing Address:** Dept Biol, State Univ NY, 44 Pierrepont Ave, Potsdam, NY 13676.

JUODKA, BENEDIKTAS, BIOCHEMISTRY. **Personal Data:** b Utena, Lithuania, January 13, 1943; m 1968, Tiina Pusse; c Robert. **Education:** Moscow State Univ, MS, 1965, PhD, 1968. **Honors & Awards:** Lithuania State Award in Sci. **Professional Experience:** Adv res & educ, Lithuanian Govt, Vilnius, 1993-1994; PRES, LITHUANIANACAD SCI, 1992-; VICE-RECTOR, VILNIUS UNIV, LITHUANIA, 1991-; mem, Sci Coun, Vilnius, 1991-1993; PROF, VILNIUS UNIV, LITHUANIA, 1982-; HEAD BIOCHEM DEPT, VILNIUS UNIV, LITHUANIA, 1971-; sr lectr, Lithuanian Acad Sci, 1969-1971; lectr, Lithuanian Acad Sci, 1968-1969. **Memberships:** Lithuanian Acad Sci; NY Acad Sci; Latvian Acad Sci. **Research Statement & Publications:** Chemistry and biochemistry of nucleic acids. **Mailing Address:** Lithuanian Acad Sci, Gedimino pr 3, Vilnius 2600, Lithuania. **Fax:** 370-261-1179. **E-Mail:** benediktas.juodka@cz.vu.lt

JUOLA, ROBERT C, STATISTICS, MATHEMATICS. **Personal Data:** b Astoria, Ore, August 8, 1940; m 1963, c 2. **Education:** Univ Ore, BS, 1962; Mich State Univ, MS, 1964, PhD (statist), 1968. **Professional Experience:** RETIRED; prof math, Boise State Univ, beginning 1970; assoc chmn dept, Boise State Univ, 1970-1977; asst prof math, Univ Tex, Austin, 1968-1970; res engr, Boeing Co, 1964-1966. **Memberships:** AAAS; Inst Math Statist; Am Statist Asn; Sigma Xi. **Research Statement & Publications:** Design of experiments; sequential experimentation. **Mailing Address:** 1526 Chrisway Dr, Boise, ID 83706. **E-Mail:** juola@diamond.idbsu.edu

JUORIO, AUGUSTO VICTOR, NEUROPHARMACOLOGY. **Personal Data:** b Buenos Aires, Arg, July 13, 1934; American citizen; m 1961, Marta; c Alex & Victor. **Education:** Univ Buenos Aires, BSP, 1958, BSc, 1961, PhD (pharmacol), 1967. **Professional Experience:** PROF EMER, DEPT PSYCHIAT, UNIV SASK, CAN, 2002-; vis scientist, NIMH, NIH, Bethesda, MD, USA, beginning 2002; prof, Dept Psychiat, 1995-1999; SR SCIENTIST, NEUROPSYCHIAT RES UNIT, UNIV SASK, SASKATOON, 1983-; head basic studies, Dept Psychiat, 1977-1983; res pharmacologist, Dept Psychiat, 1973-1977; res fel, Univ Col, Univ London, 1968-1973; asst prof, Fac Pharm Biochem, Univ Buenos Aires, 1966-1968; res fel, Inst Animal Physiol, Babraham, Cambridge, Eng, 1963-1966; demonstr pharmacol, Fac Pharm Biochem, Univ Buenos Aires, 1959-1963. **Memberships:** Am Soc Pharmacol & Exp Therapeut; Brit Pharmacol Soc; Int Soc Neurochemistry; Pharmacol Soc Can; Soc Neuroscience; Int Brain Res Orgn; Am Soc Neurochemistry. **Research Statement & Publications:** Molecular mechanisms of neurotransmitter action in the central nervous system and of drugs used to alleviate abnormal mental conditions; neuroprotective mechanisms in neural cultures and in animal models; angiotensin and hypothalamus-pituitary-adrenccortical system. **Mailing Address:** Neuropsychiat Res Unit, Univ Sask, CMR Bldg, Saskatoon, SK S7N 0W0, Can. **E-Mail:** juorio@sask.usask.ca

JURA, MICHAEL ALAN, ASTROPHYSICS. **Personal Data:** b Oakland, Calif, September 11, 1947; m 1974, c 1. **Education:** Univ Calif, Berkeley, BA, 1967; Harvard Univ, MA, 1969, PhD (astron), 1971. **Professional Experience:** PROF & VCHAIR ASTRON, UNIV CALIF, LOS ANGELES, 1981-; assoc prof, Univ Calif, Los Angeles, 1977-1981; fel, Alfred P Sloan Found, 1977-1979; asst prof, Univ Calif, Los Angeles, 1974-1977; res assoc astron, Goddard Space Flight Ctr, NASA, 1971; res assoc astron, Princeton Univ Observ, 1973-1974. **Memberships:** Int Astron Union; Am Astron Soc. **Research Statement & Publications:** Physics of the interstellar medium and problems in star formation; A Possible Massive Asteroid Belt Around Zeta Lep; Other Kuiper Belts; Direct Detection of Extrasolar Comets is Possible. **Mailing Address:** Dept Astron, Univ Calif 405 Hilgard Ave, Los Angeles, CA 90024-1594. **E-Mail:** jura@astro.ucla.edu

JURAN, JOSEPH M, QUALITY MANAGEMENT. **Personal Data:** b Braila, Romania, December 24, 1904; American citizen; m 1926, c 4. **Education:** Univ Minn, BS, 1924; Loyola Univ, JD, 1935. **Honorary Degrees:** DSc, Roch Inst Tech & Univ Minn, 1992; LLD, Univ New Haven, 1992. **Honors & Awards:** Nat Medal Technol, President of the US, 1992. **Professional Experience:** CHMN EMER, JURAN INST INC, 1987-; chmn, Juran Inst Inc, 1979-1987; consult, 1951-1979; prof & chmn indust eng, NY Univ, 1945-1951; asst adminr, Foreign Econ Admin, US Govt, 1941-1945; engr, WesternElec Co, 1924-1941; mem var int & US comts, Am Soc Qual Control. **Memberships:** Nat Acad Eng; Am Soc Mech Engrs; Am Soc Qual Control; Am Inst Indust Engrs; Sigma Xi. **Research Statement & Publications:** Pioneer in creating consulting in quality, world-wide, concept of quality improvement; author of 15 books, 40 videocassettes, numerous training manuals, and over 200 published papers. **Mailing Address:** Juran Inst, 115 Old Ridgefield Rd, Wilton, CT 06897-0811. **Fax:** 203-834-9891.

JURAND, JERRY GEORGE, PERIODONTOLOGY, IMMUNOLOGY. **Personal Data:** b Gostyn, Poland, April 23, 1923. **Education:** Univ Erlangen, DMD, 1956; Univ Tenn, Memphis, DDS, 1965. **Professional Experience:** PROF PERIODONT, COL DENT, UNIV TENN, MEMPHIS, 1970-; Consult, St Jude Children's Res Hosp, 1965-; assoc prof, Col Dent, Univ Tenn, Memphis, 1965-1970; res assoc immunol, St Jude Childrens Res Hosp, Memphis, 1962-1965; cancer res scientist, Roswell Park Mem Inst, 1958-1962. **Memberships:** AAAS; NY Acad Sci; Int Asn Dent Res; Am Dent Asn. **Research Statement & Publications:** Immunohistochemical identification and localization of antibodies in humans and animals; tumor immunology; immunological reactions in etiology of periodontal disease; growth factors in oro-facial development; collagen in normal and diseased gingiva. **Mailing Address:** Col Dent, Univ Tenn, Memphis, TN 38163.

JURASCHEK, WILLIAM A, MATHEMATICS. **Professional Experience:** STAFF, DEPT MATH SCI, UNIV COLO, as of 2005. **Memberships:** MAA. **Mailing Address:** Dept Math Sci Univ Colo, PO Box 173364, Denver, CO 80217-3364. **Fax:** 303-556-8550. **E-Mail:** wjurasc_@_arbon.cudenver.edu

JURASEK, LUBOMIR, PROTEIN CHEMISTRY, MICROBIOLOGY. **Personal Data:** b Uzhorod, Czech, June 2, 1931; m 1957, c 3. **Education:** Purkyne Univ Brno, MSc, 1954, PhD (biol), 1963. **Professional Experience:** CONSULT, 1997-; prin scientist & head, Biol Chem Sect, Pulp & Paper ResInst Can, 1975-1997; lectr, Dept Biochem, Univ Alta, 1973-1975; res assoc protein chem, UnivAlta, Edmonton, 1968-1975; res scientist microbiol, State Forest Prod Res Inst, 1966-1968; felenzymol, Nat Res Coun Can, 1964-1966; res officer mycol, State Forest Prod Res Inst, Bratislava, Czech, 1954-1964. **Research Statement & Publications:** Molecular mechanism of biological degradation of cellulose, hemicelluloses and lignin; lignin degrading enzymes; molecular modelling of eignin. **Mailing Address:** 29 Nobel, Kirkland, PQ H9H 4J5, Can.

JURASKA, JANICE MARIE, BIOPSYCHOLOGY. **Personal Data:** b Berwyn, Ill, February 9, 1949. **Education:** Lawrence Univ, BA, 1971; Univ Ill, Champaign, MA, 1975; Univ Colo, PhD (biopsychol), 1977. **Professional Experience:** PROF, DEPT PSYCHOL, UNIV ILL, 1994-; assoc prof, Dept Psychol, Univ Ill, 1986-1994; assoc prof, Dept Psychol, Ind Univ, 1985; asst prof biopsychol, Dept Psychol, Ind Univ, 1980-1985; NIMH fel, Dept Psychol, Univ Ill, 1978-1979. **Memberships:** Fel Am Psychol Soc; Int Soc Develop Psychobiol; Soc Neuroscience; Int Acad Sex Res. **Research Statement & Publications:** Plasticity and development of the nervous system (anatomy) and of behavior; sex differences in the brain; effects of the estrous cycle. **Mailing Address:** Dept Psychol Univ Ill, 735 Psychol Bldg, Champaign, IL 61820. **Fax:** 217-244-5876. **E-Mail:** jjuraska@uiuc.edu

JURCH, GEORGE RICHARD, PHYSICAL ORGANIC CHEMISTRY. **Personal Data:** b New Britain, Conn, February 1, 1934; m 1961, Molly; c George III, Steven & Carol. **Education:** Univ Fla, BS, 1957; Univ Ky, MS, 1961; Univ Calif, San Diego, PhD (chem), 1965. **Professional Experience:** RETIRED; prof chem, Univ S Fla, beginning 1980; from asst prof to assoc prof, Univ S Fla, 1966-1980; res assoc, Yale Univ, 1966; NIH fel chem, Yale Univ, 1965-1966; res chemist, IBM Corp, Ky, 1961. **Memberships:** Am Chem Soc. **Research Statement & Publications:** Radical-cation intermediates; free radicals; sulfur chemistry, nonaqueous solvent interactions with biological systems; nuclear magnetic resonance conformation studies. **Mailing Address:** Dept Chem, Univ S Fla, 4202 E Fowler Ave CHE 205A, Tampa, FL 33620-5250. **E-Mail:** gjurch@chuma.cas.usf.edu

JURD, LEONARD, chemistry; deceased, see previous edition for last biography

JURETSCHKE, HELLMUT JOSEPH, SOLID STATE PHYSICS. **Personal Data:** b Berlin, Ger, August 9, 1924; m 1950, Ruth; c Susan & Annette. **Education:** Harvard Univ, BS, 1944, MA, 1947, PhD (physics), 1950. **Professional Experience:** Vis fel, Royal Melbourne Inst Technol & Univ Melbourne, 1985; head dept, Polytech Univ, 1966-1977; actg head dept, Polytech Univ, 1965-1966; NSF Fac Fel, Grenoble, 1964-1965; PROF PHYSICS, POLYTECH UNIV, 1959-; from instr to assoc prof, PolytechUniv, 1950-1959. **Memberships:** Fel Am Phys Soc; Am Asn Physics Teachers; Sigma Xi; Am Crystallog Asn. **Research Statement & Publications:** Surface properties of metals; electronic structure of metals; dynamical theory of x-rays. **Mailing Address:** Dept Physics, Polytech Univ, Brooklyn, NY 11238. **E-Mail:** hjuretsc@photon.poly.edu

JURF, AMIN N, PHYSIOLOGY. **Personal Data:** b Syria, December 3, 1932; American citizen; m 1958, c 3. **Education:** Western Md Col, BA, 1959; Univ Md, PhD (physiol), 1966. **Professional Experience:** ASST PROF PHYSIOL, UNIV MD, BALTIMORE CITY, 1976-; assoc profrenal physiol, Univ Md, 1974-1976; from instr to asst prof, Univ Md, 1966-1974; res scientist, Univ Md, 1961-1966. **Research Statement & Publications:** Neuro-renal physiology; salt and water metabolism. **Mailing Address:** Univ Md Sch Med, Dept Physiol, Baltimore, MD 21201.

JURGELSKI, WILLIAM JR, EXPERIMENTAL CARCINOGENESIS, TOXICOLOGY. **Personal Data:** b Englishtown, NJ, May 25, 1931; m 1954, c 2. **Education:** Rutgers Univ, BS, 1953, MS, 1955, PhD (genetics), 1958; Duke Univ, MD, 1967. **Professional Experience:** EMERGENCY RM PHYSICIAN, CRAVEN COUNTY HOSP, NEWBERN, NC, 1990-; med officer, Nat Inst Environ Health Sci, 1968-; intern, Med Ctr, Duke Univ, 1967-1968; fel neuropath, Duke Univ, 1967-1968; res assoc path, Med Ctr, Duke Univ, 1963-1967; pharmacologist, Food & Drug Admin, 1960-1963; geneticist, Fed Exp Sta in PR, AgrRes Serv, USDA, 1957-1960. **Memberships:** AAAS; Am Asn Pathologists; Am Asn Cancer Res. **Research Statement & Publications:** Carcinogenesis and and pediatric cancer; the marsupial as an experimental animal. **Mailing Address:** 3211 Oak Knob Ct, Hillsborough, NC 27278.

JURGENS, MARSHALL HERMAN, ANIMAL SCIENCE & NUTRITION, ANIMAL HUSBANDRY. **Personal Data:** b Minden, Nebr, December 26, 1941; m 1964, c 2. **Education:** Univ Nebr, BS, 1964, MS, 1966, PhD (animal sci), 1969. **Professional Experience:** RETIRED; prof, animal sci dept, Iowa State Univ, 1978-2004; from asst prof to assoc prof, Animal Sci Dept, Iowa State Univ, 1968-1978; asst instr, animal sci dept, Univ Nebr, 1966; res asst, animal sci dept, Univ Nebr, 1964-1967. **Memberships:** Am Soc Animal Sci; Am Asn Feed Microscopists. **Research Statement & Publications:** Nutrient-energy relationships in diet of the growing-finishing pig. **Mailing Address:** Animal Sci, Iowa State Univ, Ames, IA 50011-2010.

JURGENSON, JAMES E, BIOLOGY. **Education:** Univ Min, BS, 1968-1972; Univ Ariz, MS, 1972-1994, PhD (genetics molecular biol), 1974-1980. **Professional Experience:** FAC, DICKINSON COL, 1985-. **Mailing Address:** Dickinson Col, Carlisle, PA 17013.

JURIC, DAMIR, FLUID DYNAMICS & HEAT TRANSFER, NUMERICAL METHODS. **Personal Data:** b Dusseldorf, Ger, June 10, 1965. **Education:** Worcester Polytech Inst, BS, 1987, MS, 1990; Univ Mich, PhD (mech eng), 1996. **Professional Experience:** AS-SOC, LIMSI, NAT SCI RES CTR, ORSAY, FRANCE, 2002-; consult, Agilent Technologies, 2001-2002; AT LOS ALAMOS NAT LAB, as of 1998; asst prof, Ga Inst Technol, Sch Mech Eng, 1998-2002; tech staff mem, Los Alamos Nat Lab, 1997-1998; postdoctrol res assoc, Los Alamos Nat Lab, 1996-1997; aerodyn engr, Pratt & Whitney Aircraft, 1987-1991. **Memberships:** Am Soc Mech Engrs; Am Inst Aeronaut & Astronaut; Am Soc Eng Educ. **Research Statement & Publications:** Fluid dynamics and heat transfer in multiphase, multicomponent processes with interdisciplinary applications in materials; chemical processing, manufacturing, combustion; thermal management, multiphase flows in micro-gravity. **Mailing Address:** Los Alamos Nat Lab, MSB216, Los Alamos, NM 87545. **Fax:** 505-665-5926. **E-Mail:** djuric@lanl.gov

JURICIC, DAVOR, MECHANICAL SYSTEMS DESIGN, COMPUTER AIDED DESIGN. **Personal Data:** b Split, Yugoslavia, August 2, 1928; m 1953, c 1. **Education:** Univ Belgrade, BS, 1952. **Honorary Degrees:** DSc, Univ Belgrade, 1964. **Professional Experience:** PROF EMER, UNIV TEX, AUSTIN, as of 2004; Southern Res Inst, Birmingham, Joy Mfg Co, Los Angeles & Dresser Industs, Houston, beginning 1978; prof mech eng, Univ Tex, Austin, beginning 1978; consult, Elec Power Res Inst, Palo Alto, Flow Res, Inc, Kent, Wash, beginning 1976; vis prof appl mech, Stanford Univ, 1975-1978; from assoc prof to prof mech eng, SDak State Univ, 1968-1975; from asst prof to assoc prof aeronaut eng, Univ Belgrade, 1963-1968; res fel aeroelasticity, Inst Aeronaut, Zarkovo-Belgrade, 1958-1963; analyst aircraft struct, Icarus-Belgrade, Yugoslavia, 1953-1958. **Memberships:** Am Soc Eng Educ; Ger Soc Appl Math & Mech; Am Soc Mech Engrs; Sigma Xi. **Research Statement & Publications:** Aircraft vibration and flutter; dynamics of railway vehicles; dynamics and stability of bipedal locomotion; modeling and simulation of dynamic systems; mechanical systems design; electrostatic precipitators. **Mailing Address:** Dept Mech Eng, Univ Tex, One Univ station C2200, Austin, TX 78712-1063. **Fax:** 512-471-3009. **E-Mail:** juricic@mail.utexas.edu

JURILOFF, DIANA M, GENETICS, BIRTH DEFECTS RESEARCH. **Personal Data:** b Nelson, BC, January 17, 1947. **Education:** Univ BC, BS, 1970, MS, 1973; McGill Univ, PhD (genetics), 1978. **Professional Experience:** PROF MED GENETICS, UNIV BC, 1994-; assoc prof, Med Genetics Dept, Univ BC, 1986-1994; med res coun scientist, Med Res Coun, 1986-1991; Asst prof, Med Genetics Dept, Univ BC, 1981-1986. **Memberships:** Teratology Soc; Mammalian Genome Soc; Can Genetics Soc. **Research Statement & Publications:** Genetics and developmental mechanisms leading to risk of common birth defects. **Mailing Address:** Dept Med Genetics, Univ BC, 300H Wesbrook Bldg, 6174 Univ Blvd, Vancouver, BC V6T 1Z3, Can. **Fax:** 604-822-5348. **E-Mail:** juriloff@interchange.ubc.ca

JURINAK, JEROME JOSEPH, SOIL PHYSICAL CHEMISTRY, ENVIRONMENTAL ASSESSMENT. **Personal Data:** b Cleveland, Ohio, June 3, 1927; m 1954, Mary A Zychowski; c Jeff, Jane, David & Victoria. **Education:** Colo State Univ, BS, 1951; Utah State Univ, MS, 1954, PhD (soil chem), 1956. **Professional Experience:** PROF EMER PLANTS & SOILS & BIOMETEOROL, COL AGR, UTAH STATE UNIV, as of 2002; visprof, Univ Calif, Davis, 1991; dept head, Col Agr, Utah State Univ, 1978-1983; visprof, Rural Univ Rio Del Janeiro, Brazil, 1975, 1977; div chmn, Soil Sci Soc Am, 1975; prof, ColAgr, Utah State Univ, 1967-1993; from asst to assoc soil chemist, Univ Calif, Davis, 1958-1967; jr soil chemist, Univ Calif, Davis, 1956-1958; vis prof, HaryanaUniv, India; consult, USAID, UNESCO, Orgn Am States & pvt indust; Danforth teaching fel. **Memberships:** Fel Am Soc Agron; fel Soil Sci Soc Am; Int Soc Soil Sci; fel Am Inst Chem; CounAgr Sci Technol; fel AAAS. **Research Statement & Publications:** Reclamation of disturbed soils and geologic material; trace element chemistry and transport in soils; salt-affected soils; environmental soil chemistry; surface chemistry. **Mailing Address:** Dept Plants & Soils & Biometeorol, Utah State Univ, Logan, UT 84322-4820.

JURINSKI, NEIL B(ERNARD), INDUSTRIAL HYGIENE, ENVIRONMENTAL CHEMISTRY. **Personal Data:** b Peekskill, NY, October 28, 1938; m 1962, Sheila; c Joseph B, Michael P & Katherine A. **Education:** State Univ NY, Albany, BS, 1960; Univ Miss, PhD (phys chem), 1963; Am Bd Indust Hyg, cert, 1974. **Professional Experience:** Indust hygienist, Tracor Jitco, Inc, 1977-1980; sr indust hygienist, SRI Int, 1976-1977; PRES, NUCHEM CO INC, 1975-; environ chemist, US Army Environ Hyg Agency, 1972-1976; res scientist, Chem Div, J M Huber Corp, 1969-1972; asst prof, Boston Col, 1964-1969; Res assoc chem, Mich State Univ, 1963-1964. **Memberships:** Fel Am Indust Hyg Asn; Acad Indust Hyg; Am Chem Soc; Royal Soc Chem; Sigma Xi; Am Soc Safety Engineers; NY Acad Sci. **Research Statement & Publications:** Industrial hygiene surveys and consultation; hazardous and toxic chemical problems; waste disposal and processing; carcinogen mutagen safety; environmental sampling and analysis; material handling and processing. **Mailing Address:** 5765-F Burke Ctr Pkwy 149, Burke, VA 22015-2233. **E-Mail:** neil@nuchemco.com

JURIST, JOHN MICHAEL, BIOPHYSICS. **Personal Data:** b Williamsport, Pa, October 13, 1943; m 1964, c 2. **Education:** Univ Calif, Los Angeles, AB, 1964, MS, 1966, PhD (biophys), 1968. **Professional Experience:** Consult, Mont State Bd Health, 1987-; consult, Deaconess Hosp, Billings, 1984-1985; PRES, CRM INC, 1982-; adj pro med sci, Mont State Univ, 1980-1982; assoc resbiophysicist, Mont State Univ, 1978-1980; sr res engr, Mont State Univ, 1977-1978; biophysicist, St Vincent Hosp, Billings, 1976-1982; res assoc, Mont State Univ, 1976-1977; asst prof orthopsurg, Univ Wis-Madison, 1971-1976; prin investr, NIH grants, 1970-1978; asst prof orthop surg& space sci & eng, Univ Wis-Madison, 1969-1971; proj assoc med physics, Univ Wis-Madison, 1968-1969; NASA fel, Univ Wis-Madison, 1968-1969. **Memberships:** AAAS; Geront Soc; NY Acad Sci; Orthop Res Soc; Aerospace Med Asn. **Research Statement & Publications:** Osteoporosis; nondestructive evaluation of skeletal status; application of computers to medical practice; medical thermography. **Mailing Address:** CRM Inc, 2520 17th St W Ste B4, Billings, MT 59102. **Fax:** 406-245-6775. **E-Mail:** jmjurist@aol.com

JURKA, JERZY W, BIOINFORMATICS, COMPUTATIONAL MOLECULAR BIOLOGY. **Personal Data:** b Ponikiew, Poland, June 4, 1950; American citizen; m 1981, Elzbieta Nowak; c Michael, Matthew & Timothy. **Education:** Jagiellonski Univ, Poland, MSc, 1973; Univ Warsaw, DSc, 1979. **Professional Experience:** PRES, GENETIC INFO RES INST, 1994-; dir bioinformatics, Linus Pauling Inst Sci & Med, 1994-1995; Prin investr, NIH, 1992-1995 & 1996-; asst dir res, Linus Pauling Inst Sci & Med, 1992-1994; Prin investr, Dept Energy, 1991-1997; dir comput resources, Linus Pauling Inst Sci & Med, 1990-1992; res scientist, Linus Pauling Inst Sci & Med, 1989-1990; scientist, Bionet, 1987-1989; res fel, Dept Biostat, Dana Farber Cancer Inst, Harvard Sch Pub Health, 1986-1987; Dept Biochem & Biophysics, Univ Houston, 1984-1986; postdoctoral fel, Dept Microbiol & Immunol, Univ Mich, 1983-1984; Vis scientist, Dept Med Physics, Karolinska Inst, Univ Stockholm, 1982-1983. **Memberships:** Int Soc Molecular Evolution; AAAS. **Research Statement & Publications:** Identification and systematic studies of mobile elements and their impact on eukaryotic genomes, using computer assisted analyses of DNA sequence data. **Mailing Address:** 1190 Eureka Ave, Los Altos, CA 94024. **E-Mail:** jurka@grinst.org

JURKAT, MARTIN PETER, MANAGEMENT SCIENCE, MATHEMATICS. **Personal Data:** b Berlin, Ger, July 23, 1935; m 1958, c 3. **Education:** Swarthmore Col, BA, 1957; Univ NC, MA, 1960; Stevens Inst Technol, PhD (math), 1972, MEng, 1983. **Professional Experience:** PROF EMER, WESLEY J. HOWE SCH TECHNOL MGT, STEVENS INST TECHNOL, as of 2001; alexander cronbic humphreys prof mgt sci, Stevens Inst Technol, beginning 1980; prof, Stevens Inst Technol, 1978-1980; dir, Ctr Munic Studies & Servs, Stevens Inst Technol, 1976-1978; staff scientist, Davidson Lab, Stevens Inst Technol, 1964-1976; sr systs analyst, ITT Info Systs Div, 1961-1964; asst engr, Res Lab, Burroughs Corp, 1960-1961; statistician, Marketer's Res Serv, Inc, 1959-1960; consult, Tank Automotive Command, US Army. **Memberships:** Opers Res Soc Am; Comput Soc Inst Elec & Electronics Engrs; Asn ComputMach. **Research Statement & Publications:** Mathematical modelling; simulation; off-road vehicle design and modelling; computer graphics; transportation systems; operations research; expert systems. **Mailing Address:** Wesley J Howe Sch Technol Mgt, Stevens Inst Technol, Kidde Bldg, Rm 324-A, Castle Pt Hudson, Hoboken, NJ 07030. **Fax:** 201-216-5385. **E-Mail:** pjurkat@stevens-tech.edu

JURKAT, WOLFGANG BERNHARD, MATHEMATICAL ANALYSIS. **Personal Data:** b Gerdauen, Ger, March 26, 1929. **Education:** Univ Tubingen, PhD (math), 1950. **Professional Experience:** PROF EMER, UNIV ULM; assoc prof, John Raymond French prof math, 1958-1990; assoc prof, Syracuse Univ, 1957-1958; assoc prof, Ohio State Univ, 1956-1957; assoc prof, Univ Cincinnati, 1954-1956; dozent, Univ Tubingen, 1952-1954; asst math, Univ Tubingen, 1950-1952. **Memberships:** Am Math Soc; Ger Math Soc. **Research Statement & Publications:** Analysis, particularly summability, Fourier series, analytic number theory, also combinatories and probability. **Mailing Address:** Abteilung F Mathmatik V, Oberer Eselsburg Germany Universita T, Ulm 7900, Ger. **Fax:** 49-0731-5023619.

JURKIEWICZ, MAURICE J, SURGERY. **Personal Data:** b Claremont, NH, September 24, 1924; m 1951, c 2. **Education:** Univ Md, DDS, 1946; Harvard Univ, MD, 1952. **Professional Experience:** PROF EMER SURG, EMORY UNIV, as of 2003; Vis prof, Soc Head & Neck Surgeons, Emory Univ, 1997; consult plastic surg, Walter Reed Hosp, Wash, DC, 1970-; lectr & consult, Naval Hosp, Orlando, 1969-1970; chiefsurg serv, Vet Admin Hosp, Gainesville, 1968-1973; mem bd sci counr, Nat InstDent Res, 1966-1971; chief plastic surg, Col Med, Univ Fla, 1964-1973; fromasst prof to prof surg, Col Med, Univ Fla, 1959-1973; clin fel plastic surg, Barnes Hosp, St Louis, Mo, 1958-1959; instr surg, Sch Med, Wash Univ, 1957-1959. **Memberships:** AAAS; Am Col Surg; AMA; Am Soc Plastic & Reconstruct Surg; Plastic Surg Res Coun. **Research Statement & Publications:** Wound healing; congenital malformations; general and reconstructive surgery; head and neck surgery. **Mailing Address:** Emory Univ, 715 Old Post Rd, NW, Atlanta, GA 30328. **Fax:** 404-686-5974.

JURKUS, ALGIRDAS PETRAS, ELECTRONICS. **Personal Data:** b Klaipeda, Lithuania, June 11, 1935; Canadian citizen. **Education:** Univ Montreal, BASc, 1957; Univ Sheffield, PhD (elec eng), 1960. **Professional Experience:** RES SCIENTIST ELECTRONICS, NAT RES COUN CAN, 1960-. **Memberships:** Inst Elec & Electronics Engrs. **Research Statement & Publications:** Establishment and maintenance of primary national standards and development of precise methods of measurement, at high and microwave frequencies, of various electromagnetic quantities. **Mailing Address:** Inst Nat Measurement Standards, Nat Res Coun, Ottawa, ON K1A 0R6, Can.

JURMAIN, ROBERT DOUGLAS, PHYSICAL ANTHROPOLOGY. **Personal Data:** b Worcester, Mass, July 20, 1948; m 1974. **Education:** Univ Calif, Los Angeles, BA, 1970; Harvard Univ, PhD (anthrop), 1975. **Professional Experience:** PROF EMER ANTHROP, SAN JOSE STATE UNIV, as of 2004; assoc prof anthrop, San Jose State Univ, beginning 1979; asst prof, San Jose State Univ, 1975-1979. **Memberships:** Am Asn Phys Anthropologists. **Research Statement & Publications:** Paleopathology of prehistoric human osteological remains; comparative biomechanical studies of primate limb skeletons; paleoanthropological research of early hominids in East Africa. **Mailing Address:** Dept Anthrop, San Jose State Univ, 1 Wash Sq, San Jose, CA 95192-0113. **E-Mail:** rjurmain@email.sjsu.edu

JURRIS, ERIC R, TECHNOLOGY TRANSFER. **Personal Data:** b Ohio. **Professional Experience:** DIR, OFFICE TECHNOL TRANSFER, CITY HOPE NAT MED CTR, 1986-. **Research Statement & Publications:** Technology transfer. **Mailing Address:** City Hope Nat Med Ctr, 1500 E Duarte Rd, Duarte, CA 91010.

JURS, PETER CHRISTIAN, ANALYTICAL CHEMISTRY. **Personal Data:** b Oakland, Calif, April 13, 1943; m 1967, c 3. **Education:** Stanford Univ, BS, 1965; Univ Wash, PhD (chem), 1969. **Honors & Awards:** Computers in Chem Award, Am Chem Soc, 1990. **Professional Experience:** Prog dir chem anal, Chem Div, NSF, 1983-1984; PROF CHEM, PA STATE UNIV, 1978-; from asst prof to assoc prof, PA State Univ, 1969-1978. **Memberships:** Am Chem Soc; AAAS. **Research Statement & Publications:** Computer methods in analytical chemistry; structure-activity studies; computer applications in chemistry; studies of relations between molecular structure and biological activity pharmacological effects; carcinogenic potential, odor; chemical applications of pattern recognition; computer-assisted structure elucidation. **Mailing Address:** Dept Chem, Pa State Univ, 336 Chem Bldg, Univ Park, PA 16802. **Fax:** 814-865-3314. **E-Mail:** pcj@psu.edu

JURSIC, BRANKO, ORGANIC CHEMISTRY. **Education:** Univ Zagreb, BS, 1978, MS, 1982 & PhD, 1985. **Professional Experience:** PROF, DEPT CHEM, UNIV NEW ORLEANS, as of 2003. **Research Statement & Publications:** Organic chemistry; synthesis and molecular recogntion. **Mailing Address:** Dept Chem, Univ New Orleans, CSB 323, New Orleans, LA 70148. **E-Mail:** bjursic1@uno.edu

JURSINIC, PAUL ANDREW, BIOPHYSICS. **Personal Data:** b Joliet, Ill, June 13, 1946. **Education:** Univ Ill, BS, 1969, MS, 1971, PhD (biophys), 1977. **Professional Experience:** ASSOC PROF RADIATION ONCOL, DEPT RADIATION ONCOL, 2003-; asst prof radiation oncol, Med Col Wis, 2000-2003; phd, Radiation Oncol, W Mich Cancer Ctr, beginning 1993; res assoc grant, USDA, 1985-1986; res scientist plant physiol, Northern Regional Res Ctr, USDA, beginning 1977; asst prof, Univ Ill, Champaign-Urbana. **Memberships:** Am Soc Photobiol. **Research Statement & Publications:** The photochemical reactions which make up the light reactions of green plant photosynthesis; author of numerous publications. **Mailing Address:** Dept Radiation Oncol, Med Col Wis, 8701 Watertown Plank Rd, Milwaukee, WI 53226. **Fax:** 414-805-4369. **E-Mail:** jursinic@mcw.edu

JURTSHUK, PETER, MICROBIAL PHYSIOLOGY, BIOCHEMISTRY. **Personal Data:** b New York, NY, July 28, 1929; m 1971, Rebecca; c Peter III & Larissa. **Education:** NY Univ, AB, 1951; Creighton Univ, MS, 1953; Univ Md, PhD (microbiol), 1957. **Honors & Awards:** Distinguished Serv Award, Am Soc Microbiol, 1982. **Professional Experience:**

PROF BIOL, UNIV HOUSTON, 1976-; undergrad chmn biol, Univ Houston, 1977-1981; assoc prof, Univ Houston, 1970-1976; from asst prof to assoc prof, UnivTex, Austin, 1963-1970; fel enzyme chem, Inst Enzyme Res, Univ Wis, 1959-1963; asst profpharmacol, Brooklyn Col Pharm, 1957-1959; asst microbiol, Univ Md, 1953-1956. **Memberships:** AAAS; fel Am Acad Microbiol; Am Soc Microbiol; Am Chem Soc; Am SocBiochem & Molecular Biol. **Research Statement & Publications:** Isolation and characterization of oxidases and oxygenating enzyme complexes from microorganisms; aspects of the microbiological oxidase reaction relating to cellular bioenergetics; microbial taxonomy specifically, on Bacillus and Azotobacter species. **Mailing Address:** Dept Biol, Univ Houston, Houston, TX 77204-5513. **Fax:** 713-743-2636. **E-Mail:** jurtshuk@uh.edu

JURY, ELIAHU I(BRAHAM), ELECTRICAL ENGINEERING. **Personal Data:** b Bagdad, Iraq, May 23, 1923; American citizen; m 1949, c 2. **Education:** Israel Inst Technol, EE, 1947; Harvard Univ, MS, 1949; Columbia Univ, EngScD, 1953. **Honorary Degrees:** DSc Tech, Swiss Fed Inst Tech, Zurich, Switz, 1982. **Honors & Awards:** Rufus Oldenburger Medal, Amer Soc Mech Engrs, 1986; Technol FounderAward, Am Technol Soc, 1990; Phoebe H Hearst Medal, Univ Calif, Berkeley, 1991; HeritageMedal, Am Contrib Coun, 1993. **Professional Experience:** EMER RES PROF, DEPT ELEC & COMPUT ENG, UNIV MIAMI, 1988-; distinguished scholar, Univ Miami, 1988; EMER PROF, UNIV CALIF, BERKELEY, 1981-; vislectr, Imperial Col Sci, London, 1964-1965; vis lectr, Univ Paris, 1958-1959; vis lectr, UnivMich, 1958; vis lectr, Northwestern Univ, 1957; consult, Bell Tel Labs, 1956 & Convair Div, GenDynamics Corp, 1957; from instr to prof elec eng, Univ Calif, Berkeley, 1953-1981; res engr, Columbia Univ, 1953-1954. **Memberships:** Fel mem Inst Elec & Electronics Engrs. **Research Statement & Publications:** Sampled-data and discrete systems; automatic control; circuit theory; transform methods; information theory; digital and sampled-data control systems. **Mailing Address:** Dept Elec Eng, Univ Miami PO Box 248294, Coral Gables, FL 33124.

JURY, WILLIAM AUSTIN, SOIL PHYSICS, ENVIRONMENTAL PHYSICS. **Personal Data:** b Highland Park, Mich, August 8, 1946; m 1972. **Education:** Univ Mich, BS, 1968; Univ Wis, MS, 1970, PhD (physics), 1973. **Honors & Awards:** Soil sci Res Award, soil sci Soc of Am, 1989; environ qual Res Award, Am Soc of agron, 1992; Appt, Water Sci & Tech board, Nat Res Coun, 1998; US DeptAg Sec's Honor Award Environ Prot, 1999. **Professional Experience:** PROF SOIL PHYSICS, DEPT SOIL & ENVIRONSCI, UNIV CALIF, RIVERSIDE, 1982-; consult, Rockwell Hanford Oper, 1976-1979 & Countyof San Diego, 1978-1979; from asst prof to assoc prof, Dept Soil & Environ Sci, Univ Calif, Riverside, 1974-1982; mem, Nat Comn, Nat Res Coun/Inst Ecol, 1974-1975; projassoc soil physics, Dept Soil Sci, Univ Wis, 1973-1974; dir, Univ Calif, Riverside, Grad Res Unit Environ Sci & Eng; dir, Univ Calif, Riverside, Grad Deg Prog Environ Sci. **Memberships:** Nat Acad Sci; Am Soc Agron; Soil Sci Soc Am; Int Soil Sci Soc; Am GeophysUnion; AAAS. **Research Statement & Publications:** Measurement and modeling of water, heat and chemical transport through and reactions in soil. **Mailing Address:** Dept Environ Sci, UC Riverside, Riverside, CA 92521-0101. **Fax:** 909-787-2954. **E-Mail:** william.jury@ucr.edu

JUSINSKI, LEONARD EDWARD, SOLID STATE PHYSICS, PHYSICAL CHEMISTRY. **Personal Data:** b Oakland, Calif, August 12, 1955. **Education:** Univ San Francisco, BS, 1977. **Professional Experience:** TECHNOLOGIST, SANDRA NAT LABS, 1996-; PHYSICIST, SRI INT, 1983-; engr, Varian Assocs, 1982; physicist, USAF Weapons Lab, 1977-1981. **Research Statement & Publications:** Laser-induced fluorescence; multi-photon ionization; author/co-author of 45 publications. **Mailing Address:** Sandia Nat Lab, PO Box 969, Livermore, CA 94551. **Fax:** 925-294-2550. **E-Mail:** lejusin@sandia.gov

JUSKO, WILLIAM JOSEPH, PHARMACY. **Personal Data:** b Salamanca, NY, October 26, 1942; m 1996, Malgorzata; c Suzanne, Majorie, Katherine, Natalie & Nicole. **Education:** State Univ NY, Buffalo, BS, 1965, PhD (pharmaceut), 1970. **Honorary Degrees:** Dr, Med Acad Crakow, 1987. **Honors & Awards:** Rawls Palmer Award, Am Soc Clin Pharmacol & Therapeut, 1987; Russell Miller Award, Am Col Clin Pharm 1988, Distinguished Serv Award, 1989, Research Achievement Award, Am Assn Pharm Sci, 1999; Volwiler Award, Am Assn Coll Pharm, 2005. **Professional Experience:** Chair, Dept Pharm Sci Sch Pharm, State Univ NY, Buffalo, 2000-present; Fulbright fel, 1978; PROF PHARMACEUT, SCH PHARM, STATE UNIV NY, BUFFALO, 1977-; Dir, Clin Pharmacokinetics Lab, Millard Fillmore Hosp, Buffalo, 1972-1981; assoc prof, Sch Pharm, State Univ NY, Buffalo, 1972-1977; Pharmacologist, Vet Admin Hosp, Boston, 1970-1972; consultant Novartis, Amgen, Eli Lilly. **Memberships:** Fel Am Pharmaceut Asn; fel AAAS; Am Soc Clin Pharmacol & Therapeut; Am Soc Microbiol; fel Am Asn Pharmaceut Sci; Am Soc Pharmacol & Exp Therapeut; fel Am Col Clin Pharmacol. **Research Statement & Publications:** Basic, theoretical, and clinical pharmacokinetics and pharmacodynamics. **Mailing Address:** Sch Pharmacy Dept Pharmaceutical Scis, State Univ NY Buffalo, Buffalo, NY 14260. **Fax:** 716-645-3693. **E-Mail:** wjjusko@buffalo.edu

JUST, GEORGE, ORGANIC CHEMISTRY. **Personal Data:** b Kobe, Japan, May 17, 1929; Canadian citizen; m 1955, c 3. **Education:** Swiss Fed Inst Technol, Ing Chim, Dl, 1951; Univ Western Ont, PhD (chem), 1956. **Professional Experience:** PROF ORG CHEM, MCGILL UNIV, 1970-; from asst prof to assoc prof, McGill Univ, 1958-1970; res chemist, Univ Calif, Los Angeles, 1956-1957 & Monsanto Can, Ltd, 1957-1958. **Memberships:** Am Chem Soc; fel Chem Inst Can. **Research Statement & Publications:** Natural products synthesis. **Mailing Address:** Dept Chem, McGill Univ, 801 Sherbrooke St W, Montreal, PQ H3A 2K6, Can. **Fax:** 514-398-3797. **E-Mail:** george.just@mcgill.ca

JUST, JOHN JOSEF, DEVELOPMENTAL BIOLOGY, ENDOCRINOLOGY. **Personal Data:** b Botschar, Banat, Yugoslavia, November 17, 1938; American citizen; m 1965, Jeannette; c Sharon, Diane & Steven. **Education:** DePaul Univ, Chicago, BS, 1962, MS, 1964; Univ Iowa, PhD (zoology), 1968. **Professional Experience:** ASSOC PROF EMER, UNIV KY as of 2004; NIH, NSF & Dept of Interior grants; vis prof, Univ Bern, 1976-1977; assoc prof biol, univ KY, beginning 1974-; asst prof biol, Univ KY, 1970-1974; fel, biochem, Fla State Univ, 1968-1970; NIH fel, Dept Chem, Fla State Univ, 1968-1970; NIH fel, Iowa Univ, 1965-1968; Schmitt fel, Dept Zool, Univ Iowa, 1963-1964; Teaching asst, DePaul Univ, 1962-1964. **Memberships:** AAAS; Am Zoologist; Sigma Xi. **Research Statement & Publications:** Biochemical and morphological methods are used to study hormonal influence on development with particular emphasis on amphibian metamorphosis; physiological triggers for hatching of embryos. **Mailing Address:** Univ Ky, 101 Morgan Bldg, Lexington, KY 40506-0225. **Fax:** 859-257-1717. **E-Mail:** jjjust@pop.uky.edu

JUST, KURT W, THEORETICAL PHYSICS. **Personal Data:** b Oels, Ger, May 19, 1927; m 1953, Sigrid Walther; c Stefan, Klemens & Felix. **Education:** Free Univ Berlin, Dr rer nat, 1954, Dr habil, 1958. **Honors & Awards:** First Prize, Gravity Res Found, 1965. **Professional Experience:** PROF EMER PHYSICS, UNIV ARIZ, 1998-; consult, Edgerton, Germeshausen & Grier, Nev, 1963-1964; from assoc prof to prof physics, Univ Ariz, 1961-1998; sci counsr, Free Univ Berlin, 1960-1963; asst physics, Free Univ Berlin, 1950-1960. **Memberships:** Int Soc Gen Relativity & Gravitation. **Research Statement & Publications:** Quantum field theory; quantized theory of gravity. **Mailing Address:** Dept Physics, Univ Ariz, Tucson, AZ 85712. **E-Mail:** just@physics.arizona.edu

JUST, RICHARD, RESOURCE ECONOMICS, PRODUCTION ECONOMICS. **Personal Data:** b Tulsa, Okla, February 18, 1948; m 1989, Janet; c Angela, David & Ronald. **Education:** Okla State Univ, BS, 1969; Univ Calif, Berkeley, MA, 1971, PhD (agr econs), 1972. **Professional Experience:** DISTINGUISHED UNIV PROF, UNIV MD, COL PARK, 1995-; prof agr econs, Univ Md, Col Park, beginning 1985; Nations Ag II, 2001-2002; US Dept of Justice, 1999; Nations Ag, 1998; Ford New Holland, 1998; Lilly Indu, 1998-1999; MicroFlo 1997-1998; Albough, 1996-1998, 2000-2002; Sostram, 1994-1995; Griffin, 1987-1988, 1993-1995; stram, 1994-1995; chmn dept, Univ Md, Col Park, 1992-1995; Price Waterhouse, 1987-1991; Agtrol, 1990; Safeway Stores, Pillsbury, 1988; Drexel, 1987-1995; Safeway Stores, Inc, 1983-1986; consult, US Gen Acct Off, 1979-1995; consult, World Bank, 1976-1993; Price Waterhouse, Oak Ridge Nat Lab, 1976-1981; prof agr econs, Univ Calif, Berkeley, 1975-1985; assoc prof, Agr Econs, Okla State Univ, 1972-1975. **Memberships:** Am Econ Asn; Econometric Soc; fel Am Agr Econ Asn; Western Agr Econ Asn. **Research Statement & Publications:** Welfare economics, production economics, risk, technical adoption distributional effects of agricultural policy; land price determination, biotechnology. **Mailing Address:** Univ Md, Dept Agr & Resource Econ, College Park, MD 20742-5535. **Fax:** 301-314-9879. **E-Mail:** rjust@umd.edu

JUSTEN, LEWIS LEO, PHYSICAL CHEMISTRY, ANALYTICAL CHEMISTRY. **Personal Data:** b Tampa, Fla, June 24, 1941; m 1971, c 2. **Education:** Univ SFla, BA, 1972; Northwestern Univ, MS, 1973, PhD (chem), 1978. **Professional Experience:** CONSULT, 1993-; at UOP Cor Res Ctr, 1977-1993; res chemist coal anal, Exxon Res & Eng Co, 1977-1980. **Memberships:** Am Chem Soc. **Research Statement & Publications:** Coal science relating to synthetic fuels; thermodynamics of liquids; optical properties of liquids; gas-liquid chromatography. **Mailing Address:** Hoffman Estates, 2004 Bayberry Lane, Schaumburg, IL 60195.

JUSTER, NORMAN JOEL, ORGANIC CHEMISTRY, SOLID-STATE ORGANIC CHEMISTRY. **Personal Data:** b New York, NY, February 19, 1924; m 1960, Marian R Friedman; c Jeanette, Debbi, Cindy, Robyn & Becky. **Education:** Univ Calif, Los Angeles, BA, 1943, MS, 1947, PhD (org chem), 1956. **Honors & Awards:** Sprenger Medal, Am Asn Consult Chemists, 1971; Mfg Chemists Asn Award, 1974; J Ray Risser Award, 1978; Res Medal, Nat Oceanic & Atmospheric Admin, 1988. **Professional Experience:** INDEPENDENT CONSULT, 1993-; vis prof, Univ Calif Los Angeles, 1984-1992; ed, Southern Calif Sect, Am Chem Soc, 1978-1984; chmn, Dept Chem & dean, Div Phys Sci, 1978-1984; vis prof chem, 1975-1977 & Univ Hawaii, 1973-1974 & 1980; McInherry Enterprises, 1969-1972 & Oncol Div, Med Res Inst Calif, 1974-1984; consult, Silverton & Silverton, 1968-1978; vis lectr, Weizmann Inst Sci, Israel, 1966; vis prof, Univ Ky, 1965-1966; res dir & consult, Energy Conversion Devices, 1964; Nat Defense Educ Act lectr, 1963; prof org chem, Pasadena City Col, 1961-1984; res dir & consult, Motorola Semiconductor Prod, Inc, 1961-1965; mgr org-polymer labs, Semiconductors Div, 1961; sr chemist & head org sect, Motorola, Inc, 1960-1961; vis prof chem, Univ Calif Los Angeles, 1959-1965; dept phys sci, Pasadena City Col, org chem, 1956-1960; consult, Witco Chem Co, 1953; res dir & consult, Photo Prod Res Lab, E I du Pont Del Nemours & Co, 1949-1952; mem chem fac, John Muir Col, 1947-1955. **Memberships:** AAAS; affil & emer mem Am Chem Soc (chmn Southern Calif Sect 1989-1991; nat coun 1990-1993); Asn Consult Chemists & Chem Eng; Soc Plastics Eng; Sigma Xi; fel NY Acad Sci. **Research Statement & Publications:** Electronic behavior of organic solids; reactions between organic solids; studies of electret phenomena; molecular modeling for electronic properties of organic solids; syntheses of small, strained molecules; polymerization of acetylenic moieties studies. **Mailing Address:** Beverly Hills, CA 90210.

JUSTESEN, DON ROBERT, NEUROPSYCHOLOGY. **Personal Data:** b Salt Lake City, Utah, March 8, 1930; m 1958, Patricia; c Richard, Jonille, Tracy & Anthony. **Education:** Univ Utah, BA, 1955, MA, 1957, PhD, 1960. **Professional Experience:** RETIRED; ed in chief, bioelectromagnetics, 1988-1992; mem, USA USSR Sci Exchange, Non Ionizing Radiation, 1984-1989; sci adv, Elec Power Res Inst, 1984-1987; mem, Comn, Nat Acad Sci Int Union Radio Sci, 1978-1979; chmn, Comt Man & Radiation, Inst Elec Electronics Engrs, 1978-1979; mem, Subcomt C 95 1 Safety Stand Non Ionizing Radiation, Am Nat Stand Inst, 1975-1989; assoc ed, J Microwave Power & Electromagnetic Energy, 1975-1988; prof psychiat & neuropsychol, Med Sch, Univ Kans, 1971-1995; consult, NASA, 1970-1972; vis prof, Univ Colo, 1965; from lectr to prof, Univ Mo, Kansas City, 1963-1975; from asst prof to prof psychiat, Med Sch, Univ Kans, 1963-1971; career res scientist & dir, Neuropsychol Res Labs, Vet Admin Hosp, 1962-1995; asst prof psychol & head dept, Westminster Col, 1959-1962. **Memberships:** Bioelectromagnetics Soc (pres, 1984-1985). **Research Statement & Publications:** Neurophysiological correlates of behavior; biothermal correlates of emotion and arousal; biological and psychological response to non-ionizing electromagnetic radiation; philosophy of science. **Mailing Address:** 12416 Ewing Ct, Grandview, MO 64030.

JUSTHAM, STEPHEN ALTON, CLIMATOLOGY, METEOROLOGY. **Personal Data:** b New Kensington, Pa, May 22, 1937; m 2001, Marian; c Kristin M & Cheryl L. **Education:** Indiana Univ Pa, BS, 1964, MA, 1970; Univ Ill, PhD (geog), 1974. **Honors & Awards:** Merit Award, Am Soc Landscape Architects, 1983. **Professional Experience:** PROF EMER GEOG, KUTZTOWN UNIV, as of 2005; actg assoc vchancellor acad & student affairs, Dept Geog, Kutztown Univ, 1991-1992; asst provost, Dept Geog, Kutztown Univ, 1989-1991; chmn, Dept Geog, Kutztown Univ, 1985-1989; prof geog, Kutztown Univ, 1983-1991; assoc prof geog, Ball State Univ, 1971-1983; teacher civics, New Kensington-Arnold Sch Dist, 1966-1968; teacher geog polit sci, Wash Twp Sch Dist, Apollo, Pa, 1964-1966. **Memberships:** Am Meteorol Soc; Am Geophys Union; Asn Am Geogr; Royal Meteorol Soc. **Research Statement & Publications:** Climatology and meteorology of severe weather phenomena, specifically tornado preparedness programs; wind resource inventory and modeling. **Mailing Address:** Dept Geog, Kutztown Univ, Kutztown, PA 19530. **Fax:** 610-683-1352. **E-Mail:** justham@kutztown.edu

JUSTICE, JAMES HORACE, EXPLORATION GEOPHYSICS. **Personal Data:** b Big Spring, Tex, August 31, 1941. **Education:** Univ Tex, BA, 1963; Univ Md, MA, 1966, PhD (math), 1968. **Professional Experience:** RES SCIENTIST, DALLAS RES LAB, MOBIL RES & DEVELOP, 1987-; geophys consult, 1982-; chair explor geophys, Univ Calgary, 1982-1987; prof, Univ Tulsa, 1978-1982; fel, Amax Inc, Colo Sch Mines, 1969-1980; consult, Amoco Prod Co, 1969-1980; from asst prof to assoc prof math, Univ Tulsa, 1968-1978. **Memberships:** Am Math Soc; Math Asn Am. **Research Statement & Publications:** Signal processing in exploration geophysics; multidimensional signal processing; digital signal processing. **Mailing Address:** 2819 Carriage Lane, Carrollton, TX 75006.

JUSTICE, KEITH EVANS, ECOLOGY. **Personal Data:** b Arkansas City, Kans, February 6, 1930; m 1957, c 3. **Education:** Univ Ariz, BS, 1955, MS, 1956, PhD (zoology), 1960. **Professional Experience:** PROF EMER ECOL & EVOLUTIONARY BIOL, UNIV CALIF,

IRVINE, 1987-; dean prof studies, Univ Calif, Irvine, 1977-1981; dean spec progs, Univ Calif, Irvine, 1974-1977; actg dean, Univ Calif, Irvine, 1969-1971; assoc dean grad div, Univ Calif, Irvine, 1968-1969; assoc prof ecol & evolutionary biol, Univ Calif, Irvine, 1967-1987; vpres, Rocky Mt Biol Lab, Crested Butte, Colo, 1966-1971; asst prof biol sci, Univ Calif, Irvine, 1965-1967; proj engr, Melpar Inc, 1962-1965; res assoc, Univ Ariz, 1960-1962; res assoc pop genetics, Columbia Univ, 1959-1960 & Ariz-Sonora Desert Mus, 1960-1962. **Memberships:** Am Soc Mammal; Sigma Xi. **Research Statement & Publications:** Population dynamics and behavior of desert rodents; computer assisted instruction. **Mailing Address:** Dept Ecol & Evolutionary Biol, Univ Calif, Irvine, CA 92697-2525.

JUSTICE, PARVIN M, PEDIATRICS. **Education:** Ill Inst Technol, PhD. **Professional Experience:** FAC, DEPT PATH, UNIV ILL, as of 2006. **Mailing Address:** Dept Pediat Univ Ill Sch Med, 840 S Wood St Rm 1240-C5B, Chicago, IL 60612-4325.

JUSTIN, JAMES ROBERT, AGRONOMY, FIELD CROPS. **Personal Data:** b Scranton, Pa, October 14, 1933; m 1957, c 2. **Education:** Pa State Univ, BS, 1955, MS, 1957; Tex A&M Univ, PhD (plant breeding), 1963. **Professional Experience:** SPECIALIST, CROPS & SOILS EXTEN, RUTGERS UNIV, NEWBRUNSWICK, 1975-; assoc specialist, Crops & Soils Exten, Rutgers Univ, New Brunswick, 1967-1975; from instr to asst prof agron, Univ Minn, 1964-1967; exten agronomist, Univ Minn, 1963-1967; instr agron, Tex A&M Univ, 1960-1963. **Memberships:** Am Forage & Grassland Coun; Am Soc Agron; Crop Sci Soc Am; Am SoybeanAsn; Asn Off Seed Certifying Agencies. **Research Statement & Publications:** Improvement of field crop and seed production; variety testing and production research with soybeans and variety testing with forages. **Mailing Address:** 35 RathLane, New Brunswick, NJ 08816.

JUSTIZ, CHARLES R, AERONAUTICS. **Education:** US Air Force Acad, BS; Univ Houston, MS, PhD (philos). **Professional Experience:** RES PILOT, JOHNSON SPACE CTR, NASA, as of 2003. **Mailing Address:** Johnson Space Ctr, NASA, CC5, Houston, TX 77058. **Fax:** 281-228-5545.

JUSTUS, DAVID ELDON, IMMUNOLOGY, PARASITOLOGY. **Personal Data:** b Van Buren, Mo, May 22, 1936; m 1960, c 5. **Education:** Southeast Mo State Col, BS, 1963; Univ Mo-Columbia, MS, 1965; Univ Okla, PhD (med parasitol), 1968. **Professional Experience:** PROF MICROBIOL & IMMUNOL, UNIV LOUISVILLE, as of 2004; asst prof microbiol & immunol, Univ Louisville, beginning 1970; fel, microbiol, Sch Med, 1969-1970. **Memberships:** Am Soc Microbiol; Am Soc Trop Med & Hyg; Reticuloendothelial Soc. **Research Statement & Publications:** Anaphylactic antibody and mast cell responses in mice infected with Trichinella spiralis. **Mailing Address:** Dept Microbiol & Immunol, Sch Med Univ Louisville, Rm 415 319 Abraham Flexner Way 55A, Louisville, KY 40202. **Fax:** 502-852-7531. **E-Mail:** dejust01@gwise.louisville.edu

JUSTUS, JERRY T, DEVELOPMENTAL BIOLOGY. **Personal Data:** b Chicago, Ill, October 13, 1932. **Education:** Franklin Col, AB, 1957; Ind Univ, MA, 1962, PhD (endocrinol, develop biol), 1965. **Professional Experience:** DISTINGUISHED PROF BIOL, GRAND CANYON UNIV, as of 2003; prof biol, Grand Canyon Univ, beginning 1991; estab investr, Am Heart Asn, 1971-1976; from asst prof to assoc prof zool, Ariz State Univ, 1968-1991; Am Heart Asn grant, 1967-1969 & 1976-1978; United Health Found grant, 1967-1968; Am Cancer Soc Inst grant, 1967-1968; sr cancer res scientist, Springville Labs, Roswell Park Mem Inst, 1966-1968; res feldevelop biol, Ind Univ, 1964-1965; res asst endocrinol, Ind Univ, 1961-1963; teacher zool, IndUniv, 1960-1961. **Memberships:** AAAS; NY Acad Sci; Am Soc Zool; Soc Develop Biol. **Mailing Address:** Nat Sci, Grand Canyon Univ, 3300 W Camelback Rd, Phoenix, AZ 85017-3030. **E-Mail:** jjustus@asu.edu

JUSTUS, PHILIP STANLEY, GEOLOGICAL HAZARDS ANALYSIS, REGULATORY GEOLOGY. **Personal Data:** b New York, NY, January 17, 1941; m 1963, c 2. **Education:** City Col NY, BS, Geology, 1962; Univ NC, Chapel Hill, MS, Geology, 1966, PhD, Geology, 1971. **Professional Experience:** SR GEOLOGIST, US NUCLEAR REGULATORY COMN, 1994-; sr on-site licensing rep, High-Level Radioactive Waste Mgt, 1992-1994; sect leader, High-Level Radioactive Waste Mgt, 1981-1992; geologist, US Nuclear Regulatory Comn, 1980-1981; res fel, Univ Col London, 1977; assoc ed, Geol Sect, NJ Acad Sci Bull & contrib ed, NJ Sci Teachers Asn Bull, 1973-1980; from asst prof to assoc prof geol, Fairleigh Dickinson Univ, 1971-1980; fel, Rice Univ, 1970-1971; asst prof astron & geol, US Mil Acad, 1968-1970; instr astron & physgeog, US Mil Acad, 1967-1968; student dir seismog sta, Univ NC, 1964-1966; teaching asst geol, Univ NC, 1962-1967. **Memberships:** Geological Soc of Washington (DC); AAAS; Geol Soc Am; Am Geophys Union; Sigma Xi; Planetary Society. **Research Statement & Publications:** regulatory geology of Yucca Mtn; evolution of Brevard fault zone, Blue Ridge Mountains; radioactive waste disposal safety; regulatory geology case studies; geological hazards risk assessment for design and performance assessments. **Mailing Address:** Div High-Level Waste Repository Safety, US Nuclear Regulatory Comm, Mailstop T-7F27, Washington, DC 20555. **E-Mail:** psj@nrc.gov

JUTAMULIA, SUGANDA, ELECTRO-OPTICS, PHOTONICS. **Personal Data:** b Muara Enim, Indonesia, July 11, 1954; m 1990, Xiaoye Sherry Li. **Education:** Bandung Inst Technol, Indonesia, BS, 1977; Univ Indonesia, MS, 1980; Hokkaido Univ, Japan, PhD (electronic eng), 1985. **Professional Experience:** AT DEPT OPTICAL & PHOTONIC ENG, UNIV NORTHERN CALIF, as of 2004; SR MEM, BLUE SKY RES, MILPITAS, as of 2002; gen mgr, Res & Develop, Kowa Co Ltd, beginning 1994; mgr prod develop, Res & Develop, Kowa CO Ltd, 1991-1993; prin investr, Quantex Corp, 1989-1991; sr scientist, Quantex Corp, 1988-1991; res assoc & instr, Pa State Univ, 1985-1988; fel, Pa State Univ, 1985-1988. **Memberships:** Optical Soc Am; Int Soc Optical Eng; Inst Elec & Electronics Engrs; Japan SocAppl Physics. **Research Statement & Publications:** Optical engineering including optical signal processing, computing, neural networks, instrumentation and medical equipment; co-authored 1 book and edited two books; numerous publications and five US patents. **Mailing Address:** Dept Optical & Photonic Eng, Univ Northern Calif, 1304 S Pt Blvd, Suite 220, Petaluma, CA 94954.

JUTILA, JOHN W, IMMUNOLOGY, MEDICAL MICROBIOLOGY. **Personal Data:** b Mullan, Idaho, May 21, 1931; m 1953, c 4. **Education:** Mont State Univ, BA, 1953, MA, 1954; Univ Wash, PhD (microbiol), 1960. **Professional Experience:** PROF EMER, MONT STATE UNIV, 1993-; coordr develop, Mont StateUniv, 1990-1993; vpres res, Mont State Univ, 1978- 1989; dean, Col Letters & Sci, Mont StateUniv, 1974-1978; NIH grants, 1962-1969 & 1970-1976; from asst prof to prof microbiol &microbiologist, Mont State Univ, 1961-1989; fel, Univ Wash, 1960-1961; bacteriologist, RockyMountain Lab, Mont, 1956-1957. **Memberships:** Fel AAAS; fel Am Acad Microbiol; Am Soc Microbiol; Soc Ext Biol & Med; AmAsn Immunol. **Research Statement & Publications:** Pathogenesis of wasting syndromes in mice; immunobiology of the congenitally athymic mouse and immune cell interactions with tumor cells in vivo and tissue culture systems. **Mailing Address:** 516 S Grand Ave, Bozeman, MT 59715.

JUTILA, MARK ARTHUR, INFLAMMATORY DISEASE, DEVELOPMENTAL IMMUNOLOGY. **Personal Data:** b Seattle, Wash, January 31, 1959; m 1981, Kathryn Campbell; c Jamie, Kelly & Aaron. **Education:** Mont State Univ, BS, 1982; Wash State Univ, MS, 1984, PhD (immunol & vet sci), 1986. **Professional Experience:** AFFIL PROF, DEPT IMMUNOL, UNIV WASH-SEATTLE, 2001-; PROF, VET Molecular BIOL, MONT ST UNIV-BOZEMAN, 2000-; asst prof immunol, Mont State Univ, 1989-1995; sr fel, Am Cancer Soc, Calif Div, 1988-1989; fel path, Stanford Univ Sch Med, 1986-1989; fel, NIH Traininggrant, Dept Path, Stanford Univ Sch Med, 1986-1988; res asst, Vet Sch, 1986; teaching asst, Wash State Univ, 1982-1986. **Research Statement & Publications:** Inflammatory disease and cancer, the molecular basis for the recruitment of host defense cells from the blood into various tissues of the body. **Mailing Address:** Vet Molecular Biol Lab, Mont State Univ S 19th & Lincoln, Bozeman, MT 59717-3610. **Fax:** 406-994-4303. **E-Mail:** uvsmj@montana.edu

JUVET, RICHARD SPALDING, PLASMA DESORPTION MASS SPECTROMETRY, CHROMATOGRAPHIC METHODS & COMPUTER INTERFACING. **Personal Data:** b Los Angeles, Calif, August 8, 1930; m 1984, Evelyn; c Victoria, David, Stephen & Richard P. **Education:** Univ Calif, Los Angeles, BS, 1952, PhD (anal chem), 1955. **Honors & Awards:** Sci Exchange Agreement Award, Czech, Hungary, Romainia & Yugoslavia, 1977. **Professional Experience:** EMER PROF ANALYTICAL CHEM, ARIZ STATE, 1995-; Univ Vienna, Austria, 1989-1990; Coun, Comt Reagent Chem, 1985-1995; nat counr, Div Anal Chem, Am Chem Soc, 1978-1989; Sci Exchange Agreement Award lect & travel Eastern Europe, 1977; Ecole Polytechnique, France, 1976-1977; chmn, Div Anal Chem, Am Chem Soc, 1972-1973; prof, Ariz State, 1970-1995; mem, Air Pollution Chem & Physics Adv Comt, US HEW, 1969-1972; Nat Taiwan Univ, 1968; NSF sr fel, Cambridge Univ, Eng, 1964-1965; Cambridge Univ, Eng, 1964-1965; vis prof, Univ Calif, Los Angeles, 1960; from instr to assoc prof anal chem, Univ Ill, Urbana, 1955-1970; res chemist, E I Du Pont de Nemours, 1955. **Memberships:** Am Chem Soc Div Anal Chem (secy-treas, 1969-1971); fel Am Inst Chemists; Sigma Xi; Am Radio Relay League; Int Platform Asn; Alpha Chi Sigma; Grand Collegiate Alchemist. **Research Statement & Publications:** New applications of gas chromatography; liquid chromatography detectors; photochemistry; organic structural determinations and functional group analysis; chelate chemistry of polyhydroxy compounds; optical rotation measurements in study of metal chelates; inorganic gas chromatography; computer interfacing; plasma desorption mass spectrometry. **Mailing Address:** Dept Chem & Biochem, Ariz State Univ, Tempe, AZ 85287-1604. **Fax:** 480-965-2747. **E-Mail:** rsjuvet@imap3.asu.edu

JWO, CHIN-HUNG, MECHANICAL SYSTEM ANALYSIS, PRODUCT RESEARCH & DEVELOPMENT. **Personal Data:** b Taiwan, November 12, 1956; m 1984, Emily; c Kevin & Doris. **Education:** Feng Chia Univ, Taiwan, BS, 1979; Univ Fla, ME, 1985, PhD (mech eng), 1989. **Professional Experience:** AT, SYMBOL TECHNOL, BOHEMIA, NY, as of 1996; SR MECH ENGR, SYMBOL TECHNOL, BOHEMIA, NY, 1993-; prin engr, NCR E&M-Atlanta, 1991-1993; advan develop engr, NCR, Ithaca, 1989-1991. **Memberships:** Am Soc Mech Engrs. **Research Statement & Publications:** Opto-mechanical systems design and analysis for bar code scanners; mechanical packaging for hand-held terminals; electronic packaging; product development for retail and industrial usages. **Mailing Address:** Symbol Technol, Inc, One Symbol Plaza, Holtsville, NY 11742-1300. **Fax:** 516-563-2831.

JYUNG, WOON HENG, PLANT PHYSIOLOGY. **Personal Data:** b Korea, March 12, 1934; m 1961, c 2. **Education:** Seoul Nat Univ, BS, 1957; Mich State Univ, MS, 1959, PhD (hort physiol), 1963. **Professional Experience:** PROF EMER BIOL, UNIV TOLEDO, 1993-; chmn dept, Univ Toledo, 1976-1991; prof biol, Univ Toledo, 1974-1993; from asst prof to assoc prof, Univ Toledo, 1964-1974; res assoc hort physiol, Mich State Univ, 1963-1964. **Memberships:** AAAS; Am Soc Plant Physiol; Japanese Soc Plant Physiol. **Research Statement & Publications:** Mechanisms of ion uptake by plant cells; zinc metabolism in higher plants; biology of aging. **Mailing Address:** Dept Biol, Univ Toledo, Toledo, OH 43606. **Fax:** 419-530-2157.

K

KAAE, JAMES LEWIS, MATERIALS SCIENCE. **Personal Data:** b Bell, Calif, October 28, 1936. **Education:** Univ Calif, Los Angeles, BS, 1959, MS, 1961, PhD (eng), 1965. **Professional Experience:** AT, GEN ATOMICS, as of 2003; Lectr, Univ Calif, San Diego, 1987-1989; Mem, Boiler & Pressure Vessel Code Comt, Am Soc Mech Engrs, 1985-1987; SR TECH ADV, GEN ATOMICS TECHNOL, 1982-; tech adv, Gen Atomic Co, 1973-1982; staff mem, metall, Gulf Energy & Environ Systs Inc, 1967-1973; Int res fel, Welding Inst, Eng, 1965-1967. **Memberships:** Am Carbon Soc; AAAS; Sigma Xi; Am Soc Metals; Am Ceramic Soc. **Research Statement & Publications:** Structure, properties and irradiation behavior of pyrolytic carbon; welding metallurgy of steels; behavior of materials under high-temperature cyclic loading; behavior of coated particle nuclear fuels; chemical vapor deposition of carbides and nitrides; mechanical properties of materials. **Mailing Address:** Inertial Fusion Technol Gen Atomics, PO Box 85608, San Diego, CA 92186-5608. **Fax:** 858-455-2838. **E-Mail:** james.kaaae@gat.com

KAARET, PHILIP, PHYSICS, ASTROPHYSICS. **Education:** Mass Inst Technol, BS, 1984; Princeton Univ, PhD (Exp particle Physics), 1989. **Professional Experience:** ASTROPHYSICIST, SMITHSONIAN ASTROPHYS OBSERV, 1998-; fac physics dept, Columbia Univ, ending 1998. **Research Statement & Publications:** Understanding the intense gravitational fields surrounding black holes and neutron stars made luminous by accreting gas from a companion star; highly luminous X-ray sources in nearby galaxies which have been interpreted as being intermediate mass black holes; jet ejection from black holesl; and the study of black hole populations to probe the star formation history of galaxies. **Mailing Address:** Harvard-Smithsonian Ctr Astrophys, 60 Garden St, Cambridge, MA 02138. **Fax:** 617-495-7356. **E-Mail:** pkaaret@cfa.harvard.edu

KAAS, JON HOWARD, PSYCHOPHYSIOLOGY NEUROANATORY BEHAVIOR & NEUROPHYSIOLOGY. **Personal Data:** b Fargo, NDak, September 13, 1937. **Education:** Northland Col, BA, 1959; Duke Univ, PhD (psychol), 1965. **Honors & Awards:** lavits-Neuroscience Investr Award, 1987; Krieg Corticol Discoverer Award, 1988; Distinguished Sci Contrib Award Am Psychol Asn, 1994. **Professional Experience:** DISTINGUISHED PROF PSYCHOL & ASSOC PROF CELL BIOL, VANDERBILT UNIV, as of 2005; CENTENNIAL PROF PSYCHOL, VANDERBILT UNIV, 1979-; assoc prof, Vanderbilt Univ, 1973-1979; asst prof, Univ Wis-Madison, 1968-1973; Trainee neurophysiol, Univ Wis-Madison, 1965-1968. **Memberships:** Soc Neuroscience; In Brain Res Orgn. **Research Statement & Publications:** Visual and sensory systems; brain functions and evolution; published over 80 articles. **Mailing Address:** Dept Psychol, Vanderbilt Univ, 061 Wilson Hall 111 21st Ave S, Nashville, TN 37240. **Fax:** 615-322-7941. **E-Mail:** jon.kaas@vanderbilt.edu

KAATTARI, STEPHEN L, COMPARATIVE IMMUNOLOGY. **Personal Data:** b Palo Alto, Calif, September 22, 1951. **Education:** Univ Calif, Davis, BS, 1973, PhD (microbiol), 1979. **Professional Experience:** CHMN, DEPT ENVIRON & AQUATIC ANIMAL HEALTH, WILLIAM & MARY, VA INST MARINE SCI, as of 2004; PROF MARINE SCI, WILLIAM & MARY, VA INST MARINE SCI, 1993-; from asst prof to prof immunol, Dept Microbiol, Ore State Univ, 1982-1992; Res fel cellular immunol, Ore Health Sci Univ, 1979-1982. **Memberships:** Int Soc Develop & Comp Immunol; Am Asn Immunol; Am Soc Microbiol. **Mailing Address:** Dept Environ & Aquatic Animal Health, William & Mary, VA Inst Marine Sci, S105 Chesapeake Bay Hall, Glouchester Point, VA 23062. **E-Mail:** slkaat@facstaff.wm.edu

KAATZ, MARTIN RICHARD, PHYSICAL GEOGRAPHY, GEOMORPHOLOGY. **Personal Data:** b Cleveland, Ohio, April 16, m Carla; c Allen, Larry & David. **Education:** Univ Mich, BA, 1948, MA, 1949, PhD (geog), 1952. **Honors & Awards:** Distinguished University Professor - Public Service, 1979-1980 Central Washington University. **Professional Experience:** PROF EMER GEOG, CENT WASH UNIV, 1983-; prof, Cent Wash Univ, 1965-1982; Fulbright prof, Trinity Col, Univ Dublin, 1965-1966; chmn dept, Cent Wash Univ, 1962-1976; From asst prof to assoc prof, Cent Wash Univ, 1952-1964. **Memberships:** Asn Am Geogr; Asn Pacific Coast Geographers; Am Quaternary Asn. **Research Statement & Publications:** Significance of mass wasting and periglacial landforms to the modern environment; irrigation, drought, flooding in Central Washington. **Mailing Address:** Dept Geography & Land Studies, Central Wash Univ, 400 E Univ Way, Ellensburg, WA 98926. **E-Mail:** marcar@elltel.net

KABACK, DAVID BRIAN, RECOMBINANT DNA, DEVELOPMENTAL BIOLOGY. **Personal Data:** b New York, NY, May 4, 1950; m 1991, Stephanie; c Alexis R & Julia I. **Education:** State Univ NY Stony Brook, BS, 1971; Brandeis Univ, PhD (biol), 1976. **Honors & Awards:** Nat Res Serv Award, Pub Health Serv. **Professional Experience:** PROF, NJ MED SCH, UNIV MED & DENT NJ, 1994-; assoc prof microbiol, NJ Med Sch, Univ Med & Dent NJ, 1985-1994; asst prof, NJ Med Sch, Univ Med & Dent NJ, 1978-1985; res fel chem, Calif Inst Technol, 1976-1978; Damon Runyon-Walter Winchell Cancer Res fel. **Memberships:** Am Soc Microbiol; Harvey Soc; Genetics Soc Am. **Research Statement & Publications:** Molecular genetics of yeast meiosis and sporulation; organization of eucaryotic genes and chromosomes; meiosis. **Mailing Address:** PO Box 1709, Dept Microbiol & Molecular Genetics, NJ Med Sch, Int Ctr for Public Health, Univ Med & Dent NJ, Newark, NJ 07101-1709. **E-Mail:** kaback@umdnj.edu

KABACK, HOWARD RONALD, BIOCHEMISTRY MEMBRANE TRANSPORT, MEMBRANE PROTEIN STRUCTURE, BIOENERGETICS. **Personal Data:** b Philadelphia, Pa, June 5, 1936. **Education:** Haverford Col, BA, 1958; Albert Einstein Col Med, MD, 1962. **Honors & Awards:** Selman A Waksman Honorary Lectureship Award, Am Soc Microbiol, 1973; Lewis Rosenstiel Award, 1974; Int Cell Res Org, UNESCO, 1976; Philips Lectr, Haverford Col, 1976-1977; Nat Lectr, Am Soc Microbiol, 1981; Nathan Kaplan Mem Lectr, Univ Calif, 1988; Kenneth Cole Award, Am Biophys Soc, 1988; Harvey Lectr, 1988; George A Feigen Mem Lectr, Stanford Univ, 1989; Philips Lectr, Haverford Col, 1989; Univ Helsinki Medal & Spec Lect, Helsinki, Finland, 1993; 3M Life Sci Award, 1993; Harold Lambert Lectr, Columbia Univ, 1993; Jacques & Giselle Weismen Lectr, Israel, 1993 & 1994; Fel Am Acad Microbiol, 1997; Coleman Fel Life Sci, Noun Shavit Mem Lect Fund, Ben-Gurion Univ, Beer-Sheva, Israel, 2000; Fel Biophys Soc, 2001; Barton Lect, Univ Okla, 2002; Melvin V Simpson Lect, Stoney Brook Univ, 2004; UCLA Fac Res Lect, 2004; Koeppe Lect, Okla State Univ, 2005. **Professional Experience:** DISTINGUISHED PROF, DEPT PHYSIOL & MICROBIOL, IMMUNOLOGY & MOLECULAR GENETICS, MEM MOLECULAR BIOL INST, UNIV CALIF, 2004-; guest speaker, Mt Sinai Deans Lect Series, 1996; distinguished lectr, Robert Wood Johnson Med Sch, 1996; vis prof prog lectr, Univ Fla, 1994; elected Chmn, Gordon Conf Transp, 1993; chmn bd, Bd Sci Coun, Nat Inst Diabetes, Digestive & Kidney Dis, 1991-1992; mem ad hoc, NIH Study Sect, 1990; prof, Depts Physiol Microbiol & Molecular Genetics, Univ Calif, Los Angeles, 1989-2004; investr, Howard Hughes Med Inst, 1989-2004; mem, Bd Sci Coun, Nat Inst Diabetes, Digestive & Kidney Dis, 1987-1991; Wellcome vis prof, Univ Idaho, 1987-1988; adj prof microbiol, NJ Med Sch, 1986-1989; adj prof, Columbia Univ, NY, 1985-1989; head, Dept Biochem, 1983-1989; nat lectr, Am Soc Microbiol, 1981; Albert Alberman vis prof, Technion-Israel Inst Technol, 1981; Lady Davis vis prof, Hebrew Univ, Israel, 1980; head, Lab Membrane Biochem, 1977-1989; adj prof, Grad Sch & Univ Ctr, City Univ NY, 1976-1989; Battelle Mem Found Fel, Seattle, WA, 1974; adj assoc prof, Columbia Univ, NY, 1973-1985; mem, Dept Biochem, Roche Inst Molecular Biol, 1972-1989; assoc mem, Dept Biochem, Roche Inst Molecular Biol, 1970-1972; sr res investr, Lab Biochem, Nat Heart Inst, NIH, 1966-1969; staff assoc, Lab Biochem, Nat Heart Inst, NIH, 1964-1966; res fel biochem, Nat Heart Inst, 1964-1966; Edward John Noble Found fel physiol, Albert Einstein Col Med, 1963-1964; Edward John Noble Found fel, 1962-1964; intern pediat, Bronx Munic Hosp Ctr, 1962-1963. **Memberships:** Nat Acad Sci; Fedn Am Socs Exp Biol; NY Acad Sci; Am Soc Microbiol; Am Biophys Soc; fel Am Acad Arts & Sci; AAAS; Am Soc Biol Chemists; Am Chem Soc; Soc Gen Physiologists. **Research Statement & Publications:** The lactose permease of Escherichia coli (LacY) couples the free energy released from downhill translocation of H+ in response to an H+ electrochemical gradient to drive the stoichiometric accumulation of D-galactopyranosides against a concentration gradient. An X-ray structure in an inward-facing conformation has been solved, which confirms many conclusions from biochemical and biophysical studies. LacY contains N- and C-terminal domains, each with six transmembrane helices, positioned pseudo-symmetrically. A large hydrophilic cavity is exposed to the cytoplasm, and ligand is bound at the two-fold axis of pseudo-symmetry at the apex of the hydrophilic cavity in the approximate middle of the molecule. By combining a large body of experimental data derived from systematic studies of site-directed mutants, residues involved in substrate binding and H+ translocation have been identified. Surprisingly, the residues involved in H+ translocation are aligned parallel to the membrane at the same level as the sugar-binding site and may be exposed to a water-filled cavity in both the inward- and outward-facing conformations, thereby allowing H+ release directly into either conformation of LacY. These structural features may explain why LacY is able to catalyze lactose/H+ symport in both directions utilizing the same residues. The data as a whole are consistent with a working that involves alternating access of both the sugar- and the H+-binding sites to either side of the membrane during turnover; pulished over 400 articles. **Mailing Address:** Dept Physiol, Howard Hughes Med Inst Univ Calif, Rm 6720B MacDonald Res Labs 675 Charles E Young Dr S, Los Angeles, CA 90095-1662. **Fax:** 310-206-8623. **E-Mail:** ronaldk@hhmi.ucla.edu

KABACK, MICHAEL M, PEDIATRICS, MEDICAL GENETICS. **Personal Data:** b September 1, 1938. **Education:** Haverford Col, BA, 1959; Univ Pa, MD, 1963; Am Bd Pediat, dipl; Am Bd Med Genetics, dipl. **Honors & Awards:** William Allen Mem Award, Am Soc Human Genetics, 1993. **Professional Experience:** PROF, DIV MED GENETICS, DEPT PEDIAT, SCH MED, UNIV CALIF, SAN DIEGO, as of 2004; CHMN, DIV MED GENETICS, DEPT PEDIAT, SCH MED, UNIV CALIF, SAN DIEGO, 1986-; chair, Dept Pediat, Univ Calif, San Diego, 1986-1991; Dir, Int Tay-Sachs Ctr, 1979; from assoc prof to prof pediat med, 1972-1986; assoc chief, Div Med Genetics, Harbor Med Ctr, Univ Calif, Los Angeles, Med Ctr, 1972-1986; Dir, Calif Tay-Sachs Dis Prev Prog, 1972; asst prof pediat, Johns Hopkins Univ, 1969-1972; instr, Johns Hopkins Univ, 1968-1969; Res assoc, Nat Inst Neurol Dis & Blindness, 1964-1966. **Memberships:** Inst Med-Nat Acad Sci; fel Am Col Med Genetics; fel Am AcadPediat; fel AAAS; Am Soc Human Genetics (pres 1991); Am Pediat Soc (pres-elect 1997). **Research Statement & Publications:** Public health considerations in human (medical) genetics; technical, psychosocial and ethics-legal aspects of genetic screening. **Mailing Address:** Children's Hosp & Health Ctr, 8110 Birmingham Way, San Diego, CA 92123. **E-Mail:** mkaback@ucsd.edu

KABACK, STUART MARK, ORGANIC CHEMISTRY. **Personal Data:** b Elizabeth, NJ, June 12, 1934; m 1955, Marilyn Feldman; c Robin N (McGowan) & Gilbert P. **Education:** Columbia Univ, BA, 1955, MA, 1956, PhD (org chem), 1960. **Honors & Awards:** Herman Skolnvik Awd, Div of Infor, Amer Chem Soc, 1999; Internat'l Patent Infor Awd, Tech - Patent Resc Inter'l, 2001. **Professional Experience:** Mem, Chem Abstracts Serv Comt, Am Chem Soc, 1996-; SCI ADV, RES SER DIV, EXXON RES & ENG CO, 1990-; sr res assoc, Anal & Info Div, 1985-1990; MEM STAFF, RES SER DIV, EXXON RES & ENG CO, 1984-; mem staff, Anal & Info Div, 1978-1983; res assoc, Res Corp Serv, 1976-1985; sr res chemist, Res Corp Serv, 1970-1976; sr res chemist, Chem Corp Serv, 1968-1970; Chem Res Div, 1963 & Tech Info Div, 1963-1968; Chemist, Tech Info Div, Esso Res & Eng Co, 1960-1963; mem, Patent Info User's Group. **Memberships:** Am Chem Soc; Chem Struct Asn. **Research Statement & Publications:** Information retrieval and analysis; patent information on petrochemicals, polymer chemistry; petroleum technology. **Mailing Address:** Info Res & Anal, Res Support Serv, ExxonMobil Res & Eng Co, Route 22 E, Annandale, NJ 08801. **Fax:** 908-730-3230. **E-Mail:** stuart.m.kaback@exxonmobil.com

KABADI, BALACHANDRA N, PHYSICAL PHARMACY, PHARMACEUTICAL CHEMISTRY. **Personal Data:** b Gadag, Mysore, India, July 15, 1933. **Education:** Karnatak Univ, India, BSc, 1958; Univ Bombay, BSc, 1960; Univ Wash, MS, 1962, PhD (pharm), 1965. **Professional Experience:** SR RES SCIENTIST ANALYSIS CONTROL, E R SQUIBB & SONS, 1968-; asst prof pharm, Col Pharm, Fla A&M Univ, 1967-1968; Fel chem, Univ SC, 1965-1966 & Sch Pharm, Univ Mich, 1966-1967. **Memberships:** Am Pharmaceut Asn; Am Chem Soc. **Research Statement & Publications:** Isolation, identification of compounds from natural plant products; pharmaceutical complexation reactions of phenols and water soluble hydrophilic polymers of nonionic nature; analytical chemistry-analysis of pharmaceutical products involving spectrophotometric methods; reference standards. **Mailing Address:** 34 Colin Dr, South River, NJ 08882-2406.

KABALKA, GEORGE WALTER, ORGANIC CHEMISTRY, ORGANOMETALLIC CHEMISTRY. **Personal Data:** b Wyandotte, Mich, February 1, 1943. **Education:** Univ Mich, BS, 1965; Purdue Univ, PhD (chem), 1970. **Professional Experience:** PROF, RH COLE FOUND ENDOWED CHAIR NEUROSCIENCE, 1994-; dir basic sci res, Inst Biomed Imaging ctr, Univ Tenn Hosp, 1988-; bd dir, Radio pharmaceut Coun Soc Nuclear Med, 1987-1989; bd dir, Int Isotope Soc, 1986-; CTI Corp, Knoxville, Tenn, 1985-; PROF RADIOL, UNIV TENN, KNOXVILLE, 1984-; consult, Brookhaven Nat Lab, 1981-; consult, Oak Ridge Assoc Univ, 1977-; consult, Oak Ridge Nat Lab, 1976-; PROF CHEM, UNIV TENN, KNOXVILLE, 1970-; Res assoc, Purdue Univ, 1969-1970. **Memberships:** Am Chem Soc; Soc Nuclear Med; Int Isotope Soc; Soc Magnetic Resonance. **Research Statement & Publications:** We are primarily interested in the development of new techniqes for preparing radiolabeled agents; Alumina as Reagent; Current Topics in the Chemistry of Boron; Bromination of Vinylboronic Acids on Alumina. **Mailing Address:** Univ Tenn, 611 Buehler Hall, Knoxville, TN 37916-1600. **E-Mail:** kabalka@novell.chem.utk.edu

KABARA, JON JOSEPH, PHARMACOLOGY, CLINICAL BIOCHEMISTRY. **Personal Data:** b Chicago, Ill, November 26, 1926. **Education:** St Mary's Col, Minn, BS, 1948; Univ Miami, MS, 1950; Univ Chicago, PhD (pharmacol), 1959. **Professional Experience:** PROF EMER MED, MICH STATE UNIV, 1987-; prof med, Col Osteop, 1970-1987; prof pharmacol & assoc dean, Mich State Univ, 1969-1970; from asst prof to prof chem, Univ Detroit, 1957-1968; asst med, Univ Chicago, 1953-1957; microbiol, Univ Miami, 1950-1953; asst chem, Univ Miami, 1948-1949; asst biochem, Univ Ill, 1948; consult, Med-Chem Labs Technol Exchange. **Memberships:** AAAS; Am Chem Soc; NY Acad Sci; Am Soc Clin Path; Am Asn Clin Chem. **Research Statement & Publications:** Cancer and virus chemotherapy; sterol biogenesis and metabolism; biochemistry of the central nervous system; radiobiology and clinical chemistry; biochemistry; venom research; pharmacology in dental research of food preservation and cosmetic; granted 19 US patents and 20 foreign patents. **Mailing Address:** 405 W Wachter Rd, Galena, IL 61036. **E-Mail:** jonkab@aol.com

KABAT, DAVID, BIOCHEMISTRY, GENETICS. **Personal Data:** b Minneapolis, Minn, October 15, 1940. **Education:** Brown Univ, ScB, 1962; Calif Inst Technol, PhD (biochem), 1967. **Professional Experience:** PROF BIOCHEM, MED SCH, UNIV ORE, 1972-; asst prof, Med Sch, Univ Ore, 1969-1972; NIH res assoc biophys, Mass Inst Technol, 1967-1969. **Memberships:** Am Soc Biol Chemists. **Research Statement & Publications:** Biochemical genetics of growth and differentiation. **Mailing Address:** Dept Biochem, Sch Med, Univ Ore Health Sci, 3181 SW Sam Jackson Park Rd, Portland, OR 97201-3098. **Fax:** 503-494-8393. **E-Mail:** kabat@ohsu.edu

KABAT, HUGH F, PHARMACY ADMINISTRATION. **Personal Data:** b Manitowoc, Wis, October 3, 1932. **Education:** Univ Mich, BS, 1954, MS, 1956; Univ Colo, PhD (pharm admin), 1961. **Honors & Awards:** Mead-Johnson Award, Am Soc Hosp Pharmacists, 1969; Hallie Bruce Mem lectr, 1969; Dorothy Dillon Mem lectr, 1990. **Professional Experience:** PROF EMER COL PHARM, UNIV NMEX, ALBUQUERQUE, 1996-; Hosp Pharm, beginning 1990; Ediciones Mayo, 1987-1990; contrib ed, Topics Hosp Pharm Mgt, 1986-; prof, Univ Nmex, Albuquerque, 1984-1996; prof, Col Pharm, 1980-1986; assoc dean, Acad Affairs, 1980-1984; asst dean admin, Univ Minn, Minneapolis, 1974-1980; prof clin pharm, Univ Minn, Minneapolis, 1969-1980; head dept clin pharm, Univ Minn, Minneapolis, 1969-1974; contrib ed, Drug Intel, 1967-1974; contrib ed, Geriatric Nursing, 1965-1968; contrib ed, Int Pharmaceut Abstr, 1964-1981; from asst prof to assoc prof pharm technol, Univ Minn, Minneapolis, 1961-1969; chief pharm serv, Alaska Native Hosp, USPHS, 1956-1958; Consult, Vet Admin Hosp, Minneapolis, Hennepin Co Med Ctr, St Paul Ramsey Med Ctr, Data Dynamics & Mkt Measurements, Vet Affairs Med Ctr, Univ NMex Hosp, Alpha Data Servs, NIH. **Memberships:** Am Pharmaceut Asn; Am Soc Hosp Pharmacists; Am Asn Cols Pharm (pres elect); Am Pub Health Asn. **Research Statement & Publications:** Drug utilization review; patient compliance; clinical pharmacy; drugs and the aging; problem based-student centered learning. **Mailing Address:** Col Pharm, Univ NMex, Albuquerque, NM 87131. **Fax:** 505-272-6749. **E-Mail:** hkabat@unm.edu

KABAYAMA, MICHIOMI ABRAHAM, POLYMER CHEMISTRY. **Personal Data:** b Kanazawa, Japan, April 18, 1926. **Education:** Sir George Williams Col, BSc, 1952; Univ

Montreal, MSc, 1956, DSc, 1958. **Professional Experience:** RETIRED; mgr environ affairs, Tetra Pak Inc, 1990-1995; mgr recycling, Twinpak Inc, 1988-1989; tech dir, Vinyl Coun Can, 1985-1988; tech dir, Soc Plastics Indust Can, 1976-1985; mgr plastics eng, Mfg Res Centre, 1974-1976; res chemist, Bell-Northern Res Labs, 1971-1974; mgr transducer & polymer mat develop, Res & Develop Labs, Northern Elec Co Ltd, 1969-1971; res chemist, Res & Develop Labs, Northern Elec Co Ltd, 1967-1969; res chemist, Ethicon, Inc, 1965-1967; res chemist, Dupont Can, 1958 & E I Dupont de Nemours & Co, 1958-1965; demonstr, Univ Montreal, 1953-1956; Control chemist, Monsanto Can, 1951-1953. **Memberships:** Soc Plastics Engrs; fel Chem Inst Can. **Research Statement & Publications:** Physical properties and structure of polymers; thermodynamics of solutions of polymers; calorimetry of polymer solutions; plastic material and processing technology; new methods and applications; combustibility and toxicity of combustion products; occupational health and safety; recycling. **Mailing Address:** 434 Winona Dr, Toronto, ON M6C 3T7, Can.

KABE, DATTATRAYA G, MATHEMATICAL STATISTICS, OPERATIONS RESEARCH. **Personal Data:** b Belgaum, India, December 30, 1926. **Education:** Univ Bombay, BSc, 1948, MSc, 1952; Univ Karnatak, India, MSc, 1955; Wayne State Univ, PhD (statist), 1964. **Professional Experience:** RETIRED; prof statist, Bowling Green State Univ, 1987-1988; prof statist, NMex State Univ, 1980-1981; prof math & statist, St Mary's Univ, NS, 1975-1992; assoc prof, St Mary's Univ, NS, 1968-1975; assoc prof math & statist, Northern Mich Univ, 1965-1966 & Dalhousie Univ, 1966-1968; assoc math, Wayne State Univ, 1961-1964; lectr statist, Vijay Col, India, 1952-1953 & Karnatak Univ, India, 1953-1961; Nat Res Coun Can grants & Can Math Cong res scholar. **Memberships:** Can Statist Asn. **Research Statement & Publications:** Distribution theory; design of experiments; multivariate analysis; Pascal computer programming language; sampling techniques; math programming. **Mailing Address:** Dept Comput Sci & Math, St Mary's Univ, Halifax, NS B3H 3C3, Can.

KABEL, RICHARD HARVEY, TRIBOLOGY, MECHANICAL ENGINEERING. **Personal Data:** b Detroit, Mich, December 18, 1932. **Education:** Gen Motors Inst, BSME, 1961. **Honors & Awards:** Coop Eng Colwell Medal, Soc Automotive Engrs. **Professional Experience:** PRES, RICH-LO-CONSULT CORP, 1987-; sr staff res engr, eng oils, Gen Motors Res Labs, 1981-1987; staff res engr eng oils, Gen Motors Res Labs, 1978-1981; group leader, Gen Motors Res Labs, 1974-1978; sr res engr, Gen Motors Res Labs, 1967-1987; Res engr eng oils, Gen Motors Res Labs, 1961-1967; Soc Automotive Engrs fel, bd dr; Gen Motors rep, Lub Rev Comt, US Army & Soc Automotive Engrs. **Memberships:** Soc Automotive Engrs; Am Soc Testing & Mat. **Research Statement & Publications:** Engine oils, formulation of engine oils, field performance, and methods to evaluate them. **Mailing Address:** 11051 Jonathan Lane, Romeo, MI 48065.

KABEL, ROBERT L(YNN), CHEMICAL REACTION ENGINEERING, SCALE-UP. **Personal Data:** b Champaign, Ill, April 3, 1932; m 1958, Barbara; c Joseph R & Douglas A. **Education:** Univ Ill, BS, 1955; Univ Wash, PhD (chem eng), 1961. **Honors & Awards:** Western Elec Fund Award Excellence Instr, Am Soc Eng Educ, 1983, Corcoran Award, Chem Eng Div, 1989; Nat Catalyst Award, Chem Mfrs Asn, 1984. **Professional Experience:** PROF EMER CHEM ENG, PA STATE UNIV, as of 2006; Erskine fel, Univ Canterbury, NZ, 1989; Chulalongkorn Univ, Thailand, 1989; vis prof, Univ NSW, Australia, 1988 & 1989; invitational prof, Ariz State Univ, 1984-1985; vis lectr, Pahlavi Univ, Iran, 1978; consult, Exxon Res & Eng, 1976-1980; prof chem eng, Pa State Univ, beginning 1974; Royal Norweg Coun Sci & Indust Res fel, Tech Univ, Norway, 1971-1972; from asst prof to assoc prof, PA State Univ, 1963-1974; staff mem, Space Systs Div, USAF, 1961-1963. **Memberships:** Am Chem Soc; fel Am Inst Chem Engrs. **Research Statement & Publications:** Reaction kinetics; adsorption; thermodynamic equilibria; heterogeneous catalysis; chemical reactor dynamics; aerospace life support systems; thermal conductivity; mathematical modeling of natural processes; mass transfer at the earth's surface; air pollution meteorology; scaleup of chemical processes. **Mailing Address:** Dept Chem, Pa State Univ, Univ Park, PA 16802. **E-Mail:** r8k@psu.edu

KABIR, PRABAHAN KEMAL, symmetry, high energy physics; deceased, see previous edition for last biography

KABLAOUI, MAHMOUD SHAFIQ, CHEMISTRY. **Personal Data:** b Tarshiha, Palestine, April 15, 1938. **Education:** Am Univ Beirut, BSc, 1960; Univ SC, PhD (org chem), 1967. **Professional Experience:** EXEC, RES FACIL, BEACON RES LAB, TEXACO INC, as of 2004; MGR CHARGE BIOTECHNOL, COAL GASIFICATION & MEMBRANE SEPARATION, BEACON RES LAB, TEXACO INC, 1987-; group leader, TEXACO INC, 1980-1987; From chemist to sr res chemist, TEXACO INC, 1967-1980. **Memberships:** Am Chem Soc; Sigma Xi; Am Soc Microbiol. **Research Statement & Publications:** Organic synthesis, petrochemicals; aromatization reactions, organic nitrogen compounds and fuels and lubricants technology; biotechnology area involving fermentation, enzyme catalysis and photobioconversion. **Mailing Address:** Texaco, Inc, 6001 Bollinger Canyon Rd, San Ramon, CA 94583.

KABLER, MILTON NORRIS, SURFACE SCIENCE, OPTICAL PROPERTIES. **Personal Data:** b Roanoke, Va, April 30, 1932. **Education:** Va Polytech Inst, BS, 1955; Univ NC, Chapel Hill, PhD (physics), 1959. **Honors & Awards:** Pure Sci Award, Sigma Xi-Naval Res Lab, 1973. **Professional Experience:** HEAD, SYNCHROTRON RAD SECT, NAVAL RES LAB, 1986-; head, Optical Probes Br, 1979-1985; assoc supt, Mat Sci Div, 1975-1977; vis scientist, Clarendon Lab, Oxford Univ, 1973-1974; head, Optical Mat Br, 1969-1979; physicist, Naval Res Lab, 1962-1969; res asst prof physics, Univ Ill, Urbana, 1959-1962. **Memberships:** Fel Am Phys Soc; Sigma Xi; AAAS; Optical Soc Am; Am Vacuum Soc. **Research Statement & Publications:** Electronic and optical properties of materials; dynamics of photochemical processes; defects, excitons, semiconductors, radiation effects, surfaces, insulators; optical technologies; synchrotron radiation; research management. **Mailing Address:** Naval Res Lab, Code 6686, Washington, DC 20375-5345.

KABOS, PAVEL, HIGH FREQUENCY MAGNETISM. **Personal Data:** b Kosice, Czech, July 24, 1947; m 1972, Dagmar; c Peter. **Education:** Slovack Tech Univ, MS, 1970, PhD (solid state physics), 1979. **Honorary Degrees:** DSc, Slovack Tech Univ, 1994. **Professional Experience:** Prof physics, Colo State Univ, beginning 1995; sr res scientist, Colo State Univ, 1992-1995; assoc prof elec eng, Slovak Tech Univ, 1983-; fel, Colo State Univ, 1982-1984; asst prof elec eng, Electro Tech Fac, Slovak Tech Univ, 1971-1983. **Memberships:** Sr mem Inst Elec & Electronics Engrs. **Research Statement & Publications:** Ferromagnetic resonance; spin wave instabilities; magnetic excitations in finite-size magnetic samples; multilayers and superlattices; Brillouin light scattering; microwave ferrites; nonlinear magnetics; microwave magnetism; solitons. **Mailing Address:** Dept Physics, Colo State Univ, Ft Collins, CO 80523. **Fax:** 970-491-7947. **E-Mail:** kabos@lamar.colostate.edu

KACEW, SAM, DRUG-INDUCED CHANGES IN NEWBORNS. **Personal Data:** b Poland, 1946. **Education:** McGill Univ, Montreal, BS, 1967; Univ Ottawa, MS, 1970, PhD (pharmacol), 1973. **Honors & Awards:** Achievement Award Soc Toxicol Canada 1983; Achievement Award Soc Toxicol 1986. **Professional Experience:** PROF, DEPT PHARMACOL, UNIV OTTAWA, as of 2006; PROF, DEPT CELLULAR & MOLECULAR MED, UNIV OTTAWA, 1975-; SCIENTIST, INST POPULATION HEALTH RISK ASSESSMENT, UNIV OTTAWA, as of 2006; ed-in-chief, J Toxicol Environ Health; assoc ed, Toxicol Appl Pharmacol. **Memberships:** Comt Toxicol Nat Acad Sci; Adv Expert Comt Canadian Network Toxicol Centres. **Research Statement & Publications:** Toxicology of newborns. **Mailing Address:** Dept Pharmacol, Univ Ottawa, Rm 2209 Health Sci Bldg 451 Smyth Rd, Ottawa, ON K1H 8M5, Can. **Fax:** 613-562-5434. **E-Mail:** skacew@uottawa.ca

KACHANOV, MARK L, FRACTURE & DAMAGE MECHANICS, MICROMECHANICS OF MATERIALS. **Personal Data:** b Moscow, USSR, August 6, 1946. **Education:** Leningrad Univ, BS & MS, 1964; Leningrad Polytech Inst, Cand Sci, 1974; Brown Univ, PhD, 1981. **Professional Experience:** PROF MECH ENG, TUFTS UNIV, 1988-; assoc prof, Tufts Univ, 1982-1988; asst prof mech & mat sci, Rutgers Univ, 1980-1982; prin investr, Dept Energy, Dept Transp, US Army & Alcoa Found; consult, SRI Int, Gen Tel Labs & Shell Labs; vis scientist, Stanford Res Inst, Nat Inst Standards & Technol, Shell Res Lab, Holland & Gen Elec Labs. **Memberships:** Am Acad Mech. **Research Statement & Publications:** Mechanics of solids with multiple cracks and other defects; micromechanics of brittle materials; fractures accompanied by damage and microcracking; mechanics of damage. **Mailing Address:** Dept Mech Eng, Tufts Univ, 200 Col Ave, Arlington, MA 02155. **Fax:** 617-627-3058. **E-Mail:** mark.kachanov@tufts.edu

KACHHAL, SWATANTRA KUMAR, INDUSTRIAL ENGINEERING, OPERATIONS RESEARCH. **Personal Data:** b India, July 7, 1947. **Education:** Univ Roorkee, India, BS, 1968; Univ Minn, MS, 1971, PhD (indust eng & opers res), 1974. **Professional Experience:** PROF & CHAIR, INDUST & MFG SYST ENG, UNIV MICH, DEARBORN, 1987-; CHMN INDUST & MFG SYST ENG, UNIV MICH, DEARBORN, 1985-; consult, Henry Ford Hosp, 1980-; consult, Corning Glass Works, 1978-; from instr to assoc prof, Univ Mich, Dearborn, 1973-1987. **Memberships:** Am Inst Indust Eng; Soc Mfg Eng; Healthcare Info & Mgt Systems Soc; Inst Indus Eng. **Research Statement & Publications:** Facilities planning; warehousing; automated and mechanized storage systems; applications of operations research in healthcare; published over 50 articles. **Mailing Address:** Dept Indust & Mfg Syst Eng, Univ Mich, 2340 Eng Complex 4901 Evergreen Rd, Dearborn, MI 48128-1491. **Fax:** 313-593-5361. **E-Mail:** kachhal@umich.edu

KACHINSKY, ROBERT JOSEPH, WATER SUPPLY & WASTEWATER DISPOSAL ENGINEERING. **Personal Data:** b Boston, Mass, May 3, 1937; m 1963, c Carolyn (Stys), Lisa (Hickey), Beth (O'Brien) & Amy (Alessi). **Education:** Northeastern Univ, BS, 1963, MS, 1975. **Professional Experience:** RETIRED; sr consult part time, Camp Dresser & McKee Inc, 2000-2003; sr vpres, Camp Dresser & McKee Inc, 1993-2000; vpres, Camp Dresser & McKee Inc, 1977-1993; proj dir, 1975-1977; staff engr, 1965-1975. **Memberships:** Fel Am Soc Civil Engrs; Am Acad Environ Engrs; Am Waterworks Asn. **Research Statement & Publications:** Wastewater treatment and disposal engineering. **Mailing Address:** Camp Dresser & McKee Inc, 50 Cambridge Ctr, Cambridge, MA 02139. **E-Mail:** kachinskyrj@cdm.com

KACHRU, RAVINDER, PHYSICS. **Professional Experience:** STAFF, MOLECULAR PHYSICS DEPT, SRI INT, as of 2000. **Memberships:** Am Phys Soc. **Mailing Address:** Molec Phys Lab SRI Int, 333 Ravenswood Ave, Menlo Park, CA 94025. **Fax:** 703-247-8569.

KACKER, RAGHU N, STATISTICAL QUALITY ENGINEERING, INDUSTRIAL EXPERIMENTATION. **Personal Data:** b India, June 24, 1951. **Education:** Univ Delhi, India, BS, 1971; Agra Univ, India, MStatist, 1973; Univ Guelph, Can, MS, 1975; Iowa State Univ, PhD (statist), 1979. **Professional Experience:** MATH STATISTICIAN, NAT INST STAND & TECHNOL, GAITHERSBURG, MD, 1988-; distinguished tech staff qual assurance, AT&T Bell Labs, Holmdel, NJ, 1985-1988; tech staff qual assurance, AT & T Bell Labs, Holmdel, NJ, 1980-1985; asst prof statist, Va Polytech Inst, Blacksburg, 1979-1980; instr statist, Iowa State Univ, Ames, Iowa, 1975-1979. **Memberships:** Am Statist Asn; Am Soc Qual Control; Am Soc Testing & Mat; Am Ceramic Soc. **Research Statement & Publications:** Accelerate advanced materials formulation and processing through statistical quality engineering; engineering designs of instruments for measurement and for processing respond linearly to changes in input signals and make such designs robust to unavoidable noise factors. **Mailing Address:** Statist Eng Div, Nat Inst Stand & Technol, Rm 353, Gaithersburg, MD 20899. **Fax:** 301-990-4127. **E-Mail:** raghu.kacker@nist.gov

KACSER, CLAUDE, THEORETICAL PHYSICS. **Personal Data:** b Paris, France, 1934; American citizen. **Education:** Oxford Univ, BA, 1955, MA & PhD (physics), 1959. **Professional Experience:** ASSOC PROF EMER PHYSICS, UNIV MD, COL PARK, 1997-; assoc prof physics, Univ MD, College Park, 1967-1997; asst prof, Univ MD, College Park, 1964-1967; asst prof, Columbia Univ, 1962-1964; res fel, Magdalen Col, Oxford Univ, 1961-1962; instr, Princeton Univ, 1959-1961; res fel physics, Magdalen Col, Oxford Univ, 1958-1959. **Memberships:** Am Asn Physics Teachers. **Research Statement & Publications:** Special theory of relativity; thermodynamics and statistical mechanics; physics teaching. **Mailing Address:** Univ Md, Dept Physics, College Park, MD 20742-4411. **E-Mail:** kacser@umd.edu

KACZMARCZYK, WALTER J, biochemical genetics; deceased, see previous edition for last biography

KACZOROWSKI, GREGORY JOHN, MEMBRANE BIOCHEMISTRY, MEMBRANE BIOPHYSICS. **Personal Data:** b South Bend, Ind, November 20, 1949; m 1982, Maria. **Education:** Univ Notre Dame, BS, 1972; Mass Inst Technol, PhD (biochem), 1977. **Professional Experience:** SR DIR, ION CHANNOLS, 1996-; dir, Dept Membrane Biochem & Biophys, Merck Inst Therapeutic Res, 1988-1996; assoc dir, Dept Membrane Biochem & Biophys, Merck Inst Therapeutic Res, 1986-1987; res fel, Dept Membrane Biochem & Biophys, Merck Inst Therapeutic Res, 1984-1986; sr res biochemist, Dept Membrane Biochem & Biophys, Merck Inst Therapeutic Res, 1980-1984; Helen Hay Whitney fel, Roche Inst Molecular biol, 1977-1980. **Memberships:** Am Soc Biol Chemists; Am Chem Soc; Biophys Soc; AAAS; NY Acad Sci Am Physicol, Soc. **Research Statement & Publications:** Membrane biochemistry; study of ion channels, especially calcium and potassium channels, as well as ion transporting; systems in electrically excitable membranes by a combination of biochemical and biophysical techniques; therapeutic drug development with ion channels as targets. **Mailing Address:** Dept ION Channels, Merck Res Lab, PO Box 2000 Rm 80n-31C, Rahway, NJ 07065-0900. **Fax:** 732-594-3925. **E-Mail:** gjk@merck.com

KACZYNSKI, DON, METALLURGICAL ENGINEERING. **Personal Data:** b Fremont, Mich, April 16, 1948. **Education:** Mich Technol Univ, BS, 1971, MS, 1973; Colo Sch Mines, PhD (metall eng), 1978. **Professional Experience:** DIR TECH, BERYLLIUM MINING, BRUSH WELLMAN ENG Mat, 1990-; Supvr res & develop, Beryllium Mining, Brush

Wellman Eng Mat, 1984-1990; sr res metallurgist, Hanna Mining Co, 1981-1984; res metallurgist, Hanna Mining Co, 1980-1981; Metallurgist, Hanna Mining Co, 1977-1980. **Memberships:** Am Soc Metals Int; Am Inst Mining; Electrochem Soc. **Research Statement & Publications:** Controlling the morphology of beryllium oxide powders, removing chlorine from copper ores, froth flotation of borate minerals and concentration of iron ores. **Mailing Address:** Brush Wellman Inc, 14710 W Portage River S Rd, Elmore, OH 43416.

KADABA, PANKAJA KOOVELI, NEUROCHEMISTRY, MEDICINAL CHEMISTRY. **Personal Data:** b Perumbavoor, India, May 15, 1928. **Education:** Travancore Univ, India, BS, 1947, MS, 1949; Univ Delhi, PhD (org chem), 1954. **Professional Experience:** RES PROF MED CHEM & PHARAMACEUT, COL PHARM, UNIV KY, 1990-; assoc, Sanders-Brown Ctr Aging, Univ Ky, 1990-1993; chmn, 9th Int Cong Heterocyclic Chem, Tokyo, Japan, 1983; prin investr, Res Proj Grant, Nat Inst Neurol Commun Dis & Stroke, NIH, 1982-1991; vis scientist, Mat Res Lab, Wright Patterson AFB, Dayton, Ohio, 1982; vis assoc prof chem, Univ Ljubljana, Yugoslavia, 1973-1974; assoc res, Col Pharm, Univ KY, 1968-1990; asst prof, Christian Bros Col, 1966-1968; assoc prof chem, Morehead State Univ, 1965-1966; instr biochem, Univ Ky, 1964-1965; res assoc, Brown Univ, 1957-1960; guest scholar, Univ Ky, 1954-1955; Fulbright-Smith-Mundt fel, 1953-1954; lectr chem, Am Mission Med Col, Vellore, India, 1949-1950 & Univ Delhi, 1950-1953; pres, Kand K Bio Sci, Inc. **Memberships:** Am Chem Soc; Int Soc Heterocyclic Chem; India Chemists & Chem Engrs Club; Am Asn Pharmaceut Scientists. **Research Statement & Publications:** Chemistry of heterocyclic compounds, their synthesis, reaction mechanisms and biological activity; 1, 2, 3-triazoles, tetrazoles, aziridinesand 1, 2, 3-triazolines; role of protic and dipolar aprotic solvents in heterocyclic synthesis via 1, 3-cycloaddition reactions; borohydride reductions of heterocyclic compounds; direct esterification of acids with alcohols using borontrifluoride-etherate catalyst; rational design of anticonvulsants, their structure-activity relationships, metabolism and pharmacology, mechanism of action and antiepileptic drug development; nmda antagonists; author of over 80 published papers and abstracts; holder of six patents; antiischemic drugs; antiparkinsonian drugs. **Mailing Address:** Div Med Chem, Univ Ky Col Pharm, Lexington, KY 40536-0082. **Fax:** 606-257-7585.

KADABA, PRASAD KRISHNA, PHYSICS, ELECTRONICS. **Personal Data:** b Bangalore, India, February 14, 1924. **Education:** Univ Mysore, BS, 1943, MS, 1944; Calif Inst Technol, MS, 1946; Univ Calif, Los Angeles, PhD (physics), 1949. **Honors & Awards:** sr Fulbright-Hays Award, Yugoslav-Am Bi-Nat Comn, 1974. **Professional Experience:** PROF EMER ELEC ENG, UNIV KY, as of 2004; Vis prof, Avionics Lab, 1981-1982; vis prof, intergovernment personnel act prog, Air Force Off Sci Res, Wright Patterson AFB Mat Lab, 1980-1981; prin investr microwave spectros proj, Ky Tobacco Res Inst, 1977-1978; prin investr proj, Off Water Resources Res Inst, 1976-; Oak Ridge Assoc Univs fel, 1976; vis scientist, Johnson Space Ctr, Houston, 1975; res fel to Yugoslavia, Int Res & Exchange Bd, 1973; prin investr microwave proj, Ky Tobacco Res Inst, 1971-1972; Ky Res Found spec fel, 1963-1964; AEC traveling fel, India, 1963-1964; prof elec eng & dir res, Univ KY, beginning 1962; assoc prof, Univ KY, 1959-1962; scholar, Univ Calif, Los Angeles, 1958-1959; consult, Fed Pac Elec Co, NJ, 1958; asst prof elec eng, Univ Ky, 1954-1957 & Newark Col Eng, 1957-1959; Alumni fel physics, Mich State Univ, 1953-1954; asst supt, Tech Develop Estab, 1952-1953; Sci officer electronics, Nat Phys Lab, India, 1950-1952; consult, IBM, Ky; mem conf elec insulation & dielec phenomena, Nat Res Coun; resident assoc, Argonne Nat Lab. **Memberships:** Am Soc Eng Educ; Brit Inst Elec Eng; sr mem Inst Elec & Electronics Engrs. **Research Statement & Publications:** Microwave absorption of organic liquids; non resonant absorption of compressed gases and molecular nature of materials; nuclear quadrupole resonance and nuclear magnetic resonance studies; biological effects of microwaves; pollution studies. **Mailing Address:** 1525 Windermere Rd Apt 104, West Chester, PA 19380.

KADABA, PRASANNA V, MECHANICAL ENGINEERING, DESIGN OF THERMAL SYSTEMS. **Personal Data:** b Gundlupet, India, July 4, 1931. **Education:** Univ Mysore, BE, 1952 & 1954, Univ Ky, MS, 1956, Ill Inst Technol, PhD (mech eng), 1964. **Honors & Awards:** Appreciation Award, Am Soc Heating, Refrig & Air-Conditioning Engrs, 1984 & 1985. **Professional Experience:** RETIRED; prof mech eng, GA Inst Technol, ending 2001; vis prof, Univ Cincinnati, 1987-1990; Lewis Res Ctr, Cleveland, Ohio, 1987; IPA fel, Lewis Res Ctr, NASA, Cleveland Ohio, 1986; Copeland Corp, Emerson Elec, Sidney, Ohio, 1984; fac fel, Marshall Space Flight Ctr, NASA, Huntsville, 1982; consult, Lawrence Berkeley Lab, Berkeley, Calif, 1979-1980; guest worker, Nat Bur Stand, Gaithersburg, MD, 1978; adv, Vol Int Tech Assistance, 1977-; vis prof, Univ Carabobo, Valencia, Venezuela, 1973 & 1975; assoc prof mech eng, Ga Inst Technol, beginning 1969; sr res scientist, Res & Develop Ctr, Westinghouse Elec Corp, Pa, 1967-1969; sr res engr, Roy C Ingersol Res Ctr, Borg-Warner Corp, 1963-1967; instr, Ill Inst Technol, 1960-1963; asst mech eng, Ill Inst Technol, 1956-1960; asst mech eng, Univ Ky, 1954-1956; mem, tech comt, TC6-3 & TC 9.6, Am Soc Heating Refrig & Air Conditioning Engrs; mem, Metric Comt, Am Soc Testing Mat. **Memberships:** Fel Am Soc Mech Engrs; fel Am Soc Heating Refrig & Air-Conditioning Engrs; Sigma Xi; Am Inst Chem Engrs; Am Soc Testing Mats. **Research Statement & Publications:** Solar energy; refrigeration; air conditioning; heat transfer; thermodynamics; mechanical systems for buildings; thermal systems design; energy conservation; productivity and efficiency; photovoltaic total energy system; heat exchangers; optimization; space power coupled photovoltaic heat engine design; thermal sciences laboratory development; second law applications to thermal systems and thermoeconomics. **Mailing Address:** Sch Mech Eng, Ga Inst Technol, Atlanta, GA 30332-0405. **E-Mail:** prasanna.kadaba@me.gatech.edu

KADAN, RANJIT SINGH, FOOD BIOCHEMISTRY, MICROBIOLOGY. **Personal Data:** b Karnal, Haryana State, India, January 1, 1935; American citizen; m 1966, Savitri; c Nina S. **Education:** Punjab Univ, DVM, 1958; Kans State Univ, MS, 1962; Rutgers Univ, New Brunswick, PhD (food sci), 1967. **Professional Experience:** SR FOOD SCIENTIST, SOUTHERN REGIONAL RES CTR, AGR RES SERV, USDA, NEW ORLEANS, 1975-; mgr, Food Products Res, Lubin Maselli Lab, Chicago, 1973-1975; sr group leader, Quaker Oats Co, Barrington, Ill, 1970-1973; sr group leader, Food Sci Dept, Rutgers Univ, 1967-1973; Consult, Volunteers Tech Assistance, 1966-; group leader food res, Quaker Oats Co, Barrington, Ill, 1966-1969; res asst food, Food Sci Dept, Rutgers Univ, 1962-1967; Vet surgeon, Punjab State, India, 1958-1960. **Memberships:** Inst Food Technologists; Am Oil Chemists Soc; Am Asn Cereal Chemists; Am Dairy Sci Asn; NY Acad Sci. **Research Statement & Publications:** Diversified food research activities in the areas of dairy, cereals, oil seeds, snacks, long shelf life food products, beverages, toxic constituents of foods including microbiological toxins, nutritional attributes of foods and value added novel foods from agricultural crops. **Mailing Address:** USDA Southern Regional Res Ctr, Food Sci Bldg, S Campus Dr, BATON ROUGE, LA 70179. **Fax:** 504-286-4419. **E-Mail:** rkadan@nrrc.ars.usda.gov

KADAN, SAVITRI SINGH, EMERGENCY MEDICINE, OBSTETRICS & GYNECOLOGY. **Personal Data:** b Sonepat, Haryana, India, August 12, 1934. **Education:** Bihar Univ, India, MD, 1958; Dipl, 1964; Patna Med Col, Patna Univ, India, MS, 1971. **Professional Experience:** Fel Family pract, Am Acad Family Pract, 1978; resident, Clarity Hosp, La State Univ, New Orleans, 1975-1977; EMERGENCY RM PHYSICIAN, ALEXIAN BROTHERS HOSP, ELKGROVE, 1974-; dir, Cook County Venereal Dis Clin, Maywood, Ill, 1974-1975; emergency rm physician, Northwest Community Hosp, 1973; resident, Lutheran Gen Hosp, Park Ridge, Ill, 1969-1970; intern, St Fransic Hosp, Evanston, Ill, 1968-1969; Asst prof obstet & gynec, Patna Med Col, 1964-1967. **Memberships:** Am Acad Family Pract. **Research Statement & Publications:** Obstetrics; gynecology. **Mailing Address:** 8554 Fordham Ct, New Orleans, LA 70127.

KADANE, JOSEPH BORN, APPLIED STATISTICS, MATHEMATICAL STATISTICS. **Personal Data:** b Washington, DC, January 10, 1941. **Education:** Harvard Univ, BA, 1962; Stanford Univ, PhD (statist), 1966. **Professional Experience:** LEONARD J SAVAGE PROF, DEPT STATIST, CARNEGIE-MELLON UNIV, 1985-; PROF STATIST & SOCIAL SCI, DEPT STATIST, CARNEGIE-MELLON UNIV, 1972-; head, Dept Statist, 1972-1981; assoc prof, Dept Statist, Carnegie-mellon Univ, 1971-1972; staff analyst, Ctr Naval Anal, 1968-1971; res staff mem, Cowles Found Res Econ, Yale Univ, 1966-1968; asst prof statist, Yale Univ, 1966-1968. **Memberships:** Fel Am Statist Asn; fel Inst Math Statist; fel Royal Statist Soc; fel AAAS; Biometric Soc; Econometric Soc. **Research Statement & Publications:** Theory and use of statistics in economics, political science, sociology, demography, law, medicine, archeology, oceanography, environment. **Mailing Address:** Dept Statist, Carnegie-Mellon Univ, Baker Hall 232E, Pittsburgh, PA 15213. **Fax:** 412-268-7828. **E-Mail:** kadane@stat.cmu.edu

KADANKA, ZDENEK KAREL, CYTOGENETICS, BIOCHEMISTRY. **Personal Data:** b Rajhrad, Czech, May 24, 1933. **Education:** Purkyne Univ, Brno, dipl chem & RNDr, 1957, dipl med & MUDr, 1963; Inst Postgrad Studies for Physicians & Pharmacists, Prague, dipl, 1966. **Professional Experience:** PVT PRACT, 1985-; sr res asst, res assoc Karyology, 1971-1985; NIH grants, 1971-1972; sr res asst, Connaught Med Res Labs, Univ Toronto, 1969-1971; Gertrude l'Anson fel, Connaught Med Res Labs, Univ Toronto, 1969-1970; intern, Sanatorium, Luhacovice, Czech, 1966-1969; physician allergy & diabetes, Sanatorium, Luhacovice, Czech, 1963-1966; Lectr histol & embryol, Med Fac, Purkyne Univ, Brno, 1959-1963. **Research Statement & Publications:** Karyologic data; cell membrane changes; transformation of human and animal cells cultured in vitro. **Mailing Address:** 64 Gwendolen Crescent, Willowdale, ON M2N 2L7, Can.

KADANOFF, LEO P, THEORETICAL PHYSICS, APPLIED MATHEMATICS. **Personal Data:** b New York, NY, January 14, 1937; m 1978, Ruth; c Michal, Betsy, Felice & & Marcia. **Education:** Harvard Univ, AB, 1957, MA, 1958, PhD (physics), 1960. **Honorary Degrees:** DSc, Copenhagen Univ, 2000. **Honors & Awards:** Buckley Prize, Am Phys Soc, 1977; Wolf Found Award, 1980; Boltzmann Medal, Int Union Pure & Appl Physics, 1989; Grande Medialle d'Or, French Acad Sci, 1998; Nat Medal Sci, US, 1999. **Professional Experience:** JOHN D MACARTHUR DISTINGUISHED SREV PROF EMER PHYSICS & MATH, UNIV CHICAGO, 1982-; Mem adv comt, Univ Minn, 1986-; mem, Bd Physics & Astron, Nat Res Coun, 1983-; vchmn, Sci & Tech Adv Comt, Argonne Nat Lab, 1983-1984; mem adv comt, Schlumberger Doll Res Lab, 1981-1986; dir, Mat Res Lab, Univ Chicago, 1981-1984; PROF PHYSICS, UNIV CHICAGO, 1978-; mem adv comt, Inst Theoret Physics, Santa Barbara, 1978-1981; prof eng, Brown Univ, 1971-1978; univ prof physics, Brown Univ, 1969-1978; prof physics, Univ Ill, 1965-1969; vis prof, Cambridge Univ, Eng, 1965; from asst prof to assoc prof physics, Univ Ill, Urbana, 1962-1964; A P Sloan Found fel, 1962-1967; Res fel, Bohr Inst Theoret Studies, Copenhagen, 1960-1962. **Memberships:** Nat Acad Sci; fel Am Phys Soc; fel Am Acad Arts & Sci; fel AAAS; fel Am Philos Soc. **Research Statement & Publications:** Solid state and many particle theory; development of urban growth models; phenomena near phase transitions; behavior of dynamical systems; turbulence; chaos; network theory, hydrodynamics; published over 350 articles. **Mailing Address:** Dept Physics, James Franck Inst Univ Chicago, Off 109 5640 S Ellis Ave, Chicago, IL 60637. **Fax:** 773-702-2172. **E-Mail:** l-kadanoff@uchicago.edu

KADAR, DEZSO, PHARMACOLOGY. **Personal Data:** b Zazar, Transylvania, July 21, 1933; Canadian citizen; m 1957, c 2. **Education:** Univ Toronto, BS, 1959, MS, 1966, PhD (pharmacol), 1968. **Professional Experience:** UNDERGRAD SECY, UNIV TORONTO, as of 1999; PROF PHARMACOL, UNIV TORONTO, as of 1998; assoc prof pharmacol, Univ Toronto, beginning 1976; Comt Drugs & Therapeut, St Joseph's Hosp, 1974- & Coun Fac Pharm, Univ Toronto, 1973-; Mem, Drug Adv Comt, Ont Col Pharmacists, 1972-; asst prof, Connaught Med Res Lab, 1970-1976; lectr, Connaught Med Res Lab, 1968-1970; demonstr, Connaught Med Res Lab, 1965-1968; Res asst pharmacol & toxicol, Connaught Med Res Lab, 1960-1965. **Memberships:** Pharmacol Soc Can. **Research Statement & Publications:** Drug metabolism and disposition in man and animals; microsomal drug oxidation in vitro. **Mailing Address:** Dept Pharmacol, Univ Toronto Fac Med, Toronto, ON M5S 1A8, Can. **Fax:** 416-978-6395.

KADAR, IVAN, AERONAUTICS. **Education:** City Col CUNY, BE; Columbia Univ, MS; Polytech Inst NY, PhD (elec eng). **Professional Experience:** TECH ADV, INFO FUSION TECHNOL, GRUMMAN NORTHROP CORP, as of 2006. **Mailing Address:** Grumman Northrop Aeronaut & Elec, M/S B35-35, Bethpage, NY 11714. **Fax:** 408-933-4956. **E-Mail:** ivan_kadar@atdc.northgrum.com

KADEKARO, MASSAKO, BODY FLUID BALANCE & VASOPRESSIN, OXYTOCIN & ANGIOTENSIN II. **Personal Data:** b Brazil, January 18, 1939. **Education:** Univ Sao Paulo, Brazil, PhD (neural regulation gastric secretion), 1970. **Professional Experience:** Dir, Neurosurg Res Lab, Med Br, Univ Tex, beginning 1984; PROF SURG, MED BR, UNIV TEX, GALVESTON, 1984-; vis scientist, Lab Cerebral Metabol, Nat Inst Mental Health, Bethesda, Md, 1977-1984; mem, Neurol Study Sect, NIH. **Memberships:** Soc Neuroscience; Am Physiol Soc; NY Acad Sci; Sigma Xi; AAAS; Integrative, Functional & Cognitive Neuroscience. **Research Statement & Publications:** Neural regulation of water balance; modulatory influence of nitric oxide on neural circuitry regulating water drinking behavior; vasopressin and oxytocin secretion and arterial blood pressure. **Mailing Address:** Dept Surg, Univ Tex Med Br, 301 Univ Blvd, Galveston, TX 77555-0517. **Fax:** 409-772-6352. **E-Mail:** mkutyna@utmb.edu

KADER, ADEL ABDEL, PLANT PHYSIOLOGY, HORTICULTURE. **Personal Data:** b Cairo, Egypt, March 1, 1941. **Education:** Univ Ain Shams, Cairo, BSc, 1959; Univ Calif, Davis, MSc, 1962, PhD (plant physiol), 1966. **Honors & Awards:** Asgrow Award, Am Soc Hort Sci, 1978; Nat Food Processors Award, Am Soc Hort Sci, 1980. **Professional Experience:** PROF POMOL, UNIV CALIF, DAVIS, 1982-; from asst prof to assoc prof, Univ Calif, Davis, 1978-1982; asst res plant physiol, Univ Calif, Davis, 1972-1977; consult, Agr Inst, Kuwait, 1971-1972; Lectr hort, Univ Ain Shams, Cairo, 1966-1971. **Memberships:** Fel Am Soc Hort Sci (pres, 1996); Am Soc Plant Physiologists; Inst Food Technologists; Int Soc Hort Sci; Coun Agr Sci & Technol. **Research Statement & Publications:** Postharvest biology and technology of horticultural crops; quality evaluation and maintenance of harvested fruits; controlled atmospheres; Effects of CO2 on ethylene biosynthesis in 'Bartlett' pears. **Mailing Address:** Dept Pomol, Univ Calif, 2049 Wickson Hall, Davis, CA 95616-8683. **Fax:** 530-752-8502. **E-Mail:** aakader@ucdavis.edu

KADESCH, ROBERT R, physics; deceased, see previous edition for last biography

KADEY, FREDERIC L, JR, economic geology, industrial minerals exploration & evaluation; deceased, see previous edition for last biography

KADIN, ALAN MITCHELL, SUPERCONDUCTING THIN FILMS & DEVICES, THIN FILM DEPOSITION & PROPERTIES. **Personal Data:** b Brooklyn, NY, December 7, 1952. **Education:** Princeton Univ, BA, 1974; Harvard Univ, MA, 1975, PhD (physics), 1979. **Professional Experience:** SR SCI, HYPRES, INC, 2000-; assoc prof elec eng, Univ Rochester, 1987-2000; res physicist, Energy ConversionDevices, Inc, 1983-1987; Res assoc, Univ Minn, 1981-1983; Res assoc, State Univ NY, Stony Brook, 1979-1980. **Memberships:** Am Phys Soc. **Research Statement & Publications:** Superconducting thin films and devices; nonequilibrium phenomena; thin film deposition and properties. **Mailing Address:** HYPRES, Inc, 175 Clearbrook Rd, Elmsford, NY 10523. **E-Mail:** kadin@hypres.com

KADIRVEL, VELMURUGAN, CIRCUIT DESIGN, LOGIC DESIGN. **Personal Data:** b Madras, India, August 15, 1967. **Education:** Anna Univ, India, BE, 1989; Tex A&M Univ, MS, 1992. **Professional Experience:** DESIGN ENGR, MOTOROLA SEMICONDUCTOR PROD SECT, 1992-. **Memberships:** Inst Elec & Electronics Engrs; Inst Elec & Electronics Engrs Comput Soc. **Mailing Address:** 3324 N Lakeharbor Lane G306, Boise, ID 81703-6255. **E-Mail:** vzgr20@email.sps.mot.com

KADIS, BARNEY MORRIS, BIOCHEMISTRY. **Personal Data:** b Omaha, Nebr, December 26, 1927. **Education:** Univ Nebr, BA, 1952; Iowa State Univ, PhD (chem), 1957. **Professional Experience:** RETIRED; prof med sci, Sch Med, Mercer Univ, 1982-1994; vis prof, Univ Calif Med Ctr, 1975-1976; prof biochem, Dept Dent Med, 1974-1982; assoc prof, Southern Ill Univ, 1970-1974; chmn, Dept Dent Med, 1970-1973; assoc prof biol sci, Southern Ill Univ, 1969-1970; fel anat, Sch Med, Stanford Univ, 1967-1969; fel, Inst Hormone Biol, Syntex Res, 1966-1967; asst prof biochem, Col Med, Univ Nebr, Omaha, 1962-1966; res asst prof obstet & gynec, Col Med, Univ Nebr, Omaha, 1961-1966; assoc prof chem, State Univ NY, Albany, 1960-1961; res chemist, Col Med, Univ Nebr, 1958-1960; asst prof, Dubuque Univ, 1957-1958; asst chem, Iowa State Univ, 1952-1957. **Memberships:** AAAS; Am Chem Soc; Endocrine Soc; Am Soc Biochem & Molecular Biol; Sigma Xi; Am Col Sports Med; Am Soc Bone & Mineral Res; Am Soc Cell Biol. **Research Statement & Publications:** Metabolism of bone cells in culture. **Mailing Address:** 13023 Frances St, Omaha, NE 68144.

KADIS, SOLOMON, microbiology; deceased, see previous edition for last biography

KADIS, VINCENT WILLIAM, MICROBIOLOGY, BIOCHEMISTRY. **Personal Data:** b Seinai, Lithuania, September 25, 1922. **Education:** Univ Sask, BA, 1955; Purdue Univ, MSc, 1957, PhD (microbiol, biochem), 1960. **Professional Experience:** RETIRED; pvt consult, 1990-1991; dir, Food Lab Serv, 1961-1990; microbiologist, Alta Dept Agr, Can, 1957-1961; consult, anal fields of foods & other agr commodities, food qual-safety anal & planning anal labs. **Memberships:** Fel Am Pub Health Asn; Am Inst Food Technologists; Sigma Xi; Can Inst Food Sci & Technol (pres, 1977-1978); Am Soc Microbiol. **Research Statement & Publications:** Bacteriophage of lactic cultures; Q-fever infection in humans and animals; detection and persistence of chlorinated insecticides in human and animal blood; insecticide residues in food; food sanitation, quality and safety; laboratory planning and design. **Mailing Address:** Unit 903 109 St, Edmonton, AB T6J 6R1, Can.

KADISH, KARL MITCHELL, ANALYTICAL CHEMISTRY. **Personal Data:** b Detroit, Mich, February 4, 1945. **Education:** Univ Mich, BS, 1967; Pa State Univ, PhD (chem), 1970. **Honors & Awards:** Sigma Xi Res Award, 1988. **Professional Experience:** Mem, Anal Div Comt, 1994-; Univ Rome La Torgavata, Italy, 1990 & 1991; secy, Comn V.5 Electroanal Chem, Int Union Pure & Appl Chem, 1988-1992; Ecole Superieure Chem, Lyon, France, 1984 & Univ Dijon, France, 1985, 1987, 1988, 1991 & 1993; PROF CHEM, UNIV HOUSTON, 1981-; vis prof, Univ Louis Pasteur, Strasbourg, France, 1980-1981; assoc chmn, Univ Houston, 1979-1984; from asst prof to assoc prof, Univ Houston, 1976-1981; pres, Inter Sci Consults, USA, 1975-; asst prof chem, Calif State Univ, Fullerton, 1972-1976; res asst, Nat Ctr Sci Res, France, 1971-1972; vis asst prof chem, Univ New Orleans, 1970-1971. **Memberships:** Am Chem Soc; Electrochem Soc; Sigma Xi; fel Royal Soc Chem. **Research Statement & Publications:** Over 450 publications; analytical chemistry; electro-and bioanalytical chemistry; rates and mechanisms of electron transferin; biologically important compounds; reactions of porphyrin metal complexes; redox reactions of transition metal complexes and dinuclears metal-metal bonded complexes; spectroelectrochemistry; fullerene chemistry; published over 35 books. **Mailing Address:** Dept Chem, Univ Houston, Houston, TX 77204-5641. **Fax:** 713-743-2745. **E-Mail:** kkadish@uh.edu

KADISON, RICHARD VINCENT, MATHEMATICS & FUNCTIONAL ANALYSIS, OPERATOR ALGEBRAS & QUANTUM MECHANICS. **Personal Data:** b New York, NY, July 25, 1925. **Education:** Univ Chicago, MS, 1947, PhD, 1950. **Honorary Degrees:** Dr, Univ d'Aix-Marseille, 1986, Univ Copenhagen, 1987. **Honors & Awards:** Steele Prize for Lifetime Achievement awarded by Am Mathematical Soc 1999. **Professional Experience:** Guggenheim fel, 1969-1970; KUEMMERLE PROF MATH, UNIV PA, 1964-; Sloan fel, 1958-1962; Fulbright res grant, Denmark, 1954-1955; from asst prof to prof, Columbia Univ, 1952-1964; mem, Off Naval Res Contract, 1951-1952; Nat Res Coun fel math, Inst Advan Study, 1950-1951. **Memberships:** Nat Acad Sci; foreign mem Royal Danish Acad Sci & Lett; Sigma Xi; foreign mem Norweg Acad Sci & Lett; Am Math Soc. **Research Statement & Publications:** Spectral theory; group representation; topological algebra; non-communtative analysis; con Neumann algebras; C- algebras; math physics. **Mailing Address:** Dept Math, Univ Pa, 209 S 33rd St, Philadelphia, PA 19104-6395. **Fax:** 215-573-4063. **E-Mail:** kadison@math.upenn.edu

KADKADE, PRAKASH GOPAL, PLANT PHYSIOLOGY, PLANT BIOCHEMISTRY. **Personal Data:** b Goa, India, September 10, 1941. **Education:** Bombay Univ, BSc, 1962, MSc, 1964; St Louis Univ, PhD (biol), 1970. **Professional Experience:** SCIENTIST, PHYTON INC, ITHACA, NY, as of 2005; MEM TECH STAFF PLANT PHYSIOL, GEN TEL & ELECTRONICS LAB, 1974-; vis prof molecular biol, Cath Univ, PR, 1974; Vis scientist plant biochem, Cent Am Res Inst, 1974; sr res chemist cereal chem, Anheuser Busch Inc, 1973-1974; vis scientist natural prod, Cent Am Res Inst, 1971-1973; Fel, plant biochem, St Louis Univ, 1970-1971. **Memberships:** AAAS; Am Inst Biol Sci; Am Inst Plant Physiologists; Int Soc Plant Cell & Tissue Cult; Sigma Xi. **Research Statement & Publications:** Understanding of mechanisms of light actions on certain plant biological and chemical processes. **Mailing Address:** Phyto Inc, 125 Langmuir Lab 95 Brown Rd, Ithaca, NY 14850-1257. **Fax:** 607-257-5515. **E-Mail:** pgkadkade@aol.com

KADKO, DAVID C, MARINE SCIENCES. **Education:** Brooklyn Col, BS, 1973; Columbia Univ, MA, 1974, MPhil, 1975, PhD (oceanog), 1981. **Professional Experience:** PROF, ROSENSTIEL SCH MARINE & ATMOSPHERIC CHEM, UNIV MIAMI, 1996-; prog mgr, nat sci found (NSF), 1999; Fulbright fel, 1996; assoc prof, Rosenstiel Sch Marine & Atmospheric Chem, Univ Miami, 1990-1996; asst prof, Ore State Univ, 1989-1990; res assoc, Ore State Univ, 1983-1988; Nat Res Coun fel, US Geol Surv, Menlo Park, Calif, 1981-1983; Doctoral fel, NSF, 1975-1978. **Memberships:** Am Soc Limnol & Oceanog; Am Geophys Union; Sigma Xi. **Research Statement & Publications:** Author of numerous publications. **Mailing Address:** Div Marine & Atmospheric Chem, Univ Miami, 4600 Rickenbacker Causeway, Miami, FL 33149-1098.

KADLEC, JOHN A, WILDLIFE MANAGEMENT, ECOLOGY. **Personal Data:** b Racine, Wis, September 22, 1931. **Education:** Univ Mich, BSF, 1952, MS, 1956, PhD (wildlife mgt), 1960. **Professional Experience:** PROF EMER WILDLIFE SCI, COL NATURAL RESOURCES, UTAH STATE UNIV, 1974-; head dept, Col Natural Resources, Utah State Univ, 1974-1980; from assoc prof to prof resource ecol, Univ Mich, Ann Arbor & prog coordr anal ecosyst, Int Biol Prog, 1971-1974; res assoc & asst prof wildlife mgt, Univ Mich, Ann Arbor & prog coordr anal ecosyst, Int Biol Prog, 1968-1971; Res biologist, Mich Dept Conserv, 1958-1963 & US Bur Sport Fisheries & Wildlife, 1963-1967. **Memberships:** AAAS; Wildlife Soc; Ecol Soc Am. **Research Statement & Publications:** Applications of population ecology and systems ecology to resource management, especially wildlife; animal habitat studies; wetland ecology. **Mailing Address:** Col Natural Resources, Utah State Univ, Logan, UT 84322-5230. **Fax:** 435-797-3976. **E-Mail:** jkadlec@cc.usu.edu

KADLEC, ROBERT HENRY, CHEMICAL ENGINEERING. **Personal Data:** b Racine, Wis, June 11, 1938. **Education:** Univ Wisconsin, BS, 1958; Univ Mich, MS, 1959, PhD (chem eng), 1962. **Professional Experience:** PROF EMER CHEM ENG, UNIV MICH, ANN ARBOR, as of 1997; ed, Am Inst Chem Engrs J, 1976-1985; prof, Univ Mich, Ann Arbor, beginning 1970; from asst prof to assoc prof, Univ Mich, Ann Arbor, 1961-1970. **Memberships:** Am Inst Chem Engrs; Water Pollution Control Fedn; Soc Wetland Sci; Nat Soc Prof Engrs; Int Asn Water Qual. **Research Statement & Publications:** Chemical reactors; water quality; mathematical modelling; simulation; wetlands; wastewater. **Mailing Address:** Dept Chem Eng, 2300 Hayward St, Rm 3074 Herbert H Dow Bldg, Ann Arbor, MI 48109-2136. **Fax:** 734-763-0459. **E-Mail:** rhkad@umich.edu

KADLUBAR, FRED F, TOXICOLOGY, ONCOLOGY. **Personal Data:** b Dallas, Tex, March 1, 1946. **Education:** Univ Dallas, BA, 1968; Univ Tex, Austin, PhD (chem), 1973. **Professional Experience:** DIR, DIV MOLECULAR EPIDEMOL, NAT CTR TOXICOL RES, 1995-; assoc dir res, Nat Ctr Toxicol Res, 1988-1995; mem, Working Cadre Nat Bladder Cancer Proj, 1980-1984; dir, Div Biochem Toxicol, 1979-1989; Adj prof, Dept Biochem, Dept Pharmacol & Toxicol, Univ Ark, Little Rock, 1977-; chemist, Div Molecular Biol, 1976-1979; fel, McArdle Lab Cancer Res, Univ Wis, Madison, 1973-1976. **Memberships:** Am Asn Cancer Res; Sigma Xi; AAAS; Am Chem Soc; Am Soc Biol Chemists. **Research Statement & Publications:** Biochemical mechanisms of chemical carcinogenesis with emphasis on aromatic amines and nitroaromatics and liver, bladder, and colon carcinogenisis; detoxification by glutathione and structure properties of carcinogen DNA adducts. **Mailing Address:** Molecular Epidemiol, Nat Ctr Toxicol Res, 3900 NCTR Rd, Jefferson, AR 72079. **Fax:** 870-543-7773. **E-Mail:** fkadlubar@nctr.fda.gov

KADNER, CARL GEORGE, INSECT PHYSIOLOGY. **Personal Data:** b Oakland, Calif, May 23, 1911; m 1939, Beth Moran; c Robert J, Grace K (Wickersham) & Carl L. **Education:** Univ San Francisco, BS, 1933; Univ Calif, Berkeley, MS, 1936, PhD (med entom), 1941. **Professional Experience:** PROF EMER BIOL, LOYOLA MARYMOUNT UNIV, 1978-; parasitologist, US Army, 1943-1946; prof & chmn dept, Loyola Marymount Univ, 1941-1978; Instr biol, Loyola Marymount Univ, 1936-1941. **Memberships:** Entom Soc Am; Sigma Xi. **Research Statement & Publications:** Nutritional requirements of Dipteran larvae. **Mailing Address:** 8100 Loyola Blvd, Los Angeles, CA 90045-2639.

KADNER, ROBERT JOSEPH, TRANSPORTER MECHANISM, GENE REGULATION. **Personal Data:** b Los Angeles, Calif, March 19, 1942; m 1967, Carole; c Kristen E & Robert J. **Education:** Loyola Univ, Los Angeles, BS, 1963; Univ Calif, Los Angeles, PhD (biol chem), 1967. **Honors & Awards:** Gradute Teaching Award, Am Soc Microbiol, 1998; Wellcome Vis Prof, 2001; Res Career develop Award, NIH, 1975-1980. **Professional Experience:** VICE CHAIR MICROBIOL, SCH MED, UNIV VA, as of 2005; Ed, Journ Bocteriology, 1998-; mem, Personal C Rev Panel, Am Cancer Soc, 1989-1993; lectr microbiol, Am Soc Microbiol Found, 1988-1989; PROF MICROBIOL, SCH MED, UNIV VA, 1980-; from asst prof to assoc prof, Sch Med, Univ VA, 1969-1980; Nat Cancer Inst, fel, microbiol Med Sch, NY Univ, 1967-1969. **Memberships:** Am Soc Microbiol; Am Soc Biol Chemists. **Research Statement & Publications:** Genetics and biochemistry of transport in Escherichia coli; bacterial genetics and regulation. **Mailing Address:** Dept Microbiol, Sch Med Univ Va, PO Box 800734 7230 Jordan Hall, Charlottesville, VA 22908-0001. **Fax:** 434-982-1071. **E-Mail:** rjk@virginia.edu

KADO, CLARENCE ISAO, MOLECULAR BIOLOGY, PLANT PATHOLOGY. **Personal Data:** b Santa Rosa, Calif, June 10, 1936. **Education:** Univ Calif, Berkeley, BS, 1959, PhD, 1964. **Honors & Awards:** Rolex Award, 1989. **Professional Experience:** PROF PLANT PATHOL, UNIV CALIF, DAVIS, as of 2005; dir, fallen leaf lake conf, 1985-; Ctr Etude Radiobiol Molecular, Belg, Univ Hawaii, Honolulu, 1982; Friedrich Miescher Inst, Basel, Switz, 1992; HEAD, DAVIS CROWN GALL GROUP, UNIV CALIF, DAVIS PROF PLANT PATHOL, UNIV CALIF, DAVIS, 1976-; sabbatical leave, Dept Molecular, Cellular & Develop Biol, Univ Colo, Boulder, 1975; NATO sr fel, Ctr Study Nuclear Energy, Mol, Belg, 1974-1975; Vis prof, Univ Colo, Boulder, 1973; asst res biochemist, Univ Calif, Berkeley, 1967-1968; from asst prof to assoc prof, Fallen Leaf Lake Conf, 1966-1976; Res fel virus lab, Univ Calif, Berkeley, 1964-1967. **Memberships:** AAAS; Am Soc Microbiol; fel Am Phytopath Soc; NY Acad Sci; Sigma Xi; fel Am Acad Microbiol; Am Soc Molecular Biol & Biochem; Am Chem Soc; Int Soc Molecular Plant-Microbe Interaction. **Research Statement & Publications:** Molecular biology of host-pathogen interactions; molecular mechanism of tumorigenesis and abnormal growth in higher cells; plant bacteriology. **Mailing Address:** Dept Plant Path, Univ Calif, 162 Robbins Off 752-0325 Lab, Davis, CA 95616. **Fax:** 530-752-5674. **E-Mail:** cikado@ucdavis.edu

KADOR, PETER FRITZ, MEDICINAL CHEMISTRY. **Personal Data:** b Regensburg, Ger, October 3, 1949; American citizen; m 1976, c 2. **Education:** Capital Univ, BA, 1972; Ohio State Univ, PhD (med chem), 1976. **Honors & Awards:** Rhoto Cataract Res Award, 1981; Alcon Res Found award, 1986; Fed Cross Merit Ger Gov, 1994; Kinoshita Lect, Nat Found Eye Res, 1995. **Professional Experience:** PROF & CHAIR DEPT PHARMACEUTICAL SCI, COL PHARMACY, UNIV NEBRASKA, 2002-; Exec Pres, nat found eye res, 1999-; Chief lab ocular theraputic, Nat Eye Inst, NIH, 1991-2002; Head Molecular Pharmacol sect, Nat, Eye ins, NIH, 1985-1991; Res Chem, Nat Eye Inst, NIH, 1979-1985; NIH, Staff Fel Res, Nat eye Inst, 1976-1979; CHIEF LAB OCULAR THERAPEUT, NAT EYE INST, NIH, 1991-; Chief Molecular Pharmacol, Nat Eye Inst, NIH, 1985-1991; res chemist, Nat Eye Inst, NIH, 1979-1985; NIH, Staff fel res, Nat Eye Inst, 1976-1979. **Memberships:** Am Chem Soc; Asn Res Vision & Ophthal; Am Diabetes Asn; Asn Ocular Pharmacol & Therapeut; Int Soc Eye Res. **Research Statement & Publications:** Cataract development; drug effects on the lens; aldose reductase inhibitors; diabetic complications; ocular pharmacology; An aldehyde scavenging enzyme in the intraneuronal metabolism of norepinephrine in human sympathetic ganglia. **Mailing Address:** Dept Pharmaceutical Sci, Univ Nebr Med ctr, 986025 Nebr Med Ctr, Omaha, NE 68198-6025. **Fax:** 402-559-9543. **E-Mail:** pkador@unmc.edu

KADOTA, T THEODORE, MATHEMATICS, COMMUNICATIONS. **Personal Data:** b Ehime-ken, Japan, November 14, 1930; American citizen; m 1978, Charlie; c Mari, Amy & Kim. **Education:** Yokohama Nat Univ, BS, 1953; Univ Calif, Berkeley, MS, 1956, PhD (elec eng), 1960. **Professional Experience:** RETIRED; mem staff math, AT&T Bell Labs Inc, 1960-1993; res asst, Univ Calif, Berkeley, 1956-1960; teaching asst, Univ Calif, Berkeley, 1955-1956. **Memberships:** Fel Inst Elec & Electronics Engrs. **Research Statement & Publications:** Mathematical research in communication and information theory, specifically, application of probability theory and stochastic processes to detection, estimation, information theory; model making; theorem proving. **Mailing Address:** 6750 Hawaii Kai Dr 904, Honolulu, HI 96825-1542.

KADOUM, AHMED MOHAMED, ENTOMOLOGY, TOXICOLOGY. **Personal Data:** b October 28, 1937. **Education:** Univ Alexandria, BSc, 1958; Univ Nebr, MSc, 1963, PhD (entom), 1966. **Professional Experience:** RETIRED; asst prof entom, Kans State Univ, beginning 1966; instr toxicol, Univ Nebr, 1965-1966; res asst entom, Univ Nebr, 1962-1965; Instr chem, Univ Alexandria, 1958-1960. **Research Statement & Publications:** Pesticidal chemistry and toxicology. **Mailing Address:** 10416 Conser St 101, Overland Park, KS 66204.

KADOWITZ, PHILLIP J, PHARMACOLOGY. **Personal Data:** b Newark, NJ, March 20, 1941; m Ellen; c Nancy & Rebacca. **Education:** Rutgers Univ, BS, 1963; Sch Med, Marquette Univ, PhD (pharmacol), 1968. **Professional Experience:** PROF PHARMACOL, TULANE UNIV MED SCH, AS OF 2006; Chmn, Cardiopulmonary Coun, Am Heart Asn, 1990-1992; from asst prof to assoc prof, Tulane Univ Med Sch, 1971-1978; Fel pharmacol, Univ Iowa, 1968-1971. **Memberships:** Am Heart Asn; Am Soc Pharmacol & Exp Therapeut. **Mailing Address:** Dept Pharmacol, Tulane Univ Sch Med, 1430 Tulane Ave, New Orleans, LA 70112-2699. **Fax:** 504-588-5283. **E-Mail:** pkadowi@tulane.edu

KADYK, JOHN AMOS, DETECTOR DEVELOPMENT. **Personal Data:** b Springfield, Ill, November 10, 1929; m Ann; c Lisa Catherine & John Christopher. **Education:** Williams Col, AB, 1952; Mass Inst Technol, BS, 1952; Calif Inst Technol, PhD (physics), 1957. **Professional Experience:** RETIRED EXP PHYSICIST, LAWRENCE BERKELEY LAB, UNIV CALIF, 1959-; Instr physics, Univ Mich, 1957-1959. **Memberships:** Am Phys Soc. **Research Statement & Publications:** High energy physics; colliding beams (at SLAC). Detector development for International Linear Collider. **Mailing Address:** Lawrence Berkeley Lab, Univ Calif, Ms 50A-2170, One Cyclotron Rd, Berkeley, CA 94720. **Fax:** 510-495-2957. **E-Mail:** jakadyk@lbl.gov

KAELBER, CHARLES THEODORE, PSYCHOPATHOLOGY. **Personal Data:** b Cardington, Ohio, February 25, 1938. **Education:** Harvard Univ, MPH, 1967, DrPH, 1969; Case Western Reserve Univ, MD, 1975. **Professional Experience:** ACTG CHIEF, EPIDEMIOL & PSYCHOPATH RES BR, EPIDEMIOL & SERV RES DIV, NIMH, NIH, as of 2004; CHIEF PSYCHOPATH RES, NIMH, NIH, 1987-. **Memberships:** Am Psychiat Asn. **Mailing Address:** Epidemiol & Serv Res Div, NIMH, NIH, Rm 8184, 6001 Exec Blvd, MSC 9663, Rockville, MD 20892-9663. **Fax:** 301-443-4279. **E-Mail:** ckaelber@nih.gov

KAELBLE, DAVID HARDIE, INTELLIGENT SYSTEMS, TECHNICAL MANAGEMENT. **Personal Data:** b Pine City, Minn, June 2, 1928. **Education:** Univ Minn, Minneapolis, BSc, 1951. **Honors & Awards:** Adhesion Award, Am Soc Test & Mat, 1963. **Professional Experience:** Chmn, Gordon Conf Thermosetts, 1981; DIR, ARROYO COMPUT CTR, 1980-; mem tech staff, group leader polymer & Composites Group, 1975-1980; chmn, Gordon Conf Adhesion, 1971; Mem comt damping nomenclature, Am Standards Asn, 1963-1965 & comt adhesion, Nat Res Coun, 1971; mem tech staff, Sci Ctr, Rockwell Int Corp, 1969-1975; res specialist, Cent Res Labs, 3M Co, 1961-1969; sr res chemist, Cent Res Labs, 3M Co, 1956-1961; Res chemist, Cent Res Labs, 3M Co, 1951-1956. **Memberships:** Am Chem Soc; Soc Rheol; Adhesion Soc. **Research Statement & Publications:** Adhesion phenomena including surface chemistry, rheology, and fracture mechanics; polymer physical chemistry and mechanical properties; biophysics and composite material properties; cognitive science; computer modeling; intelligent systems; technical management. **Mailing Address:** Arroyo Comput Ctr, 730 Blue Oak Ave, Thousand Oaks, CA 91320.

KAELBLE, EMMETT FRANK, ANALYTICAL CHEMISTRY, SPECTROSCOPY. **Personal Data:** b St Louis, Mo, July 31, 1931; m 1955, Martha; c Alan, Lynne, Steven & Tam Tang. **Education:** DePauw Univ, BA, 1953; Univ Ill, MS, 1955, PhD (anal chem), 1957. **Professional Experience:** ASSOC, CHELAN ASSOCS, 1987-; sr res group leader, appl tech, 1978-1986; res group leader, Res Dept, Inorg Chem Div, Monsanto Co, 1964-1978; From res chemist to sr res chemist, Monsanto Indust Chem Co, 1957-1964. **Memberships:** Am Chem Soc; Soc Appl Spectros. **Research Statement & Publications:** X-ray spectroscopy; chromatography; other instrumental and chemical analytical techniques. **Mailing Address:** 641 Windrush Dr, Kirkwood, MO 63122-3054.

KAELLIS, JOSEPH, HEAT TRANSFER, HEAT EXCHANGERS, MASS TRANSFER. **Personal Data:** b Philadelphia, Pa, July 6, 1925. **Education:** City Col NY, BS, 1949; Univ Mo, MS, 1950; Ill Inst Technol, PhD (chem eng), 1970. **Professional Experience:** CONSULT, PVT PRACT, 1981-; chief engr, Basic Technol Inc, 1980-1981; TRW Inc, 1977-1980; C F Braun & Co, 1974-1977; Advan Reactors Div, Westinghouse Elec Corp, 1972-1974; assoc engr, Argonne Nat Lab, 1955-1972; asst engr, Griscom Russel Co, 1950-1955; Pres, Kaellis Eng. **Memberships:** Am Inst Chem Engrs; Am Nuclear Soc; Sigma Xi. **Research Statement & Publications:** Computer technique used to determine the simultaneous transient developing mass momentum boundary layer resulting from the flow of a fluid through a channel having walls which dissolve; advanced concepts in heat exchange design. **Mailing Address:** 5700 Etiwanda Ave, Tarzana, CA 91356. **E-Mail:** hxengkaellis@aol.com

KAEMPFFER, FREDERICK AUGUSTUS, THEORETICAL PHYSICS. **Personal Data:** b Gorlitz, Ger, November 29, 1920. **Education:** Univ Gottingen, dipl physics, 1943, Dr rer nat(physics), 1948. **Professional Experience:** PROF EMER PHYSICS, UNIV BC, 1986-; from asst prof to prof, UNIV BC, 1949-1985; lectr, 1948. **Memberships:** Am Phys Soc. **Research Statement & Publications:** Theory of fields. **Mailing Address:** 2054 Western Pkwy, Vancouver, BC V6T 1V5, Can.

KAESBERG, PAUL JOSEPH, VIROLOGY. **Personal Data:** b Engers, Ger, September 26, 1923. **Education:** Univ Wis, BS, 1945, PhD (physics & math), 1949. **Honorary Degrees:** DSc, Univ Leiden, Neth, 1975. **Professional Experience:** PROF EMER MOLECULAR VIROL & BIOCHEM, UNIV WIS, MADISON, 1990-; prof molecular virol & biochem, Inst Molecular Virol, 1987-1990; chmn, Inst Molecular Virol, 1987-1988; william w beeman prof, Biophys Lab, 1982-1986; chmn, Biophys Lab, 1969-1987; res career investr, USPHS, NIH Res, beginning 1963; prof biophys & biochem, Univ Wis-Madison, 1963-1982; from asst prof to prof biochem, Univ Wis-Madison, 1955-1962; from instr to asst prof biomet & physics, Univ Wis-Madison, 1949-1954; consult, NIH, NSF & US Dept Agr; assoc ed, Virol. **Memberships:** Nat Acad Sci; Biophys Soc; Sigma Xi; Am Soc Microbiol; Am Soc Virol (pres, 1987-1988); Am Soc Biol Chem & Molecular Biol; Gt Brit Soc Gen Microbiol. **Research Statement & Publications:** Structure and synthesis of viruses and macromolecules; author of numerous publications. **Mailing Address:** Dept Biochem, Univ Wis, 821A Bock Lab 433 Babcock Dr, Madison, WI 53706-1544.

KAESER, ROBERT S, INSTRUMENT & MEASUREMENT SCIENCE. **Personal Data:** b Pittsfield, Ill, January 14, 1928. **Education:** Ill Col, BS, 1950. **Professional Experience:** RETIRED; staff scientist, Nat Inst Stand & Technol, 1962-1992. **Memberships:** Am Phys Soc. **Mailing Address:** 5800 Dimes Rd, Rockville, MD 20855-1729.

KAESLER, ROGER LEROY, MICROPALEONTOLOGY. **Personal Data:** b Ponca City, Okla, June 22, 1937; div, c 5. **Education:** Colo Sch Mines, GeolE, 1959; Univ Kans, MS, 1962, PhD (micropaleont), 1965. **Professional Experience:** PROF GEOL & DIR PALEONTOLOGICAL INST, MUS INVERT PALEONT, UNIV KANS, 1973-; from asst prof to assoc prof, Univ kans, 1965-1973. **Memberships:** Paleont Soc; Soc Syst Zool; Geol Soc Am; Am Soc Naturalists. **Research Statement & Publications:** Paleoecology of Ostracoda; quantitative methods in paleontology and applied aquatic biology. **Mailing Address:** Dept Geol, Paleontological Inst Univ Kans, 121 Lindley Hall, Lawrence, KS 66045-2911. **E-Mail:** kaesler@ku.edu

KAESZ, HERBERT DAVID, ORGANOMETALLIC CHEMISTRY. **Personal Data:** b Alexandria, Egypt, January 4, 1933. **Education:** NY Univ, BA, 1954; Harvard Univ, MA, 1956, PhD, 1959. **Honors & Awards:** US Scientist Award, Alexander von Humboldt Sr, Fed Repub Ger, 1988. **Professional Experience:** PROF INORG CHEM, UNIV CALIF, LOS ANGELES, 1968-; assoc ed, Inorg Chem, Am Chem Soc, 1968-; from asst prof to assoc prof, Univ Calif, Los Angeles, 1960-1968; fel inorg chem & adv prog high sch teachers, Harvard Univ, 1958-1960. **Memberships:** Am Chem Soc; Royal Soc Chem; fel AAAS; fel Japan Soc Prom Sci. **Research Statement & Publications:** Chemistry of transition metals, especially organometallic complexes, polynuclear metal carbonyl cluster complexes and hydrides; pathways of homogeneous catalysis; organometallic chemical deposition; coal liquefaction. **Mailing Address:** 607 Charles E Young Dr East, Box 951569, Los Angeles, CA 90095-1569. **Fax:** 310-206-4038. **E-Mail:** hdk@chem.ucla.edu

KAETZEL, MARCIA ALDYTH, CALMODULIN, CALMODULIN BINDINGS PROTEINS. **Education:** Baylor Col Med, PhD (cell biol), 1985. **Professional Experience:** ASSOC PROF, GENOME RES INST, UNIV CINCINNATI, as of 2005; fel cell biol, Sch Med, Univ Tex, 1985. **Mailing Address:** Dept Molecular & Cel Physiol, Univ Cincinnati, 231 Bethesda Ave PO Box 670576, Cincinnati, OH 45267-0576. **Fax:** 513-558-3147. **E-Mail:** marcia.kaetzel@uc.edu

KAFADAR, KAREN, DATA ANALYSIS, ROBUST METHODS. **Personal Data:** b Evergreen Park, Ill, July 6, 1953; American citizen. **Education:** Stanford Univ, BS & MS, 1975; Princeton Univ, PhD (statist), 1979. **Honors & Awards:** William G Hunter Award, Am Soc Qual, 2001; Wilcoxon Prize, Am Soc Qual Control, 1995. **Professional Experience:** PROF MATH, UNIV COLO, DENVER, 1997-; assoc prof, Univ Colo, Denver, 1993-1997; math statistician, Hewlett-Packard Co, 1983-1990; math statistician, Statist Eng Div, Nat Bur Stand, 1980-1983; asst prof, Ore State Univ, 1979-1980; Consult, OEA, Inc, 1977-. **Memberships:** Am Statist Asn; Inst Math Statist; Am Soc Qual. **Research Statement & Publications:** New methodology in data analysis particularly robust methods and treatment of outliers; experimental design; spectrum analysis; statistical engineering design. **Mailing Address:** Dept Math, Univ Colo-Denver, Campus Box 170 PO Box 173364, Denver, CO 80217-3364. **Fax:** 303-556-8550. **E-Mail:** kk@math.cudenver.edu

KAFAFI, ZAKYA HUSSEIN, LIGHT-EMITTING MATERIALS & DEVICES, NONLINEAR & LINEAR OPTICAL MATERIALS. **Personal Data:** American citizen. **Education:** Univ Houston, BSc, 1969; Rice Univ, MA, 1972, PhD (chem), 1972. **Honors & Awards:** IR-100 Award, 1986. **Professional Experience:** SR RES SCIENTIST, US NAVAL RES LAB, 1986-; pres, Spectros Assoc, 1985-1989; vis prof, Rice Univ, 1981-1986; asst prof, Ala-Azhar Univ, 1979-1981. **Memberships:** Am Chem Soc; Optical Soc Am; Soc Photo-Optical Instrumentation Engrs; Soc Info Display; Mat Res Soc. **Research Statement & Publications:** Nonlinear optical organic materials; light-emitting material and devices; matrix isolation spectroscopy; metal cluster chemistry; inert bond activation. **Mailing Address:** Naval Res Lab, Code 5611, Washington, DC 20375. **E-Mail:** kafafi@ccf.nrl.navy.mil

KAFATOS, FOTIS C, DEVELOPMENTAL BIOLOGY. **Personal Data:** b Crete, Greece, April 16, 1940. **Education:** Cornell Univ, AB, 1961; Harvard Univ, MA, 1962, PhD (biol), 1965. **Honorary Degrees:** DSc, Univ Athens, 1992, Univ Thessaloniki, 1994. **Honors & Awards:** Walter Bauer Mem Lectr, Helen Hay Whitney Found, 1978; Rosenberger Distinguished Lectr, Univ Rochester, 1981; G J Mendel Hon Gold Medal Merit Biol Sci, Acad Sci Czech Repub, 1995. **Professional Experience:** DIR-GEN, EUROP MOLECULAR BIOL LAB, 1993-; mem, Nat Sci Adv Bd, Greece, 1988-; mem, Cell Biol & Nucleic Acids & Protein Synthesis Adv Comt, Am Cancer Soc, 1983-1986; adj prof biol, Univ Crete, 1982-; prof biol & dir, Inst Molecular Biol & Biotechnol, Res Ctr Crete, 1982-1993; chmn cellular & develop biol, Harvard Univ, 1978-1981; distinguished lectr, Univ Tex, 1977; adj prof biol, Univ Athens, 1972-1982; Mem, Develop Biol Panel, NSF, 1970-1972; from instr to prof biol, Harvard Univ, 1965-1994; Tutor, Harvard Univ, 1962-1963. **Memberships:** Nat Acad Sci; fel AAAS; Am Soc Cell Biol; Soc Develop Biol (pres, 1981-1982); fel Am Acad Arts & Sci; Europ Molecular Biol Orgn; Genetics Soc Am; Am Soc Zoologists; Int Soc Develop Biologists; Hellenic Biochem & Biophys Soc; Hellenic Soc Biol Sci; Human Genome Orgn. **Research Statement & Publications:** Molecular and cellular aspects of development, cell differentiation during insect metamorphosis; molecular evolution; over 240 papers in refereed journals. **Mailing Address:** Europ Molecular Biol Lab, Meyerhofstrass Nol, 69117 Heidelberg, Ger.

KAFATOS, MINAS, ASTROPHYSICS. **Personal Data:** b Crete, Greece, March 25, 1945. **Education:** Cornell Univ, BA, 1967; Mass Inst Technol, PhD (physics), 1972. **Professional Experience:** DEAN, SCH COMPUT SCI, 2002-; DIR, CTR EARTH OBSERVING & SPACE RES, 1995-; PROF PHYSICS, GEORGE MASON UNIV, 1984-; from asst prof to assoc prof, George Mason Univ, 1975-1984; res assoc astrophys, Goddard Space Flight Ctr, NASA, 1973-1975; res assoc astrophysics, Joint Inst for Lab Astrophys, Univ Colo, 1972-1973 & Nat Res Coun, Nat Acad Sci. **Memberships:** Am Astron Soc; Am Phys Soc; Int Astron Union; Royal Astron Soc. **Research Statement & Publications:**

Black holes; quasars; active galaxies; interstellar medium; mass loss and long period variables; forbidden line calculations; symbiotic stars; cosmic rays; supernovae; quantum physics. **Mailing Address:** Dept Physics, George Mason Univ, Rm 301B Sci & Technol I Bldg, Fairfax, VA 22030-4444. **Fax:** 703-993-3628. **E-Mail:** mkafatos@compton.gmu.edu

KAFER, ENID ROSEMARY, ANESTHESIOLOGY. **Personal Data:** b Sydney, Australia, May 27, 1937. **Education:** Univ Sydney, BS, 1959, MB & BS, 1962, MD, 1970, FRACP, FRCA, ABA. **Honors & Awards:** Peter Bancroff Award, 1970. **Professional Experience:** PROF EMER ANESTHESIOL & PROF EMER MOLECULAR PHYSIOL, UNIV NC, CHAPEL HILL, as of 2004; prof anesthesiol, Sch Med, Univ NC, Chapel Hill, 1982-1998; dir Neuroanesthesiol, Sch Med, Univ Nc, Chapel Hill, beginning 1982; Mem, Res Rev Comt, NC Heart Asn, 1976-1979; assoc prof physiol & anesthesiol, Sch Med, Univ NC, Chapel Hill, 1973-1982; asst prof, Dept Anesthesia, 1972-1973; fel physiol, Univ Calif, San Francisco, 1971-1972; sr registr, Dept Anesthetics, Royal Postgrad Med Sch, London, 1969-1971; res fel, Life Ins Med Res fel, 1968-1969; lectr, Dept Med, Univ Sydney, as of 1967; res fel, Dept Med, Univ Sydney, 1965-1966; anesthetic registr, Royal Prince Alfred Hosp, Sydney, 1964; med resident, Royal Prince Alfred Hosp, Sydney, 1962-1963; consult respiratory & anesthesia dis panel, Food & Drug Admin. **Memberships:** fel Royal Australian Col Physicians; Am Physiol Soc; Am Soc Anesthesiologists; Sigma Xi; fel Royal Col Anesthetists; Am Asn Med Instrumentation. **Research Statement & Publications:** Load adjustment mechanisms of the respiratory system, including examination of neural and muscle factors, and the effects of changing chemical stimuli, chemoreceptor denervation and the effects of general anesthesia on respiratory control. **Mailing Address:** Dept Anesthesiol Sch Med, Univ NC, Chapel Hill, NC 27599-7010. **Fax:** 919-966-4873.

KAFER, ETTA (MRS E R BOOTHROYD), MITOTIC RECOMBINATION, ANEUPLOIDY. **Personal Data:** b Zurich, Switz, July 31, 1925. **Education:** Univ Zurich, dipl, 1948, PhD (genetics), 1952. **Honors & Awards:** Award of Excellence, Genetics Soc Can, 1987. **Professional Experience:** RETIRED; assoc mem, Inst Molecular Biol & Biochem, beginning 1991; from lectr to prof molecular genetics, McGill Univ, 1959-1992; res assoc, McGill Univ, 1958-1963; res fel, Carnegie Inst, 1956; res fel, Glasgow Univ, 1955-1956; res asst microbial genetics, Glasgow Univ, 1953-1955; adj prof, Biosci Dept, Simon Fraser Univ. **Memberships:** Genetics Soc Am; Genetics Soc Can; Swiss Genetics Soc; Environ Mutogen Soc. **Research Statement & Publications:** Microbial genetics; mitotic and meiotic recombination; molecular genetics of nucleases; DNA repair mutants and gene cloning in fungi; assays for environmentally induced nondisjunction; genetics of fungi used for biotechnology. **Mailing Address:** 23233 52nd Ave RR 13, Langley, BC V2Z 2R6, Can. **Fax:** 604-291-5583.

KAFESJIAN, R(ALPH), CHEMICAL ENGINEERING, PHYSICAL CHEMISTRY. **Personal Data:** b Chicago, Ill, March 28, 1934. **Education:** Purdue Univ, BS, 1955; Univ Louisville, MChE, 1957, PhD (chem eng), 1961. **Professional Experience:** AT, BAXTER INT, INC, as of 2001; SR ENGR, BAXTER HEALTHCARE, 1986-; prin scientist, Am Hosp Supply Corp, 1981-1986; sr scientist, Am Hosp Supply Corp, 1978-1980; task leader corp technol, Am Hosp Supply Corp, 1971-1977; biomed res lab, Am Hosp Supply Corp, 1969-1971; res group leader, Monsanto Res Corp, 1967-1969; sr res chem engr, Monsanto Res Corp, 1963-1967; res chem engr, Monsanto Res Corp, 1961-1963; Instr chem physics & chem eng, Univ Louisville, 1957-1960. **Memberships:** AAAS; Am Chem Soc; assoc Am Inst Chem Engrs; Nat Asn Corrosion Engrs; Biomat Soc; Sigma Xi. **Research Statement & Publications:** High temperature materials, reactions, processes and technology; electrochemical energy conversion methods; corrosion; electrochemistry; biomedical materials and devices. **Mailing Address:** Baxter Healthcare, One Baxter Pkwy, Deerfield, IL 60015-4625. **Fax:** 847-948-3642.

KAFKA, MARIAN STERN, NEUROSCIENCE, PHYSIOLOGY. **Personal Data:** b Richmond, Va, March 30, 1927; m 1952, John; c David Egon, Paul Henry & Alexander Charles Kafka. **Education:** Conn Col, BA, 1948; Univ Chicago, PhD (physiol), 1952. **Honors & Awards:** Sigma Xi, Univ Chicago 1950; Usphs postdoctoral fel nat heart blood & lung inst, 1965-1968; Adamha adminstrative award for xertorines achievement, 1989. **Professional Experience:** Chief clin, Epidemiol & Serv Rev Br, Div Extramural Activ, NIMH, USPHS, beginning 1990; exec secy, Cellular Neurobiol & Psychopharmacol, 1985-1990; physiologist, Clin Neurosci Br, 1982-1985; mem, Comt Intramural Prog Dir's Conf, NIH, 1982-1985; pres, 1982-1983 & mem, clin res rev comt, NIMH, 1982-1984; mem, coun NIMH-Nat Inst Neurol & Commun Dis Assembly Scientists, 1981-1982; mem, pub info comt, Fedn Am Socs Exp Biol, 1977-1982; sect biochem & pharmacol, Biol Psychiat Br, 1974-1982; physiologist, Hypertension-Endocrine Br, 1968-1974; USPHS fel, Endocrinol Br, Nat Heart & Lung Inst, 1965-1968; Ill Neuropsychiat Inst, Univ Ill, Chicago, 1953-1954; Sch Med, Yale Univ, 1954-1957; res asst, Sch Med, Emory Univ, 1952-1953; Marie J Mergler fel physiol, Univ Chicago, Ill, 1950; asst physiol, Sch Med, Univ Chicago, 1948-1952; reviewer, Med Res Coun Can & NSF & numerous sci publns. **Memberships:** Am Physiol Soc; Endocrine Soc; Biophys Soc; AAAS; Sigma Xi; Soc Neuroscience; Int Soc Chronobiol. **Research Statement & Publications:** Interaction between neurotransmitters, hormones and receptors on neurons and blood cells; central nervous system control of circadian rhythms. **Mailing Address:** 7834 Aberdeen Rd, Bethesda, MD 20814-1102.

KAFKA, ROBERT W(ILLIAM), DEFENSE ELECTRONICS SYSTEMS, COMMAND & CONTROL SYSTEMS. **Personal Data:** b Chicago, Ill, October 30, 1937; m 1966, Nannette; c Gregory R & Julie L. **Education:** Univ Ill, BSEE, 1958, MSEE, 1959, PhD (elec eng), 1963. **Professional Experience:** RETIRED; mgr, Advan Systs Prog Off, Systs Div, Hughes Aircraft Co, 1966-1994; mem tech staff, Guidance & Control Dept, Aerospace Corp, 1963-1966; Instr elec eng, Univ Ill, 1958-1963. **Memberships:** Inst Elec & Electronics Engrs; Sigma Xi. **Mailing Address:** 2749 Puente St, Fullerton, CA 92835.

KAFKA, TOMAS, EXPERIMENTAL ELEMENTARY PARTICLE PHYSICS. **Personal Data:** b Praha, Czech, October 15, 1936; m. **Education:** Univ Karlova, Praha, Promovany Fyzik, 1960; State Univ NY, Stony Brook, PhD (physics), 1974. **Professional Experience:** RES PROF, TUFTS UNIV, 1991-; from res asst prof to res assoc prof, Tufts Univ, 1982-1991; Res assoc, State Univ NY, Stony Brook, 1974-1982. **Memberships:** Am Phys Soc. **Research Statement & Publications:** Hadron-hadron, lepton-hadron, and photon-hadron interactions at high energies; proton decay; cosmic rays; particle astronomy. **Mailing Address:** Dept Physics & Astron, Tufts Univ, High Energy Physics, 4 Colby St, Medford, MA 02155. **E-Mail:** tomas.kafka@tufts.edu

KAFRAWY, ADEL, POLYMER & ORGANIC CHEMISTRY, CELLULOSE TECHNOLOGY. **Personal Data:** b Cairo, Egypt, October 15, 1943. **Education:** Cairo Univ, BSc, 1964; Univ Rochester, MS, 1971; Univ Mo-Columbia, PhD (org chem), 1974; Syracuse Univ, MBA, 1983. **Professional Experience:** GROUP LEADER, JOHNSON & JOHNSON, 1991-; sr scientist, Johnson & Johnson, 1981-1991; res chemist, Cellulose Res, ITT Rayonier, Inc, 1977-1981; assoc org chem, State Univ NY Col Environ Sci & Forestry, Syracuse, 1975-1977; assoc phys org chem, Syracuse Univ, 1974-1975; demonstr chem, Cairo Univ, 1964-1968. **Research Statement & Publications:** Biomedical application of polymers; controlled drug release systems; absorbable biomedical polymers. **Mailing Address:** 16 Cooke Ave, Kingston, MA 02364.

KAFRI, ODED, MOIRE EFFECT, AUTHENTICATION. **Personal Data:** b Tel-Aviv, Israel, December 13, 1944. **Education:** Technion, BSc, 1969, DSc, 1973. **Professional Experience:** PRES SYNCRONYS, ISRAEL, 1994-; pres, Fontech Ltd, 1990-1994; pres, Rotlex Optics Ltd, Arava, Israel, 1986-1989; sr physicist, Corp Technol, Allied Corp, Mt Bethel, NJ, 1983-1984; sr res scientist, Nuclear Res Ctr-Negev, Beer Sheva, 1982-1989; group leader, Optical-Non-Destructive Testing, 1978-1986; Adv energy, Nat Res Coun, Israel, 1978-1982; res scientist, Nuclear Res Ctr-Negev, Beer Sheva, 1976-1982; res scientist assoc, Dept Chem, Univ Wis-Madison, 1974-1976; instr appl physics, Hebrew Univ, Jerusalem, 1973-1974; instr, Dept Chem, Technion, 1971-1973; Asst, Dept Chem, Technion, 1969-1971. **Memberships:** Optical Soc Am; Int Soc Optical Eng. **Research Statement & Publications:** Optical metrology: invention of moire deflectometry, a method used in several industries like ophthalmological industry, wind tunnels, lasers industries and research labs; theoretical aspects of metrology and information theory; author or co-author of one book, over 100 scientific publications and holder of over 20 patents; developed a method to print data on paper and to send data from personal computer to paper fax; telecommunication. **Mailing Address:** Ehud 3, Beer Sheva 84234, Israel. **Fax:** 972-627-4695.

KAGAN, BENJAMIN, REGULATORY AFFAIRS. **Personal Data:** b New York, NY, March 9, 1921; m 1943, Helen L Hallem; c Tobias & Debra. **Education:** DePaul Univ, BS, 1947; Pa State Univ, MS, 1950. **Professional Experience:** CONSULT & LECTR, REGULATORY AFFAIRS, 1977-; supvry chemist, Div Oncol & Radiopharmaceut Drug Prod, 1973-1977; chemist, Div Oncol & Radiopharmaceut Drug Prod, 1966-1973; res anal chemist, Div Food Chem, Bur Drugs, Food & Drug Admin, 1962-1966; org res chemist, Army Chem Ctr, MD, 1950-1962. **Memberships:** Emer mem AAAS; emer mem Am Chem Soc; fel Am Inst Chemists (pres 1992-1994); NY Acad Sci; Royal Soc Chem. **Research Statement & Publications:** Organo-phosphorous and sulfur compounds; nitrogen heterocycles; radiopharmaceuticals. **Mailing Address:** PO Box 352948, Palm Coast, FL 32135-2948.

KAGAN, BRUCE L, PSYCHOPHARMACOLOGY, ELECTRO PHYSIOLOGY. **Personal Data:** b New York, NY, August 1, 1953. **Education:** Yale Univ, BA, 1975; Yeshiva Univ, MD, 1982, PhD (physiol, biophys), 1982. **Professional Experience:** PROF, UNIV CALIF, LOS ANGELES, AS OF 2006; assoc prof psychiat to Asst prof, univ calif, los angeles, 1986-1992. **Memberships:** Fel Am Psychiat Asn; Biophys Soc; Int Soc Traumatic Stress Studies; Am Soc Clin Psychopharmacol. **Research Statement & Publications:** Channel forming toxins including colicins, diphtheria toxin, yeast killer, defnsins, amylin, prions. **Mailing Address:** Psychr & Biobehav Sci, UCLA, BOX 951759, Los Angeles, CA 90095-1759. **E-Mail:** bkagan@mednet.ucla.edu

KAGAN, FRED, MEDICINAL CHEMISTRY, ORGANIC CHEMISTRY. **Personal Data:** b Chicago, Ill, December 24, 1920; m 1957, Rhoda; c Laurie, Glenn, Richard, Carolyn, Cathy & James. **Education:** Univ Ill, BS, 1942; Mass Inst Technol, PhD (org chem), 1949. **Honors & Awards:** Sigma Xi. **Professional Experience:** RETIRED; vpres therapeut, Clin Res & Biotechnol, 1982-1986; dir exp sci & therapeut, Upjohn Co, 1981-1982; group mgr, Upjohn Co, 1978-1981; mgr cent nerv syst res, Upjohn Co, 1968-1978; res org chemist, Upjohn Co, 1952-1968; res org chemist, Stand Oil Co Ind, 1949-1952. **Memberships:** Am Chem Soc; Royal Soc Chem; NY Acad Sci. **Research Statement & Publications:** Synthesis; psychopharmacology, drug development from test tube thru obtaining and obtaining international registrations. **Mailing Address:** 5922 Doral Dr, Sarasota, FL 34243.

KAGAN, HARVEY ALEXANDER, CONSTRUCTION MANAGEMENT, FORENSIC ENGINEERING. **Personal Data:** b New York, NY, September 25, 1937. **Education:** Columbia Univ, BS, 1958; Univ Ill, MS, 1959; NY Univ, Eng ScD (civil eng), 1965; Purdue Univ, MS, 1980. **Professional Experience:** FEL, AM SOC CIVILL ENGRS, as of 2005; ASSOC, S T HUDSON INT INC, 1987-; prof civil eng, Rutgers Univ, 1984-1987; pres, Construct Adv Group, Inc, 1982-1984; sr consult, Hill Int, Inc, 1981-1982; sr consult, Wagner-Hohns-Inglis, 1978-1981; assoc prof & prog chmn, Univ Evansville, 1975-1977; sr civil engr, C F Braun & Co, 1974-1975; NSF, res grant, 1967-1968; from asst prof to assoc prof civil eng, Rutgers Univ, 1966-1974; struct mech engr, Grumman Aircraft Corp, 1966; eng specialist, Martin Co Div, Martin-Marietta Corp, 1965-1966; test engr, Vertol Div, Boeing Co, 1962; struct test engr, Martin Co Div, Martin-Marietta Corp, 1961-1962; asst civil engr, NY City Bd Educ, 1961; Struct engr, Repub Aviation Corp, 1959-1961. **Memberships:** fel Am Soc Civil Engrs; Am Concrete Inst; Sigma Xi; Tau Beta Pi & Chi Epsilion Eng. **Research Statement & Publications:** Elasto-plastic analysis of reinforced plates; second-order theroy in orthotrophic plates; double acting center punch for the mechanics of materials laboratory. **Mailing Address:** 11040 Stewart Neck Rd, Princess Anne, MD 21853. **Fax:** 410-621-0476. **E-Mail:** Kagans@dmv.com

KAGAN, HERBERT MARCUS, BIOCHEMISTRY. **Personal Data:** b Boston, Mass, August 18, 1932. **Education:** Univ Mass, Amherst, BS, 1954, MS, 1956; Tufts Univ, PhD (biochem), 1966. **Professional Experience:** Merit award, NIH, 1988-; PROF BIOCHEM, SCH MED, BOSTON UNIV, 1980-; assoc prof, Sch Med, Boston Univ, 1972-1980; asst prof, Sch Med, Boston Univ, 1969-1972; Am Cancer Soc res fel biochem, Harvard Med Sch, 1966-1969; biologist, Arthur D Little, Inc, 1960-1961; res assoc pharmacol, Sch Med, Boston Univ, 1959-1960; instr microbiol, Purdue Univ, 1956-1958; fel, Arteriosclerosis Coun, Am Heart Asn. **Memberships:** AAAS; Am Soc Biol Chemists; Am Heart Asn; Sigma Xi. **Research Statement & Publications:** Enzymology; protein chemistry; structure-function relationships of enzymes; connective tissue proteins; stereospecifity in catalysis. **Mailing Address:** Dept Biochem, Boston Univ Sch Med, 715 Albany St, Boston, MA 02118-2394. **Fax:** 617-638-5339. **E-Mail:** kagan@med-biochm.bu.edu

KAGAN, IRVING GEORGE, PARASITOLOGY, IMMUNOLOGY. **Personal Data:** b New York, NY, June 1, 1919. **Education:** Brooklyn Col, AB, 1940; Univ Mich, MA, 1947, PhD (zool), 1950. **Honors & Awards:** Henry Baldwin Ward Medal, Am Soc Parasitol, 1965; Behring-Bilharz Medal, 1981. **Professional Experience:** DIR, DIAG PARASITIC & VIRAL CLIN LAB, PARASITIC DIS CONSULT, 1983-; mem, Scientific Working Group, Epidemology, WHO, 1978; dir, Div Parasitol, Ctrs Dis Control, beginning 1967; chief Parasitol Unit, Ctrs Dis Control, 1962-1966; chief Helminth Unit, Ctrs Dis Control, 1957-1962; asst prof zool, Univ Pa, 1952-1957; Nat Res Coun fel, Univ Chicago, 1950-1952. **Memberships:** Am Soc Trop Med & Hyg; Am Soc Parasitol; Am Asn Immunol; Am Micros Soc; Sci Res Soc Am. **Research Statement & Publications:** Immunodiagnosis of parasitic infections and the immunology of the host parasite interaction. **Mailing Address:** Parasitic Dis Consult, 2177 J Flintstone Dr, Tucker, GA 30084. **Fax:** 770-938-7189.

KAGAN, JACQUES, ORGANIC CHEMISTRY, BIOLOGICAL CHEMISTRY. **Personal Data:** b Paris, France, November 11, 1933. **Education:** Sorbonne, BS, 1956; Rice Univ,

PhD (chem), 1960. **Honors & Awards:** Cooley Award, Am Soc Plant Taxon, 1964. **Professional Experience:** Museum Nat d'Histoire Naturelle, Paris, 1987; Fulbright grant, 1980 & 1987; Vis prof, Univ Geneva, 1971-1972 & Univ Haute-Alsace, 1980; PROF EMER CHEM & BIOL, UNIV ILL, CHICAGO, 1973-; from asst prof to assoc prof, Univ Ill, Chicago, 1965-1973; res scientist & Welch Found fel, Univ Tex, 1962-1965; res chemist, Amoco Chem Co, Ind, 1961-1962; Res assoc, Mass Inst Technol, 1960-1961. **Memberships:** Am Chem Soc; Am Soc Photobiol. **Research Statement & Publications:** Organic synthesis and reaction mechanisms; photochemistry and photobiology; environmental chemistry. **Mailing Address:** 1620 Washington Ave, Wilmette, IL 60091-2419. **Fax:** 312-996-0431. **E-Mail:** jkagan@uic.edu

KAGAN, JEROME, DEVELOPMENTAL PSYCHOLOGY. **Personal Data:** b Newark, NJ, February 25, 1929; m 1951, Cle; c Janet. **Education:** Rutgers Univ, BS, 1950; Yale Univ, PhD (psychol), 1954; Harvard Univ, MA, 1964. **Honors & Awards:** Distinguished Sci Award, Am Psychol Asn, 1987. **Professional Experience:** DANIEL & AMY STARCH RES PROF PSYCHOL, HARVARD UNIV, as of 2002; prof, Res Dept Psychol, Harvard Univ, beginning 1964; chmn, Dept Psychol, fels res inst, 1957-1964. **Memberships:** Nat Acad Sci; Am Psychol Asn; Soc Res Child Develop; Am Asn Advan Sci. **Research Statement & Publications:** Cognitive and emotional development of children; role of temperament in personality development. **Mailing Address:** Dept Psychol, Harvard Univ, 33 Kirkland St, Cambridge, MA 02138. **Fax:** 617-495-3728.

KAGAN, JOEL (DAVID), MATHEMATICS. **Personal Data:** b New York, NY, August 18, 1943; m. **Education:** Rutgers Col, BA, 1966; Stevens Inst Technol, MS, 1967 & 1984, PhD (math), 1970. **Professional Experience:** ASSOC DEAN COL ARTS & SCI UNIV HARTFORD as of 2005; CHMN, DEPT MATH, DEPT PHYSICS, DEPT COMPUTER SCI UNIV HARTFORD, as of 2005; assoc prof math, Univ Hartford, beginning 1984; asst prof, Univ Hartford, 1970-1984; instr math, Stevens Inst Technol, 1968-1970. **Memberships:** Soc Symbolic Logic; Math Asn Am; Am math soc. **Research Statement & Publications:** Algebraic logic; algebraic structures arising from theories in the sentential and predicate calculus with identity connective. **Mailing Address:** Univ Hartford, 200 Bloomfield Ave Dana Hall Rm 220B, W Hartford, CT 06117-1545. **Fax:** 860-768-5244. **E-Mail:** kagan@hartford.edu

KAGAN, MICHAEL Z, HIGH-PERFORMANCE LIQUID CHROMATOGRAPHY, SEPARATION SCIENCES. **Personal Data:** b Moscow, USSR, February 26, 1950. **Education:** Moscow Inst Chem Technol, USSR, MS, 1973; Inst BioOrg Chem, USSR Acad Sci, PhD (bioorg chem), 1977. **Professional Experience:** RES SCIENTIST, WYETH-AYERST RES, as of 2006; fel, Harvard Univ, 1988-1990; res scientist, Inst Animal Morphol & Ecol, USSR, 1977-1988. **Memberships:** Am Chem Soc. **Research Statement & Publications:** Synthesized synthetic analogs and isolated physiologically active compounds by high-performance liquid chromatography and other separation techniques. **Mailing Address:** Wyeth-Ayerst Res, 5 Giralda Farms, Madison, NJ 07940.

KAGANSKY, LARISA, SPECTROSCOPY & SPECTROMETRY, MATERIAL PROPERTIES & PHYSICAL CHEMISTRY. **Personal Data:** b Kiev, Ukraine, June 23, 1946. **Education:** Moscow Technol Inst, ME, 1976. **Professional Experience:** CHEMIST, RUCO POLYMER CORP, 1986-; mat engr, Multiwire Div, Kollmorgen Corp, 1981-1986; sr chemist, Inst Phys Chem, Acad Sci, Kiev, Ukraine, 1974-1978. **Memberships:** Am Chem Soc; Soc Plastics Engrs. **Research Statement & Publications:** Research, development and evaluation of polyester polyols, powder toner and coating resins, polyurethane products for coatings, adhesives, waterbased polymers; design of new testing and analysis procedures for raw materials and final products. **Mailing Address:** 173 N Central Ave, Valley Stream, NY 11580.

KAGARISE, RONALD EUGENE, PHYSICS. **Personal Data:** b East Freedom, Pa, July 17, 1926. **Education:** Duke Univ, BA, 1948; Pa State Col, MS, 1949, PhD (physics), 1951. **Professional Experience:** RETIRED; div dir mat res, NSF, Wash, DC, 1979-1983; asst dir math & phys sci, NSF, Wash, DC, 1977-1979; dir div mat res, NSF, Wash, DC, 1976-1977; supt chem div, Naval Res Lab, 1968-1976; prog dir phys chem, NSF, 1966-1968; head chem spectros sect, Naval Res Lab, 1952-1966; res assoc physics, Pa State Col, 1951-1952. **Memberships:** Am Phys Soc; Sigma Xi; Am Chem Soc; Coblentz Soc. **Research Statement & Publications:** Rotational isomerism; molecular constants; structure. **Mailing Address:** 602 Pine Rd, Ft Washington, MD 20744.

KAGAWA, YUKIO, COMPUTATIONAL ACOUSTICS, NUMERICAL ANALYSIS. **Personal Data:** b Yamagata, Japan, May 8, 1935. **Education:** Tohoku Univ, Sendai, Japan, BEng, 1958, MEng, 1960, DrEng, 1963. **Honors & Awards:** Ishikawa Prize, Union Japanese Scientists & Engrs, 1989. **Professional Experience:** Vpres, Japan Soc Simulation Technol, 1996-; PROF ELEC & ELECTRONICS ENG, OKAYAMA UNIV, 1990-; EMER PROF ELEC ENG, TOYAMA UNIV, JAPAN, 1990-; mem bd dirs, Japan Soc Simulation Technol, 1986-; vis prof, Inst Acoust, Academia Sineca, China, 1984; vis prof, Indian Inst Technol, Delhi, India, 1982; Leverhulme fel, Univ NSW, Australia, 1978; prof, Okayama Univ, 1970-1990; res fel acoust eng, Inst Sound & Vibration Res, Southampton Univ, UK, 1968-1970; postdoctoral fel acoust eng, Tech Univ Norway, 1966-1968; Postdoctoral fel mech eng, Polytech Inst, Brooklyn, NY, 1964-1965. **Memberships:** Fel Inst Elec & Electronics Engrs; fel Inst Acoust UK; Inst Electronic Info & Commun Engrs Japan. **Research Statement & Publications:** Numerical modelling and simulation of electrical acoustical and vibration systems by means of finite element and boundary element method; electrical impedance and ultrasonic computed tomography as an inverse or optimization problem. **Mailing Address:** Dept Elec & Electronics Eng, Okayama Univ, Okayama 700, Japan. **Fax:** 818-625-25734. **E-Mail:** kagawa@calc.elec.okayamau.ac.jp

KAGEL, RONALD OLIVER, ANALYTICAL CHEMISTRY, ENVIRONMENTAL SCIENCE. **Personal Data:** b Milwaukee, Wis, January 16, 1936; m 1959, Lois; c Jennifer, Kathryn & Sharon. **Education:** Univ Wis, BS, 1958; Univ Minn, PhD (phys chem), 1964. **Honors & Awards:** Vern stenger award, 1974; Anachem Award, Am Inst Chem, 1988; fel, Am Inst Chem, 1986; Hon mem, crwi, 1994. **Professional Experience:** RETIRED; Environ consult, beginning 1993; environ counsult, Eng Res & Comput Serv, 1988-1993; ground water subcomt, 1984-1985; bd dirs, Coalition Responsible Waste Incineration, 1987, 1990; environ dir, Eng Res & Comput Serv, 1985-1988; mem, Environ Qual Comn, Synthetic Org Chem Mfg Asn, 1982-1985; CMA work group leader, Environ Audits, 1982-1984; dir environ qual, States Environ Activ, 1981-1985; mgr, States Environ Activ, 1981; chmn, Natural Resources Comt, State Govt Affairs Coun, 1981; mgr, Regulatory Affairs-Water, 1979-1981; liaison coordr, Am Soc Testing & Mat, 1979-1981; res mgr surface anal, Chem Res Lab, 1978-1979; environ systs group leader surface anal, Chem Res Lab, 1977-1978; secy, Int Fourier Trans Conf, 1977; CMA leader, Task Group Environ Monitoring, 1976-1981; mem adv comt, Critical Mat Register, State Mich Dept Nat Res, 1976-1979; supt environ control, Chem Res Lab, 1976-1977; assoc ed, Appl Spectros, 1975-1980; supvr spec anal group, Chem Res Lab, 1974-1976; mem, Ad-hoc Panel Micro-Raman Spectros, Nat Bur Stand, 1974; sr anal specialist, Chem Res Lab, 1972-1974; sr res chemist, Chem Res Lab, 1971-1972; mem, Numerical Data Adv Bd, Joint Comt Atomic & Molecular Structure-Subcomt Laser Raman Spectros, 1970-1980; group leader, Chem Res Lab, 1969-1971; mem adv bd, Raman Newslett, 1968-1975; secy, Adhoc Subpanel Laser Excited Raman Spectra, Nat Res Coun, 1968; proj leader, Chem Res Lab, 1967-1969; Res chemist, Dow Chem Co, 1964-1967; Mem fac, Saginaw Valley Col, 1964-1967. **Memberships:** Fel Am Inst Chemists; Sigma Xi; Am Chem Soc; AAAS; NY Acad Sci; Coblentz Soc. **Research Statement & Publications:** Molecular structure elucidation; surface catalysis and bulk mechanistic studies; remote detection of ambient air emissions by infrared Fourier transform and Raman spectroscopy; infrared chemiluminescence applications; environmental measurements of trace compounds; combustion chemistry and incineration; dioxin; Environ assesments. **Mailing Address:** 4 Hannah Ct, Midland, MI 48642. **Fax:** 989-631-4477. **E-Mail:** Kagelr@Mindnet.org

KAGEN, HERBERT PAUL, ORGANIC CHEMISTRY. **Personal Data:** b Worcester, Mass, May 6, 1929. **Education:** Mass Inst Technol, SB, 1952; Univ RI, MS, 1954; Wayne State Univ, PhD, 1960. **Professional Experience:** RETIRED; assoc dir & supvr, Anal Chem Lab, 1988-1989; field serv prof environ health & assoc dir & supvr Environ Analysis Chem Lab, Inst Environ Health, Med Ctr, Univ Cincinnati, 1987-1995; vis prof, Inst Environ Health Med Ctr, Univ Cincinnati, 1987-1988; dir chem technol, Dept Chem, 1975-1990; adj prof, Grad Studies, W Va Col, 1975-1977; dir, W Va Resa III Prog Gifted High Sch Sr, 1975; fac adv, NSF Sos Prog, Kanawha Valley, 1973; dir, NSF Coop Col Sch Sci Prog High Sch Chem Teachers, 1970-1971; adj prof, W Va Univ, 1970-1971; chmn, Dept Chem, 1968-1971, 1987; prof org chem, W Va State Col, 1967-1990; Mich Heart Asn fel, 1960; consult, Chem Serv Corp, beginning 1957; from asst prof to assoc prof chem, Detroit Inst Technol, 1957-1967; consult, Union Carbide Corp, W Va State Bd Educ & Kanawha County Bd Educ. **Memberships:** Am Chem Soc; Nat Sci Teachers Asn; Am Asn Univ Prof; Sigma Xi. **Research Statement & Publications:** Reaction of lactides; organic nitrogen chemistry; preparation of lactides; chemical education; environmental. **Mailing Address:** 8060 Springvalley Dr, Cincinnati, OH 45236.

KAGEN, LAWRENCE J, RHEUMATOLOGY, MUSCLE DISORDERS. **Personal Data:** b New York, NY, February 2, 1936. **Education:** NY Univ, MD, 1960. **Professional Experience:** PROF MED, MED COL, CORNELL UNIV, 1979-; ATTEND PHYSICIAN, NY HOSP SPEC SURG, 1979-. **Memberships:** Am Assoc Immunol; Am Col Physician; Am Col Rheumatology. **Research Statement & Publications:** Inflammatory muscle disease. **Mailing Address:** NY Hosp Spec Surg, 535 E 70th St, Seventh Floor, New York, NY 10021. **Fax:** 212-774-2358. **E-Mail:** kagenl@hss.edu

KAGETSU, T(ADASHI) J(ACK), CHEMICAL ENGINEERING. **Personal Data:** b Vancouver, BC, April 22, 1931. **Education:** Univ Toronto, BASc, 1954, MASc, 1955, PhD (appl chem), 1957. **Professional Experience:** CONSULT, 1987-; asst dir tech, Metals Div, 1978-1986; mgr design eng, process eng, 1977-1978; mgr, process eng, 1975-1977; staff engr, mining & metals div, 1967-1975; proj engr, mining & metals div, 1964-1967; assoc engr, nuclear div, 1961-1964; res chem engr, metals div, Union Carbide Corp, 1960-1961; asst res chem engr, metals div, Union Carbide Corp, 1957-1960. **Research Statement & Publications:** Kinetics of metal dissolution in aqueous media; fused salt electrolysis; gas-solid mass transfer and heat transfer; hydrometallurgy and pyrometallurgy; process simulation by computers. **Mailing Address:** 435 Dutton Dr, Lewiston, NY 14092.

KAGIWADA, HARRIET HATSUNE NATSUYAMA, APPLIED MATHEMATICS, SYSTEMS SCIENCE. **Personal Data:** b Honolulu, Hawaii, September 2, 1937. **Education:** Univ Hawaii, BA, 1959, MSc, 1960; Univ Kyoto, PhD (astrophys), 1965. **Honors & Awards:** Hughes Invention Award. **Professional Experience:** ROCKWELL INT PROF SYSTS ENG, CALIF STATE UNIV, FULLERTON, 1990-; chief engr, Infotec Develop Inc, 1987-1989; sr scientist, Hughes Aircraft Co, 1982-1987; pres, HFS Assocs, 1977-1987; from res assoc math to adj assoc prof, Univ Southern Calif 1971-1977; consult, Rand Corp, 1971-1977; mathematician, Rand Corp, 1961-1971. **Memberships:** Sr mem Inst Elec & Electronics Engrs; AAAS. **Research Statement & Publications:** Optimization; control theory; team decision theory; command and control; operations research; atmospheric temperature estimation; mathematical models; system identification, mathematical and computational methods; dynamic programming, quasilinearization and invariant imbedding; integral equations; boundary value problems; initial value problems; expert and avionics systems; numerical derivatives; nonlinear analysis; author of over 150 technical papers published in journals in the USA, USSR, UK, France and author and co-author of several textbooks on applied mathematics and computation systems science. **Mailing Address:** Sch Eng & Comput Sci, Calif State Univ Fullerton, Fullerton, CA 92634. **Fax:** 714-449-7108. **E-Mail:** kagiwada@fullerton.edu

KAGIWADA, REYNOLD SHIGERU, ELECTRONICS ENGINEERING, SOLID STATE PHYSICS. **Personal Data:** b Los Angeles, Calif, July 8, 1938. **Education:** Univ Calif, Los Angeles, BS, 1960, MS, 1963, PhD (physics), 1966. **Honors & Awards:** Gold Medal Recipient, Ramo Technol Transfer Award, 1985. **Professional Experience:** ADVAN TECHNOL MGR & ADVAN TECHNOL DIRECTORATE, TRW SPACE & ELECTRONIC GROUP, as of 2002; ADVAN TECHNOL MGR, MICROWAVE TECHNOL DEPT OPER, TRW ELECTRONIC SYSTS GROUP, 1994-; mimic chief scientist, Advan Microelectronics Lab, 1989-1994; prog mgr, Advan Microelectronics Lab, 1988-1989; asst proj mgr/dep proj mgr, Advan Microelectronics Lab, 1987-1988; mgr, Advan Microelectronics Lab, 1983-1987; mgr, Microwave Prod Dept, 1980-1983; sr scientist, TRW Systs Group, 1977-1980; sect head, TRW Systs Group, 1976-1977; scientist, TRW Systs Group, 1975-1976; mem prof staff, TRW Systs Group, 1972-1975; asst prof physics, Univ Calif, Los Angeles, 1967-1969 & Univ Southern Calif, 1969-1972. **Memberships:** Inst Elec & Electronics Engrs; Asn Old Crows. **Research Statement & Publications:** Gallium-arsenic devices; integrated circuits; millimeter-wave devices; microwave acoustic devices; low temperature physics; superconductivity; liquid helium; ultrasonics; acoustics; microwave physics. **Mailing Address:** TRW Space & Electronics Group & Electronic Systs & Technol Div, One Space Park, Redondo Beach, CA 90278. **Fax:** 310-812-7011. **E-Mail:** reynold_kagiwadg@gmail4.nloa.trw.ccm

KAGIWADE, HARRIET, SYSTEMS ENGINEERING. **Education:** Univ Hawaii, Manoa, BS, 1959, MS, 1960. **Professional Experience:** FAC MEM, COL ENG & COMPUT SCI, CALIF STATE UNIV, FULLERTON, as of 1991. **Mailing Address:** Dept Eng & Computer Sci, Calif State Univ, Fullerton, CA 92634.

KAHAN, ARCHIE M, METEOROLOGY. **Personal Data:** b Denver, Colo, January 18, 1917; m 1944, c 2. **Education:** Univ Denver, BA, 1936, MA, 1940; Calif Inst Technol, MS, 1942; Agr & Mech Col Tex, PhD (meteorol oceanog), 1959. **Honors & Awards:** Award, Am Meteorol Soc, 1962. **Professional Experience:** Sr scientist, Ophir Corp, 1987-; SR SCIENTIST, OPHIR CORP, 1987-; CONSULT METEROLOGIST, Ophir Corp, 1979-; assoc chief, div res, 1978-1979; mem, Adv Comt Weather Modification, State of Colo, 1972-1983; chief off atmospheric resources mgt, US Bur Reclamation, 1970-1979; gen phys scientist, US Bur Reclamation, 1965-1970; Consult, President's Adv Comt Weather

Control, 1954 & NSF Panel Weather Modification, 1965; dir, Univ Okla Res Inst, 1963-1965; dir, Tex Eng Exp Sta, 1962-1963; exec dir, Tex A&M Res Found, 1954-1963; asst prof meteorol, Agr & Mech Col Tex, 1953-1954; assoc dir, Am Inst Aerological Res, 1951-1953; supvr hydrologist in-chg, Mo River Forecast Ctr, 1946-1951; hydrologist, US Weather Bur, 1945-1946; Jr engr, Denison Dist, Corps Engrs, 1938-1941. **Memberships:** Am Soc Civil Engrs; AAAS; Am Meteorol Soc; Am Geophys Union fel. **Research Statement & Publications:** Hydrology; hydrometeorology; oceanography. **Mailing Address:** 610 S Eldridge, Lakewood, CO 80228.

KAHAN, BARRY D, IMMUNOLOGY, SURGERY. **Personal Data:** b Cleveland, Ohio, July 25, 1939; m 1962. **Education:** Univ Chicago, BS, 1960, PhD (physiol), 1964, MD, 1965. **Honors & Awards:** Schweppe Found Career Develop Award; First Gift Life Award. **Professional Experience:** DIR ORGAN TRANSPLANTATION CTR, UNIV TEX MED SCH, as of 2003; PROF, DEPT SURG, UNIV TEX MED SCH, 1977-; assoc prof surg, Northwestern Univ, 1974-1977; asst prof, 1972-1974; surg residency, 1968-1972; staff assoc, NIH, 1966-1968; Intern, Mass Gen Hosp, 1965-1966. **Memberships:** AAAS; Am Asn Immunol; Soc Univ Surg; fel Am Col Surg; Transplantation Soc; Am Surg Asn. **Research Statement & Publications:** Electron microscopy; protein biochemistry; transplantation antigens; delayed-typed hypersensitivity; mTOR Inhibitor Therapy; transplantation and tumor-specific antigens; published over 800 articles. **Mailing Address:** Dept Surg, Med Sch Univ Tex, 6431 Fannin MSB 6 240, Houston, TX 77030. **Fax:** 713-500-0785. **E-Mail:** Barry.D.Kahan@uth.tmc.edu

KAHAN, I HOWARD, AVIAN PATHOLOGY, BACTERIOLOGY. **Personal Data:** b New York, NY, January 7, 1923. **Education:** Queens Col, NY, BS, 1943; Univ Pa, VMD, 1949. **Professional Experience:** PROF EMER, DEL VALLEY COL, as of 2002; vet diag mgr, Dade City Animal Dis Lab, Fla Dept Agr, 1987-1992; prof poultry path, Animal Dis & Bact & Dir Poultry Diag Lab, beginning 1976; assoc prof, Del Valley Col, 1968-1976; inspector poultry, USDA, 1963-1968; instr, Pa State Univ, Ogontz Campus, 1960-1963 & Roxborough Mem Hosp, 1961-1962; dir vet med, Glenside Animal Hosp, 1951-1968. **Memberships:** AAAS; Am Asn Avian Path; US Animal Health Asn; Am Vet Med Asn. **Research Statement & Publications:** All phases of avian diseases and pathology using disciplined microbiology, virology, serology and histopathology. **Mailing Address:** Del Valley Col, 700 E Butler Ave, Doylestown, PA 18901.

KAHAN, LAWRENCE, BIOCHEMISTRY, IMMUNOLOGY. **Personal Data:** b Los Angeles, Calif, May 16, 1944. **Education:** Univ Calif, Berkeley, BA, 1965; Brandeis Univ, PhD (biochem), 1971. **Honors & Awards:** Inbusch Award, 1976. **Professional Experience:** Consult, NSF, 1987-; DIR HYBRIDOMA FAC & VCHMN, DEPT PHYSIOL CHEM, 1985-; PROF PHYSIOL CHEM, UNIV WIS, MADISON, 1983-; consult, NSF, 1982-1985; NSF, res grant, 1980-1983; Fel Fac, HI Romnes, 1979; consult, NSF, 1977-1980; res grant, NIH, 1975-; from asst prof to assoc prof, Dept Physiol Chem, 1973-1983; Fel biochem, Dept Physiol Chem, 1970-1973. **Memberships:** Fel Am Cancer Soc; Am Soc Biochem & Molecular Biol; Am Chem Soc. **Research Statement & Publications:** Structure and function of bacterial and eukaryote ribosomes; cancer associated enzymes; molecular biology; published over 200 articles. **Mailing Address:** Dept Biomolecular, Chem Univ Wis, 659 Bardeen, Madison, WI 53706-1532. **Fax:** 608-262-5253. **E-Mail:** lkahan@wisc.edu

KAHAN, LINDA BERYL, NEUROPHYSIOLOGY. **Personal Data:** b San Francisco, Calif, September 28, 1941. **Education:** Univ Calif, Berkeley, BA, 1963; Stanford Univ, MA, 1965, PhD (biol), 1967. **Professional Experience:** Mem fac, Dept Biol, Evergreen State Col, beginning 1971; asst prof, Antioch Col, 1968-1971; fel Eneurophysiol, Univ Miami, 1967-1968. **Memberships:** AAAS; Sigma Xi. **Research Statement & Publications:** Physiology and anatomy of invertebrate nervous systems; neural control of behavior. **Mailing Address:** Natural Sci, Evergreen State Col, Olympia, WA 98505-0001. **E-Mail:** kahanl@evergreen.edu

KAHAN, SIDNEY, development new food product; deceased, see previous edition for last biography

KAHAN, WILLIAM M, MATHEMATICS, COMPUTER SCIENCE. **Personal Data:** b Toronto, Ont, June 5, 1933; m 1954, Sheila; c Ari J & Simon H. **Education:** Univ Toronto, BA, 1954, MA, 1956, PhD (numerical anal), 1958. **Honorary Degrees:** Chalmers Inst, Sweden; Univ Waterloo, Can. **Honors & Awards:** ER Piore Award, IEEE, 2000; J Von Neumann Lect, Soc Indust & Appl Math, 1997; ACM fel, 1994; A M Turing Award, Asn Comput Mach, 1989. **Professional Experience:** Consult, Intel, 1977-1996; mem, Hewlett-Packard, 1974-1986; mem, IBM, 1972-1973, 1984-1986; PROF MATH & ELECT ENG & COMPUTER SCI, UNIV CALIF, BERKELEY, 1969-; vis assoc prof, Stanford, 1966; from asst prof to prof, Univ Toronto, 1960-1968; Nat Res Counc Can Fel, Cambridge Univ, 1958-1960. **Research Statement & Publications:** Large matrix calculations; trajectory problems; error analysis; design computer arithmetic units; execution-time diagnostic systems for scientific computer systems; general purpose programs to solve standard problems in numerical analysis with highest reliability on electronic computer; IEEE standards 754 and 854 for floating-point arithmetic. **Mailing Address:** Dept Elec Eng & Comput Sci, Univ Calif, 733 Soda Hall, Berkeley, CA 94720-1776. **E-Mail:** wkahan@eecs.berkeley.edu

KAHANA, SIDNEY H, THEORETICAL PHYSICS. **Personal Data:** b Winnipeg, Man, July 23, 1933. **Education:** Univ Man, BSc, 1954, MSc, 1955; Univ Edinburgh, PhD (physics), 1957. **Honors & Awards:** Sr Award, Alexander Von Humboldt Stiftone. **Professional Experience:** THEORET PHYSICIST, BROOKHAVEN NAT LAB, as of 2001; Guggenheim fel, John Simon Mem Found, 1974-1975; SCIENTIST PHYSICS, BROOKHAVEN NAT LAB, 1967-; vis scientist, Brookhaven Nat lab, 1965-1966; vis scientist, Niels Bohr Inst, 1959-1961; from asst prof to assoc prof physics, McGill Univ, 1957-1967; vis scientist, Atomic Energy Can, 1957-1962, 1963 & 1964. **Memberships:** Fel Am Phys Soc. **Research Statement & Publications:** Nuclear theory; structure and reactions; intermediate energy; baryon-anti-baryon systems; many body problems. **Mailing Address:** Dept Physics, Brookhaven Nat Lab, MS 510A, Upton, NY 11973. **Fax:** 516-344-5568. **E-Mail:** kahana@bnl.gov

KAHANER, DAVID KENNETH, APPLIED MATHEMATICS, COMPUTER METHODS. **Personal Data:** b New York, NY, September 12, 1941. **Education:** City Col New York, BS, 1962; Stevens Inst Technol, MS, 1964, PhD (math), 1968. **Professional Experience:** GROUP LEADER, NAT BUR STAND, 1981-; mem staff, Nat Bur Stand, 1979-1980; Swiss Fed Inst Technol, 1977-1978 & Vienna Tech Univ, 1978; Univ Torino, Italy, 1977; Vis prof, Univ Mich, 1972-1973; Mem staff numerical anal, Los Alamos Nat Lab, 1968-1980. **Memberships:** Am Math Soc; Asn Comput Mach. **Research Statement & Publications:** Numerical analysis; computing methods; mathematical software. **Mailing Address:** Dir Asian Tech Info Prog, Unit 45002 Box 319, APO, AP 96337-0007.

KAHL, JONATHAN D W, AIR POLLUTION METEOROLOGY, POLAR METEOROLOGY & CLIMATOLOGY. **Personal Data:** b Shirley, Mass, May 7, 1959; m 1987, Carol; c Joseph J & Samantha R. **Education:** Univ Mich, BA, 1981, MS, 1983, PhD (atmospheric sci), 1987. **Honors & Awards:** Fulbright Scholar 2003. **Professional Experience:** PROF ATMOSPHERIC SCI, UNIV WIS-MILWAUKEE, 2000-; assoc prof atmospheric sci, Univ Wis-Milwaukee, 1994-2000; asst prof, Univ Wis-Milwaukee, 1990-1994; nat res coun res assoc, Nat Oceanic & Atmospheric Admin-Geophys Monitoring Climatic Chg, 1987-1989; resident res assoc, Nat Res Coun, 1987; res assoc, Coop Inst Res Environ Sci, Univ Colo. **Memberships:** Am Meteorol Soc; Am Geophys Union. **Research Statement & Publications:** Meteorological aspects of air pollution, particularly long-range transport, polar meteorology; arctic boundary layer. **Mailing Address:** Dept Math Sci, Univ Wis-Milwaukee, PO Box 413, Milwaukee, WI 53201. **Fax:** 414-229-4907. **E-Mail:** kahl@uwm.edu

KAHLE, ANNE B, GEOPHYSICS, REMOTE SENSING. **Personal Data:** b Auburn, Wash, March 30, 1934; m 1957, James; c Sheree (Luttrel), Richard, Vicki & Jeffrey. **Education:** Univ Alaska, BS, 1955, MS, 1961; Univ Calif, Los Angeles, PhD (meteorol), 1975. **Honors & Awards:** Gen James Gordon Steese Prize. **Professional Experience:** SR RES SCIENTIST, JET PROPULSION LAB, as of 2003; US aster sci team leader, Jet Propulsion Lab, 1991-1996; SR RES SCIENTIST, 1991-; GEOL & VOLCANOLOGY PROG, 1989-; supvr, Geol Group, 1975-1991; mgr, Geol & Volcanology Prog, 1974-1996; mem tech staff, Jet Propulsion Lab, 1974-1975; sr phys scientist, Rand Corp, Calif, 1967-1974; from asst phys scientist to phys scientist, Rand Corp, Calif, 1963-1967; res asst, Rand Corp, Calif, 1961-1963. **Memberships:** Sigma Xi; Am Geophys Union; AAAS; Geol Soc Am. **Research Statement & Publications:** Remote sensing of geology; volcanology geomagnetic field; solar-terrestrial relationships; atmospheric physics; gravity; atmospheric radiation. **Mailing Address:** Jet Propulsion Lab, Mail stop 183-501, 4800 Oak Grove Dr, Pasadena, CA 90290. **Fax:** 818-354-0966. **E-Mail:** anne@aster.jpl.nasa.gov

KAHLE, CHARLES F, GEOLOGY. **Personal Data:** b Toledo, Ohio, June 2, 1930; m 1957, c 6. **Education:** St Joseph's Col, Ind, BS, 1953; Miami Univ, Ohio, MS, 1957; Univ Kans, PhD (geol), 1962. **Professional Experience:** PROF EMER GEOL, BOWLING GREEN STATE UNIV, 2000-; prof geol, Bowling Green state Univ, 1974-2000; from asst prof to assoc prof, Bowling Green State Univ, 1965-1974; asst prof geol, Okla State Univ 1962-1963 & Univ Toledo, 1963-1965; Geologist, Mobil Petrol Co, Okla, 1957-1958. **Memberships:** Geol Soc Am; Soc Econ Paleont & Mineral. **Research Statement & Publications:** Carbonate geology; stratigraphy; scanning electron microscopy; sedimentation. **Mailing Address:** Dept Geol, Bowling Green State Univ, Rm 190, Overman Hall, Bowling Green, OH 43403. **Fax:** 419-372-7205. **E-Mail:** ckahle@bgnet.bgsu.edu

KAHLER, ALBERT COMSTOCK, III, NUCLEAR PHYSICS. **Personal Data:** b Bay Shore, NY, June 10, 1951. **Education:** Gettysburg Col, BA, 1973; Univ Tenn, PhD (physics), 1978. **Professional Experience:** FEL SCIENTIST EXP PHYSICS, BETTIS ATOMIC POWER LAB, WESTINGHOUSE ELEC CORP, 1991-; sr scientist exp physics, Bettis Atomic Power Lab, Westinghouse Elec Corp, 1981-1991; Res assoc physics, Cyclotron Inst, Tex A&M Univ, 1978-1981. **Memberships:** Am Phys Soc. **Research Statement & Publications:** Nuclear structure studies using gamma-ray spectroscopy techniques. **Mailing Address:** Bettis Atomic Power Lab Bechtel Bettis Inc, PO Box 79 ZAP 34F, West Mifflin, PA 15122. **Fax:** 412-476-6924. **E-Mail:** kahlerac@bettis.gov

KAHLER, ALEX L, GENETICS, PLANT BREEDING. **Personal Data:** b Scottsbluff, Nebr, July 4, 1939. **Education:** Univ Calif, Davis, BS, 1965, MS, 1967, PhD, 1973. **Professional Experience:** PRES & FOUNDER, BIOGENETIC SERV INC, 1988-; mgr biotechnol & sr res geneticist, Garst, Slater, Iowa, 1986-1988; PROF PLANT SCI, SDAK STATE UNIV, BROOKINGS, 1980-; plant geneticist, Northern Grain Insects Res Lab, Agr Res Serv, USDA, 1980-1986, 1986-1988; staff res assoc genetics, Univ Calif, Davis, 1965-1980. **Memberships:** AAAS; Am Genetics Asn; Soc Study Evolution; Genetics Soc Am; Crop Sci Soc Am; Sigma Xi. **Research Statement & Publications:** Determining the extent and distribution of genetic variability within and between populations and with measuring the forces which are responsible for the observed variability; improving corn populations for resistance to insects and diseases. **Mailing Address:** Biogenetic Serv Inc, 801 32nd Ave, Brookings, SD 57006. **Fax:** 605-697-8507. **E-Mail:** biogene.brookings.net

KAHLER, RICHARD LEE, CARDIOVASCULAR PHYSIOLOGY. **Personal Data:** b Milltown, NJ, January 2, 1933. **Education:** YaleUniv, MD, 1957. **Professional Experience:** Assoc prof med, Sch Med, Univ Calif, San Diego, 1968-; HEAD CARDIOVASC DIV, SCRIPPS CLIN & RES FOUND, 1968-; NIH res career develop award, 1965-1968; From asst prof to assoc prof med, Yale Univ, 1965-1968. **Memberships:** AAAS; Am Physiol Soc; Am Heart Asn; Am Col Physicians; Am Col Cardiol; Sigma Xi. **Research Statement & Publications:** Cardiovascular pharmacology. **Mailing Address:** PO Box 104, Rancho Santa Fe, CA 92067-0104. **Fax:** 619-756-1485.

KAHLON, PREM SINGH, BIOLOGY, PLANT GENETICS. **Personal Data:** b Lyallpur, India, June 16, 1936; American citizen; m 1967, Darshi; c Paul & Jay. **Education:** Punjab Univ, India, BS, 1956; La State Univ, MS, 1962, PhD (plant breeding), 1964. **Professional Experience:** PROF BIOL, TENN STATE UNIV, 1966-; prof, Alcorn Agr & Mech Col, 1965-1966; asst prof biol, Talladega Col, 1964-1965. **Memberships:** Genetics Soc Am; Indian Soc Genetics & Plant Breeding; Tissue Cult Asn Am. **Research Statement & Publications:** Inheritance studies in rice, especially cooking quality; mutation genetics; chemical mutagenesis; in vitro culture of soybean and cell genetics. **Mailing Address:** Dept Biol, Tenn State Univ, 3500 John Merritt Blvd, Nashville, TN 37209-1561. **Fax:** 615-963-5785.

KAHLON, TALWINDER SINGH, NUTRITION, BIOCHEMISTRY. **Personal Data:** b Ludhiana, Punjab, India, February 25, 1945; American citizen; m Kohlon; c Ashwinder & Pushpinder. **Education:** Univ Minn, PhD (nutrit), 1974. **Professional Experience:** Assoc ed, Cereal Chem J, beginning 1991; RES CHEMIST, WESTERN REGIONAL RES CTR, USDA, 1984-; nutritionist, Western Regional Res Ctr, USDA, 1984-1987; guest staff scientist, Lawrence Berkeley Lab, beginning 1983. **Memberships:** Am Inst Nutrit; fel Am heart Asn; Am Asn Cereal Chemist. **Research Statement & Publications:** Cholesterol-lowering by cereal fibers and fractions. **Mailing Address:** Western Reg Res Ctr, 800 Buchanan St, Albany, CA 94710-1198. **Fax:** 510-559-5777. **E-Mail:** tsk@pw.usda.gov

KAHN, A CLARK, III, BIOCHEMISTRY. **Personal Data:** b Pittsburgh, Pa, December 16, 1937. **Education:** Univ NH, BA, 1961, MS, 1963; Pa State Univ, PhD (biochem), 1966. **Professional Experience:** Pres, Environ Qual Mgt Inst, 1998-1999; PRES & PRINCIPLE TEACHER ENVIRON & OCCUPATIONAL CONSUL & TRAINING, 1987-; Pres & Lab Dir Environ Evaluation & Lab Serv, 1986-1997; dir lab, ana-qual labs, 1985-1986; sr chemist, Palasades Nuclear Power Plant, 1981-1984; dir clin path, Int Res & Develop Corp, 1978-1981; dir labs, New Eng Med Labs, 1977-1978; dir res & develop, Precision Systs, 1976-1977; supvr clin path, ICI Am, 1968-1976; Lab officer clin chem & biochemist, USPHS Hosp, 1966-1968. **Memberships:** AAAS; Am Chem Soc; Am Asn Clin Chem; Am Soc Vet Clin Pathologists; Nat Registry Clin Chemists. **Research Statement & Publications:**

Clinical laboratory medicine, particularly electrolyte chemistry and intestinal absorption, malabsorption syndrome; laboratory animal clinical pathology; toxicology of hazardous materials. **Mailing Address:** Consult & Training Inc, 4000 Portage Rd Ste 201, Kalamazoo, MI 49001-4963. **Fax:** 269-383-6967. **E-Mail:** Kahn@eoct-ack.com

KAHN, ALAN RICHARD, BIOENGINEERING, PHYSIOLOGY. **Personal Data:** b Chicago, Ill, March 1, 1932. **Education:** Univ Ill, MD, 1959. **Professional Experience:** CONSULT; adj prof bioengineering & lab med, Univ Minn, beginning 2000; grad fac, Univ Minn, beginning 1994; prof elec & comput eng, Univ Cincinnati, 1984-1990; consult, Appl Electronic Consults Inc, beginning 1980; dir biomed res, Nicolet Instrument Corp, 1978-1980; pres, Andersen Med Systs, 1977-1978; sr vpres cardiovasc res, Medtronic Inc, 1970-1977; vpres res & develop, Health Technol Corp, 1968-1970; dir biophys res, Hoffman LaRoche Inc, 1966-1968; med dir, Offner Div, Beckman Instruments Inc, 1963-1966; dir physiol res, Offner Div, Beckman Instruments Inc, 1962-1963; design engr, Offner Electronics, 1958-1959; lectr, Univ Ill; chmn comt med devices, Am Nat Standards Inst; clin asst prof, Univ Minn. **Memberships:** Neuroelec Soc (vpres); AMA; Biomed Eng Soc; Inst Elec & Electronics Engrs; Asn Advan Med Instrumentation. **Research Statement & Publications:** Cardiovascular neurological and rehabilitation instrumentation; aerospace medicine; biological electrode techniques, medical device standards, management for research and development programs. **Mailing Address:** Dept Lab Med & Path, Univ Minn, 420 Del, Minneapolis, MN 55455. **Fax:** 612-377-6446. **E-Mail:** kahnx006@umn.edu

KAHN, ALBERT, DEVELOPMENTAL BIOLOGY. **Personal Data:** b Wuerburg, Ger, May 21, 1931. **Education:** Cornell Univ, BS, 1953; Univ Calif, Los Angeles, PhD (bot), 1958. **Professional Experience:** EMER PROF BIOL & LECTR, GENETICS INST, COPENHAGEN UNIV, 1992 -; assoc prof, Genetics Inst, Copenhagen Univ, 1970-1992; assoc prof, Purdue Univ, 1964-1970; res fel biol, Calif Inst Technol, 1962-1964; fels, NSF, Stockholm, 1959-1961 & USPHS, 1961-1962; Jr res botanist, Univ Calif, Los Angeles, 1958-1959. **Research Statement & Publications:** Chloroplast pigments; genetic control of chloroplast development. **Mailing Address:** Genetics Dept Copenhagen Univ Inst Molecular Biol, Oster Farimagsgade 2A, DK 1353 Copenhagen K, Denmark.

KAHN, ARTHUR B, MANAGEMENT INFORMATION SYSTEMS. **Personal Data:** b New York, NY, February 11, 1931. **Education:** City Col NY, BS, 1951; Johns Hopkins Univ, MS, 1954, PhD (dynamic meteorol), 1959. **Professional Experience:** PROF EMER, ROBERT G MERRICK SCH BUS, UNIV BALTIMORE, MD, as of 2003; assoc prof, info quant studies, Univ Baltimore, beginning 1978; adv engr, Info Processing Dept, 1971-1978; vis assoc prof, Univ Wis-Madison, 1968-1971; fel engr, Info Processing Dept, 1968-1970; fel engr, Systs Div 1963-1968; Founder & chmn prog eval & rev tech proj, SHARE, 1962-1964; sr engr, Air Arm Div, Westinghouse Elec Corp, 1958-1963; staff asst, Johns Hopkins Univ, 1954-1958; res asst dynamic meteorol, Johns Hopkins Univ, 1951-1954. **Memberships:** Asn Comput Mach; Sigma Xi; Opers Res Soc Am. **Research Statement & Publications:** Determination of what the nonspecialist should know about computers and development of ways and means to educate him; application of structured system development methods to creative activities. **Mailing Address:** Robert G Merrick Sch Bus, Univ Baltimore, 1420 N Charles St, Baltimore, MD 21201-5779. **Fax:** 410-837-4899. **E-Mail:** abkahn@ube.umd.edu

KAHN, BERND, RADIOCHEMISTRY. **Personal Data:** b Pforzheim, Ger, August 16, 1928; American citizen; m 1961, Gail; c Jennifer & Elizabeth. **Education:** Newark Col Eng, BS, 1950; Vanderbilt Univ, MS, 1952; Mass Inst Technol, PhD (chem), 1960. **Professional Experience:** DIR, ENVIRON RESOURCES CTR & PROF EMER NUCLEAR ENG & HEALTH PHYSICS, GA INST TECHNOL, 1974-; radiochemist, Radiochem & Nuclear Eng Br, Environ Protection Agency, Nat Environ Res Ctr, 1969-1974; radiochemist, USPHS, 1954-1969; assoc chemist radiochem, Oak Ridge Nat Lab, 1951-1954; mem, Nat Coun Radiation Protection & Measurements. **Memberships:** Health Physics Soc; Am Chem Soc; Am Phys Soc. **Research Statement & Publications:** Analytical radiochemical methods; behavior of radionuclides in the environment; radioactive effluents from nuclear power stations. **Mailing Address:** Environ Resources Ctr, Ga Inst Technol, Atlanta, GA 30332. **E-Mail:** bernd.kahn@me.gatech.edu

KAHN, CARL RONALD, ENDOCRINOLOGY. **Personal Data:** b Louisville, Ky, January 14, 1944; m 1966, c 2. **Education:** Univ Louisville, BA, 1964, MD, 1968. **Honors & Awards:** Davis Rumbough Mem Award, Juv Diabetes Found, 1977; Pfizer Biomed Res Award, 1986; Edwin B Astwood Lectr, Endocrine Soc, 1987. **Professional Experience:** PRES, JOSLIN DIABETES CTR, as of 2004; IACOCCA PROF MED, HARVARD MED SCH, 1984-; DIR RES, JOSLIN DIABETES CTR, 1981-; chief, Div Diabetes & Metabolism, Brigham & Women's Hosp, 1981; mem, Med Sci Adv Bd, Juv Diabetes Found, 1978-; chief cellular & molecular physiol, Diabetes Br, Nat Inst Arthritis & Metab Dis, NIH, 1978-1981; sr investr, 1973-1978. **Memberships:** Am Soc Clin Invest; Am Fedn Clin; Asn Am Physicians; Nat Coun Am Soc Clin Invest (pres-elect, 1987). **Research Statement & Publications:** Endocrine Soc; Am Diabetes Asn. Res: Insulin action and alterations in insulin action in disease states; hypoglycemia and insulin-like peptides in blood. **Mailing Address:** Joslin Diabetes Ctr, One Joslin Pl, Boston, MA 02215. **Fax:** 617-732-2593. **E-Mail:** c.ronald.kahn@joslin.harvard.edu

KAHN, DANIEL STEPHEN, MATHEMATICS. **Personal Data:** b Brooklyn, NY, November 20, 1935. **Education:** Princeton Univ, AB, 1957; Mass Inst Technol, PhD (math), 1964. **Professional Experience:** PROF EMER MATH, NORTHWESTERN UNIV, ILL, as of 2004; prof math, Northwestern Univ, ILL, beginning 1978; asst prof to assoc prof, Northwestern Univ, Ill, 1964-1978; Res instr math, Univ Chicago, 1962-1964. **Memberships:** Am Math Soc. **Research Statement & Publications:** Algebraic topology, especially field of stable homotopy theory. **Mailing Address:** Dept Math, Northwestern Univ, 2033 Sheridan Rd, Evanston, IL 60208-2730. **E-Mail:** kahn@math.nwu.edu

KAHN, DAVID, solid state physics, electrochemistry; deceased, see previous edition for last biography

KAHN, DAVID, PHYSICS. **Personal Data:** b New York, NY, April 27, 1933. **Education:** Brooklyn Col, BS, 1957; Yale Univ, MS, 1959, PhD (physics), 1962. **Professional Experience:** CONSULT, 1986-; sect chief technol, Transp Systs Ctr, 1974-1986; group head, Modelling & Anal Group, US Dept Transp, 1971-1974; Sr scientist, Raytheon Co, 1962-1966 & electronics res ctr, NASA, 1966-1971. **Memberships:** Am Phys Soc; sr mem Inst Elec & Electronics Engrs; Sigma Xi. **Research Statement & Publications:** Kinetic theory and plasma physics; wave propagation in highly rarefied gases; plasma density discontinuity wave coupling; traffic flow theory. **Mailing Address:** 238 Biddle Dr, Exton, PA 19341-1707.

KAHN, DONALD JAY, ORGANIC CHEMISTRY. **Personal Data:** b Baltimore, Md, August 10, 1930. **Education:** Princeton Univ, BA, 1952; Univ Chicago, PhD (org chem), 1957. **Professional Experience:** RETIRED; strategic planning, Exxon Enterprises Inc, 1984-1986; sr technol adv, Exxon Enterprises Inc, 1981-1984; solar energy gen mgr, Exxon Enterprises Inc, 1978-1981; environ conserv sr adv, Exxon Corp, 1971-1977; mgr aviation tech serv, Exxon Int Inc, 1968-1971; sect head, Esso Res & Eng Co, 1963-1967; proj leader & sr chemist, Esso Res & Eng Co, 1960-1963; chemist, Esso Res & Eng Co, 1957-1960; asst org chem, Univ Chicago, 1952-1955; consult, Technol Mgt. **Memberships:** Am Chem Soc; Sigma Xi. **Research Statement & Publications:** Reaction mechanisms; free radical organic chemistry and polymerization; chemical additives for lubricants; industrial lubricants, greases, wax products and asphalt products; solar photovoltics. **Mailing Address:** 62 Spring St, Metuchen, NJ 08840.

KAHN, DONALD R, CARDIOVASCULAR SURGERY, THORACIC SURGERY. **Personal Data:** b Birmingham, Ala, May 21, 1929. **Education:** Birmingham-Southern Col, BA, 1950; Univ Ala, BA, 1957, MD, 1954. **Professional Experience:** RETIRED; prof surg & chmn cardiovasc med, Univ WKis Hosp, 1971-1980; head, Div Thoracic & Cardiovasc Surg, Med Ctr, Univ Wis-Madison, 1971-1980; from asst prof to assoc prof surg, Med Sch, 1964-1971; instr thoracic surg, Med Sch, 1963-1964; Am Thoracic Soc fel, 1961-1964; dir clin invest lab, directorate med res, Chem Warfare Lab, 1956-1958; resident, Med Ctr, Univ Mich, Ann Arbor, 1955-1959; asst, Sch Med, Wash Univ, 1954-1955; intern, St Louis City Hosp, 1954-1955. **Memberships:** Fel Am Col Surg; Am Heart Asn; Am Thoracic Soc; Am Asn Thoracic Surg; Soc Thoracic Surg. **Mailing Address:** 2012 Magnolia Ave, Birmingham, AL 35205.

KAHN, DONALD W, MATHEMATICS, HOMOTOPY THEORY, CATEGORIES. **Personal Data:** b New York, NY, November 21, 1935; m 1956, Phyllis; c 2. **Education:** Cornell Univ, BA, 1957; Yale Univ, PhD (math), 1961. **Professional Experience:** Vis Fulbright prof, Univ Toulouse, 1988-1989; PROF MATH, UNIV MINN, MINNEAPOLIS, 1984-; vis Fulbright prof, Univ Heidelberg, 1965; from asst prof to assoc prof, Univ Minn, Minneapolis, 1964-1984; Ritt instr math, Columbia Univ, 1961-1964. **Memberships:** Am Math Soc, foreign mem Soc, Math de France, Foreign European Math Union. **Research Statement & Publications:** Algebraic topology. **Mailing Address:** Univ Minn Sch Math, Minneapolis, MN 55455. **E-Mail:** kahn@math.umn.edu

KAHN, ELLIOTT H, ECONOMIC STUDIES, APPLIED MECHANICS. **Personal Data:** b Brooklyn, NY, February 27, 1926; wid Laura (deceased); c 2. **Education:** City Col NY, BCE, 1945; Polytech Inst Brooklyn, MCE, 1948. **Honors & Awards:** Robert Ridgeway Award, Am Soc Civil Engrs, 1945; Tau Beta Pi. **Professional Experience:** CONSULT, 1992-; mgr, Coopers & Lybrand, 1976-1992; mgr corporate technology ctr, Kollsman Instrument Corp, Syosset, 1961-1976; mgr reliability anal sect, W L Maxson Corp, 1957-1961; sr engr, W L Maxson Corp, 1951-1957; staff engr, D B Steinman, 1947-1951; Res engr, Repub Aviation Corp, NY, 1945-1947; Lectr & consult engr, var times. **Memberships:** AAAS; NY Acad Sci; Nat Soc Prof Engrs; Am Soc Civil Engrs; Inst Elec & Electronics Engrs; Am Inst Aeronaut & Astronaut. **Research Statement & Publications:** Applied mechanics and systems engineering in the fields of structures, reliability, traffic, instruments, laser safety and electro-optical systems. **Mailing Address:** 280 Henry St, Brooklyn, NY 11201. **Fax:** 718-624-2434. **E-Mail:** lkehk@aol.com

KAHN, FREDERIC JAY, PROJECTION DISPLAYS, FLAT PANEL DISPLAYS. **Personal Data:** b Brooklyn, NY, September 1, 1941; m 1967, c 2. **Education:** Rensselaer Polytech Inst, BEE, 1962; Harvard Univ, AM, 1963, PhD (solid state physics), 1968. **Professional Experience:** PRES, KAHN INT, 1992-; vpres, Technol, Greyhawk Systs Inc, 1984-1992; dept mgr Storage Physics Dept, Mass Memory Lab, 1983-1984; dept mgr, optical mat & polymers, Mat Res Lab, 1982-1983; prin investr, Joint Serv VHSIC, 1981-1983; lab proj mgr, Hewlett Packard Lab, 1974-1982; mem tech staff liquid crystal mat, displays & related technol, Optical Control Devices Dept, Solid State Lab, Bell Labs, 1970-1973; spec researcher liquid crystal displays, Quantum Device Res Lab, Cent Res Lab, Nippon Elec Co, Kawasaki, Japan, 1968-1969; res asst magneto-optics garnets & orthoferrites, Gordon McKay Lab, Harvard Univ, 1965-1968. **Memberships:** Am Phys Soc; Inst Elec & Electronics Engrs; fel secy Soc Info Display; Int Soc Optical Eng. **Research Statement & Publications:** Liquid crystal display materials; devices and systems; electron-beam and x-ray resists for high resolution lithography; optical memory materials and systems; optical fiber properties and devices; optical disc memories and erasable media; research and developmenton very high information content (resolution) imaging systems for display; hard copy generation and optical processing based on laser and optical beam addressed liquid crystal projection light valves. **Mailing Address:** 782 Southampton Dr, Palo Alto, CA 94303-3437. **Fax:** 650-429-2035. **E-Mail:** fjkahn@post.harvard.edu

KAHN, HAROLD A, CHRONIC DISEASE, EPIDEMIOLOGY. **Personal Data:** b New York, NY, January 4, 1920. **Education:** City Col NY, BS, 1939; Am Univ, MA, 1949. **Professional Experience:** Vis prof epidemiol, Johns Hopkins Univ, 1985-; vis prof epidemiol, Loma Linda Univ, 1982; Lady Davis vis prof epidemiol, Hebrew Univ, Jerusalem, 1980; CONSULT EPIDEMIOL, 1978-; prof epidemiol, Sch Hyg & Pub Health, Johns Hopkins Univ, 1975-1978; chief off biomet & epidemiol, Nat Eye Inst, 1971-1975; Fel Coun Epidemiol, Am Heart Asn, 1964-; heart dis res, NIH, 1960-1971; res adminr, NIH, 1957-1960; USPHS award, 1957; med care needs, USPHS, 1951-1957; Statistician heart dis res, Nat Heart & Lung Inst, 1950-1951. **Memberships:** Fel Am Statist Asn; Soc Epidemiol Res. **Research Statement & Publications:** Nutrition and other risk factors in relation to chronic disease; problems of validating dietary data collected in field surveys. **Mailing Address:** 26018 S Boxwood Dr, Chandler, AZ 85248.

KAHN, HENRY SLATER, DIABETES, EPIDEMIOLOGY, OBESITY. **Personal Data:** b Poughkeepsie, NY, May 6, 1943; m 1970, Mary Gillmor; c Jeremy G & Daniel K (Gillmor). **Education:** Harvard Univ, AB, 1964, MD, 1968. **Professional Experience:** MED EPIDEMIOL, DIABETES DIV, NAT CTR CHRONIC DIS PREV & HEALTH PROM, CTR DIS CONTROL & PREV, 2001-; PROF EMER, EMORY UNIV, as of 2001. **Memberships:** fel Am Col Physicians; Am Pub Health Asn; fel Am Heart Asn; Soc Epidemiol Res; Physicians Nat Health Prog. **Research Statement & Publications:** Prevention of chronic diseases especially those related to diabetes and obesity; epidemiology of body-fat distribution; efficient, humane models of primary medical care. **Mailing Address:** Nat Ctr Chronic Dis Prev & Health Prom, Ctr Dis Control & Prev, MS K 10 4770 Buford Hwy, Atlanta, GA 30341. **Fax:** 770-488-1148. **E-Mail:** hkahn@cdc.gov

KAHN, JACK HENRY, ENGINEERING PHYSICS. **Personal Data:** b Bolivar, Tenn, November 1, 1923; m 1952, Sue; c Elizabeth, George & Andrew. **Education:** Univ Tenn, BS, 1947, MS, 1949, PhD (physics), 1951. **Professional Experience:** RETIRED; consult, SAIC, 1993-1995; consult, Hist Assocs Inc, 1988-1992; physicist, US Dept Energy, 1979-1988; asst chief, Weapons Prog Br Div Classification, 1975-1979; staff asst, Div Classification Br, US AEC, 1973-1975; chief, Declassification Br, US AEC, 1968-1973; asst chief, Declassification Br, US AEC, 1955-1968; classification analyst, Declassification Br, US AEC, 1951-1955. **Memberships:** Am Phys Soc; Sigma Xi. **Research Statement & Publications:** Nuclear physics. **Mailing Address:** 3212 Red Deer Ct, Plano, TX 75093.

KAHN, JEFFRY N, DISCRETE MATHEMATICS. **Honors & Awards:** George Polya Prize, Soc Indust & Appl Math, 1996. **Professional Experience:** PROF, DEPT MATH, RUT-

GERS UNIV, 1988-. **Mailing Address:** Dept Math, Rutgers Univ, Hill Ctr, Busch Campus Rm 226, New Brunswick, NJ 08854. **E-Mail:** jkahn@math.rutgers.edu

KAHN, JOSEPH STEPHAN, PLANT BIOCHEMISTRY. **Personal Data:** b Ger, August 12, 1929. **Education:** Univ Calif, BS, 1955; Univ Ill, PhD, 1958. **Professional Experience:** PROF EMER BOT & BIOCHEM, NC STATE UNIV, 1989-; Fulbright fel, India, 1978; from asst prof to prof, NC State Univ, 1961-1989; res assoc biol, Johns Hopkins Univ, 1959-1961; Res assoc physiol, Univ Ill, 1958-1959. **Memberships:** Am Soc Plant Physiol; AAAS; Biophys Soc; Am Soc Biol Chem. **Research Statement & Publications:** Electron transport and pathway of adenosine triphosphate formation in chloroplasts; localization of enzyme systems in chloroplasts; modification of protozoal membranes by drugs. **Mailing Address:** Dept Biochem, NC State Univ, Raleigh, NC 27695.

KAHN, KEVIN C, COMPUTER SCIENCE. **Education:** Purdue Univ, PhD, 1976. **Professional Experience:** DIR, COMMUN TECHNOL LAB, INTEL CORP, as of 1995. **Mailing Address:** Intel Corp, 5200 Elam Young Pkwy, Hillsboro, OR 97124-6497. **Fax:** 503-264-3483. **E-Mail:** kevin.kahn@intel.com

KAHN, LAWRENCE F, STRUCTURAL ENGINEERING, CIVIL ENGINEERING. **Personal Data:** b Oakland, Calif, January 26, 1945. **Education:** Stanford Univ, BS, 1966; Univ Ill, Champaign-Urbana, MS, 1967; Univ Mich, Ann Arbor, PhD (civil eng), 1976. **Honors & Awards:** Raymond Reese Res Prize, Am Soc Civil Eng, 1980; Outstanding Fac Mem, Ga Tech, 2003. **Professional Experience:** Prin investr, Georgia DOT High Performance Concrete 1995-; PROF STRUCT ENG, GA INST TECHNOL, 1976-; asst prof, Ga Inst Technol, 1976-1980; struct engr power plant, Bechtel Power Corp, 1976; Struct engr undersea struct, US Naval Civil Eng Lab, 1967-1971. **Memberships:** Fel Am Soc Civil Engrs; Fel Am Concrete Inst; Int Inst Concrete Repair; Masonry Soc. **Research Statement & Publications:** Earthquake engineering; computer aided engineering computer aided design computer aided mechanics; reinforced concrete structures; masonry structures; experimental analysis; published over 50 articles and granted several patents. **Mailing Address:** Ga Inst Technol Civil & Environ Eng, 790 Atlantic Dr NW, Atlanta, GA 30332-0355. **Fax:** 404-894-8014. **E-Mail:** lawrence.kahn@ce.gatech.edu

KAHN, LEO DAVID, BIOPHYSICAL CHEMISTRY. **Personal Data:** b Everett, Mass. **Education:** Mass Inst Technol, SB, 1954; Yale Univ, PhD (chem), 1959. **Professional Experience:** RETIRED; res chemist, Eastern Regional Res & Develop Lab, USDA, 1958-1984. **Memberships:** AAAS; Am Chem Soc; Biophys Soc; NY Acad Sci; Sigma Xi. **Research Statement & Publications:** Physical chemistry of proteins; electronic instrumentation for use in chemical investigations. **Mailing Address:** 15-38 Chandler Dr, Fairlawn, NJ 07410-2714.

KAHN, LEONARD B, SURGICAL PATHOLOGY. **Personal Data:** b Johannesburg, SAfrica, July 20, 1937. **Education:** Witwaterstrand Univ, Johannesburg, MB, BS, 1960; Univ Cape Town, M Med Path, 1965; MRCPath, 1977, FRCPath, 1986. **Professional Experience:** PROF PATH, ALBERT EINSTEIN COL, as of 2004; CHMN DEPT PATH, LONG ISLAND JEWISH MED CTR, as of 2001; prof path, State Univ NY, Stony Brook, beginning 1980; CHMN DEPT LABS, LONG ISLAND JEWISH MED CTR, 1980-; prof & dir surg & path, Sch Med, Univ NC, Chapel Hill, 1977-1980; assoc prof, Dept Path, Sch Med, Univ Cape Town, 1974-1977; resident & fel clin asst, Sch Med, Wash Univ, St Louis, 1967-1969; Cecil John Adams Mem travelling fel, Univ Cape Town, 1967; resident path, Univ Cape Town, 1962-1966; intern med & surg, Johannesburg Gen Hosp, 1961-1962. **Memberships:** Int Acad Path; Gastrointestinal Path Club; Int Skeletal Soc; Arthur Purdy Stout Soc Surg Pathologists; Col Am Pathologists. **Research Statement & Publications:** Clinical pathologic, including immunologic and ultrastructural studies of a variety of human neoplasma, especially those involving lymphoreticular tissues, bone, soft tissue and gastrointestinal tract including salivary glands. **Mailing Address:** Dept Path, Long Island Jewish Med Ctr, Albert Einstein Col Med, 718 Lakeville Rd, New Hyde Park, NY 11040. **E-Mail:** kahn@lij.edu

KAHN, MANFRED, CERAMIC SCIENCE, ELECTRICAL ENGINEERING. **Personal Data:** b Frankfurt am Main, Ger, February 21, 1926; American citizen; m 1960, Eileen; c William, Douglas & Stephen. **Education:** Univ Wis, BSEE, 1954; Rensselaer Polytech Inst, MSEE, 1959; Pa State Univ, PhD (ceramic sci), 1969. **Professional Experience:** RETIRED; consult, Naval Res Lab, 1996-2002; sect head, Naval Res Lab, Wash, DC, 1983-1996; dept head, Hurry County Tech Col, 1982-1983; sr scientist, AVX Ceramics Inc, 1974-1982; mem tech staff, Ceramic Dept, Sprague Elec Co, 1954-1974. **Memberships:** Inst Elec & Electronics Engrs; fel Am Ceramic Soc. **Research Statement & Publications:** Surface layer capacitors; ohmic contacts and hybrid microcircuits; multilayer capacitors; pilot plant production; base metal electrodes; process development; pilot plant and production; circuits and applications engineering; single crystal piezo electric sensors, programed transmission control devices; microwave heated processing and joining of ceramics. **Mailing Address:** 2912 Midiron Ct, Myrtle Beach, SC 29577. **E-Mail:** manfrew@att.net

KAHN, MARVIN WILLIAM, OTHER MEDICAL & HEALTH SCIENCES. **Personal Data:** b Cleveland, Ohio, February 1, 1926. **Education:** Pa State Univ, BS, 1948, MS, 1949, PhD (psychol), 1952. **Professional Experience:** PROF EMER PSYCHOL, UNIV ARIZ, 1995-; prof psychol, Univ Ariz, 1969-1995; prof psychol, Ohio Univ, 1964-1969; from asst prof psychol to assoc prof psychiat, Univ Colo Sch Med, 1954-1964; from instr to asst prof psychol, Yale Univ, 1952-1954. **Memberships:** Am Psychol Asn. **Mailing Address:** Dept Psychol Univ Ariz, Douglass Bldg 200W, Tucson, AZ 85721. **E-Mail:** mwkahn@email.arizona.edu

KAHN, MICHAEL LEE, MICROBIOLOGY. **Education:** Stanford Univ, PhD. **Professional Experience:** PROF MICROBIOL, WASH STATE UNIV, as of 2005. **Mailing Address:** Dept Microbiol, Wash State Univ, Clark 203, Pullman, WA 99164-6340. **Fax:** 509-335-7643. **E-Mail:** kahn@wsu.edu

KAHN, NORMAN, NEUROPHARMACOLOGY, DENTAL & MEDICAL EDUCATION. **Personal Data:** b New York, NY, December 28, 1932. **Education:** Columbia Univ, AB, 1954, DDS, 1958, PhD (pharmacol), 1964. **Professional Experience:** SPEC LECTR PHARMACOL, COL PHYSICIANS & SURGEONS, COLUMBIA UNIV, as of 2005; PROF & ASSOC DEAN EMER, DEPT DENT, SCH DENT & ORAL SURG, COLUMBIA UNIV, as of 2005; actg dean, Sch Dent & Oral Surg, 1995-1996; edwin robinson prof dent & oral surg, Col Physicians & Surgeons, Columbia Univ, beginning 1992; assoc dean acad affairs, Sch Dent & Oral Surg, 1989-1995; hon res fel, Univ Col London, beginning 1986; prof pharmacol, Col Physicians & Surgeons, Columbia Univ, beginning 1981; prof dent, Sch Dent & Oral Surg, 1981-1992; vis assoc prof anesthesiol, Univ Calif, Los Angeles, beginning 1978; assoc prof dent, Columbia Univ, 1974-1981; assoc prof pharmacol, Columbia Univ, 1972-1980; NIH career develop award, 1967-1971; Nat Inst Neurol Dis & Blindness spec fels, Pisa, 1965-1966 & Columbia Univ, 1962-1964; from instr to asst prof, Columbia Univ, 1962-1972; NIH trainee neuropharmacol, Columbia Univ, 1959-1962; dent intern, Montefiore Hosp, Bronx, NY, 1958-1959; chmn, Inst Rev Bd, Columbia Presby Med Ctr, NY. **Memberships:** Am Dent Asn; Am Physiol Soc; Int Asn Dent Res. **Research Statement & Publications:** Physiology and pharmacology of autonomic nervous system; medical and dental education. **Mailing Address:** Dept Dent, Col Physicians & Surgeons, Columbia Univ, New York, NY 10032. **Fax:** 212-243-7304. **E-Mail:** nk5@worldnet.att.net

KAHN, PETER B, THEORETICAL PHYSICS. **Personal Data:** b New York, NY, March 18, 1935. **Education:** Union Col, NY, BS, 1956; Northwestern Univ, PhD (physics), 1960. **Professional Experience:** PROF EMER, DEPT PHYSICS, STATE UNIV NY, STONY BROOK, as of 2004; Chmn dept, State Univ NY Stony Brook, 1974-1986; prof Physics, State Univ NY, Stony Brook, 1971-2003; Sr Weizmann fel, 1967-1968; from asst prof to assoc prof, State Univ NY Stony Brook, 1961-1971; res assoc physics, Univ Iowa, 1960-1961. **Memberships:** Fel Am Phys Soc. **Research Statement & Publications:** Mathematical biology; statistical theory of energy level distributions; innovation in physics curricula; dynamical systems. **Mailing Address:** Dept Physics, State Univ NY, Stony Brook, NY 11794. **Fax:** 631-632-8176. **E-Mail:** pkahn@mathlab.sunysb.edu

KAHN, PETER C, MATHEMATICS. **Education:** Harvard Col, BA, 1961; Columbia Univ, PhD (biochem), 1972. **Professional Experience:** PROF, DEPT BIOCHEM & MICROBIOL, RUTGERS UNIV, as of 2005. **Mailing Address:** Dept Biochem & Microbiol Rutgers Univ, 76 Lipman Dr Rm 120, New Brunswick, NJ 08901-8525. **Fax:** 732-932-8965. **E-Mail:** kahn@mbcl.rutgers.edu

KAHN, PETER JACK, MATHEMATICS. **Personal Data:** b Santiago, Chile, December 1, 1939. **Education:** Oberlin Col, BA, 1962; Princeton Univ, PhD (math), 1964. **Professional Experience:** PROF MATH, CORNELL UNIV, 1975-; Humboldt sr scientist, Univ Heidelberg, 1974-1975; mem, Inst Advan Study, 1969-1970; from asst prof to assoc prof, Cornell Univ, 1965-1975; instr, Univ Calif, Berkeley, 1964-1965; actg instr math, Univ Calif, Berkeley, 1963. **Memberships:** Am Math Soc. **Research Statement & Publications:** Algebraic and differential topology. **Mailing Address:** 571 Malott Hall, Cornell Univ, Ithaca, NY 14853-4201. **Fax:** 607-255-7149. **E-Mail:** kahn@math.cornell.edu

KAHN, ROBERT ELLIOT, COMPUTER SCIENCES, ELECTRICAL ENGINEERING. **Personal Data:** b Brooklyn, NY, December 23, 1938; m 1980. **Education:** City Col NY, BEE, 1960; Princeton Univ, MA, 1962, PhD (elec eng), 1964. **Honors & Awards:** Harry Goode Mem Award, Am Fedn Info Processing Soc, 1986; Marconi Award, 1994; Koji Kobayashi Comput & Commun Award, Inst Elec & Electronic Engrs, Alexander Graham Bell Medal, 1997; Nat Medal Technol, 1997. **Professional Experience:** Mem, Air Force Sci Adv Bd, 1987-; CHIEF EXEC OFFICER & PRES, CORP NAT RES INITIATIVES, 1986-; dir, deputy dir & prog mgr, Defense Advan Res Proj Agency, Info Processing Tech Off, 1972-1985; sr scientist, Bolt Beranek & Newman, 1966-1972; asst prof elec eng, Mass Inst Technol, 1964-1966; mem tech staff, Bell Tel Labs, 1960-1962; mem, Comput Sci & Technol Bd; mem, Nat Acad Sci. **Memberships:** Nat Acad Eng; fel Inst Elec & Electronics Engrs; fel Am Asn Artificial Intel, fel Assoc Comput Mach; Am Assoc Arts & Sci; Am Assoc Advan Sci. **Research Statement & Publications:** National information infrastructure including networking. **Mailing Address:** Corp Nat Res Initiatives, 1895 Preston White Dr Ste 100, Reston, VA 20191-5434.

KAHN, ROBERT PHILLIP, PLANT PATHOLOGY & PLANT QUARANTINE, PLANT PEST RISK ASSESSMENT & COMMODITY RISK ASSESSMENT. **Personal Data:** b Chicago, Ill, April 20, m Judith; c 4. **Education:** Univ Ill, BA, 1948, PhD (plant path), 1951. **Professional Experience:** CONSULT, PLANT PROTECTION & QUARANTINE, 1985-; Officer-in-chg, EAfrican Plant Quarantine Sta, Kenya, 1970-1972; plant pathologist & sr staff, Animal & Plant Health Inspection Serv, USDA, 1957-1985; from plant pathologist to supvry plant pathologist, Chem Warfare Labs, Ft Detrick, 1952-1957; Asst bot, Univ Ill, 1948-1952. **Memberships:** Am Phytopath Soc; Int Soc Plant Pathol; Am Inst Biol Sci; AAAS. **Research Statement & Publications:** Virology; plant quarantine pathology; plant tissue culture; agriculture; tropical plant pathology; international exchange of plant germplasm; plant protection and quarantine; Plant pest Risk analysis. **Mailing Address:** 14104 Flint Rock Terr, Rockville, MD 20853. **E-Mail:** rpkahn@erols.com

KAHN, ROGER, GENETICS. **Education:** Univ Calif, Santa Barbara, BS; Yale Univ, PhD (human genetics). **Professional Experience:** DIR, FORENSIC BIOL, HARRIS CO MED EXAMR OFFICE, HOUSTON, as of 2006; VICE-CHAIR, CONSORTIUM FORENSIC SCI ORGN, as of 2006; crime lab, Miami-Dade Police Dept, beginning 1988. **Memberships:** Am Soc Crime Lab Dirs. **Mailing Address:** Harris Co Med Examr, 1885 Old Spanish Trail, Houston, TX 77054-2098.

KAHN, SAMUEL GEORGE, NUTRITION SCIENCE ADMINISTRATION, NUTRITION POLICY. **Personal Data:** b Belleville, NJ, May 20, 1929. **Education:** Ill Wesleyan Univ, BS, 1951; Univ Ill, MS, 1953 & 1954, PhD (animal nutrit), 1955. **Professional Experience:** SR HEALTH-NUTRIT ADV, OFF HEALTH INFECTIOUS DIS & NUTRIT, BUR GLOBAL PROGS FIELD SUPPORT & RES, 1995-; Food Safety Workgroup, Off Sci & Technol Policy/Fed Coord Coun Sci Eng & Technol, 1991-1993; mem, Subcomt Nutrit Group Control Iron Deficiency, UN, 1989-1995; mem, Nat Comt Human Nutrit Res, beginning 1983; mem, Joint Res Comt, Pres Bd Int Food & Agr Develop, 1980-1983; ed, Am Inst Nutrit-Nutrit Notes, beginning 1979; mem, Joint Subcomt Human Nutrit Res, Exec Off Pres US, 1979-1983; secy, Int Nutrit Anemia Consult Group, beginning 1976; sr nutrit adv, Off Nutrit, Sci & Tech Bur, 1974-1995; secy, Int Vitamin A Consult Group, 1974-1977; adj prof, Va Polytech Inst & State Univ, 1974; nutrit adv, Res Off & Univ Rels, Tech Assistance Bur, 1971-1974; assoc prof nutrit, food & chmn, Drexel Inst Technol, 1969-1971; Hon prof nutrit, Rutgers Univ, 1967-1970; res supvr & head nutrit res, Div Agr Sci, 1967-1969; sr res scientist, Div Agr Sci, 1959-1967; sect head nutrit res, Div Agr Sci, 1958-1959; asst biochem, Squibb Inst Med Res, 1956-1958; res assoc, Radio Carbon Lab, 1955-1956; asst animal nutrit, Univ Ill, 1952-1955. **Memberships:** Am Soc Nutrit Sci; fel NY Acad Sci; Am Physiol Soc; Soc Exp Biol & Med; Am Soc Clin Nutrit; Am Chem Soc. **Research Statement & Publications:** Vitamin and lipid metabolism; atherosclerosis; animal nutrition; nutrition, health and population; international nutrition. **Mailing Address:** Off Health & Nutrit, Bur Global Progs Field Support & Res, USAID, Rm 1200 S-18 320 21st St NW, Washington, DC 20523. **Fax:** 703-875-4686, 202-216-3702. **E-Mail:** skahn@usaid.gov

KAHN, TRACY LYNN, CITRUS DIVERSITY & GERMPLASM, PRODUCTIVE BOTANY. **Personal Data:** b Ann Arbor, Mich, May 13, 1955. **Education:** Univ Mich, BS, 1977, PhD (bot), 1987. **Professional Experience:** SR MUS SCIENTIST & INSTR BIOL, UNIV CALIF, RIVERSIDE, 1995-; staff res assoc, Riverside, 1994-1995; Riverside Community Col, 1992 & Chaffey Col, 1993-1995; vis researcher, Swedish Agr Univ, 1993; Adj fac biol, Univ Redlands, 1990-1992; vis researcher, Riverside, 1989-1993; NIH fel, Univ Calif, Berkeley, 1987-1988. **Memberships:** Bot Soc Am. **Research Statement & Publications:** Reproductive questions associated with pollination and fruit set in citrus and another subtropical fruit, the cherimoya. **Mailing Address:** Bot & Plant Sci, Univ Calif, Riverside, CA 92521-0124. **E-Mail:** tracy.kahn@ucr.edu

KAHN, WALTER K(URT), ELECTRICAL ENGINEERING, ELECTROPHYSICS. **Personal Data:** b Mannheim, Ger, March 24, 1929. **Education:** Cooper Union, BEE, 1951; Polytech Inst Brooklyn, MEE, 1954, DEE, 1960. **Professional Experience:** Dir, Anro Eng, Inc, 1982- & Inst Info Sci & Technol, 1983-1992; ed, Trans, Antennas & Propagation, Inst Elec & Electronics Engrs, 1977-1980; PROF ENG & APPL SCI, GEORGE WASH UNIV, beginning 1969; Liaison scientist, Off Naval Res, London, 1967-1968; from assoc prof to prof electrophysics, microwave res inst, Polytech Inst Brooklyn, 1962-1969; asst prof elec eng, microwave res inst, Polytech Inst Brooklyn, 1960-1962; res assoc, microwave res inst, Polytech Inst Brooklyn, 1954-1960; Engr radar, Wheeler Labs, NY, 1951-1954; mem comn 6, Int Union Radio Sci. **Memberships:** AAAS; fel Inst Elec & Electronics Engrs; Optical Soc Am; Soc Photo Optical Instruments Engrs. **Research Statement & Publications:** Optical resonators and fiberoptics; lasers; microwave antennas and antenna arrays; waveguide junctions and directional couplers; microwave measurements; monopulse, radar systems; fiber optics. **Mailing Address:** Dept Elec Eng & Comput Sci, George Wash Univ, Washington, DC 20052. **Fax:** 202-994-0227. **E-Mail:** wkkahn@seas.gwu.edu

KAHNE, STEPHEN JAMES, CONTROL THEORY, SYSTEMS ENGINEERING. **Personal Data:** b New York, NY, April 5, 1937; m Irena; c Kasia & Christopher. **Education:** Cornell Univ, BEE, 1960; Univ Ill, MS, 1961, PhD (elec eng), 1963. **Honors & Awards:** Curtis Award, Am Soc Eng Educ, 1975; Centennial Medalist, Inst Elec & Electronics Engrs, 1984, Richard Emberson Award, 1991; Case Centennial Medal, 1981. **Professional Experience:** PROF ELEC ENG, EMBRY RIDDLE AERONAUT UNIV, 1997-; VPres, Chancellor Prescott, AZ Campus & Embry-Riddle Aeronaut Univ, 1995-1997; Exec Dir & CEO, Triangle Coalition Sci & Technol Educ, 1994; consult engr, Ctr Advan Aviation Syst Develop, 1991-1994; chief scientist, Mitre Corp, 1989-1991; prof, Ore Grad Ctr, 1985-1989; pres, Ore Grad Ctr, 1985-1986; prof & dean engr, Polytechnic Inst, NY, 1983-1985; dir, Div Elec, Comput & Systs Eng, NSF, 1980-1981; scholar, Case Western Reserve Univ, 1980; prof, Case Western Reserve Univ, 1976-1983; chmn, dept systs eng, Case Western Reserve Univ, 1976-1980; ed, Trans Automatic Control, Inst Elec & Electronics Engrs, 1975-1978; assoc prof & dir, Hybrid Comput Lab, 1969-1976; consult, Partner, Inter Design Inc, 1968-1976; asst prof elec eng, Univ Minn, Minneapolis, 1965-1969; consult, NASA Electronics Res Ctr, 1964-1965; lectr math, Northeastern Univ, 1963-1965; sr engr control, Electronics Div, Westinghouse Elec Corp, 1963; res assoc & instr elec eng, Coord Sci Lab, Univ Ill, 1962-1963; res asst control systs, Coord Sci Lab, Univ Ill, 1961-1962; Engr, Defense Syst Dept, Gen Elec Co, 1960. **Memberships:** Fel Inst Elec & Electronics Engrs; fel AAAS; Inst Elec & Electronics Engrs Control Systems Soc (pres, 1981); Am Soc Eng Educ; Air Traffic Control Asn; Int Fedn Automatic Control (pres, 1993-1996); Fel Int Fedn Automatic Control; Fel Washington Acad Sci; Eta Kappa Nu. **Research Statement & Publications:** Control theory, systems engineering, military command and control systems, air traffic control, intelligent vehicle/highway systems. **Mailing Address:** Dept Elec & Comput sci, Embry Riddle Aeronaut Univ, Rm 146 Bldg 72 3700 Willow Creek Rd, Prescott, AZ 86301. **Fax:** 928-777-6945. **E-Mail:** kahne@erau.edu

KAHNG, SEUN KWON, ELECTRICAL ENGINEERING, SOLID STATE ELECTRONICS. **Personal Data:** b Seoul, Korea, January 16, 1936. **Education:** Seoul Nat Univ, BSEE, 1958; Univ Va, MEE, 1963, PhD (elec eng), 1967. **Professional Experience:** ASST DIV CHIEF, EXP TESTING TECHNOL DIV, NASA, LANGLEY, 1989-; dir elec eng, Univ Okla, 1980-1989; prof elec eng, Univ Okla, 1978-1989; Res fel, Langley Res Ctr, NASA, 1975-1976; from asst prof to assoc prof, Univ Okla, 1968-1978; Res fel transducers, Langley Res Ctr, NASA, 1967-1968. **Memberships:** Inst Elec & Electronics Engrs; Optical Soc Am. **Research Statement & Publications:** Solid state electronic devices; piezoresistive silicon sensors; silicon-on-sapphire sensors; piezoelectric sensors. **Mailing Address:** Langley Res Ctr, NASA, MS 144 Indust Assist Off, Hampton, VA 23681-0001. **Fax:** 757-864-8315. **E-Mail:** s.k.kahng@larc.nasa.gov

KAHRIZI, MOJTABA, COMPUTER PROGRAMMING, VERY LARGE SCALE INTEGRATION TECHNOLOGY. **Personal Data:** b Arak, Iran, January 26, 1949. **Education:** BSc, Tehran Univ, 1973, MSc, 1975; MSc, Concordia Univ, 1980, PhD (physics), 1985. **Professional Experience:** ASSOC PROF, DEPT ELEC & COMPUT ENG, CONCORDIA UNIV, as of 2002; TECH OFFICER ELEC & COMPUT ENG, CONCORDIA UNIV, 1994-; RES ASSOC PHYSICS, CONCORDIA UNIV, 1990-; asst prof, St Francis Xavier Univ, 1987-1990; postdoctoral fel physics, St Francis Xavier Univ, 1985-1987; fac mem, Concordia Univ, 1983-1985; lab instr physics, Concordia Univ, 1978-1983; lectr, Arak Col Sci, Iran, 1975-1978. **Memberships:** Can Asn Physicists; Can Inst Neutron Scattering. **Research Statement & Publications:** Investigating magnetic resonance properties of electron nuclear spin coupled systems in condensed matters physics; magnetic and structural phase transitions in solid state materials, particularly high-Tc superconductors and rare-earth metals, using magnetic and dilatometric measurements. **Mailing Address:** Dept Elec & Comput Eng, Concordia Univ, 1455 de Maisonneure W, Montreal, PQ H3G 2P7, Can. **Fax:** 514-848-2802. **E-Mail:** mojtaba@ece.concordia.ca

KAHRS, MARK WILLIAM, DIGITAL AUDIO SIGNAL PROCESSING & COMPUTERMUSIC, COMPUTER-AIDED DESIGN. **Personal Data:** b Rome, Italy, October 25, 1952. **Education:** Univ Calif, San Diego, AB, 1974; Univ Rochester, MS, 1979, PhD (comput sci), 1984. **Professional Experience:** VIS ASSOC PROF, DEPT ELEC ENG, UNIV PITTSBURGH, as of 2004; res prof elec & comput eng, Rutgers Univ, beginning 1988; mem tech staff, AT&T Bell Lab, 1983-1987; researcher, Inst Res Coord Acoust Music, 1977-1978; Res programmer, Ctr Comput Res Music & Acoust, 1975-1977. **Memberships:** Inst Elec & Electronics Engrs; Asn Comput Mach; Audio Eng Soc; Acoust Soc Am. **Research Statement & Publications:** Interaction between computer architecture and hardware design of digital signal processing (especially computer music and digital audio) and programming language design and implementation particularly for use in computer aided design. **Mailing Address:** Dept Elec Eng, Univ Pittsburgh, Rm 244, 348 Benedum Hall, Pittsburgh, NJ 15261. **Fax:** 412-624-8003. **E-Mail:** kahrs@ee.pitt.edu

KAHRS, ROBERT F, VETERINARY MEDICINE, VETERINARY EPIDEMIOLOGY. **Personal Data:** b Lynbrook, NY, June 28, 1930. **Education:** Cornell Univ, DVM, 1954, MS, 1963, PhD (virol biomet), 1965. **Honors & Awards:** Nat Academias Pract. **Professional Experience:** DIR NAT CTR IMPORTS & EXPORTS, USDA, as of 2002; dean, Univ Mo, Col Vet Med, 1992; PROF VET EPIDEMIOL & CHMN, DEPT VET PREV MED, UNIV FLA, 1978-; assoc prof vet epidemiol, NY State Vet Col, Cornell Univ, 1970-1978; asst prof vet epidemiol, NY State Vet Col, Cornell Univ, 1966-1970; res assoc vet epidemiol & microbiol, NY State Vet Col, Cornell Univ, 1965-1966; res asst vet virol & biomet, NY State Vet Col, Cornell Univ, 1961-1965; vet, Attica, NY, 1955-1961; asst vet, pvt pract, Interlaken, NY, 1954-1955. **Memberships:** Am Vet Med Asn; US Animal Health Asn; Am Vet Epidemiol Soc. **Research Statement & Publications:** Epidemiology of virus diseases of livestock. **Mailing Address:** USDA Import Export Products, 4700 River Rd Unit 40, Riverdale, MD 20737.

KAIFER, ANGEL E, CHEMISTRY. **Education:** Univ PR, PhD, 1984. **Professional Experience:** PROF PHYSICAL CHEM & VICE DEAN, DEPT CHEM, UNIV MIAMI, as of 2004. **Research Statement & Publications:** General area of Supramolecular Electrochemistry. **Mailing Address:** Dept Chem, Univ Miami, 1301 Mem Dr, Coral Gables, FL 33146-0431.

KAIGHN, MORRIS EDWARD, EMBRYOLOGY, VIROLOGY. **Personal Data:** b Camden, NJ, August 6, 1922. **Education:** Brooklyn Col, BS, 1956; Mass Inst Technol, PhD (biol), 1962. **Professional Experience:** CONSULT, BIOL RES FACIL, IJAMSVILLE MD, 1995-; SR RES INVESTR, PASADENA FOUND MED RES, 1975-; sr scientist cell ctr, 1972-1975; assoc investr embryol, NY Blood Ctr, 1970-1972; res assoc, NY Blood Ctr, 1967-1970; asst investr embryol, Carnegie Inst, 1964-1967; fel virol, Univ Toronto, 1962-1964; AT FREDERICK CANCER RES FACIL, NAT CANCER INST. **Memberships:** Am Asn Cancer Res; Am Soc Cell Biol; TissueCult Asn. **Research Statement & Publications:** Isolation and characterization of epithelial cells; immortalization of epithelial cells by oncogenes; clonal culture of differentiated human liver prostate and cancer cells; growth control by steroids and peptide growth factors; cell biology. **Mailing Address:** Biol Res Facil, 10075-20 Gyler Pl, Ijamsville, MD 21754.

KAILASANATH, KAZHIKATHRA, AERONAUTICS. **Education:** Indian Inst Technol, Btech, 1976; Ga Inst Technol, MSAE, 1977; Ga Inst Technol, Phd, 1980. **Professional Experience:** HEAD, CENTER REACTIVE FLOW & DYNAMICAL SYST, NAVAL RES NAVAL RESEARCH LAB, as of 2004. **Mailing Address:** Naval Res Lab, Bldg 97 Rm 133 A, Washington, DC 20375. **Fax:** 202-767-4798. **E-Mail:** kailas@lcp.nrl.navy.mil

KAILATH, THOMAS, ELECTRICAL ENGINEERING, APPLIED MATHEMATICS. **Personal Data:** b Poona, India, June 7, 1935; American citizen; m 1962, Sarah; c Ann, Paul, Priya & Ryan. **Education:** Univ Poona, BE, 1956; Mass Inst Technol, SM, 1959, ScD(elec eng), 1961. **Honorary Degrees:** DEng, Linkoping Univ, Sweden, 1990, Strathclyde Univ, Scotland, 1992; Univ Carlos III, Madrid, Spain, 1999. **Honors & Awards:** Eng Achievement Award, Nat Fedn Asian Indian Orgns, 1986; Inst Elec & Electronics Engrs, Educ Medal, 1995, DG Fink Prize, 1996; Shannon medal, 2000. **Professional Experience:** PROF EMER, STANFORD UNIV, as of 2006; vice chmn, Integrated Systs, Inc, beginning 1989; Royal Soc guest res prof, Imp Col, London, 1989; Hitachi Am prof Eng, Stanford Univ, beginning 1988; Erna & Jacob Michael vis chair theoret math, Weizmann Inst, 1984; assoc chmn, Dept Elec Eng, 1981-1987; assoc chmn, Tech Univ, Delft, 1981; chmn bd dirs, Integrated Systs, Inc, 1980-1989; assoc chmn Katholieke Univ Leuven, 1977; Churchill fel, Statist Lab, Churchill, Eng, 1977; dir, Info Systs Lab, 1971-1981; consult, Govt India, 1970-1971; vis prof, India Inst Sci, Bangalore, 1969-1970; Guggenheim fel, Indian Inst Sci, 1969-1970; prof elec eng, Stanford Univ, beginning 1968; ed, Prentice-Hall Series on Info & Systs Sci, beginning 1963; assoc prof elec eng, Stanford Univ, 1963-1968; res specialist, Jet Propulsion Lab, Calif Inst Technol, 1961-1962. **Memberships:** Nat Acad Eng; Nat Acad Sci; Am Acad Arts & Sci; fel Inst Math Statist; fel Inst Elec & Electronics Engrs; Indian Nat Acad Eng; Nat acad sci; Am Acad Arts & Sci. **Research Statement & Publications:** Information theory; communications; computation; control; linear systems; statistical signal processing; very large scale integration systems; stochastic processes; linear algebra; operator theory; author or co-author of over 300 research papers. **Mailing Address:** Dept Elec Eng, Stanford Univ, 350 Serra Mall Packard Bldg 276, Stanford, CA 94305-9510. **Fax:** 650-723-4628. **E-Mail:** kailath@stanford.edu

KAIMAL, JAGADISH CHANDRAN, METEOROLOGY. **Personal Data:** b Kuala Lumpur, Malaysia, November 18, 1930. **Education:** Benares Hindu Univ, BSc, 1953; Univ Wash, MS, 1959, PhD (meteorol), 1961. **Professional Experience:** RETIRED; chief, Atmospheric Studies Prog, Wave Propagation Lab, Energy Res Lab, Nat Oceanic & Atmospheric Admin, 1976-1992; res physicist, Air Force Cambridge Res Labs, 1961-1976. **Memberships:** Am Meteorol Soc. **Research Statement & Publications:** Experimental investigations of turbulent fluctuations in the atmospheric boundary layer and the study of the fluxes of momentum and heat within this layer. **Mailing Address:** 13 John St, Hamilton, NY 13346-1317.

KAIN, RICHARD YERKES, ELECTRICAL ENGINEERING. **Personal Data:** b Chicago, Ill, January 20, 1936. **Education:** Mass Inst Technol, BS, 1957, MS, 1959, ScD(elec eng), 1962. **Professional Experience:** PROF EMER ELEC ENG, UNIV MINN, MINNEAPOLIS, as of 2001; Consult, Secure Computing Technol Corp, 1989-; prof elec eng, Univ Minn, Minneapolis, beginning 1977; consult, Honeywell Corp, 1975-1989; assoc prof, Univ Minn, Minneapolis, 1966-1977; Ford fel eng, 1962-1964; from instr to asst prof, Mass Inst Technol, 1960-1966; Asst elec eng, Mass Inst Technol, 1957-1960. **Memberships:** AAAS; Asn Comput Mach; Inst Elec & Electronics Engrs; Sigma Xi; Computer Prof Social Responsibility. **Research Statement & Publications:** Computer systems; computer architecture; secure computer systems. **Mailing Address:** Dept Elec Eng, Univ Minn, 200 Union St SE, Minneapolis, MN 55455. **E-Mail:** kain@ece.umn.edu

KAINE, BRIAN PAUL, EVOLUTION OF THERMOPHILIC ORGANISMS. **Education:** Northwestern Univ, PhD (biol sci), 1981. **Professional Experience:** RES ASSOC, UNIV ILL, 1981-. **Research Statement & Publications:** T RNA gene structure in archaebacteria. **Mailing Address:** B 103 Chem & Life Sci Lab, Univ Ill 601 S Goodwin Ave, Urbana, IL 61821.

KAINLAURI, EINO OLAVI, ARCHITECTURE. **Education:** Univ Mich, BArch, 1950, MArch, 1959, PhD, 1975. **Professional Experience:** EMER PROF ARCHIT, IOWA STATE UNIV, as of 2006. **Mailing Address:** Iowa State Univ, 156 Col Design, Ames, IA 50011. **Fax:** 515-294-1440. **E-Mail:** eino2gen@iastate.edu

KAINSKI, MERCEDES H, food science, nutrition; deceased, see previous edition for last biography

KAISER, ARMIN DALE, BIOCHEMISTRY, GENETICS. **Personal Data:** b Piqua, Ohio, November 10, 1927. **Education:** Purdue Univ, BS, 1950; Calif Inst Technol, PhD (biol), 1954. **Honors & Awards:** Molecular Biol Award, US Steel Found, 1970; Lasker Award, 1980; Waterford Biomed Sci Award, 1981. **Professional Experience:** PROF DEVELOP BIOL, SCH MED, STANFORD UNIV, 1989-; mem, Genetic Biol Panel, NSF, 1969-1972; PROF BIOCHEM, SCH MED, STANFORD UNIV, 1966-; NSF sr fel, 1964-1965; mem, Genetics Study Sect, NIH, 1963-1968; from asst prof to assoc prof, Sch Med, Stanford Univ, 1959-1966; from instr to asst prof microbiol, Wash Univ, 1956-1959; Am Cancer Soc fel, 1954-1956. **Memberships:** Nat Acad Sci; Genetics Soc Am; Am Soc Biol Chemists; Am Acad Arts & Sci. **Research Statement & Publications:** Bacteriophage genetics; nucleic acid biochemistry; biochemistry of morphogenesis; author and co-author of over 100 publications. **Mailing Address:** Dept Biochem, Sch Med, Stanford Univ, Rm 357A, Stanford, CA 94305-5427. **E-Mail:** kaiser@cmgm.stanford.edu

KAISER, C WILLIAM, SURGERY. **Personal Data:** b Troy, NY, December 7, 1939. **Education:** Colgate Univ, AB, 1961; Tufts Univ, MD, 1965. **Professional Experience:** CHIEF SURG, VET ADMIN MED CTR, MANCHESTER, NH, 1981-; ASST PROF SURG, HARVARD MED SCH, 1981-; chief surg, Pondville Hosp, 1978-1981; assoc chief surg, Vet Admin Med Ctr, Northport, NY, 1976-1978; assoc dir surg, Tufts Surg Serv, 1972-1976; surg resident, Boston City Hosp, 1968-1972. **Memberships:** Soc Surg Alimentary Tract; Asn Acad Surg; Asn Vet Admin Surgeons. **Research Statement & Publications:** Surgical oncology. **Mailing Address:** Vet Admin Med Ctr Lib, 718 Smyth Rd, Manchester, NH 03104-7004.

KAISER, CARL, MEDICINAL CHEMISTRY. **Personal Data:** b Baltimore, Md, February 8, 1929. **Education:** Univ Md, BS, 1951, MS, 1953, PhD (pharmaceut chem), 1955. **Professional Experience:** RETIRED; dir med chem, Nova Pharm Corp, 1986-1994; sr fel, Smith Kline & French Labs, 1981-1986; assoc sci dir, Smith Kline & French Labs, 1979-1981; asst dir chem, Smith Kline & French Labs, 1972-1979; sr investr, Smith Kline & French Labs, 1968-1972; med chem group leader, Smith Kline & French Labs, 1965-1968; sr med chemist, Smith Kline & French Labs, 1957-1965; Smith Kline & French fel, Univ Va, 1955-1957; lab asst pharmaceut chem, Univ Md, 1951-1953. **Memberships:** Am Chem Soc; Am Pharmaceut Asn. **Research Statement & Publications:** Design and synthesis of potential drug products, especially substances affecting the central and autonomic nervous systems, enzyme inhibitors, antimetabolites, drug metabolism and small ring compounds. **Mailing Address:** 8470 Woodland Rd, Millersville, MD 21108-1756.

KAISER, CHARLES FREDERICK, DEVELOPMENTAL & HEALTH PSYCHOLOGY, STRESS MANAGEMENT. **Personal Data:** b December 30, 1942; m 1966, Judith; c Edward & Michael. **Education:** City Col, City Univ NY, BS, 1964, MA, 1967; Univ Houston, PhD (psychol), 1973. **Professional Experience:** CHMN, DEPT PSYCHOL, COL CHARLESTON, 1998-; grant, Nat Hazards Res & Appln Info Ctr, 1993, 1998; PROF PSYCHOL, COL CHARLESTON, 1991-; bd mem, Asn Appl Psychophysiol & Biofeedback, 1986-1989; mem comt, Asn Appl Psychophysiol & Biofeedback, 1983-1993; adj asst prof, Dept Phys Med & Rehab, Med Univ SC, 1981-1989; assoc prof, Col Charleston, 1977-1991; asst prof, Col Charleston, 1972-1977; fel, Univ Houston, 1966-1972; fel, Dept Psychiat, Baylor Col Med, 1966-1970. **Memberships:** Int Stress Mgt Asn; Am Psychol Soc; Southeastern Psychol Asn. **Research Statement & Publications:** Research in personality and cognitive abilities of gifted adolescents; stress and depression in college students, gifted adolescents and children; published articles in various journals; personality and behaviors associated with substance abuse and natural disasters. **Mailing Address:** Dept Psychol, Col Charleston, 57 Coming St Rm 6, Charleston, SC 29424. **Fax:** 843-953-7151. **E-Mail:** kaiserc@ cofc.edu

KAISER, CHRIS A, BIOLOGY. **Education:** MIT, PhD, 1987. **Professional Experience:** PROF, DEPT BIOL, MASS INST TECHNOL, as of 2001; HEAD, DEPT BIOL, MASS INST TECHNOL, as of 2001. **Mailing Address:** Dept Biol Mass Inst Technol, Bldg 68 Rm 533 77 Mass Ave, Cambridge, MA 02139. **Fax:** 617-253-8699. **E-Mail:** ckaiser@mit.edu

KAISER, CHRISTOPHER B, HISTORY & PHILOSOPHY OF SCIENCE, PHYSICS. **Personal Data:** b Greenwich, Conn, October 16, 1941. **Education:** Harvard Univ, BA, 1963; Univ Colo, PhD (astrogeophys), 1968; Edinburgh Univ, PhD (theology), 1974. **Honors & Awards:** John Templeton Found Prize Outstanding Bks Sci & Relig, 1995. **Professional Experience:** PROF HIST SYST THEOL, WESTERN THEOL SEM, HOLLAND, 1988-; resident mem, Ctr Theol Inquiry, Princeton, NJ, 1984, 1987; from asst prof to assoc prof, Western Theol Sem, Holland, 1977-1988; with Systs Develop, QEI Inc, Bedford, Mass, 1975-1976; lectr physics, Edinburgh Univ, 1973-1974; lectr physics, Gordon Col, 1968-1971; mem, Gravity Res Found, 1968-. **Memberships:** Soc Hist Technol. **Research Statement & Publications:** History of science as influenced by religious belief and practice; history of interaction between theological beliefs and scientific progess. **Mailing Address:** Dept Hist Syst Theol, Western Theol Sem, 101 E 13th St, Holland, MI 49423. **Fax:** 616-392-7717. **E-Mail:** chrisk@westernsem.edu

KAISER, DAVID GILBERT, PHARMACEUTICAL CHEMISTRY, DRUG METABOLISM. **Personal Data:** b Detroit, Mich, August 25, 1928. **Education:** Detroit Inst Technol, BS, 1952; Purdue Univ, MS, 1954, PhD (pharmaceut chem), 1959. **Professional Experience:** SR RES CONSULT, UPJOHN CO, 1986-; dir drug metab res, Upjohn Co, 1985-1986; res mgr drug metab, Upjohn Co, 1979-1985; res head drug metab, Upjohn Co, 1969-1979; chemist, Upjohn Co, 1959-1969; Fel radiochem, Univ Mich, 1959. **Memberships:** AAAS; Am Chem Soc; Am Pharmaceut Asn; Sigma Xi; Am Soc Mass Spectrometry; NY Acad Sci. **Research Statement & Publications:** Drug metabolism and analytical chemistry. **Mailing Address:** 6605 Robinswood St, Portage, MI 49024.

KAISER, DEBRA LEE, HIGH TEMPERATURE SUPERCONDUCT CRS, FERROELECTRIC OXIDE THIN FILMS. **Personal Data:** b Hinsdale, Ill, October 9, 1957. **Education:** Lehigh Univ, BS, 1979; Colo Sch Mines, MS, 1980; Mass Inst Technol, ScD, 1985. **Professional Experience:** CHIEF, CERAMIC DIV, NIST, as of 2003; GROUP LEADER, THIN FILM CHARACTERIZATION & PROPERTIES, CERAMIC DIV, NIST, 1999-; PROG LEADER, THIN FILM MEASUREMENTS & STAND, CERAMIC DIV, NIST, 1999-; mat res engr, Nat Inst Stand & Technol, 1988-1999; fel, IBM, 1985-1987. **Memberships:** Mat Res Soc; Fedn Mat Socs; Am Asn Crystal Growth. **Research Statement & Publications:** Metal-organic chemical vapor deposition of ferroelectric oxide thin films for photonic applications; crystal growth, detwinning and magneto-optical characterization of high temperature superconductors. **Mailing Address:** Ceramic Div, Nat Inst Stand & Technol, 100 Bur Dr Stop 8520, Gaithersburg, MD 20899. **Fax:** 301-990-8729. **E-Mail:** debra.kaiser@nist.gov

KAISER, EDWARD WILLIAM, PHYSICAL CHEMISTRY. **Personal Data:** b Minneapolis, Minn, May 10, 1942; m 1968, Jacqueline; c Elizabeth. **Education:** Northwestern Univ, BA, 1964; Harvard Univ, MA, 1966, PhD (chem), 1970. **Honors & Awards:** Donald Julius Groen Prize, Inst Mech Engrs, 1986. **Professional Experience:** RES STAFF, FORD MOTOR CO, as of 1999; SR STAFF TECH SPECIALIST, FORD MOTOR CO, 1995-; staff scientist, Ford Motor Co, 1986-1995; prin res assoc, Ford Motor Co, 1980-1986; sr res scientist, Ford Motor Co, 1974-1980; assoc scientist, Xerox Corp, 1972-1974; temp mem tech staff, Bell Labs, 1970-1972; NATO fel, Southampton Univ, 1969-1970. **Memberships:** Am Phys Soc; Am Chem Soc; Combustion Inst. **Research Statement & Publications:** Chemical kinetics; combustion research; emissions from spark-ignition engines. **Mailing Address:** Ford Motor Co, SRL-E3083, 7 Windham Lane, Dearborn, MI 48120-2053. **Fax:** 313-594-2923. **E-Mail:** ekaiser@ford.com

KAISER, EDWIN MICHAEL, ORGANIC CHEMISTRY. **Personal Data:** b Youngstown, Ohio, October 15, 1938; m Judith; c Kim, Kay, Karla, Kevin, Kurt & Karenda (Deceased). **Education:** Youngstown Univ, BS, 1960; Purdue Univ, PhD (org chem), 1964. **Honors & Awards:** Fulbright Fellowship, University of Botswana, Gaborone, Botswana, 2003-2004. **Professional Experience:** CURATORS DISTINGUISHED TEACHING PROF EMER, UNIV MO, COLUMBIA, 1995-; Dir, Hon Col, 1984-1991; from asst prof to Curators distinguished teaching prof, Univ MO, Columbia, 1966-2001; 1970-1995; Res assoc org chem, Duke Univ, 1964-1966. **Memberships:** Am Chem Soc; Sigma Xi. **Research Statement & Publications:** Organometallic derivatives of methylated heterocycles; condensations and cyclizations in nonaqueous media. **Mailing Address:** Univ Mo, 125 Chem Bldg, Columbia, MO 65211. **Fax:** 573-882-2754. **E-Mail:** kaisere@missouri.edu

KAISER, GEORGE C, THORACIC SURGERY. **Personal Data:** b Bronx, NY, July 30, 1928. **Education:** Lehigh Univ, BS, 1949; Johns Hopkins Univ, MD, 1953. **Professional Experience:** CHIEF CARDIOTHORACIC SURG, ST LOUIS UNIV HEALTH SCI CTR, as of 2004; PROF EMER SURG, SCH MED, ST LOUIS UNIV, as of 2004; prof surg, Sch Med, St Louis Univ, beginning 1970; from asst prof to assoc prof, Sch Med, St Louis Univ, 1963-1970; dir St Louis Univ surg serv, Vet Admin Hosp, 1963-1965; from instr to asst prof, Med Ctr, Ind Univ, 1961-1963; Staff surgeon, Vet Admin Hosp, Indianapolis, Ind, 1961; resident surg, Med Ctr, Ind Univ, 1956-1961; clin assoc, clin surg, Nat Heart Inst, 1954-1956; resident, Vet Admin Hosp, Ft Howard, Md, 1954; Intern surg, Johns Hopkins Hosp, Baltimore, Md, 1953-1954. **Memberships:** Soc Thoracic Surg; AMA; Am Surg Asn; Int Cardiovasc Soc; Am Asn Thoracic Surg; Sigma Xi; Am Heart Asn; Am Col Surgeons. **Research Statement & Publications:** General and thoracic surgical problems, including research in cardiac physiology. **Mailing Address:** Dept Cardiothoracic Surg, St Louis Univ Hosp, PO Box 15250, 221 N Grand Blvd, St Louis, MO 63110-0250. **E-Mail:** kaisergc@slu.edu

KAISER, GERARD ALAN, THORACIC SURGERY, CARDIOVASCULAR SURGERY. **Personal Data:** b Brooklyn, NY, December 9, 1932. **Education:** Princeton Univ, BA, 1954; Columbia Univ, MD, 1958. **Professional Experience:** SR ASSOC DEAN, SCH MED, UNIV MIAMI, as of 2004; SR VICE PRES, JACKSON MEM HOSP, as of 2004; prof surg, Div Thoracic & Cardiovasc Surg, Sch Med, Univ Miami, beginning 1971; chief, Div Thoracic & Cardiovasc Surg, Sch Med, Univ Miami, beginning 1971; Otto G Storm estab investr, Am Heart Asn, 1970; vis asst surg, Elmhurst Hosp, 1968-1969 & Harlem Hosp Ctr, 1969-1971; assoc prof, Columbia Univ, 1969-1971; assoc attend surg, Columbia-Presby Med Ctr, 1969-1971; consult, Vet Admin Hosp, 1968-1971; asst prof, Mt Sinai Sch Med, 1968-1969; asst attend surg, Mt Sinai Hosp, 1968-1969; Glorney-Raisbeck fel, NY Acad Med, 1968-1969; asst vis prof, Delafield Hosp, 1968; asst attend surg, Columbia-Presby Med Ctr, 1968; instr surg, Columbia Univ, 1967-1968; resident thoracic surg, Vet Admin Hosp & Bellevue Hosp Ctr, NY, 1966 & Presby Hosp, 1967; fel, NY Tuberc & Health Asn, 1966-1967; asst surg, Columbia Univ, 1965-1967; resident, Presby Hosp, NY, 1964-1965; asst resident gen surg, Presby Hosp, NY, 1959-1962; Intern, Presby Hosp, NY, 1958-1959; active attend & chief div thoracic & cardiovasc surg, Jackson Mem Hosp. **Memberships:** Soc Univ Surgeons; Soc Thoracic Surgeons; Asn Acad Surg; Am Fedn Clin Res; Int Cardiovasc Soc; Sigma Xi. **Research Statement & Publications:** Cardiovascular physiology and pharmacology, especially electrophysiology. **Mailing Address:** Dept Surg, Univ Miami, M863, Coral Gables, FL 33124. **E-Mail:** g.kaiser@miami.edu

KAISER, HELMUT, NEUTRON SCATTERING. **Education:** Tech Univ Viena, PhD. **Professional Experience:** ADJ ASSOC PROF PHYSICS, UNIV MO-COLUMBIA, as of 2006. **Mailing Address:** Dept Physics, Univ Mo-Columbia, 424 Physics Bldg, Columbia, MO 65211. **Fax:** 573-884-5454. **E-Mail:** helmut_kaiser@neutron.murr.missouri.edu

KAISER, HINRICH, SYSTEMATICS. **Personal Data:** b February 3, 1965. **Education:** McGill Univ, BSc, 1988, PhD (biol), 1993. **Professional Experience:** FEL, UNIV WURZBURG, 1993-; Assoc mem, Redpath Mus, McGill Univ, 1993-. **Memberships:** Am Soc Ichthyologists & Herpetologists; Soc Study Amphibians & Reptiles; Herpetologists League; Soc Study Evolution; Soc Syst Biologists; Sigma Xi. **Research Statement & Publications:** Using amphibians as model organisms, study evolution using morphologicaly, morphometric, cytogenetic, and biochemical approaches; determine phylogenetic relationships of interesting amphibian assemblages and use these data to infer their biogeographic and evolutionary past. **Mailing Address:** Humangenetik Univ Wurzburg, Biozentrum Am Hubland, 97074 Wurzburg, Ger. **Fax:** 499-318-884069. **E-Mail:** hk1@vax.rz.uni-wuerzburg.d400.de

KAISER, IVAN IRVIN, BIOCHEMISTRY. **Personal Data:** b Stuart, Nebr, November 21, 1938. **Education:** Wayne State Col, BA, 1962; Iowa State Univ, PhD (biochem), 1967. **Honors & Awards:** Burlington Northern Award, Univ Wyo, 1992. **Professional Experience:** PROF EMER MOLECULAR BIOL & CHEM, UNIV WYO, 1985-; chmn biochem, UNIV WYO, 1979-1984; prof biochem & chem, UNIV WYO, 1975-1978; from asst prof to assoc prof biochem, UNIV WYO, 1967-1975. **Memberships:** Am Chem Soc; Am Soc Biol Chemists; Sigma Xi; AAAS; Int Soc Toxinology; Protein Soc. **Research Statement & Publications:** Structure and function of ribonucleic acids; selenium biochemistry; natural toxins. **Mailing Address:** Dept Molecular Biol, Univ Wyo PO Box 3944 University Sta, Laramie, WY 82071-3944. **Fax:** 307-766-5098.

KAISER, JACK ALLEN CHARLES, REMOTE SENSING, INSTRUMENTATION. **Personal Data:** b Chicago, Ill, November 15, 1935. **Education:** Ill Inst Technol, BS, 1957; Univ Chicago, PhD (geophys), 1969. **Professional Experience:** SUPVRY RES PHYSICIST, NAVAL RES LAB, 1993-; prin investr, Naval Res Lab, 1974-1981; res physisist, Naval Res Lab, 1972-1993; res assoc, Univ Chicago, 1969-1972; res asst, Univ Chicago, 1962-1969; Weather forecaster, USAF, 1958-1960. **Memberships:** Am Meterol Soc; Am Geophys Union; Sigma Xi. **Research Statement & Publications:** Experiments on air-sea interaction and upper ocean dynamics, ocean remote sensing, ocean waves, ocean measurement techniques. **Mailing Address:** 12002 Kingfield Ct, Upper Marlboro, MD 20772.

KAISER, JAMES F(REDERICK), ELECTRICAL ENGINEERING. **Personal Data:** b Piqua, Ohio, December 10, 1929. **Education:** Univ Cincinnati, EE, 1952; Mass Inst Technol, SM, 1954, ScD, 1959. **Honors & Awards:** Centennial Medal, Inst Elec & Electronics Engrs, 1984, Tech Achievement Award, Acoustics, Speech & Signal Processing, 1978, Soc Award, 1981. **Professional Experience:** RETIRED; distinguished mem tech staff, Bell Tel Labs Inc, Digital Systs Res Dept, Bell Core, 1984-1990; mem tech staff, Bell Tel Labs Inc, Digital Systs Res Dept, Bell Core, 1959-1984; from instr to asst prof elec eng, Servomech Lab, Mass Inst Technol, 1955-1960; asst, Servomech Lab, Mass Inst Technol, 1952-1955. **Memberships:** Fel Inst Elec & Electronics Engrs; Asn Comput Mach; AAAS; Soc Indust & Appl Math; Acoust Soc Am; Europ Asn Signal Processing. **Research Statement & Publications:** Theory of control and signal processing systems; system optimization; application of digital computations to continuous systems; digital signal processing; continuous system modeling; vocal tract modeling; speech technology research. **Mailing Address:** Dept Elec & Comput Eng, Rutgers Univ, Piscataway, NJ 08855.

KAISER, JOSEPH ANTHONY, PHARMACOLOGY. **Personal Data:** b Baltimore, Md, March 22, 1926; m 1951, Louise; c Joseph A Jr, Thomas M & Kathleen K (Evans). **Education:** Univ Md, BS, 1950, MS, 1952, PhD (pharmacol), 1955. **Professional Experience:** RETIRED; exec secy, Pharmacol Study Sect, Div Res Grants, 1974-1995; exec secy spec progs, Career Develop Rev Br, 1973-1974; from asst chief to dep chief, Career Develop Rev Br, 1969-1973; exec secy pharmacol & endocrinol fels rev sect, NIH, 1966-1969; res pharmacologist, Div Pharmacol, Bur Sci Res, 1964-1966; pharmacologist, Drug

Rev Br, Div Toxicol Eval, Bur Sci Stand & Eval, Food & Drug Admin, 1963-1964; exp therapeut res sect, Lederle Labs, Am Cyanamid Co, 1958-1963; sr res pharmacologist, Pfizer Therapeut Inst, NJ, 1955-1958. **Memberships:** Am Soc Pharmacol & Exp Therapeut. **Research Statement & Publications:** Pharmacology-toxicology; antibiotics; anticholinergics, antihistamines, antiparasiticides and anti-tubercular agents; health science administration; toxicological evaluation. **Mailing Address:** 1017 Tracy Dr, Colesville, MD 20904-2183.

KAISER, KLAUS L(EO) E(DUARD), ORGANIC CHEMISTRY, STRUCTURE-ACTIVITY RELATIONSHIPS. **Personal Data:** b Kempten, Ger, June 17, 1941; Canadian citizen; m Dianne E; c Anita C, Edward L & Andrew W. **Education:** Tech Univ, Munich, cand chem, 1964, dipl chem, 1966, Dr rer nat(chem), 1968. **Honors & Awards:** QSAR Award 2002, in recognition of significant contribution to the advancement of quantitative structure-activity relationships in environ sci, (2002). **Professional Experience:** Dir, Environ & Rubber Chem Div, CIC, 1997-; assoc ed, Environ Toxicol Chem, 1997-; editor-in-chief, Water Qual Res J Can, 1994-; chief, Environ Stand & Statist Proj, 1994-1996; ADJ PROF, DEPT CHEM, BROCK UNIV, 1990-; co-chair, Fate of Toxics Comt, Lake Ont-Niagara River Mgt Plan, 1989-1992; Chief, Nearshore-Offshore Interactions Proj, 1987-; pres, Int Assoc Great Lakes Res, 1987-1988; quant struct activ relationships, Environ Toxicol-II, 1987; co-ed, Acta Hydrochimica et Hydrobiologica, 1985-; ed, Quant Struct Activity Relationship in Environ Toxicol, 1984; assoc ed, J Great Lakes Res, 1980-1993; head, Org Prop Sect, 1980-1984; liaison mem, Task Force Ecol Effects Non-Phosphate Detergent Builders, Int Jt Comn, 1978-1980; mem, Task Force Polychlorinated Biphenyls, Environ Can & NHW Can, 1975-1976 & Task Force Mirex, 1976-1977; From alt mem to mem, Water Qual Objectives Subcomt, Int Jt Comn, 1974-1978; RES SCIENTIST, CAN CTR INLAND WATERS, ENVIRON CAN, 1972-; Fel organometallic chem, Fonds Ger Chem Indust, 1968-1969 & Nat Res Coun, McMaster Univ, Ont, 1969-1971. **Memberships:** Int Asn Great Lakes Res; Ger Chem Soc; Soc Environ Toxicol Chemists; fel Chem Inst Can; Asn Chem Prof Ontario. **Research Statement & Publications:** Chemistry of contaminants in the biosphere, including their analysis, bioaccumulation, metabolic and photochemical transformation and their toxicity; quantitative structure-activity correlation (QSAR) of contaminants; organometallic and environmental chemistry. **Mailing Address:** Nat Water Res Inst, PO Box 5050, Burlington, ON L7R 4A6, Can. **Fax:** 905-336-6430. **E-Mail:** klaus.kaiser@cciw.ca

KAISER, MARY AGNES, ANALYTICAL CHEMISTRY. **Personal Data:** b Pittston, Pa, June 11, 1948. **Education:** Wilkes Univ, BS, 1970; St Joseph's Univ, Pa, MS, 1972; Villanova Univ, PhD (chem), 1976. **Professional Experience:** RES FEL, CORP CTR ANAL SCI, E I DU PONT DEL NEMOURS & CO, as of 2004; prog chair, Eastern Anal Symp, 1996; SR RES ASSOC, E I DU PONT Del NEMOURS & CO, 1994-; test mgr, E I du Pont Del Nemours & Co, 1989-1994; sr supvr, E I du Pont Del Nemours & Co, 1984-1989; res supvr, E I du Pont Del Nemours & Co, 1980-1984; res chemist, E I du Pont Del Nemours & Co, 1977-1980; assoc chem, Univ Ga, 1976-1977. **Memberships:** Am Chem Soc; Sigma Xi. **Research Statement & Publications:** Analytical chemistry of separations; spectroscopy; environmental chemistry. **Mailing Address:** E I du Pont de Nemours & Co Inc, 1007 Mkt St, Wilmington, DE 19898.

KAISER, MICHAEL LEROY, RADIO ASTRONOMY. **Personal Data:** b Keokuk, Iowa, December 28, 1941. **Education:** Univ Iowa, BA, 1964; Univ Md, Col Park, MS, 1971. **Professional Experience:** RES SCIENTIST, EXTRATERRESTRIAL PHYSICS LAB, GODDARD SPACE FLIGHT CTR, NASA, as of 2004; PRINCIPAL INVESTIGATOR, WAVES, WIND SPACECRAFT, & VOYAGER PRA INSTRUMENT, NASA, as of 2004; leader & co-investigator, waves experiment nasa stero mission, nasa, as of 2004; proj scientist nasa stero mission, nasa, as of 2004; leader & co-investigator, ulysses Unified Radio & Plasma Wave Exp team & cassini radio & plasma wave sci, nasa, as of 2004; radio astronr, Goddard Space Flight Ctr, nasa, beginning 1969; sci analyst astron celestial mech, Wolf Res & Develop Corp, 1965-1969; Comput programmer astron, Nat Radio Astron Observ, 1964-1965. **Memberships:** Am Astron Soc; Am Geophys Union; Int Union Radio Scientists; Inst Elec & Electronics Engrs. **Research Statement & Publications:** Planetary radio physics; magnetospheric physics; Occurrence Rate; Polarization Character; Intensity of Broadband Jovian Kilometric Radiation; published over 190 articles. **Mailing Address:** NASA/GSFC, Code 695, Greenbelt, MD 20771-0001. **Fax:** 301-286-1683. **E-Mail:** michael.kaiser@nasa.gov

KAISER, NICHOLAS, ASTRONOMY. **Personal Data:** b September 15, 1954. **Education:** Leeds Univ, BSc, 1978; Univ Calif, PhD (astron), 1982. **Honors & Awards:** Helen Warner Prize, Am Astron Soc, 1989; Gerhard Herzberg Medal, Can Asn Physicists, 1993. **Professional Experience:** ASTRONR, INST ASTRONOMY, UNIV HAWAII, as of 2006; PROF THEORET ASTROPHYS, UNIV HAWAII, as of 2006; Steacie fel, 1991-1992; prof astron, Can Inst Theoret Astrophys, Univ Toronto, beginning 1990; fel cosmol prog, Can Inst Advan Res, 1988-; assoc prof, Can Inst Theoret Astrophys, Univ Toronto, 1988-1990; prin investr, Natural Sci & Eng Res Coun Can, 1988, 1991 & 1993; fel, Sci & Eng Res Coun advan fel, 1986-1988; fel, Univ Cambridge, 1985-1986; sr vis, Univ Sussex, 1985; fel, Univ Calif, Santa Barbara & Berkeley, 1984; Lindemann fel, Univ Calif, Berkeley, 1983. **Research Statement & Publications:** Observational cosmology; galaxy formation; large scale structure; bulk flows; gravitational lensing. **Mailing Address:** Inst Astron, 2680 Woodlawn Dr, Honolulu, HI 96822. **E-Mail:** kaiser@hawaii.edu

KAISER, PETER, ELECTRICAL ENGINEERING. **Personal Data:** b Aschaffenburg, Ger, 1938; m 1966, c 2. **Education:** Munich Tech Univ, Diplom Ing, 1963; Univ Calif, Berkeley, MS, 1965, PhD (elec eng), 1966. **Professional Experience:** SUPVR, LIGHTWAVE TECH GROUP, BELL LABS, 1979-; mem staff, Guided Waves Res Lab, 1966-1979; NATO fel, 1963-1964. **Memberships:** Inst Elec & Electronics Engrs; Optical Soc Am. **Research Statement & Publications:** Frequency independent antennas; optical communication; guided wave transmission. **Mailing Address:** Bellcore Rm 3Z379, 331 Newman Springs Rd, Red Bank, NJ 07701.

KAISER, PETER KONRAD, GEOMECHANICS & GEOTECHNICAL ENGINEERING, ROCK MECHANICS & GROUND CONTROL. **Personal Data:** b Schaffhausen, Switz, March 31, 1947. **Education:** Eidgenoessische Tech Hochschule, Zurich, dipl, 1972, Univ Alta, PhD (civil eng), 1979. **Honors & Awards:** Distinguished Serv Award, Can Inst Mining, 1991; J F Franklin Award, Can Geotech Soc, 1994; Schlumberger Award, Int Soc Rock Mech. **Professional Experience:** PRES, MIRARCO, LAURENTIAN UNIV, as of 2004; DIR, GEOMECH RES CTR, 1990-; PROF MINING ENG, LAURENTIAN UNIV, 1987-; CHMN, ROCK MECH & GROUND CONTROL, LAURENTIAN UNIV, 1987-; vis prof, Ger, Japan, France, 1983, 1989, 1993; geotech consult civil & mining applns, beginning 1980; from asst prof to prof civil eng, Univ Alta, 1977-1987; hon prof mining, Northeastern Univ, Shenyang, China. **Memberships:** Tunnelling Asn Can (vpres, 1984-1988); Int Soc Rock Mech (vpres, 1991-1995); Am Soc Civil Eng; Can Geotech Soc; Am Inst Mining Engrs; Swiss Geol Soc. **Research Statement & Publications:** Geomechanics of underground excavations; rock support under static and dynamic loading; rock mass response monitoring including microseismics for civil and mining engineering; nuclear waste disposal; ground tunnelling; dam stability; groundwater flow. **Mailing Address:** Geomech Res Ctr, Laurentian Univ, Willet Green Miller Ctr, 933 Ramsey Lake Rd, Sudbury, ON P3E 6B5, Can. **Fax:** 705-675-4862. **E-Mail:** pkaiser@mirarco.org

KAISER, QUENTIN C, SOLID STATE PHYSICS. **Personal Data:** b Ridgewood, NY, September 12, 1921. **Education:** Hofstra Col, BA, 1949; Okla Agr & Mech Col, MS, 1950. **Professional Experience:** RETIRED; br chief & supvry physicist, Microminiaturization Br, 1963-1980; supvr res & develop, Microminiaturization Br, 1961-1963; physicist, Microminiaturization Br, 1959-1961; supvry electronics scientist, Develop Lab, 1953-1959; physicist, Res Lab, Harry Diamond Labs, 1950-1953. **Memberships:** Am Phys Soc; Inst Elec & Electronics Engrs. **Research Statement & Publications:** Dielectric measurements; proximity fuze design; solid state devices. **Mailing Address:** 4114 Byrd Ct, Kensington, MD 20895.

KAISER, REINHOLD, MAGNETIC RESONANCE. **Personal Data:** b Duisburg, Ger, November 19, 1927. **Education:** Univ Gottingen, dipl physics, 1953, Dr rer nat, 1954. **Professional Experience:** RETIRED; emer prof physics, Univ NB, 1992; guest prof, Swiss Fed Inst Technol, 1971-1972; Res fel, Harvard Univ, 1964 & Shell Develop Co, Calif, 1965; from asst prof to prof, Univ NB, 1957-1991, 1966-1991; Can Res Coun fel, Dalhousie Univ, 1956; Ger Res Coun fel, Imp Col, Univ London, 1955. **Research Statement & Publications:** Acoustics; magnetic resonance. **Mailing Address:** 30 Jason Ct, Fredericton, NB E3B 6Y3, Can. **E-Mail:** reka@unb.ca

KAISER, ROBERT, CHEMICAL ENGINEERING, APPLIED CHEMISTRY. **Personal Data:** b Strasbourg, France, June 22, 1934; American citizen; m 1970, Madeleine; c Pierre J & Martine L. **Education:** Mass Inst Technol, SB, 1956, MS, 1957, ScD(chem eng), 1962. **Professional Experience:** PRES & FOUNDER, ENTROPIC SYSTEMS, INC, WINCHESTER, MASS, 1986-; vis scientist, Mass Inst Technol, 1982-1986; pres, Argos Assoc Inc, beginning 1977; consult engr, 1974-1977; group leader, Advan Processes Dept, Systs Div, 1971-1974; sr staff scientist, Res & Tech Labs, Space Systs Div, Avco Corp, Lowell, 1966-1971; res engr, Res & Develop Ctr, Pullman, Inc, NJ, 1965-1966; res chemist, Res & Develop Ctr, Pullman, Inc, NJ, 1962-1965; Res engr, M W Kellogg Co, 1961. **Memberships:** Am Chem Soc; Am Inst Chem Engrs. **Research Statement & Publications:** Oil/water separation; magnetic liquids; applied surface chemistry; fine powder technology; process development; technology assessment and forecasting; industrial market research; precision cleaning; decontamination surface cleaning. **Mailing Address:** Entropic Systems, Inc, PO Box 397, Winchester, MA 01890-0597. **Fax:** 781-938-7589. **E-Mail:** rkaiser@entropicsystems.com

KAISER, THOMAS BURTON, PLASMA PHYSICS. **Personal Data:** b St Louis, Mo, May 11, 1940; m 1967, Phyllis; c Jonathan. **Education:** St Edward's Univ, BS, 1962; Univ Md, Col Park, MS, 1971, PhD (physics), 1973. **Professional Experience:** PHYSICIST PLASMA PHYSICS, LAWRENCE LIVERMORE LAB, 1976-; res assoc space physics, Goddard Space Flight Ctr, Md, 1973-1975; Resident res assoc, Nat Acad Sci-Nat Res Coun, 1973-1975; Sr analyst programming, LTV Aerospace Corp, Mass, 1966-1968. **Memberships:** Am Phys Soc. **Research Statement & Publications:** Theoretical plasma physics; computational physics; magnetic and inertial confinement fusion. **Mailing Address:** Univ Calif Lawrence Livermore Lab, L-630 PO Box 808, Livermore, CA 94550. **Fax:** 510-423-3484. **E-Mail:** tkaiser@llnl.gov

KAISER, WILLIAM RICHARD, COAL HYDROGEOLOGY, AQUEOUS GEOCHEMISTRY. **Personal Data:** b Racine, Wis, August 15, 1937. **Education:** Univ Wis-Madison, BA, 1959, MS, 1962; Johns Hopkins Univ, PhD (geol), 1972. **Professional Experience:** Mem, Steering Comt Coal Res Assesment, Dept Energy, 1989-; chmn exec comt, Tex Univ Coal Res Consortium, 1983-1985; Lectr, Dept Geol Sci, Univ Tex, Austin, 1978-1980; mem, Lignite Subcomt & Fossil Energy Adv Comt, Dept Energy, 1978; RES SCIENTIST, BUR ECON GEOL, UNIV TEX, 1972-; geologist petrol geol, Exxon Co, USA, 1965-1968; geologist igneous & metamorphic petrog, Ghana Geol Surv, Accra, Ghana, 1963-1965; geologist micropaleont, Exxon Co, USA, 1962-1963. **Memberships:** Geol Soc Am; Am Assoc Petrol Geologists; Am Geophys Union. **Research Statement & Publications:** Depositional systems; geology of Gulf Coast (Texas) lignite; hydrogeology; underground coal gasification; low-temperature aqueous geochemistry; brine equilibria in the predication of reservoir quality; retardation of radionuclides; coalbed methane. **Mailing Address:** 4921 Strass Dr, Austin, TX 78731. **Fax:** 512-471-0140.

KAISER, WOLFGANG A, TELECOMMUNICATIONS. **Personal Data:** b Schoental, Ger, February 22, 1923. **Education:** Univ Stuttgart, dipl ing, 1951, Dr ing, 1955. **Honorary Degrees:** Dr ing Eh, Univ Munich, 1985. **Professional Experience:** Mem, Acad Sci, Heidelberg, 1982; Chmn, Res Coun, Muenchner Kreis, Munich, 1977-; PROF TELECOMMUN, UNIV STUTTGART, 1967-; res & develop dir, Stand Elektrik Lorenz, 1963-1967; lab head, Stand Elektrik Lorenz, 1957-1963; Res engr telecommun, Stand Elektrik Lorenz, 1954-1957. **Memberships:** Fel Inst Elec & Electronics Engrs. **Research Statement & Publications:** Evolution of telecommunications; optical transmission systems; wideband networks for speech, text, data, pictures; television, digital audio; data communication in local and metropolitan area networks. **Mailing Address:** Inst Fnachrichtenuebertag, Breitscheid St 2, 70563 Stuttgart, Ger.

KAISER-KUPFER, MURIEL I, OPHTHALMIC GENETICS RESEARCH. **Personal Data:** b New York, NY, May 25, 1936. **Education:** Wellesley Col, BA, 1957; Hopkins Med Sch, MD, 1961; Am Bd Pediat, cert, 1967; Am Bd Ophthal, cert, 1974. **Professional Experience:** DEP CLIN DIR, OPHTHALMIC GENETICS & CLIN SERV BR, NAT EYE INST, NIH, BETHESDA, 1991-; BR CHIEF, OPHTHALMIC GENETICS & CLIN SERV BR, NAT EYE INST, NIH, BETHESDA, 1989-; chief, Sect Ophthalmic Genetics & Pediat Ophthal, Clin Br, 1981-1989; comt mem, Pharm & Therapeut Comt Clin Ctr, NIH, 1977-1989; vis prof, Pan Am Ophthal Asn, 1976; med officer ophthal & pediat, Clin Br, Nat Eye Inst, 1974-1981; sr staff fel, Nat Inst Child Health & Human Develop, NIH, 1972-1974; asst prof, Dept Obstet & Gynec, Sch Med, George Wash Univ, 1971-1972; consult eye care delivery facill, Comprehensive Health Care Ctr, 1970-1971; residency, Ophthal & Consult Congenital Defects Clin, Sch Med, Univ Wash, 1968-1970; asst dir & instr, Comprehensive Care Clin, Dept Pediat, 1966-1968; fel child psychiat, Johns Hopkins Hosp, Baltimore, 1965-1966; residency pediat, Johns Hopkins Hosp, Baltimore, 1963-1965. **Memberships:** Am Acad Ophthal; Nat Soc Prev Blindness; Asn Res Vision & Ophthal; Am Ophthal Soc. **Research Statement & Publications:** Child psychiatry; ophthalmic genetics research. **Mailing Address:** NIH Nat Eye Inst, Ophthal Genetics & Clin Serv Br Bldg 10 Rm 10N226, Bethesda, MD 20892.

KAISERMAN, HOWARD BRUCE, ENZYME STABILIZATION, SURFACTANT & PROTEIN INTERACTIONS. **Personal Data:** b Philadelphia, Pa, October 10, 1957; m 1991, Robyn; c Rebecca & Brent. **Education:** Skidmore Col, BA, 1980; Emory Univ, PhD (chem), 1984. **Professional Experience:** INNOVATION MGR, UNILEVER HOME & PERSONAL CARE, 2001-; fel biochem, Dept Biol, Johns Hopkins Univ & NIH, 1984-1988. **Memberships:** Am

Chem Soc; Am Soc Biochem & Molecular Biol. **Research Statement & Publications:** Influence of chemical agents on protein denaturation with the ultimate goal of protecting proteins from denaturants; storage stability of proteins in aggressive environments. **Mailing Address:** Unilever Inc, 45 River Rd, Edgewater, NJ 07020. **E-Mail:** howard.b.kaiserman@unilever.co

KAISERMAN-ABRAMOF, ITA REBECA, NEUROBIOLOGY, NEUROCYTOLOGY. **Personal Data:** b Belo Horizonte, Brazil, September 11, 1933; div. **Education:** Univ Minas Gerais, BS, 1955, MS, 1956, PhD (biol sci), 1962. **Professional Experience:** PROF ANAT, SCH MED, CASE WESTERN RESERVE UNIV, as of 2000; assoc prof anat, Sch Med, Case Western Reserve Univ, beginnning 1971; asst prof anat, Sch Med, Boston Univ, 1967-1971; teaching asst histol, Sch Med, Harvard Univ, 1966-1967; assoc prof cytol, histol & embryol, 1965-1966; Actg dept chmn biol, Univ Minas Gerais, 1962-1963. **Memberships:** Am Inst Biol Sci; Am Soc Cell Biol; Am Asn Anatomists. **Research Statement & Publications:** Cytological investigations of the mammalian brain, including visual and motor cerebral cortex and cerebellum; use of electron microscopy with experimental and quantitative analysis of connectivity; anophthalmic mutant mice and mechanisms involved in epilepsy. **Mailing Address:** Dept Anat, Case Western Res Univ, Sch Med, Rm W514, 2109 Adelbert Rd, Cleveland, OH 44106. **Fax:** 216-386-8669. **E-Mail:** irk@case.edu

KAITA, ROBERT, PLASMA PHYSICS. **Personal Data:** b Tokyo, Japan, September 2, 1952; American citizen; m 1980, Chiu-Tze Lin; c Courtney L & Constance L. **Education:** State Univ NY, Stony Brook, BSc, 1973; Rutgers Univ, PhD (physics), 1978. **Professional Experience:** Chancellor's vis prof, Univ Mo, Rolla, 1994; PRIN RES PHYSICIST, PLASMA PHYSICS LAB, PRINCETON UNIV, 1990-; res physicist, Plasma Physics Lab, Princeton Univ, 1984-1990; res staff, Plasma Physics Lab, Princeton Univ, 1980-1984; res assoc, Plasma Physics Lab, Princeton Univ, 1978-1980. **Memberships:** Am Phys Soc; pres, Sigma Xi Princeton chap (2000-2002); AAAS. **Research Statement & Publications:** Tokamak heating with neutral particle beams and radiofrequency waves; probe beams and particle detectors as plasma diagnostics; computer simulations of thermonuclear plasmas. **Mailing Address:** Princeton Univ, Plasma Physics Lab Box 451, Princeton, NJ 08543. **Fax:** 609-243-2418. **E-Mail:** kaita@pppl.gov

KAIZER, HERBERT, ONCOLOGY, BONE MARROW TRANSPLANTATION. **Personal Data:** b Boston, Mass, September 30, 1930. **Education:** Boston Univ, AB, 1951, PhD (exp psychol), 1956; Stanford Univ, MD, 1965. **Professional Experience:** CLIN PROF MED, STANFORD UNIV SCH MED, as of 2004; Coleman-Fannie May Candies Found prof pediat, Med & Immunol, Rush Univ, 1985-1997; med dir, Bone Marrow Transplant Prog, Rush Presbyterian Med Ctr, St Luke's, 1983-1997; asst prof pediat & oncol, Sch Med, Johns Hopkins Univ, 1970-1988; sr fel pediat, Univ Tex M D Anderson Hosp & Tumor Inst, 1969-1970; fel microbiol, Johns Hopkins Univ, 1967-1969; intern & asst resident, Johns Hopkins Hosp, 1965-1967; mem tech staff, Thompson, Ramo, Woolridge, Inc, 1958-1959; Assoc psychologist, Int Bus Mach, Inc, 1956-1958. **Memberships:** AAAS; Am Soc Microbiol. **Research Statement & Publications:** Autologous bone marrow transplantation in cancer. **Mailing Address:** Stanford Univ Sch Med, 251 Campus Dr, MSOB X-215, Stanford, CA 94305-5479. **Fax:** 650-725-7944. **E-Mail:** kaizer@smi.stanford.edu

KAJANDER, RICHARD EMIL, SYNTHETIC & EXOTIC FIBER STRUCTURES. **Personal Data:** b Detroit, Mich, December 10, 1951. **Education:** Mich Technol Univ, BS, 1974, BS, 1975 & MS, 1976. **Professional Experience:** AT, SCHULLER INT, as of 2004; sr res engr, Johns Manville, 1990; consult coating process develop, 1984-1986; proj mgr, Tambrands Inc, 1983-1990; sr develop engr, Dexter Corp, 1981-1983; res engr, Am Can Co, 1978-1981; Process engr, Proctor & Gamble Co, 1976-1978. **Memberships:** Am Chem Soc; Tech Asn Pulp & Paper Indust. **Research Statement & Publications:** Papermaking process and specialty paper product development; granted 15 U.S. Patents. **Mailing Address:** Schuller Int, 331 N Dulton Dr, Toledo, OH 43615. **E-Mail:** kajander@jm.com

KAJFEZ, DARKO, ELECTRICAL ENGINEERING. **Personal Data:** b Delnice, Yugoslavia, July 8, 1928; m 1954, c 2. **Education:** Univ Ljubljana, EE, 1953; Univ Calif, Berkeley, PhD (eng), 1967. **Professional Experience:** Consult, Harris-Farinan, San Carlos, Calif, 1980-1983; vis prof elec eng, Univ Ljubljana, 1976-1977; res engr, Dept Elec Eng Univ Miss, beginning 1970; PROF ELEC ENG, UNIV MISS, 1970-; Assoc prof elec eng, Univ Miss, 1967-1970. **Memberships:** Inst Elec & Electronics Engrs; Int Union Radio Sci; Inst Elec Engrs Brit. **Research Statement & Publications:** Microwave circuits and antennas. **Mailing Address:** Dept Elec Eng, Univ Miss, Anderson Hall, Rm 312, Univ, MS 38677. **Fax:** 662-915-7231. **E-Mail:** eedarko@olemiss.edu

KAJI, AKIRA, BIOCHEMISTRY. **Personal Data:** b Tokyo, Japan, January 13, 1930; m 1958, Katayama; c Kenneth, Eugene, Naomi & Amy. **Education:** Univ Tokyo, BS, 1953; Johns Hopkins Univ, PhD (biochem), 1958. **Professional Experience:** Sci counr, Nat Eye Inst, 1987-1992; Fogarty int fel, 1986-1987; vis prof, Kyoto Univ, 1986-1987; PROF MICROBIOL, SCH MED, UNIV PA, 1972-; John Simmon Guggenheim Scholar, Imperial Cancer Res Fund Lab, London & prof, Tokyo Univ, 1969-; from asst prof to assoc prof, Sch Med, Univ PA, 1964-1972; Helen Hay Whitney estab investrship, 1964-1969; assoc, Sch Med, Univ PA, 1963; vis scientist, Oak Ridge Nat Lab, 1962; Helen Hay Whitney Found fel, 1961-1963; res assoc microbiol, Sch Med, Vanderbilt Univ, 1960-1961; res fel, McCollum Pratt Inst, 1959-1960; vis investr, Rockefeller Inst, 1959; Res fel ophthal, Sch Med, Johns Hopkins Univ, 1958-1959. **Memberships:** Am Soc Biol Chemists; Am Soc Microbiol; Japanese Cancer Soc; Japanese Biochem Soc. **Research Statement & Publications:** Sulfur metabolism; neurochemistry; mechanism of enzyme action; tumorgenesis; protein biosynthesis; nucleic acids; antivirus agents; anti-cancer agents. **Mailing Address:** Dept Microbiol, Sch Med, Univ PA, 319 B Johnson Pavilion, 3610 Hamilton Walk, Philadelphia, PA 19104. **Fax:** 215-573-2221. **E-Mail:** kaji@mail.med.upenn.edu

KAJI, HIDEKO (KATAYAMA), BIOCHEMISTRY, PHARMACOLOGY. **Personal Data:** b Tokyo, Japan, January 1, 1932; American citizen; m 1958, Akira; c Kenneth, Eugene, Naomi & Amy. **Education:** Tokyo Univ Pharmaceut & Life Sci, BS, 1954; Univ Nebr, MS, 1956; Purdue Univ, PhD (pharmacol), 1958. **Professional Experience:** PROF, JEFFERSON MED COL, THOMAS JEFFERSON UNIV, 1983-; consult, Nippon Paint Co Ltd, 1989-; bd mem, sci counr, NIH, 1987-1991; vis prof, Wistar Inst, 1984-1985; assoc prof, Jefferson Med Col, Thomas Jefferson Univ, 1976-1983; asst mem biochem, Inst Cancer Res, 1966-1976; res assoc, Sch Med, Univ Pa, 1965-1966; assoc, Sch Med, Univ Pa, 1963-1964; vis scientist, Oak Ridge Nat Lab, 1962-1963; from instr to asst prof, Sch Med, Vanderbilt Univ, 1960-1962; Eli Lilly fel, Sch Med, Johns Hopkins Univ, 1958-1959. **Memberships:** Am Soc Biol Chemists; Am Soc Pharmacol & Exp Therapeut. **Research Statement & Publications:** Mechanism of macromolecular synthesis; transport mechanism; genetic regulatory mechanisms of oncogenesis and AIDS. **Mailing Address:** Dept Pharmacol, Jefferson Med Col, 1020 Locust St, Philadelphia, PA 19107. **Fax:** 215-923-7343. **E-Mail:** eko.Kaji@jefferson.edu

KAK, AVINASH CARL, COMPUTER ENGINEERING. **Personal Data:** b Srinagar, Kashmir, October 22, 1944. **Education:** Indian Inst Technol, PhD (elec eng), 1970; Madras Univ, BE, 1966. **Professional Experience:** ED CHIEF, COMPUT VISION & IMAGE UNDERSTANDING J, 1995-; PROF ELEC ENG & COMPUT ENG, PURDUE UNIV, 1977-; from asst prof to assoc prof, Robot Vision Lab, Purdue Univ, 1970-1977. **Memberships:** Am Asn Artificial Intel; Inst Elec & Electronics Engrs. **Research Statement & Publications:** Sensory aspects of robotic intelligence; computer vision; spatial reasoning; robot cognition; image processing; various forms of imaging; published over 50 articles. **Mailing Address:** Sch Elec & Comput Eng, Purdue Univ, W Lafayette, IN 47907-1285. **Fax:** 765-494-6440. **E-Mail:** kak@purdue.edu

KAK, SUBHASH CHANDRA, ARTIFICIAL INTELLIGENCE, INFORMATION THEORY. **Personal Data:** b Srinagar, India, March 26, 1947; m 1979, Navnidhi; c Abhinav & Arushi. **Education:** Kashmir Univ, BS, 1967; Indian Inst Technol, Delhi, PhD (elec eng), 1970. **Honors & Awards:** Sci Acad Medal, Indian Nat Sci Acad, 1977; Kothari Award, Kothari Sci & Res Inst, 1977; Goyal Prize, 1999. **Professional Experience:** Vis prof, Harvard Univ, 1995; guest ed, Info Sci, 1993 & Circuits, Systs & Signal Processing, 1993; consult, UN Develop Prog, 1986 & 1989-1990; DELAUNE DISTINGUISHED PROF ELEC & COMPUT ENG, LA STATE UNIV, 1983-; guest ed, Inst Elec & Electronics Engrs Comput, 1983; assoc prof elec eng, LA State Univ, 1979-1983; guest researcher, Bell Labs, Murray Hill, 1976 & Tata Inst Fundamental Res, Bombay, 1977-1978; Acad visitor, Imp Col, Univ London, 1975-1976; asst prof, Indian Inst Technol, Delhi, 1974-1979; Lectr elec eng, Indian Inst Technol, Delhi, 1971-1974. **Research Statement & Publications:** Information theory; quantum physics; cognitive science; artificial intelligence; neural computing; cryptology; history and philosophy of science. **Mailing Address:** Dept Elec & Comput Eng, La State Univ, Baton Rouge, LA 70803-5901. **Fax:** 225-578-5200. **E-Mail:** kak@ece.lsu.edu

KAKAR, ANAND SWAROOP, CONDUCTIVE COATINGS, SURFACE CHEMISTRY. **Personal Data:** b India, October 14, 1937. **Education:** Banaras Hindu Univ, BSc, 1960; Indian Inst Technol, MTech, 1964; Wayne State Univ, MS, 1971, PhD (phys chem), 1978. **Professional Experience:** DIR RES, GRAFO COLLOIDS, 1981-; staff chemist, Acheson Colloids, Mich, 1978-1981; res asst, Wayne State Univ, 1974-1978; mfg develop engr, Ford Motor Co, Mt Clemons, Mich, 1972-1974; technician, Mercury Paint Co, 1971-1972; technician, Can Gen Elec, 1968-1969; lectr chem eng, Indian Inst Technol, Delhi, 1965-1968. **Memberships:** Electrochem Soc; Am Inst Chem Engrs. **Research Statement & Publications:** Heat transfer and hold-up fluidized beds; zone refining and single crystal growth; optical and electrical properties of semiconductor; photovoltaic cells; electroless deposition; size reduction; colloidal dispersion; conductive coatings; solid film lubricants; surface preparation and analysis. **Mailing Address:** 412 Boena Vista St, Emlenton, PA 16373. **Fax:** 412-867-5974.

KAKAR, RAJESH KUMAR, STATISTICS, DATA PROCESSING. **Personal Data:** b New Delhi, India, October 2, 1950. **Education:** Univ Delhi, BSc, 1970, MS, 1972; Tex Tech Univ, DBA (bus statist), 1978. **Professional Experience:** ASST PROF BUS STATIST, ARIZ STATE UNIV, 1978-; Instr bus statist, Tex Tech Univ, 1972-1978. **Memberships:** Am Statist Asn; Inst Mgt Sci; Am Inst Decision Sci. **Research Statement & Publications:** Empirical bayesian estimation; assessment of subjective probabilities; forecasting; manpower models; auditing software. **Mailing Address:** 4891 E Butler Dr, Paradise Valley, AZ 85253.

KAKEFUDA, TSUSYOSHI, INTERNATIONAL COOPERATION ON CANCER RESEARCH & TREATMENT. **Personal Data:** b January 20, 1929. **Education:** Tokyo Univ, MD, 1952, PhD (path), 1958. **Professional Experience:** MED OFFICER, NAT CANCER INST, 1967-; City Hope Med Ctr, 1960-1967. **Memberships:** Am Asn Cancer Res. **Research Statement & Publications:** Cancer etiology. **Mailing Address:** 14901 River Rd, Potomac, MD 20854.

KAKIS, FREDERIC JACOB, PHYSICAL ORGANIC CHEMISTRY, FOOD SCIENCE. **Personal Data:** b Drama, Greece, November 1, 1930. **Education:** City Col New York, BS, 1960; Stanford Univ, PhD (org chem), 1964. **Honors & Awards:** Prof Develop Award, NSF, 1977; Fulbright Award, 1980. **Professional Experience:** PROF EMER CHEM, CHAPMAN UNIV, as of 2003; INSTR, UNIV EXTENDED PROG, CALIF STATE UNIV, FULLERTON, as of 2003; PRES & CHIEF EXEC OFFICER, FORENSIC CONSULT SERVS, 1996-; exec vpres, Impact General Inc, 1989-1996; dir, Nat Inst Forensic Studies, 1989-1996; assoc vpres, Div Natural Sci, 1983-1989; chmn, Div Natural Sci, 1978-1980; grants, Union Oil Found, 1974, 1975, 1976 & 1977; prof chem, Chapman Col, 1971-1989; vis prof, Lab Org Synthesis, Polytech Sch, Paris, 1970-1971; environmentalist, Defense Contract Admin Serv, 1970; res fel, NASA-Ames Res Ctr & Stanford Univ, 1969; assoc prof, Chapman Col, 1966-1971; assoc prof, Calif State Col, Long Beach, 1966-1967 & Calif State Univ, Fullerton, 1966-1970; res fel, Oak Ridge Nat Lab, 1966; grants, Res Corp, 1966, 1967, 1970; grants, Petrol Res Fund, 1965, 1966, 1976 & 1977; grants, NSF, 1965; chmn dept, Chapman Col, 1963-1968; vis prof, Univ Calif, Los Angeles & Univ Calif, Riverside; NSF res fel, Univ Calif, Riverside. **Memberships:** AAAS; Am Chem Soc; fel Am Inst Chemists; Royal Soc Chem; NY Acad Sci; Inst Food Technologists; Soc Cosmetic Chemists. **Research Statement & Publications:** Study of reaction mechanisms by isotopic labelling; air pollution research; synthetic and mechanistic organic chemistry; heterogeneous catalysis and adsorption; food dehydration. **Mailing Address:** 1534 N Harding St, Orange, CA 92867.

KAKKAR, ASHOK, INORGANIC CHEMISTRY. **Education:** Univ Waterloo, PhD, 1990. **Professional Experience:** ASSOC PROF, DEPT CHEM, MCGILL UNIV, as of 2006. **Mailing Address:** Dept Chem, McGill Univ, 801 Sherbrooke St W, Montreal, PQ H3A 2K6, Can. **E-Mail:** ashok.kakkar@mcgill.ca

KAKO, KYOHEI JOE, PHYSIOLOGY. **Personal Data:** b Tokyo, Japan, May 29, 1928. **Education:** Tokyo Jikei Univ, MD, 1953; FRCP. **Professional Experience:** RETIRED; residency, Mt Sinai Hosp, 1981-1982; med res assoc, Mt Sinai Hosp, 1968-1988; from asst prof to prof physiol, Fac Med, Univ Ottawa, 1964-1993; Alexander von Humboldt fel, I Med Clin, Univ Munich, 1963-1964; fel, Kanton Hosp, Univ Zurich, 1961-1963; res assoc, Wayne State Univ, 1959-1961; Mo Heart Asn fel, 1957-1959; res asst med, Sch Med, Wash Univ, 1956-1957; Resident internal med, Tokyo Jikei-Kai Tokyo Hosp, 1954-1956. **Memberships:** Am Physiol Soc; Can Cardiovasc Soc; fel Am Col Cardiol; fel Am Col Physicians; fel Am Col Chest Physicians; Royal Col Physicians Can. **Research Statement & Publications:** Heart muscle biochemistry; lipid and carbohydrate metabolism; cardiomyopathies; cellular & subcellular function, membrane, calcium fluxes. **Mailing Address:** 580 Mariposa Ave, Univ Ottawa Fac Med, Rockcliffe Park, ON K1M 0S2, Can.

KAKU, MICHIO, THEORETICAL HIGH ENERGY PHYSICS, NUCLEAR PHYSICS. **Personal Data:** b San Jose, Calif, January 24, 1947. **Education:** Harvard Univ, BA, 1968; Univ Calif, Berkeley, PhD (physics), 1972. **Professional Experience:** Inst Advan Study, Princeton, 1990; vis prof, NY Univ, 1988; HENRY SEMAT PROF PHYSICS, CITY COL NEW YORK, 1982-; from asst prof to assoc prof, City Col New York, 1973-1982; Lectr physics, Princeton Univ, 1972-1973. **Memberships:** fel Am Phys Soc. **Research Statement & Publications:** High energy and nuclear physics; unified field theories; quantum gravity and supergravity; kinetics and neutron transport theory; reactor physics; gauge field theory of superstrings, which will include general covariance and SU(3)X SU(2)X U(1) as subsets; making it a candidate for a unified field theory of all known interactions. **Mailing Address:** Dept Physics, City Col New York 138th St, J 419 Convent Ave, New York, NY 10031. **Fax:** 212-650-6940. **E-Mail:** mkaku@aol.com

KAKUTANI, SHIZUO, mathematics; deceased, see previous edition for last biography

KALAB, MILOSLAV, BIOCHEMISTRY. **Personal Data:** b Urcice, Czech, June 12, 1929. **Education:** Brno Tech Univ, BSc, 1950; Slovak Tech Univ, Bratislava, MSc, 1952; Slovak Acad Sci, PhD (chem), 1957. **Honors & Awards:** Pfizer Inc Award, Am Dairy Sci Asn, 1982. **Professional Experience:** RETIRED; res scientist, Food Res Inst, Agr Can, 1968-1995; Nat Res Coun Can fel, 1966-1968; assoc prof, Dept Natural Sci, 1965-1966; from asst prof to assoc prof, Sch Med, Palacky Univ, Czech, 1958-1965; res scientist, Chem Inst, Slovak Acad Sci, 1957-1958; ed-in-chief, Food Struct. **Memberships:** Am Dairy Sci Asn; Can Inst Food Sci & Technol; Micros Soc Can; Electron Micros Soc Am; Inst Food Technologists. **Research Statement & Publications:** Food proteins; milk protein gelation, composition, texture; microstructure of dairy products using electron microscopy. **Mailing Address:** 2895 Otterson Dr, Ottawa, ON K1V 7B2, Can. **Fax:** 613-759-1734.

KALABA, ROBERT E, MATHEMATICS. **Education:** NY Univ, BA & PhD. **Professional Experience:** PROF, DEPT BIOMED ENG & ECON & ELEC ENG, UNIV SOUTHERN CALIF, as of 2004. **Mailing Address:** Dept Biomed Eng, Univ Southern Calif, OHE 500G, 3650 McClintock Ave, Los Angeles, CA 90089-1451. **Fax:** 213-740-0343.

KALABOKIDIS, KOSTAS D, FOREST FIRES, GEOGRAPHIC INFORMATION SYSTEMS. **Personal Data:** b Thessaloniki, Greece, November 2, 1958. **Education:** Aristotelian Univ, Greece, BS, 1981; Univ Mont, MS, 1985; Colo State Univ, PhD (forest fire sci/geog info systs), 1992. **Professional Experience:** ASST PROF GEOG, UNIV AEGEAN, as of 2002; asst prof forest fire sci, Colo State Univ, 1993-1994; RES ASSOC, COLO STATE UNIV, 1992-; res asst & instr, Colo State Univ, 1989-1991; Res asst, Univ Mont, 1983-1985. **Memberships:** Am Soc Photogram & Remote Sensing; Int Asn Wildland Fire; Soc Am Foresters. **Research Statement & Publications:** Wildland fire management, fire behavior modeling, fuel management, prescribed burning, fire suppression, fire ecology, geographic information systems, remote sensing and statistics. **Mailing Address:** Dept Geog, Univ Aegean, Greece. **E-Mail:** kalabokidis@aegean.gr

KALAFUS, RUDOLPH M, SATELLITE NAVIGATION ENGINEERING. **Personal Data:** b Jackson, Mich, December 17, 1937; m 1965, Lois; c 2. **Education:** Univ Mich, BS (elec eng) & BS (eng math), 1960, MS, 1963, PhD (elec eng), 1966. **Honors & Awards:** Weems award, Inst Navig, 2001; Johannes Kepler Award, Inst Navig, 1992. **Professional Experience:** CHMN, RADIO TECH SPEC COMT IOU, 1984-; mgr, GPS systems group, Trimble Navig, 1994-2002; mktg mgr landing & tracking systs, Trimble Navig, 1992-1993; dir differential GPS dept, Trimble Navig, 1988-1991; head satellite navig group, Transp Systs Ctr, US Dept Transp, 1982-1987; electronics engr, Transp Systs Ctr, US Dept Transp, 1970-1981. **Memberships:** Inst Elec & Electronics Engrs; Inst Navig. **Research Statement & Publications:** Satellite navigation development; differential GPS techniques development; integrity monitoring techniques development; GPS-based landing system development; aviation applications development. **Mailing Address:** Trimble Navigation, 645 N Mary Ave, Sunnyvale, CA 94088-3642. **Fax:** 408-481-2097.

KALAI, EHUD, GAME THEORY, MATHEMATICAL ECONOMICS. **Personal Data:** b Tel Aviv, Israel, December 7, 1942; American citizen; wid Marilyn (Deceased); c Kerren L & Adam K. **Education:** Univ Calif Berkeley, AB, 1967; Cornell Univ, MS, 1971 & PhD (math), 1972. **Professional Experience:** JAMES O'CONNOR DISTINGUISHED PROF DECISION & GAME SCI, NORTHWESTERN UNIV, 2001-; DIR, KELLOG CTR STRATEGIC DECISION MAKING, NORTHWESTERN UNIV, 1996-; vis prof econ, Sherman Fairchild distinguished scholar, Calif Inst Technol, 1994; vis prof econ, Calif Inst Technol, 1993; Oscar Morgonstern res prof math econ & game theory, NY Univ, 1991; PROF MATH, KELLOG SCH MGT, NORTHWESTERN UNIV, 1990-; ed, Games & Econ Behav, 1988-; mem bd dirs, First Savings Am & Fed Savings & Loan Asn, 1986-1989; Morrison chair prof decision sci, Kellog Sch Mgt, Northwestern Univ, 1982-2001; prin investr, NSF grants, 1979-; from asst prof to prof, Kellog Ctr Strategic Decision Making, Northwestern Univ, 1976-1982; consult, Div Common, Israeli Army, 1974-1975; asst prof decision theory & oper res, Dept Statist, Tel-Aviv Univ, 1972-1976. **Memberships:** Am Math Soc; fel Econometrics Soc. **Research Statement & Publications:** Author of over 50 journal and book articles on game-theory, decision theory, and mathematical economics; non-cooperative and cooperative games and their application to economics and other social sciences, including: bargaining and strategic interaction, social choice theory and learning in dynamic interaction. **Mailing Address:** Kellog Sch Mgt, Northwestern Univ, 2001 Sheridan Rd, Evanston, IL 60208-0001. **Fax:** 847-467-3646. **E-Mail:** kalai@nwu.edu

KALANT, HAROLD, PHARMACOLOGY, CELL PHYSIOLOGY. **Personal Data:** b Toronto, Ont, November 15, 1923. **Education:** Univ Toronto, MD, 1945, BSc, 1948, PhD (path chem), 1955. **Honors & Awards:** Jellinek Mem Award Res on Alcoholism, 1972; Int Gold Medal Res Award, Raleigh Hills Found, 1981; Ann Res Award, Res Soc Alcoholism (USA), 1983; Upjohn Award, Pharmacol Soc Can, 1985; Nathan B Eddy Mem Medal Award, 1986. **Professional Experience:** PROF EMER PHARMACOL & PATH CHEM, UNIV TORONTO, 1989-; DIR EMER RES BIOL SCI, ONT ALCOHOLISM RES FOUND, 1989-; mem, Bd Can Ctr Substance Abuse, 1989-1993; pharmacol field ed, J Stud Alcohol, 1985-; chmn, Bd Sci Counr, Nat Inst Alcohol Abuse & Alcoholism, 1983-1988; mem, Comn Prob Drug Dependence, US, 1978-; assoc ed, Can J Physiol Pharmacol, 1975-1981; mem expert adv panel on drugs dependence, WHO, 1974-1984; mem sci adv bd, Int Coun Alcoholism & Addictions, Lausanne, 1972-; memalcoholism study sect, NIMH, Wash, DC, 1970-1974; res comt non-med use drugs, Dept Nat Health & Welfare, Can, 1970-1972; from assoc prof to prof, Univ Toronto, 1964-1989; assoc res dir, Ont Alcoholism Res Found, 1962-1989; mem res comt NAm Asn Alcoholism Progs, 1962-1967; asst res dir, Ont Alcoholism Res Found, 1959-1962; sect head, Defense Res Med Labs, Can, 1956-1959; nat res coun can fel biochem, Cambridge Univ, 1955-1956. **Memberships:** Pharmacol Soc Can; Int Soc Biomed Res Alcoholism (pres, 1990-1994); fel Royal Soc Can; AAAS. **Research Statement & Publications:** Pharmacology of ethanol and other addictive drugs; cell membrane chemistry and physiology; drug-behavior interactions in drug tolerance and dependence. **Mailing Address:** Dept Pharmacol, Univ Toronto, Toronto, ON M5S 1A8, Can. **Fax:** 416-978-6395. **E-Mail:** harold.kalant@utoronto.ca

KALANTAR, ALFRED HUSAYN, DATA ANALYSIS. **Personal Data:** b Chicago, Ill, December 13, 1934. **Education:** Rutgers Univ, BSc, 1956; Cornell Univ, PhD (chem), 1963. **Professional Experience:** RETIRED; vis scientist, Nat Res Coun, Ottawa, 1985; adj assoc prof, State Univ NY Binghamton, 1970-1971; assoc prof chem, Univ Alta, beginning 1969; asst prof, Univ Alta, 1964-1969; NSF res fel chem, Calif Inst Technol, 1963-1964. **Research Statement & Publications:** Analysis of errors in parameters extracted from data; effects of weighting on efficiency of data analysis. **Mailing Address:** Dept Chem, Univ Alta, Edmonton, AB T6G 2G2, Can. **Fax:** 403-492-8231. **E-Mail:** alfred.kalantar@ualberta.ca

KALASINSKY, VICTOR FRANK, PHYSICAL CHEMISTRY, SPECTROSCOPY. **Personal Data:** b Columbus, Ohio, December 30, 1949. **Education:** Mass Inst Technol, SB, 1972; Univ SC, PhD (phys chem), 1975. **Honors & Awards:** Sigma Xi Res Award, 1983; Outstanding Chemist Award, Am Chem Soc, 1983. **Professional Experience:** CHEIF, DIV ENVIRON TOXICOL, ARMED FORCES INST PATH, 1989-; vis scientist, NIH, 1987-1988; prof chem, Miss State Univ, beginning 1985; from asst prof to assoc prof, Miss State Univ, 1977-1985; Asst prof chem, Furman Univ, 1976-1977. **Memberships:** Am Chem Soc; Am Phys Soc; Soc Appl Spectros; Coblentz Soc; Sigma Xi. **Research Statement & Publications:** Raman, infrared and microwave spectroscopy; chemical structure and conformation; intramolecular and intermolecular interactions; applications of the laboratory computer; GC/FTIR and HPLC/FTIR. **Mailing Address:** Armed Forces Inst Path, 6825 16th St NW, Washington, DC 20306-6000. **E-Mail:** kalasinv@afip.osd.mil

KALATHIL, JAMES SAKARIA, ATMOSPHERIC PHYSICS, PHYSICS. **Personal Data:** b Shertallai, India, December 4, 1935; American citizen; c 2. **Education:** Univ Madras, BS, 1956; Southern Ill Univ, MS, 1963; Univ Nev, PhD (atmospheric physics), 1977. **Professional Experience:** PROF PHYSICS, CALIF POLYTECH STATE UNIV, SAN LUIS OBISPO, 1965-; Instr physics, Frostburg State Col, Md, 1963-1965. **Memberships:** Am Meteorol Soc; Am Asn Physics Teachers; Am Geophys Union. **Research Statement & Publications:** Cumulus cloud models; history of meteorology; effects of solar activity on weather and climate; climatology. **Mailing Address:** Dept Physics, Calif Polytech State Univ, San Luis Obispo, CA 93407-0001.

KALB, G WILLIAM, MINERALOGY, ANALYTICAL CHEMISTRY. **Personal Data:** b Akron, Ohio, December 10, 1943. **Education:** Col Wooster, BA, 1965; Ohio State Univ, MS, 1967, PhD (mineral), 1969. **Honors & Awards:** Bituminous Coal Res Award, Am Chem Soc, 1972. **Professional Experience:** PRES, TRADET INC, 1970-; Lab mgr mineral, Geol Surv, 1969-1970. **Memberships:** Am Chem Soc; Am Soc Testing & Mat; Geol Soc Am. **Research Statement & Publications:** Determination of volatile trace metals in coal; development of analytical methods for the collection and measurement of volatilized mercury in high 502 concentration gas streams. **Mailing Address:** Tradet Inc, PO Box 2019, Wheeling, WV 26003. **Fax:** 304-547-9097.

KALB, JOHN W, HIGH VOLTAGE POWER EQUIPMENT. **Personal Data:** b Columbus, Ohio, June 6, 1918. **Education:** Swarthmore Col, BS, 1940. **Professional Experience:** PRES, LOW COUNTRY CANDLES, 1981-; dir res, Ohio Brass Co, 1963-1981; sr develop engr, Ohio Brass Co, 1940-1963. **Memberships:** Nat Acad Eng; fel Inst Elec & Electronics Engrs. **Mailing Address:** 101 Pier Pont Condos, 100 Floyd St, St Simons Island, GA 31522.

KALBERER, JOHN THEODORE, PHYSIOLOGY, BIOLOGY. **Personal Data:** b New York, NY, March 15, 1936. **Education:** Adelphi Univ, AB, 1956; Creighton Univ, MS, 1957; NY Univ, PhD (biol, physiol), 1966; Dartmouth Col, Inst Grad, 1981. **Professional Experience:** RETIRED; dep dir, div dis prev, off dir, NIH, beginning 1987; coordr dis prev & health prom, off dir, 1983-1986; dep dir, Off Med Appln Res, 1979-1983; assoc dir prog planning, Nat Cancer Inst, 1974-1978; spec asst to assoc dir extramural activities, Div Res Grants, NIH, 1967-1973; grants assoc, Div Res Grants, NIH, 1966-1967; res assoc path, Beth Israel Med Ctr, NY, 1957-1966. **Memberships:** Am Soc Zool; Am Asn Anat; Aerospace Med Asn; Am Acad Polit & Soc Sci; NY Acad Sci; Soc Epidemiol Res; Sigma Xi. **Research Statement & Publications:** Decompression sickness, especially as it relates to fat embolization to the lung; role of vasoactive substances as they relate to stress conditions; science and society; disease prevention and health promotion. **Mailing Address:** Dis Prev Nat Inst Health, Rm 1B03 Bldg 3 31 Ctr Dr MSC 2082, Bethesda, MD 20892-2082. **Fax:** 301-480-9654.

KALBFLEISCH, GEORGE RANDOLPH, PARTICLE PHYSICS, HIGH ENERGY PHYSICS. **Personal Data:** b Long Beach, Calif, March 14, 1931; m 1954, Ruth Ann Adams; c Karen Ruth, George R Jr, Julie Marie (Collins) & Carl W. **Education:** Loyola Univ, Calif, BS, Chem, 1952; Univ Calif, Berkeley, PhD (physics), 1961. **Honors & Awards:** Science wall of fame, Lyola-Marymount Univ, (Los Angeles), Oct, 2001. **Professional Experience:** PROF EMER PHYSICS, UNIV OKLA, as of 2003; mem bd overseers, URA Fermilab, 1989-1995; prof physics, Univ Okla, Norman, beginning 1979; physicist, Fermi Nat Accelerator Lab, 1976-1979; physicist, Brookhaven Nat Lab, 1967-1976; assoc physicist, Brookhaven Nat Lab, 1964-1967; consult, Anamet Testing Labs, 1962-1964; physicist, Lawrence Radiation Lab, Univ Calif, 1961-1964; asst, Lawrence Radiation Lab, Univ Calif, 1959-1961; technician, Lawrence Radiation Lab, Univ Calif, 1957-1959; anal chemist, Hales Testing Labs, 1957; qual control supvr, United Can & Glass, Hunt Foods, Inc, Calif, 1952-1956. **Memberships:** Am Phys Soc. **Research Statement & Publications:** Neutrino interactions; muon and pion physics; photon physics; superconducting magnets; beauty and charm physics; magnetic monopole search. **Mailing Address:** Dept Physics & Astron, Univ Okla, Norman, OK 73019. **Fax:** 405-325-7557. **E-Mail:** kalbfleisch@nhn.ou.edu

KALBFLEISCH, JAMES G, MATHEMATICAL STATISTICS. **Personal Data:** b Galt, Ont, September 12, 1940. **Education:** Univ Toronto, BSc, 1963; Univ Waterloo, MA, 1964, PhD (math), 1966. **Professional Experience:** VPRES, ACAD & PROVOST, UNIV WATERLOO, as of 1996; chmn dept, Univ Waterloo, 1975-1979; PROF STATIST, UNIV WATERLOO, 1971-; prof statist, Univ Man, 1970-1971; C D Howe fel, 1968-1969; vis prof, Univ Essex, 1968-1969; Nat Res Coun Can res grant, 1967-; Dept Univ Affairs res grant, 1967-1970; adj prof, York Univ, 1967; from asst prof to assoc prof statist, Univ Waterloo, 1966-1971; lectr math, Univ Waterloo, 1964-1966. **Memberships:** Biomet Soc; fel Int Statist Inst; Royal Statist Soc; fel Am Statist Asn. **Research Statement & Publications:** Statistical inference; combinatorial mathematics. **Mailing Address:** Dept Statist, Univ Waterloo, 200 Univ Ave W, Waterloo, ON N2L 3G1, Can.

KALBFLEISCH, JOHN DAVID, STATISTICAL INFERENCE & METHODOLOGY, APPLICATIONS IN MEDICINE & EPIDEMIOLOGY. **Personal Data:** b Grand Valley, Ont, July 16, 1943; m 1966, Sharon; c Michael Allen, Kirby Ann & Heidi Kathryn. **Education:** Univ Waterloo, BSc, 1966, MMath, 1967, PhD (statist), 1969. **Honors & Awards:** Gold Medal, Statist Soc Can, 1994. **Professional Experience:** RETIRED; dean, fac math, beginning 1990; Univ Calif, San Francisco, 1988; Univ Mich, 1987; chair, fac math, 1984-1990; assoc ed, Can J Statist, 1984-1989; sr assoc ed, Can J Statist, 1981-1984; assoc ed, Annuals Statist, 1980-1982; prof statist & actuarial sci, Univ Waterloo, beginning 1979; vis prof, Univ Wash, 1979-1980; assoc prof, Fac Math, 1973-1979; asst prof, State Univ NY, Buffalo, 1970-1973; res assoc, Univ Col, London, 1969-1970. **Memberships:** Int Statist Inst; fel Am Statist Asn; fel Inst Math Statist; fel Royal Soc Can. **Research Statement & Publications:** Mathematical statistics and statistical methodology with particular attention to applications in medicine and epidemiology. **Mailing Address:** Fac Math, Univ Waterloo, Waterloo, ON N2L 3G1, Can. **Fax:** 519-746-0274. **E-Mail:** jdkalbfl@math.uwaterloo.ca

KALBFLEISCH, PAMELA J, MATHEMATICS. **Education:** Mich State Univ, PhD, 1985. **Honors & Awards:** Extraordinary Merit Res Award, Nat Commun Asn, 2000. **Professional Experience:** PROF, DEPT COMMUN & MASS MEDIA, UNIV WYO, as of 2006. **Memberships:** Western States Commun Asn. **Mailing Address:** Dept Commun & Mass Media, Univ Wyo, PO Box 3904, Laramie, WY 82071-3904. **Fax:** 307-766-5676. **E-Mail:** PamelaK@uwyo.edu

KALDJIAN, MOVSES J(EREMY), STRUCTURAL MECHANICS, CIVIL ENGINEERING. **Personal Data:** b Beirut, Lebanon, December 26, 1925. **Education:** Am Univ, Beirut, BA, 1948, BSc, 1949; Univ Man, MSc, 1952; Univ Mich, PhD (civil eng), 1960. **Professional Experience:** PROF EMER, NAVAL ARCHIT & MARINE ENG, UNIV MICH, as of 2004; PROF EMER CIVIL & ENVIRON ENG, UNIV MICH, 1976-; vis prof, Univ Mich-US AID Prog & Indian Inst Technol, Kanpur, 1962-1964; partic, Ford Found comput proj, 1961 & Ford Fac Develop adv comt grant, 1962; from instr to assoc prof solid mech, Univ Mich, 1957-1976; lectr struct, Queen's Univ, Ont, 1953-1954; civil engr, Dom Bridge Co Ltd, Can, 1952-1953; off engr, Trans-Arabian Pipeline Co, Lebanon, 1949-1950; consult, G C Optronics & Palmer-Shile. **Memberships:** Am Soc Civil Engrs. **Research Statement & Publications:** Numerical techniques in structural mechanics including finite element methods; response of buildings and dams to earthquake forces; ship structures in ice fields and some experimentation with holography. **Mailing Address:** 111 Eng Prog Bldg, Ann Arbor, MI 48109-2140. **E-Mail:** kaldjian@engin.umich.edu

KALDOR, ANDREW, CLUSTER SCIENCE, CATALYSIS LASER PHYSICS. **Personal Data:** b Budapest, Hungary, October 11, 1944. **Education:** Univ Calif, Berkeley, BS, 1966; Cornell Univ, PhD (chem), 1970. **Honors & Awards:** Silver Medal, Dept Com, 1973; Frontiers Chem Lectr, Case Western Reserve, 1979; Edwin G Baetjer Lectr, Princeton, 1983. **Professional Experience:** MGR, RES EXXON MOBIL RES & ENG CO, as of 2005; DIR RES & DEVELOP, EXXON MOBIL RES & ENG CO, as of 2001; chmn bd trustee, Gordon Res Conf, 1989-1990; dir, resource chem lab, Corp Res Lab, Exxonres & Eng Co, beginning 1981; head chem physics group, Corp Res Lab, Exxonres & Eng CO, 1977-1981; sr res chemist appl physics, Corp Res Lab, Exxonres & Eng CO, 1974-1977; Mem staff laser chem, Nat Bur Standards, 1970-1974; Nat Acad Sci-Nat Res Coun fel, Nat Bur Standards, 1970-1972. **Memberships:** AAAS; Am Chem Soc; Am Vacuum Soc; Am Phys Soc. **Research Statement & Publications:** Laser chemistry; laser isotope separation; chemical physics; reaction dynamics; molecular spectroscopy; surface chemistry; chister science; materials science. **Mailing Address:** Exxon Mobil Res & Eng Co, Annadale, NJ 70892. **E-Mail:** a.kaldor@exxonmobil.com

KALDOR, GEORGE, PHYSIOLOGY. **Personal Data:** b Budapest, Hungary, February 10, 1926. **Education:** Med Univ Budapest, MD, 1950; Am Bd Clin Chem, dipl, 1964; Am Bd Path, dipl clin path, 1965, dipl chem path, 1978. **Professional Experience:** PROF PATH, WAYNE STATE UNIV, DETROIT, 1975-; CHIEF, CLIN LAB SERV, VETERANS ADMIN HOSP, ALLEN PARK, MICH, 1975-; clin path, Med Col Pa, 1970-1975; prof physiol & biophys, Med Col Pa, 1969-1975; assoc prof physiol, Wayne State Univ, Detroit, 1965-1969; res assoc biochem & head phys chem, Isaac Albert Res Inst, Jewish Chronic Dis Hosp, 1959-1965; mcArdle Mem Lab, Wis, 1958-1959; res fel biochem, Mass Gen Hosp, 1957-1958; asst prof clin biochem, Med Univ Budapest, 1954-1956. **Memberships:** Am Soc Biol Chem; Am Physiol Soc; Am Soc Exp Path; fel Am Soc Clin Pathologists; fel Royal Soc Health. **Research Statement & Publications:** Biochemistry of muscular contraction and relaxation; computer assisted medical decision making. **Mailing Address:** Dept Path, Vet Admin Med Ctr, 4646 John R St, Detroit, MI 48201-1916.

KALELKAR, MOHAN SATISH, PHYSICS. **Personal Data:** b Bombay, India, April 24, 1948; American citizen. **Education:** Harvard Col, BA, 1968; Columbia Univ, MA, 1970, PhD (physics), 1975. **Professional Experience:** ASSOC CHMN DEPT, RUTGERS UNIV, NEW BURNSWICK, 1998-; PROF PHYSICS & ASTRON, RUTGERS UNIV, NEW BRUNSWICK, 1995-; from asst prof to assoc prof, Rutgers Univ, New Brunswick, 1978-1995; asst prof, Columbia Univ, 1977-1978; Res assoc physics, Columbia Univ, 1975-1977. **Memberships:** Am Phys Soc; Am Asn Physics Teachers. **Research Statement & Publications:** Experimental work in elementary particle physics; neutrino interactions and electron-positron collisions. **Mailing Address:** Dept Physics & Astron, Rutgers Univ, 136 Frelinghuysen Rd, Piscataway, NJ 08854-8019. **Fax:** 732-445-4343. **E-Mail:** kalelkar@physics.rutgers.edu

KALENDA, NORMAN WAYNE, ORGANIC CHEMISTRY. **Personal Data:** b Grand Rapids, Mich, November 27, 1928; m 1957. **Education:** Univ Mich, BS, 1951; Univ Ill, PhD (chem), 1955. **Professional Experience:** RETIRED; res chemist, Eastman Kodak Co, 1957-1990; res chemist, Mellon Inst, 1954-1955. **Memberships:** Am Chem Soc. **Research Statement & Publications:** Organic chemistry; photographic chemistry. **Mailing Address:** 11 Marina View Cir, Salem, SC 29676. **E-Mail:** normkal@aol.com

KALENSHER, BERNARD EARL, POTENTIAL THEORY, FLUID MECHANICS. **Personal Data:** b Beaumont, Tex, May 4, 1927. **Education:** Univ Tex, PhD (physics), 1954. **Professional Experience:** SR ANALYTICAL PHYSICIST, PHRASOR SCI INC, 1977-; sr physicist, Electro-Optical Systs, Xerox Corp, 1961-1976; sr res engr, Jet Propulsion Lab, Calif Inst Technol, 1954-1960. **Memberships:** Am Phys Soc. **Research Statement & Publications:** Theory modification of blackbody radiation law as applied to the thermal radiation from micron size, spherical, liquid metal droplets; mathematical analysis of pressure-time history of gas flow between chambers of a dual-chamber thruster and the vacuum of outer space; statistical analyses of charged droplet distributions; determined minimum and maximum allowed twist of a rifle barrel; authored two published articles. **Mailing Address:** 551 B Linwood Ave, Monrovia, CA 91016-2659. **Fax:** 626-357-3203.

KALER, ERIC WILLIAM, COLLOIDS, SURFACTANTS. **Personal Data:** b Burlington, Vt, September 23, 1956; m 1979, c 2. **Education:** Calif Inst Technol, BS, 1978; Univ Minn, PhD (chem eng), 1982. **Honors & Awards:** McGraw Award, Am Soc Eng Educ, 1995; Chilton Award, AICHE, 2002. **Professional Experience:** DEAN, COL OF ENG, UNIV DEL, 2000-; ELIZABETH INEZ KELLEY PROF, UNIV DEL, as of 2005; chem eng dept chair, Univ Del, 1996-2000; from assoc prof to prof, Univ Del, 1989-1996; presidential young investr, 1984-1989; from asst prof to assoc prof chem eng, Univ Wash, 1982-1989; intern, Oak Ridge Nat Lab, 1979; res & teaching asst chem eng, Univ Minn, 1978-1982; res assoc, Chevron Oil Field Res Co, 1978. **Memberships:** Am Inst Chem Engrs; Am Chem Soc; Am Crystallog Asn; AAAS. **Research Statement & Publications:** Colloid and surfactant science; complex fluid thermodynamics; materials synthesis; small-angle scattering. **Mailing Address:** Dept Chem Eng, Univ Del, Newark, DE 19716. **E-Mail:** kaler@che.udel.edu

KALER, JAMES BAILEY, ASTRONOMY. **Personal Data:** b Albany, NY, December 29, 1938. **Education:** Univ Mich, Ann Arbor, AB, 1960; Univ Calif, Los Angeles, PhD (astron), 1964. **Professional Experience:** PROF EMER ASTRON, UNIV ILL, URBANA, as of 2005; prof astron, Univ Ill, Urnaba, beginning 1976; Guggenheim fel, 1972-1973; From asst prof to assoc prof, Univ Ill, Urbana, 1964-1976. **Memberships:** Am Astron Soc; Int Astron Union; Astron Soc Pac. **Research Statement & Publications:** Planetary nebulae; nebular spectrophotometry; interstellar medium; chemical abundances; published over 300 articles. **Mailing Address:** 103 Astron Bldg, Univ Ill 1002 W Green st, Urbana, IL 61801. **Fax:** 217-244-7638. **E-Mail:** kaler@astro.uiuc.edu

KALET, IRA J, COMPUTER SCIENCE. **Education:** Princeton Univ, PhD (Theoret Physics), 1968. **Professional Experience:** PROF, RADIATION ONCOL DEPT, UNIV WASH, as of 2004. **Mailing Address:** Radiation Oncol Dept, Univ Wash, PO Box 356043, Seattle, WA 98195-6043. **Fax:** 206-598-6218. **E-Mail:** ikalet@u.washington.edu

KALEY, GABOR, PHYSIOLOGY, EXPERIMENTAL PATHOLOGY. **Personal Data:** b Budapest, Hungary, November 16, 1926; American citizen; m 1969, Harriette; c Sharon & David. **Education:** Columbia Univ, BS, 1950; NY Univ, MS, 1957, PhD (exp path), 1960. **Honors & Awards:** Landis Award; 1994, Microcirculatory Soc; Brown Lectr; 1998, Am Heart Assoc Wiggers Award; 2000, Am Physiological Soc Semmelweis Award; Semmelweis Soc. **Professional Experience:** Prin investr, NIH Grants, 1974-; CHMN DEPT, NY MED COL, 1972-; PROF PHYSIOL, NY MED COL, 1970-; assoc prof, NY Med Col, 1964-1970; from instr to asst prof, NY Univ Med Ctr, 1961-1962; USPHS fel, NY Univ Med Ctr, 1960-1962; res asst path, NY Univ Med Ctr, 1956-1960; Resident asst surg, Bellevue Hosp, New York, 1955-1956. **Memberships:** AAA Microcirculatory Soc; Am Physiol Soc; fel Am Heart Assoc. **Research Statement & Publications:** Cardiovascular physiology; hypertension; juxtaglomerular cells; renal-adrenal relationships; renen-angiotens in system; erythropoietin; inflammation; microcirculation and prostaglandins; endotoxins; endothelial cells; nature and mechanisms of action of a variety of biochemical and hormonal factors that regulate the function of small blood vessels and local blood flow; nitric oxide. **Mailing Address:** Dept Physiol, NY Med Col, Valhalla, NY 10595.

KALEY, ROBERT GEORGE, II, GAS CHROMATOGRAPHY, MASS SPECTROMETRY. **Personal Data:** b Litchfield, Ill, November 8, 1945. **Education:** Purdue Univ, BS, 1968; Univ Ill, MS, 1971, PhD (anal chem), 1974. **Professional Experience:** DIR, ENVIRON AFFAIRS, SOLUTIA INC, as of 2001; mgr, Environ Tech Support, Corp Environ Policy Staff, Monsanto Co, beginning 1986; prod & environ safety mgr, Corp Res & Develop Staff, 1985-1986; sr res specialist, Corp Res & Develop Staff, 1981-1985; res group leader, Indust Chem Co, 1978-1981; sr res chemist, Indust Chem Co, 1973-1978. **Memberships:** Am Chem Soc; Am Soc Mass Spectrometry; AAAS. **Research Statement & Publications:** Spectrochemical analysis; gas chromatography-mass spectrometry; environmental analysis. **Mailing Address:** Solutia Inc, PO Box 66760, St Louis, MO 63166-6760.

KALF, GEORGE FREDERICK, BIOCHEMISTRY/PHARMACOLOGY. **Personal Data:** b New Britain, Conn, December 22, 1930; m 1966, Jeanne; c Thomas W & Charlotte A. **Education:** Upsala Col, BS, 1952; Pa State Univ, MS, (biochem)1954; Yale Univ, PhD (biochem), 1957. **Professional Experience:** ASSOC. DEAN SCI AFFAIRS, JEFFERSON MED COL, THOMAS JEFFERSON UNIV, as of 2004; DIR, DIV HUMAN SUBJECT PROTECTION, THOMAS JEFFERSON MED COL, THOMAS JEFFERSON UNIV.; PROF BIOCHEM & MOLECULAR BIOL, JEFFERSON MED COL, THOMAS JEFFERSON UNIV, 1986-; adj prof pharm & toxicol, Rutgers Univ, 1982-2000; prof path, Jefferson Med Col, Thomas Jefferson Univ, 1979-1986; prof biochem, Jefferson Med Col, Thomas Jefferson Univ, 1966-1986; investr, Am Heart Asn, 1963-1968; from asst prof to assoc prof biochem, NJ Col Med & Dent, 1960-1966; enzymologist, Chem & Physics Sect, Animal Dis & Parasite Res Div, USDA, 1959; nat Found fel, Yale Univ, 1957-1959. **Memberships:** Am Soc Biol Chem; Am Asn Cancer Res; Public Responsibility in Medicine and Research (PRIM&R). **Research Statement & Publications:** Carcinogenesis; biochemical oncology; benzene toxicity. **Mailing Address:** Office Sci Affairs Thomas Jefferson Univ, 1015 Chestnut St, Ste 1100, Philadelphia, PA 19107-5566. **Fax:** 215-503-3843. **E-Mail:** george.kalf@jefferson.edu

KALFAYAN, BERNARD, ANATOMICAL PATHOLOGY. **Education:** Am Univ, Beirut, MD, 1939. **Professional Experience:** RETIRED; pathologist, Gunderson Clinic, Ltd. **Mailing Address:** 174 S Collier Blvd Apt 902, Marco, FL 33937-4330.

KALFF, JACOB, HYDROBIOLOGY. **Personal Data:** b Velsen, Neth, December 20, 1935. **Education:** Univ Toronto, BSA, 1959, MSA, 1961; Ind Univ, PhD (limnol), 1965. **Professional Experience:** PROF EMER BIOL, MCGILL UNIV, MONTREAL, as of 2002; vis scientist, CNRS, Toulouse, France, 1986-1987; DIR, LIMNOL RES CTR, DEPT BIOL, 1982-; vis prof, Dept Bot, Univ Nairobi, Kenya, 1979-1980; prof biol, mcgill Univ, Montreal, beginning 1977; consult, Ecol Adv Comt, Baie James Energy Corp, 1977-1984; vis scientist hydrobiol, Inst Nat Rech Agron, France, 1972-1973; From asst prof to assoc prof, Limnol Res Ctr, Dept Biol, 1965-1976; regional ed, Hydrobiol; CSIC, Blanes, Spain. **Memberships:** AAAS; Am Soc Limnol & Oceanog; Int Asn Theoret & Appl Limnol. **Research Statement & Publications:** Ecology of algae, bacteria and aquatic higher plants with an emphasis on their productivity and their role in the nutrient and contaminant cycling in lakes. **Mailing Address:** Dept Biol, McGill Univ, Rm N6/9, Montreal, PQ H3A 1B1, Can. **Fax:** 514-398-5069. **E-Mail:** jacob.kalff@mcgill.ca

KALFOGLOU, GEORGE, SURFACE POLYMER CHEMISTRY, APPLICATION OF POLYMER SOLUTIONS & POLYMER GELS IN ENHANCED OIL RECOVERY. **Personal Data:** b Istanbul, Turkey, June 12, 1939. **Education:** Robert Col, Istanbul, BS, 1963; NC State Univ, PhD (chem), 1968. **Professional Experience:** RETIRED; res chemist, res assoc & sr res assoc, TEXACO INC, beginning 1968. **Memberships:** AAAS; Am Chem Soc; Soc Petrol Engrs; Sigma Xi. **Research Statement & Publications:** Solution thermodynamics; colloidal chemistry; chemical treatment of water-sensitive minerals; physical and interfacial properties of surfactants; design enhanced petroleum recovery processes in hard brines and elevated temperatures by utilizing proper surfactant systems; tertiary oil recovery by micellar/polymer systems, caustic/polymer floods, thermally stable polymers, design of polymer gels for profile modification and water shut-off treatments; granted 35 patents. **Mailing Address:** 523 Greenpark Dr, Houston, TX 77079-6415. **Fax:** 713-954-6911.

KALIA, MADHU P, NEUROBIOLOGY. **Personal Data:** b Kashmir, India, September 11, 1940. **Education:** Univ Delhi, MD, 1964, PhD (neurophysiol), 1968. **Professional Experience:** PROF, DEPT BIOCHEM & MOLECULAR PHARMACOL, JEFFERSON MED COL, THOMAS JEFFERSON UNIV, 1978-; assoc prof, Thomas Jefferson Univ, 1974-1978. **Memberships:** Soc Neuroscience; Am Physiol Soc; Am Asn Anatomists; German Physiol Soc. **Research Statement & Publications:** Respiratory control; cardiovascular control.

Mailing Address: Dept Biochem & Molecular Pharmacol, Jefferson Med Col, Thomas Jefferson Univ, 1020 Walnut St, Philadelphia, PA 19107. **E-Mail:** madhu.kalia@jefferson.edu

KALIAGUINE, SERGE, ENGINEERING EDUCATION. **Honors & Awards:** Urgel Archambault Phys Sci & Math Prize, Can-Fr Asn Advan Sci, 1994. **Professional Experience:** PROF CHEM ENG, UNIV LAVAL, as of 2006. **Research Statement & Publications:** Physical science and maths. **Mailing Address:** Dept Chem Eng, Univ Laval, Plt-1709, Adrien-Pouliot House, Quebec, PQ G1K 7P4, Can. **Fax:** 418-656-5993. **E-Mail:** serge.kaliaguine@gch.ulaval.ca

KALIAKIN, VICTOR NICHOLAS, GEOMECHANICS, STRUCTURAL MECHANICS. **Personal Data:** b Los Angeles, Calif, November 1, 1956. **Education:** Univ Calif, Davis, BS, 1978, PhD (eng mech), 1985; Univ Calif, Berkeley, MS, 1979. **Professional Experience:** ASSOC PROF CIVIL & ENVIRON ENG, UNIV DEL, 1996-; mem, Comt Inelastic Behav, Am Soc Civil Engrs, beginning 1991; mem tech staff, Sandia Nat Labs, 1987-1990; vis asst prof civil eng, Univ Ariz, 1986-1987; postdoctoral civil eng, Univ Calif, Davis, 1985-1986; mem, Comt Modeling Tech Geomech, Transp Res Bd; mem, Comt Aerospace Struct & Mat. **Memberships:** Am Soc Civil Eng; Am Acad Mech; Am Soc Eng Educ; Int Asn Comput Mech. **Research Statement & Publications:** Computational mechanics applied to problems in: geotechnical engineering, composite material and structural engineering. **Mailing Address:** Dept Civil & Environ Eng, Univ Del, 360F DuPont Hall, Newark, DE 19716-3120. **Fax:** 302-831-3640. **E-Mail:** kaliakin@ce.udel.edu

KALICA, ANTHONY R, VIROLOGY, LUNG DISEASES. **Personal Data:** b Albany, NY, June 14, 1939. **Education:** Siena Col, BS, 1962; Cath Univ Am, MS, 1964; Univ Md, PhD (microbiol), 1974. **Professional Experience:** DIR, RES ADMIN & RESOURCES, SCHEPENS EYE RES INST, as 0f 2003; chief, Nat Heart Lung & Blood Inst, NIH, beginning 1987; prog adminr, Occup & Immunol Lung Dis Prog, 1985-1987; microbiologist, Interstitial Lung Dis Br, Nat Heart Lung & Blood Inst, 1983-1985; res microbiologist, Epidemiol Sect, 1974-1983; chemist & electron microscopist, Respiratory viruses Sect, 1967-1974; Biologist, Epidemiol Sect, Lab Infectious Dis, Nat Inst Allergy & Infectious Dis, NIH, 1964-1967. **Memberships:** Am Soc Microbiol; Am Soc Virol; Int Aquired Immune Deficiency Syndrome Soc. **Research Statement & Publications:** Molecular and cellular aspects of gastrointestinal and respiratory virus infections; managed about 70 million dollars worth of biomedical research on interstitial lung disease, occupational lung disease, and lung disease associated with infection of the human immunodeficiency syndrome. **Mailing Address:** Schepens Eye Res Inst, 20th Staniford St, Boston, MA 02114.

KALIL, FORD, ENGINEERING PHYSICS. **Personal Data:** b Akron, Ohio, January 5, 1925. **Education:** Univ Akron, BEE, 1950; Vanderbilt Univ, MS, 1951, PhD (physics), 1958. **Professional Experience:** TECH ENGR & OPERS MGR & PRES, GODDARD SPACE FLIGHT CTR, NASA, 1980-; systs mgr cosmic background explorer proj, eng directorate, 1978-1980; sr tech consult, Network Procedures & Eval Div, networks directorate, 1974-1978; sr tech asst to br head, Manned Flight Planning & Anal Div, 1968-1974; mem, Apollo Exten Syst, Commun & Navig Traffic Control Panel, 1965 & Apollo Exten Syst Working Group, NASA, 1965-; aerospace technologist, Goddard Space Flight Ctr, 1963-1968; design engr, Martin Co, 1960-1963; mgr, Martin Co, 1959-1960; gen supvr test eval, Martin Co, 1959; Adj prof, Drexel Inst, 1958-; supvr lab, Martin Co, 1958-1959; staff mem, Los Alamos Sci Lab, 1953-1955; Physicist, USPHS, 1951-1953. **Memberships:** Am Inst Aeronaut & Astronaut; Am Phys Soc; Sigma Xi. **Research Statement & Publications:** Aerospace technology; mission and systems analysis; orbital mechanics; electron and radiation physics; management. **Mailing Address:** 9108 Bridgewater St, College Park, MD 20741-4008.

KALIMI, MOHAMMED YAHYA, ENDOCRINOLOGY. **Personal Data:** b Surat, India. **Education:** Bombay Univ, BS, 1961, MS, 1964, PhD (biochem), 1970. **Honors & Awards:** Res & Career Develop Award, NIH, 1980. **Professional Experience:** PROF PHYSIOL, MED COL VA, RICHMOND, 1989-; vis prof, City Hope Med Ctr, Los Angeles, 1983-1984; from asst prof to assoc prof, Dept Physiol, Med Col VA, Richmond, 1979-1989; res asst prof, dept biochem, Albert Einstein Col Med, Bronx, NY, 1975-1979; res assoc, dept cell biol, Baylor Col Med, Houston, 1974-1975; res fel, Inst Cancer Res, Columbia Univ, 1972-1974. **Memberships:** Am Physiol Soc; Endocrine Soc; AAAS. **Research Statement & Publications:** Mechanism of steroid hormone action; isolation, characterization and purification of glucocorticoid receptors; interaction of the steroid-receptor complex with genomic components; developmental and aging related changes in the steroid receptors. **Mailing Address:** Dept Physiol, VA Commonwealth Univ, PO Box 980551, Richmond, VA 23298-0551. **Fax:** 804-828-7382. **E-Mail:** mkalimi@hsc.vcu.edu

KALIN, ROBERT, MATHEMATICS EDUCATION. **Personal Data:** b Everett, Mass, December 11, 1921; wid. **Education:** Univ Chicago, BS, 1947; Harvard Univ, MAT, 1948; Fla State Univ, PhD (math educ), 1961. **Honors & Awards:** Serv Award, Math Asn Am, 1991. **Professional Experience:** EMER PROF MATH EDUC, FLA STATE UNIV, 1989-; secy & treas, Fla Sect, Math Asn Am, 1985-1991; pres, Fla Asn Math Educr, 1984-1986; pres, Nat High Sch & Jr Col Math Clubs, 1978-1980; chmn math educ prog, Fla State Univ, 1974-1978; governor, Nat High Sch & Jr Col Math Clubs, 1972-1975; Dir, NSF Acad Year Insts, 1969-1971; from instr to prof math educ, Fla State Univ, 1956-1989; exec asst, Comn Math Col Bd, 1955-1956; res assoc math educ, Educ Testing Serv, NJ, 1955; test specialist math, Educ Testing Serv, NJ, 1953-1955; statistician, Naval Air Tech Training Ctr, Okla, 1952-1953; Teacher high sch, Mass, 1948-1949 & pub sch, Mo, 1949-1952. **Memberships:** Nat Coun Teachers Math; Math Asn Am. **Research Statement & Publications:** Comparison of mathematical performance of elementary school children in Federal Republic of Germany, United Kingdom and USA since 1978; television-text instructional system for elementary school teachers; analytic geometry; elementary mathematics texts for grades 1-8; secondary geometry text. **Mailing Address:** 7 Stoneleigh Pl, Brownsville, TN 38012-2458. **Fax:** 731-772-6513. **E-Mail:** rkalin@aeneas.net

KALINA, ROBERT E, OPHTHALMOLOGY. **Personal Data:** b New Prague, Minn, November 13, 1936. **Education:** Univ Minn, BA, 1957, BS, 1960, MD, 1960. **Honors & Awards:** Sr Hon Award, Am Acad Ophth. **Professional Experience:** RETIRED; dir, Am Bd Ophthal, 1982-1989; assoc head, Ophthal Div, Children's Orthopedic Hosp, 1975-1984; actg chmn, prof & chmn Ophthal, 1970-1996; actg chmn, Univ Wash, Seattle, 1970-1971; Pub Health Hosp & Madigan Gen Hosp, US Army, 1969-; Consult, Vet Admin Hosp, 1969-; med dir, Lions Eye Bank, 1969-1993; chief, Harborview Med Ctr, 1968-1969; fel retina, Children's Hosp, San Francisco, 1966-1967 & Harvard Med Sch, 1967; resident ophthal, Univ Ore, 1961-1966; Intern med, Univ Ore, 1960-1961. **Memberships:** Am Acad Ophthal; Am Col Surgeons; Nat Soc Prev Blindness; Asn Res Vision & Ophth; AMA. **Research Statement & Publications:** Diseases and surgery of the retina. **Mailing Address:** Univ Wash Dept Ophthal, Box 356485, Seattle, WA 98195-6435.

KALINSKY, ROBERT GEORGE, PHYCOLOGY, ENVIRONMENTAL BIOLOGY. **Personal Data:** b Cleveland, Ohio, September 18, 1945. **Education:** Univ Dayton, BS, 1967; Ohio State Univ, MSc, 1969, PhD (bot), 1973. **Professional Experience:** PROF BIOL, LA STATE UNIV, SHREVEPORT, as of 2005; asst prof biol, La State Univ, Shreveport, beginning 1975; Lectr bot, Ohio State Univ, 1973-1974; Biol consult, Dames & Moore Engrs, Cincinnati, 1973-1974. **Memberships:** Sigma Xi; Phycol Soc Am; Brit Phycol Soc; Bot Soc Am. **Research Statement & Publications:** Systematic revision of the diatom genus Nitzschia; ecological studies of the major waterways of Northwestern Louisiana; Cypress Bayou Reservoir and environs. **Mailing Address:** Dept Biol Sci, La State Univ, 115 Sci One Univ Pl, Shreveport, LA 71115. **Fax:** 318-797-5230. **E-Mail:** rkalinsky@pilot.lsus.edu

KALISH, DAVID, OPTICAL FIBERS, SYSTEMS ENGINEERING. **Personal Data:** b New York, NY, August 15, 1939. **Education:** Mass Inst Technol, SB, 1960, SM, 1964, ScD, 1966. **Professional Experience:** CHIEF TECHNOL OFFICER & VPRES, RES & DEVELOP FIBER & CABLE, BELL LABS, as of 2002; optical fiber develop & eng dir, Bells Labs, beginning 1990; head mat eng & chem dept, Bell Tel Labs Inc, 1989; supvr lightguide syst eng, Bell Tel Labs Inc, 1986-1988; supvr lightguide glass technol, Bell Tel Labs Inc, 1980-1985; lectr mech eng, Ga Inst Technol, 1973-1981; supvr metall eng, Bell Tel Labs Inc, 1973-1979; mem tech staff mat eng & chem, Bell Tel Labs Inc, 1971-1973; vis assoc prof, Ga Inst Technol, 1970; scientist & team leader phys metall, Lockheed-Ga Co, 1968-1971; staff scientist, ManLabs Inc, 1965-1968; instr metall, Mass Inst Technol, 1963-1965; engr, ManLabs Inc, 1960-1963. **Memberships:** Fel Am Soc Metals. **Research Statement & Publications:** Optical fibers for communications and systems engineering, optical fibers measurements and fabrication. **Mailing Address:** OFS Lab, 2000 NE Expressway, Norcross, GA 30071. **Fax:** 770-798-4655. **E-Mail:** ofs@ofsoptics.com

KALISH, HERBERT S(AUL), METALLURGICAL ENGINEERING. **Personal Data:** b New York, NY, August 11, 1922. **Education:** Univ Mo, BS, 1943, MetE, 1953; Univ Pa, MS, 1948. **Honorary Degrees:** MetE, Univ Mo, Rolla, 1953. **Honors & Awards:** Award of Merit, Am Soc Testing & Mat; Distinguished Serv to Powder Metall Award, Metal Powder Indust Fedn. **Professional Experience:** CONSULT, 1991-; Trustee, Am Soc Metals, 1985-1988; vpres, Hertel Cutting Technologies Inc, 1971-1991; asst to pres, Hertel Cutting Technologies Inc, 1965-1971; mgr, Com Fuel Dept, United Nuclear Corp, Conn, 1962-1965; chief nuclear metall, Nuclear Fuel Res, 1960-1962; sect chief mat, Nuclear Fuel Res Labs, Olin Mathieson Chem Corp, 1957-1960; eng mgr, Sylvania-Corning Nuclear Corp, 1957; eng mgr metal fabrication & assembly, Zirconium Sect, 1955-1957; sect head appl metall, Zirconium Sect, 1952-1955; engr-in-charge, Zirconium Sect, 1950-1952; sr engr spec prod, Sylvania Elec Prod, Inc, 1948-1950; res metallurgist lead alloys, Elec Storage Battery Co, 1948; asst, Thermodyn Res Lab, Univ Pa, 1946-1948; res engr, Alloy Develop, Battelle Mem Inst, 1943-1944 & 1946; Metall observer open hearth steel, Carnegie-Ill Steel Corp, 1943; vpres & treas, Photogrs Eye Inc. **Memberships:** Fel Am Soc Metals; Sigma Xi; Am Soc Test & Mat; Am Inst Mining Metall & Petrol Engrs; Soc Mining Metall & Explor; Am Powder Metall Inst. **Research Statement & Publications:** Nuclear materials; high temperature materials; powder metallurgy, particularly alloy development; physical metallurgy; fabrication research; cemented carbide. **Mailing Address:** 65 Falmouth St, Short Hills, NJ 07078.

KALISKI, MARTIN EDWARD, MICROPROCESSOR-BASED CONTROL, SYSTEMS THEORY. **Personal Data:** b New York, NY, October 22, 1945. **Education:** Mass Inst Technol, BS, 1966 & 1968, MS, 1968, PhD (elec eng), 1971. **Professional Experience:** PROF EMER ELEC ENG, CALIF POLYTECH UNIV, as of 2005; PROF ELEC ENG, CALIF POLYTECH UNIV, as of 2002; electronic eng, Calif Polytech Univ, 1995-2001, 1989-1992; Fulbright scholar, France, 1980-1981; from asst prof to assoc prof elec eng, Northwestern Univ, 1976-1990; Prof elec & Comput Eng, 1973-1986; prof comput sci, City Col New York, 1971-1973. **Memberships:** Inst Elec & Electronics Engrs; Sigma Xi; Asn Comput Mach. **Research Statement & Publications:** Systems theory; industrial automation and robotics; microprocessor-based control; software engineering. **Mailing Address:** Dept Elec Eng, Calif Polytech State Univ, Rm 20-315, San Luis Obispo, CA 93407. **Fax:** 805-756-1458. **E-Mail:** mkaliski@calpoly.edu

KALIVODA, FRANK E, JR, MECHANICAL ENGINEERING. **Personal Data:** b Cicero, Ill, March 17, 1930. **Education:** Ill Inst Technol, BSME, 1954, MSME, 1958. **Professional Experience:** MGR ENG, COPELAND CORP, 1981-; Instr quality control & mfg processes, Edison State Univ, 1975-1978; mgr prod eval, Copeland Corp, 1973-1981; chief engr, South Wind Div, Stewart Warner Corp, 1970-1973; mgr res & develop, South Wind Div, Stewart Warner Corp, 1968-1970; mgr thermosci, Res Div, 1966-1968; mgr adv fuel systs, Eng Div, 1965-1966; mgr component develop, Res Div, Cummins Engine Co, 1965; sr res engr, Roy C Ingersoll Res Ctr, Borg-Warner Corp, 1958-1965; asst res engr, Heat-Power Res Dept, Armour Res Found, 1954-1958; Coop trainee prod, Link-Belt Corp, 1949-1952. **Memberships:** Am Soc Mech Engrs; Am Soc Heating Refrig & Air-Conditioning Engrs; Sigma Xi; Am Soc Qual Control. **Research Statement & Publications:** Development of air conditioners, heat exchangers, compressors, combustion heaters, hydraulic equipment, engine fuel injectors and pumps; research on engine heat transfer, hydrodynamic bearings; manufacturing processes; reliability engineering. **Mailing Address:** 406 E Robinwood St, Sidney, OH 45365.

KALIVRETENOS, ARISTOTLE, CHEMISTRY. **Education:** Clemson Univ, BS, 1985; Colo State Univ, PhD, 1990. **Professional Experience:** ASST PROF, DEPT CHEM & BIOCHEM, UNIV MD, BALITMORE CO, as of 2006. **Mailing Address:** Dept Chem & Biochem, Univ Md, Baltimore Co, 1000 Hilltop Circle, Baltimore, MD 21250.

KALKA, MORRIS, MATHEMATICAL ANALYSIS. **Personal Data:** b Landsberg, Ger, May 4, 1949. **Education:** Yeshiva Univ, BA, 1971; NY Univ, MS, 1973, PhD (math), 1975. **Professional Experience:** PROF MATH, TULANE UNIV, 1988-; MEM FAC MATH, TULANE UNIV, 1980-; asst prof math, Johns Hopkins Univ, 1977-1980; Instr math, Univ Utah, 1975-1977. **Memberships:** Am Math Soc. **Research Statement & Publications:** Study of holomorphic functions of several complex variables using methods of differential geometry and partial differential equations. **Mailing Address:** Dept Math, Tulane Univ, Gibson 318-B, New Orleans, LA 70118. **Fax:** 504-865-5063. **E-Mail:** mk@math.tulane.edu

KALKHORAN, IRAJ M, FLUID MECHANICS. **Education:** Univ TX, PhD, 1987. **Professional Experience:** PROF, DEPT MECH, AEROSPACE ENG POLYTECH UNIV, as of 1999. **Mailing Address:** Aerospace Eng Polytech Univ, Rte 110, Farmingdale, NY 11735. **Fax:** 516-755-4526. **E-Mail:** iraj@poly.edu

KALKOFEN, WOLFGANG, ASTROPHYSICS. **Personal Data:** b Mainz, Ger, November 15, 1931. **Education:** Univ Frankfurt, BS, 1956; Harvard Univ, MA, 1961, PhD (physics), 1963. **Honors & Awards:** sr US scientist award, Alexander vom Humboldt Found, 1979. **Professional Experience:** Vis fel, Univ Heidelberg, 1979-1980; PHYSICIST, CTR ASTROPHYS, HARVARD COL OBSERV, 1974-; lectr, Harvard Univ, 1965-; vis lectr astron, Yale Univ, 1965; Res fel, Harvard Col Observ, 1964-1966; physicist, Smithsonian Astrophys Observ, Smithsonian Inst, beginning 1963; engr, Raytheon Mfg Co, 1957-1959. **Memberships:** Am Astron Soc; AAAS; Int Astron Union. **Research Statement & Publications:** Theoretical astrophysics; radiative transfer; gas dynamics. **Mailing Address:** Ctr

Astrophys, Smithsonian Astrophys Observ, 60 Garden St, Cambridge, MA 02138. **Fax:** 617-495-7049. **E-Mail:** wolf@cfa.harvard.edu

KALKSTEIN, LAURENCE SAUL, APPLIED CLIMATOLOGY, BIOCLIMATOLOGY. **Personal Data:** b Brooklyn, NY, January 29, 1948; m 1971, Rhona; c Adam J. **Education:** Rutgers Univ, BA, 1969; La State Univ, MA, 1972, PhD (geog, climat), 1974. **Honors & Awards:** Mentor, nat coun geog edu, 2002. **Professional Experience:** Vis scientist, Environ Protection Agency Climate Change Div, 1989-1990; PROF GEOG & CLIMAT, UNIV DEL, 1988-; coordr, global warming/human health prog, Environ Protection Agency, synoptic climat pollution relationships, climate- visibility relationships, Salt River Proj & Southern pine beetle-climate anal, US Forest Serv, 1985-; vis scientist, Nat Oceanic & Atmospheric Admin, 1982-1983; prin investr, climate & socio-econ assessment, Nat Oceanic & Atmospheric Admin, 1980-1986; from asst prof to assoc prof geog & climat, Univ Del, 1975-1988; asst prof geog & ecosystems anal, Univ Calif, Los Angeles, 1973-1974; instr geog, La State Univ, 1972-1973; mem, Comt Appl Climatol, Am Meteorol Soc, Comn Climat, World Metrol Orgn; ed, Climate Res. **Memberships:** Asn Am Geographers; Am Meteorol Soc; Int soc Biometeorology(Pres-elect, 2002). **Research Statement & Publications:** Climate's impact on human health and well-being; impact of climate on organism population fluctuations; development of applied climatological indices; socio-economic impacts of a global warming; published over 100 articles. **Mailing Address:** Dept Geog, Univ Del, Newark, DE 19716-2541. **Fax:** 302-831-6654. **E-Mail:** larryk@udel.edu

KALKWARF, DONALD RILEY, BIOPHYSICAL CHEMISTRY. **Personal Data:** b Portland, Ore, August 17, 1924. **Education:** Reed Col, BA, 1947; Northwestern Univ, PhD (chem), 1951. **Professional Experience:** STAFF SCIENTIST, NAT SECURITY & DEFENSE DIRECTORATE, PAC NW NAT LAB, 1990-; staff scientist Biol & Chem Dept, Environ & Radio Sci Dept, 1978-1990; res assoc Radiol Sci Dept, Environ & Radio Sci Dept, 1968-1978; mgr Radiation Chem Unit, Environ & Radio Sci Dept, 1966-1968; res assoc Chem Dept, Pac NW Nat Labs, 1965-1966; res specialist, Gen Elec Co, 1962-1965; sr scientist, Gen Elec Co, 1954-1962; chemist, Gen Elec Co, 1951-1953. **Memberships:** Am Chem Soc; Sigma Xi. **Research Statement & Publications:** Radiation biochemistry; synthetic biomembranes; electron spin resonance spectroscopy; controlled release of pharmaceuticals; kinetics of pollutant transformation. **Mailing Address:** 1201 Birch, Richland, WA 99352.

KALKWARF, KENNETH LEE, PERIODONTOLOGY. **Personal Data:** b Lincoln, Nebr, April 12, 1946. **Education:** Univ Nebr, DDS, 1970, MS, 1973. **Professional Experience:** PROF PERIODONT, DENT SCH, UNIV TEX HEALTH SCI CTR, SAN ANTONIO, as of 2005; DEAN DENT SCH, UNIV TEX HEALTH SCI CTR, SAN ANTONIO, 1988-; assoc dean adv educ, Univ Tex Health Sci Ctr, San Antonio, 1987-1988; consult, Omaha, 1986-; mem, Nebr Bd Dent Examr, 1985-1987; Periodont Case Reports, J Periodontol, 1984-; dir grad & postgrad studies, Col Dent, Univ Nebr, 1983-1987; Cent Community Col, Hastings, Nebr, 1983-1987; Periodont Case Reports, beginnning 1982; prof periodont & dir grad periodont, Col Dent, Univ Nebr, 1981-1987; adv bd, Southeast Nebt Community Col, 1981-1987; consult, Grand Island, 1981-1987; consult, Cent Regional Dent Testing Serv, 1980-1987; vis prof, Independent Univ Guadalajara, Mex, 1980-1982; assoc prof, Col Dent, Univ Okla, 1978-1981; consult, Nebr Vet Admin Hosp, Lincoln, beginniin 1973; asst prof periodont, Col Dent, Univ Nebr, 1973-1978. **Memberships:** Int Asn Dent Res; Am Acad Periodont; Am Asn Dent Schs; Am Dent Asn; fel Am Col Dentists. **Research Statement & Publications:** Longitudinal evaluation of periodontal therapy; histologic evaluation of oral wound healing. **Mailing Address:** Dent Sch, Univ Tex Health Sci Ctr, 7703 Floyd Curl Dr, San Antonio, TX 78229-3900. **Fax:** 210-567-6721. **E-Mail:** kalkwarf@uthscsa.edu

KALLAHER, MICHAEL JOSEPH, MATHEMATICS. **Personal Data:** b Cincinnati, Ohio, September 4, 1940; m 1963, Donalyn; c Joy, Michael, Christopher, Daniel & Raymond. **Education:** Xavier Univ Ohio, BS, 1961; Syracuse Univ, MS, 1963, PhD (math), 1967. **Professional Experience:** Chmn dept, Wash State Univ, 1984-1992; assoc dean sci, Wash State Univ, 1979-1984; PROF MATH, WASH STATE UNIV, 1976-; Fulbright-Hays fel, Fulbright Comn, 1975-1976; from asst prof to assoc prof, Wash State Univ, 1969-1976; asst prof, Univ Man, 1968-1969; fel, Univ Man, 1967-1968; Instr math, Syracuse Univ, 1966-1967. **Memberships:** AAAS; Am Math Soc; Math Asn Am; Sigma Xi; fel Soc Indust & Appl Math. **Research Statement & Publications:** Non-associative algebras; finite geometries, particularly finite projective planes and finite affine planes. **Mailing Address:** Dept Math, Wash State Univ, PO Box 643113, Pullman, WA 99163-3113. **E-Mail:** mkalanher@wsu.edu

KALLAI-SANFACON, MARY-ANN, BIOCHEMISTRY, ENDOCRINOLOGY. **Personal Data:** b Montreal, Que, April 16, 1949; Canadian citizen; m Roger; c Valarie & Lorraine. **Education:** McGill Univ, Montreal, BSc, 1970; Laval Univ, Que, MSc, 1973; Univ Toronto, PhD (physiol), 1977. **Professional Experience:** HEAD BIOCHEM, JEAN-TALON HOSP, MONTREAL, 1991-; councr, Can Soc Clin Chemists, 1991-1993; Ad Hoc Comt Drugs Workplace, Order Chemists Que, 1991; tutor pharmacol & toxicol postdoctoral trainees clin chem, 1989-1990; lectr, Continuous Educ Prog Med Technologists, Pharmacol & Toxicol, 1989; sect head pharmacol & toxicol, Clin Chem Lab, Sacre-Coeur Hosp, Montreal, 1985-1991; mem, Prof Affairs Comt, Asn Biochem Que, 1985-1991; grant, Med Res Coun, 1985; dir, Clin Chem Lab, Louis-H Lafontaine Hosp, 1983-1985; dir, Lab Med Anal, BioEndo Labs, 1982-1983; sr scientist, Ayerst Res Lab Montreal, 1980-1982; res fel, Ayerst Res Lab Montreal, 1978-1980; Indust fel, Nat Res Coun Can, 1978-1980; Res fel biochem, Erindale Col, Univ Toronto, 1977-1978. **Memberships:** Can Soc Clin Chem (secy, 1995-1998); Am Asn Clin Chem; Can Acad Clin Biochem. **Research Statement & Publications:** Lipid metabolism; the development of hypolipidemic agents and the elucidation of their mode of action; carbohydrate metabolism; development of oral hypoglycaemic agents; hypertension; development of antihypertensive agents particularly those associated with angiotensin converting enzyme inhibition; pharmacology and toxicology. **Mailing Address:** Jean-Talon Hosp Biochem, 1385 Rue Jean-Talon Est, Montreal, PQ H2E 1S6, Can. **Fax:** 514-495-6772. **E-Mail:** mary-ann.kallai-sanfacon.cdi@ssss.gouv.qc.ca

KALLAL, R(OBERT) J(OHN), CHEMICAL ENGINEERING. **Personal Data:** b Chesterfield, Ill, February 1, 1921. **Education:** Univ Ill, BS, 1943, MS, 1946; Mass Inst Technol, ScD(chem eng), 1949. **Professional Experience:** PLANNING MGR, E I DU PONT DEL NEMOURS & CO, INC, 1975-; res mgr, E I Du Pont Del Nemours & CO, Inc, 1974-1975; asst plants tech mgr, E I Du Pont Del Nemours & CO, Inc, 1970-1974; sr supvr res & develop, E I Du Pont Del Nemours & CO, Inc, 1958-1970; asst tech supt, E I Du Pont Del Nemours & CO, Inc, 1955-1958; chem engr plastics develop, E I Du Pont Del Nemours & CO, Inc, 1949-1955; instr, Mass Inst Technol, 1947; asst chem eng, Mass Inst Technol, 1946-1947; Asst munitions develop, Univ Ill, 1943-1945. **Memberships:** AAAS; Am Chem Soc; Am Inst Chem Engrs. **Research Statement & Publications:** Organic and inorganic chemical process development. **Mailing Address:** 518 Kerfoot Farm Rd, Wilmington, DE 19803-2444.

KALLAND, GENE ARNOLD, REPRODUCTIVE ENDOCRINOLOGY. **Personal Data:** b Ashland, Wis, December 15, 1936; c 2. **Education:** Calif State Univ, Northridge, BA, 1962; Ind Univ, PhD (zoology), 1966. **Professional Experience:** PROF EMER BIOL, CALIF STATE UNIV DOMINGUEZ HILLS, as of 2005; prof biol, Calif State Univ Dominguez Hills, 1971-1996; res assoc endocrinol, Harbor-Univ Calif, Los Angeles Med Ctr, 1975-1980; chmn dept, Calif State Univ Dominguez Hills, 1972-1975; vis asst prof, Univ Southern Calif, 1971; from asst prof to assoc prof, Calif State Univ Dominguez Hills, 1966-1976; assoc engr, Rocketdyne Div, NAm Aviation, Inc, 1957-1962. **Memberships:** AAAS; Sigma Xi. **Research Statement & Publications:** Computer use in science instruction; biology of childhood and adolescence; amphibian hatching mechanisms. **Mailing Address:** 3603 S Walker Ave, San Pedro, CA 90731-6053.

KALLANDER, JOHN WILLIAM, COMPUTER SCIENCE. **Personal Data:** b Bessemer, Mich, June 20, 1927. **Education:** Mich Technol Univ, BS, 1948; Univ Cincinnati, MS, 1950, PhD (appl sci), 1952. **Professional Experience:** RETIRED; supvry mathematician, prog sect, 1968-1982; head prog systs sect, prog sect, 1964-1968; consult prog lang & physics to head res comput ctr, prog sect, 1963-1964; proj leader, prog sect, 1961-1963; US Naval Res Lab, high-energy radiation effects, 1956-1961; res physicist magnetic amplifiers, 1953-1956; develop engr analog computs, Gen Elec Co, 1952. **Memberships:** Sigma Xi; Inst Elec & Electronics Engrs; Asn Comput Mach. **Research Statement & Publications:** Digital computer systems analysis and programming; data base management analysis and programming. **Mailing Address:** 2436 Nolen Dr, Flint, MI 48504-4679.

KALLEN, FRANK CLEMENTS, vertebrate anatomy; deceased, see previous edition for last biography

KALLEN, ROLAND GILBERT, MEDICINE, BIOCHEMISTRY. **Personal Data:** b Glasgow, Scotland, July 3, 1935; American citizen; m 1963, Stephanie; c Jared & Caleb. **Education:** Amherst Col, AB, 1956; Columbia Univ, MD, 1960; Brandeis Univ, PhD (biochem), 1965. **Honorary Degrees:** MS, Univ Pa. **Professional Experience:** Fogerty Int fel, 1981; PROF BIOCHEM & BIOPHYS, SCH MED, UNIV PA, 1979-; from asst prof to assoc prof biochem, Sch Med, Univ PA, 1965-1977; intern, NY Univ-Bellevue Med Ctr, 1960-1961. **Memberships:** Am Chem Soc; Am Soc Biochem & Molecular Biol; Biophys Soc. **Research Statement & Publications:** Mechanisms and regulation of voltage-sensitive sodium channels; mechanisms of hormone action; mechanisms and regulation of gene expression. **Mailing Address:** Dept Biochem & Biophys, Sch Med Univ Pa, Philadelphia, PA 19104-6059. **Fax:** 215-573-7058. **E-Mail:** rgk@mbio.med.upenn.edu

KALLEN, THOMAS WILLIAM, INORGANIC CHEMISTRY. **Personal Data:** b Hammond, Ind, October 26, 1938; m 1989, Mary; c Michael, Amber & Brandon. **Education:** Beloit Col, BS, 1965; Wash State Univ, PhD (chem), 1968. **Professional Experience:** CHAIR, DEPT CHEM, STATE UNIV NY COL BROCKPORT, 1994-; from assoc prof to prof, 1986; PROF, CHEM, STATE UNIV NY COL BROCKPORT, 1980-; from asst prof to assoc prof, State Univ NY Col Brockport, 1970-1980; Res assoc chem, Georgetown Univ, 1968-1970; Lab asst, dept Chem, Col Beloit Wis, 1963-1965. **Memberships:** Sigma Xi; Am Chem Soc; Inorg Div Am Chem Soc. **Research Statement & Publications:** Kinetics and mechanisms of substitution reactions and oxidation-reduction reactions of transition-metal complex ions; catalysis by transition-metal ions; ion-exchange chromatography. **Mailing Address:** Dept Chem, State Univ Col, 350 New Campus Dr, Brockport, NY 14420. **Fax:** 716-395-5805. **E-Mail:** tkallen@brockport.edu

KALLENBACH, ERNST ADOLF THEODOR, HISTOLOGY, ELECTRON MICROSCOPY. **Personal Data:** b Minden, Ger, February 21, 1926. **Education:** George Williams Col, BSc, 1958; McGill Univ, MSc, 1960, PhD (anat), 1963. **Professional Experience:** RETIRED; prof anat, Col Med, Univ Fla, beginning 1981; assoc prof anat, Col Med, Univ Fla, 1977-1981; assoc prof path, Col Med, Univ Fla, 1967-1977; asst prof, Col Med, Univ Fla, 1964-1967; instr anat, Col Med, Univ Fla, 1963-1964; res assoc histol, McGill Univ, 1960-1963; assoc ed, Anat Rec. **Memberships:** Am Asn Anatomists; Electron Micros Soc Am. **Research Statement & Publications:** Lymphocyte production in thymus gland; presence and arrangement of cytoplasmic fibrils within epithelial cells; formation of enamel; fine structure of enamel organ. **Mailing Address:** 7903 SE County Rd 234, Gainesville, FL 32641.

KALLENBACH, NEVILLE R, BIOPHYSICAL CHEMISTRY. **Personal Data:** b Johannesburg, SAfrica, January 30, 1938. **Education:** Rutgers Univ, BS, 1958; Yale Univ, PhD (Phys chem), 1961. **Honors & Awards:** Am Inst Chemists Medal, 1958. **Professional Experience:** PROF CHEM, NY UNIV, as of 2004; NIH Fel Sr Res Biochem, 1981-1982; Guggenheim fel Weizmann Inst Sci, 1972-1973; PROF BIOL, UNIV PA, beginning 1971; from asst prof to assoc prof, Univ PA, 1964-1971; NSF fel biophys chem, NIH fel, 1962-1964; NSF fel biophys chem, Univ Calif, San Diego, 1961-1962; Woodrow Wilson fel, 1958-1959; Henry Rutgers Scholar, 1958; Etelman Found Scholar & Selman Waksman Scholar, 1954-1958. **Memberships:** Biophys Soc; Am Soc Biol Chemists. **Research Statement & Publications:** Structure and function of nucleic acids. **Mailing Address:** Dept Chem, NY Univ, 24 Waverly Pl 1170, New York, NY 10003. **Fax:** 212-260-7905. **E-Mail:** neville.kallenbach@nyu.edu

KALLENBERGER, WALDO ELBERT, LEATHER CHEMISTRY, HALOPHILIC BACTERIOLOGY. **Personal Data:** b Mercer Co, Ohio, February 25, 1950. **Education:** Valparaiso Univ, BA, 1972; Univ Cincinnati, MS, 1981, PhD (tan chem), 1985. **Honors & Awards:** Alsop Award, Am Leather Chem Asn, 1985. **Professional Experience:** CHIEF CHEMIS, LEATHER LAB, as of 2002; comt chmn, Alsop Comt, 1994; coun rep, Am Leather Chemists Asn, 1991-; Consult, 1989-; sr res assoc, tanners lab, Univ Cincinnati, beginning 1981; res assoc, Leather Industs Am Lab, 1978-1981; asst dir, Leather Industs Am Lab, 1976-2001; asst dir, 1976-2001; Jr res assoc, Leather Industs Am Lab, 1976-1978. **Memberships:** Am Leather Chemist Asn; Am Chem Soc. **Research Statement & Publications:** Leather processing, testing and product function; chromium conservation, environmental issues, analytical methods and halophilic bacteria in cured hide quality. **Mailing Address:** Leather Indust Am Res Lab, Univ Cincinnati, Cincinnati, OH 45221-0014. **Fax:** 513-242-9797. **E-Mail:** waldo.kallenberger@uc.edu

KALLEND, JOHN SCOTT, CRYSTALLOGRAPHY. **Personal Data:** b Bromley, Eng, September 30, 1945. **Education:** Univ Cambridge, BA, 1967, MA, 1970, PhD (metall), 1971. **Professional Experience:** ASSOC CHAIR MAT ENG, ILL INST TECHNOL, as of 2004; ASSOC DEAN, ARMOUR COL, as of 2004; PROF PHYSICS, ILL INST TECHNOL, as of 2004; ASSOC DEAN, ENG & SCI 1999-; dean, Undergrad Col, 1995-1999; dept chair, Undergrad Col, 1991-1995; Consult, Argonne Nat Lab, 1990; affil, Ctr Mat Sci, Los Alamos Nat Lab, 1987-1993; Consult, Naval Res Lab, 1982-1984; PROF MAT ENG, ILL INST TECHNOL, 1978-; Univ demonstr mat sci, Univ Cambridge, 1972-1977. **Memberships:** Inst Mat; Am Soc Metals; Mineral Metals & Mat Soc; Am Soc Eng Educ. **Research Statement & Publications:** Relations between crystallographic texture and anisotropy in polycrystalline materials; software development for analysis of x-ray and neutron texture data. **Mailing Address:** Undergraduate Col, Ill Inst Technol 3300 S Federal St, Chicago, IL 60616-3732. **Fax:** 312-567-3135. **E-Mail:** kallend@charlie.iit.edu

KALLER, BRIAN FRANCIS, TOTAL SYNTHESIS OF NATURAL PRODUCTS. **Personal Data:** b Regina, Sask, December 8, 1965; American & Canadian citizen. **Education:** Univ Sask, BSc, 1987, PhD (org synthesis), 1993. **Professional Experience:** Bristol-Mayers Squibb, Candiac QC, as of 2002; RES FEL, HARVARD UNIV, 1992-; Nat Sci & Eng Res Coun Can fel, 1992-1994. **Memberships:** Am Chem Soc; Can Soc Chem. **Research Statement & Publications:** Total synthesis of natural products. **E-Mail:** brian.kaller@bms.com

KALLER, CECIL LOUIS, MATHEMATICS, EDUCATION. **Personal Data:** b Humboldt, Sask, March 26, 1930. **Education:** Univ Sask, BA & BEd, 1954, MA, 1956; Purdue Univ, PhD (math statist), 1960. **Professional Experience:** RETIRED; mathematician, Okanagan Col, BC, 1976-1992; prof math & pres, Notre Dame Univ Nelson, BC, 1970-1976; from assoc prof to prof, Univ Regina, 1965-1970; chmn dept, Univ Regina, 1965-1970; from asst prof to assoc prof math, Univ Sask, 1960-1965; res statistician, UpJohn Co, Kalamazoo, 1958, 1959 & 1960; asst res statistician, Educ Div, Dom Bur Statist, Ottawa, 1955; teacher elem & high schs, Sask, 1948-1952. **Memberships:** Am Math Soc; Math Asn Am; Am Statist Asn; Biomet Soc; Sigma Xi; Can Math Soc. **Research Statement & Publications:** Mathematical statistics and probability theory; statistical models in biological sciences. **Mailing Address:** 536 Southerland Ave, Kelowna, BC V1Y 5X3, Can.

KALLFELZ, FRANCIS A, NUTRITION. **Personal Data:** b Syracuse, NY, July 17, 1938. **Education:** Cornell Univ, DVM, 1962, PhD (phys biol), 1966. **Professional Experience:** JAMES LAW PROF MED, CORNELL UNIV, as of 2005; prof clin nutrit, Dept Clin Sci, Ny State Col Vet Med, Cornell Univ, beginning 1980; from asst prof to assoc prof, dept large animal med obstet & surg, 1966-1980. **Memberships:** Am Vet Med Asn; Am Inst Nutrit; Soc Nuclear Med; Am Acad Vet Nutritionists; Am Col Vet Nutrit. **Research Statement & Publications:** Alkaline earth metabolism, the role of vitamin D in calcium metabolism; applications of radioisotopes in clinical veterinary medicine; mineral metabolism in domestic animals; metabolic diseases. **Mailing Address:** Dept Clin Sci, Col Vet Med, Cornell Univ, C2-289 VMTH, Ithaca, NY 14853. **Fax:** 607-253-3056. **E-Mail:** fak1@cornell.edu

KALLIANPUR, GOPINATH, MATHEMATICS. **Personal Data:** b Mangalore, India, April 16, 1925. **Education:** Univ Madras, BA, 1945, MA, 1946; Univ NC, PhD (math statist), 1951. **Professional Experience:** ALUMINI DISTINGUISHED PROF EMER, DEPT STATIST, UNIV NC, CHAPEL HILL, as of 2003; PROF MATH & STATIST, UNIV MINN, MINNEAPOLIS, 1963-; prof statist, Mich State Univ, 1961-1963; assoc prof math, Ind Univ, 1959-1961; vis assoc prof, Mich State Univ, 1956-1959; reader statist, Indian Statist Inst, Calcutta, 1953-1956; mem, inst Advan Study, 1952-1953; lectr statist, Univ Calif, 1951-1952. **Memberships:** AAAS; fel Inst Math Statist. **Research Statement & Publications:** Probability theory; stochastic processes; statistics. **Mailing Address:** 1301 Wildwood Dr, Chapel Hill, NC 27514. **E-Mail:** gkalk@email.unc.edu

KALLICK, DEBORAH A, BIOCHEMISTRY. **Education:** Univ Ill, PhD, 1986. **Professional Experience:** PRIN INVEST, MOLECULAR SIMULATIONS BIOMOLECULES, UNIV MINN, as of 2000; DEPT MED CHEM, UNIV MINN, as of 1999. **Mailing Address:** Dept Med Chem Col Pharm, Univ Minn, Minneapolis, MN 55455.

KALLIN, CATHERINE, STRONGLY CORRELATED ELECTRON SYSTEMS. **Personal Data:** b BC, September 4, 1954; m 1983, John; c Ann. **Education:** Univ BC, BSc, 1979; Harvard Univ, AM, 1981, PhD (physics), 1984. **Professional Experience:** PROF PHYSICS, MCMASTER UNIV, 1996-; dir acad affairs, Can Asn Physicists, 1997-; vis prof, Stanford Univ, 1996-1997; John Simon Guggenheim fel, 1996; EWR Steacie fel, Natural Sci & Eng Res Coun Can, 1996; assoc, Can Inst Advan Res, 1995-; trustee, Aspen Ctr Physics, 1994-2002; Cornell Univ, 1992-1993; Univ BC, 1991; assoc prof, McMaster Univ, 1990-1996; assoc chair, McMaster Univ, 1988-1990; vis scientist, AT&T Bell Labs, NJ, 1988; Alfred P Sloan res fel, Sloan Found, 1987; asst prof, McMaster Univ, 1986-1990; postdoctoral fel, Inst Theoret Physics, Univ Calif, Santa Barbara, 1984-1986. **Memberships:** Fel Am Phys Soc; Can Asn Physicists. **Research Statement & Publications:** Theory of highly correlated electronic systems, including high temperature super conductivity, frustrated antiferromagnets, Quantum Hall effect; Carbon nanotubes and Quantum dots; anions and the two-dimensional electron gas in the limit of large magnetic fields and low temperatures. **Mailing Address:** Dept Physics McMaster Univ, 1280 Main St W, Hamilton, ON L8S 4M1, Can. **E-Mail:** kallin@mcmaster.ca

KALLIOKOSKI, JORMA OSMO KALERVO, ECONOMIC GEOLOGY. **Personal Data:** b Harma, Finland, November 23, 1923. **Education:** Univ Western Ont, BSc, 1947; Princeton Univ, PhD (geol), 1951. **Professional Experience:** Bus ed, Econ Geol Publ Co, 1971-1977; PROF GEOL, MICH TECHNOL UNIV, 1968-; head, Geol Eng Dept, 1968-1981; from asst prof to assoc prof geol, Princeton Univ, 1956-1968; geologist, Geol Surv Can, 1949-1953 & Newmont Explor, Ltd, 1953-1956. **Memberships:** Geol Soc Am; Soc Econ Geol (secy, 1965-1967, pres elect, 1979, pres, 1980); Can Inst Mining & Metall; Geol Soc Finland; Am Inst Min Metall. **Research Statement & Publications:** Relationship between structure and mineral deposits; Precambrian geology in Canada, the United States and Venezuela; uranium geology. **Mailing Address:** 1010 Seventh Ave, Houghton, MI 49931.

KALLMAN, BURTON JAY, BIOCHEMISTRY, NUTRITION. **Personal Data:** b New York, NY, November 1, 1927; m 1958, c 2. **Education:** Bethany Col, WVa, BS, 1947; Univ Southern Calif, MS, 1951, PhD (biochem), 1958. **Honors & Awards:** Buaton Kallman Sci Achievenment Award, Nat Nutrit Foods Assoc, 1997. **Professional Experience:** RETIRED; dir, sci & technol, Nat Nutrit Foods Assoc, 1985-1996; dir, Appl Biol Sci Labs, 1982-1985; consult, NNFA, beginning 1997; Sci Appln Inc, beginning 1980; consult, IWG Corp, beginning 1980; prin, Interdisciplinary Sci Assoc Inc, 1980-1982; consult, US State Dept, 1978; sr scientist, Sci Appln Inc, 1976-1980; consult, Behav Health Serv, 1974-1976; biochemist, TRW Inc, 1967-1976; biochemist, Vet Admin Ctr, 1963-1967; biochemist, Fish Pesticide Res Lab, US Fish & Wildlife Serv, 1959-1963; consult, C Asthma Res Inst, 1962-1963; fel, Attend Staff Asn, Los Angeles County Gen Hosp, 1958-1959; res assoc, Sch Med, 1953-1958; instr chem, Sch Dent, Univ Southern Calif, 1952-1953. **Memberships:** Am Chem Soc. **Research Statement & Publications:** Adrenocorticotropic hormone release; thyroid hormone metabolism and physiology; pesticide biochemistry and pharmacology; immunochemistry; bioconversion of energy; fate and effects of petroleum on marine ecosystems; potential health effects of shale oil industry. **Mailing Address:** 23214 Robert Rd, Torrance, CA 90505. **Fax:** 310-540-2593. **E-Mail:** kallman2@aol.com

KALLMAN, KLAUS D, GENETICS, ICHTHYOLOGY. **Personal Data:** b Berlin, Ger, July 20, 1928. **Education:** Queens Col, NY, BS, 1952; NY Univ, MS, 1955, PhD (genetics), 1959. **Professional Experience:** RETIRED; head, Genetics Labs, 1986-1992; res assoc ichthyol, Am Mus Nat Hist, NY, 1965-1992; geneticist, Osborn Labs Marine Sci, 1963-1992; lectr, City Col NY, 1960-1966; res assoc, NY Aquarium, 1960-1962; fel, USPHS, 1959-1961. **Memberships:** Genetics Soc Am; Am Soc Zool; Am Soc Ichthyol & Herpet. **Research Statement & Publications:** Tissue transplantation; sex determination; evolution; pigment cell biology. **Mailing Address:** 282 Putnam Ave, Freeport, NY 11520.

KALLMAN, MARY JEANNE, PSYCHOBIOLOGY, PSYCHOPHARMACOLOGY. **Personal Data:** b Alexandria, Va, May 27, 1948. **Education:** Lynchburg Col, BS, 1970; Univ Ga, MS, 1974, PhD (biopsychol), 1976. **Professional Experience:** RES SCIENTIST, ELI LILLY & CO, GREENFIELD, IND, 1991-; adj assoc prof psychol, Pharmacol, Univ Miss, beginning 1991; assoc prof psychol & pharmacol, Eli Lilly & CO, Greenfield, Ind, 1983-1991; asst prof pharmacol, Med Col Va, 1980-1983; res assoc, Med Col Va, 1979-1980; fel, Med Col Va, 1976-1979; mem adj fac, Dept Psychol, Va Commonwealth Univ, 1975-1976; res asst psychiat, Med Ctr, Univ Miss, 1973-1974. **Memberships:** AAAS; Soc Neuroscience; Soc Stimulus Properties Drugs; Am Psychol Asn; Am Asn Pharmacol & Exp Therapeut; Behav Pharmacol Soc. **Research Statement & Publications:** State dependency of drugs and stimulus control; central nervous system function and sites of drug action; comparative and developmental central nervous system differences; central sensory processing; psychophysiology; behavioral toxicology and teratology. **Mailing Address:** Biochem Toxicol, Lilly Res Labs, PO Box 708 Drop Code GL44, Greenfield, IN 46140.

KALLMAN, RALPH ARTHUR, MATHEMATICS. **Personal Data:** b Holdrege, Nebr, September 17, 1934. **Education:** Univ Minn, BA, 1956, MA, 1961, PhD (math), 1965. **Professional Experience:** ASSOC PROF EMER, BALL STATE UNIV, as of 2004; assoc prof math, Ball State Univ, beginning 1973; asst prof, Ball State Univ, 1967-1973; asst prof math, Univ Minn, Duluth, 1965-1967. **Memberships:** Am Math Soc; Math Asn Am; Asn Comput Mach. **Research Statement & Publications:** Real and functional analysis; probability and statistics; computational combinatorics; computational probability and statistics. **Mailing Address:** Dept Math Sci, Ball State Univ, Muncie, IN 47306-0490. **Fax:** 765-285-1721.

KALLMAN, ROBERT R, MATHEMATICS. **Education:** Mass Inst Technol, PhD, 1968. **Professional Experience:** DISTINGUISHED RES PROF, DEPT MATHS UNIV N TEX, as of 2006. **Mailing Address:** Math Dept Univ N Tex, PO Box 311430, Denton, TX 76203-1430. **Fax:** 940-565-4805. **E-Mail:** kallman@unt.edu

KALLOK, MICHAEL JOHN, CARDIOVASCULAR PHYSIOLOGY, PULMONARY MECHANICS. **Personal Data:** b Gary, Ind, April 9, 1948. **Education:** Univ Colo, BS, 1970; Purdue Univ, MS, 1974; Univ Minn, PhD (biomed eng), 1978. **Honors & Awards:** Beckton Dickenson Career Achievement Award, Asn Advan Med Instrumentation, 1985. **Professional Experience:** PRES, CHIEF EXEC OFFICER & DIR, CARDIAVASC SYSTS, as of 2006; DIR RES, ANGEION CORP, as of 1999; dir res clin res, regulatory affairs, Medtronic Heart Valve Div, Medtronic Inc, beginning 1992; dir, Physiol Res Lab, 1988-1992; fel, Medtronic Inc, 1988-1989; sr res scientist, Medtronic Inc, 1987-1988; tachycordia res scientist, Medtronic Inc, 1985-1987; assoc fel, Medtronic Inc, 1983-1988; sr scientist, Medtronic Inc, 1981-1985; sr engr, Medtronic Inc, 1979-1981; instr physiol, Mayo Med Sch, 1979; res fel, Mayo Clin, 1977-1979; eng consult, Ind Health Eng Assocs, Inc, 1976; res asst, Univ Minn, 1974-1977; staff eng, Chicago Metallic Corp, 1972-1974; instr math, Andrean High Sch, 1971-1972; design engr, Pratt & Whitney Aircraft, 1970-1971. **Memberships:** Am Physiol Soc; Am Soc Mech Engrs; Biomed Eng Soc; fel Am Heart Asn; fel Am Col Cardiol; fel Am Inst Med & Biol Eng. **Research Statement & Publications:** Pulmonary mechanics; cardiac tachyarrhythmia mechanisms; detection and therapy of ventricular tachycardia and ventricular fibrillation; applications of engineering for medicine and physiology. **Mailing Address:** Cardiovasc Systs, Inc, 651 Campus Dr, St Paul, MN 55112.

KALLOS, GEORGE J, ANALYTICAL CHEMISTRY. **Personal Data:** b Greece, May 21, 1936. **Education:** Cent Mich Univ, BS, 1960; Univ Detroit, MS, 1962. **Professional Experience:** RETIRED; assoc scientist chem, Dow Chem Co, 1978-1995; Chmn, Carcinogen Safety Monograph RevPanel, Nat Cancer Inst, 1978; sr res specialist, Dow Chem Co, 1975-1978; sr res chemist, Dow Chem Co, 1971-1975; Res chemist, Dow Chem Co, 1963-1971. **Memberships:** Am Chem Soc; Sigma Xi. **Research Statement & Publications:** Development of new analytical technology for trace analysis; application of mass spectrometry to the elucidation of organic structure; monitoring of environmental pollutants. **Mailing Address:** 20 Winfred Pl, Saginaw, MI 48602.

KALLOSH, RENATA, PHYSICS. **Education:** Moscow State Univ, BS, 1966; Lebedev Phys Inst, Moscow, PhD, 1968. **Professional Experience:** PROF PHYSICS, DEPT PHYSICS, STANFORD UNIV, 1990-; sci assoc, CERN, Switz, 1989-1990; prof, Lebedev Phys Inst, Moscow, 1981-1989. **Research Statement & Publications:** published around 10 articles. **Mailing Address:** Dept Physics, Stanford Univ, Varian Bldg 342, Stanford, CA 94305-4060. **Fax:** 650-725-6544. **E-Mail:** kallosh@stanford.edu

KALLSEN, HENRY ALVIN, ENGINEERING ECONOMY, SAFETY. **Personal Data:** b Jasper, Minn, March 25, 1926; m 1950, Harriet Burger; c Margaret (Lucas), Laura (Weathers), Thomas & Alice (Weekley). **Education:** Iowa State Univ, BS, 1948; Univ Wis, MS, 1952, PhD, 1956. **Professional Experience:** EMER PROF INDUST ENG, UNIV ALA, 1991-; co-dir sch transp proj, Ala Dept Econ & Community Affairs, 1987-1990; actg head dept, Univ Ala, 1985-1986; prof, Univ Ala, 1972-1991; consult bd eng educ, Comn Higher Educ, State of Tenn, 1969; prof civil eng & asst dean eng, Univ Ala, 1965-1972; asst exec secy, Am Soc Eng Educ, 1964-1965; Mem adv res coun, La Hwy Dept, 1962-1964; actg head dept, La Polytech Inst, 1962-1963; from assoc prof to prof, La Polytech Inst, 1959-1964; from instr to asst prof civil eng, Univ Wis, 1949-1959; Asst engr, Wabash RR Co, 1948-1949. **Memberships:** Am Soc Civil Engrs fel. **Research Statement & Publications:** Engineering economy; geometronics; safety; computer science. **Mailing Address:** 3727 13th St E, Tuscaloosa, AL 35404-4313.

KALLUNKI, JACQUELYN ANN, BOTANY. **Personal Data:** b Laurium, Mich, July 3, 1948. **Education:** Univ Mich, BS, 1971; Univ Wis-Madison, MS, 1974, PhD, 1979. **Professional Experience:** Collection Serv Activ, NY Bot Garden, 1995-1998; Fulbright scholar award, 1995; grantee, Nat Geog Soc, 1993-1994; grantee, NSF, 1991-1993 & 1993-1995; ASST DIR HERBARIUM, NY BOT GARDEN, 1991-; ed-in-chief, Brittonia, 1991-1994; lectr, Yale Univ Sch Forestry, 1990 & 1991; mem, Systematics Collections Comt, Am Soc Plant Taxonomists, 1989-1991; admin cur, NY Bot Garden, 1986-1990; herbarium mgr, NY Bot Garden, 1981-1986; assoc ed, Brittonia, 1980-1990; curatorial asst, NY Bot Garden, 1979-1980; Herbarium aide, NY Bot Garden, 1975-1976. **Memberships:** Am Soc Plant Taxonomists inter assoc for plant taonomy. **Mailing Address:** NY Botl Garden, Bronx, NY 10458-5126. **Fax:** 718-817-8648. **E-Mail:** jkallunki@nybg.org

KALLWASS, HELMUT KARL WALTER, ENZYMOLOGY, MOLECULAR BIOLOGY. **Personal Data:** b Wolfenbuettel, Ger, September 21, 1959. **Education:** Univ Braunschweig, Ger, dipl, 1986, Dr rer nat(biochem), 1988. **Professional Experience:** STAFF SCIENTIST

II, GENZYME CORP, 1992-; dept chem, Univ Toronto, 1990-1992; postdoctoral fel, Ger Sci Found, 1988-1990. **Memberships:** Am Chem Soc; Am Soc Biochem & Molecular Biol. **Research Statement & Publications:** Enzyme and protein research that meets the multiple needs of an innovative biomedical company, particularly in drug discovery, diagnostic product development and chiral synthesis; multidisciplinary approach combines enzymology, protein chemistry, molecular biology and cell biology. **Mailing Address:** Genzyme Corp, One Kendall Sq, Cambridge, MA 02139-1562. **Fax:** 617-252-7550. **E-Mail:** hkallwass@genzyme.com

KALM, MAX JOHN, ORGANIC CHEMISTRY, PHARMACEUTICAL CHEMISTRY. **Personal Data:** b Munich, Ger, November 27, 1928; m 1969, Lila; c Denise & Deborah. **Education:** Univ Calif, Berkeley, BS, 1952, PhD (chem), 1954. **Professional Experience:** RETIRED; vpres qual assurance, Schering Corp, 1982-1992; vpres qual assurance, Cutter Labs, Inc, 1977-1982; Mem adv comt, Dept Health, Calif, 1976-1978; dir qual assurance, Cutter Labs, Inc, 1974-1977; dir qual control, Cutter Labs, Inc, 1971-1974; dir sci liaison, Cutter Labs, Inc, 1965-1971; sr investr, G D Searle & Co, 1955-1965; Res assoc chem, Univ Mich, 1954-1955. **Memberships:** fel Am Inst Chem; Sigma Xi. **Research Statement & Publications:** Photochemistry of benzene; psycho-stimulants and anorexics; synthesis of steroids with hormonal activity. **Mailing Address:** 2236 Viewpoint Dr, Naples, FL 34110-7951. **E-Mail:** mkalm2@juno.com

KALMA, ARNE HAERTER, NUCLEAR RADIATION EFFECTS, OPTICAL SENSORS. **Personal Data:** b Long Branch, NJ, May 26, 1941. **Education:** Rensselaer Polytech Inst, BS, 1963, MS, 1965, PhD (nuclear sci eng), 1968. **Professional Experience:** VPRES, MAXWELL TECHNOL, 1990-; group leader electro optics, Mission Res Corp, 1984-1990; mem staff, Northrop Res & Technol Ctr, 1979-1984; res scientist group leader physics, IRT Corp, 1969-1979; Res scientist physics, Univ Paris, 1968-1969. **Memberships:** Am Phys Soc; Optical Soc Am; Inst Elec & Electronics Engrs; Sigma Xi. **Research Statement & Publications:** Radiation effects in materials, particularly infrared detectors, optical materials and semiconductors; design and use of radiation hard fiber optics systems; radiation testing; nuclear radiation effects; optical sensors. **Mailing Address:** Maxwell Technol, 8888 Balboa Ave, San Diego, CA 92123. **E-Mail:** arne@maxwell.com

KALMAN, CALVIN SHEA, HIGH ENERGY PHYSICS, SCIENCE EDUCATIONAL RESEARCH. **Personal Data:** b Montreal, Que, October 29, 1944; m 1966, Rica-Judith; c Samuel A & Benjamin M. **Education:** McGill Univ, BSc, 1965; Univ Rochester, MA, 1967, PhD (physics), 1971. **Honors & Awards:** Canadian assoc of phys Medal for Excellence in Teaching 1999; Concordia univ Council on Student Life Teaching Award 1998; Teaching and Creativity Award Soc for Teaching and Learning in Higher Edu. **Professional Experience:** Chmn dept, Sir George Campus, Concordia Univ, 1983-1989; Vis assoc prof, Ind Univ, 1976-1977; PROF PHYSICS, SIR GEORGE CAMPUS, CONCORDIA UNIV, 1975-; Asst prof, Loyola Col Montreal, 1968-1975. **Memberships:** Am Asn Physics Teachers; Inst Particle Physics Canadian Assoc of phys Teachers. **Research Statement & Publications:** Supersymmetric Gauge Field Theory, subquark structure; PER. **Mailing Address:** Dept Physics, Concordia Univ, Montreal, PQ H3G 1M8, Can. **Fax:** 514-848-2828. **E-Mail:** kalman@vax2.concordia.ca

KALMAN, GABOR J, PLASMA & MANY BODY PHYSICS. **Personal Data:** b Budapest, Hungary, December 12, 1929. **Education:** Polytech Univ, Budapest, dipl, 1952; Israel Inst Technol, DSc, 1961. **Professional Experience:** DISTINGUISHED PROF PHYSICS, BOSTON COL, as of 2005; co-dir, NSF-CNRS Workshop Spectral Diag Turbulence Solar Flares, Boston, 1982; res leader, Int Ctr Theoret Physics, 1981 & 1984; dir, NATO Advan Study Inst Strongly Coupled Plasmas, Orleans, France, 1977; exchange prof, Univ Paris, 1976; sr vis fel, Univ Oxford, 1975; vis scientist, Ionosphere Res Group, Nat Ctr Sci Res, Orleans, France, 1974; assoc, Ctr Astrophys, Harvard Univ, 1973-1977; vis scientist, Paris Observ, Meudon, France, 1973-1974; res prof physics, Boston COl, beginning 1970; expert, Air Force Cambridge Res Lab, 1967-1968; vis prof, Brandeis Univ, 1966-1970; dir res, Nat Ctr Sci Res, 1966-1968; vis fel, Joint Lab Astrophys, 1965-1966; dir, Orsay Summer Inst Plasma Physics, France, 1962; prof, Univ Paris, 1961-1966; lectr physics, Israel Inst Technol, 1958-1961; res assoc, Israel Inst Technol, 1957-1958; from jr res scientist to res scientist, Cent Res Inst Physics, Budapest, Hungary, 1952-1956; prin investr grants & contracts, NSF, Dept Energy, Air Force Off Sci Res, Air Force Geophys Lab & Israel-US Binat Found NATO. **Memberships:** AAAS; European Phys Soc; fel Am Phys Soc; Fr Phys Soc; fel NY Acad Sci. **Research Statement & Publications:** Strongly coupled plasmas; plasma physics; many body response functions; plasma astrophysics; models for high density; astrophysical many body systems; solid state plasmas; many body physics. **Mailing Address:** Dept Physics, Boston Col, Higgins Hall 330B, Chestnut Hill, MA 02467. **Fax:** 617-552-3575. **E-Mail:** kalman@bc.edu

KALMAN, RUDOLF EMIL, MATHEMATICS, ENGINEERING. **Personal Data:** b Budapest, Hungary, May 19, 1930. **Education:** Mass Inst Technol, SB, 1953, SM, 1954; Columbia Univ, DSc, 1957. **Honors & Awards:** Rufus Oldenburger Medal, Am Soc Mech Eng, 1976; Steele Prize; Medal of Honor, Inst Elec & Electronics Engrs; Kyoto Prize. **Professional Experience:** GRAD RES PROF EMER & DIR, CTR MATH SYST THEORY, UNIV FLA, 1992-; prof math system theory, Swiss Fed Inst Technol, Zurich, 1973-; grad res prof & dir Ctr Math Syst Theory, Ctr Math Syst Theory, Univ Fla, 1971-1992; prof math syst theory & opers res, Stanford Univ, 1967-1971; prof eng mech & elec eng, Stanford Univ, 1964-1967; head, Ctr Control Theory, 1962-1964; staff mathematician, Res Inst Adv Studies, 1958-1962; staff engr, IBM Corp, NY, 1957-1958; instr, Columbia Univ, 1955-1957; res engr process control res, E I du Pont Del Nemours & Co, Del, 1954-1955; asst, Servo mechanisms Lab, Mass Inst Technol, 1953-1954. **Memberships:** Nat Acad Sci; Nat Acad Eng; Hungarian Acad Sci; Am Math Soc; Inst Elec & Electronics Engrs; Acad Sci Inst France. **Research Statement & Publications:** Automatic control; network and information theory; mathematical statistics; automata; nonlinear dynamic systems; calculus of variations; stochastic processes; engineering science; algebraic system theory; innovative statistics. **Mailing Address:** Dept Elec & Comput Eng Univ Fla, 527 EB PO Box 116200, Gainesville, FL 32611.

KALMAN, THOMAS IVAN, BIO-ORGANIC CHEMISTRY, ENZYMOLOGY & ANTIVIRAL. **Personal Data:** b Budapest, Hungary, January 20, 1936; American citizen; m 1963, Marietta; c Rob P & Nicolette C. **Education:** Tech Univ Budapest, Dipl Chem, BS & MS 1959; State Univ NY, Buffalo, PhD (biochem, pharmacol), 1968. **Honors & Awards:** Scholar Award, Am Cancer Soc, 1996. **Professional Experience:** Vis prof, Dept Pharmacol & Dept Med Chem, Med Col Va, 1996-1997; PROF MED CHEM, STATE UNIV NY, BUFFALO, 1993-; vis assoc prof, Dept Pharmacol, Sch Med, Yale Univ, 1975-1976, NIH res career develop award, 1971-1976; from asst prof to assoc prof biochem pharmacol, State Univ NY, Buffalo, 1970-1993; fel, NIH, 1967-1968; adj asst prof & sr res assoc health sci, State Univ NY, Buffalo, 1966-1970; res asst, Res Found, State Univ NY, 1963-1966; Res chemist, Hungary, 1959-1962. **Memberships:** AAAS; Am Chem Soc; NY Acad Sci; fel Am Inst Chem; Am Asn Cancer Res; Sigma Xi. **Research Statement & Publications:** Mechanisms of enzyme and drug action; design and synthesis of selective enzyme inhibitors; biosynthesis of purine and pyrimidine nucleotides; folic acid metabolism; drug design; experimental chemotherapy; cancer research; antiviral agents; published over 20 articles. **Mailing Address:** Dept Chem, Univ Buffalo State Univ NY, C457 Cooke Hall, Buffalo, NY 14260-3000. **Fax:** 716-645-6963. **E-Mail:** tkalman@buffalo.edu

KALMANSON, KENNETH, MATHEMATICS. **Personal Data:** b Brooklyn, NY, March 26, 1943. **Education:** Brooklyn Col, BS, 1964; City Univ NY, PhD (math), 1970. **Professional Experience:** PROF MATH, MONTCLAIR STATE UNIV, as of 2005; asst prof math, Montclair State Col, beginning 1970; Teacher high schs, NY, 1965-1966. **Memberships:** Am Math Soc; Math Asn Am. **Research Statement & Publications:** Combinatorial geometry; especially extreme Hamiltonian lines with respect to metric spaces. **Mailing Address:** Dept Math Sci, Montclair Univ, RI-208 One Normal Ave, Montclair, NJ 07043. **Fax:** 973-655-7686. **E-Mail:** kalmansonk@mail.montclair.edu

KALME, JOHN S, MATHEMATICS. **Personal Data:** b Riga, Latvia, June 20, 1938. **Education:** Univ Pa, BA, 1961, MA, 1964, PhD (math), 1966. **Professional Experience:** ASSOC PROF MATH, US NAVAL ACAD, as of 2005; CONSULT, 1982-; consult & comput prog, David Taylor, US Naval Ship Res & Develop Ctr, Annapolis, 1979-1982; asst prof math, Drexel Inst, US Naval Acad, Annapolis, 1969-1979; instr, Drexel Inst, US Naval Acad, Annapolis, 1965-1966; Teaching fel math, Univ Pa, 1961-1964. **Research Statement & Publications:** Mathematical analysis; chiefly probability theory and integral operators; stochastic processes; time series analysis; use of time series analysis in source and path identification of structure-borne noise on ships; vibration analysis. **Mailing Address:** Dept Math, US Naval Acad, 121 Blake Rd, Annapolis, MD 21402-5000. **E-Mail:** jsk@usna.edu

KALMUS, GERHARD WOLFGANG, DEVELOPMENTAL BIOLOGY. **Personal Data:** b Berlin, Ger, December 19, 1942; m 1967, Karen. **Education:** Univ Calif, Berkeley, AB, 1967; Rutgers Univ, Camden, MS, 1974; Rutgers Univ, New Brunswick, PhD (zoology), 1977. **Professional Experience:** PROF BIOL, ECAROLINA UNIV, 1993-; assoc prof, Ecarolina Univ, 1983-1993; asst prof develop, Ecarolina Univ, 1977-1983; teaching asst zool, Rutgers Univ, 1973-1977; res asst embryol, Temple Univ, 1973; teacher biol, Quakertown Community High Sch, 1972; asst proj mgr transl, Info Intersci Inc, 1969-1970; res asst physiol, Univ Pa, 1967-1968. **Memberships:** Sigma Xi Scientific Res Soc (pres, 1998-1999); AAAS; Soc Integrative Comp Biol; Am Inst Biol Sci; Soc In Vitro Biol; Soc Develop Biol; Am Inst Biol Sci; Asn Southeastern Biologists; Alpha Epsilon Dleta. **Research Statement & Publications:** Transplantation immunology; chick primordial germ cells; fetal alcohol syndrome; differentiation in cell culture; Fibroblast Chemotaxis in Response to Dexamethasone. **Mailing Address:** Dept Biol, ECarolina Univ, N-406 Howell Sci Complex, Greenville, NC 27858. **Fax:** 252-328-4178. **E-Mail:** kalmusg@mail.ecu.edu

KALNAY, EUGENIA, NUMERICAL WEATHER PREDICTION, GENERAL CIRCULATION MODELING. **Personal Data:** b Buenos Aires, Arg, October 10, 1942; American citizen; m 1981, Mal; c 1. **Education:** Univ Buenos Aires, Lic Meteorol, 1965; Mass Inst Technol, PhD (meteorol), 1971. **Honors & Awards:** Except Sci Achievement Medal, NASA, 1981; Silver Medal, Dept Com, 1990; Gold Medal, Develop Div, 1993; Jules G Charney Award, Am Meteorol Soc, 1995; Sr Exec Serv Presidential Rank Award, 1996. **Professional Experience:** DISTINGUISHED UNIV PROF, DEPT METEOROL, UNIV MD, 2001-; mem, Bd Atmospheric Sci & Climate, Nat Acad Sci, 1993; assoc ed, Quart J Royal Meteorol Soc, 1992 & Monthly Weather Rev, 1990; dir, Environ Modeling Ctr, 1987-1997; assoc ed, J Atmospheric Sci, 1984-1990; mem, First Global Atmospheric Res Prog Global Exp Panel, Nat Acad Sci, 1983-1993; head, Global Modeling & Simulation Br, 1983-1986; adj prof meteorol, Univ Md, 1980-1983; sr res meteorologist, Goddard Lab Atmosphere, NASA, 1979-1983; from asst prof to assoc prof, Mass Inst Technol, 1975-1978; prin investr, NASA res proj, 1973-; res assoc, Mass Inst Technol, 1973-1974; asst prof meteorol, Univ Montevideo, Uruguay, 1971-1973. **Memberships:** Nat Acad Eng; fel Am Meteorol Soc; Argentine Nat Acad Physical Sci. **Research Statement & Publications:** Research development division of national meteorological center, where all improvements to atmospheric models and data assimilation are developed and implemented giving guidance to the national weather service forecasts; use of satellite data; data assimilation; atmospheric predictability; ensemble forecasting; published over 50 articles. **Mailing Address:** Dept Meterol, Univ Md, 3431 Comput & Space Sci Bldg, College Park, MD 20742-2425. **Fax:** 301-314-9482. **E-Mail:** ekalnay@atmos.umd.edu

KALNIN, ILMAR L, MATERIALS SCIENCE. **Personal Data:** b Riga, Latvia, January 23, 1926. **Education:** Westminster Col, Pa, BA, 1952; Ill Inst Technol, PhD (chem), 1957. **Professional Experience:** RETIRED; res assoc, Hoechst-Celanese Co, 1986-1991; res assoc, Celanese Res Co, 1967-1986; sr res scientist, Celanese Res Co, 1966-1967; res scientist, Am-Stand Co, 1962-1966; mem tech staff, Bell Tel Labs, 1957-1962; tech consult. **Memberships:** Am Chem Soc; Am Ceramic Soc; Am Soc Testing & Mat; Mat Res Soc. **Research Statement & Publications:** Functional polymers; structural composites; fiber reinforced plastics; electronic ceramics. **Mailing Address:** 135 Haas Rd, Basking Ridge, NJ 07920-1098.

KALNINS, ARTURS, MECHANICS. **Personal Data:** b Riga, Latvia, February 13, 1931. **Education:** Univ Mich, BS, 1955, MS, 1956, PhD (eng mech), 1960. **Professional Experience:** PROF MECH, LEHIGH UNIV, 1967-; Fulbright-Hayes fel, Univ Innsbruck, 1977; assoc ed, J Acoust Soc Am, 1970-; assoc prof mech, Lehigh Univ, 1965-1967; asst prof eng & appl sci, Yale Univ, 1960-1965; res engr appl mech, Univ Calif, Berkeley, 1958-1960; res asst eng mech, Univ Mich, 1956-1958. **Memberships:** Am Soc Mech Engrs; Acoust Soc Am. **Research Statement & Publications:** Stress analysis, pressure vessel design. **Mailing Address:** 1984 Sunrise Lane, Bethlehem, PA 18015. **Fax:** 610-758-6224. **E-Mail:** ak01@lehigh.edu

KALNINS, IRENE, NURSING. **Education:** Univ ILL, BS, 1968; Boston Univ, MS, 1977. **Professional Experience:** ASSOC PROF NURSING, ST LOUIS UNIV SCH NURSING, MO, as of 2005. **Mailing Address:** Dept Continuing Educ St Louis Univ Sch Nursing, 3525 Caroline Mall, St Louis, MO 63104-1099. **Fax:** 314-977-8949. **E-Mail:** kalninsis@slu.edu

KALOGERIS, THEODORE J, GASTROINTESTINAL PHYSIOLOGY, ABSORBTION & TRANSPORT OF LIPIDS. **Personal Data:** b Salina, Kans, October 1, 1955. **Education:** Univ Calif, San Diego, BA, 1976; Univ Calif, Davis, MS, 1983, PhD (nutrit), 1988. **Professional Experience:** RES ASST PROF, DEPT SURGERY & PHYSIOL, LA STATE UNIV MED CTR, 1995-; NIH fel, Dept Surgery & Physiol, LA State Univ Med Ctr, 1992-1995; Nat Heart Asn fel, Dept Foods & Nutrit, Purdue Univ, 1988-1991. **Memberships:** Sigma Xi; Am Physiol Soc; Am Soc Nutrit Sci; Am Gastroenterol Asn; NIH first award, 1997-. **Research Statement & Publications:** Regulation of intestinal lipoproteins; role of oxidized lipoproteins in mediating endothelial dysfunction, regulation of expression of endothelial cell adhesion molecules. **Mailing Address:** Dept Surg, La State Univ Health Sci Ctr, 1501 Kings Hwy, Shreveport, LA 71130. **Fax:** 318-675-6141. **E-Mail:** tkalog@lsuhsc.edu

KALOGEROPOULOS, THEODORE E, HIGH ENERGY PHYSICS. **Personal Data:** b Megalopolis, Greece, January 20, 1931. **Education:** Dipl physics, Nat Univ Athens, 1954; dipl electronics, Radio-Eng Sch, Athens, 1951; Univ Calif, Berkeley, PhD (physics), 1959. **Professional Experience:** PROF EMER PHYSICS, SYRACUSE UNIV, as of 2004; vis prof, Nuclear Res Ctr Democritos, 1969-1970; vis physicist, Argonne Nat Lab, 1965; from asst prof to assoc prof, Syracuse Univ, 1962-1969; vis physicist, Brookhaven Nat Lab, 1960-1985; instr, Columbia Univ, 1959-1962; res assoc physics, Lawrence Radiation Lab, Univ Calif, 1959. **Memberships:** Am Phys Soc; AAAS. **Research Statement & Publications:** Elementary particle physics; investigations on antinucleon-nucleon interactions, using emulsions, bubble chambers, spark chambers, counters and drift chambers; medical applications of antiprotons; optimization algorithms and applications. **Mailing Address:** Dept Physics, Syracuse Univ, Syracuse, NY 13244.

KALONJI, GRETCHEN, ATOMISTIC COMPUTER SIMULATIONS. **Education:** Mass Inst Technol, BS, 1980, PhD (mat sci), 1982. **Honors & Awards:** Presidential Young Investr Award, NSF, 1984. **Professional Experience:** KYOCERA PROF MAT SCI, UNIV WASH, 1990-; from asst prof to assoc prof, mat sci, Mass Inst Technol, 1982-1990; mat engr, Nat Bur Standards, 1979-1981. **Memberships:** Am Ceramics Soc; Mat Res Soc; Am Phys Soc; AAAS. **Research Statement & Publications:** Theory of defects in crystalline solids; computer simulation techniques in materials science; rapid solidification of ceramics. **Mailing Address:** Dept Mat Sci & Eng, Univ Wash, 333 Roberts Hall Box 352120, Seattle, WA 98195-2120. **Fax:** 206-543-3100. **E-Mail:** kalonji@u.washington.edu

KALOOSTIAN, GEORGE H, ENTOMOLOGY. **Personal Data:** b Kaisarea, Turkey, January 12, 1912. **Education:** Fresno State Col, BA, 1935; Ore State Col, MS, 1939. **Professional Experience:** RETIRED; res leader, Calif, 1961-1979; res leader, Ga, 1957-1961; res leader, Utah, 1948-1957; res leader, Wash, 1940-1948; res leader, Calif, Fruit & Veg Insect Res, Agr Res Serv, USDA, 1938-1940. **Memberships:** Entom Soc Am; Am Phytopath Soc; Sigma Xi. **Research Statement & Publications:** Life history and control of dried fruit insects; plant and insect survey methods; insects in relation to fruit tree diseases caused by virus and mycoplasmalike organisms. **Mailing Address:** 4066 Mt Vernon Ave, Riverside, CA 92507-4804.

KALOS, MALVIN HOWARD, THEORETICAL PHYSICS, COMPUTER SCIENCE. **Personal Data:** b New York, NY, August 5, 1928. **Education:** Queens Col, NY, BS, 1948; Univ Ill, MS, 1949, PhD (physics), 1952. **Honors & Awards:** Eugene Feenberg Award, 1989. **Professional Experience:** DIR, CTR THEORY & SIMULATION SCI/ENG & PROF DEPT PHYSICS, CORNELL UNIV, 1989-; lectr, Univ Paris, 1970-1977; res prof, Courant Inst Math, 1964-1989; adv scientist, Nuclear Develop Corp, 1955-1964; res assoc physics, Cornell Univ, 1953-1955 & Univ Ill, 1952-1953. **Memberships:** Am Phys Soc; fel NY Acad Sci; AAAS; fel Am Nuclear Soc. **Research Statement & Publications:** Nuclear physics; statistical physics; neutron interactions; parallel computers; application of computers to physics, especially Monte Carlo methods. **Mailing Address:** Cornell Univ, 521 ETC Bldg, Hoy Rd, Ithaca, NY 14853-3801. **Fax:** 607-254-8888. **E-Mail:** kalos@tc.cornell.edu

KALOTA, DENNIS JEROME, ORGANIC CHEMISTRY, FLUORINECHEMISTRY. **Personal Data:** b North Tonawanda, NY, November 15, 1945. **Education:** Niagara Univ, BS, 1968; Univ Detroit, MS, 1971, PhD (chem), 1974. **Professional Experience:** AT, MONSANTO CO, as of 1996; SCI FEL, MONSANTO CO, 1988-; sr res specialist, Monsanto Co, 1984-1988; res specialist, Monsanto Co, 1980-1984; sr res chemist, Monsanto Co, 1974-1980. **Memberships:** Am Chem Soc; Sigma Xi. **Research Statement & Publications:** New products research and process development for amino acids and polyamino acids; direct fluorination of polyethers; chlorination, nitration, hydrolysis, and amination of aromatics; synthesis of polycarboxylates; electrochemistry; enzymatic and heterogeneous catalysis. **Mailing Address:** Monsanto Co, 800 N Lindbergh Blvd, St Louis, MO 63167.

KALOW, WERNER, PHARMACOLOGY, PHARMACO-GENETICS. **Personal Data:** b Cottbus, Ger, February 15, 1917; Canadian citizen; m 1991, Patricia M Arnold; c Peter & Barbara. **Education:** Univ Koenigsberg, MD, 1941. **Honors & Awards:** Upjohn Award, Pharmacol Soc Can, 1981; Oscar B Hunter Award, 1993; Res Recognition Award, Can Anaesthetists Soc, 1993; Distinguished Career Award, Drug Info Asn, 1997; Killam Prize, Can Conn Arts, 2001. **Professional Experience:** Chmn dept, Univ Toronto, 1966-1977; dir biol res, C H Boehringer Sohn, Ingelheim, WGer, 1965-1966; PROF PHARMACOL, UNIV TORONTO, 1962-; from lectr to assoc prof, Univ Toronto, 1952-1962; instr, Univ Pa, 1951; res fel pharmacol, Univ Pa, 1950; sci asst, Free Univ Berlin, 1949; sci asst, Univ Berlin, 1947-1948. **Memberships:** Am Soc Pharmacol & Exp Therapeut; NY Acad Sci; Can Physiol Soc; Pharmacol Soc Can (secy-treas, 1956-1958, pres, 1963-1964); Ger Pharmacol Soc; Can Anaesthetists Soc; Pac Rim Asn Clin Pharmacogenetics (pres, 1989-1994); fel Royal Soc Can. **Research Statement & Publications:** Bile secretion; serum cholinesterase; curare; local anesthetics; caffeine metabolism; malignant hyperthermia; genetics and drug response; ethnicity and drug metabolism. **Mailing Address:** Dept Pharmacol, Univ Toronto, Med Sci Bldg, Toronto, ON M5S 1A8, Can. **Fax:** 416-978-6395. **E-Mail:** w.kalow@utoronto.ca

KALPAKIS, KONSTANTINOS, MATHEMATICS. **Professional Experience:** ASSOC PROF, COMPUT SCI ELEC ENG DEPT, UNIV MD, BALTIMORE CO, as of 2006. **Memberships:** Asn Comput Mach. **Mailing Address:** Dept Comput Sci, Univ Md, Baltimore Co 5401 Wilkens, Baltimore, MD 21228. **Fax:** 410-455-3969.

KALPAKJIAN, SEROPE, MANUFACTURING ENGINEERING. **Personal Data:** b Istanbul, Turkey, May 6, 1928. **Education:** Robert Col, Istanbul, BSc, 1949; Harvard Univ, SM, 1951; Mass Inst Technol, SM, 1953. **Honors & Awards:** Centennial Medallion, Am Soc Mech Engrs. **Professional Experience:** PROF EMER MECH, MAT & AEROSPACE ENG, ILL INST TECHNOL, as of 2004; cor ed, J Mfg, 1990-; xerox Corp, 1979 & A Finkl & Sons, 1984-1986; consult, Continental Can Co, 1969-1976; prof mech, mat & aerospace eng, Ill Inst Technol, beginning 1963; consult, Ill Inst Technol Res Inst, 1963-1980; res supvr metal forming, Cincinnati Milacron, Inc, 1957-1963; res engr, Mass Inst Technol, 1953-1954. **Memberships:** Fel Am Soc Mech Engrs; fel Am Soc Metals; fel Soc Mfg Engrs; Int Inst Prod Eng Res. **Research Statement & Publications:** Grinding and lubrication; machining and forming; manufacturing processes. **Mailing Address:** Dept Mech Mat & Aerospace Eng, Ill Inst Technol, Room: 253C, Eng 1 Bldg, Chicago, IL 60616-3732. **Fax:** 312-567-7230. **E-Mail:** kalpakjian@iit.edu

KALRA, JAWAHAR, CLINICAL PATHOLOGY, MEDICAL BIOCHEMISTRY. **Personal Data:** b Aligarh, India, April 2, 1949; m Kamal; c Niel & Natasha. **Education:** Aligarh Univ, India, BSc, 1967, MSc, 1969; Mem Univ Nfld, 1972, PhD (biochem), 1976, MD, 1981; Can Soc Clin Chemists, cert, 1986; Royal Col Physicians & Surgeons Can, cert, 1986; FACB, 1987; FRCPC, 1987; FICA, 1988; FACA, 1989; FCACB, 1989. **Honors & Awards:** Med Chem Award, Can Soc Clin Chem, 1991, 1992; Man of Yr, Am Biog Inst Res Asn, 1994. **Professional Experience:** PROF, DEPT PATH, COL MED, UNIV SASK, AS OF 2006; STAFF, PATH LABS, ROYAL UNIV HOSP, AS OF 2006; dir path labs, royal univ hosp, 2000; dep gov, mem bd gov, Am Biog Inst Res Asn, 1995; chief, dept lab med, saskatoon dist health bd, 1993-2000; prof & head, dept path, col med, univ sask, 1991-2000; postgrad training prog, Dept Path, 1990; mem, Adv Comt Acad Enrichment Progs, Col Med, 1990; mem, Med Adv Comt, 1990; dir residency training progs gen & anat path, Univ Sask, 1990-1991; actg head, Dept Lab Med, Saskatoon Dist Health Bd, 1990-1991; Schering travelling award, Can Soc Clin Invest, 1988; active med staff, Royal Univ Hosp, 1985; From asst prof to assoc prof, Dept Lab Med, Saskatoon Dist Health Bd, 1985-1991; sr resident, Dept Med, 1984-1985 & Dept Lab Med, 1985; actg chief resident internal med, endocrinol & metab, Hosp, 1984; jr resident, Dept Med, 1983; jr resident, Dept Lab Med, Ottawa Civic Hosp, 1982-1983 & 1984; Burrough-Wellcome scholar, 1979; res assoc, Mem Univ Res Unit, Fac Med, 1976-1977; res asst, Mem Univ Res Unit, Fac Med, 1974-1976; Lab instr 3rd & 4th yr biochem lab courses, Mem Univ, Nfld, 1972-1974; mem bd dirs, Parkinson's. **Memberships:** Int Soc Free Radical Res-Oxygen Soc; Am Soc Clin Pathologists; Int Soc Heart Res; NY Acad Sci; Nat Acad Clin Biochem; Am Asn Clin Chem; Can Med Asn; Can Asn Med Biochem (pres 1993-). **Research Statement & Publications:** Role of oxygen free radicals in various clinical diseases especially heart failure, atherosclecrsis and Parkinson's disease; earlier work on cardiac glycoside (digoxin) biotransformation and thyroid function testing along with lab utilization studies. **Mailing Address:** Dept Path, Univ Sask, Saskatoon, SK S7N 0X0, Can. **Fax:** 306-655-2200.

KALRA, SATYA PAUL, NEUROSCIENCE, NEUROENDOCRINOLOY OF ENERGY HOMEOSTASIS, REPRODUCTION & ENDOCRINOLOGY OF BEHAVIOR. **Personal Data:** b Mari Indus, West Pakistan, January 1, 1939; m. **Education:** Univ Delhi, BSc, 1960, MSc, 1962, PhD (physiol), 1966. **Professional Experience:** DISTINGUISHED PROF NEUROSCIENCE, COL MED, UNIV FLA, 1982-; NIH grant, Univ Fla, 1971-; from asst prof to assoc prof, Col Med, Univ Fla, 1971-1982; ford found fel physiol, Southwestern Med Sch, Univ Tex Health Sci Ctr, Dallas, 1969-1971; ford found fel anat, Col Med, Univ Calif, Los Angeles, 1968-1969; res asst physiol reproduction, Univ Delhi, 1966-1968. **Memberships:** Endocrine Soc; Am Physiol Soc; Soc Neuroscience; AAAS. **Research Statement & Publications:** Neuroendocrinology of Energy homeostasis, obesity and eating disoerders; Energy imbalance and Impact on Reproduction; Gene therapy to control obesity. **Mailing Address:** Dept Neurosci, Univ Fla Col Med, PO Box 100244 Jhm Hc 1600 Sw Archer Rd, Gainesville, FL 32610-0294. **Fax:** 352-392-0191. **E-Mail:** skalra@mbi.ufl.edu

KALRA, S(URINDRA) N(ATH), COMMUNICATIONS. **Personal Data:** b Lahore, India, May 12, 1927. **Education:** Panjab Univ, India, BS, 1946; Univ Ill, MS, 1947, PhD, 1950. **Professional Experience:** PROF ELEC ENG, UNIV WATERLOO, 1969-; assoc prof, Univ Waterloo, 1967-1969; dir interdisciplinary studies commun, Univ Windsor, 1965-1967; assoc prof elec eng, Univ Windsor, 1962-1967; head high frequency physics lab, Div Appl Physics, 1953-1962; fel, Nat Res Coun Can, 1952-1953; reader electronics, Phys Res Lab, India, 1950-1952. **Memberships:** Sr mem Inst Elec & Electronics Engrs; Brit Inst Elec Engrs. **Research Statement & Publications:** Communication sciences; electronics; computers. **Mailing Address:** Univ Waterloo, 103-30 Blue Springs Dr, Waterloo, ON N2J 4T2, Can.

KALRA, VIJAY KUMAR, BIOCHEMISTRY. **Personal Data:** b Multan, Pakistan, August 26, 1942. **Education:** Univ Delhi, BSc, 1961, MSc, 1963, PhD (chem), 1967. **Professional Experience:** PROF BIOCHEM & SEN, FAC SENATE, SCH MED, UNIV SOUTHERN CALIF, 1984-; from asst prof to assoc prof, Fac Senate, Sch Med, Univ Southern Calif, 1971-1984; USPHS res fel, Sch Med, Univ Southern Calif, 1967-1970; USDA res fel, Ctr Advan Studies Chem Natural Prod, Univ Delhi, 1967. **Memberships:** Am Chem Soc; Am Soc Biol Chem. **Research Statement & Publications:** Structure and function of membranes; oxidative phosphorylation, mechanism of transport of amino acids in bacterial and mammalian cells; sterol metabolism in animal and human cells and relationship to atherosclerosis; structure and function of membranes of red blood cells and sickle cells; structure and function of endothelial cells. **Mailing Address:** Dept Biochem, Sch Med, Univ Southern Calif, 2011 Zonal Ave, Los Angeles, CA 90033-1034. **Fax:** 323-442-1528. **E-Mail:** vkalra@hsc.usc.edu

KALRA, YASH PAL, SOIL CHEMIST. **Personal Data:** b Gunjial, Punjab, India, October 28, 1940. **Education:** Agra Univ, Kanpur, India, BS, 1961, MS, 1963; Univ Man, Winnipeg, MS, 1967. **Professional Experience:** PRES, SOIL & PLANT ANAL COUN, CAN FORESTRY SERV, NATURAL RESOURCES CAN, as of 2004; PRES, BHOOVIGYAN VIKAS FOUND, as of 2004; Mem biol serv/environ sci adv comt, Northern Alta Inst Technol, Edmonton, 1993-; chmn, registration comt, Environ Soil Sci Conf, Can Land Reclamation Asn/Can Soc Soil Sci, 1992; exec, Edmonton Br, 1991-; mem chem exec, Professional Inst Pub Serv Can, 1984-; mem safety comt, Northern Forestry Ctr, 1970-1972; head, Anal Serv, Forestry Can, Edmonton, beginning 1967; grantee, Nat Res Coun Can, 1964-1966; Res fel, Univ Man, 1963-1964; grantee, Prime Minister India, 1963; Res fel, Indian Coun Agr Res, 1961-1963. **Memberships:** Can Soc Soil Sci (secy 1993-); Int Soc Soil Sci; Soil Sci Soc Am; Am Soc Agronomy; Indian Soc Soil Sci; Soc Ind Foresters; Asn Off Analytical Chemists; Western Inviron Agr Lab Asn (secy & treas 1981-1982 1985-1986); Prof Inst Pub Serv Can; Coun Soil Testing Plant Anal. **Mailing Address:** Can Forest Serv, 5320-122 St, Edmonton, AB T6H 3S5, Can. **Fax:** 780-435-7359. **E-Mail:** ykalra@nrcan.gc.ca

KALSBECK, JOHN EDWARD, PEDIATRIC NEUROSURGERY. **Personal Data:** b Grand Rapids, Mich, May 20, 1927. **Education:** Calvin Col, AB, 1949; Univ Mich, MD, 1953; Am Bd Neurol Surg, dipl, 1968. **Professional Experience:** PROF EMER SURG NEUROSURG, IND UNIV, INDIANAPOLIS, as of 2006; prof surg neurosurg, Ind Univ, Indianapolis, beginning 1980; consult, New Castle State Hosp, beginning 1963; from instr to assoc prof, Ind Univ, Indianapolis, 1962-1980; NIH fel, Nat Hosp, Queen Sq, London, 1960-1961. **Memberships:** Am Asn Neurol Surg; Cong Neurol Surg. **Mailing Address:** Ind Univ Med Ctr, 702 Barnhill Dr RM 2511, Indianapolis, IN 46202-5210. **Fax:** 317-274-8895.

KALSER, MARTIN, GASTROENTEROLOGY. **Personal Data:** b Pittsburgh, Pa, January 7, 1923. **Education:** Univ Pittsburgh, BS, 1942, MD, 1946; Univ Ill, MS, 1951, PhD (physiol), 1953; Am Bd Internal Med, dipl, 1955; Am Bd Gastroenterol, dipl, 1957. **Professional Experience:** PROF EMER GASTROENTEROL & PHYSIOL, SCH MED, 1963-; mem comn enteric infections, Armed Forces Epidemiol Bd, 1963-1967; CHIEF, DIV GASTROENTEROL, UNIV MIAMI, 1961-; assoc prof, Sch Med, 1959-1963; from instr to assoc prof gastroenterol, Grad Sch Med, Univ Pa, 1954-1956; res fel gastroenterol, Grad Sch Med, Univ Pa, 1954-1955; Grad Hosp, Philadelphia, 1954-1955; Cook County Hosp, Chicago, 1952-1953; Res fel clin sci, Univ Ill, 1950-1953; Vet Admin Clin, Dayton, Ohio & dean's comt, Col Med, Univ Cincinnati, 1950-1952; consult, Montefiore Hosp, Pittsburgh, 1947-1950. **Memberships:** AMA; Am Gastroenterol Asn; Am Col Physicians. **Research**

Statement & Publications: Internal medicine; physiology. **Mailing Address:** Div Gastroenterol, Univ Miami, 12145 SW 69th Pl, Miami, FL 33124. **Fax:** 305-325-9476.

KALSER, SARAH CHINN, PHARMACOLOGY. **Personal Data:** b Connellsville, Pa, June 11, 1929; m 1952. **Education:** Pa State Univ, BS, 1951; Northwestern Univ, MS, 1953; Univ Pittsburgh, PhD (pharmacol), 1961. **Professional Experience:** VOL BLIND & DYSLEXIC, NIH CLIN CTR, 1999-; liver dis prog dir, nat Inst arthritis, diabetes & digestive & kidney dis, nih, beginning 1968; from instr to asst prof, sch med, Univ pittsburgh, 1961-1968; res assoc pharmacol, sch med, Univ pittsburgh, 1958-1960; biochemist, med labs, US army chem ctr, 1953-1958. **Memberships:** AAAS; Am Gastroenterol Asn; Am Asn Study Liver dis; Am Soc Exp Pharmacol & Therapeut. **Research Statement & Publications:** Glutathione synthesis in trauma; atropine metabolism; drug metabolism in hypothermia and in cold acclimatization. **Mailing Address:** NIH Clin Ctr, NIH, Bethesda, MD 20814-2266. **Fax:** 301-402-2984.

KALSNER, STANLEY, PHARMACOLOGY. **Personal Data:** b New York, NY, August 21, 1936. **Education:** NY Univ, BA, 1958; Univ Man, PhD (pharmacol), 1966. **Professional Experience:** PROF, DEPT PHYSIOL & PHARMACOL, CITY UNIV NY, SOPHIE DAVIS SCH BIOMED EDUC, 1985-; chmn physiol, City Univ NY, Sophie Davis Sch Biomed Educ, beginning 1985; Ont Heart Found grant, beginning 1970; Med Res Coun Can grant, beginning 1967; from asst prof to prof pharmacol, Univ Ottawa, 1967-1985; fel pharmacol, Cambridge Univ, 1966-1967; asst pharmacologist, Schering Corp, 1962. **Memberships:** Pharmacol Soc Can; Am Soc Pharmacol & Exp Therapeut. **Research Statement & Publications:** Autonomic and cardiovascular pharmacology and physiology; biogenic amines; supersensitivity of autonomic effectors to drugs and denervation; receptor mechanisms; coronary artery disease; vascular smooth muscle; hypertension. **Mailing Address:** Dept Physiol & Pharmacol, Med Sch City Univ NY, Rm R-4-155 J-905 138th St & Convent Ave, New York, NY 10031. **Fax:** 212-650-7726. **E-Mail:** kalsner@med.cuny.edu

KALSOW, CAROLYN MARIE, OCULAR MICROBIOLOGY & IMMUNOLOGY. **Personal Data:** b Elgin, Ill, July 9, 1943; m Richard; c 5. **Education:** Iowa State Univ, BS, 1965; Univ Tex Med Br, MA, 1967; Univ Louisville, PhD (microbiol), 1970. **Professional Experience:** Vis scientist, C Study Sect, 1992-; RES ASSOC PROF, UNIV ROCHESTER, 1986-; SR SCIENTIST, DEPT OPHTHAL, SCH MED & DENT, UNIV ROCHESTER, 1986-; vis scientist, A Study Sect, 1982-1986; adj assoc prof, Hope Col, 1981-1985; from asst prof to assoc prof, Univ Louisville, 1973-1981; instr, Univ Louisville, 1972-1973; vis asst prof med microbiol, SFla Med Sch, 1972; res assoc ophthal, Univ Louisville, 1971-1972; lectr biol, Univ Louisville, 1970-1972; instr microbiol, Univ Louisville, 1970-1971. **Memberships:** Am Uveitis Soc; Asn Res Vision & Ophthal; Sigma Xi; AAAS; Am Asn Immunol; Int Soc Eye Res; Europ Pineal Soc; Asn Vet Immunol; Int Ocular Soc. **Research Statement & Publications:** Ocular immunology and microbiology. **Mailing Address:** Ophthal Dept, Univ Rochester, Box 314, Rochester, NY 14642. **Fax:** 585-273-1043.

KALT, MARVIN ROBERT, RESEARCH GRANTS & CONTRACTS POLICY. **Personal Data:** b Elizabeth, NJ, August 25, 1945; m 1967, c 1. **Education:** Lafayette Col, AB, 1967; Case Western Res Univ, PhD (anat), 1971. **Professional Experience:** DIR, DIV EXTRAMURAL ACTIV, NAT CANCER INST, NIH, 1994-; MEM, SR EXEC SERV, US AM, 1990-; dept dir, sci rev, 1990-1994; mem rev policy comt, Off Dir, NIH, 1982-1990; chief, sci rev, 1982-1990; referral & training officer, Nat Inst Aging, 1980-1983; exec secy grants & contracts rev, Nat Inst Aging, NIH, 1980-1982; prin investr grant awards, NSF, 1977-1980; asst prof anat, Univ Conn Health Ctr, 1973-1980; prin investr grant awards, USPHS, Nat Inst Child Health Human Develop, 1973-1977; USPHS fel cell & molecular biol, Dept Biol, Yale Univ, 1971-1973. **Memberships:** Am Soc Cell Biol; Sigma Xi. **Research Statement & Publications:** Vertebrate germ cell development; vertebrate morphogenesis; cell biology; gerontology; federal grants and contract review and administration; human subjects and animal welfare policy; national scientific research policy. **Mailing Address:** Nat Cancer Inst Nat Inst Health, Rm 8001 Eight Fl Executive Blvd, Bethesda, MD 20892-8327. **Fax:** 301-402-0956. **E-Mail:** kaltm@dea.nci.nih.gov

KALTENBACH, CARL COLIN, REPRODUCTIVE PHYSIOLOGY. **Personal Data:** b Buffalo, Wyo, March 22, 1939. **Education:** Univ Wyo, BSc, 1961; Univ Nebr, MSc, 1963; Univ Ill, PhD (animal physiol), 1967. **Professional Experience:** VDEAN & DIR, AGR EXP STA, UNIV ARIZ, 1989-; assoc dean & dir, Wyo Agr Exp Sta, 1984; assoc dir res, Col Agr, 1980; actg head, Div Animal Sci, 1978; prof animal physiol, Univ Wyo, 1969-1989; Australian Wool Bd fel, Univ Melbourne, 1967-1969. **Memberships:** AAAS; Am Soc Animal Sci; Soc Study Fertil; Soc Study Reprod; Sigma Xi. **Research Statement & Publications:** Luteotrophic and steroidogenotrophic properties of pituitary hormones; corpus luteum function; radioimmunoassay for protein and steroid hormones; experimental surgery; fetal growth and development. **Mailing Address:** Agr Exp Sta, Univ Ariz, Forbes Bldg Rm 306, Tucson, AZ 85721. **Fax:** 520-621-7196. **E-Mail:** kltnbch@ag.arizona.edu

KALTENBACH-TOWNSEND, JANE, HISTOLOGY, ENDOCRINOLOGY, THYROID HORMONE & AMPHIBIANS. **Personal Data:** b Chicago, Ill, December 21, 1922; m 1966, Robert. **Education:** Beloit Col, BS, 1944; Univ Wis, MA, 1946; Univ Iowa, PhD (zoology), 1950. **Professional Experience:** PROF EMER BIOL, MT HOLYOKE COL, 1993-; chmn dept, Mt Holyoke Col, 1980-1986; prof biol, Mt Holyoke Col, 1970-1993; guest investr, Brown Univ, 1966; guest investr, Oakland Univ, Mich, 1964; guest investr, Fla State Univ, 1960; from asst prof to prof, Mt Holyoke Col, 1958-1970; asst prof zool, Northwestern Univ, 1956-1958; guest investr, Naples Staziona Zool, Italy, 1955; guest investr, Kristinebergs Zool Sta, Swed, 1954-1955; Am Cancer Soc res fel, Wenner-Grens Inst, Univ Stockholm, 1953-1956; res asst & proj assoc path, Univ Wis, 1950-1953; teaching asst & instr, Univ Iowa, 1947-1950; teaching asst zool, Univ Wis, 1944-1947; mem, Corp Marine Biol Lab. **Memberships:** Fel AAAS; Am Asn Anatomists; Am Inst Biol Sci; Soc Integrative & Comparative Biol; Sigma Xi; Soc Exp Biol & Med. **Research Statement & Publications:** Thyroxine and other hormonal controls of amphibian metamorphosis; localization of peptides; hormones and enzymes in various larval and adult organs; (immunohistochemistry); localization of specific sugars in amphibian thyroids and skin (lectin histochemistry). **Mailing Address:** Mt Holyoke Col, Dept Biol Sci, 50 Col St, South Hadley, MA 01075.

KALTENBORN, HOWARD SCHOLL, mathematics; deceased, see previous edition for last biography

KALTENBRONN, JAMES S, ORGANIC CHEMISTRY, MEDICINAL CHEMISTRY. **Personal Data:** b New Baden, Ill, November 21, 1934. **Education:** Univ Ill, BS, 1956; Mass Inst Technol, PhD (org chem), 1960. **Professional Experience:** Res Chemist, Warner-Lambert Co, 1978-2000; Res chemist, Parke, Davis & Co, 1960-1978. **Memberships:** Am Chem Soc. **Research Statement & Publications:** Medicinal chemistry; natural products; stereochemistry.

KALTER, HAROLD, GENETICS, TERATOLOGY. **Personal Data:** b New York, NY, February 26, 1924. **Education:** Sir George Williams Col, BA, 1949; McGill Univ, MSc, 1951, PhD (genetics), 1953. **Professional Experience:** PROF EMER PEDIAT, COL MED, UNIV CINCINNATI, 1994-; ed, Issues & Rev Teratology, 1982-1994; mem, Panel Qual Criteria Water Reuse, Nat Acad Sci, 1979-1981; mem adv comt, Dept Safety Assessment, Merck Inst Therapeut Res, 1975-1980; consult, Comt Biol Effects Atmospheric Pollutants, Nat Res Coun Panel Vapor Phase Organic Air Pollutants from Hydrocarbon, 1971; adv comt, 2, 4, 5-T, Environ Protection Agency, 1971; mem Secy's Comn Pesticides, 1969; ed, Teratol, 1967-1976; mem, Human Embryol & Develop Study Sect, NIH, 1966-1970; from asst prof to prof, Col Med, Univ Cincinnati, 1958-1994; res assoc, Children's Hosp Res Found, 1955-1994; Nat Cancer Inst fel, McGill Univ, 1953-1955. **Memberships:** Teratology Soc. **Research Statement & Publications:** Experimental mammalian teratology. **Mailing Address:** Dept Pediat, Div Develop Biol, Cincinnati Children's Hosp Med Ctr, 3333 Burnet Ave, Cincinnati, OH 45229. **Fax:** 513-559-9669. **E-Mail:** harold.kalter@chmcc.org

KALTER, SEYMOUR SANFORD, VIROLOGY. **Personal Data:** b New York, NY, March 19, 1918. **Education:** St Joseph's Col, Pa, BS, 1940; Univ Kans, MA, 1943; Syracuse Univ, PhD (med bact), 1947; Am Bd Microbiol, dipl. **Professional Experience:** DIR, ESOTERIX INFECTIOUS DIS CTR, SAN ANTONIO, as of 2003; DIR VIRUS REF LAB, DIV MICROBIOL & INFECTIOUS DIS, 1988-; dir, Div Microbiol & Infectious Dis, 1966-1988; dir, Dept Virol & Infectious Dis, Southwest Found Biomed Res, 1964-1988; chmn, Dept Microbiol, 1963-1966; lectr, Med Sch, Baylor Univ, 1961-1963; chief, Virol Sect, US Air Force Sch Aerospace Med, Brooks AFB, Tex, 1961-1963; chief, Virus Diag Methodology Unit, Commun Dis Ctr, USPHS, Ga, 1956-1961; asst prof prev med, Sch Med, Emory Univ, 1956-1960; from instr to assoc prof microbiol, State Univ NY Upstate Med Ctr, 1945-1956; bacteriologist, Syracuse Dept Health, NY, 1945-1956; asst med bact, Sch Med, Univ Pa, 1943-1945; asst instr bact, Univ Kans, 1941-1943; adj prof, Trinity Univ & Univ Tex Health Sci Ctr, San Antonio, adj prof pediat & microbiol; adj prof, Dent Sci Inst, Univ Tex Health Sci Ctr, Houston; consult, Pan Am Sanit Bur; consult, Neurol Inst, Univ Cologne & Off Pesticide Progs, Environ Protection Agency; consult simian & pox viruses, WHO, chmn, comt simian viruses; consult virol, Univ Tex Syst Cancer Ctr, Houston; mem, Fedn US Culture Collections; mem bd dir, Cancer Ther & Res Found, San Antonio. **Memberships:** Fel AAAS; Am Acad Microbiol; Soc Exp Biol & Med; Am Asn Immunol; fel Am Pub Health Asn. **Research Statement & Publications:** Enteroviruses; respiratory viruses; oncogenic viruses; virus diagnosis; simian virology; comparative primate virology; oncogenic viruses; latent viruses. **Mailing Address:** Esoterix Infectious Dis Ctr, 7540 Louis Pasteur, San Antonio, TX 78229-4018. **Fax:** 210-614-7355. **E-Mail:** sy.kalter@esoterix.com

KALTHOFF, KLAUS OTTO, DEVELOPMENTAL BIOLOGY. **Personal Data:** b WGer, February 5, 1941; American citizen; m 1965, Karin; c Christian, Ulrich & Philipp. **Education:** Univ Hamburg, BA, 1964; Univ Freiburg, MA, 1967, PhD (zoology), 1971. **Professional Experience:** PROF BIOL, UNIV TEX, AUSTIN, 1980-; assoc prof, Univ Tex, Austin, 1978-1980; assoc prof, Univ Freiburg, 1976-1977; Asst prof zool, Univ Freiburg, 1971-1976. **Memberships:** Soc Develop Biol; AAAS. **Research Statement & Publications:** Role of localized cytoplasmic determinants in embryogenesis using insect embryos and ultraviolet irradiation, microinjection and molecular techniques; Published over 10 articles. **Mailing Address:** 1 Univ Station A6700, MCBD Biolabs No 311 205 W 24th St, Austin, TX 78712-1095. **Fax:** 512-232-5699. **E-Mail:** kkalthoff@mail.utexas.edu

KALTOFEN, ERICH L, COMPUTER ALGEBRA, ALGORITHM DESIGN & ANALYSIS. **Personal Data:** b Linz, Austria, December 21, 1955. **Education:** Rensselaer Polytech Inst, MS, 1979, PhD (comput sci), 1982. **Professional Experience:** PROF MATH, NC STATE UNIV, 1996-; chmn, Spec Interest Group Symbolic & Algebraic Monipolation, Asn Comput Mach, 1993-1995; prof, Rennselaer Polytech Inst, 1992-1995; vchmn, Spec Interest Group Symbolic & Algebraic Monipolation, Asn Comput Mach, 1987-1989; secy, Spec Interest Group Symbolic & Algebraic Monipolation, Asn Comput Mach, 1985-1987; vis scientist, Tektronix Inc, 1985; res fel, Math Sci Res Inst, 1985; from asst prof to assoc prof, Rennselaer Polytech Inst, 1984-1992; res assoc, Kent State Univ, 1982; Lectr comput sci, Univ Del, 1981-1982. **Memberships:** Asn Comput Mach. **Research Statement & Publications:** polynomial factorization, black box linear algebra, symbolic/numeric hybrid methods. **Mailing Address:** Dept Math, NC State Univ, PO Box 8205 312 Harrelson Hall, Raleigh, NC 27695-8205. **Fax:** 919-515-3798. **E-Mail:** kaltofen@math.ncsu.edu

KALU, DIKE NDUKWE, PHYSIOLOGY. **Personal Data:** b Nigeria, January 3, 1938. **Education:** Univ London, BS, 1967, PhD (biochem), 1971. **Honorary Degrees:** DSc, Univ London, 1998. **Professional Experience:** PROF EMER, DEPT PHYSIOL, TEX HEALTH SCI CTR, as of 2004; prof physiol, Univ Tex Health Sci Ctr, San Antonio, beginning 1980; asst prof, Univ Tex Health Sci Ctr, San Antonio, 1975-1980; fel Sch Med, Johns Hopkins Univ, 1972-1975; sci officer, Royal Postgrad Med Sch, Univ London, 1967-1971. **Memberships:** fel Inst Med Lab Sci UK; AAAS; The Endocrine Soc; Fed Am Soc Exp Biol; NY Acad Sci. **Research Statement & Publications:** Hormonal control of calcium and skeletal metabolism and the effects of aging; Modulation of bone and the calciotropic hormones by aging and diet; Evolution of the pathogenesis of postmenopausal bone loss. **Mailing Address:** Dept Physiol, Univ Tex Health Sci Ctr, 7703 Floyd Curl Dr, San Antonio, TX 78229-3900. **Fax:** 210-567-4410. **E-Mail:** kalu@uthscsa.edu

KALUZIENSKI, LOUIS JOSEPH, X-RAY ASTRONOMY. **Personal Data:** b Union Beach, NJ, July 28, 1948. **Education:** Rutgers Univ, BA, 1970; Univ Md, MS, 1974, PhD (physics), 1977. **Professional Experience:** PROG SCIENTIST, RXTE, NASA HQ, as of 2006; STAFF SCIENTIST HIGH ENERGY ASTROPHYS, NASA HQ, 1978-; res assoc, Goddard Space Flight Ctr, Univ Md, 1977-1978; Grad res asst x-ray astron, Goddard Space Flight Ctr, Univ Md, 1974-1977. **Memberships:** Am Astron Soc. **Research Statement & Publications:** Transient x-ray sources; x-ray binaries. **Mailing Address:** NASA Headquarters, Code SZ, Washington, DC 20546. **Fax:** 202-358-3097. **E-Mail:** louis.kaluzienski@hq.nasa.gov

KALYAN-RAMAN, KRISHNA, NEUROLOGY. **Personal Data:** b Madras, India, June 2, 1935; m. **Education:** Univ Madras, MBBS, 1958, DM, 1971; Univ Delhi, MD, 1962. **Professional Experience:** CLIN PROF NEUROL, UNIV CHICAGO, PRITZKER SCH MED, 1995-; Attend Neurol, Univ Ill Hosps, 1995-1996; dir, Muscular Dystrophy Asn Neuromuscular Clin, Col Med, Univ Ill, Peoria, 1979-; mem staff, St Francis Hosp Med Ctr, Methodist Med Ctr Ill & Proctor Community Hosp, Peoria, 1976-; from assoc prof to prof neurol, Col Med, Univ Ill, Peoria, 1976-1995; vis lectr, Inst Neurol, Govt Gen Hosp, 1975-; consult neurologist, West Seneca Develop Ctr, 1973-; neurologist, Outpatient Serv, Vet Admin Hosp, Buffalo, 1972-; from asst prof to assoc prof neurol, Sch Med, State Univ NY, Buffalo, 1972-1976; Neurologist, E JMeyer Mem Hosp, Buffalo, 1971-; clin asst prof, Sch Med, State Univ NY, Buffalo, 1971-1972; asst prof neurol & hon asst, Inst Neurol, Govt Gen Hosp, Madras, 1969-1971; Asst prof med, Thanjavur Med Col, Madras Univ, 1962-1965. **Memberships:** Neurol Soc India; Am Acad Neurol; fel Am Col Physicians; assoc Am Asn Electromyog & Electrodiag. **Research Statement & Publications:** Nerve and muscle involvement in systemic disorders and effects of upper motor neurone lesions on histochemical pattern of muscle. **Mailing Address:** 110 St Francis Circle, Oak Brook, IL 60521.

KAM, GAR LAI, DIGITAL SIGNAL, SPEECH ANALYSIS. **Personal Data:** b Canton, China, August 1936. **Education:** Nat Taiwan Univ, BSEE, 1961; Univ Tenn, MSEE, 1966. **Professional Experience:** AT AT&T BELL LABS, WHIPPANY, NJ, as of 2002; PRIN ENGR, XYBION CORP, 1980-; eng specialist, Singer-Kearfott Co, 1974-1980; sr engr, Martin-Marietta Aerospace Corp, 1971-1974; engr III, Jet Propulsion Lab, Calif Inst Technol, 1971; mem tech staff, Hughes Aircraft Co, 1969-1971; Sr electronics engr, Lockheed Co, Ga, 1966-1969. **Memberships:** Inst Elec & Electronics Engrs; sr mem Am Inst Aeronaut & Astronaut. **Research Statement & Publications:** Developing models and algorithms of complex aerospace engineering applications and implementing these models and algorithms in comprehensive computer simulations for system performance analyses. **Mailing Address:** 16 Cold Hill Rd, Morris Plains, NJ 07950.

KAM, JAMES TING-KONG, COMPUTER MODELING, OPERATIONS RESEARCH. **Personal Data:** b Hong Kong, July 29, 1945. **Education:** Univ Man, Can, BSc, 1968; Univ Calif, Berkeley, PhD (soil physics & hydrol), 1974. **Professional Experience:** PRIN HYDROLOGIST, MORRISON KNUDSEN, 1985-; hydro environ consult, 1984-1985; staff specialist, consult, hydrol & geol, Davy McKee Davy Inc, 1981-1985; sr engr hydrol, Sci Applns Inc, 1979-1981; hydrologist, Geol Eng, Morrison Knudsen, 1975-1979; res fel, Water Eng, Univ Calif, Davis, 1974-1975. **Memberships:** Am Soc Civil Engrs; Nat Water Well Asn; Environ Assessment Asn. **Research Statement & Publications:** Computer modeling and analyses of hydrologic and geological engineering problems; general civil (hydrologic) engineering design, contaminant transport and fate analysis, risk assessment, environmental assessment and remedial design. **Mailing Address:** 2430 35th Ave, San Francisco, CA 94116.

KAM, MOSHE, DECISION THEORY, NEURAL NETWORKS. **Personal Data:** b Tel Aviv, Israel, October 3, 1955. **Education:** Tel Aviv Univ, BS, 1977; Drexel Univ, MS, 1985, PhD (elec eng), 1987. **Professional Experience:** Assoc ed, Transactions on Systs, Man & Cybernet, Inst Elec & Electronics Engrs, 1992-; assoc ed, Pattern Recognition, 1992-; asst dept head develop, Elec & Comput Eng, beginning 1990; ROBERT G QUINN PROF ELEC & COMPUT ENG, DREXEL UNIV, 1990-; NSF presidential young investr, 1990; vpres, Reshet Inc, 1987-; asst prof, Elec & Comput Eng, 1987-1990; res & develop engr, Israeli Defense Forces, 1976-1983. **Memberships:** Inst Elec & Electronics Engrs; Int Neural Network Soc; Sigma Xi. **Research Statement & Publications:** Synthesis of optimal sensor fusion architectures; design and construction of mobile robots; design of efficient algorithms for multiaccess communications; automatic writer identification for questioned documents. **Mailing Address:** Dept Elec & Comput Eng Drexel Univ, Hess 112B, Philadelphia, PA 19104. **Fax:** 215-895-1695. **E-Mail:** kam@minerva.ece.drexel.edu

KAMACK, H(ARRY) J(OSEPH), CHEMICAL ENGINEERING. **Personal Data:** b Conn, December 5, 1918. **Education:** Ga Inst Technol, BS, 1941; Univ Del, MS, 1956. **Professional Experience:** RETIRED; prin design consult, E I DuPont de Nemours & Co, Inc, 1973-1978; sr design consult, E I DuPont de Nemours & Co, Inc, 1969-1973; process design engr, E I DuPont de Nemours & Co, Inc, 1954-1969; res engr, E I DuPont de Nemours & Co, Inc, 1946-1954; chem engr, E I DuPont de Nemours & Co, Inc, 1942-1946; chem engr, Gen Chem Co, 1941 & Ord Dept, US Army, 1942. **Memberships:** Am Inst Chem Engrs. **Research Statement & Publications:** Chemical plant design; atomic energy design; particle size reduction and measurement. **Mailing Address:** 490 Stamford Dr Apt 304, Newark, DE 19711-2774.

KAMAL, ABDUL NAIM, PARTICLE PHYSICS. **Personal Data:** b Dhaka, Bangladesh, October 28, 1935; div. **Education:** Univ Dhaka, BSc, 1955, MSc, 1956; Univ Liverpool, PhD (theoret physics), 1962. **Professional Experience:** PROF EMER PHYSICS, UNIV ALTA, as of 2006; McCalla prof, Theoret Physics Inst, 1990-1991; actg chmn, Theoret Physics Inst, 1988-1989; vis scientist, Stanford Linear Accelerator Ctr, 1984-1985; chmn physics, Theoret Physics Inst, 1980-1984; dir, Theoret Physics Inst, 1979-1980; vis prof, Stanford Linear Accelerator Ctr, 1979; prof physics, Univ Alta, beginning 1973; vis scientist, Int Ctr Theoret Physics, Trieste, Italy, 1972; vis scientist, Rutherford Lab, UK, 1971 & 1978; sr sci officer, Rutherford Lab, UK, 1968-1969; from asst prof to assoc prof physics, Univ Alta, 1964-1973; fel theoret physics, Univ Liverpool, 1963 & Theoret Physics Inst, Edmonton, Alta, 1963-1964; lectr physics, Univ Dhaka, 1962-1963. **Memberships:** Am Phys Soc; Can Asn Physicists. **Research Statement & Publications:** Theoretical particle physics; weak and strong interactions. **Mailing Address:** Dept Physics, Univ Alta, Edmonton, AB T6G 2J1, Can. **Fax:** 403-492-0714. **E-Mail:** kamal@phys.ualberta.ca

KAMAL, MEDHAT M, GEOLOGY. **Education:** Cairo Univ, BSc; Stanford Univ, PhD (Petrol Eng). **Professional Experience:** RES CONSULT, CHEVRON PETROL TECHNOL CO, as of 2006. **Mailing Address:** Chevron Petrol Technol Co, San Ramon, CA 75024.

KAMAL, MOUNIR MARK, ENGINEERING MECHANICS. **Personal Data:** b Beirut, Lebanon, February 13, 1936. **Education:** Robert Col, Istanbul, BS, 1956; Univ Mich, Ann Arbor, MS, 1958, MS, 1962, PhD (eng), 1965. **Honors & Awards:** Distinguished Serv Award, Am Soc Mech Engrs, Soc Automotive Engrs. **Professional Experience:** EXEC DIR ENG SCI, GEN MOTORS RES LABS, 1988-; tech dir mech & elec eng, Dept Eng Mech, 1982-1987; head, Dept Eng Mech, 1977-1982; asst head dept, Gen Motors Res Labs, 1971-1977; Mem, Univ Mich Indust Comt, 1970-1978; supv res engr, Gen Motors Res Labs, 1968-1971; sr res engr, Gen Motors Res Labs, 1967-1968; Assoc sr res engr, Gen Motors Res Labs, 1965-1967. **Memberships:** Sigma Xi; Soc Automotive Engrs; Am Soc Mech Engrs; Am Acad Mech; fel Soc Mfg Engrs; fel AAAS. **Research Statement & Publications:** Mechanical engineering; internal combustion engines; fluid mechanics and vehicle structural mechanics; vehicle crash dynamics. **Mailing Address:** 421 Otter Creek Dr, Venice, FL 34292.

KAMAL, MUSA RASIM, POLYMER ENGINEERING, MATERIALS SCIENCE ENGINEERING. **Personal Data:** b Tulkarm, Jordan, December 8, 1934; m Nancy; c Rammie & Basim. **Education:** Univ Ill, BS, 1958; Carnegie Inst Technol, MS, 1959, PhD (chem eng), 1962. **Honors & Awards:** Kuwait Prize, Appl Sci & Technol, 1983; Int Educ Award, Soc Plastics Engr, 1984; CanPlast Award, Soc Plastics Indust, Can, 1985, Indust Leader Yr, 1995; Allan Ganville Award, Mat Res Coun, UK, 1999; Cullimore Lect Award, NJ Inst Technol, 2002; Polymer Processing Hall Fame, 2003; Purvis Memorial Award, Soc Chem Indust Can, 2004. **Professional Experience:** PROF EMER, MCGILL UNIV, 2004-; chmn, Dept Chem Eng, McGill Univ, 1983-1993, dir, Brace Res Inst, 1987-1998, dir, McGill Int, 1995; vis prof, Ecole des Mines de Paris, Centre Mise en Form Mat (CEMEF), France, 1995-1996; vis prof, Univ Strasbourg, France, 1995; dir, Microecon & Sectoral Sect, Morocco Indust Develop Plan, Dar Ala-Handasah Consults, 1979; pres, Tulkarm Enterprises Ltd, beginning 1978; vis prof, Am Univ Beirut, 1974-1975; prof, Dept Chem Eng, McGill Univ, 1973-2004; assoc prof, Dept Chem Eng, McGill Univ, 1967-1973; group leader, Wallingford Develop Lab, Am Cyanamid Co, 1965-1967, res chem engr, Stamford Res Labs, Am Cyanamid Co, Conn, 1961-1965; teacher elem sch, Kuwait, 1952-1954; vis Distinguished Harold Morton Prof, Polymer Eng, Univ Akron. **Memberships:** Am Inst Chem Engrs; Am Chem Soc; fel Soc Plastics Engrs; Soc Rheol; NY Acad Sci; Sigma Xi; fel Chem Inst Can; Am Acad Mech; AAAS; fel Royal Soc Can; Can Acad Sci; fel Can Acad Eng; fel Plastics Acad. **Research Statement & Publications:** Polymer engineering; plastics processing; injection molding; film blowing; rheology; heat transfer; non-Newtonian flow; thermoset and thermoplastic processing; weatherability of plastics systems; polymer characterization; microstructure development and control in plastics processing; polymer crystallization and morphology; composites and nanocomposites; computer simulation; project evaluation and planning. **Mailing Address:** Dept Chem Eng, McGill Univ, 3610 Univ St, Wong Bldg, Rm 3060, Montreal, PQ H3A 2B2, Can. **Fax:** 514-398-6678. **E-Mail:** musa.kamal@mcgill.ca

KAMAN, CHARLES HURON, AERONAUTICAL ENGINEERING. **Personal Data:** b Washington, DC, June 15, 1919. **Education:** Cath Univ, BAeroE, 1940. **Honorary Degrees:** DSc, Univ Colo, 1984, Univ Hartford, 1985; LLD, Univ Conn, 1985. **Honors & Awards:** Asn Award, Navy Helicopter Asn, 1975; Dr Alexander Klemin Award, Am Helicopter Soc, 1981; Fleet Adm Chester W Nimitz Award, Navy League US, 1986; Nat President's Award, Naval Res Asn, 1987; Pioneer Award, Asn Unmanned Vehicle Systs, 1993; Nat Medal of Technol, 1996. **Professional Experience:** FOUNDER, CHMN & CHIEF EXEC OFFICER, KAMAN CORP, 1990-; pres & dir, Fidelco Guide Dog Found Coun, 1964; chmn, Helicopter Coun, Aerospace Indust Asn, 1954 & Vertical Lift Aircraft Coun, 1964; pres, Kaman Corp, 1945-1990; aerodyn, Hamilton Stand Div, United Aircraft Corp, 1940-1945; indust comt mem, Greater Hartford YMCA; founder, Univ Hartford; dir, Emhart Corp, Hartford Nat Corp, Conn Nat Bank, Inst Living & Security Conn Ins Co; corporator, Inst Living, Hartford Hosp; bd regents, Cath Univ Am, bd gov; bd dirs, Conn Bus & Indust Asn; adv bd, World Affairs Ctr Honors. **Memberships:** Nat Acad Eng; hon mem Navy Helicopter Asn; hon fel Am Helicopter Soc; fel Am Inst Aeronauts & Astronauts. **Mailing Address:** Kaman Corp, 1332 Blue Hills Ave PO Box 1, Bloomfield, CT 06002.

KAMAN, ROBERT LAWRENCE, BIOCHEMISTRY. **Personal Data:** b New York, NY, June 26, 1941; m 1986, Amy; c Geoffrey, Ken, Jessica & Perry. **Education:** Univ Pa, AB, 1963; Va Polytech Inst, MS, 1967, PhD (biochem), 1969; Texas weslyan univ sch, 1997; J.D. **Honors & Awards:** Nat sci fdn presmem, 2001; TX Wesleyan univ sch of law distinguished almmius of the Yr, 2001. **Professional Experience:** ASSOC PROF HEALTH SCI, TEX COL OSTEOP MED, NTEX STATE UNIV, 1977-; asst prof biochem, Tex Col Osteop Med, NTex State Univ, 1973-1977; res assoc, Sch Pub Health, 1972-1973; NIH fel biochem, Sch Med, Univ Mich, 1969-1972; Asst Dean, Graduate sch of biomed sci UNTHSC-FW. **Memberships:** Am Osteop Acad Sports Med; Am Col Sports Med; Am sn Fitness Dirs; Pres, 1992. **Research Statement & Publications:** Chemotherapy for atherosclerosis; effect of exercise on health and fitness; diet and exercise; exercise programs for firemen; exercise and alcohol rehabilitation; Behavioral chance for smoking cessation. **Mailing Address:** Univ of N Tx Health Sci Ctr, Grad Sch of Biomed Sci, 3500 Camp Boche Blvd, Ft Worth, TX 76107. **Fax:** 817-735-0181. **E-Mail:** kamanr@hse.unt.edu

KAMAT, PRASHANT V, COLLOID & SURFACE SCIENCE, SEMICONDUCTOR NANOCLUSTERS. **Personal Data:** b Binaga, Karnataka, India, July 6, 1953; m 1983, Shobha; c Neha & Neeta. **Education:** Bombay Univ, MS, 1974, PhD (phys chem), 1979. **Honors & Awards:** Award, Japan Soc Promotion Sci, 1996. **Professional Experience:** CONCURRENT PROF, DEPT CHEM & BIOMOLECULAR ENG, UNIV NOTRE DAME, as of 2005; SR SCIENTIST, NOTRE DAME RADIATION LAB, UNIV NOTRE DAME, as of 2005; PROF CHEM & BIOCHEM, NOTRE DAME RADIATION LAB, 1992-; reviewer, Am Chem Soc Pubs, 1983-; PRIN INVEST, NOTRE DAME RADIATION LAB, 1983-; jr scientist, Norte Dame Radiation Lab, 1983; from asst prof specialist to assoc prof specialist, Notre Dame Radiation Lab, 1983-1992; Univ Tex, Austin, 1981-1983; res assoc phys chem, chem dept, Boston Univ, 1979-1981; res asst, catalysis, Hindustan Lever Res Ctr, Bombay, 1977-1979. **Memberships:** Sigma Xi; Am Chem Soc; Soc Electroanal Chem; Electrochem Soc; Interam Photochem Soc. **Research Statement & Publications:** Investigating dynamics of interfacial processes in semiconductor particulate systems; surface photochemistry and heterogeneous photocatalysis; conducting polymers; polymer modified electrodes; excited state behavior of polymers and dyes; electrochemistry and interfacial processes; solar energy conversion; semiconductor, nanoclusters and thin films. **Mailing Address:** Dept Chem & Biochem, Radiation Lab, Univ Notre Dame, Notre Dame, IN 46556-0579. **Fax:** 219-631-8068. **E-Mail:** kamat@marconi.rad.nd.edu

KAMATH, KRISHNA, PETROLEUM ENGINEERING, PHYSICAL CHEMISTRY. **Personal Data:** b Shertallai, India, August 24, 1920. **Education:** Univ Travancore, India, BSc, 1941; Banaras Univ, MSc, 1944; Pa State Univ, MS, 1957, PhD (petrol eng), 1960. **Professional Experience:** Adj assoc prof petrol eng, WVa Univ, Morgantown, 1977-; PETROL ENGR, MORGANTOWN ENERGY TECHNOL CTR, US DEPT ENERGY, 1976-; environ protection engr, Ill Environ Protection Agency, 1974-1976; res engr, Continental Oil Co, Okla, 1966-1968 & IIT Res Inst, 1969-1972; vis assoc prof petrol eng, Stanford Univ, 1963-1966; asst prof petrol technol & chmn dept, Indian Sch Mines & Appl Geol, Dhanbad, 1961-1963; res engr, Gulf Res & Develop Co, 1959-1961; sr sci asst phys chem, Nat Chem Lab India, Poona, 1952-1954; prof chem, Petlad Col, India, 1949-1952; res chemist, Alembic Chem Works, India, 1947-1949; Anal chemist, Govt India, 1944-1946. **Memberships:** AAAS; Am Chem Soc; Soc Petrol Engrs; Am Water Works Asn. **Research Statement & Publications:** Preparative electrochemistry; education; surface and colloid chemistry relating to petroleum recovery and multiphase fluid flow through porous media; enhanced petroleum recovery; surface and colloid chemistry. **Mailing Address:** 105 Concord Cv, Clinton, MS 39056.

KAMATH, SAVITRI KRISHNA, BIOCHEMISTRY, CLINICAL NUTRITION. **Personal Data:** b Kanhangad, India, September 22, 1930. **Education:** Bombay Univ, BS, 1950; Univ Baroda, MS, 1963; Iowa State Univ, PhD (nutrit), 1967. **Professional Experience:** PROF & DEAN EMER, ADMIN, APPLIED HEALTH SCI, UNIV ILL, CHICAGO, as of 2004; prof nutrit, Univ Ill Med Ctr, Chicago, beginning 1981; dept head, Univ Ill Med Ctr, Chicago, beginning 1979; from asst prof to assoc prof, Univ Ill Med Ctr, 1972-1981; res biochemist, Hektoen Med Res Inst, Chicago, 1971-1972; reader nutrit, Univ Baroda, 1967-1969; lectr chem, St Agnes Col, India, 1951-1958. **Memberships:** Am Dietetic Asn; Soc Nutrit Educ; NY Acad Sci; fel Am Col Nutrit; Am Inst Nutrit. **Research Statement & Publications:** Ascorbic acid, lipid metabolism; nutrition and cancer; nutritional assessment of population groups; dietetic education and practice. **Mailing Address:** Dept Nutrit & Med Diet M/C 518, Univ Ill 808 S Wood St Rm 167, Chicago, IL 60612-3742. **Fax:** 312-413-0319. **E-Mail:** kamath@uic.edu

KAMATH, VENKATESH, GAS CHROMATOGRAPHY-MASS SPECTROSCOPY ANALYSIS OF FRAGRANCES & FLAVORS, GAS CHROMATOGRAPHY ANALYSIS OF FRAGRANCES & FLAVORS. **Personal Data:** b Nerlkatte, Karnataka, India, March 28, 1936; American citizen; m 1961, Ajita Nayak; c Arun, Vanita (Braver) & Sangeeta (Tyerech). **Education:** Madras Univ, India, BS, 1957. **Professional Experience:** ANALYTICAL RES DIR, ROBERTET FRAGRANCES, 1991-; tech dir, J Manheimer Inc,

NY, 1985-1987 & Takasago Inc, 1987-1991; sr chemist, Int Flavors & Fragrances, NJ, 1973-1985; asst chemist, Ciba-Geigy Ltd, NY, 1969-1973; technician, Shawinigan Chems, Can, 1967-1969; prod supvr, Union Carbide, India, 1961-1967; prod chemist, Calico Chems, India, 1957-1960. **Memberships:** Am Chem Soc. **Research Statement & Publications:** Analysis of essential oils; granted patents on sandalwood chemicals. **Mailing Address:** 125 Bauer Dr, Oakland, NJ 07436.

KAMATH, YASHAVANTH KATAPADY, PHYSICAL CHEMISTRY, POLYMER CHEMISTRY. **Personal Data:** b Katapady, India, April 15, 1938. **Education:** Univ Bombay, BSc, 1959 & 1961, MSc, 1964; Univ Conn, PhD (phys chem), 1973. **Honors & Awards:** Lit Award, Soc Cosmetic Chemists, 1986. **Professional Experience:** ADJ PROF, PHILADELPHIA UNIV, as of 1999; PRIN SCIENTIST, TEXTILE FINISHING, TEXTILE RES INST, 1987-; sr scientist, Textile Finishing, Textile Res Inst, 1976-1987; staff scientist, Textile Finishing, Textile Res Inst, 1974-1976; fel, Textile Finishing, Textile Res Inst, 1972-1974; assoc lectr plastic technol, Dept Chem Technol, Univ Bombay, 1963-1966. **Memberships:** Am Chem Soc; Fiber Soc. **Research Statement & Publications:** Surface chemical properties of human hair; effect of polymers and surfactants on the surface wettability of human hair; fractography of human hair; compressibility of fiber bundles; environmental fading of dyes in nylon; microspectrophotocetry of dyes in monofilaments; mechanisms of formaldehyde release in durable press fabric; finish distribution in fibers and textiles. **Mailing Address:** Textile Res Inst, PO Box 625 601 Prospect Ave, Princeton, NJ 08542. **Fax:** 609-683-7836. **E-Mail:** ykamath@triprinceton.org

KAMB, WALTER BARCLAY, MINERALOGY, GLACIOLOGY. **Personal Data:** b San Jose, Calif, December 17, 1931. **Education:** Calif Inst Technol, BS, 1952, PhD (geol), 1956. **Honors & Awards:** MSA Award, Mineral Soc Am, 1968; Seligman Award, Int Glaciol Soc, 1977. **Professional Experience:** BARBARA & STANLEY R RAWN JR PROF EMER GEOL & GEOPHYS, CALIF INST TECHNOL, 1999-; Barbara & Stanley R Rawn Jr prof emer Geol & Geophysics, Calif Inst Technol, 1990-1999; vpres & provost, Div Geol & Planetary Sci, 1987-1989; chmn, Div Geol & Planetary Sci, 1972-1983; Sloan fel, 1963; prof geol & geophysics, Calif Inst Technol, 1962-1990; Guggenheim mem found fel, 1960; from asst prof to assoc prof geol, Calif Inst Technol, 1956-1962. **Memberships:** Nat Acad Sci; Geol Soc Am; Am Geophys Union; Mineral Soc Am; Am Asn Petrol Geologists; AAAS; fel Am Acad Arts & Sci. **Research Statement & Publications:** Crystallography; tectonophysics; structural geology and petrology; glaciology; mineralogy and x-ray crystallography; crystal optics. **Mailing Address:** Div Geol & Planetary Sci, Calif Inst Technol, 1201 E Calif Blvd, Pasadena, CA 91125. **Fax:** 626-568-0935. **E-Mail:** barclay@gps.caltech.edu

KAMBAYASHI, TATSUJI, ALGEBRAIC GEOMETRY. **Personal Data:** b Kyoto, Japan, November 8, 1933. **Education:** Univ Tokyo, ScB, 1957; Northwestern Univ, PhD (math), 1962. **Professional Experience:** PROF MATH, TOKYO DENKI UNIV, 1987-; res grant, NSF, 1973-1980; res mem, Res Inst Math Sci, Kyoto Univ, Japan, 1972-1973; from assoc prof to prof math, Northern Ill Univ, 1967-1987; Mem res staff, Res Ctr Physics & Math, Pisa, Italy, 1965-1967; asst prof, Ind Univ, 1964-1967; lectr, Ind Univ, 1963-1964; Instr math, Brown Univ, 1961-1963. **Memberships:** Am Math Soc; Math Soc Japan. **Research Statement & Publications:** Algebraic groups. **Mailing Address:** Math Sci Dept, Tokyo Denki Univ, Hiki-gun Saitama 350-03, Japan. **Fax:** 813-332-20801. **E-Mail:** tac@r.dendai.ac.jp

KAMBOH, M ILYAS, GENETICS OF CARDIOVASCULAR DISEASE, GENETICS OF ALZHEIMER'S DISEASE & GENETICS OF LUPUS. **Personal Data:** b Punjab, Pakistan, November 1, 1956. **Education:** Univ Punjab, BS, 1976, MS, 1979; Australian Nat Univ, PhD (human genetics, 1984. **Honors & Awards:** Omicron Chap of Delta Mega Soc of Pub Health 2000. **Professional Experience:** Associate Editor, Annals of Human Genetics, 2003-present; Acting Chair, Department of Human Genetics, University of Pittsburgh, 2005-present; Chartered memeber on a Study Section, US Natiional Institutes of Health, 2003-present; Mem Univ Pittsburgh Institutional Bd Review 1998-2001; PROF, HUMAN GENETICS, UNIV PITTSBURGH, 1997-; mem, ed bd, Human Biol, 1994; Pittsburgh Cancer Inst, Nutrit Res Sci & Nat Dairy Prom & Res Bd, 1993-1996; Prin investr, Lupus Found Am, 1993-1995; Mem, Ed Bd, Ethnicity & Disease, 1991-1993; assoc prof, Univ Pittsburgh, 1991-1996; Prin investr, NIH, 1991-; Prin investr, Nat Dairy Prom Res Bd, 1990- 1995; asst prof, Univ Pittsburgh, 1987-1991; Res assoc, Univ Pittsburgh, 1985-1986. **Memberships:** AAAS; Am Soc Human Genetics; Human Genetics Soc Australasia; Am Asn Phys Anthrop; Am Heart Asn; Int Electrophoresis Soc; NY Acad Sci. **Research Statement & Publications:** Evaluate the role of genes in determining risk for cardiovascular disease, lups and Alzheimer's disease in the general population; author of 200 publications. **Mailing Address:** Dept human genetics, Univ Pittsburgh, 107 Walkers Ridge, Presto, PA 15142. **Fax:** 412-383-7844. **E-Mail:** ikamboh@hgen.pitt.edu

KAMBOUR, ROGER PEABODY, PHYSICAL CHEMISTRY & POLYMER PHYSICS, POLYMER PHYSICS & POLYMER PHYSICAL CHEMISTRY. **Personal Data:** b Wilmington, Mass, April 1, 1932; m 1984, Barbara; c Annaliese S, Christian R & Joshua V. **Education:** Amherst Col, BA, 1954; Univ NH, PhD (chem), 1960. **Honors & Awards:** Union Carbide Chem Award, Am Chem Soc, 1968; Ford High Polymer Physics Prize, Am Phys Soc, 1985. **Professional Experience:** RETIRED; cumirp res prof, Polymer Sci & Eng Dept, Univ Mass, Amherst, 1994-1999; mgr polymer studies unit, Gen Elec Res & Develop Ctr, 1970-1974; res assoc, Gen Elec Res & Develop Ctr, 1960-1970, 1975-1994. **Memberships:** Nat Acad Eng; fel Am Phys Soc; Am Chem Soc. **Research Statement & Publications:** Diffusion of gases and vapors in polymers; polymer crazing andfracture; properties of block polymers; crystallization; polymer flame retardance; polymer blend thermodynamics; mobility and toughness in plasticized resins; properties of reactive cyclic oligomers and resultant polymers. **Mailing Address:** 2572 Rosendale Rd, Schenectady, NY 12309.

KAMBYSELLIS, MICHAEL PANAGIOTIS, DEVELOPMENTAL GENETICS. **Personal Data:** b Antissa, Greece, March 1, 1935. **Education:** Nat Univ Athens, BSc, 1960; Yale Univ, MS, 1965; Univ Tex, PhD (zoology), 1967. **Professional Experience:** PROF BIOL, NY UNIV, 1980-; vis prof, Athens Univ, Greece, 1974-1975; assoc prof develop biol, NY Univ, 1973-1980; asst prof, NY Univ, 1971-1973; lectr biol, Harvard Univ, 1971; res fel insect physiol, Harvard Univ, 1968-1970; res assoc, Univ Tex, 1967-1968; res asst genetics, Univ Tex, 1965-1967. **Memberships:** AAAS; Genetics Soc Am; Am Inst Biol Sci; NY Acad Sci; Soc Develop Biol. **Research Statement & Publications:** Physiological genetics; Drosophila genetics and evolution; insect tissue transplantations; Drosophila ovarian development; insect tissue cultures; hormonal control of insect reproduction. **Mailing Address:** Dept Biol, NY Univ Brown, 29 Wash Pl 957, New York, NY 10003-6688. **Fax:** 212-998-4015. **E-Mail:** mk2@is2.nyu.edu

KAMEGAI, MINAO, COMPUTATIONAL PHYSICS. **Personal Data:** b Koshu, Korea, July 7, 1932. **Education:** Univ Hawaii, BA, 1957; Univ Chicago, MS, 1960, PhD (physics), 1963. **Professional Experience:** SCIENTIST, LAWRENCE LIVERMORE LAB, as of 1999; CONSULT, LAWRENCE LIVERMORE LAB, 1993-; sr physicist, Lawrence Livermore Lab, 1966-1993; physicist, Knolls Atomic Power Lab, Gen Elec Co, 1963-1966; Res assoc nuclear physics, Enrico Fermi Inst, Univ Chicago, 1963; consult, Kamegai & Assocs; vis scientist, Nat Chem Lab, Tsukuba Res Ctr, Tsukuba City, Ibaraki, Japan. **Memberships:** Am Phys Soc; Sigma Xi. **Research Statement & Publications:** Theoretical and computational physics; materials science, hydrodynamics and laser optics; computer modeling in shock hydrodynamics. **Mailing Address:** Lawrence Livermore Nat Lab, 7000 E Ave, Livermore, CA 94550-9234. **Fax:** 925-455-5247.

KAMEGO, ALBERT AMIL, PHYSICAL ORGANIC CHEMISTRY. **Personal Data:** b Detroit, Mich, June 11, 1941. **Education:** Wayne State Univ, BS, 1964; Calif State Univ, Long Beach, MS, 1968; Univ Calif, Santa Barbara, PhD (chem), 1974. **Professional Experience:** LORAL VOUGHT SYSTS, CORE LABS, INC, 1985-; sr eng specialist, Core Labs, Inc, 1977-1994; instr chem, Univ Tex, Arlington, 1976-1977; lectr chem, Univ Mont, 1975-1976; fel chem, State Univ NY Buffalo, 1973-1975; from teaching asst chem to staff res assoc, Univ Calif, Santa Barbara, 1968-1973; Chemist paints, Ford Motor Co, 1965-1967. **Memberships:** Am Chem Soc. **Mailing Address:** 832 Spring Brook Dr, Bedford, TX 76021-4304.

KAMEL, HUSSEIN, COMPUTER SCIENCE. **Education:** Cairo Univ, BSc, 1955; Imperial Col Sci & Technol, PhD (Aircraft Struct), 1964. **Professional Experience:** PROF EMER, DEPT AEROSPACE & MECH ENG, UNIV ARIZ, as of 2006. **Mailing Address:** Univ Ariz, AME Bldg 16 Rm 204, Tucson, AZ 85721. **Fax:** 520-621-8191. **E-Mail:** kamel@ame.arizona.edu

KAMEL, MOSTAFA M, MECHANICAL ENGINEERING. **Professional Experience:** DIR, PROD DEVELOP, CUMMINS ENGINE CO, as of 2004. **Memberships:** Inst Elec & Electronic Engrs. **Mailing Address:** Cummins Engine Co, Box 3005, Columbus, IN 47202-3005. **Fax:** 812-342-2009. **E-Mail:** mostafa.m.kamel@Cummins.com

KAMEMOTO, FRED ISAMU, ZOOLOGY, COMPARATIVE ENDOCRINOLOGY. **Personal Data:** b Honolulu, Hawaii, March 8, 1928; m 1963, Alice T Asayama; c Kenneth, Garett & Janice. **Education:** George Washington Univ, AB, 1950, MS, 1951; Purdue Univ, PhD (zool), 1954. **Professional Experience:** PROF EMER ZOOL, UNIV HAWAII, 1995-; vis foreign researcher, Trop Biosphere Res Ctr, Univ Ryukyus, Japan, 1994; vis sr scientist, Dept Fisheries, Nihon Univ, Tokyo, 1986; vis scholar, Dept Biol, Wesleyan Univ, Middletown, Conn, 1975-1976; vis res scholar, Ocean Res Inst, Univ Tokyo, 1968-1969; from asst prof to prof, Univ Hawaii, 1962-1994; asst prof zool, Univ Mo, 1959-1962; res assoc, Wash State Col, 1957-1959. **Memberships:** AAAS; Am Soc Zoologists; Sigma Xi; Zool Soc Japan. **Research Statement & Publications:** Neurosecretion and osmoregulation; crustacean biology. **Mailing Address:** Dept Zool, Univ Hawaii, 2538 The Mall, Honolulu, HI 96822. **Fax:** 808-956-9812.

KAMEMOTO, HARUYUKI, HORTICULTURE. **Personal Data:** b Honolulu, Hawaii, January 18, 1922. **Education:** Univ Hawaii, BS, 1944, MS, 1947; Cornell Univ, PhD, 1950. **Honors & Awards:** Gold Medal, Malayan Orchid Soc, 1963; Norman Jay Colman Award, 1977; Orchid Soc Thailand Medal of Honor, 1978; Alex Laurie Award, 1982; Childers Award, 1984; Gold Medal, Am Orchid Soc, 1989. **Professional Experience:** PROF EMER HORT, UNIV HAWAII, as of 2002; consult, Food & Agr Orgn, UN, 1971, 1980; prof hort & chmn dept, Univ Hawaii, 1969-1975; fulbright award, 1956-1957; from asst horticulturist to horticulturist, Univ Hawaii, 1950-1986. **Memberships:** Fel AAAS; fel Am Soc Hort Sci; fel Am Orchid Soc; Int Aroid Soc; Am Genetic Asn; Bot Soc Am. **Research Statement & Publications:** Cytogenetics and breeding of tropical ornamentals. **Mailing Address:** Dept Hort, Univ Hawaii, Honolulu, HI 96822.

KAMEN, DEAN, ELECTROMECHANICAL ENGINEERING. **Personal Data:** b April 1951. **Honorary Degrees:** DSc, Worcester Polytech Inst, 1992, NH Col, 1997. **Honors & Awards:** Hoover Medal, Am Soc Mech Engrs, 1995; John W Hyatt Award, Soc Plastics Engrs, 1996. **Professional Experience:** PRES & FOUNDER, DEKA RES & DEVELOP CORP, as of 2003; founder, US First, 1989; founder, Inspiration & Recognition Sci & Technol, 1989; owner & chmn, Enstrom Helicopter Corp, 1985-1990; founder, Sci Enrichment Encounters, 1985; founder, Auto Syringe Inc, 1976; chmn, Teletrol Energy Syst Inc. **Memberships:** Nat Acad Eng; fel Am Inst Med & Biol Engrs. **Research Statement & Publications:** Inventing and commercializing biomedical devices and fluid measurement and control systems; popularizing engineering among young people; holds more than 30 patents. **Mailing Address:** Deka Res & Develop, Ste 401 340 Com St, Manchester, NH 03101-1121. **Fax:** 603-624-0573. **E-Mail:** contactdeka@dekaresearch.com

KAMEN, EDWARD WALTER, ENGINEERING, MATHEMATICS. **Personal Data:** b Mansfield, Ohio, October 2, 1945. **Education:** Ga Inst Technol, BEE, 1967; Stanford Univ, MS, 1969, PhD (elec eng), 1971. **Professional Experience:** PROF EMER ELEC & COMPUT ENG, GA INST TECHNOL, as of 2006; CHAIRED PROF, CTR BD ASSEMPLY RES, GA INST TECNOL, as of 2006; DIR, CTR BD ASSEMBLY RES, GA INST TECHNOL, as of 2001; prof & chair elec eng, Univ Pittsburgh, 1986-1990; prof elec eng, Univ Fla, Gainesville, 1980-1986; assoc prof elec eng, Ga Inst Technol, 1976-1980; res specialist, Inst Res Info & Automatic Control, France, 1972-; NSF res initiation grant, Ga Inst Technol, 1972-1974; asst prof, GA Inst Technol, 1971-1976; engr, Argo Systs Inc, Calif, 1970-1971. **Memberships:** AAAS; Inst Elec & Electronics Engrs. **Research Statement & Publications:** Mathematical system theory; network theory; receiver systems. **Mailing Address:** Dept Elec Eng, Ga Inst Technol, Atlanta, GA 30332. **Fax:** 404-385-1436. **E-Mail:** ed.kamen@ee.gatech.edu

KAMEN, GARY P, MOTOR CONTROL, NEUROMUSCULAR PHYSIOLOGY. **Education:** Univ Mass, PhD (exercise sci), 1979. **Professional Experience:** PROF, DEPT EXERCISE SCI, UNIV MASS, as of 2002; ASSOC PROF, BOSTON UNIV, 1988-; Assoc prof, Ind Univ. **Memberships:** Soc Neuroscience; Sigma Xi; Am Physiol Soc; AAAS; fel Am Col Sports Med; Int Soc Biomech. **Research Statement & Publications:** Neuromuscular physiology and motor control with applications in gerontology, sports medicine and rehabilitation medicine; consulting in sports medicine; exercise science. **Mailing Address:** Dept Exercise Sci, Mass Univ, Amherst, MA 01003. **Fax:** 413-545-2906. **E-Mail:** kamen@excsci.umass.edu

KAMEN-KAYE, MAURICE, GLOBAL PALEOGEOGRAPHY. **Personal Data:** b London, Eng, August 17, 1905. **Education:** Royal Col Sci, London, BSc, ARES, 1926; Royal Sch Mines, London, ARSM(petrol geol), 1929. **Professional Experience:** CONSULT GEOLOGIST, 1968-; explor res geologist, Conorada Petrol Corp, NY, 1965-1967; explor res geologist, Amerada Petrol Corp, Tulsa, 1965-1967; chief geologist, Sedimentary Sect, Province Sask, Can, 1954; consult geologist, US & Canada, 1950-1953; chief geologist, Caracas Petrol Corp, Venezuela, 1940-1950; Explor geologist, Caracas Petrol Corp, Venezuela, 1930-1940. **Memberships:** Fel Geol Soc Am; Am Asn Petrol Geologists; Soc Explor Geophys. **Research Statement & Publications:** Architecture & petroleum productivity of sedimentary basins; global paleogeography; petroleum geology of African borderlands of the Indian Ocean. **Mailing Address:** 399 River Rd, Andover, MA 01810.

KAMENTSKY, LOUIS A, BIOPHYSICS, CELL BIOLOGY. **Personal Data:** b Newark, NJ, July 28, 1930; m 1955, Marcia; c Lee, Howard & Ellen. **Education:** Newark Col Eng, BS, 1952; Cornell Univ, PhD (eng physics), 1956. **Honorary Degrees:** Dr, NJ Inst Tech, 1992. **Professional Experience:** FOUNDER, CHMN & CHIEF SCIENTIST, COMPUCYTE CORP, 1992-; pres, CompuCyte Corp, 1988-1992; dir, Cambridge Res Lab, 1983-1988; vpres res, Ortho Diagnostics Systs, 1980-1988; sr res scientist, Res Lab Electronics, Mass Inst Technol, 1980-1988; vpres res & develop, Ortho Instruments, 1976-1980; consult, Dept Path, Mem Hosp for Cancer, NY, 1973-1993; adj assoc prof, Dept Path, Med Ctr, NY Univ, 1969-1973; pres, Biophysics Systs, Inc, 1968-1976; vis scientist, Karolinska Inst, 1966; mem staff, Bell Tel Labs, Inc, 1956-1960 & Watson Lab, IBM Corp, 1960-1968; mem staff, Electronics Res Lab, Columbia Univ, 1954-1955; physicist, Res Lab, US Steel Corp, 1953; res asst eng physics, Cornell Univ, 1952-1954; res asst physics, Brookhaven Nat Lab, 1951. **Memberships:** AAAS; Inst Elec & Electronics Engrs. **Research Statement & Publications:** Information and computer theories; solid state physics; optics; pattern recognition; medical instrumentation; research administration; analytic cytometry. **Mailing Address:** CompuCyte Corp, 12 Emily St, Boston, MA 02116. **Fax:** 617-492-1301. **E-Mail:** lakam@bellatlantic.net

KAMEROW, DOUGLAS B, CLINICAL DISEASE PREVENTION. **Education:** Harvard Col, AB; Univ Rochester, MD; Johns Hopkins Univ Sch, MPH (Epidemiol). **Professional Experience:** CHIEF SCIENTIST, RTI INT, WASH, 2001-. **Mailing Address:** RTI Int, 1615 M St NW Suite 740, Washington, DC 20036-3209. **Fax:** 202-728-2095. **E-Mail:** dkamerow@rti.org

KAMIEN, C ZELMAN, MECHANICAL ENGINEERING. **Personal Data:** b Bialystock, Poland, February 24, 1927. **Education:** Purdue Univ, BS, 1955, MSEng, 1956, PhD (eng), 1960. **Professional Experience:** PROF EMER & CHMN, MECH ENG DEPT, UNIV MASS, LOWELL, 1981-; assoc prof mech eng, Lowell Technol Inst, 1966-1981; proj mgr thermionics, Thermo Electron Eng Corp, 1963-1966; sr scientist, Res & Adv Develop Div, Avco Corp, 1960-1963; instr mech eng, Purdue Univ, 1958-1960. **Memberships:** AAAS; Am Soc Mech Engrs; Am Soc Eng Educ; Sigma Xi. **Research Statement & Publications:** Effect of pressure and temperature on viscosity of refrigerants; effect of rain intensity on prevention of icing on transmission cables; solar thermionic power systems development. **Mailing Address:** 29 Arbutus Ave, Chelmsford, MA 01824.

KAMIEN, ETHEL N, PLANT PHYSIOLOGY, HUMAN SEXUALITY. **Personal Data:** b New York, NY, July 1, 1930. **Education:** Brooklyn Col, BA, 1950; Univ Wis, MS, 1952, PhD (bot), 1954. **Professional Experience:** PROF EMER BIOL, UNIV LOWELL-NORTH CAMPUS, 1966-; Coop teacher, Ed Serv, Inc, 1965-; chmn dept biol & phys sci, Univ Lowell-north Campus, 1965-1975; from instr to assoc prof biol, Univ Lowell-north Campus, 1960-1966; instr hort, Purdue Univ, 1954-1958; asst bot, Univ Wis, 1950-1954; mem, US Sex Info & Educ Coun. **Memberships:** Am Soc Plant Physiol; Am Inst Biol Sci; Am Asn Sex Educrs Counrs & Therapists; Sigma Xi; AAAS. **Research Statement & Publications:** Chemical control of plant growth; plant tissue culture. **Mailing Address:** 29 Arbutus Ave, Chelmsford, MA 01824.

KAMIENSKI, CONRAD WILLIAM, ORGANIC CHEMISTRY. **Professional Experience:** CONSULT, GASTONIA, LITHIUM CORP, as of 1999. **Memberships:** Am Chem Soc. **Mailing Address:** FMC Lithium Corp, Box 795, Bessemer City, NC 28016. **Fax:** 704-868-5486.

KAMIL, ALAN CURTIS, ANIMAL BEHAVIOR, BEHAVIORAL ECOLOGY. **Personal Data:** b Bronx, NY, November 20, 1941. **Education:** Hofstra Univ, BA, 1963; Univ Wis-Madison, MS, 1966, PhD (psychol), 1967. **Professional Experience:** PROF BIOL & PSYCHOL, SCH BIOL SCI, UNIV NEBR, 1992-; prof psychol & zool, Univ Mass, Amherst, 1979-1992; prin investr grants, NSF, 1971- & NIH, 1978-1979 & 1988-; vis assoc prof psychol, Univ Calif, Berkeley, 1976-1977; from asst prof to assoc prof, Univ Mass, Amherst, 1967-1979. **Memberships:** Animal Behav Soc; Ecol Soc Am; Am Ornithologists Union; fel Am Psychol Asn. **Research Statement & Publications:** Mechanisms of foraging behavior. **Mailing Address:** Dept Biol, univ Nebr, Lincoln, NE 68502. **E-Mail:** akamil@unlserve.unl.edu

KAMILLI, DIANA CHAPMAN, ARCHAEOMETRY, PETROLOGY. **Personal Data:** b New York, NY, September 5, 1941; m 1969, c 2. **Education:** Vassar Col, BA, 1963; Rutgers Univ, MS, 1966, PhD (igneous petrol, metamorphic petrol), 1968. **Professional Experience:** INDEPENDENT CONSULT GEOL, ARCHEOL GEOL & MAT ANAL, 1983-; res assoc archaeol mat anal, Univ Colo Mus, 1977-1983; consult, Amax Molybdenum Co, 1976-1977 & 1979-1980; res assoc archeol mat anal, Mass Inst Technol & res fel archeol mat anal, Harvard Univ Peabody Mus, 1975-1977; NSF res grant, 1975; consult, Sardis Expedition, Harvard Univ, 1974-1976; Fisher fel fund & fac grants, Wellesley Col, 1971-1972; NSF grant, Colo Plateau, 1971; asst prof geol, Wellesley Col, 1969-1975; chmn dept geol, Wellesley Col, 1969-1974; asst prof mineral, City Col New York, 1968-1969; instr geol, Vassar Col, 1968. **Memberships:** Soc Am Archaeol; Geol Soc Am; Mineral Soc Am. **Research Statement & Publications:** Petrology and geochemistry of granitic and metagranitic rocks, New Jersey, Ontario and Colorado; mineralogic and chemical analysis of ancient mesopotamian, North and Central American ceramics; geochemistry and correlation of Ubaid, Samarran and Halaf ceramics, Mesopotamia. **Mailing Address:** 5050 N Siesta Dr, Tucson, AZ 85750.

KAMILLI, ROBERT JOSEPH, ECONOMIC GEOLOGY, GEOCHEMISTRY. **Personal Data:** b Philadelphia, Pa, June 14, 1947. **Education:** Rutgers Univ, BA, 1969; Harvard Univ, AM, 1971, PhD (geol), 1976. **Professional Experience:** ADJ PROF, GEOSCIENCE DEPT, UNIV ARIZ, as of 2006; CO-DIR, UNIV ARIZ CTR MINERAL RESOURCES, as of 2006; SCIENTIST-IN-CHARGE, SOUTHWEST FIELD OFF, US GEOL SURV, TUCSON, ARIZ, 1996-; secy, Soc Econ Geologists, Int Exchange Lectr Comt, beginning 1994; counr, Ariz Geol Soc, beginning 1994; res geologist, US Geol Surv Mission, Jeddah, Saudi Arabia, 1989-1996; mission chief geologist, US Geol Surv Mission, Jeddah, Saudi Arabia, 1987-1989; geologist, US Geol Surv Mission, Jeddah, Saudi Arabia, 1983-1987; adj prof, Univ Colo, Boulder, 1981-1983; proj geologist, AMAX Inc, 1980-1983; asst resident geologist, AMAX Inc, 1979-1980; geologist, AMAX Inc, 1976-1979; consult, Buenaventura Mines, 1975-1976; consult geologist, Huampar Mines, 1973-1976. **Memberships:** Fel Geol Soc Am; AAAS; fel Soc Econ Geologists; Soc Mining Engrs. **Research Statement & Publications:** Investigation of the origin of vein and intrusion-related metal deposits, especially molybdenum, tin, tungsten, gold and silver; emphasis on the geochemistry of such ore deposits. **Mailing Address:** 5050 N Siesta Dr, Tucson, AZ 85750-9652. **Fax:** 520-670-5571. **E-Mail:** bkamilli@strider.swfo.arizona.edu

KAMINER, BENJAMIN, physiology; deceased, see previous edition for last biography

KAMINETZKY, HAROLD ALEXANDER, OBSTETRICS & GYNECOLOGY. **Personal Data:** b Chicago, Ill, September 6, 1923. **Education:** Univ Ill, BS, 1948, MD, 1950; Am Bd Obstet & Gynec, dipl. **Professional Experience:** RETIRED; dir, Pract Activ, Am Col Obstet & Gynec, 1985-1994; pres, Tenth World Cong Obstet & Gynecol, 1982; pres, Am Col Obstet & Gynecologists, 1978; ed, Int J Gynaecology & Obstet, 1978; from actg dean to dean, chmn Dept Col Med & Dent NJ, Newark, 1972-1974; prog dir, Greater Newark Family Planning Prog, 1970-1981; prof obstet & Gynec & chmn dept, Col Med & Dent NJ, Newark, 1968-1985; from instr to prof, Col Med, Univ Ill, 1954-1968; mem cancer adv comt, Chicago Bd Health. **Memberships:** AMA; Am Col Obstet & Gynec; Am Col Surg; Sigma Xi; Am Gynecologists & Obstetricians Soc. **Research Statement & Publications:** Experimental dysplasia and carcinogenesis of the uterine cervix; maternal nutrition; vitamin profiles of mothers and newborns at partuition; nutrition during pregnancy. **Mailing Address:** Am Col Obstetricians & Gynecologists, 409 12th St SW, Washington, DC 20024.

KAMINKER, JEROME ALVIN, TOPOLOGY, MATHEMATICAL ANALYSIS. **Personal Data:** b Chicago, Ill, May 10, 1941. **Education:** Univ Calif, Berkeley, BA, 1963; Univ Calif, Los Angeles, MA, 1965, PhD (math), 1968. **Professional Experience:** PROF EMER, IND UNIV-PURDUE UNIV, as of 2006; mem, Math Sci Res Inst, 1984-1985; vis prof, Univ Calif, Los Angeles, 1983; prof math, ind Univ-purdue Univ, beginning 1979; from asst prof to assoc prof, Ind Univ-purdue Univ, 1973-1979; asst prof math, Ind Univ, Bloomington, 1968-1973. **Memberships:** Am Math Soc; Sigma Xi. **Research Statement & Publications:** Development of relations between algebraic topology and functional analysis; application of K-theory to the theory of linear operators on Hilbert space. **Mailing Address:** Dept Math Sci, Ind Univ-Purdue Univ, Ld224g, Indianapolis, IN 46202-3216. **E-Mail:** kaminker@math.iupui.edu

KAMINOW, IVAN PAUL, FIBER OPTICS, SEMICONDUCTOR LASERS. **Personal Data:** b Union City, NJ, March 3, 1930. **Education:** Union Univ NY, BS, 1952; Univ Calif, Los Angeles, MS, 1954; Harvard Univ, AM, 1957, PhD (appl physics), 1960. **Honors & Awards:** Quantum Electronics Award, Inst Elec & Electronics Engrs, 1983; Charles Hard Townes Award, Am Optical Soc, 1995, Tyndall Award, 1997. **Professional Experience:** Vis prof, Univ Tokyo, 1990; adj prof, Columbia Univ, 1986; DEPT HEAD, AT&T BELL LABS, INC, 1984-; mem, Ctr for Electronics & Elec Eng, 1984-1987; assoc ed, J Quantum Electronics, 1977-1983; & Univ Calif, Berkeley, 1977; mem, Eval Panel, Optical Physics Div, Nat Acad Sci-Nat Bur Stand, 1972-1975; Vis lectr, Princeton Univ, 1968; mem tech staff, Bell Labs, Inc, 1954-1984; Mem tech staff, Hughes Aircraft Co, 1952-1954. **Memberships:** Nat Acad Eng; fel Am Phys Soc; fel Optical Soc Am; fel Inst Elec & Electronics Engrs; Am Bd Laser Surg. **Research Statement & Publications:** Microwave antennas; ferrites; high pressure physics; ferroelectrics; optical lasers and communication techniques; light modulation; Raman scattering; photopolymers; integrated optics; optical fibers; semiconductor lasers; photonic networks. **Mailing Address:** Lucent Technol/Bell Labs, 791 Holmdel Rd, Holmdel, NJ 07733. **Fax:** 732-888-7007. **E-Mail:** ipk@hoh.1.att.com

KAMINS, THEODORE I, SOLID-STATE ELECTRONICS, SILICON INTEGRATED CIRCUITS. **Personal Data:** b San Francisco, Calif, November 11, 1941. **Education:** Univ Calif, Berkeley, BS, 1963, MS, 1964, PhD (elec eng), 1968. **Honors & Awards:** Electronics Div Award, Electrochem Soc, 1989. **Professional Experience:** PRIN SCIENTIST, HEWLETT-PACKARD LAB, as of 2004; DEPT SCIENTIST, HEWLETT-PACKARD LAB, 1995-; consult prof, Dept Elec Eng, 1990-; vis scholar, Ctr Integrated Systs, Stanford Univ, 1986-1987; proj leader elec eng, Hewlett-packard Lab, 1981-1995; consult, Stanford Electronic Lab, Stanford Univ, 1975-1982; mem tech staff, Hewlett-packard Lab, 1974-1981; vis lectr, Dept Elec Eng, Stanford Univ, 1974; mem res staff, Fairchild Semiconductor, 1969-1974; act asst prof elec eng, Univ Calif, Berkeley, 1968-1969. **Memberships:** Fel Inst Elec & Electronics Engrs; fel Electrochem Soc. **Research Statement & Publications:** Research and development of materials and devices for silicon integrated circuits; especially, polycrystalline silicon, silicon-on-insulator, photodiode arrays, epitaxial techniques, silicon-germanium devices; author of books on device electronics and polycrystalline silicon. **Mailing Address:** Quantum Structures Res Initiative Dep, Hewlett-Packard Co, PO Box 10350, Palo Alto, CA 94303-0867.

KAMINSKAS, EDVARDAS, PHARMOCOLOGY, MOLECULAR BIOLOGY. **Personal Data:** b Kaunas, Lithuania, September 12, 1935. **Education:** Seton Hall Univ, NJ, AB, 1955; Sch Med, Yale Univ, MD, 1959. **Professional Experience:** MED OFFICER, DIV DRUG ONCOL PRODUCTS, FOOF & DRUG ADMIN, as of 2005; assoc prof med, Harvard Med Sch, Beth Israel Hosp, 1981-; PHYSICIAN-IN-CHIEF, HEBREW REHAB CTR AGED, 1981-; from assoc prof to prof, Univ Wis, Mt Sinai Med Ctr, 1974-1981; from instr to asst prof med, Harvard Med Sch, Beth Israel Hosp, 1968-1974; res fel, Mass Inst Technol, 1965-1968; chief med, US Air Force Hosp, 1963-1965; resident med, Vet Admin Res Hosp, Chicago, Ill, 1961-1963; intern & fel hemat, Michael Reese Hosp, Chicago, Ill, 1961-1963. **Memberships:** Am Soc Biol Chemists; Am Asn Cancer Res; Am Fedn Clin Res; Geront Soc Am; Am Geriat Soc; AAAS. **Research Statement & Publications:** Regulation of tumor cell growth; effects of anti-neoplastic agents on tumor cells; molecular biology of Alzheimer's disease cells. **Mailing Address:** Hebrew Rehabil Ctr Aged Harvard Univ, 1200 Ctr St, Boston, MA 02131-1011. **Fax:** 617-325-8069.

KAMINSKI, DONALD LEON, SURGERY. **Personal Data:** b Elba, Nebr, November 9, 1940. **Education:** Creighton Univ, BS, 1962, MD, 1966. **Professional Experience:** DIR GEN SURG, ST LOUIS HEALTH SCI CTR, as of 2004; DIV DIR, GEN SURG, ST LOUIS HEALTH SCI CTR, as of 2000; PROF SURG, ST LOUIS UNIV, 1980-; assoc prof, St Louis Univ, 1975-1980; asst prof, St Louis Univ, 1971-1975. **Memberships:** Am Physiol Soc; Am Gastroenterol Soc; Soc Univ Surgeons; Asn Acad Surg; Am Col Surgeons. **Research Statement & Publications:** Gastrointestinal physiology, studying the hormonal control of hepatic bile flow. **Mailing Address:** Dept Surg, St Louis Univ Med Ctr, PO Box 15250, 3635 Vista Grand Blvd, St Louis, MO 63110-0250. **Fax:** 573-771-1945. **E-Mail:** kaminsdl@slu.edu

KAMINSKI, EDWARD JOZEF, CHEMISTRY. **Personal Data:** b Torun, Poland, March 24, 1926. **Education:** Northwestern Univ, PhB, 1960, PhD (chem), 1964, Am Bd Toxicol, dipl. **Professional Experience:** PROF EMER, NORTHWESTERN UNIVERSITY, as of 2000; prof path, dent & med sch, Northwestern Univ, beginning 1979; assoc prof, Dent Sch, Northwestern Univ, 1971-1979; asst prof, Dent Sch, Northwestern Univ, 1967-1971; Consult toxicology, 1964-; res assoc path, Dent Sch, Northwestern Univ, 1964-1967; res technologist, Dent Sch, Northwestern Univ, 1956-1960; res asst path, Mt Sinai Hosp, Toronto, Can, 1953-1956; Res technologist, Royal Cancer Hosp, London, Eng, 1951-1953. **Memberships:** Soc Toxicol; Am Chem Soc; Inst Biomed Sci; AAAS. **Research Statement & Publications:** Toxicology of materials used in the human body and the nature of the foreign body reaction; study on the mechanism of absorption of substances from the environment. **Mailing Address:** Dept Path, Dent & Med Sch, Northwestern Univ, Chicago, IL 60611-3010.

KAMINSKI, JAMES JOSEPH, MEDICINAL & THEORETICAL CHEMISTRY. **Personal Data:** b Buffalo, NY, June 5, 1947. **Education:** State Univ NY Col Fredonia, BS, 1969; Univ NH, PhD (org chem), 1972. **Professional Experience:** SR PRIN SCIENTIST, SCHERING PLOUGH CORP, 1992-; chair-elect, Med & Natural Prod Chem, Am Asn Pharmaceut Scientists, 1991; sect leader, Schering Corp, 1980-1991; res chemist, Schering Corp, 1978-1980; Sr res chemist, Interx Res Corp, 1972-1978; Adj assoc prof, Ctr Drug Discovery, Univ Fla, Gainesville, Fla. **Memberships:** Am Chem Soc; fel Am Asn Pharmaceut Scientists. **Research Statement & Publications:** Physical-chemical approach to pharmaceutical problems; chemical modification of drug to improve drug delivery and development of soft medicinal agents; computer-assisted drug design. **Mailing Address:** Schering-Plough Corp, K15-1 1800, 2015 Galloping Hill Rd, Kenilworth, NJ 07033. **E-Mail:** james.kaminski@spcorp.com

KAMINSKI, JOAN M, ORGANIC CHEMISTRY. **Personal Data:** b Darby, Pa, May 3, 1947. **Education:** West Chester State Col, BA, 1969; Drexel Univ, PhD (org chem), 1975. **Professional Experience:** SR RES ASSOC, MOBIL RES & DEVELOP CORP, 1993-; planning assoc, Mobil Res & Develop Corp, 1991-1993; res assoc, Mobil Res & Develop Corp, 1988-1991; assoc, Mobil Res & Develop Corp, 1984-1987; sr res chemist, Mobil Res & Develop Corp, 1981-1984; res chemist, Mobil Res & Develop Corp, 1977-1980; res scientist org chem, Fats & Proteins Res Found, Eastern Regional Res Ctr, Agr Res Serv, USDA, 1975-1977; Nat Res Coun-Agr Res Serv res assoc org chem, 1974-1975; teaching asst chem, Drexel Univ, 1970-1974; Asst res chemist, Univ Ill, Urbana, 1967 & 1969. **Memberships:** Am Chem Soc. **Research Statement & Publications:** Lubricants-new product development, petroleum chemistry. **Mailing Address:** Mobil Res & Develop Corp, Paulsboro, NJ 08066.

KAMINSKI, PAUL G, LOW OBSERVABLES TECHNOLOGY & APPLICATION, KALMAN FILTERING. **Personal Data:** b Cleveland, Ohio, September 16, 1942. **Education:** USAF Acad, BS, 1964; Mass Inst Technol, MS, 1966; Stanford Univ, PhD (aeronaut/astronaut eng), 1971. **Professional Experience:** CHMN & CEO, TECHNOVATION CORP, as of 2004; DIR, ANTEON CORP, as of 2004; DIR, DFI INT, as of 2004; DIR, LOGISTICS Mgt INST, as of 2004; DIR, RAND, as of 2004; CHMN, BOARD EXOSTAR, as of 2004; PARTNER, GLOBAL TECHNIOL PARTNERS, as of 2004; under secy defense acquisition & technol, Technol Strategies & Alliances, 1994-1997; chmn, Defense Sci Bd, 1993-; DIR, MICH DEVELOP CORP, 1993-; ATLANTIC AEROSPACE & ELECTRONICS CORP, 1993- & CHARLES STARK DRAPER LAB, 1993-; chmn & chief exec officer, Technol Strategies & Alliances, 1993-1994; DIR, ISY CORP, 1992-; DIR, DELFIN SYSTS, 1991-; DIR, GEO-DYNAMICS INC, 1988-; DIR, DYNCORP, 1988-; pres & chief operating officer, Technol Strategies & Alliances, 1985-1993; dir low observable technol, Off Dept Chief Staff Res & Develop, 1981-1985; spec asst under secy defense, USAF, 1977-1981. **Memberships:** Nat Acad Eng; Am Inst Aeronaut; AAAS; Sigma Xi; Inst Elec & Electronics Engrs. **Research Statement & Publications:** Kalman filtering, with application to navigation systems; internal guidance systems and terminal guidance systems for precision guided munitions; stealth technology to include design, analysis and testing; synthetic aperture radar and applications to reconnaissance and surveillance; square root filtering and smoothing; numerical methods. **Mailing Address:** Gen Dynamics Corp, 3190 Fairview Park Dr, Falls Church, VA 22042-4523. **Fax:** 703-876-3186.

KAMINSKI, ZIGMUND CHARLES, MEDICAL MICROBIOLOGY, INFECTIOUS DISEASES. **Personal Data:** b Hartford, Conn, January 15, 1929. **Education:** Univ Conn, BA, 1952; Hahnemann Med Col, MS, 1954, PhD (microbiol), 1957; Am Bd Med Microbiol, dipl pub health & med microbiol, 1972. **Professional Experience:** PROF MICROBIOL, SETON HALL COL MED & DENT, as of 2004; assoc prof microbiol & path, Med Sch, Univ Med & Dent, NJ, beginning 1971; DIR CLIN MICROBIOL, UNIV HOSP, 1968-; asst prof, Med Sch, Univ Med & Dent, NJ, 1968-1971; from instr to asst prof microbiol, Col Med, Seton Hall Univ, 1957-1965. **Memberships:** Am Soc Microbiol; Acad Clin Lab Physicians & Scientists; NY Acad Sci; Infectious Dis Soc Am. **Research Statement & Publications:** Mycobacterial infections. **Mailing Address:** Dept Microbiol, Seton Hall Col Med & Dent, NJ 150 Bergen St, Newark, NJ 07103.

KAMINSKY, LAURENCE SAMUEL, BIOLOGICAL SCIENCES, TOXICOLOGY. **Personal Data:** b Cape Town, SAfrica, December 25, 1940; m 1966, Sylvia; c Philip & Rena. **Education:** Univ Cape Town, BS, 1962, Hons, 1963, PhD (chem), 1966. **Honors & Awards:** Frank Blood Award, Soc Toxicol. **Professional Experience:** PROF, STATE UNIV NY, 1985-; CHIEF BIOCHEM GENETIC TOXICOL, NY STATE DEPT HEALTH, 1983-; dir biochem toxicol, 1978-1983; adj assoc prof, Albany Med Col, 1976-; prin res scientist biochem, 1975-1977; vis res prof biochem, State Univ NY Albany, 1974; assoc prof med biochem, Med Sch, Univ Cape Town, 1968-1975; res assoc biochem, Sch Med, Yale Univ, 1967-1968. **Memberships:** Brit Biochem Soc; Am Soc Biochem & Molecular Biol; Soc Toxicol; Int Soc Study Xenobiotics. **Research Statement & Publications:** Investigations into the role of of the heme proteins hepatic microsomal cytochrome P-450 in the metabolism of drugs; toxifying and detoxifying properties of cytochromes P-450s. **Mailing Address:** Lab Human Toxicol & Molec Epidemiol, NY State Dept Health, Wadsworth Ctr PO Box 509, Albany, NY 12201-0509. **Fax:** 518-486-1505. **E-Mail:** kaminsky@wadsworth.org

KAMINSKY, MANFRED STEPHAN, EXPERIMENTAL PHYSICS, SURFACE PHYSICS. **Personal Data:** b Koenigsberg, Ger, June 4, 1929. **Education:** Univ Rostock, Dipl, 1951, Univ Marburg, Ger, PhD (physics), 1957. **Honors & Awards:** E W Mueller Lectr, Univ Wis-Milwaukee, 1978. **Professional Experience:** AT, SURFACE TREATMENT SCI INT, as of 1988; PROP, SURFACE TREATMENT SCI INT, 1986-; Nat Res Coun, Coun Tribol, 1986-1988; consult, Off Tech Assessment, US Cong, 1986; proj mgr, US Dept Energy E Cut Tribology Proj & mgr tribology proface, Argonne Nat Lab, 1984-1986; res fel, Japanese Soc Prom Sci, 1982; chmn, Steering Comt Fusion Technol, Int Union Vacuum Sci, Technol & Appln, 1981-1983; mem, Task Group Plasma-Wall Interactions, Off Fusion Energy, Dept Energy, 1979-1980; Coop US scientist, Div Int Prog, NSF, 1978-1983; Invited prof, Inst Energy, Univ Quebec, Montreal-Varennes, 1976-1983; dir, Surface Sci Ctr, 1974-1980; sr physicist, Surface Sci Ctr, 1970-1986; assoc physicist, Argonne Nat Lab, 1962-1970; asst physicist, Argonne Nat Lab, 1959-1962; res assoc, Argonne Nat Lab, 1958-1959; sr asst, Phys Inst, Univ Marburg, 1957-1958; res asst, Phys Inst, Univ Marburg, 1953-1957; lectr, Med Tech Sch, 1952; Asst physics, Univ Rostock, 1950-1952. **Memberships:** AAAS; fel Am Phys Soc; Am Chem Soc; Sigma Xi; hon mem Am Vacuum Soc; Res Soc Am; Europ Phys Soc; Ger Phys Soc. **Research Statement & Publications:** Atomic and ionic impact phenomena on solids; channeling phenomena; nuclear polarization; surface science in thermonuclear research; mass spectrometry; tribology; ultrahigh vacuum technology; ionic processes in electrolytic solutions; radiation effects on solid surfaces; surface effects in controlled fusion devices; author of numerous books on surface physics. **Mailing Address:** 906 South Park, Hinsdale, IL 60521.

KAMINSKYJ, SUSAN GAIL WILLETS, FUNGAL BIOLOGY. **Education:** Univ Toronto, BSc, 1978, MSc, 1982; York Univ, PhD (biol), 1994. **Honors & Awards:** Alice Wilson Award, Royal Soc Can, 1995. **Professional Experience:** ASSOC PROF, DEPT BIOL, U SASKATCHEWAN, 2001-; asst prof, Dept Biol, U Saskatchewan, 1997-2001. **Research Statement & Publications:** Author of numerous articles. **Mailing Address:** Dept Biol, Univ Sask, 112 Sci Pl, Saskatoon, SK S7N 5E2, Can. **Fax:** 306-966-4461. **E-Mail:** Susan.Kaminskyj@usask.ca

KAMIYAMA, MIKIO, IMMUNOCHEMISTRY, IMMUNOHEMATOLOGY. **Personal Data:** b Kyoto, Japan, March 25, 1936; m 1971, c 3. **Education:** Kyoto Prefectural Univ, BS, 1962; Univ Tokyo, PhD (biochem) & DMSc, 1967. **Professional Experience:** Dir res, Blood Res Inst, St Michael's Med Ctr, beginning 1988; PROF, SCH GRAD MED EDUC, SETON HALL, 1988-; attend staff immunol, St Luke's Roosevelt Hosp Ctr & Columbia Univ, 1977-1988; res assoc hemat, St Luke's Roosevelt Hosp Ctr & Columbia Univ, 1974-1977; vis lectr biochem, Inst Physiol Chem, Univ Marburg, 1972-1973; sr researcher molecular biol, Inst Molecular Path, Univ Paris, 1971-1974; res assoc biochem, State Univ NY, Buffalo, 1969-1970; res assoc microbiol, Albert Einstein Med Ctr, 1968; fel biochem, Princeton Univ, 1967-1968. **Memberships:** Am Asn Immunologists; sr mem Am Fedn Clin Res; Asn Med Lab Immunologists; NY Acad Sci; Harvey Soc; Am Heart Asn Coun Thrombosis; Int Soc Thrombosis & Haemostasis. **Research Statement & Publications:** Immunological and biochemical characterization of platelet glycoproteins; cell membrane studies; monoclonal antibody preparations directed to human platelet glycoproteins; non-radioactive immune assays. **Mailing Address:** Blood Disorder Ctr Overlook Hosp, 99 Beauvoir Ave, Summit, NJ 07902-0220. **Fax:** 908-522-2977.

KAMLET, MARK S, ECONOMICS. **Education:** Stanford Univ, BA, 1974; Univ Calif, Berkeley, MS (Econ), 1976, MS (Statist), 1977 & PhD (Econ), 1980. **Professional Experience:** PROVOST, CARNEGIE MELLON UNIV, 2000-; SR VPRES, CARNEGIE MELLON UNIV, 2005-. **Mailing Address:** Heinz Sch, Carnegie Mellon Univ, Pittsburgh, PA 15213.

KAMM, DONALD E, NEPHROLOGY, PHYSIOLOGY. **Personal Data:** b Rochester, NY, July 10, 1929. **Education:** Cortland State Col, BS, 1951; Albany Med Col, MD, 1960. **Professional Experience:** ASSOC PROF MED, SCH MED & DENT, UNIV ROCHESTER, 1971-; from instr to asst prof, Sch Med & Dent, Univ Rochester, 1966-1971; NIH fel metab, Harvard Med Sch, 1964-1966; NIH res fel renal physiol, Sch Med, Boston Univ, 1962-1964; Intern & resident med, Beth Israel Hosp, Boston, 1960-1962. **Memberships:** Am Fedn Clin Res; Am Physiol Soc Nephrology; Int Soc Nephrology. **Research Statement & Publications:** Effects of potassium balance on the regulation of urea production and renal ammonia production. **Mailing Address:** Dept Med Nephrol Unit, Sch Med Univ Rochester 1425 Portland Ave, Rochester, NY 14642-0001. **E-Mail:** donald.kamm@viahealth.org

KAMM, GILBERT G(EORGE), CHEMICAL ENGINEERING. **Personal Data:** b Emington, Ill, August 6, 1925. **Education:** Univ Ill, BS, 1949. **Professional Experience:** CONSULT, 1988-; dir mat technol, Barrington Tech Ctr, 1984-1988; dir, metal mat technol, 1982-1984; assoc dir metall, Princeton Res Ctr, 1979-1981; assoc dir, Princeton Res Ctr, 1971-1978; asst to assoc dir, Mat Sci Sect, 1968-1971; mgr metals sect, Res & Develop Ctr, 1966-1968; Group leader metals, Res Div, Am Nat Can Co, Ill, 1958-1966. **Memberships:** Am Chem Soc; Electrochem Soc; Am Soc Metals. **Research Statement & Publications:** Metal cleaning and plating; corrosion, especially electrolytic tin plate and other metals used in containers; metallurgical properties of container materials; plastic-metal composites; energy related research in pulp and paper processes; organic coatings and sealing compounds. **Mailing Address:** 21032 N Crestview Dr, Barrington, IL 60010.

KAMM, JAMES A, ECONOMIC ENTOMOLOGY. **Personal Data:** b Ft Collins, Colo. **Education:** Univ Wyo, BS, 1961, MS, 1963, PhD (entom), 1967. **Professional Experience:** RETIRED; res entomologist, Agr Res Serv, USDA, 1967-1993; assoc prof, Ore State Univ, 1970-. **Memberships:** Entom Soc Am; AAAS. **Research Statement & Publications:** Grassland insects. **Mailing Address:** 440 NW Witham Dr, Corvallis, OR 97330.

KAMM, JAMES LAWRENCE, THERMODYNAMICS. **Education:** Carnegie Inst Technol, BS; Ohio State Univ, PhD. **Professional Experience:** PROF, UNIV TOLEDO, as of 2005. **Mailing Address:** Univ Toledo, Scott Park Campus, Toledo, OH 43606. **Fax:** 419-530-3068. **E-Mail:** jkamm@pop3.utoledo.edu

KAMM, JEROME J, BIOCHEMICAL PHARMACOLOGY. **Personal Data:** b New York, NY, June 4, 1933. **Education:** Brooklyn Col, BS, 1954; Georgetown Univ, MS, 1959, PhD (biochem), 1964. **Professional Experience:** SECT HEAD, HOFFMANN-LA ROCHE, INC, 1967-; sr biochemist, Smith, Kline & French Labs, 1964-1967; Chemist, Nat Heart Inst, 1955-1964. **Memberships:** AAAS; Am Chem Soc; Acad Pharmaceut Sci; NY Acad Sci; Am Soc Pharmacol & Exp Therapeut; Sigma Xi. **Research Statement & Publications:** Drug metabolism and mechanisms of drug metabolism; toxicology. **Mailing Address:** Dept Toxicol, Hoffmann-La Roche Inc, Nutley, NJ 07110-1150. **Fax:** 973-235-4795.

KAMM, ROGER DALE, BIOMEDICAL ENGINEERING, FLUID MECHANICS. **Personal Data:** b Ashland, Wis, October 10, 1950; m 1974, Judith; c Peter M. **Education:** Northwestern Univ, BS, 1972; Mass Inst Technol, SM, 1973, PhD (mech eng), 1977. **Honors & Awards:** Eschbach Distinguished Vis Scholar Award, Northwestern Univ, 2002. **Professional Experience:** GERMESHAUSEN PROF MECH & BIOL ENG & ASSOC HEAD DEPT, MASS INST TECHNOL, as of 2004; PROF BIOENGINEERING, MASS INST TECHNOL, 1998-; ASSOC DIR, CTR BIOMED ENG, MASS INST TECHNOL, 1995-; LECTR MED, HARVARD MED SCH, 1995-; PROF MECH ENG, MASS INST TECHNOL, 1988-; asst prof to assoc prof, 1978-1988; lectr & res assoc, 1977-1978; instr, 1977. **Memberships:** Am Soc Mech Engrs; Am Inst Med & Biol Eng; Biomed Eng Soc. **Research Statement & Publications:** Biomedical fluid mechanics, cell mechanics, cellular mechanotransduction. **Mailing Address:** Dept Mech Eng, Mass Inst Technol, 77 Mass Ave, Cambridge, MA 02139-4307. **Fax:** 617-258-5239. **E-Mail:** rdkamm@mit.edu

KAMMANN, KARL PHILIP, CHEMISTRY. **Personal Data:** b St Louis, Mo, March 30, 1936. **Education:** Wash Univ, AB, 1957; La State Univ, MS, 1960, PhD (chem), 1962. **Professional Experience:** PROD DEVELOP MGR, KEIL CHEM DIV, FERRO CORP, 1975-; group leader, Emery Indust, Inc, 1964-1974; sr res chemist, Cities Serv Co, 1962-1964. **Memberships:** Am Chem Soc; Am Oil Chemists Soc; Am Soc Lubrication Engrs. **Research Statement & Publications:** Sulfurization and chlorosulfurization; fats and oils, and derivatives. **Mailing Address:** 3430 W Atherton Lane, White Pine, TN 37890-4910.

KAMMASH, TERRY, NUCLEAR ENGINEERING & ENGINEERING MECHANICS, APPLIED PHYSICS. **Personal Data:** b Salt, Jordan, January 27, 1927; American citizen; m 1956. **Education:** Pa State Univ, BS, 1952, MS, 1954; Univ Mich, PhD (nuclear eng), 1958. **Honors & Awards:** Arthur Holly Compton Award & Am Nuclear Soc, 1977; Outstanding Achievement Awd, Fusiion Energy Div Am Nuclear Soc, 1977. **Professional Experience:** PROF EMER NUCLEAR ENG, UNIV MICH, ANN ARBOR, as of 2001; actg chmn, Univ Mich, Ann Arbor, 1977-; STEPHEN S ATWOOD PROF NUCLEAR ENG,

UNIV MICH, ANN ARBOR, 1977-; prof nuclear eng, Eng res inst, 1967-1977; vis scientist, Lawrence Radiation lab, 1962-1963, 1963-1967; from instr to assoc prof nuclear eng & eng mech, Eng res inst, 1955-1967; asst aircraft propulsion lab, Eng res inst, 1954-1955; instr eng mech, Pa State Univ, 1953-1954; asst aerodyn, Pa State Univ, 1952-1953. **Memberships:** Fel Am Phys Soc; fel Am Nuclear Soc; Am Soc Eng Educ; Soc Eng Sci; Assoc Fel Am Inst Aeronautucs & Astronautics. **Research Statement & Publications:** Magnetohydrodynamics; plasma physics; plasticity and physics of ionized gases; controlled fusion; space application of fusion energy. **Mailing Address:** Dept Nuclear Eng, Univ Mich, Eng Bldg, Ann Arbor, MI 48109. **Fax:** 734-763-4540. **E-Mail:** tkammash@umich.edu

KAMMEN, DANIEL M, PHYSICS. **Personal Data:** b February 13, 1962. **Education:** Cornell Univ, AB, 1984; Harvard Univ, MA, 1986, PhD (physics), 1988. **Honors & Awards:** 21st Century Earth Awd, 1993. **Professional Experience:** PROF PUB POLICY, GOLDMAN SCH PUB POLICY, UNIV CALIF, BERKELEY, 2001-; PROF, ENERGY & RESOURCES GROUP, UNIV CALIF, BERKELEY, 2001-; PROF NUCLEAR ENG, UNIV CALIF, BERKELEY, 2001-; DIR, RENEWABLE & APPROPRIATE ENERGY LAB, UNIV CALIF, BERKELEY, 1999-. **Memberships:** fel Am Phys Soc. **Mailing Address:** Energy & Resources Group, Univ Calif, 310 Barrows Hall, Berkeley, CA 94720-3050. **Fax:** 510-642-1085. **E-Mail:** kammen@opr.princeton.edu

KAMMEN, HAROLD OSCAR, BIOCHEMISTRY. **Personal Data:** b New York, NY, July 28, 1927. **Education:** Bethany Col, WVa, BS, 1946; Stanford Univ, PhD (chem), 1960. **Professional Experience:** HEALTH & SAFETY COORDR, UNIV CALIF, BERKELEY, 1990-; lectr, Univ Calif, Berkeley, 1971, 1975-1981; assoc res biochemist, Univ Calif, Berkeley, 1969-1989; asst res biochemist, Univ Calif, Berkeley, 1964-1969; res asst, Sch Med, Yale Univ, 1959; fel pharmacol, Sch Med, Yale Univ, 1959; res asst biochem, M D Anderson Hosp, Tex, 1956-1959. **Memberships:** AAAS; Am Soc Microbiol; Am Soc Biol Chem; fel Am Acad Sci. **Research Statement & Publications:** Enzymes and regulation of nucleic acid metabolism. **Mailing Address:** Univ Calif, Bldg 158 Richmond Field Sta 1301 S 46th St, Richmond, CA 94804-4603. **Fax:** 510-231-9520. **E-Mail:** kammen@uclink.berkeley.edu

KAMMER, DANIEL C, MECHANICAL ENGINEERING, ASTRONAUTICS. **Education:** Univ Wis-Madison, BS, 1976, MS, 1977, PhD, 1983. **Professional Experience:** PROF, DEPT ENG PHYSICS, UNIV WIS-MADISON, as of 2006. **Memberships:** Am Inst Aeronaut & Astronaut. **Mailing Address:** Dept Eng Physics, Univ Wis, 1500 Eng Dr 539 Eng Res Bldg, Madison, WI 53706-1687. **Fax:** 608-262-6707. **E-Mail:** kammer@engr.wisc.edu

KAMMER, GARY, IMMUNOLOGY. **Education:** Univ Akron, BA, 1966; Ohio State Univ, MD, 1970. **Professional Experience:** PROF, DEPT MICROBIOL & IMMUNOL, WAKE FOREST UNIV, as of 2003. **Mailing Address:** Dept Microbiol & Immunol, Wake Forest Univ, Med Ctr Blvd, Winston-Salem, NC 27157. **Fax:** 336-716-9821. **E-Mail:** gmkammer@wfubmc.edu

KAMMERDIENER, JOHN LUTHER, NON-PROLIFERATION, WEAPONS PHYSICS. **Personal Data:** b Perrin, Tex, July 6, 1937. **Education:** US Mil Acad, West Point, BS, 1961; Univ Calif, MS, 1966, PhD (appl sci), 1972. **Honors & Awards:** Award of Excellence, Dept Energy, 1985 & 1992. **Professional Experience:** RETIRED; fel, Los Alamos Nat Lab, beginning 1995; tech staff mem, LOS ALAMOS NAT LAB, 1972-1995. **Research Statement & Publications:** Classified weapons research and development and providing technical advice and analysis to US government policy makers. **Mailing Address:** 400 3rd St, Marble Falls, TX 78654. **Fax:** 202-665-2227. **E-Mail:** jlk@lanl.gov

KAMMERER, CANDACE MARIE, GENETIC EPIDEMIOLOGY. **Personal Data:** b Iowa City, Iowa, November 20, 1953. **Education:** Colo State Univ, BS, 1975; Ohio State Univ, PhD (genetics), 1979. **Professional Experience:** Mem, Int & Coop Proj Study Sect, NIH, 1993-1997; ASSOC SCIENTIST, Southwest FOUND BIOMED RES, 1990-2002; ASSOC PROF, UNIV TEX HEALTH SCI CTR, SAN ANTONIO, 1990-2004; from fel scientist to asst scientist, Univ Tex Health Sci Ctr, San Antonio, 1981-1989; fel scientist, Univ Cincinnati Med Sch, 1980-1981; Asst prof biol, Franklin & Marshall Col, 1979-1980. **Memberships:** Am Soc Human Genetics; Am Heart Asn; Genetics Soc Am; Int Genetics Epidemiol Soc; AAAS; Tex Genetics Soc. **Research Statement & Publications:** Genetic epidemiology of atherosclerosis, hypertension and osteoporosis using data on human families and animal models. **Mailing Address:** Dept Genetics, SW Found Biomed Res, PO Box 760549, San Antonio, TX 78245-0549. **Fax:** 210-670-3337. **E-Mail:** candy@darwin.sfbr.org

KAMMERMEIER, MARTIN A, SPEECH PATHOLOGY. **Personal Data:** b Cold Spring, Minn, October 23, 1931. **Education:** St Cloud State Col, BS, 1958, MS, 1963; Univ Minn, Minneapolis, PhD (speech path), 1969. **Professional Experience:** PROF SPEECH PATH, ST CLOUD STATE UNIV, 1973-; CHMN DEPT SPEECH SCI, PATH & AUDIOL, 1970-; from instr to asst prof, Path & Audiol, 1962-1973; Speech therapist, Pub Sch, 1958-1962. **Memberships:** Am Speech & Hearing Asn. **Research Statement & Publications:** Acoustic analysis of the voices of speakers with a variety of central nervous system disorders. **Mailing Address:** Dept Commun Disorders, St Cloud State Univ, St Cloud, MN 56301-4498.

KAMMLER, DAVID W, APPROXIMATION THEORY, FOURIER ANALYSIS. **Personal Data:** b Belleville, Ill, October 29, 1940; m 1965, Ruth; c Timothy & Daniel. **Education:** Southern Ill Univ, Carbondale, BA (chem), 1962; Southern Methodist Univ, MS (physics), 1969; Univ Mich, Ann Arbor, PhD (math), 1971. **Professional Experience:** Fel, Rome Air Develop Ctr, 1980-1981; PROF MATH, SOUTHERN ILL UNIV, CARBONDALE, 1978-; from asst prof to assoc prof, Southern Ill Univ, Carbondale, 1971-1978; mem tech staff, Tex Instruments Inc, 1965-1968; NSF grants 1977, 1989, 1990, 1992, 2002; A FOSR grants 1979, 1976, 1978. **Memberships:** Am Math Soc; Soc Indust & Appl Math; Math Asn Am; Sigma Xi. **Research Statement & Publications:** Approximation with sums of exponentials; transient analysis; numerical analysis; discrete fourier analysis; Appln of Fourier anal. **Mailing Address:** Dept Math, Southern Ill Univ, Carbondale, IL 62901-4408. **Fax:** 618-453-5300.

KAMMULA, RAJU G, TOXICOLOGY, PHYSIOLOGY. **Personal Data:** b May 1, 1935. **Education:** Madras Univ, DVM, 1957; Univ Minn, PhD (physiol), 1964. **Professional Experience:** CHMN TOXICOL, FOOD & DRUG ADMIN, as of 2001; VET MED OFFICER & TOXICOLOGIST, FOOD & DRUG ADMIN, 1979-; vet practr, Calif, 1976-1978; prof physiol, Col Vet Med, Tuskegee Univ, 1964-1976; res asst, Univ Minn, 1959-1964. **Memberships:** Am Physiol Soc; Am Vet Med Asn; Am Col Toxicol; DC Vet Med Asn. **Research Statement & Publications:** Pharmacology. **Mailing Address:** Food & Drug Admin, HFZ-470, Rm 310T, 9200 Corporate Blvd, Rockville, MD 20850. **Fax:** 301-480-4224. **E-Mail:** raju.kammula@fda.hhs.gov

KAMON, ELIEZER, ERGONOMICS, OCCUPATIONAL HEALTH. **Personal Data:** b Jerusalem, 1930. **Education:** Israel State Col, T dipl, 1952; Hebrew Univ, Jerusalem, MSc, 1959, PhD (zool), 1964. **Professional Experience:** PROF PHYSIOL, PA STATE UNIV, 1974-; res assoc, Univ Pittsburgh, 1968-1973; Res asst occup health, Univ Pittsburgh, 1966-1967; Fel ergonomics, Loughboro Univ Technolog, 1965. **Memberships:** Am Physiol Soc; Am Indust Hyg Asn; fel Am Col Sports Med; Ergonomics Soc; Human Factors Soc. **Research Statement & Publications:** Human thermal physiology and man's adaptability to his working conditions as they relate to muscular strength, cardiovascular capacity and respiratory functions. **Mailing Address:** 1244 Westerly Pkwy Apt 39, State College, PA 16801.

KAMOTANI, YASUHIRO, MECHANICAL ENGINEERING, AEROSPACE ENGINEERING. **Education:** PhD. **Honors & Awards:** Gallery Fluid Motion Video Award, Am Phys Soc, 1994. **Professional Experience:** PROF, DEPT OF MECH & AEROSPACE ENG, CASE WESTERN RESERVE UNIV, as of 2005. **Mailing Address:** Dept Mech & Aerospace Eng, Case Western Reserve Univ, Glennan Bldg Rm 412, Cleveland, OH 44106. **Fax:** 216-368-6445. **E-Mail:** yxk@po.cwru.edu

KAMOUN, MALEK, LABORATORY MEDICINE. **Education:** Pierre & Marie Curie Univ, Paris, France, MD, 1975. **Professional Experience:** PROF PATH & LAB MED, DEPT IMMUNOL & HEMAT, UNIV PA, as of 2004; asst Prof Path & Lab Med Immunol & Hemat, Univ Pa, beginning 1983. **Research Statement & Publications:** Lymphocyte growth and differentiation. **Mailing Address:** Dept Path, Univ Pa Hosp 7 Founders, Box 4283, Philadelphia, PA 19104-4274. **Fax:** 215-349-5090. **E-Mail:** malekkam@mail.med.upenn.edu

KAMOWITZ, HERBERT M, MATHEMATICS. **Personal Data:** b Brooklyn, NY, December 31, 1931; m 1955, Elaine; c David L, Sylvia J & Anne L. **Education:** City Col NY, BS, 1952; Brown Univ, MS, 1954, PhD (math), 1960. **Professional Experience:** Vis scientist, Pure Math Dept, Weizmann Inst Sci, Rehovot, Israel, 1973 & 1980; PROF MATH, UNIV MASS, BOSTON, 1970-; assoc prof, Univ Mass, Boston, 1966-1970; from staff scientist to sr staff scientist, Res & Advan Develop Div, Avco Corp, 1961-1966; sr scientist, Res & Advan Develop Div, Avco Corp, 1960-1961; assoc scientist math, Res & Advan Develop Div, Avco Corp, 1957-1960. **Memberships:** Am Math Soc. **Research Statement & Publications:** Functional analysis. **Mailing Address:** Dept Math, Univ Mass, Dorchester, MA 02125. **E-Mail:** hkamo@cs.umb.edu

KAMP, DAVID ALLEN, ORGANIC CHEMISTRY, POLYMER CHEMISTRY. **Personal Data:** b St Louis, Mo, September 26, 1947. **Education:** Univ Calif, Los Angeles, BSc, 1970; Univ Ore, PhD (chem), 1976; Univ Calif, Santa Cruz, cert hazardous mat mgt, 1991. **Professional Experience:** SCIENTIST & GROUP LEADER, LANDEC CORP, 1990-; CONSULT, ORG & POLYMER CHEM, RAYCHEM CORP, 1980-; staff scientist, Res & Develop Ctr, Gen Elec Co, 1977-1980 & Raychem Corp, 1980-1987; assoc chem, Cornell Univ, 1976-1977. **Memberships:** Am Chem Soc; Asn Consult Chemists & Chem Engrs; Prof & Tech Consults Asn; Int Soc Optical Eng. **Research Statement & Publications:** Organic synthesis; organic and polymer chemistry; materials science. **Mailing Address:** 886 Ticonderoga Dr, Sunnyvale, CA 94087-2252.

KAMPAS, FRANK JAMES, PHYSICAL CHEMISTRY, SOLID STATE PHYSICS. **Personal Data:** b Buffalo, NY, April 24, 1946. **Education:** Univ Pa, BA & MS, 1968; Stanford Univ, PhD (physics), 1974. **Professional Experience:** DIR ENCAPSULATION, AM PHYS SOC, 1990-; mgr, process develop & eng, 1988-1989; mgr, Process Develop Group, 1986-1987; sr scientist, Chronar Co, 1985-1986; from asst scientist to scientist, Dept Energy & Environ, Mat Sci Div, 1978-1985; res assoc, Molecular Sci Div, Brookhaven Nat Lab, 1977-1978; Res assoc chem, Univ Wash, 1974-1977. **Memberships:** Am Phys Soc; Mat Res Soc; Inst Elec & Electronic Engrs. **Research Statement & Publications:** Physics of organic molecules in the solid state and in solution; plasma chemistry as applied to thin film deposition; optical spectroscopy; solar cell device physics. **Mailing Address:** 1614 E Butler Pike, Ambler, PA 19002.

KAMPE, DENNIS JAMES, ELECTRON MICROSCOPY. **Personal Data:** b Brooklyn, NY, July 16, 1945; div. **Education:** State Univ NY Stony Brook, BESc, 1967; Univ Va, MMSc, 1969, PhD (mat sci), 1972. **Professional Experience:** SR RES SCIENTIST, CARBON PROD DIV, UNION CARBIDE CORP, 1995-; res scientist, Carbon Prod Div, Union Carbide Corp, 1991-1994; sr staff scientist, Carbon Prod Div, Union Carbide Corp, 1983-1990; res scientist, Carbon Prod Div, Union Carbide Corp, 1975-1982; dept head micros & phys testing, Carbon Prod Div, Union Carbide Corp, 1973-1975; Staff scientist, Carbon Prod Div, Union Carbide Corp, 1972-1973. **Memberships:** Electron Micros Soc Am; Am Soc Testing & Mat; Sigma Xi; Asn Iron & Steel Engrs; Am Inst Mech Engrs; Iron & Steel Soc. **Research Statement & Publications:** Carbon an graphite materials in steel making processes and si and p production. **Mailing Address:** UCAR Carbon, PO Box 6116, Cleveland, OH 44101. **Fax:** 216-676-2623. **E-Mail:** dennis.kampe@ucar.com

KAMPER, ROBERT ANDREW, PHYSICS. **Personal Data:** b Surbiton, Eng, March 14, 1933. **Education:** Oxford Univ, BA, 1954, MA & DPhil(physics), 1957. **Honors & Awards:** Arnold O Beckman Award, Instrument Soc Am, 1974; Gold Medal, US Dept Com, 1975. **Professional Experience:** RETIRED; dir, Boulder Labs, 1982-1994; chief electromagnetic technol div, Electromagnetics Div, 1978-1994; assoc chief, Electromagnetics Div, 1974-1978; physicist, Cryogenics Div, Nat Bur Stand, 1963-1974; physicist, Cent Elec Generating Bd, Eng, 1961-1963; Fulbright travel grant, Univ Calif, Berkeley, 1958-1959; imp Chem Industs res fel, Oxford Univ, 1957-1961. **Memberships:** Fel Inst Elec & Electronics Engrs. **Research Statement & Publications:** Cryoelectronics; superconductivity; electrical measurement technique; electron spin resonance. **Mailing Address:** 439 17th St, Boulder, CO 80302.

KAMPERMAN, GEORGE W, ENGINEERING. **Education:** Alma Col, BS. **Professional Experience:** PRES, KAMPERMAN ASSOC, as of 2005. **Memberships:** Fel Acoustical Soc Am. **Mailing Address:** Kamperman Assoc Inc, 26100 Woodland Trail, Kansasville, WI 53139. **E-Mail:** george@kamperman.com

KAMPHOEFNER, FRED J(OHN), electronics; deceased, see previous edition for last biography

KAMPHUIS, J(OHN) WILLIAM, COASTAL & OCEANOGRAPHIC ENGINEERING. **Personal Data:** b Vollenhove, Neth, September 9, 1938. **Education:** Queen's Univ, Ont, BSc, 1961, MSc, 1963, PhD (civil eng), 1966; Delft Technol Univ, dipl hydraul eng, 1964. **Professional Experience:** PROF EMER CIVIL ENG, QUEEN'S UNIV, ONT, 1974-; specialist consult coastal eng, 1969-; from asst prof to assoc prof, Queen's Univ, Ont, 1968-1972; lectr, Carleton Univ, 1965-1968; asst res officer, Nat Res Coun Can, 1965-1968. **Memberships:** Am Soc Civil Engrs; Int Asn Hydraul Res; Can Soc Civil Engrs. **Research Statement & Publications:** Wave mechanics; interaction of waves and coasts; coastal sediment transport by waves and tides; model analysis; tidal propagation and numerical analysis; marina design. **Mailing Address:** Dept Civil Eng, Queen's Univ, Ellis Hall, Kingston, ON K7L 3N6, Can. **Fax:** 613-533-2128. **E-Mail:** kamphuis@civil.queensu.ca

KAMPINE, JOHN P, ANESTHESIOLOGY, PHYSIOLOGY. **Education:** Marquette Univ, Med Col Wis, MD, 1961, PhD, 1965. **Honors & Awards:** Distinguished Serv Award, 1991. **Professional Experience:** Chmn, Dept Anesthiol, Med Col Wis, 1979-2005; PROF PHYSIOL & ANESTHIOL, MED COL WIS, 1974-; from asst prof to assoc prof, Dept Physiol & anesthiol, 1967-1974; instr physiol, Med Col Wis, 1962-1967. **Memberships:** Inst Med-Nat Acad Sci. **Mailing Address:** Dept Anesthesiol, Med Col Wis, PO Box 26099 9200 W Wis Ave, Milwaukee, WI 53226-3596. **Fax:** 414-805-6147. **E-Mail:** jpk@post.its.mcw.edu

KAMPMEIER, JACK A, ORGANIC CHEMISTRY, EDUCATION. **Personal Data:** b Cedar Rapids, Iowa, June 11, 1935; m 1958, Anne; c Scott, Margaret & Stephen. **Education:** Amherst Col, BA, 1957; Univ Ill, PhD (org chem), 1960. **Honors & Awards:** Catalyst Award for Exellence, Chem Manufacturer's Asn, 1999. **Professional Experience:** Dean, Col Arts & Sci, 1988-1991; assoc dean grad studies, Col Arts & Sci, 1982-1986; sr scientist, NATO, 1979-1980; Fulbright-Hays, sr res fel, Univ Freiburg, 1979-1980; chmn dept, Univ Rochester, 1975-1979; PROF CHEM, UNIV ROCHESTER, 1971-; NSF sci fac fel, Univ Calif, Berkeley, 1971-1972; from instr to assoc prof, Univ Rochester, 1960-1971; NSF fel, 1958-1960. **Memberships:** Am Chem Soc; Sigma Xi. **Research Statement & Publications:** Mechanistic organic chemistry; free radical reactions; organometallic reactions; photochemistry; electron transfer reactions; prep them learning. **Mailing Address:** Dept Chem, Univ Rochester, Rochester, NY 14627-1001. **Fax:** 585-506-0205. **E-Mail:** kamp@chem.rochester.edu

KAMPRATH, EUGENE JOHN, SOIL FERTILITY. **Personal Data:** b Seward, Nebr, January 9, 1926; wid Katherine (Deceased). **Education:** Univ Nebr, BS, 1950, MS, 1952; NC State Col, PhD (soils), 1955. **Honorary Degrees:** DSc, Univ Nebr, 1987. **Honors & Awards:** Soil Sci Appl Res Award, Soil Sci Soc of Am, 1986; Distinguished Serv Award, Soil Sci Soc of Am, 1997. **Professional Experience:** WILLIAM NEAL REYNOLDS EMER PROF, NC STATE UNIV, 1996-; head dept, NC State Univ, 1990-1996; William Neal Reynolds prof soil sci, NC State Univ, 1981-1996; ed-in-chief, Soil Sci Soc Am, 1969-1974; Dir, Soil Testing Div, State Dept Agr, NC, 1957-1962; From asst prof to prof, NC State Univ, 1955-1981. **Memberships:** Fel Am Soc Agron; fel Soil Sci Am; Sigma Xi. **Research Statement & Publications:** Soil fertility; soil chemistry relationships in soils as they affect availability of nutrients to plants. **Mailing Address:** Dept Soil Sci Box 7619, NC State Univ, Raleigh, NC 27695-7619. **Fax:** 919-515-2167. **E-Mail:** eugene_kamprath@ncsu.edu

KAMPSCHMIDT, RALPH FRED, BIOCHEMISTRY, IMMUNOLOGY. **Personal Data:** b Gerald, Mo, May 6, 1923; m 1954, Frances; c Kimberly, Kit, Coby & Kerry. **Education:** Univ Mo, BS, 1947, MS, 1949, PhD (agr chem) 1951. **Professional Experience:** RETIRED; sect head, Samuel Roberts Noble Found Inc, 1955-1985; res chemist biochem, Armour & Co, 1951-1955; instr animal husb, Univ Mo, 1947-1951. **Memberships:** Fel AAAS; Am Asn Cancer Res; Soc Exp Biol & Med; Reticuloendothelial Soc; NY Acad Sci. **Research Statement & Publications:** Cancer research; iron metabolism; reticuloendothelial system; endotoxin; monokines. **Mailing Address:** 2614 Ridgeway St, Ardmore, OK 73401.

KAMRA, OM PRAKASH, RADIATION GENETICS, CYTOGENETICS. **Personal Data:** b Lahore, India, March 18, 1935. **Education:** Univ Delhi, BSc, 1954; NC State Univ, MS, 1956; Wash State Univ, PhD (genetics), 1959; Univ Lund, dipl, 1959. **Honors & Awards:** Travel Award, Can Genetics Soc, 1963. **Professional Experience:** PROF EMER, DEPT INT DEVELOP STUDIES, DALHOUSIE UNIV, as of 2004; vis prof, Belgium Nuclear Res Estab, 1977, 1978, 1981; mem comt int exchange, Nat Res Coun, 1973-1976; prof radiation biol, Dalhousie Univ, beginning 1972; consult, UN Develop Prog, Indonesia, 1972; consult, Int Atomic Energy Agency, Vienna, 1969-1970; chmn biol subcomt, Atlantic Prov Inter-Univ Comt Sci, 1967-1968; assoc prof, Dalhousie Univ, 1963-1972; res assoc plant genetics, Univ Man, 1961-1963; res officer radiation genetics, Atomic Energy Estab, Trombay, India, 1960-1961; secy, Food & Agr Orgn-Swedish Int Training Ctr Genetics, Univ Lund, 1959-1960; fel, Swedish Agr Res Coun, 1959-1960; fel Swedish Agr Res Coun, 1959. **Memberships:** Sigma Xi. **Research Statement & Publications:** Cytology; genetics; mutations; food additives; effect of laser beams on biological systems. **Mailing Address:** Dept Int Develop Studies, Dalhousie Univ, 1236 Henry St, Halifax, NS B3H 3J5, Can. **E-Mail:** O.Kamra@Dal.Ca

KAMRAN, MERVYN ARTHUR, ENTOMOLOGY, ECOLOGY. **Personal Data:** b Sialkot, Pakistan, November 8, 1938. **Education:** Punjab Univ, Pakistan, BS, 1957, MS, 1959; Univ Hawaii, PhD (entom), 1965. **Professional Experience:** PROF BIOL, DOWLING COL, 1979-; asst prof biol to assoc prof, Dowling Col, 1968-1979; asst prof entom, Pa State Univ, 1968; res fel entom, Int Rice Res Inst, Philippines, 1965-1967; Pakistan AEC scholar, Cent Treaty Orgn Inst Nuclear Sci, Tehran, Iran, 1961; Lectr biol, Pakistan Ed Serv, Lahore, 1959-1961. **Memberships:** AAAS; Am Entom Soc; Entom Soc Am. **Research Statement & Publications:** Ecology and biological control of insect pests; taxonomy of tachinid flies. **Mailing Address:** Dept Math & Sci, Dowling Col, 150 Idle Hour Blvd, Oakdale, NY 11769-1906.

KAMRANY, NAKE M, ECONOMICS. **Education:** Univ Calif, BS, 1959; Univ Southern Calif, MS, 1962, PhD, 1962. **Professional Experience:** PROF & SR LECT, UNIV SOUTHERN CALIF, 1976-. **Mailing Address:** Univ Southern Calif, Rm 300, Los Angeles, CA 90089-0253. **Fax:** 310-260-7753. **E-Mail:** kamrany@usc.edu

KAMRIN, MICHAEL ARNOLD, PUBLIC EDUCATION IN SCIENCE, SCIENCE POLICY. **Personal Data:** b Brooklyn, NY, August 5, 1940; m 2004, Katherine; c Kari & Edward. **Education:** Cornell Univ, BA, 1960; Yale Univ, MS, 1962, PhD (chem), 1965. **Honors & Awards:** Mem Medal, Univ Turku, Finland; Pub Commun Award, Soc Toxicol. **Professional Experience:** PROF EMER, RES DEV, 2000-; PROF EMER, INST ENVIRON TOXICOL, MICH STATE UNIV, 2000-; DOCENT, UNIV TURKU, FINLAND, 1996-; prof, Res Develop, 1990-2000; prof, Inst Environ Toxicol, Mich State Univ, 1982-2000; vis scientist, Mich Legis Off Sci Adv, 1980-1981; from asst prof to prof, Natural Science, 1967-1989; NIH trainee, Hopkins Marine Sta, Stanford Univ, 1966-1967; consult, Biol Div, Oak Ridge Nat Lab, 1965-1966; Res assoc biol, Biol Div, Oak Ridge Nat Lab, 1963-1964. **Memberships:** Fel AAAS; Am Chem Soc; Soc Environ Toxicol & Chem; Soc Toxicol; Soc Risk Anal. **Research Statement & Publications:** Risk assessment, risk management, risk communication; science education for non-scientists; science policy. **Mailing Address:** 167 Granite Rd, Williamston, MI 48895. **E-Mail:** kamrin@msu.edu

KAMYKOWSKI, DANIEL, BIOLOGICAL OCEANOGRAPHY. **Personal Data:** b Chicago, Ill, November 23, 1945; m 1972, Sara-Joan; c Zachary & Terra-Lynn. **Education:** Loyola Univ, Chicago, BS, 1967; Univ Calif, San Diego, PhD (oceanog), 1973. **Professional Experience:** PROF MARINE EARTH & ATMOSPHERIC SCI, NC STATE UNIV, 1986-; assoc prof, Marine Earth & Atmospheric Sci, Nc State Univ, 1979-1986; TEMP ASST PROF BOT, UNIV TEXAS, AUSTIN, 1978-; asst prof bot & marine sci, Univ Tex, Austin, 1975-1979; Killam res assoc oceanog, Dalhousie Univ, 1973-1975. **Memberships:** Am Soc Limnol & Oceanog; Am Geophys Union; Oceanog Soc. **Research Statement & Publications:** Physiology and behavior of marine dinoflagellates in response to physical processes; global patterns in hydrographic factors, plant nutrients and phytoplankton species composition; Galapagos optics and oceanography. **Mailing Address:** Dept Marine Earth & Atmospheric Sci, NC State Univ Box 8208, Raleigh, NC 27695-8208. **Fax:** 919-515-7802. **E-Mail:** dan_kamykowski@ncsu.edu

KAN, JOSEPH RUCE, SPACE PLASMA PHYSICS. **Personal Data:** b Shanghai, China, February 10, 1938. **Education:** Nat Cheng-Kung Univ, Taiwan, BS, 1961; Wash State Univ, MS, 1966; Univ Calif, San Diego, PhD (appl physics), 1969. **Professional Experience:** RETIRED; dean, Grad Sch, Univ Alaska, 1994-2003; assoc ed, J Geophys Res, 1984-; prof geophys, Geophys Inst, Univ Alaska, beginning 1981; vis prof, Inst Geophys & Planetary Physics, Univ Calif, Los Angeles, 1980-1981; consult, Aerospace Corp, 1980-1981; head, Space Physics & Atmospheric Sci Prog, 1977-1980; assoc prof, Geophys Inst, Univ Alaska, 1976-1981; asst prof, Geophys Inst, Univ Alaska, 1972-1976; fel space physics, Dartmouth Col, 1969-1972. **Memberships:** AAAS; Sigma Xi; Am Phys Soc; Am Geophys Union. **Research Statement & Publications:** Space physics; plasma physics. **Mailing Address:** Dept Physics, Univ Alaska, PO Box 757520, Fairbanks, AK 99775. **Fax:** 907-474-1984. **E-Mail:** ffjrk@uaf.edu

KAN, LOU SING, PHYSICAL CHEMISTRY, BIOPHYSICS. **Personal Data:** b Honan, China, February 28, 1943; m 1970. **Education:** Nat Taiwan Univ, BS, 1964; Duquesne Univ, PhD (phys chem), 1970. **Professional Experience:** ASSOC PROF, DIV BIOPHYS, SCH HYG & PUB HEALTH, JOHNS HOPKINS UNIV, 1981-; asst prof, Div Biophys, Sch Hyg & Pub Health, Johns Hopkins Univ, 1977-1981; res assoc, Div Biophys, Sch Hyg & Pub Health, Johns Hopkins Univ, 1974-1977; fel chem, Div Biophys, Sch Hyg & Pub Health, Johns Hopkins Univ, 1971-1974; fel, Duquesne Univ, 1970-1971; Vis fel, Mellon Inst, Carnegie-Mellon Univ, 1970-1971; asst phys chem, Duquesne Univ, 1966-1970; asst chem, Nat Taiwan Univ, 1965. **Memberships:** Am Chem Soc; Biophys Soc; Sigma Xi. **Research Statement & Publications:** Studies of structure and backbone conformations of oligoribonucleotides and deoxyribonucleotides; conformation of nucleic acids; modified nucleic acids. **Mailing Address:** Inst Chem Acad Sinica, Nankang, Taipei, Taiwan.

KAN, PETER TAI YUEN, ORGANIC CHEMISTRY. **Personal Data:** b Canton, China, April 12, 1927; American citizen; m 1951, c 2. **Education:** Gannon Col, BS, 1949; Univ Mich, MS, 1951; Wayne State Univ, PhD (org chem), 1958. **Professional Experience:** RES MGR, BASF WYANDOTTE CORP, 1986-; res supvr, Wyandotte Chem Corp, 1976-1985; res assoc, Wyandotte Chem Corp, 1968-1976; from res chemist to sr res chemist, Wyandotte Chem Corp, 1957-1968; Sr anal chemist, R P Scherer Corp, Mich, 1951-1955. **Memberships:** AAAS; Am Chem Soc; fel Am Inst Chem. **Research Statement & Publications:** Isocyanates; isocyanurates; polyurethanes; organo-metallics; general organic synthesis. **Mailing Address:** 47200 Ann Arbor Rd W, Plymouth, MI 48170.

KAN, YUET WAI, GENETICS, HEMATOLOGY. **Personal Data:** b Hong Kong, China, June 11, 1936; American citizen; m 1964, c 2. **Education:** Univ Hong Kong, MB & BS, 1958, DSc, 1980; FRS, 1981; FRCP, 1983. **Honorary Degrees:** MD, Univ Cagliari, Italy, 1981; DSc, Chinese Univ, Hong Kong 1981 & Univ Hong Kong, 1987. **Honors & Awards:** Shaw Prize, Hong Kong, 2004; Helmut Horten Found Res Award, Switz, 1995; Fedn Can Chinese Professionals Award, 1994; Cotlove Award, Acad Clin Lab Physicians & Scientists, 1993; Int Award, Italy, 1989; San Remos Int Award, 1989; Warren Alpert Award, 1989; Am Col Physicians Award, 1988; Waterford Award, 1987; Gairdner Found Int Award, 1984; Allan Award, Am Soc Human Genetics, 1984; Lita Annenberg Hazen Award, 1984; Chinese Am Physicians Soc Award, 1982; George Thorn Award, Howard Hughes Med Inst, 1980; Stratton Lectr, Int Soc Hemat, 1980; Damashek Award, Am Soc Hemat, 1979. **Professional Experience:** Sr staff, Cardiovasc Res Inst, beginning 1993; hon prof, Inst Molecular Biol, Univ Hong Kong, beginning 1990; dir, Inst Molecular Biol, Univ Hong Kong, 1990-1994; CHIEF, DIV MOLECULAR MED & DIAG, DEPT LAB MED, UNIV CALIF, 1989-; LOUIS K DIAMOND PROF HEMAT, DEPT MED & LAB MED, UNIV CALIF, SAN FRANCISCO, 1983-; head, Div Genetics & Molecular Hemat, Dept Med, 1983-1989; res assoc, Cancer Res Inst, Univ Calif, San Francisco, 1980-1994; PROF, DEPT MED & LAB MED, UNIV CALIF, SAN FRANCISCO, 1977-; investr, Howard Hughes Med Inst Lab Study Human Genetic Dis, San Francisco, 1976-; chief, Hemat Serv, San Francisco Gen Hosp, 1972-1979; assoc prof, Dept Med & Lab Med, 1972-1977; asst prof pediat, Children's Hosp Med Ctr, Dept Pediat, Harvard Med Sch, 1970-1972; res assoc, Children's Hosp Med Ctr, Dept Pediat, Harvard Med Sch, 1967-1970; assoc med, Presby-Univ, Pa Hosp, Philadelphia, 1966-1967; res fel hemat, Dept Med, Royal Victoria Hosp, McGill Univ, 1964-1966; res assoc, Dept Biol, Mass Inst Technol, 1963-1964; resident med, Presby Univ Hosp, Pittsburgh, Pa, 1962-1963; resident, Univ Dept Med, Queen Mary Hosp, Hong Kong, 1959-1960; intern, Univ Dept Med, Queen Mary Hosp, Hong Kong, 1958-1959. **Memberships:** Soc Chinese Bioscientists Am (pres, 1998-1999); Am Soc Hemat (pres, 1989-1990); Asn Chinese Geneticists Am (pres, 1988-1989); Nat Acad Sci; Am Fedn Clin Res; Am Soc Clin Invest; Asn Am Physicians; fel Royal Soc London; Third World Acad Sci; Am Soc Human Genetics; foreign mem Chinese Acad Sci; fel Royal Col Physicians; fel Am Acad Arts & Sci; fel AAAS; Molecular Med Soc. **Research Statement & Publications:** Control of globin synthesis and genetic defects in homoglobinopathies and thalassemia; Published over 5 articles. **Mailing Address:** Dept Med & Lab Med, Univ Calif, PH U432 PO Box 0793, San Francisco, CA 94127. **Fax:** 415-476-2956. **E-Mail:** kanyuet@labmed2.ucsf.edu

KANA, DANIEL D(AVID), ENGINEERING MECHANICS, MECHANICAL ENGINEERING. **Personal Data:** b Cuero, Tex, September 22, 1934; m 1958, Gladys; c 3. **Education:** Univ Tex, BS, 1958, PhD (eng mech), 1967; Univ NMex, MS, 1961. **Professional Experience:** RETIRED; inst engr, SW Res Inst, 1983-1996; mgr struct dynamics & acoust, SW Res Inst, 1971-1983; group leader, SW Res Inst, 1970-1971; From res engr to sr res engr, SW Res Inst, 1961-1970. **Memberships:** Fel Am Soc Mech Engrs; fel Am Inst Aeronaut & Astronaut. **Research Statement & Publications:** Liquid and structure dynamic interaction; linear and non-linear vibrations; dynamic response and stability of structures; general structural dynamics and acoustics; environmental testing; earthquake engineering. **Mailing Address:** 10410 Mt Hope St, San Antonio, TX 78230.

KANABROCKI, EUGENE LADISLAUS, BIOCHEMISTRY. **Personal Data:** b Chicago, Ill, April 18, 1922; m 1950, c 2. **Education:** DePaul Univ, BS, 1947; Loyola Univ Chicago, MS, 1969; Jagiellonian Univ, Poland, DSc, 1983; Nat Registry Clin Chem, cert. **Professional Experience:** RES CHEMIST, NUCLEAR MED SERV, HINES VET ADMIN HOSP, 1983-; chief clin chemist, Four Hosp Complex, 1973-1983; biochemist nuclear med, Clin Lab, Hines Vet Admin Hosp, 1956-1973; Consult, 1956-; asst chief biochemist, Clin Lab, Hines Vet Admin Hosp, 1948-1956; Asst chief chemist, Clin Lab, Hines Vet Admin Hosp, 1946-1948; res assoc, Loyola Univ Chicago; chemist, US Customs Lab, Chicago; WHO investr, Int Atomic Energy Agency. **Memberships:** Am Chem Soc; Int Soc Chronobiol; Sigma Xi; Health Physics Soc. **Research Statement & Publications:** Etiology of arteriosclerosis; chronobiology; trace elements. **Mailing Address:** 151 Braddock Dr, Melrose Park, IL 60160-2406.

KANADE, TAKEO, ARTIFICIAL INTELLIGENCE. **Personal Data:** b Hyogo, Japan, October 24, 1945; c 2. **Education:** Kyoto Univ, BE, 1968, ME, 1970, PhD (elec eng), 1973. **Honors & Awards:** AVIRG Award, Audio Visual Info Res Group in Japan, 1980; AT&T Spec Group Award, 1988; Hosa Bunka Kikin Found Award, 1994; Joseph F Engelberger Award, 1995. **Professional Experience:** U A & HELEN WHITAKER CHAIRED PROF COMPUT SCI & ROBOTICS, ROBOTICS INST, CARNEGIE MELLON UNIV, 1993-; mem, Int Found Robotics Res, 1993-; dir, Robotics Inst, Carnegie Mellon Univ, 1992-; mem, Aeronaut & Space Eng Bd, Nat Res Coun, 1992-1995 & 1992-1996; found chief ed, Int J Comput Vision, 1985-; prof, Dept Comput Sci & Robotics Inst, Carnegie Mellon Univ, 1985-1994; assoc prof tenure, Dept Comput Sci & Robotics Inst, Carnegie Mellon Univ, 1982-1985; chmn, Comt Robotics, Inst Elec & Electronics Engrs Comput Soc, 1982-1983; sr res scientist, Dept Comput Sci & Robotics Inst, Carnegie Mellon Univ, 1980-1982; assoc prof, Dept Info Sci, Kyoto Univ, Japan, 1976-1980; asst prof, Dept Info Sci, Kyoto Univ, Japan, 1973-1976. **Memberships:** Nat Acad Eng; Int Soc Intelligent Automation; Asn Comput Mach; fel Inst Elec & Electronics Engrs; fel Am Asn Artificial Intel; Robotics Soc Japan; Inst Electronics & Commun Engrs Japan; Sigma Xi; Intelligent Automation Soc; Robotics & Automation Soc. **Research Statement & Publications:** Computer science; artificial intelligence; image understanding; robotics; vision; manipulator; navigation; sensors; medical imaging and graphics; granted 7 patents. **Mailing Address:** Robotics Inst, Carnegie Mellon Univ 5000 Forbes Ave, Pittsburgh, PA 15213. **Fax:** 412-268-5570. **E-Mail:** tk@cs.cmu.edu

KANAKKANATT, ANTONY, POLYMER CHEMISTRY. **Personal Data:** b Cochin, India, March 6, 1935; m 1965, c 3. **Education:** Univ Kerala, India, BSc, 1956; Marquette Univ, MS, 1960; Univ Akron, PhD, 1963. **Professional Experience:** SR ASSOC INDEXER, CHEM ABSTRACTS SERV, 1967-; res asst, Chem Abstracts Serv, 1965-1967; Sr res chemist, Monsanto Co, 1963-1965. **Memberships:** Am Chem Soc. **Research Statement & Publications:** Catalytic isomerization; sequence distribution in polypeptides; reinforcement in elastomers. **Mailing Address:** 1216 Shady Hill Dr, Columbus, OH 43221.

KANAKKANATT, SEBASTIAN VARGHESE, POLYMER PHYSICS. **Personal Data:** b Kerala, India, January 20, 1929; American citizen; m 1958, c 1. **Education:** Univ Madras, BSc, 1950; Univ Akron, MS, 1965, PhD (polymer physics), 1969. **Professional Experience:** AT, UNITED POLYMER TECHNOL, as of 2003; PRES, UNIQUE TECHNOL, INC, 1983-; bd chmn, Unique Technol, Inc, 1982-1983; prof gen technol, Univ Akron, 1980-; asst dir, Environ Mgt Lab, 1976-1980; from asst prof to assoc prof, 1969-1980; Univ Addis Ababa, 1952-1964 & Instr chem, Univ Madras, 1950-1952. **Memberships:** Am Chem Soc; Rheol Soc; Sigma Xi. **Research Statement & Publications:** Diffusion in polymeric matrices used in the controlled release of pesticides, herbicides, fertilizers and photochromic dyes; cancer therapeutic agents. **Mailing Address:** United Polymer Technol LLC, 526 S Main St, Suite 111, Akron, OH 44311.

KANAL, LAVEEN NANIK, INTELLIGENT SYSTEMS. **Personal Data:** b Dhond, India, September 29, 1931; m 1960, Agnes; c Shobhi, Jaya & Gyan. **Education:** Univ Wash, BS, 1951, MS, 1953; Univ Pa, PhD (elec eng), 1960. **Honors & Awards:** King-Sun Fu Award, Int Asn Pattern Recognition, 1992. **Professional Experience:** PROF EMER COMPUT SCI, UNIV MD, 1996-; 1977-1981 bd govs, info theory group, 1973-1979; admin comt, Systs & Cybernet, Inst Elec & Electronics Engrs, 1972-1974; MANAGING DIR L N K CORP, RIVERDALE, 1970-; porf comput sci, Univ Md, Col Park, 1970-1996; pres, Univ MD, 1969-1970; vis prof, Wharton Grad Sch, Univ Pa, 1966-1974; adj prof, Lehigh Univ, 1965-1970; mgr advan eng & res activ, Commun & Electronics Div, Philco-Ford Corp, 1965-1969; vis assoc prof, Wharton Grad Sch, Univ Pa, 1964-1966; lectr, Wharton Grad Sch, Univ Pa, 1963-1964; res mgr info sci, Philco Appl Res Lab, Philco-Ford Corp, 1962-1965; mgr mach intel lab, Gen Dynamics/Electronics, NY, 1960-1962; instr elec eng, Moore Sch Elec Eng, Univ Pa, 1955-1960; develop engr, Can Gen Elec Co, Ont, 1953-1955. **Memberships:** Fel AAAS; Asn Comput Mach; fel Int Asn Pattern Recognition Soc; Soc Mfg Engrs; fel Inst Elec & Electronics Engrs; fel Am Asn Artificial Intel; Soc Photooptical Engrs; Sigma Xi. **Research Statement & Publications:** Information science; machine recognition of patterns; stochastic learning models; statistical classification theory and applications of artificial intelligence; pattern recognition and image processing in remote sensing and automated digital cartography. **Mailing Address:** Univ Md, Dept Comput Sci, 3261 A V Williams Bldg, College Park, MD 20742-3255. **E-Mail:** kanal@cs.umd.edu, kanal@lnk.co

KANAMORI, HIROO, SEISMOLOGY, GEOPHYSICS. **Personal Data:** b Tokyo, Japan, October 17, 1936; m 1964, Keiko; c Atsushi & Tadashi. **Education:** Univ Tokyo, BS, 1959, MS, 1961, PhD (geophys), 1964. **Honors & Awards:** Medal Seismological Soc of Am, 1992; Arthur L Day Prize Lectureship, U S Nat Acad of Sci, 1993; Calif Scientist Award, 1993; The Asahi Prize, 1993; Walter H Bucher Medal, Am Geophysical Union, 1996. **Professional Experience:** Vis assoc prof geophys, Mass Inst Technol, 1969-1970; from assoc prof to prof, Univ Tokyo, 1966-1972; res fel geophys, Calif Inst Technol, 1965-1966; res assoc, Geophysics Inst, Tokyo Univ, 1962-1965; assoc prof, Earthquake res Inst, Tokyo Univ, 1966-1969; prof, Earthquake Res Inst, Tokyo Univ, 1970-1972; prof, Calif Inst of Technol, 1972-1989; JOHN E AND HAZEL S SMITS PROFESSORSHIP OF GEOPHYSICS, 1989-; dir, Seismological Lab, Calif Inst of Technol, 1990-1998. **Memberships:** Fel Am Geophys Union; Seismol Soc Am. **Research Statement & Publications:** Physics of earthquakes; application of seismology to earthquake engineering. **Mailing Address:** Geophys & Plantary Sci 252-21, Calif Inst Technol, Pasadena, CA 91125.

KANAMUELLER, JOSEPH M, INORGANIC CHEMISTRY. **Personal Data:** b Chicago, Ill, July 4, 1938. **Education:** St Joseph's Col Ind, BS, 1960; Univ Minn, PhD (inorg chem), 1965. **Professional Experience:** PROF EMER CHEM, WESTERN MICH UNIV, as of 2006; prof chem, Western Mich Univ, 1980-1999; vis prof inorg chem, Vienna Tech Univ, Austria, 1974; assoc prof, Western Mich Univ, 1972-1980; asst prof chem, Western Mich Univ, 1966-1972; res assoc inorg chloramine chem, Univ Fla, 1965-1966. **Memberships:** AAAS; Am Chem Soc. **Research Statement & Publications:** Synthetic inorganic chemistry, especially sulfur-nitrogen and phosphorus-nitrogen compounds. **Mailing Address:** Dept Chem, Western Mich Univ, Kalamazoo, MI 49008. **E-Mail:** joseph.kanamueller@wmich.edu

KANAREK, ROBIN BETH, REGULATION OF FOOD INTAKE, NUTRITION & BEHAVIOR. **Personal Data:** b April 8, 1946; m 1986, c 2. **Education:** Antioch Col, BA, Rutgers Univ, MS, PhD (psychol), 1974. **Professional Experience:** DEAN, GRAD SCH ARTS & SCI, TUFS UNIV, as of 2004; PROF PSYCHOL, TUFTS UNIV, 1989-; adj prof nutrit, Tufts Univ, beginning 1989; assoc prof, Tufts Univ, 1983-1989; ed-in-chief, Nutrit & Behav, 1980-1987; prin investr, NIH Res Grants, 1978-. **Memberships:** Am Inst Nutrit; Behav Pharmacol Soc; Am Col Nutrit; NY Acad Sci; N Am Soc Study Obesity; Soc Study Ingestive Behav. **Research Statement & Publications:** Physiological psychology; author. **Mailing Address:** Dept Psychol, Sch Med Tufts Univ, 490 Boston Ave, Medford, MA 02155-5532. **Fax:** 617-627-3181. **E-Mail:** robin.kanarek@tufts.edu

KANARIK, ROSELLA, MATHEMATICS. **Personal Data:** b Hungary, February 7, 1909; American citizen; m 1936, c 2. **Education:** Univ Pittsburgh, BA, 1930, MA, 1931, PhD (math), 1934. **Professional Experience:** PROF EMER MATH, LOS ANGELES CITY COL, 1974-; from assoc prof to prof, Los Angeles City Col, 1962-1974; counr, Los Angeles City Col, 1956-1962; instr, Los Angeles City Col, 1953-1956; teacher 1946-1953; Asst math, Univ Pittsburgh, 1931-1933. **Memberships:** Am Math Soc; Math Asn Am. **Research Statement & Publications:** Differential equations; group theory. **Mailing Address:** 238 S Mansfield Ave, Los Angeles, CA 90036-3017.

KANAROWSKI, S(TANLEY) M(ARTIN), CHEMISTRY-GENERAL, ANALYTICAL CHEMISTRY. **Personal Data:** b Beausejour, Man, December 12, 1912; American citizen; wid Pearl (Deceased); c Stanley M Jr, Nancy (Ci o ffari) & Janice E. **Education:** Univ Toledo, BS, 1934; Ohio State Univ, MS, 1938-1942. **Honors & Awards:** Army-Navy "E" Award 1943; corps of Engineers Awards 1974, 1980, 1984. **Professional Experience:** RETIRED; proj leader & prin investr, Eng Mat Div, US Army Construct Eng Res Lab, Corps Engrs, 1969-1986; proj engr & head chemist, Invests Sect, Ohio River Div Labs, Chem & Thermal Effects Br, US Army Eng Div Corps Eng, 1964-1969; sewage & indust wastes chemist, City of Toledo, 1963-1964; res & develop chem engr, Consol Paper Co, 1962-1963; chief chemist, Northern Region, Enforcement Div, Ohio, 1960-1962; chief res & develop chem engr & qual control mgr, Dairypak Butler Inc, 1953-1960; res & develop chem engr, Glass Fibers Inc, 1952-1953; lab dir & asst res & develop mgr, Fremont Rubber Co, 1949-1952; res & develop compounding chem engr, Corp Gen Lab, Ohio, 1946-1949; chief factory prod chem engr, Corp Gen Lab, Ohio, 1943-1946; asst dir, Corp Gen Lab, Ohio, 1943; consult & sr chemist, Ord Plant, Firestone Tire & Rubber Co, Nebr, 1942-1943; from chemist to chief chemist, Dept Liquor Control, Ohio, 1936-1942; new mat appln R&D chemist & engr; mat appln res chemist & engr. **Memberships:** Am Chem Soc; Am Inst Chem Engrs; Nat Defense Industrial Assoc; NY Acad Sci; Chem Soc Washington; Am Chem Soc. **Research Statement & Publications:** Construction materials application research and development including design of testing equipment; sealants application; waterproofing materials and films; reflective solar control films for windows; maple gymnasium floor finishes; paint-test kit for paint quality evaluation; prevention of windblown rain penetration; collective protection centers against chemical-biological warfare; reflection cracking in pavements; chemical hazardous materials and disposal; rubber and synthetic rubber products, elastomers, polymers, coatings, plastics, glass fibers, resins and paperboard; compo u nding; quality control; laboratory and factory operations; materials problems consultant; 30 research publications nationally and internationally. **Mailing Address:** 1329 Excaliber Lane, Sandy Spring, MD 20860-1117.

KANASEWICH, ERNEST RAYMOND, GEOPHYSICS. **Personal Data:** b Eatonia, Sask, March 4, 1931; m 1969, c 2. **Education:** Univ Alta, BSc, 1952, MSc, 1960; Univ BC, PhD (geophys), 1962. **Professional Experience:** PROF EMER PHYSICS, UNIV ALTA, as of 1998; prof physics, Univ Alta, beginning 1971; vis assoc prof, Dept Earth & Planetary Sci, Calif Inst Technol, 1970-1971; from asst chmn to actg chmn dept, Univ Alta, 1969-1974; subcomt seismol, Nat Res Coun, beginning 1967; mem adv comt explor tech, Northern Alta Inst Technol, beginning 1964; subcomt phys methods appl to geol probs, Nat Adv Comt Res Geol Sci, beginning 1965; mem cubcomt glaciol, Nat Res Coun, 1963-; from asst prof to assoc prof, Univ Alta, 1963-1971; fel, Univ BC, 1962-1963; seismologist, Tex Instruments-Geophys Serv, Inc, 1953-1958. **Memberships:** Am Geophys Union; Soc Explor Geophys; Seismol Soc Am; Can Asn Physicists. **Research Statement & Publications:** Gravity; seismology; isotope dating techniques; glaciology. **Mailing Address:** Dept Physics, Univ Alta, Edmonton, AB T6G 2M7, Can.

KANATZAR, CHARLES LEPLIE, ZOOLOGY. **Personal Data:** b St Elmo, Ill, April 12, 1914; wid, c Constance J (Buhrmann) & Phyllis R (Rock). **Education:** Eastern Ill State Teachers Col, BEduc, 1935; Univ Ill, MS, 1936, PhD (protozool), 1940. **Honorary Degrees:** DH, Mac Murray Col, 1986. **Professional Experience:** Mem bd dirs, Ill State Mus Soc, 1985-1991; EMER DEAN, MACMURRAY COL, 1974-; chmn, Ill StateMus, 1970-1974; dean col, MacMurray Col, 1967-1974; mem bd adv, Ill StateMus, 1962-1974; dean fac, MacMurray Col, 1961-1967; Pres, Ill State Acad Sci, 1959-1960; prof & head dept, MacMurray Col, 1948-1961; asst prof biol, MacMurray Col, 1946-1948; Asst zool, Univ Ill, 1935-1938. **Research Statement & Publications:** Free-living protozoa; general zoology; general education in science. **Mailing Address:** 1841 Mound Rd, Jacksonville, IL 62650.

KANATZIDIS, MERCOURI G, SOLID STATE CHEMISTRY. **Personal Data:** b Thessaloniki, Greece, August 6, 1957; m 1987. **Education:** Univ Thessaloniki, BS, 1979; Univ Iowa, PhD (chem), 1984. **Honors & Awards:** Alexander von Humboldt Prize, 2003; Morley Medal, Am Chem Soc, Cleveland Sect, 2003. **Professional Experience:** PROF CHEM, MICH STATE UNIV, 1993-; Alfred P Sloan Found fel, 1991; assoc prof chem, Mich State Univ, 1991-1993; NSF presidential young investr, 1989; asst prof chem, Mich State Univ, 1987-1991; res assoc chem, Univ Mich, 1984-1985 & Northwestern Univ, 1985-1987. **Memberships:** Am Chem Soc; Am Crystallog Soc; Mat Res Soc. **Research Statement & Publications:** Inorganic chemistry systhesis of novel molecular and solid state compounds of sulfur, selenium and tellurium; intercalation chemistry; conductive polymers; solid state chemistry; crystallography. **Mailing Address:** Dept Chem, Mich State Univ, East Lansing, MI 48824. **Fax:** 517-353-1793. **E-Mail:** kanatzid@cem.msu.edu

KANCIRUK, PAUL, SCIENTIFIC DATABASE MANAGEMENT. **Personal Data:** b New York, NY, October 10, 1947. **Education:** City Col NY, BS, 1969; Fla State Univ, PhD, 1976. **Honors & Awards:** Bronze Medal, Environ Protection Agency, 1985. **Professional Experience:** LIASON, CUDAZA COMT, NAT RES LAB, 1993-; PROG MGR, ENVIRON INFO ANAL PROG, OAK RIDGE NAT LAB, 1991-; sr res assoc, Oak Ridge Nat Lab, 1984-1990; res assoc aquatic ecol, Oak Ridge Nat Lab, 1978-1984; Marine biol, Nova Ocean Sci Ctr, 1976-1977. **Memberships:** Ecol Soc Am. **Research Statement & Publications:** Management and analysis of large environmental data bases in support of global change research including research into biogeochemical cycles general circulation model and atmospheric chemistry. **Mailing Address:** Environ Sci Div Oak Ridge Nat Lab, PO Box 2008 MS 6407, Oak Ridge, TN 37831-6407. **Fax:** 423-574-4665. **E-Mail:** pkk@ornl.gov

KANCZAK, NORBERT M, ANATOMY. **Personal Data:** b Buffalo, NY, February 12, 1931; m 1958, c 4. **Education:** State Univ NY Buffalo, BA, 1958, PhD (anat), 1964. **Professional Experience:** PROF EMER, UNIV PITTSBURGH, as of 2004; assoc prof anat, Sch Dent Med, Univ Pittsburgh, beginning 1970; asst prof, Sch Med, Tufts Univ, 1966-1970; Sr instr anat, Sch Med, Tufts Univ, 1965-1966; Nat Inst Arthritis & Metab Dis fel, Nat Cancer Inst fel, 1964-1965; Nat Inst Arthritis & Metab Dis fel, Ohio State Univ, 1963-1964.

Research Statement & Publications: Morphology and physiology of transitional epithelium; oncology of transitional cell carcinoma; electron microscopic histochemistry. **Mailing Address:** Sch Med Dent, Univ Pittsburgh, CL 801, Pittsburgh, PA 15261. **E-Mail:** nmk3@pitt.edu

KANDASAMY, SATHASIVA B, NEUROSCIENCE, MARINE PHARMACOLOGY. **Personal Data:** b Madras, India, January 16, 1945. **Education:** Univ Madras, India, BS, 1965, MS, 1968; Pasteur Inst, Paris, PhD (pharmacol), 1975. **Honors & Awards:** Int Union Pharmacologists Award, 1974. **Professional Experience:** PROJ MGR & SUPVR RES PHARMACOLOGIST, ARMED FORCES RADIOBIOL INST, 1992-; vis scientist, armed forces radiobiol Inst, 1986-1992; assoc prof pharmacol, baneras hindu Univ, India, 1984-1985; nat res coun assoc, 1983-1985; vis scientist thermoregulation, NASA, 1981-1984; vis scientist marine pharmacol, Univ Okla, 1979-1980; asst prof res, Alfaten Med Sch, Lybia, 1978-1979; asst prof pharmacol, Univ Benin, Nigeria, 1976-1978; res fel, Ciba-Geigy, Basel, switz, 1974-1975. **Memberships:** Soc Neuroscience; Am Soc Pharmacol & Exp Therapeut. **Research Statement & Publications:** Neuroscience; marine pharmacology. **Mailing Address:** Nat Inst Alcohol Abuse & Alcoholism, NIH, 6000 Exec Blvd Ste 409, Bethesda, MD 20892-7003. **Fax:** 301-443-6077. **E-Mail:** skandasa@mail.nih.gov

KANDEL, ABRAHAM, COMPUTER SCIENCES. **Personal Data:** b Tel Aviv, Israel, October 6, 1941; American citizen; m 1966, Nurit; c 3. **Education:** Technion-Israel Inst Technol, BSc, 1966; Univ Calif, Santa Barbara, MSc, 1968; Univ NMex, PhD (elec eng, comput sci), 1977. **Honors & Awards:** Gold Medal Lifetime Achv, Moisil Int Found, 1996. **Professional Experience:** DIR SOFTWARE TESTING, USF, 1999-; CHMN, DEPT CSRE, USF, 1991-; chmn dept, Fla State Univ, 1978-1991; distinguished vis, Inst Elec & Electronics Engrs-Comput Soc, 1981-1985; DIR & DISTINGUISHED RES PROF COMPUT SCI, FLA STATE UNIV, 1980-; dir comput sci, dept math & comput sci, 1978-1984; assoc prof, Fla State Univ, 1978-1980; vis sr lectr, Ben Gurion Univ Negev & Tel-Aviv Univ, Israel, 1976-1977; consult, Sandia Labs, Albuquerque, NMex, 1976; from instr to assoc prof comput sci, NMex Inst Mining & Technol, 1970-1978. **Memberships:** Fel Inst Elec & Electronics Engrs; fel Asn Comput Mach; Pattern Recognition Soc; Am Soc Eng Educ; fel AAAS; fel NY Acad Sci; Sigma Xi. **Research Statement & Publications:** Fuzzy sets and systems; computer architecture; performance evaluation; pattern recognition; fault-tolerant systems; switching, microprocessors and logic design; expert systems; applied artificial intelligence. **Mailing Address:** 4202 E Fowler Ave, CSE Dept, Univ S Fla, Tampa, FL 33620.

KANDEL, ERIC RICHARD, NEUROBIOLOGY, PSYCHIATRY. **Personal Data:** b Vienna, Austria, November 7, 1929; American citizen; m 1956, c 2. **Education:** Harvard Univ, AB, 1952; NY Univ, MD, 1956. **Honorary Degrees:** DSc, Hahnemann Univ & State Univ NY, 1986; DHL, Johns Hopkins Univ, 1986. **Honors & Awards:** Nobel Prize in Physiol/ Med, 2000; Nat Medal Sci, 1988; Moses Award, 1959; Lester N Hofheimer Prize, Am Psychiat Asn, 1977, Spec Presidential Commendation, 1986, Distinguished Serv Award, 1989; Karl Spencer Lashley Prize Neurobiol, Am Philos Soc, 1981; NY Acad Sci Award Biol & Med Sci, 1982; Albert Lasker Basic Med Res Award, 1983; Howard Crosby Warren Medal, Soc Exp Psychologists, 1984; J Murray Luck Award Sci Reviewing, Nat Acad Sci, 1988; Wolf Prize Biol & Med, Israel, 1999. **Professional Experience:** SR INVESTR, HOWARD HUGHES MED INST, 1984-; UNIV PROF, COLUMBIA UNIV, 1983-; assoc ed, J Neuroscience, 1981-1983; assoc ed, J Neurophysiology, 1977-1980; prof, Col Physicians & Surgeons, 1974-1983; mem, Neuropsychology Res Rev Comt, NIMH, 1969-1972; chief, Dept Neurobiology & Behav, Pub Health Res Inst, NY, 1968-1974; mem, Comt Life Sci, Nat Acad Sci-Nat Res Coun, 1968-1969; from assoc prof to prof physiol & psychiat, Sch Med, NY Univ, 1965-1974; res assoc, Med Sch, Harvard Univ, 1964-1965; instr, 1963-1964; USPHS spec fel, Lab Gen Neurophysiology, Col France, 1962-1963; Milton res fel, 1961-1962; dir, Mass Ment Health Ctr, 1960-1965, res psychiat, Mass Ment Health Ctr, 1960-1962 & 1963-1964; teaching fel psychiat, Harvard Med Sch, 1960-1961; Numerous lectrs, US & foreign, 1959-1990; res assoc, Lab Neurophysiology, NIH, 1957-1960; intern, Montefiore Hosp, NY, 1956-1957. **Memberships:** Nat Acad Sci; Inst Med; Am Acad Arts & Sci; fel AAAS; Am Philos Soc; hon mem Am Neurol Asn; Int Brain Res Orgn; Am Psychiat Asn; Soc Neuroscience (pres, 1980-1981). **Research Statement & Publications:** Electrophysiology of central neurons; neurosecretion; cellular mechanisms of behavior; neuronal plasticity; author or co-author of 7 books and over 220 publications. **Mailing Address:** Ctr Neurobiology & Behav-Col Physicians & Surgeons, Columbia Univ, 722 W 168th St Res Annex 1051 Riverside Dr, New York, NY 10032. **Fax:** 212-543-5474. **E-Mail:** erk5@columbia.edu

KANDEL, RICHARD JOSHUA, PHYSICAL CHEMISTRY. **Personal Data:** b New York, NY, April 30, 1924; m 1948, Jeanne; c 4. **Education:** NY Univ, BS, 1946, PhD (chem), 1950. **Professional Experience:** RETIRED; chief, Fundamental Interactions Br, Div Chem Sci, US Dept Energy, 1977-1986; chief chem & atomic physics br, div phys res, US Energy Res & Develop Admin, 1975-1977; chief radiation, Isotope & Phys Chem Br, 1969-1975; mem staff chem prog br, Div Res, 1967-1969; mem staff phys chem, Los Alamos Sci Lab, 1950-1967; instr gen chem, NY Univ, 1949-1950. **Memberships:** Am Chem Soc. **Research Statement & Publications:** Mass spectrometry; kinetics; radiation chemistry. **Mailing Address:** 818 Fordham St, Rockville, MD 20850.

KANDHAL, PRITHVI SINGH, PAVEMENT MATERIALS, ASPHALT TECHNOLOGY. **Personal Data:** b Bikaner, India, May 6, 1935; American citizen; m 1958, Ummed; c Ravindra K & Mitra S. **Education:** Univ Rajasthan, India, Bachelor Engineering, 1957; Iowa State Univ, MS, 1969. **Honors & Awards:** W J Emmons Award, Asn Asphalt Paving Technologists, 1989. **Professional Experience:** Chmn, Subcomt Bituminous Mat, Am Soc Civil Engrs, 1989-1993; ASSOC DIR EMER, NAT CTR ASPHALT TECHNOL, AUBURN UNIV, 1988-; chmn, comt road& paving mats, Am soc testing& mat, 1998-1999; chmn, Transp Res Bd Comt A2DO2 Asphalt Mixtures, 1982-1988; chief asphalt engr, Pa Dept Transp, Harrisburg, 1970-1988; hwy engr, Berger Assocs, Camp Hill, Pa, 1969-1970; dist engr, Rajasthan Pub Works Dept, India, 1965-1968; asst dist engr, Rajasthan Pub Works Dept, India, 1957-1965. **Memberships:** Asn Asphalt Paving Technologists(pres, 1999); Am Soc Testing & Mat(comt chmn, 1998-1999); emer mem Transp Res Bd; fel Am Soc Civil Engrs. **Research Statement & Publications:** Author of over 120 publications; highway pavement materials; mix design; construction; maintenance; hot mix asphalt materials. **Mailing Address:** 635 Woody Dr, Auburn, AL 36832.

KANDIL, OSAMA A, ENGINEERING. **Education:** Old Dom Univ, PhD. **Professional Experience:** PROF & CHAIR, AEROSPACE ENG, OLD DOM UNIV, as of 2006. **Memberships:** Am Inst Aeronaut & Astronaut. **Mailing Address:** Dept Aerospace, Col Eng, Old Dom Univ, Norfolk, VA 23529. **Fax:** 757-683-3200. **E-Mail:** okandil@odu.edu

KANDOIAN, A(RMIG) G(HEVONT), ENGINEERING. **Personal Data:** b Van, Armenia, November 28, 1911; nat American citizen; m 1945, c 3. **Education:** Harvard Univ, BS, 1934, MS, 1935. **Honorary Degrees:** DEng, Newark Col Eng, 1967. **Honors & Awards:** Award, Inst Elec & Electronics Engrs, 1965. **Professional Experience:** mem, Panel on Telecommun Res in US, Nat Acad Eng; Exec secy, Cable Television Tech Adv Comt, Fed Commun Comn; INDEPENDENT CONSULT, TELECOMMUN ENG, 1973-; dir off telecommun, US Dept Commerce, 1970-1973; consult telecommun, US Dept Commerce, 1970; vpres & dir, Scanwell Labs, Inc, 1968-1970; exec staff vpres, Commun Systs Inc, Comput Sci Corp, 1967-1968; pres, Commun Systs Inc, Comput Sci Corp, 1966-1967; vpres & gen mgr, Commun Systs Inc, Comput Sci Corp, 1965-1966; vpres eng, Int Tel & Tel Labs, 1964-1965; vpres & gen mgr, Int Tel & Tel Labs, 1960-1964; vpres commun systs, Int Tel & Tel Labs, 1958-1959; head radio commun lab, Fed Telecommun Labs, Inc, 1946-1958; From jr engr to head dept radio commun equip, Int Tel & Tel Corp, 1935-1946. **Memberships:** Fel Inst Elec & Electronics Engrs. **Research Statement & Publications:** Radio aids to air navigation; instrument landing systems; radio antenna systems, particularly in the range; design of radio transmitters and receivers for the very high frequency regions; radio ranges for point to point flight of aircraft; radar components; radio communication systems; satellite communication. **Mailing Address:** 195 Orchard Pl, Ridgewood, NJ 07450.

KANDULA, MAX, AERONAUTICS. **Education:** PhD, Univ Calif. **Professional Experience:** STAFF, DYNACS INC, KENNEDY SPACE CTR, as of 2006. **Mailing Address:** DYNACS Inc, Kennedy Space Ctr, FL 32899. **Fax:** 321-867-4424. **E-Mail:** max.kandula-1@ksc.nasa.gov

KANDUTSCH, ANDREW AUGUST, BIOCHEMISTRY. **Personal Data:** b Kennan, Wis, October 10, 1926; m 1952, c 2. **Education:** Ripon Col, BA, 1950; Univ Wis, MS, 1952, PhD (biochem), 1954. **Professional Experience:** STAFF EMER, JACKSON LAB, as of 2005; Dep dir, Roscoe B Jackson Mem Lab, 1981-1985; asst dir res, Roscoe B Jackson Mem Lab, 1965-1966; sr staff scientist, Jackson Lab, beginning 1964; staff scientist, Roscoe B Jackson Mem Lab, 1957-1964; res assoc, Roscoe B Jackson Mem Lab, 1955-1957; res fel biochem, Roscoe B Jackson Mem Lab, 1954-1955. **Memberships:** Am Soc Biol Chemists. **Research Statement & Publications:** Animal sterols and their metabolism; sterol biosynthesis and its regulation; membrane structure and function; relationships between sterols, cancer and atherosclerosis; regulation of dolichol biosynthesis; regulation of the cell replication cycle. **Mailing Address:** Jackson Lab, 600 Main St, Bar Harbor, ME 04609. **E-Mail:** aak@jax.org

KANE, AGNES BREZAK, CELL INJURY, EXPERIMENTAL CARCINOGENESIS. **Personal Data:** b Danbury, Conn, November 3, 1946. **Education:** Swarthmore Co, BA, 1968; Temple Univ, MD, 1974, PhD (exp path), 1976. **Professional Experience:** CHAIR, DEPT PATH & LAB MED, BROWN UNIV, 1996-; PROF, DEPT PATH & LAB MED, BROWN UNIV, 1995-; mem, Mine Health Safety Res Adv Comt, Ctr Dis Control/Nat Inst Occup Safety & Health, 1993-; mem, Environ Health Sci Rev Comt, Nat Inst Environ Health Sci, NIH, 1988-1992; consult, Identify Occup Dis, 1987-1990; sci consult, RI Comn Safety & Occup Health, 1986-; from asst prof to assoc prof path, Brown Univ, 1982-1995; staff pathologist, Temple Univ Hosp, 1979-1982; fel, Karolinska Inst, Stockholm, Swed, 1976-1977. **Memberships:** Sigma Xi; Am Asn Pathologists; Int Acad Path; AAAS; Am Med Womens Asn; Am Thoracic Soc. **Research Statement & Publications:** Experimental pathology. **Mailing Address:** Dept Path & Lab Med, Brown Univ, PO Box 6, Providence, RI 02912. **E-Mail:** agnes_kane@brown.edu

KANE, BERNARD JAMES, ORGANIC CHEMISTRY. **Personal Data:** b New York, NY, September 22, 1932; m 1955, c 6. **Education:** Iona Col, BS, 1954; Adelphi Col, MS, 1956. **Honors & Awards:** D P Joyce Award, Glidden-Durkee, Div SCM Corp, 1970. **Professional Experience:** DIR RES, GLIDDEN-DURKEE, DIV SCM CORP, 1971-; mgr develop terpene chem, 1962-1971; Chemist, 1957-1962. **Memberships:** Am Chem Soc. **Research Statement & Publications:** Terpene chemical and organic research and development. **Mailing Address:** 333 Ocean Blvd, Atlantic Beach, FL 32233-5279.

KANE, DANIEL E(DWIN), CHEMICAL ENGINEERING, STERILIZATION ENGINEERING. **Personal Data:** b Iowa Park, Tex, August 12, 1923; m 1953, Inga; c Jeffrey & Daniel. **Education:** Iowa State Univ, BS, 1947; Lawrence Col, MS, 1950, PhD (chem eng), 1953. **Professional Experience:** RETIRED; mgr sterilization eng, Miles Inc, 1982-1989; mgr process develop, Miles Inc, 1980-1982; group leader mfg technol, Miles Inc, 1976-1980; mgr pilot prod, Bus Equip Div, SCM Corp, 1973-1976; supvr paper/coatings, Bus Equip Div, SCM Corp, 1970-1973; tech mgr, NVF Co, 1966-1970; res assoc res & develop, Nat Vulcanized Fibre Co, 1959-1966; sr chem engr, Fibreboard Paper Prod Corp, 1953-1959; chem engr, Phillips Petrol Co, 1947-1948; pharmaceutical process validation, GMP. **Memberships:** Tech Asn Pulp & Paper Indust; Am Chem Soc. **Research Statement & Publications:** Kraft chemical recovery; vulcanized fibre; saturating and specialty papers; water and air pollution abatement; reprographics; coatings; hospital supplies; intravenous solutions; steam sterilization of intravenous solutions and process equipment; ETO sterilization; sterilize in place; clean in place. **Mailing Address:** 18680 Quailridge Rd, Cottonwood, CA 96022.

KANE, DANIEL JAMES, ULTRAFAST LASER DIAGNOSTICS, DIODE LASER SPECTROSCOPY. **Education:** Mont State Univ, BS, 1983; Univ Ill, MS, 1985, PhD (physics), 1989. **Professional Experience:** COORDR IMAGING TECHNOL, SOUTHWEST SCI INC, as of 2003; PRIN RES SCIENTIST, SOUTHWEST SCI INC, 2000-; sr res scientist, Southwest Sci, Inc, beginning 1992; fel, Los Alamos Nat Labs, 1989-1992. **Memberships:** Am Phys Soc; Optical Soc Am. **Research Statement & Publications:** Development of devices to measure ultrashort laser pulses and trace gas detection using diode lasers. **Mailing Address:** SW Sci, Inc, 1570 Pacheco St, Ste E-11, Santa Fe, NM 87505-3937. **Fax:** 505-988-9230. **E-Mail:** djkane@swScis.com

KANE, EDWARD R, TECHNICAL MANAGEMENT. **Personal Data:** b Schenectady, NY, September 13, 1918; m 1948, Doris; c Christine K (Plant) & Susan K (Booth). **Education:** Union Col, BS, 1940; Mass Inst Technol, PhD (phys chem), 1943. **Honors & Awards:** Int Paladium Medal, Soc Indust Chem, 1979. **Professional Experience:** RETIRED; mem gov bd, Nat Res Coun, 1990-1993; coun mem and treas, Nat Acad Eng, 1986-1993; dir, Inco Ltd, 1981-1989; dir, Tex Instruments, 1980-1989; dir, Mead Corp, 1980-1988; mem corp, Mass Inst Technol, 1979-1989; mem gov bd, JP Morgan, 1979-1988; pres, E I du Pont de Nemours & Co, 1973-1979; trustee, Union Col, 1972-1977; dir, E I du Pont de Nemours & Co, 1969-1980. **Memberships:** Soc Chem Indust (pres, 1979-1980); Nat Acad Eng (treas, 1986-1993). **Mailing Address:** Old Kennett Rd, Wilmington, DE 19807.

KANE, E(NEAS) D(ILLON), ENGINEERING. **Personal Data:** b San Francisco, Calif, January 8, 1917; m 1944, c 8. **Education:** Univ Calif, BS, 1938, PhD (mech eng), 1949; Kans State Col, MS, 1939. **Professional Experience:** RETIRED; vpres technol, Stand Oil Co, Calif, 1975-1982; vpres res, Chevron Res Co, 1970-1976; pres, Chevron Res Co, 1967-1970; vpres prod res, Chevron Res Co, 1965-1967; asst secy exec comt, Stand Oil Co, Calif, 1964-1965; mgr prod res, Chevron Res Co, 1963-1964; res, Calif Res Corp, 1954-1963; supvr process eval, Calif Res & Develop Co, 1952-1953; assoc prof, Radiation Lab, 1951-1952; assoc prof, Univ Calif, 1950-1951; lectr, Univ Calif, 1947-1948; asst prof eng design, Univ Calif, 1945-1947; group engr, Clinton Eng Works, Tenn Eastman Corp, Oak Ridge, 1943-1945; mech engr, Radiation Lab, Univ Calif, 1942-1943; Student & design engr, Westinghouse Mfg Co, Philadelphia, 1939-1940. **Memberships:** Nat Acad Eng; Am Soc Mech Engrs. **Research Statement & Publications:** Flow of gases at low pressures; process design and evaluation in nuclear energy and petroleum refining; oil field research. **Mailing Address:** 781 Balra Dr, El Cerrito, CA 94530.

KANE, FRANCIS X, AERONAUTICS. **Professional Experience:** RETIRED; US Air Force, as of 1997. **Memberships:** Am Inst Aeronaut & Astron. **Mailing Address:** USAF, Sunnyvale, CA 94085. **Fax:** 562-797-5828.

KANE, GORDON LEON, HIGH ENERGY PHYSICS, Cosmology. **Personal Data:** b St Paul, Minn, January 19, 1937; m Lois; c Hal & Mollie. **Education:** Univ Minn, BA, 1958; Univ Ill, MS, 1961, PhD (physics), 1963. **Honors & Awards:** Victor Weisskopf Collegiate Professor of Physics. **Professional Experience:** PROF PHYSICS, UNIV MICH, ANN ARBOR, 1975-; Guggenheim Mem Found fel, 1971-1972; asst prof, Univ Mich, Ann Arbor, 1965-1975; Res assoc physics, Johns Hopkins Univ, 1963-1965; ed, Phys Rev; consult, Brookhaven Nat Lab & Standord Linear Accelerator Ctr; Delphasus lectr, Univ Calif, Santa Cruz; Director, Michigan Center for Theoretical Physics. **Memberships:** Fel Am Phys Soc; Hist Sci Soc; Fel Am Asn Advan Sci; Fel British Institute of Physics. **Research Statement & Publications:** Theoretical high energy physics; supersymmetry; Higgs physics; dark matter; cosmological constant; collider physics. **Mailing Address:** Dept Physics, Univ Mich, Ann Arbor, MI 48109. **Fax:** 734-763-2213. **E-Mail:** gkane@umich.edu

KANE, GORDON PHILO, PESTICIDE FORMULATION. **Personal Data:** b New York, NY, December 8, 1926; m 1952, Saxon B; c Kathleen, Gordon & John. **Education:** Adelphi Univ, BA, 1949; Polytech Inst Brooklyn, MS, 1953. **Professional Experience:** CONSULT, 1987-; sr staff chemist, Ciba-Geigy Corp, 1978-1987; group leader, Ciba-Geigy Corp, 1973-1978; sr chemist, Ciba-Geigy Corp, 1968-1973; sr org chemist, Columbia Nitrogen Corp, 1964-1968; res scientist, Res Ctr, 1962-1964; res dir, Valchem Div, United Merchants & Mfrs, SC, 1956-1962; indust chemist, Barrett Div, Allied Chem Corp, 1956; Chemist, Warner-Lambert Pharmaceut Corp, NY, 1951-1954. **Memberships:** Am Chem Soc; fel Am Inst Chemists. **Research Statement & Publications:** Pesticide formulation and process development. **Mailing Address:** 38127 Monticello Dr, Prairieville, LA 70769.

KANE, HARRISON, GEOTECHNICAL ENGINEERING. **Personal Data:** b Brooklyn, NY, January 2, 1925; wid, c 3. **Education:** City Col New York, BCE, 1947; Columbia Univ, MS, 1948; Univ Ill, PhD (soil mech), 1961. **Professional Experience:** PROF EMER CIVIL & ENVIRON ENG, UNIV IOWA, 1993-; chmn, Civil Eng Dept, 1971-1985; prof, Civil Eng Dept, 1970-1993; NSF res grant, 1967-1972; from assoc prof to prof, Univ Iowa, 1964-1970; asst prof, Univ Ill, 1961-1964; asst prof civil eng, Pa State Univ, 1956-1961; lectr struct, City Col New York, 1956; planning engr, US Dept Army, Ger, 1951-1953; design engr, Parsons, Brinckerhoff Hall & Macdonald, 1948-1951 & 1953-1956. **Memberships:** Fel Am Soc Civil Engrs; Am Soc Eng Educ. **Research Statement & Publications:** Engineering properties of loess; earth pressures on braced excavations. **Mailing Address:** Dept Civil & Environ Eng, Univ Iowa, 260 Black Springs Circle, Iowa City, IA 52246. **E-Mail:** harrison-kane@uiowa.edu

KANE, HENRY EDWARD, GEOLOGY. **Personal Data:** b New Orleans, La, December 18, 1917; m 1953, Gertrude Mattson; c Denarie A & Karen O. **Education:** La State Univ, BS, 1945, MS, 1948; Univ Calif, Los Angeles, PhD, 1965. **Professional Experience:** EMER PROF GEOL, BALL STATE UNIV, 1983-; Univ Sci Improv Prog grant, 1970-1971; Res grant, Ball State Univ, 1970-1971 & 1968-1969 & 1965-1967; Res grant, Non-Western Studies, 1967; NSF geol Gulf Coast, Rice Univ, 1967; Res grant, Ind Acad Sci, 1966; Res grant, Univ Calif, Los Angeles, 1964-1965; from asst prof to prof, Ball State Univ, 1961-1983; Partic, NSF teachers cong, Am Univ, 1961; asst prof geol, Ft Hays Kans State Col, 1960-1961; Partic, NSF teachers cong, field geol inst, Ind Univ, 1960; Partic, NSF teachers cong, Univ Ore, 1959; Partic, NSF teachers cong, res adv undergrad res prog, 1959; asst prof geol, Lamar State Col Technol, 1956-1960; Res grant, Shell Res & Develop Co, Shell Oil Co, 1956-1959; geologist, Lloyd Corp Ltd, 1952-1956; asst, Univ Calif, Los Angeles, 1949-1951; subsurface geologist, Stanolind Oil & Gas Co, Standard Oil Co Ind, 1948; asst, La State Univ, 1946-1948; field geologist, Miss River Comn, 1945; Geol scout, Tex Co, 1944. **Memberships:** Fel Geol Soc Am. **Research Statement & Publications:** Recent sedimentation, microfaunas, quaternary geomorphology and geology of the Gulf Coast and the Southern Rockies; fluviatile geomorphology; Kentucky River Basin; geology, Eastern Indiana. **Mailing Address:** 4109 N Redding Rd, Muncie, IN 47304.

KANE, JAMES, MECHANICAL ENGINEERING. **Education:** Univ Conn, PhD. **Professional Experience:** ASSOC PROF, DEPT MECH & AERONAUT ENG, CLARKSON UNIV, NY, as of 2005. **Mailing Address:** Dept Mech & Aeronaut Eng, Clarkson Univ 207 CAMP PO Box 5725, Potsdam, NY 13699-5725. **Fax:** 315-268-6438. **E-Mail:** kane@clarkson.edu

KANE, JAMES FRANCIS, MICROBIAL PHYSIOLOGY, MICROBIAL GENETICS. **Personal Data:** b Philadelphia, Pa, November 22, 1942; m 1966, Roselyn; c Maryellen, James R & Catherine. **Education:** St Joseph's Col, BS, 1964; State Univ NY, Buffalo, PhD (biol), 1969. **Professional Experience:** SCI FEL, SMITH KLINE BEECHAM, 1992-; sci fel, Monsanto, 1988-1992; adj prof molecular biol, Wash Univ, 1988-1992; sr res group leader, Monsanto, 1984-1988; sr res specialist, Monsanto, 1982-1984; sr scientist, Bethesda Res Labs, 1981-1982; vice chmn, Dept Microbiol & Immunol, Ctr Health Sci, Univ Tenn, 1980-1981; adv & consult, Commun Media, Am Soc Microbiol, 1979-1981; NSF grant, 1973-1978; from asst prof to assoc prof, Ctr Health Sci, Univ Tenn, 1970-1981; USPHS fel, Baylor Col Med, 1968-1970; fel, Baylor Col Med, 1968-1970. **Memberships:** Am Soc Microbiol; Soc Indust Microbiol; Am Soc Biochem & Molecular Biol. **Research Statement & Publications:** Study the effects of metabolic stress on the quantity and quality of heterlogous proteins produced by E coli in high density fermentations. **Mailing Address:** Glaxo Smithkline Co, 709 Swedeland Rd, King of Prussia, PA 19406. **Fax:** 610-270-7449. **E-Mail:** james_f_kane@sbhrd.com

KANE, JAMES JOSEPH, ORGANIC CHEMISTRY. **Personal Data:** b New York, NY, March 4, 1929; m 1967, Margaret. **Education:** Upsala Col, BS, 1954; Ohio State Univ, PhD (org chem), 1960. **Professional Experience:** ASSOC PROF EMER CHEM, WRIGHT STATE UNIV, 1992-; assoc prof chem, Wright State Univ, 1970-1992; asst prof, Wright State Univ, 1966-1970; coordr, Wright State Univ, 1965-1966; asst prof, Wright State Univ, 1964-1965; res chemist, E I du Pont Del Nemours & Co, 1960-1964. **Memberships:** Am Chem Soc; Sigma Xi. **Research Statement & Publications:** Chemistry of small and medium carbocyclic and heterocyclic systems; polymers with high thermal stability. **Mailing Address:** Dept Chem, Col Sci & Math, Wright State Univ, 3640 Colonel Glenn HWY, Dayton, OH 45435-0001.

KANE, JOHN POWER, MEDICINE, BIOCHEMISTRY. **Personal Data:** b West Point, NY, July 15, 1932; m 1966, c 3. **Education:** Ore State Univ, BS, 1955; Univ Ore, MS & MD, 1957; Univ Calif, San Francisco, PhD (biochem), 1971. **Professional Experience:** ASSOC DIR, CARDIOVASC RES INST, as of 2002; PROF MED & BIOCHEM & BIOPHYSICS, CARDIOVASC RES INST, UNIV CALIF, SAN FRANCISCO, 1982-; assoc Prof Med, Cardiovasc Res Inst, Univ Calif, San Francisco, beginning 1976; asst prof, Hosps, 1971-1976; Am Heart Asn estab investr, Cardiovasc Res Inst, Univ Calif, San Francisco, 1971-1976; asst resident, Hosps, 1959-1960; asst resident internal med, Hosps, Stanford Univ, 1958-1959; intern med, Santa Clara County Hosp, San Jose, 1957-1958; mem coun arteriosclerosis, Am Heart Asn, estab investr. **Memberships:** AAAS; Am Chem Soc; Biophys Soc; Am Soc Clin Invest; Am Fedn Clin Res; Am Asn Physicians. **Research Statement & Publications:** Structure and function of serum lipoproteins; lipid and carbohydrate metabolism; arteriosclerosis; genetics. **Mailing Address:** Dept Med & Biochem, Univ Calif, Box 0130, L1337b, San Francisco, CA 94143-0130. **Fax:** 416-502-5658. **E-Mail:** kane@itsa.ucsf.edu

KANE, JOHN ROBERT, NUCLEAR PHYSICS. **Personal Data:** b Washington, DC, May 16, 1936; m Kay. **Education:** Loyola Col, Md, BS, 1959; Carnegie-Mellon Univ, MS, 1962, PhD, 1964. **Professional Experience:** PROF PHYSICS, COL WILLIAM & MARY, 1979-; assoc prof nuclear physics, 1971-1978; asst prof, 1968-1971; Res assoc, 1964-1968. **Memberships:** Am Phys Soc. **Research Statement & Publications:** Muonic and hadronic atom x-ray studies; muonium in vacuum measurements; rare kaon decays. **Mailing Address:** Dept Physics, Col William & Mary, Small Hall 339D, Williamsburg, VA 23187-8795. **Fax:** 757-221-3540. **E-Mail:** kane@physics.wm.edu

KANE, MARTIN FRANCIS, GEOPHYSICS. **Personal Data:** b Portland, Maine, September 9, 1928; m 1957, Jacqueline; c 5. **Education:** St Francis Xavier Univ, BSc, 1951; St Louis Univ, PhD, 1970. **Professional Experience:** RETIRED; consult, US Geol Surv Mission Jeddah Saudi Arabia, 1986-1990; chief geophysicist, US Geol Surv Mission Jeddah Saudi Arabia, 1984-1986; res scientist, Regional Geophys Br, 1978-1983; chief, Regional Geophys Br, 1972-1978; geologist-in-charge, Marine Geol Br, 1970-1971; supvry geophysicist, Regional Geophys Br, 1968-1970; geophysicist, Regional Geophys Br, US Geol Surv, 1952-1963; Astrogeol Br, 1964-1967. **Memberships:** Geol Soc Am; Am Geophys Union. **Research Statement & Publications:** Regional geophysics; marine geophysics; planetary geophysics. **Mailing Address:** 9998 W Fla Ave, Lakewood, CO 80232.

KANE, RICHARD M, MATHEMATICS. **Education:** Univ Waterloo, PhD, 1973. **Professional Experience:** PROF, DEPT MATHS, UNIV WESTERN ONT, CAN, as of 2005. **Mailing Address:** Dept Math, Univ Western Ont, London, ON N6A 5B7, Can. **Fax:** 519-661-3610. **E-Mail:** rkane@uwo.ca

KANE, ROBERT B, mathematics; deceased, see previous edition for last biography

KANE, RONALD S(TEVEN), THERMAL FLUID ANALYSIS, ENERGY SYSTEMS. **Personal Data:** b New York, NY, February 11, 1944; m 1968, c 2. **Education:** City Col New York, BME, 1965, MME, 1969; City Univ New York, PhD (eng), 1973. **Professional Experience:** DEAN GRAD STUDIES, NJ INST TECHNOL, as of 2004; ASST VPRES ACAD AFFAIRS, NJ INST TECHNOL, 1990-; consult, Transnuclear Corp, Gen Elec, 1985-; dean grad studies, res & continuing prod educ, prof mech eng, Stevens Inst Technol, 1985-1990; chmn dept & grad dir reactor admin, Manhattan Col, 1981-1985; consult, Burns & Roe, 1980-; reviewer, McGraw-Hill Publ Co, 1976-; consult, Polytech Design Co, Foster Wheeler Energy Corp, 1974-; from asst prof to prof mech eng, Manhattan Col, 1974-1985; consult thermal sci, Polytech Design Co, 1973-1974; grad asst fluid mech, City Col New York, 1970-1973; Res asst, City Col New York Res Found, 1970-1973; proj engr mech, Esso Res & Eng, 1966-1970; Mech engr heat transfer, Pratt & Whitney Aircraft, 1965-1966. **Memberships:** Am Soc Mech Engrs; Am Inst Chem Engrs; Sigma Xi; Am Soc Eng Educ. **Research Statement & Publications:** Drag reduction in particulate suspensions; coal gasification; liquid metal heat transfer and fluid mechanics; ocean thermal energy conversion; heat pipe development; new energy resource development; advanced reactor safety. **Mailing Address:** N J Inst Technol, 140 E Bldg, Univ Heights, Newark, NJ 07102-1982. **Fax:** 973-596-3463. **E-Mail:** ronald.kane@njit.edu

KANE, STEPHEN SHIMMON, chemistry; deceased, see previous edition for last biography

KANE, SUSAN ELIZABETH, MULTIDRUG RESISTANCE, EXPRESSION VECTORS. **Personal Data:** b Tucson, Ariz, August 8, 1957. **Education:** Stanford Univ, BS, 1979; Johns Hopkins Univ, PhD (biol), 1986. **Professional Experience:** PROF BIOL, UNIV CALIF, LOS ANGELES, as of 2003; ASSOC DEAN, GRAD STUDIES & RES, RES ADMIN, ORSP, as of 2003; assoc res scientist, City New Hope Nat Med Ctr, beginning 1996; Asst res scientist, City New Hope Nat Med Ctr, 1990-1996; staff fel, Nat Cancer Inst, NIH, 1990; Fel Am Cancer Soc, Nat Cancer Inst, NIH, 1987-1990. **Memberships:** Am Asn Cancer Res; Am Asn Advan Sci; Am Soc Cell Biol; Asn Women Sci. **Research Statement & Publications:** Multidrug resistance (MDR) which develops in cancer patients during chemotherapy, the mechanisms by which MDR works; gene therapy to protect normal cells against toxic side-effects of chemotherapy. **Mailing Address:** ORSP, 5151 State Univ Dr, Admin Bldg # 301 & 302, Los Angeles, CA 90032. **Fax:** 323-343-6430. **E-Mail:** sekane@cslanet.calstatela.edu

KANE, THOMAS R(EIF), MECHANICS, AEROSPACE ENGINEERING. **Personal Data:** b Vienna, Austria, March 23, 1924; American citizen; m 1951, Ann; c Linda & Jeffrey. **Education:** Columbia Univ, BS, 1949 & 1950, MS, 1952, PhD (appl mech), 1953. **Honorary Degrees:** Dr Tech Sci, Tech Univ Vienna, Austria, 1990. **Honors & Awards:** hon mem Am Soc Mech Engrs; Dirk Brouwer Award, Am Astron Soc; Alexander von Humboldt Prize. **Professional Experience:** PROF EMER ENG MECH, STANFORD UNIV, 1997-; vis prof, Fed Univ Rio Del Janeiro, 1971-1972; prof, Stanford Univ, 1961-1997; fulbright lectr, Victoria Univ Manchester, 1958-1959; from asst prof to assoc prof mech eng, Univ Pa, 1953-1960; res assoc, Columbia Univ, 1952-1953. **Memberships:** Am Soc Mech Engrs; Am Astronaut Soc. **Research Statement & Publications:** Dynamics; human motion; mechanics of continua. **Mailing Address:** Dept Mech Eng, Stanford Univ, 817 Lathrop Dr, Stanford, CA 94305-3030. **Fax:** 650-493-0631. **E-Mail:** tkane@stanford.edu

KANE, WALTER REILLY, NUCLEAR PHYSICS. **Personal Data:** b Ithaca, NY, November 3, 1926; m 1953, Margaret; c Katherine S. **Education:** Stanford Univ, BS, 1949; Univ Wash, MS, 1951; Harvard Univ, PhD (physics), 1959. **Professional Experience:** PHYSICIST, BROOKHAVEN NAT LAB, 1966-; from asst physicist to assoc physicist, Brookhaven Nat Lab, 1960-1966; res assoc, Brookhaven Nat Lab, 1958-1960; physicist, Avco Mfg Corp, 1956-1957; mem staff, Los Alamos Sci Lab, 1952-1954; physicist, Nat Bur Stand, 1951-1952. **Memberships:** Fel Am Phys Soc; sr mem Inst Nuclear Mat Mgt. **Research Statement & Publications:** Nuclear spectroscopy; neutron physics. **Mailing Address:** Dept Advan Technol, Brookhaven Nat Lab, Upton, NY 11973-5000. **Fax:** 516-344-7533. **E-Mail:** wkane@bnl.gov

KANE, WILLIAM J, ORTHOPEDIC SURGERY, PHYSIOLOGY. **Personal Data:** b Brooklyn, NY, February 22, 1933; m 1960, Elizabeth; c Kathleen, William, Stephen, Patricia & Anne. **Education:** Col the Holy Cross, AB, 1954; Columbia Univ, MD, 1958; Univ Minn, Minneapolis, PhD (orthop surg), 1965. **Honors & Awards:** Kappa Delta Award, Am Acad Orthop Surg, 1966. **Professional Experience:** RETIRED; prof orthop surg, med sch, Northwestern Univ, beginning 1978; Ryerson prof orthop surg & chmn dept, Med Sch, Northwestern Univ, 1971-1978; from instr to assoc prof orthop surg, Univ Minn, Minneapolis, 1964-1971. **Memberships:** Am Orthop Asn; Am Acad Orthop Surg; Scoliosis Res Soc (pres, 1979-1980); Int Soc Study Lumbar Spine; Am Col Surgeons; NAm Spine Soc. **Research Statement & Publications:** Bone blood flow; degenerative diseases of the spine; pelvic fractures; scoliosis. **Mailing Address:** 825 S Eighth St, Minneapolis, MN 55404. **Fax:** 612-333-6922.

KANE, WILLIAM THEODORE, X-RAY DIFFRACTION, SPECTROSCOPY. **Personal Data:** b Jamaica, NY, September 8, 1932; m 1954, c 4. **Education:** Univ Kans, BA, 1960; Univ Mo, PhD (x-ray crystallog), 1966. **Professional Experience:** RETIRED; res supvr, X-ray Anal, 1974-1994; supvr, X-ray Anal, 1973-1974; treas, Nat Conf Electron Probe Anal, 1969-1971; res crystallogr, Corning Glass Works, 1967-1973; crystallogr, Corning Glass Works, 1966-1967. **Memberships:** Mineral Soc Am; Am Crystallog Asn; Microbeam Anal Soc. **Research Statement & Publications:** Instrumental analysis of materials including electron probe, x-ray diffraction, scanning electron micorscopy, electron transmission microscopy; laboratory automation and computerization. **Mailing Address:** PO Box 380, Big Flats, NY 14814.

KANE-BERMAN, JOCELYNE DENISE LAMB, HEALTHCARE ADMINISTRATION. **Personal Data:** b Johannesburg, SAfrica, March 26, 1933. **Education:** Univ Cape Town, MB ChB, 1956, MPA, 1978. **Professional Experience:** CHIEF DIR, HEALTH DEPT, WEST CAPE, SAFRICA, 1996-; found mem, Coun Health Servs Accreditation, 1994-; trustee, Health Systs Trust, SAfrica, 1992-; Sr lectr, Dept Community Health, Univ Cape Town, 1978-; from med supt to chief dir, Groote Schuur Hosp, SAfrica, 1970-1995; med officer, Cape Prov Admin, 1960-1970; Intern, Groote Schuur Hosp, SAfrica, 1957. **Memberships:** Foreign assoc Inst Med-Nat Acad Sci; Med Asn SAfrica (pres, 1996-1997). **Mailing Address:** Health Dept Prov Admin, Dorp St, Cape Town West Cape, South Africa.

KANEDA, TOSHI, BIOCHEMISTRY, MICROBIOLOGY. **Personal Data:** b Utsunomiyashi, Japan, May 21, 1925; m 1959, c 2. **Education:** Tokyo Inst Technol, BEng, 1950; Univ Tokyo, DSc(biochem), 1962. **Professional Experience:** EMER RES FEL, ALTA RES COUN, 1992-; Heilongjiang Acad Sci, China, 1988-; res fel, Alta Res Coun, 1984-1992; HEAD BIOL, ALTA RES COUN, 1981-; hon prof med bact, Univ Alta, 1975-; Med Res Coun Can grant, 1964-; RES MICROBIOLOGIST, ALTA RES COUN, 1960-; fel biochem, Sch Med, Western Res Univ, 1958-1960; Fel microbiol, Prairie Regional Lab, Nat Res Coun Can, 1956-1958. **Memberships:** Am Chem Soc; Can Biochem Soc. **Research Statement & Publications:** Microbiology of fossil fuels; low temperature microbiology; biosynthesis and functions of iso and anteiso series of fatty acids in bacteria. **Mailing Address:** 312-5465 201st St, Langley, BC N3A 1P8, Can.

KANEHIRO, YOSHINORI, SOIL SCIENCE. **Personal Data:** b Puuloa, Hawaii, October 6, 1919; m 1947, c 2. **Education:** Univ Hawaii, BS, 1942, MS, 1948, PhD (soil sci), 1964. **Professional Experience:** PROF EMER SOIL SCI & SOIL SCIENTIST EMER, UNIV HAWAII, 1984-; soil scientist & prof soil sci, Univ Hawaii, 1970-1983; res soil scientist, Agr Res Serv, USDA, Ft Collins, Colo, 1968-1969; from asst soil scientist & asst prof to assoc soil scientist & assoc prof, Univ Hawaii, 1957-1970; tech consult, Olin Mathieson Chem Corp, 1957; jr soil scientist, Univ Hawaii, 1948-1957; Asst soils & agr chem, Univ Hawaii, 1942-1948. **Memberships:** Am Soc Agron; Soil Sci Soc Am; Sigma Xi. **Research Statement & Publications:** Nitrogen transformation in soils; minor elements, especially zinc in soils; clay mineralogy of soils. **Mailing Address:** Dept Agron & Soil Sci, Univ Hawaii 1910 East-West Rd, Honolulu, HI 96822.

KANEKO, HISASHI, ELECTRICAL ENGINEERING. **Personal Data:** b Tokyo, Japan, November 19, 1933; m Motoko Washino; c Satoshi, Makoto & Hajime. **Education:** Univ Tokyo, BSEE, 1956, PhD (eng), 1967; Univ Calif, MSEE, 1962. **Honors & Awards:** Kajii Mem Prize, Elec Comn Asn, Japan, 1979; Achievement Award, Inst Electronics Info & Commun Engrs, 1985; E H Armstrong Award, Inst Elec & Electronics Engrs, 1992. **Professional Experience:** Pres, NEC Corp, Tokyo, 1994-1999; exec vpres, NEC Am, NY, 1993-1994; pres & chief exec officer, NEC Am, NY, 1991-1993; bd dirs, Nat Eng Consort Corp, 1989-; sr vpres, Transmission Div, 1989-1993; vpres, Transmission Div, 1985-1989; gen mgr, Transmission Div, 1970-1985; mem tech staff, Bell Tel Labs, 1968-1970; res mgr, NEC Corp, 1962-1968; Res asst, Univ Calif, Berkeley, 1960-1962; res staff, NEC Corp, 1956-1960. **Memberships:** Foreign assoc Nat Acad Eng; fel Inst Elec & Electronics Engrs; Inst Electronics Info & Commun Engrs; Eng Acad Japan. **Research Statement & Publications:** Author of 4 publications; granted 70 Japanese patents and 4 US patents; electrical engineering. **Mailing Address:** NEC Corp, 571 Shiba Minatoku, Tokyo 108-01, Japan.

KANEKO, JIRO JERRY, PHYSIOLOGY, CLINICAL BIOCHEMISTRY. **Personal Data:** b Stockton, Calif, November 20, 1924; m 1991, Teresa; c Taro Jay, Jiro John & Saburo James. **Education:** Univ Calif, AB, 1952, DVM, 1956, PhD (comp path), 1959. **Honorary Degrees:** DVSc, Belg, 1980. **Honors & Awards:** Outstanding Achievement in Animal Clinical Chem, Int Soc Anim Clin Chem, 1995. **Professional Experience:** PROF EMER, SCH VET MED, UNIV CALIF, DAVIS, 1994-; prof clin path, Sch Vet Med, Univ Calif, Davis, 1969-1994; chmn dept, Sch Vet Med, Univ Calif, Davis, 1969-1985; from asst prof to assoc prof, Exp Sta, 1959-1969; lectr, 1957-1959; asst specialist, Exp Sta, 1956-1959. **Memberships:** Soc Exp Biol & Med; Am Physiol Soc; Am Asn Clin Chem; Am Col Vet Pathologists; Sigma Xi; Am Chem Soc. **Research Statement & Publications:** Biochemistry of erythrocyte and hemoglobin of animals; blood dyscrasias of animals; metabolic diseases; kinetics of erythropoiesis and granulopoiesis; organ functions. **Mailing Address:** Dept Path Microbiol & Immunol, Sch Vet Med, Univ Calif, Davis, CA 95616. **Fax:** 916-752-3349. **E-Mail:** jjkaneko@ucdavis.edu

KANE-MAGUIRE, NOEL ANDREW PATRICK, INORGANIC CHEMISTRY. **Personal Data:** b Brisbane, Queensland, Australia, May 4, 1942; m 1969, c 1. **Education:** Univ Queensland, BS, 1963, Hons, 1964, PhD (chem), 1969. **Professional Experience:** PROF CHEM, FURMAN UNIV, 1985-; from asst prof to assoc prof, Furman Univ, 1973-1985; assoc, Carleton Univ, 1970-1973; Assoc inorg chem, Boston Univ, 1968-1969 & Wayne State Univ, 1969-1970. **Memberships:** Am Chem Soc. **Research Statement & Publications:** Reaction mechanisms of inorganic compounds; transition metal photochemistry. **Mailing Address:** Chem Dept, Furman Univ, 122 E Plyler Hall, Greenville, SC 29613. **Fax:** 864-294-3559. **E-Mail:** noel.kane-maguire@furman.edu

KANEMASU, EDWARD TSUKASA, AGRICULTURE. **Personal Data:** b Hood River, Ore, November 16, 1940; c 3. **Education:** Mont State Univ, BS, 1962, MS, 1964; Univ Wis-Madison, PhD (soil physics), 1969. **Honors & Awards:** Agron Res Award, Am Soc Agron; fel, AAAS. **Professional Experience:** DIR INT AGR & ASST DEAN INT AFFAIRS, UNIV GA, as of 2006; REGENT'S PROF ATMOSPHERIC & ENVIRON PHYSICS, UNIV GA, as of 2004; prof & head, agron dept, Univ Ga, 1989-; prof agron, Evapo-transportation Lab, 1978-1989; from asst prof to assoc prof, Kans State Univ, 1969-1978. **Memberships:** AAAS; fel Am Soc Agron; Am Meteorol Soc. **Research Statement & Publications:** Stomatal diffusion resistance as influenced by leaf water potential and light; evapotranspiration and water use efficiency of agronomic crops. **Mailing Address:** Col Agr & Environ Sci Univ Ga, 218 Hoke Smith Bldg, Athens, GA 30602. **Fax:** 706-542-7905. **E-Mail:** ekanema@uga.edu

KANER, RICHARD B, CHEMISTRY. **Education:** Brown Univ, AB; Univ Pa, PhD. **Professional Experience:** PROF, DEPT CHEM & BIOCHEM, UNIV CALIF, LOS ANGELES, 1993-. **Research Statement & Publications:** Inorganic and materials chemistry; conjugated polymer membranes. **Mailing Address:** Dept Chem & Biochem, Univ Calif, Los Angeles, 607 Charles E Young Dr E POBox 951569, Los Angeles, CA 90095-1569. **Fax:** 310-206-4038. **E-Mail:** kaner@chem.ucla.edu

KANES, WILLIAM H, TECTONICS. **Personal Data:** b New York, NY, October 15, 1934; m 1984, c 6. **Education:** City Col NY, BS, 1956; Univ WVa, MS, 1958, PhD (geol), 1965. **Professional Experience:** DISTINGUISHED PROF EMER, UNIV SC, AS OF 2006; vis prof & adv, Postgrad Res Inst Sedimentology & exec dir, ESRI-UK, Univ Reading, beginning 1989; hon prof fel, ESRI-UK, Univ Bristol, 1986-1989; co-dir, ESRI-UK, Univ Bristol, 1986-1988; distinguished prof earth resources, Univ SC, beginning 1985; hon prof fel, Univ Col Aberystwyth, 1979-1983 & Univ Col Swansea, 1980-1986; co-dir, Earth Resources Inst, Univ Col Swansea, 1980-1986; vis prof fel, Univ Col Swansea, Univ Wales, 1977-1980; NSF resident res prof, Acad Sci Res & Technol, Cairo, Egypt, 1976-1977; PROF GEOL, UNIV SC, 1975-; dir, Earth Sci & Resource Inst, 1975; assoc prof, Univ SC, 1971-1975; asst prof geol, WVa Univ, 1969-1970; area geologist, Exxon Stan Libya, 1967-1969; Sr res geologist, Exxon Prod Res Co, 1960-1966. **Memberships:** Assoc Am Asn Petrol Geol; Soc Econ Paleontologists & Mineralogists; fel Geol Soc Am; fel AAAS; Am Geophys Union. **Research Statement & Publications:** Stratigraphy, sedimentation and structural geology in the Appalachian Region; African and circum Mediterranean regional geology and tectonics; South American tectonics and petroleum geology; tectonics and petroleum geology of Eastern Europe and the USSR. **Mailing Address:** Dept Geol, Univ SC, 901 Sumpter St, Columbia, SC 29208-0001.

KANESHIGE, HARRY MASATO, CIVIL ENGINEERING. **Personal Data:** b Aiea, Oahu, Hawaii, July 11, 1929; m 1981, Susan Fleming; c Loren & Michael. **Education:** Univ Wis, BS, 1951, MS, 1952, PhD (civil eng), 1959. **Professional Experience:** PROF EMER CIVIL ENG, OHIO UNIV, as of 1998; prof civil eng, Ohio Univ, beginning 1974; from asst prof to assoc prof, Ohio Univ, 1958-1974; proj assoc, Univ Wis, 1956-1957; Instr civil eng, Univ Wis, 1954-1956 & 1957-1958. **Memberships:** AAAS; Am Soc Civil Engrs; Am Water Works Asn; Water Pollution Control Fedn. **Research Statement & Publications:** Environmental health and sanitation; surveying and mapping; water and wastewater treatment. **Mailing Address:** Dept Civil Eng, Ohio Univ, 136 Stocker Ctr, Athens, OH 45701.

KANESHIRO, EDNA SAYOMI, CELL BIOLOGY, BIOCHEMISTRY. **Personal Data:** b Hilo, Hawaii, December 20, 1937. **Education:** Syracuse Univ, BS, 1957, MS, 1962, PhD (zoology), 1968. **Honors & Awards:** Elected fel of AAAs, 1999; Henri Warembourg Fac; Med Medal, Univ of Lille, Lille France-1997; Elected Fel of the Gradu Sch, Univ of Cincinnati, 1994; Fac Achievement Award, Univ Cincinnati, 1997; George Rieveschl Award for Distinguished Sci Res, Univ Cincinnati, 2001; Elected Fel of Am Acad of Microbiol, 2001. **Professional Experience:** DISTINGUISHED RESEARCH PROF BIOL, UNIV CINCINNATI, 1982-; sr res microbiologist, Nat Inst Allergy & Infectious Dis, 1980-1981; mem corp, Marine Biol Lab, Woods Hole, 1973-; from asst prof to assoc prof, Univ Cincinnati, 1972-1982; NSF fel biochem, Bryn Mawr Col, 1970-1972; USPHS fel cell biol, Univ Chicago, 1968-1970. **Memberships:** Am Soc Cell Biol; Soc Protozoologists; AAAS; Am Soc Trop Med & Hyg; Sigma Xi; Am Asn Univ Profs. **Research Statement & Publications:** Structure and function of protozoans; membrane structure and function; lipid biochemistry; opportunistic infections (pneumocystis). **Mailing Address:** Dept Biol Sci, Univ Cincinnati 231 Bethesda Ave, Cincinnati, OH 45221-0006. **Fax:** 513-556-5280. **E-Mail:** edna.kaneshiro@uc.edu

KANESHIRO, KENNETH YOSHIMITSU, EVOLUTIONARY BIOLOGY, BEHAVIORAL ECOLOGY. **Personal Data:** b Honolulu, Hawaii, December 15, 1943; m 1967, c 2. **Education:** Univ Hawaii, BA, 1965, MS, 1968, PhD (entom), 1976. **Honors & Awards:** Distinguished Service Award, Hawaii Conservation Alliance 2003. **Professional Experience:** DIR, CTR CONSERV RES & TRAINING, UNIV HAWAII, since 1993; dir, Hawaiian Evolutionary Biol Prog, beginning 1985; Coordr, Hawaiian Drosophila Proj, Dept Entom, Univ Hawaii, beginning 1970. **Memberships:** Soc Study Evolution. **Research Statement & Publications:** Basic mechanisms of speciation processes in Hawaiian Drosophila; tools and techniques for the formulation of a biosystematic classification of the endemic Hawaiian Drosophilidae; sexual selection theory and genetic consequences of small population size; conservation biology. **Mailing Address:** Ctr Conserv Res & Training, Univ hawaii, 3050 Maile Way, Gilmore 406, Honolulu, HI 96822. **Fax:** 808-956-2647. **E-Mail:** kykanesh@hawaii.edu

KANEY, ANTHONY ROLLAND, GENETICS. **Personal Data:** b Centralia, Ill, March 8, 1940. **Education:** Wabash Col, AB, 1961; Univ Ill, Urbana, PhD (microbiol), 1966. **Professional Experience:** PROF EMER BIOL, BRYN MAWR COL, as of 2004; prof biol, Bryn Mawar Col, beginning 1980; NATO fel, Biol Inst Carlsberg Found, Copenhagen, 1976-1977; from asst prof to assoc prof, Bryn Mawr Col, 1969-1980; asst prof biol, Univ PR, San Juan, 1967-1969; Res assoc microbiol, Univ Ill, Urbana, 1966-1967. **Memberships:** Genetics Soc Am; Soc Protozool. **Research Statement & Publications:** Developmental genetics of Tetrahymena thermophila. **Mailing Address:** Dept Biol, Bryn Mawr Col, 101 N Merion Ave, Bryn Mawr, PA 19010-2859. **E-Mail:** akaney@brynmawr.edu

KANFER, JULIAN NORMAN, BIOCHEMISTRY. **Personal Data:** b Brooklyn, NY, May 23, 1930; m 1987, Beverly McNamara; c Rachel & Brian. **Education:** Brooklyn Col, BS, 1954; George Washington Univ, MS, 1958, PhD (biochem), 1961. **Honors & Awards:** Vis Scientist Award, Med Res Coun Can, 1983, 1984 & 1986. **Professional Experience:** Vis prof, Univ Pittsburg Med Ctr, 1993-1994; PROF BIOCHEM, FAC MED UNIV MAN, 1975-; dept head, Fac Med Univ Man, 1975-1986; dir biochem, Eunice Kennedy Shriver Ctr, 1971-1975; biochemist, Mass Gen Hosp, Boston, 1971-1975; assoc biochemist, Mass Gen Hosp, Boston, 1969-1971; assoc prof, Med Sch, Duke Univ, 1968-1969; biochemist, Nat Inst Neurol Dis & Blindness, 1962-1969; NIH res fel, NSF res fel, 1962-1963; NIH res fel, Harvard Med Sch, 1961-1962; chemist, Nat Inst Neurol Dis & Blindness, 1955-1961; Lab asst biol, Brooklyn Col, 1954-1955; Harvard Med Sch; adj assoc prof Brandeis Univ; mem med adv bd, Nat Tay-Sachs Found. **Memberships:** AAAS; Am Chem Soc; Am Soc Biol Chem; Am Soc Neurochem; Int Soc Neurochem. **Research Statement & Publications:** Sphingolipid metabolism in relationship to the sphingolipidosis; membrane phosopholipids of brain; alzheimers disease, multiple sclerosis; signal transduction; second messengers. **Mailing Address:** Dept Biochem, Univ Man, 309 BMSB, Winnipeg, MB R3T 2N2, Can. **Fax:** 204-783-3548. **E-Mail:** jkanfer@cc.umanitoba.ca

KANG, C YONG, VIROLOGY, MOLECULAR BIOLOGY. **Personal Data:** b Hadong, Korea, November 28, 1940; Canadian citizen; m 1966, c 3. **Education:** Malling Agr Col, Denmark, DiplVSci, 1963; Kon-Kuk Univ, Seoul, Korea, BS, 1965; McMaster Univ, Hamilton, Can, PhD (virol), 1971. **Honorary Degrees:** Dsc, Carleton Univ, 1991. **Honors & Awards:** Korean-Canadian Heritage Award, 1989; Ho-Am Prize Med, 1999. **Professional Experience:** PROF MICROBIOL & IMMUNOL, UNIV WESTERN ONT, as of 2004; PROF EMER BIOL, UNIV WESTERN ONT, as of 2001; dean sci, Dept Microbiol & Immunol, Univ Western Ont, 1992-1999; prof & chmn, Dept Microbiol & Immunol, Fac Med, Univ Ottawa, 1982-1992; from asst prof to assoc prof virol, Southwestern Med Sch, Univ Tex, 1974-1982; asst viral oncol, McArdle Lab, Univ Wis, 1971-1974; sci consult, Virus Res Inst, Cambridge, Mass & Korea, Green Cross Corp, Seoul, Korea; res asst, Connaught Med Res Lab, Univ Toronto, Canada, 1966-1968. **Memberships:** Am Soc Virol; Am Soc Microbiol; AAAS; Can Soc Microbiologists; Genetic Soc Can; NY Acad Sci; fel Royal Soc Can. **Research Statement & Publications:** Studies of molecular mechanisms of viral interference mediated by defective interfering virus particles; investigation of molecular genetics of Hantaviruses; studies on cellular transformation by reticuloendotheliosis virus transforming gene rel; development of acquired immunodeficiency syndrome vaccine; published over 10 articles. **Mailing Address:** Dept Microbiol & Immunol, Siebens-Drake Res Inst, Univ Western Ont, 1400 Western Rd, London, ON N6G 2V4, Can. **Fax:** 519-663-3682. **E-Mail:** cykang@julian.uwo.ca

KANG, CHANG-YUIL, IDIOTYPE, VIRAL IMMUNOLOGY. **Personal Data:** b Korea, November 28, 1954; m 1984, c 2. **Education:** Seoul Nat Univ, BS, 1977, MS, 1981; State Univ NY, Buffalo, PhD (microbiol, immunol), 1986. **Professional Experience:** ASSOC PROF, DEPT PHARMACOL, SEOUL NAT UNIV, as of 2005; PRES, PANGENOMICS CO, as of 2003; scientist, Idec Pharmaceut Corp, beginning 1987; res affil, Roswell Park Mem Inst, 1983-1987; instr, Seoul Nat Univ Sch Pharm, 1981-1982; teaching asst microbiol, Seoul Nat Univ Sch Pharm, 1979-1981. **Memberships:** Am Asn Immunologists. **Research Statement & Publications:** Analysis of humoral immune response in HIV-1 infected individuals; characterization of different neutralizing antibodies with various epitope specificity and idiotype characteristics to define their roles for host defense mechanism; immunotherapy. **Mailing Address:** PanGenomics Inc, Ste 700-19 3699 Wilshire Blvd, Los Angeles, CA 90010. **Fax:** 213-385-6360. **E-Mail:** cykang@plaza.snu.ac.kr

KANG, CHIA-CHEN CHU, FUEL SCIENCE, PETROLEUM SCIENCE. **Personal Data:** b China, April 14, 1923; m 1951, c 2. **Education:** Shanghai Univ, BS, 1944; Univ Ill, MS, 1949, PhD (anal chem), 1951. **Professional Experience:** PRES, KANG ASSOCS, INC, 1981-; vpres, Catalysis Res Corp, 1978-1981; asst to sr vpres res & develop, Hydrocarbon Res, Inc, 1974-1978; Consult catalysis, United Catalysts, Inc, 1971-; consult chemist, 1970-1974; mgr sci serv, M W Kellogg Co, 1967-1970; sect head, M W Kellogg Co, 1957-1967; supvr, M W Kellogg Co, 1953-1957; Res chemist, M W Kellogg Co, 1951-1952. **Memberships:** Am Chem Soc. **Research Statement & Publications:** Catalysis; coal liquefaction process development; petroleum and petrochemical process development; trouble shooting for ammonia unit; chemical and instrumental analytical method development. **Mailing Address:** 301 Gallup Rd, Princeton, NJ 08540.

KANG, DAVID SOOSANG, PEDIATRICS, GENETICS. **Personal Data:** b Yiryong, Korea, November 7, 1931; American citizen; m 1958, c 4. **Education:** Seoul Nat Univ, MD, 1953, PhD (pharmacol), 1963. **Professional Experience:** DIR, BIOMEDICAL GENETICS, COL MED, RUSH UNIV, as of 2006; prof pediat & genetics, Col Med, Rush Univ, beginning 1988; from asst prof to assoc prof, Col Med, Rush Univ, 1977-1988; asst prof genetics, Ill Inst Technol, 1971-1975. **Memberships:** Am Soc Human Genetics. **Research Statement & Publications:** Genetic and biochemical studies of genetic disease and common diseases: interrelations of basic amino acids and their metabolites in urea cycle disorder, and role of protein-bound homocystine in common diseases. **Mailing Address:** Rush Children's Hosp, Rush Univ Med Ctr, 1650 W Harrison St, Chicago, IL 60612.

KANG, EDWARD P, SEROLOGY, INFECTIOUS DISEASES. **Personal Data:** b Chung Qing, China, August 11, 1942; American citizen; m 1970, Nancy; c Melissa. **Education:** Univ Southern Calif, BS, 1966; Howard Univ, MS, 1969, PhD (chem), 1973. **Honors & Awards:** Distingushed Alumni Award, Howard Univ Grad Sch, 1982. **Professional Experience:** SR RES SCIENTIST, BAYER DIAGNOSTICS, as of 2001; STAFF SCIENTIST, BAYER DIAGNOSTICS, 1992-; sci consult, Allen Barry & Assoc, 1991-1992; dir, Clin Sci, United Biomed Inc, 1986-1990; sr scientist & mgr, Electro-Nucleaics Inc, 1980-1986; res assoc, Blood Res Lab, Am Red Cross, 1973-1980; biochem investr, James F Mitchell Foundn, 1972-1973; lectr, Chem Dept, Howard Univ, 1972. **Memberships:** Fel Am Inst Chem; Nat Acad Clin Biochem; Am Chem Soc; Am Asn Clin Chem; N Am Chinese Clin Chem Asn (secy, 1996-1997, pres, 1998-1999); Sigma Xi. **Research Statement & Publications:** Immunodiagnostic product research and development and the applications onto automated analysis in infectious diseases, serology, coagulation and fibrinolysis and reproductive hormones. **Mailing Address:** Bayer Diagnostics, 511 Benedict Ave, Tarrytown, NY 10591. **E-Mail:** edward.kang.b@bayer.com

KANG, HONGLING, ACOUSTICS & NOISE VIBRATIONS. **Personal Data:** m 1984, Aiming; c John. **Education:** Tianjin Univ, BS, 1982, MS, 1984; Wayne State Univ, PhD (mech eng), 1990 Univ Mich (MBA), 2002. **Professional Experience:** Design & Development Engineer, Ford Motor Company, 1998-; ENG SPECIALIST, UNITED TECHNOLS, 1992-1998; struct engr, Acme Eng & Mfg Co, 1990-1992; Asst prof, Tianjin Univ, 1984-1985. **Memberships:** Am Soc Mech Engrs; Soc Automotive Engrs; Inst Noise Control Eng. **Research Statement & Publications:** Vehicle noise and vibration, noise and vibration of automobile components and their systems; noise and vibration control of automobile subsystems; finite element analysis and mechanical system analysis of the mechanical system with linear and non-linear characteristics. **Mailing Address:** 47663 Pavillon Rd, Canton, MI 48188. **E-Mail:** hkang1@ford.com

KANG, IK-JU, ATOMIC PHYSICS. **Personal Data:** b Korea, November 13, 1928; m 1955, c 3. **Education:** Yonsei Univ, Korea, BS, 1955, MS, 1957; Northwestern Univ, PhD (physics), 1962. **Professional Experience:** PROF EMER PHYSICS, SOUTHERN ILL UNIV, EDWARDSVILLE, as of 2004; chmn, Southern Ill Univ, Edwardsville, beginning 1980; prof physics, Southern Ill Univ, Edwardsville, beginning 1970; assoc prof, Edwardsville, 1969-1970; assoc prof, Carbondale, 1967-1969; asst prof, Univ Mass, Amherst, 1963-1967; res assoc, Brandeis Univ, 1962-1963; instr physics, Yonsei Univ, 1955-1959. **Memberships:** Am Phys Soc; Am Asn Physics Teachers. **Research Statement & Publications:** Theoretical atomic physics and scattering theory. **Mailing Address:** Dept Physics, Southern Ill Univ, Rm SL-2331, Box 1654, Edwardsville, IL 62026-1654. **Fax:** 618-650-3556. **E-Mail:** ikang@siue.edu

KANG, JOOHEE, SUPERCONDUCTIVITY, THIN FILM TECHNOLOGY. **Personal Data:** b Seoul, Korea. **Education:** Seoul Nat Univ, BA, 1977; Korea Advan Inst Sci, MS, 1979; Univ Minn, PhD (physics), 1987. **Professional Experience:** SR SCIENTIST, WESTINGHOUSE SCI & TECHNOL CTR, 1989-; postdoctoral superconductivity, Argonne Nat Lab, 1987-1989; asst prof physics, Ulsan Inst Technol, 1979-1982. **Memberships:** Am Phys Soc. **Research Statement & Publications:** Electromagnetic properties of exotic superconducting materials; superconducting thin films fabrication; superconducting electronic circuits design and fabrication. **Mailing Address:** Westinghouse Sci & Technol Ctr, 401-3X9B 1310 Beulah Rd, Pittsburgh, PA 15235.

KANG, JUNG WONG, POLYMER ORGANIC CHEMISTRY. **Personal Data:** b Tokyo, Japan, July 25, 1933; American citizen; m 1955, c 3. **Education:** Kinki Univ, Japan, BSc, 1956; Osaka Univ, MSc, 1959, PhD (org chem), 1962. **Professional Experience:** RETIRED; res assoc, Firestone Tire & Rubber Co, 1983-1996; res scientist chem to assoc scientist, Firestone Tire & Rubber Co, 1970-1982; res assoc, McMaster Univ, 1966-1970; fel organometallic chem, Univ NC, 1964-1966; fel org chem, Harvard Univ, 1963-1964; instr chem, Nara Med Col, Japan, 1962-1963. **Memberships:** Am Chem Soc; Japanese Chem Soc; Korean Chem & Chem Eng NAm. **Research Statement & Publications:** Polymer chemistry; organometallic chemistry. **Mailing Address:** Heritage House No 206, 6710 Hawaii Kai Dr, Honolulu, HI 96825.

KANG, KENNETH S, MICROBIAL PHYSIOLOGY. **Personal Data:** b Seoul, Korea, November 20, 1933; American citizen; m 1959, c 3. **Education:** Yonsei Univ, Korea, BS, 1957; Univ Del, MS, 1963, PhD (microbiol), 1965. **Professional Experience:** DIR, MSR, MERCK & CO, 1986-; assoc dir, Kelco Div, 1979-1986; mgr biochem res, Kelco Div, 1978-1979; Fel, Pa State Univ, 1975-1976; sect head biochem develop, Msr, Merck & CO, 1969-1978; proj leader, Msr, Merck & CO, 1968-1969; Sr res chemist, Msr, Merck & CO, 1966-1968. **Memberships:** AAAS; Am Chem Soc; Sigma Xi; Am Soc Microbiol. **Research Statement & Publications:** Development, production and characterization of microbial polysaccharides for industrial applications; authored 28 scientific publications and 19 US patents. **Mailing Address:** Merck & Co, Inc, One Merck Dr, PO Box 100, Whitehouse Station, NJ 08889-0100.

KANG, KEWON, GENETICS. **Personal Data:** b Andong, Korea, July 3, 1934; American citizen; m 1960, c 2. **Education:** Seoul Univ, Korea, BS, 1957, MS, 1960; NC State Univ, PhD (genetics), 1966. **Professional Experience:** AT KOREA INST TECH; vis researcher, Univ Hawaii, 1977; Vis assoc prof, Seoul Univ, 1977; from asst prof to assoc prof med genetics, Ind Univ, Indianapolis, 1969-1986; fel, Ind Univ, Indianapolis, 1966-1969; res asst genetics, NC State Univ, 1961-1966; Res assoc forest genetics, Inst Genetics, Korea, 1957-1960. **Memberships:** Am Soc Human Genetics; Am Soc Oil Chemists; Am Soc Genetics; Korea Soc Scientists & Engrs. **Research Statement & Publications:** Human quantitative genetics and computer application in medical genetics. **Mailing Address:** Korea Inst Technol, 400 Kusong/Dong Chung/Gu Taejon/Shi, Chung Chong Nam-Do 300-31, South Korea.

KANG, KYEHONG, MATHEMATICS. **Education:** VA Tech Univ, PhD (appl math). **Professional Experience:** ASST PROF, DEPT MATH, LAMAR UNIV, as of 2006. **Mailing Address:** Lamar Univ, 4400 MLK Blvd PO Box 10009, Beaumont, TX 77710. **Fax:** 409-880-8270. **E-Mail:** kang@math.lamar.edu

KANG, KYUNGSIK, ELEMENTARY PARTICLE PHYSICS, THEORETICAL PHYSICS. **Personal Data:** b Jochiwon, Korea, July 12, 1936; m 1963, Hai-Lanne; c Peter, Michael & David. **Education:** Seoul Nat Univ, BS, 1959; Ind Univ, PhD (theoret physics), 1964. **Honors & Awards:** Pres Award (Gold Medal), Seoul Nat Univ, 1959; Camellia Medal, Legion Honor, Korea, 1985. **Professional Experience:** PROF EMER PHYSICS, BROWN UNIV, as of 2005; adj prof, Korea Inst Advan Study, 1998-2002; invited chair prof, Ewha Womens Univ, 1997; invited chair prof, Korea Advan Inst Sci & Technol, 1993; hon prof, Yanbian Univ, Yanji, China, 1990; Los Alamos Nat Lab, 1977 & 1986; vis physicist, Fermi Nat Accelerator Lab, 1974, 1977, 1981; prof physics, Brown Univ, beginning 1973; vis scientist, Europ Orgn Nuclear Res, 1973 & 1987; vis prof, Univ Paris, 1972-1973, 1979-1980, 1986-1987 & 1994-1998; Neils Bohr Inst, 1971 & 1987; Brookhaven Nat Lab, 1968-1979; vis physicist, Argonne Nat Lab, 1968 & 1984 & 1997; from asst prof to assoc prof, Brown Univ, 1966-1973; res assoc, Brown Univ, 1964-1966; Univ Mich, 1963-1964. **Memberships:** Korean Phys Soc; Korean Scientists & Engrs Am (pres, 1982-1983); fel, Am Phys Soc; fel, Koren Acad Sci & Tech. **Research Statement & Publications:** High energy elementary particle physics and field theory and phenomenolo; grand unification theories; flavor dynamics; composite models; electroweak gauge theories; lepton-induced reactions; supersymmetric string theories; cosmology; High energy scattering and Pometon physics; Neutrino oscillations; extra dimensional brane physics. **Mailing Address:** Dept Physics Brown Univ, Barus & Holley, Rm 551, Providence, RI 02912. **E-Mail:** kang@het.brown.edu

KANG, MOHINDER SINGH, MEDICAL & HEALTH SCIENCES. **Personal Data:** c 2. **Education:** Punjab Agr Univ Ludhiana India, BS, 1966; Punjab Univ Chandigarh India, BS (Hon), 1967, MS (Hon), 1969; Tex Tech Univ, Lubbock, PhD (biochem), 1976. **Professional Experience:** SR RES BIOCHEM DEPT CELL BIOL, MARION MERRELL DOW RES INST, 1988-; biotechnol fel, Lab Molecular Biol Div Cancer Biol & Diag, Nat Cancer Inst, NIH, 1986-1988; staff fel, Lab Biochem & Metab, Nat Inst Arthritis, Diabetes, & Digestive & Kidney Dis, NIH, 1982-1986; vis fel, Lab Viral Carcinogenesis, Nat Chem Inst, NIH, 1979-1982; fel, Dept Biochem, Univ Tex Health Sci Ctr, 1976-1979; grad res asst, Dept Chem, Tex Tech Univ, 1972-1976; Vpres biochem soc, Panjab Univ Chandigarh, India, 1970-1971; Res scholar, Dept Biochem, Panjab Univ India, 1970-1971. **Memberships:** Am Soc Biol Chemists; Am Chem Soc; AAAS; Am Asn Cancer Res; Soc Complex Carbohydrates. **Research Statement & Publications:** Evaluation of glycoprotein processing inhibitors as anti human immunodeficiency virus (HIV) and anti metastatic agents; drug metabolism studies in mice and investigation of targeting of drugs to different tissues. **Mailing Address:** Dept Cell Biol, Merrell Dow Res Inst, Cincinnati, OH 45215.

KANG, MYUNG-CHOL, ORGANIC CHEMISTRY. **Education:** Ore State Univ, PhD, 1983. **Professional Experience:** Res chemist, Trimeris Co, NC, as of 2001. **Mailing Address:** Trimeris Co, Research Triangle Park, NC 27709.

KANG, SUNG-MO STEVE, COMPUTER-AIDED DESIGN, MODELING & SIMULATION OF VERY LARGE SCALE INTEGRATION. **Personal Data:** b Seoul, Korea, February 25, 1945; American citizen; m 1972, c 2. **Education:** Fairleigh Dickinson Univ, BS, 1970; State Univ NY, Buffalo, MS, 1972; Univ Calif, Berkeley, PhD (elec eng), 1975. **Honors & Awards:** Meritorious Serv Award, Inst Elec & Electronics Engrs Computer Soc, 1990; Humboldt Res Award Sr US Scientists, 1996 Third Millennium Medal, Inst Elect & Electronics engrs, 2000; SRC tech Excellence Award, 1999; Humboldt res Award Sr US 1996; fel, ACM, 2000; fel, IEEE, 1990; fel, AAAS, 1997; Foreign mem nat acad of eng, Korea, 1997. **Professional Experience:** PROF, BASKIN SCH OF ENG, UCSC, as of 2005; DEAN,

BASKIN SCH OF ENG, UCSC, 2001-; consult, Avant, 1996-; head, Dept Elec & Comput Eng, 1995-2000; mem bd dirs, Anagram Inc, 1992-1996; PROF COMPUTER SCI, UNIV ILL, URBANA-CHAMPAIGN, 1990-; consult Motorola Inc, AT&T Bell Labs, 1990; consult, Teltech, Inc, 1989-2002; Vis prof, Swiss Fed Inst Technol, Lausanne, 1989; consult, MCC, Austin, 1989; assoc dir microelectronics, Univ Ill, Urbana-Champaign, 1988-1995; prof elec & comput eng, Univ Ill, Urbana-Champaign, 1985-2000; supvr, AT&T Bell Labs, Murray Hill, 1982-1985; mem tech staff, AT&T Bell Labs, Murray Hill, 1977-1981; Asst prof elec eng, Rutgers Univ, 1975-1977. **Memberships:** Fel Inst Elec & Electronics Engrs; Inst Elec & Electronics Engrs Circuits & Systs Soc (pres, 1991); Inst Elec & Electronics Engrs Computer Soc; Inst Elec & Electronics Engrs Lasers & Electrooptical Soc; fel, AAAS; Am Soc Eng Educ; Asn Comput Mach. **Research Statement & Publications:** Computer-aided design of very-large scale integrated circuits and systems; modeling and simulation of optoelectronic and novel devices and circuits; analog and digital microelectronics; optical communications. **Mailing Address:** Baskim sch eng Univ Calif, 1156 High St, Santa Cruz, CA 95064. **Fax:** 831-459-4046. **E-Mail:** kang@soe.ucsc.edu

KANG, SUNGZONG, BIOPHYSICS, BIOCHEMISTRY. **Personal Data:** b Puyo, Korea, March 1, 1937; m 1965. **Education:** Univ Tubingen, PhD (chem), 1964. **Professional Experience:** ASSOC PROF, MT SINAI SCH MED, CITY UNIV NEW YORK, 1972- & BRONX VET ADMIN MED CTR, 1980-; Seoul Nat Univ, 1978-1979 & AID, 1978-1979; Alexander von Humboldt US sr scientist fel, 1977-1978; Max Plank Inst Physiol, Dortmund, 1977-1978; Fogarty sr int scholar, 1976-1977; Vis prof, Max Plank Inst Biophys Chem, Gottingen, 1976-1977; from instr to asst prof, MT Sinai Sch Med, City Univ New York, 1972- & Bronx Vet Admin Med Ctr, 1968-1972; Univ Notre Dame, 1966-1967 & NY Univ, 1967-1968; Res assoc chem, Chem Inst, Univ Tubingen, 1964-1966. **Memberships:** AAAS; Am Chem Soc; NY Acad Sci; Am Soc Pharmacol & Exp Therapeut. **Research Statement & Publications:** Stability, structure and function of biological macromolecules, membranes, proteins and nucleic acids; brain research; molecular pharmacology; quantum biochemistry. **Mailing Address:** Hanhyo Inst CPO Box 1751, Seoul, South Korea. **Fax:** 822-791-1705.

KANG, TAE WHA, INDUSTRIAL TOXICOLOGY, MEDICAL TECHNOLOGY. **Personal Data:** b Chejoodo, Korea, m 1973, c 2. **Education:** Yonsei Univ, BS, 1970; Ill Inst Technol, PhD (biol), 1976. **Professional Experience:** Adj prof, Pac Western Univ, 1982-; adj prof, Am Int Univ, 1979-1980; FOUNDER & DIR LAB, BIO-SCI RES INST, 1978-; chmn biochem, Bio-Technics Labs, Inc, 1977-1978; fel molecular biol, Univ Edinburgh, 1976-1977. **Memberships:** Sigma Xi; Am Soc Microbiol; AAAS. **Research Statement & Publications:** Testing of food, drug and cosmetics: product label validation and shelf-life stability studies (Rx drugs and OTC products); pre-clinical studies of new drugs and toxicological assessment of environment chemicals (acute, subchronic and chronic animal studies); mutagenicity and carcinogenicity studies of food additives and color additives; safety tests and potency assay of human leukocyte interferon; water and wastewater tests. **Mailing Address:** Bio Sci Res Inst Inc, 4813 Cheyenne Way, Chino, CA 91710-5510. **Fax:** 909-590-8948.

KANG, YUAN-HSU, CELL BIOLOGY. **Education:** Brigham Young Univ, PhD (zoology), 1972. **Professional Experience:** CHIEF ELECTRON MICROS SECT, NAVAL MED RES INST, 1984-. **Research Statement & Publications:** Natural killer cells; reticuendothelial cells in septic shock. **Mailing Address:** Div Pathobiol, Naval Med Res Inst, 8905 Wis Ave, Bethesda, MD 20889-5607. **Fax:** 301-295-0535.

KANGAS, DONALD ARNE, CHEMISTRY OF EMULSION POLYMERIZATION. **Personal Data:** b Detroit, Mich, February 12, 1929; m 1954, Sirkka; c 5. **Education:** Mich Technol Univ, BS, 1950; Mich State Univ, MS, 1958. **Professional Experience:** CONSULT, 1996-; consult, Dow Chem USA, 1993-1996; res assoc polymer, Dow Chem USA, 1980-1992; sr res specialist, Dow Chem USA, 1953-1980; develop chemist, US Army-Chem Corp, 1951-1953; anal chemist, R P Scherer Corp, 1950-1951. **Research Statement & Publications:** Hydrophobic colloids formed from vinyl monomers; kinetics of polymerization; characterization of dispersion; morphology of particles; properties of films and composites; hydrophillic polyelectrolytes from ionizable vinyl monomers; kinetics characterization and properties. **Mailing Address:** 5112 Nurmi Dr, Midland, MI 48640. **Fax:** 517-832-2959.

KANGAS, J EUGENE, ENGINEERING. **Education:** Univ Detroit, MBA. **Professional Experience:** ASST PROF, KETTERING UNIV, 1960-. **Mailing Address:** Kettering Univ, 1700 W Third Ave, Flint, MI 48504. **Fax:** 810-762-7435.

KANGOVI, SACH, COMPUTATIONAL & EXPERIMENTAL FLUID MECHANICS, FLUID FILTRATION & ABSORBENCY. **Personal Data:** b Bangalore, India, August 25, 1948; m 1978, Sita; c Shreya. **Education:** Jabalpur Univ, BE, 1969; Indian Inst Sci, ME, 1971; Rutgers Univ, PhD (mech & aeronaut eng), 1977. **Honors & Awards:** Minta Martin Award, Am Inst Aeronaut & Astronaut, 1975. **Professional Experience:** FOUNDER & CHIEF EXEC OFFICER, SIMUTEL INC, 2003-; prin scientist, Johnson & Johnson, beginning 1991; sr tech specialist, Boeing, 1989-1990; res scientist, Paramatic Filter Corp, 1982-1989; sr scientist, Nat Aeronaut Lab, 1971-1982. **Memberships:** AAAS; Am Soc Mech Engrs. **Research Statement & Publications:** Application of computational and experimental fluid mechanics, fluid absorbency and fluid filtration to problems of practical interest especially in health care industry. **Mailing Address:** Simutel Inc, POBox 252, Princeton Junction, NJ 08550. **Fax:** 609-936-0641.

KANICK, VIRGINIA, RADIOLOGY. **Personal Data:** b Coaldale, Pa, November 10, 1925. **Education:** Barnard Col, AB, 1947, Columbia Univ, MD, 1951; Am Bd Radiol, dipl, 1955. **Professional Experience:** PROF CLIN RADIOL, COLUMBIA UNIV, 1975-; assoc prof, Columbia Univ, 1974-1975; DEP DIR, DEPT RADIOL, ST LUKE'S ROOSEVELT HOSP, NY, 1964-; attend physician, Columbia Univ, 1955-1963. **Memberships:** Fel Am Col Radiol; Radiol Soc NAm; Am Roentgen Soc. **Research Statement & Publications:** Clinical research in angiology; use of contrast media in radiology. **Mailing Address:** 560 Riverside Dr, New York, NY 10027-3202.

KANICKI, JERZY, ENGINEERING & PHYSICS. **Education:** Free Univ Brussels, Belg, PhD. **Professional Experience:** PROF ELEC ENG & COMPUT SCI, DIV ELEC & COMPUT ENG, DEPT ELEC ENG & COMPUT SCI, UNIV MICH, as of 2006; PROF MACROMOLECULAR SCI & ENG, COL ENG, UNIV MICH, as of 2006; res staff mem, IBM Thomas J watson res ctr, New York, ending 1994. **Memberships:** Inst Elec & Electronics Eng. **Mailing Address:** 2307 Elec Eng Comput Sci Bldg 1301 Beal Ave, Ann Arbor, MI 48109. **E-Mail:** kanicki@umich.edu

KANIECKI, THADDEUS JOHN, ORGANIC CHEMISTRY. **Personal Data:** b Brooklyn, NY, March 24, 1931; m 1955, Florenc Florek; c Marianne, Walter & John. **Education:** NY Univ, BA, 1953, MS, 1955, PhD (org chem), 1960. **Professional Experience:** TECH DIR, DIAMOND CHEM CO INC, 1988-; dir opers, Clenesco Prod Corp, 1987-1988; dir res & develop, Clenesco Div, Chemed Corp, 1984-1987; dir res & develop, Brent Chem Corp, 1982-1984; sr tech serv rep, Brent Chem Corp, 1981-1982; sr chemist res & develop, Stauffer Chem Co, 1975-1981; sect mgr, Am Cyanamid Co, 1972-1975; res mgr, Armour-Dial Inc, Chicago, 1969-1972; res supvr, Armour-Dial Inc, Chicago, 1967-1969; Res assoc, Res & Develop Div, Lever Bros Co, NJ, 1960-1967. **Memberships:** Am Chem Soc; Soc Cosmetic Chem; Am Soc Testing & Mat. **Research Statement & Publications:** Synthesis and applications of surface active molecules; detergents, toiletries and consumer products, both basic and applied research; preparation and uses of disinfectants, sanitizers and biocides. **Mailing Address:** Two Van Alen Pl, Pompton Plains, NJ 07444.

KANIK, ISIK, ATOMIC & MOLECULAR PHYSICS, ULTRA VIOLET EMISSIONS & ABSORPTIONS IN ATMOSPHERES OF STARS & PLANETS. **Personal Data:** b Istanbul, Turkey, May 24, 1958; American citizen; m 1982, Isinsu; c Michael T. **Education:** Mid E Tech Univ, BSc, 1980; Univ Calif, MS, 1984, PhD (physics), 1988. **Professional Experience:** PRIN SCIENTIST & ELEMENT LEAD, JET PROPULSION LAB, 2002-; adj prof physics, Calif State Univ, 1996-; task mgr, USAF, 1995-; scientist, Jet Propulsion Lab, 1995-2002; prin investr, Jet Propulsion Lab, NASA, 1993-; Res adv, Nat Res Coun, 1993-; resident res assoc, Nat Res Coun, NASA, 1990-1992; asst prof physics, Erciyes Univ, Turkey, 1989-1990; postdoctoral researcher, Univ Calif, 1988-1989. **Memberships:** Am Phys Soc. **Research Statement & Publications:** Electron-impact excitation; electron-impact-induced emission and photon absorption processes to understand ultra violet emission; photoabsorption occuring in upper atmospheres of stars and solar system bodies. **Mailing Address:** Jet Propulsion Lab, Calif Inst Technol, 4800 Oak Grove Dr MS 183 301, Pasadena, CA 91109. **Fax:** 818-393-4605. **E-Mail:** Isik.Kanik@jpl.nasa.gov

KANITZ, MARY HELEN HITSELBERGER, MEDICAL RESEARCH. **Personal Data:** b Washington, DC, February 19, 1957; m 1991, David E; c Julia R. **Education:** Georgetown Univ, BS, 1979; Univ Ill, Col Med, PhD (pharmacol), 1986. **Professional Experience:** RES BIOLOGIST, DEPT HEALTH & HUMAN SERV, NAT INST OCCUP SAFETY & HEALTH, 1992-; scientist, Cancer Res Div, Lilly Res Labs, Eli Lilly & Co, 1990-1992; res fel, Dept Path & Pharmacol, Northwestern Univ Med Sch, 1987-1990; Prin investr, NIH, 1987-1990; Chemist, Agr Res Ctr, US Dept Agr, Beltsville, MD, 1979-1980. **Memberships:** Am Asn Cancer Research; Asn Women Cancer; Am Soc Cell Biol; NY Acad Sci; Asn Women Sci; AAAS. **Research Statement & Publications:** Biochemical; molecular; immunological; in vitro primary cell culture establishment. **Mailing Address:** Nat Inst Occup Safety & Health, Div Biomed & Behav Sci Mail Stop C23 44676 Columbia Pkwy, Cincinnati, OH 45226-1998. **Fax:** 513-533-0510. **E-Mail:** mhkz@niobbs1.cm.cdc.gov

KANIZAY, STEPHEN PETER, GEOLOGY. **Personal Data:** b Cleveland, Ohio, February 3, 1924; m 1948, Freda; c Jeff, Kelly & Theodore. **Education:** Miami Univ Ohio, AB, 1949, MS, 1950; Colo Sch Mines, DSc, 1956. **Professional Experience:** RETIRED; geologist, Eng Geol Br, US Geol Surv, 1958-1983; consult, 1954-1958; from instr to asst prof geol, Colo Sch Mines, 1952-1958. **Memberships:** Am Geophys Union. **Research Statement & Publications:** Engineering and structural geology; rock and soil mechanics. **Mailing Address:** 625 S Parfet St, Lakewood, CO 80226.

KANJOLIA, RAVI K, COMPOUND SEMICONDUCTORS & PRECURSOR CHARACTERIZATION, HIGH K DIELECTRICS & BARRIER LAYERS. **Personal Data:** b Raj, India, November 16, 1954; American citizen; m 1984, Sarita; c Kunal. **Education:** Univ Rajasthan, India, BS, 1973, MS, 1975; B H Univ, India, PhD (chem), 1981. **Professional Experience:** CHIEF TECHNOL OFFICER, EPICHEM, 1996-; tech mgr, Morton Int, 1987-1996; asst prof chem, Univ Ala, Birmingham, 1984-1987; postdoctoral fel, Univ Ala, Birmingham, 1982-1984. **Memberships:** Am Chem Soc; Mat Res Soc; Am Ceramic Soc. **Research Statement & Publications:** thermochemistry of volatile sources of aluminum, gallium, indium, phosphorous, arsenic and antimony; application of organometallic compounds in electronic devices; Synthesis, purification and characterization of organometallic compounds. **Mailing Address:** Epichem Inc, 1429 Hilldale Ave, Haverhill, MA 01832. **Fax:** 978-374-6474. **E-Mail:** kanjolir@epichem.com

KANKEL, DOUGLAS RAY, DEVELOPMENTALBIOLOGY, NEUROBIOLOGY. **Personal Data:** b Waterbury, Conn, January 22, 1944. **Education:** Brown Univ, PhD (biol), 1970. **Professional Experience:** CHMN, DEPT MOLECULAR, CELLULAR & DEVELOP BIOL, YALE UNIV, as of 1998; MEM, LIFE SCI RES FOUND, 1983-; MEM FAC BIOL DEPT, YALE UNIV, 1974-; res fel neurobiology, Calif Inst Technol, 1970-1974. **Mailing Address:** Dept Biol, Yale Univ, PO Box 208103, New Haven, CT 06520-8103. **E-Mail:** douglas.kankel@yale.edu

KANKI, PHYLLIS J, MEDICINE. **Honorary Degrees:** DSc, Harvard Sch Public Health, 1985. **Professional Experience:** ASSOC PROF, PATHOBIOLOGY, DEPT IMMUNOL & INFECTIOUS DIS, HARVARD SCH PUBLIC HEALTH, as of 2006. **Memberships:** Am Vet Med Asn. **Mailing Address:** Dept Immunol & Infectious Dis, Harvard Sch Public Health, 651 Huntington Avenue FXB 405, Boston, MA 02115-6023. **Fax:** 617-739-8348. **E-Mail:** pkanki@hsph.harvard.edu

KAN-MITCHELL, JUNE III, HUMAN CELLULAR IMMUNITY, TUMOR & HIV VACCINES. **Personal Data:** b Hong Kong, June 3, 1949; American citizen; m 1967, Malcolm; c Ian D. **Education:** Smith Col, BA, 1971; Yale Univ, PhD (pharmacol), 1977. **Professional Experience:** PROF Karmanos Cancer Institute and Department of IMMUNOL and MICROBIOL, WAYNE STATE UNIV SCH MED, 1999-; assoc prof path, Univ Calif, San Diego, 1994-1999; assoc prof path, Univ southern Calif Sch Med, 1990-1994; asst prof microbiol, Univ southern Calif, Sch Med, beginning 1985; Assoc ed, J Lab Clin Invests, Human Antibodies & Hybridomas & Vaccine Res; prin investr, Nat Eye Inst. **Memberships:** Am Asn Cancer Res; Asn Res Vision & Ophthal; Fedn Am Soc Exp Biol; Am Asn Immunol. **Research Statement & Publications:** T cell competition, cryoimmunology. **Mailing Address:** Karmanos Cancer Inst, Immunol & Microbiol, Sch Med, Wayne State Univ, 110 E Warren, Detroit, MI 48201. **Fax:** 313-576-8389. **E-Mail:** kanmitch@karmanos.org

KANNAN, RAVI, EDUCATION. **Honors & Awards:** Leroy P Steele Prize, Am Math Soc, 1992. **Professional Experience:** PROF MATH, CARNEGIE MELLON UNIV as of 1996. **Mailing Address:** Dept Math, Carnegie-Mellon Univ, Pittsburgh, PA 15213. **E-Mail:** ravi.kannan@cs.cmu.edu

KANNAPPAN, PALANIAPPAN, MATHEMATICS & FUNCTIONAL EQUATIONS, QUASIGRAPHS & LOOPS. **Personal Data:** b Nattarasan Kottai, India, June 28, 1934; m 1952, Ronganayaki; c 5. **Education:** Annamalai Univ, Madras, BSc(Hons), 1955, MA, 1957; Univ Wash, Seattle, MS & PhD (math), 1964. **Professional Experience:** PROF MATH, UNIV WATERLOO, 1977-; consult, Nat Res Coun Can, 1969; consult, Dept Univ Affairs, Can, 1968-1969; assoc prof, Univ Waterloo, 1967-1977; reader, Annamalai Univ, Madras, 1964-1967; asst, Univ Wash, 1961-1964; Fulbright scholar, 1961; lectr math, Annamalai Univ, Madras, 1955-1961. **Memberships:** Am Math Soc; Indian Math Soc; Indian Acad Sci; Japan Math Soc. **Research Statement & Publications:** Functional analysis and functional equations; linear algebra and quasigroups; information theory. **Mailing Address:** Dept Pure Math, Univ Waterloo, Waterloo, ON N2L 3G1, Can. **E-Mail:** plkannappan@watdragon.uwaterloo.ca

KANNE, WILLIAM R, METALLURGY. **Professional Experience:** SR FEL ENGR, WESTINGHOUSE SAVANNAH RIVER CO, as of 2005. **Memberships:** Fel Materials Info Soc. **Mailing Address:** Westinghouse Savannah River Co, Bldg 773-41A, Aiken, SC 29808. **Fax:** 803-952-6159.

KANNEL, WILLIAM B, CARDIOVASCULAR DISEASES, INTERNAL MEDICINE. **Personal Data:** b Brooklyn, NY, December 13, 1923; m 1942, c 4. **Education:** Ga Med Col, MD, 1949; Harvard Univ, MPH, 1959. **Honorary Degrees:** MD, Gothenberg Univ, 1985. **Honors & Awards:** Dana Award, 1972 & 1986; Einthoven Award, 1973; Gaidner Int Award, 1976; Paul Dudley White Award, 1977; Copernicus Award, 1977; Ciba Award, 1981; J D Bruce Award, Am Col Physicians, 1982; Distinguished Serv Award, Am Col Cardiol, 1988. **Professional Experience:** PROF MED & PUB HEALTH, SCH MED, BOSTON UNIV, 1979-; chief sect epidemiol & prev med, Sch Med, Boston Univ, 1979-1990; lectr, Harvard Med Sch, beginning 1970; dir, Framingham Unit, NIH, 1965-1979; consult, Framington Union Hosp, 1964; assoc prev med, Harvard Med Sch, 1960-1970; instr, Harvard Med Sch, 1959-1960; consult, Cushing State Hosp, 1956-1973; assoc dir, Framingham Unit, NIH, 1956-1965; asst med, Peter Bent Brigham Hosp, 1956-1962; fel, Harvard Med Sch, 1956-1959; med officer, Newton Heart Prog, Mass, 1951-1952; clin investr heart dis epidemiol study, NIH, Framingham, Mass, 1950-1951; intern & resident, USPHS Hosp, Staten Island, NY, 1949-1950 & 1953-1956; DIR, VIS SCIENTIST PROG, FRAMINGHAM HEART STUDY. **Memberships:** Fel Am Col Prev Med; fel Am Heart Asn; fel Am Col Physicians; fel Am Col Cardiol; fel Am Col Epidemiol. **Research Statement & Publications:** Cardiovascular epidemiology; investigation of factors of risk and natural history of coronary heart disease, hypertension, stroke and peripheral vascular disease; preventive medicine. **Mailing Address:** Boston Univ, Framingham Study, Five Thurber St, Framingham, MA 01701.

KANNENBERG, LLOYD C, PHYSICS, OPTICS. **Personal Data:** b Sarasota, Fla, March 23, 1939; m 1963, Susan; c Susanna. **Education:** Mass Inst Technol, BS, 1961; Univ Fla, MS, 1963; Northeastern Univ, PhD (physics), 1967. **Professional Experience:** PROF PHYSICS, UNIV MASS, LOWELL, 1977-; vis res assoc, Northeastern Univ, 1972-1980; from instr to assoc prof, Lowell Technol Inst, 1968-1977; instr physics, Lowell Technol Inst, 1966-1967 & Northeastern Univ, 1967-1968. **Memberships:** Am Phys Soc; Int Soc Gen Relativity & Gravitation; Sigma Xi; Math Asn Am. **Research Statement & Publications:** General relativity, field theory. **Mailing Address:** Dept Physics & Appl physics, Univ Mass, Lowell, MA 01854. **E-Mail:** lloyd_kannenberg@uml.edu

KANNENBERG, LYNDON WILLIAM, MAIZE BREEDING, POPULATION IMPROVEMENT. **Personal Data:** b Chicago, Ill, October 15, 1931; m Barbara; c William W, Debra A, Susan E, Jeanne M & Catherine M. **Education:** Mich State Univ, BSc, 1957, MS, 1959; Univ Calif, Davis, PhD (genetics), 1964. **Professional Experience:** PROF EMER CROP SCI, UNIV GUELPH, 1997-; CESO advsr Thailand, China 1998-pres; vis lectr, China, 1988; maize consult, Can Int Develop Agency, Bangladesh, 1985; mem, Expert Comt Plant Gene Resources, 1983-1996; mem, Grants Comt, Nat Res Coun Can, 1971-1973; from asst prof to prof, Univ Guelph, 1965-1996; NIH fel, Univ Calif, Davis, 1964-1965. **Memberships:** Am Soc Agron; Genetics Soc Can; Sigma Xi; Can Soc Agron. **Research Statement & Publications:** Development and improvement of short season corn breeding populations as sources for inbred lines with different genetic backgrounds than current commercial germplasm. **Mailing Address:** 17 Lockyer Rd, Guelph, ON N1G 1J9, Can. **E-Mail:** lkannenb@uoguelph.ca

KANNEWURF, CARL RAESIDE, SOLID STATE ELECTRONICS, ELECTRONIC MATERIALS. **Personal Data:** b Waukegan, Ill, March 24, 1931; m 1983, Patricia. **Education:** Lake Forest Col, BA, 1953; Univ Ill, MS, 1954; Northwestern Univ, PhD (physics), 1960. **Honors & Awards:** Life Senior mem for Years of serv, IEEE, 1999; Third Millennium Medal in Recognition & Appreciation of Valued serv & outstanding contrib, IEEE, 2000. **Professional Experience:** PROF EMER ELEC & COMP ENG, NORTHWESTERN UNIV, EVANSTON, 2001-; prof elec & comp eng, Northwestern univ Evanston, 1971-2001; assoc prof elec eng, Northwestern univ, Evanston, 1966-1971, asst prof elec eng, Northwestern univ, Evanston, 1963-1966. **Memberships:** Am Phys Soc; Sigma Xi; sr mem Inst Elec & Electronics Engrs; Mat Res Soc electron Devices soc of the Chicago; sect IEEE (Chmn & mem of the Chicago Exec Council, 1986-1996). **Research Statement & Publications:** Study of various electrical and optical phenomena in semiconductors, metals, molecular metals and conducting polymers; transport phenomena in superconductors; Thermoelectrics and Conducting Transparent Oxides. **Mailing Address:** Northwestern Univ, ECE, Evanston, IL 60208-3118.

KANNINEN, MELVIN FRED, ENGINEERING MECHANICS, MATERIAL SCIENCE ENGINEERING. **Personal Data:** b Ely, Minn, January 31, 1935; m 1957, c 2. **Education:** Univ Minn, BS, 1957, MS, 1959, Stanford Univ PhD (Eng Mech), 1966. **Professional Experience:** OWNER & PROPRIETOR, MFK CONSULT, 1995-; prog dir eng mech, Southwest Res Inst, 1991-1995; inst scientist, Southwest Res Inst, 1983-1991; res leader, Battelle's Columbus Lab, 1979-1983; sr researcher, Battelle's Columbus Lab, 1975-1979; Researcher, Battelle's Columbus Lab, 1966-1975; Mem, Nat Mat Adv Bd, Nat Res Coun & numerous prof soc & govt adv comts; lectr, numerous US & foreign univs. **Memberships:** Nat Acad Eng; Am Soc Testing & Mat; Int Asn Struct Mech; Am Welding Soc; fel Am Soc Mech Engrs; Soc Eng Sci. **Research Statement & Publications:** Fracture mechanics for fast fracture arrest; elastic-plastic fracture mechanics; lifetime predictions for fiber reinforced composites; residual stress and cracking of welds; applications to nuclear pressure vessels, cryogenic storage tanks, railroad equipment, gas transmission pipelines, plastic pipe and joints; author of more than 150 technical publications. **Mailing Address:** 7322 Ashton Pl, San Antonio, TX 78229.

KANNOWSKI, MARK, MATHEMATICS. **Education:** Univ Iowa, PhD. **Professional Experience:** ASSOC PROF, MATH DEPT CHAIR, DEPAUW UNIV, as of 2006. **Mailing Address:** Math Dept, Depauw Univ, Greencastle, IN 46135. **Fax:** 765-658-6084. **E-Mail:** kannowski@depauw.edu

KANNOWSKI, PAUL BRUNO, ZOOLOGY. **Personal Data:** b Grand Forks, NDak, August 11, 1927; m 1953, Phyllis; c Katherine & Mark. **Education:** Univ NDak, BS, 1949, MS, 1952; Univ Mich, PhD (zoology), 1957. **Honors & Awards:** Prof Award, Wildlife Soc, 1989. **Professional Experience:** PROF EMER BIOL, UNIV NDAK, 1991-; natural resources consult, US Congressman Mark Andrews, NDak, 1969-1970; ed, Prairie Naturalist, 1968-; entom consult, Lystads Pest Control, Inc, 1968-1975; vis scientist, Smithsonian Trop Res Inst, 1967 & 1968; NSF sr fel, 1966-1967; res assoc, Harvard Univ, 1966-1967; dir, Inst Ecol Studies, 1965-1981; chmn dept, Univ NDak, 1963-1970 & 1982-1988; from asst prof to prof biol, Univ NDak, 1957-1990; instr, Bowling Green State Univ, 1956-1957; asst biol, Univ NDak, 1950-1952. **Memberships:** Am Inst Biol Sci; Am Soc Zoologists; AAAS; Entom Soc Am; Ecol Soc Am. **Research Statement & Publications:** Ecology; biogeography; animal behavior; myrmecology; chemical communication. **Mailing Address:** Dept Biol, Univ NDak, Grand Forks, ND 58202. **Fax:** 701-777-2623.

KANO, ADELINE KYOKO, CHEMISTRY, ACADEMIC ADMINISTRATION. **Personal Data:** b Mitchell, Neb, November 22, 1927. **Education:** Univ Nebr, BA, 1948. **Professional Experience:** ADMIN ASST & FAC AFFIL, COLO STATE UNIV, 1973-; asst prof, Colo State Univ, 1960-1973; asst chemist, Colo State Univ, 1960-1966; instr chem & jr chemist, Colo State Univ, 1955-1960. **Memberships:** Am Chem Soc; Sigma Xi. **Research Statement & Publications:** Factors imposed on chicks and rats, their alleviation and relation to blood and tissue content of amino acids. **Mailing Address:** Colo State Univ, 316 Molecular & Radiol Bios, Ft Collins, CO 80523.

KANOFSKY, ALVIN SHELDON, ELEMENTARY PARTICLE PHYSICS. **Personal Data:** b Philadelphia, Pa, July 5, 1939; m 1964, Donna; c Robert & Nathan. **Education:** Univ Pa, BA, 1961, MS, 1962, PhD (physics), 1966. **Professional Experience:** PROF PHYSICS, LEHIGH UNIV, 1976-; from asst prof to assoc prof, Lehigh Univ, 1967-1976; pres, Res & Develop Co; Res collabr, Brookhaven Nat Lab, Fermilab. **Memberships:** Fel Am Phys Soc; Sigma Xi; AAAS; Rotary Int Chambers Com. **Research Statement & Publications:** Research in eta decay; proton-proton scattering; mu magnetic moment, Glauber calculations in particles, high energy particle channeling in crystals, particle-nuclei interactions, hypernuclei, jet production, cosmic rays and instrumentation; accelerator research; intermediate energy physics; radiation effects. **Mailing Address:** Dept Physics, Lehigh Univ, 410 Lewis Lab 16 Memorial Dr E, Bethlehem, PA 18015. **Fax:** 610-758-5730. **E-Mail:** ask0@lehigh.edu

KANOFSKY, JEFFREY RONALD, SINGLET OXYGEN PRODUCTION AS A FACTOR IN PHOTOSENSITIVITY DISORDERS. **Personal Data:** b Chicago, Ill, April 30, 1946; wid Donna. **Education:** Ill Inst Technol, BS, 1968, MS, 1970, PhD (chem), 1972; Rush Med Col, MD, 1975. **Professional Experience:** PROF MED, CELL BIOL, NEUROBIOLOGY & ANAT, STRITCH SCH MED, LOYOLA UNIV, 2000-; prof med, molecular & cellular biochem, Stritch Sch Med, Loyola Univ, 1991-; assoc prof med & biochem, Stritch Sch Med, Loyola Univ, 1988-1991; assoc prof, Stritch Sch Med, Loyola Univ, 1986-1988; STAFF PHYSICIAN, EDWARD HINES JR VET ADMIN HOSP, 1980-; asst prof med, Stritch Sch Med, Loyola Univ, 1980-1986; fel hemat & oncol, Univ Chicago, 1978-1980; Residency internal med, Univ Ill Hosp, 1975-1978. **Memberships:** Fel Am Col Physicians Mem; Am Soc Hemat; Am Soc Clin Oncol; Am Asn Cancer Res; Am Soc Photobiol; Oxygen Soc. **Research Statement & Publications:** Studies of synthetic carotenoid derivatives as novel cytoprotective agents for photosensitivity disorders. **Mailing Address:** Hines Vet Admin Hosp, PO Box 278, Hines, IL 60141. **Fax:** 708-202-2319. **E-Mail:** jeff.kanofsky@med.va.gov

KANOJIA, RAMESH MAGANLAL, MEDICINAL CHEMISTRY. **Personal Data:** b Mangrol, India, February 15, 1933; m 1967, c Preeti & Amee. **Education:** Bombay Univ, BSc, 1954, BScTech, 1956, MScTech, 1961; Univ Wis, PhD (pharmaceut chem), 1966. **Honors & Awards:** Philip B Hoffman Award, Johnson & Johnson Co, 1977. **Professional Experience:** AT, R W JOHNSON PHARMACEUT RES INST, as of 1998; RES FEL, ORTHO PHARMACEUT CORP, 1980-; sr scientist, Ortho Pharmaceut Corp, 1977-1979; scientist, Ortho Pharmaceut Corp, 1970-1976; assoc scientist, Ortho Pharmaceut Corp, 1966-1970; res asst pharmaceut chem, Sch Pharm, Univ Wis, 1961-1966; hon lectr tech pharmaceut & fine chem, Bombay Univ, 1959-1960; Instr pharmaceut chem, Bombay Univ, 1958-1959. **Memberships:** Am Chem Soc. **Research Statement & Publications:** Isolation, characterization and synthesis of natural and synthetic organic medicinal compounds; antifertility compounds of natural and synthetic origin; synthesis of cardiovascular-active drugs; antiinfective agents. **Mailing Address:** R W Johnson Pharmaceut Res Inst, Route 202, PO Box 300, Raritan, NJ 08869. **Fax:** 908-526-6469.

KANOPOULOS, NICK, VLSI DESIGN, INTERGRATED CIRCUIT TESTING. **Personal Data:** b Drama, Greece, August 11, 1956; American citizen; m 1990, Athiya; c Nichole & Tasos. **Education:** Univ Patras, Greece, BS, 1979; Duke Univ, MS, 1980, PhD (elect eng), 1984. **Professional Experience:** DIR, MULTIMEDIA & COMMUN PROD, ATMEL CORP, 1999-; ceo, Data Communications Technolo, 1996-1999; mgr, Res Triangle Inst, beginning 1987; adj assoc prof, Duke Univ, 1985-; coordr, Res Triangle Inst, 1985-1987; from engr to sr engr, Res Triangle Inst, 1982-1985; engr, Bendix Corp, 1981-1982; Res asst, Duke Univ, 1979-1981. **Memberships:** AAAS; sr mem Inst Elec & Electronics Engrs. **Research Statement & Publications:** Design of very large scale, application specific integrated circuits; design of parallel signal processor architectures for high-performance, real-time applications; developed design for testability and built in self-test techniques and structures; design of fault secure circuits for high reliability applications; author of various articles. **Mailing Address:** Div Multimedia & Commun, Atmel Corp, 2325 Orchard Pkwy, San Jose, CA 95131. **E-Mail:** nick@rti.rti.org

KANOST, MICHAEL ROBERT, INSECT BIOCHEMISTRY. **Personal Data:** b Cheyenne, Wyo, November 17, 1956; m 1977, c 4. **Education:** Colo State Univ, BS, 1979; Purdue Univ, PhD (entom), 1983. **Honors & Awards:** Fellow of AAAS. **Professional Experience:** PROF BIOCHEM, KANS STATE UNIV, 1999-; Assoc Prof Biochem, Kans State Univ, 1995-1999; asst prof, Kans State Univ, 1991-1995; res asst prof, Univ Ariz, 1989-1991; res assoc, Univ Ariz, 1986-1989; Postdoctoral fel, Queen's Univ, 1983-1986. **Memberships:** Am Soc Biochem & Molecular Biol; AAAS Entomological soc of Am. **Research Statement & Publications:** Structure and function of insect hemolymph proteins involved in immune responses; biochemistry of insect cuticle sclerotization. **Mailing Address:** Kans State Univ, Willard Hall 103, Manhattan, KS 65506. **Fax:** 785-532-7278. **E-Mail:** kanost@ksu.edu

KANO-SUEOKA, TAMIKO, MOLECULAR BIOLOGY. **Personal Data:** b Kyoto, Japan, June 26, 1932; m 1956, Noboru; c 1. **Education:** Kyoto Univ, Japan, BA, 1956; Radcliffe Col, MA, 1960; Univ Ill, Urbana, PhD (molecular biol), 1963. **Professional Experience:** RETIRED; sr res assoc & prof molecular celluar & develop biol, Univ Colo, 1985-2002; prof molecular cellular & develop biol, Univ Colo, beginning 1985; from asst prof to assoc prof, Univ Colo, 1973-1985; res staff, Princeton Univ, 1968-1972; res assoc biochem, Princeton Univ, 1963-1967; res asst biol, Calif Inst Technol, 1956-1958. **Memberships:** Am Soc Biochem & Molecular Biol; Am Asn Cancer Res; Am Tissue Cult Asn. **Research Statement & Publications:** Regulation of growth of normal and neoplastic mammary cells, in particular the involvement of membrane phospholipids in the control of cell proliferation. **Mailing Address:** Dept Molecular Cellular & Develop Biol, Univ Colo, Boulder, CO 80309-0347. **E-Mail:** tamiko@stripe.colorado.edu

KANT, FRED H(UGO), CHEMICAL ENGINEERING. **Personal Data:** b Vienna, Austria, January 11, 1930; American citizen; m 1952, c 2. **Education:** Columbia Univ, BS, 1951, MS, 1953, DEngSc, 1957. **Professional Experience:** RETIRED; consult, Morningside & Lamont-Doherty campuses, beginning 1984; sr tech adv, Exxon Corp, 1980-1984; sr staff adv, Corp Res, Exxon Res & Eng Co, 1978-1980; planning mgr, Govt Res, 1975-1978; sr staff adv, Corp Res Staff, 1972-1975; proj mgr, Corp Res Staff, 1969-1972; dir new invests res lab, Linden, 1966-1969; Sr staff adv, New Areas Staff, Esso Res & Eng Co, 1954-1966. **Memberships:** Am Chem Soc; AAAS; NY Acad Sci. **Research Statement & Publications:** Fuels process; staff research coordination, planning and project evaluation in new areas; research administration. **Mailing Address:** 400 W 119th St Apt 15S, New York, NY 10027-7108.

KANT, GLORIA JEAN, BIOMEDICAL RESEARCH. **Personal Data:** b Chicago, Ill, June 6, 1944. **Education:** Mich State Univ, BS, 1965; Univ Wis, PhD (physiol chem), 1969. **Professional Experience:** CHIEF, DEPT MED NEUROSCIENCE, WALTER REED ARMY INST RES, 1987-; asst chief, Neuroendocrinol & Neurochem Br, 1977-1987; neurochemist, Dept Microwave Res, 1971-1977; chemist, Dept Psychiat, Walter Reed Army Inst Res, 1970-1971; res fel, Dept Food Sci, Univ Wis, 1969-1970. **Memberships:** Sigma Xi; Soc Neurosciencence; AAAS; Women Neurosciencence; Am Soc Pharmacol & Exp Therapeut; Int Soc Psychoneuroendocrinol; Int Behav Neurosciencence Soc. **Research Statement & Publications:** Basic biomedical research; effects of stress on physiology and behavior. **Mailing Address:** 1124 Dennis Ave, Silver Spring, MD 20901-2171.

KANT, JEFFREY A, MOLECULAR DIAGNOSTICS, GENETICS, HEMATOPATHOLOGY. **Personal Data:** b Boston, Mass, October 4, 1946; m 1969, Julia; c Benjamin & Peter. **Education:** Princeton Univ, AB, 1968; Univ Chicago, PhD (biochem), 1974, MD, 1975. **Honors & Awards:** Fellow, AAAS AMP Leadership Award. **Professional Experience:** PROF, UNIV PITTSBURGH, SCH MED, DIR, MOLECULAR DIAG SECT, UNIV PA MED CTR, 1986-; dir, Hemat Sect, 1983-1993; Expert consult, Path Lab, Nat Cancer Inst, NIH, 1979-1983. **Memberships:** Am Soc Hemat; Am Soc Human Genetics; Acad Clin Lab & Physicians & Scientists; Am Acad Path; Can Acad Path; AAAS. **Research Statement & Publications:** Diagnostic applications of molecular biology inherited genetic disorder and hematopoietic neoplasia. **Mailing Address:** Dept Path, S701 Scaife Hall, Univ Pittsburgh Med Ctr 3550 Terrace St, Pittsburgh, PA 15261. **Fax:** 412-383-9594. **E-Mail:** kantja@upmc.edu

KANT, KENNETH JAMES, PHYSIOLOGY, VETERINARY MEDICINE. **Personal Data:** b Elyria, Ohio, July 14, 1935; m 1958, Elaine; c Kenneth C, Kyle J, Karyl F & Kristin M A. **Education:** Ohio State Univ, BS, 1958; Univ Ill, Urbana, MS, 1964, PhD (physiol), 1967; Univ Tenn, Knoxville, DVM, 1983. **Professional Experience:** PVT PRACT, VET MED, MOUNTAIN HWY VET HOSP, 1985-; assoc prof physiol, Univ Tenn, Knoxville, 1974-1983; from instr to asst prof physiol, State Univ NY Buffalo, 1967-1974. **Memberships:** Am Vet Med Asn. **Research Statement & Publications:** Neurophysiology and behavior, especially limbic structures. **Mailing Address:** 2216 E Lamar Alexander Pkwy, Maryville, TN 37804.

KANTACK, BENJAMIN H, ENTOMOLOGY, AGRONOMY. **Personal Data:** b Greenleaf, Kans, September 26, 1927; m 1953, c 7. **Education:** Kans State Univ, BS, 1951; Okla State Univ, MS, 1954; Univ Nebr, PhD (entom), 1963. **Honors & Awards:** F O Butler Award. **Professional Experience:** PROF EMER ENTOM, SDAK STATE UNIV, 1991-; exten entomologist, Sdak State Univ, 1963-1991; from asst prof to prof entom, Sdak State Univ, 1962-1991; instr entom, Univ Nebr, 1958-1962; entomologist, USDA, Ga, 1955-1958; instr & entomologist, Univ RI, 1954-1955; asst entom, Okla State Univ, 1952-1954; Trainee agron, Libby, McNeill & Libby, Hawaii, 1951-1952. **Memberships:** Entom Soc Am. **Research Statement & Publications:** Stored grain, vegetable and field crop insects; livestock ecto parasites. **Mailing Address:** 1907 Derdall Dr, Brookings, SD 57006.

KANTAK, KATHLEEN MARY, PSYCHOBIOLOGY. **Personal Data:** b Syracuse, NY, November 11, 1951; m 1975, c 2. **Education:** State Univ NY Potsdam, BA, 1973; Syracuse Univ, PhD (biopsychol), 1977. **Professional Experience:** PROF, DEPT PSYCHOL, BOSTON UNIV, as of 2005; RES ASSOC PHYCHOL, TUFTS UNIV, 1981-; res assoc behav neurochem, Univ Wis-Madison, 1978-1981; res asst prof biopsychol, Syracuse Univ, 1978. **Memberships:** Soc Neuroscience; Sigma Xi; Int Soc Res Aggression; Behav Pharmacol Soc. **Research Statement & Publications:** Neurochemical correlates of aggression in terms of how these measures are affected by nutritional factors; nutritional aspects of drug abuse; animal models of tardiue dyskinesia. **Mailing Address:** Dept Psychol, Boston Univ, 64 Cummington St, Boston, MA 02215. **Fax:** 617-353-6933. **E-Mail:** kkantak@bu.edu

KANTER, HELMUT, ELECTRON PHYSICS. **Personal Data:** b Hamburg, Ger, January 19, 1928; American citizen. **Education:** Univ Marburg, MS, 1953, PhD (physics), 1956. **Professional Experience:** DIR, GE JENBACHER, as of 2002; MEM STAFF, ELECTRONIC RES LAB, AEROSPACE CORP, 1974-; mem tech staff, Lab Div, 1964-1974; Res physicist, Res Labs, Westinghouse Elec Corp, 1957-1964. **Memberships:** Am Phys Soc; Ger Phys Soc. **Research Statement & Publications:** Electron scattering; photo and secondary electron emission; electron transport; photoconductivity; imaging tubes. **Mailing Address:** GE Jenbacher, Achenseestr 1-3, A-6200 Jenbach, Austria, Ger.

KANTER, IRA E, ENGINEERING PHYSICS. **Personal Data:** b Chicago, Ill, October 31, 1931; m 1968, c 2. **Education:** Ill Inst Technol, BS, 1953, MS, 1954. **Professional Experience:** SR ENGR ENVIRON CONTROL OFFICER, SOLID OXIDE FUEL CELLS, SCI & TECH CTR, WESTINGHOUSE, 1987-; sr engr chem physics, Res & Develop Labs, 1977-1987; sr engr chem eng, Astronuclear Labs, Westinghouse, 1969-1977; sr engr NERVA nuclear reactors, Astronuclear Labs, Westinghouse, 1963-1969; res staff high temperature chem, Univ Wis, 1960-1961; engr high temperature, Vanguard X405 Rocket, Flight Propulsion Lab, Gen Elec, 1957-1959; asst chem engr, US Army Chem Corps, 1954-1956. **Memberships:** Am Nuclear Soc; Inst Elec & Electronics Engrs; Air & Waste Mgt Asn; Int Technol Inst. **Research Statement & Publications:** Radio-chemical reactions for synthesis; chemical thermodynamics; inertially and magnetically confined fusion reactor blanket systems; radio-gas waste treatment and storage; glow discharge chemistry; physical chemistry; pollution control systems. **Mailing Address:** 1172 Colgate Dr, Monroeville, PA 15146.

KANTER, IRVING, RADAR, ELECTRONIC COUNTER MEASURES & COUNTER MEASURES. **Personal Data:** b New York, NY, October 30, 1924; m 1951, c 5. **Education:** Brooklyn Col, AB, 1944; Brown Univ, PhD (appl math), 1953. **Professional Experience:** RETIRED; consult engr, Raytheon Co, 1966-1992; systs engr, RCA, 1954-1966; systs specialist, Lockheed Aircraft Corp, 1951-1954; physicist, Union Carbide & US Army, 1945-1947; physicist, Kellex Corp, 1944-1945; adj lectr, Univ Calif, Los Angeles. **Memberships:** Fel Inst Elec & Electronics Engrs; Aerospace & Electronic Systs; Inst Elec & Electronics Engrs Info Theory Soc. **Research Statement & Publications:** Detection and estimation; monopulse radar. **Mailing Address:** Nine Bushnell Dr, Lexington, MA 02173.

KANTER, MANUEL ALLEN, international training; deceased, see previous edition for last biography

KANTHA, LAKSHMI, OCEANIC CIRCULATION. **Personal Data:** American citizen; m 1974, c 1. **Education:** Bangalore Univ, BE, 1967; Indian Inst Sci, ME, 1969; Mass Inst Technol, PhD (aerospace & astron), 1973. **Professional Experience:** Scientist, SACLANT Undersea Res Ctr, La Spezia, Italy, 1999-2000; PROF, PROG ATMOSPHERIC & OCEANIC SCI, UNIV COLORADO, BOULDER, COLORADO, 1993-; consult, Naval Res Lab, Stennis Space Ctr, Miss, 1991-1997; PROF, DEPT AEROSPACE ENG SCI, UNIV COLORADO, BOULDER, COLORADO, 1991-; oceanogr, Navy Oceanog & Atmospheric Res Lab, Stennis Space Ctr, Miss, 1990-1991; scientist III, Inst Naval Oceanog, Stennis Space Ctr, Miss, 1988-1990; sr vis scientist, Atmospheric & Oceanic Sci Prog, Princeton Univ, Princeton, 1986-1988; res scientist, Dynalysis Princeton, 1980-1986; res scientist, Johns Hopkins Univ, 1979-1980; assoc res scientist, Johns Hopkins Univ, 1975-1979; Fel, Johns Hopkins Univ, 1974-1975; res asst, dept Aeronaut & Astronaut, Mass Inst Technol, Cambridge, Mass, 1969-1973; jr res fel, Nat Aeronaut Lab, Bangalore, India, 1968-1969. **Memberships:** Am Meteorol Soc; Am Geophys Union. **Research Statement & Publications:** Turbulence and wave motions in the atmosphere and the oceans; ocean circulation in the coastal regions; oceanic mixing and influence of the ice cover on polar oceans; numerical and experimental modeling of oceanic and atmospheric processes. **Mailing Address:** Dept Aerospace Eng Sci, Colorado Ctr Astrodynamics Res, Univ Colorado, CB 431, Boulder, CO 80309-0431. **Fax:** 303-492-2825. **E-Mail:** kantha@colorado.edu

KANTOR, FRED STUART, IMMUNOLOGY. **Personal Data:** b New York, NY, July 2, 1931; m 1958, Linda; c 3. **Education:** Union Col NY, BS, 1952; NY Univ, MD, 1956; Am Bd Internal Med, dipl, 1964; Am Bd Allergy, dipl, 1966, Yale Univ, MA, 1973. **Professional Experience:** PAUL B BEESON PROF MED, SCH MED, YALE UNIV, beginning 1983; vis scientist with Dr Gustave Nossal, Walter & Eliza Hall Inst, Melbourne, Australia, 1968-1969; USPHS career develop awardee, 1962-; from instr to prof, Sch Med, Yale Univ, 1962-1983; Whitney fel, Sch Med, Yale Univ, 1960-1961; asst res med, Grace New Haven Hosp, Sch Med, Yale Univ, 1959-1960; res assoc, Nat Inst Allergy & Infectious Dis, 1957-1959; intern, Ward Med Serv, Barnes Hosp, St Louis, Mo, 1956-1957; mem coun, Am Heart Asn. **Memberships:** Asn Am Physicians; Am Soc Clin Invest; Am Acad Allergy; Am Asn Immunol. **Research Statement & Publications:** Immune response in man, including both delayed and immediate types of immunity; immunity to Lyme disease and other tick-borne infections. **Mailing Address:** Dept Int Med, Yale Univ, Sch Med, 333 Cedar St, New Haven, CT 06510-3219. **Fax:** 203-785-3229. **E-Mail:** philip.askenase@yale.edu

KANTOR, FREDERICK W, FOUNDATIONS OF PHYSICS, INFORMATION MECHANICS. **Personal Data:** b New York, NY, July 19, 1942. **Education:** Columbia Univ, (physics), PhD, 1973; Columbia Univ, AB, 1964. **Professional Experience:** Independent physicist, 1973-; inventor, 1961-. **Memberships:** AAAS; Am Phys Soc. **Research Statement & Publications:** Founder Information Mechanics; numerous publications and Comput programs; patents include electronics, thermodynamics, vision, water pollution control, x-ray optics. **Mailing Address:** 523 W 112 St #32, New York City, NY 10025-1619.

KANTOR, GEORGE JOSEPH, BIOPHYSICS, MOLECULAR BIOLOGY. **Personal Data:** b Titusville, Pa, January 24, 1937; m 1966, c 3. **Education:** Slippery Rock State Col, BS, 1958; NMex Highlands Univ, MS, 1962; Pa State Univ, PhD (biophys), 1967. **Professional Experience:** PROF BIOL SCI, WRIGHT STATE UNIV, 1980-; from asst prof to assoc prof, Wright State Univ, 1970-1980; fel, Biomed Res Group, Los Alamos Sci Lab, 1968-1970; NIH fel biophys, Pa State Univ, 1967-1968. **Memberships:** Biophys Soc; AAAS; Sigma Xi; Tissue Culture Asn; Am Soc Photobiol. **Research Statement & Publications:** Effects of radiation on biological systems with emphasis on human cells cultured in vitro; DNA repair in human cells. **Mailing Address:** Dept Biol Sci, Wright State Univ, 235A BH 3640 Colonel Glenn Hwy, Dayton, OH 45435. **Fax:** 937-775-3320.

KANTOR, GIDEON, NEUROMUSCULAR ELECTRICAL STIMULATION. **Personal Data:** b Vienna, Austria, March 30, 1925; American citizen; m 1967, c 2. **Education:** NY Univ, BEE, 1948; Polytech Univ NY, MEE, 1950; Cornell Univ, PhD (elec eng), 1963. **Honors & Awards:** Bicentennial Medal, Inst Elec & Electronics Engrs, 1984. **Professional Experience:** ASST PROF, DEPT BIOMED ENG, CATH UNIV, as of 2003; lectr, electroenviron eng, Cath Univ, Wash DC, beginning 1995; physicist, Ctr Devices & Radiol Health, Food & Drug Admin, Rockville, 1972-1995; staff mem, Avco, Lowell, 1965-1968 & Mitre, Bedford, 1968-1972; physicist, Air Force Cambridge Lab, 1959-1965; res asst, Cornell Univ, 1955-1959; engr, Gen Elec, Ithaca, 1955-1956; res assoc, Microwave Res Inst, Brooklyn, 1950-1955. **Memberships:** Fel Inst Elec & Electronics Engrs; Sigma Xi. **Research Statement & Publications:** Neuromuscular electrical stimulation with emphasis on the role of electrical parameters such as current and phase charge on safety and effectiveness. **Mailing Address:** Dept Biomed Eng, Sch Eng, Cath Univ, PO Box 553, Garrett Park, MD 20896. **E-Mail:** gkantor@aol.com

KANTOR, HARVEY SHERWIN, INFECTIOUS DISEASES, MICROBIOLOGY. **Personal Data:** b New York, NY, April 30, 1938; div, c Harold Frostick & Eric Frostick. **Education:** Wash Univ, MD, 1962; Am Bd Internal Med, dipl, 1968. **Professional Experience:** RETIRED, 2002; DIR, INTERNAL MED & INFECTIOUS DIS & TRAVEL HEALTH SERV, DEPT INTERNAL MED, TEX TECH UNIV, 1993-; DIR, DIV MED MICROBIOL, 1985-; CHIEF, MED MICROBIOL LAB, VET ADMIN MED CTR, NORTH CHICAGO, 1985-; ASSOC PROF PATH, CHICAGO MED SCH, 1978-; consult, Highland Park Hosp, Highland Park & US Naval Hosp, Great Lakes, Ill, 1975-; chief infectious dis sect, Vet Admin Med Ctr, North Chicago, 1975-1985; assoc prof med & dir div infectious dis, Med Microbiol Lab, Vet Admin Med Ctr, North Chicago, 1975-1985; Actg dir div infectious dis, Cook County Hosp, 1972-1974; asst prof med& microbiol, Univ Ill Med Ctr, 1971-1975; res educ assoc, Vet Admin, 1970-1971; res fel, New Eng Med Ctr Hosp, Tufts Univ, 1966-1969; asst, Sch Med, 1966-1969; Asst med, Sch Med, Wash Univ, 1962-1963. **Memberships:** Fel Am Col Physicians, assoc prof med & pathol, 1975-1993, chief, Med Microbiol Lab, 1985-1993; Sigma Xi; Am Fedn Clin Res; Am Soc Microbiol; NY Acad Sci; fel Infectious Dis Soc Am; Assoc Hosp Epidemiologists Am. **Research Statement & Publications:** Bacterial toxins and their mechanism of action; their influence on cyclic nucleotides and prostaglandin interactions; hospital infection control. **Mailing Address:** 313 Whitmore Ln, Lake Gorest, IL 60045.

KANTOR, PAUL B, VALUE INFORMATION, NETWORKED INFORMATION SYSTEMS. **Personal Data:** b Washington, DC, November 27, 1938; m 1962, Carole Kaplowitz; c Michael & David. **Education:** Columbia Univ, AB, 1959; Princeton Univ, PhD (physics), 1963. **Honors & Awards:** Fel am assoc for the Advancement of sci 2001; res Award Am soc info sci and technol 2001. **Professional Experience:** PROF, RUTGERS STATE UNIV NJ, 1991-; dist prof 2001-; vis prof, Info Systs, Rutgers Univ, 1990; distinguished vis scholar, Online Comput Libr Ctr, Ohio, 1987; sr lectr, Weatherhead Sch Mgt, Case Western Res Univ, 1981-; adj assoc prof libr & info sci, Kent State Univ, 1978-1981; PRES, TANTALUS INC, 1977-; sr res assoc systs eng, Complex Systs Inst, 1977-1981; assoc prof oper res, Libr & Info Sci, 1974-1977; prog dir, Complex Systs Inst, 1973-1974; assoc prof physics, Case Western Res Univ, 1969-1974; asst prof, Case Western Res

Univ, 1967-1969; Guest physicist, Brookhaven Nat Lab, 1965-; vis asst prof, State Univ NY, Stony Brook, 1965-1967; Res assoc physics, Brookhaven Nat Lab, 1963-1965; mem, Ctr Opers Res, Rutgers Univ. **Memberships:** Am Phys Soc; Am Statist Asn; Am Soc Info Sci; NY Acad Sci; Am Libr Asn. **Research Statement & Publications:** Value of information; information retrieval, large databases; distributed detection and decision systems; industrial learning phenomena; networked information environment. **Mailing Address:** Rutgers Univ, 4 Huntington St, New Brunswick, NJ 08903. **Fax:** 732-932-1504. **E-Mail:** kantor@scils.rutgers.edu

KANTOR, SIDNEY, PARASITOLOGY, PROTOZOOLOGY. **Personal Data:** b New York, NY, February 1, 1924; m 1973, c 5. **Education:** George Washington Univ, BA, 1947, MA, 1949; Univ Ill, PhD (zool), 1956. **Professional Experience:** RETIRED; prin res biologist, Agr Res Div, 1977-1989; sr res biologist protozool chemother, Agr Res Div, 1970-1973; from parasitologist to group leader, Am Cynamid Co, 1956-1973; coop agent, USDA, Ill, 1955-1956; asst parasitol, Col Vet Med, Univ Ill, 1953-1955; Invert zoologist, Acad Natural Sci, Pa, 1951-1953. **Memberships:** Am Soc Parasitol; Soc Protozool; Sigma Xi. **Research Statement & Publications:** Parasitic chemotherapy; veterinary entomology. **Mailing Address:** 4A Van Buren Dr, Cranbury, NJ 08512.

KANTOR, SIMON WILLIAM, POLYMER CHEMISTRY, ORGANIC CHEMISTRY. **Personal Data:** b Brussels, Belg, March 23, 1925; American citizen; m 1989, Karen C Kantor; c Michael D, Sharon, Jason, Justin. **Education:** City Col NY, BS, 1945; Duke Univ, PhD (org chem), 1949. **Honors & Awards:** Gold Patent Medallion, Gen Elec Co, 1966. **Professional Experience:** Res prof, Univ Mass, Amherst, 1982-2000; vpres res & develop, GAF Corp, Wayne, NJ, 1972-1982; br mgr, Gen Elec Co, Schenectady, NY, 1965-1972; sect mgr, Gen Elec Co, Schenectady, NY, 1960-1965; res assoc, Gen Elec Co, Schenectady, NY, 1951-1960; Fel, Duke Univ, 1949-1951; PROF EMER, UNIV MASS. **Memberships:** AAAS; Am Chem Soc. **Research Statement & Publications:** Organic reactions of carbanions; organosilicon polymers; synthesis of aromatic condensation polymers; liquid crystal polymers. **Mailing Address:** 153 Silver Lake Dr, Agawam, MA 01001. **E-Mail:** swkantor@polysci.umass.edu

KANTOR, WILLIAM M, MATHEMATICS. **Education:** Univ Wis, PhD, 1968. **Professional Experience:** PROF, DEPT MATH, UNIV ORE, as of 2004. **Mailing Address:** Dept Math, Univ Ore, 201 Deady Hall, Eugene, OR 97403-1222. **Fax:** 541-346-0987. **E-Mail:** kantor@math.uoregon.edu

KANTOROVITZ, SHMUEL, OPERATOR THEORY. **Personal Data:** b Casablanca, Morocco, September 17, 1935; m 1960, c 4. **Education:** Hebrew Univ Israel, MSc, 1956; Univ Minn, Minneapolis, PhD (math), 1962. **Professional Experience:** Dept chmn, Bar Ilan Univ, 1977-1979 & 1985-1987; PROF MATH, BAR ILAN UNIV, ISRAEL, 1972-; from assoc prof to prof math, Univ Ill, Chicago Circle, 1970-1978; asst prof, Yale Univ, 1964-1967; mem, Inst Advan Study, 1963-1964; Instr math, Princeton Univ, 1962-1963. **Memberships:** Am Math Soc. **Research Statement & Publications:** Functional analysis. **Mailing Address:** Bar Ilan Univ, 52900 Ramat Gan, Israel.

KANTOWITZ, BARRY H, ERGONOMICS, HUMAN INFORMATION PROCESSING. **Personal Data:** b New York, NY, August 25, 1943. **Education:** City Univ NY City Col, BA, 1965; City Univ NY Queens Col, MA, 1967; Univ Wis, PhD (exp psychol), 1969. **Professional Experience:** DIR TRANSP RES INST, PROF PSYCHOL, INDUST & OPER ENG, UNIV MICH, as of 2006; Ed, Transp Human Factors J, 1997; human factors sci adv, Aviation Safety Reporting Syst, 1991-; affil prof, Psychol Dept, Univ Wash, beginning 1988; chief scientist, Human Factors Transp Ctr, Batelle, beginning 1987; vis prof psychol, Univ Lulea, Sweden Tech, 1986; courtesy appointment, Dept Aeronaut & Astronaut, Stanford Univ, 1984; Am Soc Elec Engrs fel, Ames Res Ctr, NASA, 1982; prof, prof Indust Eng Dept, 1981-1987; prof, Psychol Sci Dept, 1979-1987; dir, human Factors Grad Training Prog, Psychol Dept, 1977-1987; Sr lectr ergonomics, Inst Indust Org, Univ Trodheim, Norway, 1976-1977; assoc prof, Purdue Univ, 1972-1979; Asst prof, Purdue Univ, 1969-1972. **Memberships:** Fel Am Psychol Soc; fel Am Psychol Asn; Psychonomic Soc; Human Factors Soc; Soc Automotive Engrs. **Research Statement & Publications:** Human attention; mental workload; human-machine interaction; human factors; intelligent vehicle highway systems. **Mailing Address:** Indust & Oper Eng, Univ Mich, 154 UMTRI 1205 Beal Ave, Ann Arbor, MI 48109-2117. **E-Mail:** barrykan@umich.edu

KANTOWSKI, RONALD, PHYSICS. **Personal Data:** b Shreveport, La, December 18, 1939; m 1961, Anita; c Andrew, Leila & Matthew. **Education:** Univ Tex, Austin, BS, 1962, PhD (physics), 1966. **Professional Experience:** PROF PHYSICS, UNIV OKLA, 1981-; from asst prof to assoc prof, Univ Okla, 1968-1981; res assoc, Southwest Ctr Advan Studies, 1967-1968; asst prof, Univ Tex, Austin, 1966-1967; teaching asst physics, Univ Tex, Austin, 1963-1966; res scientist med, Univ Tex Med Br, Galveston, 1962-1963. **Memberships:** Am Phys Soc. **Research Statement & Publications:** Gravity theories; quantum field theory. **Mailing Address:** Dept Physics & Astron, Univ Okla, 1318 Cherry Stone St, Norman, OK 73072. **Fax:** 405-325-7557. **E-Mail:** kantowski@nhn.ou.edu

KANTROWITZ, ADRIAN, SURGERY. **Personal Data:** b New York, NY, October 4, 1918; m 1948, c 3. **Education:** NY Univ, AB, 1940; Long Island Col Med, MD, 1943; Am Bd Surg, dipl. **Honors & Awards:** H L Moses Prize, Montefiore Alumnus, 1949; Exhibit Prize, NYState Med Soc, 1952; Gold Plate Award, Am Acad Achievement, 1966; Theodore & Susan B Cummings Award, Am Col Cardiol, 1967; Max Berg Award, 1969. **Professional Experience:** PROF EMER, COL MED, WAYNE STATE UNIV, as of 2003; chmn dept surg, Sinai Hosp, Detroit, beginning 1970; prof surg, col med, Wayne State Univ, begining 1970; dir surg, Maimonides Med Ctr, Brooklyn, 1964-1970; from asst prof to prof surg, State Univ NY Col Med, 1955-1970; dir cardiovasc surg, Maimonides Med Ctr, Brooklyn, 1955-1964; USPHS fel cardiovasc res & teaching fel physiol, Dept Physiol, Western Reserve Univ, 1951-1952; resident, Montefiore Hosp, 1948-1950; surg resident, Mt Sinai Hosp, 1947; Intern, Jewish Hosp, Brooklyn, 1944. **Memberships:** fel NY Acad Sci; Am Chem Soc; Int Soc Angiol; Am Soc Artificial Internal Organs (pres 1968-1969); Harvey Soc. **Research Statement & Publications:** Cardiac pacemakers; heart transplants; human balloon pump; partial human mechanical heart. **Mailing Address:** 70 Gallogly Rd, Auburn Hills, MI 48326-1222.

KANTROWITZ, ARTHUR (ROBERT), GAS DYNAMICS, LASER PROPULSION. **Personal Data:** b Bronx, NY, October 20, 1913; m 1980, Lee; c 3. **Education:** Columbia Univ, BS, 1934, MA, 1936, PhD (physics), 1947. **Honorary Degrees:** DE, Mont Col Mineral Sci & Technol, 1975; DSc, NJ Inst Technol, 1981. **Honors & Awards:** Fluid & Plasma Dynamics Award & Medal, Am Inst Aeronaut & Astronaut, 1981; MHD Faraday Mem Medal, UNESCO, 1983. **Professional Experience:** PROF ENG, THAYER SCH ENG, DARTHMOUTH COL, as of 2006; eng adv bd mem, Rensselaer Polytech Inst, 1981-1986; eng adv bd mem, Stanford Univ, 1966-1982; hon prof, Huazhang Inst Technol, Wuhan, China, 1980; hon life mem, Bd Gov, Technion, 1978; mem bd overseers, Thayer Sch Eng, Dartmouth Col, 1975-1982; presidential adv group, Anticipated Advances Sci & Technol, Sci Court Task Force, 1975-1976; hon trustee, Univ Rochester, 1971; mem adv coun, Dept Aeronaut Eng, Princeton Univ, 1959-1977; vis inst prof & fel, Sch Advan Study, Mass Inst Technol, 1957; sr vpres bd dir, AVCO Corp, 1956-1979; founder, dir, chief exec officer & chmn, AVCO Everett Res Lab, 1955-1978; fulbright scholar & Guggenheim fel, Cambridge Univ & Univ Manchester, 1954; vis lectr, Harvard Univ, 1952; from assoc prof to prof aeronaut eng & eng physics, Cornell Univ, 1946-1956; physicist, Nat Adv Comt Aeronaut, 1936-1946. **Memberships:** Nat Acad Sci; Nat Acad Eng; hon fel Am Phys Soc; fel Am Inst Aeronaut & Astronaut; fel Am Acad Arts & Sci; Int Acad Astronaut; founding fel Am Inst Med & Biol Eng; fel AAAS. **Research Statement & Publications:** Physical gas dynamics; magneto-hydrodynamics power; high power lasers; cardiac assist devices; application of high temperature shock tubes to earth re-entry; invention of the stagnation point experiment; interation of science and society. **Mailing Address:** Four Downing Rd, Hanover, NH 03755-1902. **E-Mail:** arthur.kantrowitz@dartmouth.edu

KANTROWITZ, EVAN R, BIOCHEMISTRY. **Personal Data:** b Fall River, Mass, August 18, 1949. **Education:** Boston Univ, BA, 1971, MS, 1973; Harvard Univ, PhD (chem), 1976. **Professional Experience:** PROF CHEM, BOSTON COL, as of 2003; CHAIR, DEPT BIOCHEM, BOSTON COL, 1992-; PROF BIOCHEM, BOSTON COL, 1984-; from asst prof to assoc prof chem & biochem, 1972-1984. **Memberships:** Am Chem Soc; AAAS; Protein Soc; Am Soc Biochem & Molecular Biol. **Mailing Address:** Dept Chem, Boston Col, Eugene F Merkert Chem Ctr 2609 Beacon St, Chestnut Hill, MA 02167. **Fax:** 617-552-2705. **E-Mail:** evan.kantrowitz@bc.edu

KANTROWITZ, IRWIN H, GEOLOGY, HYDROLOGY. **Personal Data:** b Brooklyn, NY, October 12, 1937. **Education:** Brooklyn Col, BS, 1958; Ohio State Univ, MS, 1959. **Professional Experience:** RETIRED; district chief, US Geol Surv, 1980-1995; from geologist to chief hydrologist, US Geol Surv, Fla, 1959-1980; mem, US Geol Surv Water Resources Adv Bd. **Memberships:** Fel Geol Soc Am; Am Geophys Union; Asn Groundwater Scientists & Engrs. **Mailing Address:** US Geol Surv, 227 N Bronough St, Tallahassee, FL 32301. **Fax:** 904-681-7650.

KANTZ, PAUL THOMAS, PHYCOLOGY. **Personal Data:** b Jacksonville, Tex, January 21, 1941; m 1962, c 3. **Education:** Univ Tex, BA, 1963, MA, 1965, PhD (phycol), 1967. **Professional Experience:** Dept chmn, 1988-1990; PROF BIOL, CALIF STATE UNIV, SACRAMENTO, 1981-; from asst prof to assoc prof, 1967-1981. **Memberships:** Phycol Soc Am; Bot Soc Am; NY Acad Sci; Sigma Xi. **Research Statement & Publications:** Taxonomy and morphology of blue green algae. **Mailing Address:** 525 42nd St, Sacramento, CA 95819-2818. **E-Mail:** ptkantz@csus.edu

KANTZES, JAMES (GEORGE), PLANT PATHOLOGY. **Personal Data:** b Bertha, Pa, March 29, 1924; m 1954, c 3. **Education:** Univ Md, BS, 1951, MS, 1954, PhD (plant path), 1957. **Professional Experience:** PROF EMER PLANT PATH, COL AGR, UNIV MD, as of 2003; prof plant path, Col Agr, Univ MD, 1969-; from instr to assoc prof, 1952-1969. **Memberships:** Am Phytopath Soc; Sigma Xi. **Research Statement & Publications:** Agriculture; control of vegetable diseases. **Mailing Address:** Dept Plant Path, Univ Md, 2109 H J Patterson Hall, Salisbury, MD 20742-5815.

KANWAL, RAM PRAKASH, GENERALIZED FUNCTIONS INTEGRAL EQUATIONS. **Personal Data:** b India, July 4, 1924; American citizen; m 1954, Vimla; c Neeru & Neeraj. **Education:** Punjab Univ, India, BA, 1945, MA, 1948; Ind Univ, PhD, 1957. **Professional Experience:** Vis prof, Tech Univ Denmark, 1965-1966 & Royal Inst Technol, Stockholm, 1966; PROF MATH, PA STATE UNIV, 1962-; assoc prof, PA State Univ, 1959-1962; sr scientist, Oak Ridge Nat Lab, 1959; asst prof, Math Res Ctr, Univ Wis, 1957-1959; res assoc appl math, Ind Univ, 1954-1957; asst lectr, Indian Inst Technol, Kharagpur, 1952-1954; asst prof, Birla Col, Pilani, 1951-1952; lectr math, Daynand Anglo Vernacular Col, India, 1950-1951; Asst, Ministry of Agr, Govt India, 1948-1950. **Memberships:** Soc Indust & Appl Math; Allahabed Math Soc. **Research Statement & Publications:** Hydrodynamics; aerodynamics; magnetohydrodynamics; elasticity; diffraction; integral and differential equations; General function, Assyrroptotic analysis. **Mailing Address:** Dept Math Pa State Univ, 425 McAllister Bldg, University Park, PA 16802-6401. **Fax:** 814-865-3735. **E-Mail:** kanwal@math.psu.edu

KANWAR, YASHPAL SINGH, RENAL PATHOLOGY & IMMUNOPATHOLOGY. **Personal Data:** b Punjab, India, June 1, 1947. **Education:** Univ Punjab, India, MD, 1970; Univ Ill, Chicago, PhD (biochem & path), 1976. **Professional Experience:** STEINER PROF PATH, NORTHWESTERN UNIV, as of 2004; PROF MED, NORTHWESTERN UNIV, as of 2004; PROF PATH & RENAL MED, NORTHWESTERN UNIV MED SCH, 1984-; res career develop award, NIH, 1982-1989; from asst prof to assoc prof, Northwestern Univ Med Sch, 1981-1983; fel renal cell biol & path, Yale Univ, 1976-1980; residency, Univ Ill, Chicago, 1971-1975. **Memberships:** AAAS; Am Soc Cell Biol; Am Soc Nephrology; Am Asn Path. **Research Statement & Publications:** Renal pathology and immunopathology. **Mailing Address:** Dept Path Ward 6085 Northwestern Univ Med Sch, 303 E Chicago Ave, Chicago, IL 60611-3072. **Fax:** 312-503-8240. **E-Mail:** y-kanwar@northwestern.edu

KANZELMEYER, JAMES HERBERT, ANALYTICAL CHEMISTRY. **Personal Data:** b Manila, Philippines, August 9, 1926; m 1949, c 9. **Education:** Univ Calif, AB, 1947; Ore State Col, PhD (anal chem), 1955. **Professional Experience:** CONSULT, 1987-; chief chemist, Corp Anal Serv, St Joe Minerals Corp, 1980-1987; mem, Nat Res Coun Eval Panel, Anal Chem Div, Nat Bur Standards, 1975-1978; chief chemist smelting div, St Joe Zinc Co, 1963-1980; anal res chemist, St Joe Zinc Co, 1957-1963; asst prof, NMex Highlands Univ, 1954-1957; instr chem, Ore State Col, 1953-1954; chemist, Beacon res labs, Tex Co, 1947-1949. **Memberships:** Am Soc Testing & Mat; Sigma Xi. **Research Statement & Publications:** Analytical chemistry of zinc-containing materials, including chemical, optical-emission and x-ray spectrographic methods. **Mailing Address:** 5219 Webb St, Aliquippa, PA 15001.

KANZLER, WALTER WILHELM, ANIMAL BEHAVIOR, BIOETHICS. **Personal Data:** b Jersey City, NJ, September 17, 1938. **Education:** Montclair State Col, BA, 1960, MA, 1963; Marshall Univ, MA, 1964; Univ Cincinnati, PhD (ecol, behav), 1972. **Professional Experience:** Adj prof biol, St Peter's Col, Jersey City, NJ, 1990-; adj prof biol, St John's Univ, Staten Island, NY, 1989-; PROF BIOL & CHMN, WAGNER COL, 1984-; consult, Scientists Ctr Animal Welfare, 1980-; NSF grant, Nat Primate Ctr, Univ Calif, Davis, 1971 & Am Mus Natural Hist, 1994; assoc prof biol, Wagner Col, 1976-1984; sr res assoc, Nat Ctr Bioethics, Drew Univ, 1976; NASA fel, 1969-1970; from instr to asst prof, Wagner Col, 1966-1976; asst prof, Trenton State Col, 1965-1966; Instr biol, Union City High Schs, NJ, 1960-1965. **Memberships:** Animal Behav Soc; Sigma Xi; AAAS; Nat Wildlife Fed. **Research Statement & Publications:** Insect, gerbil and primate behavior, zoo animal behavior; history of biology and medicine; social issues in biology and medicine. **Mailing Address:** Institute for Nature Study, 376 New York Avenue, Jersey City Heights, NJ 02307-1105. **E-Mail:** wknature@adl.com

KAO, CHARLES K, FIBER OPTICS. **Personal Data:** b Shanghai, China, November 4, 1933; American citizen; m 1959, Mary Wan Wong; c Simon M & Amanda M. **Education:**

Univ London, BSc, 1957, PhD (elec eng), 1965. **Honorary Degrees:** DSc, Chinese Univ Hong Kong, 1985, Univ Sussex, 1990 & Univ Durham, 1994; Dr, Soka Univ, 1991 & Univ Padova, Italy, 1996; DEng, Univ Glasgow, 1992. **Honors & Awards:** Morey Award, Am Ceramic Soc, 1976; Stewart Ballantine Medal, Franklin Inst, 1977; Morris H Liebmann Mem Award, Inst Elec & Electronics Engrs, 1978, Alexander Graham Bell Medal, 1985; L M Ericsson Int Prize, Sweden, 1979; Gold Medal, Armed Forces Commun & Electronics Asn, 1980; Int Prize New Mat, Am Phys Soc, 1989; Faraday Medal, Inst Elec Engrs, 1989; Gold Medal, Int Soc Optical Eng, 1992; Japan Prize, Sci & Tech Found, Japan, 1996; Prince Philip Medal, RAE, UK: harles Stark Draper Prize, NAE, 1999. **Professional Experience:** HON PROF ENG, CHINESE UNIV, HONG KONG, 1996-; vchancellor & pres, Chinese Univ, Hong Kong, 1987-1996; Marconi int fel, 1985; Adj prof & fel, Trumbull Col, Yale Univ, 1985; exec scientist & dir res, Advan Tech Ctr, Shelton, Conn, 1983-1987; vpres, & dir eng, 1981-1983; chief scientist, Electro-Optical Prod Div, ITT, Roanoke, Va, 1974-1981; prof, Electronics Dept, Chinese Univ Hong Kong, 1970-1974; Develop engr, Stand Tel & Cables Ltd, London, 1957-1960; prin res engr, Stand Telecommun Lab Ltd. **Memberships:** Nat Acad Eng; fel Inst Elec & Electronics Engrs; Royal Swed Acad Eng Sci; fel Inst Elec Engrs UK; fel Royal Acad Engrs UK; fel Acad Sinica Taiwan; fel, Royal Soc, UK. **Mailing Address:** c/o S K Yee Medical, Unit 1708 Office, Hong Kong, China. **Fax:** 852-2603-7663. **E-Mail:** ckao@ie.cuhk.edu.hk

KAO, FA-TEN, SOMATIC CELL & HUMAN MOLECULAR GENETICS. **Personal Data:** b Hankow, China, April 20, 1934; American citizen; m 1960, Betty; c Alan S. **Education:** Nat Taiwan Univ, BS, 1955; Univ Minn, St Paul, PhD (genetics), 1964. **Professional Experience:** Vis prof human molecular genetics, Tonji Med Univ, People's Repub China, 1988; hon consult prof med molecular genetics, Harbin Med Univ, People's Rep China, 1987; res scientist, Europ Molecular Biol Lab, Heidelberg, 1985; PROF BIOCHEM BIOPHYS & GENETICS, UNIV COLO HEALTH SCI CTR, DENVER, 1981-; Int Union Against Cancer-Eleanor Roosevelt Int Cancer fel, Univ Oxford, 1973-1974; assoc prof, Univ Col Med Ctr, 1970-1981; asst prof, Univ Col Med Ctr, 1967-1970; Nat Cancer Inst fel, Univ Colo Med Ctr, Denver, 1965-1967; sr fel, Eleanor Roosevelt Inst Cancer Res, 1965. **Memberships:** Genetics Soc Am; Am Soc Cell Biol; Am Soc Human Genetics; Am Asn Cancer Res; Tissue Cult Asn; AAAS. **Research Statement & Publications:** In vitro genetic studies of somatic mammalian cells; somatic cell and molecular genetic analysis of the human genome; mapping of human genes; use of recombinant DNA technology in human genetic studies; molecular analysis of genetic diseases. **Mailing Address:** Eleanor Roosevelt Inst Cancer Res, 1899 Gaylord St, Denver, CO 80206-1210. **Fax:** 303-333-8423.

KAO, JOHN Y, ANIMAL & EXPLORATORY DRUG METABOLISM. **Personal Data:** b Hong Kong, December 12, 1948; c 2. **Education:** Univ Surrey, Eng, BSc, 1973, PhD (biochem), 1977. **Honors & Awards:** Frank Blood Award, Soc Toxicol, 1987. **Professional Experience:** SR DIR, DEPT DRUG SAFETY & METAB, WYETH RES, as of 2003; sr res fel, Dept Animal & Explor Drug Metab, Merck Sharp & Dohme Res Labs, beginning 1991; sr investr, Dept Drug Metab, SmithKline Beecham Pharmaceut, 1986-1991; mem, Arthropod Repellent Subcomt & Bd Environ Studies & Toxicol, Nat Res Coun, 1986-1987; fac mem, Traveling Lect Prog, Oak Ridge Assoc Univs, 1984-1986; staff scientist, Biol Div, Oak Ridge Nat Lab, 1980-1986; NIH fel, Lab Reprod & Develop Toxicol, Nat Inst Environ Health Sci, 1977-1980. **Memberships:** Soc Toxicol; Int Soc Study Xenobiotics; Am Asn Pharmaceut Scientists; Am Soc Pharmacol & Exp Therapeut. **Research Statement & Publications:** Absorption, metabolism and toxicokinetics of xenobiotics; mechanisms of chemical toxicity and safety evaluation; dermatotoxicology, percutaneous absorption and transdermal delivery of drugs; drug development, drug metabolism and pharmacokinetics; author of numerous technical publications. **Mailing Address:** Dept Drug Safety & Metab, Wyeth Res, 500 Arcola Rd, Collegeville, PA 19426. **Fax:** 484-865-9403. **E-Mail:** kaoj@wyeth.com

KAO, KWAN CHI, SEMICONDUCTORS & DIELECTRICS. **Personal Data:** b Chungshan, China, October 11, 1926; Canadian citizen; m 1993, Leatrice; c 7. **Education:** Univ Nanking, BSc, 1948; Univ Mich, MSc, 1950; Univ Birmingham, Eng, PhD (elec eng), 1957. **Honorary Degrees:** DSc, Univ Birmingham, Eng, 1984. **Professional Experience:** PROF EMER ELEC & COMPUT SCI, UNIV MAN, as of 2004; Nat Univ Singapore & Xian Jiaotong Univ, China, 1981; vis prof, Nat Defense Acad Japan, 1980-1981; external referee, Res Grants Comts Can Coun & Natural Sci & Eng Res Coun Can, Ottawa, beginning 1976; prof elec eng, Univ Man, beginning 1969; assoc prof, Univ Man, 1966-1968; sr lectr elec eng, Univ Salford, Eng, 1962-1965; group leader & sr res engr dielec Mat, Brush Elec Eng Co, Ltd, Eng, 1960-1961; res engr non-linear control systs, Nelson Res Lab, Eng Elec Co Ltd, Eng, 1958-1960; res fel mat sci, Univ Col Swansea, UK, 1957-1958. **Memberships:** fel Inst Elec Engrs UK; fel Inst Physics UK; sr mem Inst Elec & Electronics Engrs; Can Asn Physicists; Sigma Xi; Asn Prof Engrs Can. **Research Statement & Publications:** Electronic and optical properties of semiconductors and insulators such as crystalline, poly-crystalline, micro-crystalline, and non-crystalline, organic and inorganic in bulk and film forms with and without doping, and their applications for devices; high-field conduction and breakdown phenomena in dielectrics; photoelectric properties of polymers and ceramics incorporated with various impurities. **Mailing Address:** Dept Elec & Comput Eng, Univ Man, Winnipeg, MB R3T 2N2, Can. **Fax:** 204-261-4639. **E-Mail:** kckao@ee.umanitoba.ca

KAO, MING-HSIUNG, ANIMAL PHYSIOLOGY. **Personal Data:** b Taipei, Taiwan, January 10, 1944; Canadian citizen; c 2. **Education:** Nat Taiwan Univ, BSc, 1964; Mem Univ Nfld, MSc, 1970, PhD (biol), 1979. **Professional Experience:** ASSOC PROF BIOL, MEM UNIV NFLD, 1988-; Asst prof, 1981-1988. **Research Statement & Publications:** Protein & glycoprotein antifreeze activities in marine teleosts. **Mailing Address:** Dept Biol Sci Mem Univ Nfld, Elizabeth Ave, St John's, NL A1C 5S7, Can.

KAO, RACE LI-CHAN, MYOCARDIAL METABOLISM, CARDIOVASCULAR DISEASES, HEART FAILURE. **Personal Data:** b Chungking, China, December 1, 1943; American citizen; m 1969, Lidia; c Elizabeth & Grace. **Education:** Nat Taiwan Univ, BS, 1965; Univ Ill, MS, 1971, PhD (biochem & physiol), 1972. **Honors & Awards:** Who's Who in Med & Healthcare, Am Man & Woman Sci, 1997; Who's Who in the South & Southwest, 1998-1999; 20th Cent Award for Achievement, 1999-2000; Lexington's Who's Who, 2000-2001; Who's Who in Med & Healthcare, 2002-2003; Strathmore's Who's Who, 2002-2003; Mem, Coun Circulation, Am Heart Asn; Who's Who in America 2004-2006. **Professional Experience:** PROF & CARROL H LONG CHMN EXCELLENCE, E TENN STATE UNIV, 1992-; prof, Med Col Pa, 1988-1992; DIR SURG RES, ALLEGHENY-SINGER RES INST, 1983-; assoc prof surg, Wash Univ, 1982-1983; asst prof surg & physiol, Univ Tex Med Br, 1977-1982; asst prof, M S Hershey Med Ctr, 1975-1977; res assoc physiol, M S Hershey Med Ctr, 1972-1975; res assoc animal sci, Univ Ill, 1972. **Memberships:** Am Heart Asn; Am Physiol Soc; AAAS; Am Soc Artificial Internal Organs; Int Soc Heart Res; NY Acad Sci; Nat Soc Med Res; Phi Tau Phi Honor Soc; Soc Chinese Biosci; Int Soc Artificial Org. **Research Statement & Publications:** Utilizing autologous myogenic stem cells to treat patients after heart attack for myocardial regeneration and to restore heart function for patients suffering heart failure. **Mailing Address:** Surg Dept, James H Quillen Col Med, E Tenn State Univ, PO Box 70575, Johnson City, TN 37614-0575. **Fax:** 423-439-8750. **E-Mail:** kao@etsu.edu

KAO, SAMUEL CHUNG-SIUNG, MATHEMATICAL STATISTICS, MATHEMATICS. **Personal Data:** b Kaohsiung, Taiwan, June 12, 1941; c 2. **Education:** Nat Taiwan Univ, BS, 1964; Nat Tsing Hua Univ, MS, 1966; Columbia Univ, PhD (statist), 1972. **Professional Experience:** STATISTICIAN, BROOKHAVEN NAT LAB, 1974-; asst prof statist, Univ Mass, Amherst, 1973-1974; statist assoc, Biomet Res, NY State Psychiat Inst, 1971-1973; Lectr math, Nat Tsing Hua Univ, 1966-1967. **Memberships:** Am Statist Asn; Inst Math Statist; Biomet Soc; Sigma Xi; NY Acad Sci. **Research Statement & Publications:** Sequential experimentation; robust statistical procedures; applied probability. **Mailing Address:** 26 Cornwallis Rd, E Setauket, NY 11733.

KAO, TAI-WU, COMMUNICATION. **Personal Data:** b China, January 5, 1935; m, c 5. **Education:** Nat Taiwan Univ, BS, 1958; Chiao Tung Univ, MS, 1961; Univ Utah, PhD (elec eng), 1965. **Professional Experience:** PROF ELEC ENG, LOYOLA MARYMOUNT UNIV, 1977-; Dept Navy, 1973-1974 & TRW, begining 1975-1992; DWP, Los Angeles, 1971-1972; from asst prof to assoc prof, Loyola Marymount Univ, 1965-1977; consult, Teledyne Systs Control Syst, 1965-1968. **Memberships:** Inst Elec & Electronics Engrs. **Research Statement & Publications:** Electromagnetics and communication systems. **Mailing Address:** Dept Elec Eng, Loyola Marymount Univ, ONE LMU Dr, Los Angeles, CA 90045. **Fax:** 310-338-5896. **E-Mail:** tkao@.lmu.edu

KAO, TIMOTHY WU, FLUID MECHANICS, CIVIL ENGINEERING. **Personal Data:** b Shanghai, China, July 20, 1937; American citizen; m 1965, c 2. **Education:** Univ Hong Kong, BS, 1959; Univ Mich, MSE, 1960, PhD (eng mech), 1963. **Professional Experience:** PROF EMER WAT RESOURCE, CATH UNIV AM, as of 2006; chmn, dept civil eng, Cath Univ Am, beginning 1981; prin investr, NSF grants, 1965-1995; prin investr, Off Naval Res Contracts, 1974-1992; prof civil eng, Cath Univ Am, beginning 1970; assoc prof atmospheric sci, dept civil eng, 1966-1970; asst prof space sci, dept civil eng, 1964-1966. **Memberships:** Am Meteorol Soc; fel Am Soc Civil Engrs. **Research Statement & Publications:** Physical oceanography; air-sea interaction; mountain waves; environmental fluid mechanics. **Mailing Address:** Dept Civil eng, Cath Univ Am, Rm G-21 Pangborn Hall, Washington, DC 20064-0001. **Fax:** 202-319-4499. **E-Mail:** kao@cua.edu

KAO, WEN-HONG, ELECTROCHEMISTRY, ENERGY STORAGE & TRANSFER SYSTEMS. **Personal Data:** b Taipei, Taiwan, March 15, 1954; m 1979, Shu-jen; c Yvonne, Peter & Jonathan. **Education:** Nat Tsing Hua Univ, Hsinchu, Taiwan, BS, 1976; Ohio State Univ, Columbus, PhD (anal chem), 1984. **Professional Experience:** SR CHEMIST, ADVAN BATTERY RES, JOHNSON CONTROLS INC, 1988-; lead scientist res & develop, Rayovac Corp, 1984-1988; res fel, Ohio State Univ, 1984. **Memberships:** Am Chem Soc; Electrochem Soc. **Research Statement & Publications:** Chemical and electrochemical analysis of battery electrode materials and systems; models of chemical and electrochemical reactions; production-related battery problems. **Mailing Address:** Johnson Controls, Inc, 5757 N Green Bay Ave, Milwaukee, WI 53201.

KAO, WINSTON WHEI-YANG, COLLAGEN & EXTRACELLULAR MATRIX COMPONENTS, CORNEAL WOUND-HEALING. **Personal Data:** b Tainam, Taiwan, American citizen; m 1972, Candace; c Edward & Charles. **Education:** Univ Pa, PhD (biochem), 1974. **Honors & Awards:** Edward McCormick Award, Res Prevent Blindness, 1986. **Professional Experience:** PROF OCULAR MOLECULAR BIOL, UNIV CINCINNATI COL MED, 1990-; assoc prof, Dept Ophthal, 1982-1990; asst prof, Dept Ophthal, Univ Pittsburgh, 1977-1982. **Memberships:** Asn Res Vision & Ophthal; Am Soc Biochem & Molecular Biol; AAAS; Int Soc Eye Res; Int Soc Matrix Biol. **Research Statement & Publications:** Metabolism of extra-cellular matrix during corneal wound healing; the role of cornea-specific K12 keratin in the maintenance of the integrity of corneal epithelium. **Mailing Address:** Dept Ophthal, 3223 Eden Ave, Cincinnati, OH 45267-0527. **Fax:** 513-558-3108. **E-Mail:** winston.kao@uc.edu

KAO, YI-HAN, PHYSICS. **Personal Data:** b Foochow, China, January 27, 1931; m 1957, c 2. **Education:** Nat Taiwan Univ, BS, 1954; Okla State Univ, MS, 1957; Columbia Univ, PhD (physics), 1962. **Professional Experience:** CEEM PROF, DEPT MAT PHYSICS, STATE UNIV NY, BUFFALO, 1990-; PROF, DEPT PHYSICS, STATE UNIV NY, BUFFALO, 1989-; prof, dept mat sci & eng, State Univ NY, Stony Brook, 1987-1992; prof Physics, State Univ NY, Stony Brook, 1971-1989; from asst prof to assoc prof, State Univ NY, Stony Brook, 1963-1971; res assoc physics, Thomas J Watson Lab, Int Bus Mach Corp, 1962-1963. **Memberships:** Am Phys Soc. **Research Statement & Publications:** Low temperature solid state physics; superconductivity; physics of thin films; transport phenomena. **Mailing Address:** Dept Physics, State Univ NY, 309 Fronczak Hall, Amherst, NY 14260. **Fax:** 716-645-2507. **E-Mail:** yhk@acsu.buffalo.edu

KAO, YUEN-KOH, CHEMICAL ENGINEERING, CONTROL ENGINEERING. **Personal Data:** b Liaoning, China, April 3, 1941; American citizen; m 1966, c 2. **Education:** Nat Taiwan Univ, BS, 1964; Northwestern Univ, MS, 1968, PhD (chem eng), 1973. **Professional Experience:** DIR GRAD STUDIES, CHEM ENG, UNIV CINCINNATI, as of 2005; PROF CHEM ENG, UNIV CINCINNATI, as of 2004; assoc prof chem eng, Univ Cincinnati, beginning 1981; consult, Mound Lab, Monsanto Res Corp, 1977; Columbia Gas, 1976 & R Katzen Asn, 1980; asst prof, Univ Cincinnati, 1975-1981; assoc chem eng, Rensselaer Polytech Inst, 1973-1975. **Memberships:** Am Inst Chem Engrs; Sigma Xi; Electrochem Soc. **Research Statement & Publications:** Process simulation and control; electrochemical engineering; boiling heat transfer; reaction engineering. **Mailing Address:** Dept Chem Mat eng, Col eng Univ Cincinnati, 497 Rhodes Hall, Cincinnati, OH 45221. **Fax:** 513-556-3473. **E-Mail:** ykao@alpha.che.uc.edu

KAPADIA, ABHAYSINGH J, PHARMACY. **Personal Data:** b Bombay, India, March 14, 1929; m 1955, c 2. **Education:** L M Col Pharm, Ahmedabad, India, 1952; Univ Mich, Ann Arbor, MS, 1958; Univ Tex, Austin, PhD (pharm), 1963. **Professional Experience:** MGR STABILITY TESTING & PROD EVAL, A H ROBINS CO INC, 1974-; res assoc, A H Robins CO Inc, 1965-1974; sect head anal res, Alcon Labs, 1963-1965; Res chemist, Univ Mich, 1957-1958. **Memberships:** Am Pharmaceut Asn. **Research Statement & Publications:** Analytical methods development; stability testing of pharmaceuticals; preformulation studies of pharmaceuticals; drug plastic interactions. **Mailing Address:** 2221 Walhala Dr, Richmond, VA 23236.

KAPANIA, RAKESH KUMAR, STRUCTURAL MECHANICS, PLATES & SHELLS. **Personal Data:** b Nakodar, Punjab, August 3, 1956; m 1985, c 1. **Education:** Punjab Univ, India, BS, 1977; Indian Inst Sci, MS, 1979; Purdue Univ, PhD (aerospace), 1985. **Professional Experience:** Boeing Welliver Fac Fel, VA Polytech Inst & State Univ, 1996; PROF AEROSPACE & OCEAN ENG, VA POLYTECH INST & STATE UNIV, 1994-; assoc prof, VA Polytech Inst & State Univ, 1990-1994; asst prof, VA Polytech Inst & State Univ, 1985-1990; NASA-ASEE fel, NASA-Langley Res Ctr, 1985; grad asst aerospace struct, Purdue

Univ, 1979-1985. **Memberships:** Am Inst Aeronaut & Astronaut; Am Soc Civil Engrs; Soc Indust & Appl Math. **Research Statement & Publications:** Application and development of state-of-the-art computational methods to solve problems in aeroelasticity, wave propagation in composites, impact response of laminated structures and plates and shells with emphasis on finite element method. **Mailing Address:** Dept Aerospace & Ocean Eng, Va Tech, 215 Randolph Hall, Blacksburg, VA 24060-7813. **Fax:** 540-231-9632. **E-Mail:** rkapania@vt.edu

KAPANY, NARINDER SINGH, PHYSICS, OPTICS. **Personal Data:** b Moga, India, October 31, 1927; American citizen; m 1954, Satinder; c Rajinder & Kiran. **Education:** DAV Col, Dehra Dun, BS, 1948; Imp Col, London, dipl, 1952; Univ London, PhD (optics), 1954. **Professional Experience:** FOUNDER & CHMN, SIKH FOUNDATION INC, as of 2006; FOUNDER & CHMN, K2 OPTRONICS INC, 2002-; dir, Ctr Innovation & Entrepreneurial Develop, 1978; regents prof, Univ Calif, Santa Cruz, 1976-1977; chmn & pres, Kaptron Inc, 1973-1990; vis scholar, Stanford Univ, 1973-1974; res assoc, Palo Alto Med Res Found, Calif, beginning 1962; founder & pres & dir res, Optics Technol, Inc, 1961-1973; mgr optics sect, Ill Inst Technol Res Inst, 1957-1961; res assoc, Inst Optics, Rochester, 1955-1957; Consult, Bausch & Lomb Optical Co, 1955-1957; res assoc physics, Imp Col, London, 1954-1955; lens designer, Barr & Stroud Optical Co, Scotland, 1952; supvr, Ord Factory, India, 1949-1951. **Memberships:** AAAS; fel Am Phys Soc; fel Optical Soc Am; sr mem Inst Elec & Electronics Engrs; fel Brit Inst Phys; Sigma Xi. **Research Statement & Publications:** Geometrical and physical optics; fiber optics with applications in medicine, photoelectronics, photography, high-speed photography; infrared fiber optics communications, local area networks; laser and its applications; image evaluation and optical information processing; photoelectronics; aspherics; interference microscopy; refractometry; solar energy; 100 patents; 100 scientific papers and 4 books on opto-electronics and entrepreneurship. **Mailing Address:** K2 Optronics Inc, 1288 Hammerwood Ave, Sunnyvale, CA 94089. **Fax:** 408-747-5921.

KAPECKI, JON ALFRED, PHYSICAL ORGANIC CHEMISTRY, PHOTOGRAPHIC SCIENCE. **Personal Data:** b Chicago, Ill, June 8, 1942; m 1982, Jeanne. **Education:** Col St Thomas, BS, 1964; Univ Vienna, Dipl, 1964; Univ Ill, Urbana, PhD (org chem), 1969. **Professional Experience:** SR LAB HEAD, EASTMAN KODAK CO, 1989-; lab head, Eastman Kodak Co, 1985-1989; vis assoc prof, Univ Rochester, 1984-1986; res assoc, Eastman Kodak Co, 1980-1985; sr lectr, Univ Rochester, 1980-1984; Mem staff, X-ray Clinic, State Univ NY, Albany, 1975-1976; sr chemist, Eastman Kodak Co, 1972-1980; lectr, Univ Rochester, 1972-1980; fel, Cornell Univ, 1971-1972; NIH fel chem, Cornell Univ, 1968-1971. **Memberships:** Am Chem Soc; Soc Imaging Sci & Technol. **Research Statement & Publications:** Organic cycloaddition mechanisms; solid state reactions; molecular orbital theory; computer applications to organic chemistry; models for reactive intermediates; reaction mechanisms; image and image modifying chemistry; qsar; information theory. **Mailing Address:** 161 Crosman Terr, Rochester, NY 14620. **Fax:** 585-588-7611. **E-Mail:** jon.kapecki@kodak.com

KAPER, HANS G, APPLIED MATHEMATICS, MATHEMATICAL ANALYSIS. **Personal Data:** b Alkmaar, Neth, June 10, 1936; American citizen; m, c 2. **Education:** State Univ Groningen, Neth, MSc, 1960, PhD (math), 1965. **Professional Experience:** PROG DIR, NSF, 2005-; Prog dir, NSF, 2001-2004; adj prof, Univ Ill Urbana-Champaign, 2003-; prof invite, Univ Bordeaux 1, france, 2000; prof invite, Univ Claude Bernard-Lyon I, france, 1993; prof invite, Univ Toulouse 3, Toulouse, france, 1996; div dir, Argonne Nat Lab, 1987-1991; adj prof, Northern Ill Univ, 1983-1990; Univ Vienna, Northwestern Univ, 1978-1980, 1984-1985; Univ Vienna, Austria, 1977; vis prof, Univ van Amsterdam, Neth, 1976-1977; SR MATHEMATICIAN, ARGONNE NAT LAB, 1969-; assoc prof, State Univ Groningen, Neth, 1967-1969; res assoc, Stanford Univ, 1966-1967; asst prof appl math, State Univ Groningen, Neth, 1965-1966. **Memberships:** Am Math Soc; Soc Indust & Appl Math; Math Soc Neth; corresp mem Royal Neth Acad Sci. **Research Statement & Publications:** Applied analysis; scientific computing. **Mailing Address:** Math & Comput Sci Div, Argonne Nat Lab, Argonne, IL 60439-4844. **Fax:** 630-252-5986. **E-Mail:** kaper@mcs.anl.gov

KAPER, JACOBUS M, BIOCHEMISTRY, MOLECULAR BIOLOGY. **Personal Data:** b Madjalenka, Indonesia, December 9, 1931; American citizen; m 1955, c 1. **Education:** Univ Leiden, BS, 1951, Drs, 1954, PhD (biochem), 1957. **Professional Experience:** RETIRED; res chemist, Plant Protection Inst, Agr Res Serv, USDA, beginning 1981; prin investr, USDA res grant, 1978-1981, 1982-1985 & 1985-1987; biochemist, Plant Sci Res Div, 1962-1969; prin investr, NIH res grants, 1962-1969; assoc res prof, George Wash Univ, 1962-1969; sr res biochemist, Univ Leiden, 1959-1962; USPHS trainee, 1958; res fel, Virus Lab, Univ Calif, 1957-1959; fel, Neth Orgn Pure Res, 1957-1958; asst biochem, Univ Leiden, 1954-1957. **Memberships:** Am Soc Virol; Am Chem Soc; Am Soc Biol Chemists; Am Soc Microbiol; corresp mem Royal Neth Acad Sci; Int Soc Plant Molecular Biol. **Research Statement & Publications:** Molecular organization and stabilizing interactions of viruses; structural biochemistry of proteins nucleic acids; divided genome viruses; mechanisms of viral disease regulation. **Mailing Address:** 115 Hedgewood Dr, Greenbelt, MD 20770-1610.

KAPER, JAMES BENNETT, VACCINE DEVELOPMENT, INFECTIOUS DISEASES. **Personal Data:** b Havre de Grace, Md, August 25, 1952; m 1997, Carol. **Education:** Univ Md, Col Park, BS, 1973, PhD (microbiol), 1979. **Honors & Awards:** Panlabs Award, Soc Indust Microbiol, 1996; MERIT award, NIH, 2004. **Professional Experience:** PROF MICROBIOL & IMMUNOL, UNIV MD, BALTIMORE, 1990-; assoc prof med, microbiol & biol chem, 1984-1990; consult, Microscience Ltd, 1998-2005; CHIEF, BACT GENETICS SECT, CTR VACCINE DEVELOP, UNIV MD, 1983-; asst prof biol chem, Univ Md, 1983-1985; consult, NIH, 1982-2005; adj prof micros, Univ RI, 1982-1983; asst prof med & microbiol, Univ Md, 1981-1984; res fel, Dept Microbiol & Immunol, Univ Wash, 1979-1981; res asst, micros dept, Univ Md, 1975-1979; lab technician, England Labs, Beltsville, Md, 1974-1975. **Memberships:** fel, Am Soc Microbiol; fel, AAAS. **Research Statement & Publications:** Molecular pathogenesis of and vaccine development for bacterial enteric diseases; published over 10 articles. **Mailing Address:** Dept Microbiol, Sch Med, Univ Md, 685 W Redwood St, Baltimore, MD 21201-1559. **Fax:** 410-706-0182. **E-Mail:** jkaper@umaryland.edu

KAPETANAKOS, CHRISTOS ANASTASIOS, INTENSE BEAMS, LASERS. **Personal Data:** b Sparta, Greece, January 2, 1936; American citizen; div, c Tassos & Yula. **Education:** Nat Univ Greece, Bachelor, 1960; Mass Inst Technol, MS, 1964; Univ Md, PhD (physics), 1970. **Honors & Awards:** Outstanding Performance Award, Naval Res Lab, 1972; Res Publ Awards, 1973, 1976, 1979, 1986, 1990. **Professional Experience:** PRES, LET CORP 1995-; prof physics, Univ Crete, 1993-1995; actg dir, Inst Plasma Physics, Univ Crete, 1993-1995; head, Adv Beam Technol Br, 1985-1989; head, Beam Dynamics Prog, 1980-1985; supvr res physicist plasma physics, Naval Res Lab, 1971-1980; res physicist plasma physics, Univ Tex, 1970-1971. **Memberships:** fel Am Phys Soc; fel Wash Acad Sci. **Research Statement & Publications:** Supervise and contact research on defense and medical devices; diagnostics technologies. **Mailing Address:** LET Corp, 4431 MacArthur Blvd, Washington, DC 20007. **Fax:** 202-337-5407. **E-Mail:** letkapetanakos@starpower.net

KAPETANOVIC, IZET MICHAEL, DRUG METABOLISM, EPILEPSY. **Education:** Northwestern Univ, Chicago, PhD (pharmacol), 1978. **Professional Experience:** PHARMACIST, PRECLIN EPILEPSY BR, NIH, 1978-. **Mailing Address:** Chemospreventive Agent Develop Res Group, NIH, 6130 Exec Blvd, Rockville, MD 20852. **Fax:** 301-402-0553. **E-Mail:** kapetani@mail.nih.gov

KAPICA, SHARON KELLY, ENVIRONMENTAL HEALTH, BIOCHEMISTRY. **Personal Data:** b Chicago, Ill, June 17, 1943; div, c Kelly, Meghan & Tracey. **Education:** Col St Elizabeth, BS, 1965; Univ Chicago, MS, 1968. **Honors & Awards:** Catalyst Award, Chem Mfr Asn, 1991. **Professional Experience:** Consult, beginning 1986; CHMN BIOL & CHEM, CO COL MORRIS, 1986-; PROF CHEM, CO COL MORRIS, 1979-; instr biol, Col St Elizabeth, 1974-1975; res assoc, Med Sch, Univ Ill, 1967-1970. **Memberships:** Am Chem Soc. **Mailing Address:** Dept Biol & Chem, County Col Morris, 214 Center Grove Rd, Randolph, NJ 07869. **Fax:** 973-328-5361. **E-Mail:** skapica@ccm.edu

KAPIKIAN, ALBERT ZAVEN, EPIDEMIOLOGY, VIROLOGY. **Personal Data:** b New York, NY, May 9, 1930; m 1960, Catherine; c Albert Kaloust, Thomas Firth & Gregory Baird. **Education:** Queens Col, NY, BS, 1952; Cornell Univ, MD, 1956. **Honors & Awards:** Kabakjian Award, Armenian Students Asn Am, 1974; Stitt Award, Asn Mil Surgeons US, 1974; Behring Diag Award, Am Soc Microbiol, 1987; Diag Virol Award (Murex), Pan Am Soc Clin Virol, 1993. **Professional Experience:** DEP CHIEF, GENOME-SCALE FUNCTIONAL INVEST SEC, NAT INST ALLERGY & INFECTIOUS DIS, as of 2003; res prof, child health & develop, sch med & health serv, George Wash Univ, 1977-; Guest worker virol, royal postgrad med sch, Univ London, 1970; HEAD, EPIDEMIOL SECT & ASST CHIEF, LAB INFECTIOUS DIS, NAT INST ALLERGY & INFECTIOUS DIS, 1967-; actg head epidemiol, epidemiol Sect & asst chief, 1964-1967; EPIDEMIOLOGIST, LAB INFECTIOUS DIS, NAT INST ALLERGY & INFECTIOUS DIS, 1957-; intern, Meadowbrook hosp, Hempstead, NY, 1956-1957. **Memberships:** Am Pub Health Asn; Am Soc Microbiol; Am Epidemiol Soc (Pres, 1996-1997); fel Infectious Dis Soc Am; fel AAAS. **Research Statement & Publications:** Epidemiologic investigations of infectious diseases; viral gastroenteritis. **Mailing Address:** Nat Inst Allergy & Infectious Dis, Rm 103 6610 Rockledge Dr MSC 6612, Bethesda, MD 20892-6612. **Fax:** 301-496-8312. **E-Mail:** ak18o@nih.gov

KAPILA, ASHWANI KUMAR, Asymptotics, computaional mathematics. **Personal Data:** b Ludhiana, India, August 26, 1946; American citizen; m 1971, c 2. **Education:** Punjabi Univ, India, BS, 1968; Univ Sask, Can, MS, 1970; Cornell Univ, PhD (theoret & appl mech), 1975. **Professional Experience:** PROF MATH, RENSSELAER POLYTECH INST, 1988-; vis prof, Inst Henri Poincare, Paris, 2001, vis assoc prof, Inst Math Appln, Univ Minn, 1986-1987; math res ctr, Univ Wis-Madison, 1979-1980; vis asst prof, Northwestern Univ, 1978; from asst prof to assoc prof, Rensselaer Polytech Inst, 1976-1988; Instr & res assoc mech, Cornell Univ, 1974-1976. **Memberships:** Combustion Inst; Soc Indust & Appl Math; fel Inst Physics. **Research Statement & Publications:** Applied mathematics, especially asymptotics, perturbation theory and numerics; application to problems in mechanics, chemically reactive flows, flame theory, detonation physics. **Mailing Address:** Dept Math Sci, Rensselaer Polytech Inst, Troy, NY 12180-3590. **Fax:** 518-276-4824. **E-Mail:** kapila@rpi.edu

KAPITULNIK, AHARON, SUPERCONDUCTORS. **Personal Data:** b Tel Aviv, Israel, July 29, 1953. **Education:** Tel Aviv Univ, BS, 1978, PhD (phys), 1984. **Honors & Awards:** Presidential Young Investr Award, NSF, 1987-1992; Distinguished Lectr in Mats Physics Award, Pa State Univ, 2000. **Professional Experience:** Vis prof, Hebrew Univ Jerusalem, Racah Inst Physics, 2000; vis scientist, Central Res Inst for Electric Power Indust, Komae, Tokyo, Japan, 1997; consult, Raychem Co, 1997; chair, Stanford Univ Dept Appl Physics, 1996-2000; PROF APPL PHYSICS & PHYSICS, STANFORD UNIV, 1994-; co-dir, Prog on Vortices, Univ Calif Inst Theoretical Physics, Santa Barbara, Calif, 1994; assoc prof appl physics & physics, Stanford Univ, 1993-1994; co-chmn, NATO/ASI on Vortices Superfluids, Cargese, Corsica, France, 1993; mem exec comt, Stanford Univ, Ctr Mat Res, 1992-; vis prof, Ecole Normale Superieure, France, 1992; vis prof, Univ Paris, XI Orsay, France, 1992; chmn, Gordon Res Conf on Condensed Matter Physics, Brewster Acad, NH, 1992; assoc prof appl physics, Stanford Univ, 1990-1994; co-chmn, Gordon Res Conf on Condensed Matter Physics, Brewster Acad, NH, 1990; chmn, local comt, Mat & Mechanisms Superconductivity, Stanford, Calif, 1989; mem, bd ed, Superconductivity Rev, 1989; consult, Conductus, Inc, 1987-1995; mem sci adv bd, Conductus, Inc, 1987-1998; Alfred P Sloan Fel, 1986-1990; mem, Stanford Univ Ctr Mat Res, 1985-; asst prof, Stanford Univ Dept Appl Physics, 1985-1990; asst prof residence, Dept Physics, Univ Calif, Santa Barbara, 1985; Chaim Weizmann Fel, Inst Postdococtoral Res Fel Univ Calif Inst for Polymers & Organic Solids, 1983-1984; assoc mem, Univ Calif, Santa Barbara, Inst Theoretical Physics, 1983-1984; instr & course develop, Israel Open Univ, Tel Aviv, 1980-1983; teaching asst, Tel Aviv Univ, Dept Physics & Math, 1978-1983; founder, Conductus, Inc. **Memberships:** Conf Elec Transport & Optical Properties of Inhomogeneous Media; Conf Series on Vortex Dynamics. **Research Statement & Publications:** Condensed Matter Physics: Superconductivity in strongly correlated systems and high temperature superconductors. Quantum phase transitions. Physics of disordered systems; in particular, the metal-insulator transition and superconductivity in materials that exhibit percolation, Anderson-localization, and strong electron-electron interaction effects. Low dimensional systems. Material science and physics of thin metallic films. Magnetism; MEMS: Physics of mesoscopic mechanical objects. Fabrication and utilization of small micro-mechanical objects. **Mailing Address:** Dept Physics, Rm 207, Stanford Univ, 316 Via Pueblo Mall, Stanford, CA 94305-4090. **Fax:** 650-725-2189. **E-Mail:** ak@loki.stanford.edu

KAPLAN, ABNER, AERONAUTICS. **Personal Data:** b New York, NY, June 21, 1923; m 1950, c 3. **Education:** Calif Inst Technol, BS, 1948, MS, 1949, PhD (aeronaut), 1954. **Professional Experience:** RETIRED; staff engr, Struct Dept, TRW Systs Group, 1970-1992; mem tech staff & mgr, Struct Dept, TRW Systs Group, 1955-1970; res engr, Struct Res Group, Northrop Aircraft Corp, 1952-1955. **Memberships:** Am Soc Mech Engrs; Am Inst Aeronaut & Astronaut. **Research Statement & Publications:** Nonlinear buckling; thin shells; pressure vessels. **Mailing Address:** 4012 Stalwart Dr, Rancho Palos Verdes Peninsu, CA 90274.

KAPLAN, ALAN MARC, IMMUNOLOGY. **Personal Data:** b Brooklyn, NY, December 10, 1940; m 1972, c 1. **Education:** Tufts Univ, BS, 1963; Purdue Univ, PhD (immunol), 1969. **Professional Experience:** PROF & CHMN, DEPT MICROBIOL, IMMUNOL & MOLECULAR GENETICS SCH MED, UNIV KY, 1982-; chmn, Dept Microbiol, 1981-1982; assoc dir res, Va Commonwealth Univ Cancer Ctr, 1980-1982; prof surg & microbiol, Tumor Immunol Sect, 1979-1982; assoc prof surg & microbiol, Med Col Va, 1975-1979; coordr, Tumor

Immunol Sect, 1974-1982; asst prof, Med Col Va, 1972-1975; can med res coun fel immunol, Univ Toronto, 1969-1972; res asst tumor immunol, Sloan-Kettering Inst, 1963-1965. **Memberships:** Am Soc Microbiol; NY Acad Sci; Can Soc Immunol; Am Asn Immunol; Am Asn Cancer Res; Reticuloendothelial Soc. **Research Statement & Publications:** Tumor and cellular immunology; autoimmunity; immunoadjuvants; immunogenetics; macrophage differentiation; Conditional macrophage ablation in transgenic mice expressing a Fas-based suicide gene. **Mailing Address:** Dept Microbiol & Immunol, Col Med Univ Ky, MS411 Med Sci Bldg 0298, Lexington, KY 40536-0298. **Fax:** 859-257-8994. **E-Mail:** akaplan@pop.uky.edu

KAPLAN, ALEX, PHYSIOLOGY, CHEMISTRY. **Personal Data:** b New York, NY, May 22, 1910; m 1940, Lena; c Annette F, Judith M & David B. **Education:** Univ Calif, Los Angeles, AB, 1932; Univ Calif, PhD (physiol), 1936. **Professional Experience:** PROF EMER LAB MED, SCH MED, UNIV WASH, 1980-; prof biochem & lab med & dir, Chem Div, 1969-1980; dir, Hosp Chem Labs, 1960-1980; assoc prof biochem, Univ Wash, 1960-1969; chief chemist, Children's Hosp, San Francisco, 1957-1960; asst dir dept biochem, Michael Reese Hosp, Ill, 1950-1957; chieflab, Vio-Bin Corp, 1946-1950; asst dir, Harold Brunn Inst Cardiovasc Res, San Francisco, 1940-1942; asst physiol, Univ Calif, 1939-1940; res assoc, Mt Zion Hosp, San Francisco, 1937-1939. **Memberships:** Emer mem AAAS; emer mem Soc Exp Biol & Med; emer mem Am Physiol Soc; emer mem Am Asn Clin Chem (pres, 1971). **Research Statement & Publications:** Lipid metabolism; clinical chemistry. **Mailing Address:** Univ Wash Med Ctr, NW 120, Seattle, WA 98115.

KAPLAN, ALEXANDER E, OPTICS, THEORETICAL PHYSICS. **Personal Data:** b Kiev, USSR, June 9, 1938; American citizen. **Education:** Moscow Phys-Tech Inst, MS, 1961; USSR Acad Sci, Moscow & Gorky State Univ, PhD (physics & math), 1967. **Professional Experience:** Von Humboldt prof Univ Ulm quantum phys dept, sabbatical 1996 1998; PROF DEPT ELEC & COMPUT ENG, JOHNS HOPKINS UNIV, 1987-; prof elec eng, Purdue Univ, 1982-1987; Honeywell, 1982; los alamos nat lab, 1981; prin investr res proj, Off sci res, USAF, 1980-; consult, Bell Labs, 1980-1981; mem res staff, Francis Bitter Nat Magnet lab, mass Inst Technol, 1979-1982; mem res staff, USSR Acad Sci, Moscow, 1963-1979; vis scientist, Max Planck Inst, Garching, WGer. **Memberships:** Am Phys Soc; fel Optical Soc Am. **Research Statement & Publications:** Quantum electronics and nonlinear optics, attosecond to zeptosecond pulses nonlinear and quantum optics of a single electron; theory of two-level systems in a strong field; self-focusing and self-bending effects; theory of solitons; interaction of light with nonlinear interfaces and theory of cavityless optical bistability; light induced nonreciprocity sagnac effect in nonlinear ring resonators and optical gyroscopes; nonlinear optical effects in superlattices; x-ray radiation by fast electron beams in periodical structrees (in particular in superlattices); four-wave mixing instabilities and multistability; the switching and steering of laser beams; x-ray nonlinear optics. **Mailing Address:** Dept Elec & Comput Eng, Johns Hopkins Univ, 34th Charles St Barton Hall, Baltimore, MD 21218. **Fax:** 410-516-5566. **E-Mail:** alexander.kaplan@jhu.edu

KAPLAN, ALLEN P, MEDICINE. **Personal Data:** b Jersey City, NJ, October 27, 1940; c 2. **Education:** Columbia Univ, BA, 1961; Downstate Med Sch, MD, 1965; Am Bd Internal Med, cert, 1972, Rheumat, cert, 1972, Allergy & Clin Immunol, cert, 1974, Diag Lab Immunol, cert, 1986. **Professional Experience:** Chmn, Allergy, Immunol & Transplantation Res Comt, Nat Inst Allergy & Infectious Dis, 1990-; mem, Allergy, Immunol & Transplantation Res Comt, Nat Inst Allergy & Infectious Dis, 1988-; Chmn Med, State Univ NY, Stony Brook Health Sci Ctr, 1987-1994; dir, Am Bd Allergy & Clin Immunol, 1985-1988; mem study sect, Am Heart Asn, 1983-1987; mem study sect, Nat Heart, Lung & Blood Inst, NIH, 1981-1985; mem study sect, Am Rheumatism Asn, 1981-1984; chmn, res Coun, Am Acad Allergy & Immunol, 1981-1984; grants, NIH, 1978-; prof med & head, div Allergy, Rheumat & Clin Immunol, State Univ NY, Stony Brook, 1978-1987; prof med & head, div Allergy, Rheumat & Clin Immunol, Northport Vet Admin Hosp, NY, 1978-1987; prof lectr, dept Biochem, Georgetown Univ, Wash, DC, 1976-1978; head, Allergic dis Sect, Lab Clin Invest, 1972-1978; Spec fel, NIH, 1970-1972; res fel med, Peter Bent & Robert B Brigham Hosps, Harvard Med Sch, 1969-1972; clin assoc, Nat Inst Arthritis & Metab dis, NIH, Bethesda, Md, 1967-1969; asst resident med, Strong Mem Hosp, Rochester, NY, 1966-1967; Intern med, Strong Mem Hosp, Rochester, NY, 1965-1966. **Memberships:** AAAS; Am Col Rheumat; Am Asn Immunologists; Am Thoracic Soc; Am Soc Exp Path; Am Soc Pharmacol & Exp Therapeut; Am Soc Hemat; Am Soc Clin Res; fel Am Acad Allergy; fel Am Col Physicians. **Research Statement & Publications:** Coagulation, fibrinolysis and inflammation; immunochemistry and immunopathology; biochemical mechanisms of allergic reactions; cytokines, mast cells and rheumatic disease; author or co-author of over 180 publications. **Mailing Address:** Dept Med, State Univ NY Health Sci Ctr, Stony Brook, NY 11794-8160.

KAPLAN, ANN ESTHER, BIOCHEMISTRY, BIOPHYSICS. **Personal Data:** b New York, NY, December 28, 1926. **Education:** Hunter Col, BA, 1947; Mt Holyoke Col, MA, 1949; Univ Pa, PhD (biochem), 1959. **Professional Experience:** Chmn & comr rep, sci manpower comn, Am Soc Exp Biol, 1978-1981; RES BIOCHEMIST, NAT CANCER INST, 1977-; biochemist, Nat Cancer Inst, 1972-1977; sr res assoc, Salk Inst Biol Studies, 1967-1972; asst prof doctoral fac biochem, City Univ New York, 1965-1967; res assoc, Rockefeller Inst, 1963-1965; Instr neurol, Albert Einstein Col Med, 1962-1963; NIH sr fel physiol, Albert Einstein Col Med, 1960-1962; Dazian Found fel microbiol, Sch Med, NY Univ, 1959-1960. **Memberships:** AAAS; Am Chem Soc; NY Acad Sci; Am Soc Biol Chem; Biophys Soc; Am Soc Physiol; Soc Gen Physiologists. **Research Statement & Publications:** Biosynthesis of lipids in biological membranes; serum lipid factors in cell growth; oxygenase pathway in heart mitochondria; lactate dehydrogenace in central nervous system and serum in experimental allergic encephalomyelitis; modification of lactate dehydrogenace in hepatocyte lines with neoplastic transformation; aerobic glycolysis in neoplastic cell lines. **Mailing Address:** Nat Cancer Inst, Valley Stream, NY 11581.

KAPLAN, ARNOLD, LYSOSOMOLOGY, ORGANELLE BIOGENESIS. **Personal Data:** b New York, NY, December 20, 1939; m 1963, c 2. **Education:** City Col NY, BS, 1961; George Wash Univ, MS, 1963, PhD (biochem), 1966; Univ Calif, PhD (biochem), 1968. **Professional Experience:** PROF EMER, BIOL SCI, UNIV ILL, CHICAGO, as of 2006; prof, dept biol sci, Univ Ill, Chicago, as of 2003; prog dir, Cell Biol Prog, NSF, 1986; prof microbiol, Med Sch, St Louis Univ, 1984-; vis assoc prof pediat, Wash Univ Med Sch, 1976; vis scientist biophys, Weissman Inst, 1972; spec res fel, NIH, 1970-1972; from asst prof to assoc prof, Med Sch, St Louis Univ, 1968-1984; fel, Nat Cancer Soc, 1966-1968; chmn, Dept Biol Sci, Univ Ark, Fayetteville; consult, Weissman Inst, Childrens Inst & Calbiochem, Monsanto. **Memberships:** Am Soc Biol Chemists; Am Soc Cell Biol. **Mailing Address:** Dept Biol Sci, Univ Ill, 4185 SEL MC 067 845 W Taylor St, Chicago, IL 60607. **Fax:** 312-413-2691. **E-Mail:** akaplan@uic.edu

KAPLAN, ARTHUR LEWIS, HEALTH PHYSICS, NUCLEAR ENGINEERING. **Personal Data:** b Boston, Mass, March 13, 1933; m 1957, c 2. **Education:** Mass Inst Technol, BS, 1954, MS, 1955. **Professional Experience:** CONSULT, ENVIRON ENG ASSOC, 1993-; sr environ eng, Gen Elec Lighting, 1991-1993; mgr environ control, Lighting Bus Group, 1981-1990; mgr licensing & compliance, Mfg Dept, 1978-1981; consult engr, Gen Elec Co Nuclear Fuel Dept, Gen Elec Co, Cleveland, 1972-1978; tech dir, Systs Sci & Eng, Inc, 1969-1972; physicist & proj leader, Tech Opers Res, 1964-1969; physicist & unit mgr, Gen Elec Co, 1960-1964; physicist, Tech Opers, Inc, 1957-1960; proj engr, Aircraft Nuclear Propulsion Prog, Wright Air Develop Ctr, Ohio, 1955-1957. **Memberships:** Health Physics Soc. **Research Statement & Publications:** Theoretical and experimental radiation shielding; biological effects of ionizing radiation; long range environmental effects of radioactive fallout; radiation effects in electronics and materials; health physics and radiation safety; health physics, licensing and compliance in uranium fabrication plants; environmental safety engineering. **Mailing Address:** 25422 Bryden Rd, Beachwood, OH 44122.

KAPLAN, BARRY B, MOLECULAR NEUROBIOLOGY. **Personal Data:** b Bronx, NY, September 28, 1946. **Education:** Hofstra Univ, BS, 1968, MS, 1969; Cornell Univ, PhD (cell & molecular biol), 1974. **Professional Experience:** PROF PSYCHIAT, UNIV PITTSBURGH SCH MED, as of 2003; ASSOC DIR, DIV INTRAMURAL RES, NAT INST MENTAL HEALTH, 1996-; PROF MOLECULAR NEUROBIOL, UNIV PITTSBURGH SCH MED, 1994-; dir, Molecular Neurobiol, Univ Pittsburgh Sch Med, 1988-1996; assoc prof, Molecular Neurobiol, Univ Pittsburgh Sch Med, 1984-1988; asst prof microscopic anat, Cornell Med Col, 1976-1984; Res fel molecular neurobiol, Andrews Geront Ctr, Univ Southern Calif, 1974-1976. **Memberships:** Soc Neuroscience; Int Brain Res Orgn; Am Soc Neurochem; Int Soc Neurochem. **Research Statement & Publications:** Molecular neurobiology. **Mailing Address:** Molecular Neurobiology Sect, Lab Molecular Biol, Nat Inst Mental Health, Rm 4N222, Bldg 10, 10 Ctr Dr, MSC 1381, Bethesda, MD 20892-1381. **Fax:** 301-480-7795. **E-Mail:** kaplanb@irp.nimh.nih.gov

KAPLAN, BARRY HUBERT, ONCOLOGY, BIOCHEMISTRY. **Personal Data:** b Brooklyn, NY, November 16, 1938; m 1962, c 2. **Education:** NY Univ, BA, 1958; Johns Hopkins Univ, MD, 1962, PhD (physiol chem), 1967. **Professional Experience:** PHYSICIAN-IN-CHARGE, MED ONCOL BOOTH MEM MED CTR, FLUSHING, 1986-; CLIN ASSOC PROF MED, ALBERT EINSTEIN COL MED, 1983-; dir, Div Oncol, 1981-1983; assoc prof med, Div Oncol, 1975-1983; actg, Div Oncol, 1974-1980; asst prof biochem, Div Oncol, 1973-1983; asst prof med, Med Oncol Booth Mem Med Ctr, Flushing, 1971-1975; Am Heart Asn estab investr, Albert Einstein Col Med, 1969-1974; attend physician, Bronx Munic Hosp Ctr, NY, 1967-; assoc, Med Oncol Booth Mem Med Ctr, Flushing, 1967-1970; USPHS training grant, Albert Einstein Col Med, 1967-1969; resident med, Bronx Munic Hosp Ctr, NY, 1966-1967; res assoc biochem, Nat Heart Inst, 1964-1966; USPHS fel physiol chem, Sch Med, Johns Hopkins Univ, 1963-1964; Intern med, Johns Hopkins Hosp, Baltimore, 1962-1963. **Memberships:** AAAS; Harvey Soc; Am Asn Cancer Res; Am Soc Clin Oncol. **Research Statement & Publications:** Hematology; Oncology; published over 40 articles. **Mailing Address:** Queens Med Associates PC, 59-16 174th St, Fresh Meadows, NY 11365. **Fax:** 718-746-3492.

KAPLAN, BERTON HARRIS, EPIDEMIOLOGY. **Personal Data:** b Winchester, Va, June 1930; m 1959, Ellen Brauer Kaplan; c David & Ron. **Education:** Va Polytech Inst, BS, 1951; Univ NC, Chapel Hill, MS, 1952, PhD (sociol), 1962. **Honors & Awards:** fel Soc Sci Res Council, Cornell Univ, 1965-1966, UNC General Alumni Distinguished Award for Facalty Sev, 1999. **Professional Experience:** Fel, Social Res Coun, 1965-1966; PROF SOCIAL EPIDEMIOL, UNIV NC, CHAPEL HILL, 1960-. **Memberships:** AAAS; Soc Behav Med; Am Anthrop Asn; Am Sociol Asn; Soc Epidemiol Res. **Research Statement & Publications:** Behavioral factors in coronary disease. **Mailing Address:** 1904 Rolling Rd, Chapel Hill, NC 27514.

KAPLAN, DANIEL ELIOT, SOLID STATE PHYSICS, PLASMA PHYSICS. **Personal Data:** b San Mateo, Calif, August 17, 1932; m 1959, c 4. **Education:** Univ Calif, AB, 1953, MA, 1955, PhD (physics), 1958. **Professional Experience:** SR STAFF SCIENTIST, LOCKHEED PALO ALTO RES LAB, 1967-; Res scientist, 1958-1967. **Memberships:** Am Phys Soc; Sigma Xi. **Research Statement & Publications:** Paramagnetic and ferrimagnetic resonance; plasma resonance phenomena. **Mailing Address:** 27000 Appaloosa Way, Los Altos Hills, CA 94022.

KAPLAN, DANIEL MOSHE, ELEMENTARY PARTICLE PHYSICS. **Personal Data:** b Philadelphia, Pa, May 21, 1953; m 1986, c 4. **Education:** Haverford Col, BA, 1974; State Univ NY, Stony Brook, PhD (physics), 1979. **Professional Experience:** DIR, IIT CTR ACCELERATOR & PARTICLE PHYSICS, ILL INST TECH, as of 2005; PROF PHYSICS, ILL INST TECH, 2002-; assoc prof physics, Ill Inst Tech, 1994-2001; from asst prof to assoc prof physics, Northern Ill Univ, 1987-1994; comput res specialist, Fla State Univ, 1984-1986; assoc scientist, Fermilab, 1982-1984; res assoc, Columbia Univ, 1979-1982; res asst, State Univ NY, Stony Brook, 1974-1978. **Memberships:** Am Phys Soc; Sigma Xi. **Research Statement & Publications:** Studies of heavy quarks in accelerator experiments; R&D on future muon accelerators. **Mailing Address:** Physics Div, Ill Inst Tech, 106A Life Sci Bldg, Chicago, IL 60616. **Fax:** 312-567-3289. **E-Mail:** kaplan@iit.edu

KAPLAN, DAVID GILBERT, PHYSICAL CHEMISTRY. **Personal Data:** b Chicago, Ill, November 13, 1944; m 1971, c 2. **Education:** Univ Ill, Urbana, BS, 1965; Univ Southern Calif, PhD (phys chem), 1972; JD, Loyola Sch Law, 1980. **Professional Experience:** TAX LAW SPECIALIST, INTERNAL REVENUE SERV, LOS ANGELES, CALIF, 1987-; sr scientist, Cilgo Inc, Pomona, Calif, 1983-1987; patent chemist, Union Oil Calif, 1981-1983; unit head gelatin res, Banner Gelatin Prod Corp, 1976-1981; res coordr radiopharm, Sch Pharm, Univ Southern Calif, 1975-1976; Fel biochem, Sch Med, Univ Calif, Los Angeles, 1972-1974. **Memberships:** Am Chem Soc. **Research Statement & Publications:** Studies on the viscoelastic behavior of connective tissue and lipid metabolism of biological systems. **Mailing Address:** 4215 Los Springs Dr, Agoura Hills, CA 91301-5328.

KAPLAN, DAVID JEREMY, OPERATIONS RESEARCH, SYSTEMS ANALYSIS. **Personal Data:** b Honolulu, Hawaii, October 8, 1934; c 3. **Education:** State Univ Iowa, BA, 1956; Univ Calif, Berkeley, MA, 1958. **Professional Experience:** OPERS RES ANALYST, NAVAL RES LAB, 1969-; mathematician syst anal, Stanford Res Inst, 1960-1969; Mathematician, Ames Res Ctr, NASA, 1958-1960. **Memberships:** Fel AAAS; Sigma Xi; Opers Res Soc Am; Math Asn Am. **Research Statement & Publications:** Developing the symbolic framework that underlies command and control systems; data-driven language representations that form the interface between signal coordinating systems and their environment. **Mailing Address:** Naval Res Lab 5583, Washington, DC 20375-0001.

KAPLAN, DAVID LEE, BIODEGRADATION-BIOTRANSFORMATIONS, BIOPOLYMERS. **Personal Data:** b Glen Cove, NY, March 18, 1953. **Education:** Univ Albany, BS, 1975; State Univ NY, PhD (biochem), 1978. **Professional Experience:** PROF & CHMN, DEPT BIOMED ENG, TUFTS UNIV, as of 2006; PROF, CHEM ENG, TUFTS UNIV, 1999-; DIR, BIOENGINEERING & BIOTECHNOL CTR, TUFTS UNIV, 1996-; AT DEPT BIOL, TUFTS UNIV, 1996-; Environ Sci & Technol, US Army Res Off grants & US Army Toxic & Hazardous Mat Agency proposals, 1983-; US Environ Protection Agency grants, 1984-; reviewer, NSF grants, 1980-; res microbiologist & chemist, Natick Res & Develop Ctr, Us Army,

1980-1991; res assoc fel, Res Found, 1978-1979; res asst, Col Environ Sci & Forestry, State Univ NY, 1976-1978; teaching asst biol, Col Environ Sci & Forestry, State Univ NY, 1976. **Memberships:** Am Soc Microbiol; Am Soc Indust Microbiol; AAAS; Water Pollution Control Fedn; Sigma Xi. **Research Statement & Publications:** Applied and environmental microbiology and biochemistry; prevention of deterioration and contamination of materials; biotransformations and biochemical reactions of natural and synthetic organic compounds in soils and waters; analytical chemistry techniques for separations and indentification of organic compounds; sewage sludge stabilization; enzymatic reactions with aromatic compounds; pollution abatement; installation restoration approaches for hazardous wastes. **Mailing Address:** Dept Biomed Eng, Tufts Univ, Sci & Technol Ctr, Medford, MA 02155. **Fax:** 617-627-3231.

KAPLAN, DONALD ROBERT, PLANT MORPHOLOGY. **Personal Data:** b Chicago, Ill, January 17, 1938. **Education:** Northwestern Univ, BA, 1960; Univ Calif, Berkeley, PhD (bot), 1965. **Honors & Awards:** Cert Merit Award, Bot Soc Am, 1984; Alexander Von Humboldt Distinguised Sr US Scientist Award, 1988; John Simm Guggenheim fel, 1989; Sigma XI Nat lectr, 1995. **Professional Experience:** Sigma Xi nat lectr, 1996-1997; Guggenheim fel, 1987-1988; PROF BOT, UNIV CALIF, BERKELEY, 1977-; from asst prof to assoc prof, Univ Calif, Berkeley, 1968-1977; asst prof biol sci, Univ Calif, Irvine, 1965-1968; NSF fel, Royal Bot Garden, Eng, 1965. **Memberships:** AAAS; Bot Soc Am; Int Soc Plant Morphol; Am Soc Cell Biol; fel Linnean Soc London; Sigma Xi. **Research Statement & Publications:** Comparative and developmental morphology of plants. **Mailing Address:** Dept Plant & Microbial Biol, Univ Calif, 434 Koshland Hall, Berkeley, CA 94720. **Fax:** 510-642-4995. **E-Mail:** koplandr@nature.berkeley.edu

KAPLAN, EDWARD LYNN, MATHEMATICAL PROGRAMMING. **Personal Data:** b Philadelphia, Pa, May 11, 1920; American citizen; div. **Education:** Carnegie Inst Technol, BS, 1941; Princeton Univ, PhD (math), 1951. **Professional Experience:** EMER PROF MATH, ORE STATE UNIV, 1981-; from assoc prof to prof, Ore State Univ, 1961-1981; mathematician, Lawrence Radiation Lab, Univ Calif, 1957-1961; mem tech staff, Bell Tel Labs, 1950-1957; asst, Princeton Univ, 1948-1950; Mathematician, US Naval Ord Lab, 1941-1948. **Memberships:** Am Math Soc emer mem. **Research Statement & Publications:** Random sequences; elliptic-integral tables; probability; statistics; Monte Carlo methods; computation; mathematical programming; optimization; musical symbology. **Mailing Address:** 727 NW 11th St, Corvallis, OR 97330.

KAPLAN, EHUD, NEUROPHYSIOLOGY, SENSORY PROCESS. **Personal Data:** b Jerusalem, Israel, December 29, 1942; American citizen; m 1966, c 2. **Education:** Hebrew Univ, Jeruselem, Israel, BA, 1967; Syracuse Univ, PhD (neurophysiol), 1973. **Professional Experience:** PROF NEUROSCI, OPTHALMOL, PHYSIOL & BIOPHYSICS, JULES & DORIS STEIN RES PREVENT BLINDNESS, MT SINAI MED SCH, 1996-; INSTR, MARINE BIOL LAB, WOODS HOLE, MASS, 1977-; asst prof to assoc prof, Rockefeller Univ, 1977-1996; fel, Rockefeller Univ, 1973-1976; res asst, Syracuse Univ, 1968-1973; res asst vision, Hadassah Hosp, Jerusalem Israel, 1963-1965. **Memberships:** NY Acad Sci; Asn Res Vision & Opthal; Sigma Xi. **Research Statement & Publications:** Information processing by the brain especially in the visual system; the way photoreceptors transduce light into electrical energy. **Mailing Address:** Mt Sinai Med Sch, One Gustave L Levy Pl Box 1065, New York, NY 10029. **E-Mail:** ehud.kaplan@mssm.edu

KAPLAN, EPHRAIM HENRY, ANALYTICAL CHEMISTRY. **Personal Data:** b New York, NY, November 16, 1918; m 1952, c 3. **Education:** City Col NY, BS, 1938; Univ Iowa, MS, 1940; Univ Pittsburgh, PhD (org chem, biochem), 1945; Northwestern Univ, MM, 1974. **Professional Experience:** RETIRED; toxicologist & supvr Biochem Sect, Chicago Bd Health, 1970-1989; res chemist, Velsicol Chem Corp, Chicago, 1960-1969; tech dir, Hodag Chem Corp, 1957-1960; res assoc, Inst Tuberc Res, Univ Ill, 1956-1957; res chemist, Vico Prod Co, 1953-1956; res assoc, Med Sch, Northwestern Univ, 1950-1953; res Corp fel enzyme chem, Inst Enzyme Res, Univ Wis, 1949-1950; res assoc, Polytech Inst Brooklyn, 1947-1949; res chemist, Sinclair Refining Co, Ind, 1945-1947; org chemist, Bur Mines, Pittsburgh, 1942-1945; asst sci aide, Eastern Regional Res Lab, Bur Agr & Indust Chem, USDA, 1941-1942. **Memberships:** Am Chem Soc. **Research Statement & Publications:** Surface active chemicals; enzymes; proteins; intermediary metabolism; sorption of vapors by and permeation through polymers; organic synthesis; analysis of hydrocarbon mixtures; pesticides; instrumental, drug and clinical analysis. **Mailing Address:** 9526 Kostner Ave, Skokie, IL 60076-1330.

KAPLAN, ERVIN, INTERNAL MEDICINE, NUCLEAR MEDICINE. **Personal Data:** b Independence, Iowa, June 19, 1918; m 1945, c Robert Louis & John. **Education:** Univ Ill, BS, 1947, MS & MD, 1949; Am Bd Internal Med, dipl; Am Bd Nuclear Med, dipl. **Honors & Awards:** Board of Trustees & Chairman, standing committe on nuclear medicine Technology, Soc of nuclear medicine 1960-1967; appointed to editorial Board Journal of Nuclear; Medicine, 1967 appointed to Ad Hoc Advisoiry committe on nuclear medicine, VA central office, Washington D C 1967 Appointed to Guest Faculty, nuclear medicine institute, Cleveland, Ohio, 1968; Scientific correspondent in the United States to Revista de biol medicine nuclear, montivideo, uruguay; appointed Senior Physician, U S First Prize Award, Gema Czerniak; Award Nuclear Med & Radiopharmacol, Ahavat Zion Found, Israel, 1974. **Professional Experience:** RETIRED; adj prof, Dept Elect Eng & Comp Sci, Coll of Eng, Univ Ill-Chicago, 1989; bd dir, Elscint Incorporated USA, 1988-1998; consult, Nuclear Medicine Service, VA Hospital, Hines, Illinois, 1998; dept dir nuclear med, Great Lakes Dist, 1986-1988; vis prof, Albert Einstein Col Med, 1982; mem, Liaison Comt between Soc Nuclear Med & World Fedn Nuclear Med & Biol, 1978; dist dir, Nat Asn Vet Admin Physicians, 1976-1980; mem, Post World Cong Nuclear Med, Vet Gen Hosp, Taiwan, 1974-1978; sr physician, Vet Admin Hosp, 1971-1975; lectr, Chicago Med Sch, 1971-1978 & Stritch Sch Med, Loyola Univ; consult nuclear med, Louis Weiss Mem Hosp, 1970-1978; consult, Radioisotope Clin & assoc attend physician, Mt Sinai Hosp, Chicago, 1967-1984; attend physician, Cook County Hosp, 1964-; bd trustees & chmn standing comt, Technol Nuclear Med, Soc Nuclear Med, 1960-1967; from clin asst prof to prof med & physiol, Univ Ill Col Med, 1959-1988; chief nuclear med serv, Vet Admin Hosp, 1959-1988; chief, Vet Admin Hosp, 1959-1970; assoc attend physician, Cook County Hosp, 1959-1964; physician-in-charge, Radioisotope Lab, Michael Reese Hosp, Chicago, 1956-1959; Physician-in-charge, Radioisotope Clin & assoc attend physician, Mt Sinai Hosp, Chicago, 1953-1959; clin instr, Univ Ill Col Med, 1953-1957; actg assoc dir radioisotope serv, Vet Admin Hosp, 1952-1959; clin asst, Univ Ill Col Med, 1952-1953; resident internal med, Vet Admin Hosp, 1950-1952; intern, Mt Sinai Hosp, Chicago, 1949-1950; sci corresp, Rev Biol & Nuclear Med, Uruguay; dep dir nuclear med, US Vet Admin Hosp Region 4; adj prof elec eng & comput sci, Col Eng, Univ Ill, Chicago. **Memberships:** AAAS; Soc Exp Biol & Med; Soc Nuclear Med; Sigma Xi; soc of Experimental Medicine & biology; soc of nuclear med; central chapter soc nuclear med; Chicago soc of Internal medicne central soc for clinical research Am asn for the Advancement of sciences; Am Medical Asn; chicago inst of medicine; central clinical research club; chicago medical soc; Illinois state medical soc; United states marine Raider Asn; Marine Corps Heritage Foud; Guadalcanal-Solomon Island War Memorial Found; United States Marine Raider Assn; Assn of Miltary Surgoens of the U S; Am College of Nuclear physicians National Computer Graphics Assn. **Research Statement & Publications:** Clinical application, research and training of biological application of radioisotopes in medicine and biological research. **Mailing Address:** 2600 Wilmette Ave, Wilmette, IL 60091. **E-Mail:** ohgng@aol.com

KAPLAN, EUGENE HERBERT, PARASITOLOGY, SCIENCE EDUCATION. **Personal Data:** b Brooklyn, NY, June 26, 1932; m 1958, Breena Lubou; c Julie & Susan. **Education:** Brooklyn Col, BS, 1954; Hofstra Col, MS, 1956; Ny Univ, PhD (sci educ), 1963. **Honors & Awards:** Marine Educ Award, Nat Marine Educr Asn, 1989. **Professional Experience:** DIR EMER, MARINE LAB, HOFSTRA UNIV, as of 2003; DIR, AQUACULT PROG, HOFSTRA UNIV, as of 2003; AXINN DISTINGUISHED PROF EMER CONSERV & ECOL, HOFSTRA UNIV, as of 2003; dir, Marine Lab, Hostra Univ, beginning 1980; prof biol, Hofstra Univ, beginning 1975; UNESCO expert elem sci, Israel, 1971-1972; NSF sci fac fel, 1963-1964; from lectr to assoc prof, Marine Lab, 1958-1974; Teacher high sch, NY, 1956-1958. **Memberships:** Am Soc Parasitol; Nat Asn Res Sci Teaching; Asn Marine Labs Caribbean; Caribbean Aquacult Asn; Sigma Xi. **Research Statement & Publications:** Marine ecology, especially coral reef invertebrates; effects of dredging on benthos; introductory science courses for non-science majors; measuring aspects of scientific thinking; comparisons of hybridfishes suitable for aquaculture. **Mailing Address:** Dept Biol, Hofstra Univ, 1000 Fulton Ave, Hempstead, NY 11550-1091. **E-Mail:** eugene.h.kaplan@hofstra.edu

KAPLAN, FRED, ORGANIC CHEMISTRY. **Personal Data:** b Brooklyn, NY, September 2, 1934; m 1973, c 4. **Education:** NY Univ, BA, 1955; Yale Univ, PhD (chem), 1960. **Professional Experience:** PROF EMER CHEM, UNIV CINCINNATI, as of 2004; prof Chem, Univ Cincinnati, beginning 1968; from instr to assoc prof, Univ Cincinnati, 1961-1968; univ fel, Calif Inst Technol, 1960-1961; USPHS res fel chem, Swiss Fed Inst Technol, 1959-1960. **Memberships:** AAAS; Am Chem Soc; Am Asn Univ Professors. **Research Statement & Publications:** Applications of ion cyclotron resonance spectroscopy; gas phase ion-molecule reactions; gas phase properties of organic species; electron deficient species. **Mailing Address:** Dept Chem, Univ Cincinnati, 2600 Clifton Ave, Cincinnati, OH 45221-2872. **Fax:** 513-556-9239. **E-Mail:** fred.kaplan@uc.edu

KAPLAN, GEORGE HARRY, ASTROMETRY RADIO & OPTICAL INTERFEROMETRY. **Personal Data:** b Hagerstown, Md, April 24, 1948; m 1972, Carol. **Education:** Univ Md, BS, 1969, MS, 1976, PhD, 1985. **Professional Experience:** ASTRONR, US NAVAL OBSERV, 1971-. **Memberships:** AAAS; Am Astron Soc; Sigma Xi; Int Astron Union. **Research Statement & Publications:** Radio and optical astrometry; radio and optical interferometry; Earth rotation; solar system dynamics and ephemerides; astronomical reference systems; celestial navigation. **Mailing Address:** US Naval Observ, 3450 Mass Ave NW, Washington, DC 20392-5420. **Fax:** 202-762-1612. **E-Mail:** gkaplan@usno.navy.mil

KAPLAN, GERALD, ANALYTICAL CHEMISTRY. **Personal Data:** b Brooklyn, NY, December 21, 1939; m 1967, Marilyn Hollender; c Andrew, Michael, Jason & Laura. **Education:** Columbia Univ, BS, 1961, MS, 1963; Rutgers Univ, PhD (pharmaceut chem), 1968. **Professional Experience:** MGR, PROD DEVELOP ORAL CARE, JOHNSON & JOHNSON CONSUMER PRODS, 1995-; mgr, Johnson & Johnson Res Ctr, 1990-1995; dir, Johnson & Johnson Res Ctr, 1989; mgr anal labs, Johnson & Johnson Res Ctr, 1979-1988; asst mgr, Johnson & Johnson Res Ctr, 1975-1979; group leader methods develop, Johnson & Johnson Res Ctr, 1972-1975; sr res scientist anal chem, Johnson & Johnson Res Ctr, 1971-1972; Res scientist, Johnson & Johnson Res Ctr, 1967-1971. **Memberships:** Am Chem Soc; Sigma Xi. **Research Statement & Publications:** Separations sciences; oral care product development, floss & toothbrushes. **Mailing Address:** Johnson & Johnson Consumer Prod, 199 Grandview Rd, Skillman, NJ 08558-9418.

KAPLAN, GILLA, IMMUNOLOGY. **Education:** Hebrew Univ, BS; Univ Tromso, MS, PhD. **Professional Experience:** FAC, PUB HEALTH RES INST, as of 2006. **Mailing Address:** Pub Health Res Inst, 225 Warren St, Newark, NJ 07103-3535. **Fax:** 973-854-3101. **E-Mail:** kaplan@phri.org

KAPLAN, HAROLD M, PHYSIOLOGY. **Personal Data:** b Boston, Mass, September 4, 1908; m 1934, c Elaine, Joyce & Lee. **Education:** Dartmouth Col, AB, 1930; Harvard Univ, AM, 1931, PhD (physiol), 1933. **Professional Experience:** RETIRED; vis prof, Sch Med, Southern Ill Univ, beginning 1977; prof physiol, Southern Ill Univ, Carbondale, 1949-1977; chmn dept, Southern Ill Univ, Carbondale, 1949-1971; assoc prof, Univ Mass, 1947-1949; writer, Wash Inst Med, 1946-1949; prof, Med Sch, 1937-1945 & Vet Sch, 1945-1947; prof physiol, Brandeis Univ, 1945-1947; Pvt res Dr E V Enzmann, Biol Labs, Harvard Univ, 1935-1937; prof physiol, Middlesex Univ, 1934-1947; asst instr zool, Harvard Univ, 1933-1934. **Memberships:** Fel AAAS; Am Physiol Soc; Am Soc Zool; Am Asn Lab Animal Sci (pres, 1996-1997); Electron Micros Soc Am. **Research Statement & Publications:** Laboratory animal medicine; About 205 papers, incl books, in human physiol Rabbit surg, Text, dir, sin vivarium. **Mailing Address:** Southern Ill Univ Sch Med, Whaler Hall, Carbondale, IL 62901. **Fax:** 618-453-1919. **E-Mail:** hkaplan@siumed.edu

KAPLAN, HARVEY, THEORETICAL PHYSICS. **Personal Data:** b New York, NY, November 29, 1924; m 1947, c 3. **Education:** City Col NY, BS, 1948; Univ Calif, PhD (physics), 1952. **Professional Experience:** PROF EMER PHYSICS, SYRACUSE UNIV, as of 1998; prof physics, Syracuse Univ, beginning 1965; from asst prof to assoc prof, Syracuse Univ, 1959-1965; asst prof physics, Univ Buffalo, 1954-1959; res assoc, Mass Inst Technol, 1952-1954. **Memberships:** Am Phys Soc. **Research Statement & Publications:** Theory of solid state; dynamical systems. **Mailing Address:** Dept Physics, Syracuse Univ, Syracuse, NY 13244.

KAPLAN, HARVEY, BIOCHEMISTRY. **Personal Data:** b New York, NY, May 24, 1940; Canadian citizen; m 1966, c 2. **Education:** Queen's Univ, Ont, BSc, 1962; Univ Ottawa, PhD (kinetics), 1966. **Professional Experience:** PROF CHEM, UNIV OTTAWA, 1988-; prof, Univ Ottawa, 1979-1988; assoc prof, Univ Ottawa, 1976-1979; asst prof biochem, Univ Ottawa, 1971-1976; asst res officer biochem, Nat Res Coun Can, 1968-1971; fel, Lab Molecular Biol, Cambridge Univ, 1967-1968; Nat Res Coun Can fel, 1966-1967. **Memberships:** Can Biochem Soc. **Research Statement & Publications:** Kinetics and mechanism of enzyme action; structure and function of serine proteases; ionization constants and reactivity of functional groups in proteins. **Mailing Address:** Dept Chem, Univ Ottawa, Ottawa, ON K1N 6N5, Can. **Fax:** 613-562-5170. **E-Mail:** hkaplan@uottawa.ca

KAPLAN, HARVEY ROBERT, PHARMACOLOGY. **Personal Data:** b New Brunswick, NJ, August 21, 1941; m 1964, c 2. **Education:** Philadelphia Col Pharm, BSc, 1963; Univ Conn, MSc, 1965, PhD (pharmacol), 1966. **Professional Experience:** ADJ PROF PHARMACOL, UNIV MICH, as of 2005; dir, Cardiovasc Sect, Warner-Lambert Res Inst, 1980-; assoc dir, Dept Pharmacol, 1967-1980; NIH fel, Univ Pittsburgh, 1966-1967. **Memberships:** AAAS; NY Acad Sci; Am Soc Pharmacol & Exp Therapeut. **Research Statement & Publications:** Cardiovascular and autonomic pharmacology; cardiac arrhythmias and antiarrhythmic drugs; central cardiovascular mechanisms; evaluation and assay of synthetics as well as natural products isolated form both plant and animals. **Mailing Address:** Univ Mich, Dept Pharmacol, 2800 Plymouth Rd, Ann Arbor, MI 48105-2430. **Fax:** 734-764-4450. **E-Mail:** hrkaplan@umich.edu

KAPLAN, HENRY J, OPHTHALMOLOGY. **Personal Data:** b New York, NY, December 29, 1942; m 1966, c 3. **Education:** Columbia Univ, AB, 1964; Cornell Univ, MD, 1968; Am Bd Ophthal, cert, 1979. **Honors & Awards:** Honor Award, Am Acad Ophthal, 1984; SciAward, Alcon Res Inst, 1987; Sr Honor Award, Am Acad Ophthal, 1994. **Professional Experience:** EVANS PROF & CHMN, DEPT OPHTHAL & VISUAL SCI, UNIV LOUIS, as of 2003; assoc examr, Am Bd Ophthal, beginning 1990; mem bd dirs, Wash Univ Physician Network, 1989-; mem bd dirs, Partners Health Plan, 1989-; ophthalmologist-in-chief, Barnes Hosp, 1988-1996 & 1996-; active staff ophthalmologist, St Louis Children's Hosp, 1988-; prof & chmn, dept ophthal & visual sci, sch med, Wash Univ, st louis, mo, beginning 1988; assoc attend ophthalmologist, Jewish Hosp, St Louis, 1988-1996; chmn, Visual Dis Study Sect A-1, Nat Eye Inst, NIH, 1987-1989; adj prof, Dept Small Animal Med, Univ Ga, Athens, 1985-; mem, Visual Dis Study Sect A-1, Nat Eye Inst, NIH, 1985-1989; assoc prof, Dept Microbiol, 1985-1988; dir res, Dept Ophthal, Sch Med, Emory Univ, Atlanta, Ga, 1984-1988; olga Keith Weiss Scholar, Res Prevent Blindness Inc, 1984; affil scientist path & immunol, Yerkes Regional Primate Res Ctr, Atlanta, Ga, 1981-; assoc prof, Dept Ophthal, Sch Med, Emory Univ, Atlanta, Ga, 1979-1984, prof, 1984-1988; asst prof, Dept Cell Biol, 1974-1975; res fel immunol, NIH, Dept Cell Biol, Univ Tex Med Sch, Dallas, 1972-1974; surg resident, Bellevue Hosp, NY Univ Med Ctr, New York, NY, 1969-1970; Intern med, Lakeside Hosp, Univ Hosps, Cleveland, Case Western Res Univ, 1968-1969. **Memberships:** Asn Res Vision & Ophthal; fel Am Acad Ophthal; AAAS; AMA; NY Acad Sci; Am Asn Immunologists; Am Uveitis Soc; fel Am Col Surgeons; Am Soc Contemp Ophthal. **Research Statement & Publications:** Retina-vitreous; immunology-uveitis; author or co-author of over 80 publications. **Mailing Address:** Dept Ophthal & & Visual Sci, Univ Louisville, 301 E Muhammad Ali Blvd, Louisville, KY 40202. **Fax:** 502-852-4595. **E-Mail:** hank.kaplan@louisville.edu

KAPLAN, ISSAC R, GEOCHEMISTRY. **Personal Data:** b Baranowicze, Poland, July 10, 1929; m 1955, c 2. **Education:** Univ Canterbury, BSc, 1952, MSc, 1953; Univ Southern Calif, PhD (biogeochem), 1961. **Professional Experience:** PRES, GLOBAL GEOCHEM CORP, 1977-; chmn, Org Geochem Div, Geochem Soc, 1976-1977; assoc ed Geochem J, beginning1976; assoc ed, Marine Chem, beginning 1972; Indust Res Orgn, Japan, New Caledonia, NZ & Australia, 1970-1971; PROF GEOL & GEOCHEM, UNIV CALIF, LOS ANGELES, 1969-; mem planetary biol subcomt, Space Sci & Appln Steering Comt, NASA, 1967-; Assoc ed, Geochem Soc, 1966-1970 & Chem Geol, 1966-1967; assoc prof geol & geophys, Global Geochem Corp, 1965-1969; guest lectr & Ziskind scholar microbiol & geochem, Hebrew Univ, Israel, 1963-1965; res fel geochem, Calif Inst Technol, 1961-1962; Res officer oceanog, Commonwealth Sci & Indust Res Orgn, Australia, 1953-1957; mem exobiol panel, Space Sci Bd, Nat Acad Sci, prin investr lunar return mat, Apollo 1911, 1912, 1914 & 1915; Guggenheim Mem Found res fel, Mineral Res Labs, Commonwealth Sci. **Memberships:** Geochem Soc; fel Am Inst Chemists; Am Asn Petrol Geologists; fel AAAS; Am Chem Soc; fel Geol Soc Am. **Research Statement & Publications:** Biogeochemistry of recent sediments; factors controlling the distribution of elements in the ocean; isotope geochemistry and organic geochemistry of terrestrial rocks and meteorites; biological fractionation of stable isotopes; atmospheric chemistry and atmospheric pollution. **Mailing Address:** ZymaX Forensics, 71 Zaca Lane, San Luis Obispo, CA 93401. **Fax:** 805-544-8226. **E-Mail:** irk@zymaxusa.com

KAPLAN, JEROME I, SOLID STATE PHYSICS. **Personal Data:** b New York, NY, July 28, 1926; m Ann; c Jeannie. **Education:** Univ Mich, BS, 1950; Univ Calif, Berkeley, PhD (physics), 1954. **Honors & Awards:** Fulbright lectr, Univ Col, Rhodesia & Nyasaland, 1963-1964. **Professional Experience:** EMER PROF PHYSICS, IND UNIV-PURDUE UNIV, INDIANAPOLIS, as of 2004; vis scientist, Naval Res Lab, 1981; sr fel, Indianapolis Ctr Advan Res, 1980-1987; prof Physics, Ind Univ-Purdue Univ, Indianapolis, beginning 1974; res assoc, Krannert Inst Cardiol, 1974-1980; res fel, Battelle-Columbus, 1967-1974; assoc res prof, Brown Univ, 1964-1967; asst prof, Brandeis Univ, 1962-1963; consult, Lincoln Lab, Mass Inst Technol, Hercules Chem Co, 1961; res assoc physics, Brandeis Univ, 1959-1962; Louis Lipsky fel physics, Weizmann Inst, 1956-1957; res scientist, Naval Res Lab, DC, 1954-1959. **Memberships:** Am Phys Soc. **Research Statement & Publications:** Magnetic properties of solids; nuclear and ferromagnetic wave resonance; electron, nuclear and ferromagnetic spin resonance phenomena; magnetic resonance in liquids and liquid crystals; nuclear magnetic resonance in heart muscle; solar heating design; nuclear magnetic resonance theory; low temperature heat conductivity in metals. **Mailing Address:** 4417 N Pa, Indianapolis, IN 46205. **E-Mail:** jkaplan@iupui.edu

KAPLAN, JERRY, CELL BIOLOGY. **Education:** Purdue Univ, PhD (biol sci), 1971. **Professional Experience:** PROF PATH, MED CTR, UNIV UTAH, 1980-. **Research Statement & Publications:** Membrane dynamics; biochemistry. **Mailing Address:** Med Ctr, Univ Utah Col Med, Rm 5C124 30 N 1900, Salt Lake City, UT 84132-0001. **Fax:** 801-581-4517. **E-Mail:** jerry.kaplan@path.utah.edu

KAPLAN, JOEL HOWARD, IMMUNOTOXICOLOGY, HEALTH RISK ASSESSMENT. **Personal Data:** b New York, NY, April 6, 1941. **Education:** City Col NY, BS, 1962; Johns Hopkins Univ, PhD (biochem), 1967. **Professional Experience:** RES SCIENTIST, BUR TOXIC SUBSTANCE ASSESSMENT, NY STATE DEPT HEALTH, 1987-; vis scientist, Johns Hopkins Sh Hyg & Pub Health, 1985-1987; staff scientist med sci, Gen Elec Res & Develop Ctr, 1969-1985; Nat Cancer Inst fel cancer biochem, McArdle Lab Cancer Res, 1967-1969. **Memberships:** Am Asn Immunol; AAAS. **Research Statement & Publications:** Health risk assessment of toxic substances, immunotoxicology; in vitro methods in cell-mediated immunity; electrokinetic properties of lymphocyte subpopulations; cancer-immunodiagnosis. **Mailing Address:** NY State Dept Health, 2 Univ Pl, Albany, NY 12203.

KAPLAN, JOEL HOWARD, CHEMICAL ENGINEERING. **Personal Data:** b Paterson, NJ, September 8, 1938; c 2. **Education:** Newark Col Eng, BS, 1961, MS, 1962, DSc(chem eng), 1966. **Professional Experience:** RETIRED; dir corp plant opers, Lonza Inc, Fairlawn, 1990-1994; mgr mat & res planning, Lonza Inc, Fairlawn, 1983-1990; proj leader process develop, Org Chem Div, 1980-1983; adj prof chem eng, NJ Inst Technol, 1978-; mgr, Systs Anal Dept, 1971-1980; group leader, Process Anal Sect, 1969-1971; res chem engr, Am Cynamid Co, Bound Brook, 1966-1969. **Memberships:** Am Inst Chem Engrs; Am Chem Soc; NY Acad Sci. **Research Statement & Publications:** Kinetics and reactor design of industrial processes; process development; application of computer control to industrial processes; research management concerned with plant and laboratory automation and development of research strategy models; inventory and production planning systems, MRP II. **Mailing Address:** 26 Bianculli Dr, South PlainfieldPlainfield, NJ 07080.

KAPLAN, JOHN ERVIN, PHAGOCYTOSIS, THROMBOSIS. **Personal Data:** b Chicago, Ill, December 4, 1950; m 1973, c 2. **Education:** Univ Ill, BS, 1972; Albany Med Col, PhD (physiol), 1976. **Professional Experience:** PROF CARDIOVASC SCI, ALBANY MED CTR, STATE UNIV NY, as of 2004; Dir, NIH Prog Proj, 1991-; ASSOC DEAN GRAD STUDIES, STATE UNIV NY, ALBANY, GRAD SCH PUB HEALTH, 1991-; PROF, STATE UNIV NY, ALBANY, GRAD SCH PUB HEALTH, 1990-; vchmn, Grad Sch Pub Health, 1990-1991; PROF PHYSIOL & CELL BIOL, ALBANY MED COL, 1986-; assoc prof, Grad Sch Pub Health, 1984-1990; res career develop award, 1980-1985; Sinsheimer Fund Scholar, 1980-1983; Prin investr res grant, Shared Instrumentation Prog, 1979-1982; Prin investr res grant, NIH, 1978; Prin investr res grant, New York Heart Asn, 1977-1978 & 1990-; from asst prof to assoc prof physiol, Albany Med Col, State Univ NY, 1977-1987; instr, Albany Med Col, State Univ NY, 1976-1977; Fel, Albany Med Col, State Univ NY, 1975-1977. **Memberships:** Sigma Xi; Reticuloendothelial Soc; Am Heart Asn; Am Physiol Soc; Am Soc Cell Biol. **Research Statement & Publications:** Mechanisms by which macrophages and adhesive proterms act as physiological anti-thrombotic mechanisms, and the role of these mechanisms in sepsis, trauma, intravascular coagulation and vascular injury; interaction of platelets and endothelial cells; fibronectin receptors; Published over 20 articles. **Mailing Address:** Dept Cardiovasc Sci, Albany Med Col, 47 New Scotland Ave, Albany, NY 12208. **Fax:** 518-262-5669. **E-Mail:** kaplanj@mail.amc.edu

KAPLAN, JOSEPH, PEDIATRICS, IMMUNOLOGY-ALLERGY. **Personal Data:** b Boston, Mass, March 7, 1941; m 1986, Carol; c Rebecca, Benjamin & Michelle. **Education:** NY Univ, BA, 1962; Johns Hopkins Univ, MD 1966. **Professional Experience:** PROF MED, IMMUNOL & MICROBIOL, WAYNE STATE UNIV, 1988-; PROF PEDIAT, IMMUNOL & MICROBIOL, WAYNE STATE UNIV, 1987-; from asst prof to assoc prof pediat, Wayne State Univ, 1972-1987. **Memberships:** Am Asn Immunologists; Am Pediat Soc; Am Soc Hematol Skin Immunol.Soc. **Research Statement & Publications:** Clinical immunology; role of natural killer cells in health and disease such as in prevention of graft-version hour disease and bone marrow graft rejection; maternal fetal cell traffic and microchromerm. **Mailing Address:** Dept Pediat, Childrens Hosp, Wayne State Univ, 3901 Beaubien Blvd, Detroit, MI 48201. **Fax:** 313-745-0282. **E-Mail:** jkaplan@med.wayne.edu

KAPLAN, LAWRENCE, BOTANY. **Personal Data:** b Chicago, Ill, April 14, 1926; m 1946, c 1. **Education:** Univ Iowa, BA, 1948, MS, 1951; Univ Chicago, PhD (bot), 1956. **Professional Experience:** Ed, Econ Bot, 1991-; PROF EMER BIOL, UNIV MASS, BOSTON, 1968-; assoc prof, Univ Mass, Boston, 1965-1968; asst prof, Roosevelt Univ, 1957-1965; instr biol, Wright Jr Col, 1956; assoc cur, Mus Useful Plants, Mo Bot Gardens, 1955. **Memberships:** Fel AAAS; Bot Soc Am; Sigma Xi; Soc Econ Bot (pres, 1987); Soc Am Archeol. **Research Statement & Publications:** Ethnobotany; systematics. **Mailing Address:** Univ Mass, Dept Biol, 100 Morrissey Blvd, Boston, MA 02125. **E-Mail:** lawrence.kaplan@umb.edu

KAPLAN, LAWRENCE JAY, BIOCHEMISTRY, FORENSIC SCIENCE. **Personal Data:** b Newark, NJ, March 20, 1943; m 1965, c 2. **Education:** Univ Pittsburgh, BS, 1965; Purdue Univ, PhD (chem), 1970. **Professional Experience:** HALFORD R CLARK PROF NATURAL SCI & CHAIRMAN, LEGAL STUDIES PROG, WILLIAMS COL, as of 2005; co-dir, Ctr workshops chem sci, 2001-; adj prof, Chem Dept, Univ Cent Fla, 1999-2000, 2002-2003; chmn, Chem Dept & Chmn, Prog Biochem & Molecular Biol, 1988-1993; PROF CHEM, WILLIAMS COL, 1984-; vis assoc prof, Biochem Dept, Brandeis Univ, 1980-1981; res scientist, Weizmann Inst, Israel, 1976-1977; From asst prof to assoc prof, Chem Dept, 1971-1984; fel, Univ Mass, Amherst, 1970-1971. **Memberships:** AAAS; Am Chem Soc; Am Soc Biochem & Molecular Biol; Am Acad Forensic Sci; Forensic Sci Soc. **Research Statement & Publications:** Physical biochemistry of proteins; Conformational transitions of macromolecules; Structure of chromatin; published over 20 articles. **Mailing Address:** Dept Chem, Williams Col, Rm 227 Bronfman Sci Ctr, Williamstown, MA 01267. **Fax:** 413-597-4116. **E-Mail:** lkaplan@williams.edu

KAPLAN, LEONARD, ORGANIC CHEMISTRY, CATALYSIS. **Personal Data:** b Brooklyn, NY, July 18, 1939. **Education:** Cooper Union, BChE, 1960; Univ Ill, PhD (org chem), 1964. **Professional Experience:** SR RES SCIENTIST, UNION CARBIDE CORP, 1979-; res scientist, Union Carbide Corp, 1975-1979; proj scientist, Union Carbide Corp, 1974-1975; asst prof, Univ Chicago, 1967-1974; instr, Univ Chicago, 1965-1967; NSF fel, 1964-1965; Res assoc org chem, Columbia Univ, 1964-1965; Alfred P Sloan Found fel. **Memberships:** Am Chem Soc; The Chem Soc. **Research Statement & Publications:** Homogeneous catalysis; organometallic chemistry; mechanistic and physical organic chemistry; exploratory synthesis; free radical chemistry. **Mailing Address:** 227 Walker Dr Apt 679, Dunbar, WV 25064.

KAPLAN, LEONARD LOUIS, PHARMACEUTICAL QUALITY ASSURANCE, CONSULTING. **Personal Data:** b New York, NY, October 10, 1928; m 1968, Susan Orent; c Robert & Marc. **Education:** NY Univ, BA, 1948, PhD (statist, mgt sci), 1968; Ohio State Univ, BScPharm, 1952; City Col New York, MBA, 1963. **Professional Experience:** PRES, PHARMA QUAL ASSOC, 1995-; sr vpres bus & tech develop, D M Graham Labs, 1991-1995; vpres res & develop, Over The Counter Drugs, Sterling Drug, 1989-1990; vpres, Advan Care Prods, 1984-1989; Adj assoc prof, Brooklyn Col Pharm, 1966-1969 & Col Pharm, Rutgers Univ, 1979-; dir res & develop, Advan Care Prods, 1978-1983; dir res & develop, Health Care Div, Ortho Pharm Corp, Johnson & Johnson-Domestic Oper Co, 1969-1978; group mgr, Vick Div Res, 1963-1969; dir develop, Walker Labs Div, Richardson-Merrell, 1959-1963; Res assoc pharm, Sterling-Winthrop Res Inst, 1955-1959. **Memberships:** Acad Pharmaceut Sci; Soc Cosmetic Chemists; Am Asn Clin Chemists; Am Asn Prof Pharmacists; Am Pharm Asn. **Research Statement & Publications:** Pharmaceutical research specializing in areas of analgesics, oral hygiene, sports medicine, dermatology and deodorancy; contraceptives; diagnostics. **Mailing Address:** 1 Minuteman Ct, East Brunswick, NJ 08816. **Fax:** 609-951-9196.

KAPLAN, MANUEL E, INTERNAL MEDICINE, HEMATOLOGY. **Personal Data:** b New York, NY, November 6, 1928; m 1955, Rita; c 3. **Education:** Univ Ariz, BS, 1950; Harvard Med Sch, MD, 1954. **Professional Experience:** PROF EMER MED, MED SCH UNIV MINN, MINNEAPOLIS, as of 2002; STAFF PHYSICIAN, VET ADMIN MED CTR, MINN, 1993-; prof med, Med Sch Univ Minn, Minneapolis, beginning 1973; chief hemat & oncol, Med Sch Univ Minn, Minneapolis, 1969-1993; assoc prof, Univ Minn, Minneapolis, 1969-1973; career develop award, 1967-1969; chief hemat, Jewish Hosp St Louis, 1965-1969; asst prof med, Sch Med, Wash Univ, 1965-1969; USPHS res grants, 1963-1964; res fel microbiol, Col Physicians & Surgeons, Columbia Univ, 1963-1965; asst dir hemat, Mt Sinai Hosp, NY, 1963-1965; res assoc, Mt Sinai Hosp, NY, 1962-1963; Fel hemat, Thorndike Mem Lab, Boston City Hosp, 1959-1962; from asst resident to sr resident, Boston City Hosp, 1955-1959; intern med, Boston City Hosp, 1954-1955. **Memberships:** AAAS; Am Fedn Clin Res; Am Soc Clin Invest; Am Soc Hemat; Am Asn Immunol. **Research Statement & Publications:** Immunohematology; lymphocyte structure and function; hematopoiesis. **Mailing Address:** Dept Hematol/Oncol, Vet Admin Med Ctr One Vet Dr, Minneapolis, MN 55417-2300. **Fax:** 612-725-2016. **E-Mail:** kapla008@umn.edu

KAPLAN, MARK STEVEN, PHOTOGRAPHIC CHEMISTRY, DRY MEDIA. **Personal Data:** b New York, NY, February 25, 1947; m 1988, Drane; c 2. **Education:** Bucknell

Univ, BS & MS, 1967; Univ Ore, PhD (org chem), 1971. **Professional Experience:** SUPV SCIENTIST, IMAGE & HARDCOPY TECHNOL, EASTMAN KODAK CO, 1994-; res assoc spec mat, 1987-1993; Sr res scientist, 1971-1987. **Memberships:** Am Chem Soc; Am Defense Preparedness Asn. **Research Statement & Publications:** Novel lithographic systems; use of lasers in graphic arts; photoresists; chemical defense research; dry or processless media; patentee in field. **Mailing Address:** Eastman Kodak Co, HE PLANT, Rochester, NY 14653-7207. **E-Mail:** markap@kodak.com

KAPLAN, MARSHALL HARVEY, AERONAUTICS, ASTRONAUTICS. **Personal Data:** b Detroit, Mich, November 5, 1939; m 1961, c 2. **Education:** Wayne State Univ, BS, 1961; Mass Inst Technol, SM, 1962; Stanford Univ, PhD (aeronaut, astronaut), 1968. **Honors & Awards:** Outstanding Res Award, Pa State Univ, 1978. **Professional Experience:** From asst prof to prof aerospace eng, Pa State Univ, 1968-1982; sr engr, Western Develop Labs, Philco Corp, 1965-1966; mem tech staff, Space Systs Div, Hughes Aircraft Co, 1964-1965; mem tech staff, Hughes Res Lab, Calif, 1962-1964; CONSULT, SPACETECH INC. **Memberships:** Am Inst Aeronaut & Astronaut; Am Astronaut Soc; Am Soc Eng Educ. **Research Statement & Publications:** Space systems synthesis and engineering; astrodynamics; propulsion; satellite dynamics and control. **Mailing Address:** 8029 Rising Ridge Rd, Bethesda, MD 20817.

KAPLAN, MARTIN CHARLES, DIGITAL IMAGE SCANNERS, COMPUTER IMAGE PROCESSING. **Personal Data:** b 1953. **Education:** Mass Inst Tech, BSc(physics) & BSc(math), 1975, PhD (physics), 1980. **Professional Experience:** RES SCIENTIST PHYSICS & IMAGE PROCESSING, KODAK RES LABS, 1982-; asst physicist, Brookhaven Nat Lab, 1980-1982; NSF grad fel physics, IBM grad fel, 1978-1979; NSF grad fel physics, Mass Inst Technol, 1975-1978. **Memberships:** Am Phys Soc; AAAS; Sigma Xi. **Research Statement & Publications:** Digital image scanning of film and paper; computer image processing and photographic science related to amateur and professional photography; color science. **Mailing Address:** Kodak Res Lab, 1/65/RL/01801, Rochester, NY 14650-1801. **Fax:** 585-477-6811. **E-Mail:** mckaplan@kodak.com

KAPLAN, MARTIN L, COMPARATIVE PHYSIOLOGY, INSECT PATHOLOGY. **Personal Data:** b New York, NY, April 7, 1923; m 1948, c 2. **Education:** Brooklyn Col, AB, 1949; NY Univ, MS, 1954, PhD (exp zool), 1958. **Professional Experience:** PROF EMER BIOL, QUEENS COL, NY, as of 2003; prof biol, Queens Col, NY, beginning 1971; asst dean Sch Gen Studies, Queens Col, NY, 1970-1975; from asst prof to assoc prof, Queens Col, NY, 1962-1971; assoc path, St Vincent's Hosp, New York, 1959-1962; lectr, Sch Gen Studies, Brooklyn Col, 1959-1962; asst prof anat, Sch Dent, 1958-1959; instr biol, Fairleigh Dickinson Univ, 1957-1958; tutor, Brooklyn Col, 1956-1957; lectr biol, Brooklyn Col, 1953-1956. **Memberships:** AAAS; Am Soc Zool; Sigma Xi. **Research Statement & Publications:** Histogenesis and biochemistry of melanotic tumors in Drosophila. **Mailing Address:** Dept Biol, Queens Col, 65-30 Kissena Blvd, Flushing, NY 11367-1597. **Fax:** 718-997-3445. **E-Mail:** mlkethics@aol.com

KAPLAN, MARTIN L, CHEMISTRY INSTRUCTOR. **Personal Data:** b New York, NY, December 27, 1935; m 1964, c 1. **Education:** City Col NY, BS, 1956; Fla State Univ, MS, 1960; Seton Hall Univ, JD, 1970. **Professional Experience:** Chem Instructor, Portland Community col, OR, 1999-; Adjunct Asst prof chem, Univ of Portland, OR, 1997-1999; RETIRED; mem staff, Bell Labs, 1977-1994; Atty at law, NJ, 1970-; assoc mem staff, Bell Labs, 1964-1977; vol sci teaching, US Peace Corps, 1962-1964; chemist, Richfield Oil Corp, 1960-1962; res assoc phys chem, Fla State Univ, 1960; Res technician microbiol, Columbia Univ, 1956-1957 & Sloan-Kettering Inst Cancer Res, 1957-1958. **Memberships:** Am Chem Soc. **Research Statement & Publications:** Mechanisms of organic reactions; rates of conformational isomerization of organic molecules by nuclear magnetic resonance; epoxy resin reactions; reactions by singlet oxygen with polymers; electrical conductivity of organic molecules and polymers. **Mailing Address:** 19436 Wilderness Dr, West Linn, OR 97068-2024.

KAPLAN, MELVIN, ORGANIC CHEMISTRY. **Personal Data:** b Brooklyn, NY, November 11, 1927; m 1953, c 4. **Education:** Brooklyn Col, BS, 1950; Ohio State Univ, PhD (org chem), 1954. **Professional Experience:** CONSULT, URETHANES & DIISOCYANATES, M KAPLAN ASSOCS, BUFFALO, 1989-; mgr res serv, Specialty Chem div, 1981-1989; mgr tech serv & develop urethanes, Specialty Chem div, 1970-1981; from proj leader to res supvr urethane applns, Indust Chem div, Allied Chem Corp, Buffalo, 1954-1970. **Memberships:** Am Chem Soc; Am Soc Testing & Mat; Int Isocyanate Inst; Soc Plastics Indust. **Research Statement & Publications:** Isocyanate and urethane polymer chemistry; plastics; organic synthesis; kinetics of chemical reactions; blowing agents; plastic foams. **Mailing Address:** 292 Culpepper Rd, Buffalo, NY 14221.

KAPLAN, MELVIN HYMAN, rheumatology, immunology; deceased, see previous edition for last biography

KAPLAN, MICHAEL, RADIATION CHEMISTRY. **Personal Data:** b New York, NY, November 7, 1937; m 1968, c 2. **Education:** Rensselaer Polytech Inst, BS, 1959; Columbia Univ, MA, 1961, PhD (electron spin resonance), 1965. **Professional Experience:** EDUC TESTING SERV, 1987-; Mem tech staff, RCA Labs, 1965-1987. **Memberships:** Am Chem Soc; Am Phys Soc; NY Acad Sci; fel Am Inst Chemists. **Research Statement & Publications:** Electron spin resonance of organic materials; interaction of charged particles with thin films; electron-beam lithography; x-ray lithography. **Mailing Address:** 45 Copper Mine Rd, Princeton, NJ 08540.

KAPLAN, MORTON, NUCLEAR REACTIONS, RELATIVISTIC HEAVY ION COLLISIONS. **Personal Data:** b Chicago, Ill, November 21, 1933; m Sandra; c David & Susan. **Education:** Univ Chicago, AB, 1954, SM, 1956; Mass Inst Technol, PhD (phys chem), 1960. **Honors & Awards:** Alfred P Sloan Research Fellow, 1965-1969 Visiting Professor of Physics, Clarendon Laboratory, University of Oxford (England), 1971-1972. **Professional Experience:** PROF PHYSICS, CARNEGIE MELLON UNIV, 2002-; PROF CHEM, CARNEGIE MELLON UNIV, 1971-; vis scientist, Oxford Univ, 1971-1972; assoc prof, Carnegie Mellon Univ, 1970; Alfred P Sloan res fel, 1965-1969; from asst prof to assoc prof, Yale Univ, 1962-1970; res staff, Lawrence Radiation Lab, 1960-1962; res assoc chem, Mass Inst Technol, 1960. **Memberships:** Am Phys Soc; Am Chem Soc; AAAS. **Research Statement & Publications:** Nuclear reactions induced by heavy ions; Mossbauer effect; perturbed angular correlations of gamma rays; magnetic properties and chemical bonding at low temperatures; nuclear spectroscopy; low temperature nuclear orientation; relativistic heavy ion collisions; primordial chemistry. **Mailing Address:** Carnegie Mellon Univ, 4400 Fifth Ave, Pittsburgh, PA 15213-2683. **Fax:** 412-268-6945. **E-Mail:** kaplan@cmchem.chem.cmu.edu

KAPLAN, MURRAY LEE, NUTRITION, METABOLISM. **Personal Data:** b Weehawken, NJ, January 9, 1941; m 1965, Helene; c Alissa & Cheryl. **Education:** Alfred Univ, NY, BA, 1962; City Univ NY, PhD (biol), 1972. **Honors & Awards:** Special Achievement Award, PhD Alumni Asn, City Univ NY, 2003. **Professional Experience:** PROF EMER, FOOD SCI & HUMAN NUTRIT IOWA STATE UNIV 2004-; vis prof pediat, Baylor Col Med, Houston, 1995; prof food sci & human nutrit, Iowa State Univ, 1990-2004; interim dir, Ctr Designing Foods Improve Nutrit, Iowa State Univ, 1988-1992; from assoc prof to prof food & nutrit, Iowa State Univ, 1981-1990; asst prof nutrit, Rutgers Univ, 1974-1980; NIH res fel, Dept food Sci & Human Nutrit, Mich State Univ, 1972-1974; res assoc nutrit, Dept Food Sci & Human Nutrit, Mich State Univ, 1971-1974; Lectr biol, Brooklyn Col, 1966-1971. **Memberships:** AAAS; Am Soc Nutrit; NY Acad Sci. **Research Statement & Publications:** Role of early nutritional experiences on the development of regulation of carbohydrate, lipid metabolism and obesity; Adipocyte metabolism; redesign of fatty acids in pork; pathways for fatty acid chain elongation. **Mailing Address:** Dept Food Sci & Human Nutrit, Iowa State Univ, 1109 Human Nutrit Sci Bldg, Ames, IA 50011-1120. **Fax:** 515-294-8181. **E-Mail:** mkaplan@iastate.edu

KAPLAN, NORMAN M, INTERNAL MEDICINE. **Personal Data:** b Dallas, Tex, January 2, 1931; m 1950, c 6. **Education:** Univ Tex, BS, 1950, MD, 1954; Am Bd Internal Med, dipl & cert endocrinol & metab. **Professional Experience:** NIH acad award, 1979-1984; HEAD HYPERTENSION SECT, HEALTH SCI CTR, UNIV TEX, DALLAS, 1978-; dep vpres res progs, Am Heart Asn, 1975-1976; PROF INTERNAL MED, SOUTHWESTERN MED CTR, UNIV TEX, DALLAS, 1970-; USPHS grants, 1962-1970; from instr to assoc prof, Health Sci Ctr, Univ Tex, Dallas, 1961-1970; USPHS res fel, Clin Endocrinol Br, Nat Heart Inst, 1960-1961; res physician, Parkland Mem Hosp, Dallas, 1955-1958. **Memberships:** Am Fedn Clin Res; Endocrine Soc; Am Col Physicians; Am Soc Clin Invest; Coun High Blood Pressure Res. **Research Statement & Publications:** Mechanisms controlling biosyntheses of adrenal cortical hormones particularly aldosterone; relationship of renin-angiotension system to hypertension; sodium restriction and other non-drug modalities in treatment of hypertension. **Mailing Address:** Univ Tex Health Sci Ctr, 5323 Harry Hines Blvd, Dallas, TX 75235-8899. **Fax:** 214-631-5340. **E-Mail:** norman.kaplan@utsouthwestern.edu

KAPLAN, PHYLLIS DEEN, CHEMISTRY, BIOCHEMISTRY. **Personal Data:** b Everett, Wash, February 9, 1931; c Harold D & Madeleine M. **Education:** Univ Wash, BA, 1953; Brandeis Univ, MA, 1956; Univ Cincinnati, PhD (chem), 1966. **Professional Experience:** Dir tech affairs, Lahaye Labs, Inc, 1992-1996; MGT CONSULT, 1990-; dir tech affairs, In-vitro Int, Inc, 1990 & 1992; adminr preclin int res & develop, dir int res & develop Europe & Middle East, 1987-1990; adminr preclin int res & develop, Allergan, 1983-1987; consult engr, Am Stand Testing Prog, 1982-1983; adj prof, NY Univ, 1982-1983; sr res toxicologist, Am Cyanamid Co, 1977-1982; lectr, Col Arts & Sci, Univ Cincinnati, 1972-1973 & Col Nursing, 1973-1974; asst prof environ health, Med Ctr, Univ Cincinnati, 1971-1977; Nat Inst Occup Safety & Health res grant, 1971-1976; res assoc, Med Ctr, Univ Cincinnati, 1968-1971; Spectroscopist chem, Syntex Corp, 1967-1968; Am Chem Soc Petrol Res Fund grant, Univ Cincinnati, 1965-1966; consult, Baker Chem Co. **Memberships:** Int Soc Ocular Toxicol; Am Chem Soc; Sigma Xi; Asn Res Vision Ophthal. **Research Statement & Publications:** Metabolism, binding and structural identity of transition metal compounds in the body, with a special interest in elucidating the mechanisms determining toxicity and essentiality of metals within living systems; pharmaceutical product development; eye and skin care; inhalation toxicology. **Mailing Address:** 526 First Ave, Suite 525, Seattle, WA 98104. **Fax:** 206-233-9072. **E-Mail:** pdkapl@eskimo.com

KAPLAN, RAPHAEL, SOLID STATE PHYSICS. **Personal Data:** b New York, NY, March 26, 1936. **Education:** Syracuse Univ, AB, 1957; Brown Univ, PhD (physics), 1963. **Professional Experience:** RETIRED; Physicist, Semiconductors Br, Solid State Div, US Naval Res Lab, 1963-. **Memberships:** Am Phys Soc. **Research Statement & Publications:** Spin resonance of color centers in irradiated crystals; far infrared and millimeter wave spectroscopy in semiconductors and other materials. **Mailing Address:** US Naval Res Lab, Code 6863, Washington, DC 20375.

KAPLAN, RAYMOND, SOLID STATE PHYSICS. **Personal Data:** b New York, NY, January 26, 1929; m 1965, c 2. **Education:** City Col New York, BS, 1950; Columbia Univ, MA, 1952, PhD (physics), 1959. **Professional Experience:** ADJ PROF PHYSICS, PACE UNIV, as of 2003; ADJ PROF PHYSICS, MARITIME COL, STATE UNIV NY, as of 2003; asst prof physics, Fordham Univ, beginning 1981; asst prof physics, Maritime Col, State Univ NY, 1979-1980; adj assoc prof physics, York Col, 1977-1979; assoc prof physics, Cooper Union, 1971-1977; asst prof, Cooper Union, 1968-1971; res physicist, US Rubber Co, NJ, 1964-1968; asst prof physics, Adelphi Univ, 1962-1964; res physicist, Airborne Instruments Lab, 1960-1962; Jr res physicist, Univ Calif, 1958-1959; consult, Info Div, Am Inst Physics & Electronic Semiconductor Co. **Memberships:** Am Phys Soc; Am Asn Physics Teachers; NY Acad Sci. **Research Statement & Publications:** Superconductivity; cryogenics. **Mailing Address:** Dept Physics, Pace Univ, Yorktown Heights, NY 10598.

KAPLAN, RICHARD E, AEROSPACE ENGINEERING, FLUID MECHANICS. **Personal Data:** b Philadelphia, Pa, July 4, 1938; m 1960, Naomi; c Hilary J Fausett & David M Kaplan. **Education:** Mass Inst Technol, BS & MS, 1961, ScD, 1964. **Professional Experience:** Provost res & acad comput, 1987-1994; assoc dean, 1984-1986; dept chmn, 1983-1986, 1997-2000; dir, Eng Comput Lab, 1982-1983; prof aerospace eng, Univ Southern Calif, 1973-2000; Fulbright lectr, 1971-1972, 1975-1976; Guggenheim fel, 1971-1972; dir, Systs Simulation Lab, 1969-1971; From asst prof to assoc prof, Univ Southern Calif, 1964-1973. **Memberships:** Am Inst Aeronaut & Astronaut; Am Phys Soc; Am Soc Eng. **Research Statement & Publications:** Fluid dynamic stability theory and turbulence experimentation; numerical methods in fluid mechanics; digital techniques in turbulence experimentation; aerosonics and jet noise. **Mailing Address:** Aerospace Eng, Univ Southern Calif, 854 W 36th Pl, Los Angeles, CA 90089. **Fax:** 909-594-7447. **E-Mail:** kaplan@usc.edu

KAPLAN, RICHARD STEPHEN, MEDICAL ONCOLOGY. **Personal Data:** b Pittsburgh, Pa, August 24, 1945; m 1970. **Education:** Univ Pittsburgh, BA, 1966; Univ Miami, MD, 1970; Am Bd Internal Med, dipl, 1974; Am Bd Med Oncol, dipl, 1975. **Professional Experience:** CHIEF, CLIN INVEST BR, NCI, as of 2003; ASSOC PROF ONCOL & MED, UNIV MD, 1979-; sr investr, Nat Cancer Inst, 1979-1981; consult oncologist, Miami Vet Admin Hosp & sr staff mem, Comprehensive Cancer Ctr, Fla, 1975-1979; asst prof oncol, Univ Miami, 1975-1979; fel, Univ Miami, 1974-1975; surgeon, USPHS, 1971-1973; clin assoc oncol, Nat Cancer Inst, 1971-1973. **Memberships:** Fel Am Col Physicians; Am Asn Cancer Res; Am Soc Clin Oncol; NY Acad Sci; AAAS; Am Soc Hemat; Am Fed Clin Res. **Research Statement & Publications:** Clinical and laboratory research in clinical oncology: neuro-oncology, malignant lymphomas and gastrointestinal malignancy. **Mailing Address:** Cancer Ther Eval Prog, Nat Cancer Inst, EPN 741, Bethesda, MD 20892-7436.

KAPLAN, ROBERT A, ENGINEERING PHYSICS. **Personal Data:** b Brooklyn, NY, June 20, 1935. **Education:** Cornell Univ, BS, 1957; Polytech Univ, PhD (physics), 1961. **Professional Experience:** OWNER, QUANTRONIX, 1965-; Res scientist, Wheeler Labs, 1957-1965. **Memberships:** Am Phys Soc. **Mailing Address:** One Gracie Terr No 6F, New York, NY 10028.

KAPLAN, ROBERT JOEL, DERMATOLOGY. **Personal Data:** b New York, NY, September 13, 1947. **Education:** Franklin & Marshall Col, BA, 1969; Univ Tenn, Memphis, MD, 1973. **Professional Experience:** PVT PRACT, MEMPHIS, TENN, 1979-; asst prof dermat, Univ Tenn, 1977-1979; residency, Univ Tenn, 1974-1977; internship, Geisinger Med Ctr, Danville, Pa, 1973-1974; tech asst, Englewood Hosp, 1968-1969. **Memberships:** Am Acad Dermat; AMA. **Research Statement & Publications:** Clinical studies involving cutaneous levels of cyclic adenosine monophate in atopic dermatitis. **Mailing Address:** 910 Madison Ste 922, Memphis, TN 38103-3460. **Fax:** 901-523-0779.

KAPLAN, ROBERT LEWIS, OPERATIONS ANALYSIS, MARKET RESEARCH. **Personal Data:** b Long Branch, NJ, October 5, 1928; m 1960, Jean; c 1. **Education:** US Mil Acad, BS, 1953; Mass Inst Technol, MS, 1960. **Professional Experience:** PRES, RUMSON CORP, 1981-; vpres opers res, Actuarial Res Corp, 1976-1980; Dep dir mat plans & prog & dep chief staff res, develop & aquisition, Hq, Dept Army, 1963-1988. **Memberships:** Am Inst Aeronaut & Astronaut; Am Helicopter Soc; Sigma Xi. **Research Statement & Publications:** Low speed aeronautical research c/w v-stol, helicopters, and aircushion vehicles; command and control operations research; quantitative measurement of subjective judgements. **Mailing Address:** Rumson's Co, Middleburg, VA 20117.

KAPLAN, ROBERT S, EXTRACTIVE METALLURGY, CHEMICAL METALLURGY. **Personal Data:** b New York, NY, July 13, 1940; m 1967, c 2. **Education:** Univ Mich, BSE, 1962, MSE, 1964; Carnegie-Mellon Univ, PhD (metall, mat sci), 1968. **Professional Experience:** MGR RECYCLING TECHNOL, BUR MINES, US DEPT INTERIOR, 1982-; mgr extractive nonfuel minerals processes, Resource Recovery, 1980-1982; staff minimum policy rev, Resource Recovery, 1978-1979; res supvr metall, Resource Recovery, 1976-1978; proj mgr res recovery, Off Tech Assess, US Cong, 1976; staff metallurgist, Bur Mines, US Dept Interior, 1971-1976; res metallurgist, Battelle Columbus Labs, 1968-1971. **Memberships:** Am Inst Mining Metall & Petrol Engrs. **Research Statement & Publications:** Iron-making slags; decarburization of steels; steel refining; inclusions in steels; recovery of metals from nonferrous metal scrap and wastes. **Mailing Address:** Horizon Eng Serv Ltd, 5436 Doral Dr, Wilmington, DE 19808.

KAPLAN, RONALD M, COMPUTER SCIENCE, COMPUTATIONAL LINGUISTICS. **Personal Data:** b Los Angeles, Calif, July 15, 1946; m 1970, c 2. **Education:** Univ Calif, Berkeley, BA, 1968; Harvard Univ, MA, 1970, PhD (social psychol), 1975. **Honors & Awards:** Software Syst Award, Asn Comput Mach, 1992. **Professional Experience:** MGR RES, NATURAL LANG THEORY & TECHNOL, as of 2002; CONSULT PROF LING, STANGORD UNIV, as of 2002; Fel residence, Neth Inst, Advan Study, Humanities & Social Sci, 1995-1996; consult prof ling, Stanford Univ, 1988-; mem adv comt sci & technol ctrs, NSF, 1988-1991; RES FEL, INTELLIGENT SYSTEMS LAB, PALO ATLO RES CTR, 1986-; vis scholar cognitive sci, Mass Inst Technol, 1978; res scientist psycholing, Palo Alto Res Ctr, 1974-1986; consult, Xerox Corp, 1973-1974; Res assoc, Harvard Univ, 1973-1974; Consult, Rand Corp, 1968-1972 & Info Sci Inst, Univ Southern Calif, 1972-1973. **Memberships:** Fel Asn Comput Mach; Asn Comput Ling (vpres 1978 pres 1979); Linguistics Soc Am. **Research Statement & Publications:** Computational models of human language comprehension; linguistics; psycholinguistics. **Mailing Address:** Intelligent Systems Lab, Palo Alto Res Ctr, 3333 Coyote Hill Rd, Palo Alto, CA 94304. **Fax:** 650-812-4374. **E-Mail:** kaplan@parc.com

KAPLAN, RONALD S, BIOENERGETICS. **Personal Data:** b New York, NY, July 12, 1951; m 1987, c 3. **Education:** NY Univ, BA, 1973, MS, 1975, PhD (biol), 1981. **Professional Experience:** PROF & VICE CHAIR BIOCHEM & MOLECULAR BIOL, CHICAGO MED SCH, FINCH UNIV HEALTH SCI, as of 2006; prof pharmacol, Col Med, Univ S Ala, beginning 1996; from asst prof to assoc prof, Col Med, Univ S Ala, 1986-1996; fel, Johns Hopkins Sch Med, 1980-1986. **Memberships:** AAAS; Am Chem Soc; Biophys Soc; Am Soc Biochem & Molecular Biol; Am Diabetes Asn. **Research Statement & Publications:** Elucidate the structure, function and mechanisms of regulation of mitochondrial transport proteins in normal and diseased States. **Mailing Address:** Dept Biochem & Molecular Biol, Chicago Med Sch, Finch Univ Health Sci, 3333 Green Bay Rd, North Chicago, IL 60064. **Fax:** 847-578-3240. **E-Mail:** kaplanr@finchcms.edu

KAPLAN, SAMUEL, MOLECULAR BIOLOGY, GENETICS. **Personal Data:** b Yonkers, NY, February 13, 1934. **Education:** Cornell Univ, BS, 1959; Univ Calif, San Diego, PhD (chem), 1963. **Honors & Awards:** A O Stark Award, Miami Univ, Ohio, 1985; Karski Award, Am Soc Microbiol, 1986; Oliver H Smith Award, Markell Univ, 1988. **Professional Experience:** PROF & CHMN, DEPT MICROBIOL & MOLECULAR GENETICS, UNIV TEX MED SCH, 1989-; prof & dir, Sch Life Sci, 1973-1989; from asst prof to assoc prof microbiol, Univ Ill, 1968-1973. **Memberships:** Am Soc Microbiol; Genetics Soc Am; AAAS. **Research Statement & Publications:** Molecular biology; genetics. **Mailing Address:** Dept Microbiol & Molecular Genetics, Univ Tex, PO Box 20708, Houston, TX 77225-0708. **Fax:** 713-500-7436. **E-Mail:** samuel.kaplan@uth.tmc.edu

KAPLAN, SAMUEL, MATHEMATICS. **Personal Data:** b Detroit, Mich, September 13, 1916; m 1953, c 2. **Education:** Univ Mich, BS, 1937, MS, 1938, PhD (math), 1942. **Professional Experience:** PROF MATH, PURDUE UNIV, 1961-; from asst prof to prof, Wayne State Univ, 1948-1961; researcher, Inst Adv Study, 1947-1948 & 1956-1957; Rackham fel, Princeton Univ, 1946-1947; Instr math, Univ Mich, 1946. **Memberships:** Am Math Soc. **Research Statement & Publications:** Homology theory; topological groups; topological spaces; duality; functional analysis. **Mailing Address:** 8516 Johnson Mill Rd, Purdue Univ, Bahama, NC 27503.

KAPLAN, SAMUEL, cardiology; deceased, see previous edition for last biography

KAPLAN, SANDRA SOLON, CLINICAL PATHOLOGY, HEMATOLOGY. **Personal Data:** b Chicago, Ill, September 9, 1934; m 1957, c David B & Susan E. **Education:** Roosevelt Univ, BS, 1955; Boston Univ, MD, 1959. **Professional Experience:** PROF PATH, SCH MED, UNIV PITTSBURGH, 1991-; dir hemat, Magee Womens Hosp, Pittsburgh, beginning 1978; from asst prof to assoc prof, Sch Med, Univ Pittsburgh, 1978-1990; res worker, Sir William Dunn Sch Path, Oxford Univ, 1971-1972; asst res prof path & med, Sch Med, Univ Pittsburgh, 1970-1978; res assoc, Yale Univ, 1965-1969; USPHS res training grant, Med Sch, Yale Univ, 1963-1964; USPHS res fel hemat, Children's Hosp, San Francisco, 1961-1962; med dir, Hemat Lab, Med Ctr, Univ Pittsburgh. **Memberships:** Am Soc Hemat; Am Soc Clin Path; Am Soc Investigative Path; Soc Leukocyte Biol. **Research Statement & Publications:** Mechanisms of leukocyte activation associated with phagocytosis; mechanisms of chemotaxis and bacterial killing by leukocytes. **Mailing Address:** Med Ctr, Univ Pittsburgh, Mt Lebanon, PA 15228. **E-Mail:** kaplanss@msx.upmc.edu

KAPLAN, SANFORD SANDY, STRATIGRAPHY, SEDIMENTATION. **Personal Data:** b New York, NY, October 2, 1950; m Connie; c Elicia, Todd, Wendi, Shira & Bryan. **Education:** Lafayette Col, AB, 1971; Lehigh Univ, MS, 1976; Univ Pittsburgh, PhD (geol), 1981; Salve Regina Col, MA, 1987. **Professional Experience:** RES ASSOC PROF, UNIV NEBR, LINCOLN, 2006-; pres, Earthsource Consult, Inc, 1987; geol, Penzoil Explor & Prod Co, 1980-1986; vis lectr coal geol, Univ Pittsburgh, 1980; geol, Coal Prep Div, Pittsburgh Mining Technol Ctr, US Dept Energy, 1979-1980; lectr gen geol, Univ Nebr, Lincoln, 1977-1978; Teaching asst, Lehigh Univ, 1975-1976; vis lectr geol, Northampton Co Area Community Col, 1974-1975; Surface Warfare Officer, USN, 1969-. **Memberships:** Am Asn Petrol Geologists; Geol Soc Am; Soc Econ Paleontologists & Mineralogists; Sigma Xi; AAAS; Am Econ Asn; Int Asn Sedimentologists. **Research Statement & Publications:** Interpreting ancient environments of deposition of sedimentary sequences especially those containing coal, oil and gas and deducing their tetonic setting from such evidence; environmental geology; site assessments; hydrology. **Mailing Address:** UNIV NEBR, LINCOLN, 5701 Judith Dr, Lincoln, NE 68517-9792. **Fax:** 402-472-4917. **E-Mail:** skaplan2@unl.edu

KAPLAN, SELIG N(EIL), NUCLEAR PHYSICS & ENGINEERING. **Personal Data:** b Chicago, Ill, June 30, 1932; m 1954, c 2. **Education:** Univ Ariz, BS, 1952; Univ Calif, MS, 1954, PhD (physics), 1957. **Professional Experience:** PROF EMER NUCLEAR ENG, LAWRENCE BERKELEY LAB, UNIV CALIF, BERKELEY, 1992-; SR PHYSICIST, LAWRENCE BERKELEY LAB, UNIV CALIF, BERKELEY, 1968-; from asst prof to prof, Lab, Univ Calif, Berkeley, 1965-1992; lectr, Lab, Univ Calif, Berkeley, 1962-1965; Physicist, Lab, Univ Calif, Berkeley, 1957-1968. **Memberships:** Am Phys Soc; Am Nuclear Soc. **Research Statement & Publications:** Nuclear instrumentation; neutronics; interaction of muons with nuclei. **Mailing Address:** Dept Nuclear Eng, Lawrence Berkeley Lab, Univ Calif, 4159 Etcheverry Hall, Berkeley, CA 94720-1730. **Fax:** 510-643-9685. **E-Mail:** kaplan@nuc.berkeley.edu

KAPLAN, SELNA L, PEDIATRICS, ENDOCRINOLOGY. **Personal Data:** b Brooklyn, NY, April 8, 1927. **Education:** Brooklyn Col, BA, 1948; Wash Univ, MA, 1950, PhD (anat), 1953, MD, 1955. **Honors & Awards:** Ayerst Award, Endocrinol Soc, 1987 & Koch Award, 1995. **Professional Experience:** PROF EMER PEDIAT, SCH MED, UNIV CALIF, SAN FRANCISCO, 1974-; from asst prof to assoc prof, Sch Med, Univ Calif, San Francisco, 1966-1974; asst prof, Col Physicians & Surgeons, Columbia Univ, 1965-1966; assoc, Col Physicians & Surgeons, Columbia Univ, 1963-1965; career develop award, 1962-1971; instr pediat, Col Physicians & Surgeons, Columbia Univ, 1961-1963; NIH fel, 1958-1961; Asst anat, Sch Med, Wash Univ, 1951-1952. **Memberships:** Endocrine Soc; Soc Pediat Res; NY Acad Sci; Am Pediat Soc. **Research Statement & Publications:** Growth disorders in children; immunochemistry of pituitary human growth hormone; ontogenesis of human fetal hormones; pubertal development. **Mailing Address:** 60 Allston Way, San Francisco, CA 94127. **Fax:** 415-476-1343. **E-Mail:** skaplan@peds.ucsf.edu

KAPLAN, SOLOMON ALEXANDER, MEDICINE. **Personal Data:** b SAfrica, February 5, 1924; American citizen; m 1957. **Education:** Univ Witwatersrand, MB & BCh, 1946. **Professional Experience:** EMER PROF PEDIAT, MED CTR, UNIV CALIF, LOS ANGELES, as of 2002; prof pediat, med ctr, Univ Calif, Los Angeles, beginning 1968; from assoc prof to prof, Sch Med, Univ Southern Calif, 1959-1968; from asst prof to assoc prof, State Univ NY, 1953-1959; instr pediat, Univ Cincinnati, 1951-1953; res fel pediat, Univ Cincinnati, 1949-1951. **Memberships:** AAAS; Am Physiol Soc; Soc Pediat Res; Am Pediat Soc; Brit Soc Endocrinol. **Research Statement & Publications:** Pediatrics; endocrinology; biochemistry. **Mailing Address:** Dept Pediat, Univ Calif Med Ctr Health Sci, Los Angeles, CA 90024-1752.

KAPLAN, STANLEY, TERATOLOGY, HUMAN DEVELOPMENT. **Personal Data:** b Canton, Ohio, April 28, 1936; div, c Wayne, Lisa & Dean. **Education:** Univ Miami, BS & BEd, 1962, PhD (teratology), 1967. **Professional Experience:** Prin investr, NIH, 1985-1986; ASSOC CHMN, MED COL WIS, 1984-; prof cellular biol & anat, Med Col Wis, 1982-1995; PROF EMER, 1995-; actg chmn, Med Col Wis, 1982-1984; vchmn, Med Col Wis, 1972-1982; vis prof, Univ Man, Can, 1974 & Hebrew Univ, Israel, 1989; from asst prof to assoc prof, Med Col Wis, 1969-1982; asst prof anat sci, Col Med, Univ Fla, 1967-1969; Instr & fel, Col Med, Univ Fla, 1966-1967. **Memberships:** Am Asn Anat; Am Soc Zool; Am Inst Biol Sci; Europ Teratology Soc; Teratology Soc; Toxicol Soc. **Research Statement & Publications:** Mechanisms by which chemical and physical environmental agents produce congenital malformations. **Mailing Address:** Dept Cellular Biol & Anat, 8701 Med Col Wis Watertown Pl, Milwaukee, WI 53226. **Fax:** 414-266-8496. **E-Mail:** skaplan@post.its.mcw.edu

KAPLAN, STANLEY A, PHARMACEUTICAL RESEARCH & DEVELOPMENT, ADMINISTRATION. **Personal Data:** b New York, NY, September 28, 1938; m 1960, Lois; c Lisa, Michelle & Martin. **Education:** Columbia Univ, BS, 1959, MS, 1961; Univ Calif, San Francisco, PhD (pharmaceut chem), 1965. **Professional Experience:** SR VPRES, ALPHARMA INC, BALTIMORE, MD, 1992-; pres & chief oper officer, Pharmetrix Corp, 1989-1992; sr vpres res & develop, Liposome Technol, Inc, 1987-1989; exec dir develop, Med Res Div, Lederle Labs, Am Cyanamid, 1984-1987; several positions, dept dir & assoc div dir exp therapeut, Hoffmann-La Roche Inc, Nutley, NJ, 1966-1984; fel, NIH, 1965. **Memberships:** Am Asn Pharmaceut Scientists; Am Soc Clin Pharmacol & Therapeut; Am Col Clin Pharmacol; Am Soc Pharmacol & Exp Therapeut; AAAS; NY Acad Sci; Controlled Release Soc. **Research Statement & Publications:** Pharmacokinetics; biopharmaceutics; drug metabolism; drug development; novel drug delivery systems; analytical methodology; design and implement programs to develop new drugs and drug products; over 90 publications, presentations or chapters in books. **Mailing Address:** 10065 Red Run Blvd, Owings Mills, MD 21117. **Fax:** 410-558-7262.

KAPLAN, STANLEY BARUCH, MEDICINE, RHEUMATOLOGY. **Personal Data:** b Memphis, Tenn, January 6, 1931. **Education:** Univ Tenn, MD, 1954. **Professional Experience:** PROF MED & RHEUMATOL, SCH MED, UNIV TENN, MEMPHIS, 1973-; attend physician, Vet Admin Hosp, 1967-; from instr to assoc prof, Sch Med, Univ Tenn, Memphis, 1961-1973; fel rheumatol, Sch Med, Univ Tenn, 1960-1962; from asst resident to chief resident, Sch Med, Univ Tenn, Memphis, 1958-1962; Intern med, Jefferson Med Col, 1955. **Memberships:** AMA; Am Col Rheumatol; Memphis Acad Internal Med; Tenn Med Asn. **Research Statement & Publications:** Clinical investigation in rheumatic diseases. **Mailing Address:** Univ Tenn, 920 Madison Ave, Suite 434, Memphis, TN 38103. **Fax:** 901-448-1123.

KAPLAN, STANLEY MEISEL, PSYCHIATRY. **Personal Data:** b Cincinnati, Ohio, May 10, 1922; m 1950, Mickey; c Steven, Barbara & Richard. **Education:** Univ Cincinnati, BS, 1943, MD, 1946. **Professional Experience:** Emer prof psychiat, Col Med, Univ Cincinnati, 1990-1992; actg dir, Col Med, Univ Cincinnati, 1975-1977; NIMH spec res fel, 1954-1956 & Inst Psychoanal, 1961-1967; from instr to prof, Col Med, Univ Cincinnati, 1952-1990; fel psychosom, Cincinnati Gen Hosp, 1951-1952; resident psychiat, Cincinnati Gen Hosp, 1949-1951; res fel, May Inst, 1948-1949; resident, Cincinnati Jewish Hosp, 1947-1948; intern med, Cincinnati Jewish Hosp, 1946-1947. **Memberships:** AAAS; Am Psychosom Soc; Am Med Asn; fel Am Psychiat Asn; Am Psychoanal Asn. **Research Statement & Publications:** Psychosomatic medicine; psychiatry; psychoanalysis. **Mailing Address:** Dept Psychiat, Univ Cincinnati Col Med, Cincinnati, OH 45267. **Fax:** 513-558-4805.

KAPLAN, THOMAS ABRAHAM, SOLID STATE THEORY, THEORY OF MAGNETISM IN SOLIDS. **Personal Data:** b Philadelphia, Pa, February 24, 1926; m 1956, Patricia; c Melissa, Andrea & Laurie. **Education:** Univ Pa, BS, 1948, PhD (physics), 1954. **Honors & Awards:** Alexander von Humboldt Sr Scientist Award, 1981. **Professional Experience:** EMER PROF PHYSICS, MICH STATE; UNIV, 1996-; prof, Mich State; Univ, 1970-1995; distinguished vis prof, Univ Tsukuba, Japan, 1989; Inst Festkorperforschung der KFA Julich, Ger, 1982; vis scientist, Max-Planck-Institut fur Festkorperforschung, Stuttgart, Ger, 1981-1982, 1983-1984, 1988-1989; consult, Naval Res Lab, Wash, DC, 1979-1980; staff mem, Lincoln Lab, Mass Inst Technol, 1959-1970; res assoc, Pa State Univ at Brookhaven Nat Lab, 1956-1959; res assoc, Eng Res Inst, 1955-1956; res asst physics, Willow Run Res Ctr, Univ Mich, 1954-1955. **Memberships:** fel Am Phys Soc; Sigma Xi; Union Concerned Scientists. **Research Statement & Publications:** Quantum theory of solids; numerical solution of models of highly-correlated-electron systems, e.g. Heisenberg spin models, Hubbard models; cluster models for spin and charge density in quantum antiferromagnets; theory of novel Mott insulators called electrides. **Mailing Address:** Dept Physics & Astron, Mich State Univ, East Lansing, MI 48824. **Fax:** 517-353-0690. **E-Mail:** kaplan@pa.msu.edu

KAPLAN, WILFRED, MATHEMATICS. **Personal Data:** b Boston, Mass, November 28, 1915; m 1938, Ida; c Roland & Muriel. **Education:** Harvard Univ, AB, 1936, AM, 1936, PhD (math), 1939. **Professional Experience:** PROF EMER MATH, UNIV MICH, ANN ARBOR, 1988-; Guggenheim Found fel, 1949-1950; res assoc, Brown Univ, 1944-1945; from instr to prof, Univ Mich, Ann Arbor, 1940-1986; instr math, Col William & Mary, 1939-1940. **Memberships:** AAAS; Am Phys Soc; Am Math Soc; Math Asn Am; Math Soc France. **Research Statement & Publications:** Non-linear differential equations; dynamics; Riemann surfaces; statistical mechanics; numerical analysis. **Mailing Address:** Univ Mich, Dept Math, 3868 E Hall, Ann Arbor, MI 48109-1109. **E-Mail:** wilkap@umich.edu

KAPLAN, WILLIAM, MEDICAL MYCOLOGY. **Personal Data:** b New York, NY, April 27, 1922; m 1953. **Education:** Cornell Univ, BS, 1943, DVM, 1946; Univ Minn, Minneapolis, MPH, 1951. **Professional Experience:** Lectr, Sch Vet Med, Univ Pa, 1971-; adj assoc prof, Ga State Univ, 1971-; adj field prof, Sch Pub Health, Univ NC, 1969-; COMMISSIONED OFFICER, MYCOL DIV, CTR DIS CONTROL, USPHS, 1951-; vet, USDA, 1947-1950; Vet, UN Relief & Rehab Admin, 1946-1947. **Memberships:** Am Soc Microbiol; Am Pub Health Asn; Int Soc Human & Animal Mycol (vpres 1967-1971); Med Mycol Soc Am; Am Vet Med Asn. **Research Statement & Publications:** Selected zoonosis, with empahsis on epidemiology; diagnostic procedures for mycotic diseases, with emphasis on immunofluorescence. **Mailing Address:** 1222 Briar Hill Dr, Atlanta, GA 30329.

KAPLAN, WILLIAM DAVID, genetics, behavior; deceased, see previous edition for last biography

KAPLANSKY, IRVING, MATHEMATICS. **Personal Data:** b Toronto, Ont, March 22, 1917; m 1951, c 3. **Education:** Univ Toronto, BA, 1938, MA, 1940; Harvard Univ, PhD (algebra), 1941. **Honorary Degrees:** DMath, Univ Waterloo, 1968; DSc, Queens Univ, Ont, 1969. **Honors & Awards:** Steele Prize, Am Math Soc. **Professional Experience:** PROF EMER MATH, UNIV CALIF, BERKELEY, as of 2004; DIR EMER MATH, MATH SCI RES INST, BERKELEY, 1992-; dir, Math Sci Res Inst, Berkeley, 1984-1992; from instr to prof math, George Herbert Mead distinguished serv prof, 1969-1984; chmn dept, Univ Chicago, 1962-1967; Guggenheim Found fel, 1948-1949; from instr to prof math, Univ Chicago, 1945-1969; res mathematician, Appl Math Group, Nat Defense Res Comt, Columbia Univ, 1944-1945; instr math, Harvard Univ, 1941-1944. **Memberships:** Nat Acad Sci; Am Math Soc; Math Asn Am. **Research Statement & Publications:** Algebra. **Mailing Address:** Dept Math, Univ Calif, 970 Evans Hall, Berkeley, CA 94720-3840. **Fax:** 510-642-8204.

KAPLER, JOSPEH EDWARD, BIOLOGY. **Personal Data:** b Cresco, Iowa, March 13, 1924; m 1959, c 4. **Education:** Loras Col, BS, 1948; Marquette Univ, MS, 1953; Univ Wis, PhD (entom), 1958. **Professional Experience:** PROF EMER BIOL, LORAS COL, 1989-; from asst prof to prof biol, Loras Col, 1957-1989; asst entom, Univ Wis, 1955-1957; instr biol, Loras Col, 1954-1955; instr, Marquette Univ, 1953-1954; asst zool, Marquette Univ, 1951-1953; Instr biol, Loras Col, 1948-1951. **Memberships:** Entom Soc Am. **Research Statement & Publications:** Biology and ecology of forest insects. **Mailing Address:** Dept Biol, Loras Col, 1450 Alta Vista, Dubuque, IA 52004-0178.

KAPLITA, PAUL V, PHARMACOLOGY. **Personal Data:** b Bridgeport, Conn. **Education:** Univ Conn, BS, 1976; State Univ NY, Buffalo, PhD (pharmacol), 1981. **Professional Experience:** AT BOEHRINGER INGELHEIM PHARMACEUT INC, as of 2004; PRIN RES INVESTR, STERLING-WINTHROP INC, 1992-; sr res investr, Sterling-winthrop Inc, 1990-1992; staff scientist, Nova Pharmaceut Corp, 1987-1990; sr res assoc, Nova Pharmaceut Corp, 1985-1987; res fel pharmacol, Dartmouth Med Sch, 1982-1985. **Memberships:** Am Soc Pharmacol & Exp Therapeut; Soc Neuroscience. **Mailing Address:** Dept Med Chem, Boehringer Ingelheim Pharmaceut Inc, PO Box 368 900 Ridgebury Rd, Ridgefield, CT 06877-0368. **Fax:** 203-798-6072. **E-Mail:** pkaplita@rdg.boehringer-ingelheim.com

KAPLON, MORTON FISCHEL, physics; deceased, see previous edition for last biography

KAPOOR, AMRIT LAL, MEDICINAL CHEMISTRY, PHARMACEUTICAL CHEMISTRY. **Personal Data:** b Amritsar, India, October 15, 1931; m 1959, c 2. **Education:** Punjab Univ, India, BS, 1952, MS, 1954; Swiss Fed Inst Technol, ScD(pharmaceut chem), 1956. **Professional Experience:** PROF PHARMACEUT CHEM, COL PHARM & ALLIED HEALTH PROFESSIONS, ST JOHN'S UNIV, NY, 1966-; res fel chem, Col Pharm & Allied Health Professions, St John's Univ, NY, 1963-1966; chief chemist, Merck, Sharpe & Dohme Int, NY, 1959-1963; sci officer, Nat Chem Labs, India, 1958-1959; fel, Wayne State Univ, 1957-1958; teaching fel, Sorbonne, 1956-1957. **Memberships:** AAAS; Am Chem Soc; Am Pharmaceut Asn. **Research Statement & Publications:** Natural products; synthesis of biologically active peptides and polypeptides. **Mailing Address:** Dept Pharm, St John's Univ, 8150 Utopia Pkwy, Jamaica, NY 11439-0001. **E-Mail:** kapoora@stjohns.edu

KAPOOR, BHUSHAN L, COMPUTER SCIENCE. **Education:** Punjab Univ, MA, PhD. **Professional Experience:** PROF INFO SYSTS & DECISION SCI, CALIF STATE UNIV, as of 2004. **Mailing Address:** Calif State Univ, 800 N State Col Blvd, Fullerton, CA 92634. **Fax:** 530-898-4070.

KAPOOR, INDER PRAKASH, METABOLISM, INSECT TOXICOLOGY. **Personal Data:** b Multan, India, September 9, 1937; m 1970, c 2. **Education:** Univ Delhi, BSc, 1957; Univ Ill, Urbana, PhD (entom), 1970. **Professional Experience:** DIR, PLANT INDUST DISCOVERY, AM CYANAMID CO, 1985-; mgr, Plant Indust Discovery, Am Cyanamid CO, 1980-1985; group leader, Plant Indust Discovery, Am Cyanamid CO, 1976-1980; res chemist, Plant Indust Discovery, Am Cyanamid CO, 1973-1975; from res asst to res assoc entom metab, Univ Ill, Urbana, 1968-1972; res asst, Univ Calif, Riverside, 1966-1968; Tech asst entom, Ministry Food & Agr, India, 1957-1966. **Memberships:** Am Chem Soc. **Research Statement & Publications:** Metabolism of pesticides in the environment and its elements; biological screening and development of new pesticides, plant growth regulants and biotechnology research. **Mailing Address:** 335 Penn-Titusville Rd, Pennington, NJ 08534.

KAPOOR, NARINDER N, ZOOLOGY, PHYSIOLOGY. **Personal Data:** b Calcutta, India, September 4, 1937; Canadian citizen; m 1969, Nitish; c 3. **Education:** Panjab Univ, India, BSc, 1960, MSc, 1961; McMaster Univ, PhD (animal behav & physiol), 1968. **Honors & Awards:** 2nd Prize Outstanding Electronmicros, Polaroid Int Competition, 1984; Grand Prize, Photomicro Graphy Contest, Bethesda Res Lab, Md, 1989; Excellence in Plecoptera Res Award, NAm Plecoptera Soc, 1990. **Professional Experience:** Grad prog dir biol, Concordia Univ, 1988-1991 & 1994-; ASSOC PROF BIOL, CONCORDIA UNIV, 1976-; asst prof, Concordia Univ, 1973-1976; asst prof, Univ Waterloo, 1969-1973; lectr, Univ Waterloo, 1968-1969; demonstr physiol, McMaster Univ, 1963-1968; Lectr zool, Govt Col, Panjab, India, 1961-1962. **Memberships:** Int Soc of Plecoptera. **Research Statement & Publications:** Respiratory physiology and behavior of stream animals; morphology, osmoregulation, scanning and transmission electron microscopy; Plecoptera; sense organs and feeding behavior. **Mailing Address:** Dept Biol, Concordia Univ, 1455 de Maisonneuve Blvd, Montreal, PQ H3G 1M8, Can. **Fax:** 514-848-2881. **E-Mail:** nkapoor@alcor.concordia.ca

KAPOOR, S F, MATHEMATICS. **Personal Data:** b Bombay, India, September 7, 1934. **Education:** Univ Bombay, BSc, 1955, MSc, 1957, LLB, 1963; Mich State Univ, PhD (math), 1967. **Professional Experience:** PROF EMER MATH, WESTERN MICH UNIV, 1996-; prof math, Western Mich Univ, 1981-1996; from asst prof to assoc prof, Western Mich Univ, 1967-1981; asst, Mich State Univ, 1963-1967; lectr math, Kirti Col, Univ Bombay, 1961-1963; Staff asst, State Bank India, 1958-1961. **Memberships:** Math Asn Am. **Research Statement & Publications:** Topology; graph theory. **Mailing Address:** Dept math, Western Mich Univ, 1903 W Mich Ave, Kalamazoo, MI 49008-5248. **Fax:** 269-387-4530.

KAPOOR, SHIV G, INDUSTRIAL ENGINEERING. **Education:** Univ Wis, Madison, PhD, 1977. **Professional Experience:** PROF MECH & INDUST ENG, UNIV ILL, URBANA-CHAMPAIGN, as of 2006. **Memberships:** Am Soc Mech Engr, Inst Indust Engrs, Soc Mfg Engr. **Mailing Address:** Univ Ill Urbana Champaign, 1206 W Green St, Urbana, IL 61801. **Fax:** 217-244-9956. **E-Mail:** s-kapoor@uiuc.edu

KAPOOR, VIKRAM J, PHYSICS. **Personal Data:** b India, July 23, 1945; American citizen. **Education:** Univ Delhi, BS, 1966, MS, 1968; Lehigh Univ, MS, 1972, PhD (physics), 1976. **Honors & Awards:** Thomas D Callinan Award, Electrochem Soc, 1991. **Professional Experience:** PROF BIOENGINEERING & ELEC ENG, TOLEDO UNIV, as of 2004; DIR, BIOMED NANOTECH RES LAB, COL ENG, TOLEDO UNIV, as of 2004; mem, Nat Comn Semiconductor Mfg & Industr Competitiveness, Dept Com, 1988-1990; dept head, Univ Cincinnati, beginning 1986; prof elec & comput eng, Univ Cincinnati, beginning 1983; mem, Subcomt State-of-the-Art Compound Semiconductor Technol, Electrochem Soc, 1983-1987; dir grad studies, Univ Cincinnati, 1983-1986; assoc prof, Solid State Integrated Circuit Lab, 1981-1983; dir, Solid State Integrated Circuit Lab, 1978-1983; asst prof elec eng, Case Western Res Univ, 1978-1981; sr design engr & mem res staff, Fairchild Semiconductor Corp, 1976-1978. **Memberships:** Am Phys Soc; sr mem Inst Elec & Electronics Engrs; Nat Soc Prof Engrs; Am Soc Eng Educ; fel Electrochem Soc; Am Vacuum Soc. **Research Statement & Publications:** Solid state electronics; microwave/millimeterwave engineering; high Tc superconductors for microwave electronics. **Mailing Address:** Dept Elec & Comput Eng, Univ Toledo, Toledo, OH 43606. **Fax:** 419-530-8007. **E-Mail:** vkapoor@utoledo.edu

KAPOR, MITCHELL DAVID, MANAGEMENT. **Personal Data:** b Brooklyn, NY, November 1, 1950; m 1983, Ellen M Poss. **Education:** Yale Univ, BA, 1971; Beacon Col, MA, 1978. **Honorary Degrees:** DHL, Boston Univ, 1985, Mass Sch Prof Psychol, 1990; DCS, Suffolk Univ, 1988. **Honors & Awards:** Distinguished Info Sci Award, Data Processing Mgt Asn, 1990. **Professional Experience:** Adj res fel, Kennedy Sch Govt, Harvard Univ, 1992-; CHMN, ELECTRONIC FRONTIER FOUND INC, 1990-; chmn, ON Tech Inc, 1987-1990; chmn, Lotus Develop Corp, 1984-1986; pres, Lotus Develop Corp, 1982-1984; prod mgr, Personal Software, 1980; Consult, 1978-1980. **Research Statement & Publications:** Computer science. **Mailing Address:** 238 Main St, Cambridge, MA 02142.

KAPOS, ERVIN, OPERATIONS RESEARCH & SYSTEMS ANALYSIS, WARGAMING & SIMULATION MILITARY COMMAND & CONTROL. **Personal Data:** b Brashov, Rumania, June 21, 1931; American citizen; m 1952, June; c Valerie. **Education:** Ind Univ, AB, 1954. **Honors & Awards:** Meritorious Pub Serv Award, Secy Navy. **Professional Experience:** PRES, KAPOS ASSOCS INC, 1984-; pres, Wash Opers, Ketron, Inc, 1980-1983; mem, adv bd, Nat Security Agency, 1979-1982; panel mem marine bd, Nat Acad Sci, 1978-1980; assoc mem, Defense Sci Bd, 1974-1976 & 1982-1987; exec vpres & dir, Wash Opers, Ketron, Inc, 1972-1980; dir, Opers Eval Group, 1969-1972; dir, Southeast Asia Combat Anal Div, Opers Eval Group, 1967-1968 & Marine Corps Anal Group, 1968-1969; rep to comdr-in-chief, US Pac Fleet, 1966-1967; head command & control sect, Ctr Naval Anal, 1962-1966; rep to oper test & eval force, rep to comdr 1st Fleet, 1960-1961; rep to oper test & eval force, US Pac Fleet, 1959-1960; analyst, Opers Eval Group, Mass Inst Technol, 1958-1959; Assoc math, Ind Univ, 1953-1958; mem, panels sci & tech policy & crisis mgt, Ctr Strategic & Int Studies. **Memberships:** Am Math Soc; Opers Res Soc Am; fel Mil Opers Res Soc. **Research Statement & Publications:** Military operations research, particularly in command, control and communications; surveillance, intelligence and electronic warfare; human information processing and problem-solving; gaming simulation; military command and control. **Mailing Address:** Kapos Assocs Ltd, 1101 Wilson Blvd Ste 1900, Arlington, VA 22209-2276. **Fax:** 703-276-1264. **E-Mail:** ekapos@kapos.com

KAPP, JUDITH A, PATHOLOGY. **Education:** Miami Univ, Ohio, BA, 1965; Indiana Univ Med Sch, MS, 1969; Harvard Univ, PhD, 1976. **Professional Experience:** PROF, DEPT OPTHOL, WINSHIP CANCER INST, 2002-; staff, Winship Cancer Ctr, beginning 1993; mem, immunobiol study sect, Nat Inst Allergy & Infectious Dis, NIH, beginning 1988; mem comt fundamental res, Nat Multiple Sclerosis Soc, beginning 1988; cancer Preclin Prog Proj Rev Comt, Nat Cancer Inst, 1986-1988; depts Path, Microbiol & Immunol, Sch Med, Wash Univ, prof, 1984-1991; mem, Transplantation Biol & Immunol Comt, Nat Inst Allergy & Infectious Dis, NIH, 1980-1984; res career develop award, NIH, 1979-1984; assoc ed, J Immunol, 1979-1983; assoc staff, Jewish Hosp, St Louis, MO, 1976-1991; from asst prof to assoc prof, 1976-1984; assoc path-immunol, Harvard Med Sch, 1973-1976. **Memberships:** Sigma Xi; Am Asn Immunologists; Am Asn Pathologists. **Research Statement & Publications:** Immunology; microbiology; author or co-author of over 140 publications. **Mailing Address:** Dept Opthal, Winship Cancer Inst, Emory Univ, N E Bldg C, 1365 Clifton Rd, Atlanta, GA 30322. **Fax:** 404-778-2109. **E-Mail:** jkapp@emory.edu

KAPP, ROBERT WESLEY, TOXICOLOGY, GENETICS. **Personal Data:** b Point Pleasant, NJ, 1945; m 1967, c 3. **Education:** Syracuse Univ, AB, 1967; George Wash Univ, MS, 1974, PhD (genetic toxicol), 1979. **Professional Experience:** PRES, BIOTOX, as of 2004; pres, Robert Kapp assocs, beginning 1989; adj prof genetic toxicol, Med Br, Univ Tex, 1985-; adj prof genetic toxicol, Cancer Ctr, Med Br, Univ Tex, 1985-; bd sci counrs, Nat Toxicol Prog, Nat Inst Occup Safety & Health, 1982-; dir, Toxicol Lab, Exxon corp, 1982-1989; rev panel, Energy Health Sci, environ protection agency, 1981-; reviewer, Nat March Dimes, 1980-; consult, Dept Health & Human Servs, 1980-1982; mem, dominant lethal comt & sperm anal comt, genetic toxicol prog, environ protection agency, 1979-; consult, Genetic toxicol Ctr, 1979-; chmn, med toxicol comt, Am Soc Testing & Mat, 1979-; assoc dir, toxicol lab, exxon corp, 1979-1982; vis fac, cancer Ctr, Med Br, Univ Tex, 1978-; sr toxicologist, Hazleton Lab Am, Va, 1978-1979; staff scientist toxicol, hazleton lab Am, Va, 1973-1978; med technician med, Group Health Asn, Wash, DC, 1969-1973; head cytogenetics, Nat Naval Med Ctr, Md, 1969-1972. **Memberships:** NY Acad sci; Soc Toxicol; Am soc Testing & Mat; Am col toxicol; Sigma Xi; environ Mutagen soc. **Research Statement & Publications:** Development of clinical and nonclinical methodology to determine occupational carcinogenesis and mutagenesis; evaluation of general and genetic toxicological procedures for safety assessment; laboratory and research management. **Mailing Address:** BioTox, 1810 A York Rd, Ste 368, Lutherville, MD 21093-5165. **Fax:** 410-472-1723. **E-Mail:** biotox@comcast.net

KAPPAGODA, C TISSA, CARDIOLOGY, PHYSIOLOGY. **Education:** Univ Ceylon, MBBS, 1965, Univ Leeds, Eng, PhD (cardiovasc physiol), 1972. **Professional Experience:** PROF MED, UNIV CALIF, DAVIS, 1990-; prof med cardiol, Univ Alta, 1978-1990. **Memberships:** Physiol Soc Am; Physiol Soc Gt Brit; fel Am Col Cardiol; Am Heart Assn. **Research Statement & Publications:** reflex regulation ofthe circulatiai and exercin physiology. **Mailing Address:** Univ Calif, TB172 One Shields Ave, Davis, CA 95616. **Fax:** 530-752-3264. **E-Mail:** ctkappagoda@ucdavis.edu

KAPPAS, ATTALLAH, METABOLISM, PHARMACOLOGY. **Personal Data:** b Union City, NJ, November 4, 1926; m 1963, c 3. **Education:** Columbia Univ, AB, 1947; Univ Chicago, MD, 1950; Am Bd Internal Med, dipl, 1958. **Honorary Degrees:** DSc, NY Med Col, 1978. **Honors & Awards:** Spec Award Clin Pharmacol, Burroughs Wellcome Fund, 1973; Sir Henry Hallet Dale Mem Lectr, Med Sch, Johns Hopkins Univ, 1975; Pfizer Lectr, Peter Bent Brigham Hosp, Harvard Med Sch, 1977; Res Award, Am Soc Pharmacol & Exp Therapeut, 1978; Pfizer Lectr, Hershey Med Ctr, Pa State Univ, 1980; Glaxo Lectr, Cornell Univ Med Col, 1984. **Professional Experience:** PROF EMER, ROCKFELLER UNIV, as of 2004; PHYSICIAN-IN-CHIEF EMER, ROCKFELLER UNIV, as of 1999; adj prof, dept Pediat, Cornell Univ Med Col, 1998-; vis prof, dept Pediat, Univ Vt Col Med, 1993-; adj prof, dept Chem Biol, State Univ NJ, Rutgers, 1988-; Nicholson exchange fel, Karolinska inst, 1985; vpres, Rockfeller Univ, 1983-1991; SHERMAN FAIRCHILD PROF, ROCKFELLER UNIV, 1981-; vincent astor prof clin sci, mem Sloan-Kettering Cancer Ctr, Cornell Univ Med Col, 1979-1981; vis prof clin pharmacol, Med Sch, Johns Hopkins Univ, 1975; physician-in-chief, 1974-1991; prof, Cornell Univ Med Col, 1972-1987; sr physician, 1971-1974; assoc prof & physician, 1967-1971; John Simon Guggenheim Found fel & guest investr, Rockefeller Univ, 1966-1967; Commonwealth Fund fel, Courtauld inst, Middlesex Hosp Med Sch, London, Eng, 1961-1962; from asst prof to assoc prof, Sch Med, Univ Chicago, 1957-1967; assoc, Sloan-Kettering inst, 1956-1957; med resident, Peter Bent Brigham Hosp, 1954-1956; res fel, Sloan-Kettering inst, 1951-1954; Intern med, Univ Serv, Kings County Hosp, New York, 1950-1951. **Memberships:** Am Soc Clin Invest; Endocrine Soc; Harvey Soc; Asn Am Physicians; Am Clin & Climat Asn; Am Soc Pharmacol & Exp Therapeut; fel Am Col Physicians. **Research Statement & Publications:** Metabolic-genetic diseases; hormone biology; drug metabolism toxicology and disorders of porphyrin-heme metabolism. **Mailing Address:** Rockefeller Univ, 1230 York Ave, New York, NY 10021-6399. **E-Mail:** kappas@rockefeller.edu

KAPPE, DAVID SYME, PHYSICAL CHEMISTRY, RADIOCHEMISTRY. **Personal Data:** b Philadelphia, Pa, September 28, 1935; c 3. **Education:** Univ Md, Col Park, BS, 1959; Pa State Univ, PhD (phys chem), 1965. **Professional Experience:** CHMN & CHIEF EXEC OFFICER, KAPPE ASSOCS INC, 1986-; tech rev res proposals, USEPA, 1975; consult, Am Acad Environ Eng-Environ Protection Agency Manpower Training Proj, 1971; res dir, Kappe Assocs, Inc, 1967-1985; chief radiation appln sect, Hittman Assocs, Inc, 1966-1967; phys sci aid, metall div, Nat Bur Standards, 1958-1959; monitoring progs hazardous waste incinerators. **Memberships:** Am Chem Soc; Am Inst Physics; Am Water Works Asn; Water Pollution Control Fedn. **Research Statement & Publications:** Reclamation of spent nuclear reactor fuels; measurement of thermal neutron cross sections; development and application of radionuclide-phosphor self-luminescent light sources; treatment of domestic, industrial and agricultural waste-waters; sludge composting. **Mailing Address:** Kappe Assoc Inc, 100 Wormans Mill Ct, Frederick, MD 21701.

KAPPEL, ELLEN SUE, MARINE GEOLOGY, GEOPHYSICS. **Personal Data:** b Brooklyn, NY, October 22, 1959; m 1989, Stuart; c Daniel C & Emily J. **Education:** Cornell Univ, AB, 1980; Columbia Univ, MA, 1982, MPhil & PhD (geol), 1985. **Professional Experience:** EDITOR, GEOSCI PROF SERV INC, as of 2005; PROG DIR, US SCII SUPPORT PROG, 1988-; ASSOC DIR, OCEAN DRILLING PROG, JOINT OCEANOG INST INC, 1986-; postdoctoral assoc res scientist, Lamont-Doharty Earth Observ, Columbia Univ, 1985-1986; Chmn, Tellers Comt, Am Geophys Union. **Memberships:** Am Geophys Union; Geol Soc Am. **Research Statement & Publications:** Relationship between midocean ridge tectonics and hydrothermal mineralization. **Mailing Address:** Joint Oceanog Inst Inc, 5610 Gloster Rd, Bethesda, MD 20816. **E-Mail:** ekappel@geo-prose.com

KAPPENMAN, RUSSELL FRANCIS, STATISTICS. **Personal Data:** b Lennox, SDak, September 2, 1938; m 1964, c 4. **Education:** Univ SDak, BA, 1960; Univ Iowa, MS, 1962; State Univ NY Buffalo, PhD (statist), 1969. **Professional Experience:** MATH STATISTICIAN, NORTHWEST & ALASKA FISHERIES CTR, SEATTLE, 1976-; Asst prof statist, Pa State Univ, 1969-1976. **Memberships:** Am Statist Asn. **Research Statement & Publications:** Statistical inference. **Mailing Address:** Alaska Fisheries Sci Ctr, Nat Marine Fisheries Serv, 7600 Sand Point Way NE, Seattle, WA 98115-0070.

KAPPERS, LAWRENCE ALLEN, SOLID STATE PHYSICS. **Personal Data:** b Hingham, Wis, May 27, 1941; m 1963, Jean. **Education:** Cent Col, Iowa, BA, 1963; Univ Mo, Columbia, MS, 1966, PhD (physics), 1970. **Professional Experience:** PROF PHYSICS, UNIV CONN, 1993-; from asst prof to assoc prof, Univ Conn, 1973-1993; NSF res assoc, Okla State Univ, 1972-1973; air Force Off Sci res fel physics, Univ Minn, Minneapolis, 1970-1972. **Memberships:** Am Phys Soc. **Research Statement & Publications:** Electronic structure of defects in ionic crystals; optical absorption; luminescence and electron paramagnetic resonance; production and decay mechanisms of color centers, additive coloration and radiation damage; lasers; high pressure diamond anvil studies. **Mailing Address:** Dept Physics, Univ Conn, Rm P-418 U-3046 2152 Hillside Rd, Storrs, CT 06269-3046. **Fax:** 860-486-3346. **E-Mail:** kappers@uconnvm.uconn.edu

KAPPLER, JOHN W, IMMUNOLOGY, MICROBIOLOGY. **Education:** Lehigh Univ, BA, 1965; Brandeis Univ, PhD (biochem), 1970. **Honors & Awards:** Louisa Gross Horwitz Prize, Columbia Univ, 1994. **Professional Experience:** SR FAC MEM MED, NAT JEWISH CTR IMMUNOL & RESPIRATORY MED, as of 2002; INVESTR, HOWARD HUGHES MED INST, DENVER, 1986-; PROF MICROBIOL & IMMUNOL & MED, UNIV COLO HEALTH SCI CTR, DENVER, 1984-; from asst prof to assoc prof oncol, Dept Microbiol & Cancer Ctr, Unive Rochester, 1973-1979; res assoc, Univ Calif, San Diego, 1972-1973; res fel, Am Cancer Soc, Dept Biol, Univ Calif, San Diego, 1970-1972. **Memberships:** Am Cancer Soc. **Mailing Address:** Nat Jewish Med & Res Ctr, 1400 Jackson St, Denver, CO 80206. **Fax:** 303-398-1396. **E-Mail:** kappler@njc.org

KAPPMEYER, KEITH K, ADMINISTRATION. **Honors & Awards:** Albert Victor Bleininger Award, Am Ceramic Soc, 1992. **Professional Experience:** VPRES ENG & RES, USX CORP, PITTSBURGH, as of 2003. **Mailing Address:** USX Corp, 600 Grant St, Pittsburgh, PA 15219-2702.

KAPPUS, KARL DANIEL, MEDICAL ENTOMOLOGY, EPIDEMIOLOGY. **Personal Data:** b Cleveland, Ohio, July 2, 1938. **Education:** Ohio State Univ, BSc, 1960, MSc, 1962, PhD (entom), 1964. **Professional Experience:** EPIDEMIOLOGIST, CTR DIS CONTROL, 1976-; biologist, Nat Commun Dis Ctr, 1969-1976; res entomologist, Nat Commun Dis Ctr, 1967-1969; res assoc mosquito biol, Res Found, Ohio State Univ, 1966-1967; Nat Res Coun fel arborvirus infection, US Army Biol Labs, 1965-1966; res asst mosquito biol, Res Found, Ohio State Univ, 1961-1964. **Memberships:** Am Soc Trop Med & Hyg; Entom Soc Am; Sigma Xi. **Research Statement & Publications:** Animal photoperiodism; viral infection in arthropods; mosquito behavior; viral zoonoses; epidemiology of viral infections; human intestinal protozoa; disease eradication. **Mailing Address:** 216 Glendale, Decatur, GA 30030-1918. **E-Mail:** kkappus@uuca.org

KAPRAL, FRANK ALBERT, BACTERIAL HOST-PARASITE INTERACTIONS. **Personal Data:** b Philadelphia, Pa, March 12, 1928; m 1951, Marina; c Frederick, Gloria & Robert. **Education:** Philadelphia Col Pharm & Sci, BS, 1952; Univ Pa, PhD (med microbiol), 1956. **Professional Experience:** PROF EMER MED MICROBIOL, OHIO STATE UNIV, as of 2004; actg chmn dept, Ohio State Univ, 1973-1978; prof Med Microbiol, Ohio State Univ, beginning 1969; NIH grants, NIH training grant, 1968-1971; NIH grants, Ohio State Univ, 1967-; chief microbiol, Philadelphia Gen Hosp, 1965-1966; chief microbiol res, Philadelphia Gen Hosp, 1964-1966; asst chief microbiol res, Vet Admin Hosp, Philadelphia, 1962-1966; assoc microbiol, Philadelphia Gen Hosp, 1962-1964; assoc prof, Ohio State Univ, 1956-1969; from asst instr to assoc microbiol, Univ Pa, 1952-1956. **Memberships:** AAAS; Am Soc Microbiol; Am Asn Immunol; Infectious Dis Soc; Soc Exp Biol & Med; Am Acad Microbiol. **Research Statement & Publications:** Pathogenesis of staphylococcal infections; bacterial host-parasite interactions; bacterial toxins; lipids as immune mechanisms. **Mailing Address:** Dept Med Microbiol & Immunol, Ohio State Univ, 333 W Tenth Ave 2166A Graves Hall, Columbus, OH 43210-1239. **Fax:** 614-292-9805.

KAPRAL, RAYMOND EDWARD, THEORETICAL CHEMISTRY. **Personal Data:** b Swoyersville, Pa, March 21, 1942; m 1964, c 1. **Education:** King's Col, Pa, BS, 1964; Princeton Univ PhD (chem), 1967. **Honors & Awards:** Noranda Award, Chem Inst Can, 1981, Joh Potanyi Award, 1996. **Professional Experience:** PROF CHEM, UNIV TORONTO, as of 2003; Killian res fell Can Coun, 1994-1996; asst prof to assoc prof, Univ Toronto, 1969-1980; res assoc chem, Mass Inst Technol, 1968-1969; res assoc chem, Princeton Univ, 1967. **Memberships:** Fel Am Phys Soc; Chem Inst Can; fel Royal Soc Can. **Research Statement & Publications:** Statistical mechanics; quantum mechanics; chemical kinetics. **Mailing Address:** Dept Chem, Univ Toronto 80 St George St, Toronto, ON M5S 3H6, Can. **Fax:** 416-978-5325. **E-Mail:** rkapral@chem.utoronto.ca

KAPRAUN, DONALD FREDERICK, PHYCOLOGY. **Personal Data:** b Spring Valley, Ill, September 13, 1945; m 1975. **Education:** Eastern Ill Univ, BS, 1966; Univ Tex, PhD (bot), 1969. **Professional Experience:** PROF BIOL SCI, UNIV NC, WILMINGTON, as of 2002; assoc prof biol, Univ Nc, Wilmington, beginning 1977; assoc prof bot & phycol, Univ NC, Wilmington, 1971-1977; Asst prof bot, Univ Southwestern La, 1969-1971. **Memberships:** Phycol Soc Am; Int Phycol Soc; Brit Phycol Soc. **Research Statement & Publications:** Ecology and reproductive periodicity of benthic marine algae in North Carolina. **Mailing Address:** Dept Biol, Univ NC 601 S College Rd, Wilmington, NC 28403-3201. **E-Mail:** kapraund@uncwil.edu

KAPRIELIAN, E F, ELECTRICAL ENGINEERING. **Professional Experience:** RETIRED; staff mem, Pacific Gas & Elec. **Mailing Address:** 39 Elmwood Ct, Walnut Creek, CA 94596. **Fax:** 925-937-1521.

KAPRON, FELIX PAUL, FIBER OPTICS. **Personal Data:** b St Catharines, Ont, November 29, 1940; m 1971. **Education:** Univ Toronto, BASc, 1962; Univ Waterloo, MSc, 1963, PhD (physics), 1967. **Professional Experience:** AT CORNING INC, as of 2004; DIR, OPTICAL SYST TECH & FIBER OPTICS DEPT, BELLCOR, 1988-; staff scientist, Electro-Optical Prod Div, Int Tel & Tel, 1982-1987; lectr, Carleton Univ, 1976-1982; sr scientist & mgr, Bell-Northern Res, 1973-1982; physicist, Corning Glass Works, 1967-1972. **Memberships:** Optical Soc Am; Soc Photo-Optical Instrumentation Engrs; Can Asn Physicists; sr mem Inst Elec & Electronics Engrs. **Research Statement & Publications:** Optical communications and sensors; fiber-optical waveguides; optical devices properties of solids, particularly emitters, modulators, detectors and couplers. **Mailing Address:** Corning Inc, MP-HQ-W1-33 One Riverfront Plaza, Corning, NY 14831. **Fax:** 607-974-4941. **E-Mail:** kapronfp@corning.com

KAPSALIS, ANDREAS A, IMMUNODIAGNOSTIC ASSAYS. **Personal Data:** b Vitina, Arkadia, Greece, November 6, 1936; m Glenda; c Terri & Effie. **Education:** Univ Athens, Bacheloris, 1960; Univ Chicago, MS, 1964; Univ Ill, PhD (immunochem), 1974. **Professional Experience:** SR RES SCIENTIST DIAGNOSTICS, ABBOTT LABS, 1976-; immunologist cancer res, West Side Vet Admin Hosp, Univ Ill, 1974-1976; res assoc, Baxter Labs, 1968-1972; res assoc allergy res, Michael Reece Hosp, Chicago, 1965-1968; res asst, Chicago Col Osteop, 1964-1965. **Memberships:** AAAS; Am Chem Soc; Am Asn Clin Chem; NY Acad Sci. **Research Statement & Publications:** Development of immunodiagnostic assays for viral diseases and for therapeutic drug monitoring. **Mailing Address:** 1005 Hinman Ave, Evanston, IL 60202.

KAPSALIS, JOHN GEORGE, FOOD SCIENCE, BIOCHEMISTRY. **Personal Data:** b Mytilene, Greece, January 27, 1927; American citizen; m 1956, Athena; c Ellen & Gina. **Education:** Athens Col Agr, BS, MS, 1954; Univ Fla, MAgr, 1955; Tex A&M Univ, PhD (food sci), 1959. **Honors & Awards:** Sci Dir Silver Key Award Res, US Army Natick Lab, 1969. **Professional Experience:** CONSULT, 1987-; chief, Biochem Br, Sci & Advan Technol Lab, 1974-1987; Secy Army res & study fel, 1965-1966; chief, food biochem lab, 1963-1974; res chemist, Armed Forces Food & Container Inst, US Army Natick Res & Develop Labs, 1962-1963; food technologist, Armed Forces Food & Container Inst, US Army Natick Res & Develop Labs, 1960-1962; asst prof & fel dairy tech, Ohio State Univ,

1959-1960. **Memberships:** Am Chem Soc; Sigma Xi; fel Am Inst Chemists; NY Acad Sci. **Research Statement & Publications:** Quality parameters of dehydrated foods; effect of water vapor equilibrium on chemical and rheological properties of foods; nondestructive methods of measurement in foods; chemical and rheological properties of lipids. **Mailing Address:** 5776 Deauville Cir, Naples, FL 34112.

KAPUR, BHUSHAN M, TOXICOLOGY, CLINICAL BIOCHEMISTRY. **Personal Data:** b Amritsar, India, February 23, 1938; m 1968, c 2. **Education:** Bombay Univ, BSc, 1959; Univ Basel, PhD (org chem), 1967; ARIC, 1972, MRIC, 1976, FRSC, 1979, FACB, 1983, FCACB, 1989. **Professional Experience:** CONSULT, TOXICOL DIV CLIN PHARMACOL & TOXICOL, HOSP SICK CHILDREN, TORONTO, 1995-; asst prof, Dept Clin Biochem, Fac Med, Univ Toronto, beginning 1978; instr, Toronto Inst Med Technol, 1974-1979; lectr, Dept Clin Biochem, Fac Med, Univ Toronto, 1974 & 1976-1978; dir labs, clin inst, 1972-1995; sr chemist, Addiction Res Found, 1971-1972; fac pharm, Univ Toronto, 1968-1971; Res assoc, Univ Basel, 1967. **Memberships:** Soc Toxicol; The Chem Soc; Can Soc Clin Chem; Am Asn Clin Chem; Can Soc Sci; Soc Forensic Toxicol. **Research Statement & Publications:** Natural product chemistry; clinical biochemistry; toxicology; biochemical changes due to alcohol use. **Mailing Address:** Hosp Sick C, 555 Univ Ave, Toronto, ON M5G 1X8, Can. **E-Mail:** bkapur@sickkids.on.ca

KAPUR, KAILASH C, QUALITY & PRODUCTIVITY IMPROVEMENT, DESIGN OF EXPERIMENTS. **Personal Data:** b India, August 17, 1941; American citizen; m 1969, Geraldine Palmer; c Anjali J & Jay P. **Education:** Delhi Univ, India, BS, 1963; India Inst Technol, MTech, 1965; Univ Calif, Berkeley, MS, 1967, PhD (oper res & indust eng), 1969. **Honors & Awards:** Allan Chop Tech Advan Award, Am Soc Qual, 1987; Craig Award, Am Soc Qual, 1989. **Professional Experience:** PROF INDUST ENG, 1992-; dir & prof indust eng, Univ Wash, Seattle, 1992-1999; dir & prof teaching & res, Univ Okla, 1989-1992; prof, Wayne State Univ, 1980-1989; sr reliability engr res, Tank Automotive Command, 1978; vis assoc prof, Univ Waterloo, 1977-1978; assoc chmn, Wayne State Univ, 1975-1976; Vis scholar, Ford Motor Co, 1973; from asst prof to assoc prof teaching & res, Wayne State Univ, 1970-1980; Sr res engr res, Gen Motors Res Labs, 1969-1970. **Memberships:** fel Inst Indust Engrs; fel Am Soc Qual, mem, Am Soc for Eng Edu; fel Inst Indust Eng. **Research Statement & Publications:** Quality engineering; product and process design optimization; reliability engineering; design of experiments; author of various publications. **Mailing Address:** Indust Eng, Univ Wash, Box 352650, Seattle, WA 98195-2650. **Fax:** 206-685-3072. **E-Mail:** kkapur@u.washington.edu

KAPUR, SHAKTI PRAKASH, HUMAN ANATOMY, HISTOLOGY. **Personal Data:** b Ludhiana, Panjab, India, August 20, 1932; m 1966, c 2. **Education:** Panjab Univ, India, BSc, 1953, MSc, 1954; McGill Univ, PhD (zool), 1964. **Professional Experience:** ASSOC PROF ANAT, GEORGETOWN UNIV, 1978-; asst prof, Georgetown Univ, 1972-1978; res assoc, Georgetown Univ, 1971-1972; asst prof zool, Panjab Univ, India, 1966-1971; exp biologist, Ayerst Drug Res Labs, Can, 1964-1966; sr teaching asst zool, McGill Univ, 1961-1964; Lectr biol, Govt Col, Panjab, 1955-1961. **Memberships:** Sigma Xi; Am Asn Anatomists; Soc Exp Biol & Med; AAAS. **Research Statement & Publications:** Electron microscopy; histochemistry of thyroid-parathyroid; endocrine mechanisms controlling calcium homeostasis; calcification in biological systems; zinc homeostasis; immunocytochemistry; radioimmunoassay. **Mailing Address:** Dept Anat Georgetown Univ Sch Med, 3900 Reservoir Rd NW, Washington, DC 20007-2187.

KAPUSCINSKI, ANNE R, GENETICS. **Education:** Ore State Univ, BA, 1976, MS, 1980, PhD (fisheries), 1984. **Professional Experience:** PROF FISHERIES & CONSERV BIOL, UNIV MINN, as of 2005. **Memberships:** Dir Inst Social Econ & Ecol Sustainability. **Mailing Address:** Dept Fisheries & Wildlife Univ Minn, 1980 Folwell Ave 200 Hodson Hall, St Paul, MN 55108-1037. **Fax:** 612-624-7719. **E-Mail:** kapus001@umn.edu

KAPUSTA, GEORGE, AGRONOMY, WEED CONTROL. **Personal Data:** b Max, NDak, November 20, 1932; m 1958, c 4. **Education:** NDak State Univ, BS, 1954; Univ Minn, MS, 1957; Southern Ill Univ, PhD (bot), 1975. **Honors & Awards:** Outstanding Res & Exten Award, Land of Lincoln Soybean Asn, 1978. **Professional Experience:** PROF AGRON, SOUTHERN ILL UNIV, 1980-; assoc prof, Southern Ill Univ, 1964-1980; agronomist, NDak State Univ, 1958-1964. **Memberships:** Agron Soc Am; Soil Sci Soc Am; fel Weed Sci Soc Am; Sigma Xi. **Research Statement & Publications:** Weed control in field and forage crops; minimum and zero-tillage; culture, especially plant density and geometry, cultivars and growth regulators; nitrification inhibition; symbiotic nitrogen fixation. **Mailing Address:** Dept agron, Univ S Ill, 1274 W No Name Rd, Carbondale, IL 62901.

KAPUSTA, JOSEPH IRVING, HIGH ENERGY NUCLEAR PHYSICS. **Personal Data:** b Antigo, Wis, June 21, 1952. **Education:** Univ Wis, Madison, BA, 1974; Univ Calif, Berkeley, MA, 1976, PhD (physics), 1978. **Professional Experience:** Prog dir, Univ Calif, Santa Barbara, 1993; PROF PHYSICS, UNIV MINN, 1986-; from asst prof to assoc prof, Univ Minn, 1982-1986; NATO-NSF fel & sci assoc, Europ Ctr Nuclear Res, 1981-1982; Post doctoral res assoc, Los Alamos Nat Lab, 1979-1981; Post doctoral res assoc, Lawrence Berkeley Lab, 1978-1979. **Memberships:** AAAS; fel Am Phys Soc. **Research Statement & Publications:** Theoretical studies of the properties of high temperature and density of nuclear and subnuclear matter and its realization in high energy nuclear collisions, stars and the early universe. **Mailing Address:** Sch Phys & Aston Univ Minn, 116 Church St SE, Minneapolis, MN 55455. **Fax:** 612-624-4578. **E-Mail:** kapusta@physics.spa.umn.edu

KAR, NARESH J, MATERIALS SCIENCE. **Education:** Univ Calif, PhD. **Professional Experience:** VPRES & PROF ENG, KARS ADVAN MAT INC, CA, as of 2005. **Memberships:** Am Soc Metals. **Mailing Address:** Kars Advan Mat Inc, 2528 W Woodland Dr, Anaheim, CA 92801-2636. **Fax:** 714-527-7169. **E-Mail:** kars@karslab.com

KAR, RAMESH J, METALLURGY. **Education:** Univ Calif, PhD. **Professional Experience:** PRES, KARS ADVAN MAT INC, CA, as of 2005. **Memberships:** Am Soc Metals. **Mailing Address:** Kars Advan Mat Inc, 2528 W Woodland Dr, Anaheim, CA 92801-2636. **Fax:** 714-527-7169. **E-Mail:** kars@karslab.com

KARAALI, ORHAN, NEURAL NETWORKS, SPEECH PROCESSING SYSTEMS. **Personal Data:** b Istanbul, Turkey, October 3, 1960; American citizen. **Education:** Univ Wis, BS, 1982, MS, 1984; Fla Atlantic Univ, PhD (comput eng), 1989. **Professional Experience:** MANAGING PARTNER, ADVAN INVESTMENT PARTNERS, as of 2004; prin staff engr, Motorola Inc, beginning 1996-; sr staff engr, Motorola Inc, 1994-1996; staff engr, Motorola Inc, 1989-1994; res engr, Modcomp/AEG, 1988-1989; sr hardware engr, ATT-Paradyne Corp, 1984-1987; lectr micro processors, Univ Wis-Milwaukee, 1983-1984. **Memberships:** Sigma Xi. **Research Statement & Publications:** Neural network architectures and algorithms, neural network implementations and applications, microprocessor and digital signal processor architectures and applications; developing neural network technologies for speech synthesis. **Mailing Address:** Advan Investment Partners, 311 Park Pl Blvd Ste 250, Clearwater, FL 33759. **Fax:** 727-799-1232.

KARABALIS, DIMITRIS L, STRUCTURAL ENGINEERING. **Professional Experience:** ASST PROF, DEPT CIVIL ENG, UNIV SC, as of 2005. **Memberships:** Am Soc Civil Eng. **Mailing Address:** Univ SC, Dept Civil Eng, Columbia, SC 29208. **Fax:** 803-777-0670.

KARABATSOS, GERASIMOS J, ORGANIC CHEMISTRY. **Personal Data:** b Chomatada, Greece, May 17, 1932; American citizen; m 1956, c 4. **Education:** Adelphi Col, AB, 1954; Harvard Univ, PhD (org chem), 1959. **Honors & Awards:** Petrol Chem Award, Am Chem Soc, 1971. **Professional Experience:** PROF EMER CHEM, MICH STATE UNIV, as of 2003; Chmn dept, Mich State Univ, 1975-1986; sci dir, Greek Atomic Energy Comn, 1974-1975; prof chem, mich state univ, beginning 1966; NSF sr fel, 1965-1966; Sloan Found res fel, 1963-1966; From asst prof to assoc prof, Mich State Univ, 1959-1966. **Memberships:** Am Chem Soc; corresp mem Acad Athens; The Chem Soc. **Research Statement & Publications:** Carbonium ions; nuclear magnetic resonance spectroscopy; isotope effects; stereochemistry of enzymatic reactions. **Mailing Address:** Dept Chem, Mich State Univ, East Lansing, MI 48823.

KARACAN, ISMET, SLEEP DISORDERS. **Personal Data:** b Istanbul, Turkey, July 23, 1927; m 1962, c 5. **Education:** Univ Istanbul, BS, 1948, MD, 1953; State Univ NY Downstate Med Ctr, DSc(med), 1965; Turkish Bd Neuropsychiat, 1960; Am Bd Psychiat & Neurol cert psychiat, 1963. **Honors & Awards:** Nathaniel Kleitman Prize, Asn Sleep Dis Ctrs, 1981. **Professional Experience:** DIR, SLEEP DISORDERS CTR, BAYLOR COL MED, as of 1991; PROF PSYCHIAT & DIR, SLEEP DISORDER & RES CTR, BAYLOR COL MED, TEX MED CTR, HOUSTON, 1973-; ASSOC CHIEF STAFF, RES & DEVELOP & DIR, SLEEP RES LAB, VET ADMIN MED CTR, HOUSTON, 1973-; from assoc prof to prof psychiat & dir, Sleep Labs, Univ Fla, Gainville, 1966-1973. **Memberships:** Fel Am Psychiat Asn; AMA; AAAS; fel Am Col Physicians; Sleep Res Soc (pres 1976-1979); NY Acad Sci; Am Col Neuropsychopharmacol; Brit Asn Psychopharmacol. **Research Statement & Publications:** Psychological and physiological mechanisms of male impotence; neurophysiological and biochemical mechanisms responsible for male erectile failure; pharmacology of human sleep. **Mailing Address:** Sleep Dis Ctr, Va Med Ctr, Baylor Col Med, One Baylor Plaza, Houston, TX 77030.

KARADBIL, LEON NATHAN, resource management; deceased, see previous edition for last biography

KARADI, GABOR M, CIVIL ENGINEERING. **Personal Data:** b Budapest, Hungary, September 12, 1924; m 1951, c 2. **Education:** Tech Univ Budapest, BSc, 1950, MSc, 1954, PhD (civil eng), 1960; Hungarian Acad Sci, DSc(hydraul), 1964. **Professional Experience:** PROF EMER, DEPT CIVIL ENG, UNIV WIS, MILWAUKEE, as of 2006; prof & chmn, Dept Civil Eng, Univ Wis, Milwaukee, as of 2004; prof eng mech, Univ Wis-milwaukee, 1969-1977; mem US comn, Int Comn Irrig & Drainage, 1968; assoc prof, Univ Wis-milwaukee, 1967-1969; inst chem eng, Budapest, Hungary, 1961-1963 & Northwestern Univ, Evanston, 1967-1968; vis assoc prof, Northwestern Univ, Evanston, 1966-1967; sr lectr, Univ Khartoum, 1965-1966; lectr civil eng, Univ Khartoum, 1963-1964; chief develop engr, Water Resources Co, 1960-1963; consult, Agr Res Inst, 1960-1963; sr engr, Water Resources Co, 1959-1960; sr engr, Inst Hwy Eng, 1958-1959; sr engr, Inst Water Resources Eng, Budapest, 1954-1958; asst hydraul engr, hungarian dept hydraul eng, 1950-1951. **Memberships:** Am Soc Civil Engrs; Am Water Resources Asn. **Research Statement & Publications:** Hydrodynamics of groundwater flow; watershed hydrology; urban hydrology. **Mailing Address:** Dept Civil Eng, Univ Wis, Rm 387 PO Box 784, Milwaukee, WI 53202. **E-Mail:** karadi@uwm.edu

KARADY, GEORGE GYORGY, POWER ELECTRONICS, TRANSMISSION & DISTRIBUTION. **Personal Data:** b Budapest, Hungary, August 17, 1930; American citizen. **Education:** Tech Univ Budapest, Dipl Eng, 1952, Dr Eng, 1960. **Honorary Degrees:** Dr, Tech Univ Budapest, Hungary, 1996. **Honors & Awards:** T&D Comt Outstanding Working Group Chmn Award, 1988; Working Group Recognition Award, Inst Elec & Electronics Engrs Power Eng Soc, 1993. **Professional Experience:** Srp chair prof, Ariz State Univ, 1986-1993; secy treas, US Nat Comt, CIGRE, 1985-1993; mgr elec systs, Ebasco Serv Inc, 1984-1986; chief engr comput technol, Ariz State Univ, 1982-1984; vpres, US Nat Comt, CIGRE, 1981-1985; chief elec consult engr, Ariz State Univ, 1979-1982; adj prof, Polytech Inst Brooklyn, 1978-1986; dir energy conversion & sr consult engr, Ariz State Univ, 1977-1978; adj prof, Univ Montreal, 1971-1977 & McGill Univ, 1972-1977; prog mgr res, Hydro Que Inst Res, Montreal, Can, 1969-1977; lectr, Univ Salford, 1968-1969; vis prof, Univ Iraq, Baghdad, 1966-1968; exec bd, Hungarian Elec Asn, 1965-1966; consult power syst anal, Elec Bd, Budapest, 1963-1966; vchmn, Hungarian Elec Asn, 1963-1965; dep secy, Hungarian Elec Asn, 1961-1962; consult, high voltage res, Inst Elec Energy Res, Budapest, 1958-1963; assoc prof elec eng, Tech Univ Budapest, 1952-1968. **Memberships:** Fel Inst Elec & Electronics Engrs; Conf Int Grandes Reseaux Electriques; Soc Aerospace Engrs; Natural Sci & Eng Res Coun Can. **Research Statement & Publications:** Power electronics, high voltage technic, insulation pollution and special insulators; high voltage thyristor valves and high voltage direct current technology; rectifier and inverter systems; pulsed power supplies. **Mailing Address:** Elec Eng Dept, Ariz State Univ, Tempe, AZ 85287-5706. **Fax:** 480-965-0745. **E-Mail:** karady@asu.edu

KARADY, SANDOR, ORGANIC CHEMISTRY. **Personal Data:** b Budapest, Hungary, August 18, 1933; American citizen; m 1963, c Jennifer & Oudine. **Education:** Eotvos Lorand Univ, Lorand, Budapest, BSc, 1956; Mass Inst Technol, PhD (org chem), 1963. **Honors & Awards:** Thomas Alva Edison Patent Award, 1985. **Professional Experience:** SR RES FEL, RES LABS, MERCK & CO, 1983-; res fel, Merck & Co, 1978-1983; sr chemist, Merck & Co, 1975-1978; SR INVESTR, RES LABS, MERCK & CO, 1966-; res chemist, Merck & Co, 1966-1975; Inst Org Chem, Gif sur Yvette, France, 1964-1965; NIH fel, Mass Inst Technol, 1963-1964; chemist, Merck & Co, 1957-1959; Chemist, Pharmaceut Res Labs, Budapest, Hungary, 1955-1956. **Memberships:** Am Chem Soc. **Research Statement & Publications:** Synthetic organic chemistry; natural products; pharmaceuticals; cephalosporin chemistry; heterocycles; synthetic electrochemistry; thienamycins. **Mailing Address:** 348 Longview Dr, Mtainside, NJ 07092-2005. **E-Mail:** sandor_karady@merc.com

KARAFIN, LESTER, UROLOGY. **Personal Data:** b Philadelphia, Pa, September 26, 1926; m 1950, c 3. **Education:** Temple Univ, MD, 1949, MSc, 1956. **Professional Experience:** PHYSICIAN, TEMPLE UNIV HOSP, as of 2004; PROF UROL, MED COL PA, 1964-; consult, Vet Admin Hosp, Philadelphia, 1964-; prof, Med Ctr, Temple Univ. **Memberships:** AMA; Am Urol Asn. **Research Statement & Publications:** General urology. **Mailing Address:** Dept Urol, Temple Univ Hosp, 3401 N Broad St, Philadelphia, PA 19140. **E-Mail:** lkarafin@astro.temple.edu

KARAGIANES, MANUEL TOM, toxicology experimental surgery, biomaterial; deceased, see previous edition for last biography

KARAGOZIAN, ANN RENEE, GASEOUS JETS. **Education:** Univ Calif, BS, 1978; Calif Inst Technol, MS, 1979, PhD (mech eng), 1982. **Professional Experience:** Assoc ed, J Propulsion & Power, beginning 1996; mem, Defense Sci Study Group, 1994-1996; PROF ENG & APPL SCI, DEPT MECH & AEROSPACE ENG, UNIV CALIF, LOS ANGELES, 1993-; mem, Panel on Molten Salt Oxidation, Dept Energy, 1991; from asst prof to assoc prof, Dept Mech & Aerospace Eng, Univ Calif, Los Angeles, 1982-1993; consult, Rand Corp & Pac-Sierra Res Corp; mem tech staff, Aerospace Corp & Hughes Aircraft Co. **Memberships:** Assoc fel Am Inst Aeronaut & Astronaut. **Research Statement & Publications:** Effects of heat release on diffusion flame-vortex pair interactions; gaseous jet in supersonic crossflow. **Mailing Address:** Dept Mech & Aerospace Eng, Univ Calif, 46-147K Eng IV PO Box 951597, Los Angeles, CA 90095-1597. **Fax:** 310-206-4830. **E-Mail:** ark@seas.ucla.edu

KARAKASH, JOHN J, ELECTRICAL ENGINEERING. **Personal Data:** b Istanbul, Turkey, June 14, 1914; American citizen; m 1945, c 1. **Education:** Duke Univ, BS, 1937; Univ Pa, MS, 1938. **Honorary Degrees:** DEng, Lehigh Univ, 1971. **Honors & Awards:** Noble Robinson Award, Lehigh Univ, 1948, Hillman Award, 1963 & 1980; Distinguished Engr Award, Nat Soc Prof Engrs, 1965; Centennial Award, Inst Elec & Electronics Engrs, 1984. **Professional Experience:** DEAN EMER, COL ENG & APPL SCI, 1981-; DISTINGUISHED PROF EMER ELEC & COMPUT ENG, LEHIGH UNIV, 1981-; resident consult, Int Bus Mach, 1980-; consult, Dept Educ, Commonwealth PR, 1972-1976 & Gen State Authority, Commonwealth Pa, 1974-1977; dean eng, Lehigh Univ, 1966-1981; distinguished prof elec eng, Lehigh Univ, 1962-1981; head dept, Lehigh Univ, 1955-1968; proj dir, Signal Corps, 1954-1961; Consult, Bell Tel Labs, NY, 1950-1955; proj engr, Signal Corps, 1950-1954; from asst prof to prof elec eng, Lehigh Univ, 1946-1962; instr & proj engr, Moore Sch Elec Eng, Univ Pa, 1944-1946; ed dir, 6th Serv Comn, Signal Corps Radar Sch, 1942-1944; with Am TV Inc, Ill, 1940-1942; Instr, Univ Pa, 1938-1940; mem, Nat Accreditation Coun Eng Cols; mem hon adv bd, Pergamon Inst. **Memberships:** Fel Inst Elec & Electronics Engrs. **Research Statement & Publications:** Electrical networks; microwaves; transmission line theory; filter networks. **Mailing Address:** Col Eng & Appl Sci, Lehigh Univ, Bldg 19, Bethlehem, PA 18015.

KARAKASHIAN, ARAM SIMON, SOLID STATE PHYSICS, OPTICAL DEVICES. **Personal Data:** b Philadelphia, Pa, November 16, 1939; m 1975, Barbara; c John & Elizabeth. **Education:** Temple Univ, BA, 1961, MA, 1963; Univ Md, PhD (physics), 1970. **Professional Experience:** CO-DIR, PHOTONICS & OPTICAL ELECTRONICS DEVICE FABRICATION CTR, 1996-; ASST CHAIR, DEPT PHYSICS & APPL PHYSICS, UNIV MASS, LOWELL, 1993-; chmn, New Eng Sect, Am Phys Soc, 1993-1994; chmn, Dept Physics & Appl Physics, Univ Mass, Lowell, 1987-1993; PROF PHYSICS, DEPT PHYSICS & APPL PHYSICS, UNIV MASS, LOWELL, 1982-; from asst prof to assoc prof, Dept Physics & Appl Physics, Univ Mass, Lowell, 1970-1982. **Memberships:** Am Phys Soc; Sigma Xi; Mat Res Soc. **Research Statement & Publications:** Optical properties of metals and semiconductors; surface plasma oscillations; photonic and optoelectronic devices. **Mailing Address:** Dept Physics & Appl Physics, Univ Mass Lowell, Lowell, MA 01854. **Fax:** 978-934-3068. **E-Mail:** aram_karakashian@uml.edu

KARAL, FRANK CHARLES, JR, APPLIED MATHEMATICS. **Personal Data:** b Philadelphia, Pa, August 3, 1926. **Education:** Univ Colo, BS, 1946; Univ Tex, Austin, PhD (physics), 1950. **Professional Experience:** UNDERGRAD CHMN DEPT, 1985-; prof math NY Univ, 1971-; from asst prof to assoc prof, Courant Inst Math Sci, 1961-1970; assoc res scientist, Courant Inst Math Sci, 1959-1961; post doctoral fel (math), NY Univ, 1957-1959; sr res technologist, Mobil Oil Corp, 1952-1957; res physicist, Defense Res Lab, 1951-1952; res engr, Hughes Aircraft Co, 1950-1951; Res physicist, Defense Res Lab, 1949-1950; Geophys consult. **Memberships:** Am Math Soc; Am Phys Soc; Am Geophys Union. **Research Statement & Publications:** Geophysics; electromagnetic theory; computer assisted instruction. **Mailing Address:** Buckner Village No 10-B, 7111 Alabama St, El Paso, TX 79904-3905.

KARALIS, JOHN PETER, COMPUTER SCIENCES. **Personal Data:** b Minneapolis, Minn, July 6, 1938; m 1963, Mary; c Amy Curtis & Theodore Curtis. **Education:** Univ Minn, BA, 1960, JD, 1963. **Professional Experience:** Secy, Tektronix Inc, as of 1997; sr vpres corp develop, Tektronix Inc, 1992-1998; adj prof, Ctr Study Law, Sci & Technol, Ariz State Univ Col Law, Tempe, 1990-1991; off coun, Brown & Bain, 1989-1992; vpres & gen coun, Apple Computer Inc, 1987-1989; sr vpres & gen coun, Sperry Corp, 1985-1987; mem bd adv, Ctr Study Law, Sci & Technol, Ariz State Univ Col Law, Tempe, 1983-; vpres, Honeywell Inc, 1982-1983; assoc gen coun, Honeywell Inc, 1970-1983; Pvt pract, Minneapolis, 1963-1970 & 1983-1985; Bd dirs, Sony, Tektronix Corp. **Mailing Address:** Tektronix, Inc, 14200 SW Karl Braun Dri, Beaverton, OR 97077. **Fax:** 503-682-3408.

KARAM, JIM DANIEL, MOLECULAR GENETICS, BIOCHEMISTRY. **Personal Data:** b Kumasi, Ghana, 1938. **Education:** Am Univ Beirut, BS, 1958; Univ NC, PhD (biochem), 1965. **Professional Experience:** PROF & CHMN BIOCHEM, TULANE UNIV, 1991-; USPHS res career develop award, 1974-; from assoc prof to prof biochem, Med Univ SC, 1971-1991; res assoc, Sloan-Kettering Inst Cancer Res, 1968-1971; res asst prof, genetics & cell biol sect, Univ Conn, 1967-1968; USPHS fel, Cold Spring Harbor Lab Quant Biol, 1965-1967; res asst biochem, Am Univ Beirut, 1959-1960. **Memberships:** Genetics Soc Am; Am Soc Biol Chemists; Am Soc Microbiol. **Research Statement & Publications:** Genetic control of DNA replication of phage T4. **Mailing Address:** Dept Biochem, Tulane Univ, 1430 Tulane Ave, Box SL-43, New Orleans, LA 70112. **Fax:** 504-584-1611. **E-Mail:** karamoff@tulane.edu

KARAM, RATIB A(BRAHAM), NUCLEAR ENGINEERING, MATHEMATICS. **Personal Data:** b Miniara, Lebanon, March 8, 1934; American citizen; m 1960, c 1. **Education:** Univ Fla, BS, 1958, MS, 1959, PhD (nuclear eng), 1963. **Professional Experience:** Prof nuclear eng, Ga Inst Technol, beginning 1972; assoc nuclear eng, Argonne Nat Lab, 1967-1972; asst nuclear engr, Argonne Nat Lab, 1963-1967; Res asst nuclear field, Fla, 1958-1963. **Memberships:** Am Nuclear Soc; Am Phys Soc. **Research Statement & Publications:** Fast reactor physics; neutron transport; alternate fuel cycles; new breeder concepts and heterogeneity effects. **Mailing Address:** Sch Mech Eng, Ga Inst Technol, Atlanta, GA 30332-0405. **Fax:** 404-894-3620. **E-Mail:** ratib.karam@nnrc.gatech.edu

KARAS, JAMES GLYNN, HORTICULTURE, BIOLOGY. **Personal Data:** b Chicago, Ill, February 24, 1933. **Education:** Univ Ill, BS, 1956; Mich State Univ, MS, 1958, PhD (hort, bot), 1962. **Professional Experience:** PROF EMER BIOL SCI, YOUNGSTOWN STATE UNIV, as of 2003; assoc prof biol Sci, Youngstown State Univ, beginning 1969; asst prof hort, NMex State Univ, 1967-1969; asst prof natural sci, hort & bot, 1964-1967; res assoc biochem, hort & bot, 1962-1964; teaching asst hort, Mich State Univ, 1956-1961. **Memberships:** Am Soc Hort Sci; Am Inst Biol Sci. **Research Statement & Publications:** Plant physiology; grauperceptions in plants; natural products; electron microscopy; plant nutrition; seed germination. **Mailing Address:** Dept Biol Sci, Youngstown State Univ, One Univ Plaza, Youngstown, OH 44555. **Fax:** 330-941-1483.

KARASAKI, SHUICHI, DEVELOPMENTAL BIOLOGY, ARTHRITIS. **Personal Data:** b Kure, Japan, November 27, 1931; m 1961, Taeko Yamamoto; c Taro. **Education:** Nagoya Univ, Japan, BSc, 1954, MSc, 1956, PhD (biol), 1959. **Professional Experience:** MEM STAFF, KORIYAMA INST MED IMMUNOL, JAPAN, 1984-; Dept Pathol, Chiba Cancer Ctr, Res Inst, Japan, 1979-1984; res assoc, Nat Cancer Inst Can, 1970-1979; From assoc prof to prof anat, Univ Montreal, 1968-1979; mem staff, Montreal Cancer Inst, Notre Dame Hosp, 1965-1979; staff mem, Putnam Mem Hosp Inst Med Res, Bennington, Vt, 1965; vis investr, Biol Div, Oak Ridge Nat Lab, Tenn, 1961-1965; Asst prof chem, Col Gen Educ, Nagoya Univ, 1959-1961. **Memberships:** Soc Develop Biol; Am Soc Cell Biol; Am Asn Cancer Res; Int Soc Differentiation; NY Acad Sci; AAAS; Histochem Soc; Micros Soc Am. **Research Statement & Publications:** Immunocytochemistry of human tissue cells in culture; cell biology of arthritis; cancer. **Mailing Address:** Koriyama Inst Med Immunol, 2-11-1 Zukei, Koriyama 963, Japan.

KARASEK, FRANCIS WARREN, ANALYTICAL CHEMISTRY. **Personal Data:** b Council Bluffs, Iowa, December 11, 1919; m 1942, c 7. **Education:** Elmhurst Col, BS, 1942; Ore State Col, PhD (chem), 1952. **Professional Experience:** PROF EMER CHEM, UNIV WATERLOO, as of 2003; prof chem, Univ Waterloo, beginning 1968; mgr instrument develop, Phillips Petrol Co, 1951-1968; sr chemist, Res & Develop Labs, Pure Oil Co, 1942-1948. **Memberships:** Am Chem Soc; Am Soc Mass Spectrometry. **Research Statement & Publications:** Mass spectroscopy; chromatography; analytical instrumentation; ion mobility spectrometry; environmental sciences. **Mailing Address:** Dept Chem, Univ Waterloo, 26209 S Nottingham Dr, Sun Lakes, AZ 85248-9287.

KARASEK, MARVIN A, BIOCHEMISTRY. **Personal Data:** b Chicago, Ill, March 8, 1931. **Education:** Purdue Univ, BS, 1953; Univ Calif, PhD (biochem), 1956. **Professional Experience:** EMER PROF BIOCHEM DERMAT, SCH MED, STANFORD UNIV, 1986-; assoc prof biochem & res dermat, Sch Med, Stanford Univ, 1968-1985; asst prof, Sch Med, Stanford Univ, 1960-1968; Boston Med Found fel, 1958-1961; asst prof biochem, Tufts Univ, 1957-1960. **Memberships:** AAAS; Soc Invest Dermat; Soc Cell Biol. **Research Statement & Publications:** Protein synthesis; nucleotide metabolism; biochemistry of virus infections; blood vessel metabolism; sebaceous gland metabolism. **Mailing Address:** CCSR 269 Campus Dr Rm 2115a, Stanford, CA 94305-5486. **Fax:** 650-723-8762. **E-Mail:** marvek@stanford.edu

KARASZ, FRANK ERWIN, POLYMER SCIENCE, BIOPHYSICAL CHEMISTRY. **Personal Data:** b Vienna, Austria, July 23, 1933; American citizen; m Ljiljana; c 2. **Education:** Univ London, BS, 1954, DSC, 1972; Univ Wash, PhD (phys chem), 1958. **Honors & Awards:** Mettler Award, NAm Thermal Anal Soc, 1975; High Polymer Physics Prize, Am Phys Soc, 1984; H F Mark Medal, Austrian Res Inst, 2002. **Professional Experience:** SILVIO O CONTE PROF, POLYMER SCI & ENG, UNIV MASS, AMHERST, 1992-; co-dir Mat Res Lab, Univ Mass, 1973-1985; from assoc prof to prof polymer sci & eng, Univ Mass, 1967-1986; res chemist, Gen Elec Co, 1961-1967; sr res fel, Basic Physics Div, Nat Phys Lab, Eng, 1959-1961; fel, Univ Ore, 1958-1959; adj prof, Mat Sci Eng Dept, Univ Fla. **Memberships:** Nat Acad Eng; Am Phys Soc; Am Chem Soc; Nat Acads India, Croatia & Serbia. **Research Statement & Publications:** Physical chemistry of polymers; thermodynamics and statistical thermodynamics of liquids; biological macromolecules. **Mailing Address:** Dept Polymer Sci & Eng, Univ Mass, Conte Res Ctr, 120 Governers Dr, Amherst, MA 01003. **Fax:** 413-253-5295. **E-Mail:** fekarasz@polysci.umass.edu

KARATHANASIS, A D, SOIL SCIENCE. **Education:** Univ Thessaloniki, Greece, BS, 1969; Univ Nebr-Lincoln, MS, 1978; Auburn Univ, PhD, 1982. **Honors & Awards:** Nat Honor Award, Soil & Water Conserv Soc Am, 1991. **Professional Experience:** PROF SOIL MORPHOL, DEPT AGRON, UNIV KY, 1983-. **Memberships:** Am Soc Agron; Soil Sci Soc Am; Sigma Xi Sci Res Soc. **Research Statement & Publications:** Acid-mine drainage quality and the use of constructed wetlands for treating various wastewater effluents; published Over 100 Articles. **Mailing Address:** Dept Agron, Univ Ky, N-122K Ag Sci N, Lexington, KY 40546-0091. **Fax:** 606-257-2185. **E-Mail:** akaratha@ca.uky.edu

KARATZAS, IOANNIS, STOCHASTIC PROCESSES & CONTROL. **Personal Data:** b Kallithea, Greece, May 29, 1952; m 1975. **Education:** Nat Tech Univ Athens, dipl, 1975; Columbia Univ, MSc, 1976, PhD (math statist), 1980. **Professional Experience:** EUGENE HIGGINS PROF, MATH STATIST, COLUMBIA UNIV, as of 2004; vis scientist, MIT, 1984-1985; assoc prof, math statist, columbia univ, beginning 1983; asst prof, Columbia Univ, 1980-1983; vis asst prof, appl math, Brown Univ, 1979-1980. **Memberships:** Sigma Xi; Inst Math Statist; Inst Elec & Electronics Engrs. **Research Statement & Publications:** Probability and Mathematical Statistics, Random Processes, Stochastic Analysis, Optimization, Mathematical Economics and Finance; Published over 15 articles. **Mailing Address:** Dept Math, Columbia Univ, 2990 Broadway Mailcode 4438, New York, NY 10027. **Fax:** 212-663-2454. **E-Mail:** ik@shire.math.columbia.edu

KARAVIFI, LEFKOTHEA P, PEDIATRIC ENDOCRINOLOGY. **Personal Data:** b Greece, August 1, 1953; American citizen; m 1990, Kimon; c Alexei, Philip, Nicholas & Eleui. **Education:** Nat Univ Athens, MD, 1977; Univ Calif, Los Angeles, PhD, (neurol/anat), 1986. **Professional Experience:** HEAD PEDIATRICIAN, TEX CLIN UNIV HOSP, 1991-; ASST PROF PEDIAT, BAYLOR COL MED, 1991-. **Research Statement & Publications:** Hormone influences for brain development and sexual disfunction. **Mailing Address:** Tex Childrens Hosp6621 Fabbin, Houston, TX 77030.

KARCHER, GUIDO GEORGE, CODES & STANDARDS FOR PRESSURE EQUIPMENT, PRESSURE VESSEL TANKAGE & PIPING DESIGN. **Personal Data:** b Brooklyn, NY, October 20, 1934; m 1961, Patricia A Ennis; c Carol A, Maureen P & Richard T. **Education:** Pratt Inst, BME, 1960; Rensselaer Polytech Inst, MSME, 1964. **Honors & Awards:** J Hall Taylor Medal, Am Soc Mech Engrs, 1995. **Professional Experience:** CONSULT ENGR, 1994-; chmn, Pressure Vessel Res Coun, 1994-; vchmn, Boiler & Pressure Vessel Main Comt, Am Soc Mech Engrs, 1992-; eng adv, Exxon Res & Eng Co, 1989-1994; Chmn, Comt Pressure Vessels & Tanks, Am Petrol Inst, 1982-1988; sr eng assoc, Exxon Res & Eng Co, 1980-1989; eng assoc, Exxon Res & Eng Co, 1975-1980; Sr engr, Exxon Res & Eng Co, 1966-1975. **Memberships:** Am Petrol Inst; fel Am Soc Mech Engrs; Am Welding Soc. **Research Statement & Publications:** Developed several unique designs for heavy wall pressure vessels, high temperature valves and storage tanks; developed design criteria for steels in the creep range and the design of thin wall expansion joints. **Mailing Address:** 38 N Boom Way, Tuckerton, NJ 08087. **Fax:** 609-294-2686. **E-Mail:** ggkaacher@aol.com

KARCHER, RAYMOND, ANALYTICAL INSTRUMENTATION FOR THE CLINICAL LABORATORY, PROCESS AUTOMATION. **Personal Data:** b Corpus Christi, Tex, December 31, 1943. **Education:** John Carroll Univ, BS, 1965; Purdue Univ, PhD (anal chem), 1971. **Professional Experience:** DIR, CLIN LAB, WILLIAM BEAUMONT HOSP, as of 2003; Adj assoc prof, Clin Lab Instrumentation, Oakland Univ, 1990-; inspector, Lab Improvement Prog, Col Am Pathol, 1980-; Adj asst prof electronics, Wayne State Univ, 1971-1986; CLIN CHEMIST, WILLIAM BEAUMONT HOSP, 1970-. **Memberships:** Am

Asn Clin Chem; Am Chem Soc; Am Soc Clin Pathologists; Clin Lab Mgt Asn. **Research Statement & Publications:** Techniques for separation of isoenzymes using electrophoretic or chromatographic methods and in automating laboratory processes for high volume testing. **Mailing Address:** Dept Clin Path, William Beaumont Hosp, 3601 W Thirteen Mile Rd, Royal Oak, MI 48073-6769. **Fax:** 248-551-3694. **E-Mail:** rkascher@smtpgw.beaumont.edu

KARCHMER, JEAN HERSCHEL, ANALYTICAL CHEMISTRY. **Personal Data:** b Dallas, Tex, December 28, 1914; m 1939, c 2. **Education:** Southern Methodist Univ, BS, 1936. **Professional Experience:** RETIRED; consult chemist, beginning 1984; consult anal chem, Exxon Res & Eng Co, 1978-1984; res assoc, Humble Oil & Refining Co, 1963-1977; res specialist, Humble Oil & Refining Co, 1955-1963; sr res chemist, Humble Oil & Refining Co, 1950-1955; sr analyst & res chemist, Humble Oil & Refining Co, 1944-1950; asst chemist, Tenn Valley Authority, Ala, 1942-1944; chief chemist, Nat Chemsearch Co, 1939-1942; jr engr, Dept Agr, Tex, 1938. **Memberships:** Am Chem Soc. **Research Statement & Publications:** Analytical chemistry of sulfur compounds; analysis of petroleum, coal, polymers; elemental analysis; polarography. **Mailing Address:** 2929 Post Oak Blvd, Apt 1201, Houston, TX 77056.

KARCZMAR, ALEXANDER GEORGE, PHARMACOLOGY, PHYSIOLOGY. **Personal Data:** b Warsaw, Poland, May 9, 1918; American citizen; m 1946, c 2. **Education:** Warsaw & Free Polish Univ, MD, 1939; Columbia Univ, MA, 1941, PhD (biophysics, embryol), 1946. **Honors & Awards:** Sixth Ann Carl F Schnidt Hon Lectr, Philadelphia, 1981; Otto Loewi Lectr, Ix Int Symp on Cholinergic Syst, Ger, 1995. **Professional Experience:** BD MEM, CHICAGO ASN RES & EDUC SCI, as of 2006; health specialist, Hines Vet Admin Hosp, Ill, 1996-; co-dir res initiative, Am Vets Reactivation Ctr, Ill, 1996-; actg med dir, Found 41, Australia, 1988-1989; sr Fulbright scholar, 1987-1988; PROF EMER PHARMACOL, LOYOLA UNIV, 1986-; inst Biol Sci, Nat Acad Sci, 1985- & Off Surgeon Gen, 1987-; alzheimer dis study sect, 1983; assoc dean res, grad sch traing, 1982-1986; assoc dean, grad sch traing, 1981-1986; toxicol comt, Nat Acad Sci, 1981; hon prof, Kurume Univ, 1980-; consult, US Army Res Develop Co, 1980-; US Defense Off 1980-1985; mem nat toxicol panel, Nat Res Coun, 1980; vis prof, Sorbonne, Paris, 1969 & 1975 & Polish Acad Sci, 1979; multi sclerosis study sect, 1972-1974; mem, Pharmacol Sect, NIH, 1968-1972; guggenheim fel, 1968-1969; sr co-dir, Inst Mind, Drugs & Behav, 1965-1985; consult, Ill State Psychiat Inst, 1960-; consult, Hines Vet Admin Hosp, 1957-; consult, Melpar Inc, 1957-1960; prof pharmacol & exp therapeut & chmn dept, Stritch Sch Med, Loyola Univ, 1956-1985; assoc mem, Sterling-Winthrop Res Inst, 1953-1956; consult, Emerson Drug Co, 1952; NIH grants, 1947-1985; from instr to assoc prof pharmacol, Sch Med, Georgetown Univ, 1946-1953; teaching fel, Columbia Univ, 1945-1946; res fel, Amherst Col, 1944-1945; Am Philos Soc grant, NY Univ, 1942-1944. **Memberships:** AAAS; Am Soc Pharmacol & Exp Therapeut; Soc Exp Biol & Med; fel Am Col Neuropsychopharmacol; Int Brain Res Orgn; Soc Neuroscience. **Research Statement & Publications:** Physiology and pharmacology of synaptic transmission; cholinesterases and anticholinesterase drugs; cholinergic system, its role in transmission, development, trophic phenomena, teratology, aging, and behavior; neuropsychopharmacology; author of over 400 publications. **Mailing Address:** Chicago Asn Res & Educ Sci, Hines, IL 60141. **Fax:** 708-216-2319.

KARDAMI, ELISSAVET, MUSCLE CELL BIOLOGY, CARDIAC MUSCLE CELL BIOLOGY. **Personal Data:** b Corinth, Greece, January 4, 1952. **Education:** Univ Athens, Greece, dipl, 1975; King's Col, London, PhD (cell biophys), 1979. **Professional Experience:** PROF & CO CHAIR, DEPT HUMAN ANAT CELL SCI & PHYSIOL, UNIV MAN, WINNIPEG, as of 2004; assoc prof cell biol, Univ Man, beginning 1992; STAFF SCIENTIST, S.B.G.H RES CTR, UNIV MAN, 1988; asst prof, Univ Man, 1987-1992; res assoc zool, Univ Calif Berkeley, 1984-1986; Res fel, Inst Del Pasteur, 1980-1983 & Univ Calif, Berkeley, 1983-1986. **Memberships:** Soc Cell Biol; Int Soc Heart Res. **Research Statement & Publications:** Muscle cell biology; cardiac muscle cell biology. **Mailing Address:** Univ Man, St Boniface Gen Hosp Res Ctr, 134 Basic Med Sc Bldg, Winnipeg, MB R3008, Can. **Fax:** 204-233-6723. **E-Mail:** ekardami@sbrc.ca

KARDOMATEAS, GEORGE A, AEROSPACE ENGINEERING. **Education:** Nat Tech Univ, BS, 1981; Mass Inst Technol, MS, 1982, PhD, 1985. **Professional Experience:** PROF, GA INST TECH, as of 2005. **Memberships:** Am Inst Aeronaut & Astronaut. **Mailing Address:** Ga Inst Tech, Aerospace Eng MC/0150, Atlanta, GA 30332. **Fax:** 404-894-2760.

KARDOS, GEZA, MECHANICAL ENGINEERING. **Personal Data:** b Tolna, Hungary, March 2, 1926; Canadian citizen; m 1949, c 3. **Education:** Univ Sask, BSc, 1948; McGill Univ, ME, 1957, PhD (mech eng), 1965. **Honors & Awards:** Fred Merryfield Design Award, Am Soc Eng Educ, 1983; vis scholar, Univ Stellenbosch, SA; vis prof, Royal Col Arts. **Professional Experience:** RETIRED; EMER PROF ENG & CONSULT, CARLETON UNIV, 1996-; Wighton fel, 1992; BBC Eng Res Ltd, 1986 & Elma Eng Serv, 1987-; consult, Nat Res Coun, Can Energy Group, 1983-1984; consult, Vitro-Tech, Monterey, Mex, 1980-1982; prof, Carleton Univ, 1971-1996; vis assoc prof, Stanford Univ, 1971; Assoc dir res, Ctr Appl Res & Eng Design, McMaster Univ, 1967-1969; assoc prof design, McMaster Univ, 1966-1971; staff engr, Aviation Elec Ltd, 1965-1966; site mgr, HARP, McGill Univ, 1962-1963; eng supvr, Aviation Elec Ltd, 1956-1962; proj engr, Aviation Elec Ltd, 1954-1956; proj engr, Tamper Ltd, 1950-1954; Jr res officer fire hazards, Nat Res Coun Can, 1948-1950. **Memberships:** Fel Am Soc Mech Engrs; Am Soc Eng Educ. **Research Statement & Publications:** Mechanical pressure elements; high strain rates; design and computer aided design; case method of engineering teaching; metal physics; fracture mechanics; creative problem solving; systematic design. **Mailing Address:** Eng Fac, Carleton Univ, Ottawa, ON K1S 5B6, Can. **E-Mail:** geza_kardos@carleton.ca

KARDOS, JOHN LOUIS, COMPOSITE MATERIALS, POLYMER ENGINEERING. **Personal Data:** b Colfax, Wash, April 19, 1939; m 1966, Janice; c Joseph, Joanna & Gina. **Education:** Pa State Univ, BS, 1961; Univ Ill, MS, 1962; Case Western Res Univ, PhD (polymer sci & eng), 1965. **Honors & Awards:** Mat Eng & Sci Div Award, Am Inst Chem Engrs, 1981; Best Tech Paper Award, Med Plastics Div Soc Plastic Engrs, 1985. **Professional Experience:** LUCY AND STANLEY LOPATA PROF CHEM ENG, WASH UNIV, 1993-; BD DIR, ZOLTEK CO, 1992-; chmn chem eng, Wash Univ, 1991-1998; chmn, Gordon Conf Composite Mat, 1983; actg chmn Chem eng, 1977-1978; prof, Mat Sci & Eng Prog, 1974-1993; chmn, Mat Sci & Eng Prog, 1971-1991; dir, Mat Res Lab, 1970-1991; from asst prof to assoc prof, Wash Univ, 1965-1974. **Memberships:** Am Chem Soc; Soc Rheology; Am Soc Test Mater; Am Inst Chem Engrs Chmn Mat Eng Sci Div 1996; Sr Mem Soc Plastics Engrs; Soc Advan Mat Process Eng. **Research Statement & Publications:** Chemistry, physics and processing science of composite materials; structure-property relations in reinforced plastics; process modelling for composite materials and carbon fibers; materials characterization techniques. **Mailing Address:** Wash Univ, Campus Box 1198, One Brookings Dr, St Louis, MO 63130. **Fax:** 314-935-7211. **E-Mail:** kardos@wustl.edu

KARECKI, DAVID RALPH, PHYSICS, INFRARED SPECTROSCOPIES. **Personal Data:** b Chicago, Ill, May 29, 1946; Canadian citizen; m 1986, Kathryn. **Education:** Mich State Univ, BS, 1968; Simon Fraser Univ, MSc, 1972, PhD (physics), 1980. **Professional Experience:** Scientist, unisearch assocs inc, beginning 1984; fel, Emory Univ, 1980-1983. **Research Statement & Publications:** Trace gas monitoring with infrared and near infrared spectroscopy. **Mailing Address:** ON M8X 2G5, Can. **E-Mail:** karecki@interlog.com

KAREEM, AHSAN, PROBABILISTIC DYNAMICS, STRUCTURAL ENGINEERING. **Personal Data:** b Lahore, Pakistan, September 29, 1947; c 2. **Education:** WPakistan Univ Eng & Technol, BSc, 1968; Univ Hawaii, Honolulu, MSc, 1975; Colo State Univ, PhD (civil eng), 1978. **Professional Experience:** CHAIR & ROBERT M MORAN PROF CIVIL ENG, COL ENG, UNIV NOTRE DAME, 2002-; robert m moran prof & chair, dept civil eng & geol sci, Univ Notre Dame, 1999-2002; prof civil eng, Univ Notre Dame, 1990-1999; pres young investr, White House Off Sci & Technol, NSF, 1983; gen consult, Aerovironment Inc, 1979-; from asst prof to prof civil eng, Univ Houston, 1978-1990; res assoc, Colo State Univ, 1977-1978; design engr, Harza Eng Co Int, Pakistan, 1968-1971. **Memberships:** Am Soc Civil Engrs; Sigma Xi; Am Inst Aeronaut & Astronaut. **Research Statement & Publications:** Analysis and design of civil engineering and ocean engineering structures subjected to stochastic excitation due to wind, waves and earthquakes; reliability based design and digital simulation of civil engineering systems; design of vibration mitigation devices; wind energy. **Mailing Address:** Dept Civil Eng & Geol Sci, Col Eng, Univ Notre Dame, 156 Fitzpatrick Hall, Notre Dame, IN 46556. **Fax:** 574-631-9236. **E-Mail:** kareem@nd.edu

KAREIVA, PETER MICHAEL, INSECT POPULATION BIOLOGY, AGRICULTURAL ECOLOGY. **Personal Data:** b Utica, NY, September 20, 1951. **Education:** Duke Univ, BS, 1973; Univ Calif, Irvine, MS, 1976; Cornell Univ, PhD (ecol & evolution), 1981. **Professional Experience:** LEAD SCIENTIST, PACIFIC WESTERN CONSERV REGION, as of 2006; PROF, DEPT ZOOL, UNIV WASH, SEATTLE, as of 2006; ASST PROF THEORET ECOL & MATH MODELLING, BROWN UNIV, 1981-; lectr environ biol, Calif State Univ, Los Angeles, 1976. **Memberships:** Ecol Soc Am; Entom Soc Am. **Research Statement & Publications:** Population biology of herbivorus insects; mathematical models of insect dispersal; the influence of vegetation texture on herbivore dynamics. **Mailing Address:** Pacific Western Conserv Region, 4722 Latona Ave NE, Seattle, WA 98105. **E-Mail:** pkareiva@tnc.org

KAREL, KARIN JOHNSON, ORGANOMETALLIC CHEMISTRY. **Personal Data:** b Portland, Ore, August 9, 1950; m 1972, c 3. **Education:** Univ Chicago, BS, 1972; Princeton Univ, MA, 1974, PhD (chem), 1978. **Professional Experience:** CHEMIST, CENT RES & DEVELOP, E I DU PONT DEL NEMOURS & CO, 1980-; NSF fel, Univ Ill, 1978-1979. **Memberships:** Am Chem Soc. **Research Statement & Publications:** Organometallic reagents for organic synthesis; preparation and characterization of novel organometallic species. **Mailing Address:** 104 Country Club Dr, Wilmington, DE 19803-2918.

KAREL, MARCUS, FOOD SCIENCE, CHEMICAL ENGINEERING. **Personal Data:** b Lwow, Poland, May 17, 1928; American citizen; m 1958, c 4. **Education:** Boston Univ, AB, 1955; Mass Inst Technol, PhD, 1960. **Honorary Degrees:** ScD, Technion Israel Inst Technol, Haifa, Israel, 1991; Dr, Univ Bergundy, Dijon, France, 1997; Dr, Univ Helsinki, Finland, 1999; DSc, Tech Univ Munich, Ger, 2003. **Honors & Awards:** William V Cruess Award, Inst Food Technol, 1970, Nicholas Appert Medal, 1986; Food Eng Award, Am Soc Agr Engrs & Dairy & Food Industs Supply Asn, 1978. **Professional Experience:** PROF EMER CHEM ENG, MASS INST TECHNOL, 1989-; prof food sci, State NJ, Rutgers Univ, 1989-1996; prof chem & food eng, Mass Inst Technol, 1988-1989; distinguished vis prof, Rutgers Univ, beginning 1986; head, Dept Nutrit Food Sci, Mass Inst Technol, 1974-1979; from asst prof to prof food eng, Mass Inst Technol, 1961-1988; consult var food & chem co, beginning 1960; res assoc food tech, Mass Inst Technol, 1957-1961. **Memberships:** Nat Acad Sci Arg; fel Inst Food Technol; fel Brit Inst Food Sci & Technol; NY Acad Sci; Am Inst Chem Eng; hon fel Int Asn Eng & Food; Am Chem Soc. **Research Statement & Publications:** Food engineering; autoxidation of lipids; diffusion of gases and vapors through polymeric membranes; physicochemical properties of foods; heat and mass transfer aspects of food processing; controlled drug release. **Mailing Address:** Mass Inst Technol, Rm 66-409, Cambridge, MA 02139. **E-Mail:** karel@comcast.net

KAREL, MARTIN LEWIS, NUMBER THEORY. **Personal Data:** b Baltimore, Md, March 15, 1944; m 1972, Karin; c 3. **Education:** Johns Hopkins Univ, BA, 1966; Univ Chicago, MA, 1967, PhD (math), 1972. **Professional Experience:** ASSOC PROF, RUTGERS UNIV, CAMDEN COL ARTS & SCI, 1983-; mem, Inst Advan Study, Princeton, 1983; asst prof, Rutgers Univ, Camden Col Arts & Sci, 1980-1983; res assoc, Univ Ill, Urbana-Champaign, 1979; NSF fel, 1975-1980, 1981-1986; asst prof math, Univ NC, Chapel Hill, 1974-1980; mem, Inst advan Study, Princeton Univ, 1973-1974; asst math, Inst Advan Study, Princeton Univ, 1972-1973. **Memberships:** Am Math Soc. **Research Statement & Publications:** Theory of vertex algebras. **Mailing Address:** Dept Math Rutgers Univ, Camden Col Arts & Sci, Armitage Hall 311 N fifth St, Camden, NJ 08102. **Fax:** 856-225-6602. **E-Mail:** karel@camden.rutgers.edu

KARFAKIS, MARIO GEORGE, ROCK MASS CHARACTERIZATION, MINE SUBSIDENCE. **Personal Data:** b Iskenderun, Turkey, September 12, 1950; m 1983, Diane; c 2. **Education:** Univ Grenoble, France, BS, 1975; Univ Wis-Madison, MS, 1978, PhD (mining eng), 1983. **Professional Experience:** ASSOC PROF MINING ENG, VA POLYTECH INST & STATE UNIV, 1993-; asst prof, VA Polytech Inst & State Univ, 1988-1993; asst prof mining eng, Univ Wyo, 1983-1988; site eval, Wash, Rockwell Int, 1980; site eval; DEQ Subsidence Eval, Wyo, 1985, 1987, 1988; consult, Chrome-Alloy Eng Instrumentation Wastewater Treatment plant, 1978; res assoc, 1977; teaching asst mining eng, 1980-1983; res asst rock mech, Univ Wis, 1976, 1978-1979. **Memberships:** Instrument Soc Am; Int Soc Rock Mech; Sigma Xi; Am Inst Mining Metall & Petrol Engrs. **Research Statement & Publications:** Rock fracture mechanics; effects of aqueous environment on fracturing; rock fragmentation; coal mine ground control; insitu stress determination. **Mailing Address:** Dept Mining & Minerals Eng, Va Polytech Inst & State Univ, 108 Holden Hall, Blacksburg, VA 24061. **Fax:** 540-231-4070. **E-Mail:** mario@vt.edu

KARG, GERHART, PHYSICAL CHEMISTRY, COSMETIC CHEMISTRY. **Personal Data:** b New York, NY, January 21, 1936; m 1966, Barbara Coyle; c Kathryn, Janet, Lawrence, Michael & Sharon. **Education:** Manhattan Col, BS, 1957; Polytech Inst Brooklyn, PhD (phys chem), 1963. **Professional Experience:** MGR FRAGRANCE & TOILETRIES PROD, BENCKISER, 1996-; mgr treatment prod, Benckiser, 1994-1996; mgr cosmetic & treat prod, Benckiser, 1992-1993; mgr cosmetic & treat prod, Coty Res & Develop, 1990-1992; sr prod develop chemist, Pfizer, Inc, 1988-1990; sr develop chemist, Avon Prod Inc, 1978-1988; sr phys chemist, Avon Prod Inc, 1971-1978; develop chemist, Avon Prod Inc, 1969-1970; res chemist, Ultra Chem Co Div, Witco Chem Co, 1964-1969; Res chemist, M W Kellogg Co, 1962-1964. **Memberships:** Soc Cosmetic Chemists. **Research State-

ment & Publications: Photochemistry; surface chemistry; hair properties; skin care. **Mailing Address:** Benckiser Int Develop Ctr, 410 American Rd, Morris Plains, NJ 07950-2451.

KARGEL, JEFF S, SEDIMENTOLOGY, PLANT GEOLOGY. **Personal Data:** b Boston, Mass, April 14, 1958; m 1979, Huong; c Joseph Van Bogner, Christopher V S & Dianna L. **Education:** Ohio State Univ, BS, 1981, MS, 1987; Univ Ariz, PhD (planetary sci), 1990. **Professional Experience:** GEOLOGIST, US GEOL SURV, 1992-; res assoc, Univ Ariz, 1991-1992; res asst, Univ Ariz, 1985-1991; teaching & res asst, Ohio State Univ, 1982-1984. **Memberships:** Corp mem Geol Soc Am; Am Geophys Union; Div Planetary Sci Am Astron Soc; Intl Geol Soc. **Research Statement & Publications:** Widley varying topics in earth and planetary sciences; glaciology and permafrost studies of earth and mars; icy satellite geology and geochemistry; natural resources of asteroids and mars; planetary geochemistry. **Mailing Address:** US Geol Surv, 2255 N Gemini Dr, Flagstaff, AZ 86001.

KARGER, BARRY LLOYD, ANALYTICAL CHEMISTRY. **Personal Data:** b Boston, Mass, April 2, 1939; m 1961, c 2. **Education:** Mass Inst Technol, BS, 1960; Cornell Univ, PhD (anal chem), 1963. **Honors & Awards:** Gulf Res Award, 1971; Steven Dal Nogare Mem Award, Delaware Valley Chromatog Form, 1975; Tswett Mem Medal, USSR, 1980; Chromatography Award, Am Chem Soc, 1982; Tswett Medal, USA, 1987; Fisher Award, Am Chem Soc, 1989; Martin Medal, 1990. **Professional Experience:** Consult, Beckman beginning 1988; consult, Genentech, beginning 1987; consult, Cambridge Anal, 1985-1987; JAMES A WATERS PROF ANALYTICAL CHEM, BARNETT INST CHEM ANALYSIS & MAT SCI, 1985-; consult, Technicon Instruments Corp, 1977-1982; dir, Barnett Inst Chem Analysis & Mat Sci, beginning 1973; sci adv, Food & Drug Admin, 1973-1976; prof chem, Northeastern Univ, 1972-1985; NIH res grant, beginning 1969; Off Naval Res grants, 1969-1974; Fed Water Pollution Control Admin res grant, 1967-1970; NSF res grant, 1966-1985; from asst prof to assoc prof, Barnett Inst Chem Analysis & Mat Sci, 1963-1972. **Memberships:** fel AAAS; Am Chem Soc; NY Acad Sci; Sigma Xi. **Research Statement & Publications:** High performance liquid chromatography; biochemical applications of high performance liquid chromatography; fundamentals of biopolymer separations; capillary electrophoresis, sequencing, electrophoresis and mass spectrometry; separation science. **Mailing Address:** Dept Chem & Chem Biol, Northeastern Univ, 341 Mugar Life Sci, Boston, MA 02115-5005. **Fax:** 617-373-2855. **E-Mail:** b.karger@neu.edu

KARGL, THOMAS E, BIOCHEMISTRY. **Personal Data:** b Des Plaines, Ill, February 25, 1932; m 1957, c 8. **Education:** St Ambrose Col, BA, 1954; Purdue Univ, MS, 1956, PhD (biochem), 1959. **Professional Experience:** PROF CHEM, BELLARMINE COL, 1970-; head dept, 1964-1968; From asst prof to assoc prof, 1959-1970. **Memberships:** Sigma Xi. **Research Statement & Publications:** Carotenoid pigments of tomatoes; Lewis acid catalyzed reactions of methyl vinyl ketone; structure determination of complex polyenes; slow release fertilizers. **Mailing Address:** Dept Chem, Bellarmine Col, 2001 Newburg Rd, Louisville, KY 40205.

KARI, LILA, THEORY & DNA COMPUTING, FORMAL LANGUAGES. **Personal Data:** b Tulcea, Romania, October 22, 1964. **Education:** Univ Bucharest, Romania, MSc, 1987; Univ Turku, Finland, PhD (math & comput sci), 1991. **Professional Experience:** CAN RES CHAIR BIOCOMPUTING, DEPT COMPUT SCI, UNIV WESTERN ONT, as of 2004; ASSOC PROF COMPUT SCI, UNIV WESTERN ONT, 2000-; asst prof comput sci, Univ Western Ont, 1996-2000; vis prof, Univ Western Ont, 1993-1996; researcher, Acad Finland, 1990-1993; researcher, Inst Informatics, Romania, 1987-1990. **Memberships:** Asn Comput Mach; Can Math Soc; Europ Asn Theoret Comput Sci. **Research Statement & Publications:** DNA computing, solving computational problems by solely manipulating DNA strands in test tubes; finding a mathematical model of DNA computing and experimentally solving hard mathematical problems using molecular biology tools. **Mailing Address:** Dept Comput Sci, Univ Western Ont, London, ON N6A 5B7, Can. **Fax:** 519-661-3515. **E-Mail:** lila@csd.uwo.ca

KARICKHOFF, SAMUEL WOODFORD, PHYSICAL CHEMISTRY. **Personal Data:** b Buckhannon, WVa, October 22, 1943; m 1964, c 2. **Education:** WVa Wesleyan Col, BS, 1965; Fla State Univ, PhD (phys chem), 1971. **Professional Experience:** RES CHEMIST, ENVIRON RES LAB, ENVIRON PROTECTION AGENCY, 1971-. **Memberships:** Am Chem Soc; SocEnviron Toxicol & Chem. **Research Statement & Publications:** Fate and transport of pollutants in the environment; computer modeling of chemical reactions. **Mailing Address:** U S Environ Res Lab, College Station Road, GA 30613.

KARIEL, HERBERT G, SOCIAL GEOGRAPHY, ENVIRONMENTAL PERCEPTION. **Personal Data:** b Plaueu, Ger, American & Canadian citizen. **Education:** Univ Ore, BS, 1949, ME, 1954; Univ Iowa, PhD (geog), 1962. **Professional Experience:** RETIRED; vis prof geog, Hebrew Univ Jerusalem, 1994; prof, Univ Calgary, beginning 1967; lectr quan methods, Inst Advan Study Geog, 1966; assoc prof, Calif State Univ, Haywood, 1965-1967; asst prof geog, Western Wash State Univ, 1962-1965. **Memberships:** Soc Sigma Xi; Asn Am Geographers. **Research Statement & Publications:** In the realm of social geography focus is on tourism and its social and cultural impact, environmental noise and its perception, news in newspapers and the circulation information. **Mailing Address:** 4500-39th St NW Apt 205, Calgary, AB T3A 0M5, Can. **Fax:** 403-282-6561. **E-Mail:** hgkariel@acs.ucalgary.ca

KARIG, DANIEL EDMUND, GEOLOGY. **Personal Data:** b Irvington, NJ, July 20, 1937; m 1971, c 1. **Education:** Colo Sch Mines, GeolE, 1959, MSc, 1964; Scripps Inst Oceanog, PhD (earth sci), 1970. **Professional Experience:** PROF EMER, EARTH & ATMOSPHERIC SCI, CORNELL UNIV, as of 2003; assoc prof, Cornell Univ, 1975-1980; asst prof, Cornell Univ, 1974-1975; asst prof geol sci, Univ Calif, Santa Barbara, 1971-1974; NSF grant & asst res geologist, Scripps Inst Oceanog, 1970-1971. **Memberships:** Am Geol Soc; Am Geophys Union; Sigma Xi; Geol Soc Malaysia. **Research Statement & Publications:** Marine geology and geophysics of marginal basins and island arc systems; genesis of rift zones; environmental problems in streams and small lagoons; structure and evolution of island arcs and young mountain belts. **Mailing Address:** Dept Earth & Atmospheric Sci, Cornell Univ, 2124 Snee Hall, Ithaca, NY 14853-1504. **Fax:** 858-534-0784. **E-Mail:** dek9@cornell.edu

KARIM, AZIZ, PHARMACEUTICAL CHEMISTRY. **Personal Data:** b Dar es Salaam, Tanzania, August 20, 1939; m 1964, c 2. **Education:** Univ London, BPharm, 1964, PhD (pharmaceut chem), 1967. **Professional Experience:** DIR CLIN BIOAVAILABILTY & PHARMACOKINETICS, G D SEARLE & CO, 1979-; res fel, Dept Drug Metab, 1974-1979; group leader, Dept Biochem Res, G D Searle & Co, 1972-1974; sr res investr drug metab, Dept Biochem Res, G D Searle & Co, 1969-1972; NIH fel, Univ Wis, 1967-1969. **Memberships:** Am Chem Soc; Pharmaceut Soc Gt Brit; Am Soc Clin Pharmacol & Therapeut; Am Soc Exp Pharmacol & Therapeut; Acad Am Pharm Sci. **Research Statement & Publications:** Drug metabolism; study of biotransformation and pharmacokinetics of drugs; isolation and structural elucidation of natural products possessing biological activities. **Mailing Address:** Dept Drug Metab, G D Searle & Co 4901 Searle Pkwy, Chicago, IL 60077-2980. **Fax:** 847-982-4734.

KARIM, GHAZI A, ENGINEERING, COMBUSTION. **Personal Data:** b Baghdad, Iraq, 1934. **Education:** Univ Durham, BSc, 1956; Univ London, DIC & PhD (mech eng), 1960. **Honorary Degrees:** DSc, Univ London, 1972. **Honors & Awards:** Unwin Award in Mech Eng, Eng, 1960; Frank Spragins Technical Award, 2002; APEGGA's Serv Award 2003; NSERC 25 Years Res Award, 2004. **Professional Experience:** Consult, Alternative Fuel Systs, 1994; consult, PetroCanada, 1985; consult, Canterra Energy Ltd, 1984; consult, Nova Corp, 1983; consult, C N G Ltd, beginning 1980; PROF MECH ENG, UNIV CALGARY, 1969-; assoc prof, Univ Calgary, 1968-1969; chmn, Combustion Res Group, 1964-1968; lectr mech eng, Imp Col, Univ London, 1962-1968; UN tech fels, 1961-1962; consult engr, Ministry Indust Repub Iraq, 1960-1961; res asstmech eng, Imp Col, Univ London, 1957-1960; trainee prime movers, Eng Elec Co, 1956-1957. **Memberships:** Soc Automotive Engrs; Combustion Inst; Am Soc Mech Engrs. **Research Statement & Publications:** Utilization of natural gas and other gaseous fuels for power in internal combustion engines; chemical kinetics of common gaseous fuels; air pollution from combustion processes; fire and explosion research; engineering education; liquid natural gas utilization; thermodynamics; coal, oil sands and heavy oil. **Mailing Address:** Dept Mech Eng, Univ Calgary, 2500 Univ Dr N W, Calgary, AB T2N 1N4, Can. **Fax:** 403-282-8406. **E-Mail:** karim@ucalgary.ca

KARIM, KHONDKAR REZAUL, ATOMIC & MOLECULAR PHYSICS, ASTROPHYSICS & THEORETICAL ATOMIC PHYSICS. **Personal Data:** b Bangladesh, February 8, 1950; c 1. **Education:** Dhaka Univ, BS, 1972, MS, 1974; Univ Ore, MS, 1980, PhD (physics), 1983. **Professional Experience:** PROF PHYSICS, ILL STATE UNIV, 2000-; vis assoc prof physics, Ill state Univ, 1994; assoc prof physics, Ill State univ, 1994-2000; asst prof physics, Ill State Univ, 1989-1994; res assoc, Kans State Univ, beginning 1985; res assoc, Univ Ore, 1983-1985. **Memberships:** Am Phys Soc. **Research Statement & Publications:** Dielectronic recombination; plasma diagnostics; x-ray and Auger transition rates; resonant transfer and excitation; electron and position scattering in rare gases. **Mailing Address:** Physics Dept, Ill State Univ, Moulton 313-A, Normal, IL 61790-4560. **Fax:** 309-438-5413. **E-Mail:** karim@phy.ilstu.edu

KARIM, MOHAMMAD A, OPTOELECTRONICS, COMPUTER & ELECTRICAL ENGINEERING. **Personal Data:** b Sylhet, Bangladesh, June 1, 1953; m 1977, Setara; c Lutfi, Lamya & Aliya. **Education:** Univ Dacca, Bangladesh, BS, 1976; Univ Ala, MS, 1978, MS, 1979, PhD (elec eng), 1981. **Professional Experience:** VPRES RES, OLD DOMINION UNIV, as of 2005; dean eng, City Col NY, ending 2004; chmn & prof elec & comput eng, Electro-Optics Prog, Univ Dayton, beginning 1994; guest ed, Optical & Laser Technol, 1994; dir, Electro-Optics Prog, Univ Dayton, beginning 1990; guest ed, Optical Eng, 1990, 1991, 1993, 1995 & 1998; assoc prof, Univ Dayton, 1989-1991; asst prof, Univ Dayton, 1986-1988; asst prof, Wichita State Univ, 1983-1986; asst prof, Univ Ark, 1981-1982. **Memberships:** Fel Optical Soc Am; fel Soc Photo-instrumentation Engrs; Am Soc Eng Educ; Inst Elec & Electronics Engrs. **Research Statement & Publications:** Pattern recognition, optical computing, information processing and optical systems design. **Mailing Address:** Old Dominion Univ, VA 10031. **E-Mail:** mkarim@engr.udayton.edu

KARIM, MUNAWAR, ELECTRO MAGNETISM. **Personal Data:** b Calcutta, India, October 7, 1945; American citizen; m 1970, Maureen. **Education:** Dacca Univ, Bangladesh, BSc, 1965, MSc, 1966; Lehigh Univ, MS, 1969; Univ Ore, PhD, 1975. **Professional Experience:** PROF PHYSICS, ST JOHN FISHER COL, 1993-; vis prof, Univ Rome, 1990; coprin investr, NSF, 1988-1994; vis prof, Inst Physics della Spazio Interplanetario, Italy, 1986-1989; vis scientist, Univ Rochester, 1983-2002; from asst prof to assoc prof, St John Fisher Col, 1983-1993; res assoc, Univ Rochester, 1980-1983; Ahmadu Bello Univ, Nigeria, 1979-1980; lectr, Univ Ife, Nigeria, 1976-1979. **Memberships:** Am Phys Soc; Am Asn Physics Teachers. **Research Statement & Publications:** Effects of gravitational curvature on the quantum electrodynamic properties of electrons; Casimir force in curved spacetime, Detection of Gravitational Radiation electronic instrumentation; high vacuum techniques; applications of solar energy. **Mailing Address:** Dept Physics, St John Fisher Col, Rochester, NY 14618. **E-Mail:** karim@sjfc.edu

KARIMAN, KHALIL, PULMONARY IMMUNOLOGY, OXYGEN TRANSPORT. **Personal Data:** b Mashad, Iran, February 1, 1944. **Education:** Mashad Med Sch, Iran, MD, 1968. **Professional Experience:** ASST PROF MED, MED CTR, DUKE UNIV, 1980-. **Memberships:** Am Fedn Clin Res; Am Thoracic Soc; fel Am Col Chest Physicians; NY Acad Sci.

KARIMI, AMIR, THERMODYNAMICS. **Education:** Univ Ky, PhD (Mech Eng), 1982. **Professional Experience:** PROF & ASSOC DEAN, DEPT MECH ENG & BIOMECHANICS, UNIV TEX, as of 2004. **Mailing Address:** Univ Tex, 6900 N Loop W, San Antonio, TX 78249-0665. **Fax:** 210-458-6504. **E-Mail:** akarimi@utsa.edu

KARIN, SIDNEY, COMPUTER SCIENCE. **Personal Data:** b Baltimore, Md, July 8, 1943; m 2002, Mary. **Education:** City Col NY, BE, 1966; Univ Mich, MSE, 1967, PhD (nuclear eng), 1973. **Professional Experience:** PROF COMPUT SCI & ENG, UNIV CALIF, SAN DIEGO, 1997-; dir, Nat partnership advan computational infrastructure, 1997-; dir, San Diego Super comput Ctr, March 1985-1995, 1997-; DIR, CTR ADV COMPUTATIONAL SCI & ENG, UNIV CALIF, SAN DIEGO, 1996-; Comput Sci Res Prog Rev Panel, Nat Res Coun-NASA, 1987 & Comput Sci & Technol Bd, Nat Res Coun, 1988-1993; vpres advan comput, San Diego Super comput Ctr, 1987-1996; Indust Liaison Coun, Dept Nuclear Eng & Eng Physics, Univ Wis, 1987-1989; chmn, Nat Res Coun Rev Panel Comput, Nat Bur Stand Comput, 1987-1988; ann rev panel, Comput Ctr, Lawrence Livermore Nat Lab, 1986; mem, Nat Res Coun Panel, Nat Bur Stand Comput, 1986; dir, San Diego Super comput Ctr, 1985-1996; mem, Sci Comput Systs Tech Adv Panel, 1984-1989; mem, Tech Adv Group Super comput Ctrs, NSF, 1984-1985; mem comput rev panel, Fusion Energy Div, Oak Ridge Nat Lab, 1980 & Plasma Physics Lab, Princeton Univ, 1983-1985; dir, Info Systs Div, 1982-1985; mgr, Fusion Div Comput Ctr, 1975-1982; sr engr & sect leader, Gen Atomics, 1973-1975; Comput programmer/nuclear engr, ESZ Assocs, Inc, 1968-1972. **Memberships:** fel AAAS; Asn comput Mach; Am Nuclear Soc; Inst Elec & Electronics Engrs comput Soc. **Research Statement & Publications:** Scientific computing; computer systems; computer hardware and software; networking and communications; distributed computing; computational science and engineering. **Mailing Address:** Univ Calif San Diego, 9500 Gilman Dr Mail Code 0505, La Jolla, CA 92093-0505. **Fax:** 619-534-5056. **E-Mail:** skarin@ucsd.edu

KARINATTU, JOSEPH J, CLINICAL BIOCHEMISTRY, PATHOLOGY. **Personal Data:** b Kerala, India, August 6, 1938; American citizen; m 1963, Raj; c Jeffrey & Jennifer Ward. **Education:** Univ Kerala, BSc, 1961; Univ Delhi, MSc, 1963; St Thomas Inst, MS, 1965, PhD (biochem), 1967; Univ Autonoma, MD, 1980. **Professional Experience:** PHYSICIAN-RESEARCHER, EAST CENT ILL EDUC FOUND & UNIV ILL, CHAMPAIGN, 1980-; vis prof clin chem, Col of Lake County, Grayslake, Ill, 1973-; biochemist, St Therese Hosp,

1969-1978; Biochemist, Jewish Hosp, Cincinnati, 1967-1969; Biochemist consult, Our Lady of Mercy Hosp, Cincinnati, Ohio, 1966-1969. **Memberships:** AMA; Am Chem Soc; fel Am Asn Clin Scientists; Am Asn Clin Chemists; NY Acad Sci. **Research Statement & Publications:** Diagnostic methods in laboratory medicine; trace metals. **Mailing Address:** 52 Maywood Dr, Danville, IL 61832-2921.

KARINEN, ARTHUR ELI, physical geography, cartography; deceased, see previous edition for last biography

KARINS, JAMES PETER, OPTICAL PROCESSING FOR PATTERN RECOGNITION, IMAGE PROCESSING. **Personal Data:** b Albany, NY, February 12, 1957; m Linda; c James III & Dylan. **Education:** State Univ NY, BS, 1978, MS, 1979, PhD (physics), 1981. **Professional Experience:** PRES, NOVASOL, as of 2004; DIR RECOGNITION SYSTS, DATA SYSTS DIV, LITTON, 1996-; prog mgr, Data Systs Div, Litton, 1992-1996; sr scientist, Mission Res Corp, 1990-1992; staff engr, GE Electronics Lab, 1983-1990; mem tech staff, Philips Lab, 1981-1983. **Memberships:** Int Soc Optical Eng; Am Phys Soc; Am Defense Preparedness Asn; Asn Old Crows. **Research Statement & Publications:** Pattern recognition, optical processing, spatial light modulators and magneto-optics; infrared systems, infrared sensors and detectors; modeling and simulation. **Mailing Address:** Novasol, 23rd Floor, 1100 Alakea St, Honolulu, HI 96813. **Fax:** 808-441-3601. **E-Mail:** jkarins@vines.littondsd.com

KARIV-MILLER, ESSIE, ORGANIC ELECTROCHEMISTRY. **Personal Data:** b Sofia, Bulgaria. **Education:** Hebrew Univ, Jerusalem, MS, 1963; Weizman Inst Sci, PhD (chem), 1969. **Honors & Awards:** Int Exchange Award, Nat Acad Sci, 1987; Career Adv Award, NSF, 1987. **Professional Experience:** RETIRED; prof chem, Univ Minn, beginning 1981; sr lectr chem, Tel Aviv Univ, 1969-1977. **Research Statement & Publications:** Studies of the electrochemical behavior of organic compounds; synthesis by means of electrochemistry; conducting organic solids; chemistry of organic radicals. **Mailing Address:** Dept Chem 139 Smith Hall, Univ Minn 207 Pleasant St SE, Minneapolis, MN 55455-0431. **E-Mail:** kariv001@umn.edu

KARIYA, TAKASHI, BIOCHEMISTRY. **Personal Data:** b Belmont, Calif, June 23, 1925; m 1951, c 2. **Education:** Drake Univ, BS, 1952, MA, 1954. **Professional Experience:** RETIRED; sr pharmacologist, Pharmacol Dept, 1980-1986; sect head, Lipid Metab Sect, Biochem Dept, Merrell-Nat Labs, Div Richardson-Merrell, Inc, 1965-1980; biochemist, Merrell Dow Res Inst, Dow Chem Co, 1961-1965; res asst atherosclerosis res, Merrell Dow Res Inst, Dow Chem Co, 1955-1961. **Memberships:** NY Acad Sci. **Research Statement & Publications:** Pharmacological control of metabolism of cholesterol and other lipids in relation to the treatment of atherosclerosis; biochemical approaches to the regulation of cardiovascular function by pharmaceutical agents. **Mailing Address:** 5809 Blue Spruce Lane, Cincinnati, OH 45224.

KARK, ROBERT ADRIAAN PIETER, NEUROLOGY, NEUROCHEMISTRY. **Personal Data:** b Boston, Mass, December 3, 1940; m 1978, Dori; c Aimee, Rebecca, Candace, Colin & Marci. **Education:** Oxford Univ, BA, 1962, MA, 1967; Harvard Univ, MD, 1965. **Professional Experience:** Fel, Aspen Inst Seminar Med & Soc, 1993; mem, Comt Bioethical Concensus, Med Soc State NY, 1991-; pres, Performing Arts Med Asn, Cent NY, 1991-1993; CLIN DIR, PERFORMING ARTS MED ASN, CENT NY, 1990-; Epilepsy clinfel, Bowman Gray Sch Med, 1988 & 1993; chief, Neurol Serv, Vet Admin Med Ctr, Shreveport, 1983-1990; assoc prof neurol, La State Univ, Sch Med, Shreveport, 1983-1990; assoc prof Neuro-Psychiat Inst Hosp, Los Angeles, & dir, Ataxia Ctr, 1980-1983; Joseph's Dis Found, 1978-; mem, Med Adv Bd, Nat Ataxia Found, Western Regional Chap, 1977-1982; mem, Med Adv Bd, Nat Ataxia Found, 1975-; dir, Friedreichs Ataxia Clin, 1975-1983; Friedreichs Ataxia Group Am, 1975-; assoc co-dir, Clin Neuromuscular Dis, 1974-1976; consult, Wadsworth Vet Admin Hosp, 1973-; investr, Neurobiochem Group, Ment Retardation Prog, Neuropsychiat Inst, Univ Calif, Los Angeles, 1972-1983; asst prof neurol, Reed Neurol Res Ctr, Neuropsychiat Inst, Univ Calif, Sch Med, 1972-1980; clin assoc & guest scientist neurol & neurochem, Med Neurol Br, Nat Inst Neurol Dis & Stroke, NIH, 1968-1971. **Memberships:** Am Acad Neurol; Am Fedn Clin Res; Am Soc Neurochem; Int Soc Neurochem; Soc Neuroscience; fel Am Col Physicians. **Research Statement & Publications:** Enzymatic defects, metabolic changes, pathophysiology and treatment of inherited forms of ataxia, mental retardation and neuromuscular disease; neurochemistry of mercurial poisoning; biochemical aspects of neuromuscular trophic effects; biomedical ethics; epilepsy clinical studies; dementias clinical studies; multiple scleroics clinical studies. **Mailing Address:** 5112 W Taft Rd Ste F, Liverpool, NY 13088. **Fax:** 315-449-2667.

KARKALITS, OLIN CARROLL, CHEMICAL ENGINEERING. **Personal Data:** b Pauls Valley, Okla, May 31, 1916; m 1961, Barbara; c Kay A & Karen S. **Education:** Rice Inst, BS, 1938; Univ Mich, MS, 1941, PhD (chem eng), 1950. **Professional Experience:** DEAN, COL ENG & TECHNOL, MCNEESE STATE UNIV, 1972-; asst dir technol, Petro-Tex Chem Corp, 1966-1972; mgr, Petro-Tex Chem Corp, 1963-1966; supvr res, Petro-Tex Chem Corp, 1956-1963; group leader process develop, Am Cyanamid Co, 1948-1956; instr chem eng, Univ Mich, 1945-1947; jr res chemist, Shell Oil Co, 1937-1942. **Memberships:** AAAS; fel Am Inst Chem Engrs; Am Soc Eng Educ; Nat Soc Prof Engrs. **Research Statement & Publications:** Catalysis; geothermal energy. **Mailing Address:** Dean Engr & Tech, McNeese State Univ 4100 Ryan St, Lake Charles, LA 70609. **Fax:** 337-475-5237. **E-Mail:** ckarkal@mail.mcneese.edu

KARKHECK, JOHN PETER, LIQUIDS, KINETIC THEORY. **Personal Data:** b New York, NY, April 26, 1945; m 1969, Kathleen Mary Shiel s; c Lorraine, Michelle & Eric. **Education:** Le Moyne Col, BS, 1966; State Univ NY Buffalo, MA, 1972; State Univ NY Stony Brook, PhD (physics), 1978. **Professional Experience:** PROF PHYSICS & DEPT CHAIR, MARQUETTE UNIV, 1993-; co-dir, NATO ASI 1998; head, Dept Sci & Math, GMI eng & mgt inst, 1989-1993; Mich State Univ, vis scholar, 1989; acad assoc, Mich st univ 1988 & 1990; dir physics, GMI Eng & Mgt Inst, 1988-1989; guest sci, Rijksuniversiteit Utrecht, 1986, 1991; guest sci, univ nat Autonomade Mex 1986 consult, BID Ctr, 1985, 1987; guest scientist, RWTH Aachen, 1983-1985; consult, STS, 1983; from asst prof to prof, GMI Eng & Mgt Inst, 1981-198 8; consult, Brookhaven Nat Lab, 1979-1985; res assoc, State Univ NY, Stony Brook, 1979-1981; Fel, State Univ NY, Stony Brook, 1978; Physics assoc, Brookhaven Nat Lab, 1975-1979. **Memberships:** Am Phys Soc; AAAS; Am Asn Physics Teachers; Sigma Xi Mmarguette chap (pres 1999-2000, vpres 1998-1999). **Research Statement & Publications:** Transport theory; liquid state thoery kinetic theory; energy modeling optical properties of composites; optoelectronics; physics education. **Mailing Address:** Dept Physics Marquette Univ, PO Box 1881, Milwaukee, WI 53201-1881. **Fax:** 414-288-3989. **E-Mail:** john.karkheck@marquette.edu

KARKLINS, OLGERTS LONGINS, GEOLOGY, PALEONTOLOGY. **Personal Data:** b Tukums, Latvia, October 3, 1924; American citizen; m 1956, Vija; c I eva. **Education:** Columbia Univ, BS, 1957, Univ Minn, MS, 1961, PhD, 1966. **Professional Experience:** RETIRED; asst prof lectr, Col Gen Studies, George Wash Univ, 1969-1972; geologist biostratig paleont, US Geol Surv, 1963-1989. **Memberships:** Emer mem Int Bryozool Asn; Sigma Xi. **Research Statement & Publications:** Invertebrate paleontology; biostratigraphy; use of paleobiology, stratigraphy and paleogeography of Paleozoic Ectoprocta in regional correlations. **Mailing Address:** 11301 Hawhill End, Potomac, MD 20854.

KARL, DAVID M, OCEANOGRAPHY. **Education:** State Univ Col, Buffalo, BA, 1971; Fla State Univ, Tallahassee, MS, 1974; Univ Calif, San Diego, PhD (oceanog), 1978. **Honors & Awards:** AG Huntsman medal(2001); GE Hutchinson medal(1998). **Professional Experience:** Mem affil fac, Bermuda Biol Sta Res, 1995-; chmn, Biol Oceanog Div, SOEST, 1990-1991; PROF OCEANOG, UNIV HAWAII, 1987-; chmn, Oceanic Biol Res Div, Hawaii Inst Geophysics, 1986-1990; from asst prof to assoc prof, Univ Hawaii, 1978-1987; fel, Am-Scand Found, 1976. **Memberships:** Am Geophys Union; Sigma Xi; Oceanog Soc; Am Soc Microbiol; Am Soc Limnol & Oceanog. **Mailing Address:** Sch Ocean & Earth Sci & Technol Univ Hawaii, 1000 Pope Rd, Honolulu, HI 96822. **Fax:** 808-956-5059. **E-Mail:** dkarl@soest.hawaii.edu

KARL, GABRIEL, THEORETICAL PHYSICS. **Personal Data:** b Cluj, Romania, April 30, 1937; Canadian citizen; m 1965, Dorothy; c Alexandra. **Education:** Univ Cluj, BA (chem), 1958; Univ Toronto, PhD (chem), 1964. **Honors & Awards:** Ger-Can Res Prize, Humboldt found 1992; CAP Medal 1993. **Professional Experience:** Vis prof, Univ Munich, 1993; PROF PHYSICS, UNIV GUELPH, 1975-; vis scientist, Europ Orgn Nuclear Res, Geneva, 1974, 1983, 1992; from asst prof to assoc prof physics, Univ Guelph, 1969-1975; fel high energy physics, Oxford Univ, 1966-1969; fel molecular physics, Univ Toronto, 1964-1966. **Memberships:** Am Phys Soc; Can Asn Physicists; fel Royal Soc Can. **Research Statement & Publications:** High energy physics; atomic physics. **Mailing Address:** Dept Physics, Univ Guelph, Guelph, ON N1G 2W1, Can. **Fax:** 519-836-9967. **E-Mail:** gk@physics.uoguelph.ca

KARL, HERMAN ADOLF, MARINE GEOLOGY, SEDIMENTOLOGY. **Personal Data:** b New York, NY, March 24, 1947; m 1970. **Education:** Colgate Univ, BS, 1969; Univ Nebr, MS, 1971; Univ Southern Calif, PhD (geol sci), 1977. **Professional Experience:** CHEIF SCIENTIST PROJ COORD, US GEOL SURV, as of 2005; VIS LECTR, MASS INST TECHNOL, as of 2004; MARINE GEOLOGIST, PAC-ARCTIC BR MARINE GEOL, US GEOL SURV, 1977-; Nat Res Coun res assoc marine geol, Pac-arctic Br Marine Geol, US Geol Surv, 1977; res geologist, Esso Prod Res Co, 1972; Explor geologist petrol explor, Humble Oil & Refining Co, 1971. **Memberships:** AAAS; Geol Soc Am; Soc Econ Paleontologists & Mineralogists; Int Asn Sedimentologists; Am Geophys Union; Sigma Xi. **Research Statement & Publications:** Dynamics of depositional processes and sediment transport on continental margins. **Mailing Address:** US Geol Surv, 655 Woodland Ave, Menlo Park, CA 80225. **E-Mail:** hkarl@usgs.gov

KARL, MICHAEL M, CLINICAL MEDICINE, HEPATOLOGIST. **Personal Data:** b Milwaukee, Wis, January 30, 1915; m 1940, Irene; c Bonnie Staffier & Terry Karl. **Education:** Univ Wis, BS, 1936; Univ Louisville, MD, 1938; Am Bd Internal Med, cert, 1946. **Honorary Degrees:** DSc, Wash Univ. **Honors & Awards:** Laureate Award, Am Col Physicians, 1988; Ralph O Claypoole Sr Mem Award, Am Col Physicians, 1990; porfship, Michael & Irene E Lectureship, WA Univ; Distinguished Aluminus, U of Louisville; Irene & Michael Karl. **Professional Experience:** Chmn, Accreditation Coun Continuing Med Educ, 1991; mem prog comt, Inst Med-Nat Acad Sci, 1988-1990; mem, Accreditation Coun Continuing Med Educ, beginning 1987; dir clin affairs, dept med, 1987-1993; am Col Physicians rep, Coun Med Specialty Socs, beginning 1986; mem, White House Conf Families, 1978-1980; chmn, Comt Serv to Elderly, Nat Coun Jewish Fedns, 1976-1981; mem exec fac, Sch Med, 1975-1976 & 1985-1986; PROF CLIN MED, SCH MED, WASH UNIV, beginning 1972; pres, Fac Ctr, Wash Univ, 1969; co-organizer, Jeff-Vander-Lou Med Clin, 1967-1972; counr, Soc Internal Med, 1967; dept Med, Jewish Hosp St Louis, 1963-1964; consult internal med, USAF, 1962-1964; mem, Munic Nursing Bd, City St Louis, 1960-1962; dir, Third Yr Med Clerkship, St Louis City Hosp, 1942-1944; pract internal med, Md Med Group, St Louis, Mo, 1942-1987; med dir, Red Cross Mobile Blood Unit, 1942-1944; resident internal med, St Louis City Hosp, Sch Med, Wash Univ, 1940-1942; Intern, St Louis City Hosp, Sch Med, Wash Univ, 1938-1942; irene & Michael Karl prof endocrinol. **Memberships:** Inst Med-Nat Acad Sci; fel & master Am Col Physicians; AMA; Cent Soc Clin Res; Am Asn Study Liver Dis; Am Soc Internal Med. **Research Statement & Publications:** Liver disease; started liver biopsy (needle). **Mailing Address:** Dept Med, Wash Univ Sch Med, 660 S Euclid Ave Box 8121, St Louis, MO 63110.

KARL, RICHARD C, SURGERY. **Personal Data:** b Albany, NY, February 16, 1920; m 1944, c 3. **Education:** Columbia Univ, AB, 1942; Cornell Univ, MD, 1944; Am Bd Surg, dipl, 1952. **Professional Experience:** RETIRED; mem, Vet Admin Hosp, White River Junction, Vt, beginning 1970; mem, USPHS Hosp, Staten Island, 1964-1970; prof surg & chmn dept, Dartmouth Med Sch, 1970-1991; dir surg, Dartmouth-Hitchcock Affil Hosps, 1970-1991; dir surg, North Shore Hosp, 1967-1970; consult, NY Vet Admin Hosp, 1963-1970; dir, Second Surg Div, Bellevue Hosp, NY, 1963-1967; from asst to assoc attend surgeon, NY Hosp, 1954-1970; from instr to assoc prof, Med Col, Cornell Univ, 1952-1970; asst surg, Med Col, Cornell Univ, 1948-1951; instr anat, Med Col, Cornell Univ, 1946-1947. **Memberships:** Fel Am Col Surg. **Research Statement & Publications:** Academic educational surgery. **Mailing Address:** Etna, NH 03750.

KARL, ROBERT RAYMOND, JR, ATMOSPHERIC CHEMISTRY, PHYSICS. **Personal Data:** b Sewickley, Pa, June 15, 1945; c 2. **Education:** Pa State Univ, BS, 1967; Cornell Univ, PhD (phys chem), 1974. **Professional Experience:** STAFF MEM & PROJ LEADER, LOS ALAMOS NAT LAB, 1976-; postdoctoral, spectros, Isotope Sepn, State Univ NY, Binghamton, 1974-1976; res asst chem laser, Chem Dept, Cornell Univ, 1973-1974; res asst molecular struct, Chem Dept, Cornell Univ, 1968-1973; Res assoc surface adsorption, Chem Dept, Pa State Univ, 1966-1967. **Memberships:** Am Inst Physics; Am Chem Soc; Am Phys Soc. **Research Statement & Publications:** Spectroscopy, photochemistry; remote atmospheric sensing; remote lidar sensing; fluorescence spectroscopy; remote beamdiagnostics; remote exoarmospheric diagnostics of weapons tests and ionospheric plasmas. **Mailing Address:** Los Alamos Nat Lab, PO Box 1663, Los Alamos, NM 87544.

KARL, SUSAN MARGARET, REGIONAL GEOLOGY OF ALASKA, MARINE GEOLOGY & GEOCHEMISTRY. **Personal Data:** b Pittsburg, Pa, October 7, 1951; m 1985, Steve; c Tamara & Rusty. **Education:** Middlebury Col, BA 1973; Stanford Univ, PhD (geol), 1982. **Honors & Awards:** Harold Stearns Award, Geol Soc Am, 1978. **Professional Experience:** RES GEOLOGIST, US GEOL SURV, as of 2004; Geologist, US Geol Surv, beginning 1977; Mem, proj 187, Int Geol Correlation Prog, ODP Leg 129. **Memberships:** Geol Asn Can; Am Geophys Union; Geol Soc Am; Am Asn Petrol Geol; Alaska Geolgical Soc (Sec 1992-3, VP 1994-5, Pres 1995-7 and 2004-5). **Research Statement & Publications:** Geochemistry and sedimentology of siliceous deposits; turbidite facies analysis; paleoenvironmental analysis of sedimentary basins; sedimentary and tectonic processes in accretionary complexes; North Pacific rim paleoceanography and tectonics and implications for ore deposits. **Mailing Address:** US Geol Surv, 4200 Univ Dr, Anchorage, AK 99508. **Fax:** 907-786-7401. **E-Mail:** skarl@usgs.gov

KARL, THOMAS RICHARD, CLIMATOLOGICAL TIME SERIES, SECULAR CLIMATE CHANGE. **Personal Data:** b Evergreen Park, Ill, November 22, 1951; m 1973, c 2. **Education:** Northern Ill Univ, BS, 1973; Univ Wis-Madison, MS, 1974. **Honors & Awards:** Bronze Medal, Dept Com, 1987; Gold Medal, 1991; Verner E Suomi Award, Am Meteorol Soc. **Professional Experience:** DIR, NAT CLIMATIC DATA CTR, NOAA, as of 2005; sr scientist, Nat Climate Data Ctr, beginning 1992; Rapporteur, Climat Time Series, World Meteorol Orgn, beginning 1983; meteorologist, Climate Res & Appln, 1980-1992; meteorologist weather forecasting & anal, Nat Weather Serv, 1979-1980; meteorologist air qual res, Environ Sci Res lab, 1975-1979. **Memberships:** fel Am Metrol Soc; fel Am Geophys Union; Nat Acad Sci. **Research Statement & Publications:** The analysis and reconstruction of the 20th century climate record for identifying climate change for basic climate research; design and management strategies of various environmentally sensitive systems; published over 200 articles. **Mailing Address:** Nat Climatic Data Ctr, Nat Oceanic Atmospheric Admin, 151 Patton Ave Rm 120, Asheville, NC 28801-5001. **Fax:** 704-271-4328. **E-Mail:** tkarl@ncdc.noaa.gov

KARLANDER, EDWARD P, BOTANY. **Personal Data:** b Manchester, Vt, November 30, 1931; wid, c 6. **Education:** Univ Vt, BS, 1960; Univ Md, MS, 1962, PhD, 1964. **Professional Experience:** RETIRED; asst chmn dept, Univ Md, College Park, 1982-1990; actg dir, Md Water Resources Res Ctr, 1980-1981; prog officer NSF, 1979-1980; assoc prof algal physiol, Univ Md, College Park, 1969-1990; asst prof, Univ Md, College Park, 1966-1969; from res asst to res assoc, Univ Md, College Park, 1960-1965. **Memberships:** Phycol Soc Am; Am Inst Biol Sci. **Research Statement & Publications:** Ecological biophysics; algal physiology; responses of organisms to light; cell growth. **Mailing Address:** 107 Lakeside Dr, Greenbelt, MD 20770.

KARLE, HARRY P, PLANT PATHOLOGY, VITICULTURE. **Personal Data:** b Sanger, Calif, January 4, 1927; wid Patsey (Deceased); c Patricia Ann (Barclay), Carolyn(Kemble), Kathryn(McDougal) & Carey L. **Education:** Fresno State Col, BS, 1950; Univ Calif, Davis, MS, 1959, PhD (plant path), 1965. **Professional Experience:** PROF EMER PLANT PATH & VITICULTURE, CALIF STATE UNIV, FRESNO, 1991-; assoc dean agr opers, Calif State Univ, Fresno, 1986-1991; prof plant path, Calif State Univ, Fresno, 1969-1986; chmn, Dept Plant Sci, Calif State Univ, Fresno, 1969-1986; consult res & study comt, Calif Raisin Adv Bd, 1965-1984; from asst prof to assoc prof, Calif State Univ, Fresno, 1962-1969; lab technician, Univ Calif, Davis, 1959-1962; res asst, Univ Calif, Davis, 1958-1959; lab asst, Univ Calif, Davis, 1955-1958; lab helper plant path, Univ Calif, Davis, 1954-1955; foreman viticulture, Fresno State Col, 1951-1953; instr, High Sch, Calif, 1950-1951. **Memberships:** AAAS; Am Phytopath Soc; Am Soc Hort Sci; Am Inst Biol Sci; Am Soc Agron; Sigma Xi. **Research Statement & Publications:** Grape diseases; non-cultivation studies. **Mailing Address:** Dept Plant Path & Viticulture, Calif State Univ, 5241 N Maple Ave, Fresno, CA 93740-8027.

KARLE, ISABELLA LUGOSKI, MOLECULAR BIOLOGY, CONFORMATION PEPTIDES. **Personal Data:** b Detroit, Mich, December 2, 1921; m 1942, Jerome; c Louise (Hanson), Jean M & Made e ine (T a wney). **Education:** Univ Mich, BS, 1941, MS, 1942, PhD (phys chem), 1944. **Honorary Degrees:** DSc, Univ Mich, 1976, Wayne State Univ, 1979 & Univ Md, 1986; LHD, Georgetown Univ, 1984; Univ Athen, Greece 1997, Univ Pennsycoania 1999; Harvard Univ, 2001. **Honors & Awards:** Sci Res Soc Am Award, 1967; Hillebrand Award, Am Chem Soc, 1969, Garvan Award, 1976; Fed Woman's Award, US Govt, 1973; Dexter Conrad Award, Off Naval Res, 1980; Pioneer Award, Am Inst Chemists, 1984; Gregori Aminoff Prize, Royal Swedish Acad Sci, 1988; Rear Admiral William S Parsons Award, Navy League of US, 1988; Mich Women's Hall Of Fame, 1989; Bijloet Medal, Univ Utrecht, Neth, 1990; Vincent du Vigneaud Award, Gordon Conf, 1992; Bower Award, Franklin Inst Philadelphia, 1993; Nat Medal of Sci, 1995; Chem Prize, Nat Acad Sci, 1995; Ralph hirachmann award, Amer chem soc, 1998. **Professional Experience:** CHIEF SCIENTIST, X RAY DIFFRACTION SECT, US NAVAL RES LIB, WASH, as of 2001; Corp Vis Comt, Mass Inst Technol, 1982-1990; mem bd, Int Orgn & Progs, Nat Acad Sci, 1980-1983; mem adv bd, Off Chem & Chem Tech, Nat Res Coun, 1978-1981; mem, Exec Comt, Am Peptide Symposium, 1976-1981; mem, Nat Comt Crystallog, Nat Acad Sci-Nat Res Coun, 1974-1977; head, X-Ray Analysis Sect, Us Naval Res Lab, beginning 1959; physicist, X-ray Analysis Sect, US Naval Res Lab, 1946-1959; instr, Univ Mich, 1944-1946; assoc chemist, Univ Chicago, 1944. **Memberships:** Nat Acad Sci; Am Philos Soc; Biophys Soc; Am Crystallog Asn (vpres, 1975, pres, 1976); Am Chem Soc; Am Acad Arts & Sci. **Research Statement & Publications:** Application of electron and x-ray diffraction to structure problems; phase determination in crystallography; elucidation of molecular formulae; peptides; configurations and conformations of natural products and biologically active materials. **Mailing Address:** Lab Struct Matter, US Naval Res Lib, Code 6030, Washington, DC 20375-5000. **Fax:** 202-767-6874.

KARLE, JEAN MARIANNE, X-RAY CRYSTALLOGRAPHY. **Personal Data:** b Washington, DC, November 14, 1950. **Education:** Univ Mich, BS, 1971; Duke Univ, PhD (chem), 1976. **Professional Experience:** DEPT PHARMACOL, WALTER REED ARMY INST RES, Wash, 1983-; staff fel, Nat CancerInst, 1978-1983; pub health serv fel, Nat Inst Arthritis, Diabetes, Digestive & Kidney Dis, NIH, 1976-1978. **Memberships:** Am Chem Soc; Am Asn Cancer Res; Int Soc Study Xenobiotics; Am Crystallographic Asn; Am Soc Trop Med Hyg. **Research Statement & Publications:** Three-dimensional structure of biologically active small molecules; chiral chromatographic methods development; drug development of antimalarials; computational chemistry. **Mailing Address:** Dept Pharmacol, Walter Reed Army Inst Res, Div Exp Therapeutics, 503 Robert Grant Ave, Silver Spring, MD 20910-7500. **Fax:** 301-319-9449. **E-Mail:** jean.karle@na.amedd.army.mil

KARLE, JEROME, CRYSTALLOGRAPHY. **Personal Data:** b New York, NY, June 18, 1918; m 1942, Isabella Lugoski; c Louise (Hanson), Jean & Madeleine (Tawney). **Education:** City Col New York, BS, 1937; Harvard Univ, MS, 1938; Univ Mich, MS, 1942, PhD (phys chem), 1944. **Honorary Degrees:** LHD, Georgetown Univ, 1984; DHC, Univ Md, City Univ NY, 1986, Univ Mich, 1989. **Honors & Awards:** Nobel Prize in chem, 1985; Sigma Xi Award, 1959; Chair of Sci Award, 1968; Hillebrand Award, Am Chem Soc, 1969; Paul Harteck Series Lectr, Rensselear Polytech Inst, 1986; Nat Libr Med Medal, 1986; Thomas Edison Mem lectr, 1986; Karl Herzfeld Mem Lectr, Cath Univ Am, 1986; Albert A Michelson Award, 1986; Rear Admiral William S Persons Award, 1986; Townsend Harris Award, 1986; Robert Dexter Conrad Award, 1986; Patterson Award, Am Crystallog Asn, 1986; numerous named lectureships, US & foreign univs, 1987-. **Professional Experience:** Mem, Comt Human Rights, 1991-; chmn, Chem Sect, Nat Acad Sci, 1988-1991; lectr, Nat Ctr Excellence Educ, 1987-1989; pres, Int Union Crystallog, 1981-1984; mem exec comt, Int Union Crystallog, 1978-1987; chmn, USA Nat Comt Crystallog, Nat Acad Sci-Nat Res Coun, 1973-1975; CHIEF SCIENTIST, LAB FOR STRUCT MATTER, US NAVAL RES LAB, 1967-; head, Diffraction Br, 1958-1967; mem, Nat Res Coun, 1954-1956, 1967-1987; lectr, Univ Col, Univ Md, 1951-1971; prof, Univ Md, 1951-1970; head, Electron Diffraction Sect, 1946-1958; res assoc, USNavy Proj, Mich, 1944-1946; res assoc, Manhattan Proj, Chicago, 1943-1944; Lab asst, State Dept Health, NY, 1939-1940. **Memberships:** Nat Acad Sci; Am Chem Soc; fel Am Phys Soc; Am Crystallog Asn (treas, 1950-1952, vpres, 1971, pres, 1972); Am Math Soc; Am Philos Soc; Sigma Xi; hon mem Int Acad Sci; fel AAAS; Int Soc Quantum Biol & Pharmacol. **Research Statement & Publications:** Structure of atoms, molecules, glasses, crystals and solid surfaces. **Mailing Address:** Lab Struct Matter, US Naval Res Lab, Bldg 35, Rm 201, Washington, DC 20375-5341. **Fax:** 202-767-6874. **E-Mail:** williams@harker.nrl.navy.mil

KARLEKAR, BHALCHANDRA VASUDEO, MECHANICAL ENGINEERING. **Personal Data:** b Baroda, India, January 19, 1939; m 1964, c 2. **Education:** Univ Baroda, BE, 1958; Univ Ill, Urbana, MS, 1959, PhD (mech eng), 1962. **Professional Experience:** Chapin Co, 1978; Xerox, 1974-1977; actg chmn, Chapin Co, 1976-1977; consult, A Burgart Inc, 1970-1971; PROF MECH ENG, ROCHESTER INST TECHNOL, 1966-; consult, Eastman Kodak Co, 1966-1970; consult, Ibcon Pvt Ltd, Bombay, 1963-1966; Lectr mech eng, Indian Inst Technol, 1962-1963; chmn energy task force, Rochester Inst Technol, prof & head mech engr dept. **Memberships:** Am Soc Mech Engrs; Am Soc Eng Educ; Sigma Xi. **Research Statement & Publications:** Heat transfer; energy conservation. **Mailing Address:** Dept Mech Eng, Univ Rochester, Rochester, NY 14627.

KARLEN, DOUGLAS LAWRENCE, SOIL & CROP MANAGEMENT, SOIL QUALITY. **Personal Data:** b Monroe, Wis, August 28, 1951; m 1973, Linda; c Sarah, Steve & Holly. **Education:** Univ Wis-Madison, BS, 1973; Mich State Univ, MS, 1975; Kans State Univ, PhD (agron), 1978. **Honors & Awards:** Scarseth Mem Award, Scarseth Mem Found, 1977 Agronomic achievement award, ASA, 1996; Agronomic res award, ASA, 2001. **Professional Experience:** RES LEADER & SOIL SCIENTIST, NAT SOIL TILTH LAB, USDA AGR RES SERV, 1987-; tech ed, Crop Sci Soc Am, 1994-; collab & prof, Agron Dept, Iowa State Univ, 1987-; assoc ed, Crop Sci Soc Am, 1987-1993; adj prof, Agron Dept, Clemson Univ, 1983-; res soil scientist, Coastal Plains Soil & Water Conserv Res Ctr, 1978-1987. **Memberships:** Fel Am Soc Agron; fel Soil Sci Soc Am; fel Crop Sci Soc Am; Coun Agr Sci & Technol; Soil & Water Conserv Soc Am; Coun Soil Testing & Plant Anal. **Research Statement & Publications:** Evaluation of the interactions among soil, crop, water and nutrient management practices as they affect nutrient losses from the soil and assessing the effects of conservation tillage and other management practices on soil tilth and soil quality. **Mailing Address:** Nat Soil Tilth Lab, USDA-ARS, 2150 Pammel Dr, Ames, IA 50011. **Fax:** 515-294-8125. **E-Mail:** karlen@nstl.gov

KARLER, RALPH, PHARMACOLOGY. **Personal Data:** b Mishawaka, Ind, November 11, 1928; m 1953. **Education:** Univ Chicago, AB, 1947; Ind Univ, BA, 1950; Univ Calif, MS, 1953, PhD (physiol), 1959. **Professional Experience:** PROF PHARMACOL, COL MED, UNIV UTAH, 1976-; from asst prof to assoc prof, Col Med, Univ Utah, 1963-1976; USPHS res career develop award, 1962-1972; USPHS spec res fel, 1961-1962; Res instr, Col Med, Univ Utah, 1959-1963. **Memberships:** Am Soc Pharmacol & Exp Therapeut; assoc Am Physiol Soc; Int Soc Biochem Pharmacol. **Research Statement & Publications:** Pharmacology of drugs affecting the nervous system and muscle; role of calcium in contraction; drug metabolism. **Mailing Address:** Dept Pharmacol Rm 2C 234, Univ Utah Sch Med, Salt Lake City, UT 84132-0001.

KARLIN, ALVAN A, EVOLUTION, SYSTEMATICS. **Personal Data:** b Newark, NJ, May 3, 1950; c 2. **Education:** Rutgers Univ, AB, 1972; Ind State Univ, MA, 1975; Miami Univ, PhD (zool), 1978. **Professional Experience:** VPRES & PROJ MGR, BIOL RES ASOC, TAMPA, as of 2003; Adj asst prof, Fla State Univ, 1979-; Staff Biologist Genetics, Tall Timbers Res Sta, 1978-; At Dept Biol, Univ Ark, Little Rock. **Memberships:** Soc Study Evolution; Soc Syst Zoologists; Am Soc Ichthyologists & Herpetologists; Soc Study Amphibians & Reptiles; Sigma Xi. **Research Statement & Publications:** Evolutionary biology, population genetics and ecological genetics; vertebrate biology and sociobiology. **Mailing Address:** Fourth Agro-Ecol Conference, St Augustine, FL 72204-1000. **E-Mail:** aakarlin@ualr.edu

KARLIN, ARTHUR, RECEPTORS, CHANNELS. **Personal Data:** b Philadelphia, Pa, January 14, 1936; m 1977, Cynthia; c 6. **Education:** Swarthmore Col, BA, 1957; Rockefeller Univ, PhD (biol), 1962. **Honors & Awards:** Louis & Bert Freedman Found Award Res Biochem, NY Acad Sci, 1985. **Professional Experience:** Mem bd rev, Neuron, 1996-2000; mem adv comt, Max-Planck Inst Med Res, Heidelberg, 1993-1999; mem bd rev, J Neuroscience, 1990-1995; HIGGINS PROF BIOCHEM, MOLECULAR BIOPHYSICS, PHSYIOL & CELLULAR BIOPHYSICS & NEUROL, 1989-; DIR, CTR MOLECULAR RECOGNITION, COLUMBIA UNIV, 1989-; mem bd rev, Proteins, 1986-1998; dir, MBL Neurobiology course, 1985-1989; Krantz lectr pharmacol & exp therapeut, Univ Md, 1985; Quastel vis prof, McGill Univ, 1984; mem bd rev, JBC, 1979-1984, 1987-1992; PROF BIOCHEM & NEUROL, COLUMBIA UNIV, 1978-; chmn, Gordon conf molecular pharmacol, 1975; assoc prof neurochem, Columbia Univ, 1974-1978; mem bd rev, Fedn Proc, 1974; New York City Health Res Coun career scientist award, Columbia Univ, 1970-1972; from asst prof to assoc prof physiol, Columbia Univ, 1965-1974; from res asst to res assoc neurol, Columbia Univ, 1962-1964. **Memberships:** Am Soc Biol Chem; Am Soc Pharmacol & Exp Therapeut; Soc Neuroscience; fel AAAS; Soc Gen Physiologists; Nat Acad Sci. **Research Statement & Publications:** Structure and function of receptors for neurotransmitters; molecular mechanisms of binding, gating and ion-conduction. **Mailing Address:** Ctr Molecular Recognition, Columbia Univ, P&S 11-401, 630 W 168th St, New York, NY 10032. **Fax:** 212-305-5594. **E-Mail:** ak12@columbia.edu

KARLIN, KENNETH DANIEL, INORGANIC CHEMISTRY. **Personal Data:** b Pasadena, Calif, October 30, 1948; c 2. **Education:** Stanford Univ, BS, 1970; Columbia Univ, PhD (inorg chem), 1975. **Honors & Awards:** Buck-Whitney Award, 1991. **Professional Experience:** PROF INORG CHEM, JOHNS HOPKINS UNIV, BALTIMORE, 1990-; prof inorg chem, State Univ NY Albany, 1977-1990; Hon US ramsey fel, 1976-1977; res assoc & NATO fel organometallic chem, Cambridge Univ, eng, 1975-1977. **Memberships:** Am Chem Soc; The Chem Soc; fel AAAS. **Research Statement & Publications:** Bioinorganic chemistry; chemistry of copper I; binuclear and trinuclear copper complexes; activation of molecular oxygen; models for copper metalloproteins; multimetal centers in hydrolysis reactions; metal-peroxide complex reactions. **Mailing Address:** Dept Chem, Johns Hopkins Univ, 3400 N Charles St New Chem 213 Remsen Hall, Baltimore, MD 21218. **Fax:** 410-516-8420. **E-Mail:** karlin@jhu.edu

KARLIN, SAMUEL, MATHEMATICAL STATISTICS, STATISTICS. **Personal Data:** b Yonava, Poland, June 8, 1924; American citizen; m 1947, c 3. **Education:** Ill Inst Technol, BS, 1944; Princeton Univ, PhD (math), 1947. **Honorary Degrees:** DSc, Technion-Israel Inst Technol, Haifa, Israel, 1985. **Honors & Awards:** Wilkes Lectr, Princeton Univ, 1977, Seymour Sherman Mem Lectr, 1978; Gibbs Lectr, 1983; Am Math Soc 1st Mahalanobis Mem Lectr, 1983; Indian Statist Inst & 11th Fisher Mem Lectr, London, 1983; Nat Medal Sci, 1989; Britton Lectr, McMasters Univ, Ont, Can, 1990. **Professional Experience:** PROF EMER MATH & STATIST, STANFORD UNIV, as of 2004; Robert Grimmitt Prof Math, Stanford Univ, beginning 1978; Andrew D White prof-at-large, Cornell Univ, 1975-1981; prof math, Stanford Univ, 1974-1978; dean, Fac Math & chmn, Dept Math, Weizmann Inst Sci, Rehovot, Israel, 1970-1976; prof math & statist, Stanford Univ, 1956-1974;

assoc prof, Calif Inst Technol, 1954-1956; vis asst prof, Princeton Univ, 1950-1951; Asst prof math, Calif Inst Technol, 1949-1950 & 1951-1954; consult, Rand Corp, Calif, beginning 1948. **Memberships:** Nat Acad Sci; Am Math Soc; Inst Math Statist (pres-elect, 1977, pres, 1978-1979); Am Statist Asn; Am Soc Human Genetics; Genetic Soc Am; Am Naturalist Soc; Human Genome Orgn; hon mem Am Philos Soc. **Research Statement & Publications:** Problems in mathematics, statistics, genetics and biology. **Mailing Address:** Dept Math, Stanford Univ, Bldg 380, Stanford, CA 94305-2125. **Fax:** 650-725-2040. **E-Mail:** karlin@math.stanford.edu

KARLINER, JERROLD, STRUCTURE ELUCIDATION, APPLIED SPECTROSCOPY. **Personal Data:** b Stanislawow, Poland, March 5, 1940; American citizen; m 1963, c 2. **Education:** City Col NY, BS, 1962; Stanford Univ, PhD (org mass spectrometry), 1966. **Professional Experience:** EXEC DEPT, ANALYTICAL DEVELOP & SERV, CIBA-VISON CORP, 1993-; dept head, Dept Spectros, 1990-1993; dept head, Dept nal Res, 1978-1990; group leader spectros, Ciba-Geigy Corp, 1968-1978; res assoc mass spectrometry, Lederle Labs Div, Am Cyanamid Co, 1966-1968. **Memberships:** Am Chem Soc; Am Soc Mass Spectrometry. **Research Statement & Publications:** Structure elucidation of organic compounds by physical methods; analysis and characterization of organic compounds and analytical and physical methods; analytical methods development. **Mailing Address:** 660 Boxwood Terr, Alpharetta, GA 30202.

KARLOF, JOHN KNOX, MATHEMATICS. **Personal Data:** b Rochester, NY, November 9, 1946; m 1969, c 2. **Education:** State Univ NY Col Oswego, BA, 1968; Univ Colo, MA, 1970, PhD (math), 1973. **Professional Experience:** PROF MATH SCI, UNIV NC, 1987-; assoc prof math & comput sci, State Univ NY, Stony Brook, 1980-1987; assoc prof, Univ Nebr, Omaha, 1977-1980; Asst prof math, Univ Nebr, Omaha, 1974-1977. **Memberships:** Am Math Soc; Math Asn Am. **Research Statement & Publications:** Gaussian channel coding theory; algebraic coding theory; group theory. **Mailing Address:** Dept Math Sci, Univ NC, Wilmington, NC 28403-3297. **E-Mail:** karlof@uncw.edu

KARLOVITZ, BELA, TURBULENT FLAMES, PLASMA. **Personal Data:** b Papa, Hungary, November 9, 1904; American citizen; m 1929, c Bela, Maria & Les. **Education:** Budapest Tech Univ, ME, 1926; Swiss Fed Inst Technol, EE, 1928. **Honors & Awards:** Gold Medal, Combustion Inst, 1970; Int MHD Faraday Mem Medal, 1986. **Professional Experience:** PARTNER, COMBUSTION & EXPLOSIVES RES, INC, 1953-; sect chief, US Bur Mines, 1947-1953; res engr, Westinghouse Elec Corp, 1938-1947; Sect engr, Elec Power Co, Hungary, 1929-1938. **Memberships:** Am Phys Soc; Combustion Inst. **Research Statement & Publications:** Magnetohydrodynamic power generation; combustion; turbulent flames; propulsion systems; electrically augmented flames; high power dispersed electrical discharge; plasma phenomena; the electromagnetic field in plasma systems. **Mailing Address:** 1290 Boyce Rd A-431, Upper St Clair, PA 15241. **Fax:** 724-941-6331.

KARLOW, EDWIN ANTHONY, PHYSICS. **Personal Data:** b Glendale, Calif, May 13, 1942; m 1964, Cross; c Marvin A & Norman E. **Education:** Walla Walla Col, BS, 1966; Wash State Univ, MS, 1968, PhD (physics), 1971. **Professional Experience:** Prof dept Physics, Lasoerra univ, 1990-; CONSULT, 1990-; chmn dept physics, Loma Linda Univ, 1978-1990; Chmn dept math & physics, Columbia Union Col, 1972-1978. **Memberships:** Am Asn Physics Teachers; Am Phys Soc; Am Sci Affil; Nat Sci Teachers Asn. **Research Statement & Publications:** Analog and digital processing of signals; acoustic reflection spectroscopy. **Mailing Address:** Dept Physics, La Sierra Univ, Riverside, CA 92515. **E-Mail:** ekarlow@lasierra.edu

KARLS, MICHAEL A, MATHEMATICS. **Education:** St Marys Col, BA; Univ Wis-Milwaukee, MA, PhD. **Professional Experience:** ASSOC PROF, DEP MATH SCI, BALL STATE UNIV, as of 2006. **Mailing Address:** Dept Math Sci, Ball State Univ, Muncie, IN 47306-0490. **Fax:** 765-285-8021. **E-Mail:** mkarls@.bsu.edu

KARLSON, ESKIL LEANNART, biophysics, zoology; deceased, see previous edition for last biography

KARLSON, RONALD HENRY, MARINE ECOLOGY, BENTHIC ECOLOGY. **Personal Data:** b Coalinga, Calif, October 13, 1947; m 1977, Susan; c James H & Tavenner A. **Education:** Pomona Col, BA, 1969; Duke Univ, MA, 1972, PhD (zoology), 1975. **Professional Experience:** PROF, BIOL SCI, UNIV, as of 2002; prin investor, Arc grant, 2002-2006; Dept Marine Biol, James Cook Univ, NQueensland, 1993-1994; travel fel, Lizard Island, 1993; prin investr, Mer Res Grant Australian Res Coun, 1993; Mountain Lake Biol Sta, Univ Va, 1990; vis scientist, Victorian Inst Marine Sci, 1986; Sch Biol Sci, Univ Sydney, 1986; Sch Biol Sci, Australian Inst Marine Sci, 1986; vis scientist, Dept Zool, Univ Adelaide, 1985; assoc prof, 1984-1999; vis fac, coral reef ecol, Discovery Bay Marine Lab, Univ WI-Jamaica, 1984; asst prof, Univ Del, 1978-1984; fel, Johns Hopkins Univ, 1976-1978. **Memberships:** Soc Int Comp Biol; AAAS; Am Soc Naturalists; Ecol Soc Am; Int Bryol Asn; Int Soc Reef Studies. **Research Statement & Publications:** Clonal life history strategies and the effects of dispersal, recruitment and disturbance on benthic invertebrates; Dynamics of coral communities. **Mailing Address:** Dept Biol Sci, Univ Del, Newark, DE 19716. **Fax:** 302-831-2281. **E-Mail:** rkarlson@udel.edu

KARLSSON, ERIC ALLAN, POWER SEMICONDUCTOR DEVICES, HIGH VOLTAGE SEMICONDUCTOR DEVICES. **Personal Data:** b San Francisco, Calif, December 3, 1950. **Education:** Univ Calif, Davis, BS, 1973; San Francisco State Univ, MS, 1980. **Professional Experience:** CONSULT, MICROSEMI CORP, 1997-; staff scientist, Sonoma Res Co, 1991-1996; tech dir, Lite-on Semiconductor, 1990-1991; consult, UDT Sensors Inc, 1990; consult, Microsemi Corp, 1990; eng mgr, Microsemi, 1989-1990; sr res scientist, Raytheon Res, 1988-1989; dir res & develop & eng, Tag Semiconductors, 1986-1988; eng mgr, Tag Semiconductors, 1985-1986; proj engr, Burroughs Corp, 1984-1985; consult, Allen-Bradley Co, 1984-1985; sr engr, Allen-Bradley Co, 1983-1984; sr engr, Fairchild Semiconductor, 1981-1983; res scientist, Lawrence Berkeley Lab, 1980-1981; process/prod engr, Fairchild Semiconductor, 1977-1979. **Research Statement & Publications:** Semiconductor device development, including process development and simulation, device design and simulation. **Mailing Address:** 1380 Thompson Ave, Napa, CA 94558. **Fax:** 714-893-2570. **E-Mail:** ekarlsson@microsemi.com

KARLSSON, STURE KARL FREDRIK, FLUID MECHANICS. **Personal Data:** b Sodra Vi, Sweden, October 11, 1925; American citizen; m 1949, c 2. **Education:** Johns Hopkins Univ, PhD (aeronaut), 1958. **Professional Experience:** PROF EMER ENG, BROWN UNIV, as of 2006; prof eng, Brown Univ, beginning 1971; from asst prof to assoc prof eng, Brown Univ, 1960-1971; NATO fel, Royal Inst Technol Sweden, 1959-1960; fel aeronaut, Johns Hopkins Univ, 1958-1959. **Memberships:** Am Phys Soc. **Research Statement & Publications:** Turbulent flows; laminar stability. **Mailing Address:** Div Eng Brown Univ, Box D 182 Hope St Prince Lab 201, Providence, RI 02912. **Fax:** 401-863-1157. **E-Mail:** sture_karlsson@brown.edu

KARLSSON, ULF LENNART, ANATOMY, NEUROBIOLOGY. **Personal Data:** b Uppsala, Sweden, September 11, 1935; m 1980, c 4. **Education:** Karolinska Inst, Sweden, MK, 1958, Doc, 1966, ML, 1968, Radiol Oncol Bd, cert, 1986. **Honorary Degrees:** DrMed, Royal Univ Umea, Sweden, 1969. **Professional Experience:** PROF, DEPT RADIATION ONCOL, BRODY SCH MED, E CAROLINA UNIV, as of 2006; asst prof radiol oncol, Hahnemann Univ, Phildelphia, beginning 1984; from assoc prof to prof anat & dent, Col Med & Dent, Univ Iosa, 1969-1984; teacher anat, Univ Umea, Sweden, 1965-1969; res zoologist, Univ Calif, Los Angeles, 1961-1965. **Memberships:** Sigma Xi; Scand Radiation Ther Soc; Am Soc Therapeut Radiol & Oncol. **Research Statement & Publications:** Brain tumor treatment. **Mailing Address:** Dept Radiation Oncol, Brody Sch Med, E Carolina Univ, Greenville, NC 27858-4354. **Fax:** 252-744-2812. **E-Mail:** karlssonu@mail.ecu.edu

KARLSTROM, ERNEST LEONARD, HERPETOLOGY, ECOLOGY. **Personal Data:** b Seattle, Wash, May 18, 1928; m 1950, c 3. **Education:** Augustana Col, AB, 1949; Univ Wash, Seattle, MS, 1952; Univ Calif, Berkeley, PhD (zoology), 1956. **Honors & Awards:** Arctic Inst NAm res grant, 1959-1961. **Professional Experience:** EMER FAC, UNIV PUGET SOUND, AS OF 2006; prof biol, Univ Puget Sound, 1964-1992; NSF basic res grants, 1962-1964; assoc prof, Univ Puget Sound, 1961-1964; from asst prof to assoc prof biol, Augustana Col, 1956-1961; assoc zool, Univ Calif, Berkeley, 1955-1956. **Memberships:** Am Soc Ichthyol & Herpet; Sigma Xi; Western Soc Naturalists. **Research Statement & Publications:** Comparative anatomy of reptiles; ecology and systematics of amphibians; basic marine ecology; radioactive tracer methods; ecological recovery Mount Saint Helens, Washington. **Mailing Address:** Dept Biol, Univ Puget Sound, 1500 N Warner St, #1088, Tacoma, WA 98416-0001. **Fax:** 253-879-3352.

KARLSTROM, KARL E, EARTH SCIENCE. **Education:** Univ Wy, PhD, 1981. **Professional Experience:** PROF STRUCT GEOL, DEPT EARTH & PANETARY SCI, UNIV NM, as of 2006. **Research Statement & Publications:** Evolution tectonic styles in the precanbrian and processes of continent accretion; assembly; and stabilization in the precanbrian and Phanerozoic orogens. **Mailing Address:** Dept Earth & Planetary Sci, Univ NM, Northrop Hall Rm 141 MSC 03 2040, Albuquerque, NM 87131. **Fax:** 505-277-8843. **E-Mail:** kek1@unm.edu

KARMALI, RASHIDA A, Cancer Therapeutics, Intellectual Property & Technology Law Practice. **Education:** Univ Newcastle-upon-Tyne, Eng, PhD (biochem), 1976, JD, 1993; Rutgers, Sch Law, Newark, NJ, JD 1993. **Professional Experience:** PATENT ATTY, 1994-; consult, Sloan-Kettering Cancer Ctr, 1990-1993; student legal specialist, City Law, Dept Tort Div, NY, 1990-1991; vis assoc prof, Sloan-Kettering Cancer Ctr, 1984-1992; Assoc res prof, Cook Col, Rutgers Univ, 1984-1989; Adj assoc prof, Sloan-Kettering Cancer Ctr, 1980-1990. **Memberships:** am asn of cancer res; am chem. soc; am bar asn; licensing exec soc; am intellectual property law asn. **Mailing Address:** 99 Wall St, 13th Floor, New York, NY 10005. **Fax:** 212-651-9654. **E-Mail:** karmali@aol.com

KARMAZYN, MORRIS, HEART RESEARCH, MYOCARDIAL ISCHEMIA & REPERFUSION. **Personal Data:** b Wloclawek, Poland, April 5, 1950; Canadian citizen; wid. **Education:** Loyola Col, BSc, 1974; McGill Univ, MSc, 1976, PhD (physiol), 1979. **Honors & Awards:** Merck Frosst Award Pharmacological Soc Canada 1990; Career Investigator Award, Heart Stroke Foundation Ontario 1990-2003; Canada Res Chair Experimental Cardiology 2004. **Professional Experience:** PROF & CANADA RES CHAIR IN EXPERIMENTAL CARDIOLOGY, AS OF 2006; prof physiol & pharmacol, career investr, heart & stroke found ont, Univ western ont, 1990-2003; assoc prof, Univ Western Ont, 1989-1990; Vis scientist, Weis Ctr Res, Geisinger Clin, Danville, Pa, 1987-1988; from asst prof to assoc prof pharmacol, Dalhousie Univ, 1981-1989; Fel physiol, Univ Man, 1978-1981. **Memberships:** Int Soc Heart Res; Am Soc Pharmacol & Exp Ther. **Research Statement & Publications:** Research in our laboratory is centered on understanding mechanisms of ischemic-reperfusion injury in the heart and myocardial remodelling and heart failure with the ultimate goal to identify novel therapeutic strategies. **Mailing Address:** Dept Physiol & Pharmacol, Univ Western Ont, Med Sci Bldg, London, ON N6A 5C1, Can. **Fax:** 519-661-3827. **E-Mail:** morris.karmazyn@schulich.uwo.ca

KARMEN, ARTHUR, MEDICINE, CLINICAL PATHOLOGY. **Personal Data:** b New York, NY, February 25, 1930; m 1955, c 3. **Education:** NY Univ, AB, 1950, MD, 1954. **Honors & Awards:** Sloan Award Cancer Res, 1957; Van Slyke Award, Am Asn Clin Chemists, 1979; Tswett Medal Chromatography, 1982. **Professional Experience:** DIR LAB, JACOBI MED CTR, as of 2004; dir clin labs, Bronx Munic Hosp Ctr & Hosp Albert Einstein Col Med, 1971-; chmn lab med, Albert Einstein Col Med, beginning 1971; PROF LAB MED, ALBERT EINSTEIN COL MED, 1971-; prof path & med, Sch Med & dir clin labs, Univ Hosp, NY Univ & Bellevue Hosp, 1968-1971; assoc prof radiol, radiol sci & med, Johns Hopkins Univ, 1963-1968; res investr, Nat Heart Inst, 1956-1963; resident & intern med, Bellevue Hosp, NY, 1954-1956. **Research Statement & Publications:** Analytical biochemistry, clinical pathology and chemistry, lipid metabolism and clinical enzymology; nuclear medicine; biochemistry. **Mailing Address:** Albert Einstein Col Med, Yeshiva Univ, 1300 Morris Park Ave, Bronx, NY 10461-1926. **E-Mail:** arthur.karmen@nbhn.net

KARMIOL, SOVERIN, DESIGN CELL CULTURE SYSTEMS. **Personal Data:** b Lodz, Poland, May 1, 1947; Canadian citizen. **Education:** Univ Toronto, BSc, 1969; Univ Windsor, MSc, 1981; Univ Guelph, PhD (nutrit biochem), 1989. **Professional Experience:** DIR RES & DEVELOP, CLONETICS CORP, BIOWHITTAKER INC, 1993-; post-doctoral fel, Dept Path, Univ Mich Med Sch, 1989-1993. **Memberships:** Am Asn Cancer Res; Soc Invest Dermat; Am Soc Cell Biol; Cell Transplantation Soc; Soc In Vitro Biol. **Research Statement & Publications:** Design in vitro cell systems. **Mailing Address:** Clonetics Corp, 9620 Chesapeake Dr, San Diego, CA 92123. **E-Mail:** sov@biowhittaker.com

KARMIS, MICHAEL E, MINING ENGINEERING. **Personal Data:** b Athens, Greece, June 9, 1948; m 1972, c 3. **Education:** Univ Strathclyde, BSc, 1971, PhD (rock mech), 1974. **Professional Experience:** DIR, VA CTR COAL & ENERGY RES, VA POLYTECH INST & STATE UNIV, as of 2004; STONIE BARKER PROF, DEPT MINING & MINERALS, VA POLYTECH INST & STATE UNIV, as of 2004; assoc prof mining eng, Va Polytech Inst & State Univ, beginning 1981; asst prof, Va Polytech Inst & State Univ, 1978-1981; asst prof mining eng, Nat Tech Univ Athens, Greece, 1975-1978; Royal Soc Brit fel rock mech, Dept Mining Eng, Univ Strathclyde, 1974-1975. **Memberships:** Am Inst Mining Metall & Petrol Engrs; Inst Mining Metall & Petrol Engrs; Int Soc Rock Mech. **Research Statement & Publications:** Stress analysis around mining excavations using theoretical and experimental methods; design of instrumentation for monitoring underground stressesand strains; in-situ investigations; mining subsidence; geotechnical techniques; mine design. **Mailing Address:** Va Ctr Coal & Energy Res, Va Tech, 460 Turner St Ste 304, Blacksburg, VA 24060. **Fax:** 540-231-4078. **E-Mail:** mkarmis@vt.edu

KARN, JAMES FREDERICK, RANGE RUMINANT NUTRITION, FORAGE EVALUATION. **Personal Data:** b Columbus, Ohio, January 28, 1939. **Education:** Ohio State Univ, BS, 1962, MS, 1964; Univ Nebr, PhD (ruminant nutrit), 1976. **Professional Experience:** RES ANIMAL SCIENTIST BEEF CATTLE NUTRIT, NORTHERN GREAT PLAINS RES

LAB, AGR RES SERV, USDA, 1976-; res technician, North Platte Sta, Univ Nebr, 1967-1976. **Memberships:** Am Soc Animal Sci; Soc Range Mgt; Am Soc Agron; Am Registry Prof Animal Scientists. **Research Statement & Publications:** Improving the efficiency of producing beef cattle on rangelands; forage nutritive quality evaluation; clarifying the nutrient requirements of range cattle. **Mailing Address:** Northern Great Plains Res Lab, PO Box 459, Mandan, ND 58554-0459. **Fax:** 701-667-3054. **E-Mail:** karnj@mandan.ars.usda.gov

KARN, RICHARD WENDALL, CIVIL ENGINEERING. **Personal Data:** b Oakland, Calif, July 19, 1927; m 1949, Peggy J; c Pamela J & Robert A. **Education:** Univ Calif, Berkeley, BS, 1950. **Honors & Awards:** Kenneth Andrew Roe Award, Am Asn Eng Soc, 1989. **Professional Experience:** SR VPRES, GREINER, INC, 1990-; pres, Bissell & Karn, Inc, 1986-1990; vpres, Bissell & Karn, Inc, 1966-1986; engr-mgr, Flood Control & Water Conserv Dist, Alameda Co, 1962-1966; Civil & hydraul engr, Flood Control & Water Conserv Dist, Alameda Co, 1950-1962; Mem, Bd Dir, Civil Eng Res Found, Wash, DC. **Memberships:** Fel Am Soc Civil Engrs (pres 1984-1985); Am Asn Eng Soc; Civil Eng Res Found; Am Pub Works Asn; Nat Soc Prof Engrs. **Mailing Address:** 7 Twelve Oaks Dr, Pleasanton, CA 94588.

KARN, ROBERT CAMERON, STRUCTURE & FUNCTION OF THE SECRETOGLOBINS, MAMMALIAN SALIVARY PROTEINS. **Personal Data:** b Berwyn, Ill, March 12, 1945; m 1997, Christina; c Colin E & Evan C. **Education:** Ind Univ, AB, 1967, MA, 1970, PhD (genetics), 1972. **Professional Experience:** PROF BIOL SCI, BUTLER UNIV, 1986-; grad adv, Dept Med Genetics, 1981-1986; career develop award, Sch Med, Ind Univ, 1977-1982; dir Genotyping Labs, Dept Med Genetics, 1975-1981; from instr to assoc prof med genetics, Sch Med, Ind Univ, 1974-1986; NIH fel, Sch Med, Ind Univ, 1974-1975. **Memberships:** Sigma Xi; Genetics Soc Am; Am Soc Biochem & Molecular Biol. **Research Statement & Publications:** Molecular genetics of salivary proteins; evolution by gene duplication. **Mailing Address:** Dept Biol Sci, Butler Univ, 4600 Sunset Ave Galllahue 271, Indianapolis, IN 46208. **Fax:** 317-940-9519. **E-Mail:** rkarn@butler.edu

KARNA, KAMAL N, AERONAUTICS. **Professional Experience:** CHAIR, CEO & PRES, CC&G CORP, as of 2005. **Memberships:** Inst Elec & Electronics. **Mailing Address:** CC&G CORP, PO Box 3189, Gaithersburg, MD 20885-3189. **Fax:** 301-330-2128. **E-Mail:** knkarna@ccagc.com

KARNAKY, KARL JOHN, EPITHELIAL TRANSPORT. **Personal Data:** b Houston, Tex, September 2, 1943. **Education:** Rice Univ, PhD (biol), 1972. **Professional Experience:** ASSOC PROF, DEPT CELL BIOL & ANAT, MED UNIV SC, 1986-; asst prof physiol, Sch Med, Univ Tex, Houston, 1980-1986; asst prof anat & cell biol, Sch Med, Temple Univ, 1976-1980. **Memberships:** Am Soc Biol Chemists. **Research Statement & Publications:** Publication on cell monolayers by apical multidrug resistance-associated protein, dissociation of the E-cadherin/B-catenin complex and changes in the tight junction during oxidant-induced disruption. **Mailing Address:** Dept Anat & Cell Biol, Med Univ SC, Rm 614 Basic Sci Bldg, Charleston, SC 29425-2204. **Fax:** 843-792-3548. **E-Mail:** karnakyk@musc.edu

KARNAUGH, MAURICE, HEURISTIC SEARCH, KNOWLEDGE REPRESENTATION. **Personal Data:** b New York, NY, October 4, 1924; m 1970, c 2. **Education:** City Col NY, BS, 1948; Yale Univ, MS, 1950, PhD (physics), 1952. **Professional Experience:** RETIRED; distinguished adj prof comput sci, Polytech Inst NY, beginning 1981; res staff, Fed Systs Div, IBM, Yorktown Heights, NY, 1970-1993; res & develop mgr, Fed Systs Div, IBM, Yorktown Heights, NY, 1966-1970; res staff, Bell Tel Labs, 1952-1966. **Memberships:** Fel Inst Elec & Electronics Engrs; Am Asn Artificial Intel; Sigma Xi. **Research Statement & Publications:** Techniques for implementing knowledge based systems in computers; knowledge representations and search methods. **Mailing Address:** Int Bus Mach Corp Res Div, Watson Res Ctr, PO Box 218, Yorktown Heights, NY 10598.

KARNER, FRANK RICHARD, GEOLOGY. **Personal Data:** b Elmhurst, Ill, August 14, 1934; m 1958, c 5. **Education:** Wheaton Col, BS, 1957; Univ Ill, PhD (geol), 1963. **Professional Experience:** RETIRED; prof geol, Univ Ndak, beginning 1969; From asst prof to assoc prof, 1962-1969. **Memberships:** AAAS; Geol Soc Am; Sigma Xi. **Research Statement & Publications:** Mineralogy and petrology of igneous, sedimentary and metamorphic rocks. **Mailing Address:** Dept Geol, Univ NDak, PO Box 8358, Grand Forks, ND 58202-8358.

KARNEY, BRYAN W, CIVIL ENGINEERING. **Education:** Univ BC, BASc, 1980, ME, 1982, PhD (civil eng), 1984. **Professional Experience:** PROF, DEPT CIVIL ENG, ENVIRON SEC, UNIV TORONTO, as of 2004. **Mailing Address:** Dept Civil Eng, Univ Toronto, Toronto, ON M5S 1A4, Can. **Fax:** 416-978-3674. **E-Mail:** karney@civ.utoronto.ca

KARNEY, CHARLES FIELDING FINCH, RADIO-FREQUENCY HEATING, DIVERTOR PHYSICS. **Personal Data:** b Eng, November 7, 1951. **Education:** Cambridge Univ, Eng, BA, 1972; Mass Inst Technol, SM, 1974, PhD (elec eng & comp sci), 1977. **Professional Experience:** BIOTECHNOLOGY SYSTS GROUP, SARNOFF CORP, as of 2000; ENG BIOWARFARE PATHOGENS, US ARMY MED RES & MAT COMMAND, as of 2000; prin res physicist, plasma physics lab & lectr/prof, dept astrophys, Princeton Univ, 1988-2000; res staff, Plasma Physics Lab & Lectr/prof, dept astrophys, Princeton Univ, 1979-1988; res assoc, Plasma Physics Lab & Lectr/prof, dept astrophys, Princeton Univ, 1977-1979; res assoc, dept elec eng & comp Sci, Mass Inst Technol, 1977. **Memberships:** Am Phys Soc. **Research Statement & Publications:** Plasma physics, especially divertor physics and radio-frequency heating; intrinsic stochasticity with application to plasma physics. **Mailing Address:** Sarnoff Corp Life Sci & Systs, 201 Wash Rd, Princeton, NJ 08543-5300. **Fax:** 609-734-2323. **E-Mail:** ckarney@sarnoff.com

KARNI, SHLOMO, ELECTRICAL ENGINEERING. **Personal Data:** b June 23, 1932; American citizen; m 1961, Michaela Jordan; c Gideon J & Sarah M. **Education:** Israel Inst Technol, BS, 1956; Yale Univ, MEng, 1957; Univ Ill, PhD (elec eng), 1960. **Professional Experience:** PROF EMER, ELEC & COMPUT ENG, as of 2003; grandner-zemke prof, Univ Nmex, beginning 1993; dir undergrad studies, Univ Nmex, beginning 1987; Tel Aviv Univ, 1970-1971 & Israel Inst Technol, 1977-1978; dir grad studies, Univ Nmex, 1971-1987; prof elec eng, Univ Nmex, beginning 1969; vis prof, Univ Hawaii, 1969-1970; from asst prof to prof, Univ Nmex, 1961-1969; Mem circuits group, Univ Ill, 1960-1961; from instr to asst prof, Univ Ill, 1957-1961; asst elec eng, Yale Univ, 1956-1957; Testing engr, Palestine Power Co, 1955-1956; consult, Los Alamos Nat Lab, Dept Energy, Westinghouse, Var Publ Houses & Kirtland AFB. **Memberships:** AAAS; fel Inst Elec & Electronics Engrs; Am Soc Eng Educ. **Research Statement & Publications:** Theory; system theory; filters; engineering education. **Mailing Address:** Dept Elec Eng & Comput Eng, Univ NMex, Albuquerque, NM 87131. **Fax:** 505-277-1439. **E-Mail:** karni@.unm.edu

KARNOK, KEITH J, AGRONOMY. **Education:** Univ Ariz, BS, 1973, MS, 1974; Tex A&M Univ, PhD (agron), 1977. **Professional Experience:** PROF AGRON, UNIV GA, 1993-; from asst prof to assoc prof agron, Univ Ga, 1983-1993; asst prof, Ohio State Univ, 1977-1982. **Mailing Address:** Dept Agron Univ Ga, 4115 Plant Sci Bldg, Athens, GA 30602. **E-Mail:** kkarnok@uga.edu

KARNOPP, BRUCE HARVEY, ENGINEERING MECHANICS, APPLIED MATHEMATICS. **Personal Data:** b Milwaukee, Wis, June 13, 1938; m 1963, c 3. **Education:** Mass Inst Technol, SB, 1960; Brown Univ, ScM, 1963; Univ Wis, PhD (eng mech), 1965. **Professional Experience:** ASSOC PROF ENG MECH & APPL MECH, UNIV MICH, ANN ARBOR, 1977-; asst prof eng mech, Univ Mich, Ann Arbor, 1968-1977; asst prof, Univ Toronto, 1965-1968; instr eng mech, Univ Wis, 1962-1965; engr, Sanders Assocs, NH, 1961; engr, AC Spark Plug, Gen Motors Corp, Wis, 1960-1961. **Memberships:** Acoust Soc Am; Tensor Soc. **Research Statement & Publications:** Variational methods in mechanics, vibrations and dynamics. **Mailing Address:** Dept Mech Eng, Univ Mich, 2350 Hayward, Ann Arbor, MI 48109-2125. **Fax:** 734-647-3170. **E-Mail:** karnopp@umich.edu

KARNOPP, DEAN CHARLES, MECHANICAL ENGINEERING, AERONAUTICAL ENGINEERING. **Personal Data:** b Milwaukee, Wis, June 12, 1934; m 1958, c 2. **Education:** Mass Inst Technol, BS & MS, 1957, PhD (mech eng), 1961. **Honors & Awards:** Levy Medal, Franklin Inst, 1969; Sr US Scientist Award, Humbolt Found, 1975. **Professional Experience:** PROF MECH ENG, UNIV CALIF, DAVIS, 1980-; vis prof, Univ Stuttgart, Ger, 1975-1976; prof syst dynamics & control, Mass Inst Technol, 1969-1980; from asst prof to assoc prof syst dynamics & control, Mass Inst Technol, 1964-1969; develop engr, Siemens Schuckert Res Ctr, Ger, 1963-1964; asst appl mech, asst prof & Ford fel, 1961-1963; instr, Mass Inst Technol, 1959-1961; asst appl mech, Mass Inst Technol, 1957-1959. **Memberships:** Am Soc Mech Engrs. **Research Statement & Publications:** Dynamic systems; random vibrations; search and optimization theory; control; computation; bond graph modeling of engineering systems. **Mailing Address:** 1217 Stanford Pl, Davis, CA 95616. **Fax:** 530-752-4158. **E-Mail:** dckarnopp@ucdavis.edu

KARNOSKY, DAVID FRANK, FOREST GENETICS. **Personal Data:** b Rhinelander, Wis, October 12, 1949; m 1970, Sheryl; c 2. **Education:** Univ Wis-Madison, BS, 1971, MS, 1972, PhD (forest genetics), 1975. **Honors & Awards:** - Michigan Tech University Researcher of the Year (1993) - IUFRO Scientific Achievement Award (2005). **Professional Experience:** PROF FOREST GENETICS & BIOTECHNOLOGY, SCH FORESTRY, MICH TECHNOL UNIV, HOUGHTON, 1983-; Forest geneticist, Cary Arboretum, NY Bot Garden, 1975-1983. **Memberships:** Int Soc Arboriculture; Tissue Culture Asn; Soc Am Foresters; Int Tissue Cult Asn; Sigma Xi; Int Plant Propagators Asn. **Research Statement & Publications:** Understanding variation in tolerance to air pollution and climate change of trees; cytogenetic and tissue culture studies of elms; developing urban hardy trees; interspecific hybridization of Ulmus and Larix species; forest biotechnology and gene transfer; increasing forest productivity in northern regions. **Mailing Address:** Sch Forestry, Mich Technol Univ, 101 U J Noblet Forestry Bldg, 1400 Townsend Dr, Houghton, MI 49931. **Fax:** 906-487-2897. **E-Mail:** karnosky@mtu.edu

KARNOVSKY, MORRIS JOHN, PATHOLOGY, CELL BIOLOGY. **Personal Data:** b Johannesburg, SAfrica, June 28, 1926; American citizen; m 1951, Shirley; c David & Nina. **Education:** Univ Witwatersrand, BSc, 1946, MB, BCh, 1950, DSc, 1984; Univ London, dipl clin path, 1954. **Honorary Degrees:** MA, Harvard Univ, 1965. **Honors & Awards:** Lederle med fac Award, 1963-1966; Rous-Whipple Award, Am Asn Pathologists, 1981; Distinguished Scientist Award, Electron Micros Soc Am, 1988; E B Wilson Award, Am Soc Cell Biol, 1990; Maude Abbott Award, US & Can Acad Path, 1994. **Professional Experience:** SHATTUCK PROF EMER PATH ANAT, HARVARD MED SCH, as of 2002; shattuck prof path anat, Harvard Med Sch, beginning 1972; prof path, Harvard Med Sch, beginning 1968; mem study group path, USPHS, 1965-1969; from asst prof to assoc prof, Harvard Med Sch, 1963-1968; sci collabr, Sch Med, Univ Geneva, 1961-1963; assoc, Harvard Med Sch, 1961-1963; assoc, Peter Bent Brigham Hosp, 1958-1960; res fel, Harvard Med Sch, 1956-1960; asst resident path, Beth Israel Hosp, 1955-1956; House officer med & surg, Johannesburg Gen Hosp, 1951. **Memberships:** Nat Acad Sci-Inst Med; fel Am Acad Arts & Sci; Am Soc Exp Path; Histochem Soc; Int Acad Path; Am Soc Cell Biol; fel AAAS; hon mem Ger Soc Cell Biol. **Research Statement & Publications:** Histochemistry; electron microscopy; ultrastructural cytochemistry; cell surface topography and modulation; cell junctions; metabolism and structure of kidney; structure and function of capillaries; growth regulation in blood vessels; reactive oxygen species. **Mailing Address:** Harvard Med Sch, Rm 101 Goldenson Bldg 200 Longwood Ave, Boston, MA 02115. **Fax:** 617-432-2793. **E-Mail:** morris_karnovsky@hms.harvard.edu

KARO, DOUGLAS PAUL, APPLIED TECHNOLOGY, INFORMATION MANAGEMENT. **Personal Data:** b Seattle, Wash, August 24, 1947; m 1971, Rebecca; c Alice J. **Education:** Stanford Univ, BS, 1969; Mass Inst Technol, PhD (physics), 1973, MS, 1980. **Professional Experience:** TECH STAFF, DRAPER LAB, 1989-; tech consult, Nat Sec, 1987-1989; staff mgt consult, Texton Defense Syst, 1980-1987; sr staff scientist physics, Avco Everett Res Lab Inc, 1973-1978; Physicist, Harry Diamond Lab, US Army, 1971. **Memberships:** Am Phys Soc; AAAS; Sigma Xi; Int Inst Strategic Studies; Am Inst Aeronaut & Astronaut. **Research Statement & Publications:** Defense science and technology; systems analysis; management of research and development. **Mailing Address:** Draper Lab, 1555 Wilson Blvd, Arlington, VA 22209. **E-Mail:** dkaro@draper.com

KARO, WOLF, INDUSTRIAL ORGANIC CHEMISTRY, POLYMER APPLICATIONSTO BIOTECHNOLOGY. **Personal Data:** b Altona-Hamburg, Ger, April 2, 1924. **Education:** Cornell Univ, AB, 1945, PhD (org chem), 1949. **Professional Experience:** Consultant: product/process development management; RETIRED; mgr res & develop, Polysci Inc, 1976-1993; res supvr, Haven Chem Co, 1975-1976; sr chemist, Rohm & Haas Co, 1975; supvr qual control, Lactona Corp Div, Warner-Lambert Pharmaceut Co, 1972-1975; new prod mgr, Sartomer Resins, Inc, 1970-1971; sr sci specialist, Scott Paper Co, 1968-1969; develop mgr, Monomer-Polymer & Dajac Labs, 1961-1968; group leader contract res, synthesis & polymerization sects, Borden Chem Co, 1955-1968; aeronaut res scientist fuel synthesis, Monomer-Polymer, Inc, 1953-1955; Aeronaut res scientist jet fuel, Nat Adv Comt Aeronaut, 1949-1953. **Memberships:** AAAS; Am Chem Soc; Sigma Xi. **Research Statement & Publications:** Reaction kinetics and mechanisms in organic chemistry; organic functional group synthesis; emulsion and anaerobic polymerization; adhesives; coatings; product and process development; materials for radiation-induced polymerization; anionic polymerization; organic polymer chemistry; monodispersed polymer latices for biotechnology; magnetizable latex and application; intraoccular materials; Publications: Books on organic functional group preparations, polymer synthesis, laboratory manual of polymer chemistry, various source movies of organic and polymer preparation. **Mailing Address:** 328 Rockledge Ave, Huntingdon Valley, PA 19006.

KAROL, FREDERICK J, POLYMER CHEMISTRY. **Personal Data:** b Norton, Mass, February 28, 1933; m 1958, Ruth Lindbom; c Mark, Donald & Cynthia. **Education:** Boston Univ, BS, 1954; Mass Inst Technol, PhD (org chem), 1962. **Honors & Awards:** Chem Pioneer Award, Am Inst Chemists, 1988; Perkin Medal, Soc Chem Indust, 1989; Int

Gold Medal, Soc Plastics Engrs, 1990; Award for Creative Invention, Am Chem Soc, 1991. **Professional Experience:** SR CORP FEL, UNION CARBIDE CORP, 1984-; corp fel, Chem & Plastics Group, Union Carbide Corp, 1981-1984; res assoc & group supvr, Chem & Plastics Group, Union Carbide Corp, 1978-1981; group leader chem & plastics, Chem & Plastics Group, Union Carbide Corp, 1969-1978; res scientist, Chem & Plastics Group, Union Carbide Corp, 1967-1969; proj scientist, Chem & Plastics Group, Union Carbide Corp, 1965-1967; Chemist, Chem & Plastics Group, Union Carbide Corp, 1956-1959 & 1962-1965. **Memberships:** Nat Acad Eng; Am Inst Chemists; Sigma Xi; Am Chem Soc. **Research Statement & Publications:** Heterogeneous and polyolefin catalyses; mechanism of polymerization; production of high density polyethylene and low density polyethylene; polypropylene; new polymers. **Mailing Address:** Union Carbide Corp, Piscataway, NJ 08854.

KAROL, MARK J, COMMUNICATIONS SYSTEMS RESEARCH, NETWORK SYSTEMS RESEARCH. **Personal Data:** b Jersey City, NJ, February 28, 1959; m 1987, Roxanne; c Robert & Kevin. **Education:** Case Inst Technol, BS & BSEE, 1981; Princeton Univ, MS, 1982, MA, 1983, PhD (elec eng), 1986. **Professional Experience:** RES SCIENTIST, AVAYA LABS RES, beginning 2000; gen chair, Commun Soc Bd Gov, 1996-; gen chair, info comt, 1994; distinguished mem tech staff, AT&T Bell Labs, 1993-2000; chmn, Tech Comt Comput Commun, Inst Elec & Electronics Engrs, 1993-1995; vchmn, Tech Comt Comput Commun, Inst Elec & Electronics Engrs, 1991-1993; assoc ed, Inst Elec & Electronics Engrs J Lightwave Technol, 1991; secy, Tech Comt Comput Commun, Inst Elec & Electronics Engrs, 1989-1991; mem tech staff, AT&T Bell Labs, 1985-1992. **Memberships:** Fel Inst Elec & Electronics Engrs; Math Asn Am. **Mailing Address:** Avaya Inc, 307 Middletown Lincroft Rd Rm 1N 239, Lincroft, NJ 07738-1526. **Fax:** 908-949-9118. **E-Mail:** mk@avaya.com, mk@bell-labs.com

KAROL, MERYL HELENE, IMMUNOCHEMISTRY, TOXICOLOGY. **Personal Data:** b New York, NY, m 1963, c 3. **Education:** Cornell Univ, BS, 1961; Columbia Univ, PhD (microbiol), 1967. **Honors & Awards:** Frank R Blood, 1981; Rachel Carson Award, 1993. **Professional Experience:** PROF & GSPH ASSOC DEAN IMMUNOTOXICOL, UNIV PITTSBURGH, 1985-; assoc prof, Univ Pittsburgh, 1979-1985; res asst prof toxicol, Univ Pittsburgh, 1976-1978; res assoc epidemiol, Univ Pittsburgh, 1974-1976; fel biochem, State Univ NY, Stony Brook, 1967-1968. **Memberships:** Am Chem Soc; Am Thoracic Soc; AAAS; Soc Toxicol (pres, 1994); NY Acad Sci; Am Asn Immunol. **Research Statement & Publications:** Chemical and industrial allergens; environmental lung disease; occupational disease; diagnostic radioimmunoassays. **Mailing Address:** Dept Environ & Occup Health, Univ Pittsburgh, 130 DeSoto St, Pittsburgh, PA 15238. **Fax:** 412-624-3040. **E-Mail:** mhk@pitt.edu

KAROL, PAUL J(ASON), PHYSICAL CHEMISTRY, ANALYTICAL CHEMISTRY. **Personal Data:** b New York, NY, March 18, 1941. **Education:** Johns Hopkins Univ, BA, 1961; Columbia Univ, MS, 1962, PhD (chem), 1967. **Professional Experience:** PROF CHEM, CARNEGIE-MELLON UNIV, 1994-; vis prof, Japan Atomic Energy Res Inst, Tokai, 2000; chmn, Div Nuclear Chem & Technol, Am Chem Soc, 1996; chmn, Comn on Radiochem, Int Union Pure & Appl Chem, 1995-1997; titular mem, Comn on Radiochem, Int Union Pure & Appl Chem, 1993-1997; vis prof, Lab Nat Di Disilia Nucleare, Padova, Italy 1991-1992; assoc mem, Comn on Radiochem, Int Union Pure & Appl Chem, 1985-1993; mem Comt Nuclear Radiochem, Nat Res Coun, 1981-1987; assoc dean sci, Carnegie-mellon Univ, 1981-1986; consult, Westinghouse Elec Corp, 1972-1985; from asst prof to assoc prof, Carnegie-mellon Univ, 1969-1994; res collabr, Brookhaven Nat Lab, 1969-1972; res assoc nuclear chem, Brookhaven Nat Lab, 1967-1969. **Memberships:** AAAS; Am Chem Soc; Am Phys Soc; Sigma Xi; fel Am Inst Chemists. **Research Statement & Publications:** Mechanisms of high and ultra-high energy nuclear reactions; rapid radiochemical separations; column chromatography; positronium quenching; wnvironmental chemistry. **Mailing Address:** Dept Chem, Carnegie Mellon Univ, 4400 Fifth Ave, Pittsburgh, PA 15213-2683. **Fax:** 412-268-6945. **E-Mail:** pk03@andrew.cmu.edu

KAROL, ROBIN A, MONOCLONAL ANTIBODY PRODUCTION. **Personal Data:** b Bronx, NY, September 29, 1951. **Professional Experience:** DIR, BOTTOMLINE INNOVATION ASSOC, WILMINGTON, DEL, as of 2004; dir, Innovation Processes Sustainability Safety Health & Environ Excellence, E I DuPont de Nemours & Co, as of 2004; sr consult, Dupont Consult Solutions, as of 2004; sr res immunol & group leader, Dept Biomed Prod, E I Du Pont Del Nemours & Co, Inc, beginning 1985; res immunologist, 1982-1985; prof, Bayer Col, Tex; fel Albert-Einstein Univ; Quality mgr, E I Du Pont Del Nemours & Co. **Memberships:** AAAS; Am Asn Immunologists. **Mailing Address:** Bottom Line Innovations Assoc Inc, 1704 Fox Grape Lane Ste 312, Annapolis, MD 21401.

KAROLY, KEITH, BIOLOGY. **Education:** Whitman Col, BA, 1985; Univ Chicago, MS, 1987, PhD, 1991. **Professional Experience:** ASSOC PROF, DEPT BIOL, REED COL, as of 2005. **Research Statement & Publications:** Ecology and evolution of flowering plants. **Mailing Address:** Dept Biol, Reed Col, Biol B240, Portland, OR 97202. **E-Mail:** Keith.Karoly@directory.reed.edu

KARON, JOHN MARSHALL, BIOSTATISTICS. **Personal Data:** b Milwaukee, Wis, November 6, 1941. **Education:** Carleton Col, BA, 1963; Stanford Univ, MS, 1965, PhD (math), 1968. **Professional Experience:** Adj Fac, Dept Biostatistics, Emory Univ, as of 2004; MATH STATISTICIAN, CTR DIS CONTROL & PREV, ATLANTA, 1984-; res assoc prof, Univ NC, 1980-1984; fel biostatist, Univ NC, 1977-1980; Vis lectr, Tel Aviv Univ, 1972-1973; asst prof math, Colo Col, 1971-1977; res assoc, Stanford Univ, 1970-1971; Asst prof math, Syracuse Univ, 1968-1970. **Memberships:** AAAS; Soc Indust & Appl Math; Am Statist Asn. **Research Statement & Publications:** Evaluation of statistical methods; statistical epidemiology. **Mailing Address:** Emory Univ, Atlanta, GA 30322.

KAROW, ARMAND MONFORT, GENERAL PHARMACOLOGY, CRYOBIOLOGY. **Personal Data:** b New Orleans, La, November 11, 1941; m 1964, Ramona; c Christopher A & Jonathan C. **Education:** Duke Univ, BA, 1962; Univ Miss, PhD (pharmacol), 1968. **Professional Experience:** Ed, Biophys Organ Cryopreservation, 1987; Fogarty sr int fel award, NIH, 1981; fel, Nat Endowment Humanities, 1980; EMER RES ASSOC PROF, DEPT SURG, MED COL GA, 1977-2000; officer, Xytex Corp, Augusta, Ga, 1975-; PROF, DEPT PHARMACOL, 1975-2000; ed, Organ Preserv for Transplantation, 1974 & 1981; dir grad studies, Dept Pharmacol, 1973-1980; res asst prof, Dept Surg, Med Col Ga, 1971-1977; assoc prof, Dept Pharmacol, 1970-1975; res instr, Dept Surg, Med Col Ga, 1968-1971; asst prof, Dept Pharmacol, 1968-1970; res grants, NIH & USPHS. **Memberships:** Fel AAAS; Am Soc Reproductive Med; Soc Cryobiol (secy, 1977-1980); Am Asn Tissue Banks; Europ Soc Human Reproduction & Embryol. **Research Statement & Publications:** Cryopreservation of mammalian organs and tissues; mammalian reproductive biology. **Mailing Address:** Dept Pharmacol, Med Col Ga, 1120 15th St, Augusta, GA 30912. **Fax:** 706-721-2347.

KAROWE, DAVID NATHAN, PLANT-INSECT INTERACTIONS, ECOLOGICAL EFFECTS OF ELEVATED CARBON DIOXIDE. **Personal Data:** b Waltham, Mass, May 27, 1957. **Education:** Harvard Univ, BA, 1979; Univ Mich, MS, 1983, PhD (ecol), 1988. **Professional Experience:** ASSOC PROF & GRAD ADV BIOL SCI, WESTERN MICH UNIV as of 1999; vis asst prof, Univ Mich Biol Sta, 1990-; asst prof biol, Va Commonwealth Univ, 1990-1996; Fel, Univ Mich, 1989-1990; Fel, NATO-NSF, 1988-1989. **Memberships:** Soc Study Evolution; Chem Ecol Soc; Entom Soc Am. **Research Statement & Publications:** Direct effects of elevated carbon dioxide on multiple trophic level systems and the potential for adaptive evolutionary response at each trophic level. **Mailing Address:** Dept Biol, Western Mich Univ, Kalamazoo, MI 49008. **Fax:** 269-387-5609. **E-Mail:** david.karowe@wmich.edu

KARP, ALAN H, COMPUTER ARCHITECTURE, COMPUTER SECURITY. **Personal Data:** b Syracuse, NY, August 6, 1946; m 1970, Nancy; c Joseph S. **Education:** Rensselaer Polytech Inst, BS, 1968; Univ Md, Col Park, PhD (astron), 1974. **Professional Experience:** Principal Scientist, Hewlett-Packard Labs, 1992-2000; SR STAFF MEM, HEWLETT-PACKARD LABS, 1992-2000; mem staff physics, IBM Sci Ctr, 1977-1992; asst prof physics, Dartmouth Col, 1976-1977; Consult, IBM Res, Yorktown Heights, NY, 1976-1977; Fel astron, IBM Res, Yorktown Heights, NY, 1974-1976. **Memberships:** Am Astron Soc; Asn Computer Mach; Soc Indust & Appl Math. **Research Statement & Publications:** Algorithms for parallel processors; radiative transfer in moving stellar atmospheres; radiative transfer in planetary atmospheres containing dust; web services; peer to peer system architecture; access control for distributed systems. **Mailing Address:** 837 Ilima Ct, Palo Alto, CA 94306. **E-Mail:** alan, karp@hp.com

KARP, ARTHUR, HIGH FREQUENCY PHYSICS, MICROWAVE ELECTRONICS. **Personal Data:** b New York, NY, April 26, 1928. **Education:** City Col New York, BEE, 1948; Mass Inst Technol, SM, 1950; Cambridge Univ, PhD (elec eng), 1962. **Honors & Awards:** B J Thompson Mem Prize, Inst Radio Engrs, 1958. **Professional Experience:** Sr engr, Varian Assocs Inc, 1977- 1989; sr res engr, SRI Int, 1964-1977; consultant Varian Assocs, 1962-1963 & Goodyear Aerospace Corp, Ariz, 1963-1964; res engr, W W Hansen Labs, Stanford, 1960-1964; Consult, Sylvania Elec Prod Inc, Calif, 1960-1962; engr lab, Cambridge Univ, 1956-1959; mem tech staff, Bell Tel Labs, Inc, 1951-1956; res asst cent lab, Int Tel & Tel, Paris, France, 1950-1951; res asst electronics, Mass Inst Technol, 1948-1950; Jr engr, A Alford Consult Engrs, Mass, 1948. **Memberships:** AAAS; Inst Elec & Electronics Engrs Life senior. **Research Statement & Publications:** Electron devices; ultrahigh frequency, microwave and millimeter-wave techniques, components, circuits, electron tubes, bio-effects; color perception and display techniques including color encryption. **Mailing Address:** 1470 Sand Mill Rd Apt 301, Palo Alto, CA 94304-2058.

KARP, BENNETT C, NUCLEAR PHYSICS. **Personal Data:** b Brooklyn, NY, May 15, 1954. **Education:** State Univ NY, Binghampton, Ba, 1976; Univ Pittsburgh, MS, 1978, PhD (physics), 1982. **Professional Experience:** DISTINGUISHED MEM TECH STAFF, AT&T BELL LABS, 1984-; res assoc, Univ NC, 1982-1984. **Memberships:** Am Phys Soc. **Mailing Address:** 812 Wellington Pl, Aberdeen, NJ 07747.

KARP, HERBERT RUBIN, NEUROLOGY. **Personal Data:** b Atlanta, Ga, April 13, 1921; m 1948, c 3. **Education:** Emory Univ, AB, 1943; MD, 1951; Am Bd Psychiat & Neurol, dipl, 1960. **Professional Experience:** PROF EMER NEUROL, SCH MED, EMORY UNIV, as of 2003; prof neurol, sch med, Emory Univ, beginning 1963; asst prof med, Sch Med, Emory Univ, 1958-1963; res fel neuropath, Harvard Med Sch, 1957-1958; Nat Inst Neurol Dis & Blindness spec trainee, 1956-1958; clin & res fel, Harvard Med Sch, 1956-1957; resident neurol, Univ Hosp, Duke Univ, 1954-1956; fel metab dis, Sch Med, Emory Univ, 1953-1954; intern & jr asst resident internal med, Grady Mem Hosp, 1951-1953; consult, Vet Admin Hosp, Atlanta, Ga. **Memberships:** AAAS; Am Neurol Asn; fel Am Acad Neurol. **Research Statement & Publications:** Cerebrovascular disease from the standpoint of further understanding of underlying pathophysiology as well as evaluation of current methods of therapy; age-dependent degenerative diseases of the nervous system. **Mailing Address:** Emory Sch Med, Emory Univ, Atlanta, GA 30322. **Fax:** 404-727-0473. **E-Mail:** hkarp02@emory.edu

KARP, HOWARD, ANALYTICAL CHEMISTRY. **Personal Data:** b Pittsburgh, Pa, September 26, 1926; m 1952, Rita; c Henry, Stuart, Robert & Laura. **Education:** Univ Pittsburgh, BS, 1949. **Professional Experience:** RETIRED; assoc res consult chem, US Steel Corp, 1949-1985. **Memberships:** Comt chem anal metals; Am Soc Testing & Mat. **Research Statement & Publications:** Analytical chemistry as it pertains to steel chemistry. **Mailing Address:** 151 Kelvington Dr, Monroeville, PA 15146.

KARP, LAURENCE EDWARD, OBSTETRICS & GYNECOLOGY, MEDICAL GENETICS. **Personal Data:** b Paterson, NJ, April 26, 1939; m 1962, c 2. **Education:** NY Univ, MD, 1963. **Professional Experience:** DIR EDUC OBSTET & GYNEC, SWED HOSP MED CTR, SEATTLE, 1977-; ASSOC PROF OBSTET & GYNEC, SCH MED, UNIV WASH, 1977-; assoc prof, Harbor Gen Hosp, Univ Calif, Los Angeles, 1976-1977; asst prof obstet & gynec, Sch Med, Univ Wash, 1972-1976; sr fel reprod genetics, Sch Med, Univ Wash, 1970-1972; instr obstet & gynec, Sch Med, Univ Tex, San Antonio, 1969-1970. **Memberships:** Fel Am Col Obstet & Gynec; AAAS; Am Soc Human Genetics. **Research Statement & Publications:** Investigation of chromosomal anomalies in gametes and preimplantation embryos; also, advancement of procedures and techniques for prenatal diagnosis. **Mailing Address:** Div Perinatal Med, Swed Hosp Med Ctr, 747 Summit, Seattle, WA 98104-2132.

KARP, RICHARD DALE, IMMUNOLOGY. **Personal Data:** b Minneapolis, Minn, June 19, 1943; m 1968, c 3. **Education:** Univ Minn, BA, 1965, MS, 1968, PhD (microbiol), 1972. **Professional Experience:** PROF BIOL SCI, UNIV CINCINNATI, 1986-; from asst prof to assoc prof, Univ Cincinnati, 1975-1986; NIH & C D Rogers fels, Univ Calif, Los Angeles, 1973-1975; Teaching Asst, microbiol, Univ Minn, 1966-1972. **Memberships:** Am Soc Microbiol; Am Soc Zoologists; Am Asn Immunologists; AAAS; NY Acad Sci; Int Soc Develop Comp Immunologists; Entom Soc Am. **Research Statement & Publications:** Evolution of humoral and cell-mediated immunity. **Mailing Address:** Dept Biol Sci, Univ Cincinnati, ML006, Cincinnati, OH 45221-0006. **Fax:** 513-556-5299. **E-Mail:** richard.karp@uc.edu

KARP, RICHARD M, COMPUTER THEORY, ALGORITHMS & COMPUTATIONAL COMPLEXITY. **Personal Data:** b Boston, Mass, January 3, 1935; m 1979, c 1. **Education:** Harvard Univ, BA, 1955, MS, 1956, PhD (appl math), 1959. **Honorary Degrees:** Dr, Univ Pa, 1986, Technion, 1989, Univ Mass, 1990 & Georgetown Univ, 1992. **Honors & Awards:** Nat Med Sci, 1996; Lanchester Prize, Opers Res Soc Am & Inst Mgt Sci, 1977; Fulkerson Prize, Am Math Soc, 1979; Turing Award, Asn Comput Mach, 1985; von Neumann Lectr, Soc Indust & Appl Math, 1987; von Neumann Theory Prize, Opers Res Soc Am, 1990; Babbage Prize, 1995; Centennial Medal, Harvard Univ, 1997. **Professional Experience:** SR RES SCIENTIST, INT COMPUT SCI INST, BERKELEY, 1999-; PROF COMPUT SCI, MATH & BIOENGINEERING, UNIV CALIF, BERKELEY, 1999-; HP vis res prof, Math Sci Res Inst, Berkeley, 1999-2000; adj prof molecular biotechnology, Univ Wash, 1995-1999; prof comput sci & eng, Univ Wash, 1995-1999; UNIV PROF EMER COMPUT SCI & OPERS RES, UNIV CALIF, BERKELEY, 1994-; chmn, Dept Comput Sci,

Math & Oper Res, Univ Calif, Berkeley, 1989-1994; mem nat adv bd, Comput Professionals Social Responsibility, 1989-; mem bd govs, Weizmann Inst Sci, 1989-; mem bd trustees, Int Comput Sci Inst, 1988-; res scientist, Int Comput Sci Inst, Berkeley, 1988-1994; fac res lectr, Univ Calif, Berkeley, 1981-1982; prof math, Univ Calif, Berkeley, 1980-1994; Miller res prof, Univ Calif, Berkeley, 1980-1981; assoc chmn dept, Univ Calif, Berkeley, 1973-1975; prof comput sci & opers res, Univ Calif, Berkeley, 1968-1994; vis prof, Polytech Inst Brooklyn, 1968; adj assoc prof indust & mgt eng, Columbia Univ, 1967-1968; vis assoc prof, Polytech Inst Brooklyn, 1965-1968; vis assoc prof elec eng, Univ Mich, 1964-1965; res staff, Watson Res Ctr, Int Bus Mach Corp, 1959-1968. **Memberships:** Nat Acad Sci; Nat Acad Eng; fel Am Acad Arts & Sci; Am Math Soc; fel Asn Comput Mach; Comput Prof Social Responsibility; Soc Indust & Appl Math; NY Acad Sci; fel AAAS. **Research Statement & Publications:** Construction of computational algorithms and the determination of the inherent computational complexity of problems with particular emphasis on combinatorial problems. **Mailing Address:** Dept Elec Eng & Comput Sci, Univ Calif, 621 Soda Hall Ste 1776, Berkeley, CA 94720-1776. **Fax:** 510-643-5775. **E-Mail:** karp@cs.berkeley.edu

KARP, SAMUEL NOAH, APPLIED MATHEMATICS. **Personal Data:** b Brooklyn, NY, February 13, 1924; m 1946, c 2. **Education:** Brown Univ, MSc, 1945, PhD, 1948. **Professional Experience:** PROF EMER MATH, COURANT INST MATH SCI, NY UNIV, WASH SQ, as of 2004; prof math, Courant Inst Math Sci, NY Univ, Wash Sq, beginning 1961; from res asst prof to res assoc prof math, Div Electromagnetic Res, 1955-1961; sr res scientist, Div Electromagnetic Res, 1948-1955; instr, Wash Sq Col, 1948-1955; res assoc compressible fluids & flutter, Brown Univ, 1946-1948; indust consult. **Memberships:** Am Math Soc. **Research Statement & Publications:** Electromagnetic theory; diffraction; boundary value problems; ship resistance and motions; surface waves; far field expansions of radiated fields; multiple impedance; higher order eigen functions of integral equations; inverse scattering. **Mailing Address:** Dept Math, NY Univ, 251 Mercer St Ste 819, New York, NY 10012. **Fax:** 212-995-4121.

KARP, STEWART, ANALYTICAL CHEMISTRY. **Personal Data:** b New York, NY, March 17, 1932; m 1957, c 2. **Education:** Queens Col, NY, BS, 1953; Polytech Inst Brooklyn, MS, 1960, PhD (chem), 1967. **Professional Experience:** PROF CHEM, C W POST COL, LONG ISLAND UNIV, 1982-; chmn, dept Chem, 1981-1988; assoc prof, C W Post Col, Long Island Univ, 1971-1982; asst prof, C W Post Col, Long Island Univ, 1968-1971; sr chemist, Am Cyanamid Co, 1967-1968; anal chemist, Colgate-Palmolive Co, 1960-1962; Chemist, Sperry Gyroscope Co, 1957-1960. **Memberships:** Am Chem Soc; Sigma Xi; AAAS. **Research Statement & Publications:** Electroanalytical chemistry; analytical methods. **Mailing Address:** Grad Prog Environ Studies, Long Island Univ, C W Post Campus, Brookville, NY 11548. **Fax:** 516-299-4140. **E-Mail:** stewart.karp@liu.edu

KARP, WARREN B, PREVENTIVE MEDICINE, NUTRITION. **Personal Data:** b Brooklyn, NY, February 12, 1944; m 1976, Nancy; c Heather & Michael. **Education:** Pace Univ, BS, 1965; Ohio State Univ, PhD (physiol chem), 1970; Med Col Ga, DMD, 1977. **Honors & Awards:** Alumnus of the Year, Pace University Elected, FASEB. **Professional Experience:** PROF EMER MED, MED COL GA, as of 2000; assoc res prof pediat, Sch Med, 1979-1988; assoc prof oral biol biochem & oral med, Sch Dent, 1979-1988; dir clin perinatal lab, 1978-; asst prof biochem, Sch Dent, 1974-1979; asst res prof pediat & asst prof cell & molecular biol, Sch Med & asst prof, Sch Grad Studies, 1973-1979; instr cell & molecular biol, Sch Med, Med Col Ga, 1972-1973; pediat res instr, Sch Med, Med Col Ga, 1971-1973; res assoc pediat, Ohio State Univ, 1970-1971; res assoc, Ohio State Univ, 1968-1970; Teaching asst physiol chem, Ohio State Univ, 1966-1968; prof pediat, oral biol, oral diag/patient serv, biochem & molecular biol, Sch Med, Dent & Grad Studi; licensed dietitian, cert nutrit spec. **Memberships:** AAAS; Sigma Xi; Am Chem Soc; NY Acad Sci; Int Dent Res Soc; Am Inst Nutrit; Am Soc Clin Nutrit. **Research Statement & Publications:** Environmental effects on human placental enzymology; human placental amino acid metabolism; the effect of bilirubin on brain metabolism; human placental lipid metabolism; human nutrition. **Mailing Address:** Dept Med Med Col Ga, 551 Cedar Rock Dr, Augusta, GA 30907. **E-Mail:** wkarp@mcg.edu

KARPATI, GEORGE, HISTOCHEMISTRY, MUSCLE BIOLOGY & NEUROSCIENCE. **Personal Data:** Canadian citizen; c 2. **Education:** Dalhousie Univ, MD, 1960. **Honors & Awards:** Can Gov Gen Award, 1993. **Professional Experience:** Chmn sci adv bd, Muscular Dystrophy Asn Can, 1991-1994; PROF PEDIAT, MONTREAL NEUROL INST, MCGILL UNIV 1990-; chmn, Bd Examiners, Royal Col Physicians & Surgeons Can, 1986-1989; KILLAM CHAIR NEUROL, MONTREAL NEUROL INST, MCGILL UNIV, 1985-; coordr, Neuromuscular Res Group, Montreal Neurol Inst, 1985-; assoc dir res, Montreal Neurol Inst, Mcgill Univ, 1985-1991; DIR NEUROMUSCULAR RES, MONTREAL NEUROL INST, MCGILL UNIV, 1984-. **Memberships:** Hon mem French Neurol Soc; Am Acad Neurol; Am Neurol Asn; Can Cong Neurol Sci; Histochem Soc; Royal Col Physicians & Surgeons Can; World Fedn Neurol. **Research Statement & Publications:** Neuromuscular system using histochemical, cytochemical, immunological and physiological techniques; cell therapy of inherited muscle diseases; gene therapy of neurological diseases. **Mailing Address:** Montreal Neurol Inst Rm 633, Montreal, PQ H3A 2B4, Can. **Fax:** 514-398-8310. **E-Mail:** george.karpati@staff.mcgill.ca

KARPATKIN, SIMON, BIOCHEMISTRY, PHYSIOLOGY. **Personal Data:** b Brooklyn, NY, September 6, 1933; m 1965. **Education:** Brooklyn Col, BS, 1954; NY Univ, MD, 1958. **Professional Experience:** DIR, HEMAT DIV, as of 2005; PROF MED, SCH MED, NY UNIV, 1974-; res grants, NY Heart Asn, 1967-1970; career scientist, Health Res Coun City NY, 1966-1971; res grants, Muscular Dystrophy Asn Am, 1966-1968; res grants, Health Res Coun City NY, 1966; from instr to prof, Sch Med, NY Univ, 1964-1974; fel biochem, 1962-1964; fel, Am Cancer Soc, 1962-1964; trainee, USPHS, 1961-1962; fel hemat, Sch Med, Wash Univ, 1961-1962; resident, Einstein Med Ctr, Bronx, 1960-1961; resident, Bellevue Hosp, NY Univ, 1959-1960; intern med, Bellevue Hosp, NY Univ, 1958-1959. **Memberships:** Am Soc Hemat; Am Asn Physicians; Am Soc Physiol; Am Soc Clin Invest; Am Soc Biol Chem. **Research Statement & Publications:** role of thrombosis, thrombin and angiogenesis in cancer; platelet biochemical interactions during hemostasis; autoimmune platelet disorders; role of platelets in cancer. **Mailing Address:** NY Univ Sch Med, 550 First Ave, New York, NY 10016-6481. **Fax:** 212-263-0695. **E-Mail:** simon.karpatkin@med.nyu.edu

KARPEL, RICHARD LESLIE, MOLECULAR BIOLOGY, BIOPHYSICS. **Personal Data:** b New York, NY, May 31, 1944; m 1968, Madeline; c Emily. **Education:** Queens Col, NY, BA, 1965; Brandeis Univ, PhD (chem), 1970. **Professional Experience:** PROF CHEM & BIOCHEM, UNIV MD, BALTIMORE CO, 1995-; Sr fel, Nat Res Coun, Nat Cancer Inst, Frederick Cancer Res Facil, NIH, 1982-1983; from asst prof to assoc prof, Univ MD, Baltimore CO, 1976-1995; res assoc, NIH res fel biochem sci, 1974-1976; res assoc, Princeton Univ, 1972-1974; res assoc, NIH res fel, 1971-1972; res assoc, Princeton Univ, 1970-1971. **Memberships:** AAAS; Am Chem Soc; Sigma Xi; Am Soc Biochem Molecular Biol. **Research Statement & Publications:** Protein-nucleic acid interactions; structure-function studies on nucleic acid helix-destabilizing proteins; retroviral nucleic acid binding proteins; nucleic acid-interactive enzymes; metal-nucleic acid interactions. **Mailing Address:** Dept Chem & Biochem, Univ Md, 1000 Hill Top Circle, Baltimore, MD 21250. **Fax:** 410-455-2608. **E-Mail:** karpel@umbc.edu

KARPETSKY, TIMOTHY PAUL, CHEMICAL WARFARE. **Education:** Johns Hopkins Univ, PhD (org chem), 1970. **Professional Experience:** PRES, ENVIRON TECHNOL GROUP INC, 1991-; vpres mkt, Environ Technol Group Inc, 1989-1991; vpres eng, Bendix Corp, 1987-1989; supvr phys scientist, Us Army Chem Res & Eng Ctr, 1982-1987. **Research Statement & Publications:** Convention compliance monitoring. **Mailing Address:** Environ Technol Group, Inc, 8219 Ruxton Crossing Ct, Baltimore, MD 21204. **Fax:** 410-339-3123.

KARPIAK, STEPHEN EDWARD, PSYCHIATRY. **Personal Data:** b Hartford, Conn, August 13, 1947. **Education:** Col the Holy Cross, BA, 1969; Fordham Univ, MA, 1971, PhD (exp psychol), 1972. **Professional Experience:** ASSOC PROF PSYCHIAT, COLUMBIA UNIV, 1978-; SR RES SCIENTIST, DIV NEUROSCIENCE, NY STATE PSYCHIAT INST, 1974-; asst prof psychol, Manhattan Col, 1972-1978; fel neuroimmunol, Parkinson Dis Found, Dept Neurol, Col Physicians & Surgeons, 1972-1974; vis fel, Dept Psychiat, Columbia Univ, 1972-1974. **Memberships:** Soc Neuroscience; Am Psychol Asn. **Research Statement & Publications:** Development of immunological tools for the study of brain function and pathology, specifically the use of brain antibodies to study behavior and electrophysiology; effects of exogenous administration of gangliosides on central nervous system pathology. **Mailing Address:** 256 W Tenth St No 2B, New York, NY 10014.

KARPILOVSKY, G, MATHEMATICS. **Professional Experience:** PROF MATH, CALIF STATE UNIV, CHICO, as of 1996. **Mailing Address:** Dept Math & Statist, Calif State Univ, 400 W First St, Chico, CA 95929-0525.

KARPINSKI, MAREK M, COMPUTER SCIENCES. **Education:** Acad Scis, Warsaw, Poland, PhD, 1973. **Honors & Awards:** Prize, Polish Math Soc, 1974; Award, Polish Acad Sci, 1976; Res Award, Humboldt Found, 1982; Max Planck Res Prize, 1994. **Professional Experience:** CHAIR PROF COMPUT SCI, UNIV BONN, GER, 1989-; Mem, Int Comput Sci Inst, Berkeley, Calif. **Memberships:** Am Math Soc; Soc Indust & Appl Math; Asn Comput Mach; Inst Elec & Electronics Engrs; AAAS. **Research Statement & Publications:** Contributed over 100 articles to professional journals; author of 5 books. **Mailing Address:** Dept Comput Sci Univ Bonn, Roemerstr 164, 53117 Bonn, Ger. **Fax:** 492-287-34440. **E-Mail:** marek@cs.uni-bonn.de

KARPLUS, MARTIN, PHYSICAL CHEMISTRY. **Personal Data:** b Vienna, Austria, March 15, 1930; American citizen; m 1981, c 3. **Education:** Harvard Univ, BA, 1950; Calif Inst Technol, PhD (chem), 1953. **Honors & Awards:** Fresenius Award, 1965; Harrison Howe Award, Am Chem Soc, 1967; Award Outstanding Contribution, Int Soc Quantum Biol, 1979; Irving Langmuir Award, Am Phys Soc, 1987; Theoret Chem Award, Am Chem Soc, 1993. **Professional Experience:** Prof, Univ Louis Pasteur, Strasbourg, 1992 & 1994-1995; nat lectr, Biophys Soc, 1991; prof, Col France, Paris, 1980-1981, 1987-1988; THEODORE WILLIAM RICHARDS PROF CHEM, HARVARD UNIV, 1979-; prof, Univ Paris, 1974-1975; vis prof, Univ Paris, 1972-1973 & 1980-1981; prof, Harvard Univ, 1966-1979; NSF sr fel, 1965-1966; from assoc prof to prof, Columbia Univ, 1960-1966; from instr to assoc prof phys chem, Univ Ill, 1955-1960; NSF fel chem, Oxford Univ, 1953-1955. **Memberships:** Nat Acad Sci; Am Acad Arts & Sci; Int Acad Quantum Molecular Sci; foreign mem Neth Acad Arts & Sci. **Research Statement & Publications:** Theory of molecular structure and spectra with emphasis on biologically important molecules; theoretical chemistry, including the electronic interpretation of nuclear magnetic resonance and spectra of molecules, the development of techniques for the evaluation of molecular properties; the formulation of detailed models for chemical reactions; author of numerous publications. **Mailing Address:** Dept Chem, Harvard Univ, 12 Oxford St, Cambridge, MA 02138. **Fax:** 617-496-3204. **E-Mail:** marci@tammy.harvard.edu

KARR, ALAN FRANCIS, INFERENCE FOR STOCHASTVCPROCESSES. **Personal Data:** b Bryn Mawr, Pa, July 12, 1947. **Education:** Northwestern Univ, BS, 1969, MS, 1970, PhD (appl math), 1973. **Professional Experience:** DIR, NAT INST STATIST SCI, 2000-; PROF STATIST & BIOSTATIST, UNIV NC, CHAPEL HILL, 1993-; assoc dir, Nat Inst Statist Sci, 1992-2000; assoc dean, GWC Whiting Sch Eng, Johns Hopkins Univ, 1986-1992; chair math sci, Johns Hopkins Univ, 1985-1986; prof math sci, Johns Hopkins Univ, 1983-1993; from asst prof to assoc prof, Johns Hopkins Univ, 1973-1983. **Memberships:** Fel Inst Math Statist; Am Statist Asn. **Research Statement & Publications:** Statistical inference for stochastic processes; image analysis and processing; statistics and materials science. **Mailing Address:** Nat Inst Statist Sci, PO Box 14152, Research Triangle Park, NC 27709-4162. **Fax:** 919-541-7102. **E-Mail:** karr@rcc.rti.org

KARR, CLARENCE, CHEMISTRY. **Personal Data:** b St Louis, Mo, May 12, 1923; m Betty; c Kathleen, Elizabeth, Laura & Jonathan. **Education:** St Louis Univ, BS, 1944; Johns Hopkins Univ, PhD (chem), 1950. **Honors & Awards:** Award, US Dept Interior, 1965 & 1966. **Professional Experience:** RETIRED; proj mgr advan gasification, Morgantown Energy Technol Ctr, 1980-1983; res chemist synthetic fuels, Energy Res & Develop Admin, US Dept Energy, 1977-1980; supvry res chemist coal liquefaction, Energy Res & Develop Admin, US Dept Energy, 1975-1977; prin investr, Apollo 11, 12, 14 & 15, Lunar Sample Prog, 1969-1972; coal chemistry, US Bur Mines, 1966-1975; supvry res chemist low temperature tar, US Bur Mines, 1955-1966; fel petrol chem, Mellon Inst, 1950-1955. **Memberships:** Fel Am Inst Chem; Am Chem Soc. **Research Statement & Publications:** Composition of low temperature coal tar, petroleum; organic synthesis; chromatography; infrared ultraviolet spectroscopy; air pollution; coal minerals; synthetic fuels from coal; lunar minerals; liquid fuels from coal; coal gasification. **Mailing Address:** 624 Vista Pl, Morgantown, WV 26505.

KARR, JAMES PRESBY, REPRODUCTIVE PHYSIOLOGY, STEROID BIOCHEMISTRY. **Personal Data:** b Nashua, NH, July 24, 1941; m 1962, c 2. **Education:** Univ Vt, BA, 1964, MS, 1966; Pa State Univ, PhD (reproductive physiol), 1970. **Professional Experience:** DIR, OFF INSTNL PROTOCOLS & SCI INTEGRITY, ROSWELL CANCER INST, 1996-; ASSOC DIR SCI AFFAIRS, ROSWELL PARK MEM INST, 1989-; dir, Organ Systs Coord Ctr, 1985-1996; assoc dir, Organ Systs Coord Ctr, 1984-1985; PROF PHYSIOL, NIAGRA UNIV, 1982-; asst prof physiol, Univ Buffalo, beginning 1982; dep dir, Sci Affairs Cancer Res, Nat Prostatic Cancer Proj, 1978-1984; asst prof animal breeding & reproductive physiol, Am Univ, Beirut, 1974-1975; cancer res scientist reproductive physiol, Roswell Park Mem Inst, 1973-1974 & 1976-1977; asst prof animal breeding, Haille Selassie I Univ, 1971-1973; res assoc reproductive physiol, Pa State Univ, 1970-1971. **Memberships:** AAAS; Am Asn Cancer Res; NY Acad Sci; Soc Basic Urol Res (pres, 1993-1994). **Research Statement & Publications:** Reproductive endocrinology, steroid biochemistry, plasma steroid binding proteins and hormone receptors in the normal physiology and disease states of the human prostate. **Mailing Address:** Roswell Park Cancer Inst, Elm & Carlton St, Buffalo, NY 14263. **Fax:** 716-845-3545.

KARR, JAMES RICHARD, WATER QUALITY, CONSERVATION BIOLOGY. **Personal Data:** b Shelby, Ohio, December 26, 1943; m 1984, Elena; c Elizabeth & Eric. **Education:** Iowa State Univ, BS, 1965; Univ Ill, Urbana-Champaign, MS, 1967, PhD (zoology), 1970. **Honors & Awards:** Carl Sullivan Fishery Conservation Award, American Fisheries Society, 2004; Environmental Stewardship Award, North American Benthological Society, 2005. **Professional Experience:** PROF FISHERIES & ZOOL, UNIV WASH, 1991-; Ecol, Ecol Appln, 1995-; Ecol, Freshwater Biol, 1993-; Ecol, Ecosyst Health, 1992-; dir, Inst Environ Studies, 1991-1995; Ecol, Conserv Biol, 1991; conserv biol, Eval Panel, Instrnl Sci Equip Prog, NSF, 1990; Harold H Bailey prof biol, Va Polytech Inst & State Univ, Blacksburg, Va, 1988-1991; actg dir, Smithsonian Trop Res Inst, Balboa, Panama, 1987-1988; Bioscience, 1985-1994; dep dir, Smithsonian Trop Res Inst, Balboa, Panama, 1984-1987; Ecol, 1981-1984; affil, Ill Natural Hist Surv, 1981-1991; consult, Orgn Am States, 1980; ed, Trop Ecol, 1977-1981; Mem, Undergrad Res Participation, 1976; from assoc prof to prof ecol, Univ Ill, Urbana-Champaign, 1975-1984; Mem, Eval Panel, Instrnl Sci Equip Prog, NSF, 1975; prin investr grants, NSF, Environ Protection Agency, Nat Geog Soc, Am Philos Soc, US Fish & Wildlife Serv, US Forest Serv & Off Water Resources Technol, Tenn Valley Authority, Dept Energy, 1973-; asst prof ecol, Purdue Univ, 1972-1975; Fel, Princeton Univ, 1970-1971 & Smithsonian Trop Res Inst, 1971-1972; adj prof civil eng, environ Health & pub affairs. **Memberships:** fel Am Ornithologists Union; Wilson Ornith Soc; fel AAAS; Am Inst Biol Sci. **Research Statement & Publications:** Community ecology from both basic and applied perspectives with emphasis on studies of tropical forest birds and stream fishes, including a wide range of land use and water resource problems; improving knowledge of biological communities and to apply that knowledge to solution of selected environmental and natural resource problems. **Mailing Address:** Univ Wash, Box 355020, Seattle, WA 98195. **Fax:** 206-528-0885. **E-Mail:** jrkarr@u.washington.edu

KARR, REYNOLD MICHAEL, JR, ALLERGY, RHEUMATOLOGY. **Personal Data:** b New York, NY, June 24, 1942; m 1976, c 2. **Education:** Johns Hopkins Univ, BA, 1964; Univ Md, MD, 1969. **Professional Experience:** FEL MEM, AM COL RHEUMATOLOGY, as of 2004; assoc prof med, Univ Wash, beginning 1980; vis physician, Charity Hosp, New Orleans, 1976-; vis consult, Vet Admin Hosp, New Orleans, 1976-; assoc prof med, Clin Immunol Sect, Sch Med, Tulane Univ, 1976-1980. **Memberships:** Fel Am Col Physicians; Am Acad Allergy; Am Thoracic Soc; Am Rheumatism Asn. **Research Statement & Publications:** Arthritis; occupational lung disease; bronchoprovocation. **Mailing Address:** Aland Arthritis Specialists, 3128 Norton Ave, Everett, WA 98201-4216. **Fax:** 425-259-1854.

KARR, STEPHEN R, BIOLOGY. **Education:** Univ Ga, PhD (biochem). **Professional Experience:** PROF & CHMN, DEPT BIOL, CARSON-NEWMAN COL, as of 2004. **Mailing Address:** Carson-Newman Col, 2130 Branner Ave, Jefferson City, TN 37760. **E-Mail:** stkarr@cn.edu

KARR, TIMOTHY LAWRENCE, BIOCONTROL OF INSECT PESTS USING BACTERIAL-INDUCED MALE STERILITY. **Personal Data:** b Phoenix, Ariz, May 1, 1953; m 1984, Wendy Weintraub; c Michael. **Education:** Univ Calif, Santa Barbara, BA, 1976, PhD (chem), 1982. **Professional Experience:** READER BIOL, UNIV BATH, 2002-; asst prof organismal biol & anat, Univ Chicago, 1994-2002; fac fel, Beckman Inst, beginning 1990; asst prof, Univ Ill, Urbana, 1987-1994; Weingart fel, Am Cancer Soc sr fel, 1986-1987; Weingart fel, Univ Calif, San Francisco, 1985-1986; fel, Jane Coffin Childs Mem Fund Med Res, 1981-1984; Res asst, Univ Calif, Santa Barbara, 1977-1981. **Memberships:** AAAS; Am Soc Cell Biol; Genetics Soc Am. **Research Statement & Publications:** Molecular mechanisms of fertilization in insects; host-symbiosis in insects; cellular and molecular mechanisms of cytoplasmic incompatibility caused by an intracellular symbiont, welbachia pipentis. **Mailing Address:** Dept Biol & Biochem, Univ Bath, Bath, UK. **E-Mail:** bsstlk@bath.ac.uk

KARRAKER, ROBERT HARRELD, INORGANIC CHEMISTRY. **Personal Data:** b Carbondale, Ill, May 6, 1931; m 1953, c 2. **Education:** Southern Ill Univ, BA, 1953; Iowa State Univ, PhD (inorg chem), 1961. **Professional Experience:** PROF CHEM, EASTERN ILL UNIV, 1980-; assoc prof chem, Eastern Ill Univ, 1967-1980; asst prof chem, Memphis State Univ, 1961-1967; Chemist, Olin-Mathieson Chem Corp, NY, 1953-1955. **Memberships:** Am Chem Soc; Sigma Xi. **Research Statement & Publications:** Chemistry of rare earth elements. **Mailing Address:** 2740 Whipoorwill Dr, Charleston, IL 61920.

KARRAS, THOMAS WILLIAM, LASERS & ELECTRO-OPTICS, COMMUNICATIONS. **Personal Data:** b Chicago, Ill, January 4, 1936; m Demetra; c Larissa E Cymerman & Wm Alexander Karras. **Education:** Univ Chicago, BS, 1957; Ill Inst Technol, MS, 1961; Univ Calif, Los Angeles, PhD (physics), 1964. **Professional Experience:** SR FEL, LOCKHEED-MARTIN SPACE SYSTEMS CO NEWTOWN, PA, 1996-; tech leader, Martin Marietta Astro-Space, 1993-1995; mgr, Electro-Optics Anal & Develop, 1988-1992; mgr electro-optic anal, Astro-Space Div, Gen Elec Co, King Prussia, Pa, 1985-1987; mgr laser res, Astro-Space Div, Gen Elec Co, King Prussia, Pa, 1979-1984; mgr laser & plasma physics, Space Div, Gen Elec Co, King Prussia, Pa, 1972-1979; physicist, Space Div, Gen Elec Co, King Prussia, Pa, 1964-1972; Physicist elec propulsion, Rocketdyne Div, N Am Aviation, 1959-1961. **Memberships:** Am Phys Soc; Am Inst Aeronaut & Astronaut; Sigma Xi; Optical Soc Am; Int Soc Optical Eng. **Research Statement & Publications:** Metal vapor lasers; nanosecond discharges; microwave photonics; space communications; electric propulsion. **Mailing Address:** 231 Wooded Way, Berwyn, PA 19312. **Fax:** 215-497-1616. **E-Mail:** thomas.w.karras@lmco.com

KARREN, KENNETH W, STRUCTURAL DESIGN. **Personal Data:** b Vernal, Utah, May 20, 1932; m 1953, c 7. **Education:** Univ Utah, BS, 1953, MS, 1961; Cornell Univ, PhD (civil eng), 1965. **Professional Experience:** CONSULT, 1979-; pres, Struct Engrs, Karren & Assocs, 1978-1979; sr engr, Hercules Inc, 1970-1971; Consult, Hercules Inc, 1966-1975; prof, Brigham Young Univ, 1965-1970; grad student civil eng, Cornell Univ, 1962-1965; asst prof civil eng, Brigham Young Univ, 1961-1962; chief engr, Otto Buehner Co, 1957-1961; Proj develop engr, Pipeline Div, Phillips Petrol, 1956-1957. **Memberships:** Am Soc Civil Engrs. **Research Statement & Publications:** Cold-forming of sheet steel led to provisions included in Am Iron and Steel Institute specifications. **Mailing Address:** 424 E 4750 N, Provo, UT 84604.

KARRENBERG, HANS K, AERODYNAMICS. **Professional Experience:** STAFF, AEROSPACE CORP, as of 1999. **Memberships:** Am Inst Aeronaut & Astronaut. **Mailing Address:** Aerospace Corp Syst & Eng Div, 2350 E El Segundo Blvd, El Segundo, CA 90245-4609. **Fax:** 310-336-7055.

KARRER, KATHLEEN MARIE, MOLECULAR BIOLOGY, DEVELOPMENTAL BIOLOGY. **Personal Data:** b Grosse Pointe Farms, Mich, June 16, 1949. **Education:** Marquette Univ, BS, 1971; Yale Univ, PhD (biol), 1976. **Honors & Awards:** John Spangler Nicholas Prize Exp Zool, Yale Univ, 1977 Fel, Am Assoc for the Advancement of Sci, 1993; John P Raynor, S J Fac Award for Teaching Excellence 1999. **Professional Experience:** PROF, MARQUETTE UNIV, as of 2006; Clare Booth Luce prof, Marquette Univ, 1989-2002; asst prof biol, Brandeis Univ, 1980-1989; NIH fel, 1978-1979; fel biol, Ind Univ, 1976-1980; Jane Coffin Childs Mem Fund Med Res fel, 1976-1978. **Memberships:** AAAS. **Research Statement & Publications:** Eukaryotic chromosome structure and function; DNA rearrangement; molecular biology of ciliates; DNA methylation; We study the cis-acting DNA sequences and trans-acting proteins required for deletion of specific DNA elements during development of the somatic macronucleus from the germ line micronucleus in Tetrahymena. **Mailing Address:** Dept Biol Marquette Univ, PO Box 1881, Milwaukee, WI 53201-1881. **Fax:** 414-288-7357. **E-Mail:** kathleen.karrer@marquette.edu

KARRON, D B, MEDICAL IMAGING & GEOMETRIC MODELING. **Personal Data:** b Brooklyn, NY, October 25, 1956; div, c Sarah. **Education:** NY Univ, BS, 1984, MS, 1988, PhD (bioeng), 1993. **Professional Experience:** PRES & CHIEF TECH OFFICER, COMPU-AIDED SURG, INC, as of 2004; Assoc, Ctr Neural Sci, 1993-; res assoc three-dimensional ultrasound comput-aidedsurg, dept surg, NY med ctr, beginning 1993; NETWORK CONSULT, DEPT SURG, NY UNIV MED CTR, 1991-; fel, Dept Appl Sci, NY Univ, 1990-1993; Database adminr, Soc Rehab Facially Disfigured, 1984-1990; Sci graphics programmer & comput syst adminr, Inst Reconstruct Plastic Surg, 1983-1991. **Memberships:** AAAS; Inst Elec & Electronics Engrs; Asn Comput Mach. **Research Statement & Publications:** Development of a topologically correct method of modeling three-dimensional structures embedded in volumetric datasets. **Mailing Address:** 300 E 33rd St, Ste 4N, New York, NY 10018. **Fax:** 212-685-0736. **E-Mail:** karron@casi.net

KARROW, PAUL FREDERICK, QUATERNARY GEOLOGY. **Personal Data:** b St Thomas, Ont, September 14, 1930; m 1962, Beth; c Douglas D, Niel A, Sheila E & Thomas P. **Education:** Queen's Univ, Ont, BS, 1954; Univ Ill, PhD (geol), 1957. **Honors & Awards:** W A Johnston Medal, Can Quaternary Asn, 1995; E B Burwell Jr Award, Geol Soc Am, 1999. **Professional Experience:** Vis scientist, & BC Geol Surv, 1992; dir, Quarternary Sci Inst, 1987-1989; vis prof, Univ SFla, Tampa, 1984; Geologist, Ont Geol Surv, 1982 & 1984-1987; vis scientist, Scripps Inst Oceanog, La Jolla, Calif, 1970 & 1976; PROF EARTH SCI, UNIV WATERLOO, 1969-; chmn dept, Univ Waterloo, 1965-1970, 1992; assoc prof earth sci, Univ Waterloo, 1965-1969; Geologist, Geol Surv Can, 1965-1968; Geologist, Ont Dept Mines, 1964 & 1973; prof civil eng, Univ Waterloo, 1963-1965; Geologist, Ont Dept Mines, 1957-1963. **Memberships:** Fel Geol Soc Am; Soc Econ Paleont & Mineral; fel Geol Asn Can; Int Asn Gt Lakes Res; Am Asn Quaternary Environ; Can Quaternary Asn. **Research Statement & Publications:** Quaternary geology; glacial geology; geomorphology; urban geology; paleoecology; great lakes history; interglacial environments. **Mailing Address:** Dept Earth Sci, Univ Waterloo, Waterloo, ON N2L 3G1, Can. **Fax:** 519-746-7484. **E-Mail:** pfkarrow@sciborg.uwaterloo.ca

KARSCH, FRED JOSEPH, REPRODUCTIVE ENDOCRINOLOGY, NEUROENDOCRINOLOGY. **Personal Data:** b New York, NY, August 8, 1942; m 1967, c 2. **Education:** Juniata Col, BS, 1964; Univ Maine, MS, 1966; Univ Ill, PhD (animal sci, biochem & physiol), 1970. **Professional Experience:** PROF PHYSIOL, UNIV MICH, ANN ARBOR, 1982-; from asst prof to assoc prof, Univ Mich, Ann Arbor, 1972-1982; Ford Found fel, NIH fel, 1971-1972; Ford Found fel, Med Sch, Univ Pittsburgh, 1970-1971. **Memberships:** Endocrine Soc; Soc Study Reprod; Soc Study Fertil. **Research Statement & Publications:** Neuroendocrine control of gonadotropin secretion; seasonal reproduction; developmental endocrinology. **Mailing Address:** Dept Physiol, Univ Mich, Ann Arbor, MI 48103. **Fax:** 734-936-8620. **E-Mail:** fjkarsch@umich.edu

KARSHNER, GARY B, ASTRONOMY & PHYSICS. **Education:** Univ Calif, Berkeley, BA, 1971; UNiv Ore, PhD (Astrophys), 1984. **Professional Experience:** ASST PROF, PHYSICS DEPT, ST MARYS UNIV, as of 2005; asst prof, Gettysburg Col, 1985-1990; Calif State Col, 1984-1985; UNiv Ore, 1976-1981; Humbolt, State Univ, 1973-1975 & 1981-1983. **Research Statement & Publications:** Stellar astronomy. **Mailing Address:** Physics Dept, St Mary's Univ, One Camino Santa Maria, San Antonio, TX 78228-8503. **E-Mail:** karshner@stmarytx.edu

KARSON, JEFFREY ALAN, STRUCTURAL GEOLOGY. **Personal Data:** b Akron, Ohio, November 3, 1949; m 1978, c 1. **Education:** Case Inst Technol, BS, 1972; State Univ NY, Albany, MS, 1975, PhD (geol), 1977. **Professional Experience:** Chmn, Div Earth & Ocean Sci, Duke Univ, 1996-2000; res fel, Danish Lithosphere Center, 1994-2000; PROF, DEPT GEOL, DUKE UNIV, 1992-; Adj res Scientist, Lamont-Doherty Earth Observatory, 1992-; assoc prof, Dept Geol, Duke Univ, 1986-1992; assoc scientist, Geol, Woods Hole Oceanog Inst, 1984-1986; Vis lectr, Bridgewater State Col, Mass, 1981-; asst scientist, Geol, Woods Hole Oceanog Inst, 1980-1984; scholar, Geol, Woods Hole Oceanog Inst, 1979-1980; fel, Erindale Col & Univ Toronto, 1977-1979; res asst, State Univ NY, Albany, 1975-1977; asst instr, State Univ NY, Albany, 1972-1975. **Memberships:** Geol Soc Am; Am Geophys Union. **Research Statement & Publications:** Internal structure of the oceanic lithosphere via direct observation of the sea floor and structural analysis of ophiolites. **Mailing Address:** Dept Geol, Duke Univ, 206A Old Chem PO Box 90230, Durham, NC 27708-0230. **Fax:** 919-684-5833. **E-Mail:** jkarson@duke.edu

KARSTEN, KENNETH STEPHEN, PLANT PHYSIOLOGY, CHEMISTRY. **Personal Data:** b Holland, Mich, July 24, 1913; m 1939, c 4. **Education:** Hope Col, AB, 1935; Univ Nev, MS, 1937; Univ Wis, PhD (plant physiol), 1939. **Professional Experience:** CONSULT, INDUST MINERALS & CHEMICALS, 1981-; vpres res & develop, R T Vanderbilt Co, Inc, 1978-1981; dir res & develop, R T Vanderbilt Co, Inc, 1972-1978; dept mgr, R T Vanderbilt Co, Inc, 1948-1972; insecticide chemist, Rohm and Haas Co, Pa, 1945-1947; dir org res, Niagara Sprayer & Chem Co, 1941-1945; tutor biol, Brooklyn Col, 1939-1941; asst, Univ Wis, 1937-1939; Chemist-analyst, Sullivan Mining Co, Idaho, 1937. **Memberships:** Am Chem Soc. **Research Statement & Publications:** Organic syntheses; insecticide and fungicide formulation and development; plant hormones; plant physiology; root activity and oxygen in relation to soil fertility; fungicides; bactericides; sap stain control chemicals; bacteriostats for soap. **Mailing Address:** 5397 Keysville Ave, Spring Hill, FL 34608-1839. **E-Mail:** kkarsten@innet.com

KARSTENS, ANDRES INGVER, AEROSPACE MEDICINE. **Personal Data:** b Pendleton, Ore, December 17, 1911; wid. **Education:** Univ Ore, BA, 1938, MD & MS, 1943; Am Bd Prev Med, dipl aerospace med, 1956. **Honors & Awards:** Hubertus Strughold Award Aerospace Med, 1973. **Professional Experience:** RETIRED; staff physician & chief flight surgeon, Med Support Serv, NASA Johnson Space Ctr, Houston, 1976; dir res & develop, Aerospace Med Div, Air Force Systs Command, Brooks AFB, Tex, 1969-1971; dir Bioastronaut, Manned Orbiting Lab, Space & Missiles Syst Orgn, Los Angeles, 1964-1969; from asst chief to chief, Aerospace Med Res Lab, Wright-Patterson AFB, 1958-1964; dir res, USAF Sch Aviation Med, Randolph AFB, Tex, 1956-1958; commanding officer, Arctic Aero Med Lab, Ladd AFB, Alaska, 1950-1955; res aviation med, high altitude physiol & environ physiol, Aero Med Lab, Wright-Patterson AFB, USAF, 1946-1950. **Memberships:**

Fel AAAS; AMA; fel Aerospace Med Asn; fel Am Col Prev Med. **Research Statement & Publications:** Autonomic control of cardiac function and intestinal motility; high altitude and environment physiology; environmental protection and life support; arctic physiology and ecology; life support in aeronautical and space flight. **Mailing Address:** 887 SE Mockingbird Dr, College Pl, WA 99324-1828.

KARTAWINATA, KUSWATA, ECOLOGY. **Education:** Univ Hawaii, PhD (plant ecol), 1971. **Professional Experience:** SR ADV, UNESCO, as of 2005; dir Bulungan Res Forest, Ctr Int Forestry Res, 1998-2002; Sr Prog Officer, Catherine T. MacArthur Found, 1992-1998. **E-Mail:** k.kartawinata@cgiar.org

KARTEN, HARVEY J, NEUROANATOMY, Evolutionary Neurobiology. **Personal Data:** b New York, NY, July 13, 1935; m 1964, Elizaabeth; c 3. **Education:** Yeshiva Col, BA, 1955, Albert Einstein Col Med, MD, 1959. **Honors & Awards:** Herrick Award, Am Asn Anat, 1968; Distinguished Professor, UCSD 2005; Krieg Cortical Award, Cajal Club, 2005; Javits Award, NINDS. **Professional Experience:** PROF NEUROSCIENCE & PSYCHIAT, UNIV CALIF, SAN DIEGO, 1986-; adj prof, Salk Inst & Univ Utah, 1986; prof neurobiology, State Univ NY, Stony Brook, 1979-1986; prof psychiat & anat sci, State Univ NY, Stony Brook, 1974-1986; sr res assoc, Mass Inst Technol, 1973-1974; Nat Inst Child Health & Human Develop career develop award, 1965-1974; res assoc neuroanat, Mass Inst Technol, 1965-1973; res assoc, Lab Neuropsychol, Wash Sch Psychiat, 1963-1965; NIMH career develop award, 1961-1965; res assoc neurophysiol, Walter Reed Army Inst Res, 1961-1965; resident psychiat, Univ Colo, 1960-1961; USPHS fel, Univ Colo, 1960-1961; Intern med, Univ Utah, 1959-1960. **Memberships:** Soc Neuroscience; Cajal Club. **Research Statement & Publications:** Evolutionary origin of mammalian cortex, neurobiology of avian brains, organization and evolution of vertebrate visual system, microscopy. **Mailing Address:** Dept NeuroSci, UCSD, Rm No 3009, 9500 Gilman Dr, La Jolla, CA 92093-0608. **Fax:** 858-534-6602. **E-Mail:** hjkarten@ucsd.edu

KARTEN, MARVIN J, MEDICINAL CHEMISTRY. **Personal Data:** b New York, NY, April 26, 1931; m 1956, c 2. **Education:** Brooklyn Col, BS, 1954; Univ Pittsburgh, PhD (chem), 1958. **Professional Experience:** HEALTH SCI ADMINR, NAT INST CHILD HEALTH & HUMAN DEVELOP, NIH, 1971-; group leader, USV Pharmaceut Corp, 1967-1970; sr res chemist, USV Pharmaceut Corp, 1960-1967; res chemist, Mass, 1959-1960; res chemist, Monsanto Chem Co, Ohio, 1958-1959. **Memberships:** Am Chem Soc. **Research Statement & Publications:** Medicinal chemistry; organic synthesis; synthesis and biological evaluation of new contraceptive agents. **Mailing Address:** Nat Inst Child Health & Human Develop, NIH, Bethesda, MD 20817-3820. **Fax:** 301-496-0962.

KARTHA, KUTTY KRISHNAN, PLANT BIOTECHNOLOGY, PLANT CELL & TISSUE CULTURE. **Personal Data:** b Shertallai, India, August 9, 1941; Canadian citizen; m 1972, c 2. **Education:** Saugar Univ, India, BS, 1962; Jawaharal Nehru Agr Univ, India, MS, 1965; India Agr Res Inst, PhD (plant path), 1969. **Honors & Awards:** George M Darrow Award, Am Soc Hort Sci, 1981; Merit Award Excellence Res, Nat Res Coun, Can, 1991; C J Bishop Award, Can Soc Hort Sci, 1992; Award of Excellence Res, Treas Bd Can, 1992. **Professional Experience:** DIR GEN, NAT RES COUN CAN, 1995-; RES DIR, CEREAL BIOTECHNOL, 1993-; mem, Can Agr Res Coun, 1990-1994; adj prof, Univ Sask, Saskatoon, beginning 1987; GROUP LEADER, CEREAL BIOTECHNOL, 1987-; ed, J Plant Physiol, 1987; head, Cell Technol Sect, 1985-1987; HEAD, CEREAL BIOTECHNOLOGY GROUP, 1985-; Nat corresp, Int Asn Plant Tissue Cult, 1982-1986; SR RES OFFICER, PLANT BIOTECHNOL INST, NAT RES COUN, 1981-; assoc res officer, Plant Biotechnol Inst, 1976-1981; asst res officer, Plant Biotechnol Inst, 1974-1976; vis scientist, Prairie Regional Lab, Nat Res Coun, Saskatoon, 1973-1974; Fel, Nat Inst Agr Res, France, 1970-1972. **Memberships:** Int Asn Plant Tissue Cult; Can Soc Plant Physiologists. **Research Statement & Publications:** Plant biotechnology especially the genetic engineering of crops such as cereals and strawberry; cryopreservation of plant cells and organs; plant tissue culture. **Mailing Address:** Nat Res Coun, 214 Old Crescent, Saskatoon, SK S7H 4W9, Can.

KARTHA, MUKUND K, RADIOLOGY, BIOPHYSICS. **Personal Data:** b Pattanakad, Kerala, India, July 31, 1936; American citizen; m 1963, c 2. **Education:** Univ Kerala, BSc, 1958; Univ Sagar, India, MSc, 1961; Univ Western Ont, PhD (radiol physics), 1969. **Professional Experience:** ASSOC PROF ALLIED MED PROF, OHIO STATE UNIV, 1976-; Am Cancer Soc fel, Nat Cancer Inst fel, 1974-1977; co-dir, Radiation Ther Consult Prog, Cancer Res Ctr, Ohio State Univ, beginning 1973; ASSOC PROF RADIOL, OHIO STATE UNIV, 1973-; Am Cancer Soc fel, Ohio State Univ, 1970-1971; asst prof, Ohio State Univ, 1968-1973; cancer res fel, Ont Cancer Found, 1963-1968; sci officer radiol physics, India Atomic Energy Comn, 1961-1963. **Memberships:** Radiol Soc NAm; Radiation Res Soc; Am Asn Physicists in Med; Am Col Radiol; Am Soc Therapeut Radiol & Oncol; Am Onocol Assoc Inc (pres). **Research Statement & Publications:** Experimental and clinical research in radiation therapy; investigation of cancer treatment using radiation; radiation therapy. **Mailing Address:** 5003 11th Ave, Vienna, WV 26105-3152.

KARTHA, SREEDHARAN, DIFFERENTIATION, GROWTH REGULATION. **Personal Data:** b Kerala, India, 1948; m 1988, Sethulaksmi; c Neelima & Malini. **Education:** Nehru Univ, India, PhD (cell biol), 1978. **Professional Experience:** ASST PROF GROWTH REGULATION, UNIV CHICAGO, as of 1999; res fel, Johns Hopkins Med Sch, Baltimore, 1980-1983. **Research Statement & Publications:** Growth factors; oncogenes. **Mailing Address:** Dept Nephrology, Univ Chicago, 5801 SEllis, Chicago, IL 60615. **Fax:** 773-702-5818. **E-Mail:** skartha@peds.bsd.uchicago.edu

KARTZMARK, ELINOR MARY, PHYSICAL CHEMISTRY. **Personal Data:** b Selkirk, Man, May 16, 1926; c 1. **Education:** Univ Man, BSc, 1949, MSc, 1950, PhD (chem), 1952. **Professional Experience:** RETIRED; from lectr to prof phys chem, Univ Man, 1951-1988; mem staff, Univ Man, 1947-1950. **Memberships:** Fel Chem Inst Can. **Research Statement & Publications:** Electrolytic conductance; heterogeneous equilibria. **Mailing Address:** Box 2 Grp 30, RR 1, Lockport, MB R0C 1W0, Can.

KARUKSTIS, KERRY KATHLEEN, PHOTOSYNTHESIS, FLUORESCENCE SPECTROSCOPY. **Personal Data:** b Buffalo, NY, 1955. **Education:** Duke Univ, BS, 1977, PhD (chem), 1981. **Honors & Awards:** NIH Nat Res Serv Award, 1981-1984; Henry T Mudd Prize, 2003. **Professional Experience:** PROF CHEM, HARVEY MUDD COL, 1993-; CHEM CONSULT, COUN UNDERGRAD RES, 1993-; from asst prof to assoc prof; Harvey Mudd Col, 1984-1993; vis res scientist, Lawerence Berkeley Lab, Calif, 1991; from asst prof to assoc prof, Harvey Mudd Col, 1984-1993; res fel chem, Lab Chem Biodynamics, Univ Calif, Berkeley, 1981-1984. **Memberships:** Am Chem Soc; Biophys Soc; Am Soc Photobiol; Sigma Xi; Coun Undergrad Res; NSF. **Research Statement & Publications:** Use of steady-state and time-resolved fluorescence and absorbance measurements to monitor the organization of chloroplast photosynthetic membranes and the processes of excitation transfer and electron transport in photosynthesis; author of various articles. **Mailing Address:** Dept Chem, Harvey Mudd Col, 301 E 12th St, Claremont, CA 91711-5990. **Fax:** 909-607-7577. **E-Mail:** kerry_karukstis@hmc.edu

KARULKAR, PRAMOD C, PHYSICS. **Personal Data:** b Maharashtra State, India, 1950; American citizen. **Education:** Univ Poona, BSc, 1969; Indian Inst Technol, MSc, 1971; Portland State Univ, MS, 1975; Univ Wis, PhD (mat sci), 1979. **Professional Experience:** FAB MGR, UNIV RES FOUND, MD, 1993-; Lincoln Lab, Mass Inst Technol, 1985-1993; Hughes Aircraft Co, Newport Beach, Calif, 1984-1985; lectr elec eng, Calif State Polytech Univ, Pomona, 1981-1985; mem staff, Rockwell Int Corp, Anaheim, Calif, 1980-1984; res scholar low temp physics, Indian Inst Technol, Bombay, 1972-1973; Res assoc, Saha Inst Nuclear Physics, India, 1971-1972. **Memberships:** Sigma Xi; Am Phys Soc; Am Vacuum Soc; Inst Elec & Electronics Engrs; Electrochem Soc. **Research Statement & Publications:** Fabrication and analysis of electronic materials; fabrication of solid state devices; fabrication of VLSI circuits; plasma processing; thin film technology; device physics; failure analysis. **Mailing Address:** 3816 Font Hills Dr, Ellicott City, MD 21042.

KARUNAKARAN, THONTHI, MOLECULAR GENETIC ANALYSIS OF VIRULENCE FACTORS & GENES, MICROBIAL PHYSIOLOGY & BIOCHEMISTRY. **Personal Data:** b Chinnamanur, Tamilnadu, India, April 20, 1962; m 1991, Bheemappa. **Education:** Vivekanda Col, Tiruvedagam West, BSc, 1982; Madurai Kamaraj Univ, MSc, 1984, PhD (microbiol), 1990. **Professional Experience:** RES SCIENTIST, UNIV TEX HEALTH SCI CTR, SAN ANTONIO, 1990-; vis fel, Nat Ctr Sci Res, France, 1988; sr res fel, Coun Sci & Indust Res, India, 1987-1990; jr res fel, Technotran Pvt Ltd, India, 1985-1986. **Memberships:** Am Soc Microbiol; Am Soc Dent Res. **Research Statement & Publications:** Isolated and characterized a few genes from pathogenically and biotechnologically important microorganisms. **Mailing Address:** Univ Tex Health Sci Ctr, San Antonio, NY 14226.

KARUNASIRI, GAMANI, SOLID STATE PHYSICS, OPTOELECTRONICS. **Personal Data:** b Colombo, Sri Lanka, April 14, 1956; m 1984, c 2. **Education:** Univ Colombo, Sri Lanka, BS, 1979; Univ Pittsburgh, MS, 1981, PhD (physics), 1984. **Professional Experience:** ASSOC PROF, PHYSICS, NAVAL POSTGRAD SCH, MONTEREY, 2000-; assoc prof, Elec Eng, Nat Univ Singapore, Singapore, 1994-2000; Research Engineer, Univ Calif, Los Angeles, 1987-1994; Research Assoc, Microtronics Assoc, Pittsburgh, 1985-1987. **Memberships:** Inst Elec & Electronics Engrs. **Research Statement & Publications:** Design and fabrication of infrared sensors using; semiconductor heterostructures and microbolometers.; Characterization of infrared sensor figure of merit. **Mailing Address:** Dept Physics, Naval Postgrad Sch, Monterey, CA 93943. **Fax:** 831-656-2834. **E-Mail:** karunasiri@nps.edu

KARUSTIS, GEORGE, CHEMISTRY. **Professional Experience:** CONSULT, CHEM CONSULT NETWORK, as of 2003. **Memberships:** mem, Am Inst Chem Engrs. **Mailing Address:** 832 Carlton Rd, Westfield, NJ 07090-1602. **Fax:** 908-232-4944. **E-Mail:** marlenek@aol.com

KARUZA, SARUNAS KAZYS, ATOMIC FREQUENCY STAND, NAVIGATION & COMMUNICATION SYSTEMS. **Personal Data:** b Kaunas, Lithuania, January 19, 1940; m 1977, c 2. **Education:** Univ Southern Calif, BS, 1963, MS, 1966, PhD (elec eng), 1972. **Professional Experience:** MEM, TECH STAFF, ELECTRONIC RES LABS, AEROSPACE CORP, 1980-; Consult, Fullerton Internal Med Clin, 1978; adj asst prof med & adj assoc prof biomed eng, Univ Southern Calif, 1975-; dir & prof staff assoc, Environ Sci Lab, Rancho Los Amigos Hosp, 1972-1980; mem, tech staff, Aeronaut Systs Div, 1966-1967; mem, tech staff, Ground Systs Div, 1965-1966; mem tech staff, Commun Div, Hughes Aircraft Co, 1963-1965. **Memberships:** Sigma Xi; Inst Elec & Electronics Engrs. **Research Statement & Publications:** Precision atomic frequency standards (cesium-rubidium) which are used in the Navstar Global Positioning System (GPS) satellites for world wide navigation; stability properties of these standards as they are influenced by their electronics and environmental factors; satellite communication systems. **Mailing Address:** Aerospace Corp, PO Box 92957, Los Angeles, CA 90009.

KARVE, MOHAN DATTATREYA, INDUSTRIAL MICROBIOLOGY, MYCOLOGY. **Personal Data:** b Kupwad, India, August 14, 1939; m 1967, c 2. **Education:** Univ Poona, BSc, 1959, Hons, 1960, MSc, 1961; Ohio State Univ, PhD (mycol), 1965. **Professional Experience:** VPRES, JAPAN/KOREA, BUCKMAN LABS, INC, 1986-; gen mgr, Northern Asia-Pac Area, 1971-1986; Asia-Pac area rep, 1965-1971. **Memberships:** Am Chem Soc; Tech Asn Pulp & Paper Indust. **Research Statement & Publications:** Microbial physiology; fungal proteins and amino acids; microbial deterioration. **Mailing Address:** Buckman Labs Inc, PO Box 80305, Memphis, TN 38108-0305.

KARWAN, KIRK R, MANUFACTURING TECHNOLOGY. **Education:** Carnegie Mellon Univ, Phd, 1979. **Professional Experience:** ASSOC PROF MGT SCI, MOORE SCH BUS, UNIV SC, as of 2006. **Mailing Address:** Col Bus Admin, Univ SC, Columbia, SC 29208. **Fax:** 803-777-6876. **E-Mail:** karwan@badm.scarolina.edu

KARWAN, MARK HENRY, MATHEMATICAL PROGRAMMING, MULTIPLE CRITERIA DECISION MAKING. **Personal Data:** b Cleveland, Ohio, November 16, 1951; m 1973, Sabina; c Maria, Melinda, Monica & Mark W. **Education:** Johns Hopkins Univ, BES, 1974, MSE, 1974; Ga Inst Technol, PhD (opers res), 1976. **Professional Experience:** DEAN, SCH ENG & APPL SCI, STATE UNIV NY, BUFFALO, 1996-; actg dean, Sch Eng & Appl Sci, 1994-1995; proj dir univ, Ctr Indust Effectiveness, Buffalo, 1993-; assoc dean, Sch Eng & Appl Sci, 1992-1994; consult, Praxair Inc, 1987-; dept chmn, Dept Indust Eng, State Univ NY, Buffalo, 1987-1992; Prof Opers Res, Dept Indust Eng, State Univ NY, Buffalo, 1986-; Prin investr, 1992-1994 & Off Naval Res, 1985-1987; consult, Health Care Plan Inc, 1984-1987; Prin investr, NSF, 1978-1982; From asst to assoc prof, Dept Indust Eng, State Univ NY, Buffalo, 1976-1986; consult, Mgt Adv Servs Inc, 1974; fac adv student chap, Inst Indust Engrs. **Memberships:** Informs ASEE. **Research Statement & Publications:** Discrete optimization, routing and scheduling; multicriteria decision making; multilevel decentralized planning; redundancy in mathematical programming; industrial inspection; contributed papers to professional journals and patentee in field. **Mailing Address:** State Univ NY, 412 Bonner Hall, N Campus, Buffalo, NY 14260. **Fax:** 716-645-2495. **E-Mail:** mkarwan@buffalo.edu

KARWE, MUKUND V, MECHANICAL ENGINEERING. **Education:** IIT, Bombay, BTech, 1981; Rutgers Univ, MS, 1983 & PhD (Mech & aerospce Eng), 1987. **Professional Experience:** PROF, DEPT FOOD SCI, RUTGERS UNIV, as of 2004; assoc prof, Dept Food Sci, Rutgers Univ, beginning 1999; UNDERGRAD PROG DIR, DEPT FOOD SCI, RUTGERS UNIV, 1999-; vis fac, Dept Chem Eng, Indian Inst Technol; CLUSTER COORDR, COOPER RES PROG CTR ADVAN FOOD TECHNOL, RUTGERS UNIV, 2003-; co-proj mgr, Cooper Res Prog Ctr Advan Food Technol, Rutgers Univ, 1997-2000; asst prof, Dept Food Sci, Rutgers Univ, 1993-1999; FAC MEM, GRAD PROG MECH ENG, RUTGERS UNIV, 1995-; asst proj mgr, Basci Res prog Ctr Advan Food technol, Rutgers Univ, 1992-1997. **Mailing Address:** Dept Food Sci Ctr Advan Food Technol, Rutgers Univ, 65 Dudley Rd, New Brunswick, NJ 08901. **Fax:** 732-932-8690. **E-Mail:** karwe@aesop.rutgers.edu

KARWEIK, DALE HERBERT, ANALYTICAL CHEMISTRY. **Personal Data:** b Milwaukee, Wis, May 27, 1948; m 1970, c 2. **Education:** Univ Wis-Milwaukee, BS, 1970; Purdue Univ, PhD (anal chem), 1975. **Professional Experience:** DIR, INSTRUMENT SUPPORT, OHIO STATE UNIV, as of 2003; MEM FAC, DEPT CHEM, OHIO STATE UNIV, 1980-; asst prof, Wayne State Univ, 1975-1980. **Memberships:** Am Chem Soc. **Research Statement & Publications:** Measurement of homogeneous electron transfer rates; electrochemistry of porphyrins and related compounds with mechanistic studies. **Mailing Address:** Dept Chem, Ohio State Univ, 100 W 18th Ave, Columbus, OH 43210-1106. **Fax:** 614-292-1865. **E-Mail:** karweik.1@osu.edu

KARZ, ROBERT STEPHEN, HEAT TRANSFER MODELLING, POLYMER RHEOLOGY & CONSTITUTIVE EQUATIONS. **Personal Data:** b Rochester, NY, June 6, 1945; m 1969, Myrna; c Sara & Lisa. **Education:** Mass Inst Technol, SB, 1967; Univ Ill, MS, 1968, PhD (metall), 1972; Univ Rochester, MBA, 1985. **Professional Experience:** PRIN SCIENTIST, XEROX CORP, 1987-; sr scientist, Xerox Corp, 1985-1987; scientist, Xerox Corp, 1977-1985; assoc scientist, Xerox Corp, 1972-1977. **Memberships:** Am Phys Soc. **Research Statement & Publications:** Development of xerographic and thermal ink jet marking technologies; modelling of toner flows, heat transfer analysis, rheological measurements and developing print quality evaluation methods. **Mailing Address:** 1202 Fox Hollow Dr, Webster, NY 14580. **Fax:** 716-422-6509. **E-Mail:** karz@wbst311.xerox.com

KARZON, DAVID T, VIROLOGY, PEDIATRICS. **Personal Data:** b New York, NY, July 8, 1920; m 1950, c 2. **Education:** Ohio State Univ, BS, 1940, MS, 1941; Johns Hopkins Univ, MD, 1944; Am Bd Pediat, dipl; Am Bd Microbiol, dipl, 1964. **Professional Experience:** PROF BIOCHEM & MED, VANDERBILT KENNEDY CTR, as of 2004; DIR, DIV GENETICS, VANDERBILT KENNEDY CTR, as of 2004; Mem biol rev steering comt, Food & Drug Admin, 1972-; MED DIR, CHILDREN'S HOSP, UNIV, 1971-; PROF PEDIAT & CHMN DEPT, SCH MED, VANDERBILT UNIV, 1968-; mem virol & rickettsiol study sect, Nat Inst Allergy & Infectious Dis, 1967-1969; assoc ed, Am J Epidemiol, 1966-1978; chmn, Nat Inst Allergy & Infectious Dis, 1966-1967; mem surgeon-gen spec adv comt immunization pract, Nat Commun Dis Ctr, USPHS, Atlanta, Ga, 1964-1970; prog consult growth & develop sect, Nat Inst Child Health & Human Develop, 1964-1968; consult res reagents comt, Nat Inst Allergy & Infectious Dis, 1963-1967; res career develop award, NIH, 1962-1968; spec consult, Nat Commun Dis Ctr, USPHS, Atlanta, Ga, 1959-1962; Markle scholar, 1956-1961; from asst prof to prof virol, Dept Bact & Immunol, 1954-1968; from asst prof to prof pediat, Sch Med, State Univ NY Buffalo, 1952-1968; dir, Virol Lab, 1952-1968; Lowell Palmer fel, 1952-1954; instr virol, Sch Med, 1949-1950; Instr contagious dis, Johns Hopkins Univ Hosp, 1945 & 1948. **Memberships:** Soc Pediat Res; Soc Exp Biol & Med; Fedn Am Soc Exp Biol; Am Epidemiol Soc; Infectious Dis Soc; Am Asn Immunologists; Am Acad Microbiol; Am Soc Virol; Am Soc Microbiol. **Research Statement & Publications:** Animal virology; tissue culture. **Mailing Address:** Dept Pediat, Vanderbilt Univ Sch Med, D7235 Med Ctr N, Nashville, TN 37232-2581. **Fax:** 615-343-9723.

KAS, ARNOLD, MATHEMATICS. **Personal Data:** b Washington, DC, July 18, 1940. **Education:** Johns Hopkins Univ, BA, 1962; Stanford Univ, PhD (math), 1966. **Professional Experience:** Prof, Ore State Univ, 1980-; assoc prof math, Ore State Univ, 1973-1980; asst prof, Univ Calif, Berkeley, 1969-1973; Air Force Off Sci Res fel, Math Inst, State Univ Leiden, 1967-1969; Instr math, Stanford Univ, 1966-1967; AT BOEING HELICOPTERS. **Research Statement & Publications:** Complex manifolds; algebraic geometry. **Mailing Address:** 171 McGraw St, Seattle, WA 98109.

KASABACH, HAIG F, SCIENCE ADMINISTRATION. **Personal Data:** b New York, NY, December 5, 1935; m 1962, Carol Rodano; c Peter & Christopher. **Education:** Univ Mich, BS, 1957, MS, 1959. **Professional Experience:** Mem, Intergovt Task Force Water Monitoring, 1992-; STATE GEOLOGIST, NJ GEOL SURV, 1985-; dep state geologist, NJ Geol Surv, 1984-1985; chief, NJ Bur Ground Water Mgt, 1980-1983; chief, NJ Bur Water Qual & Mgt, 1977-1979; Supv geologist, NJ Div Water Res, 1967-1976; sr geologist, NJ Geol Surv, 1960-1966; dir, Sterling Hill Mining Mus. **Memberships:** Asn Am State Geologists; Am Inst Prof Geologists; Asn Eng Geologists; Am Inst Hydrol; Asn Ground Water Scientists & Engrs. **Research Statement & Publications:** Hydrology and water resources. **Mailing Address:** NJ Geol Surv, CN-427, 29 Arctic Pkwy, Trenton, NJ 08625-0427. **Fax:** 609-633-1004. **E-Mail:** bgt@njgs.dep.state.nj.us

KASAHARA, AKIRA, METEOROLOGY, NUMERICAL WEATHER PREDICTIONS. **Personal Data:** b Tokyo, Japan, October 11, 1926; American citizen; m 1952, Yuko; c Alice M & Margaret R. **Education:** Univ Tokyo, BS, 1948, MS, 1950, DSc, 1954. **Honors & Awards:** Meteorol Soc; Award, Meteorol Soc Japan, 1961; Fujiwara Award, Japan Meteorol Soc, 1996. **Professional Experience:** SR RES ASSOC, NAT CTR ATMOSPHERIC RES, 1996-; adj prof, Dept Meteorol, Univ Utah, 1979-; external examr, Dept Meterol, Univ Nairobi, Kenya, 1977-1979; sr scientist, Nat Ctr Atmospheric Res, 1973-1996; vis lectr, Inst Meteorol, Univ Stockholm, Sweden, 1971-1972; assoc ed, J Appl Meteorol, 1967-1972; Affil prof dept meteorol, Tex A&M Univ, 1967-1970; prog scientist, Nat Ctr Atmospheric Res, 1963-1973; res scientist, Courant Inst Math Sci, NY Univ, 1962-1963; res assoc meteorol, Univ Chicago, 1956-1962; res assoc oceanog & meteorol, Agr & Mech Col Tex, 1954-1956; res assoc, Univ Tokyo, 1953-1954; asst geophys inst, Univ Tokyo, 1948-1953. **Memberships:** Am Geophys Union; hon mem Meteorol Soc Japan; fel Am Meteorol Soc; fel AAAS. **Research Statement & Publications:** Dynamic meteorology; development of weather prediction methods with the numerical integration of thermo-hydro-dynamical equations. **Mailing Address:** Nat Ctr Atmospheric Res, Box 3000, Boulder, CO 80307-3000. **Fax:** 303-497-1700. **E-Mail:** kasahara@ucar.edu

KASAI, PAUL HARUO, PHYSICAL CHEMISTRY. **Personal Data:** b Osaka, Japan, January 30, 1932; American citizen; m 1959, Toko; c Yumi & Miki. **Education:** Univ Denver, BS, 1955; Univ Calif, Berkeley, PhD (chem), 1959. **Professional Experience:** RES STAFF MEM, IBM ALMADEN RES CTR, 1986-; Thomas J Watson res ctr, IBM Corp, Yorktown Heights, NY, 1985-1986; mgr tech support, IBM Instruments Inc, Danbury, 1979-1985; sr scientist, Tarrytown Tech Ctr, 1977-1979; group leader, Res Inst, Union Carbide Corp, 1975-1977; mem res staff, Res Inst, Union Carbide Corp, 1967-1975; assoc prof chem, Univ Calif, Santa Cruz, 1966-1967; res inst, Union Carbide Corp, 1962-1966; mem res staff, Hitachi Cent Res Lab, Japan, 1959-1962. **Memberships:** Am Chem Soc. **Research Statement & Publications:** Magnetic resonance studies of polymer synthesis and degradation, organometallic complexes, reactions between atoms and small molecules in low temperature matrices, free radicals and surface states. **Mailing Address:** 18645 Castle Lake Dr, Morgan Hill, CA 95037. **Fax:** 408-927-3310. **E-Mail:** kasai@almaden.ibm.com

KASAMATSU, HARUMI, MOLECULAR BIOLOGY, MOLECULAR VIROLOGY. **Personal Data:** b Tokyo, Japan, August 18, 1937; m 1969, Takuji. **Education:** Osaka Univ, Japan, PhD (molecular biol), 1969. **Professional Experience:** PROF MOLECULAR BIOL, UNIV CALIF, LOS ANGELES, 1984-PRESENT ASSOCIATE PROF MOLECULAR BIOL, UNIV CALIF, LOS ANGELES, 1975-1983. **Memberships:** Member, AAAS Member, ASV Member, ASM. **Mailing Address:** Dept Molecular Cell & Develop Biol, & Mol Biol Inst, Univ Calif, Boyer Hall 456, 611 Charles E Young Dr, Los Angeles, CA 90095-1570. **Fax:** 310-206-6808. **E-Mail:** harumi_k@mbi.ucla.edu

KASAMEYER, PAUL WILLIAM, GEOPHYSICS. **Personal Data:** b Detroit, Mich, September 9, 1943; m 1965, c 3. **Education:** Mass Inst Technol, BS, 1965, PhD (geophys), 1974; Yale Univ, MS, 1966. **Professional Experience:** GEOPHYSICIST, LAWRENCE LIVERMORE NAT LAB, 1974-. **Memberships:** Soc Explor Geophysicists; Sigma Xi; Am Geophys Union. **Research Statement & Publications:** Collection and interpretation of geophysical data; thermal modeling; magnetotellurics; experimental studies of gravity; earthquake hazards. **Mailing Address:** Lawrence Livermore Nat Lab, PO Box 808 L 203, Livermore, CA 94550. **Fax:** 925-424-3886. **E-Mail:** kasameyer1@llnl.gov

KASAP, SAFA O, MATERIALS SCIENCE ENGINEERING, ELECTRICAL ENGINEERING. **Education:** Univ London, BS, 1976, MS, 1978, PhD (elec eng), 1983. **Professional Experience:** PROF ELEC ENG, UNIV SASK, 1986-; fac mem, dept elec eng, Univ London, 1983-1986. **Memberships:** Inst Elec & Electronics Engrs; Am Phys Soc. **Mailing Address:** Dept Elect Eng, Univ Sask, 57 Campus Dr, Saskatoon, SK S7N 5A9, Can. **Fax:** 306-966-5407. **E-Mail:** safa_kasap@engr.usask.ca

KASARDA, DONALD DAVID, PROTEIN CHEMISTRY. **Personal Data:** b Kingston, Pa, October 12, 1933; m 1964, c 1. **Education:** King's Col, Pa, BS, 1955; Boston Col, MS, 1957; Princeton Univ, MA, 1959, PhD (phys chem), 1961. **Honors & Awards:** Thomas Burr Osborne Medal, Am Asn Cereal Chemists, 1993; Rank prize for nutrition, J Arthur Rank foundation, 2002. **Professional Experience:** PHY SCI COLLABR, AGR RES SERV, USDA, as of 2006; RES CHEMIST, CROP IMPROV & UTILIZATION, WESTERN REGIONAL RES CTR, AGR RES SERV, USDA, 1985-; assoc, Exp Sta, Dept Agron & Range Sci, Univ Calif, Davis, 1974-; res leader, Food Qual Res Unit, 1972-1985; res chemist, Food Qual Res Unit, 1964-1972; Cardiovasc Res Inst fel, Sch Med, Univ Calif, San Francisco, 1963-1964; mem tech staff, Bell Tel Labs, NJ, 1961-1963. **Memberships:** AAAS; Am Chem Soc; Am Asn Cereal Chem. **Research Statement & Publications:** Protein chemistry; wheat genetics. **Mailing Address:** Western Regional Res Ctr, USDA, Rm 2122, 800 Buchanan St, Albany, CA 94710. **Fax:** 510-559-5818.

KASARSKIS, EDWARD JOSEPH, NEUROLOGY. **Personal Data:** b Chicago, Ill, October 9, 1946; m 1969, Mary; c Andrew, Peter, Larisa & Irina. **Education:** Col St Thomas, BA, 1968; Univ Wis-Madison, MD, 1974, PhD (biochem), 1975. **Professional Experience:** Vice Chmn, Dept Neurol, 1998; CHIEF, NEUROL SERV, VET ADMIN HOSP, LEXINGTON, KY, 1992-; PROF CHIEF, NEUROL SERV, UAMC, 1992-; from asst prof to assoc prof neurol, toxicol & nutrit, Univ Ky, 1985-1992; staff neurologist, Vet Admin Hosp, Lexington, Ky, beginning 1980; asst prof neurol, Sch Med, La State Univ, 1979-1980; resident neurol, Univ Va Hosp, 1976-1979; resident internal med, Univ Wis-Madison Hosp, 1974-1976. **Memberships:** Sigma Xi; Am Acad Neurol; Soc Neuroscience; Am Soc Neurochemistry; Int Soc Neurochemistry; Int Soc Bioinorg Sci; Am Neurol Asn. **Research Statement & Publications:** Role of trace metals in the function of the brain; Amyotrophic lateral sclerosis; nutrit in ALS, ALS in epidemiology. **Mailing Address:** Dept Neurol Univ Ky Col Med, 800 Rose St, Lexington, KY 40536-0084.

KASBEKAR, DINKAR KASHINATH, PHYSIOLOGY, BIOCHEMISTRY. **Personal Data:** b Bombay, India, April 3, 1932; American citizen; wid Gertrude (Deceased); c Anand David. **Education:** Univ Bombay, BSc, 1952 & 1954, MSc, 1957; Univ Calif, PhD (biochem), 1961. **Professional Experience:** RETIRED; prof physiol & biophys, Sch Med & Dent, Georgetown Univ, 1984-1991; vis sr fel, Nat Inst Arthritis, Metab & Digestive Dis, NIH, 1981; prin investr, NSF, beginning 1970; prin investr, Wash Heart Asn, 1970-1971; from asst prof to assoc prof physiol & biophys, Sch Med & Dent, Georgetown Univ, 1969-1984; asst res physiologist, Univ Calif, Berkeley, 1966-1968; San Francisco Heart Asn fel, 1964-1965; asst res biochemist, Cardiovasc Res Inst, 1963-1965; jr res biochemist, Univ Calif, San Francisco, 1961-1963. **Memberships:** Am Physiol Soc; AAUP. **Research Statement & Publications:** Ion transport, zymogen secretion, specifically in the area of gastric secretion. **Mailing Address:** 11330 Saddleview Ct, Raleigh, NC 27613-6807. **Fax:** 919-782-8406. **E-Mail:** drz1@aol.com

KASCSAK, RICHARD JOHN, SLOW VIRUS & PERSISTENT INFECTIONS. **Personal Data:** b Whitestone, NY, September 20, 1947; m 1972, c Matthew & Melissa. **Education:** St Francis Col, NY, BS, 1969; Adelphi Univ, MS, 1971; Cornell Univ Med Col, PhD (virol), 1976. **Professional Experience:** RES SCIENTIST, NY STATE INST BASIC RES DEVELOP DISABILITIES, 1975-; training fel, Cornell Univ, 1971-1975; teaching asst, Adelphi Univ, NY, 1969-1971. **Memberships:** Am Soc Microbiol; Am Soc Virol. **Research Statement & Publications:** Slow viral infections of the central nervous system with emphasis on the creation of model systems relevant to human disease; unconventional slow virus diseases; scrapie. **Mailing Address:** NY State Inst Basic Res Develop Disabilities, 1050 Forest Hill Rd, Staten Island, NY 10314. **Fax:** 718-698-3803.

KASE, KENNETH RAYMOND, RADIATION DOSIMETRY & SHIELDING. **Personal Data:** b Oak Park, Ill, July 13, 1938; m GRADY; c 2. **Education:** Ga Inst Technol, BS, 1961; Univ Calif, Berkeley, MS, 1963; Stanford Univ, PhD (biophys), 1975; Am Bd Health Physics, cert, 1969; Am Bd Radiol, cert, 1981. **Honors & Awards:** Elda E Anderson Award, Health Physics Soc, 1978; R S Landauer mem lecture, health physics society & Am assoc physicists in med, midwest chapters, 1992; GFailla award health physics soc & Am assoc physicists med, New York chapters, 2002. **Professional Experience:** Safety Officer, Lyncean Technologies, Inc.; Senior vpres, Nat Coun Radiation Protection & Measurement, 2002-; sr scientist, Stanford Linear Acclerator Ctr, 2001-2005; sci vpres oper radiation safety, Nat Coun Radiation Protection & Measurement, 1995-2002; assoc dir, Environ, Safety & Health, Stanford Linear Accelerator Ctr, 1995-2001; head, Radiation Physics Dept, 1992-1995; prof & dir physics, Dept Radiation & Oncol, Med Ctr, Univ Mass, 1985-1991; adj prof, Lowell Univ, 1978-1991; Ed, Health Physics J, Health Physics Soc, 1977-1982; asst prof & chief dosimetry & radiation safety radiol physics, Harvard Med Sch, 1975-1984; health physicist, Stanford Linear Accelerator, Stanford Univ, 1969-1973; chief radiation safety, Lawrence Livermore Lab, Univ Calif, 1967-1969; health physicist radiation safety, Lawrence Livermore Lab, Univ Calif, 1963-1967; Scientist reactors environ, Lockheed Missiles & Space Co, 1961-1962; mem, sci comt, Nat Coun Radiation, Protection & Measurement, 1982. **Memberships:** Fel Health Physics Soc (pres, 2003-2004); fel Am Asn Physicists Med (treas, 1986-1991); Radiation Res Soc; fel Am Col Radiol; fel Am Col Med Physics; Am Acad Health Physics (pres, 1996); nat coun radiation protection & meas (sr vpres, 2002-); Int Radiat Prot Assoc (vpres, 2004-). **Research Statement & Publications:** Radiation measurement and dosimetry; biological effects of radiation. **Mailing Address:** 955 N Calif Ave, Palo Alto, CA 94303-3407. **Fax:** 650-320-9513. **E-Mail:** kr.kase@stanfordalumni.org

KASER, J(OHN) D(ONALD), CHEMICAL ENGINEERING. **Personal Data:** b Oak Park, Ill, November 21, 1929; div, c 2. **Education:** Augustana Col, BA, 1956; Univ Iowa, BS,

1958, MS, 1960, PhD (chem eng), 1963. **Professional Experience:** RETIRED; fel eng, Westinghouse Hanford Col, 1989; prin engr, Rockwell Hanford Oper, 1980-1989; mem steering comn on shallow land burial of radioactive waste, Dept Energy, 1977-1978; staff engr, Rockwell Hanford Oper, 1976-1980; Mem fac, Joint Ctr, Grad Study, 1968-; Sr develop engr, Battelle-Northwest, 1963-1976. **Memberships:** Am Inst Chem Engrs; Am Nuclear Soc. **Research Statement & Publications:** Solidification and disposal of radioactive waste from nuclear fuel reprocessing; decontamination; solvent extraction; radioactive waste management; heat transfer. **Mailing Address:** 1140 Southeast Park Dr, Colville, WA 99114.

KASEVICH, MARK, PHYSICS. **Education:** Dartmouth Col, BA, 1985; Merton Col, Oxford Univ, MA, 1987; Stanford Univ, PhD (Appl Physics), 1992. **Professional Experience:** PROF PHYSICS, SCH HUMANITIES & SCI, STANFORD UNIV, 2002-; prof, dept physics, Yale Univ, 2001-2002. **Research Statement & Publications:** Atom optics and interferometry; quantum many-body effects in dilute atomic vapors. **Mailing Address:** Dept Physics, Stanford Univ, 382 Via Pueblo Mall, Stanford, CA 94305-4060. **Fax:** 650-723-9173. **E-Mail:** kasevich@stanford.edu

KASH, JEFFREY ALAN, OPTICAL EMISSION FROM SEMICONDUCTORS & DEVICES. **Personal Data:** b Whittier, Calif, October 14, 1953. **Education:** Univ Calif, Berkeley, BA, 1975, PhD, 1981. **Professional Experience:** RES STAFF MEM PHYS SCI, T J WATSON RES CTR, IBM, as of 2000; TECH ASST SYS, SCI & TECHNOL, IBM RES, as of 2000; res scientist, T J Watson Res Ctr, Ibm, beginning 1981. **Memberships:** Fel Am Phys Soc; Inst Elec & Electronics Engrs. **Mailing Address:** T J Watson Res Ctr, Int Bus Mach, PO Box 218, Yorktown Heights, NY 10598. **E-Mail:** jeffkash@us.ibm.com

KASH, KATHLEEN, SYSTEMS OF REDUCED DIMENSIONALITY, ULTRAFAST PHENOMENA. **Personal Data:** b Corona, Calif, November 28, 1953; m, c Nathan Amory Kash, Caroline Anne & Rebecca Katherine. **Education:** Middlebury Col, BA, 1975; Mass Inst Technol, PhD (physics), 1982. **Professional Experience:** PROF PHYSICS, CASE WESTERN RES UNIV, 1994-; adj res prof physics, Dartmouth Col, 1992-1993; mem tech staff, Bellcore, 1984-1993; fel, AT&T Bell Labs, 1982-1984. **Memberships:** Am Phys Soc. **Research Statement & Publications:** Semiconductor quantum wires and dots; carrier relaxation-diffusion in semiconductors; solid state physics; low pressure growth of III- IV nitrides; electrodeposition of semiconductors. **Mailing Address:** Dept Physics, Case Western Res Univ, 10900 Euclid Ave, Cleveland, OH 44106-7221. **Fax:** 216-368-4671. **E-Mail:** kxk43@po.cwru.edu

KASH, MICHAEL MASON, ATOMIC STRUCTURE, QUANTUM OPTICS. **Personal Data:** b Cincinnati, Ohio, August 12, 1955. **Education:** Lake Forest Col, BA, 1977; Mass Inst Technol, PhD (atomic physics), 1988. **Professional Experience:** PROF, PHYSICS, 2002-; CHMN, DEPT PHYSICS, 1995-; assoc prof physics, Lake Forest Col, 1994-2000; asst prof, 1988-1994. **Memberships:** Am Phys Soc; Sigma Xi. **Research Statement & Publications:** Rydberg atoms in strong fields, electromagnetically induced transparency and slow light. **Mailing Address:** Dept Physics, Lake Forest Col, 555 N Sheridan Rd, Lake Forest, IL 60045. **E-Mail:** kash@lfc.edu

KASHA, HENRY, HIGH ENERGY PHYSICS, COSMIC RAY PHYSICS. **Personal Data:** b Warsaw, Poland. **Education:** Hebrew Univ, Jerusalem, MSc, 1954; Israel Inst Technol, DSc(physics), 1960. **Professional Experience:** LECTR PHYSICS, YALE UNIV, as of 2002; SR RES PHYSICIST, YALE UNIV, 1973-; sr res assoc, Yale Univ, 1970-1973; assoc physicist, Brookhaven Nat Lab, 1966-1970; asst physicist, Brookhaven Nat Lab, 1964-1966; lectr physics, Israel Inst Technol, 1960-1963. **Memberships:** AAAS; Am Phys Soc. **Mailing Address:** Dept Physics, Yale Univ, PO Box 6666, New Haven, CT 06520. **Fax:** 203-432-6125. **E-Mail:** henry.kasha@yale.edu

KASHA, KENNETH JOHN, PLANT CYTOGENETICS, PLANT CELL CULTURE. **Personal Data:** b Lacombe, Alta, May 6, 1933; m 1958, Marion; c Lorelei M & David J. **Education:** Univ Alta, BSc, 1957, MSc, 1958; Univ Minn, PhD (plant genetics), 1962. **Honorary Degrees:** LLD, Univ Calgary, 1986. **Honors & Awards:** Grindley Medal, Agr Inst Can, 1977; E C Manning Award, 1983; Nilsson-Ehle Lectr, Sweden, 1987; fel Royal Soc Can, 1990; Officer of Order of Can, 1994; Award of Excellence, Genetics Soc Can, 1994; Distinguished Alumi, Univ Minn, 2000. **Professional Experience:** PROF EMER, UNIV GUELPH, 1998-; nat corresp, Int Asn Plant Cell & Tissue Cult, 1990-1994; prog chmn, XVI Int Cong Genetics, Toronto, 1988; vis scientist, Plant Indust, Commonwealth Sci & Indust Orgn, Canberra, Australia, 1985-1986; dir, Plant Biotech Ctr Guelph, Waterloo Biotech, 1984-1987; prof crop cytogenetics, Univ Guelph, 1974-1998; orgn chmn, Int Symposium Haploids Higher Plants, Guelph, 1974; assoc prof crop cytogenetics, Univ Guelph, 1969-1974; asst prof crop sci & crop cytogeneticist, Univ Guelph, 1966-1969; res scientist 1, Ottawa Res Sta, Can Dept Agr, 1966; res officer 3, Ottawa Res Sta, Can Dept Agr, 1964-1966; res officer 2, Ottawa Res Sta, Can Dept Agr, 1962-1964; Teaching asst, Univ Minn, 1960-1961. **Memberships:** Genetics Soc Am; Genetics Soc Can (secy, 1966-1969, dir 1970-1972, vpres, 1975, pres, 1976); Am Soc Agron; fel Royal Soc Can; Int Asn Plant Cell & Tissue Cult; Can Soc Plant Molecular Biol. **Research Statement & Publications:** Crop plant cytogenetics; haploidy in cereals; molecular cytology; interspecific hybridization and chromosome pairing in hordeum, linkage and RFLP mapping of barley; plant cell culture in cereals; male sterility and self-incompatibility; molecular biology. **Mailing Address:** Dept Plant Agr, Univ Guelph, Guelph, ON N1G 2W1, Can. **Fax:** 519-763-8933. **E-Mail:** kkasha@crop.uoguelph.ca

KASHA, MICHAEL, CHEMICAL PHYSICS, SPECTROSCOPY & MOLECULAR ELECTRONIC PHENOMENA. **Personal Data:** b Elizabeth, NJ, December 6, 1920; m 1947, c 1. **Education:** Univ Mich, BS, 1943; Univ Calif, PhD (phys chem), 1945. **Honorary Degrees:** DSc, Gonzaga Univ, 1988, Univ Gdansk, 1992. **Honors & Awards:** Phillips Lectr, Haverford Col, 1959; ReillyLectr, Univ Notre Dame, 1959; S C Lind Lectr, Oak Ridge Nat Lab, 1961; George Porter Medal, 1990; Robert Mulliken Medal, Univ Chicago, 1990. **Professional Experience:** PROF EMER, DEPT CHEM & BIOCHEM, FLA STATE UNIV, as of 2004; Geoffrey Frew fel, Australian Acad Sci, 1991; mem, Sci & Tech Adv Comt, Argonne Nat Lab, 1983-1988; sci adv to Gov Bob Graham, Fla, 1983-1987; foreign coun, Inst Molecular Sci, Okazaki, Japan, 1982-1985; exec comt, Inst La Vie, Paris, France, 1980-; mem, Nat Sci Bd, France, 1980-; mem, Nat Sci Bd, Pres Carter, 1979-1984; vis prof chem, Univ Mich, 1969; Charles F Kettering Res Award, Gen Motors Corp, 1963-1969; vis prof biophys, Harvard Univ, 1961; dir, Inst Molecular Biophys, 1960-1980; chmn, Dept Chem, 1959-1962; vis prof chem, Harvard Univ, 1959-1960; robert o lawton distinguished prof chem, Fla State Univ, beginning 1951; prof phys chem, Fla State Univ, beginning 1951; Guggenheim fel & spec lectr, Univ Manchester, 1950-1951; AEC fel, Univ Chicago, 1949-1950; res assoc, Plutonium Proj, Univ Calif, 1946-1949; Univ fel & instr, Plutonium Proj, Univ Calif, 1946; res chemist, Plutonium Proj, Univ Calif, 1944-1946; lab asst, Res Lab, Merck & Co, Inc, 1938-1941. **Memberships:** Nat Acad Sci; corresp mem Brazilian Acad Sci; foreign mem Ukrainian Acad Sci; fel Am Acad Arts & Sci; Int Acad Quantum Molecular Sci. **Research Statement & Publications:** Molecular biophysics and electronic spectroscopy; triplet states of molecules; emission spectroscopy of molecules; classification of electronic transitions; spin-intercombinations; n-pi transitions; radiationless transitions; theoretical photochemistry; molecular excitons and energy transfer; biological molecular interactions. **Mailing Address:** Dept Chem, Fla State Univ, Tallahassee, FL 32306-3015. **E-Mail:** kasha@sb.fsu.edu

KASHAR, LAWRENCE JOSEPH, METALLURGY, MATERIALS SCIENCE. **Personal Data:** b Brooklyn, NY, June 1, 1933; m 1981, Barbara; c Evan C, Summerlea J & Desa N. **Education:** Rensselaer Polytech Inst, BMetE, 1955; Stevens Inst Technol, MS, 1959; Carnegie Inst Technol, MS, 1961; Carnegie-Mellon Univ, PhD (metall, mat sci), 1970. **Professional Experience:** PRES, KASHAR TECH SERV, 1991-; vpres technol, Tech Serv, 1983-1991; chmn, Westec Conf, Am Soc Metals, 1983; chmn, Struct Anal Prog, Int Symp Testing & Failure Anal, 1980-1987; dir, Tech Serv, 1979-1983; vpres, Litigation Consults Int, 1978-1981; vpres & secy, ATFA, Inc, 1977-1980; Adj lectr, Univ Southern Calif, 1975-1981; dir, Metall Serv, Scanning Electron Anal Labs, Inc, 1973-1979; staff engr, Orlando Div, Martin Marietta Corp, 1973; mem tech staff, B-1 Div, Rockwell Int, 1971-1972; sr res metallurgist, US Steel Appl Res Lab, 1964-1970; res assoc, Carnegie Inst Technol, 1960-1964; assoc metallurgist, AMAX Res & Develop Co, Inc, 1955-1959. **Memberships:** Am Soc Metals; Am Soc Testing & Mat; Inst Elec & Electronics Engrs; Int Soc Testing & Failure Anal; Am Chem Soc; Electron Micros Soc Am; Am Welding Soc. **Research Statement & Publications:** Causes and prevention of failures of metal structures; development of microanalytical and surface analysis techniques for practical materials problem solving such as particulates, pollution and asbestos. **Mailing Address:** Kashar Tech Serv Inc, 6305 Ariz Pl, Los Angeles, CA 90045. **Fax:** 310-645-9859. **E-Mail:** lkashar@kts-cb.com

KASHATUS, WILLIAM C, PATHOLOGY, HEMATOLOGY. **Personal Data:** b Nanticoke, Pa, April 23, 1929; m 1954, c 2. **Education:** Wilkes Col, BS, 1951; Bucknell Univ, MS, 1953; Hahnemann Med Col, MD, 1959. **Professional Experience:** Vchmn dept, Sch Med Technol, 1973-1979; PROF PATH, HAHNEMANN MED COL, 1972-; med dir, SBCL, Philadelphia, 1971-; mem tech adv bd, Southeast Pa Div, Am Red Cross, 1968-1972 & West Co, 1969-1971; dir, Sch Med Technol, 1964-1971; dir labs, Hahnemann Hosp, 1964-1970; from instr to assoc prof path, Hahnemann Med Col, 1963-1973; Am Cancer Soc fel, 1962-1964; Mary Bailey Heart Found fel, 1956-1958; Instr chem, Bucknell Univ, 1951-1952. **Memberships:** AMA; fel Col Am Path; Am Soc Clin Path; Acad Clin Lab Physicians & Scientists. **Research Statement & Publications:** Hematology, especially cancer chemotherapy; blood banking, especially immunochematology; tissue typing. **Mailing Address:** Smith Kline Beecham Clin Lab, 400 Egypt Rd, Norristown, PA 19403-3406.

KASHDAN, DAVID STUART, APPLICATIONS OF POLYMERS, INDUSTRIAL CHEMISTRY. **Personal Data:** b New York, NY, October 21, 1950; m 1983, Letitia; c Lee H & Benjamin T. **Education:** Stevens Inst Technol, BS, 1972; Univ Vt, PhD (org chem), 1977. **Professional Experience:** DIR, POLYMERS RES, EASTMAN CHEM CO, 1988-; from res chemist to sr res chemist, Eastman Chem CO, 1979-1988; res fel, Univ Calif, Berkeley, 1977-1979; vis instr org chem, Univ Vt, 1976-1977. **Memberships:** Am Chem Soc Soc of Plastic Engineers. **Research Statement & Publications:** Organic synthesis; synthetic methods; organolithium reagents and halogenation of aromatics; synthesis of morphinans and isoquinolines; development of new polymers for use in pharmaceutical applications; polymer chemistry, especially polycondensation polymers, celulosics, polyolefins. **Mailing Address:** Eastman Chem Co, 200 S Wilcox, Kingsport, TN 37660-5027. **Fax:** 423-229-3896. **E-Mail:** dkashdan@eastman.com

KASHEF, A(BDEL-AZIZ) I(SMAIL), GEOTECHNICAL ENGINEERING, GROUNDWATER SCIENCES. **Personal Data:** b Cairo, Egypt, February 10, 1919; m 1948. **Education:** Univ Cairo, BS, 1940, MS, 1948; Purdue Univ, PhD (soil mech), 1951. **Professional Experience:** EMER PROF CIVIL ENG, NC STATE UNIV, 1980-; ed, Water Resources Bull, 1970-1973; prof, NC State Univ, 1967-1980; vis prof soil mech & ground water, NC State Univ, 1962-1967; mem tech comt, River Harbors Comt, 1960-1962; dir, Consult Eng Off, Saudi Arabia, 1959-1960; prof, Am Univ Beirut, 1956-1960; mem, Nat Hydraul Comt, 1956; sr lectr, Ein Shams Univ, 1951-1954 & Univ Cairo, 1954-1956; soil consult, High Aswan Dam Auth, Egypt, 1954-1956; mem water-well comt, Nat Prod Coun, Govt Egypt, 1953; Consult soil engr, 1952-; instr struct, Univ Cairo, 1945-1948; Irrig engr, Egyptian Govt, 1940-1945 & 1948-1951. **Memberships:** Fel Am Water Resources Asn; fel Am Soc Civil Engrs; Am Geophys Union. **Research Statement & Publications:** Water resources research, especially in ground-water field and geotechnical engineering. **Mailing Address:** 5504 N Hills Dr, Raleigh, NC 27612.

KASHGARIAN, MICHAEL, PATHOLOGY, CELL BIOLOGY. **Personal Data:** b New York, NY, September 20, 1933; m 1960, Jean; c Michaele (Rose) & Thea (Obstler). **Education:** NY Univ, BA, 1954; Yale Univ, MD, 1958. **Professional Experience:** PROF PATH & BIOL, YALE UNIV, as of 2003; vchmn dept, Yale Univ, 1976-1989; assoc chief pathologist, Yale New Haven Hosp, 1976-1986; attend pathologist, Yale New Haven Hosp, 1969-; asst attend pathologist, Yale New Haven Hosp, 1966-1969; USPHS spec fel, 1963-1965 & res career award, 1965-1975; assoc pathologist, Yale New Haven Hosp, 1963-1966; from instr to assoc prof, Yale Univ, 1962-1974; Life Ins Med Res fel physiol, Univ Gottingen, 1961-1962; asst resident path, Yale Univ, 1959-1961; asst med, Sch Med, Wash Univ, 1958-1959. **Memberships:** Am Asn Path; Am Physiol Soc; Am Soc Clin Path; Am Soc Nephrol; Int Acad Path; fel AAAS. **Research Statement & Publications:** Pathology and physiology of the kidney. **Mailing Address:** Dept Path Sch Med Yale Univ, PO Box 208023, New Haven, CT 06520-8023. **Fax:** 203-785-3348. **E-Mail:** michael.kashgarian@yale.edu

KASHIN, PHILIP, NEUROPHYSIOLOGY, CLINICAL RESEARCH. **Personal Data:** b New York, NY, October 27, 1930; m 1958, c Peter S, Thomas B & Sarah B. **Education:** Brooklyn Col, BA, 1953; Columbia Univ, MA, 1958; NY Univ, MS, 1961; Ill Inst Technol, PhD (physiol), 1970. **Honors & Awards:** I R 100 Award, 1967. **Professional Experience:** ASSOC DIR CLIN AFFAIRS, PFIZER HOSP PROD GROUP, 1986-; asst dir, Pfizer Int Corp, 1984-1986; clin monitor, Abbott Lab, 1983-1984; Consult, 1982-1983; sr asst dir clin res, USV Pharmaceut Corp, 1976-1982; asstprof biol, Queens Col, NY, 1971-1976; Nat Inst Neurol Dis & Stroke spec res fel neurophysiol, Univ Ore, 1970-1971; res biochemist, IIT Res Inst, 1969-1970; assoc biochemist, IIT Res Inst, 1964-1969; asst biochemist, IIT Res Inst, 1963-1964; res asst biochem, State Univ NY Downstate Med Ctr, 1962-1963; Res asst immunochem, Hosp for Spec Surg, New York, 1961-1962. **Memberships:** AAAS; NY Acad Sci; Am Physiol Soc. **Research Statement & Publications:** Methods to assay mosquito repellents; cardiovascular and anti-infective clinical research; mechanism of action of carbon dioxide with neurotransmitters in the central nervous system; clinical research. **Mailing Address:** 47 Glen Cove Dr, Glen Head, NY 11545.

KASHIWA, BRYAN ANDREW, NUMERICAL FLUID DYNAMICS. **Personal Data:** b Oswego, NY, February 20, 1952; m 1969, c 3. **Education:** Worcester Polytech Inst, BS, 1973; Univ Wash, MS, 1978, PhD, 1987. **Professional Experience:** MEM STAFF, LOS

ALAMOS NAT LAB, 1979-; engr, K2 Corp, 1973-1979. **Memberships:** Am Soc Mech Engrs. **Research Statement & Publications:** Application and development of methods in numerical fluid dynamics with emphasis on multifield flows. **Mailing Address:** T 3 Computational Fluid Dynamics, Los Alamos Nat Lab, B216 PO Box 1663, Los Alamos, NM 87545. **Fax:** 505-665-5926. **E-Mail:** bak@lanl.gov

KASHKARI, CHAMAN NATH, ELECTRICAL ENGINEERING. **Personal Data:** b Srinagar, India, August 27, 1933; m 1963, c 2. **Education:** Univ Jammu & Kashmir, India, BA, 1952; Univ Rajasthan, BS, 1957; Univ Detroit, MS, 1965; Univ Mich, Ann Arbor, PhD (elec eng), 1969. **Professional Experience:** ASSOC PROF ELEC ENG, UNIV AKRON, 1975-; Energy consult, Govt Nepal, NSF, 1975; asst prof elec eng, Univ Akron, 1969-1975; teaching fel, Univ Detroit, 1964-1965 & Univ Mich, Ann Arbor, 1966-1969; plant engr, India, 1961-1964; grad trainee, Eng, 1958-1960; Asst engr, Gen Elec Co, India, 1957-1958. **Memberships:** Inst Elec & Electronics Engrs; Am Soc Eng Educ; Sigma Xi. **Research Statement & Publications:** Energy planning in developing countries; solar energy; biogas plants; mini power plants; energy conservation; electric power systems engineering. **Mailing Address:** Dept Elec Eng, Akron Univ, Akron, OH 44325.

KASHKET, EVA RUTH, BACTERIOLOGY, BIOCHEMISTRY. **Personal Data:** b Zagreb, Yugoslavia, 1936; American citizen; m 1957, Shelby; c 2. **Education:** McGill Univ, BS, 1956, MS, 1957; Harvard Univ, PhD (med sci), 1963. **Honors & Awards:** Alice Evans Award, Am Soc Microbiol. **Professional Experience:** PROF EMER MICROBIOL, SCH MED, BOSTON UNIV, as of 2006; prof microbiol, Sch Med, Boston Univ, beginning 1982; assoc prof, Sch Med, Boston Univ, 1974-1982; fel biochem pharmacol, Sch Med Tufts Univ, 1962-1965; res assoc, Dept Physiol, Harvard Med Sch, 1957-1974. **Memberships:** Am Soc Microbiol. **Research Statement & Publications:** Bioenergetics, fermentations, solventogenesis; Clostridia, Lactobacilli. **Mailing Address:** Dept Microbiol, Sch Med, Boston Univ, 715 Albany St L504, Boston, MA 02118-2426. **E-Mail:** ekashket@bu.edu

KASHKET, SHELBY, ORAL BIOLOGY, NUTRITION. **Personal Data:** b Montreal, Que, February 1, 1931; American citizen; m 1957, Eva; c 2. **Education:** McGill Univ, BS, 1952, MS, 1953, PhD (biochem), 1956. **Professional Experience:** DIR, OFF TECHNOL TRANSFER, FORSYTH INST, as of 2004; PRIN INVESTR, FORSYTH DENT CTR, 1996-; assoc mem, Forsyth Dent Ctr, 1981-1996; lectr, Harvard Med Sch, 1979-; asst mem, Forsyth Dent Ctr, 1972-1980; biochemist, USPHS, 1967-1970; asst biochemist, Mass Gen Hosp, 1963-1967; res assoc, Harvard Med Sch, 1960-1977; res fel med, Harvard Med Sch, 1959-1960; res fel bact, Harvard Med Sch, 1957-1959; res fel biochem, McGill Univ, 1956-1957. **Memberships:** AAAS; Int Asn Dent Res; Am Chem Soc; AmSoc Biochem & Molecular Biol; Sigma Xi. **Research Statement & Publications:** Metabolic effects of fluoride; oral biology; intermediary metabolism; biochemical and clinical methods; foods and dental disease; mechanisms of inflammation. **Mailing Address:** Forsyth Dent Ctr, 140 Fenway, Boston, MA 02115-3799. **Fax:** 617-456-7738. **E-Mail:** skashket@forsyth.org

KASHKOUSH, ISMAIL I, UNDERWATER ACOUSTICS, MICROCONTAMINATION CONTROL. **Personal Data:** b Egypt, November 10, 1958; m 1990, c 3. **Education:** Cairo Univ, Egypt, BS, 1982, MS, 1988; Clarkson Univ, PhD (eng sci), 1993. **Professional Experience:** DIR, APPL & PROCESSING ENG, AKRION, as of 2006; DIR, SUBMICRON SYSTS, 1995-; mgr, Submicron Systs, 1994-1995; process engr, Submicron Systs, 1993-1994; instr thermodyn & fluid mech, Clarkson Univ, 1990 & 1991; res asst micro contamination control, Clarkson Univ, 1988-1993; instr solid mech, Acad Defense, Cairo, 1987-1988; assoc lectr, Dept Mech Design, Cairo Univ, 1986-1988; teaching asst, Dept Mech Design, Cairo Univ, 1982-1986. **Memberships:** Electrochem Soc; Am Vacuum Soc; Mat Res Soc; Inst Environ Sci; Am Inst Chem Engrs. **Research Statement & Publications:** Microcontamination control in the clean room environment using various removal techniques; detection of particulates on silicon wafers; research in different aspects of contamination; establishing numerical simulation of the surface cleaning using sonic methods; developing new models that accurately describe the cleaning mechanism; author of several publications. **Mailing Address:** Akiron, #150 6330 Hedgewood Dr, Allentown, PA 18106. **Fax:** 610-391-1982. **E-Mail:** kashkoush@aol.com

KASHNOW, RICHARD ALLEN, PHYSICS. **Personal Data:** b Worcester, Mass, March 26, 1942; m 1963, c 2. **Education:** Worcester Polytech Inst, BS, 1963; Tufts Univ, PhD (physics), 1968. **Professional Experience:** BD DIR, ARIBA INC, SUNNYVALE, CALIF, 2003-; pres, Tyco Ventures, 1999-2003; CONSULT, 1971-; US Army, 1968-1970. **Memberships:** Am Phys Soc; Inst Elec & Electronics Engrs. **Research Statement & Publications:** Liquid crystals; quantum electronics; lattice dynamics. **Mailing Address:** Ariba Inc, 807 11th Ave, Sunnyvale, CA 94089.

KASHY, EDWIN, EXPERIMENTAL NUCLEAR PHYSICS. **Personal Data:** b Beirut, Lebanon, July 8, 1934; American citizen; m 1957, c 2. **Education:** Rice Univ, BA, 1956, MA, 1957, PhD (physics), 1959. **Professional Experience:** DISTINGUISHED PROF EMER PHYSICS, MICH STATE UNIV, as of 2002; Guggenheim fel, Niels Bohr Inst, Copenhagen, 1970-1971; distinguished prof physics, Mich State Univ, beginning 1967; assoc prof, Mich State Univ, 1964-1967; asst prof, Princeton Univ, 1962-1964; instr, Mass Inst Technol, 1960-1962; NSF fel physics, Mass Inst Technol, 1959-1960. **Memberships:** Am Phys Soc. **Research Statement & Publications:** Experimental investigations of nuclear spectroscopy and nuclear reaction mechanisms by means of charged particle and gamma ray studies. **Mailing Address:** Cyclotron Lab Physics, Mich State Univ, East Lansing, MI 48824-1321. **Fax:** 517-353-5967. **E-Mail:** kashy@nscl.msu.edu

KASHYAP, MOTI LAL, MEDICINE ENDOCRINOLOGY, LIPIDOLOGY. **Personal Data:** b Singapore, February 19, 1939; American citizen; m 1970, Suman; c Keshni, Vikram & Ishaan. **Education:** Univ Singapore, MB, BS, 1964; McGill Univ, MS, 1967; FRCP (C), 1969, FACP, 1978. **Honors & Awards:** Distinguished Physicians Award, Indian Med Asn, USA, 1992; Distinguished Academician of the Year, Acad Med, Singapore, 1996. **Professional Experience:** Chief Gerontol & dir Atherosclerosis ctr, Dept of Vet Affairs Healthcare Sys, 1988-; PROF MED, CALIF COL MED, UNIV CALIF, IRVINE, 1986-; prof med, Col Med, Univ Cincinnati, 1981-1986; Irvine Page Young Investr Award, Am Heart Asn, 1976; assoc dir-Lipid Res Clin, Cincinnati, 1974-; dir, Apoliprotein Res Labs, Cincinnati, 1974-1986; from asst prof to assoc prof, 1974-1981; dir, Coronary Primary Prevention Trial, NIH, 1974-1978; sr lectr med physiol, Fac Med, Univ Singapore, 1971-1974; sr fel, Cardiovasc Res Inst, Moffit Hosp, Sch Med, Univ Calif, San Francisco, 1970-1971; Sr res fel, Am Heart Asn, 1970-1971; lectr, Fac Med, 1969-1970; resident internal med & fel endocrinol & metab, Royal Victoria Hosp, McGill Univ, 1965-1969; Intern med & surg, Teaching Hosps, Univ Singapore, 1964-1965; Grants, NIH 1975-1989, Dept Vet Aff 1986. **Memberships:** Sr fel Am Fedn med Clin Res; Can Soc Endocrinol & Metab; Am Geriatrics Soc; fel Am Heart Asn; fel Acad Med, Singapore fel, Soc of Geriatric cardiology. **Research Statement & Publications:** Lipoprotein metabolism and atherosclerotic cardiovascular disease; focus is Mechanism of action of lipid- regulating drugs; niacin; HDL; drug discovery. **Mailing Address:** Vet Admin Med Ctr (11-111I), 5901 E Seventh St, Long Beach, CA 90822. **Fax:** 562-826-5515. **E-Mail:** moti.kashyap@med.va.gov

KASHYAP, RANGASAMI LAKSMINARAYANA, ELECTRICAL ENGINEERING. **Personal Data:** b Mysore, India, March 28, 1938. **Education:** Univ Mysore, BSc, 1958; Indian Inst Sci, DIISc, 1961, ME, 1962; Harvard Univ, PhD (eng), 1965. **Honors & Awards:** King Sun Fu Res Award, Int Asn Pattern Recognition, 1990. **Professional Experience:** PROF ELEC & COMP ENG, PURDUE UNIV, as of 1998; Int Assoc Pattern Recognition Fel, 1995; consult, Gen Elec Co, Ind, 1967-1968; from asst prof to assoc prof, Purdue Univ, 1966-1974; res fel eng, Harvard Univ, 1965-1966; teaching fel, Harvard Univ, 1964; rs asst control systs, Harvard Univ, 1963-1965; Gordon McKay fel, 1962-1963; Indian Inst Sci Fel, 1958-1962. **Memberships:** Fel Inst Elec & Electronics Engrs; Asn Comput Mach; Sigma Xi. **Research Statement & Publications:** Systems science; pattern recognition; learning systems; statistical inference; image processing. **Mailing Address:** Sch Elec Eng, Purdue Univ, 465 Nwestern Ave, W Lafayette, IN 47907-2035. **Fax:** 765-494-0880. **E-Mail:** kashyap@ecn.purdue.edu

KASHYAP, TAPESHWAR S, POPULATION GENETICS, POULTRY BREEDING. **Personal Data:** b Kapurthala, India, October 15, 1929; American citizen; m 1959, c 2. **Education:** Punjab Agr Col, India, BSc, 1950; Univ Minn, St Paul, MSc, 1956, PhD (animal husb), 1958. **Professional Experience:** RETIRED; systs consult, Bank Am, beginning 1981; consult geneticist poultry res proj, Animal Sci Dept, Univ Nebr, beginning 1978; Food & Agr Orgn consult, Poultry Proj POL/71/515, Poznan, Poland, 1976-1978; dir genetics develop, Kimber Farms Inc, beginning 1973; geneticist & head data processing dept, Kimber Farms Inc, 1959-1973; asst animal husb, Univ Minn, St Paul, 1955-1958. **Memberships:** Genetics Soc Am; Am Genetics Asn; AAAS. **Research Statement & Publications:** Animal breeding; improving livestock performance with the aid of principles of genetics; statistical analysis of data, using modern computers, to evaluate and seek answers to various problems in poultry breeding. **Mailing Address:** 41532 Paseo Padre Pkwy, Fremont, CA 94539. **Fax:** 510-656-1776. **E-Mail:** tappykash@aol.com

KASI, LEELA PESHKAR, RADIOPHARMACEUTICAL CHEMISTRY, NUCLEAR MEDICINE. **Personal Data:** b Bombay, India, July 15, 1939; American citizen; m 1971, Kalli. **Education:** Univ Bombay, India, BS, 1958; Univ Marburg, WGer, PhD (pharmaceut chem), 1968. **Professional Experience:** RETIRED; assoc prof clin radiol, Grad Sch Biomed Sci, 1993-; mem grad fac, Grad Sch Biomed Sci, 1984-1989; asst ed, J Nuclear Med, 1984-1989; from asst prof to assoc prof nuclear med, M D Anderson Cancer Ctr, Univ Tex, 1982-1995; asst prof clin radiol, Univ Tex Med Sch, Houston, 1982-1993; from asst chemist radiopharmaceut chem to assoc chemist, M D Anderson Cancer Ctr, Univ Tex, 1979-1995; dir qual control, pharmaceut chem, Health Care Indust, Mich City, Ind, 1972-1977; sr chemist pharmaceut quality control, Boehringer-Knoll Ltd, Bombay, India, 1969-1971. **Memberships:** Soc Nuclear Med; AAAS; Sigma Xi. **Research Statement & Publications:** Development and evaluation (in vitro and in vivo) of new radiolabeled substances for use in diagnostic imaging, radioimmunotherapy or biokinetic studies in cancer patients; radioimmunoimaging, pharmacology and nuclear magnetic resonance; radiopharmaceutic chemistry. **Mailing Address:** 4710 McDermel, Houston, TX 77035.

KASIANOWICZ, JOHN JAMES, BIOSENSORS, SOFTWARE DEVELOPMENT. **Personal Data:** b Boston, Mass, April 22, 1957. **Education:** Boston Univ, BA, 1979; State Univ NY, MA, 1981, PhD (physiol & biophys), 1987. **Professional Experience:** GROUP LEADER & PRIN INVESTR, BIOMOLECULAR MAT GROUP, as of 2003; physical scientist biophys & physics, Nat Inst Sci Technol, NIH, beginning 1992; fel, Nat Inst Sci Technol, NIH, 1987-1991; lectr physics, dept physics, Eastern Nazarene Col, 1982-1983. **Memberships:** Biophys Soc; Am Phys Soc; Mats Res Soc. **Research Statement & Publications:** Experimental and theoretical investigations of ion transport in protein ion channels; developing novel methods to determine the structure-function relationship of membrane-bound proteins; emerging emphasis on potential applications of pore-forming proteins in biotechnology. **Mailing Address:** Biotechnol Div, Nat Inst Stand & Technol, 831 100 Bur Dr Stop 8313, Gaithersburg, MD 20899. **Fax:** 301-330-3447. **E-Mail:** john.kasianowicz@nist.gov

KASIK, JOHN EDWARD, MEDICINE, PHARMACOLOGY. **Personal Data:** b Chicago, Ill, August 9, 1927; m 1945, Sherle Ione; c 6. **Education:** Roosevelt Univ, BS, 1949; Univ Chicago, MS, 1953, MD, 1954, PhD (pharmacol), 1962; Am Bd Internal Med, dipl. **Honors & Awards:** Fulbrite Sch, 1966, Oxford Univ; Walter L Bierring Award, Am Thoracic Soc, Iowa, 1976; Laurant Awd, 1994; Sir William Dunn Sch of Path, Oxford England; I Am Col Phys, Iowa Chap. **Professional Experience:** Chief staff, Vet Admin Med Ctr, Iowa City, 1980-1998; assoc dean, Col Med, Univ Iowa, 1980-1998; Prof Med, Col Med, Univ Iowa, beginning 1973; assoc prof, Vet Admin Med Ctr, Iowa City, 1970-1973; Fulbright scholar, Oxford Univ, Dunn Sch, 1966-1967; from asst prof to assoc prof, Grad Sch Med, 1959-1970; Miller fel, Univ Chicago, 1957-1959; from jr asst to asst resident med, Clins Univ Chicago, 1955-1956; Intern, Clins Univ Chicago, 1954-1955; med dir, Kirchwood Col-Vet Admin Hosp Iowa City Sch Respiratory Ther; PROF EMER MED, COL MED, UNIV IOWA. **Memberships:** fel Am Col Physicians; AMA JMS. **Research Statement & Publications:** Pharmacology of immunosuppressent drugs; pharmacology of antibiotics; antituburcolosis therapy. **Mailing Address:** VA Bldg 21, IA 52333.

KASINSKY, HAROLD EDWARD, BIOCHEMISTRY, ZOOLOGY. **Education:** Columbia Univ, BA, 1961; Univ Calif, Berkeley, PhD (biochem), 1967. **Professional Experience:** ASSOC PROF EMERITUS ZOOLOGY, UNIV BC, 2003-; Vis prof, Univ Victoria, BC, 1998-1999; Vis prof, Polytech Univ Barcelona, 1984-1985; assoc prof Zoology, Univ BC, 1981-2003; Vis prof, Univ Amsterdam, 1977-1978; asst prof Zoology, Univ BC, 1969-1981; NIH fel, Dept Embryol, Carnegie Inst, 1967-1969; Vis prof, Univ Calif, Berkeley; Vis prof, Univ Calgary. **Memberships:** Soc Develop Biol; Can Soc Zoology. **Research Statement & Publications:** Sperm nuclear basic protein (SNBP) diversity in animals, plants algae protozoans; SNBP changes during spermiogenesis and temporal correlation with chromatin patterning and condensation: a physicochemical hypothesis. **Mailing Address:** Dept Zoology, Univ BC, Vancouver, BC V6T 1Z4, Can. **Fax:** 604-822-2416. **E-Mail:** kasinsky@zoology.ubc.ca

KASKA, HAROLD VICTOR, geology; deceased, see previous edition for last biography

KASKA, WILLIAM CHARLES, CHEMISTRY. **Personal Data:** b Ancon, Canal Zone, May 13, 1935; m 1964, Deborah; c 4. **Education:** Loyola Univ, Calif, BS, 1957; Univ Mich, PhD (chem), 1963. **Professional Experience:** PROF CHEM, UNIV CALIF, SANTA BARBARA, 1979-; assoc prof, Univ Calif, Santa Barbara, 1974-1979; asst prof, Univ Calif, Santa Barbara, 1965-1974; res assoc chem, Pa State Univ, 1963-1964. **Memberships:** Am Chem Soc; Sigma Xi. **Research Statement & Publications:** Synthesis and chemistry of organometallic compounds of the transition elements. **Mailing Address:** Dept Chem, Univ Calif, Santa Barbara, CA 93106. **Fax:** 805-893-4120. **E-Mail:** kaska@chem.ucsb.edu

KASKAS, JAMES, THEORETICAL PHYSICS. **Personal Data:** b Detroit, Mich, January 30, 1939. **Education:** Wayne State Univ, BS, 1960, MS, 1961, PhD (physics), 1964. **Professional Experience:** RETIRED; from instr to assoc prof physics, Detroit Inst Technol, 1963-1989. **Memberships:** Am Phys Soc; Am Asn Physics Teachers. **Research**

Statement & Publications: Elementary particle theory; quantum field theory. **Mailing Address:** 25533 Fairgrove St, Trenton, MI 48183-4447.

KASLER, FRANZ JOHANN, ANALYTICAL CHEMISTRY. **Personal Data:** b Vienna, Austria, January 1, 1930; m 1964, c 2. **Education:** Univ Vienna, PhD (org microanal), 1959. **Professional Experience:** PROF EMER CHEM, UNIV MD, COLLEGE PARK, as of 2003; assoc prof chem, Univ MD, College Park, 1965-; Asst prof, 1959-1965. **Memberships:** AAAS; Am Chem Soc; Am Microchem Soc; Austrian Chem Soc; Sigma Xi. **Research Statement & Publications:** Quantitative nuclear magnetic resonance; organic elemental analysis of classic and instrumental methods. **Mailing Address:** 1043 Hillendale Ct, Walnut Creek, CA 94596.

KASLICK, RALPH SIDNEY, PERIODONTICS, ORAL MEDICINE. **Personal Data:** b Brooklyn, NY, October 17, 1935; m 1976, Jessica; c Andrew. **Education:** Columbia Univ, AB, 1956, DDS, 1959. **Honors & Awards:** J Award, Int Col Dent, 1972; Medallion, Japan Stomatol Soc, 1978. **Professional Experience:** PRES MED STAFF, SCH DENT, 1992-; DIR DENT, GOLDWATER MEM HOSP, MED CTR, NY UNIV, 1988-; CLIN PROF SURG SCI, SCH DENT, 1988-; from asst dean to dean, Sch Dent, Fairleigh Dickinson Univ, 1972-1988; from instr to prof periodont & oral med, Sch Dent, Fairleigh Dickinson Univ, 1965-1988. **Memberships:** Fel Am Col Dent; Am Acad Periodont; Int Asn Dent Res; Sigma Xi; Am Asn Dent Schs. **Research Statement & Publications:** Genetic studies of periodontal diseases in young adults; quantitative analysis of gingival fluid; clinical testing of therapeutic dentifrices, ointments and hygiene aids. **Mailing Address:** Goldwater Mem Hosp, NY Univ Med Ctr, Roosevelt Island, New York, NY 10044. **Fax:** 212-318-4370.

KASLOW, DAVID EDWARD, AEROSPACE SYSTEM ENGINEERING. **Personal Data:** b Bloomington, Ind, September 27, 1942. **Education:** Ind Univ, Bloomington, AB, 1964, MS, 1966; Univ Mich, Ann Arbor, PhD (physics), 1971. **Professional Experience:** ANALYST & MGR, VALLEY FORGE SPACE CTR, LOCKHEED MARTIN, 1973-; Res assoc physics, Lehigh Univ, 1971-1973; SR STAFF ENGR & CHIEF ENGR. **Memberships:** Int Coun Syst Eng. **Mailing Address:** Valley Forge Space Ctr Lockheed Martin, PO Box 8555, King of Prussia, PA 19101.

KASLOW, RICHARD ALAN, MEDICINE. **Personal Data:** b Omaha, Nebr, March 1, 1943. **Education:** Yale Col, BA, 1965; Harvard Med Sch, MD, 1969; Harvard Sch Pub Health, MPH, 1976. **Professional Experience:** Adj prof, Johns Hopkins Sch Hygiene & Pub Health, 1996-; PROF EPIDEMIOL, MED & MICROBIOL, UNIV ALA, BIRMINGHAM, 1995-; DIR, PROG EPIDEMIOL INFECTION & IMMUNITY, UNIV ALA, BIRMINGHAM, 1995-; adj prof, Uniformed Serv Univ Health Sci, 1988-; adj prof, George Wash Univ, 1988-1995; Human Immuno Deficiency Virus Infection, Nat Inst Allergy & Infectious Dis, India, 1986-; capt, USPHS, 1985-1995; task force AIDS epidemiol, USPHS, 1984-1986; chmn adv comt, Study AIDS Natural Hist, NIH, 1983-1985; epidemiol comt, Reye Syndrome Task Force, 1982-; sr attend phys, Nat Inst Allergy & Infections Dis, 1981-; CHIEF, EPIDEMIOL & BIOMET BR, NAT INST ALLERGY & INFECTIONS DIS, 1980-; epidemiol comt, NIH, 1979-; diabetes mellitus coord comt, 1979-1981; sr surgeon, USPHS, 1976-1985; clin asst prof med, Emory Univ Sch Med, 1976-1979; chief, Arthritis & Immunol Dis Activ, Ctr Dis Control, 1976-1979; prev activ, Hosp Infections Prog, Ctr Dis Control, 1976-1978; Epidemiologist, Sidney Farber Cancer Ctr, 1975-1976. **Memberships:** Am Col Physicians; Infectious Dis Soc; Am Epidemiol Soc; Am Col Epidemiol; Am Fed Clin Res; AAAS. **Research Statement & Publications:** Epidemiologic research on infectious and immune disease including AIDS and other genital infections, Lyme disease, autoimmune diseases and asthma; immunogenetics of infectious and other diseases. **Mailing Address:** 212C Tidwell Hall Sch Pub Health, 720 20th St S RPHB 220A, Birmingham, AL 35294-0008. **E-Mail:** rkaslow@uab.edu

KASNER, FRED E, PHYSICAL CHEMISTRY. **Personal Data:** b New York, NY, July 8, 1926; m 1953, c 1. **Education:** City Col New York, BS, 1948; Univ Chicago, MS, 1949, PhD (phys chem), 1961. **Professional Experience:** Vis scientist, Argonne Nat Lab, 1979; PROF CHEM, OLIVE-HARVEY COL, 1971-; vis scholar, Northwestern Univ, 1971; from instr to prof chem, Fenger Jr Col, 1961-1970; consult, USAF, 1959; From instr to asst prof natural sci, Univ Chicago, 1954-1959. **Memberships:** Am Chem Soc; Am Soc Testing & Mat. **Research Statement & Publications:** Laser Raman spectroscopy of aqueous solutions; thermal conductivity and its temperature coefficient; heats of dilution of aqueous solutions of strong electrolytes. **Mailing Address:** 320 17th St, Wilmette, IL 60091-3224.

KASNER, WILLIAM HENRY, PHYSICS. **Personal Data:** b Killbuck, Ohio, January 27, 1929; m 1951, c 1. **Education:** Case Western Reserve Univ, BS, 1951; Univ Pittsburgh, PhD (physics), 1958. **Professional Experience:** FEL SCIENTIST, GAS LASERS RES & DEVELOP, WESTINGHOUSE RES & DEVELOP CTR, 1961-; asst res prof, Univ Md, 1959-1961; Res assoc physics, Univ Md, 1958-1959. **Memberships:** Am Phys Soc. **Research Statement & Publications:** Atomic physics, especially atomic and electronic collision phenomena; ultraviolet spectroscopy; gas discharges; optics; laser development and application. **Mailing Address:** 11686 Althea Dr, Pittsburgh, PA 15235.

KASOWSKI, ROBERT V, SOLID STATE PHYSICS. **Personal Data:** b Bremond, Tex, February 14, 1944; m 1969, c 1. **Education:** Tex A&M Univ, BS, 1966; Univ Chicago, PhD (physics), 1969. **Professional Experience:** AT DEPT CENT RES & DEVELOP, EI DU PONT DEL NEMOURS & CO, DEL, as of 1994; CONSULT, 1980-; Physicist, E I du Pont Del Nemours & Co Inc, 1969-1980. **Memberships:** Am Phys Soc. **Research Statement & Publications:** Calculating the electronic properties of molecules adsorbed onto metal or semiconductor surfaces using linear combination of muffin tin orbitals method. **Mailing Address:** Dept Cent Res & Develop, E I Du Pont de Nemours & Co, Exp Sta, Wilmington, DE 19898.

KASPAREK, STANLEY VACLAV, ORGANIC CHEMISTRY, MEDICINAL CHEMISTRY. **Personal Data:** b Prague, Czech, June 11, 1929. **Education:** Charles Univ, Prague, Dr rer nat, 1965. **Professional Experience:** PRES, CHEMINFO, 1985-; tech fel, Hoffmann-La Roche Inc, 1982-1985; info scientist, Hoffmann-La Roche Inc, 1968-1981; abstractor, Chem Abstracts Serv, Ohio, 1968; fel & chemist, Nat Res Coun Can, 1965-1967; Chemist, Res Inst Pharm & Biochem, Prague, 1950-1959 & Czech Acad Sci, 1962-1965. **Memberships:** Am Chem Soc. **Research Statement & Publications:** Scientific information. **Mailing Address:** 3 Rockledge Pl, Cedar Grove, NJ 07009.

KASPER, ANDREW E, PALEOBOTANY. **Personal Data:** b Bridgeport, Conn, October 29, 1942; m 1967, Nancy; c Christian & Emily. **Education:** Duquesne Univ, BA, 1965; Univ Conn, MS, 1968, PhD (bot), 1970. **Professional Experience:** ASSOC PROF BOT, RUTGERS UNIV, NEWARK, 1975-; Asst prof, 1970-1975. **Memberships:** Bot Soc Am; Sigma Xi; Paleont Soc. **Research Statement & Publications:** Description and classification of Devonian age plant fossils. **Mailing Address:** Dept Biol Sci, Rutgers Univ, 195 Univ Ave, Newark, NJ 07102. **Fax:** 973-353-5518. **E-Mail:** akasper@andromeda.rutgers.edu

KASPER, CHARLES BOYER, CELL BIOLOGY, PROTEIN STRUCTURE & FUNCTION. **Personal Data:** b Joliet, Ill, April 27, 1935; m 1957, Jeanne; c Lynda, David, Jenette & JoAnna. **Education:** Univ Ill, BS, 1958; Univ Wis, PhD (physiol chem), 1962. **Professional Experience:** PROF EMER ONCOL, MCARDLE LAB, UNIV WIS-MADISON, as of 2004; prof oncol, Mcardle Lab, Univ Wis-Madison, 1982-; from asst prof to assoc prof, Mcardle Lab, Univ Wis-Madison, 1965-1982; asst prof biol chem, Univ Calif, Los Angeles, 1964-1965; NIH fels, Univ Calif, Los Angeles, 1963-1964 & Univ Utah, 1962-1963. **Memberships:** Am Soc Biol Chemists; Am Asn Cancer Res. **Research Statement & Publications:** Structure, function and Regulation of enzymes responsible for the metabolic activation of chemical carcinogens; molecular basis of enzyme induction; molecular biology; toxicology. **Mailing Address:** Dept Oncol, Med Sch, Univ Wis, 421a McArdle Res 1420 Univ N, Madison, WI 53706-1531. **Fax:** 608-262-2824. **E-Mail:** kasper@oncology.wisc.edu

KASPER, DENNIS LEE, BACTERIAL DISEASES, IMMUNOCHEMISTRY. **Personal Data:** b February 23, 1943; 1967, c Adam, Jocelyn & Jacob. **Education:** Univ Ill, Chicago, MD, 1967. **Honorary Degrees:** MA, Harvard Univ. **Honors & Awards:** Squibb Award, Infectious Dis Soc Am; Res Career Develop Award, NIH, Merit Award, Member, Institute of Medicine. **Professional Experience:** DIR CHANNING LAB, BRIGHAM & WOMEN's HOSP, as of 1994; WILLIAM ELLERY CHANNING PROF MED, HARVARD MED SCH, as of 1985; PROF MICROBIOL & MOLECULAR GENETICS, HARVARD MED SCH, 1997-; Co- dir Channing Lab, Brigham & Women's Hosp, beginning 1989; chief infectious dis, Beth Israel Hosp, Boston, Mass, beginning 1993; President, Int Soc Infectious Dis, 2002-2004; chmn, Bd Sci Counselors, Nat Inst Allergy & Infectious Dis. **Memberships:** Am Soc Clin Invest; Asn Am Physicians; Am Fedn Clin Res; Am Asn Immunologists; Am Soc Microbiol; Infectious Dis Soc Am; Int Soc Anaerobic Bact (pres). **Research Statement & Publications:** Infectious diseases; biology of carbohydrates; bacterial pathogenesis, vaccine development and immunomodulation; primary efforts are in role of carbohydrates in immunity and pathogenesis; granted over 30 US patents. **Mailing Address:** Dept Med, Channing Lab, Brigham & Women's Hosp, Harvard Med Sch, 181 Longwood Ave, Boston, MA 02115-5889. **Fax:** 617-525-0080. **E-Mail:** dennis_kasper@hms.harvard.edu

KASPER, GERHARD, AEROSOL SCIENCE & TECHNOLOGY, CONTAMINATION CONTROL. **Personal Data:** b Salzburg, Austria, June 6, 1949; c 2. **Education:** Univ Vienna, Austria, PhD (physics), 1977. **Professional Experience:** DIR, TECHNOL, ENG & QUAL, ELECTRONICS DIV, AIR LIQUIDE, WALNUT CREEK, CA, 1993-; ed-in-chief, J Aerosol Sci, 1985-; dir res & develop, Chicago Res Ctr, 1985-1993; chmn, particulate standards subcomt Semicond Equip & Mat Inst, 1984-; Adj prof, Univ Vienna, Austria, 1983-; sr sci, Am Air Liquide Inc, Countryside, Ill, 1983-1985; from res asst prof to asst prof elec engr, State Univ NY, Buffalo, 1978-1983; asst prof physics, Inst Exp Physics, Univ Vienna, Austria, 1977-1978. **Memberships:** Europ Asn Aerosol Res; Am Asn Aerosol Res; Inst Environ Sci; Am Soc Testing & Mat. **Research Statement & Publications:** Aerosol science and particle technology including instrumentation and measurement techniques; filtration; contamination control; surface-particle interactions; aerosol generation and sampling; dynamics of irregular particles. **Mailing Address:** Inst Mech Versahrenstechnik, Univ Karlsruhe, 76128 Karlsruhe, Ger.

KASPER, HORST MANFRED, PHYSICAL CHEMISTRY, SEMICONDUCTOR DEVICES. **Personal Data:** b Dusseldorf, Ger, June 3, 1939; American citizen; c Olaf & Kathy. **Education:** Univ Bonn, Ger, dipl, 1963, Dr, 1965; Seton Hall Univ, JD, 1978. **Professional Experience:** PATENT ATTY, KASPER & LAUGHLIN, 1979-; patent atty, Allied Corp, 1977-1979; staff mem, Bell Telephone Labs, 1970-1976; Staff mem, Lincoln Lab, Mass Inst Technol, 1966-1969. **Memberships:** Fel Am Phys Soc; Electrochem Soc; Am Chem Soc; NY Acad Sci. **Research Statement & Publications:** Physical chemistry of semiconductors. **Mailing Address:** 13 Forest Dr, Warren, NJ 07060. **Fax:** 908-668-5262.

KASPER, JOHN SIMON, physical chemistry; deceased, see previous edition for last biography

KASPER, JOSEPH F, JR, QUALITY IMPROVEMENT, MANAGEMENT SCI. **Personal Data:** b Baltimore, Md, December 9, 1943; m 1986, Louise G Hersey; c Jennifer (Finfrock) & Rebecca. **Education:** Mass Inst Technol, BS, 1964, MS, 1966, SCD(instrumentation), 1968; Boston Univ, MBA, 1974. **Professional Experience:** Adj prof eng & community and family med, Darmouth col, 1990-2002; pres & chief exec officer, Found Informed Med Decision Making, 1990-1994; dir sea-launched ballistic missile, Stratig Syst Div, 1980-1990; dir, Stratig Syst Div, 1979-1980; mgr, Navig Systs, 1978-1979; Mgr spec projs, Anal Sci Corp, 1975-1978. **Research Statement & Publications:** Mathematical modeling of very low frequency propagation anomalies; statistical description of geodetic phenomena; analysis of radio and inertial navigation error behavior; applied Kalman filtering. **Mailing Address:** 338 Troon Ct, New Smyrna, FL 32168.

KASPERBAUER, MICHAEL J, PLANT PHYSIOLOGY, PHOTOBIOLOGY. **Personal Data:** b Manning, Iowa, October 8, 1929; m 1962, Isabel M Giles; c Maria, John, Paul & Sandra. **Education:** Iowa State Univ, BS, 1954, MS, 1957, PhD (plant physiol), 1961. **Honors & Awards:** L M Ware Res Award, 1990; Crop Sci Res Award, 1990; Agronomic Res Award, 1994. **Professional Experience:** Adj prof, Dept Plant Path & Physiol, Clemson Univ, as of 2000; prof plant physiol, Clemson Univ, 1983-; SR PLANT SCIENTIST, COASTAL PLAIN, WATER & PLANT RES CTR, US DEPT AGR, FLORENCE, SC, 1983-; assoc ed, Agron J, 1975-1983; adj prof agron, Univ Ky, 1965-1983; Crops Res Div, Lexington, Ky, 1963-1983; res plant physiologist, Agr Res Serv, Pioneering Res Lab Plant Physiol, Beltsville, Md, 1962-1963; NSF fel, Univ Md, 1961-1962. **Memberships:** Am Soc Plant Physiol; fel Crop Sci Soc Am; fel Am Soc Agron; Am Soc Photobiol; Sigma Xi. **Research Statement & Publications:** Interaction of light and temperature on plant growth, development and composition; phytochrome control of plant physiological processes; haploid and doubled haploid utilization in crop improvement. **Mailing Address:** Coastal Plains Soil, Water, & Plant Res Ctr, USDA, Florence, SC 29501-1241.

KASPEREK, GEORGE JAMES, BIOCHEMISTRY, EXERCISE. **Personal Data:** b Albert Lea, Minn, June 1, 1944; m 1966, Judith; c Michael & Sheila. **Education:** Mankato State Col, BS, 1966; Ore State Univ, PhD (org chem), 1969. **Professional Experience:** ASST DEAN, GRAD STUDIES, SCH MED, ECAROLINA UNIV, as of 2005; GRAD DIR, BIOCHEM & MOLECULAR BIOL, SCH MED, ECAROLINA UNIV, as of 2005; PROF, BIOCHEM & MOLECULAR BIOL, SCH MED, ECAROLINA UNIV, 1988-; vis prof, Sch Med, ECarolina Univ, 1978-1979; assoc prof, Biochem, Sch Med, ECarolina Univ, 1978-1988; assoc prof, Conn Col, 1977-1978; asst prof biochem, Conn Col, 1972-1977; fel bio org, Univ Calif, Santa Barbara, 1969-1972; NIH fel, 1969-1971. **Memberships:** Am Col Sports Med. **Research Statement & Publications:** Regulation of metabolism during exercise;

amino acid metabolism; cytoskeleton. **Mailing Address:** Dept Biochem & Molecular Biol, Sch Med ECarolina Univ, 5S 32 Brody Bldg, Greenville, NC 27858-4354. **Fax:** 252-744-3383. **E-Mail:** kasperekg@mail.ecu.edu

KASPERICK, JOSEPH E, ECONOMIC ANALYSIS. **Education:** Carroll Col, BS, 1963; Univ Calf, Riverside, MS, 1967. **Professional Experience:** PROF EMER, DEPT BUS & INFO TECHNOL, UNIV MONTANA, as of 2004; MEM BE DIRS, MONTANA TECH FOUND, as of 2004. **Mailing Address:** Dept Bus & Info Technol, Univ Montana, 300 W Park St, Butte, MT 59701.

KASPROW, BARBARA ANN, MICRO ANATOMY, REPRODUCTIVE BIOLOGY. **Personal Data:** b Hartford, Conn, April 23, 1936. **Education:** Albertus Magnus Col, BA, 1958; Loyola Univ, Ill, PhD (anat), 1969. **Professional Experience:** ASST TO PRES, UNIV RES SYSTS, 1979-; writer, Opers Specialist, 1976-1979; Co-ed, Biol Reproduction, 1973; asst prof anat, Stritch Sch Med, Loyola Univ, Chicago, 1969-1976; sr res assoc, Stritch Sch Med, Loyola Univ, Chicago, 1967-1969; from res assoc to sr res & admin assoc, Inst Study Human Reproduction, Ohio, 1962-1967; res assoc, NY Med Col, 1961-1962; res asst anat & reproductive biol, Sch Med, 1961; USPHS training scholar, Yale Univ, 1959-1960. **Memberships:** AAAS; Am Asn Anatomists; Am Soc Zoologists; NY Acad Sci; Sigma Xi. **Research Statement & Publications:** Reproductive phenomena in the mammalian female; growth mechanisms, pathologic variants in reproductive organs and endocrinologic interrelationships; cytophysiology; research administration; science education. **Mailing Address:** PO Box 385, Lombard, IL 60148.

KASRIEL, ROBERT H, MATHEMATICS. **Personal Data:** b Tampa, Fla, October 18, 1918; m 1946, c 2. **Education:** Univ Tampa, BS, 1940; Univ Va, MA, 1949, PhD (math), 1953. **Honors & Awards:** Ferst Res Award, Sigma Xi, 1962. **Professional Experience:** PROF EMER MATH, GA INST TECHNOL, 1985-; from asst prof to prof, GA Inst Technol, 1954-1984; aeronaut res scientist, Nat Adv Comt Aeronaut, 1952-1954; coordr wartraining courses, Univ Tampa, 1940-1942. **Memberships:** Am Math Soc; Math Asn Am; Sigma Xi. **Research Statement & Publications:** Analytic topology; fixed point theorems; mapping theorems. **Mailing Address:** Dept Math, Ga Inst Technol, 686 Cherry St, Atlanta, GA 30332-0160. **Fax:** 404-894-4409.

KASS, GUSS SIGMUND, COSMETIC CHEMISTRY, TOPICAL DRUGS. **Personal Data:** b Chicago, Ill, October 19, 1915; m 1938, Shirley; c Barbara (Kipnis) & Marilyn (Ring). **Education:** Univ Chicago, BS, 1938. **Professional Experience:** PRES, G S KASS & ASSOCS, LTD, 1974-; lectr, Sch Med, Univ Ill, 1965-1986; from tech dir to vpres & dir corp res & develop, Alberto-Culver Co, 1960-1974; lectr, Univ Chicago, 1958; res dir & vpres, Lanolin Plus, Inc, 1954-1960; asst res dir, Helene Curtis Industs, Inc, 1948-1954; chief chemist, Duart Mfg Co, Ltd, Calif, 1941-1942 & 1946-1948; res chemist, Acme Cosmetic Corp, 1940-1941; chemist, Prod Corp Am, 1939-1940; res chemist, Munic Tuberc Sanitarium, 1938-1939. **Memberships:** Am Acad Dermat; Am Chem Soc; fel Soc Cosmetic Chem; fel Am Inst Chem. **Research Statement & Publications:** Cosmetics; toiletries; proprietary pharmaceuticals. **Mailing Address:** 1220 Rudolph Rd Apt 4d, Northbrook, IL 60062.

KASS, LEE B, BOTANY, HISTORY OF SCIENCE. **Personal Data:** b New York, NY, May 23, 1946; m 1981, Robert. **Education:** City Col NY, BS, 1969; Cambridge Univ, MA, 1975; Cornell Univ, PhD (bot), 1975. **Honors & Awards:** Who's Who of American Women, 25th Edition, 2006; Travel Award, AAAS, 2002; Who's Who Among America's Teachers (7th edition, multiple year honoree), 2002; Who's Who Among America's Teachers (5th Edition), 1998; Everett HELM Visiting Fellowship, Lilly Library, May 1997; Mellon Resident Res Fel, Am Philosphical Soc Library, 1998; Josef Stein Award for Excellence in Teaching and Scholarly Achievement, Elmira Col, 1985. **Professional Experience:** VIS PROF, CORNELL UNIV, 2000-; Chair, Historical Section, Bot Soc of Am, 2002-; mem Archives and History Comt, Bot Soc of Am, 1999-2004; Assoc mem, Women's Studies Prog, Cornell Univ, 2000-, Development Comt mem, Women's Studies Prog, Cornell Univ, 1999-2000; Executive Comt mem, Women's Studies Prog, Cornell Univ, 1998-2000; prin investr, NSF, 1996-1997 & 1997-1998; Fulbright scholar natural sci, Col Bahamas, 1996; Bahamas Nat Herbarium, Co-founder, Assoc Staff, Consult, 1996-; adj assoc prof, Cornell Univ, 1994-2000; vis assoc prof biol & plant path, Mich State Univ, 1994; mem comt, Careers Bot, 1994; consult, Environ Mgmt Coun, Tomkins Co, 1991-1993; vis assoc prof, Cornell Univ, 1990-1991, 1996-1997, 1997-1998; PROF BOT, ELMIRA COL, 1999-2000, retired from teaching summer 2000; assoc prof, Elmira Col, 1989-1999; chair, Teaching Sect Slide Exchange, Bot Soc Am, 1984, 1987; asst prof, Elmira Col, 1982-1989; lectr biol, Elmira Col, 1979-1981; fac assoc & res technician, Sect Poultry & Avian Sci, Cornell Univ, 1979-1981; res asst pharmacol, Vanderbilt Univ, 1978-1979; Lectr biol, Univ Tenn, 1978-1979; NSF fel biol, Vanderbilt Univ, 1977-1978; supvr, Girton Col, Cambridge Univ, 1977; instr, Girton Col, Cambridge Univ, 1976; res fel, Girton Col, Cambridge Univ, 1975-1977; Teaching asst, State Univ NY, 1969-1971. **Memberships:** Am Fern Soc; Bahamas Nat Trust (BNT); Bot Soc Am; Int Soc Hist Sci & Soc Studies Biol; New York Floral Assoc (NYFA); Smithsonian Institution, Associate; Cornell Plantations. **Research Statement & Publications:** Rare plant species; ecology and reproductive biology of mangroves; history of botany and genetics; Bahama flora biodiversity; Selected Publications: An Illustrated Guide to Common Plants of San Salvador Island, Bahamas, second edition, 2005; "McClintock, Barbara, American Botanical Geneticist, 1902-1992, " In Plant Sci, 2000; Proceedings of the Fifth Symposium on the Natural History of the Bahamas, 1994 (ed.). **Mailing Address:** Dept Plant Biology, L H Bailey Hortorium, 228 Plant Sci Bldg, Cornell Univ, Ithaca, NY 14853. **Fax:** 607-255-7979. **E-Mail:** lbk7@cornell.edu

KASS, LEON RICHARD, MEDICAL ETHICS. **Personal Data:** b Chicago, Ill, February 12, 1939; m 1961, Amy; c Sarah & Miriam. **Education:** Univ Chicago, BS, 1958, MD, 1962; Harvard Univ, PhD (biochem, molecular biol), 1967. **Professional Experience:** William Brady Jr distinguished fel social thought, Am Enterprise Inst, 1991-1992; ADDIE CLARK HARDING, PROF, COL & COMT SOCIAL THOUGHT, UNIV CHICAGO, 1990-; mem, Nat Humanities Coun, 1984-1991; prof, Col & Comt Social Thought, Univ Chicago, 1984-1990; fel Nat Humanities Ctr, 1984-1985; mem bd gov, US-Israel Binat Sci Found, 1982-1988; Henry R Luce prof lib arts human biol, Col & Comt Social Thought, Univ Chicago, 1976-1984; Joseph P Kennedy, Sr res prof bioethics, Kennedy Inst & assoc prof neurol & philos, Georgetown Univ, 1974-1976; tutor, St John's Col, Md, 1972-1976; Guggenheim fel, 1972-1973; fel, Hastings Ctr, 1970-; mem bd dir, Hastings Ctr, 1970-1996; exec secy comt life sci & social policy, Nat Acad Sci, 1970-1972; sr staff fel, Nat Inst Arthritis & Metab Dis, 1969-1970; staff assoc molecular biol, Nat Inst Arthritis & Metab Dis, 1967-1969; intern med, Beth Israel Hosp, Boston, Mass, 1962-1963. **Research Statement & Publications:** Ethical and social implications of advances in biomedical science and technology; philosophy of biology and medicine; philosophical anthropology; ethics of everyday life. **Mailing Address:** 1150 17th St NW, AE1, Washington, DC 20036.

KASS, ROB, MATHEMATICS. **Education:** Univ Chicago, PhD (statistics), 1980. **Professional Experience:** FAC, DEPT STATIS, CARNEGIE MELLON UNIV, 1981-. **Mailing Address:** Dept Statist, Carnegie Mellon Univ, 5000 Forbes Ave, Pittsburgh, PA 15213-3890. **E-Mail:** kass@stat.cmu.edu

KASS, ROBERT S, MEMBRANE BIOPHYSICS. **Personal Data:** b New York, NY, June 13, 1946; m 1982, c 2. **Education:** Univ Ill, BSc, 1968; Univ Mich, MSc, 1969, PhD (physics), 1972. **Professional Experience:** DAVID HOSACK PROF & DEPT CHMN, MED CTR, UNIV COLUMBIA, as of 2004; prof physiol & pediat, Univ Rochester, beginning 1990; from asst prof to assoc prof, Univ Rochester, 1977-1990; fel physiol, Univ Yale, 1974-1977; fel membrane biophysics, Marine Biol Labs, Mass, 1973; Fel physiol, Univ Mich, 1972-1974. **Memberships:** Biophys Soc; Am Heart Asn; Soc Gen Physiologists; NY Acad Sci. **Research Statement & Publications:** Physiology and biophysics of excitable membranes with a particular interest in the membranes of heart muscle cells; regulation of ion channels by hormones and drug molecules; Published over 6 articles. **Mailing Address:** 622 W 168 St, Univ Columbia, New York, NY 10032. **Fax:** 212-342-2703. **E-Mail:** rsk20@columbia.edu

KASS, SEYMOUR, APPLICATION OF LINEAR ALGEBRA TO STATISTICS. **Personal Data:** b New York, NY, April 13, 1926; m 1955, Judith Marks; c Dan & Lia. **Education:** Brooklyn Col, BA, 1948; Stanford Univ, MS, 1957; Univ Chicago, SM, 1965; Ill Inst Technol, PhD (math), 1966. **Professional Experience:** Dir eng prog, Univ Mass, Boston, 1984-1985; PROF MATH, UNIV MASS, BOSTON, 1982-; from assoc prof to prof, Boston State Col, 1977-1982; chmn dept, Boston State Col, 1972-1975; NSF res grant, 1969 & 1970; from instr to asst prof math, Ill Inst Technol, 1960-1971; Mathematician, Curtiss Wright Corp, 1952-1955 & Stanford Res Inst, 1955-1957. **Memberships:** emer mem Am Math Soc; emer mem Math Asn Am. **Research Statement & Publications:** Algebra; geometry; statistics. **Mailing Address:** 118 York Terr, Brookline, MA 02146-2322. **E-Mail:** seymour.kass@umb.edu

KASSAKHIAN, GARABET HAROUTIOUN, ENVIRONMENTAL CHEMISTRY-REMEDIATION, QUALITY ASSURANCE. **Personal Data:** b Jerusalem, Palestine, August 15, 1944; American citizen; m 1969, Loussik; c Harutiun, Ardashes & Vazken. **Education:** Yerevan State Univ, Armenia, MS, 1967; Harvard Univ, MA, 1970, PhD (anal chem), 1975. **Honors & Awards:** Willem Rudolfs Medal, Water Pollution Control Fedn, 1982. **Professional Experience:** DIR QUAL ASSURACNCE, TETRA TECH INC, as of 2005; mgr, Qual Assurance, Shaw Environ & Infrastructure Inc, Las Vegas, Nev, beginning 2002; mgr, qual assurance, IT Corp, Las Vegas, Nev, 1999-2002; dir, Qual Assurance, Tetra Tech Inc, Pasadena, Calif, 1996-1998; mgr, qual assurance, 1992-1996; sr environ scientist, Law Environ Inc, Burbank, Calif, 1988-1991; assoc, Lockman & assocs, Monterey Park, Calif, 1985-1987; asst prof environ chem, Univ Laverne, Calif, 1985-1987; dir environ res & develop, Nayirit Syn Rubber Factory, Yerevan, Armenia, 1982-1985; mgr, Amerada Hess Corp, Woodbridge, NJ, 1980-1982; environ chemist, Eldorado Nuclear Ltd, Ottawa, 1978-1980; asst prof chem, Univ Mass, Boston, 1975-1978; Sr teaching fel chem, Harvard Univ, 1968-1974. **Memberships:** Am Soc Qual; Water Environ Fedn. **Research Statement & Publications:** Quality assurance, quality management systems ISO 9001; uranium mine and mill tailings; methane gas mitigation; radionuclides in environment; water purification; wastewater treatment; contaminated soil remediation; drinking water standards. **Mailing Address:** Tetra Tech Inc, 670 N Rosemead Blvd, Pasadena, CA 91107-2190. **Fax:** 818-351-1188. **E-Mail:** garabed.kassakhian@shawgrp.com

KASSAKIAN, JOHN GABRIEL, POWER ELECTRONICS, ELECTRICAL ENGINEERING. **Personal Data:** b New York, NY, March 27, 1943; m 1968, Wilma; c 2. **Education:** Mass Inst Technol, SB, 1965, SM, 1967, EE, 1967, ScD (elec eng), 1973. **Honors & Awards:** Centennial Medal, Inst Elec & Electronics Engrs, 1984, IEEE William E Newell Award, 1987. **Professional Experience:** Dir, Am Power Conversion Corp, 2001-; dir, ISO-NE, 1997-; TYCO Electronics Corp advisory board, 1997-; DIR, LAB ELECTROMAGNETIC & ELECTRONIC SYST, 1991-; dir, Sheldahl, Inc, 1985-2001; dir, Ault Inc, 1984-; PROF ELEC ENG, MASS INST TECHNOL, 1984-; assoc dir, Elec Power Syst Eng Lab, 1979-1983; consult, Lutron Electronics, 1978-; consult, Gould Labs, Gould Inc, 1975-1989; Sr staff scientist, Gould Labs, Gould Inc, 1975; from asst prof to assoc prof elec eng, Lab Electromagnetic & Electronic Syst, 1973-1984; tech rep to Univac naval data syst, USN, 1969-1971. **Memberships:** Fel Inst Elec & Electronics Engrs; Nat Acad Eng; Europ Power Electronics Asn; Sigma Xi; pres Inst Elec & Electronics Engrs; Power Electronics Soc. **Research Statement & Publications:** Simulation, analysis, synthesis of electronic energy conversion systems; power semiconductor devices; manufacturing technolgies for electronic apparatus; automotive electrical/electronic systems. **Mailing Address:** Mass Inst Technol, Bldg 10-172 77 Mass Ave, Cambridge, MA 02139-4301. **E-Mail:** jgk@mit.edu

KASSAL, ROBERT JAMES, PLASTICS FAILURE ANALYSIS, ORGANIC CHEMISTRY. **Personal Data:** b Berwick, Pa, October 23, 1936; m 1958, c 4. **Education:** Hofstra Univ, BA, 1958; Univ Fla, PhD (org chem), 1964. **Professional Experience:** RES FEL, POLYMER PROD DEPT, E I DU PONT DEL NEMOURS & CO INC, 1990-; sr res assoc & group leader, Polymer Prod Dept, 1985-1990; res assoc, Polymer Prod Dept, 1975-1985; mem staff, Elastomers Dept, 1975-1978; res supvr, Plastics Dept, 1969-1975; sr res chemist, Plastics Dept, 1968-1969; res chemist, E I Du Pont Del Nemours & Co Inc, 1963-1968; res asst fluorine chem, Univ Fla, 1960-1963; Chemist, Am Cyanamid Co, 1958-1960. **Memberships:** Soc Plastics Indust. **Research Statement & Publications:** Fluorine chemistry; polymer preparation; fluorocarbon heterocyclic polymers; intermediates and monomer exploratory research; new product development; polymer synthesis; polymer modification; high performance composite development; novel elastomer systems; polymer toughening; solvent resistant polymers; engineering polymers; polymer compounding and processing; failure analysis of polymer systems; accelerated test method development; environmental effects on polymers; expert witness. **Mailing Address:** E I Du Pont De Nemours & Co Legal Patent Records Ctr, 4417 Lancaster Pike, Barley Mill Plaza 25/1128, Wilmington, DE 19805.

KASSAM, SALEEM ABDULALI, SIGNAL PROCESSING, COMMUNICATION THEORY. **Personal Data:** b Dar es Salaam, Tanzania, June 16, 1949; American citizen; m 1978, c 3. **Education:** Swarthmore Col, BS, 1972; Princeton Univ, MSE & MA, 1974, PhD (elec eng), 1975. **Honorary Degrees:** MA, Univ Pa, 1980. **Professional Experience:** SOLOMON & SYLVIA CHARP PROF, MOORE SCH ELEC ENG, UNIV PA, 1993-; vis scholar, Princeton Univ, 1992; chmn dept elec eng, Moore Sch Elec Eng, Univ Pa, beginning 1992; naval air dev cen, Bio Rad Inc, 1989-1990; naval air dev cen, beginning 1987; vis assoc prof, Univ BC, 1983; consult, Interspec, 1982-1988; consult, RCA, 1980-1981; res grant, Off Naval, 1980-; naval Res Lab grants, 1978-1980; prin investr, NSF grant, 1977-1979; prin investr, Air Force Off Sci Res res grants, Univ Pa, 1976-; from asst prof to prof, Moore Sch Elec Eng, Univ PA, 1975-1993. **Memberships:** fel Inst Elec & Electronics Engrs; Sigma Xi. **Research Statement & Publications:** Signal processing and communication theory; nonparametric detection; quantization, robust signal processing; image processing; microwave and ultrasonic imaging; spectrum estimation; author of numerous technical papers and two books. **Mailing Address:** Dept Elec Eng & Systems Eng, Univ Pa, Rm 356 GRW, Moore Sch, 220 S 33rd St, Philadelphia, PA 19104. **E-Mail:** kassam@ee.upenn.edu

KASSANDER, ARNO RICHARD, RESEARCH ADMINISTRATION. **Personal Data:** b Carbondale, Pa, September 10, 1920; m 1943, Sara; c Helen (Ruskin). **Education:** Amherst Col, BA, 1941; Univ Okla, MS, 1943; Iowa State Col, PhD (physics), 1950. **Honorary Degrees:** DSc, Amherst Col, 1971, Univ Ariz, 1986. **Professional Experience:** PROF EMER ATMOSPHERIC SCI, UNIV ARIZ, as of 2004; VPRES RES EMER, UNIV ARIZ, as of 2004; prof atmospheric sci, Univ Ariz, beginning 1976; dir, Burr Brown Res Corp, 1974-1991; vpres res, Univ Ariz, beginning 1972; dir, First Interstate Bank Ariz, 1972-1992; Dir, Water Resources Res Ctr, Univ Ariz, 1964-1972; head dept atmospheric sci, Inst Atmospheric Physics, 1958-1973; chmn, Univ Corp Atmospheric Res, 1958-1968; dir, Inst Atmospheric Physics, 1957-1973; assoc dir, Inst Atmospheric Physics, 1954-1957; asst prof physics, Iowa State Col, 1950-1954; asst geophys, Magnolia Petrol Co, 1943; asst geologist, Tex Co, 1941; trustee, Ariz Sonora Desert Mus; mem panel environ, President's Sci Adv Comt. **Memberships:** Fel AAAS; Am Phys Soc; fel Am Meteorol Soc. **Research Statement & Publications:** General geophysical instrumentation; recording and automatic analysis of statistical data. **Mailing Address:** Res & Grad Studies Univ Ariz, 601 Admin Bldg, Tucson, AZ 85721-0066. **Fax:** 520-621-7507.

KASSCHAU, MARGARET RAMSEY, COMPARATIVE PHYSIOLOGY, CELL PHYSIOLOGY. **Personal Data:** b Cambridge, Mass, September 9, 1942; div, c Kristin & Michael. **Education:** Univ Rochester, AB, 1964; Univ SC, MS, 1970, PhD (biol), 1973. **Professional Experience:** ASSOC VPRES ACAD AFFAIRS, UNIV SCI PHILADELPHIA, 2004-; PROF, BIOL SCI DEPT, UNIV SCI PHILADELPHIA, as of 2004; Chair, biol sci dept, Univ sci philadelphia, 1994-2004; NSF vis prof women, Harvard Med Sch, 1990-1991; prin investr, NSF Grant, RUI Prog, 1987-1991; vis res assoc, Med Sch, Stanford Univ, 1980-1981; Prin investr, Sea Grant Col Prog, 1978-1980; from asst prof to prof biol, Univ Houston, Clearlake City, 1975-1994; fel res physics, M D Anderson Hosp & Tumor Inst, 1974-1975; guest worker parasitol, NIH, 1973-1974; res asst biol, Oak Ridge Nat Lab, 1964-1967. **Memberships:** Am soc cell biol; Am Soc Zoologists; AAAS; Biophys Soc. **Research Statement & Publications:** Cell biology invertebrates; osmotics stress on cells; hemolysis by schistosoma parasites; cell matrix adhesion; cellular toxicology. **Mailing Address:** Dept Biol Sci, Univ Sci Philadelphia, 600 S 43rd St, Philadelphia, PA 19104-4495. **Fax:** 215-596-8710. **E-Mail:** m.kassch@usip.edu

KASSIRER, JEROME PAUL, NEPHROLOGY, INTERNAL MEDICINE. **Personal Data:** b Buffalo, NY, December 19, 1932; c Amy, Richard, Wendy, Elizabeth, Winston & Samuel. **Education:** Univ Buffalo, BA, 1953, MD, 1957. **Professional Experience:** DISTINGUISHED PROF, DEPT ADMIN & MED, TUFTS UNIV SCH MED, as of 2003; adj prof med, Yale Univ Sch Med, as of 2003; ed-in-chief, New Eng J Med, 1991-1999; bd sci counr, Nat Libr Med, 1986-1989; co-ed, Clin Prob Solving Hosp Pract, 1985-1991; co-ed, Kidney Int, Nephrology Forum, 1978-1991; assoc chmn & assoc physician-in-chief, Sch Med, 1977-1991; mem, Med Sci Panel, Am Inst Biol Sci, 1977-1980; actg physician-in-chief, Sch Med, 1976-1977; prof med, Sch Med, 1974-; actg chmn, Sch Med, 1974-1975 & 1976-1977; assoc physician-in-chief & assoc chmn, Sch Med, 1971-1976; physician, Sch Med, 1969-1974; from asst prof to assoc prof med, Sch Med, 1965-1974; instr med & nephrol, Sch Med, 1962-1965; asst physician, New Eng Med Ctr Hosp, Tufts Univ, 1962-1965. **Memberships:** Inst Med-Nat Acad Sci; Am Col Informatics. **Research Statement & Publications:** Renal, electrolytes and acid-base physiology; clinical nephrology; decision analysis and clinical cognition. **Mailing Address:** Dept Med, Tufts Univ Sch Med, Sackler Cent 145 Harrison, Boston, MA 02115. **Fax:** 617-636-0375. **E-Mail:** jerome.kassirer@tufts.edu

KASSIS, SHOUKI, CELL BIOLOGY, CHEMISTRY. **Personal Data:** b Haiva, Pakistan, February 8, 1947. **Education:** Bingoway Univ, BA, 1969; Tel Aviv Univ, MS, 1973, PhD (microbiol), 1979. **Professional Experience:** STAFF MEM, DEPT BONE & CARTILAGE BIOL, SMITH-KLINE BEECHAM PHARMACEUT, as of 2000; SR INVESTR CHEM, SMITH-KLINE BEECHAM LABS, 1988-; Researcher chem, NIH, 1981-1988. **Memberships:** AAAS; Am Soc Cell Biol; Am Soc Biochem & Molecular Biol. **Research Statement & Publications:** Cell biology; chemistry. **Mailing Address:** Dept Bone & Cartilage Biol, Smith-Kline Beecham Pharmaceut, 709 Swedeland Rd MCL-101, King of Prussia, PA 19406-0939.

KASSNER, JAMES LYLE, JR, CLOUD PHYSICS, INDUSTRIAL & MANUFACTURING ENGINEERING. **Personal Data:** b Tuscaloosa, Ala, May 1, 1931; m 1956, Wanda J Hulsart; c James D (deceased), Linda J, Christine C, Peter C & Kevin C. **Education:** Univ Ala, BS, 1952, MS, 1953, PhD (physics), 1957. **Professional Experience:** FACIL MGR, NAT WOODWORKS, INC, 1991-; mfg mgt, Fibreform Containers, 1990-1991; chief exec officer, Dexter D Hulsart, Inc, 1984-1989; PRES, KASSNER WOODCRAFT, INC, 1981-; dir, Grad Ctr Cloud Physics Res, 1968-1984; prof physics, Grad Ctr Cloud Physics Res, 1966-1984; assoc prof, Univ Mo, Rolla, 1959-1966; asst prof, Mo Sch Mines, 1956-1959; res assoc, Univ Ala, 1954-1956; Asst physics, Univ Ala, 1953-1954; Mem subcomt nucleation, Int Asn Meteorol & Atmospheric Physics; mem subcomn IV, Ions, Aerosols & Radioactivity, Int Comn Atmospheric Elec. **Memberships:** Fel Am Phys Soc; Am Meteorol Soc; Am Geophys Union; Sigma Xi. **Research Statement & Publications:** Atmospheric condensation; homogeneous and heterogeneous nucleation from the vapor; mobility of cluster ions; laboratory simulation of cloud formation; measurements on atmospheric particulates; nucleation of ice. **Mailing Address:** 11947 Graceland Acres, Northport, AL 35476.

KASSNER, RICHARD J, BIOCHEMISTRY. **Personal Data:** b Chicago, Ill, July 1, 1939; m 1962, c 3. **Education:** Purdue Univ, BS, 1961; Yale Univ, MS, 1963, PhD (biophys chem), 1966. **Professional Experience:** PROF CHEM, UNIV ILL, CHICAGO, as of 2004; assoc prof chem, Univ Ill, Chicago, beginning 1974; asst prof, Univ Ill, Chicago Circle, 1969-1974; instr, Univ Calif, San Diego, 1968-1969; NIH fel chem, Univ Calif, San Diego, 1966-1968. **Research Statement & Publications:** Structural basis for the properties of heme and iron-sulfur proteins; model systems for the active sites of hemeproteins; heme and chlorophyll biosynthesis. **Mailing Address:** Dept Chem Univ M/C Ill Univ, 845 W Taylor Rm 4500, Chicago, IL 60607-7061. **Fax:** 312-996-0431. **E-Mail:** rkassner@uic.edu

KASSOY, DAVID R, FLUID MECHANICS, COMBUSTION. **Personal Data:** b Brooklyn, NY, January 29, 1938; m 1964, Carol; c Andrew R & Erin A. **Education:** Polytech Inst Brooklyn, BS, 1959; Univ Mich, MS, 1961, PhD (aerospace eng), 1965. **Professional Experience:** Interim Assoc vpres technol, Univ Colo Syst, 1997-2000; assoc vchancellor acad affairs, Univ Colo, Boulder, 1992-1997; chmn exec comt, Div Fluid Dynamics, Am Phys Soc, 1992-1993; mem exec comt, Div Fluid Dynamics, Am Phys Soc, 1989-; vchmn exec comt, Div Fluid Dynamics, Am Phys Soc, 1989-1990; asst vchancellor res, Univ Colo, Boulder, 1988-1992; Japan Soc Prom Sci, Nagoya Univ, Japan, 1985; Fulbright Res fel, Tech Univ Delft, 1983; vis fel, Sci & Eng Res Coun, Univ EAnglia, Eng, 1982-1983; PROF MECH ENG, UNIV COLO, BOULDER, 1978-; Guggenheim fel, 1973; from asst prof to assoc prof, Univ Colo, Boulder, 1969-1978; asst prof aerospace & mech eng sci, Univ Calif, San Diego, 1968-1969; asst res engr, Univ Calif, San Diego, 1965-1967. **Memberships:** fel Am Phys Soc; Soc Indust & Appl Math; Combustion Inst; assoc fel Am Inst Aeronaut & Astronaut. **Research Statement & Publications:** Combustion theory; ignition and explosion; detonation initiation and evolution; perturbation methods; theoretical fluid mechanics; solid rocket motor fluid dynamics; solidification of materials. **Mailing Address:** Dept Mech Eng, Univ Colo, 427 UCB 1111 Eng Dr, Boulder, CO 80309-0427. **Fax:** 303-492-3498. **E-Mail:** David.Kassoy@Colorado.edu

KASTELLA, KENNETH GEORGE, PHYSIOLOGY. **Personal Data:** b Kalispell, Mont, May 27, 1933; div, c 1. **Education:** Univ Wash, BS, 1959, MS, 1965, PhD (physiol), 1969. **Professional Experience:** RETIRED; teaching assoc, Dept Biol Struct, Sch Med, Univ Wash, 1987-; assoc prof, Univ Alaska, 1976-1987; asst prof physiol, Univ NMex, 1970-1976; res assoc, Univ Wash, 1970; NIH training grant neurophysiol, Univ Wash, 1969-1970. **Memberships:** AAAS; Inst Elec & Electronics Engrs; Biophys Soc. **Research Statement & Publications:** Neurophysiology, especially central control of blood pressure; temperature regulation. **Mailing Address:** 643 1/2 Meadowood Ct, Grand Junction, CO 81504.

KASTEN, FREDERICK H, CYTOLOGY. **Personal Data:** b New York, NY, March 7, 1927; m 1949, c 4. **Education:** Univ Houston, BA, 1950; Univ Tex, MS, 1951, PhD (zoology), 1954. **Professional Experience:** RETIRED; vis prof zool, Jagiellonian Univ, Krakow, Poland, 1989; Ain-Shams Univ Fac Med, Cairo Egypt, 1987 & 1990; pres, Biol Stain Comn, 1986-; vis prof histol, Alex Univ Med Sch, Alexandria, Egypt, 1986 & 1987; pres, Am Asn Dent Res, NO Sect, 1983-1984; vis prof anat, ETenn State Univ Med Sch, 1979-1980; res grants comt, Cancer Asn GNO, 1975-; rev ed, In Vitro, 1975-1978; adv bd, TCA Tech Manual, 1974-1980; trustee, Biol Stain Comn, 1973-; consult, Nat Heart & Lung Inst, 1971- & Nat Cancer Inst, 1973-; assoc coordr, La Cancer Ctr, 1973-1978; partic, W Alton Jones Cell Sci Ctr, 1971; prof anat, Med Ctr, La State Univ, 1970-1994; from asst clin prof to assoc clin prof, Loma Linda Univ, 1965-1970; res coordr & dir, Ultrastruct Cytochem Dept, Pasadena Found Med Res, 1963-1970; from adj asst prof to adj assoc prof, Univ Southern Calif, 1963-1970; NSF sr fel, NIH spec res fel, 1962-1963; NSF sr fel, Inst Cancer Res, Villejuif, France, 1962-1963; NSF sr fel, Giessen, Ger, 1961-1962; asst prof zool, Agr & Mech Col, Tex, 1956-1961; scientist cancer res, Roswell Park Mem Inst, NY, 1954-1956. **Memberships:** Biol Stain Comn; Am Soc Cell Biol; AAAS; Ger Histochem Soc; Tissue Cult Asn; Sigma Xi. **Research Statement & Publications:** Quantitative cytochemistry of nucleic acids; absorption curve analyses of stained cells; development of new staining techniques; electron microscopy; cytochemistry of viral infections; dye impurities; fluorescence microscopy; cancer; tissue culture; history of medicine. **Mailing Address:** 109 E Maple St PO Box 1157, Johnson City, TN 37605-1157.

KASTEN, PAUL R(UDOLPH), reactor evaluation, reactor technology; deceased, see previous edition for last biography

KASTENBAUM, MARVIN AARON, BIOMETRICS, BIOSTATISTICS. **Personal Data:** b New York, NY, January 16, 1926; m 1955, Helen; c Joan K (Jackson) & Robert H. **Education:** City Col NY, BS, 1948; NC State Col, MS, 1950, PhD (statist), 1956. **Professional Experience:** CONSULT, 1987-; dir statist, Tobacco Inst, 1970-1987; mem statist dept, Stanford Univ, 1969; NSF vis lectr, 1966-1971; Mem math res ctr, Univ Wis, 1965-1966; sr res statistician, Oak Ridge Nat Lab, Tenn, 1956-1970; biostatistician, Atomic Bomb Casualty Comm, 1953-1954; chief statistician mkt res, Dun & Bradstreet, Inc, 1952; asst statistician, US Bur Census, 1948 & 1950; med statist, biomet & epidemiol consult. **Memberships:** Fel AAAS; Biomet Soc (secy-treas Eastern Nam region, 1959-1960 gen treas, 1960-1963); fel Am Statist Asn; Inst Math Statist; fel Royal Statist Soc; fel NY Acad Sci. **Research Statement & Publications:** Medical statistics; biometry; epidemiology. **Mailing Address:** 16450 Fairway Woods Dr, Ft Myers, FL 33908.

KASTENBERG, WILLIAM EDWARD, NUCLEAR ENGINEERING. **Personal Data:** b New York, NY, June 25, 1939; m 1992, Gloria; c Andrew, Joshua & Lillian. **Education:** Univ Calif, Los Angeles, BS, 1962, MS, 1963; Univ Calif, Berkeley, PhD (eng), 1966. **Honors & Awards:** Arthur Holly Compton Award, Am Nuclear Soc, 2000. **Professional Experience:** DANIEL M TELLEP DISTINGUISHED PROF, NUCLEAR ENG DEPT, UNIV CALIF, BERKELY, as of 2006; PROF, NUCLEAR ENG DEPT, UNIV CALIF, BERKELY, 1995-; dept chmn, nuclear eng dept, Univ calif, berkely, 1995-; chmn, UCLA's Ctr Clean Technol, 1992-1994; mem, comt Nuclear Facility Safety, US Dept Energy, 1988-1991; dir, Risk & Syst Anal Control Toxics Prog UCLA, Univ Calif, Los Angeles, 1985-1994; chmn, Dept Aerospace & Nuclear Eng UCLA, 1985-1988; mem, Nat Res Comn Reactor Safety, 1985-1986; chmn, nuclear reactor safety, Am Nuclear Soc, 1984-1985; asst dean grad studies, Sch Eng & Appl Sci, 1981-1985; sr fel, Advisory Comt, USNRC, 1979-1980; vchmn, Dept Chem, Nuclear & Thermal Eng, 1977-1978; prof mech, aerospace & nuclear eng, 1975-1994; Guest scientist, Karlsruhe Nuclear Res, fed Repub Ger, 1972-1973; from asst prof eng to assoc prof eng & appl sci, Univ Calif, Los Angeles, 1966-1975. **Memberships:** Fel Am Nuclear Soc, 1978; fel AAAS; Nat Acad Eng. **Research Statement & Publications:** Nuclear reactor safety; engineering ethics; risk analysis; toxic waste control; environmental risk assessment; published over 150 articles. **Mailing Address:** Dept Nuclear Eng, Univ Calif, MC 1730 4155 Etchevervy Hall, Berkeley, CA 94721-1730. **Fax:** 510-643-9685. **E-Mail:** kastenbe@nuc.berkeley.edu

KASTENHOLZ, CLAUDE E(DWARD), ELECTRICAL ENGINEERING. **Personal Data:** b Milwaukee, Wis, November 27, 1936; m 1959, c 5. **Education:** Marquette Univ, BEE, 1958; Univ Southern Calif, MS, 1960; Univ Wis, PhD (elec eng), 1963; Pepperdine Univ, MBA, 1970. **Professional Experience:** RETIRED; proj mgr, Hughes Aircraft Co, Calif, 1982-1996; sr scientist, Hughes Aircraft Co, Calif, 1975-1981; sr staff engr, Hughes Aircraft Co, Calif, 1967-1975; res specialist, Autonetics Div, NAm Rockwell Corp, 1963-1967; res asst circuit design, Univ Wis, 1961-1962; res engr, Autonetics Div, NAm Aviation, Inc, 1960-1961; mem tech staff, Hughes Aircraft Co, Calif, 1958-1960. **Memberships:** Inst Elec & Electronics Engrs. **Research Statement & Publications:** Sonar systems engineering; fire control system design; system testing. **Mailing Address:** 16932 Nightingale Lane, Yorba Linda, CA 92886.

KASTENS, KIM ANNE, MARINE GEOLOGY, MARINE GEOPHYSICS. **Personal Data:** b Menlo Park, Calif, May 19, 1954. **Education:** Yale Univ, BS, 1975; Scripps Inst Oceanog, PhD (oceanog), 1981. **Professional Experience:** Chair, Collections Comt Digital Libr Earth Syst Educ, 1999-2004; SR RES SCIENTIST, LAMONT DOHERTY EARTH OBSERV, 1993-; prog Leader, Marine Geol Geophysics Group, Lamont Doherty Earth Observ, Columbia Univ, 1993-1995; Adj prof, Dept Geol Sci, Columbia Univ, 1993-; adj assoc Prof, Dept Geol Sci, Columbia Univ, 1992-1993; res scientist, Lamont Doherty Geol Observ, Columbia Univ, 1988-1991; vis lectr, Dept Geol & Geophysics, Yale Univ, 1986-1987; assoc res scientist & res rssoc, Lamont Doherty Geol Observ, Columbia Univ, 1981-1988; res teaching asst, Scripps Inst Oceanog, Univ Calif, San Diego, 1976-1981; geol technician, Marine Sci Res Ctr, Stony Brook, 1975-1976. **Memberships:** Am Geophys Union; Geol Soc Am; Sigma Xi. **Research Statement & Publications:** Tectonic and sedimentological processes in the deep sea. **Mailing Address:** Lamont Doherty Earth Observ, Palisades, NY 10964. **Fax:** 845-365-8156. **E-Mail:** kastens@ldeo.columbia.edu

KASTIN, ABBA J, PEPTIDES, BLOOD-BRAIN BARRIER. **Personal Data:** b Cleveland, Ohio, December 24, 1934. **Education:** Harvard Col, BA, 1956; Harvard Med Sch, MD, 1960. **Honorary Degrees:** DSc, Univ New Orleans, 1984. **Honors & Awards:** Edward T Tyler Fertil Award, Int Fertil Soc, 1975; Copernicus Medal, Poland, 1979; William S Middleton Award, Vet Admin, 1982; Talmage Lectr, Aspen Allergy Conf, 1986; Strand Award, 2001. **Professional Experience:** Wellcome vis prof, Fedn Am Soc Exp Biol, ET State Univ, 1989-1990; consult prof, Dept Psychol, 1986-; PROF, NEUROSCIENCE TRAINING PROG, TULANE UNIV, 1986-; CONSULT PROF, DEPT PSYCHOL, UNIV NEW ORLEANS, 1986-; ed-in-chief, Peptides, 1980-; consult, Food & Drug Admin, 1979-1980; mem res adv comt, Nat Asn Retarded Citizens, 1978-1979; assoc mem grad fac, Univ New Orleans, 1976-; PROF MED, SCH MED, TULANE UNIV, 1974-; Mem med adv bd, Nat Pituitary Agency, 1974-1977; assoc prof, Vet Admin Hosp, New Orleans, 1971-1974; CHIEF ENDOCRINOL, VET ADMIN HOSP, NEW ORLEANS, 1968-; clin investr med, Vet Admin Hosp, New Orleans, 1965-1968; NIH spec fel, Sch Med, Tulane Univ, 1964-1965; Clin assoc endocrinol, NIH, 1962-1964. **Memberships:** Endocrine Soc; Am Physiol Soc; Soc Exp Biol & Med; Soc Neurosci; Int Soc Psychoneuroendocrinol; hon mem Endocrine Socs of Chile Philippines Peru Poland & Hungary; Int Soc Neuroendocrinol; fel Int Behav Neurosci Soc; fel Am Col Endocrinol; Int Neuropeptide Soc (pres 1993-). **Research Statement & Publications:** Blood-brain barrier; brain peptides; neuroendocrinology; hypothalamic hormones; author of more thatn 650 papers. **Mailing Address:** Vet Affairs Med Ctr, 1601 Perdido St, New Orleans, LA 70146. **Fax:** 504-522-8559.

KASTING, JAMES FRASER, ATMOSPHERIC EVOLUTION, RADIATIVE TRANSFER. **Personal Data:** b Schenectady, NY, January 2, 1953; m 1980, c 2. **Education:** Harvard Univ, AB, 1975; Univ Mich, MS (phys) & MS (atmospheric sci), 1978, PhD (atmospheric sci), 1979. **Professional Experience:** DISTINGUISHED PROF, DEPT GEOSCIENCE, PA STATE UNIV, as of 2004; res scientist, Ames Res Ctr, NASA, 1983-; res fel, Ames Res Ctr, NASA, 1981-1983; Res fel, Nat Ctr Atmospheric Res, 1979-1981. **Memberships:** fel Am Geophys Union; fel Int Soc Study Origin Life; fel AAAS. **Research Statement & Publications:** Evolution of planetary atmospheres; history of the earth and why it is different from that of Mars and Venus. **Mailing Address:** Dept Geol, Pa State Univ, 443 Deike Bldg, Univ Park, PA 16802. **Fax:** 814-863-2001. **E-Mail:** jfk4@psu.edu

KASTL, PETER ROBERT, OPHTHALMOLOGY, BIOCHEMISTRY. **Personal Data:** b Alexandria, La, July 25, 1949; m 1974, c 2. **Education:** Centenary Col La, BS, 1971; Tulane Univ, MD, 1974, PhD (biochem), 1978. **Honors & Awards:** Alpha Omega Alpha. **Professional Experience:** PROF BIOCHEM & OPHTHAL, TULANE UNIV, 1989-; assoc prof biochem & ophthal, Tulane Univ, 1985-1988; asst prof, Tulane Univ, 1981-1985; NIH res grant, 1981-1983; instr ophthal, Tulane Univ, 1977-1981; instr biochem, Tulane Univ, 1975-1981; fel, Nat Inst Gen Med Sci, 1975-1976. **Memberships:** Sigma Xi; Am Acad Ophthal; Contact Lens Asn Ophthalmologists. **Research Statement & Publications:** Microsomal treatment of ingested toxins; pharmacologic prevention of cataracts; design of new types of ophthalmologic prosthetic devices; tear analysis; contact lenses. **Mailing Address:** Dept Ophthal, Tulane Med Ctr, New Orleans, LA 70112. **Fax:** 504-584-2684. **E-Mail:** pkastl@tulane.edu

KASTNER, BERNICE, MATHEMATICS. **Professional Experience:** PROF EMER, TOWSON UNIV, MD, as of 2006. **Memberships:** Math Asn Am. **Mailing Address:** Dept Math, Towson Univ, Towson, MD 21252-0001. **Fax:** 410-704-4149.

KASTNER, CURTIS LYNN, MEAT SCIENCE, MUSCLE BIOLOGY. **Personal Data:** b Altus, Okla, September 21, 1944; m 1966, Rebecca Diltz; c Jason & Justin. **Education:** Okla State Univ, BS, 1967, MS, 1969, PhD (food sci), 1972. **Honors & Awards:** US Key Res Scientist, AAAS, 1984; Teacher Fel Award, Nat Asn Cols Teachers & Agr, 1985; Signal Serv Award, Am Meat Sci Asn, 1996 advan degree grad Distinction Award, Okla State Univ, 2000. **Professional Experience:** DIR, FOOD SCI INST, 2001-; pres, Am Meat Sci Asn Ann Conf, 1993-1994; mem exec bd, Muscle & Food Div, 1991; chair, Am Meat Sci Asn Ann Conf, 1989; exec bd, Am Meat Sci Asn Ann Conf, 1988-1989; chmn, Am Meat Sci Asn Ann Conf, 1988; Sect chmn, Inst Food Technologists, 1982; PROF & RES COORDR, ANIMAL & FOOD SCI, KANS STATE UNIV, 1975-; asst prof food sci, Wash State Univ, 1972-1975. **Memberships:** Am Meat Sci Asn; Am Soc Animal Sci; Inst Food Technologists, Am assoc prof Animal ocie, Am col animal food sci; charter mem. **Research Statement & Publications:** Technology, development, processing and preservation of meat and meat products, including hot processing, tenderization, microbial sampling, shelf life extension, packaging sanitation, microbiology, chemical residues, meat safety and low fat technology. **Mailing Address:** Foods Sci Inst, Kans State Univ Call Hall, Manhattan, KS 66506-0201. **Fax:** 785-532-5861. **E-Mail:** ckastner@ksu.edu

KASTNER, MARC AARON, SEMICONDUCTORS, HIGH-TEMPERATURE SUPERCONDUCTIVITY. **Personal Data:** b Toronto, Ont, November 20, 1945; American citizen; m 1967, c 2. **Education:** Univ Chicago, BS, 1967, MS, 1969 & PhD (physics), 1973. **Honors & Awards:** David Adler Lectr Award, Am Phys Soc, 1995; Oliver E Buckley Prize, Am Phys Soc, 2000. **Professional Experience:** HEAD, DEPT PHYSICS, MASS INST TECHNOL, 1998-; dir, Ctr Mat Sci & Eng, Mass Inst Technol, 1993-1998; counr, Am Phys Soc, 1990-1994; DONNER PROF PHYSICS, MASS INST TECHNOL, 1989-; assoc dir, Consortium Superconducting Electronics, 1989-1992; head div atomic, condensed matter & plasma physics, Dept Physics, Mass Inst Technol, 1983-1987; from asst prof to prof, Mass Inst Technol, 1973-1989; res fel, Div Eng & Appl Physics, Harvard Univ, 1972-1973. **Memberships:** Fel Am Phys Soc; AAAS. **Research Statement & Publications:** Electronic and optical studies of amorphous semiconductors led to the Valence Alteration Model; measurements of conductivity of nanometer-size semiconductor devices; magnetic optical and transport studies of high-temperature superconductors; Kondo Physics with Single Electron Transistors; author of various articles. **Mailing Address:** Mass Inst Technol, Rm G 113, Cambridge, MA 02139. **Fax:** 617-253-8554. **E-Mail:** mkastner@mit.edu

KASTNER, MIRIAM, GEOLOGY, OCEANOGRAPHY. **Personal Data:** b Bratislava, Czech, American citizen; wid. **Education:** Hebrew Univ Jerusalem, Israel, BSc & MSc, 1964; Harvard Univ, PhD (geosciences/Earth Science), 1970. **Honorary Degrees:** Dr, Univ Paris XI, 1984. **Honors & Awards:** Newcomb Cleveland Prize, AAAS; Guggenheim Fel; Ocean Sci Educators Award, Off Naval Res. **Professional Experience:** Counr, Geochem Soc, 1990-1993 & 1993-1994; chmn, geol res div, Scripps Inst Oceanog, beginning 1989; chmn, Gordon Res Conf Chem Oceanog, 1989; mem-at-large, Sect Geol & Geog, AAAS, 1987-1991; mem, NSF Adv Comt, Earth Sci, 1986-1988; steering comt, 2nd Conf Sci Ocean Drilling, 1986-1987; vis prof, Hebrew Univ, Israel, 1986; planning comt mem, Ocean Drilling Proj, 1984-1990; distinguished lectr, Am Asn Petrol Geologists, 1983 & 1984; PROF GEOL, SCRIPPS INST OCEANOG, UNIV CALIF, SAN DEIGO, 1982-; assoc ed, J Sedimentary Petrol, 1980-1988 & Appl Geochem, 1986-1989; from asst prof to assoc prof, Geol Res Div, 1972-1982; fel geol, Univ Chicago, 1971-1972; fel geol, Harvard Univ, 1970-1971. **Memberships:** Fel AAAS; fel Geochem Soc and Int Asn Geochem & Cosmochem; fel Am Geophys Union; fel Geological Soc. Amer; Sigma Xi. **Research Statement & Publications:** Origin, mineralogy and geochemistry of silicates phosphates and carbonates in marine and non-marine environments; stable isotopes for diagenesis; processes that cause metal enrichment in oceanic sediments; surface chemistry in diagenesis; hydrothermal deposits in the submarine environment; the role of fluids in convergent plate margins; chemical paleoceanography. **Mailing Address:** Dept Geol, Scripps Inst Oceanog, Univ Calif, 9500 Gilman Dr, La Jolla, CA 92093-0212. **Fax:** 858-822-4945. **E-Mail:** mkastner@ucsd.edu

KASTOR, ROSS L, ENGINEERING. **Education:** Ohio State Univ, BS, MSc. **Professional Experience:** PROF MECHANICAL ENG, UNIV HOUSTON, as of 2005; PRES, ANTELOPE ENG INC, 1992-. **Mailing Address:** Antelope Eng Inc, 13514 Dripping Springs, Houston, TX 77083-1828. **Fax:** 713-743-4503. **E-Mail:** kastorr@asme.org

KASUBA, ROMUALDAS, MECHANICAL ENGINEERING, APPLIED MECHANICS. **Personal Data:** b Kaunas, Lithuania, March 23, 1931; American citizen; m 1961, Elena; c Vida R & Dalia R (Metzger). **Education:** Univ Ill, Urbana, BS, 1954, MS, 1957, PhD (mech eng), 1962. **Professional Experience:** RETIRED; invited distinguished vis researcher, Tokyo Inst Technol, 1994; dean, Col Eng & Eng Technol, Northern Ill Univ, 1986-2003; dir, Eng Doctorate Prog, 1985-1986; chairperson, Dept Mech Eng, 1978-1985; consult, Indust Fasteners Inst, 1970-1975 & Am Nat Stand Inst, 1971-1974; corp consult, Warner & Swasey Corp, 1969-1976; from assoc prof to prof mech eng, Cleveland State Univ, 1968-1986; head, Stress & Dynamics Group Power Systs Div, TRW Inc, Ohio, 1962-1968; res asst dynamics, Mech Eng Dept, Univ Ill, Urbana, 1958-1962; lectr, US, Can & Venezuela. **Memberships:** Fel Am Soc Mech Engrs; Am Soc Eng Educ; Nat Soc Prof Engrs; Mfg Asn Am Gear; Sigma Xi. **Research Statement & Publications:** Vibration and noise studies in industrial machines; dynamic loads in geared systems; development of optimum threaded fastener system; dynamic simulation of geared systems; dynamic simulation of machine tool structures and drives; application of finite element techniques; optimum fastener system; digital simulation of real rotating gear systems. **Mailing Address:** 42 W 661 Steeplechase, St Charles, IL 60175.

KASUBE, HERBERT EMIL, MATHEMATICS EDUCATION, HISTORY OF MATHEMATICS. **Personal Data:** b Chicago, Ill, March 23, 1949. **Education:** MacMurray Col, BA, 1971; Univ Ill, MA, 1973; Univ Mont, PhD (math), 1979. **Honors & Awards:** Distinguished Serv Award, Sect of Math Assoc of Am, 1999. **Professional Experience:** ASSOC PROF MATH, BRADLEY UNIV, PEORIA, ILL, 1978-; teaching asst math, Univ Ill, 1971-1975; teaching asst math, Univ Mont, 1975-1978. **Memberships:** Sigma Xi; Math Asn Am; Am Math Soc; Nat Coun Teachers Math; Can Soc Hist & Philos Math; Ill Coun Teachers Math. **Research Statement & Publications:** Discrete mathematics; number theory; college mathematics education; history of mathematics. **Mailing Address:** Dept Math, Bradley Univ, BR 436, Peoria, IL 61625. **Fax:** 309-677-3999. **E-Mail:** hkasube@hilltop.bradley.edu

KASUPSKI, GEORGE JOSEPH, DIAGNOSTIC VIROLOGY, MOLECULAR VIROLOGY. **Personal Data:** b Boston, Mass, July 26, 1946; m 1979, c 1. **Education:** McGill Univ, BSc, 1969, PhD (molecular biol), 1975. **Professional Experience:** Dir, Lakeshore Labs Ltd, 1984; asst prof, Dept Med Microbiol, Univ Toronto, 1981; adv, Wellesley Hosp Res Inst, 1981; adv, Toronto Inst Med Technol, 1981; STAFF MICROBIOLOGIST VIROL, WELLESLEY HOSP, UNIV TORONTO, 1978-; lectr, Dept Med Microbiol, Univ Toronto, 1978-1981; lectr genetics, Dept Biol, McGill Univ & fel virol, Dept Microbiol, Royal Victoria Hosp, 1975-1978. **Memberships:** Am Soc Microbiol; Pan Am Group Rapid Viral Diag; NY Acad Sci. **Research Statement & Publications:** Pathogenesis and diagnosis of viral infections of the lower respiratory tract in immunocompromised adults. **Mailing Address:** Dept Microbiol Wellesley Hosp, 160 Wellesley St E, Toronto, ON M4Y 1J3, Can.

KASVINSKY, PETER JOHN, ENZYME REGULATION, CALCIUM CONTROL. **Personal Data:** b Bridgeport, Conn, December 7, 1942; m 1974, c 2. **Education:** Bucknell Univ, BSc, 1964; Univ Vt, PhD (biochem), 1970. **Professional Experience:** DEAN GRAD STUDIES, YOUNGSTOWN STATE UNIV, as of 2005; DIR RES DEVELOP & GRAD STUDIES, SCH MED, 1988-; dir res develop, Sch Med, 1986-1988; assoc prof biochem, marshall Univ 1982-; adj assoc prof biomed sci, WVa Univ, beginning 1982; prin investr, NIH grants, 1981; adj asst prof, 1980-1982; asst prof, Sch Med, 1979-1982; instr, dept biochem, 1977-1979; sr res assoc biochem, Univ Alta, 1974-1979; instr biochem, Sch Med, Wayne State Univ, 1972-1974; radiol control officer, US Army Aeromed Res Lab, 1970-1972; Biochemist, US Army Aeromed Res Lab, 1969-1972. **Memberships:** Am Chem Soc; AAAS; Can Biochem Soc; Am Soc Biol Chemists; Sigma Xi; Nat Coun Univ res Admin. **Research Statement & Publications:** Enzymology of covalent modification of proteins, enzyme regulation, structure function and allosteric control, especially as applied to the regulation of enzymes of glycogen metabolism. **Mailing Address:** Dept Sch Grad Studies & Res, Youngstown State Univ, Tod Hall Rm 359 One Univ Plaza, Youngstown, OH 44555. **Fax:** 330-742-1580. **E-Mail:** amgrad03@ysub.ysu.edu

KASZNIAK, ALFRED WAYNE, NEUROSCIENCE. **Personal Data:** b Chicago, Ill, June 2, 1949; m 1973, Mary; c Jesse & Elizabeth. **Education:** Univ Ill, BS, 1970, MA, 1973, PhD, 1976. **Professional Experience:** HEAD PSYCHOL, UNIV ARIZ, as of 2003; Mem bd gov, Int Neuropsychol Soc, 1994; actg head, Dept Psychol, 1992-1993; chmn, Comn on Geront, Univ Ariz, 1990-1993; Ariz Gov Adv Comt on Alzheimers Dis, 1988-1992; PROF PSYCHOL, DEPT NEUROL & PSYCHIAT, UNIV ARIZ COL MED, 1987-; mem, Vet Admin Geriat & Geront Adv Comt, 1986-1989; grantee, Robert Wood Johnson Found, 1986-1989; grantee, Nat Inst Ment Health, 1984-1994; assoc prof, Dept Psychol & Psychiat, 1982-1987; mem, Human Develop & Aging Study Sect, Div Res Grants, NIH, 1981-1986; mem med & sci adv bd, Nat Alzheimers Dis & Related Disorders Asn, 1981-1984; trustee, Southern Ariz Chap, Nat Multiple Sclerosis Soc, 1980-1982; mem med adv bd, Fan Kane Fund for Brain-injured Children, Tucson, 1980-1982; res fel, Geront Soc, 1980; Univ Hosp, Tucson, 1979-; from asst prof to assoc prof, Dept Psychiat, 1979-1982; Grantee, Nat Inst Aging, 1978-1983 & 1989-1994; staff psychologist, Presby-St Lukes Hosp, 1976-1979; asst prof, Dept Psychol, 1976-1979; instr, Dept Psychol, Rush Med Col, Chicago, 1974-1976; dir & coordr, Clin Neuropsychol Prog. **Research Statement & Publications:** Author of 3 books and various articles. **Mailing Address:** Dept Psychol Univ Ariz, Rm 312 Psychol Bldg, Tucson, AZ 85721. **E-Mail:** kaszniak@u.arizona.edu

KATAPODES, NICHOLAS D, ENVIRONMENTAL ENGINEERING. **Education:** Aristotle Univ, BS, 1972; Univ Calif, MS, 1974, PhD, 1977. **Professional Experience:** PROF, DEPT CIVIL & ENVIRON ENG, UNIV MICH, MICH, as of 2005. **Mailing Address:** Dept Civil & Environ Eng, Univ Mich 121 EWRE, Ann Arbor, MI 48109-2125. **Fax:** 734-763-2275. **E-Mail:** ndk@umich.edu

KATARIA, YASH P, PULMONARY DISEASES, INTERNAL MEDICINE. **Personal Data:** b 1936. **Education:** Glancy Med Col, India, MD, 1959; Liverpool Sch Med, Eng, DTM & H, 1963; Welsh Nat Sch Med, Univ Wales, DTCD, 1965; FRCP, 1979. **Professional Experience:** DIR, SARCOIDOSIS CLIN, E CAROLINA UNIV SCH MED, as of 2004; med dir, Spec Servs, 1988; med dir, Respiratory Ther, 1988-; VCHMN DEPT MED, E CAROLINA

UNIV SCH MED, 1987-; actg chmn dept med, E Carolina Univ Sch Med, 1986-1987; PROF INTERNAL MED, E CAROLINA UNIV SCH MED, 1982-; sect head pulmonary div, E Carolina Univ Sch Med, 1978-; assoc prof, E Carolina Univ Sch Med, 1978-1982; from instr to asst prof med & pulmonary dis, Col Med, Ohio State Univ, 1972-1978; assoc med, Chicago Med Sch, 1970-1971; registr, Welsh Nat Sch Med, 1967-1969. **Memberships:** Fel Am Col Chest Physicians; Am Lung Asn; NY Acad Sci; Am Fedn Clin Res; AMA; Sigma Xi. **Research Statement & Publications:** Clinical and immunologic aspects of sarcoidosis exploring its pathogenesis and etiology; immunologic work involves studies of peripheral blood and bronchoalveolar lavage (BAL), T and B-cell quantitation; examination of sarcoidal granuloma for its cellular components and production of lymphokines, etc; production of Kreim antigen from auto logous BAL cells. **Mailing Address:** Dept Int Med & Pulmonary Dis, E Carolina Univ, 600 Moye Blvd, Greenville, NC 27858. **Fax:** 252-744-4887.

KATAYAMA, DANIEL HIDEO, MOLECULAR SPECTROSCOPY. **Personal Data:** b Honolulu, Hawaii, September 26, 1939; m 1963. **Education:** Univ Hawaii, BS, 1962, MS, 1964; Tufts Univ, PhD (physics), 1970. **Professional Experience:** Mass Inst Tech, Cambridge, 1980-1982; vis scientist, Bell Lab, Murray Hill, NJ, 1978-1979; PHYSICIST, AIR FORCE GEOPHYS LAB, 1971-; physicist solid state physics, Gillette Co, 1970-1971; physicist aeronomy, Air Force Cambridge Res Lab, 1963-1966. **Memberships:** AAAS; Am Phys Soc; Optical Soc Am. **Research Statement & Publications:** Laser induced fluorescence of molecules and ions; absorption-photoionization cross sections and spectroscopy of atmospheric gases in vacuum ultraviolet; phonon scattering in solids; elastic constants of materials. **Mailing Address:** 1525 Ohialoke St, Honolulu, HI 96821.

KATAYAMA, ROBERT W, AGRICULTURE. **Education:** Concordia Col, BA; NDak Univ, MS & PhD. **Professional Experience:** ADJ PROF, DEPT AGR, UNIV ARK, as of 2005. **Mailing Address:** Dept Entomol, Univ Ark, 1200 No Univ Dr Mail Slot 4913, Pine Bluff, AR 71601. **Fax:** 870-543-8543. **E-Mail:** katayama_r@vx4500.uapb.edu

KATCHEN, BERNARD, BIOCHEMISTRY. **Personal Data:** b New York, NY, May 20, 1928; m 1951, c 2. **Education:** City Col NY BS, 1949; Ohio State Univ, MSc, 1951; NY Univ, PhD (biochem), 1956. **Professional Experience:** RETIRED; prin scientist, Schering Corp, 1962-1991; sr chemist, Nat Cash Register, 1956-1961; chemist, Clairol Inc, 1954-1956. **Memberships:** AAAS; Am Chem Soc; NY Acad Sci. **Research Statement & Publications:** Pharmacokinetics; drug metabolism; biopharmaceutics. **Mailing Address:** 1271 Sand Castle Rd, Sanibel, FL 33957-3616.

KATCHER, DAVID ABRAHAM, writing & editing; deceased, see previous edition for last biography

KATCHMAN, ARTHUR, ORGANIC CHEMISTRY. **Personal Data:** b New York, NY, October 4, 1924; m 1960, Evelyn R Silver; c Ross N & Scott J. **Education:** NY Univ, BA, 1949; Polytech Inst Brooklyn, PhD (chem), 1956. **Professional Experience:** RETIRED; mgr, Mat & Automation Develop, 1987-1990; mgr, Anal Chem, 1984-1986; mgr, Div Qual Assurance, 1981-1984; mgr opers control & planning, Plastics Dept, 1980-1981; mgr chem develop, Plastics Dept, 1976-1979; mgr prod develop, Plastics Dept, 1970-1975; mgr advan res, Plastics Dept, 1968-1970; mgr polymer chem, Chem Develop Oper, 1966-1968; mgr mat physics & chem, Capacitor Dept, 1963-1966; res assoc, Gen Elec Res Lab, Gen Elec Co, 1959-1962; Hooker fel, 1957-1958; res assoc, Polytech Inst Brooklyn, 1957-1958; res chemist, Hooker Chem Co, 1955-1956; assoc, NY Med Col, 1952-1954; instr, NY Med Col, 1950-1952; Asst instr biochem, NY Med Col, 1949-1950. **Memberships:** Am Chem Soc; Sigma Xi. **Research Statement & Publications:** Mechanism and kinetics of polymerization; polymer structure and properties; stereospecific polymerization. **Mailing Address:** 6904 Country Lakes Circle, Sarasota, FL 34243-3803.

KATEKARU, JAMES, ANALYTICAL CHEMISTRY, NUCLEAR CHEMISTRY. **Personal Data:** b Kauai, Hawaii, June 10, 1935; m 1964, c 2. **Education:** Univ Ore, BS, 1956; Univ Ariz, MS, 1961; Univ Cincinnati, PhD (chem), 1965. **Professional Experience:** PROF EMER, CALIF POLYTECH STATE UNIV, SAN LUIS OBISPO, as of 2006; prof chem, Calif Polytech State Univ, San Luis Obispo, beginning 1980; Res consult, Trapelo West Div, Lab Electronics, 1970-1971; from asst prof to assoc prof, Calif Polytech State Univ, 1969-1980; res mgr, Naval Radiol Defense Lab, 1967-1969; index ed, Chem Abstr Serv, 1966-1967; res chemist, Rocketdyne Div, NAm Rockwell, 1965-1966; Anal chemist, Food & Drug Admin, 1962-1963. **Memberships:** Am Chem Soc; Am Inst Physics. **Research Statement & Publications:** Solvent extraction; polarography; rocket exhaust product analysis; catalysis of non-hypergollic propellant combinations; nuclear fallout phenomenology; detection and diagnosis of nuclear weapons. **Mailing Address:** Dept Chem & Biochem, Coll Arts & Sci, Calif Polytech State Univ, San Luis Obispo, CA 93407. **E-Mail:** jkatekar@calpoly.edu

KATEN, PAUL C, MICROMETEOROLOGY, AIR POLLUTION. **Personal Data:** b Lawrence, Mass, February 7, 1943; m 1968. **Education:** Lowell Technol Inst, BS, 1964; Trinity Col, MS, 1968; Colo State Univ, PhD (atmospheric sci), 1977. **Professional Experience:** STAFF MEM, KPS ASSOC, as of 2004; CONSULT, 1985-; exp scientist, Div Environ Mech, Commonwealth Sci & Indust Res Orgn, Canberra, Australia, 1984-1985; res assoc, Dept Atmospheric Sci, Ore State Univ, 1977-1984; test engr, Pratt & Whitney Aircraft, 1964-1969. **Memberships:** Am Meteorol Soc; Am Geophys Union; Air Pollution Control Asn. **Research Statement & Publications:** Instrumentation development with recent applications to the dry-deposition of gases and particles; micrometeorology; turbulence; indoor air pollution; industrial hygiene; wind power resource assessment. **Mailing Address:** KPS Assoc, Otis, OR 97368. **E-Mail:** paul-c-katen@worldnet.att.net

KATER, STANLEY B, NEUROSCIENCES. **Personal Data:** b Cleveland, Ohio, June 12, 1943; div, c 1. **Education:** Case Western Reserve Univ, BA, 1965; Univ Va, PhD (biol), 1968. **Honors & Awards:** Alexander Von Humboldt res scientist award. **Professional Experience:** RES PROF, NEUROBIOLOGY & ANAT, UNIV UTAH, as of 2006; prof Neurobiology & Anat, Sch Med, Univ Utah, beginning 1995; prof anat & neurobiology, Colo State Univ, 1990-1995; from asst prof to prof zoology, Univ Iowa, 1979-1990; NIH fel biol, Univ Ore, 1968-1969; Javits Neuroscience investr award, NIH sponsored res. **Memberships:** AAAS; Soc Neuroscience. **Research Statement & Publications:** Developmental neurobiology; control of neuronal growth cores. **Mailing Address:** Univ Utah, Sch Med, 50 N Medical Dr Rm No 527 Wintrobe Bldg, Salt Lake City, UT 84132. **E-Mail:** stanley.kater@hsc.utah.edu

KATES, JOSEF, SCIENCE POLICY, SYSTEMS SCIENCE. **Personal Data:** b Vienna, Austria, May 5, 1921; Canadian citizen; m 1944, c 4. **Education:** Univ Toronto, BA, 1948, MA, 1949, PhD (physics), 1951. **Honorary Degrees:** LLD, Concordia Univ, Can, 1981. **Professional Experience:** PRES, JOSEF KATES ASSOCS INC, 1974-; emer chancellor, Univ Waterloo, 1993-; chancellor, Univ Waterloo, 1979-1985; chmn, Teleride Sage Corp, 1978-; chmn, Sci Coun Can, 1975-1978; assoc, Kates, Peat, Marwick & Co, 1969-1973; mem, Sci Coun Can, 1968-1974; pres, Setak Comput Servs Co, 1967-; dep managing partner, Kates, Peat, Marwick & Co, 1967-1968; pres, KCS Ltd & Traffic Res Corp, 1954-1966; res engr, Univ Toronto, 1948-1954; proj engr, Rogers Electronic Tubes, 1944-1948; supvr, Imp Optical Co, 1942-1944. **Memberships:** Inst Mgt Sci; Can Oper Res Soc; fel Eng Inst Can; Sci Eng & Technol Community Can; fel Inst Mgt Consult. **Research Statement & Publications:** Application of scientific methods, especially computers and operations research to industrial, scientific and engineering problems particular to transportation and planning applications. **Mailing Address:** 3 Silverdale Crescent, North York, ON M3A 3G9, Can.

KATES, MORRIS, LIPID CHEMISTRY, BIOMEMBRANES LIPIDMETABOLISM. **Personal Data:** b Galati, Roumania, September 30, 1923; Canadian citizen; m 1957, Pirkko; c Anna L, Marja & Ilona. **Education:** Univ Toronto, BA, 1945, MA, 1946, PhD (biochem), 1948. **Honors & Awards:** Supelco Award Lipid Res, Am Oil Chemists' Soc, 1984; R A Morton Lectr, Biochem Soc London, 1994. **Professional Experience:** PROF EMER BIOCHEM, UNIV OTTAWA, as of 2003; Kansai Med Sch & Kinki Univ, Osaka, Japan, 1985; chmn dept, Univ Ottawa, 1982-1985; staff res lectr, Univ Ottawa, 1981; vdean res, Univ Ottawa, 1978-1982; Obihiro Univ, Japan, 1975 & 1985; vis prof, Univ Helsinki, 1975; co-ed, Can J Biochem, 1974-1984; prof biochem, Univ Ottawa, 1969-1989; prof chem, Univ Ottawa, 1968-1969; sr res officer, Div Appl Biol, 1961-1968; vis scientist, Nat Inst Med Res, London, Eng, 1959-1960; assoc res officer, Div Appl Biol, 1955-1961; asst res officer, Div Appl Biol, 1951-1955; Nat Res Labs fel, Nat Res Coun Can, 1949-1951; asst, Banting & Best Med Res, 1948-1949. **Memberships:** Am Chem Soc; Am Soc Biol Chem; Can Biochem Soc; Brit Biochem Soc; Royal Soc Can; Am Oil Chemists' Soc. **Research Statement & Publications:** Synthesis of lecithins and related compounds; structure of the alkaloid, gelsemine; plant lecithinases and plant phospholipids; glycerides; lipases; bacterial lipids; phospholipid desaturases; biosynthesis of phospholipids; diphytanyl glycerol ether lipids; glycolipids. **Mailing Address:** Dept Biochem, Univ Ottawa, 550 Cumberland, Ottawa, ON K1N 6N5, Can. **Fax:** 613-562-5191. **E-Mail:** mkates@oreo.uottawa.ca

KATES, ROBERT, LONG TERM POPULATION DYNAMICS, GLOBAL ENVIRONMENTAL CHANGE & SUSTAINABILITY OF BIOSPHERE. **Personal Data:** b Brooklyn, NY, January 31, 1929; m 1948, c 3. **Education:** Univ Chicago, MA, 1958, PhD (geog), 1962. **Honorary Degrees:** DSc, Clark Univ, 1993. **Honors & Awards:** Nat Medal Sci, 1991; Honors Award, Asn Am Geographers. **Professional Experience:** DIR EMER, WORLD HUNGER PROG, as of 2005; vice-chmn, bd sustainable develop, Nat Res Coun, 1995-; PROF EMER, BROWN UNIV, 1993-; mem, Comt Global Change, 1989-1992; univ prof & dir, Alan Shawn Feinstein World Hunger Prog, 1986-1993; mem, Nat Coun, Fedn Am Scientists & Bd Sci & Technol Int Develop, Nat Res Coun, 1986-1989; fel distinguished scholar exchange, Comt Scholarly Common People's Rep China, 1985; mem bd dirs, Comt Prob & Policy, Social Sci Res Coun & Comt Int Appl Syst Anal, Am Acad Arts & Sci, 1982; res prof, Ctr Technol, Environ & Develop, Clark Univ, 1981-1987; Mac Arthur Prize fel, 1981-1985; mem, Comn Human Rights, NAS, 1979-1985; fel, Woodrow Wilson Int Ctr Scholars, 1979; chmn, Comn Human Rights, NAS, 1976-1979; univ prof, Clark Univ, 1974-1980; from asst prof to prof, Grad Sch Geog, Clark Univ, 1962-1987; sr fel, econs & environ, H John Heinz III Ctr Sci; fac assoc, Col Atlantic; distinguished scientist, George Perkins Morse Inst, Clark Univ; dir, Bur Resource Assessment Land Use Planning, Univ Col, Dar Es Salaam, Tanzania. **Memberships:** Nat Acad Sci; Asn Am Geographers (pres, 1993-1994); fel AAAS; Fedn Am Sci; Am Acad Arts & Sci; Acad Europ. **Research Statement & Publications:** The prevalance and persistence of hunger; long term population dynamics; sustainability of the biosphere, climate impact assessment; theory of the human environment; author of many books on hunger, environment and technology. **Mailing Address:** Brown Univ, Providence, RI 02912. **E-Mail:** robert_kates@brown.edu

KATH, WILLIAM LAWRENCE, NONLINEAR WAVE PROPAGATION, COMPUTATIONAL NEUROSCIENCE. **Personal Data:** b Pasadena, Calif, June 23, 1957; m 1984. **Education:** Mass Inst Technol, SB, 1978; Calif Inst Technol, PhD (appl math), 1981. **Honors & Awards:** Presidential Young Investr, NSF, 1985-1990. **Professional Experience:** PROF ENG SCI & APPL MATH, McCORMICK SCH ENG, NORTHWESTERN UNIV, 1997-; CO-DIR, NORTHWESTERN INST COMPLEX SYST, as of 2005; from asst prof eng sci & appl math to assoc prof eng sci & appl math, Northwestern Univ, 1984-1996; Von Karman instr, Calif Inst Technol, 1982-1984; NSF res fel, Calif Inst Technol, 1981-1982. **Memberships:** Soc Indust & Appl Math; Optical Soc Am; Inst Elec & Electronics Engrs; Soc Neuroscience. **Research Statement & Publications:** Modeling of linear and nonlinear wave propagation in optical fibers; computational neuroscience. **Mailing Address:** ESAM, McCormick Sch Eng, Northwestern Univ, 2145 Sheridan Rd, Evanston, IL 60208-3125. **Fax:** 847-491-2178. **E-Mail:** kath@northwestern.edu

KATHAN, RALPH HERMAN, CLINICAL BIOCHEMISTRY. **Personal Data:** b Chicago, Ill, February 1, 1929; m 1993, Dorothy; c Arthur E & Kathryn (Elston). **Education:** Univ Chicago, SB, 1949; Univ Ill, MS, 1959, PhD (biochem), 1961. **Professional Experience:** RETIRED; chmn, Div Biochem, Cook Co Hosp, 1971-1991; assoc prof biol chem, Col Med, Univ Ill, 1968-1991; consult comn influenza, Armed Forces Epidemiol Bd, 1964-1968; asst prof, Col Med, Univ Ill, 1962-1968; res assoc, Col Med, Univ Ill, 1961-1962; res asst, Col Med, Univ Ill, 1957-1961; tech serv, Am Can Co, 1956-1957; biochemist res labs, Kraft Foods Div, Nat Dairy Prod Corp, 1949-1951; res asst biol chem, Univ Chicago, 1948-1949. **Memberships:** Nat Acad Clin Biochemists; Am Soc Biol Chem; Am Asn Clin Chem. **Research Statement & Publications:** Protein structure; mechanisms of viral infection; bacterial metabolism; carbohydrate absorption; plasma expanders; diagnostic biochemistry. **Mailing Address:** 38 W 086 Glenoak Lane, St Charles, IL 60175. **E-Mail:** ralphkathan@aol.com

KATHARIOU, SOPHIA, STUDY OF BACTERIAL PATHOGENESIS, SURFACE ANTIGENS OF BACTERIA. **Personal Data:** b Assos Corinth, Greece, January 1, 1954; m 1989, Edward; c Atif & Stefan. **Education:** Austin Col, BA, 1975; Univ Calif, Berkeley, PhD (genetics), 1981. **Professional Experience:** Mem grad fac, Dept Food Sci & Human Nutrit, 1993-; mem grad fac, Cell, Molecular & Neuroscience Prog, Univ Hawaii, 1990-; ASSOC PROF MICROBIOL, UNIV HAWAII, 1990-; guest researcher, Ctr Dis Control, 1988-1990; res assoc, Cornell Univ, 1981-1983; res assoc Univ Wuerzburg, 1984-1988. **Memberships:** Am Soc Microbiol; AAAS; Sigma Xi. **Research Statement & Publications:** Expression of bacterial virulence factors and surface antigens; involvement of temperature in gene expression; bacterial growth and gene expression at low temperatures. **Mailing Address:** Univ Hawaii 2538 Mall, Honolulu, HI 96822. **Fax:** 808-956-5339. **E-Mail:** ksophia@hawaii.edu

KATHMAN, R DEEDEE, TARDIGRADOLOGY, FRESHWATER POLLUTION ASSESSMENT. **Personal Data:** b Stamford, NY, April 16, 1948; m 1985. **Education:** State Univ NY, Oswego, BA, 1970; Tenn Technol Univ, MS, 1981; Univ Victoria, BC, PhD, 1989. **Professional Experience:** UNIV VICTORIA, BC, 1984-; regional dir environ conserv, EVS Consult, Ltd, 1981-1984; proj mgr environ conserv, AWARE Corp, 1978-1981; biologist environ conserv, LMS Engrs Inc, 1973-; technician, Weather Observ, Lake Ont Environ Lab, 1972-1973. **Memberships:** Int Asn Meiobenthologists; Am Micros Soc; NAm Benthological Soc; Sigma Xi. **Research Statement & Publications:** Taxonomy, ecology, evolution and distribution of tardigrades; taxonomy and ecology of oligochaetes and chironomid larvae; freshwater benthic taxonomy and ecology; freshwater pollution assessment. **Mailing Address:** 4256 Warren Rd, Franklin, TN 37064.

KATHOLI, CHARLES ROBINSON, BIOMATHEMATICS. **Personal Data:** b Charleston, WVa, January 2, 1941; m 1980, c 1. **Education:** Lehigh Univ, BA, 1963; Adelphi Univ, MS, 1965, PhD (math, appl anal), 1970. **Professional Experience:** PROF BIOSTATISTICS, UNIV ALA, BIRMINGHAM, as of 2004; assoc prof biomath, Univ Ala, Birmingham, beginning 1977; asst prof info sci, Univ Ala, Birmingham, 1973-1976; asst prof biomath, Univ Ala, Birmingham, 1970-1977; instr, Adelphi Univ, 1967-1970; instr math, Suffolk County Community Col, 1966-1967; asst, Adelphi Univ, 1964-1966. **Memberships:** AAAS; Soc Indust & Appl Math; NY Acad Sci; Asn Comput Mach; Acoust Soc Am; Sigma Xi. **Research Statement & Publications:** Mathematical modelling and computer simulations in the field of cardiovascular research; computational methods for special functions. **Mailing Address:** 315 Poinciana Dr, Birmingham, AL 35209-4127. **E-Mail:** ckatholi@uab.edu

KATHREN, RONALD LAURENCE, RADIOBIOLOGY, ENVIRONMENTAL ENGINEERING. **Personal Data:** b Windsor, Ont, June 6, 1937; American citizen; m 1964, Susan; c SallyBeth & Daniel. **Education:** Univ Calif, Los Angeles, BS, 1957; Univ Pittsburgh, MS, 1962; Univ Calif, Berkley, MS, 1964; Am Bd Health Physics, dipl, 1966; Am Acad Environ Eng, dipl, 1978; Soc Radiol Protection, cert appl health physics, 1985; Am Bd Med Physics, dipl, 1989. **Honors & Awards:** Elda E Anderson Award, Health Physics Soc, 1977, Founders Award, 1985; Arthur Humm Award, Nat Registry Radiation Protection Technologists, 1988; Hartman Orator & Medallist, Radiol Centennial, 1995. **Professional Experience:** Affil staff scientist, Pac NW Nat Lab, 1996-; chmn, Nat Coun Radiation Protection & Measurements, Sci Comt SC-1 Collective Dose, 1993-1994; PROF & DIR, US TRANSURANIUM & URANIUM REGISTRIES, WASH STATE UNIV, 1992-; ed, Radiation Pro Dosimetry, 1991-1993; chmn, SC 1-3 Comt Collective Dose, 1990-; dir res, US Transuranium & Uranium Registries, 1990-1992; dir, US Transuranium & Uranium Registries, 1989-1992; int adv bd, J Radiation Protection, 1988-; mem, Comt Film Badge Dosimetry, Nat Res Coun, 1988-1989; pres, Health Physics Soc 1988-1990; US adv comt Nuclear Wastes, 1988-; lectr, Wash State Univ, 1987-; dir, Health Physics, Hanford Environ Health Found, 1987-1989; affil prof, Tri-Cities Univ Ctr, Univ Wash, 1986-1987; bd dir, Am Acad Health Physics, 1985-1986; bd dir, US Transuranium & Uranium Registries, 1984-1987; secy-treas, Am Bd Health Physics, 1984; mem, Nat Coun Radiation Protection & Measurements Task Force Alarm & Access Control Systs, 1983-; mem, Am Bd Health Physics, 1982-1984; coordr radiol sci, Tri-Cities Univ Ctr, Univ Wash, 1980-1982; consult, US Adv Comt Reactor Safeguards, 1978-; affil assoc prof, Tri-Cities Univ Ctr, Univ Wash, 1978-1995; staff scientist, PAC Northwest Div, Battelle Mem Inst, 1978-1987; mem panel examr, Am Bd Health Physics, 1978-1980; consult, US Nuclear Regulatory Comn, 1978; mem, Radiation Adv Comt, 1977-1978; consult, Int Atomic Energy Agency tech expert, 1977; ed, Health Physics J, Health Physics Soc, 1976-1980; mem, Nat Adv Comt Nuclear Technicians, Tech Educ Res Ctr, 1975-1981; health physicist, Reed Col, 1973-1978; mem, Traineeship Adv Comt, US AEC, 1973-1974; corp health physicist, Portland Gen Elec Co, 1972-1978; adj prof, Ore State Div Continuing Educ, 1972-1977; lectr, Tri-Cities Univ Ctr, Univ Wash, 1971-1972; sect mgr & sr res scientist radiation dosimetry, Pac Northwest Div, Battelle Mem Inst, 1967-1972; abstractor, Chem Abstr, 1962-1978; physicist health, Lawrence Radiation Lab, Univ Calif, 1962-1967; supvr health physicist, Mare Island Naval Shipyard, USN, 1959-1961. **Memberships:** Fel Health Physics Soc; Am Asn Physicists Med; AAAS; fel Soc Radiol Protection; Am Acad Health Physics (pres-elect, 1997 & pres, 1998); Sigma Xi; Health Physics Soc (pres-elect, 1988-1989). **Research Statement & Publications:** Biokinetics and dosimetry of actinides; applied health physics; radiological dosimetry; environmental radioactivity; history of radiation protection and physics. **Mailing Address:** Wash State Univ at Tri-Cities, 2710 Univ Dr, Richland, WA 99354-1651. **Fax:** 509-375-5643. **E-Mail:** rkathren@tricity.wsu.edu

KATKANANT, VANVILAI, PHYSICS. **Education:** E Tex State Univ, MS, 1979; Univ Nebr, Lincoln, PhD, 1983. **Professional Experience:** PROF & CHAIR, DEPT PYHSICS, CALIF STATE UNIV, as of 2006. **Mailing Address:** Dept Physics, Calif State Univ, 2345 E San Ramon Ave, Fresno, CA 93740-0037. **Fax:** 209-278-2118. **E-Mail:** vanvilai@zimmer.CSUFresno.EDU

KATO, IKUNOSHIN, PROTEIN CHEMISTRY. **Education:** Univ Osaka, Japan, PhD (biochem), 1969. **Professional Experience:** PROTEIN CHEMIST, CENTOCOR, INC, 1983-. **Research Statement & Publications:** Sequencing of protein; monoclonal antibody. **Mailing Address:** Takara Shuzo Co 3-4-1, SETA, Otsu Shiga 520-21, Japan. **Fax:** 817-754-32312.

KATO, SUSUMU, ATMOSPHERIC PHYSICS. **Personal Data:** b Saitama, August 27, 1928; m Kyoko-Kojo. **Education:** Kyoto Univ, PhD. **Honors & Awards:** Tanakadate Prize, 1959; Yamaji Sci Prize, 1974; Appleton Prize, 1987; Hasegawa Prize, 1987; Fujiware Prize, 1989; Japan Acad Award, 1989. **Professional Experience:** Emer prof, Radio Atmospheric Sci Ctr, 1992-; VIS PROF, BANDUNG INST TECHNOL, INDONESIA, 1992-; VCHMN, JAPAN-INDONESIA SCI & TECH FORUM, 1992-; dir & prof, Radio Atmospheric Sci Ctr, 1981-1992; vis prof, Dept Meteorol, Univ Calif, Los Angeles, 1973-1974; prof, Ionosphere Res Lab, 1967-1981; Vis scientist, High Altitude Observ, Nat Ctr Atmospheric Res, 1967-1968 & 1973-1974; assoc prof, Ionosphere Res Lab, 1964-1967; res officer, Upper Atmosphere Sect, Commonwealth Sci & Indust Res Orgn, 1962-1964; asst prof, Ionosphere Res Lab, 1961-1962; Lectr, Fac Eng, Kyoto Univ, Osaka Univ, 1955-1961. **Memberships:** Nat Acad Eng. **Research Statement & Publications:** Atmospheric tidal theory; observation of atmospheric waves. **Mailing Address:** 22-15 Fujimidai Otsu, Shiga Prefecture 520, Japan.

KATO, WALTER YONEO, REACTOR SAFETY. **Personal Data:** b Chicago, Ill, August 19, 1924; m 1953, Anna Kurata; c Norman S, Cathryn J & Barbara J. **Education:** Haverford Col, BS, 1946; Univ Ill, MS, 1949; Pa State Col, PhD (physics), 1954. **Honors & Awards:** Order of Sacred Treasure, 3rd Class, Japanese Govt, 1993. **Professional Experience:** RES AFFIL, DEPT NUCLEAR ENG, MASS INST TECHNOL, as of 2002; sr scientist, Dept Advan Technol, Brookhaven Nat Lab, beginning 1993; sr scientist, Dept Nuclear Energy, 1991-1993; chmn, Dept Nuclear Energy, 1988-1991; dept chmn, Brookhaven Nat Lab, 1980-1988; assoc chmn & sr nuclear engr, Brookhaven Nat Lab, 1975-1980; consult, Off Nuclear Regulatory Res, Nuclear Regulatory Comn, 1974-1985; vis prof nuclear eng, Univ Mich, 1974-1975; sr physicist, Appl Physics Div, 1969-1975; sr physicist, Fast Reactor Exps Sect, 1968-1975; head, Fast Reactor Exps Sect, 1963-1970; assoc physicist, Reactor Physics Div, 1963-1968; Fulbright res scholar, Japan Atomic Energy Res Inst & Univ Tokyo, 1958-1959; assoc physicist, Reactor Eng Div, 1953-1963; asst physicist nuclear & reactor physics, Argonne Nat Lab, 1953; jr res assoc neutron physics, Brookhaven Nat Lab, 1952-1953; Res assoc hydrodyn, Ord Res Lab, Sch Eng, Pa State Col, 1949-1952. **Memberships:** AAAS; Am Phys Soc; fel Am Nuclear Soc. **Research Statement & Publications:** Hydrodynamics; cavitation studies; neutron resonance phenomenon; neutron total cross section measurements; neutron inelastic scattering studies; reactor physics; critical assembly experiments; fast reactor physics and safety; reactor safety research. **Mailing Address:** Dept Nuclear Eng, Mass Inst Technol, Cambridge, MA 02139.

KATO, YASUSHI, BIOMATERIALS, BIOMEDICAL ENGINEERING. **Personal Data:** b Tokyo, Japan, 1963. **Education:** Cornell Univ, BS, 1985; Rutgers Univ, PhD (biomed eng), 1991. **Professional Experience:** SR RES ENGR ARTIFICIAL INTERNAL ORGANS, CORVITA CORP, 1991-. **Memberships:** Soc Biomat; Am Soc Artificial Internal Organs. **Mailing Address:** 45 Barbour Pond Dr, Wayne, NJ 07470.

KATOCS, ANDREW STEPHEN, HYPERTENSION, ULTRASOUND. **Personal Data:** b Passaic, NJ, October 7, 1944; m 1967, c 2. **Education:** Rutgers Univ, BPh & BS, 1967; Marquette Univ, PhD (pharmacol), 1972. **Professional Experience:** SR RES PHARMACOLOGIST HYPERTENSION, LEDERLE LABS, AM CYANAMID CO, 1989-; sr res pharmacologist osteo-arthritis, Lederle Labs, Am Cyanamid CO, 1986-1989; sr res pharmacologist atherosclerosis, Lederle Labs, Am Cyanamid CO, 1973-1984; Nat Heart & Lung Inst fel & instr pharmacol, Sch Med, Ind Univ, 1972-1973. **Memberships:** Am Heart Asn; Am Soc Pharmacol & Exp Therapeut. **Research Statement & Publications:** Development of animal models of atherosclerosis; evaluation of compounds for anti-atherosclerotic activity; real-time ultrasonic imaging of arterial vasculature; development of animal models for the evaluation of compounds for anti osteo-arthritic activity; tissue culture; receptor binding assay. **Mailing Address:** Am Cyanamid Co, Med Res Div, Lederle Labs, Pearl River, NY 10965-1299.

KATOH, ARTHUR, DEVELOPMENTAL BIOLOGY. **Personal Data:** b Honolulu, Hawaii, August 24, 1933; m 1963, Dorothy Kurashige; c Ara, Austin & Ann. **Education:** Syracuse Univ, AB, 1954; Univ Ill, MS, 1956, PhD (zool), 1960; Univ Pittsburgh, MPH, 1986. **Professional Experience:** DIR, DIV NUCLEAR PATH & ONCOL, MERCY HOSP, 1973-; dir oncol lab, Dept Radiother, 1966-1973; res assoc, Argonne Nat Lab, 1963-1966; asst prof biol, Univ Toledo, 1962-1963; res assoc zool, Univ Ill, 1961-1962; NSF fel, 1960-1961. **Memberships:** Soc Develop Biol; NY Acad Sci; Am Soc Cell Biol; Am Asn Cancer Res; Metastasis Res Soc. **Research Statement & Publications:** Developmental biology; cellular differentiation in amphibian and chick embryos; cancer metastasis. **Mailing Address:** Div Nuclear Path & Oncol, Mercy Hosp, Pittsburgh, PA 15219.

KATONA, PETER GEZA, BIOMEDICAL CONTROL SYSTEMS. **Personal Data:** b Budapest, Hungary, June 25, 1937; American citizen; m 1966, Jaroslava; c Andrew & Catherine. **Education:** Univ Mich, BS, 1960; Mass Inst Technol, SM, 1962, ScD(elec eng), 1965. **Honors & Awards:** Alexander von Humboldt Sr US Scientist Award, 1987. **Professional Experience:** PRES & CHIEF EXEC OFFICER, WHITAKER FOUND, 2000-; vpres, Whitaker Found, beginning 1991; prog dir bioeng, NSF, 1989-1991; vis scientist, Univ Heidelberg, WGer, 1987-1988; chmn dept, Case Western Res Univ, 1980-1987; prof, Case Western Res Univ, 1978-1991; Fogarty sr int fel, 1978-1979; assoc prof biomed eng, Case Western Res Univ, 1969-1978; Mass Gen Hosp, Boston, 1966-1969; Ford res fel, 1965-1967; consult, Biosysts, Inc, Mass, 1965-1967; From instr to asst prof elec eng, Mass Inst Technol, 1963-1969; fel Cardiovasc Sect, Am Physiol Soc. **Memberships:** Fel AAAS; Inst Elec & Electronics Engrs; Biomed Eng Soc (pres, 1984-1985); Am Physiol Soc; Am Soc Eng Educ; fel Am Inst Med & Biomed Eng. **Research Statement & Publications:** Administration of research grant programs; neural control of the cardiovascular system; interaction of cardiovascular and respiratory control mechanisms; automated control of drug infusion. **Mailing Address:** Whitaker Fedn, 1700 N Moore St Ste 2200, Rosslyn, VA 22209. **E-Mail:** katona@whitaker.org

KATOPODES, NIKOLAOS D, CIVIL ENGINEERING. **Education:** Aristotle Univ Greece, BS, 1972; Univ Calif, Davis, MS, 1974, PhD, 1977. **Honors & Awards:** James A Robbins Award, Chi-Epsilon Nat Civil Eng Hon Soc, 2001. **Professional Experience:** PROF, CIVIL & ENVIRON ENG, UNIV MICH, as of 2005. **Mailing Address:** Univ Mich, 121 Ewre, Ann Arbor, MI 48109. **Fax:** 734-763-2275. **E-Mail:** ndk@umich.edu

KATOVIC, VLADIMIR, ELECTROCHEMISTRY. **Personal Data:** b Bihac, Croatia, December 19, 1935; American citizen; m 1971, Lois A Adcock; c Nina M. **Education:** Univ Zagreb, BS, 1961, PhD (chem), 1965. **Professional Experience:** PROF INORG CHEM, WRIGHT STATE UNIV, 1991-; assoc prof, Wright State Univ, 1978-1991; res assoc inorgchem, Iowa State Univ, 1976-1978; assoc prof anal chem, Univ Zagreb, 1971-1976; Res assoc inorg chem, Ohio State Univ, 1968-1971. **Memberships:** Am Chem Soc; Croatian Chem Soc. **Research Statement & Publications:** Synthetic and structural studies of coordination compounds of biological or catalytic interest; metal-metal bonding and metal-cluster compounds; Electrochem in room temperature ionic liquids. **Mailing Address:** Chem Dept, Wright State Univ, Dayton, OH 45435. **Fax:** 937-775-3301. **E-Mail:** vkatovic@desire.wright.edu

KATOVICH, MICHAEL J, PHARMACODYNAMICS. **Personal Data:** b San Jose, Calif, July 16, 1948; m 1990, Carol; c Megan & Sean. **Education:** Univ Calif, Davis, BS, 1970, MS, 1973, PhD (physiol), 1976. **Honors & Awards:** Irving I Hertzendorf Mem Award Physiol, 1976. **Professional Experience:** Adj prof, Dept Physiol & Functional Genomics, Col Med, Univ fla, 2000; mem, Coun Complications, Am Diabetes Asn, 1990; PROF PHARMACODYNAMICS, COL MED, UNIV FLA, 1989-; Prin investr, NIH, 1989-1992; chmn, Col Pharm, Univ Fla, 1988-1993; assoc prof, Dept Pharmaceut Biol, 1984-1988; Prin investr, Nat Inst Child Health & Human Develop, 1983-1995; Prin investr, Am Heart Asn, 1979-1981 & 1984-1994; asst prof, Dept Pharmaceut Biol, 1979-1984; Am Heart fel, Col Med, Univ Fla, 1977-1979; assoc physiol, Col Med, Univ Fla, 1976-1977; res physiologist, Dept Physiol, Univ Calif, 1975-1976; res assoc, Dept Physiol, Univ Calif, 1974-1975; assoc, Dept Physiol, Univ Calif, 1973-1974; Teaching asst, Dept Physiol, Univ Calif, 1972-1973. **Memberships:** Sigma Xi; Aerospace Med Asn; Am Physiol Soc; Endocrine Soc; Am Diabetes Asn; Am Asn Cols Pharm. **Research Statement & Publications:** Hypertension, with empahsis on the renin angiotensin system and gene therapy; metabolic phenomena; diabetes; environmental physiology with emphasis on temperature regulation; endocrinology; thirst control mechanisms; morphine dependency and withdrawal; acceleration biology; author of more than 150 technical publications. **Mailing Address:** JHMHC, Univ Fla, PO Box 100487, Gainesville, FL 32605-3965. **Fax:** 352-392-9187. **E-Mail:** katovich@cop.ufl.edu

KATRITZKY, ALAN ROY, HETEROCYCLIC CHEMISTRY. **Personal Data:** b London, Eng, August 18, 1928; American citizen; m 1952, Linde; c Margaret, Erika, Rupert & Freda. **Education:** Univ Oxford, BS, 1952, MA, 1954, DPhil, 1954; Univ Cambridge, PhD, 1958, ScD, 1963. **Honorary Degrees:** Dr, Nat Univ, Madrid, Spain, 1986, Univ Poznan, Poland, 1990, Univ Sdansk, Poland, 1994, Univ E Anglia, UK, 1995, Univ Toulouse, France, 1996, Univ St Petersburg, Russia, 1997. **Honors & Awards:** Cope Senior scholar Award, am chem soc, 2001; Hillier Medal, Inst of synthesis, Latvian acad of sci, 1999; Kametani Prize, Japan, 1999; Hyeyrovsk Medal, Czech acad of sci, 1997; Hon fel, Egyptian

Soc of heterocyclic chem, 1996; pres, Ibn Sina conf of heterocyclic chem, Egypt, 1995; Inaugural fel, Int Soc of heterocyclic chem, 1995; Hon prof, Xi'an modern chem Res inst, China, 1995; Hon prof, Beijing Inst of technol, China, 1995; 360 year commemoration medal, Tartu state univ, Estonia, 1992; Golden Tiger Award, Exxon corp, 1990; Hon fel, Polish chem soc, 1985; Foreign fel, Royal Australian Inst of chem, 1983; fel, Royal Soc of London, 1980; Hon fel, Italian chem soc, 1978; Tilden Medal, 1975; Royal Soc Chem Award in Heterocyclic Chem, 1982; Int Soc Heterocyclic Chem Award, 1993; Fla Award, Am Chem Soc, 1995. **Professional Experience:** Consult, Haughten Pharma, 1995-; consult, Bristol-Myers Squibb, 1993-; consult, Monsanto, 1989-; consult, Nutrasweet, 1987-; DIR, CTR HETEROCYCLIC COMPOUNDS, 1985-; consult, Pharmos, 1983-; consult, Reilly, 1981-; consult, Exxon, 1981-; KENAN PROF CHEM, UNIV FLA, 1980-; consult, Sandoz, 1979-1995; consult, 3M, 1964-; prof chem, dean Sch Chem Sci, 1963-1970 & 1976-1980; prof chem, Univ E Anglia, 1963-1980; lectr, Univ Cambridge, 1962-1963; fel& dir of studies, Churchill Col, 1960-1963; Univ demonstr, Univ Cambridge, 1958-1962; lectr, Pembroke Col, 1956-1958; dean, sch chem sci, Univ East Anglia, 1963-1970, 1976-1980. **Memberships:** Hon fel Italian Chem Soc; fel Royal Soc; foreign fel Royal Australian Inst Chem; hon fel Polish Chem Soc; foreign mem Polish Acad Sci; foreign mem Real Catalan Acad; Royal Soc Chem (chair, educ & training bd, 1971-1977, council, 1961-1964, 1971-1977, jour committee, 1971-1974, exec comm, 1971-1977); Heterocyclic Group Chem Soc (founder/chair, 1967-1969); Royal Inst Chem (vice pres, 1970-1973, counl, 1967-1973); Int soc heterocyclic chem. (vpres, 1973-1975); Am Chem Soc; Japanese Chem Soc; Japanese pharmaceut Soc. **Research Statement & Publications:** Heteroaromatic tautomerism and aromaticity; heteroaromatic rearrangements; electrophilic substitution; conformational analysis of heterocycles; intermolecular interactions; infrared intensites; cycloadditions to heterocyclic betaines; pyrylium and pyridinium chemistry; mechanism of nucleophlic substitution reactions. **Mailing Address:** Dept Chem Univ Fla, Chem Res Bldg PO Box 117200, Gainesville, FL 32611. **Fax:** 352-392-9199. **E-Mail:** katritzky@chem.ufl.edu

KATSAMPES, CHRIS PETER, pediatrics; deceased, see previous edition for last biography

KATSANIS, D(AVID) J(OHN), PHYSICS, PRODUCTION OPERATIONS MANAGEMENT. **Personal Data:** b Philadelphia, Pa, September 28, 1926; m 1948, c 3. **Education:** Temple Univ, BA, 1952, MA, 1954, PhD, 1962, George Washington Univ, MEng, 1980. **Professional Experience:** SR PHYSICIST MECH, SHIELDING TECHNOLOGIES, INC, 1991-; sr physicist mech, T&E Int, Inc, Bel-air, 1986-1991; physicist & chief producibility Eng Br, T&E Int, Inc, Bel-air, 1981-1986; chief mech process, Chem Systs Lab, US Army Small Arms Systs Agency, Aberdeen Proving Ground, 1977-1981; chief, suppressive shielding, Edgewood Arsenal, 1973-1977; chief physicist, US Army Small Arms Systs Agency, 1969-1973; chief physicist, laser safety team, 1968-1969; advan concepts br, 1965-1966 & spec prods lab, 1966-1968; chief, LASH Proj, 1963-1965; systs ballistics sect, gas mech sect, 1959-1963; theoret ballistics sect, gas mech sect, 1958-1959; chief, gas mech sect, 1957-1958; physicist ballistics, Frankford Arsenal, 1954-1957; Physicist fluid dynamics, Naval Air Mat Ctr, 1952-1954. **Memberships:** Am Phys Soc; Int Asn Bomb Technicians & Investigators; Asn US Army. **Research Statement & Publications:** Weapon systems analysis; fluid dynamics; mechanics; thermodynamics; design of experiments; production technology; venteted suppressive shielding. **Mailing Address:** 4047 Heaps Sch Rd, Pylesville, MD 21132.

KATSANIS, ELEFTHERIOS P, COLLOID CHEMISTRY, SURFACE CHEMISTRY. **Personal Data:** b Mytilene, Greece, September 28, 1944; American citizen; div, c 1. **Education:** Lehigh Univ, BS, 1967, MS, 1970; Clarkson Col Tech, PhD, 1981. **Professional Experience:** SR CHEMIST, PHILADELPHIA QUARTZ CO, 1975-. **Memberships:** Am Chem Soc; Sigma Xi; Soc Petrol Engrs. **Research Statement & Publications:** Preparation of hydrous metal oxide sols via precipitation techniques; zeolites; stabilization of colloidal dispersions and their application to practical systems; enhanced oil recovery; water chemistry. **Mailing Address:** 121 Green Hill Rd, King of Prussia, PA 19406-2045.

KATSANIS, THEODORE, TURBOMACHINERY FLOW ANALYSIS, NUMERICAL ANALYSIS. **Personal Data:** b North Weymouth, Mass, July 17, 1925; American citizen; m 1952, Pauline L; c Linda (Creutz), Jason & Kimberly (Ammeter). **Education:** St Louis Univ, BS, 1948; Univ Wash, MS, 1962; Case Inst Technol, PhD (math), 1967. **Professional Experience:** OWNER, THEODORE KATSANIS, 1985-; aerospace engr, NASA Lewis Res Ctr, 1963-1985; engr, Berger Eng, 1952-1962; engr, Boeing Airplane Co, 1948-1952. **Memberships:** Sigma Xi; assoc fel Am Inst Aeronaut & Astronaut; Am Soc Mech Engrs. **Research Statement & Publications:** Analysis of internal flow through rotating turbomachinery using finite difference methods to obtain a numerical solution to the appropriate partial differential equation. **Mailing Address:** 16760 NE 33th Pl, Bellevue, WA 98008. **E-Mail:** tkatsanis@cs.com

KATSAROS, KRISTINA B, ATMOSPHERIC PHYSICS. **Personal Data:** b Gothenburg, Sweden, July 24, 1938; m 1959, Michael; c Anthony & Ester S. **Education:** Univ Wash, BS, 1960, PhD (atmospheric sci), 1969. **Honors & Awards:** Sverdrup Gold Medal, Am Meteorol Soc, 1997. **Professional Experience:** DIR, NAT OCEANIC & ATMOSPHERIC ADMIN, ATLANTIC OCEANGRAPHIC & METEROL LAB, 1997-; dir, Dept Oceanog From Space, Fr Inst Explor Res Sea, Ifremer, 1992-1997; prof atmospheric sci, UnivWash, 1989-1996; vis scientist, Univ Paris, 1987 & 1990; vis scientist, Royal Dutch Meteorol Soc, 1984 & 1985; assoc prof, Univ Wash, 1983-1989; vis prof women, NSF, 1983-1985; vis scientist, Riso Nat Lab, Denmark, 1980; from res asst prof to res assoc prof, Univ Wash, 1974-1983; res assoc, Univ Wash, 1969-1974; NDEA fel, 1963-1965; res asst atmospheric sci, Univ Wash, 1960 & 1967-1968. **Memberships:** Am Geophys Union; fel AmMeteorol Soc; AAAS; Swed Geophys Soc; Europ Geophys Soc; Oceanog Soc. **Research Statement & Publications:** Air-sea transfer processes, turbulent momentum transfer and its relation to sea slate, evaporation and the effects of sea spray radiative transfers; turbulent fluxes; free convection; remote sensing of atmosphere; scatterometry of passive microwave remote sensing of surface winds and storms over the sea. **Mailing Address:** Atlantic Oceanographic & Meteorol Lab, Nat Oceanic & Atmosepheric Admn, 4301 Rickenbacker Causeway, Miami, FL 33149. **Fax:** 305-361-4449. **E-Mail:** kristina.katsaros@noaa.gov

KATSEL, PAVEL LEON, REGULATION OF GENE EXPRESSION, CHEMICAL IDENTIFICATION OF PHEROMONES & GENE THERAPY. **Personal Data:** b Irkutsk, USSR, November 19, 1960; m Bronislava; c Nora & Leonard. **Education:** Irkutsk State Univ, USSR, BS, 1981, MS, 1982, PhD (biochem & physiol), 1990. **Professional Experience:** DEPT ANESTHESIOL, MT SINAI MED CTR, as of 2001; RES COORDR, VET ADMIN MED CTR, MT SINAI SCH MED, 1992-; sr researcher, Irkutsk State Univ, Inst Biol, 1990-1992; asst prof, Irkutsk State Univ, 1990-1992; Jr researcher, Irkutsk State Univ, Inst Biol, 1982-1990. **Research Statement & Publications:** Chemical communication during reproduction in fish; steroids and phorbol ester upregulation of rat cholecystokinin gene as a model for studying the mechanisms of eukaryotic transcriptional regulation; cationic lipid mediated gene transfer into the control nervous system and gastrointestinal tract. **Mailing Address:** Dept Anesthesiol, Mt Sinai Med Ctr, One Gustave L Levy Pl, New York, NY 10029.

KATSNELSON, LEV Z, KNOWN GOOD DIE, MULTI-CHIP MODULE. **Personal Data:** m Berta; c Zinoviy & Michael. **Education:** Univ Latvia, BS, 1963, MS, 1965, PhD (appl math comput sci), 1968. **Honors & Awards:** Latvian State Award In Sci & Technol, 1980. **Professional Experience:** CHIEF SCIENTIST, MINCO TECH LABS INC, 1993-; Beer-Sheva Univ, Israel, 1990; Kar Univ Prague, Czech, 1988; head dept, Inst Math & Comput Sci, Latvia Univ, 1987-1992; Dresden Tech Univ, Ger, 1982 & 1989; head lab, Ctr Comput Sci, 1980-1987; proj leader, Ctr Comput Sci, 1977-1980; vis prof, Humboldt Univ, Berlin, 1976; sr res scientist, Ctr Comput Sci, 1973-1977; sr scientist, USSR Acad Sci, 1972; assoc prof, Univ Latvia, 1968-1992; Res scientist, Dept Math, Latvia Univ, 1968-1973. **Memberships:** Int Soc Hybrid Microelectronics; Int Elec Packaging Soc; Inst Elec & Electronics Engrs. **Research Statement & Publications:** Design and test known good die and multi chip modules; designed and developed numerical methods for analysis and optimization of linear and nonlinear integrated circuits; developed methods for optimal design of RC-filters; developed quasi-newton and adaptive algorithms for solving systems of ordinary differential equations and stiff systems. **Mailing Address:** Minco Tech Labs Inc, 1805 Rutherford Lane, Austin, TX 78754. **Fax:** 512-837-6285.

KATSOYANNIS, PANAYOTIS G, BIOCHEMISTRY. **Personal Data:** b Greece, January 7, 1924. **Education:** Nat Univ Athens, MS, 1948, PhD (chem), 1952. **Honors & Awards:** 50th Anniversary Award, Am Diabetes Asn. **Professional Experience:** CHAIR EMER, DEPT BIOL CHEM & PHARMACOL, as of 2005; DISTINGUISHED PROF, DEPT BIOL CHEM, 2001-; prof, Dept Biochem& Mol Biol, 1998-2001; prof biochem & chmn dept, Mt Sinai Sch Med, 1968-1998; head, Div Biochem, Med Res Ctr, Brookhaven Nat Lab, 1964-1968; assoc res prof, Sch Med, Univ Pittsburgh, 1958-1964; asst prof biochem, Med Col, Cornell Univ, 1956-1958; res assoc, Med Col, Cornell Univ, 1952-1956; corresp mem, Nat Acad Greece. **Memberships:** Am Chem Soc; Am Soc Biol Chem; NY Acad Sci; Royal Soc Chem; Brit Biochem Soc. **Research Statement & Publications:** Biologically active polypeptides; isolation, characterization and synthesis; insulin synthesis. **Mailing Address:** Dept Pharmacol & Biol Chem, Mt Sinai Sch Med, PO Box 1020 One Gustave L Levy Pl, New York, NY 10029-6574. **Fax:** 212-996-7214. **E-Mail:** panayotis.katsoyannis@mssm.edu

KATSUMOTO, KIYOSHI, CHEMISTRY. **Personal Data:** b Oakland, Calif, May 4, 1936; m 1968, c 2. **Education:** San Jose State Col, BS, 1964; Univ Calif, Berkeley, PhD (chem), 1968. **Professional Experience:** SR RES ASSOC, CHEVRON RES CO, 1975-; From res chemist to sr res chemist, Chevron Res Co, 1967-1975. **Memberships:** Am Chem Soc. **Research Statement & Publications:** Reaction mechanisms of cyclopropane ring openings; heterogeneous catalytic oxidations of hydrocarbons. **Mailing Address:** 2615 Brooks Ave, El Cerrito, CA 94530-1416.

KATSUURA, HIDEFUMI, MATHEMATICS. **Education:** Univ Del, PhD, 1984. **Professional Experience:** PROF MATH, SAN JOSE STATE UNIV, as of 2006. **Mailing Address:** Math Dept, San Jose State Univ, San Jose, CA 95192. **Fax:** 408-924-5080. **E-Mail:** katsuura@math.sjsu.edu

KATTA, JAYARAM REDDY, SOIL & ENVIRONMENTAL CHEMISTRY, WATER QUALITY. **Personal Data:** b Hyderabad, India, July 10, 1953; m 1980, Jyothi Reni; c Sweatha & Swathi. **Education:** Andhrapradesh Agr Univ, BS, 1977, MS, 1980; Colo State Univ, Ft Collins, PhD (soil & environ chem), 1986. **Professional Experience:** ASSOC PROF, DEPT RENEWABLE RESOURCES, UNIV WYO, 2003-; asst prof, Dept Renewable Resources, Univ Wyo, 2001-2002; Prin investr, US Environ Protection Agency, 1994-; sr res scientist, Wyo Water Resources Ctr, 1993-2000; Prin investr, US Geol Surv Merit Fund Prog, 1992-; Prin investr, Abandoned Coal Mine Land Res Prog, 1991-; res assoc IV, Wyo Water Resources Ctr, 1990-1993; adj asst prof, Wyo Water Resources Ctr, 1990-1993; Prin investr, Elec Power Res Inst, 1990-1993; res scientist, Wyo Water Resources Ctr, 1990-1992; Prin investr, US Geol Surv, 1989-1991; Prin investr, Wyo Water Resources Ctr, 1988-1991; res assoc III, Wyo Water Resources Ctr, 1987-1990; Prin investr, US Dept Energy, 1986-1989; Res assoc, Univ Wyo, 1986-1987. **Memberships:** Am Soc Agron; Soil Sci Soc Am; Am Water Resources Asn; Sigma Xi. **Research Statement & Publications:** Understanding geochemical processes of soils, groundwater systems, coal mine lands and hazardous wastes; application of chemical speciation, adsorption/disorption precipitation/dissolution processes to predict the fate of organic and inorganic contaminants in the vadose zone of contaminated soils and hazardous wastes and development of remediation methods for contaminated soils and groundwater; author of 2 books, several journal articles and publications. **Mailing Address:** Dept Renewable Resources, Univ Wyoming, PO Box 3354, Laramie, WY 82071-3354. **Fax:** 307-766-6403. **E-Mail:** katta@uwyo.edu

KATTAKUZHY, GEORGE CHACKO, RATES & PROPORTIONS, MODEL FITTING & PREDICTION. **Personal Data:** b Kottayam, South India, October 1, 1944; American citizen; m 1974, Regini; c Sandhya E, Anita M & Sarah M. **Education:** Kerala Univ, Kerala, India, BSc, 1966, MSc, 1968; Temple Univ, MA, 1973, PhD (math statist), 1975. **Professional Experience:** STATISTICIAN STATIST, HEALTH CARE FINANCING ADMIN, 1978-; asst prof math, Philadelphia Col Pharm & Sci, 1976-1978; asst prof statist, Pahlavi Univ, Shiraz, Iran, 1975-1976; lectr statist, Temple Univ, Philadelphia, Pa, 1973-1975; Instr math, Temple Univ, Philadelphia, Pa, 1972-1975. **Memberships:** Am Statist Asn (treas 1989-1990). **Research Statement & Publications:** Variation in admission rates in selected disease catagories in medicare population 1986 to present. **Mailing Address:** 6915 S Dewey Ct, Fredericksbrg, VA 22407. **Fax:** 410-966-1873.

KATTAMIS, THEODOULOS ZENON, PHYSICS, METALLURGY. **Personal Data:** b Kythrea, Cyprus, May 7, 1935; div, c Alexis & Nicholas. **Education:** Univ Liege, Mining Engr, 1960, Geol Engr, 1961, Metall Engr, 1962; Mass Inst Technol, MS, 1963, ScD(metall), 1965. **Honors & Awards:** Cert for Innovation in Metal Casting, NASA. **Professional Experience:** Contract, Continental Can Co, 1982-1985; NSF, 1973-1976 & Air Force Off Sci Res, 1977-1981; PROF METALL, UNIV CONN, 1975-; Grants, NASA, 1972-1974; from asst prof to assoc prof, Univ Conn, 1969-1975; res assoc metall, Mass Inst Technol, 1965-1969. **Memberships:** Am Soc Metals; Metall Soc; Am Foundrymen's Soc. **Research Statement & Publications:** Solidification and properties of materials, composite materials, joining, powder metallurgy, thin coatings, single crystal growth and materials processing; microstructure-property relationships; materials science engineering. **Mailing Address:** Dept Metall & Mat Eng, Univ Conn, Storrs, CT 06269-3136. **Fax:** 860-486-4745. **E-Mail:** tkattami@mail.ims.uconn.edu

KATTAN, AHMED A, HORTICULTURE, FOOD SCIENCE. **Personal Data:** b Cairo, Egypt, March 21, 1925; American citizen; m 1951, Anna; c Jeanie, Mitchell & Michael. **Education:** Cairo Univ, BSc, 1945; Univ Md, MS, 1950, PhD (hort), 1952. **Honors & Awards:** Woodbury Award, Am Soc Hort Sci, 1959; Gourley Award, 1979. **Professional Experi-**

ence: EMER UNIV PROF, DEPT FOOD SCI, UNIV ARK, FAYETTEVILLE, 1988-; head, Dept Food Sci, Univ Ark, Fayetteville, 1968-1988; exec vpres, Ozark Food Processors Assoc, 1962-1988; from asst prof to prof hort, Dept Food Sci, Univ Ark, Fayetteville, 1955-1962; asst prof, Univ Md, 1954-1955; lectr, Cairo Univ, 1953-1954; res assoc, Univ Md, 1952-1953; asst veg crops, Univ Md, 1951-1952; asst, Cairo Univ, 1946-1948. **Memberships:** Fel Am Soc Hort Sci; Inst Food Technol. **Research Statement & Publications:** Pre- and post-harvest physiology of horticultural crops; methods of quality evaluation of raw and processed fruits and vegetables; methods of handling and mechanical harvesting of fruits and vegetables. **Mailing Address:** 1625 W Halsell Rd, Fayetteville, AR 72701.

KATTAWAR, GEORGE W, OPTICAL PHYSICS. **Personal Data:** b Beaumont, Tex, August 10, 1937; m 1961, c 3. **Education:** Lamar State Col, BS, 1959; Tex A&M Univ, MS, 1961, PhD (physics), 1964. **Professional Experience:** PROF PHYSICS, TEX A&M UNIV, 1973-; assoc prof, Tex A&M Univ, 1968-1973; asst prof physics, NTex State Univ, 1966-1968; sr res physicist, Esso Prod Res, 1964-1966; theoretical physicist, Los Alamos Sci Lab, 1963-1964; consult, Navy & Jet Propulsion Lab. **Memberships:** Fel Optical Soc Am; Sigma Xi. **Research Statement & Publications:** Electromagnetic scattering theory; hydrologic optics. **Mailing Address:** 4968 Smugglers Rd, College Station, TX 77845. **Fax:** 979-845-2590. **E-Mail:** kattawar@tamu.edu

KATTELMANN, RICHARD C, SNOW HYDROLOGY. **Education:** Univ Calif, PhD. **Professional Experience:** RES HYDROLOGIST, SIERRA NEV AQUATIC RES LAB, UNIV CALIF, as of 2006. **Mailing Address:** Sierra Nev Aquatic Res Lab Box 198, Univ Calif Star Rte 1, Mammoth Lakes, CA 93546.

KATTERMAN, FRANK REINALD HUGH, PLANT PHYSIOLOGY. **Personal Data:** b Paia, Hawaii, June 28, 1929; m 1956, c 5. **Education:** Univ Hawaii, BA, 1954; Tex A&M Univ, PhD (plant physiol), 1960. **Professional Experience:** PROF EMER AGRON & PLANT GENETICS, UNIV ARIZ, as of 2000; PLANT BREEDER, AGR EXP STA, 1974-; prof agron & plant genetics, Univ Ariz, beginning 1970; assoc prof plant breeding, Agr Exp Sta, 1967-1970; plant physiologist, Agr Res Serv, USDA, 1959-1967; mem, Nat Cotton Coun Am. **Memberships:** AAAS. **Research Statement & Publications:** Composition and biochemistry of the nucleic acids in higher plants. **Mailing Address:** Dept Plant Sci Univ Ariz, Forbes 124, Tucson, AZ 85721-0001.

KATTI, KATTESH V, MAIN GROUP-TRANSITION METAL CHEMISTRY FOR THE DESIGN OF NEW CATALYSIS NEW MONOMERS & POLYMERS FOR NUCLEAR WASTE REMEDIATION. **Personal Data:** b Dharwad, Karnatak, India, November 11, 1956; m Kavita. **Education:** Karnatak Univ, India, BS, 1975; Mysore Univ India, MS, 1979; Indian Inst Sci, PhD (chem), 1985. **Professional Experience:** PROF PHYSICS & RADIOL, UNIV MO-COLUMBIA, as of 2003; Zynaxis Cell Sci Inc, 1993- & DuPont Merck, beginning 1993; asst prof radiol, Univ Mo, beginning 1993; dir, Agr Testing P-N Compounds, Monsanta, beginning 1992; co-prin investr, Dept Energy, beginning 1992; adj prof chem, Univ Mo, Columbia, beginning 1992; chief consult, Ligands Inc, beginning 1990; res asst prof, Univ MO, 1990-1993; res scientist, Univ Alta, 1987-1990; lectr several univs & industs, US, Ger, France & Neth, beginning 1985; Alexander von Humboldt fel, Univ Gottingen, Ger, 1985-1987; res fel, Dept Atomic Energy, India, 1979-1984; Merit fel, Nat Coun Educ Res & Training, New Delhi, India, 1978-1980. **Memberships:** Am Chem Soc; Soc Nuclear Med; Sigma Xi; Int Asn Radiopharmacol. **Research Statement & Publications:** Fundamental main group chemistry of phosphorus-nitrogen/sulfer-nitrogen and silicon-nitrogen compounds; application of the new main group frameworks as ligands in the coordination chemistry of transition metals which include paramagentic metals and metallic radiosisotopes; design of new main group monomers and polymers for applications in materials science and radioactive waste treatment. **Mailing Address:** Ctr Radiol Res Rm 103, 301 Business Loop 70 W, Columbia, MO 65203. **Fax:** 573-884-5679. **E-Mail:** kattik@health.missouri.edu

KATTI, SHRINIWAS KESHAV, ANALYTICAL STATISTICS, APPLIED STATISTICS. **Personal Data:** b Bijapur, India, June 20, 1936; American citizen; m 1960, c 2. **Education:** Univ Delhi, BA, 1956; Iowa State Univ, MA, 1958, PhD (statist), 1960. **Professional Experience:** PROF EMER, UNIV MO, COLUMBIA, as of 2003; vis prof, Univ New South Wales, 1971; prof, Univ Mo, Columbia, 1969-; assoc ed, Biomet Soc, 1967-1972; consult, Underwriter's Nat Assurance Co, 1962-1964 & Scot Res Lab, Perkesie, 1967-1970; USPHS fel, 1964-1966 & USDA fel, 1967-1969; from asst prof to assoc prof statist, Fla State Univ, 1960-1969; USAF fel, Fla State Univ, 1960-1962. **Memberships:** Biomet Soc; fel Am Statist Asn; Am Inst Biol Sci; Am Math Soc; Inst Math Statist; Sigma Xi. **Research Statement & Publications:** Inference; methods of tested priors; adaptive estimators. **Mailing Address:** 8290 Lake Dr Ste 249, Miami, FL 33166. **Fax:** 573-446-2209.

KATTUS, J ROBERT, FAILURE ANALYSIS, METALLOGRAPHY. **Personal Data:** b Cincinnati, Ohio, August 25, 1922; wid, c Josephine, Robert, Sandra, Laura & Patricia. **Education:** Purdue Univ, BS, 1944. **Honors & Awards:** Award of Merit, Am Soc Testing & Mat, 1971; Allen Ray Putnam Award, Am Soc Metals Int, 1990. **Professional Experience:** CONSULT METALLURGIST, AMC-VULCAN INC, 1980-; consult metallurgist, 1968-1980; gen mgr, Bethea Castings Co, 1966-1968; chmn, Comt A-4 Iron Castings, 1965-1969; mem, Eng Manpower Comn, 1965-1968; Chmn, Test Methods Panel, Joint Comt Effects Temperature Properties Metals, Am Soc Testing & Mat, 1963-1968; dir metall res, Southern Res Inst, 1952-1966; chief metallurgist, Anderson Elec Corp, 1948-1952; metallurgist, US Naval Res Lab, 1944-1946 & Aluminum Industs Inc, 1946-1948; nat trustee, Am Soc Metals Int. **Memberships:** Fel Am Soc Testing & Mat; fel Am Soc Metals Int. **Research Statement & Publications:** Elevated-temperature properties of metals under conditions of rapid heating and rapid loading simulating aerospace conditions; effects of composition and foundry practice on the quality of ferrous and non-ferrous castings. **Mailing Address:** AMC-Vulcan Inc, 810 Fifth Ave N, Birmingham, AL 35203. **Fax:** 205-328-3015. **E-Mail:** jrk825@aol.com

KATUSIC, ZVONIMIR, PHARMACOLOGY. **Personal Data:** b Belgrade, Yugoslavia, August 16, 1952. **Education:** Univ Belgrade, BS, 1977, MS, 1983, PhD (pharmacol & med), 1987. **Professional Experience:** PROF ANESTHESIOL, MAYO CLIN COL MED, as of 2004; PROF PHARMACOL, MAYO CLIN COL MED, as of 2004; sr assoc consult, Mayo clin, St Marys Hosp, beginning 1990; res assoc consult, 1987-1989. **Memberships:** Am Heart Asn; Am Physiol Soc; Am Soc Pharmacol & Exp Therapeut. **Research Statement & Publications:** Pharmacology. **Mailing Address:** Dept Anesthesiol & Pharmacol, Mayo Clin Med, 200 SW First St, Rochester, MN 55905-0001. **E-Mail:** katusic.zvonimir@mayo.edu

KATZ, ADRIAN I, INTERNAL MEDICINE, NEPHROLOGY & PHYSIOLOGY. **Personal Data:** b Bucharest, Romania, August 3, 1932; m 1965, Miriam; c Ron & Iris. **Education:** Hebrew Univ Jerusalem, MD, 1962. **Professional Experience:** PROF MED, SCH MED, UNIV CHICAGO, 1975-; head sect nephrology, Univ Chicago, 1973-1982; assoc prof, Sch Med, Univ Chicago, 1971-1974; asst prof & attend physician, Sch Med, Univ Chicago, 1968-1971; res fel, Harvard Med Sch, 1967-1968; Asst med, Peter Bent Brigham Hosp, Boston, 1967-1968; res fel med, Sch Med, Yale Univ, 1965-1967; House officer internal med, Belinson Med Ctr, Sch Med, Tel-Aviv Univ, 1962-1965. **Memberships:** Am Soc Clin Invest; Am Fedn Clin Res; Am Soc Nephrology; NY Acad Sci; fel Am Col Physicians; Asn Am Physicians. **Research Statement & Publications:** Renal physiology, especially regulation and function of Na, K-ATPase in Epithelia biochemical mechanisms of renal tubular sodium transport; renal handling of polypeptide hormones; kidney function in pregnancy; clinical nephrology; biochemistry. **Mailing Address:** Dept Med M/C 5100, Pritzker Sch Med Univ Chicago 5841 S Md Ave, Chicago, IL 60637. **Fax:** 773-702-5818. **E-Mail:** akatz@medicine.bsd.uchicago.edu

KATZ, ALAN CHARLES, REGULATORY AFFAIRS, RISK ASSESSMENT. **Personal Data:** b Kearny, NJ, November 10, 1946; m 1974, Marcia; c Bryan J & Jeffrey A. **Education:** Fairleigh Dickinson Univ, BS, 1970, MS, 1977; Am Bd Toxicol, dipl; Am Bd Forensic Examr, dipl. **Professional Experience:** PRES, TOXCEL LLC, 1999-; mgr, tech affairs, Sanachem USA Inc, 1997-1998; exec dir toxicol & anal chem, Tech Assessment Syst Inc, 1987-1997; sr toxicologist, US Environ Protection Agency, 1986-1987; toxicologist, US Environ Protection Agency, 1984-1986; toxicologist & study dir, Stauffer Chem Co, 1979-1984; sr assoc scientist, Johnson & Johnson Res Found, 1976-1979; pharmacologist, Cooper Lab Inc, 1974-1976; toxicol res asst, Ortho Pharmaceut Corp, 1972-1974; res asst, Rockefeller Univ, 1971-1972; consult toxicol. **Memberships:** Soc Comp Ophthal (pres 1992-1996); NY Acad Sci; Int Soc Study Xenobiotics; Am Col Forensic Examrs; Soc Toxicol; Can Soc Toxicol. **Research Statement & Publications:** Chemical and pharmaceutical fields; pharmacology and toxicology; program management. **Mailing Address:** TOXCEL LLC, 7545 Presidential Lane, Manassas, VA 20109. **Fax:** 703-335-0089. **E-Mail:** alan@toxcel.com

KATZ, ALAN JEFFREY, GENETIC TOXICOLOGY, BIOSTATISTICS. **Personal Data:** b Columbus, Ohio, October 2, 1947; m 1968, c 3. **Education:** Ohio State Univ, BS, 1969, MS, 1970, PhD (genetics), 1974. **Professional Experience:** Res grants, NIH, 1987-1989; PROF GENETICS, DEPT BIOL SCI, ILL STATE UNIV, 1985-; res grants, March Dimes, 1982-1986; vis res fel, Swiss Fed Inst Toxicol, Schwerzenbach, 1982; from asst prof to assoc prof, Dept Biol Sci, Ill State Univ, 1975-1985; NIH fel pop genetics, Dept Genetics & Cell Biol, Univ Minn, 1974-1975. **Memberships:** Genetics Soc Am; Biomet Soc; Environ Mutagens Soc; AAAS; Sigma Xi. **Research Statement & Publications:** Identification and study of chemical mutagens and antimutagens in the somatic tissue of drosophila. **Mailing Address:** Dept Biol Sci, Ill State Univ, Campus Box 4120, Normal, IL 61790-4120. **Fax:** 309-438-3722. **E-Mail:** ajkatz@ilstu.edu

KATZ, ALBERT BARRY, CLINICAL CHEMISTRY, DIRECTOR CLINICAL LABORATORY. **Personal Data:** b New York, NY, February 25, 1917; m 1979, Anita; c Stephanie (Greenwald) & Jeffrey H. **Education:** NY Univ, BS, 1938, MS, 1939, PhD (chem), 1942. **Professional Experience:** EMER TEACHER CHEM, PALM BEACH SCH SYST FLA, 1988-; chief lab, S Palm Beach Utilities, Boca Raton, 1981-1985; dir clin lab, Hackensack Clin Lab, 1977-1979; mem adv coun, State NJ-Gov Brendan Byrne, 1969-1971; Fel, Dept Health Ky, 1946; chief clin lab, 43rd Gen Hosp, US Army, 1943-1946; Malarial control officer, Mediter Base Sect, Europ Theatre Opers, 1942. **Memberships:** Fel Am Asn Clin Chem; Am Chem Soc; fel Am Inst Chemists; Nat Acad Clin Biochem; NY Acad Sci; Am Bd Clin Chem. **Research Statement & Publications:** Hemosiderin pigment that was found in heart failure cells; methodology found to identify the heart failure cell that appeared in sputum. **Mailing Address:** 7515 S Rosemary Cir, Englewood, CO 80112.

KATZ, ARNOLD MARTIN, MEDICINE, PHYSIOLOGY. **Personal Data:** b Chicago, Ill, July 30, 1932; m 1959, Phyllis; c Paul, Sarah, Amy & Laura. **Education:** Univ Chicago, BA, 1952; Harvard Univ, MD, 1956. **Honorary Degrees:** Dr Med, Carol Davila Univ, 1994. **Honors & Awards:** Res Achievement Award, Am Heart Asn, 1989, Sci Coun Distinguished Achievement Award, 1991, Louis N & Arnold M Katz Prize, Basic Sci Coun. **Professional Experience:** Chmn sci adv bd, Patrick & Catherin Weldon Donaghue Found, 1994-; bd dir, Am Heart Asn, 1993-1994; chmn sci bd, Sarnoff Edow Med Sci, 1992-1993; vis prof med, Dartmouth Med Sch, 1990-1991; bd sci counsellors, Nat Heart Lung Blood Inst, 1989-1992; ed chief, J Molecular & Cellular Cardiol, 1986-1992; Hartford Hosp, 1979- & New Britain Gen Hosp, 1981-; Heart Prog Proj B Comt, 1967-1969 & prog proj comt A, 1980-; consult, St Francis Hosp & Med Ctr, 1979-; assoc ed, J Molecular & Cellular Cardiol, 1979-1986; PROF MED & EMER HEAD DIV CARDIOL, HEALTH CTR, UNIV CONN, 1977-; John Dempsey Hosp, Conn, 1977-; vchmn task group cardiac failure, Nat Heart, Blood, Lung & Blood Vessel Prog, NIH, 1972; consult, Vet Admin, 1970-; Gordon Res Conf Cardiac Muscle, 1970; session chmn, Gordon Res Conf Cellular Control Cardiac Contraction, 1968; attend physician, Mt Sinai Hosp, 1969-1977; Philip J & Harriet L Goodhart prof med-cardiol, Mt Sinai Sch Med, 1969-1977; mem exec coun, Coun Basic Sci, 1968-1971; assoc prof med & physiol, Univ Chicago, 1967-1969; mem, Ad Hoc Comt Rev Proposals Myocardial Infarction Study Ctrs, 1967; mem, Comt Myocardial Infarction, Nat Heart Inst, 1966; estab investr, Am Heart Asn, 1963-1968; asst prof physiol, Col Physicians & Surgeons, Columbia Univ, 1963-1967; asst physician, Med Serv, Presby Hosp, 1963-1967; res fel med, Med Sch, Univ Calif, Los Angeles, 1961-1964; Am Heart Asn res fel, 1961-1963; Mosely traveling fel Harvard Univ, 1960-1961; hon registr, Inst Cardiol, London, 1960-1961; asst resident, Mass Gen Hosp, 1959-1960; res assoc, Nat Heart Inst, 1957-1959; intern med, Mass Gen Hosp, 1956-1957. **Memberships:** Am Physiol Soc; Am Soc Pharmacol & Exp Therapeut; Cardiac Muscle Soc (pres, 1969-1971); Am Soc Biol Chemists; Sigma Xi; Asn Univ Cardiologists; fel Am Col Cardiol. **Research Statement & Publications:** Cardiology; cardiovascular physiology; muscle biochemistry. **Mailing Address:** Cardiol Div, Univ Conn Health Ctr, 263 Farmington Ave, Farmington, CT 06030-1305. **Fax:** 860-679-3346. **E-Mail:** akatz@nso1.uchc.edu

KATZ, BARRETT, NEURO-OPHTHALMOLOGY, NEURO-SURGERY. **Personal Data:** m 1981, Deborah; c Matthew, Jacob, Nathaniel & Sarah. **Education:** Colgate Univ, AB, 1969; Case Western Res Univ, MD, 1973. **Professional Experience:** PROF & CHMN, DEPT OPTHAL, GEORGE WASH UNIV MED CTR, as of 1998; Wayne & Gladys Valley prof & vchmn, dept ophthal, Calif Pac Med Ctr, beginning 1989; sr scientist, Smith-Kettlewell Eye Res Inst, San Francisco, beginning 1984; assoc prof ophthal neurol & neurosurg, Univ Calif, San Diego, 1984-1989; asst prof ophthal neurol & neurosurg, Univ Ariz, Tucson, 1982-1984; fel neuro-ophthal, Univ Calif, San Francisco, 1981-1982; ophthal, Tufts Med Sch, Boston, 1978-1981; resident neurol, Harvard Med Sch, Boston, 1975-1978; assoc, NIH, 1974-1975; intern, Parkland Hosp, Dallas, 1973-1974. **Memberships:** Am Acad Neurol; Am Neurol Asn; Am Asn Ophthal; Asn Res Vision & Ophthal; Asn Univ Profs Ophthal. **Research Statement & Publications:** Clinical neuro-ophthalmology; ocular motility. **Mailing Address:** Dept Opthal, George Wash Univ Med ctr, 2150 Pa Ave, Washington, DC 20037. **Fax:** 202-994-6209.

KATZ, DARRYL, MATHEMATICS. **Education:** Univ Mich, BA, MA; Univ Southern Calif, PhD. **Professional Experience:** PROF EMER, DEPT MATH, CALIF STATE UNIV, FULLERTON, 1999-; prof math, Dept Math, Calif State Univ, Fullerton, 1981-1999. **Mailing Address:** Dept Math, Calif State Univ, McCarthy Hall 154, Fullerton, CA 92834.

KATZ, DAVID HARVEY, MEDICINE, IMMUNOLOGY. **Personal Data:** b Richmond, Va, February 17, 1943; m 1963, c 2. **Education:** Univ Va, AB, 1963, Duke Univ, MD, 1968. **Professional Experience:** Pres & dir, Med Biol Inst, La Jolla, 1981-1999; chief exec officer & pres, Quidel, beginning 1981; mem human cell biol adv panel, NSF, 1977-1978; mem allergy & immunol study sect, NIH, 1977; chmn & mem immunol staff, Scripps Clin & Res Found, 1976-1981; Mem adv comt cancer ctrs, Nat Cancer Inst, 1972-1974; from instr to assoc prof immunol & path, Harvard Med Sch, 1971-1976; staff assoc immunol, NIH, 1969-1971; Med house officer, Johns Hopkins Hosp, 1968-1969. **Memberships:** Am Asn Immunologists; Am Soc Clin Invest; AAAS; Am Asn Pathologists; Am Fedn Clin Res. **Research Statement & Publications:** Basic immunology; allergy; tumor immunology; developmental biology. **Mailing Address:** Dept Immunol Med Biol Inst, Lidak Pharm, 11077 N Torrey Pines Rd, La Jolla, CA 92037-1082.

KATZ, ELI JOEL, PHYSICAL OCEANOGRAPHY. **Personal Data:** b Brooklyn, NY, January 12, 1937; m 1957, c 3. **Education:** Polytech Inst Brooklyn, BSME, 1957; Pa State Univ, MS, 1959; Johns Hopkins Univ, PhD (fluid mech), 1962. **Professional Experience:** Chief ed, J Phys Oceanog, 1992-1996; co-ed, J Phys Oceanog, 1986-1991; SR SCIENTIST, LAMONT-DOHERTY EARTH OBSERV, 1984-; sr res assoc, Lamont-doherty Earth Observ, 1979-1983; assoc scientist phys oceanog, Woods Hole Oceanog Inst, 1970-1978; sr lectr mech, Tel Aviv Univ, 1969-1970; asst scientist, Woods Hole Oceanog Inst, 1966-1969; res specialist acoust, Gen Dynamics Corp, 1965-1966; vis lectr meteorol, Hebrew Univ, Jerusalem, 1963-1965; res assoc mech, Johns Hopkins Univ, 1962-1963. **Memberships:** Am Meteorol Soc. **Research Statement & Publications:** Ocean dynamics and ocean role in world climate: specifically the Tropical Oceans. **Mailing Address:** Lamont-Doherty Geol Observ, Columbia Univ, Palisades, NY 10964. **Fax:** 914-365-0718. **E-Mail:** ejk@lamont.ldgo.columbia.edu

KATZ, ERNST, SOLID STATE PHYSICS. **Personal Data:** b Maehr-Ostrau, Austria, July 23, 1913; Dutch citizen; m 1939, Katherine; c Johan M. **Education:** Univ Utrecht, BS, 1933, MS, 1937, PhD (physics), 1941. **Professional Experience:** PROF EMER PHYSICS, UNIV MICH, ANN ARBOR, 1980-; from asst prof to prof, Univ Mich, Ann Arbor, 1947-1980; dir res, Neth Instrument & Elec Apparatus Co 1945-1947; asst physics, Univ Utrecht, 1938-1947; asst physics, Rockefeller Biophys Res Group, 1937-1941. **Memberships:** Fel Am Phys Soc mem; Sigma Xi mem emer. **Mailing Address:** Univ Mich, Dept Physics, 321A W Hall, Ann Arbor, MI 48104-1120.

KATZ, EUGENE RICHARD, GENETICS. **Personal Data:** b Brooklyn, NY, April 10, 1942; m 1969, Anne; c Sarah H & David J. **Education:** Univ Wis, Madison, BS, 1962; Univ Cambridge, Eng, PhD (molecular genetics), 1969. **Professional Experience:** ASSOC DEAN, ARTS & SCI, STONY BROOK 1997-; dean, Div Biol Sci, 1988-1996; PROF MOLECULAR GENETICS & MICROBIOL, STATE UNIV NY, STONY BROOK, 1985-; dir, Grad Prog Genetics, 1980-1988; assoc prof, Dept Biol, 1980-1985; vis prof, Univ Nijmegen, Netherlands, 1977-1978; dir, Grad Prog Cellular & Develop Biol, State Univ NY at Stony Brook, 1975-1980; from asst prof to assoc prof, Dept Biol, 1970-1980; vis scientist, Mass Inst Technol, 1970. **Memberships:** AAAS. **Research Statement & Publications:** Genetic control of development using the cellular slime mold; Dictyostelium discoideum as a model system; formal genetics and biochemical analysis of mutants affecting development. **Mailing Address:** Dept Molecular Genetics & Microbiol, Sch Med, Stony Brook Univ, 130 Life Sci Bldg, Stony Brook, NY 11794-5222. **Fax:** 631-632-9797. **E-Mail:** ekatz@notes.cc.sunysb.edu

KATZ, FLORA N, GENETICS. **Education:** Kenyon Col, BA; Mass Ist Technol, PhD. **Professional Experience:** ASSOC PROF, DEPT BIOL, TEX A&M UNIV, as of 2005. **Mailing Address:** Dept Biol Tex A&M Univ, Biol Scis Bldg W Rm 348C, College Station, TX 77843-3258. **Fax:** 409-845-2891. **E-Mail:** fkatz@bio.tamu.edu

KATZ, FRANCES R, CARBOHYDRATE CHEMISTRY, PATENT AFFAIRS. **Personal Data:** b LeRoy, Ill, August 16, 1937; m 1983, Allan; c Andrew. **Education:** Ind Cent Univ, BS, 1961; Univ Chicago, MBA, 1982. **Professional Experience:** RETIRED; dir publ, Inst Food Technologists, beginning 1996; vpres res, Am Maize Prod Co, 1978-1996; ed dir, Gorman Publ Co, 1974-1978; assoc ed, Putnam Publ Co, 1969-1974; food technologist, Continental Coffee Co, 1965-1969; food technologist, Durkee Foods, SCM Corp, 1961-1965; bd govs, Food Update; fiber subcomt, Int Life Sci Inst; external adv, Food Sci Dept, Univ Ill. **Memberships:** Am Chem Soc; Inst Food Technologists; Corn Refiner Asn; Am Asn Cereal Chemists. **Research Statement & Publications:** Carbohydrate research; applications of carbohydrates; formulation of research policy; corn genetics research. **Mailing Address:** Inst Food Technologists, 525 W Van Buren Ste 1000, Chicago, IL 60607. **Fax:** 312-782-8348.

KATZ, FRANK FRED, PARASITOLOGY. **Personal Data:** b Philadelphia, Pa, July 19, 1927; m 1955, c 2. **Education:** Philadelphia Col Pharm, BS, 1951; Tulane Univ, MS, 1953; Univ Pa, PhD (parasitol), 1956. **Professional Experience:** PROF EMER BIOL, SETON HALL UNIV, as of 2004; ASSOC DEAN, COL ARTS & SCI, 1985-; actg chmn dept to chmn dept, Col Arts & Sci, 1971-1983; prof biol, Seton Hall Univ, beginning 1970; from asst prof to assoc prof, Col Arts & Sci, 1962-1970; asst prof microbiol, Jefferson Med Col, 1957-1962; sr parasitologist, Eaton Labs, Norwich Pharmacal Co, 1956-1957; jr res assoc biol, Brookhaven Nat Lab, 1955-1956; asst instr parasitol, Univ Pa, 1954-1955; Asst zool, Philadelphia Col Pharm, 1951. **Memberships:** AAAS; Am Soc Parasitol; Am Soc Trop Med & Hyg; Micros Soc Am. **Research Statement & Publications:** Helminthology; protozoology; experimental parasitology; biology of Strongyloides, Trichinella, Plasmodium and trypanosomes. **Mailing Address:** Dept Biol, Seton Hall Univ, 400 S Orange Ave, South Orange, NJ 07079. **E-Mail:** ffkatz@att.net

KATZ, FRED H, INTERNAL MEDICINE, ENDOCRINOLOGY. **Personal Data:** b Essen, Ger, April 7, 1930; American citizen; m 1960, c 3. **Education:** Columbia Univ, AB, 1952, MD, 1956; Am Bd Internal Med, dipl, 1964. **Professional Experience:** RETIRED; clin prof med, Div Endocrinol, beginning 1976; prof med, Div Endocrinol, beginning 1975; head, Div Endocrinol, 1972-1976; chief endocrinol, Vet Admin Hosp, Denver, 1969-1976; assoc prof med, Univ Colo, 1969-1975; assoc prof med & chief endocrinol, Stritch Sch Med, Loyola Univ, 1966-1969; asst prof med, Sch Med, Univ Chicago, 1963-1966; Nat Found fel & Nat Inst Arthritis & Metab Dis trainee, 1960-1961; Nat Found fel, Presby Hosp, New York, 1959-1960; mem, Med Adv Bd, Coun High Blood Pressure, Cent Soc Clin Res. **Memberships:** Endocrine Soc; Soc Exp Biol & Med; fel Am Col Physicians. **Research Statement & Publications:** Steroid hormone metabolism, physiology and pharmacology. **Mailing Address:** 3535 Cherry Creek N Dr No 307, Denver, CO 80209-3609.

KATZ, GARY VICTOR, INHALATION TOXICOLOGY, INDUSTRIAL HYGIENE. **Personal Data:** b New York, NY, July 12, 1943; m 1984, c 2. **Education:** City Col NY, BS, 1965; NY Univ, MS, 1968, PhD (biol & environ health sci), 1975. **Professional Experience:** CHIEF OPERATING OFFICER, EASTMAN KODAK CO, as of 2001; UNIT DIR CHEM & REGULATORY INFO, INHALATION TOXICOL, EASTMAN KODAK CO, 1990-; mem, CMA Integrated Risk Info Syst Task Group, 1988-; from asst to dir & div vpres, Eastman Kodak Co, 1988-; chmn, Chem Mfr Asn (CMA) Toxicol Task Group, 1984-; tech assoc, Eastman Kodak Co, 1981-; MGR, INHALATION TOXICOL, EASTMAN KODAK CO, 1981-; adj asst prof environ med, Dept Environ Med, NY Univ Med Ctr, 1977-; toxicologist, Inhalation Toxicol, Eastman Kodak CO, 1977-1981; from asst res to assoc res scientist inhalation toxicol & chem carcinogenesis, Dept Environ Med, NY Univ Med Ctr, 1969-1977; Am Indust Health Coun (ATHC) Air Toxics Work Group. **Memberships:** Am Indust Hygiene Asn; Soc Risk Anal. **Research Statement & Publications:** Chemical carcinogenesis; neurotoxicology; quantitative risk assessment. **Mailing Address:** Eastman Kodak Co, Rochester, NY 14652-6267.

KATZ, GEORGE MAXIM, engineering, neurophysiology; deceased, see previous edition for last biography

KATZ, HERBERT M(ARVIN), CHEMICAL ENGINEERING. **Personal Data:** b Brooklyn, NY, April 4, 1926; m 1954, c 2. **Education:** City Col NY, BChE, 1949; Univ Cincinnati, MS, 1950, PhD (chem eng), 1954. **Professional Experience:** RETIRED; prof chem eng, Howard Univ, 1973-1986; chmn dept, Howard Univ, 1968-1973; chem engr, Res Div, W R Grace & Co, 1967-1968; chem engr, Brookhaven Nat Lab, 1957-1967; staff engr, Eng Ctr, Univ Columbia, 1956-1957; asst chem engr, Argonne Nat Lab, 1954-1956; consult, Nuclear Safety Asn & Brookhaven Nat Lab. **Memberships:** Sigma Xi; Am Inst Chem Engrs. **Research Statement & Publications:** Chemical reprocessing of nuclear reactor fuels; treatment of radioactive wastes; fluidized bed technology. **Mailing Address:** 101 Coast Blvd, La Jolla, CA 92037.

KATZ, IRA, FOOD SCIENCE. **Personal Data:** b New York, NY, November 10, 1933; m 1955, c 3. **Education:** Univ Ga, BSA, 1957; Univ Md, MS, 1959, PhD, 1962. **Professional Experience:** VPRES & DIR, RES & DEVELOP, INT FLAVORS & FRAGRANCES, INC, 1980-; dir, Res & Develop, Int Flavors & Fragrances, Inc, 1973-1980; groupleader, Res & Develop, Int Flavors & Fragrances, Inc, 1971-1973; proj leader, Res & Develop, Int Flavors & Fragrances, Inc, 1967-1971; asst prof, Univ Md, 1965-1967; res assoc, Univ Md, 1962-1965; Res asst lipid chem, Univ Md, 1961-1962. **Memberships:** AAAS; Am Dairy Sci Asn; Am Oil Chem Soc; Am Chem Soc; Inst Food Technologists; Sigma Xi. **Research Statement & Publications:** Flavor of food and fragrance systems. **Mailing Address:** Int Flavors & Fragrances Inc, 1515 Hwy 36, Union Beach, NJ 07735.

KATZ, IRVING, MATHEMATICS. **Personal Data:** b Brooklyn, NY, October 25, 1933; m 1957, c 3. **Education:** Brooklyn Col, BS, 1956; Ohio State Univ, MA, 1958; Univ Md, PhD (math), 1964. **Professional Experience:** PROF MATH, GEORGE WASH UNIV, 1977-; from asst prof to assoc prof, George Wash Univ, 1966-1977; from instr to assoc prof, Am Univ, 1961-1966; mathematician Opers Res Inc, 1959-1960; mathematician, Nat Security Agency, 1958-1959. **Memberships:** Am Math Soc; Math Asn Am. **Research Statement & Publications:** Matrix theory. **Mailing Address:** George Wash Univ, 2121 Eye St N W, Washington, DC 20052-7528.

KATZ, ISADORE A, ELECTRICAL ENGINEERING. **Professional Experience:** PRES & CHIEF EXEC OFFICER, LIGHTCHIP INC, as of 2004. **Mailing Address:** LightChip Inc, 5 Indust Way, Salem, NH 03079. **E-Mail:** ikatz@lightchip.com

KATZ, ISRAEL NORMAN, Finite element analysis, optimal facility loation. **Personal Data:** b New York, NY, April 14, 1932; m Judith; c Avi & Maidi. **Education:** Yeshiva Univ, BA & MS, 1952 & 1954; Mass Inst Technol, PhD (math), 1959. **Honors & Awards:** Burlington Northern Foundation Faculty Award, 1991 Washington University Founders Day Award for Outstanding Teaching, 1984. **Professional Experience:** CHMN SYSTS SCI & MATH, WASH UNIV, 1991-2003; PROF APPL MATH & SYSTS SCI, WASH UNIV, 1974-; assoc prof appl math & comput sci, Wash Univ, 1967-1974; mgr math dept, Res & Adv Develop Div, Avco Corp, 1966-1967; chief math anal sect, Res & Adv Develop Div, Avco Corp, 1963-1965; sr staff scientist, Res & Adv Develop Div, Avco Corp, 1959-1963; res asst, Mass Inst Technol, 1958-1959; asst, Mass Inst Technol, 1955-1958; asst math, Yeshiva Univ, 1952-1954; lectr, Math Asn Am. **Memberships:** Am Math Soc; Math Asn Am; Soc Indust & Appl Math. **Research Statement & Publications:** Applied math; numerical analysis; facility location; finite elements; biomathematics; ordinary and partial differential equations; algorithms for parallel computation. **Mailing Address:** Dept Electrical & Systems Eng, Wash Univ, Box 1137, St Louis, MO 63130-4899. **Fax:** 314-935-7500. **E-Mail:** katz@wustl.edu

KATZ, J LAWRENCE, BONE BIOMECHANICS, BONE BIOMATERIALS. **Personal Data:** b Brooklyn, NY, December 18, 1927; m 1950, c 3. **Education:** Polytech Inst Brooklyn, BS, 1950, MS, 1951, PhD (physics), 1957. **Honors & Awards:** 3rd Annual Award for Outstanding Contributions to Tech Lit Biomat, Soc Biomat & Clemson Univ, 1975; Outstanding Biomed Eng Educator Award, Am Soc Eng Educ, 1988; George Winter Award for Outstanding Res, Europ Soc Biomat, 1989. **Professional Experience:** DISTINGUISHED RES PROF BIOMED & ORAL BIOL, UNIV MISS, as of 2003; DEAN ENG & PROF BIOMED ENG, CASE INST TECHNOL, CASE WESTERN RESERVE UNIV, 1989-; Univ London, Eng, 1985-1986 & Fac Med Lariboisiere, Paris, 1986; Lab Orthop Res, Fac Med Lariboisiere-Saint-Louis, Paris, France, 1986; NIH sr int fel, 1985-1986; vis prof, Dept Mat, Queen Mary Col, Univ London, Eng, 1985-1986; assoc ed, Biomat, Biomech & Rehab Eng, Annals Biomed Eng, 1984-1989; chmn, Dept Biomed Eng, 1983-1985; mem, Sci Rev & Eval Bd for Rehab Eng Res & Develop, Vet Admin, 1981-1983, 1990-; Orthop Panel, Food & Drug Admin, 1976-1978 & Orthop Div, Johnson & Johnson Co, 1979-1980; mem, Coun Alliance Eng Med & Biol, 1978-1981; vis lectr orthop, Sch Med, 1978; vis biophysicist, Orthopaedics Res Lab, Children's Hosp, Boston, 1978; Sao Carlos Inst Physics & Chem, Univ Sao Paulo, Brasil, 1978; Guggenheim fel, Harvard Univ, 1978; E Leon Watkins vis prof, Wichita State Univ, Kans, 1978; Jerome Fischbach travel grant, Rensselaer Polytech Inst, 1976; prof surg, Albany Med Col, 1975-1989; dir, Ctr Biomed Eng, 1974-1984; prof biophys & biomed eng, Rensselaer Polytech Inst, 1973-1989; partic vis sci prog physics, Am Asn Physics Teachers-Am Inst Physics, 1970-1971; mem equip & mat for med radiation appln & chmn subcomt diag radiol, Am Nat Standards Inst, 1969-1974; vis prof, Univ Miami, 1969-1970; mem, eng biol & med training comt, NIH, 1968-1971; Bio-Anal Labs, Inc, 1961-1983; from asst prof to prof physics, Rensselaer Polytech Inst, 1961-1973; NSF sci fac fel & hon res asst crystallog, Univ Col, London, 1959-1960; Consult, Ernest F Fullam, Inc, NY, 1958-1983; Instr math, Polytech Inst Brooklyn, 1952-1956; consult & site vis, Nat Inst Dent Res & Nat Inst Gen Med Sci. **Memberships:** Am Crystallog Asn; Am Phys Soc; Int Asn Dent Res; Sigma Xi; Soc Biomat (pres 1978-1979); Biomed Eng Soc (pres 1983-1984). **Research Statement & Publications:** Bone biomechanics and biomaterials, especially the correlation between structure and properties of the various calcified tissues and of synthetic materials used as implant biomaterials; biomechanics of calcified and connective tissues; electromechanical properties of bone and bone remodeling; rehabilitation engineering; scanning electron microscopy; X-ray diffraction and ultrasonic studies of bone and teeth; biomedical materials; rehabilitation engineering. **Mailing Address:** Univ Miss Sch Dent, 650 E 25th St, Kansas City, MO 64108. **Fax:** 816-235-5524. **E-Mail:** katzjl@umkc.edu

KATZ, JACK, AUDIOLOGY, CENTRAL AUDITORY DISORDERS & PROCESSING. **Personal Data:** b New York, NY, March 25, 1934; m 1956, Irma H Laufer; c Mark D & Miriam B. **Education:** Brooklyn Col, BA, 1956; Syracuse Univ, 1957; Univ Pittsburgh, PhD (audiol), 1961. **Honors & Awards:** Fulbright-Hays sr lectr, Ankara, Turkey, 1972-1973. **Professional Experience:** PROF EMER, DEPT COMMUN DIS & SCI, STATE UNIV NY, BUFFALO, as of 2004; Adj prof, Dept Otolaryngol, State Univ NY, 1992; assoc clin prof, vis prof Univ Kans Med Ctr, 1987-1988; mem bd dir, Orton Soc Western NY, 1987-1990 & Buffalo Hearing Speech Ctr; VETERAN ADMIN MED CTR, BUFFALO, NY, 1984-; chmn commun dis & sci, State Univ NY, Buffalo, 1982-1987; vpres univ & labs, NY State Speech Lang-Hearing Asn, 1981-1985; mem spec med staff, Chedoke-McMaster Hosps, Hamilton, Ont, 1981-1984; consult audiol, Roswell Park Mem Inst, 1979-; prof commun dis & sci, State Univ NY, buffalo, 1976-; clin prof, State Univ NY, Buffalo, 1974-1976; Consult audiol, Menorah Med Ctr, 1974-1975; assoc clin prof, Univ Mo Kansas City, 1970-1974 & Univ Kans, 1971-1974; dir audiol lab, Menorah Med Ctr, Kansas City, 1965-1974; asst prof speech path & audiol, Tulane Univ, 1962-1965; asst prof audiol, Northern Ill Univ, 1961-1962; Consult audiol, Univ Pittsburgh, 1961-1962; res audiologist, Univ Pittsburgh, 1960-1961; Therapist speech & hearing, Bd Educ, Cayuga Co, NY, 1957-1958. **Memberships:** Fel Am Speech-Lang-Hearing Asn; NY Acad Sci. **Research Statement & Publications:** Evaluation of central auditory integrity, binaural hearing, low level adaptation, auditory perception, learning disabilities, listening problems in incarcerated populations and influence of conductive hearing loss. **Mailing Address:** Dept Commun Dis & Sci, Univ State NY, 105 Park Hall, Buffalo, NY 14260-0001. **Fax:** 716-645-2216. **E-Mail:** jackkatz@buffalo.edu

KATZ, JAY, PSYCHIATRY. **Personal Data:** b Zwickau, Ger, October 20, 1922; American citizen; m 1952, c 3. **Education:** Univ Vt, BA, 1944; Harvard Univ, MD, 1949; Am Bd Psychiat & Neurol, dipl. **Honors & Awards:** Isaac Ray Award, Am Psychiat Asn, 1975; William C Menninger Award, Am Col Physicians, 1983; Am Soc Law & Med Award, 1987. **Professional Experience:** HARVEY L KARP PROF LAW PSYCHOANALYSIS, YALE UNIV, beginning 1995; ELIZABETH DOLLARD PROF EMER LAW, MED & PSYCHIAT, YALE UNIV, beginning 1993; Elizabeth Dollard prof law/med psychiat, Law Sch, 1990-1993; asst prof psychiat & law, John A Gorver prof law & psychoanalyst, 1984-1990; TRAINING & SUPV PSYCHOANALYST, WESTERN NEW ENG INST PSYCHOANAL, beginning 1972; fel, Morse Col, Yale Univ, 1968-; trustee, Psychoanal Clin, Western New Eng Inst Psychoanal, 1968-1971; fel, Ctr Advan Psychoanal Studies, 1967-; adj prof law & psychiat, Law Sch, 1967-1984; staff psychoanalyst, Psychoanal Clin, Western New Eng Inst Psychoanal, 1966-1969; chmn, Adv Comt Ment Health, Woodbridge Bd Educ, Conn, 1964-1968; assoc prof law & assoc clin prof psychiat, Law Sch, 1960-1967; asst prof psychiat & law, Law Sch, 1958-1960; attend psychiatrist, Yale-New Haven Med Ctr, 1957-; from instr to asst prof psychiat, Sch Med, Yale Univ, 1955-1958; chief resident outpatient clin, Sch Med, Yale Univ, 1954-1955; asst investr, USPHS res grant hypnotic dreams, 1953-1956; asst resident psychiat, Sch Med, Yale Univ, 1953-1954; asst resident psychiat, State Univ NY & Northport Vet Admin Hosp, Long Island, 1950-1951; intern, Mt Sinai Hosp, NY, 1949-1950. **Memberships:** Inst Med-Nat Acad Sci; fel Am Psychiat Asn; Am Orthopsychiat Asn; Am Col Psychiat; Am Psychoanal Asn. **Mailing Address:** Yale Law Sch, Yale Univ, PO Box 208215, New Haven, CT 06520.

KATZ, JONATHAN ISAAC, ASTROPHYSICS, APPLIED PHYSICS. **Personal Data:** b New York, NY, January 5, 1951; m Lilly; c Sholomo, Alexander, Isaac, Rebecca & Joseph. **Education:** Cornell Univ, AB, 1970, MA, 1971, PhD (astron), 1973. **Professional Experience:** PROF PHYSICS, WASH UNIV, 1985-; SRI Int, 1974-1982 & adv coun, NASA, 1983-1986; MITRE, 1982-; assoc prof, Wash Univ, MO, 1981-1985; Sloan Found fel, 1977-1979; assoc prof astron & geophysics, Univ Calif, Los Angeles, 1976-1981; consult, Lawrence Livermore Lab, 1973-; Mem staff astrophysics, Inst Advan Study, 1973-1976. **Memberships:** Am Phys Soc. **Research Statement & Publications:** Theoretical high energy astrophysics; capillarity, applied physics; gamma-ray astronomy including bursts, soft gamma repeaters and active galactic nuclei. **Mailing Address:** Dept Physics, Wash Univ, St Louis, MO 63130. **Fax:** 314-935-6219. **E-Mail:** katz@wuphys.wustl.edu

KATZ, JOSE, INTERNAL MEDICINE, CARDIOLOGY. **Personal Data:** b Havana, Cuba, June 6, 1944; m Anke Ebsen; c David, Rachel, Hannah & Susan. **Education:** Univ Ill, Urbana, BS, 1963, MS, 1964, PhD (theoret physics), 1967; Free Univ Berlin, MD, 1980. **Professional Experience:** ASSOC PROF MED & RADIOL, COL PHYSICIANS & SURGEONS, COLUMBIA UNIV, 1994-; staff attending, New York-presbyterian Hosp, 1988-; DIR CARDIOVASC, MAGNETIC RESONANCE IMAGING & SPECTROS, COL PHYSICIANS & SURGEONS, COLUMBIA UNIV, 1988-; Co dir of electocardiography(ECG) Laboratory, 1999-; New York-presbyterian Hosp asst prof med & radiol, Col Physicians & Surgeons, Columbia Univ, 1988-1994; cardio fel, Southwestern Med Sch, 1985-1988; resident internal med, Metrop Gen Hosp & Mt Sinai Med Ctr, Cleveland, Ohio, 1982-1985; from asst prof to prof, Free Univ, Berlin, 1971-1982; asst prof, Inst Physics, Purdue Univ, 1969-1971; Res assoc physics, Univ Hamburg, Ger, 1967-1969. **Memberships:** Fel Am Col Physicians; fel Am Col Cardiologists; fel Am Col Chest Physicians; fel Am Col Angiol; fel Am Heart Asn Coun on clinical cardiology; fel Am Heart Asn Coun on cardiovascular Radiology. **Research Statement & Publications:** Nuclear magnetic resonance Imaging and spectroscopy; technique development for the monitoring of intracellular sodium change, in biological systems without use of a shift reagent. **Mailing Address:** PO Box 637, Alpine, NJ 07620. **Fax:** 212-305-4648. **E-Mail:** jk32@columbia.edu

KATZ, JOSEPH, AEROSPACE ENGINEERING. **Education:** Technion - Israel Inst Technol, MSc, 1974; PhD. **Honorary Degrees:** DSc (aeronaut eng), Technion - Israel Inst Technol, 1976. **Professional Experience:** PROF AERO ENG, SAN DIEGO STATE UNIV, as of 2006. **Mailing Address:** Aerospace Eng, San Diego State Univ, San Diego, CA 92182. **Fax:** 619-594-6005. **E-Mail:** katz@aero.sdsu.edu

KATZ, JOSEPH, BIOCHEMISTRY. **Personal Data:** b Vilno, Lithuania, January 1915; American citizen; c 5. **Education:** Univ Calif, Berkeley, BS, 1943, PhD, 1949. **Professional Experience:** SR RES SCIENTIST, MED RES INST, CEDARS-SINAI MED CTR, 1970-; Univ Calif, Los Angeles, 1988-; adj prof, Univ Southern Calif, 1969-1988; estab investr, Am Heart Asn, 1961-1966; advan res fel, Cedars-Sinai Med Ctr, 1959-1961; from res assoc to sr res assoc, Inst Med Res, Cedars Lebanon Hosp, 1955-1970; asst res physiologist, Univ Calif, Berkeley, 1953-1955; fel physiol, Univ Calif, Berkeley, 1951-1953; res fel biochem, Univ Calif, Berkeley, 1949-1951. **Memberships:** Am Chem Soc; Am Soc Biol Chemists; Am Nutrit Soc; Am Physiol Soc; Brit Biochem Soc. **Research Statement & Publications:** Carbohydrate metabolism determination of pathways of glucose utilization; the interrelationship between lipogenesis and glucose utilization; plasma protein metabolism. **Mailing Address:** 2509 Bombadil Lane, Davis, CA 95916.

KATZ, JOSEPH J, PHYSICAL CHEMISTRY. **Personal Data:** b Detroit, Mich, April 19, 1912; m 1944, Celia; c 4. **Education:** Wayne State Univ, BS, 1932; Univ Chicago, PhD (chem), 1942. **Honors & Awards:** Nuclear Appln Award, Am Chem Soc, 1961, Midwest Award, 1969; Rumford Premium, Am Acad Arts & Sci, 1992. **Professional Experience:** SR SCIENTIST EMER, ARGONNE NAT LAB, 1982-; Guggenheim fel, 1957-1958; ed-in-chief, Inorg & Nuclear Chem Letters, 1955-1981; sr chemist, Argonne Nat Lab, 1946-1982; chemist metall lab, Univ Chicago, 1943-1946; chemist, Univ Chicago, 1942-1943; Am ed, J Inorg & Nuclear Chem. **Memberships:** Nat Acad Sci; AAAS; Am Chem Soc; Am Soc Photobiol; Sigma Xi. **Research Statement & Publications:** Chemistry of uranium and transuranium elements; deterium isotope studies; chlorophyll chemistry; photosynthesis; solar energy. **Mailing Address:** Argonne Nat Lab, 9700 S Cass Ave, Argonne, IL 60439. **Fax:** 630-252-9289. **E-Mail:** jjkatz@worldnet.att.net

KATZ, JOSEPH L, NUCLEATION & VAPOR PHASE FORMATION, FLAME REACTOR FORMATION OF CERAMIC OXIDES. **Personal Data:** b Colon, Panama, August 4, 1938; American citizen; m 1965, Liliane; c Daniel P & Alan R. **Education:** Univ Chicago, BS, 1960, PhD (phys chem), 1963. **Honors & Awards:** John W Graham Prize, 1975; Maryland Chemist Award, 1982. **Professional Experience:** Dept chmn, ChemEngineering, 1981-1984 & 2005-2006; dir, Energy Res Inst, 1981-1983; PROF CHEM ENG, JOHNS HOPKINS UNIV, 1979-; vis prof, Mass Inst Technol, 1977; Guggenheim fel, 1976-1977; prof chem eng, Clarkson Unive, 1970-1979; mem tech staff, NAm Rockwell Sci Ctr, 1964-1970; asst prof phys chem, Univ Copenhagen, 1963-1964. **Memberships:** Fel AAAS; fel Am Phys Soc; Am Chem Soc; Am Inst Chem Engrs; Sigma Xi; Mat Res Soc; Combustion Inst. **Research Statement & Publications:** Nucleation; equations of state; thermal conductivity; flame generation of ceramic powders; scale (calcite) inhibition. **Mailing Address:** Dept Chem & Biomolecular Eng, Johns Hopkins Univ, Baltimore, MD 21218. **Fax:** 410-516-5510. **E-Mail:** jlk@jhu.edu

KATZ, KAILA, MATHEMATICS. **Education:** NY Univ, PhD (math). **Professional Experience:** FAC, DEPT MATH & COMPUT SCI, MONTCLAIR STATE UNIV, as of 1997. **Mailing Address:** Montclair State Univ, 287 Beechwood Rd, Upper Montclair, NJ 07043. **Fax:** 973-655-6977.

KATZ, LARRY STEVEN, BEHAVIORAL ENDOCRINOLOGY, REPRODUCTIVE PHYSIOLOGY. **Personal Data:** b Albany, NY, December 3, 1953; m 1980, Barbara. **Education:** Cornell Univ, BS, 1976, MS, 1979; Univ Calif, Davis, PhD (animal behav), 1984. **Professional Experience:** CHAIR ANIMAL SCI, RUTGERS UNIV, 2002-; ASSOC PROF ANIMAL SCI, RUTGERS STATE UNIV NJ, 1995-; ed, Appl Animal Behav Sci, beginning 1993; sect ed, Environ & Behav, J Animal Sci, 1993-1996; asst prof, Rutgers State Univ NJ, 1989-1995; Co-founder, Coalition for Animals & Animal Res, 1988; res physiologist, Univ Calif, Berkeley, 1986-1989; researcher, Univ Calif, Davis, 1985-1986; NIH trainee, Colo State Univ, 1984-1985. **Memberships:** AAAS; Am Soc Animal Sci; Animal Behav Soc; Endocrine Soc; Soc Study Reproduction; Sigma Xi. **Research Statement & Publications:** Describe the interactions between gonadal and pituitary hormones, reproductive function, sexual behavior and seasonal environmental changes, such as photoperiod in goats, sheep and deer. **Mailing Address:** Dept Animal Sci, Cook Col, Rutgers Univ, Off 201 Bartlett Hall, New Brunswick, NJ 08901-8525. **Fax:** 732-932-6996. **E-Mail:** katz@aesop.rutgers.edu

KATZ, LAURENCE BARRY, GASTROENTEROLOGY, CARDIOVASCULAR PHARMACOLOGY. **Personal Data:** b Syracuse, NY, October 3, 1954; m 1981, c 2. **Education:** Univ Pa, BA, 1976; Philadelphia Col Pharm & Sci, MS, 1979 & PhD (pharmacol), 1982. **Professional Experience:** PROJ MGR, R W JOHNSON PHARMACEUT RES INST, 1990-; prin scientist, R W Johnson Pharmaceut Res Inst, 1989-1990; sr res scientist, Ortho Pharmaceut Corp, 1984-1989; res scientist pharmacol, Ortho Pharmaceut Corp, 1983-1984; res assoc toxicol, Univ Wis, 1981-1983. **Memberships:** Am Soc Pharmacol & Exp Therapeut; Am Asn Advan Sci; Gastrointestinal Res Group; Sigma Xi. **Research Statement & Publications:** Drugs useful in peptic ulcer disease and hypertension including prostaglandins, histamine H2-receptor antagonist and vasodilators. **Mailing Address:** Ohmeda Pharmaceut Prod Div, 100 Mountain Ave, Murray Hill, NJ 07947. **Fax:** 908-771-6161.

KATZ, LEON, science policy; deceased, see previous edition for last biography

KATZ, LEON, ORGANIC CHEMISTRY, PACKAGING. **Personal Data:** b Springfield, Mass, August 27, 1921; m 1947, c 3. **Education:** Trinity Col, Conn, BS, 1944; Univ Ill, PhD (org chem), 1947. **Honors & Awards:** Packaging Hall of Fame, 1992. **Professional Experience:** CONSULT, 1989-; vpres corp technol, James River Corp, 1987-1988; sr vpres corp res & develop, James River Corp, 1982-1986; vpres res & develop & packaging, Am Can Co, Greenwich, Conn, 1973-1982; vpres corp develop, Polychrome Corp, Yonkers, NY, 1971-1973; exec vpres, Rockwood Industs, Conn, 1969-1971; vpres, Dyestuff & Chem Div, 1966-1969; corp dir res, Dyestuff & Chem Div, 1965-1966; dir res, Dyestuff & Chem Div, 1962-1965; tech dir, Gen Aniline & Film Corp, NY, 1959-1962; prod mgr pigments, Gen Aniline & Film Corp, NY, 1958-1959; sect mgr dyes & pigments, Gen Aniline & Film Corp, NY, 1955-1958; res chemist, Gen Aniline & Film Corp, NY, 1953-1955; mgr org chem, Schenley Labs, 1949-1953; chemist, Am Cyanamid Co, 1947-1949. **Memberships:** AAAS; Indust Res Inst; Am Chem Soc; NY Acad Sci; Am Inst Chem; Sigma Xi. **Research Statement & Publications:** Alkaloids; pharmaceuticals; dyestuffs; pigments; reprographics; photography; specialty chemicals packaging; pulp paper. **Mailing Address:** 195 Dogwood Ct, Stamford, CT 06903-4500.

KATZ, LEWIS, X-RAY CRYSTALLOGRAPHY. **Personal Data:** b Fond du Lac, Wis, March 19, 1923; m 1948, Shirley Robbins; c Susan & Deborah. **Education:** Univ Minn, BChem, 1946, PhD (phys chem), 1951. **Professional Experience:** PROF EMER PHYS CHEM, UNIV CONN, 1988-; assoc provost, Univ Conn, 1985-1988; actg vpres grad educ & res, Univ Conn, 1981-1983; guest scientist, Weizmann Inst, Univ Leyden & Univ Stockholm, 1969; NSF sci fac fel, Cambridge Univ, 1961-1962; from instr to prof phys chem, Univ Conn, 1952-1988; res fel, Calif Inst Technol, 1951-1952; asst chem, Univ Minn, 1946-1950. **Memberships:** Am Chem Soc; Am Crystallog Asn. **Research Statement & Publications:** X-ray diffraction by crystals. **Mailing Address:** Dept Chem, Univ Conn, Storrs, CT 06269.

KATZ, LEWIS E, PHYSICAL METALLURGY, MATERIALS SCIENCE. **Personal Data:** b Philadelphia, Pa, July 9, 1940; m 1969, c 1. **Education:** Drexel Inst, BS, 1963; Univ Pa, MS, 1964, PhD (mat sci), 1967. **Professional Experience:** SUPVR, BELL LABS, 1980-; mem tech staff, Bell Labs, 1969-1980; fel diffusion, Lawrence Radiation Lab, Univ Calif, 1967-1969. **Memberships:** Electrochem Soc. **Research Statement & Publications:** Radiation damage; phase transformations; diffusion; electron microscopy; x-ray analysis; crystal growth; semiconductor development. **Mailing Address:** 1530 Hampton Rd, Allentown, PA 18104.

KATZ, LOUIS, MOLECULAR BIOLOGY, COMPUTER SCIENCE. **Personal Data:** b New York, NY, August 3, 1932; m 1968, c 1. **Education:** City Col NY, BS, 1953; Univ Wis, MS, 1955, PhD (physics), 1959. **Professional Experience:** Sr res assoc & dir comput graphics facil, Dept Biol Sci, Col Physicians & Surgeons, Columbia Univ, 1968-; res assoc biochem, Albert Einstein Col Med, 1964-1965 & Mass Inst Technol, 1965-1968; res assoc biol, Mass Inst Technol, 1961-1964; res physicist, Visking Co Div, Union Carbide Corp, 1960-1961; Physicist, Union Carbide Metals Co, 1958-1960; SOFTWARE ENG MGR, RGB SPECTRUM, BERKELEY, CALIF. **Memberships:** Biophys Soc; Asn Comput Mach. **Research Statement & Publications:** Small angle x-ray scattering; molecular biophysics; interactive computer graphics; macromolecular structure. **Mailing Address:** RGB Spectrum, 950 Manna Village Pkwy, Alameda, CA 94501.

KATZ, MANFRED, POLYMER CHEMISTRY, TEXTILE CHEMISTRY. **Personal Data:** b Ger, February 16, 1929; American citizen. **Education:** Okla State Univ, BS, 1950, MS, 1951; Univ Del, PhD, 1961. **Professional Experience:** Independent consult, 1995-; vis prof & dir, Polymer Sci Prog, Howard Univ, 1992-1995; res fel, E I DuPont Del Nemours & Co, Inc, 1986-1992; from res assoc to sr res assoc, E I DuPont Del Nemours & Co, Inc, 1971-1986; tech supvr, E I DuPont Del Nemours & Co, Inc, 1967-1971; Res supvr, E I DuPont Del Nemours & Co, Inc, 1961-1967. **Memberships:** AAAS; Am Chem Soc; Sci Res Soc Am; NY Acad Sci. **Research Statement & Publications:** Condensation polymers; synthetic fibers; non-woven fabrics; composites; carbon fibers. **Mailing Address:** 310 Brockton Rd, Sharpley, Wilmington, DE 19803.

KATZ, MARVIN L(AVERNE), CHEMICAL ENGINEERING. **Personal Data:** b Tulsa, Okla, December 12, 1935; m 1955, Suzanne; c Laura, Donald & Stephen. **Education:** Univ Mich, BS, 1956, MS, 1958, PhD (chem eng), 196 1. **Professional Experience:** RETIRED; vpres eng, Chief Petrol Co, 1986-1992; vpres eng, Arco Oil Gas Co Div, 1984-1986; vpres planning & eval, Arco Oil-Gas Co Div, 1982-1984; vpres res & develop dept, Arco Oil-Gas Co Div, 1979-1982; chmn, technol task group, Nat Petrol Coun Comt on enhanced recovery techniques for oil & gas in the US, 1976; mgr res & develop dept, NAm Producing Div, Atlantic Richfield Co, 1972-1978; mgr admin dept, NAm Producing Div, Atlantic Richfield Co, 1969-1972; adminr sci comput, Sinclair Res Inc, 1964-1969; res engr, Sinclair Res Inc, 1960-1964. **Memberships:** Soc Petrol Engrs (pres, 1980). **Research Statement & Publications:** Fluid flow through porous media; heat transfer; computer science. **Mailing Address:** 6924 Leameadow, Dallas, TX 75248. **E-Mail:** marvdallas@aol.com

KATZ, MAX, FISHERIES. **Personal Data:** b Seattle, Wash, March 27, 1919; m 1946, c 4. **Education:** Univ Wash, Seattle, BS, 1939, MS, 1942, PhD (fisheries biol), 1949. **Professional Experience:** AFFIL PROF FISHERIES, UNIV WASH, 73-PRES, ENVIRON INFO SERV INC, 1976-; res dir, Seattle Marine Labs, Inc, res dir, Parametrix, Inc, 1974-1976; dir water resources info ctr, Univ Wash, 1971-1973; res prof, Univ Wash, 1966-1973; Health Plating Co, Wash, 1964-1965 & various other companies; Libby, McNeil & Libby, Ill, 1963-1965; Simpson Timber Co, Wash, 1963; off resource develop, USPHS, 1962-1964; Rayonier, Northwest Pulp & Paper Asn, 1961; actg assoc prof fisheries, Univ Wash, 1960-1966; Rayonier, Inc, Wash, 1959; consult, Calif Water Pollution Control Bd, 1958; Hon assoc prof, Dept Fish & Game Mgt, Ore State Col, 1954-1960; from fisheries res biologist to pollution biologist, Corvallis, 1953-1960; from fisheries res biologist to pollution biologist, USPHS, Cincinnati, 1949-1953; asst, Inst Paper Chem, Wis, 1946-1947; Fisheries biologist, State Dept Fisheries, Wash, 1940-1942. **Memberships:** Am Fisheries Soc; Am Soc Ichthyol & Herpet; Am Inst Fishery Res Biol; Water Pollution Control Fedn; Marine Biol Asn UK; Sigma Xi. **Research Statement & Publications:** Water quality requirements of fish; fish toxicology; biological effects of water pollution; blood parasites of fish; hematology of fish; fish diseases. **Mailing Address:** 36 Kenneth Cir, Waterbury, CT 06710.

KATZ, MICHAEL, PEDIATRICS, VIROLOGY. **Personal Data:** b Lwow, Poland, February 13, 1928; m 1986, Robin; c Edward Alexander. **Education:** Univ Pa, AB, 1949; State Univ NY, MD, 1956; Columbia Univ, MS, 1963. **Honors & Awards:** Med Award, Jurzykowski Found, 1984; Sr Scientist Award, Humboldt Found, 1987. **Professional Experience:** EMER CARPENTIER PROF PEDIAT & PUB HEALTH, COLUMBIA UNIV, as of 2006; VPRES RES, MARCH OF DIMES BIRTH DEFECTS FOUND, 1992-; mem, comt exam adverse effects of vaccines, 1990-1991; vis prof, Inst Virol, Univ Wuerzbuerg, Ger, 1988; dir pediat serv, Presby Hosp, 1977-; instr, Reuben S Carpenter prof pediat & chmn dept, 1977-1992; consult, Subcomt Interactions Nutrit & Infections, Nat Acad Sci, 1975-1980; chmn, Subcomt Interactions Nutrit& Infections, Nat Acad Sci, 1974-1975; prof pediat, Col Physicians & Surgeons, Columbia Univ, 1971-1977; mem, Subcomt Interactions Nutrit & Infections, Nat Acad Sci, 1971-1974; prof trop med, Col Physicians & Surgeons, Columbia Univ, 1970-1992; attend pediatrician, Presby Hosp, 1970-1977; asst prof, Sch Med, Univ Pa, 1966-1970; assoc physician, C's Hosp Philadelphia, 1966-1970; assoc mem, Wistar Inst, Philadelphia, 1965-1970; assoc, Sch Med, Univ Pa, 1965-1966; instr, Col Physicians & Surgeons, Columbia Univ, 1964-1965; assoc vis pediatrician, Harlem Hosp Ctr, New York, & asst pediatrician, Babies Hosp, 1964-1965; consults, Peace Corps vols, Princeton Univ, 1964; hon pediat specialist, Mulago Hosp, Kampala, Uganda, 1963-1964; resident pediat, Babies Hosp, New York, 1960-1962; intern, Med Ctr, Univ Calif, Los Angeles, 1956-1957; instr biol, Queen's Col, NY, 1951-1952; hon lectr, Makerere Univ, Uganda; consult, WHO, UNICEF & USAID. **Memberships:** Inst Med-Nat Acad Sci; Am Soc Trop Med & Hyg; NY Acad Sci; Am Pediat Soc; Soc Pediat Res; Infectious Dis Soc Am; fel AAAS. **Research Statement & Publications:** Relationship of malnutrition to infection; antibody production and other host defense responses in protein deficiency; etiology of diarrhea; rubella and vaccine production; nature of slow virus infections. **Mailing Address:** March Dimes Birth Defects Found, 1275 Mamaroneck Ave, White Plains, NY 10605. **Fax:** 914-997-4560. **E-Mail:** mkatz@modimes.org

KATZ, MORRIS HOWARD, FOOD SCIENCE, BIOCHEMISTRY. **Personal Data:** b Milwaukee, Wis, January 12, 1920; m 1954, Esther Nissenkoren; c Maynard S & Larry A. **Education:** Univ Wis, BS, 1943. **Professional Experience:** PRES, M H KATZ CONSULT INC, 1980-; Int Microwave Power Inst, 1977 & Am Asn Cereal Chemists, 1979; lectr flavor technol, Univ Minn, 1976; lectr flavor technol, Ctr Prof Advan, 1974 & 1976; res assoc res labs, Pillsbury Co, 1968-1980; Guest lectr, Ill Inst Technol, 1966 & 1970; sr scientist, Pillsbury Co, 1961-1968; head flavor sect, Pillsbury Co, 1959-1961; sr chemist, Pillsbury Co, 1958-1959; flavor res chemist, Fries & Fries, Inc, 1953-1958; mfg dir, B A Railton Co, 1952-1953; asst res dir, Orange Crush Co, 1949-1952; chief chemist, Martin Food Prod, Inc, 1947-1949; Chemist, Nat Syrup Prod Co, 1946-1947. **Memberships:** Am Chem Soc; Inst Food Technol; Soc Flavor Chemists. **Research Statement & Publications:** Flavor chemistry; food texture, ingredient systems and processes; flavor and food products development. **Mailing Address:** 2700 S Yosemite Ave, Minneapolis, MN 55416-1856.

KATZ, MORTON, ORGANIC CHEMISTRY, POLYMER CHEMISTRY. **Personal Data:** b New York, NY, April 25, 1934; m 1961, c 3. **Education:** State Univ NY Albany, BS, 1956, MS, 1961; Wayne State Univ, PhD (org chem), 1968. **Professional Experience:** SR RES CHEMIST, E I DU PONT DEL NEMOURS & CO, INC, 1985-; res chemist, Plastic Prod Dept, 1970-1985; res chemist, Buffalo, 1967-1970; technician, Gen Elec Res Lab, 1959-1961; Teacher high sch, 1956-1958. **Memberships:** Am Chem Soc. **Research Statement & Publications:** Chemistry of bicyclic and tricyclic molecules; high temperature polymers; market research. **Mailing Address:** Electronics Dept, E I du Pont de Nemours & Co Inc, Circleville, OH 43113.

KATZ, MURRAY ALAN, NEPHROLOGY, MICROCIRCULATORY PATHOPHYSIOLOGY. **Personal Data:** b Albuquerque, NMex, June 15, 1941; m 1964, c 2. **Education:** Johns Hopkins Univ, BA, 1963, MD, 1966. **Professional Experience:** PROF PHYSIOL, SCH MED, UNIV ARIZ, 1987-; dir, B W Zweifach Microcirculation Labs, 1986-; Assoc Chief Staff Res, Tucson Vet Affairs Med Ctr, 1982-; ASST CHIEF STAFF RES, TUCSON VET AFFAIRS MED CTR, 1982-; PROF NEPHROL, SCH MED, UNIV ARIZ, 1981-; clin investr award, Vet Admin, 1976; staff physician med & nephrology, Vet Admin Hosp, Tucson, 1974-; from asst prof to assoc prof, Tucson Vet Affairs Med Ctr, 1974-1981; actg chief nephrol, Sch Med, Temple Univ, 1973-1974; Res career develop award, Pub Health Serv, 1971-1976; asst prof, Sch Med, Temple Univ, 1971-1974; fel nephrol, Univ Tex Southwestern Med Sch, 1968-1970; resident, Osler Ward Serv, Johns Hopkins Univ Hosp, 1967-1968; intern med, Osler Ward Serv, Johns Hopkins Univ Hosp, 1966-1967. **Memberships:** Am Soc Nephrol; Am Fedn Clin Res; AAAS; Microcirculatory Soc; Am Physiol Soc; Int Soc Lymphology; W Soc Clin Invest (pres, 1987); W Asn Physicians. **Research Statement & Publications:** General microcirculatory physiology and pathophysiology; control of microcirculatory dynamics, hypertension, capillaropathies, vasculitis; diabetes. **Mailing Address:** Dept Internal Med & Physiol Univ Ariz Col Med, Vet Admn Md Ctr Rssrv MP (0-151), Tucson, AZ 85723. **E-Mail:** murrayk@email.arizona.edu

KATZ, NORMAN L, PHARMACOLOGY. **Personal Data:** b Boston, Mass. **Education:** Mass Col Pharm, BS, 1963; Albany Med Col, Union Univ, PhD (pharmacol), 1969. **Professional Experience:** PROF PHARMACOL, UNIV ILL MED CTR, CHICAGO, as of 2004; assoc prof pharmacol, Univ Ill Med Ctr, Chicago, beginning 1981; asst prof, Univ Ill Med Ctr, 1972-1981; fel neurophysiol, State Univ NY Albany, 1969-1972. **Memberships:** Soc Neuroscience; Am Soc Pharmacol Exp Therapeut. **Research Statement & Publications:** Behavioral Pharmacology; regulation of feeding behavior. **Mailing Address:** Dept Biopharmaceut Univ Ill, 833 S Wood St M/C 865, Chicago, IL 60612-4324. **Fax:** 312-996-0098. **E-Mail:** nlkatz@uic.edu

KATZ, OWEN M, FAILURE ANALYSIS, ELECTRON MICROSCOPY. **Personal Data:** b Baltimore, Md, December 21, 1932; m 1954, Shirley; c 2. **Education:** Carnegie-Mellon Inst, BS, 1954, MS, 1958; Univ Pittsburgh, PhD (metall eng), 1963. **Honors & Awards:** ASM award, 2001. **Professional Experience:** MEM STAFF, BETTIS ATOMIC POWER LAB, ADV SCIENTIST, as of 2002; SECY, BETTIS ATOMIC POWER LAB, as of 2001; Adj prof metall eng, Univ Pittsburgh, 1970-1975. **Memberships:** Fel Am Soc Metals Int; Electron Micros Soc Am; Int Metallog Soc. **Research Statement & Publications:** Over 300 published failure analysis reports, over 20 journal articles and book contributions; metallurgy, lab management; microanalytical techniques. **Mailing Address:** Bettis Atomic Power Lab, 5600 Munhall Rd No 703, Pittsburgh, PA 15217.

KATZ, PAUL K, INTERNAL MEDICINE, IMMUNOLOGY. **Education:** Georgetown Univ, MD, 1973. **Professional Experience:** CHMN MED, GEORGETOWN UNIV, as of 2005; chief operating officer, Med Ctr, Georgetown Univ Hosp, as of 1998; asst prof med, & chief, Allergy Div, Georgetown Univ Hosp, beginning 1984. **Mailing Address:** Med Ctr, Georgetown Univ Hosp, 3800 Reservoir Rd NW, Washington, DC 20007-2197. **Fax:** 202-687-8579. **E-Mail:** katzp@georgetown.edu

KATZ, RALPH VERNE, EPIDEMIOLOGY. **Personal Data:** b Jersey City, NJ, March 20, 1944; m 1968, Frey; c Amos E. **Education:** Trinity Col, Conn, BS, 1965; Tufts Univ, DMD, 1969; Univ Minn, MPH, 1971, PhD (epidemiol), 1976. **Professional Experience:** PROF & CHMN, DEPT EPIDEMIOL & HEALTH PROM, COL DENT, NY UNIV, 2000-present; prof, Dept Behav Sci & Community Health, Univ Conn, beginning 1989; co-dir, Oral Epidemiol Training Grant, Nat Inst Dent Res, beginning 1985 & Minority Oral Health Res Ctr, beginning 1992; assoc prof & head, Dept Restorative Dent, 1982-1989; dir grad studies, Oral Health Serv Older Adults, 1981-1982; dir & prin investr, Cardiol Training Prog, 1980-1982; Dept Epidemiol, Grad Sch, 1978-1982; assoc prof, Prog Dent Pub Health, Sch Pub Health, Univ Minn, 1976-1982; assoc prof, Dept Health Ecol, Sch Dent, 1976-1982; chief, Div Prev Dent, Inst Dent Res, US Army, Wash, DC, 1974-1976; dir dent serv, Phys Med & Rehab Unit, Univ Minn, 1972-1974; NIH & Nat Res Serv Awards fel, 1970-1974; lectr, Dept Epidemiol & Biostatist, Yale Univ. **Memberships:** Am Public Health Asn; Int Asn Dent Res; Soc Epidemiol Res; Am Asn Dent Sch; Sigma Xi; fel Am Col Epidemiol. **Research Statement & Publications:** Epidimiology of root caries and coronal caries; clinical trials of preventive agents for dental caries; oral health of older adults; cancer chemoprevention trials and risk factors for oral cancer/precancerous lesions. **Mailing Address:** Dept Epidemiol & Health Prom, Col Dent, NY Univ, 132, 433 First Ave, New York, NY 10010. **Fax:** 212-995-4436. **E-Mail:** ralph.katz@nyu.edu

KATZ, RANDY H, COMPUTER SCIENCE. **Personal Data:** b August 19, 1955; American citizen. **Education:** Cornell Univ, AB, 1976; Univ Calif, Berkeley, MS, 1978, PhD (comput sci), 1980. **Honors & Awards:** Brice Colloquium Lectr, Rice Univ, 1994; Distinguished Serv Award, Comput Res Asn, 1995. **Professional Experience:** DISTINGUISHED PROF, ELEC ENG & COMPUT SCI, MICROELECTRONICS CORP, 1996-; CHMN, COMPUT SCI DIV, ELEC ENG & COMPUT SCI DEPT, UNIV CALIF, BERKELEY, 1996-; prog mgr & dep dir, Comput Systs Technol Off, Advan Res Proj Agency, Dept Defense, 1993-1994; PROF, COMPUT SCI DIV, ELEC ENG & COMPUT SCI DEPT, UNIV CALIF, BERKELEY, 1989-; consult, Microtechnol Corp, 1989-1992; consult, Teknekron Corp, 1988-1992; consult, Software Alliance Inc, 1988-1992; Univ Colo, Boulder, 1988; distinguished invited lectr, Univ Wis-Madison, 1987; consult, Electronic Design Automation Inc, 1986-1989; consult, USAF, 1985-1987; consult, Tex Instruments Cent Res Lab, 1985-1986; consult, Microelectronics & Comput Technol Corp, 1985; consult, TMC Ltd, 1984; consult, Intermetrics Inc, 1984; from asst prof to assoc prof, Comput Sci, 1983-1989; consult, Digital Equip Corp, 1983-1987; consult, Res Triangle Inst, 1983; consult, Xerox Palo Alto Res Ctr, 1982-1985; asst prof, Comput Sci Dept, Univ Wis-Madison, 1981-1983; comput scientist, Comput Corp Am Inc, 1980-1981; comput scientist, Bolt, Beranek& Newman Inc, 1980; Acad assoc, IBM Res Lab, 1978; res asst, Univ Calif, Berkeley, 1977-1980; teaching asst, Univ Calif, Berkeley, 1976-1977; consult time-sharing, Cornell Univ, 1973-1976. **Memberships:** Fel Asn Comput Mach; fel Inst Elec & Electronics Engrs. **Research Statement & Publications:** Design, implementation and integration of wireless computing systems; collaborative applications; video archive systems. **Mailing Address:** Elec Eng & Comput Sci Dept, Univ Calif, 637 Soda Hall 1776, Berkeley, CA 94720-1776. **Fax:** 510-642-5775. **E-Mail:** randy@cs.berkeley.edu

KATZ, RICHARD WHITMORE, STATISTICS, ATMOSPHERIC SCIENCE. **Personal Data:** b Williamsburg, Va, September 12, 1948. **Education:** Univ Va, BA, 1970; Pa State Univ, PhD (statist), 1974. **Honors & Awards:** Spec Achievement Award, Environ Data Serv,

1975. **Professional Experience:** ED BD EXTREMES, 1997-; ED BD CLIMATIC CHANGE, 1997-; SR SCIENTIST, NAT CTR ATMOSPHERIC RES, BOULDER, 1994-; consult, Lawrence Livermore Nat Lab, 1981; prin investr, NSF grant, 1980-; asst prof atmospheric sci, Ore State Univ, 1979-1983; adj prof, Dept Econ, Univ Colo, 1977-1979; consult, NASA, 1977; scientist & statistician environ & societal impacts, Nat Ctr Atmospheric Res, 1975-1979; Fel, Nat Ctr Atmospheric Res, 1975-1976; Statistician climatic & environ assessment, Environ Data Serv, Nat Oceanic & Atmospheric Admin, 1974-1975. **Memberships:** Am Statist Asn; Inst Math Statist; AAAS; Am Meteorol Soc. **Research Statement & Publications:** Meteorological statistics; probabilistic models for hydrological variables; applied probability theory; climatic impacts. **Mailing Address:** Nat Ctr Atmospheric Res, PO Box 3000, Boulder, CO 80307. **Fax:** 303-497-8125. **E-Mail:** rwk@ucar.edu

KATZ, ROBERT, PHYSICS. **Personal Data:** b New York, NY, July 17, 1917; div, c Steven J & John H. **Education:** Brooklyn Col, AB, 1937; Columbia Univ, AM, 1938; Univ Ill, PhD (physics), 1949. **Professional Experience:** Vchmn dept, Univ Nebr, Lincoln, 1968-1973; EMER PROF PHYSICS, UNIV NEBR, LINCOLN, 1966-; from asst prof to prof, Kans State Univ, 1949-1966; physicist, US Army Air Force, Wright Field, 1943-1946; Radiologist, US Army Air Force, Wright Field, 1939-1943. **Memberships:** fel Am Phys Soc; Radiation Res Soc. **Research Statement & Publications:** Radiography; precipitation static radio interference; cereal technology; nuclear physics; structure of particle tracks; theory of relative biological effectiveness. **Mailing Address:** 5850 Sunrise Rd, Lincoln, NE 68510-4049.

KATZ, RONALD LEWIS, ANESTHESIOLOGY. **Personal Data:** b New York, NY, April 22, 1932; div, c Richard, Laura & Margaret. **Education:** Univ Wis, BA, 1948; Boston Univ, MD, 1956; Am Bd Anesthesiol, dipl, 1962; FRCPS, 1981. **Professional Experience:** PROF ANESTHESIOL, MED SCH, UNIV CALIF, LOS ANGELES, as fo 2004; chmn dept anesthesiol, Med Sch, Univ Calif, Los Angeles, 1973-1990; mem anesthesiol res training grant comt, NIH, 1970-; Guggenheim fel, 1968-1969; vis prof, Royal Postgrad Med Sch, Univ London, 1968-1969; consult anesthesiol res grant comt, NIH, 1965-; consult, Coun Drugs, Am Med Asn, 1962-; from asst prof to prof, Col Physicians & Surgeons, Columbia Univ, 1962-1973; assoc, Col Physicians & Surgeons, Columbia Univ, 1961-1962; instr, Col Physicians & Surgeons, Columbia Univ, 1960-1961; fel pharmacol, Col Physicians & Surgeons, Columbia Univ, 1959-1960; resident anesthesiol, Columbia-Presby Med Ctr Hosp, 1957-1959; intern, Staten Island Pub Health Serv, NY, 1956-1957. **Memberships:** Am Soc Anesthesiol; fel Am Col Anesthesiol; Am Soc Pharmacol & Exp Therapeut; Am Physiol Soc; Sigma Xi. **Research Statement & Publications:** Physiology; pharmacology; respiratory neurophysiology and neuropharmacology; cardiovascular physiology and pharmacology; neuromuscular transmission. **Mailing Address:** Dept Anesthesiol, Univ Calif Sch Med, GNH 14901 120 N State St, Los Angeles, CA 90033. **Fax:** 323-226-2794. **E-Mail:** merit@usc.edu

KATZ, SAMUEL, GEOPHYSICS. **Personal Data:** b Berlin, Ger, February 13, 1923; m Jean. **Education:** Univ Mich, BS, 1943; Columbia Univ, AM, 1947, PhD, 1955. **Honors & Awards:** Kunz Prize, NY Acad Sci, 1953. **Professional Experience:** FAC MEM, DEPT EARTH SCI, REGENTS COL, STATE UNIV NY, as of 2004; PROF EMER GEOPHYS, RENSSELAER POLYTECH INST, 1986-; chmn dept, Rensselaer Polytech Inst, 1963-1968; from assoc prof to prof, Rensselaer Polytech Inst, 1957-1985; sr physicist, Stanford Res Inst, 1956-1957; physicist, Stanford Res Inst, 1953-1956; asst, Lamont Geol Observ, Columbia Univ, 1948-1953; mem staff, Radiation Lab, Mass Inst Technol, 1943-1946. **Memberships:** Sigma Xi; Am Geophys Union. **Research Statement & Publications:** Marine sciences; seismology; underwater sound propagation; high pressure; exploration geophysics. **Mailing Address:** Dept Earth & Environ Sci, Rensselaer Polytech Inst, 110 8th St, Troy, NY 12180-3522. **Fax:** 518-276-2012.

KATZ, SAMUEL LAWRENCE, PEDIATRICS VACCINOLOGY. **Personal Data:** b Manchester, NH, May 29, 1927; m 1971, Catherine; c Samuel L Jr (deceased), John S, David L, Deborah S, Susan J, Penny J, Rachel A, Catherine C & William L. **Education:** Dartmouth Col AB, 1948; Harvard Univ, MD, 1952. **Honorary Degrees:** DSc, Georgetown Univ, 1996; DSc, Dartmouth Col, 1998. **Honors & Awards:** Grulee Medal, Am Acad Pediat; Jacobi Award, Am Med Asn & Am Acad Pediat; Saint Geme Award, Am Pediat Soc & Soc Pediat Res; Bristol Award, Infectious Dis Soc Am; Distinguished Physician Award, Pediat Infectious Dis Soc neesleman award am public health asson; howland award amer pediatric soc, Gold Medal Sabin Vaccine Institute. **Professional Experience:** RETIRED; chmn bd dir, Burroughs Wellcome Fund, 1995- 2000; chmn, adv comt Immunization Pract, USPHS, 1985-1993; chmn & pres, Asn Med Sch Pediat Dept, 1977-1979; Gen Clin Res Ctr Comt, NIH, 1971-1974 & Nat Adv Coun Child Health & Human Develop, 1974-1977; prof pediat & chmn dept, Wilburt C Davison prof, 1972-1997; Armed Forces Epidemiol Bd, Comn Immunization, 1969-1973; prof pediat & chmn dept, Sch Med, Duke Univ, 1968-1990; mem, Vaccine Develop Bd, Nat Inst Allergy & Infectious Dis, 1967-1971; Nat Inst Allergy & Infectious Dis career develop award, 1965-1968; sr assoc med, Newborn Div, 1965-1968; asst prof pediat, Harvard Med Sch, 1963-1968; consult coun drugs, AMA, 1963-1965; chief, Newborn Div, 1961-1968; tutor med sci, Harvard Med Sch, 1961-1963; assoc, Harvard Med Sch, 1959-1963; res assoc, Res Div Infectious Dis, 1958-1968; assoc physician, Children's Med Ctr, 1958-1963; pediatrician-in-chief, Beth Israel Hosp, 1958-1961; instr pediat, Harvard Med Sch, 1958-1959; Nat Found Infantile Paralysis res fel pediat, Res Div Infectious Dis, Children's Hosp Med Ctr, Harvard Med Sch, 1956-1958; exchange registr from Children's Hosp Med Ctr to pediat unit, St Mary's Hosp Med Sch, London, 1956; resident, Children's Hosp Med Ctr, 1955; asst resident, Children's Med Serv, Mass Gen Hosp, 1954-1955; jr asst resident, Children's Hosp Med Ctr, 1953-1954; Intern, Med Serv, Beth Israel Hosp, Boston, Mass, 1952-1953; co-chairman Indo-US vaccive action program 2000-2004 i co-chairman nat network for immunization information 1998- i member vaccine and reloved biol products advisory committe FDA 2000-2004: Chair, Board of Trustees, International Vaccine Institute 2004-. **Memberships:** Inst Med-Nat Acad Sci; Infectious Dis Soc Am; Am Asn Immunol; Am Pediat Soc (vpres, 1985-1986, pres, 1986-1987); Am Soc Clin Invest; Am Soc Virol; Am Acad Pediat. **Research Statement & Publications:** Tissue culture studies of measles virus variants; development of live attenuated measles virus vaccine; central nervous system viral infections; AIDS and human immuno-deficiency virus infections; innunization policy communication. **Mailing Address:** Dept Pediat Duke Medical Center, Duke Univ Sch Med Box 2925, Durham, NC 27710. **Fax:** 919-681-8934. **E-Mail:** katz0004@mc.duke.edu

KATZ, SHELDON LANE, RADAR SYSTEMS, PHYSICS. **Personal Data:** b Philadelphia, Pa, October 6, 1948; m 1973, Ruth; c Michelle, Gary & Jeffrey. **Education:** Temple Univ, BA, 1969, MA, 1973, PhD (physics), 1977. **Professional Experience:** PRIN MEM ENG STAFF, LOCKHEED MARTIN, MS2 MOORESTOWN, NJ, 1992-; sr mem eng staff, GE-Govt Electronic Systs Div, GE Aerospace, 1984-1992; asst prof physics, Villanova Univ, 1983-1984; asst prof physics, Lafayette Col, 1978-1983; vis lectr, Lafayette Col, 1977-1978; res asst, Temple Univ, Philadelphia, 1974-1977; Lab instr physics, Temple Univ, Philadelphia, 1969-1974. **Memberships:** Am Phys Soc; Inst Elec & Electronics Engrs. **Research Statement & Publications:** Dynamics of first and second order phase transitions; renormalization group; Monte Carlo simulations; radar performance analysis; phased array applications to radar meteorology; radar detection of aircraft wake vortices. **Mailing Address:** Lockheed Martin MS2, 199 Borton Landing Rd, Moorestown, NJ 08057. **E-Mail:** Sheldon.L.Katz@lmco.com

KATZ, SIDNEY, PHYSIOLOGY, NEUROPHYSIOLOGY. **Personal Data:** b Brooklyn, NY, December 23, 1930; m 1957. **Education:** NY Univ, BA, 1957, MS, 1959, PhD (physiol), 1963. **Professional Experience:** PROF PHYSIOL, MED UNIV SC, 1977-; from asst prof to assoc prof, Med Univ SC, 1965-1977; Nat Heart Inst fel, 1963-1965; instr physiol, Col Dent, 1962-1963; teaching asst neuroanat, Sch Med, NY Univ, 1961-1962. **Memberships:** Am Physiol Soc; Soc Neurosci. **Research Statement & Publications:** Central control of respiration and circulation; modulation of medullary neuron discharge patterns; ionic permeabiltiy of muscle studies with electrophysiological methods; electrophysiology of spinal cord injury. **Mailing Address:** Dept Physiol, Med Univ SC 171 Ashley Ave, Charleston, SC 29425-2658. **E-Mail:** katzs@musc.edu

KATZ, SIDNEY, MEDICINE. **Personal Data:** b Cleveland, Ohio, February 4, 1924; m 1946, c 4. **Education:** Case Western Res Univ, MD, 1948; Am Col Epidemiol, cert, 1982; Brown Univ, MA, 1984. **Honors & Awards:** Robert Weiss Award. **Professional Experience:** PROF EMER GERIAT, COLUMBIA UNIV, 1989-; prof architectonic & med, Case Western Res Univ, 1987-1989; sr adv, US Prev Serv Task Force, 1985-; assoc, Pop Studies & Training Ctr, Brown Univ, 1984-1987; dir, Long Term Care Geront Ctr, 1982-1987; assoc dean med & prof community health & med, Brown Univ, 1982-1987; dir, Ctr Policy Anal Aging & Long Term Care, Col Med, Mich State Univ, 1980-1982; spec adv, White House Conf Aging, 1980-1981; prof community health & chmn dept, Off Health Serv Educ & Res, Col Human Med, Mich State Univ, 1978-1982; prof, Dept Med, 1971-1982; prof med & dir, Off Health Serv Educ & Res, Col Human Med, Mich State Univ, 1971-1977; assoc dir, Dept Community Health, 1969-1971; dir, Univ Health Serv, Sch Med, Case Western Res Univ, 1966-1971; from instr to prof, Dept Prev Med & Med, Sch Med, 1952-1971; intern & resident internal med, Am Cancer Soc fel path, 1950-1951; intern & resident internal med, Case Western Res Univ, Univ Hosp Cleveland, 1948-1950; consult, Health Care Financing Admin, Nat Ctr Health Statist, Nat Ctr Health Serv Res, Rand Corp, Dykewood Corp, Appl Mgt Sci, Inc, Morgan Mgt Systs, Inc, Geomet, Inc, Urban Inst, Herman Miller Res Corp. **Memberships:** Inst Med-Nat Acad Sci; fel Geront Soc; Am Geriatrics Soc; Int Epidemiol Asn; Soc Epidemiol Res; AMA. **Research Statement & Publications:** Clinical epidemiology; gerontology; author of 4 books and over 60 journal articles. **Mailing Address:** Stroud Ctr, Columbia Univ, New York, NY 10032.

KATZ, SIDNEY A, RADIOCHEMISTRY, ANALYTICAL CHEMISTRY. **Personal Data:** b Camden, NJ, June 4, 1935; m 1957, c 2. **Education:** Rutgers Univ, AB, 1958; Univ Pa, PhD (chem), 1962. **Professional Experience:** Vis prof, Trace Anal Res Ctr, Dalhousie Univ, 1977 & ATOMKI, Hungarian Acad Sci, 1984; Rossnagel & Assocs, 1977-1978 & Jack McCormick & Assocs, 1978; consult, John G Reutter & Assocs, 1974-1975; consult, ACCU Test & Consult Lab, 1974-1975; vis prof, Univ, Reading, Berkshire, UK, 1973; NATO sr fel sci, NSF, 1973; PROF CHEM, RUTGERS UNIV, CAMDEN, 1971-; prof, Temple Univ, 1966-1970; Res chemist, E I du Pont Del Nemours & Co, Inc, 1966; from asst prof to assoc prof, Rutgers Univ, 1962-1971; res assoc, Univ Pa Hosp, 1960-1970; instr, Rutgers Univ, 1960-1962; asst instr chem, Univ Pa, 1958-1960; Chemist, R H Hollingshead Corp, 1953-1958. **Memberships:** AAAS; Am Chem Soc; Am Nuclear Soc. **Research Statement & Publications:** Environmental and biochemical effects of trace elements. **Mailing Address:** Dept Chem, Rutgers Univ, 315 Penn St, Camden, NJ 08102-1411. **Fax:** 856-225-6506. **E-Mail:** skatz@camden.rutgers.edu

KATZ, STEPHEN I, DERMATOLOGY. **Professional Experience:** DIR, NIAMS, NIH, 1995-; CHIEF, DERMAT BR, NAT CANCER INST, NIH, 1974-. **Memberships:** Inst Med-Nat Acad Sci. **Mailing Address:** NIAMS, NIH, Rm 12N238 NIH Bldg 10 9000 Rockville Pike, Bethesda, MD 20892. **Fax:** 301-496-5370. **E-Mail:** sk48w@nih.gov

KATZ, THOMAS JOSEPH, ORGANIC SYNTHESIS, MECHANISMS OF TRANSFORMATIONS. **Personal Data:** b Prague, Czech, March 21, 1936; American citizen; m 1963, Meta; c Joshua. **Education:** Univ Wis, BA, 1956; Harvard Univ, MA, 1957, PhD (chem), 1959. **Honors & Awards:** Arthur C Cope Scholar Award, Am Chem Soc. **Professional Experience:** PROF CHEM, COLUMBIA UNIV, 1968-; Guggenheim fel, 1967-1968; Sloan fel, 1962-1966; from asst prof to assoc prof, Columbia Univ, 1961-1968; instr, Columbia Univ, 1959-1961. **Memberships:** Am Chem Soc. **Research Statement & Publications:** Non-benzenoid aromatic compounds; organometallic compounds; organic synthesis; catalysis by metals; new materials. **Mailing Address:** Dept Chem, Columbia Univ, PO Box 3112 Havemeyer Hall, New York, NY 10027. **Fax:** 212-932-1289. **E-Mail:** tjk1@columbia.edu

KATZ, VICTOR JOSEPH, HISTORY OF MATHEMATICS. **Personal Data:** b Philadelphia, Pa, December 31, 1942; m 1969, Phyllis; c Sharon, Ari & Naomi. **Education:** Princeton Univ, AB, 1963; Brandeis Univ, MS, 1965, PhD, 1968. **Honors & Awards:** Watson Davis Prize, Hist Sci Soc, 1995. **Professional Experience:** PRIN INVESTR, NSF GRANT, ON-LINE MAGAZINE CONVERGENCE, AS OF 2006; prin investr, NSF Grant, Historical Modules, 1998-2002; co-prin investr, NSF Grant Inst His Math Use Teaching, 1995-2000; vis mathematician, Math Asn Am, 2002-2003, 1994-1995; mem coun, Can Soc Hist & Philos Math, 1987-1989 & 1990-1992; vis prof, dept math, Univ MD, 2003; vis prof, dept math, Boston Univ, 1985-1986; prof math, Univ dc, 1980-2005; vis res assoc, Int Hist & Philos Sci, Univ Toronto, 1978-1979; assoc prof, Univ DC, 1973-1980; asst prof, Fed City Col, 1968-1973. **Memberships:** Am Math Soc; Math Asn Am; Can Soc Hist & Philos Math; Brit Soc Hist Math. **Research Statement & Publications:** History of mathematics; application of history to the teaching of mathematics. **Mailing Address:** Math Assoc Am, Convergence, 1529 18th St NW, Washington, DC 20036-1385. **E-Mail:** vkatz@udc.edu

KATZ, WILLIAM, SURFACE ANALYSIS, ION BEAM METHODS. **Personal Data:** b Dayton, Ohio, December 10, 1953; m 1979. **Education:** Earlham Col, Richmond, Ind, BA, 1975; Univ Ill, Urbana, MS, 1977, PhD (anal chem), 1979; State Univ NY, Albany, MBA, 1986. **Professional Experience:** CO-OWNER, KATZ ANALYTICAL CTR, 1991-; OWNER, EVANS CENT, 1990-; dir labs, Perkin Elmer Corp, 1986-1990; mgr anal chem, Gen Elec, 1984-1986; adj prof physics, State Univ NY, Albany, 1981; mat scientist, Gen Elec, 1980-1984; res chemist, Exxon Res & Develop Lab, 1978-1980; chmn, Corp Affil Comt, Mat Res Soc. **Memberships:** Am Inst Physics; Am Vacuum Soc; Am Chem Soc; Microbeam Anal Soc. **Research Statement & Publications:** Application of ion beams for the characterization of electronic materials; ion-solid interactions; sputtering; secondary ionization mechanisms. **Mailing Address:** Katz Anal Ctr, 11415 Valley View Rd, Eden Prairie, MN 55344.

KATZ, WILLIAM J(ACOB), SANITARY & CHEMICAL ENGINEERING. **Personal Data:** b Chicago, Ill, January 19, 1925; m 1948, c 3. **Education:** Univ Ill, BS, 1948; Univ Wis, MS, 1949, PhD (chem eng), 1953. **Honors & Awards:** Eddy Medal, Water Pollution Control

Fedn, 1955, Gascoigne Medal. **Professional Experience:** CONSULT, 1992-; pres, WJK Assocs, Ltd, 1981-1992; pres, Environ Planning & Sci Div, Camp Dresser & McKee Inc, 1981-1992; dir tech serv, Milwaukee Metrop Sewerage Dist, 1977-1981; vpres res & develop, Envirex Inc, 1976-1977; mgr, Ecol Div, Rex Chainbelt Inc Div, 1970-1975; vis prof civil eng, Univ Wis, 1965-1967; tech dir & mgr water treatment & water pollution control res, Envirex Inc Div, Rexnord Inc, 1963-1970; dir sanit & indust wastes res & consult, Envirex Inc Div, Rexnord Inc, 1953-1963; proj assoc indust waste & treatment, Univ Wis, 1949-1952; adj prof civil eng, Marquette Univ. **Memberships:** Water Pollution Control Fedn; Nat Soc Prof Engrs; Am Soc Civil Engrs; Am Inst Chem Engrs; Am Water Works Asn. **Research Statement & Publications:** Water and industrial waste treatment; packing plant; mechanism of activated sludge; foundries; refineries. **Mailing Address:** 220 W Cherokee Cir, Milwaukee, WI 53217.

KATZ, YALE H, METEOROLOGY. **Personal Data:** b Milwaukee, Wis, March 15, 1920; m 1945, Rosella Joseph; c Donald S & Maxine R. **Education:** Univ Wis, BS, 1947 Soils, MS, 1948 Agronomy; Pa State Col, MS, 1951 Meteorology. **Professional Experience:** DIR, INST FOR TECHNOL COMMUNICATION, 1982-; dir, Ctr Continuing Prof Educ & Training, Santa Barbara, Calif, 1982-1984; tech dir, Soc Photo-Optical Instrumentation Engrs, 1977-1981; dir, Appl Res Assocs, 1976-1977; sr systs engr, TRW Systs Group, Redondo Beach, 1973-1976; assoc ed, Optical Eng, 1972-1978; ed, J Soc Photo-Optical Instrumentation Engrs, 1970-1972; 1963 & 1965 & Univ Calif, San Diego, 1970; sr staff mem, TRW Systs Group, Redondo Beach, 1967-1973; Univ Calif, Los Angeles, 1961; phys scientist, Rand Corp, Calif, 1960-1967; sr staff meteorologist, Itek Corp, 1958-1960; res assoc, Phys Res Labs, Univ Boston, 1956-1957; Air Force Sr Technol Specialist Sch, Mather AFB, 1956; Air Force Sr Technol Specialist Sch, MIT, 1956; Partner & assoc, Appl Res Assocs, 1954-1960; tech consult, USAF Air Weather Serv, 1954-1956; lectr, Univ Chicago, 1954; specialist climatic res, USAF Air Weather Serv, 1952-1954; meteorologist, USAF Air Weather Serv, 1951; Asst, Univ Wis, 1947-1948. **Memberships:** Am Meteorol Soc; Am Geophys Union; fel Soc Photo-Optical Instrument Engrs (vpres, 1971-1975, gov, 1970-1971 & 1975); Coun Eng Sci Soc Execs. **Research Statement & Publications:** Development of educational programs for medical, legal and industrial professionals; applied optical and electro-optical engineering; environmental engineering; Remotesensing of environment applied meteorology and climatology; solar energy utilization. **Mailing Address:** 2800 Woodridge Dr, Bellingham, WA 98226.

KATZE, JON R, NEOPLASIA, Q NUCLEOSIDE. **Personal Data:** b Portland, Ore, November 21, 1939; m 1982, Kathryn; c Kendall, Prudence & Jack. **Education:** Univ Calif, Berkeley, BS, 1961; Univ Calif, Los Angeles, PhD (physiol chem), 1966. **Professional Experience:** PROF MICROBIOL & IMMUNOL, UNIV TENN, MEMPHIS, 1983-; assoc prof microbiol & immunol, Univ Tenn, Memphis, 1976-1983; asst prof microbiol, Univ Southern Calif, 1969-1976. **Memberships:** AAAS; Am Soc Microbiol; Am Soc Biochem & Molecular Biol. **Research Statement & Publications:** association of defective queuosine nucleoside metabolism with neoplasia; linkage of queuosine deficiency with tumor promotion; wide distribution of queuosine base in the biosphere but absence of synthesis in eukaryotes. **Mailing Address:** Dept Microbiol & Immunol, Univ Tenn, Rm 701 MSB 858 Madison Ave, Memphis, TN 38163. **Fax:** 901-448-8462. **E-Mail:** jkatze@utmem.edu

KATZEN, RAPHAEL, CHEMICAL ENGINEERING. **Personal Data:** b Baltimore, Md, July 28, 1915; m 1938, c 1. **Education:** Polytech Inst Brooklyn, BChE, 1936, MChE, 1938, DChE(chem eng), 1942. **Honors & Awards:** Chem Eng Prof Pract Award, Am Inst Chem Engrs, 1986, Robert L Jacks Mem Award, 1990; C D Scott Award, 1997. **Professional Experience:** CHMN, KATZEN INT INC, 1996-; mem nat panel, Am Arbit Asn, beginning 1970; mem adv bd, Expos Chem Indust, beginning 1955; pres consult & design, Raphael Katzen Assocs Int Inc, 1953-1996; prin chem process, Raphael Katzen Assocs Int Inc, 1953; proj mgr chem plant & mgr design & construct, Eng Div, Vulcan-Cincinnati, 1944-1953; tech supvr res & develop, Diamond Alkali Co, 1942-1944; dir res, Chem Prod, Northwood Chem Co, 1937-1940; instr chem eng, Polytech Inst Brooklyn. **Memberships:** Nat Acad Eng; fel Am Inst Chem Engrs; fel Am Inst Chemists; Tech Asn Pulp & Paper Indust; Can Pulp & Paper Asn; fel Am Chem Soc. **Research Statement & Publications:** Organosolv pulping process; new technology for enzymatic conversion of cellulosic materials to sugar and ethanol; advanced technology in scrubbing and recovery of sulfur dioxide emmissions; biomass conversion to fuels and chemicals technology. **Mailing Address:** Katzen Int Inc, 2300 Wall St Ste K, Cincinnati, OH 45212-2783. **Fax:** 513-351-0810.

KATZENBERG, MARY ANNE, PHYSICAL ANTHROPOLOGY. **Education:** Univ Cincinnati, BA, 1974 & MA, 1976; Univ Toronto, PhD, 1983. **Honors & Awards:** Oschinsky-McKern Award, Can Asn Phys Anthropol, 1982. **Professional Experience:** HEAD, DEPT ARCHEAOL, UNIV CALGARY, 2001-; PROF, DEPT ARCHEAOL, UNIV CALGARY, 1995-; vis assoc prof, Univ Calif, Santa Barbara, 1992; asst dean, fac Soc Sci, Univ Calgary, 1988-1991; from asst prog to assoc prof, Dept Archaeol, Univ Calgary, 1985-1995; asst prof, Scarborough Campus, Univ Toronto, 1983-1985; part time lectr, Erindale Campus, Univ Toronto, 1982. **Mailing Address:** Dept Archaeol, Univ Calgary 2500, University Drive N W, Calgary, AB T2N 1N4, Can. **Fax:** 403-282-9567.

KATZENELLENBOGEN, BENITA SCHULMAN, REPRODUCTIVE ENDOCRINOLOGY, CANCER BIOLOGY. **Personal Data:** b New York, NY, April 11, 1945; m 1967, John; c Deborah J & Rachel A. **Education:** Brooklyn Col, CUNY BA, 1965; Harvard Univ, MA, 1966, PhD (biol), 1970. **Honors & Awards:** Nat Young Scholar Award, Am Asn Univ Women, 1981; Ernst Oppenheimer Mem Award, Endocrine Soc1984; Breast Cancer Res Award, Susan G Komen Found, 1988 & 1993; Merit Award, NIH, 1991; Sci Distinction Awd, Susan G Komer Fund, 1996; Jill Rose Awd, The Breast Cancer Resc Fudn, 1998; Distingu Alumnous Awd CUNY, 2002. **Professional Experience:** PROF MED MOLECULAR INTEGRATIVE PHYS, UNIV ILL, URBANA, as of 2004; pres Endcrine Soc, 2000-2001; biochem endocninol stufy sect NIH, 1995-1999; co-chmn Gordon Res Conf Hormone Action, 1988; int org comt, Int Cong on Hormones & Cancer, 1987-; Am Asn Cancer Res Task Force Endocrinol, 1987-1989; endocrinol study sect, NIH-Nat Inst Diabetes & Digestive & Kidney Dis Bd Sci Counselors, 1985-1989; prog comt, Endocrine Soc, 1983-1987; struct biol, Col Med, Univ Ill, Physiol & biophys, Urnana, beginning 1982; publications comt, Endocrine Soc, 1981-1983; endocrinol study sect, NIH, 1979-1983; vis prof, Dept Biochem & Biophys, Univ Calif, San Francisco, 1977-1978; from assoc prof to prof, Dept Physiol & Biophys, 1970-1982; NIH res fel endocrinol, Dept Physiol & Biophys, 1970-1971. **Memberships:** Am Physiol Soc; Endocrine Soc; Am Asn Cancer Res; Soc Study Reproduction; fel Am Acad Arts & Sci; pres The Endocrine Soc 2000-2001. **Research Statement & Publications:** Regulation of the growth and function of reproductive tissues and tumors, especially breast cancer, by reproductive hormones and antihormones. **Mailing Address:** Dept Physiol & Biophys Univ Ill, 524 Burrill Hall 407 S Goodwin Ave, Urbana, IL 61801-3704. **E-Mail:** katzenel@uiuc.edu

KATZENELLENBOGEN, JOHN ALBERT, BIO-ORGANIC CHEMISTRY, SYNTHETIC ORGANIC CHEMISTRY. **Personal Data:** b Poughkeepsie, NY, May 10, 1944; m 1967, Benita; c Deborah J & Rachel A. **Education:** Harvard Univ, BA, 1966, MA, 1967, PhD (chem), 1969. **Honors & Awards:** Teacher Scholar Award, Camille & Henry Dreyfus Found, 1974-1979; Paul C A e bersold Award, Soc Nuclear Med, 1995. **Professional Experience:** SWANLUND PROF CHEM, UNIV ILL, URBANA, as of 2002; prof chem, Univ Ill, beginning 1979; Guggenheim fel, 1977-1978; Sloan fel, 1974-1976; from asst prof to assoc prof, Univ Ill, Urbana, 1969-1979; chmn, study sect, NIH. **Memberships:** Fel AAAS; Am Chem Soc; NY Acad Sci; Am Soc Biol Chemists; fel Am Acad Arts & Sci; Soc Nuclear Med; endocine soc. **Research Statement & Publications:** New synthetic methods; organometallic chemistry; natural product synthesis; mechanism of hormone action; affinity labeling; tumor localizing agents; radiopharmaceutical development; fluorescence; enzyme inhibitors; steroids; hormone receptors. **Mailing Address:** Sch Chem Sci Univ Ill, 600 S Mathews Ave, Urbana, IL 61801. **Fax:** 217-333-7325. **E-Mail:** jkatzene@uiuc.edu

KATZIN, GERALD HOWARD, PHYSICS. **Personal Data:** b Winston-Salem, NC, August 2, 1932; m 1958, c 2. **Education:** NC State Univ, BS, 1954, MS, 1956, PhD (relativity), 1963. **Professional Experience:** PROF PHYSICS, NC STATE UNIV, 1976-; NSF grant, 1967; from asst prof to assoc prof, Nc State Univ, 1963-1976; assoc nuclear reactor theory, Astra, Inc, Conn, 1957-1958. **Memberships:** Am Phys Soc. **Research Statement & Publications:** Study of the relations between symmetries and conservation laws; theoretical mechanics; Riemannian geometry and tensor analysis; differential geometry; general relativity; classical electrodynamics. **Mailing Address:** Dept Math Physics, NC State Univ, Raleigh, NC 27695-8202. **Fax:** 919-515-6538. **E-Mail:** gerald_katzin@ncsu.edu

KATZIN, LEONARD ISAAC, physical inorganic chemistry; deceased, see previous edition for last biography

KATZMAN, ROBERT, NEUROLOGY. **Personal Data:** b Denver, Colo, November 29, 1925; m 1947, c 2. **Education:** Univ Chicago, BS, 1949, MS, 1951; Harvard Med Sch, MD, 1953; Am Bd Psychiat & Neurol, dipl & cert neurol, 1959. **Honors & Awards:** S Weir Mitchell Award, Am Acad Neurol, 1960; Ann Prize, Am Asn Neuropathologists, 1962; Humanitarian Award & Allied Achievement Aging Award, Alzheimer's Dis & Related Dis Asn, 1985; Henderson Mem Award, Geriat Soc, 1986; George W Jacoby Award, Am Neurol Asn, 1989; Potamkin Prize, co-recipient, 1992; Leadership Award, Alzheimer's Asn San Diego, 1992; Rita Hayworth Gala Award, Nat Alzheimer's Asn, 1994; Crystal Tower Award, Nat Alzheimer's Asn, 1998; Luigi Amaducci Mem Award, Int Psychogeriatric Asn, 2003. **Professional Experience:** PROF EMER NEUROSCIENCE, UNIV CALIF, SAN DIEGO, 2002-; res prof neuroscience, Univ Calif, San Diego, 1995-2002; Adv Panel Alzheimer's Dis, Dept Health & Human Serv, 1987-1993; Adv Bd Alzheimer's Dis, US Cong, 1987; attend neurologist, San Diego Med Ctr & San Diego Vet Admin Med Ctr, 1984-1995; prof, Univ Calif, San Diego, 1984-1994; chmn dept, Univ Calif, San Diego, 1984-1990; Florence Riford prof res, Alzheimer's Dis, Sch Med, Univ Calif, San Diego, 1984-1990; mem, adv coun, Nat Inst Aging, 1982-1985; attend neurologist, Montefiore Hosp & Med Ctr, 1982-1984; chmn, Aging Rev Comt, 1980-1981; mem, Aging Rev Comt, 1976-1981; dir, Hosp, 1974-1984; chmn, Neurol Dis Prog Proj Rev Comt, 1972-1973; dir neurol serv, Bronx Munic Hosp Ctr, 1970-1984; mem, Neurol Prog Proj A Comn, Nat Inst Neurol & Commun Dis & Stroke, 1969-1972; consult, Montefiore Hosp & Med Ctr, 1966-1982; chmn, Neurochem Sect, Am Acad Neurol, 1965-1967; attend neurologist, Bronx Munic Hosp Ctr, 1964-1984; chmn dept, Albert Einstein Col Med, 1964-1981; mem res rev panel, Nat Mult Sclerosis Soc, 1964-1970; asst examr, Am Bd Psychiat & Neurol, 1963-1970; USPHS career res develop award, 1962-1966; assoc attend neurologist, Bronx Munic Hosp Ctr, 1962-1964; consult, Jewish Bd Guardians, 1961-1965; USPHS sr fel neurophysiol, 1961-1962; from asst prof to prof, Albert Einstein Col Med, 1960-1984; guest scholar, Polytech Inst Brooklyn, 1960-1961; assoc, Albert Einstein Col Med, 1958-1960; Nat Mult Sclerosis Soc fel, 1957-1959; instr neurol, Albert Einstein Col Med, 1957-1958; chief resident neurologist, Neurol Inst, Columbia Presby Hosp, 1956-1957; asst neurol, Columbia Univ, 1956-1957; asst resident neurol, Neurol Inst, Columbia Presby Hosp, 1954-1956; intern, Harvard Med Serv, Boston City Hosp, 1953-1954. **Memberships:** Inst Med-Nat Acad Sci; fel AAAS; fel Am Acad Neurol; Am Asn Neuropathologists; Int Soc Neurochem; Soc Neurosci; Am Neurol Asn (pres, 1984-1985); Int Soc Alzheimer's Dis Res (pres, 1996-1997). **Research Statement & Publications:** Epidemiology, clinical-pathological correlation and risk factors for Alzheimer's Disease. **Mailing Address:** Dept Neuroscience, Univ Calif, San Diego, 9500 Gilman Dr, La Jolla, CA 92093-0949. **Fax:** 619-622-1016. **E-Mail:** rkatzman@ucsd.edu

KATZOFF, SAMUEL, AERODYNAMICS. **Personal Data:** b Baltimore, Md, August 3, 1909. **Education:** Johns Hopkins Univ, BS, 1929, PhD (chem), 1934. **Professional Experience:** INSTR, GIFTED CHILDREN, CTR TALENTED YOUTH, JOHN HOPKINS UNIV, 1972-; ed, Remote Measurement Pollution, 1971; ed, Proc Symposium Thermal Radiation Solids, 1964; from sr staff scientist to chief scientist, Langley Res Ctr, NASA, 1964-1972; asst chief, Appl Mat & Physics Div, 1960-1964; res scientist, Nat Adv Comt Aeronaut, NASA, 1958-1960; physicist, Nat Adv Comt Aeronaut, NASA, 1936-1958; Jones fel biophys, Cold Spring Harbor, 1935-1936; res chemist, Baltimore Paint & Color Works, 1934-1953; lab technician, Rockefeller Inst, 1929-1930. **Memberships:** AAAS. **Research Statement & Publications:** X-ray crystallography; x-ray studies of the molecular arrangements in liquids; colloids; general aerodynamics; stability; electrical analogies; wind-tunnel interference; cascades; helicopters; space sciences; thermal control of spacecraft. **Mailing Address:** Ctr Talented Youth, 5801 Smith Ave Ste 400 McAuley Hall, Baltimore, MD 21209.

KATZUNG, BERTRAM GEORGE, PHARMACOLOGY, MEDICINE. **Personal Data:** b Floral Park, NY, June 11, 1932; m 1957, Alice; c Katharine & Brian. **Education:** Syracuse Univ, BA, 1953; State Univ NY, MD, 1957; Univ Calif, PhD, 1962. **Professional Experience:** Periodic guest lectr, Sch Med, Stanford Univ, Univ Hawaii & Univ Calif, Berkeley; ed, Basic & Clin Pharmacol; act chmn, Univ Calif, San Francisco, 1980-1983; PROF PHARMACOL, MED CTR, UNIV CALIF, SAN FRANCISCO, 1971-; VCHMN DEPT, MED CTR, UNIV CALIF, SAN FRANCISCO, 1967-; Markle Scholar, 1966-1971; from asst prof to assoc prof, Univ Calif, San Francisco, 1962-1971; lectr, Univ Calif, San Francisco, 1960-1962. **Memberships:** AAAS; Am Soc Pharmacol & Exp Therapeut; Biophys Soc; Soc Gen Physiologists; NY Acad Sci. **Research Statement & Publications:** Cardiovascular pharmacology; electrophysiology; author and editor of 3 books. **Mailing Address:** 65 Knoll Rd, San Rafael, CA 94901-3626.

KAUDER, OTTO SAMUEL, ORGANIC CHEMISTRY. **Personal Data:** b Vienna, Austria, November 26, 1926; American citizen; m 1956, c 2. **Education:** City Col New York, BS, 1946; Polytech Inst Brooklyn, MS, 1949; Oxford Univ, DPhil(org chem), 1952. **Professional Experience:** AT, LERNER & GREENBERG, 1995-; TECH VPRES, ARGUS CHEM CORP, 1979-; vpres res & develop, Argus Chem Corp, 1968-1979; patent liaison & toxicol supvr, Argus Chem Corp, 1962-1968; res group leader, Argus Chem Corp, 1959-1968; chemist plastics additives, Argus Chem Corp, 1952-1959; Chemist, Polychem Labs, NY,

1946-1948. **Memberships:** Am Chem Soc. **Research Statement & Publications:** Time-dependent properties of organic compounds and effect of additives and contaminants thereon; synthesis of organic compounds containing phosphorus, cadmium, tin and antimony. **Mailing Address:** Lerner & Greenberg, 2445 Hollywood Blvd, Hollywood, FL 33020. **Fax:** 954-925-1101. **E-Mail:** okauder@patentusa.com

KAUER, JAMES CHARLES, ORGANIC CHEMISTRY, NEUROCHEMISTRY. **Personal Data:** b Cleveland, Ohio, January 17, 1927; m 1954, c Julie, Catherine, James, Frederic & Susanne. **Education:** Case Western Res Univ, BS, 1951; Univ Ill, PhD (chem), 1955. **Professional Experience:** VPRES CHEM TECHNOL, CEPHALON INC, 1994-; dir chem, Cephalon Inc, 1988-1993; prin investr med chem, Dupont, 1985-1987; Res chemist, E I du Pont Del Nemours & Co, Inc, 1955-1985. **Memberships:** Am Chem Soc; Soc Neurosci; AAAS. **Research Statement & Publications:** Organic synthesis; heterocycles; peptides; antiviral agents; neurotransmitter analogs; Neuropeptides; growth factors; enzyme inhibitors. **Mailing Address:** Savorys Mill Rd, Kennett Square, PA 19348. **E-Mail:** kauer@shrys.hslc.org

KAUER, JOHN STUART, SENSORY PHYSIOLOGY, BIOMIMICRY. **Personal Data:** b New York, NY, December 26, 1943; m 1985, Barbara R Talamo; c Jane & Joshua. **Education:** Clark Univ, BA, 1967, MA, 1969; Univ Pa, PhD (anat), 1973. **Honors & Awards:** Javits Award, NIH, 1988; wright awad sr, Fraser Univ, 1996; mannheimer award monell Ctr, Univ PA, 1998; achems award, 2002. **Professional Experience:** PROF NEUROSCI, TUFTS UNIV MED SCH, 1993-; prof neurosci, anat & cell biol & dir neurosurg res, 1983-1993; asst prof, Sect Neurosurg, 1978-1980; res assoc & dir lab studies, Sch Med, Yale Univ, 1976-1978; Fel neurophysiol, Sch Med, Yale Univ, 1973-1975. **Memberships:** Soc Neurosci; Asn Chemoreception Sci; Europ Chemoreception Res Orgn; Executive Chairman, 1994; Program Chairman, 1990. **Research Statement & Publications:** Central synaptic organization of the olfactory and other sensory systems; mathematical models of neurophysiology; artificial olfactory systems. **Mailing Address:** Tufts Univ Med Sch Dept Neurosci, 136 Harrison Ave, Boston, MA 02111. **E-Mail:** john.kautr@tufils.edu

KAUFERT, JOSEPH MOSSMAN, MEDICAL ANTHROPOLOGY. **Personal Data:** b Minneapolis, Minn, February 10, 1943; m 1970, c 1. **Education:** Univ Minn, BA, 1966; Northwestern Univ, MA, 1968, PhD (polit sci, anthrop), 1973. **Honors & Awards:** Keith L Were Award, Nat Media Develop Trust, 1972. **Professional Experience:** Vis health scientist, Univ Toronto, 1985; prof, Dept Social & Prev Med, 1985; adj prof, Dept Anthrop, Univ Man, 1977-; Nat Haemophilia Soc, UK, 1974-1976 & Ment Health Man, 1977-1978; PROF COMMUNITY MED, COMMUNITY HEALTH SCI, FAC MED, UNIV MAN, 1976-; head soc sci sect, St Thomas Hosp Med Sch, Univ London, 1974-1976; consult, Welsh Off, Brit Health & Social Serv, UK, 1974-1976; Leverhulme fel, Univ Birmingham, 1973-1974; asst prof med sociol & social psychiat, Med Sch, Univ Tex, San Antonio, 1972-1974; asst prof health admin, Baylor Univ, 1971-1972; vis prof Can Studies, Leeds Univ. **Memberships:** Soc Social Med; fel Soc Appl Anthrop; Brit Sociol Asn; Soc Med Anthrop; Can Asn Med Anthrop (pres). **Research Statement & Publications:** Social epidemiology; medical sociology; illness behavior; the sociology of disability; social gerontology. **Mailing Address:** Dept Community Health Sci, Fac Med Univ Man, Winnipeg, MB R3T 2N2, Can. **Fax:** 204-772-8748. **E-Mail:** kaufertj@ms.umanitoba.ca

KAUFFELD, NORBERT M, entomology, apiculture; deceased, see previous edition for last biography

KAUFFMAN, CAROL A, INFECTIOUS DISEASES, FUNGAL INFECTIONS. **Personal Data:** b Columbia, Pa, October 9, 1943; m Charles; c 0. **Education:** Penn State Univ, BS, 1965; Univ Mich, MD, 1969. **Professional Experience:** Asst dean student affairs, Univ Mich, 1986-1991; PROF, DEPT INTERNAL MED, HEALTH SYSTEM, UNIV MICH, 1981-; CHIEF, DIV INFECTIOUS DIS, VET ADMIN MED CTR, ANN ARBOR, MICH, 1977-; fel, Univ Cincinnati, 1973. **Memberships:** Int Imunocompromised Host Soc (pres, 2002-2004); Infectious Dis Soc Am; Am Soc Microbiol; Am Fedn Clin Res; Am Col Physicians; Cent Soc Clin Res. **Research Statement & Publications:** Infections in the elderly; antifungal therapy. **Mailing Address:** Vet Affairs Ann Arbor Healthcare Syst, Rm 838A(111-I) 2215 Fuller Rd, Ann Arbor, MI 48105-2399. **Fax:** 734-769-7039. **E-Mail:** ckauff@umich.edu

KAUFFMAN, ELLWOOD, DIGITAL COMPUTER PROGRAMMING, COMPUTER APPLICATIONS. **Personal Data:** b Philadelphia, Pa, March 18, 1928; m 1950, Shirley Rosengarten; c Scott L, Geoffrey N, Jane R & Matthew W. **Education:** Temple Univ, AB, 1952. **Professional Experience:** DIR, PARHAM GROUP, 1988-; PRES, MAINTENANCE DATABASE SYSTS, INC, 1985-; exec vpres, K-Squared Systs, Inc, 1978-1984; exec vpres, Mainstem, Inc, 1965-1978; tech dir, Mgt Info Systs, Inc, 1965-1969; pres, Appl Data Res, Inc, 1959-1963 & Comput Mgt Corp, 1963-1965; comput consult, 1958-1959; sr programmer digital comput, Elec Assocs, Inc, 1957-1958; comput applns officer, Chesapeake & Ohio Rwy Co, Va, 1955-1957; Sr analyst, Remington Rand, Inc, NY, 1952-1955. **Memberships:** Am Pub Work Asn. **Research Statement & Publications:** Utility concept of computer problem solving; application of digital computing systems to the solutions of commercial and scientific problems; automatic programming procedures for digital computers; application of mainframe, mini- & personal computers to maintenance management applications. **Mailing Address:** 35 Richard Ct, Princeton, NJ 08540.

KAUFFMAN, ERLE GALEN, PALEOBIOLOGY, PALEOECOLOGY. **Personal Data:** b Washington, DC, February 9, 1933; m 1956, c 3. **Education:** Univ Mich, BS, 1955, MS, 1956, PhD (geol, paleont, stratig), 1961. **Honorary Degrees:** MS, Oxford Univ, 1970. **Professional Experience:** PROF EMER GEOBIOLOGY & SEDIMENTARY SYSTS, IND UNIV, as of 2005; geol sci stop, Univ Colo, Boulder, as of 2002; adj prof, Univ Colo, beginning 1976; mem, Univ Colo, 1976-1978; res assoc, Mus Paleontol, Univ Mich, beginning 1975; mem, Univ Tubingen, 1974; vis prof, Oxford Univ, 1970-1971; cur dept paleobiol, beginning 1967; Smithsonian Res Found grants, beginning 1965; adj prof, George Wash Univ, beginning 1965; Paleont Soc rep, Comt Earth Sci, Nat Res Coun-Nat Acad Sci, 1965-1971; Am Geol Inst vis lectr, 1965-1966; NSF res grant, 1963-1971; lectr, George Wash Univ, 1963-1964; assoc cur, 1961-1967; asst cur, US Nat Mus, Smithsonian Inst 1960-1961. **Memberships:** AAAS; Brit Palaeont Asn; Malacol Soc London; Int Palaeont Union; Paleont Soc. **Research Statement & Publications:** Systematics, evolution and paleoecology of Mesozoic-Cenozoic Mollusca; ecology of Recent Mollusca; Mesozoic-Cenozoic stratigraphy, biostratigraphy and sedimentation. **Mailing Address:** Dept Geol Sci, Ind Univ 1005 E Tenth St, Bloomington, IN 47405. **E-Mail:** kauffman@indiana.edu

KAUFFMAN, FREDERICK C, BIOCHEMISTRY, PHARMACOLOGY. **Personal Data:** b Chicago, Ill, July 9, 1936; m 1961, c 2. **Education:** Knox Col, Ill, BA, 1958; Univ Ill, Chicago, PhD (pharmacol), 1965. **Professional Experience:** DISTINGUISHED PROF PHARMACOL TOXICOL, RUTGERS UNIV, 1988-; prof pharmacol, Sch Med, Univ MD, Baltimore, 1978-1988; assoc prof, State Univ NY, Buffalo, 1974-1978; asst prof & assoc pharmacol, State Univ NY, Buffalo, 1967-1974; USPHS fel pharmacol, Wash Univ, 1965-1967. **Memberships:** AAAS; Am Chem Soc; Am Toxicol Soc; Am Pharmacol Soc. **Research Statement & Publications:** Biochemical pharmacology; neurochemistry. **Mailing Address:** Dept Toxicol, Rutgers Univ, 41 Gordon Rd, Piscataway, NJ 08854-5930. **Fax:** 732-445-6905. **E-Mail:** kauffma@rci.rutgers.edu

KAUFFMAN, GEORGE BERNARD, INORGANIC CHEMISTRY, HISTORY OF SCIENCE, COORDINATION CHEMISTRY. **Personal Data:** b Philadelphia, Pa, September 4, 1930; m 1969, Laurie; c Ruth D(Bryskier), Judith M(Reposo), Robert Papazian, Teresa Lynn(Baron) & Mary Papazian. **Education:** Univ Pa, BA, 1951; Univ Fla, PhD (chem), 1956. **Honors & Awards:** Lev Aleksandrovich Chugaev Jubilee Dipl & Bronze Medal, USSR Acad Sci, 1976, Nikolai Semenovich Kurnakov Jubilee Dipl & Bronze Medal, 1990, Ilya Ilyich Chernyaev Jubilee Dipl & Bronze Medal, 1991; Catalyst Award, Mfg Chemists Asn, 1976; Dexter Award Hist of Chem, 1978; Marc-Aguste Pictet Medal, Physics Soc Natural Hist Geneve, 1992; George C Pimentel Award Chem Educ, Am Chem Soc, 1993; Laudatory Decree, S I Vavilov Inst for History of Natural Sci & Tech, Russian Acad of Sci, 2000; Award for Res at an Undergraduate Institution, Am chem Soc, 2000; Helen M Free Award for Public Outreach, Am Chem Soc 2002. **Professional Experience:** PROF EMER CHEM, CALIF STATE UNIV, FRESNO, as of 1999; contributing ed, Chem 13 News, beginning 1998; contributing ed, Chem Educ, beginning 1996; contributing ed, Chem Heritage, beginnning 1996; contributing ed, chem intelligencer, 1995-2000; contributing ed, Today's Chemist at Work, beginning 1995; contributing ed, Today's Chemist, beginning 1989; contributing ed, J Chem Educ, beginning 1987; contrib ed, Indust Chemist, 1985; contrib ed, Polyhedron, 1982-1985; Nat Endowment Humanities grant, 1982-1983; Strindberg fel, Svenska Inst, 1982-1983; contrib ed, Hexagon, beginnning 1980; ed, Topics Hist Chem, Lectures on Tape Series, Am Chem Soc, 1978-1981; vis scholar, Univ Calif, Berkeley, 1976 & Univ Puget Sound, 1978; NSF res grants, Berkeley, 1976-1977; co-ed, Topics Hist Chem, Lectures on Tape Series, Am Chem Soc, 1975-1978; grant, John Simon Guggenheim Mem Found, 1975; CONTRIBUTING ED, J COL SCI TEACHING, 1973-; fel, John Simon Guggenheim Mem Found, 1972-1973; NSF undergrad res partic dir, 1972; tour speaker, Am Chem Soc, 1971; chmn, Div Hist Chem, Am Chem Soc, 1969; prof chem, calif state univ, fresno, beginning 1966; Am Philos Soc grant, 1963 & 1969; NSF res grants, Zurich, 1963; Am Chem Soc Petrol Res Fund grant, 1962 & 1965; NSF res grants, 1960 & 1967-1969; from asst prof to assoc prof, Calif State Univ, Fresno, 1956-1966; instr, Univ Tex, 1955-1956; res corp grant, 1955, 1957, 1959 & 1969; asst chem, Univ Fla, 1951-1955. **Memberships:** Fel Amer Assoc for Advan Sci; AAAS; Am Chem Soc; Hist Sci Soc; Soc Study Alchemy & Chem; Sigma Xi. **Research Statement & Publications:** Inorganic synthesis; stereochemistry; coordination compounds; chromatography separations; ion exchange; platinum metals; lanthanides; chemical education; unusual oxidation states; history of chemistry; biographies of chemists; translations of classics of chemistry. **Mailing Address:** Dept Chem, Calif State Univ, Fresno, CA 93740-8034. **Fax:** 559-278-4402. **E-Mail:** georgek@csufresno.edu

KAUFFMAN, GLENN MONROE, PHYSICAL ORGANIC CHEMISTRY. **Personal Data:** b Goshen, Ind, April 8, 1938. **Education:** Goshen Col, BA, 1961; Univ Pa, PhD (org chem), 1966. **Professional Experience:** PROF EMER CHEM, EASTERN MENNONITE COL, as of 2004; res fel, Univ Fla, 1975-1976; acad exten grant, Univ Fla & Eastern Mennonite Col, 1968-1970; res corp res grant, Eastern Mennonite Col, 1968-1969; chmn dept chem, Eastern Mennonite Col, beginning 1966; prof chem, Eastern Mennonite Col, beginning 1965. **Memberships:** AAAS; Am Chem Soc. **Research Statement & Publications:** Conformational analysis of cyclopentane compounds; mechanisms of epoxidation reactions and ring-opening reaction of epoxides; hydrogen-deuterium exchange of pyridine-N-oxides. **Mailing Address:** Dept Chem, Eastern Mennonite Col, 1200 Park Rd, Harrisonburg, VA 22802. **Fax:** 540-432-4488. **E-Mail:** kauffgm@emu.edu

KAUFFMAN, GORDON LEE, PHYSIOLOGY. **Personal Data:** b Grand Rapids, Mich, March 30, 1946; m Christie; c Gordon L III & Christian A. **Education:** Wheaton Col, BS, 1968; Univ Mich Med Sch, MD, 1972. **Professional Experience:** PROF CELLULAR & MOLECULAR PHYSIOL, DIV GEN SURG, MILTON S HERSHEY MED CTR, PA STATE UNIV, 1985-; from asst prof to assoc prof, Sch Med, Univ Calif, Los Angeles, 1979-1985; investr, Ctr Ulcer Res & Educ, Los Angeles, 1979-1981; staff surgeon, VA Wadsworth, Los Angeles, 1977-1985. **Memberships:** Am Physiol Soc; fel Am Col Surgeons; Am Surg Asn; Soc Surg Alimentary Tract. **Research Statement & Publications:** Control of brain peptides on gastro-intestinal function. **Mailing Address:** Milton S Hershey Med Ctr Dept Surg, PO Box 850, Hershey, PA 17033-0850. **Fax:** 717-531-4335. **E-Mail:** gkauffman@psu.edu

KAUFFMAN, HAROLD E, PHYTOPATHOLOGY, AGRONOMY. **Personal Data:** b West Liberty, Ohio, April 23, 1939; m 1961, c 3. **Education:** Goshen Col, BS, 1961; Mich State Univ, PhD (plant path), 1967. **Professional Experience:** EMER PROF & INTERIM ASST DEAN, UNIV ILL, URBANA-CHAMPAIGN, as of 2006; prof emer, Univ Ill, as of 2002; co-ordr, Winrock Int, 1992-1995; dir, Int Soybean Prog, Univ Ill, Urbana, 1981-1992; joint co-ordr, Int Rice Testing Prog, 1975-1981; plant pathologist, Int Rice Res Inst, 1967-1981. **Memberships:** Am Phytopath Soc. **Research Statement & Publications:** International agriculture; bacterial diseases of rice plants; crop improvement. **Mailing Address:** Dept Crop Sci, Univ Ill, 210 Mumford Hall MC-710 1301 W Gregory, Urbana, IL 61801. **E-Mail:** kauffmanh@uiuc.edu

KAUFFMAN, JAMES FRANK, ELECTRICAL ENGINEERING. **Personal Data:** b St Joseph, Mo, January 29, 1937; m 1964, c 2. **Education:** Univ Mo, Rolla, BS, 1960; Univ Ill, Urbana, MS, 1964; NC State Univ, PhD (elec eng), 1970. **Professional Experience:** PROF EMER ELEC & COMPUT ENG, NC STATE UNIV, as of 2005; prof elec eng, NC State Univ, beginning 1989; from asst prof to assoc prof, NC State Univ, 1970-1989; sr engr, Electronics Res Lab, Corning Glass Works, 1967-1970; res asst lens antennas, Antenna lab, Univ Ill, Urbana, 1964-1965; engr airborne radar, Westinghouse Elec Corp, 1960-1962. **Memberships:** Inst Elec & Electronics Engrs; Sigma Xi. **Research Statement & Publications:** Electromagnetics, especially antennas and microwave transmission. **Mailing Address:** Elec Eng Dept, NC State Univ, Box 7911, Raleigh, NC 27695.

KAUFFMAN, JOEL MERVIN, LASER DYES & FLUORESCENT TAGS, SCINTILLATION FLUORS. **Personal Data:** b Philadelphia, Pa, January 3, 1937. **Education:** Philadelphia Col Pharm, BS, 1958; Mass Inst Technol, PhD (org chem), 1963. **Professional Experience:** PROF EMER CHEM, DEPT CHEM & BIOCHEM, UNIV SCI, PHILADELPHIA, 2002-; res prof chem, Univ Sci, Philadelphia, 1997-2002; prof chem, Philadelphia Col Pharm & Sci, 1991-1997; consult laser dyes, 1982-; from asst prof to assoc prof, Philadelphia Col Pharm & Sci, 1979-1991; res assoc, Mass Col Pharm, 1977-1979; consult liquid scintillation counting, 1976-; res & develop dir, Pilot Chem Div, New Eng Nuclear Corp, Watertown, 1969-1976; res chemist, ICI Am Inc, Mass, 1966-1969; USPHS fel antiradiation drugs, Mass Col Pharm, 1964-1966; chemist, Reaction Motors Div, Thiokol Chem Corp, 1963-1964. **Memberships:** Am Asn Univ Prof; Soc Sci Exploration; Doctors Disaster Preparedness; Nat Motorist Asn. **Research Statement & Publications:** Synthesis of fluors, fluorescent dyes, laser dyes, scintillators, antiallergenic drugs, antimalarials, antimicrobials drugs and other medicinal chemicals; laser dyes; scintillators;

blocked amino acids; heterocyclics; vinyl monomers; photochemical reactions; terpenes; peptides; boron cage compounds; antiradiation-anticancer drugs; radiation sensitizers; plasticizers; fatty acid derivatives; formulation of liquid scintillators, solubilizers, decontaminants. **Mailing Address:** Dept Chem & Biochem, Univ Sci, 600 S 43rd St, Philadelphia, PA 19104-4495. **E-Mail:** kauffman@hslc.org

KAUFFMAN, JOHN W, BIOPHYSICS. **Personal Data:** b Washington, DC, March 28, 1925; m 1959, c Steven W & Lee A (deceased). **Education:** George Wash Univ, BS, 1947; Univ Md, MS, 1949; Univ Ill, PhD, 1955. **Professional Experience:** RETIRED; prof biomed eng, Northwestern Univ, 1955-1990; asst, Univ Ill, 1950-1955; res physicist, US Naval Res Lab, 1948-1950. **Research Statement & Publications:** Biomaterials; consciousness studies. **Mailing Address:** 621 W Pl Nueva, Green Valley, AZ 85614.

KAUFFMAN, LEON A, PULMONARY DISEASES, INTERNAL MEDICINE. **Personal Data:** b Philadelphia, Pa, July 26, 1934; m 1969, c 2. **Education:** Temple Univ, AB, 1957, MD, 1961; Am Bd Internal Med, dipl, 1973, cert pulmonary med, 1978. **Professional Experience:** ASSOC PROF MED, HAHNEMANN UNIV, 1977-; attend pulmonary med, St Agnes Hosp, 1973-; chmn, Div Pulmonary Med, Metrop Hosp, Philadelphia, 1973-1983; med dir sect respiratory ther, St Agnes Hosp, 1973-1978; pulmonary consult, Shock & Trauma Unit, Hahnemann Med Col & Hosp, 1970-1982; asst prof med, Hahnemann Med Col & Hosp, 1970-1977; asst dir pulmonary dis div & dir respiratory intensive care unit, Hahnemann Med Col & Hosp, 1969-1973; mem fel & res comt, Pa Thoracic Soc, 1968-1974; sr instr & dir pulmonary function lab, Hahnemann Med Col & Hosp, 1968-1970; mem ad hoc comt to evaluate med care state tuberc hosp syst, Pa, 1967; clin asst pulmonary med, Hahnemann Div, Philadelphia Gen Hosp, Pa, 1966-1978; instr med, Hahnemann Med Col & Hosp, 1966-1968; Pa Thoracic Soc fel pulmonary physiol & clin chest dis, 1965-1966; fel pulmonary med & pulmonary physiol, Hahnemann Med Col & Hosp, 1965-1966; resident internal med, Hahnemann Med Col & Hosp, 1963-1965; Resident path, SDiv, Einstein Med Ctr, Philadelphia, 1962-1963. **Memberships:** AMA; Am Thoracic Soc; fel Am Col Physicians; Am Soc Internal Med. **Research Statement & Publications:** Respiratory intensive care and respiratory failure in man; design of systems for delivery of care and treatment of repiratory failure; respiratory therapy; clinical pulmonary physiology. **Mailing Address:** 1930 Pine St, Philadelphia, PA 19103.

KAUFFMAN, MARVIN EARL, GEOLOGY. **Personal Data:** b Lancaster, Pa, August 31, 1933; m 1953, c 7. **Education:** Franklin & Marshall Col, BS, 1955; Northwestern Univ, MS, 1957; Princeton Univ, PhD, 1960. **Professional Experience:** PROF EMER GEOL, FRANKLIN & MARSHALL COL, as of 2005; prog dir, Nat Sci Found, 1991-1994; exec dir, Learning Ctr Appl Environ Technol, 1990-1991; exec dir, Am Geol Inst, 1985-1990; NSF sci fel, State Univ Utrecht, 1965-1966; prof geol, Franklin & Marshall Col, 1959-1988; asst geologist, Bethlehem Steel Co, 1953-1955; asst geologist, Alaskan Br, US Geol Surv, 1953; pres, Yellowstone-Bighorn Res Asn; consult geologist various cos. **Memberships:** Nat Asn Geol Teachers; Int Asn Sedimentologists; Geol Soc Am; Am Inst Prof Geol; Am Asn Petrol Geol; AAAS. **Research Statement & Publications:** Structure and stratigraphy of the Garnet Range and Marine Jurassic of western Montana; cambrian stratigraphy of southeastern Pennsylvania. **Mailing Address:** 540 Upper Continental Dr, Red Lodge, MT 59068.

KAUFFMAN, RALPH EZRA, DRUG METABOLISM, PHARMACOKINETICS. **Education:** Univ Kans, MD, 1965. **Professional Experience:** PROF PEDIAT & PHARMACOL, UNIV MO, KANS, 1995-; DIR MED RES, C MERCY HOSP & CLIN, KANS, 1995-; prof pediat & pharmacol, Sch Med, Wayne State Univ, 1979-1995. **Mailing Address:** Children's Mercy Hosp, 2401 Gillham Rd, Kansas City, MO 64108. **Fax:** 816-855-1703. **E-Mail:** rkauffman@cmh.edu

KAUFFMAN, RAYMOND F, CARDIOVASCULAR PHARMACOLOGY, ATHEROSCLEROSIS. **Personal Data:** b Dayton, Ohio, August 20, 1952; m 1974, Jane; c Christopher & Carolyn. **Education:** Univ Dayton, BS, 1973; Univ Wis-Madison, PhD (biochem), 1978. **Professional Experience:** SR RES SCIENTIST CARDIOVASC RES, LILLY RES LABS, ELI LILLY & CO, 1993-; res scientist, Lilly Res Labs, Eli Lilly & CO, 1987-1992; sr pharmacologist cardiovasc res, Lilly Res Labs, Eli Lilly & CO, 1981-1986; fel, Hormel Inst, Univ Minn, 1979-1981; fel biochem, Enzyme Inst, Univ Wis, 1979. **Memberships:** Am Chem Soc; Am Soc Pharmacol & Exp Therapeut; Sigma Xi; Am Heart Asn Arteriosclerosis Coun; NAm Vascular Biol Orgn. **Research Statement & Publications:** Vascular occlusive disorders, including atherosclerosis and chronic restenosis following balloon angioplasty; discovery of new mechanisms/drugs for prevention of vascular proliferative disorders and for modulating serum lipoproteins. **Mailing Address:** Cardiovasc Res, Lilly Corp Ctr, Eli Lilly & Co, Indianapolis, IN 46285. **Fax:** 317-277-0892. **E-Mail:** kauffman_raymond_f@lilly.com

KAUFFMAN, ROBERT GILLER, MEAT SCIENCE. **Personal Data:** b St Joseph, Mo, December 29, 1932; m 1955, Phyllis; c Rebecca Ruth (Henly) & Ellen (Campbell). **Education:** Iowa State Univ, BS, 1954; Univ Wis, MS, 1958, PhD (animal sci), 1961. **Honors & Awards:** Signal Serv Award, Am Meat Sci Asn. **Professional Experience:** PROF EMER ANIMAL SCI, UNIV WIS, MADISON, 1996-; prof, Univ Wis-madison, 1966-1996; asst prof animal sci, Univ Ill, 1961-1966. **Memberships:** Fel Am Soc Animal Sci; Am Meat Sci Asn; Inst Food Technol. **Research Statement & Publications:** Lipid transport in striated muscle; composition of meat animals; re-and post rigor quality modification for meat animals. **Mailing Address:** Muscle Biol Lab, Univ Wis, 1805 Linden Dr, Madison, WI 53706-1205. **Fax:** 608-265-3110. **E-Mail:** rgkauffm@facstaff.wisc.edu

KAUFFMAN, SHIRLEY LOUISE, PATHOLOGY. **Personal Data:** b Grand Junction, Colo, September 10, 1924. **Education:** Univ Chicago, BS, 1946, MS, 1948; Univ Kans, MD, 1955. **Professional Experience:** Inst Cancer Res Royal Marsden, Sutton Surrey, UK, 1977; Path Inst Rikshospitalet, Oslo, Norway, 1976-; PROF PATH, SU NY DOWNSTATE MED CTR, 1970-; vis prof, Dept Anat, Univ Berne, 1969; from asst prof to assoc prof, Su NY Downstate Med Ctr, 1961-1970; fel, Su NY Downstate Med Ctr, 1960; instr, Albert Einstein Col Med, 1959-1960; Nat Cancer Inst trainee path, Francis Delafield Hosp, 1957-1959; Provisional asst pathologist, NY Hosp, 1955-1957; Asst path, Med Col, Cornell Univ, 1955-1957. **Memberships:** Am Soc Exp Path; NY Acad Sci; Int Soc Stereology; Am Asn Path & Bact. **Research Statement & Publications:** Mammalian embryogenesis; lung morphometry; cell differentiation and proliferation; neoplasia. **Mailing Address:** 680 Hudson Terr, Cliffside Park, NJ 07010-3020.

KAUFFMAN, STUART ALAN, MEDICINE, THEORETICAL BIOLOGY. **Personal Data:** b Sacramento, Calif, September 28, 1939; m 1967, c 1. **Education:** Dartmouth Col, BA, 1960; Oxford Univ, BA, 1963; Univ Calif, San Francisco, MD, 1968. **Honors & Awards:** Norbert Wiener Gold Medal, Am Soc Cybernet, 1970. **Professional Experience:** PROF EMER BIOCHEM & BIOPHYS, UNIV PA, as of 2004; GENERAL PARTNER, BIOS GROUP, SANTAFE, as of 2004; EXTEN PROF, SANTA FE INST, as of 2004; assoc prof biochem & biophys, Univ PA, beginning 1981; assoc prof biochem-biol, Univ PA, 1975-1981; res assoc, Lab Theoret Biol, Nat Cancer Inst, 1973-1975; asst prof med, Univ Chicago, 1970-1973; asst prof theoret biol, Univ Chicago, 1969-1973; intern, Cincinnati Gen Hosp, 1968-1969; fel genetics, Univ Cincinnati, 1968-1969; vis scientist, Mass Inst Technol, 1967-1968. **Memberships:** Philos Sci Asn. **Research Statement & Publications:** Theory of organization of eukaryotic gene regulation networks; control of DNA synthesis. **Mailing Address:** Bios Group LP, 317 Paseo de Peralta, Santa Fe, NM 87501. **Fax:** 505-988-2229. **E-Mail:** stu@santafe.edu

KAUFMAN, ALBERT IRVING, MEDICAL PHYSIOLOGY, EPITHELIAL TRANSPORT. **Personal Data:** b New York, NY, July 22, 1938; m 1962, Jeannetta; c Joshua & Rachel. **Education:** Cooper Union, BEE, 1961; Drexel Inst Technol, MS, 1962; Temple Univ, PhD (physiol), 1968. **Professional Experience:** ASST DEAN, STATE UNIV NY DOWNSTATE MED CTR, 1990-; ASSOC PROF PHYSIOL, STATE UNIV NY DOWNSTATE MED CTR, 1980-; vis prof, Tokyo Metrop Inst Geront, 1975-1976; asst prof, State Univ NY Downstate Med Ctr, 1969-1980; instr, State Univ NY Downstate Med Ctr, 1966-1969. **Memberships:** Sigma Xi; NY Acad Sci; AAAS; Am Physiolog Soc. **Research Statement & Publications:** Transepithelial water and electrolyte movement. **Mailing Address:** State Univ NY Health Sci Ctr, 450 Clarkson Ave Box 31, Brooklyn, NY 11203.

KAUFMAN, ALLAN N, PLASMA PHYSICS THEORY. **Personal Data:** b Chicago, Ill, July 21, 1927; m 1957, Louise; c Joel & Janet. **Education:** Univ Chicago, PhB, 1947, BS, 1949, MS, 1951, PhD (physics), 1953. **Professional Experience:** Chmn, Div Plasma Physics, Am Phys Soc, 1981-1982; PROF PHYSICS, UNIV CALIF, BERKELEY, 1967-; sr fel, Goddard Space Flight Ctr, 1967; STAFF PHYSICIST, LAWRENCE BERKELEY LAB, 1965-; assoc, Lawrence Berkeley Lab, 1965-1967; vis prof physics, Univ Calif, Los Angeles, 1964-1965; staff physicist, Lawrence Livermore Lab, 1953-1964. **Memberships:** Fel Am Phys Soc. **Research Statement & Publications:** Basic plasma physics theory. **Mailing Address:** Bldg 4/230 Lawrence Berkeley Lab, 1 Cyclotron Rd, Berkeley, CA 94720. **Fax:** 510-495-2111, 510-486-4773.

KAUFMAN, ALVIN B(ERYL), electrical engineering, electronic engineering; deceased, see previous edition for last biography

KAUFMAN, BORIS, MECHANICAL ENGINEERING. **Personal Data:** b New York, NY, January 10, 1926; m 1949, c 1. **Education:** Univ Cincinnati, BS, 1950, MechEng, 1960; Ill Inst Technol, MS, 1952. **Professional Experience:** PROF EMER MECH ENG, CALIF STATE UNIV, SACRAMENTO, 1992-; prof mech eng, Calif State Univ, Sacramento, 1969-1992; co-dir, Bio-Eng Sect, Cardio-Pulmonary Div, Sutter Hosps Med Res Found, Sacramento, beginning 1962; from asst prof to assoc prof, Calif State Univ, Sacramento, 1961-1969; asst prof mech eng, Univ Idaho, 1959-1961; chief engr, US Air Conditioning Corp, Ohio, 1957-1959; design engr, US Air Conditioning Corp, Ohio, 1953-1957; asst engr, Armour Res Found, Ill Inst Technol, 1950-1953. **Memberships:** Am Soc Heating Refrig & Air-Conditioning Engrs. **Research Statement & Publications:** Air conditioning theory and design; bio-engineering aspects of prosthetic heart devices. **Mailing Address:** Dept Mech Eng, Calif State Univ 6000 J St, Sacramento, CA 95819-2605.

KAUFMAN, CHARLES, THEORETICAL PHYSICS. **Personal Data:** b Brooklyn, NY, June 4, 1937; m Carol D Kaufman; c Eleanor D & Amelia D. **Education:** Univ Wis, BS, 1956; Pa State Univ, MS, 1959, PhD (physics), 1963. **Professional Experience:** Fel, Off Naval Res-Am Soc Eng Educ, Naval Underwater Systs Ctr, New London, 1991, 1992 & 1993; sr visitor, DAMTP, Univ Cambridge, 1985-1986; fel, Off Naval Res-Am Soc Eng Educ, Naval Underwater Systs Ctr, New London, 1983, 1984; PROF PHYSICS, UNIV RI, 1981-; consult, Raytheon Corp, 1978-1981; guest lectr, Univ Vienna, 1971-1972; Physicist, US Naval Underwater Systs Ctr, 1969-1971; from asst prof to assoc prof, Univ RI, 1964-1981; Instr physics, Pa State Univ, 1963-1964. **Memberships:** NY Acad Sci; Acoust Soc Am; Am Phys Soc; Am Asn Univ Professors. **Research Statement & Publications:** Electrodynamics; quantum field theory; atomic and elementary particle physics; turbulence theory; Classical & Quantum chaos; underwater acoustics. **Mailing Address:** Dept Physics, Univ RI, Kingston, RI 02881-0817. **Fax:** 401-874-2380. **E-Mail:** chuck@uri.edu

KAUFMAN, DANIEL, ORGANIC CHEMISTRY. **Personal Data:** b Washington, DC, March 8, 1920; m 1943, Florence Esten; c 5. **Education:** Univ Md, MS, 1941. **Professional Experience:** Sr Scientist, Coating Supply, Inc. 1999; res dir, Kaufman Develop Co, 1975-1999; US mem, Fedn Dentaire Int Comn, 1975-1977; vpres res & develop, Kerr Mfg Co Div, Sybron Corp, 1971-1975; dir res & develop, Kerr Mfg Co Div, Sybron Corp, 1969-1971; res assoc, Kerr Mfg Co Div, Ritter Pfaudler Corp, 1968-1969; supvr inorg res, Res Div, Wyandotte Chem Corp, 1959-1968; res chemist, Nat Lead Co, 1947-1959; chemist, NC, 1946-1947; chemist, Manhattan Proj, Los Alamos, NMex, 1944-1946; chemist, US Bur Mines, Utah, 1942-1944; Asst, Univ Md, 1941-1942; Mem nat adv bd biomat res, Clemson Univ. **Memberships:** Am Chem Soc; Int Asn Dent Res; AAAS. **Research Statement & Publications:** Hydrogenation and hydrogenolysis of furfural; production of elemental boron; hydrometallurgy of manganese ores; titanium chemistry; cyclopentadienyl metal compounds; catalysis and olefin polymerization; metallurgical chemistry; dental materials; powder coating of vegetable seed. **Mailing Address:** 2242 Newquist Ct, Camarillo, CA 93010-1166. **E-Mail:** floridan@juno.com

KAUFMAN, DARRELL S, GEOLOGY. **Education:** Univ Calif, Santa Cruz, BA, BS, 1982; Univ Wash, MS, 1987; Univ Colo, PhD (Geol Sci), 1991. **Professional Experience:** ASSOC PROF, GEOL & ENVIRON SCI, DEPT GEOL, NORTHERN ARIZ UNIV, 1998-; from asst to assoc prof, dept geol, Utah State Univ, 1993-1998. **Mailing Address:** Dept Geol & Environ Sci, Northern Ariz Univ, Flagstaff, AZ 86011-4099. **Fax:** 928-523-9220. **E-Mail:** darrell.kaufman@nau.edu

KAUFMAN, DAVID GORDON, PATHOLOGY, BIOCHEMISTRY. **Personal Data:** b Jersey City, NJ, May 28, 1943; m 1966, c 2. **Education:** Reed Col, BA, 1966; Wash Univ, MD, 1968, PhD (exp path), 1973. **Professional Experience:** DIR PATH, UNIV NC, as of 2006; res career develop award, mem Cancer Ctr support rev comt, beginning 1984; PROF PATH, UNIV NC, 1980-; Mem, Chem Path Study Sect, 1979-1983; res career develop award, Nat Cancer Inst, 1978-1983; mem prototype explicit anal pesticides comt, Nat Acad Sci, 1978-1980; mem, Path B Study Sect, NIH, 1977-1979; assoc prof, Univ NC, 1975-1980; res scientist, Nat Cancer Inst, 1973-1975; res assoc carcinogenesis, Nat Cancer Inst, 1970-1973; resident, Barnes Hosp, Wash Univ, 1969-1970; intern path, Barnes Hosp, Wash Univ, 1968-1969. **Memberships:** Am Asn Cancer Res; Am Asn Pathologists; Am Soc Cell Biol; Am Col Toxicol; NY Acad Sci; Soc Toxicol. **Research Statement & Publications:** Chemical carcinogenesis; eukaryotic DNA replication and repair; cell biology of respiratory tract and female genital tract tissues; toxicology. **Mailing Address:** Dept Path 228H, Univ NC Med Sch 515 Brinkhaus-Bullitt Bldg, Chapel Hill, NC 27599-7525. **E-Mail:** uncdgk@med.unc.edu

KAUFMAN, DON ALLEN, ORGANIC CHEMISTRY. **Personal Data:** b Wahoo, Nebr, August 4, 1940; m 1963, c 1. **Education:** Univ Nebr, BS, 1961; Univ Colo, MBS, 1965; Colo State Univ, PhD (chem), 1969. **Professional Experience:** PROF CHEM, UNIV NEBR, KEARNEY, as of 2004; NSF fac prof develop grant, Univ Nebr-Lincoln, 1977-

1978; prof org chem, Kearney State Col, beginning 1969; instr chem, Chandler High Sch, Ariz, 1963-1964; instr gen sci, Omaha Pub Schs, Nebr, 1961-1963. **Memberships:** Am Chem Soc. **Research Statement & Publications:** Use of crown ethers in organic synthesis; stability of vinyl cations; pH of precipitation; synthesis and reactions of Bunte salts. **Mailing Address:** Dept Chem, Univ Nebr, 905 W 25th St, Kearney, NE 68849-1150. **Fax:** 308-865-8399. **E-Mail:** kaufmand@ @unk.edu

KAUFMAN, DONALD BARRY, IMMUNOLOGY, NEPHROLOGY. **Personal Data:** b Los Angeles, Calif, August 5, 1937. **Education:** Univ Calif, MD, 1963. **Professional Experience:** PROF EMER, COL HUMAN MED, MICH STATE UNIV, AS OF 2006; prof med, Col Human Med, Mich State Univ, beginning 1981. **Memberships:** Am Acad Pediat; Am Soc Nephrology; Int Pediat Nephrology Asn; Am Soc Pediatric Nephrology; Am Fedn Clin Res; Soc Pediatric Res; Am Asn Immunologists; Am Asn Advan Sci; NY Acad Sci. **Research Statement & Publications:** Pediatric Nephrology, Pediatrics. **Mailing Address:** Dept Pediat & Human Develop, Mich State Univ, B-140 Life Sci, East Lansing, MI 48824-1317. **Fax:** 517-483-3994. **E-Mail:** kaufmand@msu.edu

KAUFMAN, DONALD DEVERE, SOIL MICROBIOLOGY, AGRICULTURAL CHEMISTRY. **Personal Data:** b Wooster, Ohio, December 2, 1933; m 1981, Joye Sutton; c Colin, Eve, Sharon, Shawn, Tom, John, Matt & Lisa, David. **Education:** Kent State Univ, BA, 1955, MA, 1958; Ohio State Univ, PhD (plant path), 1962. **Honors & Awards:** distinguished Alumnae Award, Ohio st univ March 15, 1980. **Professional Experience:** Owner & manager, Joyedon farm, Supervisor; West manheim twp; mem, York county agri preservation bd RETIRED; res leader & soil microbiologist, Soil-Microbiol Systs Lab, Agr Environ Qual Inst, Agr Res Serv, 1984-1996; soil microbiologist, Agr Environ Qual Inst, Beltsville Agr Res Ctr W, Sci & Educ Admin-Agr Res, 1973-1984; Fulbright lectr soil microbiol, Khonkaen Univ, Thailand, 1967-1968; soil microbiologist pesticides, Plant Indust Sta, USDA, 1962-1973; res asst, Ohio Agr Exp Sta, 1958-1962; Res technician plant path, Ohio Agr Exp Sta, 1956-1957. **Memberships:** AAAS; Am Phytopath Soc; Am Soc Microbiol; Am Chem Soc; Weed Sci Soc Am. **Research Statement & Publications:** Microbial decomposition of pesticides; effects of pesticides on soil microorganisms; soil microbiology of root diseases. **Mailing Address:** 1294 Grand Valley Rd, Joyedon Farm, Hanover, PA 17331.

KAUFMAN, DONALD WAYNE, MAMMALIAN ECOLOGY, WILDLIFE ECOLOGY. **Personal Data:** b Abilene, Tex, June 7, 1943; m 1967, Glennis; c Dawn Michelle. **Education:** Ft Hays Kans State Col, BS, 1965, MS, 1967; Univ Ga, PhD (zoology), 1972. **Honors & Awards:** Fort Hays State University Alumni Achievement Award, 2005; Am Soc Mammalogists Award, 1972. **Professional Experience:** Adjunct curator mammals, Sternberg Museum Nat Hist, Fort Hays State Univ, 2000-; adjunct prof biol, Univ New Mexico, 1998; Mem rev panel, Environ Protection Agency, 1981-1985 & US Dept Agr, 1995-1996; PROF BIOL, KANS STATE UNIV, 1991-; dir, Konza Prairie Res Natural Area, 1990-1991; mem bd dirs, Am Soc Mammalogists, 1989-1992; proj dir, Konza Prairie Long-term Ecol Res Prog, 1985-1990; mem Kans Nongame Wildlife Adv Coun, 1985-1988; mem Kans Natural & Sci Areas Adv Bd, 1985-1988; actg dir, Konza Prairie Res Natural Area, 1985-1986; mem, External Oversight Comt Pop Biol & Ecol Progs, NSF, 1984; assoc dir, Konza Prairie Res Natural Area, 1981-1985; from asst prof to assoc prof, Kans State Univ, 1980-1991; dir, Pop Biol & Physiol Ecol Prog, NSF, 1977-1980; asst prof biol, State Univ NY, Binghamton, 1975-1977; asst prof zool, Univ Ark, 1974-1975; vis scientist, Savannah River Ecol Lab, Aiken, SC, 1973-1974; Fel genetics, Univ Tex, 1971-1973. **Memberships:** Am Soc Mammalogists, Patron & Life Member; Board of Directors, 1989-1992; Ecol Soc Am; AAAS; Central Plains Soc Mammalogists, Patron & Life Member; Board of Governors, 2000-2006; Soc Study Evolution; Am Inst Biol Scientists; Soc Conserv Biol. **Research Statement & Publications:** Ecology of rodents, evolutionary ecology; grassland ecology; ecological effects of disturbances in grasslands; physical impacts of mammals on grassland ecosystems; mammalian herbivory; plant-mammal interactions; conservation biology. **Mailing Address:** Div Biol, Ackert Hall Kans State Univ, Manhattan, KS 66506-4901. **Fax:** 785-532-6653. **E-Mail:** dwkaufma@ksu.edu

KAUFMAN, DWIGHT, CANCER RESEARCH ADMINISTRATION. **Education:** MD, PhD. **Professional Experience:** JACKSON CLIN, TENN, as of 2006. **Mailing Address:** Jackson Clin, 616 W Forest Ave, Jackson, TN 38301. **Fax:** 901-422-0442.

KAUFMAN, EDWARD GODFREY, DENTISTRY. **Personal Data:** b New York, NY, June 8, 1919; m 1938, c 3. **Education:** UCLA 1939, NY Univ, DDs, 1943. **Professional Experience:** DEAN, COL DENT, NY UNIV, 1984-; CHMN DEPT, COL DENT, NY UNIV, 1974-; from asst dean to assoc dean, Col Dent, NY Univ, 1969-1984; PROF PROSTHODONT, COL DENT, NY UNIV, 1967-; consult outpatient clin USPHS, 1966-; co-prin investr, NIH Grant, 1966-1971; Williams Ref Corp grant, 1964-; consult dent asst training prog, NIH, 1960-; Gordon Res Found grant, 1957-1960; res assoc, Mat Res Lab, Murry & Leone Guggenheim Inst Dent Res, 1956-; pvt pract, 1946-; pvt practice, 1946-; from instr to assoc prof prosthodont, Col Dent, NY Univ, 1946-1966. **Memberships:** AAAS; Am Dent Asn; Am Soc Metals; Am Ceramic Soc; Sigma Xi. **Research Statement & Publications:** Clinical and laboratory research in fields of dental materials, stress analysis and applied technology. **Mailing Address:** New York Col Dent, NY Univ, 345 E 24th St, New York, NY 10010.

KAUFMAN, ELAINE ELKINS, BIOSYNTHESIS. **Personal Data:** b Cincinnati, Ohio, June 23, 1923; m 1948, Seymour; c Allan S, Emily (Watkins) & Leslie (Barrick). **Education:** Wellesley Col, BA, 1945; Duke Univ, PhD (biochem), 1949. **Professional Experience:** RES CHEMIST, Nat Inst Mental Health, 1970-; res chemist, NIH, 1967-1969; res chemist, NIMH, 1965-1967; fel, USPHS, 1947-1948. **Memberships:** Sigma Xi; Am Soc Neurochem; Int Soc Neurochem; Am Soc Biochem & Molecular Biol. **Research Statement & Publications:** Neuronal-astroglial interactions and interdependence; biosynthesis and degradation of the neuromodulator-hydroxybutyrate; biochemical basis for the physiological effects of -hydroxybutyrate. **Mailing Address:** Nat Inst Mental Health, NIH, Bldg 36 Rm 1A21 9000 Rockville Pike, Bethesda, MD 20892-0001. **Fax:** 301-480-1668.

KAUFMAN, FRANK B, PHYSICAL CHEMISTRY, ORGANIC CHEMISTRY. **Personal Data:** b June 23, 1943; American citizen. **Education:** Univ Rochester, BS, 1965; Johns Hopkins Univ, PhD (chem), 1971. **Professional Experience:** CHEM MECH PLANARIZATIONENG FEL, DIV MICROELECTRONICS MAT, CABOT MICROELECTRONICS CORP, as of 2004; MEM RES STAFF PHYS CHEM, T J WATSON RES CTR, IBM CORP, 1973-; vis prof, Univ Ill, 1972-1973; NIH fel phys chem, Royal Inst Great Brit, 1970-1972. **Memberships:** Am Chem Soc; NY Acad Sci. **Research Statement & Publications:** Design, synthesis and properties of new monomeric and polymeric materials with novel electronic properties. **Mailing Address:** IBM Corp, 1133 Westchester Ave, White Plains, NY 10604.

KAUFMAN, GLENNIS ANN, SOCIAL ORGANIZATION, PLANT-ANIMAL INTERACTION. **Personal Data:** b Deshler, Nebr, November 13, 1947; m 1967, Donald; c Dawn M. **Education:** Kans State Univ, BS, (Wildlife biol) 1984, PhD (biol), 1990. **Honors & Awards:** Vice President, Am Soc Mammalogists, 2005-2006; Board of Directors, Am Soc Mammalogists, 1997-2005; A Brazier Howell Award, Am Soc Mammalogists, 1989. **Professional Experience:** RES ASST PROF, KANS STATE UNIV, 1996-; asst scientist, Kans State Univ, 1991-1995; instr gen biol, Kans State Univ, 1991-1992; grad asst, Kans State Univ, 1984-1990; res asst biol, Kans State Univ, 1981-1984; res asst zool, Univ Tex, 1971-1973; Res asst, Savannah River Ecol Lab, 1968-1971 & 1973-1974. **Memberships:** Am Soc Mammalogists; Life & Patron Member; Board of Directors, 1997-2005; Vice President, 2005-2006; Am Behav Soc; Ecol Soc Am; Soc Study Evolution; Sigma Xi; Int Soc Behav Ecol Am Institue of Biological Sciences; Am Soc of Naturalists; Central Plains Soc of Mammalogists, Patron & Life Member; President Elect, 2001-2003; President, 2003-2005; Past President, 2005-2007; Phi Kappa Phi; Soc for Study of Evolution; Soc of Conservation Biology; Southwestern Asn of Naturalists. **Research Statement & Publications:** Mammalian behavior and population biology; community organization of small mammals in grasslands; plant-small mammal interactions; fire ecology of small mammals; human effects on populations and communities of small mammals. **Mailing Address:** Div Biol, Kans State Univ Ackert Hall, Manhattan, KS 66506-4901. **Fax:** 785-532-6653. **E-Mail:** gkaufman@ksu.edu

KAUFMAN, HAROLD ALEXANDER, ORGANIC CHEMISTRY, AGRICULTURAL. **Personal Data:** b Brooklyn, NY, January 27, 1933; m 1956, Elaine; c Michele B & Roy S. **Education:** Brooklyn Col, BS, 1955; Univ Pittsburgh, PhD (chem), 1961. **Professional Experience:** RETIRED; vpres res & develop, J T Baker Chem Co, 1976-1995; mgr pesticides synthesis, screening & develop, Mobil Chem Co, 1961-1976; res chemist, AMP, Inc, 1955-1956; instr chem, Brooklyn Col, 1955. **Memberships:** Am Chem Soc; The Chem Soc; AAAS. **Mailing Address:** 142 Fountain Ave, Piscataway, NJ 08854.

KAUFMAN, HAROLD RICHARD, PLASMA PHYSICS, MECHANICAL ENGINEERING. **Personal Data:** b Audubon, Iowa, November 24, 1926; m 1948, Elinor; c Brian C, Karin T, Bruce R & Cynthia A. **Education:** Northwestern Univ, BS, 1951; Colo State Univ, PhD (mech eng), 1971. **Honors & Awards:** James H Wyld Award, Am Inst Aeronaut & Astronaut, 1969; Medal Except Sci Achievement, NASA, 1971; Albert Nerken Award, Am Vacuum Soc, 1991. **Professional Experience:** PRES, FRONT RANGE RES, 1984-; EMER PROF, COLO STATE UNIV, 1984-; chmn, Physics dept, 1979-1984; prof mech eng & physics, Front Range Res, 1974-1984; mgr, Space Propulsion Res, 1958-1974; res engr, Nat Adv Comt Aeronaut, NASA, Cleveland, Ohio, 1951-1958. **Memberships:** Assoc fel, Am Inst Aeronaut & Astronaut; Am Phys Soc; fel Am Vacuum Soc. **Research Statement & Publications:** Electric space propulsion; industrial broad-beam ion sources. **Mailing Address:** Front Range Res, 1306 Blue Spruce Unit A, Ft Collins, CO 80524-2067. **Fax:** 970-484-9350.

KAUFMAN, HERBERT EDWARD, OPHTHALMOLOGY, PHARMACOLOGY. **Personal Data:** b New York, NY, September 28, 1931; m 1977, c 3. **Education:** Princeton Univ, AB, 1952; Harvard Med Sch, MD, 1956; Am Bd Ophthal, dipl, 1963. **Honors & Awards:** Albion O Bernstein Award, NY State Med Soc, 1963; Knapp Award, AMA, 1963; Lions Int Humanitarian Award, 1968; Conrad Berens Award, 1975; Proctor Award, Asn Res Vision & Ophthal, 1978; Jackson Mem Lectr, 1979; Pocklington Lectr, 1979; Proctor Lectr, Asn Res In vision & Ophthal, 1981; R Townley Paton Award, 1983; Twentieth Annual Edwin B Dunphy Lectr, Harvard 1983; First Ann Wohl Lectr Ophthal, Isreal 1983; G Victor Simpson Lectr, 1984; Peter Kronfeld Mem Lectr, 1984; Lifetime Achievement Award, Int Soc Refractive Surg, 2000; Weisenfeld Award, Asn Res Vision & Ophthal, 2001. **Professional Experience:** Med dir, Eye & Ear Inst La, 1979-1984; BOYD PROF OPHTHAL & PHARMACOL & MICROBIOL, LA STATE UNIV MED CTR, NEW ORLEANS, 1978-; prof ophthal & pharmacol & chmn Ophthal&Dean Col Med, Univ Fla, 1962-1977; head & lectr ophthal, Uveitis Lab, Mass Eye & Ear Infirmary, 1959-1962; ed, Invest Ophthal; ed, Am J Ophthal & Chemotherapy, Metabolic Ophthal & Ann Ophthal; bd dir, Tissue Banks Int; dr outpatient clins, Univ Fla. **Memberships:** AAAS; AMA; Asn Res Vision & Ophthal (secy-treas, 1964-1973, pres, 1975); Am Asn Immunol; Am Fedn Clin Res; Am Acad Ophthal; Asn Univ Prof Ophthal; Contact Lens Soc Ophthalmologists; Int Soc Refractory Surg. **Mailing Address:** La State Univ Med Ctr, 2020 Gravier St Ste B, New Orleans, LA 70112. **E-Mail:** hkaufm@lsuhsc.edu

KAUFMAN, HERBERT S, MEDICINE, ALLERGY. **Personal Data:** b Salina, Kans, April 30, 1935; m Vivian Janho; c 3. **Education:** Univ Kans, BA, 1957; Baylor Univ, MD, 1961; Am Bd Pediat, dipl, 1966, Am Acad Pediat Allergy, cert, 1967; Am Bd Allergy & Immunol, dipl, 1972, cert, 1978. **Professional Experience:** Mem prog clin immunol, Brit Allergy Soc, Oxford Univ, 1977; chief allergy & immunol clin, Dept Pediat, Children's Hosp, San Francisco, 1968-1971; consult, Dept Rehab, State Calif & Letterman Gen Hosp, 1966-; comt mem & course chmn, Continuing Educ Dept, Pac Presby Med Ctr, 1966-; Res grant, Univ Calif, San Francisco, 1966-; CLIN INSTR DERMAT, MED CTR, UNIV CALIF, SAN FRANCISCO, 1966-; dir pediat allergy clin, Continuing Educ Dept, Pac Presby Med Ctr, 1966-1968; NIH fel allergy & immunol, Med Ctr, Univ Calif, San Francisco, 1964-1966; resident, Tex Childrens Hosp, 1963-1964; resident, St Louis Childrens Hosp, Mo, 1962-1963; Intern pediat, St Louis Childrens Hosp, Mo, 1961-1962. **Memberships:** AMA; Am Acad Allergy; Am Col Allergists; Brit Soc Allergy; Brit Soc Immunol; Am Thermography Asn. **Research Statement & Publications:** Immunoglobin defects in allergic individuals; complement levels in allergic disease; organic components of mental illness; author of 60 peer reviewed published papers. **Mailing Address:** 2211 Post St Suite 301, San Francisco, CA 94115. **Fax:** 415-921-5990.

KAUFMAN, HOWARD NORMAN, MECHANICAL ENGINEERING, TRIBOLOGY. **Personal Data:** b Boston, Mass, January 2, 1926; m 1947, c 3. **Education:** Northeastern Univ, BS, 1945; Carnegie-Mellon Univ, MS, 1952. **Honors & Awards:** Walter D Hodson Award, Am Soc Lubrication Engrs, 1955. **Professional Experience:** PVT CONSULT, 1987-; lectr, Am Soc Lubrication Engrs, beginning 1982; instr mech eng, Carnegie-Mellon Univ, 1952-1956 & Allegheny County Community Col, 1966-1969; res fel engr mech eng & tribology, Westinghouse Sci & Technol Ctr, Westinghouse Elec Corp, 1947-1986. **Memberships:** Am Soc Lubrication Engrs. **Research Statement & Publications:** Research and development in the field of friction, wear, and lubrication mechanics encompassing the theory, test, and application of journal and thrust bearings, rolling contact bearings and seals. **Mailing Address:** 1233 Northwestern Dr, Monroeville, PA 15146.

KAUFMAN, HYMAN, MATHEMATICS. **Personal Data:** b Lachine, Que, February 2, 1920; m 1959. **Education:** McGill Univ, BSc, 1941, MSc, 1945, PhD (physics), 1948. **Professional Experience:** RETIRED; prof math, McGill Univ, 1952-1980; engr, Lab, Fox Electronics Inc, 1951-1952; geophysicist, Continental Oil Co, 1949-1951; fel & asst instr elec eng, Yale Univ, 1948-1949; lectr math, McGill Univ, 1941-1948. **Memberships:** Soc Indust & ApplMath; Soc Explor Geophys; Asn Comput Mach; Math Asn Am; Inst Elec & Electronics Engrs. **Research Statement & Publications:** Applied mathematics in engineering. **Mailing Address:** 400 Stewart Apt 2211, Ottawa, ON K1N 6L2, Can.

KAUFMAN, IRVING, ELECTRONICS ENGINEERING, MICROWAVES. **Personal Data:** b Geinsheim, Ger, January 11, 1925; American citizen; m 1950, Ruby; c Eve Deborah, Sharon Anne & Julie Ellen. **Education:** Vanderbilt Univ, BE, 1945; Univ Ill, MS, 1949, PhD (elec eng), 1957. **Professional Experience:** PROF EMER ELEC ENG, ARIZ STATE UNIV, as of 2006; collabr, Los Alamos Nat Lab, 1989, 1991; distinguished res award, Grad Col, Ariz State Univ, 1986-1987; liaison scientist, Off Naval Res, London, 1978-1980; vis prof, Univ Auckland, NZ, 1974; collaborating scientist, Consiglio Nazionale delle Ricerche, Florence, Italy, 1973-1974; dir, Solid State Res Lab, 1968-1978; prof eng, Ariz State Univ, 1965-1994; sr res fel, Italy, 1964-1965, 1973-1974; head microwave res, Ramo-Wooldridge & Space Tech Labs, TRW Inc, 1961-1964; mem tech staff, Ramo-Wooldridge & Space Tech Labs, TRW Inc, 1957-1964; res assoc, Univ Ill, 1953-1956; instr, Univ Ill, 1949-1953; asst elec eng, Univ Ill, 1948-1949; engr, RCA Victor, 1945-1948. **Memberships:** Fel Inst Elec & Electronics Engrs; Sigma Xi. **Research Statement & Publications:** Microwave electronics; electronic and optical device research; displays; non-destructive evaluation. **Mailing Address:** Dept Elec Eng, Ariz State Univ, Tempe, AZ 85287-5706.

KAUFMAN, JANICE NORTON, PSYCHIATRY. **Personal Data:** b Denver, Colo, June 22, 1923; m 1972, Charles. **Education:** Univ Utah, BA, 1948, MD, 1951; Am Bd Psychiat & Neurol, dipl, 1958. **Professional Experience:** RETIRED; prof psychiat, Med Ctr, Univ Colo, Denver, 1972-1979; mem fac, Denver Inst Psychoanal, 1972-1979; dir, Denver Inst Psychoanal, 1969-1972; mem fac, Chicago Inst Psychoanal, 1963-1979; USPHS career teacher fel, 1956-1958; from instr to assoc prof, Med Ctr, Univ Colo, Denver, 1955-1972; resident psychiat, Strong Mem Hosp, Rochester, NY, 1952-1955; Strong Mem Hosp, Rochester, NY, 1951-1952. **Memberships:** Fel Am Psychiat Asn; Am Psychoanal Asn. **Research Statement & Publications:** Practice and teaching of psychoanalysis and psychiatry. **Mailing Address:** 2404 Loring St 250, San Diego, CA 92109.

KAUFMAN, JEROME, MATHEMATICS. **Education:** Ohio State Univ, Sch Med, MD. **Professional Experience:** ASSOC, PSYCHOPHARMACOLOGY & MED MGT, OCD RESOURCE CTR FLA, 2004-. **Memberships:** Am Psychiatric Asn. **Mailing Address:** OCD Res Ctr Fla, 3475 Sheridan St Suite 310, Hollywood, FL 33021. **Fax:** 954-962-6164.

KAUFMAN, JOHN GILBERT, COMPUTERIZED MATERIAL SCIENCE DATA, FRACTURE MECHANICS. **Personal Data:** b Baltimore, Md, October 14, 1931; m 1953, Ruth; c John G III, Ruth A & Keith C. **Education:** Carnegie Inst Technol, BSCE, 1953, MS, 1954; Carnegie Mellon Univ, MS, 1975. **Honors & Awards:** Award of Merit, Am Soc Testing & Mat; Award of Merit, Am Soc Metals Int. **Professional Experience:** Mat Database Comt, Am Soc Metals, beginning 1996; DIR, ALUMINUM ASN, 1996-; chmn, Codata Mat Property Database Comt, beginning 1995; chmn, Mat Property Databases Mgt Comt, 1995; vpres technol, Aluminum Asn, 1993-1996; mem, Struct Comt, Nat Res Coun, 1980-1985 & Nat Mat Adv Bd Comt Appln Computers Mat Sci, beginning 1991; technol develop, 1984-1989 & fabrication technol, 1989-1990; pres, Mat Property Databases Mgt Comt, 1987-1993; pres, Nat Mat Properties Data Network, 1985-1993; dir res & develop, Anaconda Aluminum Co, 1980-1983 & Arco Metals, Atlantic Richfield, 1983-1985; chmn, Comt E24, Am Soc Testing & Mat, 1980-1984 & Comt E49, 1986-1988; mgr, eng properties, Aluminum Co Am, 1954-1983. **Memberships:** Fel Am Soc Testing & Mat; fel Am Soc Metals; SigmaXi; Am Soc Mech Engrs; Comt Data Sci & Technol; Asn Comput Mach; Aluminum Asn; Am Soc Testing & Mat. **Research Statement & Publications:** Materials development, notably aluminum alloys; fracture mechanics and applications; networking of materials databases; metallurgy of aluminum alloys. **Mailing Address:** Aluminum Asn Inc, 3662 Pevensey Dr, Columbus, OH 43220. **Fax:** 614-459-3949. **E-Mail:** gkaufman@aluminum.org

KAUFMAN, JOYCE J, QUANTUM CHEMISTRY, PSYCHOPHARMACOLOGY. **Personal Data:** b New York, NY, June 21, 1929; m 1948, Stanley; c Jan C. **Education:** Johns Hopkins Univ, BS, 1949, MA, 1959, PhD (chem, chem physics), 1960; Sorbonne Univ, DES(theoret physics), 1963. **Honors & Awards:** Gold Medal, Martin Co, 1964, 1965 & 1966; Dame Chevalier, Nat Ctr Sci Res, France, 1969; Md Chemist Award, 1974; Garvan Medal, Am Chem Soc, 1974; Lucy Pickett Award, 1975. **Professional Experience:** RETIRED; mem heavy ion sources comt, Nat Acad Sci, 1973-1975; assoc Prof Anesthesiol, Sch Med & Prin Res Scientist Chem, Johns Hopkins Univ, beginning of, 1969; US deleg, Int Atomic Energy Symp, Vienna, Austria, 1964; head quantum chem group, Res Inst Advan Studies, 1962-1969; Soroptimist fel int study, 1962; Vis staff mem, Ctr Appl Quantum Mech, France, 1962; staff scientist, Res Inst Advan Studies, 1960-1962; res asst, Johns Hopkins Univ, 1952-1960; chemist, US Army Chem Ctr, Md, 1949-1952; mem corresp, Acad Europ Sci, Arts & Letters. **Memberships:** Am Chem Soc; fel Am Phys Soc; fel Am Inst Chem; Int Soc Quantum Biol. **Research Statement & Publications:** Physicochemistry and theory of drugs which affect the central nervous system; computer systems; experimental chemical physics; chemical effects of nuclear transformation; isotopic exchange reactions of boron hydrides; quantum chemistry. **Mailing Address:** Dept Chem, Johns Hopkins Univ, Baltimore, MD 21218. **Fax:** 410-516-8420. **E-Mail:** chm_zjjk@jhunix.hcf.jhu.edu

KAUFMAN, KENTON RICHARD, BIOENGINEERING. **Education:** Univ SDak State Univ, BS, MS (Agr Eng) & PhD (Biomech Eng); Mayo Grad Sch, PhD (Biomech Eng). **Professional Experience:** ORTHOP SURG, MAYO CLIN, as of 2006; PROF PYSIOL & BIOMED ENG, MAYO CLIN COL MED, as of 2006. **Mailing Address:** Mayo Clin, 200 First St S W, Rochester, MN 55905.

KAUFMAN, LARRY, THERMODYNAMICS, MATERIALS SCIENCE. **Personal Data:** b Brooklyn, NY, June 6, 1931; m 1955, c 3. **Education:** Polytech Inst Brooklyn, BMetE, 1952; Mass Inst Technol, ScD(metall), 1955. **Honors & Awards:** Rossiter Raymond Award, Am Inst Mining, Metall & Petrol Engrs, 1964; Gibbs Triangle Award, Calphad, Inc, 1989; Hume Rothery Prize, Inst Metals, London, 1996. **Professional Experience:** LECTR, DEPT MAT SCI & ENG, MASS INST TECHNOL, 1996-; CONSULT, DEPT MAT SCI & ENG, MASS INST TECHNOL, 1996-; prin scientist, Mfg Labs, Inc, Alcan Aluminum Corp, 1991-1996; pres, Mfg Labs, Inc, Alcan Aluminum Corp, 1984-1991; Ed-in-chief, Calphad, 1977-1995; founding ed, Calphad Jour, 1977-; vpres, Mfg Labs, Inc, Alcan Aluminum Corp, 1976-1984; ORGANIZER, CALPHAD INC, 1973-; dir res, Mfg Labs, Inc, Alcan Aluminum Corp, 1963-1976; sr metallurgist, Mfg Labs, Inc, Alcan Aluminum Corp, 1958-1963; mem res staff, Lincoln Lab, Mass Inst Technol, 1955-1958. **Memberships:** Am Soc Metals; Am Inst Mining Metall & Petrol Engrs; Sigma Xi. **Research Statement & Publications:** Kinetics; phase equilibria; high pressure and temperature; transformations; computer calculation of phase diagrams. **Mailing Address:** Mass Inst Tech, Dept Mat Sci & Eng, 77 Mass Ave, Cambridge, MA 02139-4307. **Fax:** 617-258-9344. **E-Mail:** calphad@mit.edu

KAUFMAN, LEO, MEDICAL MYCOLOGY. **Personal Data:** b New York, NY, January 20, 1930; m 1952, c 3. **Education:** Brooklyn Col, BS, 1952; Univ Ky, MS, 1955, PhD (bact), 1959. **Honors & Awards:** Kimble Methodology Res Award, 1974; Meridian Award, Med Mycol Soc Am, 1984; Int Soc Human Animal Mycol Award, 1985. **Professional Experience:** Asst chief mycotic dis br, Div Bact & Mycotic Dis, USPHS, beginning 1990; chief fungus immunol br, Mycol Div, Ctr Dis Control, 1967-1990; in-chg, Fungus Serol Lab, Mycol Unit, 1963-1967; microbiologist med res, USPHS, 1959-1962; instr bact, Univ Ky, 1958-1959; mem fac, Univ NC, Sch Pub Health, Ga State Univ & Emory Univ; dir, Nat Ctr Fungal Serol. **Memberships:** Am Asn Immunol; Am Thoracic Soc; Am Soc Microbiol; Int Soc Human & Animal Mycol; Sigma Xi. **Research Statement & Publications:** Immunological procedures for diagnosis of systemic fungus infections and for identification of fungal pathogens. **Mailing Address:** Div Bact & Mycotic Dis, Mycoses Immunodiagnosis Lab, G-11 Bldg 5 B-13, Atlanta, GA 30333.

KAUFMAN, LINDA, NUMERICAL ANALYSIS, COMPUTER SCIENCE. **Personal Data:** b Fall River, Mass, March 20, 1947; m 1981. **Education:** Brown Univ, ScB, 1969; Stanford Univ, MS, 1971, PhD (comput sci), 1973. **Professional Experience:** Prin investr, NSF Grant, 1976-; mem tech staff, Bell Labs, beginning 1976; ast prof comput sci, Univ Colo, Boulder, 1973-1976; vis lectr comput sci, Univ Aarhus, 1973-1974; assoc ed, J Matrix Anal & Applns; RESEARCHER, SCIENTIFIC COMPUT RES DIV, BELL LABS. **Memberships:** Asn Comput Mach; Soc Indust & Appl Math. **Research Statement & Publications:** Development of algorithms in numerical linear algebra and function minimization. **Mailing Address:** Bell Labs, Lucent Technol, Rm 2C461, 600 Mountain Ave, MurrayHill, NJ 07974. **E-Mail:** lck@bell-labs.com

KAUFMAN, MARC P, PHYSIOLOGY & PSYCHOLOGY. **Personal Data:** b December 10, 1947; m 1974, c Scott & Michael. **Education:** Univ Miami, PhD (physiol & psychol), 1977. **Professional Experience:** PROF INTERNAL MED & HUMAN PHYSIOL, DIV CARDIOVASCULAR MED, UNIV CALIF, DAVIS, 1991-; assoc prof, Univ Calif, Davis, 1987-1991; asst prof physiol, Health Sci Ctr, Univ Tex, Dallas, 1980-1987. **Memberships:** Am Physiol Soc. **Research Statement & Publications:** Neural control of cardiovascular and respiratory system. **Mailing Address:** Dept Internal Med, Div Cardiovasc Med, Univ Calif Davis, TB 172 One Shields Ave, Davis, CA 95616-8636. **Fax:** 530-752-3265. **E-Mail:** mpkaufman@ucdavis.edu

KAUFMAN, MIRON, POLYMER PHYSICS, STATISTICAL PHYSICS. **Personal Data:** b October 31, 1950; American citizen; m 1975, c 2. **Education:** Tel Aviv Univ, Israel, BSc, 1973, MSc, 1977; Carnegie Mellon Univ, PhD (physics), 1981. **Professional Experience:** Chair Physics Dept 2000-; PROF, CLEVELAND STATE UNIV, 1995-; from asst prof to assoc prof, Cleveland State Univ, 1985-1995; Bantrell fel surface physics, Mass Inst Technol, 1983-1985. **Memberships:** Am Phys Soc. **Research Statement & Publications:** Research activity on condensed matter and statistical physics focused on following topics: random magnets, liquid mixtures, spin (ISING-POTTS) models, percolation, superconductivity, polymers and fractals; research methods: scaling theory of critical phenomena, renormalization-group technique. **Mailing Address:** Physics Dept, Cleveland State Univ, Cleveland, OH 44115. **Fax:** 216-523-7268. **E-Mail:** m.kaufman@csuohio.edu

KAUFMAN, MYRON JAY, PHYSICAL CHEMISTRY. **Personal Data:** b New York, NY, March 24, 1937; m 1967. **Education:** Harvard Univ, MS, 1963, PhD (chem physics), 1965; Rensselaer Polytech Inst, BS, 1958. **Professional Experience:** PROF CHEM, EMORY UNIV, 1978-; assoc prof, Emory Univ, 1972-1978; asst prof, Princeton Univ, 1966-1972; res fel chem, Harvard Univ, 1964-1966; Trainee, Gen Elec Co, 1958-1959. **Memberships:** Am Chem Soc. **Research Statement & Publications:** Chemical kinetics; molecular beams; atmospheric chemistry; combustion; coal chemistry. **Mailing Address:** Dept Chem, Emory Univ, Atlanta, GA 30322. **Fax:** 404-727-6586. **E-Mail:** chemmjk@emory.edu

KAUFMAN, NATHAN, PATHOLOGY. **Personal Data:** b Lachine, Que, August 3, 1915; m 1946, c 5. **Education:** McGill Univ, BSc, 1937, MD & CM, 1941; Am Bd Path, dipl, 1950. **Professional Experience:** HEAD DEPT PATH, QUEEN'S UNIV, ONT, as of 1997; PROF EMER PATH, QUEEN'S UNIV, ONT, 1981-; secy-treas, US-Can Div, Int Acad Path, 1979; ed, Lab Invest, 1972-1975; consult, Ont Cancer Treatment & Res Found, Kingston Clin, 1971-1979; consult, Lennox & Addington Co Gen Hosp, Napanee, Ont & Hotel Dieu Hosp, 1969-1979; mem coun, Med Res Coun, 1971-1977; exec, Med Res Coun, 1971-1974; chmn, Med Res Coun, 1971-1974; mem grants panel, Nat Cancer Inst Can, 1970-1974; mem grants comt path & morphol, Med Res Coun, 1968-1974; prof & head dept, Queen's Univ, Ont, 1967-1979; pathologist-in-chief, Kingston Gen Hosp, 1967-1979; prof, Sch Med, Duke Univ, 1960-1967; pathologist chg, Cleveland Metrop Gen Hosp, 1952-1960; from instr to assoc prof, Med Sch, Western Res Univ, 1948-1960; asst pathologist, Cleveland Metrop Gen Hosp, 1948-1952; asst resident, Cleveland City Hosp, 1947-1948; resident path, Jewish Gen Hosp, 1946-1947; intern, Royal Victoria Hosp, Montreal, 1941-1942. **Memberships:** Int Acad Path (vpres, 1972-1974, pres-elect, 1974-1976, pres, 1976-1978); Can Asn Path; Am Asn Path; Soc Exp Biol & Med; US & Can Acad Path (pres, 1973-1974, secy-treas, 1979). **Mailing Address:** Dept Path, Richardson Lab, Queen's Univ, Kingston, ON K7L 3N6, Can. **Fax:** 613-533-2907.

KAUFMAN, PAUL LEON, OPHTHALMOLOGY, GLAUCOMA. **Personal Data:** b New York, NY, September 16, 1943; m 1970, c 1. **Education:** Univ NY, MD, 1967. **Honors & Awards:** Alcon Res Inst Award, Outstanding Contrib Vision Res, 1985. **Professional Experience:** DIR, GLAUCOMA SERV, as of 2004; AFFIL PROF, VET SCI, ANIMAL HEALTH & BIOMED SCI, UNIV WIS, as of 2004; AFFIL SCIENTIST, WIS REGIONAL PVT RES CTR, UNIV WIS, as of 2004; Trustee, Asn Res Vision Opthal, 1993-; counr, Int Soc Eye Res, 1992-; mem, Nat Adv Eye Coun, 1991-1994; PROF OPHTHAL, UNIV WIS, MADISON, 1983-; Mem, Vis Sci study Sect, 1982-1985; Mem, Special Study Sects & Site Visit Teams, 1980-1982; Mem, Glaucoma Prog Planning Panel, Nat Adv Eye Coun, Nat Eye Inst, NIH, 1980-1982; prin investr, Nat Eye Inst Res Grants, 1979-; consult, Retinal & Choroidal Dis Prog Planning Panel, Nat Adv Eye Coun, NIH, 1977; from asst prof to assoc prof, Univ Wis-Madison, 1975-1983; res fel, Univ Uppsala, Sweden, 1973-1975; resident ophthal, Univ Wash, 1970-1973; Staff assoc, Nat Cancer Inst, 1968-1970. **Memberships:** Asn Res Vision & Ophthal; Am Acad Ophtal; Am Glaucoma Soc; Int Soc Eye Res. **Research Statement & Publications:** Anatomy, physiology, pharmacology, neural control and aging of aqueous humor formation, drainage, and accommodation as related to pathophysiology and treatment of glaucoma and presbyopia; Published over 10 articles. **Mailing Address:** Dept Ophthal & Visual Sci, Univ Wis, 600 Highland Ave, Madison, WI 53792. **Fax:** 608-263-1466. **E-Mail:** kaufmanp@mhub.ophth.wisc.edu

KAUFMAN, PETER BISHOP, PLANT PHYSIOLOGY. **Personal Data:** b San Francisco, Calif, February 25, 1928; m 1958, Hazel; c Linda & Laura. **Education:** Cornell Univ, BS, 1949; Univ Calif, PhD (bot), 1954. **Honors & Awards:** Orr E Reynolds Award Distinguished Serv, Am Soc Gravitational & Space Biol. **Professional Experience:** PROF EMER BIOL, UNIV MICH, ANN ARBOR, as of 2005; US Dept Agr, Univ Calgary, 1985; prof cell & molecular biol & bioengineering prog, Univ Mich, Ann Arbor, beginning 1983; vis scientist, Int Rice Res Inst, Los Banos, Philippines, 1981; US Dept Agr, Beltsville, Md, 1981; vis prof cell, Molecular & Develop Biol, Univ Colo, Boulder, 1974; Nagoya Univ,

Japan, 1981; inst Environ Qual, Univ Mich, 1971-1972; NASA, 1979-1988; prof bot, Univ Mich, Ann Arbor, beginning 1973; grants, Am Cancer Soc, 1968-1971; grants, Inst Plant Physiol, Univ Lund, 1964-1966; NSF grants, 1959-1961, 1975 & 1980-1983; cur, Bot Gardens, 1957-1973; from instr to assoc prof bot, Univ Mich, Ann Arbor, 1956-1973; res assoc, Univ Mich, Ann Arbor, 1956-1957; Muellhaupt scholar, Ohio State Univ, 1954; res technician & asst bot, Univ Calif, 1949-1954; res technician, Shell Develop Co, 1949; res technician hort, Cornell Univ, 1945-1949. **Memberships:** Am Soc Plant Physiol; Soc Develop Biol; fel AAAS; Am Soc Gravitational & Space Biol; Int Plant Growth Substances Asn; Int Soc Plant & Molecular Biol. **Research Statement & Publications:** Scanning electron microscopy, electron microprobe analysis and neutron activation analysis as related to silicification mechanisms in rice, oats, sugarcane and other grasses; studies on hormonal interactions and primary mode of action of gibberellin hormone regulation of stem elongation in grasses; mechanism of negative gravitropic response in grasses under NASA Space Biology programs; molecular biology of rice seedproteins, heat-shock proteins in rice; use of plant cell cultures for production of useful secondary compounds; development of life support systems for NASA space station and moon-mars bases; gravitropic response mechanism in snapdragon flowering shoots and in cereal grass shoots; natural products of medicinal value in plants. **Mailing Address:** Univ Mich, Dept Biol, Ann Arbor, MI 48109-1048. **E-Mail:** pbk@umich.edu

KAUFMAN, RANDAL J, MEDICAL RESEARCH. **Education:** Univ Colo, BA; Stanford Univ, PhD. **Professional Experience:** PROF BIOL CHEM, UNIV MICH MED SCH, as of 2005; FEL, HOWARD HUGHES MED INST, as of 2005. **Mailing Address:** Univ Mich, 4570 MSRB II, Ann Arbor, MI 48109-0606. **Fax:** 734-763-4581. **E-Mail:** kaufmanr@umich.edu

KAUFMAN, RAYMOND H, OBSTETRICS & GYNECOLOGY, GYNECOLOGICAL PATHOLOGY & CYTOPATHOLOGY. **Personal Data:** b Brooklyn, NY, November 24, 1925; m 1946, Patricia; c Susan, Wendy, Murri & Elisabeth. **Education:** Univ Md, MD, 1948; Am Bd Obstet & Gynec, dipl. **Professional Experience:** PROF PATH, OBSTET & GYNEC, BAYLOR MED COL, 1973-; Ernst W Bertner chmn obstet & gynec, Dept Obstet & Gynec, 1973-1993; actg chmn, Dept Obstet & Gynec, 1968-1972; from asst prof to assoc prof obstet, gynec & path, Baylor Med Col, 1958-1973; fel path, Methodist Hosp, Houston, 1955-1958; resident obstet & gynec, Beth Israel Hosp, NY, 1948-1953. **Memberships:** Am Col Obstet & Gynec; fel Am Col Surg; Am Gynec & Obstet Soc; Am Cytol Soc; Ctr Asn Obstet & Gynec; Soc Gynec & Oncol. **Research Statement & Publications:** Gynecologic pathology; cytopathology; relationship of virus to lower genital tract carcinoma. **Mailing Address:** Dept Obstet & Gynec, Baylor Col Med, 6550 Fannin St Ste 701 One Baylor Plaza, Houston, TX 77030. **Fax:** 713-798-3692. **E-Mail:** rkaufman@bcm.tmc.edu

KAUFMAN, SAMUEL, PHYSICAL & ANALYTICAL CHEMISTRY, CHEMICAL EDUCATION. **Personal Data:** b Toledo, Ohio, January 29, 1913; wid Julia (Deceased). **Education:** Univ Toledo, BEd, 1937, BSc, 1940, MSc, 1947. **Professional Experience:** RETIRED; consult, Univ Md, 1982-1995; consult, US Naval Res Lab, 1976-1982; res chemist, US Naval Res Lab, 1948-1975; instr, Montgomery Jr Col, 1946-1947; chemist, Nat Bur Stand, 1945-1948; chemist, Engr Corps, US Army, 1941-1945; control analyst, US Gypsum Co, 1941; Control & prod supvr ceramics, Save Elec Corp, 1937-1938. **Memberships:** Am Chem Soc; Sigma Xi. **Research Statement & Publications:** Isopycnic ultracentrifugation; lubricant additives; water pollution abatement; nonaqueous micelle formation and solubilization; reactions of amines in nonaqueous media; analysis of fluorine-bearing silicates; concrete curing agents; nonaqueous titrations; carbon fiber composites. **Mailing Address:** 919 Hyde Rd, Silver Spring, MD 20902.

KAUFMAN, SEYMOUR, BIOCHEMISTRY, NEUROSCIENCES. **Personal Data:** b NY, March 13, 1924; m 1948, Elaine; c Allan, Emily & Leslie. **Education:** Univ Ill, BS, 1945, MS, 1946; Duke Univ, PhD (biochem), 1949. **Honors & Awards:** Hillebrand prize, 1991. **Professional Experience:** STAFF, LAB NEUROCHEM, NIMH, as of 2004; chief lab neurochem, NIMH, beginning 1968; chief sect cellular regulatory mechanisms, NIMH, 1954-1968; NSF travel award, Int Cong biochem, Paris, 1952; from instr to asst prof, Sch Med, NY Univ, 1950-1953; res fel, sch Med, NY Univ, 1949. **Memberships:** Nat Acad Sci; Am Chem Soc; Harvey Soc; Am Soc Neurochem; Int Soc Neurochem; Am Soc Biol Chemists; Am Acad Arts & Sci. **Research Statement & Publications:** Mechanism of action of enzymes; intermediary metabolism of amino acids phenylketonuria neurotransmitter biosynthesis tetrahydrobiopterin. **Mailing Address:** Lab Neurochem, NIMH, 9000 Rockville Pike Bldg 36 Rm 3d32, Bethesda, MD 20892. **Fax:** 301-480-9284.

KAUFMAN, SHELDON BERNARD, NUCLEAR CHEMISTRY. **Personal Data:** b Los Angeles, Calif, June 7, 1929; wid, c 2. **Education:** Univ Chicago, MS, 1951, PhD, 1953. **Professional Experience:** SR PHYSICIST, ARGONNE NAT LAB, 1986-; from assoc chemist to chemist, Argonne Nat Lab, 1966-1986; from instr to asst prof, Princeton Univ, 1957-1966; Res assoc chem, Columbia Univ, 1955-1957. **Memberships:** Am Phys Soc; AAAS; Am Chem Soc. **Research Statement & Publications:** Radiochemical studies of low and high energy nuclear reactions; hot-atom chemistry; tracer applications to inorganic chemistry; high-energy nuclear reactions; nuclear fission; pi-meson reactions; reactions of complex nuclei with energetic protons, pi-mesons, and heavy ions; nuclear fission. **Mailing Address:** Argonne Nat Lab, 9700 S Cass Ave, Argonne, IL 60439.

KAUFMAN, SIDNEY, CRUSTAL STUDIES, GEOTHERMAL STUDIES. **Personal Data:** b Passaic, NJ, August 10, 1908; wid, c Martha A (Selzman) & Susan J. **Education:** Cornell Univ, AB, 1930, PhD (physics, math), 1934. **Honors & Awards:** Gold Medal Award, Soc Explor Geophys, 1983; Hedberg Award, Southern Methodist Univ, 1990. **Professional Experience:** RETIRED; adj prof geophys, Cornell Univ, beginning1991; consult, Energy Res & Develop Admin, beginning 1975; prof, Cornell Univ, 1974-1991; dir, Geothermal Resources Coun, 1973-1977; mem comt seismol, Nat Acad Sci-Nat Res Coun, 1966-1971 & 1974-1977; asst to vpres, Shell Develop Co, 1965-1974; chmn, Air Force Off Sci Res, 1964-1966; mem geophys adv panel, Air Force Off Sci Res, 1961-1974; consult, Adv Res Projs Agency, US Dept Defense, 1961-1973; sr res assoc, Shell Develop Co, 1961-1965; head geophys instrumentation dept, Shell Develop Co, 1958-1961; sr physicist, Shell Develop Co, 1946-1958; prin physicist, Naval Res Labs, 1946; geophysicist, Shell Oil Co, 1936-1941; asst physics, Coffin Found fel, 1935; asst physics, Cornell Univ, 1930-1933. **Memberships:** Hon mem Soc Explor Geophys; Seismol Soc Am; Am Geophys Union; Sigma Xi; Europ Asn Explor Geophysicists. **Research Statement & Publications:** Geophysical exploration; deep crustal seismic profiling; geothermal resource assessment. **Mailing Address:** 651 Bering Dr No 605, Houston, TX 77057-2134. **E-Mail:** sk651605@aol.com

KAUFMAN, SOL, SIMULATION MODELING, BIOSTATISTICS. **Personal Data:** b New York, NY, March 2, 1928; m 1954, Joyce; c Bruce A, Wayne M, Jay S, Jessica L & Daniel K. **Education:** Wash Univ, AB, 1951; Cornell Univ, PhD (math), 1965. **Professional Experience:** INDEPENDENT CONSULT, 1990-; Anal & Simulation, Inc, 1986-1993; systs analyst, XMCO, Inc, 1984-1986; res asst prof otolaryngol, State Univ NY, Buffalo, 1980-; mem staff, Falcon Res & Develop Co, 1979-1984; cancer control network coordr, State Univ NY Buffalo, 1974-1979; coordr res & eval, Niagara Falls Community Ment Health Ctr, 1973-1974; lectr indust eng & social & prev med, State Univ NY, Buffalo, 1970-1982; systs analyst & asst head opers, Res Dept, Cornell Aeronaut Lab/Calspan Corp, 1953-1962 & 1965-1973; physicist, Nat Bur Stand, 1951-1952. **Memberships:** Math Asn Am. **Research Statement & Publications:** Causal modeling in social epidemiology; Expert system application to simulation modeling; discrete event simulation, statistical analysis of complex survey data; cancer epidemiology and outcome analysis. **Mailing Address:** 1201 Stolle Rd, Elma, NY 14059. **E-Mail:** skaufma@buffalo.edu

KAUFMAN, STANLEY, MATERIALS SCIENCE. **Personal Data:** b New York, NY, October 30, 1941; m 1964, c 2. **Education:** City Col NY, BS, 1963; Brown Univ, PhD (chem), 1970. **Honors & Awards:** Akzo Chemie Award, UK, 1980. **Professional Experience:** ENVIRON & SAFETY OFFICER, CHEM GROUP, AT&T BELL LABS, 1992-; SUPVR CHEM ENVIRON & SAFETY, CHEM GROUP, AT&T BELL LABS, 1977-; mem tech staff, Chem Group, AT&T Bell Labs, 1970-1977; Res scientist, Uniroyal Res Ctr, 1968-1970. **Memberships:** Am Phys Soc; Nat Fire Protection Asn; Am Chem Soc. **Research Statement & Publications:** Materials for communications use. **Mailing Address:** Bell Labs Lucent Technol, 2000 Northeast Expressway, Norcross, GA 30071. **Fax:** 770-798-4655. **E-Mail:** stankaufman@lucent.com

KAUFMAN, STEPHEN J, CELL BIOLOGY, DEVELOPMENTAL BIOLOGY. **Personal Data:** b New York, NY, January 3, 1943; div, c 2. **Education:** State Univ NY, Binghamton, BA, 1964, MA, 1966; Univ Colo, PhD (microbiol), 1971. **Professional Experience:** Adj prof, Kwang-Ju Inst Technol, Korea, 1994-; PROF CELL & STRUCT BIOL, UNIV ILL, URBANA, 1993-; ed, Exp Cell Res, 1985-1991; vis scientist, Max Planck Inst for Biophys Chem, Goettingen, FRG, 1984-1985; sr fel, Fogarty Int Ctr, 1984-1985; assoc prof microbiol & cell biol, Univ Ill, 1981-1993; prin investr, NIH grant, 1979-; consult, Nat Birth Defect Found, 1978-1981; asst prof cell biol, Univ Ill, 1977-1981; prin investr, 1975-1978; prin investr, Basil O'Connor Grant, 1975-1978; asst prof microbiol, Univ Ill, 1974-1981; Muscular Dystrophy Asn fel, 1973-1974; fel molecular biol, Mass Inst Technol, 1971-1974; Jane Coffin Childs Found fel, 1971-1973. **Memberships:** AAAS; Soc Develop Biol; Am Soc Cell Biol; Am Soc Microbiol; Am Soc Biol Chem. **Research Statement & Publications:** Muscle differentiation; development of specialized cells; role of integrins and extracellular matrix in muscle development. **Mailing Address:** Dept Cell & Struct Biol, Univ Ill, B107 CLSL, Urbana, IL 61801. **E-Mail:** stephenk@uiuc.edu

KAUFMAN, STEPHEN P, ELECTRONICS. **Personal Data:** b Cambridge, Mass, November 19, 1941; m 1969, Sharon; c Jeremy S. **Education:** Mass Inst Technol, BS, 1963; Harvard Univ, MBA, 1965. **Professional Experience:** DIR, KLA TENCOR INC, 2002-; SR LECTR, HARVARD BUS SCH, 2001-; chmn, Arrow Electronics Inc, 1994-2002; chief exec officer, Arrow Electronics Inc, 1986-2000; pres, Arrow Electronics Inc, 1985-1999; chief oper officer, Arrow Electronics Inc, 1984-1986; exec vpres, Arrow Electronics Inc, 1982-1984; group vpres, Midland Ross Corp, 1980-1982; from assoc to partner, McKinsey & Co, 1969-1980; group controller, Chase Brass & Copper Co, 1967-1969; asst to pres, Grand Steel & Mfg Co, 1965-1967. **Mailing Address:** KLA Tencor Corp, 160 Rio Robles, San Jose, CA 95134.

KAUFMAN, THOMAS CHARLES, GENETICS, DEVELOPMENT & EVOLUTION. **Personal Data:** b Chicago, Ill, July 28, 1944; m 1967, Trudy; c Erin. **Education:** Calif State Un., BA, 1967; Univ Tex, Austin, MA, 1969, PhD (genetics), 1970. **Honors & Awards:** Welshons Lecture, Iowa State University, 1991; D Allan Harmon Lectureship, Oklahoma Medical Research Foundation, 1993; The Edwin Grant Conklin Medal, Society for Developmental Biology, 1998; The John C Davis Memorial Lecture, University of Kansas, 1998; The John H Blaffer Lecture, The University of Texas, MD Anderson Cancer Center, 1999; American Academy of Arts and Sciences, fellow, 1999-; Singer Medal, Midwest Development Biology Meeting, Columbia, Missouri, 2002; GSA Beadle Medal for contributions to genetics research, 2005; Distinguished Lecturer, University of Manchester, UK, 2005. **Professional Experience:** DIST. PROF GENETICS, IND UNIV, BLOOMINGTON, 1993-; prof genetics, 1981-1993; investr. hhmi, 1990-2003; assoc prof biology, 1980-1983; asst prof biology, 1975-1980; lectr, Univ BC, 1973-1974; Nat Res Coun Can res assoc zool, Univ BC, 1971-1973; Adj prof med genetics, Med Sch, Ind Univ. **Memberships:** AAAS; Genetics Soc Am; Soc for Devel. Biol. **Research Statement & Publications:** Mutagenesis; genetic fine structure in eucaryotic organisms; cytology of dipterin polytene salivary gland chromosomes; position effect variegation and developmental genetics of drosophila; genetics and control of redundant genes; evolution of developmentally important genes. **Mailing Address:** Dept Biology, Ind Univ, Bloomington, IN 47405. **Fax:** 812-855-2577. **E-Mail:** kaufman@bio.indiana.edu

KAUFMAN, VICTOR, atomic physics; deceased, see previous edition for last biography

KAUFMAN, WILLIAM CARL, JR, HUMAN PHYSIOLOGY, BIOPHYSICS. **Personal Data:** b Appleton, Minn, January 21, 1923; m 1946, Patricia Hurley; c Jane & William C III. **Education:** Univ Minn, BA, 1948; Univ Ill, MS, 1953; Univ Wash, PhD (physiol), 1961. **Professional Experience:** RETIRED; prof, Univ Wis, 1978-1986; chmn res coun, Univ Wis, 1978-1981; prof human adaptability & chmn dept, Univ Wis, 1969-1978; Nat Inst Med Res spec res fel, Hampstead Labs, London, Eng, 1968-1969; NIH special res fel, London, Eng, 1968-1969; chief, Byodynamics Br, Aeromed Res Lab, Holloman AFB, 1966-1968; mem nuclear weapons effects res comt, Defense Atomic Support Agency, 1965-1968; Asst prof prev med, Ohio State Univ, 1962-1967; res biologist thermal environ, Aerospace Med Res Labs, 1958-1966; proj officer altitude suits, Aeromed Lab, 1953-1956; Instr aviation physiol, Wright-Patterson AFB, 1950-1951; consult to pvt indust. **Memberships:** AAAS; Aerospace Med Asn; Am Physiol Soc. **Research Statement & Publications:** Temperature regulation and peripheral circulation; thermal and space environments; respiration; evaluation and development of cold weather protective equipment; evaluation and development of protective and recreational clothing. **Mailing Address:** Dept Physiol, Univ Wis, 2420 Nicolet Dr, Green Bay, WA 54311-7001.

KAUFMAN, WILLIAM MORRIS, ELECTRICAL ENGINEERING, AUTOMATED INSPECTION & TRANSPORTATION SAFETY. **Personal Data:** b Pittsburgh, Pa, December 31, 1931; m 1953, Iris F Picovsky; c Nathan, Marjorie & Emily. **Education:** Carnegie Inst Technol, BS & MS, 1953, PhD (elec eng), 1955. **Professional Experience:** Consult technol Acquisition, 1997-; vpres appl res, Carnegie Mellon Univ, 1985-1997; dir, Carnegie Mellon Res Inst, 1985-1997; vpres new prod develop, Ocean Data Systs, Inc, 1984-1985; vpres eng, Ensco, Inc, 1971-1984; mgr, Med Eng Dept, Hittman Assocs, Inc, 1966-1971; consult engr, Gen Elec Co, 1965-1966; dir res, Gen Instrument Corp, 1962-1965; supvry engr, Westinghouse Elec Corp, 1959-1962; res mathematician, Westinghouse Elec Corp, 1957-1959; engr, Westinghouse Elec Corp, 1955-1957; res engr, Carnegie Inst Technol, 1954-1955; Instr, Carnegie Inst Technol, 1953-1954. **Memberships:** Fel, Inst Elec & Electronics Engrs. **Research Statement & Publications:** Transportation safety res and develop; automated inspection of RR track; med instr; distributed R-C Circuit theory; solid state device applications; artificial internal organs; 17 patents. **Mailing Address:** 38 Sheridan Rd, Swampscott, MA 01907. **Fax:** 781-596-2966. **E-Mail:** wk0e@andrew.cmu.edu

KAUFMAN-JACOBS, SUSAN E, BLOOD PRESSURE REGULATION, BODY FLUID HOMEOSTASIS. **Personal Data:** b Ottawa, Ont, August 5, 1943; m 1988, Harold; c Naomi, Rachel & Oren. **Education:** Univ Col, London, BS, 1965; McGill Univ, Montreal, MS, 1967; Univ BC, PhD (zoology), 1971. **Professional Experience:** PROF PHYSIOLOGY, UNIV ALTA, 1992-; Alta Heritage Foundation Scholar, 1983-1995; Can Heart Foundation Scholar, 1980-1983; assoc prof med, Univ Alta, 1979-1992; res assoc, Univ Alta, 1977-1979; premier asst, Univ Lausanne, 1975-1977; sr res worker, Univ Cambridge, 1973-1974; Sci res coun fel, Univ Cambridge, 1971-1972. **Memberships:** Am Physiol Soc; AAAS; NY Acad Sci; Can Physiol Soc. **Research Statement & Publications:** Integrative cardiovascular/renal physiology; mechanisms underlying control of blood pressure and intravascular volume with special reference to influence of gender on cardiovascular homeostasis. **Mailing Address:** Univ Alta, 475 HMRC, Edmonton, AB T6G 2S2, Can. **Fax:** 403-492-7522. **E-Mail:** susan.jacobs@ualberta.ca

KAUFMANN, ALVERN WALTER, MATHEMATICS. **Personal Data:** b Cleveland, Ohio, February 21, 1924; m 1946, c 3. **Education:** Greenville Col, BA, 1947; Ohio State Univ, MA, 1948, PhD, 1960. **Professional Experience:** RETIRED; prof math, Mt Vernon Nazarene Col, Ohio, 1981-1986; acad dean, Roberts Wesleyan Col, 1974-1981; prof math, Roberts Wesleyan Col, 1965-1981; assoc prof math & physics, Roberts Wesleyan Col, 1957-1965; asst instr math, Ohio State Univ, 1954-1957; teacher, Pub Sch, Ohio, 1952-1954; instr math & physics, Cent Col, Kans, 1950-1952; instr math, Aurora Col, 1948-1950. **Memberships:** Math Asn Am; Am Sci Affil; Nat Coun Teachers Math. **Research Statement & Publications:** Meaning and definition in mathematics. **Mailing Address:** 39 Kester Dr, Mt Vernon, OH 43050.

KAUFMANN, ANTHONY J, MICROBIOLOGY, BIOCHEMISTRY. **Personal Data:** b Millen, Ga, August 19, 1936; m 1966. **Education:** Univ Ga, BS, 1959, MS, 1961; La State Univ, PhD (microbiol), 1967. **Professional Experience:** DEAN SCH SCI ENG TECH, ST MARYS UNIV, SAN ANTONIO, as of 2003; PROF BIOL, ST MARYS UNIV, SAN ANTONIO, 1974-; consult, Southwest Res Found & Inst, San Antonio, 1971-; assoc prof, St Mary's Univ, San Antonio, 1969-1974; assoc prof health sci, Etenn State Univ, 1967-1969; res assoc, La State Univ, 1967; fel microbiol, La State Univ, 1963-1967; med microbiologist, Nat Communicable Dis Ctr, 1962-1963. **Memberships:** AAAS; Am Soc Microbiol; Am Inst Biol Sci. **Research Statement & Publications:** Microorganisms capable of degrading certain solid waste products such as cellulose, paper products and certain plastics. **Mailing Address:** Dept Biol, St Marys Univ, Math 203, One Camino Santa Maria, San Antonio, TX 78228-5433. **E-Mail:** setdean@stmarytx.edu

KAUFMANN, ARNOLD FRANCIS, EPIDEMIOLOGY. **Personal Data:** b Dubuque, Iowa, February 24, 1936; div, c 3. **Education:** Iowa State Univ, DVM, 1960; Univ Minn, MS, 1968; Am Col Vet Path, dipl. **Professional Experience:** RETIRED; chief, Mycotic Dis Br, Ctr Dis Control, beginning 1990; chief, Bact Zoonoses Act, Ctr Dis Control, 1971-1990; vet pathologist, Ctr Dis Control, 1968-1970; vet epidemiologist, Ctr Dis Control, 1963-1967; vet, 1962-1963. **Memberships:** Am Vet Med Asn; Am Asn Lab Animal Sci; Am Col Vet Pathologists. **Research Statement & Publications:** Pathology and epidemiology of infectious diseases; molecular biology of leptospires. **Mailing Address:** 2155 Mountclaire Ct, Stone Mtain, GA 30087.

KAUFMANN, ELTON NEIL, SCIENCE POLICY, MATERIALS SCIENCE. **Personal Data:** b Cleveland, Ohio, March 18, 1943. **Education:** Rensselaer Polytech Inst, BS, 1964; Calif Inst Technol, PhD (physics), 1969. **Professional Experience:** Secy, Intl Union of Materials res soc, 2001-2002; Exec Editor, IUMRS Facets, 2001-; Ed, Ann Rev Mat Sci, 1993-2001; ASSOC DIR, STRATEGIC PLANNING GROUP, OFF DIR, ARGONNE NAT LAB, 1991-; dir, Superconductivity Pilot Ctr, 1989-1991; Mats Div Leader, Lawrence Livermore Nat Lab, 1981-1989; Ed, Hyperfine Interactions, 1980-1989; Mem tech staff, Bell Tel Labs, 1968-1981. **Memberships:** Fel Am Phys Soc; Metall Soc; Mat Res Soc (pres, 1985); AAAS; Mat Res Soc Japan. **Research Statement & Publications:** Hyperfine interactions using nuclear spectroscopic methods; particle-solid interactions including ion-beam channeling and ion-implantation; directed energy beam materials modification; superconductivity; research administration and policy. **Mailing Address:** Off Dir Argonne Nat Lab, 9700 S Cass Ave, Argonne, IL 60439-4832. **Fax:** 630-252-5149. **E-Mail:** eltonk@anl.gov

KAUFMANN, JOHN HENRY, VERTEBRATE ZOOLOGY, BEHAVIORAL ECOLOGY. **Personal Data:** b Baltimore, Md, January 7, 1934; div, c 3. **Education:** Cornell Univ, BS, 1956; Univ Calif, Berkeley, PhD (vert zool), 1961. **Professional Experience:** PROF ZOOL, UNIV FLA, 1974-; from asst prof to assoc prof zool, Univ Fla, 1963-1974; biologist animal ecol, Nat Inst Neurol Dis & Blindness, 1961-1963. **Memberships:** Am Soc Mammal; Ecol Soc Am; Animal Behav Soc. **Research Statement & Publications:** Social behavior and ecology of Emydidae, Procyonidae, Mustelidae, Primates and Macropodidae, including home range, movements and dominance behavior including territoriality, food habits and activity cycles. **Mailing Address:** Dept Zool Univ Fla, 223 Bartram Hall PO Box 118525, Gainesville, FL 32611-8525. **Fax:** 352-392-3704.

KAUFMANN, KENNETH JAMES, INSTRUMENTATION. **Personal Data:** b New York, NY, May 2, 1947. **Education:** City Col NY, BS, 1968; Mass Inst Technol, PhD (chem), 1973. **Professional Experience:** MKT MGR, HAMAMATSU CORP, as of 1999; mem staff, Worthington Group, Mcgraw Edison Co, beginning 1980; asst prof chem, Univ Ill, Urbana, 1976-1980; Fel chem, Bell Tel Labs, 1974-1975; Fel chem, Calif Inst Technol, 1973-1974. **Memberships:** Am Phys Soc; Am Chem Soc; Sigma Xi. **Research Statement & Publications:** Picosecond kinetics of biological and chemical reaction. **Mailing Address:** Hamamatsu Corp, 360 Foothill Rd, Bridgewater, NJ 08807. **Fax:** 908-231-9374. **E-Mail:** kkaufmann@hamamatsu.com

KAUFMANN, MAURICE JOHN, PLANT PATHOLOGY. **Personal Data:** b Hopedale, Ill, November 11, 1929. **Education:** Bluffton Col, BS, 1952; Univ Ill, MS, 1955, PhD (plant path, bot), 1957. **Professional Experience:** PROF EMER BIOL, BLUFFTON COL, 1994-; from assoc prof to prof, Bluffton Col, 1970-1994; mem fac biol, Bluffton Col, 1963-1970; Plant pathologist, Agr Res Serv, USDA, Wis, 1957-1963. **Memberships:** Am Phytopath Soc. **Research Statement & Publications:** Diseases of soybeans and forage grasses. **Mailing Address:** Dept Biol, Bluffton Col, 280 W Col Ave, Bluffton, OH 45817-1196. **E-Mail:** kaufmannm@bluffton.edu

KAUFMANN, MERRILL R, PHYSIOLOGICAL ECOLOGY, FOREST HYDROLOGY. **Personal Data:** b Paxton, Ill, June 17, 1941; m 1993, Evelyn; c 2. **Education:** Univ Ill, BS, 1963; Duke Univ, MF, 1965, PhD (forestry), 1967. **Professional Experience:** RETIRED; chmn, Whole Plant Physiol Working Party, Int Union Forestry Res Orgn, 1991-; prin plant physiologist, Rocky Mountain Forest & Range Exp Sta, US Forest Serv, USDA, 1977-2006; assoc prof plant physiol & assoc plant physiologist, Univ Calif, Riverside, 1973-1977; asst prof plant physiol & asst plant physiologist, Univ Calif, Riverside, 1967-1973. **Memberships:** Int Union Forestry Res Orgn; Ecol Soc Am. **Research Statement & Publications:** Physiological ecology of old-growth trees; plant-environment interaction; plant water relations; physiological effects on subalpine forest watersheds; ecosystem management strategies. **Mailing Address:** USDA Forest Serv Rocky Mountain Forest & Range, 240 W Prospect Rd, Ft Collins, CO 80526. **Fax:** 970-498-1297. **E-Mail:** mkauf@lamar.colostate.edu

KAUFMANN, PETER G, STRESS PHYSIOLOGY PSYCHOSOMATIC MEDICINE & HEALTH PSYCHOLOGY. **Personal Data:** b Europe, February 5, 1942; American citizen; m Aukse; c Vikoras, Arius & Vyga. **Education:** Loyola Univ, BS, 1964, MA, 1966; Univ Chicago, PhD (psychol), 1970. **Honors & Awards:** Natl Leadership Award, Soc of Behavioral Medicine, 2002. **Professional Experience:** Acting Dir, Office of Behavioral& Social Sci, Res Natl Inst of Health, 2000-; CHIEF, BEHAV MED BR, NAT HEART LUNG & BLOOD INST, 1992-; adj assoc prof, George Mason Univ, 1992; lectr psychol, Montgomery Col, 1991-1992; SPEC EXPERT TO CHIEF, BEHAV MED BR, NAT HEART LUNG & BLOOD INST, 1983-; assoc to asst med res prof, Duke Univ Med Ctr, 1975-1983; scholar neurosci, Duke Univ Med Ctr, 1972-1975; asst prof psychol, Emory & Henry Col, 1970-1972; lectr psychol, Loyola Univ, Chicago, 1966-1967. **Memberships:** Am Psychol Soc; Am Psychol Asn; fel Soc Behav Med; Am Psychosomatic Soc; Acad Behav Med Res. **Research Statement & Publications:** Clinical trials of behavioral and physological interventions for preventions and rehabilitation; behavioral and neurol aspects of cardiovascular function; basic and clinical research related to biopsychosocial and sociocultural factors in somatic illness and stress-related disorders; treatment and prevention of cardiovascular diseases. **Mailing Address:** Nat Heart Lung & Blood Inst, 6701 Rockledge Dr MSC 7936, Bethesda, MD 20892-7936. **E-Mail:** pvk@cu.nih.gov

KAUFMANN, PETER G, NEUROSCIENCE. **Education:** PhD. **Professional Experience:** BEHAVIORAL MED SCI RES GROUP LEADER, CLIN APPL 7 PREV PROG, DIV EPIDEMIOL & CLIN APPL, NAT HEART, LUNG & BLOOD INST, MD, as of 2005. **Memberships:** Assoc Appl psychophysiol & Biofeedback. **Mailing Address:** Nat Heart, Lung & Blood Inst, Div Epidemiol & Clin Appl PO Box 30105, Bethesda, Md 20824-0105.

KAUFMANN, PETER JOHN, COSMETIC CHEMISTRY. **Personal Data:** b Amsterdam, Holland, October 30, 1935; m 1963, Arlene; c Mark & Cybele. **Education:** Univ Ill, Urbana, BS, 1959. **Honors & Awards:** Nat chairman, Soc of Cormetic chem, 1983. **Professional Experience:** VPRES, RQD ESTEELANDER CO, 1991-; vpres prod develop & res & develop, Almay Inc, 1980-1991; dir prod develop, Max Factor & Co, 1970-1980; lab dir, Marcelle Cosmetics Div, Borden, Inc, 1967-1970; res chemist cosmetics, Alberto-Culver Co, Ill, 1965-1967; chief chem, Dr P Fahrney & Sons, Chicago, 1963-1965. **Memberships:** Am Chem Soc; Soc Cosmetic Chemists; Inst Food Technol. **Research Statement & Publications:** Emulsion technology; formulation, development and manufacture of makeup and skin care products; efficacy and safety of cosmetics. **Mailing Address:** Estee Lauder, 125 Pinelawn Rd, Melville, NY 11747-3145. **Fax:** 516-531-1565.

KAUFMANN, RICHARD L, PHYSICS. **Personal Data:** b Honolulu, Hawaii, June 11, 1935; m 1963, c 2. **Education:** Calif Inst Technol, BS, 1957; Yale Univ, MS, 1958, PhD (chem), 1960. **Professional Experience:** PROF PHYSICS, UNIV NH, 1973-; from asst prof to assoc prof, 1963-1973. **Memberships:** Am Phys Soc. **Research Statement & Publications:** Space physics. **Mailing Address:** Dept Physics, Univ NH, DeMeritt Hall Rm 209D 9 Libr Way, Durham, NH 03824. **E-Mail:** dick.kaufmann@unh.edu

KAUFMANN, WILLIAM B, ELEMENTARY PARTICLE PHYSICS. **Personal Data:** b San Francisco, Calif, November 11, 1936; m 1968, c 2. **Education:** Univ Calif, Berkeley, PhD (physics), 1968. **Professional Experience:** PROF EMER PHYSICS, ARIZ STATE UNIV, AS OF 2005; prof physics, Ariz State Univ, beginning 1987; from asst prof to assoc prof, 1969-1987. **Memberships:** Am Phys Soc; AAAS. **Research Statement & Publications:** Theoretical medium-energy nuclear physics. **Mailing Address:** Dept Physics, PSF 433B, Ariz State Univ, Tempe, AZ 85287-1504. **Fax:** 480-965-7954. **E-Mail:** william.kaufmann@asu.edu

KAUFMANN, WILLIAM KARL, MOLECULAR BIOLOGY. **Personal Data:** b Richland, Wash, August 13, 1951. **Education:** Yale Univ, BS, 1973; Univ NC, PhD (path), 1979. **Professional Experience:** PROF, DEPT PATH & LAB MED, UNIV NC, CHAPEL HILL, as of 2004; asst prof, Dept Path & Lab Med, Univ NC, Chapel Hill, beginning 1988; fel biol, Lab Radiol & Environ Health, Univ Calif, San Francisco, 1982-1987. **Memberships:** AAAS; Sigma Xi. **Research Statement & Publications:** Mechanisms of DNA replication and repair and their importance in carcinogenesis. **Mailing Address:** Dept Path & Lab Med, Sch Med, Univ NC, 31 325 Lineberger Comprehensive Cancer Ctr, Chapel Hill, NC 27599-7295. **Fax:** 919-966-9673. **E-Mail:** Bill_kaufmann@med.unc.edu

KAUGERTS, JURIS E, LOW TEMPERATURE PHYSICS. **Personal Data:** b Riga, Latvia, September 24, 1940; American citizen; m 1969, c 3. **Education:** Stevens Inst Technol, BS, 1962, MS, 1964, PhD (physics), 1972. **Professional Experience:** SUPERCOLLIDER CENT DESIGN GROUP, 1987-; sr scientist, Oxford Superconducting Technol, 1984-1987; physicist, Brookhaven Nat Lab, 1980-1982; assoc physicist superconductivity, Brookhaven Nat Lab, 1977-1979; asst physicist superconductivity, Brookhaven Nat Lab, 1975-1977; res assoc, Plasma Physics Lab, Princeton Univ, 1973-1975; Presidential intern superconductivity, Lawrence Berkeley Lab, Univ Calif, 1972-1973. **Memberships:** Am Phys Soc. **Research Statement & Publications:** Superconducting accelerator magnet research, design and development. **Mailing Address:** 104 Hamburg Turnpike, Pompton Lakes, NJ 07442.

KAUKER, MICHAEL LAJOS, PHARMACOLOGY, GENERAL & ANIMAL PHYSIOLOGY. **Personal Data:** b Szerecseny, Hungary, January 24, 1935; American citizen; m 1994, Linda M Brahms; c 4. **Education:** Univ Ala, Birmingham, PhD (pharmacol), 1967. **Professional Experience:** Fulbright scholar, Semmelweis Univ Med, 1995; PROF PHYSIOL & PHARMACOL, UNIV SDAK, VERMILLION, 1983-; from asst prof to assoc prof pharmacol, Ctr Health Sci, Univ Tenn, Memphis, 1969-1983; NIH fel, Univ NC Chapel Hill, 1967-1979. **Memberships:** Am Soc Pharmacol & Exp Therapeut; Soc Exp Biol & Med; Am Soc Nephrology; Int Soc Nephrology. **Research Statement & Publications:** Electrolyte and water metabolism; renal micropuncture; mechanism of action of antidiuretic hormone; renal effects of diuretic drugs; regulation of body fluid compartments. **Mailing Address:** Dept Physiol & Pharmacol, Sch Med, Univ SDak, Vermillion, SD 57069. **E-Mail:** mkauker@usd.edu

KAUL, MAHARAJ KRISHEN, ENGINEERING MECHANICS, APPLIED MATHEMATICS. **Personal Data:** b India, November 11, 1940; m 1969, c 1. **Education:** Punjab Univ, India, BS, 1962; SUNY, Stony Brook, MS, 1967; Univ Calif, Berkeley, PhD (civil eng), 1972. **Professional Experience:** Consult, Nuclear Energy Div, Gen Elec, 1987-1988; PRES,

ENG MECH RES, INC, 1981-; vpres, Enconi, Inc, 1980; consult engr, Quadrex Corp, 1977-1980; Sr engr, EDS Nuclear, Inc, 1972-1977. **Research Statement & Publications:** Vibrations; earthquake engineering; finite elements; probabilistic and stochastic methods; numerical analysis; applied mathematics. **Mailing Address:** 43670 Vista Del Mar, Fremont, CA 94539.

KAUL, PUSHKAR NATH, PHARMACOLOGY, CLINICAL PHARMACOLOGY. **Personal Data:** b Srinagar, India, June 29, 1933; m 1961, Leela; c Meena, Venita & Reema. **Education:** Banaras Hindu Univ, BPharm, 1954, MPharm, 1955; Univ Calif, San Francisco, PhD (pharmacol, pharmaceut chem), 1960. **Honors & Awards:** Aruna & Malaviya Prizes, 1954; Lunsford Richardson Pharm Award, 1960; Ebert Prize Cert, 1962; Univ Okla Alumni Res Award, 1969 & 1970; Acharya Oration Gold Medal, 1997; Dandiya Oration Award, 1999. **Professional Experience:** Prof biol sci & Assoc vpres; Atlantic Univ, 1984-1987; Assoc vpres res, Wichita State Univ, 1987-1989; PROF BIOL SCI, CLARK ATLANTIC UNIV, 1989-; prof & chmn pharmacol & asst to pres, Res & Spec progs, Sch Med, Morehouse Univ, 1981-1984; prof pharmacodyn & toxicol, res med & res pediat, Univ Okla, 1977-1981; prof pharmacol, res med & res pediat, Univ Okla, 1975-1977; assoc prof pharmacol, res med & res pediat, Univ Okla, 1968-1975; group leader, Farbwerke Hoechst, Ger, 1965-1968; Lectr, Univ Poona, 1962-1963; chief res pharmacol, Antibiotics Res Ctr, India, 1961-1965; res assoc pharmacol & vis scientist, Med Sch, Univ Melbourne, 1960-1961; asst pharmacol, Med Ctr, Univ Calif, San Francisco, 1958-1960; asst pharmaceut chem, Med Ctr, Univ Calif, San Francisco, 1957-1958; Asst prof pharmaceut, Birla Inst Technol, India, 1955-1957; dir drug metab, Cent State Hosp, Norman; chmn, Nat Task force Marine Biomed; dir marine Pharmacol & adj prof pediat & res med, Univ Okla. **Memberships:** Assocfel Royal Australian Chem Inst; Am Soc Pharmacol & Exp Therapeut; Int Soc Biochem Pharmacol; Acad Pharmaceut Sci. **Research Statement & Publications:** Biotransformation of drugs; mechanism of drug action; screening of pharmacologically active substances from the sea; antibiotics; psychotropic drugs. **Mailing Address:** 385 Longwood Pl, Jonesboro, GA 30236. **Fax:** 404-880-8941. **E-Mail:** pkaul@cau.edu

KAUL, RAJINDER K, MOLECULAR BASIS OF INHERITED DISORDERS, ENZYMOLOGY & PROTEIN CHEMISTRY. **Personal Data:** b Banihal, India, March 3, 1951; American citizen; m 1979, Chandrika; c Abhinau & Anand. **Education:** Lucknow Univ, India, PhD (biochem), 1978. **Professional Experience:** PROJ LEADER, AEIVEOS SCI GROUP, as of 1997; ACTG CHIEF SCI OFFICER, AEIVEOS SCI GROUP, 1996-; assoc prof biol, Fla Int Univ, 1990-1996; sr res scientist, Miami Children's Hosp Res Inst, 1989-1996; sr res fel, Chicago Heart Asn, 1985-1987; from instr to asst prof genetics, Univ Ill, 1984-1989; res assoc, Univ Chicago, 1979-1984; lectr, Indian Inst Technol, 1978-1979. **Memberships:** Soc Inherited Metab Dis; Am Soc Human Genetics; NY Acad Sci; AAAS. **Research Statement & Publications:** Molecular basis of canavan disease; identification of mutations that lead to canavan disease; creation of a mouse model for canavan disease; gene organization and regulation of aspartoacylase. **Mailing Address:** Aeiveos Sci Group, 4010 Stone Way N Ste 220, Seattle, WA 98103. **Fax:** 305-663-2461. **E-Mail:** Kaul@Aeiveos.com

KAUL, ROBERT BRUCE, BOTANY, TAXONOMY. **Personal Data:** b Faribault, Minn, January 28, 1935; m 1976, Martha. **Education:** Univ Minn, 1957, PhD (bot), 1964. **Professional Experience:** PROF EMER, UNIV NEBR, LINCOLN, AS OF 2003; vice dir biol sci, 1989-1991; ed, Trans Nebr Acad Sci, beginning 1988; prof bot, Univ Nebr, Lincoln, beginning 1972; from asst prof to assoc prof, Univ Nebr, Lincoln, 1964-1972; instr, Univ Minn, 1961-1962; asst bot, Univ Minn, 1957-1960. **Memberships:** Bot Soc Am; Am Soc Plant Taxon; Am Inst Biol Sci. **Research Statement & Publications:** Morphology and life history of angiosperms, especially trees and aquatic plants; floristics of the Great Plains. **Mailing Address:** Sch Biol Sci, Univ Nebr, Lincoln, NE 68588-0118. **Fax:** 402-472-2083. **E-Mail:** rkaul@unlinfo.unl.edu

KAUL, S K, PURE MATHEMATICS. **Personal Data:** b Lucknow, India, December 25, 1936; Canadian citizen; m 1963, Radha; c 2. **Education:** Univ Lucknow, BSc, 1954, MSc, 1955; Univ Delhi, PhD (math), 1959. **Professional Experience:** PROF EMER MATH, UNIV REGINA, as of 2004; prof math, Univ Regina, beginning 1971; from asst prof to assoc prof, Univ Regina, 1963-1971; instr math, Univ Utah, 1962; Univ fel, Univ Rochester, 1960-1961; instr math, Univ Rochester, 1959-1960; Instr math, Hampton Inst, 1958-1959. **Memberships:** Am Math Soc; Can Math Cong; Math Asn Am. **Research Statement & Publications:** Studying topological structures associated with differential equations, like flows, semi-flows and generalized dynamical systems and various stability notions using a flow associated with a semiflow and a semiflow associated with a generalized dynamical system; impulsive differential equations. **Mailing Address:** Dept Math, Univ Regina, Rm 307 14 Col W Bldg, Regina, SK S4S 0A2, Can. **Fax:** 306-585-4020. **E-Mail:** kaul@math.uregina.ca

KAUL, SANJIV, CARDIOLOGY. **Personal Data:** b Kashmir, India, August 18, 1951; m 1981, c 1. **Education:** Univ Delhi, MBBS, 1975. **Professional Experience:** PROF INTERNAL MED, UNIV VA, as of 2004; DIR, CARDIAC IMAGING CTR, as of 2004; assoc prof med, Univ Va, beginning 1988; Mem, Coun Clin Cardiol, Am Heart Asn, 1985; asst prof, Univ VA, 1984-1988; fel cardiol, Univ Calif Sch Med, Los Angeles, 1980-1982; fel cardiol Harvard Med Sch, 1982-1984; resident med, Univ Vt, 1978-1980; Intern med, Chicago Med Sch, 1977-1978. **Memberships:** Fel Am Col Physicians; fel Am Col Cardiol; fel Am Col Chest Physicians; Physicians for Social Responsibility; Am Fedn Clin Res; fel Am Heart Asn; Am Soc Echocardiography. **Research Statement & Publications:** Assessment of regional myocardial flow-function relationships using non-invasive techniques. **Mailing Address:** Cardiol Div, Univ VA Health Sci Ctr, Box 158, Charlottesville, VA 22908. **Fax:** 434-982-3183. **E-Mail:** sk@virginia.edu

KAUMA, SCOTT W, MEDICINE. **Education:** MD, Univ Wis. **Professional Experience:** CLIN PROG DIR, JONES INST, W PENN ALLEGHENY HEALTH SYST, 2003-; DIR, DIV REPRODUCTIVE ENDOCRINOL, WESTERN PA HOSP & ALLEGHENY GENERAL HOSP, as of 2006. **Mailing Address:** W Penn Allegheny Health Syst, Pittsburgh, PA 15224. **Fax:** 866-305-6637. **E-Mail:** Kauma@jonesinstitutepittsburgh.org

KAUNE, WILLIAM TYLER, BIOENGINEERING. **Personal Data:** b Everett, Wash, August 31, 1940; m 1972, c 2. **Education:** Univ Wash, BS, 1966; Stanford Univ, PhD (physics), 1973. **Professional Experience:** PRES, EM FACTORS, 1993-; vpres, Enertech Consults, Campbell, Calif, 1988-1993; physicist, Nat Bur Standards, Boulder, Colo, 1987-1988; staff engr Bioengineering, Pac Northwest Div, Battelle Mem Inst, 1980-1987; sr res engr, 1975-1980; asst prof physics, Loyola Marymount Univ, 1973-1975; res assoc, Univ Wash, 1972-1973; Res asst high energy physics, Stanford Linear Accelerator Ctr, 1968-1972. **Memberships:** Bioelectromagnetics Soc; Inst Elec & Electronics Engrs. **Research Statement & Publications:** Biological effectsof electromagnetic radiation; exposure systems and dosimetry. **Mailing Address:** EM Factors, 640 Jadwin Ave, Suite F, Richland, WA 99352. **Fax:** 509-943-9707.

KAUP, DAVID JAMES, INTEGRABLE SYSTEMS, NONLINEAR STUDIES. **Personal Data:** b Marionville, Mo, April 8, 1939; m 1982, c 3. **Education:** Univ Okla, BS, 1960, MS, 1962; Univ Md, PhD (physics), 1967. **Professional Experience:** PROF MATH & PHYSICS, CLARKSON UNIV, 1987-; vis prof math, Lab Physics Math, Univ Sci & Tech Langs, Montpellier, France, 1987; prof comput sci, Clarkson Univ, beginning 1987; consult, Varian Assocs, 1983; vis res geophysicist, Univ Calif Los Angeles, 1981; res scientist, Dynamics Technol, 1980-1981; from res asst prof to res assoc prof, Comput Sci & Physics, Clarkson Univ, 1974-1976; from asst prof to prof physics, Comput Sci & Physics, Clarkson Univ, 1967-1987. **Memberships:** Am Phys Soc; Sigma Xi; Am Math Soc; Soc Indust Appl Math. **Research Statement & Publications:** Soliton theory; inverse scattering; nonlinear optics; plasma physics; mathematical physics. **Mailing Address:** Dept Physics, Clarkson Univ, Sci Ctr 353 PO Box 5815, Potsdam, NY 13699-5820. **Fax:** 315-268-6610. **E-Mail:** kaup@sun.mcs.clarkson.edu

KAUP, EDGAR GEORGE, CHEMICAL ENGINEERING. **Personal Data:** b Irvington, NJ, October 5, 1927; m 1953, c 2. **Education:** Lehigh Univ, BS, 1950; Neward Col Eng, BS, 1958, MS, 1963. **Professional Experience:** MEM, PLANNING BD, BOROUGH ESSEX FELLS, as of 2004; sr chem engr, Burns & Roe, Inc, Burns & Roe Construct Corp Div, Contractor To Off Saline Water, Us Dept Interior, beginning 1976; resident eng mgr, 1969-1976; sr chem engr, 1965-1969; develop engr, Celanese Plastic Co, 1962-1965; res chem engr, Air Reduction Lab, 1955-1962; spectroscopist, Air Reduction Lab, 1954-1955; Phys chemist, Hoffmann-La Roche, NJ, 1952-1954. **Memberships:** Am Chem Soc; Am Inst Chem Engrs; Am Soc Test & Mat. **Research Statement & Publications:** Desalting and water pollution abatement; reverse osmosis evaluations and applications; water and waste treatment by ion exchange and evaporative methods. **Mailing Address:** Borough Essex Fells, Eight Essex Rd, Essex Fells, NJ 07021-1104.

KAUPP, VERNE H, ELECTRICAL ENGINEERING. **Personal Data:** b Denver, Colo, April 15, 1940; m 1966, c 2. **Education:** Univ Md, BS, 1971; Univ Kans, DEng, 1979. **Professional Experience:** PROF ELEC ENG, UNIV ARK, 1980-2005; Ark Res Consults Inc, 1980-; consult, Systs Technol/Appl Res Corp, 1977-1980; sr res engr microwave remote sensing, Ctr Res Inc, 1975-1980; eng consult microwave sensor, Earth Resources Technol, 1975; engr microwave sensor, Martin Marietta Corp, 1971-1975. **Memberships:** Inst Elec & Electronics Engrs; Sigma Xi; Am Soc Photogram & Remote Sensing; Am Soc Eng Educ. **Research Statement & Publications:** Microwave remote sensing; electromagnetics; digital signal processing. **Mailing Address:** Dept Elec Eng, Univ Ark, Fayetteville, AR 72701.

KAUPPILA, RAYMOND WILLIAM, ENGINEERING MECHANICS. **Personal Data:** b Iron Mountain, Mich, February 17, 1929; m 1952, c 4. **Education:** Univ Mich, BS (mech eng) & BS (eng math), 1951; Mich Col Mining & Technol, MS, 1961; Univ Mich, PhD, 1968. **Professional Experience:** PROF EMER MECH ENG, MICH TECHNOL UNIV, 1989-; from asst prof to prof, Mich Technol Univ, 1957-1989; plant engr, Cliffs Dow Chem Co, Mich, 1955-1957; maintenance, develop & inspection engr, Standard Oil Div, Am Oil Co, Ind, 1951-1955; expert witness, failure analysis; Design Consult. **Research Statement & Publications:** Machine design; dynamics and vibrations of machinery; stress analysis; thermal stresses; plasticity in forming operations. **Mailing Address:** Dept Mech Eng, Mich Technol Univ, 1400 Townsend Dr, Houghton, MI 49931-1295.

KAUPPILA, WALTER ERIC, POSITRON & ELECTRON SCATTERING EXPERIMENTS. **Personal Data:** b Hancock, Mich, September 11, 1942; m 1966, Margaret; c Eric & David. **Education:** Mich Technol Univ, BS, 1964; Univ Pittsburgh, PhD (physics), 1969. **Professional Experience:** PROF PHYSICS, WAYNE STATE UNIV, 1983-; co-prin investr, NSF supported res grants, beginning 1975; from asst prof to assoc prof, Wayne State Univ, 1972-1983; asst prof physics, Univ Mo-Rolla, 1971-1972; res assoc, Joint Inst Lab Astrophys, Univ Colo, 1969-1971. **Memberships:** fel Am Phys Soc; fel Sigma Xi. **Research Statement & Publications:** Experimental studies of elastic, inelastic and total scattering for positrons and electrons colliding with atoms and molecules. **Mailing Address:** Dept Physics & Astron, Wayne State Univ, 266 Physics Res Bldg, Detroit, MI 48202. **Fax:** 313-577-3932. **E-Mail:** kauppila@physics.wayne.edu

KAUS, PETER EDWARD, THEORETICAL PHYSICS. **Personal Data:** b Vienna, Austria, October 9, 1924; American citizen; m 1950, c 3. **Education:** Univ Calif, Los Angeles, BA, 1947, MA, 1952, PhD, 1954. **Honors & Awards:** Sarnof Achievement Medal, 1956. **Professional Experience:** PROF EMER PHYSICS, UNIV CALIF, as of 2004; pres, Aspen Ctr Physics, 1981-1983; Jet Propulsion Lab, Pasadena, 1959-1961 & Los Alamos Nat Lab, 1980-; vpres, Aspen Ctr Physics, 1970-1982; prof physics, Univ Calif, Riverside, beginning 1967; fulbright res scholar, Denmark, 1965-1966; trustee, Aspen Ctr Physics, 1964-; assoc prof, Univ Calif, Riverside, 1962-1967; asst prof physics, Univ Southern Calif, 1958-1962; consult, Hughes Aircraft Co, 1958-1959; res physicist, Labs, Radio Corp Am, NJ, 1954-1958; asst physics, Univ Calif, Los Angeles, 1951-1953. **Memberships:** Fel Am Phys Soc. **Research Statement & Publications:** Field theory; elementary particle theory; biophysics; biologic rhythms. **Mailing Address:** Dept Physics, Univ Calf, 3047 Physics Bldg, Riverside, CA 92521. **E-Mail:** peter.kaus@ucr.edu

KAUSER, FAZAL B, AERONAUTICS. **Education:** Emerson Col, BS, 1961; USAF Inst Technol, MS, 1976. **Professional Experience:** PROF, CALIF STATE POLYTECH UNIV, as of 2005. **Memberships:** Fel Am Inst Aeronaut & Astronaut. **Mailing Address:** Calif State Poytech Univ, 4533 Pleasant St, La Verne, CA 91750. **Fax:** 909-869-5475.

KAUSHIK, AZAD KUMAR, IMMUNOLOGY, VETERINARY CLINICAL IMMUNOLOGY. **Personal Data:** b Dhauj, Haryana, India, September 8, 1955; American citizen; m 1982, Archana; c Manu. **Education:** Pasteur Inst (Univ Paris VII), DSc, 1987; Haryana Agril Univ, MVSc, 1978, BVSc, 1976. **Honors & Awards:** Greenberg vis prof, 1998, Oklahoma Med Res Found, Oklahama City, USA. **Professional Experience:** ASSOC PROF IMMUNOL, 2000-; ASST PROF IMMUNOL, UNIV GUELPH, CAN, 1999-; ASST PROF IMMUNOL, UNIV GUELPH, CAN, 1991-2000; asst prof, Med Sch, Univ Geneva, 1990-1991; res scientist, Mt Sinai Sch Med, NY, 1987-1990; res assoc, Pasteur Inst, Paris, France, 1983-1987; asst prof immunol, Haryana Agril Univ, Hisar, India, 1979-1983. **Memberships:** Am Asn Immunologists; NY Acad Sci; Canadian Soc Immunol. **Research Statement & Publications:** Natural autoimmunity and autoimmune disorders; molecular immunoglobulin genetics; idiotypy; protective immunity and clinical veterinary immunology. **Mailing Address:** Dept Molec & Cellular Biol, Univ Guelph, Guelph, ON N1G 2W1, Can. **Fax:** 519-837-1802. **E-Mail:** akaushik@uoguelph.ca

KAUSHIK, NARINDER KUMAR, ECOLOGY, HYDROBIOLOGY. **Personal Data:** Canadian citizen; c 2. **Education:** Univ Delhi, India, BS, 1954, MS, 1956; Univ Waterloo, MS, 1966, PhD (biol), 1969. **Professional Experience:** PROF EMER ENVIRON BIOL, UNIV GUELPH, as of 2004; assoc prof Environ Biol, Univ Guelph, beginning 1977; asst prof, Univ Guelph, 1973-1977; asst prof biol, Univ Waterloo, 1971-1972; fel ecol, Univ Toronto, 1969-1971; res & sr res asst sanit biol, Cent Pub Health Eng Res Inst, 1961-1964. **Memberships:** Can Water Resource Asn; NAm Benthol Soc; Can Soc Zoologists;

Int Soc Theoret & Appl Limnol. **Research Statement & Publications:** Role of autumn shed leaves in secondary production in streams; nitrogen transport and transformations in streams; use of limnocorrals for pesticide impact assessment; ecotoxicology. **Mailing Address:** Dept Environ Biol, Ont Agr Col, Univ Guelph, Guelph, ON N1G 2W1, Can. **Fax:** 519-837-0442. **E-Mail:** nkaushik@evb.uoguelph.ca

KAUSHIK, ROY, LOW POWER ELECTRONICS FOR PORTABLE COMPUTING & WIRELESS COMMUNICATION, VERY LARGE SCALE INTEGRATION TESTING & FAULT TOLERANCE. **Personal Data:** b Calcutta, India, August 30, 1961. **Education:** Indian Inst Technol, BTech, 1983; Univ Ill, Urbana-Champaign, PhD (elec & comput eng), 1990. **Honors & Awards:** NSF Career Award, 1995. **Professional Experience:** PROF ELEC & COMPUT ENG, PURDUE UNIV, as of 2002; assoc ed, Trans Circuits & Systs, 1997-; assoc prof elec eng, Purdue Univ, beginning 1997; vis prof, Intel Corp, 1996; assoc ed, Design & Test Comput, inst Elec & Electronics Engrs, 1995-; prin investr, numerous govt & corp contracts & grants, 1993-; asst prof, Purdue Univ, 1993-1997; adj fac, Univ Tex, Dallas, 1992-1993; mem tech staff, Tex Instruments, 1990-1993. **Memberships:** Sr mem Inst Elec & Electronics Engrs. **Research Statement & Publications:** Low energy computing for portable applications where battery life is very important; reconfigurable/adaptive computing; very large scale integration testing, fault tolerance and nanoscale electronics. **Mailing Address:** Sch Elec Eng, Purdue Univ, 1285 Elec Eng Bldg, West Lafayette, IN 47907-1285. **Fax:** 765-494-3371. **E-Mail:** kaushik@ecn.purdue.edu

KAUTZ, FREDERICK ALTON, II, LOW DENSITY GAS DYNAMICS, AERO THERMODYNAMICS. **Personal Data:** b Knoxville, Tenn, August 27, 1950; m 1977, Carol; c Catherine & Elizabeth. **Education:** Univ Tenn, BSc, 1972; Mass Inst Technol, SM & NucE, 1983. **Professional Experience:** STAFF MEM, LINCOLN LAB, MASS INST TECHNOL, 1986-; reviewer, J Spacecraft & Rockets, Am Inst Aeronaut & Astronaut, 1989-1992; mem, NASA-Langley ad hoc comt reentry plasmas, 1988-; mem, Themophys Tech Comt, Am Inst Aeronaut & Astronaut, 1987-1990; secy, Themophys Tech Comt, Am Inst Aeronaut & Astronaut, 1987; staff scientist, Off Sci & Weapons Res, Cent Intel Agency, 1977-1986; res asst, Lincoln Lab, Mass Inst Technol, 1974-1977; staff mem, Oak Ridge Nat Lab, 1972-1973. **Memberships:** NY Acad Sci; Am Inst Aeronaut & Astronaut; Am Phys Soc; Inst Elec & Electronics Engrs; Soc Indust & Appl Math; AAAS; Sigma Xi. **Research Statement & Publications:** Low density gas dynamics; physics and chemistry of reentry and planetary entry plasmas; computational aerothermodynamics; spacecraft-environment interactions; missile aerodynamics. **Mailing Address:** Carnegie-Mellon Univ Grad Sch Indust Admin, Pittsburgh, PA 15213-3890. **Fax:** 781-981-0783. **E-Mail:** kautz@andrew.cmu.edu

KAUTZ, STEVEN M, MATHEMATICS. **Education:** Univ Ill, PhD (Randomness & Genericity), 1981; Cornell Univ, PhD (Random Sets), 1991. **Professional Experience:** STAFF, DEPT MATH RANDOLPH-MACON WOMAN'S COL, as of 2005. **Mailing Address:** Randolph-Macon Woman's Col, 2500 Rivermont Ave, Lynchburg, VA 24503. **Fax:** 434-947-8996. **E-Mail:** skautz@rmwc.edu

KAUZLARICH, JAMES J(OSEPH), MECHANICAL ENGINEERING, TRIBOLOGY. **Personal Data:** b Des Moines, Iowa, September 27, 1927; m 1952, Sally; c Ann, John, Susan & Jane. **Education:** Univ Iowa, BS, 1950; Columbia Univ, MS, 1952; Northwestern Univ, PhD (mech eng), 1958. **Professional Experience:** Prof emer, Univ VA, 1998; vis res, Cambridge Univ, 1970-1971, 1996, 1997, 1999, 2001, 2002, & Swansea Univ, 1984-1985 & 1988-1989; prof mech eng, Univ Va, 1963-1998; chmn dept, Univ VA, 1963-1975; engr, Boeing Corp, 1962 & 1963; assoc prof, Univ Wash, Seattle, 1961-1963; from asst prof to assoc prof, Worcester Polytech Inst, 1958-1961; instr mech eng, Northwestern Univ, 1954-1957; develop engr, Gen Elec Co, NY, 1952-1954; lab asst, Columbia Univ, 1950-1952. **Memberships:** Am Soc Eng Educ; fel Am Soc Mech Engrs; Am Soc Lubrication Engrs; Sigma Xi. **Research Statement & Publications:** Fluid mechanics; hear transfer; rehabilitation engineering; tribology; applied mechanics. **Mailing Address:** Dept Mech Eng, Univ Va, Charlottesville, VA 22904-4746. **Fax:** 434-982-2037. **E-Mail:** jjk@virginia.edu

KAUZMANN, WALTER (JOSEPH), PHYSICAL CHEMISTRY, PROTEIN CHEMISTRY. **Personal Data:** b Mt Vernon, NY, August 18, 1916; m 1951, Elizabeth; c Charles P, Eric F & Katherine E J. **Education:** Cornell Univ, BA, 1937; Princeton Univ, PhD (phys chem), 1940. **Honorary Degrees:** PhD, Univ Stockholm, 1962. **Honors & Awards:** Linderstrom-Lang Medal, 1966; Stein-Moore Award, Protein Soc, 93. **Professional Experience:** RETIRED; vis scientist, Nat Res Coun Can, Halifax, 1983; chmn, Dept Biochem Sci, 1980-1982; vis prof, Univ Ibadan, 1975; chmn dept, Princeton Univ, 1964-1968; from asst to assoc prof chem, David B Jones prof chem, 1963-1982; Guggenheim fel, 1957 & 1974-1975; from asst to assoc prof chem, Princeton Univ, 1946-1963; engr, Manhattan Dist Proj, Los Alamos, 1944-1946; chemist, Nat Defense Res Comt, Bruceton, Pa, 1942-1943; fel, Westinghouse Elec & Mfg Co, 1940-1942. **Memberships:** Nat Acad Sci; Am Geophys Union; Am Acad Arts & Sci; Am Chem Soc; fel Am Phys Soc; fel AAAS; Protein Soc. **Research Statement & Publications:** Physical chemistry of proteins; theory of water; properties of matter at high pressures; geochemistry; muscle physiology. **Mailing Address:** 302 N Harriston St Ste 152, Princeton, NJ 08540-3512.

KAVALER, FREDERIC, physiology; deceased, see previous edition for last biography

KAVALJIAN, LEE GREGORY, PLANT MORPHOLOGY. **Personal Data:** b Chicago, Ill, February 6, 1926. **Education:** Univ Chicago, PhB, 1947, BS, 1948, PhD (bot), 1951. **Professional Experience:** PROF EMER BIOL SCI, CALIF STATE UNIV, SACRAMENTO, as of 2004; prof biol sci, calif state univ, sacramento, begining 1964; from instr to assoc prof biol sci, Calif State Univ, Sacramento, 1954-1964; instr, Univ Chicago, 1954; Ford Found teaching intern natural sci, Univ Chicago, 1953-1954; asst to chief chemist, Modern Agr Crop Serv, Calif, 1953; vis res assoc, Brookhaven Nat Lab, NY, 1952; res assoc bot, Brooklyn Bot Garden, NY, 1951-1952. **Research Statement & Publications:** Plant tissue cultures; floral morphology; cytochemistry; ethnobotany. **Mailing Address:** Dept Biol 6077, Calif State Univ 6000 Jay St, Sacramento, CA 95819-6077. **E-Mail:** leek@csus.edu

KAVANAGH, KAREN L, MATERIAL SCIENCE ENGINEERING. **Personal Data:** b Halifax, NS, May 3, 1956. **Education:** Queens Univ, BSc, 1978; Cornell Univ, MSc, 1984, PhD (mat sci & eng), 1987. **Honors & Awards:** Presidential Young Investr Award, NSF, 1991. **Professional Experience:** PROF GRAD CHAIR, DEPT PHYSICS, SIMON FRASER UNIV, as of 2005; assoc prof elec eng & mat sci, Univ Calif, San Diego, beginning 1993; fel, IBM Corp, 1988; fel, Mass Inst Technol, 1987-1988; tech staff, Bell-Northern Res, 1978-1981. **Memberships:** Mat Res Soc; Am Phys Soc; Am Vacuum Soc; Electron Micros Soc Am. **Research Statement & Publications:** Electronic materials science defects and diffusion at semiconductor interfaces; structure-electronic property correlations. **Mailing Address:** Shrum Sci Centre Rm P8443, 8888 Univ Dr, Simon Fraser Univ, BC V5A 1S6, Can. **Fax:** 604-291-3592. **E-Mail:** kavanagh@sfu.ca

KAVANAGH, RALPH WILLIAM, NUCLEAR PHYSICS. **Personal Data:** b Seattle, Wash, July 15, 1924; m 1948, c 5. **Education:** Reed Col, BA, 1950; Univ Ore, MA, 1952; Calif Inst Technol, PhD, 1956. **Professional Experience:** PROF EMER PHYSICS, KELLOGG LAB, CALIF INST TECHNOL, 2000-; prof physics, Calif Inst Technol, 1970-2000; from asst prof to assoc prof, 1960-1970; from res fel to sr res fel, 1956-1960. **Memberships:** Am Phys Soc. **Research Statement & Publications:** Spectroscopy of light nuclei using electrostatic accelerators. **Mailing Address:** Dept Physics, Calif Inst Tehnol, Pasadena, CA 91125. **Fax:** 626-564-8708. **E-Mail:** kav@krl.caltech.edu

KAVANAGH, ROBERT JOHN, RESEARCH MANPOWER. **Personal Data:** b Whitchurch, Hants, Eng, October 7, 1931; m 1956, c 2. **Education:** Univ NB, BSc, 1953; Univ Toronto, MASc, 1954, PhD (elec eng), 1957; Imp Col, London, DIC, 1960. **Professional Experience:** RETIRED; dir-gen, Scholarships & Int Prog, Natural Sci & Eng, Res Coun, 1984-1995; vis scientist, Natural Sci & Eng Res Coun, 1982-1983; actg vpres acad, Univ NB, 1978-1980; dean grad studies & res, Univ NB, 1971-1984; assoc dean, Univ NB, 1969-1971; guest worker, Control Eng Div, Warren Spring Lab Eng, 1968-1969; from assoc prof to prof elec eng, Univ NB, 1962-1984; asst prof, Univ Toronto, 1960-1962; NATO fel, Imp Col, Univ London, 1959-1960; lectr elec eng, Univ Toronto, 1957-1959. **Memberships:** Sr mem Inst Elec & Electronics Engrs; fel NY Acad Sci. **Mailing Address:** 849 Mary's Island Ave, Ottawa, ON K2C 0H9, Can. **E-Mail:** rjk@nserc.ca

KAVANAU, JULIAN LEE, ETHOLOGY & NEUROSCIENCE, MEMORY & SLEEP. **Personal Data:** b Detroit, Mich, January 21, 1922; m 1987, Marisa; c Warren, Christopher & Kristina. **Education:** Univ Mich, BS, 1943; Univ Calif, MS & PhD (zoology), 1952. **Professional Experience:** PROF EMER BIOL, UNIV CALIF, LOS ANGELES, 1991-; from asst prof to prof, Univ Calif, Los Angeles, 1957-1991; res assoc develop, Rockefeller Inst, 1955-1957; USPHS fel, Wenner-Gren Inst, Stockholm, Sweden, 1952-1954; asst zoology, Univ Calif, Los Angeles, 1949-1951; asst math, Univ Calif, Los Angeles, 1946-1947; mem res staff physics, Calif Inst Technol, 1943-1945; physicist, Univ Calif, 1943; asst prof physics, Univ Mich, 1941-1943. **Memberships:** Fel AAAS; Animal Behav Soc; Am Ornithol Union. **Research Statement & Publications:** Instrumentation for behavior research; influences of environmental variables on mammalian activity; symmetry of curves and figures; behavior and evolution of psittaciforms; origin, evolution and functions of sleep; evolution of synaptic efficacy maintenance. **Mailing Address:** Dept Biol, Univ Calif, Slichter Hall 2851 621 Charles E Young Dr S, Los Angeles, CA 90095-1606. **Fax:** 310-206-3987. **E-Mail:** lkavanau@biology.ucla.edu

KAVANAUGH, DAVID HENRY, SYSTEMATIC ENTOMOLOGY, BIOGEOGRAPHY. **Personal Data:** b San Francisco, Calif, April 7, 1945. **Education:** San Jose State Univ, BA, 1967; Univ Colo, Denver, MA, 1970; Univ Alta, PhD (entom), 1978. **Professional Experience:** RES PROF BIOL, SAN FRANCISO STATE UNIV, 1998-; chmn dept, Calif Acad Sci 1996-1998; SR CUR ENTOM, CALIF ACAD SCI, 1988-; res Prof, San Francisco State Univ, beginning 1988; dir res, Calif Acad Sci, 1986-1988; cur, dept entom, Calif Acad Sci, 1984-1988; chmn dept, Calif Acad Sci, 1979-1983, 1990-1992; from asst cur to assoc cur, Calif Acad Sci, 1974-1984; fel, Nat Res Con Can, 1972-1974, 2000-; adj prof, Sonoma State Univ, Rohnert Park, Calif. **Memberships:** Soc Syst Zool; Entom Soc Am; Coleopterists Soc; Am Entom Soc. **Research Statement & Publications:** Classification, phylogeny, zoogeography and natural history of ground beetles; biogeography and evolution of high altitude biota, especially the coleoptera faunas of western North America; theory and practice of systematic zoology. **Mailing Address:** Dept Entom, Calif Acad Sci, Golden Gate Park, San Francisco, CA 94118. **Fax:** 415-750-7228. **E-Mail:** dkavanaugh@calacademy.org

KAVARNOS, GEORGE JAMES, SOLID STATE MATERIALS. **Personal Data:** b New London, Conn. **Education:** Clark Univ, BA, 1964; Univ RI, PhD (org chem), 1968; Dipl, Am Bd Clin Chem. **Professional Experience:** EMER, AM BD CLIN CHEM, as of 2004; DIR, THAMES TESTING LAB, as of 2001; RES CHEMIST, NAVAL UNDERWATER SYSTS CHIEF NAVAL TRAINING, 1989-; lectr, St Joseph Col, 1985-; adj prof chem, Univ RI, 1978-; assoc dir & clin chemist, Cyto Med Lab Inc, Norwich, 1974-1989; vpres, Bio-Anal Labs, 1973-; chief chemist, New London, Cyto-Roche, Div Hoffmann La-Roche, 1971-1974; NIH fel, Columbia Univ, 1968-1971. **Memberships:** Am Chem Soc; Am Asn Clin Chemists. **Research Statement & Publications:** Photochemistry; clinical chemistry; photoinduced electron transfer material; science molecular modeling. **Mailing Address:** Thames Testing Lab, 118 Riverview Ave, New London, CT 06320.

KAVASSALIS, TOM A, PHYSICAL CHEMISTRY. **Personal Data:** b Toronto, Ont, February 3, 1958; m 1983, c 2. **Education:** Univ Toronto, BSc, 1980; Mass Inst Technol, PhD (phys chem), 1985. **Professional Experience:** DIR, STRATEGY & INTEGRATION, XEROX INNOVATION GROUP, 2002-; ASSOC CTR MGR, XEROX RES CTR, CAN, 1996-; mgr planning & bus processes, Xerox Res Ctr, Can, 1995-1996; MEM RES, XEROX RES CTR, CAN, 1987-; Chemist, Ont Hydro Res, 1985-1987. **Memberships:** Am Chem Soc; Am Phys Soc. **Research Statement & Publications:** Theoretical and computational methods for material science applications; simulation of surfactants; theories of polymer structure, morphology and dynamics; mechanical properties of polymers; theory of transport in fluids. **Mailing Address:** Xerox Res Ctr Can, 5650 Yonge St, North York, ON M2M 4G7, Can. **Fax:** 416-229-3769.

KAVATHAS, PAULA B, IMMUNOLOGY, GENETICS. **Personal Data:** b Evanston, Ill, May 30, 1950; c 2. **Education:** Univ Wis-Madison, BA, 1972, PhD (genetics), 1980. **Professional Experience:** PROF, LAB MED, IMMUNOBIOL & GENETICS, SCH MED, YALE UNIV, beginning 1986. **Research Statement & Publications:** Immunobiology of T lymphocyte co-receptor molecule CD8. **Mailing Address:** Dept Lab Med Fitkin 617 Yale Univ Sch Med, 333 Cedar St PO Box 208035, New Haven, CT 06520-8035.

KAVEH, MOSTAFA, STATISTICAL SIGNAL PROCESSING, IMAGE PROCESSING. **Personal Data:** b Karadj, Iran, April 18, 1947. **Education:** Purdue Univ, BS, 1969, PhD (elec eng), 1974; Univ Calif, Berkeley, MS, 1970. **Professional Experience:** CENANTIAL CHAIR ELEC ENG, UNIV MINN, as of 2005; DEPT HEAD ELEC & COMPUT ENG, UNIV MINN, 1990-; PROF ELEC ENG, UNIV MINN, 1985-; various ranks, Univ Minn, 1975-1985; res assoc, Purdue Univ, 1975; consult. **Memberships:** Fel Inst Elec & Electronics Engrs. **Research Statement & Publications:** Sensor array signal processing. **Mailing Address:** Dept Elec & Comput Eng, Univ Minn, Minneapolis, MN 55108. **E-Mail:** mos@ece.umn.edu

KAVESH, SHELDON, POLYMER PROCESSING, STRUCTURE & PROPERTIES. **Personal Data:** b New York, NY, January 15, 1933; m 1957, c 2. **Education:** Mass Inst Technol, BSChE, 1957; Polytech Inst Brooklyn, MChE, 1960; Univ Del, PhD (chem eng), 1968. **Honors & Awards:** Gold Medal, Nat Assoc Sci Technol & Soc, 1994. **Professional Experience:** Sr PRIN scientist, consult, 1999-; allied chem corp, Morristown, 1980-1999; Allied Chem Corp, Morristown, 1970-1980; proj leader polymers, Films Packaging Div, Union Carbide Corp, 1968-1970; Foster Grant Co, Inc, 1960-1962 & Avisun Corp, 1962-1965; Res engr, Celanese Corp Am, 1957-1960. **Memberships:** Am Inst Chem Engrs;

Am Phys Soc; Am Chem Soc. **Research Statement & Publications:** Polymer physics; transport phenomena; materials science; fiber processing. **Mailing Address:** 16 N Pond Rd, Whippany, NJ 07981-1277. **Fax:** 973-386-0429. **E-Mail:** skavesh@att.net

KAVI, KRISHNA M, COMPUTER SCIENCE. **Education:** Andhra Univ, India, BSc, 1972; Indian Inst Sci, BE, 1975; Southern Methodist Univ, MS, 1977, PhD (Comput Sci & Eng), 1980. **Professional Experience:** PROF & CHAIR, COMPUT SCI & ENG DEPT, UNIV N TEX, as of 2005. **Mailing Address:** Univ N Tex, PO Box 19015, Arlington, TX 76019. **Fax:** 940-565-2799. **E-Mail:** kavi@cse.unt.edu

KAVLOCK, ROBERT J, TOXICOLOGY. **Education:** Univ Miami, PhD (Biol), 1977. **Professional Experience:** DIR, REPRODUCTIVE TOXICOL DIV, NAT HEALTH & ENVIRON EFFECTS RES LAB, as of 2002. **Memberships:** Soc Toxicol (pres, 2000-2001). **Mailing Address:** US Environ Protection Agency, 86 T W Alexander Dr, MD 71, Research Triangle Park, NC 27711. **Fax:** 919-541-1499. **E-Mail:** kavlock.robert@epa.gov

KAVVAS, LEVENT M, HYDROLOGY & WATER RESOURCES. **Personal Data:** b Ankara, Turkey, May 24, 1948; American citizen; m 1976, Jale; c Eren & Erol. **Education:** Mid E Tech Univ, Turkey, BS, 1970; Colo State Univ, MS, 1972; Purdue Univ, PhD (civil eng), 1975. **Honors & Awards:** Res Award Foreign Specialists, Ministry Construct, Japan, 1989; Richard Torrens Award, Am Soc Civil Engr, 1999; Arid Lands Hydraulic Eng Award, Am Soc Civil Engr, 2001. **Professional Experience:** Founding ed, J Hydrol Eng, Am Soc Civil Engrs, 1994-2004; consult assoc ed, Hydrol Sci J, 1994-2000; Hydrol Eng Ctr, US Army Engrs, 1994-1995; assoc ed, J Hydrol, 1991-1997; consult, USAF, 1991-1992; PROF HYDROL ENG, DEPT CIVIL & ENVIRON ENG, UNIV CALIF, DAVIS, 1990-; consult, PWRI, Ministry Construct, Japan, 1990-; assoc prof, Dept Civil & Environ Eng, Univ Calif, Davis, 1985-1990; assoc prof, Dept Civil Eng, Univ Ky, 1982-1985; vis assoc prof hydrol eng, Sch Civil Eng, Purdue Univ, 1980-1982; assoc prof math & probability, stochastic processes, Indust Eng Dept, Mid E Tech Univ, 1980; asst prof math, probability, stochastic processes, Indust Eng Dept, Mid E Tech Univ, 1975-1980. **Memberships:** Am Soc Civil Engrs; Am Geophys Union; Am Meteor Soc; Int. Assoc Hydrol Sci. **Research Statement & Publications:** Mathematical modeling of hydrometeorological processes; regional scale modeling of coupled hydrologic-atmospheric processes; mathematical modeling of hydrologic processes such as overland flow, channel flow, unsaturated-saturated subsurface flow, snow melt runoff, contaminant transport, erosion; stochastic modeling of hydrologic processes, published over 15 articles. **Mailing Address:** Dept Civil & Environ Eng, Univ Calif, 2001 Eng III, Davis, CA 95616. **Fax:** 530-753-9584. **E-Mail:** mlkavvas@ucdavis.edu

KAWAHARA, FRED KATSUMI, ENVIRONMENTAL RISK MANAGEMENT, CONTAMINANT MEDIA REMEDIATION. **Personal Data:** b Penngrove, Calif, February 26, 1921; m 1991, Anrea L Eary; c Robert K, Kiku S & Richard H. **Education:** Univ Tex, BS Honors, 1944; Univ Wis, MS, 1946, PhD (chem), 1948 post PhD (chem), univ of Chicago, 1950. **Honors & Awards:** Group Super Serv Award, Bur Agr & Indust Chem, USDA, 1952; Int Order Merit, IBC Cambridge, Eng, 1988, First Five Hundred Gold Medal, 1989 IBC Combridge, England, 1988; Sci & Technol Achivement Award II, US EPA, 1998; World Biographical Hall of fame, Am Biographical inst, Raleigh, North Carolina, 1987, (Historical Preservation of Am, Inc). **Professional Experience:** EXPERT WITNESS, nat Risk mgt Risk lab, ENVIRON PROTECTION AGENCY, 1980-; spec consult, Sustainable techonol div, indust multimedia Branch, 1985-Lab, 1972-1984; SPEC CONSULT OIL IDENTIFICATION, ENVIRON PROTECTION AGENCY, 1985-; res sci Sust Tech div, 1968-1971, 1985-; res chemist, Stand Oil Co, Ind, 1966-1968; sr res scientist, Stand Oil Co, Ind, 1953-1965; fel org chem, Univ Chicago, 1951-1953; Assoc chemist, USDA, 1948-1951; dep gov, Am Biographic Inst Res Asn; Expert witness petroleum fuels. **Memberships:** Fel Am Inst Chem 1968-; Am Biographic Inst Res Asn, 1980; fel Int Biographic Asn, 1985. **Research Statement & Publications:** Synthetic fuels, coal liquefaction; lubricants; phosphorus; fluorocarbons; gasoline additives; waxes; carcinogens; chromatography, infrared, ultraviolet, synthesis, identification; insecticides; greases; phenols; mercaptans; oil pollution; soy bean oil flavor reversion; aromatic amines; peroxides; methods development; auto-oxidation; laser-fiber optics; freon 113 substitute solvent; hydrodechlorinization of polychlorobiphenyls reaction mechanism; methods develop, synthetic & natural inorganic synthesis. **Mailing Address:** Environ Protection Agency nat Resh mgr res lab, 26 W Martin Luther King, Cincinnati, OH 45268. **Fax:** 513-569-7471.

KAWAI, MASATAKA, ELECTRICAL ENGINEERING, COMPUTER CONTROLLED EXPERIMENTS. **Personal Data:** b Gifu, Japan, June 13, 1943; m 1969, c 2. **Education:** Tokyo Univ, BS, 1966; Princeton Univ, PhD (biol), 1971. **Professional Experience:** PROF ANAT, UNIV IOWA, as of 2002; assoc prof anat, Univ Iowa, beginning 1987; asst prof anat & cell biol, Dept Neurol, 1983-1987; asst prof muscle physiol, Dept Neurol, 1978-1983; Prin investr, Dept Neurol, Columbia Univ, 1976-; res assoc, Columbia Univ, 1971-1978. **Memberships:** Biophys Soc; Gen Physiol Soc. **Research Statement & Publications:** Cross-bridge kinetics in chemically skinned muscle fibers by use of sinnsoidal analysis which changes the length and detects concomitant amplitude and phase shift in tension. **Mailing Address:** Dept Anat & Cell Biol, Univ Iowa, 1 670 Bowen Sci Bldg, Iowa City, IA 52242. **E-Mail:** masataka-kawai@uiowa.edu

KAWAKAMIT, TOSHIAKI, IMMUNOLOGY, METABOLISM. **Personal Data:** b Matfu, Japan, October 25, 1950. **Education:** Univ Tokyo, BS, 1976, MS, 1978, PhD (immunol), 1983. **Professional Experience:** FAC & RES, LA JOLLA INST, as of 2006; ASSOC MEM IMMUNOL, LA JOLLA INST, 1993-; asst mem allergy res, 1987-1993; fel immunol & allergy res, 1984-1986. **Memberships:** Am Asn Immunol; Am Chem Soc. **Research Statement & Publications:** Immunology; metabolism. **Mailing Address:** La Jolla Inst Allergy & Immunol, 10355 Sci Ctr Dr, San Diego, CA 92121. **E-Mail:** toshi@liai.org

KAWALEK, JOSEPH CASIMIR, BIOCHEMISTRY, BIOCHEMICAL PHARMACOLOGY. **Personal Data:** b Stockton, Calif, December 21, 1945; m 1972, Rosella; c Kiera A & James A. **Education:** St Francis Col, BS, 1967; Univ Pittsburgh, PhD (biochem), 1973. **Professional Experience:** RES CHEMIST, OFF RES, CTR VET MED, FOOD & DRUG ADMIN, 1980-; staff scientist chem carcinogen, Frederick Cancer Res Ctr, Litton Bionetics Inc, 1976-1980; res assoc, Hoffmann-La Roche Inc, 1974-1976; res asst biochem, Univ Pittsburgh, 1970-1973. **Memberships:** Am Chem Soc; Am Inst Biol Sci; Sigma Xi; NY Acad Sci; Soc Toxicol; Am Col Toxicol; Am Acad Vet Comp Toxicol. **Research Statement & Publications:** Factors affecting drug metabolism in food producing and companion animals. **Mailing Address:** US Food & Drug Admin Ctr Vet Med, 7500 Standish Pl, Rockville, MD 20855-2773. **Fax:** 301-827-8250. **E-Mail:** jkawalek@cvm.fda.gov

KAWAMURA, HIROSHI, BRAIN MECHANISMS OF BEHAVIOR, CIRCADIAN RHYTHMS. **Personal Data:** b Antong, China, January 26, 1927; Japanese citizen; m 1971, Keiko Tsuruta; c 2. **Education:** Univ Tokyo, MD, 1954, DMed Sc(neurophysiol), 1959. **Honors & Awards:** Mainischi Award, Mainischi Shinbunsha, Tokyo. **Professional Experience:** Vis prof, Toho Univ Med Sch, 1993-1997; PROF NEUROSCI, UNIV EASIA GRAD SCH, 1992-; distingusihed scientist, Dept Neurosci, 1990-1992; dir, Dept Neurosci, 1981-1990; chief, Neurophysiol Lab, Mitsubishi Kasei Inst Life Sci, 1972-1981; vis scientist, Dept Res Anesthesia, McGill Univ, 1971-1972; Chief, Neurophysiol Sect, Lafayette Clin, 1967-1971; res assoc, Dept Pharmacol, Univ Mich, 1966-1971; UNESCO fel neurophysiol, Inst Physiol, Univ Pisa, 1965-1966; asst res anatomist, Dept Anat, Univ Calif, Los Angeles, 1963-1965; assoc prof, Yokohama Univ Sch Med, 1961-1963; Instr neurophysiol, Brain Res Inst, Univ Tokyo, 1959-1961. **Memberships:** Am Physiol Soc; Soc Neurosci; AAAS; Soc Study Biol Rhythms. **Research Statement & Publications:** Hypothalmic mechanisms of sleep-wakefulness and circadian rhythm generation of the suprachiasmatic nucleus; brain tissue transplantation, learning after brainstem transection. **Mailing Address:** 2-1-2 Ichigaya Sadoharacho Apt 208, Shinjuku-ku, Tokyo 162, Japan.

KAWAMURA, KAZUHIKO, INTELLIGENT ROBOTICS, INTELLIGENT TRAINING SYSTEMS. **Personal Data:** b Nagoya, Japan, February 4, 1939; m 1971. **Education:** Waseda Univ, Japan, BEng, 1963; Univ Calif, Berkeley, MS, 1966; Univ Mich, Ann Arbor, PhD (elec eng), 1971. **Professional Experience:** PROF MGT TECHNOL, DEPT ELEC ENG, 1988-; PROF, DEPT ELEC ENG & COMPUT SCI & DIR GRAD STUDIES, CTR INTEL SYSTS, VANDERBILT UNIV, 1988-; assoc dir, ctr intel systs, Vanderbilt Univ, beginning 1985; mem, AAAS Comt Sci, Eng, & Pub Policy, beginning 1983; orgn coordr, Int Asn Impact Assessment, 1981-1983; consult, Saudi Arabian Nat Ctr Sci & Technol, 1981-1983; assoc prof elec eng & mgt technol, dept elec eng, 1980-1988; vis prof, Kyoto Univ, Japan, 1980-1981; sr res fel, Japan Soc Prom Sci, 1980; prin researcher tech assessment, Columbus Div, Battelle Mem Inst, 1973-1981; res specialist exp vehicles, Ford Motor Co, 1973; Lectr elec eng, Univ Mich-Dearborn, 1972-1973. **Memberships:** Inst Elec & Electronics Engrs; AAAS; Sigma Xi; Am Asn Artificial Intel. **Research Statement & Publications:** Expert systems; intelligent robotics; intelligent tutoring systems; risk analysis; computer vision. **Mailing Address:** Dept Elec Eng & Comput Sci, Sch Eng Vanderbilt Univ, 324 Featheringill Hall VU Station B 351674, Nashville, TN 37215-1674. **Fax:** 615-343-6702. **E-Mail:** kawamura@vuse.vanderbilt.edu

KAWANISHI, HIDENORI, CELLULAR IMMUNOLOGY, IMMUNOCHEMISTRY. **Education:** Kyoto Med Sch, Japan, MD & PhD (exp path), 1960. **Professional Experience:** PROF MED, UNIV MED & DENT NJ, ROBERT WOOD JOHNSON MED SCH, as of 2004; CHMN & PROF, DEPT MED, RESIDENCE KAMEDA FOUND & MED CTR, as of 2004; prof med, Rutgers Univ, beginning 2002; assoc prof med, Health Sci Ctr, State Univ Ny, Stony Brook, beginning 1982. **Mailing Address:** Residence Kameda Found & Med Ctr, 929 Higashi-Machi, Kamogawa, 296, Japan.

KAWASAKI, EDWIN POPE, CHEMICAL ENGINEERING, PHYSICAL CHEMISTRY. **Personal Data:** b Sikeston, Mo, January 25, 1926; m 1948, c 2. **Education:** Case Inst Technol, BS, 1954, MS, 1958, PhD (chem eng), 1960. **Professional Experience:** RETIRED; asst dir res, Repub Steel Res Ctr, 1975-1984; div head processing, res ctr, 1973-1975; div head surface chem, res ctr, 1963-1973; supvr chem processing, res ctr, 1958-1963; res engr, res ctr, 1954-1958. **Memberships:** Nat Asn Corrosion Engrs. **Research Statement & Publications:** Corrosion of ferrous metals; chemical processing; environmental control; iron and steel making. **Mailing Address:** 4250 Meadow Gateway, Broadview Heights, OH 44147.

KAWATA, KAZUYOSHI, SANITARY ENGINEERING, ENVIRONMENTAL HEALTH. **Personal Data:** b Portland, Ore, January 2, 1924; m 1949, Marion; c David, Ray & Jean. **Education:** Ore State Col, BS, 1949; Univ Minn, MS, 1950; Univ Calif, Berkeley, MPH, 1958; Johns Hopkins Univ, DrPH (sanit eng), 1965. **Professional Experience:** PROF EMER ENVIRON HEALTH ENG, JOHNS HOPKINS UNIV, as of 2006; World Bank consult, 1990-1997; prof environ health eng & prof int health, Johns Hopkins Univ, 1980-1989; consult, AID, 1979-1995; expert health sci, AID, 1976-1978; consult & lectr, Egypt, 1976; consult, WHO, Philippines, 1975; consult, WHO, Bangladesh, 1973; from asst prof to assoc prof, Johns Hopkins Univ, 1966-1980; civil sanit engr, Bd Missions, Methodist Church, 1950-1966. **Memberships:** Am Soc Civil Engrs; Am Pub Health Asn; Am Water Works Asn; Water Environ Fedn; Am Acad Environ Engrs; Int Asn Water Qual. **Research Statement & Publications:** Water and waste-water treatment processes; disinfection kinetics; tropical environmental health. **Mailing Address:** Dept Environ Health Eng, Johns Hopkins Univ, Baltimore, MD 21205.

KAWATERS, WOODY H, AIR POLLUTION IMPACTS, WASTE MANAGEMENT IMPACTS. **Personal Data:** b Hoboken, NJ, January 14, 1951; m 1966, c 5. **Education:** Univ Md, BA, 1974. **Professional Experience:** AIR GROUP MGR, ENVIRON SCI SERVS, 1994-; consult, Gov Infostructure Taskforce, 1985-1987; vpres Environ Sci Div Dir, TRC Environ Consult, 1982-1987; prin consult, TRC Environ Consult, 1978-1982; sr anal, Chi-Comput Horizons, 1974-1978. **Memberships:** Air Pollution Control Asn; Nat Asbestos Coun; Nat Asn Manufacturers. **Research Statement & Publications:** Research physical and engineering science aspects of air and waste pollution; environmental policy analysis; data tracking system design for pollution information; research designs; cost of complying with regulations; management of technical personnel and projects. **Mailing Address:** Environ Sci Servs, 532 Atwells Ave, Providence, RI 02909.

KAWATRA, MAHENDRA P, PHYSICS. **Personal Data:** b Wazirabad, India, June 22, 1935; American citizen; m 1962, Ved; c Anjali, Anita & Sandhya. **Education:** Univ Delhi, BSc, 1955, MSc, 1957, PhD (physics), 1962. **Professional Experience:** PROF MATH, MEDGAR EVERS COL, CITY UNIV NEW YORK, 1991-; dir educ & computtechnol, Medgar Evers Col, City Univ New York, 1980-1983; PROF PHYSICS, MEDGAR EVERS COL, CITY UNIV NEW YORK, 1971-; asst prof, Fordham Univ, 1966-1971; assoc res scientist, Courant Inst Math Sci, NY Univ, 1964-1966; Res assoc, Univ Ill, 1964; Smith-Mundt scholar & Fulbright grant, Mass Inst Technol, 1963-1964; Lectr physics, Univ Delhi, 1957-1963; Smith-Mundt scholar, Mass Inst Technol. **Memberships:** Am Phys Soc; NY Acad Sci. **Research Statement & Publications:** Quantum-statistical mechanics; many-body problem; liquid helium; thin film and theory of superconductivity; low-temperature physics. **Mailing Address:** Hilldale Lane, Sands Point, NY 11050.

KAWOOYA, JOHN KASAJJA, PROTEIN FOLDING, RECONSTITUTION OF PROTEINS WITH LIPIDS. **Personal Data:** b Ft Portal, Uganda, May 16, 1952. **Education:** Makerere Univ Kampala, BSc, 1973; Univ Nairobi, MSc, 1979; Univ Ill, Urbana-Champagne, PhD (entomol), 1982. **Professional Experience:** LEADING RES SCIENTIST, UPJOHN CO, 1989-; Univ Rio Del Jeneiro, Brazil, 1988-1989; Vis scientist, Univ Utrecht, Holland, 1987-1988; res asst prof, Univ Ariz, 1986-1988; Res assoc, Univ Ariz, 1983-1984 & Univ Chicago, 1984-1986. **Memberships:** Am Soc Biochem & Molecular Biol; AAAS. **Research Statement & Publications:** Isolation and refolding of recounbinant proteins-these proteins represent a new generation of biopharmaceutical therapeutics designed to combat various ailments. **Mailing Address:** Upjohn Co Bldg No 89, Kalamazoo, MI 49001.

KAXIRAS, EFTHIMIOS, PHYSICS. **Education:** Mass Inst Technol, PhD, 1987. **Professional Experience:** GORDON MCKAY PROF APPL PHYSICS & PROF PHYSICS, HARVARD UNIV, as of 2005. **Mailing Address:** Dept Physics Harvard Univ, Lyman 333 17 Oxford St, Cambridge, MA 02138. **E-Mail:** kaxiras@physics.harvard.edu

KAY, ALAN, PERSONAL COMPUTING. **Personal Data:** b May 17, 1940; m 1983, Bonnie Lynn. **Education:** Univ Colo, BS, 1966; Univ Utah, PhD, 1969. **Honors & Awards:** J D Warnier Prize; Software Systs Award, Asn Comput Mach. **Professional Experience:** PRES, VEW PT RE INST, as of 2004; SR FEL, HEWLETT PACKARD LAB, as of 2004; disney fel, Walt Disney Imagineering Res & Develop Inc, beginning 1996; Chief scientist, Atari Inc, 1984-; Apple fel, Apple Comput Inc, 1984-1996. **Memberships:** fel Royal Soc Arts; fel AAAS; Nat Acad Eng. **Research Statement & Publications:** Help children learn to think better. **Mailing Address:** Viewpt Res Inst, 1209 Grand Cent Ave, Glendale, CA 91201. **Fax:** 818-244-976.

KAY, ALVIN JOHN, MATHEMATICAL ANALYSIS. **Personal Data:** b Luling, Tex, June 10, 1938; m 1967, Mary; c John, Mike, Lisa & Will. **Education:** Southwest Tex State Univ, BS, 1961, MA, 1965; Univ Houston, PhD (math), 1975. **Professional Experience:** CHAIR, DEPT MATH, TEX A&M UNIV KINGSVILLE, as of 1999; PROF MATH, TEX A&M UNIV KINGSVILLE, 1992-; from instr to assoc prof, Tex A&I Univ, 1970-1992; asst, Univ Houston, 1969-1970; instr, San Jacinto Col, 1965-1969; asst, SW Tex State Univ, 1964-1965; Teacher math, Woodsboro High Sch, 1961-1964. **Memberships:** Am Math Soc; Math Asn Am. **Research Statement & Publications:** Integral equations and product integral. **Mailing Address:** Dept Math, Tex A&M Univ, N Armstrong St 1055 Univ Blvd, Kingsville, TX 78363-8201. **Fax:** 512-593-3518. **E-Mail:** kfajk00@tamuk.edu

KAY, CYRIL MAX, BIOCHEMISTRY. **Personal Data:** b Calgary, Alta, October 3, 1931; m 1953, Faye; c Lewis E & Lisa (Sherman). **Education:** McGill Univ, BS, 1952; Harvard Univ, PhD (biochem), 1956. **Honors & Awards:** Ayerst Award Biochem, 1970. **Professional Experience:** Vpres, Res Alta Cancer Bd, 1999-; PROF EMER BIOCHEM, UNIV ALTA, as of 1999; mem, Protein Eng Network Ctr Excellence, 1990-; co-dir, Med Res Coun Group Protein Struct & Function, Univ Alta, 1974-1995; vis prof, Med Res Coun Can, Weizmann Inst Sci, Rehovot, Israel, 1969-1970; prof biochem, Univ Alta, beginning 1967; from asst prof to assoc prof, Univ Alta, 1958-1967; res phys biochemist, Eli Lilly & Co, 1957-1958; fel, Life Ins Med Res Fund, Cambridge Univ, 1956-1957. **Memberships:** Fel NY Acad Sci; fel Royal Soc Can; Brit Biochem Soc; Am Soc Biol Chem; Can Biochem Soc; Biophys Soc; Order Can. **Research Statement & Publications:** Protein physical chemistry; hydrodynamic and optical properties of macromolecules; correlation of physicochemical properties with biological function for muscle proteins; de novo design of proteins. **Mailing Address:** Dept Biochem, Univ Alta, 3-36 Med Sci Bldg, Edmonton, AB T6G 2H7, Can. **Fax:** 403-492-0095. **E-Mail:** ckay@gpu.srv.ualberta.ca

KAY, DAVID CLIFFORD, COMBINATORICS, FINITE MATHEMATICS. **Personal Data:** b Oklahoma City, Okla, July 26, 1933; m 1978, c 3. **Education:** Otterbein Col, BS, 1955; Univ Pittsburgh, MS, 1959; Mich State Univ, PhD (math), 1963. **Professional Experience:** Dir, Reg NSF Conf, Convexity, Nat Sci Found, 1971; Res Coun award, Univ Wyo, 1965; Asst prof math, Univ Wyo, 1963-1966; AT DEPT MATH, UNIV NC. **Memberships:** Sigma Xi; Am Math Soc; Math Asn Am. **Research Statement & Publications:** Problems regarding curve-curvature in metric spaces; axiomatic convexity, matroids and geometric problems in topological linear spaces. **Mailing Address:** 201 Golden Autumn Dr, Dahlonega, GA 30533.

KAY, DAVID CYRIL, PSYCHIAT, PSYCHOPHARMACOLOGY. **Personal Data:** b Sault Ste Marie, Mich, September 5, 1932; American & Canadian citizen; m 1961, Carla; c David, Andrew, Rachel & Thomas. **Education:** Wheaton Col, Ill, BS, 1954; Univ Ill, Chicago, MD, 1958; Am Bd Psychiat & Neurol, dipl, 1969; Am Bd Psychiat & Neurol Addn Qualification Addiction Psychiat, 1994. **Honors & Awards:** NIMH Ment Health Career Devel Fel, 1961-1966; Life Fel, Am Psychiat Asn, 1997; Distinguished Life Fel, Am Psychiat Asn. **Professional Experience:** PVT PRACT, PSYCHIAT & PSYCHOPHARMACOLOGY, 1985-; dir drug abuse prog, Houston Vet Admin Hosp, 1980-1987; assoc prof psychiat & pharmacol, Baylor Col Med, 1980-1988; chief exp psychiat sect, Addiction Res Ctr, Nat Inst Drug Abuse, 1969-1980; chief exp psychiat unit, Addiction Res Ctr, Nat Inst Drug Abuse, 1966-1969; clin instr, Med Ctr, Univ Ky, 1964-1980; vis lectr, Asbury Theol Sem, 1964-1966; fel, Addiction Res Ctr, Nat Inst Ment Health, 1964-1966; NIMH Ment health career develop fel, 1961-1966; res psychiatrist, Ill State Psychiat Inst, 1961-1964; staff physician, USPHS Hosp, Ft Worth, Tex, 1959-1961; intern, Presby-St Luke's Hosp, Chicago, 1958-1959. **Memberships:** Am Soc Pharmacol & Exp Therapeut; Int Brain Res Orgn; Sigma Xi; Am Psychiat Asn; Am Soc Clin Pharmacol & Therapeut; Soc Neuroscience. **Research Statement & Publications:** Behav physiological invest of psychoactive drugs and individuals who abuse them:interaction of sleep with drugs and sexual dysfunction. **Mailing Address:** 1313 Campbell Rd Bldg C, Houston, TX 77055-6429. **Fax:** 713-973-0545. **E-Mail:** dckay1@pol.net

KAY, DENIS G, MOLECULAR BIOLOGY. **Personal Data:** b PEI, August 14, 1956. **Education:** Dalhousie Univ, BS, 1978, MS, 1981; McGill Univ, PhD (biochem), 1987. **Professional Experience:** ASSOC SCIENTIST MOLECULAR BIOL, CLIN RES INST MONTREAL, as of 2004; sr res scientist molecular biol, clin res inst montreal, beginning 1990; res fel, 1987-1990. **Memberships:** Am Soc Cell Biol; Am Soc Biochem & Molecular Biol. **Research Statement & Publications:** Molecular biology. **Mailing Address:** Lab Molecular Biol, Clin Res Inst Montreal, Rm 502, 110 Pine Ave W, Montreal, PQ H2W 1R7, Can. **Fax:** 514-987-5675. **E-Mail:** kayd@ircm.qc.ca

KAY, ELIZABETH ALISON, BIOLOGY. **Personal Data:** b Kauai, Hawaii, September 27, 1928. **Education:** Mills Col, BA, 1950; Cambridge Univ, BA, 1952, MA, 1956; Univ Hawaii, PhD, 1957. **Professional Experience:** PROF EMER ZOOL, UNIV HAWAII, MANOA, as of 2002; actg vice chancellor, Grad Div, 1984-1985; assoc dean, Grad Div, 1975-1979; prof zool, Univ Hawaii, Manoa, beginning 1970; HON ASSOC MALACOL, B P BISHOP MUS, 1958-; from asst prof to assoc prof sci, Univ Hawaii, Manoa, 1957-1966; Fulbright scholar, 1950-1952. **Memberships:** Fel AAAS; Soc Syst Zool; Marine Biol Asn UK; Challenger Soc; Malacol Soc Australia; fel Linnean Soc. **Research Statement & Publications:** Functional morphology of marine gastropods; molluscan ecology and systematics; biogeography. **Mailing Address:** Dept Zool, Univ Hawaii, Manoa, 2538 McCarthy Mall, Edmondson 152, Honolulu, HI 96822. **Fax:** 808-956-9812. **E-Mail:** ekay@hawaii.edu

KAY, ERIC, PLASMA SCIENCE, THIN FILM POLYMERS. **Personal Data:** b Heidelberg, Ger, November 23, 1926; American citizen; m 1953, Lorel Lu; c David, Erica, Andrew. **Education:** Univ Calif, BS, 1953; Univ Wash, Seattle, PhD (chem), 1958. **Honorary Degrees:** Dr, Univ Karlsruhe, Ger, 1989. **Honors & Awards:** John Thornton Mem Award, Am Vacuum Soc, 1989. **Professional Experience:** CONSULT PROF, STANFORD UNIV, 1993-; PROF, DEPT MAT SCI & TECHNOL, STANFORD UNIV, 1992-; US Sr Scientist Von Humboldt Award, 1987-1988; Technol Div, Argonne Nat Lab, 1981-1986 & Tech Rev bd, Nat Submicron Facil, Cornell Univ, 1985-; mem, Tech Rev Panel, Nat Bur Stand, 1976-1979, rev comt, Argonne Univ Asn Math Sci; Vis prof, Univ Calif, Berkeley, 1968-1969; head, Mat Sci Dept, Res Lab, 1965-1992; staff res chemist, IBM Corp, 1958-1965; asst phys chem, Univ Wash, Seattle, 1954-1955; Lawrence Radiation Lab, Univ Calif, 1952-1954; Res chemist, Best Co, Oakland, Calif, 1948-1952. **Memberships:** Fel Am Vacuum Soc; fel Am Phys Soc; Sigma Xi. **Research Statement & Publications:** Ion impact phenomena on condensed phases; plasma chemistry; surface phenomena; chemistry and physics of thin films; surface magnetism; cluster science. **Mailing Address:** PO Box 28, Mendocino, CA 95460. **Fax:** 707-937-3467. **E-Mail:** kayeric@almaden.ibm.com

KAY, FENTON RAY, T-E SPECIES MANAGEMENT, VERTEBRATE ZOOLOGY. **Personal Data:** b Pacoima, Calif, October 10, 1942; div, c Aelene B & Jennifer M. **Education:** Nev Southern Univ, BS, 1967; Univ Nev, Las Vegas, MS, 1969; NMex State Univ, PhD (biol), 1975. **Professional Experience:** RES ASSOC, EL PASO COMMUNITY COL, 2000-; Sr Scientist, SWCA Inc, environ Consult, 1998-2000; sci specialist, Jornada Exp Range, Nmex state Univ, 1996-1998; sr biologist & regional mgr, ECG Inc, 1995-1996; ADJ ASSOC PROF, DEPT FISHERY & WILDLIFE SCI, NMEX STATE UNIV, 1995-; sr environ scientist, Proteus Corp, 1993-1995; supvr, Natural Resource Data Bases, Ariz Game & Fish Dept, 1992-1993; W Coast Univ, Los Angeles, 1992; ind consult, Biol & Environ, 1990-1992; Univ Nev, Reno, 1988-1989; Western Nev Community Col, Carson City, 1988; habitat staff biol, Nev Dept Wildlife, 1984-1990; instr, Truckee Meadows Community Col, Reno, 1984-1989; independent comput consult, 1983-1984; Comput programmer & opers mgr, OAO Corp, 1980-1983; Pvt Consul, 1978-1996; asst prof biol, Calif State Univ, Los Angeles, 1976-1978; NIH trainee, Dept Physiol, Col Med, Univ Fla, 1974-1976; US Int Biol Prog, Desert Biome, Dept Biol, NMex State Univ, 1970-1974; res asst, Desert Res Inst, Univ Nev, Las Vegas, 1970. **Memberships:** Ecol Soc Am; Am Soc Mammalogists; Sigma Xi. **Research Statement & Publications:** Thermal biology of desert animals; desert animal community composition; economic value of wildlife; application of geographic information systems to environmental problems effects of rodents on desert grassland structure. **Mailing Address:** Dept Fishery & Wildlife Sci, Nmex State Univ, 4100 Cholla Rd, Las Cruces, NM 88011. **Fax:** 505-646-1281. **E-Mail:** kayrat@lascruces.com

KAY, H DAVID, CELLULAR IMMUNOLOGY, LEUKEMIA. **Personal Data:** b Glendale, Ohio, September 6, 1943; m 1968, Judy; c Carrie S & Emily J. **Education:** Rensselaer Polytech Inst, BS, 1966; Iowa State Univ, MS, 1969, PhD (immunobiol), 1972. **Professional Experience:** RES COORDR & CO-DIR, DEPT INTERNAL MED, LAB GENE REGULATION RES, 1991-; legal consult, 1990-1991; lectr cellular immunol, Univ Nebr, Omaha, 1988; chmn, Immunol Coun, 1984-1990; assoc prof med & dir, Exp Immunol Lab, Med Ctr, Univ Nebr, 1983-1990; asst tumor immunol, M D Anderson Hosp & Tumor Inst, Univ Tex, 1972-1973. **Memberships:** Am Asn Immunologists; Am Rheumatism Asn; Am Asn Cancer Res; Am Fedn Clin Res; Int League Against Rheumatism. **Research Statement & Publications:** Design and testing of novel antisense oligonucleotides for use in clinical research trials to treat and cure certain cancers such as leukemia, lymphoma and breast cancer. **Mailing Address:** 5206 Underwood Ave, Omaha, NE 68132. **Fax:** 402-559-8101. **E-Mail:** hdkay@unmcvm.unmc.edu

KAY, IRVIN (WILLIAM), APPLIED MATHEMATICS, ELECTROMAGNETISM. **Personal Data:** b Savannah, Ga, April 19, 1924; m 1954, Marjorie; c Lily & Eli. **Education:** NY Univ, BA, 1948, MS, 1949, PhD (math), 1953. **Professional Experience:** SR CONSULT, VERTECH INC, 1996-; staff mem, Inst Defense Anal, 1973-1996; prof elec eng, Wayne State Univ, 1971-1973; dir independent res & develop, Conductron Corp, 1968-1971; dept head advan systs, Conductron Corp, 1964-1968; sr res mathematician, Conductron Corp, 1962-1964; from asst prof to assoc prof, NY Univ, 1959-1962; Res assoc math, NY Univ, 1952-1958. **Memberships:** Am Math Soc; Am Phys Soc. **Research Statement & Publications:** Electromagnetic theory; systems analysis; optics. **Mailing Address:** 6111 Wooten Dr, Falls Church, VA 22044.

KAY, JACK GARVIN, PHYSICAL & INORGANIC CHEMISTRY, NUCLEAR & ATMOSPHERIC CHEMISTRY. **Personal Data:** b Scott City, Kans, July 11, 1930; m 1952, c 2. **Education:** Univ Kans, AB, 1952, PhD (phys chem), 1960. **Professional Experience:** PROF EMER CHEM, DREXEL UNIV, 1969-; HEAD, DEPT CHEM, DREXEL UNIV, as of 2006; prin investr, Atomic Energy Comn, 1960-1969 & NSF, 1984-; Rep Pa Asn Cols & Univs Task Force to Develop Pa Right-to-Know legis, 1983-1984; rep Coun Chem Res, 1980-; head dept, Drexel Univ, 1969-1985; prof chem, Univ Toledo, 1966-1969; chmn dept, Univ Toledo, 1966-1968; from instr to asst prof inorg chem, Univ Ill, Urbana, 1959-1966; consult, Chemotronics, Inc, Avco, Inc, Charlestown Twp, Chester County, Pa, Alex C Fergusson Co & Dwight & Wilson Co. **Memberships:** AAAS; Am Chem Soc; Am Phys Soc; Faraday Soc; fel Am Inst Chem; Am Geophys Union. **Research Statement & Publications:** Electronic spectroscopy of gaseous diatomic molecules; matrix-isolation spectroscopy; flash heating and kinetic spectroscopy; flash photolysis; high temperature chemistry; solar furnaces; radiation chemistry; hot atom chemistry in inorganic crystals; nuclear and radiochemistry; radon and decay products in the atmosphere and oceans. **Mailing Address:** Dept Chem, Drexel Univ, Philadelphia, PA 19104.

KAY, KENNETH GEORGE, INTRAMOLECULAR ENERGY TRANSFER, SEMICLASSICAL APPROXIMATIONS. **Personal Data:** b New York, NY, October 13, 1943; m 1968, Katherine Brody; c Victoria, Elizabeth & Jennifer. **Education:** Polytech Inst, Brooklyn, BS, & MS, 1965; Johns Hopkins Univ, PhD (chem), 1970. **Professional Experience:** PROF CHEM, BAR-ILAN UNIV, 1987-; vis prof, Univ Toronto, 1982-1983; Vis assoc prof, Tel-Aviv Univ, 1979-1980; from asst prof to prof, Kans State Univ, 1971-1981; Res assoc chem, Univ Chicago, 1970-1971. **Memberships:** Am Phys Soc; Am Chem Soc. **Research Statement & Publications:** Theory of molecular reaction dynamics; unimolecular dissociation; intramolecular vibrational energy transfer; quantum ergodic theory; theoretical models for photodecomposition reactions; Semiclassical approximations. **Mailing Address:** Chem Dept, Bar Ilan Univ, Ramat Gan, Israel. **Fax:** 972-535-1250. **E-Mail:** kay@fen.cc.biu.ac.il

KAY, MARGUERITE M B, GERIATRICS & GERONTOLOGY, MEMBRANE BIOLOGY. **Personal Data:** b Washington, DC, May 13, 1947. **Education:** Univ Calif, Berkeley, BA, 1970; Univ Calif, San Francisco, MD, 1974; Nat Inst Aging, NIH, cert, 1976. **Professional Experience:** REGENTS PROF, MICROBIOL & IMMUNOL & MED, COL MED, UNIV ARIZ, 1990-; nam ed, Geront, 1988-; prof micro biol & immunol, Col Med, 1981-1991; prof med & prof med biochem & genetics & dir, Div Geriat Med, Tex A & M Univ, Col Med, 1981-1990; reviewer, NSF & US-Israel Binational Sci Found, 1977-, reviewer, NIH; USPHS Off & chief, High Resolution Membrane Lab, 1975-1977; consult, immuno-electron micros, Dept Basic & Clin Immunol & Microbiol, Med Univ SC, 1974-1981; biol consult, Electron Micros Lab, Enrico Fermi Inst, Univ Chicago, 1974-1975; Staff fel, Geront Res Ctr, Nat Inst Child Health & Human Develop, NIH Baltimore City Hosp, 1974; chief, Lab Molecular & Clinical Immunol, Veterans Admin Wadsworth Med Ctr, Los Angeles Calif. **Memberships:** Am Soc Clin Invest; Am Soc Biol Chem; Am Asn Immunologists; Am Geriat Soc; Am Soc Cell Biol; Am Soc Hemat. **Research Statement & Publications:** Molecular and cell biology of aging. **Mailing Address:** Dept Microbiol & Immunol, Univ Ariz, Rm 644 LSN Med 1501 N Campbell Ave, Tucson, AZ 85724-0001. **Fax:** 520-626-2100.

KAY, MICHAEL AARON, RADIOACTIME MATERIALS LICENSING & MANAGEMENT PROGRAMS, HEALTH-SAFETY & ENVIRONMENTAL CONSULTING. **Personal Data:** b San Francisco, Calif, May 7, 1943; m 2001, Sabina. **Education:** Univ Calif, Berkeley, BS, 1965; Mass Inst Technol, Cambridge, ScD, 1970. **Honors & Awards:** Champion Excellence, Acad Cert hazardous Materials Managers, 2005. **Professional Experience:** INSTR, CHEM LIBERAL ARTS & SCI PORTLAND STATE UNIV, as of 2006; adj prof anal chem, Portland State Univ, 1991-2003; Sr environ scientist, environ div, DESCO indust group, 1990-1995; PRES, AMBRY INC, 1988-; mgr chem res & develop, Hannah Car Wash Int, 1986-1988; Consult forensic sci & health physics, Radiation Systs assoc, 1981-; assoc prof chem & dir, Reed Reactor Facil, Reed Col, 1980-1986; sr scientist, Rockwell Hanford Opers, Wash, 1978-1980; sr res scientist, Res Reactor Facility, Univ Mo, Columbia, 1975-1978; mem fac, Univ Mo, Columbia, 1975-1978; sr chemist, Res Reactor Facility, Univ Mo, Columbia, 1970-1975; Radiochemist, US Naval Radiol Defense Lab, Calif, 1965. **Memberships:** Acad cert hazardous mat mgrs; Am Chem Soc; Health Physics Soc; Inst hazardous Mats Mgt; fel Am Instit Chemists. **Research Statement & Publications:** Health safety and environment compliance; radioactive mat management and training; data quality assurance and quality control; expert witness; certified hazardous mat mgr; licensed health physics consultant. **Mailing Address:** Chem Liberal Arts & Sci Portland State Univ, PO Box 751, Portland, OR 97207. **Fax:** 503-725-3888. **E-Mail:** kaym@pdx.edu

KAY, MORTIMER ISAIA, CRYSTALLOGRAPHY. **Personal Data:** b Bronx, NY, August 27, 1930; m 1964. **Education:** Brooklyn Col, BA, 1952; Purdue Univ, MS, 1953; Univ Conn, PhD (phys chem), 1958. **Professional Experience:** PHYS SCIENTIST, US DEPT ENERGY, 1981-; head sea water-surfactant project, ocean thermal energy conversion, 1979-1980; head, Mat Sci Div, PR Ctr Energy & Environ Res, 1976-1979; sr scientist & head neutron diffraction prog, PR Nuclear Ctr, 1964-1977; res assoc prof, Ga Inst Technol, 1962-1964; res scientist, NASA, 1960-1961; fel, Royal Norweg Coun Sci & Indust Res, 1959-1960; res assoc, Pa State Univ, 1957-1959; Vis assoc physicist, Brookhaven Nat Lab, 1957-1959; asst, Univ Conn, 1953-1957; Asst chem, Purdue Univ, 1952-1953. **Memberships:** AAAS; Am Chem Soc; Am Phys Soc; Am Crystallog Asn; Sigma Xi. **Research Statement & Publications:** Molecular and crystal structure; diffraction studies of ferroelectric transitions; ocean thermal energy; pyroelectric energy conversion; surface chemistry; atomic energy. **Mailing Address:** 70 Oak Shade Rd, Gaithersburg, MD 20878-1048.

KAY, PETER STEVEN, CLINICAL CHEMISTRY, INSTRUMENTATION. **Personal Data:** b Milwaukee, Wis, September 24, 1937. **Education:** Cornell Univ, AB, 1959; Purdue Univ, PhD (org chem), 1966. **Professional Experience:** CONSULT, as of 2003; prin, Strategic Mgr Adv Group, beginning 1986; gen mgr x-ray prod, Picker Int, 1985-1986; dir mkt Harshaw Chem Co (Gulf Oil), 1982-1984; nat sales mgr, Electronic Div, 1980-1982; mgr liquid chromatography, Sci Instruments, Inst Prod, 1979-1980; mgr thermal anal, Sci Instruments, Inst Prod, 1977-1979; nat sales mgr, Sci Instruments, Inst Prod, 1976-1977; dist mgr, Textile Fibers Dept, E I Du Pont Del Nemours & Co, Inc, 1973-1976; mkt rep, Textile Fibers Dept, E I Du Pont Del Nemours & Co, Inc, 1972-1973; res chemist, Textile Fibers Dept, E I Du Pont Del Nemours & Co, Inc, 1970-1972; col rels rep, Employee Rels Dept, 1969-1970; res chemist, Textile Fibers Dept, 1966-1969; teaching asst chem, Purdue Univ, 1960-1962; Tech asst coal chem, US Steel Res Ctr, 1959-1960. **Memberships:** AAAS; Am Chem Soc; Sigma Xi; fel Am Inst Chemists. **Research Statement & Publications:** Kinetics and product distributions in solvolyses of allylic halides and esters; polyamide fibers; biocomponent fibers; polyamide textile fibers; robotics; digital x-ray techniques; clinical laboratory automated analyzers and medical imaging devices; general management consultation. **Mailing Address:** Purdue Cancer Ctr, Purdue Univ, Hansen Life Sci Res Bldg, 201 S Univ St, West Lafayette, IN 47907-2064.

KAY, ROBERT EUGENE, EPITAXIAL CRYSTAL GROWTH, INFRARED DETECTORS. **Personal Data:** b Missoula, Mont, December 23, 1925; m 1951, Beverly Buell; c Kimberly, Roberta & Gregory. **Education:** Univ Calif, Los Angeles, BS, 1948, PhD (bot sci), 1952. **Professional Experience:** Tech consult, Semiconductor Technol Dept Aeronutronic Div, Ford Aerospace Corp, 1980-1988; mgr, Biosci Dept, 1961-1980; supvry chemist, US Naval Radiol Defense Lab, 1954-1961; Asst bot, Univ Calif, Los Angeles, 1951-1952. **Research Statement & Publications:** Radiobiology; lipid metabolism; isolated perfused organs; adaptive enzyme systems; olfactory transduction in insects; model membrane systems; interactions of dyes with biological macromolecules; immobilized enzymes; organic semiconductors; infrared detectors; missile-vehicle integration; missile systs mgt; high temperature batteries; hetero epitaxial crystal growth. **Mailing Address:** 1515 Warwick Ln, Newport Beach, CA 92660. **E-Mail:** weyak@earthlink.net

KAY, ROBERT LEO, PHYSICAL CHEMISTRY, SOLUTION CHEMISTRY. **Personal Data:** b Hamilton, Ont, December 13, 1924; m 1952, Ann; c David (deceased), Theresa, Joanne & Robert Jr. **Education:** Univ Toronto, MA, 1950, PhD (phys chem), 1952. **Professional Experience:** PROF EMER CHEM, CARNEGIE-MELLOW UNIV, 1990-; head dept, Ctr Spec Studies, 1974-1983; actg dir, Ctr Spec Studies, 1973-1974; ed, J Solution Chem, 1971-; prof, Ctr Spec Studies, 1967-1990; sr fel, Mellon Inst, 1963-1967; asst prof chem, Brown Univ, 1956-1963; res asst, Rockefeller Inst, 1953-1956; merck fel, Rockefeller Inst, 1952. **Memberships:** Am Chem Soc; Biophys Soc. **Research Statement & Publications:** Transport properties of electrolyte solutions; structure of liquids; electrophoresis; solutions at high pressure and temperature; dielectrics; thermodynamics; computer generation of scientific information. **Mailing Address:** Carnegie Mellon Univ, 4400 Fifth Ave, Pittsburgh, PA 15213. **Fax:** 412-268-6945. **E-Mail:** rk6a@andrew.cmu.edu

KAY, ROBERT WOODBURY, GEOCHEMISTRY. **Personal Data:** b New York, NY, January 21, 1943; m 1975, Suzanne; c Jennifer & Alexander. **Education:** Brown Univ, AB, 1964; Columbia Univ, PhD (geol), 1970. **Professional Experience:** DIR, UNDERGRAD STUDIES, CORNELL UNIV, as of 2005; PROF EARTH & ATMOSPHERIC SCI, CORNELL UNIV, 1986-; from asst prof to assoc prof, Cornell Univ, 1976-1986; asst res geophysicist, Univ Calif, Los Angeles, 1975-1976; asst prof geol, Columbia Univ, 1970-1975; consult geochem. **Memberships:** Fel Geol Soc Am; Am Geophys Union; Geochem Soc. **Research Statement & Publications:** Geochemistry of rare earth elements in volcanic rocks; regional geology of the Aleutian Islands, Alaska; chemistry of the lower crust. **Mailing Address:** Dept Geol Sci, Cornell Univ, 3142 Snee Hall, Ithaca, NY 14853. **E-Mail:** rwk6@cornell.edu

KAY, RONALD D, PHYSICAL CHEMISTRY. **Education:** Gordon Col, BA; Ohio State Univ, PhD (Phys Chem). **Professional Experience:** FAC, DEPT CHEM, GORDON COL, as of 2005. **Mailing Address:** Dept Chem Gordon Col, 255 Grapevine Rd, Wenham, MA 01984.

KAY, SAUL, surgical pathology; deceased, see previous edition for last biography

KAY, SUZANNE MAHLBURG, PETROLOGY, MINERALOGY, GEOCHEMISTRY. **Personal Data:** b Rockford, Ill, May 30, 1947; American citizen; m 1975, Robert; c Jennifer & Alexander. **Education:** Univ Ill, Urbana, BS, 1969, MS, 1972; Brown Univ, PhD (geol), 1975. **Professional Experience:** PROF, DEPT EARTH & ATMOSPHERIC SCI, CORNELL UNIV, 1999-; assoc prof, Dept Earth & Atmospheric Sci, Cornell Univ, 1993-1999; Fulbright fel, 1989-1990; vis prof, Univ Buenos Aires, Arg, 1989; sr res assoc, Inst Study Continents, 1983-1993; vis assoc petrol, Calif Inst Technol, 1983; res assoc geol, Cornell Univ, 1976-1982; fel geol, Univ Calif, Los Angeles, 1975-1976. **Memberships:** fel Geol Soc Am; fel Mineral Soc Am; Am Geophys Union; Sigma Xi; hon mem Asn Geol Arg. **Research Statement & Publications:** Application of geochemical techniques to study of the origin and evolution of continental crust at continental margins with special emphasis in the Chilean-Argentine Andes and Aleutian Islands Alaska. **Mailing Address:** Dept Earth & Atmospheric Sci, Cornell Univ, 3140 Snee Hall, Ithaca, NY 14853. **Fax:** 607-254-4780. **E-Mail:** smk16@cornell.edu

KAYA, CALVIN MASAYUKI, ENVIRONMENTAL BIOLOGY OF FISHES. **Personal Data:** b Maui, Hawaii, September 4, 1942; m 1967, Kathryn; c Brandon & Rachel. **Education:** Univ Hawaii, Manoa, BA, 1964; Univ Wis-Madison, MA, 1967, PhD (zoology), 1971. **Professional Experience:** PROF EMER BIOL, MONT STATE UNIV, 2002-; prof biol, Mont State Univ, 1982-2002; Vis scientist fishery biol, Nat Marine Fisheries Serv, Honolulu Lab, 1978-1980 & 1983; from asst prof to assoc prof zool, Mont State Univ, 1971-1982. **Memberships:** Am Fisheries Soc. **Research Statement & Publications:** Ecology, reproduction and behavior of fishes, with recent focus on rare or threatened freshwater fishes. **Mailing Address:** Biol Dept, Mont State Univ, Bozeman, MT 59717. **Fax:** 406-994-3190. **E-Mail:** ubick@gemini.oscs.montana.edu

KAYA, HARRY KAZUYOSHI, INSECT PATHOLOGY & NEMATOLOGY. **Personal Data:** b Honolulu, Hawaii, November 20, 1940; m 1964, c 2. **Education:** Univ Hawaii, BS, 1962, MS, 1966; Univ Calif, Berkeley, PhD (insect path), 1970. **Professional Experience:** PROF, DEPT NEMATOL, UNIV CALIF, DAVIS, 1984-; from asst prof to assoc prof, Dept Nematol, Univ Calif, Davis, 1976-1984; asst entomologist, Conn Agr Exp Sta, 1971-1976. **Memberships:** Soc Invert Path; Entom Soc Am; Int Orgn Biol Control; Soc Nematol; fel Japan Soc Promotion Sci. **Research Statement & Publications:** Biological control of insects; epizootiology in insect populations; use of microorganisms to control insects; insect nematology. **Mailing Address:** Dept Entom, Univ Calif, Davis, CA 95616-5200. **Fax:** 530-752-5809. **E-Mail:** hkkaya@ucdavis.edu

KAYANI, JOSEPH THOMAS, APPLIED MECHANICS, STRESS ANALYSIS. **Personal Data:** b Kuravilangad, India, March 8, 1945; American citizen; m 1969, c 2. **Education:** Univ Kerala, India, BSc, 1967; Polytech Inst Brooklyn, MS, 1971; Polytech Inst NY, PhD (mech eng), 1975. **Professional Experience:** PRIN ENGR APPL MECH, EBASCO SERV INC, 1978-; res fel, Polytech Inst New York, 1975-; Burns & Roe Inc, 1975-1978; stress analysis, Nuclear Power Servs, Inc, New York, 1974-1975; res asst, Polytech Inst Brooklyn, 1973-1975; mech engr, Acoust & Vibrations Lab, Souncoat Co, Inc, Brooklyn, 1972-1974; engr supvr construct, Telecommun Dept, Govt India, 1967-1969. **Memberships:** Am Soc Mech Engrs; Am Acad Mech. **Research Statement & Publications:** Stress and vibration analysis of pressure vessels and piping; nonlinear random vibrations; acoustics and noise control of machines and structural components. **Mailing Address:** 300 Ellen Pl, Jericho, NY 11753.

KAYAR, SUSAN RENNIE, RESPIRATORY PHYSIOLOGY, MICROCIRCULATION & DIVING PHYSIOLOGY. **Personal Data:** b Highland, Ill, May 17, 1953. **Education:** Univ Miami, BS, 1974, PhD (biol), 1978. **Honors & Awards:** Arne Zetterstrom Award Hydrogen Diving Res. **Professional Experience:** HEALTH SCIENTIST ADMINR, NAT CTR RES RESOURCES, NIH, as of 2006; RES PHYSIOLOGIST, NAVAL MED RES INST, NAT NAVAL MED CTR, BETHESDA, MD, 1990-; instr, Univ Med Dent, NJ, 1989-1990; res asst prof, Univ Bern, Switz, 1984-1989; fel, Med Sch, Univ Colo, Denver, 1981-1984; res assoc, Univ Colo, Boulder, 1979-1981; res asst, Everglades Nat Park, 1978-1979. **Memberships:** Am Physiol Soc; Microcirculatory Soc; AAAS. **Research Statement & Publications:** Patented a process for facilitating diving decompression by biochemical elimnation of gases in divers. **Mailing Address:** Nat Ctr Res Resources, NIH, One Rockledge Ctr Ste 6030 6705 Rockledge Dr MSC 7965, Bethesda, MD 20892-7965. **Fax:** 301-480-3770. **E-Mail:** kayars@ncrr.nih.gov

KAYDEN, HERBERT J, MEDICINE. **Personal Data:** b New York, NY, January 30, 1920; m 1951, c 2. **Education:** Columbia Col, AB, 1940; NY Univ, MD, 1943. **Professional Experience:** Vis physician, Bellevue Hosp, 1971-; attend physician, NY Univ Hosp, 1971-; PROF MED, SCH MED, NY UNIV, 1970-; assoc dir, Goldwater Mem Hosp, 1958-1962; vis physician, Goldwater Mem Hosp, 1956-; attend physician, Manhattan Vet Admin Hosp, 1956-; from asst prof to assoc prof, NY Univ, 1954-1970; from asst vis physician to assoc vis physician, Bellevue Hosp, 1952-1971; from asst attend physician to assoc attend physician, NY Univ Hosp, 1951-1971; clin instr, NY Univ, 1951-1954; from asst vis physician to assoc vis physician, Goldwater Mem Hosp, 1950-1956; asst, NY Univ, 1949-1951; mem coun arteriosclerosis, Am Heart Asn. **Memberships:** Am Soc Pharmacol & Exp Therapeut; Harvey Soc; Am Fedn Clin Res; fel Am Col Physicians; fel NY Acad Med. **Research Statement & Publications:** Cardiovascular diseases, especially disorders of cardiac rhythm; pharmacology of antiarrhythmic drugs; lipid metabolism in humans, including studies of serum and tissue lipoproteins; vitamin E metabolism in humans. **Mailing Address:** Dept Med, NY Univ Col Med, 550 First Ave, New York, NY 10016-6402. **Fax:** 212-263-6571. **E-Mail:** kaydeh01@popmail.med.nyu.edu

KAYE, ALVIN MAURICE, REPRODUCTIVE ENDROCRINOLOGY, DEVELOPMENTAL BIOLOGY. **Personal Data:** b New York, NY, September 18, 1930; m 1958, Myra Ockrent. **Education:** Columbia Univ, AB, 1951, AM, 1955; Univ Pa, PhD, 1956. **Honors & Awards:** Bernhard Zondek Mem Plenary Lectr, VI Int Cong Hormonal Steroids, 1982. **Professional Experience:** PROF MOLECULAR GENETICS, WEIZMANN INST SCI, 1995-; Joseph Moss prof molecular endocrinol & hormone res, Weizmann Inst Sci, 1985-1995; assoc prof & hormone res, Weizmann Inst Sci, 1977-1986; sr scientist biodynamics, Weizmann Inst Sci, 1968-1977; mem res staff biochem cancer, Weizmann Inst Sci, 1956-1968; asst cell physiol, Univ Pa, 1953-1955; Asst cytol, Columbia Univ, 1951-1952; chmn, Int Orgn Comt, Hormones & Cancer Congresses & mem, Prog Comt, Int Study Group Steroid Hormones; Corresp ed, J Steroid Biochem, Molecular Biol. **Memberships:** Israel Chem Soc; Biochem Soc Israel; Am Soc Cell Biol; Endocrine Soc; Sigma Xi; Biochem Soc UK. **Research Statement & Publications:** Enzymic modification of nucleic acids and proteins; hormonal induction of protein synthesis; enzyme catabolism; mechanism of carcinogenesis by ethyl carbamate regulation of creatine kinase amd ornithine decarboxylase genes; hormones & osteoporosis; selective estrogen receptor modulators and cancer. **Mailing Address:** Dept Molecular Genetics, Weizmann Inst Sci, Rehovot, 76100, Israel. **Fax:** 972-893-44108. **E-Mail:** lhkaye@weizmann.weizmann.ae.il

KAYE, BRIAN H, PHYSICS. **Personal Data:** b Hull, Eng, July 8, 1932; m 1957, c 4. **Education:** Univ Hull, BSc, 1953, MSc, 1955; Univ London, PhD (physics), 1962. **Professional Experience:** PROF EMER PHYSICS, LAURENTIAN UNIV, as of 1995; prof physics, Laurentian Univ, beginning 1968; sr physicist, IIT Res Inst, 1963-1968; res officer, Welwyn Res Asn, 1962-1963; consult, Brit Atomic Energy Authority, 1961-1963; lectr physics, Univ Nottingham, 1959-1962; sci officer, Brit Atomic Weapons Res Estab, 1955-1959; managing dir, Brian Kaye Assocs Ltd; educ & res consult. **Memberships:** Am Soc Testing & Mat. **Research Statement & Publications:** Particle size analysis of powders; physical and chemical properties of powder systems and aerosols; fractal geometry powder mixing; author of two books. **Mailing Address:** Dept Physics, Laurentian Univ, Fraser Bldg F518, Sudbury, ON P3E 2C6, Can. **Fax:** 705-675-4856. **E-Mail:** bkaye@nickel.laurentian.ca

KAYE, DONALD, INFECTIOUS DISEASE, INTERNAL MEDICINE. **Personal Data:** b New York, NY, August 12, 1931; m 1955, Janet; c Kenneth, Karen, Kendra & Keith. **Education:** Yale Univ, AB, 1953; NY Univ, MD, 1957; Am Bd Internal Med, dipl, 1964, cert infectious dis, 1974. **Honorary Degrees:** Honorary Prof, Federal Univ of Bahia, Salvador, Brazil 1990. **Honors & Awards:** Strittmatter Award, Philadelphia County Med Soc 1997; Solomon Berson Alumn Award, Npu Sch Med 1996; Emilio Ribas Medal, Brazilian Soc Infectious Disease 1994; Distinguished Achievement Award, NY Hosp Cornell Med Center Alumn Coun 1994; Lindback Award 1972. **Professional Experience:** PROF MED, HCP HAHNEMANN SCH MED 1995-; prof med & chmn dept, Med Col Pa & Chief Med, Hosp, 1969-1995; NIH fel, NY Health Res Coun career scientist award, 1966-1969; from asst attend physician to assoc attend physician, NY Hosp, 1963-1969; From asst prof to assoc prof med, Cornell Univ, 1963-1969; spec fel, Cornell Univ Med Col, 1962-1963; NIH fel, Cornell Univ Med Col, 1960-1962; Intern and Resident, NY Hosp Cornell Med Center 1957-1960. **Memberships:** Asn Am Physicians; Infectious Dis Soc Am; master Am Col Physicians; Am Soc Clin Invest, Amer Clin Climatological Asn. **Research Statement & Publications:** Research in infectious diseases with special interest in pathogenesis of bacterial infections and host defense mechanisms against bacterial infection. **Mailing Address:** Med Col Penn, 1535 Sweet Briar Rd, Gladwine, PA 19035. **E-Mail:** donjank@aol.com

KAYE, GEORGE THOMAS, SYSTEMS DESIGN. **Personal Data:** b Lorain, Ohio, December 11, 1944; m 1967, c 2. **Education:** US Naval Acad, BS, 1966; Univ Mich, MS, 1972, PhD (oceanog), 1974. **Professional Experience:** DEP EXEC DIR, SCI TECH ENG, SPACE & NAVAL WARFARE SYSTEMS CTR, SAN DIEGO, as of 2004; MGR PROG, NAVAL OCEAN SYSTS CTR, SAN DIEGO, 1985-; br head, Naval Ocean Systs Ctr, San Diego, 1979-1984; asst res oceanogr, Marine Phys Lab, Scripps Inst Oceanog, Univ Calif, San Diego, 1974-1978; Asst res oceanogr, Sea Grant Prog, Univ Mich, 1971-1974. **Memberships:** Acoust Soc Am. **Research Statement & Publications:** High-frequency sound scattering from biota and water density structures; theoretical acoustics; upper-ocean measurements with drifting arrays; acoustic noise generation by storms; model decomposition of internal waves; information processing and data fusion for systems application; optical propagation in the upper ocean. **Mailing Address:** Dept Navy, Space & Naval Warfare Systems Ctr, 53560 Hull St, San Diego, CA 92152-3127.

KAYE, GORDON I, WASTE MANAGEMENT, CELL BIOLOGY. **Personal Data:** b New York, NY, August 13, 1935; m Nancy; c Jacqueline & Vivienne. **Education:** Columbia Col, AB, 1955; Columbia Univ, AM, 1957, PhD (anat), 1961. **Honors & Awards:** Charles Huebschman Prize, Columbia Univ, 1954; Tousimis Prize, 1981; Raymond C Truex Distinguished lectr, Hahneman Med Col, 1987. **Professional Experience:** ALDEN MARCH PROF EMER PATH, ALBANY MED COL, 1999-; pres & chief exec officer, Waste Reduction Waste Reduction Inc, Troy, NY 1993-1998; chmn, NY State Low-Level Waste Group, 1986-1995; prof, Sch Pub Health, State Univ NY, Albany, 1985-1998; prof path, Dept Anat, Albany Med Col, 1981-1999; affil attend surg, Albany Med Ctr Hosp, 1978-1993; Alden March prof anat, cell biol & Neurobiology, 1976-1999; prof & chmn, Dept Anat, Albany Med Col, 1976-1987; consult surg, 1976-1978; metab & digestive dis res career award, Nat Inst Arthritis, 1972-1976; from asst prof to assoc prof, Columbia Univ, 1966-1976; consult, NY Vet Admin Hosp, 1965-1999; dir, F H Cabot Lab Electron Micros, Columbia Univ, 1963-1976; Career scientist, Health Res Coun New York, 1963-1972; assoc surg path, Columbia Univ, 1963-1966; Res assoc anat, Columbia Univ, 1961-1963; CHMN BD & EXEC VPRES, WASTE REDUCTION WASTE REDUCTION, INC. **Memberships:** Am Soc Cell Biol; Am Asn Anat; Asn Anat Cell Biol & Neurobiol Chmn (pres 1980-1981); Harvey Soc; Sigma Xi; Arthur Purdy Stout Soc. Surg. Pathologists, Am Asn Lab Animal Sci, Laboratory Animal Managment Assn., Amer. Assn. Vet. Lab. Diagnosticians. **Research Statement & Publications:** Electron microscopy; fluid transport; epithelial-mesenchymal interactions in gastrointestinal tissue differentiation; collagen-glycoconjugate interaction in cornea; cell biology of soft tissue tumors; waste management technology. **Mailing Address:** 212 Pinewood Ave, Troy, NY 12180-7244. **Fax:** 518-271-2040. **E-Mail:** wr2kaye@aol.com

KAYE, HOWARD, POLYMER CHEMISTRY, INDUSTRIAL CHEMISTRY. **Personal Data:** b New York, NY, December 9, 1938; m 1966, c 2. **Education:** Polytech Inst Brooklyn, BS, 1960, PhD (polymer chem), 1965. **Professional Experience:** DIR, POLYHEDRON LABS INC, 1980-; pres, Howard Kaye & Assoc, 1973-1980; asst prof chem, Tex A&M Univ, 1967-1973; NIH fel, Cambridge Univ, 1965-1967; consult chem indust. **Memberships:** Fel Am Inst Chemists; Am Chem Soc; Soc Plastic Engrs; Royal Soc Chem; Am Soc Testing Mat; Royal Micros Soc. **Research Statement & Publications:** Synthesis and properties of macromolecules; new syntheses for the manufacture of industrially important materials and chemicals; process and product improvement research; characterization of high polymers; automatic chemical analysis; chemical, physical and thermal testing of plastics. **Mailing Address:** Polyhedron Lab, 10626 Kinghurst, Houston, TX 77099.

KAYE, JACK ALAN, SciencE Management, Science program development. **Personal Data:** b Brooklyn, NY, November 3, 1954; m 1984, Dawn; c Rebecca, Hannah & Allison. **Education:** Adelphi Univ, BA, 1976; Calif Inst Technol, PhD (chem), 1982. **Honors & Awards:** Meritorious Senior Executive, 2004; Citation for Excellence in Refereeing, Am Geophysical Union (awarded twice); NASA Exceptional Service Medal; NASA Exceptional Achievement Medal; several NASA Group Achievement Awards. **Professional Experience:** Director, R&A Program, Earth-Sun System Division, NASA SMD, 2004-; Dir. Res. Div., NASA Office of Earth Sci., 1999-2004; Mgr., Atmospheric Chem Modeling & Analysis Prog, NASA Hq, 1991-1999; Space Scientist, Goddard Space Flight Ctr, 1983-1991; Res assoc, Plasma Physics Div, Naval Res Lab, Washington, DC, 1982-1983. **Memberships:** Mem, Am Chem Soc; Mem. Amer. Assoc. for the Advancement of SCi; Mem., Amer. Geophysical Union (Co-secy, atmospheric Sci sect, 1998-2000). **Research Statement & Publications:** Director of research program on Earth system science; Earth system modeling and remote sensing; coordination of interagency and international environmental research programs. **Mailing Address:** NASA Hq, Sci Mission Directorate - Mail Ste 5H79, Washington, DC 20546. **Fax:** 202-358-2770. **E-Mail:** Jack.A.Kaye@nasa.gov

KAYE, JAMES HERBERT, RADIOCHEMISTRY. **Personal Data:** b Seattle, Wash, September 3, 1937; m 1965, c 3. **Education:** Univ Wash, BS, 1958; Carnegie Inst Technol, MS, 1961, PhD (nuclear chem), 1963. **Professional Experience:** RES SCIENTIST RADIOCHEM, PAC NORTHWEST LABS, BATTELLE MEM INST, 1963-. **Memberships:** Am Chem Soc; Am Nuclear Soc; AAAS. **Research Statement & Publications:** Development of highly sensitive instrumentation and techniques for measurement of trace substances in the environment. **Mailing Address:** 2119 Newcomer Ave, Richland, WA 99352.

KAYE, JEROME SIDNEY, CELL BIOLOGY. **Personal Data:** b Hartford, Conn, June 15, 1930; m 1955. **Education:** Columbia Univ, AB, 1952, MA, 1954, PhD, 1957. **Professional Experience:** EMER PROF BIOL, UNIV ROCHESTER, 1992-; from asst prof to prof biol, Univ Rochester, 1959-1992; Lalor Found fel, 1958; Instr zool, Univ Calif, Los Angeles, 1957-1959. **Research Statement & Publications:** Transacting factors controlling gene transcription. **Mailing Address:** 160 Commonwealth Rd, Rochester, NY 14618.

KAYE, MICHAEL PETER, PHYSIOLOGY, SURGERY. **Personal Data:** b Chicago, Ill, February 10, 1935; m 1960, c 5. **Education:** Loyola Univ, Chicago, MS & MD, 1959. **Professional Experience:** PVT CONSULT, 1991-; prof surg, Med Ctr, Univ Calif, San Diego, 1989-1991; prof surg & dir res, Heart & Lung Inst, 1985-1989; from assoc prof to prof surg, Mayo Med Sch, Univ Minn, 1974-1985; dir cardiovasc res, Mayo Clin, 1974-1985; sci dir artificial heart prog, Res Inst, Ill Inst Technol, 1971-1974; adj assoc prof physiol, Loyola Univ, 1971-1974; Assoc thoracic & cardiovasc, Cook County Hosp, Chicago, 1967-1974; from asst prof to assoc prof surg & physiol, Med Ctr, 1967-1971; Clin assoc physiol, Stritch Sch Med, Loyola Univ, 1961-1962. **Memberships:** Am Asn Thoracic Surg; Am Col Surg; Am Col Cardiol; Int Soc Heart Transplantation; Am Physiol Soc; Soc Thoracic Surg. **Research Statement & Publications:** Cardiovascular surgery and physiology; neural control of the heart. **Mailing Address:** 10079 Norell Ave N, Stillwater, MN 55082.

KAYE, NANCY WEBER, EMBRYOLOGY, ANIMAL PHYSIOLOGY. **Personal Data:** b Englewood, NJ, September 14, 1929; m 1956, Gordon; c Jacqueline & Vivienne. **Education:** Swarthmore Col, BA, 1951; Hunter Col, MEd, 1954; Columbia Univ, MA, 1958, PhD (zoology), 1960. **Professional Experience:** Asst secy, Waste Reduction by Waste by Waste Reduction, Inc, 1993-; consults, EM Consult Serv, 1990-; CONSULT, DEPT MED, ALBANY MED COL, 1989-; vis lectr, dept Biol, Rensselaer Polytech inst, 1984; res asst prof, dept Med, 1982-1989; asst prof, dept Anat, 1982-1989; res assoc, Albany Med Col, 1976-1982; res worker, Col Physicians & Surgeons, Columbia Univ, 1962-1976; fel neuroanat, Columbia Univ, 1960-1961. **Memberships:** Sigma Xi; AAAS; Am Soc Cell Biol; Asn Res Vision & Ophthal; Am Asn Anatomists; NY Acad Sci. **Research Statement & Publications:** Spleen and liver pathobiology and fine structure; gene mapping connective tissue genes; fine structure of connective tissue; corneal fine structure and physiology. **Mailing Address:** 212 Pinewoods Ave, Troy, NY 12180. **Fax:** 518-271-2040.

KAYE, NORMAN JOSEPH, applied business statistics, math applied to business; deceased, see previous edition for last biography

KAYE, ROBERT, PEDIATRICS. **Personal Data:** b New York, NY, July 17, 1917; m 1942, c 3. **Education:** Johns Hopkins Univ, AB, 1939, MD, 1943. **Professional Experience:** PROF PEDIAT & CHMN DEPT, HAHNEMANN MED COL & HOSP, 1973-; chmn, Nat Med Adv Bd, Juvenile Diabetes Found, 1973-1976; asst chmn dept, Sch Med, Univ Pa, 1964-1973; dep physician-in-chief, Children's Hosp, 1964; dir clins & clin teaching, Children's Hosp, 1952-1957; sr physician, Children's Hosp, 1951-; from asst prof to prof, Sch Med, Univ Pa, 1951-1973; assoc, Sch Med, Univ Pa, 1950-1951; asst physician, Children's Hosp, 1948-1951; instr pediat, Sch Med, Univ Pa, 1948-1950; assoc physiol, Sch Pub Health, Harvard Univ, 1946-1947; asst, Harvard Med Sch, 1946-1947; instr, Med Sch, Johns Hopkins Univ, 1945; from intern to chief resident pediat, Johns Hopkins Hosp, 1943-1945. **Memberships:** AAAS; Am Pediat Soc; Soc Pediat Res; AMA; Am Diabetes Asn. **Research Statement & Publications:** Nutrition and metabolism. **Mailing Address:** 34 Civic Ctr Blvd, Philadelphia, PA 19104.

KAYE, SAMUEL, ORGANIC CHEMISTRY. **Personal Data:** b Canton, Ohio, December 18, 1917; m 1941, Aline; c Donald, Michael, Robert & Ellen. **Education:** Mt Union Col, BS, 1940; Ohio State Univ, MS, 1941, PhD (chem), 1948. **Professional Experience:** RETIRED; consult, Space Sci Dept, Gen Dynamics/Convair, 1981-1983; staff scientist, Space Sci Dept, Gen Dynamics/Convair, 1957-1981; tech specialist, Aerojet Gen Corp, 1956-1957; aeronaut res scientist chem, Nat Adv Comt Aeronaut, 1948-1956; inspector powder & explosives, Ind Ord Works, 1942; anal chemist, Repub Steel Corp, 1941. **Memberships:** Am Chem Soc; Am Inst Aeronaut & Astronaut; Fel Am Inst Chem; Combustion Inst. **Research Statement & Publications:** Pollution detection; materials sciences; space manufacturing; high energy propellants. **Mailing Address:** 5626 Albalone Pl, La Jolla, CA 92037-7501.

KAYE, SAUL, sterilization, asepsis; deceased, see previous edition for last biography

KAYE, SIDNEY, TOXICOLOGY. **Personal Data:** b Brooklyn, NY, March 10, 1912; m 1951, Carmen M; c Cynthia & Frederic. **Education:** NY Univ, BS, 1935, MSc, 1939; Med Col Va, PhD (pharmacol), 1956; Am Bd Clin Chem, dipl, 1952; Nat Registry Clin Chem, cert, 1968. **Honors & Awards:** Award of Merit, Am Acad Forensic Soc, 1973, Gettler Outstanding Achievement Medal, 1985; Milton Helpern Award, Nat Asn Med Examnrs, 1989. **Professional Experience:** RETIRED; emer prof pharmacol, Toxicol & Path, 1982; exec res liaison officer, Defense Civil Prep Agency, Fed Emergency Mgt Admin, Dept Defense, 1973-; USAF Hosp, 1971-1975 & USN Hosp, 1971-1982; emer consult toxicol, Dept of US Army, 1970-; Vet Admin Hosp, San Juan, 1969-; coordr poison control ctrs, Community PR, 1964-1984; consult toxicologist, Vet Admin Hosp, Richmond, US Army Hosp, San Juan, 1964-1970; prof toxicol, Pharmacol and Legal med & assoc dir, Inst Legal Med, Univ PR, San Juan, 1962-1982; lectr, Armed Forces Inst Path, 1958-1962 & 1971; dir, Richmond Poison Control Ctr, 1958-1962; mem subcomt alcohol & drugs, Nat Safety Coun, 1952-; toxicologist & dir toxicol labs, Off Chief Med Exam, Va, 1947-1962; from asst prof to assoc prof, Med Col Va, 1947-1962; instr path, Wash Univ, Sch Med, 1946-1947; Toxicologist & assoc dir, Sci Crime Detection Lab, St Louis Police Dept, 1946-1947; res asst toxicol lab, City Off Chief Med Exam, New York, 1938-1941; Teaching fel, NY Univ, 1935-1938. **Memberships:** Assoc fel Am Soc Clin Path; Asn Mil Surg US; Soc Toxicol; Pan Am Med Asn; Sigma Xi; fel Am Acad Forensic Sci. **Research Statement & Publications:** Analytical method for detection of lead poisoning; identification of seminal stains; diagnosis of poisoning; alcohol and its effects on man. **Mailing Address:** Med Sch Univ PR, PO Box 865067, San Juan, PR 00936-5067. **Fax:** 787-754-0710. **E-Mail:** skaye@rcm.upr.edu

KAYE, STEPHEN VINCENT, HEALTH PHYSICS, RADIOECOLOGY. **Personal Data:** b Rahway, NJ, September 17, 1935; m 1959, c 3. **Education:** Rutgers Univ, BS, 1957; NC State Univ, MS, 1959; Univ Rochester, PhD (radiation biol), 1966. **Professional Experience:** MFR REP, APPALACHIAN ENVIRON EQUIP INC, as of 2001; gen mgr, Anal Corp, beginning 1993; consult, US Vet Admin, 1990-; div dir, Biol Div, 1987-1988; mem, Tech Adv, Fla Phosphate Res Inst, 1986-1987; mem, Environ Protection Agency High Level

Radioactive Waste Comt, Sci Adv Bd, 1982-1984; mem support group to develop proc guide for probabilistic risk assessment, Inst Elec & Electronics Engrs, Am Nuclear Soc, Nuclear Regulatory Comn, & nuclear indust, 1981-1982; div dir, Health & Safety Res, 1977-1992; chmn radiol data working group, US Dept Energy Reactor Safety Data Coord Group, 1976-1979; mem nuclear fuel subgroup, Comt Nuclear & Alternative Energy Systs, Nat Res Coun, 1976-1978; sect head radiol assessments, Environ Sci Div, 1975-1977; proj supvr environ impacts, Environ Sci Div, 1973-1975; Adv health physics fel, Univ Rochester, 1963-1966; Res staff health physics & radioecol, Ecol Div & Health Physics Div, Oak Ridge Nat Labs, 1960-1972. **Memberships:** Health Physics Soc; Soc Risk Anal; Am Nuclear Soc; Sigma Xi; AAAS. **Research Statement & Publications:** Transport of radionuclides in the environment and estimation of dose to man from ingestion or external exposure; assessments and comparisons of health and environmental issues related to all energy technologies. **Mailing Address:** Appalachian Environ Equip, 109 Timberline Dr, Kingston, TN 37763. **Fax:** 865-376-5667. **E-Mail:** svkaye@usit.net

KAYE, WILBUR (IRVING), CHEMISTRY, INSTRUMENTATION. **Personal Data:** b Pelham Manor, NY, January 28, 1922; m 1944, Virginia; c Roy A & Elsa K (Campbell). **Education:** Stetson Univ, BS, 1942; Univ Ill, PhD (chem), 1945. **Professional Experience:** RETIRED; prin staff scientist, Irvine, 1980-1987; sr scientist, Corp Res Activ, 1973-1980; dir sci res, Corp Res Activ, 1968-1973; dir res, Sci Instruments Div, Beckman Instruments, Inc, Fullerton, 1956-1968; sr res chemist, Tenn Eastman Corp, 1945-1955; asst chem, Univ Ill, 1942-1944; Beckman fel; consult. **Memberships:** Am Chem Soc; Optical Soc Am; Soc Appl Spectros; fel AAAS. **Research Statement & Publications:** Infrared and ultraviolet spectroscopy; chromatography; instrument development. **Mailing Address:** PO Box 3034, Princeville, HI 96722.

KAYES, STEPHEN GEOFFREY, IMMUNOPARASITOLOGY. **Personal Data:** b Madison, Wis, May 1, 1946. **Education:** Univ Wis-Madison, BS, 1971; Tulane Univ, MS, 1973; Univ Iowa, PhD (anat), 1977. **Professional Experience:** PROF, DEPT MICROBIOL, UNIV S ALA, 1991-; PROF, DEPT STRUCT & CELLULAR BIOL, UNIV S ALA, 1990-; from asst prof to assoc prof, Univ S Ala, 1981-1991; asst prof neuroanat, Dept Anat & asst prof parasitol, 1981-1987; Res assoc, Vet Admin Med Ctr, 1977-1981; Fel immunol, Sch Med, Vanderbilt Univ, 1977-1981. **Memberships:** Am Soc Trop Med & Hyg; Am Soc Parasitologists; AAAS; Am Assoc Anat; Am Asn Immunol. **Research Statement & Publications:** Immunologic basis of the host-parasite relationship by correlation of the host's immune status with the pathology elicited by the parasite. **Mailing Address:** Dept Struct & Cellular Biol, Univ S Ala, Rm 2042 MSB, Mobile, AL 36688-0002. **Fax:** 251-460-6771. **E-Mail:** kayes@sungcg.usouthal.edu

KAYHART, MARION, GENETICS. **Personal Data:** b Butler, NJ, September 14, 1926. **Education:** Drew Univ, BA, 1947; Univ Pa, MA, 1949, PhD (zoology), 1954. **Professional Experience:** PROF EMER BIOL, CEDAR CREST COL, as of 2004; prof biol & chmn dept, Cedar Crest Col, beginning 1957; from asst prof to assoc prof, Cedar Crest Col, 1954-1957; from instr to asst prof biol, Roanoke Col, 1949-1952. **Memberships:** AAAS; Genetics Soc Am; Nat Asn Biol Teachers; Sigma Xi. **Research Statement & Publications:** Radiation genetics. **Mailing Address:** Dept Biol, Cedar Crest Col, 100 Col Dr Curtis Hall, Allentown, PA 18104. **Fax:** 610-740-3764.

KAYLL, ALBERT JAMES, FORESTRY. **Personal Data:** b Vancouver, BC, January 21, 1935; m 1962, c 2. **Education:** Univ BC, BSF, 1959; Duke Univ, MF, 1960; Aberdeen Univ, PhD (fire ecol), 1964. **Honors & Awards:** H R MacMillan Prize, 1959. **Professional Experience:** PROF EMER FORESTRY, LAKEHEAD UNIV, as of 2004; Can Forestry Accreditation Bd, 1989-; prof, Lakehead Univ, beginning 1987; prof & dir, Sch Forestry, 1981-1987; prof fire ecol & chmn, Dept Forest Resources, 1977-1980; actg chmn, Dept Forest Resources, 1975-1976; Mem fire mgt working group, NAm Forestry Comn, Food & Agr Orgn, UN, 1973-1975; assoc prof fire ecol, Dept Forest Resources, 1971-1977; co-dir, Fire Sci Ctr, 1970-1978; asst prof fire ecol, Univ NB, 1968-1971; Res scientist fire ecol, Can Dept Forestry, 1960-1968. **Memberships:** Soc Am Foresters; Can Inst Forestry (pres 1987-1988); Asn Univ Forestry Schs Can. **Research Statement & Publications:** Ecological and physiological effects of fire on forest vegetation. **Mailing Address:** Sch Forestry, Lakehead Univ, 955 Oliver Rd, Thunder Bay, ON P7B 5E1, Can. **Fax:** 807-343-8023.

KAYLOR, HOYT MCCOY, OPTICAL PHYSICS. **Personal Data:** b Alexander City, Ala, August 17, 1923; m 1957, c 2. **Education:** Birmingham-Southern Col, BS, 1943; Univ Tenn, MS, 1949, PhD (physics), 1953. **Professional Experience:** PROF EMER PHYSICS & MATH, BIRMINGHAM-SOUTHERN COL, as of 2003; prof physics & math, Birmingham-Southern Col, 1981-1889; prof physics, 1958-1981; assoc prof, 1952-1958. **Memberships:** Fel AAAS; Am Phys Soc; Optical Soc Am; Am Asn Physics Teachers. **Research Statement & Publications:** High dispersion infrared spectroscopy; physical properties of optical materials. **Mailing Address:** Dept Sci & Math, Birmingham-Southern Col, 900 Arkadelphia Rd, Birmingham, AL 35254.

KAYNE, FREDRICK JAY, BIOCHEMISTRY, CLINICAL CHEMISTRY. **Personal Data:** b Washington, DC, January 19, 1941; m 1965, Marlene; c Jonathan. **Education:** Ill Inst Technol, BS, 1962; Mich State Univ, PhD (biochem), 1966. **Professional Experience:** PROF PATH & LAB MED, MED COL HOSP, DREXEL UNIV, as of 2005; Fulbright res fel, Max Planck Inst Biophys, 1985-1986; assoc prof path & lab med, Hahnemann Med Col, beginning 1977; assoc prof biochem & biophys, Univ Pa, 1974-1977; asst prof phys biochem, Johnson Res Found, 1969-1974; res assoc phys chem, Max Planck Inst Phys Chem, 1967-1969; NATO fel, Max Planck Inst Phys Chem, 1967. **Memberships:** Am Asn Clin Chemists; Am Soc Biochem & Molecular Biol. **Research Statement & Publications:** Enzyme mechanisms; chemical relaxation; clinical chemistry; laboratory medicine. **Mailing Address:** Dept Path, Med Col Hosp Drexel Univ, 3300 Henry Ave, Philadelphia, PA 19129. **Fax:** 215-246-5433. **E-Mail:** fredrick.kayne@drexel.edu

KAYNE, HERBERT LAWRENCE, PHYSIOLOGY. **Personal Data:** b Chicago, Ill, September 22, 1934; m 1962, c 2. **Education:** Univ Ill, BS, 1955, MS, 1958, PhD (physiol), 1962. **Professional Experience:** ASSOC PROF PUBLIC HEALTH, SCH PUB HEALTH, as of 2003; ASSOC PROF PHYSIOL, SCH MED, BOSTON UNIV, 1969-; From instr to asst prof, 1962-1969. **Memberships:** Am Physiol Soc; Biomet Soc. **Research Statement & Publications:** Biostatistics. **Mailing Address:** Dept Physiol, Boston Univ Sch Med 80 E Conard St, Boston, MA 02118-2307.

KAYNE, MARLENE STEINMETZ, BIOCHEMISTRY, MOLECULAR BIOLOGY. **Personal Data:** b Bronx, NY, July 6, 1941; m 1965. **Education:** St John's Univ, BS, 1962; Mich State Univ, PhD (biochem), 1966. **Professional Experience:** Fulbright fel, Wolfgang Goethe Univ, Frankfurt, Ger, 1985-1986; PROF MOLECULAR BIOL COL NJ, 1977-; asst prof molecular biol & chmn dept biol, Trenton State Col, beginning 1977; NSF res grants, 1976-1977, 1978-; res assoc, Biol Dept, Univ Pa, 1975-1977; res assoc enzym, Dept Biol, 1974-1977; res assoc, Johnson res Found, Univ Pa, 1970-1974; res assoc enzym, Dept Biophysics, Univ Pa, 1970-1974; ger Res Asn fel, 1967-1969; fel immunol, Max Planck Inst Exp Med, 1967-1969; Teaching Asst, Biochem Dept, Mich State Univ 1962-1964. **Memberships:** Sigma Xi. **Research Statement & Publications:** Purification and characterization of procaryotic enzymes required in protein biosynthesis. **Mailing Address:** Dept Biol, Col NJ, Biol Bldg 241 PO Box 7718, Ewing, NJ 08628-0718. **E-Mail:** mkayne@tcnj.edu

KAYS, M ALLAN, GEOLOGY, PETROLOGY. **Personal Data:** b Princeton, Ind, May 13, 1934; m 1955, Dorothy Tucker; c David, Timothy & Mary. **Education:** Southern Ill Univ, BA, 1956; Univ Washington, St Louis, MA, 1958, PhD (geol), 1961. **Professional Experience:** PROF EMER GEOL SCI, UNIV ORE, as of 1996; prof geol sci, Univ Ore, beginning 1980; part-time geologist, US Geol Surv, 1979, 1980; vis geologist, Precambrian Geol Div, Dept Mineral Resources, Prov Sask, Can, 1970-1971; From asst prof to assoc prof, Univ Ore, 1961-1980. **Memberships:** Am Geophys Union; Geol Soc Am; Am Asn Univ Prof. **Research Statement & Publications:** Petrology of xenoliths and their fused products in margins of basic intrusions; petrology and structural relations of Archaean supracrustal metamorphic and plutonic rocks, East Greenland; petrology of migmatized gneisses of Canada, Finland and East Greenland; metamorphism and structure of convergent plate marginal sequences in cordillera of western North America. **Mailing Address:** Dept Geol Sci, Univ Ore, Eugene, OR 97403-1272. **Fax:** 541-346-4692. **E-Mail:** makays@oregon.uoregon.edu

KAYS, STANLEY J, HORTICULTURE, VEGETABLE CROP PHYSIOLOGY. **Personal Data:** b Stillwater, Okla, February 3, 1945. **Education:** Okla State Univ, BS, 1968; Mich State Univ, MS, 1969, PhD (hort), 1971. **Professional Experience:** PROF, DEPT HORT, UNIV GA, as of 2006; Sci Educ Adm, AID 1986; Sci Educ Adm, USDA, 1981; Grants, Woolfolk Chem Works Inc, 1978; Grants, Gilroy Foods Inc, 1978; assoc prof veg crops & post-harvest, dept hort, Univ GA, beginning 1977; assoc prof, Dept Hort Food Sci, Univ Ark, 1976-1977; Grants, Nat Pecan Shellers, 1976; asst prof veg crops, Dept Hort, Univ Ga, Tifton, 1973-1975; researcher, Sch Plant Biol, Univ Col Northern Wales, UK, 1971-1972; researcher plant biol, Dept Biol, Tex A&M Univ, 1971; vis scientist, Dept Appl Biol, Cambridge Univ, Cambridge, Eng; vis scholar, Wolfson Col, Cambridge. **Memberships:** Am Soc Hort Sci; Int Hort Soc; AAAS; Int Trop Root Crops Soc; Sigma Xi. **Research Statement & Publications:** Developmental and post-harvest physiology of vegetable crops. **Mailing Address:** Dept Hort, Univ Ga Col Agr & Environ Sci, 1111 Plant Sci Bldg, Athens, GA 30602-7273. **Fax:** 706-542-0624. **E-Mail:** kaysstan@uga.edu

KAYS, WILLIAM MORROW, MECHANICAL ENGINEERING. **Personal Data:** b Norfolk, Va, July 29, 1920; m 1983, Judith; c Nancy, Leslie, Margaret & Elizabeth. **Education:** Stanford Univ, AB, 1942, MS, 1947, PhD (mech eng), 1951. **Honors & Awards:** Am Soc Mech Engrs Mem Award, 1965; Max Jacob Award, 1992. **Professional Experience:** PROF EMER, DEPT MECH ENG, STANFORD UNIV, as of 2003; dean eng, from asst prof to assoc prof, 1972-1984; NSF sr fel, 1966-1967; head dept, from asst prof to assoc prof, 1961-1972; fulbright lectr, Imp Col London, 1959-1960; prof mech Eng, Stanford Univ, beginning 1957; from asst prof to assoc prof, Stanford Univ, 1951-1957; res assoc, Stanford Univ, 1947-1951. **Memberships:** Nat Acad Eng; Fel Am Soc Mech Engrs; fel Am Soc Eng Educ. **Research Statement & Publications:** Heat transfer to fluids, especially turbulent boundary layers. **Mailing Address:** Dept Mech Eng, Stanford Univ, Stanford, CA 94305. **E-Mail:** kays@sierra.stanford.edu

KAYSER, BORIS JULES, THEORETICAL ELEMENTARY PARTICLE PHYSICS. **Personal Data:** b New York, NY, June 2, 1938; m 1960. **Education:** Princeton Univ, AB, 1960; Calif Inst Technol, PhD (physics), 1964. **Professional Experience:** PROG DIR THEORET PHYSICS, NSF, 1975-; assoc prog dir theoret physics, NSF, 1972-1975; asst prof, Northwestern Univ, Evanston, 1969-1974; asst prof, State Univ NY Stony Brook, 1966-1969; res assoc physics, Univ Calif, Berkeley, 1964-1966. **Memberships:** fel Am Phys Soc. **Research Statement & Publications:** Weak interactions. **Mailing Address:** Physics Div, NSF, Rm 1015N 4201 Wilson Blvd, Arlington, VA 22230. **E-Mail:** bkayser@nsf.gov

KAYSER, RICHARD FRANCIS, TECHNICAL MANAGEMENT. **Personal Data:** b Toledo, Ohio, February 24, 1925; m 1950, c 9. **Education:** Univ Cincinnati, PhD (chem eng), 1952. **Professional Experience:** ACTG DEP DIR CTR CHEM TECHNOL, NAT BUR STAND & TECHNOL, GAITHERSBURG, as of 2002; VPRES TECHNOL, ETHYLENE OXIDE/GLYCOL DIV, beginning 1980; dir, Res & Develop, Chem & Plastics Div, 1974-1980; opers mgr, Silicones Div, 1972-1974; prod mgr, Silicones Div, 1965-1972; engr, Linde Div, Union Carbide Corp, 1952-1965. **Memberships:** Sigma Xi. **Research Statement & Publications:** Silicones processes; low pressure oxo process and oxo alcohols; new ethylene oxide catalyst developments. **Mailing Address:** Nat Inst Stand & Technol, A111 Phys Bldg, Gaithersburg, MD 20899.

KAYSER, ROBERT HELMUT, Hazardous Waste Evaluation, Regulatory Experience. **Personal Data:** b Orange, NJ, August 21, 1948; m 1972, c 2. **Education:** Stevens Inst Technol, BS, 1970; Georgetown Univ, PhD (org chem), 1975. **Professional Experience:** US ENVIRON PROTECTION AGENCY, Office of Solid Waste, Wash, DC, 1980-; res assoc bio-org chem, Univ Md, Baltimore County, 1974-1980; Res asst org chem, Georgetown Univ, 1974. **Memberships:** Am Chem Soc. **Research Statement & Publications:** Hazardous Waste evaluation; organic mechanisms. **Mailing Address:** US Environ Protection Agency, Mail Code 5304W, 1200 Pa Ave, NW, Washington, DC 20460. **E-Mail:** kayser.robert@epamail.epa.gov

KAYTON, MYRON, VEHICLE SYSTEM DESIGN, VEHICLE ELECTRONICS, CONTROL OF INDUSTRIAL MACHINERY. **Personal Data:** b New York, NY, 1934; m Paula; c Elizabeth & Susan. **Education:** Cooper Union, BS, 1955; Harvard Univ, SM, 1956; Mass Inst Technol, PhD (instrumentation), 1960. **Honors & Awards:** Gano Dunn Medal, Cooper Union, 1975; M B Carlton Award, Inst Elec & Electronics Engrs, 1988; Millennium Medal, Inst Elect, Inst Elect & Elec Engr, 2000. **Professional Experience:** Dir, Electronic Conventions Inc 2000-2001; Bd Dir of, Inst Elec & Electronics Engrs, 1996-1997; Pres, Aerospace & Electronic Systs Soc, Inst Elec & Electronics Engrs, 1993-1994; distinguished lectr, Aerospace & Electronic Systs Soc, Inst Elec & Electronics Engrs, 1988-; PRES, KAYTON ENG CO, 1981-; Lectr, Univ Calif, Los Angeles, 1969-1988; sr staff mem, TRW Defense & Space Sector, 1969-1981; mgr, NASA Space Ctr, 1965-1969; sect head, Guid & Control Div, Litton, 1960-1965; res asst navig systs, Draper Lab, Mass Inst Technol, 1958-1960; Design engr, Res & Develop Div, Avco, 1956-1958. **Memberships:** Life Fellow Inst Electrical and Electronics Engrs; Am Soc Mech Engrs Life Mem; Inst Navig mem; Soc Automotive Engrs. **Research Statement & Publications:** Electronic system design and testing for high-value vehicles and plants, emphasizing navigation, communications, control, fault-tolerance; authored books, articles and 70 technical papers. **Mailing Address:** Kayton Eng Co, PO Box 802, Santa Monica, CA 90406. **E-Mail:** m.kayton@ieee.org

KAZAHAYA, MASAHIRO MATT, MANAGING EXPERIENCE OF RESEARCH & DEVELOPMENT ENGINEERS, COMPUTER-TO-COMPUTER COMMUNICATION. **Per-**

sonal Data: b Yonago, Japan, January 24, 1932; American citizen; m 1960, c 3. **Education:** Okayama Univ-Japan, BS, 1954, PhD (technol), 1989; Univ Pa, MBA, 1977. **Professional Experience:** Vpres technol Mkt & Strategy, Fischer & Porter co, Warminster, Pa, beginning 1991; voting mem & US Rep, Int Electro-Tech Comn, SC65 WG6 Comt, 1986-; voting mem, SP50 Fieldbu Standard Making Comt, Instrument Soc Am, 1985-; Dir res, Fischer & Porter CO, Warminster, PA, 1985-1991; lectr corp planning, Wharton Grad Sch, Univ Pa, 1978-1989. **Memberships:** Sr mem Instrument Soc Am; sr mem Inst Elec & Electronics Engrs; Soc Mfg Engrs. **Research Statement & Publications:** Develop new measuring instruments and control systems; corporate planning and business modeling. **Mailing Address:** Fisher & Porter Co, Co Line Rd, Warminster, PA 18974.

KAZAKIA, JACOB YAKOVOS, APPLIED MECHANICS. **Personal Data:** b Istanbul, Turkey, February 27, 1945; American citizen; m 1972, c 2. **Education:** Istanbul Tech Univ, MS, 1968; Lehigh Univ, PhD (appl mech), 1972. **Professional Experience:** PROF ENG MATH & MECH, LEHIGH UNIV, 1989-; assoc prof Dept Mech Eng & Mech, Dept Math, Lehigh Univ, 1983-1989; from asst prof to assoc prof, Ctr Appln Math, Lehigh Univ, 1974-1979; from res asst to res assoc, Ctr Appln Math, Lehigh Univ, 1969-1972. **Memberships:** Am Acad Mech; Am Soc Mech Engrs. **Research Statement & Publications:** Nonlinear wave propagation in fluids; viscoelastic fluid flows; stability of liquid filled shells; run-up and spin-up problems. **Mailing Address:** Dept Mech Eng & Mech, Lehigh Univ, Packard Lab 19 Mem Dr W, Bethlehem, PA 18015. **Fax:** 610-758-6224. **E-Mail:** jyk0@lehigh.edu

KAZAKS, PETER ALEXANDER, SCATTERING THEORY IN LOW & HIGH ENERGY PHYSICS. **Personal Data:** b Riga, Latvia, February 22, 1940; American citizen; m 1968, c 6. **Education:** McGill Univ, BSc, 1962; Yale Univ, MS, 1963; Univ Calif, Davis, PhD (physics), 1968. **Professional Experience:** RETIRED; prof physics, Univ Sfla, beginning 1980; vis scholar, Harvard Univ, 1991 & 1996; vis prof/scholar, Univ Pa, 1985; chmn, Div Natural Sci, New Col, Univ SFla, 1980-1985; Res Corp grant, 1975; asst prof, Univ Sfla, 1973-1975; NSF grant, St Lawrence Univ, 1971-1972; NSF res partic, Univ Fla, 1971; asst prof physics, St Lawrence Univ, 1970-1973; res assoc, Ohio Univ, 1968-1970. **Memberships:** Am Phys Soc. **Research Statement & Publications:** Three-body models of nuclear reactions; electron-atom collision collisions; pion-nucleus scattering; proton-proton scattering; spin physics. **Mailing Address:** Div Nat Sci, New Col Univ SFla, Sarasota, FL 34243.

KAZAL, LOUIS ANTHONY, BIOCHEMISTRY, HEMATOLOGY. **Personal Data:** b Newark, NJ, July 2, 1912; m 1942, Marie T Barry; c Marianne K (Livingston), Susan K (Bove), Alicia K (Ricci) & Louis A Kazal, Jr. **Education:** Seton Hall Col, BS, 1935; Rutgers Univ, PhD (biochem, physiol), 1940. **Honors & Awards:** Co-recipient Rorer Award, Am J Gastroenterol, 1966. **Professional Experience:** HON PROF PHYSIOL & HON ASSOC PROF MED, JEFFERSON MED COL, THOMAS JEFFERSON UNIV, 1978-; prof physiol, Col Grad Studies, 1970-1978; Chmn blood coagulation sessions, Fed Am Soc Exp Biol, 1963-1968; assoc prof med & assoc dir Cardeza Found Hemat Res, Cardeza Found, Jefferson Med Col, 1960-1978; from asst prof to prof physiol, Cardeza Found, Jefferson Med Col, 1957-1978; head sect blood plasma fractionation, Cardeza Found, Jefferson Med Col, 1956-1960; tech asst to med dir, Merck Sharp & Dohme Inc, 1955-1956; mgr tech info, Merck Sharp & Dohme Inc, 1954-1955; dir biol develop, Merck Sharp & Dohme Inc, 1950-1954; res biochemist, Merck Sharp & Dohme Inc, 1940-1950; Asst physiol & biochem, Rutgers Univ, 1937-1940. **Memberships:** Am Chem Soc; emer mem Soc Exp Biol & Med; emer emer mem mem Am Soc Biol Chem; fel NY Acad Sci; emer mem Int Soc Thrombosis & Homeostasis; emer mem fel AAAS; emer mem Sigma Xi (Club, Jetterson Med Col, pres, 1967); Asn Clin Scientists, 1971-1979 Editorial Board. **Research Statement & Publications:** Blood coagulation; proteins; blood group specific substances; ion-exchange resins; erythropoietin inhibitors; lipids; trypsin inhibitor; isolation and crystalization of Kazal pancreatic secretory trypsin inhibitor; gastric juice and saliva thromboplastin; fibrinogen-glycine; human typing serum; author of numerous publications and recipient of one US patent. **Mailing Address:** 18215 Organ Pipe Dr, Sun City, AZ 85373-1773.

KAZAN, BENJAMIN, MEDICAL PHYSICS. **Personal Data:** b New York, NY, May 8, 1917; div, c David L. **Education:** Calif Inst Technol, BS, 1938; Columbia Univ, MA, 1940; Munich Tech Univ, Dr rer nat, 1961. **Honors & Awards:** Silver Medal, Am Roentgen Ray Soc, 1957; Coolidge Award, Gen Elec Co, 1958. **Professional Experience:** CONSULT, 1984-; assoc ed, Advan Electronics & Electron Physics, beginning 1985 & Inst Elec & Electronics Engrs, Trans Electron Devices, 1978-1984; head, Display Group, Xerox Corp, 1974-1984; consult adv group electron devices, Defense Dept, 1973-1982; ed, Advan Image Pickup & Display, 1972-1984; adj prof, Univ RI, 1970-1974; mgr explor display dept, Thomas J Watson Res Ctr, IBM Corp, 1968-1974; chief scientist aerospace electronics div, Electro-Optical Systs, Inc, 1961-1968; head solid-state display sect, Res Labs, Hughes Aircraft Co, 1958-1961; physicist, RCA Labs, 1950-1958; chief spec purpose tube sect, Signal Corps Eng Labs, 1944-1950; radio engr, Signal Corps Eng Labs, 1940-1944. **Memberships:** Sigma Xi; Am Phys Soc; fel Inst Elec & Electronics Engrs; fel Soc Info Display. **Research Statement & Publications:** Research and development on new types of electronic devices for image pickup; wavelength conversion and display purposes, based on solid-state, electron-beam and gas-plasma phenomena. **Mailing Address:** 800 Blossom Hill Rd, Los Gatos, CA 95032.

KAZANJIAN, ARMEN ROUPEN, PHYSICAL CHEMISTRY. **Personal Data:** b New Haven, Conn, February 13, 1928; m 1962, c 3. **Education:** Northeastern Univ, BS, 1951; Univ Calif, Los Angeles, PhD (phys chem), 1965. **Professional Experience:** RETIRED; res chemist, Rocky Flats Div, Rockwell Int, 1975-1990; res chemist, Rocky Flats Div, Dow Chem Co, 1966-1975; res chemist, Rocket Power Inc, 1966; res chemist, Rocketdyne Div, NAm Aviation Inc, 1956-1960; chemist, Raw Mat Develop Lab, AEC, 1951-1956. **Memberships:** AAAS; Radiation Res Soc; Sigma Xi; Nuclear Soc Am. **Research Statement & Publications:** Chemical effects of nuclear transformations; radiation chemistry; plutonium chemistry. **Mailing Address:** 1596 Snee-Oosh Rd, La Conner, WA 98257.

KAZARIAN, LEON EDWARD, BIOMECHANICS. **Personal Data:** b Norwalk, Conn. **Education:** Northrop Inst Technol, BS, 1966; Karolinska Inst, Sweden, Dr (orthop biomech), 1972. **Professional Experience:** RETIRED; res scientist biomech, Aerospace Med Res Labs, Wright Patterson AFB, 1967-1991. **Memberships:** Orthop Res Soc; Aerospace Med Asn. **Research Statement & Publications:** Hard and soft tissue mechanics as related to dynamic environments. **Mailing Address:** 1062 Geneva Rd, Beaver Creek, OH 45385.

KAZARINOFF, MICHAEL N, BIOCHEMISTRY. **Personal Data:** b Ann Arbor, Mich, March 24, 1949; m 1970, c 3. **Education:** Yale Univ, BS, 1970; Cornell Univ, PhD (biochem), 1975. **Professional Experience:** Assoc dir, Pew Nat Nutrit Prog, 1987-1993; actg Dir, Div Nutrit Sci, Cornell Univ, 1987-1988; ASSOC PROF NUTRIT SCI, CORNELL UNIV, 1985-; asst prof, Cornell Univ, 1978-1984; fel microbiol, Univ Tex, Austin, 1976-1978; fel biochem, Univ Calif, Berkeley, 1975-1976. **Memberships:** Am Chem Soc; AAAS; Am Inst Nutrit; Am Soc Biol Chem. **Research Statement & Publications:** Enzymology; protein-coenzyme interactions; protein turnover; coenzyme mechanisms; purification and properties of enzymes of vitamin metabolism; nutrition and cancer. **Mailing Address:** Div Nutrit Sci, Col Human Ecol, Cornell Univ, 230 Savage Hall, Ithaca, NY 14853. **Fax:** 607-255-1033. **E-Mail:** mnk1@cornell.edu

KAZAZIAN, HAIG H, PEDIATRIC GENETICS, HUMAN MOLECULAR GENETICS. **Personal Data:** b Toledo, Ohio, July 30, 1937. **Education:** Dartmouth Col, BA, 1959; Johns Hopkins Univ, MD, 1962. **Honors & Awards:** Mead Johnson Award, Am Acad Pediat, 1976. **Professional Experience:** SEYMOUR GREY PROF MOLECULAR MED GENETICS & CHMN, DEPT GENETICS, UNIV PA, PHILADELPHIA, 1994-; dir, Ctr Med Genetics, 1989-1993; prof med, Johns Hopkins Univ, 1988-1994; prof obstet & gynec, Johns Hopkins Univ, 1985-1994; prof biol, Johns Hopkins Univ, 1982-1994; from asst prof to assoc prof pediat, Johns Hopkins Univ, 1969-1994; pediat genetics residency, Johns Hopkins Univ, 1968-1969; staff assoc, NIH, 1966-1968; fel genetics, Johns Hopkins Univ, 1964-1968; pediat intern, Univ Minn, 1962-1964. **Memberships:** Inst Med-Nat Acad Sci; Am Pediat Soc; Am Soc Clin Invest; Am Soc Human Genetics; Asn Am Physicians. **Mailing Address:** Dept Genetics, Univ Pa, 475 Clin Res Bldg 412 Curie Blvd, Philadelphia, PA 19104-6145. **Fax:** 215-573-7760. **E-Mail:** kazazian@mail.med.upenn.edu

KAZDA, LOUIS F(RANK), ELECTRICAL ENGINEERING. **Personal Data:** b Dayton, Ohio, September 21, 1916; m 1940, Jane; c Judith, Sally & Joan. **Education:** Univ Cincinnati, EE, 1940, MSE, 1943; Syracuse Univ, PhD (elec eng), 1962. **Professional Experience:** PROF ELEC & COMPUT ENG, UNIV MICH, ANN ARBOR, 1981-; Conduction Corp, 1963; Ford Motor Co, 1962; prof elec eng, Univ Mich, Ann Arbor, 1960-1981; Willow Run Labs, Clark Equipment Co, 1960-1962; Willow Run Labs, Maxitrol Corp, 1958-1968; Willow Run Labs, USAF, 1957-1959; Willow Run Labs, Mich, 1954-; consult, Cook Res Labs, 1951-1953; from instr to assoc prof, Univ Mich, Ann Arbor, 1947-1960; res & develop engr elec eng, Bendix Aviation Corp, 1943-1946. **Memberships:** AAAS; fel Inst Elec & Electronics Engrs; Sigma Xi; Rotary International Fel. **Research Statement & Publications:** Feedback control systems of linear, nonlinear or adaptive type; inertial navigation systems; application of system engineering techniques to societal problems. **Mailing Address:** Klipsch Sch Elec & Comput Eng, Dept 3-O, Thomas & Brown 113, Las Cruces, NM 88003. **Fax:** 505-646-1435. **E-Mail:** lkazda@nmsu.edu

KAZDAN, JERRY LAWRENCE, DIFFERENTIAL GEOMETRY, PARTIAL DIFFERENTIAL EQUATIONS. **Personal Data:** b Detroit, Mich, October 31, 1937. **Education:** Rensselaer Polytech Inst, BS, 1959; NY Univ, MS, 1961, PhD (math), 1963. **Honors & Awards:** 1999 Lester R Ford Award, Math Asn Am. **Professional Experience:** Dept head, Cent Europ Univ, 2002-2004; chmn, Univ PA, 1989-1992; vis prof, Univ Paris, 1981; PROF MATH, UNIV PA, 1974-; vis prof RIMS Kyoto, 1986-1987; vis prof, Univ Calif, Berkeley, 1974-1976; vis assoc prof, Harvard Univ, 1971-1972; from asst prof to assoc prof, Univ PA, 1966-1974; Benjamin Peirce instr, Harvard Univ, 1963-1966; Instr math, NY Univ, 1963. **Memberships:** Am Math Soc. **Research Statement & Publications:** Partial differential equations; differential geometry. **Mailing Address:** Dept Math, Univ Pa, 2095 33rd St, Philadelphia, PA 19104-6395. **E-Mail:** kazdan@math.upenn.edu

KAZEMI, HOMAYOUN, PULMONARY MEDICINE. **Personal Data:** b Teheran, Iran, September 28, 1934; American citizen; m 1958, Katheryne; c Paul A & Laili N. **Education:** Univ London, MB, 1953; Lafayette Col, BA, 1954; Columbia Univ, MD, 1958. **Honorary Degrees:** MSc, Harvard Univ, 1990. **Honors & Awards:** P D Agarwal Orator, Calcutta, India, 1987; R J Carabasi lectr, Texas A&M Sch Med, 1991. **Professional Experience:** PHYSICIAN & MGH POROF MED, MASS GEN HOSP, BOSTON, as of 2005; CHIEF EMER PULMONARY & CRITICAL CARE UNIT, MASS GEN HOSP, as of 2005; hon consult, Internal Med, Shang Hai First People's Hosp, China, 1991-; vis prof, Peking Union Med Col, Beijing, China, 1991; chief, Pulmonary & Critical Care Unit, Mass Gen Hosp, beginning 1988; consult, Fed Aviation Agency, 1987-1988; prof med, harvard med sch, Harvard-Mass Inst Technol Div Health Sci & Technol, beginni 1980; consult, Nat Heart Lung & Blood Inst, 1973-; chief pulmonary unit, Mass Gen Hosp, 1967-1988; consult, Brigham & Women's Hosp, Boston, 1965-1982; Vis fel, Hammersmith Hosp, Royal Postgrad Med Sch, London, 1965; Am Heart Asn res fel, Mass Gen Hosp, 1964; resident med, Mass Gen Hosp, 1963; asst res med, Am Heart Asn res fel, 1961-1962; res fel, Bassett Hosp, 1960-1961; asst res med, Bassett Hosp, 1959-1960; Intern, 1958-1959. **Memberships:** Am Thoracic Soc; Am Physiol Soc; Am Heart Asn; Am Soc Clin Invest. **Research Statement & Publications:** Central chemical control of ventilation as it relates to biochemistry of the respiratory centers; role of brain metabolism and amino acid neurotransmitters in determining the central ventilatory drive; control of cardiorespiratory function during exercise; occupational lung disease. **Mailing Address:** Mass Gen Hosp Pulmonary Unit, 55 Fruit St, Boston, MA 02114. **Fax:** 617-726-6878.

KAZEMI, HOSSEIN, PETROLEUM ENGINEERING. **Personal Data:** b Iran, March 11, 1938; m 1964, c 3. **Education:** Univ Tex, BS, 1961, PhD (petrol eng), 1963. **Honors & Awards:** Henry Matlson Technical Award, Soc Petrol Engrs, 1980; John Franklin Carll Award, 1987. **Professional Experience:** ADJ PROF, DEPT PETROL ENG, COLO SCH MINES, as of 2003; ASSOC DIR, PROD TECHNOL, PROD TECHNOL CTR, MARATHON OIL CO, 1988-; mgr, Reservoir Mgt Dept, Explor & Prod Technol Ctr, 1986-1988; adj prof petrol eng, Colo Sch Mines, beginning 1981; mgr eng dept, sr res scientist & res assoc, Marathon Oil Co, 1981-1986; adv res scientist, sr res scientist & res assoc, Marathon Oil Co, 1969-1980; res scientist, Atlantic Richfield Co, 1969; lectr math, Univ Tulsa, 1967-1969; sr res scientist, reservoir eng, Tulas Res Ctr, Sinclair Oil & Gas Co, 1963-1969; Eng fel, Univ Tex, 1961. **Memberships:** Soc Petrol Engrs. **Research Statement & Publications:** Solution mining; pressure transient testing of oil and gas wells; reservoir simulation; enhanced oil recovery, naturally fractured reservoirs. **Mailing Address:** Dept Petrol Eng, Colo Sch Mines, Rm 229 Alderson Hall, Golden, CO 80401. **Fax:** 303-273-3189.

KAZEROUNI, LEWA, MICROBIAL FERMENTATION & FREEZE DRYING, MEDIA DEVELOPMENT FOR MICROBIAL FERMENTATION. **Personal Data:** b Kuwait, October 18, 1956; American citizen. **Education:** Kuwait Univ, BS, 1977; Ore State Univ, PhD (microbiol), 1985. **Professional Experience:** MICROBIOL CONSULT, ORE FREEZEDRY, 1989-; Consult, K & K Inc, 1989-; res assoc, Ore State Univ, 1987-1988; res assoc, Southwestern Univ, Tex, 1986-1987; res asst, Ore State Univ, 1982-1986; Res microbiologist, Kuwait Inst Sci Res, 1978-1982. **Memberships:** Am Soc Microbiol; Inst Food Technologists. **Research Statement & Publications:** Optimizing the fermentation conditions for growing microorganisms of industrial value; finding the best way to keep these cultures viable for long periods of time after being freeze dried and held at ambient temperature. **Mailing Address:** Ore Freeze Dry, 525 25th Ave SW, Albany, OR 97321. **Fax:** 541-967-8768.

KAZEROUNIAN, KAZEM, OPTIMIZATION, REDUNDANCY RESOLUTION. **Personal Data:** b Shiraz, Iran, November 3, 1956; m 1976, c 2. **Education:** Univ Ill, BS, 1980, MS,

1981, PhD (mech design). **Professional Experience:** PROF MECH ENG, UNIV CONN, as of 2003; assoc prof design & robotics, Univ Conn, beginning 1989; reviewer, Inst Elec & Electronics Engrs, Int J Robotics Res, Robotics & Automation, Am Soc Mech Engrs, 1984-1991; consult, specialized mechanics, Gen Elec, Bran Rex & Rogers, Inc, 1984-1991; asst prof, Univ Conn, 1984-1989; res asst, Univ Ill, 1980-1984. **Research Statement & Publications:** Analysis and design optimization of robotic systems and mechanisms, theoretical and applied kinematics. **Mailing Address:** Dept Mech Eng, Univ Conn, 309 Eng II Bldg 191 Auditorium Rd U-139, Storrs, CT 06269-3139. **Fax:** 860-486-0318. **E-Mail:** kazem@engr.uconn.edu

KAZES, EMIL, THEORETICAL PHYSICS. **Personal Data:** b Istanbul, Turkey, June 13, 1926; American citizen; m 1954, c 3. **Education:** Univ Wis, BS, 1949, MS, 1950; Univ Chicago, PhD (physics), 1956. **Professional Experience:** PROF EMER PHYSICS, PA STATE UNIV, 1966-; from asst prof to assoc prof, PA State Univ, 1959-1966; proj assoc physics, Univ Wis, 1957-1959. **Memberships:** Fel Am Phys Soc. **Research Statement & Publications:** Electrodynamics; general relativity; soluble field theories; elementary particle theory; pion nucleon interaction, current algebra. **Mailing Address:** Dept Physics, Pa State Univ, 104 Davey Lab, Univ Park, PA 16802-6300. **E-Mail:** kazez@phys.psu.edu

KAZHDAN, DAVID, MATHEMATICS. **Education:** Moscow State Univ, MA, 1967, PhD, 1969. **Honorary Degrees:** BA, Harvard Univ, 1977. **Professional Experience:** PROF EMER MATH, HARVARD UNIV, as of 2004; prof math, Harvard Univ, beginning 1977; vis prof, Moscow State Univ, 1975-1977; researcher, Moscow State Univ, 1969-1975. **Memberships:** Nat Acad Sci. **Research Statement & Publications:** Algebraic aspects of analysis. **Mailing Address:** Dept Math, Harvard Univ, 338 One Oxford St, Cambridge, MA 02138. **Fax:** 617-495-5132. **E-Mail:** kazhdan@math.harvard.edu

KAZI, ABDUL HALIM, RADIATION EFFECTS, NEUTRON SOURCES. **Personal Data:** b Kreuzlingen, Switz, January 12, 1935; American citizen; m 1959, Patricia; c Aaron & Ethan. **Education:** Am Univ, Cairo, Egypt, BSc, 1954; Rensselaer Polytech Inst, MS, 1956; Mass Inst Technol, SM, 1959, PhD (nuclear eng), 1961. **Professional Experience:** DIR, RADIATION SIMULATION ANAL DIRECTORATE, ABERDEEN TEST CTR, 1995-; Radiation Dosimetry Standards Comt, Am Soc Testing & Mat, 1984- & Multi Serv Test & Res Investment Comt Nuclear Effects, 1989-; dir, Nuclear Effects Directorate, US Army Combat Systs Test Activ, 1987-1995; Mem, NATO Panel VII & VIII Res Study Groups, 1976-; prin investr, Army Pulse Radiation Facil, 1966-1987; sect chief, United Nuclear, White Plains, NY, 1963-1966; Staff mem, Gen Atomics, La Jolla, Calif, 1961-1963. **Memberships:** Am Nuclear Soc. **Research Statement & Publications:** Design, operation and utilization of nuclear weapon radiation simulators; neutron sources; flash gamma accelerators; radiation dosimetry; radiation effects. **Mailing Address:** 2813 Rocks Rd, Jarrettsville, MD 21084.

KAZIM, A LATIF, MEDICAL RESEARCH. **Education:** Boston Univ, BA, 1971; Wayne State Univ, Detroit, MI, MA, 1974; Univ Minn, PhD, 1979. **Professional Experience:** FACIL DIR BIOPOLYMER FACIL & MASS SPECTROMETRY, ROSWELL PARK CANCER INST, as of 2005. **Mailing Address:** Biopolymer Facil Roswell Park Cancer Inst, CCC-514Elm & Carlton St, Buffalo, NY 14263-0001. **Fax:** 716-845-7621. **E-Mail:** latif.kazim@roswellpark.org

KAZIMI, MUJID S, THERMAL ENGINEERING, SAFETY ENGINEERING. **Personal Data:** b Jerusalem, Palestine, November 20, 1947; American citizen; m Nozik; c Marwan, Yasmeen & Omar. **Education:** Univ Alexandria, Egypt, BS, 1969; Mass Inst Technol, MS, 1971, PhD (nuclear eng), 1973. **Professional Experience:** PROF MECH ENG, MASS INST TECHNOL, as of 2004; DIR, CTR ADVAN NUCLEAR ENERGY SYSTS, MASS INST TECHNOL, as of 2004; TOKYO ELEC POWER PROF NUCLEAR ENG, MASS INST TECHNOL, 2000-; chmn, High Level Waste Tech Adv Panel, Dept Energy, 1990-1995; dept head, Nuclear Eng, Mass Inst Technol, beginning 1989; prof nuclear eng, Mass Inst Technol, 1986-2000; pres, Asn Arab Am Univ Graduates, Inc, 1980 & 1987; from asst prof to assoc prof, Mass Inst Technol, 1976-1986; assoc scientist, Brookhaven Nat Lab, 1974-1976; Sr engr, Westinghouse Elec Corp, 1973-1974. **Memberships:** Am Nuclear Soc; Am Soc Mech Engrs; Am Inst Chem Engrs; Am Soc Eng Educ. **Research Statement & Publications:** Thermal design and safety of nuclear facilities, including nuclear power reactors, nuclear waste storage facilities and nuclear fusion research facilities. **Mailing Address:** Dept Nuclear Eng, Mass Inst Technol, Rm 24-219 77 Mass Ave, Cambridge, MA 02139-4307. **Fax:** 617-258-8863. **E-Mail:** kazimi@mit.edu

KAZIMIERCZUK, MARIAN K, POWER ELECTRONICS, RADIO FREQUENCY TECHNOLOGY. **Personal Data:** b Smolugi, Poland, March 3, 1948; m 1973, Alicja Nowowiejska; c Anna & Andrew. **Education:** Tech Univ Warsaw, MSc, 1972, PhD (electronics eng), 1978, DSCi, 1984. **Honors & Awards:** Outstanding Engr & Scientists Award, Eng & Sci Found & Affil Socs Coun, 1995. **Professional Experience:** PROF ELEC ENG, WRIGHT STATE UNIV, 1994-; from asst prof to assoc prof, Wright State Univ, 1985-1994; design engr, Design Automation, Inc, 1984-1985; vis prof, Va Polytech Inst & State Univ, 1984-1985; res award, Ministry Sci & Higher Educ, Poland, 1984; res award, Polish Acad Sci, 1983; Asst prof, Dept Electronics, Tech Univ Warsaw, 1978-1984. **Memberships:** Sr mem Inst Elec & Electronics Engrs. **Research Statement & Publications:** Energy conversion; published over 190 articles and granted 5 patents. **Mailing Address:** Dept Elec Eng, Russ Eng Ctr, Wright State Univ, 311, 3640 Colonel Glenn Hwy, Dayton, OH 45435-0001. **Fax:** 937-775-3936. **E-Mail:** mkazim@cs.wright.edu

KAZIRO, YOSHITO, MEDICAL RESEARCH. **Education:** Univ Tokyo, MD, 1954, PhD, 1959. **Professional Experience:** PROF, HORIZONTAL MED RES ORGN, KYOTO UNIV, 2003-. **Mailing Address:** Horizontal Med Res Orgn Kyoto Univ, Yoshida Konoe-cho, Sakyo-ku, 606-8501, Japan. **Fax:** 81-75-753-9282. **E-Mail:** ykaziro@hmro.med.kyoto-u.ac.jp

KAZLAUSKAS, ROMAS J, ORGANIC CHEMISTRY. **Education:** Mass Inst Technol, PhD, 1982. **Professional Experience:** ASSOC PROF, DEPT BIOCHEM, MOLECULAR BIOL & BIOPHYS UNIV MINN, as of 2006. **Research Statement & Publications:** Nature uses enzymes to make complex natural products. **Mailing Address:** Univ Minn Rochester, 855 30th Ave SE 174A Gortner Lab, Rochester, MN 55904. **Fax:** 612-625-5780. **E-Mail:** rjk@umn.edu

KAZMAIER, HAROLD EUGENE, ENVIRONMENTAL SCIENCES, ENVIRONMENTAL MANAGEMENT. **Personal Data:** b Bowling Green, Ohio, February 17, 1924; m 1949, c 3. **Education:** Ohio State Univ, BS, 1949, MS, 1951, PhD (bot), 1960. **Professional Experience:** CHIEF TECH ASSISTANCE, PESTICIDE BR, US ENVIRON PROTECTION AGENCY, 1972-; sr res plant pathologist, Battelle-Columbus, 1952-1972; Asst plant path, Agr Exp Sta, Ohio State Univ, 1950-1952. **Memberships:** Am Phytopath Soc; Soc Nematol; Sigma Xi. **Research Statement & Publications:** Pesticides; plant pest control; registration support data. **Mailing Address:** Four Evans Dr, Wilmington, MA 01887.

KAZMAIER, PETER MICHAEL, ELECTRONIC MATERIALS & MOLECULAR MODELING, LIVING FREE RADICAL POLYMERIZATION. **Personal Data:** b Neustadt, Ger, April 19, 1951; Canadian citizen; m Kathy; c 3. **Education:** Univ Calgary, BSc Hons, 1973; Queen's Univ, PhD (chem), 1978. **Honors & Awards:** Chem Inst Can Prize, Chem Inst Can, 1972; Arthur K Doolittle Award, Am Chem Soc, 1993. **Professional Experience:** AREA MGR, XEROX RES CTR CAN, XEROX CORP, 1998-, vis fel, Cornell Univ; adj assoc prof chem, Queen's Univ Kingston, 1993-1999; SR MEM RES STAFF, XEROX RES CTR CAN, XEROX CORP, 1992-1998; mem comt, Can Soc Chem Publ, 1991-; mem res staff chem, Xerox Res Ctr Can, Xerox Corp, 1979-1992; Killam fel chem, Univ BC, 1978-1979. **Memberships:** Chem Inst Can; Am Chem Soc. **Research Statement & Publications:** Electronic materials; novel photogenerator materials; living free-radical polymerization; hole and electron; transport; use of molecular orbital calculations; author of more than 60 publication; granted 57 patents. **Mailing Address:** Xerox Res Ctr, 2660 Speakman Dr, Mississauga, ON L5K 2L1, Can. **Fax:** 905-822-7022. **E-Mail:** peter.kazmaier@crt.xerox.com

KAZMAR, RICHARD R, AERONAUTICS. **Professional Experience:** PRATT & WHITNEY SPACE PROPULSION, as of 2005. **Memberships:** Am Inst Aeronaut & Astronaut. **Mailing Address:** Pratt & Whitney Space Propulsion, PO Box 109600, West Palm Beach, FL 33410-9600. **Fax:** 561-796-5099. **E-Mail:** Richard.Kazmar@pw.utc.com

KAZMERSKI, LAWRENCE L, PHOTOVOLTAICS, SURFACE SCIENCE. **Personal Data:** b Chicago, Ill, June 9, 1945; m 1968, Kathleen; c Keira E & Timothy L. **Education:** Univ Notre Dame, BSEE, 1967, MSEE, 1968, PhD (elec eng), 1970. **Honors & Awards:** Peter Mark Mem Award, Am Vacuum Soc, 1980; Res Develop IR 100 Award, 1985; Res Develop R & D 100 Award, 1989, 1992; William R Cherry Award, Inst Elec & Electronics Engrs, 1993. **Professional Experience:** DIR, NAT CTR PHOTOVOLTAIC, as of 2005; COLLABR, NAT RENEWABLE ENERGY LAB, as of 2004; HEAD, US NAT CTR PHOTOVOLTAIC, as of 2004; chmn, Inst Elec & Electronics Engrs PVSC, 1987; chmn, Nat Am Vacuum Soc Symposium, 1982; BR MGR, NAT RENEWABLE ENERGY LAB, SOLAR ENERGY RES INST, 1980-; Adj prof, Colo Sch Mines, 1980-; ed, Polycrystalline & Amorphous Thin Films & Devices, 1980; PRIN SCIENTIST, NAT RENEWABLE ENERGY LAB, SOLAR ENERGY RES INST, 1979-; Adj prof, Univ Colo, 1979-; ed, J Solar Cells, 1979-1991; sr scientist, Nat Renewable Energy Lab, Solar Energy Res Inst, 1977-1979; assoc prof, Univ Maine, Orono, 1974-1977; asst prof teaching res, Univ Maine, Orono, 1971-1974; res fel, Am Eng Coun, Notre Dame Radiation Lab, 1971. **Memberships:** Am Vacuum Soc (pres, 1991); fel Inst Elec & Electronics Engrs; fel Am Phys Soc; Sigma Xi. **Research Statement & Publications:** Photovoltaic devices and solid state physics, with emphasis on the correlation of compositional and chemical properties and electrical characteristics of interfaces in solar cells and other semiconductor devices; scanning tunneling microscopy and surface analysis. **Mailing Address:** Nat Renewable Energy Lab, 1617 Cole Blvd, Golden, CO 80401-3393. **Fax:** 303-384-6601. **E-Mail:** kaz@nrel.gov

KAZNOFF, ALEXIS I(VAN), METALLURGICAL ENGINEERING, CHEMICAL ENGINEERING. **Personal Data:** b Harbin, China, October 22, 1933; American citizen; m 1980. **Education:** Univ Calif, Berkeley, BS, 1955, PhD (phys metall), 1961; Calif Inst Technol, MS, 1956. **Professional Experience:** DIR MAT ENG, NAVAL SEA SYSTS COMMAND, 1982-; mgr, prod & qual assurance oper, nuclear energy bus group, 1975-1982; consult engr, prod & qual assurance oper, nuclear energy bus group, 1973-1975; metall & ceramics lab, Nuclear Technol & Appln Oper, 1969-1973; mat sci & develop, Nucleonics Lab, 1966-1969; mgr ceramics & electronic mat, Gen Elec Co, 1964-1966; scientist mat sci, Gen Elec Co, 1960-1964. **Memberships:** Am Soc Metals; Am Ceramic Soc; Am Chem Soc; Am Welding Soc; Am Mgt Asn. **Research Statement & Publications:** Nuclear fuel technology; structural materials for nuclear plants and ships; nuclear materials; welding and materials processing; marine corrosion; corrosion control; fuels and lubricants. **Mailing Address:** Dept Mat & Environ Eng, Naval Sea Systs Command, 1333 Isaac Hull Ave SE, Washington, DC 20376. **Fax:** 202-781-4734. **E-Mail:** KaznoffAI@navsea.navy.mil

KAZURA, JAMES, ONCOLOGY, TROPICAL HEALTH. **Personal Data:** b Cleveland, Ohio, 1946. **Education:** Wash Univ, AB, 1968; Ohio State Univ, MD, 1972. **Professional Experience:** PROF MED, DEPT PATH, CASE WESTERN RESERVE UNIV, 1989-; CHIEF, DIV GEOG MED, CASE WESTERN RESERVE UNIV, as of 2005; DIR, CTR GLOBAL HEALTH & DIS, SCH MED, CASE WESTERN RESERVE UNIV, as of 2005; assoc prof med, Univ Hosp, Case Western Reserve Univ, beginning 1983. **Memberships:** Am Soc Trop Med & Hyg; Am Fedn Clin Res; Infectious Dis Soc Am. **Research Statement & Publications:** molecular mechanisms by which antigen-specific white blood cells differentiate in vivo, and to apply this information to the development of immunologic approaches to control parasitic diseases important in tropical countries; publications on filarial protein in human bancroftian filariasis, modulation of murine cytokine responses to mycobacterial antigens by helminth-induced responses, t helper responses to the filarial helminth, brugia malayi, interleukin 4 and t helper type 2 cells are required for development of experimental onchocercal keratitis. **Mailing Address:** Div Geog Med, Case Western Reserve Univ, Rm W 137 2109 Adelbert Rd, Cleveland, OH 44106-4983. **Fax:** 219-368-1825. **E-Mail:** james.kazura@case.edu

KE, HUA ZHU, OSTEOPOROSIS, PHYSICAL FRAILTY. **Personal Data:** b Maoming, China, August 25, 1962; m Juan; c Qiao Han, Hunter & Jason. **Education:** Zhanjiang Med Col, BS, 1981; Guangdong Med Col, MD, 1984. **Honors & Awards:** Am Soc Bone & Mineral Res Award outstanding res pathophysiol osteoporosis, 2001. **Professional Experience:** Vis prof, Guangdong Med Col, 1996-; PRIN RES INVESTR, GLOBAL RES & DEVELOP, PFIZER INC, 1996-; vis assoc prof bone biol & med, Guangdong Med Col, 1995-1996; young investr travel award, Int Bone & Mineral Soc, 1995; sr res scientist, Div Ctr Res, Pfizer Inc, 1992-1995; res assoc osteoporosis, Univ Utah, 1990-1992; postdoctoral fel bone biol, Univ Utah, 1988-1990; teaching asst anat, Guangdong Med Col, 1984-1988. **Memberships:** Am Soc Bone & Mineral Res; Int Bone & Mineral Soc; Int Soc Bone Morphometry; Endocrine Soc; Soc Chinese Bioscientists Am; Int Chinese Hard Tissue Soc. **Research Statement & Publications:** Pathophysiology of osteoporosis and physical frailty; discovery and development of new therapies for osteoporosis, frailty and related diseases. **Mailing Address:** Div Metab Dis, Global Res & Develop, Pfizer, Inc, Eastern Pt Rd, Groton, CT 06340. **Fax:** 860-686-0170. **E-Mail:** huazhu_ke@groton.pfizer.com

KE, PAUL JENN, ANALYTICAL BIOCHEMISTRY, FOOD TECHNOLOGY. **Personal Data:** b Ahwei Prov, China, January 16, 1934; Canadian citizen; m 1961, c 2. **Education:** Nat Cheng-Kung Univ, Taiwan, BEng, 1959; Nat Taiwan Univ, MSc, 1963; Mem Univ Nfld, MSc, 1966; Univ Windsor, PhD (anal biochem), 1972. **Professional Experience:** RETIRED; prof biochem, Mem Univ, 1988-1998; sr scientist & head tech studies dept, Halifax Lab, Fisheries & Oceans Can, 1983-1993; res scientist, Halifax Lab, Fisheries & Oceans Can, 1972-1983; anal chemist, Fish Res Bd Can, 1966-1969; instr, Nat Taiwan Univ, 1962-1964; res & develop chem engr, Taiwan Sugar Res Inst, Taiwan, 1959-1961. **Memberships:** Chem Inst Can; Can Soc Chem Engrs; Inst Food Technologists; Can Inst

Food Sci & Technol; Am Oil Chemists Soc; fel Can Sci Coun. **Research Statement & Publications:** Biochemical study on kinetics of lipid oxidation and various rancidity reactions; methodological studies for determination of biochemical parameters and contaminates in various fishery products and waters; quality science studies for sea foods; preservation biochemistry investigation; fish engineering sciences. **Mailing Address:** Biochem Dept, Mem Univ Nfld, St John's, NL A1C 3X9, Can. **Fax:** 709-737-4000.

KEAGY, PAMELA M, FOLIC ACID & NUTRIENT BIOAVAILABILITY. **Education:** Univ Calif, Berkeley, PhD, 1981. **Professional Experience:** AT US DEPT AGR-WRRC, BERKELEY, CALIF, as of 2004; proj leader food qual res, Agr Res Serv-Usda, 1978-. **Memberships:** Am Inst Nutrit; Inst Food Technologists; Am Asn Cereal Chemists. **Mailing Address:** US Dept Agr-WRRC, 800 Buchanan St, Berkeley, CA 94710. **Fax:** 510-559-5626. **E-Mail:** pkeagy@pw.usda.gov

KEAHEY, KENNETH KARL, VETERINARY PATHOLOGY. **Personal Data:** b Covington, Okla, September 17, 1923; m 1956, c 3. **Education:** Okla State Univ, BS, 1948, DVM, 1954; Mich State Univ, PhD (vet path), 1963. **Honors & Awards:** EP Pope Mem Award. **Professional Experience:** RETIRED; dir, Anal Health Diag Lab, 1977-1990; from asst prof to prof vet path, Mich State Univ, 1963-1990; NIH fel, Mich State Univ, 1960-1963; actg pres, Imp Ethiopian Col Agr & Mech Arts, 1958-1960; dean, Imp Ethiopian Col Agr & Mech Arts, 1957-1958; head dept animal sci, Imp Ethiopian Col Agr & Mech Arts, 1956-1957; adv vet med, Imp Ethiopian Col Agr & Mech Arts, 1954-1956. **Memberships:** AAAS; Am Vet Med Asn. **Research Statement & Publications:** Infectious diseases and nutritional deficiencies in swine. **Mailing Address:** 1817 Cahill Dr, East Lansing, MI 48823.

KEAIRNS, DALE LEE, CHEMICAL ENGINEERING, RESEARCH ADMINISTRATION. **Personal Data:** b Vincennes, Ind, November 20, 1940; m 1967, c 1. **Education:** Okla State Univ, BS, 1962; Carnegie Inst Technol, MS, 1964, PhD (chem eng), 1967. **Professional Experience:** SR ADV ENGR, SCI APPLN INT CORP, as of 2004; Mem, adv panel, chem eng dept, Univ Pittsburgh, 1984-; coun, Carnegie Mus Nat Hist, 1984-; mem, adv comt, Carnegie Inst & Carnegie Libr, 1984-1985; mgr, Chem & Process Eng, Res & Develop Ctr, Westinghouse Elec Corp, beginning 1983; chem & process eng adv comt, NSF, 1982-1983; mem, fossil fuel adv comt, Oak Ridge Nat Lab, 1979-1983; mgr, fossil fuel & fluidized bed processing, 1978-1983; co-chmn, First Int Fluidization Conf, Eng Found, 1978; Chmn, First Int Fluidization Conf, Eng Found, 1975; mgr, Fluidized Bed Eng, 1973-1978; sr engr, Res & Develop Ctr, 1967-1973; Assoc develop engr, Oak Ridge Nat Lab, 1962 & Gaseous Diffusion Plant, Tenn, 1963; mem, tech comt, Particulate Solids Res Inst. **Memberships:** Am Inst Chem Engrs; Am Chem Soc; AAAS; Soc Hist Technol. **Research Statement & Publications:** Hydrodynamic, heat transfer and reaction rate studies on fluidized bed systems; pilot plant engineering and design; gasification and fluidized bed combustion systems development; gas cleaning. **Mailing Address:** Sci Appln Int Corp, 626 Cochrans Mill Rd, PO Box 10940, Pittsburgh, PA 15236-0940. **Fax:** 412-386-4822. **E-Mail:** dale.keairns@netl.doe.gov

KEAMMERER, WARREN ROY, PLANT ECOLOGY. **Personal Data:** b Gary, Ind, November 25, 1946; m 1970, Deborah; c Holly. **Education:** Capital Univ, BS, 1968; NDak State Univ, PhD (bot), 1972. **Professional Experience:** ECOL CONSULT, KEAMMERER ECOL CONSULT, 1973-; fel ecol, Univ Colo, 1972-1973; lectr biol, Capital Univ, 1971-1972. **Memberships:** Ecol Soc Am; Brit Ecol Soc; Sigma Xi; Wilderness Soc; Soc Range Mgt. **Research Statement & Publications:** Preparation of baseline plant ecological reports designed to provide necessary data for impact analysis and permit applications; study areas are located in eastern Wyoming, western Colorado, Utah, New Mexico, North Dakota and Montana; monitoring revegetation success on reclaimed lands using comprehensive microcomputer program; Remediation of metals enriched soils. **Mailing Address:** 5858 Woodbourne Hollow Rd, Boulder, CO 80301. **E-Mail:** wrkeam@comcast.net

KEAN, CHESTER EUGENE, FOOD CHEMISTRY. **Personal Data:** b Chicago, Ill, October 16, 1925; m 1972, Betty; c John M, Carolyn E (Reichman), Jeffry J, Janice (Gilmour), Richard C Graden & Jeffery R Graden. **Education:** Univ Ill, BS, 1948; Ore State Col, MS, 1950; Univ Calif, PhD (agr chem), 1954. **Professional Experience:** RETIRED; chief chemist prod develop, C&H Sugar Co, Crockett, 1978-1986; sr technologist, Calif & Hawaiian Sugar Refining Corp, 1966-1978; new prod technologist, Calif & Hawaiian Sugar Refining Corp, 1961-1966; technologist, Calif & Hawaiian Sugar Refining Corp, 1958-1961; assoc technologist, Calif & Hawaiian Sugar Refining Corp, 1953-1958; food technologist, Univ Calif, 1950-1953; asst chem, Ore State Col, 1948-1950. **Memberships:** Inst Food Technologists. **Research Statement & Publications:** Copper clouding in wines; fungal amylases in butanol acetone fermentation; organic acids in wine; method for determining the sub-sieve particle size distribution of pulverized sugar; carbohydrate chemistry; product development based on sugar properties. **Mailing Address:** 667 Byrdee Way, Lafayette, CA 94549.

KEAN, EDWARD LOUIS, GLYCOPROTEINS & GLYCOLIPIDS, RHODOPSIN GLYCOSYLATION. **Personal Data:** b Philadelphia, Pa, October 19, 1925; m 1962, c 4. **Education:** Univ Pa, BA, 1949, PhD (biochem), 1961; Drexel Univ, MS, 1956. **Professional Experience:** PROF EMER OPTHALI & BIOCHEM, SCH MED, CASE WESTERN RES UNIV, 1998-; DIR EMER CTR VISION RES, CASE WESTERN RES UNIV, 1998-; dir, Ctr Vision Res, beginning 1991; Fogarty sr int res fel, 1986-1987; Erna & Jakob Michael, Vis Professorship Award, Weizman Inst Sci, Israel, 1986-1987; exchange scientist, Japan, 1981; exchange scientist fel, Japan Soc Prom Sci, 1981; Prof Opthal & Biochem, Sch Med, Case Western Res Univ, beginning 1979; Nat Inst Neurol Dis & Stroke & Nat Eye Inst res grants, 1968-; from sr instr to assoc prof, Ctr Vision Res, 1965-1979; sr cancer res scientist, Roswell Park Mem Inst, NY, 1964-1965; Arthritis & Rheumatism Found fel, 1961-1964; res assoc, Univ Mich, 1961-1964; asst instr biochem, Univ Pa, 1956-1957; Chemist, Sharp & Dohme Inc, 1949-1952 & Smith Kline & French Labs, 1952-1956. **Memberships:** Am Chem Soc; Asn Res Vision & Ophthal; Int Soc Eye Res; Soc Glycobiol; Am Soc Biochem Molecular Biol; AAAS. **Research Statement & Publications:** Biosynthesis, subcellular location and degradation of cytosine monophosphate-sialic acid; glycolipid sulfation and vitamin A deficiency; glycosylation, oligosaccharide structure and degradation of rhodospin; activation, regulation, topography and kinetics of initial reactions of the dolichol pathway. **Mailing Address:** Case Western Res Unit, 11100 Euclid Ave, Rm 653 Wearn Bldg, Cleveland, OH 44106. **Fax:** 216-844-7899. **E-Mail:** elk2@po.cwru.edu

KEAN, VANORA MABEL, FORENSIC SEROLOGY, BLOODSTAIN PATTERN INTERPRETATION. **Personal Data:** b Manchester, Eng, June 3, 1955; m 1988, William. **Education:** Univ Manchester, Eng, Hons BSc, 1976; Univ Aberdeen, Scotland, PhD (genetics), 1981. **Professional Experience:** FORENSIC BIOLOGIST, CTR FORENSIC SCI, MINISTRY SOLICITOR GEN, GOVT ONT, as of 2003; res asst, Dept Optom & Vision Sci, Univ Manchester Inst Sci & Technol, Eng, 1985-1987; tutor molecular biol, Univ Manchester Inst Sci & Technol, 1985-1987; res assoc, Dept Genetics, Hosp Sick Children, Toronto, 1984-1985; teaching asst med genetics, Dept Genetics, Hosp Sick Children, Toronto, 1984; res fel, Dept Genetics, Hosp Sick Children, Toronto, 1983-1984; res fel, Fac Med, Univ Nfld, 1981-1983; tutor molecular biol, Fac Med, Univ Nfld, 1981-1983; teaching asst genetics, Dept Genetics, Univ Aberdeen, Scotland, 1977-1980. **Memberships:** Am Soc Human Genetics; Brit Soc Cell Biol; Genetical Soc UK; Can Soc Forensic Sci; Int Asn Bloodstain Pattern Analysts. **Research Statement & Publications:** Plant and human cytogenetics; human genetic diseases, including Duchenne muscular dystrophy and retinitis pigmentosa; DNA recombinant technology. **Mailing Address:** Biol Sect Ctr Forensic Sci, RR2 Site78 Comp30, Summerland, BC V0H 1Z0, Can. **Fax:** 250-494-1746. **E-Mail:** bio4nsk@yahoo.com

KEANA, JOHN F W, ORGANIC CHEMISTRY. **Personal Data:** b St Joseph, Mich, September 14, 1939; m 1966, c 2. **Education:** Kalamazoo Col, BA, 1961; Stanford Univ, PhD (chem), 1965. **Professional Experience:** PROF CHEM, UNIV ORE, 1977-; from asst prof to assoc prof, Univ Ore, 1965-1977; NSF fel, Columbia Univ, 1964-1965; res career award, NIH; Guggenheim fel; A P Sloan fel. **Memberships:** Am Chem Soc; Soc Magnetic Res Med; Int Soc Heterocyclic Chem. **Research Statement & Publications:** Synthetic organic and medicinal chemistry, molecular tips for atomic force miscroscopy, surface and functionalization of polymers, novel phospholipase C enzyme substrates and inhibitors. **Mailing Address:** Dept Chem, Univ Ore, Eugene, OR 97403.

KEANE, J R, NEURO-OPHTHALMOLOGY, BRAIN STEM NEUROLOGY. **Personal Data:** b Washington, DC, March 12, 1937. **Education:** Univ Utah, BS, 1958; Harvard Med Sch, MD, 1961. **Professional Experience:** PROF NEUROL, UNIV SOUTHERN CALIF SCH MED, LOS ANGELES, 1982-; Bd examr, Am Bd Neurol & Psychiat, 1974-; from instr to assoc prof, Univ Southern Calif Sch Med, Los Angeles, 1970-1982; fel neuro-ophthal, Univ Calif Med Ctr, San Francisco, 1968-1969; fel res, Mt Sinai Hosp, NY, 1967-1968; resident neurol, NY Neurol Inst, Columbia-Presby, 1965-1967; intern, Bellevue Hosp, Univ Calif Med Ctr, 1961-1962; intern, Bellevue Hosp, Univ Calif Med Ctr, 1964-1965. **Memberships:** Am Acad Neurol; Am Neurol Asn. **Research Statement & Publications:** Clinical-anatomic correlations, with emphasis on eye movement neuropathology. **Mailing Address:** Dept Neurol, Keck Sch Med, Univ Southern Caif, GNH 5641 9315, Los Angeles, CA 90033-4525. **Fax:** 323-226-5869. **E-Mail:** jkeane@usc.edu

KEANE, JOHN FRANCIS, BIOPHYSICS, PHYSIOLOGY. **Personal Data:** b Milford, Mass, February 3, 1922; m 1948, c 2. **Education:** Boston Col, BS, 1943; Fordham Univ, MS, 1949; Univ St Louis, PhD (biol chem), 1954. **Professional Experience:** RETIRED; from instr to assoc prof physics, St Louis Col Pharm, 1955-1980; res assoc, Biophys Inst, Univ St Louis, 1954-1956; asst biol, Biophys Inst, Univ St Louis, 1950-1954; asst biol, Cytochem Sect, Sloan-Kettering Inst, 1949-1950; asst biol, Fordham Univ, 1948-1949. **Memberships:** AAAS; NY Acad Sci. **Research Statement & Publications:** Physical properties and chemical constitution of crystalline inclusions in giant Amoebae; ultraviolet microspectrography of normal and malignant, desquammated and cultured cells; protective and other action of chemical agents particularly aliphatic amides on biological and physical systems subjected to subfreezing temperatures. **Mailing Address:** 1105 Mo Ave, Kirkwood, MO 63122-1013.

KEANE, ROBERT W, NEUROIMMUNOLOGY, DEVELOPMENTAL NEUROBIOLOGY. **Education:** Univ Calif, Davis, PhD, 1976. **Professional Experience:** ASSOC PROF PHYSIOL, SCH MED, UNIV MIAMI, as o f 2006. **Memberships:** Soc Neuroscience; Soc Develop Biol; Soc Cell Biol. **Mailing Address:** Dept Physiol & Biophys R430, Univ Miami Sch Med, 1600 NW Tenth Ave, Miami, FL 33136-1015. **Fax:** 305-243-5931. **E-Mail:** rkeane@miami.edu

KEANE, WILLIAM FRANCIS, NEPHROLOGY. **Personal Data:** b New York, NY, September 21, 1942; m 1967, Stephanie; c Alicia A & Elizabeth G. **Education:** Fordham Univ, BS, 1964; Yale Univ, MD, 1968. **Professional Experience:** VPRES, CLIN DEVELOP, MERK & CO, as of 2003; PRES, NAT KIDNEY FOUND, MINN, as of 1998; chmn, dept med, Hennepin Co Med Ctr, beginning 1992; pres, Minn Med res Found, beginning 1989; prof med, Univ Minn, Minneapolis, beginning 1987; from asst prof to assoc prof, Univ Minn, Minneapolis, 1976-1987; intern, resident then chief med resident, Cornell NY Hosp Med Ctr, 1968-1973. **Research Statement & Publications:** Nephrology. **Mailing Address:** Nat Kidney Found, 30 E 33rd St, Ste 1100, New York, NY 10016. **Fax:** 212-689-9261.

KEAR, BERNARD HENRY, MATERIALS & TECHNOLOGY. **Personal Data:** b Port Talbot, South Wales, July 5, 1931; American citizen; m 1959, Jacqueline; c Andrew, Gareth, Edward & Gwyneth. **Education:** Birmingham Univ, BSc, 1954, PhD (mat sci), 1957, DSc, 1970. **Honors & Awards:** Howe Medal, Am Soc Metals, 1970; Mathewson Gold Medal, Am Inst Mining, Metall & Petrol Engrs, 1971; John Dorn Mem Lectr, 1980; Henry Krumb Mem Lectr, 1983. **Professional Experience:** DIR, CTR FOR NANOMAT RES, RUTGERS UNIV, 1995-; chmn, dept mech & mat sci & dir advan technol, ctr surface eng mat, rutgers univ, beginning 1986; chmn, Nat Mat Adv Bd, Nat Res Coun, 1986-1989; PROF, DEPT CERAMIC & MAT ENG, RUTGERS UNIV, 1986-; sci adv, Exxon Res & Eng Co, 1981-1986; sr consult scientist, United Technologies Res Ctr, 1977-1981; Chmn, Gordon Res Conf Phys Metall, 1974; mem staff, Com Prod Div, Pratt & Whitney Aircraft, 1963-1981; fel, Franklin Inst, Philadelphia, 1959-1963; res metallurgist, Tube Investments Ltd, UK, 1957-1959; co-ed, J Nanostructured Mat. **Memberships:** Nat Acad Eng; fel Am Soc Metals; Am Inst Mining Metall & Petrol Engrs; Mat Res Soc; Am Ceramic Soc. **Research Statement & Publications:** New phenomena associated with chemical vapor deposition and solidification of materials surfaces; laser processing of materials; structure and property relationships in nickel base superalloys; chemically synthesized nanophase materials; chemical vapor deposition, surface modification and structure-properties-processing relationships in crystalline solids; author of 230 technical publications; awarded 30 patents. **Mailing Address:** Dept Ceramics & Mat Eng, Rutgers Univ, 607 Taylor Rd, Piscataway, NJ 08854. **Fax:** 732-445-5977. **E-Mail:** bkear@ric.rutgers.edu

KEAR, EDWARD B, MECHANICAL ENGINEERING, SYSTEMS ANALYSIS. **Personal Data:** b Yonkers, NY, March 23, 1932; m 1954, c 3. **Education:** Clarkson Tech Univ, BME, 1954; Cornell Univ, MS, 1956, PhD, 1969. **Professional Experience:** REGISTR & DEAN SPEC PROG SUMMER SCH, CLARKSON UNIV, as of 2002; PRES, CLARKSON DEVELOP CORP, as of 2002; ASSOC PROF MECH & INDUST ENG, CLARKSON COL TECHNOL, beginning 1976; EXEC OFFICER, MECH ENG DEPT, 1971-; from asst prof to assoc prof control systs anal, Clarkson Col Technol, 1958-1976. **Memberships:** Am Soc Eng Educ. **Research Statement & Publications:** Control systems analysis; variation of hand-eye coordination with age. **Mailing Address:** 12 Bradley Dr, Potsdam, NY 13676.

KEARBY, WILLIAM H, TECHNOLOGY. **Personal Data:** b Green Bay, Wis, October 2, 1923; m 1956, Esther; c Todd & Mark. **Education:** Univ WI, Stevens Pt, BS, 1960; Univ WI-Madison, MS (entom), 1962; Univ WI-Madison, PhD (Foved/entom), 1965. **Professional Experience:** RETIRED, prof fovest, Univ WI, 1985-1996; prof Univ WI, Stevens

Pt, 1983-1985; prof, Univ Miss, Columbia, 1969-1980; asst prof, PENN State, 1964-1969. **Mailing Address:** Kearby Christmas Tree Farm, WI4959 Christmas Tree Ln, Sheldon, WI 54766. **E-Mail:** ckearby@centurytel.com

KEARL, WILLIS GORDON, FARM & RANCH MANAGEMENT, MARKETING & PRICES. **Personal Data:** b Laketown, Utah, May 11, 1927. **Education:** Utah State Univ, BS, 1949, MS, 1951; Univ Calif, Berkeley, PhD (agr econ), 1968. **Professional Experience:** RETIRED; prof ranch mgt, Range Econ & Livestock Mkt, Univ Wyo, 1962-1990; agr econ res, Econ Res Serv, USDA, Calif & Wyo, 1958-1962; Res Fluoride Damage, Res Water Develop, Bur Agr Econ USDA, Utah State Univ, 1954-1955; first lieutenant radar maintenance, USAF, 1951-1953; digest staff, Doan Agr Serv, 1951; agr economist, res water develop, Bur Agr Econ USDA, Utah State Univ, 1950-1951. **Memberships:** Am Agr Econ Asn; Am Soc Range Mgt; Am Soc Animal Sci; Am Agr Law Asn. **Research Statement & Publications:** Ranch management and economics of range improvements. **Mailing Address:** Dept Agr Econs, Univ Wyo, Box 3983 Univ Sta, Laramie, WY 82071.

KEARLEY, ERIC, BIOPHYSICS. **Education:** Univ Tex, BS, 1972; NTex State Univ, MS, 1974; Univ Wis-Madison, PhD (radiol physics), 1982; Am Bd Health Physics, cert. **Professional Experience:** CAPT, ARMED FORCES RADIOBIOL RES INST, USN, as of 1996; DIR, ARMED FORCES RADIOBIOL RES INST, USN, 1995-; dep sci dir, radiation biophysics dept, 1993-1994; plasma physics lab, USN Bur Med & Surg Dosimetry Ctr, 1992-1994, naval sea systs Command; plasma physics lab, Princeton Univ, 1991; Consult, Nat Vol lab accreditation prog, 1990-1994; chair, radiation biophysics dept, 1990-1993; head, Mil Req & Appln Depts, 1989-1990; asst dir radiation health, puget sound naval shipyard, 1986-1989; sci dir, USN Dosimetry Ctr, 1980-1986; radiation physicist, armed forces radiobiol res Inst, USN, 1975-1978. **Memberships:** Health Physics Soc; Am Asn Physicists Med; Radiation res Soc; Am Acad Health Physics. **Research Statement & Publications:** Author several publications in field. **Mailing Address:** Armed Forces Radiobiol Res Inst, 8901 Wis Ave, Bethesda, MD 20889-5603. **Fax:** 301-295-4967. **E-Mail:** ekearsley@vax.afrri.usuhs.mil

KEARLEY, FRANCIS JOSEPH, JR, organic chemistry; deceased, see previous edition for last biography

KEARNEY, JOHN F, IMMUNOBIOLOGY, MICROBIOLOGY. **Personal Data:** b Orrorroo, SAustralia, March 30, 1945. **Education:** Univ Adelaide, SAustralia, BDS Hons, 1969; Univ Melbourne, PhD, 1973. **Professional Experience:** Consult, Becton-Dickinson, 1979-1984 & Idec Inc, Calif, 1986-; Basel Inst Immunol, 1985-1986 & Allergy & Immunol Study Sect, 1986-; Am Cancer Soc & Eleanor Roosevelt int cancer fels, 1985-1986; mem adv bd, Am Type Cult Asn, 1984-; ASSOC PROF, CELLULAR IMMUNOBIOL UNIT, SR SCIENTIST, COMPREHENSIVE CANCER CTR & PROF, DIV DEVELOP & CLIN IMMUNOL, DEPT MICROBIOL, UNIV ALA, BIRMINGHAM, 1983-; assoc scientist, Multipurpose Arthritis Ctr, Univ Ala, Birmingham, 1979; Europ Molecular Biol Orgn vis sr fel, Dept Genetics, Univ Cologne, WGer, 1978; assoc scientist, Comprehensive Cancer Ctr, 1976-1983; asst prof, Dept Microbiol, 1976-1980; res assoc, Dept Pediat, Univ Ala, Birmingham, 1974-1976; vis foreign dent scientist, Dept Pediat, Univ Ala, Birmingham, 1973-1974. **Memberships:** Am Asn Univ Prof; Am Asn Immunologists; Am Asn Pathologists; AAAS. **Mailing Address:** Dept Microbiol Univ Ala, 378 Tumor Inst, Birmingham, AL 35294-3300. **Fax:** 205-934-1875.

KEARNEY, JOSEPH K, COMPUTER SCIENCE. **Personal Data:** b January 2, 1951. **Education:** Univ Minn, BA, 1975, MS, 1981, PhD (comput sci), 1983; Univ Tex, MA, 1979. **Professional Experience:** ASSOC DEAN RES & DEVELOP, COL LIBERAL ARTS & SCI, UNIV IOWA, as of 2004; PROF, DEPT COMPUT SCI, UNIV IOWA, 1996-; chair, Dept Comput Sci, Univ Iowa, 1993-1996; assoc ed, Asn Comput Mach Comput Surveys, 1990-1994; grantee, NSF, 1988-1989, 1992-1995, 1994-1997 & 1995-1998; grantee, NIH, 1988; Vis scientist, Robotics Lab, Dept Comput Sci, Cornell Univ, 1986-1987; From asst prof to assoc prof, Dept Comput Sci, Univ Iowa, 1983-1996. **Memberships:** Asn Comput Mach; Inst Elec & Electronics Engrs; Inst Elec & Electronics Engrs Comput Soc. **Research Statement & Publications:** Author of several published articles. **Mailing Address:** Dept Comput Sci, Univ Iowa, Iowa City, IA 52242-1419. **Fax:** 319-335-3624. **E-Mail:** kearney@cs.uiowa.edu

KEARNEY, MICHAEL SEAN, COASTALGEOMORPHOLOGY, PALYNOLOGY. **Personal Data:** b Chicago, Ill, May 12, 1947; m 1980, Mary; c Moira. **Education:** Univ Ill, Urbana, AB, 1973; Western Ill Univ, MA, 1976; Univ Western Ont, PhD (geog), 1981. **Professional Experience:** Prin investr, US Fish & Wildlife Serv, 1987-; ASSOC PROF, GEOMORPHOL, UNIV MD, COL PARK, 1987-; prin investr, US Fish & Wildlife Serv, 1984-1985 & Cult Triangle Proj, UNESCO, 1984-; prin investr, US Environ Protection Agency, 1983-1984; prin investr, Off Water Policy, US Dept Interior, 1983-1985; asst prof, Geomorphol, Univ MD, College Park, 1981-1987; lectr geomorphol, Univ MD, Col Park, 1980-1981; Consult, Environ Can, 1977-1978. **Memberships:** AAAS; Am Asn Geogr; Am GEO Phys union, Estuarine res fedn, Coasta educ res found. **Research Statement & Publications:** Coastal and quaternary geomorphology and paleoecology, with emphasis on the Holocene; coastal marshes; estuaries; sea-level rise. **Mailing Address:** Dept Geog Lab Coastal Res, Univ Md, College Park, MD 20742-0001. **E-Mail:** mk11@umail.umd.edu

KEARNEY, PHILIP C, BIOCHEMISTRY, AGRICULTURE. **Personal Data:** b Baltimore, Md, December 31, 1932; m 1955, c 2. **Education:** Univ Md, BS, 1955, MS, 1957; Cornell Univ, PhD (agr), 1960. **Honors & Awards:** Int Award Res Pesticide Chem, Am Chem Soc, 1981. **Professional Experience:** RETIRED; ctr assoc dir, Md Water Resource Res Ctr, as of 2003; dep area dir, Nat Resource Inst, beginning 1988; adj prof chem & biochem, Univ Md, 1983; chief pesticide degradation lab, Nat Resources Inst, 1972-1988; Unit leader, Pesticide Degradation Lab, 1965-1972; BIOCHEMIST PESTICIDES, AGR RES CTR-WEST, USDA, 1962-; NSF fel biochem, 1960-1962; dir, Nat Resource Inst. **Memberships:** Am Chem Soc; Int Union Pure & Appl Chem; AAAS; Weed Sci Soc Am; Asn Off Anal Chemists. **Research Statement & Publications:** Pesticides; metabolism of organic pesticides by soil microorganisms; enzymology of pesticides. **Mailing Address:** Agr Res Serv, Nat Res Bldg, USDA, 3 Rm 10810300, Baltimore Ave BARC W, Beltsville, MD 20705-2350.

KEARNEY, PHILIP DANIEL, PHYSICS, ENVIRONMENTAL RADIATION PROTECTION, RADON. **Personal Data:** b Detroit, Mich, November 21, 1933; m 1958, Elizebeth; c Michael, David, Thomas & Charlotte (Mason). **Education:** Univ Mich, BS, 1958, MS, 1960, PhD (physics), 1964. **Professional Experience:** PROF EMER PHYSICS, COLO STATE UNIV, as of 2005; core lab, Argonne Nat Lab, 1987-2000; chem-nuclear corp, Argonne Nat Lab, 1984-2000; consult, Argonne Nat Lab, 1981-; Environ Radiation Measurements, Argonne Nat Lab, 1980-1981; assoc prof physics, Colo State Univ, beginning 1974; Sabbatical leave, Solar Particle Physics, Los Alamos Sci Lab, 1971-1972. **Memberships:** Health Physics Soc; emer, Board dir of radon sect of health physics soc. **Research Statement & Publications:** Environmental radiation measurements, radon, radon flux density, soil radium measurements. **Mailing Address:** Dept Physics, Colo State Univ, Ft Collins, CO 80523. **E-Mail:** kearneype@earthlink.net

KEARNEY, ROBERT EDWARD, BIOMEDICAL ENGINEERING. **Personal Data:** b Montreal, Que, January 19, 1947. **Education:** McGill Univ, BEng, 1968, MEng, 1971, PhD (biomed eng), 1976. **Honors & Awards:** Geddes Prize Biomed Eng, 1972. **Professional Experience:** PROF, PROF, DEPT BIOMED ENG & PHYSIOL, MCGILL UNIV, 1990-; CHMN BIOMED ENG, MCGILL UNIV, 1990-; mem Med Res Coun Grants Comt Biomed Eng, 1989-; actg chmn, Dept Biomed Eng, 1989-1990; assoc mem, Dept Elec Eng, 1989; assoc mem, Dept Mech Eng, 1986-; dir, Biomed eng Unit, 1985-1989; assoc prof, Biomed Eng & Dept Physiol, 1983-1990; Assoc mem, Sch Phys & Occup Therapy, McGill Univ, 1981-; asst prof Biomed Eng, 1978-1983 & Dept Physiol, 1979-1983; fac lectr, Dept Physiol, 1978-1979; lectr, Biomed Eng Unit, 1978; fel, Aviation Med Res Unit, 1977-1978; res asst, Biomed Eng Unit, McGill Univ, 1976-1977; Comput systs engr, Div Neurol, Montreal Gen Hosp, 1974-1977; assoc ed, Inst Elec & Electronics Engrs Trans Biomed Eng. **Memberships:** Inst Elec & Electronics Engrs; Soc Neuroscience; Biomed Eng Soc. **Research Statement & Publications:** Biomedical engineering; medical imaging; human joint dynamics; motor control system; medical and biological engineering and computing; numerous technical publications. **Mailing Address:** Dept Biomed Eng, McGill Univ, 3775 Univ St Rm 309, Montreal, PQ H3A 2B4, Can. **Fax:** 514-398-7461. **E-Mail:** robert.kearney@mcgill.ca

KEARNEY, ROBERT JAMES, SOLID STATE PHYSICS. **Personal Data:** b Manchester, NH, October 5, 1935; m 1961, c 4. **Education:** Univ NH, BS, 1957, MS, 1959; Iowa State Univ, PhD (physics), 1964. **Professional Experience:** RETIRED; prof emer physics, Univ Idaho, as of 2003; prof physics, Univ Idaho, beginning 1973; Vis prof, Univ Milan, Italy, 1972-1973; from asst prof to assoc prof, Univ Idaho, 1964-1973; Asst physics, Ames Lab, AEC, 1960-1964. **Memberships:** AAAS; Am Asn Physics Teachers; Am Phys Soc. **Research Statement & Publications:** Electronic structure of metals and semiconductors; optical spectroscopy of molecules. **Mailing Address:** Dept Physics, Univ Idaho, 718 E Eighth St, Moscow, ID 83843. **E-Mail:** bkearney@uidaho.edu

KEARNS, DAVID R, BIOPHYSICAL CHEMISTRY. **Personal Data:** b Urbana, Ill, March 20, 1935; m 1958, Alice; c 2. **Education:** Univ Ill, BS, 1956; Univ Calif, Berkeley, PhD (phys chem), 1960. **Professional Experience:** PROF EMER CHEM, UNIV CALIF, SAN DIEGO, as of 2005; chmn, Chem Dept, 1988-1989; chem rev, Anal Biochem, 1977-1982; prof chem, Univ Calif, San Diego, beginning 1975; adv bd, Biopolymers, 1974; molecular photochem, photochem & photobiol, 1972-1978; assoc ed, photochem & photobiol, 1971-1975; Guggenheim fel, 1969-1970; A P Sloan fel, 1965-1967; lectr comt biophys, Harvard Med Sch, 1965; from asst prof to prof phys chem, Univ Calif, Riverside, 1962-1975; fel, Mass Inst Technol, 1961-1962; fel theoret chem, Univ Chicago, 1960-1961. **Memberships:** Am Chem Soc; Am Photobiol Soc; Biophys Soc; Protein Soc. **Research Statement & Publications:** Physical biochemistry; spectroscopy; nuclear magnetic resonance, protein and DNA. **Mailing Address:** Dept Chem, Univ Calif San Diego, La Jolla, CA 92093-0342.

KEARNS, DAVID TODD, FEDERAL AGENCY ADMINISTRATION. **Personal Data:** b Rochester, NY, August 11, 1930; m 1954, Shirley V Cox; c Katherine, Elizabeth, Anne, Susan, David T & Andrew. **Education:** Univ Rochester, BS, 1952. **Honors & Awards:** Chairman's Award, Am Asn Eng Soc, 1992. **Professional Experience:** DAVID T KEARNS CTR, UNIV ROCHESTER, as of 2004; DEP SECY EDUC, US DEPT EDUC, 1991-; chmn, Xerox Corp, 1990-1991; chmn & chief exec officer, Xerox Corp, 1985-1990; pres & chief exec officer, Xerox Corp, 1977-1985; chief oper officer, Xerox Corp, 1977-1982; exec vpres int opers, Rank Xerox & Fuji Xerox, 1977; group vpres charge, Rank Xerox & Fuji Xerox, 1975-1977; group vpres info syst, Xerox Corp, 1972-1975; staff, Xerox Corp, 1971-1972; vpres, Mkt Opers Data Processing Div, 1971; Staff, IBM, 1954-1971; Mem, Pres Educ Policy Adv Comn. **Memberships:** Am Philos Asn. **Mailing Address:** US Dept Educ, 400 Maryland Ave SW No 4015, Washington, DC 20202.

KEARNS, DONALD ALLEN, MATHEMATICS. **Personal Data:** b New Bedford, Mass, September 10, 1923; m 1947, c 7. **Education:** Boston Univ, AB, 1947, PhD (math), 1955; Brown Univ, MA, 1950. **Professional Experience:** PROF MATH, MERRIMACK COL, 1958-; asst prof math, Univ Maine, 1953-1958; From instr to asst prof math, Merrimack Col, 1948-1953. **Memberships:** Am Math Soc; Math Asn Am. **Research Statement & Publications:** Differential equations. **Mailing Address:** 23 Pleasant St, Andover, MA 01810.

KEARNS, LANCE EDWARD, GEOLOGY, MINERALOGY. **Personal Data:** b Greensburg, Pa, May 22, 1949; m 1991, Cynthia; c Jessica C & Janel L. **Education:** Waynesburg Col, BS, 1971; Univ Del, MS, 1973, PhD (mineral), 1977. **Professional Experience:** PROF GEOL, JAMES MADISON UNIV, as of 2003; DIR, SUMMER GEOL FIELD PROG, JAMES MADISON UNIV, as of 2003; CUR, JAMES MADISON UNIV MINERAL MUS, as of 2003; assoc prof geol, James Madison Univ, beginning 1976. **Memberships:** Am Mineral Soc. **Research Statement & Publications:** Mineral chemistry, especially fluorine effects in high temperature metacarbonates; minerals of Amelia Pegmatite Dist, Va, USA. **Mailing Address:** Dept Geol & Environ Sci, James Madison Univ, MSC 7703 Miller Hall 226 800 S Main St, Harrisonburg, VA 22807-0001. **Fax:** 540-568-7938. **E-Mail:** kearnsle@jmu.edu

KEARNS, ROBERT J, CELLULAR IMMUNOLOGY. **Personal Data:** b February 9, 1946; c 3. **Education:** Wash State Univ, PhD, 1978. **Professional Experience:** PROF BIOL, UNIV DAYTON, as of 2002; DIR, PREMEDICAL & PREDENTAL STUDIES PROG, as of 2002; assoc prof biol, Univ Dayton, beginning 1990; asst prof, 1984-1990. **Memberships:** Am Soc Microbiologists; Am Asn Immunologists; Reticuloendothial Soc. **Research Statement & Publications:** Cellular immunology. **Mailing Address:** Dept Biol, Univ Dayton, SC-307B/137 300 Col Park, Dayton, OH 45469-2320. **Fax:** 937-229-2021. **E-Mail:** kearns@udayton.edu

KEARNS, ROBERT WILLIAM, mechanical engineering; deceased, see previous edition for last biography

KEARNS, THOMAS J, ALGEBRA. **Personal Data:** b Evanston, Ill, June 1, 1940; m 1963, c 3. **Education:** Univ Santa Clara, BS, 1962; Univ Ill, MS, 1964, PhD (math), 1968. **Professional Experience:** CHMN, DEPT MATH, NORTHERN KY UNIV, 1981-; ASSOC PROF MATH, NORTHERN KY UNIV, 1977-; asst prof, Northern Ky Univ, 1975-1977; from instr to asst prof math, Univ Del, 1967-1975. **Memberships:** Am Math Soc; Math Asn Am. **Research Statement & Publications:** Representation theory for Lie algebras of classical type. **Mailing Address:** Dept Math & Comput Sci, Northern Ky Univ, Suite 336, Highland Heights, KY 41099-0000. **E-Mail:** kearns@nku.edu

KEARNS, THOMAS P, OPHTHALMOLOGY. **Personal Data:** b Louisville, Ky, April 2, 1922; m 1944, c 2. **Education:** Univ Louisville, AB, 1944, MD, 1946; Univ Minn, MS, 1952. **Professional Experience:** RETIRED; emer consult, Mayo Clin, beginning 1987;

mem fac ophthal, Mayo Med Sch, Univ Minn, 1977-1987; consult, Mayo Clin, 1953-1987; from asst prof to assoc prof, Mayo Med Sch Univ Minn, 1953-1977. **Research Statement & Publications:** Diseases of the brain and eye. **Mailing Address:** Mayo Clin, Rochester, MN 55905.

KEARNS, WILLIAM G, GENETICS. **Professional Experience:** DIR, SHADY GROVE CTR PREIMPLANTATION GENETIC DIAG, as of 2002. **Memberships:** Am Soc Human Genetics. **Mailing Address:** Shady Grove Ctr Preimplantation Genetic Diag, Rockville, MD 20850.

KEAST, CRAIG LEWIS, ADVANCED MICROELECTRONICS RESEARCH IN SILICON TECHNOLOGIES, DEEP SUBMICRON LITHOGRAPHY. **Personal Data:** b Los Angeles, Calif, November 6, 1958; m Rev. **Education:** Hamilton Col, BA, 1980; Mass Inst Technol, SM, 1989, Eng, 1990, PhD (elec eng & comput sci), 1992. **Professional Experience:** LEADER, ADVAN SILICON TECHNOL, MASS INST TECHNOL LINCOLN LAB, as of 2005; dir opers, Microelectronic Lab, Mass Inst Technol Lincoln Lab, beginning 1994; mem tech staff, Mass Inst Technol, 1992-1994; Kodak res fel, Mass Inst Technol, 1988-1992; asst staff, Mass Inst Technol Lincoln Lab, 1983-1988; semiconductor process technician, Mass Inst Technol Lincoln Lab, 1981-1983; math & sci teacher, Concord Pub Schs, 1980-1981. **Memberships:** Inst Elec & Electronics Engrs; Sigma Xi; Int Soc Optical Eng. **Research Statement & Publications:** Advanced optical lithography; three-dimensional silicon device fabrication and characterization; chemical-mechanical planarization; focal plane analog signal processing; advanced process development. **Mailing Address:** Mass Inst Technol, Lincoln Lab, 244 Wood St, Lexington, MA 02420-9108. **Fax:** 781-981-7889. **E-Mail:** keast@ll.mit.edu

KEAST, DAVID N(ORRIS), ENVIRONMENTAL NOISE. **Personal Data:** b Pittsburgh, Pa, January 8, 1931; m 1955, Estelle; c 4. **Education:** Amherst Col, BA, 1952; Mass Inst Technol, BS & MS, 1954. **Professional Experience:** CONSULT, 1988-; vpres, HMM Assocs, Inc, 1983-1988; mgr, environ dept, Bolt Beranek & Newman, 1973-1983; vpres develop, MFE Corp, Wilmington, 1971-1973; consult acoust & instrumentation, vpres Data Equip Div, 1966-1971; supvr consult, Calif, 1964-1966; consult acoust & instrumentation, Calif, 1960-1964; sr engr, Bolt Beranek & Newman, Inc, Los Angeles, 1957-1960; engr acoust, Bolt Beranek & Newman, Inc, Los Angeles, 1954-1957. **Memberships:** fel Acoust Soc Am; sr mem Inst Elec & Electronics Engrs; Inst Noise Control Engrs. **Research Statement & Publications:** Acoustic-meteorological interactions and processing techniques for high-frequency dynamic data; effects of sound on the human environment; community noise and emergency warning. **Mailing Address:** 657 Westford Rd, Carlisle, MA 01741-1542. **E-Mail:** dnk@world.std.com

KEASTER, ARMON JOSEPH, ENTOMOLOGY. **Personal Data:** b Lilbourn, Mo, March 12, 1933; m 1956, c 2. **Education:** Univ Mo, BS, 1959, MS, 1961, PhD (entom), 1965. **Professional Experience:** PROF EMER ENTOM, UNIV MO-COLUMBIA, as of 2001; prof entom, Univ Mo-Columbia, beginning 1976; From instr to assoc prof, 1970-1976. **Memberships:** Sigma Xi; Entom Soc Am. **Research Statement & Publications:** Biology and management of soil and foliar pests attacking corn and other field crops; dispersal migration of Noctuidae. **Mailing Address:** Dept Entom, Univ Mo, Columbia, MO 65211.

KEAT, PAUL POWELL, CERAMICS, PHYSICAL CHEMISTRY. **Personal Data:** b Elizabeth, NJ, November 29, 1923; m 1952, c 3. **Education:** Rutgers Univ, BSc, 1947, MSc, 1950, PhD (ceramics), 1956. **Professional Experience:** RETIRED; sr res assoc, Norton Co, 1986-1992; res assoc, Norton Co, 1963-1986; sr res engr, Norton Co, 1958-1963; res engr, Norton Co, 1953-1958. **Research Statement & Publications:** Design of ultrahigh pressure equipment; synthesis at ultrahigh pressure; hydrothermal synthesis; abrasive bond development. **Mailing Address:** 22 Heatherwood Dr, Shrewsbury, MA 01545.

KEATING, BARBARA HELEN, PALEOMAGNETISM, ARCHAEOLOGY. **Personal Data:** b Brooksville, Fla, December 25, 1950. **Education:** Fla State Univ, BA, 1971; Univ Tex, Dallas, MS, 1975, PhD (geosci), 1976. **Professional Experience:** ASSOC GEOPHYS, UNIV HAWAII, as of 2000; PROF OCEANOG, UNIV HAWAII, 1981-; researcher geophys, Univ Hawaii, beginning 1976. **Memberships:** Geol Soc Am; Am Geophys Union; Int Asn Geomagnetism & Aeronomy; Soc Econ Paleontologist & Mineralogist. **Research Statement & Publications:** Paleomagnetism and marine geology of the Pacific Ocean basin. **Mailing Address:** Hawaii Inst Geophys & Paleantol, Univ Hawaii, 2525 Correa Rd, Honolulu, HI 96822. **Fax:** 808-956-3189. **E-Mail:** keating@soest.hawaii.edu

KEATING, EUGENE KNEELAND, AGRICULTURAL BIOCHEMISTRY, NUTRITION. **Personal Data:** b Liberal, Kans, February 15, 1928; m 1951, Iris L Myers; c Denise L (Schnagl) & Kimberly A. **Education:** Kans State Univ, BS, 1953, MS, 1954; Univ Ariz, PhD (ruminant nutrit), 1964. **Professional Experience:** PROF RUMINANT NUTRIT, CALIF STATE POLYTECH UNIV, POMONA, 1978-; chmn dept animal sci, Calif State Polytech Univ, Pomona, 1971-1978; from asst prof to assoc prof, Calif State Polytech Univ, Pomona, 1964-1971; farm mgr, Midwestern Univ, 1959-1960; Instr animal sci, Midwestern Univ, 1957-1960; asst farm mgr, Midwestern Univ, 1957-1959; mem coun, Agr Sci & Technol, Am Inst Chem. **Memberships:** Am Soc Animal Sci; Brit Soc Animal Prod; fel Am Inst Chem. **Research Statement & Publications:** Ruminant nutrition, particularly in cattle. **Mailing Address:** Dept Animal Sci, Calif State Polytech Univ, Pomona, CA 91768.

KEATING, GERALD M, AERONAUTICS. **Professional Experience:** SCIENTIST, LANGLEY RESEARCH CTR, as of 2006. **Memberships:** Asia Oceania Geosciences Soc. **Mailing Address:** 401B, NASA Langley Res Ctr, Hampton, VA 23665. **Fax:** 804-864-6326.

KEATING, JAMES T, ORGANIC CHEMISTRY, POLYMER CHEMISTRY. **Personal Data:** b Oak Park, Ill, January 21, 1941; m 1970, Mimi; c 3. **Education:** St Mary's Col, Minn, BA, 1962; Pa State Univ, PhD (chem), 1968. **Professional Experience:** SR RES ASSOC, E I DU PONT DEL NEMOURS & CO INC, WILMINGTON, DEL, 1989-; res assoc, Seneca, Ill, 1983-1989; sr chemist, Seneca, Ill, 1981-1983; sr chemist, Seneca, Ill, 1977-1981; res chemist, Plastic Prod & Resins Dept, Exp Sta, Wilmington, Del, 1968-1976; NSF fel, 1962-1966. **Research Statement & Publications:** Carbene chemistry; aliphatic carbonium ion reactions; fluorinated free radicals; electrochemistry; Friedel-Crafts-type polymerizations; organic and inorganic coatings; emulsion polymerization; occupational safety and health; ion exchange membranes; fluoropolymers chloralkali. **Mailing Address:** E I duPont de Nemours & Co, 1007 Mkt St, Wilmington, DE 19898.

KEATING, JEROME P, MATHEMATICS. **Honors & Awards:** Don Owen Award, 2006. **Professional Experience:** PROF, DEPT MGT SCI & STATIST COL BUS, UNIV TEX, SAN ANTONIO, as of 2006. **Mailing Address:** Div Math, Univ Tex San Antonio, San Antonio, TX 78429-0664. **Fax:** 810-551-3694.

KEATING, JOHN JOSEPH, NUCLEAR REACTOR FUELS. **Personal Data:** b Montrose, SDak, January 17, 1938; m 1961, c 4. **Education:** SDak State Col, BS, 1960; Iowa State Univ, MS, 1966, PhD (nuclear eng), 1968. **Professional Experience:** RETIRED; asst mgr tech support, Fuels Supply Div, Richland Opers Off, 1989-1994; dir, Fuels Supply Div, Richland Opers Off, 1981-1989; dir, Reactor Technol Div, Fast Flux Test Fac Prog Off, US Dept Energy, 1978-1981; asst dir engr technol & fuels, Fast Flux Test Fac Proj Off, US Energy Res & Develop Agency, 1974-1978; reactor fuels engr, Div Reactor Develop & Technol, 1973-1974; nuclear engr, Idaho Opers Off, US AEC 1968-1973. **Memberships:** Am Nuclear Soc. **Research Statement & Publications:** Development and production of core components for liquid metal fast breeder reactors; core components include fuel, blanket, absorber and reflector assemblies. **Mailing Address:** 2611 Harris Ave, Richland, WA 99352.

KEATING, KATHLEEN IRWIN, PLANKTON CULTURE, TRACE ELEMENT NUTRITION. **Personal Data:** b NJ, March 7, 1938; m 1962, Martin; c Sean Michael. **Education:** Cornell Univ, BA, 1960; William Patterson Col, MS, 1970; Yale Univ, MPh, 1972, PhD (limnol), 1975. **Professional Experience:** Consult, Dow Chem Co, 1982-1989; prin investr, NSF Ecol Prog, 1979-1982; prin investr, NJ Agr Exp Sta, 1976-; PROF LIMNOL & ENVIRON SCI, DEPT ENVIRON SCI, RUTGERS UNIV, 1974-; teacher sci & math, Dumont Pub Sch Syst, 1962-1968. **Memberships:** AAAS; Am Soc Limnol & Oceanog; Crustacean Soc; Ecol Soc Am; Soc Environ Toxicol & Chem; Am Inst Nutrit. **Research Statement & Publications:** Roles of trace element nutrition and allelochemistry in plankton (phytoplankton and zooplankton) community structure; use of highly controlled, defined cultures to isolate critical factors significant to in situ community structure; in vivo trace element interaction; publications on the headings selenium deficiency induced by zinc deprivation, allelopathy, blue-green algal inhibition of diatom growth, transition from mesotrophic to eutrophic community structure. **Mailing Address:** Dept Environ Sci, Cook Col, Rutgers Univ, EENR 013 14 Col Farm Rd, New Brunswick, NJ 08901. **Fax:** 732-932-8644. **E-Mail:** kkeating@rci.rutgers.edu

KEATING, KENNETH L(EE), MATERIALS SCIENCE ENGINEERING. **Personal Data:** b Chicago, Ill, May 19, 1923. **Education:** Mass Inst Technol, SB, 1947; Univ Mo, MS, 1950; Stanford Univ, PhD (metall), 1954. **Professional Experience:** PROF EMER METALL ENG, UNIV ARIZ, 1990-; consult, Cabot Corp, 1978-1986; prof, Univ Ariz, 1967-1990; assoc prof, Univ Ariz, 1961-1967; metallurgist, Semiconductor Prod Div, Motorola, Inc, Ariz, 1955-1961; metallurgist, Bell Tel Labs, Inc, 1954-1955; instr, Stanford Univ, 1951-1954; instr, Univ Mo, 1949-1950; asst metall, Univ Mo, 1948-1949; metallurgist, Titanium Div, Nat Lead Co, 1947-1948. **Memberships:** Am Soc Metals; Electrochem Soc; Am Inst Mining Metall & Petrol Engrs; Am Ceramic Soc; Nat Asn Corrosion Engrs. **Research Statement & Publications:** Corrosion of metals; phase relations between materials; solid state metallurgy. **Mailing Address:** Dept Mat Sci & Eng, Univ Ariz, Tucson, AZ 85715-1506.

KEATING, PATRICK NORMAN, APPLIED PHYSICS, ELECTRONICS ENGINEERING. **Personal Data:** b Newcastle, UK, February 18, 1939; div, c 2. **Education:** Univ Nottingham, BSc, 1959, MSc, 1961; Univ Mich, PhD (physics), 1969. **Professional Experience:** DIR & GEN MGR, ALLIED-SIGNAL AEROSPACE TECHNOL CTR, 1983-; assoc dir res, Bendix Advan Technol Ctr, 1980-1983; dir, Appl Physics Dept, Bendix Res Lab, 1974-1979; head Laser Optics & Acoustics Dept, Allied-Signal Aerospace Technol Ctr, 1970-1974; proj physicist, Allied-Signal Aerospace Technol Ctr, 1965-1970; physicist, Tyco Labs, Inc, Waltham, Mass, 1963-1965; physicist, Assoc Elec Industs, UK, 1960-1963. **Memberships:** Am Mgt Asn; Inst Elec & Electronics Engrs. **Research Statement & Publications:** Computer science, acoustics, underwater acoustics, and acoustic signal processing; sensors, optics; lattice dynamics; solid state physics. **Mailing Address:** Allied-Signal Aerospace Technol Ctr, Ellicott City, MD 21042.

KEATING, RICHARD CLARK, SYSTEMATIC BOTANY. **Personal Data:** b St Paul, Minn, August 6, 1937; m 1961, c 2. **Education:** Colgate Univ, AB, 1959; Univ Cincinnati, MS, 1962, PhD (bot), 1965. **Professional Experience:** PROF EMER BIOL, SOUTHERN ILL UNIV, EDWARDSVILLE, as of 2004; RES ASSOC, MO BOT GARDEN, 2000-; actg cordr, Deans Col, beginning 1990; elected fel, Ill State Acad Sci, 1984; consult, Syst Panel, NSF, 1982-1984; prof biol, Southern Ill Univ, Edwardsville, beginning 1975; res assoc, Marie Selby Bot Garden, Sarasota, 1974-1980; dir, Trop Biol Prog, Assoc Univs Int Educ, 1970; res assoc, Mo Bot Garden, St Louis, beginning 1969; from asst prof to assoc prof, Dean's Col, 1966-1975; vis asst prof bot, Univ Cincinnati, 1965-1966; asst prof biol, Wis State Univ, Platteville, 1964-1965. **Memberships:** AAAS; Bot Soc Am; Int Asn Wood Anatomists; Int Asn Plant Taxon; Int Aroid Soc; Soc Conserv Biol; Am Soc Plant Taxon. **Research Statement & Publications:** Anatomical investigations on the evolution and classification of vascular plants; Ranales, Solanaceae and Araceae. **Mailing Address:** Mo Bot Garden, PO Box 299, St Louis, MO 63166-0299. **Fax:** 314-577-9596. **E-Mail:** rkeatin@siue.edu

KEATON, PAUL W, NUCLEAR PHYSICS. **Personal Data:** b Roanoke, Va, October 1, 1935; m 1957, c 3. **Education:** Emory & Henry Col, BS, 1957; Johns Hopkins Univ, PhD (physics), 1963. **Professional Experience:** RETIRED; strategic planning & policy analysis, Los Alamos Nat Lab, beginning 1980; adj prof, dept physics, Colo Sch Mines, as of 2004; asst to dir, Electron Div, 1979-1980; leader, Electron Div, 1973-1979; vis scientist, Ctr Europ Nuclear Res, Geneva, Switz, 1972-1973; staff mem, Physics Div, 1965-1973; res assoc nuclear physics, Johns Hopkins Univ, 1963-1965. **Memberships:** Fel Am Phys Soc; sr mem Inst Elec & Electronics Engrs. **Research Statement & Publications:** Experimental research with charged particle polarization, Mossbauer effect, direct reactions, electronics and fast neutron cross sections. **Mailing Address:** Los Alamos Nat Lab, Los Alamos, NM 87545.

KEATS, ARTHUR STANLEY, PHARMACOLOGY. **Personal Data:** b New Brunswick, NJ, May 31, 1923; m 1946, c 4. **Education:** Rutgers Univ, BS, 1943; Univ Pa, MD, 1946. **Professional Experience:** CLIN PROF ANESTHESIOL, UNIV TEX HEALTH SCI CTR, HOUSTON, 1978-; CHIEF ANESTHESIA, DIV CARDIOVASC ANESTHESIA, TEX HEART INST, 1974-; clin prof, Baylor Col Med, 1974-1975; dir anesthesiol, Ben Taub Gen Hosp, 1955-; prof anesthesiol & chmn dept, Baylor Col Med, 1955-1974; anesthesiologist, House Sisters Red Cross, Switz, 1952-1953 & Mary Imogene Bassett Hosp, 1953-1955; assoc anesthesiol, Col Physicians & Surgeons, Columbia Univ, 1953-1955; asst anesthetist, Mass Gen Hosp, 1951; Asst instr, Sch Med, Univ Pa, 1946. **Memberships:** AAAS; Am Soc Pharmacol & Exp Therapeut; Am Soc Anesthesiol. **Research Statement & Publications:** Opiates; analgesics. **Mailing Address:** Div Cardiovasc Anesthesia, Tex Heart Inst, THI MC 1-226, PO Box 20345, Houston, TX 77225-0345. **Fax:** 832-355-6500. **E-Mail:** dcamp@heart.thi.tmc.edu

KEATS, BRONYA J, GENETICS. **Professional Experience:** PROF & HEAD, DEPT GENETICS, LA STATE UNIV HEALTH SCI CTR, as of 2005. **Memberships:** Am Soc Human Genetics; Asn Res Otolaryngol; Int Genetic Epidemiol Soc. **Mailing Address:** Dept Biometry & Genetics La State Univ Med Ctr, 1901 Perdido St, New Orleans, LA 70112-1328.

KEATS, JOHN BERT, INDUSTRIAL ENGINEERING, STATISTICS. **Personal Data:** b New York, NY, September 14, 1936; m 1968, c 2. **Education:** Lehigh Univ, BS, 1959; Fla State Univ, MS, 1964, PhD (educ res), 1970; Okla State Univ, PhD, 1983. **Professional Experience:** PROF INDUST & MGT SYSTS ENG, ARIZ STATE UNIV, 1997-; DIR, STATIST & ENG APPLN QUAL LAB, ARIZ STATE UNIV, 1997-; vis prof, Univ Christchurch, 1995; assoc prof, Ariz State Univ, 1984-1996; mem fac, Sch Indust Eng & Mgt, Okla State Univ, 1980-1983; consult, Southern Regional Off, Col Entrance Exam Bd, Ga, beginning 1970; assoc prof, La Tech Univ, 1969-1980; assoc, Advan Proj Dept, Syst Develop Corp, Calif, 1968; asst prof indust eng, La Tech Univ, 1964-1966; Indust engr, US Steel Corp, Ill, 1959-1961. **Memberships:** Sr mem Am Inst Indust Engrs; Am Statist Asn; Am Educ Res Asn. **Research Statement & Publications:** Educational and operations research; computer assisted instruction. **Mailing Address:** Dept Indust & Mgt Systs Eng, Ariz State Univ, PO Box 875906, Tempe, AZ 85287-5906. **Fax:** 602-965-2910. **E-Mail:** keats@asuvax.eas.asu.edu

KEATS, THEODORE ELIOT, RADIOLOGY. **Personal Data:** b New Brunswick, NJ, June 26, 1924; m 1974, Patricia; c Matthew & Ian. **Education:** Rutgers Univ, BS, 1945; Univ Pa, MD, 1947; Am Bd Radiol, dipl. **Honors & Awards:** Gold Medal, Am Col Radiol; Medal, Int Skeletal Soc; Medal Am Soc Energy Radiology. **Professional Experience:** VIS PROF RADIOL, UNIV VA HEALTH SYST, 2001-; trustee, Am Bd Radiol, 1973-1985; prof radiol, Univ Hosp, Univ Va Sch Med, 1964-2001; chmn dept, Univ Hosp, Univ VA Sch Med, 1964-1991; vis prof, Karolinska Inst, Sweden, 1963-1964; from assoc prof to prof, Sch Med, Univ Mo, 1956-1963; from instr to asst prof, Sch Med, Univ Calif, 1953-1956; resident radiol, Univ Mich Hosp, 1948-1951; intern, Hosp Univ Pa, 1947-1948; ed, J Skeletal Radio, J Appl Radiol, J Energy Radiol, J Current Prob Diag Radiol. **Memberships:** Radiol Soc NAm; Roentgen Ray Soc; AMA; fel Am Col Radiol; Asn Univ Radiol; Int Skeletal Soc; Am Soc Energy Radiol; hon mem Soc Pediat Radiol. **Research Statement & Publications:** Pediatric and skeletal radiology; name variants; musculo skeletal strain injury. **Mailing Address:** Dept Radiol, Univ Va Health Syst, Charlottesville, VA 22908. **Fax:** 434-982-1618. **E-Mail:** tek@virginia.edu

KEAVENEY, WILLIAM PATRICK, ORGANIC CHEMISTRY. **Personal Data:** b New York, December 25, 1936; m 1961, c 5. **Education:** Manhattan Col, BS, 1958; Fordham Univ, PhD (org chem), 1964. **Professional Experience:** SCIENTIST, SUN CHEM CORP, CARLSTADT, 1991-; Res assoc, Inmont Corp, Clifton, 1962-1990. **Memberships:** Am Chem Soc; affil Int Union Pure & Appl Chem. **Research Statement & Publications:** Pyrodoxine determination; synthesis of dichloro-diphenyl-trichlorethane analogs; norbornylene polymerization; ozonolysis; radiation curing; polymer chemistry. **Mailing Address:** Sun Chem Corp Tech Ctr, 631 Central Ave, Carlstadt, NJ 07072.

KEAVENY, TONY M, BIO-MECHANICS. **Personal Data:** b Dublin, Ireland, June 14, 1962. **Education:** Univ Col Dublin, Ireland, BE, 1984; Cornell Univ, MS, 1988, PhD (mech eng), 1991. **Honors & Awards:** Y C Fung Young Investr Award, Bioeng Div, Am Soc Mech Engrs, 1996. **Professional Experience:** PROF DEPT MECH ENG & BIOENGINEERING, UNIV CALIF, BERKELEY, as of 2005; ASSOC ED, JOURNAL BIOENGINEERING, UNIV CALIF, BERKERLY, 1999-; assoc prof, Dept Bioengineering, Univ Calif, Berkerly, beginning 1999-; assoc prof, Dept Mech Eng, Univ Calif, Berkeley, beginning 1997-; NSF Career Award, 1996-; ASST PROF, DEPT ORTHOP SURG, UNIV CALIF, SAN FRANCISCO, 1994-; FAC MEM, JOINT GRAD GROUP BIOENGINEERING, UNIV CALIF, BERKELEY, 1993-; adj asst prof, Dept Ceramic Eng, Clemson Univ, 1993-1998; asst prof, Dept Orthop Surg, Univ Calif, San Francisco, 1993-1997; DIR, ORTHOP BIOMECHANICS LAB, DEPT MECH ENG, UNIV CALIF, BERKELEY, CALIF, 1993-; NIH First Award, 1992-1997; health sci & technol affil fac mem, Div Health Sci & Technol, Harvard Univ-Mass Inst Technol, 1992-1993; sr res assoc, Orthop Biomech Lab, Dept Orthop Surg, Beth Israel Hosp, Mass, 1991-1993; Instr, Dept Orthop Surg, Harvard Med Sch, 1991-1993; Maurice E Muller Found postdoctoral fel orthop biomech, Orthop Biomech Lab, Dept Orthop Surg, Beth Israel Hosp, Mass, 1990-1991; res asst, E I Dupont Del Nemours & Co, Del, 1987; Asst lectr, Dublin Inst Technol, Ireland, 1984-1985. **Memberships:** Orthop Res Soc; Am Soc Mech Engrs; Am Soc Biomech; Biomed Eng Soc; Am Soc Bone & Mineral Res. **Mailing Address:** Dept Mech Eng, Univ Calif, 6175 Etcheverry Hall, Berkeley, CA 94720-1740. **Fax:** 510-642-6163. **E-Mail:** tmk@me.berkeley.edu

KEAY, BRIAN A, ORGANIC CHEMISTRY. **Education:** Univ Waterloo, BSc, 1979 & PhD, 1983. **Professional Experience:** PROF, DEPT CHEM, UNIV CALGARY, as of 2003. **Research Statement & Publications:** Development of new chiral ligands; catalysts; and reagents for asymmetric transformations at both 1 atm (1 x 105Pa) and high pressures (1-2 GPa); asymmetric ligands; catalysts; reactions and syntheses; palladium-catalyzed reactions; chiral Lewis acids; natural product syntheses; solid phase organic syntheses. **Mailing Address:** Dept Chem, Univ Calgary, 2500 University Drive NW, Calgary, AB T2N 1N4, Can. **Fax:** 403-289-9488. **E-Mail:** keay@ucalgary.ca

KEBABIAN, JOHN WILLIS, ENDOCRINOLOGY, DOPAMINE RECEPTORS. **Personal Data:** b New York, NY, September 20, 1946; m 1975, Procy; c 2. **Education:** Yale Univ, BS, 1968, MPhil, 1970, PhD (pharmacol), 1973. **Professional Experience:** VPRES RES & DEVELOP, RES BIOCHEM INT, 1992-; from proj leader to sr proj leader Neurosci, Abbott Labs, 1986-1992; Bd dirs, Yale Alumni Fund, 1983-; sect chief, NIH, 1981-1986; pharmacologist, NIH, 1978-1981; sr staff fel, NIH, 1976-1978; res assoc, NIH, 1974-1976. **Memberships:** Am Soc Biol Chemists; Am Soc Pharm & Exp Therapeut; Brit Pharmacol Soc; Endocrine Soc; AAAS. **Research Statement & Publications:** Receptors for neurotransmitters; dopamine receptors; pituitary gland; author of three citation classics. **Mailing Address:** Res Biochem Int, One Strathmore Rd, Natick, MA 01778.

KEBARLE, PAUL, PHYSICAL CHEMISTRY. **Personal Data:** b Sofia, Bulgaria, September 21, 1926; m, c 1. **Education:** Swiss Fed Inst Technol, Dipl Ing Chem, 1952; Univ BC, PhD, 1955. **Honors & Awards:** American Chemical Society, The Field and Franklin Award for Outstanding Achevement in Mass Spectrometry 1994 The Canadian Institute of Canada (CIC) Medal for Outstanding Contribution to Chemistry of Chemical Engineering 1986 The F P Lossing Award of Canadian Society for Mass Spectrometry 1994. **Professional Experience:** PROF EMER CHEM, UNIV ALTA, as of 2003; prof chem, Univ Alta, beginning 1968; from asst prof to assoc prof, Univ Alta, 1958-1968; Nat Res Coun Can fel, 1955-1958. **Memberships:** Fel Royal Soc Can. **Research Statement & Publications:** Application of mass spectrometry to reaction kinetics in the gas phase; ion-molecule interactions at high pressure; ionic solvation and ionic reactivity in the gas phase; ion-molecule equilibria; Mechaninsm of Electrospray and Applications to the study of Proteins. **Mailing Address:** Dept Chem, Univ Alta, Edmonton, AB T6G 2G2, Can. **Fax:** 403-492-8231. **E-Mail:** paul.kebarle@ualberta.ca

KEBLAWI, FEISAL SAID, COMMUNICATIONS SYSTEMS ENGINEERING. **Personal Data:** b Acre, Palestine, July 11, 1935; American citizen; m 1973, c 4. **Education:** Am Univ Beirut, BS, 1957; NC State Univ, MS, 1962, PhD (elec eng), 1965. **Professional Experience:** PROJ MGR, FED AVIATION ADMIN, WASH, DC, 1990-; staff asst defense, Senator Thurmond, beginning 1981; cong fel, Inst Elec & Electronics Engrs, 1981-1982; US deleg, US/USSR Working Group Air Traffic Control, Moscow, 1978; satellite commun systs engr, Mitre Corp, 1968-1990; mem tech staff satellite systs eng, RCA Corp, 1965-1968; US deleg, US/Ger group air defense. **Memberships:** Sr mem Inst Elec & Electronics Engrs; Planetary Soc. **Research Statement & Publications:** Satellite communications deep space and tactical systems; tactical communications systems; air traffic control; forward air defense; control systems engineering; stabilization of heat transfer process in nuclear reactors; legislation in civil defense; researcher of major foreign policy and arms sales issues. **Mailing Address:** Syst Archit & Investment Anal, Fed Aviation Admin, 800 Independence Ave S W, Washington, DC 20591. **E-Mail:** feisal.keblawi@faa.gov

KEBLER, RICHARD WILLIAM, applied physics; deceased, see previous edition for last biography

KECECIOGLU, D(IMITRI) B(ASIL), ENGINEERING MECHANICS, RELIABILITY ENGINEERING, AEROSPACE OF MECHANICAL ENGINEERING. **Personal Data:** b Istanbul, Turkey, December 26, 1922; American citizen; m 1951, Lorene; c Dr Zoe D Kececioglu, Draelos &John D Kececioglu. **Education:** Robert Col, Istanbul, BS, 1942; Purdue Univ, MS, 1948, PhD (eng mech), 1953. **Honors & Awards:** Ralph Teetor Award, Soc Automotive Engrs, 1977; Allen Chop Award, Am Soc Qual Control, 1981; Excellence Award, Soc Reliability Eng; Reliability Educ Advan Award, Am Soc Qual Control; Anderson Prize, Univ Ariz Col Eng & Mines. **Professional Experience:** Fulbright scholar, Greece, 1971-1972; PROF, RELIABILITY ENG PROG, 1969-; PROF AEROSPACE & MECH ENG, UNIV ARIZ, 1963-; dir reliability & corp consult, Res Labs, Allis-Chalmers Mfg Co, 1960-1963; from asst to dir mech eng industs group, Res Labs, Allis-Chalmers Mfg Co, 1957-1963; eng scientist-in-chg mech lab, Res Labs, Allis-Chalmers Mfg Co, 1952-1957; asst instr mach tool lab, Purdue Univ, 1951; asst instr eng drawing & descriptive geom, Purdue Univ, 1950-1952; asst metal cutting, Purdue Univ, 1949-1952; instr mech, Purdue Univ, 1947; hon prof, Phi Kappa Phi, Shangai Univ Technol; dir, Reliability Eng & Mgt Insts; consult reliability & maintainability eng, indust & govt. **Memberships:** AAAS; Am Soc Mech Engrs; Am Soc Eng Educ; Soc Exp Stress Anal; Inst Elec & Electronics Engrs; Sigma Xi; Soc Reliability Engrs; Inst Environ Sci; Soc Automotive Engrs. **Research Statement & Publications:** System effectiveness, reliability, maintainability; quality control; statistics; probability; design; production engineering; design by reliability; tooling engineering; applied mathematics. **Mailing Address:** Dept Aerospace & Mech Eng Col Eng Univ Ariz, 1130 N Mountain Rm N614, Tucson, AZ 85721-0119. **Fax:** 520-521-8191. **E-Mail:** dimitri@u.arizona.edu

KECK, DONALD BRUCE, PHYSICS. **Personal Data:** b Lansing, Mich, January 2, 1941; m 1965, Ruth; c Lynne & Brian. **Education:** Mich State Univ, BS, 1962, MS, 1964, PhD (physics), 1967. **Honors & Awards:** Technol Achievement Award, Soc Photo-optical Instrumentation Engrs, 1981; IR-100 Award, 1981; Eng Achievement Award, Am Soc Metall, 1983; John Tyndall Award, Inst Elec & Electronics Engrs/Optical Soc Am, 1992, Nat Inventores Hall of Fame, 1993, Nat Acad Eng, 1993; Am Innovation, US Dept Commerce, 1994; Distng Alumni Mich State Univ, 1996; US Pres Nat Medal of Tech, 2000. **Professional Experience:** CTO, INFOTONICS TECHNOL CTR INC, as of 2004; PRES, CEDARWOOD CONSULT, 2002-; vp, exec dir, res, Corning, Inc, 1996-2002; dir optics & photonics res, Corning Glass Works, 1986-1996; DIR APPL PHYSICS RES, CORNING GLASS WORKS, 1986-; mgr Appl Physics dept, Corning Glass Works, 1976-1986; res assoc physics, Corning Glass Works, 1974-1976; res physicist, Corning Glass Works, 1968-1974. **Memberships:** Fel Optical Soc Am; fel Inst Elec & Electronics Engrs; Soc Photo-optical Instrumentation Engrs; Nat Acad Eng. **Research Statement & Publications:** Near infrared molecular spectroscopy; magnetic rotation spectroscopy; fiber optics; propagation in fiber optic waveguides; gradient index imaging; guided wave optics; optical couplers; optical amplifiers; optical fiber sensors; optical networks. **Mailing Address:** Infotonics Technol Ctr Inc, 5450 Campus Dr, Canandaigua, NY 14424. **Fax:** 585-919-3011.

KECK, JAMES COLLYER, PHYSICS. **Personal Data:** b New York, NY, June 11, 1924; m 1947, c 2. **Education:** Cornell Univ, BA, 1947, PhD, 1951. **Professional Experience:** PROF EMER & SR LECTR, MASS INST TECHNOL, 1989-; Ford prof mech eng, Mass Inst Technol, 1965-1989; dep dir, Avco-Everett Res Lab, Mass, 1960-1964; prin scientist, Avco-Everett Res Lab, Mass, 1955-1965; res fel, Calif Inst Technol, 1952-1955; res assoc physics, Cornell Univ, 1951-1952. **Memberships:** Am Phys Soc; AAAS; Sigma Xi; fel Am Acad Arts & Sci; Combustion Inst. **Research Statement & Publications:** Atomic and molecular kinetics; high temperature gas dynamics; combustion; nonequilibrium thermodynamics; high energy nuclear physics. **Mailing Address:** Dept Mech Eng, Mass Inst Technol, 77 Mass Ave 31-168A, Cambridge, MA 02139-4307.

KECK, MAX HANS, POLYMER CHEMISTRY. **Personal Data:** b Konstanz, Ger, May 7, 1919; American citizen; m 1949, c 2. **Education:** Col Wooster, BA, 1941; Univ Akron, MSc, 1945. **Professional Experience:** RETIRED; res scientist, Fiber Tech Ctr, 1967-1983; sr res chemist polyester chem, Goodyear Tire & Rubber Co, 1942-1967. **Memberships:** Am Chem Soc. **Research Statement & Publications:** Linear polyester research, preparation of new linear polyesters and new monomers; catalysis studies; dyeable and specialty polyester fibers; cross-linkable polyesters for coatings. **Mailing Address:** 3117 Mayfield Rd, Silver Lake, OH 44224-3097.

KECK, MAX JOHANN, VISUAL PSYCHOPHYSICS. **Personal Data:** b February 22, 1939; American citizen; m 1968, Roberta; c 2. **Education:** Mass Inst Technol, BS, 1961; Purdue Univ, MS, 1964, PhD (physics), 1968. **Professional Experience:** DISTINGUISHED PROF EMER, DEPT PHYSICS, XAVIER UNIV, as of 2004; dean stud develop, John Carrol Univ, as of 2002; prof emer, Dept Physics, Xavier Univ, as of 2001; dean, Col Arts & Sci, Xavier Univ 1992-1999; prin investr res grant, Nat Eye Inst, NIH, 1979-; prof physics, John Carroll Univ, beginning 1978; adj staff mem ophthalmol, Cleveland Clin Found, Ohio, beginning 1978; vis prof, Dept Physiol Sci, Ohio State Univ, 1976-1977; from asst prof to assoc prof, John Carroll Univ, 1968-1978. **Memberships:** Am Phys Soc. **Research Statement & Publications:** Binocular vision; spatial vision; amblyopia and strabismus. **Mailing Address:** Dept Physics, Xavier Univ, 110 Lindner Hall, Cincinnati, OH 45207. **Fax:** 513745-2070. **E-Mail:** keck@xu.edu

KECK, ROBERT WILLIAM, SCIENCE ADMINISTRATION, RESEARCH ADMINISTRATION. **Personal Data:** b Manchester, Iowa, January 2, 1941; m 1964, Juanita; c Robert A & Julie K. **Education:** Univ Iowa, BS, 1962, MS, 1964; Ohio State Univ, PhD (plant physiol), 1968. **Professional Experience:** PROF BIOL, IND UNIV-PURDUE UNIV, 1990-; actg dean, Ind Univ-Purdue Univ, 1988-1989; assoc dean, Ind Univ-Purdue Univ, 1984-1988, 1987-1990; asst dean, Ind Univ-Purdue Univ, 1982-1984; from asst to prof biol, Ind Univ-Purdue Univ, 1972-1982; lectr bot, Univ Ill, 1972; researcher bot, Univ Ill, 1971-1972; researcher hort, Univ Ill, 1970-1971; Researcher photosynthesis, Charles F Kettering Res Lab, 1968-1970. **Memberships:** Am Soc Plant Physiologists; Crop Sci Soc Am. **Research Statement & Publications:** Photosynthesis, membrane physiology. **Mailing Address:** Dept Biol, Ind Univ Purdue Univ, 1201 E 38th St, Indianapolis, IN 46205. **E-Mail:** rkeck@iupui.edu

KECK, WINFIELD, PHYSICS. **Personal Data:** b Clifton Heights, Pa, September 15, 1917; m 1944, Margaret; c Peter, Lindsey, Jonathan & Timothy. **Education:** Amherst Col, AB, 1937; Univ Pa, MA, 1938; Brown Univ, PhD (physics), 1949. **Professional Experience:** PROF EMER PHYSICS, LAFAYETTE COL, as of 2003; prof physics, Lafayette Col, 1961-1983; chmn dept, Lafayette Col, 1960-1982; vis assoc prof, Brown Univ, 1958-1959; from asst prof to assoc prof, Lafayette Col, 1949-1961; instr, Brown Univ, 1946-1948; instr physics, Muhlenberg Col, 1941-1946; Instr math, Franklin & Marshall Col, 1939-1940. **Memberships:** Am Asn Physics Teachers; Sigma Xi. **Research Statement & Publications:** Acoustic wave propagation. **Mailing Address:** Dept Physics, Lafayette Col, 17 Watson Hall, Easton, PA 18042.

KEDDIE, B A, INSECT PATHOLOGY. **Education:** Seattle Univ, BS, 1976; Univ Calif, Berkeley, PhD, 1989. **Professional Experience:** ASSOC PROF, DEPT BIOL SCI, UNIV ALTA, as of 2006. **Mailing Address:** Dept Biol Sci, Univ Alta, Rm ES 221, Earth Sci Bldg, Edmonton, AB T6G 2E9, Can. **Fax:** 780-492-9234. **E-Mail:** akeddie@ualberta.ca

KEDDY, JAMES RICHARD, COMPUTER SCIENCES. **Personal Data:** b Boston, Mass, October 18, 1936; m 1961, c 3. **Education:** Colby Col, BA, 1958. **Professional Experience:** RETIRED; dir eng, Teradata Corp, 1985-1994; proj leader, Teradata Corp, 1980-1984; prin engr off systs, Xerox Corp, 1974-1980; mem advan design staff, Xerox Data Systs, 1972-1973; sect mgr oper systs, Sci Data Systs, 1968-1971; sect mgr satellite control, Syst Develop Corp, 1963-1967; Mem staff air defense, Syst Develop Corp, 1960-1962. **Research Statement & Publications:** Word processing systems; information storage and retrieval; operating systems; database management systems; communications. **Mailing Address:** 16331 Serenade Lane, Huntington Beach, CA 92646.

KEDDY, PAUL ANTHONY, BOTANY, WETLAND ECOLOGY. **Personal Data:** b London, Ont, May 29, 1953; c 2. **Education:** York Univ, Toronto, BSc, 1974; Dalhousie Univ, Halifax, PhD (ecol), 1978. **Honors & Awards:** Gleason Prize, 1990; Lawson Medal, 1991. **Professional Experience:** PROF ECOL, DEPT BIOL, UNIV OTTAWA, 1989-; coordr, Inst Res Environ & Econ, Univ Ottawa, 1989-1990; mem, Sci Adv Comt, World Wildlife Fund, Can, 1986-1990; chmn, Sci Comt, Can Coun Ecol Areas, 1986-1990; grant comt, Population Biol Grant Selection Comt, Nat Sci & Eng Res Coun, Can, 1986-1989; vis lectr, dept bot & microbiol, Univ London, 1985-1986; vis lectr, Comp Plant Ecol Unit, Univ Sheffield, 1986; mem, Subcomt Plants, Comt Status Endangered Wildlife Can, 1985-1991; from asst prof to assoc prof, dept biol, Univ Ottawa, 1982-1989; asst prof ecol, dept bot & genetics, Univ Guelph, 1978-1982. **Memberships:** Ecol Soc Am; Brit Ecol Soc; Can Bot Asn; Int Asn Veg Sci. **Research Statement & Publications:** Plant community ecology; competition and plant traits; assembly rules; wetland ecology; conservation of endangered wetland plants and habitats; author of various articles. **Mailing Address:** Dept Biol, Univ Ottawa, PO Box 450 Station A, Ottawa, ON K1N 6N5, Can. **Fax:** 613-562-5486. **E-Mail:** pkeddy@uottawa.ca

KEDES, LAURENCE H, MOLECULAR GENETIC RESEARCH, GENE EXPRESSION. **Personal Data:** b Hartford, Conn, July 19, 1937; m 1958, Shirley Beck; c Dean H, Maureen J & Todd R. **Education:** Stanford Univ, BS, 1961, MD, 1962; Wesleyan Univ 1955-1958. **Professional Experience:** WILLIAM KECK PROF & CHMN, DEPT BIOCHEM & DIR, INST GENETIC MED, UNIV SOUTHERN CALIF, 1988-; vis scientist, Imp Cancer Res Fund, London, 1976-1977; fel, John Simon Guggenheim Found, 1976-1977; investr, Howard Hughes MedInst, 1974-1982; staff physician, Vet Admin Med Ctr, Palo Alto, 1970-1989; from asst prof to prof med, Stanford Univ, 1970-1989; Leukemia Soc, Am scholar, 1969-1974; lectr, Mass Inst Technol, 1967-1969; Res assoc, Lab Biochem, Nat Cancer Inst, 1964-1966. **Memberships:** Am Soc Microbiol; Am Soc Biochem & Molecular Biol; Int Soc Develop Biol; Am Soc Clin Invest; Asn Am Physicians; Am Soc Hemat. **Research Statement & Publications:** Biotechnology; gene expression in animal cell differentiation. **Mailing Address:** Dept Biochem HMR No 413, Univ Southern Calif 2011 Zonal Ave, Los Angeles, CA 90033. **Fax:** 323-442-2764. **E-Mail:** kedes@usc.edu

KEDWARD, KEITH T, MECHANICAL ENGINEERING. **Education:** Univ Wales, UK, PhD, 1966. **Professional Experience:** PROF, UNIV CALIF, 1990-. **Mailing Address:** Dept Mech Eng, Univ Calif, Rm 2347 Eng II Bldg, Santa Barbara, CA 93106-5070. **Fax:** 805-893-8651. **E-Mail:** kedward@engineering.ucsb.edu

KEDZIE, DONALD P, ENGINEERING ADMINISTRATION. **Professional Experience:** Prof mech eng, Ark State Univ, 1984-1996. **Mailing Address:** 17830 Desert Glen Dr, Sun City West, AZ 85375.

KEEDY, CURTIS RUSSELL, PHYSICAL CHEMISTRY, RADIOCHEMISTRY. **Personal Data:** b Selma, Calif, September 14, 1938; m 1976, c 3. **Education:** Occidental Col, BA, 1960; Univ Wis, PhD (phys chem), 1965. **Professional Experience:** PROF EMER CHEM, LEWIS & CLARK COL, as of 2002; prof chem, Lewis & Clark Col, beginning 1985; chmn dept, Lewis & Clark Col, beginning 1982; assoc prof, Lewis & Clark Col, 1975-1985; asst prof, Lewis & Clark Col, 1972-1975; vis lectr, Lewis & Clark Col, 1971-1972; reactor supvr, Reed Col, 1968-1972; asst prof chem, Reed Col, 1966-1970; resident res assoc nuclear chem, chem eng div, Argonne Nat Lab, 1964-1966. **Memberships:** Am Chem Soc; Sigma Xi; Am Asn Univ Prof. **Research Statement & Publications:** Nuclear chemistry; neutron activation analysis as applied to geochemical systems and environmental areas. **Mailing Address:** Dept Chem, Lewis & Clark Col, 0666C SW Palatine Hill Rd, Mail Stop 55, Portland, OR 97219-7831.

KEEDY, HUGH F(ORREST), ENGINEERING MECHANICS. **Personal Data:** b Berkeley Springs, WVa, September 22, 1926; m 1948, c 2. **Education:** George Peabody Col, BS, 1951, MA, 1952; Univ Mich, MSE, 1962, PhD, 1967. **Professional Experience:** PROF EMER ENG SCI, VANDERBILT UNIV, as of 2005; prof eng sci, Vanderbilt Univ, beginning 1974; pres, Southeastern Sect, Am Soc Eng Educ, Zone II chmn, 1988-1990; tech ed & writer, Lawrence Livermore Nat Lab, 1980-1981; assoc dean instr, Vanderbilt Univ, 1969-1971; assoc prof eng sci, Vanderbilt Univ, 1968-1974; instr, Univ Mich, 1963-1965; asst, Univ Mich, 1962-1963; consult various industs, beginning 1954; asst prof appl math, Vanderbilt Univ, 1951-1968. **Memberships:** Am Soc Eng Educ; Soc Tech Commun. **Research Statement & Publications:** Fluid mechanics; engineering education; technical communication. **Mailing Address:** Vanderbilt Univ, 2201 W End Ave, Nashville, TN 37235.

KEEFE, DEBORAH LYNN, CARDIOVASCULAR PHARMACOLOGY, NONINVASIVE CARDIOLOGY. **Personal Data:** b Oklahoma City, Okla, November 23, 1950; m 1971, Richard; c Jennifer, Colin & Corwin. **Education:** Rice Univ, BA, 1973; NY Med Col, MD, 1976; Columbia Univ, MPH, 1990. **Professional Experience:** PROF MED, MED COL, CORNELL UNIV, 1995-; ATTEND PHYSICIAN, MEM SLOAN-KETTERING HOSP, 1994-; assoc mem & assoc attending physician, Mem Sloan Kettering Hosp, 1988-1994; asst clin prof, Albert Einstein Col Med, 1987-1988; assoc dir clin invest, Am Cynamid Med Res, 1987-1988; assoc ed, J Clin Pharamacol, 1985-; assoc prof, Mem Sloan-kettering Hosp, 1985-1995; attend physician, Hosp Albert Einstein Col Med, 1981-1987; asst prof med, Albert Einstein Col Med, 1981-1987; dir coronary care, Bronx Munic Hosp Ctr, 1981-1987; fel cardiol, Stanford Univ, 1979-1981; resident internal med, St Vincents Hosp, NY, 1976-1979. **Memberships:** Fel Am Col Cardiol; fel Am Col Chest Physicians; fel Am Heart Asn; fel Am Col Angiolog; fel Am Col Clin Pharmacol; fel Am Soc Clin Pharmacol & Therapeut; fel Am Col Critical Care Med. **Research Statement & Publications:** Clinical investigation of cardiovascular therapeutic agents including clinical trials; pharmacokinetics and pharmacodynamics; epidemiology and the prevention of heart disease. **Mailing Address:** J Clin Pharamacol, PO Box 500, New York, NY 10804-0500. **Fax:** 914-636-0711. **E-Mail:** dkclinpharm@aol.com

KEEFE, LAURENCE, MATHEMATICS. **Education:** Univ Southern Calif, PhD (Fluid Dynam & Appl Math). **Professional Experience:** SR RES SCIENTIST, NIELSEN ENG & RES, as of 2006. **Mailing Address:** Nielsen Eng & Res, 526 Clyde Ave, Mtain View, CA 94043-2212. **Fax:** 650-968-1410. **E-Mail:** lrk@nearinc.com

KEEFE, THOMAS J, VETERINARY MEDICINE. **Personal Data:** b Algona, Iowa, December 4, 1937; m 1965, c 4. **Education:** Univ Mo, BS & DVM, 1963; Iowa State Univ, PhD (Statist), 1972. **Professional Experience:** PROF, DEPT ENVIRON & RADIOL HEALTH SCI, as of 2005; DIR VET MED, BEECHAM LABS, 1974-; mgr clin res, Bristol Labs, 1969-1974; livestock consult, Livestock Servs, Ralston Purina, 1967-1969; Pvt vet pract, 1966-1967. **Memberships:** Am Vet Med Asn; Am Asn Swine Practitioners (pres, 1971); Am Asn Bovine Practitioners; fel Am Col Pharmacol & Therapeut; Indust Vet Asn; Sigma Xi. **Research Statement & Publications:** Pharmacology; pathology; diagnostic medicine. **Mailing Address:** Dept Environ Radiol Health Sci, Col Vet Med & Biomed Sci, Colo State Univ, 145 Environ Health Bldg 1681 Campus Delivery, Ft Collins, CO 80523. **Fax:** 970-491-2940. **E-Mail:** thomas.keefe@colostate.edu

KEEFE, THOMAS LEEVEN, BOTANY, BIOLOGY. **Personal Data:** b Columbia, SC, January 22, 1937; m 1964. **Education:** Univ SC, BS, 1959, MS, 1961; Univ Ga, PhD (bot), 1967. **Professional Experience:** ASST PROF, DEPT BIOL SCI, EASTERN KY UNIV, 1966-; asst prof biol, Newberry Col, 1962. **Memberships:** Am Forestry Asn; Am Inst Biol Sci. **Research Statement & Publications:** Shoot development in forest trees; radiation inducted mutations in insects. **Mailing Address:** Dept Biol Sci, Eastern Ky Univ, Moore 235, Richmond, KY 40475. **Fax:** 606-622-1020. **E-Mail:** biokeefe@acs.eku.edu

KEEFE, WILLIAM EDWARD, BIOPHYSICS, CRYSTALLOGRAPHY. **Personal Data:** b Norfolk, Va, February 23, 1923; m 1946, c 2. **Education:** Va Polytech Inst, BS, 1959, MS, 1964; Med Col Va, PhD (biophys), 1967. **Professional Experience:** ASSOC PROF MICROBIOL, MED COL VA, VA COMMONWEALTH UNIV, 1981-; asst prof, 1976-1981; asst prof biophys, 1966-1976. **Memberships:** Am Crystallog Asn; Am Inst Physics; Am Phys Soc; Sigma Xi; Int Solar Energy Soc. **Research Statement & Publications:** Formation of kidney stone nuclei; interaction of fast neutrons with biological materials; determination of molecular structure of biologically important compounds; computer programming to solve crystal structures; model building of proteins. **Mailing Address:** 107 Fairway Lane, Ashland, VA 23005.

KEEFER, CAROL LYNDON, IN VITRO FERTILIZATION, PREIMPLANTATION DEVELOPMENT. **Personal Data:** b Columbia, SC, January 20, 1953. **Education:** Univ SC, BS, 1974; Univ Del, PhD (biol sci), 1981. **Professional Experience:** ASSOC PROF, ANIMAL & AVIAN SCI, UNIV MD, as of 2005; res scientist, Am Breeders Serv Specialty Genetics, beginning 1989; asst prof, Col Vet Med, Univ Ga, 1985-1989; asst physiologist reproductive physiol, Col Vet Med, Univ Ga, 1984-1985; reproductive biologist, Reproductive Biol Assocs, 1983-1986; Postdoctoral fel reproductive physiol, Sch Hyg & Pub Health, Johns Hopkins, 1981-1982 & Sch Vet Med, Univ Pa, 1982-1983. **Memberships:** Soc Develop Biol; Int Embryo Transfer Soc; Soc Study Reproduction; Am Soc Cell Biol. **Research Statement & Publications:** Bovine oocyte maturation; in vitro fertilization and embryo culture; bovine embryo nuclear transfer; assisted fertilization. **Mailing Address:** Univ Md, Animal & Avian Sci, 1413A AnSc AgEn Bldg, College Park, MD 20742-2311. **Fax:** 301-314-9059. **E-Mail:** ckeefer@umd.edu

KEEFER, DENNIS RALPH, AEROSPACE ENGINEERING, LASER PROPULSION. **Personal Data:** b Winter Haven, Fla, September 22, 1938; m 1957, c 3. **Education:** Univ Fla, BES, 1962, MSE, 1963, PhD (aerospace eng), 1967. **Professional Experience:** PROF ENG SCI & MECH, UNIV TENN, 1978-; assoc prof aerospace eng, Univ Fla, 1976-1978; asst prof, 1967-1976. **Memberships:** Am Phys Soc; Sigma Xi; Am Inst Aeronaut & Astronautics; Inst Elec & Electronic Engrs. **Research Statement & Publications:** Electrodeless arcs and discharges; gas lasers; plasma spectroscopy. **Mailing Address:** Univ Tenn Space Inst, Tullahoma, TN 37388. **E-Mail:** dkeefer@utsi.edu

KEEFER, DONALD WALKER, METALLURGY. **Personal Data:** b Idaho Falls, Idaho, November 7, 1931; m 1954, c 2. **Education:** Univ Idaho, BS, 1954; Univ Ill, MS, 1957, PhD (metall), 1961. **Professional Experience:** MGR MAT SCI BR, MAT TECH DIV, EG&G IDAHO INC, 1981-; mgr, Off Res Mgt, Fuels & Mat Div, 1977-1981; Mem tech staff, Atomics Int, 1961-1977. **Memberships:** Am Asn Advan Sci; Am Soc Metals. **Research Statement & Publications:** Studies of point defects in metals and alloys by means of anelastic techniques; studies of void formation in irradiated reactor cladding materials; environmental effects on materials. **Mailing Address:** 6731 E Lincoln Rd, Idaho Falls, ID 83401.

KEEFER, LARRY KAY, NITRIC OXIDE, CHEMISTRY & PHARMACOLOGY OF NITRIC OXIDE-RELEASING COMPOUNDS. **Personal Data:** b Akron, Ohio, October 28, 1939; m 1962, Julie; c Steven H & Simona N. **Education:** Oberlin Col, AB, (Chem) 1961; Univ NH, PhD (org chem), 1965. **Professional Experience:** CHIEF, LAB COMP CARCINOGENESIS, NAT CANCER INST, 1997-; CHIEF, CHEM SECT, LAB COMP CARCINOGENESIS, NAT CANCER INST, 1983-; head, Anal Chem Sect, Lab Carcinogen Metab, 1971-1983; asst prof biochem, Col Med, Univ Nebr, 1968-1971; asst prof oncol, Inst Med Res, Chicago Med Sch, 1965-1968. **Memberships:** Am Chem Soc; AAAS; Am Asn Cancer Res. **Research Statement & Publications:** Chemistry and pharmacology of nitric oxide and its progenitors. **Mailing Address:** Nat Cancer Inst-Frederick, Bldg 538, Frederick, MD 21702. **Fax:** 301-846-5946. **E-Mail:** keefer@mail.ncifcrf.gov

KEEFER, RAYMOND MARSH, PHYSICAL ORGANIC CHEMISTRY, MOLECULAR COMPLEXES. **Personal Data:** b Twin Falls, Idaho, April 29, 1913; m 1943, c 3. **Education:** Univ Calif, BS, 1934, PhD (chem), 1940. **Professional Experience:** PROF EMER CHEM, UNIV CALIF, DAVIS, 1981-; chmn dept, 1962-1974; prof, 1956-1981; from instr to assoc prof, 1941-1956; From asst to assoc, 1936-1941. **Memberships:** Am Chem Soc; Sigma Xi. **Research Statement & Publications:** Molecular complexes; electrophilic aromatic halogenation; participation by ortho substituents in reactions at aromatic side chains; medium effects on nucleophilic solvolytic displacement reactions. **Mailing Address:** Dept Chem, Univ Calif, Davis, CA 95616. **Fax:** 530-752-8995.

KEEFER, ROBERT FARIS, SOIL SCIENCE. **Personal Data:** b Wheeling, WVa, May 27, 1930; c 6. **Education:** Cornell Univ, BS, 1952; Ohio State Univ, MS, 1961, PhD (agron), 1963. **Professional Experience:** PROF EMER AGRON & AGRONOMIST, WVA UNIV, as of 2001; prof agron & agronomist, Wva Univ, beginning 1976; assoc prof & assoc agronomist, Wva Univ, 1974-1976; HEW grant, 1966-1970; from asst prof to assoc prof soil sci, Wva Univ, 1965-1974; Res agronomist, Hercules Powder Co, 1963-1965. **Memberships:** Am Soc Agron; Soil Sci Soc Am; Int Soil Sci Soc; Int Humic Sub Soc. **Research Statement & Publications:** Soil organic matter; soil fertility, particularly micronutrient nutrition; sewage sludge, fly ash and strip mine reclamation. **Mailing Address:** Dept Plant Sci, WVa Univ, PO Box 6018, Morgantown, WV 26506-0001.

KEEFER, WILLIAM RICHARD, GEOLOGY. **Personal Data:** b Fayette, Ohio, June 7, 1924; m Eleanor. **Education:** Univ Wyo, BA, 1948, MA, 1952, PhD, 1957. **Professional Experience:** RETIRED; explor adv, Mitchell Energy Corp, 1981-1986; geologist, US Geol Surv, Denver, 1948-1981. **Memberships:** Geol Soc Am. **Research Statement & Publications:** Regional stratigraphy and structure, especially in sedimentary rocks. **Mailing Address:** 5693 Xeno Way, Arvada, CO 80002.

KEEFFE, JAMES RICHARD, ORGANIC CHEMISTRY. **Personal Data:** b Visalia, Calif, November 13, 1937; m 1961, c 1. **Education:** Univ Calif, Santa Barbara, BA, 1959; Univ Wash, Seattle, PhD (chem), 1964. **Professional Experience:** PROF CHEM, SAN FRANCISCO STATE UNIV, 1974-; res grants, Petrol Res Fund, 1965-1966 & Res Corp, 1966-1968; from asst prof to assoc prof, San Francisco State Univ, 1965-1974; NIH res fel, 1964-1965. **Research Statement & Publications:** Kinetic hydrogen isotope effects; acid-base catalysis; organic reaction mechanisms. **Mailing Address:** Dept Chem & Biochem, San Francisco State Univ, 1600 Holloway Ave, San Francisco, CA 94132-4163. **Fax:** 415-338-2384. **E-Mail:** keeffe@sfsu.edu

KEEGAN, ACHSAH D, RESEARCH. **Personal Data:** m 1984, James; c Simon H, Eleanore L & James D. **Education:** Duke Univ, BS, 1983; Johns Hopkins Univ, PhD (immunol), 1989. **Professional Experience:** SR SCIENTIST IMMUNOL, HOLLAND LAB, GEORGE WASH UNIV, as of 2004; res assoc, Nat Inst Allergy & Infectious Dis, NIH, beginning 1989. **Memberships:** Am Asn Immunologists. **Research Statement & Publications:** Lymphocyte activation and clonal expansion forms the basis of a productive immune response to an antigenic challenge and often involves the collaboration between B and T cells. **Mailing Address:** Dept Immunol, Holland Lab, George Wash Univ, Am Red Cross, 15601 Crabbs Br Way, Rockville, MD 20855. **E-Mail:** keegana@usa.redcross.org

KEEGSTRA, KENNETH G, Chloroplast biogenesis, Biosynthesis of plant cell walls. **Personal Data:** b Grand Rapids, Mich, August 10, 1945; m 1965, c 3. **Education:** Hope Col, BA, 1967; Univ Colo, PhD (biochem), 1971. **Honors & Awards:** George Olmsted Award, Am Paper Inst, 1973; Fulbright Scholar, 1985. **Professional Experience:** UNIV DISTINGUISHED PROF, DEPT PLANT BIOL, DEPT BIOCHEM, MICH STATE UNIV, as of 2004; DIR & PROF, PLANT RES LAB, MICH STATE UNIV, 1993-; from asst prof to prof plant physiol, Univ Wis-Madison, 1977-1993; fac Mem, Univ Wis, 1974-1993; asst prof microbiol, State Univ NY, 1973-1977; fel biochem, Mass Inst Technol, 1971-1973. **Memberships:** Am Soc Plant Physiologists; Am Soc Biochem Mol Bio; AAAS; Am Soc Cell Biol. **Research Statement & Publications:** Structure, function and biogenesis of plastid envelope membranes; import of cytoplasmically synthesized proteins into chloroplasts; biosynthesis of plant cell wall polysaccharides in the Golgi. **Mailing Address:** Dept Biochem & Molecular Biol, Mich State Univ, 106 Plant Biol Lab, East Lansing, MI 48824. **Fax:** 517-353-9168. **E-Mail:** keegstra@msu.edu

KEEHN, PHILIP MOSES, ORGANIC CHEMISTRY, PHYSICAL-ORGANIC CHEMISTRY. **Personal Data:** b Brooklyn, NY, March 22, 1943. **Education:** Yeshiva Col, BA, 1964; Yale Univ, MA, 1967, PhD (chem), 1969. **Honors & Awards:** Alfred Bader Award, 1980. **Professional Experience:** Fulbright scholar, 1988; Acad Sinica Lecturship, 1987; PROF CHEM, BRANDEIS UNIV, 1986-; Nat Acad Sci E Europ Exchange fel, Yugoslavia, 1985; Consult, Olive Corp, 1982-1985; Dreyfus teacher-scholar, 1979-1984; Wolfson Professorship, Weizman Inst Sci, 1979-1980; Consult, US Army, 1979-1980; assoc prof chem, Brandeis Univ, 1978-1986; Consult, Am Optical Corp, 1976-; asst prof, Brandeis Univ, 1971-1978; NIH res fel chem, Harvard Univ, 1969-1971. **Memberships:** Am Chem Soc; Sigma Xi. **Research Statement & Publications:** Synthesis of strained rings and theoretically interesting molecules; synthetic methods; application of nuclear magnetic resonance spectroscopy to organic systems; photooxidation; thermal chemistry; pure and applied laser chemistry of organic systems; host-guest chemistry. **Mailing Address:** Dept Chem, Brandeis Univ, MS 015 415 S St, Waltham, MA 02454. **Fax:** 781-736-2516. **E-Mail:** keehn@brandeis.edu

KEELER, CALVIN LEE, AVIAN VIROLOGY, RECOMBINANT VACCINE DEVELOPMENT. **Personal Data:** b Boston, Mass, November 22, 1954; m 1987, Sharon; c Timothy L & Jeremy J. **Education:** Tufts Univ, BS, 1976; Va Commonwealth Univ, Richmond, MS, 1979; Univ Md, Baltimore Co, PhD (biol), 1987. **Professional Experience:** PROF, DEPT ANIMAL & FOOD SCI, UNIV DEL, NEWARK, 1993-; asst prof, Dept Animal Sci & Agr Biochem, Univ Del, Newark, 1987-1993; assoc, E I du Pont de Nemours & Co, Wilmington, Del, 1985-1987; sr scientist, Igene Biotechnol, Inc, Columbia, Md, 1981-1985. **Memberships:** Am Soc Microbiol; A ssoc Am Soc Virol; Poultry Sci Asn; assoc Am Asn Avian Pathologists; AAAS. **Research Statement & Publications:** Use an avian herpes virus as a model to study murosal cell-mediated immunity; molecular basis of viral pathogenesis and immunity; mucosal cell-mediated immunity. **Mailing Address:** Dept Animal & Food Sci, Univ Del, 040 Townsend Hall, Newark, DE 19717-1303. **Fax:** 302-831-2822. **E-Mail:** ckeeler@udel.edu

KEELER, EMMETT BROWN, HEALTH MODELING, HEALTH SERVICES RESEARCH. **Personal Data:** b West Point, NY, September 28, 1941; m 1975, Shan; c Mikala, Lauren & Alexis. **Education:** Oberlin Col, BA, 1962; Harvard Univ, MA, 1967, PhD (math), 1969. **Honors & Awards:** Distinguished Investigator Award, Academy Health 2003. **Professional Experience:** ADJ PROF UCLA Public Health School as of 1999-, PROF, PARDEE RAND GRAD SCH, 1980- vis res assoc, Sch Pub Health, Harvard Univ, 1974-1975 & 1982; Vis assoc prof econ, Univ Chicago, 1973; SR MATHEMATICIAN, RAND, 1968-. **Memberships:** Math Asn Am; AcademyHealth. **Research Statement & Publications:** Utility theory; mathematical statistics; healtheconomics; operations research; medical decision-making. **Mailing Address:** Rand, 1776 Main Str, Santa Monica, CA 90407-2138. **Fax:** 310-260-8013. **E-Mail:** emmett@rand.org

KEELER, JOHN S(COTT), ELECTRICAL ENGINEERING. **Personal Data:** b Toronto, Ont, August 12, 1929; m 1951, c 3. **Education:** Univ Toronto, BASc, 1951, MASc, 1963. **Professional Experience:** RETIRED; consult, 1990-1997; from lectr to assoc prof elec eng, Univ Waterloo, 1960-1990; Acoust consult, 1959-; chief engr, Hallman Organs, Ont, 1955-1959; Res officer, Nat Res Coun Can, 1951-1955. **Memberships:** Sr mem Inst Elec & Electronics Engrs; Audio Eng Soc. **Research Statement & Publications:** Numerical analysis and synthesis of sound particularly noise and music; effects of noise on man; acoustical instrumentation; environmental noise. **Mailing Address:** RR 8, Owen Sound, ON N4K 5W4, Can.

KEELER, JUDITH ADELE, ANIMAL BEHAVIOR, BIOLOGICAL RHYTHMS. **Personal Data:** b Providence, RI, December 30, 1944; m 1973. **Education:** Whittier Col, BA, 1966; Northwestern Univ, MS, 1969, PhD (biol), 1973. **Professional Experience:** Field res, Calif Fish & Wildlife Agency, 1975-; ASSOC PROF BIOL, CALIF STATE COL, STANISLAUS, 1975-; Res assoc, Inst Cult Resources, Calif State Col, Stanislaus, 1973-; Asst prof, Calif State Col, Stanislaus, 1969-1975. **Memberships:** AAAS; Animal Behav Soc; Int Audio-Tutorial Cong. **Research Statement & Publications:** Field research in animal behavior and laboratory research in patterns of biorhythmicity. **Mailing Address:** Dept Biol Sci, Calif State Univ 801 W Monte Vista Stanislaus, Turlock, CA 95382-0299.

KEELER, KATHLEEN HOWARD, PLANT POPULATION CYTOGENETICS, PLANT DEMOGRAPHY. **Personal Data:** b Hackensack, NJ, January 17, 1947; m 1975, (Richard). **Education:** Univ Mich, Ann Arbor, BS, 1969; Univ Calif, Berkeley, PhD (genetics), 1975. **Professional Experience:** Mem, Sci Adv Panel Biotechnol, US Environ Protection Agency, 1992-; dir, Cedar Point Biol Sta, 1992-1994; PROF BIOL SCI, SCH NATURAL RESOURCES, UNIV NEBR, LINCOLN, 1991-; consult, Nat Audubon Soc, Calgene, 1988-1990; prin investr, NSF, 1987-; chair biol sci, Ecol Sect, Univ Nebr, Lincoln, 1985-1988; from asst prof to assoc prof, Univ Nebr, Lincoln, 1975-1991. **Memberships:** Soc Study Evolution; Bot Soc Am; Ecol Soc Am; Am Soc Naturalists. **Research Statement & Publications:** Function of polyploid variation with native plant populations, pioneering use of flow cytometry for population cytogenetics; longevity of prairie plants; role of extreme events (flood, drought) in evolution. **Mailing Address:** Dept Biol Sci, Sch Natural Resources, Univ Nebr, 302A Manter Hall, Lincoln, NE 68588-0118. **Fax:** 402-472-2083. **E-Mail:** kkeeler1@unl.edu

KEELER, MARTIN HARVEY, MEDICINE. **Personal Data:** b New York, NY, June 16, 1927; m 1953, c 3. **Education:** NY Univ, BA, 1949; NY Med Col, MD, 1953; Am Bd Psychiat & Neurol, dipl, 1959. **Professional Experience:** DIR ALCOHOLIC TREAT PROG HOUSTON, VET ADMIN HOSP, 1977-; prof psychiat, Baylor Col Med, 1977-1992; prof psychiat, Med Univ, SC, 1970-1977; prof, NY Med Col, 1969-1970; res grants, 1961 & beginning 1962; from instr to assoc prof, Sch Med, Univ NC, Chapel Hill, 1957-1969; from asst resident to resident psychiat, Sch Med, Univ NC, Chapel Hill, 1954-1957; intern, State Univ NY Upstate Med Ctr, 1953-1954. **Memberships:** AMA; Am Psychoanal Asn; Am Med Soc Alcoholism; Am Psychiat Asn. **Research Statement & Publications:** Defining of the psychological abnormalities in schizophrenia as specific to the individual or to the disease process and the pharmacological manipulation of these differences in schizophrenic and normal populations. **Mailing Address:** 5230 Ariel St, Houston, TX 77096.

KEELER, RALPH, PHYSIOLOGY. **Personal Data:** b Norwich, Eng, January 11, 1930; m 1956, c 2. **Education:** Univ Birmingham, BSc, 1953, PhD (physiol), 1956. **Professional Experience:** PROF EMER PHYSIOL, UNIV BC, as of 2006; prof physiol, Univ Bc, beginning 1974; from asst prof to assoc prof, Univ Bc, 1966-1974; lectr, Univ Newcastle, 1959-1966; lectr, Univ Ibadan, 1956-1959; asst lectr physiol, Univ Birmingham, 1955-1956. **Memberships:** Can Physiol Soc; Am Physiol Soc. **Research Statement & Publications:** Pathophysiology of renal function; control of sodium excretion. **Mailing Address:** Dept Physiol, Univ BC 2146 Health Sci Mall, Vancouver, BC V6T 1W5, Can. **E-Mail:** rkeeler@vip.net

KEELER, RICHARD FAIRBANKS, NATURAL PRODUCTS CHEMISTRY. **Personal Data:** b Provo, Utah, January 24, 1930; m 1952, c 5. **Education:** Brigham Young Univ, BS, 1954; Ohio State Univ, MS, 1955, PhD (biochem), 1957. **Professional Experience:** RES CHEMIST BIOCHEM, USDA, UTAH STATE UNIV, 1965-; res chemist biochem, Nat Animal Dis Lab, 1961-1965; Asst biochemist, Mont State Col, 1957-1961. **Memberships:** Am Chem Soc; Soc Exp Biol & Med; AAAS; Teratol Soc. **Research Statement & Publications:** Molybdenum-tungsten metabolism; silicon-mucoprotein interaction in urolithiasis; muscular dystrophy; cytochemistry of Listeria and Vibrio; products of Nocardia; steroidal, quinolizidine and piperidine alkaloid chemistry and metabolic effects; chemistry of poisonous and teratogenic plants. **Mailing Address:** 125 Quarter Circle, 1150 E 14th N, Logan, UT 84321-6315.

KEELER, ROGER NORRIS, SHOCK WAVE PHYSICAL & OPTICAL OCEANOGRAPHY, OCEAN LIDAR SYSTEMS. **Personal Data:** b Houston, Tex, August 12, 1930; m 1987, Miriam S; c Catherine, John, Roger & Carolyn. **Education:** Rice Univ, Houston, BA, BS, 1947-1951; Univ Colo, Boulder, MS, 1957-1958; Univ Calif, PhD (chem eng), 1963. **Honors & Awards:** Ford Found Prof Chem Eng, Univ Mex City, Mex City, DF, 1968; Gold Medal Eng, Am Soc Naval Engrs, Armed Forces Commun & Electronics Asn. **Professional Experience:** DIR TECH MKT, KAMAN DIVERSIFIED TECHNOL CORP, WASH, DC & BLOOMFIELD, CONN, 1988-; prin sci adv, Kaman Diversified Technol Corp, Wash, DC & Bloomfield, Conn, 1987-1988; lectr, Nat Strategy Info Ctr, Wash, DC, 1987; adj prof, Physics & Chem, US Naval postgrad Sch, Calif, 1979- 1981; staff dir, Lawrence Livermore Lab, Univ Calif, 1978-1980; lectr, Int Sch Physics, Enrico Fermi, Varenna, Italy, 1968, 1970; lectr, Dept Applied Sci, Univ Calif, 1967-1975; From staff mem to head, Physics Dept, Lawrence Livermore Lab, Livermore, Calif, 1963-1975; lectr, Dept Chem Eng, 1960-; Consult, Nat Tech & various orgns, 1960-; 7; dir technol, US Navy Dept. **Memberships:** Sigma Xi; Res Soc Am; fel Am Inst Chemists; fel Am Phys Soc. **Research Statement & Publications:** Turbulence, chemical kinetics, catalysis, cryogenics and cryogenic engineering; thermodynamics of Phase Equilibria; high pressure equation of state; optical and electronic properties of condensed media at high pressure; high pressure geophysics; high pressure fabrication of materials, anti-submarine warfare; advanced sensor technology; holds over 20 patents on submarine laser communications and ocean lidar systems. **Mailing Address:** 6652 Hampton Park Ct, McLean, VA 22101.

KEELER, STUART P, MECHANICAL METALLURGY, SHEET METAL FORMABILITY. **Personal Data:** b Wausau, Wis, September 1, 1934; m 1961, Denise; c Suzanne. **Education:** Ripon Col, BA, 1956; Mass Inst Technol, BS, 1957, DSc(mech metal), 1961. **Honors & Awards:** William Hunt Eisenman Award, Advan Semi Conductor Mat Int, 1992. **Professional Experience:** PRES, KEELER TECHNOL LLC, as of 2002; mgr tech develop, Budd Co Tech Ctr, beginning 1996; mgr metals, Budd CO Tech Ctr, 1987-1996; instr, Sheet Metal Formability, Univ Wis, 1984-; Nat Steel Corp, Mgr Automotive res, 1973-1987; Supvr Tech Develop, 1963-1972. **Memberships:** Fel Am Soc Metal; Fel Soc Automotive Engrs; Amer Inst Mining Metal & Petrol Engrs; Int Deep Drawing Res Group (pres 1972-1974 & 1988-1990). **Research Statement & Publications:** Transforming sheet metal formability from an art to a science; discovered forming limit programs; developed circle grid analysis, statistical deformation control and other press shop analysis technologies. **Mailing Address:** Keeler Technol LLC, PO Box 283, Grosse Ile, MI 48138. **Fax:** 734-671-2271. **E-Mail:** keeltech@comcast.net

KEELEY, DEAN FRANCIS, ANALYTICAL CHEMISTRY, HEADSPACE ANALYSIS. **Personal Data:** b Chicago, Ill, November 16, 1926; m 1951, Mary Ruth; c Mary Patricia. **Education:** Univ Ill, BS, 1952; Fla State Univ, PhD (chem), 1957. **Professional Experience:** PROF CHEM, UNIV LA, 1977-; from asst prof to assoc prof, UNIV LA, 1957-1977. **Memberships:** Am Chem Soc; Am Asn Univ Prof. **Research Statement & Publications:** Physical properties by headspace analysis. **Mailing Address:** Univ Southwestern La, Lafayette, LA 70504-0001. **E-Mail:** deankeeles@aol.com

KEELEY, FRED W, BIOCHEMISTRY. **Personal Data:** b Winnipeg, Man, March 21, 1944; m 1966, c 3. **Education:** Univ Man, BSc, 1965, PhD (pharmacol), 1970. **Professional Experience:** PROF BIOCHEM, UNIV TORONTO, as of 2005; prof clin biochem, Univ Toronto, beginning 1990; prof biochem, Univ Toronto, beginning 1990; PROF, RES INST, HOSP SICK C, TORONTO, 1990-; assoc prof, Univ Toronto, 1987-1990; assoc prof 1983-1990; assoc prof, Res Inst, Hosp Sick C, Toronto, 1983-1990; Med Res Coun Can scholar, Res Inst, Hosp Sick C, beginning 1973; res Inst, Hosp Sick Children, Toronto, 1972-1973; Med Res Coun Can fels, Agr Res Coun, Langford, Eng, 1970-1972. **Memberships:** Can Biochem Soc; NY Acad Sci. **Research Statement & Publications:** Biosynthesis of elastin; calcification of aortic tissue in atherosclerosis; effects of hypertension on vascular connective tissue. **Mailing Address:** Dept Biochem, Univ Toronto, Hosp Sick C, Rm 7003 McMaster Bldg, Toronto, ON M5G 1X8, Can. **Fax:** 416-978-8548. **E-Mail:** fwk@sickkids.on.ca

KEELEY, JON E, POPULATION ECOLOGY. **Personal Data:** b Chula Vista, Calif, August 11, 1949; m 1990. **Education:** San Diego State Univ, BS, 1971, MS, 1973; Univ Ga, PhD (bot), 1977. **Professional Experience:** RES ECOLOGIST, US GEOL SURV, as of 2003; prof biol, Occidental Col, beginning 1988; Guggenheim fel, 1985; assoc prof, Occidental Col, 1983-1988; res grants, NSF, 1979-1988; asst prof, Occidental Col, 1977-1983; lectr bot, Univ Ga, 1976-1977; consult, EIRs Publ; fel, Southern Calif Acad Sci. **Memberships:** Ecol Soc Am; Bot Soc Am; Am Soc Plant Physiologists; Am Soc Naturalists; Int Asn Veg Sci; Int Asn Wildland Fire. **Research Statement & Publications:** Aquatic plant photosynthesis; reproductive biology and demography of plants; fire ecology of mediterranean vegetation. **Mailing Address:** US Geol Surv, Sequoia & Kings Canyon Field Sta, HCR 89, Box 4, 47050 Generals Hwy, Three Rivers, CA 93271-9651. **Fax:** 559-565-3177. **E-Mail:** jon_keeley@usgs.gov

KEELEY, LARRY LEE, INSECT PHYSIOLOGY & NEUROENDOCRINOLOGY. **Personal Data:** b South Bend, Ind, January 3, 1939; m, c Lawrence, Brian, Erin, Brendan & Shannon. **Education:** Univ Notre Dame, BS, 1962; Purdue Univ, PhD (entom), 1966. **Professional Experience:** RETIRED; PROF EMER, TEX A&M UNIV, 2004-; NIH grants, 1993-1997; NSF grants, 1991-1994; NOAA sea grants, 1985-1997; NSF grants, 1985-1988 & 1981-1983; NIH grants, 1984-1987; NIH grants, 1978-1981; prof entom, Tex A&M Univ, beginning 1976; NSF grants, 1974-1978; from asst prof to prof, Tex A&M Univ, 1966-1976. **Memberships:** Fel AAAS; Entom Soc Am. **Research Statement & Publications:** Hormonal regulation of metabolism; identification and action of neurohormones on physiological functions of insects and other invertebrates. **Mailing Address:** Dept Entom, Tex A&M Univ, College Station, TX 77843. **Fax:** 979-845-6305. **E-Mail:** llkeeley@tamu.edu

KEELEY, STERLING CARTER, SYSTEMATIC BOTANY, MOLECULAR SYSTEMATICS. **Personal Data:** b San Francisco, Calif, October 23, 1948. **Education:** Stanford Univ, AB, 1970; San Diego State Univ, MS, 1973; Univ Ga, PhD (bot), 1977. **Professional Experience:** PROF BOT, UNIV HAWAII, 1991-; NSF vis prof biol, Univ Conn, 1988-1990; chloroplast DNA, Vernonia, NSF grant, 1988-1989; from assoc prof to prof biol, Whittier Col, 1979-1991; consult salt marsh veg, Port Los Angeles, 1979-1981; NSF grants, Systs Neotrop Vernonia, 1979-1981, 1982-1986; res assoc, Los Angeles County Mus Natural Hist, 1978-; consult flora, Southern Calif Ocean Studies Consortium Calif State Univ & Cols, 1978-; lectr bot, Calif State Univ, Long Beach, 1978-1979; NSF dissertation improv grant, 1974-1977; res asst ecol, Int Biol Prog Struct Ecosysts, 1970-1973. **Memberships:** Soc Study Evolution; Am Soc Plant Taxonomists; Am Bot Soc; AAAS; Sigma Xi; Ecol Soc Am. **Research Statement & Publications:** Systematics and biogeography of neotropical species of the genus Vernonia Compositae molecular systematics genetic diversity in island ecosystems; ecology and reproductive biology of mediterranean climate plants in relation to fire. **Mailing Address:** Dept Bot, Univ Hawaii, St John 508A, 3190 Maile Way, Honolulu, HI 96822. **Fax:** 808-956-3539. **E-Mail:** sterling@hawaii.edu

KEELING, CHARLES DAVID, physical chemistry, marine geochemistry; deceased, see previous edition for last biography

KEELING, RICHARD PAIRE, MYCOLOGY. **Personal Data:** b Crawfordsville, Ind, September 17, 1931; m 1952, c 2. **Education:** Wabash Col, AB, 1957; Purdue Univ, MS, 1960, PhD (bot), 1963. **Professional Experience:** RETIRED; prof biol, Emporia Kans State Col, 1974-1997; assoc prof biol, 1970-1974; asst prof microbiol, 1963-1970. **Memberships:** AAAS; Mycol Soc Am; AmSoc Microbiol; Soc Indust Microbiol; Japanese Mycol Soc; Sigma Xi. **Research Statement & Publications:** Fungus physiology; metabolism. **Mailing Address:** Dept Biol Sci, Emporia State Univ, Box 4050, Emporia, KS 66801. **Fax:** 620-341-5607.

KEELUNG, HONG, MEMBRANE FUSION. **Education:** Univ Calif, Berkeley, PhD (chem), 1975. **Professional Experience:** SCIENTIST, CALIF PAC MED CTR RES INST, as of 2003; RES BIOCHEMIST, CANCER RES INST, UNIV CALIF, SAN FRANCISCO, 1981-. **Memberships:** Biophys Soc; Am Chem Soc. **Mailing Address:** Cancer Res Inst, Univ Calif, San Francisco, CA 94143. **E-Mail:** khong@cooper.cpmc.org

KEEM, JOHN EDWARD, SOLID STATE PHYSICS. **Personal Data:** b Buffalo, NY, May 31, 1948; m 1980. **Education:** Syracuse Univ, BS, 1970; Purdue Univ, PhD (physics), 1976. **Professional Experience:** DIR RES & DEVELOP, OVONIC SYNTHETIC MAT CO, 1984-; mgr, Superconductivity Res, Energy Conversion, 1980-1983; devices phys dept, Gen Motors Res, 1977-1980; fel dept physics, Purdue Univ, 1976-1977; RES SCIENTIST, DIV MAT SCI, ARGONNE NAT LAB, 1974-; Mat res adv bd mat sub-micron struct, Nat Acad Sci. **Memberships:** Am Phys Soc; Am Soc Metals; Mat Res Soc. **Research Statement & Publications:** Synthesis of multilayer structures by sputtering and ion beam deposition; x-ray scattering from multilayer structures; melt spinning of Nd2 Fel4B permanent magnets; magnetic interactions between grains in Wd2 Fel4B materials; solid lubricating materials. **Mailing Address:** Argonne Nat Lab, 9700 S Cass Ave, Argonne, IL 60439.

KEEN, CARL L, DEVELOPMENTAL NUTRITION, MINERALS. **Education:** Univ Calif, Davis, PhD, 1979. **Professional Experience:** DISTINGUISHED PROF NUTRIT & INTERNAL MED, UNIV CALIF, DAVIS, as of 2004; MARS CHAIR, DEVELOP NUTRIT, UNIV CALIF, DAVIS, as of 2004, CHAIR, DEPT NUTRIT, AGRI EXP STA, UNIV CALIF, DAVIS, as of 2004; assoc prof nutrit, Univ Calif, Davis, beginning 1984. **Memberships:** Am Inst Nutrit; Teratology Soc; Soc Exp Biol & Med. **Mailing Address:** Dept Nutrit, Univ Calif, 3135B Meyer Hall, Davis, CA 95616. **E-Mail:** clkeen@ucdavis.edu

KEEN, CHARLOTTE ELIZABETH, MARINE GEOPHYSICS. **Personal Data:** b Halifax, NS, June 22, 1943; m 1963. **Education:** Dalhousie Univ, BSc, 1964, MSc, 1966; Cambridge Univ, PhD (geophys), 1970. **Professional Experience:** Chmn, Can Nat Lithosphere Comn, beginning 1981; mem working group 8 inter-union comn on geodynamics, Int Union Geod & Geophys & Int Union Geol Sci, beginning 1972; res scientist marine geophys, Atlantic Geoscience Centre, Bedford Inst, beginning 1970; chmn study group Northwest Atlantic Continental Margin, Inter-Union Comn Geodynamics; assoc ed, Can J Earth Sci. **Memberships:** Geol Asn Can; Royal Soc Can; Am Geophys Union. **Research Statement & Publications:** Surface wave propagation in Canadian shield and along mid-ocean ridges; plate tectonics of Baffin Bay region; continental-oceanic transition in the North West Atlantic; application of Backus-Gilbert inversion to upper mantle properties at ocean-continent transition; subsidence and thermal history of continental margins. **Mailing Address:** Geol Surv Can, Bedford Inst Oceanog, PO Box 1006, One Challenger Dr, Dartmouth, NS B2Y 4A2, Can. **Fax:** 902-426-6152. **E-Mail:** ckeen@agc.bio.ns.ca

KEEN, DOROTHY JEAN, PHYSICAL OCEANOGRAPHY. **Personal Data:** b Lancaster, Pa, June 19, 1922. **Education:** Swarthmore Col, BA, 1944. **Professional Experience:** RETIRED; phys sci adminr, Naval Ocean Res & Develop Activ, 1978-1982; sci staff asst, Ocean Sci Dept, Plans & Requirements Off, 1971-1978; head systs anal group, Ocean Prediction, 1966-1971; oceanogr ocean prediction, Hydrographic Off, US Naval Oceanog Off, 1958-1966; phys oceanogr mil appln, Hydrographic Off, US Naval Oceanog Off, 1953-1958; res asst chem & phys oceanog, Woods Hole Oceanog Inst, 1944-1953. **Memberships:** AAAS; Marine Tech Soc; Am Geophys Union. **Research Statement & Publications:** Military oceanography, plans and analysis; ocean prediction; fleet environmental support programs; effects on acoustic systems and tactics; ocean and estuarine dynamics; chemical analyses of sea water. **Mailing Address:** 6 Kendal Dr, Kennett Square, PA 19348.

KEEN, JAMES H, CELL BIOLOGY, MEMBRANE TRAFFICkING. **Personal Data:** b New York, NY, February 14, 1948; m 1973, Gwen; c 2. **Education:** Cornell Univ, PhD, 1976. **Professional Experience:** PROF, DEPT BIOCHEM & MOLECULAR BIOL, JEFFERSON MED COL, THOMAS JEFFERSON UNIV, as of 2005; DEAN, JEFFERSON COL GRAD STUDIES, as of 2005; ASSOC DIR, KIMMEL CANCER CTR, THOMAS JEFFERSON UNIV, PHILA, PA, 2002-; PROF PHARMACOL, JEFFERSON CANCER INST, PHILADELPHIA, PA, 1991-; prof, Dept Microbiol & Immunol, Thomas Jefferson Univ, as of 2001; assoc prof, Fels Res Inst, Sch Med, Temple Univ, 1985-1991; chmn grad studies, Prog Molecular Biol & Genetics, Sch Med, Temple Univ. **Memberships:** AAAS; Am Soc Cell Biol; Am Soc Biol Chem. **Research Statement & Publications:** Structure and function of clathrin coated membranes; role in receptor-mediated endocytosis and membrane dynamics; biochemistry; biophysics; cell biology; developmental biology; genetics; human physiology; pharmacology; neuron; antibody; clathrin; mast cell; exocytosis; macrophage; radiotracer; calcium flux; cytoskeleton; cell membrane; stoichiometry; immune complex; molecular site; phosphorylation; laboratory mouse; light microscopy; membrane protein; fluorescence microscopy; site directed mutagenesis; platelet activating factor; protein structure function; confocal scanning microscopy; receptor mediated endocytosis; publications on based on endocytic clathrin-coated pit formation. **Mailing Address:** Dept Biochem & Molecular Biol, Jefferson Med Col, Thomas Jefferson Univ, BLSB 915 233 S 10th St, Philadelphia, PA 19107-5541. **Fax:** 215-503-0622. **E-Mail:** jim.keen@mail.jci.tju.edu

KEEN, LINDA, MATHEMATICS. **Personal Data:** b New York, NY, August 9, 1940; m Jonathan; c 2. **Education:** City Col NY, BS, 1960; NY Univ, MS, 1962, PhD (math), 1964. **Honors & Awards:** Abby Mauze Rockefeller Award, Mass Inst Technol, 1990. **Professional Experience:** PROF COMPUT SCI, CITY UNIV NY, LEHMAN COL, GRAD CTR, AS OF 2003; State Univ NY, Stony Brook, 1993; vis prof, Mass Inst Technol, 1991; vis prof, Princeton, 1989-1990; vis scientist, Max Planck Inst, 1988; vis scientist, IBM, 1988; vis prof, Boston Univ, 1987; vis scientist, vis mem Nat Sci Res Inst, 1986; NSF partial res grant, 1982-1988, 1989-1992, 1993-1998; vis prof, 1980-1981; PROF MATH, CITY UNIV NY, LEHMAN COL, GRAD CTR, 1974-; from asst prof to assoc prof, City Univ NY, Lehman Col, Grad Ctr, 1967-1974; asst prof, Hunter Col, 1965-1967; NSF fel math, Inst Advan Study, 1964-1965. **Memberships:** Am Math Soc (vpres, 1990-1993); Asn Women Math (pres, 1985-1986). **Research Statement & Publications:** Complex analysis; Riemann surfaces; discontinuous groups; Teichmuller spaces; dynamical systems. **Mailing Address:** Dept Math & Comput Sci, Lehman Col, City Univ NY, Gillet Hall Rm 137 E250 Bedford Pk Blvd, Bronx, NY 10468. **Fax:** 718-960-8969. **E-Mail:** linda.keen@lehman.cuny.edu

KEEN, ROBERT ERIC, LIMNOLOGY, POPULATION ECOLOGY. **Personal Data:** b Oakland, Calif, May 29, 1944; m 1972, c 2. **Education:** Kans State Univ, BS, 1965; Mich State Univ, MS, 1967, PhD (zoology), 1970. **Professional Experience:** ASSOC PROF BIOL, MICH TECHNOL UNIV, 1981-; asst prof, Mich Technol Univ, 1977-1981; vis asst prof zool, Ind Univ, 1977; vis asst prof biol, Kans State Univ, 1976-1977; consult, Vt Inst Water Resources Res, 1976-1977; staff consult, Nat Comn Water Qual, 1975; partic, Advan Inst Statist Ecol, Pa State Univ, 1972; asst prof zool, Univ Vt, 1971-1976; fel, Philadelphia Acad Natural Sci, 1970-1971. **Memberships:** Am Soc Limnol & Oceanog; Ecol Soc Am; Int Soc Limnol; Soc Pop Ecol. **Research Statement & Publications:** Population ecology of zooplankton; limnology of Lake Superior; toxicity tests with Ceriodaphnia. **Mailing Address:** Dept Biol Sci, Mich Technol Univ, 1400 Townsend Dr Dow 740, Houghton, MI 49931. **Fax:** 906-487-3167. **E-Mail:** rekeen@mtu.edu

KEEN, WILLIAM HUBERT, ECOLOGY, ZOOLOGY. **Personal Data:** b Jewell Ridge, Va, September 2, 1944; m 1968, c 1. **Education:** Pikeville Col, BA, 1967; Eastern Ky Univ, MS, 1971; Kent State Univ, PhD (ecol), 1975. **Professional Experience:** INTERIM PRES, YORK COL, CITY UNIV NY, as of 1999; vpres acad affairs, York Col, City Univ NY, beginning, 1994; dean arts & sci, State Univ NY, Cortland, 1988-1994; chmn dept, State Univ NY, Cortland, 1983-1988; from asst prof to prof biol, State Univ NY, Cortland, 1976-1994; instr, Kent State Univ, Ohio, 1975-1976; lectr, Cuyahoga Community Col, Cleveland, Ohio, 1975-1976; teacher biol & sci, Jefferson Co Pub Sch, Louisville, Ky, 1969-1970; coordr interdisciplinary field studies, Pikeville Col, Ky, 1968-1969; teacher biol & sci, Buchanan Co Pub Sch, Grundy, Va, 1967-1968. **Memberships:** Sigma Xi; AAAS; Am Asn Higher Educ; Soc Study Amphibians & Reptiles; Am Soc Ichthyologists & Herpetologists; Asn Gen & Lib Studies. **Research Statement & Publications:** Population ecology and behavior of lower vertebrates; thermoregulation in amphibians; functions of fish schooling; interspecific interactions. **Mailing Address:** Vpres Acad Affairs York Col, City Univ NY 94-20 Guy R Brewer Blvd, Jamaica, NY 11451. **Fax:** 607-753-5999.

KEENAN, EDWARD JAMES, PHARMACOLOGY, ENDOCRINOLOGY. **Personal Data:** b Shelton, Wash, September 6, 1948. **Education:** Creighton Univ, BS, 1970, MS, 1972; WVa Univ, PhD (pharmacol), 1975. **Professional Experience:** PROF & ASSOC DEAN MED EDUC, DEPT PHARMACOL, ORE HEALTH SCI UNIV, SCH MED, as of 2005; asst prof pharmacol, Org Health Sci Univ, beginning 1978; instr pharmacol, Clin Res Ctr Lab & Hormone Res Lab, Univ Ore Health Sci Ctr, 1977-1978; Dir, Clin Res Ctr Lab & Hormone

Res Lab, Univ Ore Health Sci Ctr, 1976-; asst prof surg, Univ Ore Health Sci Ctr, beginning 1976; res assoc, Univ Ore Health Sci Ctr, 1975-1976. **Memberships:** Am Soc Andrology; AAAS; Sigma Xi. **Research Statement & Publications:** Significance of steroid hormones in cancer of the breast and prostate gland; mechanism of steroid hormone action; role of prolactin in male accessory sex organ function. **Mailing Address:** Dept Pharmacol, Ore Health Sci Univ Sch Med, Dean's Off L-102 3181 SW Sam Jackson Park Rd, Portland, OR 97201-3098. **E-Mail:** keenane@ohsu.edu

KEENAN, EDWARD L, MATHEMATICS. **Personal Data:** American citizen. **Education:** Swarthmore Col, BA, 1959; George Wash Univ, MA, 1966, Univ Pa, Phd (ling), 1969. **Professional Experience:** CHAIR, DEPT LING, UNIV CALIF, LOS ANGELES, 1998-; prof, Dept Ling, Univ Claif, Los Angeles, 1976-1995. **Memberships:** Ling Soc Am; Am Math Soc; NY Acad Sci; Am Acad Arts & Sci; AAAS. **Mailing Address:** Dept Ling, Univ Calif, 3125 Campbell Hall PO Box 951543, Los Angeles, CA 90095-1543. **E-Mail:** ekeenan@ucla.edu

KEENAN, JOHN DOUGLAS, WATER & WASTEWATER TREATMENT, ALTERNATIVE ENERGY SOURCES. **Personal Data:** b Sarnia, Ont, March 16, 1944; American citizen; m 1963, Martha; c Mark, Sean, Patrick & Matthew. **Education:** State Univ NY, Buffalo, BA, 1967; Syracuse Univ, MS, 1970, PhD (civil eng), 1972. **Honorary Degrees:** MA, Univ Pa, 1978. **Professional Experience:** DIR, UNDERGRAD FACULTY ADV, 1994-; prof civil eng systs & assoc dean undergrad educ, Univ Pa, 1990-1994; assoc prof, Univ Pa, 1986-1990; from asst prof to assoc prof civil eng, Univ Pa, 1973-1986; vis asst prof civil eng, Univ Pa, 1972-1973; Instr water & wastewater treat, Syracuse Univ, 1970-1972. **Research Statement & Publications:** Environmental systems engineering; water and wastewater engineering; biological and health effects of pollutants; alternative energy sources. **Mailing Address:** Dept elec & systs Engr, Univ Pa, Philadelphia, PA 19104-6391. **Fax:** 215-898-1130. **E-Mail:** keenan@seas.upenn.edu

KEENAN, JOSEPH ALOYSIUS, NUCLEAR CHEMISTRY. **Personal Data:** b Washington, DC, August 5, 1938; m 1968, c 2. **Education:** Spring Hill Col, BS, 1964; Clark Univ, PhD (nuclear chem), 1971. **Professional Experience:** SR MEM TECH STAFF, MAT SCI LAB, TEX INSTRUMENTS INC, 1980-; mem res staff, 1969-1980. **Memberships:** Am Chem Soc; Electro Chem Soc; Am Vacuum Soc. **Research Statement & Publications:** Instrumental neutron activation analysis, radiotracer techniques and x-ray fluorescence analysis in materials characterization; design and building of mini computer systems for manufacturing and laboratory automation; auger spectroscopy; surface science ion backseat housing; nuclear reaction analysis. **Mailing Address:** Mat Characterization Lab Tex Instruments Inc, Dallas, TX 75222.

KEENAN, KATHLEEN MARGARET, BIOSTATISTICS. **Personal Data:** b St Paul, Minn, May 24, 1934. **Education:** St Catherine Col, BA, 1956; Univ Minn, MS, 1958, PhD (biostatist), 1964. **Professional Experience:** PROF EMER ORAL SCI, SCH DENT, UNIV MINN, as of 1999; assoc prof oral sci, Sch Dent, Univ Minn, beginning 1969; Asst prof, 1964-1969. **Memberships:** AAAS; Am Statist Asn; Biom Soc; fel Am Pub Health Asn; Am Soc Human Genetics; Sigma Xi. **Research Statement & Publications:** Biostatistical applications in dental research. **Mailing Address:** 1768 Field Ave, Dept Oral Sci, St Paul, MN 55116-2726. **Fax:** 612-626-2651. **E-Mail:** kmkeenan@umn.edu

KEENAN, PHILIP T, MATHEMATHICS. **Professional Experience:** STAFF, RICE UNIV, as of 2005. **Memberships:** Nat Sci Found. **Mailing Address:** Dept Comput & Appl Math, Rice Univ, PO Box 1892, Houston, TX 77251. **Fax:** 713-285-5273.

KEENAN, ROBERT GREGORY, ENVIRONMENTAL CHEMISTRY. **Personal Data:** b St Albans, Vt, December 19, 1915; m 1944, Yvonne; c Patricia, Richard & Eileen (Herzog). **Education:** Catholic Univ, BS, 1937; Univ Md, MS, 1952; Am Bd Indust Hyg, cert indust hyg, 1962. **Honors & Awards:** Moyer D Thomas Award, Am Soc Testing & Mat, 1977. **Professional Experience:** RETIRED; vpres & dir lab serv, George D Clayton & Assocs, 1969-1976; assoc chief div occup health, Div Occup Health, USPHS, 1967-1969; dep chief res & med affairs, Div Occup Health, USPHS, 1966-1967; guest worker, Anal Chem Div, Radiochem Anal Sect, Nat Bur Standards, 1963-1964; chief, Div Occup Health, USPHS, 1960-1969; asst chief anal serv, Div Occup Health, USPHS, 1956-1960; chief phys anal unit, Div Occup Health, USPHS, 1953-1956; scientist, Div Occup Health, USPHS, 1949-1953; sr asst scientist, Div Occup Health, USPHS, 1945-1949; from jr chemist to assoc chemist, Div Occup Health, USPHS, 1940-1945; lab helper chem, Div Occup Health, USPHS, 1938-1940. **Memberships:** Emer mem Am Chem Soc; hon mem Am Indust Hyg Asn; Am Soc Testing & Mat. **Research Statement & Publications:** Spectrography; determination of cobalt in dust samples; determination of iron in welding fume samples; quantitative analytical methods in emission spectroscopy and suppression of cyanogen bands in emission spectra; activation analysis; atomic absorption; beryllium in air; biological materials and ores; analytical techniques for industrial hygiene and air pollution; author or coauthor of over 75 scientific publications. **Mailing Address:** 5333 N Sheridan Rd 18t, Chicago, IL 60640.

KEENAN, ROY W, METABOLISM. **Education:** Ohio State Univ, PhD, 1960. **Professional Experience:** PROF BIOCHEM, UNIV TEX HEALTH SCI CTR, 1982-. **Mailing Address:** Univ Tex Health Sci Ctr, 7703 Floyd Curl Dr, San Antonio, TX 78284-7700.

KEENAN, THOMAS AQUINAS, COMPUTER SCIENCE. **Personal Data:** b Rochester, NY, March 8, 1927; m 1993, Marcelline; c 3. **Education:** Univ Rochester, BS, 1947; Purdue Univ, MS, 1950, PhD (physics), 1955. **Professional Experience:** RETIRED; prog dir software systs sci, NSF, 1969-1990; exec dir educ info network, Interuniv, Commun Coun, 1968-1969; dir systs planning, Interuniv, Commun Coun, 1966-1968; consult, Sch Math Study Group, 1965-1966; exec dir, comt on uses of comput, Nat Acad Sci-Nat Res Coun, 1962-1963; chmn prog appl math, Rochester Univ, 1958-1966; asst prof physics, Rochester Univ, 1957-1962; dir comput ctr, Rochester Univ, 1956-1966; instr physics, Purdue Univ, 1950-1955. **Memberships:** AAAS. **Research Statement & Publications:** Computation; formal languages; symbol manipulation; information retrieval; data structure; phase transitions; combinatorial mathematics. **Mailing Address:** 12433 Over Ridge Rd, Potomac, MD 20854-3047.

KEENAN, THOMAS K, INORGANIC CHEMISTRY. **Personal Data:** b Ft Dodge, Iowa, October 8, 1924; m 1952, Beverly; c Jacqueline Petersen, Kathi Gardner, Michelle Melton & Robert. **Education:** SDak Sch Mines & Technol, BS, 1949; Univ NMex, MS, 1950, PhD (chem), 1954. **Professional Experience:** RETIRED; assoc group leader waste mgt, Los Alamos Nat Lab, 1984-1986; asst assoc dir, Los Alamos Nat Lab, 1981-1984; group leader waste mgt, Los Alamos Nat Lab, 1975-1981; mem staff, Los Alamos Nat Lab, 1954-1975; asst, Univ NMex, 1949-1953. **Memberships:** Am Nuclear Soc. **Research Statement & Publications:** Basic Res on Actinide elements, Primary Phytonium, Americaium and Custum. **Mailing Address:** 289 Venado St, Los Alamos, NM 87544.

KEENAN, THOMAS WILLIAM, FOOD SCIENCE. **Personal Data:** b Johnstown, Pa, May 12, 1942; m 1964, c 3. **Education:** Pa State Univ, BS, 1964; Ore State Univ, MS, 1965, PhD (food sci), 1967. **Professional Experience:** PROF EMER BIOCHEM, VA POLYTECH INST, as of 2002; ASST DEAN GRAD SCH, PURDUE UNIV, 1977-; PROF ANIMAL SCI, PURDUE UNIV, 1973-; assoc prof food sci, 1967-1973. **Memberships:** Am Chem Soc; Am Dairy Sci Asn; Inst Food Technol. **Research Statement & Publications:** Membrane function; microbial biochemistry; lipid metabolism. **Mailing Address:** Dept Biochem, Va Polytech Inst & State Univ, 315 Engel Hall, Blacksburg, VA 24061-0308. **Fax:** 540-231-9070. **E-Mail:** twkeenan@vt.edu

KEENAN, WILLIAM JEROME, PEDIATRICS, NEONATAL-PERINATAL MEDICINE. **Personal Data:** b Rawlins, Wyo, September 8, 1939; m 1965, c 7. **Education:** Loyola-Stritch Sch Med, MD, 1964. **Professional Experience:** Consult, Mo Dept Health, 1985; dir, Southern Ill grant, 1984-; dir pediat, St Mary's Health Ctr, 1981-; PROF PEDIAT, ST LOUIS UNIV, 1980-; DIR, DIV NEONANTOLOGY, CARDINAL GLENNON C HOSP, ST LOUIS UNIV, 1980-; from asst prof to prof, Univ Cincinnati, 1969-1980; fel pediat, Univ Cincinnati, 1967-1969. **Memberships:** Soc Pediat Res; Am Fedn Clin Res; AAAS; Sigma Xi; Am Acad Pediat. **Research Statement & Publications:** Neonatal hyperbilirubinemia; critical care of neonatal patients; developmental biology. **Mailing Address:** Div Neonatology, Cardinal Glennon C Hosp, St Louis Univ, 1465 S Grand Blvd, St Louis, MO 63104. **Fax:** 314-268-6410.

KEENE, HARRIS J, ORAL PATHOLOGY. **Personal Data:** b Brooklyn, NY, April 13, 1931; m 1956, c 3. **Education:** Univ Md, DDS, 1955. **Professional Experience:** PROF, HEALTH SCI CTR, UNIV TEX, HOUSTON, as of 2000; MEM STAFF, UNIV TEX DENT BR, DENT SCI INST, 1977-; dir, Naval Dent Res Inst, 1968-1977; res officer dent, US Navy, 1960-1977. **Memberships:** fel AAAS; Am Dent Asn; Am Asn Phys Anthrop; Int Asn Dent Res. **Research Statement & Publications:** Epidemiology of oral diseases; dental oncology; dental anthropology; paleopathology; oral physiology. **Mailing Address:** Univ Tex Health Sci Ctr, 7000 Fannin Ste 1200, Houston, TX 77030. **E-Mail:** harris.j.keene@uth.tmc.edu

KEENE, JACK DONALD, MOLECULAR VIROLOGY, GENE EXPRESSION. **Personal Data:** b Jacksonville, Fla, June 21, 1947; m 1969, Judith; c Michael & Lisa. **Education:** Univ Calif, Riverside, AB, 1969; Univ Wash, Seattle, PhD (microbiol & immunol), 1974. **Honors & Awards:** Fac Res Award, Am Can Soc, 1981-1986. **Professional Experience:** CO-DIR, CTR RNA BIOL, MED CTR, DUKE UINV, as of 2005; JAMES B DUKE PROF, DEPT MOLECULAR GENETICS & MICROBIOL, MED CTR, DUKE UNIV, 1997-; prof, Dept Molecular genetics & Microbiol, Med Ctr, 1988-1997; Pew scholar biomed sci, 1986-1990; asst prof rheumatol & immunol, Dept med, Med Ctr, Duke Univ, beginning 1985-; mem, Exp Virol Study Sect, 1985-1988; spec reviewer, Virol Study Sect, NIH, 1984-; assoc ed, Virol, 1983-; from asst prof to assoc prof virol & molecular genetics, Dept Microbiol & Immunol, 1979-1988; staff fel molecular virol, Lab Molecular Genetics, Nat Inst Neurol Dis & Stroke, NIH, 1974-1978; mem, Molecular Biol Study Sect & Arthritis Found Study Sect; fel Comn & Res Comn. **Memberships:** Fel Am Soc Microbiol; Am Soc Virol; Am Soc Biochem & Molecular Biol; RNA Soc; Henry Kunkel Soc. **Research Statement & Publications:** RNA metabolism and processing; nature of autoimmunity and genetic regulation; virus-host interactions as models of cellular gene expression. **Mailing Address:** Dept Microbiol, Med Ctr, Duke Univ, 414 Jones Bldg Box 3020, Durham, NC 27710-0001. **Fax:** 919-684-8735. **E-Mail:** keene001@mcdvke.edu

KEENE, JAMES H, POULTRY NUTRITION. **Personal Data:** b Epps, La, May 8, 1930; m 1958, c 2. **Education:** Univ Ark, BS, 1957; La State Univ, MS, 1959, PhD (poultry nutrit), 1962. **Professional Experience:** RETIRED; from asst prof to prof poultry & dairying, Ark State Univ, 1964-1963; nutritionist, George B Matthews & Sons Inc, 1962-1964. **Memberships:** Poultry Sci Asn. **Research Statement & Publications:** Poultry production and physiology. **Mailing Address:** 1103 Fernwood Cove, Jonesboro, AR 72401.

KEENE, OWEN DAVID, POULTRY NUTRITION. **Personal Data:** b New Eagle, Pa, April 28, 1934; m 1997, Shirley. **Education:** Pa State Univ, BS, 1955; Univ Md, MS, 1959, PhD (poultry nutrit), 1963. **Professional Experience:** POULTRY NUTRITIONIST, HERITAGE PMS INC, 1990-; Agr prog leader, Residual Avoidance Prog, 1985; Agr prog leader, Poultry Exten Prog, USDA/Exten Serv, Washington, DC, 1984-1985; assoc prof poultry sci exten, Pa State Univ, 1975-1990; asst prof, Pa State Univ, 1969-1975; Sr biochemist, Abbott Labs, 1963-1969. **Memberships:** Poultry Sci Asn; World Poultry Sci Asn. **Research Statement & Publications:** Product development relating to the nutrition of poultry; extension publicatioons related to poultry nutrition & mgt. **Mailing Address:** Heritage PMS Inc, 2043 Horsehoe Pike, Annville, PA 17003.

KEENE, WILLIS RIGGS, INTERNAL MEDICINE, HEMATOLOGY. **Personal Data:** b Woodbine, Ga, January 30, 1932; c 4. **Education:** Emory Univ, BA, 1953; Johns Hopkins Univ, MD, 1957. **Professional Experience:** CLIN PRACT, 1975-; assoc chmn dept internal med, Col Med, Univ Fla, 1974-1975; prof med, Col Med, Univ Fla, 1971-1975; staff physician, Dept Internal Med, Lahey Clin, 1964-1968; instr, Harvard Univ, 1963-1964; fel med, Harvard Univ, 1961-1963; with USPHS Hosp, Boston, 1960-1961& Nat Cancer Inst, 1959-1960; from intern to resident, Johns Hopkins Hosp, 1957-1959. **Memberships:** Am Col Physicians; Am Soc Hemat. **Research Statement & Publications:** Blood platelet physiology; iron metabolism. **Mailing Address:** 130 N Gross Rd No 205, Kingsland, GA 31548.

KEENER, CARL SAMUEL, BOTANY. **Personal Data:** b Columbia, Pa, April 12, 1931; m 1955, Gladys; c Carl, Dorothy & Joyce. **Education:** Eastern Mennonite Col, AB, 1957; Univ Pa, MS, 1960; NC State Univ, PhD (bot), 1966. **Honors & Awards:** Jesse M Greeman Award, 1968; Henry Allan Gleason Award, 1984. **Professional Experience:** PROF EMER BIOL, PA STATE UNIV, as of 2006; CUR SEED PLANTS HERBARIUM, PA STATE UNIV, 1978-; prof biol, Pa State Univ, beginning 1991; from asst prof to assoc prof, PA State Univ, 1966-1991; vis lectr, Univ Va, 1966, 1968, 1972, 1976, & 1978; NFS grad fel bot, 1963-1966; asst prof biol, Eastern Mennonite Col, 1960-1963. **Memberships:** Am Soc Plant Taxon; Int Asn Plant Taxon; Int Orgn Biosyst; Systs Asn; Sigma Xi. **Research Statement & Publications:** Evolutionary patterns in the shale barren endemics of eastern US; floristics of Pennsylvania; Ranunculaceae of North America. **Mailing Address:** Dept Biol, Pa State Univ, 208 Mueller Lab, Univ Park, PA 16802-5301. **Fax:** 814-865-9193. **E-Mail:** kux@psuvm.psu.edu

KEENER, E(VERETT) L(EE), ELECTRICAL ENGINEERING. **Personal Data:** b Grafton, WVa, January 30, 1922; m Naomi. **Education:** Univ WVa, BSEE, 1944; Purdue Univ, MSEE, 1949. **Professional Experience:** RETIRED; sales, beginning 1987; assoc res consult, Res Ctr, 1966-1982; sr res engr, US Steel Corp, 1955-1966; sr res engr, Analog & Hybrid Comput, 1955-1966; instr, Purdue Univ, 1947-1948; from instr to asst prof elec eng, Univ WVa, 1946-1955; test engr, Gen Elec Co, 1944. **Memberships:** Inst Elec & Electronics Engrs; Soc Comput Simulation. **Research Statement & Publications:** Instrumentation, control and electrical analogs for steel industry processes; development of micro-computers for data acquisition and control. **Mailing Address:** 303 McGraw Ave, Grafton, WV 26354. **E-Mail:** elk266@aol.com

KEENER, HAROLD MARION, AGRICULTURAL ENGINEERING. **Personal Data:** b Ashland, Ohio, July 28, 1943; m 1965, Nancy; c Kevin, Myra, Kathy & Clinton. **Education:** Ohio State Univ, BS, 1967, MS, 1968, PhD (agr eng), 1973. **Professional Experience:** PROF AGR ENG, OHIO AGR RES & DEVELOP CTR, as of 2004; assoc prof agr eng, Ohio Agr Res & Develop Ctr, beginning 1980; from inst to asst prof, 1968-1980. **Memberships:** Am Soc Agr Engrs. **Research Statement & Publications:** Biomass combustion systems; fluidized bed combustion applied to small scale energy systems; grain and solar grain drying; analysis of total energy consumption in crop production systems and livestock enterprises; composting agricultural and yard waste. **Mailing Address:** Dept Agr Eng, Ohio Agr Res & Develop Ctr, 105 Agr Eng Bldg 1680 Madison Ave, Wooster, OH 44691. **Fax:** 330-263-3670. **E-Mail:** keener.3@osu.edu

KEENER, HARRY ALLAN, ANIMAL NUTRITION. **Personal Data:** b Greensboro, Pa, December 22, 1913; m 1941, Elizabeth Hartley; c Allan & William. **Education:** Pa State Univ, BS, 1936, PhD (animal nutrit, dairy husb), 1941; WVa Univ, MS, 1938. **Professional Experience:** EMER PROF ANIMAL SCI & EMER DEAN, COL LIFE SCI & AGR, UNIV NH, 1978-; dean, Col Life Sci & Agr, 1961-1978; dir agr exp sta, Col Life Sci & Agr, Univ NH, 1958-1978; prof animal sci, Col Life Sci & Agr, Univ NH, 1950-1978; assoc prof dairy husb, Col Life Sci & Agr, Univ NH, 1945-1950; from instr to asst prof animal & dairy husb, Col Life Sci & Agr, Univ NH, 1941-1945; Asst dairy husb, WVa Univ, 1936-1938 & Pa State Univ, 1938-1941. **Memberships:** Am Soc Animal Sci; Am Dairy Sci Asn; NY Acad Sci. **Research Statement & Publications:** Trace elements; cobalt; vitamin D; nitrogen and energy metabolism. **Mailing Address:** PO Box 165, Durham, NH 03824-0165.

KEENER, JAMES PAUL, MATHEMATHICS. **Education:** Calif Inst Technol, PhD (Maths), 1972. **Professional Experience:** DISTINGUISHED PROF MATH, UNIV UTAH, as of 2005; ADJ PROF BIOENGINEERING, UNIV UTAH, as of 2005. **Memberships:** Soc Math Biol; Biophys Soc; Soc Indust & Appl Math. **Mailing Address:** Univ Utah, Dept Maths, 155 S 1400 E, Salt Lake City, UT 84112. **Fax:** 801-581-4148. **E-Mail:** keener@math.utah.edu

KEENER, MARVIN STANFORD, MATHEMATICAL ANALYSIS. **Personal Data:** b Birmingham, Ala, October 25, 1943; m 1965, Margaret; c Susan (Lavergne) & Ross S. **Education:** Birmingham-Southern Col, BS, 1965; Univ Mo-Columbia, MA, 1967, PhD (math), 1970. **Professional Experience:** REGENTS SERV PROF, OKLA STATE UNIV, as of 2003; exec vpres, Okla State Univ, beginning 1996; interim provost & vpres acad affairs, Dept Maths, 1993-1996; assoc dean arts & sci, Dept Maths, 1990-1993; head, Dept Maths, 1987-1990; PROF MATH, OKLA STATE UNIV, 1979-; from asst prof to assoc prof, Okla State Univ, 1970-1979. **Memberships:** Am Math Soc; Sigma Xi; Soc Indust & Appl Math; Math Asn Am. **Research Statement & Publications:** Ordinary differential equations. **Mailing Address:** Dept Math, Okla State Univ, 401 Mathematical Sci, Stillwater, OK 74078-1058. **Fax:** 405-744-8275. **E-Mail:** mkeener@okway.okstate.edu

KEENEY, CLIFFORD EMERSON, PHYSIOLOGY. **Personal Data:** b Springfield, Mass, June 28, 1921; m 1950, c 2. **Education:** Springfield Col, BS, 1948, MEd, 1949; Rutgers Univ, MS, 1951; NY UNiv, PhD (phys ed), 1959. **Professional Experience:** PROF EMER BIOL, SPRINGFIELD COL, as of 2004; prof biol, Springfield Col, beginning 1965; NSF sci fac fel, 1964-1965; dir Div Arts & Sci, Springfield Col, 1962-1964; from asst prof to assoc prof biol, Springfield Col, 1957-1965; asst prof physiol, Springfield Col, 1955-1957; biologist, Lederle Labs Div, Am Cyanamid Co, NY, 1952-1955; instr biol, Springfield Col, 1951-1952; Teacher high sch, Mass, 1949-1950. **Memberships:** AAAS; Nat Asn Biol Teachers; NY Acad Sci. **Research Statement & Publications:** Cytological changes induced by exercise. **Mailing Address:** 47 Old Coach Rd, Hampden, MA 01109.

KEENEY, DENNIS RAYMOND, SOIL FERTILITY, BIOCHEMISTRY. **Personal Data:** b Osceola, Iowa, July 2, 1937; m 1959, c 2. **Education:** Iowa State Univ, BS, 1959, PhD (soil fertil), 1965; Univ Wis, MS, 1961. **Honors & Awards:** Soil Sci Res Award, Soil Sci Soc Am, 1981; Soil Sci Prof Serv Award, 1994; Environ Qual Res Award, Am Soc Agron, 1986. **Professional Experience:** SR FEL, INST AGR & TRADE POLICY, IOWA STATE UNIV, as of 2005; DIR EMER LEOPOLD CTR SUSTAINABLE AGR, IOWA STATE UNIV, as of 2004; DIR, IOWA STATE WATER RESOURCES RES INSTS, 1992-; PROF AGRON, IOWA STATE UNIV, 1988-; dir leopold ctr sustainable agr, Iowa State Univ, beginning 1988; chmn land resources, Inst Environ Sci, 1985-1988; chmn dept, Univ Wis, 1979-1984; sr res fel, Dept Sci & Indust Res, Grasslands, Palmerston N, NZ, 1976-1977; Romnes grad sch fel, Univ Wis Grad Sch, 1975; from asst prof to prof soils, Univ Wis, 1966-1988; fel soil biochem, Iowa State Univ, 1965-1966. **Memberships:** fel Am Soc Agron (pres, 1992-1993); fel Soil Sci Soc Am (pres, 1988); Soil Conserv Soc Am; fel AAAS. **Research Statement & Publications:** Sustainable agriculture; agricultural systems; modeling of N cycle; elucidation of nitrogen transformation in soils and waters; sustainable agriculture; land application of solid and liquid municipal and industrial wastes. **Mailing Address:** Leopold Ctr Sustainable Agr, Iowa State Univ, 209 Curtiss Hall, Ames, IA 50011-1050. **Fax:** 515-294-9696. **E-Mail:** drkeeney@iastate.edu

KEENEY, NORWOOD HENRY, CHEMICAL ENGINEERING, PULP & PAPER-FOREST PRODUCTS. **Personal Data:** b Hartford, Conn, July 10, 1924; m 1946, Phyllis; c Norwood H III. **Education:** Trinity Col, Conn, BS, 1948; Univ Maine, Orono, MS, 1950; Victoria Univ, Manchester, PhD, 1962. **Professional Experience:** RETIRED; chmn dept, Univ Lowell, 1976-1983; from asst prof to prof chem eng, Univ Lowell, 1953-1986; paper chemist, Fram Corp, 1950-1953. **Memberships:** Tech Asn Pulp & Paper Indust. **Research Statement & Publications:** Chemical engineering applications to pulp and paper industry; porous media; filtration of compressibles; zeta potentials; stress-strain properties of fibers and fibrous structures. **Mailing Address:** PO Box 695, Unity, NH 03773.

KEENEY, PHILIP G, FOOD SCIENCE. **Personal Data:** b Caldwell, NJ, February 28, 1925; m 1957, Elsie Bamesberger; c Philip G II. **Education:** Univ Nebr, BSc, 1949; Ohio State Univ, MSc, 1953; Pa State Univ, PhD (dairy sci), 1955. **Honors & Awards:** Distinguished Aluminus, The Pennsylvania State Univ; Fellow AAAS; Fellow Am Dairy Sci Assoc. **Professional Experience:** PROF EMER, PA STATE UNIV, 1985-; prof food sci, Pa State Univ, 1968-1985; assoc prof, Pa State Univ, 1963-1968; Asst prof dairy sci, Pa State Univ, 1955-1963; Consult, sci & technol ice cream & chocolate. **Memberships:** Fel AAAS; Am Chem Soc; Am Dairy Sci Asn; Inst Food Technol. **Research Statement & Publications:** Food technology andchemistry; ice cream; chocolate products. **Mailing Address:** Dept Food Sci, Pa State Univ, State College, PA 16803. **Fax:** 814-238-8157. **E-Mail:** pgk1@psu.edu

KEENEY, RALPH LYONS, RISK ANALYSIS, DECISION ANALYSIS. **Personal Data:** b Lewistown, Mont, January 29, 1944. **Education:** Univ Calif, Los Angeles, BS, 1966; Mass Inst Technol, MS, 1967, EE, 1968, PhD (opers res), 1969. **Professional Experience:** PROF EMER INDUST SYSTS ENG, UNIV SOUTHERN CALIF, as of 2001; prof systs sci, Univ Southern Calif, beginning 1983; vpres, Decision Anal, Woodward-Cycle Consults, 1980-1983; head, Decision Anal, Woodward-Cycle Consults, 1976-1983; res scholar, Int Inst Appl Systs Anal, Laxenburg, Austria, 1974-1976; assoc prof mgt & opers res, Opers Res Ctr, Mass Inst Technol, 1972-1974; pvt consult, 1969-; asst prof civil eng & staff mem, Opers Res Ctr, Mass Inst Technol, 1969-1972; engr, Bell Tel Labs, 1966-1969. **Memberships:** Nat Acad Eng; Soc Risk Anal; Inst Opers Res & Mgt Sci. **Research Statement & Publications:** Decision analysis, risk analysis; probabilistic models. **Mailing Address:** 101 Lombard St No 704W, San Francisco, CA 94111.

KEENLEYSIDE, MILES HUGH ALSTON, FISH BEHAVIOR. **Personal Data:** b Ottawa, Ont, April 8, 1929; m 1951, Hilda; c Joel H & Eric M. **Education:** Univ BC, BA, 1952, MA, 1953; Univ Groningen, PhD (zoology), 1955. **Professional Experience:** PROF EMER, UNIV WESTERN ONT, as of 2005; sr Queen's Fel Marine Sci, Australia, 1983; prof zool, Univ Western Ont, beginning 1972; from asst prof to assoc prof, Univ Western Ont, 1961-1972; assoc scientist, Biol Sta, Fisheries Res Bd Can, 1957-1961; asst scientist fisheries biol, Biol Sta, Fisheries Res Bd Can, 1955-1957. **Memberships:** Can Soc Zoologists; fel Animal Behav Soc; Int Soc Behav Ecol. **Research Statement & Publications:** Social and reproductive behavior of fishes; parent-young interactions; social organization, mating systems and ecology; mate choice; correlates of reproductive success. **Mailing Address:** Dept Zool, Univ Western Ont, London, ON N6A 5B7, Can. **Fax:** 519-661-2014.

KEENLYNE, KENT DOUGLAS, WILDLIFE ECOLOGY, GEOLOGY. **Personal Data:** b Durand, Wis, May 28, 1941; m 1964, c 2. **Education:** Univ Wis-River Falls, BS, 1964; Univ Minn, MS, 1968, MAPA, 1971, PhD (wildlife ecol), 1976. **Honors & Awards:** Spec Achievement Award, US Fish & Wildlife Serv, 1989, 1993, 1994, 1995; Nat Wildlife Vol Award, 1991, Star Award, 1996. **Professional Experience:** RETIRED; sr staff biologist, off mgr, Bluestem Inc, beginning 1997; adj prof wildlife, Pallid Sturgeon Recovery Team, 1995-; adj prof wildlife, SDak State Univ, Brookings, 1987-; Mo River Natural Resources Comt, Coordr, 1987-1997; Interior Coal rep, Interior Task Force Strip Mine Legis Coal Develop, 1978; Big game biologist, Minn Dept Natural Resources, 1978; area supvr, Pierre, SDak, 1977-1987; coal coordr mineral develop, Casper, Wyo, 1976-1977; fish & wildlife biologist ecol serv & proj planning, US Fish Wildlife Serv, Rock Island, Ill, 1976; herpetologist herpetol studies & res, Fla Game & Fresh Water Fish Comn, 1975-1976; coordr interagency coord, Upper Miss River Conserv Comt, 1972-1974; wildlife mgr, US Fish & Wildlife Serv, 1971-1996; Wildlife biologist river basin studies, US Fish & Wildlife Serv, Minneapolis, Minn, 1970-1972; Int Union Conserv, Nature & Natural Resources. **Memberships:** Am Fisheries Soc. **Research Statement & Publications:** Whitetailed deer reproduction; reproduction and life history of rattlesnakes; alligator attacks; physiology of whitetailed deer; sturgeon reproduction and life history; large river ecology. **Mailing Address:** Bluestem, Inc, 105 S Euclid Ste D, Pierre, SD 57501. **Fax:** 701-223-4645. **E-Mail:** bluestem@tic.bisman.com

KEENMON, KENDALL ANDREWS, PETROLEUM GEOLOGY, REMOTE SENSING. **Personal Data:** b Detroit, Mich, September 13, 1920; m 1942, Elizabeth; c Janet S (Gamble), John S, Joanne S (Parker) & Judith S (Janik). **Education:** Univ Mich, BS, 1947, MS, 1948, PhD (geol), 1950. **Professional Experience:** OWNER & CONSULT, K-TECHNOL, 1985-; staff geologist, Pecten Int Co, 1978-1985; sr geologist, Int Region, 1972-1977; sr geologist, Shell Oil Co, 1967-1969 & Shell Develop Co, 1969-1972; sr res geologist, Shell Develop Co, 1961-1967; sr geologist, Shell Oil Co, 1960-1961; div geologist, Shell Oil Co, 1950-1960. **Memberships:** Geol Soc Am; Am Asn Petrol Geol. **Research Statement & Publications:** Structural geology; stratigraphy. **Mailing Address:** 5158 Imogene St, Houston, TX 77096.

KEENS, THOMAS GEORGE, PEDIATRIC PULMONOLOGY, RESPIRATORY PHYSIOLOGY. **Personal Data:** b Altadena, Calif, November 22, 1946; m 1972, Susan; c Jenny & Peter. **Education:** St John's Col, Santa Fe, NMex, BA, 1968; Univ Calif, San Diego, MD, 1972. **Honors & Awards:** Danile E Boatwright Award, SIDS, 1992; Apnea Infancy Award, Annenberg Ctr, 1997. **Professional Experience:** PROF PHYSIOL & BIOPHYS, KECK SCH MED, UNIV SOUTHERN CALIF, LOS ANGELES, as of 2004; PROF PEDIAT, KECK SCH MED, UNIV SOUTHERN CALIF & CHILDRENS HOSP, LOS ANGELES, 1979-; Pediat pulmonologist & neonatologist, Childrens Hosp Los Angeles, 1977-; from asst prof to assoc prof pediat, Sch Med, Univ Southern Calif & Childrens Hosp, Los Angeles, 1977-1983; res fel pediat respiratory physiol, Res Inst, Hosp Sick Children, Toronto, Ont, 1975-1977; pediat intern & resident, Childrens Hosp Los Angeles, Calif, 1972-1975. **Memberships:** Am Physiol Soc; Soc Pediat Res; Am Pediatr Soc; fel Am Acad Pediat; Am Thoracic Soc; fel, Am Col Chest Physicians; Sleep Res Soc. **Research Statement & Publications:** Sudden infant death syndrome; congenital central hypoventilation syndrome; development of cardiorespiratory control; chronic lung disease; ventilatory muscle function; pediatric pulmonary function; exercise in chronic lung disease; published over 50 articles. **Mailing Address:** Childrens Hosp Los Angeles, 4650 Sunset Blvd MS 83, Los Angeles, CA 90027-6062. **Fax:** 323-664-9758. **E-Mail:** tkeens@chla.usc.edu

KEENY, SPURGEON MILTON, PHYSICS. **Personal Data:** b New York, NY, October 24, 1924; m 1952, c 3. **Education:** Columbia Univ, BA, 1944, MA, 1946. **Professional Experience:** SR FEL, NAT ACAD SCI, as of 2005; pres & exec dir, Arms Control Asn, as of 2002; mem, Comt Int Security & Arms Control, Nat Acad Sci, beginning 1981; scholar-in-residence, Nat Acad Sci, beginning 1981; head US deleg, US/Soviet Theater Nuclear Force Talks, 1980; dep dir, US Arms Control & Disarmament Agency, 1977-1981; chmn, Ford-Mitre Nuclear Energy Policy Study, 1975-1977; Am Phys Soc Study Group Light-Water Reactor Safety, 1974-1975; dep chmn, Nat Acad Sci, Comt Environ Decision Making, 1974; dir policy & prog develop, Mitre Corp, 1973-1977; asst dir sci & technol, US Arms Control & Disarmament Agency, 1969-1973; sr staff mem, Nat Security Coun, 1963-1969; tech asst, President's Sci Adv, 1958-1969; mem US del, Conf Discontinuance Nuclear Weapon Tests, 1958-1960; mem US del, Geneva Conf Experts Nuclear Test Detection, 1958; mem, Gaither Security Resources Panel, 1957; chief atomic energy div, Off Asst Secy Defense Res & Eng, 1956-1957; mem staff, Panel Peaceful Uses Atomic Energy, 1955-1956; intel analyst, chief Spec Weapons Sect, 1952-1955; intel analyst, Directorate Intel Hq, US Air Force, 1950-1952; asst physics, Columbia Univ, 1944-1946. **Memberships:** Fel Am Acad Arts & Sci; Coun Foreign Relations; Am Phys Soc. **Research Statement & Publications:** Arms control and disarmament; defense policy; military and civilian applications of atomic energy; energy and environmental policy. **Mailing Address:** Nat Acad Sci, 500 Fifth St N W, Washington, DC 20036.

KEEPIN, GEORGE ROBERT, NUCLEAR PHYSICS, INSTRUMENTATION. **Personal Data:** b Oak Park, Ill, December 5, 1923; m 1948, Madge; c G Robert, William N, Ardis E (Davis), Mavis E & Denice C. **Education:** Univ Chicago, PhB, 1945; Mass Inst Technol, BS & MS, 1947; Northwestern Univ, PhD (physics), 1949. **Honors & Awards:** Am Nuclear Soc Spec Award, 1973; Distinguished Serv Award, Inst Nuclear Mat Mgmt, 1984. **Professional Experience:** RETIRED; fel, Los Alamos Nat Lab, beginning 1985; App fel, Los Alamos Nat Lab, beginning 1985; sr adv, Los Alamos Safeguards & Security Prog, 1985-1990; spec adv dep dir gen, Int Atomic Energy Agency, Vienna, 1982-1985; prog mgr, nuclear safeguards affairs, 1979-1982; nat chmn, Inst Nuclear Mat Mgt, 1978-1980; prog dir nuclear safeguards, Los Alamos Sci Lab, 1975-1979; nat prog chmn, Inst Nuclear Mat Mgt, 1974-1976; group leader nuclear assay res, Los Alamos Sci Lab, 1966-1975; tech adv, Int Atomic Energy Agency, Geneva, 1964; head physics sect, Int Atomic Energy Agency, Vienna, 1963-1965; deleg, Atoms for Peace Conf, Geneva, 1955, 1964 & 1971; res physicist, Los Alamos Sci Lab, 1952-1962; AEC fel radiation lab, Univ Calif, 1950; consult, Argonne Nat Lab, 1948-1949. **Memberships:** NY Acad Sci; fel Am Phys Soc; fel Am Nuclear Soc; fel Inst Nuclear Mat Mgt. **Research Statement & Publications:** Fission physics; reactor dynamics; pulsed neutron research, nuclear safeguards research and development; development of non-destructive assay techniques for domestic and international inspection and safeguards of fissionable materials; development and implementation of nondestructive assay technology for stringent nuclear safeguards and nonproliferation of nuclear weapons. **Mailing Address:** Los Alamos Nat Lab, Los Alamos, NM 87544.

KEEPORTS, DAVID, PHYSICS & CHEMISTRY EDUCATION, SOFTWARE DEVELOPMENT. **Personal Data:** b York, Pa, June 15, 1951. **Education:** Univ Del, BS, 1973; Yale Univ, MS, 1974; Univ Wash, PhD (phys chem), 1982. **Professional Experience:** PROF PHYSICS & CHEM, MILLS COL, 1993-; from asst prof to assoc prof, Mills Col, 1982-1993; lectr physics/math, Univ New Haven, 1976-1979; lectr math, Southern Conn State Col, 1976-1978; lectr physics/chem/math, Quinnipiac Col, 1975-1979. **Memberships:** Am Chem Soc; Am Asn Physics Teachers; Sigma Xi. **Research Statement & Publications:** Author of numerous publications on the practice and theory of molecular spectroscopy and numerous publications in physics, chemistry and math education journals; development of software for physics education. **Mailing Address:** Dept Chem & Physics Mills Col, CPM 108, Oakland, CA 94613. **E-Mail:** dave@mills.edu

KEER, LEON M, CIVIL ENGINEERING, ENGINEERING MECHANICS. **Personal Data:** b Los Angeles, Calif, September 13, 1934; m 1956, Barbara Sara; c PatriciaR. Munro, Jacqueline S. Keer, Harold N. Keer, Michael D. Keer. **Education:** Calif Inst Technol, BS, 1956, MS, 1958; Univ Minn, PhD (Eng Mech), 1962. **Honors & Awards:** Innovative Res Award, Am Soc Mech Engrs, Tribology Div, 2001; Daniel C Drucker Medal, Am Soc Mech Engrs, 2003. **Professional Experience:** WALTER P MURPHY PROF CIVIL ENG, NORTHWESTERN UNIV, 1994-; prof & chmn dept, Northwester Univ, 1992-; tech ed, J Appl Mech, Am Soc Mech Engrs, 1988-1992; JSPS fel, Tohoku Univ, Japan, 1986; fel, Japan Soc Prom Sci, 1986; assoc dean grad studies & res, Northwestern Univ, 1985-1992; sr vis fel, Dept Math, Univ Glasgow, 1975; Guggenheim sr vis fel, Dept Math, Univ Glasgow, 1972-1973; prof civil eng, Northwestern Univ, 1970-1985; from asst prof to assoc prof, Northwester Univ, 1964-1970; preceptor, Columbia Univ, 1963-1964; NATO fel, 1962-1963; NATO fel eng mech, Newcastle, 1962-1963; mem tech staff, Hughes Aircraft Co, 1956-1959. **Memberships:** Fel Am Soc Mech Engrs; Fel Acoust Soc Am; Fel Am Soc Civil Engrs; Fel Am Acad Mech (secy, 1981-1985; pres, 1988-1989); Ame Soc Civil Engrs; Am Acad Mech. **Research Statement & Publications:** Contact stress and fracture problems; contact mechanics; composite materials; wave propagation. **Mailing Address:** Dept Civil Eng, Northwestern Univ, A319 Technological Inst 2145 Sheridan Rd, Evanston, IL 60208-3109. **Fax:** 847-491-4011. **E-Mail:** l-keer@northwestern.edu

KEES, KENNETH LEWIS, SYNTHESIS OF NON-INSULIN RELEASING ANTIDIABETIC AGENTS & NOVEL ANTIINFLAMMATORY AGENTS. **Personal Data:** b Highland Park, Mich, January 17, 1950. **Education:** Wayne State Univ, BS, 1973; Univ Calif, Santa Cruz, PhD (chem), 1979. **Professional Experience:** Contrib bd mem, Chemtracts, Org Chem, 1989-; PRIN SCIENTIST METAB DISORDERS, AM HOME PROD, WYETH-AYERST RES, 1988-; res scientist & supvr diabetes, Am Home Prod, Wyeth-ayerst Res, 1985-1988; res scientist immunoinflammatory, Am Home Prod, Wyeth-ayerst Res, 1983-1985; res assoc & adj lectr chem, Univ Santa Clara, Calif, 1982; fel chem, Univ Calif, Berkeley, 1981; Vis lectr chem, Univ Calif, Santa Cruz, 1980. **Memberships:** Am Chem Soc; Int Soc Heterocyclic Chem. **Research Statement & Publications:** Design and synthesis of novel (patentable) medicinal chemicals using state of the art synthetic and analytical techniques; synthesis of lipophillic, acidic heterocycles-some are new bioisosteres of carboxylic acids-for application to diabetes, inflammation and cardiovascular metabolic derangements. **Mailing Address:** 1015 Aspen Dr, Plainsboro, NJ 08536.

KEESE, CHARLES RICHARD, CELL BEHAVIOR, CELL MOTILITY. **Personal Data:** b Cooperstown, NY, March 4, 1944; m Kathleen; c Dan & Jody. **Education:** State Univ NY, Albany, BS, 1967; Rensselaer Polytech Inst, PhD (biol), 1971. **Honors & Awards:** IR-100 Award, 1984, Sci Digest, Outstanding Investr, 1984, 1985. **Professional Experience:** VPRES, APPL BIOPHYSICS INC, 1991-; SR RES SCIENTIST, DEPT BIOL, RENSSELAER POLYTECH INST, 1989-; staff scientist, Res & Develop, Gen Elec Corp, 1983-1989; assoc investr, Nat Found Cancer Res, 1981-1982; NSF fel sci fac prof develop award, Gen Elec Corp Res & Develop, 1977-1978; prof biol, State Univ NY, Cobleskill, 1971-1983; from asst prof to assoc prof physics, State Univ NY, Cobleskill, 1971-1979. **Memberships:** Sigma Xi; AAAS; Soc In Vitro Biol. **Research Statement & Publications:** Behavior of cells in culture; properties of proteins on surfaces; biosensors; electric cell-substrate impedance sensing. **Mailing Address:** Applied Biophysics, Inc, 185 Jordan Rd, Troy, NY 12180. **Fax:** 518-276-2907. **E-Mail:** keese@biophysics.com

KEESEE, ROBERT GEORGE, ION CHEMISTRY, AEROSOL SCIENCE. **Personal Data:** b Spokane, Wash, November 10, 1953. **Education:** Univ Ariz, BS, 1975; Univ Colo, PhD (phys chem), 1979. **Professional Experience:** Res assoc, Atmospheric Sci Res Ctr, Albany, NY, 1992-; ASSOC PROF CHEM, STATE UNIV NY, 1992-; ASSOC PROF ATMOSPHERIC SCI, STATE UNIV NY, 1991-; assoc prog dir, Atmospheric Chem Prog, NSF, 1988-1989; res asst prof chem, Pa State Univ, 1982-1991; sr res assoc chem, Univ Colo, 1982; Nat Res Coun res assoc, Space Sci Div, Ames Res Ctr, NASA, 1979-1981. **Memberships:** Am Chem Soc; Am Geophys Union; AAAS; Sigma Xi. **Research Statement & Publications:** Chemistry of planetary atmospheres; nucleation phenomena; ion solvation; gas-surface interactions; ion-molecule and ion-aerosol interactions; chemical and physical properties of molecular clusters and aerosols. **Mailing Address:** Dept Chem, Univ Albany, State Univ NY, 1400 Wash Ave, Albany, NY 12222-0001. **Fax:** 518-442-5825. **E-Mail:** rgk@atmos.albany.edu

KEESEY, RICHARD E, NUTRITION. **Personal Data:** b York, Pa, October 14, 1934. **Education:** Dartmouth Col, AB, 1956; Brown Univ, ScM, 1958, PhD, 1960. **Professional Experience:** PROF EMER PSYCHOL, UNIV WIS-MADISON, 1999-; vis lectr, Sydney Univ, beginning 1974; prof psychol, Univ Wis-Madison, beginning 1969; from asst prof to assoc prof, Univ Wis-madison, 1962-1969. **Memberships:** Am Inst Nutrit; NAm Soc Study Obesity; Am Psychol Soc; Soc Study Ingestive Behav. **Research Statement & Publications:** Physiology of body weight regulation; central nervous control of energy expentiture; obesity and other disorders of body energy regulation. **Mailing Address:** Dept Psychol, Univ Wis-Madison, 1202 W Johnson St, Madison, WI 53706. **Fax:** 608-262-4029. **E-Mail:** rekeesey@wisc.edu

KEESLING, JAMES EDGAR, TOPOLOGY, APPLIED MATHEMATICS. **Personal Data:** b Indianapolis, Ind, June 26, 1942; m 1963, Marian; c James E Jr, Timothy C, Marian E & Ruth E. **Education:** Univ Miami, Fla, BSIE, 1964, MS, 1966, PhD (math), 1968. **Professional Experience:** Managing ed, Toplogy & Appli, 2000-; vis prof, Univ Utah, 1991-1992; vis lectr, Univ Ga, 1976-1977; PROF MATH, UNIV FLA, 1975-; from asst prof to assoc prof, Univ Fla, 1967-1975; NASA fel, Univ Miami, 1965-1967; teaching asst, Univ Miami, Fla, 1964-1965. **Memberships:** AAAS; Am Math Soc; Math Asn Am; Soc Indust & Appl Math; The Soc for Math Biol. **Research Statement & Publications:** Topology; numerical analysis; biomathematics; over 70 professional publications; dynamical systems. **Mailing Address:** Dept Math Univ Fla, PO Box 118105 440 Little Hall, Gainesville, FL 32611-8105. **Fax:** 352-392-8357. **E-Mail:** jek@math.ufl.edu

KEETING, PHILIP E, ENDOCRINOLOGY. **Education:** Univ Med & Dent NJ, PhD, 1986. **Professional Experience:** ASSOC PROF, DEPT BIOL, W VA, as of 2005. **Mailing Address:** Dept Biol, W Va Univ, Morgantown, WV 26506-6057. **E-Mail:** pkeeting@wvu.edu

KEETON, T KENT, ANTIHYPERTENSIVE DRUGS, CARDIOVASCULAR PHARMACOLOGY. **Education:** Univ Tex, Dallas, PhD (pharmacol), 1975. **Professional Experience:** ASSOC PROF PHARMACOL, UNIV TEX HEALTH SCI CTR, 1983-. **Memberships:** Am Fed Clin Res; Am Soc Pharmacol & Exp Therapeut. **Mailing Address:** Dept Pharmacol, Univ Tex, 7703 Floyd Curl Dr, San Antonio, TX 78284-7764. **Fax:** 210-567-4303. **E-Mail:** keeton@uthscsa.edu

KEEVER, CAROLYN ANNE, CELLULAR IMMUNOLOGY, IMMUNOGENETICS. **Personal Data:** b Norfolk, Va, March 17, 1948. **Education:** Old Dominion Univ, BS, 1970; Wake Forest Univ, PhD (immunol), 1984. **Professional Experience:** RES ASSOC IMMUNOL, AMTEST, 1990-; res assoc immunol, Sloan-Kettering Cancer Ctr, 1987-1990; Prin investr, res grants, 1986-; res fel, Sloan-Kettering Cancer Ctr, 1984-1987; chmn, Am Bd Histocompatability & Immunogenetics. **Memberships:** Am Soc Histocompatibility & Immunogenetics; NY Acad. **Research Statement & Publications:** Immunology of bone marrow transplantation; the effects of interleukin Z on T-cell and NK-cell activities; the role of NK-cells in graft rejection and leukemia relapse; the kinetics of immune reconstitution following bone marrow transplantation; donor-host and host-donor tolerance. **Mailing Address:** 5325 Tara Hill Dr, Dublin, OH 43017.

KEEVER, DAVID BRUCE, SYSTEMS DESIGN & SYSTEMS SCIENCE. **Personal Data:** b Oakland, Calif, June 29, 1953; m 1985, Deborah. **Education:** Purdue Univ, BS, 1975, MS, 1976; Univ Va, PhD (syst eng), 1984. **Professional Experience:** SR SYST ENGR, SCI APPLN INT ORGN, 1990-; vis prof, City Univ, London, Eng, 1986-; asst prof & assoc dir, Ctr Interactive Mgt, George Mason Univ, 1984-1989; res & develop engr, Aerojet Liquid Rocket Corp, 1976-1978. **Memberships:** Inst Elec & Electronics Engrs. **Research Statement & Publications:** Design theory and methodology using structure methods, group processes and selective computer assisted methodologies. **Mailing Address:** Sci Appln Int Corp, M/S CV-48 7980 Sci Appln Court M/S CV-48, Vienna, VA 22183. **Fax:** 703-394-4270. **E-Mail:** david.b.keever@saic.com

KEEVIL, NORMAN BELL, MINING & METALLURGY. **Personal Data:** b Cambridge, Mass, February 28, 1938; m 1990, Joan E Macdonald; c Scott, Laura, Jill & Norman B III. **Education:** Univ Toronto, BA, 1959; Univ Calif, Berkeley, PhD, 1964. **Honorary Degrees:** LLD, Univ BC, 1993. **Honors & Awards:** Selwyn G Blaylock Medal, Can Inst Mining & Metall, 1990. **Professional Experience:** DIR, FORDING INC, as of 2004; pres & Chief exec officer, Teck Corp, Can, 1994-2001; DIR, AUR RESOURCES INC, 1992-; chmn, pres & chief exec officer, 1989-1994; CHMN, TECK COMINCO LTD, 1986-; pres & chief exec officer, explor, Teck Corp, Can, 1981-1989; exec vpres, explor, Teck Corp, Can, 1968-1981; Vpres, explor, Teck Corp, Can, 1962-1968. **Memberships:** Can Inst Mining & Metall; Prospectors & Develop Asn; Soc Explor Geophysicists. **Mailing Address:** Aur Resources Inc, One Adelaide St E Suite 2501, Toronto, ON M5C 2V9, Can. **Fax:** 416-367-0427.

KEEVIL, THOMAS ALAN, ORGANIC CHEMISTRY, BIOCHEMISTRY. **Personal Data:** b Long Branch, NJ, February 11, 1947; m 1969, Jean; c Derek & Melissa. **Education:** Bucknell Univ, BS, 1968; Univ Calif, Berkeley, PhD (chem), 1972. **Professional Experience:** Vis scholar, Oxford Univ, 1989-1990; res assoc, Univ Calif, San Diego, 1982-1983; PROF CHEM, SOUTHERN ORE UNIV, 1974-; res assoc biochem, Med Sch, Ore Health Sci Univ, 1972-1974. **Memberships:** Am Chem Soc; AAAS. **Research Statement & Publications:** Nickel biochemistry; A Kinetic Study of the Isomerization of Eugenol. **Mailing Address:** Dept Chem, Southern Ore Univ, 1250 Siskiyou Blvd, Ashland, OR 97520. **Fax:** 541-552-6415. **E-Mail:** keevil@sou.edu

KEFALIDES, NICHOLAS ALEXANDER, BIOLOGICAL CHEMISTRY, INTERNAL MEDICINE. **Personal Data:** b Alexandroupolis, Greece, January 17, 1927; American citizen; m 1949, Eugeia; c Alexandra (deceased), Patricia & Paul. **Education:** Augustana Col, Ill, AB, 1951; Univ Ill, BS, 1954, MD & MS, 1956, PhD (biochem), 1965. **Honorary Degrees:** MA, Univ Pa, 1971; Dr, Univ Reims, France, 1987. **Honors & Awards:** Borden Award, 1956; Award for Pioneering Res on Connective Tissues, Coll Gordon Conf, 1997. **Professional Experience:** PROF EMER MED, UNIV PA, as of 2004; Exec chair, IRBS, Univ PA, 1998-; assoc dean res, Univ PA, 1994-1995; mem & chair NIH Pathobiochem Study Sect, 1982-1986; chair Gordon res Conf Basement Membranes, 1982; DIR CONNECTIVE TISSUE RES INST, UNIV PA, 1977-; vis prof, Oxford Univ, Eng, 1977-1978 & 1984-1985; Guggenheim fel, 1977-1978; PROF BIOCHEM & BIOPHYSICS, UNIV PA, 1975-; dir, Connective Tissue Res Sect, Univ Pa, 1975-; prof med, Univ Pa, beginning 1974; dir, Gen Clin res Ctr, 1972-1976; attend physician, Philadelphia Gen Hosp, 1970-1977; assoc prof, Univ PA, 1970-1974; from asst prof to assoc prof, La Rabida Inst & dept Med, Univ Chicago, 1965-1970; chief infectious dis consult serv, Univ Chicago Hosp, 1965-1970; instr, Col Med, 1964-1965; chief infectious dis sect, Vet Admin Hosp, Hines, 1964-1965; assoc attend physician, Cook County Hosp, Chicago, Ill, 1962-1965; USPHS fel, Infectious Disease, 1962-1964; resident internal med, res & Educ Hosps, Univ Ill, 1960-1963; dir res proj burns, USPHS, Peru, 1957-1960; Intern med, res & Educ Hosps, Univ Ill, 1956-1957. **Memberships:** Int Soc Nephrology; Am Chem Soc; Am Soc Invest Path; Am Soc Clin Invest; Am Soc Biochem & Molecular Biol; Am Soc Cell Biol; fel AAAS. **Research Statement & Publications:** Chemistry of glycoproteins and basement membranes; molecular biology of collagen; metabolism of endothelial cells; angiogenesis. **Mailing Address:** Connective Tissue Res Inst, Univ Pa, 3624 Market St, Fifth Floor, Philadelphia, PA 19104-2614. **Fax:** 215-966-6101. **E-Mail:** kefalide@mail.med.upenn.edu

KEFFER, CHARLES JOSEPH, SOLID STATE PHYSICS, CRYSTALLOGRAPHY. **Personal Data:** b Philadelphia, Pa, August 7, 1941; m 1966, Barbara; c Susan, David, Peter & Dennis. **Education:** Univ Scranton, BS (physics), 1963; Harvard Univ, AM, 1964, PhD (solid state physics), 1969. **Professional Experience:** EXEC VP & CHEIF ADMIN OFFICER, UNIV ST THOMAS, as of 2004; Consult, 1998-; provost, Univ St Thomas, 1977-

1998; dean, Univ St Thomas, 1973-1977; from instr to asst prof physics, Univ Scranton, 1969-1973. **Mailing Address:** Univ St Thomas, 2115 Summit Ave, St Paul, MN 55105. **E-Mail:** Cjkeffer@stthomas.edu

KEFFER, JAMES F, MECHANICAL ENGINEERING. **Personal Data:** b Toronto, Ont, December 15, 1933; m 1955, c 2. **Education:** Univ Toronto, BASc, 1956, MASc, 1958, PhD (mech eng), 1962. **Professional Experience:** PROF EMER MECH ENG, UNIV TORONTO, as of 2004; Univ Tarragova, Spain, beginning 1997; vpres res, Univ Toronto, 1973-1990; vis prof, Inst Mechnique Statisique Turbulence, Marseille, France, 1973-1974; prof mech eng, Univ Toronto, beginning 1973; consult, Pulp & Paper Res Co Can, 1965-; from asst prof to assoc prof, Univ Toronto, 1964-1973; Nat Res Coun Can fel physics, Cambridge Univ, 1962-1964. **Memberships:** Sigma Xi. **Research Statement & Publications:** Fluid mechanics; heat and mass transfer; turbulent flows; wind erosion, building aerodynamics turbulent combustion; environmental pollution. **Mailing Address:** Dept Mech Eng, Univ Toronto, Kings Col Rd, Toronto, ON M5S 1A1, Can. **E-Mail:** keffer@mie.utoronto.ca

KEGEL, GUNTER HEINRICH REINHARD, NUCLEAR PHYSICS. **Personal Data:** b Herborn, Ger, June 16, 1929; m 1957, c 2. **Education:** Rio de Janeiro, BS, 1951; Mass Inst Technol, PhD (physics), 1961. **Professional Experience:** PROF PHYSICS, UNIV MASS, LOWELL, 1971-; chmn dept physics & appl physics, Univ Lowell, 1971-1981; consult, Millipore Corp, Bedford, Mass, 1969-1970; prof nuclear eng, Univ Lowell, 1966-1971; prof physics, Univ Mass, Lowell, 1964-1966; prof physics, Cath Univ, Rio Del Janeiro, 1961-1964; res asst, Lab Nuclear Sci, Mass Inst Technol, 1958-1961; prof, Rio Del Janeiro, 1952-1956 & 1961-1964; engr, Nat Inst Technol, Brazil, 1951-1956. **Memberships:** Brazilian Acad Sci; Am Phys Soc; Electrochem Soc; Am Nuclear Soc; Inst Elec & Electronics Engrs; Am Vacuum Soc; Mat Res Soc. **Research Statement & Publications:** Nuclear spectroscopy; rutherford backscattering spectroscopy; proton induced x-ray emission; neutron physics; neutron radiation damage. **Mailing Address:** Dept Physics, Univ Mass, One Univ Ave, Lowell, MA 01854. **E-Mail:** gunter_kegel@uml.edu

KEGELES, GERSON, BIOPHYSICAL CHEMISTRY. **Personal Data:** b New Haven, Conn, April 23, 1917; m 1944, Bertha; c Winifred, Lawrence, Stanley, Gloria & Joyce. **Education:** Yale Univ, BS, 1937, PhD (phys chem), 1940. **Professional Experience:** PROF EMER SECT BIOCHEM & BIOPHYS, UNIV CONN, 1982-; prof, Univ Conn, 1968-1982; Vis prof chem, Yale Univ, 1968; mem, Study Sect Biophys Chem, NIH, 1967-1970; chmn, Chem Dept, 1958-1961; from assoc prof to prof chem, Clark Univ, 1951-1968; phys chemist, Nat Cancer Inst, 1947-1951; fel, Univ Wis, 1945-1947; fel, Yale Univ, 1940-1941. **Memberships:** Am Chem Soc; Biophys Soc; Am Acad Arts & Sci. **Research Statement & Publications:** Ultracentrifugation; countercurrent distribution; equilibria and kinetics of protein interactions; diffusion and optical methods for its study; pressure effects in protein transport experiments. **Mailing Address:** Dept Biophysics & Biochem, Univ Conn, 369 Fairfield Rd, Storrs, CT 06269.

KEGELES, LAWRENCE STEVEN, BRAIN IMAGING, THEORETICAL ASTROPHYSICS. **Personal Data:** b Madison, Wis, February 9, 1947; m 1987, Wendy; c Laura. **Education:** Princeton Univ, AB, 1969; Univ Pa, PhD (physics), 1974, Mt Sinai Sch Med, MD, 1991. **Honors & Awards:** Florence & Herbert Irving clin Res Career Award, 2000-2003; Clin Scientist Develop Award, Nat Inst Mental Health, 1999-2004; ACNP/Bristol-Myers Squibb Travel Award, 2000; Young investr Awards, Nat alliance schizophrenia & Depression, 1995-1997, 1997-1999; Eli Lilly/Soc Biolog Psychiatry fel, 1995. **Professional Experience:** RES PSYCHIATRIST, COLUMBIA PRESBY HOSP, 1991-; mem tech staff, Bell labs, 1981-1987; res assoc, Stevens Inst Technol, 1978-1980; res assoc physics, Univ Pa & Naval res lab, 1974-1976 & Univ Alta, 1976-1978. **Memberships:** Sigma Xi; Soc Nuclear med; soc for Neuroscience; Am med asn. **Research Statement & Publications:** Perturbations of spacetimes; equations of motion and radiation damping; tracer kinetics in nuclear medicine; PET and MRS neurochemistry brain imaging. **Mailing Address:** 127 W 96th St Apt 13D, New York, NY 10025-6430.

KEGELMAN, MATTHEW ROLAND, ELECTROCHEMISTRY, POLYMER CHEMISTRY. **Personal Data:** b New York, NY, June 24, 1928; m 1953, c 10. **Education:** Fordham Univ, BS, 1948, MS, 1949, PhD (org chem), 1953. **Professional Experience:** RETIRED; sr res assoc, E I du Pont de Nemours & Co, 1971-1990; res assoc petrochem dept, E I du Pont de Nemours & Co, 1971-1978; from res chemist to sr res chemist, E I du Pont de Nemours & Co, 1953-1971; prin investr, Dielectric Gases Proj, Elec Power Res Inst. **Memberships:** AAAS; Am Chem Soc; Sigma Xi. **Research Statement & Publications:** Heterocyclics; pinacol rearrangement; petroleum chemicals; dielectric fluids; high-energy batteries; electro-organic synthesis; polymer intermediates; polyesters; polyamides. **Mailing Address:** 204 N Pembrey Dr, Wilmington, DE 19803-2005.

KEGG, RICHARD L, MECHANICAL ENGINEERING. **Education:** Univ Cincinnati, BS, MS, PhD (Mech Eng). **Professional Experience:** RETIRED; vpres, Technol & Mfg Develop, Milacron Inc, 1999. **Memberships:** Fel Soc Mfg Engrs; fel Am Soc Mech Engrs. **Mailing Address:** Cincinnati Milacron, 4701 Marburg Ave, Cincinnati, OH 45209. **Fax:** 513-556-5056. **E-Mail:** casquestions@uc.edu

KEGLEY, ELIZABETH BRIGHT, NUTRITIONAL MODIFICATION OF IMMUNE FUNCTION, BEEF CATTLE NUTRITION. **Personal Data:** b Staunton, Va, October 22, 1963; m 1995, Tim. **Education:** Va Inst Technol, BS, 1986; NC State Univ, MS, 1989, PhD (nutrit), 1996. **Professional Experience:** ASSOC PROF, DEPT ANIMAL SCI, UNIV ARK, as of 2006; asst prof, dept animal sci, Univ Ark, beginning 1996. **Memberships:** Am Soc Animal Sci; Am Dairy Sci Asn. **Research Statement & Publications:** Nutritional modification of the immune response of cattle. **Mailing Address:** Dept Animal Sci, B114 AFLS, Fayetteville, AR 72701. **E-Mail:** ekegley@uark.edu

KEHEW, ALAN EVERETT, HYDROGEOCHEMISTRY, GEOMORPHOLOGY. **Personal Data:** b Pittsburgh, Pa, September 17, 1947; m 1974, c 3. **Education:** Bucknell Univ, BS, 1969; Montana State Univ, MS, 1971; Univ Idaho, PhD (geol), 1977. **Professional Experience:** PROF, DEPT GEOL, WESTERN MICH UNIV, & HYDROGEOCHEM & GLACIAL GEOL, ASSOC PROF GEOL, WESTERN MICH UNIV, 1986-; from asst prof to assoc prof geol, Univ NDak, 1980-1986; Geologist, NDak Geol Surv, 1977-1980. **Memberships:** Geol Soc Am; Nat Water Well Asn; Am Geophys Union; Am Quaternary Asn, Int Quaternary Asn. **Research Statement & Publications:** Groundwater contamination by waste disposal; chemical evolution of groundwater in glacial terrains; glacial landforms and processes. **Mailing Address:** Dept Geol, Western Mich Univ, 1185, Rood Hall, 1201 Oliver St, Kalamazoo, MI 49008. **Fax:** 269-387-5513. **E-Mail:** alan.kehew@wmich.edu

KEHL, THEODORE H, COMPUTER SCIENCE, BIOPHYSICS. **Personal Data:** b Racine, Wis, April 1, 1933; m 1954, c 2. **Education:** Univ Wis, BS, 1956, MS, 1958, PhD (zool), 1961. **Professional Experience:** PROF PHYSIOL, BIOPHYS & COMPUT SCI, SCH MED, UNIV WASH, 1977-; assoc prof, Biophys & Comput Sci, Sch Med, Univ Wash, 1973-1977; from instr to assoc prof physiol & biophys, Biophys & Comput Sci, Sch Med, Univ Wash, 1963-1973; NIH fel, Sch Med, Univ Wash 1961-1963; Wis Alumni Res Found res assoc, NIH fel, 1961; Wis Alumni Res Found res assoc, Univ Wis, 1956-1961. **Memberships:** AAAS; Asn Comput Mach. **Research Statement & Publications:** Implementation of computer science to quantitative physiology and biophysics. **Mailing Address:** 9116 20th Ave NE, Seattle, WA 98115.

KEHL, WILLIAM BRUNNER, COMPUTER SCIENCE. **Personal Data:** b Pittsburgh, Pa, April 8, 1919; m 1944, c 2. **Education:** Harvard Univ, SB, 1940, AM, 1942 & 1948. **Professional Experience:** RETIRED; dir academic computing, Univ Calif, Los Angeles, 1967-1993; assoc prof elec eng & assoc dir comput ctr, Mass Inst Technol, 1966-1967; consult, USAF, 1957-1959 & comt use of comput, Nat Acad Sci; prof comput sci & dir comput & data processing ctr, Univ Pittsburgh, 1956-1966; head anal group, Instrumentation Lab, 1954-1956; instr, Mass Inst Technol, 1948-1954; instr math, Ga Inst Tech, 1943-1946; mem sci adv bd, Regional Indust Develop Corp; consult, NSF & NIH. **Memberships:** Asn Comput Mach. **Research Statement & Publications:** Computers; applied mathematics. **Mailing Address:** 1201 Corsica Dr, Pacific Palisades, CA 90272.

KEHLENBECK, MANFRED MAX, STRUCTURAL GEOLOGY, METAMORPHIC GEOLOGY. **Personal Data:** b Bremen, Ger, January 16, 1937; m 1968, Elenore E Kehlenbeck. **Education:** Hofstra Univ, BA, 1959; Syracuse Univ, MS, 1964; Queen's Univ, PhD (geol), 1971. **Professional Experience:** Prof Emer, lakehead univ, 2000; Energy Mines & Resources grant, 1986-; prof geol, Lakehead Univ, 1986-2000; Northern Ont Rural Develop Agreement grant, 1983-1985; dept chmn, Lakehead Univ, 1976-1982 & 1991-1997; Nat Res Coun Can grant, 1972-; from asst prof to assoc prof, Lakehead Univ, 1971-1986; Vis prof geol, Univ NB, 1969-1970. **Memberships:** Am Geol Inst; Geol Asn Can. **Research Statement & Publications:** Structural evolution of Archean gneissic terrains; polyphase folding in volcano sedimentary belts in northwestern Ontario; archean subprovince margins and boundaries; transpressional basins. **Mailing Address:** 149 Bentwood Drive, Thunder Bay, ON P7A 7A7, Can. **E-Mail:** mkehlenb@tbaytel.net

KEHLER, PHILIP LEROY, STRATIGRAPHY, SEDIMENTOLOGY. **Personal Data:** b Lyons, NY, June 15, 1936; m 1965, c 2. **Education:** Purdue Univ, BS, 1959, MS, 1961; Southern Methodist Univ, PhD (geol), 1970. **Professional Experience:** PROF EMER, DEPT EARTH SCI, UNIV ARK, LITTLE ROCK, as of 2005; Young scholar, NSF, 1989-1990; chmn, Univ Ark, Little Rock, beginning 1983; lignite consult, Shell Mining, 1979-1981; NSF student originated studies grant, 1975; chairperson, Univ Ark, Little Rock, 1973-1978; assoc prof earth sci, Univ Ark, Little Rock, beginning 1973; fac res grant, ETex State Univ, 1971-1972; asst prof geol, ETex State Univ, 1969-1973; asst, Southern Methodist Univ, 1965-1969. **Memberships:** Geol Soc Am; Soc Econ Paleontologists & Mineralogists; Nat Asn Geol Teachers. **Research Statement & Publications:** Regional studies of Jurassic and Cretaceous rocks in western North America; stratigraphic relationships associated with widespread unconformities within these rocks; statigraphic relationships, Ouachita Mountains of Arkansas and Oklahoma; earthquake mitigation in northeast Arkansas. **Mailing Address:** Dept Earth Sci, Univ Ark, FH 309 2801 S Univ Ave, Little Rock, AR 72204-1099. **Fax:** 501-569-3271. **E-Mail:** plkehler@ualr.edu

KEHLET, ALAN B, AERONAUTICS. **Education:** Univ Ill, BS, 1951; Univ Va, MS, 1961; Calif state Univ, MBA, 1976. **Professional Experience:** PRES, ROCKWELL INT, 1991-. **Mailing Address:** Rockwell Int, 1201 S 2nd St, Milwaukee, WI 53204-2496. **Fax:** 414-382-4444.

KEHOE, BRANDT. **Personal Data:** b Cleveland, Ohio, November 20, 1933; m Sandra; c Noel E & Christopher J. **Education:** Cornell Univ, BA, 1956; Univ Wis, MS, 1959, PhD (physics), 1963. **Professional Experience:** Retired, 2004. Dir, Off of Institutional Res, Planning & Assessment, Calif St Univ, Fresno, 2000-2004; Interim Ass Provost, Calif State Univ, Fresno, 1996-2000; DEPT CHMN PHYSICS, CALIF STATE UNIV, FRESNO, 1989-; dept chmn comput sci, Sch Natural Sci, 1987-1989; pres, Deep Springs Col, 1983-1987; PROF PHYSICS, CALIF STATE UNIV, FRESNO, 1972-; dean, Sch Natural Sci, 1972-1983; from asst prof to assoc prof, Univ Md, 1962-1972; Res asst physics, Los Alamos Sci Lab, 1956-1957. **Mailing Address:** 680 Canterbury Lane, Cambria, CA 93428. **E-Mail:** brandtk@csufresno.edu

KEHR, CLIFTON LEROY, ORGANIC CHEMISTRY, POLYMER CHEMISTRY & TECHNOLOGY. **Personal Data:** b Brodbecks, Pa, May 25, 1926; m Louise; c Alan D, David D & Alison J. **Education:** Gettysburg Col, AB, 1949; Univ Del, MS, 1950, PhD (org chem), 1952. **Honors & Awards:** Phi Beta Kappa, 1949 Sigma Xi, 1960. **Professional Experience:** RETIRED, 1998; consult polymer technol, 1991-1998; res dir, Res Div, Washington Res Ctr, W R Grace & Co, 1969-1991; res chemist, Res Div, Washington Res Ctr, W R Grace & Co, 1959-1969; elastomers chem dept, Org Chem Dept, E I du Pont de Nemours & Co, 1957-1959; res chemist, Org Chem Dept, E I du Pont de Nemours & Co, 1953-1957; Res asst synthetic org chem, Forrestal Res Ctr, Princeton Univ, 1952-1953. **Memberships:** Am Chem Soc. **Research Statement & Publications:** 79 U.S. Patents; seven technical publications. Mechanisms of organic reactions; polyurethanes; elastomers; polyolefins; isocyanate chemistry; polymers from chloroprene and related monomers; foam technology; radiation curable polymers; water based coatings; biocompatible polymers; medical polymers. **Mailing Address:** 1929 Weisgerber Way, York, PA 17404. **Fax:** 717-764-7058. **E-Mail:** clkehr@juno.com

KEHRER, JAMES PAUL, toxicology, apoptosis. **Personal Data:** b Watertown, Wis, August 25, 1951; m 1977, Debra; c Paul & Marc. **Education:** Purdue Univ, BS, 1974; Univ Iowa, PhD (pharmacology), 1978. **Honors & Awards:** University of Texas Summer Research Award - 1981 Research Career Development Award - National Institutes of Health (NHLBI) 1984-1989 Gustavus Pfeiffer Centennial Endowed Fellowship in Pharmacology - 1985-1991 Achievement Award - Society of Toxicology 1989 Gustavus and Louise Pfeiffer Professorship in Toxicology - 1991-2005 Zeneca Traveling Lectureship Award, Society of Toxicology 1996 Univ of Texas College of Pharmacy Alumni Association "Best Friend" Award, Nov 1, 2001 Distinguished Alumnus Award, Purdue Univ School of Pharmacy, 2004. **Professional Experience:** Dean, College of Pharmacy, Washington State University 2005 - present Adjunct Professor, University of Texas College of Pharmacy 2005 - present Director, Center for Molecular and Cellular Toxicology 2003 - 2005 Member, US-EPA Science Advisory Board Environmental Health Committee 2003-2006 Adjunct Professor, Dept. Carcinogenesis, M.D. Anderson Cancer Center, 1997 - present Science Park Research Division Head, Division of Pharmacology and Toxicology, College of Pharmacy 1991 - 2004 Professor of Pharmacology - University of Texas at Austin 1990 - 2005 Guest Scientist - UniversitSt Dnsseldorf May-June 1990 and 1997 Visiting Professor - Institut Fnr Physiologische Chemie I, UniversitSt Dnsseldorf, Dnsseldorf, West Germany Jan. - Dec. 1986 Associate Professor of Pharmacology - University of Texas at Austin 1985 - 1990 Assistant Professor of Pharmacology - University of Texas at Austin 1980 - 1985 Postdoctoral Investigator-Biology Div., Oak Ridge National Laboratory 1978 - 1980 NIH Predoctoral Fellow, Univ. of Iowa 1974 - 1978 Editor for the Americas and Japan - Toxicology Letters (1993-present) Associate Editor for Reviews - Toxicology

Letters (1988-93) Associate Editor - Journal of Toxicology and Environmental Health (1992-93) Deputy Chairman of the Editorial Board - Biochemical Journal (2000-present). **Memberships:** Am Asn for the Advancement of Science (1975-present) American Asn for Cancer Research (1999-present) American Soc for Pharmacology and Experimental Therapeutics (1984-present). Chairman, Toxicology Division 2006-2007 Society of Toxicology (1982-present); President of Mechanisms Specialty Section, 1998-1999 Society for Free Radical Biology and Medicine (1988-present; formerly the Oxygen Society) International Soc for Free Radical Research (1986-present) Gulf Coast Chapter Soc of Toxicology (1989-present) Vice-President 1989; President 1990 International Soc for the Study of Xenobiotics (ISSX) (1993-97) Western Pharmacology Soc (1984-1998) American Pharmacy Asn (2005-present) American Soc of Health System Pharmacists (2005-present) American Asn of Colleges of Pharmacy (2005-present). **Research Statement & Publications:** Apoptosis cell signaling pathways, oxidative stress, free radical toxicology. **Mailing Address:** Wash State Univ, 105 Wegner Hall - PO Box 646510, Pullman, WA 99164-6510. **E-Mail:** kehrer@wsu.edu

KEHRL, HOWARD H, MECHANICAL ENGINEERING. **Personal Data:** b Detroit, Mich, February 2, 1923. **Education:** Ill Inst Technol, BS, 1944; Univ Notre Dame, MS, 1948; Mass Inst Technol, MS, 1960. **Professional Experience:** RETIRED; vchmn, Oldsmobile Div, Gen Motors Corp, 1981-1991; exec vpres, Oldsmobile Div, Gen Motors Corp, 1974-1981; vpres & group exec, Oldsmobile Div, Gen Motors Corp, 1973-1974; Vpres & gen mgr, Oldsmobile Div, Gen Motors Corp, 1972-1973. **Memberships:** Nat Acad Eng; Soc Automotive Engrs; Motor Vehicle Mfrs Asn US. **Mailing Address:** 5157 Country Club Shores, Walloon Lake, MI 49796.

KEHS, R ALAN, PHYSICS. **Education:** Univ Md, BS, 1970, MS (elec eng), 1973, MS (physics), 1984, PhD (physics), 1987. **Professional Experience:** SR SCIENTIST, DIRECTED ENERGY & POWER GENERATION DIV, US ARMY RES LAB, as of 2005. **Memberships:** Sigma Xi; Am Phys Soc; Inst Elec & Electronics Engrs. **Mailing Address:** Directed Energy & Power Generation Div, US Army Res Lab, 2800 Powder Mill Rd, Adelphi, MD 20783-1197. **Fax:** 301-394-4704. **E-Mail:** kehs@arl.army.mil

KEICHER, WILLIAM EUGENE, LASER RADAR SYSTEMS, LASER COMMUNICATION STSTEMS. **Personal Data:** b Pittsburgh, Pa, December 28, 1947; m 1972, Barbara; c Lisa A, Kathy M & William M. **Education:** Carnegie Mellon Univ, BS, 1969, MS, 1970, PhD (elec eng), 1974. **Professional Experience:** ASSOC LEADER, AIR DEFENSE SYTS GROUP, LINCOLN LAB MASS INST TECHNOL, as of 2006; GROUP LEADER, LINCOLN LAB, MASS INST TECHNOL, 2000-; assoc group leader, Lincoln Lab, Mass Inst Technol, 1993-2000; group leader, Lincoln Labs, Mass Inst Technol, 1985-1993; asst group leader, Lincoln Lab, Mass Inst Technol, 1983-1985; staff mem, Lincoln Lab, Mass Inst Technol, 1975-1983; sr elec engr, CBS Lab, 1973-1975; tech asst, Kodak Res Lab, 1970; elec engr, Manned Spacecraft Ctr, NASA, 1969. **Memberships:** Sr mem Inst Elec & Electronics Engrs; Mem Optical Soc Am Assoc Old Crows. **Research Statement & Publications:** laser communicaton system; fiber optic communication systems; laser radar systems; imaging radar; infrared detection systems; electro optic modulators; atmospheric propagation; microwave radar. **Mailing Address:** Lincoln Lab Mass Inst Technol, 244 Wood St, Lexington, MA 02420-9108. **Fax:** 781-981-4129. **E-Mail:** keicher@ll.mit.edu

KEIDERLING, TIMOTHY ALLEN, SPECTROSCOPY, PROTEIN & PEPTIDE CONFORMATION. **Personal Data:** b Waterloo, Iowa, June 22, 1947; m 1976, Candace; c Michael. **Education:** Loras Col, BS, 1969; Princeton Univ, MA, 1971, PhD (phys chem), 1974. **Professional Experience:** John Simon Guggenheim Mem Found fel, Univ. Freiburg 2004 and Univ. Padova 2005; sr vis, Oxford Univ, 1994; PROF CHEM, UNIV ILL, CHICAGO, 1985-; Fulbright fel, WGer, 1984; guest prof, Max Planck Inst Quantenoptik, 1984; from asst prof to assoc prof, Univ Ill, Chicago, 1976-1985; res assoc optical activity, Univ Southern Calif, 1973-1976. **Memberships:** Am Chem Soc; Am Phys Soc; Biophys Soc; Soc Appl Spectros. **Research Statement & Publications:** Spectroscopic studies of protein and peptide; conformations and folding; theoretical simulations of vibrational optical activity of peptides; magnetic vibrational circular dichroism and associated vibronic coupling effects. **Mailing Address:** Univ Ill, Dept Chem, M/C 111, 845 W Taylor, Chicago, IL 60607-7061. **Fax:** 312-996-0431. **E-Mail:** tak@uic.edu

KEIFER, LEONARD C, CHEMISTRY. **Professional Experience:** CHEMIST, US ENVIRON PROTECTION AGENCY, as of 1998. **Memberships:** Quant Struct Activ Relationship Modelling Soc. **Mailing Address:** US Environ Protection Agency 7403, 401 M St SW, Washington, DC 20460. **Fax:** 202-260-1279. **E-Mail:** keifer.leonard@epa.gov

KEIFFER, DAVID GOFORTH, PHYSICS. **Personal Data:** b New Orleans, La, July 24, 1931; m 1956, c 6. **Education:** Loyola Univ, La, BS, 1952; Univ Notre Dame, MS, 1954, PhD (physics), 1956. **Professional Experience:** Chmn dept physics, Loyola Univ, La, beginning 1973; ASSOC PROF PHYSICS, LOYOLA UNIV, LA, 1964-; asst prof physics, Canisius Col, 1956-1964. **Memberships:** Am Phys Soc. **Research Statement & Publications:** Radiation damage in glass. **Mailing Address:** Dept Physics, Loyola Univ, Rm 453, Monroe Hall, New Orleans, LA 70118.

KEIGHER, WILLIAM FRANCIS, ALGEBRA. **Personal Data:** b Montclair, NJ, October 28, 1945; m 1968, c 3. **Education:** Montclair State Col, BA, 1967; Univ Ill, AM, 1969, PhD (math), 1973. **Professional Experience:** ASSOC PROF MATH & COMPUT SCI, RUTGERS UNIV, as of 2005; asst prof math, Rutgers Univ, beginning 1978; asst prof mat, Univ Tenn, Knoxville, 1974-1978; Lectr math, Southern Ill Univ, Carbondale, 1973-1974. **Memberships:** Am Math Soc; Math Asn Am. **Research Statement & Publications:** Category theory and its applications to differential algebra. **Mailing Address:** Dept Math & Comput Sci, Rutgers Univ, Newark Coll Arts & Sci, 101 Warren St Smith Hall 216, Newark, NJ 07102. **Fax:** 973-353-5270.

KEIGHIN, CHARLES WILLIAM, GEOCHEMISTRY, ECONOMIC GEOLOGY. **Personal Data:** b Pontiac, Ill, August 29, 1932; m 1960, c 3. **Education:** Oberlin Col, BA, 1954; Univ Colo, MS, 1960, PhD (geol), 1966. **Professional Experience:** GEOLOGIST, US GEOL SURV, DENVER, 1974-; asst prof Geoscience, Northeastern La Univ, 1973-1974; vis asst prof geol & mineral, Ohio State Univ, 1972-1973; asst prof geol, Northern Ill Univ, 1966-1972; geologist, Cerro Del Pasco Corp, La Oroya, Peru, SAm, 1962-1963; Res mineralogist, Cerro Del Pasco Corp, La Oroya, Peru, SAm, 1960-1962. **Memberships:** Am Asn Petrol Geologists; Soc Econ Paleontologists & Mineralogists; Soc Petrol Engrs; Can Soc Petrol Geologists. **Research Statement & Publications:** Trace element migration; diagenesis of clastic rocks; inorganic geochemistry; oil shale resource evaluation. **Mailing Address:** 1666 S Holland Ct, Lakewood, CO 80232.

KEIHN, FREDERICK GEORGE, SOLID STATE CHEMISTRY. **Personal Data:** b Scranton, Pa, August 29, 1923; m 1948, c 4. **Education:** Randolph Macon Col, BS, 1947; Lehigh Univ, MS, 1949; Syracuse Univ, PhD (chem), 1953. **Professional Experience:** PROF EMER CHEM, BRIDGEWATER COL, as of 2003; prof chem, Bridgewater Col, 1967-1986; assoc prof chem, Presby Col, SC, 1965-1967; mem staff, Union Carbide Res Inst, NY, 1959-1965; res chemist ceramics lab, Corning Glass Works, 1957-1959; inorg chemist electronics lab, Gen Elec Co, 1952-1957; asst chem, Syracuse Univ, 1949-1951; asst electrochem, Lehigh Univ, 1948-1949. **Memberships:** AAAS; Am Chem Soc; Am Crystallog Asn. **Research Statement & Publications:** Double crystal x-ray diffractometry high temperature phase and mechanical properties studies; physical science curriculum development; applied ecology. **Mailing Address:** Dept Chem, Bridgewater Col, 402 E Col St, Bridgewater, VA 22812. **Fax:** 540-828-5661.

KEIL, DAVID JOHN, PLANT TAXONOMY. **Personal Data:** b Elmhurst, Ill, December 13, 1946; m 1989, Kathleen; c Michaela Alice & Kaitlyn Ruth. **Education:** Ariz State Univ, BS, 1968, MS, 1970; Ohio State Univ, PhD (bot), 1973. **Professional Experience:** Ed, Madrono, 1988-1990; PROF BIOL, CALIF POLYTECH STATE UNIV, 1985-; DIR ROBERT F HOOVER HERBARIUM & CURATOR VASCULAR PLANTS, CALIF POLYTECH STATE UNIV, 1978-; vis assoc prof bot, Ohio State Univ, 1980; from asst prof to assoc prof, Calif Polytech State Univ, 1978-1985; lectr, Calif Polytech State Univ, 1976-1978; asst prof, Franklin Col, 1975; vis asst prof biol, Grand Valley State Col, 1973-1974. **Memberships:** Bot Soc Am; Am Soc Plant Taxon; Int Asn Plant Taxon; Calif Bot Soc; Sigma Xi; Soc Syst Biologists; Willi Henning Soc. **Research Statement & Publications:** Systematics of compositae; cytology, taxonomy, evolution and biogeography of genus Pectis; systematics of genus Cirsium; floristics. **Mailing Address:** Dept Biol Sci, Calif Polytech State Univ, San Luis Obispo, CA 93407-0401. **Fax:** 805-756-1419. **E-Mail:** dkeil@calpoly.edu

KEIL, JULIAN E, EPIDEMIOLOGY, CARDIOVASCULAR EPIDEMIOLOGY. **Personal Data:** b Charleston, SC, October 30, 1926; m 1948, Barbara Willis; c Barbara A (Burgis), Christopher A & Jean M (Rigsby). **Education:** Clemson Univ, BS, 1949, MS, 1968; Univ NC, Chapel Hill, PhD (epidemiol), 1975. **Professional Experience:** PROF EMER EPIDEMIOL, SCH PUB HEALTH, UNIV SC, 1993-; from assoc prof to prof, Sch Pub Health, Univ SC, 1977-1992; asst prof prev med, Sch Pub Health, Univ SC, 1973-1977; assoc, Sch Pub Health, Univ SC, 1970-1972; instr, Sch Pub Health, Univ SC, 1967-1969; mgr, Pesticide Dept, 1956-1967; Entomologist, W R Grace & Co, 1949-1955; Coun epidemiol, Am Heart Asn. **Memberships:** Am Pub Health Asn; Soc Epidemiol Res; Int Epidemiol Asn. **Research Statement & Publications:** Cardiovascular epidemiology; environmental epidemiology; epidemiology of coronary disease in blacks and whites. **Mailing Address:** 16 Sheridan Rd, Charleston, SC 29407.

KEIL, KLAUS, METEORITICS, PETROLOGY. **Personal Data:** b Hamburg, Ger, November 15, 1934; American citizen; m 1984, Linde; c 2. **Education:** Univ Jena, MSc, 1958; Univ Mainz, PhD (mineral, meteoritics), 1961. **Honorary Degrees:** Dt retuim natutalium horis causa, Friedtich-schiller univ, Jena, Ger, 2002. **Honors & Awards:** Apollo Achievement Award, NASA, 1970; George P Merrill Award, Nat Acad Sci, 1970; John Wesley Powell invited lectr, Ariz Acad Sci, 1971; Plaque Am Fedn Mineral Socs hq, Wash, DC, 1974; NASA Except Sci Achievement Medal, 1977; Regents Meritorious Serv Medal, Univ NMex, 1983; Group Achievement Award, NASA, 1984; Leonard Medal, Meteoritical Soc, 1988; Asteroid 5054 named in honor, Int Astron Union, 1993; Cosslett Award, Microbeam Analysis Society, Pres Sci Award, Microbeam Anal Soc, 2002; New extraterrestrial mineral (Fe, Mg)S named keilite approved by the Commission on New Minerals and Mineral Names of the Int Mineral Asn, 2002. **Professional Experience:** INTERIM DEAN, SCH OCEAN & EARTH SCIENCE & TECH, UNIV HAWAII MANOA, HONOLULU, 2003-; from interim dir to dir, Hawaii Inst Geophys & Planetology, Univ Hawaii Manoa, Honolulu, 1994-2003; head & prof geol geophys, Univ Hawaii, 1990-; mem panel, Lunar & Planetology, Geoscience Rev, 1987-; chmn, Dept Geol, Univ NMex, 1986-1989; Presidential prof geol, Univ NMex, 1985-1990; chmn rev panel, space sta planetology exp & Mars observer, NASA, 1985; Inst Geophys, Planet, Physics, Los Alamos Nat Lab, Univ Calif, 1984-1990; assoc ed, J Earth Chem, 1984-1986; mem, NASA adv comt, minority grad researchers, 1984; assoc ed, J Geophys Res, 1982-1985; mem adv comt, Comp Planetology, Inst Geol Sci, 1981-1982; distinguished vis scientist, Jet Propulsion Lab, Pasadena, 1981; ann res lectr, Univ NMex, 1981; distinguished vis prof, Dept Astonomy & Geophys, Univ Sao Paulo, Brazil, 1981; dir, Caswell Silver Found, Univ NMex, 1980-1990; chmn, Lunar & Planet, Sci Coun, 1980-1984; mem, Antarctic Meteorite Working Group, NSF, 1978-1984; HON RES ASSOC, DEPT MINERAL SCI, AM MUS NATURAL HIST, 1977-; mem, Lunar & Planet, Sci Coun, 1977-1979, 1987-1990; mem, Viking Mars Flight Team, 1976-1978; vis assoc geochem, Div Geol Planet Sci, Calif Inst Technol, 1976-1977; chmn facil subcomt, Lunar Sample Anal Planning Team, 1975-1976; mem & chmn, Lunar Sample Anal Planning Team, 1974-1978; mem geophys res bd, Nat Acad Sci, 1974-1975; distinguished vis prof, Inst Earth Sci, 1974, 1976, 1977 & 1978; assoc ed, Chem Geol, 1973-1985; invited speaker, Int Geol Cong, 1972; mem & chmn, US Nat Comt Geochem, Nat Acad Sci, 1971-1975; mem lunar sci rev bd, 1971-1973; secy, Comt Cosmic Mineral, Int Mineral Asn, 1970-; prof geol & dir, Inst meteoritics, Univ NMex, 1968-1990; rep, Comt Meteorites, Int Union Geol Sci, 1968-1972; mem planetology adv subcomt, space sci & applns steering comt, 1968; prin investr, Electron Microprobe Study Returned Lunar Sample, NASA, 1967-1968; mem, Nat Steering Comt, 1966-1968; lectr, Dept Geol, San Jose State Col, 1966-1967; staff res scientist, Space Sci Div, Ames Res Ctr, NASA, 1964-1968; Nat Acad Sci-Nat Res Coun resident res assoc, Space Sci Div, Ames Res Ctr, NASA, 1963-1964; res assoc, Max Planck Inst Chem, Mainz, Ger, 1961; res assoc, Univ Calif, San Diego, 1961-1963; res assoc & instr mineral meteoritics, Mineral Inst, Univ Jena, Ger, 1958-1960. **Memberships:** Fel AAAS; Ger Mineral Soc; Corresp Mem, Natural Hist Mus, Vienna, Minster Educ & Sci the Repub Austria & the Dir Mus, 1976 Microbeam Anal Soc; Int Asn Geochem & Cosmochem (secy, 1972-1976); Planetary Soc; fel Mineral Soc; fel, Am Geophys Union; Geochemical Soc; fel Meteoritical Soc (pres, 1968-1970); Corresp (Foreign) Mem Sachisische Akademie der Wissenschaften (Saxony Academy of Sciences), Leipzing, Ger (1996). **Research Statement & Publications:** Lunar geology; chemistry, geology and mineralogy of extraterrestrial materials, such as meteorites, cosmic dust and lunar surface; application of electron microprobe, laser microprobe and ion microprobe to study of rocks and minerals; geology of mars. **Mailing Address:** Sch Ocean & Earth Sci & Technol, Univ Hawaii, 1618 EW Rd, Honolulu, HI 96822. **Fax:** 808-956-9152. **E-Mail:** keil@hawaii.edu

KEIL, LANNY CHARLES, PHYSIOLOGY, ENDOCRINOLOGY. **Personal Data:** b Elgin, Nebr, April 16, 1936; m 1966, c 3. **Education:** Creighton Univ, BS, 1963, MS, 1966; Univ Calif, Davis, PhD (physiol), 1973. **Professional Experience:** RETIRED; res scientist endocrinol, Biomed Res Div, 1972-1992; res scientist, Physiol Br, Ames Res Ctr NASA, 1967-1972. **Memberships:** Edocrine Soc; AAAS; Am Physiol Soc. **Research Statement & Publications:** Hormonal control of water and electrolyte metabolism; gravitational biology; acceleration stress physiology. **Mailing Address:** 1637 Kennewick Dr, Sunnyvale, CA 94087-4129.

KEIL, RALPH L, BIOLOGICAL CHEMISTRY. **Education:** Ohio State Univ, B.S, 1976; Cornell Univ, PhD, 1982. **Professional Experience:** ASSOC PROF BIOCHEM & MOLECULAR BIOL, COL MED, MILTON S. HERSHEY MED CTR, PA STATE UNIV, as of

2005. **Mailing Address:** Dept Biol Chem, Milton S Hershey Med Ctr, Pa State Univ, 500 Univ Dr, Hershey, PA 17033. **Fax:** 717-531-7072. **E-Mail:** rkeil@psu.edu

KEIL, ROBERT GERALD, PHYSICAL CHEMISTRY. **Personal Data:** b New Rochelle, NY, May 7, 1941; m 1982, Paula R Preskih; c 2. **Education:** Villanova Univ, BS, 1963; Temple Univ, PhD (phys chem), 1967. **Professional Experience:** ASSOC DEAN, UNIV DAYTON, 1991-; chmn, Univ Dayton, 1988-1991; PROF CHEM, UNIV DAYTON, 1984-; from asst prof to assoc prof, Univ Dayton, 1969-1984; Res chemist, Org Chem Dept, E I du Pont Del Nemours & Co, Inc, 1967-1969; Alt counr, Dayton Sect, Am Chem Soc. **Memberships:** Electrochem Soc; Am Chem Soc; Soc Electroanal Chem. **Research Statement & Publications:** Anodic oxide films; voltammety in aqueous and nonaqueous solutions; physical chemistry; infrared spectroscopy. **Mailing Address:** Dept Chem, Univ Dayton 300 College Park, Dayton, OH 45469-2357. **Fax:** 513-229-2635.

KEIL, STEPHEN LESLEY, SOLAR PHYSICS. **Personal Data:** b Billings, Mont, February 21, 1947; m 1971, Alice; c Pamela & Wesley. **Education:** Univ Calif, Berkeley, AB, 1969; Boston Univ, AM, 1971, PhD (physics & astron), 1975. **Professional Experience:** DIR, NAT SOLAR OBSERV, 1999-; tech adv, Air Force Res Lab, Space Hazards Br, 1997-1999; Task Scientist, Air Force Off Sci Res, 1983-1999; Br Chief, Air Force Res Lab., 1983-1997; Capt USAF, Res Scientist, Air Force Geophys Lab, 1980-1983; Nat Res Coun Res Fel, Air Force Geophys Lab, 1978-1979. **Memberships:** Am Astron Soc; Int Astron Union; Am Phy Soc; Am Geophy Union; Am Asn Adv Sci. **Research Statement & Publications:** Solar atmospheric inhomogenonities; multidimensional stellar atmospheres; high resolution solar observations; mathematical models of solar atmospheric structure; solar activity and variability; solar telescopes. **Mailing Address:** National Solar Observ, PO Box 57, Sunspot, NM 88349. **Fax:** 505-434-7029. **E-Mail:** skeil@nso.edu

KEIL, THOMAS H, SOLID STATE PHYSICS. **Personal Data:** b Philadelphia, Pa, July 24, 1939; m 1964, c Seth & Perry. **Education:** Calif Inst Technol, BS, 1961; Univ Rochester, PhD (optics), 1965. **Professional Experience:** HEAD, DEPT PHYSICS, WORCHESTER POLYTECH INST, as of 2004; PROF PHYSICS, WORCESTER POLYTECH INST, 1978-; chmn dept physics, Worcester Polytech Inst, 1972-1978; from asst prof to assoc prof physics, Worcester Polytech Inst, 1967-1978; Sloan fel solid state physics, Sloan vis lectr, 1966-1967; Sloan fel solid state physics, Princeton Univ, 1965-1966. **Memberships:** Am Phys Soc; Sigma Xi. **Research Statement & Publications:** Solid state theory; optics. **Mailing Address:** Dept Physics, Worcester Polytech Inst, Olin Hall 120 100 Inst Rd, Worcester, MA 01609-2280. **Fax:** 508-831-5886. **E-Mail:** thkeil@wpi.edu

KEILY, HUBERT JOSEPH, DRUG REGULATORY AFFAIRS & QUALITY OPERATIONS. **Personal Data:** b Worcester, Mass, January 29, 1921; m 1971, Rosemary K Almer; c Mark & Lea. **Education:** Niagra Univ, BS, 1949; Union Col, MS, 1951; Mass Inst Technol, PhD (anal chem), 1956. **Professional Experience:** CONSULT DRUG REGULATORY AFFAIRS, 1993-; rev chemist, Food & Drug Admin, 1984-1992; mgr, Submissions & Develop Qual Control, Adria Lab Inc, 1982- 1984; Adj asst prof pharmaceut chem, Col Pharm, Univ Cincinnati, 1982-1983; dept head anal chem, Merrell Dow Pharmaceut Inc, 1964-1982; sect chief anal methods, Res Ctr, Lever Bros Co, 1958-1964; anal chemist, Gen Elec Co, 1956-1958; asst, Union Col, 1949-1951 & Mass Inst Technol, 1951-1955; Lab asst, Res Lab, Linde Co, 1940-1943. **Memberships:** Am Chem Soc; fel Am Inst Chem. **Research Statement & Publications:** Evaluations of manufacturing and controls information submitted in support of investigational new drugs and new drug applications for drug products; analytical methods; packaging guidelines; computer assisted reviews. **Mailing Address:** 5052 S Ridge Dr, Cincinnati, OH 45224. **Fax:** 513-853-2703.

KEIM, BARBARA HOWELL, ECOLOGICAL GENETICS. **Personal Data:** b Detroit, Mich, March 9, 1946; m James A. **Education:** Univ NC, Greensboro, BA, 1967; Rutgers Univ, MS, 1969; Univ Va, PhD (genetics), 1976; Bradley Univ, MBA, 1988. **Professional Experience:** DEAN, BUS & SOCIAL SCI, ST CHARLES COMMUNITY COL, 2000-; dir exec & prof develop, Bradley Univ, 1991- 2000; dir financial develop, Am Red Cross, 1989-1991; from asst prof to assoc prof biol, Eureka Col, Ill, 1980-1987; adj prof, Dept Biol, 1979-1980; asst prof, Dept Nursing, 1977-1978; asst prof, Dept Biol, Bradley Univ, 1976-1977; instr, Dept Biol, Wheaton Col, Norton, Mass, 1975-1976; asst ed biol, Biol Sci Info Serv, Philadelphia, 1969-1970. **Research Statement & Publications:** Disruptive selection; speciation; polymorphisms. **Mailing Address:** Div Bus & Social Sci, St Charles Community Col, Tech 105 4601 Mid River Mall Dr, St Peters, MO 63376-2865. **E-Mail:** bkeim@stchas.edu

KEIM, CHRISTOPHER PETER, CHEMISTRY. **Personal Data:** b Tecumseh, Nebr, April 6, 1906; m 1929, c 2. **Education:** Nebr Wesleyan Univ, AB, 1927; Univ Nebr, MSc, 1932, PhD (chem), 1940. **Honorary Degrees:** DSc, Nebr Wesleyan Univ, 1959. **Professional Experience:** RETIRED; dir rowing, Spec Olympics Int, 1986-1989; consult, Hiwassee Col, 1978-1979; pres & gen mgr, Mgt Servs Inc, 1973-1975; consult, Roane State CommunityCol, 1971-1981; tech info div, Oak Ridge Nat Lab, 1957-1971; dir stable isotope res & prod div, Oak Ridge Nat Lab, 1947-1957; res physicist & adminr, Tenn Eastman Corp, 1944-1947; res chemist & fel, Mellon Inst, 1942-1944; res engr, Sylvania Corp, Mass, 1941-1942; instr chem, Univ Tulsa, 1940-1941; head dept phys sci, York Col, 1933-1937. **Memberships:** Fel AAAS; Am Chem Soc; fel Am Phys Soc; Sigma Xi. **Research Statement & Publications:** Isotope separations and properties; monomolecular surface films; electrical discharge in gases; surface chemistry; spreading of organic liquids and mixtures on water in the presence of monomolecular surface films; technical information. **Mailing Address:** 102 Orchard Lane, Oak Ridge, TN 37830-3803.

KEIM, GERALD INMAN, paper chemistry; deceased, see previous edition for last biography

KEIM, JOHN EUGENE, ELECTRONICS ENGINEERING. **Personal Data:** b Columbus, Ohio, December 3, 1941; m 1965, c 3. **Education:** Valparaiso Tech Inst, BS, 1969; Pac Western Univ, MS, 1984, PhD (appl physics), 1985. **Professional Experience:** CORP VPRES ENG, CIRCLE PRIME MFG CO, 1990-; sr develop engr, Westinghouse Corp, 1981-1989; res & develop engr, Scott & Fetzer, 1978-1981; chief engr, Advan Weight Systs, 1976-1978; Consult, Advan Weight Systs, 1975-; Consult, Inservco, 1972; Proj engr, Gilford Instrument Labs, 1967-1976. **Memberships:** Inst Elec & Electronics Engrs. **Research Statement & Publications:** Medical electronics; power controls; RF, military communications devices; seven patents. **Mailing Address:** 9319 Avon Lake Rd, Lodi, OH 44254.

KEIM, KATHRYN SARAH, COOPERATIVE EXTENSION, NUTRITION EDUCATION. **Personal Data:** b Glencoe, Minn, October 20, 1951; m 1973, Kent Richard; c Lee R. **Education:** Univ Minn, BS, 1973; Univ Nebr, MS; Tex Tech Univ, PhD (nutrit), 1983. **Honors & Awards:** Sigma Xi; Am Home Econs Asn; Am Inst Nutrit; Nat Asn Exten Home Econs; Am Asn Diabetes Educators; Am Diabetes Asn; Am Dietetic Asn. **Professional Experience:** ASSOC PROF NUTRIT SCI, OKLA STATE UNIV, as of 2004; PROG CO-ORD, EXTEN WIC NUTRIT EDUC INITIATIVE, 1993-; COORD PROG DIETETICS, CONSULT, 1993-; EXPANDED FOOD & NUTRIT EDUC PROG COORDR, NUTRIT, DIET & HEALTH, 1992-; PROG LEADER, NUTRIT, DIET & HEALTH, 1991-; asst exten prof, Univ Idaho, Boise, 1991-1995; asst prof & dir, Didactic Prog Dietetics, Dept Foods & Nutrit, Univ Ill, Urbana, 1985-1988; Asst prof, Human Nutrit, Food & Food Syst Mgt, La State Univ, Baton Rouge, 1983-1984. **Research Statement & Publications:** Nutrition education methods that result in behavior change, determining which methods work with specific target groups. **Mailing Address:** Dept Nutrit Sci, Okla State Univ, 039 HES, Stillwater, OK 74078. **Fax:** 405-744-1357. **E-Mail:** kkathry@okstate.edu

KEIM, LON WILLIAM, PULMONARY DISEASE. **Personal Data:** b Washington, DC, June 1, 1943; m, c 2. **Education:** Med Col Va, BS, 1966, MD, 1970. **Professional Experience:** AM COL CHEST PHYSICIANS REP, NAT BD RESPIRATORY CARE, 1997-; asst prof internal med, Univ Nebr, beginning 1976; MEM MED STAFF, BISHOP CLARKSON MEM HOSP, 1976-; assoc pulmonary dis, Col Med, Univ Iowa, 1975-1976; fel, Col Med, Univ Iowa, 1973-1975; resident, Med Col Va, 1971-1973; intern med, Univ Kans Med Ctr, Kansas City, 1970-1971. **Memberships:** Fel Am Col Physicians; fel Am Col Chest Physicians; Am Thoracic Soc; Undersea Med Soc; Int Union Aganist Tuberc; Am Med Asn. **Research Statement & Publications:** Tuberculosis and atypical mycobacteria; pulmonary diagnostic techniques, fiberoptic bronchoscopy; hyperbaric oxygen therapy. **Mailing Address:** 4242 Farnham St, Omaha, NE 68131-2850. **E-Mail:** info@imaomaha.com

KEIM, ROBERT GERALD, ORTHODONTICS, CRANIOFACIAL ANOMALIES. **Personal Data:** b Joplin, Mo, November 19, 1954; m 1975, Cynthia Calahan; c Jason A, Eric R, Theresa R & Jennifer L. **Education:** Univ NMex, BS, 1977; Marquette, DDS, 1981; Eastman Dent Ctr, Specialist Cert Orthod, 1990. **Professional Experience:** ASSOC DEAN, ADVAN STUDIES, SCH DENT, UNIV SC, as of 2003; CLIN DIR, CRANIOFACIAL ANOMALIES CLIN, BOLING CTR DEVELOP DISABILITIES, 1993-; assoc, Plastic Clin, Tenn Dept Health, 1992-; Faustin Neff Weber fel, 1992; ASSOC PROF ORTHOD, COL DENT, UNIV TENN, 1990-; Res award, Northeastern Soc Orthodontists, 1990. **Memberships:** Am Asn Dent Schs; Am Asn Orthod; Am DentAsn. **Research Statement & Publications:** Developmental biology of craniofacial anomalies and histopathology in the temporomandibular joint; biological changes associated with orthodontic treatment. **Mailing Address:** 875 Union Ave Suite 301, Grad Orthodontic Clin Univ Tenn, Memphis, TN 38163. **Fax:** 213-740-5715. **E-Mail:** rkeim@usc.edu

KEIM, WAYNE FRANKLIN, PLANT BREEDING & GENETICS, GENETICS INSTRUCTION. **Personal Data:** b Ithaca, NY, May 14, 1923; m 1947, Joyce; c Kathryn K (Logsdon), David W & Julie K (Hughes). **Education:** Univ Nebr, BS, 1947; Cornell Univ, MS, 1949, PhD (plant genetics & breeding), 1952. **Honors & Awards:** Agron Educ Award, Am Soc Agron, 1971, Agron Serv Award, 1991. **Professional Experience:** Bil dirs, Agron Sci Found, 1999-; bil dirs, Coun Agr Sci & Technol, 1996-2000; EMER PROF SOIL & CROP SCI, COLO STATE UNIV, 1992-; prof, Colo State Univ, 1985-1992; head dept, Colo State Univ, 1975-1985; NSF sci fac fel, Inst Genetics, Univ Lund, 1962-1963; from asst prof to prof agron, Purdue Univ, 1956-1975; from instr to asst prof bot, Iowa State Col, 1952-1956. **Memberships:** Fel AAAS; fel Am Soc Agron; AIBS; fel Crop Sci Soc Am (pres, 1983-1984). **Research Statement & Publications:** Breeding and genetics of forage and grain legumes. **Mailing Address:** Dept Soil & Crop Sci, Colo State Univ, Ft Collins, CO 80523. **Fax:** 970-491-0564.

KEINATH, GERALD E, mechanical engineering; deceased, see previous edition for last biography

KEINATH, JOHN ALLEN, MARINE VERTEBRATE BIOLOGY, HERPETOLOGY. **Personal Data:** b New London, Conn, October 6, 1959; m 1984, Debra. **Education:** Univ RI, BS, 1981, BA, 1984, MS, 1986; Col William & Mary, PhD (marine sci), 1993. **Professional Experience:** ADJ PROF, THOMAS NELSON COMMUNITY COL, as of 1998; postdoctoral assoc, Va Inst Marine Sci, 1993-1994; res asst, Va Inst Marine Sci, 1986-1993; fisheries tech, State Univ Col NY, Buffalo, 1984-1985; teaching asst intro zool & human anat, Univ RI, 1981-1984; mem, Marine Turtle Specialist Group, Int Union Conserv Nature & Natural Resources. **Memberships:** Am Soc Ichtheyologists & Herpetologists; Ecol Soc Am; Herpet League; Soc Study Amphibians & Reptiles; Soc Conserv Biol. **Research Statement & Publications:** Behavior, ecology and biology of marine vertebrates, primarily sea turtles, and how movements, distribution, ecology and behavior can be utilized for species conservation. **Mailing Address:** PO Box 1478, Bluffton, SC 29910. **Fax:** 804-642-7327. **E-Mail:** jak@vims.edu

KEINATH, STEVEN ERNEST, POLYMER SCIENCE. **Personal Data:** b Saginaw, Mich, September 10, 1954; m 1987, Carol. **Education:** Saginaw Valley State Col, BS, 1976, MBA, 1981; Univ Mass, MS, 1978; Cent Mich Univ, MA, 1985; Mich Technol Univ, PhD (chem), 1992. **Professional Experience:** RES SCI, MICH MOLECULAR INST, 2001-; ASSOC PROF, MICHI MOLECULAR INST, 2001-; REGISTR, MICH MOLECULAR INST, 2001-; RES SCI & ASSOC PROF, MICH MOLECULAR INST, 1999-2001; sr assoc scientist, Mich Molecular Inst, 1994-1999; adj asst res prof, Cent Mich Univ, 1993-; asst prof, Mich molecular inst, 1994-1999; asst res prof, Mich Molecular Inst, 1992-1994; assoc res scientist, MMI Press, 1992-1994; instr, MMI Press, 1985-1992; consult, 1984-; independent res, MMI Press, 1984-1992; ed, Midland Chemist, 1984-1987; adminr grants & contracts, MMI Press, 1983-1984; asst ed, MMI Press, 1981-1982; sr res asst, Mich Molecular Inst, 1978-1984; asst to dir instrumentation, Dept Polymer Sci & Eng, Univ Mass, 1978; res asst, Chem Dept, Siginaw Valley State Col, Mich, 1974-1976. **Memberships:** Am Chem Soc; Soc Advan Mat & Process Eng; NY Acad Sci; Sigma Xi; Soc Plastics Engrs; Internet Soc; Phi Lambda Upsilon; Am Soc Composites; N Am Thermal Anal Soc. **Research Statement & Publications:** Thermal analysis; polymer transitions and relaxations; binary and ternary polymer blends; composites; effects of absorbed moisture on high performance organic fibers; molecular modeling; plastics recycling; sensor polymers; author of 3 edited books, 23 publications and 43 presentations. **Mailing Address:** Mich Molecular Inst, 1910 W St Andrews Rd, Midland, MI 48640-2696. **E-Mail:** keinath@mmi.org

KEINATH, THOMAS M, ENVIRONMENTAL ENGINEERING. **Personal Data:** b Frankenmuth, Mich, January 5, 1941; m 1963, c 1. **Education:** Univ Mich, Ann Arbor, BSE, 1963, MSE, 1964, PhD (water resources eng), 1968. **Honors & Awards:** Walter L Huber Prize, Am Soc Civil Engrs, 1985; Gordon Maskew Fair Award, Water Environ Fedn, 1997. **Professional Experience:** DEAN ENG & SCI, CLEMSON UNIV, 1992-; Eng Sci Inc, UNESCO, 1980; expert sci adv, Environ Protection Agency, 1975-1976; Eng Sci Inc, beginning 1974; Gaston Co, Dyeing Mach Co, 1971-; consult, Westvaco Inc, beginning 1970; prof environ systs eng & head dept, Clemson Univ, 1969-1992; inst sci & technol fel, Univ Mich, 1968-1969; consult, Waverly Assocs, 1968-1969. **Memberships:** Am Chem Soc; Am Inst Chem Engrs; Am Water Works Asn; Am Soc Civil Engrs; Asn Environ Eng Prof; Sigma Xi; Water Pollution Control Fedn; Int Asn Water Pollution Res & Control; Am Soc Engr Educ. **Research Statement & Publications:** Physiochemical processes of water and waterwaste treatment; automation and control of water and wastewater treatment systems. **Mailing Address:** Col Eng & Sci, Clemson Univ, 109 Riggs Hall PO Box 340901, Clemson, SC 29634-0901. **Fax:** 864-656-0859. **E-Mail:** tom.keinath@ces.clemson.edu

KEIPER, RONALD R, ANIMAL BEHAVIOR. **Personal Data:** b Allentown, Pa, September 21, 1941; m 1964, c 2. **Education:** Muhlenberg Col, BS, 1963; Univ Mass, MS, 1966, PhD (zoology), 1968. **Professional Experience:** DEAN SCI DEPT, VALENCIA COMMUNITY COL, ORLANDO, FLA, as of 2002; dir acad affairs, Pa State Univ 1990-1996; distinguished prof biol, Pa State Univ, 1990-1996; Fulbright fel, 1984-1985; prof zool, Pa State Univ, 1982-1990; assoc prof zool, PA State Univ, 1973-1982; Asst prof zool & biol, PA State Univ, 1968-1973; Frank M Chapman Mem Fund-Am Mus Natural Hist grant, 1968-1970; Theodore Roosevelt Mem Fund-Am Mus Natural Hist grant, 1968-1969; Nat Park Serv study grants. **Memberships:** Animal Behav Soc; Lepidopterists Soc. **Research Statement & Publications:** Causes and functions of the abnormal stereotyped behaviors shown by caged birds; effects of early experience on bird behavior; natural behavior of cyptic moths; studying the behavior, ecology and social organization of feral horses and Prezewalski horses. **Mailing Address:** 8141 St Andrew Circle, Valencia Community Col, Orlando, FL 32835. **E-Mail:** rkeiper@gwmail.valencia.cc.fl.us

KEIRANS, JAMES EDWARD, MEDICAL ENTOMOLOGY, ACAROLOGY. **Personal Data:** b Worcester, Mass, April 4, 1935; m 1963, c 2. **Education:** Boston Univ, AB, 1960, AM, 1963; Univ NH, PhD (zoology), 1966. **Professional Experience:** RES PROF & CUR, US NAT TICK COLLECTION, GA SOUTHERN UNIV, 1990-; res entomologist, Brit Mus Nat Hist, 1977-1978; res entomologist, NIH, 1969-1990; res entomologist, Commun Dis Ctr, USPHS, 1966-1969; res asst entom, Univ NH, 1965-1966; res asst parasitol, Boston Univ, 1960-1963. **Memberships:** Am Soc Parasitol; Entom Soc Am; Acarological Soc Am. **Research Statement & Publications:** Arthropods of public health significance; Ixodoidea taxonomy. **Mailing Address:** Inst Arthropodology & Parasitol, Ga Southern Univ, PO Box 8056, Statesboro, GA 30460-8056. **Fax:** 912-681-0559. **E-Mail:** jkeirans@georgiasouthern.edu

KEIRNS, JAMES JEFFERY, BIOCHEMISTRY. **Personal Data:** b New Haven, Conn, July 1, 1947; m 1975, c 3. **Education:** Rice Univ, BA, 1968; Yale Univ, MPhil, 1970, PhD (molecular biophys & biochem), 1972. **Professional Experience:** DIR, DEPT DRUG METAB & PHARMACOKINETICS, BOEHRINGER INGELHEIM LTD, 1988-; dir, dept biochem, 1979-1988; sr res biochemist & proj leader allergy res, Lederle Labs Div, Am Cyanamid Co, 1975-1979; Jane Coffin Childs Mem Fund Med Res fel biochem, dept path, Sch Med, Yale Univ, 1972-1975. **Memberships:** Am Chem Soc; AAAS; NY Acad Sci; Am Acad Allergy; Health Physics Soc. **Research Statement & Publications:** Biochemical aspects of metabolic immunological and viral diseases; cyclic nucleotides; mechanism of enzyme reactions; inflammation; immediate hypersensitivity; pharmacokinetics and drug metabolism. **Mailing Address:** Dept R&D Strategic Planning, Boehringer Ingelheim Pharmaceut Inc, 900 Ridgebury Rd PO Box 368, Ridgefield, CT 06877-0368. **Fax:** 203-798-5595. **E-Mail:** jkeirns@rdg.boehringer-ingelheim.com

KEISCH, BERNARD, RADIOCHEMISTRY. **Personal Data:** b Brooklyn, NY, August 1, 1932; m 1954, c 3. **Education:** Rensselaer Polytech Inst, BS, 1953; Wash Univ, St Louis, PhD (chem), 1957. **Professional Experience:** NUCLEAR CHEMIST, BROOKHAVEN NAT LAB, as of 1994; SCIENTIST, BROOKHAVEN NAT LAB, 1978-; sr fel, Carnegie-Mellon Inst Res, 1974-1978; from fel to sr fel, Carnegie-Mellon Univ, 1966-1974; sr scientist, Nuclear Sci & Eng Corp, 1962-1966; mat testing reactor, Idaho Chem Processing Plant, Phillips Petrol Co, 1959-1962; Res chemist, Idaho Chem Processing Plant, Phillips Petrol Co, 1957-1959. **Memberships:** Sigma Xi; AAAS; Am Chem Soc. **Research Statement & Publications:** Nuclear applications in art and archaeology; activation analysis; isotope mass spectrometry; carbon-14 dating; Mossbauer effect; nuclear safeguards. **Mailing Address:** Brookhaven Nat Lab, Box 5000, Upton, NY 11973-5000.

KEISER, BERNHARD E(DWARD), TELECOMMUNICATIONS ENGINEERING, RADIO ENGINEERING. **Personal Data:** b Richmond Heights, Mo, November 14, 1928; m 1955, Evelyn; c Sandra, Carol, Nancy, Linda & Paul. **Education:** Wash Univ, St Louis, BS, 1950, MS, 1951, DSc, 1953. **Honors & Awards:** Centennial Medal, IEEE, 1984. **Professional Experience:** PRES, KEISER ENG, INC, 1975-; dir anal, Fairchild Space & Electronics Co, 1972-1975; dir advan systs electronics & commun, Atlantic Res Corp, Alexandria, 1971-1972; vpres systs res & eng, Page Commun Engrs, Va, 1969-1970; adminr advan tech planning, RCA Missile & Surface Radar Div, NJ, 1967-1969; mgr plans & prog sect, Kennedy Space Ctr Commun Proj, RCA Serv Co, Fla, 1964-1967; group leader new commun systs, RCA Corp, 1959-1964; Petrolite Corp, 1956-1957 & Mo Res Labs, 1957-1959; Proj engr, White-Rodgers Elec Co, Mo, 1953-1956. **Memberships:** Fel Inst Elec & Electronics Engrs. **Research Statement & Publications:** Telecommunications; electronic systems; Broadband and Wireless Commun syst. **Mailing Address:** 2046 Carrhill Rd, Vienna, VA 22181-2917. **Fax:** 703-281-9582. **E-Mail:** keiser@ieee.org

KEISER, EDMUND DAVIS, VERTEBRATE ZOOLOGY, WETLANDS ECOLOGY. **Personal Data:** b Appalachia, Va, February 18, 1934; m Sue; c Mark E, Julie A, Louis A & Jenifer M. **Education:** Southern Ill Univ, BA, 1956, MS, 1961; La State Univ, PhD (vert zoology), 1967. **Professional Experience:** Res assoc Miss Museum Natural Sci, 2001-; Consul, US Army C.E. 2005-; consul, US Fish & Wildlife Serv 2000-; consul, MS Dept. Wildlife, Fisheries, and Parks 1989-; Consul Nat Park Serv, 2001-4; Tetra Tech Inc Atlanta, 2000-2001; consul, NASA/GB Tech, 1998-2000; NASA Sverdrup Engr, 1994-1995; US Army Corps Engrs, 1998-1999, 1992-1995 & NAA, 1994-1995; NASA/Lockheed Sci & Engr, 1990-1991; environ consult, Lockheed Eng, Advanced Solid Rocket Motor Proj, NASA, 1990-1991 & 1994-1995; chmn and Comnr, Miss Dept Wildlife Conserv, 1983-1984; mem, Miss Wildlife Heritage Comnr, 1980-1984; mem, Governor's Select Comm Radioactive Waste & Waste Depository, 1979; comnr, Miss Dept Wildlife Conserv, 1978-1979 & 1980-1984; consult, La Chenier Plain Study, US Fish & Wildlife Serv, 1978; Prof Emeritus & Chmn Emeritus, Univ. Miss, 2005-; Prof Biol, Univ Miss, 1976-2005; chmn dept, Univ Miss, 1976-1987; assoc prof, Univ Miss, 1976; consult & proj dir, US Fish & Wildlife Serv, Atchafalaya Basin Surv, 1973-1976; dir, Lafayette Natural Hist Mus, 1973; res assoc, Gulf South Res Inst, Baton Rouge, 1972-1975; dir biol, Physics & Chem, NSF Coop Col-Sch Sci Prog biol, 1969-1970; from asst prof to prof comp anat & syst zool, Univ Southwestern La, 1966-1976; sci ed consult, Southwestern La Parish Schs, 1966-1971; teaching asst zool, La State Univ, 1964-1966; instr zool & anat, La Salle-Peru-Oglesby Jr Col, 1962-1964; Teaching asst, Southern Ill Univ, 1961; Dist Sci. Coord, Freeburg, Ill, 1958-1962; Mt. Venon pub schs, Ill, 1957; Teacher Kinmundy High sch, Ill, 1956-1957. **Memberships:** Soc Study Amphibians & Reptiles; Herpetologist League. **Research Statement & Publications:** Ecology of amphibians. reptiles, and mammals of the southeastern United States; wetlands ecology and management. **Mailing Address:** Ecological Consulting, 211 St Andrews Circle, Oxford, MS 38655. **E-Mail:** bykeiser@olemiss.edu

KEISER, GEORGE MCCURRACH, GRAVITATIONAL & ATOMIC PHYSICS. **Personal Data:** b Plainfield, NJ, July 21, 1947. **Education:** Middlebury Col, AB, 1969; Duke Univ, PhD (physics), 1976. **Professional Experience:** SR RES SCIENTIST, DEPT PHYSICS, STANFORD UNIV, as of 2004; mem fac, Dept Physics, stanford Univ, beginning 1980; Nat Res Coun fel, Nat Bur Stand, 1977-1980; Lectr, Univ Colo, 1977-1978; res assoc, Joint Inst Lab Astrophys, 1976-1977. **Memberships:** Am Phys Soc; Nat res Coun. **Research Statement & Publications:** High precision measurements in gravitational and atomic physics. **Mailing Address:** Hansen Labs GP-B, Stanford Univ, Stanford, CA 94305. **E-Mail:** mac@relgyro.stanford.edu

KEISER, GERD E, TELECOMMUNICATIONS. **Education:** Northeastern Univ, PhD (solid state physics). **Honors & Awards:** Leslie Warner Award. **Professional Experience:** FOUNDER & PRES, PHOTONICSCOMM SOLUTIONS INC, as of 2005. **Memberships:** fel Inst Elect & Electronic Engrs. **Mailing Address:** PhotonicsComm Solutions Inc, 65 Rachel Rd Newton Ctr, Newton Ctr, MA 02459-2923. **Fax:** 617-332-4851. **E-Mail:** gkeiser@PhotonicsComm.com

KEISER, HAROLD D, RHEUMATOLOGY. **Education:** NY Univ, MD, 1964. **Professional Experience:** PROF MED, ALBERT EINSTEIN COL MED, 1983-. **Memberships:** Am Rheumatism Asn; Am Asn Immunologists; Am Asn Clin Res; Soc Complex Carbohydrates; Am Soc Clin Invest. **Mailing Address:** Montefiore Med Park, Albert Einstein Col Med, Rm 200 1575 Blondell Ave, Bronx, NY 10461-1975. **Fax:** 718-430-8789. **E-Mail:** orebh@aol.com

KEISER, HARRY ROBERT, CLINICAL PHARMACOLOGY, HIGH BLOOD PRESSURE. **Personal Data:** b Chicago, Ill, August 9, 1933; m 1992, Phyllis; c Harry R II & Robert H. **Education:** Northwestern Univ, BA, 1955, MD, 1958. **Professional Experience:** Clin prof med, Georgetown Univ, 1991-; CHIEF, HYPERTENSION-ENDOCRINE BR, 1985-1998; CLIN DIR, NAT HEART, LUNG & BLOOD INST, NIH, 1976-1998. **Memberships:** Am Col Physicians; Am Fedn Clin Res; Am Heart Asn; Am Soc Pharmacol & Exp Therapeut; Am Soc Hypertension. **Research Statement & Publications:** Etiology and therapy of high blood pressure. **Mailing Address:** Nat Heart Lung & Blood Inst, NIH, 10 Ctr Dr MSC 1754, Bethesda, MD 20892-1754. **Fax:** 301-402-1679.

KEISER, JEFFREY E, ORGANIC CHEMISTRY. **Personal Data:** b Kalamazoo, Mich, February 25, 1941; m 1988, c 5. **Education:** Kalamazoo Col, AB, 1962; Wayne State Univ, PhD (org chem), 1966. **Professional Experience:** RETIRED; sr res assoc, Penford Prod Co, beginning 1988; chmn dept, Coe Col, 1976-1988; from asst prof to prof chem, Coe Col, 1966-1988. **Memberships:** Am Chem Soc; AAAS. **Research Statement & Publications:** Organic analytical chemistry; starch chemistry. **Mailing Address:** Penford Prod Co, PO Box 428, Cedar Rapids, IA 52406-0428.

KEISER, JOAN A, CARDIOVASCULAR RESEARCH. **Personal Data:** b Muskegon, Mich, October 26, 1953. **Education:** Mich State Univ, BS, 1976; Univ Mich, PhD (physiol), 1982. **Professional Experience:** ADJ PROF PHYSIOL, UNIV MICH, as of 2005; adj assoc prof physiol, Univ Mich, as of 2004; assoc res fel cardiovasc, Parke-Davis Pharmaceut, beginning 1988; res scientist cardiovasc, Ortho Pharmaceut, 1985-1988; res fel physiol, Mayo Clin, 1982-1985; mem, High Blood Pressure Coun, Am Heart Asn. **Memberships:** Am Physiol Soc; Am Soc Exp Biol; Am Heart Asn; Am Soc Pharmacol & Exp Therapeut. **Mailing Address:** Univ Mich, Dept Physiol, Warner-Lambert 2800 Plymouth Rd, Ann Arbor, MI 48105. **E-Mail:** joan.keiser@pfizer.com

KEISER, TERRY DEAN, ICHTHYOLOGY, HERPETOLOGY. **Personal Data:** b Canton, Ohio, October 27, 1942; m 1984, Christine. **Education:** Ohio Northern Univ, BS, 1964; Bowling Green State Univ, MA, 1966. **Honors & Awards:** Fellow, Ohio Acad of Sci. **Professional Experience:** 1992-PROF & CHAIR, DEPT BIOL SCI, OHIO NORTHERN UNIV, 1966-; Dir, Metzger Nature Center; Pres, OH Sci Edu Research Assoc 2001-2003 Acting Dir, OBS 2001-2003; Chair Bd, Ohio Biol Surv. **Memberships:** Am Fisheries Soc; ASIH, SSAR, Asian Fisheries Soc NFC, N Am Native Fish Assoc, MBA. **Research Statement & Publications:** Stream fish distributions in Ohio; herptile populations-distributions in Hardin County Ohio. **Mailing Address:** Dept Biol Sci, Ohio Northern Univ, Ada, OH 45810. **Fax:** 419-772-2330. **E-Mail:** t-keiser@onu.edu

KEISLER, HOWARD JEROME, MATHEMATICAL LOGIC. **Personal Data:** b Seattle, Wash, December 3, 1936; m 1959, Lois; c Randall B, Jeffrey M & Thomas D. **Education:** Calif Inst Technol, BS, 1959; Univ Calif, Berkeley, PhD (math), 1961. **Professional Experience:** VILAS PROF MATH EMER, UNIV WIS, MADISON, as of 2005; vis prof, Univ Colo, 1985; John S Guggenheim fel, 1976-1977; prof math, Univ wis, madsion, beginning 1967; vis prof, Univ Calif, Los Angeles, 1967-1968; Alfred P Sloan fel, 1966-1969; from asst prof to assoc prof, Univ Wis, Madison, 1962-1967; vis res assoc, Princeton Univ, 1961-1962; Mathematician, Commun Res Div, Inst Defense Anal, 1961-1962. **Memberships:** Am Math Soc; Asn Symbolic Logic (vpres, 1977-1980). **Research Statement & Publications:** Model theory; set theory; applications of model theory to probability theory and mathematical economics. **Mailing Address:** Dept Math, Univ Wis-Madison, 480 Lincoln Dr, Madison, WI 53706-1388. **Fax:** 608-263-8891. **E-Mail:** keisler@math.wisc.edu

KEISLER, JAMES EDWIN, MATHEMATICS. **Personal Data:** b Spartanburg, SC, August 20, 1929; m 1950, Patience W Keisler; c James Jr, William Bryon & Paul T. **Education:** Midland Col, BS, 1949; Univ Mich, MA, 1954, PhD (math), 1959. **Professional Experience:** EMER PROF, LA STATE UNIV, 1994-; prof math, La State Univ, Baton Rouge, 1973- 1994; from asst prof to assoc prof, LA State Univ, Baton Rouge, 1959-1973; Teacher high sch, Nebr, 1949-1951. **Memberships:** Am Math Soc; Math Asn Am. **Research Statement & Publications:** Point-set topology; fixed point problems and characterizations of spaces. **Mailing Address:** 215 Stanford Ave, Baton Rouge, LA 70808-4666.

KEISTER, DONALD LEE, PLANT-MICROBE INTERACTIONS. **Personal Data:** b Beckley, WVa, December 10, 1933. **Education:** WVa Wesleyan Col, BS, 1954; Univ Md, MS, 1956, PhD, 1959. **Professional Experience:** Chmn, Beltsville Symp Agr, 1989; RES LEADER, SOYBEAN & ALFALFA RES LAB, USDA AGR RES SERV, 1984-; assoc prof, Wright State Univ, 1980-1984; chmn, Gordon Res Conf Photosynthesis, 1969; sr investr, Charles F Kettering Res Lab, 1962-1984; assoc prof biochem, Antioch Col, 1962-1980; fel, Res Inst Adv Study, Md, 1961-1962; fel, McCollum-PrattInst, Johns Hopkins Univ, 1958-1961; Nat Found fel, 1958-1960. **Memberships:** Am Soc Plant Physiol; Am Soc Microbiol; Int Soc Molecular Plant-Microbe Interactions. **Research Statement & Publications:** Mechanisms of pyridine nucleotide reduction in photosynthetic organisms; structure and function in photosynthetic organelles; control mechanisms in nitrogen fixation; symbiotic nitrogen fixation in legumes; author or co-author of over 100 publications. **Mailing Address:** Soybean & Alfalfa Res Lab, USDA Agr Res Serv, Bldg 006 BARC-W, Beltsville, MD 20705. **Fax:** 301-504-5728. **E-Mail:** dkeister@asrr.arsusda.gov

KEISTER, JAMES E, ELECTRICAL ENGINEERING, ELECTRONIC ENGINEERING. **Personal Data:** b Coburg, Iowa, July 11, 1914; m 1935, Ila; c Jamieson C, Holly J

(Crandall) & Bradley D. **Education:** Cornell Univ, BS, 1935. **Honors & Awards:** Apollo Achievement Award, NASA, 1969. **Professional Experience:** RETIRED; mem, Semiconductor Stand Comt, US Radio Tech Planning Bd & Nat TV Systs Comt. **Memberships:** Fel Inst Elec & Electronics Engrs; Sigma Xi. **Research Statement & Publications:** Development of television transmitters; radar counter measures, semiconductors; ground support equipment for Apollo and Skylab Prog. **Mailing Address:** 5566 Dry Ridge Rd, Cincinnati, OH 45252-1856.

KEISTER, JAMIESON CHARLES, DIFFERENTIAL EQUATIONS. **Personal Data:** b Schenectady, NY, February 28, 1938; m 1960, c 4. **Education:** Cornell Univ, BS, 1960; Georgetown Univ, MS, 1967, PhD (physics), 1970. **Professional Experience:** AT, 3M SOFTWARE, ELECTRO MECH SYST TECH CTR, as of 2006; res specialist, 3m pharmaceut, 1992; prin scientist basic res, Alcon Lab, 1984-1991; math consult, Miami Valley Labs, Procter & Gamble, Inc, beginning 1981; prof physics & math, Covenant Col, 1970-1984; sr field res physicist, Melpar Div, West Airbrake Co, 1966-1967; jr tech assoc, NUS Corp, 1964-1966; engr, Nuclear Prop Div, Buships, 1960-1964. **Memberships:** Electrochem Soc. **Research Statement & Publications:** Tunneling in super conductors; mathematical modeling and experiments for diffusion problems; complex variables; conformal mapping; transdevual drug delivery systems. **Mailing Address:** 3M Software, Electro-Mech Syst Tech Ctr, St Paul, MN 55144-1000.

KEISTER, JEROME BAIRD, INORGANIC CHEMISTRY, ORGANOMETALLIC CHEMISTRY. **Personal Data:** b Baton Rouge, La, March 28, 1953. **Education:** La State Univ, Baton Rouge, BS, 1973; Univ Ill, Urbana-Champaign, PhD (chem), 1978. **Professional Experience:** CHMN, DEPT CHEM, STATE UNIV NY, BUFFALO, as of 2003; PROF INORG CHEM, STATE UNIV NY, BUFFALO, 1991-; Alfred P Sloan fel, 1987-1989; from asst prof to assoc prof, State Univ NY, Buffalo, 1980-1991; res chemist organometallic catalysis, Corp Pioneering res, Exxon res & Eng Co, 1977-1980. **Memberships:** Am Chem Soc. **Research Statement & Publications:** Homogeneous catalysis, organometallic chemistry; metal cluster chemistry. **Mailing Address:** Dept Chem, State Univ NY, 562 Natural Sci Complex, Buffalo, NY 14260-3000. **Fax:** 716-645-6963. **E-Mail:** keister@acsu.buffalo.edu

KEITER, ELLEN ANN, INORGANIC CHEMISTRY. **Education:** Augsburg Col, BA, 1964; Univ Md, MS, 1968; Univ Ill, PhD (inorg chem), 1986. **Professional Experience:** CHAIR, DEPT CHEM, 1994-; PROF CHEM EASTERN ILL UNIV, Dept Chem, 1992-; vis prof, Colo State Univ, 1990; from instr to assoc prof, Dept Chem, 1978-1992. **Memberships:** Am Chem Soc; AAAS. **Research Statement & Publications:** Nuclear magnetic invest(s) of structure and dynamics of transition metal complexes. **Mailing Address:** Dept Chem, Eastern Ill Univ, 600 Lincoln Ave, Charleston, IL 61920. **E-Mail:** cfeak@eiu.edu

KEITER, RICHARD LEE, INORGANIC CHEMISTRY. **Personal Data:** b Winchester, Va, January 10, 1939; m 1966, c 2. **Education:** Shepherd Col, BS, 1961; WVa Univ, MS, 1964; Univ Md, PhD (inorg chem), 1967. **Professional Experience:** Univ Ill, 1980 & Colo State Univ, 1990; DISTINGUISHED PROF, EASTERN ILL UNIV, 1988-; PROF INORG CHEM, EASTERN ILL UNIV, 1979-; Univ Exeter, Eng, 1975; vis prof, Univ Wis, 1972 & 1977; assoc prof, Eastern Ill Univ, 1969-1979; assoc inorg chem, Iowa State Univ, 1967-1969. **Memberships:** Am Chem Soc; AAAS. **Research Statement & Publications:** Coordination chemistry of trivalent phosphorous ligands; transition metal carbonyls; polydentate phosphorus ligand control; synthetic inorganic and organometallic chemistry; phosphido-bridged complexes. **Mailing Address:** Dept Chem, Eastern Ill Univ, Charleston, IL 61920. **E-Mail:** cfrlk@eiu.edu

KEITH, BRIAN D, GENETICS. **Education:** Rockefeller Univ, PhD. **Professional Experience:** ASSOC INVESTR & ADJ FAC, DEPT CANCER BIOL, ABRAMSON FAMILY CANCER RES INST, UNIV PA, as of 2005. **Mailing Address:** Dept Cancer Cell Biol, Abramson Family Cancer Res Inst, 421 Curie Blvd 453 BRB II/III, Philadelphia, PA 19104-6160. **Fax:** 215-746-5511.

KEITH, DAVID ALEXANDER, ORAL & MAXILLOFACIAL SURGERY. **Personal Data:** b Chelmsford, Essex, Eng, August 28, 1944; m 1976, Barbara; c Sean & Lisa. **Education:** Univ London, BDS, 1966; FDSRCS(Eng), 1970; Harvard Univ, DMD, 1983. **Honors & Awards:** Malleson Prize, 1966; Brit Asn Oral Surgeons Award, 1973. **Professional Experience:** PROF, ORAL & MAXILLOFACIAL SURGERY, HARVARD SCH DENT MED, as of 2005; DENT DIR, HOWARD COMMUN HEALTH PLAN, 1996-; chief oral & maxillofacial surg, Harvard Community Health Plan, 1995-1996; DIR, POST-DOCTORAL PROG OROFACIAL PAIN & TEMPOROMANDIBULAR DISORDERS, HARVARD SCH DENT MED, 1993-; DIR, FACIAL PAIN SERV, SPAULDING REHAB HOSP, BOSTON, MA, 1993-; ADJ STAFF DENT, SPAULDING REHAB HOSP, BOSTON, MA, 1992-; DIR, OROFACIAL PAIN & TEMPOROMANDIBULAR DISORDERS, HARVARD SCH DENT MED, BOSTON, 1991-; VIS ORAL & MAXILLOFACIAL SUR, MASS GEN HOSP, BOSTON, MA, 1990-; ASSOC PROF ORAL & MAXILLOFACIAL SURG, HARVARD SCH DENT MED, 1985-; asst surgeon, Oral & Maxillofacial Surg, beginning 1984; clin assoc oral surg, Mass Gen Hosp, 1978-1984; asst prof, Howard Commun Health Plan, 1978-1984; res assoc orthop surg, Children's Hosp Med Ctr, 1977; res fel, Howard Commun Health Plan, 1975-1977; res fel, Mass Gen Hosp, Boston, 1973-1974; lectr oral surg, Hosp Dent Sch, Kings Col, London, 1971-1973. **Memberships:** Brit Dent Asn; Brit Asn Oral Surgeons; Int Asn Dent Res; Am Dent Asn; Int Asn Oral Surgeons; Am Acad Orofacial Pain. **Research Statement & Publications:** Craniofacial development; orofacial pain and temporo mandibular disorders. **Mailing Address:** Mass Gen Hosp, 55 Fruit St Ambulatory Care Ctr No 230, Boston, MA 02114.

KEITH, DAVID LEE, ENTOMOLOGY. **Personal Data:** b Mankato, Minn, December 7, 1940; m 1961, Brenda; c Beeky, Jennifer, Nulissh & Rochele. **Education:** Gustavus Adolphus Col, BS, 1962; Univ Minn, MS, 1965; Univ Nebr, Lincoln, PhD (entom/zoology), 1971. **Professional Experience:** PROF EMER, DEPT ENTOM, UNIV NEBR, LINCOLN, as of 2005; exten entomologist, Univ nebr, lincoln, beginning 1967. **Memberships:** Entom Soc Am. **Research Statement & Publications:** Biology, ecology and control of cutworms; development of integrated pest management projects on Nebraska field crops. **Mailing Address:** Dept Entom, Univ Nebr-Lincoln, 202 Plant Indust Bldg, Lincoln, NE 68583-0816. **Fax:** 402-472-4687. **E-Mail:** dkeith1@unl.edu

KEITH, DENNIS DALTON, ORGANIC SYNTHESIS, ANTIBIOTICS. **Personal Data:** b Hartford, Conn, July 11, 1943; c 2. **Education:** Bates Col, BS, 1965; Yale Univ, MS, 1967, MPh, 1969, PhD (org chem), 1969. **Professional Experience:** VPRES CHEM DEVELOP, CUBIST PHARMACEUT INC, as of 2003; res group chief, Hoffmann-La Roche Inc, beginning 1981; res fel, Hoffmann-la Roche Inc, 1976-1981; sr res chemist, Hoffmann-la Roche Inc, 1971-1976; NIH fel, Harvard Univ, 1969-1971. **Memberships:** Am Chem Soc; Am Soc Microbiol; Sigma Xi. **Research Statement & Publications:** Synthesis of natural products; heterocyclic chemistry; synthetic methods. **Mailing Address:** Cubist Pharmaceut Inc, 65 Hayden Ave, Lexington, MA 02421. **Fax:** 781-861-0566.

KEITH, DONALD EDWARDS, INVERTEBRATE ECOLOGY. **Personal Data:** b Ft Worth, Tex, October 7, 1938; m 1959, Lanita; c Dean & Wayne. **Education:** Tex Christian Univ, BA, 1962, MS, 1964; Univ Southern Calif, PhD (biol), 1968. **Professional Experience:** PROF BIOL, TARLETON STATE UNIV, 1985-; fel, Tex Acad Sci, 1977; consult, US Army CEngrs, Lake Proctor, 1976-; res grant, Tarleton State Univ, 1975-1988; asst prof to assoc prof, 1975-1985; dir environ sci prog, Tex Christian Univ, 1969-1971; asst prof biol, Tex Christian Univ, 1968-1975; NSF res grant, summer, 1961. **Memberships:** AAAS; Sigma Xi. **Research Statement & Publications:** Benthic ecology; substrate selection feeding and functional digestive tract morphology of Caprellid amphipods; amphipod phylogeny; effects of industrial effluents on benthic invertebrate communities; corals of the Swan Islands, Honduras; brachyuran crabs of Roatan and The Swan Islands Honduras; octocorals of Roatan. **Mailing Address:** Dept Biol Sci, Tarleton State Univ, Stephenville, TX 76402. **Fax:** 254-968-9157. **E-Mail:** keith@tarleton.edu

KEITH, ERNEST ALEXANDER, RUMINANT NUTRITION. **Personal Data:** b Fayetteville, Tenn, December 19, 1951; m 1972. **Education:** Univ Ark, BS, 1973, MS, 1974; Purdue Univ, PhD (ruminant nutrit), 1978. **Professional Experience:** ASST PROF DAIRY NUTRIT, DEPT DAIRY SCI, LA STATE UNIV, 1978-. **Memberships:** Sigma Xi; Am Dairy Sci Asn; Am Soc Animal Sci; Am Forage & Grassland Coun. **Research Statement & Publications:** Forage nutrition of dairy cattle. **Mailing Address:** 5015 S Rochelle Ct, Springfield, MO 65804.

KEITH, FREDERICK W(ALTER), CHEMICAL ENGINEERING. **Personal Data:** b Chicago, Ill, January 20, 1921. **Education:** Yale Univ, BS, 1942; Univ Pa, PhD (chem eng), 1951. **Professional Experience:** RETIRED; consult, 1979-1988; dir environ technol, Sharples Div, Pennwalt Corp, Warminster, 1971-1979; chem engr process develop, Pennwalt Chem Equip Div, Sharples Corp, 1950-1971; asst instr, Univ Pa, 1949; chem engr res & develop, Sharples Res Lab, 1944-1948; chem engr process develop, E I du Pont de Nemours & Co, 1942-1944. **Memberships:** Am Chem Soc; Am Inst Chem Engrs; Sigma Xi. **Research Statement & Publications:** Development and evaluation of centrifuges; waste and sewage process development; separations in synfuel processing. **Mailing Address:** 3300 Darby Rd, Haverford, PA 19041.

KEITH, H(ARVEY) DOUGLAS, CRYSTALLINE MORPHOLOGY. **Personal Data:** b Belfast, Northern Ireland, March 10, 1927; American citizen; m 1984, Gerhild; c Sheela H & Brian. **Education:** Queen's Univ, Belfast, BSc, 1948; Univ Bristol, Eng, PhD (physics), 1951. **Honors & Awards:** High-Polymer Physics Prize, Am Phys Soc, 1973. **Professional Experience:** PROF EMER MAT SCI, UNIV CONN, 1996-; res prof, Univ Conn, 1988-1996; consult, AT & T Bell Labs, 1988-1996; div counr, Am Phys Soc, 1977-1985; mem tech staff, Bell Tel Labs, 1960-1988; lectr physics, St Joseph's Col, Philadelphia, Pa, 1958-1960; res physicist, Am Viscose Corp, 1957-1960; lectr physics, Univ Bristol, 1951-1956. **Memberships:** Fel Am Phys Soc. **Research Statement & Publications:** Optical and electron microscopy; x-ray and electron diffraction of structure and morphology of crystalline polymers and relationships to properties. **Mailing Address:** Dept Mat Sci, Univ Conn, South Windsor, CT 06074-4224.

KEITH, JAMES OLIVER, WILDLIFE ECOLOGY, ECOTOXICOLOGY. **Personal Data:** b Pasadena, Calif, March 20, 1932; m 1950, Berniece; c Edward, Paul, Joan, Ellen & Ann. **Education:** Univ Calif, Berkeley, AB, 1953; Univ Ariz, MS, 1956; Ohio State Univ, PhD (ecol), 1978. **Professional Experience:** CONSULT, 1991-; wildlife res biologist, Int Prog, Denver Wildlife Res Ctr, 1981-1990; wildlife res biologist environ contaminants, Patuxent Wildlife Res Ctr, 1976-1981; chief, Denver Wildlife Res Ctr, US Fish & Wildlife Serv, 1969-1973; wildlife res biologist, Denver Wildlife Res Ctr, US Fish & Wildlife Serv, 1961-1976; Res assoc, Agr Exp Sta, Univ Calif, 1961-1965; Wildlife res biologist, Rocky Mt Forest & Range Exp Sta, US Forest Serv, 1956-1961; consult, World Wildlife Fund, Galapagos Islands, Food & Agr Orgn, Sudan, Kenya & Argentina, US Aid, Haiti, Sudan, Kenya, Senegal & Morocco, Nat Geog, Chile, govt Bahamas. **Memberships:** Am Soc Mammalogists; Soc Conserv Biol; Wildlife Soc; Am Ornith Union; Soc Ecosyst Restoration & Mgt. **Research Statement & Publications:** Ecological effects of land management practices; influence of logging, grazing, agriculture and pesticides on wildlife and their habitats; restoring altered ecosystems; control of introduced predators. **Mailing Address:** USDA Wildlife Res Ctr, Bldg 16 Denver Fed Ctr, Denver, CO 80225.

KEITH, JENNIE, GERONTOLOGY, ANTHROPOLOGY. **Personal Data:** b Carmel, Calif, November 15, 1942; m 1980, Roy; c Aaron, Kate, Leslie & Robert. **Education:** Pomona Col, BA, 1964; Northwestern Univ, MA, 1966, PhD (anthrop), 1968. **Honorary Degrees:** Dr Humane Letters, Pomoa Col, 2002. **Professional Experience:** DIR, EUGENE M LANG CTR CIVIC & SOCIAL RESPONSIBILITY, SWARTHMORE COL, as of 2004; provost, Swarthmore Col, 1992-2001; PROF ANTHROP, SWARTHMORE COL, 1990-; chair, Geront Soc Am, 1990; sr adv coun, Brookdale Found, 1989-1992; prog chair, Geront Soc Am, 1989; assoc ed, J Geront, 1986-1992; mem, Aging & Human Develop Rev Panel, NIH, 1985-1990; exec, Comt Behav & Social Sci Sect, Geront Soc Am, 1985-1987; co-dir, Proj AGE, Nat Inst Aging, 1982-1990; task group leader, Nat Res Plan Aging, 1981; mem, Res Rev Comt, NIMH, 1979-1982; from asst prof to prof, Swarthmore Col, 1970-1990. **Memberships:** fel Geront Soc Am; fel Am Anthrop Asn; Asn Anthrop & Geront. **Research Statement & Publications:** Cross-cultural comparative research on social and cultural influences on aging and old age. **Mailing Address:** Dept Sociol & Anthrop, Swarthmore Col, Train Sta 500 Col Ave, Swarthmore, PA 19081. **E-Mail:** jkeith1@swarthmore.edu

KEITH, JERRY M, ENZYMOLOGY, VIROLOGY. **Personal Data:** b Salt Lake City, Utah, October 22, 1940; m 1992, Kim; c Stephanie D, Marlowe D & Jonathan K. **Education:** Univ Calif, Berkeley, BA, 1973, PhD (comp biochem), 1976. **Professional Experience:** SR SCIENTIST, BIOMED CONSULT, 2003; CHIEF, LAB MICROBIAL ECOL, NIH, BETHESDA, MD, as of 2002; adj asst prof biol doctoral fac, Univ New York, beginning 1981; prin investr, gen med-biochem, NIH, 1981-1984; ASST PROF, BIOCHEM, COL DENT, UNIV NY, 1978-; staff fel, Lab Biol Viruses, Nat Inst Allergy & Infectious Dis, NIH, 1976-1978; sect chief, Dept Path, Rocky Mountain Labs, Nat Inst Allergy & Infectious Dis, NIH, Hamilton, Mont; indust consult, vaccine develop, Biotech. **Memberships:** Sigma Xi; AAAS; Am Soc Microbiol; Am Soc Virol; Am Soc Biol Chem. **Research Statement & Publications:** Molecular mechanisms of bacterial pathogens and the development of new generation vaccines; structure and function of biologically active nucleic acids and proteins, with a particular interest in the isolation and characerization of the enzymes related to the synthesis, processing and post-transcriptional modification of MRNA's; Published over 6 articles. **Mailing Address:** Biomed Consult, 18510 Snowberry Way, Olney, MD 20832-1570. **Fax:** 301-774-7163. **E-Mail:** jmkeith@dca.net

KEITH, LAWRENCE H, ENVIRONMENTAL CHEMISTRY, ELECTRONIC PUBLISHING. **Personal Data:** b Morris, Ill, April 5, 1938; m 1969, c Jack. **Education:** Stetson Univ, BS, 1960; Clemson Univ, MS, 1963; Univ Ga, PhD (natural prod chem), 1966. **Honors & Awards:** Chemist of the Year, Am Chem Soc, 1975; Distinguished Serv Award, Am Chem

Soc Div Environ Chem, 1986. **Professional Experience:** PRES & CEO, INSTANT REF SOURCES INC, as of 2004; adv bd, Environ Protection, beginning 1990; adv bd, Environ Lab, beginning 1989; corp fel, Radian Int, beginning 1986; prin scientist, Radian Corp, beginning 1985; sr prog mgr, Anal Chem Div, 1985-1992; adv bd, ES&T, 1982-1985; chmn, Am Chem Soc Subcomt on Environ Monitoring & Anal, 1981-; chem develop coordr, Anal Chem Div, 1981-1984; mem, Comt Mil Environ Res & Subcomt Indust Hyg, Nat Res Coun, 1981; mgr, Anal Chem Div, 1979-1981; chmn, Am Chem Soc Div Environ Chem, beginning 1979; head, Org Chem Dept, Radian Corp, 1977-1978; vchmn, Gordon Res Conf Environ Sci & Water, beginning 1973; pres, KCP, 1973-1983; Res chemist, Environ Protection Agency, 1966-1977. **Memberships:** Am Chem Soc; Sigma Xi; Am Soc Testing & Mat. **Research Statement & Publications:** Chemical changes produced by pollution treatment; nuclear magnetic resonance of pesticides; mass spectrometry; identification of organic chemical pollutants; computerized GC-MS analysis of pollutants; industrial pollutants; electronic book publishing; artificial intelligence. **Mailing Address:** Instant Ref Sources Inc, 329 Claiborne Way, Monroe, GA 30655. **Fax:** 253-595-7268. **E-Mail:** larrykeith@earthlink.net

KEITH, LLOYD BURROWS, WILDLIFE MANAGEMENT. **Personal Data:** b Victoria, BC, November 29, 1931; m 1954, c 4. **Education:** Univ Alta, BSc, 1953, MSc, 1955; Univ Wis, PhD (wildlife mgt), 1959. **Professional Experience:** PROF EMER WILDLIFE ECOL, UNIV WIS, MADISON, as of 2002; Prof Wildlife Ecol, Univ Wis, Madison, beginning 1970; from instr to assoc prof, 1960-1970; fel, 1959-1960; Asst forestry & wildlife mgt, 1955-1959. **Memberships:** Wildlife Soc; Am Soc Mammal; Ecol Soc Am. **Research Statement & Publications:** Natural regulation of animal populations; ten-year cycle of northern furbearers and grouse. **Mailing Address:** 9344 Boxturtle Rd, Mazomanie, WI 53560.

KEITH, LONNIE, MATHEMATICS. **Education:** Kans State Univ, PhD (Maths), 1970. **Professional Experience:** INSTR, CENT PIEDMONT COMMUNITY COL, as of 2005. **Mailing Address:** Cent Piedmont Community Col, PO Box 35009 Giles Bldg 206 Cent Campus, Charlotte, NC 28235. **Fax:** 704-330-6560. **E-Mail:** Lonnie.Keith@cpcc.edu

KEITH, ROBERT ALLEN, PSYCHOLOGY, MEDICAL REHABILITATION. **Personal Data:** b Brea, Calif, March 16, 1924; m 1949, c 2. **Education:** Univ Calif, Los Angeles, BA, 1948, MA, 1951, PhD (psychol), 1953; Am Bd Prof Psychol, dipl psychol. **Professional Experience:** PROF EMER PHYCHOL, CLAREMONT GRAD SCH, 1989-; Int Exchange Experts & Info Rehab, World Rehab Fund, 1987; fel, Div Rehab Psychol, Am Psychol Asn, 1984; vis scholar, Dept Child Develop, Univ London, 1967-1968; dir, Ctr Rehab Res & Planning, 1965-1995; res fel, Dept Nutrit, Sch Pub Health, Harvard Univ, 1960-1961; psychol consult, Casa Colina Hosp, 1955-1967; from asst prof to prof, Claremont Grad Sch, 1953-1989. **Memberships:** Am Psychol Asn; Am Congr Rehab Med. **Research Statement & Publications:** Treatment effectiveness for brain injury, strokes, spinal cord injury; organizational analysis of operations of the rehabilitation hospital; market research and strategic planning. **Mailing Address:** Dept Psychol, Claremont Grad Univ, 150 E Tenth St, Claremont, CA 91711.

KEITH, SAMUEL J, CLINICAL TREATMENT RESEARCH. **Education:** Emory Univ Sch Med, MD. **Professional Experience:** PROF & CHAIR, DEPT PSYCHIAT & PSYCHOL, UNIV NMEX, NMEX, as of 2005. **Mailing Address:** Univ NMex Dept Psychiat, MSC09-5030, Albuquerque, NM 87131.

KEITH, SANDRA ZAROODNY, MATHEMATICS. **Education:** Brown Univ, BA, 1966; Univ Pa, MA, PhD, 1971. **Professional Experience:** PROF, DEPT MATH & STATIST, ST CLOUD STATE UNIV, 1989-; vis lect, Univ Va, 1975-1976. **Mailing Address:** Eng & Comput Ctr 157, St Cloud State Univ, 720 S Fourth Ave S, St Cloud, MN 56301. **Fax:** 320-255-4269. **E-Mail:** szkeith@stcloudstate.edu

KEITH, TERRY EUGENE CLARK, HYDROTHERMAL ALTERATION, MINERALOGY. **Personal Data:** b Redlands, Calif, January 28, 1940; m 1966, William; c David & Caven. **Education:** Univ Ariz, BS, 1962; Univ Ore, MS, 1964. **Professional Experience:** SCIENTIST-IN-CHG ALASKA VOLCANO OBSERV, US GEOL SURV, 1993-; assoc chief, Br Igneous & Geothermal Processes, 1987-1990; RES GEOLOGIST, US GEOL SURV, 1964-. **Memberships:** Am Geophys Union; Geothermal Res Coun; Clay Mineral Soc. **Research Statement & Publications:** Hydrothermal and fumarolic alteration mineralogy, primarily in Yellowstone National Park the Pacific Northwest Cascade Range and Alaskan volcanoes; field distribution and petrography of ultramafic rocks in the Yukon-Tanana Upland Alaska. **Mailing Address:** US Geol Surv, 4200 Univ Dr, Anchorage, AK 99508-4667. **Fax:** 907-786-7425. **E-Mail:** tkeith@doodlepig.com

KEITH, THEO GORDON, THERMAL SCIENCES, NUMERICAL ANALYSIS. **Personal Data:** b Cleveland, Ohio, July 2, 1939; m 1960, c 2. **Education:** Fen Col, BME, 1964; Univ Md, MSME, 1968, PhD (mech eng). **Honors & Awards:** Ralph R Teetor Award, Soc Automotive Engrs, 1978. **Professional Experience:** DISTINGUISHED PROF MECH, INDUST & MFG ENG, UNIV TOLEDO, as of 2004; VPRES, WORKFORCE ENHANCEMENT, OHIO AEROSPACE INST, as of 2004; co-prin investr devicing grant, Lewis Res Ctr, NASA, 1977-1981; wind energy grant, beginning 1980; prin investr, pumping ring seal grant, Lewis Res Ctr, NASA, 1977-1981; wind energy grant, 1979; prof & chmn, mech eng, Univ Toledo, beginning 1971; mech engr, Naval Ship Res & Develop Ctr, Annapolis, Md, 1964-1971; assoc fel, AIAA. **Memberships:** Am Soc Mech Engrs; Am Soc Eng Educ; Am Inst Aeronaut & Astronaut; Soc Automotive Engrs; Sigma Xi. **Mailing Address:** Dept Mech, Indust & Mfg Eng, Univ Toledo, Nitschke Hall 4054, Toledo, OH 43606. **Fax:** 419-530-8206. **E-Mail:** tkeith@eng.utoledo.edu

KEITHLY, JANET SUE, MICROBIOLOGY. **Personal Data:** b Jefferson City, Mo, November 29, 1941; m 1973, c 2. **Education:** Cent Mo State Univ, BSc, 1963; Iowa State Univ, PhD (zoology), 1968. **Professional Experience:** ASSOC PROF, DEPT BIOMED SCI, UNIV ALBANY, STATE UNIV NY, as of 2005; Vis asst prof, Seattle Biomed Res Inst, 1986-1987; ASST PROF MICROBIOL MED, MED COL, CORNELL UNIV, 1981-; res assoc med, Med Col, Cornell Univ, 1979-1980; vis assoc prof microbiol, Med Col, Cornell Univ, 1979; Adj asst prof biochem cytol, Rockefeller Univ, 1978-1980; from asst prof to assoc prof biol, Herbert H Lehman Col, City Univ New York, 1972-1978; fel parasitol, Rockefeller Univ, 1970-1972; fel parasitol, Rutgers Univ, 1968-1970. **Memberships:** Am Soc Microbiol. **Research Statement & Publications:** Chemotherapeutic strategies in treatment of leishmaniasis; drug mode of action against the human blood protozoa; factors influencing virulence of leishmania species; metabolic pathways of Leishmania as unique targets for chemotherapy; cloning the genes for and studying the expression of the rate-controlling enzymes in these pathways eg polyamine and trypanothione metabolism; ornithine decarboxylase and trypanothione reductase genes. **Mailing Address:** Dept Biomed Sci, Wadsworth Ctr, NY State Univ, PO Box 509, Albany, NY 12208. **Fax:** 518-473-8520. **E-Mail:** keithly@wadsworth.org

KEITT, GEORGE WANNAMAKER, PLANT PHYSIOLOGY, PESTICIDE REGULATION. **Personal Data:** b Madison, Wis, September 11, 1928; m 1957, Gretchen; c Anne L (Spell), Elizabeth P (Nowak), George W III & Edward N. **Education:** Harvard Univ, AB, 1950; Univ Wis, MS, 1952, PhD (bot). 1957. **Professional Experience:** BIOL ANALYSIS BR, BIOL & ECON ANALYSIS DIV, US ENVIRON PROTECTION AGENCY, as of 2002; PLANT PHYSIOLOGIST, BIOL & ECON ANALYSIS DIV, PESTICIDE PROG, ENVIRON PROTECTION AGENCY, 1975-; res dept, Brooklyn Botanic Garden, 1970-1975; chmn, Brooklyn Botanic Garden, 1970-1974; vis investr, Princeton Univ, 1970; sr fel, Mackinac Col, 1967-1970; asst prof bot, Fla State Univ, 1959-1967; rRes assoc, Ford Agr Plant Nutrit Proj, Mich, 1957-1959. **Memberships:** NY Acad Sci; Sigma Xi; Bot Soc Am; Am Inst Biol Sci; Scand Soc Plant Physiol; Am Soc Plant Physiol. **Research Statement & Publications:** Chemical control of plant growth and differentiation. **Mailing Address:** US Environ Protection Agency, Ariel Rios Bldg 1200 Pa Ave N W, Washington, DC 20460. **E-Mail:** keitt.george@epamail.epa.gov

KEIZER, EUGENE O(RVILLE), video systems, color television; deceased, see previous edition for last biography

KELBER, CHARLES NORMAN, PHYSICS, MATHEMATICS. **Personal Data:** b Minneapolis, Minn, June 2, 1928; m 1950, Rhonda; c Jeffrey A & Steven G. **Education:** Univ Minn, BS, 1947, MS, 1948, PhD (physics), 1951. **Professional Experience:** MEM, ATOMIC SAFETY & LICENSING BD PANEL, US NUCLEAR REGULATORY COMN, 1990-; sr tech adv, Atomic Energy Comn, Nuclear Regulatory Comn, 1988-1990; PHYSICIST & ADV REACTOR SAFETY RES, NUCLEAR REGULATORY COMN, 1973-; physicist, Frankford Arsenal, Pa, 1951-1955; physicist, Argonne Nat Lab, 1955-1974. **Memberships:** Fel Am Phys Soc; Am Nuclear Soc. **Research Statement & Publications:** Reactor physics and safety; reactor computation. **Mailing Address:** Off Pub Affairs, US Nuclear Regulatory Comn, Washington, DC 20555. **Fax:** 301-415-5575. **E-Mail:** cnk@mnc.gov

KELCH, ROBERT P, PEDIATRIC ENDOCRINOLOGY. **Education:** Wayne State Univ, PhB, 1963; Univ Mich, MD, 1967. **Professional Experience:** EXEC VICE PRES, MED AFFAIRS, MICH UNIV, as of 2003; chmn, Am Bd Pediat, 1995; PROF & DEAN, DEPT PEDIAT, UNIV IOWA COL MED, 1994-; Univ Iowa distinguished fel, 1994; chief clin affairs, Univ Mich Hosp, 1989-1992; asst dean clin affairs, Univ Mich Med Sch, 1989-1992; mem, Gen Clin Res Ctrs Comt, NIH, 1987-1989; chmn, Dept Pediat, 1981-1994; actg chmn, Dept Pediat, 1979-1980; from asst prof to prof pediat, Univ Mich, 1972-1994; NIH trainee pediat endocrinol, Univ Calif, San Francisco, 1970-1972; Res fel, Dept Obstet & Gynec, Univ Mich, 1969-1970; from intern to resident pediat, Univ Hosp, Mich, 1967-1970. **Memberships:** Inst Med-Nat Acad Sci; Soc Pediat Res (pres 1987). **Research Statement & Publications:** Contributed numerous articles to professional publications. **Mailing Address:** Univ Iowa Col Med, 212 CMAB, Iowa City, IA 52242-1101. **E-Mail:** robert-kelch@uiowa.edu

KELCH, WALTER L, MANAGEMENT OF RESEARCH, ENGINEERING. **Personal Data:** b Dayton, Ohio, October 27, 1948; m 1970, Tina Ziegler; c Matthew J. **Education:** Miami Univ, AB, 1970; Ind Univ, MA, 1973, PhD (astrophys). 1975. **Professional Experience:** ENGR & ANALYST, CENT INTEL AGENCY, LANGLEY, VA, 1978-; res assoc, Joint Inst Lab Astrophys, Univ Colo, 1976-1978; Instr astron, Kean Col, NJ, 1975-1976. **Memberships:** Am Astron Soc. **Research Statement & Publications:** Spectral line formation in stellar atmospheres; solar and stellar atmosphere models; radiative transport; astrophysics. **Mailing Address:** 2103 Sugarloaf Ct, Herndon, VA 22070.

KELCHNER, BURTON L(EWIS), CHEMICAL ENGINEERING. **Personal Data:** b Bethlehem, Pa, November 15, 1921; m 1944, Ann; c 3. **Education:** Moravian Col, BS, 1943; Va Polytech Inst, BS, 1944. **Professional Experience:** RETIRED; consult, Los Alamos Tech Assocs, beginning 1983; proj mgr, Long-Range Rocky Flats Utilization Study, 1979-1983; mgr nuclear waste processing, Rockwell Int Corp, 1975-1979; proj mgr, Rocky Flats Div, Dow Chem Co, 1970-1975; sr res engr facil eng, Rocky Flats Div, Dow Chem Co, 1968-1970; mfg tech mgr, Rocky Flats Div, Dow Chem Co, 1965-1968; supt dept, Rocky Flats Div, Dow Chem Co, 1952-1965; sect leader, Los Alamos Sci Lab, 1946-1951; consult, uranium & plutonium processing. **Research Statement & Publications:** Nuclear waste processing; uranium and plutonium processing. **Mailing Address:** 5357 S Cody St, Littleton, CO 80123.

KELDYSH, LEONID, THEORETICAL PHYSICS, CONDENSEDMATTER PHYSICS. **Personal Data:** b Moscow, Russia, July 4, 1931. **Education:** Moscow State Univ, MSc, 1954; P N Lebedev Physics Inst Russ Acad Sci, PhD, 1965. **Honors & Awards:** Lenin Prize, USSR, 1974; Hewlett-Packard Prize, Europ Phys Soc, 1975; Humboldt Res Award, 1994. **Professional Experience:** Roentgen prof, Univ Wuerzburg, 1997; SR SCI RESEARCHER, PN LEBEDEV PHYS INST RUSS ACAD SCI, 1994-; managing dir, P N Levedev Phys Inst Acad Sci, 1989-1993; HEAD QUANTUM RADIOPHYSICS, CHAIR, PHYSICS DEPT, 1978-; head sector, P N Levedev Phys Inst Acad Sci, 1968-1989; PROF, MOSCOW STATE UNIV, 1965-; Sr sci researcher, P N Levedev Phys Inst Acad Sci, 1965-1968; Asst prof, Phys-Technol Inst, Moscow, 1962-1964; chmn, Gen Physics & Astron Sect, Russ Acad Sci. **Memberships:** Foreign assoc Nat Acad Sci; Acad Sci USSR. **Research Statement & Publications:** Many-body theory; semiconductors; superconductors; nonlinear optics; low-dimensional systems. **Mailing Address:** Lebedev Inst Physics Russ Acad Sci, Leninskiy Prospect 53 117924GSP, Moscow B-333, Russia.

KELE, ROGER ALAN, INDUSTRIAL MICROBIOLOGY. **Personal Data:** b Waterbury, Conn, January 24, 1943; m 1972, c 2. **Education:** Clark Univ, BA, 1964; Harvard Univ, MA, 1966; Univ Wis, PhD (bact), 1970. **Honors & Awards:** Am Cyanamid Sci Achievement Award, 1980. **Professional Experience:** RES MICROBIOLOGIST, LEDERLE LABS DIV, AM CYANAMID CO, 1970-. **Memberships:** Am Soc Microbiol; Soc Indust Microbiol. **Research Statement & Publications:** Strain improvement work on the tetracycline antibiotics. **Mailing Address:** Lederle Labs, Pearl River, NY 10965.

KELEHER, J J, ENVIRONMENTAL SCIENCES. **Personal Data:** b Winnipeg, Man, February 9, 1926; m 1953, c 3. **Education:** Univ Man, BA, 1948; Univ Toronto, MA, 1950. **Professional Experience:** RETIRED; environ officer, Man Dept Consumer, Corp Affairs & Environ, 1983-1985; Exec secy, Man Environ Coun, 1973-1983; spec asst, Fisheries Opers, 1972-1982; chief, Fisheries Opers, 1970-1971; chief fisheries biologist, Man Dept Mines & Natural Resources, 1968-1969; biologist, Fisheries Res Bd Can, 1950-1968. **Memberships:** Am Fisheries Soc; Am Inst Fishery Res Biol. **Research Statement & Publications:** Environmental management. **Mailing Address:** 10 Baldry Bay, Winnipeg, MB R3T 3C4, Can.

KELEMEN, CHARLES F, COMPUTER SCIENCE EDUCATION. **Personal Data:** b Mt Vernon, NY, January 7, 1943; m 1975, Sylvia Brown; c Rebecca, Colin & Elizabeth. **Education:** Valparaiso Univ, BA, 1964; Pa State Univ, MA, 1966, PhD (math), 1969. **Professional Experience:** PROF COMPUT SCI, DIR, COMPUT SCI PROG PROG, SWARTHMORE COL, 1984-; from assoc prof to prof comput sci, Lemoyne Col, 1980-1984; NSF grant, 1977-1981; vis assoc prof, Dept Comput Sci, Cornell Univ, 1977-1981;

Res assoc, Dept Comput Sci, Cornell Univ, 1975-1976; From asst prof to assoc prof math, Ithaca Col, 1969-1980. **Memberships:** Inst Elec & Electronics Engrs; Math Asn Am; Asn Comput Mach; Soc Indust & Appl Math; Sigma Xi. **Research Statement & Publications:** Computational complexity; analysis of algorithms; computer science education. **Mailing Address:** Comput Sci Prog Swarthmore Col, 500 College Ave, Swarthmore, PA 19081-1397.

KELEMEN, DENIS GEORGE, CHEMISTRY OF SOLIDS, ELECTRONIC MATERIALS. **Personal Data:** b Budapest, Hungary, June 18, 1925; American citizen; m 1994, Joanne; c Peter B. **Education:** Princeton Univ, PhD (chem), 1951. **Professional Experience:** INDEPENDENT CONSULT, TECHNOL APPRAISALS, 1988-; sr consult, Electronic Mat Div, 1984-1987; prin consult, Electronic Prod Div, Photoprod Dept, 1980-1984; develop mgr, Electronic Prod Div, Photoprod Dept, 1978-1980; prod mgr, Photoprod Dept, 1972-1978; planning mgr, Photoprod Dept, 1970-1972; res mgr electronic prod div, Electrochem Dept, 1968-1970; res supvr, E I Du Pont De Nemours & Co Inc, 1957-1968; res chemist, E I Du Pont De Nemours & Co Inc, 1950-1957; ed asst tables chem kinetics, Nat Res Coun, 1948-1950. **Memberships:** Am Chem Soc; Am Solar Energy Soc; Inst Elec & Electronics Engrs. **Research Statement & Publications:** Physical chemistry of solids. **Mailing Address:** Eight Smith Rd, Hanover, NH 03755-1540.

KELISKY, RICHARD PAUL, MATHEMATICS, DATA PROCESSING. **Personal Data:** b St Louis, Mo, November 27, 1929; wid, c Jeffrey. **Education:** Tex Tech Col, BS, 1951; Univ Tex, MA, 1953, PhD (math), 1957. **Professional Experience:** RETIRED; res mathematician dir plan & qual, Comput Systs Dept, Thomas J Watson Res Ctr, IBM Corp, 1986-1991; dir lab opers, Comput Systs Dept, Thomas J Watson Res Ctr, IBM Corp, 1982-1986; dir, Comput Systs Dept, Thomas J Watson Res Ctr, IBM Corp, 1971-1982; adj prof, Grad Div, City Univ New York, 1965-1972; asst prof, Univ Tex, 1957-1958; lectr, Univ Tex, 1955-1957; asst appl math, Univ Tex, 1952-1955. **Memberships:** Math Asn Am. **Research Statement & Publications:** Theory of numbers; numerical analysis; computing center management. **Mailing Address:** 24 Coolidge Ave, White Plains, NY 10606.

KELKER, DOUGLAS, STATISTICS. **Personal Data:** b Logan, Utah, March 23, 1940; m 1975, c 2. **Education:** Hiram Col, BA, 1961; Univ Ore, MA, 1963, PhD (math), 1968. **Professional Experience:** Assoc prof statist, Univ Alta, 1976-1981; asst prof math, Univ Alta, 1976-1981; vis asst prof, Univ Alta, 1973-1976; asst prof math, Wash State Univ, 1968-1973; asst prof probability & statist, Mich State Univ, 1968. **Memberships:** Inst Math Statist; Am Statist Asn; Can Statist Soc. **Research Statement & Publications:** Characterization theorems; infinite divisibility; distributions on the unit sphere applied to geological data. **Mailing Address:** Math Sci, Univ Alta, Edmonton, AB T6G 2G1, Can. **Fax:** 780-492-2927. **E-Mail:** kelk@fisher.stat.ualberta.ca

KELL, ROBERT M, EMULSION POLYMERIZATION, EXPERIMENTAL DESIGN. **Personal Data:** b Piqua, Ohio, November 27, 1922; m 1949, c 3. **Education:** Ohio State Univ, BChE, 1947, MSc, 1948. **Professional Experience:** SR RES ASSOC, FRANKLIN INT, 1979-; res chemist, Franklin Int, 1968-1979; sr res chemist, Battelle Mem Inst, 1962-1968; res chemist, Battelle Mem Inst, 1952-1962; jr chem engr, Olin Corp, 1948-1952. **Memberships:** Am Chem Soc; Tech Asn Pulp & Paper Indust. **Research Statement & Publications:** Adhesives; physical chemistry of polymers; plastics applications; vinyl polymerization. **Mailing Address:** Franklin Int, 2020 Bruck St, Columbus, OH 43207. **Fax:** 614-445-1813.

KELLAND, DAVID ROSS, PHYSICS, MAGNETISM. **Personal Data:** b East Orange, NJ, July 29, 1935; m 1989, Marjorie; c 3. **Education:** Montclair State Col, BA, 1957, MA, 1960; Salford Univ, PhD, 1989. **Professional Experience:** RETIRED, 1998; chmn, Forum Int Physics, Am Phys Soc, 1994-1996; Vis Scientist, Mass Inst Technol, 1991-1998; Prog mgr, NSF, 1987-1991; group leader, Francis Bitter Nat Magnet Lab, 1980-1991; co-group leader, Mass Inst Technol, 1978-1980; asst group leader, Mass Inst Technol, 1977-1978; staff mem, Mass Inst Technol, 1967-1977; asst prof, Emmanuel Col, Mass, 1963-1967; Instr physics, Simmons Col, 1961-1963. **Memberships:** Am Phys Soc; Inst Elec & Electronics Engrs. **Research Statement & Publications:** Applied magnetism and low temperature physics. **Mailing Address:** 884 Massachusetts Ave, Lexington, MA 02173. **E-Mail:** kelland@mit.edu

KELLAR, KENNETH JON, NEUROPHARMACOLOGY, MOLECULAR PHARMACOLOGY. **Personal Data:** b Baltimore, Md, February 13, 1945; m 1972, c 2. **Education:** Univ Johns Hopkins, BS, 1966; Univ Ohio State, PhD (pharmacol), 1974. **Honors & Awards:** Anna Monika Prize, Res Into Causes & Treat Depression. **Professional Experience:** PROF PHARMACOL, SCH MED, UNIV GEORGETOWN, 1985-; asst prof to assoc prof, Sch Med, Univ Georgetown, 1976-1985; prof psychiat, Univ Georgetown, Med Ctr. **Memberships:** Soc Neuroscience; Am Soc Pharmacol Exp Therapeut; Int Soc Neurochemistry. **Research Statement & Publications:** Nicotinic cholinergic receptors in the nervous system. Regulation of neurotransmission; signal transduction; Published over 15 articles. **Mailing Address:** Dept Pharmacol Georgetown Univ Sch Med, 3900 Reservoir Rd NW, Washington, DC 20057-2195. **Fax:** 202-687-5390. **E-Mail:** kellark@georgetown.edu

KELLAS, SOTIRIS, MECHANICAL ENGINEERING. **Professional Experience:** AT LANGLEY RES CTR, NASA, as of 2003. **Mailing Address:** Langley Res Ctr, NASA, Hampton, VA 23681.

KELLEHER, DENNIS L, ENVIRONMENTAL PHYSIOLOGY. **Education:** Univ Fla, PhD (physiol), 1978. **Professional Experience:** HEAD TRAUMA RES, FAIRFAX HOSP, FALLS CHURCH, VA, 1992-; asst prof, Dept Physiol, Uniformed Serv Univ, Bethesda, 1985-1990. **Memberships:** Am Physiol Soc; Aerospace Med Asn; Sigma Xi. **Mailing Address:** Antiviral Clin Res, Glaxo Wellcome Inc, 5 Moore Dr, Research Triangle Park, NC 27709.

KELLEHER, HERBERT DAVID, AVIATION. **Personal Data:** b Camden, NJ, March 12, 1931; m 1955, Joan Negley; c Julie, Michael, Ruth & David. **Education:** Wesleyan Univ, BA, 1953; New York Univ, LLB, 1956. **Honors & Awards:** Aircraft Opers Excellence Award, Am Inst Aeronaut & Astronaut, 1994. **Professional Experience:** FOUNDER, GEN COUNR, CHMN & DIR, SOUTHWEST AIRLINES, 1967-. **Mailing Address:** SW Airlines Co, Box 36611 Love Field, Dallas, TX 75235-1611.

KELLEHER, JAMES JOSEPH, MOLECULAR BIOLOGY, IMMUNOLOGY. **Personal Data:** b Hudson, Mass, September 12, 1938; m 1963, c 4. **Education:** Boston Col, BS, 1960, MS, 1963; Rutgers Univ, PhD (microbiol), 1968. **Professional Experience:** PROF EMER MICROBIOL/IMMUNOL, SCH MED, UNIV NDAK, 1996-; chmn, sch med, Univ Ndak, beginning 1989; prof microbiol/immunol, sch med, Univ Ndak, 1980-1996; environ virol, 1974-1978; consult diag virol, beginning 1972; from asst prof to assoc prof microbiol, Sch Med, Univ Ndak, 1968-1980; res asst, Woods Hole Oceanog Inst, 1967-1968; fel, Woods Hole Oceanog Inst, 1967-1968; instr microbiol, Rutgers Univ, 1966-1967. **Memberships:** AAAS; Am Soc Microbiol; Sigma Xi; NY Acad Sci; Am Heart Asn. **Research Statement & Publications:** Nutrition, viral infection and immune response; clinical diagnosis of viral infections; herpes virus latency in cell culture and animal model systems; virus transmission by the water route; virology; nucleic acid probes; immunological diagnosis. **Mailing Address:** Dept Microbiol & Immunol, Sch Med, Univ NDak, 411 Twamley Hall, Grand Forks, ND 58202.

KELLEHER, MATTHEW D(ENNIS), MECHANICAL ENGINEERING, HEAT TRANSFER. **Personal Data:** b Flushing, NY, February 1, 1939; m 1969, Jean; c Genevieve & Veronica. **Education:** Univ Notre Dame, BS, 1961, MS, 1963, PhD (mech eng), 1966. **Professional Experience:** Assoc Dir, Off of Naval Res Int Field Off, London, 2001-2003; Chmn Dept, Naval Postgrad Sch, 1992-1995; sr acad visitor, Oxford Univ, 1988-1989; vis prof, Univ Notre Dame, 1987; Consult, Apple Comput, 1984 & Kaiser Engrs, 1985; coord comt, Nat Heat Transfer Conf, 1984-1988; PROF MECH ENG, NAVAL POSTGRAD SCH, 1982-; from asst prof to assoc prof, Naval Postgrad Sch, 1967-1982; Ford Found fel eng, Dartmouth Col, 1966-1967; asst prof mech eng, Univ Notre Dame, 1965-1966. **Memberships:** Fel Am Soc Mech Engrs; Sigma Xi; Am Soc Eng Educ. **Research Statement & Publications:** Heat transfer and fluid mechanics, specifically convection and radiation; heat pipes; electronics cooling. **Mailing Address:** Dept Mech Eng, Naval Postgrad Sch Code ME Kk, Monterey, CA 93943. **Fax:** 408-656-2238. **E-Mail:** mkelleher@nps.navy.mil

KELLEHER, RAYMOND JOSEPH, GENETICS, IMMUNOLOGY. **Personal Data:** b Fall River, Mass, September 27, 1939; m 1964, Maura; c Raymond Joseph III, Patricia Anne & Kevin Francis. **Education:** Col Holy Cross, AB, 1961; Boston Col, MS, 1964; Univ NC, Chapel Hill, PhD (genetics), 1969. **Professional Experience:** RES PROF, STATE UNIV NY, BUFFALO, 2001-; cancer res sci, Roswell Park Ctr, Park Cancer Inst, 1997-2002; sr res scientist, Lederle-Praxis Biol, 1993- 1996; res scientist, Roswell Park Cancer Inst, 1991-1993; vpres res, T & B Bioclone Corp, 1987-1991; Asst prof, SUNY College, Geneseo, 1984-1987; asst prof, State Univ NY, Buffalo, 1977-1984; res fel, Univ Calif, San Diego, 1976-1977; sr res assoc, Salk Inst Biol Studies, 1973 -1976; NIH fel genetics & biochem, 1969-1973; fel, Biochemi & Immunol Salk Inst Biol Studies. **Memberships:** AAAS. **Research Statement & Publications:** Molecular and cellular immunology; cancer research vaccine development. **Mailing Address:** Dept Microbiol & Immunol, State Univ NY, 211 Biomed Res Bldg, Buffalo, NY 14214. **Fax:** 716-829-2662. **E-Mail:** rjk6@buffalo.edu

KELLEHER, ROBERT NEAL, ASBESTOS REMEDIATION, HAZ-MAT REMEDIATION & INCIDENT RESPONSE. **Personal Data:** b Teaneck, NJ, June 26, 1943; wid, c Scott & Kristen. **Education:** Univ Eastern Fla, BS (chem eng), 1965. **Honors & Awards:** Innovative Eng Award, 1996. **Professional Experience:** Mem, Washoe Co/Reno Environ Adv Bd, 1992-1994; ENVIRON & CHEM CONSULT, CLEAN-AGRI FRUIT CHEM, 1983-; vpres opers mgr, Cyclo Chem Corp, 1981-1984; opers mgr, Trojan Chem Co, 1979-1981; vpres & opers mgr, Ajax Div, Biscayne Chem, 1971-1979; opers coodr, Jefferson Chem Co, 1969-1971; asst res & develop chemist, Penetone Div, Amerace-Esna, 1967-1969; pharmacist med supply, USAF, 1965-1967. **Memberships:** Am Chem Soc; AAAS; Am Inst Plant Engrs. **Research Statement & Publications:** Agricultural/chemical formulation of environmentally safe products for the farm community and the development of non-toxic adjuvents and insecticides. **Mailing Address:** PO Box 2408, Fallon, NV 89407-2408. **E-Mail:** r-agent3@aol.com

KELLEHER, WILLIAM JOSEPH, BIOCHEMISTRY, PHARMACOGNOSY. **Personal Data:** b Hartford, Conn, July 18, 1929. **Education:** Univ Conn, BS, 1951, MS, 1953; Univ Wis, PhD (biochem), 1960. **Professional Experience:** RETIRED; consult, Copley Pharmaceut, 1992-1995; consult, Vicks Res Ctr, 1985-1992; vis scientist, Vicks Res Ctr, 1984-1985; asst dean, Med Chem & Pharmacog Sect, 1976-1981; chmn, Med Chem & Pharmacog Sect, 1971-1976; assoc ed, Lloydia, 1971-1976; prof pharmacog, 1970-1988; guest prof, Univ Freiburg, 1970-1971, 1977-1978; mem, Nat Formulary Adv Panel Pharmacog, 1964-1971; from asst prof to assoc prof, Sch Pharm, Univ 1960-1970; asst biochem, Univ Wis, 1956-1960; asst pharm, Univ Conn, 1951-1953. **Memberships:** Am Chem Soc; Am Soc Pharmacog; Brit Biochem Soc. **Research Statement & Publications:** Microbial chemistry and the production and biosynthesis of alkaloids and other medicinal products by fermentation processes; formulation and dosage form development. **Mailing Address:** PO Box 205, Storrs, CT 06268.

KELLEMS, RODNEY E, MOLECULAR GENETICS. **Education:** Princeton Univ, PhD (biochem), 1975. **Professional Experience:** PROF & CHMN BIOCHEM & MOLECULAR BIOL, UNIV TEX, HOUSTON, as of 2005; assoc prof biochem, Baylor Col Med, beginning 1984. **Memberships:** Am Soc Biol Chem; Am Chem Soc; Am Soc Cell Biol; Am Soc Human Genetics. **Mailing Address:** Dept Biochem & Molecular Biol, Med Sch, Univ Tex Health Sci Ctr, PO Box 20708, Houston, TX 77225. **Fax:** 713-500-0652. **E-Mail:** rodney.e.kellems@uth.tmc.edu

KELLER, ANDREW, PHYSICS. **Personal Data:** b Budapest, Hungary, August 22, 1925; m 1951, Eva Bulhack; c Peter & Nicola. **Education:** Univ Eotvos Lorant, Hungary, BS, 1947; Univ Bristol, Eng, PhD (physics), 1958. **Honors & Awards:** High Polymer Prize, Am Phys Soc, 1964; Max Born Medal Physics, Inst Physics London, 1983; Rumford Medal, Royal Soc, 1994. **Professional Experience:** RETIRED; Morton res prof, Univ Akron, 1993; emer prof, Univ Bristol, Eng, 1991-1997; chmn, Macromolecular Sect, Europ Physicists Soc, 1984-1988; Clyde res prof, Univ Utah, 1982-1983; Vis prof, Case Western Res Univ, Cleveland, 1969-; prof, Univ Bristol, Eng, 1966-1991; reader, Univ Bristol, Eng, 1966-1969; lectr, Univ Bristol, Eng, 1962-1966; res assoc, Univ Bristol, Eng, 1955-1962; Tech officer, Imp Chem Indust, Eng, 1948-1955. **Memberships:** Fel Royal Soc; Am Phys Soc; Acad Europaea; Europ Physicists Soc. **Research Statement & Publications:** Contributed numerous articles to journals. **Mailing Address:** 41 Westbury Rd, Bristol, UK.

KELLER, BERNARD GERARD, PHARMACY. **Personal Data:** b New Orleans, La, December 18, 1936. **Education:** Loyola Univ, BS, 1959; Univ Miss, MS, 64, PhD (pharm admin), 1966. **Professional Experience:** PROF EMER, SCH PHARM, SOUTHWESTERN OKLA STATE UNIV, as of 2005; prof pharm admin, Sch Pharm, Southwestern Okla State Univ, beginning 1981; from asst dean clin progs to dean, Okla State Univ, 1972-1987; chmn, Div Pharmaceut & Pharm Admin, Okla State Univ, 1970-1981; prof pharmaceut & chmn dept, Okla State Univ, 1969-1981; assoc prof pharm admin, Southern Col Pharm, 1967-1969; asst prof pharm & pharm admin, Southern Col Pharm, 1965-1967. **Memberships:** Am Pharmaceut Asn; Am Soc Hosp Pharmacists; Am Col Apothecaries; Nat Asn Retail Druggists. **Research Statement & Publications:** Pharmacy administration; motivation research; the pharmacist's relationship to the terminal patient; medical ethics. **Mailing Address:** Sch Pharm, Southwestern Okla State Univ, 100 Campus Dr, Weatherford, OK 73096. **Fax:** 580-774-3795.

KELLER, C KENT, HYDROGEOCHEMISTRY, VADOSE ZONE. **Personal Data:** b Ashland, Ohio, September 6, 1955; m 1984, Teresa. **Education:** Stanford Univ, BS, 1977; Univ Waterloo, Ont, MS, 1985, PhD (earth sci), 1987. **Professional Experience:** PROF

GEOL, WASH STATE UNIV, as of 2005; vis prof, NMex Inst Mining & Technol, 1994-1995; assoc prof geol, Wash State Univ, beginning 1988; res assoc, Sask Res Coun, 1985-1987; consult, USAID, 1982-1983. **Memberships:** Am Geophys Union; Nat Ground Water Asn; Geol Soc Am; Am Chem Soc. **Research Statement & Publications:** Carbon cycling in groundwater systems and the soil-vadose continuum; chemical weathering and the carbon cycle; groundwater chemical evolution. **Mailing Address:** Dept Geol, Wash State Univ, Pullman, WA 99164.

KELLER, D STEVEN, FORMATION & STRUCTURE OF FIBROUS WEBS & FINE PARTICLE SCIENCE & SURFACE CHEMISTRY, WETTABILITY/ADHESION COLLOID SCIENCE. **Personal Data:** b Syracuse, NY, July 15, 1958; m 1981, c 1. **Education:** Syracuse Univ, BS, 1980; State Univ NY, PhD, 1996. **Professional Experience:** ASSOC PROF, COL ENVIRON SCI & FORESTRY, STATE UNIV NY, as of 2004; asst prof, Col Environ Sci & Forestry, State Univ Ny, beginning 1997; Staff Scientist, COL ENVIRON SCI & FORESTRY, STATE UNIV NY, 1990-; prin investr, SBIR Res Proj, Dept Energy, 1989-1990; assoc res chemist, Otisca Industs, Ltd, 1982-1990; regional tech serv coordr, Asst chemist, Champion Chem, 1980-1982. **Memberships:** Am Chem Soc; Soc Rheol; Technol Asn Pulp & Paper, Soc. of Rheology. **Research Statement & Publications:** Investigation of surface properties of micron size precipitated and naturally occuring calcium carbonate compounds using inverse gas chromatography; kinetics of rheological instabilities in shear-thickening, non-Newtonian concentrated fine particle suspensions. **Mailing Address:** Dept Paper Sci, State Univ NY, 419 Walters Hall, Syracuse, NY 13210-2778. **Fax:** 315-470-6945. **E-Mail:** dskeller@syr.edu

KELLER, DOLORES ELAINE, REPRODUCTIVE PHYSIOLOGY, MICROBIOLOGY. **Personal Data:** b New York, NY, October 29, 1926. **Education:** Long Island Univ, BS, 1945; NY Univ, MA, 1947, PhD (sex educ), 1956; Univ Hawaii, cert, 1964; Univ Calif, Berkeley, cert, 1966. **Professional Experience:** Sr therapist, Payne Whitney Sexual Disorder Clin & pvt pract licensed marriage counr sexual dysfunction, NJ, 1974-; clin asst prof biol psychiat, Dept Psychiat, Med Col, Cornell Univ, 1974-; spec consult, UN Comt Human Environ, 1971-1972; res assoc, Lamont Geol Lab, Columbia Univ, Davis, 1971; NSF partic, Conf Primate Behav, Univ Calif, Davis, 1971; dir, NSF Inserv Inst Cell Physiol & Genetics, 1966-1992; prof biol & dir allied health progs, Chair, Dept Biol, Pace Univ, Westchester Campus, 1965-1992; curric chmn, Bergen Co Community Col, 1964-; consult, Rennselaer Polytech Prog Intgerdisciplinary Col Sci, Charles Kettering Found, 1964-; NSF-AEC grant marine & radiation biol, Univ Hawaii, 1964-; res assoc, Haskins Labs, Carnegie Found, 1963-; US deleg, Int Oceanog Conf, 1959 & NSF grants, 1963-; from instr to assoc prof & chmn, Dept Sci, Fairleigh Dickinson Univ, 1956-1965; instr biol, Fr& lang & asst dean women, Long Island Univ, 1952-1956; Teacher biol & chmn dept, NY Pub Sch, 1949-1952; PSYCHOTHER, PVT PRACT. **Memberships:** Fel AAAS; Nat Sci Teachers Asn; Soc Protozool; Int Soc Clin & Exp Hypnosis; Am Asn Sex Educ Counrs. **Research Statement & Publications:** Protozoology; fresh water and marine microbiology; science curriculum and education; sex education; human sexuality. **E-Mail:** deekkk5@aol.com

KELLER, DONALD V, EXPERIMENTAL PHYSICS. **Personal Data:** b Centralia, Wash, August 17, 1930; m 1959, c 2. **Education:** Harvard Univ, AB, 1952; Univ Calif, Berkeley, PhD (physics), 1957. **Professional Experience:** CHMN, KTECH CORP, as of 2004; pres, Ktech Corp, beginning 1971; pres, Effects Technol, Inc, 1969-1971; mem tech staff, Defense Res Corp, 1966-1969; chief tech exp physics, Northrop Corp, Calif, 1962-1966; Chief shock dynamics, Boeing Co, 1957-1962. **Memberships:** Am Phys Soc. **Research Statement & Publications:** High energy nuclear physics; shock hydrodynamics; laser physics; dynamic mechanic and thermal properties of materials. **Mailing Address:** Ktech Corp, 1300 Eubank Blvd S E, Albuquerque, NM 87123-3336. **Fax:** 505-998-5848. **E-Mail:** dvkeller@ktech.com

KELLER, DOUGLAS VERN, PHYSICAL CHEMISTRY, MATERIAL SCIENCE. **Personal Data:** b Syracuse, NY, February 8, 1928; m 1953, Patricia; c Brian A, Jennifer A, Douglas S & Diana L. **Education:** Univ Buffalo, BA, 1955; Syracuse Univ, PhD (chem), 1958. **Professional Experience:** RES PROF, SYRACUSE UNIV, 1991-; adj prof math sci, Syracuse Univ, 1978-; vpres technol, Otisca Industs Ltd, 1978-1991; Bd dirs, Otisca Industs Ltd, NY, 1973-1991; prof, Syracuse Univ, 1969-1978; from asst prof to assoc prof metall eng, Syracuse Univ, 1959-1969; asst prof metall, Mont Sch Mines, 1958-1959. **Memberships:** emer mem Am Soc Metals. **Research Statement & Publications:** Physical chemistry of surfaces; coal physical chemistry and fuels benification. **Mailing Address:** Dept Elect Eng, Syracuse Univ, 339 Link Hall, Syracuse, NY 13244. **Fax:** 315-443-4936. **E-Mail:** dvkeller@mailbox.syr.edu

KELLER, EDWARD ANTHONY, GEOMORPHOLOGY. **Personal Data:** b Los Angeles, Calif, June 6, 1942; m 1966, c 2. **Education:** Calif State Univ, Fresno, BS, 1965, BA, 1968; Univ Calif, Davis, MS, 1969; Purdue Univ, PhD (geol), 1973. **Professional Experience:** PROF ENVIRON STUDIES & GEOL SCI, UNIV CALIF, SANTA BARBARA, 1976-; asst prof, Univ NC, Charlotte, 1973-1976; res asst, Purdue Univ, 1971-1973; instr, Purdue Univ, 1970-1973; asst prof geol, Calif State Univ, Fresno, 1969-1970; Hartley vis prof, Southampton Univ, UK. **Memberships:** Geol Soc Am; Sigma Xi. **Research Statement & Publications:** Fluvial processes in geomorphology; environmental geology; tectonic geomorphology. **Mailing Address:** Dept Geol Sci, Univ Calif, Santa Barbara, CA 93106. **Fax:** 805-893-2314. **E-Mail:** keller@geol.ucsb.edu

KELLER, EDWARD CLARENCE, ECOLOGY, BIOSTATISTICS, SCIENCE EDUCATION. **Personal Data:** b Freehold, NJ, October 8, 1932; c Edward C III & Kim L. **Education:** Pa State Univ, BSc, 1956, MSc, 1959, PhD (genetics), 1961. **Honorary Degrees:** DSc, Salem Col, 1978. **Professional Experience:** Coordr equity & access, WVa Dept Educ, 1995-; expert, disabled affairs, EHR Directorate, NSF, 1991-1992; pres, Found Sci & the Handicapped, 1977; pres, WVa Acad Sci, 1975-1976; vpres, Ecometrics Corp, 1973-1979; chmn dept, Wva Univ, 1969-1974; PROF BIOL, WVA UNIV, 1968-; mgr biostatist, NUS Corp, 1966-1968; staff biologist, Comn Undergrad Educ Biol Sci, 1965-1966; asst prof zool, Univ Md, Col Park, 1964-1967; NIH trainee, NIH fel, 1962-1964; res assoc, Med Sch, Univ NC, 1962; NIH trainee, Med Sch, Univ NC, 1961-1962; asst genetics, Pa State Univ, 1956-1961; chmn, spec ed adv comt, Nat Sci Teachers Asn. **Memberships:** AAAS; Nat Sci Teachers Asn; Ecol Soc Am; Am Statist Asn; Am Inst Biol Sci; Found Sci & Disability; Asn Sci & Disabled Persons, WV Acad Sci (WVAS) (pres, treas, Fsd, pres, SESD, pres); Nat Sci Teach Asn; Am Asn Adv Sci. **Research Statement & Publications:** Aquatic ecology; quantitative inheritance of biochemical traits in Drosophila; vibration stress in organisms; ecosystem analysis and simulation; environmental influences on human health; disabled persons in science; science education; genetics. **Mailing Address:** Dept Biol, WVa Univ, PO Box 6057, Morgantown, WV 26501-6057. **Fax:** 304-293-6363. **E-Mail:** u0072@wvnvm.wvnet.edu

KELLER, EDWARD LEE, APPLIED MATHEMATICS. **Personal Data:** b Glade Springs, Va, November 23, 1941; m 1968, Esther; c 2. **Education:** Duke Univ, BS, 1964; Univ Mich, Ann Arbor, MA, 1966, PhD (math), 1969. **Professional Experience:** ASSOC CHAIRMAN, CALIF STATE UNIV, HAYWARD, as of 2005; Dept chair, Calif State Univ, Hayward, 1989-2001; PROF MATH, CALIF STATE UNIV, HAYWARD, 1980-; from asst prof to assoc prof, Calif State Univ, Hayward, 1969-1980; res asst, Univ Mich, Ann Arbor, 1964-1968. **Memberships:** Am Math Soc; Math Asn Am; Soc Indust & Appl Math. **Research Statement & Publications:** Mathematical programming, particularly quadratic programming; matrix theory; mathematics of population; The following information is not for publication. **Mailing Address:** Dept Math & Comput Sci, Calif State Univ E Bay, 25800 Carlos Bee Blvd, Hayward, CA 94542-3092. **Fax:** 510-885-4169. **E-Mail:** ekeller@csuhayward.edu

KELLER, EDWARD LOWELL, BIOMEDICAL ENGINEERING, NEUROBIOLOGY. **Personal Data:** b Rapid City, SDak, March 6, 1939; m 1965, c 3. **Education:** US Naval Acad, BS, 1961; Johns Hopkins Univ, PhD (biomed eng), 1971. **Professional Experience:** Dir, Smith-Kettlewell Ctr for Vision Res & sr scientist, Smith-Kettlewell Inst Visual Sci, 1980; PROF ELEC ENG, UNIV CALIF, BERKELEY, 1979-; from asst prof to assoc prof, Univ Calif, Berkeley, 1971-1979. **Memberships:** AAAS; Asn Res Vision & Ophthal; Inst Elec & Electronic Engrs; Soc Neuroscience. **Research Statement & Publications:** Neurophysiological studies of the central organization of the primate oculomotor system; mathematical modelling of neuromuscular control systems. **Mailing Address:** Smith-Kettlewell Inst Visual Sci, Eecs 278 Cory, San Francisco, CA 94720. **Fax:** 415-561-1656. **E-Mail:** keller@eecs.berkeley.edu

KELLER, ELDON LEWIS, NUCLEAR PHYSICS, RESEARCH ADMINISTRATION. **Personal Data:** b Tiffin, Ohio, December 25, 1934; m 1961, c 1. **Education:** Heidelberg Col, BS, 1956; Univ Pittsburgh, MS, 1960. **Professional Experience:** ASST TO RES DIR, WESTINGHOUSE RES & DEVELOP CTR, 1974-; res prog adminr, 1969-1974; from assoc scientist to sr scientist, 1960-1969. **Memberships:** Am Phys Soc; Am Nuclear Soc. **Research Statement & Publications:** Low-temperature radiation effects in superconductors; gamma-ray imaging using image intensifiers; semiconductorgamma-ray monitor; thickness gauging; gamma-ray spectrometry. **Mailing Address:** 629 Burden Lake Rd, Aiken, SC 29803.

KELLER, EVELYN FOX, HISTORY & PHILOSOPHY OF SCIENCE, GENDER & SCIENCE. **Personal Data:** b New York, NY, March 20, 1936. **Education:** Brandeis Univ, BA, 1957; Harvard Univ, PhD (physics), 1963. **Honorary Degrees:** DHH, Mt Holyoke Col, 1991; Dr, Amsterdam, 1993, Tech Univ Lulea, Sweden, 1996; LHD, Rensselaer Polytech Inst, 1995; DSc, Simmons Col, 1995. **Honors & Awards:** Welle K Lectr, Univ Calif, 1993. **Professional Experience:** PROF HIST & PHILOS SCI, MASS INST TECHNOL, 1992-; prof, Univ Calif, Berkeley, 1988-1992; mem, Inst Advan Study, Princeton Univ, 1987-1988; sr fel, Cornell Univ, 1987; vis prof, Prog Sci, 1985-1986; prof, Kreegerb Wolf distinguished prof, Nebr Univ, 1982-1988; vis prof math & humanites, Kreegerb Wolf distinguished prof, Nebr Univ, 1981-1982; vis scholar, Mass Inst Technol, 1980-1984; vis fel, Mass Inst Technol, 1979-1980; mem, Ctr Policy Res, beginning 1976; assoc prof, Col Purchase, State Univ NY, 1972-1981; from asst prof to assoc prof, Grad Sch Med Sci, Cornell Univ, 1966-1972; asst res scientist, NY Univ, 1963-1966; instr, NY Univ, 1962-1963. **Memberships:** Hist Sci Soc. **Research Statement & Publications:** Meanings of explanation in developmental biology. **Mailing Address:** Dept Hist & Philos Sci, Mass Inst Technol, E51 171, Cambridge, MA 02139-4307. **E-Mail:** efkeller@mit.edu

KELLER, FREDERICK ALBERT, BIOCHEMICAL ENGINEERING, BIOCHEMISTRY. **Personal Data:** b New York, NY, m 1966, Judith; c 2. **Education:** Stevens Inst Technol, BE, 1961; Rutgers Univ, New Brunswick, MS, 1967, PhD (microbial biochem & eng), 1968. **Professional Experience:** TASK LEADER & SR BIOCHEM ENGR, NAT RENEWABLE ENERGY LAB, 1991-; sr consult, M G Pappas Co, 1990-1991; dir bioprocessing, Cambridge Bioscience Corp, 1987-1990; vis prof biochem eng, Ill Inst Technol, 1985-1987; sect leader, CPC Int, 1979-1987; sr biochem engr, Union Carbide Corp, 1975-1979; biochem engr, Biol & Med Sci Lab, Gen Elec Co, 1970-1975; USPHS fel, 1968-1970; chemist, Polymerization Develop Lab, Hercules Inc, 1961-1962. **Memberships:** Am Inst Chem Engrs; Am Chem Soc; Am Soc Microbiol; Soc Indust Microbiol. **Research Statement & Publications:** Biosynthesis, bioregulation and biodegradation of structural and storage macromolecules, including cellulo-lignins, starch, hemicellulose, chitin, glycogen; biochemical engineering processing; separation processes; regenerable raw materials; SCP; commercialization of chemicals by fermentation processes; biotechnology process development. **Mailing Address:** Nat Renewable Energy Lab, 1617 Cole Blvd, Golden, CO 80401-3393. **Fax:** 303-384-6877. **E-Mail:** kellerf@tcplinkk.nrel.gov

KELLER, FREDERICK JACOB, EXPERIMENTAL SOLID STATE PHYSICS. **Personal Data:** b Huntington, WVa, May 10, 1934; m 1954, c 4. **Education:** Marshall Univ, BS, 1960; Univ Tenn, MS, 1962, PhD (physics), 1966. **Professional Experience:** PROF EMER, CLEMSON UNIV, 1993-; prof physics, Clemson Univ, 1977-1993; from asst prof to assoc prof, Clemson Univ, 1966-1977; physicist, Oak Ridge Nat Lab, 1966; Teaching asst physics, Univ Tenn, 1963-1964. **Memberships:** Am Phys Soc. **Research Statement & Publications:** Color centers in alkali halides. **Mailing Address:** 140 McCracken Dr, Seneca, SC 29678. **Fax:** 864-972-2293. **E-Mail:** fkeller@clemson.edu

KELLER, GEOFFREY, ASTRONOMY. **Personal Data:** b New York, NY, June 12, 1918; m 1950, c 2. **Education:** Swarthmore Col, BS, 1938; Columbia Univ, PhD (astron), 1948. **Professional Experience:** RETIRED; prof astron, Col Math & Phys Sci, Ohio State Univ, 1972-1989; dean, Col Math & Phys Sci, Ohio State Univ, 1968-1971; dep planning dir, NSF, 1966-1968; div dir math & phys sci, NSF, 1961-1966; prog dir astron, NSF, 1959-1961; from instr to prof physics, Dir Perkins Observ, 1953-1959; from instr to prof physics, Ohio State Univ, 1948-1959; instr, Ohio Wesleyan Univ, 1948-1949; assoc physicist, Bur Ord, USN, 1941-1945; asst physics, Columbia Univ, 1938-1941. **Memberships:** Am Astron Soc. **Research Statement & Publications:** Internal constitution of stars; fluid turbulence. **Mailing Address:** 103 Abbey Cross Lane, Westerville, OH 43082-7309.

KELLER, GEORGE E, II, ENGINEERING ADMINISTRATION, CHEMICAL ENGINEERING. **Personal Data:** b Charleston, WVa, June 4, 1933. **Education:** Va Polytech Inst, BS, 1955; Pa State Univ, MS, 1958, PhD (chem eng), 1964. **Honors & Awards:** Clarence Gerhold, Am Inst Chem Engrs, 1995, Chem Pioneer Award, 1996. **Professional Experience:** RETIRED; chair, Eng Found Int Conf Separation Technol, 1991; regents prof eng, State Univ WVa; adj prof, Dept Chem Eng, Univ WVa; sr corp res fel, Union Carbide Corp, beginning 1987; lectr, Am Chem Inst, 1985; chair, Gordon Res Conf Separation & Purification, 1985; corp res fel, Union Carbide Corp, 1981-1987; res assoc res & develop, Union Carbide Corp, 1976-1981; adj assoc prof reaction eng, WVa Col Grad Studies, beginning 1963. **Memberships:** Nat Acad Eng; fel Am Inst Chem Engrs; Am Chem Soc. **Research Statement & Publications:** Advanced technique hydrocarbon cracking; separation, process research and development; development of medical oxygen technology. **Mailing Address:** Union Carbide Corp, PO Box 8361, S Charleston, WV 25303.

KELLER, GEORGE EARL, NUCLEAR PHYSICS. **Personal Data:** b Baton Rouge, La, November 6, 1940; m 1964. **Education:** La State Univ, BS, 1962, PhD (physics), 1969.

Professional Experience: RETIRED; assoc prof physics, W Ga Col, as of 2004; asst prof, beginning 1969. **Memberships:** Am Phys Soc; Am Asn Physics Teachers; Am Inst Physics; Sigma Xi. **Research Statement & Publications:** Gamma ray spectroscopy; determination of the properties of the excited states of the doubly even deformed nuclei. **Mailing Address:** Dept Physics, W Ga Col, 1600 Maple St, Carrollton, GA 30118. **E-Mail:** gkeller@westga.edu

KELLER, GEORGE H, MARINE GEOLOGY. **Personal Data:** b Hartford, Conn, September 9, 1931; m 1955, c 2. **Education:** Univ Conn, AB, 1954; Univ Utah, MS, 1956; Univ Ill, PhD (marine geol), 1966. **Professional Experience:** VICE PROVOST EMER RES, ORE STATE UNIV, as of 2004; vpres res & grad studies, Ore State Univ, beginning 1985; dean res, Sch Oceanog, 1981-1985; assoc dean, Sch Oceanog, 1975-1981; mem Mid-Atlantic Ridge explor, Nat Oceanic & Atmospheric Admin & others, 1974-1977; res oceanog, Atlantic & Meteorol Oceanog Labs, Nat Oceanic & Atmospheric Admin, Fla, 1969-1975; res oceanogr, Inst Oceanog, Md, 1967-1969; geol oceanogr, US Naval Oceanog Off, DC, 1959-1967; geologist, Stand Oil Co Tex, 1957-1959. **Memberships:** Geol Soc Am; Int Asn Sedimentol; Am Geophys Union. **Research Statement & Publications:** Marine geology and oceanography of the Malacca Strait, Malaysia; marine geotechnique, study of the mass physical and engineering properties of deep sea sediments and bottom material stability. **Mailing Address:** Res Off, Ore State Univ, 312 Kerr Admin Bldg, Corvallis, OR 97331-2140. **Fax:** 514-737-2064. **E-Mail:** george.keller@orst.edu

KELLER, GEORGE HENRY, BIOCHEMISTRY. **Personal Data:** b Harrisburg, Pa, October 21, 1950; m 1974, Nancy; c Laura & Emily. **Education:** Univ Md, BS, 1972; Pa State Univ, Hershey, PhD (biochem), 1978. **Professional Experience:** TECHNOL LICENSING SPECIALIST, OFF TECHNOL TRANSFER, NIH, 1995-; dir proj mgt, Cambridge Biotech Corp, 1990-1995; dir com develop, Biotech res labs Inc, 1989-1990; consult biochemist, Keller res servs, 1983-1989; staff fel, NIH, 1981-1983; fel, Am lung asn, 1979; res assoc, M S Hershey med ctr, 1978-1981. **Memberships:** Am Soc Microbiol; Asn Consult Chemists & Chem Engrs. **Research Statement & Publications:** DNA probes. **Mailing Address:** NIH, 6011 Exec Blvd, Ste 325, Rockville, MD 17078. **Fax:** 301-402-0220. **E-Mail:** kellerg@mail.nih.gov

KELLER, GEORGE MATTHEW, PETROLEUM ENGINEERING. **Personal Data:** b Kansas City, Mo, December 3, 1923; m 1946, Adelaide; c William G, Robert A & Barry R. **Education:** Mass Inst Technol, BS, 1948. **Professional Experience:** RETIRED; chmn & chief exec officer, Stand Oil, Chevron Corp, Calif, 1981-1988; vchmn, Stand Oil, Chevron Corp, Calif, 1974-1981; dir, Stand Oil, Chevron Corp, Calif, 1970-1988; vpres, Stand Oil, Chevron Corp, Calif, 1969-1974; asst vpres, Stand Oil, Chevron Corp, Calif, 1967-1969; foreign opers staff, Stand Oil, Chevron Corp, Calif, 1963-1967; engr, Stand Oil, Chevron Corp, Calif, 1948-1963. **Mailing Address:** 30 El Cerrito Ave, San Mateo, CA 94402-1210.

KELLER, GEORGE RANDY, SEISMOLOGY. **Personal Data:** b Muskogee, Okla, April 17, 1946; m 1967, c William & Nicole. **Education:** Tex Tech Univ, BS, 1968, MS, 1969, PhD (geophys), 1973. **Professional Experience:** CHiEF SCIENTIST & CO-PRIN INVESTR UTEP'S NASA EARTH SCI RES CTR, as of 2004; LA Nelson Professorship Dept Geol Sci Univ Tex, El Paso, as of 2004; PROF GEOPHYS, UNIV TEX, EL PASO, 1982-; CHMN, UNIV TEX, EL PASO, 1981-; from asst prof to assoc prof, Univ Tex, El Paso, 1976-1982; asst prof, Univ Ky, 1973-1976; res asst prof, Univ Utah, 1972-1973; Instr geophys, Tex Tech Univ, 1970-1971. **Memberships:** Am Geophys Union; Am Asn Petrol Geologists; Geol Soc Am; Seismol Soc Am; Soc Explor Geophysicist; Royal Astron Soc. **Research Statement & Publications:** Solid earth geophysics (seismology, gravity and geomagnetism); specifically the crustal structure, tectonics of North America and extensional terrains; published over 200 scientific papers, reports and book chapters. **Mailing Address:** Dept Geol Sci, Univ Tex El Paso, El Paso, TX 79912. **Fax:** 915-747-5073. **E-Mail:** keller@geo.utep.edu

KELLER, HAROLD WILLARD, MYCOLOGY, TREE CANOPY ECOLOGY & BIODIVERSITY. **Personal Data:** b Newton, Kans, December 10, 1937; m 1965, Brenda J Griffith; c David B & Brian L. **Education:** Kans Wesleyan Col, BA, 1960; Univ Kans, MA, 1963; Univ Iowa, PhD (bot), 1971. **Professional Experience:** Prof, Dept Biol, Cent Mo State Univ, 1998-; Living Sci Ctr trail guide, 1994-1998; bd trustess, Kans Wesleyan Univ, 1992-2002; RES OFFICER, OFF RES & BIOTECHNOL, UNIV N TEX HEALTH SCI CTR, 1990-; RES ASSOC, BOT RES INST TEX, 1990-; bd consult, N Tex Poison Ctr, 1986-; field reader & reviewer G-pop proposals, Dept Educ, 1985-1995; dir off sponsored projs & assoc prof biol, Univ Tex, Arlington, 1983-1990; mem, NC Bd Sci & Technol, 1983; chmn planning team, Southeastern NC Regional Forum Sci & Technol, 1983; gov's appointment, State NC Marine Res Ctr Admin Bd, 1982-1983; dir res & assoc prof biol, Univ NC, Wilmington, 1982-1983; adj assoc prof, Dept Microbiol & Immunol, 1980-1982; panel reviewer, Comprehensive Assistance Undergrad Sci Educ, NSF, 1981 & Instrnl Sci Equip Prog, 1980; from asst dir to assoc dir, Univ Res Serv, 1978-1982; NSF grants, 1975-1978 & 1983-1984; Ohio Biol Surv, 1974-1975; asst prof biol, Wright State Univ, Ohio, 1972-1978; Fel bot, Grad Sch, Univ Fla, 1971-1972; NSF fel, Summer Inst Systematics V, 1971; Conf partic, Comn Undergrad Educ Biol Sci, 1970. **Memberships:** Asn Southeastern Biologists; Mycol Soc Am; Sigma Xi; NAm Mycol Soc. **Research Statement & Publications:** Systematics, floristics and ecology of coricolous myxomycetes; floristic studies-US southeastern Gulf states and middle latitude states and Myxomycetes from Mexico; systematic world monographs are in preparation for the genera Perichaena, Licea and related taxa; scanning and transmission electron microscopy and energy dispersive spectroscopy are being used to study the formation, deposition and composition of mineral deposits in the Myxomycetes; development and use of K-12 teaching materials for fungi and Myxomycetes represented by hands on laboratory exercises and videos. **Mailing Address:** 2228 Stafford Dr, Arlington, TX 76012-4141. **Fax:** 660-543-4355. **E-Mail:** keller@cmsu1.cmsu.edu

KELLER, HERBERT BISHOP, APPLIED MATHEMATICS, NUMERICAL ANALYSIS. **Personal Data:** b Paterson, NJ, June 19, 1925; m 1953, c 2. **Education:** Ga Inst Technol, BEE, 1945; NY Univ, MA, 1948, PhD (math), 1954. **Honors & Awards:** Theodore von Karman Prize, Soc Indust & Appl Math, 1994. **Professional Experience:** PROF EMER APPL MATH, CALIF INST TECHNOL, 2000-; Ed, 1974- & Japan J Appl Math, 1984-; J Numerical Anal, 1964-1971 & Numerical Math, 1981-; Guggenheim fel, 1979-1980; assoc ed, J Comput & Systs Sci, 1971-1974; mem coun, Conf Bd Math Sci, 1971-1973; mem math div, Nat Res Coun, 1969-1972; prof appl math, Calif Inst Technol, 1967-2000; vis prof, Calif Inst Technol, 1965-1966; assoc dir, AEC Comput & Appl Math Ctr, 1964-1967; ed, Monogr Ser, Asn Comput Mach, 1963-1965; prof appl math, Courant Inst Math Sci, 1961-1967; assoc ed, J Appl Math, Soc Indust & Appl Math, 1961-1966; assoc prof, Univ, 1959-1961; lectr math, Wash Sq Col, 1957-1959; Head dept math, Sarah Lawrence Col, 1951-1953; res scientist, Div Electromagnetic Res, Inst Math Sci, NY Univ, 1948-1953; Instr physics & math, Ga Inst Technol, 1946-1947; consult, var indust & govt concerns. **Memberships:** Soc Indust & Appl Math (pres 1975-1976); Asn Comput Mach; Am Math Soc; Math Asn Am; fel Am Acad Arts & Sci. **Research Statement & Publications:** Numerical analysis; fluid mechanics; nuclear and chemical reactors; applied mechanics; computing machinery; bifurcation theory. **Mailing Address:** Dept Appl Math, Calif Inst Technol, MC 217-50, 311 Firestone, Pasadena, CA 91125. **E-Mail:** hbk@acm.caltech.edu

KELLER, JACK, AGRICULTURAL & IRRIGATION ENGINEERING AND CONSERVATION & WATER RESOURCES PLANNING. **Personal Data:** b Roanoke, Va, January 5, 1928; m 1954, Sara Altick Keller; c Andrew A, Jeffery S, & Judith. **Education:** Univ Colo, BS, 1953; Colo State Univ, MS, 1955; Utah State Univ, PhD (irrigation eng), 1967. **Honors & Awards:** Man of the Year, Irrigation Asn, 1965; Engineer of the Year, Utah Engr Coun, 1993; Advancement in Surface Irrigation, Am Soc Ag Eng, 2002. **Professional Experience:** Mem Exec Sci Bd, CLFED Bay-Delta Authority, 2003-; Sr Scientist Water Use Efficiency Prog, CALFED Bay-Delta Auhority, 1999-; Bd Mem, Int Develop Enterprises, 1999-; Sr Irrigation Adv, Int Develop Enterprises, 1999-; Team Leader Conserv Verification Consult, IID/MWD Conserv Agreement, 1994-; vis prof, fac agr sci & fac appl sic, KU Leuven, Belg, 1986, 1991, 1990; assoc ed, Irrigation & Drainage Systs J, Hague, Neth, 1984-; mem comt water resources res, Water Sci Technol Bd, Nat Res Coun, 1984-1986; head dept agr & irrigation eng, Utah State Univ, 1979-1985; co-dir water mgt synthesis proj, Utah State Univ, 1978-; mem tech control bd, Jordan Valley Irrigation Proj, Jordan, 1978-1980; mem comt consult eng, Soil & Water Br, Am Asn Agr Eng, 1976-; mem, Soil & Water Br, Am Asn Agr Eng, 1972-; chmn sprinkler irrigation comt, Soil & Water Br, Am Asn Agr Eng, 1966-1972; CHIEF EXEC OFFICER, KELLER-BLIESNER ENG, LOGAN, UTAH, 1962-; prof agr & irrigation eng, Utah State Univ, 1960-1990; asst irrigation engr, indust sales mgr & eng coordr, WR Ames Co, Denver, Colo & San Jose, Calif, 1956-1960; Sales engr, South Irrigation Co, Miss, 1955-1956; mem Int Comn Irrigation & Drainage. **Memberships:** Nat Acad Eng; Am Soc Agr Engrs; Am Soc Civil Engrs; Am Soc Eng Educ; AAAS; Irrigation Asn; Sigma Xi. **Research Statement & Publications:** Sprinkle and trickle irrigation; socio-technical assistance for transferring irrigation technologies worldwide; improving irrigated agriculture in developing countries; author of 85 technical papers, 15 articles and 6 books. **Mailing Address:** Keller-Bliesner Eng, 78 E Ctr St, Logan, UT 84321. **Fax:** 435-753-6139. **E-Mail:** jkeller@kelbli.com

KELLER, JAIME, MATERIALS SCIENCE, PHYSICS & CHEMISTRY. **Personal Data:** b Mexico, DF, Mex, November 10, 1936; m 1967, c 3. **Education:** Nat Autonomous Univ Mex, Chem Eng, 1959; Univ Bristol, UK, PhD (physics), 1972. **Honors & Awards:** Nat Prize Chem, Chem Soc Mex, 1980; Nat Award Chem Sci, Mex Fed Govt, 1982; Jose Gomez-Ibanez Lectr, Wesleyan Univ, 1982. **Professional Experience:** DEAN, HIGHER STUDIES FAC, 1989-; mem vd, Mex Nat Res Syst & fel, 1984-; dir, Fac Study, Super Cuauthlan, Nat Automous Univ Mex; HEAD, DEPT THEORET CHEM, 1974-; res visitor, Fed Polytech Inst, Zurich, 1973- & Univ Geneve; PROF THEORET PHYSICS, NAT AUTONOMOUS UNIV MEX, 1972-; Fac, IBM Res Lab, San Jose, Calif, 1972; res fel physics, Univ Bristol, UK, 1970-1971; tech dir chem process, Der Macrochem, 1963-1969; res engr chem physics, Indust Chem Pennsalt, 1959-1963. **Memberships:** Am Phys Soc; Chem Soc Mex; Mex Soc Physics; Ital Soc Physics; Mex Acad Sci Invest; Europ Acad Art & Sci. **Research Statement & Publications:** Chemistry and physics of condensed matter especially of metals in the liquid, amorphous and crystalline state; fundamental theory behind chemistry and physics; foundations of quantum and elementary particles theory. **Mailing Address:** Col Fuente de la Juventud, Mexico City DF 11000, Mex.

KELLER, JEFFREY THOMAS, NEUROANATOMY, NEUROSURGICAL RESEARCH. **Personal Data:** b Cincinnati, Ohio, October 17, 1946; m 1976, Adele; c Jocelyn & Susan. **Education:** Univ Cincinnati, BA, 1969, MS, 1972, PhD (anat), 1975. **Honors & Awards:** Distinguished Teacher Res Award, Col of Med, Univ Cincinnati; 1986. **Professional Experience:** Dir, Neurosurg Residency Training Prog, 1991-; RES PROF NEUROSURG & ADJ PROF ANAT, COL MED, UNIV CINCINNATI, 1990-; DIR, DIV NEUROSURG EDUC, DEPT NEUROSURG, COL MED, UNIV CINCINNATI, 1989-; Co-dir, Goodyr Microsurgery Lab, 1988-; res assoc prof neurosurg, Col Med, Univ Cincinnati, 1984-1990; dir, Div Neurosurg Res, dept neurosurg 1984-1989; adj assoc prof, Col Med, Univ Cincinnati, 1979-; Instr, Neuroanat, 1979-1980; NIH fel, Uniformed Serv Univ, 1978-1980; fel, Col Med, Univ Cincinnati, 1978, 1979-1980; dir Neuroanat res, mayfield neurol inst, 1975-; adj asst prof anat, Col Med, Univ Cincinnati, 1975-1979; asst anat, Col Med, 1971-1975; asst biol, Univ Cincinnati, 1969-1971. **Memberships:** Sigma Xi; fel Am Heart Asn; Am Asn Anatomists; Soc Neuroscience; NAm Skull Base Soc Int Headache Soc; Am Asn Study of Headache; Int Brain Res orgn; Frank H Mayfield Soc. **Research Statement & Publications:** Surgical anatomy of the skull base Post-operative cicatrix and the spinal dura; spinal dura repair; basal ganglia; trigeminal system; cephalgias; facial neuralgias; cranial nerves and their brainstem circuitry; applying state of the art neuroanatomical tract tracing techniques and immunocytochemistry to examine the neuronal circuitry of cranial nerves involved with cerebral vasculature including the dura mater and cephalgias. **Mailing Address:** Dept Neurosurg, Univ Cincinnati Col Med, 231 Albert Sabin Way Rm 4313, Cincinnati, OH 45267-0515. **Fax:** 513-558-7702. **E-Mail:** jkeller@mayfieldclinic.com

KELLER, JOSEPH BISHOP, MATHEMATICS. **Personal Data:** b Paterson, NJ, July 31, 1923; m 1963, c 2. **Education:** NY Univ, BA, 1943, MS, 1946, PhD (math), 1948. **Honorary Degrees:** Dr (tech), Tech Univ, Copenhagen, 1977; PhD, Univ Crete, 1993; DSc, NY Univ, 2002. **Honors & Awards:** Gibbs Lectr, Am Math Soc; Von Karman Prize, Soc Ind Appl Math; Timoshenko Medal, Am Soc Mech Eng; Hedric Lectr, Math Asn Am; Von Neuman Lectr, Soc Ind Appl Math; Wolf Found Prize Math, 1997; nat Medal of sci, 1988; nat acad of sci Award in applied math & numerical analysis, 1995; Frederic Esser Nemmers prize in math, Northwestern univ, 1996. **Professional Experience:** EMER PROF MATH, STANFORD UNIV, 1993-; hon prof math sci, Univ Cambridge, 1989-1993; prof, Stanford Univ, 1979-1993; vis scholar, Calif Inst Technol, 1973-1974; res assoc, Woods Hole Oceanog Inst, 1969-; vis prof, Stanford Univ, 1969-1970 & 1976-1978; chmn dept, NY Univ, 1967-1973; dir, Div Electromagnetic Res, Courant Inst Math Sci, 1966-1979; prof, NY Univ, 1956-1979; head, Math Br, Off Naval Res, 1953-1954; assoc res prof, NY Univ, 1952-1956; asst prof, NY Univ, 1948-1952; Lectr, Grad Sch, Stevens Inst Technol, 1948; asst, Wash Sq Col, 1946-1947; mathematician, Inst Math & Mech, 1945-1952; asst, Div War Res, Columbia Univ, 1944-1945; Instr physics, Princeton Univ, 1943-1944; consult, var indust & govt concerns. **Memberships:** Nat Acad Sci; Am Phys Soc; Am Math Soc; Soc Indust & Appl Math (vpres, 1978-1979); Am Acad Arts & Sci; Royal Soc London. **Research Statement & Publications:** Applied mathematics; acoustics; electromagnetic theory; fluid dynamics; geometrical optics. **Mailing Address:** Dept Math, Stanford Univ, Stanford, CA 94303-2125.

KELLER, JOSEPH EDWARD, APPLIED MECHANICS & MECHANICAL ENGINEERING, RESEARCH ADMINISTRATION & TECHNICAL MANAGEMENT. **Personal Data:** b La Crosse, Wis, March 31, 1936; m 1974, Eleanor; c Lowrey Evan & Andrew Joseph. **Education:** Swarthmore Col, BS, 1958; Univ Kans, MS, 1960, PhD (eng mech), 1964. **Professional Experience:** RETIRED; asst assoc dir defense systs, SIS Prog, 1989-1996; proj mgr, SIS Prog, 1986-1989; div leader, Lasers Prog, 1977-1987; dep div leader, Lawrence Livermore Nat Lab, 1974-1977; dep leader weapons prog, Lawrence Livermore Nat Lab,

1974; engr, Lawrence Livermore Nat Lab, 1964-1974. **Memberships:** Am Soc Mech Engrs; Sigma Xi; AAAS. **Research Statement & Publications:** Development and implementation of numerical techniques. **Mailing Address:** 786 Mirador Ct, Pleasanton, CA 94566.

KELLER, JOSEPH HERBERT, PHYSICAL CHEMISTRY. **Personal Data:** b Bristol, Va, September 25, 1946; m 1969, c 2. **Education:** King Col, BS, 1968; Univ Ill, Urbana, MS, 1970, PhD (phys chem), 1974. **Professional Experience:** INDEPENDENT CONSULT, CATALYSIS & PLATINUM METAL SALTS, 1994-; mgr catalysts develop, Johnson Matthey, 1992-1995; mgr, mgr plant & Dept Catalysts, 1985-1992; mgr, Catalyst Dept, Met-Pro Corp, 1980-1985; sr res assoc, Oxy-Catalyst, Inc, 1977-1980; res assoc catalysis, Oxy-Catalyst Inc, 1975-1977; res assoc & NSF fel chem, Univ Tenn, Knoxville, 1973-1975. **Memberships:** Am Chem Soc; Sigma Xi; Catalysis Club; Org Reactions Catalysis Soc. **Research Statement & Publications:** Heterogeneous catalysis; kinetic isotope effects of hydrogen and carbon; vapor pressure isotope effects; surface and media effect on reaction rates; wastewater analysis and treatment; catalyst manufacturing; nitrogen-oxygen catalyst; woodstove catalyst; volatile organic compound and polycyclic organic matter catalyst abatement, testing and manufacture; hydrogenation reactions involving supported catalysts phosphoglucomutase catalysts. **Mailing Address:** 522 N Md Ave, West Chester, PA 19380. **Fax:** 610-4364374. **E-Mail:** jhkeller@bellatlantic.net

KELLER, KENNETH F, microbiology; deceased, see previous edition for last biography

KELLER, KENNETH H(ARRISON), SCIENCE POLICY. **Personal Data:** b New York, NY, October 19, 1934; m 1981, c 4. **Education:** Columbia Univ, BA, 1956, BS, 1957; Johns Hopkins Univ, MSE, 1963, PhD (chem eng), 1964. **Honors & Awards:** Food, Pharmaceut & Bioeng Award, Am Inst Chem Engrs, 1980. **Professional Experience:** CHARLES M DENNY JR PROF & CHMN, SCI & TECHNOL POLICY, HUBERT H HUMPHERY INST PUBLIC AFFAIRS, UNIV MINN, as of 2004; sr vpres, Coun Foreign Rels, Ny, 1993-1995; philip d reed sr fel sci & technol, Coun Foreign Rels, Ny, 1990-1996; vis fel, Woodrow Wilson Sch Pub & Int Affairs, Princeton Univ, 1988-1990; pres, dept chem eng & mat sci, Univ Minn, 1985-1988; vpres acad affairs, Dept Chem Eng & Mat Sci, Univ Minn, 1980-1984; head, Dept Chem Eng & Mat Sci, Univ Minn, 1978-1980; Sigma Xi nat lectr, 1978-1979; mem surg & Bioengineering study sect, NIH, 1976-1980; actg dean, Grad Sch, Univ Minn, 1974-1975; assoc dean, grad sch, Univ Minn, 1973-1974; NIH spec fel, 1972-1973; PROF CHEM ENG, UNIV MINN, MINNEAPOLIS, 1972-; chmn biomed eng prog, Univ Minn, 1971-1973; from asst prof to assoc prof chem eng, Univ Minn, 1964-1971; engr, Div Reactor Develop, AEC, Wash, DC, 1957-1961. **Memberships:** Am Inst Chem Engrs; Am Soc Artificial Internal Organs; Am Inst Med & Biol Eng. **Research Statement & Publications:** Transport phenomena in biological systems; artificial internal organ development. **Mailing Address:** Hubert H Humphery Inst Public Affairs, Univ Minn, 301 19th Ave S, 248 Humphrey Ctr, Minneapolis, NJ 55455. **E-Mail:** kkeller@hhh.umn.edu

KELLER, LAURA R, CELL BIOLOGY, DEVELOPMENTAL BIOLOGY. **Education:** Univ Va, PhD, 1980. **Professional Experience:** ASSOC PROF BIOL, FLA STATE UNIV, as of 2003; asst prof biol, Fla State Univ, beginning 1986. **Memberships:** Am Soc Cell Biol; Soc Develop Biol. **Mailing Address:** Dept Biol Sci, Fla State Univ, Tallahassee, FL 32306-3050. **Fax:** 850-644-0481. **E-Mail:** lkeller@bio.fsu.edu

KELLER, MARGARET AGNELLO, HEMATOLOGIC DISEASES RESEARCH, DNA ANALYSIS CORE FACILITY. **Personal Data:** b Rockville Center, NY, August 15, 1966; m 1990, Grant. **Education:** Rutgers State Univ, NJ, BA, 1988; Univ Pa, PhD (molecular biol), 1994. **Honors & Awards:** NIH; Comprehensive Sickle Cell Center Scholar's Award, 2003. **Professional Experience:** ASST PROF, DEPT MED, UNIV JEFFERSON, 2000-; res scientist & core dir, dupont hosp c, 1996-2000; admin dir, Core Facil, Children's Hosp Philadelphia, 1995-1996; postdoctoral fel, DuPont Merck Pharm Co, 1994-1995. **Memberships:** AAAS; Am Soc hemat; Am Soc Human Genetics; Assoc Biomolecular Resource Facilities; Genetic Alliance. **Research Statement & Publications:** Molecular approaches to thetreatment of sickle cell anemia and other hematologic disorders affecting children. **Mailing Address:** 1015 Walnut St, Philadelphia, PA 19107. **E-Mail:** margaret.keller@jefferson.edu

KELLER, MARGARET ANNE, INFECTIOUS DISEASES, PEDIATRIC AIDS. **Personal Data:** b Boston, Mass, May 29, 1947; m 1971, Robert; c 2. **Education:** Mass Inst Technol, SB, 1968; Albert Einstein Col Med, MD, 1972. **Professional Experience:** PROF PEDIAT, HARBOR-UNIV CALIF LOS ANGELES MED CTR, as of 2001; ACTG CHIEF PEDIAT INFECTIOUS DIS, DEPT PEDIAT, HARBOR-UNIV CALIF LOS ANGELES MED CTR, as of 2001; DIR, PROG PEDIAT ACQUIRED IMMUNE DEFICIENCY SYNDROME, 1991-; assoc prof pediat, Harbor-Univ Calif, Los Angeles Med Ctr, beginning 1985; asst prof, Dept Pediat, 1978-1985; fel immunol & infectious dis, Dept Pediat, 1976-1978; fel infectious dis, Dept Pediat, 1975-1976; chief resident, Med Ctr, Univ Calif, San Diego, 1975; From intern to resident pediat, Med Ctr, Univ Calif, San Diego, 1972-1975. **Memberships:** Fel Am Acad Pediat; Am Fedn Clin Res; Soc Pediat Res; Am Phys Soc; Am Soc Microbiol; fel Infectious Dis Soc Am; Am Asn Immunol. **Research Statement & Publications:** Pediatric AIDS; magnetic resonance spectroscopy of the brain, cerebral metabolites in HIV-infected children. **Mailing Address:** Harbor-UCLA Med Ctr, 100 W Carson St, N-25, Box 468, Torrance, CA 90509. **Fax:** 310-320-2271. **E-Mail:** keller@labiomed.org

KELLER, MARTIN DAVID, EPIDEMIOLOGY. **Personal Data:** b New York, NY, April 7, 1923; m 1953, c 3. **Education:** Yeshiva Univ, BA, 1944; NY Univ, MS, 1946, PhD (biol), 1953; Cornell Univ, MD, 1952; Columbia Univ, MPH, 1958. **Professional Experience:** PROF EMER PUB HEALTH, OHIO STATE UNIV, 1992-; head div community health, Ohio State Univ, 1967-1992; prof prev med, Ohio State Univ, 1966-1992; head div epidemiol & biomet, Ohio State Univ, 1966-1967; consult, Ohio Dept Health, 1964-; asst prof med, Ohio State Univ, 1962-1966; assoc prof prev med, Ohio State Univ, 1962-1966; dir clin serv, Beth Israel Hosp, Boston, Mass, 1960-1962; Lectr, Harvard Med Sch, 1960-1962; dir res training, Ohio Dept Health, 1958-1960; actg dir chronic dis div, Ohio Dept Health, 1957-1958; resident med serv, Columbia Univ, 1957; med resident internal med, Vet Admin Hosp, Ny, 1955-1956; Intern pediat, Ny Hosp-Cornell Med Ctr, 1952-1953. **Memberships:** Am Pub Health Asn; Am Col Prev Med; NY Acad Sci. **Research Statement & Publications:** Environmental and host factors affecting distribution of human disease entities. **Mailing Address:** Dept Prev Med, Ohio State Univ Med Ctr 320 W Tenth Ave, Columbus, OH 43210-1236. **E-Mail:** keller.1@osu.edu

KELLER, OSWALD LEWIN, ACTINIDES, SPECTROSCOPY. **Personal Data:** b New York, NY, May 24, 1930; m Dona; c Christopher, Claire (Ohshiro), Elaine (Roberts) & Elizabeth. **Education:** SewaneeUniv the South, BS, 1951; Mass Inst Technol, PhD (phys chem), 1959. **Honors & Awards:** Exchange Scientist, US Nat Acad Sci & Acad Sci USSR, 1972; Invited Speaker, Robert A Welch Found, 1969, 1975, 1978. **Professional Experience:** RETIRED; dir, Transuranium Res Lab, 1967-1974 & 1984-1990 & Chem Div, 1974-1984; Mem nuclear physics panel, Physics Surv Comt, Nat Acad Sci, 1969-1972; chemist, Oak Ridge Nat Lab, 1960-1967; USPHS res fel, MIT, 1959-1960; fel, Rockefeller Found, MIT, 1951. **Research Statement & Publications:** Physical chemistry of proteins; chemistry of transuranium elements; molecular spectroscopy; preparation and characterization of compounds; heavy ion reactions; administration of nuclear and chemical research. **Mailing Address:** 734 Peachtree Hills Circle, Atlanta, GA 30305. **E-Mail:** olewk@bellsouth.net

KELLER, PATRICIA J, BIOCHEMISTRY. **Personal Data:** b Detroit, Mich, November 16, 1923. **Education:** Univ Detroit, BS, 1945; Wash Univ, PhD (biochem), 1953. **Professional Experience:** CHMN ORAL BIOL, SCH DENT, UNIV WASH, 1979-; vis fel, Inst Marine Biochem, Aberdeen, Scotland, 1978-1979; assoc dean, Grad Sch, 1974-1977; PROF ORAL BIOL, SCH DENT, UNIV WASH, 1967-; assoc prof, Sch Dent, 1962-1967; res asst prof, Sch Med, 1957-1962; instr, Sch Med, 1956-1957; res assoc biochem, Sch Med, 1955-1956; USPHS fels, Wash Univ, 1953-1954 & Univ Wash, 1954-1955. **Memberships:** AAAS; Am Soc Biol Chem; Am Soc Cell Biol; Am Chem Soc; Int Asn Dent Res. **Research Statement & Publications:** Structure, function and biosynthesis of enzyme proteins. **Mailing Address:** Dept Oral Biol, Univ Wash Sch Dent, SB22, Seattle, WA 98195-0001.

KELLER, PHILIP CHARLES, INORGANIC CHEMISTRY. **Personal Data:** b San Francisco, Calif, March 10, 1939; m 1965. **Education:** Univ Calif, Berkeley, BA, 1961; Ind Univ, PhD (boron chem), 1966. **Professional Experience:** PROF CHEM, UNIV ARIZ, 1975-; from asst prof to assoc prof, 1966-1975. **Memberships:** Am Chem Soc; Royal Soc Chem. **Research Statement & Publications:** Boron hydride chemistry; chemistry of Group III elements. **Mailing Address:** Dept Chem, Univ Ariz, Old Chemi 216A PO Box 210041 1306 E Univ Blvd, Tucson, AZ 85721-0002. **Fax:** 520-621-8407. **E-Mail:** kellerp@email.arizona.edu

KELLER, PHILIP JOSEPH, PHYSICAL CHEMISTRY. **Personal Data:** b New Brunswick, NJ, September 21, 1941; m 1963, c 2. **Education:** Temple Univ, AB, 1964, PhD (phys chem), 1970. **Professional Experience:** MGR PROCUREMENT PROCESS, SOURCING, E I DU PONT DEL NEMOURS & CO, 1991-; mgr eng procurement, Mat & Logistics Dept, 1989-1991; mgr imaging med & electronics purchasing, Mat & Logistics Dept, 1984-1989; regional mgr, Indust Chem Dept, 1982-1984; sr purchasing agt, Indust Chem Dept, 1979-1982; purchasing agt, Indust Chem Dept, 1976-1979; planning specialist, Indust Chem Dept, 1975-1976; mkt res specialist, E I Du Pont Del Nemours & Co, 1975; prod technologist, E I Du Pont Del Nemours & Co, 1973-1974; develop rep, E I Du Pont Del Nemours & Co, 1971-1972; res chemist, E I Du Pont Del Nemours & Co, 1969-1972; Adj asst prof, Temple Univ, 1969-1970; Sr anal chemist, Merck Sharp & Dohme Res Labs, Pa, 1964-1966. **Memberships:** Am Chem Soc. **Research Statement & Publications:** Waste water chemistry; fused salts; electrochemistry; polyelectrolytes; surface chemistry. **Mailing Address:** E I du Pont de Nemours & Co, Sourcing B-8342-5, Wilmington, DE 19898-0001.

KELLER, R KENNEDY, BIOCHEMISTRY. **Personal Data:** b New Rochelle, NY, October 15, 1945. **Education:** Fla Atlantic Univ, BS, 1968; Vanderbilt Univ, PhD (biochem), 1973. **Professional Experience:** PROF CHEM, UNIV SFLA COL MED, 1989-; assoc prof 1982-1989; fel chem, Baylor Col Med, 1975-1980; NIH Career Develop award. **Memberships:** AAAS; Am Soc Biochem & Molecular Biol; NY Acad Sci. **Research Statement & Publications:** Biochemistry. **Mailing Address:** Dept Biochem Univ SFla Col Med, 12901 Bruce B Downs Blvd MDC 87 Box 7, Tampa, FL 36612-4742. **Fax:** 813-974-7357. **E-Mail:** rkeller@hsc.usf.edu

KELLER, RAYMOND E, DEVELOPMENTAL BIOLOGY, CELL BIOLOGY. **Personal Data:** b Cape Girardeau, Mo, May 25, 1945; c 2. **Education:** Southeast Mo State Univ, BS, 1967; Univ Ill, Urbana, MS, 1969, PhD (develop), 1975. **Professional Experience:** PROF & CHMN BIOL, UNIV VA, as of 2004; ASSOC PROF, DEPT ZOOL, UNIV CALIF, BERKELEY, 1980-; vis scientist, Univ Ind, 1977-1980; assoc, Am Cancer Soc fel, 1976-1977; Assoc, Lab Prof J P Trinkaus, Dept Biol, Univ Yale, 1975-1976. **Memberships:** Soc Cell Biol; Soc Zool. **Research Statement & Publications:** Analysis of the mechanisms of metazoan morphogenetic cell movements; Published ove 10 articles. **Mailing Address:** Dept Biol Univ Va, PO Box 400328 Rm 241 Gilmer Hall, Charlottesville, VA 22904-4328. **Fax:** 434-982-5626. **E-Mail:** rek3k@virginia.edu

KELLER, REED THEODORE, GASTROENTEROLOGY, INTERNAL MEDICINE. **Personal Data:** b Aberdeen, SDak, May 26, 1938; m 1959, c 3. **Education:** Univ NDak, BA, 1960, BS, 1961; Harvard Med Sch, MD, 1963; cert, Am Bd Internal Med, 1966 & 1977; cert, Am Bd Gastroenterol, 1975. **Honors & Awards:** Physicians Recognition Award, AMA, 1988; Laureate Award, Am Col Physicians. **Professional Experience:** Mem, NDak State Bd Med Examrs, 1987-; mem, Nat Bd Med Examrs, 1984-1988; consult gastroenterol, Fargo Vet Admin Hosp, 1974-1975 & 1976-; CHIEF MED, MED CTR REHAB HOSP, 1974-; chief med, Fargo Vet Admin Hosp, 1974-1976; vis prof med, Univ Guadalajara, 1974; grant, Univ NDak, 1973-; PROF MED & CHMN DEPT, SCH MED, UNIV NDAK, 1973-; Fel gastroenterol, Vet Admin grant, 1972-1973; asst prof, Med Sch, Case Western Reserve Univ, 1970-1973; chief resident, Univ Hosp, Cleveland, 1967-1968; Fel gastroenterol, Vet Admin Hosp, Cleveland, 1966-1967; From intern to resident med, Univ Hosp, Cleveland, 1963-1966. **Memberships:** Am Soc Gastrointestinal Endoscopy; Soc Exp Biol & Med; AMA; fel Am Col Gastroenterol; fel Am Col Physicians. **Research Statement & Publications:** Use of acrylic polymers to control gastrointestinal hemorrhage. **Mailing Address:** 4919 Belmont Rd, Grand Forks, ND 58201.

KELLER, RICHARD ALAN, ANALYTICAL CHEMISTRY. **Personal Data:** b Pittsburgh, Pa, November 28, 1934; m 1956, Mary; c Natalie, Bruce & Alan. **Education:** Allegheny Col, BS, 1956; Univ Calif, Berkeley, PhD (phys chem), 1961. **Honors & Awards:** Anal Chem Award for Spectrochem Anal, Am Chem Soc, 1993; Lester Strock Award, Soc Appl Spectros, 1996. **Professional Experience:** FEL, LOS ALAMOS NAT LAB, 1983-; STAFF MEM CHEM, LOS ALAMOS NAT LABS, 1976-; staff mem, Div Phys Chem, Nat Bur Stand, 1963-1976; asst prof chem, Univ Ore, 1959-1963. **Memberships:** Am Chem Soc. **Research Statement & Publications:** Laser induced chemistry; laser induced isotope enrichment; laser based analytical techniques. **Mailing Address:** Los Alamos Nat Lab, PO Box 1663, Los Alamos, NM 87545. **Fax:** 505-665-3024. **E-Mail:** keller@lanl.gov

KELLER, ROBERT B, MECHANICAL ENGINEERING. **Personal Data:** b Wichita, Kans, November 8, 1924; m 1952, c 2. **Education:** Univ Wichita, BS, 1948; Univ Mich, MS, 1951, PhD (mech eng), 1962. **Professional Experience:** ASSOC PROF EMER MECH ENG, UNIV MICH, ANN ARBOR, as of 2005; assoc prof mech eng, Univ Mich, Ann Arbor, beginning 1962; supvr turbine engines, Allison Div, Gen Motors Corp, 1954-1959; res engr, NAm Aviation, Inc, 1951-1954; consult, Ford Motor Co, Babcock & Wilcox, Clark Equip Co, Navistar Corp. **Memberships:** AAAS; Am Soc Mech Engrs; Am Inst Aeronaut & Astronaut; Soc Automotive Engrs. **Research Statement & Publications:** Rocket propulsion systems; gas turbine technology; fluid control systems; micro-processor real-time control. **Mailing Address:** Univ Mich, Dept Mech Eng, 2026 GGB, Ann Arbor, MI 48109-2125. **E-Mail:** rbk@umich.edu

KELLER, ROBERT ELLIS, ANALYTICAL INSTRUMENTATION, SPECTROSCOPY. **Personal Data:** b Marshalltown, Iowa, January 10, 1923; wid, c James R & Karen L (Miller). **Education:** Univ Iowa, BA, 1947, MS, 1949, PhD (anal chem), 1951. **Professional Experience:** RETIRED; independent contractor & investr, St Louis Sci Ctr & NSF, 1990-1992; consult, 1986-1990; mgr appl technol, Monsanto Co, 1982-1986; mgr appl sci, Monsanto Co, 1969-1982; sect mgr, Monsanto Co, 1967-1969; from group leader to sr res group leader, Monsanto Co, 1955-1967; proj leader, Monsanto Co, 1954-1955; res chemist, Monsanto Co, 1952-1954; res chemist anal chem, Smith, Kline & French Labs, 1950-1952. **Memberships:** Am Chem Soc; Soc Appl Spectros. **Research Statement & Publications:** Analytical and physical chemistry-separation; characterization and measurement of chemical species by chromatography, spectroscopy, general instrumental and chemical techniques; on line process; process monitoring and control, computerized data management. **Mailing Address:** 10142 Glenfield Terr, St Louis, MO 63126-2348.

KELLER, ROBERT H, HEMATOLOGY, IMMUNOLOGY. **Personal Data:** b Brooklyn, NY, October 3, 1945; div, c Stacie, Chiara, Magan & Robert. **Education:** Fordham Univ, Bronx, BA, 1966, MS, 1966; Temple Univ, MD, 1970; Mayo Grad Sch Med, Minn, MS, 1976; Am Bd Internal Med, cert, 1974. **Professional Experience:** DIR RES, VIT IMMUNE INC, as of 2006; CHMN, CHIEF EXEC OFFICER & Co-FOUNDER, PHOENIX BIOSCIENCES, 1996-; FOUNDER, BIODORON, WILSON BODE CTR, 1995-; consult immunol & hemat, Health Prof Inc & Ctr Spec Immunol, 1994-1995; med dir & dir immune reconstitution prog, Ctr Spec Immunol, 1992-1995; pres & med dir, Wilson Bode Ctr, beginning 1987; assoc dir res & develop Coulter Immunol, 1986-1987; assoc dir res develop, Coulter Immunol, 1986-1987; Nat Cancer Inst, Food & Drug Admin IND, 1986-1987; co-prin investr, Hillman Found, 1985-1986; Nat Cancer Inst, NIH RR Shared Equip Prog, 1984-1986; Max Planck Inst Biochemie, Munich, 1984; clin investr, 1983-1986; vis prof, Wilford Hall Air Force Res Ctr, 1983; assoc prof immunol & flow cytometry 1982-1986; co-prin investr, Nat Inst Allergy & Infectious Dis, NIH, 1982-1986; clin investr, Zablocki Bet Admin Med Ctr, 1982-1986; assoc dir clin diag lab & med dir hemat immunol res, Chief Exec Officer & Dir Res, Immune Balance Technol, 1982-1986; vis prof, Univ Tex Med Br, 1982; Nat Cancer Inst, NIH, 1981-1986; vis prof, Univ Calif, 1981; dir immunol, Midwest Children's Cancer Ctr, Milwaukee Children's Hosp, 1980-1982; assoc prof, Dept Pediat, 1980-1982; vis prof, Univ Miss, 1980; vet admin career develop award res assoc, 1978-1981; res assoc & staff physician, Zablocki Bet Admin Med Ctr, 1978-1980; prin investr, Vet Admin Res, 1978-1980; asst prof hemat & oncol, Med Col Wis, 1977-1980; asst prof, Mayo Sch Med, 1977; Nat Arthritis Found fel, 1975-1978; fel & sr res fel immunol, Mayo Sch Med, 1974-1977; Mayo Found res fel, Mayo Grad Sch Med, 1974-1975; intern, resident & sr resident, Univ Rochester, 1970-1974. **Memberships:** Nat Acad Sci; Fel Am Col Physicians; Int Soc Hemat; Am Soc Hemat; Am Soc Immunol; AAAS; Soc Anal Cytol; Am Fed Clin Res; Am Soc Clin Path; NY Acad Sci. **Research Statement & Publications:** Basic and clinical research in immune regulation, specifically the development of new testing modalities and new therapeutic strategies and agents using immunologicprinciples to heat human diseases. **Mailing Address:** Biodoron, 5821 Hollywood Blvd, Hollywood, FL 33021. **Fax:** 305-672-7160.

KELLER, RODERICH, PHYSICS. **Education:** Univ Kiel, Ger, PhD (physics). **Professional Experience:** STAFF PHYSICIST & SR TEAM LEADER, SPALLATION NEUTRON SOURCE FRONT-END GROUP, E O LAWRENCE BERKELEY NAT LAB, as of 1998. **Mailing Address:** Spallation Neutron Source Front-End Group, E O Lawrence Berkeley Nat Lab, One Cyclotron Rd, Berkeley, CA 94720. **Fax:** 510-486-5788. **E-Mail:** r_keller@lbl.gov

KELLER, ROY FRED, MATHEMATICS, COMPUTER SCIENCE. **Personal Data:** b Cape Girardeau, Mo, April 3, 1927; m 1949, Eldora; c Clifford & Jana. **Education:** Southeast Mo State Univ, BS, 1950; Univ Mo, AM, 1958, PhD (math), 1962. **Honors & Awards:** Outstanding Amer Educator, 1972; Alumni Merit Award, Sotheast Missouri State Univ, 2001. **Professional Experience:** PROF EMER, COMPUT SCI & ENG, UNIV NEBR, 1990-; prof & chmn dept, Comput Sci & Eng, Univ Nebr, 1981-1990; prof, Iowa State Univ, 1971-1981; assoc prof math & comput sci, Iowa State Univ, 1967-1971; asst prof math & dir, Comput Ctr, 1962-1967; instr math, actg dir Comput Res Ctr, 1959-1962; instr math, Univ Mo Columbia, 1956-1957. **Memberships:** Asn Comput Mach; Inst Elec & Electronics Engrs. **Research Statement & Publications:** Iterative methods for solving systems of equations; programming and programming languages. **Mailing Address:** Dept Comput Sci & Eng, Ferguson Hall, Lincoln, NE 68588-0115.

KELLER, RUDOLF, ELECTROMETALLURGY, ELECTROCHEMISTRY. **Personal Data:** b Winterthur, Switz, December 27, 1933; American & Swiss citizen; m 1962, Elisabeth Langhard; c Andrea K & Eva S. **Education:** Kantonsschule Winterthur, Matura, 1952; Swiss Fed Inst Technol, Zuerich, dipl, 1956, DSc nat, 1960. **Professional Experience:** PRES, ELECTROSTRIP CORP, 1997-; SOLE PROPRIETOR, EMEC CONSULT, 1984-; staff scientist, Alcoa Labs, 1979-1983; group leader, Argonne Nat Lab, 1977-1979; group leader, Swiss Aluminium Ltd, 1970-1977; mem tech staff, Rocketdyne Div, Rockwell Int, 1963-1970; Scientist, Stanford Res Inst, 1961-1963. **Memberships:** Int Soc Electrochem (treas, 1976-1979); Electrochem Soc; Minerals, Metals & Mat Soc; Am Chem Soc; Space Studies Inst; Soc of Protective Coatings (SSPC). **Research Statement & Publications:** Research and consulting in electrometallurgy, electrochemistry and related areas; principal investigator on government funded research, and development efforts on topics such as electrochemical processes to utilize lunar resources, neodymium oxide electrolysis; cyanide formation in Hall-Heroult cells; metal hydride battery electrodes and paint removal from steel structures. **Mailing Address:** 4221 Roundtop Rd, Export, PA 15632.

KELLER, SAMUEL W, AERONAUTICS. **Education:** Univ MD, BSc; George Wash Univ, BL. **Honors & Awards:** NASA Distinguished Serv Medal, 1985; Presidential Rank Distinguished Exec Medal, 1985. **Professional Experience:** ASSOC ADMINR, SPACE SCI & APPLN, as of 2001. **Mailing Address:** NASA Space Sci Ctr, Suite 1M32, Washington, DC 20546. **Fax:** 202-358-3469.

KELLER, SEYMOUR PAUL, SOLID STATE PHYSICS. **Personal Data:** b New York, NY, July 5, 1922; m 1949, Peal; c Jan, David, Richard & Lisa. **Education:** Univ Chicago, BS, 1947, MS, 1948, PhD (chem, physics), 1951. **Professional Experience:** RETIRED; consult to dir res, Thomas J Watson Res Ctr, IBM Corp, 1972-1994; dir phys sci dept, Thomas J Watson Res Ctr, IBM Corp, 1966-1972; dir tech planning res, Thomas J Watson Res Ctr, IBM Corp, 1964-1966; mgr solid state physics & chem, Thomas J Watson Res Ctr, IBM Corp, 1962-1964; staff mem, Thomas J Watson Res Ctr, IBM Corp, 1953-1963; res assoc, Columbia Univ, 1952-1953; Du Pont fel chem, Univ Wis, 1951-1952. **Memberships:** Fel Am Phys Soc. **Research Statement & Publications:** Optical and electrical properties of dielectric and semiconducting solids; luminescent materials; paramagnetic resonance of solids; wave function calculations. **Mailing Address:** 29 Gary Dr, Chappaqua, NY 10514. **Fax:** 914-241-7366. **E-Mail:** skeller@us.ibm.com

KELLER, STANLEY E, dentistry; deceased, see previous edition for last biography

KELLER, STEPHEN JAY, MOLECULAR BIOLOGY, BIOCHEMISTRY. **Personal Data:** b Philadelphia, Pa, July 30, 1940; m 1962, Ching; c Lisa & Michele. **Education:** Univ Pa, AB, 1963; State Univ NY Stony Brook, PhD (biol), 1970. **Professional Experience:** Pres, The Lotus-Group Inc 1989-; consult biotechnol, Protatek Inc, Sperti Drug, MDH Labs, Arel Pharmaceut, Promega Corp & Hy-Gene Inc, 1984-; Grantee, Environ Protection Agency, 1980-1984; vis assoc prof microbiol, State Univ NY, Stony Brook, 1978-1979; ASSOC PROF BIOL, UNIV CINCINNATI, 1975-; NIHGrantee, 1975-1977; NSF Grantee, 1970-1978; asst prof, Univ Cincinnati, 1969-1975; Grantee, Am Cancer Soc, 1969-1971. **Memberships:** Sigma Xi; Am Soc Virol; AAAS; Am Chem Soc; Am Cancer Soc. **Research Statement & Publications:** Molecular biology of development and differentiation of animal cell cultures and viruses. **Mailing Address:** Dept Biol sci, Univ Cincinnati, ML006, Cincinnati, OH 45221-0006. **Fax:** 513-556-5299. **E-Mail:** kellersj@uc.edu

KELLER, TEDDY MONROE, POLYMER & ORGANIC CHEMISTRY, SYNTHETIC INORGANIC & ORGANOMETALLIC CHEMISTRY. **Personal Data:** b Parrottsville, Tenn, November 20, 1944; m 1988, Molly. **Education:** ETenn State Univ, BS, 1966; Univ SC, PhD (org chem), 1972. **Professional Experience:** RES CHEMIST POLYMER CHEM, NAVAL RES LAB, 1977-; chief chemist leather, A C Lawrence Leather Co, 1974-1975; fel, Univ Fla, 1972-1974; Nat Defense Educ Act fel, Univ SC, 1966-1969. **Memberships:** Am Chem Soc; Soc Aerospace Mat & Process Engrs. **Research Statement & Publications:** Monomer synthesis, polymerization, and unusual polymer properties such as exceptional thermal and oxidative stability of phthalonitrile resins and polyamides; electrical conductivity of infinite network, fully conjugated polymers; fluoropolymers; inorganic-organic hybrid polymers; ceramics. **Mailing Address:** Dept Navy, Naval Res Lab, Code 6127, Washington, DC 20375-5320.

KELLER, THOMAS C S, III, CYTOSKELETON. **Personal Data:** b June 20, 1950; c 1. **Education:** Univ Va, PhD, 1981. **Professional Experience:** ASSOC PROF BIOL SCI, FLA STATE UNIV, 1993-; asst prof, Fla State Univ, 1986-1992; asst prof biol, Wesleyan Univ, Conn, 1984-1986. **Memberships:** AAAS; Am Soc Cell Biol. **Research Statement & Publications:** Cell and molecular biology of the cytoskeleton. **Mailing Address:** Dept Biol Sci, Fla State Univ, Tallahassee, FL 32306-4370. **Fax:** 850-644-0481. **E-Mail:** tkeller@bio.fsu.edu

KELLER, TONY S, BIOMECHANICS, ORTHOPAEDIC BIOMECHANICS. **Personal Data:** b Salzburg, Austria, August 13, 1955; American citizen; m 1983, Sally; c Jeffrey S, Sarah E & Erin L. **Education:** Ore State Univ, BS (sci) & BS (eng), 1978, Univ Wash, MS, 1983; Vanderbilt Univ, PhD (mech eng), 1988. **Honors & Awards:** Young Scientist Award, Am Soc Biomech, 1987; Volvo Award Exp Studies, Int Soc Study Lumbar Spine, 1990. **Professional Experience:** PROF MECH ENG & ORTHOPAEDICS & REHAB, UNIV VT, 2002-; interim chair, dept mech eng, Univ Vt, 2000-2003; assoc prof mech eng & orthop & rehab, Univ Vt, 1995-2002; ASSOC DIR, BIOMED ENG PROG, UNIV VT, 1994-; prin investr, Whitaker Found, 1993-1996; prin investr, Nat Inst Chiropractic Res, 1993-1995; co-dir, Vt Space Grant Consortium, 1992-2003; asst prof mech eng & orthop & rehab, Univ Vt, 1991-1995; res asst prof orthop & mech eng, Vanderbilt Univ, 1988-1991; vis scientist, Sahlgren Hosp, Sweden, 1984; dir orthop biomech, Vanderbilt Univ, 1983-1991; res biomed engr, Veterans Admin Med Ctr, 1983-1991; res biomed engr, Veterans Admin Med Ctr, Seattle, Wash, 1981-1983; res asst, dept Bioengineering, Univ Wash, Seattle, 1979-1981. **Memberships:** Inst Elec & Electronics Engrs; Am Soc Biomech; Am Soc Mech Engrs; Orthop Res Soc; Europ Soc Biomech. **Research Statement & Publications:** Spine mechanics, material and structural properties of biologic tissues, orthopaedic implant-biomechanics and design, and skeletal growth and remodelling. **Mailing Address:** Dept Mech Eng, Univ Vt, 119 C Votey Bldg, Burlington, VT 05405-0156. **Fax:** 802-656-4441. **E-Mail:** tkeller@zoo.uvm.edu

KELLER, WALDO FRANK, VETERINARY SURGERY. **Personal Data:** b Hicksville, Ohio, April 13, 1929; m 1958, c 2. **Education:** Ohio State Univ, DVM, 1953; Mich State Univ, MS, 1961; Am Col Vet Ophthal, dipl. **Professional Experience:** RETIRED; prof, ophthal, Dept Small Animal Surg & Med, 1988-1997; actg dean, Mich State Univ, 1983-1984; assoc dean, Mich State Univ, 1979-1983 & 1984-1988; prof, researcher vet surg & med, Mich State Univ, 1970-1997; chmn, Dept Small Animal Surg & Med, 1968-1997; trainee, Div Ophthal, Sch Med, Stanford Univ, 1965-1966; from asst prof to assoc prof vet surg & med, Mich State Univ, 1961-1970; univ clin res grant, Mich State Univ, 1961-1965; instr, Mich State Univ, 1953-1955 & 1957-1961. **Memberships:** Am Asn Vet Clinicians; Am Soc Vet Ophthal; Am Col Vet Ophthalmologists. **Research Statement & Publications:** Veterinary ophthalmology; growth of cornea in tissue culture and pathology of eye tissues in evaluating surgical techniques. **Mailing Address:** 615 Baily St, East Lansing, MI 48823.

KELLER, WILLIAM EDWARD, QUANTUM PHYSICS. **Personal Data:** b Cleveland, Ohio, March 11, 1925; m 1961, c William Eric, Ann (Hinnen), Margaret & Amber (Archer). **Education:** Harvard Univ, AB, 1945, AM, 1947, PhD (chem), 1948. **Professional Experience:** RETIRED; asst div leader physics, Los Alamos Sci Lab, 1983-1987; chair, Appl Superconductivity Conf, 1979-1980; US/USSR comt superconducting power transmission, Pres Nixon's Sci Exchange Prog, 1972-1978; group leader cryogenics, 1970-1983; Nat Acad Sci/Nat Res Coun Panel to evaluate Nat Bur Standards, 1970-1976; vis scientist, Univ Sussex, England, 1967-1968; mem staff, Res Found, 1950-1970; assoc supvr mil sponsored res, Res Found, Ohio State Univ, 1948-1950. **Memberships:** Am Chem Soc; fel Am Phys Soc; fel Am Inst Chemists; Sigma Xi. **Research Statement & Publications:** Infrared spectroscopy; low temperature physics; liquid helium hydrodynamics; applications of superconductivity to electric power systems. **Mailing Address:** 1090 Old Taos Hwy, Santa Fe, NM 87501.

KELLERHALS, GLEN E, PHYSICAL CHEMISTRY. **Personal Data:** b Vinton, Iowa, September 29, 1945; m 1973, c 2. **Education:** Upper Iowa Col, BS, 1967; Okla State Univ, PhD (chem), 1974, Tulsa Univ, MBA, 1980. **Professional Experience:** Sect Dir, Sco Petrol Eng, Permian Basin, 1988; SPECIAL PROJ ENGR, CITIES SERV CO, 1981-; strategic planner, Cities Serv Co, 1980-1981; group leader, Cities Serv Co, 1977-1980; res chemist, Cities Serv Co, 1974-1977. **Memberships:** Am Chem Soc; Soc Petrol Engrs; Am Petrol Inst. **Research Statement & Publications:** Enhanced oil recovery. **Mailing Address:** 10908 Craigton Ct, Bakersfield, CA 93311.

KELLERMAN, MARTIN, PHYSICAL CHEMISTRY. **Personal Data:** b New York, NY, February 11, 1932; m Livia; c Kathryn Alene & David Scott. **Education:** Polytech Inst Brooklyn, BS, 1953; Univ Wash, PhD (chem), 1966. **Professional Experience:** PROF EMER CHEM, CALIF POLYTECH STATE UNIV, SAN LUIS OBISPO, as of 2004; assoc prof chem, Calif Polytech State Univ, San Luis Obispo, beginning 1968; NIH res traineeship, Univ Calif, San Diego, 1966-1968; Anal chemist, Continental Baking Co, 1958-1961. **Memberships:** AAAS. **Research Statement & Publications:** X-ray crystal structure analysis; structure of metal chelate compounds; circular dichroism studies on structure of molecules of biological interest. **Mailing Address:** Dept Chem, Coll Arts & Sci, Calif Polytech State Univ, San Luis Obispo, CA 93407-0001. **E-Mail:** mkellerm@calpoly.edu

KELLERMANN, KENNETH IRWIN, RADIO ASTRONOMY. **Personal Data:** b New York, NY, July 1, 1937; wid, c 1. **Education:** Mass Inst Technol, SB, 1959; Calif Inst Technol, PhD (physics & astron), 1963. **Honors & Awards:** Calif Inst Technol-Eastman Kodak Corp Eastman Kodak Prize, 1963; Rumford Prize, Am Acad Arts & Sci, 1970; Helen B Warner Prize, Am Astron Soc, 1971; B A Gould Prize, Nat Acad Sci, 1973. **Professional Experience:** RES PROF, UNIV VA, as of 2003; pres, 1982-1985; vpres, Comn 40, Int Radio Sci Union, 1979-1982; SR SCIENTIST, NAT RADIO ASTRON OBSERV, 1978-; dir, Max Planck Inst Radio Astron, 1977-1979; asst dir, Nat Radio Astron Observ, beginning 1977; adj prof, Univ Ariz, 1970-1973; scientist, Nat Radio Astron Observ, 1969-1977; res assoc, Calif Inst Technol, beginning 1969; lectr, Leiden Univ, beginning 1967; from asst scientist to assoc scientist, Nat Radio Astron Observ, 1965-1969; NSF fel, 1965-1966; res scientist, Radiophys Lab, Commonwealth Sci & Indust Res Orgn, 1963-1965; chmn, Comn J, US Nat Comt. **Memberships:** Nat Acad Sci; Am Astron Soc; Am Acad Arts & Sci; Int Astron Union; Int Radio Sci Union. **Research Statement & Publications:** Extragalactic radio sources; galaxies; quasars; cosmology; instrumentation. **Mailing Address:** Nat Radio Astron Observ, 520 Edgemont Rd, Charlottesville, VA 22902. **Fax:** 804-296-0278. **E-Mail:** kkellerm@nrao.edu

KELLERMEIER, JOHN K, MATHEMATICS. **Education:** Univ Toledo, BA, 1973, MS, 1973; Bowling Green State Univ, PhD (probability & statist), 1979. **Professional Experience:** PROF, TACOMA COMMUNITY COL, WA, as of 2005. **Mailing Address:** Tacoma Community Col, 6501 S 19th St., Tacoma, WA 98466. **Fax:** 253-566-6027.

KELLERSTRASS, ERNST JUNIOR, CIVIL ENGINEERING, GEOPHYSICS. **Personal Data:** b Peoria, Ill, January 9, 1933; m 1954, c 5. **Education:** Bradley Univ, BSCE, 1954; St Louis Univ, MS, 1962; George Washington Univ, MS, 1967. **Professional Experience:** CONSULT, SYSTECH CORP, 1997-; sr res scientist, Systs Res Lab, 1982-1997; civil engr environ, Sanit Landfills, Bowse Morner Testing Lab, Systech Corp, 1981-1982; civil engr, Sanit Landfills, Bowse Morner Testing Lab, Systech Corp, 1980-1981; Instr, Univ Dayton, 1979-1980; staff scientist, Advan Res Br, Foreign Technol Div, Wright-Patterson AFB, 1974-1979; chief planning, Remote Piloted Vehicle Syst Prog Off, Aeronaut Systs Div, 1971-1974; geophysicist, VELA Prog, 1967-1971; geophysicist, Electronic Syst Div, 1964-1966; asst staff meteorologist for environ eng, Weather Cent Japan, 1962-1964; analyst & forecaster, Weather Cent Japan, 1957-1960; aeronaut meteorologist, US Army Corps Engrs, 1955-1957; Engr, USAF, 1954-; Engr, US Army Corps Engrs, 1954. **Memberships:** Am Meteorol Soc; Am Geophys Union; Am Soc Civil Engrs; Sigma Xi. **Research Statement & Publications:** Meteorology, forecasting and environmental engineering; management of research in meteorological sensors, environmental effects, electric systems survivability-vulnerability, seismological instrumentation-field experiments and aeronautical systems; research and development management; geotechnical engineering; hydrology; environmental engineering. **Mailing Address:** 2547 Sugarloaf Ct, Dayton, OH 45434.

KELLETT, CLAUD MARVIN, RESEARCH ADMINISTRATION. **Personal Data:** b Memphis, Tenn, September 5, 1928; m 1948, Janice; c Claudia, Richard, Daniel & Cynthia. **Education:** Ga Inst Technol, BEE, 1950; Purdue Univ, MS, 1957. **Professional Experience:** RETIRED; prog mgt officer, NSF, 1972-1988; sr res scientist, Tyco Corp Technol Ctr, 1971; physicist, Electronics Res Ctr, NASA, 1966-1970; sr res physicist, Ion Physics Corp, 1965-1966; prod supvr transistor mfg, Crystalonics, Inc, 1964-1965; prod eng supvr, Sperry Semiconductor Div, Sperry Rand Corp, 1963-1964; develop engr, Semiconductor Div, Raytheon Co, 1962-1963; sr engr, Tex Instruments, Inc, 1956-1962; res test engr, Allison Div, Gen Motors Corp, 1950-1954. **Research Statement & Publications:** Electrical measurements, especially Hall and photoelectromagnetic effects of semiconductor materials; modificationof electrical properties of semiconductor materials by ion implantation. **Mailing Address:** 5203 Faraday Ct, Fairfax, VA 22032-2708.

KELLETT, JOHN M, MATHEMATICS. **Education:** Univ Fla, PhD (Maths), 1968. **Professional Experience:** PROF EMER MATH, GETTYSBURG COL, PA, as of 2005. **Memberships:** Math Asn Am. **Mailing Address:** Gettysburg Col, Dept Math, 300 N Wash St, Gettysburg, PA 17325. **Fax:** 717-337-6666.

KELLEY, ALBERT J(OSEPH), strategic management, technology investment; deceased, see previous edition for last biography

KELLEY, ALLEN FREDERICK, MATHEMATICS, FORESTRY. **Personal Data:** b Franklin, NH, July 1, 1933. **Education:** Mont State Univ, BS, 1955; Univ Calif, Berkeley, PhD (math), 1963. **Professional Experience:** PROF EMER MATH, UNIV CALIF, SANTA CRUZ, as of 2003; assoc prof math, Univ Calif, Santa Cruz, beginning 1969; asst prof, Univ Calif, Santa Cruz, 1966-1969; mem fac, Inst Advan Study, 1965-1966; partic, Exchange Prog, US Nat Acad Sci-USSR Acad Sci, 1964-1965; instr math, Univ Calif, Berkeley, 1963-1964. **Memberships:** Soc Am Foresters; Am Math Soc. **Research Statement & Publications:** Differential equations and celestial mechanics; wood technology and engineering. **Mailing Address:** Dept Math, Univ Calif, Santa Cruz, CA 95064-1099. **E-Mail:** blufox@cats.ucsc.edu

KELLEY, BENJAMIN S, BIOMEDICAL ENGINEERING. **Education:** Auburn Univ, BS; Univ Ky, MS; PhD. **Professional Experience:** ASSOC PROF ENG, MERCER UNIV, GA, as of 2005. **Mailing Address:** Biomed & Environ Eng Sch Eng, Mercer Univ 1400 Coleman Ave, Macon, GA 31207. **Fax:** 912-752-2166. **E-Mail:** kelley_bs@mercer.edu

KELLEY, C STUART, NUCLEAR PHYSICS, COMPUTATIONAL PHYSICS. **Education:** Union Col, BS, 1964; Univ Del, MS, 1966, PhD (solid state physics), 1970. **Professional Experience:** RETIRED; prog mgr, Defence Threat Reduction Agency, 1983-2005; phys scientist, Defense Intel Agency, 1980-1983; Physicist, Edgewood Arsenal, 1970-1973; Physicis, Harry Diamond Labs, 1976-1980; analyst, Gen Res Corp, 1973-1976. **Research Statement & Publications:** Optical properties of impurities in solids; combustion physics; optical properties of ocean layers; effects of nuclear weapons. **Mailing Address:** HQDSWA, 6801 Telegraph Rd, Alexandria, VA 22310-3398.

KELLEY, CARL T, MATHEMATICS. **Education:** Vanderbilt Univ, BA, 1973; Purdue Univ, PhD, 1976. **Professional Experience:** DREXEL PROF, DEPT MATHS, NC STATE UNIV, 2002-. **Mailing Address:** NC State Univ, Math Dept, PO Box 8205, Raleigh, NC 27607-8205. **Fax:** 919-515-3798. **E-Mail:** Tim_Kelley@ncsu.edu

KELLEY, CHARLES JOSEPH, SYNTHESIS OF FLUORESCENT COMPOUNDS. **Personal Data:** b Akron, Ohio, February 2, 1943; c Eurydice & Anthe. **Education:** St Joseph's Col, Ind, BA, 1964; Ind Univ, Bloomington, PhD (org chem), 1970. **Professional Experience:** ASSOC PROF CHEM, MASS COL PHARM & HEALTH SCI, 1983-; asst prof, Mass Col Pharm, 1977-1983; res assoc natural prod, Northeastern Univ, 1976-1977; asst prof chem, Ball State Univ, 1975-1976; res assoc org synthesis, Ind Univ, 1970-1975. **Memberships:** Am Chem Soc; Am Soc Pharmacog. **Research Statement & Publications:** Isolation from plant sources of potential pharmaceutical agents; synthesis of oligophenylenes and proton-transfer fluors as laser dyes and scintillators. **Mailing Address:** Dept Chem, Sch Arts & Sci, Mass Col Pharm & Health Sci, 179 Longwood Ave, Boston, MA 02115. **Fax:** 617-732-2801. **E-Mail:** charles.kelley@bos.mcphs.edu

KELLEY, CHARLES THOMAS, SYSTEMS ANALYSIS, PHYSICS. **Personal Data:** b Boston, Mass, February 9, 1940; m 1964, c 3. **Education:** Univ Notre Dame, BS, 1961; Univ Mass, MS, 1963; Ind Univ, PhD (nuclear physics), 1967. **Professional Experience:** DIR AIR FORCE, FORCE MODERIZATION & EMPLOYMENT PROG, RAND CORP, 1994-; from dir to sr phys scientist, Ground Warfare Prog, 1977-1994; phys scientist, Wash Defense Res Div, Rand Corp, Wash, DC, 1973-1977; analyst, Wash Defense Res Div, Rand Corp, Wash, DC, 1971-1973; physicist, Anal Serv Inc, Falls Church, Va, 1967-1971; res asst nuclear physics, Cyclotron Lab, Ind Univ, 1965-1967. **Memberships:** Am Phys Soc; Opers Res Soc Am; Sigma Xi. **Research Statement & Publications:** Weapon systems analysis; operations research; nuclear physics. **Mailing Address:** RAND Corp, 1700 Main St, PO Box 2138, Santa Monica, CA 90407-2138. **Fax:** 310-451-7065. **E-Mail:** kelley@rand.org

KELLEY, DARSHAN SINGH, DIET & IMMUNO-COMPETENCE, NUTRIENT REQUIREMENTS. **Personal Data:** b Ludhiana, Punjab, India, February 5, 1947; American citizen; m 1980, c 2. **Education:** Punjab Agr Univ Ludhiana, India, BSc, 1967, MSc, 1969; Okla Univ, PhD (biochem), 1974. **Professional Experience:** Adj Fac, Nutrit Dept, UC Davis, as of 2004; RES CHEMIST, PROJECT LEADER, DIETARY LIPIDS & HEALTH, WESTERN HUMAN NUTRIT RES CTR, 1990-; Agr Res Serv, USDA, 1996-; res Leader Bioenergetics, Western Human Nutrit Res Ctr, Agr Res Serv, USDA, 1990-1996; res chemist, Western Human Nutrit Res Ctr, Agr Res Serv, Usda, 1983-1990; asst prof, biochem, WVa Univ Med Ctr, 1980-1983; postdoctoral res assoc, McArdle Lab, Univ Wis, 1975-1980; consult, res, Okla Med Res Found, 1974-1975. **Memberships:** Am Instit Nutrit; Am Soc Biochem & Molecular Biol; AAAS; Sigma Xi. **Research Statement & Publications:** Nutritional regulation of immune-status in humans and animals; nutritional and hormonal regulation of hepatic gene expression; Long-term high copper intake: effects on indices of copper status, antioxidant status, and immune function in young men; author of various articles. **Mailing Address:** UC Davis W Human Nutrit Res Ctr, One Shields Ave, Davis, CA 95616. **Fax:** 530-752-8966. **E-Mail:** dkelley@whnrc.usda.gov

KELLEY, FRANK NICHOLAS, ADVANCED NON-METALLIC MATERIALS, SOLID ROCKET PROPELLANTS. **Personal Data:** b Akron, Ohio, January 19, 1935; m 1960, c 3. **Education:** Univ Akron, BS, 1958, MS, 1959, PhD (polymer chem), 1961. **Honors & Awards:** Rubber Age Award; Outstanding Tech Contrib Award, Am Inst Aeronaut & Astronaut. **Professional Experience:** Consult, NSF, beginning 1979; dept energy progs, Jet Propulsion Lab, Midwest Res Inst, Solar Energy Res Inst, beginning 1979; DEAN & PROF, INST POLYMER SCI, UNIV AKRON, 1978-; dir, Air Force Mat Lab, 1976-1978; chief scientist, Dept Defense, Wright-Patterson AFB, 1973-1976; chief scientist, Air Force Rocket Propulsion Lab, 1971-1973; chief advan plans, Air Force Rocket Propulsion Lab, 1970-1971; br chief solid rockets, Air Force Rocket Propulsion Lab, 1966-1970; res chemist, Air Force Rocket Propulsion Lab, 1964-1966; Chmn, Interagency Working Group Mech Behav, 1963-1965. **Memberships:** Assoc fel Am Inst Aeronaut & Astronaut; Am Chem Soc. **Research Statement & Publications:** Polymer physics; structure-property relationships of elastomersand thermosetting resins; mechanical properties of solid propellants. **Mailing Address:** Coll Polymer Sci & Polymer Eng, Univ Akron, Akron, OH 44325-3909. **Fax:** 330-972-5290. **E-Mail:** fkelley@uakron.edu

KELLEY, GAYNOR NATHANIEL, INSTRUMENTATION. **Personal Data:** b New Canaan, Conn, May 12, 1931; m 1974, Diane; c Gaynor Jr, Russell, Theodore, Ronald & Victoria. **Education:** Delehanty Inst, BSME, 1951. **Professional Experience:** RETIRED; chmn & chief exec officer, Perkin-Elmer Corp, 1990-2001; pres & chief oper officer, Perkin-Elmer Corp, 1985-1990; mgr, Perkin-Elmer Corp, 1951-1985. **Mailing Address:** 1801 Ponus Ridge, New Canaan, CT 06840-2524.

KELLEY, GEORGE GREENE, BIOLOGICAL CHEMISTRY. **Personal Data:** b Philadelphia, Pa, November 6, 1918; m 1947, c 4. **Education:** Fla State Univ, BS, 1950, MS, 1951, PhD (biochem, food, nutrit), 1956. **Professional Experience:** RETIRED; prof chem, Jacksonville Univ, 1967-1988; chmn div sci & math, Jacksonville Univ, 1964-1973; assoc prof chem, Jacksonville Univ, 1963-1967; guest lectr, Med & Dent Schs, 1961; instr, Exten Ctr, Univ Ala, 1959-1962; instr pharmacol, Howard Col, 1958-1961; sr biochemist, Southern Res Inst, 1957-1962; asst prof, Univ Mo, 1956-1957; tech res asst chem, Fla State Univ, 1952-1954. **Memberships:** AAAS; Am ChemSoc; Am Soc Limnol & Oceanog; NY Acad Sci; fel Am Inst Chemists. **Research Statement & Publications:** Study of the life cycle, the propagation and large scale cultivation of three species of the large fresh water shrimp, genus Macrobrachium. **Mailing Address:** 5353 Arlington Expy Apt 5a, Jacksonville, FL 32211.

KELLEY, GREGORY M, DESIGN ENGINEERING, VACUUM SYSTEM DESIGN. **Personal Data:** b Boston, Mass, November 18, 1933; m 1996, Karen; c Michael R, Gregory M & Alice A. **Education:** Wentworth Inst Technol, Boston, AEng, 1958 & 1965; Col Santa Fe, BCS, 1985. **Honors & Awards:** Award of Excellence, US Dept Energy, 1989. **Professional Experience:** INSTR VACUUM TECHNOL, UNIV NMEX, LOS ALAMOS, as of 2002; tech liaison, Icon Corp, Shreveport, La, 1995-1996; group criticality safety officer, Los Alamos Nat Lab, 1991-1993; sr prod technologist, Nuclear Weapons Diag, Los Alamos Nat Lab, 1989-1994; sr technologist, Nuclear Mat Mgt, 1989-1993; sr technologist, Nuclear Weapons Diag, Los Alamos Nat Lab, 1966-1989; sr technician, Avco Everett Res Lab, 1961-1966. **Memberships:** Soc Mfg Engrs. **Research Statement & Publications:** Automated measurement of radioactive samples by gamma and neutron counting and calorimetry; robotic applications; nuclear shielding; ionsource design vacuum system design; weapons diagnostics; nuclear criticality safety. **Mailing Address:** 1710-37th St, Los Alamos, NM 87544-2152. **E-Mail:** gmkelley@zianet.com

KELLEY, J, ENGINEERING. **Professional Experience:** PRES, CHIEF EXEC OFFICER & CHMN, MCDATA CORP, as of 2004. **Mailing Address:** McData Corp, 380 Interlocken Crescent, Broomfield, CO 80021. **Fax:** 720-558-3860.

KELLEY, JAMES CHARLES, OCEANOGRAPHY. **Personal Data:** b Los Angeles, Calif, October 5, 1940; m 1963, Susan; c Jason & Megan. **Education:** Pomona Col, BA, 1963; Univ Wyo, PhD (geol), 1966. **Honors & Awards:** Fellows' Medal, Calif Acad Sci, 2000. **Professional Experience:** Pres, Calif Acad Sci, 1986-1993; dean, Sci & Eng, San Francisco State Univ, 1975-2001; Fulbright prof, Univ Athens, 1971; From asst prof to assoc prof oceanog, Biomath & Geol Sci, Univ Wash, 1966-1975; DEAN & PROF EMER, SAN FRANCISCO STATE UNIV. **Memberships:** AAAS; Am Geophys Union; Pac Sci Cong; Am Soc Limnology & Oceanog; Oceanog Soc. **Research Statement & Publications:** Coastal upwelling; structural petrology; statistics; computer science. **Mailing Address:** PO Box 909, Montara, CA 94037. **E-Mail:** jkelley@sfsu.edu

KELLEY, JAMES LEROY, MEDICINAL CHEMISTRY. **Personal Data:** b San Diego, Calif, November 12, 1943; m 1967, c 3. **Education:** Fresno State Col, BS, 1967; Univ Calif, Santa Barbara, PhD (chem), 1970. **Professional Experience:** ASSOC DIR, DIV ORGANIC CHEM, KRENITSKY PHARMACEUT INC, 1991-; asst div dir, Burroughs Wellcome & Co, 1970-1990. **Memberships:** Am Chem Soc; AAAS; NY Acad Sci. **Research Statement & Publications:** Chemistry on purine, pyrimidine and imidazole heterocycles and antiviral agents especially acyclic nucleosides; design and synthesis of enzyme inhibitors and novel CNS active agents. **Mailing Address:** Krenitsky Pharmaceut Inc, Four Univ Pl, 4611 Univ Dr, Durham, NC 27707. **Fax:** 919-403-0456.

KELLEY, JASON, CELL BIOLOGY. **Personal Data:** b Buffalo, NY, September 8, 1943; m 1965, c 3. **Education:** Harvard Univ, AB, 1966; Univ Tex, Dallas, MD, 1972. **Professional Experience:** Prof, pulmonary dis sect, univ vt, 1988-1990; from asst prof to prof cell biol & med, Univ Vt, 1983-1988. **Memberships:** NY Acad Sci; Biochem Soc; Am Soc Cell Biol; Reticuloendothelial Soc; Am Thoracic Soc; AAAS. **Research Statement & Publications:** Cellular and molecular mechanisms of tissue remodelling in growth and disease. **Mailing Address:** Pulmonary Unit, Univ Vt, Col Med Given C-305, Burlington, VT 05405-0001. **Fax:** 802-656-3854. **E-Mail:** JASON.KELLEY.1@uvm.edu

KELLEY, JAY HILARY, MINING ENGINEERING, COMPUTER SCIENCE. **Personal Data:** b Greensburg, Pa, March 9, 1920; m 1949, c 9. **Education:** Pa State Univ, BS, 1942, MS, 1947, PhD, 1952. **Professional Experience:** DISTINGUISHED PROF EMER COL MINERAL & ENERGY RESOURCES, WVA UNIV, 1987-; chmn, Coal Mining Sect, Nat Safety Coun, Chicago, 1979-1980; distinguisehd prof, Col Mineral & Energy Resources, Wva Univ, 1978-1987; pres, Engrs Index, Inc, 1976-1978; dean, Col Mineral & Energy Resources, Wva Univ, 1970-1978; pres, Kelastic Mine Beam Co, Greensburg, 1969-1986; pres, Urbdata Inc, Pa, 1969-1980; dir, Engrs Index, Inc, 1969-1978; trustee, Engrs Index, Inc, 1967-1980; mgr comput & asst instr, Philco-Ford Corp, Pa, 1966-1969; prof info sci & assoc dir, Bur Info Sci Res, Rutgers Univ, 1965-1966; panel drug info, President's Sci Adv Comt, 1964-1966; staff scientist, Off Sci & Technol, Exec Off President, Wash, DC, 1962-1965; comt sci & technol info, Fed Coun Sci & Technol, 1962-1965; exec secy panel sci info, President's Sci Adv Comt, 1962-1963; sr engr, Westinghouse Elec Corp, 1957-1962; dir, Leonard Express, Inc, 1954-; sr res engr, Joy Mfg Co, Pa, 1952-1957; instr, Pa State Univ, 1949-1952; Vpres, Mammoth Coal & Coke Co, 1946-1954; Res asst, Pa State Univ, 1946-1949; chmn proj comt, Eng Found, New York; ptnr, Mining Eng Consult, Greensburg, Pa. **Memberships:** AAAS; Inst Elec & Electronics Engrs; Opers Res Soc Am; Am Soc Info Sci; Am Inst Mining Metall & Petrol Engrs; Am Mining Congress; Asn Comput Mach; Cosmos Club. **Research Statement & Publications:** Mine design; mineral resource economics; entropic systems; computer science and applications; mine roof control; machinery design and development; bulk handling; spontaneous combustion. **Mailing Address:** Col Mineral & Energy Resources, WVa Univ, PO Box 6201, Morgantown, WV 26506. **E-Mail:** jhilk@access.mountain.net

KELLEY, JIM LEE, BIOCHEMISTRY, CHEMISTRY. **Personal Data:** b Ada, Okla, October 20, 1947; m 1968, Louise; c 3. **Education:** Bethany Nazarene Col, BS, 1969; Univ Okla, PhD (biochem), 1973. **Professional Experience:** PROF, E TENN STATE UNIV, as of 2005; assoc prof, E Tenn State Univ, beginning 1994; asst prof, Univ Tex Health Sci Ctr, San Antonio, 1980-1993; grant, HEW Pub Health Serv, beginning 1978; grants, Am Heart Asn, Okla Affil Inc, 1976-1978; staff scientist med res, Okla Med Res Found, 1976-1979; fel, 1973-1976. **Memberships:** AAAS; Am Soc Cell Biol; Am Heart Asn; Am Soc Invest Path. **Research Statement & Publications:** Metabolism of plasma lipoproteins by macrophages; role of antioxidants in atherosclerosis. **Mailing Address:** Dept Internal Med, E Tenn State Univ Box 70622, Johnson City, TN 37614. **Fax:** 423-929-6459. **E-Mail:** kelleyj@etsu.edu

KELLEY, JOHN DANIEL, CHEMICAL PHYSICS. **Personal Data:** b Chicago, Ill, July 30, 1937; m 1960, Elizabeth McDermott; c John, James & Ann. **Education:** St Louis Univ, BS, 1959; Georgetown Univ, PhD (phys chem), 1964. **Honors & Awards:** St Louis award, Am chemical soc, 1996. **Professional Experience:** VISITING SCHOLAR, STANFORD UNIV, 2001-; chief scientist, McDonnell Douglas Res Labs, 1989-2001; prin scientist, McDonnell Douglas Res Labs, 1981-1989; adj prof, Dept Chem & Physics, Univ Mo, St Louis, 1977-; sr scientist, McDonnell Douglas Res Labs, 1973-1981; assoc scientist, McDonnell Douglas Res Labs, 1970-1973; res scientist, McDonnell Douglas Res Labs, 1967-1970; res fel, Brookhaven Nat Lab, 1964-1967; Res assoc theoret chem, Georgetown Univ, 1963-1964. **Memberships:** Am Chem Soc; Sigma Xi; AIAA, sr mem. **Research Statement & Publications:** Theoretical and experimental reaction kinetics; molecular quantum mechanics; inter-molecular energy transfer processes. **Mailing Address:** 13103 Gascogne Ct, St Louis, MO 63141. **Fax:** 775-618-1050. **E-Mail:** jdkelley@telocity.com

KELLEY, JOHN ERNEST, MATHEMATICS. **Personal Data:** b Milwaukee, Wis, June 27, 1919; m 1950, c 4. **Education:** Univ Wis, BS, 1941; Marquette Univ, MS, 1948; Univ Mich, PhD (math), 1960. **Professional Experience:** Chmn dept, Univ Sfla, 1966-1969; ASSOC PROF MATH, UNIV SFLA, 1964-; from instr to asst prof math & chmn dept, Marquette Univ, 1954-1964; analyst, US Dept Defense, 1953-1954; Instr math, Univ Miami, 1949-1951. **Memberships:** Math Asn Am; Nat Coun Teachers of Math. **Research Statement & Publications:** Mathematical logic. **Mailing Address:** 1120 Michigan Blvd, Dunedin, FL 34698-2711.

KELLEY, JOHN FRANCIS, biochemistry, academic administraton; deceased, see previous edition for last biography

KELLEY, JOHN FREDRIC, PSYCHIATRY. **Personal Data:** b Gay, WVa, September 17, 1931; m 1960, c 3. **Education:** Marietta Col, AB, 1954; McGill Univ, MD, 1958; Am Bd Psychiat & Neurol, cert psychiat, 1966, cert child psychiat, 1971. **Professional Experience:** PROF BEHAV MED, PSYCHIAT & PEDIAT, MED SCH, WVA UNIV, 1974-; dir child psychiat prog, Med Ctr, 1968-1983 & 1987-1990; assoc prof, Psychiat & Pediat, Med Sch, Wva Univ, 1968-1974; fel child psychiat, Worcester Youth Guid Ctr, Mass, 1966-1968; staff psychiatrist, Patuxent Inst, Md, 1964-1966; resident psychiat, Health Ctr, Ohio State Univ, 1959-1962. **Memberships:** Am Psychiat Asn; AMA; Am Acad Child Psychiat. **Research Statement & Publications:** Child psychiatry. **Mailing Address:** WVa Univ Med Ctr, Morgantown, WV 26506.

KELLEY, JOHN JOSEPH, II, OCEANOGRAPHY, METEOROLOGY. **Personal Data:** b Philadelphia, Pa, January 4, 1933; m 1970, Eleanor. **Education:** Pa State Univ, BS, 1958; Univ Nagoya, Japan, PhD (oceanog), 1974. **Professional Experience:** CHMN, N SLOPE BOR SCI ADV, as of 2003; VPRES, US CORP, ARCTIC INST N AM, as of 2003; PROF MARINE SCI, UNIV ALASKA, 1993-; dir, NSF Polar Ice Coring Off, 1989-; chmn, Sci Adv Comt, Northslope Borough/Alaska Eskimo Whaling Comn, 1980-; assoc prof, Naval Arctic Res Lab, 1980-1993; dir, Naval Arctic Res Lab, 1977-1980; prog mgr, NSF Off Polar Prog, 1974-1976; asst prof oceanog, Univ Alaska, 1973-1977; oceanogr, Univ Alaska, 1968-1973; sr scientist meteorol, Univ Wash, 1960-1968; prog mgr, Ocean/Meteoro, Div Polar Prog, NSF, Wash, DC. **Memberships:** Am Geophys Union; Am Soc Limnol & Oceanog; Am Polar Soc; Arctic Inst NAm; Sigma Xi. **Research Statement & Publications:** Exchange processes; polar ecosystems; coastal upwelling phenomena; air-sea exchange processes; ice coring-drilling technology. **Mailing Address:** Inst Marine Sci Univ Alaska, Rm 331 O'Neill Bldg, Fairbanks, AK 99775. **Fax:** 907-474-7204. **E-Mail:** ffjjk@uaf.edu

KELLEY, JOSEPH MATTHEW, POLYMER CHEMISTRY. **Personal Data:** b Baltimore, Md, December 10, 1929; m 1955, c 3. **Education:** Loyola Col, Md, BS, 1950; Fordham Univ, MS, 1952, PhD (chem), 1956; NY Univ, BSChE, 1966. **Professional Experience:** VPRES, MOJAVE RES & DEVELOP CO, 1984-; vpres res & develop, El Paso Polyolefins Co, 1979-1984; vpres res & develop, ABS res & develop, 1970-1979; dir mkt admin rexene polymers, ABS res & develop, 1969-1970; dir, ABS res & develop, 1967-1969; asst dir styrenic polymer develop, Dart Industs Chem Group, 1966-1967; mgr polymer res, Dart Industs Chem Group, 1965-1966; mgr develop res, Dart Industs Chem Group, 1963-1965; supvr polyolefins res, Rexall Chem Co, Paramus, 1961-1963; proj leader polyolefins, Chem Res Div, Esso Res & Eng Co, NJ, 1957-1961; Res chemist, Chem Res Div, Esso Res & Eng Co, NJ, 1955-1957. **Memberships:** Am Chem Soc; Sigma Xi. **Research Statement & Publications:** Polymerization of olefins; stabilization of polymers; organic synthesis; enzyme chemistry; heterogeneous catalysis; styrene type polymers; chlorine oxide chemistry.

KELLEY, KEITH WAYNE, IMMUNOPHYSIOLOGY. **Personal Data:** b Bloomington, Ill, November 5, 1947; m 1978, c 1. **Education:** Ill State Univ, BS, 1969; Univ Ill, MS, 1973, PhD (animal physiol), 1976. **Honors & Awards:** Animal Mgt Award, Am Soc Animal Sci, 1987. **Professional Experience:** Nat Inst Med Res, Bordeaux, France, 1987; PROF NUTRITIONAL SCI, UNIV ILL, URBANA, 1984-; invited res scientist, Nat Inst Agron Res, Paris, France, 1982-1983; from asst prof to assoc prof, Wash State Univ, 1976-1984. **Memberships:** Am Asn Immunologists; Am Soc Animal Sci; Soc Exp Biol & Med; AAAS; Am Asn Vet Immunologists. **Research Statement & Publications:** Neuroimmunomodulation; influence of hormones and neurotransmitters on regulation of T and B cell function in young and aged mammals. **Mailing Address:** Dept Animal Sci, Univ Ill, 1201 W Gregory Dr, Urbana, IL 61801-3838. **Fax:** 217-333-8804. **E-Mail:** kwkelley@uiuc.edu

KELLEY, LEON A, BIOCHEMISTRY. **Personal Data:** b Madison, Wis, June 28, 1923; m 1945, c 4. **Education:** Univ Wis, BS, 1948, MS, 1949, PhD (agr chem), 1951. **Professional Experience:** PROF EMER CHEM, SAN JOSE STATE UNIV, 1994-; prof chem, San Jose State Univ, beginning 1963; from asst prof to assoc prof, San Jose State Univ, 1954-1963; Asst prof agr chem, Univ Calif, Davis, 1953-1954. **Memberships:** Am Chem Soc; Am Dairy Sci Asn. **Research Statement & Publications:** Dairy chemistry; factors affecting rennet coagulation; rancidity in milk; development of instant milk products. **Mailing Address:** Dept Chem, San Jose State Univ, One Washington Sq, San Jose, CA 95192.

KELLEY, LORETTA A, MATHEMATICS. **Education:** Stanford Univ, PhD (Math), 1993. **Professional Experience:** LEAD EVALUATOR, NSF, WASH UNIV, of 2005. **Mailing Address:** 20 De Soto St, San Francisco, CA 94127. **Fax:** 415-239-3804. **E-Mail:** LKelley@kpacm.com

KELLEY, MAURICE LESLIE, MEDICINE. **Personal Data:** b Indianapolis, Ind, June 29, 1924; m Carol; c Elizabeth & Mary. **Education:** Univ Rochester, MD, 1949. **Professional Experience:** PROF CLIN MED, DARTMOUTH MED SCH, 1974-; STAFF MEM, MARY HITCHCOCK MEM HOSP CLIN, 1967-; assoc prof, Mary Hitchcock Mem Hosp Clin, 1967-1974; sr assoc physician, Strong Mem Hosp, 1963-; Fel, Mayo Clin, 1957-1959; from instr to assoc prof med, Univ Rochester, 1955-1967; from asst physician to assoc physician, Strong Mem Hosp, 1955-1959; consult, Vet Admin Hosp, Canandaigua, NY, Genesee Hosp & Rochester Gen Hosp. **Memberships:** AMA; Am Gastroenterol Asn; Am Fedn Clin Res; Am Col Physicians; Am Physiol Soc. **Research Statement & Publications:** Gastroenterology; motility of the esophagus. **Mailing Address:** Dept Med, Dartmouth Hitchcock Med Ctr, One Med Ctr Dr, Lebanon, NH 03756-0001. **Fax:** 603-650-0567.

KELLEY, MICHAEL C, GEOPHYSICS. **Personal Data:** b Toledo, Ohio, December 21, 1943; m 1966, c 3. **Education:** Kent State Univ, Ohio, 1964; Univ Calif, Berkeley, PhD (physics), 1970. **Honors & Awards:** James MacElware Award, Am Geophys Union, 1979. **Professional Experience:** JAMES A FRIEND FAMILY DISTINGUISHED PROF ENG, CORNELL UNIV, ITHACA, 2001-; CHMN, NSF, GLOBAL CHANGE PROGS, CEDAR, 1991-; investr, NASA-Combined Release Radiation Effects Satellite working group, 1986-; proj scientist, Greenland II, 1986-1987; proj scientist, NASA-Greenland I Rocket campaign, 1984-1985; prof, Sch Elec Eng, Cornell Univ, Ithaca, 1982-; NSF Atmospheric Sci Adv Comt, 1982-1984; proj scientist, NASA-Peru Rocket campaign, 1981-1983; Nat Acad Sci Comt, Solar Space Plasmas, 1980-1983; assoc ed, J Geophys Res, 1979-1983; mem, Nat Res Coun Comt, Jicamara Radar Observ, 1976-1979; from asst prof to assoc prof, Sch Elec Eng, Cornell Univ, Ithaca, 1975-1982; alexander von Humboldt fel, 1974-1975; from assoc res physicist to assoc physicist, Space Sci Lab, Univ Calif, 1970-1974. **Memberships:** Fel Am Geophys Union. **Research Statement & Publications:** AC-DC electrical field experiments in space; supplied electron and/or analyzing results for sixty rocket flights, four satellite missions and numerous balloon flights; author of two textbooks and over 100 articles; published over 10 articles. **Mailing Address:** Sch Elec Engr, Cornell Univ, 318 Rhodes Hall, Ithaca, NY 14853-3801. **Fax:** 607-255-9606. **E-Mail:** mikek@ece.cornell.edu

KELLEY, MICHAEL H, ELECTRON PHYSICS. **Education:** PhD (physics), Univ Tex, Austin. **Professional Experience:** PHYSICIST, NAT INST STAND & TECHNOL, GAITHERSBURG, as of 2006. **Mailing Address:** Nat Inst Stand & Technol, 325 Broadway PO BOX 818.01, Boulder, CO 20899. **Fax:** 303-497-3122. **E-Mail:** michael.kelley@nist.gov

KELLEY, MICHAEL J, CHEMISTRY. **Professional Experience:** RES SCIENTIST, AMGEN INC, THOUSAND OAKS, CALIF, 1992-; Researcher, Dept Chem, Univ Calif, San Diego, 1989-1992. **Mailing Address:** Dept Protein Chem, AMGEN Inc, 1840 Oak Terrace Lane, Thousand Oaks, CA 91320-1789. **Fax:** 805-499-7464.

KELLEY, MYRON TRUMAN, ANALYTICAL CHEMISTRY. **Personal Data:** b Allerton, Iowa, March 9, 1912; m 1937. **Education:** Univ Nebr, BSc, 1932, MSc, 1933; Iowa State Univ, PhD (phys chem), 1937. **Honors & Awards:** Chem Instrumentation Award, 1973. **Professional Experience:** CONSULT, HARSHAW CHEMICAL CO, 1981-; CONSULT, OAK RIDGE NAT LAB, 1973-; Consult, Tennecomp Systs, Inc, 1973-1979; Dir anal chem div, Harshaw Chemical CO, 1948-1972; asst sect chief chem process develop sect, Clinton Lab, 1945-1948; chief anal chemist, Queeny Plant Monsanto Chem Co, Mo, 1941-1945; Asst chief anal chemist, Queeny Plant Monsanto Chem Co, Mo, 1937-1941. **Memberships:** AAAS; Am Nuclear Soc; Am Chem Soc; Sigma Xi. **Research Statement & Publications:** Analytical instrumentation; instrumental methods of analysis, especially applications of small computers; analysis of highly radioactive materials. **Mailing Address:** 1814 Village Lane, Naples, FL 33963.

KELLEY, NEIL DAVIS, METEOROLOGICAL MEASUREMENTS, ACOUSTICS. **Personal Data:** b Clayton, Mo, January 8, 1942. **Education:** St Louis Univ, BS, 1963; Pa State Univ, MS, 1968. **Professional Experience:** AT, NAT WIND TECHNOL CTR, NAT RENEWABLE ENERGY LAB, as of 2002; PRIN SCIENTIST WIND ENERGY, SOLAR ENERGY RES INST, 1980-; br chief measurements, Solar Energy Res Inst, 1977-1980; group chief airborne measurements, Nat Ctr Atmospheric Res, 1972-1977; prog supvr, ESSO (Exxon) Res & Eng Co, 1967-1968; instr meteorol, Pa State Univ, 1966-1971; Meteorologist, Meteorol Res Inc, 1963-1966. **Memberships:** Am Meteorol Soc; Instrument Soc Am; Am Inst Aeronaut & Astronaut; AAAS; Sigma Xi; Inst Environ Sci. **Research Statement & Publications:** Developing a physical understanding of the role of atmospheric turbulence on the energy conversion efficiency and structural component lifetime of wind energy conversion systems. **Mailing Address:** Nat Wind Technol Ctr, Nat Renewable Energy Lab, 1617 Cole Blvd, Golden, CO 80401-3393. **Fax:** 303-384-6901. **E-Mail:** neil_kelley@nrel.gov

KELLEY, PATRICIA HAGELIN, INVERTEBRATE PALEONTOLOGY, EVOLUTIONARY PALEOECOLOGY. **Personal Data:** b Cleveland, Ohio, December 8, 1953; m 1977, Jonathan; c Timothy D & Katherine L. **Education:** Col Wooster, BA, 1975; Harvard Univ, AM, 1977, PhD (geol), 1979. **Honors & Awards:** FELLOW, AAAS 2005; OUTSTANDING EDUCATOR AWARD, ASSOCIATION FOR WOMEN GEOSCIENTISTS, 2003. **Professional Experience:** PROF OF GEOLOGY, UNIV NC WILMINGTON, 1997-; CHAIR, DEPT EARTH SCIENCES, UNIV NC WILMINGTON, 1997-2003; CHAIR, DEPT GEOL & GEOL ENG, UNIV NDAK, 1992-1997; PROF, DEPT GEOL & GEOL ENG, UNIV NDAK, 1992-1997; prog dir, geol & paleontol, NSF, 1990-1992; from asst prof to prof geol, Univ Miss, 1979-1990; instr, New Eng Col, 1979; prin investr, NSF Grant. **Memberships:** Paleont Soc; Geol Soc Am; AAAS; Sigma Xi; Paleont Res Inst; Asn for Women Geoscientists. **Research Statement & Publications:** Evolutionary patterns, including modes and rates of evolution; origin of macroevolutionary trends in Miocene molluscs; coevolution; carboniferous biogeography; predator-prey interactions in the fossil record, especially gastropod predation, coevolution and escalation. **Mailing Address:** Dept Earth Scis, Univ N Carolina Wilmington, Wilmington, NC 28403-5944. **Fax:** 910-962-7077. **E-Mail:** kelleyp@uncw.edu

KELLEY, PAUL LEON, LASERS, NONLINEAR OPTICS. **Personal Data:** b Philadelphia, Pa, December 8, 1934; m 1958, Patricia L Pieretti; c Matthew W & Diana R. **Education:** Rutgers Univ, BA, 1956; Cornell Univ, MS, 1959; Mass Inst Technol, PhD (physics), 1962. **Honors & Awards:** Distinguished Service Award, Optical Soc Am, 1998. **Professional Experience:** CHAIRPERSON, PUBLICATIONS COUNC, OPTICAL SOC AM, 1993-1995 PROF ELEC ENGR & COMPUT SCI 1992- & DIR, ELECTRO-OPTICS TECHNOL CTR, TUFTS UNIV, 1992-; 1999 CHAIR BD ED, OPTICAL SOC AM, 1990-; 1993 VIS INDUST PROF, TUFTS UNIV, 1985-; ed, Optics Lett, Optical Soc Am, 1984-1989; assoc group leader, Lincoln Lab, Mass Inst Technol, 1971-1992; asst group leader, Lincoln Lab, Mass Inst Technol, 1969-1971; vis lectr, Univ Calif, Berkeley, 1968-1969; Lectr, Mass Inst Technol, 1966-1967; Lectr, Northeastern Univ, 1963-1964; staff mem, Lincoln Lab, Mass Inst Technol, 1962-1969; staff assoc, Lincoln Lab, Mass Inst Technol, 1958-1962; Teaching asst physics, Cornell Univ, 1956-1958. **Memberships:** Am Phys Soc; fel Optical Soc Am; fel Sigma Xi. **Research Statement & Publications:** Las s er, nonlinear optics; ultrafast electro-optical devices. **Mailing Address:** 236 Varick Rd, Waban, MA 02168. **Fax:** 617-627-3151. **E-Mail:** pkelley@tufts.edu

KELLEY, RALPH EDWARD, ATOMIC PHYSICS, MOLECULAR PHYSICS. **Personal Data:** b Greenville, SC, March 6, 1930; m 1968, Martha; c Mary, David & Robert. **Education:** Furman Univ, BA, 1951, BS, 1955; Univ Va, MS, 1957, PhD (physics), 1960. **Professional Experience:** RETIRED; prog mgr, physics directorate, Off Sci Res, USAF, 1966-2002; sr scientist theoret anal, Res Labs Eng Sci, Univ Va, 1960-1966. **Memberships:** Am Phys Soc; Sigma Xi. **Research Statement & Publications:** Annihilation radiation of positrons in crystals; polarization effects in scattering. **Mailing Address:** 7551 Marshall Dr, Annandale, VA 22003.

KELLEY, RAYMOND H, NUCLEAR PHYSICS. **Personal Data:** b Roscoe, Mont, July 10, 1922; m 1951, c 1. **Education:** Mont State Col, BS, 1950; Ohio State Univ, MS, 1955, PhD (nuclear physics), 1963. **Professional Experience:** PROF EMER PHYSICS & MATH, SOUTHWESTERN ORE COMMUNITY COL, 1983-; from assoc prof to prof, Southwestern Ore Community Col, 1971-1983; part-time instr math, Southwestern Ore Community Col, 1969-1971; from instr to assoc prof physics, USAF Acad, 1962-1969; nuclear res officer, Modern Physics Br, Wright-Patterson AFB, Ohio, 1955 & Aeronaut Res Lab, 1957-1960; staff scientist, Brookhaven Nat Lab, 1955-1957; Instr electronics, Ellington AFB, Tex, USAF, 1951-1954. **Memberships:** Am Phys Soc; Am Asn Physics Teachers. **Research Statement & Publications:** Helium filled scintillation detectors; radiation damage to semiconductor materials; particle accelerators; gamma ray spectroscopy. **Mailing Address:** PO Box 335, Bandon, OR 97411.

KELLEY, RICHARD I, GENETICS. **Education:** Univ Pa, MD, PhD. **Professional Experience:** ASSOC PROF PEDIAT, JOHNS HOPKINS UNIV, as of 2005; DIR CLIN MASS SPECTROMETRY LAB, KENNEDY KRIEGER INST, as of 2005. **Mailing Address:** Kennedy Krieger Inst, 707 N Broadway Suite 500, Baltimore, MD 21205-1832. **Fax:** 443-923-2781. **E-Mail:** rkelley3@jhmi.edu

KELLEY, RICHARD L, ZOOLOGY. **Education:** Univ Tex, BS, 1979; Stanford Univ, PhD, 1984. **Professional Experience:** ASSOC PROF, DEPT MOLECULAR & CELLULAR BIOL & MOLECULAR & HUMAN GENETICS, BAYLOR COL MED, as of 2005. **Mailing Address:** Dept Molecular & Human Genetics Baylor Col Med, One Baylor Plaza Rm T734, Houston, TX 77030. **Fax:** 713-798-8515. **E-Mail:** rkelley@bcm.tmc.edu

KELLEY, ROBERT LEE, MATHEMATICAL PHYSICS. **Personal Data:** b East St Louis, Ill, March 20, 1937. **Education:** Univ Ill, Urbana, BS, 1958; Univ Miami, MS, 1960; Univ Mich, PhD (math), 1966. **Professional Experience:** ASSOC CHAIR, DEPT MATH, UNIV MIAMI, as of 2004; ASSOC PROF MATH, UNIV MIAMI, 1972-; from instr to asst prof, Univ Miami, 1964-1972. **Memberships:** Am Math Soc; Math Asn Am; Sigma Xi; Soc Indust & Appl Math; Asn Comput Mach. **Research Statement & Publications:** Mathematical physics; functional analysis; mathematical biology; theory of algorithms. **Mailing Address:** Dept Math, Univ Miami, PO Box 249085, Coral Gables, FL 33124-4250. **E-Mail:** r.kelley@miami.edu

KELLEY, ROBERT OTIS, DEVELOPMENTAL BIOLOGY, CELL BIOLOGY. **Personal Data:** b Santa Monica, Calif, April 30, 1944; m 1994, c 2. **Education:** Abilene Christian Col, BS, 1965; Univ Calif, Berkeley, MA, 1966, PhD (zoology), 1969. **Professional Experience:** Distinguished res prof, Nat Inst Basic Biol, Okazaki Nat Res Inst, Japan, 1985; CHMN DEPT ANAT, SCH MED, UNIV NMEX, 1981-; PROF ANAT, SCH MED, UNIV NMEX, 1979-; res fel, Hubrecht Lab, Utrecht, Neth, 1972-1973; NIH grant, 1970-; from instr to assoc prof, Sch Med, Univ Nmex, 1969-1979; actg asst prof, Univ Calif, Berkeley, 1969; assoc zoology, Univ Calif, Berkeley, 1967-1968. **Memberships:** Soc Develop biol; Am Soc Cell Biologists; Am Asn Anat; Electron Micros Soc Am; Biophys Soc. **Research Statement & Publications:** Fine structural associations between interacting cell layers during early amphibian development; ultrastructure and cell biology of vertebrate limb mesenchyme and associated limb morphogenesis; biology of the aging cell surface; organization of the cytoskeleton, cell imaging. **Mailing Address:** Dept Anat, Sch Med, Univ NMex, N Campus, Albuquerque, NM 87131. **Fax:** 505-277-1754.

KELLEY, RUSSELL VICTOR, BIOLOGY, SCIENCE EDUCATION. **Personal Data:** b Norfolk, Va, December 21, 1934; m 1956, c 3. **Education:** Va State Col, BS, 1957; NY Univ, MA, 1964; Purdue Univ, PhD (biol sci), 1972. **Professional Experience:** ASSOC PROF, DEPT BIOL, MORGAN STATE UNIV, as of 2005; ASST CHMN BIOL SCI, MORGAN STATE UNIV, as of 2003; PROF BIOL SCI, MORGAN STATE UNIV, as of 2003; consult sci, md state dept educ bicentennial comt, Baltimore City Pub sch syst, 1978-; chmn bd adv, Math Eng Sci achievement, 1977-; lectr zoology & biol, Community Col Baltimore, 1974-; lectr contemp biol, Towson State Univ, 1972, 1975; consult, NASA, 1967, 1968; assoc prof biol sci, Morgan State Univ, beginning 1966; teacher biol, Plainview, long island pub schs, 1962-1966; teacher chem & biol, Baltimore Pub Schs, 1960-1962. **Memberships:** Nat Sci Teachers Asn; AAAS. **Research Statement & Publications:** Instructional strategies in science teaching and population genetics. **Mailing Address:** Dept Biol, Sch Comput, Math & Natural Sci, Morgan State Univ, 1700 E Coldspring Lane Carnegie G65, Baltimore, MD 21251. **E-Mail:** rkelley@morgan.edu

KELLEY, THOMAS E, MATHEMATICS. **Education:** Boston Col, BA, 1972, MA, 1973; Ore State Univ, PhD, 1977. **Professional Experience:** INSTR MATH, HENRY FORD COMMUNITY COL, MI, 2000-. **Mailing Address:** Henry Ford Community Col, 5101 Evergreen Rd 5101 Evergreen Rd, Dearborn, MI 48128-1495. **Fax:** 313-317-4089. **E-Mail:** tkelley@hfcc.edu

KELLEY, THOMAS F, BIOMEDICAL ENGINEERING, CLINICAL CHEMISTRY. **Personal Data:** b Melrose, Mass, March 23, 1932; m 1956, c 3. **Education:** Boston Univ, AB, 1954, MA, 1955; Brown Univ, PhD (biol), 1959. **Professional Experience:** RETIRED; dir appl res, Instrumentation Lab Inc, 1980-1992; prog mgr, Instrumentation Lab Inc, 1968-1980; sr res assoc, Bio-Res Inst Inc, 1958-1968. **Memberships:** Am Asn Clin Chemists; Am Soc Clin Path; Sigma Xi. **Research Statement & Publications:** Development of hospital, medical and laboratory instrumentation. **Mailing Address:** 460 N Tenth St, Albemarle, NC 28001.

KELLEY, VICKI E, AUTOIMMUNITY. **Education:** Univ Pittsburgh, PhD, 1977. **Professional Experience:** ASSOC PROF MED, SCH MED, HARVARD UNIV, 1981-. **Memberships:** Am Asn Immunologists; Am Asn Pathologists. **Mailing Address:** Brigham & Women's Hosp, Dept Med, 75 Francis St, Boston, MA 02115-6195. **Fax:** 617-732-6392.

KELLEY, WILLIAM NIMMONS, INTERNAL MEDICINE, RHEUMATOLOGY. **Personal Data:** b Atlanta, Ga, June 23, 1939; m 1959, Lois; c Margaret P, Virginia L (Yost), Lori A & William M. **Education:** Emory Univ, MD, 1963. **Honorary Degrees:** MA, Univ Pa, 1989. **Honors & Awards:** Mosby Scholar Award, 1963-; John D Lane Award, USPHS, 1969; Geigy Int Prize Rheumatology, 1969; Res Career Develop Award, 1972-1975; Numerous Named Lectr, US & Foreign Univs, 1973-1994; Heinz Karger Prize, 1973; John Phillips Mem Award & Medal, Am Col Physicians, 1990. **Professional Experience:** DIR, ADVAN BIOSURFACES INC, as of 2003; DIR, GENVEC INC, as of 2003; PROF MED, BIOCHEM & BIOPHYS, SCH MED, UNIV PA, 1998; DIR, BECKMAN COULTER INC, 1994-; DIR, MERCK & CO INC, 1992-; exec vpres, Univ Pa, 1989-2000; dean sch med & Robert G Dunlop prof med, biochem & biophys, Univ Pa, 1989-2000; chief exec officer, Med Ctr & Health Syst, Univ Pa, 1989-2000; master, Am Col Physicians, 1988; chmn, Am Bd Int Med, 1985-1986 & Sect 4, Inst Med Nat Acad Sci, 1987-1989; pres, Cent Soc Clin Res, 1986-1987; consult med, numerous univs & indust, 1982-1994; vis prof & lectr, numerous univs, 1979-1994; John G Searle prof & chmn, dept Internal Med & prof biol chem, Med Sch, Univ Mich, 1975-1989; mem, numerous sci comts & councils, NIH, 1974-; Macy Fac scholar, Oxford Univ, 1974-1975; chief div rheumatic & genetic dis, Med Ctr, Duke Univ, 1970-1975; Am Rheumatism Asn clin scholar, 1969-1972; from asst prof to prof med, Med Ctr, Duke Univ, 1968-1975; from asst prof to assoc prof biochem, Med Ctr, Duke Univ, 1968-1975; Am Col Physicians Mead-Johnson scholar, 1967-1968; teaching fel med, Harvard Med Sch, 1967-1968; sr resident med, Mass Gen Hosp, 1967-1968; clin assoc, Nat Inst Arthritis & Metab Dis, 1965-1967; resident, Parkland Mem Hosp, 1964-1965; Intern med, Parkland Mem Hosp, 1963-1964. **Memberships:** Inst Med-Nat Acad Sci; Am Fedn Clin Res (pres, 1979-1980); Am Rheumatism Asn (pres, 1986-1987); Am Soc Biol Chemists; Am Soc Clin Invest (pres, 1983-1984); AAAS; Asn Am Physicians; Am Soc Human Genetics. **Research Statement & Publications:** Human biochemical genetics; rheumatology; author of numerous articles and books. **Mailing Address:** Sch Med, Univ Pa, 2002 Penn Tower, 399 S 34th St, Philadelphia, PA 19104-4385. **Fax:** 215-898-5607. **E-Mail:** kelleyw@mail.med.upenn.edu

KELLEY, WILLIAM S, MICROBIAL GENETICS. **Personal Data:** b Washington, Pa, November 30, 1941; m 1968, c 1. **Education:** Haverford Col, BS, 1963; Mass Inst Technol, MS; Tufts Univ, PhD (microbiol), 1968. **Professional Experience:** VPRES, VERTEX PHARMACEUT, as of 2003; vpres, Prod & Process Develop, Biogen Res Corp, Cambridge, Mass, beginning 1984; asst dir res for admin & molecular biol, Prod & Process Develop, Biogen Res Corp, Cambridge, Mass, 1982-1983; sr scientist, Prod & Process Develop, Biogen Res Corp, Cambridge, Mass, 1981-1982; from asst prof to assoc prof biol, Dept Biol Sci, Carnegie-Mellon Univ, Pittsburgh, Pa, 1971-1980; dept fel, grad dept biochem, Brandeis Univ, Mass, 1970-1971; US Pub Health Serv, postdoc fel, Dept Molecular Biol, Edinburgh Univ, Scotland, 1968-1970. **Memberships:** Am Chem Soc; Am Soc Microbiol; AAAS. **Research Statement & Publications:** Responsible for transfer of projects from research into pharmaceutical development, overseeing the groups who devise the manufacturing processes and implement them at pilot scale sufficiently large to support clinical trials; head technology transfer teams for interaction with other companies. **Mailing Address:** Vertex Pharmaceut, 130 Waverly St, Cambridge, MA 02139-4211. **Fax:** 617-444-6680.

KELLGREN, JOHN, ORGANIC CHEMISTRY, RUBBER CHEMISTRY. **Personal Data:** b New York, NY, December 26, 1940; m 1971, Joanne; c Carl & Eric. **Education:** Rutgers Univ, BS, 1962; Columbia Univ, PhD (org chem), 1966; Univ New Haven, MBA, 1977 & MS, 1984. **Professional Experience:** Process mgr, Rhein-Chemie, 1987-2005; process mgr, Wyrough-Loser Inc, 1984-1987; res scientist indust prod, Uniroyal Inc, 1979-1984; tech supt, Uniroyal Inc, 1976-1979; res chemist, Uniroyal Res Ctr, 1967-1975. **Memberships:** Sigma Xi; Am Chem Soc. **Research Statement & Publications:** Free radical reactions; polyurethane chemistry; oxidation of organic compounds; aging; vulcanization. **Mailing Address:** Rhein-Chemie, 1008 Whitehead Rd Ext, Trenton, NJ 08638. **Fax:** 609-771-9539.

KELLIHER, GERALD JAMES, PHARMACOLOGY. **Personal Data:** b Taunton, Mass, May 31, 1942; m 1965, c 2. **Education:** Univ RI, BS, 1965; Duquesne Univ, MS, 1967; Univ Pittsburgh, PhD (pharmacol), 1969. **Professional Experience:** Consult, Vet Admin, 1978-1980; Nat Inst Age grant, 1976-1980; ASSOC PROF MED, MED COL PA, 1975-; Nat Inst Child Health & Human Develop grant, 1972-1976; Southeast Pa Heart Asn, Del Heart Asn, Heart & Lung Found, Ayerst Co & Shering Co grants, Med Col Pa, 1971-1981; Whitehall Found grants, 1971-1977; Nat Heart & Lung Inst grants, 1971-1975, 1973-1977 & 1976-1980; from asst prof to prof pharmacol, Med Col PA, 1970-1978; fel pharmacol, Sch Med, Univ Pittsburgh, 1969-1970; educ consult, Smith Kline Corp; ASSOC DEAN, MED EDUC. **Memberships:** Am Soc Pharmacol & Exp Therapeut; assoc fel Am Col Cardiol; Geront Soc; fel Am Col Clin Pharmacol; Am Fedn Clin Res. **Research Statement & Publications:** Cardiovascular and autonomic pharmacology with emphasis on the mechanisms and treatment of cardiac arrhythmias and hypertension. **Mailing Address:** Dept Pharm Med Col Pa, 3300 Henry Ave, Philadelphia, PA 19129-1121. **Fax:** 215-843-5495.

KELLING, CLAYTON LYNN, VETERINARY VIROLOGY. **Personal Data:** b Killdeer, NDak, March 26, 1946; m 1974. **Education:** NDak State Univ, BS, 1968, MS, 1971, PhD (pharm chem), 1975; Iowa State Univ, PhD (Vet med), 1987. **Professional Experience:** PROF, DEPT VET & BIOMED SCI, UNIV NEBR, LINCOLN, as of 2006; technician vet virol, dept Vet Sci, NDak State Univ, beginning 1968. **Memberships:** Am Soc Microbiol; Sigma Xi. **Research Statement & Publications:** Veterinary microbiology concerned with respiratory and reproductive diseases of animals; antiviral agents; virological diagnostic techniques. **Mailing Address:** Dept Vet & BioMed Sci, Univ Nebr, PO Box 830905, Lincoln, NE 68583-0905. **Fax:** 402-472-9690. **E-Mail:** ckelling@unl.edu

KELLISON, ROBERT CLAY, FOREST GENETICS. **Personal Data:** b Marlinton, WVa, November 20, 1931; m 1965, c 2. **Education:** WVa Univ, BSF, 1959; NC State Univ, MS, 1966, PhD (forest genetics), 1970. **Professional Experience:** Adv forestry, Taiwan, 1985; adv forestry, Port, 1983 & 1985; mem Panel Forest Tree Breeding, Peoples Repub China, 1981, 1983; adv forestry, Brazil, 1980; PROF EMER DIR HARDWOOD COOP, NC STATE UNIV, 1977-; adv forestry, Venezuela, 1975 & 1977; scientist, NZ Forest Serv, 1973-1974; panel expert, Food & Agr Orgn-Int Breeding Prog for Preserv Forest Gene Resources, 1968; assoc dir coop prog, NC State Univ, 1966-1977; Fel, Am-Scand Found, 1965; liaison geneticist, NC State Univ, 1963-1967; forest supt, WVa Univ, 1959-1961. **Research Statement & Publications:** Selection and breeding of forest trees for improved volume yields, quality, adaptability and resistance to frost, drought and environmental pollution; preservation of forest gene resources. **Mailing Address:** 3035 Biltmore Hall, NC State Univ, Box 8001, Raleigh, NC 27695-0001. **Fax:** 919-786-1579. **E-Mail:** kellib@champint.com

KELLMAN, RAYMOND, POLYMER CHEMISTRY, ORGANIC CHEMISTRY. **Personal Data:** b Staten Island, NY, February 27, 1942; m 1978, Kathryn; c 2. **Education:** St Peter's Col, NJ, BS, 1963; Univ Colo, Boulder, PhD (org chem), 1968. **Professional Experience:** SR ASSOC, RES CORP, as of 2004; VPRES, RES CORP, as of 2004; PROG OFFICER, RES CORP, 1992-; fulbright res scholar, Univ Queensland, Australia, 1988-1989; prof chem, San Jose State Univ, 1982-1992; asst prof polymer chem, Univ Tex, 1977-1982; lectr chem, Univ Ariz, 1975-1977; res assoc, 1972-1975; res chemist, Uniroyal Inc, 1969-1972; res assoc chem, Univ Wis-Madison, 1967-1969. **Memberships:** AAAS; Am Chem Soc; Am Phys Soc. **Research Statement & Publications:** Synthesis of new monomers; new methods of condensation polymerization; synthesis of thermally stable electroactive and biocompatable polymers; radiation effect on polymers. **Mailing Address:** Res Corp, 4703 E Camp Lowell Dr, Ste 201, Tucson, AZ 85712. **E-Mail:** ray@rescorp.org

KELLMEL, DONALD J, TECHNOLOGY. **Education:** Pa State Univ, BS, MS, PhD (Elec Eng). **Professional Experience:** CHIEF TECH OFFICER, HADRON INC, 1999-. **Mailing Address:** Hadron Inc, 7611 Little River Tpke Suite 404W, Annandale, VA 22003. **Fax:** 703-329-8187.

KELLN, ELMER, ORAL PATHOLOGY, CANCER. **Personal Data:** b Sask, November 6, 1926; m 1951, c 3. **Education:** Univ Nebr, BSc & DDS, 1949; Univ Minn, MSD(path), 1960. **Professional Experience:** PROF ORAL MED, GRAD SCH & ASSOC DEAN SCH DENT, LOMA LINDA UNIV, 1971-; prof oral med, Univ, 1966-1971; cancer coordr, Sch Dent, WVa Univ & mem tumor bd, WVa Univ Hosp, 1963-1966; Grants wound healing, 1960-1963 & age studies, 1961-; Assoc prof path, Sch Med, WVa Univ, 1960-1966. **Memberships:** Fel Am Acad Oral Path; Am Dent Asn; Int Asn Dent Res. **Research Statement & Publications:** Cancer behavior; disease processes of oral diseases, particularly wound healing, cancer treatment and behavior, and vascular degeneration. **Mailing Address:** 25246 Lawton Ave, Loma Linda, CA 92354.

KELLNER, JORDAN DAVID, PHYSICAL CHEMISTRY. **Personal Data:** b New York, NY, August 25, 1938; m 1960, c 2. **Education:** City Col New York, BS, 1958; NY Univ, MS, 1962, PhD (phys chem), 1964; Rensselaer Polytech Inst, MS, 1972. **Honors & Awards:** SAm Tour Award, Am Soc Testing & Mat. **Professional Experience:** SR SCIENTIST, KENDALL RES LAB, 1991-; career develop chmn, Northeast Region, 1990-; trustee, Boston sect, Nat Asn Corrosion Engrs, 1987-1990; sr res assoc, Kendall Res Lab, 1983-1991; res assoc, Kendall Res Lab, 1981-1982; supvr, Res Ctr, 1980-1981; Adj prof chem, Univ Hartford, 1980-1981; supvr chem processes, Res Ctr, 1978-1980; sr res scientist, Hamilton Standard Div, United Technologies Corp, 1971-1978; res scientist, Hamilton Standard Div, United Technologies Corp, 1968-1971; sr chemist, Atomics Int Div, NAm Aviation, 1964-1968; res asst phys chem, NY Univ, 1961-1964; res asst biochem res, St Catherine's Hosp, 1959-1961; Jr chemist, Kings County Hosp, 1958-1959. **Memberships:** Sigma Xi; Am Chem Soc; Nat Asn Corrosion Engrs; Am Soc Testing & Mat. **Research Statement & Publications:** Transport processes in fused salts and metal-metal salt mixtures; Soret effect and viscosity; electrodeposition of semi-metals and their compounds from fused fluorides; electrochemical techniques of corrosion measurement including electrochemical impedance spectroscopy. **Mailing Address:** 1489 Carrio Dr, Vista, CA 92084.

KELLNER, STEPHAN MARIA EDUARD, PHYSICAL CHEMISTRY. **Personal Data:** b Friedberg, Ger, February 1, 1933; American citizen; m 1960, Jane; c Paul, Mark, Ted, Mary J, Elizabeth, Margaret, Bernard, Monica, Christine, Christopher, Julie & John. **Education:** Univ Rochester, BS, 1955, PhD (phys chem), 1960. **Professional Experience:** PROF EMER CHEM, ST MICHAEL'S COL, VT, as of 2004; chmn dept, St Michael's Col, 1971-1975; prof chem, St Michael's Col, VT, beginning 1969; from asst prof to assoc prof, St Michael's Col, 1959-1969. **Memberships:** Am Chem Soc; Sigma Xi. **Research Statement & Publications:** Rates and mechanisms of homogeneous gas phase reactions. **Mailing Address:** Dept Chem, St Michael's Col, One Winsooki Park, Colchester, VT 05439.

KELLOGG, CHARLES NATHANIEL, MATHEMATICS. **Personal Data:** b Albuquerque, NMex, June 29, 1938; m 1957, c 3. **Education:** NMex Inst Mining & Technol, BS, 1960; La State Univ, PhD (math), 1964. **Professional Experience:** ASSOC PROF MATH, TEX TECH UNIV, 1970-2003; asst prof, Univ Ky, 1964-1970; teaching asst math, La State Univ, 1963-1964. **Memberships:** Am Math Soc; Math Asn Am. **Research Statement & Publications:** Harmonic analysis; theory of multiplier operators; Banach algebras. **Mailing Address:** Dept Math, Tex Tech Univ, Lubbock, TX 79409-1042. **E-Mail:** kellogg@math.ttu.edu

KELLOGG, CRAIG KENT, ORGANIC CHEMISTRY. **Personal Data:** b Westfield, Mass, December 3, 1937; m 1960, Bernice; c 3. **Education:** Ga Inst Technol, BS, 1959, PhD (org chem), 1963. **Professional Experience:** RETIRED; assoc prof emer chem, dept chem, GA Souther Col, as of 1999; assoc prof chem, GA Southern Col, beginning 1970; asst prof, GA Southern Col, 1966-1970; res chemist, E I du Pont Del Nemours & Co Inc, 1963-1966. **Memberships:** Am Chem Soc. **Research Statement & Publications:** Natural products; dioxetanes. **Mailing Address:** 113 Herty Dr, Statesboro, GA 30458. **E-Mail:** carigk@gsaix2.cc.gasou.edu

KELLOGG, DAVID WAYNE, NUTRITION, ANIMAL PHYSIOLOGY. **Personal Data:** b Seymour, Mo, August 19, 1941; m 1964, Mary; c Kirk D, Susan J (Franz), Kimberley A (Vanvacter) & Gregory W. **Education:** Univ Mo Columbia, BS, 1963, MS, 1964; Univ Nebr, Lincoln, PhD (nutrit), 1968. **Honors & Awards:** Charter Diplomats, Am Coll of Animal Nutrition, Am Regist Prof Animal Scientists, 1995. **Professional Experience:** PROF, DEPT ANIMAL SCI, UNIV ARK, FAYETTEVILLE, 1986-; head, Dept Animal Sci, 1981-1986; from asst prof to prof dairy sci, NMex State Univ, 1967-1981. **Memberships:** Am Dairy Sci Asn; Am Regist Prof Animal Scientists (pres, 1994-1995, pres elect, 1993-1994). **Research Statement & Publications:** Nutrition of dairy calves; nutritive value of alfalfa varieties; mineral nutrition; improvement of forage digestion by ruminants. **Mailing Address:** Dept Animal Sci, Univ Ark, Fayetteville, AR 72701.

KELLOGG, EDWIN M, ELECTRON & ION BEAM SYSTEMS, X-RAY DETECTION. **Personal Data:** b New York, NY, February 3, 1939; m 1981, Diane; c Andrew, Gregory, Russell, Amelia, Jeffrey & Bradford. **Education:** Rensselaer Polytech Inst, BS, 1960; Univ Pa, MS, 1963, PhD (physics), 1966. **Honors & Awards:** Newton Lacey Pierce Prize, Am Astron Soc, 1974. **Professional Experience:** ASTROPHYSICIST, HARVARD-SMITHSONIAN ASTROPHYS OBSERV, 1988-; vpres eng, Ion Beam Technol Inc, 1983-1986; vpres develop, Ion Beam Technol Inc, 1982-1986; staff scientist, Ion Beam Technol Inc, 1982-1983; software mgr, Micro-Bit Div, Control Data Corp, Mass, 1981-1982; proj mgr, Micro-Bit Div, Control Data Corp, Mass, 1979-1981; astrophysicist, Harvard-Smithsonian Astrophys Observ, 1973-1979; Lectr astron, Harvard Univ, 1973-1979; mem, Inst Advan Study, 1973; sr staff scientist, Am Sci & Eng, Mass, 1969-1973; sr scientist, Am Sci & Eng, Mass, 1965-1969; Physicist, Radiation Dynamics Inc, 1961-1962. **Memberships:** Fel Am Phys Soc; Inst Elec & Electronics Engrs; Am Vacuum Soc; Sigma Xi; Am Astron Soc. **Research Statement & Publications:** Ion beam assisted surface phenomena; liquid metal ion sources; electron beam lithography; x-ray astronomy. **Mailing Address:** Harvard-Smithsonian Astrophys Observ, Ctr Astrophys, 60 Garden St MS-29, Cambridge, MA 02138. **Fax:** 617-495-7040. **E-Mail:** emk@cfa.harvard.edu

KELLOGG, GARY LEE, SURFACE SCIENCE, MICROSCOPY. **Personal Data:** b Meadville, Pa, January 16, 1950; m 1971, Susan; c Brian & Justin. **Education:** Pa State Univ, BS, 1971, PhD (physics), 1976. **Honors & Awards:** Award for Outstanding Accomplishment in Solid State Physics, Off Basic Energy Sci, Dept Energy, 1991. **Professional Experience:** Chmn, Surface Sci Div, Am Vacuum Soc, 1992-1993; SR MEM TECH STAFF, SANDIA NAT LABS, 1976-. **Memberships:** Fel Am Phys Soc; Am Vacuum Soc; Int Field Emission Soc (vpres, 1992-1993); Microbeam Anal Soc. **Research Statement & Publications:** Application of field ion microscope, atom-probe mass spectrometer and low energy electron microscope to problems in surface physics and surface chemistry; single-atom surface diffusion, cluster nucleation, thin film growth and surface chemical reactions. **Mailing Address:** 917 La Charles Dr NE, Albuquerque, NM 87112. **Fax:** 505-844-5470. **E-Mail:** glkello@sandia.gov

KELLOGG, HERBERT H(UMPHREY), EXTRACTIVE METALLURGY. **Personal Data:** b New York, NY, February 24, 1920; m Jeanette. **Education:** Columbia Univ, BS, 1941, MS, 1943. **Honors & Awards:** James Douglas Gold Medal, Am Inst Mining, Metall & Petrol Engrs, 1973. **Professional Experience:** STANLEY-THOMPSON PROF EMER CHEM METALL, COLUMBIA UNIV, 1990-; consult, Int Nickel Co & Am Smelting & Refining Co, beginning 1969; stanley-thompson prof chem metall, Columbia Univ, 1968-1990; prof, Columbia Univ, 1956-1968; chmn, titanium adv comt, Off Defense Mobilization, 1954-1958; assoc prof extractive metall, Columbia Univ, 1946-1956; asst prof mineral preparation, Pa State Col, 1944-1946; instr, Pa State Col, 1942-1944; asst mineral dressing, Columbia Univ, 1941-1942; jr engr, Dorr Co, Conn, 1941. **Memberships:** Nat Acad Eng; Am Inst Mining Metall & Petrol Engrs; fel Inst Mining & Metall London. **Research Statement & Publications:** Thermodynamics and kinetics of metallurgical reactions; high-temperature chemistry; equilibria in the systems Cu-S-O, Ni-Fe-S; slag chemistry; computer modeling of metallurgical processes. **Mailing Address:** Dept Chem Eng, Sch Eng Appl Sci, Columbia Univ, 801 S W Mudd, MC 4721, Palisades, NY 10964. **Fax:** 212-854-3054.

KELLOGG, LILLIAN MARIE, SOLID STATE CHEMISTRY. **Personal Data:** b Detroit, Mich, March 6, 1939. **Education:** Ariz State Univ, BS, 1961; Wayne State Univ, PhD (phys chem), 1967. **Professional Experience:** RETIRED; adj fac, Rochester Inst Technol, 1970-1975; res assoc res labs, Eastman Kodak Co, 1968-2002; assoc scientist chem, Aeroneutronic Div, Ford Motor Co, 1961-1962. **Memberships:** AAAS; Am Chem Soc; Am Phys Soc; Soc Photog Scientists & Engrs; NY Acad Sci. **Research Statement & Publications:** Solid state chemistry; light interactions in solids; photoconductivity, photochemical and photographic studies. **Mailing Address:** 1786 Lake Rd, Webster, NY 14580.

KELLOGG, LOUISE HELEN, GEOPHYSICS. **Education:** Cornell Univ, BA & BS, 1982, MS, 1985, PhD (geol sci), 1988. **Professional Experience:** CHMN GEOL, UNIV CALIF, 2000-; PROF GEOL, UNIV CALIF, 1998-; assoc prof geol, Univ calif, 1993-1998. **Mailing Address:** Dept Geol, Univ Calif, One Shields Ave, Davis, CA 95616-8605. **E-Mail:** kellogg@geology.ucdavis.edu

KELLOGG, PAUL JESSE, PLASMA PHYSICS. **Personal Data:** b Tacoma, Wash, November 6, 1927; m 1969, Janet; c 4. **Education:** Mass Inst Technol, BS, 1950; Cornell Univ, PhD (theoret physics), 1955. **Professional Experience:** PROF EMER PHYSICS, UNIV MINN, MINNEAPOLIS, as of 1962; Guggenheim Mem Found fel, 1962-1963; NATO fel; from asst prof to assoc prof, Univ Minn, Minneapolis, 1957-1964; res assoc, Univ Minn, Minneapolis, 1956-1957; Nat Res Coun fel, Naval Res Lab, 1955-1956. **Memberships:** Fel Am Phys Soc. **Research Statement & Publications:** Invented balloon measurements of electric fields, predicted earth's bow shock; plasma physics as applied to space; beam-plasma interaction, waves in plasma; antennas in flowing plasma. **Mailing Address:** Sch Physics & Astron, Univ Minn, Minneapolis, MN 55455. **Fax:** 612-626-2029. **E-Mail:** kellogg@waves.space.umn.edu

KELLOGG, RALPH HENDERSON, PHYSIOLOGY. **Personal Data:** b New London, Conn, June 7, 1920. **Education:** Univ Rochester, BA, 1940, MD, 1943; Harvard Med Sch, PhD (physiol), 1953. **Professional Experience:** EMER PROF PHYSIOL, UNIV CALIF, SAN FRANCISCO, 1990-; actg chmn, Hist Health Sci Dept, Univ Calif, 1984-1985; adj lectr, Hist Health Sci Dept, Univ Calif, 1978-1993; vis scientist, Lab Physiol Respiratory, Cent Nat Res Sci, Strasbourg, France, 1977; vis fel, Corpus Christi Col, Oxford Univ, 1970-1971; physiol test comt, Nat Bd Med Examrs, 1966-1973 & chmn, 1969-1973; mem physiol study sect, NIH, 1966-1970; actg chmn dept physiol, Univ Calif, San Francisco, 1966-1970; sr res fel, Sch Pub Health, Harvard Univ, 1962-1963; from asst prof to prof, Sch Med, 1953-1990; instr, Harvard Med Sch, 1947-1953; investr physiol, Naval Med Res Inst, 1946; intern med, Cleveland Univ Hosps, 1944. **Memberships:** AAAS; Am Physiol Soc; Am Asn Hist Med; History Sci Soc; Sigma Xi. **Research Statement & Publications:** Isotonic and osmotic diuresis in rats; respiration at altitude; history of physiology. **Mailing Address:** 1400 Geary Blvd Apt 2103, San Francisco, CA 94109-9313.

KELLOGG, RICHARD MORRISON, ORGANIC CHEMISTRY. **Personal Data:** b Los Angeles, Calif, December 24, 1939; m 1967, c 2. **Education:** Kans State Teachers Col, AB, 1961; Univ Kans, PhD (org chem), 1965. **Professional Experience:** PROF CHEM, STATE UNIV GRONINGEN, 1975-; assoc prof, State Univ Groningen, 1970-1975; res fel, State Univ Groningen, 1965-1970; Res fel chem, Univ Kans, 1965. **Memberships:** Am Chem Soc; Royal Dutch Chem Soc. **Research Statement & Publications:** Synthetic organic chemistry; photochemistry; bio-organic chemistry; synthesis of unusual organic molecules and models for mechanisms of enzymic reactions. **Mailing Address:** Dept Org Chem, Nyenborgh 4, 9747 A6 Groningen, Netherlands.

KELLOGG, ROYAL BRUCE, APPLIED MATHEMATICS. **Personal Data:** b Chicago, Ill, December 28, 1930; m 1956, c 3. **Education:** Mass Inst Technol, BS, 1952; Univ Chicago, MS, 1953, PhD (math), 1959. **Professional Experience:** PROF EMER RES PROF MATH & INST PHYS SCI & TECHNOL, UNIV MD, COLLEGE PARK, 1980-; res prof, Inst Fluid Dynamics & Appl Math, 1974-1980; from assoc prof to prof math, Univ MD, College Park, 1966-1974; mathematician, Westinghouse Elec Corp, 1961-1966; mathematician, Combustion Eng, Inc, 1958-1961. **Memberships:** Am Math Soc; Soc Indust & Appl Math. **Research Statement & Publications:** Numerical analysis. **Mailing Address:** PO Box 698, 4311A Comput & Space Sci Bldg, Landrum, SC 29356. **E-Mail:** kellogg@umd.edu

KELLOGG, SPENCER II, AERONAUTICAL ENGINEERING. **Personal Data:** b Buffalo, NY, December 9, 1913; m 1938, c 5. **Education:** Cornell Univ, ME, 1937; Polytech Inst Brooklyn, MSEE, 1967. **Honors & Awards:** Pioneer Award, Inst Elec & Electronics Engrs Aerospace & Elec Systs Soc, 1976. **Professional Experience:** RETIRED; independent aviation consult, 1967-1995; asst chief engr, Aeronaut Equip Div, 1959-1967; dept head flight instrument eng, Sperry Gyroscope Co, 1950-1959; from gyropilot engr to dept head, Sperry Gyroscope Co, 1940-1950; flight test engr, Sperry Gyroscope Co, 1939-1940; field serv engr, Sperry Gyroscope Co, 1937-1939. **Research Statement & Publications:** Gyropilot and gyroscopic flight instruments; altitude control for aircraft; turn error control of gyroscopes; erection mechanism for gyroscopes; flight directors. **Mailing Address:** 25 Valentine Ln, Glen Head, NY 11545.

KELLOGG, THOMAS B, PALEO-OCEANOGRAPHY, PALEO-CLIMATOLOGY. **Personal Data:** b New York, NY, April 30, 1942; m 1967, c 3. **Education:** Columbia Univ, BA, 1968, PhD (geol), 1973. **Honors & Awards:** Antarctic Serv Medal, US Cong, 1979. **Professional Experience:** PROF GEOL SCI & QUARTERNARY STUDIES, UNIV MAINE, ORONO 1989-; from asst prof to assoc prof, Univ Maine, 1978-1989; res assoc, Univ Maine, 1975-1978; res assoc, geol sci, Brown Univ, 1973-1975; mem, Cushman Found Foraminiferal Res, Climap Long Range Invest, Mapping & Prediction, 1971-1980. **Memberships:** Fel Geol Soc Am. **Research Statement & Publications:** High latitude marine sediment and how it is used to determine the past extent of ice sheets, ice shelves and icebergs; published over 10 articles. **Mailing Address:** Dept Geol, Univ Maine, Boardman Hall, Orono, ME 04469-5790. **Fax:** 207-581-1203. **E-Mail:** tomk@iceage.umeqs.maine.edu

KELLOGG, THOMAS FLOYD, BIOCHEMISTRY. **Personal Data:** b Aurora, Ill, April 7, 1934; m 1982, c 3. **Education:** Iowa State Univ, BS, 1959, MS, 1960; Univ Wis-Madison, PhD (biochem), 1964. **Professional Experience:** PROF EMER BIOCHEM, MISS STATE UNIV, 2001-; prof biochem, Miss State Univ, beginning 1978; assoc prof, Miss State Univ, 1970-1978; asst prof, Lobund Lab, Univ Notre Dame, 1968-1970; NIH Spec Res fel, 1967-1968; res scientist, Lobund Lab, Univ Notre Dame, 1965-1968; fel microbiol, Lobund Lab, Univ Notre Dame, 1964-1965; res asst biochem, Univ Wis, 1960-1964. **Memberships:** Am Physiol Soc; Asn Gnotobiotics (vpres & pres-elect 1981-1982 pres 1982-1983). **Research Statement & Publications:** Cholesterol and bile acid metabolism; liquid scintillation counting. **Mailing Address:** Dept Biochem, Miss State Univ, Drawer BB, Mississippi State, MS 39762-9999. **Fax:** 601-325-8664.

KELLOGG, WILLIAM WELCH, METEOROLOGY. **Personal Data:** b New York Mills, NY, February 14, 1917; m 1942, Elizabeth; c Karl, Judith, Joseph, Jane & Thomas. **Education:** Yale Univ, AB, 1939; Univ Calif, Los Angeles, MS, 1942, PhD (meteorol), 1949. **Honors & Awards:** Special Award, Am Meteorol Soc, 1961; Decoration Except Civilian Serv, Dept Air Force, 1966; Commemorative Medal, SovietGeophys Comt, 1985; Spec Citation, Garden Club Am, 1988. **Professional Experience:** RETIRED; sr res assoc, Nat Ctr Atmospheric Res, beginning 1987; chmn adv comt, Div Polar Progs, NSF, 1982-1985; Spec Comt Int Years Quiet Sun, 1963-1966 & Polar Res Bd, 1975-1978; sr scientist, Nat Ctr Atmospheric Res, 1973-1987; chmn meteorol adv comt, Environ Protection Agency, 1970-1974; mem panel on environ, President's Sci Adv Comt, 1968-1970; mem sci adv group, Off Aerospace Res, 1965-1970; mem adv group supporting tech oper meteorol satellites, NASA-US Weather Bur, 1964-1975; assoc dir, Nat Ctr Atmospheric Res, 1964-1973; mem, Comt Atmospheric Sci, 1963-1967; mem consult group potentially harmful effects of space exp, Comt Space Res, 1962-1968; mem tech adv bd, US Dept Com, 1962-1964; mem planetary atmospheres subcomt, NASA, 1961-1965; chmn working group upper atmosphere, World Meteorol Orgn, 1961-1965; chmn int comn meteorol upper atmosphere, Int Union Geod & Geophys, 1960-1975; mem, Space Sci Bd, 1959-1966; chmn meteorol satellite comt, Adv Res Projs Agency, 1958-1959; consult & mem sci adv bd, US Air Force, 1957-1965; Rocket & Satellite Res Panel, 1957-1962; mem tech panel, Earth Satellite Prog, Int Geophys Year, 1957-1958; mem, Comt Meteorol Aspects Effects Atomic Radiation, Nat Acad Sci, 1956-1964; Mem, Upper Atmosphere Comt, Nat Adv Comt Aeronaut, 1953-1955; asst prof, Inst Geophys, 1949-1952; res assoc, Inst Geophys, 1948-1949; phys scientist & dept head, Rand Corp, Calif, 1947-1964; res asst, Univ Calif, Los Angeles, 1947-1948; instr meteorol, Univ Calif, Los Angeles, 1942-1943; asst optics lab, Univ Calif, Berkeley, 1940-1941; teacher prep sch, Mass, 1939-1940. **Memberships:** Fel AAAS; fel Am Geophys Union; Sigma Xi; fel Am Meteorol Soc (pres, 1973-1974). **Research Statement & Publications:** Physics of the atmosphere; turbulence and structure of the upper atmosphere; scientific uses of rockets, satellites and space probes; atmospheres of Mars and Venus; causes of climate change. **Mailing Address:** 445 Col Ave, Boulder, CO 80302.

KELLS, LYMAN FRANCIS, general science, theory; deceased, see previous edition for last biography

KELLY, ALAN M, DEVELOPMENTAL BIOLOGY. **Education:** Univ Pa, PhD (path), 1968. **Professional Experience:** GILBERT S KAHN DEAN, SCH VET MED, UNIV PA, 1994-; PROF PATH, SCH VET MED, UNIV PA, 1980-. **Memberships:** Am Soc Cell Biol; Biophys Soc Am. **Mailing Address:** Dept Path, 110 Rosenthal, 3800 Spruce St, Univ Pa Sch Vet Med, Philadelphia, PA 19104-4192.

KELLY, AMY SCHICK, NEUROBIOLOGY, NEUROPHYSIOLOGY. **Personal Data:** b Rochester, NY, November 11, 1940; m 1971, c 2. **Education:** Mt Holyoke Col, AB, 1962; Brown Univ, MSc, 1964, PhD (psychol), 1967. **Professional Experience:** PSYCHOLOGIST, ROCKINGHAM CO PUB SCH(S), as of 2004; Asst Prof Physiol, Univ Calif, San Francisco, beginning 1978; fel neurobiology, Med Ctr, Stanford Univ, 1974-1978; spec res fel, Med Sch, Stanford Univ, 1974-1977; fel neurobiology, Univ Calif, Berkeley, 1972-1974; asst prof, Northeastern Univ, 1968-1971; Fel, Northeastern Univ, 1967-1968; Fel psychol, Northeastern Univ, 1967-1968. **Memberships:** Soc Neurosci; Asn Res Vision & Ophthal; AAAS. **Research Statement & Publications:** Organization of the mammalian central visual system; development of the central visual pathways and visual centers; plasticity of central connections in the mammalian visual system. **Mailing Address:** Rockingham Co Pub Sch(s), 2 S Main St, Harrisonburg, VA 22801.

KELLY, B(ERNARD) WAYNE, AGRICULTURAL ECONOMICS, HORTICULTURE PRODUCTION ECONOMICS. **Personal Data:** b Corning, NY, October 7, 1918; m 1945, Wilma; c Bruce W, Elizabeth A & Barbara L. **Education:** Pa State Univ, BS, 1949, MS, 1950. **Professional Experience:** Financial consult, 1983-; EMER PROF FARM MGT EXTEN, PA STATE UNIV, UNIV PARK, 1983-; from asst prof to prof, Pa State Univ, Univ Park, 1956-1983; asst prof & county agt, Agr Exten, Univ Md, 1954-1956; instr & asst county agt, Agr Exten, Univ Md, 1950-1953. **Memberships:** Am Agr Econ Asn; Am Soc Farm Mgrs & Rural Appraisors. **Research Statement & Publications:** Cost of production; fruits and vegetable crops; taxation, insurance, investments and credits. **Mailing Address:** Dept Farm Mgt Exten, 1427 S Pugh St, State College, PA 16801.

KELLY, BRENDAN PATRICK, ZOOLOGY & ECOLOGY. **Education:** Univ Calif, Santa Cruz, BA, 1975; Univ Alaska, MS, 1979; Purdue Univ, PhD, 1996. **Professional Experience:** DEAN ARTS & SCI, UNIV ALASKA SOUTHEAST, 2003-; ASSOC PROF MARINE BIOL, UNIV ALASKA FAIRBANKS, 1996-; ASSOC PROF BIOL, UNIV ALASKA SOUTHEAST, 1996-; res assoc, Inst Marine Sci, Univ Alaska, Fairbanks, 1982-1996. **Memberships:** Life mem Arctic Inst NAm; Int Soc Behav Ecol; Soc Marine Mammal; Nat Ctr Sci Educ; Sigma Xi; Nat Asn Underwater Instrs. **Mailing Address:** Sch Arts & Sci, Univ Alaska Southeast 11120 Glacier Hwy, Juneau, AK 99801. **Fax:** 907-796-6406. **E-Mail:** brendan.kelly@uas.alaska.edu

KELLY, CAROL ANNE, ECOLOGY. **Education:** Univ Ill, PhD. **Professional Experience:** DEPT BIOL, UNIV MO-ST LOUIS, as of 2000. **Mailing Address:** Dept Biol, Univ Mo-St Louis, 8001 Natural Bridge Rd, St Louis, MO 63121. **E-Mail:** ckelly@umsl.edu

KELLY, CLARK ANDREW, ANALYTICAL CHEMISTRY, PHARMACEUTICAL CHEMISTRY. **Personal Data:** b Rocky Ford, Colo, September 14, 1925; m 1954, Ruth; c Bret A. **Education:** Univ Colo, BS, 1946; Temple Univ, MS, 1951; Univ Minn, PhD (anal pharm chem), 1958. **Professional Experience:** ASST EDITOR ELECTROANALYSIS, CHEM DEPT, NMEX STATE UNIV, LAS CRUCES, 1991-; sr res chemist & group leader, Sterling Res Group, 1988-1991; sr res chemist & group leader, Sterling-Winthrop Res Inst, Rensselaer, 1968-1988; res chemist, Sterling-Winthrop Res Inst, Rensselaer, 1963-1968; res assoc, Sterling-Winthrop Res Inst, Rensselaer, 1956-1963; res asst, summers 1951-1954; res asst, Sterling-Winthrop Res Inst, Rensselaer, 1946-1948. **Memberships:** Am Chem Soc; Am Pharmaceut Asn; fel Acad Pharmaceut Sci. **Research Statement & Publications:** Polarography of organic compounds; ion exchange separations of organic compounds; colorimetric and spectrophotometric studies. **Mailing Address:** 4024 Shadow Run, Las Cruces, NM 88011-7696.

KELLY, CONRAD MICHAEL, CHEMICAL ENGINEERING. **Personal Data:** b Bradford, Pa, November 26, 1944; m 1966, c 1. **Education:** Mich State Univ, BS, 1966, MS, 1967, PhD (chem eng), 1970. **Professional Experience:** CHAIR, DEPT CHEM ENG, VILLANOVA UNIV, as of 2004; PROF CHEM ENG, VILLANOVA UNIV, 1980-; assoc prof, Air Prod & Chem Inc, beginning 1980; assoc prof, Villanova Univ, 1975-1980; asst prof, Villanova Univ, 1969-1975. **Memberships:** Am Inst Chem Engrs; Am Soc Eng Educ; Sigma Xi. **Research Statement & Publications:** Molecular diffusion; air and water pollution abatement; mathematical modeling. **Mailing Address:** Dept Chem Eng, Villanova Univ, 800 Lancaster Ave, Villanova, PA 19085. **Fax:** 610-519-7354. **E-Mail:** c.michael.kelly@villanova.edu

KELLY, DONALD C, THEORETICAL PHYSICS. **Personal Data:** b Poland, Ohio, August 18, 1933; m 1955, c 4. **Education:** Miami Univ, Ohio, AB, 1955, MA, 1956; Yale Univ, PhD (physics), 1959. **Professional Experience:** RETIRED; Nat Acad Sci sr res assoc, Inst Space Studies, 1970-1971; from asst prof to prof physics, Miami Univ, Ohio, 1960-1993; res assoc physics, Yale Lab Marine Physics, 1959-1960. **Memberships:** Am Phys Soc; Am Asn Physics Teachers. **Research Statement & Publications:** Classical and quantum kinetic theory; scattering theory; theoretical plasma physics. **Mailing Address:** Dept Physics, Miami Univ, Oxford, OH 45056-1618.

KELLY, DONALD G, AERONAUTICAL & ASTRONAUTICAL ENGINEERING. **Education:** Va Inst Technol, BS, 1964. **Professional Experience:** CEO, INTELLECTUAL ASSET MGT ASSOC, as of 2003; EXEC DIR, CHARTERED NY INST, as of 2003; BD DIR, PATENT CAFE INC, as of 2003; patent exam group dir, sr exec servs, US Patent & Trademark Off, 1988-2000; exec asst to comnr patents & trademarks, Sr Exec Servs, US Patent & Trademark Off, 1985-1988; mktg dir, Pergamon Press, Ltd, 1981-1983; patent info dir, Nat Tech Info Serv, 1980-1981; Wash & Geneva coordr, Tokyo Round Gen Agreements Tariffs & Trade Negotiations, 1976-1978; sci adv to US congressman, 1975-1976; patent examr, US Patent & Trademark Off, 1964-1975. **Research Statement & Publications:** Heat transfer; combustion engines; turbines; rocket propulsion systems; textile manufacturing; hydraulic/pneumatic engineering devices. **Mailing Address:** Intellectual Asset Mgt Assoc, LLC, 515 King St Ste 420, Alexandria, VA 22314. **Fax:** 703-684-6048.

KELLY, DONALD J, MATHEMATICS. **Education:** Polytech Univ, PhD (Oper Res). **Professional Experience:** ASST PROF MATH, SCH COMPUT SCI & MATHS, MARIST

COL, NY, as of 2005. **Mailing Address:** Marist Col, Dept Math, 3399 N Rd Lowell Thomas 120, Poughkeepsie, NY 12601. **Fax:** 845-575-3645. **E-Mail:** Donald.Kelly@marist.edu

KELLY, DOROTHY HELEN, PEDIATRICS, PULMONOLOGY. **Personal Data:** b Fitchburg, Mass, July 29, 1944. **Education:** Fitchburg State Col, BSN, 1966; Wayne State Univ, BS, 1968, MD, 1972. **Professional Experience:** Assoc dir, Pediat Pulmonary Unit, 1988; FDA, Health Devices, 1988; ECRI, Apnea Monitoring Stand, 1987-1988; ASSOC PEDIATRICIAN, MASS GEN HOSP, 1985-; prof, Orgn Soc Pediat Res, beginning 1985; FDA, Health Devices, 1985; mem, Sci Rev Comt, 1981; chmn, Apnea Adv Comt, Nat Sudden Infant Death Syndrome Found, 1979-1981; consult, Sudden Infant Death Syndrome Proj, Bur Commun Health Serv, Dept Health, Educ & Welfare, 1979-1980; co-dir, Pediat Pulmonary Lab, 1977-1986, asst pediatrician, 1979-1984; fel pediat pulmonary med, Mass Gen Hosp, 1976-1979; from instr to assoc prof pediat, Harvard Med Sch, 1975-1989; asst pediat, Mass Gen Hosp, 1975-1979; resident, Dept Pediat, Mass Gen Hosp, 1973-1975; intern, Dept Pediat, Mass Gen Hosp, 1972-1973. **Memberships:** fel Am Acad Pediat; Asn Psychophysiol Study; Int Pediat Soc; Am Med Women's Asn; Am Thoracic Soc; Soc Pediat Res. **Research Statement & Publications:** Control of ventilation; Sudden Infant Death Syndrome; sleep apnea. **Mailing Address:** Hermann Hosp, SW SIDS Res Inst Fannin St, Houston, TX 77030. **Fax:** 617-726-1036.

KELLY, DOUGLAS ELLIOTT, DEVELOPMENTAL ANATOMY, MICROSCOPIC ANATOMY. **Personal Data:** b Cheyenne, Wyo, November 13, 1932; m 1954, c 5. **Education:** Colo State Univ, BS, 1954; Stanford Univ, PhD (biol sci), 1958. **Honors & Awards:** Medal, Japan Asn Anat, 1984. **Professional Experience:** ASSOC VPRES BIOMED RES, ASN AM MED COLS, 1989-; chmn, coun acad sci, Asn Am Med Col, 1987-1988; pres, Asn Anat Chmn, 1979-1980; pres, Am Asn Anat, 1986-1987; NIH Human Embryol & Develop Study Sect, 1978-1982 & chmn, 1983-1985; mem admin bd, coun acad sci, Asn Am Med Col, 1982-1984 & 1985-1988; NSF & NIH res grants & Univ Southern Calif, beginning 1977; prof anat & cell biol & chmn dept, Sch Med, Univ Southern Calif, 1974-1989; prof & chmn dept, Sch Med, Univ Miami, 1970-1974; mem anat comt, Nat Bd Med Exam, 1970-1974; NSF & NIH res grants, Univ Miami, 1970-1974; from asst prof to assoc prof biol struct, Sch Med, Univ Wash, 1963-1970; NSF & NIH res grants, Univ Wash, 1963-1970; Univ Colo fac res fel, Univ Wash, 1962-1963; NSF & NIH res grants, Univ Colo, 1960-1963; USPHS res fel, Zoology Lab, State Univ Utrecht, 1959-1960; from instr to asst prof biol, Univ Colo, 1958-1963. **Memberships:** Am Asn Anat; Soc Develop Biol; Am Soc Zool; Am Soc Cell Biol. **Research Statement & Publications:** Electron microscopy; development and ultrastructure of junctional complexes; ultrastructure of muscle and eye. **Mailing Address:** Div Biomed & Health Sci Res, Asn Am Med Cols, One Dupont Circle N W, Washington, DC 20037-1126. **Fax:** 202-828-1125.

KELLY, DOUGLAS G, MATHEMATICS. **Education:** Princeton Univ, BA, 1961, PhD (Math), 1967. **Professional Experience:** PROF, DEPT STATIST, UNIV NC, as of 2005; SR ASSOC DEAN, COL ARTS & SCI, UNIV NC, as of 2005. **Mailing Address:** Univ NC, Dept Statist, 302 New W, Chapel Hill, NC 27599-7545. **Fax:** 919-962-1279. **E-Mail:** kelly@stat.unc.edu

KELLY, EDWARD JOSEPH, PHYSICAL CHEMISTRY. **Personal Data:** b Baltimore, Md, March 4, 1934; m 1967, c 2. **Education:** Johns Hopkins Univ, BES, 1956, MAT, 1962, MS, 1968; Purdue Univ, MS, 1967, PhD (chem, physics), 1972. **Professional Experience:** ASSOC PROF CHEM, MARIAN COL, 1980-; asst prof, Marian Col, 1975-1980; asst prof math & physics, Mt Marty Col, 1972-1975; teacher, Mt St Joseph High Sch, Md, 1962-1965; Engr, Bendix Radio Corp, 1960-1961. **Memberships:** AAAS; Am Chem Soc; Am Asn Physics Teachers; Sigma Xi. **Research Statement & Publications:** Exploring alternatives in science teaching; quantum mechanics of small molecules. **Mailing Address:** 4440 Manning Rd, Indianapolis, IN 46208-2726.

KELLY, ERNEST L, PHYSICAL PHARMACY, ANALYTICAL METHODS DEVELOPMENT. **Personal Data:** b DuBois, Pa, January 6, 1950; m 1969, Glenna; c Richard, David & Matthew. **Education:** Millersville State Col, BA, 1971; Villanova Univ, MS, 1974, PhD (phys chem), 1977. **Professional Experience:** VPRES WORLDWIDE QUAL CONTROL, CEPHALON INC, as of 2006; SR VPRES QUAL ASSURANCE & REGULATORY AFFAIRS, SAVIENT PHARAMA INC, as of 2004; sr dir qual assurance, Rhore Poulenc Rorer, beginning 1990; sect head, Wm H Rorer, Inc, 1979-1981; vpres qual assurance, Rhore Poulenc Rorer, 1979-1996; sr anal chem, Merck Sharp & Dohme Res Labs, 1974-1979; res asst, McNeil Labs, 1972-1974; adj prof pharmaceut, Temple Univ; panel mem, US Pharmacepol Aerosol. **Memberships:** Am Chem Soc; Am Pharmaceut Asn; Acad Pharmaceut Sci; Am Asn Pharmaceut Soc. **Research Statement & Publications:** Development of analytical and microscopic methods for the analysis of pharmaceutical drug substances and raw materials; evaluation of physical chemical properties of pharmaceutical drug substances in relationship to the formulation and stability of the drug; pharmaceutical quality assurance and compliance. **Mailing Address:** Cephalon Inc, 41 Moores Rd, Frazer, PA 19355. **Fax:** 610-738-6590.

KELLY, FLOYD W, ORGANIC CHEMISTRY. **Personal Data:** b Greeley, Colo, December 30, 1941; m 1965, c 2. **Education:** Colo State Univ, BS, 1963; Univ Ore, MS, 1965; Univ Idaho, PhD (org chem), 1968. **Professional Experience:** FAC CHEM, CASPER COL, as of 2006; INSTR CHEM, CASPER COL, 1969-; fel chem, Utah State Univ, 1968-1969. **Memberships:** Am Chem Soc. **Research Statement & Publications:** Organic synthesis; organic photochemistry; gas phase homolyses. **Mailing Address:** Dept Chem, Casper Col, PS311 125 Col Dr, Casper, WY 82601. **E-Mail:** fkelly@caspercollege.edu

KELLY, FRANCIS JOSEPH, LONG WAVE PROPAGATION, MAGNETOSPHERIC PROPAGATION. **Personal Data:** b Baltimore, Md, October 12, 1940; m 1964, c 3. **Education:** Cath Univ Am, Wash, DC, BA, 1962, PhD (physics), 1966. **Professional Experience:** SR RES ASSOC, CATH UNIV AM, 1994-; lectr, Va Polytech Inst, 1976-1984; physicist, Naval Res Lab, Wash, DC, 1968-1994; Naval Ord Lab, White Oak, Silver Spring, Md, 1965-1968; physicist, Nat Bur Stand, Wash, DC, 1962-1965. **Memberships:** Am Phys Soc; Inst Elec & Electronics Engrs; Union Radio Sci Int. **Research Statement & Publications:** Propagation of long electromagnetic waves and systems for transmitting and receiving them; constructed models of atmospheric noise and studied the propagation of such waves from a satellite to the earth; nuclear structure effects on electron and neutrino reactions; author of various publications. **Mailing Address:** Dept Physics, Cath Univ Am, Washington, DC 20064. **Fax:** 301-422-9021.

KELLY, GEORGE EUGENE, MECHANICAL ENGINEERING, STATISTICAL MECHANICS. **Personal Data:** b Brooklyn, NY, March 28, 1928; m 1970, c 3. **Education:** State Univ NY, Stony Brook, BES, 1965; Northwestern Univ, PhD (mech eng), 1970. **Honors & Awards:** Silver Medal, Dept Commerce, 1978. **Professional Experience:** CHIEF, BLDG ENVIRON DIV, BLDG & FIRE RES LAB, NIST, as of 2001; mech engr, NIST, beginning 1972; res assoc, Nat Res Coun, Nat Bur Standards 1970-1972. **Memberships:** Am Phys Soc; Am Soc Heating Refrig & Air-Conditioning Engrs. **Research Statement & Publications:** Theoretical, laboratory and field research on the performance of heating and cooling equipment and systems, controls, and energy management systems in buildings and residences; thermodynamics, fluid mechanics, heat transfer and methods of numerical and analytical analysis. **Mailing Address:** Nat Inst Stand & Technol, 100 Bureau Dr, Stop 8630, Gaithersburg, MD 20899-8630. **E-Mail:** george.kelly@nist.gov

KELLY, GREGORY, CELL-CYCLE REGULATION, CARCINOGENESIS. **Personal Data:** b McKeesport, Pa, December 7, 1954; m 1976, c 2. **Education:** Univ Pittsburgh, BS, 1977; Purdue Univ, PhD (biochem), 1983. **Professional Experience:** PRES SOUTHWEST SCI RESOURCES, 1995-; adj prof exp path, Dept Vet Path, Purdue Univ, 1992-; clin asst prof, Toxicol Prog, Univ NMex, Sch Pharm, 1990-; adj asst prof, Dept Vet Path, Purdue Univ, 1989-1992; staff scientist, Inhalation Toxicol Res Inst, 1986-1995; fel, Dept Biochem, Univ Iowa, Sch Med, 1983-1986. **Memberships:** Am Asn Cancer Res; Radiation Res Soc; AAAS. **Research Statement & Publications:** Pulmonary carcinogenesis; development of the tracheo-bronchial epithelium; role of cell-cycle controlling genes in the development of neoplasia. **Mailing Address:** SW Sci Resources Inc, 5300 Sequoia NW Ste 150, Albuquerque, NM 87120. **Fax:** 505-831-2635.

KELLY, GREGORY M, Paediatrics. **Professional Experience:** ASSOC PROF BIOLOGY, UNIV WESTERN ONT, as of 2003; asst prof zool, Univ Western Ont, beginning 1995; Sr fel, Dept Pharmacol, Univ Wash, 1989-1994. **Mailing Address:** Dept Biology, Univ Western Ont, London, ON N6A 5B7, Can. **Fax:** 519-661-3935. **E-Mail:** gkelly@uwo.ca

KELLY, HENRY CHARLES, TECHNOLOGY & ECONOMIC GROWTH, ENERGY EFFICIENCY. **Personal Data:** b Boston, Mass, July 10, 1945; m 1969, c 2. **Education:** Cornell Univ, BA, 1967; Harvard Univ, PhD (physics), 1972. **Honors & Awards:** Szilard Award, Am Phys Soc, 2002; Champion Energy Efficiency, Am Council Energy Efficiet Econo, 2000. **Professional Experience:** Chmn, Lawrence Berkely Lab, Appl Sci Div Rev Comt, 1989, 1990; SR ASSOC, OFF TECHNOL ASSESSMENT, 1981-; assoc dir, Solar Energy Res Inst, 1979-1981; dir technol & int rels, Off Technol Assessment, 1978-1979; tech adv to dir, Off Technol Assessment, 1975-1978; AAAS Cong Sci fel, 1974-1975; Physicist, US Arms Control & Disarmament Agency, 1971-1974; mem sci adv bd, Risk Reduction Subcomt, Environ Protection Agency. **Memberships:** Fel AAAS; fel Am Phys Soc; Fedn Am Specialists. **Research Statement & Publications:** photovoltaic and other solar energy equipment; energy conservation technologies; international relations; technology and structural economic change including publications on federal statistics, textiles and apparel, information technolgy, technology and education, energy efficiency technology, construction, and renewable energy; strategic arms control, nuclear effects, and quantumelectrodynamics. **Mailing Address:** 2210 N Nelson St, Arlington, VA 22207.

KELLY, HENRY CURTIS, INORGANIC CHEMISTRY. **Personal Data:** b Providence, RI, May 17, 1930; m 1956, Lucille Mainland; c Luanne, Nancy & Curtis. **Education:** Bates Col, BS, 1951; Brown Univ, PhD (chem), 1962. **Honors & Awards:** TCU Honors Professor 1975. **Professional Experience:** PROF EMER, TEX CHRISTIAN UNIV, 1998-; Chmn, Dept Chem, 1989-1995; Dir, Honors Prog, Tex Christian Univ, 1981-1987; Prof Chem, Tex Christian Univ, 1974-1997; Assoc Prof, Texas Christian University 1967-1974; Asst prof, Tex Christian Univ, 1964-1967; sr res chemist, Metal Hydrides Inc, 1962-1964; Instr chem, Brown Univ, 1958-1962; res chemist, Metal Hydrides Inc, 1952-1958; Anal chemist, Metal Hydrides Inc, 1951-1952. **Memberships:** Am Chem Soc; Sigma Xi; Royal Soc Chem. **Research Statement & Publications:** Chemistry of boron and silicon hydrides; boron-nitrogen compounds; kinetics and mechanisms of hydride reactions in solution; amineborane solvolysis and oxidation; kinetics of peroxidatic activity of metal-porphyrins and enzymes; cyclodextrin inclusion compound formation and function. **Mailing Address:** Dept Chem, Tex Christian Univ, Ft Worth, TX 76129. **Fax:** 817-257-7110. **E-Mail:** h.kelly@tcu.edu

KELLY, JAMES L(ESLIE), CHEMICAL ENGINEERING, MATERIALS SCIENCE ENGINEERING. **Personal Data:** b New Orleans, La, December 20, 1932; m 1956, Aileen; c Kevin Wilson, Megan Elizabeth, Michael Wilson & Katherine (Wren). **Education:** Tulane Univ, BS, 1954; La State Univ, MS, 1960, PhD (chem eng), 1962. **Professional Experience:** PROF EMER NUCLEAR ENG, SCH ENG & APPL SCI, UNIV VA, as of 2000; asst dean undergrad prog, Sch Eng & Appl Sci, Univ VA, 1991-1996; prof Nuclear Eng, Sch Eng & Appl Sci, Univ Va, beginning 1972; assoc prof, Sch Eng & Appl Sci, Univ VA, 1964-1972; chem tech div, Oak Ridge Nat Lab, 1962-1964; process engr, Kaiser Aluminum & Chem Corp, 1956-1957 & Ormet Corp, 1957-1959. **Memberships:** Am Inst Chem Engrs; Am Nuclear Soc; Nat Asn Corrosion Engrs. **Research Statement & Publications:** Radiation processing; reactor materials; nuclear chemical engineering; radioactive waste disposal. **Mailing Address:** Sch Eng & Appl Sci, Univ Va, 122 Eng Way PO Box 400746, Charlottesville, VA 22904-4746. **E-Mail:** jlk@virginia.edu

KELLY, JAMES MICHAEL, PLANT NUTRITION, FOREST SOILS. **Personal Data:** b Knoxville, Tenn, February 2, 1944; m 1968, Susan; c John K & Christopher K. **Education:** ETenn State Univ, BS (biology), 1966; Univ Tenn, MS, (plant & soil sci), 1968, PhD (forest ecol), 1973. **Honors & Awards:** gold award res achievement environmental sci, Tenn Valley Authority, 1988; fel, Soil Sci Soc Am, 1993; Environment sector delivery & applications award, Elect Power Res Inst, 2001. **Professional Experience:** PROF & CHMN, DEPT FORESTRY, IOWA STATE UNIV, 1995-; sr tech specialist, Tenn Valley Authority, 1989-1995; vis prof agron, Purdue Univ, 1988-1989; adj prof, Purdue Univ, 1987-1995; adj prof, Univ Tenn, 1978-1995; tech specialist, Tenn Valley Authority, 1976-1988; postdoctoral res assoc, Purdue Univ, 1974-1976; predoc fel, Oak Ridge Nat Lab, 1970-1973; asst prof biol, Ferrum Col, 1969-1970. **Memberships:** Soil Sci Soc Am; Soc Am Foresters; Am Soc Agron; AAAS; Ecol Soc Am. **Research Statement & Publications:** Cycling and availability of nutrients in forests, nutrient uptake by trees and the impacts of air pollution on forests and soils. **Mailing Address:** Forestry Dept, Iowa State Univ, 253 Bessey Hall, Ames, IA 50011-1021. **E-Mail:** jmkelly@iastate.edu

KELLY, JEFFREY JOHN, BIOCHEMISTRY, CHEMISTRY. **Personal Data:** b Portland, Ore, November 2, 1942; m 1966, c 3. **Education:** Harvey Mudd Col, BS, 1964; Univ Calif, Berkeley, PhD (chem), 1968. **Professional Experience:** DIR RES, BARLOW SCI INC, as of 2003; vis prof chem, Ctr Process Anal Chem, Univ Wash, 1987-1988; vis sci, Ctr Process Anal Chem, Dept Chem, Univ Wash, 1986-1987, 1988-1992; RES BIOCHEMIST, BARLOW SCI INC, 1984-; Vis prof chem, Harvey Mudd Col, 1980-1981; FAC MEM, DEPT CHEM, EVERGREEN STATE COL, 1972-; asst prof chem, Reed Col, 1968-1972. **Memberships:** AAAS; Sigma Xi. **Research Statement & Publications:** Physical and chemical processes of photosynthesis; biomedical spectroscopy; analytical near infrared spectroscopy. **Mailing Address:** Evergreen State Col, Rm 054 Lab I 2700 Evergreen Pkwy NW, Olympia, WA 98505-0002. **Fax:** 360-866-6794. **E-Mail:** kellyj@evergreen.edu

KELLY, JOHN BECKWITH, MATHEMATICS. **Personal Data:** b New York, NY, August 30, 1921. **Education:** Columbia Univ, AB, 1942; Mass Inst Technol, PhD, 1948. **Professional Experience:** PROF EMER MATH, ARIZ STATE UNIV, TEMPE, as of 2004; prof math, Ariz State Univ, Tempe, beginning 1966; assoc prof, Ariz State Univ, Tempe, 1962-1966; from instr to assoc prof, Mich State Univ, 1951-1962; mem, Inst Advan Study, 1950-

1951; instr math, Univ Wis, 1948-1950. **Memberships:** Sigma Xi. **Research Statement & Publications:** Number theory; graph theory; combinatorial analysis. **Mailing Address:** Ariz State Univ, Tempe, AZ 85281.

KELLY, JOHN C, MATHEMATICS. **Education:** Univ Warwick, PhD (Maths), 1975. **Professional Experience:** STAFF, JET PROPULSION LAB, CA, as of 2000. **Mailing Address:** Calif Technol, Jet Propulsion Lab, 4800 Oak Grove Dr, Pasadena, CA 91109. **Fax:** 310-377-2463. **E-Mail:** john.c.kellyw@jpl.nasa.gov

KELLY, JOHN FRANCIS, HORTICULTURE, OLERICULTURE. **Personal Data:** b Chicago, Ill, November 28, 1931; m 1959, Janet; c Marcia, Andrea, Shaun, Claudia, Daniel, Timothy, Michael, Kurt & Kristine. **Education:** Mich State Univ, BS, 1953, MS, 1957; Univ Wis, PhD (hort, plant physiol), 1960. **Honorary Degrees:** Dr, Univ Hort & Food Indust, Budapest, Hungary, 1988. **Professional Experience:** PROF EMER HORT, MICH STATE UNIV, 1978-; chmn dept, Mich State Univ, 1978-1990; prof veg crops & chmn dept, Univ Fla, 1972-1978; vpres pioneer res, Campbell Inst Agr Res, 1966-1972; dir pioneer plant res, Campbell Soup Co, 1965-1966; soils technologist, Campbell Soup Co, 1962-1964; asst prof veg crops & soils, Southern Ill Univ, 1959-1962; asst, Mich State Univ, 1956 & Univ Wis, 1957-1959; Agr res asst, Campbell Soup Co, 1952-1953. **Memberships:** Fel AAAS; fel Am Soc Hort Sci (pres, 1985-1986); Int Soc Hort Sci. **Research Statement & Publications:** Culture, physiology, nutrition and chemical composition of vegetable crops; quality of food crops. **Mailing Address:** Dept Hort, Mich State Univ, 428 Plant Sci Bldg, East Lansing, MI 48824-7325. **E-Mail:** jkelly@msu.edu

KELLY, JOHN HENRY, DIFFRACTION, NON-LINEAR PROPAGATION. **Personal Data:** b Tonawanda, NY, September 26, 1952. **Education:** Univ Buffalo, BS, 1974; Univ Rochester, MS, 1976, PhD (optics), 1980. **Professional Experience:** Res assoc, Lab Laser Energetics, 1980-; SEMICONDUCTER RES CORP. **Memberships:** Inst Elec & Electronics Engrs; Optical Soc Am; Sigma Xi. **Research Statement & Publications:** Diffraction and the propagation of light in large laser systems; resonant energy transfer in both crystalline and amorphous materials. **Mailing Address:** 306 Rutherglen Dr, Cary, NC 27511-6439.

KELLY, JOHN RUSSELL, OCEANOGRAPHY. **Personal Data:** b Nashua, NH, January 25, 1952. **Education:** Univ NH, BA, 1974; Univ RI, PhD (oceanog), 1982. **Professional Experience:** AT, ENVIRON PROTECTION AGENCY, as of 2003; RES ASSOC, ECOSYSTS RES CTR, CORNELL UNIV, 1981-; res asst, Grad Sch Oceanog, Univ RI, 1975-1981. **Memberships:** Am Soc Limnol & Oceanog; Sigma Xi. **Research Statement & Publications:** Elemental cycling in marine, aquatic and terrestrial systems. **Mailing Address:** Environ Protection Agency, Mid Continent Ecol Div, 6201 Congdon Blvd, Duluth, MN 55804. **E-Mail:** kelly.johnr@epa.gov

KELLY, JOHN V, OBSTETRICS, GYNECOLOGY. **Personal Data:** b London, Ont, August 21, 1926; American citizen. **Education:** Wayne State Univ, BS, 1948, MD, 1951; Am Bd Obstet & Gynec, dipl, 1961. **Professional Experience:** MED MISSIONARY, MAKIUNGU HOSP, SINGIDA, TANZANIA, E AFRICA, 1997-; adj prof obstet & gynec, Sch Med, Univ Ariz, 1975-1996; chmn dept obstet & gynec, Maricopa County Hosp, Phoenix, 1975-1996; prof obstet & gynec, Sch Med, Univ Pa, 1967-1975; med missionary, St Luke's Hosp, Anua, ENigeria, 1964-1966; from instr to asst prof, Sch Med, Univ Calif, Los Angeles, 1957-1964; Fulbright fel, Stockholm, Sweden, 1956; Res fel, Harvard Med Sch, 1955; Graves fel, Free Hosp Women, Brookline, Mass, 1955; resident obstet & gynec, Metrop Hosp, NY Med Col, 1952-1955; Intern, Metrop Hosp, NY Med Col, 1951-1952. **Memberships:** Am Fertil Soc; Am Med Asn; Am Fedn Clin Res. **Research Statement & Publications:** Dynamics of uterine muscle contraction. **Mailing Address:** Makiungu Hosp, Box 3124, Arusha, Tanzania.

KELLY, KENNETH C, ARRAY ANTENNAS FOR MICROWAVES, MICROWAVE FILTERS. **Personal Data:** b New York, NY, March 6, 1928; div, c 2. **Education:** Polytech Inst Brooklyn, BSEE, 1953; Univ Calif, Los Angeles, MS, 1963. **Honors & Awards:** Community Serv Award, Inst Elec & Electronics Engrs, 1975. **Professional Experience:** AT, JET PROPULSION LAB, CALIF INST TECHNOL, as of 1999; SR SCIENTIST, HUGHES AIRCRAFT CO, 1986-; consult, 1973-1986; dept head, Rantec Div, Emerson Elec Co, 1970-1973; mem tech staff, Rantec Div, Emerson Elec Co, 1962-1970; section head, Hughes Aircraft Co, 1958-1962; mem tech staff, Hughes Aircraft Co, 1953-1958; Engr, Polytech Res & Develop, 1951-1953. **Memberships:** Res Engrs Soc Am; Inst Elec & Electronics Engrs. **Research Statement & Publications:** Microwave optics, microwave antennas and various passive microwave components and devices. **Mailing Address:** Jet Propulsion Lab, Calif Inst Technol, Pasadena, CA 91125. **E-Mail:** ken.kelly@earthlink.net

KELLY, KENNETH WILLIAM, ORGANIC CHEMISTRY. **Personal Data:** b New York, NY. **Education:** St John's Univ, NY, BS, 1961, MS, 1963; Rutgers Univ, PhD (chem), 1969. **Professional Experience:** DIR RES & DEVELOP, KAY-FRIES, INC, 1969-; Chemist synthesis, Merck & Co, Rahway, NJ, 1963-1969. **Memberships:** Am Chem Soc. **Research Statement & Publications:** Organic synthesis; organic analysis. **Mailing Address:** 6 Herbert Ct, Tomkins Cove, NY 10986.

KELLY, MARTIN JOSEPH, PHYSICS. **Personal Data:** b New York, NY, September 27, 1924. **Education:** St John's Univ, NY, BS, 1949; NY Univ, PhD, 1958. **Professional Experience:** RETIRED; prof physics, C W Post Col, Long Island Univ, 1964-1997; chmn dept, C W Post Col, Long Island Univ, 1964-1974; mem fac, Manhattan Col, 1959-1964; assoc, Tech Res Group Inc, 1959; assoc, Nucleonics Inc, 1954-1959; physicist, Naval Mat Lab, 1951-1953. **Memberships:** Am Phys Soc. **Research Statement & Publications:** Neutron physics; reactors; shielding. **Mailing Address:** Dept Physics, C W Post Col, Greenvale, NY 11548-1300.

KELLY, MICHAEL THOMAS, CLINICAL MICROBIOLOGY, IMMUNOLOGY. **Personal Data:** b Indianapolis, Ind, March 8, 1943; m 1965, c 4. **Education:** Purdue Univ, BS, 1965; Ind Univ, PhD (microbiol), 1969, MD, 1973. **Professional Experience:** MED DIR, LAB SERV, MDS METRO'S MED, as of 2004; assoc prof path, Univ Tex Med Br, Galveston, 1978-; asst prof path, Sch Med, Univ Utah, 1976-1978; comn officer res, Rocky Mt Lab, NIH, USPHS, 1974-1976; intern path, Scg Med, Univ Minn, 1973-1974; res assoc infectious dis, Sch Med, Ind Univ, 1971-1973; fel, Sch Med, Ind Univ, 1969-1971; HEAD, MICROBIOL DEPT, METRO MCNAIR CLIN LAB. **Memberships:** AAAS; Reticuloendothelial Soc; Am Asn Immunologists; Am Soc Microbiol; Am Fedn Clin Res. **Research Statement & Publications:** Host-parasite relationships; modulation of macrophage function by microbial agents; immunopotentiation by microbial agents; mechanism of macrophage activation; clinical microbiology; antimicrobial susceptibility testing; marine microbiology. **Mailing Address:** Metro McNair Clin Lab, 660 W Seventh Ave, Vancouver, BC V5Z 1B5, Can.

KELLY, MINTON J, HIGH TEMPERATURE CHEMISTRY. **Personal Data:** b Liberty, Mo, February 14, 1921; m 1949, c 3. **Education:** Tex A&M Univ, BS, 1947, MS, 1950, PhD (phys chem), 1956. **Professional Experience:** RES ASSOC, CHEM TECHNOL DIV, OAK RIDGE NAT LAB, 1974-; chemist, Reactor Chem Div, 1963-1974; group supvr instrumentation, Aerospace Div, Boeing Co, 1962-1963; group leader reactor chem div, Oak Ridge Nat Lab, 1959-1962; develop engr instrumentation & controls div, Oak Ridge Nat Lab, 1955-1959; teaching fel chem univ, Tex A&M Univ, 1954-1955; consult instrumentation, Tex A&M Univ, 1950-1954; Engr, Arabian-Am Oil Co, 1948-1949; Field party chief oceanog res found, Tex A&M Univ, 1947-1948. **Memberships:** AAAS; Sigma Xi; fel Am Inst Chemists. **Research Statement & Publications:** Instrumental measurements under nuclear conditions. **Mailing Address:** 114 Lewis Lane, Oak Ridge, TN 37830.

KELLY, NELSON ALLEN, RENEWABLE ENERGY, ENVIRONMENTAL CHEMISTRY & AIR QUALITY. **Personal Data:** b Lakewood, Ohio, August 6, 1951; m 1982, Suzanne; c Ben, Bryan & Dan. **Education:** Miami Univ, Ohio, BS, 1973; Pa State Univ, PhD (phys chem), 1977. **Honors & Awards:** Joseph P Culler Prize. **Professional Experience:** STAFF RES SCIENTIST, GEN MOTORS RES LABS, 1982-; mem, Chem Comt, Air Pollution Control Asn, 1982-; sr res scientist, Gen Motors Res Labs, 1977-1982. **Memberships:** Sigma Xi; Am Chem Soc; InterAm Photochem Soc; Air Pollution Control Asn. **Research Statement & Publications:** Solar energy and sustainable transportation; reducing vehicle pollution by using fuel cells and hydrogen generated from renewable energy sources; environmental pollution and ozone formation; vehicle cabin-air quality. **Mailing Address:** Gen Motors Res & Develop Ctr, MC480-106-269 30500 Mound Rd, Warren, MI 48090-9055. **Fax:** 586-986-1910. **E-Mail:** nelson.a.kelly@gm.com

KELLY, PATRICK JOSEPH, ORTHOPEDIC SURGERY. **Personal Data:** b Minneapolis, Minn, February 12, 1926; m 1950, c 8. **Education:** St Lawrence Univ, BS, 1945; St Louis Univ, MD, 1949; Univ Minn, MS, 1958. **Professional Experience:** Prof orthop surg, Mayo Med Sch, 1973-1990; prof orthop surg, Mayo Grad Sch, 1969-1973; CONSULT, MAYO CLIN, 1957-; pres, Bd Trustees, Orthopaedic Res & Educ Found; mem, Am Inst Biol Sci Adv Panel, NASA; mem, Am Bd Orthop Surg; Am Orthop Asn Traveling Fel. **Memberships:** Am Acad Orthop Surg; Am Orthop Asn; Orthop Res Soc (past pres); Am Physiol Soc. **Research Statement & Publications:** Circulation and physiology of bone; bone metabolism. **Mailing Address:** Dept Orthop Surg, Mayo Clin & Found, 200 First St SW, Rochester, MN 55905.

KELLY, PAUL ALAN, MEDICAL RESEARCH. **Personal Data:** b Washington, DC, June 3, 1943; m 1991, c Daniel. **Education:** Western Mich Univ, BS, 1966, MS, 1968; Univ Wis, PhD (endocrinol & reprod physiol), 1972. **Professional Experience:** PROF & DIR, INSERM UNITE 344; ENDOCRINOL MOLECULAR FAC MED NECKER, 1991-; prof, Dept Med & Physiol, 1983-1991; dir, Lab Molecular Endocrinol, Royal Victoria Hosp, Montreal, 1983-1991; dir, Lab Molecular Endocrinol, 1983-1991; assoc prof physiol, Laval Univ, 1980-1982; Sr mem, Med Res Coun Group Molecular Endocrinol, 1975-; asst prof, Laval Univ, 1975-1980; Med Res Coun Can scholar, 1975-1980; fel, Laval Univ, 1974-1975; Fel endocrinol, McGill Univ, 1972-1974. **Memberships:** Endocrine Soc; Can Soc Clin Invest; Int Soc Neuroendocrinol; Int Soc Neurodendocrinol; Am Soc Biochem & Molecular Biol. **Research Statement & Publications:** signal transduction pathways of growth hormone and prolacton receptors; phenotypes associated with receptor knockouts. **Mailing Address:** INSERM Unite 344 Endocrinologie Moleculaire Faculte de Medicine Necker Enfants Malades, 156 rue de Vaugirard, 75730 Paris Cedex 15, France. **Fax:** 331-430-60443. **E-Mail:** kelly@necker.fr

KELLY, PAUL J, mathematics; deceased, see previous edition for last biography

KELLY, PAUL JAMES, PHYSICS. **Personal Data:** b Montreal, Que, July 19, 1934; m 1960, c 5. **Education:** Sir George Williams Univ, BSc, 1960; Carleton Univ, MSc, 1962, PhD (physics), 1965. **Professional Experience:** Air Force consult grant, Wash State Univ, 1978-; SR RES OFFICER PHYSICS, NAT RES COUN, 1976-; Asst invest officer, Energy Res & Develop Admin consult grant, Wash State Univ, 1975-1977; From asst res officer to assoc res officer, Nat Res Coun, 1965-1976. **Memberships:** Am Phys Soc. **Research Statement & Publications:** Thermally stimulated processes; interaction of high-intensity laser pulses with solids. **Mailing Address:** 310 Smyth Rd, Ottawa, ON K1H 5A3, Can.

KELLY, PAUL SHERWOOD, ATOMIC PHYSICS, QUANTUM MECHANICS. **Personal Data:** b Erie, Pa, December 22, 1927; m 1956, c 3. **Education:** Haverford Col, AB, 1949; Yale Univ, MS, 1950; Univ Calif, Los Angeles, PhD (physics), 1961. **Professional Experience:** RETIRED; prof physics, Humboldt State Univ, 1968-1997; res scientist, Lockheed Missiles & Space Co, Palo Alto, 1960-1968; electronic scientist, Nat Bur Stand, Calif, 1951-1953; physicist, US Naval Ord Lab, Md, 1950-1951. **Memberships:** Am Phys Soc; Sigma Xi. **Research Statement & Publications:** Calculation of atomic wave functions and related atomic parameters; nuclear structure calculations. **Mailing Address:** 2670 Kelly Ave, McKinleyville, CA 95519.

KELLY, PETER MICHAEL, PHYSICS, ELECTRICAL ENGINEERING. **Personal Data:** b New York, NY, July 6, 1922; m 1946, c 3. **Education:** Union Col, NY, BS, 1950; Calif Inst Technol, MS, 1952, PhD (physics) & PhD (elec eng), 1960. **Professional Experience:** RETIRED; consult, 1993; prof elec eng & dir, Telecommun Ctr, George Wash Univ, Wash, DC, 1980-1993; pres & chmn bd, Kelly Sci Corp, 1969-1980; consult, Pres Commun Task Force, 1968; consult, Pres Crime Comn, 1966; from assoc dir res to chief engr, Systs Tech Ctr, Philco, Ford, 1962-1969; mgr elec dept, Astropower, Douglas Aircraft Co, 1961-1962; consult, NSF, 1960-1961; from design engr to prin scientist, Aeronutronic Div, Ford Motor Co, 1956-1961; mem tech staff, Hughes Aircraft Co, 1954-1956; proj engr, Electronics Div, Century Metalcraft Co, 1953-1954; design engr, Jet Propulsion Lab, Calif Inst Technol, 1951-1952. **Memberships:** AAAS; Asn Comput Mach. **Research Statement & Publications:** Radar; network synthesis; data processing. **Mailing Address:** 901 N Monroe St Apt 1406, Arlington, VA 22201.

KELLY, RAYMOND CRAIN, ANALYTICAL TOXICOLOGY. **Personal Data:** b Portland, Ore, September 4, 1945; m 1994, Connie; c Leif, Nicole, Clinton & Joel. **Education:** Wash State Univ, BS, 1967; Univ Ore, PhD (chem), 1975. **Professional Experience:** Mem, Subcomt Perinatal Substance Abuse, State Nev & lab dir, 1997-; forensic toxicologist, NY, 1995-; DIR TOXICOL, ASSOC PATHOLOGISTS LABS, LAS VEGAS, 1993-2003; consult, Substance Abuse & Ment Health Serv Admin, 1991-; clin lab toxicologist, Calif, 1989-; lab & sci dir, Medtox Lab Inc, 1989-1993; pres, State Toxicol Ctr, 1985-1989; pres, Willow Toxicol Group, 1985; chief toxicologist, Specialty Labs, 1984; asst dir, Dept Clin & Indust Toxicol, Bio-Sci Lab, Van Nuys, Calif, 1978-1983; head toxicol, Lab Procedures, Upjohn Co, 1977-1978; Nat Res Serv fel, Nat Inst Drug Abuse, NIH, 1976; assoc toxicologist, Cuyahoga Co Coroners Off, Ohio, 1975-1977; develop chemist, Sacred Heart Gen Hosp, 1969-1971. **Memberships:** Am Acad Forensic Sci; Am Asn Clin Chem; Soc Forensic Toxicologists; Col Am Pathologists. **Research Statement & Publications:**

Devising of novel methods for the analysis of drugs in biological samples, characterization of drug metabolites, mechanisms of drug toxicity and monitoring of therapeutic drug concentrations in man; pharmacology of drug abuse in man; laboratory automation; analysis for drugs in hair. **Mailing Address:** Assoc Pathologists Labs, 4230 Burnham Ave Ste 250, Las Vegas, NV 89119. **Fax:** 702-733-0318. **E-Mail:** rkelly@apllabs.com

KELLY, REGIS BAKER, CELL BIOLOGY. **Personal Data:** b Edinburgh, Scotland, May 26, 1940; m 1992, Rae; c Gordon, Alison & Colin. **Education:** Univ Edinburgh, BSc, 1961, dipl, 1962; Calif Inst Technol, PhD (biophys), 1967. **Honors & Awards:** Javitz Investr Award, 1985 & 1992. **Professional Experience:** DISTINGUISHED NEUROSCIENTIST, UNIV CALIF, SAN FRANCISCO, as of 2006; exec vice chancellor, Univ Calif, San Francisco, 2001-2004; DIR, HORMONE RES INST, 1992-; DIR, CELL BIOL PROG, 1988-; vis prof, Mass Inst Technol, 1986; PROF BIOCHEM & BIOPHYS, UNIV CALIF, SAN FRANCISCO, 1978-; from asst prof to assoc prof, Hormone Res Inst, 1971-1978; Mult Sclerosis fel, 1970-1971; instr neurobiology, Harvard Med Sch, 1969-1971; Helen Hay Whitney Found fel, Sch Med, Stanford Univ, 1967-1969 & Harvard Med Sch, 1969-1970; rev, Am Cancer Soc; mem, Study Sect, NIH; mem adv panel, NEI. **Memberships:** Soc Neuroscience; Am Soc Biol Chem; Am Soc Cell Biol. **Research Statement & Publications:** Membrane traffice in cells; protein sorting; molecular events in nerve terminals; synaptic vesicles; development of the neuron. **Mailing Address:** Dept Biochem & Biophys, Univ Calif, 513 Parnassus Ave 1090 HSW, San Francisco, CA 94143-0534. **Fax:** 415-731-3612. **E-Mail:** rkelly@biochem.ucsf.edu

KELLY, RICHARD DELMER, BIOLOGY, SCIENCE EDUCATION. **Personal Data:** b Kingston, NY, August 24, 1935; m 1954, c 4. **Education:** State Univ NY Albany, BS, 1955, MS, 1956; Syracuse Univ, EdD(biol, sci educ), 1965. **Professional Experience:** Vis fel, Col Educ, Kingston Upon Hull, Eng, 1973-1974 & Rosentiel Inst, Univ Miami, 1982; prof biol, State Univ NY Albany, 1963-; consult, NY State Educ Dept, 1960- & NSF Summer Progs, 1960-1965; high sch teacher, NY, 1956-1963; PROF EMER PROF BIOL, STATE UNIV NY, ALBANY; prof biol, Univ WFla, Pensacola. **Memberships:** AAAS; Am Inst Biol Sci. **Research Statement & Publications:** Instructional technology; television, audio-tutorial; cetaceans and whaling history. **Mailing Address:** Dept Biol State Univ NY, 1400 Wash Ave, Albany, NY 12222.

KELLY, RICHARD W(ALTER), ELECTRICAL ENGINEERING. **Personal Data:** b Iowa City, Iowa, September 6, 1935; m 1964. **Education:** Univ Iowa, BSEE, 1958, MS, 1962, PhD (elec eng), 1965. **Professional Experience:** PROF EMER ASST DEAN, ARIZ STATE UNIV, as of 2006; PROF ELEC ENG, ARIZ STATE UNIV, 1970-; sr Fulbright-Hays lectureship, Trinity Col, Dublin, 1972-1973; assoc prof, Ariz State Univ, 1965-1970; from instr to asst prof elec eng, Univ Iowa, 1958-1965. **Memberships:** Inst Elec & Electronics Engrs; Am Soc Eng Educ. **Research Statement & Publications:** Application of modern signal theory; detection and estimation theory. **Mailing Address:** Dept Elec Eng, Ariz State Univ, GWC 424, Tempe, AZ 85281. **E-Mail:** richard.kelly@asu.edu

KELLY, ROBERT CHARLES, ORGANIC CHEMISTRY. **Personal Data:** b St Joseph, Mich, November 28, 1939; m 1960, c 2. **Education:** Kalamazoo Col, BA, 1961; Harvard Univ, MA, 1963, PhD (chem), 1966. **Professional Experience:** RES ASSOC ORG CHEM, UPJOHN CO, 1965-. **Memberships:** Am Chem Soc. **Research Statement & Publications:** Organic synthesis and structure determination, particularly of cyclic hydrocarbons; terpenes and oxygen heterocycles; natural products chemistry; prostaglandins. **Mailing Address:** Dept Chem 7246-209-6, Upjohn Co 301 Henrietta St, Kalamazoo, MI 49001-0199.

KELLY, ROBERT EDWARD, FLUID MECHANICS, HEAT TRANSFER. **Personal Data:** b Abington, Pa, October 20, 1934; m 1964, Karin E Lampert; c Nicholas & Jennifer. **Education:** Franklin & Marshall Col, BA, 1957; Rensselaer Polytech Inst, BS, 1957; Mass Inst Technol, AE, 1959, ScD (aeronaut eng), 1964. **Professional Experience:** PROF EMER, UNIV CALIF, LOS ANGELES, as of 2005; vis prof, Manchester Univ, UK, 1994; vis scientist, Japan Atomic Res Inst, 1991; vis prof, Northwestern Univ, 1985; assoc ed, Physics Fluids, 1981-1983 & 1992-; chmn, Div Fluid Dynamics, Am Phy Soc, 1980-1981; consult, Hughes Aircraft Co, 1976-1983; prof eng, Univ Calif, Los Angeles, beginning 1975; Sci Res Coun sr vis fel, Dept Math, Imp Col, London, 1973-1974; from asst prof to assoc prof, Univ Calif, Los Angeles, 1967-1975; asst res geophysicist, Inst Geophys & Planetary Physics, Univ Calif, San Diego, 1966-1967; guest scientist, UK Civil Serv sr res fel fluid mech, 1964-1966; res asst aeronaut eng, Mass Inst Technol, 1961-1964; guest scientist, Nat Phys Lab, UK, 1960-1961. **Memberships:** Fel Am Phys Soc; Am Inst Aeronaut & Aeronaut; fel Am Soc Mech Engrs; Sigma Xi; Am Acad Mech. **Research Statement & Publications:** Viscous flow; flow instabilities; fluid wave motion; stratified and rotating flow phenomena; thermal convection; thermocapillary flow. **Mailing Address:** Dept Mech & Aeronaut Eng, Univ Calif, Engr IV Rm 46-147B, Los Angeles, CA 90095-1597. **Fax:** 310-206-4830. **E-Mail:** rekhome@ucla.edu

KELLY, ROBERT EMMETT, PHYSICS. **Personal Data:** b Cape Girardeau, Mo, November 26, 1929; m 1962, Sarah Combs; c Katelyn, Frank & Tara. **Education:** Southeast Mo State Univ, BS, 1950; Univ Mo-Rolla, MS, 1952; Univ Conn, PhD (physics), 1959. **Professional Experience:** PHYSICIST, LOS ALAMOS NAT LAB, 1988-; vis scientist, Ctr d'Etudes Bruyeres-le-Chatel, Serv Physique Nucleaire, France, 1981 & 1982; consult, Los Alamos Sci Lab, 1975-1982 & Lawrence Livermore Lab, 1975-1979; Physicist, Gen Elec Co, 1952 & Marshall Space Flight Ctr, NASA, 1970 & 1971; prof, NMex Highlands Univ, 1968; is investr oceanog, Woods Hole Oceanog Inst, 1967; Richland fac fel, Hanford Lab, 1965; Prof physics, Univ Miss, 1959-1988; E I du Pont Del Nemours & Co, Inc, 1957 & Am Optical Co, 1959; consult, Boeing Co, 1954. **Memberships:** Am Geophys Union; Acoust Soc Am; Int Soc Optical Eng. **Research Statement & Publications:** Electromagnetic theory; physical optics; atmospheric and mathematical physics; mathematical approach to transient radiation damage in optical fibers; energy deposition and profiles of particle beams, plus topics in musical acoustics. **Mailing Address:** Los Alamos Nat Lab, PO Box 1663, Los Alamos, NM 87544. **Fax:** 505-667-7684. **E-Mail:** bkelly@lanl.gov

KELLY, ROBERT FRANK, BIOCHEMISTRY, ANIMAL HUSBANDRY. **Personal Data:** b Fond du Lac, Wis, May 21, 1919; m 1944, c 6. **Education:** Univ Wis, BS, 1948, MS, 1953, PhD (biochem, animal husb), 1955. **Honors & Awards:** Signal Serv Award, Am Meat Sci Asn, 1984. **Professional Experience:** AED prof, Sri Lanka, 1986; Williams-Waterman scientist, Haiti, 1963; PROF FOOD SCI & TECHNOL, VA POLYTECH INST & STATE UNIV, 1958-; assoc prof, VA Polytech Inst & State Univ, 1955-1958; asst, Univ Wis, 1951-1955; Pub sch instr, Wis, 1948-1951. **Memberships:** Am Inst Food Technologists; NY Acad Sci; Am Coun Sci & Health; Fel AAAS; Am Meat Sci Asn; Am Soc Animal Sci. **Research Statement & Publications:** Food science and nutrition. **Mailing Address:** 2801 Shadowlake Rd, Blacksburg, VA 24060.

KELLY, ROBERT JAMES, ORGANIC CHEMISTRY. **Personal Data:** b New York, NY, December 2, 1923; m 1952, c 7. **Education:** Trinity Col, BS, 1943; NY Univ, MS, 1947, PhD (chem), 1952. **Professional Experience:** TECH DIR UNIROYAL FIBER & TEXTILE DIV, UNIROYAL FIBER & TEXTILE DIV, 1976-; mgr tire cord res & develop, Uniroyal Fiber & Textile Div, 1969-1976; mgr new fiber res & develop, Uniroyal Fiber & Textile Div, 1965-1969; sr res scientist, 1962-1965; res chemist, 1951-1962; asst, NY Univ, 1946-1951. **Memberships:** Am Chem Soc. **Research Statement & Publications:** Synthetic rubber and fibers. **Mailing Address:** 4018 Sandwood Dr, Columbia, SC 29206-2222.

KELLY, ROBERT P, CELL PHYSIOLOGY. **Personal Data:** b Dover, NJ, March 17, 1938; m 1963. **Education:** Fairleigh Dickinson Univ, BS, 1962; Fordham Univ, MS, 1965, PhD (biol), 1966. **Professional Experience:** PROF BIOL & CHMN DEPT & COORDR PROG BIOL CHEM, ST PETER'S COL, NJ, 1980-; From instr to assoc prof, St Peter's Col, NJ, 1964-1980; Fac res grant, St Peter's Col, NJ, 1964-1965 & 1967. **Research Statement & Publications:** Insect and cell physiology with emphasis on nutrition and enzyme chemistry. **Mailing Address:** Dept Biol, St Peter's Col, 2641 Kennedy Blvd, Jersey City, NJ 07306-5943.

KELLY, ROBERT WITHERS, ZOOLOGY, ECOLOGY. **Personal Data:** b Stanford, Ky, October 20, 1926; m 1948, c 2. **Education:** Centre Col, BA, 1949; Univ Ore, MS, 1950; Univ Mo, PhD (zoology), 1956. **Professional Experience:** RETIRED; chmn dept, Furman Univ, 1974-1985; prof biol, Furman Univ, 1964-1988; assoc prof biol, Ariz State Col, 1963-1964; assoc prof biol, Southeastern La Col, 1956-1963; head sci dept, Campbellsville Jr Col, 1951-1953. **Memberships:** Am Soc Zool. **Research Statement & Publications:** Invertebrate ecology, especially freshwater forms. **Mailing Address:** 101 Redspire Dr, Greenville, SC 29617.

KELLY, RONALD BURGER, ORGANIC CHEMISTRY. **Personal Data:** b Fairvale, NB, May 26, 1920; m 1945. **Education:** Univ NB, MSc, 1951, PhD (chem), 1953. **Professional Experience:** PROF EMER CHEM, UNIV NB, 1985-; chmn Div Sci & Math, Univ Nb, 1973-1979; prof, Univ Nb, 1967-1985; res assoc chem, Upjohn Co, 1958-1967; sr res chemist, Merck & Co, Ltd, Can, 1955-1958; Nat Res Coun Can fel, Queen's Univ, Ont, 1954-1955; Beaverbrook overseas scholar, Univ London, 1953-1954. **Memberships:** AAAS; Am Chem Soc; Royal Soc Chem; fel Chem Inst Can; NY Acad Sci. **Research Statement & Publications:** Structure determination of organic molecules; synthesis of natural products. **Mailing Address:** Ft Worth, TX 76129.

KELLY, SALLY MARIE, CLINICAL PATHOLOGY, BIOCHEMICAL MEDICAL GENETICS. **Personal Data:** b Bridgeport, Conn. **Education:** Conn Col, AB, 1943; Univ Wis, MA, 1944, PhD (bot), 1946; NY Univ, MD, 1963; Am Bd Path, dipl, 1971. **Professional Experience:** RES ASSOC PROF PEDIAT, ALBANY MED COL, 1968-; RES PHYSICIAN, WADSWORTH CTR LABS & RES, NY STATE DEPT HEALTH, 1967-; assoc res scientist, Wadsworth Ctr Labs & Res, NY State Dept Health, 1964-1967; Brown-Hazen Fund fel, 1958-1959 & 1960-1963; sr res scientist, Wadsworth Ctr Labs & Res, NY State Dept Health, 1951-1964; asst prof plant sci, Vassar Col, 1948-1951; fel, Harvard Univ, 1947-1948; Instr, Simmons Col, 1947-1948; Fel, Brooklyn Bot Garden, 1945-1947. **Memberships:** Col Am Pathologist; fel AAAS. **Research Statement & Publications:** Cell physiology; enteroviruses; biochemical medical genetics; clincal pathology. **Mailing Address:** Wadsworth Ctr Labs & Res, NY State Dept Health, Albany, NY 12201.

KELLY, SUSAN JEAN, ENZYMOLOGY, BIOCHEMICAL ENGINEERING. **Personal Data:** b Cincinnati, Ohio, October 2, 1947; div, c 2. **Education:** Col Mt St Joseph, AB, 1969; Purdue Univ, PhD (biochem), 1974. **Professional Experience:** BIOL, DURHAM NC, 1990-; workshop coordr, Carolina Workshop, 1984-1990; consult, 1980-; res assoc, Univ NC, Chapel Hill, 1980-1984; res assoc enzyme eng, Dept Biochem, Purdue Univ, 1974-1980; lectr & lab mgr, Duke Univ, Howard Hughes Lab Molecular. **Memberships:** Sigma Xi. **Research Statement & Publications:** Enzyme-catalyzed synthesis of sucrose and other economically important physiological compounds; enzymic mechanism of phosphatases; phosphonate analogs of phosphatase substrates; relationship of phosphatases to developmental changes and to cancer. **Mailing Address:** 8104 Lair Ct, Chapel Hill, NC 27516.

KELLY, THADDEUS ELLIOTT, MEDICAL GENETICS. **Personal Data:** b New York, NY, October 7, 1937; m 1960, c 3. **Education:** Davidson Col, BS, 1959; Med Col SC, MD, 1963; Johns Hopkins Univ, PhD (genetics), 1975. **Professional Experience:** PROF PEDIAT, UNIV VA, 1980-as of today; pres, Am Bd Med Genetics, 1993-1994; dir, Div Med Genetics, Univ Va, 1975-; assoc prof, Univ VA, 1975-1980; asst prof med & pediat, Sch Med, Johns Hopkins Univ, 1973-1975. **Memberships:** Soc Pediat Res; Am Pediat Soc; Am Soc Human Genetics; Am Col Med Genetics. **Research Statement & Publications:** Biochemical genetic analysis of genetic heterogenity; genetic disorders in large family studies; molecular biology of X chromosome. **Mailing Address:** Univ Va Hosp, PO Box 800386, Charlottesville, VA 22908-0001. **Fax:** 434-982-3850. **E-Mail:** tek8s@virginia.edu

KELLY, THOMAS J, MOLECULAR BIOLOGY. **Personal Data:** b Birmingham, Ala, November 21, 1941; m 1969, c 2. **Education:** Johns Hopkins Univ, BA, 1962, PhD (biophys), 1968, MD, 1969. **Professional Experience:** DIR, SLOAN-KETTERING INST, 2001-; chair, Dept Molecular Biol & Genetics, Sch Med, Johns Hopkins Univ, ending 2001; Harvey Soc lectr, 1990; chmn, Virol Study Sect, NIH, 1988-1990; bd dirs, Passano Found, 1987-; mem, Awards Assembly, Gen Motors Cancer Prize, 1986-1989; chmn dept, Johns Hopkins Univ, sch med, beginning 1982; prof, Dept Molecular Biol & Genetics, Sch Med, Johns Hopkins Univ, 1981-2001; mem, Virol Study Sect, NIH, 1980-1984; from asst prof to assoc prof microbiol, Johns Hopkins Univ, Sch Med, 1972-1979; NIH career develop award, 1972-1977; staff assoc, NIH, 1970-1972; Bd Sci Counr, Nat Ctr Biotechnol Info; found dir, Inst Basics Biomed Sci, Johns Hopkins Univ. **Memberships:** Am Soc Microbiol; Am Soc Biol Chemists; Am Soc Virol; fel Am Acad Arts & Sci; Nat Acad Sci; Inst Med; Am Philos Soc. **Research Statement & Publications:** Molecular genetics of animal cells and viruses; duplication of the genes in normal and cancer cells. **Mailing Address:** Sloan-Kettering Inst, 1275 York Ave, New York, NY 10021. **Fax:** 646-422-2189. **E-Mail:** tkelly@mskcc.org

KELLY, THOMAS MICHAEL, PHYSICS, SOLID STATE SCIENCE. **Personal Data:** b Watertown, NY, May 16, 1941; m 1962, Ann; c Mary A, John & T Michael. **Education:** Le Moyne Col, NY, BS, 1962; Wayne State Univ, PhD (physics), 1966. **Professional Experience:** DIR SILICON FILM, DIGIT PROD CTR, EASTMAN KODAK RES LABS, 1994-; vpres & dir res develop, Eastman Kodak Res Labs, 1988-1993; from lab head to asst div dir, Eastman Kodak Res Labs, 1982-1988; from sr res physicist to res assoc, Eastman Kodak Res Labs, 1968-1988; AEC res assoc positron annihilation, New Eng Inst Med Res, 1966-1968. **Memberships:** Inst Elec & Electronics Engrs. **Research Statement & Publications:** Physics of solid state imaging; design and fabrication. **Mailing Address:** Eastman Kodak Co, 901 Elmgrove Rd, Rochester, NY 14653-9053.

KELLY, THOMAS ROSS, ORGANIC CHEMISTRY. **Personal Data:** b New York, NY, April 26, 1942; c 2. **Education:** BS, Holy Cross Col, 1964; Univ Calif, Berkeley, PhD (org chem), 1968. **Honors & Awards:** res career develop award, NIH, 1975-1980; Arthur C

Cope Scholar Award, Am Chem Soc, 1996. **Professional Experience:** THOMAS A & MARGARET A VANDERSLICE PROF CHEM, BOSTON COL, 1989-; from asst prof to prof, Boston Col, 1969-1989; NIH postdoctoral fel, 1968-1969. **Research Statement & Publications:** Organic synthesis; natural products. **Mailing Address:** Dept Chem, Boston Col, 140 Commonwealth Ave, Chestnut Hill, MA 02467. **Fax:** 617-552-2705. **E-Mail:** ross.kelly@bc.edu

KELLY, WALTER JAMES, ORGANIC CHEMISTRY, POLYMER CHEMISTRY. **Personal Data:** b Cleveland, Ohio, February 25, 1941; m 1971. **Education:** Case Inst Technol, BS, 1963, Case Western Reserve Univ, PhD (phys org chem), 1970. **Professional Experience:** PROJ MGR, FOIL DIV, GOULD INC, 1981-; proj engr, Polymer Technol, 1980-1981; staff scientist, Polymer Technol, 1978-1980; Sr res chemist, Polymer Res, Goodyear Tire & Rubber Co, 1969-1978. **Memberships:** Am Chem Soc; Electrochemical Soc. **Research Statement & Publications:** Dynamic properties of elastomers; structure-property correlations; polymer rheology and processing; crosslinking mechanisms; post polymerization reactions; adhesion, polymer modification electrodeposition. **Mailing Address:** 1545 Forest Lane, Marion, IN 46952-9810.

KELLY, WILLIAM ALBERT, NEUROSURGERY. **Personal Data:** b Cincinnati, Ohio, July 16, 1927; m 1952, c 2. **Education:** Ohio Wesleyan Univ, BA, 1950; Univ Cincinnati, MD, 1954. **Professional Experience:** PROF EMER NEUROL SURG, UNIV WASH, as of 2005; prof neurosurg, Univ Wash, beginning 1977; from instr to assoc prof, Univ Wash, 1961-1977; chief resident & clin asst, Univ Wash, 1960-1961; res fel, Univ Wash, 1959-1960; resident, Univ Wash, 1957-1959; res fel neurosurg, Univ Chicago Clins, 1956-1957. **Memberships:** Am Asn Neurol Surg. **Research Statement & Publications:** Pituitary tumors; medical education on student and resident level. **Mailing Address:** Dept Neurol Surg, Sch Med, Univ Wash, R1 20, Seattle, WA 98195.

KELLY, WILLIAM ALVA, VETERINARY PATHOLOGY. **Personal Data:** b Cullman, Ala, February 24, 1937; div, c 5. **Education:** Auburn Univ, DVM, 1962; Purdue Univ, PhD (vet path), 1971. **Professional Experience:** SR VET PATHOLOGIST, BRISTOL MYERS SQUIBB, 1987-; vet pathologist, Mead Johnson & Co, 1970-1981; instr vet path, Purdue Univ, 1966-1970; Vet, pvt pract, 1962-1966. **Memberships:** Am Col Vet Pathologists; Int Acad Path. **Research Statement & Publications:** Experimental toxicologic pathology; pathology of laboratory animals; nutritionally-induced pathology; chemical carcinogenesis. **Mailing Address:** 3249 Lower New Harmony Rd, Mt Vernon, IN 47620.

KELLY, WILLIAM B, MATHEMATICS. **Education:** Ga Inst Technol, PhD (Maths), 1992. **Professional Experience:** PROF, DEPT MATH & COMPUT SCI, MARYVILLE UNIV, as of 2002. **Mailing Address:** Maryville Col, Dept Math & Comput Sci, PO Box 2875, Maryville, TN 37804-5907. **Fax:** 865-981-1175.

KELLY, WILLIAM CLARK, PHYSICS. **Personal Data:** b Braddock, Pa, March 18, 1922; m 1947, Gertrude; c Emily (Szumowski) & William B. **Education:** Univ Pittsburgh, BS, 1943, MS, 1946, PhD (physics), 1951. **Professional Experience:** RETIRED; spec asst, Am Asn Physics Teachers, 1984-1989; mem coun on teaching sci, Int Coun Sci Unions, 1975-1978; exec dir comn human resources, Nat Res Coun, 1974-1983; chmn, Int Union Pure & Appl Physics, 1972-1975; mem subcomt prof sci & technol manpower, Dept Labor, 1971-1972; dir off sci personnel, Nat Acad Sci-Nat Res Coun, 1967-1974; secy comn physics educ, Int Union Pure & Appl Physics, 1966-1972; fel officer, Nat Acad Sci-Nat Res Coun, 1965-1967; dir dept educ & manpower, Am Inst Physics, 1958-1965; Ford fac fel, 1954-1955; from asst to assoc prof physics, Univ Pittsburgh, 1946-1958. **Memberships:** AAAS; Am Asn Physics Teachers. **Research Statement & Publications:** Measurement of spectral emissivities of metals; beta and gamma ray spectroscopy; improvements in the teaching of science; manpower studies; human-resource supply and demand, especially in science and engineering. **Mailing Address:** 9320 Renshaw Dr, Bethesda, MD 20817.

KELLY, WILLIAM CROWLEY, ECONOMIC GEOLOGY. **Personal Data:** b Philadelphia, Pa, May 10, 1929; m 1959. **Education:** Columbia Univ, AB, 1951, MA, 1953, PhD (geol), 1954. **Professional Experience:** PROF EMER GEOL, UNIV MICH, ANN ARBOR, as of 2001; VPRES, DEPT GEOL, UNIV MICH, ANN ARBOR, 1993-; vpres res, Univ Mich, Ann Arbor, 1990-1993; prof & chmn geol sci, Univ Mich, Ann Arbor, 1980-1990; prof geol & mineral, Univ Mich, Ann Arbor, 1967-1980; Ed, Geochem News, 1961-1963; from instr to assoc prof geol, Univ Mich, Ann Arbor, 1956-1967; opers analyst, Opers res Off, Johns Hopkins Univ, 1954-1956; instr geol, Hunter Col, 1954; asst econ geol, Columbia Univ, 1951-1953. **Memberships:** Geol Soc Am; Geochem Soc; Mineral Soc Am; Soc Econ Geol; Geol Soc France. **Research Statement & Publications:** Chemical weathering; telluride ore deposits; oxidation of lead-zinc ores; mineralogy of iron oxides; ore microscopy. **Mailing Address:** Dept Geol Sci, Univ Mich, 1063, 2534 C C Little Bldg, 425 E Univ, Ann Arbor, MI 48109-1063. **E-Mail:** billkell@umich.edu

KELLY, WILLIAM DANIEL, SURGERY. **Personal Data:** b St Paul, Minn, October 28, 1922; m 1951, c 6. **Education:** Univ Minn, BS, 1943, MB, 1945, MD, 1946, PhD (surg), 1955; Am Bd Surg, dipl, 1955; Am Bd Thoracic Surg, dipl, 1959. **Professional Experience:** CLIN PROF SURG, UNIV HOSPS, 1980-; mem surg staff, Univ Hosps, 1962-1980; prof surg, Univ Hosps, 1961-1980; chief surg, Vet Admin Hosp, Minneapolis, 1960-1962; Dir exp surg lab, Vet Admin Hosp, Minneapolis, 1959-1960; From instr to assoc prof, Univ Hosps, 1953-1961. **Memberships:** AAAS; Soc Exp Biol & Med; Soc Univ Surgeons; AMA; NY Acad Sci. **Research Statement & Publications:** Homotransplantation; cardiovascular physiology and surgery. **Mailing Address:** 3838 Zenith Ave S, Minneapolis, MN 55410-1167.

KELLY, WILLIAM ROBERT, GEOCHEMISTRY, ANALYTICAL CHEMISTRY. **Personal Data:** b Norfolk, Va, July 24, 1944; m 1969, c 1. **Education:** Old Dominion Col, BS, 1968; Ariz State Univ, PhD, 1974. **Honors & Awards:** Nininger Meteorite Award, 1974; IR100 Award, 1984; Outstanding Support Serv Award, Sigma Xi, 1992. **Professional Experience:** RES CHEMIST, ANALYTICAL CHEM, NAT INST STAND & TECHNOL, 1979-; res fel, Calif Inst Technol, 1977-1979; vis assoc geochem, Calif Inst Technol, 1975-1977. **Memberships:** Am Chem Soc; Meteoritical Soc; Geochem Soc; Sigma Xi. **Research Statement & Publications:** Cosmochemistry; thermal ionization mass spectrometry; environmental chemistry; analytical chemistry. **Mailing Address:** Anal Chem Div, Nat Inst Stand & Technol, 100 Bureau Dr Stop 8397, Gaithersburg, MD 20899. **Fax:** 301-869-0413. **E-Mail:** william.kelly@nist.gov

KELLY-FRY, ELIZABETH, BIOACOUSTICS, MEDICAL ULTRASOUND. **Personal Data:** wid, c 2. **Education:** Howard Univ, ScM, 1953; Sarasota Univ, EdD(sci educ), 1975. **Honors & Awards:** Japan Soc US Med Award, 1976; Presidential Award, Am Inst Ultrasound Med, 1980; World Fedn US Med Award, 1988. **Professional Experience:** EMER PROF RADIOL, IND UNIV, INDIANAPOLIS, as of 2004; RES SCIENTIST & PHYSICIST MED ULTRASOUND, INDIANAPOLIS BREAST CTR, 1992-; prof radiol, Sch Med, Ind Univ, Indianapolis, beginning 1991; Med Physics Dept, Univ Wis, 1983-1987; assoc prof radiol, Sch Med, Ind Univ, Indianapolis, 1982-1991; consult, Ultrasound Corp, 1980-1986; mem, NIH Diag Res Adv Comt, 1980-1981; consult, Nat Heart, Lung & Blood Inst, NIH, 1976-1979; assoc ed, J Clin Ultrasound, 1975-1979; Consult, Bur Radiol Health, 1973-1981; res scientist, Ind Ctr Advan Res, 1972-1992; assoc prof surg, Sch Med, Ind Univ, Indianapolis, 1972-1991; vpres, Intersci Res Inst, 1968-1971; assoc dir res, Intersci Res Inst, 1964-1967; Biophys Res Lab, Univ Ill, 1954-1964. **Memberships:** Am Phys Soc; Acoust Soc Am; Biophys Soc; fel Am Inst Ultrasound Med; Am Asn Univ Prof. **Research Statement & Publications:** Ultrasound breast examination; design of ultrasoundinstrumentation for breast imaging; development of advanced ultrasound imaging techniques for detection of breast. **Mailing Address:** Indpolis Breast Ctr, 1950 W 86th St, Indianapolis, IN 46260. **Fax:** 317-872-9856.

KELMAN, ARTHUR, PHYTOBACTERIOLOGY. **Personal Data:** b Providence, RI, December 11, 1918; m 1949, c 1. **Education:** Univ RI, BS, 1941; NC State Univ, MS, 1946, PhD (plant path), 1949. **Honorary Degrees:** DSc, Univ RI, 1977. **Honors & Awards:** Stakman Award, 1987. **Professional Experience:** UNIV DISTINGUISHED SCHOLAR, NC STATE UNIV, 1990-; chmn, Class VI, Appl Biol & Agr Sci, Nat Acad Sci, 1988-1991; coun, Nat Acad Sci, 1986-1989; prof & chmn dept, Wis Alumni Res Found sr distinguished prof plant path, 1985-1989; chmn, Bd Basic Biol, 1984-1985; chmn, Div Biol Sci, Assembly Life Sci, Nat Res Coun, 1981-1984; chmn, Sect Appl Biol & Agr Sci, Comn Life Sci, 1981-1983; prof bact, Univ Wis-Madison, 1978-1989; prof & chmn dept, L R Jones distinguished prof, 1975-1985; vis prof, Dept Biochem, 1971-1972; NSF sr fel, Cambridge Univ, 1971-1972; prof & chmn dept, Univ Wis-Madison, 1965-1975; from instr to prof plant path, Reynolds distinguished prof, 1962-1965; vis lectr, Am Inst Biol Sci, 1958-1960; vis investr, Rockefeller Inst, 1953-1954; from instr to prof plant path, NC State Univ, 1948-1962; mem US nat comt, Int Union Biol Sci. **Memberships:** Nat Acad Sci; Am Acad Arts & Sci; Am Inst Biol Sci; Soc Gen Microbiol; hon mem Int Soc Plant Path (vpres, 1968-1973, pres, 1973-1978); Am Phytopath Soc (vpres, 1966, pres, 1967); fel AAAS; Sigma Xi. **Research Statement & Publications:** Physiology of parasitism; bacterial diseases of plants; nature of resistance to bacterial soft rot of potatoes. **Mailing Address:** Dept Plant Path NC StateUniv, 3411 Gardner Hall, Raleigh, NC 27695-7616. **Fax:** 919-515-7716. **E-Mail:** arthur_kelman@ncsu.edu

KELMAN, BRUCE JERRY, TOXICOLOGY, TERATOLOGY. **Personal Data:** b Chicago, Ill, July 1, 1947; m 1972, Jacqueline; c Aaron Wayne, Diantha Renee & Coreyanne L. **Education:** Univ Ill, BS, 1969, MS, 1971, PhD (vet med sci), 1975; Am Bd Toxicol, cert, 1980, 1985, 1990, 1995, 2000, 2005. **Professional Experience:** PRES, VERITOX INC, 2005-; PRES, GLOBALTOX INC, 1998-2005; National Director, Health and Environmental Sciences, Golder Associates Inc., 1993-1998; dept toxicol, Failure Analysis Assoc, 1990-1993; mgr biol & chem dept, Pac Northwest Labs, Battelle Mem Inst, 1985-1990; from assoc mgr to mgr, dev toxicol, Pac Northwest Labs, Battelle Mem Inst, 1980-1984; sr res scientist develop toxicol, Pac Northwest Labs, Battelle Mem Inst, 1979-1980; asst prof prenatal toxicol, Comp Animal Res Lab, Oak Ridge, Tenn, 1976-1979; res assoc toxicol, Comp Animal Res Lab, Oak Ridge, Tenn, 1974-1976; Res asst physiol, Univ Ill, 1969-1974. **Memberships:** Soc Toxicol; Soc Exp Biol & Med; Teratol Soc; Am Soc Pharmacol & Exp Therapeut; Am Coll of Occup & Env Med; Am Acad Vet & Comp Toxicol; Am College of Toxicology. **Research Statement & Publications:** Toxicology of chemicals (including chemical mixtures and metals) and radiation; teratology and other developmental effects of toxic materials including radionuclides. **Mailing Address:** VeriTox, 18372 Redmond Fall City Rd, Redmond, WA 98052. **Fax:** 425-556-5556. **E-Mail:** bkelman@veritox.com

KELMAN, CHARLES D, ophthalmology; deceased, see previous edition for last biography

KELMAN, L(EROY) R, ENGINEERING OF MATERIALS FOR NUCLEAR POWER. **Personal Data:** b Minneapolis, Minn, August 16, 1919; m 1984, Elizabeth; c Bruce, Keith & Scott. **Education:** Univ Minn, BS, 1942. **Professional Experience:** RETIRED; proj leader & prog coodr, Safety Light Water Reactor Fuels, 1975-1978; prog planner, Mat Sci Div, 1970-1973; mgr fuels & mat sect, Liquid Metal Fast Breeder Reactor Prog Off, 1966-1970; sr metallurgist, Safety Light Water Reactor Fuels, 1959-1989; group leader, Metall Div, 1947-1966; metallurgist anal, Argonne Nat Lab, 1944-1959; metallurgist, Caterpillar Tractor Co, 1942-1944. **Memberships:** Am Nuclear Soc; Am Soc Metals; Am Inst Mining, Metal & Petrol Engrs; Sigma Xi. **Research Statement & Publications:** Metallurgy for nuclear reactors; fuels, structural materials and liquid metal coolants; behavior of nuclear fuels and structural materials under transient and hypothetical accident conditions; materials behavior in liquid metal coolants. **Mailing Address:** 1030 Prairie Ave, Naperville, IL 60540.

KELMAN, LORI MACELLARO, HISTONE GENE TRANSCRIPTION. **Personal Data:** b New York, NY, May 16, 1960; m 1996, Zvi. **Education:** Mt Holyoke Col, AB, 1982; St Johns Univ, MS, 1984; Cornell Univ, PhD (molecular biol), 1994. **Professional Experience:** Sci writer, Online Mendelian Inheritance Man, 1996-; ASSOC PROF BIOL, IONA COL, 1996-; asst prof, Iona Col, 1991-1996. **Memberships:** AAAS; Asn Women Sci. **Research Statement & Publications:** New developments in molecular biology that effect knowledge about human genes and diseases. **Mailing Address:** Iona Col, 715 N Ave, New Rochelle, NY 10801. **Fax:** 914-633-2240.

KELMAN, ROBERT BERNARD, MATHEMATICS, COMPUTER SCIENCE. **Personal Data:** b Ansonia, Conn, August 12, 1930; m 1957, c Karl & Daniel. **Education:** Univ Calif, Berkeley, AB, 1953, MA, 1955, PhD (math), 1958. **Professional Experience:** CHAIR & PROF EMER, DEPT COMPUT SCI, COLO STATE UNIV, as of 2006; owner, heel & toe publ, beginning 1994; dir, klmn consult, beginning 1988; chmn, Colo State Univ, 1981-1988; prof comput sci, Colo State Univ, 1972-1988; prof, Univ Colo Med Ctr, 1972-1980; assoc prof prev med, Univ Colo Med Ctr, 1967-1972; assoc prof math, Colo State Univ, 1966-1968; res asst prof math, Univ Md, 1963-1966; Lectr, Howard Univ, 1961-1965; mgr biomath res, Univac Div, Sperry Rand Corp, 1961-1963; consult, Exec Off President Eisenhower, 1960-1961; mathematician, Int Bus Mach Corp, 1958-1961; instr, Univ Ill, 1957-1958; Comput engr, NAm Aviation, Inc, 1955-1956. **Memberships:** Fel AAAS; Math Asn Am; Soc Indust & Appl Math; Am Soc Nephrology. **Research Statement & Publications:** Differential equations; theoretical renal physiology; computer modeling. **Mailing Address:** 1312 Robertson St, Ft Collins, CO 80524. **Fax:** 970-482-0974. **E-Mail:** klmn@compuserve.com

KELNHOFER, WILLIAM JOSEPH, MECHANICAL ENGINEERING, FLUID MECHANICS. **Personal Data:** b Manitowoc, Wis, November 24, 1930. **Education:** Marquette Univ, BME, 1956; Cath Univ, MME, 1960, DEng, 1966. **Professional Experience:** PROF EMER MECH ENG, CATH UNIV AM, as of 2004; Dept chmn, Cath Univ Am, 1983-1992; prin investr, Off NavalRes contract, 1966 & Nat Bur Stand contracts, 1974-; ord prof mech eng, Cath Univ Am, beginning 1973; res prof, Max Planck Inst, Goettingen, 1966-1967 & Munich Tech Univ, 1969-1970; assoc, US Army contract, 1963-1964; Prin investr, US Navy contract, 1962-1968; from instr to assoc prof, Cath Univ Am, 1960-1973; Proj engr,

US Navy Bur Ships, 1956-1959. **Memberships:** Am Soc Mech Engrs; Nat Soc Prof Engrs; Am Soc Heating Refrig & Air Conditioning Engrs; Sigma Xi. **Research Statement & Publications:** Heat transfer; boundary layer theory; thermal systems; energy conservation; applied thermodynamics. **Mailing Address:** Dept Mech Eng, Cath Univ, Washington, DC 20017.

KELSAY, JUNE LAVELLE, NUTRITION. **Personal Data:** b Jacksboro, Tex, June 29, 1925. **Education:** NTex State Univ, BS, 1946, MS, 1947; Univ Wis, PhD (foods & nutrit), 1967. **Honors & Awards:** Borden Award, Am Home Econ Asn, 1982. **Professional Experience:** RETIRED; res nutritionist, Agr Res Serv, 1967-1987; nutrit specialist, USDA, 1954-1962; technician nutrit res, Tex Agr Exp Sta, 1951-1952; instr nutrit, NTex State Univ, 1947-1950. **Memberships:** Am Inst Nutrit; Am Soc Clin Nutrit; Am Home Econ Asn. **Research Statement & Publications:** Preadolescent children; folic and pantothenic acid; vitamin B-6 deficiency in man; effect of protein level; forms of vitamin B-6; excretion of niacin metabolites; nutritional status; carbohydrate response in human subjects; effects of fiber in human subjects; mineral balances; oxalic acid and mineral bioavailability; fiber and nutrient intakes. **Mailing Address:** 312 E Col St Apt 12, Gunter, TX 75058.

KELSEY, CHARLES ANDREW, MEDICAL PHYSICS. **Personal Data:** b Norfolk, Nebr, July 9, 1935; m 1960, c 4. **Education:** St Edward's Col, BS, 1957; Univ Notre Dame, PhD (physics), 1962; Am Bd Radiol, dipl. **Professional Experience:** PROF EMER, UNIV NMEX, as of 2002; prof radiol, Univ Nmex, beginning 1975; chief biomed physics, Univ Nmex, 1975-1980; from asst prof to prof radiol, Univ Wis-Madison, 1965-1975; from instr to asst prof physics, Univ Wis-Madison, 1963-1965; res assoc, Univ Wis-Madison, 1962-1963; Res assoc physics, Univ Notre Dame, 1962. **Memberships:** AAAS; Am Phys Soc; Am Acad Phys Med & Rehab; Am Inst Ultrasonics in Med; Radiol Soc NAm; fel Am Col Radiol. **Research Statement & Publications:** Application of physics technology to medical problems. **Mailing Address:** Dept Radiol, Univ NMex Med Sch 1 Univ Campus, Albuquerque, NM 87131-0001.

KELSEY, DONALD ROSS, HIGH PERFORMANCE POLYMERS, RING-OPENING METATHESIS POLYMERIZATIONS. **Personal Data:** b Windsor, Mo, September 30, 1945. **Education:** Cent Mo State Univ, BS, 1968; Calif Inst Technol, PhD (phys orgchem), 1973. **Honors & Awards:** ALS Award for Team innoation, Amer chem soc, 2000; Distinguished Alumni Award, Central Mo state univ, 1996. **Professional Experience:** STAFF RES CHEMIST, SHELL DEVELOP CO, 1995-; sr res chemist, Shell Develop CO, 1987-1995; sr res scientist, Amoco Peformance Prod, Inc, 1986-1987; sr res scientist, Union Carbide Corp, 1984-1986; res scientist, Union Carbide Corp, 1978-1984; proj scientist, Union Carbide Corp, 1977-1978; chemist, Union Carbide Corp, 1974-1977; fel, Chem Dept, Yale Univ, 1972-1974. **Memberships:** Am Chem Soc; Am Inst Chem. **Research Statement & Publications:** Design and synthesis of polymers and polymerization catalysts; polyarylethers, ring-opening metathesis polymers, polyesters; mechanisms of nucleophilic displacement and aryl coupling reactions, orbital topology analysis of thermal reactions; granted 51 US patents and publications. **Mailing Address:** PO Box 1380, Whollow Res Ctr, Houston, TX 77441-1380. **E-Mail:** Donkelsey@shellus.com

KELSEY, EDWARD JOSEPH, SOFTWARE SYSTEMS, ATOMIC & MOLECULAR PHYSICS. **Personal Data:** b Washington, DC, December 10, 1948. **Education:** Wesleyan Univ, BA, 1970; Univ Md, MS, 1972, PhD (physics), 1974. **Professional Experience:** ADJ LECTR, MONMOUTH UNIV, as of 2005; mem tech staff comput sci, At&T Bell Labs, beginning 1979; assoc res scientist, NY Univ, 1976-1978; res assoc physics, Univ Nebr, Lincoln, 1974-1976. **Memberships:** Am Phys Soc; Asn Comput Mach. **Research Statement & Publications:** Quantum electrodynamic theory applied to problems concerning one and two electron systems; operation systems which maintain and test the telephone network. **Mailing Address:** 220 Conifer Crest Way, Eatontown, NJ 07724. **E-Mail:** ekelsey@monmouth.edu

KELSEY, EUGENE LLOYD, ELECTRICAL ENGINEERING, AERO-SPACE ENGINEERING. **Personal Data:** b Ponca City, Okla, May 10, 1932; m 1973, c 2. **Education:** Okla State Univ, BSEE, 1958; Va Polytech Inst, MSEE, 1966. **Professional Experience:** RETIRED; adj instr math, Christopher Newport Col, 1976-1979; eng supvr systs develop-elec flight systs, NASA, 1972-1994; aerospace technologist, NASA, 1962-1972; test engr B-58 radar guidance, Gen Dynamics, Fort Worth, 1958-1962; jr engr guidance, Autonetics-NAm Aviation, 1956-1957. **Memberships:** Soc Automotive Engrs-Aerospace. **Research Statement & Publications:** Design, development and analysis of aerospace stabilization control and pointing systems for aircraft, satellite and research projects; unique requirements-unique solutions. **Mailing Address:** 101 McClellan Ct, Yorktown, VA 23692.

KELSEY, FRANCES OLDHAM, PHARMACOLOGY. **Personal Data:** b Cobble Hill, BC, July 24, 1914; American citizen; m 1943, c 2. **Education:** McGill Univ, BSc, 1934, MSc, 1935; Univ Chicago, PhD (pharmacol), 1938, MD, 1950. **Honorary Degrees:** DSc, Hood Col, 1962, Univ NB, 1964, Western Col Women, 1964, Middlebury Col, 1966, Wilson Col, 1967, St Mary's Col, 1969, Drexel Univ, 1973, Univ SDak, 1982, McGill Univ, 1984. **Honors & Awards:** Lederle Award, 1954, 1957. **Professional Experience:** Res, dept health & human serv, Food & drug admin, beginning 1960; pvt pract, 1957-1960; assoc prof med, Sch Med, Univ SDak, 1954-1957; asst prof pharmacol, Univ Chicago, 1946; dir, div sci invest, Off sci Compliance, Ctr drug eval. **Memberships:** Am Soc Pharmacol & Exp Therapeut; Soc Exp Biol & Med; Teratol Soc; Am Women Sci; Am Med Writers' Asn; Sigma Xi. **Research Statement & Publications:** Posterior pituitary; chemotherapy of malaria; radioisotopes. **Mailing Address:** 5811 Brookside Dr, Chevy Chase, MD 20815. **Fax:** 301-594-1204.

KELSEY, JOHN EDWARD, SCIENTIFIC INFORMATION, ENVIRONMENTAL HEALTH. **Personal Data:** b Beloit, Wisc, October 28, 1942; m 1965, c 3. **Education:** Univ Wis, BS, 1965, PhD (pharm chem), 1969. **Professional Experience:** RETIRED; dir tech & admin opers, Tech Serv Div, 1984-1994; dir, Tech Serv Div, 1981-1984; dir occup health, Burroughs Wellcome Co, Inc, 1978-1980; sr res chemist, Burroughs Wellcome Co, Inc, 1975-1978; res chemist, Burroughs Wellcome Co, Inc, 1970-1974; Nat Cancer Inst overseas fel, 1968-1970. **Memberships:** Am Chem Soc. **Research Statement & Publications:** Management of science information, automation, administration, radiation, and unit facilities services functions in the pharmaceutical research, development and manufacturing industry. **Mailing Address:** 106 Greenock Ct, Cary, NC 27511.

KELSEY, KARL, OCCUPATIONAL MEDICINE. **Education:** Harvard Sch Pub Health, MOH, 1984; Univ Minn, MD, 1981. **Professional Experience:** PROF CANCER BIOL & ENVIRON HEALTH, DEPT GENETICS & COMPLEX DIS & ENVIRON HEALTH, HARVARD UNIV, as of 2006; ASSOC PROF MED, HARVARD MED SCH. **Research Statement & Publications:** Application of laboratory-based biomarkers in chronic disease epidemiology and tumor biology; mechanistic understanding of individual susceptibility to exposure-related cancers; tumor biology; investigating somatic alterations in tumor tissue. **Mailing Address:** Dept Genetics & Complex Dis & Environ Health, Harvard Sch Pub Health, Bldg One 6nd Floor Rm 607 665 Huntington Ave, Boston, MA 02115. **E-Mail:** kelsey@hsph.harvard.edu

KELSEY, MORRIS IRWIN, IMMUNOLOGY. **Personal Data:** b Easton, Pa, August 14, 1939; m 1964, c 2. **Education:** Lehigh Univ, BA, 1961; Univ Mass, MS, 1964; Univ Pittsburgh, PhD (biochem), 1969. **Professional Experience:** PROG DIR, BIOL RESPONSE MODIFIERS PROG, 1989-; exec secy, Exp Therapeut Study Sect, Div Res Grants, 1985-1989; ASST COORDR ENVIRON CANCER, NAT CANCER INST, NIH, 1980-; adj assoc prof agr biochem, WVa Univ, 1977-1979; sect head chem carcinogenesis prog, Biol Response Modifiers Prog, 1975-1980; sr scientist, Frederick Cancer Res Ctr, 1973-1975; adj asst prof, Univ Mo, 1972-1973; asst prof biochem, Mo Inst Psychiat, 1971-1973; fel biochem, St Louis Univ, 1969-1971; Chemist starch chem, Nat Starch & Chem Corp, 1963-1965. **Memberships:** Am Chem Soc; AAAS; Sigma Xi; Am Soc Biol Chemists. **Research Statement & Publications:** Biotransformation of neutral sterols and bile acids by enterohepatic enzyme systems; effects of metabolism of endogenous steroid metabolites on the metabolic activation of chemical carcinogens; mechanism of action of chemotherapeutic agents. **Mailing Address:** Nat Cancer Inst-Frederick Cancer Res & Develop Ctr, Bldg 1052 Rm 253, Frederick, MD 21702-1201. **Fax:** 301-846-5429. **E-Mail:** kelsey@mail.ncifcrf.gov

KELSEY, RICK G, PLANT CHEMISTRY, FOREST HEALTH. **Personal Data:** b Libby, Mont, August 14, 1948; m 1982, c 4. **Education:** Univ Mont, BS, 1970, PhD (forestry), 1974. **Professional Experience:** TEAM LEADER, BEHAV & CHEM & ECOL FOREST INSECTS DIS TEAM, USDA, as of 2005; res scientist, Pnw Res Sta, Usda Forest Serv, beginning 1989; res assoc prof, Entomol Dept, Ore State Univ, 1986-1989; Prin investr, McKnight Found Individual Award plant biol, 1983-1986; from res asst prof to res assoc prof, Dept Chem, Univ Mont, 1981-1986; res assoc plant chem, Wood Chem Lab, 1974-1980. **Memberships:** NAm Phytochem Soc; AAAS. **Research Statement & Publications:** Isolation and identification of plant allelochemicals, their physiological and ecological function in forest health and their potential use to man. **Mailing Address:** Pac NW Res Sta, Forest Serv Lab, USDA, 3200 Jefferson Way, Corvallis, OR 97331. **Fax:** 541-750-7329. **E-Mail:** rkelsey@fs.fed.us

KELSEY, RONALD A(LBERT), MATERIALS SCIENCE ENGINEERING. **Personal Data:** b Oakville, Conn, March 29, 1923. **Education:** Polytech Inst Brooklyn, BS, 1949; Carnegie Inst Technol, MS, 1952. **Professional Experience:** RETIRED; pres, Seniors Helping Seniors, Inc, 1990-1995; sr tech specialist, Alcoa Res Lab, 1981-1983; chmn, Int Comt Fatigue Data Exchange & Eval, 1980-1984; mem, Tech Adv Comt Metals Prop Coun, 1980-1983; mem, Joint USA/USSR Comn Properties Welds, Low Temp Appln, 1975-1981; sect head, ALCOA RES LAB, 1974-1981; eng assoc, Alcoa Res Lab, 1970-1974; chmn, Aluminum Alloys Comn, Welding Res Coun, 1968-1984; sr res engr, ALCOA RES LAB, 1960-1970; nuclear engr, Gen Dynamics Corp, 1955-1960; res engr, Alcoa Res Labs, Aluminum Co Am, 1949-1955. **Memberships:** Soc Exp Stress Anal; fel Am Soc Metals; Am Welding Soc. **Research Statement & Publications:** Deformation and fracture mechanics of materials and structures; development of metal deformation process; armor development. **Mailing Address:** 27 Naushon N Rd, Falmouth, MA 02540. **E-Mail:** RAKEELSEY27@AOL.COM

KELSEY, RUBEN CLIFFORD, COMPARATIVE ENDOCRINOLOGY. **Personal Data:** b Park Falls, Wis, May 26, 1923; m 1960, Margaret; c Janet R & Leonard D. **Education:** Univ Wis, PhB, 1949, MS, 1950, PhD (zoology), 1959. **Professional Experience:** RETIRED; prof biol, E Stroudsburg Univ, 1968-1988; head dept, E Stroudsburg Univ, 1968-1974, 1980-1983; asst prof biol sci, Drexel Inst Technol, 1963-1968; sr res scientist biochem, Smith, Kline & French Labs, 1959-1963. **Memberships:** AAAS; Am Soc Zool; Am Inst Biol Sci. **Research Statement & Publications:** Physiology of mammalian reproduction; function. **Mailing Address:** 51 Club Ct, Stroudsburg, PA 18360.

KELSEY, STEPHEN JORGENSEN, DESIGN & DEVELOPMENT, CONSTRUCTION OF CHEMICAL PLANTS. **Personal Data:** b Salt Lake City, Utah, January 15, 1940; m 1965, Justine; c Lydia K (Creager), Richard, Bruce, Mary & Julie. **Education:** Univ Utah, BSChE, 1965, MES, 1969, PhD (chem eng), 1971. **Professional Experience:** MGR ENG, THATCHER CO, SALT LAKE CITY, UTAH, 1978-; plant supt, Wasatch Chem Co, Salt Lake City, Utah, 1976-1978; asst res prof, Div Mat Sci Mech Eng, Col Eng, Univ Utah, 1971-1976; asst res prof, Div Artificial Surg, Organs, Col Med, 1971-1976; assoc res prof, Computer Sci, Dept Elec Eng, Col Eng, 1971-1976; GS-4, GS-9, US Bur Mines, Salt Lake City, Utah, 1966-1967; process engr, Celanese Chem Co, Pampa, Tex, 1965-1966. **Memberships:** Am Inst Chem Engrs. **Research Statement & Publications:** Numerical analysis; chlorine and sulfur dioxide handling and facility design; sulfur dioxide manufacturing; plant design and construction. **Mailing Address:** 5368 Cottonwood Club Dr, Salt Lake City, UT 84117. **Fax:** 801-972-4606.

KELSH, DENNIS J, PHYSICAL CHEMISTRY. **Personal Data:** b Valley City, NDak, December 24, 1936. **Education:** St John's Univ, Minn, BA & BS, 1958; Iowa State Univ, PhD (phys chem), 1962. **Professional Experience:** EMER PROF, GONZAGA UNIV, 1999-; prof chem & chair, Gonzaga Univ, 1997-1999; Sr chemist, Sci Appl Int Corp, 1993-1996; scientist in residence, US Dept Energy Hq, 1991-1992; vis scientist, Univ Wash, 1985; coun mem, Am Chem Soc, 1974-1991; Am Coun Educ fel acad admin & spec asst to dean, Grad Sch, Wash State Univ, 1974-1975; prof, Gonzaga Univ, 1972-1999; chmn dept, Gonzaga Univ, 1968-1974, 1981-1986 & 1989-1990; assoc res scientist, NY Univ, 1966-1967; Res chemist, Spokane Mining Res Ctr, US Bur Mines, 1965-1993; from instr to assoc prof, Gonzaga Univ, 1962-1972. **Memberships:** Am Chem Soc; AAAS. **Research Statement & Publications:** Electrical properties of surfaces; adsorption from solution; solid-liquid separations by electrokinetics; electrokinetic remediation of soils. **Mailing Address:** Dept Chem Gonzaga Univ, E 502 Boone Ave Box 13, Spokane, WA 99258. **E-Mail:** kelsh@barney.gonzaga.edu

KELSO, ALBERT FREDERICK, PHYSIOLOGY. **Personal Data:** b Ft Wayne, Ind, November 19, 1917; m 1943, c 3. **Education:** George Williams Col, BA, 1943, MS, 1946; Loyola Univ, PhD, 1959. **Honorary Degrees:** DSc, Kirksville Col Osteop & Surg, 1970. **Honors & Awards:** Louisa Burns Mem Lectr, 1981; Guttensohn-Denslow Prize, 1984; Phillips Medal Honor. **Professional Experience:** RETIRED; dir res affairs, Chicago Col Osteop Med, 1976-1990; consult, Nat Bd Osteopath Exam, 1965-1978; chmn dept, Chicago Col Osteop Med, 1958-1990; actg chmn dept, Chicago Col Osteop Med, 1954-1959; from instr to prof physiol, Chicago Col Osteop Med, 1946-1990; instr physiol, George Williams Col, 1946-1947; res consult, Am Acad Osteop; educ consult, Am Osteopath Asn. **Memberships:** AAAS; Am Physiol Soc; Soc Exp Biol & Med; Am Heart Asn; Inst Elec & Electronics Eng; Sigma Xi. **Research Statement & Publications:** Sensorimotor performance; circulation; tissue respiration; family medicine theory and practice. **Mailing Address:** Chicago Col Osteop Med, Dolton, IL 60419-2728.

KELSO, ALEC JOHN (JACK), PHYSICAL ANTHROPOLOGY. **Personal Data:** b Chicago, Ill, December 5, 1930; m 1951, c 2. **Education:** Northern Ill Univ, BS, 1952; Univ Mich, MA, 1954, PhD, 1958. **Professional Experience:** PROF EMER ANTHROP, UNIV COLO, BOULDER, as of 2001; presidents teaching scholar, 1990; dir, Honors Prog, beginning 1988; dir, Young Scholars Summer Session, 1985-1989; chmn biol unit, Am Anthrop Asn, 1985-1987; dir, Farrand Hall Residential Acad Prog, 1983-1988; dir, Semester at Sea Prog, 1978-1979; prof anthrop, univ colo, boulder, beginning 1975; vchancellor acad affairs, Univ Colo, Colorado Springs, 1975-1977; distinguished vis prof, Ore State Univ, 1971; NIH spec fel, Univ Hawaii, 1965-1966; consult, Coun Grad Schs US, 1964-1978; mem training comt, Nat Inst Child Health & Human Develop, 1964-1966; chmn dept, Univ Colo, Boulder, 1963-1968 & 1971-1981; from instr to assoc prof anthrop, Univ Colo, Boulder, 1958-1975. **Memberships:** fel Am Anthrop Asn; Am Asn Phys Anthropologists (vpres, 1972-1974). **Research Statement & Publications:** Selection and blood groups; human sexuality; healthy people. **Mailing Address:** Dept Anthrop, Univ Colo Box 233, Boulder, CO 80309-0233. **E-Mail:** kelso@colorado.edu

KELSO, DONALD PRESTON, MARINE ECOLOGY. **Personal Data:** b Pulaski, Va, August 12, 1940; m 1963, c 2. **Education:** Univ Tenn, Knoxville, BS, 1962; Univ Fla, MS, 1965; Univ Hawaii, PhD (zoology), 1970. **Professional Experience:** ASSOC PROF BIOL, GEORGE MASON UNIV, 1977-; asst prof, George Mason Univ, 1970-1977. **Memberships:** Am Inst Biol Sci; Am Soc Zool; Ecol Soc Am. **Research Statement & Publications:** Inshore marine ecology; evolution of echinoderms; reproductive cycles of tropical animals. **Mailing Address:** Dept biol, George Mason Univ, Rm 3046 David King Hall 4400 Univ Dr, Fairfax, VA 22030-4443. **Fax:** 703-993-1046. **E-Mail:** dkelso@gmu.edu

KELSO, JOHN RICHARD MURRAY, ENVIRONMENTAL SCIENCE. **Personal Data:** b Kingston, Ont, February 9, 1945; m 1966, c 2. **Education:** Univ Guelph, BS, 1967, MS, 1969; Univ Man, PhD (zoology), 1971. **Honors & Awards:** Chandler-Misener Award, Int Asn Great Lakes Res, 1982. **Professional Experience:** AT, DEPT FISHERIES & OCEANS, GREAT LAKES LAB FISHERIES & AQUATIC SCI, as of 2000; assoc ed, Can J Fishery Aquatic Sci, 1988-; RES SCIENTIST, CAN DEPT FISHERIES & OCEANS, 1973-; dir, Nanticoke Proj, Ont Ministry Natural Resources, 1971-1973. **Memberships:** Can Soc Zoologists; Am Fisheries Soc; Int Asn Great Lakes Res. **Research Statement & Publications:** Effects of environmental perturbations and natural factors on the community structure, biomass and production of freshwater fish communities. **Mailing Address:** Great Lakes Lab Fisheries & Aquatic Sci, One Canal Dr, Sault St Marie, ON P6A 6W4, Can. **Fax:** 705-941-3025. **E-Mail:** kelsoj@dfo-mpo.gc.ca

KELSO, RICHARD MILES, HEATING VENTILATION & AIR CONDITIONING, BUILDING SYSTEMS. **Personal Data:** b Knoxville, Tenn, January 20, 1937; m 1960, c Suzanne S (Logan), Richard A & Robert M. **Education:** Univ Tenn, BS, 1960, MS, 1961. **Professional Experience:** Mem, Bd Assessment, Bldg & Fire Res Panel, Nat Inst Stand & Technol, 1996-1999; coun mem, Am Soc Heating Refrig & Air Conditioning Engrs, 1995-1997; pres, Richard Kelso & Assoc, 1974-1989; consult Engrs, Kelso-Regen Assoc, 1989-; PROF ENVIRON CONTROLS, SCH ARCHIT, UNIV TENN, 1976-; mech engr, Facil Planning, 1971-1976; vpres, George S Campbell & Assoc, 1968-1971; sales engr, Trane Corp, 1960-1968. **Memberships:** Fel Am Soc Heating Refrig & Air Conditioning Engrs; Am Soc Plumbing Engrs; Illum Eng Soc. **Research Statement & Publications:** Thermal and moisture transfer in buildings; indoor air quality; energy consumption; numerical modeling of building systems; automated commissioning of building systems. **Mailing Address:** Sch Archit, Univ Tenn, 1715 Volunteer Blvd, Knoxville, TN 37996-2400. **Fax:** 423-974-0656. **E-Mail:** rkelso@utk.edu

KELTIE, RICHARD FRANCIS, STRUCTURAL DYNAMICS. **Personal Data:** b Alexandria, Va, August 1, 1951; m 1973, c 1. **Education:** NC State Univ, BS, 1973, MS, 1975, PhD (mech eng), 1978. **Professional Experience:** ASSOC DEAN ACAD AFFAIRS, DEPT MECH & AEROSPACE ENG, NC STATE UNIV, as of 2004; assoc dept head, Dept Mech & Aerospace Eng, NC State Univ, 1994-195; PROF MECH & AEROSPACE ENG, NC STATE UNIV, 1990-; from asst prof to assoc prof, NC State Univ, 1981-1990; engr, Appl Physics Lab, Johns Hopkins Univ, 1978-1981. **Memberships:** Acoust Soc Am; Am Soc Mech Engrs; Sipna Xi; Phi Kappa Phi. **Research Statement & Publications:** Mechanical design; structural dynamics; forced acoustics radiation from large structures; structural acoustics; structural dynamics, acoustic radiation and acoustic emission. **Mailing Address:** Dept Mech & Aerospace Eng, NC State Univ, Rm 120C Page Hall PO Box 7910, Raleigh, NC 27695. **Fax:** 919-515-8702. **E-Mail:** keltie@eos.ncsu.edu

KELTNER, LLEW, TECHNOLOGY ACQUISITION & MONITORING, CLINICAL DUE DILIGENCE. **Personal Data:** b Norman, Okla, February 5, 1950; m 1978, Leila; c Reed, Tiel, Mera & Case. **Education:** Case Western Res Univ, MS, 1982, PhD (med informatics), 1983, MD, 1984. **Professional Experience:** CHMN, METASTAT LIGHT SCI CORP, as of 2004; chief exec dir, Oncol Drug Develop, beginning 1994; dir, Organ Life Sci, beginning 1993; dir, Thesis Tech, beginning 1991; chmn, Epistat Financial, beginning 1991; dir, Vital Choice, 1990-1993; dir, Infostat, beginning 1988; chmn, Drilling Data Stand Comt, Int Asn Drilling Contractors, 1985-1988; CHEIF EXEC OFFICER, EPISTAT, 1981-; fel, Nat Libr Med, Case Western Res Univ, 1981-1983; vis prof, Univ Ore, 1976-1978. **Memberships:** Am Asn Clin Chem; AMA; Int Asn Tumor Marker Oncol. **Research Statement & Publications:** Requirements for adequate clinical due diligence; implications of US health policy on the Japanese health care industry; biotechnology transfer; antimetastatic drugs; appropriate use oftumor markers. **Mailing Address:** Light Sci Corp, 34931 SE Douglas St, Ste 200, Snoqualmie, WA 98065. **Fax:** 425-369-2801.

KELTON, DIANE ELIZABETH, GENETICS, CANCER. **Personal Data:** b Holden, Mass, December 4, 1924. **Education:** Univ Mass, BS, 1945, PhD (zoology), 1961. **Professional Experience:** RETIRED; staff scientist, Mason Res Inst, 1974-1983; res assoc, genetics, 1961-1974; res assoc genetics & neuropath, 1956-1958; histol, 1956-1958 & genetics, 1958-1961; res asst cancer res, Univ Mass, Amherst, 1953-1956; sr res asst, Jackson Lab, 1950-1953; res asst genetics, Jackson Lab, 1947-1950. **Memberships:** AAAS; Am Inst Biol Sci; Am Genetic Asn; Genetics Soc Am; Environ Mutagen Soc; Sigma Xi. **Research Statement & Publications:** Genetics; tumor biology; cancer chemotherapy. **Mailing Address:** 15 Heatherstone Rd, Amherst, MA 01002-1634.

KELTS, LARRY JIM, MARINE BIOLOGY, ENTOMOLOGY. **Personal Data:** b Westfield, Pa, August 13, 1937; m 1967, c 2. **Education:** Cornell Univ, BS, 1959; Southeastern Mass Univ, MS, 1971; Univ NH, PhD (zoology), 1977. **Professional Experience:** ASSOC PROF BIOL & ALLIED HEALTH, MERRIMACK COL, as of 2005; asst prof Biol, Merrimack Col, beginning 1977; res asst plant path, Agr Exp Sta, Cornell Univ, 1964-1969; res asst marine biol, Marine Lab, Duke Univ, 1960-1961. **Memberships:** Am Inst Biol Sci; Ecol Soc Am; Nat Wildlife Fedn. **Research Statement & Publications:** Faunal and floral community structure and composition in stressed aquatic environments; such as saltmarsh pannes; supratidal rock pools, mixohaline and oligohaline lotic systems; bogs; temporary woodland pools and creek beds; salt-marsh dragonfly ecology. **Mailing Address:** Dept Biol, Merrimack Col, 315 Turnpike St, North Andover, MA 01845. **E-Mail:** larry.kelts@merrimack.edu

KELTY, MIRIAM C FRIEDMAN, PSYCHOLOGY & PSYCHOBIOLOGY, AGING. **Personal Data:** b New York, NY, November 4, 1938; m 1966, Edward; c Joel P & Ruth A. **Education:** City Col NY, BA, 1960, MA, 1962; Rutgers Univ, PhD (psychol & psychobiol), 1965. **Professional Experience:** ASSOC DIR EXTRAMULAR ACTIV, NAT INST AGING, NIH, 1986-; asst chief, Referral & Review, 1981-1986; exec secy, Human Develop Study Sect, Div Res Grants, 1978-1981; psychologist, Nat Comn Protect Human Subj Res, Bethesda, Md, 1974-1978; admin officer, Sci Affairs, Am Psychol Asn, Wash, DC, 1970-1974; psychologist, NIMH, Bethesda, Md, 1968-1970; res assoc, Sch Pub Health, Harvard Univ, 1966-1968; psychologist, Vet Admin Med Ctr, Boston, 1966-1968; lectr, City Col New York, 1962-1965; ed, Contemp Psychol. **Memberships:** Fel Am Psychol Asn; fel AAAS; World Future Soc; Geront Asn Am. **Research Statement & Publications:** Aging, hormones and behavior; health research; ethics of research; science policy. **Mailing Address:** Off Extramural Affairs Nat Inst Aging NIH, Rm 2C218 Gateway Bldg 7201 Wis Ave, Bethesda, MD 20892-9205. **Fax:** 301-402-2945. **E-Mail:** mk46u@nih.gov

KEMBLOWSKI, MARIAN, CIVIL & ENVIRONMENTAL ENGINEERING. **Education:** Inst Land Reclamation, PhD. **Professional Experience:** PROF, UAH STATE UNIV, as of 1996. **Mailing Address:** Utah State Univ, Logan, UT 84322-8200.

KEMELHOR, ROBERT ELIAS, MECHANICAL ENGINEERING. **Personal Data:** b New York, NY, May 19, 1919; m 1947, Shirley P Tennen; c Judy E, Joel M & Barry M. **Education:** George Washington Univ, BSME, 1949. **Professional Experience:** CONSULT ENG MECH, 1991-; chief engr, Appl Physics Lab, Tech Serv Dept, Johns Hopkins Univ, 1986-1991; br supvr, Design & Fabrication Br, 1982-1985; prog mgr, Ocean Data Acquisition Prog, 1976-1982; prog mgr, Pershing Weapon Syst, 1966-1976; proj engr, Landing Force Support Weapon, 1962-1966; Cleveland Pneumatic, Inc, 1962-1963; Consult, Thompson Ramo Wooldridge, Inc, 1961-1962; sect supvr, Polaris Prog, 1958-1962; dir res & develop, Pesco Div, Borg Warner Corp, 1957-1958; chief engr, McLean Develop Lab, 1952-1957; Design engr, Dept Navy, 1939-1952; US del, Int Stand Orgn Tech Comt; mem, Comput Automation Systs Asn Soc Mfg Engrs; chmn, DC Chap Soc Man Eng, Wash; consult, Nat Inst Stand & Technol & NASA. **Memberships:** Assoc fel Am Inst Aeronaut & Astronaut; sr mem Soc Mfg Engrs; sr mem Am Astronaut Soc; Senior Scientists & Engineers, amer assoc, advancement of sci (exec.com). **Research Statement & Publications:** Magnetic fluids and mechanisms for use in shock and vibration absorbing devices; demonstrate the feasibility of electrically controlling spring rates and damping constants by electronically reactive fluids; methods of checking hazardous circuits, flow around pylons of sub and supersonic aircraft; Effects of nuclear and conventional weapons, manufacturing & design using comput aided devices. **Mailing Address:** 6211 Redwing Ct, Bethesda, MD 20817-5914.

KEMENY, GABOR, THEORETICAL PHYSICS. **Personal Data:** b Budapest, Hungary, February 6, 1933; American citizen; m 1958, c 2. **Education:** Eotvos Lorand Univ, Budapest, dipl, 1956; NY Univ, PhD (physics), 1962. **Professional Experience:** PROF BIOPHYS, MICH STATE UNIV, 1974-; assoc prof, mech & mat sci, 1970-1974; assoc prof metall, mech & mat sci, 1968-1974; assoc prof elec eng, Mich State Univ, 1968-1970; Sr vis, Cavendish Lab, Cambridge Univ, 1966; res scientist, Ledgemont Lab, Kennecott Copper Corp, 1963-1968; res scientist, Am-Stand, 1961-1962; assoc scientist, Res Dept, Lamp Div, Westinghouse Elec Corp, 1957-1961; Assoc scientist, Cent Res Inst Physics, Hungarian Acad Sci, 1955-1956. **Memberships:** AAAS; Am Phys Soc. **Research Statement & Publications:** Quantum mechanics and electronics; many-body problem; solid state and mathematical physics; electrical conductivity in biomacromolecules; protein denaturation; microwave interactions with biological systems. **Mailing Address:** Dept Physics, Michigan State Univ, East Lansing, MI 48824-1116. **E-Mail:** kemeny@pa.msu.edu

KEMENY, NANCY E, COLORECTAL CARCINOMA. **Personal Data:** b Elizabeth, NJ, January 18, 1945; m 1977, Daniel; c Jackie, Laura & Vicki. **Education:** Univ Pa, BA, 1967; NJ Col Med, MD, 1971. **Honors & Awards:** Ancell Fund Award, 1981. **Professional Experience:** PROF MED, CORNELL UNIV MED COL, 1992-; chairperson, Spec Awards, 1991; mem, Oncol Drug Adv Comt, Food & Drug Admin, 1990-1994; dir, Am Soc Clin Oncol, 1990-1993; chmn mem comt, Am Soc Clin Oncol, 1987-; Professor of Medicine, Cornell Univ Med Col, 1992-Present; ATTEND PHYSICIAN, MEM SLOAN-KETTERING CANCER CTR, 1976-Present. **Memberships:** Am Soc Clin Oncol; Am Asn Cancer Res. **Research Statement & Publications:** Chemotherapeutic treatments for metastatic colorectal carcinoma; hepatic arterial infusion of hepatic metastases. **Mailing Address:** Mem Sloan-Kettering Cancer Ctr, 1275 York Ave, New York, NY 10021. **Fax:** 212-794-7186. **E-Mail:** kemenyn@mskcc.org

KEMIC, STEPHEN BRUCE, ASTROPHYSICS. **Personal Data:** b Boston, Mass, December 31, 1946. **Education:** Univ NC, BS, 1968; Univ Colo, MS, 1970, PhD (astrophys), 1973. **Professional Experience:** STAFF MEM PHYSICS, LOS ALAMOS NAT LAB, 1974-. **Memberships:** Am Astron Soc. **Research Statement & Publications:** Spectroscopy of magnetic white dwarfs; laser fusion. **Mailing Address:** Los Alamos Nat Lab, PO Box 1663, Los Alamos, NM 87545. **Fax:** 505-665-2227. **E-Mail:** sbk@lanl.gov

KEMNITZ, JOSEPH WILLIAM, PHYSIOLOGICAL PSYCHOLOGY. **Personal Data:** b Baltimore, Md, March 15, 1947; m 1990, Amanda; c Julia E. **Education:** Univ Wis, BA, 1969, MS, 1974, PhD (physiol psychol), 1976. **Professional Experience:** DIR, NAT PRIMATE RES CTR, UNIV WIS MADISON, as of 2004; PROF, DEPT PHYSIOL, UNIV WIS MADISON, as of 2000; assoc scientist, Dept Med, beginning 1990; affil scientist, Inst Aging & Adult Life, beginning 1989; mem, Spec Study Sect, NIH, 1987-; assoc ed, Hormones & Behav, 1987-; Div Comp Med, Caribbean Primate Res Ctr, 1985-; consult, Div Diabetes & Clin Nutrit, Univ Southern Calif Med Ctr, 1984-; assoc scientist, Wis Regional Primate Res Ctr, Univ Wis, beginning 1984; vis scientist, Div Endocrinol, Med Ctr, Univ Calif, Los Angeles, 1981; mem task force animal models diabetes res, NIH, 1980-1981; asst scientist, Dept Med, 1979-1984; res assoc, Dept Med, 1977-1979; teaching & res asst, Univ Wis, 1971-1976; proj specialist psychol, Univ Wis, 1969-1971. **Memberships:** Am Diabetes Asn; Am Soc Primatologists; Int Primatological Asn; NAm Asn Study Obesity; fel Gerontol Soc Am; Am Inst Nutrit; NY Acad Sci; Am Physiol Soc; Sigma Xi. **Research Statement & Publications:** Regulation of energy balance, emphasizing obesity, diabetes, caloric restriction and aging, particularly in Rhesus monkeys. **Mailing Address:** Wis Primate Res Ctr, Univ Wis, 1220 Capitol Ct, Madison, WI 53715-1299. **Fax:** 608-263-4031. **E-Mail:** kemnitz@primate.wisc.edu

KEMP, ARNE K, FOREST PRODUCTS. **Personal Data:** b Kajaani, Finland, March 5, 1918; American citizen; m 1943, c 2. **Education:** Univ Ga, BSF, 1948; Duke Univ, MF, 1949; Univ Minn, PhD (wood tech), 1957. **Professional Experience:** RETIRED; asst dir res, N Cent Forest Exp Sta, 1973-1984; asst dir mkt & eng res, Lake State Forest Exp Sta, US Forest Serv, 1965-1973; chief div forest prod utilization & mkt & eng res, Lake

State Forest Exp Sta, US Forest Serv, 1963-1965; NSF grant, 1962; head dept forestry, Stephen F Austin State Col, 1955-1963; assoc prof, La State Univ, 1953-1955; instr wood tech, Sch Forestry, Univ Minn, 1949-1953. **Memberships:** Forest Prod Res Soc; Soc Wood Sci & Technol; Int Union Forest Res Orgns. **Research Statement & Publications:** Wood seasoning, preservation and anatomy; wood liquid relationships; forest products marketing. **Mailing Address:** Six Cap Dunbar Lane, Savannah, GA 31411.

KEMP, DANIEL SCHAEFFER, ORGANIC CHEMISTRY, PROTEIN SCIENCE. **Personal Data:** b Portland, Ore, October 20, 1936. **Education:** Reed Col, BA, 1958; Harvard Univ, PhD (org chem), 1964. **Professional Experience:** PROF CHEM, MASS INST TECHNOL, 1972-; Camile & Henry Dreyfus fel, 1970; vis asst prof, Univ Calif, San Diego, 1969; A P Sloan Found fel, 1968-1970; from asst prof to assoc prof, Mass Inst Technol, 1964-1972. **Memberships:** Am Chem Soc. **Research Statement & Publications:** Peptide chemistry. **Mailing Address:** Dept Chem, Mass Inst Technol, 77 Mass Ave Rm 18-584, Cambridge, MA 02139-4307. **Fax:** 617-252-1609. **E-Mail:** kemp@ucockatoo.mit.edu

KEMP, EMORY LELAND, STRUCTURAL ENGINEERING. **Personal Data:** b Chicago, Ill, October 1, 1931; m 1958, Janet; c Mark, Alison & Geoffrey. **Education:** Univ Ill, BSc, 1952, PhD (theoret & appl mech), 1962; Univ London, DIC, 1955, MSc, 1958. **Honors & Awards:** Buxton Award, Inst Struct Engrs, 1980; Hist & Heritage Award, Am Soc Civil Engrs, 1981. **Professional Experience:** DIR EMER, INST HIST SCI & INDUST ARCHAEOL, WVA UNIV, as of 2005; Regents fel, Smithsonian Inst, 1983-1984; prof hist sci & technol, Wva Univ, beginning 1977; fel, Am Coun Learned Socs, 1975-1976; chmn dept, Wva Univ, 1967-1974; prof Civil Eng, Wva Univ, beginning 1965; assoc prof, Wva Univ, 1962-1965; instr theoret & appl mech, Univ Ill, 1959-1962; struct engr, consult firms, London, 1956-1959; asst engr, Ill State Water Surv, 1952. **Memberships:** fel Am Soc Civil Engrs; fel Brit Inst Civil Engrs; fel Am Concrete Inst; Brit Inst Struct Engrs. **Research Statement & Publications:** History of technology; industrial archeology; structural engineering. **Mailing Address:** Inst Hist Technol & Indust Archaeol, WVa Univ, 1535 Mileground, Morgantown, WV 26505. **Fax:** 304-293-2499. **E-Mail:** elkemp31@aol.com

KEMP, GORDON ARTHUR, MICROBIOLOGY, RESEARCH ADMINISTRATION. **Personal Data:** b Newark, NJ, December 12, 1932; m 1958, c 3. **Education:** Lehigh Univ, AB, 1954; Rutgers Univ, PhD (microbiol), 1961. **Professional Experience:** DIR SCI POLICY AFFAIRS, PFIZER CENT RES, PFIZER INC, as of 2004; dir, animal indust res & develop, Am Cyanamid Co, 1976-1982; mgr animal indust res, 1973-1976; mgr chemother res, 1970-1973; group leader chemother, 1964-1970; res scientist microbiol, 1961-1964. **Memberships:** Fel AAAS; Am Soc Microbiol; Sigma Xi. **Research Statement & Publications:** Pathogenesis of disease; prophylaxis and therapy of experimental infections; veterinary microbiology and immunology; protozoal and helminth infections of domestic animals; non-medical uses of antibiotics. **Mailing Address:** Pfizer Cent Res, Pfizer Inc, Eastern Pt Rd, Groton, CT 06340.

KEMP, GRAHAM ELMORE, VETERINARY PUBLIC HEALTH. **Personal Data:** b Alta, January 8, 1927; American citizen; m 1948. **Education:** Univ Toronto, DVM, 1951; Univ Calif, Berkeley, MPH, 1958. **Professional Experience:** RETIRED; dir, Bur Labs, Vector-Borne Dis Div, Commun Dis Ctr, USPHS, 1975-1980; chief virol unit, San Juan Trop Dis Labs, PR, 1973-1975; mem animal res comt, San Juan Vet Admin Hosp, 1973-1974; hon sr scientist, PR Nuclear Ctr, 1973-1974; staff mem, Rockefeller Found, Virus Res Lab, Fac Med, Univ Ibadan, 1964-1972; mem staff, Epidemiol Bur Commun Dis, Div Prev Med Serv, Calif State Dept Pub Health, 1958-1964; consult zoonoses, State Calif, 1958-1964; Sch Vet Med, Univ Calif, Davis, 1957-1964; pvt pract, Ill, 1952-1957; mem staff, Div Livestock Indust, Univ Ill, 1951-1952; lectr, Sch Pub Health, Univ Calif, Berkeley. **Memberships:** Am Vet Med Asn; Am Pub Health Asn; Conf Pub Health Vets; Am Soc Trop Med &Hyg. **Research Statement & Publications:** Arbovirus; food-borne disease and zoonoses. **Mailing Address:** 808 Inverness St, Ft Collins, CO 80524.

KEMP, JAMES DILLON, ANIMAL SCIENCE, FOOD SERVICE & TECHNOLOGY. **Personal Data:** b Pickett, Ky, February 6, 1923; m 1947, Helen; c Bonnie (Collins) & James W. **Education:** Univ Ky, BS, 1948, MS, 1949; Univ Ill, PhD (animal sci), 1952. **Honors & Awards:** Am Meat Sci ASN, 1968; Res Award, Am Soc Animal Sci, 1971; Pollock Award, Am Meat Sci Asn, 1988; Teaching Award. **Professional Experience:** PROF EMER ANIMAL SCI, UNIV KY, 1989-; consult, Thailand, 1974 & Italy, 1985; coord, food sci prog, 1966-1989; Fulbright res scholar, NZ, 1964; prof animal sci, Univ Ky, 1959-1989; from asst prof to assoc prof animal husb, Univ Ky, 1952-1959; asst animal sci, Univ Ill, 1949-1952. **Memberships:** Fel Am Soc Animal Sci; fel Inst Food Technologists; Sigma Xi; Am Meat Sci Asn (pres 1975-1976). **Research Statement & Publications:** Meats teaching and research; composition and processing characteristics of red meats. **Mailing Address:** 778 Hildeen Rd, Lexington, KY 40502. **E-Mail:** jdkmeati@aol.com

KEMP, JOHN DANIEL, MOLECULAR GENETICS. **Personal Data:** b Minneapolis, Minn, January 20, 1940; div, c Todd, Laura & Christine. **Education:** Univ Calif, Los Angeles, BS, 1962, PhD (biochem), 1965. **Professional Experience:** PROF PLANT PATHOL & CHMN, INSTNL BIOSAFETY COMT, NMEX STATE UNIV, as of 2004; prof plant path, NMex State Univ, Las Cruces, 1985-; prof plant path, Univ Wis-Madison, 1977-1985; assoc prof, Univ Wis-Madison, 1972-1977; res chemist, USDA, 1968-1981; asst prof, Univ Wis-Madison, 1968-1972; res assoc, Univ Wash, 1967-1968; NIH fel biochem, Univ Wash, 1965-1967. **Memberships:** Am Soc Plant Physiologists; Sigma Xi; Int Soc Molecular Plant-Microbe Interactions. **Research Statement & Publications:** Molecular mechanisms of normal and abnormal plant growth and development; plant genetic engineering by novel approaches. **Mailing Address:** Instnl Biosafety Comt, Nmex State Univ, PO Box 30001, Las Cruces, NM 88003-8001. **Fax:** 505-646-1302. **E-Mail:** jkemp@nmsu.edu

KEMP, JOHN WILMER, PHYSIOLOGICAL CHEMISTRY, PHARMACOLOGY. **Personal Data:** b Midvale, Utah, July 28, 1920; m 1952, c 2. **Education:** Westminster Col, AB, 1950; Univ Calif, PhD (physiol chem), 1957. **Professional Experience:** ASSOC PROF PHYSIOL, COL MED, UNIV UTAH, 1983-; assoc prof pharmacol, Col Med, Univ Utah, 1959-1983; res pharmacologist metab heroin, Sch Med, Univ Calif, 1957-1959. **Memberships:** Am Soc Pharmacol & Exp Therapeut. **Research Statement & Publications:** Biochemistry and pharmacology of the central nervous system; nucleic acids; membrane transport; neuronal excitability; anticonvulsants; physiology. **Mailing Address:** Dept Physiol, Sch Med, Univ Utah, 410 Chipeta Way, 167 Stangl, Salt Lake City, UT 84108-1209.

KEMP, KENNETH COURTNEY, PHYSICAL ORGANIC CHEMISTRY. **Personal Data:** b Chicago, Ill, August 7, 1925. **Education:** Nwestern Univ, BS, 1950; Ill Inst Technol, PhD (chem), 1956. **Professional Experience:** PROF EMER CHEM, UNIV NEV, 1990-; vchmn dept, Univ Nev, 1976-1980; from instr to prof, Univ Nev, 1955-1990; asst chem, Ill Inst Technol, 1950-1955. **Memberships:** Am Chem Soc; Chem Soc London; Sigma Xi. **Research Statement & Publications:** Organic mechanisms; neighboring group reactions. **Mailing Address:** Dept Chem, Univ Nev, Reno, NV 89557-8075. **Fax:** 775-784-6804. **E-Mail:** kemp@chem.unr.edu

KEMP, KENNETH E, STATISTICS. **Personal Data:** b Detroit, Mich, August 24, 1941; m 1978, c 2. **Education:** Mich State Univ, BS, 1963, MS, 1965, PhD (animal husb), 1967. **Professional Experience:** PROF STATIST, KANS STATE UNIV, 1979-; from asst prof to assoc prof, Kans State Univ, 1968-1979; Sr statist programmer, Biomet Serv, Agr Res Serv, USDA, 1967-1968. **Memberships:** Biomet Soc; Am Statist Asn. **Research Statement & Publications:** Algorithms and techniques for statistical analysis. **Mailing Address:** Dept Statist, Kans State Univ, 109B Dickens Hall, Manhattan, KS 66506. **Fax:** 785-532-7736. **E-Mail:** kekemp@stat.ksu.edu

KEMP, MARWIN K, PHYSICAL CHEMISTRY, GEOCHEMISTRY. **Personal Data:** b Strong, Ark, November 23, 1942; m 1961, c 2. **Education:** Univ Ark, BS, 1964; Univ Ill, MS, 1965, PhD (phys chem), 1968. **Honors & Awards:** Okla Chemist Award, 1988. **Professional Experience:** RES SUPVR, AMOCO PROD CO, as of 1999; staff res scientist, Amoco Prod Co, 1985-1988; sr res scientist, Amoco Prod Co, 1981-1985; from asst prof to assoc prof, phys chem, Univ Tulsa, 1968-1981. **Memberships:** Am Chem Soc; AAAS; Sigma Xi. **Research Statement & Publications:** Geochemistry; statistical analysis of organic geochemistry data; thermodynamics; infrared spectroscopy. **Mailing Address:** 4335 S Allegheny Ave, Tulsa, OK 74135. **E-Mail:** mkemp@trc.amoco.com

KEMP, PAUL JAMES, IDENTIFICATION OF ODOPHORIC COMPOUNDS, DETOXIFICATION REACTIONS. **Personal Data:** b Inglewood, Calif, June 26, 1942; m 1990, Hsu N Shieh; c James, Eran, Sean & Hong-ru. **Education:** Iowa State Univ, BS, 1965; Ore State Univ, MS, 1969. **Professional Experience:** AT BREWER ENVIRON INDUST, as of 2003; INDUST APPLNS CHEMIST, INDUST CHEM DIV, BREWER ENVIRON INDUSTS, INC, 1990-; regional mgr food processing & water treatment, Assoc Chem & Serv, Inc, 1981-1989; dist mgr food processing & water treatment, Olin Water Serv, Olin Corp, 1977-1981; grad teaching fel anal chem, Univ Hawaii, 1975-1977; gen mgr & chief exec officer food packaging prod, Outrite Plastics Inc, 1969-1974; Grad teaching asst gen & anal chem, Ore State Univ, 1965-1969; Tech Dir, Lens, Inc, Sunset Terr Wastewater Reclamation Facil. **Memberships:** Am Chem Soc; Am Waterworks Asn; Water Environ Fedn; Sigma Xi. **Research Statement & Publications:** Industrial odor control chemistry; nonhalogen oxidative sterilants for industrial and potable water; industrial wastewater management. **Mailing Address:** Brewer Environ Indust, PO Box 48, Honolulu, HI 96810. **Fax:** 808-532-7500. **E-Mail:** kempp001@hawaii.rr.com

KEMP, PAULA ANN, MATHEMATICS, NUMBER THEORY. **Personal Data:** b Jonesbow, Ark, August 14, 1947. **Education:** Ark State Univ, BS, 1968; Kans State Univ, MS, 1970, PhD, 1974. **Professional Experience:** DISTINGUISHED PROF, SOUTHWEST MO STATE UNIV as of 2003; prof math, Southwest MO State Univ, beginning 1977. **Memberships:** Am Math Soc; Mathh Asn Am. **Research Statement & Publications:** Fix point theory; analysis; set theory; number theory. **Mailing Address:** Dept Math, SW MO State Univ, Cheek Hall 047M 901 S Nat Ave, Springfield, MO 65804. **E-Mail:** PaulaKemp@MissouriState.edu

KEMP, ROBERT GRANT, BIOCHEMISTRY. **Personal Data:** b Massillon, Ohio, February 12, 1937; m 1985, c 2. **Education:** Col Wooster, BA, 1959, Yale Univ, PhD (biochem), 1964. **Professional Experience:** PROF BIOCHEM, CHICAGO MED SCH, FINCH UNIV HEALTH SCI, beginning 1976; chmn, Univ Health Sci, Chicago Med Sch, 1976-1988; fulbright fel, 1971; estab investr, Am Heart Asn, 1968-1973; from asst prof to prof biochem, Med Col Wis, 1966-1976; res assoc biochem, Univ Wash, 1964-1966. **Memberships:** AAAS; Am Chem Soc; Am Soc Biol Chem; Sigma Xi; Protein Soc. **Research Statement & Publications:** Control of carbohydrate metabolism; structure-activity relationships of enzymes. **Mailing Address:** Dept Biochem, Chicago Med Sch, Finch Univ Health Sci, 3333 Green Bay Rd, North Chicago, IL 60064-3095. **Fax:** 847-578-3240. **E-Mail:** robert.kemp@finchcms.edu

KEMP, WALTER MICHAEL, IMMUNOBIOLOGY, PARASITOLOGY. **Personal Data:** b Big Spring, Tex, August 26, 1944; m 1983, c 4. **Education:** Abilene Christian Col, BSE, 1966; Tulane Univ, PhD (biol), 1970. **Honors & Awards:** Henry Baldwin Ward Medal, Am Soc Parasitologists, 1983. **Professional Experience:** ASSOC DEAN SCI, TEX A&M UNIV, 1989-; chmn, Study Sect Trop Med Parasitol, NIH, 1983-1985; PROF BIOL, TEX A&M UNIV, 1982-; mem, Study Sect Trop Med Parasitol, NIH, 1981-1985; Clark Found grants, 1976-1978, 1978-1982 & 1982-1985; from asst prof to assoc prof, Tex A&M Univ, 1975-1982; NIH grants, 1972-1975, 1978-1983 & 1986-1989; res assoc immunol, Southwest Found Res & Educ, 1970-1973 & Univ Ga, 1974; asst prof, Abilene Christian Col, 1970-1975; Res Corp res grant, 1970-1971; cell biol trainee biol, Tulane Univ, 1968-1970. **Memberships:** AAAS; Am Soc Parasitologists (pres 1989); Am Soc Trop Med & Hyg; Am Asn Immunologists. **Research Statement & Publications:** Immune responses to parasites, particularly schistosomes and trypanosomes; host-parasite antigen sharing and parasite immune escape mechanisms. **Mailing Address:** Dept Biol, Tex A&M Univ, 312 Admin Bldg, College Station, TX 77843-1112. **Fax:** 979-845-6077. **E-Mail:** m-kemp1@tamu.edu

KEMP, WILLIAM MICHAEL, ECOLOGY. **Personal Data:** b Washington, DC, May 16, 1947. **Education:** Ga Inst Technol, BA, 1969, MA, 1971; Univ Fla, PhD (environ sci), 1976. **Professional Experience:** PROF ENVIRON SCI, UNIV MD, as of 2004; SYSTS ECOLOGIST ENVIRON RES, CTR ENVIRON & ESTUARINE STUDIES, UNIV MD, 1977-; environ engr eval, US Environ Protection Agency, 1971-1972. **Memberships:** Ecol Soc Am; Am Soc Limnol & Oceanog; AAAS; Sigma Xi. **Research Statement & Publications:** Ecosystem modeling; productivity and nutrient dynamics of estuaries; structure of ecological trophic webs; economics and energetics of environment. **Mailing Address:** Univ Md, PO Box 775, Cambridge, MD 21613. **Fax:** 410-221-8490. **E-Mail:** kemp@hpl.umces.edu

KEMPE, LUDWIG GEORGE, NEUROSURGERY, NEUROANATOMY. **Personal Data:** b Brandenburg, Ger, October 16, 1915; American citizen; m 1955. **Education:** Univ Berne, MD, 1942. **Professional Experience:** PROF NEUROSURG & ANAT, MED UNIV SC, 1973-; mem adv bd, Coun Neurosurg, beginning 1968; assoc clin prof neurosurg, George Wash Univ, 1960-1973. **Memberships:** Am Asn Neurol Surgeons; Cong Neurol Surgeons; Soc Neurol Surgeons; Am Asn Anatomists; Am Col Surgeons. **Research Statement & Publications:** Mesoscopic neuroanatomy. **Mailing Address:** 12 Valley View Dr, Pisgah Forest, NC 28768-9509.

KEMPEN, RENE RICHARD, PHARMACOLOGY. **Personal Data:** b Kankakee, Ill, March 24, 1928; m 1969, c 1. **Education:** St Joseph's Col, Ind, BS, 1950; Loyola Univ Chicago, MS, 1955, PhD (pharmacol), 1962. **Professional Experience:** ADJ PROF, DEPT PHARMACOL & TOXICOL, as of 2006; ASST PROF, SCH ALLIED HEALTH, 1976-; ASSOC DIR TOXICOL LAB, SCH MED, UNIV TEX MED BR GALVESTON, 1973-; asst prof, Sch Med, Univ Tex Med Br, beginning 1963; instr, Col Med, Baylor Univ, 1961-1963; Loyola Univ Sch Nursing, 1956 & St Elizabeth's Hosp Sch Nursing, 1957; lab instr pharmacol, Stritch Sch Med, Loyola Univ Chicago, 1956-1959; instr, St Anne's Hosp Sch Nursing, 1955-1957; chemist, Chicago Biol Res Lab, 1954-1955. **Memberships:** AAAS; Am Asn

Lab Animal Sci; Am Heart Asn; Sigma Xi. **Research Statement & Publications:** Action of drugs on cardiac electrophysiological parameters; muscle contraction; toxicology; effect of drugs on endocrine pancrease. **Mailing Address:** Dept Pharmacol, Med Sch, Univ Tex, 301 Univ Blvd, Galveston, TX 77550-2708. **Fax:** 409-772-9642. **E-Mail:** rkempen@utmb.edu

KEMPER, BYRON W, MOLECULAR BIOLOGY. **Personal Data:** b Evansville, Ind, October 10, 1943; m 1992, Kim; c Jason, Hanna & Esther. **Education:** Wabash Col, BA, 1965; Stanford Univ, PhD (pharmacol), 1969. **Professional Experience:** DEPT HEAD PHARMACOL, UNIV ILL, URBANA, 1996-; PROF CELLULAR & STRUCT BIOL, UNIV ILL, URBANA, 1989-; PROF PHYSIOL & PHARMACOL, UNIV ILL, URBANA, 1986-; From asst to assoc prof pharmacol/physiol, Univ Ill, Urbana, 1974-1986. **Memberships:** AAAS; Am Soc Biochem & Molecular Biol. **Research Statement & Publications:** Our studies focus on the regulation of the expression of cytochrome p450 genes and on the protein structural determinants of cellular targeting, membrane interaction, and assembly of cytochrome p450. **Mailing Address:** Dept Molecular & Integrative Physiol, Univ Ill 524 Burrill 407 S Goodwin, Urbana, IL 61801-3704. **Fax:** 217-333-1133. **E-Mail:** byronkem@uiuc.edu

KEMPER, GENE ALLEN, NUMERICAL ANALYSIS, PERFORMANCE ANALYSIS. **Personal Data:** b Drake, NDak, April 12, 1933; m 1969, c 1. **Education:** Univ NDak, BS, 1956, MS, 1959; Iowa State Univ, PhD (appl math), 1965. **Professional Experience:** Vice chancellor acad affairs, Comput Ctr, Univ NDak, 1993-1992; PROF EMER MATH & ASSOC VPRES EMER ACAD AFFAIRS, UNIV NDAK, 1992-; assoc vpres acad affairs, Comput Ctr, Univ NDak, 1982-1992; asst vpres acad affairs, Comput Ctr, Univ NDak, 1981-1982; assoc dir, Comput Ctr, Univ NDak, 1979-1981; vis soc indust & appl math lectr, 1975-1977, 1979-1980 & 1980-1982; dir, Inst Comput Use Educ, 1974-1981; prof math, Comput Ctr, Univ NDak, 1972-1992; sr consult, Comput Ctr, 1969-1979; NSF Col Sci Improv Prog grant, Univ NDak, 1968-1971; assoc prof, Univ NDak, 1966-1972; sr res specialist & vis staff mem, Boeing Sci Res Labs, 1965-1966; instr math, Iowa State Univ, 1961-1965; exten lectr math, Univ Wash, Seattle, 1960-1961 & 1965-1966; mathematician, Boeing Co, 1960-1961; instr math, Univ NDak, 1956-1959; vis scientist, Atomic Energy Comn Lab, Iowa State Univ, Ames, Iowa. **Memberships:** Soc Indust & Appl Math; Asn Comput Mach. **Research Statement & Publications:** Numerical solution of functional differential equations and integral equations; mathematical modeling of biological systems. **Mailing Address:** Off Acad Affairs, Univ NDak, Box 8176, Grand Forks, ND 58202.

KEMPER, JOHN D(USTIN), MECHANICAL ENGINEERING. **Personal Data:** b Portland, Ore, May 29, 1924; m 1947, Barbara; c Kathleen. **Education:** Univ Calif, Los Angeles, BS, 1949, MS, 1959; Univ Colo, PhD (struct mech), 1969. **Honors & Awards:** Alex Laurie Award, Am Soc Hort Sci, 1974; John D Kemper Hall of Eng Named in Honor, Univ Calif Davis, 2003. **Professional Experience:** EMER PROF ENG, UNIV CALIF DAVIS, 1991-; Task Force Prep Teaching Eng, Am Soc Eng Educ, 1984-1986; dir, Plantronics Inc, 1983-1986; chmn, Panel Grad Educ & Res, Nat Res Coun, 1983-1985; dean, Col Eng, 1969-1983; prof, Col Eng, 1967-1991; assoc prof, Univ Calif Davis, 1962-1967; vpres eng, Marchant Div, Smith-Corona Marchant Inc, 1959-1962; chief engr, Marchant Div, Smith-Corona Marchant Inc, 1958-1959; asst to vpres eng, Marchant Calculators, Inc, 1956-1958; chief mech engr, H A Wagner Co, 1955-1956; chief mech engr, Telecomput Corp, Calif, 1952-1955; proj engr, Telecomput Corp, Calif, 1950-1952; engr, Telecomput Corp, Calif, 1949-1950. **Memberships:** Fel AAAS; fel Am Soc Mech Engrs; Am Soc Eng Educ. **Research Statement & Publications:** Mechanical design; structural mechanics; writings on engineering profession, introduction to engineering profession, ethics, creativity, graduation education and research, preparation for teaching. **Mailing Address:** 1316 Peartree Ln, Medford, OR 97504. **E-Mail:** jdkemperrvm@charter.net

KEMPER, JOHN THOMAS, BIOMATHEMATICS, MATHEMATICAL FINANCE, MATHEMATICS EDUCATION. **Personal Data:** b San Francisco, Calif, March 7, 1944. **Education:** Rice Univ, BA, 1966, PhD (math), 1970. **Honors & Awards:** Prof of the year, Univ of St Thomas, 2001 Nat Res Serv Award, Univ Minn, 1976-1978. **Professional Experience:** Fund Improv Post Sec Educ, US Dept Educ, 1995-1997; PROF, DEPT MATH, UNIV ST THOMAS, 1987-; dept chair, Dept Math, Univ St Thomas, 1987-1994; proj dir, Inst Sec Teachers, NSF, 1984-1985; Prin investr, NSF, 1981-1983; fac mem, Dept Math, Univ St Thomas, 1978-1987; Nat Res Serv award, Univ Minn, 1976-1978; City Col, Univ Minn, 1974-1976; City Col, New York, 1973-1974; Asst prof math, NY Univ, 1970-1973. **Memberships:** Am Math Soc; Math Asn Am; Mathematicians Educ Reform; Coun Undergrad Res. **Research Statement & Publications:** Development and analysis of deterministic models in population biology and finance. **Mailing Address:** 221 Woodlawn Ave, St Paul, MN 55105.

KEMPER, KIRBY WAYNE, NUCLEAR PHYSICS, ION SOURCE DEVELOPMENT. **Personal Data:** b New York, NY, April 13, 1940. **Education:** Va Polytech Inst, BS, 1962; Ind Univ, MS, 1964, PhD (physics), 1968. **Honors & Awards:** Jesse W Beans Medal, SE Sect Am Phys Soc. **Professional Experience:** VPRES RES, FLA STATE UNIV, as of 2006; chair, Dept Physics, Fla State Univ, 1997-2003; ROBERT B LAWSON DISTINGUISHED PROF, FLA STATE UNIV, 1994-; prof physics, Fla State Univ, 1979-1994; from asst prof to assoc prof, Fla State Univ, 1971-1979; res assoc nuclear physics, Fla State Univ, 1968-1971. **Memberships:** Sigma Xi; fel Am Phys Soc (Chmn SE Sect); SIgma Pi Sigma. **Research Statement & Publications:** Selective population of states with heavy ions; polarized ion source development; laser induced atomic polarizations; spin effects in nuclear reactions; implantation of heavy-ions; radiation damage. **Mailing Address:** Phys Dept, Fla State Univ, Tallahassee, FL 32306. **Fax:** 850-644-8630. **E-Mail:** kirby@phy.fsu.edu

KEMPER, WILLIAM ALEXANDER, ENVIRONMENTAL CHEMISTRY, BALLISTICS. **Personal Data:** b Baltimore, Md, January 1, 1911; m 1973, Marcia. **Education:** Johns Hopkins Univ, PhD (phys chem), 1934. **Professional Experience:** RETIRED; asst prof physics, Metrop State Col, 1976-1977; sr ballistician, Navy Surface Warfare Ctr-Dahlgren Lab, 1973-1975; sci adv, Comdr Cruiser Destroyer Forces Atlantic Fleet, 1972-1973; chmn, USN Aeroballistics Adv Comt, 1967, 1968; physicist, US Naval Weapons Lab, 1946-1972; chemist, Res Dept, Baltimore Gas & Elec Co, 1934-1943. **Memberships:** AAAS. **Research Statement & Publications:** Ballistics; fire control; investigated sulphur and nitrogen compounds in heating gas; flight characteristics of missiles directed preparation of firecontrol data; radiologic measurements at Crossroads tests. **Mailing Address:** 7363 W 26th Pl, Denver, CO 80033.

KEMPERMAN, JOHANNES HENRICUS BERNARDUS, PROBABILITY, MATHEMATICAL STATISTICS. **Personal Data:** b Amsterdam, Neth, July 16, 1924; wid, c Steven, Bruce, Hubert, Ingrid & Eric. **Education:** Univ Amsterdam, BS, 1945, MS, 1948, PhD (math), 1950. **Professional Experience:** PROF EMER STATIST, RUTGERS UNIV, 1995-; prof statist, Rutgers Univ, 1986-1995; & Stanford Univ, 1966-1967 & Univ Tex, Austin, 1977-1978; prof, Univ Rochester, 1961-1985; on leave, Univ Wis, 1960-1961; on leave, Univ Amsterdam, 1958-1959 & 1972-1973; from asst prof to prof math, Purdue Univ, 1951-1961; Res assoc appl math, Math Ctr, Amsterdam, 1948-1951. **Memberships:** Am Statist Asn; fel Inst Math Statist; Dutch Math Soc; Math Asn Am; fel Am Asn Advan Sci; corresp mem Royal Neth Acad Sci. **Research Statement & Publications:** Analysis; probability; statistics. **Mailing Address:** Dept Statist, Rutgers Univ, 501 Hill Ctr, Busch Campus, Piscataway, NJ 08854-8019. **Fax:** 732-445-3428.

KEMPH, JOHN PATTERSON, PSYCHIATRY, PHYSIOLOGY. **Personal Data:** b Lima, Ohio, December 17, 1919; m 1943, c 4. **Education:** Ohio Northern Univ, AB, 1947; Ohio State Univ, BSc, 1947, MSc, 1948, MD, 1953; Am Bd Psychiat & Neurol, dipl psychiat, 1960, dipl child psychiat, 1962. **Professional Experience:** EMER DEAN, MED COL OHIO, 1996-; PROF EMER, DEPT PSYCHIAT, MED COL OHIO, 1986-; PROF PSYCHIAT, UNIV FLA, 1986-; vpres acad affairs, dean med fac & prof psychiat, 1974-1986; prof psychiat & chmn dept, Med Col Ohio, 1972-1974; prof psychiat & dir child & adolescent psychiat, State Univ NY Downstate Med Ctr, 1968-1972; clin dir, Children's Psychiat Hosp, 1965-1968; chmn clin serv comt, Children's Psychiat Hosp, 1965-1968; consult, Cent Mich Coun Continuing Psychiat Educ, 1964-1968; mem clin serv comt, Sch Social Work & lectr psychosom med, Univ Hosp, 1963-1968; lectr human growth & behav, Sch Social Work & lectr psychosom med, Univ Hosp, 1962-1968; infections control officer, Med Ctr, Univ Mich, Ann Arbor, 1961-1968; dir in-patient serv & coord res, Children's Psychiat Hosp, 1961-1965; from instr to assoc prof psychiat, Univ Mich, 1960-1968; instr child psychiat, Med Ctr, Univ Mich, Ann Arbor, 1960-1961; fel child psychiat, Med Ctr, Univ Mich, Ann Arbor, 1960-1961; vice chief staff psychiat, St Rita's Hosp, 1958-1960; mem active staff, Mem Hosp, Lima, Ohio, 1957-1960; dir, Ohio Northwest Guid Ctr, 1957-1960; jr clin instr, Med Ctr, Univ Mich, 1956-1957; resident psychiat, Med Ctr, Univ Mich, 1955-1956; resident psychiat, Columbus State Hosp, 1954-1955; intern, Mt Carmel Hosp, Columbus, Ohio, 1953-1954; res assoc, Res Found, Ohio State Univ, 1951-1955; Res fel, Ohio State Univ, 1948-1951; Res asst, Res Found, Ohio State Univ, 1947-1948. **Memberships:** Fel Am Psychiat Asn; AMA; Am Orthopsychiat Asn; Am Asn Ment Deficiency; Am Psychosom Soc; Sigma Xi. **Research Statement & Publications:** Child psychiatry; applied cardiovascular and respiratory physiology; study of physiological and psychological correlates of behavior. **Mailing Address:** Med Col, 3000 Arlington Ave, Toledo, OH 43614.

KEMPHUES, KENNETH J, ANIMAL DEVELOPMENT. **Personal Data:** b Cincinnati, Ohio, July 3, 1950; m 1984, Diane; c Zachary & Amanda. **Education:** Northern Va Community Col, AS, 1974; Univ Va, BS, 1976; Ind Univ, PhD (genetics), 1981. **Professional Experience:** PROF DEVELOP BIOL, CORNELL UNIV, 1996-; from asst prof to assoc prof, Cornell Univ, 1984-1996; teaching fel, Univ Colo, 1981-1984; postdoctoral fel, NIH, Univ Colo, 1981-1984. **Memberships:** Genetics Soc Am; Soc Develop Am; AAAS. **Research Statement & Publications:** The problem of determination in animal development; identification and characterization of gene encoding functions necessary for determination; the use of molecular, ultrastructural and biochemical techniques to exploit mutations in the genes; author of various articles. **Mailing Address:** Dept Develop Biol, Cornell Univ, 435 Biotech Bldg, Ithaca, NY 14853-2703. **Fax:** 607-255-6249. **E-Mail:** kjk1@cornell.edu

KEMPLE, MARVIN DAVID, MAGNETIC RESONANCE. **Personal Data:** b Indianapolis, Ind, September 2, 1942; m 1964, c 2. **Education:** Purdue Univ, BS, 1964; Univ Ill, Urbana-Champaign, MS, 1965, PhD (physics), 1971. **Professional Experience:** PROF PHYSICS, IND UNIV-PURDUE UNIV, INDIANAPOLIS, as of 2004; asst prof physics, Ind Univ-purdue Univ, Indianapolis, beginning 1977; Nat Res Coun res assoc, Nat Bur Standards, 1976-1977; res assoc, Dept Chem, 1972-1976; Enrico Fermi fel chem & physics, Enrico Fermi Inst, Univ Chicago, 1971-1972. **Memberships:** Am Phys Soc; AAAS; Sigma Xi. **Research Statement & Publications:** Application of electron paramagnetic resonance and electron nuclear double resonance to the study of ions and molecules in ionic crystals, organic crystals, protein crystals, and intact, live biological systems. **Mailing Address:** Dept Physics, Ind Univ-Purdue Univ Indpolis, 402 N Blackford St, Indianapolis, IN 46205-3273. **E-Mail:** mkemple@iupui.edu

KEMPLER, WALTER, FAMILY COUNSELING. **Personal Data:** b New York, NY, September 9, 1923; c 5. **Education:** Univ Tex, BS, 1946, MD, 1947. **Professional Experience:** RETIRED; founder & dir family coun, Kempler Inst, 1960-. **Research Statement & Publications:** The structure, dynamics and treatment of the family. **Mailing Address:** Kempler Inst, PO Box 2185, Laguna Hills, CA 92654-2185.

KEMPNER, DAVID H, IMMUNOCHEMISTRY, BIOCHEMISTRY. **Education:** Tufts Univ, PhD (chem), 1975. **Professional Experience:** PRES, IMTA, INC, 1992-; sr assoc, Strategic Tech Int, 1988-1992; prin consult, Bernard Wolnak & Assocs. 1983-1988. **Mailing Address:** 42 E Depot St, Vernon Hills, IL 60061.

KEMPNER, ELLIS STANLEY, RADIATION TARGET ANALYSIS. **Personal Data:** b New York, NY, March 20, 1932; m 1961, c 3. **Education:** Brooklyn Col, BS, 1953; Yale Univ, MS, 1955, PhD (biophys), 1959. **Professional Experience:** CHIEF, SECT MACROMOLECULAR BIOPHYSICS, NIAMS, 1986-; lectr, Univ Calif, Davis, 1968-1969; physicist, Nat Inst Arthritis, Diabetes & Digestive & Kidney Dis, NIH, 1961-1986; asst scientist bionucleonics, 1958-1961. **Memberships:** Biophys Soc. **Research Statement & Publications:** Radiation effects on macromolecules; macromolecular synthesis; growth under extreme conditions; cellular organization. **Mailing Address:** Radiation Biophysics Sec, Lab Muscle Biol, NIAMS, Bldg 50, Rm 1345, Bethesda, MD 20892. **Fax:** 301-402-0009. **E-Mail:** kempnere@mail.nih.gov

KEMPNER, JOSEPH, APPLIED MECHANICS, AEROSPACE ENGINEERING. **Personal Data:** b Brooklyn, NY, April 25, 1923; m 1947, c 2. **Education:** Polytech Inst Brooklyn, BAeE, 1943, MEE, 1947, PhD (appl mech), 1950. **Honors & Awards:** Citation Distinguished Res, Sigma Xi, 1973; Laskowitz Gold Medal Res Aerospace Eng, NY Acad Sci, 1973. **Professional Experience:** PROF EMER MECH, AEROSPACE, INDUST MFG & MAT ENG, POLYTECH INST NY, 1990-; mem comt basic res, Adv Army res Off, 1973-1976 & 1982-1985; mem adv group, Ship res Comt, Maritime Transp res Bd, Nat Acad Sci, 1973-1976; consult, USN, 1970-; head, dept Aerospace & Appl Mech, 1966-1976; prin investr, Off Naval res & Air Force Off Sci res grants & contracts, 1958-1977; prof appl mech, dept Aerospace & Appl Mech, 1957-1990; from instr to assoc prof, Polytech inst NY, 1950-1957; from res asst to res assoc appl mech, Polytech inst NY, 1947-1950; Aeronaut engr struct res, Nat Adv Comt Aeronaut, 1943-1947. **Memberships:** Assoc fel Am Inst Aeronaut & Astronaut; Am Soc Mech Eng; fel Am Acad Mech; fel NY Acad Sci; Am Soc Eng Educ. **Research Statement & Publications:** Structural research related to aerospace vehicles, submersible vessels and pressure vessels; statics and dynamics of plates and shells, including large deformation and elevated temperature effects; applied mechanics. **Mailing Address:** Dept Mech Eng, Polytech Univ, Brooklyn, NY 11201. **Fax:** 718-260-3532.

KEMPSON, STEPHEN ALLAN, MEMBRANE & EPITHELIAL TRANSPORT, OSMOTIC STRESS & KIDNEY PHYSIOLOGY. **Personal Data:** b Walsall, Eng, July 2, 1948; American citizen. **Education:** Lancaster Univ, UK, BA, 1970; Warwick Univ, MS, 1971; London Univ, PhD (biochem), 1975. **Honors & Awards:** Fellow of the American Society of Nephrology 2004-2009. **Professional Experience:** PROF PHYSIOL, IND UNIV MED SCH, 1993-; from asst prof to assoc prof, Ind Univ Med Sch, 1982-1993; asst prof med, Univ Pittsburgh, 1980-1982; asst prof, Mayo Med Sch, 1979-1980; fel physiol, Mayo Clinic Found, 1977-1980; Fel biochem, Univ Rochester, 1975-1977. **Memberships:** Am Physiol Soc; Am Soc Renal Biochem & Metab; Am Soc Nephrol. **Research Statement & Publications:** Biochemistry and physiology of the kidney, specifically the cellular control mechanisms which allow adaptation to stresses such as hypertonicity. **Mailing Address:** Dept Cellular & Integrative Physiol, Ind Univ Sch Med, Rm 306, 635 Barnhill Dr, Indianapolis, IN 46202-5120. **Fax:** 317-274-3318. **E-Mail:** skempson@iupui.edu

KEMPTER, CHARLES PRENTISS, TOXICOLOGY. **Personal Data:** b Burlington, Vt, February 12, 1925; m 1977, Judith; c Colin, Eric & Reid. **Education:** Stanford Univ, BS, 1949, MS, 1950, PhD (chem), 1956. **Professional Experience:** RETIRED; sci adv, Kempter-Rossman Int, 1975-1993; tech dir, Kempter-Rossman Int, 1973-1975; sci consult, 1971-1973; gov's adv, NMex State Crime Lab, 1971-1973; vis scientist, Inst Phys Chem, Vienna, 1963-1964; thesis adv, Los Alamos Grad Ctr, Univ NMex, 1959-1971; staff mem, Los Alamos Sci Lab, Univ Calif, 1956-1971; phys chemist, Dow Chem Co, 1950-1953; asst phys sci, Stanford Univ, 1949-1950. **Memberships:** Fel Inst Chemists; Am Chem Soc; AAAS; Sigma Xi. **Research Statement & Publications:** Biomedical literature research primarily in toxicology. **Mailing Address:** 6202 Agee St, San Diego, CA 92122.

KEMPTON, JOHN P(AUL), GROUNDWATER GEOLOGY. **Personal Data:** b Buffalo, NY, August 14, 1932; m 1954, c 2. **Education:** Denison Univ, BS, 1954; Ohio State Univ, MA, 1956; Univ Ill, PhD, 1962. **Professional Experience:** SR EMERITUS GEOLOGIST & HEAD, QUATERNARY FRAMEWORK STUDIES SECT, ILL GEOL SURV, as of 2004; sr geologist & head, quaternary framework studies sect, Ill Geol Surv, beginning 1988; sr geologist & spec proj leader, Hydrogeol & Geophys Sect, 1986-1988; SSC geol task force leader, Hydrogeol & Geophys Sect, 1984-1986; Vis prof, Northern Ill Univ, 1973; geologist, Hydrogeol & Geophys Sect, 1971-1984; from asst geologist to assoc geologist, Ill Geol Surv, 1956-1971; geologist, Ohio Div Water, 1955-1956; Asst, Ohio State Univ, 1954-1956. **Memberships:** AAAS; Geol Soc Am; Asn Eng Geologists; Sigma Xi; Am Quaternary Asn. **Research Statement & Publications:** Quaternary stratigraphy and mapping, environmental and groundwater geology; three-dimensional, lithostratigraphic stackunit geologic maps of quaternary sediments for direct interpretation for ground-water resources development and protection, siting, and other land uses. **Mailing Address:** Illinois State Geol Surv, 615 E Peabody Dr, Champaign, IL 61820.

KENAGA, DUANE LEROY, WOOD TECHNOLOGY, PULP & PAPER TECHNOLOGY. **Personal Data:** b Midland, Mich, March 9, 1920. **Education:** Univ Mich, BSChe, 1943, MWT, 1948. **Professional Experience:** RETIRED; res assoc, Designed Prod Dept, 1978-1985; res specialist, Biochem Res Lab, Dow Chem Co, 1969-1978; sr res wood chemist, Biochem Res Lab, Dow Chem Co, 1965-1969; wood technologist, Biochem Res Lab, Dow Chem Co, 1951-1965; wood technologist, Wood & Paper Sect, Southern Res Inst, 1948-1951; asst, Univ Mich, 1947-1948. **Memberships:** Forest Prod Res Soc; Soc Wood Sci & Tech; Tech Asn Pulp & Paper Indust. **Research Statement & Publications:** Chemical utilization of wood; chemical modification of wood to promote dimensional stability; paper and fiber treatments; wet end additives in paper systems, including bulking aids, retention aids and high filler sheets. **Mailing Address:** 4622 Chatham Court, Midland, MI 48642. **E-Mail:** dlkenaga@aol.com

KENAGY, GEORGE JAMES, ECOLOGY & BEHAVIOR PHYSIOLOGY, EVOLUTION. **Personal Data:** b Los Angeles, Calif, July 9, 1945; m 1969, c 2. **Education:** Pomona Col, BA, 1967; Univ Calif, Los Angeles, PhD (zoology), 1972. **Professional Experience:** Vis prof, Univ Catalica Chile, 1996-; CUR MAMMALS, BURKE MUS, 1994-; vis scholar, Univ Calif, Berkeley, 1989-1990; PROF, DEPT ZOOLOGY, UNIV WASH, 1986-; vis scientist, Commonwealth Sci & Res Orgn Wildlife, Australia, 1983-1984; from asst prof to assoc prof, Burke Mus, 1976-1986; res biologist, Univ Calif, Los Angeles, 1974; fel, Max Planck Inst Behav Physiol, Ger, 1972-1973. **Memberships:** AAAS; Animal Behav Soc; Am Soc Mammalogists; Soc Study Evolution. **Research Statement & Publications:** Bahavior and population biology of small mammals; daily and seasonal rhythms; reproduction; hibernation; energetics. **Mailing Address:** Dept Zoology, Univ Wash, 438 Kincaid 205B Burke Museum PO Box 353010, Seattle, WA 98195. **Fax:** 206-543-3041. **E-Mail:** kenagy@u.washington.edu

KENAN, RICHARD P, INTEGRATED OPTICS, FIBER OPTICS, & NONLINEAR OPTICS. **Personal Data:** b Waycross, Ga, December 25, 1931; m 1968, Jane; c Jeffrey C, Diane L & Richard A. **Education:** Ga Inst Technol, BS (physics) 1955; Ohio State Univ, PhD (physics), 1962. **Professional Experience:** PROF EMERITUS, GA INST TECHNOL, 1999-; PROF, ELEC & COMPUTER ENG, GA INST TECHNOL, 1986-1999; assoc sect mgr, Battelle Mem Inst, 1981-1986; prin res scientist, Battelle Mem Inst, 1975-1981; fel, Battelle Mem Inst, 1969-1975; sr physicist, Battelle Mem Inst, 1963-1969; Res physicist, Battelle Mem Inst, 1962-1963. **Memberships:** Am Phys Soc; Am Asn Physics Teachers; Optical Soc Am; Inst Elec & Electronics Engrs. **Research Statement & Publications:** nonlinear optics; diffractive optics; integrated optics; optical processing. **Mailing Address:** Sch Elec & Comput Eng, Ga Inst Technol 777 Atlantic Dr NW, Atlanta, GA 30338-5944. **E-Mail:** dick.kenan@ece.gatech.edu

KENAT, THOMAS ARTHUR, CHEMICAL ENGINEERING, POLYMER SCIENCE. **Personal Data:** b Cleveland, Ohio, August 6, 1942; m 1964, Wynne; c Steven T & Lisa M. **Education:** Carnegie-Mellon Univ, BS, 1964, MS, 1965, PhD (chem eng), 1968. **Professional Experience:** PRIN CONSULT, KENA TECH PROCESS ENG, 1992-; sr prog mgr, Quantum Technol Inc, 1989-1992; sr res & develop assoc, Camet Co, 1988-1989; sr res & develop assoc, B F Goodrich Co, 1983-1988; sr eng scientist, B F Goodrich Co, 1981-1983; sr res & develop engr, B F Goodrich Co, 1974-1980; res engr, B F Goodrich Co, 1969-1974; res engr, Chemstrand Res Ctr Inc, NC, 1968-1969. **Memberships:** Am Inst Chem Engrs; Am Chem Soc. **Research Statement & Publications:** Dynamics and control of polymerization reactions; design and development of chemical reaction systems; processing of polymer composites; corrosion testing to select materials of construction for chemical process applications; design and development of chemical process concepts; synthetic rubber research and development; paper pulp bleaching chemicals; process engineering. **Mailing Address:** 3573 Autumn Tree Dr, Medina, OH 44256. **Fax:** 330-725-7091. **E-Mail:** tak@kenatech.com

KENDALL, BRUCE REGINALD FRANCIS, VACUUM TECHNOLOGY, SPACE PHYSICS. **Personal Data:** b Guildford, Western Australia, July 23, 1934; m 1988, Carolyn Ruwitch; c 3. **Education:** Univ Western Australia, BSc, 1954, PhD (physics), 1960. **Professional Experience:** Chmn, hist comt, 1994-1999; trustee, Vacuum Technol Div, Am Vacuum Soc, 1992-1995; EMER PROF PHYSICS, PA STATE UNIV, 1991-; chmn, Vacuum Technol Div, Am Vacuum Soc, 1988-1989; prof, PA State Univ, 1969-1991; Consult, 1964-; assoc prof, PA State Univ, 1964-1969; dir new prod develop, Nuclide Corp, 1962-1964; sr res scientist, Nuclide Corp, 1961-1962; asst res officer, Nuclide Corp, 1960-1961; Nat Res Coun Can, 1959-1960. **Memberships:** Am Phys Soc; Am Vacuum Soc. **Research Statement & Publications:** Electron, vacuum and space physics; mass spectrometry; vacuum and electrical properties of spacecraft materials; measurement and production of high vacuum. **Mailing Address:** Dept Physics, Pa State Univ, University Park, PA 16802.

KENDALL, BURTON NATHANIEL, NETWORKS, DISTRIBUTED DATA BASES. **Personal Data:** b San Francisco, Calif, December 15, 1940; m 1979, Sally; c Anne, James & Samuel. **Education:** Stanford Univ, BS, 1962; Brown Univ, PhD (physics), 1969. **Professional Experience:** PRIN ENG/MANAGER, QUALCOMM, 2000-; chief technol officer, lifemasters, inc, 1996-2000; dir technol, Octel Commun Corp, 1993-1996; syst archit, Octel Commun Corp, 1989-1993; mem, NASA Adv Panel Knowledge Based Systs Verification & Validation, 1987-1989; PRES, DELTA RES FOUND, 1980-; prin scientist, Measurex Corp, 1980-1989; consult, Libr Automation, 1979-; sr staff scientist, Measurex Corp, 1978-1980; sr res scientist, Systs Control Inc, 1973-1978; asst prof, Univ Calif, Santa Barbara, 1971-1973; lectr, Univ Calif, Santa Barbara, 1969-1971; res asst physics, Brown Univ, 1962-1969; Res aide microwave design, Stanford Univ, 1959-1962. **Memberships:** AAAS; Am Phys Soc; Sigma Xi. **Research Statement & Publications:** Computer hardware and software design; large scale systems design and modelling; indust process control system design; voice processing and multimedia system design; distributed medical information systems; wireless location technology. **Mailing Address:** 675 Campbell Technol Parkway, Campbell, CA 95008. **Fax:** 408-626-0550. **E-Mail:** bkendall@qualcomm.com

KENDALL, H(AROLD) B(ENNE), CHEMICAL ENGINEERING. **Personal Data:** b Midland, Mich, April 27, 1923; m 1948, c 4. **Education:** Grove City Col, BS, 1948; Case Inst Technol, MS, 1950, PhD (chem eng), 1956. **Professional Experience:** Chmn, Dept Chem Engr, Ohio Univ, 1961-1967, 1971-1972 & 1982-1983; PROF CHEM ENG, OHIO UNIV, 1960-; asst prof chem eng, Case Inst Technol, 1955-1960; instr chem & chem eng, Case Inst Technol, 1951-1955; instr chem & metall eng, Univ Mich, 1950-1951. **Memberships:** Am Chem Soc; Soc Hist Technol; Am Inst Chem Engrs. **Research Statement & Publications:** Reaction kinetics in flow reactors; catalytic processing; heterogeneous catalysis; history of technology. **Mailing Address:** 69 Morris Ave, Athens, OH 45701.

KENDALL, HARRY WHITE, PHYSICS. **Personal Data:** b Sopchoppy, Fla, October 9, 1924; m 1950, c 3. **Education:** Tusculum Col, BA, 1948; Fla State Univ, MS, 1950; Univ Fla, PhD (electronics, physics), 1961. **Professional Experience:** RETIRED; actg chmn dept, Univ S Fla, 1978-1984; prof, Univ S Fla, 1963-1984; assoc prof & chmn dept physics, Univ S Fla, 1960-1963; teaching asst, NSF, 1959-1960; assoc prof & head dept, Emory & Henry Col, 1957-1959; teaching asst, Univ Fla, 1954-1957; asst prof, Emory & Henry Col, 1951-1954; instr physics, Chipola Jr Col, 1950-1951. **Memberships:** Am Phys Soc; Am Asn Physics Teachers; Sigma Xi. **Research Statement & Publications:** Electrical breakdown of gases. **Mailing Address:** Grand Ridge, FL 32442.

KENDALL, JOHN HUGH, FOOD SCIENCE, CEREAL CHEMISTRY. **Personal Data:** b Mt Pleasant, Tex, September 30, 1942; m 1965, c 2. **Education:** La State Univ, BS, 1964, MS, 1969, PhD (food sci), 1973. **Professional Experience:** DIR PROCESS DEVELOP, RIVIANA FOODS INC, 1993-; adj asst prof, Univ Houston, 1975-1993; sr food technologist, 1973-1975; qual control rep, Borden Inc, 1971-1973. **Memberships:** Inst Food Technologists; Am Asn Cereal Chemists; Int Asn Milk Food & Environ Sanitarians; Am Soc Microbiol. **Research Statement & Publications:** Rice processing and by-product utilization. **Mailing Address:** Riviana Foods Inc, 1702 Taylor St, Houston, TX 77007.

KENDALL, JOHN WALKER, ENDOCRINOLOGY. **Personal Data:** b Bellingham, Wash, March 19, 1929; m 1954, Betty; c John, Kay & Victoria. **Education:** Yale Univ, BA, 1952; Univ Wash, MD, 1956. **Honors & Awards:** Mentor Award, Med Res Found Ore, 1993. **Professional Experience:** Distinguished physician, Dept Vet Affairs, 1993-1996; EMER DEAN, SCH MED, ORE HEALTH SCI UNIV, 1992-; pres, Ore Found Med Excellence, 1989-1991; prof med & asst dean res, dean, Ore Health Sci Univ, 1983-1992; Div Metab, Med Sch, 1980-1983; mem, Vet Admin Res Adv Comt, 1980-1983; chmn pro tem, Dept Med, Med Sch, Univ Ore, 1975-1976; assoc chief of staff for res, Vet Admin Hosp, Portland, 1971-1983; prof med & head, Div Metab, Med Sch, 1971-1980; from prof to assoc prof, Sch Med, Ore Health Sci Univ, 1962-1971; USPHS trainee, 1959-1962; instr med, Sch Med, Vanderbilt Univ, 1959-1960; acad affil liason officer VISN20. **Memberships:** Asn Am Physicians; Endocrine Soc; Am Soc Clin Invest; Am Fedn Clin Res. **Research Statement & Publications:** Neural control of pituitary function. **Mailing Address:** PO Box 1034, Portland, OR 97207.

KENDALL, KATHERINE CLEMENT, GRIZZLY BEAR ECOLOGY, COMMUNITY ECOLOGY OF PLANTS & ANIMALS. **Personal Data:** b Morristown, NJ, December 9, 1951; m 1982, George; c Jack & Samuel. **Education:** Univ Va, BA, 1974; Mont State Univ, MS, 1981. **Professional Experience:** RES ECOLOGIST, BIOL RESOURCES DIV, US GEOL SURV, 1996-; chmn, Interagency Grizzly Bear Res Subcomt, Nat Park Serv, 1993-; res ecologist, Nat Biol Serv, US Dept Interior, 1993-1996; rep, Interagency Grizzly Bear Res Subcomt, Nat Park Serv, 1989-; Adj prof, Univ Mont, 1982-; res ecologist, W Glacier, Mont, 1982-1993; res biologist, Bozeman, Mont, 1977-1982; environ specialist, Nat Park Serv, DC, 1974-1977. **Memberships:** Int Bear Asn; Wildlife Soc; Sigma Xi; George Wright Soc. **Research Statement & Publications:** Monitoring long-term population trends, community ecology and interaction between climate and community processes; focus on grizzly and black bears, huckleberry, whitebark pine; conservation biology. **Mailing Address:** Glacier Nat Park Sci Ctr, West Glacier, MT 59936-0128. **Fax:** 406-888-7990. **E-Mail:** kkendall@usgs.gov

KENDALL, MICHAEL WELT, GROSS ANATOMY, MICROSCOPIC ANATOMY. **Personal Data:** b Glendale, Ariz, January 30, 1943; m 1965, c 1. **Education:** Univ Northern Iowa, BA, 1965; Univ Louisville, MS, 1969, PhD (anat), 1972. **Professional Experience:** CONSULT, 1984-; consult gross anat, Int Cong Col Physicians & Surgeons, 1976-; chmn dept, Sch Med Sci, Univ Nev, Reno, 1975-1977; pesticide consult, Dept Agr, Univ Nev, 1975-1976; from asst prof to assoc prof anat, Sch Med Sci, Univ Nev, Reno, 1974-1984; Asst prof anat, Med Ctr, Univ Miss, 1972-1974. **Memberships:** AAAS; Am Asn Anatomists; Am Heart Asn. **Research Statement & Publications:** Ultrastructural descriptive analysis of carcinogenesis induced by aflatoxin-B, in rat liver; ultrastructural hepatotoxic effects of mirex in rats; scanning electron microscopy of human knee joints. **Mailing Address:** 4800 Olsen Blvd, Amarillo, TX 76106.

KENDALL, NORMAN, PEDIATRICS. **Personal Data:** b Philadelphia, Pa, May 7, 1912; m 1944, c 2. **Education:** Temple Univ, MD, 1936, MS, 1941. **Professional Experience:** RETIRED; chmn dept neonatology, Temple Univ Hosp; attend pediatrician, St Christopher's Hosp for Children; consult, 1982; consult, NJ Dept Health, 1979-1982; prof pediat, Sch Med, 1967-1979; from asst prof to assoc prof, Sch Med, 1947-1967; instr pediat, Sch Med, 1941-1947; resident, Hosp, Temple Univ, 1941; intern, Hosp, Temple Univ, 1938. **Memberships:** Am Acad Pediat. **Research Statement & Publications:** Newborn infants. **Mailing Address:** 2401 Pennsylvania Ave Apt 20-B-22, Philadelphia, PA 19130.

KENDALL, PHILIP C, CHILD & ADOLESCENT CLINICAL PSYCHOLOGY. **Personal Data:** m 1974, Sue; c Mark & Reed. **Education:** Old Dominion Univ, BS, 1972; Va Commonwealth Univ, PhD (clin psychol), 1977. **Professional Experience:** LAURA H CARNELL PROF PSYCHOL, TEMPLE UNIV, as of 2003; head div psychol, Temple Univ, 1984-; PROF PSYCHOL, TEMPLE UNIV, 1984-; DIR CHILD & ADOLESCENT ANXIETY DISORDERS CLIN, TEMPLE UNIV, 1984-; prof psychol, Univ Minn, 1977-1984; fel, Ctr Advan Study Behav Sci, Stanford, Calif, 1977. **Memberships:** Am Psychol Asn; Asn Advan Behav Ther (pres-elect, 1988). **Research Statement & Publications:** Child and adolescent clinical psychology with a special focus on the cognitive and behavioral aspects of psychopathology; design and evaluation of psychotherapeutic programs; self control, anxiety and depression. **Mailing Address:** Dept Psychol, Temple Univ, 1701 N 13th St, Philadelphia, PA 19122. **Fax:** 215-204-5539. **E-Mail:** pkendall@temple.edu

KENDALL, RONALD J, WILDLIFE & ENVIRONMENTAL TOXICOLOGY. **Education:** Clemson Univ, MS; Va Polytech Inst, PhD. **Professional Experience:** DIR, INST ENVIRON & HUMAN HEALTH, TEX TECH UNIV, TEX, 1997-. **Mailing Address:** Tex Tech Univ Health Sci Ctr, Reese Ctr, Box 41163, Lubbock, TX 79409-1163. **Fax:** 806-885-2132. **E-Mail:** ron.kendall@tiehh.ttu.edu

KENDE, ANDREW S, ORGANIC CHEMISTRY, ORGANIC SYNTHESIS. **Personal Data:** b Budapest, Hungary, July 17, 1932; American citizen; m 1954, Frances; c Mark. **Education:** Univ Chicago, BA, 1950; Harvard Univ, MA, 1954, PhD, 1957; Glasgow Univ, postdoc, 1958; Univ Munchen, postdoc, 1960. **Professional Experience:** PRES, ORG SYNTHESES INC, 1991-; Dow Chem Co, 1974- & Eastman Kodak, 1988-; Japan Soc Prom Sci Award, 1985-1986; PROF EMER HOUGHTON CHEM, UNIV ROCHESTER, 1981-; chmn, Org Syntheses, Inc, 1979-1983; Guggenheim fel, 1978-1979; chmn, Org div, Am Chem Soc, 1978-1979; chmn, Med Chem Study Sect, NIH, 1974-1976; consult, Med Chem Study Sect, NIH, 1972-1976 & 1985-1986; vis prof, Mich State Univ, 1968 & Univ Geneve, 1974; consult, Lederle labs, 1968-; prof chem, Org Syntheses, Inc, 1968-1981; res fel, Lederle labs, Am Cyanamid Co, 1967-1968; res assoc, Lederle labs, Am Cyanamid Co, 1963-1967; res chemist, Lederle labs, Am Cyanamid Co, 1957-1962. **Memberships:** Am Chem Soc; Am Asn Univ profs. **Research Statement & Publications:** Thermal and photochemical rearrangements, total synthesis of alkaloids and antibiotics, synthetic methods; chemistry of antitumor compounds. **Mailing Address:** Dept Chem, Univ Rochester, PO Box 270216, Rochester, NY 14627-0216. **Fax:** 585-473-6889. **E-Mail:** kende@chem.rochester.edu

KENDE, HANS JANOS, PLANT HORMONE ACTION. **Personal Data:** b Szekesfehervar, Hungary, January 18, 1937; American citizen; m 1960, Gabriele Guggenheim; c Benjamin, Michael & Judith. **Education:** Univ Zurich, PhD (bot), 1960. **Honorary Degrees:** DSc, Univ Fribourg, Switz. **Honors & Awards:** Medal Res Excellence, Int Plant Growth Substances Asn, 1995; Stephen Hales Prize, Am Soc Plant Biol, 1998. **Professional Experience:** Vis prof, Fedn Inst Technol, Inst Plant Sci, 2000; vis scientist, Friedrich Miescher Inst Basel, Switz, 1991; DISTINGUISHED UNIV PROF PLANT BIOL, DEPT ENERGY PLANT RES LAB, MICH STATE UNIV, 1990-; dir, Dept Energy Plant Res Lab, Mich State Univ, 1985-1988; actg dir, Mich State Univ, Dept Energy, Plant Res Lab, 1984-1985; vis prof, Swiss Fed Inst Technol, 1979-1980; Guggenheim Mem Found fel & vis prof, Swiss Fed Inst Technol, 1972-1973; from assoc prof to prof, Dept Energy Plant Res Lab, Mich State Univ, 1965-1990; plant physiologist, Negev Inst Arid Zone Res, Israel, 1963-1965; res fel, Div Biol, Calif Inst Technol, 1961-1963; res fel, plant physiol, Nat Res Coun Can, 1960-1961. **Memberships:** Nat Acad Sci; Am Soc Plant Biol; fel AAAS; Ger Acad Nat Sci Leopoldina. **Research Statement & Publications:** Function, biosynthesis and action mechanism of plant growth regulators. **Mailing Address:** Dept Energy, Plant Res Lab, Mich State Univ, S236 Plant Biol Lab, East Lansing, MI 48824-1312. **Fax:** 517-353-9168. **E-Mail:** hkende@msu.edu

KENDER, DONALD NICHOLAS, ANALYTICAL CHEMISTRY. **Personal Data:** b Passaic, NJ, August 30, 1948; m 1971. **Education:** Ohio State Univ, BA, 1970; Georgetown Univ, PhD (chem), 1975. **Professional Experience:** MGR, CIBA-GEIGY CORP, 1976-; Chemist & Nat Res Coun assoc, Naval Surface Weapons Ctr, 1975-1976. **Memberships:** Am Chem Soc; Soc Appl Spectros; Sigma Xi. **Research Statement & Publications:** Isolation, identification and physical organic chemistry of pharmaceuticals. **Mailing Address:** CIBA-GEIGY Pharm, 556 Morris Ave, Summit, NJ 07901-1330.

KENDER, WALTER JOHN, AGRICULTURAL ADMINISTRATION, CITRUS. **Personal Data:** b Camden, NJ, December 20, 1935; m 1957, Carole; c David & Lily. **Education:** Del Valley Col, BS, 1957; Rutgers Univ, MS, 1959, PhD (plant nutrit), 1962. **Honorary Degrees:** DSc, Del Valley Col, 1993. **Honors & Awards:** Darrow Award, Am Soc Hort Sci, 1983. **Professional Experience:** PROF EMER, UNIV FLA, 2002-; consult, World Bank, Indonesia, 1991; prin investor, Agr Res Serv Coop Agreement Citrus Exotic Dis, 1989-1994; consult, US-AID-Pakistan, 1989; ADV COMT, FARM BUR CITRUS, 1985-; prof, Univ Fla, 1982-2001; dir, Citrus Res & Educ Ctr, Lake Alfred, 1982-1996; prof pomol & chmn dept, Cornell Univ, 1975-1982; bd dir, Am Soc Hort Sci, 1975-1980, 1982-1985; distinguished scientist, ARIC Univ, Wageningen Netherlands, 1974; head dept pomol & viticult, NY Agr Exp Sta 1972-1982; assoc ed, Am Soc Hort Sci, 1972-1976; assoc prof, 1969-1975; from asst prof to assoc prof hort, Univ Maine, Orono, 1962-1969. **Memberships:** Am Pomol Soc; fel AAAS; fel Am Soc Hort Sci; Sigma Xi; Fla State Horticultural Soc. **Research Statement & Publications:** Physiology and culture of fruit crops; air pollution effects on agricultural crops; emphasis on impacts of fossil fuel effluents and acid rain on fruit crop productivity and economic assessment; citrus; agricultural administration; abscission chemicals for mechanically harvesting citrus fruit. **Mailing Address:** Citrus Res & Educ Ctr Univ Fla, 700 Exp Sta Rd, Lake Alfred, FL 33850. **Fax:** 941-956-4631. **E-Mail:** kender@icon.lal.ufl.edu

KENDIG, EDWIN LAWRENCE, JR, pediatrics, respiratory disorders; deceased, see previous edition for last biography

KENDIG, JOAN JOHNSTON, NEUROBIOLOGY. **Personal Data:** b Derby, Conn, May 1, 1939; m 1964, c Scott J & Leslie A. **Education:** Smith Col, BA, 1960; Stanford Univ, PhD (biol sci), 1966. **Honors & Awards:** Javits Neurosci Investr Award, 1988-1995. **Professional Experience:** Mem, Surg, Anethesia & Trauma Study Sect, NIH, 1996-; vis prof, Ben Gurion Univ, Israel, 1988; PROF ANESTHESIA, SCH MED, STANFORD UNIV, 1986-; vis scientist, Clin Res Ctr Northwick Park, UK, 1984; NIH physiol study sect, 1981-1985; Mellon fac fel, Stanford Univ, 1976; from asst prof to assoc prof, Sch Med, Stanford Univ, 1971-1986; res assoc, Sch Med, Stanford Univ, 1967-1971; NSF fel neurophysiol, Univ Calif, Berkeley, 1965-1967. **Memberships:** Soc Neurosci; Int Asn Study Pain; Am Pain Soc; Am Soc Anethesiologists. **Research Statement & Publications:** Neuropharmacology of anesthetic and analgesic drugs; cellular effects of anesthetic and analgesic agents. **Mailing Address:** Dept Anesthesia, Sch Med, Stanford Univ, 300 Pasteur Dr, Stanford, CA 94305. **Fax:** 650-725-8052. **E-Mail:** kendig@leland.stanford.edu

KENDIG, MARTIN WILLIAM, PHYSICAL CHEMISTRY, CORROSION SCIENCE. **Personal Data:** b Danville, Pa, October 20, 1945; m 1969, Michele L Mulligan; c Rebecca L & Jamie A. **Education:** Franklin & Marshall Col, AB, 1967; Brown Univ, PhD (phys chem), 1974. **Honors & Awards:** Melvin Romanoff Award, Nat Asn Corrosion Engrs. **Professional Experience:** SR SCIENTIST & MEM TECH STAFF, ROCKWELL INT SCI CTR, 1980-; assoc chemist corrosion sci, Brookhaven Nat Lab, 1978-1980; asst chemist, 1976-1978; Res assoc, Ctr Surface & Coatings Res, Lehigh Univ, 1973-1976; Chmn, Corrosion Div, Electrochem Soc. **Memberships:** Electrochem Soc; Am Chem Soc; Sigma Xi; Am Soc Testing & Mat; Nat Asn Corrosion Engrs. **Research Statement & Publications:** Electrochemical aspects of surface energy, wetting wear and environmental fracture; the chemistry and physics of localized corrosion and corrosion protection; corrosion monitoring; polymer coatings. **Mailing Address:** Rockwell Sci Ctr, Thousand Oaks, CA 91360. **Fax:** 805-373-4383. **E-Mail:** mwkendig@scimail.risc.rockwell.com

KENDRICK, BRYCE, MYCOLOGY. **Personal Data:** b Liverpool, Eng, December 3, 1933; m 1977, Laureen; c Clinton & Kelly. **Education:** Univ Liverpool, BSc, 1955, PhD (mycol), 1958. **Honorary Degrees:** DSc, Univ Liverpool, 1980. **Honors & Awards:** Distinguished Mycologist Award, Mycol Soc Am, 1995. **Professional Experience:** Adj prof, Univ Victoria, BC, beginning 1994; DISTINGUISHED PROF EMER, UNIV WATERLOO, 1994-; Sir CV Raman fel, 1993; distinguished res fel, Found Res Development, SAfrica, 1990; hon prof, Nanjing Forestry Univ, Nanjing, China, 1988; assoc dean grad studies, Univ Waterloo, 1985-1993; secy, Acad Sci, Royal Soc Can, 1985-1991; Guggenheim fel, 1979-1980; chmn, Plant Biol Grant Selection Comt, Nat Sci & Eng Res Coun, Can, 1979; from asst prof to prof biol, Univ Waterloo, 1965-1994; mycologist, Plant Res Inst, Res Br, Can Dept Agr, 1959-1965; fel taxonomic mycol, Nat Res Coun Can, 1958-1959. **Memberships:** Mycol Soc Am; Brit Mycol Soc; fel Royal Soc Can; fel Brit Mycol Soc. **Research Statement & Publications:** Computer simulations; systematics of hyphomycetes; development, ecology, karyology, and toxicology of microfungi; mycorrhizae; fungal biodiversity. **Mailing Address:** Dept Biol, Univ Waterloo, 8727 Lochside Dr, Sidney, BC V8L 1M8, Can. **Fax:** 250-655-0755. **E-Mail:** mycolog@pacificcoast.net

KENDRICK, FRANCIS JOSEPH, PATHOLOGY, DENTISTRY. **Personal Data:** b St Petersburg, Fla, October 19, 1926; m 1953, c 2. **Education:** Northwestern Univ, DDS, 1952, PhD (path), 1963. **Professional Experience:** DEPT CHIEF REV, DIV RES RESOURCES, NIH, 1983-; asst dir, manpower & resource develop, 1981-1982; dir, biomed res support prog, 1975-1980; actg dir gen res support prog, div res resources, 1974-1975; spec asst prog planning & eval, Nat Inst Child Health & Human Develop, 1970-1974; asst to chief gen res support br, Nat Inst Child Health & Human Develop, 1969-1970; pathologist, Nat Inst Child Health & Human Develop, 1963-1969; res assoc teratology, Nat Inst Dent Res, 1960-1963; instr dent, Northwestern Univ, 1955-1956; pvt practr, 1953-1955; intern dent, USPHS Hosp, Seattle, 1952-1953. **Memberships:** AAAS; Teratology Soc; fel Am Acad Oral Path; Int Asn Dent; NY Acad Sci. **Research Statement & Publications:** Experimental carcinogenesis and teratology; oral and general pathology. **Mailing Address:** NIH, Potomac, MD 20854.

KENDRICK, HUGH, NUCLEAR ENGINEERING, SOLID STATE PHYSICS. **Personal Data:** b Ewell, Eng, January 25, 1940; m 1963, Diana W Adams; c Stuart & Amanda K. **Education:** Univ London, BSc, 1961; Calif Inst Technol, MS, 1962; Univ Mich, PhD (nuclear eng), 1968. **Professional Experience:** ASST PRES, SCI APPLICATIONS INT CORP, 1989-; dep chief operating officer, Sci Applications Int Corp, 1985-1989; CORP VPRES, SCI APPLICATIONS INT CORP, 1984-; vpres, Sci Applications Int Corp, 1981-1984; dir, Off Plans & Anal, 1979-1981; spec asst, Off Fuel Cycle Eval, US Dept Energy, 1977-1979; mgr, Div Safeguards & Nuclear Fuels, 1975-1977; dep mgr, Div Environ & Safety, Sci Applns, Inc, 1972-1975; sr physicist, Radiation Transport Group, Gulf Radiation Technol, 1968-1972; scientist, Vickers Res Ltd, 1962-1963; Teaching res asst mech eng, Calif Inst Technol, 1961-1962. **Memberships:** Am Phys Soc; Inst Nuclear Mat Mgt; Am Nuclear Soc; Sigma Xi. **Research Statement & Publications:** Investigation of magnetic materials through neutron diffraction; pulsed neutron investigation of radiation transport in shields; spectroscopy and unfolding techniques; nuclear materials assay; assessment of proliferation risks of nuclear technology; nuclear safeguards system effectiveness evaluation; environmental economic safety assessment of technology. **Mailing Address:** 13062 Caminito Pt, Del Mar, CA 92014-3853. **Fax:** 619-458-2739. **E-Mail:** hugh_kendrick@cpqm.saic.com

KENDZIORSKI, FRANCIS RICHARD, NUCLEAR PHYSICS. **Personal Data:** b Alpena, Mich, April 2, 1931; m 1964, c 2. **Education:** Univ Detroit, BS, 1953; Cornell Univ, PhD (physics), 1961. **Professional Experience:** Chmn Dept Physics & Astron, Western Conn State Col, 1978-1985; PROF PHYSICS, WESTERN CONN STATE COL, 1977-; assoc prof, Western Conn State Col, 1967-1977; asst prof, Univ Dayton, 1963-1967; Asst prof physics, Univ Detroit, 1961-1963. **Memberships:** AAAS; Am Phys Soc; Am Asn Physics Teachers. **Research Statement & Publications:** Lowenergy studies of nuclear structure in intermediate weight nuclei; extensive cosmic ray air showers; elementary education. **Mailing Address:** Dept Physics, Western Conn State Univ, 181 White St, Danbury, CT 06810.

KENEALY, MICHAEL DOUGLAS, ANIMAL NUTRITION, PHYSIOLOGY. **Personal Data:** b Council Bluffs, Iowa, May 7, 1947; m 1969, c 2. **Education:** Iowa State Univ, BS, 1969, PhD (animal nutrit & physiol), 1974. **Professional Experience:** PROF ANIMAL SCI, IOWA STATE UNIV, 1984-; from asst prof to assoc prof, Iowa State Univ, 1975-1984; nutritionist, Dr Macdonalds Feed Co, 1974-1975. **Memberships:** Sigma Xi; Am Dairy Sci Asn; Am Soc Animal Sci. **Research Statement & Publications:** International work in China, Costa Rica, Taiwan, andthe Soviet Union. **Mailing Address:** Dept Animal Sci, Iowa State Univ, 119 Kildee, Ames, IA 50011-2010. **Fax:** 515-294-0018. **E-Mail:** dkenealy@iastate.edu

KENEALY, PATRICK FRANCIS, MATHEMATICS EDUCATION. **Personal Data:** b Chicago, Ill, August 4, 1939. **Education:** Loyola Univ, Ill, BS, 1961; Univ Notre Dame, PhD (physics), 1967. **Professional Experience:** PROF PHYSICS & SCI EDUC, CALIF STATE UNIV, LONG BEACH, 1988-; sr sci consult, Detroit Sci Ctr, 1988; NSF fac fel sci, 1976-1977; vis assoc prof, Stanford Univ, 1976-1977; from asst prof to assoc prof physics, Wayne State Univ, 1967-1988; vis scholar, Grad Group Sci & Math Educ, Univ Calif, Berkeley. **Memberships:** AAAS; Am Phys Soc; Am Asn Physics Teachers; Am Educ Res Asn. **Research Statement & Publications:** Research on the role of language in science and mathematics learning; teacher training in science and mathematics; informal science and mathematics instruction in museum settings; use of computers in teaching physics; theoretical and experimental analysis of physics instruction and learning. **Mailing Ad-

dress: Dept Physics Sci Calif State Univ, 1250 Bellflower Blvd, Long Beach, CA 90840-3901. **Fax:** 562-985-2315. **E-Mail:** kenealyp@csulb.edu

KENEFICK, ROBERT ARTHUR, TRAPPED IONS. **Personal Data:** b Syracuse, NY, March 9, 1937; m 1960, Kathleen; c 3. **Education:** Mass Inst Technol, BS, 1959; Fla State Univ, PhD (physics), 1962. **Professional Experience:** PROF, DEPT PHYSICS, TEX A&M UNIV, 1974-; from asst prof to assoc prof, Tex A&M Univ, 1965-1974; asst prof, Univ Mich, 1964-1965; asst prof, Univ Colo, 1963-1964; res assoc nuclear physics, Univ Colo, 1962-1963. **Memberships:** Am Phys Soc; AAAS; Am Asn Physics Teachers. **Research Statement & Publications:** Atomic collisions; particle detectors; ion sources; musical acoustics. **Mailing Address:** Dept Physics, Tex A&M Univ, College Station, TX 77843. **Fax:** 979-845-2590. **E-Mail:** bob-kenefick@tamu.edu

KENELLY, JOHN WILLIS, MATHEMATICS. **Personal Data:** b Bogalusa, La, November 22, 1935; m 2000, Vicki; c Deidre & Trent. **Education:** Southeastern La Col, BS, 1957; Univ Miss, MS, 1957; Univ Fla, PhD (math), 1961. **Professional Experience:** Treasurer, Mathematical Association of America, 2002- Pres, inst math Olympied, 2001; interim dir, Col & Advan Placement Prog, 1989-1990; prog officer, NSF, 1988; dir advan placement reading, Advan placement Prog Math, Educ Testing Serv, 1985-; ALUMNI DISTINGUISHED PROF MATH SCI, CLEMSON UNIV, 1985-; chmn, Southeastern Sect, Math Asn Am, bd govs, 1985-1996; Math Sci Adv Comt, 1983- & coun acad affairs, 1985-1987; ed, Placement Test Newslett, 1979-1985; chmn, Advan Placement Math Comt, Col Bd, 1979-1983; chief reader, Advan placement Prog Math, Educ Testing Serv, 1975-1979; Vis lectr & curric consult, Math Asn Am, 1970-; prof, Clemson Univ, 1969-1985; head dept, Clemson Univ, 1969-1977; prof & chmn dept, La State Univ, 1968-1969; assoc prof, Clemson Univ, 1963-1968; asst prof, Univ Southwestern La, 1961-1963; Instr math, Univ Fla, 1959-1961. **Memberships:** Am Math Soc; Math Asn Am; Nat Coun Teachers Math; Math ASN Am (treas, 2002-2007); Mu alpha theta (nat pres, 1989-1991). **Research Statement & Publications:** Geometry; convexity; operations research. **Mailing Address:** 303 Eagles View Dr, Seneca, SC 29678-1627. **Fax:** 864-886-1226. **E-Mail:** kenellj@clemson.edu

KENESHEA, FRANCIS JOSEPH, INORGANIC CHEMISTRY. **Personal Data:** b Providence, RI, June 25, 1921; wid, c Ellen & Jane. **Education:** RI State Col, BS, 1943, MS, 1948; Univ NMex, PhD (chem), 1951. **Professional Experience:** RETIRED; sr consult, Quadrex Corp, 1980-1985; consult engr, Quadrex Corp, 1974-1980; sr res assoc, Ore State Univ, 1963-1964; sr chemist, Stanford Res Inst, 1955-1971; sr res engr, NAm Aviation Inc, 1951-1955; asst, Cornell Univ, 1947-1948; instr chem, RI State Col, 1946-1947. **Memberships:** Sigma Xi; Am Chem Soc. **Research Statement & Publications:** Thermodynamics of vaporization; chemical diffusion; chemistry of molten salts and metal-salt solutions; nuclear and radiochemistry; nuclear technology. **Mailing Address:** 20 Bear Paw, Portola Valley, CA 94028-8014.

KENETT, RON, STATISTICAL METHODS, DESIGN OF EXPERIMENTS. **Personal Data:** b Zurich, Switz, October 20, 1950; Israeli citizen; m 1976, c 4. **Education:** London Univ, BS, 1974; Weizmann Inst Sci, PhD (math), 1978. **Professional Experience:** PROF, TEL AVIV UNIV, as of 2004; CHIEF EXEC OFFICER, KPA LTD, as of 2003; prof qual mgt, Sch Mgt, State Univ Ny, 1987-1992; consult statist methods & qual mgt, 1987-; adj prof, Technion, 1986; adj prof, Tel Aviv Univ, 1982-1989; dir statist methods, indust statist, Tadiran Co, 1981-1990; mem tech staff statist, Bell Labs, NJ, 1980-1981; lectr, Dept Statist, Univ Wis-Madison, 1978-1980. **Memberships:** Am Statist Asn; Am Soc Qual Control. **Research Statement & Publications:** Quality management; industrial statistics; statistical process control; design of experiments; performance appraisal systems; software reliability; multivariate quality control. **Mailing Address:** KPA Ltd, PO Box 2525, Raanana, Israel. **E-Mail:** ron@kpa.co.il

KENG, PETER C, CELL SEPARATION, RADIATION BIOLOGY. **Personal Data:** b Kinagsu, China, August 12, 1946; m 1972, Suzan; c 3. **Education:** Tunghai Univ, BS, 1968; Colo State Univ, PhD (radiation biol), 1978. **Professional Experience:** PROF, DEPT RADIATION ONCOL & BIOPHYS & BIOCHEM, UNIV ROCHESTER, 1993-; assoc prof, Dept Radiation Oncol & Dept Radiation Biol & Biophys, 1985-1992; DIR RES, CELL SEPARATION & FLOW CYTOMETRY FACIL, UNIV ROCHESTER, 1981-; asst prof, Dept Radiation Biol & Biophys, 1981-1985; asst prof, Dept Radiation Oncol, Univ Rochester, 1980-1985. **Memberships:** Radiation Res Soc; Anal Cytometry; Am Soc Cell Biol; AAAS. **Research Statement & Publications:** Separation of cell subpopulations from solid tumors, bone marrow and tissue culture cells into various host cells; neoplastic cells and cells at different stages of the cell cycle to study the DNA damage of these cells. **Mailing Address:** Dept Radiation Oncol, Univ Rochester Sch Med, 601 Elmwood Ave Rm 3 4103A, Rochester, NY 14642-0001. **E-Mail:** peter_keng@urmc.rochester.edu

KENIG, MARVIN JERRY, APPLIED MECHANICS, MATERIALS SCIENCE. **Personal Data:** b Philadelphia, Pa, September 20, 1936; m 1959, c 2. **Education:** Drexel Univ, BSME, 1959, MSME, 1963; Princeton Univ, MA, 1963, PhD (eng), 1965. **Professional Experience:** DEAN ENG & APPL SCI, UNIV NEW HAVEN, 1989-; prof & chmn, Dept Aircraft & Automotive Eng, 1987-1989; prof & chmn, Dept Mech Eng, Western Mich Univ, 1983-1987; asst to pres, Drexel Univ, 1974-1983; Consult, J P Oat & Sons, Inc, 1968- & US Army Frankford Arsenal, 1970-1975; From assoc prof to prof mech eng, Drexel Univ, 1969-1982. **Memberships:** Am Soc Mech Engrs; Am Acad Mech; Am Soc Eng Educr; Am Defense Preparedness Asn; AAAS; Sigma Xi. **Research Statement & Publications:** Effect Portevin-Le Chatalier phenomenon on plastic potential theory of yielding; implications with respect to propagation of small stress increments; creep; fatigue; quantum mechanics modeling of dislocation motion; response of orthotropic plates under lateral pressure pulse; inelastic buckling of non-prismatic columns; bending of prismatic unsymmetric eccentrically loaded columns; forensic engineering. **Mailing Address:** 380 Hitchcock Rd Unit 129, Waterbury, CT 06705-3954. **Fax:** 203-932-7394. **E-Mail:** mjkenig@chager.newhaven.edu

KENK, VIDA CARMEN, INVERTEBRATE ZOOLOGY, BIVALVE MOLLUSKS. **Personal Data:** b San Juan, PR, December 24, 1939; m 1974, William; c Chris & Lauren. **Education:** Col William & Mary, BS, 1961; Radcliffe Col, AM, 1962; Harvard Univ, PhD (biol), 1967. **Professional Experience:** INTERIM DEAN, COL SCI, SAN JOSE STATE UNIV, as of 2005; assoc Dean, coll of sci San Jose State univ beginning 1999; PROF BIOL, SAN JOSE STATE UNIV, 1977-; assoc prof, San Jose State Univ, 1970-1977; asst prof, San Jose State Univ, 1966-1970. **Memberships:** AAAS; Am Malacol Union; Western Soc Malacologists (pres, 1980). **Research Statement & Publications:** Systematics, ecology and functional anatomy of bivalve molluscs. **Mailing Address:** Dep Biol Sci, San Jose State Univ, One Wash Square Duncan Hall Rm 214, San Jose, CA 95192-0100.

KENKARE, DIVAKER B, BIOLOGICAL CHEMISTRY, PHYSICAL CHEMISTRY. **Personal Data:** b Goa, India, May 25, 1936; American citizen; m 1966, c 2. **Education:** Univ Poona, BSc, 1959; Sardar Patel Univ, India, MSc, 1961; Ohio State Univ, MSc, 1963, PhD (food chem), 1966. **Professional Experience:** ASSOC DIR TECH, COLGATE PAL-MOLIVE RES CTR, 1994-; sr assoc, Colgate Palmolive Res Ctr, Piscataway, 1985-1994; res assoc, Colgate Palmolive Res Ctr, Piscataway, 1978-1985; sr res chemist, Colgate Palmolive Res Ctr, Piscataway, 1971-1978; res chemist, Colgate Palmolive Res Ctr, Piscataway, 1968-1971; Res assoc protein chem, Univ Ill, Urbana, 1966-1968. **Memberships:** Am Chem Soc. **Research Statement & Publications:** Changes of protein at elevated temperatures; characterization, physical chemical behavior, and modification of proteins. **Mailing Address:** Mountain View Rd, Ashbury, NJ 08802.

KENKEL, JOHN V, ANALYTICAL CHEMISTRY. **Personal Data:** b Harlan, Iowa, April 20, 1948; m 1975, c 3. **Education:** Iowa State Univ, BS, 1970; Univ Tex, Austin, MA, 1972. **Honors & Awards:** Gustav Ohans Award, Nat Sci Teachers Asn, 1990. **Professional Experience:** PROF SUPVR CHEM, SOUTHEAST COMMUNITY COL, AS OF 2006; comt Educ, Div Anal Chem, 1988; chem Mfg Asn regional catalyst award, 1988; Burlington Northern Found fac achievement award, 1985; mem, Comt Chem 2 Yr Col, Am Chem Soc, 1982; sr staff assoc, Sci Ctr, Rockwell Int, 1973-1977. **Memberships:** Am Chem Soc. **Research Statement & Publications:** Analytical chemistry; author of 2 books and 2 publications. **Mailing Address:** Southeast Community Col, 8800 O St, Lincoln, NE 68520-1227. **E-Mail:** jkenkel@scc.cc.ne.us

KENKNIGHT, GLENN, PLANT PATHOLOGY. **Personal Data:** b Canby, Ore, November 26, 1910; m 1940, c 2. **Education:** Carleton Col, BA, 1934; Mich State Col, MS, 1937, PhD (bot, plant path), 1939. **Professional Experience:** CONSULT, 1973-; res plant pathologist, Pecan Field Lab, 1962-1973; plant pathologist, Hort Field Lab, USDA, 1948-1962; assoc plant pathologist, Calif Dept Agr, Indio, 1945-1948; assoc plant pathologist, Exp Sta, Univ Idaho, 1942-1945; plant pathologist, Exp Sta, Agr & Mech Col Tex, 1940-1942; asst, Exp Sta, Mich State Col, 1935-1939; asst plant path, Univ Minn, 1935. **Memberships:** Am Phytopath Soc. **Research Statement & Publications:** Soil actinomyces in relation to potato scab; fungicidal action of mercury compounds; breeding vegetable crops for disease resistance; virus diseases of stone fruits; witches' broom diseaseof trees; pecan diseases. **Mailing Address:** 9517 Palmetto Lane, Shreveport, LA 71118.

KENKRE, VASUDEV MANGESH, THEORETICAL CONDENSED MATTER PHYSICS, BIOLOGICAL & OTHER INTEDISCIPLINARY PHYSICS. **Personal Data:** b Panjim, India, September 21, 1946; m 1969, Shaila; c Niman, Prabhav & Salil. **Education:** Indian Inst Technol, Bombay, BTech, 1968; State Univ NY, Stony Brook, MA, 1971, PhD (physics), 1971. **Professional Experience:** DISTINGUISHED PROFESSOR, 2005-; DIR, CONSORTIUM AMERICAS INTERDISCIPLINARY SCI, 2000-; DIR, Center Advanced Studies, Univ New Mexico, 1996-2000; PROF PHYSICS, UNIV NEW MEXICO, 1984-2005; Assoc Prof physics, Univ Rochester, 1979-1984; Asst Prof, Inst Fundamental Studies, 1974-1979; FELLOW, INST FUNDAMENTAL STUDIES, 1972-; res assoc, Inst Fundamental Studies, 1972-1974; Instr physics, State Univ NY, Stony Brook, 1971-1972. **Memberships:** Am Physical Society, American Asn for the Advancement of Science. **Research Statement & Publications:** Theory of the spread of epidemics, transport/response theories, pattern formation, nonlinear dynamics, granular materials, quasiparticle dynamics in organic materials, interaction of light with matter, polarons, statistical mechanics. **Mailing Address:** Univ NMex, 800 Yale Blvd NE, Albuquerque, NM 87131. **Fax:** 505-277-1520. **E-Mail:** kenkre@unm.edu

KENLEY, RICHARD ALAN, ORGANIC CHEMISTRY. **Personal Data:** b Chicago, Ill, January 17, 1947; m 1973. **Education:** Univ Ill, Champaign, BS, 1969; Univ Calif, San Diego, PhD (org chem), 1973. **Professional Experience:** SR VPRES & MANAGING DIR, MAGELLAN LABS CABRILLO FACILITY, as of 2004; dir, pharmaceut develop, Genetics Inst, beginning 1990; assoc dir parenteral res & develop, Baxter Health Care Corp, 1985-1990; phys org chem, SRI Int, beginning 1975. **Memberships:** Am Chem Soc. **Research Statement & Publications:** Free radical reactions in gas and solution phase. **Mailing Address:** Am Assoc Pharmaceut Scientists, 2107 Wilson Blvd Ste 700, Arlington, VA 22201. **Fax:** 703-243-9650.

KENNAMER, JAMES EARL, WILDLIFE ECOLOGY. **Personal Data:** b Fairfield, Ala, August 6, 1942; m 1967, c 2. **Education:** Auburn Univ, BS, 1964; Miss State Univ, MS, 1967, PhD (wildlife mgt), 1970. **Honors & Awards:** Henry Hardtner Award, Southern Group State Foresters, 2005. **Professional Experience:** SR VPRES CONSERV PROGS, NAT WILD TURKEY FEDN, as of 2004; DIR RES & MGT, NAT WILD TURKEY FEDN, 1980-; from asst prof to assoc prof wild life ecol, Auburn Univ, 1970-1980; instr wildlife mgt, Miss State Univ, 1969-1970. **Memberships:** Wildlife Soc; Sigma Xi. **Research Statement & Publications:** Wild turkey ecology and physiology; Canada goose, white-tailed deer and fallow deer ecology and physiology. **Mailing Address:** Nat Wild Turkey Fedn, PO Box 530, Edgefield, SC 29824. **Fax:** 803-637-0034.

KENNARD, KENNETH CLAYTON, ORGANIC CHEMISTY, BIOCHEMISTY. **Personal Data:** b Battle Creek, Mich, December 18, 1926; m 1949, Albert; c Norman J, Kathleen M (Hurst) & Elaine M (Schoch). **Education:** Univ Notre Dame, BS, 1949; Univ Nebr, MS, 1952, PhD (org chem), 1954; Mass Inst Technol, SM, 1964. **Professional Experience:** RETIRED; gen mgr & vpres, Bio-Prod Div, 1984-1987; dir, Biosci Div, Kodak Res Labs, 1975-1984; staff asst to dir res, Emulsion Res Div, 1969-1975; asst div head, Emulsion Res Div, 1965-1969; res chemist, Eastman Kodak Co, 1954-1965. **Memberships:** Am Chem Soc; Am Asn Clin Chemists; AAAS. **Research Statement & Publications:** Organic chemistry of phosphorous and sulfur compounds; preparation and properties of light sensitive materials; biotechnology. **Mailing Address:** 19 Veldor Park, Rochester, NY 14612.

KENNARD, WILLIAM CRAWFORD, PLANT PHYSIOLOGY, HORTICULTURE. **Personal Data:** b Centreville, Md, November 29, 1921; m 1943, c 3. **Education:** Univ Del, BS, 1943; Pa State Univ, MS, 1948, PhD (plant physiol, soils), 1956; Oak Ridge Inst Nuclear Studies, cert, 1960. **Professional Experience:** RETIRED; assoc seminars, Columbia Univ, beginning 1969; dir inst water resources, Univ Conn, 1965-1974; actg dir, Inst Water Resources, Univ Conn, 1964-1965; prof plant physiol, Univ Conn, 1962-1991; prof hort & assoc dir res admin, Univ Conn, 1962-1974; prin horticulturist & res adminr, US Off Exp Sta, Wash, DC, 1957-1962; vis prof, Univ PR, 1956; horticulturist, Mayaguez Inst Trop Agr, Mayaguez, PR, 1952-1957; instr, Pa State Univ, 1948-1952; res fel pomol, Pa State Univ, 1946-1948. **Memberships:** Fel AAAS; Am Inst Biol Sci; Am Soc Hort Sci. **Research Statement & Publications:** Physiology and culture of temperate zone fruit crops; physiology of flowering; growth and development of tropical plants, including fruits, drug crops, insecticidal crops and bamboo; remote sensing of the environment. **Mailing Address:** 70 Lynnwood Rd, Storrs Mansfield, CT 06268.

KENNAWAY, NANCY G, GENETICS. **Honorary Degrees:** Dphil, Univ Oxford, 1967. **Professional Experience:** PROF, DEPT MOLECULAR & MED GENETICS, ORE HEALTH & SCI UNIV, as of 2005. **Mailing Address:** Dept Molecular-Med Genetics Ore Health Sci Univ, 3181 SW Sam Jackson Park Rd L-473, Portland, OR 97201-3011.

KENNEALLY, DANIEL J, ENGINEERING. **Professional Experience:** AT BROOKSIDE ASSOC, as of 2004. **Mailing Address:** Brookside Assoc, 7976 Brookside Dr, Rome, NY 13440-2050.

KENNEDY, ALBERT JOSEPH, RADIOCHEMISTRY, CORROSION. **Personal Data:** b Spring Valley, Ill, July 2, 1943; m 1967, c 4. **Education:** Univ Ill, Champaign, BS, 1966; Purdue Univ, PhD (nuclear chem), 1972. **Professional Experience:** ADJ INSTR, CHEM, JOLIET JR COL, 1998-; chem assessment adminr, Commonwealth Edison, 1989-1998; supvr chem, Commonwealth Edison, 1980-1989; prin chemist, Commonwealth Edison, 1978-1980; sr res chemist, Babcock & Wilcox Co, 1973-1978; fel nuclear chem, Lawrence Berkeley Lab, 1972-1973. **Memberships:** Am Chem Soc; Am Nuclear Soc. **Research Statement & Publications:** Corrosion chemistry; corrosion product deposition; activation analysis, radiochemistry, quality control and nuclear fuel evaluation. **Mailing Address:** 415 Manor Hill Lane, Lombard, IL 60148-4437.

KENNEDY, ANDREW JOHN, SOLID STATE PHYSICS, PHYSICAL ELECTRONICS. **Personal Data:** b Budapest, Hungary, May 16, 1935; American citizen; m 1958, c 2. **Education:** Wash State Univ, BS, 1961; Univ Wash, MS, 1964. **Professional Experience:** RES PHYSICIST, CTR NIGHT VISION & ELECTRO-OPTICS, 1964-; assoc res engr A, boeing Co, 1961-1964. **Memberships:** Inst Elec & Electronics Engrs; Am Inst Physics. **Research Statement & Publications:** Solid state infrared detector physics and technology, intensified charge coupled devices; imaging focal plane technology. **Mailing Address:** US Army Res Lab AMSRL-SE-R, 2800 Powder Mill Rd, Adelphia, MD 20783-1197.

KENNEDY, ANN RANDTKE, CARCINOGENESIS. **Personal Data:** b Rochester, NY, December 24, 1946; m 1973, c 2. **Education:** Vassar Col, AB, 1969; Harvard Univ, SM, 1971, SD, 1973. **Professional Experience:** RICHARD CHAMBERLAIN PROF RES ONCOL, DEPT RADIATION ONCOL, UNIV PA SCH MED, as of 2005; mem, chem pathol study sect, consult, workshops & prin investr grants, NIH, 1981-1988; comt mem, Nat Coun Radiation Protection Pub Educ, 1980-; ASSOC PROF RADIOBIOL, HARVARD UNIV, 1980-; asst prof, Harvard Univ, 1976-1980; res assoc, Harvard Univ, 1973-1975. **Memberships:** Am Asn Cancer Res & Radiation Res; Sigma Xi; Free Radical Res Soc. **Research Statement & Publications:** Radiobiology; mechanism of carcinogenesis with the ultimate aim of preventing cancer in human populations. **Mailing Address:** Dept Radiation Oncol, Univ Pa Sch Med, 195 John Morgan Bldg 3620 Hamilton Walk, Philadelphia, PA 19104. **Fax:** 215-898-0090. **E-Mail:** akennedy@mail.med.upenn.edu

KENNEDY, ANTHONY JOHN, DIGITAL SIGNAL PROCESSING, ADOPTIVE CONROL SYSTEMS. **Personal Data:** b Brooklyn, NY, December 1, 1932; m 1960, c 6. **Education:** Univ Notre Dame, BS, 1954; Carnegie Inst Technol, MS, 1956, PhD (physics), 1962. **Professional Experience:** PRIN SCIENTIST, XYBION CORP, 1977-; scientist, Space Sci Lab, Gen Elec Co, 1974-1977; consult, Boland & Boyce, Inc, 1970-1974; Scientist, Nuclear Div, Martin Marietta Corp, 1960-1965 & Space Div, Chrysler Corp, 1965-1970. **Research Statement & Publications:** Design of signal processing systems for the detection of signals in ocean noise; computer systems for processing oceanographic information. **Mailing Address:** Xybion Corp, 240 Cedar Knolls Rd, Cedar Knolls, NJ 07927.

KENNEDY, BILL WADE, PLANT PATHOLOGY. **Personal Data:** b Dallas, Tex, March 21, 1929; m 1951, c 4. **Education:** Southeastern State Col, BS, 1951; Okla State Univ, MS, 1955; Univ Minn, PhD (plant path), 1961. **Professional Experience:** RETIRED; sr ed, Phytopath, 1973-1976; coop, US Regional Soybean Lab, Ill, beginning 1964; res grants, Grad Sch, 1964-1966; from asst prof to prof plant path, Univ Minn, 1963-1993; res assoc, Univ Minn, 1961-1963; res fel, Univ Minn, 1959-1960; res asst, Univ Minn, 1958-1959; sr technician, Univ Calif, 1955-1958; asst plant path, Okla State Univ, 1951-1952 & 1954-1955. **Memberships:** Am Phytopath Soc; Am Inst Biol Sci; Am Soybean Asn. **Research Statement & Publications:** Chemical control of cotton seedling blight; root-rot studies; physiology of reproduction in Phytophthora, identity and epidemiology of bacterial blight on strawberry; seed pathology; ecology of bacteria associated with soybean. **Mailing Address:** 1987 E Singing Bow Way, Tucson, AZ 85737.

KENNEDY, BURTON MACK, ISOTOPE GEOLOGY, GEOCHRONOLOGY. **Personal Data:** b St Louis, Mo, April 15, 1949; m 1974, c 1. **Education:** Wash Univ, BA, 1974, PhD (earth & planetary sci), 1981. **Professional Experience:** STAFF SCIENTIST, EARTH SCI DIV, LAWRENCE BERKELEY LAB, BERKELEY, CALIF, 1992-; res geophysicist, Dept Physics, 1985-1992; res assoc, Univ Calif, Berkeley, 1981-1985. **Memberships:** Meteoritical Soc; Am Geophys Union; AAAS. **Research Statement & Publications:** High sensitivity rare gas mass spectrometry as applied to meteoritic, lunar and terrestrial samples to investigate the origin and early history of the earth and solar system. **Mailing Address:** Earth Sci Div, Ctr Isotope GeoChem, Lawrence Berkeley Lab, MS 70A 4418, Berkeley, CA 94720. **Fax:** 510-486-5496. **E-Mail:** bmkennedy@lbl.gov

KENNEDY, BYRL JAMES, INTERNAL MEDICINE, ONCOLOGY. **Personal Data:** b Plainview, Minn, June 24, 1921; m 1950, Margaret; c Sharon, Brad, Scott & Grant. **Education:** Univ Minn, BA & BS, 1943, BM, 1945, MD, 1946; McGill Univ, MSc, 1951; Am Bd Internal Med, dipl, 1958, Am Bd Med Oncol, cert, 1979. **Honors & Awards:** Nat Div Award, Am Cancer Soc, 1975; Medal of Honor Clin Res, 1996; Margaret H Edwards Achievement Medal, Am Asn Cancer Educ, 1990; Sci Achievement Award, AMA, 1992; Laureate Award, Am Col Phys, Minn, 1992; Charles Bolles Bolles-Roger Award, Hennepin Med Soc, 1996. **Professional Experience:** EMER MASONIC PROF ONCOL, UNIV MINN, MINNEAPOLIS, 1991-; regents prof med, Sch Med, 1988-1991; masonic prof oncol, Dept Med, Health Sci Ctr, 1970-1991; prof med, Dept Med, Health Sci Ctr, 1970-1988; from asst prof to assoc prof, Med Ctr, Univ Minn, 1952-1967; resident, Mass Gen Hosp & Harvard Univ, 1951-1952; Med Sch, NY Hosp, 1950-1951; Med Sch, Cornell Univ, 1950-1951; Med Sch, McGill Univ & Royal Victoria Hosp, 1949-1950; fel, Mass Gen Hosp & Harvard Univ, 1947-1949; intern & asst resident med, Mass Gen Hosp, 1945-1946. **Memberships:** Master Am Col Phys; Am Asn Cancer Res; AMA; Am Asn Cancer Educ; Am Soc Clin Oncol. **Research Statement & Publications:** Medical oncology, breast cancer, testis cancer, aging and cancer, chemotherapy of cancer and clinical research. **Mailing Address:** Univ Hosps mmc 286, 420 Del St SE, Minneapolis, MN 55455. **Fax:** 612-625-8966. **E-Mail:** kenne018@tc.umn.edu

KENNEDY, CHARLES, PEDIATRIC NEUROLOGY. **Personal Data:** b Buffalo, NY, August 27, 1920; m 1946, c 3. **Education:** Princeton Univ, AB, 1942; Univ Rochester, MD, 1945. **Professional Experience:** MED OFFICER, LAB CEREBRAL METAB, NIMH, 1990-; EMER PROF PEDIAT, SCH MED, GEORGETOWN UNIV, 1990-; sr res scientist, NIMH, 1979-; prof, Lab Cerebral Metab, Nimh, 1971-1990; vis prof, Stanford Univ, 1969; guest worker, Lab Cerebral Metab, NIMH, 1968-; from asst prof to assoc prof neurol pediat, Sch Med, Univ Pa, 1958-1970; neurologist, Children's Hosp, Philadelphia, 1958-1967; vis fel, Neurol Inst, Columbia-Presby Med Ctr, 1957-1958; asst neurologist, Children's Hosp, Philadelphia, 1956-1958; resident neurol, Hosp Univ Pa, 1953-1954; fel physiol, Grad Sch Med, Univ Pa, 1951-1953; Life Ins Med Res Fund fel, 1951-1952; resident pediat, Children's Hosp, Buffalo, 1948-1951; instr path, Sch Med, Yale Univ, 1945-1946. **Memberships:** AAAS; Soc Pediat Res; Am Neurol Asn; Am Pediat Soc; Soc Neuroscience. **Research Statement & Publications:** Cerebral circulation; developmental neurology; energy metabolism of developing brain. **Mailing Address:** HC71 Box 830, Machias, ME 04654. **E-Mail:** kennedyc@georgetown.edu

KENNEDY, CHRISTOPHER JESSE, AQUATIC TOXICOLOGY, BIOCHEMICAL & PHYSIOLOGICAL TOXICOLOGY. **Personal Data:** b Las Vegas, Nev, February 6, 1960. **Education:** Simon Fraser Univ, BSc, 1982, PhD (environ toxicol), 1990. **Professional Experience:** ASSOC PROF BIOL SCI, SIMON FRASER UNIV, 2003-; asst prof biol sci, Simon Fraser Univ, beginning 1991; fel, Univ Miami, 1989-1990; res assoc, Univ Miami, 1987; res asst, Dept Biol Sci, Simon Fraser Univ, 1983-1988. **Memberships:** AAAS; Am Fisheries Soc. **Research Statement & Publications:** Environmental modulators of xenobiotic toxicity in aquatic organisms; life history modifications of xenobiotic toxicokinetics; biochemistry of toxicant metabolism; development of in vitro tests in toxicological research. **Mailing Address:** Dept Biol Sci, Simon Fraser Univ, Rm SSB6157 8888 Univ Dr, Burnaby, BC V5A 1S6, Can. **Fax:** 604-291-3496. **E-Mail:** ckennedy@sfu.ca

KENNEDY, D J LAURIE, CIVIL ENGINEERING. **Education:** Univ Toronto, BA, 1951; Univ Ill, MS, 1952, PhD (civil eng), 1961. **Honors & Awards:** Casimir Gzowski Medal, Can Soc Civil Eng, 1980 & 1992, Le Prix P L Pratley Award, 1992; A B Sanderson Award, 1989; Shortridge Hardesty Award, Am Soc Civil Engrs, 1994; John Jenkins Award, Can Stand Asn, 1995. **Professional Experience:** PROF EMER CIVIL ENG, UNIV ALTA, CAN, 1982-. **Mailing Address:** Dept Civil Eng, Univ Alta, 220F, Edmonton, AB T6G 2G7, Can. **Fax:** 780-492-0249. **E-Mail:** djlaurie.kennedy@ualberta.ca

KENNEDY, DANIEL, MATHEMATICS. **Education:** Col Holy Cross, BA; Univ NC, Chaper Hill, MS & PhD. **Professional Experience:** INSTR MATHS, BAYLOR SCH, TENN, as of 2005; chmn, Dept Math, Baylor Sch, 1990-1994. **Mailing Address:** Baylor Sch, 171 Baylor Sch Rd, Chattanooga, TN 37405. **Fax:** 713-799-8544. **E-Mail:** Dan_Kennedy@BaylorSchool.org

KENNEDY, DAVID P, electrical engineering; deceased, see previous edition for last biography

KENNEDY, DIANE L, PHARMACOLOGY. **Education:** Purdue Univ, MS; Johns Hopkins Univ, MPH. **Professional Experience:** MGR, CTR DRUG EVAL & RES, DIV EPIDEMIOL & SURVEILLANCE, FOOD & DRUG ADMIN, 1993-; DIR MEDWATCH, MED PROD REPORTING PROG, FOOD & DRUG ADMIN, 1993-. **Mailing Address:** Food & Drug Admin, 5600 Fishers Lane, Rockville, MD 20857-0001. **Fax:** 301-443-5776. **E-Mail:** dlkfoxy@pce.net

KENNEDY, DONALD, BIOLOGY, SCIENCE & PUBLIC POLICY. **Personal Data:** b New York, NY, August 18, 1931; m 1953, c 2. **Education:** Harvard Univ, AB, 1952, AM, 1954, PhD (biol sci), 1956. **Honorary Degrees:** DSc, Columbia Univ, 1979, Williams Col, 1980, Univ Mich, 1982, Univ Rochester, 1984, Univ Ariz, 1985; LLD, Reed Col, 1986, Whitman Col, 1994. **Honors & Awards:** Bowditch Lectr, Am Physiol Soc, 1970. **Professional Experience:** BING EMER PROF ENVIRON SCI, STANFORD UNIV, as of 2005; PRES EMER BIOL SCI, STANFORD UNIV, as of 2005; pres, Stanford Univ, 1980-1992; vpres & provost, Stanford Univ, 1979-1980; comnr, Food & Drug Admin, 1977-1979; ed bd, Science, 1973-1978; ed bd, J Neurophysiol, 1970-1976; Nat lectr, Sigma Xi, 1969-1970; ed bd, J Comp Physiol, 1966-1977; chmn dept, Stanford Univ, 1965-1972; ed bd, J Exp Zool, 1965-1970; from asst prof to prof biol sci, Stanford Univ, 1960-1977; from asstprof to assoc prof zool, Syracuse Univ, 1956-1960. **Memberships:** Nat Acad Sci; Inst Med-Nat Acad Sci; Am Soc Zool; Soc Gen Physiol; fel Am Acad Arts & Sci; Soc Exp Biol UK; Am Physiol Soc; Am Inst Biol Sci; fel AAAS; Marine Biol Asn UK. **Research Statement & Publications:** Comparative physiology of sense organs, especially visual systems; central nervous system of crustacea; over 60 articles and publications; environmental policy studies. **Mailing Address:** CESP, Stanford Univ, Encina Hall E401, Stanford, CA 94305-2060. **Fax:** 650-725-1992. **E-Mail:** kennedyd@stanford.edu

KENNEDY, EDWARD EARL, ANALYTICAL CHEMISTRY. **Personal Data:** b Evansville, Ind, January 7, 1925; m 1950, Julia; c Jay D & Matthew C. **Education:** Purdue Univ, BS, 1945; Ind Univ, MA, 1948. **Professional Experience:** RETIRED; dir qual assurance, Park Fletcher Plant, 1983-1985; dir biosynthetic oper, Park Fletcher Plant, 1980-1983; dir biochem mfg, Park Fletcher Plant, 1970-1980; dir, Park Fletcher Plant, 1970; dir qual assurance, 1962-1966; head anal develop & spec servs, Dept Assay Methods Develop, 1956-1962; head anal res & develop, Dept Assay Methods Develop, 1952-1956; head, Dept Assay Methods Develop, 1950-1952; anal chemist, Eli Lilly & Co, 1948-1950; instr, Ind Univ, 1947-1948; anal chemist, Eli Lilly & Co, 1945-1946. **Memberships:** AAAS; Am Pharmaceut Asn; Am Soc Qual Control; Am Chem Soc. **Research Statement & Publications:** Instrumentation of analytical chemistry, particularly field of spectrophotometry; several scientific papers on spectrophotometric analysis of pharmaceutical products. **Mailing Address:** 8305 Reef Ct, Indianapolis, IN 46236-9539.

KENNEDY, EDWARD FRANCIS, NUCLEAR PHYSICS. **Personal Data:** b Chicago, Ill, January 2, 1932; m 1956, Marcia; c Kathryn, Edward III, Maribeth, Christopher, Marcia & John. **Education:** Loyola Univ, Ill, BS, 1954; Univ Notre Dame, PhD (nuclear physics), 1960. **Professional Experience:** PROF EMER PHYSICS, HOLY CROSS COL, as of 2005; vis scientist, Univ Aarhus, Denmark, 1990; vis res physicist, Univ Calif, San Diego, 1987; vis prof, Cornell Univ, 1983-1985; vis scientist, Fraunhofer Inst, Munich, Ger, 1982-1983; vis assoc, Calif Inst Technol, 1975-1976, 1977, 1978; prof physics, Holy Cross Col, beginning 1970; vis scientist, Cavendish Lab, Cambridge, 1968-1969; chmn dept, Holy Cross Col, 1964-1976; actg chmn dept, Holy Cross Col, 1963-1964; consult, Air Force Cambridge Res Labs, 1962-1971; from asst prof to assoc prof physics, Holy Cross Col, 1960-1970; res assoc, Univ Notre Dame, 1958-1960; asst physics, Univ Notre Dame, 1954-1958; technician, Argonne Nat Lab, 1952-1954. **Memberships:** Am Phys Soc; Am Asn Physics Teachers; Sigma Xi. **Research Statement & Publications:** Ion channeling in crystals; surface physics; nuclear fluorescence; radiation damage. **Mailing Address:** Dept Physics, Holy Cross Col, Worcester, MA 01610. **E-Mail:** kennedy@hcacad.holycross.edu

KENNEDY, EDWIN RUSSELL, ENVIRONMENTAL CHEMISTRY. **Personal Data:** b Los Angeles, Calif, November 4, 1911; wid, c 5. **Education:** Calif Inst Technol, BS, 1933, MS, 1934, PhD (chem), 1936. **Professional Experience:** CONSULT, 1977-; sr technologist, Shell Chem Co, 1956-1962; res coordr, Shell Chem Co, 1948-1956; group leader res, Shell Chem Co, 1946-1948; Technologist, Shell Oil Co, 1936-1942. **Memberships:** Am Chem Soc; Am Inst Aeronaut & Astronaut; Am Ord Asn; Nat Asn Corrosion Eng. **Research Statement & Publications:** Air pollution; corrosion; protective coatings; petrochemicals; rocket propellants; metallurgy; petroleum technology. **Mailing Address:** 240 Forest Ave, Rye, NY 10580-4124.

KENNEDY, ELDREDGE JOHNSON, SOLID STATE ELECTRONICS, ELECTRICAL ENGINEERING. **Personal Data:** b Fayetteville, Tenn, September 19, 1935; m 1961, c 3. **Education:** Univ Tenn, BS, 1958, MS, 1959, PhD (eng sci), 1967. **Professional Experience:** PROF EMER ELEC & COMPUT ENG, UNIV TENN, KNOXVILLE, 1975-; consult, Oak Ridge Nat Lab, 1970-; assoc prof, Univ Tenn, Knoxville, 1969-1975; ford found assoc prof, 1968-1969; design engr, Instrumentation & Controls Div, Oak Ridge Nat Lab, 1963-1970; res engr, Exp Sta, 1960-1963; instr, Univ Tenn, 1959-1963; asst elec eng, Univ Tenn, 1958-1959; Coop stud, Arnold Eng Develop Ctr, ARO Inc, Tenn, 1953-1957. **Memberships:** Inst Elec & Electronics Engrs; Sigma Xi; Int Soc Hybrid Microelectronics. **Research Statement & Publications:** Electronic solid state circuit design; low-current meaurements; hybrid thick-film integrated circuits; high-speed pulse amplifiers, low-noise electronics; radiation effects in integrated circuits and devices. **Mailing Address:** Dept Elec Eng, Univ Tenn, 414 Ferris Hall, Knoxville, TN 37996-2100. **Fax:** 865-974-5483. **E-Mail:** ejk@utk.edu

KENNEDY, EUGENE P, BIOCHEMISTRY. **Personal Data:** b Chicago, Ill, September 4, 1919; m 1943, Adelaide; c Lisa (Helprin), Sheila (Violich) & Katherine (Diller). **Education:** Univ Chicago, PhD (biochem), 1949. **Honorary Degrees:** MA, Harvard Univ, 1960; DSc, Univ Chicago, 1977. **Honors & Awards:** Paul Lewis Award, Am Chem Soc, 1958; Lipid Res Award, Am Oil Chem Soc, 1970; Ledlie Prize, 1976; Gairdner Found Award, 1976; Passano Award, 1986; Wieland Prize, 1986. **Professional Experience:** HAMILTON KUHN PROF EMER BIOL, HARVARD MED SCH, 1991-; Hamilton Kuhn prof, Harvard Med Sch, 1990-1991; von Humboldt sr fel, 1984; NSF fel, 1959-1960; Am Chem Soc res award, 1955; from asst prof to prof, Dept Biochem & Ben May Lab, Univ Chicago, 1951-1960; Am Cancer Soc fel, Univ Calif, 1949-1950. **Memberships:** Nat Acad Sci; Am Acad Arts & Sci; Am Chem Soc; Am Soc Biol Chemists (pres, 1970-1971); Am Philos Soc. **Research Statement & Publications:** Metabolism and function of lipids; membrane function. **Mailing Address:** Dept Biol Chem & Molecular Pharmacol, Harvard Med Sch, 25 Shattuck St, Boston, MA 02115. **E-Mail:** eugene_kennedy@hms.harvard.edu

KENNEDY, EUGENE RICHARD, BACTERIOLOGY. **Personal Data:** b Scranton, Pa, July 3, 1919; m 1945, c 3. **Education:** Univ Scranton, BS, 1941; Cath Univ Am, MS, 1943; Brown Univ, PhD, 1949; Am Bd Med Microbiol, dipl, 1964. **Professional Experience:** PROF EMER, DEPT BIOL, CATH UNIV AM, 1985-; consult microbiologist, Providence Hosp, DC, beginning 1981; dean, Sch Arts & Sci, 1973-1985; staff microbiologist, Providence Hosp, DC, 1958-1977; consult bacteriologist, Providence Hosp, DC, 1954-1958; from instr to prof bact & immunol, Cath Univ Am, 1949-1985; bacteriologist, US Food & Drug Admin, 1949; instr, RI Hosp, 1946-1948; instr, Brown Univ, 1946-1948; Serologist, US Army Med Ctr, DC, 1942; asst bact, Cath Univ Am, 1941-1943. **Memberships:** AAAS; Am Soc Microbiol; Sigma Xi. **Research Statement & Publications:** Vi antigen; quantitative dye adsorption; quantitative gram reaction; staphylococcus autogenous vaccine; in vivo and in vitro staphylococci. **Mailing Address:** Dept Biol, Cath Univ, 620 Mich Ave NE, Washington, DC 20064.

KENNEDY, FLYNT, ORGANIC CHEMISTRY. **Personal Data:** b Chillicothe, Tex, May 25, 1931; m 1957, c 1. **Education:** Tex Christian Univ, BA, 1952; Rice Univ, PhD (org chem), 1956. **Professional Experience:** RETIRED; vpres res & develop, Consol Coal Co, 1987-1996; gen mgr coal & chem res develop, Consol Coal Co, 1984-1987; mgr, Chem Res Div, 1969-1982; supv res scientist, Conoco, Inc, 1964-1969; res group leader, Conoco, Inc, 1961-1964; sr res chemist, Conoco, Inc, 1960-1961; res chemist, Conoco, Inc, 1957-1960; res corp fel, Calif Inst Technol, 1956-1957. **Memberships:** Am Chem Soc. **Research Statement & Publications:** Investigation of reactions of organometallic compounds; synthesis of three and four membered compounds; upgrading of hydrocarbons; chemicals from coal, polyvinyl chloride and polyolefins; coal seam degasification; improved coal mining technology; coal processing and combustion; sulfurdioxide. **Mailing Address:** 110 Waterside Dr, Canonsburg, PA 15317.

KENNEDY, FRANCIS E, JR, ENGINEERING. **Education:** Worcester Polytech Inst, BS, 1963; Stanford Univ, MS, 1965; Rensselaer Polytech Univ, PhD (mech), 1973. **Professional Experience:** PROF ENG, THAYER SCH ENG, DARTMOUTH COL, NH, as of 2005. **Memberships:** Am Soc Mech Engrs; Sigma Xi. **Mailing Address:** Thayer Sch Eng, Darmouth Col, Hanover, NH 03755-8000. **Fax:** 603-646-3856. **E-Mail:** Francis.Kennedy@Dartmouth.EDU

KENNEDY, FRANK SCOTT, METALLOENZYMES, TRACE METALS. **Personal Data:** b Washington, DC, October 16, 1944; m 1980, c 2. **Education:** Wash Lee Univ, BS, 1966; Univ Ill, Urbana, PhD (biochem), 1970. **Professional Experience:** ASST DEAN STUDENT ADMIS, SCH MED, LA STATE UNIV, SHREVEPORT, 1988-; ASSOC PROF BIOCHEM, SCH MED, LA STATE UNIV, SHREVEPORT, 1978-; asst prof, Sch Med, LA State Univ, Shreveport, 1976-1978; res assoc biochem, Harvard Med Sch, 1974-1976. **Research Statement & Publications:** Intermediary metabolism in cardiac tissue; role of copper in normal iron metabolism. **Mailing Address:** PO Box 33932, Shreveport, LA 71130-3932. **E-Mail:** fkenne@lsumc.edu

KENNEDY, FREDERICK JAMES, THEORETICAL PHYSICS. **Personal Data:** b Lowell, Mass, March 20, 1937; m 1967, Joyce Deveau; c Simon, David & Frederick. **Education:** Lowell Tech Inst, BS, 1960; Univ Del, MS, 1965, PhD (physics), 1967. **Professional Experience:** Lectr, Dept Math, Statist & Comput Sci, Dalhousie Univ, 1982-1986; SCI LIBRN, KILLAM LIBR SCI, DALHOUSIE UNIV, 1973-; fel, Theoret Physics Inst, Univ Alta, 1968-1973; Asst prof physics, Univ Bridgeport, 1967-1968. **Research Statement & Publications:** Classical mechanics and electrodynamics. **Mailing Address:** Killam Libr Sci, Dalhousie Univ, Halifax, NS B3H 4M8, Can. **E-Mail:** frederick.kennedy@dal.ca

KENNEDY, GEORGE ARLIE, VETERINARY PATHOLOGY. **Personal Data:** b Chicago, Ill, January 11, 1940; m 1972. **Education:** Univ NMex, BS, 1962; Wast State Univ, DVM, 1967; Kans State Univ, PhD (path), 1975. **Professional Experience:** PROF EMER, KANS STATE UNIV, as of 2004; prof path, Kans State Univ, as of 2003; dir, diag lab, Kans State Univ, as of 2003; asst prof, Vet Diag Lab, Kans State Univ, beginning 1972; instr vet path, Dept Path, Col Vet Med, 1970-1975; clinician, Kans State Univ Vet Teaching Hosp, 1970-1972; res pathologist, US Army Med Res& Nutrit Lab, 1967-1970. **Memberships:** Am Vet Med Asn; Am Col Vet Path; Sigma Xi. **Research Statement & Publications:** Transmission and scanning electron microscipic study of swine enteric diseases, particularly swine dysentery and diseases of the large intestine. **Mailing Address:** Col Vet Med, Kans State Univ, 101 Trotter Hall, Manhattan, KS 66506-5601. **Fax:** 785-532-4481. **E-Mail:** kennedy@vet.k-state.edu

KENNEDY, GEORGE GRADY, ECONOMIC ENTOMOLOGY, PEST MANAGEMENT & INSECT ECOLOGY. **Personal Data:** b Amityville, NY, March 23, 1948; m 1973, Leslie; c 2. **Education:** Ore State Univ, BS, 1970; Cornell Univ, PhD (entom), 1974. **Honors & Awards:** L M Ware Res Award, Am Soc Hort Sci. **Professional Experience:** Mem, Sci Adv Subpanel Pesticidal Plants, US Environ Protection Agency, 1993 & 1994; WILLIAM NEAL PROF, NC STATE UNIV, 1992-; external consult, Merck Sharp & Dohme, 1990-1994; mem, assessment panel, US Off Technol, 1985 & 1990; Prog mgr, USDA Competitive Grants Prog Entom/Nematol, 1984-1986; from asst prof to prof entom, NC State Univ, 1976-1992; Asst prof entom, Univ Calif, Riverside, 1974-1975. **Memberships:** Entom Soc Am; Am Inst Biol Sci. **Research Statement & Publications:** Pest management; insect and plant interactions. **Mailing Address:** Dept Entom, NC State Univ, Box 7630, Raleigh, NC 27695-7630. **Fax:** 919-515-3748. **E-Mail:** george_kennedy@ncsu.edu

KENNEDY, GEORGE HUNT, SURFACE CHEMISTRY. **Personal Data:** b Seattle, Wash, April 24, 1936; m 1961, c 2. **Education:** Univ Ore, BS, 1959; Ore State Univ, MS, 1962, PhD (phys chem), 1966. **Professional Experience:** PROF EMER CHEM, COLO SCH MINES, as of 2002; prof chem, Colo Sch Mines, beginning 1977; head, dept chem & geochem, Colo Sch Mines, 1976-1988; from asst prof to assoc prof, Colo Sch Mines, 1965-1976; res chemist, Chevron Res Corp Div, Chevron Oil Co, 1961-1962. **Memberships:** Am Chem Soc. **Research Statement & Publications:** Physical adsorption of gases on solid adsorbents; gas chromatography; sorption of vapors on liquid coated adsorbents. **Mailing Address:** Dept Chem, Colo Sch Mines, Coolbaugh Hall 254, Golden, CO 80401. **Fax:** 303-273-3629. **E-Mail:** gkennedy@mines.edu

KENNEDY, HARVEY EDWARD, MICROBIOLOGY, INFORMATION SCIENCE. **Personal Data:** b Goldsboro, NC, October 2, 1928; m 1951, c 2. **Education:** Atlantic Christian Col, BA, 1948; NC State Univ, MS, 1952, PhD microbiol, 1954. **Honors & Awards:** Bronze Medal, Zoology Soc London. **Professional Experience:** RETIRED; pres, Biosci Info Serv, 1980-1993; exec dir, Biosci Info Serv, 1975-1979; pres, Nat Fedn Abstracting & Info Serv, 1974-1975; asst dir-dir sci affairs, Biosci Info Serv, 1967-1975; dir prod develop, Vetco Div, 1965-1967; dir dairy prod res, Johnson & Johnson, 1961-1965; asst prof & res assoc, Ohio State Univ, 1959-1961; sr res scientist, NC Sanatorium Syst, Med Ctr, Univ NC, 1957-1959; USPHS res grants, 1954-1958, 1959-1961; assoc res bacteriologist, NC Sanatorium Syst, Med Ctr, Univ NC, 1954-1957. **Memberships:** AAAS; Am Soc Microbiol; Am Inst Biol Sci (pres, 1986-1987); AmSoc Info Sci; Coun Biol Ed (secy, 1973-1974, pres, 1978-1979); Int Coun Sci & Tech Info (pres, 1990-1992). **Research Statement & Publications:** Information science and communications applied to biological and biomedical research literature; bacterial nutrition and metabolism; virulence of pathogens; antimicrobial agents; pharmaceutical and agricultural product development. **Mailing Address:** 205 Haverford Ave, Swarthmore, PA 19081.

KENNEDY, IAN MANNING, COMBUSTION. **Personal Data:** b Brisbane, Australia, September 11, 1952; m 1981, c 2. **Education:** Sydney Univ, BEng, 1975, PhD (mech eng), 1980. **Honors & Awards:** Pres Young Investr Award, NSF, 1988. **Professional Experience:** PROF ENG, UNIV CALIF, DAVIS, as of 2001; from asst prof to assoc prof, Univ Calif, Davis, 1986-1993; res scientist, Aeronaut Res Labs, 1983-1986; mem res staff, Princeton Univ, 1980-1983. **Memberships:** Am Inst Aeronaut & Astronaut; Combustion Inst; Am Asn Aerosol Res. **Research Statement & Publications:** Fundamental combustion phenomena; turbulent reacting flows; formation of pollutants such as soot in flames; application of laser and optics to measurements in flames; dynamics of aerosol systems. **Mailing Address:** Mech & Aero Eng Univ Calif, 1347 Eng II, Davis, CA 95616. **Fax:** 530-752-4158. **E-Mail:** imkennedy@ucdavis.edu

KENNEDY, JAMES A, ENZYMOLOGY. **Personal Data:** b Rochester, Minn, July 3, 1935; m 1965. **Education:** Univ Notre Dame, BS, 1957; St Louis Univ, MD, 1961. **Professional Experience:** ASSOC DEAN, UNIV KANS MED CTR, as of 2006; Chrmn, VA Res Adv Group A, 1985-; mem, VA Res Adv Group A, beginning 1983; assoc Ed, J Lab Clin Med, beginning 1982; prof med, Univ Kans Med Ctr, beginning 1981; assoc prof, Univ Kans Med Ctr, 1973-1981; asst prof, Col Physicians & Surgeons, Columbia Univ, 1971-1973; assoc internal med, Col Physicians & Surgeons, Columbia Univ, 1968-1971; NIH fel med, Med Sch, Univ Kans, 1963-1965. **Memberships:** Am Soc Biol Chemists. **Research Statement & Publications:** Urea cycle; superoxide; regulation of pyrimidine biosynthesis in mammals; electron transport. **Mailing Address:** Res Serv, Va Hosp 4801 Linwood Blvd, Kansas City, MO 64128-2295.

KENNEDY, JAMES CECIL, EXPERIMENTAL CANCER THERAPIES. **Personal Data:** b Toronto, Ont, March 14, 1935; m 1966, Ruth; c David, Andrew, Marta, Peter, Sara, Samuel & Joseph. **Education:** Univ Toronto, BA, 1957, MD, 1961, PhD (biophys), 1966. **Honorary Degrees:** BA, Univ Toronto, 1957. **Professional Experience:** PROF PATH, QUEENS UNIV, ONT, as of 2005; ADJ PROF, ROYAL MIL COL, 1991-; PROF ONCOL, QUEENS UNIV, ONT, 1991-; adj assoc prof chem & chem eng, Royal Mil Col, 1989-1991; career scientist, Ont Cancer Treat & Res Found, beginning 1983; assoc prof radiation oncol, Queens Univ, Ont, 1977-1991; res assoc, Ont Cancer Treat & Res Found, 1977-1983; assoc prof path, Queens Univ, Ont, beginning 1974; res assoc, Nat Cancer Inst Can, 1972-1977; asst prof, Queens Univ, Ont, 1969-1974; res scholar, Nat Cancer Inst Can, 1969-1972; res fel, Nat Cancer Inst Can, 1966-1968; intern, Wellesley Hosp, Toronto, 1961. **Memberships:** Am Soc Photobiol; Europ Soc Photobiol; Am Asn Cancer Res. **Research Statement & Publications:** Photoradiation therapy for cancer; fluorescence detection of cancer; chemistry and pharmacology of photosensitizing agents. **Mailing Address:** Dept Oncol & Path, Queen's Univ, 25 King St W, Kingston, ON K7L 5P9, Can. **Fax:** 613-544-9708. **E-Mail:** kennedyj@post.queensu.ca

KENNEDY, JAMES H, AQUATIC ECOSYSTEMS POLLUTANT EFFECTS, ECOLOGY AQUATIC INSECTS. **Personal Data:** b Garrett, Ind, May 20, 1947; m 1970, Virginia; c Amanda T. **Education:** Mansfield State Col, BS, 1969; Ind Univ Pa, MS, 1973; Va Polytech Inst & State Univ, PhD (zoology), 1980. **Professional Experience:** ADJ PROF, UNIV NTEX, as of 2004; prin investr numerous grants, CIBA, 1992-1997; Prin investr numerous grants, Hoechst-Roussel Agr-Vet, 1989; prin investr numerous grants, Bayer, 1988-1992; DIR, WATER RES FIELD STA, UNIV NTEX, 1987-; prin investr numerous grants, US Environ Protection Agency, 1987-1993; ecotoxicologist, Water Sci Assocs Inc, 1982-1987, pres; sr ecologist, mgr aquatic toxicol, NUS Corp, 1981-1982; res biologist, Ichthyol Assocs Inc, 1973-1975; fisheries biologist, Pa Fish Comn, 1972-1973; consult, Zeneca, Intevep, Venezuela. **Memberships:** Am Entom Soc; Entom Soc Am; Soc Environ Toxicol & Chem; NAm Benthological Soc; Sigma Xi. **Research Statement & Publications:** Ecology of macroinvertebrates; pollution ecology of lakes, streams and estuaries; fate and effects of pesticides in aquatic ecosystems. **Mailing Address:** Dept Biol Sci PO Box 310559, Univ NTex, Denton, TX 76203-3078. **Fax:** 940-565-4297.

KENNEDY, JAMES J, FOREST RESOURCES. **Professional Experience:** PROF ENVIRON SOC, COL NATURAL RESOURCES, UTAH STATE UNIV, as of 2004. **Mailing Address:** Dept Environ & Soc, Utah State Univ, Logan, UT 84322-5215. **Fax:** 435-797-4048. **E-Mail:** jkennedy@cc.usu.edu

KENNEDY, JAMES M, COMPUTER SCIENCE, ADMINISTRATION. **Personal Data:** b Ottawa, Ont, April 25, 1928; m 1950, Norah. **Education:** Univ Toronto, BA, 1949, MA, 1950; Princeton Univ, PhD (physics), 1953. **Professional Experience:** PROF EMER COMPUT SCI, UNIV BC, as of 2004; vpres, Comput Ctr, Univ BC, 1980-1984; prof comput sci, Comput Ctr, Univ BC, 1968-1993; dir, Comput Ctr, Univ BC, 1966-1980; supvr,

Comput Ctr, 1956-1966; res officer, Theoret Physics Br, Atomic Energy Can Ltd, 1952-1966. **Memberships:** Can Math Soc; Can Info Processing Soc (pres, 1971-1972); Can Asn Physicists. **Research Statement & Publications:** Numerical and non-numerical computer methods. **Mailing Address:** Dept Comput Sci, Univ BC, Vancouver, BC V6T 1Z4, Can.

KENNEDY, JAMES VERN, CHEMISTRY, RESEARCH ADMINISTRATION. **Personal Data:** b Jessup, Pa, May 4, 1934; m 1962, c 2. **Education:** Pa State Univ, BS, 1955; Univ Pittsburgh, PhD (chem), 1972. **Professional Experience:** SR RES ASSOC, CHEVRON RES CO, CHEVRON OIL CORP, 1985-; dir catalysis res, Chemicals & Minerals Div, Gulf Sci & Technol Co, 1980-1985; dir res-new bus, Minerals & Chem Div, 1979-1980; dir res-existing bus, Minerals & Chem Div, 1978; mgr prod res, Minerals & Chem Div, 1974-1978; group leader petrol prod res, Engelhard Minerals & Chem Corp, 1973-1974; catalyst prod mgr, Baroid Div, 1972-1973; tech mgr mineral synthesis dept, NL Industs, Inc, 1971-1973; supvr catalysis labs, Baroid Div, Nat Lead Co, 1970-1971; sect leader catalysis res, Baroid Div, Nat Lead Co, 1970; technologist, Baroid Div, Nat Lead Co, 1963-1969; Res assoc phys chem, Mellon Inst, 1955-1963. **Memberships:** Am Chem Soc; fel Am Inst Chem; Catalysis Soc; Clay Minerals Soc; NY Acad Sci. **Research Statement & Publications:** Fluidized cracking catalyst research and development for petroleum redefining; catalysis by layer-lattice silicates; alteration and synthesis of clay minerals; infrared characterization of synthetic clays; applications of minerals; new product development in catalyst, ceramic, industrial and paper products. **Mailing Address:** Chevron Res Co, PO Box 1627, Richmond, CA 94802-0627.

KENNEDY, JERRY DEAN, PHYSICS. **Personal Data:** b Oklahoma City, Okla, June 23, 1934; m 1957, c 2. **Education:** Univ Okla, BS, 1956; Univ Calif, Berkeley, MA, 1959; Lehigh Univ, PhD (physics), 1963. **Professional Experience:** RETIRED; mgr, Eng Sci Dept, 1973-1993; supvr, Exp Planning Div, 1971-1973; supvr, Test Exp Div, 1969-1971; mem tech staff physics, Sandia Labs, 1963-1969; engr, Autonetics Div, N Am Aviation, Inc, 1959; adv study scientist, Lockheed Missile & Space Co, 1956-1959. **Memberships:** Am Phys Soc. **Research Statement & Publications:** Dynamic high pressure solid state physics in semiconductors; shock wave phenomena in solids. **Mailing Address:** 8904 Crestwood Ave NE, Albuquerque, NM 87112.

KENNEDY, JOHN B, ENGINEERING MECHANICS, STRUCTURAL ENGINEERING. **Personal Data:** b Baghdad, Iraq, January 7, 1932; m 1957, c 3. **Education:** Univ Wales, BSc, 1955; Univ Toronto, PhD (civil eng), 1961. **Honorary Degrees:** DSc, Univ Wales, 1984. **Honors & Awards:** Duggan Medal, Eng Inst Can, 1978; T Y Lin Award, Am Soc Civil Engrs, 1982; Arthur M Wellington Prize, 1995 & 1999. **Professional Experience:** PROF EMER CIVIL ENG, UNIV WINDSOR, as of 2004; head dept, Univ Windsor, 1966-1976; prof civil eng, Univ Windsor, beginning 1966; assoc prof, Univ Windsor, 1963-1966; asst prof civil eng, Univ Sask, 1961-1963; res asst skewed bridges, Univ Toronto, 1957-1961; asst engr, Develop Bd Iraq, 1955-1957; consult engr, Ministry Transp & Commun, Ont. **Memberships:** Am Soc Civil Engrs; Am Concrete Inst; Eng Inst Can. **Research Statement & Publications:** Structural mechanics; skewed slab structures; waffle-slab bridges; cold-bending of HSS beams; reinforced-earth supporting soil-steel arch structures. **Mailing Address:** Dept Civil Eng, Univ Windsor, 362 Dillon Hall, Windsor, ON N9B 3P4, Can. **E-Mail:** cjk@uwindsor.ca

KENNEDY, JOHN EDWARD, physics, astronomy; deceased, see previous edition for last biography

KENNEDY, JOHN ELMO, JR, MANUFACTURING TECHNOLOGY, ENVIRONMENTAL SCIENCE. **Personal Data:** b Louisville, Ky, June 21, 1932; div, c Kevin, Eric, John III & Brian. **Education:** Univ Louisville, BS, 1959, PhD (org chem), 1963. **Professional Experience:** PVT CONSULT, 1977-; instr org chem, Univ Louisville, 1976-1977; res area supvr, Brown & Williamson Tobacco Corp, 1970-1976; sr group leader biol chem, Brown & Williamson Tobacco Corp, 1967-1970; group leader org chem, Brown & Williamson Tobacco Corp, 1964-1967; res chemist, Brown & Williamson Tobacco Corp, 1963-1964; chemist, Dept Exp Med, Sch Med, Univ Louisville, 1959-1961; chemist, Ky Color & Chem Co, 1956-1959; Lab technician anal chem, Schenley Distillers, Inc, 1955-1956; Expert witness, Liability & Environ Litigation, Gen, Forensic & Environ Toxicol. **Memberships:** AAAS; fel Am Inst Chem; NY Acad Sci; Am Chem Soc; Phytochem Soc NAm; Sigma Xi. **Research Statement & Publications:** Biological chemistry; pharmacology; natural products; synthesis; steroids; alkaloids; alicyclics; biosynthetic routes; reaction mechanisms; psychopharmacology; information science; science writing; toxicology. **Mailing Address:** 3501 Pimlico Pkwy No 124, Lexington, KY 40517.

KENNEDY, JOHN HARVEY, ELECTROCHEMISTRY, ANALYTICAL CHEMISTRY. **Personal Data:** b Oak Park, Ill, April 24, 1933; m 1970, Victoria; c 5. **Education:** Univ Calif, Los Angeles, BS, 1954; Harvard Univ, PhD (anal chem), 1957. **Professional Experience:** EMER PROF CHEM, UNIV CALIF, SANTA BARBARA, 1993-; Univ NC, 1981 & 1982 & China Acad Sci, 1990; chmn dept, Bissett-Berman Corp, 1982-1985; Japan Soc Advan Sci, 1974 & 1975; vis prof, Japan Soc Prom Sci, 1974 & 1975; from asst prof to prof, Univ Calif, Santa Barbara, 1967-1993; Tech adv, Bissett-Berman Corp, 1967-1971; head inorg chem, Gen Motors Defense Res Labs, 1964-1967; assoc prof, Boston Col, 1963-1964; asst prof, Univ Calif, Santa Barbara, 1961-1963; Res chemist, E I du Pont Del Nemours & Co, Del, 1957-1961. **Memberships:** Am Chem Soc; Electrochem Soc. **Research Statement & Publications:** Solid electrolytes; fused salts; electrochemistry; instrumental methods of analysis; photoelectrochemistry. **Mailing Address:** Dept Chem, Univ Calif, Phys Sci n 1631, Santa Barbara, CA 93106. **Fax:** 805-893-4120. **E-Mail:** jvkennedy@aol.com

KENNEDY, JOHN HINES, THORACIC SURGERY, CARDIOVASCULAR SURGERY. **Personal Data:** b Washington, DC, November 1, 1925; m 1977, Shirley A J Watson; c Anne, John, Mark & Joan. **Education:** Harvard Med Sch, MD, 1949; Am Bd Surg, dipl, 1957; Am Bd Surg, 1960; Imp Col, London, MPhil, 1990. **Professional Experience:** VIS SCIENTIST, DEPT MOLECULAR PHYSIOL, BABRAHAM INST, CAMBRIDGE, ENG, 1987-; vis scientist, Nat Inst Health & Med Res, Paris, France, 1986; Physiol Flow Studies Unit, Imp Col, Univ London, 1982-1985; med dir, Moat House Hosp, Gt Easton, Dunmow, Essex, 1980-1986; consult surgeon, Middlesex Hosp Med Sch, Wembley & Cent Middlesex Hosps, London, 1978-1982; fac mem, Dept Macro Molecular Sci, Case Western Res Univ, 1976-1977; consult, Pres Panel Biomed Res, 1975-; vis prof, Dept Macromolecular Sci, 1975-1976; adj prof, Biomed Eng, Rice Univ, 1975-1976; mem, Admis Comt, 1971-1976; dir, Taub Labs Mech Circulatory Support, 1970-1976; prin investr grant, Tech Adv Group, Artificial Heart-Myocardial Infarction Prog, Nat Heart & Lung Inst, 1970; consult site visitor prog proj grants, Tech Adv Group, Artificial Heart-Myocardial Infarction Prog, Nat Heart & Lung Inst, 1970; prof surg, Baylor Col Med, 1969-1976; adj prof, Rice Univ, 1969-1975; USPHS grant, Baylor Col Med, 1969-1972; dir, Baylor Med Col, 1969-1971; mem, Coun Cardiovasc Surg & ed, Surg Supplement Circulation, Am Heart Asn, 1968-1970; mem, Tech Adv Group, Artificial Heart-Myocardial Infarction Prog, Nat Heart & Lung Inst, 1968; dir, Circulatory Assistance Prog Group, Artificial Heart-Myocardial Infarction Prog, NIH contract, Case Western Res Univ, 1967-1969; res assoc, Eng Design Ctr, Case Western Res Univ, 1966-1969; dir, Div Thoracic Surg, Cleveland Metrop Gen Hosp, 1962-1969; asst prof thoracic surg, Sch Med, Case Western Res Univ, 1962-1969; sr registr, Thoracic Unit, Frenchay Hosp, Bristol, Eng, 1959-1960; Clin asst, Bristol Royal Infirm, Bristol Univ, 1959-1960; resident, Mass Gen Hosp, 1954-1955; asst resident, Mass Gen Hosp, 1950-1951 & 1953-1954; Intern, Mass Gen Hosp, 1949-1950. **Memberships:** Am Asn Thoracic Surg; Soc Thoracic Surgeons; Western Surg Asn; fel Am Col Surg; Royal Soc Med. **Research Statement & Publications:** Physiology; interstitium; physiology. **Mailing Address:** Dept Molecular Physiol, Babraham Inst, Cambridge CB2 4A5, UK.

KENNEDY, JOHN M, MECHANICS. **Education:** Va Tech, BS, 1975, MS, 1977; Clemson Univ, PhD, 1984. **Professional Experience:** DIR, CTR ADV ENG FIBERS & FILMS, CLEMSON UNIV, as of 2005. **Mailing Address:** Clemson Univ, PO Box 340921, Clemson, SC 29634-0921. **Fax:** 864-656-4557. **E-Mail:** kennedy@utsc utoronto.ca

KENNEDY, J(OHN) R(OBERT), INDUSTRIAL & MANUFACTURING ENGINEERING. **Personal Data:** b Frederick, Md, March 25, 1925; m 1945, MaryAnn; c John Jr, Eileen, Katherine & Michael. **Education:** Vincennes Univ, AA, 1947; Purdue Univ, BS, 1949. **Honorary Degrees:** Vincennes Univ AS, 1997. **Professional Experience:** CONSULT ENGR, 1979-; supvry gen engr, Eng & Plant Mgt, 1960-1979; chief, Eng & Plant Mgt, 1958-1979; gen engr, Nat Animal Disease Ctr, USDA, 1958-1960; mech engr, Chem Corps, Ft Detrick, Md, 1955-1958; biol test engr, Chem Corps, Ft Detrick, Md, 1951-1955; physicist, Chem Corps, Ft Detrick, Md, 1950-1951; aeronaut engr, Chem Corps, Ft Detrick, Md, 1949-1950. **Research Statement & Publications:** Maintenance engineering; design of containment laboratory facilities. **Mailing Address:** 510 Nicholas St, Vincennes, IN 47591.

KENNEDY, JOHN ROBERT, CELL BIOLOGY. **Personal Data:** b Cleveland, Ohio, July 17, 1937. **Education:** Univ Mich, BS, 1959, MS, 1961; Univ Iowa, PhD (zoology), 1964. **Professional Experience:** PROF EMERITUS, BIOCHEM & CELLULAR & MOLECULAR BIOL, UNIV TENN, KNOXVILLE, 1995-; from assoc prof to prof zool, Univ Tenn, Knoxville, 1969-1995; from instr to asst prof anat, Bowman Gray Sch Med, 1964-1969. **Memberships:** Am Soc Cell Biol; Electron Micros Soc Am. **Research Statement & Publications:** Effect of physiological factors on tracheal cell fine structure and function; ciliary cell physiology; consulting in electron microscopy and toxicology. **Mailing Address:** Dept Biochem & Cellular & Molecular Biol, Univ Tenn, Knoxville, TN 37996. **E-Mail:** jnrkenad@utk.edu

KENNEDY, JOSEPH PATRICK, ANATOMY, ECOLOGY. **Personal Data:** b Houston, Tex, March 9, 1932; c Justice. **Education:** Univ St Thomas, Tex, BA, 1954; Univ Tex, MA, 1955, PhD (zoology), 1958. **Honors & Awards:** Species named in hon, Hyla Kennedy, 1973. **Professional Experience:** Prof anat, Univ Tex Health Sci Ctr, Houston Med Sch, 1976-1977; mem exec comt & bd trustees, Armand Bayou Nature Ctr, Inc, 1974-1977; dir, Adv Comt, Univ Tex Environ Sci Park, 1971-1976; prof animal ecol & chmn dept, Grad Sch Biomed Sci, 1969-1977; prof ecol, M D Anderson Hosp & Tumor Inst, 1969-1976; chmn, Adv Comt, Univ Tex Environ Sci Park, 1969-1971; PROF ANAT, BASIC SCI DENT BR, UNIV TEX, HOUSTON, 1968-; ed, J Herpet, 1968-1979; Terra Alta Biol Sta, WVa Univ, 1968; lectr, Univ Houston, 1963; vis prof, Mt Lake Biol Sta, Univ Va, 1962; from asst prof to assoc prof, Univ Tex, 1960-1968; chmn, Dept Biol, Univ St Thomas, Tex, 1958-1960; mem, Coun Biol Eds. **Memberships:** Soc Study Amphibians & Reptiles; Sigma Xi. **Research Statement & Publications:** Ecology, evolution and behavior; herpetology; literary criticism. **Mailing Address:** Basic Sci Dent Br, Univ Tex Health Sci Ctr, PO Box 20068, Houston, TX 77225-0068.

KENNEDY, JOSEPH PAUL, POLYMER CHEMISTRY. **Personal Data:** b Budapest, Hungary, May 18, 1928; American citizen; m 1957, Ingrid; c Katherine, Cynthia & Julie. **Education:** Univ Vienna, PhD (chem), 1955; Rutgers Univ, MBA, 1961. **Honorary Degrees:** DHC, Kossuth Sci Univ, Debrecen, Hungary, 1989. **Honors & Awards:** Polymer Chem Award, Am Chem Soc, 1985, Appl Polymr Sci, 1995, G S Whitby Award, 1996, Dist Svc Polymer Sci, Soc Polymer Sci, Japan, 2000. **Professional Experience:** DISTINGUISHED PROF POLYMER SCI & CHEM & RES ASSOC INST POLYMER SCI, UNIV AKRON, 1970-; sr res assoc, Exxon Res & Eng Col, 1969-1970; res assoc, Exxon Res & Eng Col, 1965-1969; sr res chemist, Exxon Res & Eng Col, 1962-1965; guest prof polymer chem, Kyoto Univ, Japan, 1960; res chemist, Exxon Res & Eng Col, 1959-1962; res chemist, Celanese Corp Am, 1957-1959; res assoc, McGill Univ, 1956-1957; fel biochem, Sorbonne, 1955-1956. **Memberships:** Am Chem Soc. **Research Statement & Publications:** Cationic polymerizations; Friedel-Crafts chemistry; polymer synthesis; polymerization mechanisms; elastomer chemistry, particularly butyl rubber and polyisobutylene; blocks and grafts; terminally functional liquids; derivatization of polymers; living polymerizations; biomaterials. **Mailing Address:** Inst Polymer Sci, Univ Akron, Akron, OH 44325. **Fax:** 330-972-5290. **E-Mail:** kennedy@polymer.uakron.edu

KENNEDY, KATHERINE ASH, TOXICOLOGY, CANCER CHEMOTHERAPY. **Personal Data:** b Bryn Mawr, Pa, March 24, 1950; m 1987. **Education:** Vanderbilt Univ, BA, 1973; Univ Iowa, PhD (pharmacol), 1977. **Professional Experience:** PROF PHARMACOL, SCH MED, GEORGE WASH UNIV, as of 2003; assoc prof, Sch Med, George Wash Univ, beginning 1987; asst prof pharmacol, Sch Med, George Wash Univ, 1981-1987; fel, Sch Med, Yale Univ, 1978-1981. **Memberships:** AAAS; Am Asn Cancer Res; NY Acad Sci; Radiation Res Soc; Am Soc Pharmacol & Exp Ther. **Research Statement & Publications:** Role of biotransformation for drug activity and toxicity; mechanisms for antitumor agents in normally aerated and hypozic cells; mechanisms of drug induced cytotoxicity; tumor microenvironmental effects on drug induced toxicity. **Mailing Address:** Dept Pharmacol George Wash Univ, 2300 I St NW, Washington, DC 20037-2337. **Fax:** 202-994-2870. **E-Mail:** phmkak@gwumc.edu

KENNEDY, KEN, SOFTWARE SYSTEMS, RESEARCH ADMINISTRATION. **Personal Data:** b Washington, DC, August 12, 1945; m 1998, Carol; c Caitlin Lohrenz (stepdaughter). **Education:** Rice Univ, BA, 1967; NY Univ, MS, 1969, PhD (comput sci), 1971. **Honors & Awards:** National Acad Engineering, 1991; W W McDowell Award, Inst Elec & Electronics Engrs Comput Soc, 1995; Programming Languages Achievement Award, ACM SIGPLAN, 1999; CRA Distinguished Service Award, 1999; Seymour Cray HPCC Industry Recognition Award, 1999; Dist Alumnus, Rice University, 2002; American Acad Arts and Sciences, 2005. **Professional Experience:** University Professor, Rice University, 2002-; dir, Center for High Performance Software Research, Rice University, 2000-, co chmn, President's Information Technology Advisory Committee, 1997-1999; John and Ann Doerr Professor, Comp Sci, Rice University, 1997-; chmn, Dept Comput Sci, 1990-1992; director, Tera Computer Corp (now Cray, Inc.), 1990-; dir, Comput & Info Tech Inst, 1989-1992; dir, Ctr Res Parallel Computing, 1989-2000; Noah Harding Prof Comp Sci, Rice Univ, mem board Computing Res Assn, 1986-1991; 1985-1997; chmn, Dept Comput Sci, 1984-1988; mem NSF advisory comm for computer research, 1984-

1988 (chair, 1985-1987); pres, R M Thrall &Assoc, Inc, 1981-; Noah Harding prof math sci, 1980-1984; vis sci, IBM Watson Res Lab, 1978-1979; vis staff mem, Comput Div, Los Alamos Sci Lab, 1977-1985; mem, Panel Comput Sci & Eng Res, Div Comput Res, NSF, 1975-1977 & Adv Comt Comput Res, NSF, 1984-; vis scientist, Space Shuttle Prog Lead Off, NASA, 1975; vpres, R M Thrall &Assoc, Inc, 1974-1981; prin investr, numerous grants, 1973-; From asst prof to prof, Dept Math Sci, Rice Univ, 1971-1984. **Memberships:** Nat Acad Eng; fel Assn Comput Mach; Soc Indust & Appl Math; fel Inst Elec & Electronics Engrs; Sigma Xi; fel AAAS, Amer Acad Arts & Sci. **Research Statement & Publications:** Numerous publications; computer science; theory and practice of programming language implementation, especially optimization of compiled code for scientific languages; programming systems for high-performance computers and computational grids. **Mailing Address:** Dept Comput Sci, Rice Univ, 6100 Main St, Houston, TX 77005-1892. **Fax:** 713-348-5136. **E-Mail:** ken@rice.edu

KENNEDY, KENNETH ADRIAN RAINE, PHYSICAL & FORENSIC ANTHROPOLOGY, ARCHAEOLOGY. **Personal Data:** b Oakland, Calif, June 26, 1930; m 1969, Margaret C Fairlie. **Education:** Univ Calif, Berkeley, BA, 1953, MA, 1954, PhD (anthrop), 1962; Am Bd Forensic Anthrop, dipl, 1978. **Honors & Awards:** T Dale Stewart Award, Am Acad Forensic Sci, 1987; Book Award, Am Anthrop Asn, 2003. **Professional Experience:** PROF EMER, DEPT ECOL & EVOL BIOL, ANTHROP & ASIAN STUDIES, CORNELL UNIV, 2005-; secy, Am Bd Forensic Anthrop, 1999-2002; mem ed bd, Am Phys Anthrop, 1998-2001; chair, Phys Anthrop Sect, Am Acad Forensic Sci, 1994-1995; secy, Phys Anthrop Sect, Am Acad Forensic Sci, 1993-1994; elected chmn, Biol Anthrop Unit, Am Anthrop Asn, 1986-1988; vis prof, Dept Anthropol, Univ Ariz, 1985; actg ed-in-chief, Am J Phys Anthrop, 1985; prof, Dept Ecol & Evol Biol, Anthrop & Asian Studies, Cornell Univ, 1981-2005; vis fel, Kings Col, Cambridge Univ, 1981; fel, Am Inst Indian Studies, 1980-1988; NSF fel, Deccan Col Post-Grad & Res Inst, Univ Poona, India, 1980-1981; vis prof, Dept Anthropol, Univ Ariz, 1979; vis prof, Cornell Univ, 1972; fel, Am Inst Indian Studies, 1971-1972; NSF fel, Deccan Col Post-Grad & Res Inst, Univ Poona, India, 1971; assoc prof div biol sci, Anthrop & Asian Studies, Cornell Univ, 1969-1981; vis prof, Univ Calif, Berkeley, 1968-1969; fel, Am Inst Indian Studies, 1966; Cornell Univ fac res grant, Brit Mus Natural Hist, London, 1965-1966; from asst prof to assoc prof anthrop, Anthrop & Asian Studies, Cornell Univ, 1964-1981; NSF fel, Deccan Col Post-Grad & Res Inst, Univ Poona, India, 1963-1964; vis prof, Deccan Col Post-Grad & Res Inst, 1963-1964; actg instr phys anthrop, Univ Calif, Berkeley, 1962-1963. **Memberships:** Fel AAAS; fel Am Anthrop Asn; Am Asn Phys Anthrop (vpres, 1994-1996); fel Royal Anthrop Inst Gt Brit; Int Asn Human Biol. **Research Statement & Publications:** Human evolution in South Asia, particularly the hominid osteological fossil record; history of biological sciences, especially human evolution and physical anthropology; palaeodemography of South Asia; forensic anthropology; paleoanthropology of South Asia (India, Pakistan, Sri Lanka); forensic anthropology with special emphasis on markers of occupational stress; human palaeontology; evolutionary biology. **Mailing Address:** Ecol & Evol Biol, Cornell Univ, Corson Hall, Ithaca, NY 14853-2701. **Fax:** 607-255-8088. **E-Mail:** kak10@cornell.edu

KENNEDY, KEVIN JOSEPH, ANAEROBIC TREATMENT PROCESS DESIGN, BIOREMEDIATION. **Personal Data:** b Clitheroe, UK, December 2, 1954; Canadian citizen; m 1980, Linda A Manila; c Erica, Jordan & Dean. **Education:** Univ Western Ont, BSc, 1977, MESc, 1980; Univ Ottawa, PhD (civil & environ eng), 1985. **Honors & Awards:** Innovative Wastewater Treatment Process Award, Que Ministry Environ, 1986; Award Excellence Wastewater, Can Asn Environ Sci & Eng, 1989. **Professional Experience:** PROF CIVIL & CHEM ENG, UNIV OTTAWA, as of 2004; Consult various cos, 1991-; secy, Spec Group Anaerobic Digestion, Int Asn Water Qual, 1991-; assoc prof civil & chem eng, Univ Ottawa, beginning 1991; res officer, Nat Res Coun Can, 1982-1991; Process engr, Eco-Res (CIL), 1980-1982. **Memberships:** Int Asn Water Qual; Water Pollution Control Fedn; Am Soc Microbiol; Can Asn Water Qual. **Research Statement & Publications:** Biological treatment of industrial and municipal wastewater; advanced anaerobic process for treatment of recalcitrant toxic wastewaters. **Mailing Address:** Dept Civil & Chem Eng, Univ Ottawa, 161 Louis Pasteur, Rm A106, Ottawa, ON K1N 6N5, Can. **E-Mail:** kennedy@eng.uottawa.ca

KENNEDY, KRISTIN, MATHEMATICS. **Education:** Brown Univ, MS, 1983; Univ RI, PhD (appl sci), 1989. **Professional Experience:** ASSOC PROF, DEPT MATH, BRYANT COL, as of 2005. **Mailing Address:** Bryant Col, 1150 Douglas Pike, Smithfield, RI 02917-1291. **Fax:** 401-232-6319. **E-Mail:** kkennedy@bryant.edu

KENNEDY, LAWRENCE A, FLUID MECHANICS, COMBUSTION. **Personal Data:** b Detroit, Mich, May 31, 1937; m 1957, c 6. **Education:** Univ Detroit, BS, 1960; Northwestern Univ, MS, 1962, PhD (mech eng), 1964. **Honors & Awards:** AT&T Found Award, Am Soc Eng Educ; Ralph R Teetor Award, Soc Auto Engrs. **Professional Experience:** DEAN EMER & PROF EMER, COL ENG, UNIV ILL, CHICAGO, 2005-; dean & prof, Col Eng, Univ Ill, Chicago, 1994-2005; dept mech eng, Ohio State Univ, Columbus, 1983-1994; Air Preheater Div, Combustion Eng Corp, 1978-; MGB Res Corp, 1976-; NATO sr fel sci, 1971-1972; adv Group Aerospace Res & Develop, NATO, 1971; dir aerospace eng, State Univ NY, Buffalo, 1969-1971; NSF sci fac fel, 1968-1969; Consult, Cornell Aero Labs, 1966-1971; prof mech eng, State Univ NY, Buffalo, 1964-1983; res engr, Mech Res & Develop Div, Gen Am Transp Corp, Ill, 1963-1964; ed, J Exp Methods Thermal & Fluid Sci. **Memberships:** Combustion Inst; assoc fel Am Inst Aeronaut & Astronaut; Am Phys Soc; fel Am Soc Mech Engrs; Soc Automotive Engrs; Am Soc Engr Educ. **Research Statement & Publications:** High temperature gas dynamics; chemical reacting flow; magnetohydrodynamics and combustion; radiative transfer; combustion generated pollutants; manufacturing processes; extensive work in the areas of reacting flows and optical dragnistics; specific studies turbulent combustion, radiation transfer with application to coal combustion and catalytic combustion. **Mailing Address:** Univ Ill, 851 S Morgan St M/C159, Chicago, IL 60607-7043. **Fax:** 312-996-8664. **E-Mail:** lkennedy@ulc.edu

KENNEDY, M(ALDON) KEITH, ENTOMOLOGY. **Personal Data:** b Little Rock, Ark, July 26, 1947. **Education:** Hendrix Col, BA, 1969; Cornell Univ, MS, 1971, PhD (insect ecol), 1976. **Professional Experience:** SECT MGR, ENTOM RES CTR, SC JOHNSON WAX CO, 1984-; asst prof entom, Mich State Univ, 1975-1981. **Memberships:** Entom Soc Am; Ecol Soc Am; Acarological Soc Am. **Research Statement & Publications:** Biology of the Sciaridae Diptera, especially those of economic importance. **Mailing Address:** Sc Johnson, 1525 Howe St, Racine, WI 53403-5011.

KENNEDY, MARY BERNADETTE, BRAIN BIOCHEMISTRY, LEARNING MECHANISMS. **Personal Data:** b Pontiac, Mich, July 4, 1947. **Education:** St Mary's Col, BS, 1969; Johns Hopkins Univ, PhD (biochem), 1975. **Honors & Awards:** McKnight Neuroscience Develop Award, 1984; Fac Award, Women Scientist & Engrs, NSF, 1991; Javits Neuroscience Invest Award, NIH, 1992. **Professional Experience:** Chmn, Gordon Conf Neural Plasticity, 1993; ALLEN & LENABELLE DAVIS PROF BIOL, KENNEDY LAB, CALIF INST TECHNOL, 1992-; vchmn, Gordon Conf Neural Plasticity, 1991; mem & consult, ss1 study sect, NIH Neurol Sci, 1990-1993; assoc ed, J Neuroscience, 1986-1989; chmn, Hereditary Dis Found, 1986-1987; mem sci adv bd, Hereditary Dis Found, 1984-1987; from asst prof to assoc prof, Calif Inst Technol, 1981-1992; fel, Yale Med Sch, 1978-1980; fel, Harvard Med Sch, 1975-1978. **Memberships:** Soc Neuroscience; Am Soc Biochem & Molecular Biol; Am Soc Cell Biol; fel AAAS. **Research Statement & Publications:** Biochemical mechanisms by which calcium regulates neuronal function in the central nervous system; regulation of type II calcium/calmodulin-dependent protein kinase and the molecular structure of the postsynaptic density; published numerous articles. **Mailing Address:** Div Biol, Kennedy Lab, Calif Inst Technol, MC 216-76, Pasadena, CA 91125. **Fax:** 626-395-8474. **E-Mail:** kennedym@caltech.edu

KENNEDY, MAURICE VENSON, BIOCHEMISTRY. **Personal Data:** b Pontotoc, Miss, November 23, 1925; m 1948, c 2. **Education:** Miss State Univ, BS, 1949, MS, 1954, PhD (biochem), 1967. **Professional Experience:** RETIRED; prof biochem, Miss State Univ, 1984-1986; consult, NATO Sponsored Symp Pesticides, Lethbridge, Can, 1970; assoc prof biochem, Miss State Univ, 1966-1983; instr microbiol, Miss State Univ, 1962-1966; dir microbiol & chem, Miss Dept Agr Lab, 1949-1962. **Memberships:** AAAS; Am Chem Soc; Am Soc Microbiol; Sigma Xi. **Research Statement & Publications:** Biochemical mechanisms of toxic substances, metabolic pathways in food poisoning microorganisms, production of useful substances from animal waste, and degradation and disposal of waste pesticides. **Mailing Address:** 1027 Brandywine Rd, Tuscaloosa, AL 35406.

KENNEDY, MICHAEL CRAIG, NEUROBIOLOGY. **Personal Data:** b Buffalo, NY, December 5, 1946; c 3. **Education:** Rice Univ BA, 1968; Univ Rochester, MS, 1971, PhD (biol, neurobiol), 1974. **Professional Experience:** PROG DIR & PROF ANAT, HAHNEMANN UNIV, as of 2004; assoc prof anat, Hahnemann Univ, beginning 1981; asst prof biol, NY Univ, 1976-1981; fel comp neuroanat, NY Univ Med Ctr, 1974-1976. **Memberships:** AAAS; Am Asn Anatomists; Soc Neuroscience. **Research Statement & Publications:** Investigations of the anatomy and physiology of neural pathways in nonmammalian vertebrates; neural substrates of auditory communication in the Tokay Gecko; developmental neurobiology of the reptilian auditory system; the visual system in the sea lamprey, Petromyzon marinus; influence of norepinephrine on blood-forming cells in bone marrow. **Mailing Address:** Dept Anat, Hahnemann Univ Sch Med, Rm 1204 Bellet Bldg, Philadelphia, PA 19102. **Fax:** 215-762-3973. **E-Mail:** michael.kennedy@drexel.edu

KENNEDY, MICHAEL JOHN, STRUCTURAL GEOLOGY, TECTONICS. **Personal Data:** b London, Eng, January 21, 1940; m 1966, Deirdre; c Robin J, Maru C & Emma S. **Education:** Univ Dublin, BS, 1963, MA & PhD (struct geol), 1966. **Honors & Awards:** Young Award, Atlantic Provinces Inter-Univ Comt on the Sciences, 1973. **Professional Experience:** PROF & HEAD, DEPT GEOL, UNIV COL, DUBLIN, 1980-; prof & chmn, Dept Geol Sci, Brock Univ, 1976-1980; prof geol, Mem Univ Nfld, 1974-1976; Co-chmn, Int Geodynamics Working Group 9, Appalachian-Caledonian Group, 1972-1980; from asst prof to assoc prof, 1967-1974; Nat Res Coun Can fel, Geol Surv Can, 1966-1967; chmn, invest comt IGCP Proj 233. **Memberships:** Fel Geol Asn Can; fel Geol Soc London; fel Geol Soc Am. **Research Statement & Publications:** Structural geology of metamorphic rocks, particularly Caledonian and Appalachian systems; petrofabrics and the relationship of deformation with metamorphism; metamorphic complexes of Appalachians and Caledonides; structural development of south east Ireland; terwanes in Caledonian and Appalachian orogens. **Mailing Address:** Dept Geol Univ Col, Belfield, Dublin 4, Ireland. **Fax:** 353-128-37733.

KENNEDY, MICHAEL LYNN, VERTEBRATE ZOOLOGY. **Personal Data:** b Scotts Hill, Tenn, January 31, 1942. **Education:** Memphis State Univ, BS, 1966, MS, 1968; Univ Okla, PhD (vert zool), 1975. **Professional Experience:** PROF BIOL, MEMPHIS STATE UNIV, as of 2003; assoc prof biol, Memphis, State Univ, beginning 1980; asst prof, Memphis State Univ, 1974-1980; Asst vert zool, Univ Okla, 1969-1974. **Memberships:** Am Soc Mammalogists; Soc Syst Zool; Am Ornithologists Union. **Research Statement & Publications:** Mammalian systematics; geographic variation studies with small mammals. **Mailing Address:** Dept Biol, Univ Memphis, Ellington Hall, 3700 Walker Ave, Memphis, TN 38152. **Fax:** 901-678-4746. **E-Mail:** mlkenndy@memphis.edu

KENNEDY, PAUL A, MATHEMATICS. **Professional Experience:** PROF MATH, SOUTHWEST TEX STATE UNIV, as of 2005. **Memberships:** Am Math Soc. **Mailing Address:** Southwest Tex State Univ, Dept Math, San Marcos, TX 78666. **Fax:** 512-245-1469. **E-Mail:** pkennedy@swt.edu

KENNEDY, PETER CARLETON, VETERINARY PATHOLOGY. **Personal Data:** b Berkeley, Calif, June 19, 1923; m 1946, c 4. **Education:** Kans State Univ, DVM, 1949; Cornell Univ, PhD (vet path), 1954. **Professional Experience:** PROF EMER VET PATH, UNIV CALIF, DAVIS, 1992-; pathologist, Exp Sta, 1970-1992; lectr path, Med Sch, 1957-1992; from lectr to prof, Univ Calif, Davis, 1954-1992; asst path, Cornell Univ, 1952-1953; asst large animal surg, Cornell Univ, 1951; intern, Angell Mem Animal Hosp, Mass, 1950. **Memberships:** Am Col Vet Path. **Research Statement & Publications:** Pathology of infectious diseases and endocrinopathies of domestic animals. **Mailing Address:** Vet Med, Univ Calif-Davis, 1120B Haring Hall, Davis, CA 95616. **E-Mail:** pdkennedy@ucdavis.edu

KENNEDY, ROBERT ALAN, PLANT STRESS PHYSIOLOGY. **Personal Data:** b Benson, Minn, September 29, 1946; m 1984, c 4. **Education:** Univ Minn, BS, 1968; Univ Calif, Berkeley, PhD (bot), 1974. **Honors & Awards:** Kenneth Post Award, Am Soc Hort Sci, 1983. **Professional Experience:** PROF, DEPT BIOL, TEX A&M UNIV, as of 1999; VPRES RES & ASSOC PROVOST GRAD STUDIES, TEX A&M UNIV, 1992-; assoc vchair & dir agr res, Univ Md, 1989-1992; consult, NSF, 1989-1990; prog dir, NSF, 1987-1989; mem fac, Biotechnol Ctr, Ohio State Univ, 1986-1988; prof hort & chair, Ohio State Univ, 1985-1987; asst dir res, Wash State Univ, 1984-1985; from assoc prof to prof plant physiol, Wash State Univ, 1979-1985; asst prof bot, Univ Iowa, 1974-1978; res assoc, US Army Med Res & Nutrit Lab, 1969-1971. **Memberships:** Am Soc Plant Physiologists; AAAS; Bot Soc Am; Sigma Xi; Am Inst Biol Sci. **Research Statement & Publications:** Plant biochemistry and physiology, especially anaerobic or flooding metabolism; metabolic adaptation to flooding; induction and coordination of metabolic pathways during anoxia; energy relations and regulations of protein synthesis without oxygen. **Mailing Address:** Dept Biol Tex A&M Univ, 312 Admin Bldg, College Station, TX 77843-3258. **Fax:** 409-845-1855. **E-Mail:** kennedy@bio.tamu.edu

KENNEDY, ROBERT DELMONT, MECHANICAL ENGINEERING. **Personal Data:** b Pittsburgh, Pa, November 8, 1932; m 1956, Sally; c Robert Boyd, Kathleen Tyson, Thomas Alexander & Melissa Kristine. **Education:** Cornell Univ, BSME, 1955. **Honors & Awards:** Palladium Medal, Soc Chem Indust, 1991, Chem Indust Medal, 1995. **Professional Experience:** RETIRED; pres, chief exec officer & chmn, Union Carbide Corp, 1986-1995; chmn, Inroads Inc; pres & chief exec officer, Chem & Plastics, 1985-1986; sr vpres corp & exec vpres, Linde Div, 1982; pres, Linde Div, 1977-1982; staff, Nat Carbon Div, 1957-

1977; staff mem, Union Carbide Corp, 1955-1957. **Memberships:** Hon fel Am Inst Chem Engrs; Chem Mfr Asn. **Mailing Address:** Union Carbide Corp, 39 Old Ridgebury Rd, Danbury, CT 06817.

KENNEDY, ROBERT E, THEORETICAL PHYSICS, THERMAL PHYSICS. **Personal Data:** b Santa Monica, Calif, June 5, 1939; m 1961, c 5. **Education:** Loyola Univ, BS, 1961; Univ Notre Dame, PhD (physics), 1966. **Professional Experience:** CHMN, DEPT PHYSICS, CREIGHTON UNIV, 1993-; ASSOC PROF PHYSICS, CREIGHTON UNIV, 1973-; chmn dept, Creighton Univ, 1973-1981; asst prof, Creighton Univ, 1966-1972. **Memberships:** Am Inst Physics; Am Phys Soc; Am Asn Physics Teachers. **Research Statement & Publications:** Non-equilibrium thermodynamics; impact of Albert Einstein on modern physics. **Mailing Address:** Dept Physics, Creighton Univ, Omaha, NE 68178-0001. **E-Mail:** re.kennedy@creighton.edu

KENNEDY, ROBERT P, SEISMIC LOADING. **Personal Data:** b Glendale, Calif, April 2, 1939. **Education:** Stamford Univ, BA, 1960, MA, 1961, PhD (struct eng), 1967. **Honors & Awards:** Stephen Bechtel Energy Eng Award, Am Soc Civil Engrs, 1992. **Professional Experience:** CONSULT ENGR, RPK STRUCT MECH CONSULT INC, as of 2004; BD ADV, NC STATE UNIV, as of 2003; PRES, RPK STRUCT MECH CONSULT, 1986-; pres, Struct Mech Assoc, 1980-1986; vpres, Eng Div, Anal Corp, 1976-1980; dir eng mech, Holmes & Narber, 1966-1976; res engr, Northrop Corp, 1961-1964. **Memberships:** Nat Acad Eng; Am Concrete Inst; Earthquake Eng Res Inst; Am Soc Civil Engrs. **Mailing Address:** R P K Struct Mech Consult, Inc, 18971 Villa Terr, Yorba Linda, CA 92686. **Fax:** 714-777-8299. **E-Mail:** rpkstruct@earthlink.net

KENNEDY, ROBERT SAMUEL, EXPERIMENTAL PSYCHOLOGY. **Personal Data:** b Bronxville, NY, January 10, 1936; div, c Kathryn J, Robert C, Richard M & Kristyne E. **Education:** Iona Col, BA, 1957; Fordham Univ, MA, 1959; Univ Rochester, PhD (sensation & perception), 1972. **Honors & Awards:** Franklin Taylor Award, Am Psychol Asn, 1996; Raymond F Longacre Award, Aerospace Med Asn, 93. **Professional Experience:** AT RSK ASSESSMENTS INC, as of 2000; VPRES, ESSEX CORP, ORLANDO, FLA, 1987-; PROF, UNIV CENT FLA, 1987-; consult, NASA/Johnson Space Ctr, Houston, 1985-, Systems Tech Inc, Univ Space Res Asn, Momterey Tech Inc, Battelle, Am Inst Biol Sci, Performance Metrics, Bolt, Beranek & Newman, NAS/Nat Sci Res Coun, NASA/Ames Res Ctr, US Navy Med Res & Develop Command; FAC DIR, ESSEX CORP, COLUMBIA, MD, 1981-; head, Dept Human Performance, Naval Biomed Lab, New Orleans, 1979-1981; head, Dept Human Performance, 1977-1979; officer-in-charge, Dept Bioengineering Sci, Naval Aerospace Med Res Lab Detachment, New Orleans, 1976-1979; head, Human Div Human Factors, Naval Air Develop Ctr, Warminster, Pa, 1976; Syst Mgt Dept, Univ SCalif, 1975-1976; lectr grad, Psychol Dept, Laverne Col, Pt Mugu, 1973-1976; head, Br Human Factors Eng, Naval Missile Ctr, Pt Mugu, Calif, 1972-1976; head diver div eval, Naval Med Res Inst, Pensacola, 1968-1970; res psychologist, Psychol Div, Naval Sch Aviation Med, Pensacola, Fla, 1959-1965; consult ed, Aviation, Space & Environ Med, Behav Res Methods, Instruments & Computers, J Exp Psychol; bd dirs, Aviation, Space & Environ Med. **Memberships:** Fel Am Psychol Asn; fel Am Psychol Soc; Am Soc Safety Engrs; fel Aerospace Med Asn; AAAS; Aerospace Human Factors Asn; Soc Neuroscience; NY Acad Sci. **Research Statement & Publications:** Development of microcomputer based test battery, motion sickness data base and prediction tools. **Mailing Address:** Rsk Assessments Inc, 1040 Woodcock Rd, Ste 227, Orlando, FL 32803. **Fax:** 407-896-0638. **E-Mail:** rkennedy@msis.dmso.mil

KENNEDY, ROBERT SPAYDE, ELECTRICAL ENGINEERING, COMMUNICATIONS. **Personal Data:** b Augusta, Kans, December 9, 1933; m 1955, c 3. **Education:** Univ Kans, BS, 1955; Mass Inst Technol, SM, 1959, ScD(info theory), 1963. **Professional Experience:** Dir, Commun Form, Mass Inst Technol, 1984-1988; PROF EMER ELEC ENG, MASS INST TECHNOL, 1976-; from asst prof to assoc prof, Lincoln Lab, 1964-1976; Ford fel, Mass Inst Technol, 1964-1965; staff mem, Lincoln Lab, 1963-1964; Ford Found grad fel, 1959-1960; nuclear engr, Naval Reactors Br, US AEC, 1955-1957. **Memberships:** fel Inst Elec & Electronics Engrs; Optical Soc Am. **Research Statement & Publications:** Extraordinary wide band fiber optic networks. **Mailing Address:** Dept Elect Eng, Mass Inst Technol, Cambridge, MA 02139.

KENNEDY, ROBERT WILLIAM, WOOD SCIENCE, TECHNOLOGY. **Personal Data:** b Syracuse, NY, September 13, 1931; m 1956, c 3. **Education:** State Univ NY, BS, 1953; Univ BC, MF, 1955; Yale Univ, PhD (wood tech), 1962. **Professional Experience:** RETIRED; prof wood sci, Fac Forestry, 1990; dean, Fac Forestry, 1983-1990; prof wood sci & indust, Univ BC, 1979-1983; from assoc dir to dir, Protection & Prod Div, 1971-1979; prog mgr, Protection & Prod Div, 1969-1971; head wood biol sect, Western Forest Prod Lab, 1966-1969; consult, Forestry & Forest Prod Div, Food & Agr Orgn, UN, 1964 & 1982; from asst prof to assoc prof, Univ Toronto, 1962-1966; instr wood tech, Univ BC, 1955-1956 & 1957-1961. **Memberships:** Forest Prod Res Soc; fel Int Acad Wood Sci (pres 1987-); Can Inst Forestry; fel Inst Wood Sci. **Research Statement & Publications:** Physiology of wood formation; wood structure and properties at micro level; wood utilization. **Mailing Address:** 6303 Salish Dr, Vancouver, BC V6N 4C2, Can.

KENNEDY, ROBERT WILSON, ORGANIC CHEMISTRY. **Personal Data:** b Tampa, Fla, September 9, 1927; div, c 1. **Education:** Emory Univ, AB, 1953, MS, 1954, PhD (chem), 1956. **Professional Experience:** RETIRED; proj mgr, New Prod Div, 1979-1986; proj mgr, New Prod Div, 1974-1979; asst to the works mgr, Polymers Div, 1974; asst div supt, Polymers Div, 1973-1974; dept supt, Intermediates Dept, 1972-1973; sr chemist, Org Chem Div, Tenn Eastman Co, 1959-1972; Develop res chemist, Org Chem Div, Tenn Eastman Co, 1956-1958. **Memberships:** Am Chem Soc; Sigma Xi. **Research Statement & Publications:** Developmental research in industrial organic chemistry; mechanisms of organic reactions; naturally occurring organic compounds, particularly pine resin acids; new products marketing aspects; new products development. **Mailing Address:** 3357 Ridgeview St, Kingsport, TN 37764-3467.

KENNEDY, ROBIN JOHN, MATERIALS SCIENCE. **Personal Data:** b NZ, May 12, 1950. **Education:** Univ Canterbury, BSc, 1971, PhD (physics), 1977. **Professional Experience:** PROF PHYSICS, FLA A&M UNIV, 1990-; prof, Dept Physics, Fla State Univ, 1968-1990. **Memberships:** Am Phys Soc. **Mailing Address:** Dept Physics, Fla A&M Univ, Tallahassee, FL 32301. **E-Mail:** kennedy@cennas.nhmfl.gov

KENNEDY, RUSSELL JORDAN, CIVIL ENGINEERING, HYDRAULICS. **Personal Data:** b Dunrobin, Ont, November 23, 1917; m 1968, Marjorie; c Ian, Robert, Nancy & Barbara. **Education:** Queen's Univ, Ont, BSc, 1941; Univ Iowa, MS, 1949. **Honorary Degrees:** DSc, Queen's Univ, 1993. **Honors & Awards:** Angus Medal, Eng Inst Can, 1958. **Professional Experience:** RETIRED; exec dir, Alumni Asn, 1981-1986; NW Hydraul Consults, Vancouver, BC, 1979-1980; Irving Pulp & Paper Ltd, St John, NB, 1979-1980; vprin admin, Queen's Univ, 1970-1976; Dept Energy, Mines & Resources, 1968-1971; assoc dean sch grad studies, Queen's Univ, 1968-1970; consult, Pulp & Paper Res Inst Can, 1951-1964; from asst prof to prof civil eng, Queen's Univ, 1949-1984; consult, Ont Paper Co, 1948-1951; lectr, Queen's Univ, 1946-1948. **Memberships:** Eng Inst Can; Int Asn Hydraul Res. **Research Statement & Publications:** Ice control; improvement of design criteria for air bubbler systems. **Mailing Address:** Ellis Hall, Queen's Univ, Kingston, ON K7L 3N6, Can.

KENNEDY, STEPHEN DANDRIDGE, ECONOMICS, STATISTICS. **Personal Data:** b New York, NY, February 25, 1942; m 1965, Joanna; c Julia (Paca) & Benjamin Bartlett. **Education:** Harvard Univ, BA, 1963; Mass Inst Technol, PhD (econ), 1972. **Professional Experience:** Adj lectr, John F Kennedy Sch Govt, Harvard Univ, 1995; CHIEF SCIENTIST, ABT ASSOCS INC, MASS, 1986-; vpres, Abt Assocs Inc, Mass, 1975-1988; analyst, Abt Assocs Inc, Mass, 1970-1975. **Research Statement & Publications:** Evaluation and research design. **Mailing Address:** Abt Assoc Inc, 55 Wheeler St, Cambridge, MA 02138. **Fax:** 617-492-5219.

KENNEDY, THELMA TEMY, NEUROPHYSIOLOGY. **Personal Data:** b Chicago, Ill, October 18, 1925; m 1964, Richard. **Education:** Univ Chicago, PhB & BS, 1947, MS, 1949, PhD (biopsychol), 1955. **Professional Experience:** RETIRED; emer prof physiol, Univ Wash, 1988; assoc dean grad sch, Univ Wash, 1969-1972; from instr to prof, Univ Wash, 1958-1988; USPHS fel neurophysiol, Univ Wash, 1956-1958; asst neurosurg, Univ Chicago, 1951-1956. **Memberships:** AAAS. **Research Statement & Publications:** Cerebral cortex organization; unit activity; motor systems; sensory physiology. **Mailing Address:** Dept Physiol & Biophys SJ-40, Univ Wash MS357290, Seattle, WA 98195.

KENNEDY, THOMAS JAMES, PHYSIOLOGY, NEPHROLOGY. **Personal Data:** b Washington, DC, June 24, 1920; m 1950, Elaine; c Thomas J III, Ann E, Joan F, Paul E & Christopher. **Education:** Cath Univ, BS, 1940; Johns Hopkins Univ, MD, 1943; Am Bd Internal Med, dipl, 1956. **Professional Experience:** RETIRED; consult, Dept Planning & Policy Develop, Asn Am Med Col, 1990-1995; assoc vpres, Dept Planning & Policy Develop, Asn Am Med Col, 1986-1990; dir, Dept Planning & Policy Develop, Asn Am Med Col, 1976-1986; exec dir assembly life sci, Nat Acad Sci, Nat Res Coun, 1974-1976; assoc dir prog planning & eval, Nat Inst Healing, 1968-1974; chief, Div Res Facil & Resources, 1965-1968; mem staff, Off Dir, NIH, 1960-1965; res assoc, Sch Med, George Wash Univ, 1951-1965; investr, Lab Kidney & Electrolyte Physiol, Nat Heart Inst, 1950-1960; asst med, Col Physicians & Surgeons, Columbia Univ, 1947-1950; asst med, Col Med, NY Univ, 1945-1947. **Memberships:** Am Physiol Soc; Am Fedn Clin Res. **Research Statement & Publications:** Renal physiology, especially mechanisms for excretion of electrolytes; electrolyte physiology; clinical disorders of renal and electrolyte physiology; administration of research. **Mailing Address:** 10703 Weymouth St, Box 427, Garrett Park, MD 20896-0427. **Fax:** 301-949-8173. **E-Mail:** dreroica@erols.com

KENNEDY, THOMAS WILLIAM, CIVIL ENGINEERING. **Personal Data:** b Danville, Ill, January 7, 1938; div, c 2. **Education:** Univ Ill, BS, 1960, MS, 1962, PhD (civil eng), 1965. **Professional Experience:** ENG FOUND PROF, UNIV TEX, AUSTIN, 1985-; ASSOC DEAN ENG RES PLANNING, UNIV TEX, AUSTIN, 1979-; asst vpres res, Coun Advan Transp Studies, 1978-1979; dir, Coun Advan Transp Studies, 1975-1978; PROF CIVIL ENG, UNIV TEX, AUSTIN, 1974-; Hwy Res Bd, Nat Acad Sci-Nat Res Coun, 1965-; from asst prof to assoc prof, Univ Tex, Austin, 1965-1974; from asst to instr civil eng, Univ Ill, 1962-1965; mem, Transp Res Bd. **Memberships:** Am Soc Civil Engrs; Am Concrete Inst; Am Soc Testing & Mat; Asn Asphalt Paving Technologists. **Research Statement & Publications:** Materials; pavements; transportation; civil engineering. **Mailing Address:** Dept Civil Eng, Univ Tex, Austin, TX 78712-1076. **Fax:** 512-475-8744. **E-Mail:** twk@mail.utexas.edu

KENNEDY, TIMOTHY C, MECHANICAL ENGINEERING. **Education:** State Univ NY, Buffalo, BS, 1968; Stanford Univ, MS, 1969, PhD, 1972. **Professional Experience:** PROF, SOLID MECHANICS, DEPT MECH ENG, ORE STATE UNIV, as of 2006. **Mailing Address:** Dept Mech Eng Rogers Hall 204, Ore State Univ, Corvallis, OR 97331-6001. **Fax:** 541-737-2600. **E-Mail:** kennedy@engr.orst.edu

KENNEDY, VANCE CLIFFORD, GEOCHEMISTRY, HYDROLOGY. **Personal Data:** b Big Run, Pa, May 18, 1923; wid deceased; c Warren, Lynne, Mary, Nancy. **Education:** Pa State Univ, BS, 1948, MS, 1949; Univ Colo, PhD (geol), 1961. **Honors & Awards:** Distinguished Serrioe Award, US Dept Interior, 1994. **Professional Experience:** ANNUITANT, US GEOL SURV, 1984-; res geologist geochem & hydrol, US Geol Surv, 1960-1984; Geologist geochem, US Geol Surv, 1949-1952 & 1955-1960. **Memberships:** Amer Geophy Union. **Research Statement & Publications:** Geochemical prospecting; uranium geology and geochemistry; transport of stream sediment; effects of stream sediment on the chemistry of water; chemistry of rainfall-runoff. **Mailing Address:** 5052 Tully Rd, Modesto, CA 95356.

KENNEDY, W KEITH, ELECTRICAL ENGINEERING, SOLID STATE PHYSICS. **Personal Data:** b Phoenix, Ariz, September 19, 1943; m 1965, c 2. **Education:** Cornell Univ, BEE & MS, 1965, PhD (elec eng), 1968. **Professional Experience:** INTERIM CHIEF EXEC OFFICER, CNF INC, as of 2006; CHMN, CNF INC, 2004-; vchmn, CNF Inc, 2002-2004; dir, Transp/ Trucking, CNF Inc, as of 1996; pres & chief exec officer, Watkins-Johnson Co, 1988-2000; shareowner relations & planning Coord, Solid State Res & Develop Dept, Watkins-Johnson Co, 1986-1988; vpres devices group, Solid State Res & Develop Dept, Watkins-Johnson Co, 1978-1986; vpres, Solid State Res & Develop Dept, Watkins-Johnson Co, 1977; solid state div, Solid State Res & Develop Dept, Watkins-Johnson Co, 1974-1978; mgr, Solid State Res & Develop Dept, Watkins-Johnson Co, 1971-1974; mem tech staff, Watkins-Johnson Co, 1968-1969. **Memberships:** Inst Elec & Electronics Engrs. **Research Statement & Publications:** Microwave power generation and amplication with semiconductor devices; microwave integrated circuits; microwave systems. **Mailing Address:** CNF Inc, 2855 Campus Dr, Ste 300, San Mateo, CA 94403.

KENNEDY, WILBERT KEITH, AGRONOMY. **Personal Data:** b Vancouver, Wash, January 4, 1919; m 1941, c 2. **Education:** State Col Wash, BS, 1940; Cornell Univ, MSA, 1941, PhD (agron), 1947. **Professional Experience:** PROVOST EMER, CORNELL UNIV, as of 2003; provost univ, Res & Agr Exp Sta, Col Agr, Cornell Univ, 1978-1984; dean col, Res & Agr Exp Sta, Col Agr, Cornell Univ, 1972-1978; vprovost univ, Res & Agr Exp Sta, Col Agr, Cornell Univ, 1967-1972; assoc dean col, Res & Agr Exp Sta, Col Agr, Cornell Univ, 1965-1967; dir, Res & Agr Exp Sta, Col Agr, Cornell Univ, 1959-1965; assoc dir, Res & Agr Exp Sta, Col Agr, Cornell Univ, 1959; Fulbright res scholar & Guggenheim fel, 1956-1957; prof agron, NY State Col Agr & Life Sci, 1949-1984; from asst prof & asst agronomist to assoc prof & assoc agronomist, exp sta, State Col, Wash, 1947-1949; asst, Cornell Univ, 1940-1942 & 1946-1947. **Memberships:** Fel AAAS; fel Am Soc Agron; Sigma Xi. **Research Statement & Publications:** Chemistry; botany; factors influencing yield and nutritive value of farm crops; grazing management practices and their relationship to the behavior and grazing habits of cattle; measuring, harvesting and storage losses in hay and silage; accumulation of nitrates in forage plants; nitrate toxicity. **Mailing Address:** Off Provost, Cornell Univ, 300 Day Hall, Ithaca, NY 14853. **Fax:** 607-255-9924.

KENNEDY, WILLIAM E, HEALTH PHYSICS. **Education:** Kan Univ, BS 1973, MS (Nuclear Eng) 1975. **Professional Experience:** VPRES & SECY, DADE MOELLER & ASSOC INC, as of 2006; mem bd dirs, Dade Moeller & Assoc Inc, beginning 1995. **Mailing Address:** Dade Moeller & Assoc Inc, 1845 Terminal Dr, Ste 140, Richland, WA 99352. **Fax:** 509-946-4412.

KENNEDY, WILLIAM ROBERT, NEUROLOGY. **Personal Data:** b Chicago, Ill, November 2, 1927; m 1957, c 5. **Education:** Univ Ill, BS, 1951; Univ Wis, MS, 1952; Marquette Univ, MD, 1958. **Professional Experience:** PROF NEUROL, MED CTR, UNIV MINN, MINNEAPOLIS, 1971-; from asst prof to assoc prof, Med Ctr, Univ Minn, Minneapolis, 1964-1971; fel neurol, Mayo Clin, 1960-1964; fel internal med, Mayo Clin, 1959-1960. **Memberships:** AMA; Am Neurol Asn; Am Electroencephalog Soc; Am Asn Electromyog & Electrodiag (past pres); Am Acad Neurol. **Research Statement & Publications:** Clinical-pathological-physiological research on neuromuscular disorders; patho-physiology of cutaneous nerves. **Mailing Address:** Box 187 UMHC, 505 Essex St SE, Minneapolis, MN 55455. **E-Mail:** kenne001@umn.edu

KENNEL, CHARLES FREDERICK, PLASMA & SPACE PHYSICS, GLOBAL ENVIRONMENTAL SCIENCE. **Personal Data:** b Cambridge, Mass, August 20, 1939; m 1991, Ellen Lehmon; c 2. **Education:** Harvard Univ, AB, 1959; Princeton Univ, PhD (astrophys sci), 1964. **Honors & Awards:** Fulbright Sr lectr, Brazil, 1985; Fairchild Prof, Calif Inst Technol, 1987; Aurelio Peccei Prize for Environ Sci, Accademia Lincei (Ital Acad Sci), Rome, 1996; Distinguished Serv Medal, NASA, 1996; The James Clerk Maxwell Prize, Am Phys Soc, 1997; Hannes Alfven Medal, Europ Geophys Soc, 1998; William T Pecora Award for Group Achievement, Topex/Poseidon Team, 1998. **Professional Experience:** Bd mem, Calif Climate Action Registry, 2001-2003; Pew Oceans Comn, 2000-; vis Comt Jet Propulsion, Calif Inst Technol 2000-; bd trustees exec comt, Univ Corp Atmospheric Res, 2000-; bd trustees, San Diego Natural History Museum, 1999-2002; dir, dean & vice Chancellor, Marine Sci Div, Univ Calif, San Diego, 1998-; DIR, GRAD DEPT, SCRIPPS INST OCEANOG, UNIV CALIF, SAN DIEGO, 1998-; Nasa-Goddard Space Flight Ctr, 1998-; chair, Comt Global Change Res, 1998-2001; bd trustees, Joint Oceanog Inst, 1998-; public policy comt, Consortium Ocean Res & Educ, 1998; bd dir, Cecil H & Ida M Green Found, 1998-; eval comt, Nat Space Develop Agency of Japan, 1998-; chair, Nasa Adv Coun, 1998-; found bd trustees, Univ Calif, San Diego, 1998-; exec vice chancellor, Inst Geophys & Planetary Physics, Univ Calif, 1996-1998; assoc adminr, Mission Planet Earth, NASA, 1994-1996; bd adv, Geophys Inst, Univ Alaska, 1991-; mem, Fusion Policy Adv Comt, Dept Energy, 1990; vis scientist, Space Res Ctr, Moscow, 1988-; Guggenheim fel, 1988; vis scholar, Univ Alaska, 1988, 1989 & 1990; Space & Earth Sci adv comt, NASA, 1987-1989; Fairchild prof, Calif Inst Tech, 1987; chmn, Inst Geophys & Planetary Physics, 1983-1986; mem, Space Sci Bd, Nat Acad Sci-Nat Res Coun, 1977-1980; chmn, Comt Space Physics, 1977-1980; vis prof, Ctr Phys Theory, Polytech Sch, Paris, 1974-1975; PROF PHYSICS, UNIV CALIF, LOS ANGELES, 1971-; MEM, INST GEOPHYS & PLANETARY PHYSICS, 1971-; mem sci adv group, NASA, 1971-1972; mem, Physics res eval group, Air Force Off Sci Res, 1970-1978; Alfred P Sloan Found fac fel, 1968-1970; consult, TRW Systs Group, Calif, 1967-; assoc prof, Inst Geophys & Planetary Physics, 1967-1971; prin res scientist, Avco-Everett Res Lab, 1966-1967; NSF fel, 1965-1966; vis scientist, Int Ctr Theoret Physics, Trieste, 1965-1966; staff mem, Avco-Everett Res Lab, 1964-1965; asst res scientist, Avco-Everett Res Lab, 1960-1961; assoc dir, Inst Plasma Physics & Fusion Res, Univ Calif, Los Angeles. **Memberships:** Fel Am Phys Soc; fel Am Geophys Union; Am Acad Arts & Sci; AAAS; Int Acad Astronaut (Basic Sci); Int Union Radio Sci; Comn H; Nat Acad Sci; fel, Calif Coun Sci & Technol (2000). **Research Statement & Publications:** Plasma turbulence theory; solar system and astrophysical plasma physics. **Mailing Address:** Scripps Inst Oceanog, 9500 Gilman Dr 0210, La Jolla, CA 92093-0210. **E-Mail:** ckennel@ucsd.edu

KENNEL, JOHN MAURICE, AEROSPACE NAVIGATION & GUIDANCE SYSTEM DEVELOPMENT, STAR TRACKERS & INERTIAL INSTRUMENT DEVELOPMENT. **Personal Data:** b Sioux City, Iowa, October 7, 1927; m 1952, Clara; c Susan J, Sandra L (Camp), John F & William P. **Education:** Miami Univ, Ohio, AB, 1948; Univ Tex, PhD (physics), 1955. **Professional Experience:** RETIRED; res eng star trackers, Astro Inertial Navigation Res & Develop, Northrop Corp, 1989-1993; eng mgr, Astro Inertial Navigation Res & Develop, Northrop Corp, 1985-1989; staff engr accurancy assurance, Peacekeeper MX ICBM Missile Guid Inertial Instrument & Syst Develop, 1975-1985; mgr liquid crystal display design & develop, Autonetics Div, Rockwell Int, 1971-1975; proj mgr microelectronic process & device res & develop, Autonetics Div, 1967-1971; res specialist inertial navig & proj mgr N 40 navig syst develop, 1964-1967; sr scientist navig req definition, Autonetics Div, 1962-1964; mgr adv inertial navig & missile guid syst, Autonetics Div, 1960-1962; mgr gyro & accelerometer res, Autonetics Div, 1958-1960; res specialist inertial navig, Autonetics Div, 1955-1958; res eng, Aerophys Lab, N Am Aviation, 1951-1952; physicist, US Naval Ord Lab, Md, 1949-1951. **Memberships:** AAAS; Am Phys Soc; Am Inst Aeronaut & Astronaut; Inst Navig. **Research Statement & Publications:** Precision measurement and the development of precision instruments; applications to navigation, missile guidance, attitude measurement and control; development of precision accelerometers, gyroscopes, star trackers and ancillary equipment. **Mailing Address:** 11591 Suburnas Way, Santa Ana, CA 92705. **E-Mail:** kennel@cok.net

KENNEL, STEPHEN JOHN, TUMOR IMMUNOLOGY, IMAGING. **Personal Data:** b Peoria, Ill, January 15, 1945; m 1966, Ellen; c Jennifer, Jill & Ted. **Education:** Univ Ill, BS, 1967; Univ Calif, San Diego, MS, 1968, PhD (chem), 1971. **Professional Experience:** Associate Professor, University of TN Graduate School of Medicine, 2005-; Distinguished Sr. Staff Scientist Oak Ridge National Lab, 1999-2005; SR STAFF SCIENTIST, BIOL DIV, OAK RIDGE NAT LAB, 1981-1999; staff mem, Biol Div, Oak Ridge Nat Lab, 1976-1981; res assoc, Dept Immunopath, 1974-1976; res asst, Dept Exp Path, Scripps Clin & Res Found, 1973-1974; res fel, Dept Exp Path, Scripps Clin & Res Found, 1971-1973; USPHS Grad fel trainee fel, 1967-1971. **Memberships:** Am Asn Cancer Res. **Research Statement & Publications:** Antibody directed specific radioimmunotherapy of malignancies; vascular targeting; phage display and antibody engineering. **Mailing Address:** Univ Tenn Graduate Sch Med, 1924 Alcoa Hwy, Knoxville, TN 37920. **Fax:** 865-544-6865. **E-Mail:** skennel@mc.utmck.edu

KENNEL, WILLIAM E(LMER), CHEMICAL ENGINEERING. **Personal Data:** b St Louis, Mo, August 11, 1917; m 1939, c 2. **Education:** Univ Ill, BS, 1940; Mass Inst Technol, MS, 1947, DSc(chem eng), 1949. **Professional Experience:** EXEC VPRES & DIR, AMOCO CHEM CORP, 1975-; vpres mkt & dir, Amoco Chem Corp, 1972-1975; group vpres & dir, Amoco Chem Corp, 1970-1972; vpres plastics, Amoco Chem Corp, 1968-1970; vpres & dir, Amoco Chem Corp, 1967-1968; vpres res & develop & dir, Amoco Chem Corp, 1961-1967; dir chem res, Amoco Chem Corp, 1960-1961; mgr tech develop, Amoco Chem Corp, 1957-1960; res sect leader, Stand Oil Co, Ind, 1952-1957; res group leader, Stand Oil Co, Ind, 1951-1952; chem engr, Stand Oil Co, Ind, 1948-1951; Chem engr, A E Staley Mfg Co, 1939-1941. **Memberships:** Am Chem Soc; Am Inst Chem Engrs. **Research Statement & Publications:** Technical development of petrochemicals.

KENNELL, DAVID EPPERSON, MOLECULAR BIOLOGY. **Personal Data:** b Syracuse, NY, May 23, 1932; m Tanner; c Charles, Frederick & Laura. **Education:** Univ Calif, Berkeley, AB, 1954, PhD (biophysics), 1959. **Professional Experience:** PROF EMER 1998-; mem, Microbial Physiol Study Sect, NIH, 1981-1985; prof microbiol, Sch Med, Wash Univ, 1973-1998; NIH res career develop award, 1969-1974; from instr to assoc prof, Sch Med, Wash Univ, 1961-1973; res assoc, Mass Inst Technol, 1960-1961; res fel bact & immunol, Harvard Med Sch, 1959-1960; Nat Cancer Inst fel, 1957-1961; Res engr mineral tech, Univ Calif, Berkeley, 1956-1957. **Memberships:** Am Soc Biol Chem. **Research Statement & Publications:** Ribonucleic acid metabolism in bacteria and reaction mechanisms of ribonucleases; energy metabolism in cultured cells. **Mailing Address:** Dept Molecular Microbiol, Box 8230 Wash Univ Sch Med, St Louis, MO 63110-1093. **Fax:** 314-362-1232. **E-Mail:** kennell@borcim.wustl.edu

KENNELL, JOHN HAWKS, PEDIATRICS, DEVELOPMENTAL-BEHAVIORAL PEDIATRICS. **Personal Data:** b Reading, Pa, January 9, m Margaret; c David, Susan & Jack. **Education:** Univ Rochester, BS, 1944, MD, 1946. **Honors & Awards:** George Armstrong Award, Ambulatory Pediat Asn; Aldrich Award, Am Acad Pediat. **Professional Experience:** PROF EMER PEDIAT, CASE WESTERN RES UNIV, as of 2003; Dir, Neonatal Nurseries, Univ Hosp, Cleveland, 1982-1967; Child Develop, Rainbow Babies & Childrens Hosp, 1980-; prof pediat, Case Western Res Univ, beginning 1973; consult, Headstart, 1968-; Nat Inst Child Health & Human Develop spec res fel, Univ London, 1966-1967; dir, Pediat Clin, 1960-1970; ASSOC PEDIATRICIAN, CASE WESTERN RES UNIV, 1956-; from asst prof to assoc prof, Pediat Clin, 1955-1973; dir, Family Clin, Case Western Res Univ, 1952-1960; sr instr, Pediat Clin, 1952-1955; dir dept, Children's Hosp Med Ctr, 1952; chief med resident, Children's Hosp Med Ctr, 1951; chief resident med out-patient dept, Children's Hosp Med Ctr, 1950; asst resident, Children's Hosp Med Ctr, 1949-1950; Intern pediat, Children's Hosp, Boston, 1946-1947. **Memberships:** Am Acad Pediat; Am Pediat Soc; Asn Child Care Hosps (vpres 1973-1975); Soc Res Child Develop; Ambulatory Pediat Asn (pres 1970); Soc Develop Behav Pediat (pres 1989). **Research Statement & Publications:** Child development; medical education; social and psychological factors in medicine; effects of mother-infant early contact on maternal attachment; effects of perinatal death on parents; effect of supportive companion during labor and delivery; parent to infant bonding for full term, premature, sick, malformed infants and stillborn and perinatal death; effects of continuous emotional support by a doula during labor on early and later mother-infant interaction; on mother-partner relationship and on the infant's secure attachment. **Mailing Address:** Rainbow Babies & Childrens Hosp, 2101 Adelbert Rd, Cleveland, OH 44106. **E-Mail:** jhk3@po.cwru.edu

KENNELLEY, JAMES A, METALLURGY, EXECUTIVE EDUCATION & DEVELOPMENT. **Personal Data:** b Rochester, NY, August 23, 1928; m 1955, Sarah T Wade; c Kevin, Mark & Judith Ann. **Education:** Col Wooster, BA, 1945; Mich State Univ, PhD (chem), 1955. **Professional Experience:** CONSULT, 1992-, assoc dir exec educ, Columbia Bus Sch, 1983-1992; pres, Direct Reduction Corp, 1978-1983; group vpres, Que Iron & Titanium Corp, 1975-1978; vpres, Que Iron & Titanium Corp, 1973-1975; asst to pres, Que Iron & Titanium Corp, 1965-1973; tech dir div, Mallinckrodt, Inc, 1962-1965; mgr res, Mallinckrodt, Inc, 1959-1962; group leader res, Mallinckrodt, Inc, 1957-1959; Res chemist uranium, Mallinckrodt, Inc, 1955-1957. **Memberships:** Sr mem Am Chem Soc; Sr mem Am Soc Metals; Sr mem Am Inst Mining, Metall & Petrol Engrs. **Research Statement & Publications:** Rare earths; uranium chemistry and metallurgy; titanium; raw materials; ilmenite smelting; titanium dioxide pigments; direct reduction of iron ore. **Mailing Address:** 8774 SE Riverfront Terr, Tequesta, FL 33469-1813. **E-Mail:** jimkennel@msn.com

KENNELLEY, KEVIN JAMES, NONMETALLICS, ELASTOMERICS. **Personal Data:** b St Louis, Mo, August 6, 1958; m 1982, Emily J Cromley; c Robert, Sarah & Natalie. **Education:** Univ Okla, BS, 1980, MS, 1985, PhD (metall eng & mat sci), 1986. **Honors & Awards:** AB Cambell Award, Nat Asn Corrosion Engrs, 1993, 1994. **Professional Experience:** Corrosion specialist, Mat Sect, Arco Explor & Prod Technol, 1994-1995; MGR TECHNOL SUPPORT SERV, ARCO INDONESIA, 1991-; Prin res engr, Mat Sect, Arco Explor & Prod Technol, 1990-1994; Prog chmn, Ann Conf Nat Asn Corrosion Engrs, 1988-1989 & 1989-1990; res specialist, Mat Sect, Exxon Prod Res Co, 1986-1990; Sr field engr, Duncan Dist, Schlumberger Well Serv, 1980-1982. **Memberships:** Sigma Xi; Metall Soc; Am Soc Metals; Nat Asn Corrosion Engrs. **Research Statement & Publications:** Controlling corrosion of materials in oil and gas production that are exposed to high temperature, high pressure sour hydrocarbon fluids; cathodic protection; nonmetallics. **Mailing Address:** ARCO Explor & Prod Technol, 2300 W Plano Pkwy, Plano, TX 75075. **Fax:** 214-754-3565. **E-Mail:** kkennel@arco.fs.com

KENNELLY, MARY MARINA, INORGANIC CHEMISTRY, ORGANIC CHEMISTRY. **Personal Data:** b Chicago, Ill, November 12, 1919. **Education:** Mundelein Col, BS, 1942; Univ Notre Dame, MS, 1950, PhD (chem), 1959. **Professional Experience:** RETIRED; Seattle, 1962; Fla State, 1961; NSF sci fac summer fels, London, 1960; prof chem, Mundelein Col, 1959-1974; chmn dept, Mundelein Col, 1959-1969; asst prof, Mundelein Col, 1950-1957. **Memberships:** AAAS; Am Chem Soc; Nat Sci Teachers Asn; Sigma Xi. **Research Statement & Publications:** Coordination chemistry; infrared studies of metal complexes of amino acids. **Mailing Address:** Five Forest Park E, Jacksonville, IL 62650.

KENNELLY, WILLIAM J, CHEMISTRY. **Personal Data:** b Cleveland, Ohio, August 22, 1949; m 1977, c 2. **Education:** Mass Inst Technol, BS, 1970; Northwestern Univ, PhD (chem), 1975; Temple Univ, MBA, 1986. **Professional Experience:** DIR, TECHNOL & OPERS, CYPRUS AMAX POLYMER ADDITIVES GROUP, ANN ARBOR, MICH, 1987-; sr res chemist, Amax Mat Res Ctr, 1984-1987; res scientist, Rohm & Haas Co, 1977-1984; fel, Mass Inst Technol, 1976-1977; fel, Univ NDak, Grand Forks, 1975-1976. **Memberships:** Am Chem Soc; Soc Plastics Eng; Am Soc Testing & Mat. **Research Statement & Publications:** Polymer additives especially flame retardants and smoke suppressants. **Mailing Address:** 2481 Windmill Way, Saline, MI 48176.

KENNER, MORTON ROY, MATHEMATICS. **Personal Data:** b Rochester, NY, June 10, 1925; m 1954, c 2. **Education:** Univ Rochester, BA, 1949; Univ Minn, MA, 1951; PhD (math, math ed), 1958. **Professional Experience:** PROF EMER MATH, NORTHWEST MO STATE UNIV, 1987-; chmn div math & comput sci, Northwest Mo State Univ, 1978-1987; prof math & chmn dept, Northwest Mo State Univ, beginning 1970; prof math & chmn dept, Stephens Col, 1967-1970; dir nairobi math ctr, Kenya, 1964 & 1965; consult, opers res group, Ohio State Univ, 1960-; dir develop proj sec math, Southern Ill Univ, 1958-1967; from asst prof to assoc prof math, Southern Ill Univ, 1952-1967. **Memberships:** Hist Sci Soc; Math Asn Am; Sigma Xi. **Research Statement & Publications:** Foundations of mathematics; systems models; mathematical education; history of mathematics. **Mailing Address:** Dept Math, NW Mo State Univ, 800 Univ Dr, Maryville, MO 64468-6001.

KENNERLY, GEORGE WARREN, INDUSTRIAL CHEMISTRY. **Personal Data:** b Boston, Mass, March 11, 1922; m 1949, Sarah; c 2. **Education:** Harvard Univ, BS, 1944, MA,

1947, PhD, 1949. **Professional Experience:** RETIRED; dir, Am Cyanamid Co, 1968-1984; mgr, 1959-1968; group leader, 1954-1959; res chemist, 1949-1954. **Memberships:** AAAS; Am Chem Soc. **Research Statement & Publications:** Auto-oxidation; peroxide chemistry; photochemistry; electrochemistry; luminescence; reaction kinetics. **Mailing Address:** 4910 Mill Creek Rd, Dallas, TX 75244. **E-Mail:** gwkennerly@aol.com

KENNET, HAIM, aeronautics, astronautics; deceased, see previous edition for last biography

KENNETT, JAMES PETER, MICROPALEONTOLOGY, PALEOECOLOGY. **Personal Data:** b Wellington, NZ, September 3, 1940; American citizen; m 1964, Diana; c Douglas & Mary. **Education:** New Zealand Univ, BSc, 1962; Victoria Univ, Hons, 1963, PhD (geol), 1965, DSc, 1976. **Honors & Awards:** McKay Hammer Award, Geol Soc NZ, 1968. **Professional Experience:** PROF, DEPT GEOL SCI, UNIV CALIF, SANTA BARBARA, 1987-; dir, Marine Sci Inst, Univ Calif, Santa Barbara, 1987-1997; prof, grad sch oceanog, Univ RI, 1974-1987; assoc prof, Grad Sch Oceanog, Univ RI, 1970-1974; asst prof, Fla State Univ, 1968-1970; NSF fel micropaleont, Allan Hancock Found, Univ Southern Calif, 1966-1968; sci officer, NZ Oceanog Inst, 1965-1966. **Memberships:** AAAS; Geol Soc Am; Am Asn Petrol Geol; Soc Econ Paleont & Mineral; Int Quaternary Asn.; fel Am Geophys Union. **Research Statement & Publications:** Marine geology; foraminiferal ecology and paleoecology; stratigraphic paleontology and stratigraphy of the Cenozoic; climate evolution of the cenozoic, including the quatenam; role of methone hydrates in climate change and paleoceanography. **Mailing Address:** Dept Geol Sci, Univ Calif, Webb Hall 1037A, Santa Barbara, CA 93106. **Fax:** 805-893-2314. **E-Mail:** kennett@geol.ucsb.edu

KENNETT, ROGER H, GENETICS, IMMUNOLOGY. **Personal Data:** b Lakewood, NJ, December 27, 1940; m 1966, Carol; c Ted, David & Timothy. **Education:** Eastern Col, AB, 1964; Princeton Univ, PhD (biochem sci), 1969; Univ Pa, MSEd, 1988. **Professional Experience:** DEPT CHAIR CELL BIOL, RUTH KRAFT STROHSCHEIN PROF BIOL, WHEATON COL, as of 2005; RUTH KRAFT STROHSCHEIN PROF BIOL, WHEATON COL, as of 2004; assoc prof genetics, Sch Med, Univ PA, beginning 1980; asst prof, Human Genetics Cell Ctr, 1976-1980; dir, Human Genetics Cell Ctr, 1973-1996; res officer, Genetics Lab, Oxford Univ, 1973-1976; demonstr, Genetics Lab, Oxford Univ, 1972-1973. **Memberships:** Fel AAAS; Am Asn Immunologists; Am Soc Microbiol. **Research Statement & Publications:** Use of combination of immunological, biochemical and molecular genetic techniques to study molecular changes related to oncogenesis, and to the growth and differentiation of human neuroblastoma cells. **Mailing Address:** Dept Biol, Wheaton Col, 501 Col Ave, Wheaton, IL 60187-5593. **Fax:** 630-752-5996. **E-Mail:** roger.h.kennett@wheaton.edu

KENNETT, TERENCE JAMES, NUCLEAR PHYSICS. **Personal Data:** b Toronto, Ont, August 8, 1927; m 1949, c 2. **Education:** McMaster Univ, BSc, 1953, MSc, 1954, PhD (physics), 1956. **Professional Experience:** PROF EMER ENG PHYSICS, McMASTER UNIV, as of 2003; from asst prof to prof eng physics & physics, McMaster Univ, 1959-1976; assoc physicist, Argonne Nat Lab, 1957-1959; fel physics, McMaster Univ, 1956-1957. **Memberships:** Am Phys Soc. **Research Statement & Publications:** Neutron physics; decay scheme studies; neutron capture gamma rays; instrumentation and detector development. **Mailing Address:** Dept Physics & Astron, McMaster Univ 1280 Main St W, Hamilton, ON L8S 4K1, Can. **E-Mail:** Kennett@mcmaster.ca

KENNEY, CHARLES S, MATHEMATICS. **Education:** Univ Md, PhD. **Professional Experience:** RES ENGR, DEPT ELEC & COMPUT ENG, UNIV CALIF, as of 2004. **Mailing Address:** Univ Calif, Dept Elec & Comput Eng, Rm 3102 Eng I, Santa Barbara, CA 93106-9560. **Fax:** 805-893-3262. **E-Mail:** kenney@ece.ucsb.edu

KENNEY, CHRIS, PHYSICS. **Professional Experience:** AT DIV RES, SLAC, STANFORD UNIV, as of 1999. **Mailing Address:** SLAC, PO Box 78, Stanford, CA 94305. **E-Mail:** kenney@slac.stanford.edu

KENNEY, DONALD J, PHYSICAL CHEMISTRY. **Personal Data:** b Chicago, Ill, August 26, 1925; m 1948, c 7. **Education:** Loyola Univ, Ill, BS, 1949; Iowa State Univ, PhD (phys chem), 1953. **Professional Experience:** RETIRED; prof chem, Univ Detroit, 1954-1994; dir govt projs, 1954-1965; res engr, Steel Div, Ford Motor Co, 1953-1954. **Memberships:** Am Chem Soc. **Research Statement & Publications:** Iron complexes; metallurgy. **Mailing Address:** 1840 E Morten Ave No 240, Phoenix, AZ 85020.

KENNEY, GERALD, SURGERY, MEDICINE. **Personal Data:** b Seattle, Wash, December 14, 1934; c 4. **Education:** Notre Dame Univ, BS, 1956; Northwestern Univ, MD, 1960. **Professional Experience:** Overlake Urol, Inc, beginning 1985; treas, Seattle Surg Soc, 1985-1986; med rev bd, Nat Transplant Prog, beginning 1984; bd dirs, Northwest Kidney Ctr, beginning 1985; Lake Wash Kidney Ctr, beginning 1984; pres, Northwest Urol Soc, 1984; Urol Adv Coun, Nat Kidney Found, 1982-1985; secy-treas, Northwest Urol Soc, 1980-1983; Belleuve Urol, Inc, 1972-1985; clin instr urol, beginning 1971; chief transplantation serv, Swed Hosp Med Ctr, beginning 1971; priv pract, OA Nelson Med Group, 1971-1972; asst prof, State Univ NY, 1968-1971; fel, Inst Urol, Univ London, 1967-1968; resident gen surg, 1961-1962 & urol, 1964-1967; gen med officer, Ft Sam Houston, 1962 & Little Rock AFB, 1962 & 1964; intern, Cook Co Hosp, 1960-1961; ASST PROF, UNIV WASH; PVT PRACT, UROLOGY RESOURCE CTR, SEATTLE. **Memberships:** Am Med Asn; Am Urol Asn; Am Col Surgeons; Am Soc Transplant Surgens; Soc Univ Urol; Soc Acad Surg; Am Soc Clin Urologists; Int Urol Soc. **Research Statement & Publications:** Evaluation of diagnostic modalities for urological cancer which includes transrectal prostatic ultrasound and serum blood studies; methods for early detection of organ transplantation rejection. **Mailing Address:** 1560 N 115th St Ste 209, Seattle, WA 98133.

KENNEY, JAMES FRANCIS, GEOPHYSICS. **Personal Data:** b Buffalo, NY, September 3, 1926; m 1957, c 3. **Education:** Union Col, NY, BS, 1951; Univ NMex, MS, 1953, PhD (physics), 1957. **Professional Experience:** PROF, CITY UNIV, 1993-; chief, Eng Missiles Systs, 1990-1993; chief scientist, radiation physics, 1979-1990; mgr, radiation physics, 1976-1979; resources develop mgr, Laser & Environ Sci Lab, 1975-1976; mgr, Laser & Environ Sci Lab, 1973-1975; head, Environ Sci Dept, 1970-1973; head, Geoastrophys Dept, 1969-1970; staff mem geoastrophys res, Boeing Sci Res Lab, Boeing Aerospace Co, 1960-1969; instr, Univ NMex, 1959-1960; res fel, Univ NMex, 1958-1959; res fel, Lab Cosmic Physics, La Paz, 1958-1959; res assoc physics, Univ NMex, 1957-1958; BSD technol mgr, Boeing Aerospace Co. **Memberships:** Am Inst Aeronaut & Astronaut; AAAS; Am Geophys Union. **Research Statement & Publications:** Cosmic rays; ionospheric properties and radio propagation; nuclear, space and solar physics; magnetic fields and micropulsations; environmental science, urban studies; remote sensing, laser physics; military sciences; radiation physics; countermeasures. **Mailing Address:** 26203 Marine View Dr SW, Kent, WA 98032.

KENNEY, JAMES FRANKLIN, POLYMER SYNTHESIS. **Personal Data:** b Richmond, Va, August 4, 1934. **Education:** Howard Univ, BS, 1956, MS, 1958; Univ Akron, PhD (polymer chem), 1964. **Professional Experience:** MGR POLYMER & ANALYTICAL CHEM, VISTAKON DIV, JOHNSON & JOHNSON VISION PRODS, INC, 1990-; mgr polymers & mat sci, Johnson & Johnson, Inc, 1979-1990; sr proj leader, Johnson & Johnson 1978-1979; res assoc, Plastics Div, Allied Chem Corp, 1968-1971 & M & T Chem, Inc, 1971-1978; res chemist, Chemstrand Res Ctr, Inc, 1964-1968; res fel, Inst Rubber Res, Akron, 1961-1964; Res chemist, US Air Force Mat Lab, 1958-1961. **Memberships:** Am Chem Soc. **Research Statement & Publications:** Synthesis, structure, property and performance of polymers; adhesion to skin; adhesive tapes; emulsion, condensation and addition polymerization; graft and block copolymers; polyblends; impact modification; processing characteristics of polymers; economic and technical evaluation of research; developing catalysts for polyesters and polyurethanes; emulsion and hot melt adhesives; hydrogel soft contact lens materials; synthesis and evaluation; acrylic adhesives. **Mailing Address:** 13153 Cricket Cove Rd N, Jacksonville, FL 32224.

KENNEY, MALCOLM EDWARD, ORGANOSILICON CHEMISTRY. **Personal Data:** b Berkeley, Calif, October 7, 1928; m 1951. **Education:** Univ Redlands, BS, 1950; Cornell Univ, PhD (chem), 1954. **Professional Experience:** HINMAN HURLBUT PROF CHEM, CASE WESTERN RES UNIV, 1991-; PROF CHEM, CASE WESTERN RES UNIV, 1966-; John Teagle prof fel, 1964-1966; from instr to assoc prof, Case Western Res Univ, 1956-1966; fel, Cornell Univ, 1954; asst, Cornell Univ, 1950-1952. **Memberships:** Am Chem Soc. **Research Statement & Publications:** Metal complexes and inorganic polymers. **Mailing Address:** Dept Chem, Case Western Res Univ, 2040 Adelbert Rd, Cleveland, OH 44106-7078. **E-Mail:** mek9@case.edu

KENNEY, MARGARET JUNE, MATHEMATICS. **Personal Data:** b Boston, Mass, June 7, 1935. **Education:** Boston Col, Chestnut Hill, BS, 1957, MA, 1959; Boston Univ, PhD (math), 1977. **Honors & Awards:** Glenn Gilbert Nat Leadership Award; Nat Coun Supvrs Math, 2001. **Professional Experience:** ASST DIR, MATHEMATICS INST, BOSTON COL, as of 2003; PROF MATH, BOSTON COL, 1992-; from instr to assoc prof, Boston Col, 1959-1992; asst dir, Math Inst, Boston Col, 1957-. **Memberships:** Nat Coun Teachers Math; Math Asn Am; Am Math Soc; Nat Coun Supvrs Math; Asn Women Math. **Research Statement & Publications:** Mathematics education at the pre-college level; number theoretic applications of mathematics to art; discrete mathematics for pre-college students. **Mailing Address:** Math Inst, Boston Col, Chestnut Hill, MA 02467-3814. **Fax:** 617-552-3789. **E-Mail:** peg.kenney@bc.edu

KENNEY, MARY ALICE, NUTRITIONAL STATUS, NUTRITION & IMMUNOCOMPETENCE, MINERAL NUTRITION & BONE. **Personal Data:** b Lubbock, Tex, May 16, 1938. **Education:** Tex Tech Univ, BS, 1958; Iowa State Univ, MS, 1960, PhD (nutrit), 1963. **Professional Experience:** PROF EMER HUMAN ENVIRON SCI & FOOD SCI, 2001-; prof home econ, Univ Ark, 1985-2001; prof food, nutrit & inst admin, Okla State Univ, 1978-1984; prof food & nutrit, Tex Tech Univ, 1973-1978; from asst prof to assoc prof, Iowa State Univ, 1963-1973; Instr nutrit, Purdue Univ, 1960-1961. **Memberships:** AAAS; Am Inst Nutrit; NY Acad Sci; Am Dietetic Asn; Am Pub Health Asn; Am Col Nutrit. **Research Statement & Publications:** Immunoglobulin levels; assessment of nutritional status; magnesium, calcium, boron, zinc nutrition. **Mailing Address:** Sch Human Environ Sci, Univ Ark, 118 HOEC Bldg, Fayetteville, AR 72701. **E-Mail:** kenney@uark.edu

KENNEY, NANCY JANE, PSYCHOBIOLOGY, BEHAVIORAL ENDOCRINOLOGY. **Personal Data:** b Wilkes-Barre, Pa. **Education:** Wilkes Col, BA, 1970; Univ Va, MA, 1972, PhD (psychol), 1974. **Professional Experience:** ACTG CHAIR, PSYCHOL, UNIV WASH, 1998-; ASSOC PROF PSYCHOL & WOMEN STUDIES, UNIV WASH, 1983-; prin investr, Nat Inst Arthritis, Metab & Digestive Dis, 1978-1984; asst prof, Univ Wash, 1976-1982; NIH res fel, Nat Inst Child Health & Human Develop, 1974-1976; fel neurol sci, Univ Pa, 1974-1976. **Memberships:** Soc Neuroscience; Am Psychol Asn; Nat Women Studies Asn. **Research Statement & Publications:** Neural, endocrine and behavioral control of food intake and body weight. **Mailing Address:** Grad Sch, Univ Wash, 3900 Seventh Ave Northeast, Seattle, WA 98195-0001. **Fax:** 206-685-3157. **E-Mail:** nkenney@u.washington.edu

KENNEY, ROBERT WARNER, HIGH ENERGY PHYSICS, PARTICLE PHYSICS. **Personal Data:** b Portland, Ore, November 9, 1922; m 1950, Alice; c Jane & Wanda. **Education:** Univ Calif, Los Angeles, BA, 1944; Calif Inst Technol, BS, 1947; Univ Calif, PhD (physics), 1952. **Professional Experience:** EMER SR PHYSICIST, LAWRENCE BERKELEY LAB, UNIV CALIF, BERKELEY, 1990-; sr staff physicist, Lawrence Berkeley Lab, Univ Calif, Berkeley, 1953-1990; mem staff, Los Alamos Sci Lab, 1952-1953; consult, Marquardt Corp; staff mem, NASA; lectr, Univ Calif, Berkeley. **Memberships:** Am Phys Soc; AAAS; Sigma Xi. **Research Statement & Publications:** High energy particle physics; electromagnetic interactions at high energies; particle accelerators; pion nuclear interaction; weak interaction and symmetry principles; double beta decay and nature of the neutrino. **Mailing Address:** 122 Scenic Dr, LBNL-Physics 50-4037A - 5230, Orinda, CA 94563. **Fax:** 510-486-5401. **E-Mail:** kenney@lbl.gov

KENNEY, T CAMERON, CIVIL & GEOTECHNICAL ENGINEERING. **Personal Data:** b Montreal, Que, March 26, 1931; m 1960, c 4. **Education:** McGill Univ, BEng, 1953; Univ London, DIC, 1954, MSc, 1956, PhD (civil eng), 1967. **Honors & Awards:** Walter L Huber Prize, Am Soc Civil Engrs, 1967; First Bjerrum Lectr, Norweg Geotech Soc, 1975; Silver Jubilee Medal, Govt Can, 1977; Keefer Medal, Can Soc Civil Eng, 1983; Can Geotech Prize, Can Geotech Soc, 1985. **Professional Experience:** PROF EMER CIVIL ENG, UNIV TORONTO, as of 2000; eng consult, beginning 1968; prof civil eng, Univ Toronto, beginning 1968; chmn dept, Univ Toronto, 1968-1974; assoc prof civil eng, Univ Toronto, 1967-1968; res engr, Norweg Geotech Inst, Oslo, 1961-1967; geotech engr, Acres Ltd, Niagara Falls, Ont, 1956-1961. **Memberships:** Fel Eng Inst Can; Can Geotech Soc (pres 1974-1976). **Research Statement & Publications:** Engineering properties of natural soils; landslides; engineering geology; dams; tailings dams. **Mailing Address:** Dept Civil Eng, Univ Toronto, Toronto, ON M5S 1A1, Can.

KENNEY, VINCENT PAUL, PHYSICS, ELEMENTARY PARTICLE PHYSICS. **Personal Data:** b New York, NY, September 15, 1927; m 1954, Margaret; c Ann, Charles, John & Mary E. **Education:** Iona Col, AB, 1948; Fordham Univ, MS, 1950, PhD (physics), 1956. **Professional Experience:** Sr physicist, Dept Energy, 1986-1988; life mem, Clare Hall, Cambridge Univ, as of 1985; sr vis fel, Cavendish Lab, Cambridge Univ, 1982-1983; Fermi Nat Accelerator Lab, 1971-; PROF EMER PHYSICS, UNIV NOTRE DAME, as of 1966; Argonne Nat Lab, 1965-1982; assoc prof, Univ Notre Dame, 1963-1966; European Orgn Nuclear Res, 1961-1962 & 1982-1985; fel, Max Planck Inst Physics & Astrophys, Munich, 1961-1962 & 1972; Oak Ridge Inst Nuclear Studies, 1958-1964; vis physicist, Brookhaven Nat Lab, 1957-; from prof to assoc prof physics, Univ Ky, 1955-1963; res assoc, Brookhaven Nat Lab, 1953-1955. **Memberships:** Fel Am Phys Soc; AAAS; Sigma Xi. **Research Statement & Publications:** High energy particle physics; energy studies. **Mailing Address:** Dept Physics, Univ Notre Dame, 413 Nieuwland Sci, Notre Dame, IN 46556. **E-Mail:** vincent.p.kenney.1@nd.edu

KENNEY, WILLIAM CLARK, BIOCHEMISTRY, PROTEIN SCIENCE. **Personal Data:** b Grand Forks, NDak, February 25, 1940. **Education:** Carleton Col, BA, 1962; Univ Calif, Berkeley, PhD (biochem), 1967. **Honors & Awards:** Alcoholism Res Award, Vet Admin, 1979. **Professional Experience:** Dir, Protein Chem, beginning 1992; lab head, Protein Chem, 1989-1992; RES SCIENTIST, AMGEN, THOUSAND OAKS, CALIF, 1984-; res chemist, Vet Admin Med Ctr, 1979-1984; adj assoc prof biochem med, Univ Calif, San Francisco, 1979-1984; asst & assoc res biochemist, Univ Calif, San Francisco, 1970-1979; fel, Am Cancer Soc, 1968-1969; Teaching & res asst, Univ Calif, Berkeley, 1963-1967. **Memberships:** Am Soc Biochem & Molecular Biol; AAAS; Am Chem Soc; NY Acad Sci; Res Soc Alcoholism; Sigma Xi; Am Cancer Soc; Protein Soc. **Research Statement & Publications:** Enzymology; protein biochemistry and biophysics; molecular biology; structure and function of enzymes; biological oxidations; biotechnology. **Mailing Address:** 2654 Castillo Circle, Thousand Oaks, CA 91360-1301.

KENNEY, WILLIAM LAWRENCE, ENVIRONMENTAL PHYSIOLOGY, BIOPHYSICS OF HEAT EXCHANGE. **Personal Data:** b Latrobe, Pa, January 3, 1957; m 1982, Patricia; c Matthew, Alex & Lauren. **Education:** Ind Univ, Pa, BS, 1978, MS, 1980; Pa State Univ, PhD (physiol), 1983. **Honors & Awards:** New Investr Award, NIH, 1986. **Professional Experience:** PROF PHYSIOL & KINESIOL, PA STATE UNIV, 1989-; assoc prof appl physiol, Pa State Univ, 1989-; res assoc, Pa State Univ, 1983; assoc ed, J Appl Physiol. **Memberships:** Fel Am Col Sports Med; Am Physiol Soc; Sigma Xi. **Research Statement & Publications:** Effects of high heat and humidity on the human body with a special emphasis on age; biophysics of heat exchange. **Mailing Address:** Dept Kinesiol, Pa State Univ, 102 Noll Lab, Univ Park, PA 16802-6900. **Fax:** 814-865-4602. **E-Mail:** w7k@psu.edu

KENNEY-WALLACE, GERALDINE ANNE, CHEMICAL PHYSICS, CHEMICAL DYNAMICS OPTICS. **Personal Data:** b London, Eng, March 29, 1943. **Education:** Royal Inst Chem, ARIC, 1965; Univ BC, MS, 1968, PhD (chem), 1970. **Honorary Degrees:** DSc, DLitt, Univ Toronto, 1988. **Honors & Awards:** Corday-Morgan Medal, UK, 1979; Noranda Award, 1984; E W R Steacie Award, 1984. **Professional Experience:** Pres, Univ MacMaster, 1990-1995; chmn, Sci Coun Can, 1987-1992; chmn, Res Bd, Univ Toronto, 1985-1987; vis prof, Stanford Univ, 1985-1986; Guggenheim fel, 1983; vis scientist, Ecole Polytech Paris, 1981; PROF CHEM & PHYSICS, UNIV TORONTO, 1980-; Killam Res fel, 1979-1981; Alfred P Sloan fel, 1977-1979; from asst to assoc prof, Univ Toronto, 1974-1980; vis scientist chem, Argonne Nat Lab, 1973-; from instr to asst prof, Yale Univ, 1972-1974; assoc, Radiation Lab, Univ Notre Dame, 1971-1972; fel chem, Univ BC, 1970-1971; res assoc biophys, Oxford Univ, 1964-1966. **Memberships:** Royal Soc Chem; Am Chem Soc; Am Phys Soc; Sigma Xi; Optical Soc Am; InterAm Photochem Soc; Nat Adv Bd Sci & Technol. **Research Statement & Publications:** Molecular photophysics, energy transfer and molecular dynamics studied via picosecond, femtosecond laser spectroscopy; electronic and molecular structure of electrons in fluids; laser-induced electron transfer; holography, picosecond non linear optics. **Mailing Address:** Univ Toronto, Toronto, ON M5S 1A1, Can.

KENNINGTON, GARTH STANFORD, animal ecology, animal physiology; deceased, see previous edition for last biography

KENNISH, JOHN M, ANALYTICAL CHEMISTRY. **Personal Data:** b Vineland, NJ, October 6, 1945; m 1967, c 1. **Education:** Rutgers Univ, AB, 1967; Shippensburg Univ, MS, 1973; Portland State Univ, PhD (environ chem), 1978. **Professional Experience:** PROF CHEM, UNIV ALASKA, ANCHORAGE, 1988-; vis prof res, Ore State Univ, 1988-1989; vis fel res, Univ Colo, Boulder, 1982-1983; from asst prof to assoc prof, Univ Alaska, Anchorage, 1979-1988; res assoc res, Ore Health Sci Ctr, 1977-1979. **Memberships:** Am Chem Soc; Sigma Xi. **Research Statement & Publications:** Fish biochemistry related to evaluating the response of major hepatic enzymes to toxic agents; the biochemistry of post-mortem changes in fish tissue especially lipids and the application of analytical methods to environmental chemistry. **Mailing Address:** Dept Chem Univ Alaska, Rm 301 Eng Bldg, Anchorage, AK 99508. **E-Mail:** afjmk@uaa.alaska.edu

KENNISH, MICHAEL JOSEPH, ECOLOGICAL RESEARCH ON ESTUARINE & COASTAL MARINE ECOSYSTEMS, GEOLOGICAL & BIOLOGICAL RESEARCH ON DEEP-SEA MID-OCEAN RIDGE SYSTEMS. **Personal Data:** b Vineland, NJ, April 1950. **Education:** Rutgers Univ, BA, 1972, MS, 1974, PhD (geol), 1977. **Professional Experience:** RES PROF, INST MARINE & COASTAL SCI, RUTGERS UNIV, as of 2005; RES COORD, JACQUES COUSTEAU NAT ESTUARINE RES RESERVE, as of 2005; grad fac, Dept Oceanog, 1996-; mgr, res labs, Deep-sea & Biotechnol Ctr, Inst Marine & Coastal Sci, Rutgers Univ, beginning 1996; res marine scientist, Inst Marine & Coastal Sci, 1993-1996; grad fac, Dept Geol Sci, Inst Marine & Coastal Sci, Rutgers Univ, 1992-; supv res scientist, Inst Marine & Coastal Sci, 1990-1993; vis prof, Inst Marine & Coastal Sci, 1988-1990; sr environ scientist, GPU Nuclear Corp, Forked River, 1982-1990; environ scientist, Jersey Cent Power & Light Co, Morristown, 1977-1982; res asst, Geol Dept, Rutgers Univ, 1974-1977. **Memberships:** Sigma Xi; Am Geophys Union; Am Fisheries Soc; Atlantic Estuarine Res Soc; Estuarine Research Federation. **Research Statement & Publications:** Biological and geological investigations on estuarine and coastal marine ecosystems; pollution studies on these regions; assessment of fisheries and shellfisheries in coastal habitats; geological and biological research on deep-sea mid-ocean ridge systems. **Mailing Address:** Inst Marine & Coastal Sci, Rutgers Univ, New Brunswick, NJ 08901. **Fax:** 732-932-6557. **E-Mail:** kennish@imcs.rutgers.edu

KENNISON, JOHN FREDERICK, MATHEMATICS. **Personal Data:** b New York, NY, October 7, 1938; m 1964, Cynthia; c Kendall & Jane. **Education:** Queens Col, NY, BS, 1959; Harvard Univ, AM, 1960, PhD (topology), 1963. **Professional Experience:** PROF MATH, CLARK UNIV, 1963-. **Memberships:** Am Math Soc. **Research Statement & Publications:** Category theory. **Mailing Address:** Dept Math, Clark Univ, Carson Hall 116 950 Main St, Worcester, MA 01610. **Fax:** 508-421-3715. **E-Mail:** jkennison@clarku.edu

KENNY, ANDREW AUGUSTINE, AUTOMOTIVE CONTROL DESIGN & DEVELOPMENT, FACILITATE QUALITY FUNCTION DEPLOYMENT. **Personal Data:** b Chicago, Ill, July 21, 1934; m 1966, c 2. **Education:** Univ Ill, BS, 1961. **Professional Experience:** Qual assurance mgr, Controls Div, Eaton, 1989-1991; chief engr, Controls Div, Eaton, 1986-1989; eng supvr, Controls Div, Eaton, 1981-1986; proj engr, Controls Div, Eaton, 1970-1986; proj engr, Bastian-Blessing, 1963-1970. **Memberships:** Soc Automotive Engrs; Am Soc Qual Control. **Research Statement & Publications:** Nineteen patents in a variety of automotive control fields; published many articles on engineering, management and quality control. **Mailing Address:** N 57 W 26515 Mt DuLac Dr, Sussex, WI 53089.

KENNY, DAVID HERMAN, ORGANIC CHEMISTRY. **Personal Data:** b Lake Linden, Mich, October 6, 1927; m 1976, Judith Archibald; c Melanie, Amber & Emily. **Education:** Cornell Univ, AB, 1949; Univ Mich, MS, 1955, PhD, 1959. **Professional Experience:** ASSOC PROF EMER CHEM, MICH TECHNOL UNIV, 1989-; chmn, Org Chem Dept, 1974-1981; assoc prof, Org Chem Dept, 1962-1989; Smith-Mundt lectr, Baghdad, 1960-1962; Asst prof chem, Eastern Mich Univ, 1958-1960. **Memberships:** AAAS; Am Chem Soc. **Research Statement & Publications:** Organic nitrogen chemistry. **Mailing Address:** Dept Chem, Mich Technol Univ, 1400 Townsend Dr, Houghton, MI 49931-1295.

KENNY, GEORGE EDWARD, INFECTIOUS DISEASES. **Personal Data:** b Dickinson, NDak, September 23, 1930; m Mary; c Frank, Michael, John, Maureen & Edward. **Education:** Fordham Univ, BS, 1952; Univ NDak, MS, 1957; Univ Minn, Minneapolis, PhD (microbiol), 1961. **Honors & Awards:** Kimble Methodol Award, Am Pub Health Asn, 1971. **Professional Experience:** PROF Emeritus, DEPT PATHOBIOL, UNIV WASH, 2003 -; Professor 1991-2003; chmn, Dept Pathobiol, 1971-1991; from asst prof to assoc prof, Univ Wash, 1963-1971; Res instr prev med, Univ Wash, 1961-1963. **Memberships:** Am Soc Microbiol; Infectious Dis Soc Am; Int Orgn Mycoplasmol; Sigma Xi; fel Am Acad Microbiol. **Research Statement & Publications:** Antigenic analysis of microorganisms; host-parasite relationships of animal cells and microorganisms; biology of the mycoplasmatales; human mycoplasmal diseases; blood borne viral diseases. **Mailing Address:** 1504 37th Ave, Seattle, WA 98122. **Fax:** 206-543-3873. **E-Mail:** kennyg@u.washington.edu

KENNY, JAMES JOSEPH, IMMUNE DEFICIENCY, B-LYMPHOCYTES. **Education:** Univ Calif, Los Angeles, PhD (immunol), 1977. **Professional Experience:** ASST PROF MICROBIOL & IMMUNOL, UNIFORMED SERV UNIV HEALTH SCI, 1979-. **Mailing Address:** NIA NIH Gerontol Res Ctr, 4940 Eastern Ave, Baltimore, MD 21224. **Fax:** 410-558-8137.

KENNY, MICHAEL THOMAS, ANTIBIOTICS, ANTIVIRALS. **Personal Data:** b San Francisco, Calif, October 3, 1938; m 1963, c 1. **Education:** Univ San Francisco, BS, 1960; Univ Del, PhD (microbiol), 1964. **Professional Experience:** SR RES MICROBIOLOGIST & MICROBIOL DEPT HEAD, HOECHST MARION ROUSSEL, 1992-; assoc scientist, Pharmacol Dept, 1981-1992; clin res assoc, Med Dept, 1978-1981; sr res immunologist, Dow Diag Res & Develop, 1974-1978; sr res virologist, Dept Infectious Dis, 1971-1974; res virologist, Dow Human Health Res & Develop Labs, 1967-1971; Sr virologist, Biohazards Dept, Pitman-Moore Div, Marion Merrell Dow Pharmaceut Inc, 1966-1967. **Memberships:** Am Soc Microbiol; Am Asn Immunologists; AAAS; Int Soc Antiviral Res; Soc Leukocyte Biol; Anaerobe Soc. **Research Statement & Publications:** Invertebrate microbiology and invertebrate tissue culture; diagnostic virology; radioimmunoassay; laboratory safety; viral immunology; virus vaccine development; development of antibiotics and anti-viral compounds; immunomodulation and inflammatory disease. **Mailing Address:** Hoescht Marion Roussell Inc, 10236 Marion Park Dri, Kansas City, MO 64137-1405.

KENNY, RAY, STABLE ISOTOPE GEOCHEMISTRY, ENVIRONMENTAL GEOLOGY, GEOMORPHOLOGY. **Personal Data:** b Chicago, Ill, June 13, 1955. **Education:** Northeastern Ill Univ, BSc, 1983; Ariz State Univ, MSc, 1986, PhD (geochem), 1991. **Professional Experience:** PROF, DEPT Geoscience, FORTLEWIS COL, 2001-; RES PROF GEOL, NMEX HIGHLANDS UNIV, 2001-; asst prof Geol, NMEX Highlands Univ, beginning 1993; Prof res asst, Inst Arctic & Alpine Res, Univ Colo, 1991-1995. **Memberships:** Geol Soc Am. **Research Statement & Publications:** Paleotemperature determinations using stable isotope geochemistry on geologic materials and biological materials; paleoclimate change; field geology studies on paleosols and carbonate sediments; slope instability. **Mailing Address:** Dept Geosci, Fort Lewis Col, 321 BH, 1000 Rim Dr, Durango, CO 81301-3999. **E-Mail:** kenny_r@fortlewis.edu

KENSEK, RONALD P, NUCLEAR ENGINEERING, COMPUTER SIMULATION. **Personal Data:** b Buffalo, NY, July 9, 1958. **Education:** State Univ, NY, Buffalo, BA, 1980, BS, 1980; Univ Mich, PhD (nuclear eng), 1986. **Professional Experience:** MEM TECH STAFF, SANDIA NAT LAB, 1986-. **Memberships:** AAAS; Am Phys Soc. **Research Statement & Publications:** Pursuing the development of inertial confinement fusion and developing new methods of radiation transport computer simulation. **Mailing Address:** Sandia Nat Lab, Org 9341, Albuquerque, NM 87185. **E-Mail:** rpkense@sandia.gov

KENSHALO, DANIEL RALPH, PSYCHOPHYSIOLOGY. **Personal Data:** b West Frankfort, Ill, July 27, 1922; m 1970, c 4. **Education:** Wash Univ, BA, 1947, PhD (exp psychol), 1953. **Professional Experience:** RETIRED; prof psychol, Fla State Univ, beginning 1959; distinguished prof, Fla State Univ, 1974-1975; Univ Claude Bernard, France, 1973; vis prof physiol, Univ Marburg, Ger, 1969; from asst prof to assoc prof, Fla State Univ, 1953-1959; actg asst prof, Fla State Univ, 1950-1953; instr psychol, Wash Univ, St Louis, 1948-1949. **Memberships:** Soc Neuroscience; Fel Am Psychol Asn; Fel AAAS; Fel NY Acad Sci; Am Physiol Soc. **Research Statement & Publications:** Psychophysical and electrophysiological investigation of the skin senses. **Mailing Address:** 2414 Delgado Dr, Tallahassee, FL 32304-1304.

KENSON, ROBERT EARL, PHYSICAL CHEMISTRY, AIR POLLUTION CONTROL. **Personal Data:** b Stoneham, Mass, April 15, 1939; m 1968, c Brian & Bruce. **Education:** Boston Univ, AB, 1961; Purdue Univ, PhD (phys chem), 1965. **Professional Experience:** PRIN, KENSON ASSOC, 1996-; prin Mclarenihart Environ Eng Corp, 1995-1996; develop dir, Met-Pro Corp, 1980-1995; mgr engineered systs div, Oxy-Catalyst Inc, 1978-1980; sr proj scientist, TRC, Res Corp New Eng, 1974-1978; sr res chemist, Olin Mathieson Chem Corp, 1965-1969 & Engelhard Minerals & Chem Corp, Newark, 1969-1974. **Memberships:** Am Chem Soc; Am Inst Chem Eng; Air Pollution Control Asn; Soc Mfg Engrs; Soc Pharml Engrs. **Research Statement & Publications:** Catalysis; kinetics of gas and solution reactions; petroleum chemistry and petrochemicals; energy systems; environmental control. **Mailing Address:** 1126 E Cardinal Dr, West Chester, PA 19382. **Fax:** 610-399-1127.

KENT, ALLEN, INFORMATION SCIENCE. **Personal Data:** b New York, NY, October 24, 1921; m 1943, Rosalind Kossoff; c Merryl F (Samuels), Emily B (Yeager), Jacqueline (Maryak) & Carolyn (Hall). **Education:** City Col New York, BS, 1942. **Honors & Awards:** Info Technol Award, Eastman Kodak Co, 1968; Award of Merit, Am Soc Info Sci, 1976, Pioneer of Info Sci Award, 1984. **Professional Experience:** RETIRED; interim dean, Interdisciplinary Dept Info Sci, 1985-1986; mem bd dirs, Marcel Dekker Inc, 1979-1993; distinguished serv prof, Interdisciplinary Dept Info Sci, 1976-1982; chmn, Interdisciplinary Dept Info Sci, 1968-1980; chmn nat adv comt, Nat Inst Neurol Dis & Stroke, 1967-1970; coun mem, Ctr Res Libr, 1966-1986; dir, Off Commun Progs, Univ Pittsburgh, 1963-1980; consult info sci ment retardation, Spec Asst to Presidents Kennedy & Johnson, 1963-1964; Consult, Diebold, Inc, 1962-1972; assoc dir & prof, Ctr for Doc & Commun Res, Western Res Univ, 1955-1963; prin doc engr, Battelle Mem Inst, 1953-1955; Res assoc info sci, Mass Inst Technol, 1951-1953. **Memberships:** Am Soc Info Sci; fel AAAS; Asn Comput Mach; Am Libr Asn. **Research Statement & Publications:** Quantitative studies of information transfer; modelling and simulation of library networks. **Mailing Address:** Rm 519 LIS Bldg, Univ Pittsburgh, Pittsburgh, PA 15260.

KENT, BARBARA, PHYSIOLOGY, GENERAL MEDICAL SCIENCES. **Personal Data:** b Decatur, Ill, July 29, 1940. **Education:** Emory Univ, BA, 1962, MS, 1964, PhD (physiol), 1970. **Professional Experience:** DIR, TRAINING & MENTORING CORE, MT DESERT BIOL LAB, as of 2001; ADMIN DIR, MT DESERT ISLAND BIOL LAB, 1991-; assoc prof geriat & adv develop, Dept Physiol, Mt Sinai Sch Med, NY, 1983-1991; vis scientist, Jackson Lab, 1982; assoc prof physiol, Mt Sinai Sch Med, NY, 1978; dir surg res, Mt Sinai Sch Med, NY, 1972-1983; res assoc prof surg, Mt Sinai Sch Med, NY, beginning 1971; res physiologist, Bronx Vet Admin Hosp, 1970-1983; investr, Mt Desert Island Biol Lab, beginning 1968. **Memberships:** Am Physiol Soc; NY Acad Sci. **Research Statement & Publications:** Cardiovascular control systems; patho physiology of respiration; comparative cardiovascular physiology. **Mailing Address:** Mt Desert Island Biol Lab, PO Box 35, Salsbury Cove, ME 04672. **Fax:** 207-288-2130. **E-Mail:** bkb@mdibl.org

KENT, BION H, STRATIGRAPHY, COAL GEOLOGY. **Personal Data:** b Utica, NY, October 19, 1925. **Education:** Cornell Univ, BA, 1949; Stanford Univ, MS, 1952. **Professional Experience:** RETIRED; geologist, US Geol Surv, 1949-1986. **Memberships:** Fel Geol Soc Am; Am Asn Petrol Geologists. **Mailing Address:** 13511 W Alaska Pl, Denver, CO 80228.

KENT, CLAUDIA, BIOCHEMISTRY. **Personal Data:** b South Bend, Ind, October 6, 1945; m 1981, c 2. **Education:** St Mary's Col, Ind, BS, 1967; Johns Hopkins Univ, PhD (biochem), 1972. **Professional Experience:** PROF BIOCHEM, UNIV MICH, 1991-; from asst prof to prof biochem, Purdue Univ, 1975-1991; NIH fel, 1974-1975; Am Cancer Soc fel biochem, Dept Biol Chem, Sch Med, Wash Univ, 1972-1975; Physiol Chem Study Sect, NIH; bd sci counrs, Nat Inst Heart Lungs & Blood; assoc ed, J Biol Chem. **Memberships:** Am Soc Biochem Molecular Biol; Am Soc Cell Biol; fel AAAS. **Research Statement & Publications:** Regulation of phospholipid metabolism. **Mailing Address:** Dept Biol Chem, Univ Mich Sch Med, Ann Arbor, MI 48109-0606. **Fax:** 734-763-4581. **E-Mail:** ckent@umich.edu

KENT, CLEMENT F, THEORETICAL COMPUTER SCIENCE, LOGIC. **Personal Data:** b Charleston, SC, March 15, 1927; m 1948, c 3. **Education:** Ga Inst Technol, BS, 1948, MS, 1950; Mass Inst Technol, PhD (math), 1960. **Professional Experience:** PROF EMER MATH SCI & CHMN MATH COMPETITION COMT, LAKEHEAD UNIV, as of 2006; vis prof, Univ Laval, 1979-1980; vis prof, Univ Bristol, 1972-1973; prof math sci, Lakehead Univ, beginning 1968; chmn dept math, Lakehead Univ, 1968-1972, 1976-1979 & 1985-1987; assoc prof math, Case Western Reserve Univ, 1962-1968; sci staff mem, Opers Eval Group, Mass Inst Technol, 1951-1962; instr physics, Ga Inst Technol, 1948-1950. **Memberships:** Math Asn Am; Am Math Soc; Asn Symbolic Logic; Can Math Cong; Asn Comput Mach. **Research Statement & Publications:** Mathematical logic; theoretical computer science; proof theory; recursive functions. **Mailing Address:** Dept Math Sci, Lakehead Univ, RB 2018 955 Oliver Rd, Thunder Bay, ON P7B 5E1, Can. **E-Mail:** cfkent@shaw.ca

KENT, CLIFFORD EUGENE, CHEMICAL ENGINEERING, ELECTROCHEMISTRY, DIRECT ENERGY CONVERSION. **Personal Data:** b Butler Co, Kans, 11, 1920; m 1942, Elizabeth; c Jane, Peter & Richard. **Education:** Purdue Univ, BSChE, 1942, BA (Theol), 1980. **Professional Experience:** RETIRED; asst rector, St Patricks, Kenwood, Calif, 1992-1997; interim rector, St Patricks, Kenwood, Calif, 1989-1990; priest assoc, 1983-1989, 1998-2002; prof placement counsellor, 1981-1982; mgr chem systs design, Nuclear Energy Div, 1967-1982; prog mgr electrochem eng, Gen Elec Co, 1965-1967; prog mgr advan fuel cell technol, Gen Elec Co, 1961-1965; mgr proj eng, Gen Elec Co, 1956-1961; prog planning supvr, Gen Elec Co, 1952-1956; design engr, Gen Elec Co, 1949-1952; develop engr, Gen Elec Co, 1946-1949; develop engr, Western Prod Inc, 1945-1946; pilot plant supvr, Merck & Co, NJ, 1942-1945. **Memberships:** Am Inst Chem Engrs; Am Chem Soc; Am Nuclear Soc; Electrochem Soc. **Research Statement & Publications:** Fuel cell and batteries radiochemical plants; equipment design; chemical and gas processes; nuclear plant effluent control; water treatment; personnel development; granted three US patents. **Mailing Address:** 5555 Montgomery Dr, Santa Rosa, CA 95409-8818. **E-Mail:** ckent801@mac.com

KENT, D RANDALL, ENGINEERING. **Honors & Awards:** Aircraft Design Award, Am Inst Aeronaut & Astronaut, 1992. **Professional Experience:** Vpres, Gen Dynamics Corp, Tex, ending 2004; CONSULT, LOCKHEED-MARTIN CORP, as of 2004; DIR, QUICKSILVER RESOURCES INC, 1999-. **Mailing Address:** Quicksilver Resources Inc, 777 West Rosedale St, Suite 300, Ft Worth, TX 76104. **Fax:** 817-665-5004.

KENT, DARRELL C, MATHEMATICS. **Professional Experience:** PROF, DEPT MATH, WASH STATE UNIV, as of 2003. **Mailing Address:** Dept Math, Wash State Univ, PO Box 643113, Pullman, WA 99163-3113. **E-Mail:** dkent@wsunix.wsu.edu

KENT, DENNIS V, PALEOMAGNETISM. **Personal Data:** b Prague, Czech, November 4, 1946; American citizen; m 1971, Carolyn; c Amanda Grace. **Education:** City Col NY, BS, 1968; Columbia Univ, PhD (geophys), 1974. **Honorary Degrees:** Dr Honoris Causa, Sorbonne, Univ Paris-IPGP (2005). **Honors & Awards:** Arthur L Day Medal, Geol Soc Am, 2003; Vening Meinesz Sch Geodynamics Medal, Delft Univ, Holland, 2003. **Professional Experience:** Vis scholar, Scripps Inst Oceanog, Univ Calif, San Diego, 2003; ADJ ST RES SCIENTIST, LAMONT-DOLERTY EARTH OBSERV, COLUMBIA UNIV, 1999-; PROF, DEPT GEOL SCI, RUTGERS UNIV, 1998-; dir res, Lamont-Doherty Earth Observ, Columbia Univ, 1993-1998; interim dir, Lamont Doherty Earth Observ, 1989-1990; adj prof, Dept Earth & Environ Sci, Columbia univ, 1987-1998; assoc dir, Lamont Doherty Earth Observ, 1987-1989; Doherty sr scientist, Lamont Doherty Earth Observ, Columbia Univ, 1984-1999; guest prof, Inst Geophys, ETH, Zurich, 1982; adj assoc prof geol sci, Dept Earth & Environ Sci, Columbia Univ, 1981-1987; sr res scientist, Columbia Univ, 1979-1984; res assoc, Columbia Univ, 1974-1979. **Memberships:** Integrated Ocean Drilling Prog Mgt Int, bd Gov 2003-; Joint oceanog inst (chair, 2004-2006); Nat Acad Sci; fel Am Geophys Union (pres elect & pres, 1992-1996, chair, fel comt, 2000-2002); Joint oceanog Inst (board gov, 1989-); fel Geol Soc Am; fel AAAS. **Research Statement & Publications:** Paleomagnetism and rock magnetism and their application to the history of earth's magnetic field and geologic problems; published over 200 articles. **Mailing Address:** Dept Geol Sci, Rutgers Univ, Piscataway, NJ 08854-8066. **Fax:** 732-445-3374. **E-Mail:** dvk@rci.rutgers.edu

KENT, DONALD MARTIN, SCANNING ELECTRON MICROSCOPE, CARBONATE ROCKS. **Personal Data:** b Medicine Hat, Alta, January 25, 1933; m 1987, Joyce Barton; c Mark, Christopher, Paul, Teresa, Carmel, Crystal, Terri & Doug. **Education:** Univ Sask, BS, 1957, MS, 1959; Univ Alta, PhD (geol), 1968. **Professional Experience:** Adj prof, Dept Geol, Univ Regina, as of 2004; CONSULT GEOL, D M KENT CONSULT GEOLOGIST LTD, as of 2004; PROF EMER GEOL, UNIV REGINA, 1996-; CONSULT GEOL, UNIV REGINA, 1996-; head dept, Univ Regina, 1991-1996; assoc ed, Bull Can Petrol Geol, 1986-1988 & Geol Atlas Western Can Sedimentary Basin, 1989-1993; head dept, Univ Regina, 1982-1988; pres, D M Kent Consult Geologist Ltd, 1981-; prof geol, Univ Regina, 1977-1996; consult, Can Occidental Petrol, Union Oil Can, 1976-1981; assoc prof, Univ Regina, 1971-1977; sr res geologist, Sask Dept Mineral Resources, 1968-1971; Res geologist, Sask Dept Mineral Resources, 1958-1968. **Memberships:** Am Asn Petrol Geologists; Int Asn Sedimentologists; Can Soc Petrol Geologists; Geol Asn Can; Sask Geol Soc (pres 1965 1969 & 1978); Soc Sedimentary Geol. **Research Statement & Publications:** Microfacies, diagenesis and nature ofpore systems in carbonate hydrocarbon reservoir rocks; depositional settings of mixed carbonate-siliciclastic and carbonate-evaporite sequences; application of scanning electron microscope to diagenetic studies of carbonate rocks; paleotectonic controls on sedimentation; application of cathodo luminescence to carbonate diagenesis. **Mailing Address:** D M Kent Consult Geologist Ltd, 86 Metcalfe Rd, Regina, SK S4V 0H8, Can. **Fax:** 306-761-1567. **E-Mail:** donald.kent@uregina.ca

KENT, DONALD WETHERALD, PHYSICS. **Personal Data:** b Philadelphia, Pa, June 26, 1926; m 1958, c 3. **Education:** Yale Univ, BSc, 1949; Temple Univ, PhD (physics), 1960. **Professional Experience:** RETIRED; res physicist, Bartol Res Found, Franklin Inst, beginning 1952; researcher cosmic radiation, H H Wills Lab, Eng, 1949-1952. **Memberships:** Am Phys Soc; Am Geophys Union; Sigma Xi. **Research Statement & Publications:** Cosmic ray physics. **Mailing Address:** 510 Walnut Lane, Swarthmore, PA 19081.

KENT, DOUGLAS CHARLES, GEOLOGY. **Personal Data:** b Hastings, Nebr, September 26, 1939; m 1962, c 2. **Education:** Univ Nebr, BSc, 1961, MSc, 1963; Iowa State Univ, PhD (water resources, geol), 1969. **Professional Experience:** PROF EMER ASSOC PROF GEOL, OKLA STATE UNIV, 1972-; groundwater consult, 1971-; asst prof, Okla State Univ, 1969-1972; res assoc, Iowa State Univ, 1968-1969; instr, Iowa State Univ, 1967-1968; prod geologist, Gulf Oil Corp, 1964-1966. **Memberships:** Geol Soc Am; Am Geophys Union; Am Water Resources Asn; Nat Water Well Asn; Sigma Xi. **Research Statement & Publications:** Application of remote sensing to groundwater exploration and water resources; geochemistry of aquifers; application of mathematical modeling to groundwater management; stratigraphy; groundwater geology; applied geophysics and water resources. **Mailing Address:** Dept Geol Main Campus, Okla State Univ, Stillwater, OK 74078.

KENT, GEOFFREY, PATHOLOGY. **Personal Data:** b Amsterdam, Holland, January 30, 1914; American citizen; m 1944, c 4. **Education:** Univ Amsterdam, MD, 1939; Univ Manchester, MSc, 1944; Northwestern Univ, PhD (path), 1957. **Professional Experience:** PROF EMER PATH, MED SCH, NORTHWESTERN UNIV, 1984-; chmn dept, Med Sch, Northwestern Univ, 1972-1977; chmn dept path, Chicago Wesley Mem Hosp, 1969-1972; from asst prof to prof, Med Sch, Northwestern Univ, 1960-1984; Chief pathologist, WSuburban Hosp, 1958-1969; assoc dir path, Cook County Hosp, Chicago, 1956-1957; sr pathologist, Cook County Hosp, Chicago, 1953-1956; pathologist, London Hosp, 1947-1950; asst dir, Res Dept, Manchester Royal Infirmary, 1943-1944; Chief asst hemat, Res Dept, Manchester Royal Infirmary, 1940-1943. **Memberships:** AAAS; Am Soc Exp Path; Am Asn Pathologists; Col Am Path; Am Soc Cell Biol. **Research Statement & Publications:** Iron metabolism; liver disease. **Mailing Address:** Dept Path Northwestern Univ Med Sch, 303 E Chicago Ave, Chicago, IL 60611-3072.

KENT, GORDON, ELECTRICAL ENGINEERING. **Personal Data:** b Pittsfield, Mass, October 1, 1920; m 1957, c 1. **Education:** Univ Wis, BS, 1947; Stanford Univ, MS, 1949, PhD (elec eng), 1952. **Professional Experience:** CONSULT, 1983-; prof, Syracuse Univ, 1963-1985; assoc prof elec eng, Syracuse Univ, 1957-1963; res fel electronics, Gordon McKay Lab, Harvard Univ, 1953-1957; res engr comput design, Inst Adv Study, 1951-1953; Proprietor, GDK Prod. **Memberships:** Inst Elec & Electronics Engrs. **Research Statement & Publications:** Development of measuring techniques and hardware for microwave properties of materials. **Mailing Address:** 473 Savage Farm Dr, Ithaca, NY 14850.

KENT, HENRY JOHANN, ROBOTIC SYSTEMS FOR AUTOMATED PAPER PRODUCT QUALITY TESTING, PARTICLE MORPHOLOGY & SUSPENSION RHEOLOGY. **Personal Data:** b Plymouth, Eng, February 2, 1953. **Education:** Sussex Univ, Eng, BSc, 1974, PhD (theoret phys), 1979. **Professional Experience:** Chmn coating fundamentals comt, Tech Asn Pulp & Paper Indust, 1991-1992; PRIN SCIENTIST, INT PAPER, 1986-; Head paper coating res, ECC Int, 1977-1986. **Memberships:** Tech Asn Pulp & Paper Indust. **Research Statement & Publications:** Equilibrium and stability of fluid bodies in gravitational fields; measurement and analysis of surface topography; characterization of physical systems by fractal descriptors; numerical modelling of capillary flow in complex pore systems. **Mailing Address:** 2 Wildwood Circle, Bloomingburg, NY 12721. **Fax:** 914-577-7307.

KENT, JOSEPH C(HAN), CIVIL ENGINEERING. **Personal Data:** b Victoria, BC, January 16, 1922; American citizen; m 1952, c 3. **Education:** Univ BC, BS, 1945; Stanford Univ, MS, 1948; Univ Calif, PhD (fluid mech), 1952. **Professional Experience:** EMER PROF CIVIL ENG, UNIV WASH, 1990-; assoc prof, Univ Wash, 1961-1990; from instr to asst prof, Univ Wash, 1952-1961; asst civil eng, Univ Calif, 1949-1952; hydrographic surveyor, Dept Mines & Resources, Can, 1945-1947. **Memberships:** Am Soc Eng Educ. **Research Statement & Publications:** Fluid mechanics specializing in waves; drag of submerged bodies and fluid flow. **Mailing Address:** 3600 Island Crest Way, Box 352700 132F More Hall, Mercer Island, WA 98040-3529. **Fax:** 206-685-9185.

KENT, JOSEPH FRANCIS, TOPOLOGY. **Personal Data:** b Richmond, Va, February 13, 1944; m 1966. **Education:** Univ Va, BA, 1966, MA, 1967, PhD (math), 1970. **Professional Experience:** PROF EMER COMPUT SCI, UNIV RICHMOND, as of 2005; ASSOC PROVOST, UNIV RICHMOND, 2005-; actg chair, Dept Physics, Univ Richmond, 2002-2003; assoc dean arts & sci acad oper, Univ Richmond, 2000-2003; prof comput sci, Univ Richmond, beginning 1987; chmn, Dept Math & Comput Sci, Univ Richmond, 1982-1992; from asst prof to assoc prof, Univ Richmond, 1973-1987; asst prof math, Univ Fla, 1970-1973. **Memberships:** Am Math Soc; Math Asn Am; Sigma Xi. **Research Statement & Publications:** Topological dynamics and the study of ergodic flows; differentiability of norms on Banach spaces. **Mailing Address:** Dept Math & Comput Sci, Univ Richmond, Provost Office Md Hall 15 Quail Run Dr, Manakin-Sabot, VA 23173-0001. **E-Mail:** jkent@richmond.edu

KENT, RAYMOND D, COMMUNICATIVE DISORDERS, SPEECH DEVELOPMENT. **Personal Data:** b Red Lodge, Mont, December 21, 1942. **Education:** Univ Mont, BA, 1965; Univ Iowa, MA, 1969, PhD (speech path), 1970. **Professional Experience:** PROF COMMUNICATIVE DIS, WAISMAN CTR, UNIV WIS-MADISON, as of 2003; mem, Ad Hoc Adv Comt Commun Dis Prog, Nat Inst Neurol & Commun Dis & Stroke, 1981-; sr res assoc, Boys Town Inst Commun Dis Children, 1979-; ed, J Speech & Hearing Res, 1977-1981; prin investr, NIH grants, 1973-; prof commun dis, Univ Wis-Madison, 1971-1979; Fel, Res Lab Electronics, Mass Inst Technol, 1970-1971. **Memberships:** Am Speech-Language-Hearing Asn; Am Asn Phonetic Sci; Acoust Soc Am; Sigma Xi; NY Acad Sci. **Research Statement & Publications:** Production and perception of speech, especially to speech development in children, neurologic speech and language disorders, and theories of speech production; Published over 10 articles. **Mailing Address:** Waisman Ctr Univ Wis-Madison, Rm 435 1500 Highland Ave, Madison, WI 53705. **Fax:** 608-263-0529. **E-Mail:** kent@waisman.wisc.edu

KENT, ROBERT D, COMPUTER SCIENCE. **Professional Experience:** PROF & GRAD PROG COORDR, SCH COMPUT SCI, UNIV WINDSOR, as of 2004. **Mailing Address:** Dept Comput Sci, Univ Windsor, 401 Sunset Ave, Windsor, ON N9B 3P4, Can. **Fax:** 519-973-7093. **E-Mail:** rkent@uwindsor.ca

KENT, RONALD ALLAN, CATALYSIS, INORGANIC CHEMISTRY. **Personal Data:** b New York, NY, February 23, 1935; m 1960, c 2. **Education:** Cornell Univ, AB, 1954. **Professional Experience:** PRES, TECHNOL NETWORK, 1987-; tech mgr, Process Develop, PQ Corp, 1986-1987; dir com develop, Phillips Petrol, 1983-1985; dir tech & develop, Dart Industs, 1981-1983; dir systs technol res & appl catalytic chem, Dart Industs, 1978-1981; sr res assoc catalysis, Dart Industs, 1975-1978; prin chemist heterogeneous catalysis, Dart Industs, 1971-1975; res chemist platinum metal catalysis, Matthey Bishop Inc, 1968-1971; chief chemist, Chem Info & Doc Serv, Univ Pa, 1965-1967; Instr chem, Spring Garden Inst Technol, 1960-1961; res assoc inorg sulfur & nitrogen, Dept Chem, Univ Pa, 1957-1968; Develop chemist catalytic chlorination, Gen Chem Res Lab, Allied Chem, 1955-1957. **Memberships:** Am Chem Soc (secy treas inorg sect 1970); NY Acad Sci; AAAS; Com Develop Asn; Catalysis Soc NAm. **Research Statement & Publications:** Hydrogenation and isomerization catalysis; polymerization catalysis; oxide catalyst processes; ozone preparation and utilization; sulfur dioxide control; noble metal utilization and recovery; secondary copper recovery processes; polyolefins; silica products; composites for invivo use. **Mailing Address:** PO Box 23131, Federal Way, WA 98093-0131.

KENT, STEPHEN MATTHEW, EXTRAGALACTIC ASTRONOMY. **Personal Data:** b West Orange, NJ, December 2, 1952. **Education:** Mass Inst Technol, BS, 1974; Calif Tech, PhD (astron), 1980. **Professional Experience:** HEAD, EXP ASTROPHYS GROUP, FERMILAB, as of 2002; ASSOC PROF, DEPT ASTRON & ASTROPHYS PHYSICS, ENRICO FERMI INST, as of 2002; SCIENTIST, FERMI NAT ACCELERATOR LAB, 1991-; asst prof astron, Harvard Univ, 1983-1991; teaching fel astron, Mass Inst Technol, 1981-1983; res fel astron, Ctr Astrophys, 1979-1981. **Memberships:** Am Astron Soc; Int Astron Union. **Research Statement & Publications:** Extragalactic astronomy; internal dynamics of galaxies and clusters of galaxies. **Mailing Address:** Fermi Nat Accelerator Lab, PO Box 500 MS 127, Batavia, IL 60510. **Fax:** 630-840-8274. **E-Mail:** skent@fnal.gov

KENT, THOMAS HUGH, PATHOLOGY. **Personal Data:** b Iowa City, Iowa, August 17, 1934; m 1957, c 3. **Education:** Univ Iowa, BA, 1956, MD, 1959; Am Bd Path, dipl, 1965. **Professional Experience:** PROF PATH, COL MED, UNIV IOWA, 1972-; from asst prof to assoc prof, Col Med, Univ Iowa, 1966-1972; assoc pathologist, Walter Reed Army Inst Res, 1964-1966; resident path, Univ Iowa, 1960-1964; intern, Methodist Hosp, Indianapolis, 1959-1960. **Memberships:** AMA; Col Am Path; Am Asn Pathologists & Bacteriologists; Am Soc Clin Path. **Research Statement & Publications:** Gastroenterology. **Mailing Address:** Univ Iowa Col Med, 158 ML, Iowa City, IA 52240.

KENTFIELD, JOHN ALAN CHARLES, MECHANICAL ENGINEERING. **Personal Data:** b Hitchin, Eng, March 4, 1930; m 1966, Amelia. **Education:** Univ Southampton, BSc, 1959; Univ London, DIC & PhD (mech eng), 1963. **Honors & Awards:** R J Templin Award, Can Wind Energy Asn, 1992. **Professional Experience:** PROF EMER MECH & MANUFACTURE ENG, UNIV CALGARY, 1981-; Killam Resident fel, Univ Calgary, 1980; operating grant, 1977 & 1980 & Nat Sci & Eng Rec Coun Can grant, 1983, 1986, 1989 & 1993; Nat Res Coun grant, Univ Calgary, 1971-1972; assoc prof, Univ Calgary, 1970-1979; lectr res & educ, Imp Col, Univ London, 1966-1970; proj engr, Curtiss-Wright Corp, 1963-1966; asst lectr res & educ, Imp Col, Univ London, 1962-1963; asst tester, Ricardo & Co Ltd, 1952-1956; trainee, C V A Kearney & Trecker Ltd, Eng, 1950-1952. **Memberships:** Am Inst Aeronaut & Astronaut; Am Soc Mech Engrs; Brit Inst Mech Engrs; Am Wind Energy Asn; Can Wind Energy Asn. **Research Statement & Publications:** Non-steady flow of compressible fluid and the application of non-steady flow phenomena in engineering equipment, such as pressure exchangers and pulsating combustors; wind-turbines and wind-energy systems; author of over 140 research publications plus a graduate level text/reference book. **Mailing Address:** Dept Mech & Manufacture Eng, Univ Calgary, 2500 Univ Dr NW, Calgary, AB T2N 1N4, Can. **Fax:** 403-282-8406. **E-Mail:** kentfield@ucalgary.ca

KENTZER, CZESLAW P(AWEL), GAS DYNAMICS, COMPUTATIONAL FLUID MECHANICS. **Personal Data:** b Poland, June 29, 1925; American citizen; m 1958, c 3. **Education:** San Diego State Col, BS, 1952; Purdue Univ, MS, 1954, PhD (aerospace eng), 1958. **Professional Experience:** PROF EMER, PURDUE UNIV, 1991-; prom asst prof to assoc prof aerodyn, Purdue Univ, 1958-1991; Consult, Missiles & Space Systs Div, Douglas Aircraft Corp. **Memberships:** Am Math Soc; Am Acad Mech; Am Inst Aeronaut & Astronaut. **Research Statement & Publications:** Fluid mechanics; transonic aerodynamics; acoustics; nonlinear waves; turbulence theories; computational fluid mechanics; geophysical fluid mechanics.

KENY, SHARAD V, MATHEMATICS, GROUP THEORY. **Personal Data:** b Panaji, India, January 21, 1946; American citizen; m 1969, Vasant; c Hemant, Shilpa, Shveta & Ameet. **Education:** Univ Bombay, BSc, 1966; Univ Bombay, MSc, 1968; Univ Calif, Los Angeles, MA, 1973; Univ Calif, Los Angeles, PhD (math), 1976. **Professional Experience:** PROF, WHITTIER COL, 1995-; assoc prof, Whittier Col, 1989-1995; asst prof, Whittier Col, 1986-1989; lectr, dept math, Orange Coast Col, Calif, 1983-1984; inst, Calif State Univ Long Beach, 1977-1986; lectr, Golden West Community Col, Calif, 1977-1978; lectr, Univ Calif Los Angeles, 1976-1977; grad teaching asst, Univ Calif, Los Angeles, 1971-1976; lectr, Dhempe Col, India, 1968-1969. **Memberships:** Amer Math Soc; Math Assoc Amer. **Mailing Address:** Dept Math, Whittier Coll, PO Box 634, 13406 E Philadelphia, Whittier, CA 90608-0634. **Fax:** 562-698-4067. **E-Mail:** skeny@whittier.edu

KENYON, ALAN J, BIOCHEMISTRY, IMMUNOLOGY. **Personal Data:** b Whitehall, Wis, September 10, 1929; m 1954, c 3. **Education:** Univ Minn, BS, 1954, DVM, 1957, PhD (bact & biochem), 1961. **Professional Experience:** RETIRED; mem, Walker Lab, Sloan-Kettering Inst Cancer Res, 1973-1997; prof biol, Med Sch, Cornell Univ, 1973-1980; res inst, Ill Inst Technol, beginning 1971; res inst, Path Dept, Hartford Hosp, beginning 1970; sabbatical leave pediat & path, Sch Med, Univ Minn, Minneapolis, 1971-1972; consult, Manned Spacecraft Ctr, Apollo Prog, NASA, beginning 1968; career develop award, 1965-1975; NIH res grants, beginning 1963; from assoc prof to prof biochem, Univ Conn, 1961-1973. **Memberships:** AAAS; NY Acad Sci; Am Soc Exp Path; Reticuloendothelial Soc; Am Asn Lab Animal Sci. **Research Statement & Publications:** Immunochemistry as applied to lymphoproliferative diseases and neoplasias of man and animals; comparative biochemistry of Mustelidae; diseases of marine mammals; immunological deficiency. **Mailing Address:** Cross Link Technol, 822 The Parkway, Mamaroneck, NY 10543.

KENYON, CYNTHIA JANE, BIOCHEMISTRY. **Education:** Univ Ga, Athens, BS, 1976; Mass Inst Technol, PhD (biol), 1981. **Professional Experience:** Weirsma vis prof, Cal Tech, 2004; HERBERT BOYER PROF BIOCHEM & BIOPHYS, UNIV CALIF, SAN FRANCISCO, as of 2003; David & Lucille Packard Found fel, 1989; Searle scholar, 1986. **Memberships:** Nat Acad Sci; Genetics Soc Am (pres, 2003). **Mailing Address:** Dept Biochem & Biophys, Univ Calif, Genentech Hall 600 16th St Box 2200, San Francisco, CA 94143-2200. **Fax:** 415-476-3892. **E-Mail:** ckenyon@biochem.ucsf.edu

KENYON, GEORGE LOMMEL, BIOCHEMISTRY. **Personal Data:** b Wilmington, Del, August 29, 1939; m 1981, c 1. **Education:** Univ Bucknell, BS, 1961; Univ Harvard, MA, 1963, PhD (org chem), 1965. **Honors & Awards:** Merit Award, NIH, 1986. **Professional Experience:** PROF, COL PHARM, UNIV MICH, 1993-; Dean, Col Pharm, Univ Mich, 1998-2004; PROF EMER, SCH PHARM, UNIV CALIF, SAN FRANCISCO, 1998-; dean, sch pharm, Univ Calif, San Francisco, 1994-1998; prof, Pharm Chem, Univ Calif, San Francisco, 1977-1998; assoc prof, Univ Calif, San Francisco, 1974-1977; asst prof, pharm chem, Univ Calif, San Francisco, 1972-1974; asst prof chem, Univ Calif, Berkeley, 1966-1972; Fel biochem, Mass Inst Technol, 1965-1966. **Memberships:** Fel AAAS; Am Chem Soc; Am Soc Biol Chemists; fel NY Acad Sci. **Research Statement & Publications:** Enzyme mechanisms; organophosphorus chemistry; bio-organic chemistry of nucleotides; application of nuclear magnetic resonance spectroscopy to biological problems; design of reagents for protein modification; design of specific enzyme inhibitors. **Mailing Address:** Col Pharm Univ Mich, 428 Church St, Ann Arbor, MI 48109-1065. **Fax:** 734-615-3079. **E-Mail:** gkenyon@umich.edu

KENYON, HEWITT, mathematics; deceased, see previous edition for last biography

KENYON, KAY A, ZOOLOGY. **Personal Data:** b Monterey Park, Calif, March 12, 1955; m Peregrine. **Education:** Cedar Crest Col, BA, 1977; Univ Denver, MA, 1978. **Professional Experience:** BR LIBRARIAN, NAT ZOOL PARK BR, SMITHSONIAN INST, 1981-; actg chief librarian, Smithsonian Inst Libr, 1981; asst librarian, Smithsonian Inst Libr, 1979-1981; ref librarian, Smithsonian Inst Libr, 1978-1979; libr intern, Denver Mus Natural Hist Libr, 1978. **Memberships:** Am Zoo & Aquarium Asn; Spec Libr Asn. **Research Statement & Publications:** Author of numerous publications in field. **Mailing Address:** Nat Zoology Park Libr, Smithsonian Inst, 3001 Conn Ave NW, Washington, DC 20008. **Fax:** 202-673-4900. **E-Mail:** tko@kaykenyon.com

KENYON, KERN ELLSWORTH, PHYSICAL OCEANOGRAPHY, WAVES. **Personal Data:** b Kansas City, Mo, May 24, 1938; m 1966, Julie; c Douglas & Pamela. **Education:** Mass Inst Technol, BS & MS, 1961; Scripps Inst Oceanog, PhD (oceanog), 1966. **Professional Experience:** Asst res oceanogr, Scripps Inst Oceanog, 1973-1982; Asst prof, Grad Sch Oceanog, Univ RI, 1967-1973. **Memberships:** Am Geophys Union; AAAS; Oceanog Soc Japan; Sigma Xi. **Research Statement & Publications:** Large-scale ocean circulation and air sea interaction; Physics of gravity waves. **Mailing Address:** 4632 North Lane, Del Mar, CA 92014-4134. **E-Mail:** kernken@aol.com

KENYON, PATRICIA MAY, TECTONICS & GEODYNAMICS, ENVIRONMENTAL GEOPHYSICS. **Personal Data:** b Binghamton, NY, March 16, 1952. **Education:** Rensselaer Polytech Inst, BS, 1974; Cornell Univ, PhD (geophys), 1986. **Professional Experience:** Mem, CCLI Proposal Review Panel, DUE, National Science Foundation, 2000-2001; Fac mem, Earth and Environ Sci Prog, City Univ NY Graduate Ctr, 1995-; assoc prof, City Col NY, beginning 1994; mem, Marine Geol & Geophysics Proposal Rev Panel, Ocean Sci Div, NSF, 1994; mem, Basic Energy Sci Prog Rev Panel, Dept Energy, 1993; asst prof geophys, Univ Ala, 1988-1994; asst prof geol, Cent Conn State Univ, 1987-1988; res assoc, Carnegie Inst Wash, 1985-1987; res physicist, Eastman Kodak Co, 1974-1980. **Memberships:** Am Geophys Union; Geol Soc Am; Sigma Xi; Environ & Eng Geophys Soc. **Research Statement & Publications:** Magma migration and the influence of this migration on geochemistry, particularly on the midocean ridges; near surface resistivity and seismic studies; problems in sediment deposition and mantle convection. **Mailing Address:** Dept Earth & Atmospheric Sci, City Col NY, Convent Ave at 138th St, New York, NY 10031. **Fax:** 212-650-6482. **E-Mail:** pkenyon@sci.ccny.cuny.edu

KENYON, RICHARD H, VIROLOGY, IMMUNOLOGY. **Personal Data:** b Blakely, Pa, November 22, 1942; m 1968. **Education:** Bucknell Univ, BS, 1964; Pa State Univ, MS, 1966, PhD (microbiol), 1968. **Professional Experience:** PROG MGR, BREAST CANCER RES PROG, US ARMY MED RES & MAT COMMAND, as of 2003; VIROL DIV, 1980- & DIS ASSESSMENT DIV, 1988-; MED MAT DEVELOP, 1980- & DIS ASSESSMENT DIV, 1988-; ASST CHIEF, RICKETTSIOLOGY DIV, US ARMY MED RES INST INFECTIOUS DIS, 1978-; rickettsiologist-immunologist, Virol Lab, 1971-1977; Virol Lab, US Army Med Res Inst Infectious Dis, 1971; virologist-immunologist, US Army Biol Labs, Ft Detrick, 1969-1971. **Research Statement & Publications:** Vaccine development; Rocky Mountain spotted fever; Rickettsiae; Junn virus; Argentine hemorrhagic fever. **Mailing Address:** US Army Med Res & Mat Command, Ft Detrick, MD 21773.

KENYON, RICHARD R(EID), ELECTRICAL ENGINEERING, COMPUTER SCIENCE. **Personal Data:** b Middletown, Ohio, October 6, 1928. **Education:** Purdue Univ, BS, 1950, MS, 1951, PhD (elec eng), 1961. **Professional Experience:** PVT CONSULT, 1986-; consult comput sci, McDonnell Douglas Astronaut Co, 1980-1986; asst prof, Purdue Univ, 1961-1965; instr, Purdue Univ, 1958-1961; res asst comput sci, Purdue Univ, 1955-1958; mem tech staff, Bell Tel Labs, NJ, 1951-1955. **Memberships:** Asn Comput Mach; Inst Elec & Electronics Engrs; Sigma Xi. **Research Statement & Publications:** Circuit theory; numerical methods of approximation; computer architecture, programming languages. **Mailing Address:** 17781 Crestmoor Lane, Huntington Beach, CA 92649. **E-Mail:** richardrkenyon@msn.com

KENYON, STEPHEN C, DIGITAL SIGNAL PROCESSING, NEURAL NETWORKS. **Personal Data:** b Coronado, Calif, May 9, 1948; m 1970, c 1. **Education:** Va Polytech Inst, BS, 1971. **Professional Experience:** PRES & COFOUNDER, CREATIVE ENG CONCEPTS INC, 1990-; vpres eng, Digital Signal Corp, 1983-1990; chief eng, Ensco Inc, 1975-1983; elec engr, US Army, 1971-1975. **Memberships:** Inst Elec & Electronics Engrs Systs Man & Cybernet Soc; Inst Elec & Electronics Engrs Control Systs Soc; Inst Elec & Electronics Engrs Acoust Speech & Signal Processing Soc; Inst Elec & Electronics Engrs Comput Soc; Inst Elec & Electronics Engrs Commun Soc; Int Neural Network Soc. **Research Statement & Publications:** Research and Development in electronic, optical and software signal processing; intelligent sensors, pattern recognition and machine intelligence; adaptive control for autonomous systems; 3 US patents. **Mailing Address:** Creative Eng Concepts Inc, 3545 Chain Bridge Rd Ste Six, Fairfax, VA 22030. **Fax:** 703-359-8154.

KEOGH, MICHAEL JOHN, ORGANIC CHEMISTRY, POLYMER CHEMISTRY. **Personal Data:** b Bronx, NY, May 26, 1937; m 1975, Paula; c Michael, Laura & Christine. **Education:** Manhattan Col, BS, 1959; Purdue Univ, PhD (org chem), 1963. **Professional Experience:** CORP RES FEL, UNION CARBIDE CORP, 1988-; res assoc, Polyolefins

Div, 1982-1988; sr res scientist, Union Carbide Corp, 1978-1982; res scientist, Union Carbide Corp, 1970-1978; proj scientist, Union Carbide Corp, 1967-1970; chemist, Union Carbide Corp, 1963-1967. **Memberships:** Am Chem Soc; Fire Retardant Chem Asn; Soc Plastic Eng. **Research Statement & Publications:** Synthetic, organic and polymer chemistry; fluorocarbons; condensation monomer synthesis; organometallic and anionic polymerization systems; epoxide and other thermosetting polymerization systems; polymers engineered for pollution control; wire and cable technology; flame retardant and polymer stabilization technology. **Mailing Address:** Res & Develop Dept, Union Carbide Corp, 1 Riverview Dr, Somerset, NJ 08875-0450.

KEOGH, RICHARD NEIL, CELL BIOLOGY. **Personal Data:** b Nashua, NH, April 21, 1940. **Education:** Tufts Univ, BS, 1962; Brown Univ, PhD (biol), 1967. **Professional Experience:** DIR, OFF RES & GRANTS ADMIN, RI COL, as of 1996; PROF BIOL, RI COL, 1977-; from asst prof to assoc prof, 1966-1977. **Memberships:** AAAS; Am Asn Biol Teachers; Am Inst Biol Sci; Sigma Xi. **Research Statement & Publications:** Mammalian pigment cell biology; teaching of biology via television; multimedia methods of instruction. **Mailing Address:** Off Res & Grants Admin, RI Col, Providence, RI 02908. **E-Mail:** rkeogh@ric.edu

KEON, WILBERT JOSEPH, CARDIOVASCULAR SURGERY, DISEASE COSTING. **Personal Data:** b Sheenboro, Que, May 17, 1935; m 1960, c 3. **Education:** St Pat's Col, Ottawa, BSc, 1957; Univ Ottawa, MD, 1961; McGill Univ, MSc, 1963; FRCPS(C), 1966. **Honors & Awards:** Officer, Order of Can, Can Govt, 1985; Hippocrates Award, Am Hellenic Educ Progressive Asn, 1985. **Professional Experience:** Sen, govt Can, 1990; vpres, Med Res Coun Can, 1985-1990; assoc ed, Can J Cardiol, 1984-; med vpres, med adv bd, Can Heart Found, 1983-1985; chmn, med adv bd, Can Heart Found, 1980-1983; vchmn, med adv bd, Can Heart Found, 1979-1980; surg fel, James IV Asn Surgeons, 1979; surgeon-in-chief, Ottawa Civic Hosp, 1977-1983; prof surg & chmn dept, Cardiac Unit, 1976-1991; sr fel, Ont Heart Found, 1970-1976; chmn, Div Cardiovasc & Thoracic Surg, 1969-; FOUNDER & CHIEF & DIV CARDIOTHORACIC SURG, OTTAWA CIVIC HOSP, 1969-; dir, Cardiac Unit, 1969-1983; assoc prof surg, Univ Ottawa, 1969-1976; FOUNDER & DIR, UNIV OTTAWA HEART INST, 1969-; mem bd dirs, Transplant Int Inc; chmn, div cardiovasc & thoracic surg, Univ Ottawa, begining. **Memberships:** Am Surg Soc; Am Asn Thoracic Surg; Int Asn Cardiac Biol Implants; Int Cardiovasc Soc; Can Cardiovasc Soc (pres 1988-1989); Soc Cardiothoracic Surgeons. **Research Statement & Publications:** Surgical treatment in the presence of acute myocardial infarction; cardiac muscle mechanics; lasers for treatment of coronary artery disease; artificial heart as a bridge to transplantation. **Mailing Address:** Univ Ottawa Heart Inst, 40 Ruskin St, Ottawa, ON K1Y 4W7, Can. **Fax:** 613-761-5323. **E-Mail:** wjkeon@ottawaheart.ca

KEOUGH, ALLEN HENRY, ORGANIC CHEMISTRY. **Personal Data:** b Chelsea, Mass, April 24, 1929; m 1952, c 6. **Education:** Univ Mass, BS, 1950; Univ NH, MS, 1952; Mass Inst Technol, PhD (org chem), 1956. **Professional Experience:** Bd dir, Vitronics Corp, 1989-; TECH DIR, METALLIZED PRODS INC, 1986-; bd dirs, Rad Tech Int, 1986, 1987-1988; pres, Rad Tech Int, 1986; chmn, Radiation Curing Div, Asn Finishing Processes, Soc Mfg Engrs, 1985-1986; tech dir, Metall Prods Div, Household Mfg, Inc, 1981-1986; pres, Design Cote Co, 1978-1981; sect head advan develop div, Dennison Mfg Co, 1974-1978; sect head, Res Div, 1971-1974; pres, Chem-Tech Assocs, Inc, Mass, 1968-1971; asst dir res, Nat Res Corp, 1966-1968; res assoc, Nat Res Corp, 1963-1966; asst dir res & develop, Explor Res Div, Norton Co, Worcester, 1962-1963; res assoc, Explor Res Div, Norton Co, Worcester, 1962; sr res engr, Explor Res Div, Norton Co, Worcester, 1958-1962; res chemist, Johnson & Johnson, 1955-1958. **Memberships:** AAAS; Am Chem Soc; Asn Finishing Processes Soc Mfg Engrs. **Research Statement & Publications:** Synthetic organic chemistry; organometallic compounds; heterogeneous catalysis surface active agents; polymer chemistry; radiation curing printing inks and coatings. **Mailing Address:** 3 Elizabeth Dr, Northborough, MA 01532.

KEOUGH, GERARD E, MATHEMATICS. **Education:** Ind Univ, PhD (Maths), 1979. **Professional Experience:** CHMN MATH, BOSTON COL, as of 2005. **Memberships:** Am Math Soc. **Mailing Address:** Boston Col, Dept Maths & Comput Sci, Carney Hall, Chestnut Hill, MA 02167-3806. **Fax:** 617-552-3789. **E-Mail:** keough@bc.edu

KEOUGH, KEVIN MICHAEL WILLIAM, BIOCHEMISTRY. **Personal Data:** b St George's, Nfld, August 2, 1943; m 1967, c 2. **Education:** Univ Toronto, BSc, 1965, MSc, 1967, PhD (biochem), 1971. **Professional Experience:** CHIEF SCIENTIST, HEALTH CAN, as of 2003; Mem, Med Res Coun Can, 1992-; vpres res, Mem Univ Nfld, beginning 1992; dir, Seabright Corp, Can Ctr Fisheries Innovation & Can Ctr Marine Commun, beginning 1992; head, Dept Biochem, 1986-1992; PROF BIOCHEM & PEDIAT, MEM UNIV NFLD, 1982-; assoc prof pediat, Mem Univ Nfld, 1980-1982; from asst prof to assoc prof biochem, Mem Univ Nfld, 1972-1982; Muscular Dystrophy Asn Can fel phys biochem, Univ Sheffield, 1971-1972. **Memberships:** Can Biochem Soc (pres 1988-1989); Can Lung Asn; Biochem Soc; Am Soc Biol Chemists; Am Chem Soc; Biophys Soc; Sigma Xi; Biophys Soc Can; Am Oil Chem Soc. **Research Statement & Publications:** Molecular organization in membranes and lung surfactant; synthetic lung surfactant; liposomal biotechnology. **Mailing Address:** Dept Biochem, Mem Univ Nfld, St Johns, NL A1B 3X9, Can. **Fax:** 709-737-2552. **E-Mail:** kkeough@mun.ca

KEOWN, ERNEST RAY, APPLIED MATHEMATICS. **Personal Data:** b Thurber, Tex, March 17, 1921; m 1943, Ruby; c 2. **Education:** Univ Tex, BS, 1946; Mass Inst Technol, PhD (math), 1950. **Professional Experience:** RETIRED; vis prof, Tex A & M Univ, 1991-1992; prof math, Univ Ark, Fayetteville, 1967-1991; mem, Solid State & Molecular Theory Group, Mass Inst Technol, 1963-1964; prof math, Tex A & M Univ, 1960-1967; tech specialist, Aerojet Gen Corp Div, Gen Tire & Rubber Co, 1959-1960; comput specialist, Douglas Aircraft Co, 1957-1959; asst prof math, Tex A & M, 1952-1957; sr aerophysics engr, Consol Vultee Aircraft Co, 1951-1952; consult, AEC, Stand Oil Co, Tex & Magnolia Petrol Co. **Memberships:** Am Math Soc. **Research Statement & Publications:** Group representation theory; applications of group representation theory in physics; numerical analysis; computers and law; gauge theory. **Mailing Address:** PO Box K-10, College Station, TX 77844.

KEOWN, ROBERT WILLIAM, PACKAGING CHEMISTRY, FOOD CHEMISTRY. **Personal Data:** b Louisville, Ky, April 23, 1929; m 1993, Yan Shi; c 3. **Education:** Univ Louisville, BS, 1951, MS, 1952, PhD (chem), 1954. **Professional Experience:** PROF EMER, DEPT FOOD SCI, UNIV DEL, as of 2004; CHAIR, DEPT FOOD SCI, UNIV DEL, 1988-; prof & actg chair, dept food sci, Univ Del, 1987-1988; prof, dept food sci, Univ Del, 1985-1987; from res assoc to sr res assoc, Adhesives & Fluids Div, 1981-1985; supvr, Adhesives & Fluids Div, 1974-1981; tech assoc, E I du Pont Del Nemours & Co, Inc, 1971-1974; res chemist, E I du Pont Del Nemours & Co, Inc, 1954-1971; pres, Isomer Corp. **Memberships:** Am Chem Soc; AAAS; Adhesion Soc; Inst Food Technologists; Soc Packaging Engrs. **Research Statement & Publications:** Polymer chemistry; food interactions with polymeric packaging materials, specifically flavor loss and adhesion effects. **Mailing Address:** Dept Food Sci, Univ Del, 19 Townsend Hall, Wilmington, DE 19803-2226. **Fax:** 302-831-6763. **E-Mail:** meyer@udel.edu

KEPECS, JOSEPH GOODMAN, PSYCHIATRY, PSYCHOANALYSIS. **Personal Data:** b Philadelphia, Pa, October 8, 1912; m 1944, c 2. **Education:** Univ Chicago, BS, 1935, MD, 1937; Chicago Inst Psychoanal, cert, 1949. **Professional Experience:** PROF EMER PSYCHIAT, MED SCH, UNIV WIS, MADISON, 1965-; prof lectr, Univ Chicago, 1960-1965; consult, Univ Wis, 1960-1965; lectr, Chicago Inst Psychoanal, 1957-1960; vis lectr, Univ Cincinnati, 1956; pvt practr, 1946-1965. **Memberships:** Am Psychiat Asn; Am Psychoanal Asn; Am Psychosom Soc. **Research Statement & Publications:** Applications of psychiatry to medicine; sociological studies of changes in therapists and patients; psychiatry in developing countries. **Mailing Address:** 3230 Univ Ave, 250 Clin Sci Ctr, Madison, WI 53705.

KEPES, JOHN J, PATHOLOGY, NEUROPATHOLOGY. **Personal Data:** b Budapest, Hungary, March 31, 1928; American citizen; m 1950, c 1. **Education:** Univ Budapest, MD, 1952. **Professional Experience:** PROF EMER PATH, UNIV KANS MED CTR, KANSAS CITY, beginning 1968; vis prof, Neurol Inst, Univ Vienna, 1968-1969; consult, Vet Admin Hosp, Kansas City, beginning 1960; from asst prof to assoc prof, Univ Kans Med Ctr, Kansas City, 1960-1968; spec fel neuropath, Mayo Found, Univ Minn, 1957-1958; pathologist-in-chief, Nat Inst Neurosurg, Hungary, 1954-1956. **Memberships:** Am Acad Neurol; Am Asn Neuropathol (vpres 1978-1979 pres 1984-1985); Am Asn Neurol Surgeons. **Research Statement & Publications:** Histological differential diagnosis of brain tumors; electron microscopic studies of meningiomas; spinal cord circulation; primary malignant lymphomas of central nervous system; histiocytosis and xanthosarcomas of central nervous system; pathogenesis of central pontine myelinolysis; etiology and pathogenesis of the Arnold-Chiari malformation. **Mailing Address:** Dept Path & Lab Med, Univ Kans Med Ctr, 3901 Rainbow Blvd, 2017 Wahl Hall W, Kansas City, KS 66160-7410. **Fax:** 913-588-7073.

KEPES, JOSEPH JOHN, NUCLEAR & REACTOR PHYSICS. **Personal Data:** b Cleveland, Ohio, January 25, 1931; m 1954, c 6. **Education:** Case Inst Technol, BS, 1953; Univ Notre Dame, PhD (nuclear physics), 1958. **Professional Experience:** PROF EMER PHYSICS, UNIV DAYTON, as of 2002; prof physics, Univ Dayton, beginning 1971; chmn dept, Univ Dayton, 1962-1975; assoc prof, Univ Dayton, 1962-1971; Sr scientist, BettisAtomic Power Lab, 1957-1962. **Memberships:** Am Phys Soc; Am Asn Physics Teachers. **Research Statement & Publications:** Electron-electron scattering at low energies; resonance escape probabilities in natural uranium plates. **Mailing Address:** Dept Physics, Univ Dayton, Dayton, OH 45409. **E-Mail:** joseph.kepes@notes.udayton.edu

KEPHART, ROBERT DAVID, HIGH ENERGY PHYSICS, Superconducting magnets, CRYOGENICS. **Personal Data:** b Phillipsburg, Pa, November 27, 1949; m 1971, c 2. **Education:** Va Polytech Inst & State Univ, BS, 1971; State Univ NY, Stony Brook, MS, 1973, PhD (physics), 1975. **Honors & Awards:** APS Fellow. **Professional Experience:** 2005-present, Director, International Linear Collider R&D Program, 2002-2005, HEAD, Technical DIV, FERMI NAT ACCELERATOR LAB, 1988-2002, staff physicist & Department head, Fermi Nat Accelerator Lab, 1977-1988; fel, Dept Physics, State Univ NY, Stony Brook, 1975-1977; res asst, Dept Physics, State Univ NY, Stony Brook, 1971-1975; res asst physics, Dept Physics, Va Polytech Inst & State Univ, 1969-1971; proj mgr, Chicago Cyclotron Super Conducting Magnet Proj & leader, Fermilab Superconducting Analysis Magnetic Group; proj physicist, Collider Defector Facil, 3M0X5M Superconditioning Solenoid Proj Project Manager $ 110 M upgrade of CDF detector. **Memberships:** Am Phys Soc. **Research Statement & Publications:** Project Management, Accelerator component development, Detector development; liquid argon calorimetry; super conducting magnet development; high purity gas systems; dimuon high energy physics; engineering physics; p collider physics; super conducting solenoid; vertex detectors. **Mailing Address:** Fermil Nat Accelerator Lab, PO Box 500, MS 105, Batavia, IL 60510-0500. **Fax:** 630-840-2700. **E-Mail:** kephart@fnal.gov

KEPHART, SUSAN R, RESEARCH SCIENCE. **Education:** Ohio Wesleyan Univ, BA; Ind Univ, PhD. **Professional Experience:** PROF, DEPT BIOL, WILLAMETTE UNIV, QRE, as of 2006. **Mailing Address:** Williamette Univ, 900 State St, Salem, OR 97301. **E-Mail:** skephart@willamette.edu

KEPLER, CAROL R, LIPID CHEMISTRY. **Personal Data:** b Berea, Ohio, October 21, 1937; m 1959, c 2. **Education:** Oberlin Col, BA, 1959; Univ NC, PhD (zoology), 1965. **Professional Experience:** ASST PURCHASING ADMINR, STATE NC, 1984-; asst prof, Meredith Col, 1981-1984; asst prof biochem, NC State Univ, 1966-1981; NIH fel, 1965-1966; asst prof nutrit, NC State Univ, 1965-1966. **Memberships:** Sigma Xi; Am Soc Zoologists. **Research Statement & Publications:** Rumen bacteria; hydrogenation and isomerization of unsaturated fatty acids; specificity of triglyceride synthesis. **Mailing Address:** Dept Admin, State NC 116 W Jones St, Raleigh, NC 27603-8002.

KEPLER, GRACE M, MATHEMATICS. **Education:** Brandeis Univ, PhD (Physics), 1992. **Professional Experience:** RES ASSOC PROF, CTR RES SCI COMPUT MATHS DEPT, NC STATE UNIV, 2005-. **Memberships:** Am Phys Soc; Soc Math Biol. **Mailing Address:** NC State Univ, Ctr Res Sci Comput, PO Box 8205, Raleigh, NC 27695-8205. **Fax:** 919-515-8967. **E-Mail:** gmkepler@ncsu.edu

KEPLER, HAROLD BENTON, MECHANICAL ENGINEERING. **Personal Data:** b Dayton, Ohio, January 3, 1922; m 1946, c 2. **Education:** Sinclair Col, AEA, 1953, BBA, 1956; Xavier Univ, Ohio, MBA, 1958. **Honors & Awards:** Except Civilian Serv Award, USAF, 1967. **Professional Experience:** Lectr, Univ Dayton, beginning 1984; EMER PROF, USAF INST TECHNOL, 1977-; lectr, Sinclair Col, Ohio, beginning 1960; from instr to assoc prof mech eng, USAF Inst Technol, 1948-1977; prod designer, Ohmer Corp, 1947-1948; design checker, Aircraft Lab, Wright-Patterson AFB, 1946-1947; eng draftsman, Eng Div, Wright Field, Ohio, 1940-1942. **Memberships:** Am Soc Eng Educ. **Research Statement & Publications:** Engineering graphics; mechanisms and reliability engineering; Text book Basic Graphical Kinematics Mcgraw-Hill 1960, 1973. **Mailing Address:** 90 Sheldon Dr, Dayton, OH 45459. **E-Mail:** h.kepler@att.net

KEPLER, RAYMOND GLEN, EXPERIMENTAL SOLID STATE PHYSICS. **Personal Data:** b Long Beach, Calif, September 10, 1928; m 1953, Carol; c Julianne, Linda, Russell & David. **Education:** Stanford Univ, BS, 1950; Univ Calif, MS, 1955, PhD (physics), 1957. **Professional Experience:** RETIRED; res scientist, Sandia Nat Labs, 1989-1995; mem, Eval Panel Mat Sci, Nat Bur Stand, 1982-1988; mem, Applns Physics Comt, 1979-1981; chmn, Comt Educ, Am Phys Soc, 1979-1980; mem, Comt Educ, Am Phys Soc, 1978-1980; mem, Solid State Sci Panel, Nat Acad Sci, 1977-1982; dept mgr, Sandia Nat Labs, 1969-1989; div supvr, Sandia Nat Labs, 1964-1969; res physicist, Cent Res Dept, E I du Pont de Nemours & Co, 1957-1964; vchmn, Panel 2 Comt Mat Sci & Eng, Nat Acad Sci, Nat Res Coun. **Memberships:** AAAS; fel Am Phys Soc. **Research Statement & Publica-**

tions: Photoconductivity; conductivity; excitons and other solid state properties, primarily of organic solids; piezoelectricity, pyroelectricity and ferroelectricity in polymers. **Mailing Address:** 4908 Danube Ct N E, Albuquerque, NM 87111. **E-Mail:** glen_skepler@compuserve.com

KEPLINGER, MORENO LAVON, TOXICOLOGY. **Personal Data:** b Ulysses, Kans, May 25, 1929; m 1950, c 3. **Education:** Univ Kans, BS, 1951, MS, 1952; Northwestern Univ, PhD (pharmacol), 1956; Am Bd Toxicol, dipl, 1980. **Professional Experience:** CONSULT TOXICOL, 1978-; mgr toxicol, Indust Bio-Test Labs, Inc, 1970-1977; asst dir, Indust Bio-Test Labs, Inc, 1968-1970; pharmacol, Univ Miami, 1964-1968; toxicologist, Hercules Powder Co, 1960-1964; asst prof, Univ Miami, 1959-1960; res instr pharmacol, Univ Miami, 1956-1959. **Memberships:** Europ Soc Toxicol; Soc Toxicol; Am Soc Pharmacol & Exp Therapeut; Am Indust Hyg Asn. **Research Statement & Publications:** Experimental and industrial toxicology; pharmacology. **Mailing Address:** Keplinger, PO Box 1299, Hilltop Lakes, TX 77871-1299.

KEPNER, JAMES L, MATHEMATICS. **Professional Experience:** DIR, DIV STATIST & EVALUATION, AM CANCER SOC, as of 2006. **Memberships:** Am Cancer Soc. **Mailing Address:** Am Cancer Soc, 1599 Clifton Rd NE, Atlanta, GA 30329-4251. **Fax:** 404-982-3677. **E-Mail:** james.kepner@cancer.org

KEPPEL, KENNETH G, PUBLIC HEALTH, EPIDEMIOLOGY. **Personal Data:** b Somers Point, NJ, January 19, 1949. **Education:** Col William & Mary, 1971, BA; Pa State Univ, MA, 1980, PhD (sociol), 1980. **Professional Experience:** CHIEF, STATE & LOCAL SUPPORT BR, DIV HEALTH PROM & STATIS, NAT CTR HEALTH STATIST, CTR DIS CONTROL, 1992-; statistician, Maternal Child Health Bur, 1979-1990. **Memberships:** Am Pub Health Asn. **Mailing Address:** Nat Ctr Health Statist, Ctr Dis Control & Prev, 65-25 Belcrest Rd, Rm 770, Hyattsville, MD 20782. **Fax:** 301-436-3572. **E-Mail:** kkeppel@cdc.gov

KEPPEN, LAURA DAVIS, PEDIATRIC GENETICS, PEDIATRIC ENDOCRINOLOGY. **Personal Data:** b Sioux Falls, SDak, March 13, 1954; div, c David, Sarah, Thomas & Joseph. **Education:** Cornell Univ, BS, 1975; Univ SDak Sch Med, MD, 1979. **Honors & Awards:** Janet M Glasgow Award, Am Med Women's Asn, 1979. **Professional Experience:** PROD PEDIAT, SCH MED, UNIV SDAK, 1996-; assoc prof, Sch Med, Univ Sdak, 1990-1996; Ark Genetics Serv, 1984-1990; asst prof pediat, Univ Ark Med Sci, 1984-1990; Young Investr Award, Southern Soc Pediat Res. **Memberships:** Am Acad Pediat; Am Soc Human Genetics; Lawson Wilkins Pediat Endocrine Soc. **Research Statement & Publications:** Clinical genetics; author of various publications. **Mailing Address:** Dept pediat, S Dak Univ, 1305 w 18TH St, Sioux Falls, SD 57117-5039. **Fax:** 605-333-1585. **E-Mail:** lkeppen@usd.edu

KEPPIE, JOHN D, TECTONICS. **Personal Data:** b Nakuru, Kenya, October 3, 1942. **Education:** Univ Glasgow, BSc, 1964, PhD (geol), 1967. **Professional Experience:** CONSULT, 1994-; mgr, surv sect, Mineral Resources Div, NS Dept Mines & Energy, 1974-1994; regional geologist, Geol Surv Zambia, 1970-1973; asst prof geol, Bryn Mawr Col, 1967-1970; co-leader, Terrains Circum-Atlantic Paleozoic Orogens, Int Geol Correlation Prog, UNESCO. **Memberships:** Fel Geol Soc Am; Geol Asn Can. **Research Statement & Publications:** Tectonics of the circum-Atlantic area. **Mailing Address:** RR 3, Wolfville, NS B0P 1X0, Can.

KEPPLE, PAUL C, PHYSICS. **Personal Data:** b San Luis Potosi, Mex, February 6, 1936; American citizen; m 1962, c 2. **Education:** Univ Okla, BS, 1958, MS, 1961; NMex State Univ, PhD (physics), 1966. **Professional Experience:** RETIRED; res physicist, Naval Res Lab, 1969-2006; res assoc plasma physics, Univ Md, 1966-1969. **Memberships:** Am Phys Soc. **Research Statement & Publications:** Plasma physics; atomic physics. **Mailing Address:** Naval Res Lab, Code 6720 4555 Overlook Ave SW, Washington, DC 20375.

KEPPLER, WILLIAM J, GENETICS, EVOLUTION. **Personal Data:** b Teaneck, NJ, January 20, 1937; m 1960, c 1. **Education:** Univ Miami, Fla, BS, 1959; Univ Ill, MS, 1961, PhD (genetics), 1965. **Professional Experience:** PRES, NAT COL NATUROPATHIC MED, as of 2003; dean col health & prof genetics, Fla Int Univ, 1988-2003; vchancellor, Univ Alaska, 1985-1988; dean arts & sch, Boise State Univ, 1977-1985; asst provost, Eastern Ill Univ, 1973-1976; from asst prof to prof zool, Eastern Ill Univ, 1965-1976. **Memberships:** Sigma Xi. **Research Statement & Publications:** Cytochemistry of chromosomes. **Mailing Address:** Nat Col Naturopathic Med, 049 SW Porter St, Portland, OR 97201.

KEPRON, MICHAEL RAYMOND, DIAGNOSTICS. **Personal Data:** b Ann Arbor, Mich, February 15, 1955; American & Canadian citizen; m 1982, Ruth; c Marla A, Nicole J & Jared M. **Education:** McGill Univ, BSc, 1977; Univ Man, PhD (immunol), 1989. **Professional Experience:** RES SCIENTIST, IDEXX LABS INC, 1991-; instr, Univ Tex Southwestern Med Ctr, 1986-1991. **Memberships:** Am Asn Immunologists. **Research Statement & Publications:** Development of diagnostic products for the veterinary market. **Mailing Address:** IDEXX Labs Inc, One IDEXX Dr, Westbrook, ME 04092. **Fax:** 207-856-0474.

KEPRON, WAYNE, IMMUNOLOGY, PHYSIOLOGY. **Personal Data:** b Winnipeg, Man, March 31, 1942; m 1966, c 3. **Education:** Univ Man, BSc & MD, 1967. **Professional Experience:** Prin investr, Med Res Coun Group Allergy Res, Dept Immunol, Univ Man, 1978-; ASSOC PROF IMMUNOL, FAC MED, UNIV MAN, 1978-; ASSOC PROF INTERNAL MED, FAC MED, UNIV MAN, 1975-; Attend physician, Respiratory Ctr, Health Sci Ctr. **Memberships:** Am Acad Allergy; Am Thoracic Soc; Can Lung Asn. **Research Statement & Publications:** Studies in the pathogenesis of Ige, Ige mediated asthma with specific reference to the role of local immune mechanisims in the lung; the modification of Ige metabolism with tolerogenic conjugates. **Mailing Address:** Dept Med, Univ Man Lung Transplant Prog, 810 Sherbrook St, Winnipeg, MB R3A 1R8, Can. **Fax:** 204-787-2420. **E-Mail:** wkepron@hsc.mb.ca

KER, JOHN WILLIAM, FORESTRY. **Personal Data:** b Chilliwack, BC, August 27, 1915; m 1943, Marguerite; c John G, Kerry A (Markle) & Wendy R (Andrews). **Education:** Univ BC, BASc, 1941; Yale Univ, MF, 1951, DF (forestry), 1957. **Honorary Degrees:** DSc, Univ BC, 1971. **Professional Experience:** RETIRED; consult, Int Develop Res Ctr, People's Repub China, 1987; mem, Natural Sci & Eng Res Coun Can, 1980-1983; chmn, Forest Mgt Task Force, NB Dept Natural Resources, 1978-1981; Can deleg, Food & Agr Orgn, Adv Comt Forestry Educ, 1975-1978; expert univ educ, Can Int Develop Agency, 1973-1974; consult, IntBank Reconstruct & Develop, 1972-1973; consult, Can Coun Rural Develop, 1972-1973; consult, Prov NB Land Compensation Bd, 1970-1971; consult, Atlantic Develop Bd, 1966-1968; consult, Royal Comn Econ State & Prospects of Nfld & Labrador, 1966-1967; consult, H G Acres & Agr Rehab & Develop Act, 1964-1965; prof forest mensuration & econ & dean, Fac Forestry, Univ NB, 1961-1982; assoc prof forest mensuration & econ, Univ BC, 1953-1961; asst prof forest mensuration, Univ BC, 1948-1953; asst forester, BC Forest Serv, 1945-1948; forest ranger, BC Forest Serv, 1941-1945. **Memberships:** Can Forestry Asn (vpres, 1972-1973); Can Inst Forestry (pres, 1972-1973). **Research Statement & Publications:** Forest economics and valuation; forest measurements and biometry; university-level forestry education in both Canada and developing countries. **Mailing Address:** 760 Golf Club Rd RR3, Fredericton, NB E3B 4X4, Can.

KERAMAS, JAMES G, MECHANICAL ENGINEERING. **Personal Data:** b Athens, Greece, October 13, 1928; American citizen; m 1952, Virginia; c George & Renita (Johnson). **Education:** Athens Polytech Inst, BS, 1952, MS, 1953; Fitchburg State Col, MEd, 1979; Univ Mass, EdD, 1989. **Honorary Degrees:** LHD, Hellenic Soc Amer, 1967. **Professional Experience:** Prof robotics, Mass Inst Technol, 1992-1998; prof complex integrated manufacturing, Mass Inst Technol, 1992-1998; prof electromechanical technol, Univ Mass, 1984-1993; prof machine design, Univ Mass, 1984-1993; prof indust electronics, Univ Mass, 1984-1993; prof manufacturing process, Middlesex Community Col, 1976-1984; prof design auto mechanics, Middlesex Community Col, 1976-1984; prof indust automotion, Middlesex Community Col, 1976-1984. **Memberships:** Mem Inst Elect & Electronics Engrs; mem Nat Asn Indust Technol; mem Mass Soc Prof Engrs; mem Robotic Indust Asn; mem AAAS. **Research Statement & Publications:** Curricular development for high technology programs, automated manufacturing systems, product development and high-tech innovations, robotics art intelligence, CAD/CAM, CIM. **Mailing Address:** 343 Nye Rd, PO Box 554, Centerville, MA 02632.

KERAMIDAS, VASSILIS GEORGE, APPLIED PHYSICS, MATERIALS SCIENCE. **Personal Data:** b Moudros, Greece, June 27, 1938; American citizen; m 1967, Elaine Marikakis; c Jason & Kimon. **Education:** Rockford Col, BA, 1960; Univ Ill, BS, 1962; John Carroll Univ, MS, 1969; Pa State Univ, PhD (solid state sci), 1973. **Professional Experience:** VPRES, APPLIED RES, FORMATIVE TECHNOLOGIES COMMERCIALIZATION, TELCORDIA TECHNOLOGIES, INC, as of 2002; exec dir, info access & energy storage res, Bellcore, beginning 1991; chmn, Int Compound Semiconductor Comt, 1991-1994; chmn, Electronic Mat Comt, 1991-1993; div mgr, Photonics & Electronics Mat Res, 1985-1991; dist res mgr, photonic & electronic mat res, 1983-1985; supvr III-V semiconductor mat devices & integrated circuits, Bell Lab, 1980-1983; mem tech staff optoelectronic mat & devices, Bellcore, 1973-1980; Res staff mem cadmium sulfide solar cells, Crystal Solid State Div, Harshaw Chem Co, 1963-1967. **Memberships:** Mat Res Soc; Electrochem Soc; Am Phys Soc; Am Asn Crystal Growth; sr mem Inst Elec & Electronics Engrs; Minerals Metals & Mat Soc. **Research Statement & Publications:** Leadership, technical management and personal research contributions in the fields of: optoelectronic materials research for fiber optic communications, novel materials and systems for information storage (memory research) and energy storage (rechargeable batteries). **Mailing Address:** Telcordia Technologies, Inc, One Telcordia Dr, Piscataway, NJ 08854-4157.

KERANS, CHARLES, RESERVOIR CHARACTERIZATION, SEQUENCE STRATIGRAPHY. **Personal Data:** b Boston, Mass, October 11, 1954; m 1983, Pamela; c Peter D & Graham M. **Education:** St Lawrence Univ, BS, 1977; Carleton Univ, Can, PhD (geol), 1982. **Professional Experience:** PROF & ROBERT K GOLDHAMMER CHAIR, CARBONATE GEOL, DEPT GEOL SCI, UNIV TEX, ASUTIN, as of 2006; SR RES SCIENTIST, BUR ECON GEOL, UNIV TEX, AUSTIN, 1993-; sr geologist, Marathon Oil Co, 1992; distinguished lectr, Am Asn Petrol Geologists, 1990; from res assoc to res scientist, Bur Econ Geol, Univ Tex, Austin, 1985-1994; sr res fel, Western Australian Mining & Petrol Res Inst, 1982-1985; actg asst prof geol, Univ Kans, 1981-1982. **Memberships:** Am Asn Petrol Geologists; Soc Sedimentary Geol. **Research Statement & Publications:** Integrated reservoir characterization providing stratigraphic frameworks for quantification by engineers and petrophysicists; development and testing of new concepts in the area of carbonate sequence stratigraphy. **Mailing Address:** Jackson Sch Geo Sci, Univ Tex, One Univ Sta C1100, Austin, TX 78712-0254. **Fax:** 512-471-0140. **E-Mail:** charles.kerans@beg.utexas.edu

KERBEL, ROBERT STEPHEN, CANCER. **Personal Data:** b Toronto, Ont, April 5, 1945; m 1970, c 1. **Education:** Univ Toronto, BS, 1968; Queen's Univ, Ont, PhD (microbiol & immunol), 1972. **Honors & Awards:** Wild Leitz Jr Sci Award, Exp Path, 1980. **Professional Experience:** SR SCIENTIST, MOLECULAR & CELL BIOL, S&W, as of 2005; ADJ PROF, CANCER BIOL, MD ANDERSON CANCER CTR, UNIV TEX, as of 2005; PROF MED BIOPHYS, UNIV TORONTO, as of 2005; PROF, LAB MED & PATHOBIOL, MED, UNIV TORONTO, as of 2005; prof Antiogenesis, Antiangiogenic Ther & Drug Resistance, Univ Toronto, beginning 2002; dir Canver Biol, S&W, beginning 1991; res assoc, Nat Cancer Inst Can, beginning 1981; assoc ed, Inv & Metastasis, Cancer Metastasis Rev, beginning 1981; mem study sect B, NIH, 1981-1982; from asst prof to assoc prof, Dept Path, Queen's Univ, 1980-1991; mem, Grants Panel B, Nat Cancer Inst Can, 1977-1981; res scholar, Nat Cancer Inst Can, 1975-1981; King George V Silver Jubilee Cancer Res fel, Nat Cancer Inst Can, 1973-1974; res fel, Nat Cancer Inst Can, Chester Beatty Res Inst, London, 1972-1974. **Memberships:** Brit Soc Immunol; Can Soc Immunol; Am Asn Immunologists; Can Assoc Pathol. **Research Statement & Publications:** Cancer; tumor biology; immunology; cell biology of cancer metastasis studied using membrane mutant tumor sublines; tumor progression and heterogeneity; membrane biology of activated lymphocyte and macrophage cell populations. **Mailing Address:** Div Cancer Biol, Sunnybrook & Women's Coll Health Sci Ctr, Rm S218, Res Bldg, 2075 Bayview Ave, Toronto, ON M4N 3M5, Can. **Fax:** 416-480-5703. **E-Mail:** kerbel@srcl.sunnybrook.utoronto.ca

KERBER, ERICH RUDOLPH, CYTOGENETICS. **Personal Data:** b Langham, Sask, April 2, 1926; m 1956, c 2. **Education:** Univ Sask, BSA, 1950, MSc, 1953; Univ Alta, PhD (cytogenetics), 1958. **Honors & Awards:** Gold Medal, Prof Inst Pub Serv Can, 1983. **Professional Experience:** WHEAT CYTOGENETICIST, RES STA, CAN DEPT AGR, 1960-; Res officer, plant breeding, 1956-1960. **Memberships:** AAAS; Genetics Soc Can; Am Soc Agron; Am Soc Crop Sci. **Research Statement & Publications:** Plant cytology and genetics; cytogenetic investigations on the transfer of rust resistance to common wheat from related species and endosperm proteins of wheat related to baking quality. **Mailing Address:** 195 Dafoe Rd, Winnipeg, MB R3T 2M9, Can.

KERBER, RICHARD E, CARDIOVASCULAR DISEASES. **Personal Data:** b New York, NY, May 10, 1939; m Linda K; c Ross & Justin. **Education:** Columbia Univ, AB, 1960; NY Univ, MD, 1964. **Honors & Awards:** Award Merit Achievement, Am Heart Asn, Scientific Coucils Distinguished Achievement Award, Am HEart Asn. **Professional Experience:** PROF & ASSOC DIV DIR INT MED, COL MED, UNIV IOWA, 1978-; From asst prof to assoc prof, Col Med, Univ Iowa, 1971-1978; Asn dir, Cardiol Div, Univ Iowa. **Memberships:** Am Soc Echocardiography Pres; Am Heart Asn; fel Am Col Cardiol; Am Soc Clin Invest; Asn Am Physicians; Asn Univ Cardiologists. **Research Statement & Publications:** Echocardiography; resuscitation; defibrillation and cardioversion; cardiovascular pharmacology. **Mailing Address:** Dept Int Med, Univ Iowa Hosps & Clins, Iowa City, IA 52242-0001. **Fax:** 319-356-4552. **E-Mail:** richard_kerber@uiowa.edu

KERBER, ROBERT CHARLES, CHEMICAL EDUCATION. **Personal Data:** b Hartford, Conn, November 29, 1938; American citizen. **Education:** Mass Inst Technol, SB, 1960; Purdue Univ, PhD (org chem), 1965. **Professional Experience:** DIST TEACHING PROF, STATE UNIV NY, STONY BROOK, 2001-; vis scientist, Brookhaven Nat Lab, 1983; fel, Humboldt Found, WGer, 1973-1974; from asst prof to prof, State Univ NY, Stony Brook, 1965-2001; fel org chem, Purdue Univ, 1965. **Memberships:** AAAS; Am Chem Soc; Royal Soc Chem. **Research Statement & Publications:** Effects of terminology on student comprehension; historical development of ideas. **Mailing Address:** Dept Chem, State Univ NY, 775 Chem Bldg, Stony Brook, NY 11794-3400. **Fax:** 516-632-7960. **E-Mail:** robert.kerber@stonybrook.edu

KERBER, RONALD LEE, MECHANICAL ENGINEERING, ELECTRICAL ENGINEERING. **Personal Data:** b Lafayette, Ind, July 2, 1943; m 1963. **Education:** Purdue Univ, BS, 1965; Calif Inst Technol, MS, 1966, PhD (eng sci), 1970. **Professional Experience:** RETIRED; exec vpres & chief tech officer, Whirlpool Corp, 1991-2004; vpres tech bus develop, McDonnell Douglas Corp, 1988-1991; dep undersecretary, Dept Defense, 1985-1988; assoc dean eng & dir, Div Eng Res, 1980-1983; prof mech & elec eng, Div Eng, 1978-1985; assoc dir, Div Eng, 1978-1980; mem tech staff, Aerospace Corp, 1970-1972; from asst prof to assoc prof mech eng, Mich State Univ, 1969-1978. **Memberships:** Am Soc Mech Engrs; Inst Elec & Electronics Engrs. **Research Statement & Publications:** Theory of phase transitions and liquids, gas-surface interaction, chemical and molecular lasers. **Mailing Address:** Whirlpool Corp R & E Ctr, Monte Rd, Benton Harbor, MI 49022.

KERBISPETERHANS, JULIAN C, DISTRIBUTION & SYSTEMATICS OF SMALL AFRICAN MAMMALS, TAPHONOMY IN AFRICAN SAVANNAH & RAIN FOREST CONTEXTS. **Personal Data:** b Chicago, Ill, December 13, 1952; m 1993, Pamela K Austin. **Education:** Beloit Col, Wis, BSc, 1974; Univ Chicago, MA, 1979, PhD (anthropol), 1990. **Professional Experience:** ASSOC PROF NATURAL SCI, ROOSEVELT UNIV, as of 2004; adj cur, div mammals, Roosevelt Univ, as of 2004; Adj fac anthrop, Univ Chicago, 1993-; RES ASSOC, COMT EVOLUTIONARY & ENVIRON BIOL, 1993-; consult, Forensic Lab, US Fish & Wildlife Serv, 1992-; prog developer & coordr, Minority Undergrad Training Prog, 1992-1993; CURATORIAL ASSOC, FIELD MUS, 1990-; Co-prin investr, NSF, 1989 & 1992-1993; collection mgr, Comt Evolutionary & Environ Biol, 1987-1989; Lectr, Loyola Univ Chicago, 1981-1982. **Memberships:** Am Soc Mammalogists. **Research Statement & Publications:** Systematics and distribution of African mammals, especially those confined to the Albertine Rift mountaintops of central Africa; taphonomy of mammals in African contexts; establishing a suite of fingerprints necessary in identifying agents of predation; making inferences on the sociobiology of the prey species; taphonomy; paleoanthropology. **Mailing Address:** Div Mammals, Roosevelt Univ, Rm CPA205-L, PO Box CPA205, Schaumburg, IL 60173. **Fax:** 312-281-3132. **E-Mail:** jkerbis@roosevelt.edu

KERCE, ROBERT H, MATHEMATICS. **Personal Data:** b Bartow, Fla, November 29, 1925; m 1946, c 3. **Education:** Ga Inst Tech, BME, 1946; Vanderbilt Univ, MS, 1957; George Peabody Col, PhD (math), 1965. **Professional Experience:** RETIRED; prof math, David Lipscomb Univ, as of 2002; adj prof math, David Lipscomb Col, beginning 1990; prof, David Lipscomb Col, 1985-1990; chmn dept, David Lipscomb Col, beginning 1965; chmn dept, David Lipscomb Col, 1965-1985; from instr to assoc prof, David Lipscomb Col, 1946-1966. **Memberships:** Math Asn Am; Nat Coun Teachers Math. **Mailing Address:** Dept Math, Lipscomb Univ, 3901 Granny White Pike, Nashville, TN 37204-3951.

KERCHER, CONRAD J, ANIMAL NUTRITION. **Personal Data:** b Yakima, Wash, June 17, 1926; m 1946, Lydia; c Kathryn A, Nina L, Jane M & Kise S. **Education:** Mont State Col, BS, 1950; Cornell Univ, MS, 1952, PhD (animal nutrit), 1954. **Professional Experience:** PROF EMER, COL AGR, UNIV WYO, 1996-; head, Animal Sci Dept, 1987-1988; actg vpres, Acad Affairs, 1975-1976; animal nutritionist, Univ Wyo, 1954-1996; assoc animal nutrit, Cornell Univ, 1950-1954; consult, Agency Int Develop. **Memberships:** AAAS; fel Am Soc Animal Sci; Am Dairy Sci Asn; Am Registry Prof Animal Scientists (pres); Am Forage & Grassland Coun. **Research Statement & Publications:** Forage harvesting systems; sources of dietary fat for ruminants; alternate crops for ruminants; feed additives for cattle; replacement value of feeds for ruminants. **Mailing Address:** Dept Animal Sci, Col Agr, Univ Wyo, PO Box 3684 1000 E Univ Ave, Laramie, WY 82071. **Fax:** 307-766-2355. **E-Mail:** kercher@uwyo.edu

KERCHNER, HAROLD RICHARD, EXPERIMENTAL SOLID-STATE PHYSICS, MAGNETIC AND TRANSPORT-CURRENT CHARACTERIZATION OF TYPE-II SUPERCONDUCTORS. **Personal Data:** b Lewistown, Pa, March 5, 1946; m 1968, Ruth Fisher; c Geoffrey A & Nichole D. **Education:** Harvard Univ, AB, 1968; Univ Ill, MS, 1972, PhD (physics), 1974. **Professional Experience:** Dir, Nat Low-Temp Neutron Irradiation Facil, Oak Ridge Nat Lab, 1985-1988; RES STAFF MEM, SOLID STATE PHYSICS, OAK RIDGE NAT LAB, 1976-; Res Assoc, Martin Marietta Energy Syst, 1974-1976. **Memberships:** Am Phys Soc; Mat Res Soc. **Research Statement & Publications:** Type II superconductivity; radiation effects in materials. **Mailing Address:** MS 061 Oak Ridge Nat Lab, PO Box 2008 Bldg 3115, Oak Ridge, TN 37831-2008. **Fax:** 423-574-6270. **E-Mail:** hrk@ornl.gov

KERDESKY, FRANCIS A J, CHEMISTRY. **Personal Data:** b Wilkes-Barre, Pa, March 10, 1953. **Education:** Wilkes Col, BS, 1975; Univ Pa, PhD (org chem), 1980. **Professional Experience:** RES INVESTR, ABBOTT LABS, N CHICAGO, 1981-as of today; res assoc, Mass Inst Technol, 1980-1981. **Memberships:** Am Chem Soc; Sigma Xi. **Research Statement & Publications:** Design and synthesis of drugs; process research; synthesis of natural products. **Mailing Address:** Abbott Labs, 100 Abbott Park Rd, Abbott Park, IL 60064-6124. **Fax:** 847-937-1511. **E-Mail:** kerdesky@aol.com

KEREIAKES, JAMES GUS, PHYSICS. **Personal Data:** b Columbus, Ohio, August 15, 1924; m 1950, c 4. **Education:** Western Ky State Col, BS, 1945; Univ Cincinnati, MS, 1947, PhD (physics), 1950; Am Bd Radiol, dipl radiol physics, 1960. **Honors & Awards:** Coolidge Award, Am Asn Physicists in Med, 1981, Gold Medal, 1985; Gold Medal, Radiol Soc N Am, 1988. **Professional Experience:** PROF EMER RADIOL, COL MED, UNIV CINCINNATI, 1991-; prof, Col Med, Univ Cincinnati, 1968-1991; from asst prof to assoc prof, Col Med, Univ Cincinnati, 1959-1968; dep dir, dept radiobiol, 1957-1959; supvy physicist, dept radiobiol, 1953-1957; res physicist, Environ Med Br, Med Res Lab, US Army, Ky, 1950-1953. **Memberships:** AAAS; Am Soc Therapeut Radiol Oncol; Biophys Soc; Radiation Res Soc; Am Asn Physicists Med (pres, 1969-1970); Radiol Soc North Am (vpres, 1981-1982). **Research Statement & Publications:** Radiation physics and biology; radiopharmaceutical dosimetry. **Mailing Address:** Dept Radiol, Univ Cincinnati, E555 Med Sci Bldg, PO Box 670579, Cincinnati, OH 45267-0579. **Fax:** 513-558-0300.

KEREKES, RICHARD JOSEPH, FLUID MECHANICS, SUSPENSIONS. **Personal Data:** b Welland, Ont, July 9, 1940; m 1978. **Education:** Univ Toronto, BASc, 1963, MASc, 1965; McGill Univ, PhD (chem eng), 1970. **Honors & Awards:** Beloit Award, Tech Asn Pulp Paper & converting Indust Eng Div, 1997. **Professional Experience:** PAPRICAN PROF PULP & PAPER ENG, UNIV BC, as of 2004; DIR, PULP & PAPER CTR, UNIV BC, 1983-; HON PROF CHEM ENG, UNIV BC, 1978-; sect head, Pulp & Paper Res Inst Can, 1977-1983; scientist, Pulp & Paper Res Inst Can, 1971-1977. **Memberships:** Can Soc Chem Eng; Can Pulp & Paper Asn. **Research Statement & Publications:** Fibre flocculation; mixing in pulp suspensions; pulp screening. **Mailing Address:** Dept Chem & Bio Eng, Univ Bc, 2216 Main Mall, Vancouver, BC V6T 1Z2, Can. **Fax:** 604822-8563. **E-Mail:** kerekes@ppc.ubc.ca

KEREN, JOSEPH, PHYSICS. **Personal Data:** b Czech, February 28, 1930; m 1964. **Education:** Univ Melbourne, BSc, 1954, MSc, 1956; Columbia Univ, PhD (physics), 1963. **Professional Experience:** ASSOC PROF PHYSICS, NORTHWESTERN UNIV, 1969-; asst prof, Northwestern Univ, 1965-1969; res assoc, Australian Nat Univ, 1963-1964; Instr physics, Agr & Mech Col Tex, 1956-1957. **Memberships:** Am Phys Soc. **Research Statement & Publications:** Theoretical investigations of charge transfer reactions in helium-helium scattering; experimental work in elementary particles. **Mailing Address:** Dept Physics Northwestern Univ, 1373 Tech Inst 2145 Sheridan Rd, Evanston, IL 60201-5506.

KERFOOT, CHARLES, ECOLOGY. **Education:** Univ Mich, PhD, 1972. **Professional Experience:** PROF, DEPT ECOL & BOT, MICH TECHNOL UNIV as of 2005; DIR, LAKE SUPERIRO ECOSYSTS RES CTR, as of 2005. **Research Statement & Publications:** Aquatic ecology; groundwater coupling; sediment transport; how different zooplankton populations develop in nearshore and offshore waters; the importance of recruitment from resting eggs; how the Keweenaw current transports individuals and resting eggs around the lake; creating a coastal corridor. **Mailing Address:** Dept Biol Sci, Mich Technol Univ, 1400 Townsend Dr Rm 722 Dow, Houghton, MI 49931-1295. **Fax:** 906-487-3371. **E-Mail:** wkerfoot@mtu.edu

KERFOOT, WILSON CHARLES, LIMNOLOGY, EVOLUTIONARY ECOLOGY. **Personal Data:** b Staten Island, NY, March 13, 1944; m 1978, Lucille; c Alex & Katherine. **Education:** Univ Kans, BA (zoology) & BA (geol), 1966; Univ Mich, PhD (zoology), 1972. **Honors & Awards:** Hon Woodrow Wilson Scholar. **Professional Experience:** DIR, LAKE SUPERIOR ECOSYSTS RES CTR, 1992-; PROF AQUATIC ECOL, DEPT BIOL SCI, MICH TECHNOL UNIV, AS OF 2006; co-dir, Lake Superior Ecosysts Res Ctr, 1990-1992; on leave assoc prof aquatic ecol, Dept Biol, Sch Natural Resources, Univ Mich, 1989; assoc prof, Mich State Technol Univ, 1989-1991; adj assoc prof, Dept Biol, Sch Natural Resources, Univ Mich, 1985-1989; assoc res scientist, Great Lakes Res Div, Univ Mich, 1984-1990; vis assoc res scientist, Great Lakes Res Div, Univ Mich, 1983-1984; assoc prof res ecol, Dept Biol Sci, Dartmouth Col, 1982-1983; vis sr scientist, Ctr Ecosysts Studies, Cornell Univ, 1981-1983; asst prof aquatic ecol, Dept Biol Sci, Dartmouth Col, 1975-1982; res assoc, Dept Zool, Univ Wash, 1973-1976; NSF fel limnol, Dept Zool, Univ Wash, 1972-1973. **Memberships:** Ecol Soc Am; Am Soc Limnol & Oceanog; Am Soc Naturalists; Int Asn Theoret &Appl Limnol; Int Asn Ecol; Int Asn Great Lakes Res. **Research Statement & Publications:** Aquatic ecology of large and small lakes; zooplankton population biology and evolution; paleoecology of zooplankton; limnology; community ecology. **Mailing Address:** Dept Biol Sci, Mich Technol Univ, 722 DOW Bldg 1400 Townsend Dr, Houghton, MI 49931-1200. **Fax:** 906-487-3371. **E-Mail:** wkerfoot@mtu.edu

KERJASCHKI, DONTSCHO, IMMUNOPATHOLOGY. **Personal Data:** b Vienna, Austria, February 8, 1947; m 1981, c 2. **Education:** Albertus Magnus Sch, Vienna, Natura, 1965, Univ Vienna, MD, 1972. **Honors & Awards:** Vollhard Prize, Ger Nephrology Soc, 1990. **Professional Experience:** DIR, DIV ULTRASTRUCT PATH & CELL BIOL, 1990-; vis res scientist cell biol, Div Cellular & Molecular Med, Univ Calif, San Diego, 1989-; PROF PATH & CELL BIOL, DEPT PATH, UNIV VIENNA, 1986-; vis prof cell biol, Yale Univ Sch Med, 1980-1988; mem, Comn Cell Biol, Int Soc Nephrology. **Memberships:** Int Soc Nephrology. **Research Statement & Publications:** Molecular aspects of autoimmune diseases, especially kidney. **Mailing Address:** Dept Clin Path, Univ Vienna AKH Wahringer Gurtel 18-20, Vienna A-1090, Austria. **Fax:** 431-404-005193.

KERKA, WILLIAM (FRANK), MECHANICAL ENGINEERING. **Personal Data:** b Cleveland, Ohio, April 5, 1921; m 1953, c 1. **Education:** Fenn Col, BS, 1948; Case Inst Technol, MS, 1952. **Professional Experience:** ASSOC PROF EMER, CLEVELAND STATE UNIV, as of 2006; assoc prof mech eng, Cleveland State Univ, 1977-1981; assoc dean eng, Cleveland State Univ, 1961-1977; res engr res lab, Am Soc Heating, Refrig & Air-Conditioning Engrs, 1954-1961; instr mech eng, Ore State Col, 1952-1954; instr graphics, Case Inst Technol, 1951-1952. **Research Statement & Publications:** Odor control and acoustics as related to air conditioning. **Mailing Address:** 2913 Priscilla Ave, Cleveland, OH 44134.

KERKAR, AWDHOOT VASANT, POLYMER ENGINEERING. **Personal Data:** b Bombay, India, September 20, 1963; m 1990. **Education:** Univ Bombay, BChemE, 1984; Univ Pittsburgh, MS, 1986; Case Western Reserve Univ, PhD (chem eng), 1990. **Professional Experience:** RES ENGR, W R GRACE & CO, 1990-; res asst chem eng, Case Western Reserve Univ, 1986-1990; res asst chem eng, Univ Pittsburgh, 1984-1986. **Memberships:** Am Ceramic Soc. **Research Statement & Publications:** Products and processes for materials application such as ceramics, polymers and their composites; chemical engineering, colloid science and polymer processing to develop novel processing strategies for materials. **Mailing Address:** W R Grace Co, Columbia, MD 21045.

KERKAY, JULIUS, CLINICAL CHEMISTRY. **Personal Data:** b Sopron, Hungary, April 27, 1934; American citizen; c 2. **Education:** Veszprem Tech Univ, BS, 1955, MS, 1956; Univ Louisville, PhD (biochem), 1969; Am Bd Clin Chem, dipl. **Honors & Awards:** Outstanding Contrib in Educ, Am Assoc Clin Chem, 1988. **Professional Experience:** PROF EMER CHEM & BIOL, CLEVELAND STATE UNIV, 1981-; affil staff, St Luke's Hosp Cleveland, 1977-1985; assoc prof & dir clin chem, Cleveland State Univ, 1974-1981; adj consult, Cleveland Clin Found, 1970-1985; asst prof, Cleveland State Univ, 1970-1974; speaker, Health Careers Info, Cleveland Hosp Coun, 1969-; consult, Diamond Shamrock Health Sci Labs, 74-76. sci vpres, Euclid Clin Res Found, 1969-1986; dir lab, Euclid Clin Found, 1968-1970; Adj prof, Cleveland State Univ, 1968-1970; chief anal sect, US Army Res Inst Environ Med, 1962-1964; asst in res, Cleveland Clin Found, 1958-1959; technician, Alloys & Chem Mfg Co, Ohio, 1957-1958; Chief chem engr, Alcohol Factory Gyor, Hungary, 1956. **Memberships:** AAAS; fel Am Asn Clin Chem; fel Am Inst Chem; NY Acad Sci; Am Chem Soc; Sigma Xi; Nat Registry Clin Chem. **Research Statement & Publications:** protein electrophoresis; protein and steroid hormone interactions; serum constituents of mothers of down syndrome children; clinical chemistry methodology, computerization in clinical chemistry; changes in body fluid constituents of hemodialysis patients; development of radiobioassays for vitamins and isoenzymes; plasticizers and their metabolites in human organs and body fluids; awarded one US patent. **Mailing Address:** Tatorjan U 11, Veszprem, H-8200, Hungary.

KERKER, MILTON, PHYSICAL CHEMISTRY, LIGHT SCATTERING. **Personal Data:** b Utica, NY, September 25, 1920; m 1946, Reva Stemerman; c Ruth A, Martin, Susan & Joel. **Education:** Columbia Univ, AB, 1941, MA, 1947, PhD (chem), 1949. **Honorary Degrees:** DSc, Lehigh Univ, 1975 & Clarkson Univ, 1985. **Honors & Awards:** Kendall

Award, Am Chem Soc, 1971; Langmuir Lectr, Div Coloid Chem, Am Chem Soc, 1981. **Professional Experience:** EMER PROF, CLARKSON UNIV, 1991-; titular mem & secy comn on colloids & surfaces, Int Union Pure & Appl Chem, 1978-1983; Thomas S Clarkson prof, Clarkson Univ, 1974-1991; vis prof, Hebrew Univ & Technion, 1974-1975; chmn, Nat Acad Sci-Nat Res Coun Comt Colloids & Surface Chem, 1970-1974; Unilever prof, Univ Bristol, 1967-1968; dean sch arts & sci, Clarkson Univ, 1966-1974; Ed-in-chief, J Colloid & Interface Sci, 1965-1993; dean sch sci, Clarkson Univ, 1964-1966 & 1981-1985; chmn dept, Clarkson Univ, 1960-1964; fel, Ford Found, 1952-1953; from instr to prof, Clarkson Univ, 1949-1960; Asst chem, Columbia Univ, 1946-1949. **Memberships:** Am Chem Soc; Hist Sci Soc; fel Optical Soc Am; Sigma Xi. **Research Statement & Publications:** Light scattering; aerosols; history of science; surface enhanced; Raman scattering; heteropoly acids. **Mailing Address:** 7291 W Country Club Dr N 119, Sarasota, FL 34243.

KERKMAN, DANIEL JOSEPH, CHEMISTRY. **Personal Data:** b Milwaukee, Wis, September 17, 1951; m 1973, c 2. **Education:** Johns Hopkins Univ, MA, 1976; Mass Inst Technol, PhD (chem), 1979. **Professional Experience:** MED CHEMIST, ABBOTT LABS, 1980-; Assoc fel, Mass Inst Technol, 1979-1980. **Memberships:** Am Chem Soc. **Research Statement & Publications:** Medicinal chemistry. **Mailing Address:** 21 Cremin Dr, Lake Villa, IL 60046-8864.

KERKMAN, RUSSEL JOHN, ELECTRICAL ENGINEERING. **Personal Data:** b Burlington, Wis, August 11, 1948; m 1971. **Education:** Purdue Univ, BS, 1971, MS, 1973, PhD (elec eng), 1976. **Professional Experience:** ENG CONSULT, ALLEN-BRADLEY CO, as of 2000; PRIN ENGR, ALLEN-BRADLEY CO, 1986-; sr proj engr, Allen-bradley CO, 1980-1986; Elec engr mach anal, Gen Elec Co, 1976-1980. **Memberships:** Inst Elec & Electronics Engrs. **Research Statement & Publications:** Electric machine design and analysis; power systems; control systems; solid state power conditioning; AC motor drives. **Mailing Address:** 6815 W Howard Ave, Milwaukee, WI 53220. **Fax:** 262-512-8300. **E-Mail:** rjkerkman@ra.rockwell.com

KERLAN, JOEL THOMAS, ENDOCRINOLOGY. **Personal Data:** b Minneapolis, Minn, February 23, 1940. **Education:** Col St Thomas, Minn, BS, 1952; Univ Utah, MS, 1965; Univ Mich, Ann Arbor, PhD (zoology), 1972. **Professional Experience:** PROF EMER BIOL, HOBART & WILLIAM SMITH COL, as of 2004; assoc prof biol, Hobart & William Smith Cols, 1981-2001; vis prof, Dept Obstet & Gynec, Univ Mich, 1975; asst prof, Hobart & William Smith Cols, 1971-1981; instr, Hobart & William Smith Cols, 1970-1971. **Memberships:** Sigma Xi; Am Soc Zoologists. **Research Statement & Publications:** Regulation and biosynthesis of sex steroid hormones in vertebrate testes. **Mailing Address:** Dept Biol, Hobart & William Smith Col, Geneva, NY 14456. **Fax:** 315-781-3860. **E-Mail:** kerlan@hws.edu

KERLEE, DONALD D, NUCLEAR PHYSICS, MANAGEMENT INFORMATION. **Personal Data:** b Ryderwood, Wash, December 22, 1926; m 1950, c 4. **Education:** Seattle Pac Col, BS, 1951; Univ Wash, PhD (physics), 1956. **Professional Experience:** PROF EMER PHYSICS, SEATTLE PAC COL, 1990-; dir planning res, Seattle Pac Col, 1979-1984; dir res, Seattle Pac Col, 1976-1979; vpres admin, Seattle Pac Col, 1974-1976; acad vpres, Roberts Wesleyan Col, 1969-1974; Am Inst Physics & Am Asn Physics Teachers regional counsr, Wash State, 1965-1969; sci fac fel, Univ Manchester, 1963-1964; chmn dept, Seattle Pac Col, 1962-1969; dir inst res, Seattle Pac Col, 1959-1969; from asst prof to prof, Seattle Pac Col, 1956-1969; res instr physics, Univ Wash, 1956. **Memberships:** AAAS; Am Asn Physics Teachers; Am Phys Soc; Sigma Xi; Asn Comput Mach. **Research Statement & Publications:** Heavy ion, nuclear and cosmic ray physics; institutional planning; forecasting models; Elastic scattering; alpha particles. **Mailing Address:** Dept Physics, Seattle Pac Col, Otto Miller Hall 3307 Third Ave W, Seattle, WA 98119-1997.

KERLEY, GERALD IRWIN, STATISTICAL MECHANICS, EQUATIONS OF STATE. **Personal Data:** b Houston, Tex, March 23, 1941. **Education:** Ohio Univ, BS, 1963; Univ Ill, PhD (chem physics), 1966. **Professional Experience:** SCI TECH CONSULT, APPOMATOX, VA, 1995-; sr mem tech staff, Computational Physics & Mech Dept, Sandia Nat Lab, 1984-1995; staff mem phys chem, Los Alamos Nat Lab, Univ Calif, 1969-1984; US Army Officer, 1967-1969; fel chem, Univ Ill, 1966-1967. **Research Statement & Publications:** Theory and calculation of equations of state of gases, liquids, and solids; statistical mechanics; theory of electrons in condensed matter; atomic physics; shock wave physics; theory of explosives. **Mailing Address:** PO Box 709, Appomattox, VA 24522. **Fax:** 434-352-4973. **E-Mail:** gkerley@compuserve.com

KERLEY, MICHAEL A, ANATOMY. **Personal Data:** b Crockett, Tex, April 17, 1941; m 1985, Jordana; c Timothy, Erin, Arista, Blayne & Graham. **Education:** Stephen F Austin State Col, BS, 1964; Tex A&M Univ, MS, 1969, PhD (zoology), 1971. **Professional Experience:** PROF BIOL, SOUTHWESTERN OKLA STATE UNIV, as of 2003; CHAIR, SOUTHWESTERN OKLA STATE UNIV, 1993-; fel, Health Ctr, Univ Conn, 1975-1977; assoc prof biol, Southwestern Okla State Univ, beginning 1971. **Memberships:** Am Asn Anatomists. **Research Statement & Publications:** Embryonic development of mammalian dentitions. **Mailing Address:** Dept Biol Sci, Southwestern Okla State Univ, 100 Campus Dr, Weatherford, OK 73096.

KERLEY, TROY LAMAR, PHARMACOLOGY. **Personal Data:** b Allen, Okla, August 20, 1929; m 1950, c 1. **Education:** Univ Okla, BS, 1953, MS, 1955; Purdue Univ, PhD (pharmacol), 1958. **Professional Experience:** PHARMACEUT CONSULT, 1992-; dir tech eval-licensing, 3M Pharmaceut, 1989-1992; dir new bus develop, 3M Health Care Ltd, Tokyo, 1984-1989; dir int new bus develop, Riker Labs Res & Develop, 1981-1984; tech dir, Riker Labs Res & Develop, 1973-1980; dir biol res, 3M Co, 1971-1973; dir biol sci sect, Riker Labs, Calif, 1966-1971; head biomed res dept, Dow Chem Co, 1964-1966; Pharmacologist, Dow Chem Co, 1957-1964. **Memberships:** AAAS; Sigma Xi; Am Pharmaceut Asn; Am Found Pharmaceut Educ; Am Soc Pharmacol & Exp Therapeut. **Research Statement & Publications:** Pharmacologic aspects of the blood-brain barrier; neuromuscular pharmacology; pharmacology and physiology of tremor and rigidity syndromes; asthmatic pharmacology. **Mailing Address:** 1926 Cypress Pt W, Austin, TX 78746.

KERLICK, GEORGE DAVID, THEORETICAL PHYSICS. **Personal Data:** b Sharon, Pa, June 24, 1949. **Education:** Rensselaer Polytech Inst, BS, 1970; Princeton Univ, MA, 1972, PhD (physics), 1975. **Professional Experience:** RETIRED; consult, 1990-2004; prin scientist, Tektronix Inc, 1989-1990; res scientist Sterling Software, Comput Sci Coordr, 1989; res scientist Sterling Software, NASA Ames Res Ctr, 1983-1988; res scientist, Comput Fluid Dynamics Dept, Nielsen Eng & Res Inc, 1979-1983; adj asst prof physics, Univ San Francisco, 1978-1979; vis asst prof math, Ore State Univ, 1977-1978; fel physics, Max-Planck Inst, Munich, 1976-1977; res fel physics, Alexander von Humboldt Found, Univ Cologne, 1975-1976; res res assoc physics, Mont State Univ, 1975. **Memberships:** Am Phys Soc; Asn Comput Mach; Soc Indust & Appl Math; Sigma Xi. **Research Statement & Publications:** Scientific visualization; computer graphics; computational geometry. **Mailing Address:** 6342 34th Ave SW, Seattle, WA 98126. **E-Mail:** davidk@eskimo.com

KERLIN, THOMAS W, NUCLEAR ENGINEERING. **Personal Data:** b Charlotte, NC, April 7, 1936; m 1954, c 3. **Education:** Univ SC, BSChE, 1958; Univ Tenn, MS, 1959, PhD (eng sci), 1965. **Honors & Awards:** Glenn Murphy Award, Am Soc Eng Educ, 1978. **Professional Experience:** PROF EMER NUCLEAR ENG, UNIV TENN, KNOXVILLE, 1976-; consult, Oak Ridge Nat Lab, 1966-; assoc prof, Univ Tenn, Knoxville, 1966-1976; res engr, Atomics Int Div, NAm Aviation, 1959-1961; res engr, Oak Ridge Nat Lab, 1961-1966. **Memberships:** Am Nuclear Soc; Instrument Soc Am; Am Soc Eng Educ. **Research Statement & Publications:** Instrumentation, thermometry and process simulation. **Mailing Address:** Keltic Fla, PO Box 2917, Ft Walton Beach, FL 32549. **E-Mail:** jkerlin@utk.edu

KERMAN, ARTHUR KENT, THEORETICAL PHYSICS. **Personal Data:** b Montreal, Que, May 3, 1929; American citizen; m 1952, Enid; c Ben, Daniel, Elisabeth, Melissa & Andrew. **Education:** McGill Univ, BS, 1950; Mass Inst Technol, PhD, 1953. **Honors & Awards:** Humboldt Sr US Scientist Award, Max Planck Inst, 1985. **Professional Experience:** Comt sci, Nat Res Coun, 1985; dir, Lab Nuclear Sci, 1983-1992; comt sci & technol, Exec Off Pres, White House Sci Coun, 1982-1985 & Argonne Nat Lab, Univ Chicago, 1984-; comt nuclear sci, Dept Energy & NSF, 1982-1985; mem, comt sci & acad, Lawrence Livermore Nat Lab & Los Alamos Sci Lab, 1981-; Oak Ridge Nat Lab, 1979- & Nat Bur Standards, 1980-1981; theory div, Los Alamos Sci Lab, 1977-1985 & Physics Div, 1984; dir, Ctr Theoret Physics, 1976-1983; chmn, Lawrence Berkeley Nat Lab, 1976-1978 & 1981; assoc prof, Inst Nuclear Physics, Univ Paris-South, beginning 1975; consult, Lawrence Berkeley Nat Lab, 1975-1980; mem adv comt high energy, Brookhaven Nat Lab, 1975; foreign mem, Sci Coun Nat Inst Nuclear & Particle Physics, Nat Ctr Sci Res, Paris, France, 1972-1976; adj prof, Brooklyn Col, City Univ New York, 1971-1975 & Argonne Nat Lab; vis prof physics, State Univ NY, Stony Brook, 1970-1971; consult, Brookhaven Nat Lab, 1965-1981; PROF PHYSICS, MASS INST TECHNOL, 1964-; consult, Lawrence Livermore Nat Lab, 1964-; consult, Los Alamos Sci Lab, 1961-; consult, Argonne Nat Lab, 1961-1983; exchange prof, Guggeheim mem fel, Univ Paris, 1961-1962; from asst prof to assoc prof, Lab Nuclear Sci, 1956-1964; mem res staff, Calif Inst Technol, 1953-1954 & Inst Theoret Physics, Copenhagen, 1955-1956; Nat Res Coun Can res fel theoret physics, Calif Inst Technol, 1953-1954 & Inst Theoret Physics, Copenhagen, 1954-1955; Consult, Educ Serv Inc, Shell Develop Co Div, Shell Oil Co, 1953-1958; mem, physics surv comt, Panels Nuclear Data & Heavy Ion Physics, Nat Acad Sci. **Memberships:** fel Am Phys Soc; fel Am Acad Arts & Sci; fel NY Acad Sci. **Research Statement & Publications:** Theoretical nuclear physics. **Mailing Address:** Dept Physics, Mass Inst Technol, Rm 6-302A 77 Mass Ave, Cambridge, MA 02139. **Fax:** 617-253-8554. **E-Mail:** kerman@mitlns.mit.edu

KERMAN, RON A, ANALYSIS & FUNCTIONAL ANALYSIS. **Personal Data:** b Winnipeg, Man, May 31, 1943; m 1967, c 2. **Education:** Univ Manitoba, BA, 1965, MA, 1966; Univ Toronto, PhD (math), 1969. **Professional Experience:** PROF MATH, BROCK UNIV, 1986-; from asst prof to assoc prof math, Brock Univ, 1970-1985. **Memberships:** Am math soc. **Research Statement & Publications:** Weighted norm inequalities with applications to differential equations; approximation theory in weighted lebesgue spaces; weighted convolution algebras. **Mailing Address:** Dept Math, Brock Univ, MC J412, St Catharines, ON L2S 3A1, Can. **Fax:** 905-682-9020. **E-Mail:** rkerman@brocku.ca

KERMANI-ARAB, VALI, REGULATION OF IMMUNE SYSTEM. **Personal Data:** b Bombay, India, January 29, 1939. **Education:** Wash State Univ, PhD (immunol & microbiol), 1975. **Professional Experience:** PRES & TECH SUPVR, IMMUNO BIOGENE, INC, as of 2003; RES SCIENTIST IMMUNOL. **Memberships:** Am Immunol Asn; Am Soc Microbiologist; AAAS. **Mailing Address:** Immunol-Biogene Inc, 22030 Sherman Way, Canoga Park, CA 91303-1855. **Fax:** 310-470-2155.

KERMICLE, JERRY LEE, CORN GENETICS, PLANT MOLECULAR GENETICS. **Personal Data:** b Dundas, Ill, March 8, 1936; m 1957, c 5. **Education:** Univ Ill, BS, 1957; Univ Wis, MS, 1959, PhD (genetics), 1963. **Professional Experience:** PROF EMER GENETICS, UNIV WIS, MADISON, as of 2006; Prof, Genetics, Univ Wis, Madison, beginning 1977; from asst prof to assoc prof, Univ Wis, madison, 1963-1977; fel genetics & biochem, Univ Wis-madison, 1963; NSF & Dept Energy grantee. **Memberships:** AAAS; Genetics Soc Am. **Research Statement & Publications:** Maize genetics, cytogenetics and development; analysis of spontaneous mutation; paramutation and complex loci. **Mailing Address:** Lab Genetics, Univ Wis, 445 G Henry Mall, Madison, WI 53706. **Fax:** 608-262-2976. **E-Mail:** kermicle@wisc.edu

KERMISCH, DORIAN, OPTICS, ELECTROMAGNETICS. **Personal Data:** b Bucharest, Romania, November 13, 1931; m 1962, c 2. **Education:** Israel Inst Technol, BSc, 1955; Polytech Inst Brooklyn, MS, 1964, PhD (elec eng), 1968. **Professional Experience:** SR SCIENTIST OPTICS, XEROX CORP, 1968-; lectr, City Col New York, 1967-1968; res fel, Polytech Inst Brooklyn, 1962-1966; elec engr, Israeli Ministry Defense, 1960-1962. **Memberships:** Optical Soc Am. **Research Statement & Publications:** Theoretical investigations of blazed holograms, volume holograms and phase imaging; optical and computer image processing. **Mailing Address:** Xerox Corp, Penfield, NY 14526.

KERN, BERNARD DONALD, NUCLEAR PHYSICS GAMMA-RAY SPECTROCOPY. **Personal Data:** b New Castle, Ind, October 31, 1919; m 1946, Nedda; c Richard B, Jonathan K & Arthur R. **Education:** Univ Ind, BS, 1942, MS, 1947, PhD (physics), 1949. **Professional Experience:** PROF EMER PHYSICS, UNIV KY, 1985-; vis, Stanford Univ, 1971 & Inst Nuclear Physics, KFA WGer, 1978; chmn, dept physics & astron, 1967-1969; prof, Univ Ky Overseas Prog, Bandung Tech Inst, 1961-1962; vis physicist, US Naval Radiol Defense Lab, 1957-1958; from asst prof to prof, Univ KY, 1950-1985; sr physicist, Nuclear Physics, Oak Ridge Nat Lab, 1949-1950; physics, Ind Univ, 1946-1949; asst nuclear physics, Metall Lab, Chicago, 1943; jr physicist radar, Signal Corps, US Army, 1942-1943. **Memberships:** Am Phys Soc; Am Asn Physics Teachers. **Research Statement & Publications:** Nuclear energy level studies with Van de Graaff accelerator; beta and gamma-ray spectroscopy; radioactive ion induced reactions; nuclear orientation. **Mailing Address:** Dept Physics & Astron, Univ Ky, Lexington, KY 40506-0055. **E-Mail:** blrcamera@aol.com

KERN, CHARLES WILLIAM, THEORETICAL CHEMISTRY. **Personal Data:** b Middletown, Ohio, July 13, 1935; m Regine Bouchard. **Education:** Carnegie Inst Technol, BS, 1957; Univ Minn, PhD (chem), 1961. **Professional Experience:** Vpres res & grad studies, Northwestern Univ, 1992-1997; sect head phys chem & dynamics, Chem Div, 1985-1992; actg dir, Chem Div, 1984-1985; proj mgr, CSNET, 1980-1983; prog dir, NSF, 1978-1980 & 1983-1984; prof chem, Ohio State Univ, 1976-1992; mgr chem phys sect, dir Battelle Inst Prog, 1974-1976; mgr chem phys sect, Battelle Mem Inst, 1972-1976; acad vchmn, Dept Chem, 1972-1973; adj prof, Ohio State Univ, 1971-1976; res scientist, Battelle Mem Inst, 1966-1972; Adj assoc prof, Ohio State Univ, 1966-1971; asst prof chem, State Univ NY Stony Brook, 1964-1966; Fel theoret chem, Dept Chem & IBM Watson Lab, Columbia Univ, 1961-1964. **Memberships:** Am Phys Soc; Am Chem Soc; Sigma Xi. **Research Statement & Publications:** Theoretical chemistry; theory of molecular structure and spectra; quantum and computational chemistry. **Mailing Address:** 1910 Viriginia Ave No. 301, Ft Myers, FL 33901.

KERN, CLIFFORD DALTON, METEOROLOGY. **Personal Data:** b Oakland, Calif, January 6, 1928; m 1951, c 3. **Education:** Univ Calif, Berkeley, AB, 1952; Univ Calif, Los Angeles, MA, 1958; Univ Wash, Seattle, PhD (atmospheric sci), 1965. **Professional Experience:** SR STAFF ENGR & GROUP LEADER, PROPAGATION SCI, LOCKHEED MISSILES & SPACE C0, 1980-; staff engr & group leader, Atmospheric Effects Group, 1978-1980; res supvr, Environ Transp Div, Savannah River Lab, E I du Pont Del Nemours & Co, Inc, 1972-1978; staff meteorologist, Space & Missile Systs Orgn, 1971-1972; chief spec proj br, Air Force Global Weather Ctr, Offutt AFB, Nebr, 1969-1970 & develop activ sci & numerical area, 1970-1971; adv weather officer, Satellite Control Facil, Calif, 1967-1969; tech serv officer, Southeast Asia, 1965-1967; adv weather officer, Cambridge Res Lab & Electronics Systs Div, 1958-1965; weather officer, USAF, 1952-1958. **Memberships:** AAAS; Am Meteorol Soc; Am Geophys Union; Sigma Xi. **Research Statement & Publications:** Infrared emission of the earth and its cloud fields as seen by weather satellites; satellites considering solar interactions with the earth, its upper atmosphere and geomagnetic field; propagation of electromagnetic radiation through the atmosphere and ionosphere. **Mailing Address:** 1879 Cole Rd, Aromas, CA 95004.

KERN, CLIFFORD H, III, DEVELOPMENTAL GENETICS, IMMUNE REGULATION. **Personal Data:** b New Orleans, La, August 30, 1948; m 1972, Arvilla; c Daniel & David. **Education:** Wash & Lee Univ, BS, 1970; Ind Univ, MA, 1972, PhD (zoology), 1979. **Professional Experience:** BIOMED CONSULT, 1998-; res fel, Tulane Univ Sch Med, 1996-1998; Off Pres, Imreg Inc, 1985-1996; lectr, Ind Univ & Purdue Univ, 1981; vis asst prof, Ind Univ, Bloomington, 1981 & 1980; asst prof, genetics and biochem, DePauw Univ, 1979-1981; instr genetics & biochem, DePauw Univ, 1976-1979; prog coordr, Diabetes Proj/Sect Chief, LA Office of Pub Health 1981-1985. **Memberships:** Sigma Xi. **Research Statement & Publications:** Diabetes; genetics and development of female-sterile mutants in Drosophila; development of biological immunomodulators and cancer diagnostics. **Mailing Address:** 1309 Richland Ave, Metairie, LA 70001-3634. **E-Mail:** chkern@bellsouth.net

KERN, ERNEST L, METEOROLOGY. **Education:** Univ S Calif, PhD, 1984. **Professional Experience:** PROF, DEPT GOESCI, SE MO STATE UNIV, as of 2004; DIR, NASA EDCUATOR RESOURCE CTR, SE MO STATE UNIV, as of 2004; DIR, GODWIN CTR SCI & MATH EDU, MO STATE UNIV, as of 2004. **Research Statement & Publications:** Meteorology; oceanography; earth-science/geological education; atmospheric science. **Mailing Address:** Dept Geosci, SE Mo State Univ, Cape Girardeau, MS 0100. **Fax:** 573-290-5255. **E-Mail:** ekern@semovm.semo.edu

KERN, FRANK HOWARD, PEDIATRIC CARDIAC ANESTHESIA, PEDIATRIC CRITICAL CARE MEDICINE. **Personal Data:** b Newark, NJ, July 24, 1956; m Sharon; c David & Aaron. **Education:** George Wash Univ, BS, 1978; Univ Pa, MD, 1982. **Professional Experience:** PROF ANESTHESIOL & PEDIAT, DUKE UNIV, as of 2005; Cecilie Grieg vis prof, Hammersmith Hosp, London, 1992; DIR PEDIAT CARDIAC ANESTHESIOL, DUKE UNIV, 1992-; CHIEF, DIV PEDIAT ANESTHESIOL, DUKE UNIV, 1991-; ASSOC DIR PEDIAT INTENSIVE CARE UNIT, DUKE UNIV, 1991-; lectr pediat crit care & cardiac anesthesiol, Duke Univ Med Ctr, 1991-; assoc prof pediat, Duke Univ Med Ctr, 1991-; instr anesthesia, Children's Hosp & Harvard Med Sch, 1990-1991; assoc prof anesthesiol, Duke Univ med ctr, beginning 1988; fel pediat anesthesiol & critical care, Children's Hosp Philadelphia, 1987-1988; residency anesthesiol, Hosp Univ Pa, 1985-1987; residency pediat, Baylor Col Med, 1982-1985; chmn, First George Wash Conf Biomed Ethics, 1977-1978. **Memberships:** Am Heart Asn; Am Acad Pediat; Am Soc Anesthesiologists; Soc Pediat Anesthesia; fel Soc Critical Care Med; Soc Cardiovascular Anesthesia. **Research Statement & Publications:** Cerebral injury during cardiopulmonary bypass; cardiopulmonary effects of cardiopulmonary bypass; ventilatory strategies in patients with cardiac and respiratory disease. **Mailing Address:** Dept Anesthesiol & Pediat, Duke Univ Med Ctr, PO Box 3046, Durham, NC 27710. **Fax:** 919-681-8357.

KERN, JEROME, VIROLOGY. **Personal Data:** b New York, NY, November 2, 1927; m 1952, c 3. **Education:** Brooklyn Col, BSc, 1950; Ohio State Univ, MSc, 1954; George Wash Univ, PhD (virol), 1962. **Professional Experience:** RETIRED; lab dir, Veridien Corp, 1996-2001 res assoc, Am Type Cult Collection, 1976-1992; sr scientist, Flow Labs, Inc, 1966-1976; res microbiologist, Nat Cancer Inst, 1965-1966; bacteriologist, Nat Inst Allergy & Infectious Dis, 1958-1965; bacteriologist, Walter Reed Army Inst Res, 1957-1958; bacteriologist, US Dept Interior, 1956-1957; res assoc, Smithsonian Inst, 1954-1956; asst bact, Ohio State Univ, 1951-1954. **Memberships:** AAAS; Am Soc Microbiol; Sigma Xi. **Research Statement & Publications:** Serological methods of virus identification; immunological relationships between human and animal viruses; virus purification. **Mailing Address:** 315 S Edison Ave Apt 11, Tampa, FL 33606.

KERN, JOHN PHILIP, INVERTEBRATE PALEONTOLOGY. **Personal Data:** b Springfield, Mass, January 3, 1939; m 1969. **Education:** Univ Calif, Los Angeles, AB, 1963, PhD (geol), 1968. **Professional Experience:** PROF EMER GEOL, SAN DIEGO STATE UNIV, as of 1998; prof geol, San Diego State Univ, beginning 1977; from asst prof to assoc prof, 1968-1977. **Memberships:** Paleont Soc; Paleont Res Inst. **Research Statement & Publications:** Paleoenvironmental studies of late Cenozoic marine invertebrates; trace fossils. **Mailing Address:** Dept Geol Sci, San Diego State Univ, San Diego, CA 92182-1020.

KERN, JOHN W, PETROLEUM ENGINEERING, SPACE RADIATION. **Personal Data:** b Mansfield, Ohio, December 16, 1930; m 1962, c Wesley & Meredyth. **Education:** Univ Calif, Berkeley, BS, 1956, MA, 1958, PhD (geophys), 1960. **Professional Experience:** TECH STAFF, DYNACS ENG INC, 1995-; tech staff, petrophysics & reservoir eng, Rockwell Int, 1991-1995; consult, petrophysics & reservoir eng, Rockwell Int, 1991-1995; dir training, mgr Intepretational Support, 1989-1990; dir training, Atlas Wireline Serv, 1987-1989; staff petrophysicist, Info & Interpretation Systs, Dresser Atlas, Houston, 1984-1987; dir, Info & Interpretation Systs, Dresser Atlas, Houston, 1981-1984; sr res specialist, Exxon Prod Res Co, Houston, 1975-1981; adj prof, Univ Houston, 1975-1978; consult phys scientist, Rand Corp, 1964-1975; from asst prof to prof physics, Univ Houston, 1964-1974; mem working group data anal, comn II, Int Union Geod & Geophys, beginning 1963; Mem comn 4, Int Sci Radio Union, 1962; phys scientist, Rand Corp, Calif, 1960-1964. **Research Statement & Publications:** Rock magnetism; geomagnetism; auroral and magnetospheric physics; solar and planetary physics; well log analysis; well log methods development; well log instrument theory and applications; reservoir description; environment design verification for international space station; ionizing radiation. **Mailing Address:** 18307 Cape Bahamas Ln, Houston, TX 77058. **E-Mail:** jkem@ssfg.jsc.nasa.gov

KERN, MICHAEL DON, AVIAN PHYSIOLOGY. **Personal Data:** b Los Angeles, Calif, November 25, 1938; m 1961, Alice; c Robert, Jeffrey & Sean. **Education:** Whittier Col, BA, 1962; Wash State Univ, MS, 1965, PhD (zoophysiol), 1970. **Professional Experience:** MATEER PROF EMER BIOL, COL WOOSTER, 2003-; prof biol, Col Wooster, beginning 1989-2003; asst prof biol, Col Wooster, 1983-1988; asst prof animal physiol, Col Wooster, 1976-1982; asst prof chordate morphogenesis, Fordham Univ, 1971-1975; USPHS trainee avian reproductive physiol, Cornell Univ, 1969-1971. **Memberships:** Cooper Ornith Soc; Asn Field Ornithologists; Am Ornithologists Union; Sigma Xi. **Research Statement & Publications:** Photoperiodism in birds; annual cycles of birds; avian reproductive physiology, particularly incubation, nests, eggs; alligator eggshells. **Mailing Address:** Dept Biol, Col Wooster, Wooster, OH 44691. **Fax:** 330-263-2378. **E-Mail:** mkern@wooster.edu

KERN, RALPH DONALD, JR, PHYSICAL CHEMISTRY. **Personal Data:** b New Orleans, La, August 8, 1935; m 1961, c 3. **Education:** Univ Tex, Austin, BS, 1957 & 1960, PhD (chem), 1965. **Professional Experience:** CHMN DEPT, UNIV NEW ORLEANS, LAKEFRONT, 1980-; PROF CHEM, UNIV NEW ORLEANS, LAKEFRONT, 1977-; from asst prof to assoc prof, Univ New Orleans, Lakefront, 1967-1977; res fel, Harvard Univ, 1965-1967. **Memberships:** Am Chem Soc; Am Phys Soc; Combustion Inst. **Research Statement & Publications:** Rates of gas phase reactions in shock tubes monitored by infrared emission and time-of-flight mass spectrometry. **Mailing Address:** Dept Chem, Univ New Orleans Lakefront, New Orleans, LA 70122. **E-Mail:** rdkern@uno.edu

KERN, ROLAND JAMES, CHEMISTRY. **Personal Data:** b Bay City, Mich, October 29, 1925; m 1953, c 2. **Education:** Univ Mich, BS, 1948; Northwestern Univ, PhD (chem), 1952. **Professional Experience:** RES CHEMIST, MONSANTO CO, 1952-; fac, Univ Col, Wash Univ. **Memberships:** Am Chem Soc. **Research Statement & Publications:** Polymerization; polymer technology. **Mailing Address:** 50 Forest Crest Dr, Chesterfield, MO 63017.

KERN, WERNER, CHEMICAL VAPOR DEPOSITION, SEMICONDUCTOR PROCESSING. **Personal Data:** b Basel, Switz, March 18, 1925; American citizen; m 1955, Mildred C Patti; c Jeffrey K, Vanessa A & Peter R. **Education:** Univ Basel, Cert chem, 1944; Polyglot Sch Lang, Switz, dipl lang, 1947; Rutgers Univ, AB, 1955. **Honors & Awards:** T C Callinan Award, Electrochem Soc Inc, 1972. **Professional Experience:** Fel, Electrochem Soc, 1991-; sr scientist & tech consult, Teltech, Inc, Minneapolis, 1988-; fel tech staff, David Sarnoff Res Ctr, RCA Corp, 1964-1987 & Lam Res Corp, 1988-1992; PRES, WERNER KERN ASSOC, 1987-; chem vapor deposition course lectr, Am Vacuum Soc, 1981- & Electrochem Soc, 1985-; adv, Electrochem Soc, 1985-1986; chmn, Electrochem Soc, 1983-1984; vchmn, Electrochem Soc, 1981-1982; Safety coun rep, RCA Labs, RCA Corp, 1970-1987; engr & div health physicist, Electronics Component & Devices Div, Somerville, 1959-1964; chief chemist & radiol safety off, Nuclear Corp Am, 1958-1959; anal res chemist, Dept Radioisotope Biochem, 1955-1957; anal res chemist, NJ, 1948-1955; Jr chemist, Hoffmann-LaRoche, Ltd, Switz, 1942-1948. **Memberships:** fel Electrochem Soc; emer mem Am Vacuum Soc. **Research Statement & Publications:** Semiconductor process research; chemical vapor deposition; silicon wafer cleaning technology; chemical etching of microelectronic materials; analytical process control methods; radioactive tracer applications; surface decontamination research; preparation and properties of dielectric films. **Mailing Address:** 22 Greenways Lane, Lakewood, NJ 08701-7501.

KERN, WILLIAM H, PATHOLOGY, CANCER. **Personal Data:** b Nuermberg, Ger, December 25, 1927; c 2. **Education:** Univ Munich, MD, 1952. **Honors & Awards:** Papanicolaou Award, Am Soc Cytol, 1987. **Professional Experience:** DIR LABS, HOSP GOOD SAMARITAN, 1966-. **Memberships:** Col Am Path; Am Asn Cytol; Int Acad Path; Int Acad Cytol. **Research Statement & Publications:** cytopathology of cancer; urinary tract pathology; pathology of vascular bypass grafts. **Mailing Address:** Univ Southern Calif, Sch Med, 2321 Chislehurst Dr, Los Angeles, CA 96027-1046.

KERN, WOLFHARD, HIGH ENERGY PHYSICS. **Personal Data:** b Berlin, Ger, February 18, 1927; m 1952, Hille; c Rainer, Jurgen & Anne. **Education:** Univ Frankfurt, BS, 1948, MS, 1951; Univ Bonn, PhD (physics), 1958. **Professional Experience:** CO-PRIN INVESTR, UNIV MASS DARTMOUTH, as of 2004; vis scientist, Brookhave Nar Lab, 1982-1983 & 1989-1990; vis scientist, Max-Planck Inst, 1975-1976; prof physics, Univ Mass Dartmouth, beginning 1967; scientist, Deutsches Elektronen-Synchrotron, 1965-1967; assoc prof, Univ Mass Dartmouth, 1964-1965; res assoc physics, Mass Inst Tech, 1963-1964; res assoc, Deutsches Elektronen-Synchrotron, 1960-1963; asst prof physics, Univ Bonn, 1958-1960. **Memberships:** Am Phys Soc; Am Asn Physics Teachers; Sigma Xi; AAAS. **Research Statement & Publications:** Experimental high energy physics; meson spectroscopy. **Mailing Address:** Dept Physics, Univ Mass, N Dartmouth, MA 02747. **Fax:** 508-999-9115. **E-Mail:** wkern@umassd.edu

KERNAGHAN, ROY PETER, BIOLOGY, GENETICS. **Personal Data:** b Schenectady, NY, March 26, 1933; m 1956. **Education:** Dartmouth Univ, BA, 1955, MA, 1957; Univ Conn, PhD (genetics), 1963. **Professional Experience:** PROF BIOL & CHMN DEPT, SALISBURY STATE COL, 1974-; asst prof biol sci, State Univ NY, Stony Brook, 1965-1974; NIH trainee electron micros, Col Physicians & Surgeons, Columbia Univ, 1963-1965. **Memberships:** Genetics Soc Am; Am Soc Cell Biol. **Research Statement & Publications:** Developmental genetics. **Mailing Address:** Continuing Educ, Salisbury State Univ 1101 Camden Ave, Salisbury, MD 21801-6800.

KERNAN, ANNE, PHYSICS. **Personal Data:** b Dublin, Ireland, January 15, 1933; American citizen. **Education:** Univ Col, Dublin, BSc, 1953, PhD (physics), 1957. **Honorary Degrees:** DSc, Nat Univ Ireland, 1995. **Professional Experience:** PROF EMER PHYSICS, UNIV CALIF, RIVERSIDE, 1994-; dean, Grad Div & vice chancellor res, 1991-1994; exec Comt, Users Orgn SSC, 1989-1992; Fermilab Prog Adv Comt, 1986-1990; Dept Energy, high energy physics adv panel, 1986-1990; counciller-at-large, Am Phys Soc, 1985-1989; Sci & Educ Adv Comt, Lawrence Berkeley Lab, 1983-1987; mem, Adv Comt Physics, NSF, 1978-1982; chmn dept, Univ Calif, Riverside, 1973-1976; prof physics, Univ Calif, Riverside, 1970-1994; prin investr, Dept Energy, res contract, 1969-1994; assoc prof, Univ Calif, Riverside, 1967-1970; res physicist, Lawrence Berkeley Lab, 1962-1966 & Stanford Linear Accelerator Ctr, Stanford Univ, 1966-1967; asst lectr physics, Univ Col, Dublin, 1958-1962. **Memberships:** AAAS; fel, Council Delegate, 1998-2001; Am Phys Soc fel. **Research Statement & Publications:** Experimental high energy physics. **Mailing Address:** Dept Physics, Univ Calif, 3001 Physics Bldg, Riverside, CA 92521. **Fax:** 909-787-3345. **E-Mail:** kernan@citrus.ucr.edu

KERNAN, MAURICE, GENETICS. **Education:** Univ Wis, PhD. **Professional Experience:** ASSOC PROF, DEPT NEUROBIOLOGY & BEHAV, STATE UNIV NY, as of 2005. **Mailing Address:** Ctr Molecular Med State Univ NY, Rm 447, Stony Brook, NY 11794-5110. **Fax:** 631-632-9182. **E-Mail:** mkernan@notes.cc.sunysb.edu

KERNBERG, OTTO F, PSYCHOANALYSIS. **Personal Data:** b Vienna, Austria, September 10, 1928; American citizen; m Paulina; c Martin, Karen & Adine. **Education:** Univ Chile, BS, 1947, MD, 1953. **Honors & Awards:** Heinz Hartman Award, 1972; Edward A Strecker Award, 1975; William F Schonfeld Award, 1982; Van Geison Award, 1986; Mary S Sigourney Award, 1990. **Professional Experience:** Vis prof, Menninger Sch Psychiat & Mass Gen Hosp, Harvard Med Sch, 1974-1975 & Albert Einstein Col Med, 1977-; assoc ed, J Am Psychoanal Asn, 1977-1993; PROF PSYCHIAT, CORNELL UNIV MED COL, 1976-; TRAINING & SUPV ANALYST, COLUMBIA UNIV CTR PSYCHOANALYTICAL TRAINING & RES, 1974-; fac mem, NY Psychoanal inst, 1974-1981; asst ed, J Am Psychoanal Asn, 1974-1977; attend psychiatrist, Serv Psychiat, Presby Hosp, NY, 1974-1976; prof clin psychiat, Col Physicians & Surgeons, Columbia Univ, 1973-1976; dir gen clin serv, NY State Psychiat Inst, 1973-1976; mem staff, A K Rice inst, Group Rels Conf, Wash Sch Psychiat, 1972-1975; assoc clin prof psychiat, Univ Kans Med Ctr, Kansas City, Kans, 1971-1973; dir, C F Menninger mem Hosp, 1969-1973; treas, Topeka inst Psychoanal, 1968-1973; staff psychiatrist, Adult Outpatient Serv, Menninger Found, 1968-1969; consult, C F Menninger mem Hosp, Topeka, 1968-1969; chief investr, Psychother res Proj, 1967-1969; training analyst, Topeka inst Psychoanal, 1966-1973; resident psychiat, C F Menninger mem Hosp, Topeka, 1965-1968; fac mem, Menninger Sch Psychiat & Topeka inst Psychoanal, 1964-1973; consult, Topeka State Hosp, Kans, 1964-1968; staff psychiatrist, res dept, Menninger Found, 1962-1967; staff psychiatrist, C F Menninger mem Hosp, Topeka, Kans, 1961-1962; Rockefeller Found fel psychiat, Henry Phipps Clin, Johns Hopkins Hosp, Baltimore, 1959-1960; prof ment health & prof psychol diag, Sch Psychol, Cath Univ Chile, 1958-1961; prof ment health, Sch Social Work, Nat Health Serv, Santiago, 1958-1959; asst prof, dept Psychiat, 1958-1959; staff mem, dept Psychiat, 1957-1961; prof psychopath, Sch Social Work, Nat Health Serv, Santiago, 1957-1959; resident psychiat, Psychiat Clin, Univ Chile, 1954-1957; Intern, Hosp J J Aquirre, Santiago, Chile, 1953. **Memberships:** Fel Am Psychiat Asn; AMA; fel Am Col Physicians; Sigma Xi; fel NY Acad Med; NY Acad Sci; AAAS; Int Psychoanal Asn (vpres 1983-); Cent Neuropsychiat Hosp Asn (pres 1988-); Asn Psychoanal Med (pres 1991-1992). **Research Statement & Publications:** Diagnosis of severe personality disorders with particular reference to borderline conditions and narcissistic pathology; the process and outcome of psychoanalytic psychotherapy with severe personality disorders; psychoanalytic object relations theory, institutional dynamics, psychopathology of love relations and psychoanalytic technique. **Mailing Address:** 21 Bloomingdale Rd, White Plains, NY 10605-1504. **Fax:** 914-997-5997.

KERNELL, ROBERT LEE, PHYSICS OF SPORTS, SCIENCE COURSES FOR NON-SCIENCE MAJORS. **Personal Data:** b Greer, SC, March 24, 1929; m 1959, Judith; c Robert William & Charles Lee. **Education:** Wofford Col, AB, 1950; Univ SC, MS, 1958; Univ Tenn, PhD (physics), 1968. **Honors & Awards:** Bronze Medalist, Nat Prof of 1989, Council for Advancement and Support of Education (CASE). **Professional Experience:** PROF PHYSICS, OLD DOM UNIV, 1979-; assoc prof, Old Dom Univ, 1967-1979; Asst prof physics, Col William & Mary, 1958-1962. **Memberships:** Am Asn Physics Teachers; NY Acad Sci; Sigma Xi. **Research Statement & Publications:** Nuclear structure physics; radiation effects induced by charged particles; published book: "Instructor's Manual for College Physics (ISBN 0-471-04057-6). **Mailing Address:** 1725 W 49th St, Norfolk, VA 23508. **E-Mail:** lkernell@odu.edu

KERNEY, PETER JOSEPH, MECHANICAL ENGINEERING. **Personal Data:** b Philadelphia, Pa, April 7, 1940; m 1968, c 3. **Education:** Univ Notre Dame, BS, 1962, MS, 1964; Pa State Univ, PhD (mech eng), 1970. **Professional Experience:** CHMN ADVAN TECHNOL, CTI-CRYOGENICS; adj prof mech eng, Tufts Univ, beginning 1977; mgr advan technol, Cti-Cryogenics, beginning 1977; res staff engr, Draper Lab, Mass Inst Technol, 1972-1977; consult, US Army Frankford Arsenal, 1971; asst prof, Lafayette Col, 1970-1972; res asst, Ord Res Lab, 1968-1970; Instr mech eng, Tri-State Col, 1965-1966; Pa State Univ, 1966-1970. **Memberships:** Am Soc Mech Engrs; Am Soc Eng Educ; Am Soc Heating Refrig & Air Conditioning Engrs; Sigma Xi. **Research Statement & Publications:** Two phase flow and turbulent jet mixing; jet penetration characteristics of a submerged steam jet; energy and momentum characteristics of liquid bath downstream of steam jet; convection and cryogenic heat transfer. **Mailing Address:** Mansfield Corp Ctr, CTI Cryogenics, 266 Second Ave, Waltham, MA 02254-9171. **Fax:** 508-337-5180.

KERNIS, MARTEN MURRAY, ANATOMY, TERATOLOGY. **Personal Data:** b Chicago, Ill, September 21, 1941; m 1982, Janet; c Ariel. **Education:** Roosevelt Univ, BS, 1963; Univ Fla, PhD (anat sci), 1968. **Professional Experience:** ASSOC PROF EMER HEALTH POLICY & ADMIN, SCH PUB HEALTH, UNIV ILL, CHICAGO, as of 2004; asssoc prof health policy & admin, Sch Pub Health, beginning 1993; assoc vchancellor acad affairs, Col Med, 1991-1993; vdean, Col Med, 1983-1991; actg exec dean, Sch Basic Med Sci & dep exec dean, Univ Ill, 1982-1983; assoc prof anat, Sch Basic Med Sci & dep exec dean, Univ Ill, 1978-1982; assoc prof anat & dean, Col Allied Health Sci, 1976-1978; from asst dean to assoc dean, Sch Basic Med Sci, Jefferson Med Col, 1972-1976; from asst prof to assoc prof anat obstet & gynec, Abraham Lincoln Sch Med, 1968-1976; from asst prof to assoc prof anat, Sch Basic Med Sci, Univ Ill, 1968-1976. **Memberships:** Teratology Soc; Asn Am Med Cols. **Research Statement & Publications:** Transport across the placenta during normal and abnormal embryogenesis; effects of teratogens on function; distribution of teratogens; mechanism of malformations. **Mailing Address:** Sch Pub Health Univ Ill, 2035 W Taylor St, Chicago, IL 60612-7259. **Fax:** 312-996-5356. **E-Mail:** mmkernis@uic.edu

KERNS, CARL M, MATHEMATICS. **Education:** BA, MS, EdD. **Professional Experience:** EMER, MESA STATE COL, as of 2005. **Mailing Address:** Mesa State Col, 12th St, N Ave, Grand Jct, CO 81502. **Fax:** 970-248-1973.

KERNS, DAVID MARLOW, electromagnetics; deceased, see previous edition for last biography

KERNS, MICHAEL LESTER, ELASTOMER SYNTHESIS, FUNCTIONAL INITIATOR SYNTHESIS. **Personal Data:** m 1991, Connie Elaine Emerson. **Education:** Oberlin Col, BS, 1991; Ohio State Univ, PhD (org chem), 1995. **Professional Experience:** SCIENTIST, BRIDGESTONE-FIRESTONE CENT RES, 1995-. **Memberships:** Am Chem Soc. **Research Statement & Publications:** Organic synthesis; national product synthesis, electrochemical organic synthesis methodology development; organic polymer synthesis including anionic and Ziegler-Natta systems. **Mailing Address:** 41869 Oberlin Rd, Elyria, OH 44035-7405. **E-Mail:** mkbuckeye@aol.com

KERNS, SHERRA E, ENGINEERING EDUCATION, RESEARCH, CONSULTING. **Personal Data:** b Ann Arbor, Mich, May 27, 1947; m David; c Sarah Horan (Lange), Melissa Caryl & David V III. **Education:** Mt Holyoke Col, AB; Univ Wis, MA; Univ NC, PhD. **Honors & Awards:** Fellow IEEE (technical); Fellow ASEE (education); IEEE Centennial Medal; H P Rigas Award. **Professional Experience:** PRES, ASEE 2004-2005; VPRES INNOVATION RES, FRANKLIN W. OLIN COL ENG, 1999-; F. W. OLIN PROF ELEC & COMPUT ENG, FRANKLIN W. OLIN COL ENG, 1999-; Eng Accreditation Commission, 1996-; dir, Univ Consoritum Res Elec Space, Vanderbilt Univ, 1989-1999; chmn, Dept Elec & Comput Eng, Vanderbilt Univ, 1993-1998; prof comput & Elec Eng, Vanderbilt Univ, 1987-2000; Pres, Radiation Microsci Inc, 1985-; assoc prof elec & comput eng, NC State Univ, 1982-1987; asst prof elec eng, Auburn Univ, 1979-1982; NIH postdoctoral biomed eng, Duke Univ, 1977-1979. **Memberships:** Inst Elec & Electronics Engrs; Am Soc for Engineering Education; Nat Asn Elec & Eng Dept Heads (pres 1995-); Am Asn Eng Educ. **Research Statement & Publications:** design solutions enhancing information integrity in complex systems; detection, prevention of information corruption; detection of nuclear materials. **Mailing Address:** Franklin W Olin Col Eng, Needham, MA 02492. **Fax:** 781-292-2380. **E-Mail:** sherra.kerns@olin.edu

KERPER, MATTHEW J(ULIUS), CERAMICS. **Personal Data:** b St Louis, Mo, April 9, 1922; m 1948, c 1. **Education:** Univ Mo, BS, 1943, MS, 1947; George Wash Univ, MS, 1959; Am Univ, MPA. **Professional Experience:** RETIRED; ceramic engr, Air Force Off Sci Res, 1972-1988; Off Aerospace Res, 1966-1970 & Air Force Systs Command, 1970-1972; ceramic engr, Nat Bur Stand, 1952-1966; ceramic engr, Laclede Christy Co, Mo, 1947-1952. **Memberships:** Am Ceramic Soc; Am Inst Ceramic Engrs. **Research Statement & Publications:** Physical properties of ceramics and glass at elevated temperatures; science administration. **Mailing Address:** 4620 N Park Ave, Chevy Chase, MD 20815.

KERR, ANTHONY ROBERT, MILLIMETER-WAVE ELECTRONICS, RADIO ASTRONOMY. **Personal Data:** b Farnborough, Eng, August 30, 1941; American citizen; m 1974, Tanya; c Tristan. **Education:** Univ Melbourne, BE, 1963, MESc, 1967, PhD (elec eng), 1969. **Honors & Awards:** Microwave Prize, Inst Elec & ELectronics Engrs, 1978; Except Eng Achievement Medal, NASA, 1983. **Professional Experience:** Adj fac, Dept Astron, Univ Va, as of 2004; consult, NASA, 1987-1990; SCIENTIST, NAT RADIO ASTRON OBSERV, CHARLOTTESVILLE, VA, 1984-; vis prof, Univ Va, beginning 1984; consult, Macom Inc, 1980-1983; physicist millimeter-wave electronics, Goddard Inst Space Studies, NASA, 1974-1984; electronics engr millimeter-wave electronics, Nat Radio Astron Observ, Charlottesville, Va, 1971-1974; res scientist radio astron, Div Radiophys, Commonwealth Sci & Indust Res Orgn, Sydney, Australia, 1969-1971. **Memberships:** Fel Inst Elec & Electronics Engrs; Int Union Radio Sci; Sigma Xi; Am Phys Soc. **Research Statement & Publications:** Development of low-noise receivers at millimeter and submillimeter wavelengths; and their application in radio astronomy; atmospheric physics, and space communications. **Mailing Address:** Nat Radio Astron Observ, 2015 Ivy Rd, Ste four, Charlottesville, VA 22903-4164. **Fax:** 804-296-0324. **E-Mail:** akerr@nrao.edu

KERR, ARNOLD D, ENGINEERING MECHANICS & ICE COVER MECHANICS, RAILROAD ENGINEERING. **Personal Data:** b Suwalki, Poland, March 9, 1928; American citizen; m 1966, Berta; c Regina & Orin. **Education:** Tech Univ, Munich, Dipl Ing, 1952; Northwestern Univ, MS, 1956, PhD (theoret & appl mech), 1958. **Professional Experience:** Fel, Ctr Advan Study, Univ Del, 1989-1990; pres, Inst Railroad Eng, beginning 1980; PROF CIVIL & ENVIRON ENG, UNIV DEL, 1978-; vis prof civil eng, Princeton Univ, 1973-1978; dir, Lab Mech Solids, 1967-1973; prof, Courant Inst Math & Sci, NY Univ, 1966-1973; consult to US govt agencies & indust, beginning 1959; from asst prof aeronaut to assoc prof aeronaut & astronaut, Courant Inst Math & Sci, NY Univ, 1959-1966; asst res scientist mech solids, Courant Inst Math & Sci, NY Univ, 1958-1959; engr design & anal, Hazelet & Erdal Consult Engrs, 1955. **Memberships:** Fel Am Soc Mech Engrs; Am Railway Eng Asn; Int Soc Interaction Mech & Math. **Research Statement & Publications:** Structural mechanics; continuously supported structures; dynamics and stability of structures; bearing capacity and dynamics of floating ice covers; railroad track analyses and technology. **Mailing Address:** Dept Civil & Environ Eng, Univ Del, Newark, DE 19716. **Fax:** 302-831-3640. **E-Mail:** adkerr@ce.udel.edu

KERR, CARL E, MATHEMATICS. **Personal Data:** b Corsicana, Tex, September 16, 1926; m 1950, c 1. **Education:** La Salle Col, BA, 1950; Univ Del, MA, 1953; Lehigh Univ, PhD (math), 1959. **Professional Experience:** PROF EMER MATH & COMPUT SCI, SHIPPENSBURG STATE COL, 1976-1991; prof math, Shippensburg State Col, 1969-1976; asst prof, Dickinson Col, 1959-1969; mathematician, Convair Div, Gen Dynamics Corp, 1956; asst prof math, Lafayette Col, 1953-1959; Mathematician, Frankford Arsenal, 1952-1954. **Memberships:** Am Math Soc; Math Asn Am. **Research Statement & Publications:** Linear spaces; summability. **Mailing Address:** Dept Math & Comput Sci, Shippensburg Univ PA, 1871 Old Main Dr, Shippensburg, PA 17257.

KERR, DONALD L(AURENS), CHEMICAL ENGINEERING. **Personal Data:** b Putnam, Conn, June 28, 1943; m 1966, c 1. **Education:** Worcester Polytech Inst, BS, 1965; Univ Del, MChE, 1968, PhD (chem eng, phys chem), 1970. **Professional Experience:** RES ASSOC PHOTOG PROCESSES LAB, RES LABS, EASTMAN KODAK CO, 1975-; sr chemist, Photog Eng lab, 1969-1975. **Memberships:** Am Inst Chem Engrs. **Research Statement & Publications:** Mass tranfer; chemical kinetics; drying; photographic processing. **Mailing Address:** 177 Long Pond Rd, Rochester, NY 14612.

KERR, DONALD M, TECHNICAL MANAGEMENT, GEOPHYSICS. **Personal Data:** b Philadelphia, Pa, April 8, 1939; m 1961, Alison; c Margot K. **Education:** Cornell Univ, BEE, 1963, MS, 1964, PhD (elec eng, physics), 1966. **Honors & Awards:** Outstanding Serv Award, Dept Energy, 1979. **Professional Experience:** DIR, NAT RECONNAISSANCE OFF, as of 2006; dir, Dep Sci & Technol, Fed Bur Invest, beginning 2001; asst dir, Fed Bur Invest, ending 2000; dir & exec vpres, Info Systs Labs, Inc, San Diego, Calif, 1996-1997; mem, Defense Sci Bd, beginning 1993; dir & corp exec vpres, Sci Applns Int Corp, San Diego, Calif, 1993-1996; dir, Ktaadn Inc, beginning 1992; consult, Lawrence Livermore Nat Lab, beginning 1992; dir, Resources Future, beginning 1990; dir, Mirage Systs Inc, 1988-1991; dir, Nat Asn Mfrs, 1987-1992; from sr vpres to pres, EG&G Inc, Wellesley, Mass, 1985-1992; consult, Los Alamos Nat Lab, 1985; mem corp, Cornell Univ Eng Col Coun, beginning 1984; mem corp, Charles Stark Draper Lab, beginning 1982; mem, Joint Strategic Target Planning Staff, Sci Adv Group, beginning 1981; mem corp, SRI Nat Security Adv Coun, 1980-1989; dir, Los Alamos Nat Lab, 1979-1985; chmn, Comt Res & Develop, Int Energy Agency, OECD, 1979-1985; dep & actg asst secy energy technol, Nev Opers, Dept Energy, 1979; dep & actg asst secy defense progs, Nev Opers, Dept Energy, 1977-1979; dep mgr, Nev Opers, Dept Energy, 1976-1977; mem, US Army Sci Adv Panel, 1975-1978; alt energy div leader, Dir Off, 1975-1976; consult, Navajo Sci Comt, 1974-1977; asst, Dir Off, 1973-1975; group leader, Los Alamos Nat Lab, Univ Calif, 1971-1973; staff mem, Los Alamos Nat Lab, Univ Calif, 1966-1971. **Memberships:** Fel AAAS; Am Phys Soc; Am Geophys Union. **Research Statement & Publications:** Nuclear weapons research and development testing; laser, heavy ion, and electron beam fusion; nuclear safeguards and security; ionospheric physics; international activities relating to nuclear technology and political, military, economic and energy affairs. **Mailing Address:** Nat Reconnaissance Off, Off Corp Commun 14675 Lee Rd, Chantilly, VA 20151-1715. **Fax:** 703-808-1171. **E-Mail:** donkerr@islinc.com

KERR, DONALD PHILIP, ATOMIC PHYSICS, MOLECULAR PHYSICS. **Personal Data:** b Winnipeg, Man, October 22, 1938; m 1962, c 2. **Education:** Univ Man, BS, 1960, MS, 1961, PhD (physics), 1965. **Professional Experience:** CONSULT, UNIV WINNIPEG, 1979-; prof physics, Univ Winnipeg, beginning 1976; from asst prof to assoc prof, Univ Winnipeg, 1969-1976; res assoc, Harvard Univ, 1967-1969; Nat Res Coun Can fel, Univ Giessen, 1965-1967. **Memberships:** Can Asn Physicists. **Research Statement & Publications:** Positron annihilation in organic liquids and solids; high resolution mass spectrometry; heavy ion scattering. **Mailing Address:** Dept Physics, Univ Winnipeg, 515 Portage Ave 2C31, Winnipeg, MB R3B 2E9, Can. **Fax:** 204-774-4134. **E-Mail:** d.kerr@uwinnipeg.ca

KERR, DONALD R, MATHEMATICS. **Personal Data:** b Chicago, Ill, March 12, 1938; m 1960, c 1. **Education:** Univ Ariz, BS, 1960, MS, 1962; Lehigh Univ, PhD (math), 1967; Fla State Univ, PhD (clin psychol). **Professional Experience:** CLIN PSYCHOLOGIST, PSYCHOL ASSOCS TALLAHASSEE, 1987-; acad officer & basic skills coordr math, Ind Univ, Bloomington, 1978-1982; assoc prof educ & asst dir math educ develop ctr, 1971-1978; vis prof math, 1969-1971; asst prof, State Univ NY Albany, 1967-1969; Instr math, Lafayette Col, 1963-1967. **Memberships:** Am Math Soc; Math Asn Am; Nat Coun Teachers Math. **Research Statement & Publications:** Elementary education in mathematics and the mathematics training of elementary teachers; problem solving of children; grades 4 5 6; basic skills in mathematics for college students. **Mailing Address:** FL State Univ Psychol Clin, 214 Regional Rehab Ctr, Tallahassee, FL 32312.

KERR, DOUGLAS S, COMPUTER SCIENCES. **Personal Data:** b Washington, DC, November 19, 1940; m 1968. **Education:** Yale Univ, BA, 1962; Purdue Univ, MS, 1964, PhD (computer sci), 1967. **Professional Experience:** ASSOC PROF, COMPUT & INFO SCI, OHIO STATE UNIV, 1971-; asst prof, 1967-1971. **Memberships:** Asn Comput Mach; Inst Elec & Electronics Engrs. **Research Statement & Publications:** Data base systems; software engineering. **Mailing Address:** 695 Dreese Lab, 2015 Neil Ave, Columbus, OH 43201. **E-Mail:** kerr.2@osu.edu

KERR, ERIC DONALD, PHYTOPATHOLOGY. **Personal Data:** b Gipsy, Mo, February 21, 1930; m 1971, Joyce; c Robin E (Clark) & Joleanna M (Williams). **Education:** Univ Mo, Columbia, BS (agr), 1951, MS (field crops), 1960; Univ Nebr, Lincoln, PhD (plant path), 1967. **Professional Experience:** EXTEN PLANT PATHOLOGIST, PANHANDLE RES & EXT CTR, UNIV NEBR, 1967-; res plant pathologist, Agr Res Serv, 1967. **Memberships:** Emer mem Soc Nematol. **Research Statement & Publications:** Control of Cercospora leaf spot on sugar beet; control of wheat disease; dry bean yield losses caused by white mold; control of nematodes on sugar beet. **Mailing Address:** 2460 Valencia, Gering, NE 69341.

KERR, ERNEST ANDREW, PHYTOPATHOLOGY. **Personal Data:** b Guelph, Ont, August 24, 1917; m 1945, Olive; c Gordon E, Douglas J & Elizabeth L (Simms). **Education:** McMaster Univ, BA, 1940; McGill Univ, MSc, 1941; Univ Wis, PhD (genetics, plant path), 1944. **Honors & Awards:** Award of Merit, Can Soc Hort Sci, 1983; H R MacMillan Laureate Agr Award, 1989 & 1994. **Professional Experience:** RETIRED; dir plant breeding & res, Stokes Seeds, 1983-1994; res scientist, Hort Res Inst Ont, 1972-1982; res coordr prod systs, Hort Res Inst Ont, 1970-1972; chief res scientist plant breeding, Hort Exp Sta, Ont Ministry Agr & Food, 1954-1970; res assoc, Hort Exp Sta, Ont Ministry Agr & Food, 1952-1954; asst, Hort Exp Sta, Ont Ministry Agr & Food, 1944-1952. **Memberships:** fel Agr Inst Can; Can Soc Hort Sci; hon mem Can Phytopathological Soc. **Research Statement & Publications:** Horticultural plant breeding, particularly tomatoes, sweet peppers and sweet corn; trilliums and rhododendrons. **Mailing Address:** 8 Eden Pl, Simcoe, ON N3Y 3K9, Can.

KERR, GEORGE R, PUBLIC HEALTH NUTRITION, PEDIATRICS. **Personal Data:** b Winnipeg, Man, May 15, 1930; m 1954, c 6. **Education:** Dalhousie Univ, MD & CM, 1955. **Professional Experience:** PROF SCH PUB HEALTH, UNIV TEX HEALTH SCI CTR, 1977-; dir, Human Nutrit Ctr, Univ Tex, Health Sci Ctr, 1977-1988; assoc prof nutrit, Sch Pub Health, Harvard Univ, 1971-1977; res assoc, Joseph P Kennedy, Jr Mem Lab & Wis Regional Primate Res Ctr, 1963-1971; from asst prof to assoc prof, Sch Med, Univ Wis-Madison, 1963-1971; asst prof pediat, Med Sch, Univ Ore, 1962-1963; asst dir, Ore Regional Primate Res Ctr, 1962-1963; instr, Univ BC, 1961-1962; Queen Elizabeth II Can res fel, 1960-1961; res fel pediat endocrinol & metab, Med Sch, Univ Ore, 1959-1961; R Samuel McLaughlin traveling fel, 1959-1960; asst resident med, Vancouver Gen Hosp, BC, 1959; res fel, Vancouver Gen Hosp, BC, 1959; asst resident pediat, Vancouver Gen Hosp, BC, 1957-1958; resident pediat & orthop, Gen Hosp, St Johns, Nfld, 1956-1957; gen pract, 1955-1956; intern med & surg, Victoria Gen Hosp, Halifax, NS, 1954-1955. **Research Statement & Publications:** Public health maternal-child health program needs and effectiveness, nutrition and child development. **Mailing Address:** Sch Pub Health, Univ Tex Health Sci Ctr, PO Box 20186, Houston, TX 77225. **Fax:** 713-500-9264. **E-Mail:** gkerr@utsph.sph.uth.tmc.edu

KERR, GEORGE THOMSON, surface chemistry; deceased, see previous edition for last biography

KERR, J RICHARD, TECHNOLOGY. **Education:** Stanford Univ, PhD (elec eng). **Professional Experience:** VPRES & CHIEF TECHNOL OFFICER, MAX-VIZ INC, as of 2005. **Mailing Address:** Max-Viz Inc, 11615 SW Cloud Ct, Tigard, OR 97224. **Fax:** 503-968-7615. **E-Mail:** dick.kerr@max-viz.com

KERR, J(AMES) S(ANFORD) STEPHENSON, ELECTRICAL ENGINEERING, ELECTROMAGNETISM. **Personal Data:** b Vancouver, BC, March 9, 1926; American citizen; m 1949, Jean; c John S & Jane E. **Education:** Univ BC, BASc, 1948; Univ Ill, MS, 1949, PhD, 1951. **Professional Experience:** RETIRED; sr staff engr, Appl Technol Div, TRW Electronics Systs Group, 1986-1990; sr staff engr, Space Commun Div, 1980-1986; sr staff engr spec proj, TRW Defense & Space Systs Group, 1976-1980; sr staff engr, Ballistic Missile Defense Prog Off, Redondo Beach, 1971-1976; sr staff engr to gen mgr electronics systs div, Guid & Control Opers, TRW Systs Group, 1967-1971; asst mgr, Guid & Control Opers, TRW Systs Group, 1966-1967; asst lab dir antisubmarine warfare, tracking & eval dept, TRW Space Technol Labs, 1965-1966; mgr guid, tracking & eval dept, TRW Space Technol Labs, 1956-1965; eng analyst elec eng, Gen Elec Co, NY, 1951-1956. **Memberships:** Sr mem Inst Elec & Electronics Engrs. **Research Statement & Publications:** Application of electromagnetic theory to space program: analysis of advanced radar systems and data therefrom; management of radio guidance system and radio guidance equation development for space programs such as Mercury, Ranger and Mariner. **Mailing Address:** 1564 Prospect Pl, Victoria, BC V8R 5X8, Can.

KERR, JANET SPENCE, DEVELOPMENT NOVEL THERAPEUTICS. **Personal Data:** b New Haven, Conn, m Thomas; c Sarah, Matthew & Timothy. **Education:** Beaver Col, BA, 1964; Rutgers State Univ, MS, 1969, PhD (physiol), 1973. **Professional Experience:** Adj assoc prof, Philadelphia Sch Osteop Med, beginning 1994; mem, Orgn Comt, Inflammatory Res Asn, 1988-1994; SR RES SCIENTIST, DUPONT MERCK PHARMACEUT CO, 1985-; adj assoc prof, Sch Med, Univ Pa, 1985-1989; assoc mem, Grad Fac & Bur Biol Res, Rutgers Univ, 1980-1985; asst prof med & physiol, Rutgers Med Sch, Univ Med & Dent NJ, 1979-1985; NIH trainee & res assoc physiol, Sch Med, Univ Pa, 1976-1979; asst prof physiol, Camden Col Arts & Sci, Rutgers Univ, 1973-1976. **Memberships:** Am Physiol Soc; Am Thoracic Soc; Inflammatory Res Asn; AAAS; Am Soc Bone Mineral Res. **Research Statement & Publications:** Modulators of tissue injury: including cytokires and oxygen- derived free radicals and their localization in the disease process. **Mailing Address:** Du Pont Merck Pharmaceut Co, PO Box 80400, E400/4223, Wilmington, DE 19880-0400. **Fax:** 302-695-7873. **E-Mail:** janet.s.kerr@dupontpharma.com

KERR, JOHN (JACK) M(ARTIN), CERAMIC & CHEMICAL ENGINEERING. **Personal Data:** b Normal, Ill, January 31, 1934; m 1956, c 4. **Education:** Univ Ill, BS, 1956. **Professional Experience:** RETIRED; adv engr, Advan Energy Components Eng, 1994-1995; mgr, Fuels & Mat Unit, 1987-1994; mgr, Systs Design & Eng Sect, 1981-1987; mgr, Nuclear Fuel Cycle Sect, 1974-1981; mgr, Ceramics Sect, 1971-1974; supvr nuclear ceramics, Babcock & Wilcox Co, 1966-1971; sr engr, Babcock & Wilcox Co, 1961-1966; metallurgist, Oak Ridge Nat Lab, 1956-1961. **Memberships:** Fel Am Ceramic Soc; Am Soc Testing & Mat. **Research Statement & Publications:** Ceramic bodies for waste disposal; ceramic fuel-metal compatibility studies; ceramic fuels development and development of fuels fabrication methods; nuclear ceramics; nuclear fuel cycle studies. **Mailing Address:** 1425 Brookville Lane, Lynchburg, VA 24502.

KERR, JOHN POLK, ZOOLOGY, AQUATIC BIOLOGY. **Personal Data:** b Little Rock, Ark, July 14, 1931; m 1956, c 4. **Education:** Rutgers Univ, BA, 1956; Univ Calif, MS, 1957; Univ Mich, PhD (zool), 1962. **Professional Experience:** ENVIRON MGR, DEPT ENVIRON REG, STATE FLA, 1986-; prof biol, Salem Col, 1983-1986; head, New South Ecosyst, Inc, 1978-1986; gen mgr & pres, Baseline, Inc, 1976-1978; vpres & sr ecol consult, Baseline, Inc, 1973-1976; Fac fel, Systs Design Prog, NASA & Am Soc Eng Educ, AuburnUniv, 1970; assoc prof biol & marine sci, Univ WFla, 1969-1973; partic, Electronics for Scientists Prof, Univ Ill, 1968; vis asst prof, Ore Inst Marine Biol, Univ Ore, 1965; asst prof zool, Univ Ga, 1963-1969; res assoc fisheries, Univ Mich, 1962-1963; Rackham fel fisheries, Univ Mich, 1962-1963; instr biol, Adrian Col, 1961-1962; teaching asst zool, Univ Mich, 1958-1959; researcher animal behavior, Ciba Pharmaceut Co, 1957-1958; Asst biol, Rutgers Univ, 1955-1956. **Memberships:** Am Soc Zool; Ecol Soc Am; Am Fisheries Soc; Am Soc Ichthyol & Herpet; Am Soc Limnol & Oceanog. **Research Statement & Publications:** Aquatic ecology; biology of vertebrates, especially fishes; ichthyology and herpetology; fisheries; marine and freshwater ecosystems, especially rivers, estuaries, wetlands, and lakes; animal behavior, especially under field conditions. **Mailing Address:** 4770 Velasquez St, Pensacola, FL 32504.

KERR, KIRKLYN M, VETERINARY PATHOLOGY, EDUCATIONAL ADMINISTRATION -DEAN. **Personal Data:** b Green Bank, WVa, May 1, 1936; m 1957, Anna; c Kirklyn Todd & Travis Leighton. **Education:** Univ WVa, BS, 1961, MS, 1966; Ohio State Univ, DVM, 1961; Tex A&M Univ, PhD (vet path), 1970; Am Col Vet Path, dipl, 1968. **Professional Experience:** DEAN & DIR, SCH AGR, UNIV CONN, 1993-; prof vet prev med & fac mem, Dept Prev Med, 1991-1993; dir, Ohio Agr Res & Develop Ctr & prof poultry sci, Col Vet Med, Ohio State Univ, 1987-1990; asst dean res & advan studies, Sch Vet Med & Head Vet Sci, La State Univ, 1978-1987; assoc prof vet pathobiol & dir div appl path, Col Vet Med, Ohio State Univ, 1972-1978; from instr to assoc prof vet path, Col Vet Med, Tex A&M Univ, 1965-1972; res assoc vet microbiol & path, Univ WVa, 1962-1965; vet practr, North Side Vet Clin, Carlisle, Pa, 1961-1962. **Memberships:** Am Vet Med Asn; Am Col Vet Path; Ct Farm Bur; Am Asn Avian Path. **Research Statement & Publications:** Veterinary pathology; mycoplasmatacea; cancer research in animals. **Mailing Address:** Col Agr & Natural Res, Univ Conn, 1376 Storrs Rd, Storrs, CT 06269-4066. **E-Mail:** kirklyn.kerr@uconn.edu

KERR, MARILYN SUE, DEVELOPMENTAL BIOLOGY. **Personal Data:** b Sumner, Ill. **Education:** Gettysburg Col, BA, 1959; Duke Univ, MA, 1961, PhD (zoology), 1966. **Professional Experience:** ASST PROF BIOL, SYRACUSE UNIV, 1970-; USPHS fel vitellogenesis, Nat inst Child Health & Human Develop trainee biophys, 1969-1970; USPHS fel vitellogenesis, Biol div, Oak Ridge Nat lab, 1966-1969. **Memberships:** Am Soc Zoologists; Soc Develop Biol; AAAS; Sigma Xi. **Research Statement & Publications:** Vitellogenesis and limb regeneration correlated with studies of hemocyte origin, differentiation and functions in arthropods; hemocyanin synthesis, its isolation and characterization. **Mailing Address:** Dept Biol, Syracuse Univ, 214B Lyman Hall, Syracuse, NY 13244-0002. **Fax:** 315-443-2156. **E-Mail:** mskerr@syr.edu

KERR, MILLER H, PUBLIC HEALTH. **Personal Data:** b St Augustine, Fla, August 3, 1940. **Education:** Univ Fla, BS, 1962; Univ Ga, MPA, 1971. **Professional Experience:** DEP DIR, DIV DIABETES TRANSLATION, CTR DIS CONTROL & PREV, 1989-; pub health adv & asst dir pub health pract, Nat Ctr Prev Serv, 1984-1989; planning & eval officer, Nat Ctr Prev Serv, 1971-1984; pub health adv, Ga, 1967-1971; pub health adv, NJ, 1966-1967; Pub health adv, Mont, 1964-1966; pub health adv, State Health Dept, NC, 1962-1964. **Memberships:** Am Pub Health Asn. **Mailing Address:** 781 Gilda Dr, St Augustine, FL 32086. **E-Mail:** kerr.4044@juno.com

KERR, PETER DONALD, GEOGRAPHY. **Personal Data:** b Toronto, Ont, April 19, 1920. **Education:** Univ BC, BA, 1941; Univ Toronto, MA, 1943, PhD (geog), 1950. **Professional Experience:** EMER PROF GEOG, UNIV TORONTO, 1985-; mem exec comt, Hist Atlas Can, 1980-; Grantee, Hist Atlas Can Proj, 1980-1989; assoc dean, Sch Grad Studies, 1976-1979; Publ Comt Social Sci Res Coun, Can, 1974-1977; Grantee, Can Coun, 1973-1975; chmn dept, Univ Toronto, 1968-1973; mem, Nat Adv Comt Geog Res, 1967-1970; Grantee, Dept Treas & Econ, 1966-1968; Grantee, Emergency Measures Org, 1962-1964; partic, Pugwash Int Conf Chem & Biol Warfare, 1959; Grantee, Dept Mines & Tech Surveys, 1955-1961; from asst prof to prof, Univ Toronto, 1951-1985; lectr, Univ Toronto, 1946-1951; Grantee, Defense Res Bd, 1946-1949; teaching Asst, Univ Calif, Berkeley, 1945-1946; Meterol officer, RCAF, 1943-1945. **Memberships:** Asn Am Geogr; Can Asn Geogr (vpres 1959 pres 1960); Int Geog Union; Sigma Xi. **Research Statement & Publications:** Climatology of British Columbia; industrial and urban geography of southern Ontario, especially metro Ontario; land use and industrial change in Metropolitan Toronto; changing wholesale trade in Winnipeg; changing status in Canadian ports; various aspects of wholesale trade in Canada; resource development in Canada. **Mailing Address:** Dept Geog Univ Toronto, 100 St George St, Toronto, ON M5S 1A1, Can.

KERR, ROBERT LOWELL, AIRBREATHING PROPULSION, ENERGY CONVERSION & AEROSPACE POWER. **Personal Data:** b Dayton, Ohio, March 31, 1936; m 1991, Camille; c Mary, Donald, Brian, Kelly & Kendra. **Education:** Ohio State Univ, BS, 1959; Univ Dayton, MS, 1970, PhD (mech eng), 1986. **Professional Experience:** CONSULT, 1992-; adj assoc prof mech eng, Wright State Univ, 1991-1992; asst chief scientist, APL, 1981-1991; electrochem res task mgr, APL, 1978-1981; advan develop prog mgr, APL, 1973-

1978; battery task mgr, APL, 1968-1972; aerospace engr, APL, 1966-1968 & 1972-1973; develop engr, Foreign Technol Div, 1965-1966; Apollo-LM subsyst mgr, NASA Manned Spacecraft Ctr, Tex, 1964-1965; Instr physics, Wilberforce Univ, 1962-1964; fuel cell task mgr, Aero Propulsion Lab, Wright Patterson AFB, Ohio, 1959-1964; APL-Aero Propulsion Lab, Wright-Patterson AFB, Ohio. **Research Statement & Publications:** Investigation of the electrochemistry of batteries and fuel cells such as nickel-cadmium, nickel hydrogen and lithium rechargeable batteries along with hydrogen-oxygen fuel cells; heat transfer in cells and fundamental electrochemical studies of lithium couples. **Mailing Address:** 14236 Palm St, Madeira Beach, FL 33708. **E-Mail:** kerrbob3@aol.com

KERR, ROBERT MCDOUGALL, TURBULENCE, NUMERICAL METHODS. **Personal Data:** b Harvey, Ill, March 22, 1954; m 1984, c 2. **Education:** Univ Chicago, BS, 1975, MS, 1975; Cornell Univ, PhD (physics), 1981. **Professional Experience:** CHAIR & PROF, COMPUTATIONAL FLUID DYNAMICS, UNIV WARWICK, 2002-; visiting prof, atmospheric sci/math, Univ Ariz, 2000-2002; scientist, Nat Ctr Atmospheric Res, 1986-2000; Lawrence Livermore Nat Lab, 1983-1986; postdoctoral, Ames Res Ctr, NASA, 1981-1983. **Memberships:** Am Phys Soc; Soc Indust & Appl Math. **Research Statement & Publications:** Three-dimensional direct simulations to study isotropic turbulence, convective turbulence and vortex interactions; produced numerical evidence for a singularity of the three-dimensional, incompressible, Euler equations. **Mailing Address:** Nat Ctr Atmospheric Res, PO Box 3000, Boulder, CO 80307. **Fax:** 303-497-8181. **E-Mail:** kerrrobt@ncar.ucar.edu

KERR, SANDRIA NEIDUS, SCIENTIFIC PROGRAMMING. **Personal Data:** b Youngstown, Ohio, October 1, 1940; m 1963, William; c Tamara J & Elizabeth L. **Education:** Col Wooster, BA, 1962; Bryn Mawr Col, MA, 1964; Cornell Univ, PhD (math), 1971. **Professional Experience:** Consult, 1992-; collabr, Los Alamos Nat Lab, 1985-1992; PROF MATH, WINSTON-SALEM STATE UNIV, 1982-; from asst prof to assoc prof, Winston-salem State Univ, 1971-1982; vis lectr, Chalmers Univ Technol, Sweden, 1967; teaching asst, Dept Math, Cornell Univ, 1963-1967; instr math, Col Wooster, 1963. **Memberships:** Am Math Soc; Asn Comput Mach; Inst Elec & Electronics Engrs Comput Soc. **Research Statement & Publications:** Analysis on infinite-dimensional manifolds; studies involving placement of students in math courses; scientific programming. **Mailing Address:** Dept Comput Sci, Winston Salem State Univ, 3203 Jones Comput Sci Bldg 601 Martin Luther King Jr Dr, Winston-Salem, NC 27110. **Fax:** 336-750-2499. **E-Mail:** kerrs@wssu.edu

KERR, SYLVIA JEAN, BIOCHEMISTRY. **Personal Data:** b St Louis, Mo, July 2, 1941. **Education:** Smith Col, AB, 1962; Columbia Univ, PhD, 1967. **Professional Experience:** ASSOC PROF BIOCHEM, UNIV COLO MED CTR, DENVER, 1976-; Nat Cancer Inst career develop award, 1971-; asst prof surg, Univ Colo Med Ctr, Denver, 1970-1975. **Memberships:** Am Chem Soc; Am Soc Biol Chemists; Am Asn Cancer Res. **Research Statement & Publications:** Biochemical control mechanisms; transfer RNA metabolism. **Mailing Address:** Univ Colo Health Sci Ctr, Denver, CO 80220. **Fax:** 303-315-8215.

KERR, SYLVIA JOANN, DEVELOPMENTAL BIOLOGY, MICROBIOLOGY. **Personal Data:** b Detroit, Mich, June 19, 1941; m 1965, c David & Kathleen. **Education:** Carleton Col, BA, 1963; Univ Minn, Minneapolis, MS, 1966, PhD (zoology), 1968. **Professional Experience:** PROF BIOL, HAMLINE UNIV, 1989-; from asst prof to assoc prof, Hamline Univ, 1976-1989; med fel cell biol, Univ Minn, 1974-1975; asst prof biol, Anoka-Ramsey Community Col, Augsburg Col & Hamline Univ, 1972-1974; res fel pharmacog, Univ Minn, 1972; asst prof biol, Augsburg Col, 1968-1971. **Memberships:** AAAS; Soc Develop Biol; Am Inst Biol Sci. **Research Statement & Publications:** Developmental biology-myxomycetes; planarian regeneration; population genetics-mutant allele frequencies in cats. **Mailing Address:** Dept Biol, Hamline Univ, St Paul, MN 55108. **Fax:** 651-523-2620. **E-Mail:** skerr@piper.hamline.edu

KERR, THOMAS HENDERSON, III, KALMAN FILTER TRACKING, FAILURE DETECTION IN NAVIGATION SYSTEMS. **Personal Data:** b Washington, DC, November 9, 1945; m 1975, Aniece; c Thomas Henderson IV & Stephen McAllister. **Education:** Howard Univ, BSEE, 1967; Univ Iowa, MSEE, 1969, PhD (elec eng), 1971. **Professional Experience:** CHIEF EXEC OFFICER & PRIN INVESTR, TEK ASSOCS, 1992-; instr, Northeastern Univ, 1990-1995; mem tech staff, Lincoln Lab, Mass Inst Technol, 1986-1992; sr syst analyst, Intermetrics Inc, 1979-1986; control engr, General Electric, 1971-1973; circuits res & teaching asst, Univ Iowa, 1969-1971; res asst, Howard Univ, 1966-1967. **Memberships:** Sr mem Inst Elect & Electronics Engrs (pres, 1990-1992, 2001-); Am Inst Aeornaut & Astronaut; Inst Navig; SPIE; Asn Comput Mach; AAAS. **Research Statement & Publications:** Centralized and decentralized Kalman filter theory and applications in GPS/INS navigation failure detection; radar and IR target tracking, sensor fustion, submarine navaid utilization trade-off of accuracy vs ASW exposure. **Mailing Address:** Tek Assoc, PO Box 459 Meriam St Ste 7-R, Lexington, MA 02420. **Fax:** 781-862-8680. **E-Mail:** tkerr@tiac.net

KERR, THOMAS JAMES, MICROBIOLOGY. **Personal Data:** b Muskogee, Okla, October 7, 1927; m 1951, c 7. **Education:** Okla A & M Univ, BS, 1950; Okla State Univ, MS, 1963; Univ Ga, PhD (microbiol), 1976. **Professional Experience:** RETIRED; dir lab studies, Univ Ga, 1976-1990; res asst microbiol, Univ Ga, 1971-1976; proj officer, US Army Test & Eval Command, Aberdeen, Md, 1967-1970; dep dir med res, US Biol Warfare Ctr, Frederick, Md, 1963-1964; asst dir biol res, US Biol Warfare Ctr, Frederick, Md, 1958-1960. **Memberships:** Am Soc Microbiol; Sigma Xi. **Research Statement & Publications:** Biological inhibition of fusarium moniliforme various subglutinans; the casual agent of pine pitch canker; production of single cell protein from agricultural waste products. **Mailing Address:** 430 Cherokee Ridge, Athens, GA 30606.

KERR, WARWICK ESTEVAM, GENETICS, BEE BIOLOGY. **Personal Data:** b Santana de Parnaiba, Brazil, September 9, 1922; m 1956, c 7. **Education:** Univ Sao Paulo, MSc, 1948, PhD (genetics), 1950. **Honorary Degrees:** Prof Hon Causa, Univ Fed Amazonas, 1980, UNESP, Rio Claro, 1992. **Honors & Awards:** Souzandrade Gold Medal, Univ Fed Maranhao. **Professional Experience:** PROF GENETICS, UNIV FED UBERLANDIA, 1988-; pres, State Univ Maranhao, 1987-1988; prof biol, Fed Univ Maranhao, Sao Luis, 1981-1988; dir, Nat Res Inst Amazon, 1975-1979; State ofSao Paulo Res Found grants, 1965-1967; prof genetics, Col Med, Univ Sao Paulo, 1964-1975; Brazilian Nat Res Coun grants, USDA, 1961-1966; prof biol, Col Sci UNESP-Rio-Claro, 1959-1964; Rockefeller Found Fel, 1951-1952; from asst prof to assoc prof, Univ Sao Paulo, 1948-1958; Biologist genetics, Grad Sch Agr, 1946-1948; hon pres, Brazilian Asn Advan Sci. **Memberships:** Foreign assoc Nat Acad Sci; Brazilian Genetics Soc (pres, 1964-1966 & 1994-1996); Brazilian Soc Advan Sci (pres, 1969-1973); Soc Study Evolution. **Research Statement & Publications:** Bee genetics; cytology and evolution; plant breeding. **Mailing Address:** Dept Genetics & Biochem, Univ Fed Uberlandia, Uberlandia, 38400-902, Brazil.

KERR, WILLIAM, REACTOR SAFETY, REACTOR SHIELDING. **Personal Data:** b Sawyer, Kans, August 19, 1919; m 1945, c 3. **Education:** Univ Tenn, BS, 1942, MS, 1947; Univ Mich, PhD (elec eng), 1954. **Honors & Awards:** Arthur Holly Compton Award, Am Nuclear Soc, 1974. **Professional Experience:** PROF EMER NUCLEAR ENG, UNIV MICH, 1989-; dir, Off Energy Res, 1977-1984; mem gov task force nuclear waste disposal, State Mich, 1976-1984; mem adv comt reactor safeguards, US Nuclear Regulatory Comn, 1972-1992; pres bd dir, Assoc Midwest Univs, 1965; chmn, Dept Nuclear Eng, 1961-1974; from assoc dir to dir, Mich Mem Phoenix Proj, 1960-1989; from assoc prof to prof nuclear eng, Univ Mich, Ann Arbor, 1956-1989; proj supvr nuclear energy proj, USAID, 1956-1965; USAID, 1956-1965; Union Carbide Nuclear Corp, 1954; consult, Atomic Power Develop Assocs, 1954-1959; asst prof elec eng, Univ Mich, Ann Arbor, 1953-1956; asst prof elec eng, Univ Tenn, 1947-1948. **Memberships:** Fel Am Nuclear Soc; Inst Elec & Electronics Engrs; Am Soc Eng Educ; Sigma Xi. **Research Statement & Publications:** Application of telemetering to power systems; autoradiography; nuclear reactor system dynamics; reactor control; reactor shielding; reactor safety analysis. **Mailing Address:** Dept Nuclear Eng, Univ Mich, 108 Cooley Bldg N Campus 2355 Bonisteel Blvd, Ann Arbor, MI 48109-2104.

KERR, WILLIAM B, HOSPITAL ADMINISTRATION. **Personal Data:** b Chicago, Ill, December 21, 1943; c 3. **Education:** Loyola Univ, BS, 1964; Univ Minn, MS, 1969. **Professional Experience:** SR V PRES, HUNTER GROUP, as of 2004; dir Med Ctr, Univ Calif, San Francisco, 1977-1996; adminr, Inpatient Serv, 1974-1977; asst dir, Univ Calif, San Francisco, 1970-1974; exec asst hosp admin, New York City Health & Hosp Corp, 1969-1970; asst comnr, Comnr Off, New York City Dept Hosps, 1969-1970; admin resident, Comnr Off, New York City Dept Hosps, 1968-1969; US Army Mil Intel, 1965-1967; lectr, Inst Health Policy Studies, Univ Calif, San Francisco. **Memberships:** Inst Med-NatAcad Sci; Asn Am Med Col; Am Hosp Asn. **Mailing Address:** 825 Albatross, Box 1205, Novato, CA 94945. **Fax:** 415-353-4520.

KERR, WILLIAM CLAYTON, COMPUTER SIMULATION. **Personal Data:** b Steubenville, Ohio, March 8, 1940; m 1963, Sandria; c Tamara & Elizabeth. **Education:** Col Wooster, BA, 1962; Cornell Univ, PhD (theoret physics), 1967. **Professional Experience:** Collabr, Los Alamos Nat Lab, 1984-1985 & 1995-1996; PROF PHYSICS, WAKE FOREST UNIV, 1983-; Univ Paris, 1976-1977 & Los Alamos Nat Lab, 1981, 1986-1988, 1991, 1992 & 1994; vis scientist, Chalmers Univ Technol, 1974; vis scientist, Argonne Nat Lab, 1971, 1972 & 1980; from asst prof to assoc prof, Wake Forest Univ, 1970-1983; Res assoc physics, Inst Theoret Physics, Chalmers Univ Technol, Sweden, 1967-1968 & Solid State Sci Div, Argonne Nat Lab, 1968-1970. **Memberships:** Am Phys Soc; Am Asn Physics Teachers; Sigma Xi. **Research Statement & Publications:** Theory of nonlinear systems; computer simulation of nonlinear, low dimensional systems of interest in statistical physics, including structural phase transitions, sine-Gordon chains and biological molecules. **Mailing Address:** Dept Physics, Wake Forest Univ, Box 7507, Olin Physics Lab 311, Winston-Salem, NC 27109-7507. **Fax:** 336-758-6142. **E-Mail:** wck@wfu.edu

KERREBROCK, JACK LEO, AERONAUTICS, ASTRONAUTICS. **Personal Data:** b Los Angeles, Calif, February 6, 1928; m 1953, c 3. **Education:** Ore State Col, BS, 1950; Yale Univ, MS, 1951; Calif Inst Technol, PhD (mech eng), 1956. **Honors & Awards:** Dryden Lectr, Am Inst Aeronaut & Astronaut, 1980. **Professional Experience:** Fairchild scholar, Calif Inst Tech, 1990; assoc dean eng, Space Propulsion Lab, 1985-1990; mem, Nat Comn Space, 1985; hon prof, Beijing Inst Aeronaut & Astronaut, China, 1980; assoc adminr, Off Aeronaut & Space Technol, NASA, 1980; head dept, Space Propulsion Lab, 1978-1981, 1983-1985; Richard Cockburn Maclaurin prof aeronaut & astronaut, Space Propulsion Lab, beginning 1975; Gas Turbine Lab, Space Propulsion Lab, 1968-1978; dir, Space Propulsion Lab, 1962-1976; PROF EMER AERONAUT & ASTRONAUT, MASS INST TECHNOL, 1960-; from asst prof to prof, Mass Inst Technol, 1960-1975; sr res fel, Calif Inst Technol, 1958-1960; res engr, Oak Ridge Nat Lab, 1956-1958; mem, Nat Res Coun Aeronaut & Space Eng Bd; mem, Am Soc Mech Engrs Turbomach Comt; NASA Adv Bd Aircraft Fuel Conserv Technol; chmn, Sci & Technol Adv Group, USAF Sci Adv Bd. **Memberships:** Nat Acad Eng; fel Am Inst Aeronaut & Astronaut; fel Explorers Club; Am Phys Soc; sr mem Am Astronaut Soc; fel Am Acad Arts & Sci. **Research Statement & Publications:** Aircraft propulsion; space propulsion and power generation systems; magnetohydrodynamics; nuclear rockets. **Mailing Address:** Mass Inst Technol, Aeronaut & Astronaut, Rm 31-261G, Cambridge, MA 02139. **E-Mail:** kerbrock@mit.edu

KERRI, KENNETH D, CIVIL & SANITARY ENGINEERING. **Personal Data:** b Napa, Calif, April 25, 1934; m 1958, Judith Reeves; c Christopher & Kathleen. **Education:** Ore State Univ, BS, 1956, PhD (civil eng), 1965; Univ Calif, Berkeley, MS, 1959. **Honors & Awards:** Collection Syst Award, Water Pollution Control Fedn, 1977. **Professional Experience:** PROF EMER CIVIL ENG, CALIF STATE UNIV, SACRAMENTO, 1997-; Asn Bds Cert, 1983 & Calif Water Pollution Fedn, 1983-1984; pres, Nat Environ Training Asn, 1979-1980; prof civil eng, Calif State Univ, Sacramento, beginning 1968; assoc prof, Calif State Univ, Sacramento, 1959-1968. **Memberships:** Water Pollution Control Fedn; Am Soc Civil Engrs; Am Water Works Asn; Am Soc Eng Educ. **Research Statement & Publications:** Water quality economics; training manuals for operators of water and wastewater facilities. **Mailing Address:** Dept Civil Eng, Calif State Univ 6000 J St, Sacramento, CA 95819-6025. **E-Mail:** kerrik@saclink.csus.edu

KERRICH, ROBERT, GEOCHEMISTRY, GEODYNAMICS. **Personal Data:** b December 15, 1948; m Beverly. **Honorary Degrees:** DSc, Univ Saskatchewan, 1996. **Honors & Awards:** Duncan Derry Medal, Geol Asn Can, 2003; Distinguished Researcher Award, Uni Sask, 2000; Willett G Miller Medal, Royal Soc Can, 1999. **Professional Experience:** McLeod Res Chair, Univ of Saskatchewan, 1987-2006-; Prof, Univ of Western Ont, 1979-1986. **Research Statement & Publications:** My philosophy is to attempt to identify unknowns in Earth Sciences, and bring all the necessary field, analytical, and theoretical tools to bear to resolve those unknowns. **Mailing Address:** Dept Geol Sci Rm 246, Univ Sask 114 Sci Pl, Saskatoon, SK S7N 5E2, Can. **Fax:** 306-966-8593. **E-Mail:** robert.kerrich@usask.ca

KERRICK, DERRILL M, PETROLOGY, GEOCHEMISTRY. **Personal Data:** b Santa Cruz, Calif, December 27, 1940; m 1961, c 3. **Education:** San Jose State Col, BS, 1963; Univ Calif, Berkeley, PhD (geol), 1968. **Professional Experience:** PROF EMER GEOCHEM, PA STATE UNIV, as of 2005; prof geophysics, PA State Univ, beginning 1992; prof petrol, PA State Univ, beginning 1979; chmn geochem & mineral grad prog, PA State Univ, 1978-1983; from asst prof to assoc prof petrol, PA State Univ, 1969-1979; Lectr geol, Victoria Univ Manchester, 1967-1969; assoc ed, Geochimica et Cosmochimica Acta. **Memberships:** Fel Mineral Soc Am; Geochem Soc. **Research Statement & Publications:** Laboratory and field investigations of metamorphic reactions and stability relations of metamorphic assemblages. **Mailing Address:** Dept Geophysics, Pa State Univ, 243 Deike Bldg, Univ Park, PA 16802. **Fax:** 814-863-7823. **E-Mail:** kerrick@geosc.psu.edu

KERRICK, JERRIL D, MATHEMATICS. **Education:** Calif State Univ, Sanjose, BA, 1962, MS, 1967; Ore State Univ, PhD, 1971. **Professional Experience:** RETIRED; prof math &

comput sci, Univ Puget Sound, ending 2003. **Mailing Address:** Dept Math & Comp Sci, Univ Puget Sound, Tacoma, WA 98416-0001.

KERRICK, WALLACE GLENN LEE, PHYSIOLOGY, BIOPHYSICS. **Education:** Univ Puget Sound, Tacoma, BS, 1961; Univ Wash, Seattle, PhD (physiol & biophysics), 1971. **Professional Experience:** PROF PHYSIOL & BIOPHYSICS, UNIV MIAMI, 1983-; Wash Univ, St Louis, 1985 & Univ Calgary, 1988; res grants, NIH, 1987; mem, Nat Peer Rev, Am Heart Asn, 1986-; res grants, Am Heart Asn, 1982-1992; res grants, Muscular Dystrophy Asn, 1982-1991; assoc prof, Univ Miami, 1981-1983; lectr, Univ Cincinnati, 1980; lectr, Wash State Univ, 1977; lectr, Univ Calif, San Diego, 1976; from asst prof to assoc prof, Dept Physiol & Biophys, Univ Wash, 1974-1981; actg asst prof, Dept Physiol & Biophys, Univ Wash, 1972-1974; Postdoctoral fel, Dept Physiol & Biophys, Univ Wash, 1971-1972. **Memberships:** Fedn Am Socs Exp Biol; Biophys Soc; Am Heart Asn; Sigma Xi. **Research Statement & Publications:** Mechanism of cardiac muscle regulation by troponin; effects of weightlessness on physiological and biochemical properties of single muscle cells; author of numerous technical publications. **Mailing Address:** Dept Physiol & Biophysics, Univ Miami, 5065 Gautier Med Res Bldg 1011 NW 15th St, Miami, FL 33136. **Fax:** 305-243-1134. **E-Mail:** wkerrick@miami.edu

KERSCHENSTEINER, DANIEL A, DENTAL DIAGNOSTICS, IMMUNOCHEMISTRY. **Personal Data:** b Corning, NY, September 29, 1949; c 1. **Education:** Syracuse Univ, BS, 1971, MS, 1973; Univ NH, PhD (biochem), 1979. **Professional Experience:** PRES & FOUNDER, CHERRYSTONE & CO, 1983-; mgr, Warner-Lambert, 1981-1983; sr scientist, Carter Wallace, 1979-1981; postdocoral fel, Univ Wis-Madison, 1979; biologist, Corning Inc, 1973. **Research Statement & Publications:** Primary structure and sequence of superoxide dismutase; collagenase assay by colloidal flocculation (patent); sensitive tests for periodontal disease, dental caries, and oral malodor (patents). **Mailing Address:** 5 Briarcliff Dr, Corning, NY 14830. **E-Mail:** dankerschensteiner@yahoo.com

KERSCHNER, JEAN, GENETICS. **Personal Data:** b Baltimore, Md, May 31, 1922. **Education:** Hood Col, AB, 1943; Univ Pa, PhD (zoology), 1950. **Professional Experience:** EMER PROF, Western Md Col, as of 2005; prof biol, Western Md Col, 1968-1980; fac fel, NSF, Columbia Univ, 1960-1961; from asst prof to assoc prof, Western Md Col, 1952-1968; histologist, Army Chem Ctr, 1951-1952; asst prof biol, Elmira Col, 1950-1951; lab asst, Univ Pa, 1945-1946; chemist, E I du Pont de Nemours & Co, 1943-1945. **Memberships:** Genetics Soc Am; Sigma Xi. **Research Statement & Publications:** X-ray induced mutations in Drosophila. **Mailing Address:** 231 Geisky Creek Rd, Hayesville, NC 28904.

KERSEY, JOHN H, LEUKEMIA. **Personal Data:** b April 22, 1964. **Education:** Darmouth Col, BA; Darmouth Med Sch, BMS; Univ Minn, MD, 1964. **Professional Experience:** FOUND DIR, CANCER CTR, UNIV MINN, as of 2005; C CENCER RES FUND ENDOWED CHAIR, PEDIAT ONCOL, UNIV MINN, as of 2005; C CENCER RES FUND LAND GRANT PROF LAB MED, PATH & PEDIAT, SCH MED, UNIV MINN, 1977-; dir, Blood & Marrow Transplant Prog, Univ Minn, 1974-1995; ed bd, Biol Blood & Marrow Transplantation, Bone Marrow Transplantation, British J Hemat, Clinical Transplantation, Exp Hemat; assoc ed, Blood; assoc ed, Cancer Res. **Memberships:** Am Soc Blood & Marrow Transplantation(pres, 1997-1998; Int Soc Exp Hemat(pres, 1995-1996); Am Asn Cancer Res; Am Soc Hemat; Am Soc Clin Investrs; Am Asn Pathologists; Nat Cancer Inst; Am Cancer Soc Adv. **Research Statement & Publications:** Lymphoma; childhood leukemia; Immune based therapies; publications around ten numbers basically on leukemia and its treatment. **Mailing Address:** Dept Cancer Ctr, Univ Minn Health Ctr, Mayo Mail Code 8 420 Del St SE, Minneapolis, MN 55455. **Fax:** 612-624-3069. **E-Mail:** kerse001@umn.edu

KERSEY, MATTHEW T, ANALYTICAL CHEMISTRY. **Education:** PhD. **Professional Experience:** GLAXO SMITHKLINE, NC, as of 2005. **Memberships:** Am Asn Pharmaceut Sci. **Mailing Address:** GlaxoSmithKline Corp, Five Moore Dr, Research Triangle Park, NC 27709. **Fax:** 919-315-8735.

KERSHAW, DAVID STANLEY, THEORETICAL PHYSICS, COMPUTER SCIENCE. **Personal Data:** b Missoula, Mont, May 20, 1943; m 1966, Winifred Shaw; c Miriam, Jeremy & Elizabeth. **Education:** Harvard Univ, BA, 1965; Univ Calif, Berkeley, PhD (physics), 1970. **Professional Experience:** PHYSICIST LASER FUSION, LAWRENCE LIVERMORE LAB, UNIV CALIF, 1974-; Fel theoret partical physics, Stanford Linear Accelerator Ctr, 1970-1972 & Dept Physics & Astron, Univ Md, College Park, 1972-1974. **Memberships:** Am Phys Soc. **Research Statement & Publications:** Computer simulation of the physics of laser fusion. **Mailing Address:** 1827 Newcastle Ct, Walnut Creek, CA 94595. **E-Mail:** dsk@icf.llnl.gov

KERSHAW, KENNETH ANDREW, PLANT ECOLOGY, LICHENOLOGY. **Personal Data:** b Morecambe, Eng, September 5, 1930; m 1967, c 3. **Education:** Manchester Univ, BS, 1952; Univ Wales, PhD (ecol), 1957, DSc, 1968. **Professional Experience:** PROF EMER BIOL, MCMASTER UNIV, as of 2004; prof Biol, Mcmaster Univ, 1969-; lectr, Imp Col, Univ London, 1965-1968; sr lectr, Secondment to Ahmadu Bell Univ, N Nigeria, 1963-1965; Lectr, Imp Col, Univ London, 1957-1963. **Memberships:** Brit Lichen Soc; fel Royal Soc Can. **Research Statement & Publications:** Ecology of northern plant systems with special emphasis on the interaction of microclimate and plant physiology; lichen physiology. **Mailing Address:** Dept Biol, Univ Mcmaster, 1280 Main St W, ON L8S 4K1, Can. **Fax:** 905-522-6066.

KERSHENBAUM, AARON, ALGORITHMS, NETWORK DESIGN. **Personal Data:** b Brooklyn, NY, October 9, 1948; m 1970, c 2. **Education:** Polytech Inst NY, BS & MS, 1970, PhD (elec eng), 1976. **Professional Experience:** RES STAFF MEM, TJ WATSON RES CTR, as of 2005; res mgr, IBM, 1990-1997; Systems Biolo, Comput Security, Nat Language Processing, Anti-virus, Network Design Anal Groups, IBM TJ Watson Res Center, 1988-; dir, Network Design Lab, Polytech Univ, 1984-; PROF COMPUT SCI, POLYTECH UNIV, BROOKLYN NY, 1984-; assoc ed, Networks, 1983-1985; assoc ed, J Telecommun Networks, 1983-1985; from asst prof to prof elec & comput sci, Polytech Univ, 1978-1990; vpres software, Network Anal Corp, 1969-1978; programmer, Network Anal Corp, 1969-1978; dir, Network Anal Corp, 1969-1978. **Memberships:** Asn Comput Mach; Inst Elec & Electronics Engrs. **Research Statement & Publications:** The Encyclopedia of Genetics, Genomics, Proteomics and Bioinformatics; Discovering Motifs in Biological Networks Using Subgraph Isomorphism; Reconstructing Synthetic Biological Networks Using Pairwise Correlation Analysis; author of various articles. **Mailing Address:** Comput Security Functional Genomics & Systems Biol Group, Int Bus Mach res TJ Watson Res Ctr, Brooklyn, NY 11201. **Fax:** 914-945-4104. **E-Mail:** aaronk@us.ibm.com

KERSHENSTEIN, JOHN CHARLES, PHYSICS, ELECTROOPTICS. **Personal Data:** b New York, NY, September 23, 1941; m 1968, c 1. **Education:** Georgetown Univ, BS, 1964, MS, 1967, PhD (physics), 1969. **Professional Experience:** CHEIF SCIENTIST NAVAL RES LAB, as of 2005; Br head, Optical Sci Div US Naval Res Lab, as of 2004; res physicist, US Naval Res Lab, beginning 1969; fel physics, US Naval Res Lab, 1968-1969. **Mailing Address:** US Naval Res Lab, 4555 Overlook Ave SW, Washington, VA 22039. **E-Mail:** kershenstein@nrl.navy.mil

KERSHNER, CARL JOHN, PHYSICAL CHEMISTRY, RADIOCHEMISTRY. **Personal Data:** b Lima, Ohio, December 15, 1934; m 1958, c 2. **Education:** Capital Univ, BS, 1956; Univ Ohio, PhD (inorg chem), 1961. **Professional Experience:** VPRES, FEMTO-TECH, INC, 1986-; adj prof, Ohio State Univ, 1980-1981; sr sci fel, Mound Lab, 1979-1985; sci fel, Mound Lab, 1970-1979; sr res specialist, Monsanto Res Corp, 1968-1970; sect mgr, Monsanto Res Corp, 1966-1968; group leader radiochem res, Monsanto Res Corp, 1964-1966; Sr res chemist, Monsanto Res Corp, 1961-1964. **Memberships:** Am Inst Physics; Am Chem Soc; Am Nuclear Soc; Sigma Xi. **Research Statement & Publications:** High temperature radiochemical research; syntheses and physical property determinations; isotope separation; radioactive waste and emission control; laser photochemistry; radiation detection instrumentation.

KERST, A(L) FRED, ORGANIC CHEMISTRY, PHYSICAL CHEMISTRY. **Personal Data:** b Greeley, Colo, June 3, 1940; m 1962, c 3. **Education:** Colo State Univ, BS, 1962, MS, 1963; Harvard Univ, PhD (chem), 1967. **Professional Experience:** CHIEF OPERATING OFF & BOARD MEM, AUROGEN INC, as of 2004; pres & ceo, Calgon Corp, beginning 1989; vpres mkt, Calgon Corp, 1984-1989; vpres res & develop, Calgon Corp, 1977-1984; eval panel, Nat Bur Standards Ctr Fire Res, 1976-1979; vpres res & develop, Velsicol Chem Corp, 1976-1977; vpres res & develop, Mich Chem Corp, 1971-1976; mgr, Gates Rubber Co, 1969-1971; Sr chemist, Monsanto Co, 1967-1968. **Memberships:** Am Chem Soc. **Research Statement & Publications:** Chemistry of phosphorus compounds, flame retardants, polymers; agriculture pesticides and industrial biocides; water treatment chemicals. **Mailing Address:** Aurogen Inc, PO Box B 202 Remington St, Ft Collins, CO 80522. **Fax:** 970-482-5990.

KERSTEIN, MORRIS D, VASCULAR TRAUMA. **Personal Data:** b Trenton, NJ, January 13, 1938; m 1980, c 1. **Education:** Colgate Univ, AB, 1959; Chicago Med Sch, 1963. **Professional Experience:** DEISSLER PROF & CHMN, DEPT SURG, HAHNEMANN UNIV, PHILADELPHIA, PA, 1988-; assoc dean, acad affairs & dir, grad & postgrad prog, 1986-1988; clin prof, surg, Tulane Univ Sch Med, 1983-; surgeon, 1981-; prof surg, Tulane Univ Sch Med, 1979-1988; chief, peripheral vascular surg, Michael Reese Hosp, Chicago, 1977-1979; assoc prof, surg, Pritzker Sch Med, Univ Chicago, 1977-1979; staff surgeon, Vet Admin Hosp, West Haven, Conn, 1971-1977; from asst prof to assoc prof surg, Yale Univ Sch Med, 1971-1977; chief resident, Boston City Hosp, 1970-1971; instr surg, Tufts Univ Sch Med, 1970-1971; resident surg serv, Boston City Hosp, 1969-1970. **Memberships:** Am Col Surgeons; Am Heart Asn; AMA; Soc Vascular Surg; Am Surg Asn; Soc Univ Surgeons. **Research Statement & Publications:** Prostoglandin metabolism in human vessels; vascular trauma; non-invasive laboratory. **Mailing Address:** Dept Surg, Hahnemann Univ, Broad & Vine St MS 413, Philadelphia, PA 19102-1192. **Fax:** 215-762-8389.

KERSTEN, MILES S(TOKES), ENGINEERING. **Personal Data:** b St Paul, Minn, August 12, 1913; m 1938, c Cynthia K (Doran) & Thomas L. **Education:** Univ Minn, BCE, 1934, MS, 1936, PhD (hwys, soils), 1945. **Honors & Awards:** Harold R Peyton Award, Am Soc Civil Eng, 1989. **Professional Experience:** PROF EMER SOIL MECH, HWYS & SOILS, UNIV MINN, MINNEAPOLIS, as of 2002; prof soil mech, hwys & soils, Univ Minn, Minneapolis, beginning 1978; from asst prof to prof, Hwys & Soils, Univ Minn, Minneapolis, 1945-1978; spec investr, Hwy Res Bd, Wash, DC, 1944-1945; instr hwys & soils, Univ Minn, 1937-1944; Soils engr, State Hwy Dept, Minn, 1936-1937. **Memberships:** Hon mem Am Soc Civil Eng; Am Soc Eng Educ; Nat Asn Prof Engrs. **Research Statement & Publications:** Thermal conductivity of soil; soil stabilization; sub-grade moisture conditions and their role in flexible pavement design; airport engineering; general civil engineering; surveying and mapping. **Mailing Address:** 4300 W River Pkwy Apt 619, Minneapolis, MN 55406-3662. **E-Mail:** kerst002@umn.edu

KERSTEN, ROBERT D(ONAVON), ENGINEERING EDUCATION & WATER RESOURCES. **Personal Data:** b Carlinville, Ill, January 30, 1927; m 1950, c Susan & John. **Education:** Okla State Univ, BS, 1949, MS, 1956; Northwestern Univ, PhD (fluid mech), 1961. **Professional Experience:** DEAN EMER ENG, UNIC CENT FLA, as of 2005; PROF EMER ENG, UNIV CENT FLA, as of 2005; vpres, Pan Am Union Eng Socs, Eng Educ Comt, 1992-; mem, US Coun Int Eng Practice, 1989-1993; mem, Pan Am Union Eng Socs, Eng Educ Comt, 1986-; mem, Eng Accreditation Comn, 1982-1989; mem, Fla Bd Prof Engrs, 1980-1986; chmn bd trustees, Inst Cert Eng Technicians, 1978-1980; actg dir, Fla Solar Energy Ctr, 1975; prof eng, Univ Cent Fla, beginning 1968; dean, Col Eng, 1968-1987; dir univ res, Univ Cent Fla, 1968-1969; vis scholar, Stanford Univ, 1966; mem, Col Bus Exchange Prog Found Econ Ed, 1963; mem, NASA-Cambridge Conf Explor Mars & Venus, 1965; mem, NASA-NSF Conf Lunar Explor, 1962; mem, Flight Safety Found, 1962; prof civil eng & chmn, Ariz State Univ, 1960-1968; from asst prof to assoc prof eng, Ariz State Univ, 1957-1960; res engr, Jersey Prod Res Co, Stand Oil NJ, 1956-1957; asst prof, Okla State Univ, 1956; res assoc civil eng, Okla State Univ, 1953-1956; Hydraul engr, US Dept Interior, 1949-1953. **Memberships:** AAAS; Am Soc Eng Educ; Am Soc Civil Engrs; Nat Soc Prof Engrs (vpres, 1984-1985); Sigma Xi; NatCoun Examr Eng & Surv; Fla Eng Soc (pres, 1993-1994). **Research Statement & Publications:** Fluid mechanics, including fluid turbulence, turbulent diffusion, non-Newtonian flow, two phase flow; water resources engineering; applied mathematics. **Mailing Address:** 590 Demmerich Dr, Maitland, FL 32751. **Fax:** 407-823-3315.

KERSTEN, THOMAS L, MATHEMATICS. **Education:** Univ Minn, MS, 1973, PhD (Maths), 1976. **Professional Experience:** PROF & INSTR, DEPT COMPUT SCI & MATHS, NORMANDALE COMMUNITY COL, as of 2006. **Memberships:** Am Math Soc. **Mailing Address:** Normandale Commun Col, 9700 France Ave S, Bloomington, MN 55431-4309. **Fax:** 952-487-8101. **E-Mail:** thomas.kersten@normandale.edu

KERSTETTER, REX E, PLANT PHYSIOLOGY. **Personal Data:** b Ashland, Kans, November 22, 1938; div, c Kelvin T & Derek E. **Education:** Ft Hays Kans State Col, BS, 1960, MS, 1963; Fla State Univ, PhD (plant physiol), 1967. **Professional Experience:** RETIRED; prof biol, furman Univ, beginning 1980; from asst prof to assoc prof, furman Univ, 1967-1980; Instr biol, Fla State Univ, 1967. **Memberships:** AAAS; Am Soc Plant Physiologists; Bot Soc Am; Sigma Xi. **Research Statement & Publications:** Plant hormone physiology; plant tissue culture; peroxidase isoenzymes. **Mailing Address:** 16 Zelma Dr, Greenville, SC 29617. **E-Mail:** rex.kerstetter@furman.edu

KERSTETTER, THEODORE HARVEY, FISH PHYSIOLOGY, ELECTROLYTE BALANCE. **Personal Data:** b Milwaukee, Wis, December 16, 1930; div, c 2. **Education:** Univ Nev, Reno, BS, 1959; Wash State Univ, MS, 1962, PhD (zoo physiol), 1969. **Professional Experience:** PROF EMER ZOOL, HUMBOLDT STATE UNIV, 1986-; chmn, dept fisheries, beginning 1992; prof zool, Humboldt State Univ, 1979-1986; dir, Marine Lab & Sea Grant Prog, 1974-1979; from asst prof to assoc prof, Marine Lab & Sea Grant Prog,

1970-1979; NIH fel, Wash State Univ, 1969-1970; instr biol, Peninsula Col, 1963-1964. **Memberships:** Am Inst Fisheries Res Biologists. **Research Statement & Publications:** Water and ion balance in lower vertebrates; mechanisms of ion transport through epithelia; fish physiology; heavy metal toxicity in fish. **Mailing Address:** Dept Zool, Humboldt State Univ, 1 Harpst St, Arcata, CA 95521-8299. **E-Mail:** kerstettert@axe.humboldt.edu

KERTAMUS, NORBERT JOHN, FUEL & CHEMICAL ENGINEERING. **Personal Data:** b Murray City, Utah, October 12, 1932; m 1956, c 3. **Education:** Univ Utah, BS, 1960, PhD (fuels eng), 1964. **Professional Experience:** SR RES SCIENTIST, SOUTHERN CALIF EDISON, 1979-; sr process engr, C F Braun Engrs, 1975-1979; res specialist chem & combustion, Babcock & Wilcox Co, 1970-1975; sr res chemist nuclear fuels, Idaho Nuclear Co, 1966-1970; Res engr, Phillips Petrol Co, 1964-1966. **Memberships:** Am Chem Soc; Am Inst Chem Engrs. **Research Statement & Publications:** Conversion of coal to gases and/or liquids; hydrogen processing and catalysis; combustion. **Mailing Address:** Southern Calif Edison Co, Rosemead, CA 84094.

KERTESZ, ANDREW (ENDRE), VISION, BIOMEDICAL ENGINEERING. **Personal Data:** b Budapest, Hungary, October 10, 1938; American citizen; m 1963, c 2. **Education:** McGill Univ, BEng, 1963; Northwestern Univ, Evanston, MS, 1966, PhD (bioeng), 1969. **Professional Experience:** Chmn biomed eng, psychol & biomed eng, Northwestern Univ, Evanston, beginning 1983; clin assoc ophthal, Evanston Hosp, 1977; 1974; PROF ELEC ENG, PSYCHOL & BIOMED ENG, NORTHWESTERN UNIV, EVANSTON, 1972-; sr res fel appl sci, Calif Inst Technol & prin investr, USPHS res grant, 1970-; asst prof elec eng, Univ Pittsburgh, 1969-1972. **Memberships:** Inst Elec & Electronics Engrs; Asn Res Vision & Ophthal; Biomed Eng Soc; Optical Soc Am. **Research Statement & Publications:** Human binocular information processing; binocular vision. **Mailing Address:** Dept Biomed Eng, Northwestern Univ, 2145 Sheridan Rd, Evanston, IL 60208-3107. **Fax:** 847-491-5299. **E-Mail:** a-kertesz@northwestern.edu

KERTESZ, DENNIS, CHEMISTRY. **Mailing Address:** 2329 W 2nd St Apt 7, Los Angeles, CA 90057-2037.

KERTESZ, JEAN CONSTANCE, PHARMACEUTICAL CHEMISTRY. **Personal Data:** b New York, NY, September 3, 1943. **Education:** Northwestern Univ, BA, 1963; Univ Southern Calif, PhD (pharmaceut chem), 1970. **Professional Experience:** ASST RES PROF, SCH PHARM, UNIV SOUTHERN CALIF, 1977-; res assoc biomed chem, Sch Med, 1968-1977; Res asst biochem, Sch Med, 1965-1966. **Memberships:** Am Chem Soc; Intra-Sci Res Found; Int Soc Magnetic Resonance; Sigma Xi. **Research Statement & Publications:** Free radical intermediates in biological systems; utilization of electron spin resonance techniques for biomedical applications; molecular mechanisms of radiation damage; protection processes; carcinogenesis. **Mailing Address:** 2329 W Second St Apt 7, Los Angeles, CA 90057.

KERTESZ, MIKLOS, QUANTUM CHEMISTRY OF SOLIDS & POLYMERS, CONDUCTING POLYMERS & CARBON NANOTUBES. **Personal Data:** b Budapest, Hungary, July 15, 1948; m 1969, Eva; c Anna & Kata. **Education:** Eotvos L Univ, Budapest, dipl, 1971, Dr rer nat, 1979; Hungarian Acad Sci, Cand phys sci, 1978. **Professional Experience:** PROF, DEPT CHEM, GEORGETOWN UNIV, 1983-; res assoc, Dept Chem, Cornell Univ, 1982-1983; sr scientist, Cent Res Inst, Hungarian Acad Sci, 1981; res fel, Quantum Theory Proj, Univ Fla, 1979-1980 & Dept Chem, Cornell Univ, 1980; Res scientist, Cent Res Inst, Hungarian Acad Sci, 1971-1979. **Memberships:** Am Chem Soc; Am Phys Soc. **Research Statement & Publications:** Theoretical solid state chemistry; structure and electronic structure of conducting polymers; vibrational spectrum of polymers. **Mailing Address:** Dept Chem, Georgetown Univ, Washington, DC 20057-1227. **Fax:** 202-687-6209. **E-Mail:** kertesz@georgetown.edu

KERTH, LEROY THOMAS, PHYSICS. **Personal Data:** b Visalia, Calif, November 23, 1928; m 1950, Ruth; c Norman L, Randall T, Christine G & Bradlley N. **Education:** Univ Calif, BA, 1950, PhD (physics), 1957. **Professional Experience:** PROF EMER PHYSICS, LAWRENCE BERKELEY LAB, UNIV CALIF, 1993-; assoc lab dir, Sci & Tech Resources, 1989-1991; assoc lab dir gen sci, 1987-1989; assoc dir & div head comput sci, 1983-1987; assoc dean, Col Lett & Sci, 1966-1970; prof, Col Lett & Sci, 1965-1993; res physicist, Lawrence Berkeley Lab, Univ Calif, 1957-1965; asst, Lawrence Berkeley Lab, Univ Calif, 1950-1957. **Memberships:** Fel Am Phys Soc. **Research Statement & Publications:** High energy physics; weak interactions; CP Violation; instrumentation. **Mailing Address:** Dept Physics, Lawrence Berkeley Lab, Univ Calif, One Cyclotron Rd, Berkeley, CA 94720. **Fax:** 510-486-4047. **E-Mail:** ltkerth@lbl.gov

KERTZ, ALOIS FRANCIS, ANIMAL NUTRITION. **Personal Data:** b Bloomsdale, Mo, September 15, 1945; m 1969, c 4. **Education:** Univ Mo-Columbia, BS, 1967, MS, 1968; Cornell Univ, PhD (animal nutrit), 1974. **Professional Experience:** FOUNDER & PRIN, ANDHIL LLC, 2001-; CO-FOUNDED KKC TECHNOLOGIES LLC, as of 2003; res Mgr, Ruminant Res Dept, Purina Mills Inc, 1985-1991; mgr res, Dept Dairy Res, 1975-1985; res nutritionist, Ruminant Res Dept, Purina Mills Inc, 1973-1975; res asst animal nutrit, Cornell Univ, 1970-1973; food supply & mgt officer, US Army Depot, Sattahip, Thailand, 1969-1970; Nutrit officer, US Army Natick Labs, 1968-1969. **Memberships:** Am Dairy Sci Asn; Am Soc Animal Sci; AAAS; Nutrit Today Soc; Am Inst Nutrit. **Research Statement & Publications:** Efficiency of nitrogen and energy utilization by calves and dairy cattle; evaluation and utilization of common feedstuffs and other by-products. **Mailing Address:** Andhil LLC, 9999 Manchester Rd, Ste 366, St Louis, MO 63122-1928. **Fax:** 314-821-7239. **E-Mail:** andhil@andhil.com

KERTZ, GEORGE J, MATHEMATICS, COMPUTER SCIENCE. **Personal Data:** b Bloomsdale, Mo, December 10, 1933; m 1968. **Education:** Cardinal Glennon Col, AB, 1955; St Louis Univ, MA, 1963, PhD (math), 1966; Univ Mich, MSE, 1978. **Professional Experience:** PROF EMER MATH, UNIV TOLEDO, 1999-; prof math, Univ Toledo, 1978-1999; from asst prof to assoc prof, Univ Toledo, 1966-1978; Mem staff, Int Bus Mach Corp, 1958-1960. **Memberships:** Asn Comput Mach; Math Asn Am. **Research Statement & Publications:** Database. **Mailing Address:** Dept Math, Univ Toledo, Toledo, OH 43606-3390.

KERWAR, SURESH, MOLECULAR BIOLOGY. **Personal Data:** b Madras, India, May 9, 1937; American citizen; m 1964, c 2. **Education:** Univ Madras, BS, 1956; Univ Nagpur, MS, 1958; Ore State Univ, PhD (microbiol), 1964. **Professional Experience:** GROUP LEADER, CONNECTIVE TISSUES RES SECT, LEDERLE LABS, 1977-; sr scientist, Div Metab Dis, Ciba-Geigy Inc, 1975-1977; Am Soc Biol Chemists travel grant, 1973 & 1976; asst mem staff, Roche Inst Molecular Biol, NJ, 1971-1975; res assoc, Roche Inst Molecular Biol, NJ, 1969-1971; fel, Brandeis Univ, 1967-1969; Res assoc biochem, Scripps Clin & Res Found, 1963-1967. **Memberships:** Am Soc Biol Chemists. **Research Statement & Publications:** Protein synthesis; regulation of connective tissue metabolism; animal models of joint diseases. **Mailing Address:** Lederle Labs, Pearl River, NY 10965.

KERWIN, EDWARD MICHAEL, JR, acoustics; deceased, see previous edition for last biography

KERWIN, JOHN LARKIN, PHYSICS. **Personal Data:** b Quebec City, Que, June 22, 1924; m 1950, Maria Guadalupe Turcot; c Lupita, Alan, Larkin, Terence, Rosa Maria, Gregory, Timothy & Guillermina. **Education:** St Francis Xavier Univ, BSc, 1944; Mass Inst Technol, MSc, 1946; Laval Univ, DSc, 1949. **Honorary Degrees:** LLD, St Francis Xavier Univ, 1970, Univ Toronto, 1973, Concordia Univ, 1976, Univ Alta, 1983, Dalhousie Univ, 1983; DSc, Univ BC, 1973, McGill Univ, 1974, Mem Univ & DCL, Bishops Univ, 1978, Univ Ottawa, 1981, Royal Mil Col, Kingston, 1982, Univ Winnipeg. **Honors & Awards:** Gov Gen Medal, 1944; Laureate of Lit & Sci Competition of Prov of Que, 1951; Pariseau Medal, Fr-Can Asn Advan Sci, 1965; Centenary Medal, Romania, 1967; Gold Medal, Can Asn Physicists, 1969; Companion, Order Can, 1980; Gold Medal, Can Coun Prof Engrs, 1982; National Order Quebec, 1988. **Professional Experience:** EMER PROF, LAVAL UNIV, 1992-; pres, Can Space Agency, 1989-1992; Can rep, working group res & develop, Int Econ Summit, 1982-; Pres, Nat Res Coun Can, 1980-1989; pres, Asn Univs & Cols Can, 1974; mem bd dirs, Can-France-Hawaii Telescope Corp, Nat Res Coun Can, 1973-1978; mem standing comt int rels, Nat Res Coun Can, 1972-1980; rector, Laval Univ, 1972-1977; Mem, Defence Res Bd Can, 1971-1977; acad vrector, Laval Univ, 1969-1972; vdean fac sci, Laval Univ, 1967-1968; chmn dept, Laval Univ, 1961-1967; from asst prof to prof physics, Laval Univ, 1948-1980; lectr, Laval Univ, 1946; pres, Int Union Pure & Appl Physics. **Memberships:** Am Phys Soc; Can Asn Physicists (vpres 1953 pres 1954); Fr-Can Asn Advan Sci; fel Royal Soc Can (pres 1976); Nat Sci & Eng Coun Can (vpres 1978-1980); fel Royal Soc Arts; fel AAAS; fel Am Inst Physics; Can Acad Eng (vpres 1987 pres 1989). **Research Statement & Publications:** Mass spectrometry; atomic and molecular structure. **Mailing Address:** 2166 Parc Bourbonniere, Sillery, PQ G1T 1B4, Can.

KERWIN, JOSEPH PETER, ASTRONAUTICAL ENGINEERING, MEDICAL & HEALTH SCIENCES. **Personal Data:** b Oak Park, Ill, February 19, 1932; c 3. **Education:** Col Holy Cross, BA, 1953; Northwestern Univ, MD, 1957. **Professional Experience:** CAPTAIN, LYNDON B JOHNSON SPACE CTR, NASA, as of 2002; mgr houston manned progs, Eva Systs, Lockheed Missiles & Space Co, NASA, beginning 1990; mgr, Eva Systs, Lockheed Missiles & Space Co, NASA, beginning 1987; dir, Space-Life Sci, 1984-1987; rep, Australia, 1982-1983; mem, Skylab Crew, 1973; astronaut, NASA, 1965; aviator, 1962. **Research Statement & Publications:** Space exploration; medical sciences. **Mailing Address:** Lyndon B Johnson Space Ctr, Houston, TX 77062.

KERWIN, WILLIAM J(AMES), ELECTRICAL ENGINEERING, PHYSICS. **Personal Data:** b Portage, Wis, September 27, 1922; m 1947, Madolyn Lyons; c Dorothy, Deborah & David. **Education:** Univ Redlands, BS, 1948; Stanford Univ, MS, 1954, PhD (elec eng), 1967. **Honors & Awards:** Centennial Medal, Inst Elec & Electronics Engrs, 1984. **Professional Experience:** EMER PROF ELEC & COMPUT ENG, UNIV ARIZ, 1986-; NASA res awards, 1970 & 1975; prof elec eng, Univ Ariz, 1969-1986; chief, Electronics Res Br, 1964-1969; asst prof, San Jose State Col, 1963-1968; chief, Space Tech Br, Ames Res Ctr, NASA, 1962-1964; head, Electronics Dept, Stanford Linear Accelerator Ctr, 1962; Lectr, Stanford Univ, 1956-1961 & 1968; Aeronaut res scientist, Nat Adv Comt Aeronaut & NASA, Ames Res Ctr, 1948-1962. **Memberships:** Fel Inst Elec & Electronics Engrs; AAAS. **Research Statement & Publications:** Network and circuit theory, especially synthesis of active resistance-capacitance networks; DC-DC power conversion; switched-mode converters. **Mailing Address:** 1981 W Shalimar Way, Tucson, AZ 85704.

KERZMAN, NORBERTO LUIS MARIA, ANALYSIS, COMPLEX VARIABLES. **Personal Data:** b Buenos Aires, Arg, February 1, 1943. **Education:** Univ Buenos Aires, Lic, 1966; NY Univ, PhD (math), 1970. **Honors & Awards:** Krakauer Award in Sci, Courant Inst, NY Univ, 1971. **Professional Experience:** PROF MATH, UNIV NC, CHAPEL HILL, 1982-; assoc prof, Univ NC, Chapel Hill, 1979-1982; from asst prof to assoc prof, Mass Inst Technol, 1973-1979; Sloan fel, 1973-1975; asst prof math, Princeton Univ, 1971-1973; Lectr, Princeton Univ, 1970-1971; vis mem staff, Gottingen, Munster, Florence, Paris, Marseille, Grenoble, Stockholm, Amsterdam, Zurich, Buenes Aires, Mex. **Memberships:** Am Math Soc. **Research Statement & Publications:** Complex analysis in particular several complex variables, involving methods of partial differential equations and singular integrals; conformal mapping. **Mailing Address:** Dept Math, Univ NC, Phillips Hall Ste 302, Chapel Hill, NC 27599-3250. **Fax:** 919-962-2568. **E-Mail:** kerzman@math.unc.edu

KESAVAN, SUNIL KUMAR, REACTIVE POLYMERS, CHEMICAL ENGINEERING. **Personal Data:** b Kanpur, India, May 29, 1961; American citizen; c 1. **Education:** Univ Madras, India, BTech, 1982; Univ Akron, Ohio, MSChE, 1985, PhD (chem eng), 1987. **Honors & Awards:** Soc Plastics Engrs Award, 1994. **Professional Experience:** MGR CORE TECHNOL, HONEYWELL FRICTION MAT, 1993-; Adj prof, Dept Chem Eng, Univ Akron, 1990-; prin engr, Allied Signal Friction Mat, 1990-1993; Res assoc, Chem Eng Dept, Univ Akron, 1987-1990. **Memberships:** Soc Plastics Engrs; Am Chem Soc; Am Inst Chem Engrs; Soc Automotive Engrs. **Research Statement & Publications:** Reactive polymers; conductive plastics; friction materials, biomaterials; slurry technologies, process design. **Mailing Address:** Allied Signal, 900 W Maple, Troy, MI 48084. **Fax:** 248-362-7228. **E-Mail:** sunilk7@hotmail.com

KESHAVA, CHANNA K C, GENETIC TOXICOLOGY, CANCER BIOLOGY. **Personal Data:** b Kaiwara, India, May 5, 1965; m 1996, Nagalakshmi Ramachandra. **Education:** Univ Agr Sci, Bangalore, India, BS, 1989, MS, 1991; WVa Univ, PhD (genetics & develop biol), 1995. **Honors & Awards:** Nat Travel Award, Environ Mutagen Soc, 1995, 1996. **Professional Experience:** ASSOC SERV FEL, NAT INST OCCUP SAFETY & HEALTH, CTR DIS CONTROL, as of 1998; RES FEL, FOX CHASE CANCER CTR, 1997-; Postdoctoral fel, Sch Med, Emory Univ, 1996-1997. **Memberships:** AAAS; Environ Mutagen Soc; Sigma Xi. **Research Statement & Publications:** Radiation and chemically inducedDNA damage and prevention of its damage by antigenotoxic agents; preneoplastic and neoplastic potential of morphologically distinct transformed foci. **Mailing Address:** Nat Inst Occup Safety & Health, Ctr Dis Control, 1095 Willowdale Rd, Morgantown, WV 26505. **Fax:** 304-285-5708. **E-Mail:** ckeshava@cdc.gov

KESHAVA, NAGALAKSHMI, CARCINOGENESIS & TUMOR BIOLOGY, ESTROGEN & BREAST CANCER. **Personal Data:** b Bangalore, India, March 30, 1967; m 1996, Channa. **Education:** Univ Agr Sci, Bangalore, BS, 1989, MS, 1991; WVa Univ, PhD (genetics), 1995. **Professional Experience:** Int travel award, Environ Mutagen Soc, 1997; mem, Spec Interest Group, beginning 1996; mem, Publ Comt, Environ Mutagen Soc, beginning 1996; mem, Educ Comt, beginning 1996; RES FEL, SCH MED, EMORY UNIV, 1995-; Nat travel award, Environ Mutagen Soc, 1994, 1995, 1996; sr res assoc, Univ Agr Sci, 1991-1992; asst agr officer, Dept Agr, 1989-1990. **Memberships:** Environ Mutagen Soc; Am Asn Cancer Res; Sigma Xi. **Research Statement & Publications:** Overexpression of int-5/aromatose in transgenic mice leads to preneoplastic and neoplastic lesions; increased in situ estrogen increases the risk for breast cancer. **Mailing Address:** Sch Med Emory Univ, WMB Rm 4331 1639 Pierce Dr, Atlanta, GA 30322. **Fax:** 404-727-8615. **E-Mail:** rnagala@emory.edu

KESHAVAN, H R, GENERAL COMPUTER SCIENCES, ELECTRICAL ENGINEERING. **Personal Data:** b Bangalore, India, April 20, 1949; American citizen; m 1979, c 3. **Education:** Bangalore Univ, BS, 1969; Southern Methodist Univ, PhD (elec eng), 1977. **Professional Experience:** Vis prof, Univ Southern Calif, beginning 1989; MGR, AUTOMATION SCI LAB, NORTHROP RES, 1985-; sr mem tech staff, Northrop Corp, 1980-1985; scientist, Rockwell Int, 1977-1980; Asst prof, Bangalore Univ, 1971-1974. **Memberships:** Sr mem Inst Elec & Electronics Engrs. **Research Statement & Publications:** Computer science; intelligent systems; artificial intelligence; automation. **Mailing Address:** Automation Sci Lab, Northrop Grumman 8900 E Wash Blvd, Pico Rivera, CA 90660.

KESHAVAN, KRISHNASWAMIENGAR, CIVIL ENGINEERING, ENVIRONMENTAL ENGINEERING. **Personal Data:** b Hassan, India, June 5, 1929; m 1957, Sita; c Rangaswamy, Padma M & Leela. **Education:** Univ Mysore, BS, 1950, BE, 1955; Univ Iowa, MS, 1960; Cornell Univ, PhD (sanit eng), 1963. **Professional Experience:** PROF EMER CIVIL ENG, WORCESTER POLYTECH INST, as of 2003; consult, UNESCO, beginning 1976; prof civil eng, Worcester Polytech Inst, beginning 1976; head dept, Worcester Polytech Inst, 1976-1986; sr adv, UNESCO, 1975-1976; Off Water Resources Res grant thermal pollution & NSF grant & chlorination, 1971; assoc prof, Worcester Polytech Inst, 1967-1976; Water Resources Ctr res grant, Univ Maine, Orono, 1965-1967; assoc prof, Univ Maine, Orono, 1963-1967; asst civil eng, Cornell Univ, 1960-1963; sect officer, Cent Pub Works Dept, Govt India, 1955-1958; co-dir, Environ Systs Study Prog, Sloan Found. **Memberships:** Am Soc Civil Engrs; Am Soc Eng Educ; Water Pollution Control Fedn; Am Water Works Asn. **Research Statement & Publications:** Kinetics of biological treatment of organic liquid wastes; nitrification of natural bodies of water and its effect on oxygen utilization; combined effects of thermal and organic pollution; hazardous chlorinated compounds due to chlorination. **Mailing Address:** Dept Civil & Environ Eng, Worcester Polytech Inst, Worcester, MA 01609. **E-Mail:** keshavan@wpi.edu

KESHAVIAH, PRAKASH RAMNATHPUR, ARTIFICIAL ORGANS, END-STAGE RENAL DISEASE. **Personal Data:** b Bangalore, India, February 15, 1945; c 2. **Education:** Indian Inst Technol, Madras, BTech, 1967; Univ Minn, MS, 1970, PhD (mech eng), 1974, MS, 1980. **Professional Experience:** DIR CLIN ONCOL, BAXTER HEALTH CARE CORP, as of 1998; SR RES ASSOC, DEPT MED, HENNEPIN COUNTY MED CTR & UNIV MINN, 1981-; Consult & mem, Artificial Kidney-Chronic Uremia Adv Comt, Nat Inst Arthritis, Metab & Digestive Dis, 1978-1979; res assoc, Dept Med, Hennepin County Med Ctr & Univ Minn, 1977-1981; prin investr, Dept Health Educ & Welfare, Food & Drug Admin, 1977-1981; MGR BIOENGINEERING, REGIONAL KIDNEY DIS CTR, 1976-; BIOMED ENGR, REGIONAL KIDNEY DIS CTR, 1973-; res asst, Dept Mech Eng, Univ Minn, 1968-1973; Process Planning Engr, Larsen & Toubro Ltd, India, 1967-1968. **Memberships:** Am Soc Artificial Internal Organs; Int Soc Artificial Organs. **Research Statement & Publications:** Basic physiology, kinetic modeling and engineering design aspects of therapies for end-state renal disease and kinetic modeling of biological systems. **Mailing Address:** 10840 41st Ave N, Minneapolis, MN 55441.

KESHGEGIAN, ALBERT ARAKEL, CLINICAL PATHOLOGY. **Personal Data:** b Brooklyn, Ny, January 22, 1949; m Patrice; c Gregory, Mark & James. **Education:** Univ Pa, BA, 1969, PhD (biochem), 1974, MD, 1975. **Professional Experience:** CLIN PROF PATH, ANATOMY & CELL BIOL, JEFFERSON MED COL, 1999-; SYST CHMN, DEPT PATH, MAIN LINE HOSP, 1998-; MED DIR, MAIN LINE CLIN LABS, 1997-; assoc dir path & chief clin path, Bryn Mawr Hosp, 1988-1998; assoc prof path, Thomas Jefferson Univ, 1985-1999; adj assoc prof path & lab med, Univ Pa Sch Med, 1985-1994; asst pathologist, dir Hemat Sect, 1984-1987; adj asst prof microbiol & cell biol, Pa State Univ, 1982-1987; asst pathologist, dir immunopath & co-dir, Clin Chem Sections, 1981-1987; assoc pathologist, Lankenau Hosp, 1981-1987; adj asst prof path & lab med, Univ Pa, 1981-1985; asst pathologist, Lankenau Hosp, 1981-1982; dir, Protein Chem Div, William Pepper Lab, Hosp Univ Pa, 1979-1981; asst prof path, Univ Pa, 1979-1981; actg assoc dir, Protein Chem Div, William Pepper Lab, Hosp Univ Pa, 1978-1979; asst instr path, Univ Pa, 1975-1979. **Memberships:** Fel Col Am Pathologists; fel Am Soc Clin Pathologists; Am Asn Clin Chem. **Research Statement & Publications:** Molecular markers detected by immunohistochemistry in cancer; clinical pathology. **Mailing Address:** Dept Path, Bryn Mawr Hosp, 130 S Bryn Mawr Ave, Bryn Mawr, PA 19010-3158.

KESHOCK, EDWARD G, FLUID MECHANICS, THERMODYNAMICS. **Personal Data:** b Campbell, Ohio, March 2, 1935; m 1959, c 3. **Education:** Univ Detroit, BME, 1958; Okla State Univ, MS, 1966, PhD (mech eng), 1968. **Professional Experience:** PROF MECH ENG, FENN COL ENG, CLEVELAND STATE UNIV, as of 2001; vis prof, Univ Petrol & Minerals, Saudi Arabia, 1983-1985; prof mech & aerospace eng, Univ Tenn, beginning 1980; assoc prof, Univ Tenn, 1977-1980; vis scientist, Nat Sci Coun, Repub China & Nat Tsing Hua Univ, Taiwan, 1974-1975; assoc prof thermal eng, Old Dominion Univ, 1969-1977; asst prof mech eng, Cleveland State Univ, 1967-1969; res asst film boiling heat transfer, Okla State Univ, 1964-1967; Res engr, Lewis Res Ctr, NASA, 1958-1964. **Memberships:** Am Soc Mech Engrs; Am Soc Eng Educ; Am Inst Chem Engrs. **Research Statement & Publications:** Boiling heat transfer and two-phase flow; condensation heat transfer; thermophysical properties; phase change heat transfer; multiphase flow and heat transfer; energy systems; measurement techniques in heat transfer and fluid mechanics. **Mailing Address:** Dept Mech Eng, Cleveland State Univ, Rm 235, Stilwell Hall, 1960 E 24th St, Cleveland, OH 44115-2425. **Fax:** 216-687-5375. **E-Mail:** e.keshock@csvax.egr.csuohio.edu

KESIK, ANDRZEJ B, PHYSICAL GEOGRAPHY, REMOTE SENSING. **Personal Data:** b Warsaw, Poland, October 27, 1930; m 1964, c 2. **Education:** Marie Curie-Sklodowska Univ, MSc, 1951, PhD (geog), 1959; Int Training Centre Aerial Surv, Holland, dipl geomorphol, 1963. **Professional Experience:** PROF GEOG, UNIV WATERLOO, 1971-; assoc prof photo interpretation, Univ Waterloo, 1971-1981; vis prof photo interpretation & geomorphol, Univ Waterloo, 1970-1971; Brit Coun scholar, 1970; nat reporter, Comn VII, Int Soc Photogram, 1968-1970; lectr cartog & photo interpretation, Marie Curie-Sklodowska Univ, 1964-1970; govt training grant, Univ Amsterdam, 1963; lectr, Marie Curie-Sklodowska Univ, 1960-1964; sr asst phys geog, Marie Curie-Sklodowska Univ, 1955-1960. **Memberships:** Can Inst Surveying; Am Soc Photogram; Can Asn Geogr; Am Asn Geogr. **Research Statement & Publications:** Physical elements of the environment; application of remote sensing techniques to the land evaluation; geomorphological mapping. **Mailing Address:** Dept Geog, Univ Waterloo, Waterloo, ON N2L 3G1, Can.

KESKKULA, HENNO, MATERIAL SCIENCE. **Personal Data:** b Tartu, Estonia, March 25, 1926; American citizen; m 1952, Carol; c Linda-Louise (Sorensen) & Lesli-Ann (Pitts). **Education:** Davis & Elkins Col, BS, 1949; Univ Cincinnati, MS, 1951, PhD (org chem), 1953. **Professional Experience:** RES FEL, UNIV TEX, 1983-; vis scholar, Univ Tex, 1982-1983; sr vis res fel, Queen Mary Col, Univ London, 1969-1970; assoc scientist, Dow Chem Co, 1968-1982; group leader, Dow Chem Co, 1956-1968; chemist, Dow Chem Co, 1953-1956. **Memberships:** emer mem Am Chem Soc. **Research Statement & Publications:** Elastomers; polymer chemistry; mechanical behavior of polymers; miscibility of polymers; toughened plastics. **Mailing Address:** 6205 Quail Hollow, Austin, TX 78750-8229. **Fax:** 512-471-0542. **E-Mail:** keskkula@che.utexas.edu

KESLER, CLYDE E(RVIN), CONCRETE. **Personal Data:** b Champaign, Ill, May 7, 1922; m 1947, Mary; c Philip R & David C. **Education:** Univ Ill, BS, 1943, MS, 1946. **Honors & Awards:** Thompson Award, Am Soc Testing & Mat, 1958; Lindau Award, Am Concrete Inst, 1971. **Professional Experience:** PROF EMER CIVIL ENG, THEORET & APPL MECH, UNIV ILL, URBANA, 1982-; prof civil eng, Univ Ill, Urbana, 1963-1982; from instr to prof, Theoret & Appl Mech, Univ Ill, Urbana, 1948-1982; res assoc, Theoret & Appl Mech, Univ Ill, Urbana, 1947-1948; jr eng aide, Ill Cent RR, 1946-1947. **Memberships:** Nat Acad Eng; fel Am Soc Civil Engrs; hon mem Am Concrete Inst (pres, 1967-1968); Am Soc Eng Educ; hon mem Wire Reinforcement Inst. **Research Statement & Publications:** Plain and reinforced concrete; cracking and crack control; freeze-thaw durability; fracture; creeps; fiber reinforcement; diffusion; expansion; quick-setting; history and future; United States patentee. **Mailing Address:** Dept Civil Eng Univ Ill, 205 N Mathews St, Urbana, IL 61801. **Fax:** 217-356-7808. **E-Mail:** cekes@prairienet.org

KESLER, DARREL J, REPRODUCTIVE BIOLOGY. **Personal Data:** b Portland, Ind, September 21, 1949; m 1973, Cheryl; c Cheralyn E & D Phillip. **Education:** Purdue Univ, BS, 1971, MS, 1974; Univ Mo, PhD, 1977. **Honors & Awards:** Broadrick-Allen Award, Univ Ill, Urbana, 2000; Karl R Natho Award, Univ Ill, 1999; D E Becker Award, Univ Ill, Urbana, 1998; Karl E Gardner Award, Univ Ill, 1996. **Professional Experience:** PROF ANIMAL SCI, CAMPUS HONORS PROG & ACAD OUTREACH & EXTENSION REPRODUCTIVE BIOL, UNIV ILL, URBANA, 2000-; dir, Enteron Inc, 1992-1993; consult, Sanoti Animal Health, 1988-1991 & Ballistivet, Inc, 1989-1992; chmn, Antech Lab, Inc, 1984-; biochemist, Abbott Labs, Inc, 1983-1984; assoc prof reproductive biol & biotechnol, dept animal sci, Univ Ill, Urbana, beginning 1981-; asst prof, dept animal sci, Univ Ill, Urbana, 1977-1981; res asst reprod & lactation physiol, dept dairy husb, Univ Mo, 1974-1977; teaching asst acad coun & admin, deans off, Sch Agr, Purdue Univ, 1971-1974; prof, dept animal sci, Univ Ill, Urbana, 1997-1999; prof animal sci & campus honors prog & extension reproductive biol, Univ Ill, Urbana, 1999-2000. **Memberships:** AAAS; Am Soc Animal Sci; Controlled Release Soc; Am Asn Bovine Pract; Am Dairy Sci Asn; Ill Coun Food Agr Res; Ill State Acad Sci; Int Embryo Transfer Soc; Nat Asn Col Teachers Agr; Nat Dairy Shrine. **Research Statement & Publications:** Infertility and assisted reproductive technol, synchronization of ovulation, contraception/contragestation, embryonic signaling and maintenance of pregnancy, immunoassay diagnostics, androgen-induced sexual dimorphism, and controlled release and drug delivery systs. **Mailing Address:** Dept Animal Sci, Univ Ill, Urbana, IL 61801. **Fax:** 217-244-3169. **E-Mail:** d-kesler@uiuc.edu

KESLER, EARL MARSHALL, DAIRY SCIENCE. **Personal Data:** b Dunmore, WVa, December 3, 1920; m 1945, c 3. **Education:** WVa Univ, BS, 1943; Pa State Univ, MS, 1948, PhD, 1951. **Professional Experience:** Prof dairy sci, Pa State Univ, University Park, beginning 1964; PROF EMER DAIRY SCI, PA STATE UNIV, UNIVERSITY PARK, beginning 1964; From instr to assoc prof, 1948-1964. **Memberships:** AAAS; Am Soc Animal Sci; Am Dairy Sci Asn; Sigma Xi. **Research Statement & Publications:** Dairy cattle nutrition, physiology of digestion; calf nutrition rumen metabolism and intermediary metabolism of the bovine; forage production; physiology of milk secretion; management of cows. **Mailing Address:** Dept Animal Sci, Pa State Univ, State College, PA 16801.

KESLER, G(EORGE) H(ENRY), HEAT TRANSFERS, METALS TECHNOLOGY. **Personal Data:** b West Terre Haute, Ind, October 29, 1920; m 1942, Wilma; c David (deceased), Deborah (deceased) & Sandra J (Hodge). **Education:** Rose Polytech Inst, BS, 1942; Mass Inst Technol, MS, 1949, ScD, 1952. **Professional Experience:** RETIRED; eng consult, 1977-1983; dept mgr, Mat Lab Dept, McDonnell Aircraft Co, St Louis, 1965-1977; assoc dir res, Nat Steel Corp, 1959-1965; asst div chief, Battelle Mem Inst, 1955-1959; prin chem engr, Battelle Mem Inst, 1951-1955; chem engr distillation, Tex Co, 1942-1948. **Memberships:** Am Soc Metals. **Research Statement & Publications:** Mass transport in spray-laden turbulent air streams; titanium production; laboratory distillation column evaluation; heat and mass transfer; steelmaking fundamentals; materials testing. **Mailing Address:** 600 Bennett Lane, West Terre Haute, IN 47885-0255. **E-Mail:** bigsquard@aol.com

KESLER, OREN BYRL, ELECTRICAL ENGINEERING, APPLIED ELECTROMAGNETIC THEORY. **Personal Data:** b Crawford Co, Ill, August 28, 1939; m 1967, c 1. **Education:** Univ Ill, BS, 1961, MS, 62, PhD (elec eng), 1965; Univ Wis, MA, 1968. **Professional Experience:** AT RAYTHEON SYST CO, as of 1999; DISTINGUISHED MEM TECH STAFF, ANTENNA & MICROWAVE LAB, EQUIP GROUP, TEX INSTRUMENTS INC, 1997-; sr mem tech staff, Antenna & Microwave Lab, Equip Group, Tex Instruments Inc, 1981-1996; mem tech staff, Antenna & Microwave Lab, Equip Group, Tex Instruments Inc, 1972-1981; NSF sci fac fel, 1970-1971; asst prof elec eng, Univ Tex, Austin, 1965-1972. **Memberships:** Sr mem Inst Elec & Electronics Engrs; Am Math Asn. **Research Statement & Publications:** Electromagnetic field; antennas; microwaves; radar; information processing; mathematical and computational techniques for engineering analysis. **Mailing Address:** 3305 Dibrell Dr, Plano, TX 75023-5653. **Fax:** 972-952-3773. **E-Mail:** obk@timsg.csc.ti.com

KESLER, STEPHEN EDWARD, ECONOMIC GEOLOGY, EXPLORATION GEOCHEMISTRY. **Personal Data:** b Washington, DC, October 5, 1940; m 1965, c 2. **Education:** Univ NC, BS, 1962; Stanford Univ, PhD (geol), 1966. **Professional Experience:** Int lectr, Soc Econ Geologists, 1989-1990; assoc ed, J Geochem Expl, 1985-; fulbright panel, coun int exchange scholars, 1984-1987; assoc ed, econ geol, 1980-1990; PROF GEOL, UNIV MICH, 1977-; assoc chair, Univ Mich, 1977-; vis scientist, Consejo Del Recursos Minerales, Mex, 1975-1976; assoc prof geol, Univ Toronto, 1971-1977; asst prof, 1970-1971; asst prof geol, La State Univ, Baton Rouge, 1966-1970. **Memberships:** Soc Econ Geologists (vpres, 1990-1991, pres, 1998-1999); Asn Explor Geochemists; Geochem Soc; fel Geol Soc Am. **Research Statement & Publications:** Tectonic petrologic and geochemical framework of ore deposition; ore deposit and exploration geochemistry; geology of Central America, Mexico and West Indies. **Mailing Address:** Dept Geol, Univ Mich, 2534 CC Little Bldg 1100 N Univ Ave, Ann Arbor, MI 48109-1005. **Fax:** 734-763-4690. **E-Mail:** skesler@umich.edu

KESLING, ROBERT VERNON, PALEONTOLOGY. **Personal Data:** b Cass Co, Ind, September 11, 1917; m 1942, c 3. **Education:** DePauw Univ, AB, 1939; Univ Ill, MS, 1941, PhD (geol), 1949. **Professional Experience:** PROF EMER GEOL, UNIV MICH, ANN ARBOR, as of 2001; dir, Mus Paleont, 1966-1974; cur, Mus Paleont, beginning 1958; ed, J Paleont, 1958-1964; from asst prof to assoc prof geol, Mus Paleont, 1949-1959; assoc cur micropaleont, Mus Paleont, 1949-1958. **Memberships:** Paleont Soc;

Sigma Xi; AAAS. **Research Statement & Publications:** Living and fossil Ostracoda; middle Devonian stratigraphy; Paleozoic echinoderms. **Mailing Address:** Univ Mich, Dept Geol, LSA, 505 S State St, Ann Arbor, MI 48109.

KESMODEL, LARRY LEE, SOLID STATE PHYSICS, SURFACE SCIENCE. **Personal Data:** b Ft Worth, Tex, March 5, 1947; m 1970, c 3. **Education:** Calif Inst Technol, BS, 1969; Univ Tex, Austin, PhD (physics), 1974. **Professional Experience:** PROF PHYSICS, IND UNIV, BLOOMINGTOM, as of 2004; pres, LK Technologies, beginning 1985; prin investr, US Dept Energy Grant, beginning 1984 & Off Naval Res Contract, beginning 1980; assoc prof Physics, Ind Univ, Bloomington, beginning 1983; asst prof, Ind Univ, Bloomington, 1978-1983; staff scientist surface physics, Mat & Molecular Res Div, Lawrence Berkeley Lab, 1975-1978; fel phys chem, Univ Calif, Berkeley, 1973-1975. **Memberships:** Am Phys Soc. **Research Statement & Publications:** Experimental studies of solid surfaces and chemisorption; low-energy electron diffraction; high-resolution electron energy loss spectroscopy. **Mailing Address:** Dept Physics Swain Hall W Rm 117, Ind Univ, Bloomington, IN 47401. **E-Mail:** lkesmode@indiana.edu

KESNER, JAY, PLASMA PHYSICS. **Personal Data:** b New York, NY, March 17, 1943. **Education:** Cornell Univ, BS, 1965, MEng, 1966; Columbia Univ, PhD (physics), 1970. **Professional Experience:** SR RES SCIENTIST, PLASMA FUSION CTR, MASS INST TECHNOL, 1981-; prof, Dept Physics, Univ Wis, 1973-1981. **Memberships:** Am Phys Soc. **Mailing Address:** Plasma Sci & Fusion Ctr, 167 Albany St Rm NW17-213, Cambridge, MA 02139.

KESNER, LEO, BIOCHEMISTRY, ANALYTICAL CHEMISTRY. **Personal Data:** b New York, NY, February 22, 1931; m 1954, c 3. **Education:** City Col NY, BS, 1954; State Univ NY, PhD (biochem), 1961. **Professional Experience:** PROF EMER BIOCHEM, STATE UNIV NY, DOWNSTATE MED CTR, as of 2004; assoc prof, State Univ NY, Downstate Med Ctr, 1969-1989; prof biochem, State Univ NY, Downstate Med Ctr, beginning 1969; from instr to asst prof, State Univ NY, Downstate Med Ctr, 1961-1969; asst, State Univ NY, Downstate Med Ctr, 1956-1960; jr biochemist, State Univ NY, Downstate Med Ctr, 1954-1956; Sr technician biophys, Sloan-Kettering Inst, 1954. **Memberships:** AAAS; Am Asn Clin Chem; Am Chem Soc; NY Acad Sci; Am Soc Biol Chemists. **Research Statement & Publications:** Relationship of acid-base balance to intermediary metabolism; nutrition; design of analytical techniques in biochemistry; protein chemistry; inborn errors of metabolism; membrane phospholipids; growth promotion; proteases; protease inhibitors. **Mailing Address:** Dept Biochem State Univ NY Health Sci Ctr, 450 Clarkson Ave Box 8, Brooklyn, NY 11203-2012. **Fax:** 718-270-3316.

KESNER, MICHAEL H, SYSTEMATICS, MAMMALOGY. **Personal Data:** b Pawtucket, RI, November 30, 1945; m 1969, c 1. **Education:** Northwestern Univ, BA, 1969, MS, 1972; Univ Mass, PhD (zoology), 1978. **Professional Experience:** PROF BIOL, IND UNIV, as of 2004; Theodore Roosevelt Grant, Am Mus Natural Hist, 1976 & Univ Res Grant, Ind Univ Pa, 1977, 1978, 1981; assoc prof human anat & comp anat, Ind Univ Pa, beginning 1976. **Memberships:** Am Soc Mammalogists; Soc Syst Zool; Sigma Xi, 1976. **Research Statement & Publications:** Mammalian Rodent functional morphology and systematics primarily of the subfamily microtinae; biogeography and systematics of insular populations of the genus Microtus from off the coast of Northeastern North America. **Mailing Address:** Dept Biol, Ind Univ, 330 Weyandt Hall, Indiana, PA 15705. **E-Mail:** mkesner@iup.edu

KESNER, RAYMOND PIERRE, PHYSIOLOGICAL PSYCHOLOGY, NEUROSCIENCE. **Personal Data:** b Oran, Algeria, December 19, 1940; American citizen; m 1965, c 2. **Education:** Wayne State Univ, BS, 1962; Univ Ill, MS, 1964, PhD (psychol), 1965. **Professional Experience:** PROF PSYCHOL, UNIV UTAH, 1975-; fel, Ctr Advan Study Behav Sci, 1971-1972; from asst prof to assoc prof, Univ Utah, 1967-1975; fel physiol, Ctr Brain Res, Rochester, NY, 1965-1967. **Memberships:** Soc Neuroscience; Psychonomic Soc. **Research Statement & Publications:** Neurobiological mechanisms of memory. **Mailing Address:** Dept Psychol, Univ Utah, 380 S 1530 E Rm No 502, Salt Lake City, UT 84112-0251. **Fax:** 801-581-5841. **E-Mail:** rpkesner@behsci.utah.edu

KESSEL, BRINA, ORNITHOLOGY, VERTEBRATE ZOOLOGY. **Personal Data:** b Ithaca, NY, November 20, 1925; wid. **Education:** Cornell Univ, BS, 1947, PhD (ornith), 1951; Univ Wis, MS, 1949. **Professional Experience:** PROF EMER ZOOL & CUR EMER ORNITHOL, UNIV ALASKA, 2000-; DEAN EMER, COL BIOL SCI & RENEWABLE RESOURCES, UNIV ALASKA, 2000-; cur, Ornith Collection, Univ Mus, 1990-1995; ornithologist, Sustina Hydroelec Proj, Alaska, 1980-1983; ornithologist, invests Northwest Alaska pipeline, 1976-1981; admin assoc, Acad Progs, Off Chancellor, 1973-1980; cur terrestrial vert mus collections, Univ Mus, 1972-1990; dean, Col Biol Sci & Renewable Resources, 1961-1972; prof zool, Univ Alaska, Fairbanks, 1959-1996; Proj dir, Ecol Invests, AEC Proj Chariot, Univ Alaska, 1959-1963; head, Dept Biol Sci, 1957-1966; assoc prof zool, Univ Alaska, 1954-1959; asst prof biol sci, Univ Alaska, 1951-1954; asst ornith & conserv, Cornell Univ, 1947-1948 & 1949-1951. **Memberships:** Fel AAAS; fel Am Ornithologists' Union (pres-elect, 1990-1992, pres, 1992-1994); fel Arctic Inst NAm; Wilson Ornith Soc; Cooper Ornith Soc; Sigma Xi. **Research Statement & Publications:** European starling in North America; biodiversity and natural history of Alaska birds; wildlife conservation management. **Mailing Address:** Univ Alaska Mus, PO Box 756960 13 UA Mus, Fairbanks, AK 99775-6960. **Fax:** 907-474-5469. **E-Mail:** ffbxk@uaf.edu

KESSEL, CHARLES, PLASMA PHYSICS. **Education:** Univ Calif, Los Angeles, PhD (fusion eng & appl plasma physics), 1987. **Honors & Awards:** Fusion Eng Award, Fusion Power Assocs, 1994. **Professional Experience:** PROJ SCIENTIST, PRINCETON PLASMA PHYSICS LAB, NJ, 1988-. **Mailing Address:** Princeton Plasma Physics Lab, PO Box 451, Princeton, NJ 08543.

KESSEL, DAVID HARRY, BIOCHEMISTRY. **Personal Data:** b Monroe, Mich, January 8, 1931; c 2. **Education:** Mass Inst Technol, BS, 1952; Univ Mich, MS, 1954, PhD (biochem), 1959. **Professional Experience:** PROF PHARMACOL & MED, SCH MED, WAYNE STATE UNIV, as of 2000; secy-treas, Am Soc Photobiol, beginning 1988; res scientist, Mich Cancer Found, 1974; from asst prof to assoc prof pharmacol, Sch Med, Univ Rochester, 1969-1973; res assoc, Children's Cancer Res Found & asst path, Harvard Med Sch, 1965-1968; NIH fel, Harvard Univ, 1959-1963. **Memberships:** AAAS; Biochem Soc; Am Asn Cancer Res; Am Soc Pharmacol & Exp Therapeut; Am Soc Biol Chemists. **Research Statement & Publications:** Development of anti-tumor agents; mode of action of anti-neoplastic drugs and photosensitizing agents. **Mailing Address:** Pharmacol Dept, Wayne State Univ Sch Med, 540 E Canfield St, Detroit, MI 48201. **Fax:** 313-577-6739. **E-Mail:** dhkessel@med.wayne.edu

KESSEL, QUENTIN CATTELL, EXPERIMENTAL ATOMIC MOLECULAR & SURFACE PHYSICS, ACCELERATOR BASED MATERIALS SCIENCE. **Personal Data:** b Boston, Mass, August 15, 1938; m 1960, Margaret; c Lori E & Scott M. **Education:** Yale Univ, BS, 1960; Univ Mich, MS, 1962; Univ Conn, PhD (physics), 1966. **Professional Experience:** PROF PHYSICS, UNIV CONN, 1994-; GUEST SCIENTIST, FOM-INST VOOR ATOM-EN MOLECULFYSICA, AMSTERDAM, NETHERLANDS 1978-; guest prof, Univ Freiburg, Ger, 1977-1978; assoc prof, Univ Conn, 1973-1978; asst prof, Univ Conn, 1971-1973; guest Scientist, Inst Physics, Aarhus Univ, 1970-1971; physicist, Robert J Van de Graaff Lab, High Voltage Eng Corp, 1966-1970; res assoc, Univ Conn, 1965-1966; res asst physics, Univ Conn, 1962-1965. **Memberships:** Fel Am Phys Soc; Europ Phys Soc; Mat Res Soc; Bohmische Phys Soc; Sigma Xi; Sigma Pi Sigma. **Research Statement & Publications:** Interaction of accelerated ions and molecules with matter for the investigation and creation of new materials especially thin films and interfaces; measurement of ion, electron and x-ray cross sections of astrophysical interest. **Mailing Address:** Dept Physics, Univ Conn, Storrs, CT 06269. **Fax:** 860-486-3346. **E-Mail:** kessel@uconnvm.uconn.edu

KESSEL, RICHARD GLEN, ANATOMY, CELL BIOLOGY. **Personal Data:** b Fairfield, Iowa, July 19, 1931. **Education:** Parsons Col, BS, 1953; Univ Iowa, MS, 1956, PhD (zoology), 1959. **Professional Experience:** PROF EMER BIOL, UNIV IOWA, as of 2005; assoc ed, J Exp Zool, 1978-1982; prof Biol, Univ Iowa, beginning 1968; NSF res grant, 1968-1971; prog dir, NIH Training grant develop biol, 1966-1978; career develop award, 1964-1969; Nat Inst Child Health & Human Develop res grant, 1964-1969; from asst prof to assoc prof, Univ Iowa, 1961-1968; Nat Inst Gen Med Sci res grant, 1960-1965; NIH fel, 1960-1961; From instr to asst prof anat, Bowman Gray Sch Med, 1959-1961. **Memberships:** Soc Study Reproduction; Am Asn Anat; Soc Develop Biologists; Am Soc Cell Biol; Am Phys Soc; Electron Micros Soc Am. **Research Statement & Publications:** Electron microscopic, autoradiographic, cytochemical and freeze-fracture studies on oocyte growth and differentiation; origin, structure and function of cell organelles; mechanisms of secretion; scanning electron microscopy of tissues and organs; immunocytochemistry. **Mailing Address:** Dept Biol Scis, Univ Iowa, 110 BB, Iowa City, IA 52242-1324. **Fax:** 319-335-1069. **E-Mail:** richard-kessel@uiowa.edu

KESSEL, SAMUEL SHERWOOD, MATERNAL & CHILD HEALTH. **Personal Data:** b Philadelphia, Pa, November 30, 1948; c 2. **Education:** Drexel Univ, BS, 1970; Yeshiva Univ, MD, 1974; Johns Hopkins Univ, MPH, 1982. **Honors & Awards:** Maternal & Child Health Young Prof Award, Am Pub Health Asn, 1989; Job Lewis Smith Award, Am Acad Pediat, 1996. **Professional Experience:** Dir, div sci, educ & analysis, maternal & child health bur, health resources & servs admin, dept health & human servs, usphs, 1995-2001; dir Div Systs, Educ & Sci, 1990-1995; staff dir, Task Force Infant Mortality, White House, 1989-1990; liaison rep, Fedn Pediat Orgn, 1988; secy staff rep, Nat Comn to Prevent Infant Mortality, 1988-1992; Expert Panel, USPHS, 1987-1994; dir, Div Maternal & Child Health Prog Coord & Systs Develop, Off Maternal & Child Health, Bur Maternal & Child Health & Resources Develop, 1987-1990; liaison rep, Coun Pediat Res, Am Acad Pediat, 1985-; chief, Res & Training Br, Div Maternal & Child Health, Bur Health Care & Delivery Assistance, Health Resources & Servs Admin, 1983-1987; asst clin prof, Dept Pediat, Uniformed Univ Health Sci, Md, 1981-; med officer epidemiol & biomet res prog, Nat Inst Child Health & Human Develop, NIH, 1981-1983; spec asst to asst secy health & surgeon gen, Dept Health & Human Servs, USPHS, 1979-1981; asst secy health's staff rep, USPHS, 1979-1981; Bur Community Health Servs, Nat Capital Med Found Inc, 1979; clin instr, Dept Child Health & Develop, Children's Hosp & Nat Med Ctr, George Wash Sch Med, 1978-; spec fel ambulatory pediat, Dept Child Health & Develop, Childrens Hosp & Nat Med Ctr, George Wash Univ Sch Med, 1977-1979; Consult, US Gen Accounting Off, 1977-1979; Bur Community Health Servs, Health Servs Admin, Dept Health & Human Servs, USPHS, 1977-1978; Consult, Off Comnr Health, City Boston, 1977; sr asst resident & fel, Dept Pediat, Boston City Hosp, Boston Univ Sch Med, 1976-1977; jr asst resident, Dept Pediat, Boston City Hosp, Boston Univ Sch Med, 1975-1976; Intern, Dept Pediat, Boston City Hosp, Boston Univ Sch Med, 1974-1975. **Memberships:** Am Pub Health Asn; Ambulatory Pediat Asn. **Research Statement & Publications:** Hygiene and public health. **Mailing Address:** Maternal & Child Health Bur USPHS, 5600 Fishers Ln Parklawn Bldg Rm 18A-55, Rockville, MD 20857.

KESSELMAN, WARREN ARTHUR, ELECTROMAGNETIC COMPATIBILITY, COMMUNICATIONS SECURITY. **Personal Data:** b Newark, NJ, April 8, 1927; m 1950, c 3. **Education:** Newark Col Eng, BS, 1950. **Professional Experience:** DEP DIR RES & DEVELOP, MGT CTR C3 SYST, 1984-; chief comsec div, commun security, US Army Commun Electron Comd, 1981-1984; chief, Electro Magnetic Compatibility Team, electron US Army Comn Res & Develop, Comd, 1976-1981; eng supvr electron, US Army Electron Comd, 1958-1976; Engr electron, US Army Signal Corps Eng Lab, 1949-1958. **Memberships:** Fel Inst Elec & Electronics Engrs; Armed Forces Commun & Electron Asn. **Research Statement & Publications:** Electromagnetic compatibility and interference measurement techniques, analysis methodology, standardization and interference reduction techniques. **Mailing Address:** US Army Commun Elec Command, C3sd/Amsel-Rd-CS-Dd, Ft Monmouth, NJ 07703.

KESSELRING, JOHN PAUL, ENERGY ANALYSES, HVAC EQUIPMENT. **Personal Data:** b Detroit, Mich, March 26, 1940; m 1966, Jane; c Joan P & Thomas M. **Education:** Univ Mich, BS, 1961; Stanford Univ, MS, 1962, PhD (aeronaut & astronaut sci), 1968. **Professional Experience:** SR PROJ MGR, ELEC POWER RES INST, as of 1998; MGR, RESIDENTIAL SYSTS, ELEC POWER RES INST, 1992-; sr proj mgr, Residential Systs, Elec Power Res Inst, 1986-1991; lectr, Soviet Acad Sci, 1986; vpres, Alzeta Corp, 1982-1986; assoc mgr combustion technol, Acurex Corp, 1981-1982; Instr aeronaut & astronaut, Stanford Univ, 1977; mgr catalytic combustion progs, Acurex Corp, 1974-1980; asst prof mech & aerospace eng, Univ Tenn, Knoxville, 1969-1974; mem tech staff, NAm Rockwell Corp, 1967-1969; Res engr, Rocketdyne Div, NAm Aviation, Inc, 1962-1963. **Memberships:** Combustion Inst; Am Soc Mech Engrs; Sigma Xi. **Research Statement & Publications:** Residential building energy analysis; HVAC equipment; heat pumps; residential appliances. **Mailing Address:** Elec Power Res Inst, 3412 Hillview Ave, Palo Alto, CA 94304. **Fax:** 415-855-2954. **E-Mail:** jkesselr@epri.com

KESSIN, RICHARD HARRY, DEVELOPMENTAL GENETICS, SIGNAL TRANSDUCTION. **Personal Data:** b Bayonne, NJ, February 24, 1944; c 2. **Education:** Yale Univ, BA, 1966; Brandeis Univ, PhD (biol), 1971. **Professional Experience:** PROF DEPT ANAT & CELL BIOL, COLUMBIA UNIV, as of 1998; ASSOC PROF BIOL, HARVARD UNIV, 1980-; asst prof, Harvard Univ, 1974-1980. **Research Statement & Publications:** Development and regulation of signal transduction. **Mailing Address:** Dept Anat & Cell Biol, Columbia Univ, New York, NY 10027. **E-Mail:** rhk2@columbia.edu

KESSINGER, MARGARET ANNE, MEDICINE, MEDICAL ONCOLOGY. **Personal Data:** b Beckley, WVa, June 4, 1941; m 1971, Loyd. **Education:** WVa Univ, BA, 1963, MD, 1967. **Professional Experience:** Chair, Human Embryonic Stem Cell Scientific Rev Comt, as of 2006; ASSOC DEP DIR CLIN RES, UNIV NEBR MED CTR EPPLEY CANCER CTR, 1996-; chief, Sect Oncol Hematol, Univ Nebr Med Ctr, 1991-1999; PROF INTERNAL MED, SECT HEMATOL & ONCOL, UNIV NEBR MED CTR, 1990-; from asst prof to assoc prof med oncol, Sect Oncol hematol, 1972-1990. **Memberships:** Am Col

Physicians; Am Soc Clin Oncol; Am Asn Cancer Res; Am Asn Cancer Educ; Am Med Soc; Am Fedn Clin Res. **Research Statement & Publications:** peripheral hematopietic stem cell transfusion. **Mailing Address:** Oncol Hematol Sect, Univ Nebr Med Ctr, PO Box 987680, Omaha, NE 68198-7680. **Fax:** 402-559-6520.

KESSINGER, WALTER PAUL, MICROPALEONTOLOGY. **Personal Data:** b Corsicana, Tex, July 9, 1930; m 1962, Dorothy; c Walter P III, Charles H & Linda K. **Education:** Tex Technol Col, BS, 1951, MS, 1953; La State Univ, PhD (geol), 1974. **Professional Experience:** RETIRED; head dept, Univ Southwestern La, 1956-1986; from asst prof to prof, Univ Southwestern La, 1953-1986. **Memberships:** Geol Soc Am; Am Asn Petrol Geologists; Paleont Soc; Soc Econ Paleontologists & Mineralogists; Nat Asn Geol Teachers; Sigma Xi. **Research Statement & Publications:** Ostracoda of the Comanche Series of north Texas. **Mailing Address:** 406 Orangewood Dr, Lafayette, LA 70503-5228.

KESSLER, ALEXANDER, MEDICINE, PUBLIC HEALTH. **Personal Data:** b Vienna, Austria, March 19, 1931; British citizen; m 1992, Constance C Offen; c Daniel, Anne, David & Jonathan. **Education:** NY Univ, BA, 1951; Columbia Univ, MD, 1955; Rockefeller Univ, PhD (pop biol), 1966. **Professional Experience:** RETIRED; dir spec leave, Spec Prog Res Human Reprod, WHO, Geneva, 1984-1986; dir, Spec Prog Res Human Reprod, WHO, Geneva, 1966-1984; Walter Reed Hosp & Res Inst, 1957-1960 & Georgetown Univ Hosp, 1960-1961; physician, Albert Einstein Med Ctr, NY, 1956-1957; Physician, Bellevue Hosp Cornell Serv, 1955-1956. **Research Statement & Publications:** International public health; family planning; reproductive biology and contraceptive technology; research administration. **Mailing Address:** 4 Ellerdale Close, London NW3 6BE, UK.

KESSLER, BERNARD V, lasers, stock market analyses; deceased, see previous edition for last biography

KESSLER, DAN, high energy physics; deceased, see previous edition for last biography

KESSLER, DAVID, MEDICAL ADMINISTRATION. **Personal Data:** b New York, NY, May 31, 1951. **Education:** Amherst Col, BA, 1973; Univ Chicago, JD, 1978; Harvard Univ, MD, 1979. **Honors & Awards:** Trumpeter award, nat consumers league; award courage, Am found AIDS res. **Professional Experience:** DEAN, MED SCH, YALE UNIV SCH MED, 1997-; comnr food & drug, Food & Drug admin, 1990-1997; instr food & drug law, Columbia Univ, 1986-1990; med dir, hosp albert einstein col med, 1984-1990; consult, Senate labor & human resources comt, 1981-1984. **Memberships:** Inst Med-Nat Acad Sci. **Mailing Address:** Food & Drug Admin, 5600 Fishers Lane, Rockville, MD 20857. **Fax:** 202-785-7437.

KESSLER, DAVID PHILLIP, chemical engineering, bioengineering; deceased, see previous edition for last biography

KESSLER, DIETRICH, CELL BIOLOGY, MOLECULAR BIOLOGY. **Personal Data:** b Hamilton, NY, May 28, 1936; m 1990, Johanna; c Jonathan F & Melissa B. **Education:** Swarthmore Col, BA, 1958; Univ Wis, MS, 1960, PhD (zoology), 1964. **Professional Experience:** PROF EMER, DEPT BIOL, COLGATE UNIV, 1999-; vis scientist, Genetics Dept, Univ Leicester, Eng, 1990-1991; vis prof, McArdle Lab Cancer Res, Dept Oncol Med Sch, Univ Wis-Madison, 1988; prof, dept biol, colgate univ, 1984-1999; head, Dept Biol, 1984-1990; Fulbright res grant, Bonn, Ger, 1980-1981; NSF sci fac fel, Swiss Inst Exp Cancer Res, Lausanne, 1971-1972; Am Cancer Soc fel, Brandeis Univ, 1966-1967; from asst prof to prof, Dept Biol, Haverford Col, 1964-1984. **Memberships:** AAAS; Am Soc Cell Biol. **Research Statement & Publications:** Molecular mechanism of amoeboid movement in Physarum polycephalum using techniques of molecular and cell biology. **Mailing Address:** Dept Biol, Colgate Univ, 13 Oak Dr, Hamilton, NY 13346-1398.

KESSLER, DONALD J, ORBITAL MECHANICS. **Honors & Awards:** Losey Atmospheric Sci Award, AIAA, 2000. **Professional Experience:** RETIRED; sr scientist, Johnson Space Ctr, NASA. **Mailing Address:** NASA Johnson Space Ctr, Mail Code SN3, Houston, TX 77058.

KESSLER, EDWIN III, METEOROLOGY, SUSTAINABLE AGRICULTURE. **Personal Data:** b New York, NY, December 2, 1928; m 1950, Lottie; c Austin R & Thomas R. **Education:** Columbia Univ, AB, 1950; Mass Inst Technol, SM, 1952, ScD(meteorol), 1957. **Honors & Awards:** Cleveland Abbe Award, Am Meteorol Soc, 1989. **Professional Experience:** RETIRED; consult, private sector, beginning 1996; chair, Common Cause Okla, 1993-1999; adj prof geog, Univ Okla, beginning 1997; consult, Saudi Arabia, 1987; adj prof & consult meteorol, Univ Okla, 1964-2002; vis lectr, McGill Univ, 1980; vis prof, Mass Inst Technol, 1975-1976; dir, Nat Severe Storms Lab, US Weather Bur, 1964-1986; dir, Atmospheric Physics Div, Travelers Res Ctr, 1961-1964; chief synoptic sect, Weather Radar Br, Air Force Cambridge Res Ctr, 1954-1961; adj prof, Depts of Geography & Meteorology, Univ Okla, Norman, beginning 1964; mem, USDA Sustainable Agr, Res & Educ Prog. **Memberships:** Fel AAAS; Am Geophys Union; fel Am Meteorol Soc; Royal Meteorol Soc; Sigma Xi; Am Inst Aeronaut & Astronaut. **Research Statement & Publications:** Synthesis of varied observations and theory to improve understanding of meteorological phenomena and to develop and apply technology in the public interest; sustainable agriculture; edited a three-volume definitive work on thunderstorms (thunderstorms; a social, scientific, and technological documentary) published in a second edition by the university of oklahoma press. **Mailing Address:** Depts Geog & Meteorol, Univ Okla 100 E Boyd Energy Ctr, Norman, OK 73019. **Fax:** 405-360-3246. **E-Mail:** kess3@swbell.net

KESSLER, ERNEST GEORGE, PRECISION MEASUREMENTS, X-RAY SPECTROSCOPY. **Personal Data:** b Hanover, Pa, September 12, 1940; m 1962, c 4. **Education:** Shippensburg State Col, BS, 1962; Univ Wis-Madison, MS, 1964, PhD (physics), 1969. **Professional Experience:** PHYSICIST, CTR ATOMIC, MOLECULAR & OPTICAL PHYSICS, NAT INST STAND & TECHNOL, 1971-; Nat Res Coun-Nat Bur Stand res assoc spectros, 1969-1971. **Memberships:** Am Phys Soc. **Research Statement & Publications:** High resolution studies of the ionized helium spectrum; determination of the Rydberg constant from wavelength measurements on ionized helium; precise x-ray and gamma ray wavelength measurements. **Mailing Address:** Nat Inst Stand & Technol, Bldg 221 Rm A267 100 Bureau Dr, Gaithersburg, MD 20899-8422. **Fax:** 301-990-1350. **E-Mail:** ernest.kessler@nist.gov

KESSLER, FREDERICK MELVYN, ENGINEERING ACOUSTICS, ELECTROMECHANICAL ENGINEERING. **Personal Data:** b Brooklyn, NY, May 15, 1932; m 1954, c 3. **Education:** City Col NY, BME, 1954; Rutgers Univ, MS, 1967, PhD (elec eng), 1971. **Professional Experience:** CONSULT, 1996-; managing partner eng acoust, Dames & Moore, 1980-1983; Adj prof, Dept Mech Eng, Stevens Inst Technol, Hoboken, NJ, 1978-; partner, Dames & Moore, 1973-1980; vpres eng acoust, Lewis S Goodfriend & Assoc, 1971-1973; fac mem elec eng, Rutgers Univ, 1968-1971; sr develop engr eng acoust, Ingersoll-Rand Co, 1961-1968; sr proj mgr acoust, David Taylor Model Basin, Wash, DC, 1959-1961; at TMK Technol Inc, Bound Brook; jr test engr, Curtiss-Wr. **Memberships:** Acoust Soc Am; Inst Elec & Electronics Engrs; Inst Noise Control Eng (pres 1988). **Research Statement & Publications:** Optimization muffler design parameters using conjugate gradient search techniques. **Mailing Address:** 102 Miller Rd, Delray Beach, FL 33483.

KESSLER, GEORGE MORTON, HORTICULTURE. **Personal Data:** b Philadelphia, Pa, July 26, 1917; m 1943, c 2. **Education:** Pa State Univ, BS, 1946, MS, 1947; Mich State Col, PhD (hort), 1953. **Professional Experience:** EMER ASSOC PROF HORT, MICH STATE UNIV, 1982-; Ed, Fruit Varieties & Hort Digest, Am Pomol Soc, 1953-1972; From instr to assoc prof, Mich State Univ, 1947-1982. **Memberships:** Am Soc Hort Sci; Am Pomol Soc (secy-treas 1957-1964 pres 1967-1968). **Research Statement & Publications:** Teaching and evaluating of fruit varieties. **Mailing Address:** 1127 Lilac, East Lansing, MI 48823.

KESSLER, GERALD, CLINICAL CHEMISTRY. **Personal Data:** b New York, NY, March 27, 1930; m 1952, c 4. **Education:** City Col NY, BS, 1950; Univ Md, MS, 1952, PhD (biochem), 1954. **Professional Experience:** CHIEF EXEC OFFICER, NATURES PLUS, as of 2002; prof, Sch Med, Wash Univ, 1982; dir div biochem, Jjewish Hosp St Louis, beginning 1967; assoc prof, Sch Med, Wash Univ, 1967-1982; chief automation div, Bio-Sci Labs, Los Angeles, 1965-1967; consult automation res prog, Vet Admin Hosp, Bronx, NY, 1963-1964; head clin ctr core lab, Montefiore Hosp, NY, 1961-1964; assoc scientist, dept biochem, Sloan-Kettering inst Cancer res, 1959-1961; biochemist, Technicon Instruments Corp, NY, 1957-1961; Clin biochemist, Albert Einstein Med Ctr, 1954-1957. **Memberships:** AAAS; Am Chem Soc; Am Asn Clin Chem; NY Acad Sci; Acad Clin Lab Physicians & Scientists; Nat Acad Clin Biochem. **Research Statement & Publications:** Clinical biochemistry; methodological instrumentation research as applied to automation of analytical procedures. **Mailing Address:** Natures Plus, 548 Broadhollow Rd, Melville, NY 11747. **Fax:** 516-293-0349.

KESSLER, HAROLD D, TITANIUM. **Personal Data:** b Toledo, Ohio, December 28, 1921. **Education:** Case Inst Technol, BS, 1942; Ill Inst Technol, MS, 1949. **Honors & Awards:** Russ Ogden Award, Am Soc Testing & Mat, 1985. **Professional Experience:** CONSULT, 1986-; mgr titanium opers, Cabot Corp, 1981-1986; tech dir, DH Titanium, 1979-1981; vpres technol, Reactive Metals Co, 1969-1979; chief metallurgist, Reactive Metals Co, 1964-1969; mgr, Metall Res Lab, Titanium Metals Corp Am, 1954-1957 & Tech Develop Lab, 1957-1964; Air Force, Wright Field, 1944-1945 & Armour Res Found, 1945-1954; Mem staff, Nat Advan Comt Aeronaut, 1943-1944; mem bd dirs, Am Soc Metals. **Memberships:** Am Inst Mining Metall & Petrol Engrs; Am Soc Metals. **Research Statement & Publications:** Processes for manufacture of titanium; titanium alloys. **Mailing Address:** KesCo Inc, 18010 Alyssum Dr, Sun City West, AZ 85375.

KESSLER, IRVING ISAR, PREVENTIVE MEDICINE, EPIDEMIOLOGY. **Personal Data:** b Chelsea, Mass, March 22, 1931; m 1970, Laure; c Amelia & Abigail. **Education:** NY Univ, AB, 1952; Harvard Univ, MA, 1955, DrPH, 1969; Stanford Univ, MD, 1960; Columbia Univ, MPH, 1962; Am Bd Prev Med, dipl. **Professional Experience:** PROF EMER, UNIV MD, as of 2005; vpres health Sci, ECRI, 1992-1993; prof dermat & med, Univ Md, 1984-; exec dir, Md Cancer Registry, 1982; chmn epidemiol & prev med, Univ MD, 1978-1988; prof, Johns Hopkins Univ, 1973-1978; Fac res award, Am Cancer Soc, 1972-1977; assoc prof prev med, Univ MD, 1970-1978; assoc prof epidemiol, Johns Hopkins Univ, 1970-1972; asst prof chronic dis, Johns Hopkins Univ, 1966-1969; instr environ med, State Univ NY, 1964-1966; med dir res, USPHS; mem exec comn, Gov Coun Toxic Substances, Md; scientific res bd, Ctr Indoor Dir Res. **Memberships:** AAAS; Am Epidemiol Soc; Am Asn Cancer Res; Am Pub Health Asn; Asn Teachers Prev Med; Sigma Xi. **Research Statement & Publications:** Epidemiological research in cancer, diabetes mellitus, birth defects and Parkinson's disease; epidemiological principles; community studies of health; gerontology; environmental and occupational health; health regulation. **Mailing Address:** Dept Epidemiol & Prev Med, Sch Med Univ Md, Baltimore, MD 21201. **Fax:** 410-706-8013. **E-Mail:** ikessler@erols.com

KESSLER, IRVING JACK, MATHEMATICS. **Personal Data:** b Brooklyn, NY, May 14, 1940; c 2. **Education:** Brooklyn Col, BA, 1962; Univ Wis, MS, 1963, PhD (math), 1966. **Professional Experience:** Prof math, Southern Ill Univ, 1978-1980; RES STAFF MATH, INST DEFENSE ANALYSIS, 1977-, PRES; Res staff math, Inst Defense Anal, 1974-1975 & 1977-; from asst prof to assoc prof, Southern Ill Univ, 1968-1978; Asst prof math, Univ Mich, 1966-1968. **Memberships:** Am Math Soc; Math Asn Am. **Research Statement & Publications:** Combinatorial mathematics; number theory; applying mathematics to problems in speech recognition. **Mailing Address:** Inst Defense Analysis Thanet Rd, Princeton, NJ 08540.

KESSLER, JOHN OTTO, MICROBIOLOGY, STOKES FLOWS. **Personal Data:** b Vienna, Austria, November 26, 1928; American citizen; m 1950, Eva; c Helen & Steven. **Education:** Columbia Univ, BA, 1949, MS, 1950, PhD (physics), 1953. **Professional Experience:** PROF EMER, DEPT PHYSICS, UNIV ARIZ, as of 2004; Fulbright fel, Cult Ctr Algae & Protozoa, 1985-; Fulbright fel, Dept Appl Math & Theoret Phys, Cambridge Univ, 1983-1984; vis prof physics, Univ Leeds, 1972-1973 & T H Delft, Neth, 1979; Dept Physics, Univ Arizona 1966-1995, prof 1995- prof Emeritus active Dept Appl Math, Univ Leeds, 1990-1991; prof physics, Univ Ariz, beginning 1966; mgr grad recruiting, RCA Corp, 1965-1966; Physicist labs, Radio Corp Am, 1952-1962 & Princeton Univ, 1963-1965; asst physics, Columbia Univ, 1948-1952. **Memberships:** Fel AAAS; Am Phys Soc. **Research Statement & Publications:** Applied phycology; biophysics; plant physiology; fluid mechanics of microorganisms; concentrative and cooperative phenomena of microrganism populations for practical applications in cell separation and phycoculture for investigating phase transformations in biosystems self organizing systems. **Mailing Address:** Dept Physics Univ Ariz, PAS 471, Tucson, AZ 85721. **Fax:** 520-621-4721. **E-Mail:** kessler@physics.arizona.edu

KESSLER, KENNETH J, JR, PLANT PATHOLOGY. **Personal Data:** b Wheeling, WVa, March 15, 1933; m 1954, c 4. **Education:** WVa Univ, BS, 1955, MS, 1957, PhD (plant path), 1960. **Professional Experience:** PLANT PATHOLOGIST, NORTH CENT FOREST EXP STA, US FOREST SERV, 1959-. **Memberships:** Am Phytopath Soc; Mycol Soc Am. **Research Statement & Publications:** Hardwood tree diseases. **Mailing Address:** N Cent Forest Exp Sta, Carbondale, IL 62901.

KESSLER, LAWRENCE W, ULTRASOUND, NONDESTRUCTIVE TESTING. **Personal Data:** b Chicago, Ill, September 26, 1942; m 1985, Francesca; c Jeffrey, Brett, Corey, Brandy, Lindsay, Bryan & Bradley. **Education:** Purdue Univ, BS, 1964; Univ Ill, Urbana-Champaign, MS, 1965, PhD (elec eng), 1968. **Professional Experience:** Nat lectr, Inst Elec & Electronics Engrs, 1981-1982; PRES & FOUNDER ACOUST MICROS, SONOSCAN INC, 1974-; mem adv panel, Tech Electronic Prod Radiation Safety Stand Comt, Dept Health, Educ & Welfare, 1972-1975; mem res staff acoust visualization, Zenith Radio Corp, 1968-1974. **Memberships:** Sr mem Inst Elec & Electronics Engrs; Am Inst Ultrasound Med; fel Acoust Soc Am; Am Soc Nondestructive Testing. **Research State-

ment & Publications: Acoustic microscopy and ultrasonic visualization applications in life and materials sciences; quality assurance inspection equipment; biomedical engineering; laser scanning systems. **Mailing Address:** Sonoscan Inc, 2149-T E Pratt Blvd, Elk Grove Village, IL 60007. **Fax:** 847-437-1550. **E-Mail:** lkessler@soncscin.com

KESSLER, NATHAN, CHEMICAL ENGINEERING. **Personal Data:** b St Louis, Mo, August 19, 1923; m 1947, c 3. **Education:** Wash Univ, BSChE & MS, 1944. **Professional Experience:** Mem, Indust Adv Bd, Fed Lab Consortium, beginning 1987; chmn, Indust Adv Comt, Mich Biotechnol Inst, beginning 1987; CONSULT, TECHNOL INC, ST LOUIS, 1985-; assoc dir, Biotech Resources Inc, 1985-1989; technol consult, Biotech Resources Inc, 1985-1987; mem bd, Technol Transfer Soc, beginning 1983; Univ Ill, 1982-1987; mem, Jr Eng & Technol Soc Bd & pres, 1982-1985; mem, Biotechnical Resources Bd, 1982-1985; mem eng adv bd, Rice Univ, 1971; mem bd dirs, Wastech Inc, Tex, 1970-1976; mem bd dirs & tech group vpres, A E Staley Mfg Co, 1967-1985; pres, Staley Techventures, 1964-1986; gen supt, Ill, 1962-1967; plant supt, Ill, 1961-1962; dir process eng, Ill, 1960-1961; chief chem engr, Ill, 1957-1960; sr chem eng, Ill, 1953-1957; tech supvr, Ohio, 1951-1953; chem engr, A E Staley Mfg Inc, 1944-1951; White-Rodgers fel. **Memberships:** Am Inst Chem Engrs; Am Chem Soc; Technol Transfer Soc (pres 1985-1988, chmn 1988-1990). **Research Statement & Publications:** Engineering, research and development; food processes; biotechnology; technology transfer. **Mailing Address:** 232 N KingsHwy Blvd # 1405, St Louis, MO 63108.

KESSLER, RICHARD HOWARD, MEDICINE, PHYSIOLOGY. **Personal Data:** b Paterson, NJ, December 15, 1923; m 1944, c 3. **Education:** Rutgers Univ, BSc, 1948; NY Univ, MD, 1952. **Professional Experience:** RETIRED; prof med, Mt Sinai Sch Med, NY, 1984-1988; sr vpres, Michael Reese Hosp & Med Ctr, 1978-1983; prof med, Pritzker Sch Med, Univ Chicago, 1978-1983; assoc dean, Med Sch, 1970-1978; prof med, Med Sch, Northwestern Univ, Chicago, 1968-1978; Hofheimer Found fel, 1957-1962; from instr to assoc prof physiol, Cornell Univ, 1955-1968; Life inst med res fel, 1955-1956; asst med, NY Univ, 1952-1955; asst chem, Rutgers Univ, 1947-1948; mem, Sect Renal Dis, Coun Circulation, Am Heart Asn; mem, Health Econ Adv Comt, Nat Bur Econ Res; vpres, Kidney Found Ill; fel, Hastings Inst Soc, Ethics & Life Sci; consult, Educ Serv, Vet Admin; comnr, Chicago Health Systs Agency; comnr, Health & Hosps Gov Comn Cook Co. **Memberships:** AAAS; Harvey Soc; Soc Exp Biol & Med; Am Physiol Soc; fel Am Col Physicians. **Research Statement & Publications:** Cardiovascular and renal physiology; fluid balance; electrolyte transport; diuretics; renal disease; hypertension. **Mailing Address:** 349 S Wash Dr, Sarasota, FL 34236.

KESSLER, ROBERT, AERONAUTICS. **Education:** Stanford Univ, ME. **Professional Experience:** CHIEF TECHNOL OFFICER, TEXTRON SYSTS CORP, as of 2006; CHMN, INDUST ADV BD, CENSSIS, as of 2006. **Mailing Address:** Textron Systs Corp, Avco Res Lab, 201 Lowell St, Wilmington, MA 02149-5900. **Fax:** 978-657-6644.

KESSLER, SEYMOUR, GENETICS. **Personal Data:** b New York, NY, September 3, 1928; m 1953, c 2. **Education:** City Col NY, BS, 1960; Columbia Univ, MA, 1962, PhD (zoology), 1965; PhD (soc-clin psychol). **Professional Experience:** CONSULT, 1985-; dir & sr lectr, Univ Calif, Berkeley, 1975-1985; adj prof psychiat, Sch Med, Stanford Univ, 1974-1975; sr scientist, Sch Med, Stanford Univ, 1973-1974; asst prof, Sch Med, Stanford Univ, 1967-1973; fel psychiat, Sch Med, Stanford Univ, 1965-1967; assoc clin prof, Univ Calif, San Francisco. **Memberships:** Am Soc Human Genetics; Sigma Xi; Am Psychol Asn; Nat Soc Genetic Counselors. **Research Statement & Publications:** Behavior and psychiatric genetics; genetic counseling. **Mailing Address:** PO Box 7702, Berkeley, CA 94707. **Fax:** 510-525-1996.

KESSLER, WILLIAM J(OSEPH), COMMUNICATIONS ENGINEERING. **Personal Data:** b Roebling, NY, February 28, 1917; c 4. **Honors & Awards:** Cert Off Sci & Res & Develop & Ord Develop Award, 1945. **Professional Experience:** OWNER, KESSLER & GEHMAN ASSOCS, as of 1998; OWNER, W J KESSLER ASSOC, 1967-; asst prof, Univ Fla, 1945-1967; asst res engr, Univ Fla, 1945-1953; Lab instr elec eng, Univ Fla, 1943-1945; Microwave, TV & commun consult, eng forensics. **Memberships:** Nat Soc Prof Engrs; Am Electronic Soc. **Research Statement & Publications:** Thunderstorm electricity; propagation of low frequency electromagnetic radiations; special instrumentation for radio location of thunder-storms for meteorological forecasting purposes. **Mailing Address:** 1625 SW 35th Pl, Gainesville, FL 32608.

KESSNER, DAVID MORTON, INTERNAL MEDICINE. **Personal Data:** b New York, NY, August 23, 1932; m 1959, c 2. **Education:** Univ Ariz, BS, 1954; Wash Univ, MD, 1958; Am Bd Internal Med, dipl, 1967. **Professional Experience:** PROF & VCHMN COMMUNITY & FAMILY MED, UNIV MASS MED CTR, 1975-; dir, Health Serv Res Off; assoc prof community med & int health, Georgetown Univ, 1973-1975; attend physician, Hosp, 1970-; asst clin prof, Sch Med, George Wash Univ, 1970-1973; study dir & res assoc, Inst Med, Nat Acad Sci, 1969-1973; consult internist, Yale Psychiat Inst, 1967-1969; assoc physician, Dept Med, 1966-1969; from instr to asst prof med & epidemiol, Sch Med, Yale Univ, 1965-1969; attend physician, Metab Sect, Yale-New Haven Hosp, 1965-1969; second year resident internal med, Sch Med, Yale Univ, 1964-1965; fel, Nat Inst Arthritis & Metab Dis, 1963-1964; fel med, Sch Med, Yale Univ, 1962-1964; jr attend physician, Med Clin, Univ Ill, 1961-1962; fel prev med, Sch Med, Univ Ill, 1960-1962; asst resident internal med, Mary Imogene Bassett Hosp, 1959-1960; intern med, Mary Imogene Bassett Hosp, 1958-1959. **Memberships:** Am Fedn Clin Res; Am Pub Health Asn; Int Epidemiol Asn; fel Am Col Physicians. **Research Statement & Publications:** Chronic disease epidemiology; the use of epidemiology in health services research. **Mailing Address:** 401 The Hl Ste 201, Portsmouth, NH 03801.

KESTEN, ARTHUR S(IDNEY), RESEARCH ADMINISTRATION. **Personal Data:** b New York, NY, September 10, 1934. **Education:** NY Univ, BS, 1955; Univ Pittsburgh, MS, 1958, PhD (chem eng), 1961. **Professional Experience:** Dir res, Progs United Technol Res Ctr, 1996-1997; assoc dir res, United Technol Res Ctr, 1993-1995; assoc dir res, indust systs & technol, 1992-1993; asst dir, United Technol Res Ctr, 1990-1992; CHMN, SOLAR ENERGY RES INST ADV BD, 1984-; asst dir res power indust systs technol, United Technol Res Ctr, 1981-1990; mgr energy res, United Technol Res Ctr, 1977-1981; mgr combustion sci, United Technol Res Ctr, 1976-1977; prin scientist kinetics & environ sci, United Technol Res Ctr, 1972-1976; supvr kinetics & heat transfer, United Technol Res Ctr, 1968-1972; ADJ ASSOC PROF, RENSSELAER POLYTECH INST, 1965-; sr res engr, United Technol Res Ctr, 1965-1968; res engr, United Technol Res Ctr, 1963-1965; sr engr, Bettis Atomic Power Lab, Westinghouse Elec Corp, 1961-1963; engr, Bettis Atomic Power Lab, Westinghouse Elec Corp, 1957-1961; assoc engr res & develop, Bettis Atomic Power Lab, Westinghouse Elec Corp, 1955-1957. **Memberships:** Fel Am Inst Chem; Sigma Xi; Am Inst Chem Engrs; Am Chem Soc; Combustion Inst; Res Soc Am. **Research Statement & Publications:** Hydrogen energy systems, chemical reactors, transport processes, combustion; sixteen patents awarded in area of chemical heat pumps and gas transporting systems. **Mailing Address:** Rensselear Polytech Inst, 17 Morning Crest Dr, West Hartford, CT 06117.

KESTEN, HARRY, MATHEMATICS. **Personal Data:** b November 19, 1931. **Education:** Cornell Univ, PhD, 1958. **Honors & Awards:** Rietz Lectr, Inst Math Statist, 1971, Wald Lectr, 1986; Brouwer Mem Lectr & Medal, Dutch Math Soc, 1981; George Polya Prize, Soc Indust & Appl Math, 1994, Leroy P Steele Prize, 2001. **Professional Experience:** PROF EMER MATH, DEPT MATH, UNIV CORNELL, as of 2003; guggenheim fel, 1972-1973; prof math, Cornell Univ, beginning 1965; alfred P Sloan fel, 1963-1965; from asst prof to assoc prof, Cornell Univ, 1961-1965; hebrew Univ, Jerusalem, 1959-1961; instr, Princetown Univ, 1958-1959. **Memberships:** Nat Acad Sci; Am Math Soc; Inst Math Statist; corresp mem Royal Dutch Acad Sci; Amer. Acad. of Arts and Sciences. **Research Statement & Publications:** Author of numerous publications. **Mailing Address:** Dept Math, Cornell Univ, 410 Malott Hall, Ithaca, NY 14853. **Fax:** 607-255-7149. **E-Mail:** kesten@math.cornell.edu

KESTENBAUM, RICHARD CHARLES, BACTERIOLOGY. **Personal Data:** b New York, NY, April 3, 1931; m 1954, Rhoda Mutterperl; c Edward, Jeffrey & Roberta. **Education:** City Col New York, BS, 1952; Rutgers Univ, MS, 1954, PhD (bact), 1959. **Professional Experience:** RETIRED; assoc dir technol planning, Colgate-Palmolive Co, Piscataway, 1988-1990; assoc dir res & develop planning, Colgate-Palmolive Co, Piscataway, 1983-1988; assoc dir personal care prod, Colgate-Palmolive Co, Piscataway, 1981-1983; mgr oral prod, Colgate-Palmolive Co, Piscataway, 1978-1981; sr sect head oral prod & appl res, Colgate-Palmolive Co, Piscataway, 1977-1978; sect head oral prod, Colgate-Palmolive Co, Piscataway, 1969-1971; sect head oral res, Colgate-Palmolive Co, Piscataway, 1966-1969 & 1971-1975; sect head microbiol, Colgate-Palmolive Co, Piscataway, 1963-1966; sr res microbiologist, Colgate-Palmolive Co, Piscataway, 1961-1963; bacteriologist, Colgate-Palmolive Co, Piscataway, 1959-1961; Asst bact, Rutgers Univ, 1952-1954 & 1956-1959. **Memberships:** Am Soc Microbiol; Int Asn Dent Res. **Research Statement & Publications:** Dental medicine; bacterial metabolism; microbial quality control; antimicrobial agents; oral and clinical research; oral products. **Mailing Address:** 18 Bradford Rd, East Brunswick, NJ 08816.

KESTENBAUM, RICHARD STEVEN, NEUROPSYCHOPHARMACOLOGY, PSYCHOTHERAPY. **Personal Data:** b New York, NY, March 20, 1942; m 1970, c 1. **Education:** NY Univ, BA, 1963, PhD (psychol), 1968. **Professional Experience:** ADJ ASST PROF PSYCHOL & EDUC, as of 2005; PRES, PSYCHOL NETWORKS, 1980-; assoc prof psychol & clin supvr, teacher's col, columbia Univ, beginning 1980; assoc dir res, Dept Psychiat, NY Med Col, 1974-1979; fel, Nat Inst Psychother, 1974-1979; asst prof, State Univ NY Stony Brook, 1968-1973; res fel psychol, NIMH, 1966-1968. **Memberships:** AAAS; Am Psychol Asn; NY Acad Sci. **Research Statement & Publications:** Neural coding of pain and neuropsychopharmacology of pain perception; chopharmacology of opiates and implications for treatment; neuropsychopharmacology of cocaine in man; psychotherapy outcome evaluation. **Mailing Address:** Teachers Col Columbia Univ, 525 W 120th St, New York, NY 10027. **Fax:** 212-678-4089.

KESTER, ANDREW STEPHEN, BACTERIOLOGY. **Personal Data:** b Abington, Pa, September 1, 1932; m 1960, c 2. **Education:** Pa State Univ, BS, 1954; Univ Tex, PhD (bact), 1961. **Professional Experience:** ASSOC PROF BIOL, NTEX STATE UNIV, 1974-; asst prof, Ntex State Univ, 1967-1974; Res microbiologist, Miles Chem Co, Ind, 1961-1967. **Memberships:** Am Soc Microbiol; Am Chem Soc. **Research Statement & Publications:** Microbial oxidation of hydrocarbons; industrial microbiology. **Mailing Address:** 387 7147 Kesterson Chad 619, Denton, TX 76201.

KESTER, DALE EMMERT, pomology; deceased, see previous edition for last biography

KESTER, DANA R, CHEMICAL OCEANOGRAPHY, PHYSICAL CHEMISTRY. **Personal Data:** b Los Angeles, Calif, January 26, 1943; m 1963, c 1. **Education:** Univ Wash, BS, 1964; Ore State Univ, MS, 1966, PhD (oceanog), 1969. **Professional Experience:** PROF OCEANOG, UNIV RI, 1976-; Ed, J Marine Res, 1973-1980; Ed, Marine Chem, 1973-1978; from asst prof to assoc prof, Univ RI, 1969-1976. **Memberships:** Am Geophys Union; Sigma Xi; Amer soc linnology & oceangraphy. **Research Statement & Publications:** Physical chemistry of seawater; effects of temperature and pressure on ionic equilibria; transition metal marine chemistry; oceanic chemical distributions; Satellite remote sensing; coastal time series. **Mailing Address:** Grad Sch Oceanog, Univ RI, S Ferry Rd, Narragansett, RI 02882-1197. **Fax:** 401-874-6818. **E-Mail:** dkester@gso.uri.edu

KESTER, DENNIS EARL, ORGANIC POLYMER CHEMISTRY. **Personal Data:** b Eureka, Kans, August 21, 1947; m 1968, c 1. **Education:** Col Emporia, BS, 1969; Univ Ark, PhD (org chem), 1975. **Professional Experience:** SR VPRES, PLASTICS DIV, AM NAT CAN CO, 1991-2002; vpres res & develop, coatings & eng, Am Nat Can Co, 1984-1991; supvr organic res & dir prod develop, coatings & eng, Am Nat Can Co, 1980-1984; Res scientist polymers, coatings & eng, Am Nat Can Co, 1974-1980. **Memberships:** Am Chem Soc. **Research Statement & Publications:** Polymer characterization and polymer synthesis; anionic, condensation and free radical polymerizations for the preparation of materials for specific coatings applications; radiation curable resins and coatings, adhesion; film and sheet laminating and extrusion, printing. **Mailing Address:** Am Nat Can Co, MS 06K, 770 W Bryn Mawr Ave, Chicago, IL 60631-3542.

KESTER, MONTY C, MATHEMATICS. **Education:** Okla State Univ, EdD (maths), 1972. **Professional Experience:** PROF MATH, LIBERTY UNIV, VA, as of 2005. **Memberships:** Am Math Soc. **Mailing Address:** Liberty Univ, Dept Math, 1971 Univ Blvd, Lynchburg, VA 24502. **Fax:** 434-522-0430. **E-Mail:** mkester@liberty.edu

KESTING, ROBERT E, polymer chemistry; deceased, see previous edition for last biography

KESTNER, MARK OTTO, INORGANIC CHEMISTRY, DUST CONTROL. **Personal Data:** b Berea, Ohio, December 10, 1947; m 1971, c 1. **Education:** Carnegie-Mellon Univ, BS, 1969; Northwestern Univ, MS, 1970, PhD (chem), 1974. **Professional Experience:** PRES, NAT ENVIRON SERV CO INC, 1988-; pres, Chemicoal Inc, 1983-1988; mgr, prod develop, 1980-1983; group leader, Apollo Chem Corp, 1978-1980; res chemist, Borg-Warner Corp, 1974-1978. **Memberships:** Am Chem Soc; NY Acad Sci; Sigma Xi. **Research Statement & Publications:** Handling, storage and combustion of coal and other fossil fuel; air pollution control and chemical treatments for control of particulate and gaseous emissions; solid waste disposal. **Mailing Address:** Nat Environ Serv Co, Inc, Seven Hampshire Dr, Mendham, NJ 07945. **Fax:** 973-543-4588.

KESTNER, MELVIN MICHAEL, ORGANIC CHEMISTRY. **Personal Data:** b Wooster, Ohio, October 20, 1945; m 1971. **Education:** Heidelberg Col, BS, 1967; Purdue Univ, PhD (org chem), 1973. **Professional Experience:** SR CHEMIST ORG CHEM, EASTMAN KODAK CO, 1973-. **Memberships:** Am Chem Soc. **Research Statement & Publications:** Synthesis of compounds used in photographic products. **Mailing Address:** 590 Parma Ctr Rd, Hilton, NY 14468.

KESTNER, NEIL R, CHEMICAL PHYSICS. **Personal Data:** b Milwaukee, Wis, December 11, 1937; m 1967, Arlene; c Lars. **Education:** Univ Wis-Milwaukee, BS, 1960; Yale Univ, MS, 1962, PhD (theoret chem), 1964. **Professional Experience:** CHARLES BARRE DISTINGUISHED PROF CHEM, LA STATE UNIV, BATON ROUGE, as of 1998; Res collabr, Brookhaven Nat Lab, 1981; chmn dept, La State Univ, 1976-1981; chmn freshman chem, La State Univ, 1973-1976; prof chem, La State Univ, Baton Rouge, beginning 1972; vis prof, Tel-Aviv Univ, 1972; A P Sloan fel, 1967-1969; assoc prof, La State Univ, 1966-1972; asst prof chem, Stanford Univ, 1964-1966; Res assoc, Inst Study Metals, Univ Chicago, 1963-1964. **Memberships:** Am Chem Soc; Am Phys Soc; Sigma Xi; AAAS. **Research Statement & Publications:** Quantum chemistry; intermolecular forces; electrons in disordered media; electron transfer reactions; quantum statistical mechanics; electronically mediated education. **Mailing Address:** Dept Chem, La State Univ, Baton Rouge, LA 70803-0001. **Fax:** 225-578-3458. **E-Mail:** kestner@lsu.edu

KETCHA, DANIEL MICHAEL, HETEROCYCLIC CHEMISTRY. **Personal Data:** b Newark, NJ, January 12, 1956; c 1. **Education:** King's Col, Wilkes-Barre, BS, 1977; Temple Univ, Philadelphia, PhD (org chem), 1984. **Professional Experience:** ASSOC PROF CHEM, WRIGHT STATE UNIV, 1991-; asst prof, Wright State Univ, Dayton, Ohio, 1985-1991; res instr chem, Dartmouth Col, Hanover, NH, 1985; res assoc, Dartmouth Col, Hanover, NH, 1983-1985. **Memberships:** Am Chem Soc. **Research Statement & Publications:** Development of novel synthetic methodologies and their subsequent application towards the synthesis of molecules of biological importance. **Mailing Address:** Dept Chem, Wright State Univ, 3640 Colonel Glenn Hwy, Dayton, OH 45435-0001. **Fax:** 937-775-2717. **E-Mail:** daniel.ketcha@wright.edu

KETCHAM, ALFRED SCHUTT, SURGERY. **Personal Data:** b Newark, NY, October 7, 1924; m 1946, c 6. **Education:** Hobart Col, BS, 1945; Univ Rochester, MD, 1949; Am Bd Surg, dipl, 1959. **Honorary Degrees:** DSc, Hobart Col, 1970. **Honors & Awards:** Meritorious Serv Medal, USPHS. **Professional Experience:** PROF SURG & CHIEF DIV ONCOL, SCH MED, UNIV MIAMI, 1974-; assoc sci dir clin res, Gen Labs & Clins & clin dir, Inst, 1971-1974; chief, Dept Surg, Nat Cancer Inst, 1962-1974; resident, Seattle, 1952-1955; resident, USPHS Hosps, San Francisco, 1950-1952; Intern surg, US Naval Med Ctr, Bethesda, 1949-1950. **Memberships:** Fel Am Col Surg; Am Asn Cancer Res; Am Radium Soc; Soc Head & Neck Surgeons; Am Surg Asn. **Research Statement & Publications:** Cancer surgery; experimental metastases; clinical and laboratory investigation. **Mailing Address:** Dept Surg, Sch Med Univ Miami, PO Box 016310, Miami, FL 33101-6310.

KETCHAM, BRUCE V(ALENTINE), aerospace engineering; deceased, see previous edition for last biography

KETCHAM, ROGER, ORGANIC CHEMISTRY, HETEROCYCLIC CHEMISTRY. **Personal Data:** b Berea, Ohio, September 2, 1926; m 1950, c 4. **Education:** Antioch Col, BS, 1951; Cornell Univ, PhD (chem), 1956. **Professional Experience:** EMER FAC, UNIV CALIF, SAN FRANCISCO, AS OF 2004; vis prof, Univ Graz, Austria, 1971-1972; from instr to prof chem & pharmaceut chem, Sch Pharm, Univ Calif, San Francisco, 1969-1991; mem, Orgn Am States Prof, Monterrey Inst Technol & Higher Educ, 1964-1965. **Memberships:** Am Chem Soc; Am Pharmaceut Asn; Chem Soc; Sigma Xi. **Research Statement & Publications:** Three-membered rings; nitrogen and sulfur heterocycles; reaction mechanisms; organo-sulfur chemistry. **Mailing Address:** Sch Pharm, Univ Calif, San Francisco, CA 94143-0446.

KETCHEL, MELVIN M, REPRODUCTIVE PHYSIOLOGY. **Personal Data:** b Pontiac, Mich, June 1, 1922; m 1958, c 3. **Education:** Olivet Col, AB, 1948; Western Reserve Univ, MS, 1949; Harvard Univ, PhD (biol), 1954. **Professional Experience:** RETIRED; exec secy, div res grants, NIH, 1981-; owner, Shelter Co, 1977-1981; scientist, Human Reprod Unit, WHO, 1975-1977; prof zool, Univ Tenn, 1974-1975; dir, Oak Ridge Pop Res Inst, 1972-1975; NSF sr fel, 1971-1972; from assoc prof to prof, Sch Med, Tufts Univ, 1965-1972; srscientist, Worcester Found Exp Biol, 1963-1965; staff scientist physiol, Worcester Found Exp Biol, 1959-1963; res assoc surg, Harvard Med Sch, 1956-1959; res assoc cytol, Protein Found Labs, 1955-1956; Res asst biophys chem, Harvard Univ, 1954-1955. **Research Statement & Publications:** Hormonal aspects of pregnancy and pseudopregnancy; immunological aspects of the relationships between the fetus and its mother. **Mailing Address:** Div Res Grants, NIH, Rm 1040, MSC 7710, 6701 Rockledge Dr, Bethesda, MD 20892-7710.

KETCHEN, EUGENE EARL, PHYSICAL CHEMISTRY. **Personal Data:** b Miami, Fla, May 3, 1921; m 1951, c 3. **Education:** Univ Miami, BS, 1943; Univ Pittsburgh, PhD (phys chem), 1950. **Professional Experience:** INDUST HYG CHEMIST, OAK RIDGE NAT LAB, 1974-; chemist, Isotope Div, 1951-1974; asst prof chem, Wash & Jefferson Col, 1950-1951; Asst, Univ Pittsburgh, 1946-1950. **Memberships:** Am Chem Soc; Am Indust Hyg Asn; Am Acad Indust Hyg. **Research Statement & Publications:** Radio-isotopes; industrial hygiene chemistry; industrial toxicology. **Mailing Address:** 654 Lakeshore Dr, Kingston, TN 37763-2010.

KETCHEN, MARK B, CRYOGENIC DIGITAL DEVICES. **Personal Data:** b St Stephen, NB, September 15, 1948. **Education:** Mass Inst Technol, BS, 1970; Univ Calif, Berkeley, MA, 1971, PhD (physics), 1977. **Professional Experience:** RES STAFF MEM & MGR, THOMAS J WATSON RES CTR, IBM, 1977-; officer, Physics Thermodynamics Reactor Oper, US Naval Nuclear Power Prog, 1972-1976. **Memberships:** Am Phys Soc; Inst Elec & Electronics Engrs. **Research Statement & Publications:** Electrical design and evaluation of superconducting quantum interference devices for digital and analog applications; logic and power circuits for an ultra-high-speed cryogenic computer. **Mailing Address:** Int Bus Mach Corp, Hopewell Junction, NY 10604. **E-Mail:** mketchen@us.ibm.com

KETCHIE, DELMER O, PLANT PHYSIOLOGY, BIOCHEMISTRY. **Personal Data:** b Salisbury, NC, July 7, 1932; m 1979, c 4. **Education:** Wash State Univ, BS, 1959; Univ Idaho, MS, 1961; Cornell Univ, PhD (pomol), 1965. **Honors & Awards:** Stark Award, 1973; Paul Howe Sheppard Award, 1984. **Professional Experience:** HORTICULTURIST, TREE FRUIT RES CTR, WASH STATE UNIV, 1980-; from asst horticulturist to assoc horticulturist, Tree Fruit Res Ctr, Wash State Univ, 1967-1980; Plant physiologist, Date & Citrus Sta, USDA, Calif, 1965-1967. **Memberships:** Am Soc Hort Sci; Soc Cryobiol; Int Soc Hort Sci; Sigma Xi. **Research Statement & Publications:** Winter hardiness of deciduous fruit trees, including biochemical and physical aspects; rest dormancy of deciduous fruit trees. **Mailing Address:** Tree Fruit Res Ctr, Wash State Univ, 1100 N, Western Ave, Wenatchee, WA 98801-1230.

KETCHMAN, JEFFREY P E, MECHANICAL ENGINEERING & SAFETY ENGINEERING, ENGINEERING MANAGEMENT. **Personal Data:** b New York, NY, November 23, 1942; m Niki; c Linda & Karen. **Education:** City Col NY, BSME, 1964; Ohio State Univ, MSME, 1967; Columbia Univ, Dr Eng Sci, 1972. **Professional Experience:** DIR, MECH & SAFETY ENG, INTERCITY TESTING & CONSULT CORP, 1987-; vp design, Eng & Res, Lightolier Inc, 1985-1987; dir, Eng & Res, Genlyte Group, 1985; dir, Eng & Res, AMF Inc, 1976-1985; mem, Tech Staff, Bell Labs, 1967-1976; proj & task leader, Battelle Mem Inst, 1964-1967; consult, new prod develop, eng mgt & forensic eng; adj prof, The Cooper Union sch eng, NY. **Memberships:** Am Ceramics Soc; Accreditation Comn Traffic Accident Reconstruction; Am Soc Testing & Mat; fel Inst Diag, Engrs, UK; ACFE; AAAS; NY Acad Sci; Assn Res Dirs; Am Soc Mech Eng; Am Soc Safety Eng; Sys Safety Soc; Soc Automotive Engrs. **Research Statement & Publications:** Optimizing radioisotope thermoelectric generators; design and development of submarine sonar systems; exercise and sports equipment; oil-field equipment; lighting systems; product safety; forensic engineering and accident reconstruction. **Mailing Address:** 14 Caccamo Lane, Westport, CT 06880. **Fax:** 203-227-3164. **E-Mail:** Ketchman@Optonline.net

KETCHUM, PAUL ABBOTT, MICROBIAL PHYSIOLOGY. **Personal Data:** b Hyannis, Mass, August 11, 1942; m 1996, Robin; c Geoffrey Stephen & Jennifer Louise. **Education:** Bates Col, BS, 1964; Univ Mass, PhD (microbiol), 1969. **Professional Experience:** Dir, Res Assocs Cape Cod Inc, 1994-2002; prof, Oakland Univ, 1993-1995; guest scientist, Univ Ga, Athens, 1989-1990; from asst prof to full prof biol sci, NSF grant, 1971-1977; NIH fel biochem, Johns Hopkins Univ, 1968-1970; CHMN ASM MEM COMT, COM A AAUP. **Memberships:** AAAS; Am Soc Microbiol; Sigma Xi; Int Endotoxin Soc. **Research Statement & Publications:** Inorganic nitrogen metabolism; biochemistry of nitrate reductase; role of molybdenum in inorganic nitrogen metabolism; biochemistry of limulus amebocyte lysate; glucan assay for detecting fungal infections. **Mailing Address:** 31 Moorland Rd, Falmouth, MA 02540. **Fax:** 508-540-8680. **E-Mail:** paketchum@verizon.net

KETELLAPPER, HENDRIK JAN, PLANT PHYSIOLOGY. **Personal Data:** b Ridderkerk, Neth, December 23, 1925; American citizen; m 1951, c 3. **Education:** Univ Utrecht, BSc, 1947, PhC, 1951, PhD (plant physiol), 1953. **Professional Experience:** EMER PROF BOT, UNIV CALIF, DAVIS, 1991-; prof, Col Lett & Sci, 1969-1991; assoc dean, Col Lett & Sci, 1967-1983; assoc prof, Univ Calif, Davis, 1965-1969; lectr, Univ Calif, Davis, 1964-1965; Nat Acad Sci exchange scientist, USSR, 1963; res fel biol, Calif Inst Technol, 1957-1964; res officer, Div Plant Indust, Commonwealth Sci & Indust Res Orgn, Canberra, Australia, 1954-1957; instr gen bot, Univ Utrecht, 1948-1951. **Memberships:** AAAS; Japanese Soc Plant Physiol; NY Acad Sci; Royal Neth Bot Soc; Sigma Xi. **Research Statement & Publications:** Climate and plant growth and development; algal physiology; physiological ecology; environmental ethics. **Mailing Address:** 621 Francisco Pl, Davis, CA 95606.

KETHLEY, THOMAS WILLIAM, biology; deceased, see previous edition for last biography

KETLEY, ARTHUR DONALD, PHOTOCHEMISTRY, POLYMER CHEMISTRY. **Personal Data:** b London, Eng, December 27, 1930; c 3. **Education:** Univ London, BSc, 1951, PhD (chem), 1953. **Professional Experience:** MANAGING DIR, JAPAN RES CTR, 1988-; dir technol prod res, W W Grace & Co, 1979-1988; mgr mat develop photopolymer systs, W W Grace & Co, 1973-1979; chemist, W W Grace & Co, 1959-1973; chemist, Esso Res & Eng Co, 1958-1959; res fel, Ga Inst Technol, 1957-1958; lectr, Univ Sydney, 1956-1957; Res assoc chem, Mass Inst Technol, 1953-1955. **Memberships:** Am Chem Soc; Int Am Photochem Soc; Soc Photog Scientists & Engrs. **Research Statement & Publications:** Mechanisms of organic reactions; organometallic chemistry; photochemistry; development and applications of photopolymerizable materials; imaging science. **Mailing Address:** 2777 9th St Suite 101, Berkeley, CA 94710.

KETLEY, JEANNE NELSON, ENZYMOLOGY, DRUG METABOLISM. **Personal Data:** b New York, NY, c Alex. **Education:** Queens Col, NY, BS, 1962; Cornell Univ, MS, 1967; Johns Hopkins Univ, PhD (biochem), 1973. **Professional Experience:** CONSULT, 2002-; Chief, Cardiovasc Sci Irg, Ctr for sci review, NIH, 1996-2002; chief, Clin Sci Rev Sect, 1994-1996; chief, Phys Sci Rev Sect, Div Res Grants, 1989-1993; chief, Spec Rev Sect, 1985-1989; exec secy, Phys Biochem Study Sect, NIH, 1979-1985; chemist, Bur Foods, Food & Drug Admin, 1977-1979; sr staff fel, Nat Inst Aging, 1976-1977; staff fel enzyme biochem, lab biochem & metab, Nat Inst Arthritis, Metab & Digestive Dis, 1974-1976; Muscular Dystrophy Asn Am fel, 1973-1974; vis scientist develop biol, Nat Inst Dent Res, NIH, 1973-1974; Res asst enzym & biochem, Med Col, Cornell Univ, 1968-1969. **Memberships:** AAAS; Am Chem Soc. **Research Statement & Publications:** Drug metabolism; mammalian biochemical processes at the molecular level; changes in biological structure and function of proteins; physical biochemistry. **Mailing Address:** 5659 Vantage Point Road, Columbia, MD 21044. **Fax:** 301-596-1097. **E-Mail:** jnketley@sumstat.com

KETNER, KEITH B, GEOLOGY OF NEVADA. **Personal Data:** b Boscobel, Wis, February 5, 1921; m 1946, Donna; c 3. **Education:** Univ Wis, BA, 1947, MA, 1952, PhD (geol), 1968. **Professional Experience:** EMER GEOLOGIST, US GEOL SURV, 1994-; Geologist & res geologist, 1950-1994. **Memberships:** AAAS mem; fel Geol Soc fel Am. **Mailing Address:** US Geol Surv MS 939 Box 25046, Fed Ctr, Denver, CO 80225. **E-Mail:** kketner@usgs.gov

KETOLA, H GEORGE, FISH NUTRITION. **Education:** Cornell Univ, BS, 1965, MS, 1967, PhD (nutrit), 1973. **Professional Experience:** RES PHYSIOLOGIST, EASTERN BASIN ECOSYS BR, TUNISON LAB AQUATIC SCI, as of 2003; US Fish & Wildlife Serv res grant, 1984-1985 & Dept Natural Resources, beginning 1991; adj asst prof, Dept Poultry & Avian Sci, Cornell Univ, 1976-1991; res physiologist, Tunison Lab Fish Nutrit, Us Fish & Wildlife Serv, beginning 1973; consult fish nutrit, feed mfrs. **Memberships:** Am Inst Nutrit; Poultry Sci Asn; Am Fisheries Soc; Am Soc Animal Sci; Sigma Xi; Animal Nutrit Res Coun. **Research Statement & Publications:** Nutritional studies to reduce nutrient discharges in effluent waters from fish hatcheries; improvement of nutritional quality of diets for fry and fingerling salmon and trout. **Mailing Address:** Tunison Lab Aquatic Sci, USGS Great Lake Sci ctr, 3075 Gracie Rd, Cortland, NY 13045-9457. **Fax:** 607-753-0259. **E-Mail:** george_ketola@usgs.gov

KETRING, DAROLD L, PLANT PHYSIOLOGY, BIOCHEMISTRY. **Personal Data:** b Van Nuys, Calif, March 14, 1930; m 1950, c 2. **Education:** Univ Calif, Los Angeles, BS, 1963, PhD (plant sci), 1967. **Professional Experience:** EMER FAC, DEPT PLANT & SOIL SCI, OKLA STATE UNIV, as of 2002; PLANT PHYSIOLOGIST, USDA, 1967-. **Memberships:** Am Soc Plant Physiologists; Am Soc Agron; Am Peanut Res & Educ Asn; Plant Growth Regulator Soc Am; Sigma Xi. **Research Statement & Publications:** Relation of ethylene and other plant hormones to plant growth, development, senescence and accompanying biochemistry; effect of environmental stress on plant growth and development. **Mailing Address:** Dept Plant & Soil Sci, Okla State Univ, 368 Ag Hall, Stillwater, OK 74078. **Fax:** 405-744-5269.

KETTELKAMP, DONALD B, ORTHOPEDIC SURGERY. **Personal Data:** b Anamosa, Iowa, January 21, 1930; m 1954, c 4. **Education:** Cornell Col, BA, 1952; Univ Iowa, MD, 1955, MS, 1960. **Professional Experience:** Pres, Am Orthop Assoc, 1990; EXEC DIR, AM BD ORTHOP SURGEONS, 1986-; assoc dean, Tex Tech Univ Regional Acad Med Ctr, 1984-1987; prof orthop surg & chmn dept, Ind Univ Med Ctr, Indianapolis, 1974-1984;

prof & chmn dept, Med Ctr, Univ Ark, Little Rock, 1971-1974; Consult, Vet Admin Hosp, Little Rock, 1971-1974; assoc prof, Univ Iowa, 1968-1971; From asst prof to assoc prof orthop surg, Albany Med Col, 1964-1968. **Memberships:** Fel Am Acad Orthop Surg; fel Am Col Surg; Am Orthop Asn. **Research Statement & Publications:** Knee and hand reconstruction and biomechanics. **Mailing Address:** 400 Silver Cedar Ct, Chapel Hill, NC 27514.

KETTERER, JOHN JOSEPH, zoology; deceased, see previous edition for last biography

KETTERER, PAUL ANTHONY, ANALYSIS & CHARACTERIZATION OF POLYMERS, ADDITIVES & CATALYSTS. **Personal Data:** b Warwick, NY, August 2, 1941; m 1962, Mary; c Nancy & Paul. **Education:** Syracuse Univ, AB, 1964; Seton Hall Univ, MS, 1973. **Professional Experience:** SR MGR CHARACTERIZATION & ANALYSIS, MONTELL INC, 1992-; res scientist, Montell Inc, 1989-1992; sr res chemist, Montell Inc, 1986-1989; mgr anal serv, Tenneco Polymers Inc, 1982-1986; lab mgr polymer characterization & anal, Tenneco Chem Inc, 1976-1981; group leader anal chem, Tenneco Chem Inc, 1974-1975; sr chemist, Tenneco Chem Inc, 1968-1973; chemist, Polaks Frutal Works Inc, 1964-1968. **Memberships:** Am Chem Soc; Soc Appl Spectros; Soc Plastics Indust. **Research Statement & Publications:** Polymer characterization and analysis, determination of structure-property relationships of polymers and additives; development of analytical methods for trace analysis of air and water pollutants; trace residual monomers in polymers. **Mailing Address:** 3308 Coachman Rd, Wilmington, DE 19803-1946.

KETTERING, JAMES DAVID, MEDICAL MICROBIOLOGY, VIROLOGY, TUMOR IMMUNOLOGY. **Personal Data:** b Pekin, Ill, March 27, 1942; m 1963, Betty; c Brian D, Pamela S & David E. **Education:** Andrews Univ, BA, 1964; Loma Linda Univ, MS, 1968, PhD (microbiol), 1974. **Professional Experience:** PROF & ASST CHAIR MICROBIOL, SCH MED, LOMA LINDA UNIV, 1989-; assoc prof microbiol, Sch Med, Loma Linda Univ, 1980-1989; fel med microbiol, Calif State Dept Health, Berkeley, 1975-1977; asst prof, Sch Med, Loma Linda Univ, 1974-1980; instr, Sch Med, Loma Linda Univ, 1972-1974; Microbiologist, Abott Labs Inc, 1966; Microbiologist, Indust Bio-Test Labs, 1964-1966. **Memberships:** Am Soc Microbiol; Sigma Xi; Am Asn Dent Schs; Am Asn Dent Res; Am Soc Virol. **Research Statement & Publications:** diagnostic virology-clinical; tumor immunology; dental immunology; published in areas of tumor immunology; virology and dental microbiology and immunology research. **Mailing Address:** Dept Microbiol & molecular genetics, Loma Linda Univ, Sch med, 11021 Campus St Alumni Hall Basic Sci 119, Loma Linda, CA 92350. **Fax:** 909-558-4035. **E-Mail:** jkettering@llu.edu

KETTERSON, ELLEN D, ORNITHOLOGY. **Education:** Ind Univ, AB, 1966, MA, 1968 PhD, 1974. **Professional Experience:** CO-DIR, CTR INTEGRATIVE STUDY ANIMAL BEHAV, OFF RES & UNIV GRAD SCH, IND UNIV, as of 2003; PROF BIOL, BIOL DEPT, COL ARTS & SCI, IND UNIV, as of 2003. **Mailing Address:** Dept Biol Ind Univ, 142 Jordan Hall 1001 E Thrid St, Bloomington, IN 47405. **Fax:** 812-855-6705. **E-Mail:** ketterso@indiana.edu

KETTERSON, JOHN BOYD, PHYSICS. **Personal Data:** b Orange, NJ, October 2, 1934; m 1961, c 3. **Education:** Univ Chicago, BS, 1957, MS, 1959, PhD (physics), 1962. **Professional Experience:** PROF, DEPT ECE, NORTHWESTERN UNIV, 1992-; chmn dep, Argonne Nat Lab, 1985-1990; FAYERWEATHER PROF, DEPT PHYSICS, NORTHWESTERN UNIV, 1974-; consult Argonne Nat Lab, beginning 1974; sr physicist, Argonne Nat Lab, 1974; assoc physicist, Argonne Nat Lab, Ill, 1962-1972. **Memberships:** Fel Am Phys Soc. **Research Statement & Publications:** Low and ultra low temperature technique; properties of monomolecular films; physics of liquid crystals; properties of composition modulated structures; properties of liquid and solid helium; electronic properties of metals and Fermi surfaces; semiconducting films; nonlinear optical films; thermoelectric materials. **Mailing Address:** Robert R McCormick Sch Eng Appl Sci, Northwestern Univ, Rm FG19, Evanston, IL 60201. **E-Mail:** jbk@northwestern.edu

KETTMAN, JOHN RUTHERFORD, IMMUNOLOGY. **Personal Data:** b Niles, Calif, November 29, 1939; m 1968, c 2. **Education:** Univ Calif, Berkeley, BA, 1961; Ore State Univ, PhD (biochem), 1968. **Professional Experience:** Vis prof, 1985; PROF MICROBIOL, SOUTHWESTERN MED SCH, SOUTHWESTERN MED CTR, UNIV TEX, DALLAS, 1980-; mem, Immunol Sci Study Group, 1980-1983; assoc prof, Southwestern Med Sch, Southwestern Med Ctr, Univ Tex, Dallas, 1975-1980; asst prof, Southwestern Med Sch, Southwestern Med Ctr, Univ Tex, Dallas, 1973-1975; asst res biologist, Univ Calif, San Diego, 1969-1972; NIH trainee immunochem, Kaiser Res Found, San Francisco, 1967-1969. **Memberships:** Am Chem Soc; Am Asn Immunologists; Soc Anal Cytol; AAAS. **Research Statement & Publications:** Cellular immunology; cell cooperation in the immune response; development of lymphoid systems. **Mailing Address:** Microbiol Dept, Southwestern Med Ctr Univ Tex, Dallas, TX 75235-9048. **Fax:** 214-648-5963.

KETTNER, CHARLES ADRIAN, ENZYMOLOGY, PEPTIDE CHEMISTRY. **Personal Data:** b Fredericksburg, Tex, October 27, 1946; m 1969, Janet; c 2. **Education:** Southwest Tex State Univ, BSE, 1969, MA, 1971; Tex A&M Univ, PhD (biochem), 1974. **Professional Experience:** RES FEL, BRISTOL-MYERS SQUIBB CO, 2001-; res fel, Dupont Pharmaceuticals Co, beginning 1998; res fel, Du Pont Merck Pharmaceut Co, 1992-1998; prin investr biochem, CR&D Dept, 1991-1992; prin investr biochem, CR&D Dept, 1980-1990; from asst biologist to assoc biologist biochem, Brookhaven Nat Lab, 1978-1980; sr res assoc biochem, Brookhaven Nat Lab, 1977-1978; res collabr biochem, Brookhaven Nat Lab, 1974-1977; res asst, Tex A&M Univ, 1971-1974; asst instr chem, Southwest Tex State Univ, 1971. **Memberships:** Am Soc Biochem & Molecular Biol; Am Chem Soc. **Research Statement & Publications:** Design and synthesis of inhibitors of proteolytic enzymes; identification of target proteases where control of proteolysis can be theropeutically useful. **Mailing Address:** DuPont Merck Pharmaceut Co, E 500/2404B, Wilmington, DE 19880-0328. **Fax:** 302-467-5877. **E-Mail:** charles.kettner@6ms.com

KEUDELL, KENNETH CARSON, MICROBIOLOGY, IMMUNOL. **Personal Data:** b Oklahoma City, Okla, May 3, 1941; m 1967, Marion L; c 2. **Education:** Okla State Univ, BS, 1963, MS, 1967; Univ Mo, PhD (microbiol), 1969. **Professional Experience:** PROF, WESTERN ILL UNIV, 1989-; assoc prof microbiol, Western Ill Univ, 1978-1989; Nat Inst Dent Res grant, 1974-1976; asst prof, Sch Dent Med, Wash Univ, 1971-1978; Fel microbiol, Albert Einstein Col Med, 1969-1971. **Memberships:** Am Soc Microbiol; Sigma Xi. **Research Statement & Publications:** Medical microbiology, general microbial, bioconversion of fatty acids, bacterial taxonomy. **Mailing Address:** 40 Briarwood Pl, Macomb, IL 61455-1243.

KEUSCH, GERALD TILDEN, INFECTIOUS DISEASES. **Personal Data:** b New York, NY, April 30, 1938; m 1985, Kathleen; c Lawrence, Lyssa & Alana. **Education:** Columbia Col, AB, 1958; Harvard Univ, MD, 1963. **Honors & Awards:** Squibb Award, Infectious Dis Soc Am, 1981; Finland Lectr, Infectious Dis Soc Am, 1997; Bristol Award, Infectious Dis Soc Am, 2002. **Professional Experience:** ASST PROVOST GLOBAL HEALTH, BOSTON UNIV, MED CTR, as of 2004; ASSOC DEAN GLOBAL HEALTH, BOSTON UNIV SCH PUB HEALTH, as of 2004; PROF, BOSTON UNIV SCH MED, as of 2004; ASSOC DIR, INT RES, NIH, 1998-2003; DIR, FOGARTY INT CTR, NIH, 1998-2003; prof med, Tufts-New Eng Med Ctr, 1978-2003; mem comt int nutrit progs, 1975- & comn int rels, beginning 1976; chmn, Nat Acad Sci, beginning 1976; mem subcomt interactions nutrit & infection, Nat Acad Sci, beginning 1971; from asst prof to prof med, Mt Sinai Sch Med, 1970-1978. **Memberships:** IOM; AAAS; Am Soc Microbiol; Am Soc Clin Invest; Infectious Dis Soc Am; Asn Am Physicians. **Research Statement & Publications:** Microbial pathogenesis, particularly enteric infections; effect of malnutrition on the immune response and host defenses; HIV/AIDS. **Mailing Address:** Sch Pub Health, Boston Univ, 715 Albany St T4W, P O Box 041, Boston, MA 02111. **Fax:** 617-638-4476. **E-Mail:** keusch@bu.edu

KEVAN, LARRY, PHYSICAL CHEMISTRY. **Personal Data:** b Kansas City, Mo, December 12, 1938. **Education:** Univ Kans, BS, 1960; Univ Calif, Los Angeles, PhD (chem), 1963. **Honors & Awards:** Polish Soc Radiation Res Award, 1979; Am Chem Soc Tex Award, 1986; Nat Honor Soc Res Award, 1986; Rector's Medal, Poland, 1987; Sigma Xi Res Award, 1989; Marie Curie Medal, 1995. **Professional Experience:** PROF CHEM, UNIV HOUSTON, as of 2005; vis prof, Univ Florence, Italy, 1987, 1990; Hokkaido Univ, Japan, 1987; chmn, Southwest Catalysis Soc, 1986-1988; dir, Southwest Catalysis Soc, 1982-1984, 1996-1998; chmn, Argonne Nat Lab, 1982; CULLEN PROF CHEM, UNIV HOUSTON, 1980-; Chem Div Rev Comt, Argonne Nat Lab, 1980-1986; Armed Forces Tech Univ, Munich, 1979; chmn, Brookhaven Nat Lab, 1978; Univ Paris, 1977; vis scientist, Japan Soc Prom Sci, 1976; Univ Nagoya, Japan, 1976; chmn, Gordon Conf Radiation Chem, 1975; vis comt chem, Brookhaven Nat Lab, 1974-1978; exchange fel USSR, Nat Acad Sci, 1974, 1975, 1977; vis prof, Univ Utah, 1971; Guggenheim fel, 1970-1971; vis scientist, Danish Atomic Energy Lab, 1970; prof chem, Wayne State Univ, beginning 1969; Exchange fel, Czech, 1969; from asst prof to assoc prof, Univ Kans, 1965-1969; instr, Univ Chicago, 1963-1965; vis res assoc chem, Univ Newcastle, 1963. **Memberships:** Fel AAAS; Am Chem Soc; fel Am Phys Soc; Int Soc Magnetic Resonance; fel Royal Soc Chem; Int Electron Paramagnetic Resonance Soc. **Research Statement & Publications:** Electron magnetic resonance and relaxation; electron spin echo spectrometry; photoredox reactions in constrained media; electron localization and solvation; radiation damage in materials; synthesis and characterization of metal species in microporous oxide materials. **Mailing Address:** Dept Chem, Univ Houston, Houston, TX 77204. **Fax:** 713-743-2709. **E-Mail:** kevan@uh.edu

KEVAN, PETER GRAHAM, ENTOMOLOGY, BOTANY ECOLOGY EVOLUTION. **Personal Data:** b Edinburgh, Scotland, June 17, 1944; Canadian citizen; m 1984, Sherrene; c Colin & Kayte. **Education:** McGill Univ, BSc (hons Zool), 1965; Univ Alta, PhD (entom), 1970. **Honors & Awards:** Ent Soc Canada Gold Medal 2005 Synergy Award (NSERC Canada) 2001 Alum Pride Award (U Alberta) 2003. **Professional Experience:** Vpres, Enviroquest Ltd, as of 1998; PROF ENVIRON BIOL, UNIV GUELPH, CAN, 1991-; mem bd dirs, Entom Soc Can, 1990-; mem bd dirs & ed, Entom Soc Ont, 1986-; prin investr, Nat Sci & Eng Res Coun Grants, Univ Guelph, 1983-; Consult, Palm Oil Res Inst Malaysia, 1983-; Consult, Can Int Develop Agency, 1983-; Can Int Develop Res Ctr, 1983- & Food & Agr Orgn, Rome, 1983-1984 & 1989-1990; US Nat Acad Sci 2005-6; various others; prin investr NSF grants, Colo Springs, 1976-1982; grad fac asst prof biol & assoc, Inst Arctic & Alpine Res, Boulder, 1975-1983; asst prof biol, Univ Colo, Colo Springs, 1975-1982; proj mgr ecol, Mem Univ Nfld, Can, 1972-1975; fel, Plant Res Inst, Can Agr, Ottawa, Can, 1971-1972; contract biologist, Can Wildlife Serv, Inuvik, NT, Can, 1970-1971; Consult, Can Wildlife Serv, 1970-1971; Nat coordr, Int Biol Prog, Univ Alta, Can, 1969-1970; ed, Can Entomologist. **Memberships:** Brit Ecol Soc; Bot Soc Am; Entom Soc Can; Sigma Xi; fel Royal Entom Soc London. **Research Statement & Publications:** Botanical and entomological research in co-evolutionary and conservation ecology; pollination biology; arctic and alpine ecology; apiculture and agriculture in developing countries; sustainable and ecological agriculture and development. **Mailing Address:** Dept Environ Biol, Univ Guelph, Guelph, ON N1G 2W1, Can. **Fax:** 519-837-0442. **E-Mail:** pkevan@uoguelph.ca

KEVANE, CLEMENT JOSEPH, physics; deceased, see previous edition for last biography

KEVERN, NILES RUSSELL, AQUATIC ECOLOGY, FISHERIES SCIENCE. **Personal Data:** b Elizabeth, Ill, May 15, 1931; m 1955, c 3. **Education:** Univ Mont, BS, 1958; Mich State Univ, MS, 1961, PhD (limnol), 1963. **Professional Experience:** ASSOC DIR, SEA GRANT PROG, 1978-; PROF EMER FISHERIES & WILDLIFE, MICH STATE UNIV, 1969-; chmn dept, Mich State Univ, 1969-1992; Asst dir, Inst Water Res, Mich State Univ, 1967-1969; from asst prof to assoc prof, Mich State Univ, 1966-1969; Limnologist, Oak Ridge Nat Lab, Union Carbide Corp, 1963-1966. **Memberships:** Am Fisheries Soc; AAAS; Wildlife Soc. **Research Statement & Publications:** Aquatic ecology, particularly bioenergetics and mineral cycling of flowing water ecosystems; fisheries. **Mailing Address:** Dept Fisheries & Wildlife, Mich State Univ Nat Resources Bldg, East Lansing, MI 48824-1222. **Fax:** 517-336-1699.

KEVILL, DENNIS NEIL, PHYSICAL ORGANIC CHEMISTRY. **Personal Data:** b Walton-le-Dale, Eng, May 27, 1935. **Education:** Univ Col London, BS, 1956, PhD (chem), 1960. **Honorary Degrees:** DSc, London Univ, 1982. **Professional Experience:** DISTINGUISHED RES PROF EMER, NORTHERN ILL UNIV, as of 2003; vis prof, Univ Munich, 1990 & Univ Wales, Swansea, 1996; res prof, Northern Ill Univ, beginning 1989; vis prof, Univ Freiburg, 1987; presidential res prof, Northern Ill Univ, 1985-1989; vis prof, Univ Tuebingen, 1983; Nat Acad Sci Exchange Partic, Yugoslavia, 1983; NIH, 1975-1976 & NASA, 1982; hon res fel, Univ Col London, 1975-1976; prof chem, Northern Ill Univ, beginning 1970; grants, NSF, 1967-1971, 1974-1975, 1984-1988; consult, Carus Chem Co, Inc, 1965-1968; from asst prof to assoc prof, Northern Ill Univ, 1963-1970; grants, Petrol Res Fund, 1963-1964 & 1965-1970; res assoc, Univ Nebr, 1960-1963; asst lectr chem, Univ Col London, 1959-1960. **Memberships:** Am Chem Soc; The Chem Soc. **Research Statement & Publications:** Organic reaction mechanisms; nucleophilicity; reaction mechanisms in solvents of low polarity; elimination reactions; electrophilic assistance to nucleophilic substitutions; perchlorate esters; adamantane derivatives; boron-carbon compounds; chemical vapor deposition. **Mailing Address:** Dept Chem, Northern Ill Univ, De Kalb, IL 60115-2862. **Fax:** 815-753-4802. **E-Mail:** dkevill@niu.edu

KEVLES, DANIEL JEROME, HISTORY OF SCIENCE & ITS RELATIONSHIP TO SOCIETY, MODERN AMERICAN HISTORY. **Personal Data:** b Philadelphia, Pa, March 2, 1939; m Bettyann; c Beth & Jonathan. **Education:** Princeton Univ, BA, 1960, PhD (hist), 1964; Oxford Univ, 1961. **Honors & Awards:** Nat Hist Soc Prize, 1979; Watson Davis Prize, 1999; George Sarton Medal, 2002. **Professional Experience:** STANLEY WOODWARD PROF HISTORY, YALE U, 2001-; dir graduate students, Program in History of Science& Medicine, 2002-2005; Chair, of Program, 2005-; prof humanities, J O & Juliette Koepfli, Calif Inst Tech, ending 2001; chmn fac, Calif Inst Technol, 1995-1997; koepfli prof humanities, Calif Inst Technol, 1986-2001; educ adv comt, Guggenheim Found, 1986-1995; fel, Ctr Adv Study Behav Sci, 1986-1987; mem, adv comt sci autobiog, Sloan

Found, 1980-1990; vis prof, Univ Pa, 1979; exec officer humanities, Calif Inst Technol, 1978-1981; vis res fel, Univ Sussex, 1976; from assoc prof to prof hist, Calif Inst Technol, 1964-1986; instr hist, Princeton Univ, 1964. **Memberships:** Hist Sci Soc; Am Hist Asn; Am Acad Arts & Sci; Orgn Am Historians; fel AAAS; Am Philos Soc; Soc Am Historians; Int Acad Hist Sci. **Research Statement & Publications:** Social and political history of modern science, especially physics, eugenics, and genetics in the United States and Britain; environmentalism, scientific fraud and misconduct; intellectual property. **Mailing Address:** Dept Hist, PO Box 208324, New Haven, CT 06520-8324. **E-Mail:** daniel.kevles@yale.edu

KEVORKIAN, ARAM K, LARGE-SCALE SCIENTIFIC COMPUTATIONS, SPARSE MATRIX COMPUTATIONS, GRAPH THEORY. **Personal Data:** b August 27, 1942; American citizen; div, c 4. **Education:** Univ London, BS, 1965, PhD (appl math), 1968. **Honors & Awards:** Meritorious Civilian Service Award, Department of the Navy, 1991. **Professional Experience:** Adj prof, San Diego State Univ, 2005-; chair, DoD High Performance Computing Modernization Program Metacomputing Working Group, 2001-; sr fel, San Diego Supercomputer Ctr, 1991-1995; assoc dir, Cornell Nat Supercomputer Ctr, Cornell Univ, 1988-1989; vis scientist, T J Watson Res Ctr, IBM Corp, Yorktown Heights, NY, 1986-1987; head comput, GA Technologies, 1980-1986; sr mathematician, Royal Dutch Shell Res Lab, Amsterdam, Holland, 1968-1980. **Memberships:** Soc Indust & Appl Math. **Research Statement & Publications:** Large-scale scientific computations with emphasis on combining graph theory and numerical analysis to solve very large, complex, nonlinear/linear systems of equations of type encountered in industry. **Mailing Address:** 730 Rushville St, La Jolla, CA 92037. **E-Mail:** kevork@spawar.navy.mil

KEVORKIAN, JIRAIR, PERTURBATION METHODS, NONLINEAR WAVES. **Personal Data:** b Jerusalem, Israel, May 14, 1933; American citizen; m 1980, Seta. **Education:** Ga Inst Technol, BS, 1955, MS, 1956; Calif Inst Technol, PhD (aeronaut, math), 1961. **Professional Experience:** Fulbright-Hays Award, Coun Int Exchange of Scholars, 1975; PROF APPL MATH, AERONAUT & ASTRONAUT, UNIV WASH, 1971-2002; Emer prof 2002-; Vis prof, Univ Paris, 1971-1972; from asst prof to assoc prof, Aeronaut & Astronaut, Univ Wash, 1964-1971; res fel aeronaut, Calif Inst Technol, 1961-1964; Aerodynamicist, Gen Dynamics/Convair, 1956-1957. **Research Statement & Publications:** Development and application of perturbation techniques to problems in nonlinear systems. **Mailing Address:** Dept Appl Math Univ Wash, Box 352420, Seattle, WA 98195-2420. **Fax:** 206-685-1440. **E-Mail:** kevork@amath.washington.edu

KEW, DAVID, ENDOCRINOLOGY, MOLECULAR BIOLOGY. **Personal Data:** b Mattapan, Mass, May 14, 1954. **Education:** Mass Inst Technol, BS, 1976; Western Univ Mass, PhD (biol), 1984. **Professional Experience:** SR SCIENTIST, GRENPHARMA LLC, WALTHAM, 2003-; scientist molecular biol, Baystate Med Ctr, beginning 1991; researcher, Baystate Med Ctr, 1986-1991; res fel chem, Univ Med Ctr, 1984-1986. **Memberships:** AAAS; Am Soc Biochem & Molecular Biol; NY Acad Sci; Develop Biol Soc. **Research Statement & Publications:** Endocrinology; molecular biology. **Mailing Address:** GrenPharma LLC, Waltham, MA 02453. **E-Mail:** kew@alum.mit.edu

KEY, ANTHONY W, PHYSICS EDUCATION, PARTICLE PHYSICS. **Personal Data:** b Edinburgh, Scotland, March 3, 1939; m 1963, c 2. **Education:** Aberdeen Univ, MA, 1960; Oxford Univ, DPhil(physics), 1964. **Honors & Awards:** Canadian Association of Physicists Medal for Excellence in Teaching (2003). **Professional Experience:** PROF EMERITUS, UNIV TORONTO. PROF PHYSICS 1973-2005. Acting chmn Physics Dept 1992; Chmn Grad Studies, 1986-1992; Chmn Undergrad Studies, 1980-1986. Psychotherapist, pvt practice & faculty Gestalt Institutes of Toronto, Tokyo, Taiwan 1973-. **Memberships:** Can Asn Physicists; Brit Inst Physics. **Research Statement & Publications:** Higher Education; Experimental particle physics. **Mailing Address:** Dept Physics, Univ Toronto, Sir George St, Rm 401, Toronto, ON M5S 1A7, Can. **E-Mail:** key@physics.utoronto.ca

KEY, CHARLES R, PATHOLOGY, CANCER EPIDEMIOLOGY. **Personal Data:** b Oklahoma City, Okla, August 4, 1934; m 1958, c 3. **Education:** Okla State Univ, BS, 1956; Univ Okla, MD, 1959, MS, 1962, PhD (med sci), 1966; Am Bd Path, dipl, 1964. **Honors & Awards:** Div Ann Award, Am Cancer Soc, 1985. **Professional Experience:** PROF ENER PATH, SCH MED, UNIV NMEX, 1983-; assoc path, Sch Med, Univ Nmex, 1973-1983; Med dir, NMex Tumor Registry, 1969-; asst prof, Sch Med, Univ Nmex, 1969-1973; pathologist, Atomic Bomb Casualty Comn, Hiroshima, Japan, 1966-1969; pathologist, Div Air Pollution, USPHS, Ohio, 1964-1966; resident, Med Ctr, Univ Okla, 1960-1964; Intern path, Med Ctr, Univ Okla, 1959-1960. **Memberships:** Col Am Path; Int Acad Path; Am Asn Pathologists; Am Soc Prev Oncol. **Research Statement & Publications:** epidemiological pathology of cancer; tumor registry. **Mailing Address:** Dept Path Univ NMex Sch Med, 915 Stanford Dr NE, Albuquerque, NM 87131-0001.

KEY, JOE LYNN, PLANT PHYSIOLOGY. **Personal Data:** b Troy, Tenn, September 10, 1933; m 1956, c 2. **Education:** Univ Tenn, BS, 1955; Univ Ill, MS, 1957, PhD (plant physiol), 1959. **Professional Experience:** PROF EMER BOT, UNIV GA, as of 2003; vpres res, Agrigenetics Corp, Boulder, Colo, 1984, 1985; dir, Competitive Grants Prog, Sci & Educ Admin, USDA, 1978-1979; res prof bot, Univ GA, beginning 1969; from assoc prof to prof, plant physiol, Purdue Univ, 1962-1969; asst prof, Univ Calif, Davis, 1960-1962; NSF fel, Univ Calif, Davis, 1960; fel biochem, Univ Ill, 1959-1960; asst agron, Univ Ill, 1955-1959. **Research Statement & Publications:** Biochemistry of auxin action; nucleic acid metabolism; developmental regulation in plants; RNA metabolism; control of protein synthesis; stress-regulated RNA and protein synthesis. **Mailing Address:** Dept Bot Univ Ga, A420A Life Scis, Athens, GA 30602. **E-Mail:** jkey@arches.uga.edu

KEYES, DAVID ELLIOT, COMPUTATIONAL SCIENCES & ENGINEERING, PARALLEL COMPUTATION. **Personal Data:** b Brooklyn, NY, December 4, 1956; m 1980, Wendy; c Sarah & Nathan. **Education:** Princeton Univ, BS, 1978; Harvard Univ, MS, 1979, PhD (appl math), 1984. **Honors & Awards:** Gordon Bell Prize, IEEE Comput Soc, 1999. **Professional Experience:** FU FOUND PROF APPL MATH, COLUMBIA UNIV, 2003-; ATG DIR, LAWRENCE LIVERMORE NAT LAB, as of 2003; Richard F Barry prof math, Old Dominion Univ, 1993-2003; Maths & Comput Sci Div, Argonne Nat Lab, Argonne, Ill, 1991; assoc prof mech eng, Yale Univ, beginning 1990; vis scientist, Inst Comput Appl Sci & Engr, NASA Langley Res Ctr, Hampton, Va, 1990, 1993-1994; NSF pres young investr, 1989; asst prof, Yale Univ, 1986-1990; res assoc comput sci, Yale Univ, 1984-1985. **Memberships:** Am Inst Aeronaut & Astronaut; (Chairman, Connectnut Section 1991-1993) Am Soc Mech Engrs; Combustion Inst; Soc Indust & Appl Math; Coun, 2000-present Asn for Computing Machinery (ACM), Math Soc (AMS). **Research Statement & Publications:** Numerical methods for partial differential equations; domain decomposition algorithms; parallel computation; computational modelling of combustion, heat transfer aerodynamics; Radiation Transport, Magnetohydrodynamics, and geophysics-; computer Performance Modelling. **Mailing Address:** Inst Sci Computing Res Lawrence Livermore Nat Lab, Box 808 L-419, Livermore, CA 94551. **Fax:** 925-422-7819. **E-Mail:** dekeyes@llnl.gov

KEYES, JACK LYNN, PHYSIOLOGY. **Personal Data:** b St Johns, Mich, November 15, 1941; m 1968, Connie; c James & Tanya. **Education:** Linfield Col, BA, 1963; Univ Ore Med Sch, PhD (physiol), 1970. **Professional Experience:** DEPT BIOL, LINFIELD COL, as of 2004; PROF BIOL, LINFIELD COL, PORTLAND, 1994-; prof & chmnn sci, Linfield Col, Portland, 1988-1994; assoc prof, Linfield Col, Portland, 1983-1988; from asst prof to assoc prof physiol, Med Sch, Ore Health Sci Univ, 1971-1983; Instr physiol, Med Col, Cornell Univ, 1970-1971. **Memberships:** Am Physiol Soc. **Research Statement & Publications:** Renal physiology; acid-base regulation; venous blood-gas composition. **Mailing Address:** Sci Dept, Linfield Col, Peterson 317, 2255 NW Northrup St, Portland, OR 97210. **E-Mail:** jkeyes@linfield.edu

KEYES, MARION ALVAH, IV, REAL-TIME MISSION CRITICAL SYSTEMS, ARTIFICIAL INTELLIGENCE. **Personal Data:** b Bellingham, Wash, May 11, 1938; m 1962, c 3. **Education:** Stanford Univ, BS, 1960; Univ Ill, MS, 1968; Baldwin Wallace Col, MBA, 1981. **Professional Experience:** SR VPRES TECHNOL, BUS DEVELOP & PLANNING, FISHER-ROSEMOUNT INC, as of 2002; PRES, ROSEMOUNT INC, as of 2002; SR VPRES TECHNOL & DEVELOP, EMERSON ELEC CO, 1993-; officer, Instrument Soc Am, 1992-; bd dirs, Ohio Acad Sci, 1991-; PRES, TRICE ENGRS, 1991-; chmn, DCOM Corp, 1990-1993; pres & chief exec officer, res & develop, Bailey Controls Co, 1989-1990; sr vpres & group exec, McDermott Int Inc, 1985-1989; trustee, Baldwin Wallace Col, 1983-; pres, res & develop, Bailey Controls Co, 1980-1985; vpres eng, res & develop, Bailey Controls Co, 1975-1980; dir & secy, Am Automatic Control Coun, 1972-1980; gen mgr digital systs, Div Taylor Instrument Co, 1970-1975; Mem, Automation Res Coun, NSF, 1970-1973; Dir eng, Control Systs Div, Beloit Corp, 1963-1970; dir, Fact Inc. **Memberships:** Fel Tech Asn Pulp & Paper Indust; fel Inst Elec & Electronics Engrs; fel Instrument Soc Am; Am Inst Chem Engrs; Soc Mfg Engrs; Soc Am Mil Engrs; Am Chem Soc. **Research Statement & Publications:** Computers; process controls; information systems; electronics; process design and development automation; holder of over 50 US patents in these fields and have 17 patents pending. **Mailing Address:** 8 Washington Terr, St Louis, MO 63112. **Fax:** 314-746-9816.

KEYES, PAUL HOLT, LIQUID CRYSTALS, PHASE TRANSITIONS. **Personal Data:** b Hartford, Conn, October 23, 1943; m 1987, Mary; c Robert. **Education:** Rensselaer Polytech Inst, BS, 1965; Univ MD, PhD (physics), 1972. **Professional Experience:** PROF, WAYNE STATE UNIV, 1991-; assoc prof, Wayne State Univ, 1987-1991; from asst prof to assoc prof, Bartol Res Found, Univ Del, 1979-1987; asst prof physics, Univ Mass, Boston, 1975-1979; fel physics, Univ Del, 1972-1975. **Memberships:** Am Phys Soc; Sigma Xi. **Research Statement & Publications:** Critical phenomena; liquid crystals; phase transitions. **Mailing Address:** Dept Physics & Astron, Wayne State Univ, 239 Physics Res Bldg, Detroit, MI 48202. **Fax:** 313-577-3932. **E-Mail:** keyes@physics.wayne.edu

KEYES, PAUL LANDIS, REPRODUCTIVE ENDOCRINOLOGY, PHYSIOLOGY. **Personal Data:** b Thomasville, NC, July 7, 1938; m 1966, Sharon; c Jeffrey L & Christopher A. **Education:** NC State Univ, BS, 1960, MS, 1962; Univ Ill, PhD (animal sci, physiol), 1966. **Professional Experience:** RES SCIENTIST, REPRODUCTIVE SCI PROG, UNIV MICH, as of 2005; dir, Soc Study Reproduction, 1985-1988; mem, Clin Sci Study Sect, NIH, 1985-1989; PROF PHYSIOL UNIV MICH, ANN ARBOR, 1984-; ed, Endocrinol, 1979-1982; assoc prof path & physiol, Univ Mich, Ann Arbor, 1975-1984; from asst prof to assoc prof physiol, Univ Mich, Ann Arbor, 1975-1984; asst prof path, Univ Mich, Ann Arbor, 1972-1975; res asst prof, Dept Obstet & Gynec, Albany Med Col, 1968-1972; res asst prof, Dept Obstet & Gynec, Albany Med Col, 1968-1972; NIH fel, Med Sch, Harvard Univ, 1966-1968. **Memberships:** Endocrine Soc; Soc Study Reproduction; Am Physiol Soc; Soc Study Fertil Soc Study Reprod (Dir, 1995-1998; Treas, 1994-1997, Pres Elect, 2001-2002, Pres, 2002-2003); Clin Sci Study Sect; Reprod Biol Study Sect (Chair, 1998-2000). **Research Statement & Publications:** Endocrine regulation of the ovary; regulation of the corpus luteum by growth factors and cytokines. **Mailing Address:** Univ Mich, Dept Physiol, M7793 Med Sci II, Ann Arbor, MI 48109-0622. **Fax:** 734-936-8813. **E-Mail:** plkey@umich.edu

KEYES, ROBERT W, PHYSICS, APPLICATION OF PHYSICS TO INFORMATION TECHONLOGY. **Personal Data:** b Chicago, Ill, December 2, 1921; m 1966, c 2. **Education:** Univ Chicago, BS, 1942, MS, 1949, PhD (physics), 1953. **Honors & Awards:** WRG Baker Prize, Inst Elec & Electronics Engrs, 1976. **Professional Experience:** Vis prof, Univ Sydney, 1996; EMER RES STAFF MEM, IBM, 1993-; Comt Applications Physics, Am Phys Soc, 76-78 Int Conf Heavy Doping & Metal-Insulator Transition in Semiconductors, 1984; chmn, Comt Ion Implantation, Nat Mat Adv Bd, 1979; assoc ed, Rev Mod Physics, 1976-1995; Corresp, Comments on Solid State Physics, 1970-1983; consult, Physics Surv Comt, Nat Acad Sci, 1970-1972; physicist, IBM, 1960-1993; consult physicist, Res Lab, Westinghouse Elec Corp, 1960; adv physicist, Res Lab, Westinghouse Elec Corp, 1957-1960; res physicist, Res Lab, Westinghouse Elec Corp, 1953-1956; Jr physicist, Argonne Nat Lab, 1946-1950. **Memberships:** Nat Acad Eng; fel Am Phys Soc; fel Inst Elec & Electronics Engrs; AAAS; Sigma Xi. **Research Statement & Publications:** Solid state physics and its applications to electronics. **Mailing Address:** T J Watson Res Ctr, IBM Corp PO Box 218, Yorktown Heights, NY 10598.

KEYES, SUSAN RILEY, BIOCHEMISTRY, CELL BIOLOGY. **Education:** Marymount Col, BS, 1967; Univ Conn Health Ctr, 1980. **Professional Experience:** AT LUCENT TECH INC, as of 2002; ASSOC DIR PROJ MGT, BIOMEASURE, INC, 1994-; dir cell biol, Primary Eval Unit, Biol Dept, 1989-1994; assoc res scientist, Dept Pharmacol, Develop Therapeut Prog, Yale Univ Sch Med, 1983-1989; assoc, Dept Pharmacol, Develop Therapeut Prog, Yale Univ Sch Med, 1982-1983; Fel, Dept Pharmacol, Develop Therapeut Prog, Yale Univ Sch Med, 1980-1982. **Memberships:** Am Asn Cancer Res; AAAS; Am Soc Biochem & Molecular Biol. **Research Statement & Publications:** Cell biology; biochemistry; co-author of numerous scientific publications. **Mailing Address:** Lucent Tech Inc, 600 Mountain Ave, Murray Hill, NJ 07974-0636.

KEYES, THOMAS FRANCIS, THEORETICAL CHEMISTRY. **Personal Data:** b New Haven, Conn, September 21, 1945; m 1968. **Education:** Yale Univ, BS, 1967; Univ Calif, Los Angeles, PhD (chem), 1971. **Professional Experience:** PROF CHEM, BOSTON UNIV, as of 2002; assoc Prof Chem, Yale Univ, beginning 1981; asst prof, Yale Univ, 1974-1981; NSF fel chem, Mass Inst Technol, 1971-1974. **Research Statement & Publications:** Statistical mechanics, emphasizing theory of light scattering, dynamics of fluctuations in fluids and kinetic theory. **Mailing Address:** Dept Chem, Boston Univ, 685 Commonwealth Ave, Boston, MA 02215-1406. **Fax:** 617-353-6466. **E-Mail:** keyes@bu.edu

KEYNES, HARVEY BAYARD, ERGODIC THEORY & DYNAMICAL SYSTEMS, MATHEMATICS EDUCATION. **Personal Data:** b Philadelphia, Pa, December 27, 1940; m 1964, Cheryl; c Davin, Michael & Alana. **Education:** Univ Pa, BA, 1962, MA, 1963; Wesleyan Univ, PhD (math), 1966. **Honors & Awards:** Distinguished Pub Ser Award, Am Math Soc; G Taylor Award, Distinguished Pub Serv Inst Tech; Univ of Minnesota Presidential Award for Outstanding Service. **Professional Experience:** DIR, INST TECH

CTR EDUCAT PROGRAMS, 1996-; assoc dir educ, geom ctr, 1991-1994; dir, Outreach Projs, 1984-1996; prog dir, NSF, 1982-1983; assoc head math, Univ Minn, Minneapolis, 1979-1982; PROF MATH, UNIV MINN, MINNEAPOLIS, 1978-; vis prof math, Univ Witwatersrand, SAfrica, 1977-1996; HEW grant, 1973-1975; from asst prof to assoc prof, Univ Minn, Minneapolis, 1969-1978; vis asst prof, Univ Minn, Minneapolis, 1968-1969; NSF grants, 1967-; Asst prof math, Univ Calif, Santa Barbara, 1966-1968; Trainee math, US Naval Air Develop Ctr, Pa, 1958-1962; proj dir, Math & Educ Reform Network, Minn Math Mobilization. **Memberships:** Nat Coun Teachers Math; Am Math Soc; Math Asn Am. **Research Statement & Publications:** Topological dynamics; dynamical systems; ergodic theory; mathematics education. **Mailing Address:** Dept Math Univ Minn, 127 Vincent Hall, Minneapolis, MN 55455.

KEYOMARSI, KHANDAN, MOLECULAR BIOLOGY. **Education:** Univ Southern Calif, PhD, 1989. **Professional Experience:** ASST PROF, DEPT HEALTH, WADSWORTH CTR, NY, as of 1995. **Mailing Address:** Wadsworth Ctr Labs & Res, PO Box 509, Albany, NY 12201-0509. **Fax:** 518-486-5798. **E-Mail:** Keyomars@wadsworth.org

KEYS, ANCEL (BENJAMIN), physiology, nutrition; deceased, see previous edition for last biography

KEYS, JOHN DAVID, PHYSICS. **Personal Data:** b Toronto, Ont, September 30, 1922; m 1945, c 2. **Education:** McGill Univ, BSc, 1947, MSc, 1948, PhD (nuclear physics), 1951. **Professional Experience:** CONSULT, 1981-; asst dep minister, Sci & Technol Sector, Dept Energy, 1976-1981; vpres, Nat Res Coun Can, 1973-1976; asst vpres, Nat Res Coun Can, 1971-1973; sci adv, Treasury Bd Secretariat, 1970-1971; chief hydrol sci div, Inland Waters Br, 1967-1970; head mineral physics sect, Dept Energy, Mines & Resources, Ont, 1963-1967; sr sci off, Dept Energy, Mines & Resources, Ont, 1958-1967; head dept, Can Serv Col, Royal Roads, 1957-1958; From asst prof to prof physics, Can Serv Col, Royal Roads, 1951-1958. **Memberships:** AAAS; Am Phys Soc; Can Asn Physicists; Royal Astron Soc. **Research Statement & Publications:** Application of radiotracers to industrial problems associated with mining; solid state physics studies applied to minerals and semiconductors. **Mailing Address:** 39 Ridean Terr, Ottawa, ON K1M 2A2, Can.

KEYS, L KEN, MATERIALS SCIENCE ENGINEERING, CHEMISTRY. **Personal Data:** b Cincinnati, Ohio, November 6, 1939; m 1961, Carol; c Kevin J, Gian D & Perryn M. **Education:** Univ Cincinnati, BS, 1961; Pa State Univ, PhD (solid state sci), 1965. **Professional Experience:** PROF & DEPT CHMN, INDUST & MFG SYSTS ENG, LA STATE UNIV, BATON ROUGE, 1989-; assoc prof indust eng, Instrumentation Systs Ctr, Univ Wis-Madison, 1987-1989; dir, Instrumentation Systs Ctr, Univ Wis-Madison, 1984-1987; prog mgr, DBX progs & dir technol, United Technols Lexar Corp, 1981-1984; mgr, Tel Progs, Stromberg-Carlson Corp, 1977-1978; mgr, Advan Electronic Tel Develop, 1977-1978; mgr, Advan Mfg Develop, Northern Telecom Ltd, 1975-1977; mgr microelectronics technol, Bell-Northern Res, 1973-1975; mgr advan microelectronics eng, Magnavox Co, 1969-1973; prin engr, Nuclear Systs Progs Div, Gen Elec Co, 1966-1968; res assoc, solid state sci, Pa State Univ, 1965-1966. **Memberships:** Sr mem Inst Elec & Electronics Engrs; sr mem Soc Mfg Engrs; Sigma Xi; sr mem Inst Indust Engrs; NY Acad Sci; Soc Eng & Mgt Systs. **Research Statement & Publications:** New technology, product development and transfer into production-market place, including follow-up support, life cycle process; management of technology, intelligent, enterprise, virtual enterprise. **Mailing Address:** 5946 Hickory Ridge Blvd, Baton Rouge, LA 70817. **Fax:** 504-388-5990.

KEYS, RICHARD TAYLOR, PHYSICAL CHEMISTRY. **Personal Data:** b Salina, Kans, February 11, 1931. **Education:** Harvard Univ, AB, 1953; Iowa State Col, PhD (chem), 1958. **Professional Experience:** PROF EMER CHEM, CALIF STATE UNIV, LOS ANGELES, as of 2003; vis prof, Univ Southern Calif, 1984-1985; vis prof, Nat Auro Univ Mex, 1975-1976; prof chem, Calif State Univ, Los Angeles, beginning 1972; NIH spec fel, Univ Calif, Riverside, 1966-1967; from asst prof to assoc prof, Calif State Univ, Los Angeles, 1959-1972; res fel, Calif Inst Technol, 1958-1959; asst chem, Iowa State Col, 1953-1958. **Memberships:** Am Chem Soc; Am Phys Soc. **Research Statement & Publications:** Chemistry of free radicals; magnetic resonance. **Mailing Address:** Dept Chem, Calif State Univ, 5151 State Univ Dr, Los Angeles, CA 90032-8202.

KEYSER, DAVID RICHARD, MECHANICAL ENGINEERING, AEROSPACE ENGINEERING. **Personal Data:** b Ft Wayne, Ind, December 5, 1941; m 1992, Eleanor; c Wendy & Orion. **Education:** Swathmore Col, BS, 1963; Univ Pa, MS, 1965; Eurotech Res Univ, PhD, 1991. **Honors & Awards:** Independent Engr Develop Award, USN, 1984; Cert Award Code & Stands, Am Soc Mech Engrs, 1991. **Professional Experience:** AIRCRAFT SUBSYSTS, AIRCRAFT DIV PATUXENT RIVER, MD, 1996-; aerospace engr fluidic flight control, Aircraft Div Patuxent River, MD, 1980-1996; mem, Stand Comt, Measurement Fluid Flow, beginning 1978; secy, Res Comt Fluid Meters, Am Soc Mech Engrs, beginning 1978; sr proj engr fluid dynamics & control systs, Naval Ship Engr Ctr, Philadelphia, 1972-1980; res engr flow & temperature measurement, Naval Ship Engr Ctr, Philadelphia, 1968-1972; Res engr fluid dynamics & flow measurement, Naval Boiler & Turbine Lab, 1965-1968; vpres & chair, BPTC, 1995-1998; chair, Exe Committee, 1995-1998; chair, PTC 19.5 Comt, Flow Measurement, beginning 1980; chair, PTC 2, Definitions& Values, beginning 1994; chair, PTC 55, Aircraft Engines, beginning 2001; lead, Task group on Sustainable Develop, beginning 2000; mem, PTC 25, Pressure Relief Devices, beginning 1992; mem, PTC 19.2, Pressure Measurement, 1985-1990; mem, PTC 1, gen instr, beginning 1995; mem, Coun on Codes& Standards, 1995-; Vice Chair, Board Int stand, beginning 2000; Steering Commitee, Codes& Standards Redesign Team, 1997-1998; Coun on Mem Affairs; Board on Prof Practice& Ethics, beginning 1998; Stand comt Fluid Meters; sys & design assoc ed, ASME Transact, J Dyn Syst, Meas & Cntrl, 1993-1995; exe comm, Fluid Power Sys& technol Div 1994-1997; chair, Fluid Power Control Sys Panel, DS&C, 1981-1987; chmn, Fluid Power Control Systs Panel & vpres, Bd Performance Test Codes, Exec Comt, Fluid Power Syst & Technol Div; mem, Comn A-6D Flight Controls Panel, Soc Automotive Engrs. **Memberships:** Fel Am Soc Mech Engrs; Soc Automotive Engrs. **Research Statement & Publications:** Flight controls and flying qualities; fluidics; advanced actuation systems; unsteady flow measurements; new methods of flow measurement; two US patents; fire sci, aircraft fire suppression sys. **Mailing Address:** 185 Calvert Beach Rd, St Leonard, MD 20685. **Fax:** 301-862-5093. **E-Mail:** dkeyser@pax.ins.com

KEYSER, N(AAMAN) H(ENRY), METALLURGY. **Personal Data:** b Philadelphia, Pa, December 5, 1918; m 1942, c 4. **Education:** Antioch Col, BS, 1941; Ohio State Univ, MS, 1943. **Professional Experience:** CONSULT, 1980-; dir res, Interlake Inc, 1962-1980; asst chief process metall, Battelle Mem Inst, 1948-1962; asst group leader fabrication group, Los Alamos Sci Lab, Univ Calif, 1947-1948; Res engr process metall, Battelle Mem Inst, 1941-1947; master gardener, Coop Exten Serv, Univ Ill; exec consult, Exec Serv Corps Chicago. **Memberships:** Am Soc Metals; Am Foundrymen's Soc (secy 1948-1960); Am Inst Mining Metall & Petrol Engrs; Iron & Steel Soc. **Research Statement & Publications:** Economic studies and new processes for metals and inorganic chemicals using elevated temperatures produced by electric and blast furnaces; making, forming and treating of steel and steel products especially in silicon and silicon alloys. **Mailing Address:** 122 W Walnut, Hinsdale, IL 60521-3350.

KEYSER, PETER D, MEDICAL MICROBIOLOGY. **Personal Data:** b Columbus, Ohio, October 26, 1945; m 1969, c 1. **Education:** Ohio State Univ, BS, 1968, MS, 1970, PhD (microbiol), 1972. **Professional Experience:** PVT PRACT, 1991-; asst prof microbiol & immunol, Tex Col Osteop Med, 1981-1991; adj prof biol sci, Tex Col Osteop Med, 1975-1991; asst prof microbiol, NTex State Univ Health Sci Ctr, 1973-1981; res fel microbiol, Univ Ky & Fla State Univ, 1972-1973. **Memberships:** Sigma Xi; Am Soc Microbiol. **Research Statement & Publications:** Role of lipases in pathogenicity of gram negative organisms, particularly those species isolated from burn wound sepsis. **Mailing Address:** Chesterfield Family Med, 500 W Blvd, Chesterfield, SC 29709. **Fax:** 803-623-2843.

KEYT, DONALD E, mechanical engineering; deceased, see previous edition for last biography

KEYWORTH, GEORGE A, II, EXPERIMENTAL NUCLEAR PHYSICS. **Personal Data:** b Boston, Mass, November 30, 1939; m 1962, c 2. **Education:** Yale Univ, BS, 1963; Duke Univ, PhD (physics), 1968. **Professional Experience:** CHMN & SR FEL, PROGRESS & FREEDOM FOUND, 1995-; DIR TECHNOL & COMPUT PERIPHERALS, HEWLETT PACKARD CO, PALO ALTO, 1986-; CHMN, KEYWORTH CO, 1986-; sci adv to pres & dir, White House Off Sci & Technol Policy 1981-1986; laser fusion div leader, Los Alamos Sci Lab, 1980-1981; alt physics div leader & physics div leader, Los Alamos Sci Lab, 1978-1981; group leader, Los Alamos Sci Lab, 1974-1978; staff mem, Los Alamos Sci Lab, 1968-1974; res assoc, Duke Univ, 1968; hon prof, Fudan Univ Shanghai. **Memberships:** AAAS; Am Phys Soc; Sigma Xi. **Research Statement & Publications:** Nuclear structure problems; isobaric analogue states; polarization experiments; fission physics; neutron physics; fusion physics; science policy. **Mailing Address:** Hewlett-Packard Co, 3000 Hanover St, Palo Alto, CA 94304-1181. **Fax:** 650-857-3962.

KEYZER, HENDRIK, PHYSICAL CHEMISTRY, SOLID STATE CHEMISTRY. **Personal Data:** b Djakarta, Indonesia, December 7, 1931; m 1954, c 7. **Education:** Univ NSW, BS, 1963, PhD (chem), 1966. **Honors & Awards:** NASA Award, 1971. **Professional Experience:** PROF EMER CHEM, CALIF STATE UNIV, LOS ANGELES, as of 2006; Dept Educ, training grants, 1981-1986; prof chem, Calif State Univ, Los Angeles, beginning 1979; Health & Human Welfare, res grant, 1976-1980; reader, Victoria Univ, Wellington, 1972-1973; consult, Jet Propulsion Lab, beginning 1968; NIMH res grant, 1968-1969 & 1971-1972; from asst prof to assoc prof, Calif State Univ, Los Angeles, 1967-1979; res grant, Calif State Univ, Los Angeles, 1967-1968; univ fel & NIH fel, Calif State Univ, Los Angeles, 1967; lectr, Sydney Tech Col, 1964-1966; res chemist, Mus Appl Arts & Sci, 1962-1963. **Memberships:** Am Chem Soc. **Research Statement & Publications:** Physical-organic chemistry of natural compounds and compounds of biological importance; psychotropic drugs; polymer chemistry; electrochemistry; micro-analysis; natural products. **Mailing Address:** Dept Chem, Calif State Univ, 5151 State Univ Dr, Los Angeles, CA 90032-8000.

KEZDY, FERENC J, BIOCHEMISTRY. **Personal Data:** b Budapest, Hungary, July 28, 1929; American citizen; m 1958, Marie T Colas; c John F, Pierre G & Andre E. **Education:** Univ Louvain, DrSci(phys org chem), 1957. **Honors & Awards:** Stas-Spring Prize, Belg Royal Acad Sci, 1958; Woutes Prize, Chem Soc Belg, 1960. **Professional Experience:** DISTINGUISHED SCIENTIST, UPJOHN CO, 1988-1996; from asst prof to prof biochem, Univ Chicago, 1966-1988; assoc biochem, Northwestern Univ, 1961-1965; Asst phys & org chem, Univ Louvain, 1957-1961. **Memberships:** Am Chem Soc; Sigma Xi; Emeritus member for both. **Research Statement & Publications:** Physical organic chemistry; surface biochemistry; enzymology; protein chemistry. **Mailing Address:** 3805 Robin Lane, Kalamazoo, MI 49008-3148. **E-Mail:** fj.mt.kezdy@att.net

KEZIOS, STOTHE PETER, thermodynamics; deceased, see previous edition for last biography

KEZLAN, THOMAS PHILLIP, MATHEMATICS. **Personal Data:** b Omaha, Nebr, August 6, 1935. **Education:** Univ Omaha, 1957; Univ Kans, MA, 1959, PhD (math), 1964. **Professional Experience:** PROF MATH, UNIV MO, KANSAS CITY, as of 2004; assoc prof math, Univ Mo, Kansas City, beginning 1968; asst prof, Univ Tex, Austin, 1964-1968; Asst prof math, Univ Mo, Kansas City, 1963-1964. **Memberships:** Math Asn Am; Am Math Soc. **Research Statement & Publications:** Theory of rings. **Mailing Address:** Dept Math, Univ Mo, Kansas City, MO 64110-2499.

KHABBAZ, SAMIR ANTON, MATHEMATICS. **Personal Data:** b Tel Aviv, Palestine, March 31, 1932; American citizen; m 1959, c 3. **Education:** Bethel Col, BA, 1954; Univ Kans, MA, 1956, PhD, 1960. **Professional Experience:** PROF MATH, LEHIGH UNIV, 1968-; assoc prof, Lehigh Univ, 1964-1968; univ res fel, Yale Univ, 1963-1964; Off Naval Res res fel, Yale Univ, 1962-1963; asst prof, Lehigh Univ, 1960-1962; instr math, Univ Mass, 1960. **Memberships:** Am Math Soc. **Research Statement & Publications:** Algebra and topology. **Mailing Address:** Dept Math, Lehigh Univ, Bethlehem, PA 18015. **E-Mail:** sak2@lehigh.edu

KHACHADURIAN, AVEDIS K, MEDICINE ENDOCRINOLOGY METABOLISM, NUTRTION. **Personal Data:** b Aleppo, Syria, January 6, 1926; m 1961, Hadidian; c Cynthia & Linda. **Education:** Am Univ Beirut, BA, 1949, MD, 1953. **Professional Experience:** PROF MED, UNIV MED & DENT NJ-R W JOHNSON MED SCH, 1973-; CHIEF DIV ENDOCRINE, METAB DIS & NUTRIT, 1973-; prof, Northwestern Univ, Chicago, 1971-1973; dir, Clin Res Ctr, Children's Mem Hosp, 1971-1973; lectr pediat, Northwestern Univ, Chicago, 1965-1966; from asst prof to prof biochem & internal med, Sch Med, 1959-1971; Res fel, Harvard Med Sch & Joslin Clin, Mass, 1957-1959; fel biochem, Am Univ Beirut, 1956-1957; Resident internal med, Am Univ Beirut, 1953-1956. **Memberships:** Am Diabetes Asn; Endocrine Soc; Am Fedn Clin Res; Am Heart Asn; NY Acad Sci; Am Inst Nutrit. **Research Statement & Publications:** Clinical and biochemical aspects of familial hypercholesterolemia; effect of excercise on metabolic parameters in diabetes mellitus. **Mailing Address:** Dept Med Univ Med & Dent NJ, R W Johnson Med Sch C N 19, New Brunswick, NJ 08903. **Fax:** 732-235-7096.

KHACHATOURIANS, GEORGE G, TOXICOLOGY, BIOTECHNOLOGY. **Personal Data:** b 1940; m 1974, c 1. **Education:** Calif State Univ, BA, 1966, MA, 1969; Univ BC, PhD (Microbiol), 1971. **Professional Experience:** Vis prof, Univ BC, 1992; dir, Biotechnology, 1984-1986; DIR, BIOINSECTICIDE RES LAB, 1982-; PROF APPL MICROBIOL, UNIV SASK, 1981-; chmn genetics, Univ Sask, 1980-1983; mem, fed task force biotechnology, Govt Can, Ottawa, Ont, 1980-1981; asst prof, Univ Sask, 1974-1981; res assoc, Univ Mass, 1973-1974. **Memberships:** Am Soc Microbiol; Can Soc Microbiol; Int Soc Toxins; Soc Invert Path; AAAS; Am Chem Soc; Asn Integrative Studies; Am Soc Indust Microbiol. **Research Statement & Publications:** Agricultural biotechnologies including microbial insect control system development and testing; microbial release and gene tracking in the environment; environmental toxicology and production of fungal toxins in agricultural products; effects of combination of food toxicants and additives; food biotechnology and transgeric plants; microbiology. **Mailing Address:** Dept Appl Microbiol & Food Sci, Univ Sask, Col Agr Campus Dr, Saskatoon, SK S7N 5A8, Can. **Fax:** 306-966-8898. **E-Mail:** khachatouria@sask.usask.ca

KHACHATURIAN, NARBEY, CIVIL ENGINEERING, STRUCTURAL ENGINEERING. **Personal Data:** b Teheran, Iran, January 12, 1924; American citizen; m 1952, Margaret; c Gregory M, Jon E, Mary D (Thrift) & Steven J. **Education:** Univ Ill, BS, 1947, MS, 1948, PhD (eng), 1952. **Honors & Awards:** Parmer Award, 1986; Halliburton Award, 1988. **Professional Experience:** EMER PROF CIVIL ENG, UNIV ILL, URBANA, 1989-; pres, Struct Engrs Asn Ill, 1989-1990; assoc head, Dept Civil Eng, 1983-1989; chmn, Ill Struct Engr Exam Comt, 1971; NSF sr fel, Univ Calif, Los Angeles, 1963-1964; From instr to prof, Univ Ill, Urbana, 1949-1989. **Memberships:** Hon mem Am Soc Civil Engrs; Am Soc Eng Educ; Am Concrete Inst; Nat Soc Prof Engrs; Sigma Xi; Struct Engrs Asn. **Research Statement & Publications:** Experimental and analytical structural engineering, especially reinforced and prestressed concrete; structural optimization; structural concrete. **Mailing Address:** PO Box 26, Philo, IL 61864-0026. **E-Mail:** nkhachat@uiuc.edu

KHACHATURIAN, ZAVEN SETRAK, NEUROSCIENCE, SCIENCE COMMUNICATION. **Personal Data:** b Alleppo, Syria, April 15, 1937; American citizen; m 1963, c 1. **Education:** Yale Univ, BA, 1961; Case Western Reserve Univ, PhD (neurobiol), 1967. **Honors & Awards:** Dir Award, Nat Inst Health, 1983; Aalgheimer's Asn, 1993. **Professional Experience:** DIR, RONALD & NANCY REAGAN RES INST, 1995-; CONSULT ALZHEIMERS DIS, KR ASSOC INC, 1995-; assoc dir, Neurosci & Neuropsychol of Aging & dir, Off Alzheimer's Dis Res, 1986-1995; prof, Health Serv Admin, 1986; Interim sci dir, Pittsburgh Biotechnol Ctr, 1985-1986; vpres res, Health Sci Univ Pittsburgh Med Ctr, 1985; chief, Nat Inst Aging, NIH, Physiol Aging Br, 1981-1985; spec asst dir, Nat Inst Aging, NIH, Physiol Aging Br, 1980-1981; health policy coordr, Off Secy, Dept Health, Educ & Welfare, 1979-1980; prog dir, Neurosci Aging, Nat Inst Aging, NIH, 1978-1979; grants assoc, Div Res Grants, NIH, 1977-1978; prog dir neurophysiol, Dept Psychiat, 1972-1977; asst prof develop neurobiol, Div Child Psychiat, Med Sch, Univ Pittsburgh, 1969-1972; fel neurophysiol, Col Physicians & Surgeons, Columbia Univ, 1967-1969. **Memberships:** Soc Neuroscience. **Research Statement & Publications:** Alzheimer's disease; neuroscience of aging; neural plasticity; science policy; calcium regulation in agingneurine. **Mailing Address:** 8912 Copenhaver Dr, Potomac, MD 20854.

KHAIR, ABDUL WAHAB, ROCK MECHANICS, ACOUSTICS EMISSION. **Personal Data:** b Kabul, Afghanistan, March 20, 1941; m 1969. **Education:** WVa Univ, BS, 1967, MS, 1968; Pa, State Univ, PhD (miningeng), 1972. **Professional Experience:** PROF MINING ENG, WVA UNIV, 1986-; assoc prof mining eng, Wva Univ, 1981-1986; res assoc rock mech, Pa State Univ, 1979-1981; pres, Ministry Mines & Ind, Afghanistan, 1975-1979; res assoc rock mech, Pa, State Univ, 1972-1975. **Memberships:** Soc Mining Eng; Int Soc Rock Mech; Am Rock Mechanics Assoc; Int Bur Strata Mechanics; WVa Coal Mining Inst; Water Jet Technol Assn; Fullbright Assn; AAAS. **Research Statement & Publications:** Respirable dust generation in underground coal mines, coal bump and gas outburst; subsidence due to underground excavations, monitoring, and prediction; structural stability analysis of mines and design of mine layout and support system; rock mechanics and ground control relation problems, and physical and analytical modeling of geotechnical problems; author of various articles. **Mailing Address:** Dept Mining Eng, WVa Univ, 359B Mineral Resources BLDG, Morgantown, WV 26506-6070. **Fax:** 304-293-5708. **E-Mail:** wakhair@mail.wvu.edu

KHAIRALLAH, PHILIP ASAD, PHYSIOLOGY, PHARMACOLOGY. **Personal Data:** b New York, NY, February 3, 1928; m 1963, c 4. **Education:** Am Univ Beirut, BA, 1947; Columbia Univ, MD, 1951. **Professional Experience:** DIR ANESTHESIA RES, CLEVELAND CLIN FOUND, 1986-; staff res div, Found, 1980-1986; sci dir res div & head dept cardiovasc res, Found, 1970-1980; mem staff res div, Found, 1963-1970; Am Heart Asn estab investr, Found, 1958-1963; Cleveland Clin Found, 1956-1957 & Am Univ Beirut, 1957-1958; Am Heart Asn fel, Duke Univ, 1951-1953; mem, Coun High Blood Pressure Res, Am Heart Asn; adj prof, John Carroll Univ & Cleveland State Univ. **Memberships:** Am Soc Pharmacol & Exp Therapeut; Am Physiol Soc; Am Soc Nephrology; AMA; Int Anesthesia Res Soc. **Research Statement & Publications:** Cardiovascular research in biochemistry, physiology and pharmacology; cardiac and blood vessel contraction; medical ethics; narcotic anesthetics. **Mailing Address:** Cleveland Clin Found, 9500 Euclid Ave, Cleveland, OH 44195-0002.

KHAKOO, MURTADHA A, ELECTRON-ATOM, -MOLECULE SCATTERING, LASER EXCITED ATOMS. **Personal Data:** b Zanzibar, Tanzania, April 29, 1953; British citizen; m 1983, Sherbanu; c Naushad & Sabaha. **Education:** Univ London, BS (Hons), 1975, PhD (physics), 1980. **Honors & Awards:** NASA Award, 1988. **Professional Experience:** PROF PHYSICS, CALIF STATE UNIV, FULLERTON, as of 2006; consult, Jet Propulsion Labs, Pasadena, 1989-; res asst prof physics, Univ Mo, Rolla, 1987-1989; postdoctoral fel, Univ Col London, 1980-1981 & Univ Windsor, Ont, 1984-1987; visiting fel, Jet Propulsion Lab, NASA-Nat Res Coun, 1981-1984; reviewer, J Physics B, J Geophys Res, Phys Rev A & Phys Rev Lett. **Memberships:** Am Phys Soc; Inst Physics; Coun Undergraduate Res. **Research Statement & Publications:** Electron impact studies of fundamental gaseous targets; Low energy electron scattering from atomic and molecular targets-elastic, inelastic and ionization; Electron-photon coincidence studies; Fragmentation of molecules, lifetime studies; Spin polarized electron scattering. **Mailing Address:** Dept Physics, Calif State Univ, Fullerton, CA 92834-9480. **Fax:** 714-449-5810. **E-Mail:** mkhakoo@fullerton.edu

KHALAF, KAMEL T, ZOOLOGY, MEDICAL ENTOMOLOGY. **Personal Data:** b Mosul, Iraq, 1923; American citizen; m 1958, Layla; c Suhad, Ramiz & Samir. **Education:** Univ Baghdad, BS, 1944; Univ Okla, MS, 1950, PhD (zoology), 1952. **Professional Experience:** RETIRED; prof entom, Loyola Univ, La, 1969-1986; NIH res grant, 1965-1968; from asst prof to assoc prof, Loyola Univ, La, 1963-1969; res prof, Iraq Natural Hist Inst, 1962-1963; from asst prof to prof, Univ Baghdad, 1956-1962; instr high teachers col, Univ Baghdad, 1953-1956; acad grant fund, Loyola Univ. **Research Statement & Publications:** Surveys of biting gnats; biology of puss caterpillar and its parasites; animal surveys; micromorphology of Arthropods Integument. **Mailing Address:** 5811 S Claiborne Ave, New Orleans, LA 70125.

KHALAFALLA, SANAA E, PHYSICAL CHEMISTRY, CHEMICAL METALLURGY. **Personal Data:** b Mit Yaish, Egypt, July 1, 1924; American citizen; m 1957, Aida; c Ashraf & Sammy. **Education:** Cairo Univ, BSc, 1944; Univ Minn, Minneapolis, MS, 1949, PhD (phys chem), 1953. **Honors & Awards:** Spec Act of Serv Award, Twin Cities Metall Res Ctr, US Bur Mines, 1966. **Professional Experience:** CHIEF SCIENTIST, US DEPT INTERIOR, 1987-; res supvr, Twin Cities Metall Res Ctr, Bur Mines, 1966-1987; proj leader, US Dept Interior, 1964-1966; Hill Family Found res fel & res assoc, Univ Minn, 1961-1964; Vis prof, Bristol Univ, 1960-1961; from asst prof to assoc prof phys chem, Cairo Univ, 1953-1961; Demonstr chem fac sci, Cairo Univ, 1944-1948. **Memberships:** Am Inst Mining Metall & Petrol Engrs; Am Inst Elec & Electronics Engrs. **Research Statement & Publications:** Process and extractive metallurgy; kinetics and mechanisms of mineral reactions; electrochemistry and polarography; catalytic reactions; magneto chemistry; plasma chemistry; leaching processes; asbestos fibers; mine water and wastes; magnetic fluids; water conservation; minerals and mining. **Mailing Address:** 2551 37th Ave, Minneapolis, MN 55406-1745. **Fax:** 612-721-5542.

KHALED, MOHAMMAD ABU, BIOPHYSICS, PHYSICAL CHEMISTRY & NUTRITIONAL BIOCHEMISTRY. **Personal Data:** b Murshidabad, India, November 1, 1942; American citizen; m 1976. **Education:** Univ Calcutta, BS, 1964; Aligarh Muslim Univ, India, MS, 1966; Univ London, PhD (biophys, chem), 1975. **Professional Experience:** PROF NUTRIT SCI, UNIV ALA, beginning 1999; assoc prof Nutrit Sci, Univ Ala, 1984-1999; asst prof, Univ Ala, 1983-1984; from instr to asst prof biochem, Univ Ala, 1977-1983; fel, Univ Ala, 1975-1977; lectr, Cadet Col, Rajshahi, Bangladesh, 1966-1971; lectr chem, Polytech Inst, Chittagong, Bangladesh, 1964-1965. **Research Statement & Publications:** Spectroscopic approach in determining biomolecular conformations and structure-function relationships; body composition measurements. **Mailing Address:** Dept Nutrit Sci Univ Ala, Univ Sta, Birmingham, AL 35294. **Fax:** 205-934-7049.

KHALIFA, RAMZI A, ACOUSTICS, METAL FABRICATING. **Personal Data:** b Cairo, Egypt, July 20, 1940; American citizen; c 3. **Education:** Cairo Univ, BSME, 1964; NJ Inst Technol, MS, 1974, MS, 1989. **Professional Experience:** DIR CORP MFG ACOUST, INDUST ACOUST CO, 1985-; prog chmn, Precision Metal Stamping Asn, 1981-1985; dir eng electronics, Edson Tool & Mfg Co, 1970-1989; Teacher, Cairo Univ, 1964-1969; Mfg eng mgr, HVAC, Delta Indust Co, 1964-1969. **Research Statement & Publications:** Developed cable enclosures with patented self-locking devices; new metal stamping tooling concepts; universal mount dies; modular correctional security ceiling system; acoustical windows; modular track wall panels and highway barrier panels; five patents. **Mailing Address:** 448 Lincoln Ave, Rutherford, NJ 07070.

KHALIFAH, RAJA GABRIEL, CHEMISTRY, BIOCHEMISTRY. **Personal Data:** b Tripoli, Lebanon, May 5, 1942; American citizen; m 1971, c 2. **Education:** Am Univ Beirut, BS, 1962; Princeton Univ, PhD (phys chem), 1969. **Professional Experience:** MEM STAFF, VET ADMIN MED CTR, 1980-; RES ASSOC PROF, DEPT BIOCHEM, SCH MED, UNIV KANS, 1979-; asst prof chem, Univ Va, 1973-1980; res assoc pharmacol, Sch Med, Stanford Univ, 1970-1973; res assoc biochem, Harvard Univ, 1968-1970. **Memberships:** Am Chem Soc; Am Soc Biol Chemists; Sigma Xi. **Research Statement & Publications:** Biophysical chemistry; kinetics and thermodynamics of protein conformation changes; enzyme kinetics and mechanism; chemical modification of active sites; nuclear magnetic resonance applications to proteins and enzymes. **Mailing Address:** Dept Biochem & Molecular biol, Univ Kans Med Ctr, 3901 Rainbow Blvd, Kansas City, KS 66160-7421. **Fax:** 913-588-7963.

KHALIL, M ASLAM KHAN, ATMOSPHERIC CHEMISTRY & PHYSICS. **Personal Data:** b Jhansi, India, January 7, 1950; American citizen; m 1973, Giti; c Kathayoon & Kaviyaan. **Education:** Univ Minn, BPhys, BA (math) & BA (psychol), 1970; Va Polytech Inst & State Univ, MS, 1972; Univ Tex, Austin, PhD (physics), 1976; Ore Grad Ctr, MS & PhD (environ sci), 1979. **Professional Experience:** PROF PHYSICS, PORTLAND STATE UNIV, 1995-; dir, Global Change Res Ctr, 1990-1995; prof, Dept Environ Sci & Eng, Ore Grad Inst, 1987-1995; prof chem, biol & environ sci, 1984-1987; OWNER, ANDARZ CO, 1981-; prin investr, NSF, NASA, Environ Protection Agency & Dept Energy, beginning 1980; from asst prof to assoc prof, environ sci, 1980-1984; sr res assoc, Inst Atmosphere Sci, Ore Grad Ctr, 1979-1980; res asst, Inst Atmosphere Sci, Ore Grad Ctr, 1977-1979; instr physics, Pac Univ, 1977-1978; teaching asst physics, Univ Tex, Austin, 1972-1976; res scientist asst, Ctr Particle Theory, 1972-1976; grad asst math & physics, Univ Tex, Austin, 1971-1972; teach asst physics, Va Polytech Inst & State Univ, 1970-1971. **Memberships:** Am Phys Soc; Am Chem Soc; Am Geophys Union; Air & Waste Mgt Asn. **Research Statement & Publications:** Elementary particles with spin (theoretical physics); author or coauthor of 150 publications; atmospheric physics and chemistry; models for global dispersion of trace gases; effects of man-made trace gases; long-distance transport of pollution; receptor models for urban pollution; mathematical and statistical techniques in environmental sciences; biogeochemical cycles; climate models. **Mailing Address:** Dept Physics, Portland State Univ, Rm SBII 410, PO Box 751, Portland, OR 97207-0751. **Fax:** 503-725-8550. **E-Mail:** aslam@global.phy.pdx.edu

KHALIL, MICHEL, ORGANOHALOGENATED COMPOUNDS. **Personal Data:** b Alexandria, Egypt, June 30, 1935; Canadian citizen; m 1967, c 3. **Education:** Univ Alexandria, Egypt, BSc, 1957, MSc, 1964; Univ Laval, Can, PhD (chem), 1970. **Professional Experience:** PROF CHEM, UNIV QUE, RIMOUSKI, 1970-; provincial, Dept Transports, 1984-1985 & PCB studies, Hydro-Que, 1984-1986; consult, Provincial Dept Environ, 1982; vis prof chem oceanog, Univ Marie Curie, Paris, 1974 & Univ Miami, 1977-1978; chemist, El-Nasr Spinning, Egypt, 1957-1965 & Dionne Spinning, Can, 1965-1967. **Memberships:** Am Chem Soc; Can Meterol & Oceanog Soc. **Research Statement & Publications:** Bioconcentration and contamination studies in marine and estuarine ecosystems regarding halogenated and polyaromatic hydrocarbons. **Mailing Address:** UQAR, 300 Ave Ursulines, Rimouski, PQ G5L 3A1, Can.

KHALIL, MOHAMED THANAA, BIOPHYSICS, MATHEMATICS. **Personal Data:** b Al-Kosair, Egypt, February 8, 1933; m 1960, c 2. **Education:** Cairo Univ, BSc, 1953; Univ Pittsburgh, BS, 1974, PhD (biophys), 1966; Univ Alexandria, MSc, 1961. **Professional Experience:** PROF NATURAL SCI & ENG TECHNOL, POINT PARK COL, 1974-; dean int students, Point Park Col, 1974-1977; from asst prof to prof phys sci, Point Park Col, 1969-1974; res prof biophys & microbiol, Univ Pittsburgh, 1966-1971; res assoc biophys, Univ Pittsburgh, 1961-1966; Instr & res asst physics, Univ Alexandria, 1953-1961. **Memberships:** AAAS; Biophys Soc; NY Acad Sci; Am Chem Soc; Am Inst Physics. **Research Statement & Publications:** Effect of laser beam on the system of polymerization of virus protein; thermodynamics of the reconstitution of virus particles in deuterium; structure and function of tobacco mosaic virus interferon and plant viruses. **Mailing Address:** Dept Natural Sci Eng Tech, Point Park Col, 201 Wood St Rm 404 Acad Hall, Pittsburgh, PA 15222.

KHALIL, SHOUKRY KHALIL WAHBA, PHARMACOGNOSY. **Personal Data:** b Cairo, Egypt, December 7, 1930; American citizen; m 1964. **Education:** Cairo Univ, BPharm, 1953, MPharm, 1956, PhD (pharmacog), 1960. **Professional Experience:** PROF EMER PHARMACEUT SCI, N DAK STATE UNIV, 1994-; prof pharmacog, N Dak State Univ, 1975-1994; from asst prof to assoc prof, N Dak State Univ, 1968-1975; Egyptian govt fel, Univ Mich, Ann Arbor, 1962-1963; from instr to assoc prof pharmacog, Cairo Univ, 1954-1968. **Memberships:** Am Pharmaceut Asn; Am Soc Pharmacog; Soc Cosmetic Chemists;

Sigma Xi. **Research Statement & Publications:** Plant chemistry; analysis of medicinal plants; pharmacokinetic. **Mailing Address:** Col Pharm, NDak State Univ, PO Box 5454, Fargo, ND 58105-9986.

KHALIL, TAREK M, ERGONOMICS. **Education:** Cairo Univ, BS, 1964; Tex Tech Univ, MSIE, 1968, PhD, 1969. **Honors & Awards:** Phil Carol Awd, Inst Indust Engrs, 1990. **Professional Experience:** PROF, Univ Miami, as of 2006. **Memberships:** Int Asn Mgt Technol. **Mailing Address:** Univ Miami, PO Box 248294 McArthur Eng Bldg, Coral Gables, FL 33124. **Fax:** 305-284-4040. **E-Mail:** tkhalil@miami.edu

KHALIMSKY, EFIM D, GENERAL TOPOLOGY, GENERALIZED HOMOLOGY & HOMOTOPY THEORY. **Personal Data:** b Odessa, USSR, June 23, 1938; American citizen; m 1962, Elena Merems; c Olga. **Education:** Pedagogical Inst, Odessa, MS, 1960; Pedagogical Inst, Moscow, USSR, PhD (math), 1969. **Professional Experience:** PROF MATH, CENT STATE UNIV, 1989-; assoc prof comput sci, Col Staten Island, City Univ NY, 1985-1989; assoc prof math & comput sci, Manhattan Col, Riverdale, NY, 1980-1985; assoc prof math, City Univ NY, 1979-1980; sr res scientist appl math & OS, Econ Inst, Acad Sci, Odessa, USSR, 1973-1977; sr res scientist, Opers Res Math Econ, Food Indust, Res & Prod Inst, 1972-1973; assoc prof math, Pedagogical Inst, Magnitogorsk, USSR, 1969-1972; Postdoctoral studies, Pedagogical Inst, Moscow, USSR, 1969; Teacher math & physics, Miss, Odessa, USSR, 1960-1966; ed-at-large, Marcel Dekker Publ Co; assoc ed, J Appl Math & Stochastic Anal. **Memberships:** Am Math Soc; Soc Indust & Appl Math; Asn Comput Mach; Inst Elec & Electronics Engrs Systs Man & Cybernetics Soc. **Research Statement & Publications:** Defined and investigated properties of ordered topological spaces and have used them in developing the generalized homotopy and homology groups, digital topology, topological cell complexes and used those theories in cmputer graphics, systems analysis and design. **Mailing Address:** 1260 Brentwood Dr, Dayton, OH 45406.

KHALONA, RAMON ANTONIO, TELECOMMUNICATION SYSTEMS ENGINEERING, DIGITAL TRANSMISSION SYSTEMS. **Personal Data:** b Managua, Nicaragua, September 14, 1961. **Education:** Ill Inst Technol, BS, 1982, MS, 1984, PhD (elec eng), 1990. **Professional Experience:** ASST PROF LECTR, GEORGE Wash UNIV, 1991-; mem tech staff, Com Sat Lab, 1990-; instr elec eng, Ill Inst Technol, 1987-1990. **Memberships:** Inst Elec & Electronics Engrs Commun Soc; Inst Elec & Electronics Engrs Info Theory Soc. **Research Statement & Publications:** Digital transmission systems; modulation and coding techniques. **Mailing Address:** 2585 Jefferson St, Carlsbad, CA 92008.

KHAMIS, HARRY JOSEPH, LOG-LINEAR MODEL THEORY. **Personal Data:** b San Jose, Calif, December 20, 1951. **Education:** Santa Clara Univ, BS, 1974; Va Tech, MS, 1976, PhD (statist), 1980. **Professional Experience:** PROF, DEPT COMMUNITY HEALTH, SCH MED, WRIGHT STATE UNIV, 1993-; DIR, STATIST CONSULT CTR, WRIGHT STATE UNIV, 1993-; PROF MATH & STATIST, WRIGHT STATE UNIV, 1993-; Wright State Univ, dir, Statist Consult Ctr, 1990-1993; assoc prof, Wright State Univ, 1987-1993; adj instr ethnic dance, Dept Health, Phys Educ & Recreation, consult, 1982-1990. **Memberships:** Am Statist Asn; Biomet Soc; Inst Math Statist. **Research Statement & Publications:** Loglinear model analysis and applications to genetic data; goodness of fit tests. **Mailing Address:** Lifespan Health Res Ctr, Wright State Univ, Boonshoft Sch Med, 3171 Res Blvd, Kettering, OH 45420-4014. **Fax:** 937-775-2081. **E-Mail:** Harry.Khamis@wright.edu

KHAN, ABDUL JAMIL, PEDIATRIC MEDICINE, PEDIATRIC NEPHROLOGY. **Personal Data:** b Allahabad, India, May 5, 1940; m 1968, Farida; c Faiz & Faiza. **Education:** Univ Allahabad, BSc, 1957; Univ Lucknow, MB & BS, 1962; Agra Univ, DCH, 1964; Panjab Univ, India, MD, 1967; Am Bd Pediat, cert, 1973, cert pediat nephrol, 1985. **Professional Experience:** Clin prof, Health Sci Ctr, 1994-; CHMN & PROG DIR, MEHARRY MED COL, BROOKLYN, 1992-; ASSOC DIR, DEPT PEDIAT, INTER FAITH MED CTR, BROOKLYN, 1990-; prof pediat, Meharry Med Col, 1987-1992; assoc prof, State Univ NY Downstate Med Ctr, 1978-1994; chief Div Pediat Nephrol, Meharry Med Col, Brooklyn, 1973-1987; From instr to asst prof clin pediat, State Univ NY Downstate Med Ctr, 1973-1978; fel, Meharry Med Col, Brooklyn, 1971-1973; resident, Kings Co, State Univ Hosp, Brooklyn, 1969-1970; registr pediat, Med Col, Aligarh Muslim Univ, India, 1968-1969; teaching fel pediat, Inst Post-Grad Med, Panjab Univ, India, 1966-1967; physician med & pediat, Northern Railway Hosp, India, 1964-1965; intern, King George Med Col, Univ Lucknow, 1962-1963. **Memberships:** Am Fedn Clin Res; Soc Pediat Res; Am Soc Pediat Nephrol; Asn PedProg Dirs; fel Am Acad Pediat. **Research Statement & Publications:** White blood cell functions including Chemotaxis; studies on efficacy and pharmacokinetics of newer antibiotics; renal diseases in infants and children; medical education. **Mailing Address:** Dept Pediat, Interfaith Med Ctr, 1545 Atlantic Ave, Glen Head, CT 11545-3303. **Fax:** 718-604-6630.

KHAN, ABDUL WAHEED, BIOCHEMISTRY, MICROBIOLOGY. **Personal Data:** b Lahore, West Pakistan, April 16, 1928; Canadian citizen; m 1960, c 2. **Education:** Univ Panjab, Pakistan, MSc, 1952, PhD (biochem), 1956; Manchester Col Sci & Technol, Eng, PhD (microbiol), 1958. **Professional Experience:** RETIRED; sr res officer, Div Biosci, Nat Res Coun Can, 1972-1989; from asst res officer to assoc res officer, Div Biosci, Nat Res Coun Can, 1960-1972; fel biophys, Div Biosci, Nat Res Coun Can, 1958-1960; res fel microbiol, Manchester Col Sci & Technol, Eng, 1955-1958; lectr org chem, Univ Panjab, Pakistan, 1954-1955; res fel biochem, Univ Panjab, Pakistan, 1952-1954. **Memberships:** Inst Food Technologists; Can Biochem Soc; Can Soc Microbiol; fel Royal Soc Chem. **Research Statement & Publications:** Conversion of biomass to fuels and chemical feed stock; anaerobic degradation of cellulose; methanogensis; meat biochemistry; effect of freezing and storage on muscle proteins; biosynthesis of cellulose; studies in bacterial cell wall components; microbiological synthesis of fat from carbohydrates; nutritive values of foods and dietary standards. **Mailing Address:** 2155 Tawney Rd, Ottawa, ON K1G 1C2, Can.

KHAN, ADAM, MICRONUTRIENTS, SORPTION OF ORGANIC POLLUTANTS. **Personal Data:** b Harrori, Pakistan, January 27, 1946; American citizen; c Isaac A & David A. **Education:** Peshawar Univ, Pakistan, BS, 1967; Am Univ Beirut, MS, 1972; Colo State Univ, PhD (agron), 1977. **Professional Experience:** CHMN, DEPT AGR SCI, DAIRY & AGR BUS, STATE UNIV NY, MORRISVILLE, 1998-; ASSOC PROF AGRON, MORRISVILLE STATE COL, 1995-; prof agron, Mo Western State Col, 1988-1994; asst to assoc prof agron, Mo Western State Col, 1979-988; Postdoctoral soils, Univ Ill, 1977-1979; tech dir, Mey Soil Testing lab. **Memberships:** Am Soc Agron; Soil Sci Soc Am; Crop Sci Soc; Nat Asn Cols & Teachers Agr. **Research Statement & Publications:** Sorption of organic pollutants on soil and sediments; zinc in soil; soil testing; teaching; maximum economic yield. **Mailing Address:** Dept Agr Sci, Morrisville State Col, 104 Marshall Hall, Hamilton, NY 13346. **Fax:** 315-684-6125. **E-Mail:** khana@morrisville.edu

KHAN, AKHTAR SALAMAT, SOLID MECHANICS, MECHANICAL ENGINEERING. **Personal Data:** b Aligarh, India, June 8, 1944; m 1972, c 2. **Education:** Aligarh Univ, India, BS, 1961, BS, 1965; Johns Hopkins Univ, PhD (solid mech), 1972. **Professional Experience:** PROF MECH & NUCLEAR ENG, UNIV MD, BALTIMORE, 1994-; from asst prof to prof aerospace, Mech & Nuclear Eng, Univ Okla, 1978-1994; sr staff engr, Bechtel Power Corp, 1974-1978; staff engr stress anal, Arthur McKee, Cleveland, 1973-1974; from res asst to res assoc mech, Johns Hopkins Univ, 1967-1973; lectr mech eng, Aligarh Univ, India, 1965-1967; ed-in-chief, Int J Plasticity. **Memberships:** Fel Am Soc Mech Engrs; Am Acad Mech; Soc Exp Mech; Soc Natural Philos. **Research Statement & Publications:** Dynamic and quasi-static behavior of metallic solids; finite amplitude wave propagation in solids; use of finite element techniques to study stresses in shell-to-shell intersections; fracture mechanics; rock mechanics. **Mailing Address:** Dept Mech Eng, Univ Md-Baltimore, 1000 Hilltop Circle, Catonsville, MD 21250. **E-Mail:** khan@umbc.edu

KHAN, ALI ATHER, RESEARCH ADMINISTRATION, HEALTH SCIENCES. **Personal Data:** b Dhaka, Bangladesh, January 31, 1948; American citizen; m Sultana Ahmed; c Ahmed M. **Education:** Dhaka Univ, Bangladlesh, BPharm. 1969, MPharm, 1972; Grenoble Univ, DPharm, 1977. **Professional Experience:** PROF PHYS SCI, ELIZABETH CITY STATE UNIV, as of 2004; DIR, SUMMER SCH, ELIZABETH CITY STATE UNIV, 2003-; trainee fel, 1992 & prin investr, beginning 1996; prin investr, Dept Energy, beginning 1993; res fel, Nat Inst Drug Addiction, beginning 1992; extramural assoc, NIH, 1991 & 1996; assoc prof phys sci, Elizabeth City State Univ, beginning 1990; asst prof chem, Elizabeth City State Univ, 1980-1990; pharm asst, Maryview Hosp, Va, 1979-1980; lectr chem, Dhaka Univ, Bangladesh, 1973-1974. **Memberships:** Am Chem Soc; Nat Coun Univ Res Adminrs; Nat Coun Undergrad Res; Soc Res Adminrs. **Research Statement & Publications:** Undergradute research; extraction, purification and identification of natural products. **Mailing Address:** Dept Chem & Physics, Elizabeth City State Univ, 406 Jimmy R Jenkins Sci Ctr, Campus Box 925, Elizabeth City, NC 27909. **Fax:** 252-335-3520. **E-Mail:** aakhan@mail.ecsu.edu

KHAN, AMANULLAH RASHID, CHEMICAL ENGINEERING. **Personal Data:** b Bhavnagar, India, March 1, 1927; American citizen; m 1952, c 2. **Education:** Univ Bombay, BS, 1947; Ill Inst Technol, MS, 1951. **Professional Experience:** PRES, GDC, INC, INST GAS TECHNOL, ILL INST TECHNOL, 1970-; mgr gas opers res, Gdc, Inc, Inst Gas Technol, Ill Inst Technol, 1962-1970; opers engr, Universal Oil Prod Co, 1961-1962; supvr refinery processing, Attock Oil Co, 1954-1961; fel, French Petrol Inst, 1953-1954; res engr, Inst Gas Technol, Ill Inst Technol, 1952-1953; Develop engr, Dry Freeze Corp, 1951-1952. **Memberships:** Am Chem Soc; Am Inst Chem Engrs; Am Gas Asn. **Research Statement & Publications:** Liquefaction, storage and utilization of liquefied natural gas; gas distribution and transmission research; hydrocarbon processing. **Mailing Address:** 249 Westmoreland Dr, Wilmette, IL 60091-3059.

KHAN, ATA M, TRANSPORTATION & TRAFFIC ENGINEERING. **Personal Data:** b Khan, West Pakistan, December 15, 1941; m 1969. **Education:** Am Univ Beirut, BEng, 1963, MEng, 1965; Univ Waterloo, PhD (transp planning), 1970. **Professional Experience:** PROF CIVIL & ENVIRON ENG, CARLETON UNIV, as of 2006; assoc prof eng, Carleton Univ, beginning 1977; spec consult, N D Lea & assocs, 1971; asst prof, Carleton Univ, 1969-1977; Individual supporting mem, Hwy Res Bd, Nat Res Coun-Nat Acad Sci, 1968-; Nat Res Coun Can fel, 1968-1969; teaching asst transp eng, Univ Waterloo, 1967-1969; transp engr, Del Leuw, Cather & Co, Chicago, 1965-1967; engr, Trans Arabian Pipeline Co, 1964; asst civil eng, Am Univ Beirut, 1963-1965. **Memberships:** Am Soc Civil Engrs; Inst Traffic Eng. **Research Statement & Publications:** Development of transport planning methodology for the evaluation of policy and investment alternatives and for the analysis of transport subsidy policy in Canada; published over 20 articles. **Mailing Address:** Dept Civil & Environ Eng, Carlton Univ, 3044 Minto 1125 Colonel Dr, Ottawa, ON K1S 5Z6, Can. **E-Mail:** ata_khan@carleton.ca

KHAN, FAIZ MOHAMMAD, BIOPHYSICS, RADIOLOGICAL PHYSICS. **Personal Data:** b Multan, Pakistan, November 1, 1938; m 1966, c 3. **Education:** Univ Minn, Minneapolis, PhD (biophys), 1969. **Honorary Degrees:** BS, Univ Punjab, Multan, Pakistan, 1957; MS, Univ Punjab, 1959. **Professional Experience:** PROF EMER THERAPEUT RADIOL, UNIV MINN, MINNEAPOLIS, 2001-; prof therapeut radiol, Univ Minn, Minneapolis, 1979-2001; HEAD SECT RADIATION PHYSICS, UNIV MINN, MINNEAPOLIS, 1974-; Consult physicist, Vet Admin Hosp, Minneapolis, 1971-; from asst prof to assoc prof, Univ Minn, Minneapolis, 1969-1979; instr radiol, Univ Minn, Minneapolis, 1968-1969; Health physicist, Radiother Inst, Mayo Hosp, Lahore, Pakistan, 1960-1963. **Memberships:** Am Asn Physicists Med; Sigma Xi. **Research Statement & Publications:** Radiation dosimetry and treatment techniques in radiation therapy; application of computers in radiotherapy; biological effects of radiation. **Mailing Address:** Dept Radiation, Med Sch, Univ Minn, 424 Harvard St SE, Minneapolis, MN 55455-0374. **E-Mail:** khanx001@umn.edu

KHAN, FAZAL R, ANALYTICAL CHEMISTRY, PROTEIN CHEMISTRY. **Personal Data:** b Varanasi, India, October 30, 1949; m Fathun; c Nareena, Abbasia & Asim. **Education:** Aligarh Univ, BS, 1969, MS, 1971, MPh, 1973, PhD (biochem), 1976. **Professional Experience:** VPRES MFG OPERS, HUMAN GENOME SCI, 1999-; dir human genome sci, Hoffmann-La Roche, Inc, 1996-1999; dir, Hoffmann-La Roche, Inc, 1990-1995; res leader, Hoffmann-La Roche, Inc, 1988-1990; res investr, Hoffmann-La Roche, Inc, 1986-1988; sr scientist, Hoffmann-La Roche, Inc, 1984-1986. **Memberships:** Fedn Am Soc Exp Biol. **Research Statement & Publications:** Heading a group of scientists involved in developing a process to produce proteins for clinical trials and market needs. **Mailing Address:** Human Genome Sci Inc, 9410 Key W Ave, Rockville, MD 20850-3338. **Fax:** 301-309-8512.

KHAN, HAMEED A, DNA BINDING AGENTS, HUMAN GENOME, DISCOVERER OF AZQ. **Personal Data:** b Hyerabad, Andhra Pradesh, India, January 3, 1941; American citizen; m 1972, Vijayluxmi. **Education:** Univ London, PhD (org chem), 1969. **Professional Experience:** HEALTH SCIENTIST ADMINR, NAT INST CHILD HEALTH & HUMAN DEVELOP, NIH, 1989-; consumer safety officer, US Food & Drug Admin, Rockville, Md, 1978-1989; sr scientist, Microbiol Assocs, Md, 1976-1977; assoc found scientist, SW Res Found, San Antonio, 1974-1976; vis fel, Nat Cancer Inst, 1971-1974; Univ London fel, Chester Beaty Cancer Res Inst, 1969-1971. **Memberships:** Am Chem Soc; fel Am Inst Chem; NIH-EEO Adv Cont, NIH. **Research Statement & Publications:** Worked on a ten-year project started at the Royal Cancer Hospital, London University, and completed at the National Cancer Institute in the US; made over 200 anti-cancer drugs, forty-five of them are patented. **Mailing Address:** NIH, 11965 Old Columbia Pike, Silver Spring, MD 20904. **E-Mail:** hk22h@nih.gov

KHAN, HYDER M, MEDICINE. **Education:** Universidad Autonoma de Ciudad, Juarez, Mexico. **Professional Experience:** STAFF MEM, HENNEPIN FAC ASSOC, HENNEPIN CARE-NORTH. **Research Statement & Publications:** General pediatrics; asthma; and allergy. **Mailing Address:** Hennipen Fac Assoc, Hennepin Care-North, 914 S Eighth St, Minneapolis, MN 55404.

KHAN, IKHLAS AHMAD, CHEMISTRY. **Education:** Aligarh Muslim Univ, Aligarh, India, BS, 1980, MS 1982; Inst Pharmaceut Biol, Munich, PhD (pharm), 1987. **Professional**

Experience: RES PROF, NAT CTR NAT PROD RES, RES INST PHARMACEUT SCI & PROF PHARMACOG, UNIV MISS, as of 2006. **Mailing Address:** Dept Pharmacog, Univ Miss, 443 Faser Hall, University, MS 38677-1848. **Fax:** 662-915-7989. **E-Mail:** ikhan@olemiss.edu

KHAN, IQBAL M, TEACHING PHYSIOLOGY. **Personal Data:** b Karachi, Pakistan, December 27, 1950; American citizen; m 1980, Shahida; c Sohail, Imran, Nida & Adnan. **Education:** Univ Karachi, BS, 1969, MS, 1970; Univ G^ot♣borg, PhD (physiol), 1980. **Professional Experience:** PROF, DEPT OBSTET & GYNEC, MED COL GA, AUGUSTA, as of 2003; PROF, DEPT CELLULAR BIOL & ANAT, MED COL GA, AUGUSTA, as of 2003; PRES, SURE INST, as of 2001; assoc prof, dept obstet & gynec, Med Col Ga, Augusta, beginning 1990; DIR IVF & ANDROLOGY LAB, DEPT OBSTET & GYNEC, MED COL GA, AUGUSTA, 1990-; res asst prof, Univ Ill, Chicago, 1981-1989; res assoc physiol, Univ Ill, Chicago, 1981-1982; Postdoctoral fel, Ford Found, 1980-1981; Postdoctoral fel physiol, Univ Ill, Urbana, 1980-1981. **Memberships:** Soc Study Reproduction Fertil & Steril; Endocrine Soc. **Research Statement & Publications:** Pituitary-ovarian axis; corpus luteum function; hormonal control of luteal steroidogenesis; in vitro fertilization. **Mailing Address:** Dept Obstet & Gynec, Med Col Ga, 1459 Laney Walker Blvd, Augusta, GA 30907. **E-Mail:** ikhan@mail.mcg.edu

KHAN, ISHRAT MAHMOOD, POLYMER SYNTHESIS & CHARACTERIZATION, ELECTROACTIVE POLYMERS & SMART MATERIALS. **Personal Data:** b Sylhet, Bangladesh, February 24, 1956; m 1990, Farhana; c Irfan. **Education:** Susquehanna Univ, BA, 1979; Univ Fla, PhD (org chem), 1984. **Professional Experience:** PROF CHEM, CLARK ATLANTA UNIV, as of 2003; vis scientist, McGill Univ, 1991-1992; asst prof chem, Clark Atlanta Univ, beginning 1988; fel, Col Forestry, State Univ NY, Syracuse, 1985-1988. **Research Statement & Publications:** Development of new electroactive polymers for sensors, nano-electronics, membranes for biological electron transfer processes; new methodologies for helix-sense selective polymerizations; chiral materials as smart materials. **Mailing Address:** Dept Chem, Clark Atlanta Univ, 223 James P Brawley Dr SW, Atlanta, GA 30314. **Fax:** 404-880-6849. **E-Mail:** ikhan@cau.edu

KHAN, JAMIL AKBER, ORGANOMETALLIC CHEMISTRY. **Personal Data:** b Hyderabad, Pakistan, May 17, 1952; American citizen; m 1981, Susan; c Farooq J & Omar J. **Education:** Univ Sind, Pakistan, BSc, 1971, MSc, 1973; Univ London, Eng, PhD (org chem), 1979; Univ New Haven, MBA, 1985. **Professional Experience:** DIR SALES, ENICHEM AM INC, 1990-; prod mgr, Sales & Mkt Div, 1987-1990; dir technol & mkt int, Ausimont USA, 1986-1987; dir mkt, Ausimont USA, 1985-1986; res scientist, Uniroyal Inc, 1984-1985; res chemist, Uniroyal Inc, 1981-1984; res assoc chem, Duke Univ, 1979-1981; demonstr chem, Univ Col London, Eng, 1976-1979; joint secy, Sind Lectr Asn, 1976-1977; Secy gen, Inst Pub Affairs, Pakistan, 1975-1978; lectr chem, D J Sci Col, Pakistan, 1974-1976; chemist qual control, Eastman Chem Co, 1973-1974; mem, Republican Presidential Task Force, Sen Inner Circle & Health Reforms Task Force; mem, Presidential Task Force & Pub Educ Fund Comt, Am Inst Chemists; mem, Int Org Chem Sci Develop Network, UNESCO, bd educ, Mt Arlington, NJ; guest fac, Opers Enterprize, Am Mgt Asn. **Memberships:** Am Chem Soc; Royal Soc Chem; Sigma Xi; Am Inst Chemists; Chem Mkt Res Asn; Am Mgt Asn; Soc Automotive Eng. **Research Statement & Publications:** Synthesis and development of activators and catalysts, which can be used in polymerization, autoxidation of unsaturated fatty acids; synthesis of antioxidants, which can be used to inhibit the autoxidation of phospholipid biomembranes; Ziegler-Natta catalysis; organometallic chemistry; free radical chemistry polymerization; polymerization kinetics; reaction mechanism; polypeptides; bio compatible polymers; synthetic lubricants; higher performance polymers and their application to high technology industry. **Mailing Address:** Enichem Am Inc, 2000 W Loop St Ste 2010, Houston, TX 77027. **Fax:** 713-940-0733. **E-Mail:** j.khan@enichem-americas.com

KHAN, MAHBUB R, MAGNETIC THIN FILMS, DIGITAL MAGNETIC RECORDING. **Personal Data:** b Dhaka, Bangladesh, September 11, 1949; American citizen; m 1976, Reena; c Madhury, Kamal, Jamal & Monika. **Education:** Dhaka Univ, BSc, 1969, MSc, 1970; Boston Col, PhD (solid state physics), 1979. **Professional Experience:** Appl mats, 2000-; mem of tech Staff SR SCIENTIST, IBM CORP, 1996-2000; mem tech staff, Appl Mat, 1994-1996; mgr, Seagate Magnetics, 1986-1993; sr scientist magnetic rec, Alcoa-Stolie Corp, 1985-1986; sr scientist magnetic rec, Control Data Corp-MPI, 1983-1985; fel, Argonne Nat Lab, 1981-1983; teaching fel, Univ Nebr, Lincoln, 1979-1981; grad asst, Boston Col, 1974-1979; lectr physics, Jahangirnagar Univ, Bangladesh, 1972-1974. **Memberships:** Am Phys Soc; Inst Elec & Electronics Engrs. **Research Statement & Publications:** Preparation, characterization, magnetic properties, anisotropy, surface analysis, electron microscopy of magnetic thin films; longitudinal and vertical high density digital magnetic recording; metallic superlattice; optical and electro-optical properties of layered materials. **Mailing Address:** 3463 Sagewood Lane, San Jose, CA 95132. **Fax:** 408-986-7630. **E-Mail:** mahbubkhan@ieee.org

KHAN, MAHMOOD AHMED, FOOD SCIENCE, HOTEL RESTAURANT & INSTITUTIONAL MANAGEMENT. **Personal Data:** b Hyderabad, India, September 16, 1945; American citizen; m 1975, c Samala, Feras & Nufayl. **Education:** Osmania Univ, BS, 1966; Andhra Pradesh Agr Univ, BS, 1969; La State Univ, MS, 1972, PhD (food sci), 1975. **Honors & Awards:** Donald K Tessler Res Award; Cesar Ritz Award. **Professional Experience:** PROF & DIR, HOSPITALITY & TOURISM MGT, 1998-; dept head, dept hotel & restaurant, VA Polyytech & State Univ, 1992-1998; prof, dept hotel & restaurant, VA Polyytech & state Univ, 1987-1998; asst head, Dept Hotel & Restaurant, VA Polyytech & State Univ, 1987-1992; from asst prof to assoc prof, Univ Ill, Urbana, 1978-1987; asst prof foods & nutrit, Albright Col, 1975-1978; res asst food sci, La State Univ, 1971-1975; vis prof, Catering Res Ctr, Huddersfield Polytech, UK. **Memberships:** Inst Food Technologists; Am Dietetic Asn; Coun Hotel Restaurant & Inst Educ; Nat Restaurant Asn; Am Inst Nutrit; Int Nat Acad Hospitality Res. **Research Statement & Publications:** Food quality in food service systems; concepts of nutrition and obesity; nutritional evaluation of food processing; international food patterns; food habits; food service consultant; food snacking and eating away from home; franchising in hospitality and tourism industry. **Mailing Address:** Dept hospity & Tourism Mgt, Northern VA Ctr, 7054 Haycock Rd, Falls Church, VA 22043. **E-Mail:** mahmood@vt.edu

KHAN, MANZOOR M, IMMUNOPHARMACOLOGY, CELLULAR IMMUNOLOGY. **Personal Data:** b Karachi, Pakistan, July 3, 1953; American citizen; m 1985, Sadia; c Zoya & Taimoor. **Education:** Univ Karachi, BSc & MSc, 1972; Univ Bridgeport, MS, 1975; Univ Ariz, PhD (pharmacol), 1980. **Honors & Awards:** Res award, Health Future Found, 1991 & 1992. **Professional Experience:** PROF PHARMACEUT & PHARMACOL, CRIEGHTON UNIV, as of 2004; assoc prof pharmaceut & Pharmacol, Creighton Univ, beginning 1990; from res assoc to sr res assoc, Stanford Univ, 1983-1990; Am Heart Asn advan res fel, 1983; fel, Stanford Univ, 1982-1983; Arthritis Found res fel, 1981; fel, Univ Colo, 1980-1982. **Memberships:** Am Asn Immunol; Am Soc Pharmacol & Exp Therapeut. **Research Statement & Publications:** Regulation of helper T cell function by endogenous mediators; investigating the effects of histamine, prostaglandins and phosphodiesterase inhibitors on synthesis and secretion of interleukin-4 and interleukin-5; role of cytokines in allergic disease and asthma. **Mailing Address:** Dept Pharmaceut & Pharmacol, Creighton Univ, Omaha, NE 68178. **Fax:** 402-280-2334. **E-Mail:** mmkhan@creighton.edu

KHAN, MASOOD, BIOCHEMISTRY, INTERNAL MEDICINE. **Personal Data:** b Amrobe, India, August 2, 1948. **Education:** Aligalgh Univ, India, BSc, 1968, MSc, 1970, PhD (biochem), 1975. **Professional Experience:** DIR, CHEM DEPT, PHOENIX INT, 1991-; assoc prof med, McGill Univ, 1986-1991; fel chem, McGill Univ, 1979-1984; res fel chem, NIH, 1976-1979. **Memberships:** Am Soc Clin Chem; Am Soc Cell Biol; Biomed Mkt Asn; Am Endocrine Soc. **Mailing Address:** Phoenix Int, 2330 Cohen St, St Laurent, PQ H4R 9Z7, Can.

KHAN, MIZAN RAHMAN, MATHEMATICS. **Education:** London Sch Econs, BS, MS; Univ Mass, PhD. **Professional Experience:** ASSOC PROF MATH, EASTERN CONN STATE UNIV, as of 2005. **Memberships:** Am Math Soc. **Mailing Address:** Dept Math, Eastern Conn State Univ, WH 333, Willimantic, CT 06226. **Fax:** 203-345-3977. **E-Mail:** khanm@easternct.edu

KHAN, MOHAMED SHAHEED, PLANT PATHOLOGY, AGRICULTURE. **Personal Data:** b Bloomfield, Guyana, December 29, 1933; American citizen; m 1958, c 3. **Education:** Eastern Caribbean Inst, Trinidad, dipl, 1957; Iowa State Univ, BS, 1964, MS, 1966, PhD (plant path & hort), 1968. **Professional Experience:** ACTG STATE PROG LEADER EXTEN SPECIALIST, UNIV DC, as of 2005; pest mgt specialist, Soma Lia, 1979-1980; consult res agronomist, JWK Int Corp, Govt Chad, Africa, 1978-1979; consult trop agr, Indonesia USAID, 1977; coordr training, Environ Protection Agency grant, beginning 1974; teacher pesticide applicators, DC Coop Exten Serv, Wash, DC, beginning 1973; teacher hort & landscaping, Spingarn-Phelp's Voc Sch, Wash, DC, 1973-1977; exten specialist & pesticide coordr path, Entom Pesticides, Univ DC & USDA, beginning 1972; assoc prof biol & physical sci, Morris Col SC, 1972; plant pathologist res, Ministry Agr Govt Guyana, 1969-1971; res asst, Iowa State Univ, 1963-1968; agr res asst, McGill Univ, 1960-1963; agr exten agent agr educ, Govt Brit Guyana, 1957-1960. **Memberships:** Am Phytopath Soc; Am Hort Soc; Am Entom Soc; Am Chem Soc; Sigma Xi. **Research Statement & Publications:** Mycorrhizal associates of Juglans Nigra with special emphasis on nitrogen and phosphorous uptake; pesticide screening; chemical and biological control of pests; environmental preservation. **Mailing Address:** Coop Exten Serv, Univ DC, Bldg 52 Rm B-17 4200 Conn Ave NW, Washington, DC 20008. **Fax:** 202-274-7130. **E-Mail:** jhazel@esusda.gov

KHAN, MOHAMMAD ASAD, GEODESY, RESEARCH ADMINISTRATION. **Personal Data:** b Pakistan, m 1974, c 1. **Education:** Univ Punjab, W Pakistan, BS, 1957, MS, 1963; Univ Hawaii, PhD (geophys), 1967. **Professional Experience:** PROF EMER GEOPHYS & GEOL, HAWAII INST GEOPHYS, UNIV HAWAII, MANOA, as of 2004; Senator, Nat Econ Coun, 1985-1986; chmn, Hydrocarbon Develop Inst, 1984-1986; chmn, Attock Oil Refinery, 1984-1986; minister, Petrol & Natural Resources, Govt Pakistan, 1983-1986; cabinet mem, Nat Econ Coun, 1983-1986; chmn, Environ Coun Exec Comn, 1979-1983 & vchmn, Environ Coun, 1981-1983; mem, Hawaii State Environ Coun, 1979-1983; sr consult, Comput Sci Corp, 1976-1977; prof geophys & geol, Hawaii Inst Geophys, Univ Hawaii, Manoa, beginning 1974; sr scientist, Comput Sci Corp, 1974-1976; adv resource surv, Gov Pakistan, 1974-1976; sr vis scientist, Nat Acad Sci, Goddard Space Flight Ctr, NASA, 1972-1974; from asst prof to assoc prof, Hawaii Inst Geophys, Univ Hawaii, 1967-1974; Lectr geophys, Univ Panjab, WPakistan, 1963-1964. **Memberships:** Am Geophys Union; Am Geol Inst; Pakistan Asn Advan Sci. **Research Statement & Publications:** Geophysics; Satellite altimetry; earth density modelling; geophysical, geodetic and geodynamical applications of satellites; plate tectonics; gravity and isostasy; geophysical exploration; resource surveys; geodesy; geodynamics; core-mantle boundary problems; technology transfer; technical management. **Mailing Address:** Hawaii Inst Geophys & Planetology, Univ Hawaii, Manoa, 2525 Correa Rd, Honolulu, HI 96822. **Fax:** 808-956-3188. **E-Mail:** khan@soest.hawaii.edu

KHAN, MOHAMMAD IQBAL, ENDOCRINOLOGY, REPRODUCTIVE PHYSIOLOGY. **Personal Data:** b Karachi, Pakistan, December 27, 1950; m 1980, c 2. **Education:** Univ Karachi, Pakistan, BS Hons, 1969, MS, 1970; Univ Goteborg, Sweden, PhD, 1980. **Professional Experience:** ASST DEAN ADMIN MED, MED COL GA, as of 2005; PROF, DEPT CELLULAR BIOL & ANAT, MED COL GA, as of 2004; DIR, UNDERGRAD EDUC, SCH MED, MED COL GA, as of 2004; dir Ivf Andrology Labs, Med Col Ga, beginning 1989; assoc prof, Med Col Ga, beginning 1989; res asst & prof endocrinol, Dept Physiol & Biophys, Med Ctr, Univ Ill, Chicago, 1981-1989; fel endocrinol, Dept Animal Sci, Univ Ill, Urbana-Champaign, 1980-1981; fel endocrinol, Dept Physiol, Univ Goteborg, Sweden, 1980; asst lectr, Dept Physiol, Sch Med, Univ Goteborg, Swed, 1976-1979. **Memberships:** Soc Study Reprod; Scand Soc Physiologists; Swed Med Asn; Endocrine Soc; Am Fertil Soc. **Research Statement & Publications:** Mechanism of action of gonadotropins in the maintenance and function of the corpus luteum as well as the role of prostaglandins in the regression of the corpus luteum; endocrinology. **Mailing Address:** Dept Cellular Biol & Anat, Sch Med, Med Col Ga, 1120 15th St, Augusta, GA 30912. **E-Mail:** IKHAN@MCG.EDU

KHAN, MOHAMMAD K, MATHEMATICS. **Education:** Case Western Reserve Univ, PhD (math statist), 1980. **Professional Experience:** PROF, DEPT MATH SCI, KENT STATE UNIV, as of 2006. **Mailing Address:** Dept Math & Comput Sci, Kent State Univ, Kent, OH 44242. **Fax:** 330-672-7824. **E-Mail:** mkkhan@kent.edu

KHAN, MOHAMMED ABDUL QUDDUS, BIOCHEMICAL & ENVIRONMENTAL TOXICOLOGY, INSECTICIDE TOXICOLOGY. **Personal Data:** b India, March 10, 1939; American citizen; m 1974, Anwarun; c Sara, Samreen & Yaseen. **Education:** Univ Karachi, BSc, 1957, MSc, 1959; Univ Western Ont, PhD (zoology), 1964; Univ Auto de Cd Juarez, MD, 1984. **Professional Experience:** Res assoc sr Fulbright Scholar, 1992-1993; Eastern Res Group, 1985; Continental Chemists, 1985; Univ Wageniegen fel, 1982; expert toxicol, UN Develop Prog, Pakistan, 1980-1981; vis chemist, US Environ Protection Agency, Corvallis, 1980; consult, Environ Protection Agency, 1980; consult, NSF, 1977-1978; vis scientist, Nat Inst Environ Health Sci, NIH, 1975-1976; vis sciengtist, NAEHS, 1975-1976; consult, Velsicol Chem Corp, Chicago, 1975; PROF BIOL SCI, UNIV ILL, CHICAGO, 1974-; vis prof, Univ Wis, 1970; assoc prof, Univ Ill, Chicago, 1969-1974; Ore State Univ, 1967-1968; Rutgers Univ, 1968-1969; fel entom, NC State Univ, 1965-1967; ed, J Biochem Toxicol. **Memberships:** AAAS; Environ. Soc Toxicol & Chem; Am Chem Soc; Sigma Xi; Soc Toxicol; Int Soc Study Xenobiotics. **Research Statement & Publications:** Metabolism of insecticides, drugs and lipids; biochemistry and genetics of insecticide resistance; environmental toxicology; metabolism of xenobiotics including pesticides; in vitro detoxication and mechanisms; induction of drug metabolizing enzymes; effects on steriodogenesis. **Mailing Address:** Dept Bio-Sci, Univ Ill, 845 W Taylor St, Chicago, IL 60607-7060. **Fax:** 312-413-2435. **E-Mail:** maqkhen@uic.edu

KHAN, MOHAMMED NASRULLAH, PHYSIOLOGY, VETERINARY SCIENCE. **Personal Data:** b Hyderabad, India, October 11, 1933; c 2. **Education:** Osmania Univ, India, BVSc, 1955; La State Univ, Baton Rouge, MS, 1963, PhD (environ physiol), 1970. **Professional Experience:** PROF ANAT & PHYSIOL, RAVENSWOOD HOSP, RADIOL SCH, 1990-; prof biol, Truman Col, 1987-; assoc prof, Truman Col, 1977-1987; assoc prof anat, physiol, microbiol & chem, Little Co Mary Hosp Sch Nursing, 1975-1983; instr microbiol, Schs Nursing, Michael Reese Hosp & Med Ctr, Chicago, 1973-1974; instr anat, physiol & microbiol, South Chicago Community Hosp Schs Nursing & Radiol, 1972-1977; asst prof biol, City Cols Chicago, Mayfair Col & Southwest Col, 1970-1972; asst lectr reproductive physiol, Tirupati & Hyderabad Vet Cols, India, 1963-1967; res asst, La State Univ, Baton Rouge, 1961-1963, 1967-1970; asst lectr anat, State Vet Sch, Hyderabad, India, 1958-1961; Vet, Govts Hyderabad & Andhra Pradesh, India, 1955-1958; HEH Nizam fel; Ford Found res scholar. **Research Statement & Publications:** Stress. **Mailing Address:** 2904 W Greenleaf Ave, Chicago, IL 60645-2916.

KHAN, MUSHTAQ A, MATHEMATICS. **Education:** Punjab Univ, MS; Quaid-I-Azam Univ, MS; Old Dominion Univ, Phd (Maths). **Professional Experience:** ASSOC PROF, DEPT MATH, NORFOLK STATE UNIV, as of 2006. **Mailing Address:** Dept Math Norfolk State Univ, 700 Park Ave B 182 Brown Mem Hall, Norfolk, VA 23504. **Fax:** 757-823-8427. **E-Mail:** makhan@nsu.edu

KHAN, MUSHTAQ AHMAD, PERINATAL TOXICOLOGY, ENDOCRINOLOGY. **Personal Data:** b Lyallpur, Pakistan, December 12, 1939; American citizen; m 1959, Jamila; c Shahid, Tahira, Zahid & Nasir. **Education:** Univ Punjab, Pakistan, BSc, 1960; Mont State Univ, MS, 1962; Wash State Univ, PhD (vet sci & physiol), 1968. **Professional Experience:** ASSOC PROF, DEPT MATH, NORFOLK STATE UNIV, as of 2006; CHIEF PATHOPHYSIOL SCI IRG, SCIENTIFIC REV ADMIN, NIH, as of 2004; health scientific adminr, Gen Med A 2 Study Sect, Food & Drug Admin, beginning 1988; supvr res physiologist & head, Perinatal Toxicol, Bur Foods, 1981-1988; adj asst prof, Univ RI, 1980-; res physiologist perinatal toxicol, Metab Br, 1980-1981; physiologist food additives, Div Toxicol, Food & Drug Admin, 1978-1980; asst prof path, Med Sch, Univ Md, Baltimore, 1977-1978; asst prof, Med Sch, Univ Md, Baltimore, 1974-1978; prin investr, Sch Med, Univ Md, Baltimore, 1972-1978; res assoc pediat, Med Sch, Univ Md, Baltimore, 1972-1974; asst prof vet physiol, Univ Agr, Pakistan, 1965-1972; chemist steroid biochem, Syntex Res Ctr, Calif, 1964-1965. **Memberships:** Am Physiol Soc; Am Inst Nutrit; Am Col Toxicol; Am Soc Vet Physiologists & Pharmacologists; World Asn Physiol Pharmacol & Biochem. **Research Statement & Publications:** Endocrine and nutritional factors in obesity and atherosclerosis; perinatal toxicology; perinatal nutrition and delayed effects imprinting; cholesterol metabolism; age and sex related changes in metabolic responses. **Mailing Address:** Dept Math, Norfolk State Univ, B 182 Brown Memorial Hall 700 Park Ave, Norfolk, VA 23504. **E-Mail:** makhan@nsu.edu

KHAN, NASIM A, GENE REGULATION, MITOCHONDRIAL GENETICS. **Personal Data:** b Benares, India, June 1, 1938; American citizen; m 1977. **Education:** Univ Dacca, BSc, 1958, MSc, 1960; City Univ NY, PhD (genetics), 1967. **Professional Experience:** PROF EMER BIOL, BROOKLYN COL, CITY UNIV NY, as of 2004; prof genetics, Brooklyn Col, City Univ NY, beginning 1985; from asst prof to assoc prof, Genetics Lab, 1970-1984; instr, Genetics Lab, 1968-1969; lectr gen biol, Brooklyn Col, City Univ NY, 1964-1968; fel, gen biol, Brooklyn Col, City Univ NY, 1962-1964; Lectr bot, Univ Dacca, 1961-1962. **Memberships:** Sigma Xi; Am Soc Microbiol. **Research Statement & Publications:** Construction of yeast strains exhibiting elevated levels of ethanol production using genetic selection procedures and certain recombinant DNA technique; interaction of nuclear and cytoplasmic genes in the utilization of fermentive sugars in yeast; regulation of maltase and alpha-methylglucosidose synthesis in yeast. **Mailing Address:** Dept Biol Brooklyn Col City Univ NY, 2900 Bedford Ave, Brooklyn, NY 11210.

KHAN, PARWAIZ ASHRAF ALI, HIGH ENERGY LASER MATERIALS PROCESSING, SEMI SOLID METALWORKING. **Personal Data:** b Hyderabad, Pakistan, March 4, 1955; m 1988, Ghazala; c Reema P & Bushra P. **Education:** Nat Col Eng & Technol, BE, 1978; Pa State Univ, MS, 1983, PhD (metall-mat sci), 1987. **Professional Experience:** SR ENGR, CONCURRENT TECHNOL CORP, 1992-; engr, Concurrent Technol Corp, 1991-1992; res prof, Mich State Univ, 1990-1991; res assoc laser processing, Mich State Univ, 1987-1991; Lectr, Nat Col Eng & Technol, 1980-1981; metall engr, Resources Develop Corp, 1978-1981; Proj engr, Boomer Engrs & Technocrates Ltd, 1978. **Memberships:** Laser Inst Am; Am Welding Soc; Am Soc Mat; Mining Metals & Mat Soc; Sigma Xi. **Research Statement & Publications:** High energy laser welding, machining, surface treatment and laser fabrication of superconductors; characterization of thixtropic feed alloys and parts made by semi-solid metalworking. **Mailing Address:** C67 Block 4, Gulshan-E-lobal, Karachi, Pakistan.

KHAN, RASUL AZIM, PARASITOLOGY. **Personal Data:** b Port Mourant, Guyana, October 31, 1934; Canadian citizen; m 1966, c 3. **Education:** Univ Toronto, Can, BSA, 1964, MSc, 1966, PhD (parasitol), 1969. **Professional Experience:** PROF EMER BIOL, MEM UNIV NFLD, 1999-; vis prof, Univ Concepcion, Chile, 1999-; Prof biol, Mem Univ Nfld, 1982-1999; assoc prof, Mem Univ Nfld, 1974-1981; Res scientist, Marine Sci Res Lab, 1972-; Asst prof, Mem Univ Nfld, 1969-1974. **Memberships:** Am Soc Parasitilogists; Am Soc Protozoologists; Can Soc Zoologists. **Research Statement & Publications:** Studies on the effects of parasites and pollutants as causative agents of disease in commercial fish in Eastern Canada; long term effects of petroleum on fish. **Mailing Address:** Marine Sci Res Lab, Mem Univ Nfld, St John's, NL A1C 5S7, Can.

KHAN, SEKENDER ALI, PLANT PATHOLOGY. **Personal Data:** b Bogra, Bangladesh, February 1, 1933; m 1963, c 2. **Education:** Univ Dacca, BAgr, 1953, MAgr, 1954; La State Univ, PhD (plant path), 1959. **Professional Experience:** Chmn dept, Elizabeth City State Univ, 1965-1978; PROF BIOL, ELIZABETH CITY STATE UNIV, 1964-; actg chmn dept, Elizabeth City State Univ, 1964-1965; chmn sci & math, Tex Col, 1960-1963; prof biol, Tex Col, 1959-1963; asst cane develop officer, M/S Carew & Co, 1957; sect officer, EPakistan Indust Develop Corp, 1955-1957. **Memberships:** Phytochem Soc Nam; Phy & Chem Soc Nam; Helminthological Soc Wash DC. **Research Statement & Publications:** Plant hormones; plant alkaloids extraction of active chemicals from Vitex negundo L; science education; tropical vegetable plants. **Mailing Address:** Dept Biol, Elizabeth City State Univ, 423 Jenkins Sci Ctr, Elizabeth City, NC 27909. **E-Mail:** sakhan@mail.ecsu.edu

KHAN, SHABBIR AHMED, MOLECULAR BIOLOGY, BIOCHEMISTRY. **Personal Data:** b December 24, 1945; c 1. **Education:** Bangalore Univ, India, PhD (peptide chem), 1977. **Professional Experience:** ASSOC PROF CHEM, WISTAR INST, 1986-; asst prof chem, Rockefeller Univ, 1980-1986. **Memberships:** Am Soc Biochem & Molecular Biol; Am Chem Soc; AAAS. **Research Statement & Publications:** Structure-function studies of the transacting proteins of human immuno virus. **Mailing Address:** Infinity Biotech Res, 610 Upland Ave, Upland, PA 19015. **Fax:** 610-499-8871.

KHAN, SHAHAMAT ULLAH, ENVIRONMENTAL SCIENCES. **Personal Data:** b Rampur, India, April 1937; Canadian citizen; m 1967, Nighat; c Saira & Zia. **Education:** Agra Univ, BSc, 1957; Aligarh Muslim Univ, India, MSc, 1959; Univ Alta, MSc, 1963, PhD (soil chem), 1967. **Professional Experience:** RETIRED; Can Dept Agr, 1997; AFFIL RES PROF, DEPT CHEM & BIOCHEM, GEORGE MASON UNIV, 1999-; prin res scientist, Can Dept Agr, beginning 1982; res scientist org matter & environ sci, Can Dept Agr, 1968-1982; Res asst soil chem, Univ Alta, 1963-1964; ed, J Environ Sci & Health, Part A, and J. Environ Sci & Health, Part B. **Memberships:** Am Chem Soc; fel Chem Inst Canada. **Research Statement & Publications:** Development of analytical techniques applicable to residues of pesticides and their metabolites in the environmental, biological and food samples; persistence, binding, degradation and metabolic fate of pesticides in soil, sediments, crops and food products; bound pesticide residues; and humic substances and their interaction with pesticides. **Mailing Address:** Dept Chem & Biochem, MSN 3E2, George Mason Univ, Sci & Technol I, Rm 358, Fairfax, VA 22030-4444. **Fax:** 703-993-1055. **E-Mail:** skhan6@gmu.edu

KHAN, SHAKIL AHMAD, PHYSICAL CHEMISTRY. **Personal Data:** b Bareilly, India, American citizen; m 1974, c 2. **Education:** Univ Karachi, Pakistan, BS, 1967, MS, 1968; Univ Islamabad, MPhil, 1969; Northwestern Univ, Evanston, Ill, PhD (phys org chem), 1974. **Professional Experience:** RES SPECIALIST NUCLEAR MAGNETIC RENOSANCE SPECTROS & ANALYSIS, MOBAY CHEM CORP, 1978-; fel, Fla State Univ, 1977-1978; asst prof spectros quantum chem, Univ Islamabad, Pakistan, 1974-1977; Fel molecular orbital theory, Univ SC, 1974. **Memberships:** Am Chem Soc; Soc Plastic Industs. **Research Statement & Publications:** Use of nuclear magnetic renosance spectroscopy to study polymers especially polyurethanes, polycarbonates; laboratory and office automation; personal computer in chemistry. **Mailing Address:** Bayer Corp Bldg 8, Pittsburgh, PA 15205-9741.

KHAN, SULTANA A, SOLID STATE PHYSICS, ASTRONOMY. **Personal Data:** b Dacca, Bangladesh, December 13, 1947; m 1974, c 1. **Education:** Univ Dacca, BS, 1970, MS, 1972; Univ Grenoble, PhD (solid state physics), 1977. **Professional Experience:** PROF PHYSICS, ELIZABETH CITY STATE UNIV, 1994-; assoc prof, Elizabeth City State Univ, 1978-1994. **Memberships:** Bangladesh Phys Soc; Am Phys Soc. **Research Statement & Publications:** Involved in a project to measure solar radiation in southeastern United States in cooperation with the Solar Energy Research Institute Department of Energy and National Oceanic and Atmospheric Administration. **Mailing Address:** Dept Chem & Physics, Elizabeth City State Univ, 403 Jenkins Sci Ctr, Elizabeth City, NC 27909. **Fax:** 252-335-3775. **E-Mail:** sakhan2@mail.ecsu.edu

KHAN, WINSTON, APPLIED MATHEMATICS, MATHEMATICAL PHYSICS. **Personal Data:** b San Fernando, Trinidad, March 12, 1934; American citizen; m 1961, Joan A Aziz; c Alima, Selina, Shereeza, Winston Jr & Alim. **Education:** Univ London, BSc, 1956, MSc, 1958; Univ Birmingham, Eng, dipl, 1961, PhD (mat Physics), 1964. **Honorary Degrees:** 6. **Honors & Awards:** Commemorative Medal of Honor, ABI, 1984. **Professional Experience:** Coordr, US Army Mat Command, Rep, Univ PR, 1984-1987; PROF PHYSICS, UNIV PR, MAYAQUEZ, 1982-; dir, US Army grants, 1982-1985; exec adv mem, Nat Sci Comn, 1982-1983; Adv, Comn Educ Reform, NSF, 1981-1983; assoc prof, Univ PR, Cayey, 1974-1982; from asst prof to assoc prof mat, Univ PR, Cayey, 1970-1974; lectr & dir mat, Univ WI-Trinidad, 1964-1969; Asst prof mat, Univ WI-London, 1958-1959. **Memberships:** Am Mat Soc; Am Phys Soc; AAAS; Soc Inst & Appl Math; Int Asn Mat & Comput Modeling; Int Asn Math and Comput Simulation. **Research Statement & Publications:** Fluid dynamics involving mathematics, physics and engineering sciences. **Mailing Address:** 1020 Ave Los Corazones, Mayaguez, PR 00680. **Fax:** 787-832-1135.

KHAN, ZAFRULA, MAXILLOFACIAL PROSTHODONTICS, ORAL DENTAL ONCOLOGY. **Personal Data:** b Myoore, India, April 26, 1949; American citizen; m 1978, Zareen; c Omar & Shaheen. **Education:** Govt Dent Col, DDS, 1972; Univ Louisville, MS, 1995. **Professional Experience:** Assoc, Dept Med & Radiation Oncol, beginning 1998; adj prof, Tufts Univ Dent Sch, beginning 1998; vis prof, RG Univ Health Sci, India, beginning 1998; prof & chmn, Univ Louisville Dent Sch, 1992-1998; assoc prof & actg chmn, Univ Louisville Dent Sch, 1989-1992; PROF & DIR, UNIV LOUISVILLE, BROWN CANCER CTR, 1988-; dir, post grad, Univ Louisville Dent Sch, 1984-1989. **Memberships:** Int Asn Dent Res; Am Asn Dent Res; Univ Tex MID Anderon Asn; Karnataka Med Dent Asn; Am Acad Maxillofacial Prothetics. **Research Statement & Publications:** Maxillofacial and dental materials; pharmaceutical studies including head and neck radiation; stogren's syndrome; advanced head and neck cancers. **Mailing Address:** Maxillofacial Dent Oncol Brown Cancer Ctr, 529 S Jackson St No 127, Louisville, KY 40202-3267. **E-Mail:** zafkhan@louisville.edu

KHANA, RAJIVE KUMAR, CHEMISTRY. **Education:** Univ Delhi, BSc, 1974; Indian Inst Technol, Delhi, MSc; Indian Inst Technol, Kanpur, PhD. **Professional Experience:** ASSOC PROF, DEPT CHEM & BIOCHEM, as of 2005. **Mailing Address:** Dept Chem & Biochem, Univ Southern Miss, Hattiesburg, MS 39406-5043. **E-Mail:** rkhanna@ocean.st.usm.edu

KHANAL, PUNYA PRASAD, PAVEMENT DESIGN ANALYSIS & MANAGEMENT SYSTEMS, CONSTRUCTION MATERIALS. **Personal Data:** b Ilam, Nepal, March 29, 1956; m 1986, Saraswati; c Gaurav & Garima. **Education:** Univ Rajasthan, BE, 1980; Strathclyde Univ, MSc, 1985; Ariz State Univ, PhD (civil eng), 1995. **Professional Experience:** RES ENGR, REED & GRAHAM LAB SERV, 1996-; proj engr, Appl Paving Technol, 1995-1996; transp engr assoc, Ariz Dept Transp, 1993-1995; civil engr, Dept Roads, Nepal, 1980-1989. **Memberships:** Asn Asphalt Paving Technologist; Am Soc Testing & Mat; Am Soc Civil Engrs; Nat Soc Prof Engrs. **Research Statement & Publications:** Design and analysis of pavements; use of available and innovative materials in highway and airport pavements; pavement management. **Mailing Address:** Reed & Graham Lab Serv, 550 Sunol St, San Jose, CA 95126. **Fax:** 408-294-1959. **E-Mail:** ppkhanal@worldnet.att.net

KHANDAN, NIRMALA N, QUANTITATIVE STRUCTURE-ACTIVITY RELATIONSHIPS MODELING, REMEDIATION TECHNOLOGIES. **Personal Data:** b Badulla, Sri Lanka, June 21, 1947; m 1975, Mary; c Rajeer & Sanjeer. **Education:** UnivCeylon, BS, 1970; Drexel Univ, MS, 1985, PhD (environ eng), 1988. **Professional Experience:** Consult, beginning 1989; prin investr, NMex State Univ, beginning 1989; ASSOC PROF CIVIL & ENVIRON ENG, NMEX STATE UNIV, 1989-; res asst prof, Vanderbilt Univ, beginning 1988; mgr, Eng Dept, Hayleys Ltd, Sri Lanka, 1975-1983. **Memberships:** Int Asn Water Qual; Asn Environ Eng Profs; Am Chem Soc. **Research Statement & Publications:** Control and management of environmental hazards of organic chemicals; physical/biological processes. **Mailing Address:** Civil Eng Dept, NMex State Univ, Las Cruces, NM 88003. **Fax:** 505-646-6049. **E-Mail:** nkhandan@nmsu.edu

KHANDEKAR, MADHAV LAXMAN, NUMERICAL MODELLING OF OCEAN SURFACE WAVES, LARGE SCALE ATMOSPHERIC CIRCULATION AND INDIAN MONSOON. **Personal Data:** b Dohad, India, July 12, 1935; Canadian citizen; m 1968, Shalan Damle;

c Nitin & Seema. **Education:** Poona Univ, India, BSc, 1955, MSc, 1957; Fla State Univ, MS, 1964, PhD (meterol), 1968. **Honors & Awards:** Sci Contrib Award, Int Natural Hazards Soc, 1993; Prize Appl Oceanog, Can Meteorol & Oceanog Soc, 1994. **Professional Experience:** CONSULT, as of 2004; res scientist, Atmospheric Environ Serv, Environ Can, beginning 1982; expert aeronaut meteorol, Int Civil Aviation Orgn, UN, 1980-1982; lectr meteorol, World Meteorol Orgn, UN, 1975-1977; res assoc, Univ Alta, Can, 1971-1974; fel, Nat Res Coun, Can, 1969-1970; Sci asst, India Meterol Dept, Poona, India, 1957-1962. **Memberships:** Can Meteorol & Oceanog Soc; Can Soc Agrometeorol; Am Meteorol Soc; Am Geophys Union. **Research Statement & Publications:** Numerical modelling of ocean surface waves, impact of large-scale atmospheric and oceanic anomalies on Indian Monsoon droughts and floods and on world grain yields; statistical analysis of atmospheric and oceanic data. **Mailing Address:** 52 Montrose Crescent, Unionville, ON L3R 7Z5, Can. **E-Mail:** mkhandekar@rogers.com

KHANDELWAL, RAMJI LAL, BIOCHEMISTRY OF DIABETES, SIGNAL TRANSDUCTION ENZYMES. **Personal Data:** b Dausa, India, June 2, 1944; Canadian citizen; m 1962, Vimla; c Deepak. **Education:** Univ Udaipur, India, BSc, 1963; Punjab, Agr Univ, India, MSc, 1966; Univ Man, PhD (biochem), 1972. **Professional Experience:** HEAD, DEPT BIOCHEM, UNIV SASK, as of 2006; PROF BIOCHEM, UNIV SASK, 1985-; Med res Coun Can, develop grant, 1981-1992; assoc prof, Univ Sask, 1980-1985; Med Res Coun Can scholar, 1975-1980; asst prof oral biol, Univ Man, 1975-1980; res biochem, Univ Calif, Davis, 1973-1975; res asst, Univ Man, 1972-1973; teaching asst biochem, Univ Man, 1969-1970; res asst, Govt Rajasthan, India, 1966-1968; Demonstr agr, Univ Udaipur, India, 1963-1964. **Memberships:** Can Biochem Soc; Am Soc Biochem & Molecular Biol. **Research Statement & Publications:** Role of insulin and cyclic adenosine monophosphate in the regulation of glycogen metabolism in normal and diabetic animals; regulation of protein phosphorylation/dephosphorylation in biological systems. **Mailing Address:** Dept Biochem, Univ Sask, Rm A10-1 Health Sci Bldg, Saskatoon, SK S7N 5E5, Can. **Fax:** 306-966-4390. **E-Mail:** ramji.khandelwal@usask.ca

KHANDWALA, ATUL S, SCIENCE. **Professional Experience:** EXEC VPRES RES & DEVELOP, CHEMEX PHARMACEUT INC, 1986-. **Mailing Address:** Chemex Pharmaceut Inc, One Executive Dr, Ft Lee, NJ 07024-3309.

KHANG, SOON-JAI, CHEMICAL ENGINEERING. **Personal Data:** b Seoul, Korea, February 26, 1944; m 1973, c 2. **Education:** Yonsei Univ, Korea, BE, 1966; Ore State Univ, MS, 1972, PhD (chem eng), 1975. **Professional Experience:** PROF CHEM ENG, UNIV CINCINNATI, as of 2004; Amoco Oil, 1980- & Exxon, 1981; Assoc Prof Chem Eng, Univ Cincinnati, beginning 1980; Consult, Procter & Gamble Co, 1978-1980; asst prof, Univ Cincinnati, 1975-1979; Instr chem eng, Ore State Univ, 1974-1975. **Memberships:** Am Inst Chem Engrs; Sigma Xi. **Research Statement & Publications:** Chemical reaction engineering, including residence time distribution, mixing and catalyst deactivation; energy conversion and coal gasification; application of statistical methods for process control; mathematical modeling. **Mailing Address:** Dept Chem & Mat eng, Col eng, Univ Cincinnati, Cincinnati, OH 45236. **Fax:** 513-556-3473. **E-Mail:** soon-jai.khang@uc.edu

KHANNA, FAQIR CHAND, NUCLEAR PHYSICS & MANY BODY PHYSICS, GALILEAN SYMMETRY & FLUIDS. **Personal Data:** b Lyallpur, India, January 23, 1935; m 1966, Swara; c Shrawan F & Varun F. **Education:** Univ Panjab, India, BSc, 1955, MSc, 1956; Fla State Univ, PhD (physics), 1962. **Professional Experience:** AEC Labs, dir, Theoret Physics Inst, 1986-1993; PROF PHYSICS, UNIV ALTA, 1984-; from assoc to sr res physicist, Univ Alta, 1967-1984; Nat Res Coun Can fel, Univ Alta, 1966-1967; fel, Univ Iowa, 1961-1963 & Rice Univ, 1963-1965; Lectr physics, Univ Panjab, India, 1956-1958. **Memberships:** Fel Am Phys Soc; Can Asn Physics. **Research Statement & Publications:** Nuclear physics, many body problem with emphasis on nuclear physics and solid state physics; quantum liquids and solids; Galilean symmetry, Fluids, Casimir effect, Finite temperature field theory and its applications, Quarkonium, Chaos at finite temperature. **Mailing Address:** Univ Alta, Theort Physics Inst, Edmonton, AB T6G 2J1, Can. **Fax:** 780-492-0714. **E-Mail:** khanna@phys.ualberta.ca

KHANNA, JATINDER MOHAN, BIOCHEMICAL PHARMACOLOGY. **Personal Data:** b Amritsar, India, April 15, 1936; m 1966, c 2. **Education:** Punjab Univ, India, BSc, 1958, MSc, 1960; Univ Conn, PhD (pharmacol), 1964. **Professional Experience:** PROF EMER PHARMACOL, UNIV TORONTO, as of 2006; prof pharmacol, fac med, Univ Toronto, beginning 1977; Scientist IV, Alcohol & Drug Addiction Res Found, 1969-; from asst prof to assoc prof, Fac Med, Univ Toronto, 1966-1977; lectr, Fac Med, Univ Toronto, 1965-1966; Res fel pharmacol, Fac Med, Univ Toronto, 1964-1965; mem ed bd, J Alcohol; head, Behav Pharmacol & Drug Anal Sect; Lederle Res fel, Univ Conn, Starrs. **Memberships:** Soc Neuroscience; Can Pharmacol Soc; Am Soc Pharmacol & Exp Therapeut; Res Soc Alcoholism; Int Soc Biomed Res Alcoholism; Sigma Xi. **Research Statement & Publications:** Biochemical and behavioral mechanisms of alcohol and drug addiction. **Mailing Address:** Dept Pharmacol, Univ Toronto, Rm 4207 Med Sci Bldg one King's Col Circle, Toronto, ON M5S 1A8, Can. **Fax:** 416-978-6395. **E-Mail:** j.khanna@utoronto.ca

KHANNA, KRISHAN L, phytochemistry, pharmaceutical chemistry; deceased, see previous edition for last biography

KHANNA, PYARE LAL, BIO-ORGANIC CHEMISTRY, SYNTHETIC CHEMISTRY & IMMUNOCHEMISTRY. **Personal Data:** b Lahore, March 28, 1945; American citizen; m 1973, Swatanter; c Sonia & Pavan. **Education:** Univ Delhi, BSc, 1965, MSc, 1967, PhD (chem), 1970. **Honors & Awards:** Syntex Sci Award, 1984. **Professional Experience:** PRES & CHIEF EXEC OFFICER, DISCOVERX, 2000-; vpres, res & develop, Boehringer Mannheim Corp, beginning 1992; vpres res & develop, Microgenics, 1986-1991; asst dir res, Microgenics, 1980-1986; res group leader, Microgenics, 1977-1980; res assoc, Columbia Univ, 1974-1977; asst prof chem, Ramjas Col, Univ Delhi, 1971-1974; res assoc natural prod, Indian Nat Sci Acad, 1970-1971. **Memberships:** Am Chem Soc; Am Asn Clin Chem; NY Acad Sci; AAAS. **Research Statement & Publications:** Natural products isolation and synthesis; steroids; small ring compounds; fluorescent dyes; protein modifications; development of new immunoassay techniques; dipstick immunoassays; homogenous and heterogenous immunoassays; future research and development strategy. **Mailing Address:** Boehringer Mannheim Corp, 42501 Albrae St, Fremont, CA 94538. **Fax:** 510-979-1650. **E-Mail:** pyarekhanna@aol.com

KHANNA, RAVI, POLYMER CHEMISTRY, CHEMICAL ENGINEERING. **Personal Data:** b Kapurthala, India, September 27, 1944; m 1974. **Education:** Indian Inst Technol, Kanpur, BTech, 1967; Mass Inst Technol, SM, 1968. **Professional Experience:** TECH ASST TO DIR RES, EASTMAN KODAK CO RES LABS, 1981-; lab head, Eastman Kodak Co Res Labs, 1977-1981; res assoc, Eastman Kodak Co Res Labs, 1976-1977; sr res chemist polymer chem, Eastman Kodak Co Res Labs, 1972-1976; res chemist, Eastman Kodak Co Res Labs, 1968-1972. **Memberships:** Am Chem Soc; Am Inst Chem Engrs. **Research Statement & Publications:** Investigation of the mechanism and kinetics of batch and continuous free radical polymerization. **Mailing Address:** Eastman Kodak Co, 343 State St, Rochester, NY 14650. **Fax:** 585-724-1089.

KHANNA, SARDARI LAL, PHYSICS. **Personal Data:** b Amritsar, India, April 15, 1937; m 1963, c 2. **Education:** Panjab Univ India, BA, 1956; Univ Saugar, MSc, 1959, PhD (physics), 1963. **Professional Experience:** PROF PHYSICS, YORK COL, PA, 1978-; assoc prof, York Col, PA, 1970-1978; sci pooloff, Panjab Univ, 1968-1969; from asst prof to assoc prof, York Jr Col, Pa, 1965-1968; lectr, Panjab Univ, 1962-1964; Lectr physics, DAV Col, Amritsar, India, 1959-1960. **Memberships:** Am Phys Soc; Am Asn Physics Teachers. **Research Statement & Publications:** Electrets; solid state physics; study of dielectrics subjected to electric and magnetic fields. **Mailing Address:** Dept Phys Sci, York Col Pa, C-107C Country Club Rd, York, PA 17405-7199. **Fax:** 717-849-1607. **E-Mail:** skhanna@ycp.edu

KHANNA, SHYAM MOHAN, PHYSIOLOGY, BIOPHYSICS. **Personal Data:** b Agra, India, May 10, 1932; m 1959, Shirley; c Ravi & Shyama. **Education:** Univ Lucknow, BS, 1951; St Xavier's Col, India, DRE, 1954; City Univ NY, PhD (hearing), 1970. **Honors & Awards:** Res career develop award, Nat Inst Neurol Commun Dis & Stroke, 1977-1994. **Professional Experience:** SPEC LECTR OTOLARYNGOL, HEAD & NECK SURG, COLUMBIA UNIV, as of 2006; PROF EMER, COLUMBIA UNIV, 2001-; prin investr, prog proj grants, 1985-; prof otolaryngol, Col Physicians & Surgeons, Columbia Univ, 1983-2001; dir res, Fowler Mem Labs, 1983-2001; prin investr, beginning 1979; from asst prof to assoc prof, Fowler Mem Labs, 1970-1983; NIH RES GRANTS, 1964-; res assoc hearing, Fowler Mem Labs, 1964-1970; adv engr commun, IBM Corp, 1961-1964; sr engr avionics, Int Tel & Tel Labs, 1958-1961; design engr commun, Can Westinghouse Ltd, Ont, 1955-1958; develop engr instrumentation, Pye Ltd, Eng, 1954-1955. **Memberships:** Sr mem Inst Elec & Electronics Engrs; fel Acoust Soc Am; Sigma Xi; Asn Res Otolaryngol; AAAS; Int Soc Optics Life Sci (pres, 1992-1994). **Research Statement & Publications:** Physics of hearing; mechanics of the middle and inner ear; transducer action and coding in the peripheral auditory system. **Mailing Address:** Col Physicians & Surgeons Rm 11-452, Columbia Univ 630 W 168th St, New York, NY 10032. **Fax:** 212-305-4045. **E-Mail:** smk3@columbia.edu

KHARAKA, YOUSIF KHOSHU, GEOCHEMISTRY, HYDROGEOLOGY. **Personal Data:** b Mosul, Iraq, May 15, 1941; c 2. **Education:** King's Col, Univ London, BSc, 1963; Univ Calif, Berkeley, PhD (geol), 1971. **Honors & Awards:** Spec Award, Soc Econ Paleontologists & Mineralogists, 1985. **Professional Experience:** HYDROLOGIST WATER RESOURCES DIV, US GEOL SURV, 1975-; consult explor, Mining & Metals Div, Union Carbide Corp, 1974-1975; asst res geologist, Univ Calif, Berkeley, 1971-1975; asst geologist explor & res dept, Ministry Oil, Baghdad, Iraq, 1963-1967; asst geol, Univ Baghdad, 1963-1964. **Memberships:** Int Asn Geochemistry & Cosmochemistry; Geochemical Soc; Am Asn Petrol Geologists; Am Geophys Union; Geol Soc Am. **Research Statement & Publications:** Geochemistry of sediments, sedimentary rocks and their associated fluids; computer modelling of water-rock interactions; membrane properties of fine grained sediments; stable isotopes. **Mailing Address:** 3385 St Michael Dr, Palo Alto, CA 94306.

KHARAS, GREGORY B, BIODEGRADABLE POLYESTERS, POLYMERIC MATERIALS. **Personal Data:** b Moscow, USSR, September 6, 1946; American citizen; m 1973, Cecilya; c Boris & Michael. **Education:** Moscow Inst Petrochem & Gas Indust, BS & MS, 1968; Technion-Israel Inst Technol, PhD (chem), 1981. **Professional Experience:** PROF DEPT CHEM, DEPAUL UNIV, as of 2005; asst prof, org chem & polymer sci, Depaul Univ, 1992-; adj prof, Univ Mass, Lowell, 1989-1992; assoc scientist, Novacor Chem Inc, 1985-1992; res assoc, Albany Int, 1983-1985; Univ Mass, Lowell, 1982-1983; fel, Case Western Res Univ, 1981-1982; res assoc, Inst Petrochem Synthesis, Acad Sci USSR, 1968-1978. **Memberships:** Am Chem Soc. **Research Statement & Publications:** Synthesis and characterization of copolymers of trisubstituted ethylenes; biodegradable polyesters for packaging and biomedical applications; analysis of microstructure of copolymers thermal and environmental degradation of polymeric materials. **Mailing Address:** Dept Chem DePaul Univ, 1036 W Belden Ave, Chicago, IL 60604-2218. **Fax:** 773-362-6636. **E-Mail:** gkharas@depaul.edu

KHARE, ASHOK KUMAR, FORGINGS & EXTRUSIONS. **Personal Data:** b Kanpur, India, August 7, 1948; American citizen; m 1974, c 2. **Education:** Agra Univ, India, BS, 1964; Indian Inst Tech, BTech, 1969; Stevens Inst Tech, MS, NJ, 1971. **Professional Experience:** PRES, ASM INT, as of 2000; sr develop metallurgist, Res & Develop Corp, Nat Forge Co, Irvine, PA, beginning 1982; sr prod metallurgist, Dept Metall, Nat Forge Co, Irvine, Pa, 1975-1982. **Memberships:** AAAS; fel Am Soc Metals; Am Soc Mech Eng. **Research Statement & Publications:** Product and process develpment for new and existing ferrous non ferrous forgings and extrusions. **Mailing Address:** Off Pres, ASM Int, Materials Park, OH 44073-0002. **E-Mail:** akhare@po.asm-intl.org

KHARE, BISHUN NARAIN, PHYSICS, PHYSICAL CHEMISTRY. **Personal Data:** b Varanasi, India, June 27, 1933; m 1962, Jyoti; c Reena & Archana. **Education:** Banaras Hindu Univ, BSc, 1953, MSc, 1955; Syracuse Univ, PhD (physics), 1961. **Professional Experience:** RES SCIENTIST, SETI INST, NASA AMES RES CTR, as of 1997; NAT RES COUN SR RESIDENT RES ASSOC, AMES RES CTR, NASA, MOFFETT FIELD, CALIF, 1996-; sr res physicist, Lab Planetary Studies, Ctr Radiophys & Space Res, Cornell Univ, 1968-1996; physicist, Smithsonian Astrophys Observ, Mass, 1966-1968; Assoc, Harvard Observ, 1966-1968; assoc res scientist, Ont Res Found, Can, 1964-1966; res assoc, Univ Toronto, 1961-1962 & State Univ NY, Stony Brook, 1962-1964. **Memberships:** AAAS; Am Phys Soc; Am Astron Soc; Int Soc Study Origin of Life; Astron Soc India; Am Chem Soc; Int Astron Union; Sigma Xi; Planetary Soc. **Research Statement & Publications:** Interdisciplinary research; molecular structure and spectroscopy; synthesis of organic compounds in primitive terrestrial and contemporary planetary atmospheres by photochemical reaction; hydrogen bonding among molecules of biological interest; planetary surfaces and atmospheres; interstellar and cometary chemistry; optical constants of materials of astronomical interest. **Mailing Address:** SETI Inst, NASA Ames Res Lab, Mtain View, CA 94035-1000. **Fax:** 650-604-1088. **E-Mail:** bkhare@mail.arc.nasa.gov

KHARE, MOHAN, PHYSICAL CHEMISTRY, ENVIRONMENTAL CHEMISTRY. **Personal Data:** b Varanasi, India, May 15, 1942; American citizen; m 1973, Meena; c Rohit. **Education:** Banaras Hindu Univ, BSc, 1961, MSc, 1963 & PhD (chem), 1967. **Professional Experience:** PRES & CHIEF EXEC OFFICER, ENVIROSYST INC, 1989-; sr vpres, Recra Environ Inc, 1987-1989; dir, Anal Chem Lab, EA Eng, Sci & Technol Inc, 1985-1987; mgr, Environ Monitoring Servs Lab, Rockwell Int, 1984-1985; res prof chem, Univ Nev, Las Vegas & mgr, Qual Assurance Lab, under contract with US Environ Protection Agency, 1982-1984; sr anal specialist & technologist, IT Corp, 1978-1982; sr res assoc, Cornell Univ, 1970-1978; res assoc & fel, Univ Md, 1967-1969; res assoc, Radiation Ctr, Ore State Univ, 1969-1970; Lectr chem, Banaras Hindu Univ, 1967. **Memberships:** Am Chem Soc; AAAS; Am Water Works Asn; Int Union Pure & Appl Chem; Int Asn Environ Testing

Lab. **Research Statement & Publications:** Radiochemical separation of isotopes; kinetics of annealing of radiation damage; energy transfer in solids; photolysis and radiolysis of aqueous systems and interstellar molecules; water pollution characterization and environmental research; analytical methods development for trace and toxic materials, organic and inorganic, in diverse matrices; water quality and hazardous waste management; detoxification and disposal; analytical methods development for air water soil and sediment biota. **Mailing Address:** Envirosystems Inc, 9200 Rumser Rd Ste B102, Columbia, MD 21045-1900. **Fax:** 410-740-9306.

KHARGONEKAR, PRAMOD P, CONTROL THEORY, SYSTEM THEORY. **Personal Data:** b Indore, India, August 24, 1956; m 1983, Seema; c Aditya & Shivangi. **Education:** Indian Inst Technol, Bombay, BTech, 1977; Univ Fla, Gainesville, MS, 1980, PhD (elec eng), 1981. **Honors & Awards:** George Taylor res award, 1987; D Eckmann Award, 1989; Axelby Award, Inst Elec & Electronics Engrs, 1990, W R G Baker Prize, 1991. **Professional Experience:** DEAN COL ENG, UNIV FLA, as of 2004; ASSOC VPRES ENG & INDUST EXP STA, UNIV FLA, as of 2004; ECIKS PROF ELEC & COMPUT ENG, UINV FLA, as of 2004; PROF ELEC ENG & COMPUT SCI, UNIVMICH, ANN ARBOR, 1989-; prin young investr award, NSF, 1985; consult, Honeywell Corp, 1984-; from assoc prof to prof elec eng, Univ Minn, Minneapolis, 1984-1989; vis prof, Swiss Fed Inst Technol, Zurich, 1983; vis asst prof, Tex Tech Univ, Lubbock, 1982; prin investr, Air Force Off Sci Res, Army Res Off, NSF, 1981-; asst prof elec eng, Univ Fla, Gainesville, 1981-1984. **Memberships:** Inst Elec & Electronics Engrs. **Research Statement & Publications:** Control and systems theory; robust control, optimal control, infinite dimensional systems, adaptive control, algebraic system theory, control of electronics manufacturing. **Mailing Address:** Col Eng, Univ Fla, 300 Weil Hall PO Box 116550, Gainesville, FL 32611-6550. **Fax:** 352-392-9673. **E-Mail:** ppk@ufl.edu

KHASNABIS, SNEHAMAY, TRANSPORTATION ENGINEERING, SYSTEMS ANALYSIS. **Personal Data:** b Dacca, India, November 4, 1939; American citizen; m 1967, c 2. **Education:** Univ Calcutta, India, BE, 1962; NC State Univ, Raleigh, MCE, 1970, PhD (civil eng), 1973. **Professional Experience:** INTERIM ASSOC DEAN RES, WAYNE STATE UNIV, as of 2004; actg dir, Urban Transp Inst, Wayne State Univ, 1985-; chmn dept, Wayne State Univ, Detroit, 1984-1987; chmn, NSF Educ Proj, 1984-1987; prin investr, US Dept Transp Res Projs, Wayne State Univ, 1977-1991 & NSF Educ Proj, 1983-1986; actg chmn dept, Wayne State Univ, Detroit, 1983-1984; PROF CIVIL ENG, WAYNE STATE UNIV, DETROIT, 1982-; chmn dept, US Dept Transp Res Projs, Wayne State Univ, 1977-1991; from asst prof to assoc prof, Wayne State Univ, Detroit, 1975-1982; transp engr, Barton-Aschman Assocs, Inc, Wash, DC, 1974-1975. **Memberships:** Am Soc Civil Engrs; Inst Transp Engrs; Transp Res Bd. **Research Statement & Publications:** Land-use models, simulation, transit station location, traffic safety and operation, transportation logistics; computer techniques for bus system planning and expansion, and financial strategies for transit system development; transit drivatization and intelligent vehicles highway systems; published over 100 articles. **Mailing Address:** Wayne State Univ, 2168 Eng, Troy, MI 48098. **Fax:** 313-578-5755. **E-Mail:** skhas@eng.wayne.edu

KHATAMI, MAHIN, PROTEIN CHEMISTRY, ENZYMOLOGY. **Personal Data:** b Tehran, Iran, May 9, 1943. **Education:** Teachers Training Col, BS, 1964; State Univ NY Buffalo, MS, 1977; Univ Pa, PhD (molecular biol), 1980. **Professional Experience:** MOLECULAR, CELLULAR BIOLOGIST & IMMUNOLOGIST TECHNOL TRANSFER BR, 2005-; prof docent, dept opthal, Univ Tampere Finland Sch Med, beginning 1992; dir, Res Pasteur Inst, Iran, 1992-1993; adv, Res Pasteur Inst, Iran, 1992-1993; panalist fel grants, Nat Res Coun, Wash, DC, 1992; sci rev, Coronary Heart Dis Res, Am Health Asst Found, 1987-1992; ad hoc ed revs, Current Eye Res, 1987-1992; mem, Cell Biol Grad Group, Univ Pa, 1987-1992; asst prof, Dept Ophthal, Univ Pa, 1985-1992; res assoc dept physiol, Univ Va, 1980-1981; instr chem, Philadelphia Community Col, 1974-1975; instr biochem, Philadelphia Col Podiatric Med, 1974-1975; Instr chem & physics, Teachers Training Col, Tehran, Iran, 1964-1969. **Memberships:** Asn Res Vision & Ophthal; AAAS; Soc Exp Biol & Med; Am Diabetes Asn. **Research Statement & Publications:** Biochemistry and molecular aspects of diabetic retinopathy; role of hyperglycemia in retinal metabolism; cellular transport and metabolism of vital metabolites (e.g., sugars, ascorbate, myo-inositol); mechanism of signal transduction and receptor function; immunology; mechanisms of ocular allergic reactions; author of various articles. **Mailing Address:** Technol Transfer Br, Nat Cancer Insti, 6120 Exe Blvd Ste 450, Rockville, MD 20852.

KHATIB, HISHAM M, ENERGY & ELECTRICITY GLOBAL IMPACT, ENVIRONMENTAL EFFECTS OF ENERGY. **Personal Data:** b Palestine, January 5, 1936; Jordanian citizen; m 1968, Maha; c Mohamed, Lynn & Issam. **Education:** Univ Ain Shams, Cairo, BSc, 1959; Univ Birmingham, MSc 1962; Univ London, BSc, 1967, PhD (elec eng), 1974. **Honors & Awards:** Achievement Medal 1998 IEE (UK). **Professional Experience:** CONSULT INT ORGN, 1995-; hon vchmn, World Energy Coun, 1993-; minister of planning, 1993-1995; consult ed, Int J Elec & Energy Systs, 1985- & Environ Policy, 1990-; chmn, Inst Elec Engrs Ctr, Jordan, 1989-; vchmn, World Energy Coun, 1988-; minister energy, Govt Jordan, 1984-1989; Mem, Int Comt Availability Generating Plant, 1982-; dir gen, Jordan Elec Authority, 1980-1984; energy adv, Arab Fund, Kuwait, 1976-1980; dep dir gen, Jordan Elec Authority, 1974-1976; res fel elec eng, Univ London, 1973-1974; chief engr, Jerusalem Dist Elec Co, 1966-1973; engr, Jerusalem Dist Elec Co, 1962-1966; Asst engr, Jerusalem Dist Elec Co, 1959-1962; Bd World Energy Efficiency Asn. **Memberships:** Fel Inst Elec & Electronics Engrs; World Energy Coun; fel Inst Elec Eng UK. **Research Statement & Publications:** Book on "Financial and Economic Evaluation of projects" UK 1997 Global energy matters, demand and supply, effect on the environment; future of electrical energy and its environmental impact. **Mailing Address:** PO Box 925387, Amman, Jordan.

KHATIB-RAHBAR, MOHSEN, CHEMICAL ENGINEERING, NUCLEAR ENGINEERING. **Personal Data:** b Rafsandjan, Iran, February 21, 1954; m 1985, Maryam; c Dara & Dina. **Education:** Univ Minn, BS, 1974; Cornell Univ, PhD (nuclear eng), 1978. **Professional Experience:** PRES, ENERGY RES INC, 1989-; group leader accident anal group, Brookhaven Nat Lab, 1985-1988; vis scientist, Ger Res Satellite, WGerm, 1982; mem sci staff, Brookhaven Nat Lab, 1978-1988; Cornell McMullin fel, 1975; prin investr, US Nuclear Regulatory Comn; consult, US Nuclear Regulatory Comm, US Dept Energy, Int Atomic Energy Lab, Los Alamos Nat Lab, Pac Northwest Lab, Swiss Nuclear Safety Inspecterate, Finnish Nuclear Safety Authority, Dutch Ministry Social Affairs & Swedish Nuclear Safety Inspectorate. **Memberships:** Am Inst Chem Engrs; Am Nuclear Soc. **Research Statement & Publications:** Nuclear reactor dynamics and safety; heat transfer; fluid dynamics; numerical methods; probabilistic risk assessment; severe nuclear reactor accident analysis; mathematical methods for propagation of stochastic and physical uncertainty. **Mailing Address:** Energy Res Inc, 6167 Executive Blvd PO Box 2034, Rockville, MD 20847. **Fax:** 301-881-0867. **E-Mail:** mkr@eri-world.com

KHATRA, BALWANT SINGH, BIOCHEMISTRY. **Personal Data:** b Nabha, India, February 2, 1945; American citizen; m 1968, c 2. **Education:** Univ Punjab, BS, 1965, MS, 1967; Univ Leeds, PhD (biochem), 1972. **Professional Experience:** PROF PHYSIOL, UNIV VANDERBILT, as of 2004; asst prof physiol, Univ Vanderbilt, 1978-; res assoc, Dept Physiol, Univ Vanderbilt, 1975-1978; res fel, Clin Res Facil, Univ Emory, 1972-1975. **Memberships:** Am Soc Biol Chemists. **Research Statement & Publications:** Phosphoprotein phosphatases: isolation, characterization and their role in the regulation of glycogen metabolism. **Mailing Address:** Dept Biol Calif State Univ, 1250 Bellflower Blvd, Long Beach, CA 90840-3702. **Fax:** 562-985-2315. **E-Mail:** bskhatra@csulb.edu

KHATRI, HIRALAL C, MECHANICAL ENGINEERING. **Personal Data:** b Navsari, India, February 6, 1936; m 1965, c 1. **Education:** Imp Col Eng, Addis Ababa, Ethiopia, BS, 1958; Purdue Univ, MS, 1963, PhD (mech eng), 1966. **Professional Experience:** PHYS SCIENTIST, HARRY DIAMOND LABS, 1980-; mech engr, Harry Diamond Labs, 1971-1980; assoc prof mech eng, Cath Univ Am, 1967-1971; NSF res grant, 1966-1968; asst prof elec eng, Mont State Univ, 1965-1967; engr, Imp Hwy Authority, Ethiopia, 1958-1961. **Memberships:** Am Soc Mech Engrs; Inst Elec & Electronics Engrs. **Research Statement & Publications:** Automatic control systems; optimal filter, identification and control of distributed systems; stability and sensitivity of distributed parameter systems; radar systems and signal processing. **Mailing Address:** US Army Res Lab, 2800 Powder Mill Rd, Adelphi, MD 20783-1197.

KHATTAB, GHAZI M A, POLYMER CHEMIST. **Personal Data:** b Baghdad, Iraq, November 20, 1930; c 1. **Education:** Univ Baghad, BS, 1953; Univ Ill, Urbana, MS, 1958; Polytech Inst Brooklyn, PhD (polymer sci), 1965. **Professional Experience:** RES MGR, ITW, INC, 1987-; vpres, Res & Develop Corp, 1984-1987; tech dir res & develop, Wellman, Inc, 1981-1984; sr res chemist res & develop, Allied Chem Corp, 1976-1980; res assoc, GAF Corp, 1973-1975; prog mgr, BiomedSci, 1972-1973; Sr res chemist res & develop, Allied Chem Corp, 1965-1971. **Memberships:** Soc Plastics Engrs; Sigma Xi; Am Chem Soc. **Research Statement & Publications:** New polymeric materials; engineering plastics including fluoropolymers; polyamides; polyesters and polysulfones; synthetic fibers. **Mailing Address:** ITW Inc, 3650 W Lake Ave, Glenview, IL 60025.

KHATTAK, CHANDRA PRAKASH, SOLID STATE PHYSICS, MATERIALS SCIENCE. **Personal Data:** b Rawalpindi, Pakistan, May 19, 1944; m 1970, Veena; c Payal & Gautam. **Education:** Indian Inst Technol, Bombay, BTech, 1965; State Univ NY, Stony Brook, MS, 1971, PhD (mat sci), 1973. **Honors & Awards:** IR-100 Award, 1979, 2 NASA Innovation Awards. **Professional Experience:** DIR, RES & DEVELOP & SILICON OPER, as of 2003; EXEC VPRES, CRYSTAL SYSTS INC, 1989-; sr vpres, Crystal Systs Inc, 1987-1989; vpres technol, Crystal Systs Inc, 1980-1986; dir res & develop, Crystal Systs Inc, 1977-1980; asst physicist, Brookhaven Nat Lab, 1975-1977; res assoc solid state physics, Brookhaven Nat Lab, 1974-1975; asst mat sci, State Univ NY, Stony Brook, 1968-1973; Jr sci officer magnetism, DMR Lab, Hyderabad, India, 1965-1968. **Memberships:** Am Ceramic Soc; Am Phys Soc; Am Asn Crystal Growth; Electrochemical Soc; Am Soc Metals; Materials Res Soc. **Research Statement & Publications:** Growth of large diameter sapphire for optical application, directional solidification of silicon crystals for photovoltaic applications and laser crystals growth by heat exchanger method; low-cost slicing of silicon by multi-ware fixed abrasive slicing technique; characterization and evaluation of silicon material for solar cells; thermodynamic evaluation of vacuum processing ofsilicon; single crystal growth of compound semiconductors and non-linear crystals. **Mailing Address:** Crystal Systems, Inc, 27 Congress St, Salem, MA 01970. **Fax:** 978-744-5059. **E-Mail:** chandra@crystalsystems.com

KHAW, BAN-AN, MODIFICATION OF ANTIBODIES, RADIOIMMUNOSCINTIGRAPHY. **Personal Data:** b Bassein, Burma, July 25, 1947; American citizen; m 1976, c 4. **Education:** State Univ NY, Oswego, BA, 1969; Boston Col, MS, 1970 & PhD (immunol), 1973. **Honors & Awards:** Berson-Yalow Award, Soc Nuclear Med, 1991. **Professional Experience:** GEORGE D BEHRAKIS PROF PHARMACEUT SCI & DIR, CTR CARDIOVASC TARGETING & ANAL, NORTHEASTERN UNIV, 1991-; ASSOC RADIO CHEMIST, DEPT RADIOL, MASS GEN HOSP E, 1990-; consult, Vasocor, beginning 1989; assoc prof, Dept Radiol, Harvard Med Sch, 1984-; asst radio chemist, Dept Radiol, 1983-1989; dept radiol, dept path, Harvard Med Sch, 1983-1984; consult, Centocor, beginning 1982; assoc biochemist, Dept Med, Mass Inst Technol, 1981-1983; asst biochemist, Dept Med, Mass Inst Technol, 1980-1981; asst prof, dept path, Harvard Med Sch, 1978-1983; asst biochem, Mass Gen Hosp, 1976-1979; instr, Harvard Med Sch, 1976-1978; res fel, Mass Gen Hosp & Harvard Med Sch, 1973-1976. **Memberships:** Soc Nuclear Med; Am Heart Asn Basic Sci; Chinese Am Soc Nuclear Med (pres, 1990-); Am Chem Soc; Am Soc Nuclear Cardiol. **Research Statement & Publications:** Application of antibodies in vivo diagnosis of cardiovascular diseases; modification of charge of proteins to affect changes in biodistribution and enhancement in vivo target localization; general application of radioimmunoscintigraphy; targeting with proteins, peptides and carbohydrates for diagnosis and therapy; autoimmune myocarditis; myocardial salvages, regeneration and gene therapy; published over 10 articles. **Mailing Address:** Dept Pharmaceut Sci, Ctr Cardiovasc Targeting, Northeastern Univ, 205 Mugar Hall 360 Huntington Ave, Boston, MA 02115. **Fax:** 617-373-3663. **E-Mail:** b.khaw@neu.edu

KHAWAJA, IKRAM ULLAH, ECONOMIC GEOLOGY. **Personal Data:** b Delhi, India, December 25, 1942; m 1968. **Education:** Univ Karachi, BS, 1962, MS, 1963; Southern Ill Univ, MS, 1968; Ind Univ, Bloomington, PhD (geol), 1969. **Professional Experience:** PROF EMER GEOL, YOUNGSTOWN STATE UNIV, as of 2006; prof geol, youngstown state univ, beginning 1981; from asst prof to assoc prof, Youngstown State Univ, 1968-1981. **Memberships:** Geol Soc Am; Sigma Xi. **Research Statement & Publications:** Coal geology; petrology; sulphides in coal. **Mailing Address:** Dept Geol, Youngstown State Univ, Moser Hall 2120 One Univ Plaza, Youngstown, OH 44555. **Fax:** 330-941-1754. **E-Mail:** ikhawaja@cis.ysu.edu

KHAYAT, ALI, AGRICULTURAL CHEMISTRY, FOOD SCIENCE. **Personal Data:** b Tehran, Iran, February 2, 1938; American citizen; m 1966, c 2. **Education:** Univ Tehran, BS, 1961; Univ Calif, Davis, MS, 1964, PhD (agr chem), 1968. **Professional Experience:** ASSOC DIR RES, BEATRICE, 1982-; sr scientist res dept, Van Camp Div, 1977-1982; assoc scientist, Ralston Purina Co, 1972-1977; res biochemist, Ralston Purina Co, 1970-1972; asst prof, Med Sch, Pahlavi Univ, Iran, 1968-1970; Res asst biochem, Univ Calif, Davis, 1964-1968. **Memberships:** Am Chem Soc; Sigma Xi; Inst Food Technologists; AAAS. **Research Statement & Publications:** Chemical modification of proteins; flavor chemistry; studies on vegetable oils; food texture; sensory and microbiological evaluation of foods. **Mailing Address:** Hunt Wesson Food Inc, 1645 W Valencia Dr, Fullerton, CA 92833.

KHAZAN, NAIM, PHARMACOLOGY. **Personal Data:** b Baghdad, Iraq, February 15, 1921; American citizen; m 1952, c 2. **Education:** Col Pharm & Chem, Baghdad, PhC, 1943; Hebrew Univ Jerusalem, PhD (pharmacol), 1960. **Honors & Awards:** Ellis Grollman Lectr Award, 1990. **Professional Experience:** EMERSON PROF, PHARMACOL & TOXICOL, UNIV MD, 1980-; Mem, Grad Coun, Univ Md, Baltimore City, 1978-; Nat Inst Drug Abuse grants, 1975-1978, 1978-1988; chmn, Dept Pharmacol & Toxicol & dir, Grad

Prog Pharmacol, 1974-1986; prof pharmacol & toxicol, Pharmacol & Toxicol, Univ MD, 1974-1980; head dept pharmacol, Merrell Nat Labs, Cincinnati & assoc clin prof, Col Med, Univ Cincinnati, 1972-1974; assoc prof pharmacol, Mt Sinai Sch Med, 1968-1972; USPHS int fel, 1968; assoc prof, Columbia Univ, 1967-1968; NIMH grants, 1967, 1968-1972, 1972-1975; asst prof, Med Sch, Univ Ore, 1966-1967; sr lectr, Hadassah Med Sch & Sch Pharm, Hebrew Univ, Jerusalem, 1966; lectr, Hadassah Med Sch & Sch Pharm, Hebrew Univ, Jerusalem, 1964; Res assoc cent nerv syst pharmacol, Upjohn Co, 1963-1964. **Memberships:** Am Pharmaceut Asn; Am Soc Pharmacol & Exp Therapeut; NY Acad Sci; Soc Neurosci; Sigma Xi. **Research Statement & Publications:** Electroencephalographic and behavioral studies of experimental drug dependence on narcotics; electroencephalographic effects of cannabinoids; pharmacology of rapid eye movement sleep; opioid multiple receptors and electroencephalograph power spectra. **Mailing Address:** Dept Pharmacol & Toxicol, Sch Pharm, Baltimore, MD 21209. **Fax:** 410-363-0225.

KHESHGI, HAROON S, CLIMATE CHANGE, FLUID MECHANICS. **Personal Data:** b Bay Shore, NY, September 25, 1957. **Education:** Univ Ill, Champaign Urbana, BS, 1978; Univ Minn, Minneapolis, PhD (chem eng), 1984. **Professional Experience:** AT EXXON RES & ENG CO, as of 1999; Vis researcher climate change prog, Lawrence Livermore Nat Lab, 1994; Adj assoc prof dept earth sys sci, NY Univ, 1993-; STAFF ENGR CORP RES, EXXON RES & ENG CO, 1986-; Engr laser isotope separating prog, Lawrence Livermore Nat Lab, 1983-1986. **Memberships:** Am Inst Chem Eng; Am Phys Soc; Am Geophs Union. **Research Statement & Publications:** Global climate change, mitigation of greenhouse gas emissions, fluid mechanics, coating operations and reaction engineering. **Mailing Address:** Exxon Res & Eng Co, Route 22 E, Annandale, NJ 08801. **Fax:** 908-730-3301. **E-Mail:** hskhesh@erenj.com

KHO, BOEN TONG, ANALYTICAL CHEMISTRY. **Personal Data:** b Tegal, Indonesia, December 3, 1919; American citizen; m 1960, Helen; c John, Andrew, Peter, Suzanne. **Education:** Univ Utrecht, BS, 1942; State Univ Leiden, Drs, 1947, apotheker, 1949; Philadelphia Col Pharm, MS, 1952; Univ Wis, PhD (pharm), 1957. **Professional Experience:** RETIRED; at Wyeth Inc, 1985-1990; dir anal res & develop, Ayerst Labs, Inc, 1971-1985; asst dir anal res & develop, Ayerst Labs, Inc, 1968-1971; mgr analytical res, Ciba-Agrochem Co, 1967-1968; head analytical res, Toms River Res Lab, Ciba Chem & Dye Co, 1964-1967; head methods develop, Merck Sharp & Dohme, 1960-1964; res chemist, Cent Res Labs, Gen Aniline & Film Co, Pa, 1957-1960. **Memberships:** Am Chem Soc; Am Pharmaceut Asn; NY Acad Sci; Sigma Xi. **Mailing Address:** 37 Adirondack Lane, Plattsburgh, NY 12901-3213.

KHO, JAMES W, COMPUTER SCIENCE. **Education:** Univ Philippines, BS; Univ Wis-Madison, MS, PhD (comput sci); Calif State Uinv, Sacremento, MBA. **Professional Experience:** VPRES OPERS, DEVRY UNIV, 2005-. **Mailing Address:** Devry Univ, 6600 Dumbarton Cir, Fremont, CA 94555. **Fax:** 510-742-0868. **E-Mail:** jkho@fre.devry.edu

KHODADAD, JENA KHADEM, ULTRASTRUCTURE, MEMBRANES. **Personal Data:** b Tehran, Iran, American citizen; c 3. **Education:** Mt Union Col, BS, 1960; Northwestern Univ, MS, 1971, PhD (biol sci), 1975. **Professional Experience:** PROF & SCI RESEARCHER, MED COL, RUSH UNIV, as of 2004; assoc prof anat, Med Col, Rush Univ, as of 2003; asst prof anat & path, Med Col, Rush Univ, beginning 1979; instr cell biol, Dept Path, Rush Univ, 1978-1979; fel membrane, Rush Univ, 1977-1978. **Memberships:** Am Soc Cell Biol; Am Asn Anatomists; AAAS. **Research Statement & Publications:** Membrane research; biological membranes and the correlationship of ultrastructure with biochemical studies; red blood cell is the model membrane system used. **Mailing Address:** Dept Anat, Med Sch, Rush Univ, 600 S Paulina St, Chicago, IL 60612. **Fax:** 312-942-5744. **E-Mail:** jena_k_khodadad@rush.edu

KHONDKER, ABUL N, ELECTRICAL ENGINEERING. **Education:** Rice Univ, PhD. **Professional Experience:** ASSOC PROF, DEPT ELEC & COMPUT SCI, CLARKSON UNIV, NY, as of 2006. **Mailing Address:** Dept Elec & Comput Eng, Clarkson Univ 134 Camp Bldg PO Box 5720, Potsdam, NY 13699-5720. **E-Mail:** khondker@clarkson.edu

KHONSARI, MICHAEL M, MECHANICAL ENGINEERING. **Personal Data:** b August 17, 1957; m 1990, Karen S Troy. **Education:** Univ Tex, BS, 1978, MS, 1979, PhD (mech eng), 1983. **Honors & Awards:** Newark Award, Am Soc Mech Engrs, 1990. **Professional Experience:** DIR, CTR ROTATING MACHINERY, as of 2004; PROF MECH ENG & DOW CHEM ENDOWED CHMN, LA STATE UNIV, as of 2004; Wright-Patterson AFB, 1990 & US Dept Energy, 1993; assoc ed, J Tribology Trans, 1990-; Assoc Prof, Univ Pittsburgh, beginning 1990; William Whiteford fac fel, Univ Pittsburgh, 1990-1992; Found award, Alcoa, 1990-1991; MEM FAC, CTR MOTION CONTROL, 1989-; asst prof, Ctr Motion Control, 1988-1990; Prof Mech Eng, Univ Pitt, 1988-1996; fac res fel, NASA Lewis Res Ctr, 1986, 1987, 1988; asst prof, Ohio State Univ, Columbus, 1984-1988; Res & teaching asst, Univ Tex, Austin, 1978-1983; reviewer, NSF, NASA, Am Chem Soc Books, McGraw Hill Books, Addison Wesley Books, Prentice-Hall Books, Holt Rinehart & Winston books. **Memberships:** Am Soc Mech Engrs; Soc Tribology & Lubrication Engrs. **Research Statement & Publications:** Thermal effects in hydrodynamic bearings; multi-phase flows in bearings; friction associated with instrument pointing mechanisms operating under ultra low speeds; elastohydrodynamic lubrication; non-Newtonian fluid mechanics and heat transfer analysis. **Mailing Address:** Dept Mech Eng, La State Univ, Baton Rouge, LA 70803-6413. **Fax:** 225-578-5924. **E-Mail:** khonsari@me.lsu.edu

KHOO, MICHAEL C K, BIOMEDICAL ENGINEERING. **Personal Data:** b Kowloon, Hong Kong, September 15, 1954; c 2. **Education:** Univ London, BSc, 1976; Harvard Univ, MS, 1977, PhD (bioeng), 1981. **Honors & Awards:** biomed eng res award, Whitaker Found, 1985-1988; NSF res initiation award, 1985-1987; new investr award, NIH, 1985-1989; res career develop award, NIH, 1990-1996; career investr award, Am Lung Asn, 1991-1996. **Professional Experience:** Co-dir educ, UNIV SOUTHERN CALIF, as of 2005; PROF BIOMED ENG, UNIV SOUTHERN CALIF, 1997-; assoc prof biomed eng, Univ Southern Calif, 1990-1997; asst prof, Univ Southern Calif, 1983-1990; res assoc biomed eng, Vet Admin Med Ctr, W Roxbury & Brigham & Women's Hosp, Boston, 1981-1983; fel, Am Inst Med & Biol Eng. **Memberships:** Biomed Eng Soc; Am Physiol Soc; Inst Elec & Electronics Engrs; Am Thoracic Soc; Am Sleep Disorders Asn. **Research Statement & Publications:** Modeling of physiological control systems; cardiopulmonary physiology during sleep; biomedical signal processing. **Mailing Address:** Biomed Eng Dept, Univ Southern Calif, OHE 530C, Los Angeles, CA 90089-1451. **Fax:** 213-740-0343. **E-Mail:** khoo@bmsr.usc.edu

KHOO, TENG LEK, NUCLEAR PHYSICS. **Personal Data:** b Penang, Malaysia, June 1, 1943; m 1972, c 2. **Education:** Dalhousie Univ, BSc, 1965, MSc, 1967; McMaster Univ, PhD (physics), 1972. **Professional Experience:** SR PHYSICIST, NUCLEAR PHYSICS, ARGONNE NAT LAB, 1979-; from asst physicist to physicist, Nuclear Physics, Argonne Nat Lab, 1977-1985; asst prof, Mich State Univ, 1974-1977; res assoc nuclear physics, Mich State Univ, 1972-1974. **Memberships:** Fel Am Phys Soc. **Research Statement & Publications:** Experimental nuclear structure physics, especially properties of deformed nuclei, effective nucleon interaction and nuclei at high angular momentum and high temperature; formation and decay of compound nucleus. **Mailing Address:** Argonne Nat Lab, 9700 S Cass Ave Bldg 203, Argonne, IL 60439. **Fax:** 630-252-6210. **E-Mail:** khoo@anl.gov

KHOOBYARIAN, NEWTON, virology; deceased, see previous edition for last biography

KHORANA, BRIJ MOHAN, APPLIED OPTICS, RESEARCH & MANAGEMENT. **Personal Data:** b Multan, India, April 11, 1939; m 1967, Renu; c 3. **Education:** Univ Delhi, BSc, 1958, MSc, 1960; Indian Inst Technol, Kharagpur, MTech, 1961; Univ Chicago, MS, 1964; Case Western Res Univ, PhD (physics), 1968. **Professional Experience:** VPRES, ROSE-HULMAN INST VENTURES, as of 2006; dir, Tech Assistance Servs Ctr, Rose-Hulman Inst Technol, 1993-; DIR, CTR APPL OPTICS STUDIES, 1985-; PROF PHYSICS & APPL OPTICS, ROSE-HULMAN INST TECHNOL, 1984-; head, Ctr Appl Optics Studies, 1980-1991; assoc prof physics, Ctr Appl Optics Studies, 1977-1984; asst prof physics, Univ Notre Dame, 1970-1977; res assoc physics, Univ Rochester, 1968-1970; res assoc physics, James Franck Inst, Univ Chicago, 1967-1968. **Memberships:** Sr mem Soc Mfg Engrs; fel Int Soc Optical Eng; Optical Soc Am; Machine Vision Asn. **Research Statement & Publications:** Machine vision applications; quality inspection systems; design of automotive lighting (external); design of luminares; biomedical optic. **Mailing Address:** Ctr Appl Optics Studies, Rose-Hulman Inst Technol, 5500 Wabash Ave, Terre Haute, IN 47803. **Fax:** 812-877-8817. **E-Mail:** brij.khorana@rose_hulman.edu

KHORANA, HAR GOBIND, ORGANIC CHEMISTRY. **Personal Data:** b Raipur, India, January 9, 1922; m 1952, Esther; c Julia, Emily Anne & Dave Roy. **Education:** Punjab Univ, India, BS, 1943, MS, 1945; Univ Liverpool, PhD, 1948. **Honorary Degrees:** DSc, Univ Chicago, 1966, Simon Fraser Univ, 1969, Univ Liverpool, 1971, Univ Wis, 1976, Univ BC, 1977, New Eng Col, 1984, Hokkaido Univ, 1993, Univ Miami, 1994, Univ Bergen, 1996; Dr, Adam Mickiewicz Univ, 1994. **Honors & Awards:** Nobel Prize in Med, 1968; Nat Medal of Sci, 1987; Merck Award, Chem Inst Can, 1958; Gold Medal, Prof Inst Can Pub Serv, 1960; Dannie Heinneman Prize, 1967; Lasker Found Award, 1968; Louisa Gross Horwitz Prize, 1968; Paul Kayser Int Award of Merit in Retina Res, 1987; David E Green Lectr, Wis; First Phillip Handler Lectr, Duke Univ; John T Edsau Lectr, Harvard Univ; Hans Neurath Lectr, Univ Wash. **Professional Experience:** ALFRED P SLOAN PROF EMER, BIOL & CHEM, MASS INST TECHNOL, as of 1998; Andrew D White prof, Cornell Univ, 1974-1980; Alfred P Sloan Prof, Mass Inst Technol, beginning 1970; vis prof, Harvard Med Sch, 1966; prof & group leader, Conrad A Elvejhem prof life sci, 1964-1971; vis prof, Stanford Univ, 1964; prof, Inst Enzyme Res, Univ Wis-Madison, 1962-1971; prof & group leader, Inst Enzyme Res, Univ Wis-Madison, 1960-1962; vis prof, Rockefeller Inst, 1959; head org chem group, BC Res Coun & res prof fac grad studies, Univ BC, 1952-1960; Nuffield fel, with Prof Sir Alexander Todd, Cambridge Univ, 1950-1952; Govt India fel, with Prof V Prelog, Swiss Fed Inst Technol, 1948-1949. **Memberships:** Nat Acad Sci; fel AAAS; Am Chem Soc; Am Soc Biol Chem; fel Am Acad Arts & Sci; foreign mem Royal Soc; Am Philos Soc; Indian Acad Sci; Pontifical Acad Sci; Royal Soc Edinburgh; hon fel Indian Soc Genetics & Plant Breeding; hon mem Pharmaceut Soc Japan; hon mem Japanese Biochem Soc. **Research Statement & Publications:** Peptides and proteins; chemistry of phosphate esters of biological interest; nucleic acids; chemical synthesis and structure; enzymes of nucleic acid metabolism; viruses and chemical genetics; chemistry and biochemistry of bilogical membranes; polynucleotide syntheas and the elucidation of the genetic code. **Mailing Address:** Mass Inst Technol, Dept Biol & Chem, 77 Mass Ave Rm 68-680, Cambridge, MA 02139. **Fax:** 617-253-0533. **E-Mail:** khorana@mit.edu

KHORRAM, SIAMAK, ELECTRICAL ENGINEERING. **Education:** Univ Calif, Davis, MS & MS; Univ Calif, Berkeley, PhD, 1975. **Professional Experience:** PROF FORESTRY & OF ELEC & COMPUT ENG, NC STATE UNIV, as of 2006; DIR, CTR EARTH OBSERV, NC STATE UNIV, as of 2006. **Mailing Address:** NC State Univ, PO Box 7106, Raleigh, NC 27695. **E-Mail:** khorram@ncsu.edu

KHOSAH, ROBINSON PANGANAI, CHROMATOGRAPHY, MASS SPECTROMETRY. **Personal Data:** b Marondera, Zimbabwe, January 1, 1954; American citizen. **Education:** Univ Rhodesia, BS, 1976; Univ Mass Amherst, MS, 1981, PhD (chem), 1985. **Professional Experience:** PRIN INVESTR, ADVAN TECHNOL SYST INC, as of 2000; TECH SPECIALIST, ALCOA, 1989-; staff scientist, Alcoa, 1987-1989; sr scientist, Alcoa, 1986-1987; pres & coatings consult, Diverse Technologies Inc, 1985-; scientist, Alcoa, 1984-1986. **Memberships:** Am Chem Soc. **Research Statement & Publications:** Separation mechanisms under supercritical fluids; analytical chromatography; preparative scale supercritical fluid extraction. **Mailing Address:** Advan Technol Syst Inc, 639 Alpha Dr RIDC Park, Pittsburgh, PA 15238. **Fax:** 412-967-1911. **E-Mail:** rkhosah@atsengineers.com

KHOSHNEVIS, BEHROKH, INDUSTRIAL ROBOTICS. **Education:** Univ SC, BS. **Professional Experience:** PROF, INDUST & SYST ENG, UNIV SOUTHERN CALIF, as of 2006; DIR, CTR RAPID AUTOMATED FABRICATION TECHNOL, UNIV SOUTHERN CALIF, as of 2006; DIR, MFG ENG GRAD PROG, UNIV SOUTHERN CALIF, as of 2006. **Memberships:** Inst Indust Engrs; Soc Comput Simulation. **Mailing Address:** Dept Indust & Syst Eng, Univ Southern Calif, Los Angeles, CA 90089-0193. **Fax:** 213-740-1120. **E-Mail:** khoshnev@rcf.usc.edu

KHOSHNEVISAN, MOHSEN MONTE, ELECTROOPTICS, NONLINEAR OPTICS. **Personal Data:** b 1945; American citizen; m 1970, c 2. **Education:** Calif State Univ, San Jose, BS & BA, 1968; Mich State Univ, MS, 1971, PhD (physics), 1973. **Professional Experience:** DIR OPTICS, SCI CTR, ROCKWELL INT, 1988-; mem tech staff, Electro-Optics Dept, 1978-1988; vis asst prof, Mich State Univ, Lansing, 1977-1978; asst prof phys, Arya-Mehr Univ Technol, Iran, 1973-1977. **Memberships:** Am Phys Soc; Optical Soc Am; Soc Photo-Instrumentation Engrs. **Research Statement & Publications:** Electro-optics; nonlinear optics; thin films. **Mailing Address:** Rockwell Int Sci Ctr, 1049 Camino do Rios, Thousand Oaks, CA 91360.

KHOSLA, MAHESH C, HYPERTENSION, NEUROSCIENCES. **Personal Data:** b Rajoya, Hazara, India, July 6, 1925; m 1957, Santosh; c Renu, Rajan & Rajesh. **Education:** Panjab Univ, India, BS, 1950, MS, 1952, PhD, 1957. **Professional Experience:** NIH grantee, beginning 1978; STAFF, CLEVELAND CLIN FOUND, beginning 1971; fel med adv bd, Coun High Blood Pressure Res, Am Heart Asn, beginning 1971; assoc staff, Cleveland Clin Found, 1971; sr sci officer, Cent Drug Res Inst, Lucknow, Uttar Pardesh, India, 1957-1969. **Memberships:** Am Chem Soc; Am Soc Biochem & Molecular Biol; Int Soc Hypertension; Am Soc Hypertension; AAAS; Am Heart Asn; NY Acad Sci; Inter-Am Soc Hypertension; Am Peptide Soc. **Research Statement & Publications:** Synthesis of angiotensin II antagonists with minimum agonist activity; synthesis of tissue selective congeners of angiotensin II; hypertension; granted nine patents; author of various publications. **Mailing Address:** Health Sci Ctr, Cleveland Clin Found, REBV/NC3-147, 9500 Euclid Ave, Cleveland, OH 44195-5286.

KHOSLA, PRADEEP, INDUSTRIAL ROBOTICS. **Education:** Indian Inst Technol, Kharagpur, India, BTech, 1980; Carnegie-Mellon Univ, MS, 1984, PhD, 1986. **Professional Experience:** DEAN & PHILIP & MARSHA DOWD PROF ELEC & COMPUT ENG, CARNEGIE-MELLON UNIV, as of 2005. **Memberships:** Robotics & Automation Soc. **Mailing Address:** Dept Elec & Comput Eng, Carnegie-Mellon Univ, 2107 Collab Innovation Ctr Hamerschlag Hall, Pittsburgh, PA 15213. **Fax:** 412-268-6421. **E-Mail:** pkk@ece.cmu.edu

KHOSLA, RAJINDER PAUL, SOLID STATE PHYSICS, NANOTECHNOLOGY. **Personal Data:** b Phillaur, India, July 25, 1933; m 1966, Linda; c Ronald, Priya & Sunita. **Education:** Univ Delhi, BSc, 1953; Benaras Hindu Univ, MSc, 1955; Purdue Univ, PhD (physics), 1966 Harvard Univ, Advanced management Program, 1989. **Honors & Awards:** Frederick Philips Award, Inst Elec & Electronics Engrs; Director's Superior Accomplishment Award, National Science Foundation. **Professional Experience:** PROG Director, Electronics, Photonics, and Device Technologies, NAT SCI FOUND, as of 1996; Acting Division DIR, Electrical & Communications Systems, NAT SCI FOUND (2000-2002), Embassy Fellow at the US Embassy in Tokyo (3/02-6/02); gen mgr, microelectronics technol div, Eastman Kodak Co, 1985-1995; asst dir, Physics Div, 1982-1985; sr res lab head, Solid State Lab, 1979-1982; lab head, Solid State Lab, 1976-1979; group leader device technol, Solid State Lab, 1975-1976; vis scholar, Dept Elec Eng & Comput Sci, Univ Calif, Santa Barbara, 1974-1975; Lectr, Eve Sch, Univ Rochester, 1972-1974; res assoc, Microelectronics Technol Div, Eastman Kodak CO, 1971-1976; sr physicist, Microelectronics Technol Div, Eastman Kodak CO, 1966-1970; teaching & res asst, Purdue Univ, 1959-1966; sci asst, Nat Phys Lab India, New Delhi, 1956-1959; Lectr physics, Govt Col, Narnaul, India, 1955-1956. **Memberships:** Fel Am Phys Soc; fel Inst Elec & Electronics Engrs; fel Optical Soc of America. **Research Statement & Publications:** Applications of micro/nanotechnologies in biology and medicine; molecular electronics; micro/nanoelectronic devices and processing technologies; micro/nano electro mechanical systems; development of biocompatible and implantable devices for diagnosis and treatment. **Mailing Address:** Nat Sci Found, 4201 Wilson Blvd, Ste 675, Arlington, VA 22230. **Fax:** 703-292-9147. **E-Mail:** rkhosla@nsf.gov

KHOSRAVIYANI, FIROOZ, GROUP REPRESENTATION THEORY, ALGORITHMS. **Personal Data:** b Tehran, Iran, April 21, 1952; American citizen; m 1975, Mahvash; c Kourosh & Anahita. **Education:** Tehran Univ, BSc (math), 1974; Univ Wales, MSc (math), 1977, PhD (math), 1981. **Professional Experience:** ASSOC PROF COMPUT Sci & MATH, TEX A&M INT UNIV, 1995-; asst prof, Tex A&M Int Univ, 1992-1995; asst prof comput sci & math, Univ Tex, 1985-1992; adj fac res, San Diego State Univ, 1984-1985; Asst prof comput sci & math, Univ Gezira, Sudan, 1981-1984. **Memberships:** London Math Soc; Math Asn Am (Life, Dept Liaison); South Texas Mathematics Consortium (Member Exec Comm, 1992-). **Research Statement & Publications:** Group character tables over a finite field and the inter-relationship of group character tables over fields of different characteristic; algorithms and data structures, e g extension of binary and fibonacci search to linear linked list. **Mailing Address:** Dept Mathematical & Physical Scis, Tex A&M Int Univ, 5201 Univ Blvd, Laredo, TX 78041-1900. **E-Mail:** FiroozKh@tamiu.edu

KHOT, NARENDRA S, AEROSPACE ENGINEERING. **Education:** Stanford Univ, Phd. **Professional Experience:** RES SCI, AIR FORCE RES LAB, OHIO, as of 1999. **Mailing Address:** USAF AFWAL/FIBRA, Flight Dynamics Lab, Wright-Patt AFB, OH 45433. **Fax:** 513-255-6992.

KHOURY, MUIN J, GENETICS. **Education:** Am Univ Beirut, BS; Johns Hopkins Univ, PhD (genetic Epidemiol). **Professional Experience:** DIR, OFF GENOMICS & DIS PREV CTR DIS CONTROL & PREV, as of 2005. **Mailing Address:** Genomics & Dis Prev Ctr Dis Control & Prev, 1600 Clifton Rd NE, Atlanta, GA 30333.

KHRAIBI, ALI A, CARDIOVASCULAR PHYSIOLOGY, RENAL PHYSIOLOGY. **Personal Data:** b Sidon, Lebanon, November 21, 1956; American citizen. **Education:** Univ Miss Sch Med, BS, 1978, MS, 1980, PhD (physiol), 1984. **Professional Experience:** PROF PHYSIOL, EASTERN VA MED SCH, NORFOLK, 2000-; asst prof physiol, Mayo Clin & Found, Rochester, 1990-1995; sr res fel, Mayo Clin & Found, 1986-1990; fel, Bowman Gray Sch Med, 1984-1986. **Memberships:** Fel Am Heart Asn; Am Physiol Soc; Am Soc Nephrology. **Research Statement & Publications:** Study the handling of regulation of sodium and water excretion by the kidneys in hypertension. **Mailing Address:** Dept Physiol, Eastern Va Med Sch, Norfolk, VA 23507. **E-Mail:** khraibaa@evms.edu

KHURANA, ANIL, PHYSICS. **Professional Experience:** ADJ PROF, DEPT MATH SCI, STEVENS INST TECH, as of 2005. **Memberships:** Am Phys Soc. **Mailing Address:** Dept Math Sci, Stevens Inst Technol, Kidde 111, Hoboken, NJ 07728. **Fax:** 201-216-8321. **E-Mail:** akhurana@stevens.edu

KHURANA, KRISHAN KUMAR, SPACE PHYSICS, MAGNETOSPHERIC PHYSICS. **Personal Data:** b New Delhi, India, June 1, 1955. **Education:** Delhi Univ, India, BSc, 1974; Osmania Univ, India, MSc, 1977, PhD (appl geophys), 1981; Durham Univ, UK, PhD (pure geophys), 1984. **Professional Experience:** Prin investr, NASA, beginning 1990; ASST RES GEOPHYSICIST SPACE PHYSICS, UNIV CALIF, LOS ANGELES, 1985-. **Memberships:** Am Geophys Soc; Am Phys Soc; Am Astron Soc. **Research Statement & Publications:** Magnetospheres of Venus, Earth, Jupiter, Saturn and Uranus; structure and motion of Jupiter's magnetosphere; spherical harmonic models of planetary magnetic fields; data processing for the Galileo mission to Jupiter. **Mailing Address:** Inst Geophys & Planetary Physics, Univ Calif, 405 Hilgard Ave Slichter Hall, Los Angeles, CA 90095-1567. **Fax:** 310-206-8042. **E-Mail:** kkhurana@igpp.ucla.edu

KHURANA, SURJIT SINGH, MATHEMATICS. **Personal Data:** b Tandlianwala, Pakistan, June 15, 1931; m 1962, c 3. **Education:** Panjab Univ, India, BA, 1953, MA, 1955; Univ Ill, Urbana, PhD (math), 1968. **Professional Experience:** PROF MATH, UNIV IOWA, 1979-; assoc prof, Univ Iowa, 1974-1979; asst prof, Univ Iowa, 1968-1974; lectr math, Postgrad Inst, Univ Delhi, 1959-1964; lectr math, Camp Col, Panjab Univ, India, 1956-1959. **Memberships:** Am Math Soc. **Research Statement & Publications:** Measure theory; functional analysis; general topology; probability theory; topological vector spaces. **Mailing Address:** Univ Iowa, 14 MLH, Iowa City, IA 52242. **E-Mail:** surjit-khurana@uiowa.edu

KHURGIN, JACOB B, PHYSICS. **Education:** Inst Fine Mech & Optics, Russia, BS, 1977 & MS 1979; Polytech Univ Ny, PhD (Electro Physics), 1987. **Professional Experience:** PROF ELEC ENG, JOHNS HOPKINS UNIV, 1995-; asst to assoc prof, Johns Hopkins Univ, 1988-1995; from res staff to sr mem res staff, Philips Labs, Briarcliff Ma, NY, 1980-1988. **Research Statement & Publications:** Theoretical and experimental studies of electronic; optical; and magnetic properties of the semiconductors and their heterostructures - quantum wells; and superlattices. **Mailing Address:** Dept Elect & Comp Eng, Johns Hopkins Univ, 315 Barton Hall 3400 N Charles St, Baltimore, MD 21218. **Fax:** 410-516-5566. **E-Mail:** jakek@jhu.edu

KHURI, NICOLA NAJIB, THEORETICAL PHYSICS. **Personal Data:** b Beirut, Lebanon, May 27, 1933; m 1955, c 2. **Education:** Am Univ, Beirut, BA, 1952; Princeton Univ, PhD (physics), 1957. **Professional Experience:** PROF EMER PHYSICS, ROCKFELLER UNIV, as of 2004; Trustee, Brearley Sch, 1970-1979; trustee, Am Univ Beirut, 1969-; prof physics, Rockefeller Univ, beginning 1968; assoc prof, Rockefeller Univ, 1964-1968; Brookhaven Nat Lab, 1963-1973; vis assoc prof, Columbia Univ, 1963-1964; assoc prof physics, Am Univ, Beirut, 1961-1962; mem Inst Adv Study, 1959-1960, 1962-1963; asst prof physics, Am Univ, Beirut, 1957-1958. **Memberships:** Fel Am Phys Soc. **Research Statement & Publications:** Quantum field theory; scattering theory; theory of dispersion relations and their applications; high energy particle physics. **Mailing Address:** Dept Physics, Rockefeller Univ, 1230 York Ave, New York, NY 10021. **Fax:** 212-327-7974. **E-Mail:** khuri@rockefeller.edu

KHURI, SAMI, COMPUTER SCIENCE. **Education:** Syracuse Univ, BS, MS, PhD (Comput Sci). **Professional Experience:** PROF, DEPT COMPUT SCI, SAN JOSE STATE UNIV, 1992-. **Mailing Address:** Comput Sci Dept, Wellesley Col, Wellesley, MA 02181. **Fax:** 408-924-5062. **E-Mail:** khuri@cs.sjsu.edu

KHUSH, GURDEV S, PLANT BREEDING, GENETICS. **Personal Data:** b Rurki, India, August 22, 1935; m 1961, Marwant K Grewal; c Ranjiv S, Manjeev K, Sonia K & Kiran K. **Education:** Punjab Univ, India, BSc, 1955; Univ Calif, Davis, PhD (genetics), 1960. **Honorary Degrees:** Dr, Punjab Agr Univ, India, 1987, Tamil Nadu Agri Univ, 1995, C S Azad Univ Agr Technol, 1995, G B Pant Univ Agr & Technol, 1996. **Honors & Awards:** Borlaung Award, 1977; Japan Prize, 1987; ASA Fel Award, 1987; Int Agron Award, 1989; Emil M Marak Int Award, 1990; World Food Prize, 1996. **Professional Experience:** PRIN PLANT BREEDER & HEAD, DIV PLANT BREEDING, GENETICS & BIOCHEM, INT RICE RES INST, 1986-; Vis prof, Univ Philippines, Los Banos, 1968- & Colo State Univ, 1975-1976; head, Varietal Improv Dept, 1972-1985; plant breeder, Div Plant Breeding, Genetics & Biochem, Int Rice Res Inst, 1967-1972; asst res geneticist, Univ Calif, Davis, 1962-1967; jr res geneticist, Univ Calif, Davis, 1961-1962; Asst genetics, Univ Calif, Davis, 1957-1961. **Memberships:** Foreign assoc Nat Acad Sci; Genetics Soc Am; Bot Soc Am; NY Acad Sci; Indian Nat Sci Acad; Third World Acad Sci. **Research Statement & Publications:** Cytogenetic studies of genus Secale and origin of cultivated rye and genus Lycopersicon particularly gene location, chromosome mapping and centromere location in the cultivated tomato; rice genetics and breeding. **Mailing Address:** Int Rice Res Inst, PO Box 933, Manila, Philippines. **Fax:** 632-818-2087; 632-891-1292. **E-Mail:** g.khosh@cgnet.com

KHWAJA, TASNEEM AFZAL, CANCER, CHEMOTHERAPY. **Personal Data:** b Pakistan, April 20, 1936; m 1965, c 2. **Education:** Univ Panjab, WPakistan, BSc, 1955, MSc, 1957; Cambridge Univ, MA, 1961, PhD (synthetic nucleic acid chem), 1964. **Professional Experience:** ASSOC PROF PATH, SCH MED, UNIV SOUTHERN CALIF, 1976-; SR RES SCIENTIST & DIR ANIMAL TUMOR RESOURCE FACIL & PHARMACOANALYTIC FACIL, LOS ANGELES CO-UNIV SOUTHERN CALIF CANCER CTR, 1973-; asst prof, Los Angeles Co-univ Southern Calif Cancer Ctr, 1973-1975; head, Dept Cancer Chemother, ICN Nucleic Acid Res Inst, 1970-1973; res asst, Max Planck Inst Exp Med, Ger, 1969-1970; NIH proj assoc grant, McArdle Lab Cancer Res, Univ Wis-Madison, 1966-1968; NIH res assoc grant, Univ Utah, 1965-1966. **Memberships:** Am Asn Cancer Res; fel Royal Chem Soc; Am Chem Soc. **Research Statement & Publications:** Synthesis of nucleoside antimetabolites as antitumor agents; biochemical mechanisms of drug action; use of animal tumor models. **Mailing Address:** Dept Path, Sch Med, Univ Southern Calif, HMR 209, 2011 Zonal Ave, Los Angeles, CA 90089-9092. **Fax:** 949-760-6817. **E-Mail:** takhwaja@aol.com

KIAER, C LYNN, MATHEMATICS. **Education:** PhD (appl math), 1992. **Professional Experience:** ASST PROF MATH, ROSE-HULMAN INST TECH, as of 2006. **Memberships:** Am Math Soc. **Mailing Address:** Rose-Hulman Inst Technol, 5500 Wabash Ave, Terre Haute, IN 47803. **Fax:** 812-877-8256. **E-Mail:** kiaer@nextwork.rose-hulman.edu

KIANG, CHIA SZU, ATMOSPHERIC SCIENCES, PHYSICS. **Personal Data:** b Shanghai, China, September 9, 1939; American citizen; m 1968, Marilyn; c Mia & Lara. **Education:** Nat Taiwan Univ, BS, 1962; Ga Inst Technol, MS, 1964, PhD (physics), 1970. **Honors & Awards:** Henry A Hill Distinguished Lectr Award, 1986. **Professional Experience:** PROF EMER EARTH & ATMOSPHERIC SCI, GA INST TECHNOL, as of 2006; Dir, Off Environ Sci Technol & Policy, 1991-1992; inst prof earth & atmospheric sci, Ga inst technol, beginning 1988; dir, Southern Oxidants Study, 1988-1992; nat lectr, Sigma Xi, 1982-1984; dir, Sch Geophys Sci, 1981-1988; prof geophys sci, Ga Inst Technol, beginning 1978; aerosol proj leader, Nat Ctr Atmospheric Res, 1976-1978; adj prof physics, Ga Inst Technol, 1976-1977; adj prof, Dept Chem, Atlanta Univ, 1974-1976; adj prof, Dept Atmospheric Sci, Colo State Univ, 1974-1978; res scientist, Nat Ctr Atmospheric Res, 1974-1976; Sr res assoc, Atmospheric Sci Res Ctr, State Univ NY, Albany, 1971-; assoc prof physics, Clark Col, 1967-1974. **Memberships:** Am Chem Soc; Am Physics Soc; Am Meteorol Soc; AAAS. **Research Statement & Publications:** Nucleation; aerosol physics; aerosol chemistry; atmospheric chemistry; surface science; phase transition; critical phenomena; statistical physics; planetary atmosphere; environmental science and planning; natural phenomena. **Mailing Address:** Ga Inst Technol, Sch Earth & Atmospheric Sci, 311 Ferst Dr, Atlanta, GA 30332-0340. **Fax:** 404-894-5638.

KIANG, DAVID TEH-MING, INTERNAL MEDICINE, ONCOLOGY. **Personal Data:** b Chekiang, China, November 13, 1935; m 1968, c 3. **Education:** Nat Defense Med Ctr Taiwan, MB, 1960; Columbia Univ, MS, 1964; Univ Minn, PhD, 1973. **Professional Experience:** AT CANCER CTR, UNIV MINN, as of 2005; PROF EMER MED, MED SCH, UNIV MINN, MINNEAPOLIS, as of 2005; prof med, med sch, Univ Minn, Minneapolis, beginning 1990; assoc prof, Univ Minn, Minneapolis, 1981-1990; asst prof, Univ Minn, Minneapolis, 1973-1981; instr, Univ Minn, Minneapolis, 1970-1973; USPHS fel oncol, Univ Minn, Minneapolis, 1968-1970; resident, Francis Delafield Hosp, 1966-1968; resident, Beekman-Downtown Hosp, NY, 1965-1966; intern med, Beekman-Downtown Hosp, NY, 1964-1965. **Memberships:** Soc Exp Biol & Med; Am Fedn Clin Res; Am Asn Cancer Res; Am Soc Clin Oncol; Sigma Xi. **Research Statement & Publications:** Treatment of mammary cancer. **Mailing Address:** Dept Med, Univ Minn, Box 286 Mayo 420 Del St SE, Minneapolis, MN 55455-0392. **Fax:** 612-624-1443. **E-Mail:** kiang001@tn.umn.edu

KIANG, JULIANN G, SIGNAL TRANSDUCTION, HEAT SHOCK PROTEINS. **Personal Data:** b Taiwan, December 3, 1952; American citizen; m 1977, Peter; c Sharon & Andrew. **Education:** Fu-Jen Cath Univ, Taiwan, BS, 1975; Univ Nebr, Omaha, MS, 1977; Univ Calif, Berkely, PhD (toxicol), 1983. **Honors & Awards:** Henry Christian Mem Award, Am Fedn Clin Res, 1990 & 1993. **Professional Experience:** ASST CHIEF, DEPT CLIN PHYSIOL, WALTER REED ARMY INST RES, 1994-; asst prof pharmacol, Uniformed Serv Univ Health Sci, 1992-; jr investr travel award, Am Soc Gastroenterol, 1992; res physiologist, Dept Clin Physiol, Walter Reed Army Inst Res, 1989-1994; res physiologist,

Armed Forces Radiobiol Res Inst, 1988-1989; asst toxicol specialist, Univ Calif, Berkeley, 1984-1988; Travel award, Nat Inst Drug Abuse, 1982-1987; Res technologist, Creighton Univ Hosp, Omaha, 1977-1978. **Memberships:** Am Soc Cell Biol; Am Soc Pharmacol & Exp Therapeut; Soc Chinese Biologists Am. **Research Statement & Publications:** Characterize heat shock proteins in cultured cell lines; investigate the relationship between heat shock protein and signal transduction; study the protective role of heat shock protein from environmental toxins toxicity. **Mailing Address:** Dept Clin Physiol, Walter Reed Army Inst, Res Bldg 40 Rm 3078, Washington, DC 20307.

KIANG, NELSON YUAN-SHENG, NEUROPHYSIOLOGY. **Personal Data:** b Wuxi, China, July 6, 1929; American citizen; m 1976, Barbara Norris; c Peter Nien-chu. **Education:** Univ Chicago, PhB, 1947, PhD (biopsychol), 1955. **Honorary Degrees:** MD, Univ Geneva, Switz, 1981; MS, Harvard Univ, 1984. **Honors & Awards:** Beltone Award, 1968; prof Achievement Citation, univ of Chicago, 1991; Am Acad Arts & sci. **Professional Experience:** Sr adv, Am Chinese vet med frontiers, inc, 2002-; sr adv, china found, 2001-; Hon prof, Sun Yat-sen med univ, China, 2001-; hon prof, Peking union med col, China, 2001-; adv, center for Am studies, fudan univ, China, 1999-; Hon chair, Chinese med asn, 1998-2001; Hon adv, Chinese med asn, 1997-; adv, Center for brain res, fudan univ, China, 1997-; adv prof, school of life sci, fudan univ, China, 1997-; Chair and hon prof, acad and inst committee, Int higher inst of biomed eng, Zhejiang univ, China, 1997-; RETIRED; comn, Sci Freedom & Responsibility, AAAS, 1995; mem, Behav & Neurosci Study Sect, 1985-1989; prof, Dept Otol & Laryngol, Harvard Med Sch, 1984-1996; Health Sci & Technol, Res Lab Electronics, 1983-1996; neurophysiologist, Neurol Serv, Mass Gen Hosp, 1977-1996; Sr res assoc otolaryngol & physiol, Harvard Med Sch, 1969-; lectr elec eng, Res Lab Electronics, Mass Inst Technol, 1968-1983; mem, Commun Sci Study Sect, Div Res Grants, NIH, 1968-1972; Dir, Eaton Peabody Lab, Mass Eye & Ear Infirmary, 1962-1996; Res asst otolaryngol, Harvard Med Sch, 1961-1969; Res asst otol, Harvard Med Sch, 1957-1961; staff mem, Res Lab Electronics, Mass Inst Technol, 1955-1996; mem, Comt Hearing Bioacoust & Biomech, Nat Acad Sci-Nat Res Coun, Collegium Otorhinol-Laryngol Amiticiam Sacrum, Deafness Res Found & Int Brain Res Orgn. **Memberships:** AAAS; Soc Neurosci; Am Physiol Soc; fel Acoust Soc Am; Am Otol Soc; NY Acad Sci; Psychonomic Soc; Sigma Xi; Asn Res Otolaryngol; Royal Soc Med. **Research Statement & Publications:** Physiology of auditory and other sensory systems; relation of brain to behavior. **Mailing Address:** 18 Cedar Lane Way, Boston, MA 02108. **Fax:** 617-720-4408. **E-Mail:** bnk@epl.mcci.harvard.edu

KIANG, ROBERT L, MECHANICAL ENGINEERING, AERONAUTICAL ENG, GAS TURBINS ENGINES. **Personal Data:** b Chungking, China, November 30, 1939; American citizen; m 1986, Ming D; c Leland & Jennifer. **Education:** Nat Taiwan Univ, BS, 1961; Stanford Univ, MS, 1964, PhD (aeronaut eng), 1970. **Honors & Awards:** fel ASME. **Professional Experience:** Mech Engr, Naval Air syst command, 1996-; MECH ENGR, DAVID TAYLOR RES CTR, 1987-; sr res engr, Stanford Res Inst, 1971-1987; Res engr, Stanford Res Inst, 1963-1971; Teacher, USN Acad, Johns Hopkins Univ & San Jose State Univ. **Memberships:** Am Soc Mech Engrs. **Research Statement & Publications:** Fluid dynamics; dynamic modeling; nuclear safety; heat transfer; noise and vibration; friction and lubrication; Gas Turbine. **Mailing Address:** 408 Hartman Dr, Severna Park, MD 21146.

KIANG, YING CHAO, FIBER OPTICS, LASERS. **Personal Data:** b China, American citizen; c 2. **Education:** Nat Cheng Kung Univ, BS; Univ Ill, MS; Univ Md, PhD (elec eng). **Professional Experience:** CHMN, OPTICAL FIBER COMMUN STEERING COMT, FIBER OPTICS, DATA SYST DIV, IBM, 1967-; adj prof, Polytech Univ NY, 1966-1969; res mem lasers, Electronics div, Gen Dynamics, 1960-1966. **Memberships:** Sr mem Inst Elec & Electronics Engrs; Optical Soc Am. **Research Statement & Publications:** Analysis and experimentation on reflection induced intensity noise from laser diode and its effect on optical system performance. **Mailing Address:** Int Bus Mech, PO Box 950 F05a/052-A1, Poughkeepsie, NY 12602.

KIANG, YUN-TZU, POPULATION GENETICS, PLANT BREEDING. **Personal Data:** b Taiwan, February 1, 1932; American citizen; m 1957, c 3. **Education:** Taiwan Normal Univ, BS, 1956; Ohio State Univ, MA, 1962; Univ Calif, Berkeley, PhD (genetics), 1970. **Professional Experience:** Assoc ed, J Hered, 1987-; PROF PLANT SCI & GENETICS, UNIV NH, 1983-; vis scientist, Academia Sinica, 1978 & 1986; Vis prof, Taiwan Normal Univ, 1978; from asst prof to assoc prof, Univ NH, 1970-1983; teaching assoc, Univ Calif, Berkeley, 1969-1970; teaching asst, Univ Calif, Berkeley, 1968-1969; Res asst genetics, Univ Calif, Berkeley, 1967-1968. **Memberships:** Soc Study Evolution; Bot Soc Am; Am Soc Agron; Am Soc Naturalists; Genetics Soc Can; AAAS; Genetics Soc Am; Am Genetic Asn. **Research Statement & Publications:** Genetics and evolution of economic and natural plant populations. **Mailing Address:** 3 Magrath Rd, Durham, NH 03824.

KIANI, MOHAMMAD F, BIOPHYSICS. **Education:** Univ Okla, BSc, 1983; La Tech Univ, MS, 1987, PhD (biomed eng), 1990. **Honors & Awards:** August Krough Young Investr Award, Am Microcirculatory Soc, 1991, Young Investr Travel Award, 1991. **Professional Experience:** ACTG CHAR, DEPT BIOMED ENG, UNIV TENN, 2003; PROF, DEPT RADIATION ONCOL & BIOMED ENG, UNIV TENN, 2002-; dir graduate studies, Dept Biomed Eng, Univ Tenn, 2000-2003; assoc prof, Dept Biomed Eng, Univ Tenn, 1998-2002; assoc prof, Dept Radiation Oncol, Univ Tenn, 1998-2002; dir res, Dept Bio Med Eng, Univ Tenn, 1997-2000; asst prof, Dept Biomed Eng, Univ Tenn, 1995-1998; asst prof, Dept Radiation Oncol, Univ Tenn, 1995-1998; res sci, Dept Radiation, Oncol & Biophys, Univ Rochester, 1994-1995; nih fel, Dept Biophys, Univ Rochester, beginning 1990; res teaching asst, Dept Biomed Eng, La Tech Univ, 1984-1990; teaching asst, Dept Elec Eng, Univ Okla, 1981-1983. **Memberships:** Biomed Eng Soc; Microcirculatory Soc; Sigma Xi. **Research Statement & Publications:** Mathematical modeling and simulation of network blood flow; microvascular growth and adaptation of hemodynamic factors; blood rheology and hemodynamics; in vitro cell culturing; in vivo hamster cremaster muscle preparations; high impedance instrumentation-microelectrode measurements; development of expert systems for biomedical applications; numerical methods, high performance computing and computer applications. **Mailing Address:** Dept Biomed Eng, Univ Tenn, 920 Madison Ave Suite 1005, Memphis, TN 38163. **E-Mail:** mkiani@utmem.edu

KIANIAN, SHAHRYAR F, AGRONOMY. **Education:** Univ Calif, Irvine, BS, 1984; Univ Calif, Davis, PhD (Genetics), 1990. **Professional Experience:** ASST PROF, DEPT PLANT SCI, NDAK STATE UNIV, 1997-. **Mailing Address:** Dept Plant Scis NDak State Univ, Loftsgard Hall 470G, Fargo, ND 58105-5051. **Fax:** 701-231-8474. **E-Mail:** s.kianian@ndsu.edu

KIBBEL, WILLIAM H, INORGANIC CHEMISTRY, PEROXYGEN CHEMICALS. **Personal Data:** b Buffalo, NY, August 31, 1923; m 1949, Anja; c Candace R & William H III. **Education:** Case Inst Technol, MS, 1948; Case Sch Appl Sci, BS, 1944. **Professional Experience:** RETIRED; tech admin, 1982-1985; tech serv, 1977-1982; mgr indust appln develop, FMC Corp, 1958-1977; mgr mkt res, Becco Chem Div, 1957-1958; sales mgr peroxy chem, Becco Sales Corp, 1952-1957; chem eng reactor design, Buffalo Electro Chem Co, 1947-1952. **Memberships:** Sigma Xi. **Research Statement & Publications:** Pulp and paper; textiles; pollution control; metal surface treatments. **Mailing Address:** 24 Dublin Rd, Pennington, NJ 08534-2501.

KIBBEY, MAURA CHRISTINE, CANCER, ASSAY DEVELOPMENT. **Personal Data:** b Pittsburgh, Pa, March 13, 1962; m 1988, Timothy; c Siobhan & Nicholas. **Education:** State Univ NY, Albany, BS, 1983; Albany Med Col, PhD (anat & cell biol), 1989. **Professional Experience:** DIR, IGEN INT, as of 1998; dir, Scientific Mkt & Res, IGEN Int Inc, 1995-; STAFF FEL, LAB DEVELOP BIOL, NAT INST DENT RES, NIH, 1992-; Inst med gross anat, Georgetown Univ Med Sch, 1990; res biologist, Lab Develop Biol, Nat Inst Dent Res, NIH, 1989-1992; teaching asst med gross anat & med histol, Albany Med Col, 1987; teaching asst histol, Va Polytech Inst & State Univ, 1985; teaching asst gen biol, Va Polytech Inst & State Univ, 1984. **Memberships:** Am Soc Cell Biol; Sigma Xi; Soc Biomolecular Screening Am Asn Pharmaceut Sci; Clin Ligand Assay Soc. **Research Statement & Publications:** Investigating the biological activity of laminin, as well as its receptors and proteases, with regard to tumor cell growth and metastasis and in the progression of Alzheimer's disease. **Mailing Address:** Igen Inc, 16020 Industrial Dr, Gaithersburg, MD 20877. **Fax:** 301-947-6990.

KIBBY, CHARLES LEONARD, CHEMICAL KINETICS, SURFACE CHEMISTRY. **Personal Data:** b Wenatchee, Wash, January 2, 1938; m 1970, Diana; c Kenneth. **Education:** Reed Col, BA, 1959; Purdue Univ, PhD, 1964. **Professional Experience:** STAFF SCIENTIST, CHEVRON RES & TECHNOL CO, RICHMOND, CA, 1991-; sr staff scientist, Chevron Texaco, Richmond, Ca 2000-; sr res assoc, Chevron Res & Technol CO, Richmond, CA, 1985-1991; res assoc, Pittsburgh Energy Res Ctr, 1981-1985; sr res chemist, Pittsburgh Energy Res Ctr, 1977-1980; res chemist, Pittsburgh Energy Res Ctr, 1976-1977; vis scientist catalysis, Inst Org Chem, Moscow, USSR, 1974; res chemist, Gulf Res & Develop Co, Pittsburgh, 1970-1975; fel catalysis, Mellon Inst Sci, Carnegie-Mellon Univ, 1967-1969; res assoc, Brookhaven Nat Lab, 1965-1967; Fel chem, Harvard Univ, 1963-1965. **Memberships:** Am Chem Soc; AAAS; Catalysis Soc. **Research Statement & Publications:** Characterization of heterogeneous catalysts for hydrocarbon processing and chemicals production, by chemical and physical methods; Fischer-Tropsch chem. **Mailing Address:** 846 Clifton Ct, Benicia, CA 94510. **E-Mail:** ckib@chevron.com

KIBENS, VALDIS, AEROACOUSTICS, TURBULENCE. **Personal Data:** b Riga, Latvia, October 22, 1936; American citizen; m 1988, c 2. **Education:** Univ Yale, BE, 1957; UnivJ ohns Hopkins, PhD (mech), 1968. **Honors & Awards:** Lewis F Moody Award, Am Soc Mech Eng Int, 2002. **Professional Experience:** PRIN SCIENTIST, RES LABS, MCDONNELL DOUGLAS CORP, 1985-; sr scientist aeroacoust, Res Labs, Mcdonnell Douglas Corp, 1974-1985; consult & vis res scientist, Res Labs, Gen Motors Corp, Mich, 1973; asst prof, aerospace eng, Univ Mich, Ann Arbor, 1968-1974; Res engr, Gen Dynamics Corp, Conn, 1957-1960. **Memberships:** Am Phys Soc; assoc fel Am Inst Aeronaut & Astronaut; Sigma Xi. **Research Statement & Publications:** Control of the development of turbulent structures in flow fields as the basis for technological devices to reduce aerodynamic noise, enhance mixing, and control buffeting. **Mailing Address:** McDonnell Douglas Res Lab, St Louis, MO 63166-0516.

KIBLER, JAMES F, AERONAUTICS. **Professional Experience:** MGR, NASA LANGLEY RES CTR, as of 2004. **Memberships:** Am Inst Aeronaut & Astronaut. **Mailing Address:** NASA Langley Res Ctr, DMO/ASD M/S 423, Hampton, VA 23681. **Fax:** 804-864-5386.

KIBLER, KENNETH G, GEOPHYSICS, ENVIRONMENTAL SCIENCE. **Personal Data:** b Peoria, Ill, April 15, 1940; m 1961, c 2. **Education:** Univ Iowa, MS, 1964, PhD (nuclear physics), 1966. **Professional Experience:** ENG CHIEF STRUCT & MAT, LOCKHEED MARTIN, 1995-; SR RES SCIENTIST, GEN DYNAMICS-CONVAIR AEROSPACE, 1969-; asst prof, Tex Wesleyan Col, 1969-; res assoc, Case Western Res Univ, 1966-1969; res asst nuclear physics, Univ Iowa, 1962-1966. **Memberships:** AAAS; Am Phys Soc; Am Geophys Union. **Research Statement & Publications:** Heavy-ion nuclear reactions; gravity measurement; remote sensing of earth resources; enhancement techniques for aerial or orbital images; physics of materials. **Mailing Address:** General Dynamics Corp, Ft Worth, TX 76116.

KIBLER, RUTHANN, IMMUNOLOGY, VIROLOGY. **Personal Data:** b Mansfield, Ohio, December 1, 1942. **Education:** Marietta Col, BS, 1964; Purdue Univ, MS, 1967; Univ Calif, Berkeley, PhD (immunol), 1973. **Professional Experience:** ASSOC PROF BIOL SCI, SAN JOSE STATE UNIV, as of 2006; asst prof biol sci, San Jose State Univ, beginning 1990; sr res scientist, Bio-Rad Lab, 1987-1989; asst prof microbiol & immunol, Dept Microbiol, Col Med, Univ Ariz, 1980-1987; mem staff, Calif State Dept Health Serv, Berkeley, 1979-1980; res scientist immmunol, Dept Microbiol, Col Med, Univ Ariz, 1976-1979. **Memberships:** Am Soc Microbiol; Sigma Xi; Am Asn Immunologists. **Research Statement & Publications:** Flow cytometry-cell analysis. **Mailing Address:** Dept Biol Sci, San Jose State Univ, Duncan Hall Rm 251 One Wash Sq, San Jose, CA 95192-0100. **Fax:** 408-924-4840. **E-Mail:** rkibler@email.sjsu.edu

KIBRICK, ANNE K, EDUCATION. **Personal Data:** b Palmer, Mass, June 1, 1919; wid Sidney (deceased); c Joan & John. **Education:** Boston Univ, BS, 1945; Columbia Teachers Col, 1948; Harvard Univ, EdD, 1958. **Honorary Degrees:** DLitt, St Josephs Col. **Honors & Awards:** Nutting Award Leadership Nursing, Distin Serv Award, Nat League Nursing, Stewart Award; Nat Hadassah Org Serv Award; Hall of Fame, Columbus Teachers Col, MA Nurses Assoc. **Professional Experience:** PROF EMER, UNIV MASS, 1993-; prof, Univ Mass, 1982-1993; dean, Univ Mass, 1982-1988; chmn, Dept Nursing, Boston Col Grad Sch Arts & Sci, 1970-1974 & Boston State Col, 1974-1982; mem staff, USPHS, NIH, 1968-1973; prof, dean, Boston Univ Sch Nursing, 1963-1968; dir, Grad Div Nursing, Boston Univ Sch Nursing, 1958-1963; asst prof nursing, Simmons Col, 1949-1955; Asst educ dir, Cushing Mass Hosp, Framingham, 1948-1949; bd dir exec comt, Post Grad Med Inst, Mass Med Soc; consult, Nat League Nursing, China, Soviet Union, Israel, Egypt, Australia, Africa. **Memberships:** Nat Acad Sci; Inst Med; Nat League Nursing (pres 1971-1973); fel Am Acad Nursing; Nat Acad Pract. **Research Statement & Publications:** Self concept; role perception; occupational choice; minorities in nursing; co-author "Explanations of Nursing Research"; nursing education. **Mailing Address:** 381 Clinton Rd, Brookline, MA 02146.

KICE, JOHN LORD, ORGANIC CHEMISTRY. **Personal Data:** b Colorado Springs, Colo, February 18, 1930; m 1953, Ellen Bass; c Virginia & Joanne. **Education:** Harvard Univ, AB, 50, MA, 1953, PhD (chem), 1954. **Professional Experience:** EMER PROF SCI, MATH & ENG, UNIV DENVER, 1995-; dean, sci, math & eng, Univ Denver, 1988-1995; prof & chmn, dept chem, Univ Denver, 1985-1988; Fel, Japan Soc Prom Sci, 1983; chmn dept, chem prof, Tex Tech Univ, 1975-1985; prof & chmn dept, Univ Vt, 1970-1975; NIH spec fel, 1968-1969; from assoc prof to prof, Ore State Univ, 1960-1970; from asst prof to assoc prof chem, Univ SC, 1956-1960; Sr chemist, Rohm and Haas Co, 1953-1956. **Memberships:** Am Chem Soc; Sigma Xi. **Research Statement & Publications:** Organic reaction mechanisms; free radical reactions; organic sulfur chemistry; organic selenium chemistry. **Mailing Address:** Dept Chem, Univ Denver, Denver, CO 80208.

KICHER, THOMAS PATRICK, ENGINEERING MECHANICS. **Personal Data:** b Johnsonburg, Pa, October 20, 1937; m Janet; c Rita (Deceased), Paul & Laura. **Education:** Case West Res Univ, BS, 1959, MS, 1962, PhD (eng mech), 1964. **Honors & Awards:** Honarary Member; Theta Tau, Tau Beta Pi. **Professional Experience:** ARTHUR P. ARMINGTON PROF Emeritus, DEPT MECH & AEROSPACE ENG, CASE WESTERN RES UNIV, as of 2004; CHMN DEPT MECH & AEROSPACE ENG, CASE WESTERN RES UNIV, 1985-1992; prof mech eng, Case Western Res Univ, 1981-1987; Armington Professor of Engineering, 1987-2004; assoc dean sci & eng, Case Western Res Univ, 1974-1979; Dean of the Case School of Engineering, 1992-1997; assoc prof mech eng, Case Western Res Univ, 1968-1981; Consult, 1965-; asst prof eng, Case Western Res Univ, 1965-1968; design engr, Douglas Aircraft Co, Inc, Calif, 1964-1965; res asst, Case Western Res Univ, 1959-1964; Res engr, Aeronca Mfg Co, 1959. **Memberships:** Am Inst Aeronaut & Astronaut; Am Soc Mech Engrs; Soc Exp Mech. **Research Statement & Publications:** Computer methods of optimum design; basic phenomena of buckling of elastic systems; analysis and testing of composite materials; analysis and testing of plates and shells; failure analysis and design; design methodology. **Mailing Address:** Dept Mech & Aerospace eng, Case Western Res Univ, Rm 616, Glennan Bldg, 10900 Euclid Ave, Cleveland, OH 44106-1749. **Fax:** 216-368-6445. **E-Mail:** tpk@case.edu

KICKLER, THOMAS STEVEN, HEMATOLOGY. **Personal Data:** b Pittsburgh, Pa, July 7, 1947. **Education:** WVa Univ, BA, 1969, MD, 1973. **Professional Experience:** DIR, EUGENE & MARY B MEYER CTR BLOOD RES, 1999-; PROF PATH, JOHNS HOPKINS SCH MED, 1995-; DIR HEMAT & COAGULATION LAB, 1996-; from asst prof to assoc prof, Johns Hopkins Sch Med, 1980-1996; fel hemat, Univ Rochester, 1978-1980; fel med, Mayo Grad Sch, 1976-1978; fel path, Johns Hopkins Univ, 1974-1976. **Memberships:** Am Soc Hemat; Am Asn Blood Banks; Col Am Path. **Research Statement & Publications:** Platelet immunology; blood transfusion therapy; blood coagulation; laboratory testing for blood disorders; Measurement of tissue factor expression in whole blood; Tissue factor in patients with systemic lupus erythematosus: Association with disease activity; author of various articles. **Mailing Address:** Dept Path, Johns Hopkins Univ Sch Med, 720 Rutland Ave, Baltimore, MD 21205. **Fax:** 410-955-0767. **E-Mail:** tkickler@jhmi.edu

KICKLIGHTER, CLOIS E, ENERGY ENGINEERING. **Education:** Univ Fla, BS; Ind State Univ, MS, 1963; Univ MD, EdD, 1966. **Professional Experience:** RETIRED; prof, Construct Technol, Ind State Univ, 1983-1998. **Memberships:** Natl Asn Indust Technol. **Mailing Address:** Ind State Univ, 6th & Cherry Sts, Terre Haute, IN 47809. **Fax:** 812-237-7797. **E-Mail:** cloiskicklighter@juno.com

KICLITER, ERNEST EARL, NEUROANATOMY, COLOR VISION. **Personal Data:** b Ft Pierce, Fla, June 19, 1945; m 1993, Nidza; c Jennifer A. **Education:** Univ Fla, BA, 1968; State Univ NY Upstate Med Ctr, PhD (anat), 1973. **Professional Experience:** PROF ANAT, SCH MED, UNIV PR, 1984-; assoc prof, Sch Med, Univ PR, 1977-1984; vis prof, Univ Med Sch, Pecs, Hungary, 1976; asst prof physiol, Col Lib Arts & Sci, Univ Ill, Urbana-Champaign, 1974-1977; asst prof neuroanat, Col Med, Sch Basic Med Sci univ Ill Urbana-Champaign, 1974-1977; NIH fel neurol surg, Sch Med, Univ Va, 1972-1974. **Memberships:** Fel AAAS; Soc Neuroscience; Am Asn Anatomists; Cajal Club. **Research Statement & Publications:** Comparative studies of structure and function in vertebrate visual systems; color vision and neuronal plasticity in visual systems. **Mailing Address:** Dept Anat, Univ PR, Med Sci Campus, San Juan, PR 00936-5067. **Fax:** 787-721-1236. **E-Mail:** e_Kicliter@rcmaca.upr.clu.edu

KIDAWA, ANTHONY STANLEY, PODIATRIC MEDICINE & SURGERY, ANGIOLOGY. **Personal Data:** b Philadelphia, Pa, April 1, 1942; m 1969, Nancy; c Kevin & Lori. **Education:** Villanova Univ, BS, 1964, Pa Col Pediat Med, DPM, 1969. **Honors & Awards:** William J Stickel Silver Medal, Am Podiatry Asn, 1982, William J Stickel Bronze Medal, 1985. **Professional Experience:** PROF PODIATRIC MED, TEMPLE UNIV, as of 2001; pres & dir angiol, Clindialab Inc, Cherry Hill, NJ, beginning 1984; ed podiatry, J Am Podiatric Med Asn, beginning 1984; dir, Vascular Lab, beginning 1984; NJ State Bd Med Examrs, 1982 & Advan Diag, Inc, Oak Ridge, Tenn, 1983-1985; vis lectr angiol, Logan Col Chiropractic, St Louis, 1981-1983; vis lectr podiatry, Ohio Col Podiatric Med, Cleveland, 1980-1981; Vascular Diag Instruments, Cherry Hill, 1976-1982; dir res educ podiatry, John F Kennedy Wash Div Hosp, Turnersville, 1976-1980; chmn med, Vascular Lab, 1974-1984; Sentry Instruments, Inc, Atlanta, Ga, 1974-1976; consult, Pa Blue Shield, 1974; staff podiatrist, James C Guiuffre Med Ctr, 1971-1982 & JFK Wash Div Hosp, Turnersville, 1973-1984; consult, Bionic Instruments, Bala Cynwyd, Pa, 1972-1974; prof med, pa col podiatric med, beginning 1970; resident podiatric med & surg, James C Guiffre Med Ctr, Philadelphia, 1969-1970. **Memberships:** Am Podiatry Med Asn; Am Asn Hosp Podiatrists; Am Asn Col Podiatric Med; Am Soc Podiatric Angiol (pres, 1983-); Am Diabetes Asn. **Research Statement & Publications:** Effects of hypothermia and anesthetic blocks on the peripheral circulation; physiological studies for determining various parameters of circulation in the lower extremities; clinical trials for antifungal medication in the treatment of pedal fungus infections and vasodilators in the treatment of peripheral vascular diseases. **Mailing Address:** Sch Podiatric Med & Foot & Ankle Inst Temple Univ, Eighth Race St, Philadelphia, PA 19107-2496.

KIDD, BERNARD SEAN LANGFORD, CARDIOVASCULAR PHYSIOLOGY. **Personal Data:** b Belfast, Northern Ireland, July 7, 1931; m 1958, c 4. **Education:** Queen's Univ Belfast, MB, BCh & BAO, 1954, MD, 1957. **Professional Experience:** RETIRED; dir, Div Pediat Cardiol, 1996; Harriet Lane Home prof pediat cardiol &dir div, Sch Med, 1975-1996; dep dir, Johns Hopkins Univ, 1973-1975; Physician & assoc scientist, Hosp Sick Children, 1967-1975; assoc prof pediat physiol, Univ Toronto, 1961-1975; physician & assoc scientist, Hosp for Sick Children, 1961-1967; tutor & registr, Royal Victoria Hosp, Belfast, 1957-1960; Asst lectr physiol, Queen's Univ Belfast, 1955-1957. **Memberships:** Am Pediat Soc; Can Soc Clin Invest; Am Col Cardiol; Am Heart Asn; Soc Pediat Res. **Research Statement & Publications:** Circulatory physiology, hemodynamics in congenital heart disease. **Mailing Address:** Helen B Taussig Children's Cardiac Ctr, Johns Hopkins Univ Hosp 600 N Wolfe St, Baltimore, MD 21205.

KIDD, DAVID EUGENE, PHYCOLOGY, RESERVOIR WATER QUALITY. **Personal Data:** b Evanston, Ill, April 13, 1930; m 1955, Dolores Dichtenmiller; c David, Dennis & Deborah. **Education:** Ariz State Col, BS, 1951; Northwestern Univ, MS, 1952; Univ NH, MST, 1960; Mich State Univ, PhD (bot), 1963. **Professional Experience:** EMER PROF SCI EDUC & BIOL, UNIV NMEX, 1989-; fel, NSF, 1971-1977; fel, Water Resources Inst, 1969-1972; fel, NSF Undergrad Equip, 1969-1971; from assoc prof to prof biol, Univ Nmex, 1967-1989; fel, Sigma Xi, 1965-1966; Grants, Am Philos Soc, 1964-1966; asst prof natural sci, Mich State Univ, 1960-1967; sci teacher high sch, Ariz, 1956-1960; prof chem, Lindsey Wilson Col, 1955-1956; Sci teacher high sch, Ariz, 1954-1955; vol exec dir, Ajo Ariz Dist Chamber Com. **Memberships:** Am Micros Soc; Am Chem Soc; Nat Sci Teachers Asn; Sigma Xi. **Research Statement & Publications:** Taxonomy and ecology of algae in polluted ranch ponds in northern Arizona; carbon-14 primary productivity and population dynamics of phytoplankton in Elephant Butte Reservoir and Lake Powell; nutrient loading models and their modification as applied to Southwestern reservoirs. **Mailing Address:** 9408 Regal Ridge Dr Ne, Albuquerque, NM 87111.

KIDD, FRANK ALAN, PLANT PHYSIOLOGY. **Personal Data:** b Dodge City, Kans, July 24, 1952; m 1973. **Education:** Ore State Univ, BS, 1974; Colo State Univ, MS, 1976, PhD (tree physiol), 1982. **Professional Experience:** MEM STAFF, DOW CHEM USA, as of 1998; RES FORESTER, POTLATCH CORP, 1981-; instr forest ecol, econ & physiol, Colo State Univ, 1980-1981; Consult, Repub Nat Bank, Dallas, Tex, 1976-1982; contributing researcher, Lightwood Res Coord Coun, US Forest Serv, 1976-1978; teaching asst forest biomet, econ & physiol, Colo State Univ, 1974-1981; res asst forest tree physiol, econ & physiol, Colo State Univ, 1974-1980; Teaching asst forestry, Ore State Univ, 1973-1974. **Memberships:** AAAS; Soc Am Foresters; Am Forestry Asn; Sigma Xi. **Research Statement & Publications:** Forest tree physiology; mycorrhizal relationships; physiological consequences of silvicultural treatment of conifers. **Mailing Address:** 10381 S Sunup Ave, Yuma, AZ 85367.

KIDD, GEORGE JOSEPH, JR, MECHANICAL ENGINEERING. **Personal Data:** b Grand Rapids, Mich, May 6, 1934; m 1956, c 3. **Education:** Northwestern Univ, BS, 1956, MS, 1957; Univ Tenn, PhD (eng sci), 1966. **Professional Experience:** DEPT SUPVR, OAK RIDGE GASEOUS DIFFUSION PLANT, MARTIN MARIETTA ENERGY SYSTS, INC, 1977-; develop engr, Oak Ridge Nat Lab, 1968-1977; res staff mem reactor develop, Oak Ridge Nat Lab, 1958-1968; Assoc engr, Y-12 Plant, Martin Marietta Energy Systs Inc, 1957-1958. **Memberships:** Am Soc Mech Engrs; Am Inst Chem Engrs; Nat Soc Prof Engrs. **Research Statement & Publications:** Heat transfer; fluid mechanics. **Mailing Address:** 120 Windham Rd, Oak Ridge, TN 37830.

KIDD, HAROLD J, CYTOGENETICS, PLANT MORPHOLOGY. **Personal Data:** b Billings, Okla, January 30, 1924; m 1955, c 2. **Education:** Okla State Univ, BS, 1949, MS, 1951; Wash Univ, PhD (bot), 1956. **Professional Experience:** RETIRED; br plant mgr, Plant Breeding, Pioneer Hi-Bred Int Inc, 1955-1983; instr bot, Okla State Univ, 1951-1953. **Memberships:** Am Genetics Asn; Sigma Xi; AAAS; Bot Soc Am; Am Inst Biol Sci. **Research Statement & Publications:** Cultivated sorghum; plant breeding; morphology. **Mailing Address:** 1617 Dallas St, Plainview, TX 79072.

KIDD, KENNETH KAY, POPULATION GENETICS, HUMAN GENETICS. **Personal Data:** b Bakersfield, Calif, September 5, 1941; m 1964. **Education:** Univ Southern Calif, AB, 1965; Univ Wis, MS, 1967, PhD (genetics), 1969; Am Bd Med Genetics, dipl, 1982. **Professional Experience:** PROF HUMAN GENETICS & PSYCHIATRY & BIOL, SCH MED, YALE UNIV, as of 2005; ed bd, J Genetics, J Genomics, 1987-; bd dir, Am Bd Med Genetics, 1982-1984; vis scientist, Mass Inst Technol, 1982; assoc prof human genetics & psychiat, Sch Med, Yale Univ, 1981-1986; vis assoc prof, Harvard Univ, 1981-1982; mem, NIH Study Sect, Mammalian Genetics, 1979-1983; assoc prof human genetics, Sch Med, Yale Univ, 1978-1981; asst prof, Sch Med, Yale Univ, 1973-1978; asst prof anthrop genetics, Sch Med, Wash Univ, 1972-1973; res assoc genetics, Sch Med, Stanford Univ, 1971-1972; NIH fel, Sch Med, Stanford Univ, 1971; Univ Pavia, 1969-1971. **Memberships:** Genetics Soc Am; Soc Study Evolution; Am Soc Human Genetics; Am Asn Phys Anthrop; Behav Genetics Asn; fel AAAS. **Research Statement & Publications:** Genetics of human behavioral disorders; genetic relationships of human populations; human gene mapping. **Mailing Address:** Dept Genetics, Yale Univ Sch Med, 333 Cedar St, New Haven, CT 06510-8005.

KIDD, RICHARD WAYNE, PHYSICAL CHEMISTRY. **Personal Data:** b Westminster, Md, June 16, 1947; m 1969, c 1. **Education:** Western Md Col, BA, 1969; Univ Ill, MS, 1971, PhD (chem), 1975. **Professional Experience:** STAFF MEM, HITCO INC, 1997-; prin res scientist, Ceramics & Mat Processing Sect, Columbus Lab, 1980-; res scientist, Mat Technol Sect, Battelle Mem Inst, 1977-1980; res assoc chem, Univ Ill, Urbana, 1975-1977; Teaching & res asst, Univ Ill, Urbana, 1969-1975; staff mem, San Fernando Labs, Pacoima. **Memberships:** Am Chem Soc; Sigma Xi. **Research Statement & Publications:** Mathematical modeling and experimental determination of isotope effects in chemical reactions; mechanisms of reactions; chemical vapor deposition of coatings to enhance the properties of the substrate material. **Mailing Address:** 63 Rockinghorse Rd, Rancho Palos Verde, CA 90275-6569.

KIDD, ROBERT GARTH, INORGANIC CHEMISTRY. **Personal Data:** b Stockton-on-Tees, Eng, July 19, 1936; Canadian citizen; m 1959, Edna; c Jon, Dale & Warren. **Education:** Univ Man, BSc, 1958, MSc, 1960; Univ London, PhD (chem), 1962. **Professional Experience:** PROF EMER, UNIV WESTERN ONT, as of 2001; asst dean grad studies, Univ Western Ont, 1970-1983; assoc prof chem, Univ Western Ont, beginning 1969; asst prof, Univ Western Ont, 1963-1969. **Memberships:** Chem Inst Can; Am Chem Soc. **Research Statement & Publications:** Nature of bonding in transition metal complexes; nuclear magnetic resonance spectroscopy of inorganic compounds; philosophy of science. **Mailing Address:** Dept Chem, Univ Western Ont, London, ON N6A 5B7, Can. **E-Mail:** rkidd@uwo.ca

KIDD, WILLIAM SPENCER FRANCIS, GEOLOGY. **Personal Data:** b Shawford, Eng, February 23, 1947; m 1984, c 1. **Education:** Univ Cambridge, Eng, BA, 1969, PhD (geol), 1974. **Professional Experience:** PROF GEOL, STATE UNIV NY, ALBANY, 1998-; assoc prof geol, State Univ NY, Albany, 1981- 1998; asst prof, State Univ NY, Albany, 1975-1981; lectr, State Univ NY, Albany, 1974; Vis lectr geol, Erindale Col, Univ Toronto, 1972-1973. **Memberships:** Am Geophys Union; Geol Soc Am; AAAS. **Research Statement & Publications:** Tectonics; structural geology; orogenic belts; Tibet; Appalachian geology. **Mailing Address:** Dept Earth & Atmos Sci, Univ at Albany, 1400 Washington Ave, Albany, NY 12222-0100. **E-Mail:** wkidd@albany.edu

KIDDER, ERNEST H(IGLEY), ENGINEERING. **Personal Data:** b Amiret, Minn, July 14, 1912; m 1939, Maxine M Horn; c Sharon M (Tuttle) & Steven R. **Education:** Univ Minn, BAgrEng, 1935; Univ Ill, MSCE, 1947; US Naval Acad, CMet, 1945. **Honors & Awards:** Hancor Award, Am Soc Agr Engrs, 1971. **Professional Experience:** EMER PROF AGR ENG, MICH STATE UNIV, 1979-; from assoc prof to prof, Mich State Univ, 1950-1979; proj supvr, Auburn, Ala, 1948-1949; assoc hydraul engr, Univ Ill, 1946-1948; asst hydraul engr, Univ Ill, 1941-1943; jr hydraul engr, Univ Ill, 1939-1941; Jr soil conservationist, Soil Conserv Serv, USDA, Minn, 1935-1939. **Memberships:** Fel Am Soc Agr Engrs. **Research Statement & Publications:** Hydraulic, hydrologic, meteorologic, soil physical and agronomic phases of soil and water conservation. **Mailing Address:** 4471 S 1625 W, Roy, UT 84067-3008.

KIDDER, GEORGE WALLACE, III, PHYSIOLOGY, BIOPHYSICS. **Personal Data:** b New York, NY, September 24, 1934; m 1957, c 2. **Education:** Amherst Col, AB, 1956; Univ Pa,

PhD (bot), 1961. **Professional Experience:** SR INVESTR, MT DESERT ISLAND BIOL LAB, ILL STATE UNIV, as of 2003; prof, dept biol sci, Ill State Univ, beginning 1984; chmn, Dept Biol Sci, Ill State Univ, 1984-1991; from assoc prof to prof physiol, Univ Md Sch Dent, 1973-1984; asst prof biol, Wesleyan Univ, 1964-1973; USPHS fel, Harvard Univ, 1964; res fel biophys labs, Harvard Med Sch, 1962-1964; res fel, Johnson Found, Univ Pa, 1961-1962. **Memberships:** AAAS; Am Physiol Soc; Biophys Soc. **Research Statement & Publications:** Gastric acid secretion; electrophysiology; active transport of ions in relation to aerobic metabolism. **Mailing Address:** Mt Desert Island Biol Lab, Ill State Univ, PO Box 35, Salsbury Cove, ME 04672. **E-Mail:** gkidder@mdibl.org

KIDDER, GERALD, SOIL FERTILITY, LAND APPLICATION OF NON-HAZARDOUS WASTES. **Personal Data:** b Leonville, La, January 2, 1940; m 1966, Kathryn; c Andrew W, Daniel P & Elizabeth Y. **Education:** Univ Southwestern La, BS, 1961; Univ Ill, MS, 1964; Okla State Univ, PhD (soil sci), 1969. **Professional Experience:** PROF EMER SOIL SCI, INST FOOD & AGR SCI, UNIV FLA, as of 2006; prof soil sci, Inst Food & Agr Sci, Univ Fla, beginning 1988; assoc prof, Inst Food & Agr Sci, Univ Fla, 1980-1988; asst prof agron, Inst Food & Agr Sci, Univ Fla, 1975-1980; mgr agr serv, Standard Fruit Co, Castle & Cooke, Inc, 1972-1975; res agronomist, Standard Fruit Co, Castle & Cooke, Inc, 1969-1972; vol, Papal Vol Latin Am, US Cath Bishops' Conf, 1964-1966; lab asst soil nitrogen, Univ Ill, 1963-1964. **Memberships:** Am Soc Agron; Soil Sci Soc Am; Sigma Xi. **Research Statement & Publications:** Beneficial utilization of non-hazardous wastes through application to land. **Mailing Address:** Univ Fla, PO Box 110510, Gainesville, FL 32611-0290. **Fax:** 352-392-3399. **E-Mail:** kidder@ufl.edu

KIDDER, GERALD MARSHALL, DEVELOPMENTAL BIOLOGY, DEVELOPMENTAL GENETICS. **Personal Data:** b Harlingen, Tex, December 26, 1944; m 1983, Brigitte; c Joanna & Andrew. **Education:** Hiram Col, BA, 1966; Univ Yale, PhD (biol), 1971. **Honors & Awards:** Millipore Can Res Team Award, 1991. **Professional Experience:** PROF PAEDIAT, OBSTET & GYNEC, UNIV WESTERN ONT, as of 2004; CHMN, DEVELOP BIOL PROG, CHILD HEALTH RES INST, as of 2004; PROF PHYSIOL & PHARMACOL, UNIV WESTERN ONT, 1996-; mem, sci officer, Pathol & Morphol Grants Comt, Med Res Coun Can, 1995-; distinguished res prof, Univ Western Ont, 1990-1991; prof zool, Univ Western Ont, 1989-1996; vis scientist, Mass Inst Technol, 1986-1987; mem, Spec Study Sect, Nat Inst Child Health & Human Develop, 1986; vis res assoc radiobiol, Med Sch, Univ Calif, San Francisco, 1979-1980; mem, bd trustees, Soc Develop Biol, 1977-1980 & 1986-1991; res scientist, Alpha Helix Exped, Honduras Reef, 1977; from asst prof to assoc prof, Univ Western Ont, 1972-1989; Res fel biol sci, Reed Col, Ore, 1971-1972. **Memberships:** Fel AAAS; Am Soc Cell Biol; Can Soc Biochem Cellular & Molecular Biol; Soc Develop Biol; Can Fedn Biol Sci; Genetics Soc Am. **Research Statement & Publications:** Developmental genetics of the early embryo: genetic control of morphogenesis and the early events of cell differentiation; control of gene expression in early mammalian development; development of the female gene line. **Mailing Address:** Dept Physiol & Pharmacol, Univ Western Ont, Off 00061B, Dent Sci Bldg, London, ON N6A 5C1, Can. **Fax:** 519-850-2562. **E-Mail:** gerald.kidder@fmd.uwo.ca

KIDDER, RAY EDWARD, APPLIED MATHEMATICS, PHYSICS. **Personal Data:** b New York, NY, November 12, 1923; m 1947, c 3. **Education:** Ohio State Univ, PhD (physics), 1950. **Honors & Awards:** Alexander von Humboldt Award, 1989. **Professional Experience:** ASSOC STAFF, LAWRENCE LIVERMORE NAT LAB, UNIV CALIF, 1990-; assoc div leader, Theoret Div, 1956-1990; Sr physicist, Calif Res Corp, 1950-1956. **Memberships:** Fel Am Phys Soc. **Research Statement & Publications:** Thermonuclear physics; astrophysics; quantum electronics. **Mailing Address:** Lawrence Livermore Nat Lab, PO Box 808, 7000 E Ave, Livermore, CA 94550. **Fax:** 510-422-0435.

KIDMAN, KENT O, MATHEMATICS. **Education:** Weber State Col, BA, 1978; Univ Calif, Santa Barbara, MA, 1980, PhD (Maths), 1983. **Professional Experience:** PROF & CHMN, DEPT MATHS, WEBER STATE UNIV, as of 2000. **Mailing Address:** Weber State Univ Math Dept, Ogden, UT 84408-1702. **Fax:** 801-626-6427. **E-Mail:** kkidman@weber.edu

KIDNAY, ARTHUR J, CHEMICAL ENGINEERING, PHYSICAL CHEMISTRY. **Personal Data:** b Milwaukee, Wis, April 4, 1934; m 1960, c 3. **Education:** Colo Sch Mines, BS, 1956, DSc(chem eng), 1968; Univ Colo, MS, 1961. **Professional Experience:** PROF EMER, DEPT CHEM ENG, COLO SCH MINES, as of 2005; dean grad studies & res, Colo Sch Mines, 1990-1998; dept head Chem Eng, Colo Sch Mines, 1983-1990; prof chem & petrol refining eng, Colo Sch Mines, 1977-1983; from asst prof to assoc prof, Colo Sch Mines, 1968-1976; res engr, Cryogenics Div, Nat Bur Standards, Colo, 1959-1968; Proj engr, Monsanto Chem Co, Mass, 1956-1958. **Memberships:** Am Inst Chem Engrs; Am Soc Eng Educ. **Research Statement & Publications:** Solid-vapor and liquid vapor equilibria at cryogenic temperatures; physical adsorption at cryogenic temperatures. **Mailing Address:** Dept Chem Eng, Colo Sch Mines, Golden, CO 80401. **Fax:** 303-273-3730. **E-Mail:** akidnay@mines.edu

KIDWELL, ALBERT LAWS, PETROLEUM GEOLOGY. **Personal Data:** b Auxvasse, Mo, January 1, 1943; m 1943, c 4. **Education:** Mo Sch Mines, BS, 1940; Wash Univ, MS, 1942; Univ Chicago, PhD (geol), 1949. **Professional Experience:** RETIRED; sr res assoc, Exxon Prod Res Co, 1973-1984; res assoc, Esso Prod Res Co, 1965-1973; sect head, Jersey Prod Res Co, 1958-1965; res geologist, Carter Oil Co, 1950-1958; geologist, Mo Geol Surv, 1944-1947; Photogrammetric engr, US Coast & Geod Surv, 1942-1944. **Memberships:** Geol Soc Am; Mineral Soc Am; Am Asn Petrol Geol; Soc Econ Geol. **Research Statement & Publications:** Igneous and economic geology. **Mailing Address:** 14403 Carolcrest Dr, Houston, TX 77079.

KIDWELL, DAVID, ORGANIC CHEMISTRY. **Professional Experience:** RES CHEMIST, NAVAL RES LAB, as of 2006. **Memberships:** Nat Res Coun Comt. **Mailing Address:** Naval Res Lab, 4555 Overlook Ave SW Code 6177, Washington, DC 20375. **Fax:** 202-767-3321. **E-Mail:** kidwell@ccf.nrl.navy.mil

KIDWELL, GEORGE H, AERONAUTICS. **Professional Experience:** DIR, NASA AMES RES CTR, as of 2003. **Memberships:** Am Inst Aeronaut & Astronaut. **Mailing Address:** NASA Ames Res Ctr, MS 237-11, Moffett Field, CA 94035. **Fax:** 650-604-3068.

KIDWELL, MARGARET GALE, EVOLUTIONARY GENETICS, DROSOPHILA. **Personal Data:** b Askham, Eng, August 17, 1933; wid, c Mary R & Stella M. **Education:** Nottingham Univ, BS, 1953; Iowa State Univ, MS, 1962; Brown Univ, PhD (genetics), 1973. **Professional Experience:** REGENTS PROF EMER ECOL & EVOLUTIONARY BIOL, UNIV ARIZ, 2001-; regents prof ecol evolution biol, Univ Ariz, 1994-2001; head ecol & evolutionary biol, Univ Ariz, 1992-1996; prof ecol & evolutionary biol, Univ Ariz, 1985-1994; from asst prof to prof biol, Brown Univ, 1977-1985; investr, Brown Univ, 1975-1977; res assoc, Brown Univ, 1974-1975; res fel, Brown Univ, 1973-1974; assoc res, Brown Univ, 1966-1970; adv officer agr, Ministry Agr, London, 1955-1960. **Memberships:** Nat Acad Sci; Am Genetic Asn (pres, 1991); Am Soc Naturalists (vpres, 1984); Genetics Soc Am; Soc Study Evolution; Sigma Xi; fel AAAS; fel Am Acad Arts & Lett; Soc Molecular Biol & Evolution. **Research Statement & Publications:** Drosophila genetics and evolution; recombination transposable elements; speciation. **Mailing Address:** Dept Ecol & Evolutionary Biol Univ Ariz, Biol Sci W 116, Tucson, AZ 85721-0001. **Fax:** 520-621-9190. **E-Mail:** kidwell@email.arizona.edu

KIDWELL, ROGER LYNN, SYNTHETIC ORGANIC CHEMISTRY. **Personal Data:** b Nevada City, Calif, February 24, 1938; m 1961, c 1. **Education:** Chapman Col, BS, 1962; Univ Southern Calif, PhD (org chem), 1966. **Professional Experience:** RES GROUP LEADER SURFACTANTS, MONSANTO CO, 1973-; res specialist, Monsanto Co, 1971-1973; res chemist, Monsanto Co, 1966-1971. **Memberships:** Am Chem Soc; Sigma Xi. **Research Statement & Publications:** Synthesis and process development for new surface active agents. **Mailing Address:** Diamonex-Diamond Protective Coatings-Unit Monsanto, 7150 Windsor Dr, Allentown, PA 18106-9328. **Fax:** 610-366-7111.

KIDWELL, SUSAN M, STRATIGRAPHY. **Education:** Col William and Mary, BS; Univ Yale, PhD (geol). **Honors & Awards:** Charles Schuchert Award, Paleontological Soc. **Professional Experience:** WILLAIM RAINEY HARPER PROF, DEPT GEOPHY SCI, UNIV CHICAGO, as of 2006; COMT EVOLUTIONARY BIOL, UNIV CHICAGO, as of 2006. **Memberships:** Earth Sci Bd, Nat Res Coun. **Research Statement & Publications:** Unconformities and condensed intervals in stratigraphic records; rates and selectivities in organic recycling and modification; increasingly, the practical application of death assemblages to modern conservation issues and the testing of biological principles. **Mailing Address:** Dept Geol Sci, Univ Chicago, Off Hinds 261 5734 S Ellis Ave, Chicago, IL 60637. **Fax:** 773-702-9505. **E-Mail:** skidwell@uchicago.edu

KIEBER, ROBERT JOHN, ENVIRONMENTAL CHEMISTRY. **Personal Data:** b Red Bank, NJ, June 10, 1960; m 1985, Cecilia Baylouny; c Marissa & Robert. **Education:** Rutgers Univ, BS, 1982; Univ Md, PhD (environ chem), 1987. **Professional Experience:** PROF CHEM, UNIV NC, WILMINGTON, 1999-; Prin investr, NSF, 1995-; assoc prof chem, Univ NC, Wilmington, 1994-1999; asst prof, Univ NC, Wilmington, 1989-1994; Postdoctoral fel, Rosenthiel Sch Marine & Atmospheric Sci, Univ Miami, 1988-1989. **Memberships:** Am Chem Soc; Am Soc Limnol & Oceanog; Am Geophys Union. **Research Statement & Publications:** Air-sea exchange processes including hydrogen ion and carbon deposition; trace metal photchemistry in seawater. **Mailing Address:** Dept Chem, Univ NC, Wilmington, NC 28403-3297. **Fax:** 910-962-3013. **E-Mail:** kieberr@uncwil.edu

KIEBLER, JOHN W(ILLIAM), COMMUNICATION SATELLITES, ORBIT & SPECTRUM UTILIZATION. **Personal Data:** b Hershey, Pa, April 1, 1928; m 1981, Barbara; c Ruth K, Robert K & Jean (O'Donnell). **Education:** Lafayette Col, BS, 1950. **Honors & Awards:** Except Serv Medal, NASA, 1985. **Professional Experience:** RETIRED; consult, Comt Radio Frequencies, Nat Acad Sci, beginning 1998; consult, Computer sci Corp, 1996-1998; lead engr, Mitre Corp, 1992-1996; sr adv, Atlantic Res Corp, 1991-1992; telecommun consult, 1990-1991; head, Tech Consult Serv, NASA HQ, 1985-1989; sr commun engr, NASA Hq, 1979-1985; sr engr, Commun Div, NASA Goddard space flight ctr, 1973-1979; proj mgr, Satellite Tracking & Data Acquistion, NASA Goddard space flight ctr, 1970-1973; asst chief, Proj Opers Support Div, NASA Goddard space flight ctr, 1966-1970; actg chief, Proj Opers Support Div, 1965-1966; head, Network Implementation Br, Goddard Space Flight Ctr, NASA, 1960-1965; prin engr, Emerson Res Labs, 1959-1960; sr engr, Appl Physics Lab, Johns Hopkins Univ, 1958-1959; assoc engr, Appl Physics Lab, Johns Hopkins Univ, 1953-1958; proj engr, Off Chief Ord, 1952-1953; Electronic scientist, Nat Bur Stand, 1951-1952. **Memberships:** Inst Elec & Electronics Engrs. **Research Statement & Publications:** Communications systems; remote sensing; regulatory filings; radio wave propagation. **Mailing Address:** 15 Purple Martin Ln, Hilton Head, SC 29926. **E-Mail:** jkiebler@cpcmg.org

KIEBURTZ, RICHARD B(RUCE), COMPUTER SCIENCE. **Personal Data:** b Spokane, Wash, November 28, 1933; m 1959, c 2. **Education:** Univ Wash, BSEE, 1955, MSEE, 1957, PhD (elec eng), 1961. **Professional Experience:** PROF EMER, DEPT COMPUT SCI & ENG, ORE SCH SCI & ENGI, ORE HEALTH & SCI UNIV, as of 2004; SUPVR DATA NETWORKING GROUP, AT&T BELL LABS, WHIPPANY, NJ, 1985-; eng staff mgr info systs, Prin Res Lab, Bell Labs, dist eng mgr prod planning & support, 1983-1985; dist mgr, Prin Res Lab, Bell Labs, dist eng mgr prod planning & support, 1980-1983; mem tech staff, Prin Res Lab, Bell Labs, dist eng mgr prod planning & support, 1977-1980; NSF sci fac fel, 1968-1969; Consult, CBS Labs, Conn, 1962-1963 & Rome Air Develop Ctr, USAF, 1963-1968; from res engr to group mgr ballistic missile defense, Boeing Co, 1957-1967; Develop engr, Gen Elec Co, 1954-1957. **Memberships:** AAAS; sr mem Inst Elec & Electronics Engrs; NY Acad Sci. **Research Statement & Publications:** programming languages; distributed computing. **Mailing Address:** Dept Comput Sci & Eng, Sch Sci & Eng, Ore Health Sci Univ, 20000 NW Walker Rd, Beaverton, OR 97006. **Fax:** 503-748-1553. **E-Mail:** dick@cse.ogi.edu

KIEBURTZ, R(OBERT) BRUCE, ELECTRICAL ENGINEERING, TELECOMMUNICATIONS SYSTEM ENGINEERING. **Personal Data:** b Seattle, Wash, March 22, 1931; m 1954, Alvena; c Geoffrey B & Karl D. **Education:** Univ Wash, BSEE, 1952, MSEE, 1963, PhD (elec eng), 1966. **Professional Experience:** PRIN, KIEBURTZ ENG CONSULTS, 1990-; mgr, AT&T Bell Labs, 1988-1989; asst eng mgr, Network Planning & Bus Serv, AT&T Co, 1977-1983; mem tech staff, Bell Tel Labs, 1967-1977; supvr, Boeing Co, 1966-1967; res engr, Boeing Co, 1957-1965; Proj engr, Gen Elec Co, 1954-1957. **Memberships:** mem AAAS; sr mem Inst Elec & Electronics Engrs; mem NY Acad Sci; mem Sigma Xi. **Research Statement & Publications:** Ballistic missile defense; balanced magnetic circuits for logic and memory; digital processing of signals, including digital filtering. **Mailing Address:** 14 Cramer Dr Rm 1A12, Chester, NJ 07930-2717.

KIECH, EARL LOCKETT, ARTIFICIAL INTELLIGENCE. **Personal Data:** b Jonesboro, Ark, January 29, 1949. **Education:** Southwestern Memphis, BS, 1971; Memphis State Univ, MS, 1973. **Professional Experience:** ARNOLD ENG DEVELOP CTR, as of 2003; sci programmer, Univ Tenn Space Inst, 1987-; SCI PROGRAMMER, CALSPAN CORP, 1973-. **Memberships:** Am Phys Soc; Sigma Xi. **Research Statement & Publications:** Researching a program to diagnose mechanical problems or faults with the main engine in the space shuttle. **Mailing Address:** Arnold Eng Develop Ctr, Bldg 685 Second St, Arnold AFB, TN 37389-6900. **E-Mail:** earl.kiech@arnold.af.mil

KIECHLE, FREDERICK LEONARD, CLINICAL CHEMISTRY, INSULIN ACTION. **Personal Data:** b Indianapolis, Ind, March 26, 1946; m 1975, Janet; c Rachel, Elizabeth & Jonathan. **Education:** Evansville Col, BA, 1968; Ind Univ, PhD (biochem), 1973, MD, 1975. **Honors & Awards:** Clin Scientist Year Award, Asn Clin Scientist, 1996. **Professional Experience:** Mem, Therapeut Drug & Resource Comt, Col Am Pathologists, 1990-1995; chmn & adv, Patient Prep & Specimen Handling Comt, 1989-1996; CLIN ASSOC PROF PATH, WAYNE STATE UNIV SCH MED, 1988-; CHMN DEPT CLIN PATH, WILLIAM BEAUMONT HOSP, 1988-; mem coun spec topics, Am Soc Clin Path, 1988-1994; adv & mem, subcomt, Nat Comt Clin Lab Stand, 1987-1994; clin asst prof path, Wayne

State Univ Sch Med, 1984-1988; vis lectr, Nat Univ Singapore, 1984; chief clin chem, Dept Clin Path, William Beaumont Hosp, 1983-1988; fel, Hartford Found, 1982-1983; asst prof path, Univ Pa Sch Med, 1980-1983; res fel clin chem, Barnes Hosp, 1979-1980; resident path, William Beaumont Hosp, 1975-1979. **Memberships:** Fel Am Soc Clin Pathologists; Am Soc Invest Path; Am Asn Clin Chem; Am Diabetes Asn; Col Am Pathologists; Am Fedn Clin Res; Asn Clin Scientists (pres, 1999); Am Med Asn; Am Chem Soc; Clin Legend Assay Soc. **Research Statement & Publications:** Unraveling the temporal sequence of rapid events which occur following the binding of insulin to its receptor; membrane polarization; phospholipid metabolism; fatty acid metabolism; redox potential and impedance changes induced by insulin; detection of nitric oxide; metabolism in peroxisomal diseases, apoptosis, autoimmunity and endomtriosis. **Mailing Address:** William Beaumont Hosp, 3601 W 13 Mile Rd, Royal Oak, MI 48073. **Fax:** 248-551-3694. **E-Mail:** fkiechle@beaumont.edu

KIECKHEFER, ROBERT WILLIAM, INSECT ECOLOGY. **Personal Data:** b Milwaukee, Wis, March 13, 1933; m 1969, Janice; c Karla, Jon & Joel. **Education:** Univ Wis, BS, 1955, PhD (entom), 1962; Univ Minn, MS, 1958. **Professional Experience:** RETIRED; res entomologist, Northern Grain Insects Res Lab, USDA, beginning 1963. **Memberships:** Entom Soc Am; Ecol Soc Am; Int Orgn Biol Control; Michigan Entom Soc. **Research Statement & Publications:** Aphid biology and ecology; ecology and biological control of cereal insects. **Mailing Address:** 3226 Sunnyview Dr, Brookings, SD 57006-4282. **Fax:** 605-693-5240.

KIEDA, DAVID BARAK, COSMIC RAY PHYSICS, INTERMEDIATE & ULTRA HIGH ENERGY GAMMA RAY ASTRONOMY. **Personal Data:** b Johnson City, NY, March 22, 1960; m 1988, Lisa; c Daniel J & Zachary A & Benjamin. **Education:** Mass Inst Technol, SB, 1982; Univ Pa, PhD (physics), 1989. **Professional Experience:** Prof of Physics, Univ of Utah, 2002-; Dir, Utah High Energy Astropics Inst, 1999-2004; ASSOC PROF PHYSICS, UNIV UTAH, 1996-; prin investr, NSF, 1995-; prin investr, NASA, 1993-1996; pres, Wildcat Sci Consult, 1991-; asst prof, Univ Utah, 1990-1996; res assoc, Univ Utah, 1989; Lectr physics, SDak Sch Mines & Technol, 1984; res asst, Univ Pa, 1983-1988; Teaching asst physics, Univ Pa, 1982-1983. **Memberships:** Sigma Xi; AAAS; Am Phys Soc. **Research Statement & Publications:** High energy astrophysics; sources of ultra-high energy particles and radiation; experimental measurement of source spectra; high energy gamma ray astronomy; sources of gamma ray bursts; sources above one giga electron volt; scientific and medical instrumentation; power conduction in electrosurgical environment; simulation of particles interactions; design/analysis of instrumentation software/hardware. **Mailing Address:** Univ Utah Dept Physics, 115 S 1400 E #201, Salt Lake City, UT 84112-0830. **Fax:** 801-581-6256. **E-Mail:** kieda@physics.utah.edu

KIEFER, CHARLES R(ANDOLPH), ATHEROGENESIS. **Personal Data:** b Minneapolis, Minn, November 24, 1947; m 1973, Samira; c Alexandra. **Education:** Univ Cincinnati, BS (Bacteriol), 1969; Med Col Ga, PhD (Microbiol), 1981. **Professional Experience:** ASSOC PROF PATHOL, UNIV MASS MED SCH, 1995-; DIR, ANDROLOGY & CLIN ASSAY RES, DEPT HOSP LABS, UNIV MASS MEM MED CTR, 1995-; asst prof immunol & microbiol, Med Col Ga, 1991-1995; prin investr, Am Heart Asn, Ga Affil, 1990-1991; asst res scientist, Med Col Ga, 1987-1991; consult, Med Diag Technol Inc, Augusta, Ga, 1987-1990; res fel, Med Col Ga, 1981-1987. **Memberships:** Am Asn Immunologists; Am Asn Clin Chem. **Research Statement & Publications:** Investigation of hypercholesterolemic effect on juvenile arterial development; development of a quantitative assay for early stage (preclinical/reversible) atherosclerosis. **Mailing Address:** Hosp Labs Clin Path, Univ Mass Mem Med Ctr 365 Plantation St, Worcester, MA 01605-2376. **Fax:** 508-334-0270. **E-Mail:** kieferc@ummhc.org

KIEFER, DALE, TECHNOLOGY. **Education:** Yale Univ, BS; Univ Calif, San Diego, Scripps Inst Oceanog, PhD. **Professional Experience:** PROF BIOL SCI, UNIV SOUTHERN CALIF, as of 2006. **Mailing Address:** Univ Southern Calif, Los Angeles, CA 90033. **Fax:** 213-740-8123. **E-Mail:** kiefer@physics.usc.edu

KIEFER, DAVID JOHN, MICROBIOLOGY, IMMUNOLOGY. **Personal Data:** b Sewickley, Pa, October 1, 1938; m 1962, Muriel. **Education:** Univ Pittsburgh, BS, 1968; Univ Miami, PhD (microbiol), 1977. **Professional Experience:** CHIEF OPERATING OFFICER, DIAMEDIX CORP, 1993-; vpres, Prod Develop, 1990-1993; dir, Diamedix Corp, 1986-1990; prin immunologist, Cordis Labs Inc, 1983-1986; sr staff immunologist, Cordis Labs Inc, 1980-1983; staff immunologist, Cordis Labs Inc, 1977-1980; res technician immunol, Sch Med, Univ Miami, 1968-1977. **Memberships:** Am Soc Microbiol; Nat Comt Clin Lab Standards. **Research Statement & Publications:** Pregnancy associated plasma proteins; immunology of pregnancy; immunosuppressive properties of pregnancy serum; enzyme-labeled immunoassays for the detection and quantitation of humoral constituents for example antibodies to rubella herpes simplex virus cytomegalovirus; Human T-Cell Leukemia or Lymphoma Virus I and HIV-1; Epstein Barr Virus and autoantigens in systemic rheumatic diseases. **Mailing Address:** Diamedix Corp, 2140 N Miami Ave, Miami, FL 33127. **Fax:** 305-324-2385.

KIEFER, HAROLD MILTON, THEORETICAL PHYSICS. **Personal Data:** b Detroit, Mich, March 9, 1933; m 1966, c 1. **Education:** Wayne State Univ, PhD (physics), 1969. **Professional Experience:** ASSOC PROF PHYSICS, NORFOLK STATE COL, 1981-; asst prof, Norfolk State Col, 1969-1981; Personnel exam, City Detroit, 1958-1962. **Memberships:** Am Phys Soc; Sigma Xi. **Research Statement & Publications:** Applications of group theory to coulomb potential problems. **Mailing Address:** 116 W Government Ave, Norfolk, VA 23503.

KIEFER, JOHN DAVID, GEOLOGIC HAZARDS, ENERGY RESOURCES. **Personal Data:** b Evansville, Ind, January 2, 1940; m 1964, c 5. **Education:** St Josephs Col, BS, 1961; Univ Ill, MS, 1965, PhD (eng geol), 1970. **Professional Experience:** ADJ PROF, GEOL SCI, UNIV KY, as of 2004; ASST STATE GEOLOGIST, KY GEOL SURV, UNIV KY, 1981-; head, Water Resources Div, 1979-1982; eng geologist, Geol Surv Ala, 1978-1979; head, Eng Geol Div, Geotech Eng Assoc, 1971-1978; assoc prof, Eastern Ky Univ, 1967-1971; instr geol, Univ Ill, 1965-1967. **Memberships:** Geol Soc Am; Am Asn Petrol Geologists; Soc Econ Paleontologists & Mineralogists; AAAS; Sigma Xi; Soc Sedimentary Geol; Seismol Soc Am; Nat Soc Professional Engrs. **Research Statement & Publications:** Engineering geology and hydrogeology; Published over 5 articles. **Mailing Address:** Dept Geol Sci, Univ Ky, 226B Mining Mineral Resources Bldg, Lexington, KY 40506. **Fax:** 859-257-1147. **E-Mail:** kiefer@kgs.mm.uky.edu

KIEFER, JOHN HAROLD, COMBUSTION & KINETICS, ENERGY TRANSFER. **Personal Data:** b New Ulm, Minn, August 27, 1932; m 1971, Barbara; c Steven, Amy & Andrew. **Education:** Univ Minn, BS, 1954; Cornell Univ, PhD (phys chem), 1961. **Professional Experience:** Prof & head emer, 2001-; Head or actg head, Univ Ill, Chicago, 1989- 2001; joint appointment, Argonne Nat Lab, 1985-1991; STA 2002-. Consult, Ill Tool Works, 1975-1977; Shell res fel, Thorton, UK, 1973-1974; PROF CHEM ENG & CHEM, UNIV ILL, CHICAGO, 1972-; Consult, Los Alamos Nat Lab, 1967-; assoc prof, Univ Ill, Chicago, 1967-1972; res staff mem, Los Alamos Sci Lab, Univ Calif, 1961-1967; Fel, Cornell Univ, 1959-1960. **Memberships:** Combustion Inst. **Research Statement & Publications:** Shock tube studies of kinetics; energy transfer in high temperature gases; laser diagnostics; unimolecular rate theory. **Mailing Address:** Univ Ill, 810 S Clinton, Chicago, IL 60607. **Fax:** 312-996-0808. **E-Mail:** kiefer@uic.edu

KIEFER, RALPH W, CIVIL ENGINEERING, REMOTE SENSING & IMAGE INTERPRETATION. **Personal Data:** b Somerville, NJ, November 28, 1934; m 1983, Lois; c Hope, Joy, Lynn & Jennifer. **Education:** Cornell Univ, BCE, 1956, MS, 1960, PhD (civil eng), 1964. **Professional Experience:** PROF EMER CIVIL ENG, UNIV WIS, MADISON, 1996-; vis prof, Univ Hawaii, 1970-1971; from asst prof to prof, Univ Wis-madison, 1962-1996; asst civil eng, Cornell Univ, 1958-1962; asst hwy engr, NJ State Hwy Dept, 1958. **Memberships:** Am Soc Civil Engrs; Am Soc Photogram & Remote Sensing. **Research Statement & Publications:** Remote sensing of the environment; engineering applications of airphoto interpretation; land use suitability evaluation. **Mailing Address:** Dept Civil Eng, Univ Wis, 1210 Eng Hall 1415 Eng Dr, Madison, WI 53706. **E-Mail:** rwkiefer@facstaff.wisc.edu

KIEFER, RICHARD L, POLYMER CHEMISTRY. **Personal Data:** b Columbia, Pa, December 14, 1937; m 1962, Sharon E; c 3. **Education:** Drew Univ, AB, 1959; Univ Calif, Berkeley, PhD (nuclear chem), 1964. **Professional Experience:** PROF CHEM, COL WILLIAM & MARY, 1981-; asst prof to assoc prof, Col William & Mary, 1965-1981; Res assoc, Brookhaven Nat Lab, 1963-1965. **Memberships:** Am Chem Soc; Sigma Xi. **Research Statement & Publications:** Space radiation effects on polymers. **Mailing Address:** Dept Chem, Col William & Mary, PO Box 8795, Williamsburg, VA 23185-8795. **E-Mail:** rlkief@chem1.chem.wm.edu

KIEFF, ELLIOTT DAN, INFECTIOUS DISEASES & VIROLOGY, MICROBIOLOGY & CANCER. **Personal Data:** b Philadelphia, Pa, February 2, 1943; m 1965, Jacqueline; c David, Scott & Elizabeth. **Education:** Univ Pa, AB, 1963; Johns Hopkins Univ, MD, 1966; Univ Chicago, PhD (virol), 1971. **Honorary Degrees:** MA, Harvard Univ, 1986. **Honors & Awards:** University Scholar, Univ of Pennsylvania 1960-1963 American Cancer Society Post Doctoral Scholar, University of Chicago 1967-1971 American Cancer Society Faculty Research Award 1980-1985 Member National Academy of Sciences 1996- Member Institute of Medicine, NAS, 2000- Member American Academy of Arts and Sciences, 2001- Howard Taylor Ricketts Award, Univ of Chicago 1996. **Professional Experience:** ALBEE PROF MED, MICROBIOL & MOLECULAR GENETICS, HARVARD UNIV, 1987-; Director Division of Infectious Diseases Brigham and Women's Hospital 1987-; Chief, Sect Infectious Dis, 1971-1987; Mem, Comt Virol, Univ Chicago, 1971-; from Asst Prof to Louis Block Prof, Sch Med, 1970-1987; Resident, Hosp, Sch Med, Univ Chicago, 1969-1970; from jr resident to sr asst resident, Hosp, Sch Med, Univ Chicago, 1967-1969; Intern, Hosp, Sch Med, Univ Chicago, 1966-1967; fac res award, Am Cancer Soc; Carl Hartford vis prof, Wash Univ. **Memberships:** Nat Acad Sci; IOM; Am Academy of Arts and Sciences; Am Academy of Microbiology; AAP; Infectious Dis Soc Am; Am Soc Clin Invest; Am Asn Cancer Res; Am Soc Microbiol. **Research Statement & Publications:** Molecular biology of animal viruses, particularly herpes viruses. **Mailing Address:** Dept Med & Microbiol, Infectious Dis Div-Channing Lab, Harvard Univ, 181 Longwood Ave, Boston, MA 02115. **Fax:** 617-525-4257. **E-Mail:** ekieff@rics.bwh.harvard.edu

KIEFFER, HUGH HARTMAN, PLANETARY SCIENCE, INFRARED INSTRUMENTATION. **Personal Data:** b Norwich, Conn, October 31, 1939; m 1993, Victoria; c 1. **Education:** Calif Inst Technol, BS, 1961, PhD (planetary sci), 1968. **Honors & Awards:** Antarctic Serv Medal, 1968; Sci Achievement Medal, NASA, 1977. **Professional Experience:** SCIENTIST EMER, CELESTIAL REASONING, US GEOL SURV, as of 2004; US partic scientist, Soviet Mars mission, 1994; Chmn, Fourth Int Conf Mars, 1989; chief, Br Astrogeology, Geol Div, US Geol Surv, 1986-1990; Nat Acad Sci, Comt Lunar & Planetary Explor, 1979-1983; res geophysicist, br astrogeology, geol div, US geol surv, beginning 1978; adj prof planetary sci, Univ Calif, Los Angeles, 1978-1981; assoc prof planetary sci, Univ Calif, Los Angeles, 1975-1978; vis assoc planetary physics, Calif Inst Technol, 1975-1977; asst prof, Univ Calif, Los Angeles, 1969-1975; res fel planetary sci, Calif Inst Technol, 1968-1969; team mem, Earth Observing Syst High Resolution Imaging Spectrometer; prin investr, Viking Infrared Thermal Mapper; coinvestr, Mariner 6 & 7 Infrared Radiometer, Mariner 9 Infrared Radiometer, Galileo Near Infrared Mapping Spectrometer, Mars Observer Thermal Emission Spectrometer; US team mem, Earth Observing Syst Advan Spaceborne Thermal Emission Radiometer (Japan). **Memberships:** AAAS; Am Astron Soc; Am Meteorol Soc; Am Optical Soc; fel Am Geophys Union; Am Soc Photogram & Remote Sensing. **Research Statement & Publications:** Planetary atmospheres and surfaces; spectra of the moon and planets; atmospheric condensation processes; infrared instrumentation, observations and thermal models; thermal infrared and radar observations of volcanos; remote sensing calibration. **Mailing Address:** US Geol Serv, 2256 Christmas Tree Lane, Carson City, NV 89703. **E-Mail:** hkieffer@charter.net

KIEFFER, JOHN C, MATHEMATICS. **Education:** Univ MO, Rolla, BS, 1967; Univ Ill Urbana-Champaign, MS, PhD (math). **Professional Experience:** RES DIR & PROF, DEPT ELEC & COMPUT ENG, UNIV MINN, as of 2005. **Mailing Address:** Dept Elec Eng Univ Minn, EE CS Bldg 200 Union St SE, Minneapolis, MN 55455. **Fax:** 612-625-4583. **E-Mail:** kieffer@ece.umn.edu

KIEFFER, NAT, GENETICS. **Personal Data:** b Montgomery, La, July 13, 1930; m 1951, c 3. **Education:** Univ Southwestern La, BS, 1952; La State Univ, MS, 1956; Okla State Univ, PhD (animal breeding), 1959. **Professional Experience:** PROF EMER ANIMAL SCI, TEX A&M UNIV, 1987-; prof, Tex A&M Univ, 1977-1987; assoc prof mammalian cytogenetics, Tex A&M Univ, 1969-1977; asst prof, Tex A&M Univ, 1965-1969; res assoc & fel molecular biol, Univ Calif, Berkeley, 1964-1965; supt beef cattle res, Range Livestock Exp Sta, USDA, 1962-1964; Animal geneticist, Range Livestock Exp Sta, USDA, 1959-1962. **Memberships:** Genetics Soc Am; Am Soc Animal Sci. **Research Statement & Publications:** Population genetics; beef cattle breeding; molecular biology, gene action in bacteria on molecular level; mammalian cytogenetics, beef cattle. **Mailing Address:** 1212 Winding Rd, College Station, TX 77840.

KIEFFER, STEPHEN A, RADIOLOGY, NEURORADIOLOGY. **Personal Data:** b Minneapolis, Minn, December 20, 1935; m 1958, Cyrille; c Alisa, Mitchell, Stuart & Paula. **Education:** Univ Minn, BA, 1956, BS, 1957, MD, 1959. **Professional Experience:** Consult to ed, Radiol, 1987-1993; panelist & subcomt chair, NIH Consensus Develop Conf Magnetic Resonance & Imaging, 1987; assoc ed, Radiol, 1986; assoc ed, Year Book Diag Radiol, 1981-1987; PROF RADIOL & CHMN DEPT, STATE UNIV NY HEALTH SCI CTR, SYRACUSE, 1974-; chief radiol, Minneapolis Vet Admin Hosp, 1968-1974; from instr to prof, Univ Minn, 1966-1974; Nat Heart Inst cardiovasc trainee, James Picker Found scholar radiol res, 1966-1968; Nat Heart Inst cardiovasc trainee, Nat Inst Neurol Dis & Blindness fel neuroradiol, 1966; Nat Heart Inst cardiovasc trainee, Univ Minn, 1961-1962 & 1964-1965. **Memberships:** Am Col Radiol; Am Soc Neuroradiol (pres 1978-1979); Radiol Soc NAm; Am Roentgen Ray Soc; Asn Univ Radiologists. **Research State-**

ment & Publications: Neuroradiology; utility of diagnostic imaging in evaluation and management of lowback pain; clinical outcomes research; MR engiography. **Mailing Address:** Dept Radiol, State Univ NY Health Sci Ctr, 750 E Adams St, Syracuse, NY 13210. **Fax:** 315-464-7458. **E-Mail:** kieffers@vax.cs.hscsyr.edu

KIEFFER, SUSAN WERNER, VOLCANOLOGY, MINERAL PHYSICS. **Personal Data:** b Warren, Pa, November 17, 1942; m 1966, c 1. **Education:** Allegheny Col, BS, 1964; Calif Inst Technol, MS, 1967, PhD (planetary sci), 1971. **Honorary Degrees:** DSc, Allegheny Col, 1987. **Honors & Awards:** Mineral Soc Am Award, 1980; W H Mendenhall Lectr, US Geol Surv, 1980; Meritorious Serv Award, Dept Interior, 1987; Int Geol Spendiarov Prize, 1989; Day Medal, Geol Soc Am, 1992; MacArthur Fel, John D & Catharine T MacArthur Found, 1995. **Professional Experience:** PROF GEOL, UNIV ILL, URBANA-CHAMPAIGN, as of 2003; CO FOUNDER, KIEFFER & WOO INC, 1996-; prof & head, Dept Geol Sci, Univ BC, 1993-1995; regents prof, Ariz State Univ, 1991-1993; prof, Ariz State Univ, 1989-1993; geologist, US Geol Surv, 1978-1990; Alfred P Sloan res fel, 1977-1979; from asst prof to assoc prof geol, Univ Calif, Los Angeles, 1973-1979; res geophysicist, Univ Calif, Los Angeles, 1971-1973. **Memberships:** Nat Acad Sci; Am Geophys Union; Meteoritical Soc; Sigma Xi; Geol Soc Am; Am Acad Arts & Sci; Mineral Soc Am; Geol Asn Can. **Research Statement & Publications:** Geological physics; high pressure geophysics and impact processes; shock metamorphism of natural materials; thermodynamic properties of minerals; mechanisms of geyser and volcano eruptions; river hydraulics. **Mailing Address:** Dept Geol Univ Ill, 1207 S Oak St, Champaign, IL 61820.

KIEFFER, WILLIAM FRANKLIN, GENERAL CHEMISTRY. **Personal Data:** b Trenton, NJ, March 16, 1915. **Education:** Col Wooster, BA, 1936; Ohio State Univ, MSc, 1938; Brown Univ, PhD (photochem), 1940. **Honors & Awards:** Award Chem Educ, Mfg Chem Asn, 1965 & Am Chem Soc, 1968. **Professional Experience:** Vis prof, US Naval Acad, 1981; EMER PROF CHEM, COL WOOSTER, 1980-; vis scholar, Stanford Univ, 1969-1970 & Univ Calif, Santa Cruz, 1974-1975; NSF fac fel, Mass Inst Technol, 1963-1964; ed J Chem Educ, Am Chem Soc, 1955-1967; Res partic, Chem Div, Oak Ridge Nat Lab, 1951-1952; prof, Col Wooster, 1946-1980; from instr to asst prof, Western Reserve Univ, 1942-1946; instr, Col Wooster, 1940-1942; Asst chem, Ohio State Univ, 1936-1938 & Brown Univ, 1938-1939. **Memberships:** emer mem AAAS; Am Chem Soc; Am Inst Chemists; NY Acad Sci. **Research Statement & Publications:** Photochemistry; radiation chemistry; chemical education. **Mailing Address:** 1873 Golden Rain Rd 3, Walnut Creek, CA 94595.

KIEFL, ROBERT FRANCES, PHYSICS. **Personal Data:** b October 28, 1953. **Education:** Carleton Univ, BSc, 1976; Univ BC, MSc, 1978, PhD, 1982. **Honors & Awards:** Gerhard Herzberg Medal, Can Asn Physicists, 1992; Killiam Res Prize, 1992; McDowell Medal, 1993. **Professional Experience:** PROF, DEPT PHYSICS, UNIV BC, 1992-; asst prof, Dept Physics, Univ BC, 1990-1992; assoc superconductivity, Can Inst Advan Res, 1990; Nat Sci & Eng Res Coun Can univ res fel, Dept Physics, Univ BC, 1987-1990; Grantee, Univ BC, 1987; grantee, nat sci & eng res coun can, 1986, 1990-1991, 1992-; res scientist II, Tri-Univ-Meson Facil, 1984-1987; nat sci & eng res coun can fel, Dept Physics, Univ Zurich, 1982-1984; res assoc, Dept Physics, Univ BC, 1982. **Research Statement & Publications:** Superconductivity. **Mailing Address:** Dept Physics & Astron, Univ BC, Hennings 407 6224 Agricultural Rd, Vancouver, BC V6T 1Z1, Can. **E-Mail:** kiefl@triumf.ca

KIEFT, JOHN A, PHYSICAL CHEMISTRY, INORGANIC CHEMISTRY. **Personal Data:** b Oak Park, Ill, February 27, 1941; m 1965, c 1. **Education:** Hope Col, BA, 1963; Ill Inst Technol, PhD (chem), 1968. **Professional Experience:** SITE MGR, ZENECA INC, as of 2005; res & develop opers lead, Zeneca, beginning 1994; mgr environ sci, Zeneca, 1993-1994; mgr envirn sci, Zeneca, 1991-1993; mgr regist, Zeneca, 1987-1991; dir, regulatory affairs, 1985-1987; dept mgr res serv, Western Res Lab, 1979-1985; sr sect mgr anal, Stauffer Chem Co, 1976-1979; sect mgr, Stauffer Chem Co, 1974-1976; supvr prod develop, Stauffer Chem Co, 1972-1974; res chemist anal chem, Stauffer Chem Co, 1970-1971; Chemist, Shell Chem Co, 1967-1970. **Memberships:** Am Chem Soc. **Research Statement & Publications:** New product development; analytical chemistry; agricultural chemicals; research administration. **Mailing Address:** Zeneca Inc, PO Box 15438, Wilmington, DE 19850-5458. **Fax:** 302-886-3000.

KIEFT, LESTER, ANALYTICAL CHEMISTRY. **Personal Data:** b Grand Haven, Mich, September 18, 1912; m 1941, c 3. **Education:** Hope Col, AB, 1934; Pa State Col, MS, 1936, PhD (anal chem), 1939. **Professional Experience:** PROF EMER CHEM, BUCKNELL UNIV, 1981-; secy fac, Bucknell Univ, 1968-1980; head dept, Bucknell Univ, 1944-1970; from asst prof to prof, Bucknell Univ, 1942-1981; asst prof chem, Pa State Jr Col, 1937-1942; asst, Pa State Col, 1934-1937. **Memberships:** AAAS; Am Chem Soc; Nat Sci Teachers Asn. **Research Statement & Publications:** Analytical properties of salts of the iodometallic acids. **Mailing Address:** 319 Buffalo Rd, Lewisburg, PA 17837-1134.

KIEFT, RICHARD LEONARD, INORGANIC CHEMISTRY, ANALYTICAL CHEMISTRY. **Personal Data:** b Lewisburg, Pa, April 27, 1945. **Education:** Dickinson Col, BS, 1967; Univ Ill, Urbana, PhD (inorg chem), 1973. **Honors & Awards:** Sears-Roebuck Found Award, 1988. **Professional Experience:** DEPT CHAIR CHEM, MONMOUTH COL, as of 2005; PROF CHEM, MONMOUTH COL, ILL, 1989-; from asst prof to assoc prof, Monmouth Col, Ill, 1975-1989; teaching res assoc chem, Tulane Univ, 1973-1975. **Memberships:** Am Chem Soc. **Research Statement & Publications:** Synthesis and identification of organometallic compounds; environmental analysis. **Mailing Address:** Dept Chem, Monmouth Col, Rm 302 Haldeman-Thiessen 700 E Broadway, Monmouth, IL 61462. **Fax:** 309-457-2141. **E-Mail:** richardk@monm.edu

KIEHL, JEFFREY THEODORE, RADIATIVE TRANSFER, CLIMATE MODELING. **Personal Data:** b Harrisburg, Pa, June 10, 1952; m 1980, c 2. **Education:** Elizabethtown Col, BS, 1974; Ind Univ, MS, 1977; State Univ NY, Albany, PhD (atmospheric sci), 1981. **Professional Experience:** CO DIR, NSF SCI & TECHNOL CTR CLOUDS, CHEM & CLIMATE, SCRIPPS INST OCENOG, as of 1999; RES SCIENTIST, ATMOSPHERIC SCI, NAT CTR ATMOSPHERIC RES, 1984-; fel adv studies, 1982-1984; vis scientist, 1981-1982. **Memberships:** Am Meteorol Soc; Am Geophys Union. **Research Statement & Publications:** General circulation modeling, aerosols and climate; infrared transfer in the atmosphere with applications to the carbon dioxide climate problems. **Mailing Address:** Nat Ctr Atmospheric Res, 1850 Table Mesa Dr, Boulder, CO 80303. **Fax:** 303-497-1324.

KIEHL, RICHARD ARTHUR, PHYSICAL ELECTRONICS. **Personal Data:** b Akron, Ohio, February 14, 1948. **Education:** Purdue Univ, BS & MS, 1970, PhD (elec eng), 1974. **Professional Experience:** PROF, ELEC & COMPUT ENG, UNIV MINN, 1999-; actg prof, elec eng, Stanford Univ, 1996-1999; asst dir, Quantum Electron Device Lab, Fujitsu Lab Ltd, Japan, 1992 to 1995; mem tech staff, IBM T J Watson Res Ctr, 1985-1992; mem tech staff, Explor High-Speed Device Group, Bell Labs, 1980-1985; mem tech staff, Div Solid-State Device Physics Res, Sandia Labs, 1974-1980; asst elec eng, Sch Elec Eng, Purdue Univ, 1971-1974. **Memberships:** Inst Elec & Electronics Engrs; Am Phys Soc. **Research Statement & Publications:** Microwave and optical active semiconductor devices; high-speed logic devices in compound semiconductors. **Mailing Address:** Dept Elec & Comput Eng, Univ Minn, 200 Union St, SE, Minneapolis, MN 55455-0154. **Fax:** 612-625-4583. **E-Mail:** kiehl@ece.umn.edu

KIEHLMANN, EBERHARD, ORGANIC CHEMISTRY. **Personal Data:** b Grosshartmannsdorf, Ger, February 9, 1937. **Education:** Univ Tuebingen, Vordiplom, Ger, 1959; Univ Md, Col Park, PhD (org chem), 1964. **Professional Experience:** RETIRED; assoc prof chem, Simon Fraser Univ, beginning 1972; asst prof, Simon Fraser Univ, 1966-1972; res fel, Dartmouth Col, 1965-1966; res fel, Univ Calif, Berkeley, 1964-1965. **Memberships:** Am Chem Soc; Ger Soc Chem; Chem Inst Can. **Research Statement & Publications:** Synthesis and reactions of flavanoids. **Mailing Address:** 7292 Ridge Dr, Burnaby, BC V5A 1B5, Can. **E-Mail:** ekie@sfu.ca

KIEHN, ROBERT MITCHELL, PHYSICS. **Personal Data:** b Oak Park, Ill, December 29, 1929; m 1958. **Education:** Mass Inst Technol, BS, 1950, PhD, 1954. **Professional Experience:** PROF EMER PHYSICS, UNIV HOUSTON, as of 2000; prof physics, Univ Houston, beginning 1972; assoc prof, Univ Houston, 1962-1972; staff physicist, Los Alamos Sci Lab, 1954-1962. **Memberships:** Am Phys Soc; Am Nuclear Soc. **Research Statement & Publications:** Neutron reactor physics; hydrodynamics; thermodynamics. **Mailing Address:** Dept Physics, Univ Houston, 4800 Calhoun Rd, Houston, TX 78755.

KIEL, JOHNATHAN LLOYD, BIOCHEMICAL IMMUNOLOGY, BACTERIOLOGY. **Personal Data:** b Houston, Tex, September 4, 1949; m 1973, c 2. **Education:** Tex A&M Univ, BS, 1973, DVM, 1974, Health Sci Ctr, PhD (microbiol & biochem), 1981. **Professional Experience:** CHIEF, BIOPHYS MECHANISM FUNCTION RADIO FREQUENCY, RADIATION BR, ENERGY DIV, OCCUP & ENVIRON HEALTH DIRECTORATE, USAF, 1991-; adj asst prof, Tex Tech, 1981; res immunol, Physics Br, Radiation Sci Div, Sch Aerospace Med, Brooks AFB, Tex, 1981-1991; vet, Vet Pub Health, Grissom AFB, Ind, 1975-1977; instr, vet microbiol, Sch Vet Med, Tex A&M Univ, 1974-1975. **Memberships:** Am Vet Med Asn; Bioelectromagnetics Soc; Am Col Vet Microbiologists. **Research Statement & Publications:** Oxidative metabolism of the various cells of the immune system and how it influences the immune response and cytotoxic mechanisms; influence of radiofrequency radiation on this metabolism. **Mailing Address:** Usaf Res Lab, 8315 Hawks Rd bldg 1162, Brooks, TX 78235. **Fax:** 210-536-4716. **E-Mail:** johnathan.kiel@aloer.brooks.af

KIEL, OTIS GERALD, ENGINEERING SCIENCES, MATHEMATICS. **Personal Data:** b Wichita Falls, Tex, February 10, 1931; m 1953, c 3. **Education:** NTex State Univ, BS, 1949; Univ Okla, BS, 1956, MS, 1957, PhD (eng sci), 1963. **Honors & Awards:** C K Ferguson Award, Am Inst Mining, Metall & Petrol Engrs, 1963. **Professional Experience:** CHIEF RESERVOIR ENGR, CONOCO, INC, 1980-; Sect supvr, Continental Oil Co, 1959-1980. **Memberships:** Am Inst Mining Metall & Petrol Engrs; Soc Petrol Engrs. **Research Statement & Publications:** Reservoir mechanics, mathematical modeling; reserve determination enhanced recovery projects. **Mailing Address:** 807 Soboda Ct, Houston, TX 77079.

KIELKOPF, JOHN F, Radiative transport, spectroscopy. **Personal Data:** b Louisville, Ky, August 1, 1945; m 1970, Helen; c Clara L. **Education:** Univ Louisville, BS & MS, 1966; Johns Hopkins Univ, PhD (physics), 1969. **Professional Experience:** Scientist resident, Argonne Nat Lab, 1981; astron, Observ Paris, Meudon, 1979-1980; PROF PHYSICS, UNIV LOUISVILLE, 1977-; vis scientist, Argonne Nat Lab, 1974-1975; Assoc res scientist, Johns Hopkins Univ, 1974; From asst prof to assoc prof, Univ Louisville, 1969-1977. **Memberships:** Am Phys Soc; Optical Soc Am; Am Astron Soc. **Research Statement & Publications:** Radiative atomic and molecular processes with applications to astrophysics; detection and analysis of time-dependent optical phenomena. **Mailing Address:** Moore Observ, Univ Louisville, 8000 Old Zaring Rd, Crestwood, KY 40014. **Fax:** 502-852-0742. **E-Mail:** kielkopf@louisville.edu

KIELY, DONALD EDWARD, SYNTHETIC ORGANIC CHEMISTRY. **Personal Data:** b Waterbury, Conn, January 5, 1938; m 1963, c 3. **Education:** Fairfield Univ, BS, 1960; Univ Conn, PhD (org chem), 1965. **Professional Experience:** PROF CHEM, UNIV MONT, beginning 1997; Ed, J Carbohydrate Chem, 1981-; resident prof, Staley Mfg Co, 1981-1982; prof Chem, Univ Ala, Birmingham, beginning 1977; Vis fel, Res Sch Chem, Australian Nat Univ, 1974; from asst prof to assoc prof, Univ Ala, Birmingham, 1968-1977; staff fel, Nat Inst Arthritis & Metab Dis, 1966-1968; Vis asst prof org chem, Wofford Col, 1965-1966. **Memberships:** Am Chem Soc; Sigma Xi. **Research Statement & Publications:** Synthesis of biologically interesting carbohydrates, cyclitols and other carbocyclic and heterocyclic compounds; chemical studies related to cyclitol biosynthesis; synthetic carbohydrate chemistry; industrially related carbohydrate chemistry; synthetic carbohydrate based polymer synthesis. **Mailing Address:** 2521 Chatwood Rd, Birmingham, AL 35226-3503.

KIELY, JOHN STEVEN, PHARMACOLOGY. **Personal Data:** b Missoula, Mont, October 11, 1951; m 1974, c 2. **Education:** Mont State Univ, BSc, 1974; NDak State Univ, PhD (organ chem), 1979. **Professional Experience:** DIR MED CHEM, ISIS PHARMACEUT, 1993-; from res assoc to sr res assoc, Parke Davis/Warner Lambert Res, Warner Lambert Co, 1987-1993; from scientist to sr scientist, Parke Davis/Warner Lambert Res, Warner Lambert Co, 1981-1987; Assoc res fel, Lawrence Berkeley Lab, Univ Calif, 1979-1981. **Memberships:** Am Chem Soc; Sigma Xi; AAAS. **Research Statement & Publications:** Quinolone antibacterials; cognition activators; peptide nucleic acid; antisense technology; oligonucleotide synthesis and sarcosine. **Mailing Address:** 12460 Saddle Rd, Carmel Valley, CA 93924. **E-Mail:** john_kiely@isisph.com

KIELY, MICHAEL LAWRENCE, ANATOMY. **Personal Data:** b Springfield, Ill, June 17, 1938; m 1967, c 2. **Education:** Lewis Col, BS, 1960; Loyola Univ Ill, MS, 1964, PhD (anat), 1967. **Professional Experience:** PROF, NAT UNIV HEALTH SCIENCES, 1994-; from asst prof to prof anat, Sch Dent, 1967-1994; Res assoc, Stritch Sch Med, Loyola Univ, Chicago, 1967. **Memberships:** Am Asn Anatomists; Int Asn Dent Res; Am Asn Dent Res; Am Asn Clin Anatomists. **Research Statement & Publications:** Gross and oral anatomy; temporomandibulow joint; morphologic variations in the human skull and cranial soft tissue. **Mailing Address:** 200 E Roosevelt Rd, Lombard, IL 60148. **Fax:** 630-889-6554. **E-Mail:** mkiely@national.chiropractic.edu

KIEMELE, MARK J, MATHEMATICS. **Education:** NDak State Univ, BS, MS; Texas A&M Univ, Phd (comput sci). **Professional Experience:** PRES & CHAIR, AIR ACAD ASSOC, CO, as of 2005. **Mailing Address:** 2065 Mulligan Dr, Colorado Springs, CO 80920-1603. **Fax:** 719 531-0778.

KIEN, C LAWRENCE, STABLE ISOTOPIC TRACERS, CARBOHYDRATE & PROTEIN METABOLISM. **Personal Data:** b October 5, 1946; m Patricia; c 2. **Education:** Duke Univ, BS, 1968; Univ Cincinnati, MD, 1972; Mass Inst Technol, PhD (nutrit & biochem), 1977. **Professional Experience:** PROF PEDIAT, OHIO STATE UNIV, 1988-; C E Compton prof nutrit, Sch Med, Univ Wva, 1984-1987; from asst prof to assoc prof pediat & biochem, Med Col Wis, Milwaukee, 1977-1984; med consult, Amino Acid/Org Acid Lab, C Hosp; assoc dir, Gen Clin Res Ctr; mem, Div Gastroenterol & Human Molecular Genetics, Ohio State Univ Hosp; fel med, C Hosp Med Ctr, Boston, Massachusetts, 1976-1977; fel, Mass Inst Technol, 1977. **Memberships:** AAAS; Am Physiol Soc; Am Soc Clin Nutrit; Am Inst Nutrit; Am Soc Parenteral & Enterol Nutrit; Soc Pediat Res; Am Pediat Soc; fel Am Acad Pediat; fel Am Col Nutrit; spec fel Leukemia Soc; Am Gastroenterol Asn; Sigma Xi; Milwaukee Pediat Soc; Am Soc Nutrit Sci; Monongalia Med Soc; Central Ohio Pediat Soc; N Am Soc Pediat Gastroenterol & Nutrit; European Soc Pediat Res; N Am Asn Study Obesity. **Research Statement & Publications:** Nutrition; study of protein and energy; use stable, non-radioactive isotopes to study lactose utilization, carbohydrate and amino acid metabolism, and energy expenditure in the newborn and in children with cystic fibrosis or obesity; effects of caloric fermentation on cell proliferation and apoptosis in colon and intestine; diagnosis and treatment of disorders of nutrition and inburn errors of metabolism. **Mailing Address:** Children's Hosp, Rm W209 700 Children's Dr, Columbus, OH 43205. **Fax:** 409-772-4599. **E-Mail:** clkien@utmb.edu

KIENER, PETER A, IMMUNOLOGY. **Education:** Lancaster Univ, BS. **Professional Experience:** SR VPRES, MEDIMMUNE INC, as of 2006. **Memberships:** Nat Acad Sci. **Mailing Address:** Medimmune Inc, One Medimmune Way, Gaithersburg, MD 20878. **Fax:** 301-398-9000.

KIENTZ, MARVIN L, BIOCHEMISTRY. **Personal Data:** b Clovis, Calif, January 28, 1936; m 1984, Sharon; c Randal & Jane. **Education:** Fresno State Col, BA, 1958, MA, 1961; Western Ont Univ, PhD (biochem), 1966. **Professional Experience:** PROF EMER CHEM, SONOMA STATE UNIV, as of 2006; prof chem, Sonoma State Univ, beginning 1974; inst dir, NSF, 1971-1973; assoc prof, Sonoma State Univ, 1967-1974; res biochemist, Med Ctr, Univ Calif, San Francisco, 1966-1967; teacher high sch, 1959-1963. **Research Statement & Publications:** Determination of the structure of proteins; protein polymorphism. **Mailing Address:** Dept Chem, Sonoma State Univ, 1801 E Cotati Ave, Rohnert Park, CA 94928.

KIER, ANN B, GENE TARGETING & COMPARATIVE PATHOLOGY. **Personal Data:** b Littlefield, Tex, June 26, 1949; m 1979, Friedhelm; c Hilary. **Education:** Univ Tex, Austin, BA, 1971; Tex A&M Univ, BS, 1973, DVM, 1974; Univ Mo, Columbia, PhD (path), 1979; Am Col Lab Animal Med, dipl. **Professional Experience:** PROF & HEAD, DEPT PATHOBIOL, TEX A&M UNIV, 1994-; dir & prof, Div Comparative Path, Univ Cincinatti Col Med, 1991-1993; head, Div Comparative Path, 1990-1993; from assoc prof to prof path, Univ Cincinnati Med Sch, 1987-1993; dir, Histopath Lab, Vet Med Diag Lab, 1980-1987; from asst prof to assoc prof path & microbiol, Lab Animal Med & Comp Path, Univ Mo, Columbia, 1979-1987; NIH fel, Lab Animal Med & Comp Path, Univ Mo, Columbia, 1976-1979. **Memberships:** Am Vet Med Asn; Am Asn Vet Med Col; Am Col Lab Animal Med; Am Soc Invest Path; Am Asn Exp Pathologist. **Research Statement & Publications:** Immunpathology, Corpartive Pathology; cholesterol and fattyacid intracelluler transport transgenic mice and gene targeting; genetics; Published over 100 articles. **Mailing Address:** Dept Pathobiol, TVMC Tex A&M Univ, College Station, TX 77843-4467. **Fax:** 979-845-9231.

KIER, LEMONT BURWELL, MEDICINAL CHEMISTRY. **Personal Data:** b Cleveland, Ohio, September 13, 1930; m 1953, c 5. **Education:** Ohio State Univ, BS, 1954; Univ Minn, PhD (med chem), 1958. **Professional Experience:** PROF EMER, DEPT PHARMACEUT CHEM, MED COL VA, VA COMMONWEALTH UNIV as of 2005; vis prof, Univ Lausanne, Switz, 1992; prof, Dept Pharmaceut Chem, Va Commonwealth Univ, beginning 1977; chmn, Dept Pharmaceut Chem, Med Col VA, Va Commonwealth Univ, 1977-1987; prof chem, Mass Col Pharm, 1972-1977; chmn, Dept Chem, Mass Col Pharm, 1972-1974; assoc fel med chem, Columbus Labs, Battelle Mem Inst, 1969-1972; adj prof, Univ Mich, 1969-1972; sr med chemist, Columbus Labs, Battelle Mem Inst, 1966-1969; assoc prof, Ohio State Univ, 1963-1966; asst prof pharmaceut chem, Univ Fla, 1959-1963. **Memberships:** Fel Am Asn Pharmaceut Scientists; Am Chem Soc; fel Acad Pharmaceut Sci; fel Am Pharmaceut Asn. **Research Statement & Publications:** Theoretical approaches to drug structure activity relationships; topological structure indices; cellular automata models of dynamic solution phenomena. **Mailing Address:** Dept Med Chem, Va Commonwealth Univ, 410 N 12th St PO Box 980540, Richmond, VA 23298. **E-Mail:** kier@hsc.vcu.edu

KIERAS, FRED J, CONNECTIVE TISSUE BIOCHEMISTRY, GENETIC DISEASES. **Education:** Univ Chicago, PhD (biochem), 1968. **Professional Experience:** RES SCIENTIST, NY INST BASIC RES, 1971-. **Mailing Address:** NY State Inst Basic Res, 1050 Forest Hill Rd, Staten Island, NY 10314-6330. **Fax:** 718-698-3803.

KIERNAN, JOHN ALAN, NEUROHISTOLOGY & HISTOCHEMISTRY. **Personal Data:** b Kidderminstar, Eng, 1942; m 1967, Tessa; c Julia, Edward, Susan, Jeffrey & Philip. **Education:** Univ Birmingham, BSc, 1963, MB & ChB, 1966, MA, PhD (neuroanat), 1969; DSc, (anat) Univ Birmingham, Eng, 1979. **Professional Experience:** CORE FAC MEM, NEUROSCIENCE GRAD PROG, UNIV WESTERN ONT, CAN, 1990-; commonwealth med fel & vis prof, dept Anat & Cell Biol, Univ Sheffield, Eng, 1985-1986; PROF, DEPT ANAT, UNIV WESTERN ONT, 1981-; from asst prof to assoc prof, dept Anat, Univ Western Ont, 1972-1981; Univ demonstr, dept Anat, Univ Cambridge, 1971-1972; dir studies med, Sidney Sussex Col, Cambridge, 1970-1972; fel, Sidney Sussex Col, Cambridge, Eng, 1969-1972; sr res fel, Sidney Sussex Col, Cambridge, 1969-1971; res fel, dept Anat, Univ Birmingham, Eng, 1967-1969; house physician, Worcester Royal Infirmary, 1967; house surgeon, E Birmingham Hosp, 1966. **Memberships:** Anat Soc Brit; Bot Soc Brit Isles; Histochem Soc; fel Royal Microscopical Soc; Soc mem biol Stain comn; Soc Histotech; Southern Ont Neuroscience Asn; Soc Neuroscience. **Research Statement & Publications:** Reactions of nervous tissue to injury and disease; histology and histochemistry; human neuroanatomy; Published over 20 articles. **Mailing Address:** Dept Anat & Cell Biol, Univ Western Ont, London, ON N6A 5C1, Can.

KIERSTEAD, DAVID P, MATHEMATICS. **Education:** Univ Wis-Mad, PhD (Maths), 1979. **Professional Experience:** VPRES MGR, DANIEL H WAGNER ASSOCS, VA, as of 2005. **Memberships:** Mil Opers Res Soc. **Mailing Address:** Daniel H Wagner Assocs, 450 Maple Ave E 206, Vienna, VA 22180. **Fax:** 703-255-4781. **E-Mail:** kierstead@nva.wagner.com

KIERSTEAD, RICHARD WIGHTMAN, ORGANIC CHEMISTRY, PHARMACEUICAL CHEMISTRY. **Personal Data:** b Fredericton, NB, February 17, 1927; American & Canadian citizen; m 1964, c 3. **Education:** Univ NB, BSc, 1948, MSc, 1950; Univ London, PhD (org chem), 1952. **Professional Experience:** RETIRED; dir, Chem Synthesis Dept, 1993-1994; dir med chem, Hoffman-La Roche Inc, 1978-1992; sect chief, Hoffman-La Roche Inc, 1969-1977; group chief, Hoffman-La Roche Inc, 1963-1969; sr res chemist, Hoffman-La Roche Inc, 1956-1963; res chemist, Harvard Univ, 1955-1956; res chemist, E I Du Pont De Nemours & Co, 1954-1955; res assoc, Univ Calif, Los Angeles, 1953-1954; res assoc, Univ Toronto, 1952-1953. **Memberships:** Am Chem Soc. **Research Statement & Publications:** Synthesis of medicinal compounds. **Mailing Address:** 30 Willowbrook Dr, North Caldwell, NJ 07006.

KIERSZEBAUM, FELIPE, MEDICAL RESEARCH. **Education:** Univ Buenos Aires, PhD, 1966. **Professional Experience:** PROF, DEPT MICROBIOL & MOLECULAR GENETICS, MICH STATE UNIV, as of 2005. **Mailing Address:** Dept Microbiol & Pub Health Mich State Univ, 148 Giltner Hall 5175 Biomed Physi Scis, East Lansing, MI 48824-0001. **E-Mail:** kierszen@msu.edu

KIERSZENBAUM, FELIPE, MICROBIOLOGY. **Education:** Univ Buenos Aires, PhD, 1966. **Professional Experience:** PROF, DEPT MICROBIOL & MOLECULAR GENETICS, MICH STATE UNIV, as of 2006. **Mailing Address:** Dept Microbiol & Molecular Genetics, Mich State Univ, 5175 Biomed Phys Sci, East Lansing, MI 48824-1101. **Fax:** 561-658-0856. **E-Mail:** kierszen@msu.edu

KIESCHNICK, W(ILLIAM) F(REDERICK), CHEMICAL ENGINEERING. **Personal Data:** b Dallas, Tex, January 5, 1923; m 1979, c 2. **Education:** Rice Univ, BS, 1947. **Professional Experience:** CHIEF EXEC OFFICER EMER, ATLANTIC RICHFIELD CORP, as of 1997; DIR, PRES EMER & CHIEF OPERATING OFFICER, ATLANTIC RICHFIELD CORP, 1985-; pres & chief exec officer, Tex, 1982-1985; pres & chief opers officer, Tex, 1981; vice chmn, Tex, 1979; mem bd dirs, Atlantic Richfield Co, beginning 1973; exec vpres, Tex, 1973-1979; vpres & head corp planning, Tex, 1972-1973; vpres chem opers, Tex, 1970-1972; vpres synthetic crude & mineral opers, Tex, 1969-1970; vpres & mgr cent region, Tex, 1966-1969; div mgr dists, Res Sect, 1963-1966; mgr explor prod dist, Res Sect, 1961-1963; asst to gen mgr explor, Res Sect, 1959-1961; head, Res Sect, 1954-1959; supv engr, Res Dept Admin, 1951-1954; sr chem engr, Res Dept Admin, 1949-1951; admin asst, Res Dept Admin, 1948-1949; from jr engr to theoret oil reservoir engr, Atlantic Refining Co, Atlantic Richfield Co, 1947-1948; vice chmn bd trustees, Calif Inst Technol; trustee, Carnegie Inst Wash; dir, Atlantic Richfield, TRW, First Interstate Bancorp, Pac Mutual Life Ins; chmn, Biotech Group Inc; chmn bd, Coun Health, Safety & Environ. **Memberships:** Am Inst Mining Metall & Petrol Engrs; Am Inst Chem Engrs; Am Asn Petrol Geologists; Am Petrol Inst. **Mailing Address:** Atlantic Richfield Corp, 515 S Flower St, Los Angeles, CA 90017.

KIESLING, ERNST W(ILLIE), STRUCTURAL MECHANICS. **Personal Data:** b Eola, Tex, April 8, 1934; m 1956, Juanita Haseloff; c Carol, Chris & Max. **Education:** Tex Tech Col, BS, 1955; Mich State Univ, MS, 1958, PhD (appl mech), 1966. **Professional Experience:** PROF CIVIL ENG, COL ENG, TEX TECH UNIV, 1993-; assoc dean res, Col Eng, Tex Tech Univ, 1988-1993; Dir, Ctr Advan Res & Eng Res Found, 1988-1993; prof civil eng & chmn dept, Col Eng, Tex Tech Univ, 1969-1988; sr res engr, Struct Res Dept, Southwest Res Inst, 1966-1969; From instr to asst prof civil eng, Tex Tech Col, 1956-1963. **Memberships:** Am Soc Eng Educ; Am Soc Civil Engrs; Nat Soc Prof Engrs; Sigma Xi. **Research Statement & Publications:** Housing; earth sheltered buildings; occupant protection form serve winds; Storm Shelter design. **Mailing Address:** Dept Civil Eng, Tex Tech Univ, Lubbock, TX 79409.

KIESOW, LUTZ A, BIOLOGY. **Education:** MD, PhD. **Professional Experience:** RETIRED; legacy chief res, Good Samaritan Found, as of 2001. **Memberships:** Am Soc Microbiol. **Mailing Address:** Good Samaritan Found, PO Box 4484, Portland, OR 97208. **Fax:** 503-413-6930.

KIESS, EDWARD MARION, PHYSICS. **Personal Data:** b Washington, DC, March 10, 1933; m 1959, c 3. **Education:** Mass Inst Technol, 1955; Pa State Univ, MS, 1962, PhD (physics), 1965. **Professional Experience:** Cotrell grant, 1971-; ASSOC PROF PHYSICS, HAMPDEN-SYDNEY COL, 1968-; physicist, Battelle Mem Inst, 1965-1967; Asst prof physics, Lycoming Col, 1965. **Memberships:** Optical Soc Am. **Research Statement & Publications:** Brillouin scattering; Fourier spectroscopy. **Mailing Address:** Hwy 658, Hampden-Sydney, VA 23943.

KIESSLING, GEORGE ANTHONY, ELECTRICAL ENGINEERING. **Personal Data:** b New York, NY, December 2, 1920; m 1951, c 6. **Education:** Manhattan Col, BSEE, 1951; Stevens Inst Technol, MSIE, 1953. **Professional Experience:** RETIRED; dir prod safety-plans & progs, RCA Corp, 1970-1985; dir prof eng serv, RCA Corp, 1969-1970; mgr prod eng prof develop, RCA Corp, 1963-1969; mgr prod admin, RCA Corp, 1962-1963; staff engr, RCA Corp, 1961; mgr eng stand & serv, RCA Corp, 1956-1961; adminr eng financial planning, RCA Corp, 1954-1955; mem tech staff, Physics Lab, Sylvania Electronics Prod, Inc, 1951-1954. **Memberships:** Inst Elec & Electronics Engrs. **Research Statement & Publications:** Product safety programs, including policy, management, systems, audit, standards, legislation and regulations; product ionizing and nonionizing radiation safety; laser safety including standards, legislation and regulations. **Mailing Address:** 412 Longwood Dr, Haddonfield, NJ 08033.

KIEWIET DE JONGE, JOOST H A, ASTRONOMY. **Personal Data:** b Leiden, Neth, September 4, 1919; m 1954, c 1. **Education:** Harvard Univ, PhD (astron), 1954. **Professional Experience:** PROF EMER PHYSICS & ASTRON, UNIV PITTSBURGH, as of 2003; MEM STAFF, ALLEGHENY OBSERV, 1977-; actg dir, Allegheny Observ, 1970-1977; actg chmn, Univ Pittsburgh, 1970-1975; assoc prof astron, Univ Pittsburgh, beginning 1966; consult, J W Fecker Div, Am Optical, 1960-1970; lectr, Chatham Col, 1956-1970; asst prof, Univ Pittsburgh, 1954-1965; instr, Univ Pittsburgh, 1950-1954. **Memberships:** Am Astron Soc. **Research Statement & Publications:** Astronomical navigation; stellar statistics; celestial mechanics; astronomical instrumentation. **Mailing Address:** Dept Physics & Astron, Univ Pittsburgh, Pittsburgh, PA 15214.

KIEWIT, DAVID ARNOLD, APPLIED PHYSICS, MATERIALS SCIENCE. **Personal Data:** b Cincinnati, Ohio, February 25, 1940; m 1963, Michelle; c Douglas & Devra. **Education:** Northwestern Univ, Evanston, BA, 1962, PhD (mat sci), 1968. **Professional Experience:** CONSULT & REGIST PATENT AGENT, 1990-; dir eng & advan develop, A C Nielsen Co, 1981-1990; mgr device develop, Gould Lab, Elec & Electronic Res, Gould Inc, 1973-1981; mem tech staff, Hughes Res Labs, Hughes Aircraft Co, 1967-1973. **Memberships:** Am Phys Soc; Inst Elec & Electronics Engrs. **Research Statement & Publications:** Development of intelligent instrumentation systems for statistical measurements; preparation and prosecution of patent applications. **Mailing Address:** 5901 Third St S, St Petersburg, FL 33705-5305. **Fax:** 727-866-0669. **E-Mail:** dak@patent-faq.com

KIFER, EDWARD W, INORGANIC CHEMISTRY, PHYSICAL CHEMISTRY. **Personal Data:** b Penn, Pa, October 31, 1938; m 1963, c 2. **Education:** Ind State Col, BSEd, 1960; George Wash Univ, MS, 1965; Carnegie-Mellon Univ, PhD (inorg chem), 1969. **Professional Experience:** RETIRED; mgr res, Phenolic Prod Dept, 1980-1988; sr res group mgr physics & phys chem, Res Dept, 1975-1980; res group mgr physics & phys chem, Res Dept, Koppers Co, Inc, 1969-1975; sr res scientist, Res Dept, Koppers Co, Inc, 1968-1969; asst res scientist phys chem, Res Dept, Koppers Co, Inc, 1965-1968;

asst chem, George Wash Univ, 1963-1965; teacher, Norwin Sch Syst, Pa, 1960-1963. **Memberships:** AAAS; Am Chem Soc; fel Am Inst Chemists. **Research Statement & Publications:** Synthesis and characterization of compounds of the group IV elements, especially silicon hydrides; inorganic coordination polymer behavior; fire retardant systems for wood and plastics. **Mailing Address:** 106 Ardennes Ct, Trafford, PA 15085-1219.

KIFER, MICHAEL, MATHEMATICS, COMPUTER SCIENCE. **Education:** Moscow Univ, Russia, MS, 1976; Hebrew Univ Jerusalem, Israel, PhD (comput sci), 1985. **Professional Experience:** PROF COMPUT SCI, STATE UNIV NY, STONY BROOK, as of 2003; prof comput sci, Univ Toronto, Can, 1991-1992; assoc prof comput sci, State Univ Ny, Stony Brook, beginning 1984. **Research Statement & Publications:** Declarative languages for data and knowledge manipulation; integration of object-oriented and deductive paradigms; object-oriented data bases; query optimization; logic programming; artificial intelligence. **Mailing Address:** Dept Comput Sci, 1413 Comput Sci, State Univ NY Stony Brook, Stony Brook, NY 11794-4400. **E-Mail:** kifer@cs.stonybrook.edu

KIFER, PAUL EDGAR, FOOD SCIENCE. **Personal Data:** b Grove City, Pa, August 16, 1924; m 1950, D Joan; c 3. **Education:** Mich State Univ, BS, 1950, MS, 1953, PhD (animal nutrit), 1956. **Professional Experience:** PROF EMER INTERNAL RES & DEVELOP, ORE STATE UNIV, 1985-; assoc dean, int agr, 1983-1985; head dept food sci & technol, Ore State Univ, 1973-1983; asst dir corp res, Pet Food Res & Develop, 1969-1973; asst to vpres corp res, Pet Food Res & Develop, 1967-1969; dir, Pet Food Res & Develop, 1964-1967; mgr, Spec Chows Res Div, 1959-1964; asst mgr poultry res div, Ralston Purina Co, 1957-1959; Asst prof poultry, Univ Ga, 1956-1957. **Memberships:** Poultry Sci Asn; Inst Food Technologists; Am Inst Nutrit. **Research Statement & Publications:** Nutrition as related to food science, food safety. **Mailing Address:** Dept Internal Res & Develop, Ore State Univ, 400 Snell Hall, Corvallis, OR 97331-1641.

KIFF, LLOYD F, ORNITHOLOGY. **Professional Experience:** SCI DIR, THE PEREGRINE FUND, as of 2001. **Memberships:** Cooper Ornith Soc. **Mailing Address:** The Peregrine Fund, 5668 W Flying Hawk Lane, Boise, ID 83709. **Fax:** 208-362-2376. **E-Mail:** lkiff@peregrinefund.org

KIGER, JOHN ANDREW, DEVELOPMENTAL GENETICS, CYCLIC NUCLEOTIDE ACTION. **Personal Data:** b Dayton, Ohio, February 6, 1941. **Education:** Calif Inst Technol, BS, 1963, PhD (biophys), 1968. **Professional Experience:** NIH Fogarty fel, 1993 & 1994; chair, Dept Genetics, 1987-1991; PROF GENETICS, UNIV CALIF, DAVIS, 1982-; from asst prof to assoc prof, Univ Calif, Davis, 1973-1982; asst prof biochem, Ore State Univ, 1969-1973; Am Cancer Soc fel, 1969; Instr biol, Mass Inst Technol, 1968-1969. **Memberships:** AAAS; Genetics Soc Am; Soc Develop Biol. **Research Statement & Publications:** Biochemical and developmental genetics of Drosophila; cyclic nucleotide metabolism and action. **Mailing Address:** Molecular & Cellular Biol, Univ Calif, 1 Shields Ave, Davis, CA 95616. **E-Mail:** jakiger@ucdavis.edu

KIGER, ROBERT WILLIAM, SYSTEMATIC BOTANY, HISTORY OF BIOLOGY. **Personal Data:** b Washington, DC, October 4, 1940; m 1968, Suellen; c David & James. **Education:** Tulane Univ, BA, 1966; Univ Md, MA (hist sci), 1971, PhD (bot), 1972. **Professional Experience:** DIR & PRIN RES SCIENTIST, HUNT INST BOT DOC, CARNEGIE MELLON UNIV, 1977-; adj scientist, Pittsburgh Poison Ctr, 1990-; adj prof botany, Dept Biol Sci, Carnegie Mellon Univ, 1984-1999; disting serv prof botany, Dept Biol Sci, Carnegie Mellon Univ, 1999-; adj prof hist sci, Dept Hist, Carnegie Mellon Univ, 1979-; Res assoc, Bot Sect, Carnegie Mus Nat Hist, 1978-; asst dir & sr res scientist, Hunt Inst Bot Doc, Carnegie Mellon Univ, 1974-1977; dir develop, Sea Kal Develop Cor, 1973-1974; res botanist, Smithsonian Inst, 1972-1973; teacher elem schs, Montgomery Co, Md, 1966-1967. **Memberships:** Bot Soc Am; Am Soc Plant Taxonomists; Int Asn Plant Taxon. **Research Statement & Publications:** Floristic and monographic study of various New World angiosperms, especially Flacourtiaceae and Talinum; history, philosophy and theory of biological systematics; evolutionary philosophy, especially in relation to theory of evolutionary mechanism and change, and to systematics; Flora of North America project; botanical documentation and databanking. **Mailing Address:** Hunt Inst, Carnegie Mellon Univ, Pittsburgh, PA 15213. **Fax:** 412-268-5677. **E-Mail:** rkiger@andrew.cmu.edu

KIGGINS, EDWARD M, MICROBIOLOGY. **Personal Data:** b Stamford, Conn, March 26, 1929; m 1958, c 2. **Education:** Univ Conn, AB, 1952, MS, 1954, PhD (microbiol), 1958. **Professional Experience:** DIR RES, LUBRIZOL ENTERPRISES INC, 1985-; with Diamond Shamrock Corp, 1980-1985; dir & prod develop, Rhodia, Hess & Clark Div, 1975-1980; dir res & develop, Agr & Vet Prod Div, 1970-1975; mgr animal health res, Amdal Co Div, 1967-1970; sect head, Abbott Labs, 1966-1967; group leader, Abbott Labs, 1961-1966; mem staff microbiol, Abbott Labs, 1958-1960; Asst animal dis, Univ Conn, 1952-1957. **Memberships:** AAAS; Am Soc Microbiol; US Animal Health Asn; Sigma Xi; NY Acad Sci. **Research Statement & Publications:** Veterinary microbiology. **Mailing Address:** 8950 Woodland Pl, Mentor, OH 44060.

KIHARA, HAYATO, BIOCHEMISTRY, BIOCHEMICAL GENETICS. **Personal Data:** b Oakland, Calif, February 28, 1922; m 1950, c 2. **Education:** Univ Tex, BS, 1944; Univ Wis, MS, 1951, PhD (biochem), 1952. **Professional Experience:** PROF EMER BIOCHEM, UNIV CALIF, LOS ANGELES, 1987-; vis prof, Sch Med, Nihon Univ, Tokyo, 1980; prof biochem, Biochem Lab, Ment Retardation Res Ctr, Univ Calif, Los Angeles-lanterman State Hosp, 1975-1987; CHIEF, BIOCHEM LAB, MENT RETARDATION RES CTR, UNIV CALIF, LOS ANGELES-LANTERMAN STATE HOSP, 1973-; assoc res biochemist, Biochem Lab, Ment Retardation Res Ctr, Univ Calif, Los Angeles-lanterman State Hosp, 1973-1975; chief res biochemist, Pac State Hosp, 1963-1973; res specialist, Sonoma State Hosp, Eldridge, Calif, 1960-1963; asst res biochemist, Univ Calif, 1956-1960; res scientist, Biochem Inst, Univ Tex, 1951-1956; asst biochem, Univ Wis, 1948-1951; chemist, US Army, 406th Med Gen Lab, Japan, 1946-1948. **Memberships:** Am Chem Soc; Am Soc Biol Chem; Am Soc Human Genetics; Am Asn Ment Deficiency. **Research Statement & Publications:** Biochemistry of inborn errors of metabolism; tissue culture; enzyme purification; diagnosis of genetic disorders; heterozygote identification; prenatal diagnosis. **Mailing Address:** Lanterman Develop Ctr, 3530 W Pomona Blvd, Pomona, CA 91768.

KIHLSTROM, KENNETH EDWARD, THIN FILM SUPERCONDUCTIVITY, SUPERCONDUCTING TUNNELING. **Personal Data:** b Buffalo, NY, May 11, 1954; m 1978, Kim Potter Kihlstrom; c Katherine, Karen & Kevin. **Education:** Stanford Univ, BS, 1976, MS, 1979, PhD (physics), 1982. **Honors & Awards:** Teacher of yr (Sci) westmont coll 1989, 1995. **Professional Experience:** PROF, WESTMONT COL, 1994-; vis scholar, Stanford Univ, 1992-1993; Conductus, Inc, 1992-1993; consult, Santa Barbara Res Ctr, 1988-1989; Prin investr, Off Naval Res, 1985-1987 & NSF, 1987-; consult, R G Hansen & Assoc, 1987-1988; PHYSICS DEPT CHAIR, WESTMONT COL, 1984-; from asst prof to assoc prof, Westmont Col, 1984-1994; Res assoc, Nat Res Coun-Naval Res Lab, 1982-1984. **Memberships:** Am Phys Soc. **Research Statement & Publications:** Thin film superconductivity; superconducting tunneling on high-core temperature materials. **Mailing Address:** Dept Physics Westmont Col, 955 La Paz Rd, Santa Barbara, CA 93108. **Fax:** 805-565-6220. **E-Mail:** kihlstr@westmont.edu

KIHN, HARRY, ELECTRONICS. **Personal Data:** b Tarnow, Austria, January 24, 1912; American citizen; m 1937, c 2. **Education:** Cooper Union, BSEE, 1934; Univ Pa, MSEE, 1952. **Honors & Awards:** Centennial Award, Inst Elec & Electronics Engr. **Professional Experience:** PRES, KIHN ASSOCS, INC, 1977-; sr tech adv patent opers, RCA Corp, Camden, 1939-1942 & Princeton, NJ, 1975-1977; staff tech adv corp licensing, RCA Corp, Camden, 1939-1942 & Princeton, NJ, 1971-1975; Mem mat adv bd, Nat Acad Sci-Nat Res Coun, 1960-; staff engr to vpres res & eng, RCA Corp, Camden, 1939-1942 & Princeton, NJ, 1960-1970; group head space systs res, RCA Corp, Camden, 1939-1942 & Princeton, NJ, 1958-1960; res engr, RCA Corp, Camden, 1939-1942 & Princeton, NJ, 1942-1958; res engr, Ferris Instrument Co, 1938-1939; chief engr, Polytherm, Inc, 1937-1938; Res engr, Hygrade Sylvania Corp, 1935-1937; mem comm sr ed, Gov Comn Sci Technol. **Memberships:** AAAS; Sigma Xi; fel Inst Elec & Electronics Engrs; NY Acad Sci; Am Defense Preparedness Asn; Am Mgt Asn; Nat Soc Prof Engrs. **Research Statement & Publications:** Electronics and systems research; television communication theory and devices; electromagnetics; radar; infrared; space physics and instrumentation; solid state circuits and devices; integrated circuits; computer design; information processing systems; medical electronics; nuclear energy and waste isolation; industrial electronics; robotics. **Mailing Address:** 30 Green Ave, Lawrenceville, NJ 08648.

KIILSGAARD, THOR H, ECONOMIC GEOLOGY. **Personal Data:** b Honeyville, Utah, June 10, 1919; m 1946, c 3. **Education:** Univ Idaho, BS, 1942; Univ Calif, MA, 1949. **Professional Experience:** RETIRED; Sudan, 1977 & Yemen, 1979; geologist-in-chg, US Geol Surv, Wash, 1976-1989; chief, US Geol Surv-Saudi Arabia Proj, 1972-1976; dep asst chief geologist, US Geol Surv, 1969-1972; chief br resources res, US Geol Surv, 1963-1969; US Geol Surv adv, Iran, 1963; commodity geologist, US Geol Surv, 1959-1969; Int Coop Admin consult, Bolivia, 1959-1960 & Peru, 1958-1959; staff asst, US Geol Surv, 1954-1959; proj geologist, US Geol Surv, 1951-1954; assoc geologist, State Bur Mines & Geol, Idaho, 1949-1951; asst geologist, State Bur Mines & Geol, Idaho, 1948-1949; jr geologist, State Bur Mines & Geol, Idaho, 1946-1947. **Memberships:** Soc Econ Geol; Geol Soc Am; distinguished mem Am Inst Mining, Metal & Petrol Engrs; Northwest Mining Asn. **Research Statement & Publications:** Challis 2 geologic map, Idaho; Hailey 2 geologic map, Idaho; trans-Challis fault system and its control on gold and silver deposits. **Mailing Address:** 4604 S Napa St, Spokane, WA 99223.

KIJEWSKI, LOUIS JOSEPH, THEORETICAL PHYSICS. **Personal Data:** b Philadelphia, Pa, March 20, 1936; m 1975, c 1. **Education:** LaSalle Col, BA, 1958; Columbia Univ, MA, 1961; NY Univ, PhD (physics), 1967. **Professional Experience:** PROF PHYSICS, MONMOUTH COL, NJ, 1968-; assoc res scientist, NY Univ, 1967-1968; res asst atomic physics, NY Univ, 1964-1967; physicist, RCA Corp, Moorestown & Princeton, 1961-1964; asst physics, Columbia Univ, 1958-1961. **Memberships:** Am Phys Soc; Math Asn Am. **Research Statement & Publications:** Calculations for the energy of atomic systems using density matrices. **Mailing Address:** Dept Physics, Monmouth Univ, 400 Cedar Ave, West Long Branch, NJ 07764-1898. **E-Mail:** kijewski@monmouth.edu

KIKER, CLYDE F, ECOLOGY. **Education:** Univ Fla, BS, 1962, MS, 1965, PhD, 1973 1965 M.S. in Engineering. Univ of Florida, Gainesville 1962 B.S. in Ag. Engineering. Univ of Florida, Gainesville. **Professional Experience:** PROF, UNIV FLA, as of 2005. **Mailing Address:** Univ Fla, G086A McCarty Hall B PO Box 110240 IFAS, Gainesville, FL 32611-0240. **Fax:** 352-846-0988. **E-Mail:** cfkiker@ufl.edu

KIKKAWA, YUTAKA, PATHOLOGY. **Personal Data:** b January 30, 1932; c 4. **Education:** Univ Tokyo, BS, 1953, MD, 1957. **Professional Experience:** PROF EMER, DEPT PATH, UNIV CALIF, IRVINE, as of 2003; prof & chmn, Dept Path, Univ Calif, Irvine, beginning 1988; prof, Dept Path, NY Med Col, 1976-1988; from instr to prof, Dept Path, Albert Einstein Col Med, 1963-1976; mem, Coun Acad Socs, Am Asn Med Cols. **Memberships:** Fel Col Am Pathologists; fel Int Acad Path; Am Asn Pathologists & Bacteriologists; Am Thoracic Soc; Fedn Am Soc Exp Biol; Int Acad Path. **Research Statement & Publications:** Pathology of pulmonary oxygen toxicity; pulmonary benzo(a)pyrene metabolism and tobacco smoking; tobacco related disease. **Mailing Address:** Dept Path Med Sci, Univ Calif, D440 Med Sci, Irvine, CA 92717-4800. **E-Mail:** ykikkawa@uci.edu

KIKTA, DIANNE C, BIOLOGY. **Professional Experience:** ASST VPRES, WYETH RES, PA, as of 2005. **Memberships:** Biol Soc Am. **Mailing Address:** Dept Clin Comm Wyeth-Averst Res, PO Box 8299, Philadelphia, PA 19101-1245. **Fax:** 610-989-4854.

KIKTA, EDWARD JOSEPH, JR, ANALYTICAL CHEMISTRY, CHROMATOGRAPHY. **Personal Data:** b Buffalo, NY, June 11, 1948. **Education:** State Univ NY, Buffalo, BA, 1970, PhD (anal chem), 1978; Canisius Col, MS, 1972. **Honors & Awards:** Chromatography Award, Am Chem Soc, 1981. **Professional Experience:** MGR ANAL SCI, AGR CHEM GROUP, FMC CORP, 1980-; Anal res chemist & lab supvr, FCM Corp, 1976-1980. **Memberships:** Am Chem Soc; Am Inst Chemists; AAAS; Am Soc Testing & Mat; NY Acad Sci. **Research Statement & Publications:** Chromographic methods and systems development; application of hplc to high resolution and high sensitivity analysis; optimization of hplc and gc systems; new hplc bonded phases. **Mailing Address:** FMC Corp, 1735 Mkt St, Philadelphia, PA 19103. **Fax:** 215-299-5998.

KIKUCHI, NOBORU, MATHEMATICS. **Education:** Tokyo Inst Technol, BS (civil), 1974; Univ Tex, Austin, MS, 1975; Univ Tex, Austin, Phd (Eng Mech), 1977. **Professional Experience:** PROF, DEPT MECH ENG & APPL MECH, UNIV MICH, 1985-. **Memberships:** Am Soc Mech Engrs. **Mailing Address:** Mech Eng & Appl Mech, Univ Mich, 2250 GGBrown Lab, 2350 Hayward, Ann Arbor, MI 48109-2125. **Fax:** 734-647-3170. **E-Mail:** kikuchi@engin.umich.edu

KIKUCHI, SHINYA, FUZZY SET THEORY APPLICATION, LOGISTICS. **Personal Data:** b Kobe, Japan, May 5, 1943; m 1975, Laura. **Education:** Hokkaido Univ, Japan, BS, 1967, MS, 1969; Univ Pa, PhD (transp), 1974. **Professional Experience:** PROF & DIR, INTELLIGENT TRANSP SYSTS LAB, UNIV DEL, 1993-; dir, Del Transp Ctr, 1989-; from asst prof to assoc prof, Univ Del, 1982-1993; staff asst, Logistics Opers, 1979-1982; sr proj engr, Transp Systs Div, Gen Motors Corp, 1977-1979; assoc, Transp Develop Assocs, Seattle, Wash, 1974-1977. **Memberships:** Am Soc Civil Engrs; Inst Transp Engrs; Soc Logistics Engrs; Transp Res Bd. **Research Statement & Publications:** Analysis of transportation systems and application of operations research; urban public transportation systems design and operation; application of fuzzy set theory; routing and scheduling of transportation system; traffic engineering; development of systems analysis methodologies. **Mailing Address:** Dept Civil & Environ Eng, Univ Del, 342B DuPont Hall, Newark, DE 19716-3120. **Fax:** 302-831-3640. **E-Mail:** kikuchi@ce.udel.edu

KILAKOS, KYRIAKOS, MATHEMATICS. **Education:** Univ Waterloo, PhD, 1993. **Professional Experience:** PROF, DEPT MATH, LONDON SCH ECON, UNIV QUE, MONT, as of 2005. **Mailing Address:** Math Dept, Univ Que Mont, Montreal, PQ H3C 3P8, Can. **Fax:** 514-343-5700.

KILAMBI, RAJ VARAD, FISHERIES, ZOOLOGY. **Personal Data:** b India, February 1, 1933; m 1957, c 3. **Education:** Univ Wash, PhD (fisheries), 1965. **Professional Experience:** PROF EMER ZOOL, UNIV ARK, as of 2003; prof zool, Univ Ark, Fayetteville, beginning 1977; From asst prof to assoc prof, Univ Ark, Fayetteville, 1966-1971. **Memberships:** Am Fisheries Soc; Sigma Xi. **Research Statement & Publications:** Fish biology and population dynamics; reservoir fisheries. **Mailing Address:** Dept Biol Sci, Univ Ark, Fayetteville, AR 72701. **E-Mail:** rkilambi@uark.edu

KILAMBI, SRINVASACHARYULU, BARACH ALGEBRA, TOPOLOGY OF COMPLEX MANIFOLDS. **Education:** Univ Paris, DSc(math), 1962. **Professional Experience:** PROF MATH, UNIV MONTREAL, 1984-; from asst prof to assoc prof, Univ Montreal, 1965-1984; asst prof, math, Univ Md, 1962-1965. **Memberships:** Am Math Soc. **Mailing Address:** Math Dept, Univ Montreal, Montreal, PQ H3C 3J7, Can.

KILBERG, MICHAEL STEVEN, REGULATION OF NUTRIENT TRANSPORT. **Personal Data:** b November 21, 1951; c 3. **Education:** Morningside Col, Sioux City, BS, 1973; Univ SDak, MS, 1975, PhD (biochem), 1977. **Professional Experience:** PROF BIOCHEM & MOLECULAR BIOL, UNIV FLA GENETICS INST, 1989-; from assoc prof to prof & chmn, Dept biochem & Molecular Biol, Univ Fla, 1986-1996; from asst to assoc prof, Dept Biochem & Molecular Biol, Univ Fla, 1980-1986; ed bd, J Biol Chem. **Memberships:** Am Phys Soc; Am Soc Biochem & Molecular Biol; Am Soc Cell Biol. **Research Statement & Publications:** Regulation of hepatic amino acid transport and transcriptional control of gene expression by amino acids; epigenetics; gene expression. **Mailing Address:** Dept Biochem & Molecular Biol, Sch Med, Univ Fla, PO Box 100245 R3 116 B, Gainesville, FL 32610-0245. **Fax:** 352-392-6511. **E-Mail:** mkilberg@ufl.edu

KILBOURN, JOAN PRISCILLA PAYNE, MEDICAL MICROBIOLOGY. **Personal Data:** b Juneau, Alaska, June 15, 1936; m 1961, Lee; c Laurie J & Ellen M. **Education:** Univ Ore, BS, 1958, MS, 1960; Ore State Univ, PhD (microbiol), 1963. **Honors & Awards:** Women Achievement Award, Ore Comn Women, 1998. **Professional Experience:** LAB DIR, TREATMENT ALTERNATIVES TO ST CRIME, 1996-; OWNER, PRES & LAB DIR, CONSULT CLIN & MICROBIOL LAB INC, 1984-; consult microbiologist, 1978-1984; instr, Clackamas Community Col, 1978; instr, Portland State Univ Cont Educ Div, 1977; assoc dir, ICN Med Labs, 1974-1976; instr, Med Sch, Univ Ore, 1973-1974; tutor, Portland Community Col, 1971-; microbiologist, Clin Path Lab, Vet Admin Hosp, 1971-1974; tutor sci & math, Portland Community Col, 1968-1971; pediat, Med Sch, 1966-1968; consult, Choice, Books for Col Libraries, 1964-; Instr bact, Univ Ore, 1963-1966; Am Cancer Soc res grant, 1963-1965. **Memberships:** Fel AAAS; Am Soc Clin Pathologists; Am Soc Microbiol; Nat Registry Microbiologist; Am Bd Bioanalysis. **Research Statement & Publications:** Use of a radiation resistant microorganism as a protectant and therapeutic agent from the lethal effects of irradiation; automation of clinical medical microbiology; bacterial flora of chronic lung diseases; over the counter test for vaginal yeast infections. **Mailing Address:** Consult Clin & Microbiol Lab Inc, 1033 SW Yamhill No 101, Portland, OR 97205. **Fax:** 503-244-1778.

KILBOURNE, EDWIN DENNIS, MEDICINE, PUBLIC HEALTH & EPIDEMIOLOGY. **Personal Data:** b Buffalo, NY, July 10, 1920; m 1952, Joy; c Edwin M, Richard S, Christopher N & Paul A. **Education:** Cornell Univ, AB, 1942, MD, 1944. **Honorary Degrees:** DSc, Rockefeller Univ, 1986. **Honors & Awards:** R E Dyer lectr Award, NIH, 1973; Borden Award, Asn Am Med Cols, 1974; Thomas Francis Jr mem lectr, 1976; Harry F Dowling lect Award, 1976; Henry Brainerd mem lectr, 1976; Bernard A Briody mem lectr, 1977; Harvey Soc lectr, 1978; Harry M Rose mem lectr, 1980. **Professional Experience:** RES PROF, NY MED COL, 1992-; DISTINGUISHED SERV PROF, MT SINAI SCH MED, 1986-; Virol Task Force chmn, NIH & mem, Adv Comt Immunization Pract, CDC, 1976-1980; chmn, Subcomt Influenza, 1971-1974; mem, Infectious Dis Adv Comt, Nat inst Allergy & Infectious Dis, 1969-1973; chmn, dept Microbiol, 1968-1986; NIH res career award, 1961-1968; mem, Comn Influenza, US Armed Forces Epidemiol Bd, 1959-1971; from assoc prof pub health to prof, Med Col, Cornell Univ, 1955-1969; dir, div Virus res, 1955-1969; assoc prof med & dir, div Infectious Dis, Tulane Univ, 1951-1955; asst resident physician, Hosp Rockefeller inst, 1948-1951; asst, Rockefeller inst, 1948-1951; asst resident, NY Hosp, 1945-1946; Intern med, NY Hosp, 1944-1945. **Memberships:** Nat Acad Sci; Am Acad Microbiol; Asn Am Physicians; Am Asn Immunologists; Am Epidemiol Soc; Am Soc Clin Invest; fel NY Acad Sci. **Research Statement & Publications:** Influenza virus genetics; host determinants of viral virulence; viral genetics and immunology; experimental epidemiology; vaccines; major research activities involve continuing studies of the genetics and virulence mechanisms of influenza viruses with special emphasis on the development of new vaccines. **Mailing Address:** Dept Microbiol & Immunol, NY Med Col Basic Sci Bldg Rm 315, Valhalla, NY 10595. **Fax:** 914-993-4176. **E-Mail:** kilbourn@ct1.nai.net

KILBOURNE, EDWIN MICHAEL, ENVIRONMENTAL EPIDEMIOLOGY, TOXICOLOGY & IMMUNIZATION INFORMATION SYSTEMS. **Personal Data:** b New Orleans, La, October 1, 1953; m 1982, Barbara; c David, Michael, Rebecca & Kate. **Education:** Cornell Univ, AB, 1974, MD, 1978; Am Bd Internal Med, cert, 1984; Am Bd Prev Med, cert, 1988. **Honors & Awards:** Alexander D Longmuir Award, 1982. **Professional Experience:** MEM, ED BD AM JOUR PREV MED, 1999-; CHIEF MED OFF, DIV ENVIRON HAZARDS & HEALTH EFFECTS, NAT CTR ENVIRON HEALTH, 1998-; MED TOXICOLOGIST, GA POISON CTR, 1998-; CLIN ASST PROF, DEPT MED, SCH MED, EMORY UNIV, GA, 1997-; dir data mgt div, Nat Immunization Prog, Ctr Dis Control & Prev, 1996-1998; adj assoc prof, Div Environ & Occup Health, Rollins Sch Public Health, Emory Univ, Ga, 1991-; asst dir sci, epidemiol prog off, Ctr Dis Control & Prev, Ga, 1990-1996; chief, Health Studies Br, Div Environ Hazards & Health Effects, Ctr Environ Health & Injury Control, 1989-1990; med epidemiologist, Ctr Environ Health & Injury Control, 1987-1989; med epidemiologist, Foreign Assignment, 1985-1987; chief, invests sect, Spec Studies Br, Ctr Environ Health, 1983-1985; epidemic intel serv officer, Ctr Dis Control, Atlanta, 1980-1982; resident internal med, Univ Ala Hosps, Birmingham, 1982-1983, 1978-1980. **Memberships:** Am Acad Clin Toxicol; Am Pub Health Asn; fel Am Col Physicians; fel Am Col Prev Med; Am Med Informatics Asn. **Research Statement & Publications:** Epidemiologic research regarding the adverse effects on human health of physical and chemical environmental agents; effects of heat and cold, the newly discovered toxic oil syndrome in Spain, and the eosinophilia myalgia syndrome in the United States; technical and logistical problems of implementing computerized registries of children to ensure that they are properly immunized. **Mailing Address:** Nat Ctr Environ Health, Ctr Dis Control & Prev, 1600 Clifton Rd N E Mail Stop E 60, Atlanta, GA 30333. **Fax:** 404-521-5077. **E-Mail:** ekilbourne@cdc.gov

KILBURN, KAYE HATCH, INTERNAL & PREVENTIVE MEDICINE. **Personal Data:** b Logan, Utah, September 20, 1931; m Gerrie; c Ann L (Ingram), Scott K & Jean M. **Education:** Univ Utah, BS, 1951, MD, 1954. **Professional Experience:** PRES & DIR, NEURO TEST, INC, PASADENA, 1994-; pres, Workers Dis Detection Serv, 1986-1994; DIR, SOUTHERN CALIF ENVIRON MED CLIN, LONG BEACH, 1984-1997; dir, Barlow Occup Health Ctr, 1982-1984; chief, pulmonary & environ med sect, LAC-USC Med Ctr, 1982-1984; RALPH EDGINGTON PROF MED, UNIV SOUTHERN CALIF SCH MED, LOS ANGELES, 1980-; prof med & community Med, Mt Sinai Sch Med, City Univ New York, 1977-1980; prof med, assoc prof anat & dir, Div Pulmonary & Environ Med, Med Ctr, Univ Mo-Columbia, 1973-1977; dir, div pulmonary & environ med, 1973-1977; dir, Div Environ Med, Med Ctr, 1968-1973; consult, Vet Admin Hosps, Durham, Fayetteville & Oteen, 1968-1973; asst prof anat, Med Ctr, Duke Univ, 1968-1973; chief med serv, Durham Vet Admin Hosp, 1963-1968; Nat Heart Inst res grant & USPHS training grants, beginning 1962; from assoc prof to prof, Med Ctr, Duke Univ, 1962-1973; asst prof med, Wash Univ, 1961-1962; USPHS fel cardiol, Brompton Hosp, Univ London, 1960-1961; dir, cardiopulmonary div, Sch Med, Wash Univ, 1960-1962; Am Trudeau Soc fel, 1958; fel cardiopulmonary physiol, Duke Univ, 1957-1958; resident, Univ Utah Hosps, 1955-1957; Intern med, Univ Hosps, Cleveland, 1954-1955. **Memberships:** Am Fedn Clin Res; Am Thoracic Soc; Am Phys Soc; AAP; ASCB. **Research Statement & Publications:** Pulmonary structure and function, particularly pulmonary circulation; early detection of dysfunction; respiratory failure causing cerebral and circulatory dysfunction; pulmonary responses to environmental and occupational agents; alveolar surfactant; structure and function of cilia, mechanism of inflammation; proteolytic enzymes and antienzymes; mediators of leukocyte response; experimental pathology of lung; epidemiology of occupational diseases, byssinosis, asbestosis, and effects of exposure to formaldehyde, trichlorolthylene, welding gases and fumes; neurobehavioral toxicology of solvents, formaldehydes and PCB's; methods for measuring neurological functions in populations, toxic effects of chemicals associated with birth defects associated with metals, metal chelating agents and enzyme blockers, smoking cessation intervention in blue collar workers. **Mailing Address:** Dept Med, Keck Sch Med, Univ Southern Calif, 1000 S Fremont St #7-401, Alhambra, CA 91803. **Fax:** 626-457-4203. **E-Mail:** kilburn@usc.edu

KILBY, JACK ST CLAIR, electrical engineering; deceased, see previous edition for last biography

KILDAL, HELGE, APPLIED PHYSICS. **Personal Data:** b Oslo, Norway, June 23, 1942; American citizen; m 1967, Unni Rasmussen; c Tronol, Tore & Audreas. **Education:** Norweg Inst Technol, sivil 1967; Stanford Univ, MS, 1969, PhD (appl physics), 1972. **Professional Experience:** PROF, UNIV OSLO, 1990-; RES DIR, SINTEF, 1988-; sect head, Norweg Coun Sci & Indust Res, 1981-1988; mem staff, Forsvarets Forsknings Inst, 1980-1981; mem staff, Lincoln Lab, Mass Inst Technol, 1974-1980; Res asst appl physics, Stanford Univ, 1972-1974. **Memberships:** Optical Soc Am; Inst Elec & Electronics Engrs. **Research Statement & Publications:** Development and applications of infrared nonlinear materials; laser spectroscopy; integrated optics. **Mailing Address:** SINTEF, PO Box 124 Blindern, Oslo, 0314, Norway.

KILDAY, WARREN D, ORGANIC CHEMISTRY. **Personal Data:** b Westminster, Calif, July 10, 1929; m 1958, c 3. **Education:** Fresno State Col, BA, 1959; Wash State Univ, PhD (org chem), 1964. **Professional Experience:** PROF CHEM, PEPPERDINE UNIV, 1974-; assoc prof chem, Pepperdine Univ, 1967-1974; asst prof org chem, Pepperdine Univ, 1963-1967. **Memberships:** Am Chem Soc; Sigma Xi. **Research Statement & Publications:** Papain catalyzed reactions of acylated amino acids. **Mailing Address:** Pepperdine Univ, Malibu, CA 90265-4321.

KILDSIG, DANE OLIN, PHYSICAL PHARMACY. **Personal Data:** b Oshkosh, Wis, August 3, 1935; m 1958, c 2. **Education:** Univ Wis, Madison, BS, 1957, PhD (phys pharm), 1965. **Professional Experience:** ASSOC DIR, CTR PHARMACEUT PROCESSING RES, PURDUE UNIV, as of 2003; PROF PHYS PHARM, PURDUE UNIV, 1985-; head, Dept Indust & Phys Pharma, Purdue Univ, beginning 1985; assoc head dept, Purdue Univ, 1981-1985; from asst prof to assoc prof, Purdue Univ, 1966-1975; res scientist, Wyeth Labs, 1965-1966. **Memberships:** Am Asn Pharmaceut Scientists; fel Am Asn Pharmaceut Scientists. **Research Statement & Publications:** Mechanism of dissolution of solids and drug binding to protein; drug targeting; liposomes, pulmonary drug delivery. **Mailing Address:** Dept Indust & Phys Pharm, Purdue Univ, Rm RHPH 105 B Heine Pharm Bldg, 575 Stadium Mall Dr, West Lafayette, IN 47907-2091. **Fax:** 765-494-6545. **E-Mail:** kildsig@purdue.edu

KILEDJIAN, MEGERDITCH, REGULATION OF EUKARYOTIC GENE EXPRESSION, RNA-PROTEIN INTERACTIONS. **Personal Data:** b Aleppo, Syria, March 24, 1963; American citizen; m 1996, Paneyiota Trifillis. **Education:** Rutgers Univ, BA, 1985; Univ Pa, PhD (molecular biol), 1990. **Professional Experience:** ASSOC PROF, RUTGERS UNIV, as of 2004; asst prof, Rutgers Univ, beginning 1995; Postdoctoral assoc, Univ Pa, 1990-1995. **Memberships:** AAAS; Am Soc Biochem & Molecular Biol. **Research Statement & Publications:** Structural and functional characterization of RNA-protein interactions in the regulation of RNA turnover and eukaryotic gene expression. **Mailing Address:** Dept Cell Develop & Neurobiol, Rutgers Univ, Rm B303, Piscataway, NJ 08854. **Fax:** 732-445-0104. **E-Mail:** kiledjia@biology.rutgers.edu

KILEN, THOMAS CLARENCE, PLANT GENETICS, HOST PLANT RESISTANCE TO PESTS. **Personal Data:** b Jackson, Minn, January 24, 1933; m 1965, Nancy A Kollath. **Education:** Univ Wis, BS, 1963, MS, 1966, PhD (agron, genetics), 1968. **Professional Experience:** RES LEADER, AGR RES SERV, USDA, as of 2002; PLANT RES GENETICIST, AGR RES SERV, USDA, 1967-. **Memberships:** Am Soc Agron; Crop Sci Soc Am; Am Genetic Asn. **Research Statement & Publications:** Inheritance of disease resistance in soybeans; inheritance of characters modifying plant type and their effect upon seed yield; genetics of resistance to foliar feeding insects of soybeans. **Mailing Address:** Dept Plant & Soil Sci, Miss State Univ, Mississippi, MS 39762. **Fax:** 601-686-5465.

KILEY, CHARLES WALTER, ICHTHYOLOGY. **Personal Data:** b Staten Island, NY, February 25, 1944; m 1970, c 2. **Education:** Wagner Col, BS, 1966; NY Univ, MS, 1969, PhD (biol, ichthyol), 1973, DDS, 1980. **Professional Experience:** PVT PRACT DENT, as of 1998; DIR DENT, NY SHIPPING-PORT POLICE UNION, 1985-; adj teaching staff, Staten Island Hosp, 1981-; ST JOHN'S UNIV, 1976- & INT MED EDUC, 1976-; CHMN DEPT, WAGNER COL, 1975-; ASST PROF BIOL, WAGNER COL, 1974-; adj asst prof, Staten Island Community Col, 1974-1975; instr biol, Wagner Col, 1969-1974. **Memberships:** Am Inst Biol Sci; AAAS; Am Fisheries Soc; Am Soc Ichthyologists & Herpetologists; NY Acad Sci. **Research Statement & Publications:** Histology and ultrastructure of immunocompetent organs in fishes; field collection and identification of fishes. **Mailing Address:** 11 Ralph Pl Ste 303, Staten Island, NY 10304.

KILEY, JAMES P, RESPIRATORY PHYSIOLOGY, NEUROPHYSIOLOGY. **Personal Data:** b Medford, Mass, April 16, 1952; m 1977, Randi; c Lori, Karen & Steven. **Education:** Kans State Univ, PhD (physiol), 1982. **Professional Experience:** DIR LUNG DIS DIV, NAT HEART LUNG & BLOOD INST, NIH, as of 2004; chief airways dis, Nat Heart Lung & Blood Inst, NIH, beginning 1984; fel physiol, Univ NC, Chapel Hill, 1982-1984; adj asst prof physiol, Georgetown Univ, Wash, DC. **Memberships:** Am Physiol Soc; Sigma Xi. **Mailing Address:** Nat Heart Lung & Blood Inst, NIH, Silver Spring, MD 20901.

KILEY, LEO AUSTIN, nuclear chemistry, meteorology; deceased, see previous edition for last biography

KILEY, SUSAN CAROL, BIOLOGY. **Professional Experience:** ASST PROF RES, UNIV VA, as of 2004. **Memberships:** Am Soc Microbiol. **Mailing Address:** Dept Pediatrics, Univ Va, PO Box 801334, Charlottesville, VA 22901. **Fax:** 434-982-4328. **E-Mail:** sck3k@virginia.edu

KILGORE, BRUCE MOODY, FOREST ECOLOGY, FIRE ECOLOGY. **Personal Data:** b Los Angeles, Calif, March 26, 1930; m 1952, Elaine; c David B & Steven P. **Education:** Univ Calif, Berkeley, AB, 1952, PhD (zoology), 1968; Univ Okla, MA, 1954. **Professional Experience:** RETIRED; assoc reg dir stewardship & sci, Div Nat Res & Res, Western Region, Nat Park Serv, San Francisco, 1996-1997; assoc reg dir res mgt & planning, Div Nat Res, Western Region, Nat Park Serv, San Francisco, 1993-1996; chief, Div Nat Res & Res, Western Region, Nat Park Serv, San Francisco, 1985-1993; res proj leader, Northern Forest Fire Lab, Intermountain Forest & Range Exp Sta, US Forest Serv, Montana, 1981-1985; assoc regional dir prof serv, Western Region, 1972-1981; res biologist, Off Chief Scientist, Nat Park Serv, 1968-1972; teaching asst zool, Univ Calif, Berkeley, 1963-1968; managing ed, Sierra Club Pub & ed, Sierra Club Bull, Sierra Club, Calif, 1960-1965; ed, Nat Parks Mag, Nat Parks Asn, 1957-1960; info asst, Nature Conserv, DC, 1956-1957. **Research Statement & Publications:** Fire ecology of giant sequoia-mixed conifer forests; crown fire potential; fire history frequency; impact of prescribed burning on vegetation, fuels, and breeding birds; role of fire in wilderness/parks; understory burning in pine-larch-fir forests. **Mailing Address:** Nat Park Serv Western Reg, 600 Harrison St Ste 600, San Francisco, CA 94107. **Fax:** 650-427-1485.

KILGORE, DELBERT LYLE, ENVIRONMENTAL PHYSIOLOGY, RESPIRATORY PHYSIOLOGY. **Personal Data:** b Hutchinson, Kans, September 28, 1942; m 1966, Judith; c Alison & Trevor. **Education:** Univ Kans, BA, 1964, MA, 1967, PhD (physiol, cell biol), 1972. **Professional Experience:** Res fel, Sch Biol Sci, Flinders Univ S Australia, Adelaide, 1992; ASSOC DEAN BIOL SCI, UNIV MONT, 1991-; vis scholar, Dept Med, Univ Califm, San Diego, La Jolla, 1990; PROF ZOOLOGY, UNIV MONT, 1983-; vis adj prof, Col Vet Med, Kans State Univ, 1982-1983, 1984; from asst prof to assoc prof, Univ Mont, 1973-1983; res assoc physiol, Duke Univ, 1971-1973. **Memberships:** Sigma Xi; Am Physiol Soc; Am Soc Zoologists. **Research Statement & Publications:** Respiratory adaptations of birds toextreme environments; physiology of temperature regulation, control of respiration, acid-base balance and water balance. **Mailing Address:** Div Biol Sci, Univ Mont, Missoula, MT 59812-1002. **Fax:** 406-243-4184. **E-Mail:** del.kilgore@mso.umt.edu

KILGORE, LOIS TAYLOR, NUTRITION. **Personal Data:** b Starkville, Miss, February 9, 1922; wid, c Marcia K (Newsom) & Susan K (Booker). **Education:** Miss State Univ, BS, 1955, MS, 1963, PhD (physiol), 1968. **Professional Experience:** EMER PROF HOME ECON, MISS STATE UNIV, 1984-; prof, Miss State Univ, 1969-1984; asst home economist, Miss State Univ, 1955-1969; jr chemist, Petrol Prod Lab, Motor Vehicle Controller, 1953-1955; med technologist with Dr Hunt Cleveland, 1946-1948; med technologist, Vicksburg Hosp, 1943-1944 & Scales Clin, 1944-1946. **Memberships:** AAAS; Home Econ Asn Am; Am Soc Clin Path; Am Inst Nutrit; Am Dietetic Asn. **Research Statement & Publications:** Nutrition of pre-school children; interrelationships of nutrients; international nutrition; breakdown of fats during cooking. **Mailing Address:** 1378 Kilgore Dr, Starkville, MS 39759.

KILGOUR, D MARC, MATHEMATICS. **Education:** Univ Toronto, PhD (Maths) 1973. **Professional Experience:** PROF, DEPT MATHS, LAURIER CTR MIL STRATEGIC & DISARMAMENT STUDIES, as of 2005; ASSOC DIR, LAURIER CTR MIL STRATEGIC & DISARMAMENT STUDIES, as of 2005. **Mailing Address:** Math Dept, Wilfrid Laurier Univ, Waterloo, ON N2L 3C5, Can. **Fax:** 519-886-5057. **E-Mail:** mkilgour@wlu.ca

KILGOUR, GORDON LESLIE, BIOCHEMISTRY. **Personal Data:** b Vancouver, BC, April 24, 1929; m 1949, c 2. **Education:** Univ BC, BA, 1951, MSc, 1953; Univ Wash, PhD (biochem), 1956. **Professional Experience:** PROF EMER BIOCHEM, DEPT CHEM, PORTLAND STATE COL, as of 2003; prof chem, Portland State Col, beginning 1968; head dept chem, Portland State Col, 1968-1974; from assoc prof to prof, San Fernando Valley State Col, 1963-1968; asst prof biochem, Mich State Univ, 1957-1963; jr res biochemist, Univ Calif, Berkeley, 1956-1957. **Memberships:** Am Chem Soc. **Research Statement & Publications:** Oxidative enzymes and coenzymes; chemistry and biochemistry of phosphorylated carbohydrate compounds. **Mailing Address:** Dept Chem, Portland State Col, Lake Oswego, OR 97034.

KILHAM, SUSAN SOLTAU, ECOLOGY, AQUATIC BIOLOGY. **Personal Data:** b Duluth, Minn, January 22, 1943; American citizen; wid Peter (deceased). **Education:** Eckerd Col, BS, 1965; Duke Univ, PhD (zoology), 1971. **Professional Experience:** INTERIM DIR, SCH OF ENVIRON SCI, ENG & POLICY, DREXEL UNIV, 2000-; PROF BIOSCI & BIOTECHNOL, DREXEL UNIV, 1994-; assoc prof, Drexel Univ, Philadelphia, 1991-1994; Quinney Scholar, UT state univ, 1998-1999; VIS ASSOC PROF, UNIV WASH, 1990-; vis scientist, Max Panck Soc scholar, 1988; vis scientist, Max Planck Inst Limnol, 1987-1988; nat lectr, Phycological Soc Am, 1985-1987; assoc res scientist biol, Univ Mich, Ann Arbor, 1979-1990; asst res scientist, Univ Mich, Ann Arbor, 1975-1978; asst res scientist natural resources, Univ Mich, Ann Arbor, 1973-1975; lectr, Univ Mich, Ann Arbor, 1973; guest investr oceanog, Woods Hole Oceanog Inst, 1972, 1979-1980; res assoc microbiol, Duke Univ, 1970-1972; oceanog trainee, NSF, 1967-1970. **Memberships:** Am Soc Limnol & Oceanog; Phycol Soc Am; AAAS; Int Soc Limnol; SigmaXi; Ecol Soc Am. **Research Statement & Publications:** Aquatic ecology; freshwater phytoplankton; algal physiology and ecology; population dynamics and competition; food webs; tropical Streams; urban waterheds; climate change. **Mailing Address:** Sch Environ Sci, Drexel Univ, Philadelphia, PA 19104. **Fax:** 215-895-2267. **E-Mail:** kilhams@drexel.edu

KILHEFNER, DALE Z, MATHEMATICS. **Education:** Pa State Univ, PhD. **Professional Experience:** PROF, ARMSTRONG ATLANTIC STATE UNIV, GA, as of 2005. **Memberships:** Ga Coun Teachers Math. **Mailing Address:** Armstrong State Univ UH 287, Savannah, GA 31419. **Fax:** 912-927-5209. **E-Mail:** kilhefda@mail.armstrong.edu

KILINC, ATTILA ISHAK, GEOCHEMISTRY, VOLCANOLOGY. **Personal Data:** b Mersin, Turkey, February 15, 1936; American citizen; m Ulku; c Ayse & Beril. **Education:** Istanbul Univ, BS, 1960; Pa State Univ, MSc, 1966, PhD (geol), 1969. **Professional Experience:** HEAD DEPT, UNIV CINCINNATI, 1991-; PROF GEOL, UNIV CINCINNATI, 1979-; head dept, Univ Cincinnati, 1975-1983; asst head, Dept Geol, Univ Cincinnati, 1972-1975; from asst prof to assoc prof, Univ Cincinnati, 1970-1979; res assoc, Stanford Univ, 1968-1970. **Memberships:** Am Geophys Union; Sigma Xi. **Research Statement & Publications:** Geochemistry of magmatic and hydrothermal systems at high temps and pressures; explosive volcanism. **Mailing Address:** Dept Geol, Univ Cincinnati, Cincinnati, OH 45221-0013. **Fax:** 513-556-6931. **E-Mail:** atilla.kilinc@uc.edu

KILKENNY, JOSEPH DAVID, PHYSICS. **Personal Data:** b Eng, July 7, 1947. **Education:** Imp Col, London, BS, 1968, MS, 1970, PhD (physics), 1972. **Professional Experience:** VPRES, INERTIAL FUSION TECHNOL DIV, GENERAL ATOMICS ENERGY GROUP, as of 2005-; SR PHYSICIST, LAWRENCE LIVERMORE NAT LAB, UNIV CALIF, as of 2003; ASSOC DIR SCI & TECHNOL, LAB LASER ENERGETICS, UNIV ROCHESTER, as of 2003; MGR, INERTIAL FUSION TECHNOL DIV, GENERAL ATOMICS ENERGY GROUP, 2003-; res scientist, lawrence livermorenat lab, beginning 1985; dep assoc dir ICF & NIH prog, lawrence livermore nat lab, beginning 1985. **Memberships:** Am Phys Soc. **Mailing Address:** Fusion Power Assocs, Two Prof Dr Ste 248, Gaithersburg, MD 20879. **Fax:** 301-975-9869.

KILKSON, HENN, CHEMICAL ENGINEERING, PHYSICAL CHEMISTRY. **Personal Data:** b Tartu, Estonia, December 30, 1930; American citizen; m 1963, Reet; c Tiia & Eero. **Education:** Univ Colo, BS, 1952, MS, 1954; Cornell Univ, PhD (chem eng), 1957. **Honors & Awards:** T H Chilton Award, Am Inst Chem Engrs, 1989. **Professional Experience:** CONSULT, E I DU PONT DEL NEMOURS & CO, 1996-; fel, Dupont 1990-1996; sr res fel, Eng Tech Lab, 1985-1990; res fel, Eng Tech Lab, 1972-1955; res assoc, Eng Tech Lab, 1966-1972; sr res engr, Eng Tech Lab, 1965-1966; res engr, Eng Res Lab, 1960-1965; res engr, Eastern Lab, E I DuPont Del Nemours & Co, Inc, 1957-1959; leadership team mem, Eng Res & Develop, DuPont. **Memberships:** Am Chem Soc; Am Inst Chem Engrs; BEPS; EX. **Research Statement & Publications:** Mathematical aspects of polymerizations; chemical kinetics; chemical reactor design and stability. **Mailing Address:** Northminster, 5 Birch Knoll Rd, Wilmington, DE 19810. **E-Mail:** hkilkson@aol.com

KILKSON, REIN, BIOPHYSICS. **Personal Data:** b Tartu, Estonia, August 1, 1927; American citizen. **Education:** Yale Univ, BS, 1953, MS, 1954, PhD (physics), 1956. **Professional Experience:** PROF EMER MICROBIOL & IMMUNOL, UNIV ARIZ, 1999-; PROF EMER PHYSICS, UNIV ARIZ, 1999-; prof microbiol & immunol, Univ Ariz, 1976-1999; prof physics, Univ Ariz, 1972-1999; vis prof chem & physics, Univ Ariz, 1970-1972; guest researcher, Dept Med Physics, Karolinska Inst, Stockholm, 1964-1970; asst prof physics, Wayne State Univ, 1958-1959 & biophysics, Yale Univ, 1959-1966; mem tech staff, Bell Tel Labs, Inc, 1956-1958. **Memberships:** AAAS; Biophys Soc; Am Soc Microbiol; Sigma Xi; Am Phys Soc; Int Soc Molecular Evolution. **Research Statement & Publications:** Molecular biophysics; virus structure; macromolecular arrangements in cell organelles; molecular regulation; molecular evolution; theoretical biology and biophysics; biological systems; light scattering and nerve conduction; general laws of the biological state of matter. **Mailing Address:** Dept Physics Univ Ariz, PAS 253, Tucson, AZ 85721. **E-Mail:** kilkson@physics.arizona.edu

KILLAM, ELEANOR, MATHEMATICS. **Personal Data:** b Whitefield, NH, May 18, 1933. **Education:** Univ NH, BS, 1955, MS, 1956; Yale Univ, PhD (math), 1961. **Professional Experience:** PROF EMER MATH, UNIV MASS, AMHERST, 1991-; from asst prof to assoc prof, 1960-1991. **Memberships:** Am Math Soc; Math Asn Am. **Research Statement & Publications:** Ring theory; banach algebras; locally m-convex algebras. **Mailing Address:** 26 Valley Lane, Amherst, MA 01002. **E-Mail:** killam@math.umass.edu

KILLAM, EVA KING, PHARMACOLOGY, NEUROPHARMACOLOGY. **Personal Data:** b New York, NY, November 16, 1921; m 1955, c 3. **Education:** Sarah Lawrence Col, AB, 1942; Mt Holyoke Col, AM, 1944; Univ Ill, PhD (pharmacol), 1953. **Honors & Awards:** Abel Award, Soc Pharm Exp Therapist, 1954. **Professional Experience:** PROF EMER PHARMACOL, SCH MED, UNIV CALIF, DAVIS, as of 2004; Pres, Western Pharmacol Soc, 1984; Prof Pharmacol, Sch Med, Univ Calif, Davis, beginning 1978; Ed-in-chief, J Pharmacol & Exp Therapeut, 1978-; prof residence, Sch Med, Univ Calif, Davis, 1968-1978; res assoc pharmacol, Sch Med, Stanford Univ, 1959-1968; res pharmacologist, Univ Cal, Los Angeles, 1953-1959; instr pharmacol, Univ Ill, 1952-1953; pharmacologist & toxicologist, Army Chem Ctr, Md, 1948-1951; asst therapeut, Col Med, NY Univ, 1947-1948; instr biol, Albertus Magnus Col, 1946-1947; Instr, Sarah Lawrence Col, 1944-1946. **Memberships:** Am Soc Pharmacol & Exp Therapeut (pres 1989-1990); Am Col Neuropsychopharmacol (pres 1988); Soc Exp Biol & Med; Am Epilepsy Soc. **Research Statement & Publications:** Neuropharmacology, especially central nervous system; influence of drugs on epilepsy; eletrophysiological correlations of behavior and influence of drugs thereon. **Mailing Address:** 2225 Anza Ave, Davis, CA 95616.

KILLAM, EVERETT HERBERT, RESEARCH & DEVELOPMENT OF WASTE DISPOSAL METHODS. **Personal Data:** b Whitefield, NH, February 2, 1938; c 2. **Education:** Univ NH, BS, 1961; Univ Wyo, MS, 1965, PhD (civil eng), 1973. **Professional Experience:** CONSULT, FORENSIC ENG, 1990-; consult, Waste Mgt, 1988-1990; engr mgr, Custodis-Cotrell, 1983-1988; eng mgr indust chimneys, Custodis Construct Co, 1982; mgr res & develop, Custodis Construct Co, 1977-1982; asst prof mech, Rose-Hulman Inst Technol, 1974-1977; stress engr, Earl & Wright, 1973-1974; stress engr, Boeing Co, 1967-1968; instr mech, Univ Wyo, 1968-1972. **Memberships:** Am Soc Civil Engrs. **Research Statement & Publications:** Dynamic and thermal effects on large industrial chimneys; new cooling tower designs using theoretical and experimental data; seperation of trash into useful end products. **Mailing Address:** 14 Fieldstone Pl, Flemington, NJ 08822.

KILLAR, LORAN, INFLAMMATORY DISEASES. **Education:** Temple Univ, PhD (Immunol). **Professional Experience:** VPRES, INFLAMMATION RES ASN, as of 2006. **Mailing Address:** Bristol Myers Squibb, PO Box 4000, Princeton, NJ 08543. **Fax:** 208-875-2421. **E-Mail:** loran.killar@bms.com

KILLEBREW, FLAVIUS CHARLES, MAMMALOGY. **Personal Data:** b Canadian, Tex, April 2, 1949; m 1978, c 1. **Education:** WTex State Univ, BS, 1970, MS, 1972; PhD (zool), 1976. **Professional Experience:** PROVOST & VICE PRES ACAD AFFAIRS, W T A&M UNIV, 1994-; res prof grant, US Dept Interior, 1978-1979; asst prof biol, Wtex State Univ, beginning 1976; res prof grant, Killgore Comt, 1976-1977; res asst, Univ Ark Mus, 1974-1976; instr zool, Univ Ark, 1972-1976; res asst grant-in-aid, Sigma Xi, 1971-1972; res asst grant, Killgore Comt, 1971-1972. **Memberships:** Sigma Xi (vpres 1977-1978 pres 1978-1979); Soc Study Amphibians & Reptiles; Herpetologists League; Am Soc Ichthyologists & Herpetologists. **Research Statement & Publications:** Systematics and ecology of reptiles. **Mailing Address:** Dept Biol, WTex State Univ, 2501 Fourth Ave, Canyon, TX 79016-0001.

KILLEEN, JOHN, PLASMA PHYSICS, MAGNETOHYDRODYNAMICS. **Personal Data:** b Guam, July 28, 1925; m 1950, c 6. **Education:** Univ Calif, AB, 1949, MA, 1951, PhD (math), 1955. **Professional Experience:** PROF EMER, UNIV CALIF, DAVIS, as of 2005; dir, Nat Magnetic Fusion Energy Comput Ctr, 1974-1990; prof appl sci, Math Radiation Lab, Lawrence Livermore Lab, Univ Calif, 1968-1990; Ed, J Comput Physics, 1968-1990; mathematician, Math Radiation Lab, Lawrence Livermore Lab, Univ Calif, 1957-1968; Inst

Math Sci, NY Univ, 1956 & Bell Tel Labs, Inc, 1955; mathematician, Radiation Lab, Univ Calif, 1950-1955. **Memberships:** Am Math Soc; Am Phys Soc; Sigma Xi. **Research Statement & Publications:** Mathematical physics; computation; computer applications to controlled thermonuclear research. **Mailing Address:** Dept Appl Sci, Univ Calif, One Shields Ave, Davis, CA 95616.

KILLEN, JOHN YOUNG, MEDICAL RESEARCH. **Personal Data:** b July 20, 1949. **Education:** Kenyon Col, BA, 1971; Tufts Univ, MD, 1975. **Professional Experience:** DIR, OFF INT HEALTH RES, NIH, 2003-; dir div AIDS, Nat Inst Allergy & Infectious Dis, NIH, 1994-; actg dir, Div Aids, Nat Inst Allergy & Infectious Dis, NIH, 1993-1994; dep dir, Div Aids, Nat Inst Allergy & Infectious Dis, NIH, 1987-1993; med dir, Whitman-Walker Clin, Wash, DC, 1986-1987; dep chief, Clin Invest Br & prog dir, Coop Clin Trials Group, 1984-1986; head, Med Sect, 1981-1984; sr investr, Clin Invest Br, Cancer Ther Eval Prog, Div Cancer Treat, Nat Cancer Inst, 1980-1981; physician, Moses Taylor Hosp, Scranton, 1977-1980. **Memberships:** Am Col Physicians; Am Soc Clin Oncol; Int AIDS Soc; Am Asn Physicians Human Rights. **Research Statement & Publications:** Medicine. **Mailing Address:** Off Int Health Res NIH, 401Ste 6707 Democracy Blvd, Bethesda, MD 20892-5475.

KILLEN, ROSEMARY MARGARET, ASTRONOMY, PHYSICS. **Personal Data:** b Denver, Colo, m 1979, c 1. **Education:** Rice Univ, PhD (space physics & astron), 1987. **Professional Experience:** ASSOC RES SCIENTIST, DEPT ASTRON, UNIV MD, as of 2005; STAFF, GODDARD SPACE FLIGHT CTR, 1989-; res assoc planetary atmospheres, Rice Univ, 1986-1989; engr guidance & control mechs, McDonnell Douglas Corp, 1976-1980; analyst earth resources, Lockheed Electronics Co, 1974-1976. **Mailing Address:** Univ Md, Dept Astron, 2213 Computland Space Sci, College Park, MD 20742. **E-Mail:** rkillen@swri.edu

KILLGOAR, PAUL CHARLES, ELASTOMERS. **Personal Data:** b Boston, Mass, August 3, 1946; m 1969, c 2. **Education:** State Col, Bridgewater, BA, 1968; Mich State Univ, PhD (chem), 1972. **Professional Experience:** DIR, PHYS SCI & SYSTS RES LAB, FORD MOTOR CO, as of 2006; mgr, Vehicle Crash Safety Res, Prod Develop Ctr, Ford Motor Co, 2000; mgr, Fuels & Lubricants Dept, Ford Motor Co, 1990-1992; scientist, 1972-1990; res assoc, Mich State Univ, 1972; scientist, Cabot Corp, 1968. **Memberships:** Am Chem Soc; Sigma Xi; Soc Plastic Engrs. **Research Statement & Publications:** Physical properties of elastomers; dynamic mechanical and fatigue properties; use of elastomers in automotive applications; polymer processing. **Mailing Address:** Ford Motor Co, Ford Res Lab, 15455 Ashurst Rd, Livonia, MI 48154-2603. **E-Mail:** pkillgoa@ford.com

KILLGORE, CHARLES A, MEDICAL PHYSICS & ENGINEERING. **Personal Data:** b Lisbon, La, August 19, 1934; m 1954, c 3. **Education:** La Polytech Inst, BS, 1956, MS, 1963. **Honors & Awards:** Am Soc Eng Educ Award, 1970. **Professional Experience:** PRES, KILLGORE'S, INC, RADIATION & ENG CONSULTS, 1976-; assoc dean eng & dir eng res, Nuclear Ctr, 1972-1976; dir, Nuclear Ctr, 1963-1976; from instr to prof chem eng, La Tech Univ, 1959-1976; chemist, Claiborne Gasoline Co, La, 1959; Chem engr, Am Oil Co, Ark, 1956; NSF sci fac fel. **Memberships:** Am Inst Chem Engrs; Am Soc Eng Educ; Am Nuclear Soc; Health Physics Soc; Am Asn Physicists Med; Am Col Radiol. **Research Statement & Publications:** Industrial applications of radioactive isotopes. **Mailing Address:** 506-100 Oaks Dr, Ruston, LA 71270.

KILLIAN, CARL STANLEY, CHEMICAL PATHOLOGY, DIAGNOSTIC IMMUNOLOGY. **Personal Data:** b Cleveland, Ohio, April 13, 1933. **Education:** Daemen Col, BS, 1973; State Univ NY, Buffalo, MA, 1977, PhD (chem path), 1981. **Professional Experience:** Lectr, Div Grad Sch, Roswell Park Mem Inst, State Univ NY, Buffalo, 1977-; CANCER RES SCIENTIST, DIAG IMMUNOL RES & BIOCHEM, ROSWELL PARK MEM INST, BUFFALO, NY, 1976-; sr technologist, Clin Chem, 1964-1976; technologist, Hemat, Blood Banking & Urinalysis, 1962-1964; Res technologist, Corning Glass Works, NY, 1959-1961. **Research Statement & Publications:** Methods of detection and application of biologic tumor markers in prostate cancer. **Mailing Address:** Roswell Park Mem Inst, 666 Elm St, Buffalo, NY 14263-0002.

KILLIAN, FREDERICK LUTHER, POLYMER CHEMISTRY. **Personal Data:** b Lancaster, Pa, May 31, 1942; m 1963, c 2. **Education:** Franklin & Marshall Col, AB, 1963; Northwestern Univ, Ill, PhD (org chem), 1967. **Professional Experience:** PATENT ASSOC, E I DU PONT DEL NEMOURS & CO, 1992-; sr financial adv, E I Du Pont Del Nemours & Co, 1981-1992; from res chemist to sr res chemist, E I Du Pont Del Nemours & Co, 1967-1981. **Memberships:** Am Chem Soc. **Research Statement & Publications:** Physical-organic chemistry; reaction mechanisms; polymer synthesis and conversion to synthetic fibers; fiber structure; organic polymer chemistry. **Mailing Address:** DuPont, 1007 Market St, Wilmington, DE 19898. **Fax:** 302-892-7819. **E-Mail:** fk42@aol.com

KILLIAN, GARY JOSEPH, REPRODUCTIVE PHYSIOLOGY. **Personal Data:** b Rockville Centre, NY, December 6, 1945; m 1965, c 3. **Education:** Kans State Univ, BS, 1967, MS, 1969; Pa State Univ, PhD (reprod biol), 1973. **Professional Experience:** PROF REPRODUCTIVE PHYSIOL, DEPT DAIRY & ANIMAL SCI, PA STATE UNIV, 1984-; assoc prof reprod physiol, Dept Biol Sci, Kent State Univ, 1979-1984; asst prof, Kent State Univ, 1976-1979; asst prof reprod physiol, Dept Dairy & Animal Sci, 1975-1976; asst prof anat physiol, Dept Biol, Pa State Univ, 1973-1974; from res asst to res assoc, Dept Biol, Pa State Univ, 1972-1975. **Memberships:** Soc Study Reproduction; AAAS. **Research Statement & Publications:** Male reproductive physiology, endocrine regulation and effects of contraceptives on epididymal physiology and sperm maturation; biology of spermatozoa and sperm capacitation. **Mailing Address:** Dept Dairy & Animal Sci, Pa State Univ, 109 Almquist Res Ctr, Univ Park, PA 16802. **E-Mail:** gkillian@psu.edu

KILLICK, KATHLEEN ANN, MICROBIAL BIOCHEMISTRY. **Personal Data:** b Chicago, Ill, January 22, 1942. **Education:** Ill Inst Technol, BS, 1964, MS, 1966, PhD (biochem), 1969. **Professional Experience:** FEL RES, DEPT PHYSIOL, TUFTS UNIV, 1990-; Instr develop biol, Harvard Univ, 1975-1977; staff scientist develop biol, Boston Biomed Res Inst, 1974-; NIH trainee develop biol, NIH spec fel, 1972-1974; NIH trainee develop biol, Boston Biomed Res Inst, 1970-1972; AEC res assoc biochem, Argonne Nat Lab, 1969-1970. **Memberships:** AAAS; Am Soc Microbiol; Am Chem Soc; Am Soc Biol Chemists; Sigma Xi. **Research Statement & Publications:** Biochemical basis of cellular differentiation in the slime mold, Dictyostelium discoideum. **Mailing Address:** 12 Pond Lane, Arlington, MA 02174-6604.

KILLILEA, S DEREK, BIOCHEMISTRY. **Education:** Nat Univ Ireland, Galway, BS, 1966, PhD, 1972. **Professional Experience:** PROF & CHMN BIOCHEM, NDAK STATE UNIV, as of 2006. **Mailing Address:** Dept Biochem, NDak State Univ, Fargo, ND 58105-5051. **Fax:** 701-231-8324. **E-Mail:** derek.killilea@ndsu.edu

KILLINGBECK, STANLEY, PHYSICAL CHEMISTRY. **Personal Data:** b Blackburn, Eng, May 20, 1929; American citizen. **Education:** Blackburn Tech Col, BS, 1951; Cornell Univ, MS, 1956, PhD (chem), Univ Kans, 1964. **Professional Experience:** ASSOC PROF CHEM, CENT MO STATE COL, 1971-; asst prof, Cent MO State Col, 1963-1971; asst tech off, Imp Chem Indust, Eng, 1952-1954; Lab asst, Walpamur Paint Co, Eng, 1946-1952. **Research Statement & Publications:** Analytical chemistry. **Mailing Address:** 623 Eusbus Hwy, Warrensburg, MO 64093.

KILLINGER, DENNIS K, LASER REMOTE SENSING, QUANTUM OPTICS. **Personal Data:** b Boone, Iowa, September 23, 1945; m 1969, c 2. **Education:** Univ Iowa, BA, 1967; DePauw Univ, MA, 1969; Univ Mich, PhD (physics), 1978. **Professional Experience:** PROF PHYSICS, UNIV SFLA, 1987-; prog mgr laser remote sensing, Lincoln Lab, 1981-1987; quantum electronics staff, Lincoln Lab, Mass Inst Technol, 1979-1981; res assoc, physics, Univ Mich, 1974-1978; Res physicist, Naval Avionics Fac, 1968-1974. **Memberships:** Am Phys Soc; Optical Soc Am. **Research Statement & Publications:** Physics of new optical and laser sources, quantum electronics and non-linear optical techniques with applications toward laser remote sensing; lidar. **Mailing Address:** Dept Physics, Univ SFla, Tampa, FL 33620.

KILLINGSWORTH, LAWRENCE MADISON, CLINICAL CHEMISTRY, PATHOLOGY. **Personal Data:** b Cuthbert, Ga, March 9, 1946; m 1966, c 1. **Education:** Emory Univ, BS, 1968; Univ Fla, PhD (path, clin chem), 1973. **Professional Experience:** CHIEF SCI & TECHN OFFICER, SACRED HEART MED CTR, as of 2004; DIR CLIN CHEM & IMMUNOL LABS, SACRED HEART MED CTR, 1977-; assoc dir, Radioassay Lab, 1974-1976; assoc dir clin chem, NC Mem Hosp, 1973-1977; Asst prof med & path, Sch Med, Univ NC, Chapel Hill, 1973-1977. **Memberships:** Am Asn Clin Chem; Asn Clin Scientists. **Research Statement & Publications:** Application of light-scattering techniques to the measurement of immunochemical reactions; application of immunochemical techniques to the clinical chemistry laboratory; study of protein physiology in health and disease. **Mailing Address:** 2704 E Player Dr, 101 W Eighth Ave, Spokane, WA 99223.

KILLINGSWORTH, R(OY) W(ILLIAM), CIVIL ENGINEERING, ENGINEERING MECHANICS. **Personal Data:** b Headland, Ala, April 8, 1925; m 1950, c 2. **Education:** Univ Ala, BS, 1948, MS, 1956. **Professional Experience:** EMER PROF CIVIL ENG, UNIV ALA, 1990-; sr consult engr new proj, 70-85 prof civil eng, 1985-1980; dir phys planning & facil, 70-85 prof civil eng, 1967-1990; consult, US Army, 1963-; from asst dean to assoc dean, Col Eng, 1963-1970; from asst prof to prof eng, Col Eng, Univ Ala, 1956-1967; asst dean, Col Eng, Univ Ala, 1954-1956; vpres, Pressure Concrete Co, 1950-1952; fieldengr, Pressure Concrete Co, 1949-1950; Gen contractor, Ala, 1948-1949; Asst col eng, Univ Ala, 1948-1949. **Memberships:** AAAS; Am Soc Civil Engrs; Am Soc Eng Educ; Nat Soc Prof Engrs. **Research Statement & Publications:** Properties of materials; soil mechanics; hydrology. **Mailing Address:** 731 13th St, Tuscaloosa, AL 35401.

KILLION, JERALD JAY, IMMUNOBIOLOGY, CANCER. **Personal Data:** b Wichita, Kans, October 4, 1942; c 2. **Education:** Wichita State Univ, BS, 1970, MS, 1971; Univ Okla, PhD (biophys), 1973. **Professional Experience:** PROF, DEPT CANCER BIOL, MD ANDERSON CANCER CTR, UNIV TEX, as of 2006; assoc prof dept cell biol, Md Anderson Cancer Ctr, Univ Tex, beginning 1987; assoc prof, Dept Physiol, 1981-1987; mem fac, Sch Med, Oral Roberts Univ, 1978-1981; asst mem, Cancer Res Prog, Okla Med Res Found, 1975-; asst prof, Dept Radiol Sci, Health Sci Ctr, Univ Okla, 1974-1978; staff scientist, Cancer Res Prog, Okla Med Res Found, 1974-1975; instr biophys, Univ Okla, 1973-1974; affil instr, Cancer Res Prog, Okla Med Res Found, 1973-1974. **Memberships:** Sigma Xi; Am Asn Cancer Res; Am Soc Cell Biol; Biophys Soc; Tissue Cult Asn. **Research Statement & Publications:** Membrane properties of tumor cells and tumor cell subpopulations; the influence of biological and biochemical properties of tumor on the tumor-host relationship; antigenic topography of tumor cell membranes. **Mailing Address:** MD Anderson Cancer Ctr, Univ Tex, 1515 Holcombe Blvd, Houston, TX 77030. **Fax:** 713-792-8747. **E-Mail:** jkillion@mdanderson.org

KILLION, KURT, MATHEMATICS. **Education:** Univ Ga, EdD, 1990. **Professional Experience:** PROF MATH, MO STATE UNIV, as of 2005. **Mailing Address:** Math Dept, Southwest Mo State Univ, Springfield, MO 65804-0094. **Fax:** 417-836-6966. **E-Mail:** KurtKillion@MissouriState.edu

KILLION, LAWRENCE EUGENE, LASERS, COMPUTER SCIENCE. **Personal Data:** b Ross, Tex, March 28, 1924; m 1948, c 2. **Education:** Baylor Univ, BA, 1944; Univ Ind, MS, 1948; Washington Univ, PhD (physics), 1955. **Professional Experience:** DIR, LASER FUSION DIV, DEPT ENERGY, 1977-; actg asst dir laser & isotope separation technol, Div Mil Appln, Energy Res & Develop Admin, 1975-1977; dep asst dir laser & isotope separation technol, Div Mil Appln, Energy Res & Develop Admin, 1974-1975; dep asst dir res & develop, Div Mil Appln, Energy Res & Develop Admin, 1973-1974; spec asst to asst gen mgr, Div Mil Appln, Energy Res & Develop Admin, 1969-1973; dep asst controller info systs, US AEC, DC, 1967-1969; chief scientist, US Army Electronics Proving Ground, 1965-1967; sci adv electronics, US Army Electronics Proving Ground, 1964-1965; chief, Nuclear Qual Assurance Agency, Albuquerque Opers Off, US AEC, 1958-1964; tech asst to dir defense weapons effects tests, Blast & Shock Prog, Defense Atomic Support Agency, US Dept Defense, 1956-1958; Asst dir, Nuclear Prog, 1955-1956; Asst dir, Blast & Shock Prog, Defense Atomic Support Agency, US Dept Defense, 1951-1952. **Memberships:** Am Phys Soc; sr mem Inst Elec & Electronics Engrs; Am Statist Asn. **Research Statement & Publications:** Computer controls and computation; communications electronics; laser technology for laser fusion and laser isotope separation; electron and ion beam technology and application to fusion. **Mailing Address:** Off Inertial Fusion, US Dept Energy, Washington, DC 20545.

KILLION, MEAD C, AUDIOLOGY. **Education:** Northwestern Col, PhD (audiol), 1979. **Professional Experience:** FOUNDER, ETYMOTIC RES, as of 2006. **Mailing Address:** Etymotic Res Inc, 61 Martin Ln, Elk Grove Village, IL 60007. **Fax:** 847-228-6836. **E-Mail:** abonso@aol.com

KILLOUGH, JOHN EDWIN, Reservoir Simulation, Environmental Engineering. **Personal Data:** b Goose Creek, Texas, June 19, 1947; m 1970, Dianne; c Alex & Claire. **Education:** Rice Univ, BA, MS (Chem Eng), PhD (Math Sci). **Honors & Awards:** Rossiter W Raymond Award, AIME, 1977 Alfred Noble Prize, IEEE, AICE, AIME, Western Society of Engineers, ASME, 1977. **Professional Experience:** HALLIBURTON RESEARCH FELLOW, 1996-. **Memberships:** Society of Petroleum Engineers. **Research Statement & Publications:** The quest for reality in reservoir simulation has been the goal of Dr. Killough's research for the past thirty years including parallel computing applications to increase model sizes and enhanced model physics. **Mailing Address:** Halliburton Digital & Consulting Solutions, 2101 City W Blvd, Bldg 2, Houston, TX 77042. **Fax:** 713-839-2015. **E-Mail:** jkillough@lgc.com

KILLPATRICK, JOSEPH E, ELECTRICAL ENGINEERING, PHYSICS. **Personal Data:** b Hillsboro, Ill, February 15, 1933; m 1955, c 3. **Education:** Univ Ill, BS, 1955. **Professional Experience:** RES MGR, SYSTS & RES CTR, HONEYWELL INC, 1974-; mem staff, Aeronaut Div, 1969-1974; sect head electro-optics, Systs & Res Ctr, 1967-1969; supvr optics, MPG Res, 1962-1967; sr res engr, MPG Res, 1959-1962; Res engr, Aero Res, 1955-1959. **Memberships:** Optical Soc Am; Inst Elec & Electronics Engrs. **Research Statement & Publications:** Electronic devices and circuitry; optical scanning and detection systems; horizon scanners; sun seekers; lasers; laser devices and systems; laser gyro; frequency stability and precision control of lasers. **Mailing Address:** Honeywell Inc, Minneapolis, MN 55413.

KILMAN, JAMES WILLIAM, CARDIOVASCULAR SURGERY, THORACIC SURGERY. **Personal Data:** b Terre Haute, Ind, January 22, 1931; m 1968, c 3. **Education:** Ind State Univ, BS, 1956; Ind Univ, Indianapolis, MD, 1960; Am Bd Surg, dipl 1967; Am Bd Thoracic Surg, dipl, 1967. **Professional Experience:** PROF EMER SURG, MED COL, OHIO STATE UNIV, 1991-; dir Thoracic Surg Div, Med Col, Ohio State Univ, 1973-1981; consult, Vet Admin Hosp, Dayton, Ohio, 1966-; attend surgeon, Ohio State Univ & Children's Hosp, Columbus, 1966-; from asst prof to prof surg, Med Col, Ohio State Univ, 1966-1991; USPHS fel cardiovasc surg, Med Ctr, Ind Univ, Indianapolis, 1963-1964; resident, Med Ctr, Ind Univ, Indianapolis, 1961-1966; Intern, Med Ctr, Ind Univ, Indianapolis, 1960-1961. **Memberships:** Am Col Surg; Am Acad Pediat; Am Col Chest Physicians; Am Col Cardiol; Am Surg Asn. **Research Statement & Publications:** Infant cardiopulmonary bypass and peripheral blood flow. **Mailing Address:** Dept Surg, Med Col, Ohio State Univ, Columbus, OH 43210.

KILMER, LOUIS CHARLES, SOLAR CELLS, SEMICONDUCTOR PHYSICS. **Personal Data:** b Baltimore, Md, October 5, 1966; m 1991, Krista. **Education:** Univ Del, BEE, 1987, MEE, 1989, PhD (elec eng), 1992. **Professional Experience:** PROG MGR, IMAGING DEVICES, ROCKWELL SCIENTIFIC CORP, 1999-; mem tech staff, Aerospace Corp, 1992-1996; res asst, Dept Elec Eng, Univ Del, 1989-1992; Teaching asst, Dept Elec Eng, Univ Del, 1987-1989. **Memberships:** Inst Elec & Electronics Engrs; Optical Soc Am; Am Inst Aeronaut & Astronaut; The Planetary Soc. **Research Statement & Publications:** Research and development of advanced technologies for satellite power systems, specifically concentrating in solar cells and battery subsystem components. **Mailing Address:** Rockwell Sci Co, 1049 Camino Dos Rios, Thousand Oaks, CA 91360. **Fax:** 805-373-4775.

KILP, TOOMAS, PHOTOPHYSICS, PHOTOCHEMISTRY. **Personal Data:** b Charleroi, Belg, October 24, 1948; Canadian citizen. **Education:** Univ Toronto, BSc, 1974, MSc, 1975, PhD (chem), 1979. **Professional Experience:** MGR POLYMER CHEM & MICROS, ORTECH INT, 1988-; consult, 1983-1988; asst prof, Univ Notre Dame, 1979-1983; chemist, Lumonics Res Ltd, 1978-1979; Chemist, Inmont Can Ltd, 1970-1972. **Memberships:** Am Chem Soc; Can Thermal Anal Soc. **Research Statement & Publications:** Polymer photochemistry; photophysics including degradation; polymerization; photoconductivity; intramolecular energy migration; excited state complex formation. **Mailing Address:** Can Ortech Environ, Inc, 2395 Speakman Dr, Mississauga, ON L5K 1B3, Can. **Fax:** 905-855-0406.

KILPATRICK, CHARLES WILLIAM, EVOLUTION, MOLECULAR SYSTEMATICS. **Personal Data:** b Wichita Falls, Tex, June 10, 1944; wid, c 3. **Education:** Midwestern Univ, BS, 1968, MS, 1969; N Tex State Univ, PhD (zoology), 1973. **Professional Experience:** Res assoc, Fla State Mus, Univ Fla, 1980-1981; vis prof, Dept Zool, Univ Fla, 1980-1981; ASSOC PROF, DEPT BIOL, UNIV VT, 1978-; asst prof, Dept Biol, Univ Vt, 1973-1978; vis asst prof, Dept Biol, Univ St Lawrence, 1973-1974; instr, human biol, Midwestern Univ, 1969-1970. **Memberships:** Am Soc Mammalogists; Soc Study Evolution; Soc Syst Zoologists; Am Genetic Asn. **Research Statement & Publications:** Genetic changes and evolutionary processes associated with speciation; effects of isolation on the genetic structure of populations; evolutionary relationships based upon analysis of morphology, protein electrophovesis, restriction fragments, DNA-DNA hybridization and karyology of vertebrates. **Mailing Address:** Dept Biol Univ Vt, 120A Marsh Life Sci Bldg, Burlington, VT 05405. **E-Mail:** c-william.kilpatrick@uvm.edu

KILPATRICK, DANIEL LEE, BIOCHEMISTRY. **Personal Data:** b Los Angeles, Calif, April 2, 1951; m 1979. **Education:** Univ Calif, San Diego, BA, 1974; Duke Univ PhD (biochem), 1980. **Professional Experience:** ASSOC PROF PHYSIOL, UNIV MASS, as of 2005; lectr, 1988 & 1990 & Ore Regional Primate Ctr, 1990; sr scientist, Worcester Found Exp Biol, beginning 1989; ad hoc reviewer, Biochem Endocrinol Study Sect, 1989; Lectr, Univ Mass, 1987; lectr, Harvard Univ, 1987; Lectr, Tufts Univ, 1986, 1988; lectr, Univ Miami & Columbia Univ, 1986; staff scientist, Worcester Found Exp Biol, 1984-1989; lectr, Seventh Int Cong Endocrinol, Can, 1984; res assoc, Roche Inst Molecular Biol, 1982-1984; sr scientist, Unigene Labs, 1981-1982; dept physiol chem & pharmacol, Roche Inst Molecular Biol, 1980-1981. **Memberships:** AAAS; NY Acad Sci; Am Soc Neurochem; Am Soc Biol Chemists; Endocrine Soc. **Research Statement & Publications:** Author of numerous publications in medical journals. **Mailing Address:** Univ Mass, Sch Med, Dept Physiol, S4-139, 55 Lake Ave N, Worcester, MA 01655-0127. **Fax:** 508-842-9362. **E-Mail:** daniel.kilpatrick@umassmed.edu

KILPATRICK, EARL BUDDY, FISH BIOLOGY. **Personal Data:** b Burkburnett, Tex, June 21, 1920; m 1956, c 6. **Education:** Univ Okla, BS, 1942, MS, 1949, PhD (zoology), 1959. **Professional Experience:** RETIRED; prof & head dept, Southeastern Okla State Univ, 1962-1983; dir, NSF Res Partic Prog, 1959-1960; from asst prof to assoc prof biol, Southeastern Okla State Univ, 1949-1962; asst zool, Univ Okla, 1946-1949. **Memberships:** AAAS. **Research Statement & Publications:** Cytology, seasonal gonadal cycles of the fresh water fishes. **Mailing Address:** 1223 N Fifth Ave, Durant, OK 74701.

KILPATRICK, JEREMY, MATHEMATICS EDUCATION RESEARCH, MATHEMATICS CURRICULUM. **Personal Data:** b Fairfield, Iowa, September 21, 1935; m 1962, Carlene; c Judson C & Barton P. **Education:** Univ Calif, Berkeley, AB, 1956, MA, 1960; Stanford Univ MS, 1962 PhD (educ), 1967. **Honorary Degrees:** Dr Honoris Causa, Gothenburg Univ, Sweden, 1995. **Honors & Awards:** Fulbright Sr Lectr, Spain, 1989. **Professional Experience:** REGENTS PROF, UNIV GA, 1993-; Fulbright res scholar, Sweden, 1993; distinguished scholar, San Diego State Univ, 1988; distinguishedvisitor, NZ Asn Res Educ, 1987; guest prof, Institute Fr Didactik Der Mathematics, WGer, 1976; PROF MATH EDUC, UNIV GA, 1975-; vis lectr, Univ Cambridge, Eng, 1973-1974; res assoc, Sec Sch Math Curric Improv Study, Teachers Col, 1969-1975; from asst prof to assoc prof math, Teachers Col, Columbia Univ, 1967-1975; res asst, Sch Math Study Group, Stanford Univ, 1962-1967; Supvr math interns, Sec Educ Proj, Stanford Univ, 1962-1963; Teaching asst math educ, Sch Math Study Group, Stanford Univ, 1961-1963. **Memberships:** Nat Coun Teachers Math; Math Asn Am; Am Educ Res Asn; Nat Coun Measurement Educ. **Research Statement & Publications:** Evaluations of math curricula; studies in testing and assessment; problem solving and mathematical abilities; editing translations of Soviet studies in mathematics education; surveys of research in mathematics education. **Mailing Address:** 227 Woodlawn Ave, Athens, GA 30606-4353. **E-Mail:** jkilpat@core.uga.edu

KILPATRICK, JOHN MICHAEL, Pharmaceutical Development. **Personal Data:** b Chickamauga, GA, February 2, 1953; American citizen; m Kathleen; c Alyson M, John M & Christopher M. **Education:** Col Charleston, BS, 1975; Med Univ SC, PhD (immunol & microbiol), 1981. **Professional Experience:** EXECUTIVE DIRECTOR, PHARMACEUTICAL DEVELOPMENT, PRECLIN BIOL SCI, BIOANALYTICAL CHEMISTRY BIOCRYST PHARMACEUT, 2005-; Director, Preclinical Biology, Biocryst Pharmaceut, 2001-2005, section head, dept of biol, BioCryst pharmaceut, 1997-2001; sr biol II, dept of biol, BioCryst, 1995-1997; sr scientist II, Crystallography, BioCryst, 1993-1994; Asst prof, dept of med, div of clin immunology & Rheumatology, Univ of Ala Birmingham, 1989-1983; Assoc Sci, Multipurpose Arthritis Center, UAB, 1989-1993; Lab dir, Biotherapeuties Inc, Cininnati, Ohio & Birminham, Ala, 1987-1989; Asst prof, dept of microbiology and immunol, mem grad fac, mem molecular and cellular biol and biopathol fac, med Univ of SC, 1985-1987; res assoc, dept if basic & clinical immunology & Microbiol, med Univ of SC, 1984-1985; postdoc fel, NIH inst training prog in immunol diseases and basic immunology, UAB, 1981-1984; instrutor microbiology, dept of biol, Col of Charleston, 1979. **Memberships:** AAAS; Am Soc Hematology, Am Asn Immunologists, Ame Asn Pharmaceutical Sci, Am Chem Soc. **Research Statement & Publications:** Preclinical and Clinical Development of drugs based on the three dimensional structure of proteins important for the development or exacerbation of diseases of the immune system. **Mailing Address:** 401 Park Lake Terrace, Helena, AL 35080. **Fax:** 205-444-4640. **E-Mail:** jkilpatrick@biocryst.com

KILPATRICK, KERRY EDWARDS, INDUSTRIAL ENGINEERING, OPERATIONS RESEARCH. **Personal Data:** b Baltimore, Md, March 17, 1939; m 1965, c 2. **Education:** Univ Mich, Ann Arbor, BSE(mech eng) & BSE(eng math), 1961, MS, 1967, PhD (indust eng), 1970; Harvard Univ, MBA, 1963. **Professional Experience:** DIR, CTR HEALTH POLICY RES, 1981-; Consult, World Health Orgn & Vet Admin, 1977-; PROF COMMUNITY HEALTH & FAMILY MED, COL BUS ADMIN, 1972-; DIR, HEALTH SYSTS RES DIV, J HILLIS MILLER HEALTH CTR, 1972-; PROF HEALTH & HOSP ADMIN, COL BUS ADMIN, 1971-; PROF INDUST & SYSTS ENG, UNIV FLA, 1970-; res asst indust eng, Univ Mich, Ann Arbor, 1967-1970; Methods engr, Buick Motor Div, Gen Motors Corp, 1963-1965. **Memberships:** Inst Mgt Sci; Opers Res Soc Am; Am Inst Indust Engrs. **Research Statement & Publications:** Industrial and systems engineering, analysis of production and health service systems; analysis of extended function auxiliaries in health care delivery systems; evaluation of international health services delivery programs. **Mailing Address:** Dept Health Policy & Admin, Univ NC, CB 7400, Chapel Hill, NC 27599-7400.

KILPATRICK, LAURIE E, CELL BIOLOGY, IMMUNOLOGY. **Personal Data:** b Philadelphia, Pa, October 1, 1953; m 1990, William Fox; c Lauren. **Education:** Hampshire Col, BA, 1976; Univ Pa, PhD (biochem), 1983. **Professional Experience:** ASSOC MEM, JOSEPH STOKES JR RES INST CHILDREN'S HOSP, 1993-; Med dent staff mem, Children's Hosp Philadelphia, 1987-; res asst prof pediat, Univ Pa Med Sch, 1986-1993; Res fel pharmacol, Univ Pa Med Sch, 1983-1986. **Memberships:** Am Soc Cell Biol; Sigma Xi; Shock Soc. **Research Statement & Publications:** Molecular mechanisms underlying cytokine; mediated cellular dysfunction in sepsis and host defense against infections; pharmacological approaches to protection in sepsis and inflammatory diseases. **Mailing Address:** Div Immunol & Infectious Dis, 34th St & Civic Center Blvd, Philadelphia, PA 19104. **Fax:** 215-590-3044. **E-Mail:** kilpatrick@email.chop.edu

KILPATRICK, S JAMES, BIOSTATISTICS, Quantitative EPIDEMIOLOGY. **Personal Data:** b Belfast, Northern Ireland, American citizen. **Education:** Queen's Univ Belfast, BSc (Honors i.e. a 4 year degree) Pure & Applied Mathematics, 1954; MSc, 1957, Human Genetics; PhD (Med Statist), 1960. **Honors & Awards:** Fellow of the Royal Statistical Society. **Professional Experience:** PROF EMER BIOSTATIST, MED COLL VA, V.C.U.; Currently: Mem, Gerson Lehrman Council of Advisers, consultant to pharmaceutical firms. Formerly: Mem. F.D.A. C.D.E.R. Advisory Cttee, Mem. N.I.H. Oral Biol Med Study Section. Founding Chairman, Dept. of Biostatistics, M.C.V./V.C.U., Director of Graduate Affairs, School of Basic Health Sciences. Former: Mem. Indoor Air Pollution Adv Cttee. Former prof family pract, Med Col VA, Former chmn, Va Health Statist Adv Coun, U.S-.Public Health fel statist, Iowa State Univ. Graduate Queen's U. Belfast. B.S. (Mathematics), M.S. (Human Genetics), Ph.D. (Medical Statistics). **Research Statement & Publications:** Mortality Indices, Genetics of Kidney Transplant Histocompatibility, Family Practice Research (text and papers), Meta Analysis, Health Services Research, Statistical Methods (text). **Mailing Address:** Dept Biostatist, VA Commonwealth Univ, PO Box 980032, Richmond, VA 23298-0032. **Fax:** 804-828-8900. **E-Mail:** sjkilpat@vcu.edu

KILPPER, ROBERT WILLIAM, TOXICOLOGY, BIOMATHEMATICS. **Personal Data:** b Houston, Tex, October 21, 1938; m 1960, c 3. **Education:** Univ Houston, BS, 1961, MS, 1963, PhD (biophys), 1967. **Professional Experience:** SR TOXICOLOGIST, XEROX CORP, as of 1998; toxicologist, Xerox Corp, beginning 1981; assoc prof, radiation biol & biophys, Sch Med & Dent, Univ Rochester, 1975-1981; asst prof biomath, radiation biol & biophys, Sch Med & Dent, Univ Rochester, 1967-1975. **Memberships:** Soc Toxicol. **Research Statement & Publications:** Mathematical model analysis of physiological systems, especially the mechanical behavior of some mammalian lung models and the compartmental distribution of various compounds. **Mailing Address:** 144 Branford Rd, Rochester, NY 14618.

KILSHEIMER, JOHN ROBERT, AGRICULTURAL CHEMISTRY. **Personal Data:** b Mt Vernon, NY, September 21, 1923; m 1946, Betty Carraher; c Joan, Jean, Kathleen, Mary, Elizabeth & Jacqueline. **Education:** Col Holy Cross, BS, 1944; Fordham Univ, MS, 1948; Syracuse Univ, PhD (chem), 1951. **Professional Experience:** CONSULT, 1982-; sr vpres res, mfg & sales, 1980-1982; Mem bd dirs, Fertilizer Inst, 1977-1980; Mem bd dirs, Nat Agr Chem Asn, 1972-1981; vpres res & develop, OM Scott & Sons Co, 1971-1980; head pesticides res & develop, Esso Res & Eng Co, 1967-1971; sr staff adv agr prods, Esso Res & Eng Co, 1966-1967; mgr org chem, Mobil Chem Co, 1963-1966; supvr agr chem, Mobil Chem Co, 1961-1963; org-agr, Polymer Div, Union Carbide Chem Co, 1954-1961; res chemist, Polymer Div, Union Carbide Chem Co, 1950-1954; asst, Syracuse Univ, 1947-1948; Instr chem, Fordham prep sch, 1946-1947. **Memberships:** Am Chem Soc; Nat Agr Chem Asn; Fertil Inst. **Research Statement & Publications:** Pesticides; fertilizers; oxidation reactions; synthetic organics; vinyl polymers; turf research. **Mailing Address:** 683 Bella Vis, Edgewater, FL 32141.

KILSHEIMER, SIDNEY ARTHUR, ORGANIC CHEMISTRY. **Personal Data:** b New Rochelle, NY, October 19, 1930; wid. **Education:** Wagner Col, BS, 1952; NC State Col, MS, 1954; Purdue Univ, PhD (chem), 1959. **Professional Experience:** PROF EMER CHEM, BUTLER UNIV, 1996-; prof chem, Butler Univ, 1972-1996; from asst prof to assoc prof, Butler Univ, 1958-1972; instr, Purdue Univ, 1956-1958; asst, Purdue Univ, 1954-1956;

asst chem, NC State Col, 1952-1954. **Memberships:** Fel AAAS; Am Chem Soc; fel The Chem Soc; fel Am Inst Chemists. **Research Statement & Publications:** Chemical reductions; natural products. **Mailing Address:** Dept Chem, Butler Univ, 751 W 46th St, Indianapolis, IN 46208. **Fax:** 317-940-8434.

KIM, AGNES KYUNG-HEE, CLINICAL PATHOLOGY, HEMATOLOGY. **Personal Data:** b Seoul, Korea, May 17, 1937; American citizen; m 1965, c 3. **Education:** Yonsei Univ, BS, 1958, MD, 1962. **Professional Experience:** ASSOC PATHOLOGIST, NEW ENG DEACONESS HOSP & NEW ENG BAPTIST HOSP, 1973-; assoc pathologist, Vet Admin Hosp, WRoxbury, Mass, 1971-1973; asst pathologist, Lenox Hill Hosp, 1971; asst pathologist, St Barnabas Med Col, 1969-1970; DEPT PATH, HARVARD MED SCH. **Memberships:** fel Col Am Pathologists; Am Soc Clin Pathologists. **Mailing Address:** New Eng Baptist Hosp, 91 Parker Hill Ave, Boston, MA 02120-3215.

KIM, BENJAMIN K, TRANSDERMAL DELIVERY SYSTEMS, CONTROLLED RELEASE DELIVERY SYSTEMS. **Personal Data:** b Seoul, Korea, April 27, 1933; American citizen; m Soon S; c John, Henry, Cheryl & Martie. **Education:** Seoul Nat Univ, BS, 1959; Kyung Hee Univ, MS, 1969; Univ Southern Calif, PhD (pharmaceut chem), 1977. **Professional Experience:** VPRES RES & DEVELOP, DDS RES, 1991-; develop vpres, Paco Res Inc, 1984-1991; res & develop dir, Nelson Res, 1983-1984; sr res scientist, G D Searle, 1980-1983; tech dir, Rich Life Inc, 1976-1980; res scientist, Rochelle Labs, 1970-1976; sect head, NIH, 1965-1969; dir res & develop, Seoul Pharmaceut Co, 1961-1965; Scientist, Nat Chem Lab, 1959-1961. **Memberships:** Am Pharmaceut Asn; Am Pharmaceut Scientist Asn; Am Chem Soc; Control Release Soc. **Research Statement & Publications:** New drug delivery systems; oral, transdermal implant and nasal delivery systems. **Mailing Address:** DDS Res Inc, 226 Middle Dr, Toms River, NJ 08753. **Fax:** 732-255-7907.

KIM, BORIS FINCANNON, MOLECULAR SPECTROSCOPY, LASERS. **Personal Data:** b Commerce, Ga, November 19, 1938; m 1962, c 2. **Education:** Johns Hopkins Univ, BES, 1960, PhD (physics), 1967. **Professional Experience:** Prin investr, Dept Health, Educ & Welfare Res Grant, 1975-1981; Instr physics, Evening Col, Johns Hopkins Univ, 1970-; PRIN PROF STAFF PHYSICIST, JOHNS HOPKINS UNIV APPL PHYSICS LAB, 1969-. **Memberships:** Am Phys Soc. **Research Statement & Publications:** High resolution, low temperature optical spectroscopy, and electron spin resonance studies of the class of porphyrin compounds; high temperature superconductivity; computer vision. **Mailing Address:** Johns Hopkins Univ Appl Phys Lab, Johns Hopkins Rd, Laurel, MD 20723. **E-Mail:** bkim@aplcomm.jhuapl.edu

KIM, BYUNG CHO, PROCESS DEVELOPMENT, PROCESS DESIGN. **Personal Data:** b Pyongyang, Korea, November 2, 1934; American citizen; m 1960, Dolores; c Julian, Joseph, Ann, Helen & Robert. **Education:** Ripon Col, AB, 1956; Mass Inst Technol, BS, 1958, MS, 1961. **Honors & Awards:** R&D 100 Award, Res & Develop Mag, 1992. **Professional Experience:** PROG MGR, BATTELLE MEM INST, 1992-; proj mgr, Battelle Mem Inst, 1982-1992; assoc sect mgr, Battelle Mem Inst, 1979-1982; sr chem engr, Battelle Mem Inst, 1966-1979; prin chem engr, Battelle Mem Inst, 1961-1966. **Memberships:** Am Inst Chem Engrs; Sigma Xi; Am Chem Soc. **Research Statement & Publications:** Fluidized bed combustion; biomass gasification; bioreactors; microencapsulation; hydrothermal process; separation processes; soil remediation; groundwater remediation; pollution prevention; waste minimization; solid waste management; hazardous waste management; radioactive waste management. **Mailing Address:** 55 W Livingston Ave, Columbus, OH 43215. **Fax:** 614-424-3321.

KIM, BYUNG J, HAZARDOUS WASTE TREATMENT TECHNOLOGIES WASTEWATER TREATMENT TECHNOLOGIES. **Personal Data:** b Seoul, Korea, January 25, 1947; American citizen; m 1974, Yangs; c Peter & NaYoung. **Education:** Seoul Nat Univ, BS, 1970; Polytech Univ, MS, 1976, PhD (civil & environ eng), 1980. **Professional Experience:** SR PROJ MGR, ENG RES DEVELOP CTR, US ARMY, as of 2005; PRIN INVESTR, CONSTRUCT ENG RES LAB, US ARMY, as of 2002; TEAM LEADER, CONSTRUCT ENG RES LAB, US ARMY, 1987-; chief, Utilities Div, Facil Eng Activ, Korea, 1982-1987; lectr, Korea Univ, Seoul Nat Univ & City Col Seoul, 1981-1987; chief, Sanit Br, Eight US Army, Yongsan, 1981-1982; environ engr, NY State Environ Conserv Dept, 1977-1981; civil engr, Seoul Metrop Transit Authority, 1971-1975; civil engr, Korea Hwy Corp, 1969-1971. **Memberships:** Water Environ Fedn; Am Water Works Asn; Soc Am Mil Engrs; Int Asn Water Qual; Am Soc Civil Engrs. **Research Statement & Publications:** Army's effective hazardous waste management and wastewater treatment; domestic sludge dewatering using reed beds, energetic waste separation and treatment from munition production, and Army's industrial sludge treatment. **Mailing Address:** Construct Eng Res Lab, US Army, Champaign, IL 61826-9005. **Fax:** 217-373-3490. **E-Mail:** b-kim@cecer.army.mil

KIM, BYUNG RO, TREATMENT OF MANUFACTURING WASTES & WASTEWATER, PROCESS & WATER QUALITY MODELING. **Personal Data:** c Hahn G & Hahna B. **Education:** Seoul Nat Univ, CE, 1971; Univ Ill, Urbana, MS, 1974, PhD (environ eng), 1976. **Honors & Awards:** Willem Rudolfs Medal, Water Environ Fedn, 1990. **Professional Experience:** STAFF TECH SPECIALIST, DEPT PHYSICS & ENVIRON SCI, FORD RES LAB, FORD MOTOR CO, as of 2002; lectr environ eng, Wayne State Univ, 1993-; PRIN STAFF ENGR, FORD RES LAB, 1990-; assoc ed, J Environ Eng, Am Soc Civil Engrs, 1990-; staff res engr, Gen Motors Res Labs, 1985-1990; asst prof environ eng, Ga Inst Technol, 1980-1985; environ engr, Tenn Valley Authority, 1976-1980. **Memberships:** Am Soc Civil Engrs; Asn Environ Eng Profs; Am Water Works Asn; Int Asn Water Qual; Water Environ Fedn. **Research Statement & Publications:** Industrial waste treatment, adsorption, mathematical modeling of treatment processes and natural water systems. **Mailing Address:** Dept Physical & Environ Sci, Ford Res Lab, Ford Motor Co, PO Box 2053, Dearborn, MI 3083. **Fax:** 313-594-2923. **E-Mail:** bkim@mail.srl.ford.com

KIM, BYUNG SUK, IMMUNOLOGY. **Personal Data:** b Korea, March 20, 1942; American citizen; m 1967, Oak; c Peggy & Charles. **Education:** Seoul Nat Univ, BS, 1967; Va State Univ, MS, 1969; Univ Ill, PhD (microbiol), 1973. **Professional Experience:** PROF IMMUNOL, NORTHWESTERN UNIV, CHICAGO, 1991-; Mem, Korean Acad Sci Tech, 1997-; Mem, Study Sect, NIH, 1985-1989, 1992-1995; Assoc Ed, J Immunol, 1999-2003; from asst prof to assoc prof, Northwestern Univ, Chicago, 1976-1991; res asst prof immunol, Univ Chicago, 1974-1976; sr staff assoc, Columbia Univ, 1973-1974; sr res technician genetics, Univ Chicago, 1969-1970; Res assoc radiation biol, Atomic Energy Res Inst, Korea, 1967-1968. **Memberships:** Am Soc Microbiol; Am Asn Immunol; Sigma Xi. **Research Statement & Publications:** Pathogenic mechanisms of virus-induced neurodegerative diseases; mouse model for multiple sclerosis. **Mailing Address:** Dept Microbiol & Immunol, Med Sch Northwestern Univ, Chicago, IL 60611. **Fax:** 312-503-1339. **E-Mail:** bskim@northwestern.edu

KIM, CHANGHYUN, ULSI DESIGN, SOLID STATE SEMICONDUCTOR. **Personal Data:** b Seoul, Korea, January 1, 1961; m 1987, c 1. **Education:** Seoul Nat Univ, Korea, BS, 1982, MS, 1984. **Professional Experience:** RES ASST, UNIV MICH, ANN ARBOR, 1989-; mgr, MOS Device Develop, Samsung Electronics Co, Ltd, 1989; asst mgr, Samsung Semiconductor Tech Co, Ltd, 1986-1988; Researcher dynamic random access memory design, Samsung Semiconductor Tech Co, Ltd, 1984-1986. **Memberships:** Inst Elec & Electronics Engrs. **Research Statement & Publications:** Dynamic random access memory from 64K bit to 16M bit dynamic random access memory; MOS device characterization for submicron devices and reliability problems; circuit design and BiCMOS process development for sensors. **Mailing Address:** Samsung Electronics Co, San 24 Nogseo-R1 Kiheung Eup, Kyungki-do 449-900, South Korea.

KIM, CHANG-SIK, ANTENNAS, PASSIVE MICROWAVE COMPONENTS. **Personal Data:** b Korea, March 8, 1939; c 2. **Education:** Ohio State Univ, MSc, 1980; Univ Miss, PhD (electromagnetics), 1983. **Professional Experience:** PRIN ENGR, PRODELIN CORP, 1984-; radar engr, Radio Res Inst, 1983-1984. **Memberships:** Inst Elec & Electronics Engrs; Korean Scientists & Engrs Asn. **Research Statement & Publications:** Research in electromagnetics including horn antenna, reflector antenna, microwave passive components. **Mailing Address:** Prodelin Corp, PO Box 368 1700 NE Cable Dr, Conover, NC 28613.

KIM, CHARLES WESLEY, IMMUNOLOGY, PARASITOLOGY. **Personal Data:** b Nashville, Tenn, March 20, 1926; m 1956, Soo; c Charles Jr. **Education:** Univ Calif, BA, 1949; Univ NC, MSPH, 1952, PhD (parasitol, bact), 1956. **Professional Experience:** PROF EMER MICROBIOL & MED, HEALTH SCI CTR, STATE UNIV NY, STONY BROOK; pres, Int Comn Trichinellosis, 1988-1992; prof microbiol & med, Health Sci Ctr, State Univ Ny, Stony Brook, beginning 1987; assoc vice provost, Grad Sch, 1981-1983; assoc dean, Grad Sch, State Univ NY Stony Brook, 1974-1981; assoc dean, Sch Basic Health Sci, Health Sci Ctr, State Univ NY Stony Brook, 1972-1974; res collabr, Med Dept, Brookhaven Nat Lab, beginning 1970; assoc prof microbiol, Health Sci Ctr, 1970-1987; scientist, Brookhaven Nat Lab, 1968-1970; assoc scientist, Brookhaven Nat Lab, 1965-1968; USPHS fel, Argonne Nat Lab & Univ Chicago, 1964-1965; asst prof, NY Med Col, 1959-1964; La State Univ Trop Med fel, Cent Am, 1958; Instr microbiol, NY Med Col, 1956-1959. **Memberships:** Am Soc Parasitol; Am Soc Trop Med & Hyg; fel Royal Soc Trop Med & Hyg; Sigma Xi. **Research Statement & Publications:** Immune response to parasites; mechanism of immunity to parasites, including Trichinella spiralis; Cryptosporiduim; pathogenesis and chemotherapy of cryptosporidiosis; chemotherapy of trichinellosis; complement activity of Trichinella spiralis. **Mailing Address:** State Univ NY, Health Sci Ctr, Div Infectious Dis, Stony Brook, NY 11794-8153. **Fax:** 516-444-7518.

KIM, CHERNG-JU, PHARMACOLOGY & CHEMICAL ENGINEERIN. **Education:** McMaster Univ, PhD. **Professional Experience:** ASSOC PROF PHARMACEUT SCI, SCH PHARM, TEMPLE UNIV, as of 2002; DIR, GRAD STUDIES, TEMPLE UNIV, as of 1998. **Mailing Address:** Grad Progs, Temple Univ, 3307 N Broad St, Philadelphia, PA 19140. **Fax:** 215-707-3678. **E-Mail:** ckim0006@astro.temple.edu

KIM, CHUNG SUL (SUE), POLYMER CONCRETES, PROPELLANT CHEMISTRY. **Personal Data:** b Seoul, Korea, December 21, 1932; American citizen; m 1957, c 2. **Education:** Univ Ill, BS, 1955; Cornell Univ, PhD (org chem), 1960. **Professional Experience:** PROF EMER CHEM, CALIF STATE UNIV, SACRAMENTO, 1994-; Consult, unsaturated polyesters, vinyl esters & polymer concretes, beginning 1986; Prof Chem, Calif State Univ, Sacramento, beginning 1981; Consult, Aerojet Solid Propulsion Co, 1974-1986; from asst prof to assoc prof, Calif State Univ, Sacramento, 1973-1981; sr chem specialist, Aerojet Solid Propulsion Co, 1966-1973; res chemist, Ga Pac Corp, 1963-1965; Proj leader polymer chem, Stand Oil, Ohio, 1959-1962. **Memberships:** Am Chem Soc; Soc Advan Mat & Process Eng; Soc Plastics Engrs. **Research Statement & Publications:** Chemistry and behavior of polymers incomposite; propellant binders; polymer synthesis; bonding (coupling) agents; polymer concretes. **Mailing Address:** Dept Chem, Calif State Univ 6000 J St, Sacramento, CA 95819-2605.

KIM, CHUNG W, THEORETICAL HIGH ENERGY PHYSICS, THEORETICAL NUCLEAR PHYSICS. **Personal Data:** b Hiroshima, Japan, January 8, 1934; m 1960, c 1. **Education:** Seoul Nat Univ, BS, 1958; Univ Ind, PhD (physics), 1963. **Honors & Awards:** Presidential award, Seol Nat Univ, 1958; Nat order Merit, Morean award 1998 (Korean); Chong-Am Sci Award, Korea Acad Sci & Technol, 2001. **Professional Experience:** PROF EMER, JOHNS HOPKINS UNIV, as of 2005; prof physics, Johns hopkins Univ, beginning 1973; from asst prof to assoc prof, Johns Hopkins Univ, 1966-1973; res assoc physics, Univ Pa, 1963-1966. **Memberships:** Fel Am Phys Soc; Korean Acad Sci & Technol. **Research Statement & Publications:** Nuclear and elementary particle physics; cosmology. **Mailing Address:** Dept Physics & Astron, Johns Hopkins Univ, Bloomberg Ctr Rm 366 3400 N Charles St, Baltimore, MD 21218-2686. **Fax:** 410-516-7239. **E-Mail:** kim@eta.pha.jhu.edu

KIM, DAE MANN, ATOMIC PHYSICS, QUANTUM ELECTRONICS. **Personal Data:** b Seoul, Korea, April 22, 1938; m 1967, c 1. **Education:** Seoul Nat Univ, BS, 1960; Yale Univ, MS, 1965, PhD (physics), 1967. **Professional Experience:** DEPT APPL PHYSICS & ELEC ENG, ORE GRAD CTR, BEAVERETON, AS OF 1998; ASSOC PROF, RICE UNIV, 1974-; asst prof elec eng, Rice Univ, 1970-1974; instr, Mass Inst Technol, 1969-1970; Res assoc physics, Mass Inst Technol, 1967-1969; Dept Elec-Comput Eng Rice Univ. **Memberships:** Am Phys Soc. **Research Statement & Publications:** Modelocked laser pulses and their detection processes; photorefractive phase holography, dye lasers, light scattering study. **Mailing Address:** Pohang Inst Sci & Technol, PO Box 125 Pohang, Kyungbuk, 790-600, South Korea.

KIM, DONG HAN, MOLECULAR RECOGNITION, ENZYME INHIBITOR DESIGN. **Personal Data:** b Korea, August 10, 1934; American citizen; m 1960, Yong N Yang; c Wook, Jean & John. **Education:** Seoul Nat Univ, BS, 1957; Univ NC, PhD (org chem), 1965. **Honors & Awards:** Medal of Camellia, Pres Repub Korea, 1988. **Professional Experience:** DIR, CTR BIOFUNCTIONAL MOLECULES, 1991-; vpres sci & eng, Res Inst Indust Sci & Technol, 1987-1988; PROF ORG CHEM & MED CHEM, POHANG UNIV SCI & TECHNOL, 1986-; Sr res chemist, group leader & prin scientist, Res Div, Wyeth Labs, Inc, 1965-1986. **Memberships:** Korean Scientists & Engrs Asn Am (pres, 1985); Am Chem Soc; AAAS; Int Soc Heterocyclic Chem; Korean Chem Soc (vpres, 1991); Korean Pharmacol Soc. **Research Statement & Publications:** Novel types of enzyme inhibitor development; host-guest chemistry (chiral molecular recognition) and medicinal and heterocyclic chemistry (synthesis of structurally novel guinolone antibacterials). **Mailing Address:** Dept Chem Pohang Univ Sci & Technol, San/31 Hyojatong Nampu Pohang 790-784, Pohang 790-600, South Korea. **Fax:** 825-622-795877.

KIM, DONG KWANG, TIRE REINFORCEMENT, STEEL TIRE CORD. **Personal Data:** b Korea, March 18, 1943; American citizen; m 1972, Soojaa Lee; c Eugene & Norman. **Education:** Seoul Nat Univ, Korea, BS, 1967; NC State Univ, MS, 1970, PhD (mat eng), 1973. **Honors & Awards:** Arch T Colwell Award, Soc Automotive Engrs, 1979. **Professional Experience:** Steering comt, Edison Mat Technol Ctr, 1991-; RES & DEVELOP AS-

SOC, GOODYEAR TIRE & RUBBER CO, 1986-; prin engr, Goodyear Tire & Rubber CO, 1982-1986; sr metallurgist, Goodyear Tire & Rubber CO, 1978-1982; res scientist, Lehigh Univ, 1976-1978; Postdoctoral res assoc, Lehigh Univ, 1973-1976. **Memberships:** Am Inst Mech Engrs; Am Soc Metal; Tire Soc. **Research Statement & Publications:** Steel tire cords for tire reinforcing; ultra high strength steel cord development; steel cord process; adhesion between rubber and steel tire cord; cord mechanics and steel cord in tire or tire failure mechanisms. **Mailing Address:** 4194 Big Spruce Dr, Akron, OH 44333. **Fax:** 330-796-3947. **E-Mail:** dkkim@goodyear.com

KIM, DONG YUN, ELEMENTARY PARTICLE PHYSICS. **Personal Data:** b Korea, May 6, 1929; Canadian citizen; m 1962, Elisabeth; c 3. **Education:** Univ Seoul, Korea, BSc, 1953; Aachen Tech Univ, Ger, PhD (theoret physics), 1962. **Professional Experience:** PROF PHYSICS, DEPT PHYSICS, UNIV REGINA, SASK, 1990-; Dept Appl Math & Theoret Physics, Univ Cambridge, Eng & Bohr Inst, Denmark, 1971-1979; assoc prof, Dept Physics, Univ Regina, Sask, 1965-1990; asst prof physics, Dept Physics, Mont State Univ, 1963-1965; fel, Radiation Lab, New York Univ, 1962-1963; vis scientist, Var Orgn, Int Ctr Theoret Physics, Trieste, Italy; inst theoret physics, Univ Heidelberg, Ger; theory group, Stanford Univ; theory group, Fermi Nat Lab. **Memberships:** Can Asn Physicists; Am Phys Soc. **Research Statement & Publications:** Theoretical nuclear and elementary particle physics. **Mailing Address:** Dept Physics & Astron, Univ Regina, Regina, SK S4S 0A2, Can.

KIM, DONGHEE, PHYSIOLOGY. **Education:** Mich State, PhD, 1982. **Professional Experience:** PROF PHYSIOL & BIOPHYS, DEPT PHYSIOL & BIOPHYS, ROSALIND FRANKLIN UNIV MED & SCI, as of 2006. **Research Statement & Publications:** Molecular physiology of potassium channels in excitable cells. **Mailing Address:** Dept Physiol & Biophysics, Rosalind franklin Univ Med Sci, 3333 Green Bay Rd, North Chicago, IL 60064. **Fax:** 847-578-3265. **E-Mail:** donghee.kim@rosalindfranklin.edu

KIM, GIHO, CLINICAL BIOCHEMISTRY. **Personal Data:** b Seoul, Korea, May 15, 1937; m 1968, c 2. **Education:** Simpson Col, BA, 1963, Iowa State Univ, MS, 1969, PhD (biochem), 1971. **Professional Experience:** Clin instr, Downstate Med Ctr, 1976-; RES ASSOC MED RES, DOWNSTATE MED CTR, 1973-; Res assoc biochem, Iowa State Univ, 1971-1972. **Memberships:** Am Chem Soc. **Research Statement & Publications:** Biochemical effect of environmental pollutants on intestinal transport. **Mailing Address:** 81 Morewood Oaks, Port Washington, NY 11050.

KIM, HAN JOONG, METALLURGY, CERAMICS ENGINEERING. **Personal Data:** b Seoul, Korea, November 3, 1937; m 1962, c 2. **Education:** Seoul Nat Univ, BS, 1960; San Jose State Col, MS, 1966; Lehigh Univ, PhD (metall), 1969. **Professional Experience:** Mgr res & develop, Gibson Elec, Subsid GTE, 1976-1996; Mem tech staff electronic mat, GTE Labs Inc, 1969-1976. **Memberships:** Am Ceramic Soc; Am Soc Metals; Am Inst Mining Metall & Petrol Engrs. **Research Statement & Publications:** Oxidation of metals; glass-metal sealing; crystal growth; electrical contact materials. **Mailing Address:** 342 Silver Hill Rd, Concord, MA 01742.

KIM, HAN-SEOB, PATHOLOGY. **Personal Data:** b Seoul, Korea, September 5, 1934; m 1963, c 2. **Education:** Seoul Nat Univ, MD, 1959, MS, 1962, PhD (biochem), 1968. **Professional Experience:** PROF ANAT PATH, BAYLOR COL MED, 1993-; from instr to asst prof path, Baylor Col Med, 1971-1993; from instr to asst prof, Col Med, Seoul Nat Univ, 1967-1969; asst biochem, Col Med, Seoul Nat Univ, 1963-1967; dir cytopath, Ben Taub Gen Hosp. **Memberships:** Am Asn Invest Path; Int Acad Path; Am Soc Cytol. **Research Statement & Publications:** Anatomic pathology relating to cardiovascular and cytopathology. **Mailing Address:** Dept Path, Baylor Col Med, Houston, TX 77030-3498. **Fax:** 713-798-5838. **E-Mail:** hs_kim@hchd.tmc.edu

KIM, HAN-SOO, IMMUNOLOGY. **Education:** Col Pharm Chonnam Nat Univ, Korea, MS. **Professional Experience:** RES FEL, MOLECULAR NEUROBIOLOGY LAB, MCLEAN HOSP, MASS, as of 2006. **Mailing Address:** Molecular Neurobiology Lab, Mclean Hosp, 115 Mill St, Belmont, MA 02478. **Fax:** 617-855-3479. **E-Mail:** hkim@mclean.harvard.edu

KIM, HARRY HI-SOO, PATHOLOGY. **Personal Data:** b Taegu, Korea, January 23, 1922; American citizen; m 1947, c 3. **Education:** Yonsei Univ, Korea, MD, 1945; Univ Pa, MSc, 1959. **Professional Experience:** ASSOC PATHOLOGIST, FLOWER & FIFTH AVE HOSPS, 1968-; consult pathologist, NIH maternal & child health prog, NY Med Col Unit, 1967-; ASSOC PROF PATH, NY MED COL, 1967-; pathologist, NIH maternal & child health prog, NY Med Col Unit, 1961-1967; asst prof, Flower & Fifth Ave Hosps, 1961-1967; assoc pathologist, Metrop Hosp, NY, 1960-1967; clin instr, Sch Med, Univ Wash & Children's Orthop Hosp, 1960-1961; res assoc, Sch Med, Univ Wash & Children's Orthop Hosp, 1958-1959; res assoc, Sch Med, Univ Wash & Children's Orthop Hosp, Philadelphia, Pa, 1957-1958; res asst path, Children's Hosp, Philadelphia, Pa, 1957-1958; fel, Grad Sch Med, Univ Pa, 1956-1958. **Memberships:** Int Acad Path; fel Am Soc Clin Path; fel Am Col Path. **Research Statement & Publications:** Pediatric-pathology; genetics. **Mailing Address:** NYMC Metro Hosp, 1901 First Ave Rm 2A47, New York, NY 10029-7418.

KIM, HEE JOONG, NUCLEAR PHYSICS. **Personal Data:** b Seoul, Korea, February 10, 1934; American citizen; m 1963, c 2. **Education:** Case Inst Technol, MS, 1959, PhD (physics), 1962. **Professional Experience:** PHYSICIST, PHYSICS DIV, OAK RIDGE NAT LAB, 1962-. **Memberships:** Am Phys Soc. **Research Statement & Publications:** Experimental nuclear physics. **Mailing Address:** Physics Div Oak Ridge Nat Lab, PO Box 2008, Bldg 6000, Oak Ridge, TN 37831. **E-Mail:** kim@orph01.phy.ornl.gov

KIM, HEE-YONG, BIOCHEMISTRY, BIOANALYTICAL CHEMISTRY. **Personal Data:** b Seoul, Korea, February 18, 1956; m. **Education:** Seoul Nat Univ, BS, 1978, MS, 1980; Univ Houston, PhD (chem), 1984. **Professional Experience:** SEC CHIEF ALCOHOL ABUSE & ALCOHOLISM, LAB MEMBRANE BIOCHEM & BIOPHYS, NIH, 1991-. **Memberships:** Am Soc Mass Spectrometry; Am Soc Neurochem; Am Chem Soc. **Mailing Address:** Lab Membrane Biochem & Biophys, NIH, 12501 Wash Ave, Rockville, MD 20852. **Fax:** 301-594-0035. **E-Mail:** hykim@nih.gov

KIM, HELEN, BIOLOGY. **Education:** Mary Wash Col, Chem, BS; Yale Univ Sch Forestry, Environ Studies, MS; Univ Va, PhD (BioPhys). **Professional Experience:** RES ASSOC PROF, DEPT PHARMACOL & TOXICOL, UNIV ALA, as of 2005. **Mailing Address:** Univ Ala, Birmingham, AL 35294. **Fax:** 205-934-8240. **E-Mail:** helen.kim@ccc.uab.edu

KIM, HONG C, PLASTICS & COMPOSITES, FATIGUE BEHAVIOR OF COMPOSITE MATERIALS. **Personal Data:** b Seoul, Korea, March 26, 1949; American citizen; m 1977, c 2. **Education:** Seoul Nat Univ, BS, 1971; Case Western Res Univ, MS, 1976, PhD (metall & mat sci), 1978. **Professional Experience:** AT KOREA ADVAN INST SCI & TECHNOL, as of 1999; RES & DEVELOP LAB MGR, LNP ENG PLASTICS, 1989-; mat lab supvr advan mat, ICI Americas, 1986-1989; sr mat scientist, ICI Americas, 1980-1986; Staff develop engr, Goodyear Tire & Rubber Co, 1978-1980. **Memberships:** Soc Plastics Engrs; Soc Advan Mat & Process Eng; Am Soc Testing & Mat. **Research Statement & Publications:** Sheet molding compounds; reaction injection molding materials; advanced composites; filament wound composites; pultruded fiberglas-reinforced plastic; engineering plastics. **Mailing Address:** Korea Advan Res Inst Sci & TechnoL, South Korea.

KIM, HYEONG LAK, NATURAL PRODUCTS CHEMISTRY. **Personal Data:** b Korea, January 18, 1933; American citizen; m 1967, c 5. **Education:** Seoul Nat Univ, BS, 1956; St Louis Univ, MS, 1968; Tex A&M Univ, PhD (biochem), 1970. **Professional Experience:** ASSOC PROF EMER, DEPT VET PHYSIOL & PHARMACOL, TEX A&M UNIV, as of 2004; assoc prof, dept vet physiol & pharmacol, Tex A&M Univ, beginning 1989; asst prof, Tex A&M Univ, 1979-1989; MEM GRAD FAC, DEPT VET PHYSIOL & PHARMACOL, TEX A&M UNIV, 1975-; RES CHEMIST, TEX AGR STA, TEX A&M UNIV, 1969-. **Memberships:** Am Chem Soc; AAAS; NY Acad Sci. **Research Statement & Publications:** Chemical constituents of poisonous plants; naturally occurring toxicants in food chain; metabolism of toxicants. **Mailing Address:** Dept Vet Physiol & Pharmacol, Tex A&M Univ, College Station, TX 77840.

KIM, HYUN DJU, PHYSIOLOGY, BIOCHEMISTRY. **Personal Data:** b Ham Buk, Korea, January 4, 1937; American citizen; m 1969, c 2. **Education:** Duke Univ, AB, 1962, PhD (physiol), 1968. **Professional Experience:** PROF & CHMN DEPT PHARMACOL, UNIV MO, COLUMBIA, as of 2004; prof pharmacol & physiol, Univ Ala, Birmingham, beginning 1980; assoc prof physiol, Univ Ariz, 1972-1980; Alexander von Humboldt fel, Div Med Physiol, Aachen Tech Univ, 1971-1972; Muscular Dystrophy Asn Am fel physiol, Univ Calif, Los Angeles, 1969-1971. **Memberships:** Biophys Soc; Am Soc Cell Biol; Am Physiol Soc. **Research Statement & Publications:** Membrane transport and energy metabolism in red blood cells; protein metabolism in muscle development. **Mailing Address:** Dept Pharmacol, Univ Mo-Columbia, M-517B Med Sci Bldg, Columbia, MO 65212-0001. **Fax:** 573-884-4558. **E-Mail:** kimh@health.missouri.edu

KIM, IN C, BIOLOGY. **Education:** Univ Nmex Sch Med, PhD. **Professional Experience:** STAFF, INGEN LABS INC, as of 1996. **Mailing Address:** Ingen Labs Inc, 6303 4th St NW Ste 4, Albuquerque, NM 87107. **Fax:** 505-345-8157. **E-Mail:** ingen@ingenlabs.com

KIM, J JOHN, TURBULENCE, COMPUTATIONAL FLUID DYNAMICS. **Personal Data:** b Seoul, Korea, October 20, 1947; m 2003, Stacy; c June Kim. **Education:** Seoul Nat Univ, BS, 1970; Brown Univ, MS, 1974; Stanford Univ, PhD (mech eng), 1978. **Honors & Awards:** Medal for, Except Sci Achievement, NASA, 1985; Otto Laporte Award, APS, 2001; Hoam Prize in Engineering, 2002. **Professional Experience:** ROCKWELL INT PROF MECH ENG, UNIV CALIF, LOS ANGELES, AS OF 2006; Chief, Turbulence & Transition Physics Br, 1992-1993; consult prof, Stanford Univ, 1987-1993; head, Turbulence Physics Sect, 1987-1992; res scientist, Ames Res Ctr, NASA, 1982-1987; Consult, Nielson Eng, 1980-1985; actg asst prof, Stanford Univ, 1980-1982; Nat Res Coun fel, Ames Res Ctr, NASA, 1978-1980. **Memberships:** Fel Am Phys Soc; assoc fel Inst Aeronaut & Astronaut; Am Soc Mech Engrs. **Research Statement & Publications:** Investigate the fundamental physics of turbulence and transition to turbulence using large-scale computations on super computers. **Mailing Address:** MAE/UCLA, 420 Westwood Plz, Los Angeles, CA 90095-1597. **Fax:** 310-206-4830. **E-Mail:** jkim@seas.ucla.edu

KIM, JAE HO, RADIOBIOLOGY, RADIOTHERAPY. **Personal Data:** b Taegu, Korea, December 17, 1935; American citizen; m 1963, c 2. **Education:** Kyung-Pook Nat Univ, Korea, MD, 1959; Univ Iowa, PhD (radiobiol), 1963. **Professional Experience:** Adj prof physics, Oakland Univ, as of 2003; CHMN, DEPT RADIATION ONCOL, HENRY FORD HEALTH SYST, as of 2003; PROF RADIOL, MED COL, CORNELL UNIV, 1980-; ATTEND, MEM HOSP, 1978-; assoc attend, Mem Hosp, 1975-1977; ASSOC PROF BIOPHYS, MED COL, CORNELL UNIV, 1972-; ASSOC MEM, SLOAN-KETTERING INST, 1972-; from asst prof to assoc prof radiol, Med Col, Cornell Univ, 1972-1979; asst attend, Mem Hosp, 1972-1975; resident radiother, Mem Hosp, NY, 1969-1972; intern med, Montefiore Hosp, Bronx, 1968-1969; asst prof biophys, Sloan-Kettering Div, Cornell Univ, 1967-1968; Res assoc, Sloan-Kettering Inst Cancer Res, 1963-1968. **Memberships:** AMA; NY Acad Sci; Radiation Res Soc; Am Asn Cancer Res; Am Radium Soc. **Research Statement & Publications:** Cellular radio and chemo-biology; metabolic studies occurring during the cell cycle of mammalian cells in vitro; effects of ionizing radiation, metabolic inhibitors, hyperthermia on nucleic acid metabolism and cell viability in various tumors in culture. **Mailing Address:** Dept Radiation Oncol, Henry Ford Health Syst, 2799 W Grand Blvd, Detroit, MI 48202. **Fax:** 313-916-3235. **E-Mail:** jkim1@hfhs.org

KIM, JAE HOON, PHOTOTONICS & OPTOELECTRONICS, COMPOUND SEMICONDUCTOR DEVICE & PHYSICS. **Personal Data:** b Seoul, Korea, January 8, 1952; m 1979, c 1. **Education:** Seoul Nat Univ, BS, 1976, MS, 1978; Univ Fla, PhD (elec eng), 1987. **Professional Experience:** AFFIL ASSOC PROF & GRAD FAC, DEPT ELEC ENG, UNIV WASH, as of 2003; MGR/ASSOC TECH FEL, PHANTOM WORKS, BOEING CO, as of 2003; PRIN STAFF ENGR PHOTONICS, BOEING HIGH TECHNOL CTR, 1991-; task mgr photonics, Jet Propulsion Lab, 1989-1991; Prin investr, Jet Propulsion Lab, 1989-1991; mem tech staff, Jet Propulsion Lab, 1987-1989; res asst elec eng, Univ Fla, 1984-1987; teaching asst elec eng, Univ Minn, 1982-1983; dept head, Korea Naval Acad, 1980-1981; instr elec eng, Korea Naval Acad, 1978-1980; teaching asst elec eng, Seoul Nat Univ, 1976-1978. **Memberships:** Inst Elec & Electronics Engrs; Am Phys Soc; Japan Soc Appl Physics; Korea Inst Elec Engrs. **Research Statement & Publications:** Development of optoelectronic integrated circuits for applications to neural networks, optical signal processing, and optical communications; development of integrated optoelectronic receivers and transmitters for fiber-optic avionics networks. **Mailing Address:** Boeing Co, Seattle, WA 98124-2499. **E-Mail:** jae.h.kim@boeing.com

KIM, JAI BIN, CIVIL ENGINEERING. **Personal Data:** b Seoul, Korea, May 17, 1934; m 1960, c 4. **Education:** Ore State Univ, BS, 1959, MS, 1960; Univ Md, PhD (civil eng), 1965. **Professional Experience:** PROF CIVIL & ENVIRON ENG, BUCKNELL UNIV, 1977-; chmn, Dept Civil Eng, Bucknell Univ, 1976-; res engr, Nat Bur Stand, 1976-1977; from asst prof to assoc prof civil eng, Bucknell Univ, 1966-1977; chief hwy res engr, DC Dept Transp, 1964-1966. **Memberships:** Am Soc Testing & Mat; Am Concrete Inst; Am Soc Civil Engrs; Sigma Xi. **Research Statement & Publications:** Structural mechanics; engineering analysis; foundation engineering; nonlinear structural analysis; pile foundations; shallow excavations; pile caps. **Mailing Address:** Dept Civil Eng, Bucknell Univ, Moore Ave, Lewisburg, PA 17837. **Fax:** 570-577-3415. **E-Mail:** jaikim@bucknell.edu

KIM, JAI SOO, ATMOSPHERIC PHYSICS, SPACE PHYSICS. **Personal Data:** b Korea, November 1, 1925; American citizen; m 1952, Hai; c Kami, Tomi, Kihyun & Himi. **Education:** Seoul Nat Univ, BSc, 1949; Univ Sask, MSc, 1957, PhD (physics), 1958. **Professional Experience:** PROF EMER ATMOSPHERIC SCI & PHYSICS, STATE UNIV NY ALBANY, 1994-; KOREAN ANTARCTIC PROG, 1988-; Korean Studies prog, State Univ NY Stony Brook, 1983-1985; vis prof, Advan Inst Sci & Tech, Seoul, Korea, 1983; consult, Norlite Corp, 1982-1984; consult, US Army Res Off, 1978-1980; consult, Battelle mem Inst, 1977-1980; consult, NY State Environ Conserv dept & Environ One Corp, 1976-

1982; res, Univ Corp Atmospheric res, Boulder, CO 1971-1976; chmn dept, State Univ NY Albany, 1969-1976; prof, State Univ NY Albany, 1967-1994; from asst prof to prof, Univ Idaho, 1959-1967; asst prof, Clarkson Univ, 1958-1959; instr, Sung Kyun Kwan Univ, Korea, 1953-1954; instr physics, Tonga Col, Pusan, 1952-1953. **Research Statement & Publications:** Upper atmospheric physics; solar-terrestrial relations; plasma physics; magneto-hydrodynamics. **Mailing Address:** Dept Earth & Atmospheric Sci, State Univ NY Albany, Albany, NY 12222. **Fax:** 518-442-5825.

KIM, JEAN BARTHOLOMEW, ORGANIC CHEMISTRY. **Personal Data:** b Philadelphia, Pa, October 12, 1940; m 1965, c 2. **Education:** Eastern Baptist Col, BA, 1961; Bryn Mawr Col, PhD (chem), 1968. **Professional Experience:** EXEC DIR BD EDUC MINISTRIES, AM BAPTIST CHURCHES, 1989-; vpres & acad dean, Eastern Co, 1980-1989; prof chem & head dept, Eastern Co, 1970; res assoc chem, Drexel Univ, 1968-1970; asst prof chem, Haverford Col, 1967-1968. **Memberships:** AAAS; Am Chem Soc; Sigma Xi; Nat Sci Teachers Asn. **Research Statement & Publications:** Electrophilic substitution on electronic properties of porphin derivatives. **Mailing Address:** 131 Waterloo Ave, Berwyn, PA 19312.

KIM, JIN BAI, ALGEBRA. **Personal Data:** b Sangju, Korea, June 23, 1921; wid, c 1. **Education:** Yonsei Univ, Korea, BS, 1950; Univ Chicago, MS, 1956; Va Polytech Inst, PhD (math), 1965. **Professional Experience:** GRAD FAC, WVA UNIV, 1989-; Barnara Hindu Univ, India, 1979-1980; PROF MATH, WVA UNIV, 1976-; asst prof, George Wash Univ, 1969-1971; asst prof, Mich State Univ, 1965-1967; from instr to asst prof math, Yonsei Univ, Korea, 1949-1961. **Memberships:** Am Math Soc; Math Asn Am. **Research Statement & Publications:** Algebraic semigroups; linear algebra; matrices; tensors and differential manifolds. **Mailing Address:** Dept Math 311 Armstrong Hall, WVa Univ, Morgantown, WV 26506. **E-Mail:** kim@mathwvu.edu

KIM, JINCHOON, NUCLEAR FUSION, PARTICLE ACCELERATOR. **Personal Data:** b Choon-Chun, Korea, March 5, 1943; American citizen; m 1970, Yoonchung; c Nina, Margaret & Angela. **Education:** Seoul Nat Univ, BS, 1965; Univ Calif, Berkeley, MS, 1968, PhD (plasma physics), 1971. **Professional Experience:** Adj fac, Mesa Col, 1989-1992; Vis scientist, Jet Joint Undertaking, 1988; PRIN SCIENTIST, GEN ATOMICS, 1980-; res staff, Oak Ridge Nat Lab, 1974-1980; Physicist, Cyclotron Corp, 1971-1974. **Memberships:** Am Phys Soc; Korean Nuclear Soc. **Research Statement & Publications:** Thermonuclear fusion research, including tokamak plasma transport, spectroscopic diagnostics of plasma ions, neutral beam injection heating of plasma, particle accelerators, neutron dosimetry and shielding, and vacuum technology. **Mailing Address:** PO Box 85608, 3550 Gen Atomics Ct, San Diego, CA 92138. **Fax:** 619-455-4156. **E-Mail:** kimj@gav.gat.com

KIM, JIN-SOO, PHYSICS. **Education:** Seoul Nat Univ, BS, 1991, MS, 1993, PhD, 1999. **Professional Experience:** ASST PROF, DIV COMPUT SCI, KOREA ADVANCED INST SCI & TECHNOL, 2002-. **Mailing Address:** 3146 Bunche Ave, San Diego, CA 92122. **Fax:** 822-884-3002.

KIM, JOHN K, ELECTRICAL ENGINEERING, MATERIAL SCIENCE. **Personal Data:** b Seoul, Korea, October 26, 1937; American citizen; m 1961, c 2. **Education:** Ohio Univ, BS, 1963; Ohio State Univ, MS, 1963, PhD (elec eng), 1967. **Professional Experience:** PRES, SUPERTEK CO, 1975-; head dept semiconductor res & develop, Raytheon Co, 1970-1975; head sect semiconductor eng, Micro State, 1968-1970; sr engr solid state, Semiconductor Group, Motorola, 1967-1968; mem tech staff electronics, Lincoln Lab, Mass Inst Technol, 1966-1967. **Memberships:** Sigma Xi; Inst Elec & Electronics Engrs; Korean Sci Eng Asn. **Research Statement & Publications:** Analysis and development of solid state devices for high efficiency and high power generation of microwave energy. **Mailing Address:** Supertek Co, 2231 Colby Ave, Los Angeles, CA 90064. **Fax:** 310-444-1164.

KIM, JONATHAN JANG-HO, METALLURGICAL ENGINEERING. **Personal Data:** b Kwang-Ju, Korea, June 11, 1932; m 1958, c 1. **Education:** Seoul Nat Univ, BS, 1955; Carnegie-Mellon Univ, MS, 1961 Univ Okla, PhD (metall eng), 1966. **Professional Experience:** RETIRED; mgr process technol, Carborundum Co, 1980-1991; staff metall engr, Lexington Develop Ctr, 1975-1980; sr proj engr, Ledgemont Lab, Kennecott Copper Corp, 1967-1975; process design engr, Lummus Co, 1965-1967; res engr, Sci Res Lab, Ministry Nat Defense, Korea, 1955-1959. **Memberships:** Am Inst Mining, Metall & Petrol Engrs; Am Ceramic Soc. **Research Statement & Publications:** Smelting and refining of nonferrous metals; extractive metallurgy; ceramic manufacturing processes via fusion and sintering; ceramic grains synthesis. **Mailing Address:** 79 Brandywine Dr, Williamsville, NY 14221.

KIM, JONGSOO, MATHEMATICS. **Education:** Yonsei Univ, Korea, BS, MS; Lehigh Univ, PhD (Chem Eng), 2002. **Professional Experience:** RES SCIENTIST, CTR NANOSCALE SCI & ENG, 2004-; VIS SCIENTIST, NAVAL RES LAB, WASH, DC. **Mailing Address:** 1805 NDSU Res Pk Dr., Fargo, ND 58102. **Fax:** 701-231-5306.

KIM, JUHEE, MICROBIOLOGY. **Personal Data:** b Osan, Korea, September 13, 1935; m 1968, c 2. **Education:** Seoul Nat Univ, BS, 1958; Cornell Univ, MS, 1962, PhD (food sci & microbiol), 1966. **Professional Experience:** PROF EMER MICROBIOL, CALIF STATE UNIV, LONG BEACH, 1997-; Prof Microbiol, Calif State Univ, Long Beach, beginning 1975; environ specialist, Southern Calif Coastal Water Res Proj, 1974; Vis investr, Scripps Inst Oceanog, 1970-1971 & Wood Hole Oceanog Inst, 1973; from asst prof to assoc prof, Calif State Univ, Long Beach, 1966-1975; Researcher food & nutrit, Sci Res Inst, Ministry Defense, Seoul, Korea, 1958-1959. **Memberships:** AAAS; Am Soc Microbiol; Am Chem Soc; NY Acad Sci. **Research Statement & Publications:** Food and industrial microbiology; public health. **Mailing Address:** Dept Biol, Calif State Univ 3702 CSULB, Long Beach, CA 90840-0004.

KIM, JUNG-JA P, BIOCHEMISTRY. **Education:** Cornell Univ, PhD, 1969. **Professional Experience:** PROF BIOCHEM, MED COL WIS, as of 2005. **Mailing Address:** Dept Biochem, Med Col WI, 8701 Watertown Plank Rd, Milwaukee, WI 53226-4801. **Fax:** 414-456-6510. **E-Mail:** jjkim@mcw.edu

KIM, KAY KWANGE-AE, BIOLOGY. **Education:** Univ Md, PhD (biochem). **Professional Experience:** DIR, OFF PATENT QUAL REV, beginning 1999. **Mailing Address:** Off Patent Qual Rev, 1911 Jefferson Davis Hwy, Arlington, VA 22202. **Fax:** 703-305-9265.

KIM, KE CHUNG, ENTOMOLOGY & FORENSIC SCIENCE, SYSTEMATICS & BIODIVERSITY SCIENCE. **Personal Data:** b Korea, March 7, 1934; American citizen; m 1964, Young; c Stuart K & Sally A Kim. **Education:** Seoul Nat Univ, BS, 1956; Univ Mont, MA, 1959; Univ Minn, PhD (Entom), 1964. **Honors & Awards:** Fulbright Lectr & Researcher, Korea, 1975; L O Howard Distinguished Achievement Award, Entom Soc Am EB, 1988; Fulbright Sr Scholar, 1993-1994. **Professional Experience:** Chair, Am Board of Forensic Entomol, 2000-2002; Chair/Director, Pa Invertebrate Biodiversity Project, 2001-; Pres, Pa Biol Surv, 1996-1999; Sr Fulbright Scholar, South Korea, 1993-1994; DIR, CTR BIODIVERSITY RES, 1989-; Entom Coll. Network, 1989-1990 & Intern. Advisory Council f. Biosystst. Serv.in Entom, 1985-1986; Chair, Sect A, Entom Soc Am, 1985; Chair, Coun Appl Syst., Assn. Systs. Collections, 1982-1985; Chmn, Council f. Systs. & Soc., 1981-1987; PROF ENTOM & CURATOR, FROST ENTOM MUS PA STATE UNIV, UNIVERSITY PARK, 1979-; Visit. Prof, Seoul Nat Univ, 1975 & 1993-1994 & Univ Heidelberg, 1976; Fulbright-Hays \ Lectr & Researcher Award, 1975-1976; Visit. Scientist, Atomic Energy Res Inst, Seoul, 1975-1976; CUR, FROST ENTOM MUS PA STATE UNIV, UNIVERSITY PARK, 1968-; from Asst prof to Assoc prof to Full Prof; Director, Ctr Biodiversity Res, 1968-1979; Res Assoc, Univ Minn, 1967-1968; Nat. Inst. Allergy & Infectious Dis res grants, 1964-; Res Fellow Entom, Univ Minn, 1964-1967; Consult, Smithsonian Inst, 1964-1967. **Memberships:** Sigma Xi (pres, 1992-1995); Entom Soc Am; Entom Soc WA; Soc Syst Biologists; Soc Conserv Biol; Korean Acad Sci & Technol. **Research Statement & Publications:** Biodiversity science, systematics and ecology of sucking lice; ecology and evolution of ectoparasites-mammalian host relationships; forensic entomology; contributed over 150 articles to professional journals; books, 30 book chapters, 14 books authored, co-atuthored or edited. **Mailing Address:** 213 Momingside Circle, State College, PA 16803. **Fax:** 814-865-3048. **E-Mail:** kck@psu.edu

KIM, KENNETH, MICROBIOLOGY. **Personal Data:** b Honolulu, Hawaii, December 24, 1931. **Education:** Univ Hawaii, BA, 1953; Wash Univ, MS, 1960, PhD (microbiol), 1964. **Professional Experience:** ASSOC PROF CLIN PATH, BACT DIV, MED SCH, UNIV ORE, 1980-; asst prof, Bact Div, Med Sch, Univ Ore, 1971-1980; Instr prev med, Univ Wash, 1964-1971. **Memberships:** Am Soc Microbiol; NY Acad Sci. **Research Statement & Publications:** Relationship of diphtheria toxin to the diphtheria phage-bacterium relationship and the mode of action of toxin on cultured cells; biology of Rubella virus. **Mailing Address:** Dept Clin Path Sch Med, Ore Health Sci Univ 3181 SW Sam Jackson Park Rd, Portland, OR 97201-3011.

KIM, KEUN YOUNG, CHEMICAL ENGINEERING, INORGANIC CHEMISTRY. **Personal Data:** b Kaesong, Korea, May 29, 1928; American citizen; m 1958, c 2. **Education:** Seoul Nat Univ, BS, 1951; Univ Wis, MS, 1956, PhD (chem eng), 1959. **Professional Experience:** FEL, DEPT RES & DEVELOP, DETERGENT & PHOSPHATE DIV, MONSANTO INDUST CHEM CO, 1970-; res specialist, Dept Res & Develop, Detergent & Phosphate Div, Monsanto Indust Chem CO, 1966-1970; res chem engr, Dept Res & Develop, Detergent & Phosphate Div, Monsanto Indust Chem CO, 1962-1966; Res investr, Inst Sci Res & Technol, Korea, 1950-1953. **Memberships:** Am Inst Chem Engrs; Am Chem Soc. **Research Statement & Publications:** Phosphates product and process research; calcium phosphates, particularly dentifrices. **Mailing Address:** 237 Ladue Lake Dr, St Louis, MO 63141-7412.

KIM, KI HANG, MATHEMATICS. **Personal Data:** b Mundok, Pyongando, Korea, August 5, 1936; American citizen; m 1963, Myong; c John & Linda. **Education:** Univ Southern Miss, BS, 1960, MS, 1961; George Wash Univ, MP, 1970, PhD (math), 1971. **Professional Experience:** Vis prof math, USSR Acad Sci, 1990-1991; DISTINGUISHED PROF MATH, ALA STATE UNIV, 1988-; assoc ed, Future Generations Comput Systs, beginning 1983 & Pure Math & Applns, beginning 1990; vis prof math, Chinese Acad Sci, 1983-1984; managing ed, Math Social Sci, 1980-1994; vis prof math, Univ Stuttgart, 1978-1979; prof, Ala State Univ, 1974-1987; grants, US Army Res Off, 1972-1976 & NSF, beginning 1983; vis prof math, Portugal Inst Physics & Math, 1971-1974; assoc prof, St Mary's Col, MD, 1968-1970 & Pembroke State Univ, 1970-1973; lectr, George Wash Univ, 1966-1968; instr math, Univ Hartford, 1961-1966. **Memberships:** fel Korean Acad Sci & Technol. **Research Statement & Publications:** Diophantine decidability; symbolic dynamics; decision and game theory; elliptic curves; algebraic varieties; Boolean matrices. **Mailing Address:** Dept Math, Ala State Univ, PO Box 69, Montgomery, AL 36101-0271. **Fax:** 334-229-4982. **E-Mail:** kkim@asunet.alasu.edu

KIM, KI HONG, ANALYTICAL CHEMISTRY. **Personal Data:** b Seoul, Korea, American citizen; m 1968, c 2. **Education:** Ohio State Univ, BS, 1959; Ohio Univ, MS, 1962; George Wash Univ, MPH, 1973, PhD (chem), 1976. **Professional Experience:** CHIEF EXEC OFFICER, SAMSUNG SDS, as of 2001; tech dir electromech, Samsung, beginning 1988; consult, Samsung, beginning 1985; tech adv, Kyocerra Int Inc, San Diego, 1984-1985; mat mgr, Kyocerra Int Inc, San Diego, 1981-1984; mgr metal systs, Emcon Div, 1978-1980; proj leader, Paktron Div, Ill Tool Works Inc, 1973-1978; res chemist, Paktron Div, Ill Tool Works Inc, 1966-1973; Res assoc biochem, Med Ctr, Univ Ky, 1963-1966. **Memberships:** Am Chem Soc; Soc Appl Spectros; Am Ceramic Soc. **Research Statement & Publications:** Spectrophotometric and photopolarographic studies of organometallic compounds; research and development of precious metal powder and electrode ink systems for ceramic chip capacitor. **Mailing Address:** Samsung Sds, 85 W Tasman Dr, San Jose, CA 95134. **Fax:** 408-544-4966.

KIM, KI HWAN, COMPUTER ASSISTED MOLECULAR DESIGN, TWO-DIMENSIONAL & THREE-DIMENSIONAL QUANTITATIVE STRUCTURE-ACTIVITY RELATIONSHIP STUDY. **Personal Data:** b Pyung-Yang, Korea, May 12, 1946; American citizen; m 1970, Esther; c Daniel, Angela & Jane. **Education:** Yonsei Univ, Seoul, Korea, BS, 1969, MS, 1971; Univ Kans, Lawrence, MS, 1976, PhD (med chem), 1981. **Professional Experience:** RES INVESTR, DEPT STRUCT BIOL, ABBOTT LABS, 1980-; res assoc, Chem Dept, Pomona Col, 1976-1980; res & teaching asst, Med Chem Dept, Univ Kans, 1973-1976; res asst, Chem Dept, Pomona Col, 1971-1973; res asst, Yonsei Univ, Seoul, Korea, 1969-1971. **Memberships:** Am Chem Soc; Drug Info Soc; Korean Scientists & Engrs Asn Am; Quant Struct Activ Relationships Soc. **Research Statement & Publications:** Quantitative correlation of chemical structure and biological activity; conformational and quantum chemical calculations; application of computer graphics to drug design; mechanism of action of biologically active compounds; protein modeling and de novo drug design; over 80 research papers published in major scientific journals. **Mailing Address:** Dept Structural Biol, Abbott Labs, D46Y AP10-2 100 Abbott Park Rd, Abbott Park, IL 60064. **Fax:** 847-937-2625. **E-Mail:** ki.h.kim@abbott.com

KIM, KI WOOK, ELECTRONICS. **Education:** Seoul Nat Univ, BS, 1983; Univ Ill, Urbana, MS, 1985 & PhD (Elec Eng), 1988. **Professional Experience:** PROF, DEPT ELEC & COMPUT ENG, NC STATE UNIV, as of 2006; DIR, NANOSCALE QUANTUM ENG GROUP, NC STATE UNIV, as of 2006. **Research Statement & Publications:** Nanoelectronics and photonics including device simulation and modeling; III - V materials and devices; optical materials and photonic devices; silicon devices and fabrication; semiconductor physics and modeling of electronic and optoelectronic devices; carrier transport in heterostructures; low dimensional effects; quantum transport; quantum computing; Monte Carlo simulations; magnetoelectronics; and bioelectronics. **Mailing Address:** Dept Elec & Compu Eng, NC State Univ, 234 D Monteith POBox 7911, Raleigh, NC 27695-7911. **Fax:** 919-515-3027. **E-Mail:** kwk@eos.ncsu.edu

KIM, KI-HAN, BIOCHEMISTRY. **Personal Data:** b Seoul, Korea, June 20, 1932; American citizen; m 1958, Lois; c Thomas, James & Oliver. **Education:** Univ Calif, Berkeley, BA,

1957; Wayne State Univ, PhD (chem), 1961. **Professional Experience:** PROF EMER BIOCHEM, PURDUE UNIV, as of 2004; prof Biochem, Purdue Univ, beginning 1973; from asst prof to assoc prof, Purdue Univ, 1967-1973; res assoc biochem, Wayne State Univ, 1961-1965 & Univ Wis-Madison, 1965-1967. **Memberships:** AAAS; Am Soc Biol Chem. **Research Statement & Publications:** Mechanism of hormone action; biochemical basis of cellular differentiation. **Mailing Address:** Dept Biochem, Purdue Univ, West Lafayette, IN 47907-1968. **Fax:** 765-494-7897. **E-Mail:** khkkim@purdue.edu

KIM, KI-HYON, MEDICAL PHYSICS, NUCLEAR MEDICINE. **Personal Data:** b Ui ju City, Korea, April 20, 1933; m 1965, c 3. **Education:** Seoul Nat Univ, BSc, 1956; Univ Vienna, PhD (nuclear physics), 1963. **Professional Experience:** PROF APPL PHYSICS, NC CENT UNIV, 1972-; consult, Oak Ridge Assoc Univs, beginning 1971; lectr-consult, NASA-Langley Res Ctr, beginning 1968; assoc prof nuclear physics, NC Cent Univ, 1968-1972; resident res assoc, NASA-Langley Res Ctr, 1966-1968; res off, Atomic Energy Res Inst, Seoul, 1963-1966. **Memberships:** Am Phys Soc; Korean Phys Soc; Am Asn Physicists Med; Soc Nuclear Med; Korean Scientists & Engrs Am. **Research Statement & Publications:** Nuclear spectrometry; high-flux pulsed neutron sources; biomedical applications of nuclear electronics; organ visualization by means of radiopharmaceuticals and computer based scanning. **Mailing Address:** Dept Physics, NC Cent Univ, 1805 Fayetteville St, Durham, NC 27707-3129. **E-Mail:** kihyonkim@aol.com

KIM, KI-SOO, POLYMER CHEMISTRY. **Personal Data:** b Korea, November 6, 1942; m 1970, Cecilia Lee; c John, Julie & Peter. **Education:** Seoul Nat Univ, BS, 1965; City Univ New York, PhD (chem), 1972. **Professional Experience:** Adj fac, Mercy Col, 1994-; SCIENTIST, AKZO CHEM, 1988-; res assoc, Eastern Res Ctr, Stauffer Chem Co, 1974-1987; assoc, Res Inst, City Univ New York, 1972-1974; Res asst chem, Atomic Energy Res Inst Korea, 1966-1968. **Memberships:** Am Chem Soc; Korean Chem Soc. **Research Statement & Publications:** Condensation and vinyl polymerization; synthesis of phosphorus and sulfur-containing polymers; engineering plastics; adhesive formulation, materials research for microelectronics, liquid crystalline polymers. **Mailing Address:** 104 Lily Pond Lane, Katonah, NY 10536-1814.

KIM, KWANG SHIN, MEDICAL MICROBIOLOGY, HORTICULTURE. **Personal Data:** b Seoul, Korea, November 15, 1937; American citizen; m 1965, Bu-Choon; c Edwin C & Andrew K. **Education:** Seoul Nat Univ, BS, 1959; Rutgers Univ, NB, MS, 1963, PhD (hort), 1967. **Professional Experience:** Adj prof, Sch Med, Med Ctr, NY Univ, 1998-; ASSOC PROF MICROBIOL, SCH MED, MED CTR, NY UNIV, 1975-; Merck Co Found grantee, 1974-1976; Mellon Found fel, 1973-1974; asst prof, Sch Med, Med Ctr, NY Univ, 1971-1975; from asst res scientist to assoc res scientist microbiol, Sch Med, Med Ctr, NY Univ, 1967-1971; res assoc, Rutgers Univ, NB, 1966-1967; res asst hort, Rutgers Univ, NB, 1965-1966. **Memberships:** AAAS; Am Soc Microbiol; Sigma Xi; NY Acad Sci. **Research Statement & Publications:** Ultrastructure and cytochemistry of bacteria, especially human pathogenes and their interactions with the host cells using immunoelectron-microscopy. **Mailing Address:** Dept Microbiol, NY Univ Sch Med, New York, NY 10016.

KIM, KWANG-HAE, COMPUTER ENGINEERING. **Education:** Seoul Nat Univ, Korea, BS, 1969; Univ Tex, Austin, MA, 1972; Univ Calif, Berkeley, PhD (Comput sci), 1972. **Professional Experience:** PROF, DEPT ELEC ENG & COMPUT SCI, UNIV CALIF, IRVINE, as of 2006. **Research Statement & Publications:** Real-time object-based software and system engineering; and ultra-reliable distributed and parallel computing. **Mailing Address:** Dept Elect Eng & Computer Sci, Univ Calif-Irvine, Irvine, CA 92697-2625. **Fax:** 949-824-2321. **E-Mail:** khkim@uci.edu

KIM, KWANG-JE, PHYSICS. **Education:** Univ Md, PhD (physics), 1970. **Professional Experience:** PROF, DEPT PHYSICS, UNIV CHICAGO & ASSOC DIV DIR, ACCELERATOR SYSTS DIV/ADVAN PHOTON SOURCE, ARGONNE NAT LAB, as of 2005. **Mailing Address:** Argonne Nat Lab, Clayton, CA 94517. **Fax:** 630-252-7369. **E-Mail:** kwangje@aps.anl.gov

KIM, KWANG-JIN, ELECTROPHYSIOLOGY OF EPITHELIUM, PULMONARY DRUG DELIVERY. **Personal Data:** b Hamyang, Korea, March 22, 1949; m 1972, Soon-Ja; c Min-Soo & Shirley. **Education:** Seoul Nat Univ, BSEE, 1971, MSEE, 1973; Univ Pa, PhD (bioeng), 1980. **Professional Experience:** ASSOC PROF, UNIV SOUTHERN CALIF, 1991-; prin investr, Am Lung Asn, 1989-1992; asst prof, Cornell Univ Med Col, 1986-1990; prin investr, Nat Heart Lung & Blood Inst, 1985-1988; prin investr, NIH, 1984-1994; asst res physiologist, Univ Calif, Los Angeles, 1982-1986; prin investr, Am Heart Asn, 1980-1985; fel, Univ Calif, Los Angeles, 1980-1982; res fel, Univ Pa, 1976-1980; Lectr electroncs, Korea Mil Acad, 1973-1976. **Memberships:** Biomed Soc; NY Acad Sci; Asn Res Vision & Ophthal; AAAS. **Research Statement & Publications:** Study of the alveolar epithelial barrier properties in health and disease; mechanisms of injury and recovery of epithelial barrier. **Mailing Address:** Univ Southern Calif Med Sch, 2011 Zonla Ave HMR914, Los Angeles, CA 90033. **Fax:** 213-342-2611. **E-Mail:** kjkins@hsc.usc.edu

KIM, KYEKYOON K(EVIN), COMPOUND SEMICONDUCTOR MICROELECTRONICS, ELECTROHYDRODYNAMIC SPRAYING. **Personal Data:** b Seoul, Korea, October 5, 1941; American citizen; m 1969, c 2. **Education:** Seoul Nat Univ, BS, 1966; Cornell Univ, MS, 1968, PhD (appl physics), 1971. **Professional Experience:** ADJ PROF NUCLEAR ENG, UNIV ILL, as of 2005; Argonne Nat Lab, 1986-; Lab Laser Energetics, Univ Rochester, 1986-; PROF ELEC & COMPUT ENG, MECH & INDUST ENG & NUCLEAR ENG MAT SCI & ENG, UNIV ILL, 1985-; chmn, Comt Fueling Plasma Devices, Am Vacuum Soc, 1981-1986; Consult, Elec Power Res Inst, 1981-1986; Consult, NASA, 1980-1986; Consult, Y Div, Lawrence Livermore Lab, 1978-; from asst prof to assoc prof, Univ Ill, 1976-1985; fel elec eng, Univ Ill, 1974-1976; fel phys chem, Univ Ill, 1972-1974; fel appl physics, Cornell Univ, 1971-1972; res asst nuclear sci & appl physics, Cornell Univ, 1966-1971. **Memberships:** Am Phys Soc; Inst Elec & Electronics Engrs; Am Vacuum Soc. **Research Statement & Publications:** Fusion technology; plasma engineering; cryogenic laser fusion targets; lectrohydrodynamics; monodispersed micro-particle generation from insulators; polymers and metals; compound semiconductor microelectronics. **Mailing Address:** Dept Elec & Comput Eng, Univ Ill, 1406 W Green St 45 William L Everitt Lab, Urbana, IL 61801. **Fax:** 217-333-2906. **E-Mail:** kevinkim@uiuc.edu

KIM, KYUNG SOO, PLANT CELL VIRUS INTERACTION, VIRUS-INDUCED INCLUSION. **Personal Data:** b Seoul, Korea, June 6, 1933. **Education:** BS, Kyungpook Nat Univ, 1957; MS, Univ Ark, 1963; Univ Ark, PhD (plant path), 1971. **Professional Experience:** UNIV PROF PLANT PATH, UNIV ARK, 1993-; prof plant path, Univ Ark, 1982-1993. **Research Statement & Publications:** Plant pathology; electron microscopy. **Mailing Address:** Dept Plant Pathol Plant Sci Bldg No 217, Univ Ark, Fayetteville, AR 72701. **Fax:** 501-575-3348. **E-Mail:** kskim@comp.uark.edu

KIM, KYUNGHA HYDE, PHYSICS. **Professional Experience:** PROF PHYS, UNIV WASH, as of 1995. **Memberships:** fel Am Phys Soc. **Mailing Address:** Univ Wash, 7021 Sand Point Way NE, Seattle, WA 98115. **Fax:** 206-685-4258.

KIM, MAHN WON, PHYSICS. **Education:** Seoul Nat Univ, BA, 1969; Univ Calif, MA, 1972; Univ Calif, PhD, 1975. **Professional Experience:** PROF, DEPT PHYSICS, KAIST, 1996-. **Mailing Address:** Exxon Res & Engr Co, Clinton Township Rte 22 E, Annandale, NJ 08801. **Fax:** 242-869-2510. **E-Mail:** mwkim@kaist.ac.kr

KIM, MATTHEW HIDONG, COMPOUND SEMICONDUCTOR HETEROJUNCTION ELECTRONIC DEVICES, VERTICAL CAVITY SURFACE EMITTING LASERS. **Personal Data:** b Seoul, Korea, September 21, 1958. **Education:** Cornell Univ, BS, 1980; Univ Ill, MS, 1981, PhD (physics), 1988. **Professional Experience:** SCIENTIST, MOTOROLA, 1994-; device scientist, Bandgap Technol, 1989-1993. **Memberships:** Am Phys Soc; NY Acad Sci. **Research Statement & Publications:** Electronic and opto-electronic properties of hetero-junction compound semiconductors. **Mailing Address:** Motorola Phoenix Corp Res Lab, MD-EL703 2100 E Elliot Rd, Tempe, AZ 85284.

KIM, MEUNG J, MECHANICAL ENGINEERING. **Education:** Seoul Nat Univ, BS, 1977; Univ Okla, MS, 1980; PHD, Va Polytechnic Inst & State Univ, PhD, 1985. **Professional Experience:** ASSC PROF, DEPT MECH ENG, NORTHERN ILL UNIV, 1985. **Mailing Address:** Northern Ill Univ, Mech Eng EB 112, DeKalb, IL 60115. **Fax:** 815-753-0416. **E-Mail:** kim@ceet.niu.edu

KIM, MI JA, PHYSIOLOGY, NURSING. **Education:** Univ Ill, PhD (physiol), 1975. **Professional Experience:** PROF & DEAN EMER, COL NURSING, UNIV ILL, as of 2004; DIR, ACAD INT LEADERSHIP DEVELOP, UNIV ILL, as of 2004; vice chancellor res, Univ Ill, Chicago, beginning 1995; prof med surg nursing & dean, Col Nursing, 1978-1995. **Memberships:** Fel Am Acad Nursing. **Research Statement & Publications:** Respiratory muscle training. **Mailing Address:** Univ Ill, 1737 W Polk M/C 672, Chicago, IL 60612-7227. **E-Mail:** mjkuic@uic.edu

KIM, MINBO, MATHEMATICS. **Professional Experience:** STAFF, SAS INST INC, NC, as of 2004. **Memberships:** Am Statist Asn. **Mailing Address:** SAS Inst, SAS Campus Dr, Cary, NC 27513. **Fax:** 919-677-4444.

KIM, MOON W, MATHEMATICAL ANALYSIS. **Personal Data:** b Seoul, Korea. **Education:** Univ NH, BA, 1964; Polytech Inst Brooklyn, MS, 1968, PhD (math), 1969. **Professional Experience:** ASSOC PROF, SETON HALL UNIV, 1969-; instr, Polytech Inst Brooklyn, 1967-1969; teaching fel math, Polytech Inst Brooklyn, 1966-1967. **Memberships:** Am Math Soc; Math Asn Am. **Research Statement & Publications:** Functional analysis; fixed points theorems in non-linear analysis; analytic sets in Banach spaces. **Mailing Address:** Dept Math, Seton Hall Univ, 400 S Orange Ave, South Orange, NJ 07079. **Fax:** 973-275-2366. **E-Mail:** kimmoon@shu.edu

KIM, PETER S, BIOCHEMISTRY. **Personal Data:** b Atlanta, Ga, April 27, 1958; m Kathryn; c Michael, Jeremy & Alexander. **Education:** Cornell Univ, BA, 1979; Stanford Univ, PhD (biochem), 1985. **Honors & Awards:** Excellence Chem Award, ICI Pharmaceut Group, 1989; Walter J Johnson Prize Molecular Biol, J Molecular Biol, 1989; Nat Acad Sci Award Molecular Biol, Nat Acad Sci, 1993; Eli Lilly Award Biol Chem, Am Chem Soc, 1994; Du Pont Merck Young Investr Award, Protein Soc, 1994; Hans Neurath Award The Protein Soc, 1999; Ho-Am Prize Basic Sci, Samsung Found, 1998; Eli Lilly Biol Chemistry Award, Am Chem Soc, 1994; Dupont Merck Young Investr Award, Protein Soc, 1994; Molecular Biology Award, Nat Acad Sci, 1990. **Professional Experience:** PRES, RES & DEVELOP, MERCK RES LABS, W POINT, PA, 2001-; investr, 1997-2001; assoc investr, 1993-1997; mem, Whitehead Inst, 1992-2001; prof biol, Mass Inst Technol, 1995-2001; assoc investr, Howard Hughes Med Inst, 1993-1997; asst investr, Howard Hughes Med Inst, 1990-1993; from asst prof to assoc prof, MIT, 1988-1995; assoc mem, Whitehead Inst Biomed Res, 1988-1992; Whitehead fel, Whitehead Inst Biomed Res, 1985-1988. **Memberships:** Nat Acad Sci. **Research Statement & Publications:** Structural biology and physical biochemistry; mechanisms of protein folding, macromolecular recognition and protein-induced membrane fusion; peptide design and protein engineering; published over 80 publications. **Mailing Address:** Merck Research Laboratories, 770 Sumneytown Pike, W Point, PA 19486. **Fax:** 617-258-5737. **E-Mail:** kimadmin@wi.mit.edu

KIM, RHYN H(YUN), MECHANICAL & CHEMICAL ENGINEERING. **Personal Data:** b Seoul, Korea, February 4, 1936; m 1966, c 3. **Education:** Seoul Nat Univ, BSME, 1958; Mich State Univ, MS, 1961, PhD (mech eng), 1965. **Professional Experience:** PROF EMER, COL ENG, UNIV NC, CHARLOTTE, as of 2005; bd mem, NC State Bd Examiners, Plumbing, Heating & Sprinkler's Contractors, 1988-1991; consult, Duke Power Co, NC, Westinghouse Steam Turbine Plant & Teledyne Allvac, 1980; prof, Col Eng, Univ NC, Charlotte, beginning 1978; consult, Indust Environ Res Lab, Off Res & Develop, Environ Protection Agency, 1978-; mech engr, Indust Environ Res Lab, Off Res & Develop, 1977-1978; staff engr, Off Air Qual Planning & Stand, Environ Protection Agency, 1976-1977; assoc prof mech eng, Univ NC, Charlotte, 1965-1976. **Memberships:** Am Soc Mech Engrs; Am Soc Heating Refrig & Air-Conditioning Engrs; Instrument Soc Am. **Research Statement & Publications:** Combustion, energy conservation and utilization; environmental emission controls; mass transfer in porous media; thermal system optimization and simulations; computer aided heat exchanger design; flow phenomenon visualization; computational fluid mechanics. **Mailing Address:** Dept Mach Eng & Eng Sci, Univ NC, Charlotte, NC 28223. **Fax:** 704-547-2352.

KIM, SANG HYUNG, PHOTOGRAPHIC SCIENCE ENGINEERING, INTERFACIAL SCIENCE. **Personal Data:** b Kyunggi, Korea, October 18, 1942; m 1968, c 2. **Education:** Seoul Nat Univ, BS, 1964; Univ Utah, PhD (phys chem), 1971. **Professional Experience:** RES ASSOC RES DEVELOP, RES LABS, EASTMAN KODAK CO, 1986-; sr res chemist, Res Labs, Eastman Kodak CO, 1979-1985; res chemist, Res Labs, Eastman Kodak CO, 1974-1978; fel membrane biophys, Northwestern Univ, 1971-1974; fel electrochem, Univ Pa, 1970-1971; res asst, Univ Utah, 1967-1970; Asst teaching & res, Seoul Nat Univ, 1966-1967. **Memberships:** Am Chem Soc; Soc Imaging Sci Tech. **Research Statement & Publications:** Ion-selective electrodes; solution and interfacial electrochemistry; membrane biophysics; electrochemistry applied to biological and medical sciences; emulsion and polymer coatings; photographic sciences. **Mailing Address:** 19 Sutton Pt, Pittsford, NY 14534-1729.

KIM, SANG SOO, CIVIL ENGINEERING MATERIALS, TRANSPORTATION ENGINEERING. **Personal Data:** b Chungsan, Chungbuk, Korea, November 28, 1961; m 1986, Hyunsun; c Dennis & Elliot. **Education:** Hanyang Univ, Korea, BS, 1984; Iowa State Univ, MS, 1988, PhD (civil eng), 1994. **Professional Experience:** ASST PROF, CIVIL ENG, OHIO UNIV, as of 2005; res engr, Western Res Inst, beginning 1992; scientist, Western Res Inst, 1991-1992; res asst, Iowa State Univ, 1985-1990. **Memberships:** Asn Asphalt Paving Technologist; Am Soc Civil Engrs. **Research Statement & Publications:** Characterizing asphalt properties for better use in highway construction; identifying chemical properties of asphalt which influence physical and engineering properties of asphalt. **Mailing Address:** Civil Eng Dep, Ohio Univ, 137 Stocker Ctr, Athens, OH 45701. **Fax:** 740-593-0625. **E-Mail:** skim@bobcat.ent.ohiou.edu

KIM, SANGDUK, ENZYMOLOGY, NEUROCHEMISTRY. **Personal Data:** b Seoul, Korea, June 15, 1930; American citizen; m 1959, c 3. **Education:** Korea Univ Med Col, MD, 1953; Univ Wis, PhD (biochem), 1959. **Professional Experience:** PROF BIOCHEM, FELS RES INST, SCH MED, TEMPLE UNIV, 1990-; assoc prof, Fels Res Inst, Sch Med, Temple Univ, 1978-1990; res assoc biochem, Fels Res Inst, Sch Med, Temple Univ, 1965-1978; res assoc biochem, Univ Ottawa, 1962-1965; res assoc physiol chem, Univ Wis, 1959-1961. **Memberships:** Am Soc Biol Chemist; Am Asn Cancer Res; Am Soc Neurochemistry; Am Chem Soc. **Research Statement & Publications:** Biochemistry of protein methylation; enzymatic modification of protein molecule, biology of myelination. **Mailing Address:** Fels Res Inst, Temple Univ Sch Med, Philadelphia, PA 19140.

KIM, SANGTAE, COMPUTER SCIENCE. **Personal Data:** b Seoul, Korea, August 2, 1958; American citizen; c 2. **Education:** Calif Inst Technol, BS, 1979, MS, 1979; Princeton Univ, PhD, 1983. **Honors & Awards:** Allan P Colburn Mem lectr, Univ Del, 1989; Robert W Vaughan lectr, Calif Inst Technol, 1991; Plenary lectr, Korean Inst Chem Engrs, 1991; Award Initiatives Res, Nat Acad Sci, 1992; Allan P Colburn Award, Am Inst Chem Engrs, 1993. **Professional Experience:** VPRES & INFO OFFICER, LILLY RES LABS, as of 1999; ADJ PROF, DEPT CHEM & BIOL ENG, UNIV WIS-MADISON, as of 1999; prin invester, Off Naval Res, 1993-; prin invester, NSF, 1993-; prin invester, Am Chem Soc, 1992-; prof comput sci & distinguished prof chem eng, Univ Wis-Madison, beginning 1991; vis prof, Pohang Inst Sci Tech, Korea, 1991; romnes fac fel, Univ Wis, 1990; distinguished vis scholar, Univ Mass, Amherst, 1989; George A Miller vis scholar, Univ Ill, Urbana-Champaign, 1987; pres young investr award, Nat Acad Sci, 1985; from asst prof to prof, Univ Wis-Madison, 1983-1990; consult, Amoco Oil Corp, Ill, 1983; process engr, Intel Corp, Santa Clara, Calif. **Research Statement & Publications:** Dynamics of particulate suspensions; protein dynamics and simulations; computational methods on high performance computers; author of 1 publication. **Mailing Address:** Lilly Res Labs, Indianapolis, IN 46285. **Fax:** 317-276-4127. **E-Mail:** kim_sangtae@lilly.com

KIM, SEUNG U, NEUROPATHOLOGY, NEUROBIOLOGY. **Personal Data:** b Osaka, Japan, October 28, 1936; American citizen; m 1962, c 2. **Education:** Univ Seoul, Korea, MD, 1960; Kyoto Univ, Japan, PhD (neurobiol), 1965. **Professional Experience:** PROF EMER NEUROL, UNIV BC, as of 2006; prof neurol, Univ Hosp, Vancouver, beginning 1981; from asst prof to assoc prof neuropath, Univ Hosp, Vancouver, 1972-1981; assoc prof neurobiology, Univ Sask, Saskatoon, 1970-1972; Multiple Sclerosis Soc fel, Col Physicians & Surgeons, Columbia Univ, 1966-1969. **Memberships:** Tissue Cult Asn; Am Asn Neuropathologists; Histochem Soc; Soc Neuroscience; Am Soc Cell Biol. **Research Statement & Publications:** Experimental neurology; neural tissue culture. **Mailing Address:** Univ Hosp, 2211 Wesbrook Mall, Vancouver, BC V6T 2B5, Can. **Fax:** 604-822-7897. **E-Mail:** sukim@interchange.ubc.ca

KIM, SHOON KYUNG, theoretical chemistry; deceased, see previous edition for last biography

KIM, SOO MYUNG, SOLID STATE PHYSICS. **Personal Data:** b Chaeryung, Korea, October 24, 1936; m 1970, c 1. **Education:** Seoul Nat Univ, BS, 1959; Univ NC, Chapel Hill, PhD (physics), 1968. **Professional Experience:** RES OFFICER, ATOMIC ENERGY CAN RES CO, CHALK RIVER, 1985-; assoc res officer, Atomic Energy Can Res CO, Chalk River, 1977-1984; asst res officer, Atomic Energy Can Res CO, Chalk River, 1972-1976; Nat Res Coun fel neutron physics br, Atomic Energy Can Res CO, Chalk River, 1970-1972; fel dept physics, Univ Guelph, 1968-1970; Res assoc physics, Univ NC, Chapel Hill, 1967-1968. **Memberships:** Am Phys Soc; Can Asn Physicists; Asn Korean Scientists & Engrs Am. **Research Statement & Publications:** Positron annihilation in metals; defects in metals. **Mailing Address:** Neutron & Mat Sci Br, Atomic Energy Can Res Co, Chalk River, ON K0J 1J0, Can.

KIM, SOOJA K, Dietetics, Gerontology, Epidemiology. **Personal Data:** b Seoul, Korea, American citizen. **Education:** Humboldt State Univ, BS, 1967; Tex Woman's Univ, MS, 1973, PhD (Nutritional Science & Biochemistry), 1975. **Honors & Awards:** Excellent Faculty Award from Bowling Green State Univ, 1982; NIH Director's Awards, NIH Merit Awards, 1995, 1999, 2002. **Professional Experience:** CHIEF, Endocrinology, Metabolism, Nutrition & Reproductive Sciences IRG, CSR, NIH, as of 1998; Health Scientist Administrator of Nutrition and Metabolism; Prog director in Nutrition, National Institute on Aging; Inst Aging, 1985-1986; Assist, Associate, and Professor of Nutrition, Bowling Green State Univ, Ohio, 1977-19879; Adjunct Res. Prof, Med Col Ohio, Toledo, 1980-1987; Nutrit consult, Med Col Ohio, Toledo, Asst prof nutrit & food sci, Ga Col, 1975-1977. **Memberships:** Am Soci for Nutri Sci., Am Dietetic Asn. **Research Statement & Publications:** Dietary energy consumption in relation to longevity and health; age related metabolic changes during trauma and illness; nutritional status of elderly. **Mailing Address:** Ctr for Sci Review, NIH, 6701 Rockledge Dr, Rm 6182, MSC 7892, Bethesda, MD 20892-7892. **Fax:** 301-402-2065. **E-Mail:** kims@csr.nih.gov

KIM, SOON-KYU, MATHEMATICS. **Personal Data:** b Hadong, Korea, October 3, 1932; m 1959, Kang-Un; c Jin-Chul, Jin-Kyung & Jin-Wook. **Education:** Seoul Nat Univ, BS, 1957, MS, 1959; Univ Mich, PhD (math), 1967. **Professional Experience:** PROF EMER MATH, UNIV CONN, as of 1999; Vis prof, Pohang Univ Sci & Technol, 1994; hon prof, Yanbian Univ, Jilin, People's Repub China, 1992; DEPT HEAD, UNIV CONN, 1988-; assoc dept head, Univ Conn, 1985-1988; prof math, Univ Conn, beginning 1983; vis lectr, Seoul Nat Univ, Korea, 1983; Vis assoc prof, Mich State Univ, 1975-1976; from asst prof to assoc prof, Univ Conn, 1969-1983; instr, Univ Ill, Urbana, 1966-1969; instr math, Seoul Univ & Kunkook Univ, 1959-1962. **Memberships:** Am Math Soc; Korean Math Soc; Korean Scientists & Engrs Asn Am (vpres, 1984, pres, 1987). **Research Statement & Publications:** Fiberings and transformation groups; fixed point theory; infinite dimensional topology. **Mailing Address:** Dept Math, Univ Conn, Storrs, CT 06269. **Fax:** 860-486-4238. **E-Mail:** kim@math.uconn.edu

KIM, STUART, GENETICS. **Education:** Dartmouth Col, BA, 1979; Calif Inst Technol, PhD (molecular biol). **Professional Experience:** HEAD SECT PATTERN FORMATION, STANFORD UNIV, as of 2005; PROF DEVELOP BIOL, STANFORD UNIV SCH MED, as of 2005. **Mailing Address:** Dept Develop Biol Stanford Univ Sch Med, Beckman Ctr Rm B300, Stanford, CA 94305. **Fax:** 650-725-7739. **E-Mail:** kim@cmgm.stanford.edu

KIM, SUKYOUNG, BIOMATERIALS-BIOCERAMICS, STRUCTURAL CERAMICS. **Personal Data:** b Korea, June 7, 1954; m 1982, c 2. **Education:** Inha Univ, Korea, BS, 1980; Seoul Nat Univ, Korea, MS, 1982; Alfred Univ, NY, MS, 1985; Univ Vt, PhD (mat sci), 1990. **Professional Experience:** RES ASSOC, CTR BIOMAT, UNIV TORONTO, 1991-; res asst mos devices, res assoc DLC coating & wear study, 1990-1991; NSF grant, 1987; aluminatool wear, Univ Vt, 1986-1990; Libr asst, Cook Sci Libr, Univ Vt, 1986; res asst mos devices, Univ Vt, 1985-1986; crystal structure anal, Alfred Univ, 1983-1985; Res asst diezoelec ceramic, Seoul Nat Univ, Korea, 1980-1982. **Memberships:** Am Ceramic Asn; Am Crystallog Asn; Electron Micros Soc Am. **Research Statement & Publications:** Development of load bearing materials for dentals & orthopaedics; development of totally biodegradable biomaterial for internal fracture fixation devices; surface coating/modification of mental implants; development of structural ceramics; author of various publications. **Mailing Address:** Univ Toronto Ctr Biomat, 170 College St, Toronto, ON M5S 1A1, Can. **Fax:** 416-978-1462.

KIM, SUNG KYU, THEORETICAL PHYSICS. **Personal Data:** b Chulla Namdo, Korea, January 12, 1939; m 1968, Sherry; c Robert, Jennifer, Alicia & Alexander. **Education:** Davidson Col, BS, 1960; Duke Univ, AM, 1964, PhD (physics), 1965. **Professional Experience:** Astron & Astrophys, Univ Chicago, 1994-1995; PROF PHYSICS, MACALESTER COL, as of 1991; Astron & Astrophys, Univ Chicago, 1987-1988; vis scholar, Fermi Inst, Univ Chicago, 1980-1981; asst prof, Univ Calif, Irvine, 1970-1971; master teacher, Twin City Inst Talented Youth, 1968-1969; from asst prof to assoc prof, Macalester Col, 1965-1975. **Memberships:** Am Phys Soc; Am Asn Physics Teachers. **Research Statement & Publications:** Cosmology; astrophysics. **Mailing Address:** 1 Sparrow Lane, St Paul, MN 55127.

KIM, SUNG WAN, BIOMATERIALS, PHARMACEUTICS. **Personal Data:** b Pusan, Korea, August 21, 1940; m 1966, c 2. **Education:** Seoul Nat Univ, BS, 1963, MS, 1965; Univ Utah, PhD, 1969. **Professional Experience:** DISTINGUISHED PROF, DEPT BIOENGINEERING, PHARMACEUT, PHARMACEUT CHEM, UNIV UTAH, as of 2006; prof pharmaceut, Col Pharm, Univ Utah, beginning 1980; NIH res career develop award, 1977-1981; from asst prof to assoc prof pharmaceut, Univ Utah, 1973-1980; asst res prof mat sci & eng, Univ Utah, 1970-1973; res assoc mat sci, Univ Utah, 1969-1970; fel, Univ Utah, 1969; res asst chem, Univ Utah, 1966-1969; res asst, Seoul Nat Univ, 1963-1965. **Memberships:** AAAS; Am Chem Soc; Korean Chem Soc; Am Soc Artificial Internal Organs; Am Pharm Asn. **Research Statement & Publications:** Blood compatible polymers; membrane diffusion; interface induced thrombosis; polymeric drug delivery system. **Mailing Address:** Col Pharm, Univ Utah, 205A Bio-Polymer, Salt Lake City, UT 81412. **Fax:** 801-581-7848.

KIM, SUNG-HOU, BIOPHYSICAL CHEMISTRY, STRUCTURAL MOLECULAR BIOLOGY. **Personal Data:** b Taegu, Korea, December 12, 1937; American citizen; m 1968, c 2. **Education:** Seoul Nat Univ, Korea, BS, 1960, MS, 1962; Univ Pittsburgh, PhD (phys chem), 1966. **Honors & Awards:** Pres Serv Merit Award, Repub Korea, 1985; Ernest O Lawrence Award, Dept Energy, 1987; Javits Neuroscience Investr Award, Dept Health & Human Servs, 1988; Princess Takamatsu Award, Princess Takamatsu Cancer Found, Tokyo, Japan, 1989. **Professional Experience:** Mem, US Nat Comt Crystallog, Nat Res Coun, Nat Acad Sci, 1990-; chmn, Adv Comt, Ctr Korean Studies, Inst EAsian Studies, Univ Calif, Berkeley, 1989-; DIR, STRUCT BIOL LAB, LAWRENCE BERKELEY NAT LAB, 1989-; coun mem, Korean Scientists & Engrs Asn Am, 1988-; vis prof, Univ Paris, France, 1986; Guggenheim fel, NY, 1985-1986; mem, Sci Planning Comt, Nat Found Cancer Res, 1983-; ed bd, Nucleic Acids Res, 1983-; Miller res prof, Univ Calif, Berkleley, 1983-1984; exchange prof, Peking Univ, Peking, China, 1982; Lansdowne scholar, Univ Victoria, Can, 1980; FAC SR SCIENTIST, LAWRENCE BERKELEY NAT LAB, BERKELEY, 1979-; ed bd, J Biol Chemistry, 1979-1983; PROF, DEPT CHEM, UNIV CALIF, BERKELEY, 1978-; biophys, NIH consult, 1976-1980; assoc prof, Sch Med, Duke Univ, 1973-1978; asst prof biochem, Sch Med, Duke Univ, 1972-1973; sr res scientist, Mass Inst Tech, 1970-1972; biophys, Dept Biol, Mass Inst Technol, Cambridge, Mass, 1966-1970; res assoc biol, Mass Inst Tech, 1966-1970; Fulbright fel, Fulbright Found, 1962. **Memberships:** Nat Acad Sci; Am Crystallog Asn; Am Chem Soc; AAAS; Korean Scientists & Engrs Am; Biophys Soc; Protein Soc; Am Soc Biochem & Molecular Biol. **Research Statement & Publications:** Structure and function of DNA, RNA and proteins; reviewer for several scientific journals. **Mailing Address:** Dept Chem, Univ Calif, 220 Melvin Calvin Lab, Berkeley, CA 94720-1460. **Fax:** 510-486-5272. **E-Mail:** shkim@lbl.gov

KIM, SUN-KEE, CELL BIOLOGY, ANATOMY. **Personal Data:** b Seoul, Korea, December 11, 1937; American citizen; m 1963, c 2. **Education:** Yon-sei Univ, Korea, BS, 1960; Univ Rochester, MS, 1964, PhD (biol), 1970. **Professional Experience:** ASSOC PROF ANAT & CELL BIOL, UNIV ROCHESTER, as of 2003; Adj assoc prof oral biol, Sch Dent, 1982-; assoc prof, Sch Med, Univ Mich, 1981-; proj dir aging studies salivary gland, Nat Inst Aging, NIH, 1978-1982, 1987-; asst prof anat & cell biol, Sch Med, Univ Mich, 1974-1981; COORDR ELECTRON MICROS, RES SERV, 1973-; Co-dir, Advan Spec Training Dent Res, Vet Admin Med Ctr, 1970- 1975; res assoc anat, Sch Med, Univ Mich, 1970-1974; RES BIOLOGIST, VET ADMIN MED CTR, 1968-; pre-doctoral trainee, NIH, 1965-1968; Asst cancer res scientist endocrinol, Rosewell Park Mem Inst, Buffalo, 1964-1965. **Memberships:** Am Soc Cell Biol; Am Asn Anatomists; Int Asn Dent Res; AAAS; Sigma Xi. **Research Statement & Publications:** Age-related changes in secretory function of exocrine glands; ultrastructure and protein synthesis in secretory cells of the salivary gland. **Mailing Address:** Res Serv Vet Admin Med Ctr, 2215 Fuller Rd, Ann Arbor, MI 48105-2300. **Fax:** 734-761-7693.

KIM, THOMAS JOON-MOCK, MECHANICAL ENGINEERING, APPLIED MECHANICS. **Personal Data:** b Seoul, Korea, October 13, 1936; American citizen; m 1967, c 2. **Education:** Seoul Nat Univ, BS, 1959; Villanova Univ, MS, 1964; Univ Ill, PhD (mech), 1967. **Honors & Awards:** Advan Technol Award, Am Waterjet Soc, 1995. **Professional Experience:** VINCENT AND ESTELLE MURPHY PROF MECH ENG & APPL MECH & DIR NUWC STUD SERV CTR, UNIV RI, as of 2006; dean eng, Univ RI, 1991-2002; dir, Waterjet Res Lab Univ RI, 1984-1999; chmn mech eng, Univ RI, 1979-1991; consult, US Naval Underwater Systs Ctr, 1977-1984; from asst prof to prof, Univ RI, 1968-1991; asst prof math, Villanova Univ, 1967-1968; instr mech, Univ Ill, 1965-1967. **Memberships:** Am Soc Mech Engrs; Am Ceramic Soc; Soc Mfg Engrs; Am Water Jet Technol Asn; Int Soc Water Jet Technol. **Research Statement & Publications:** Solid mechanics; ceramic processing; dynamic face seals; water jet machining. **Mailing Address:** Dept Mech Eng & Appl Mech, Univ RI, 105 Wales Hall, Kingston, RI 02881. **Fax:** 401-874-4182. **E-Mail:** tomkim3@egr.uri.edu

KIM, UNTAE, CANCER RESEARCH, TUMOR IMMUNOLOGY. **Personal Data:** b December 16, 1926. **Education:** Seoul Univ, Korea, MD, 1952. **Professional Experience:** HEAD PATH RES, ROSWELL PARK MEM INST, 1963-. **Memberships:** Am Asn Pathologists; Am Asn Immunologists; Am Asn Cancer Res; NY Acad Sci; Int Soc Differentiation; Int Soc Metastasis Res; Int Asn Breast Cancer Res. **Research Statement & Publications:** Breast cancer research on carcinogenesis and evolution of neoplastic state; hormone dependency, immunology of tumor cells and acquisition of metastatic potential and its patterns; interaction between tumor and lymphoid cells. **Mailing Address:** Res Path, 4720 Main St, Snyder, NY 14226. **Fax:** 716-845-8017.

KIM, WON, DATABASE & DISTRIBUTED SYSTEMS. **Personal Data:** b Korea, 1948. **Education:** Mass Inst Technol, BS & MS, 1971; Univ Ill, Urbana-Champaign, PhD (computer sci), 1980. **Professional Experience:** FOUNDER & CHIEF EXEC OFFICER, CYBER DATABASE SOLUTIONS, as of 2005; pres, Unisql Inc, beginning 1990; CHMN, SPEC INTEREST GROUP MGT DATA, ASN COMPUT MACH, 1989-; dir, Object-Oriented

Distrib Syst Lab, 1987-1990; prin scientist, MCC, 1984-1990. **Memberships:** Asn Comput Mach. **Mailing Address:** Cyber Database Solutions, 3445 Exec Ctr Dr, Austin, TX 78731. **Fax:** 512-329-0244. **E-Mail:** won.kimacm.org

KIM, WOO JONG, MATHEMATICS. **Personal Data:** b Seoul, Korea, January 15, 1937. **Education:** Seoul Nat Univ, BS, 1958; Okla State Univ, MS, 1960; Carnegie-Mellon Univ, MS & PhD (chem eng), 1964, PhD (math), 1968. **Professional Experience:** PROF APPL MATH & STATIST, STATE UNIV NY, STONY BROOK, 1985-; from asst prof to assoc prof appl math, State Univ NY, Stony Brook, 1968-1984. **Memberships:** Am Math Soc. **Research Statement & Publications:** Disconjugacy, oscillation and asymptotic behavior of ordinary differential equations. **Mailing Address:** Dept Math Educ & Statist, Chungbak Nat Univ, Cheongiu Chungbak, 360-763, Korea.

KIM, YEE SIK, BIOCHEMISTRY, PHARMACOLOGY. **Personal Data:** b Seoul, Korea, April 15, 1928; American citizen; m 1950, Young; c Karl, Ruth, Grace & Elizabeth. **Education:** Kans State Univ, BS, 1957, MS, 1960; St Louis Univ, PhD (pharmacol), 1965. **Professional Experience:** PROF PHARMACOL & PHYSIOL SCI, ST LOUIS UNIV, 1976-; USPHS res grant, 1967-; gen res support grant & Cancer Inst res grant, 1966-; from asst prof to prof, St Louis Univ, 1966-1976; USPHS fel biochem, State Univ NY Buffalo, 1965-1966; res chemist, Union Starch & Refining Co, Ill, 1960-1963; Instr chem, Kans State Univ, 1960. **Memberships:** AAAS; Am Soc Pharmacol & Exp Therapeut; Am Chem Soc; NY Acad Sci. **Research Statement & Publications:** Molecular mechanism of hormone action; enzyme reaction mechanisms; metabolisms of macromolecules; diabetic pregnancy; mechanisms of vitamin D metabolites. **Mailing Address:** Dept Pharmacol & Physiol Sci, Sch Med, St Louis Univ, 1402 S Grand Blvd, St Louis, MO 63104. **Fax:** 314-977-6410. **E-Mail:** kimyee@slu.edu

KIM, YEONG ELL, THEORETICAL NUCLEAR PHYSICS. **Personal Data:** b South Korea, American citizen; m 1961, c 2. **Education:** Lincoln Mem Univ, BS, 1959; Univ Calif, Berkeley, PhD, 1963. **Honors & Awards:** US Sr Scientist Humboldt Award, 1977. **Professional Experience:** DIR, CTR SENSING SCI & TECHNOL, beginning 2001; RES DIR, PHYSICAL SCI, PURDUE RES FOUNDATION, beginning 2001; DIR, INTEGRATED DETCTION HAZARDOUS MAT PROG, beginning 2000; dir, Div Sponsored Prog Develop, Purdue Res Found, 1999-2001; res Dir, Physical Sci, Purdue Res Foundation, 1993-1998; vis prof, Seoul Nat Univ, 1979 & 1980; PROF PHYSICS, PURDUE UNIV, 1977-; chmn, Gordon Res Conf, 1977; consult, Los Alamos Nat Lab, Univ Calif, 1974-1979, 1987-1993; vis staff mem, Los Alamos Nat Lab, Univ Calif, 1973-1974; assoc prof, Purdue Univ, 1973-1977; Proj dir, Purdue Nuclear Theory Group, 1971-; from asst prof to assoc prof, Purdue Univ, 1967-1977; asst prof, Purdue Univ, 1967-1973; fel physics, Oak Ridge Nat Lab, 1965-1967; fel physics, Bell Tel Labs Inc, 1963-1965. **Memberships:** Korean Scientists & Engrs Asn Am; fel Korean Phys Soc; fel Am Phys Soc. **Research Statement & Publications:** Quantum theory of scattering; theory of the three-nucleon systems; intermediate energy physics; theories of meson-exchange currents; parity violations in nuclear physics; photonuclear reactions; nuclear structure and reactions; quark degrees of freedom in nuclei; geodesy; geodynamics; gravitational theory; exploration geophysics; nuclear fusion; astrophysics. **Mailing Address:** Dept Physics, Purdue Univ, Physics 258, West Lafayette, IN 47907-1396. **Fax:** 765-494-0706. **E-Mail:** yekim@physics.purdue.edu

KIM, YEONG WOOK, SOLID STATE PHYSICS, ATOMIC & MOLECULAR PHYSICS. **Personal Data:** b July 21, 1925; c 3. **Education:** Seoul Nat Univ, Korea, BS, 1948, MS, 1950; Brown Univ, Providence, RI, PhD (physics), 1961. **Professional Experience:** PROF EMER PHYSICS, WAYNE STATE UNIV, as of 2001; NIH cancer sci fel, 1976-1978; Sigma Xi award, Wayne State Univ, 1976; prof physics, Wayne State Univ, beginning 1960. **Memberships:** Fel Am Phys Soc; Am Asn Physics Teachers; Sigma Xi; Inst Elec & Electronics Engrs; Am Asn Univ Professors. **Research Statement & Publications:** Solid State experiments; spatial pairing effects in high temperature superconductors. **Mailing Address:** Dept Physics & Astron, Wayne State Univ, 372 Physics, Detroit, MI 48202. **Fax:** 313-577-3932. **E-Mail:** kim@physics.wayne.edu

KIM, YESOOK, PHARMACEUTICAL CHEMISTRY. **Mailing Address:** 47 Quarry Dock Rd, Branford, CT 06405.

KIM, YONG BAEK, PHYSICS. **Education:** Seoul Nat Univ, BSc, 1989; Mass Inst Technol, PhD, 1995. **Professional Experience:** CAN RES CHAIR, THEORET CONDENSED MATTER PHYSICS, UNIV TORONTO, as of 2002. **Mailing Address:** Univ Toronto, 60 St George St, Toronto, ON M5S 1A7, Can. **Fax:** 416-978-2537. **E-Mail:** ybkim@physics.utoronto.ca

KIM, YONG HAK, PHYSICS. **Education:** Univ Calif, Berkeley, PhD. **Professional Experience:** PROF ASTRON & PHYSICS, SADDLEBACK COL, as of 2005. **Mailing Address:** Dept Astron & Physics, Saddleback Col, Mission Viejo, CA 92692. **Fax:** 949-347-1936. **E-Mail:** ykim@saddleback.edu

KIM, YONG IL, BIOMEDICAL ENGINEERING, NEUROMUSCULAR TRANSMISSION. **Personal Data:** b Seoul, Korea, June 5, 1945; m 1975, c 3. **Education:** Seoul Nat Univ, BS, 1968; Cornell Univ, MS, 1973, PhD (biomed eng), 1977. **Professional Experience:** PROF, BIOMED ENG & NEUROL, SCH MED, UNIV VA, 1995-; vis scientist, Dept Pharmacol, Univ Lund, Sweden, 1983-1984; new investr res award, NIH, 1982-1985; asst prof, dept neurol, Jerry Lewis Neuromuscular Ctr, 1979-1995; instr, Bioengineering & elec systs, Cornell Univ, 1977; res assoc, Dept Neurol & Jerry Lewis Neuromuscular Ctr, 1977-1979; systs analyst trainee, Korea Comput Ctr, 1968; systs engr, Gadelius & Co, Ltd, 1968-1970. **Memberships:** Inst Elec & Electronics Engrs; Biomed Eng Soc; AAAS; Soc Neuroscience; Korean Scientists & Engrs Am. **Research Statement & Publications:** Neuromuscular transmission in disease states; bioelectric systems; biomedical instrumentation. **Mailing Address:** Dept Biomed eng, Univ Va PO Box 800759, Charlottesville, VA 22908. **Fax:** 804-982-3870. **E-Mail:** yik@virginia.edu

KIM, YONG WOOK, STATISTICAL PHYSICS. **Personal Data:** b Seoul, Korea, September 30, 1938; American citizen; m 1966, Sook; c Irene, Christopher & Michelle. **Education:** Seoul Nat Univ, BS, 1960, MS, 1962; Univ Mich, PhD (physics), 1968. **Honors & Awards:** Elected a fellow of the Am Physical Soc, 1982. **Professional Experience:** Lectr, USSR Acad Sci, 1991; chmn dept, Lehigh Univ, 1984-1987; PROF PHYSICS, LEHIGH UNIV, 1977-; from asst prof to assoc prof, Lehigh Univ, 1968-1977. **Memberships:** Fel Am Phys Soc; Sigma Xi; AAAS; Metall Soc; Electrochem Soc. **Research Statement & Publications:** Non-linear phenomena in molecular and Brownian fluctuation; radiative transport in nonideal plasmas; spectroscopy of light scattering from small particle suspension and fractals; shock wave generation; interfacial instability in laser-produced plasmas; thermal diffusion. **Mailing Address:** Dept Physics, Lehigh Univ, Bldg 16, Bethlehem, PA 18015. **Fax:** 610-758-5730. **E-Mail:** ywk0@lehigh.edu

KIM, YONG-KI, ATOMIC PHYSICS. **Personal Data:** b Seoul, Korea, February 20, 1932; m 1963, Younghee; c Edward & Charlotte. **Education:** Seoul Nat Univ, BS, 1957; Univ Del, MS, 1961; Univ Chicago, PhD (physics), 1966. **Professional Experience:** CONTRACTOR, NAT INST STAND & TECHNOL, 2002-; physicist, Nat Inst Stand & Technol, 1995-2002; supvry physicist, Nat Bur Stand, 1988-1995; physicist, Nat Bur Stand, 1983-1988; sr, physicist, 1979-1983; physicist, Argonne Nat Lab, 1970-1979; asst physicist, Argonne Nat Lab, 1968-1970; Lectr, Univ Chicago, 1967-1968; res assoc, Argonne Nat Lab, 1966-1968; Instr physics, Korean Air Force Acad, 1957-1959. **Memberships:** Fel Am Phys Soc. **Research Statement & Publications:** Atomic structure theory; atomic collision theory; radiation physics. **Mailing Address:** Nat Inst Stand & Technol, Atomic Physics Div, 100 Bureau Dr, Stop 8422, Gaithersburg, MD 20899-8422. **Fax:** 301-975-3038. **E-Mail:** yong-ki.kim@nist.gov

KIM, YOON BERM, IMMUNOLOGY. **Personal Data:** b Soon Chun, Korea, April 25, 1929; m 1959, c 3. **Education:** Seoul Nat Univ, MD, 1958; Univ Minn, PhD (microbiol), 1965. **Professional Experience:** AT DEPT MICROBIOL & IMMUNOL, CHICAGO MED SCH, N CHICAGO, AS OF 1998; CHMN, IMMUNOL UNIT, 1980-; HEAD, LAB ONTOGENY IMMUNE SYST, SLOAN-KETTERING INST CANCER RES, NY, 1973-; PROF BIOL & IMMUNOL, GRAD SCH MED SCI, CORNELL UNIV, 1973-; USPHS career develop res award, 1968-1973; from instr to assoc prof microbiol, Med Sch, Univ Minn, Minneapolis, 1965-1973; from asst teaching & res to assoc teaching & res, Med Sch, Univ Minn, Minneapolis, 1960-1964; res fel, 1960-1964; Intern med, Univ Hosp, Seoul Nat Univ, 1958-1959. **Memberships:** Asn Gnotobiotics (pres, 1979-1980); Am Asn Immunol; Am Soc Microbiol; Reticuloendothelial Soc; Am Asn Path. **Research Statement & Publications:** Immunobiology and immunochemistry; ontogeny of the immune system; mechanism of the immune response, regulation of the immune system; tumor immunity; immunochemistry and biology of bacterial toxins and host-parasite relationships; gnotobiology. **Mailing Address:** Dept Microbiol & Immunol Finch Univ Health Sci, Chicago Med Sch 3333 Green Bay Rd, North Chicago, IL 60064-3095. **Fax:** 847-578-3349.

KIM, YOONKEE, MICROACOUSTICS, FREQUENCY CONTROL. **Personal Data:** b Seoul, Korea, April 18, 1958; m 1987, Soae; c Junho & Jiho. **Education:** Seoul Nat Univ, BS, 1981; Korean Advan Inst Sci Technol, MS, 1984, Ga Inst Technol, MS, 1991, PhD (elec eng), 1993. **Professional Experience:** ELECTRONICS ENGR, US ARMY RES LAB, 1996-; res assoc, Nat Res Coun, 1995-1996; postdoctoral fel, Ga Inst Technol, 1993-1994; consult, Motorola, 1992; consult, Bon-Ohio Electronics, 1987; Electronics engr, Goldstar Inc, 1984-1986. **Memberships:** Inst Elec & Electronics Engrs. **Research Statement & Publications:** High precision clocks and smart sensors based upon bulk acoustic wave devices and surface acoustic devices; author of more than 20 technical publications. **Mailing Address:** US Army Commun Electronics Command, Ft Monmouth, NJ 07724. **Fax:** 732-427-4805. **E-Mail:** ykim@ieee.org

KIM, YOUNG C, COASTAL ENGINEERING, HYDRAULIC ENGINEERING. **Personal Data:** b Seoul, Korea, May 25, 1936; American citizen; m 1965, Janet; c Raymond, Susan & Harold. **Education:** Univ Southern Calif, BS, 1958, PhD (civil eng), 1964; Calif Inst Technol, MS, 1959. **Professional Experience:** CHMN, DEPT CIVIL ENG, CALIF STATE UNIV, LOS ANGELES, 1993-; reviewer, Sci Develop Countries Prog, NSF, 1980; ACTG ASSOC DEAN, SCH ENG, 1978-; mem bd gov, Southern Calif Ocean Studies Consortium, 1978; chmn, Dept Civil Eng, Calif State Univ, Los Angeles, 1976-1979; vis scientist, US-Japan Coop Sci Prog, Osaka City Univ, 1976; resident consult, Sci Eng Assocs, 1975-1980; NATO sr fel sci, Delft Technol Univ, Neth, 1975; prof civil eng, Dept Civil Eng, Calif State Univ, Los Angeles, beginning 1973; vis scholar, Univ Calif, Berkeley, 1971; sr res engr, Sci Eng Assocs, 1969; Res Corp, travel grant, 1968; resident consult, Sci Eng Assocs, beginning 1967; resident consult, US Naval Civil Eng Lab, 1967 & 1969; prin investr, NSF, Res Corp & Defense Atomic Support Agency, beginning 1965; from asst prof to assoc prof, Dept Civil Eng, Calif State Univ, Los Angeles, 1965-1973; sr lectr, Univ Southern Calif, 1965-1970; NSF res grant, 1965; Res Corp res grants, 1964 & 1967; lectr civil eng, Univ Southern Calif, 1961-1964; civil engr, Daniel, Mann, Johnson & Mendenhall, 1959-1961. **Memberships:** AAAS; Am Soc Civil Engrs; Int Asn Hydraul Res; Am Soc Eng Educ; Sigma Xi; Permanent Int Asn Navig Congresses. **Research Statement & Publications:** Underwater explosions; wave forces; interaction of structures and sea waves; hydraulic model studies; oil slick transport on coastal waters; wave energy absorption in coastal structures; extraction of energy from the sea; hydraulic model studies; oil slick transport in coastal waters; wave energy absorption in coastal structures; extraction of energy from the sea; sea level rue. **Mailing Address:** Dept Civil Eng, Calif State Univ, Los Angeles, CA 90032. **E-Mail:** ykim@calstatela.edu

KIM, YOUNG DUC, ELECTRICAL ENGINEERING. **Personal Data:** b Korea, October 28, 1932; m 1965, c 1. **Education:** Newark Col Eng, MSEE, 1963, ScD, 1968. **Professional Experience:** RES ELECTRONIC ENGR, US NAVAL AMMUNITION DEPOT, 1968-. **Memberships:** Inst Elec & Electronics Engrs. **Research Statement & Publications:** Investigation of noise spectral density observed in solid state devices. **Mailing Address:** 2922 N Ramble Rd W, Bloomington, IN 47408-1050.

KIM, YOUNG GUL, CHEMICAL ENGINEERING. **Education:** Seoul Nat Univ, BS (Pharma), 1951; Princeton Univ, PhD, 1963. **Professional Experience:** PROF EMER CHEM ENG, POHANG UNIV SCI & TECHNOL, 2001-. **Mailing Address:** Dept Chem Eng, Pohang Inst Sci & Technol, Kyungbuk, Korea. **E-Mail:** ygkim@postech.ac.kr

KIM, YOUNG JOO, BIOSEPARATION, SEPARATION PROCESS. **Personal Data:** b Kwangju, December 12, 1960; m 1986, c 1. **Education:** Chonnam Nat Univ, Korea, BE, 1983; Seoul Nat Univ, Korea, ME, 1985. **Professional Experience:** ASST RESEARCHER CHEM ENG, RENSSELAER POLYTECH INST, 1989-; Ssangyong Oil Refinery, Korea, 1987-1989; Res engr chem eng, Orient Chem Indust Res Ctr, 1986. **Memberships:** Am Inst Chem Engrs. **Research Statement & Publications:** Separation and purification of various pharmaceutical proteins and biochemicals by preparative chromatography; scale-up; mathematical modeling. **Mailing Address:** 400 McChesney Ave Bldg 6 No 3, Troy, NY 12180.

KIM, YOUNG NOK, THEORETICAL PHYSICS. **Personal Data:** b Seoul, Korea, January 30, 1921; m 1960, c 3. **Education:** Seoul Nat Univ, BS, 1947, MS, 1949; Univ Birmingham, PhD (math physics), 1957. **Professional Experience:** PROF EMER PHYSICS, TEX TECH UNIV, 1991-; prof physics, Tex Tech Univ, 1964-1992; prof physics, Mem Univ, 1963-1964; edmonton, Can, 1962-1963; inst Henri Poincare, Paris, France, 1958-1959 & Univ Wash, 1960-1962; heidelberg, Ger, 1958; Res grants, Inst Theoret Physics, Copenhagen, Denmark, 1956-1958. **Memberships:** Am Phys Soc; Italian Phys Soc. **Research Statement & Publications:** Nuclear structure; collision; mesonic atoms. **Mailing Address:** Dept Physics, Tex Tech Univ, Lubbock, TX 79423.

KIM, YOUNG SHIK, MEDICINE. **Personal Data:** b Seoul, Korea, February 5, 1933; American citizen; c 2. **Education:** Stanford Univ, AB, 1956; Cornell Univ, MD, 1960. **Honors & Awards:** Western Gastroenterol Res Award, 1978; Vet Admin Med Investr

Award, 1984-1990; NIH Merit Award, 1988. **Professional Experience:** SR RES SCIENTIST, NORTHERN CALIF INST RES & EDUC, 1996-; clin sci I Study Sect, NIH, 1989-; cancer res, Gastronenterol, 1987-; large bowel cancer working group, Nat Cancer Inst, 1985-1989; assoc ed, Gastronenterol, 1981-1986; PROF PATHOL, UNIV CALIF, SAN FRANCISCO, 1981-; PROF MED, UNIV CALIF, SAN FRANCISCO, 1976-; mem gen med study sect A, NIH, 1976-1979; DIR, GI RES LAB, VET ADMIN HOSP, SAN FRANCISCO, 1968-; from asst prof to assoc prof, Gi Res Lab, Vet Admin Hosp, San Francisco, 1968-1976; asst prof biochem, New York Med Col, 1967-1968; Am Cancer Soc res scholar, 1965-1968; res assoc path, Stanford Univ, 1965-1966; instr med, Med Col, Cornell Univ, 1964-1965. **Memberships:** Am Asn Cancer Res; Am Soc Clin Invest; Am Gastroenterol Asn; Biochem Soc; Asn Am Physicians. **Research Statement & Publications:** Glycoprotein and glycolipid chemistry, immunochemistry and metabolism of the gastrointestinal tract; biology and molecular biology of gastrointestinal cancer. **Mailing Address:** Univ Calif, PO Box 0120, San Francisco, CA 94143-0120. **Fax:** 415-750-6972. **E-Mail:** youngk@itsa.ucsf.edu

KIM, YOUNG TAI, BIOCHEMISTRY, IMMUNOLOGY. **Personal Data:** b Seoul, Korea, November 10, 1930; m 1955, c 3. **Education:** Seoul Nat Univ, BS, 1953, MS, 1957; Univ Calif, Los Angeles, PhD (plant biochem), 1963. **Professional Experience:** ASSOC PROF MED, MED COL, CORNELL UNIV, 1980-; asst prof, Med Col, Cornell Univ, 1970-1980; biochem specialist, Growth Sci Ctr, Int Minerals & Chem Corp, 1965-1970; res assoc bot, Univ Calif, Los Angeles, 1963-1964; Asst prof biochem, Kyung Hee Univ, Korea, 1957-1960. **Memberships:** AAAS; Am Chem Soc; Am Inst Chemists; NY Acad Sci; Am Asn Immunologists. **Research Statement & Publications:** Virology; molecular biology; relationship between immunological response and genetics; immune response in aging. **Mailing Address:** 1205 Lexington Ave No 2C, New York, NY 10028.

KIM, YOUNG-GIL, ALLOY DESIGN & DEVELOPMENT, HIGH TEMPERATURE ALLOYS. **Personal Data:** b Andong, Korea, October 3, 1939; m 1970, Young-Ae; c James H & Joanne J. **Education:** Seoul Nat Univ, BS, 1964; Univ Mo, Rolla, 1969; Rensselaer Polytech Inst, PhD (mat eng), 1973. **Honors & Awards:** IR-100, Inco Alloys Int, 1980; King Sejang Sci Award, Korea Govt, 1986. **Professional Experience:** Consult, Nickel Develop Inst, 1990-; Vis prof, Dept Mat, Univ Calif, Los Angeles, 1984-1985; PROF MAT ENG, KOREA ADVAN INST SCI & TECHNOL, 1978-; res metallurgist, Inco Alloys Res & Develop Ctr, 1976-1978; Nat Res Coun res assoc, Lewis Res Ctr, NASA, 1974-1976; res assoc, US Army Const Eng Res Lab, 1973-1974; from res asst to res assoc, Mat Div, Rensselaer Polytech Inst, 1969-1973; Res asst, Univ Mo, Rolla, 1967-1969. **Memberships:** Fel Am Soc Metals; Mineral Metals & Mat Soc; Korea Inst Metals. **Research Statement & Publications:** Alloy development of oxide dispersion strengthened Nickel-base super alloys for gas turbine by mechanical alloying process; development of high strength automotive structural alloys and high strength-good electrical conductivity copper alloys for electronic applications. **Mailing Address:** Banpo Dong, 7411 Kyungnam Apt Seochokuy, Seoul 137047, South Korea. **Fax:** 824-286-93310.

KIM, YOUNGMIN, ELECTRICAL ENGINEERING. **Education:** Seoul Nat Univ, BS, 1975; Univ Wis-Madison, MS, 1979, PhD, 1982. **Professional Experience:** PROF & CHMN, DEPT BIOENGINEERING, UNIV WASH, 1999-; adj prof, Dept Radiol & Comput Sci & Eng, 1999-; PROF ELEC ENG, UNIV WASH, 1999-; DIR, UNIV WASH IMAGE COMPUT LIBR CONSORTIUM, beginning 1995. **Mailing Address:** Dept BioEng, Univ Wash, PO Box 357962 Rm 309E, Seattle, WA 98195. **Fax:** 206-685-3300. **E-Mail:** ykim@u.washington.edu

KIM, YUNG DAI, TUMOR IMMUNOLOGY, CLINICAL CHEMISTRY. **Personal Data:** b Seoul, Korea, March 24, 1936; American citizen; m 1967, Young; c Jean & Sue. **Education:** Wash State Univ, BS, 1961; Univ Idaho, MS, 1963; Univ Minn, PhD (biophys chem), 1968. **Professional Experience:** PROBE DIAGS, RES & DEVELOP, ABBOTT LABS, 1993-; assoc res fel, Cancer Res Lab, 1988-1992; sr scientist immunol, Res & Develop, Abbott Labs, 1974-1988; NIH res fel, Univ Pa, 1971-1973; NIH fel, Northwestern Univ, 1969-1971; vis scientist, C F Kettering Res Inst, 1968-1969. **Memberships:** Am Asn Immunologists; Am Chem Soc; Sigma Xi; Am Asn Cancer Res. **Research Statement & Publications:** Cancer research in immunology and immunochemistry; isolation and characterization of tumor-associated antigens; research and development of clinical diagnostic tests; DNA probe technology. **Mailing Address:** Dept 907, Abbott Lab, N Chicago, IL 60064.

KIM, YUNGKI, ORGANIC CHEMISTRY, POLYMER CHEMISTRY. **Personal Data:** b Korea, December 11, 1935; American citizen; m 1961, c 2. **Education:** Tex Christian Univ, BA, 1959; Univ Colo, Boulder, MS, 1961; Ariz State Univ, PhD (org chem), 1965. **Professional Experience:** RES & DEVELOP DIR, FRPL, DOW CORNING CORP, 1989-; TS&D dir, Silicone Polymers & Intermediates, 1986-1989; develop mgr, Silicone Polymers & Intermediates, 1984-1986; res mgr, Silicone Polymers & Intermediates, 1983-1984; process eng mgr, Silicone Polymers & Intermediates, 1977-1983; res group leader, Silicone Polymers & Intermediates, 1970-1977; sr res chemist, Dow Corning Corp, 1968-1970; res chemist, Dow Corning Corp, 1965-1968; Fac res assoc chem, Ariz State Univ, 1964-1965. **Memberships:** Am Chem Soc; Sigma Xi. **Research Statement & Publications:** Synthetic organic and polymer chemistry; silicone fluorosilicone and hybrid of silicone and organic/fluoro-organic leading to sealants, rubbers, resins and fluids. **Mailing Address:** Mail Stop CO-2406, Dow Corning Corp, Midland, MI 48686-0994.

KIM, ZAEZEUNG, IMMUNOLOGY, ALLERGY. **Personal Data:** b Hamhung, Korea, February 21, 1929; American citizen; m 1961, c 2. **Education:** Seoul Nat Univ, MD, 1960; Univ Cologne, PhD (immunol), 1968. **Professional Experience:** CLIN ASSOC PROF, DEPT MED ALLERGY SECT, MED COL WIS, 1980-; from instr to assoc prof med, Dept Med Allergy Sect, Med Col Wis, 1972-1980; Travel grants, AAAS, 1967 & Am Acad Allergy, 1970; fel allergy-immunol, Col Med, Ohio State Univ, 1969-1971; resident physician allergy-immunol, Temple Univ Hosp, 1968-1969; clin fel hematol, Univ Tex M D Anderson Hosp, 1967-1968; res fel immunol, Max Planck Inst, 1965-1967; resident physician, Heidelberg Univ Hosp, 1963-1964; Resident physician, Seoul Nat Univ Hosp, 1961-1963; pvt pract. **Memberships:** AAAS; Am Acad Allergy; AMA. **Research Statement & Publications:** Modification (change) of cellular antigenicity by enzyme treatment. **Mailing Address:** 1300 Green Bay Rd, Racine, WI 53406-4469.

KIMBALL, ALLYN WINTHROP, PUBLIC HEALTH & EPIDEMIOLOGY. **Personal Data:** b Buffalo, NY, October 2, 1921; m 1944, c 2. **Education:** Univ Buffalo, BS, 1943; NC State Univ, PhD (statist), 1950. **Professional Experience:** PROF EMER, DEPT BIOSTATISTICS, SCH PUB HEALTH, JOHNS HOPKINS UNIV, 1994-; dean, Fac Arts & Sci, 1966-1970; prof, Fac Arts & Sci, beginning 1962; chmn, Dept Statist, 1962-1966; prof, Sch Med, beginning 1960; prof, Sch Hyg & Pub Health, Johns Hopkins Univ, 1960-1984; chmn, Dept Biostatist, Johns Hopkins Univ, 1960-1966; chief statist sect, Math Panel, Oak Ridge Nat Lab, 1950-1960; exp statistician aerospace med, USAF Sch Aviation Med, 1948-1950. **Memberships:** Biomet Soc (treas, 1955-1960); Am Statist Asn. **Research Statement & Publications:** Statistics and mathematics applied to biology and medicine. **Mailing Address:** Dept Biostatistics, Sch Pub Health, Johns Hopkins Bloomberg, 615 N Wolfe St, Baltimore, MD 21205-2179. **Fax:** 410-955-0958.

KIMBALL, AMY SARAH, DNA REPLICATION, SITE-SPECIFIC RECOMBINATION. **Personal Data:** b Palo Alto, Calif, April 25, 1964; m 1989, David. **Education:** Univ Calif, Santa Cruz, BA, 1985, Johns Hopkins Univ, PhD (biol), 1990. **Professional Experience:** At dept biol, Johns Hopkins Univ, as of 1995-1998; fel, Johns Hopkins Univ, 1991-1998. **Memberships:** AAAS. **Research Statement & Publications:** Bactiophage and DNA replication. **Mailing Address:** Dept Biol, Johns Hopkins Univ, Baltimore, MD 21218.

KIMBALL, BRUCE ARNOLD, CARBON DIOXIDE EFFECTS ON PLANTS, MICROMETEOROLOGY. **Personal Data:** b Aitkin, Minn, September 27, 1941; m 1966, Laurel; c Britt, Rica & Megan. **Education:** Univ Minn, St Paul, BS, 1963; Iowa State Univ, MS, 1965; Cornell Univ, PhD (soil physics), 1970. **Professional Experience:** RES LEADER, US WATER CONSERV LAB, AGR RES SERV, USDA, 1990-; soil Scientist, US Water Conserv Lab, Agr Res Serv, USDA, 1970-1990; adj prof, Dept Plant Biol & Dept Geog, Ariz State Univ, Tempe. **Memberships:** Fel Am Soc Agron; fel Soil Sci Soc Am; AAAS; Int Soc Advan Indust Crops. **Research Statement & Publications:** Carbon dioxide effects on plants; energy relationships of greenhouses; evaporation and transpiration; soil air movement. **Mailing Address:** US Water Conserv Lab, 4331 E Broadway Rd, Phoenix, AZ 85040.

KIMBALL, CLYDE WILLIAM, SOLID STATE PHYSICS. **Personal Data:** b Laurium, Mich, April 20, 1928. **Education:** Mich Tech Univ, BS, 1950, MS, 1952; St Louis Univ, PhD (physics), 1959. **Professional Experience:** DISTINGUISHED PROF EMER, NORTHERN ILL UNIV, as of 2003; distinguished prof, Northern Ill Univ, beginning 1990; univ res prof, Northern Ill Univ, 1986-1990; sci & technol adv to pres, Northern Ill Univ, 1982-1988; prog dir low temperature physics, Div Mat Res, NSF, 1977-1978; prof physics, Northern Ill Univ, 1968-1990; consult, Argonne Nat Lab, 1964-; assoc prof physics, Northern Ill Univ, 1964-1968; assoc physicist, Solid State Div, Argonne Nat Lab, 1962-1964; mem res staff res opers, Aeronutronics Div, Ford Motor Co, Calif, 1960-1962; res physicist solid state physics, Autonetics Div, NAm Aviation, Inc, 1959-1960; res assoc, Argonne Nat Lab, 1957-1959; asst physicist, Argonne Nat Lab, 1950-1953. **Memberships:** AAAS; fel Am Phys Soc; Sigma Xi; Am Asn Physics Teachers. **Research Statement & Publications:** Experimental reactor physics; photodisintegration cross sections; neutron cross sections and nuclear reactions; magnetic and electronic properties of metals and alloys; Mossbauer effect; superconductivity; amorphous solids; lattice properties; optoelectronics. **Mailing Address:** Dept Physics, Northern Ill Univ, Faraday W 217, De Kalb, IL 60115. **Fax:** 815-753-8565. **E-Mail:** kimball@physics.niu.edu

KIMBALL, FRANCES ADRIENNE, REPRODUCTIVE ENDOCRINOLOGY. **Personal Data:** b Oakland, Calif, May 2, 1939. **Education:** Univ Calif, Berkeley, BA, 1961; Calif State Univ, Chico, MA, 1970; Cornell Univ, PhD (physiol), 1973. **Professional Experience:** RETIRED; consult drug develop, 1996-2003; dir proj mgt, Upjohn Co, 1991-1995; actg dir, Upjohn Co, 1989-1991; sr proj mgr prod develop, Upjohn Co, 1985-1989; scientist, Sr Res Scientist III Reproductive Endocrinol & Fertil Res, 1980-1985; scientist, res scientist II, 1975-1980; scientist, Upjohn Co, 1974-1975; NIH fel, Upjohn Co, 1973-1974; USPHS fel, Cornell Univ, 1970-1973; instr biol, Calif State Univ, Chico, 1968-1970; res technician, Med Sch, Univ Calif, San Francisco, 1968; res asst endocrinol, Reed Col, 1961-1968. **Memberships:** Am Soc Zoologists; Soc Study Reproduction; Am Soc Microbiol; Drug Info Asn. **Research Statement & Publications:** Mechanism of hormone action in the uterus and corpus luteum; action of prostaglandins in uterine contractility; physiology of antimicrobial agents. **Mailing Address:** 402 Michael Pl, Sebastopol, CA 95472.

KIMBALL, JOHN WARD, BIOLOGY. **Personal Data:** b Portland, Maine, January 13, 1931; m 1953, Margaret; c Christopher & Nicholas. **Education:** Harvard Univ, AB, 1953, AM, 1970, PhD (biol), 1972. **Professional Experience:** RETIRED; vis lectr biol, Harvard Univ, 1990-1991; assoc prof biol, Bradford Col, 1988-1989; vis lectr biol, Harvard Univ, 1982-1986; assoc prof biol, Tufts Univ, 1977-1981. **Memberships:** Fel AAAS; emer mem Am Asn Immunologists. **Research Statement & Publications:** Author of biology textbooks; currently online text. **Mailing Address:** 89 Prospect Rd, Andover, MA 01810. **E-Mail:** jkimball@mcb.harvard.com

KIMBALL, PAUL CLARK, MOLECULAR GENETICS, VIROLOGY. **Personal Data:** b New London, Conn, January 26, 1946; m 1985, c 1. **Education:** Mass Inst Technol, BS, 1968; Univ Calif, Berkeley, PhD (molecular biol), 1972. **Professional Experience:** CONSULT, FOLEY & LORDNER, ALEXANDRIA, VA, 1990-; consult, Cushman, Darby & Cushman, Wash, DC, 1988-1990; res leader, Battelle, Columbus, 1984-1988; sr res scientist, Battelle, Columbus, 1983; prin res scientist, Battelle, Columbus, 1981-1982; asst prof microbiol, Ohio State Univ & molecular virologist, Cancer Res Ctr, 1975-1981; sr scientist tumor virol, Meloy Labs Inc, 1973-1975; instr microbiol, Univ Ill Med Ctr, 1972-1973. **Memberships:** AAAS; Am Soc Microbiol; Am Soc Virol. **Research Statement & Publications:** Patenting of biotechnologies, especially genetic engineering products and processes; microbial production of biologicals with medical/veterinary/industrial import; use of microcomputers in biotechnology research; protein/peptide engineering. **Mailing Address:** 8908 Brierly Rd, Chevy Chase, MD 20815.

KIMBELL, JULIA S, MATHEMATICS. **Personal Data:** b Waltham, Mass, September 11, 1960. **Education:** Middlebury Col, BA, 1982; Duke Univ, MA, 1984, PhD (math), 1988. **Professional Experience:** APPL MATHEMATICIAN, CHEM INDUST INST TOXICOL, 1992-. **Memberships:** Am Math Soc; Math Asn Am; SocRisk Anal; Soc Indust & Appl Math. **Mailing Address:** Ctr Health Res, PO Box 12137, Research Triangle Park, NC 27709-2137. **E-Mail:** kimbell@ciit.org

KIMBER, CLARISSA THERESE, GLOBAL CHANGE, ETHNO-MEDICINE. **Personal Data:** b Merced, Calif, February 1, 1929. **Education:** Univ Calif, Berkeley, AB, 1949; Univ Wis-Madison, MS, 1962, PhD (geog), 1969. **Professional Experience:** PROF EMER GEOG, TEX A&M UNIV, as of 2006; fulbright res scholar, 1995-1996; mem bd gov, Orgn Trop Studies, beginning 1981; prof geog, Tex A&M Univ, 1981-1996; co-prin investr, Fish & Wildlife Serv, US Dept Interior, 1978-1982; HEW, NIH, 1971-1972; prin investr, Res Coun Fiscal Grant, Tex A&M Univ, 1971; from asst prof to assoc prof, Tex A&M Univ, 1968-1981; asst prof, Calif State Col, Hayward, 1967-1968; lectr, Univ Calif, Riverside, 1966-1967; actg asst prof, Univ Calif, Riverside, 1964-1966; res asst, Univ Wis-Madison, 1962-1964; teaching asst geog, Univ Wis-Madison, 1961. **Memberships:** Sigma Xi; Soc Women Geogrs; AAAS; Asn Am Geogrs; Orgn Trop Studies; fel Royal Geog Soc. **Research Statement & Publications:** Island biogeography; people-plant relations as in domestication of plants and ethno-medical systems; human impacts on isolated environments, sustainable strategie in context of global change. **Mailing Address:** Dept Geog, Tex A&M Univ, Col Station, TX 77843.

KIMBER, GORDON, CYTOGENETICS. **Personal Data:** b Manchester, Eng, July 21, 1932; m 1957, c 1. **Education:** Univ London, BSc, 1954; Univ Manchester, PhD (genetics), 1961. **Honorary Degrees:** DSc, Univ London, 1986. **Professional Experience:** PROF EMER, UNIV MO, as of 2004; prof agron, Univ Mo, Columbia, 1972-1995; expert, Int Atomic Energy Agency, Indian Agr Res Inst, New Delhi, 1970-1971; assoc prof, Univ Mo, Columbia, 1967-1972; sr sci off, Plant Breeding Inst, 1963-1967; fel, Kellogg Found, 1963-1964; sci officer, Plant Breeding Inst, 1958-1963; res asst genetics, Univ Manchester, 1954-1958. **Memberships:** Genetics Soc Am; Brit Genetical Soc; Sigma Xi; Genetics Soc Can. **Research Statement & Publications:** Wheat cytogenetics. **Mailing Address:** 12237 Alcosta Blvd, San Ramon, CA 94583. **Fax:** 510-803-5928. **E-Mail:** gkimber@attbi.com

KIMBERLEY, JOHN A, MECHANICAL ENGINEERING. **Education:** Lehigh Univ, BS, 1942. **Honors & Awards:** Internal combustion Engine Award, Am Soc Mech Engrs, 1992. **Professional Experience:** MGR ADVAN PROD GROUP, AM BOSCH, CONSULT, AMBAC, 1986-; develop engr, Curtis Wright. **Memberships:** Am Soc Mech Engrs; Soc Automotive Engrs. **Research Statement & Publications:** Development of a gas carburetor, electric governor for generator sets, hydraulically-powered, electronically controlled unit injector research diesel fuel system, optical start to injection timing, automobile diesel injection pump with variable injection rate, system to control injection pressure in a pumpline-injection system independent of engine speed, fuel system for injecting a slurry of coal and water and a pilot diesel injector for gas/diesel engines; granted 15 patents. **Mailing Address:** 149 Crescent Dr, East Hartford, CT 06118.

KIMBERLING, WILLIAM J, GENE LINKAGE, COMMUNICATION DISORDERS. **Personal Data:** b Logansport, Ind, October 16, 1940; m 1962, Rose; c Susan E (Kannawin), Mary T (Dougherty), Patricia D, William J & Thomas D. **Education:** Univ Ind Sch Med, PhD (med genetics), 1967. **Professional Experience:** CTR DIR, BOYS TOWN INST HERED COMMUN DIS, 1990-; RES ASSOC, BOYS TOWN INST HERED COMMUN DIS, 1979-; assoc prof, Med Genetics, Med Sch, Univ Creighton, 1979-; PROF, OTOLARYNGOL & PATH, MED SCH, UNIV CREIGHTON, 1979-; asst prof, Med Sch, Univ Colo, 1972-1979; instr, med genetics, Med Sch, Univ Ore, 1971-1972; Fel, Med Sch, Univ Ore, 1967-1971. **Memberships:** AAAS; Am Soc Human Genetics. **Research Statement & Publications:** Gene linkage and localization in humans; Published over 10 articles. **Mailing Address:** Dept Biomed Sci Creighton Univ, 2500 Calif Plaza, Omaha, NE 68178. **Fax:** 402-498-6331. **E-Mail:** kimber@boystown.org

KIMBERLY, ROBERT PARKER, INTERNAL MEDICINE, RHEUMATOLOGY. **Personal Data:** b New Haven, Conn, m 1972, Susan; c Christopher, Taylor, Sarah, Michael & Thomas. **Education:** Princeton Univ, BA, 1968; Oxford Univ, BA & MA, 1970; Harvard Univ, MD, 1973. **Professional Experience:** SR SCIENTIST, COMPREHENSIVE CANCER CTR, 1996-; PROF MED, MICROBIOL, SCH MED, UNIV ALA, 1996-; DIR & SR SCIENTIST ARTHRITIS CTR, MICROBIOL, SCH MED, UNIV ALA, 1996-; prof med, Cornell Univ Med Col, 1991-1996; assoc prof, Hosp Spec Surg, NY Hosp, 1984-1991; asst prof, Hosp Spec Surg, NY Hosp, 1979-1984; fel, Hosp Spec Surg, NY Hosp, 1977-1979; clin assoc, Nat Inst Arthritis, Metab & Digestive Dis, NIH, 1975-1977; attending physician, Hosp Spec Surg, NY Hosp; Howard L Holley Prof Med. **Memberships:** Fel Am Col Physicians; fel Am Col Rheumatology; Am Asn Immunologists; Am Soc Clin Invest. **Research Statement & Publications:** Immunology. **Mailing Address:** Dept Microbiol Univ Ala, 1900 Univ Blvd, Birmingham, AL 35294-0006. **Fax:** 205-934-1564. **E-Mail:** Robert.Kimberly@ccc.uab.edu

KIMBLE, ALLAN WAYNE, IMAGE ANALYSIS, ANALYTICAL INSTRUMENTATION DESIGN. **Personal Data:** b Washington, DC, January 2, 1960; m 1986, Maura; c Rebecca L & Rachel A. **Education:** State Univ NY, Albany, BS, 1989. **Professional Experience:** SR SCIENTIST, MICROS & SPECTROS LAB, VISTAKON, JOHNSON & JOHNSON VISION CARE, as of 1997; staff scientist New Prod Res & Develop, Vistakon, Johnson & Johnson Vision Prods, beginning 1989; anal instrumentation instr, 1986-. **Memberships:** AAAS; Asn Off Anal Chemists; Coblentz Soc; Int Soc Optical Eng; Micros Soc Am. **Research Statement & Publications:** Development of integrated image-spectral data analysis systems including ultraviolet, visible, near and mid infrared regions of the spectrum; functional analysis of polymers by spectral imaging techniques. **Mailing Address:** Micros & Spectros Lab, Vistakon Johnson & Johnson Vision Care, Jacksonville, FL 32217. **Fax:** 904-443-3433. **E-Mail:** awkimble@aol.com

KIMBLE, GERALD WAYNE, NUMERICAL ANALYSIS. **Personal Data:** b Bakersfield, Calif, April 24, 1928; m 1965, Isabel Clemeshaw; c Craig L (Hill). **Education:** Univ Calif, Berkeley, AB, 1949, Univ Calif, Los Angeles, MA, 1958, PhD (math), 1962. **Professional Experience:** PROF EMER MATH & COMPUT SCI, UNIV NEV, RENO, 1988-; prof, Univ Nev, Reno, 1975-1988; assoc prof, Univ Nev, Reno, 1967-1975; mathematician, TRW, Inc, Calif, 1963-1967; assoc prof math & dir comput ctr, Univ Mont, 1963; asst prof math, Calif State Col, Long Beach, 1961-1963; res asst numerical anal, Univ Calif, Los Angeles, 1959-1961; engr, Hughes Aircraft Co, 1955-1958; Mathematician, Nat Bur Stand Inst Numerical Anal, Univ Calif, Los Angeles, 1949-1951. **Memberships:** Math Asn Am. **Research Statement & Publications:** Calculus of variations; computer science; random permutations; history of mathematics. **Mailing Address:** Dept Math & Comput Sci, Univ Nev, Reno, NV 89557. **Fax:** 775-784-1080.

KIMBLE, HARRY JEFFREY, PHYSICS. **Personal Data:** b Floydada, Tex, April 23, 1949. **Education:** Abilene Christian Univ, BS, 1971; Univ Rochester, MA, 1973, PhD (physics), 1978. **Professional Experience:** PRIN INVESTER, QUANTUM OPTICS GROUP, as of 2006; valentine prof physics, calif inst technol, beginning 1997; PROF PHYSICS, CALIF INST TECHNOL, 1989-; prof physics, Univ Tex, Austin, 1979-1985; assoc sr res physicist, Gen Motors Res Labs, 1977-1979. **Memberships:** Am Phys Soc; Optical Soc Am; AAAS. **Research Statement & Publications:** Quantum optics; theory of coherence; atomic physics; infrared spectroscopy; semiconductor diode lasers; laser intracavity absorption spectroscopy; optoacoustic spectroscopy; theory of resonance fluorescence; photostatistics. **Mailing Address:** Quantum optics group, Norman Bridge Lab Physics, Calif Inst Technol MC 12-33, Pasadena, CA 91125. **Fax:** 626-793-9506.

KIMBLE, JUDITH E, MOLECULAR & CELLULAR BIOLOGY. **Personal Data:** b Providence, RI, April 24, 1949. **Education:** Univ Calif, Berkeley, BA, 1971; Univ Colo, Boulder, PhD (molecular, cellular & develop biol), 1978. **Professional Experience:** INVESTR MED GENETICS, HOWARD HUGHES MED INST, 1994-; PROF BIOCHEM & LAB MOLECULAR BIOL, HOWARD HUGHES MED INST, 1992-; from asst prof to assoc prof, Univ Wis, 1983-1992; Postdoctorate, Univ Wis, 1978-1982. **Memberships:** Nat Acad Sci; Am Acad Arts & Sci; Am Soc Cell Biol; Am Soc Biochem & Molecular Biol; Genetic Soc. **Mailing Address:** Dept Biochem, Howard Hughes Med Inst, Rm 341 E, 433 Babcock Dr, Madison, WI 53706-1544. **Fax:** 608-265-5820. **E-Mail:** jekimble@facstaff.wisc.edu

KIMBLE, ROBERT J, JR, MATHEMATICS. **Education:** Mass Inst Technol, PhD (Maths), 1973. **Honors & Awards:** Prof Henry M. Robert Jr. award, 1970. **Professional Experience:** PROF, US NAVAL ACAD, VA, as of 2006. **Mailing Address:** 4379 Spillway Lane, Dumfries, VA 22026-1604. **Fax:** 410-293-3074.

KIMBLER, DELBERT LEE, WORK DESIGN, ERGONOMICS. **Personal Data:** b Whitman, WVa, September 8, 1945; m 1967, Elisabeth. **Education:** Univ SFla, BSE, 1976; Va Polytech Inst & State Univ, MS, 1978, PhD (indust engr & opers res), 1980. **Professional Experience:** PROF INDUST ENGR, CLEMSON UNIV, 1990-; chair indust eng, Clemson Univ, 1995-2002; coordr continuous qual improv, Col Eng, 1993-1994; consult eng, Ciba Viscon Corp, 1992-1993; actg dept head, Indust Engr, Clemson Univ, 1989-1990; assoc prof, Clemson Univ, 1986-1990; from asst prof to assoc prof indust engr, Univ SFla, 1980-1986; instr indust eng & opers res, Va Polytech Inst & State Univ, 1978-1980. **Memberships:** fel Inst Indust Engrs; Sigma Xi; Am soc engr edu. **Research Statement & Publications:** Design and analysis of work system with emphasis indust ergonomics. **Mailing Address:** Clemson Univ, 110 Freeman Hall, Clemson, SC 29634-0920. **E-Mail:** kimbler@clemson.edu

KIMBLIN, CLIVE WILLIAM, ARC & INTERRUPTION PHYSICS. **Personal Data:** b Stockport, Eng, December 25, 1938; m 1968, Judy; c Sally, Clare & Hilary. **Education:** Univ Liverpool, BSc, 1960, PhD (elec eng), 1964, Univ Pittsburgh, MSIE, 1976. **Honors & Awards:** Kite and Key Award, National Electrical Manufacturers Association, 2005. **Professional Experience:** Consultant, Applications Codes and Standards, Eaton Electrical 2004 to date; Manager Application Codes and Standards, Eaton/Cutler-Hammer 1994-to 2004; Manager Applications Codes and Standards Westinghouse Electric 1991-1994; dir, Technol Develop, Begemann, 1990-1991; dir, Prod Develop, Holec, 1986-1989; mgr, Power Interruption Res, 1975-1986; fel engr, Westinghouse Res & Develop Ctr, 1974-1975; sr engr, Westinghouse Res & Develop Ctr, 1965-1974; Res engr arc physics, Westinghouse Res & Develop Ctr, 1964-1965. **Memberships:** Fel Inst Elec & Electronics Engrs. **Research Statement & Publications:** Physics of arcing and interruption in vacuum and air with particular reference to electrode mechanisms, properties of the interelectrode metallic plasma and development of high power switching devices. **Mailing Address:** 225 Tech Rd, Pittsburgh, PA 15205. **Fax:** 412-494-3417. **E-Mail:** clivewkimblin@eaton.com

KIMBRELL, DEBORAH ANN, INSECT IMMUNITY. **Personal Data:** b Goodfellow AFB, Tex, July 22, 1950; m 1991, S Ingemar Olsson. **Education:** Mills Col, BA, 1972; Univ Calif, Berkeley, PhD (genetics), 1985. **Professional Experience:** PROF GENETICS, UNIV HOUSTON, as of 2004; Prin investr, Am Cancer Soc, 1993-; prin investr, Univ Houston, 1992-1993; asst prof, Dept Biol & Inst Molecular Biol, Univ Houston, bgeginning 1991; Swed Med Res Coun vis scientist, Dept Microbiol, Univ Stockholm, Sweden 1988-1990; Am Cancer Soc fel, Dept Genetics, Univ Cambridge, 1985-1988; res technician, Dept Respiration Physiol, Max Planck Inst Exp Med, Ger, 1973-1974. **Memberships:** Genetics Soc Am; AAAS. **Research Statement & Publications:** Immune response and regulation of tumor formation; author of several publications. **Mailing Address:** Dept Biol, Univ Houston, Houston, TX 77204-5513. **Fax:** 713-743-2636. **E-Mail:** kimbrell@uh.edu

KIMBRELL, JACK T(HEODORE), MECHANICAL ENGINEERING. **Personal Data:** b Peoria, Ill, April 23, 1921; m 1948, c 4. **Education:** Purdue Univ, BS, 1943; Univ Mo-Columbia, MS, 1947. **Professional Experience:** Chmn dept mech eng, Wash State Univ, 1970-1977; dean col eng, Wash State Univ, 1969-1970; ALCOA PROF, WASH STATE UNIV, 1966-; PROF MECH ENG, WASH STATE UNIV, 1954-; sr res engr, Midwest Res Inst, 1951-1954; asst prof mech eng, Univ Mo, 1947-1951; Prod engr, Eversharp Corp, 1943-1944. **Memberships:** Am Soc Eng Educ; Am Soc Mech Engrs. **Research Statement & Publications:** Machinery design with emphasis on the kinematic synthesis of mechanisms. **Mailing Address:** 7401 Parkwood NW, Albuquerque, NM 87120.

KIMBROUGH, DAVID L, GEOCHRONOLOGY, TECTONICS OF CIRCUM-PACIFIC OROGENIC BELTS. **Education:** Univ Calif, Santa Cruz, BS, 1976; Univ Calif, Santa Barbara, PhD, 1982. **Honors & Awards:** Antarctic Serv Medal, NSF, 1990. **Professional Experience:** PROF, DEPT GEOL SCI, SAN DIEGO STATE UNIV, as of 2003; J William Fulbright grantee, 1995-1996; assoc prof, dept geol sci, San Diego State Univ, beginning 1992; dir, baylor brook inst isotope geol, col sci, San Diego State Univ, 1989-; asst prof, dept geol sci, San Diego State Univ, 1989-1992; postdoctoral fel, William Evans Teaching fel, 1987; res assoc, Univ Calif, Santa Barbara, 1983-1988; postdoctoral fel, Otago Univ, NZ, 1982-1983; Geol Soc Am Harold T Stearns fel, 1980; penrose grantee, 1979; sigma Xi res grantee, 1978; Geologist Ashland Explor Inc, Houston, 1976. **Memberships:** Geol Soc Am; Am Geophys Union; Nat Asn Geosci Teachers. **Research Statement & Publications:** Author of numerous publications. **Mailing Address:** Dept Geol Sci, San Diego State Univ, PS-117A, 5500 Campanile Dr, San Diego, CA 92182-1020. **Fax:** 619-594-4372. **E-Mail:** david.kimbrough@geology.sdsu.edu

KIMBROUGH, JAMES W, MYCOLOGY. **Personal Data:** b Eupora, Miss, November 7, 1934; m 1961, c Virginia Dawn, John Jeffery & William Jay. **Education:** Miss State Univ, BS, 1957, MS, 1960; Cornell Univ, PhD (mycol), 1964. **Honors & Awards:** Award excellence res supervision, 1975-1991; Distinguished prof, univ fl, 1992; Superior accomplishment award, univ fl, 19963; Westin award excellence teaching, mycological soc amer, 2001; Distinguished mycologist award, mycological soc am, 2001. **Professional Experience:** PROF PLANT PATH, UNIV FLA, 1987-; actg chmn, Univ Fla, 1985-1986; panelist, NSF, 1982-1985; prof bot, Univ Fla, 1976-1987; assoc chmn dept, Univ Fla, 1974-1975; from asst prof to assoc prof, Univ Fla, 1964-1976; teaching asst mycol, Cornell Univ, 1962-1964; instr bot, Vet Sci Dept, Miss State Univ, 1961-1962; asst bacteriologist, Vet Sci Dept, Miss State Univ, 1960-1961. **Memberships:** Mycol Soc Am (secy-treas, 1974-1977, vpres, 1977-1978, pres elect, 1978-1979, pres, 1979-1980); Bot Soc Am; Int Asn Plant Taxon; Brit Mycol Soc; Linnean Soc. **Research Statement & Publications:** Developmental and taxonomic studies in the powdery mildews; morphological, developmental and taxonomic studies of operculate Discomycetes; fungi as biocontrol agents of termites; fungi involved in indoor house pollution. **Mailing Address:** Dept Plant Path Univ Fla, PO Box 110680, Gainesville, FL 32611-2002. **Fax:** 352-392-7670. **E-Mail:** jwk@gnv.ifas.ufl.edu

KIMBROUGH, RENATE DORA, PATHOLOGY TOXICOLOGY. **Personal Data:** b Hannover, Ger, January 14, 1933; American citizen; div, c Doris, Erich & Lucy. **Education:** Univ Gottingen, MD, 1957. **Honors & Awards:** Clinton H Thienes Award, Am Acad Clin Toxicol, 1987; Herbert E Stockinger Award, Am Conf Govt & Indust Hygienists, 1991. **Professional Experience:** SR MED ASSOC, INST EVALUATING HEALTH RISKS, as of 2003; US Environ Protection Agency, consult, as of 2000; mem, Sci Adv Board, USAF, 1992-1994; sr med assoc, Inst Evaluating Health Risks, 1991-1999; advisor, 1987-1991; res med officer, Toxicol Br, Ctr Dis Control, 1973-1987; pathologist, Atlanta Toxicol Br, US Food & Drug Admin, 1968-1970; pathologist, Environ Protection Agency, 1970-1973; consult, St Joseph's Infirmary, 1962-1974; res pathologist, Pesticide Prog, Toxicol Lab,

Nat Commun Dis Ctr, Ctr Dis Control, USPHS, 1962-1969; resident path, St Joseph's Infirmary, Atlanta, Ga, 1960-1962; intern, Evanston Hosp, Ill, 1958-1959. **Memberships:** Fel Am Acad Clin Toxicol; hon fel Am Acad Pediat; Am Asn Clin Pathologists; Soc Toxicol. **Research Statement & Publications:** Risk assessment; human exposure; human health effects of chemical exposure; extrapolating data on chemicals from laboratory animals to humans. **Mailing Address:** Inst Evaluating Health Risk, 1629 K St NW Ste 402, Washington, DC 20006.

KIMBROUGH, THEO DANIEL, JR, PHYSIOLOGY, BIOCHEMISTRY. **Personal Data:** b Lafayette, Ala, September 17, 1933; m 1965, Christine Mary Kimbrough; c Philip Daniel & Kathryn Mary. **Education:** Univ Ala, BS, 1955, MA, 1959; Auburn Univ, PhD (zoology), 1965. **Professional Experience:** RETIRED; NSF grant, Res Small Col Fac, Univ NC, 1983; assoc prof biol, Va Commonwealth Univ, beginning 1974; asst prof, VA Commonwealth Univ, 1967-1974; asst prof biol, Birmingham-Southern Col, 1964-1967; teaching asst zoology, NIH fel physiol, 1963-1964; teaching asst zoology, Auburn Univ, 1962-1963. **Memberships:** fel Am Inst Chem; Soc Indust Microbiol; Sigma Xi; Am Entom Soc. **Research Statement & Publications:** Physiology of intestinal serotonin; animal physiology; histology; physiology of intestinal serotonin; insect physiology, characterization of serotonin receptors in the cockroach digestive tract; neurophysiology, study of effects of aspartame on serotonin levels in brain and on behavior in mice. **Mailing Address:** 10300 Waltham Dr, Richmond, VA 23233-4823. **Fax:** 804-784-5183. **E-Mail:** dkimbrou@hotmail.com

KIMEL, JACOB DANIEL, PARTICLE PHYSICS, THEORETICAL & COMPUTATIONAL PHYSICS. **Personal Data:** b Winston-Salem, NC, August 11, 1937; m Lau. **Education:** Univ NC, Chapel Hill, BS, 1959; Univ Wis-Madison, MS, 1960, PhD (physics), 1966. **Professional Experience:** Adj Prof, Dept Physics, Fla State Univ, as of 2006; PROF PHYSICS, FLA STATE UNIV, 1988-; dir grad affairs, Physics Dept, 1989-1991; from asst prof to assoc prof, Fla State Univ, 1967-1988; res assoc, Fla State Univ, 1966-1967; res assoc physics, Univ Wis-Madison, 1966. **Memberships:** Sigma Xi; Am Phys Soc. **Research Statement & Publications:** Theoretical physics with emphasis on studies of elementary particle properties and intearctions; computational and simulational physics. **Mailing Address:** Dept Physics, Fla State Univ, Tallahassee, FL 32306-4350. **Fax:** 850-644-6735. **E-Mail:** kimel@fsuhep.physics.fsu.edu

KIMELBERG, HAROLD KEITH, ASTROGLIA. **Personal Data:** b Hertford, Eng, December 5, 1941; div, c David & Michael. **Education:** Univ London, BS, 1963; State Univ NY, Buffalo, PhD (biochem), 1968. **Honors & Awards:** Fukbright Sr Prof, Univ Heideberg, 1988. **Professional Experience:** PROF, CTR NEUROPHARM & NEUROSCIENCE, ALBANY MED COL, UNION UNIV, as of 2003; prof biochem, Albany Med Col, Union Univ, 1988-; fulbright grantee, Univ Heidelberg, Ger, 1988; res prof neurosurg, Albany Med Col, Union Univ, 1980-; prof anat, Albany Med Col, Union Univ, 1980-1988; adj assoc prof biol, State Univ NY, Albany, 1978-1988; assoc prof biochem, Albany Med Col, Union Univ, 1974-1988; res assoc prof neurosurg, Albany Med Col, Union Univ, 1974-1980; asst res prof, Roswell Park Div, Grad Sch, State Univ NY, 1972-1974; sr cancer res scientist, Roswell Park Mem Inst, 1970-1974; NIH fel, Roswell Park Mem Inst, 1969-1970; fel, Johnson Res Found, Univ Pa, 1968-1969; adj prof biol, State Univ NY, Albany. **Memberships:** Am Soc Biol Chemists; Am Soc Neurochem; Soc Neuroscience; AAAS. **Research Statement & Publications:** Ion transport, electrical properties, transmitter responsiveness and uptake systems of astroglial cells; roles of astrocytes in trauma and ishemia especially in regard to cerebral cellular edema and excitotoxcity. **Mailing Address:** Ctr Neuropharm & Neurosci, Albany Med Col, 47 New Scotland Ave, Albany, NY 12208. **Fax:** 518-262-6178. **E-Mail:** kimbelbh@mail.amc.edu

KIMELDORF, GEORGE S, STATISTICS, MATHEMATICS. **Personal Data:** b New York, NY, September 3, 1940; m 1964, Carol Shulman; c Joyce & Joel. **Education:** Univ Rochester, AB, 1960; Univ Mich, MA, 1961, PhD (math), 1965. **Professional Experience:** RETIRED; prof math sci, Univ Tex, Dallas, 1976-1995; assoc prof, Univ Tex, Dallas, 1975-1976; from asst prof to assoc prof statist, Fla State Univ, 1969-1975; vis assoc prof, Math Res Ctr, Univ Wis, 1968-1969; vis asst prof, Math Res Ctr, Univ Wis, 1967-1968; from asst prof to assoc prof math, Calif State Univ, Hayward, 1965-1969. **Research Statement & Publications:** Mathematical statistics; probability; operations research. **Mailing Address:** 7612 Queens Ferry Lane, Dallas, TX 75248.

KIMERLING, LIONEL COOPER, SOLID STATE SCIENCE, PHYSICS. **Personal Data:** b Birmingham, Ala, December 2, 1943; m 1966, c 2. **Education:** Mass Inst Technol, SB, 1965, PhD (mat sci), 1969. **Professional Experience:** THOMAS LORD PROF MAT SCI & ENG, MASS INST TECHNOL, as of 2006; DIR, MAT PROCESSING CTR, MASS INST TECHNOL, as of 2006; head, Mat Physics Res Dept, Bell Labs, beginning 1981; lectr, Welsh Found, 1979; adj prof phys, Lehigh Univ, beginning 1977; vis fel, Inst Study Defects Solids, beginning 1975; mem tech staff, Mat Physics Res Dept, Bell Labs, 1972-1981; res physicist, Air Force Cambridge Res Labs, USAF, 1969-1972; res asst, Dept Metall & Mat Sci, Mass Inst Technol, 1965-1969. **Memberships:** AAAS; Am Inst Mining Metall & Petrol Engrs; Am Phys Soc; Electrochem Soc; Sigma Xi. **Research Statement & Publications:** Defects in solids: structure; electrical properties and chemical reactions; elemental and III-V semiconductor systems. **Mailing Address:** Dept mat sci & Eng, Mass Inst Technol, Rm 13-4118 77 Mass Ave Bldg, Cambridge, MA 02139. **Fax:** 617-253-6782. **E-Mail:** lckim@mit.edu

KIMES, BRIAN WILLIAM, CANCER RESEARCH. **Personal Data:** b Tampa, Fla, September 7, 1943. **Education:** Stanford Univ, BS, 1966; Univ Wash, PhD (biochem), 1971. **Professional Experience:** RETIRED; assoc dir, Nat Cancer Inst, NIH, beginning 1989; assoc dir, Extramural Res Prog, 1982-1988; chief, Extramural Cancer Biol Br, 1979-1985; prog dir, Extramural Tumor Biol Prog, Div Cancer Resources Ctr & Div Cancer Biol & Diag, Nat Cancer Inst, 1976-1979; grants assoc, Div Res Grants, NIH, 1975-1976; res assoc, Salk Inst Biol Studies, San Diego, 1973-1975; Am Cancer Soc fel, Salk Inst Biol Studies, San Diego, 1971-1973; NIH grant & contract prog. **Research Statement & Publications:** Structure and function of ribosomes; vitro protein synthesis; vitro macromolecular synthesis; tissue culture of nerve; muscle and fibroblast cell lines; electron microscopy; cell-cell communication. **Mailing Address:** 8201 Kentbury Dr, Bethesda, MD 20814. **E-Mail:** kimesb@mail.nih.gov

KIMES, THOMAS FREDRIC, NUMERICAL ANALYSIS, MATHEMATICAL ANALYSIS. **Personal Data:** b Phoenixville, Pa, July 24, 1928. **Education:** Ursinus Col, BS, 1949; Univ Tex, MA, 1956; Carnegie Inst Technol, PhD, 1962. **Professional Experience:** EMER PROF MATH, AUSTIN COL, 1992-; chmn dept, Mathematics, 1984-1990; dir, Jan Term Prog, 1981-1990; vis scholar, Cambridge Univ, 1980; Chadwick prof math, Jan Term Prog, 1976-1990; dir interactive comput serv, Austin Col, 1973-1976; Vis prof math, Furness Col, Univ Lancaster, 1970; from asst prof to prof math, Austin Col, 1962-1976; chmn dept, Austin Col, 1962-1973; sr mathematician, Bettis Atomic Power Lab, Westinghouse Elec Corp, 1960-1962; mathematician, Bettis Atomic Power Lab, Westinghouse Elec Corp, 1959-1960; proj mathematician, Carnegie Inst Technol, 1958-1959; asst, Carnegie Inst Technol, 1956-1958; Asst math, Univ Tex, 1954-1956. **Research Statement & Publications:** Ordinaryand partial differential equations. **Mailing Address:** 4600 Ocean Dr Apt 402, Crp Christi, TX 78412. **E-Mail:** tfkimes4600@cs.com

KIMLER, BRUCE FRANKLIN, RADIATION BIOLOGY, CANCER BIOLOGY. **Personal Data:** b St Paul, Minn, September 23, 1948; m 1975, Susan; c Laura J & Britton F. **Education:** Univ Tex, Austin, BA, 1970, MA, 1971, PhD (radiation biol), 1973. **Professional Experience:** Councillor, Radiation Res Soc, 1991-1994; adj prof, Dept Pharmacol, Toxicol & Therapeut, Univ Kans Med Ctr, beginning 1990; PROF DEPT RADIATION ONCOL, UNIV KANS MED CTR, KANSAS CITY, 1984-; from asst prof to assoc prof radiation ther, Univ Kans Med Ctr, Kansas City, 1977-1984; adj prof, Dept Radiation Biophys, Univ Kans, 1977-1982; assoc scientist, Mid-Am Cancer Ctr Prog, 1977-1981; fel, Thomas Jefferson Univ Hosp, 1975-1977; Appointee radiation biol, Argonne Nat Lab, 1973-1975. **Memberships:** Radiation Res Soc; Am Asn Cancer Res; Cell Kinetics Soc (secy, 1981-1983, vpres, 1991-1992, pres, 1992-1993); Am Soc Therapeut Radiol & Oncol; Sigma Xi; Int Soc Anal Cytol. **Research Statement & Publications:** Preclinical experimental radiation oncology; cancer chemotherapeutic agents; flow cytometry; in utero effects of radiation; brain tumor therapy; breast cancer prediction and chemoprevention. **Mailing Address:** Dept Radiation Oncol, Univ Kans Med Ctr, 3901 Rainbow Blvd, Kansas City, KS 66160-7321. **Fax:** 913-588-3663. **E-Mail:** bfkimler@kumc.edu

KIMLER, VICTORIA ANN, CARDIOLOGY. **Education:** Wayne State Univ, PhD (cell biol). **Professional Experience:** ASST PROF BASIC CLIN SCI, UNIV DETROIT-MERCY, beginning 1998. **Mailing Address:** Dept Basic Clin Sci, Univ Detroit Mercy, 4001 W McNichols Rd, Detroit, MI 48219-0900. **Fax:** 313-993-1003.

KIMMEL, ALAN R, MOLECULAR BIOLOGY. **Personal Data:** b New York, NY, January 22, 1949. **Education:** Rutgers Univ, BA, 1970; Univ Rochester, PhD (biol), 1977. **Professional Experience:** CHIEF, LAB CELLULAR & DEVELOP BIOL, NIH, as of 2004; CHIEF, NAT INST DIABETES & DIGESTIVE & KIDNEY DIS, as of 2004; CHIEF, MOLECULAR MECHANISMS DEVELOP SEC, NIH, 1992-; sr investr molecular biol, NIH, 1980-1992. **Memberships:** Fedn Am Socs Exp Biol; AAAS. **Mailing Address:** Nat Inst Diabetes & Digestive & Kidney Dis, NIH, Rm 3351 Bldg 50, Bethesda, MD 20892-2715. **Fax:** 301-496-5239. **E-Mail:** ark1@helix.nih.gov

KIMMEL, BRUCE LEE, LIMNOLOGY, AQUATIC ECOLOGY. **Personal Data:** b Poplar Bluff, Mo, November 6, 1945; m 1987, c 2. **Education:** Baylor Univ, BS, 1967, MS, 1969; Univ Calif, Davis, PhD (ecol), 1977. **Professional Experience:** DIR PROG PLANNING & INTEGRATION, LMES ENVIRON MGT, as of 1997; prog mgr, Off-Site Environ Restoration Prog, Environ Sci Div, Oak Ridge Nat Lab, beginning 1990; proj dir, RCRA Facil Invest, Environ Sci Div, Oak Ridge Nat Lab, 1987-; prin & co-prin investr res contracts, Dept Energy, US Army CEngrs & Tenn Valley Authority, NSF Ecosysts Progs, 1980-; res staff mem & group leader ecosysts dynamics, Mat Transport & Fate, 1980-1990; Prin investr res grant, Okla Water Resources Inst, Off Water Res & Technol, Dept Interior, 1978-1980; asst prof zool & asst dir, biol sta, Univ Okla, 1977-1980; instr chem, Div Math Sci, US Naval Acad, 1971-1972; Proj officer oceanic biol, Ocean Sci & Technol Group, Off Naval Res, 1970-1971. **Memberships:** Am Soc Limnol & Oceanog; Int Asn Theoret & Appl Limnol; Ecol Soc Am; Am Inst Biol Sci; AAAS; Sigma Xi. **Research Statement & Publications:** Biological productivity and foodweb interactions in lakes and reservoirs; energy flow and nutrient cycling in aquatic systems; contaminant transport, fate, and effects in river-reservoir ecosystems; reservoir and lake liminology and ecology; water resources management. **Mailing Address:** LMES, ORNL, Oak Ridge, TN 37830.

KIMMEL, CAROLE ANNE, DEVELOPMENTAL & REPRODUCTIVE TOXICOLOGY. **Personal Data:** b Lexington, Ky, April 26, 1944; m 1970, Gary; c Rebecca A. **Education:** Georgetown Col, BS, 1966; Univ Cincinnati, PhD (anat), 1970. **Honors & Awards:** Commissioner's Commendable Serv Award, Food & Drug Admin, 1983; Spec Achievement Award, US Environ Protection Agency, 1985 & 1986; Spec Achievement Award, US Environ Protection Agency, Bronze Medals, 1986; Sci Achievement Award, Health Sci, 1990 & 1994; Sci Technol Achievement Award, 1991. **Professional Experience:** SR SCIENTIST, OFF RES & DEVELOP, NAT CTR ENVIRON ASSESSMENT, US ENVIRON PROTECTION AGENCY, as of 2004; SR DEVELOP TOXICOLOGIST, ENVIRON PROTECTION AGENCY, 1992-; adj prof, Univ Md, beginning 1989; guest worker, Food & Drug Admin, beginning 1984; develop toxicologist, US Environ Protection Agency, 1984-1992; adj assoc prof, Interdis Toxicol Div, Univ Ark Med Sci, 1982-1989; prog mgr, Reproductive & Develop Toxicol, Nat Toxicol Prog, 1979-1986; chief, Perinatal & Postnatal Eval Br, 1979-1984; res pharmacologist, Div Teratogenesis Res, Nat Ctr Toxicol Res, NIH, beginning 1977; adj asst prof, Sch Med, Univ NC, 1975-1976; sr staff fel teratology, Nat Inst Environ Health Sci, 1973-1977; instr anat, Sch Med, Harvard Univ, 1972-1973; consult, Environ Protection Agency, 1972-1973; sect head teratology, Environ Protection Agency, 1972; fel toxicol, Col Med, Univ Cincinnati, 1970-1972. **Memberships:** Soc Toxicol; Neurobehav Teratology Soc; Teratology Soc; Europ Teratology Soc; Int Fedn Teratology Socs; Soc Experimental Biol & Med. **Research Statement & Publications:** The effects of developmental exposures to drugs and environmental agents on the behavior and function of offspring; test methodology in teratology; extrapolation of animal data for human risk assessment; Hyperthermia effects on developing enbryo; early molecular markers of heat stress and abnormal development; patterning of segmentation. **Mailing Address:** Nat Ctr Environ Assessment, US Environ Protection Agency, Ariel Rios Bldg 8623D 1200 Pa Ave, Washington, DC 20460. **Fax:** 202-565-0050, 202-260-8719. **E-Mail:** kimmel.carole@epa.gov

KIMMEL, CHARLES BROWN, DEVELOPMENTAL BIOLOGY. **Personal Data:** b New Orleans, La, May 3, 1940; m 1962, Reida; c Seth. **Education:** Swarthmore Col, BA, 1962; Johns Hopkins Univ, PhD (biol), 1966. **Professional Experience:** DIR, INST NEUROSCIENCE, UNIV ORE, as of 2003; Javits Investr Award, NIH, Nat Inst Neurol Dis & Stroke, 1991-; PROF, DEPT BIOL, UNIV ORE, 1983-; mem, Inst Neuroscience, 1983; assoc prof, Inst Neuroscience, 1975-1983; asst prof biol, Inst Neuroscience, 1969-1975; NIH fel immunol, Salk Inst Biol Studies, 1966-1968. **Memberships:** Fel AAAS; NY Acad Sci; Soc Develop Biol(pres 1993-1994); Soc Neuroscience. **Research Statement & Publications:** Experimental neurogenesis; vertebrate neural development; cell lineage; developmental genetics. **Mailing Address:** Dept Biol, Univ Ore, 1210 Univ Ore, Eugene, OR 97403-1210. **Fax:** 541-346-6056. **E-Mail:** kimmel@uoneuro.uoregon.edu

KIMMEL, DONALD LORAINE, DEVELOPMENTAL BIOLOGY. **Personal Data:** b Swedesboro, NJ, April 15, 1935. **Education:** Swarthmore Col, BA, 1956; Temple Univ, MD, 1960, MSc, 1962; Johns Hopkins Univ, PhD (develop genetics), 1964. **Professional Experience:** PROF EMER BIOL, DAVIDSON COL, 2000-; prof biol, Davidson Col, 1978-2000; res scientist, Div Res NC Dept Mental Health, 1978-1979; assoc prof & chmn dept, Davidson Col, 1971-1978; res fel, Calif Inst Technol, 1970-1971; asst prof, Div Med Sci, Brown Univ, 1964-1971. **Memberships:** emer mem Am Soc Cell Biol. **Research State-**

ment & Publications: Web building behavior, neural control of web building and web geometry during development of orb weaving spiders. **Mailing Address:** Dept Biol, Davidson Col, Davidson, NC 28035. **Fax:** 704-892-2512. **E-Mail:** dokimmel@davidson.edu

KIMMEL, GARY LEWIS, BIOCHEMICAL TERATOLOGY. **Personal Data:** b Dayton, Ohio, November 20, 1945; m 1970, Carole; c Rebecca. **Education:** Miami Univ, AB, 1967; Univ Cincinnati, MS, 1969, PhD (physiol), 1972. **Professional Experience:** DEVELOP TOXICOLOGIST, NAT CTR TOXICOL RES, ENVIRON PROTECTION AGENCY, 1984-; reproductive toxicologist, Nat Ctr Toxicol Res, Environ Protection Agency, 1977-1984; reproduction biologist, Res Triangle Inst, 1973-1975; fel steroid biochem, Worcester Found Exp Biol, 1972-1973. **Memberships:** Teratology Soc. **Research Statement & Publications:** Relationship of toxic exposures and developmental alterations in relation to risk assessment. **Mailing Address:** USEPA, Off Res & Develop 8623-D, 401 M St, Washington, DC 20460. **Fax:** 202-260-8719.

KIMMEL, HOWARD S, PHYSICAL CHEMISTRY. **Personal Data:** b Brooklyn, NY, February 2, 1938; m 1964, c 1. **Education:** Brooklyn Col, BS, 1959; WVa Univ, 1961; City Univ New York, PhD (phys chem), 1967. **Professional Experience:** EXEC DIR, CTR PRE-COL PROG, NJ INST TECHNOL, as of 2004; PROF CHEM, NJ INST TECHNOL, 1980-; assoc chmn dept, Nj Inst Technol, beginning 1980; assoc prof, NJ Inst Technol, 1970-1980; asst prof, NJ Inst Technol, 1966-1970; res assoc chem, Isaac Albert Res Inst, Jewish Chronic Dis Hosp, Brooklyn, NY, 1962-1963. **Memberships:** Am Chem Soc. **Research Statement & Publications:** Vibrational spectra of inorganic coordination compounds, tin compounds, olefinic compounds, monosubstituted benzene derivatives and biochemicals; kinetics studies using infrared spectroscopy. **Mailing Address:** Dept Chem, NJ Inst Technol, Cypress Hall Annex, 180 Bleeker St, Newark, NJ 07102. **Fax:** 973-642-1847. **E-Mail:** kimmel@adm.njit.edu

KIMMEL, PAUL LAWRENCE, NEPHROLOGY. **Personal Data:** b New York, NY, November 12, 1951. **Education:** Yale Col, AB, 1972; NY Univ, MD, 1976. **Professional Experience:** DIR DIV NEPHROLOGY, GEORGE WASH UNIV MED CTR, as of 2005; dir, division of renal dis& Hypertension, dept of medicine, George Wash Univ med ctr, as of 2002; prin investr HIV & kidney, NIH, 1989-1994 & depression hemodialysis patients, 1992-1998; PROF MED, GEORGE WASH UNIV MED CTR, 1992-; from asst prof to assoc prof, George Wash Univ Med Ctr, 1983-1992; asst prof med, Sch Med, Univ Pa, 1982-1983. **Memberships:** Am Soc Nephrology; fel Am Col Physicians. **Research Statement & Publications:** Effect of HIV infection on kidney function; pathogenesis and treatment of HIV associated renal diseases; immune and psychologic adaptations to chronic renal diseases. **Mailing Address:** George Wash Univ Med Ctr, 2150 Pa Ave NW, Washington, DC 20037.

KIMMEL, ROBERT MICHAEL, MATERIALS ENGINEERING, POLYMER PHYSICS. **Personal Data:** b Beverly, Mass, February 6, 1943; m 1965, c 3. **Education:** Mass Inst Technol, BS, 1964, MS, 1965, Mat Engr, 1967, ScD(mat eng), 1968. **Professional Experience:** ASSOC PROF, CLEMSON UNIV, as of 2004; INDUST MGR, AM HOECHST CORP, 1980-; prod supvr, Celanese Plastics Co, 1976-1979; group leader, Celanese Plastics Co, 1973-1975; sr res chemist, Celanese Res Co, 1971-1973; res chemist, Celanese Res Co, 1968-1971. **Memberships:** Am Phys Soc; Fiber Soc; Sigma Xi. **Research Statement & Publications:** Fiber physics; physics of acrylic polymers; formation structure and properties of graphite fibers; effects of high pressure on materials; nature of the glassy state; structure properties of oriented films. **Mailing Address:** Clemson Univ, Clemson, SC 29634.

KIMMEL, WILLIAM GRIFFITHS, WATER POLLUTION BIOLOGY. **Personal Data:** b Scranton, Pa, August 27, 1945; m 1969, Janet; c David & Christina. **Education:** Wilkes Col, BA, 1967; Pa State Univ, MS, 1970, PhD (zoology), 1972. **Professional Experience:** Chmn, dept Biol & Environ Sci, 1987-1993; PROF BIOL & ENVIRON SCI, CALIF UNIV, 1982-; from asst prof to assoc prof, Calif Univ, 1976-1982; consult aquatic ecol. **Memberships:** Sigma Xi; Am Fisheries Soc; PA Acad Sci. **Research Statement & Publications:** Responses of headwater streams to acidification; bioassessment of mitigation strategies. **Mailing Address:** Dept Biol, Calif Univ Pa, 250 Univ Ave, California, PA 15419-1394. **Fax:** 724-938-1514. **E-Mail:** kimmel@cup.edu

KIMMERER, ROBIN WALL, BRYOECOLOGY, DISTURBANCE ECOLOGY. **Personal Data:** b Schenectady, NY, September 13, 1953. **Education:** State Univ NY, BS, 1975; Univ Wis, MS, 1978, PhD (bot), 1983. **Professional Experience:** ASST PROF BOT & ECOL, DEPT ENVIRON SCI & FORESTRY, STATE UNIV NY, SYRACUSE, 1993-; asst prof bot & ecol, Centre Col, 1985-1993. **Research Statement & Publications:** Community ecology of bryophytes; response of ecological communities to disturbance. **Mailing Address:** Dept Environ & Forest Biol, State Univ NY, 350 Illick Hall One Forestry Dr, Syracuse, NY 13210-2723. **Fax:** 315-470-6934. **E-Mail:** rwkimmer@syr.edu

KIMMERER, THOMAS W, ENVIRONMENTAL SCIENCES. **Education:** Univ Wis, PhD (forestry & bot). **Professional Experience:** PRES & CHIEF EXEC OFFICER, TREE-GUIDE, as of 2006. **Mailing Address:** 330 E Main St, Suite 205, Lexington, KY 40507. **Fax:** 859-254-7605. **E-Mail:** Kimmerer@athenic.com

KIMMERLE, FRANK, ELECTROCHEMISTRY. **Personal Data:** b Tuebingen, Ger, March 27, 1940; Canadian citizen; m 1963, c 3. **Education:** Univ Toronto, BS, 1963, MS, 1964, PhD (electrochem), 1967. **Professional Experience:** CHIEF ANALYTICAL CHEM, ALCAN INT LTD, 1984-; from asst prof to assoc prof chem, Univ Sherbrooke, 1968-1984; NATO fel, Free Univ Brussels, 1967-1968; Can Res Coun fel, 1967. **Memberships:** Electrochem Soc. **Research Statement & Publications:** Thermodynamics and kinetics of adsorption and reaction of organic compounds at the electrode-electrolyte interface; electro-organic synthesis; non-aqueous battery systems. **Mailing Address:** Alcan Int Ltd, Res & Develop Ctr, PO Box 1250, Jonquiere, PQ G7S 4K8, Can.

KIMMEY, JAMES WILLIAM, FOREST PATHOLOGY. **Personal Data:** b St Johns, Ore, January 24, 1907; m 1932, c 2. **Education:** Ore State Col, BSF, 1931, MS, 1932; Yale Univ, PhD (forestry), 1940. **Professional Experience:** RETIRED; consult, 1965-1975; proj leader, Intermountain Forest & Range Exp Sta, 1963-1965; chief div forest dis res, Intermountain Forest & Range Exp Sta, 1957-1963; sr pathologist, US Forest Serv, 1956-1957; pathologist, US Forest Serv, 1953-1956; pathologist, Bur Plant Indust, Soils & Agr Eng, Agr Res Admin, 1947-1953; assoc pathologist, Bur Plant Indust, Soils & Agr Eng, Agr Res Admin, 1942-1947; asst pathologist, Bur Plant Indust, Agr Res Admin, USDA, 1935-1942; field asst div forest path, Bur Plant Indust, Agr Res Admin, USDA, 1928-1935; field asst, US Forest Serv, 1927. **Memberships:** Fel AAAS; Soc Am Foresters; Am Phytopath Soc; Am Forestry Asn; Arctic Inst NAm; Sigma Xi. **Research Statement & Publications:** White pine blister rust in western United States and Canada; decay of wood in use; deterioration of fire-killed timber in Pacific Coast States; decay and other cull in timber stands of California and Alaska; forest disease survey in California and Alaska; dwarf mistletoes. **Mailing Address:** 620 E Elizabeth Ave, Westport, WA 98595.

KIMMICH, GEORGE ARTHUR, BIOCHEMISTRY, CELL PHYSIOLOGY. **Personal Data:** b Cortland, NY, December 8, 1941; m 1963, c 2. **Education:** Cornell Univ, BS, 1963; Univ Wis-Madison, MS, 1965; Univ Pa, PhD (biochem), 1968. **Honors & Awards:** NIH Res Career Develop Award, 1972-1977. **Professional Experience:** PROF BIOCHEM & BIOPHYS, SCH MED & DENT, UNIV ROCHESTER, 1983-; prof radiation biol & assoc chmn biochem, sch med & dent, Univ Rochester, beginning 1983; vis lectr biochem, Univ Manchester Inst Sci & Technol, Manchester, Eng, 1975-1976; prin investr, NIH grant, 1971; from asst prof to assoc prof radiation biol & biophys, Radiation Biol & Biophys & Assoc Chmn Biochem, Sch Med & Dent, Univ Rochester, 1970-1983; Nat Inst Dent Res fel biophys, Radiation Biol & Biophys & Assoc Chmn Biochem, Sch Med & Dent, Univ Rochester, 1968-1970. **Memberships:** Am Soc Biol Chemists; Am Physiol Soc. **Research Statement & Publications:** Epithelial ion transport; metabolic regulation; sodium-dependent transport systems for sugars and amino acids; bioenergetics. **Mailing Address:** Dept Biochem & Biophysics, Sch Med & Dent, Univ Rochester, 601 Elmwood Ave Box 712, Rochester, NY 14642. **Fax:** 585-275-6007. **E-Mail:** george_kimmich@urmc.rochester.edu

KIMMINS, JAMES PETER (HAMISH), FOREST ECOLOGY, ENVIRONMENTAL SCIENCES. **Personal Data:** b Jerusalem, Israel, July 31, 1942; m 1964, Ann; c Mark & Shaun. **Education:** Univ Wales, BSc, 1964; Univ Calif, MSc, 1966; Yale Univ, MPhil, 1968, PhD (ecol), 1970. **Honors & Awards:** Gold Medal Sci Achievement, Int Union Forest Res Orgns, 1986 & Can Inst Forestry, 1987. **Professional Experience:** PROF FOREST ECOL, DEPT FOREST SERV, UNIV BC, 1979-; moderator, Forestry Roundtable, Can Nat Roundtable Environ & Econ, 1990-1993; vis scientist, Kyoto, Japan, 1982; Killam fel, Can Coun, 1975-1976; chmn nat forest ecol working group, Can Inst Forestry, 1974-1976; consult, Environ Res Consults, 1971-; BC Govt Ecol Res Comt, 1969-; from asst prof to assoc prof, Dept Forest Serv, Univ Bc, 1969-1979. **Memberships:** Commonwealth Forestry Asn; Can Inst Forestry. **Research Statement & Publications:** Nutrient cycling in forest ecosystems; effects of forest management on ecosystem function; response of forest ecosystems to management-related and natural disturbance; forcyte, forecast, forcee, fortoon and horizon ecologically-based forest management computer simulation models. **Mailing Address:** Dept Forest Sci, Univ BC 2357 Main Mall, Vancouver, BC V6T 1Z4, Can. **Fax:** 604-822-9133. **E-Mail:** kimmins@interchg.ubc.ca

KIMMINS, WARWICK CHARLES, MARINE MAMMALS. **Personal Data:** b London, Eng, July 20, 1941; m 1964, c 2. **Education:** Univ London, BSc, 1962, PhD, 1965. **Professional Experience:** PRES, CHIEF EXEC OFFICER & CHMN BD, IMMUNOVACCINE TECHNOLOGIES, INC, as of 2004; dean, Fac Sci, Dalhousie Univ, beginning 1990; chmn dept, Fac Sci, Dalhousie Univ, 1981-1982 & 1985-1990; PROF BIOL, FAC SCI, DALHOUSIE UNIV, 1974-; from asst prof to assoc prof, Fac Sci, Dalhousie Univ, 1965-1974; asst lectr, Southeast Essex Col Technol, Eng, 1963-1964; Consult res dept, Encyclop Britannica, 1962-1965. **Memberships:** Soc Exp Biol & Med; Brit Asn Appl Biol; Can Soc Zool. **Research Statement & Publications:** Marine mammals; large predator prey impact on fisheries; parasitology; population control. **Mailing Address:** ImmunoVaccine Technologies, Inc, 1819 Granville St, Halifax, NS B3J 3R1, Can. **Fax:** 902-492-0888.

KIMMONS, GEORGE H, engineering; deceased, see previous edition for last biography

KIMOTO, MASAO, IMMUNOLOGY, GENETICS. **Personal Data:** b Osaka, Japan, August 24, 1947; m 1974, c 3. **Education:** Osaka Univ, MD, 1972, PhD (med), 1981. **Professional Experience:** PROF IMMUNOL, SAGA MED SCH, 1986-; asst prof internal med, Osaka Univ, 1981-1985; res fel immunol, Mayo Clin, 1978-1981; Res assoc immunol, Osaka Univ, 1972-1978. **Memberships:** Am Asn Immunol. **Research Statement & Publications:** Structure and function of major histocompatibility complex. **Mailing Address:** Dept Immunol, Saga Med Sch 5-1-1 Nabeshima, Saga 849, Japan. **Fax:** 819-523-32518.

KIMOTO, WALTER IWAO, FOOD CHEMISTRY. **Personal Data:** b Honolulu, Hawaii, March 25, 1932. **Education:** Univ Hawaii, BA, 1954; Univ Wis, PhD (org chem), 1961. **Professional Experience:** RETIRED; res chemist, Eastern Regional Res Ctr, 1971-1985; res chemist, Sci & Educ Admin-Agr Res, USDA, Beltsville, 1963-1971; res chemist, Am Oil Co, 1961-1963. **Memberships:** Am Chem Soc; Sigma Xi. **Research Statement & Publications:** Flavor and aroma of cured meat products. **Mailing Address:** 15790 E Alameda Pkwy, Apt 4-210, Aurora, CO 80017-2034.

KIMPEL, JAMES FROOME, METEOROLOGY. **Personal Data:** b Cincinnati, Ohio, April 18, 1942; m 1986, M'lou; c J Andrew, Thomas J, Mollie A, Zoe A & Hanna A. **Education:** Denison Univ, BS, 1964; Univ Wis-Madison, MS, 1970, PhD (meteorol), 1973. **Professional Experience:** DIR, NAT SEVERE STORMS LAB, UNIV OKLA, 1997-; mem, Bd Natural Disasters, Nat Res Coun, 1994-; sr vpres & provost, Col Geoscience, 1992-1995; chair, bd trustees, 1991-1993; fel explor res, Elec Power Res Inst, 1989-1991; chair, Adv Comt Atmospheric Sci, NSF, 1989-1991; dean, Col Geoscience, 1987-1992; prof meteorol, Univ Okla, beginning 1986; elected trustee, Univ Corp Atmospheric Res, 1986-1993; pres, Appl Systs Inst Inc, 1986-1988; mem, Adv Comt Atmospheric Sci, NSF, 1983-1986; dir, Sch Meteorol, 1981-1987; assoc dean eng, Col Eng, 1978-1981; prin investr, Nat Oceanic & Atmospheric Admin, NSF, 1974-1990; asst prof, Univ Okla, 1973-1979; res asst, Univ Wis-Madison, 1968-1973; weather officer meteorol, USAF, 1964-1968. **Memberships:** Am Meteorol Soc; Nat Weather Asn; Am Asn Geog; Sigma Xi. **Research Statement & Publications:** Synoptic and severe storms research for hydrometeorological applications. **Mailing Address:** Dept Meteorol, Univ Okla, Rm 1310 100 E Boyd, Norman, OK 73019. **Fax:** 405-325-7689. **E-Mail:** jkimpel@ou.edu

KIMPEL, RICHARD R, METALLURGY. **Personal Data:** b 1939; m 1958, c Richard & Steven. **Education:** NDak State Univ, BS, 1961, MS, 1962; Pa State Univ, PhD (mat sci), 1964. **Honors & Awards:** Robert H Richards Award, Soc Mining, Metall & Explor, 1988, Arthur F Taggart Award, 1992 & Antoine M Gaudin Award, 1994. **Professional Experience:** Adj prof mat sci, Univ Fla, 1996-; PRIN, R K ASSOCS, MICH, 1995-; sr res scientist, Eng Anal Div, Dow Chem, 1980-1995; Mgr, Eng Anal Div, Dow Chem, 1970-1980. **Memberships:** Am Inst Chem Engrs; Am Chem Soc; Soc Mining Metall & Explor (pres 1997). **Research Statement & Publications:** Particle processing; mineral processing; froth flotation reagents and plant optimization; size reduction methodology. **Mailing Address:** R K Assocs, 4805 Oak Ridge Dr, Midland, MI 48640-1917. **Fax:** 517-835-3141.

KIMSEY, LYNN SIRI, SYSTEMATICS, FUNCTIONAL MORPHOLOGY EVOLUTION. **Personal Data:** b Oakland, Calif, February 1, 1953; m 1976, Robert; c Erin & Benjamin. **Education:** Univ Calif, Davis, BS, 1975, PhD (entomol), 1979. **Professional Experience:** PROF ENTOM, UNIV CALIF, DAVIS, as of 2004; DIR, BOHART MUS ENTOMOL & CTR BIOSYSTEMATICS, as of 2004; RES ASSOC, MUS COMP ZOOLOGY, HARVARD UNIV, 1989-; dir, Bohart Mus Entom, 1989-; assoc prof, Univ Calif, Davis, beginning 1989; CONSULT, UNIV CALIF, DAVIS, 1983-; lectr, Dept Entom, 1982-1983; res fel, Smithsonian Trop Res Inst, Panama, 1981-1982; res fel, Mus Comp Zoology, Harvard Univ, 1979-1980 & 1983-1986. **Memberships:** Asn Systs Collections; Int Hymenopterists Soc.

Research Statement & Publications: Systematics, biogeography and evolution of wasp families chrysididae, pompilidae, Tiphiidae and sphecidae. **Mailing Address:** Bohart Mus Entomol, Univ Calif, 1124 Acad Surge Bldg, Davis, CA 95616-5200. **Fax:** 530-752-9464. **E-Mail:** lskimsey@ucdavis.edu

KIMURA, DOREEN, NEUROPSYCHOLOGY, BEHAVIORAL ENDOCRINOLOGY. **Personal Data:** b Winnipeg, Man, February 15, 1933; div, c Charlotte Vanderwolf. **Education:** McGill Univ, BA, 1956, MA, 1957, PhD (physiol psychol), 1961. **Honorary Degrees:** LLD, Simon Fraser Univ, BC, 1993; LLD, Queen's Univ, Ont, 1999. **Honors & Awards:** Distinguished Contrib to Can Psychol Sci Award, Can Psychol Asn, 1985; Outstanding Sci Achievement Award, Can Asn Women Sci, 1986; John Dewan Award, Ont Ment Health Found, 1992; Furedy award for academic freedom, 2001; DO Hebb distinguished scientist award, CSBBCS, 2005. **Professional Experience:** Visiting prof, Simon Fraser U., 1998-; coordr, Clin Neuropsychology, Dept Psychol, 1984-1998; hon lectr, Dept Clin Neurol Sci, Univ Western Ont, 1982-1998; Supvr clin neuropsychol, Univ Hosp, London, 1975-1983; PROF PSYCHOL, UNIV WESTERN ONT, 1974-1998; assoc prof, Univ Western Ont, 1967-1974; res assoc II, Col Med, McMaster Univ, 1964-1967; Geigy fel & res assoc, Neurochirurgische Klinik, Kantonsspital, Zurich, 1963-1964; res assoc, Otologic Res Lab, Univ Calif, Los Angeles, 1962-1963; fel, Montreal Neurol Inst, 1960-1962; Prin investr, Med Res Coun & Natural Sci & Eng Res Coun. **Memberships:** Fel Am Psychol Soc; fel Can Psychol Asn; Can Soc Brain Behav & Cognitive Sci; Soc Neuroscience; fel Royal Soc Can. **Research Statement & Publications:** Research into the biological basis of human cognitive and motor function, including neural and hormonal mechanisms; emphasis on the neurobiology of brain asymmetry and sex differences in human problem-solving abilities. **Mailing Address:** Dept Psychol, Simon Fraser Univ, 8888 Univ Dr, Burnaby, BC V5A 1S6, Can. **Fax:** 604-291-3427. **E-Mail:** dkimura@sfu.ca

KIMURA, EUGENE TATSURU, PHARMACOLOGY, TOXICOLOGY. **Personal Data:** b Sheridan, Wyo, September 19, 1922; m 1950, c 3. **Education:** Univ Nebr, BS, 1944, MS, 1946; Univ Chicago, PhD (pharmacol), 1948. **Professional Experience:** ASSOC RES FEL, ABBOTT LABS, 1980-; SR TOXICOLOGIST, ABBOTT LABS, 1976-; mgr corp res develop dept, Corp Res & Exp Ther, 1972-1976; mgr dept autonomic pharmacol, Sci Div, 1971-1972; sect head, Abbott Labs, 1962-1971; group leader, Abbott Labs, 1960-1962; res pharmacologist, Abbott Labs, 1955-1960; res pharmacologist, Nepera Chem Co, NY, 1949-1955; Fel pharmacol, Univ Chicago, 1948-1949; Lab instr inorg chem & microbiol, Sch Nursing, St Elizabeth Hosp, Nebr, 1945-1946; asst, Univ Nebr, 1944-1946. **Memberships:** Am Soc Pharmacol & Exp Therapeut; Am Pharmaceut Asn; NY Acad Sci; Soc Exp Biol & Med; Soc Toxicol. **Research Statement & Publications:** Pharmacology and toxicology of antihistamines and antiserotonins; bronchial asthma and allergy; drugs affecting ciliary motility; antiheparin agents; analeptics; antispasmodics; blood coagulants; anti-inflammatory compounds; toxicology and carcinogenicity of experimental drugs. **Mailing Address:** 4 Oak Brook Club Dr, Oak Brook, IL 60521-1314.

KIMURA, HIDENORI, CONTROL ENGINEERING. **Personal Data:** b Tokyo, Japan, November 3, 1941; m 1971, Michiko; c Naofumi, Taeko & Kazufumi. **Education:** Univ Tokyo, BEng, 1965, MEng, 1967, DEng, 1970. **Honors & Awards:** George Axelby Awards, Inst Elec & Electronics Engrs, 1985. **Professional Experience:** PROF, DEPT MATH ENG & INFO PHYSICS, UNIV TOKYO, 1997-; prof control eng, Dept Mech Eng, 1987-1997; assoc prof, Dept Control Eng, 1973-1987; lectr, Osaka Univ, 1971-1973; Res asst control eng, Osaka Univ, 1970-1971. **Memberships:** Fel Soc Instrument & Control Engrs; fel Inst Elec & Electronics Engrs. **Research Statement & Publications:** Control engineering; theory; mechanical control systems; robotics. **Mailing Address:** Dept Math Eng & Info Physics, Univ Tokyo 7-3-1 Hongo Bunkyo-ku, Tokyo 113, Japan.

KIMURA, JAMES HIROSHI, BIOCHEMISTRY. **Personal Data:** b Kona, Hawaii, October 29, 1944; div, c Melissa H & Daniel T. **Education:** Univ Hawaii, BS, 1971; Case Western Res Univ, PhD (developbiology), 1976. **Professional Experience:** HEAD, DIV RES, 1995-; SR STAFF, BONE & JOINT CTR, HENRY FORD HOSP, 1990-; from asst prof to prof, Dept Biochem, Rush Presby St Luke's Med Ctr, 1981-1990; from asst prof to prof biochem, Dept Ortho Surg, Rush Presby St Luke's Med Ctr, 1981-1990; sr staff fel, Nat Inst Dent Res, NIH, 1980-1981; staff fel, Nat Inst Dent Res, NIH, 1978-1980; fel, Nat Inst Dent Res, NIH, 1976-1978. **Memberships:** Orthop Res Soc; Am Soc Biochem & Molecular Biol; AAAS; Soc Complex Carbohydrates. **Research Statement & Publications:** Biochemistry of proteoglycans and mechanisms for the control of their synthesis; organization in cartilage. **Mailing Address:** Henry Ford Hosp, 2799 W Grand Blvd, Detroit, MI 48202-2689. **Fax:** 313-876-8064. **E-Mail:** kimura@bjc.hfh.edu

KIMURA, KEN-ICHI, NATURAL ENERGY UTILIZATION, DESICCANT COOLING & DEHUMIDIFICATION WITH SOLAR ENERGY. **Personal Data:** b Fushun, China, March 5, 1933; Japanese citizen; m 1961, Aiko Takasaki; c Mari & Tomo. **Education:** Waseda Univ, BArch, 1957, MSc, 1959, DEng, 1964. **Honorary Degrees:** DEng, Waseda Univ, 1965. **Professional Experience:** Pres, Japan Solar Energy Soc, 1984-1986; mem bd dirs, Int Solar Energy Soc, 1973-1979 & Archit Inst Japan, 1980-1982; PROF ENVIRON ENG & ARCHIT, WASEDA UNIV, 1973-; fel, Nat Res Coun, 1967-1969; From asst prof to assoc prof, Waseda Univ, 1964-1973; Teaching asst, Mass Inst Technol, 1960-1962. **Memberships:** Int Solar Energy Soc; fel Am Soc Heating, Refrig & Air Conditioning Engrs; Archit Inst Japan; Soc Heating, Air Conditioning & Sanitary Engrs Japan (vpres, 1980-1982 & 1992-1994, pres, 1994-1996); Japan Solar Energy Soc; Int Soc Indoor Air Qual & Climate; Acad Indoor Air Sci. **Research Statement & Publications:** Architectural utilization of solar energy; energy conservation in buildings; thermal comfort; indoor air quality; visual comfort in interiors; heat and moisture transfer in buildings; environmental engineering; architectural design; building science; vernacular architecture. **Mailing Address:** 13-21 Enoki-cho, Tokorozawa, Saitama 359, Japan. **Fax:** 81-3-3209-8316. **E-Mail:** kimura@kimura.arch.waseda.ac.jp

KIMURA, MINEO, CHEMICAL PHYSICS, CONDENSED MATTER PHYSICS. **Personal Data:** b Tokyo, Japan, November 15, 1946; m 1973, Keiko; c Kana, Mari & Nao. **Education:** Waseda Univ, Japan, BSc, 1970; Univ Tokyo, MSc, 1972; Univ Alta, Can, PhD (chem physics), 1981. **Professional Experience:** PHYSICIST, ARGONNE NAT LAB, 1986-; adj prof, Dept Physics, Rice Univ, 1986-; scientist, Joint Inst Lab Astrophys, Univ Colo & Nat Bur Standards, 1984-1986; asst prof atomic physics, Univ Mo, Rolla, 1981-1984. **Memberships:** Am Phys Soc; Radiation Res Soc; Sigma Xi. **Research Statement & Publications:** Theoretical atomic physics; radiation physics and biology; theoretical condensed matter physics. **Mailing Address:** Argonne Nat Lab, 9700 S Cass Ave Bldg 203, Argonne, IL 60439. **Fax:** 630-252-7415.

KIMURA, NAOKI, MATHEMATICS. **Personal Data:** b Wakayama City, Japan, May 20, 1922; m 1947, c 3. **Education:** Osaka Univ, DSc, 1944; Tulane Univ, PhD, 1957. **Professional Experience:** PROF EMER MATH, UNIV ARK, as of 1996; prof math, Univ Ark, Fayetteville, beginning 1965; assoc prof, Univ Okla, 1962-1965; asst prof, Univ Wash, 1958-1960 & Univ Sask, 1960-1962; Lectr math, Tokyo Inst Technol, Japan, 1949-1955.

Memberships: Am Math Soc; Math Soc Japan; Swed Math Soc. **Research Statement & Publications:** Functional analysis and general algebra. **Mailing Address:** Dept Math, Univ Ark, Fayetteville, AR 72701.

KIMURA, ROBERT S, BIOLOGY. **Education:** Hokkaido Univ, Sapporo, PhD (chem), 1979. **Professional Experience:** HEAD, ENDOCRINAL SECT, NAT CANCER INST, 1996-. **Mailing Address:** Nat Cancer Inst, Bldg 37 Rm 3112B, Bethesda, MD 20892. **Fax:** 301-496-8419. **E-Mail:** shioko@helix.nih.gov

KIMURA, TOKUJI, ENZYMOLOGY, BIOPHYSICS. **Personal Data:** b Osaka, Japan, November 14, 1925; m 1951, c 2. **Education:** Osaka Univ, BS, 1950, PhD (chem), 1960. **Professional Experience:** PROF CHEM, WAYNE STATE UNIV, 1968-; Prof chem, St Paul's Univ, Tokyo, 1965-1968; NIH res grant, 1965. **Memberships:** Am Soc Biol Chemists; Am Soc Chem; Sigma Xi. **Research Statement & Publications:** Adrenal cortex mitochondrial steroid hydroxylases. **Mailing Address:** Osaka Biosci Inst, Fusuedai, Osaka 565, Japan.

KIMURA, WAYNE D, LASERS. **Education:** Stanford Univ, PhD, 1981. **Professional Experience:** VPRES RES & DEVELOP, STI OPTRONICS, as of 2005. **Mailing Address:** STI Optronics, 2755 Northup Way, Bellvue, WA 98004-1495. **Fax:** 425-828-3517. **E-Mail:** wkimura@stioptronics.com

KIMZEY, WILLIAM F, AERONAUTICS. **Professional Experience:** GEN MGR, SVERDRUP TECH, as of 2005. **Memberships:** Am Inst Aeronaut & Astronaut. **Mailing Address:** Sverdrup Tech Inc, 600 William Northern Blvd, Tullahoma, TN 37389-5051. **Fax:** 931-393-6389.

KINACH, BARBARA M, MATHEMATICS. **Education:** Harvard Univ, EdD, 1992. **Professional Experience:** ASSOC PROF, DEPT MATHS EDUC, UNIV MD BALTIMORE CO, as of 2005. **Mailing Address:** Vanderbilt Univ, Math Dept, Box 330 GPC ACIV Bldg Off 414, Nashville, TN 37221. **Fax:** 410-455-1075. **E-Mail:** kinach@umbc.edu

KINARD, FRANK EFIRD, RESEARCH ADMINISTRATION. **Personal Data:** b Newberry, SC, January 15, 1924; m 1952, Mary McNease; c Sally K (Bayless) & Anne D. **Education:** Newberry Col, BS, 1946, AB, 1947; Univ NC, MS, 1950, PhD (physics), 1954. **Professional Experience:** CONSULT, 1990-; sr assoc comnr, SC Comn Higher Educ, 1987-1990; assoc dir, SC Comn Higher Educ, 1968-1987; exec dir, SC Comn Higher Educ, 1967-1968; head univ rels off, Savannah River Lab, E I du Pont Del Nemours & Co, 1963-1967; physicist tech div, Savannah River Lab, E I du Pont Del Nemours & Co, 1953-1963; instr physics, Univ NC, 1949-1952. **Memberships:** Am Phys Soc. **Research Statement & Publications:** Research in higher education generally; especially graduate education. **Mailing Address:** 801 Albion Rd, Columbia, SC 29205.

KINARD, W FRANK, NUCLEAR CHEMISTRY. **Personal Data:** b Greenville, SC, November 16, 1942. **Education:** Duke Univ, BS, 1964; Univ SC, PhD (anal chem), 1968. **Professional Experience:** Vis scientist, Westinghouse Savannah River Lab, 1990-1991; MEBANE PROF CHEM & BIOCHEM, COL CHARLESTON, 1983-; guest scientist, Lawrence Livermore Nat Lab, 1983-1989; sr scientist, Oak Ridge Nat Lab, 1978-1979; from asst prof to assoc prof, Col Charleston, 1972-1983; res assoc chem oceanog, Univ PR, 1970-1972; Nuclear chem, US AEC, Fla State Univ, 1968-1970. **Memberships:** Am Chem Soc; AAAS; Sigma Xi. **Research Statement & Publications:** Research in solution chemistry of lanthanide and actinide elements; applications of ICP-MS to radiochemical problems. **Mailing Address:** Dept Chem & Biochem, Col Charleston, SCIC 310, Rm 310, 58 Coming St, Charleston, SC 29424. **Fax:** 843-953-1404. **E-Mail:** kinardf@cofc.edu

KINARIWALA, BHARAT K, ALGORITHMS, DATABASE SYSTEMS. **Personal Data:** b Ahmedabad, India, October 14, 1926; American citizen; m 1953, c 2. **Education:** Benares Hindu Univ, BS, 1951; Univ Calif, Berkeley, MS, 1954, PhD (elec eng), 1957. **Professional Experience:** PROF EMER ELEC ENG, UNIV HAWAII, MANOA, as of 1997; chmn, Dept Elec Eng, 1969-1975 & 1978-1981; prog chmn, Int Symp Circuit Theory, 1968; prog chmn, Hawaiian Int Conf Systs Sci, 1967; Inst Educ Exchange Serv deleg, Popov Soc Meeting, USSR, 1967; prof elec eng, Univ Hawaii, beginning 1966; mem tech staff, Bell Tel Labs, 1957-1966; comput consult, Marchant, Inc, 1956-1957; actg asst prof elec eng, Univ Calif, Berkeley, 1956-1957. **Memberships:** Fel Inst Elec & Electronics Engrs. **Research Statement & Publications:** System and computer sciences. **Mailing Address:** Dept Elec Eng, Univ Hawaii, 2540 Dole St, Honolulu, HI 96822. **Fax:** 808-956-3427. **E-Mail:** bk@spectra.eng.hawaii.edu

KINASEWITZ, GARY THEODORE, PULMONARY DISEASE, CRITICAL CARE. **Personal Data:** b New York, NY, August 17, 1946; m 1969, c 3. **Education:** Boston Col, BS, 1968, MEd, 1969; Wayne State Univ, MD, 1973. **Honors & Awards:** Albert Hyman Award, Am Heart Asn, La, 1981, Annual Sci Award, Soc Critical Care Med, 2005. **Professional Experience:** CHIEF, PULMONARY & CRITICAL CARE MED, OKLA UNIV HEALTH SCI CTR, OKLAHOMA CITY, OKLA, as of 1988; mem Okla Res Found, 1994; prof med & physiol & biophys, Med Ctr, La State Univ, Shreveport, 1988-; head, Pulmonary & Critical Care Med, Okla Univ Health Sci Ctr, beginning 1988; PROF, PULMONARY & CRIT CARE MED, OKLA UNIV HEALTH CTR, OKLAHOMA CITY, OKLA, 1988-; from asst prof to assoc prof, 1980-1988; asst prof med, Dept Med, Cardiovasc Pulmonary Div, Univ Pa, 1979-1980; res assoc med, Dept Med, Cardiovasc Pulmonary Div, Univ Pa, 1978-1979; fel pulmonary dis, Dept Med, Cardiovasc Pulmonary Div, Univ Pa, 1976-1978; resident med, Univ Pa Hosp, 1973-1976; Counr cardiopulmonary dis, Am Heart Asn. **Memberships:** Am Thoracic Soc; Am Col Chest Physicians; Am Fedn Clin Res; Am Col Physicians; Am Physiol Soc. **Research Statement & Publications:** Coagulopathic and inflammatory resonse to sepsis in patients and experimental models.Quantitative analysis of fluid exchanges across the pulmonary capillaries of the visceral pleura; cardiopulmonary adjustments to exercise in patients with lung disease; mesothelial cell glycosaminoglycans. **Mailing Address:** Dept Med, Pulmonary & Critical Care Med, Univ Okla Health Sci Ctr, WP1310, PO Box 26901, Oklahoma City, OK 73190. **Fax:** 405-271-5892. **E-Mail:** gary-kinasewitz@ouhsc.edu

KINBACHER, EDWARD JOHN, PLANT PHYSIOLOGY. **Personal Data:** b Brooklyn, NY, November 19, 1927; m 1955, c 3. **Education:** Cornell Univ, BS, 1949; Purdue Univ, MS, 1951; Univ Calif, PhD (plant physiol), 1955. **Professional Experience:** PROF HORT, UNIV NEBR, LINCOLN, 1971-; assoc prof hort, Univ Nebr, Lincoln, 1963-1971; assoc prof plant breeding & agron, Cornell Univ, 1955-1963; Plant physiologist crops res div, Agr Res Serv, USDA, 1955-1962; Asst, Purdue Univ, 1949-1951 & Univ Calif, 1951-1955. **Memberships:** Am Soc Plant Physiol; Am Soc Agron. **Research Statement & Publications:** Heat, drought and cold resistance of horticultural crops and specifically turfgrasses. **Mailing Address:** 3816 Orchard St, Lincoln, NE 68503.

KINCADE, PAUL W, IMMUNOBIOLOGY, MICROBIOLOGY. **Personal Data:** b Moorhead, Miss, October 10, 1944; div, c 1. **Education:** Miss State Univ, BS, 1966, MS, 1968; Univ Ala, PhD (microbiol & immunol), 1971. **Professional Experience:** Adj prof microbiol & immunol, Health Sci Ctr, Univ Okla, as of 2004; WILLIAM H & RITA BELL CHAIR, BIOMED RES, as of 2004; mem, Prog Comt, Am Asn Immunologists, 1989-; Mem, Immunobiol Study Sect, 1984-1988; MEM & HEAD, DEPT IMMUNOBIOL, OKLA MED RES FOUND, OKLAHOMA CITY, 1982-; assoc prof, Grad Sch Med Sci, Cornell Univ, 1980-1982; assoc mem, Sloan Kettering Inst, 1979-1982; assoc, Sloan Kettering Inst, 1974-1979; Walter & Eliza Hall Inst, Melbourne, 1972-1974; fel, Univ Ala, 1971-1972; res asst, Lobund Lab, Univ Notre Dame, 1968-1969. **Memberships:** Am Asn Immunologists; Am Soc Hemat; Sigma Xi; Am Soc Microbiologists; Int Soc Develop Comparative Immunologists; Am Soc Invest Pathol. **Research Statement & Publications:** Humoral immune system with particular emphasis on relationships between stem cells and B lymphocytes and utilizing normal and genetically defective animal models. **Mailing Address:** Dept Microbiol & Immunol, Health Sci Ctr, Univ Okla, 825 N E 13th St, Oklahoma City, OK 73104. **Fax:** 405-271-8568. **E-Mail:** Paul-Kincade@omrf.ouhsc.edu

KINCADE, ROBERT TYRUS, ENTOMOLOGY, WEED SCIENCE. **Personal Data:** b Indianola, Miss, May 16, 1941; m 1968, c 3. **Education:** Miss State Univ, BS, 1963, MS, 1966, PhD (entom), 1970. **Professional Experience:** MGR FIELD RES STAS & FIELD RES SPECIALIST, BIOL RES INSECTICIDES, HERBICIDES, FUNGICIDES, VALENT USA, 1977-; supvr herbicides, fungicides & insecticides, 1975-1977; Field res specialist weed control, Chevron Chem Co, 1969-1975. **Memberships:** Sigma Xi. **Research Statement & Publications:** Development of herbicides, fungicides and insecticides for agricultural use. **Mailing Address:** Valent USA Corp, 3800 Old Leland Road, PO Box 5008, Greenville, MS 38702.

KINCAID, DENNIS CAMPBELL, IRRIGATION SYSTEMS. **Personal Data:** b Deer Park, Wash, June 17, 1944; m 1975, c 3. **Education:** Wash State Univ, BS, 1966; Colo State Univ, MS, 1968, PhD (agr eng), 1970. **Professional Experience:** Affil prof, Univ Idaho, 1979-; agr engr, agr res serv, USDA, beginning 1970. **Memberships:** Am Soc Agr Engrs; Am Soc Civil Engrs; Irrigation Asn; Sigma Xi; US comt Irrig & drainage. **Research Statement & Publications:** Basic and applied research in irrigation system improvement and water management; sprinkler droplet energy effects on sugarbeet emergence and surface soil aggregate size distribution; author of various articles. **Mailing Address:** USDA-ARS, 3793 N 3600 E, Kimberly, ID 83341. **E-Mail:** kincaid@nwisrl.ars.usda.gov

KINCAID, JAMES ROBERT, ANALYTICAL CHEMISTRY, BIOPHYSICAL CHEMISTRY. **Personal Data:** b Covington, Ky, February 11, 1945; m 1968, c 1. **Education:** Xavier Univ, Ohio, BS, 1970; Marquette Univ, PhD (chem), 1974. **Professional Experience:** PFLETSCHINGER HABERMANN PROF CHEM, MARQUETTE UNIV, as of 2004; asst prof chem, Univ Ky, 1978-; Nat Res Serv award, NIH, 1975-1977 & Nat Cancer Inst, 1977-1978; vis fel chem, Princeton Univ, 1974-1978. **Memberships:** Am Chem Soc. **Research Statement & Publications:** Applications of Raman spectroscopy to biologically significant systems; structure and function relationships in heme proteins; role of trace metals in biochemistry and medicine. **Mailing Address:** Dept Chem, Marquette Univ, Wehr Chem Bldg PO Box 1881, Milwaukee, WI 53201-1881. **Fax:** 414-288-7066. **E-Mail:** james.kincaid@mu.edu

KINCAID, RANDALL L, PHARMACOLOGY, CALMODULIN PHOSPHODIESTERASE. **Education:** Stanford Univ, PhD (pharmacol), 1978. **Professional Experience:** PRES, VERITAS INC, 1994-; res pharmacologist, NIH, 1979-1994. **Mailing Address:** Veritas Inc, 679 S Lawn Maine, Rockville, MD 20850. **Fax:** 301-838-8650.

KINCAID, RONALD LEE, ANIMAL NUTRITION, BIOCHEMISTRY. **Personal Data:** b St Joseph, Mo, October 29, 1950; m 1970, c 4. **Education:** Univ Mo, BS, 1971, MS, 1973; Univ Ga, PhD (animal nutrit), 1976. **Professional Experience:** PROF ANIMAL NUTRIT, WASH STATE UNIV, 1977-; lectr animal nutrit, Lincoln Col, Univ Canterbury, 1976-1977. **Memberships:** Am Dairy Sci Asn; Am Soc Animal Sci; Am Inst Nutrit; Coun Agr Sci & Technol; Soc Exp Biol & Med. **Research Statement & Publications:** Mineral metabolism in animals; phyto estrogens; dairy cattle nutrition. **Mailing Address:** Dept Animal Sci, Animal Sci Lab, Wash State Univ, 226, Pullman, WA 99164-6353. **Fax:** 509-335-1082. **E-Mail:** rkincaid@wsu.edu

KINCAID, STEVEN ALAN, ANATOMY. **Personal Data:** b Indianapolis, Ind, July 6, 1943; m 1977, Nancy; c Amy Elizabeth, Jeremy Brent, Cheryl Ann & Scott Alan. **Education:** Purdue Univ, BS, 1965, DVM, 1969, MS, 1971, PhD (anat), 1977. **Professional Experience:** PROF ANAT, AUBURN UNIV, 1996-; assoc prof anat, Auburn Univ, 1989-1996; mgr physiol & sr scientist, Collagen Corp, Palo Alto, Calif, 1984-1989; assoc prof, Purdue Univ, 1982-1984; asst prof anat, Univ Tenn, 1977-1981; veterinarian, South Bend, Ind, 1972-1973; NIH fel, 1971-1972; Seeing Eye Found, Inc grant, 1969-1971. **Memberships:** Sigma Xi; Am Asn Vet Anatomists; Am Vet Med Asn; Am Soc Animal Sci. **Research Statement & Publications:** Pathobiology of articular cartilage; comparative arthrology; copper metabolism. **Mailing Address:** Dept Anat & Histol Auburn Univ, Rm 109 Greene Hall, Auburn, AL 36849-5510. **E-Mail:** kincasa@vetmed.auburn.edu

KINCAID, THOMAS GARDINER, NONDESTRUCTIVE EVALUATION. **Personal Data:** b Hamilton, Ont, September 18, 1937; m 1962, c 3. **Education:** Queens Univ Kingston, BSc, 1959; Mass Inst Technol, SM, 1961, PhD (elec eng), 1965. **Professional Experience:** PROF ELEC & COMPUT ENG, BOSTON UNIV, as of 2005; systs engr, Gen Elec Co, beginning 1965. **Memberships:** Inst Elec & Electronics Engrs; Am Soc Nondestructive Testing. **Research Statement & Publications:** Investigation of methods of evaluating materials for structural defects, including ultrasonic and electromagnetic techniques and x-ray. **Mailing Address:** Dept Elec & Comput Eng, Col Eng, Boston Univ, PHO520 Eight St Mary's St, Boston, MA 02215. **Fax:** 617-353-5769. **E-Mail:** tgk@bu.edu

KINCAID, WILFRED MACDONALD, STATISTICS, NUMERICAL ANALYSIS. **Personal Data:** b Cornhill, Scotland, September 13, American citizen; wid Fay (Deceased); c William A, W James (deceased) & David A. **Education:** Univ Calif, Berkeley AB, 1940; Brown Univ, PhD (appl math), 1946. **Professional Experience:** EMER PROF MATH, UNIV MICH, ANN ARBOR, 1984-; from asst prof to prof, math, Univ Mich, 1960-1984; lectr, math, 1958-1960; res mathematician, Vision Res Lab, Univ Mich, Ann Arbor, 1950-1958; instr math, Univ Mich, Ann Arbor, 1946-1951; physicist, Nat Adv Comt Aeronaut, Langley Field, 1944-1946; instr math & eng, Brown Univ, 1943-1944. **Memberships:** fel AAAS; emer mem Am Math Soc; emer mem Math Asn Am; emer mem Asn Res Vision & Ophthal; emer mem Soc Sci Explor. **Research Statement & Publications:** Numerical analysis; statistics; vision; psychophysics. **Mailing Address:** Dept Math, Univ Mich, 530 Church St, Ann Arbor, MI 48109-1043. **E-Mail:** wkincaid@umich.edu

KINCANNON, DONNY FRANK, BIOENVIRONMENTAL ENGINEERING. **Personal Data:** b Olustee, Okla, January 17, 1933; m 1957, c 2. **Education:** Okla State Univ, BS, 1959, MS, 1960, PhD (bioeng), 1966. **Professional Experience:** RETIRED; from asst prof to prof civil eng, Okla State Univ, 1966-1980; asst prof, Univ Mo, Rolla, 1965-1966; instr civil eng, Arlington State Col, 1961-1963; Sanit engr, Tex State Dept Health, 1960-1961. **Memberships:** Am Soc Civil Engrs; Am Soc Eng Educ; Water Pollution Control Fedn. **Research Statement & Publications:** Water pollution control; biological treatment; industrial wastes; solid wastes. **Mailing Address:** 4606 Fairfield, Stillwater, OK 74074.

KINCH, MICHAEL ANTHONY, INFRARED DEVICES, SENSOR PHYSICS. **Personal Data:** b Northampton, Eng, November 14, 1936; American citizen; wid, c Lisa Nicol & Mark Anthony. **Education:** Oxford Univ, BA, 1960, MA, 1961, DPhil(solid state physics), 1965. **Honors & Awards:** Jack A Morton Award, Inst Elec & Electronics Engrs, 1987. **Professional Experience:** AT DRS INFRARED TECHNOL, as of 1998; res fel, Tex Instruments Inc, beginning 1985; sr mem, Tex Instruments Inc, 1978-1985; mem tech staff, Tex Instruments Inc, 1966-1978; Postdoctoral fel, Oxford Univ, 1964-1966. **Memberships:** Fel Am Phys Soc. **Research Statement & Publications:** All aspects of the physics of infrared materials, devices and process development. **Mailing Address:** DRS Infrared Technol, 13544 N Cent Expressway, PO Box 740188, Dallas, TX 75374. **E-Mail:** makinch@drs-irtech.com

KINCHEN, DAVID G, MATERIALS LABORATORY TESTING & CONSULTING, STATISTICAL ANALYSIS FOR PROCESS & PROBLEM EVALUATION. **Personal Data:** b Hammond, La, March 7, 1953; m 1979, Laurie; c Adrianne, Travis & Lauren. **Education:** La State Univ, BE, 1980. **Professional Experience:** SR MAT ENGR, LOCKHEED MARTIN, 1994-; chief process eval, Martin Marietta Qual Advan Technol, 1993-1994; group engr, Martin Marietta Qual Advan Technol, 1991-1992; Prin investr, Martin Marietta Qual Eval Lab, Qual Control Performance Criteria Aerospace Aluminum Alloys, Martin Marietta Manned SpaceSysts, 1984-1985; Eval Straight Line X-Ray Radiographic Indications, 1988; sr qual engr, Martin Marietta Qual Eval Lab, Martin Marietta Manned Space Systs, 1985-1991; qual engr, Martin Marietta Qual Eval Lab, Martin Marietta Manned Space Systs, 1983-1985; tech mgr, Mat Eval Lab, Inc, 1981-1983. **Memberships:** Am Soc Metals Int; Am Soc Qual Control. **Research Statement & Publications:** Laboratory identification and investigation of unknown x-ray indications in aluminum alloy weldments; statistical study to characterise weld process performance; develop and train quality control weld inspectors to implement SPC based on study. **Mailing Address:** Lockheed Martin Manned Space Systs, PO Box 29304 MS 3713, New Orleans, LA 70189. **Fax:** 504-257-4403. **E-Mail:** davidkinchen@maf.nasa.gov

KIND, CHARLES ALBERT, BIOCHEMISTRY. **Personal Data:** b Philadelphia, Pa, April 17, 1917; m 1944. **Education:** Lafayette Col, BS, 1939, Yale Univ, PhD (chem), 1942. **Professional Experience:** CONSULT, 1977-; actg dean, Col Lib Arts & Sci, Univ Conn, 1970-1971; from instr to asst prof chem, prof biol & assoc dean Col Lib Arts & Sci, 1967-1977; asst dean, Univ Conn, 1963-1967; from assoc prof to prof zoology, Univ Conn, 1957-1967; Am Philos Soc fel, Bermuda Biol Sta, 1951; Lalor fel, Marine Biol Lab, Woods Hole, Mass, 1949-1950; from instr to asst prof chem, Univ Conn, 1942-1957; res chemist, Nat Defense Res Comt, Yale Univ, 1942; mem corp, Marine Biol Lab, Woods Hole & Bermuda Biol Sta. **Memberships:** AAAS; Am Chem Soc; Am Inst Chemists. **Research Statement & Publications:** Lipids of marine invertebrate animals; sterols of vegetable oils; phosphatases. **Mailing Address:** 47 Willowbrook Rd, Storrs Mansfield, CT 06268.

KIND, LEON SAUL, MICROBIOLOGY. **Personal Data:** b Boston, Mass, December 26, 1922. **Education:** Harvard Univ, AB, 1947; Yale Univ, PhD (microbiol), 1951. **Professional Experience:** RETIRED; prof microbiol, Dalhousie Univ, beginning 1978; assoc prof, Dalhousie Univ, 1970-1978; asst prof, Sch Med, Univ Calif, San Francisco, 1958-1970; res grants, NIH, 1953-; from asst prof to assoc prof, Med Col SC, 1951-1958. **Memberships:** Soc Exp Biol & Med; Am Soc Immunol. **Research Statement & Publications:** Immunology; experimental allergy; sensitivity of pertussis inoculated mice to histamine; anaphylaxis. **Mailing Address:** Eight Heffler, Bedford, NS B4A 1N3, Can.

KIND, PHYLLIS DAWN, CELLULAR IMMUNOLOGY. **Personal Data:** b Sidney, Mont, July 31, 1933. **Education:** Univ Mont, BA, 1955; Univ Mich, MS, 1956, PhD (bact), 1960. **Professional Experience:** PROF EMER MICROBIOL & IMMUNOL, GEORGE WASH UNIV, as of 2003; mem, Drug Abuse Aids Res Comt, Nat Inst Drug Abuse, 1988-1990; fel, Prog Evaluation Panel, 1988; mem, Drug Abuse Biomed Res Review Comt, Nat Inst Drug Abuse, 1986-1988; vis prof, Nat Cheng Kung Med Col, Tainan, Taiwan, 1986; coun, immunol div, Am Soc Microbiol, 1985-1988; prof microbiol & med, george Wash univ, beginning 1979; fel mem, evauluation panel for NSF, 1979-1981; ASSOC DIR, TISSUE TYPING LAB, beginning 1978; chairperson, Immunol Div, Am Soc Microbiol, 1975-1976; assoc prof microbiol, Tissue Typing Lab, 1974-1979; res microbiologist, Nat Cancer Inst, 1971-1974; from instr to asst prof path, Univ Colo, 1963-1971; fel dermat, Univ Mich, 1960-1963. **Memberships:** AAAS; Am Asn Immunol; Am Soc Microbiol; Soc Exp Biol & Med; Sigma Xi; Am Soc Histol Compatability & Immunogenetics. **Research Statement & Publications:** Regulation of antibody synthesis. **Mailing Address:** Dept Microbiol & Immunol, George Wash Univ, Washington, DC 20052. **Fax:** 202-223-3691.

KIND, RICHARD JOHN, AERODYNAMICS OF AIRCRAFT & TURBOMACHINERY WIND ENGINEERING. **Personal Data:** m 1967, Lorraine; c David & Donna. **Education:** Loyola Col, BSc, 1962; McGill Univ, BEng, 1964; Univ Cambridge, PhD (aerodyn), 1967. **Honors & Awards:** Casey-Baldwin Award, Can Aeronaut & Space Inst, 1993. **Professional Experience:** PROF ENG, CARLETON UNIV, 1980-; mem, Fluid Dynamics Panel, NATO Adv Group Aerospace Res & Develop, 1991-; chmn, Dept Mech & Aerospace Eng, Carleton Univ, 1986-1992; vis res officer, Nat Res Coun, 1973-1974; vis asst prof, WVa Univ, 1969; from asst prof to assoc prof, Carleton Univ, 1967-1980. **Memberships:** Fel Can Aeronaut & Space Inst; assoc fel Am Inst Aeronaut & Astronaut; Am Soc Mech Engrs. **Research Statement & Publications:** Low speed aerodynamics with applications to aircraft, turbomachinery and wind engineering; boundary-layer flow, turbulence modelling, wind damage mechanisms, effects of surface roughness. **Mailing Address:** Dept Mech & Aerospace Eng, Carleton Univ, 1125 Colonel By Dr, Ottawa, ON K1S 5B6, Can. **Fax:** 613-520-5715. **E-Mail:** dkind@mae.carleton.ca

KINDEL, JOSEPH MARTIN, PLASMA PHYSICS. **Personal Data:** b Barberton, Ohio, March 10, 1943; c 2. **Education:** Univ Akron, BS, 1965; Univ Calif, Los Angeles, MS, 1966, PhD (physics), 1970. **Professional Experience:** GROUP LEADER INERTIAL FUSION & PLASMA THEORY, APPL THEORET PHYSICS DIV, LOS ALAMOS NAT LAB, 1980-; assoc group leader, Plasma Theory Sect, 1979-1980; head, Plasma Theory Sect, 1978-1979; assoc group leader laser theory, Laser Div, 1975-1978; mem staff controlled thermonuclear res group, Physics Div, Los Alamos Nat Lab, 1971-1972 & laser theory group, Theoret Div, 1972-1975; res assoc plasma physics, Princeton Univ, 1970-1971. **Memberships:** Am Phys Soc. **Research Statement & Publications:** Space plasma physics; radio frequency heating of plasmas; nonlinear theory; controlled thermonuclear fusion; laser plasma interaction; plasma simulation studies; hydrodynamics of laser fusion. **Mailing Address:** Los Alamos Nat Lab, MS F630, PO Box 1663, Los Alamos, NM 87545. **Fax:** 505-665-1093. **E-Mail:** jkindel@lanl.gov

KINDEL, PAUL KURT, BIOCHEMISTRY. **Personal Data:** b Milwaukee, Wis, September 6, 1934; m 1961, c 3. **Education:** Univ Wis, BS, 1956; Cornell Univ, PhD (biochem), 1961. **Professional Experience:** PROF EMER BIOCHEM, MICH STATE UNIV, as of

2001; prof biochem, Mich Stste Univ, 1977-2001; from asst prof to assoc prof biochem, Mich State Univ, 1963-1977; NIH fel, Max Planck Inst Cell Chem, Munich, 1961-1963. **Memberships:** AAAS; Am Soc Biol Chemists; Am Soc Plant Physiol. **Research Statement & Publications:** Isolation and structure of plant cell wall polysaccharides, particularly pectic polysaccharides; biosynthesis of pectic polysaccharides. **Mailing Address:** Dept Biochem, Mich State Univ 212 Biol Chem, East Lansing, MI 48824-1319.

KINDER, THOMAS HARTLEY, PHYSICAL OCEANOGRAPHY. **Personal Data:** b Riverside, Calif, September 6, 1943; m 1970. **Education:** US Naval Acad, BS, 1965; Univ Wash, MS, 1974, PhD (phys oceanog), 1976. **Professional Experience:** TEAM LEADER, COASTER DYNAMIC PROG, OFF NAVAL RES, 1989-; scientific officer, Coatal Sci Prog, Off Naval Res, 1987-1989; guest investr, Woods Hole Oceanog Inst, 1984-1985; oceanogr, Naval Ocean Res & Develop Activ, 1978-1987; res assoc, dept oceanog, Univ Wash, 1976-1978; res asst, dept oceanog, Univ Wash, 1971-1976. **Memberships:** Am Geophys Union; Am Meteorol Soc; AAAS; Sigma Xi. **Research Statement & Publications:** Measurements of mesoscale features on shelves and in semi-enclosed seas (Bering, Caribbean, Mediterranean), especially fronts and eddies formed by flows exiting straits and flows within straits. **Mailing Address:** Coastal Dynamic Prog, Off Naval Res, 800 N Quincy St, Springfield, VA 22217-1206. **E-Mail:** kindert@onr.navy.mil

KINDERLEHRER, DAVID (SAMUEL), MATHEMATICS. **Personal Data:** b Allentown, Pa, October 23, 1941. **Education:** Mass Inst Technol, SB, 1963; Univ Calif, Berkeley, PhD (math), 1968. **Professional Experience:** PROF MATH SCI, CARNEGIE MELLON UNIV, as of 2003; prof math, Univ Minn, Minneapolis, beginning 1975; researcher math, Ital Govt Advan Training Sch, Pisa, 1971-1972; from instr to asst prof, Univ Minn, Minneapolis, 1968-1975. **Research Statement & Publications:** Partial differential equations; minimal surfaces; variational inequalities; mechanics. **Mailing Address:** Dept Math, Carnegie Mellon Univ, Wean Hall 7208, Pittsburgh, PA 15213-3890. **E-Mail:** davidk@andrew.cmu.edu

KINDERMAN, EDWIN MAX, ENERGY & ENVIRONMENTAL CONTROL TECHNOLOGIES, ENVIRONMENTAL REGULATION. **Personal Data:** b Cincinnati, Ohio, August 21, 1916; m Jean; c Gibbs V, Albert J, Mary M & Joel F. **Education:** Oberlin Col, AB, 1937; Univ Notre Dame, MS, 1938, PhD (phys chem), 1941. **Professional Experience:** RETIRED; independant consult energy & environ, 1994-2005; sr scientist, mgr energy planning, 1986-1994; mgr nuclear & utility systs, mgr energy planning, 1980-1986; sr scientist, mgr mkt Europe, 1975-1977; sr scientist, Sci Int, 1973-1975; dir mkt, Phys Sci, 1971-1973; dir, Appl Physics Lab, 1968-1971; mgr, Nuclear Physics Dept, 1957-1968; sr physicist, 1956-1957; chemist, Gen Elec Co, Wash, 1949-1956; from asst prof to assoc prof chem, Univ Portland, 1945-1949; chemist, Radiation Lab, Univ Calif, 1943-1945; res chemist, Res & Develop Div, H J Kaiser Co, Calif, 1943; Chemist, Columbia Steel Casting Co, Ore, 1943; instr chem, Univ Portland, 1941-1943. **Memberships:** Am Chem Soc; Am Phys Soc; Am Nuclear Soc; Sigma Xi; Inst Nuclear Math Mgt. **Research Statement & Publications:** Analytical chemistry; radiation chemistry and radiation damage effect; nuclear materials management; energy economics and planning; non fossil energy technologies; nuclear energy and weapons proliferation; environmental regulation and techonologies. **Mailing Address:** 855 Marshall Dr, Palo Alto, CA 94303. **Fax:** 650-856-7414. **E-Mail:** ekinderman@aol.com

KINDERMANN, ROSS P, MATHEMATICS. **Education:** Univ Ill, PhD (Maths), 1978. **Professional Experience:** PROF, DEPT MATH, SDAK STATE UNIV, as on 2006. **Memberships:** Am Math Soc. **Mailing Address:** Math Dept, SDak State Univ Box 2220, Brookings, SD 57007-0001. **Fax:** 605-688-6814. **E-Mail:** Ross_Kindermann@sdstate.edu

KINDERS, ROBERT JAMES, TUMOR MARKERS, BREAST CANCER & BLADDER CANCER. **Personal Data:** b February 12, 1948; m 1980, Patricia. **Education:** Loyola Univ Chicago, BS, 1970, MS, 1976; Kans State Univ, PhD (biol), 1980. **Professional Experience:** DIR, RES & DEVELOP, ALIDEX INC, 1998-; dir, Reagents Res & Develop, Bard Daig Sci, 1994-1998; head, Molecular Diag Appn Lab, Abbott Diag, Abbott Lab, 1991-1994; MEM ADV COUN, CTR BASIC CANCER RES, KANS STATE UNIV, 1990-; proj mgr, Abbott Lab, 1989-1991; prof mgr, Abbott Lab, 1985-1989; res scientist, Abbott Lab, 1983-1985; res assoc, Div Biol, Kans State Univ, 1980-1983; staff, Dept Immunochem Res, Evanston Hosp, 1976-1977. **Memberships:** Am Asn Cancer Res; AAAS; Am Asn Clin Chem. **Research Statement & Publications:** Application of monoclonal antibodies in cancer diagnosis and therapy; use of alternative binding agents in In Vitro Diagnostics; diagnostic immunoassays and their interferents; molecular diagnostics. **Mailing Address:** Bard Diag, 12277 134th Ct NE, Redmond, WA 98052. **Fax:** 425-814-1520. **E-Mail:** bobkatbb@aol.com

KINDIG, DAVID A, PEDIATRICS, HEALTH POLICY. **Personal Data:** b May 19, 1940; m 1962, Mary; c Mark, Laura Elizabeth & Brian David. **Education:** Carleton Col, BA, 1962; Univ Chicago, MD, 1968, PhD (exp path), 1968. **Professional Experience:** PROF EMER POP HEALTH SCI & VCHANCELLOR HEALTH SCI, WIS SCH MED, as of 2005; Dir Wis Network Health Policy Res, Univ Wis-Madison Sch Med, 1994-; vis prof health mgt, Beijing Med Univ, Sch Pub Health, beginning 1988 & Shanghi Second Med Univ, 1987-; dir progs health mgt, Sch Med, 1985-1994; chair, Wis Gov Task Force AIDS, 1985-1986; bd dirs, Am Med Student Asn Found, 1984-1986; prof Prev Med, Univ Wis-Madison Sch Med, 1980-; vchancellor health sci, Univ Wis-Madison, 1980-1985; sr prog consult, Rural Prod Proj, Robert Wood Johnson Found, 1979-1982; assoc prof, Dept Community Health, Albert Einstein Col Med, 1978-1980; dir, Montefiore Hosp & Med Ctr, 1976-1980; bd dirs, Rural Prod Proj, Robert Wood Johnson Found, 1975-1979; dep dir, Bur Health Manpower, HEW, 1974-1976; co-dir, Inst Health Team Develop, Montefiore Hosp & Med Ctr, 1973-1974; dir, Div Prof Servs, Nat Health Servs Corp, HEW, 1971-1973; instr, Dept Community Health, Albert Einstein Col Med, 1970-1971; actg med dir, Martin Luther King Jr Neighborhood Health Ctr, 1970-1971; from resident pediat to chief resident, Dept Pediat & Social Med, Montefiore Hosp & Med Ctr, NY, 1969-1971; prog coordr, Montefiore Hosp & Med Ctr, 1969-1970; intern, Dept Pediat, Univ Chicago, 1968-1969. **Memberships:** Inst Med-Nat Acad Sci; Asn Health Servs Res (treas, 1993-1996; pres-elect, 1996); Am Col Physician Execs; Soc Med Adminr. **Mailing Address:** Dept Pop Health Sci, Univ Wis-Madison, 229 Bradley Mem 1300 Univ Ave, Madison, WI 53706-2397. **Fax:** 608-262-6404. **E-Mail:** dakindig@facstaff.wisc.edu

KINDLER, SHARON DEAN, ENTOMOLOGY. **Personal Data:** b Omaha, Nebr, April 27, 1930; m 1964, c 2. **Education:** Univ Nebr, BSc, 1959, PhD (entom), 1967. **Professional Experience:** Adj prof entom, Okla State Univ, as of 2003; SR RES ENTOMOLOGIST, AGR RES SERV, USDA, OKLA STATE UNIV, 1987-; res entomologist, Agr Res Serv, USDA, Univ Nebr, 1964-1987. **Memberships:** Entom Soc Am; Sigma Xi. **Research Statement & Publications:** Biology, ecology and control of sorghum and grass insects; plant resistance to sorghum and grass insects. **Mailing Address:** Dept Entom, Okla State Univ, 1301 N Western Rd, Stillwater, OK 74075-2714. **Fax:** 405-624-4142. **E-Mail:** dean.kindler@ars.usda.gov

KINDT, GLENN W, NEUROSURGERY. **Personal Data:** b Alpena, Mich, September 10, 1930; m 1960, c 4. **Education:** Mich State Univ, BS, 1951; Pa State Univ, BS, 1952; Univ Mich, MD, 1959. **Professional Experience:** DIR NEUROSURG SERV, VET ADMIN MED CTR, as of 2004; head, Dept Neurosurg, Univ Colo Health Sci Ctr, 1981-1999; PROF, DEPT NEUROSURG, UNIV COLO MED CTR, 1980-; from asst prof to assoc prof neurosurg, Univ Mich Med Ctr, Ann Arbor, 1969-1980; co-investr, NIH res grant, 1967-; asst prof, Univ Calif, Davis, 1967-1969; Chief investr, US Vet Admin res grant, 1966-; assoc, Med Col SC, 1966-1967; instr, Med Col SC, 1965-1966; resident neurosurg, Univ Mich Hosp, 1962-1965; resident, Harvard Med Sch & Peter Bent Brigham Hosp, Boston, 1961-1962; resident surg, Univ Mich Hosp, 1960-1961; Intern med, Univ Mich Hosp, 1959-1960. **Memberships:** AMA; Cong Neurol Surg. **Research Statement & Publications:** Regional hypothermia and vascular insufficiency of the brain; intracerebral hematomas. **Mailing Address:** Dept Neurosurg, Health Sci Ctr, Univ Colo, 4200 E Ninth Ave C-307, Denver, CO 80262-0001. **E-Mail:** glenn.kindt@uchsc.edu

KINDT, THOMAS JAMES, BIOCHEMISTRY, IMMUNOGENETICS. **Personal Data:** b Cincinnati, Ohio, May 18, 1939; m 1964, c Rachel & James. **Education:** Thomas More Col, AB, 1963; Univ Ill, Urbana, PhD (biochem), 1967. **Professional Experience:** SEC HEAD MOLECULAR & CELLULAR IMMUNOGENETICS SEC, NAT INST ALLERGY & INFECTIOUS DIS, NIH, as of 2004; DIR, DIV INTRAMURAL RES, 1995-; vis scientist, Inst Pasteur, Paris, 1982-1983; adj prof micro & pediatrics, Sch Med & Dent, Georgetown Univ, 1981-; adv ed, J Exp Med, 1977-; Immunochem, 1977-; chief lab immunogenetics, Nat Inst Allergy & Infectious Dis, NIH, beginning 1977; assoc ed, J Immunol, beginning 1973; assoc prof biol, Rockefeller Univ, 1973-1977; adj assoc prof med, Cornell Univ Med Col, 1973-1977; asst prof, Rockefeller Univ, 1971-1973; fel, Rockefeller Univ, 1970-1971; asst res scientist, City Hope Med Ctr, 1969-1970; NIH fel biol, City Hope Med Ctr, 1967-1969. **Memberships:** Am Heart Asn; Harvey Soc; Sigma Xi; Am Asn Immunol; Am Soc Biol Chemists. **Research Statement & Publications:** Genetic determinants on immunoglobulins and histocompatibility antigens; protein and polysaccharide structure. **Mailing Address:** Sec Molecular & Cellular Immunogenetics, Nat Inst Allergy & Infectious Dis, NIH, Bethesda, MD 20817. **Fax:** 301-402-0259. **E-Mail:** tk9c@nih.gov

KINEKE, J H, JR, TERMINAL BALLISTICS. **Personal Data:** b Rockville Center, NY, April 27, 1933. **Education:** St Johns Univ, BS, 1954; Univ Del, MS, 1968. **Professional Experience:** RES PHYSICIST, US ARMY RES LAB, MD, 1954-. **Memberships:** Am Phys Soc. **Mailing Address:** 3403 Crosswood Dr, Aberdeen, MD 21001.

KINERSLY, THORN, DENTISTRY, DENTAL RESEARCH. **Personal Data:** b The Dalles, Ore, September 15, 1923; m 1954, c 3. **Education:** Univ Ore, DMD, 1948. **Professional Experience:** Consult on-site invest res appl, Dent Sect, NIH, 1970; prin investr, Educ & Res Found Prosthodont, 1969; ASSOC PROF DENT, DENT SCH, UNIV ORE HEALTH SCI CTR, 1967-; abstractor, Oral Res Abstr, 1966-; asst prof, Dent Sch, Univ Ore Health Sci Ctr, 1964-1967; res assoc, Dent Sch, Univ Ore Health Sci Ctr, 1964; pvt pract, 1956-1964; res fel, Nobel Inst, 1954; res fel dent, Sch Med, Yale Univ, 1952-1956; lectr, Forsyth Dent Infirmary, 1952-1956; asst resident, Sch Med, Yale Univ & Grace-New Haven Community Hosp, 1950; intern children's dent, Forsyth Dent Infirmary, 1949-1950; pvt pract, 1948-1949. **Memberships:** Fel AAAS; Soc Exp Biol & Med; Int Asn Dent Res; Am Dent Asn; Sigma Xi. **Research Statement & Publications:** Paper electrophoresis of saliva and salivary glands for identification of enzymes, blood group factors and anti-bacterial factors; track radioautography of teeth with Ca-45 isotopes; lasers and their relation to dentistry. **Mailing Address:** 10720 SW 30th Ave, Portland, OR 97219.

KING, ALAN JONATHAN, OPTIMIZATION, STOCHASTIC PROGRAMMING, RISK MANAGEMENT, GENERALIZED EQUATION, DECOMPOSITION METHODS, COMPUTER IMPLEMENTATIONS. **Personal Data:** b Northampton, Eng, October 20, 1954; Canadian citizen. **Education:** Univ Wash, BS, 1981, MS, 1984, PhD (appl math), 1986. **Professional Experience:** AT IBM T J WATSON RES CTR, as of 2004; Vis lectr, Dept Math, Univ Wash, 1989; RES STAFF MEM, INT BUS MACH RES, 1988-; actg asst prof, Dept Math, Univ Wash, 1988; res scholar, Int Inst Appl Systs Anal, 1987-1988; Postdoctoral fel math, Univ BC, 1986-1987; assoc ed math, J Optimization, Soc Indust & Appl Math. **Memberships:** Math Prog Soc; Opers Res Soc Am; Soc Indust & Appl Math. **Research Statement & Publications:** Stochastic programming; applications to engineering and economic systems; optimization theory; statistical estimation; robustness and sensitivity analysis; large scale optimization. **Mailing Address:** IBM T J Watson Res Ctr, PO Box 218, Yorktown Heights, NY 10598. **E-Mail:** kingaj@watson.ibm.com

KING, ALBERT IGNATIUS, BIOENGINEERING. **Personal Data:** b Tokyo, Japan, June 12, 1934; American citizen; m 1960, c 2. **Education:** Univ Hong Kong, BSc, 1955; Wayne State Univ, MS, 1960, PhD (eng mech), 1966. **Honors & Awards:** Charles Russ Richards Mem Award, Am Soc Mech Engrs, 1980; Volvo Award, 1984. **Professional Experience:** DISTINGUISHED PROF MECH ENG, SCH MED, WAYNE STATE UNIV, beginning 1990; DIR & DISTINGUISHED PROF BIOENGINEERING, SCH MED, WAYNE STATE UNIV, 1976-; ASSOC NEUROSURG, SCH MED, WAYNE STATE UNIV, beginnning 1971; from instr to assoc prof, Sch Med, Wayne State Univ, 1960-1976; demonstr civil eng, Hong Kong, 1955-1958; NIH Career develop award. **Memberships:** Am Soc Eng Educ; Am Soc Mech Engrs; Am Acad Orthop Surg; Sigma Xi. **Research Statement & Publications:** Human response to acceleration and vibration, automotive and aircraft safety; biomechanics of the spine; mathematical modelling of impact events; low back pain research. **Mailing Address:** Mech Eng Wayne State Univ, 818 W Hancock, Detroit, MI 48202. **Fax:** 313-578-5703. **E-Mail:** king@eng.wayne.edu

KING, ALEXANDER HARVEY, ELECTRON MICROSCOPY, CRYSTALLOGRAPHY. **Personal Data:** b London, Eng, July 1, 1954; m 1977, Christine; c 2. **Education:** Univ Sheffield, BMet, 1975; Univ Oxford, DPhil(metall), 1979. **Professional Experience:** PROF & HEAD, MAT SCI & ENG, PURDUE UNIV, as of 2005; PROF MAT SCI & ENG, STATE UNIV NY, STONY BROOK, 1990-; vprovost grad studies, Dept Mat Sci & Eng, State Univ NY, Stony Brook, 1990-1992; assoc vprovost grad studies, Dept Mat Sci & Eng, State Univ NY, Stony Brook, 1987-1990; from asst prof to assoc prof, Dept Mat Sci & Eng, State Univ NY, Stony Brook, 1981-1990; Harwell fel, Dept Metall & Sci Mat, Univ Oxford, 1979. **Memberships:** Inst Metall; Am Inst Mining Metall & Petrol Engrs; Electron Microscope Soc Am; Am Soc Metals; Mat Res Soc; Am Phys Soc. **Research Statement & Publications:** Crystal lattice defects, particularly grain boundaries; electron microscopy, electron and x-ray diffraction. **Mailing Address:** Dept Mat Sci & Eng, Purdue Univ, West Lafayette, IN 47907. **E-Mail:** alexking@ecn.purdue.edu

KING, ALFRED DOUGLAS, FOOD MICROBIOLOGY. **Personal Data:** b Portland, Ore, May 11, 1933; m 1959, c 2. **Education:** Wash State Univ, BS, 1955, PhD (food sci), 1965; Univ Calif, Davis, MS, 1961. **Professional Experience:** RES MICROBIOLOGIST, WESTERN REGIONAL RES LAB, USDA, 1978-; vis scientist, Commonwealth Sci & Indust Res Orgn Div Food Res, Sydney, Australia, 1977-1978, 1989; res leader microbiol, USDA, 1973-1977; microbiologist, USDA, 1965-1972; from assoc chemist to chemist,

USDA, 1961-1965; food technologist, Nalley's Inc, 1957-1959. **Memberships:** Inst Food Technologists; Am Soc Microbiol; Asn Off Anal Chemists; Am Acad Microbiol; vpres Int Comn Food Mycol. **Research Statement & Publications:** Microbial physiology; food sanitation and public health; wine flavor; human and microbial nutrition; food mycology. **Mailing Address:** USDA Western Regional Res Lab, 800 Buchanan St, Albany, CA 94710.

KING, ALLEN LEWIS, history of physics, biophysics; deceased, see previous edition for last biography

KING, AMY C P, ANALYSIS. **Personal Data:** b Douglas, Wyo, December 30, 1928; m 1949. **Education:** Univ Mo, BS, 1949; Wichita State Univ, MA, 1960; Univ Ky, PhD, 1970. **Professional Experience:** PROF EMER MATH, EASTERN KY UNIV, as of 2004; Found Professorship, Eastern Ky Univ, Richmond, 1993; prof math, Eastern Ky Univ, beginning 1979; from asst prof to assoc prof, Eastern KY Univ, 1970-1979; teaching asst, Univ Ky, 1967-1970; instr math, Washburn Univ, 1966-1967; asst instr, Univ Kans, 1962-1965; instr, Wichita State Univ, 1960-1962; teaching fel, Wichita State Univ, 1958-1960; Teacher pub schs, Goddard, Kans, 1956-1958. **Memberships:** Am Math Soc; Math Asn Am; Nat Coun Teachers Math. **Research Statement & Publications:** Complex variables; mathematics education. **Mailing Address:** Dept MAth & Statist, Eastern Ky Univ, Wallace 313, Richmond, KY 40475. **Fax:** 859-622-3051. **E-Mail:** amyking@infi.net

KING, ANN CHRISTIE, BIOCHEMISTRY, MOLECULAR BIOLOGY. **Education:** Wash Univ, PhD (molecular biol), 1979. **Professional Experience:** SR RES SCIENTIST, WELLCOME RES LABS, 1987-; Asst prof biochem, Sch Med, Univ Ill, 1982-1987. **Research Statement & Publications:** Mechanism of growth factor. **Mailing Address:** Div Molecular Genetics Burroughs Wellcome Co, 3030 Cornwallis Rd, Research Triangle Park, NC 27709-4416.

KING, ANTHONY WAYNE, ECOLOGY. **Education:** Univ Tenn, PhD (Ecol), 1986. **Professional Experience:** RES STAFF MEM, CARBON-CLIMATE SIMULATION SCI GROUP, ENVIRON SCI DIV, OAK RIDGE NAT LAB, as of 2005. **Research Statement & Publications:** Systems ecology; ecosystem dynamics and ecosystem modeling; global biogeochemistry; landscape ecology; spatially structured population dynamics; model analysis. **Mailing Address:** Environ Sci Div, Oak Ridge Nat Lab, PO Box 2008, Oak Ridge, TN 37831-6335. **Fax:** 865-574-2232. **E-Mail:** kingaw@ornl.gov

KING, ARTHUR FRANCIS, GEOLOGY. **Personal Data:** b St John's, Nfld, February 11, 1937; m 1963, Muriel; c Peter & Jennifer. **Education:** Mem Univ, BSc, 1961, MSc, 1963; Univ Reading, PhD (geol), 1967. **Professional Experience:** DEPT HEAD EARTH SCI, UNIV NFLD, 1987-; dep head, Acad Earth Sci, 1987-1992; PROF GEOL, MEM UNIV NFLD, 1980-; from asst prof to assoc prof, 1967-1980. **Memberships:** Geol Asn Can. **Research Statement & Publications:** Late precambrian clastic sequences in avalon zone of Newfoundland and the Appalachian-Caledonian Orogen. **Mailing Address:** Dept Earth Sci, Mem Univ NFld, St John's, NL A1C 5S7, Can. **Fax:** 709-737-4569. **E-Mail:** aking@esd.mun.ca

KING, BELINDA B, MATHEMATICS. **Education:** Univ Md, BS, 1985; Univ Md Baltimore, MS, 1987; Clemnson Univ, PhD, 1991. **Professional Experience:** PROF MATH, VA TECH, VA, 2002-. **Mailing Address:** Va Tech 518 McBryde, Interdisciplinary Ctr Appl Math, Blacksburg, VA 24061. **Fax:** 540-231-5960. **E-Mail:** bbking@vt.edu

KING, B(ERNARD) G(EORGE), ELECTRICAL ENGINEERING. **Personal Data:** b Kitchener, Ont, December 22, 1922; American citizen; m 1949, Joan Townsend; c Charles, Bernard, Adam, Philip & Quintas. **Education:** Univ Southern Calif, BE, 1944; Univ Wis, MS, 1951, PhD (elec eng), 1955. **Professional Experience:** CONSULT, 1989-; prof, Stevens Inst Technol, 1987-1989; ed, Bell Syst Tech J, 1981-1984; mem tech staff, Bell Tel Labs, Inc, 1955-1988; instr elec eng, Univ Southern Calif, 1944-1948 & Univ Wis, 1948-1955. **Memberships:** Sigma Xi; Inst Elec & Electronics Engrs. **Research Statement & Publications:** Atmospheric optical transmission; radio physics; microwave radio. **Mailing Address:** 5 Monmouth Ave, Rumson, NJ 07760.

KING, BETTY LOUISE, METABOLISM. **Personal Data:** b Atlanta, Ga, November 26, 1943; c 1. **Education:** Brandeis Univ, BA, 1965; Harvard Univ, PhD (microbiol, molecular genetics), 1972. **Professional Experience:** Asst div chmn nat sci, Northern VA Community Col, 1983-1985; PROF BIOL, NORTHERN VA COMMUNITY COL, 1978-; from asst prof to assoc prof, Northern VA Community Col, 1978-1984; asst prof biol, Skidmore Col, 1976-1977; Asst prof biol, Bard Col, 1972-1975. **Research Statement & Publications:** Genetics and regulation of primary and secondary metabolism in bacteria, fungi and plants; chemical communication; biochemistry and ecology of alkaloids; drug use and abuse. **Mailing Address:** Div Sci & Appl Tech, Northern Va Community Col 3001 N Beauregard St, Alexandria, VA 22311-5065. **E-Mail:** bking@nvcc.vccs.edu

KING, BLAKE, MECHANICAL ENGINEERING, PHYSICAL METALLURGY. **Personal Data:** b Atlanta, Ga, February 4, 1921; m 1948, c 2. **Education:** Univ Fla, BME, 1948; Calif Inst Technol, MSME, 1949. **Professional Experience:** RETIRED; from assoc prof to prof mech eng, Univ Miami, 1958-1987; unit supvr, Nuclear Div, 1956-1958; sr engr, Design Integration Dept, Martin Co, Md, 1954-1956; asst prof mech eng, Univ Miami, 1949-1951, 1953-1954. **Memberships:** Am Soc Metals; Metall Soc; Am Soc Mech Engrs. **Research Statement & Publications:** Dispersion-strengthened high temperature alloys; creative mechanical design. **Mailing Address:** 4102 Alhambra Circle, Miami, FL 33146.

KING, CALVIN ELIJAH, MATHEMATICS. **Personal Data:** b Chicago, Ill, June 5, 1928. **Education:** Morehouse Col, AB, 1949; Atlanta Univ, MA, 1950; Ohio State Univ, PhD (math educ), 1959. **Professional Experience:** RETIRED; head, Dept Physics & Math, Tenn State Univ, 1974-1979; specialist math & head dept, Fed Adv Teachers Col, Nigeria, 1962-1964; head, Prof Math, 1958-1988; asst instr, Ohio State Univ, 1955-1958; instr math, Jackson Col, 1953-1955. **Research Statement & Publications:** Methods of teaching remedial mathematics; teaching elementary mathematics by television; the relation of modern mathematics to traditional mathematics. **Mailing Address:** 626 N Fifth St, Nashville, TN 37207.

KING, C(ARY) JUDSON, III, SEPARATION PROCESSES. **Personal Data:** b Ft Monmouth, NJ, September 27, 1934; m 1957, Jeanne; c Mary E, Cary J IV & Catherine J. **Education:** Yale Univ, BE, 1956; Mass Inst Technol, SM, 1958, ScD(chem eng), 1960. **Honors & Awards:** 25th Ann Inst Lectr, 1973; Food, Pharmaceut & Bioeng Div Award, 1975; William H Walker Award, 1976; Warren K Lewis Award; 1990, Clarence Gerhold Award, 1992; Am Inst Chem Engrs; George Westinghouse Award; 1978, Am Soc Eng Educ; Mac Pruitt Award, Coun Chem Res, 1990; Award Separations Sci & Technol, Am Chem Soc, 1997. **Professional Experience:** PROF CHEM ENG EMER & UC SYSTEM-WIDE PROVOST & SR VPRES ACAD AFFAIRS EMER, UNIV CALIF, as of 2005; provost & sr vpres Acad Affairs, Univ Calif, beginning 1996; vice provost res, prof schs & cols, 1994-1996; provost, prof schs & cols, 1987-1994; dean col chem, Univ Calif, Berkeley, 1981-1987; chmn dept, Univ Calif, Berkeley, 1972-1981; prof chem eng, Univ Calif, beginning 1969; vice chmn dept, Univ Calif, Berkeley, 1967-1972; consult, Procter & Gamble Co, 1965-1993; from asst prof to assoc prof, Univ Calif, Berkeley, 1963-1969; asst prof chem eng, Mass Inst Technol, 1959-1963; dir Bayway Sta, Sch Chem Eng Pract, Mass Inst Technol, 1959-1961. **Memberships:** Nat Acad Eng; Am Chem Soc; fel Am Inst Chem Engrs; AAAS. **Research Statement & Publications:** Synthesis and analysis of chemical processes; drying and concentration of foods; separation processes; water pollution abatement. **Mailing Address:** Dept Chem Eng, Univ Calif, 320 Gilman, Kensington, CA 94707-1009. **Fax:** 510-987-9209. **E-Mail:** jud.king@ucop.edu

KING, CHARLES C, NATURAL HISTORY, NATURAL AREAS MANAGEMENT. **Personal Data:** b Kittanning, Pa, January 12, 1933; m 1981, Anita Colton; c Connie, Jerry, Linda, Sylvia, Eric & Victor. **Education:** Marietta Col, BS, 1954; Ohio State Univ, MSc, 1956, PhD (entom), 1961. **Honors & Awards:** Herbert Osborn Awd, Ohio Biolo Survy, 1992; Ohio Convers Hall of Fame, Ohio Dept of Natural Resou, 1992. **Professional Experience:** DIR EMER, OHIO BIOL SURV, 1993-; coordr, 38th Meeting Am Inst Biol Sci, 1987; mem, Ohio Natural Areas Coun, 1984-1990; NAm Prairie Conf, Ohio State Univ, 1978 & Ann Conf Lepidopterists Soc, 1983; exec dir, Ohio Biol Surv, 1972-1992; coordr, Geobot Conf, Malone Col, 1970; consult, Dept Geol, Univ Calgary, 1968 & Dept Geol, Univ Calgary, 1968; consult, Dept Bot, Okla State Univ, 1963; consult radiation biol, Univ Wash, 1962; from asst prof to prof biol, Malone Col, 1961-1972; res technician entom, Ohio Agr Res & Develop, 1956-1961; mem, Orgn Biol Field Sta, Ohio Acad Sci; mem, Ohio Acad Sci. **Memberships:** Am Quaternary Asn; Nature Conserv. **Research Statement & Publications:** Effects of herbicides and fungicides on honeybees, metabolism of 2, 4-D in blackjack oak; effects of 2, 4-D on nectar secretion; peat bog palynology; environmental analysis; distribution and ecology of prairies in central Ohio. **Mailing Address:** 483 Cliffside Pl, Pagosa Springs, CO 81147.

KING, CHARLES EVERETT, POPULATION BIOLOGY. **Personal Data:** b Oak Park, Ill, May 8, 1934; c 2. **Education:** Emory Univ, AB, 1958; Fla State Univ, MS, 1960; Univ Wash, PhD (zool), 1965. **Professional Experience:** PROF EMER ZOOL, ORE STATE UNIV, 2002-; Univ Milan, Italy, 1992; Vis prof, Shandong Col Oceanog, People's RepubChina, 1984-1985 & Univ Valencia, Spain, 1991-1992; vis scholar, Univ Wash, 1985; prof zool, Ore State Univ, 1977-2002; chmn dept, Ore State Univ, 1977-1986; from assoc prof to prof biol, Univ SFla, 1972-1977; asst prof biol, Yale Univ, 1968-1972; asst prof zool, Univ Ill, Urbana, 1966-1968; instr biol, Yale Univ, 1965-1966; Res assoc zool, Col Fisheries, Univ Wash, 1965. **Memberships:** Fel AAAS; Soc Study Evolution; Sigma Xi. **Research Statement & Publications:** Laboratory and field investigation of zooplankton population dynamics; interaction of genetical and ecological phenomena within populations; relation of life history characteristics to ecological adaptation. **Mailing Address:** Dept Zool, Ore State Univ, Corvallis, OR 97331-2914. **Fax:** 541-737-0501. **E-Mail:** kingc@science.oregonstate.edu

KING, CHARLES MILLER, BIOCHEMISTRY, ONCOLOGY. **Personal Data:** b West Salem, Ill, October 2, 1932; m 1954, c 2. **Education:** Univ Ill, Urbana, BA, 1954; Univ Minn, Minneapolis, PhD (biochem), 1962. **Professional Experience:** ADJ PROF CHEM, WAYNE STATE UNIV, 1982-; mem, Coun Res & Clin Invest Awards, 1988-1991; mem, Metab Path Study Sect, NIH, 1986-1990; assoc ed, Cancer Res, 1983-1987; mem, Chem Path Study Sect, NIH, 1979-1983; mem, Amines Comt, Nat Res Coun, Nat Acad Sci, 1979-1980; dir carcinogenesis prog, Comprehensive Cancer Ctr Metrop Detroit, beginning 1977; chmn Dept Chem Carcinogenisis, Mich Cancer Found, beginning 1977; expert, Nat Cancer Inst, Nat Ctr Toxicol Res, 1975-1977; assoc prof biochem, Univ Ark for Med Sci, 1975-1977; mem, Nat Bladder Cancer Proj, Nat Cancer Inst, 1973-1978; asst prof med, Pritzker Sch Med, Univ Chicago, 1973-1975; from actg dir to dir div cancer res, Michael Reese Hosp & Med Ctr, 1965-1975; res assoc, Michael Reese Hosp & Med Ctr, 1965-1968; Am Cancer Soc fel, Neth Cancer Inst, 1963-1965; res fel oncol, Med Sch, Univ Minn, Minneapolis, 1962-1963. **Memberships:** Am Asn Cancer Res; Am Chem Soc; Am Soc Biochem & Molecular Biol; Japanese Cancer Soc; Environ Mutagen Soc. **Research Statement & Publications:** Mechanism of action of chemical carcinogens; metabolism in covalent interaction with protein and nucleic acid. **Mailing Address:** Mich Cancer Found, 110 E Warren, Detroit, MI 48201-1379.

KING, CHARLES O(RRIN), CHEMICAL ENGINEERING. **Personal Data:** b Rochester, NY, January 9, 1916; m 1943, Mary; c Marilyn, Marjorie & Charles W. **Education:** Univ Rochester, BS, 1937; Univ Mich, MS, 1939. **Honorary Degrees:** DSc (chem eng), Univ Mich, 1943. **Professional Experience:** RETIRED; asst tech dir, Textile Fiber Dept, 1967-1982; sr engr, Tenn, 1961-1967; process supvr, Va, 1960-1961; planning engr, DE, 1956-1960; asst to tech mgr, DE, 1952-1956; process develop supvr, Tenn, 1948-1952; res engr, E I Du Pont De Nemours & Co Inc, 1943-1948; asst chem eng, Univ Mich, 1939-1941. **Memberships:** Am Chem Soc; Am Inst Chem Engrs; Am Inst Chem; Sigma Xi. **Research Statement & Publications:** Solvent extraction; polyamide textile fibers. **Mailing Address:** 1514 Woodsdale Rd, Wilmington, DE 19809-2247.

KING, CHERYL E, PHYSIOLOGY. **Personal Data:** b Ont, September 3, 1954. **Education:** Queens Univ, PhD (physiol), 1983. **Professional Experience:** CHAIR, GRAD PROG REHAB SCI, QUEEN'S UNIV, as of 2005; ASSOC PROF, SCH REHAB THER, QUEEN'S UNIV, as of 2005; asst prof physiol, Queen's Univ, beginning 1986; fel, Queen's Univ, 1983-1986. **Memberships:** Can Physics Soc; Am Physics Soc; Sigma Xi. **Research Statement & Publications:** Oxygen transport during hypoxia. **Mailing Address:** Sch Rehab Ther, Queens Univ, Louise D Acton Bldg, Kingston, ON K7L 3N6, Can. **Fax:** 613-545-6776. **E-Mail:** kingce@post.queensu.ca

KING, CHI-YU, SEISMOLOGY, TECTONOPHYSICS, GAS & HYDRO-GEOCHEMISTRY. **Personal Data:** b Nanking, China, August 14, 1934; American citizen; m Bi-Shia; c Tsu-Jae, Hans & Henry. **Education:** Univ Taiwan, BEE, 1956; Duke Univ, MS, 1961; Cornell Univ, PhD (appl physics), 1965. **Honors & Awards:** Spec Achievement Award, US Geol Surv, 1970; Japanese Govt Res Award, 1992. **Professional Experience:** Chair, Earthquake Prediction res Inc, Los Altos, CA 1995-; Guest res, Univ of Tokyo, 1997-1999; GEOPHYSICIST, US GEOL SURV, 1973-1995; geophysicist, US Earthquake Mechanism Lab, Nat Oceanic & Atmospheric Admin, 1970-1973; geophysicist, US Geol Surv, 1968-1970; asst res geophysicist, Univ Calif, Los Angeles, 1966-1968; Res fel geophys, Calif Inst Technol, 1965-1966; Proj chief, Earthquake Mech & Chem. **Memberships:** Am Geophys Union. **Research Statement & Publications:** Earthquake source mechanisms and prediction; hydrologic and geochemical methods for earthquake study; fracture of solids; heat transfer; geomagnetism; geophysical fracture phenomena. **Mailing Address:** 381 Hawthorne Ave, Los Altos, CA 94022. **Fax:** 650-948-4438. **E-Mail:** chiyuking@aol.com

KING, CRESTON ALEXANDER, LOW TEMPERATURE PHYSICS. **Personal Data:** b San Antonio, Tex, July 9, 1935; m 1962, c 3. **Education:** Rice Univ, AB, 1958, MA, 1963, PhD (physics), 1965; Duke Univ, MA, 1962. **Professional Experience:** CHMN, DEPT PHYSICS, LOYOLA UNIV, LA, 1980-; ASSOC PROF PHYSICS, LOYOLA UNIV, LA,

1973-; asst prof, Loyola Univ, LA, 1966-1973; asst physics, Rice Univ, 1962-1964. **Memberships:** Am Phys Soc; Am Asn Physics Teachers. **Research Statement & Publications:** Superconductivity; solid state physics. **Mailing Address:** Dept Physics, Loyola Univ, 451 Monroe, 6363 St Charles Ave, Box 92, New Orleans, LA 70118-6195. **Fax:** 504-865-2453. **E-Mail:** mking@loyno.edu

KING, DARRELL LEE, LIMNOLOGY. **Personal Data:** b Hall, Mont, January 10, 1937; m 1962, c 3. **Education:** Mont State Col, BS, 1959; Mich State Univ, MS, 1962, PhD (limnol), 1964. **Professional Experience:** EMER PROF, FISHERIES & WILDLIFE, MICH STATE UNIV, as of 2004; ACTG DIR, INST WATER RES, 1978-; Harland Bartholomew & Assocs, 1973-1974 & A P Green Refractories Co, 1975; prof fisheries & wildlife, Mich State Univ, beginning 1974; Consult, Campbell Soup Co, 1970-1971; Consult, St Louis Co Water Co, 1967-1969 & 1973-1974; From asst prof to prof civil eng, Univ Mo, Columbia, 1964-1974; Consult, Ralston Purina, 1964-1965 & 1972-1973. **Memberships:** AAAS; Am Soc Limnol & Oceanog; Am Fisheries Soc; Water Pollution Control Fedn. **Research Statement & Publications:** Interrelationships between physical, chemical and biological factors with specific reference to detailing interacting mechanisms which govern aquatic ecosystems. **Mailing Address:** Dept Wildlife Mgmt, Mich State Univ 13 Natural Resources, East Lansing, MI 48824-1222. **E-Mail:** dlking@msu.edu

KING, DAVID BEEMAN, ENDOCRINOLOGY, ANIMAL PHYSIOLOGY. **Personal Data:** b Ware, Mass, March 12, 1937; m 1961, Christine Ross; c Marcia & Linda. **Education:** Univ Mass, BS, 1959, MA, 1961; Ind Univ, PhD (zool), 1965. **Professional Experience:** DR E PAUL & FRANCES H REIFF PROF EMER BIOL, FRANKLIN & MARSHALL COL, 1996-; Dr E. Paul & Frances H. Reiff prof biol, Franklin & Marshall Col, 1988-1996; Nat Inst Arthritis & Metab Dis res grant, 1966-1978; from asst prof to prof, Franklin & Marshall Col, 1965-1988. **Memberships:** AAAS; Am Soc Zoologists; Sigma Xi. **Research Statement & Publications:** Comparative endocrinology; hormonal regulation of growth in chickens; thyroidal influence on muscle growth and development. **Mailing Address:** Dept Biol, Franklin & Marshall Col, PO Box 3003, Lancaster, PA 17604-3003.

KING, DAVID GEORGE, NERVE CELLS, EVOLUTION. **Education:** Purdue Univ, BS, 1970; Univ Calif, PhD (neuroscience), 1975. **Professional Experience:** ASSOC PROF ANAT, COL SCI, SOUTHERN ILL UNIV, as of 2004; ASSOC PROF HISTOL, SOUTHERN ILL UNIV, 1978-. **Research Statement & Publications:** Neurobiology. **Mailing Address:** Dept Zoology, Southern Ill Univ, Mail Code 6523, Carbondale, IL 62901. **Fax:** 618-453-1527. **E-Mail:** dgking@siu.edu

KING, DAVID S(COTT), PHOTO-DISSOCIATION. **Personal Data:** b Hartford, Conn, November 5, 1949. **Education:** Univ Pa, BA, 1971, PhD (phys chem), 1976. **Professional Experience:** CO-CHMN, ADVANCED TECHNNOLOGY GROUP, as of 2005; DIR, ALTAIR NANOTECHNOLOGIES INC, as of 2004; sci advr, Under Secy Commerce Technol, 2000-; sci adv, Nat Inst Standards & Technol, Physics Lab, 1999-2000; prog mgr, Nat Inst Standards & Technol, Advanced Technol Prog, 1994-1999; res chemist, Nat Inst Standards & Technol Physics lab, 1976-1994. **Memberships:** Am Chem Soc; Optical Soc Am. **Research Statement & Publications:** State-resolved and time-resolved laser studies of the mechanisms and rates of energy flow within model molecular systems, including relaxation and bond rupture. **Mailing Address:** Altair Nanotechnologies, Inc, 204 Edison Way, Reno, NV 89502. **E-Mail:** david.king@nist.gov

KING, DAVID THANE, PHYSICS. **Personal Data:** b Wellington, NZ, January 16, 1923; American citizen; m 1950, c 4. **Education:** Univ NZ, BSc, 1944, MSc, 1947; Bristol Univ, PhD (physics), 1951. **Professional Experience:** RETIRED; consult, Oak Ridge Nat Lab, beginning 1965; mem users group zero gradient synchrotron, Argonne Nat Lab, beginning 1962; from asst prof to prof physics, Univ Tenn, Knoxville, 1955-1961; physicist, US Naval Res Lab, 1951-1955. **Memberships:** Am Phys Soc; Italian Phys Soc. **Research Statement & Publications:** High energy physics. **Mailing Address:** 117 Park Hill Circle, Knoxville, TN 37909.

KING, DONALD WEST, PATHOLOGY. **Personal Data:** b Cochranton, Pa, June 30, 1927; m 1952, c 3. **Education:** Syracuse Univ, MD, 1949. **Professional Experience:** CONSULT, 1987-; Delafield prof path & chmn dept, Col Physicians & Surgeons, Columbia Univ, 1967-1982; prof & chmn dept, Univ Colo, Denver, 1961-1967; USPHS fel, Univ Chicago, 1954-1955 & Carlsberg Lab, 1955-1956; resident & instr path, Col Physicians & Surgeons, Columbia Univ, 1949-1952. **Memberships:** Am Soc Exp Path; Am Soc Cell Biol; Human Genetics Soc; Am Asn Path; NY Acad Sci; AAAS. **Research Statement & Publications:** Cell injury; membrane transport. **Mailing Address:** 2122 Mass Ave NW, Washington, DC 20008.

KING, DOROTHY WEI (CHENG), NUTRITION, PHYSIOLOGY. **Personal Data:** b Hankow, China, March 3, 1914; American citizen; m 1961. **Education:** Yenching Univ, China, BS, 1936; Mt Holyoke Col, MA, 1948; Iowa State Univ, PhD (animal nutrit), 1954. **Professional Experience:** EMER PROF ZOOL, NAT TAIWAN UNIV, 1984-; prof, Nat Taiwan Univ, 1970-1984; vis prof, Nat Taiwan Univ, 1967-1970; Sr lectr biol, Chung Chi Col, Hong Kong, 1961-1962; from instr to asst prof histol, Univ Iowa, 1954-1967; asst zool, Iowa State Univ, 1950-1951; instr, Nat Med Col, Shanghai, 1945-1946; teacher, China, 1938-1945; Asst biol, Yenching Univ, China, 1936-1937. **Memberships:** AAAS; Am Asn Anatomists; Am Soc Zoologists; Am Soc Animal Sci; Am Inst Nutrit. **Research Statement & Publications:** Effects of mitomycin C, monosodium glutamate, antihistaminic drugs and heavy metals on chick embryos. **Mailing Address:** Dept Zool, Nat Taiwan Univ, Taipei, 107, Taiwan.

KING, EDWARD FRAZIER, INORGANIC CHEMISTRY. **Personal Data:** b Lake Providence, La, December 3, 1935; m 1966, c 5. **Education:** Gregorian Univ, BA, 1958; Loyola Univ, BS, 1965; La State Univ, New Orleans, PhD (chem), 1969. **Professional Experience:** ASST PROF & CHMN SCI DEPT, S PLAINS COL, 1989-; mem, fac chem & physics, Cent Tex Col, 1975-1989; asst prof chem, Tex Woman's Univ, 1970-1975; Instr, Tex Woman's Univ, 1968-1979. **Research Statement & Publications:** Complexes of the first row transition metals, particularly their preparation and visible infrared spectra; halogen complexes of vanadium and copper. **Mailing Address:** Sci Dept, S Plains Col 1401 College Ave, Levelland, TX 79336-6503.

KING, EDWARD LOUIS, INORGANIC CHEMISTRY. **Personal Data:** b Grand Forks, NDak, March 15, 1920; m 1952, c 2. **Education:** Univ Calif, Berkeley, BS, 1943, PhD (chem), 1945. **Professional Experience:** PROF EMER, UNIV COLO, BOULDER, 1986-; chmn dept, Univ Colo, Boulder, 1970-1972; ed, Inorg Chem, Am Chem Soc, 1964-1968; prof chem, Univ Colo, Boulder, 1963-1986; Guggenheim fel, Calif Inst Technol, 1957-1958; from asst prof to prof, Univ Wis, 1948-1963; instr, Harvard Univ, 1947-1948; du Pont fel & lectr chem, Harvard Univ, 1946-1947; res assoc, Manhattan Dist Proj, 1945-1946; asst chem, Manhattan Dist Proj, 1944-1945; at Off Sci Res & Develop, 1944; asst chem, Univ Calif, 1942-1944. **Memberships:** Am Chem Soc. **Research Statement & Publications:** Chemistry of chromium and other transition metals in solution; ion solvation in mixed solvents; mechanisms of reactions in solution. **Mailing Address:** Dept Chem, Univ Colo, Campus Box 215, Ekeley Chem M347, Boulder, CO 80309-0215. **Fax:** 303-492-5894.

KING, ELIZABETH NORFLEET, CELL PHYSIOLOGY. **Personal Data:** b Concord, NC, May 22, 1925. **Education:** Randolph-Macon Woman's Col, AB, 1946; Wellesley Col, MA, 1951; Duke Univ, PhD (cell physiol), 1963. **Professional Experience:** EMER ASSOC PROF BIOL, WINTHROP UNIV, as of 2001; assoc prof biol, Winthrop Col, 1969-1994; asst prof biol, Vassar Col, 1963-1969; instr physiol, Vassar Col, 1961-1963; instr biol, Bucknell Univ, 1960-1961 & Woman's Col, NC, 1953-1956; instr zoology, Wellesley Col, 1951-1953. **Memberships:** Emer mem AAAS. **Research Statement & Publications:** Cellular physiology; separation of cellular organelles. **Mailing Address:** Dept biol, Winthrop Univ, Rock Hill, SC 29733.

KING, ELIZABETH RAYMOND, GEOLOGY. **Personal Data:** b Halifax, NS, December 5, 1923; American citizen. **Education:** Smith Col, AB, 1947. **Professional Experience:** SCIENTIST EMER, US GEOL SURV, 1993-; res geophysicist, US Geol Surv, 1974-1993; geophysicist, US Geol Surv, 1951-1974; geologist, US Geol Surv, 1948-1951. **Memberships:** AAAS; Soc Explor Geophys; Am Geophys Union; fel Geol Soc Am. **Research Statement & Publications:** Airborne magnetometer surveys; analysis of magnetic and gravity anomalies by modeling techniques; geologic interpretation of data from geophysical studies of continents and oceans. **Mailing Address:** US Geol Surv, 954 Nat Ctr, Reston, VA 20192. **Fax:** 703-648-6383. **E-Mail:** eking@usgs.gov

KING, FRANKLIN G, CHEMICAL ENGINEERING, BIOCHEMICAL ENGINEERING. **Personal Data:** b Mahanoy City, Pa, September 23, 1939; m 1959, Phyllis; c Jeffrey, Samantha & Timothy. **Education:** Penn State Univ, BS, 1961; Kansas State Univ, MS, 1962; Stevens Inst Technol, DSc, 1966; Howard Univ, MEd, 1976. **Professional Experience:** CHMN PROF CHEM ENG, NC A&T STATE UNIV, 1985-; prof & Dept Chmn, 1985-2002, assoc prof & prof, Howard Univ, 1972-1985; asst prof chem eng, Lafayette Col, 1966-1972; process engr, Am Cyanamid Co, 1965-1966; res engr, Uniroyal Res Ctr, 1962-1965. **Memberships:** Am Inst Chem Eng; Am Soc Eng Educ; Mat Res Soc. **Research Statement & Publications:** Permeation and diffusion of gases through barriers, including volcanic tuff, food packaging materials and high temperature membranes; process control; physiological pharmacokinetic modeling of drug distribution in mammals. **Mailing Address:** Dept Mech & Chem Eng, NC A&T State Univ, Greensboro, NC 27411. **Fax:** 336-334-7417. **E-Mail:** king@ncat.edu

KING, FREDERICK ALEXANDER, NEUROSCIENCE. **Personal Data:** b Paterson, NJ, October 3, 1925; m 1991, Sally Wolff; c Elizabeth G & Alexander K. **Education:** Stanford Univ, AB, 1953; Johns Hopkins Univ, MA, 1955, PhD (psychol, med sci), 1956. **Honors & Awards:** Spec Leadership & Serv Citation, Am Psychol Asn, 1984 & 1992; Pres Award, Soc Neurosci, 1994; Commendation, AMA, 1994, NIH, 1994, Incurably Ill Animal Res, 1994. **Professional Experience:** DIR EMER, YERKES NAT PRIMATE RES CTR, EMORY UNIV, as of 2002; chmn, Govt & Pub Affairs Comn, 1990-1993; mem adv bd & dir, NIH, 1989-1992; mem bd trustees, Am Asn Accreditation Lab Animal Care, 1987-1990; mem bd dir, Nat Asn Biomed Res, 1987-1990; chmn, Comn Animal Res, Soc Neuroscience, 1987; bd sci affairs, Comn Animals Res & Experimentation, Am Psychol Asn, 1986-1988; mem Int Adv Bd, Nat Mus Kenya & Kenyan Inst Primate Res, 1983-; chmn, Comn Animals Res & Experimentation, Am Psychol Asn, 1983-1985; adj prof psychol, Emory Univ, 1978-; PROF EMER ANAT & CELL BIOL, SCH MED, EMORY UNIV, 1978-; res emer prof neurobiology, Yerkes Regional Primate Res Ctr, 1978-1996; mem Nat Res Coun-Nat Acad Sci brain sci comt, 1974-; mem bd sci adv, Yerkes Regional Primate Res Ctr, 1974-1978; mem & chmn res scientist develop rev comt, Biol Sci Training Prog, NIMH, 1974-1978; chmn & mem comt educ, Soc Neuroscience, 1974-1977; chmn comt commun & coord, Biol Sci Training Prog, NIMH, 1972-1978; mem ed adv bd, Behav Biol, 1971-; ed, Physiol & Animal Psychol & J Suppl Abstr Serv, 1971- prof neuroscience & chmn dept, Col Med, Univ Fla, 1969-1978; mem adv comt, Primate Res Ctr, NIH, 1969-1973; dir, Ctr Neurobiology Sci, Col Med, Univ Fla, 1968-1978; div biol sci training grant, 1965-; dir & scientist, Ctr Neurobiology Sci, Univ Fla, 1964-1968; vis scientist, Neuroanat Prog, NIH, 1963-1970; vis scientist, Am Psychol Asn-NSF Prog, 1962-1967; NIMH fel & vis prof, Inst Physiol, Sch Med, Univ Pisa, 1961-1962; Nat Inst Neurol Dis & Stroke grant, 1959-1971; from asst prof to prof psychol & neurosurg, Col Med, Univ Fla, 1959-1969 NIMH grant, 1957-1960; res mem psychobiol adv panel, Biol & Med Sci Div, NSF, 1963-1967; from instr to asst prof psychiat, Col Med, Ohio State Univ, 1956-1959; consult, Battelle Mem Inst, 1956-1959; instr psychol, Johns Hopkins Univ, 1955-1956. **Memberships:** Fel AAAS; fel Am Psychol Asn; Am Physiol Soc; Soc Neurosci; Int Neuropsychol Soc (secy-treas 1969-1973); Asn Clin Scientists; Int Brain Res Orgn. **Research Statement & Publications:** Effects of subcortical brain lesions on motivated behavior; analysis of cortical functions by use of ablation and brain stimulation techniques; electrophysiological and conditioning analysis of recovery of function in the isolated forebrain. **Mailing Address:** Yerkes Nat Primate Res Ctr, Emory Univ, Atlanta, GA 30322. **Fax:** 404-634-6148. **E-Mail:** swolff@emory.edu

KING, FREDERICK JESSOP, FOOD SCIENCE. **Personal Data:** b Niagara Falls, NY, July 4, 1928; m 1956, c 3. **Education:** Cornell Univ, BS, 1951, MFS, 1952; Mass Inst Technol, PhD, 1960. **Professional Experience:** RETIRED; exec secy, New Eng Fisheries Inst, 1970-1989; biochemist, Northeast Utilization Res Ctr, Nat Marine Fisheries Serv, Nat Oceanic & Atmospheric Admin, 1960-1989. **Memberships:** Am Chem Soc; Inst Food Technologists; fel Am Inst Chemists; fel Asn Anal Chemists. **Research Statement & Publications:** Denaturation of fish proteins; irradiation preservation of fish; flavor chemistry of fish; nutritive value; fishery technology; process and product improvements; quality assurance. **Mailing Address:** 84 Cherry St, Wenham, MA 01984.

KING, FREDERICK WARREN, LOWER BOUNDS FOR ENERGY LEVELS & HIGH PRECISION CALCULATIONS ON THREE & FOUR-ELECTRON SYSTEMS, THEORY OF HILBERT TRANSFORMS. **Personal Data:** b Sydney, Australia, April 15, 1947. **Education:** Univ Sydney, BS (Hons), 1969; Univ Calgary, MS, 1971; Queen's Univ, PhD (chem), 1975. **Honors & Awards:** Camille & Henry Dreyfus Teacher-Scholar Award, Dreyfus Found, 1983, Camille & Henry Dreyfus Scholar Award, 1991; Outstanding Contrib Chem Award, Am Chem Soc, Cent Wis Sect, 1984. **Professional Experience:** PROF CHEM, UNIV WIS-EAU CLAIRE, 1979-; fel chem, Brock Univ, 1978-1979; fel, Oxford Univ, 1975-1976; fel, Northwestern Univ, 1977-1978. **Memberships:** Am Chem Soc; Am Phys Soc. **Research Statement & Publications:** Efforts focus on problems in theoretical chemistry and atomic physics; bounds on the electronic density on the energy levels in three-electron systems and mathematical problems associated with these problems; Theory and applications of Hilbert transforms. **Mailing Address:** Dept Chem, Univ Wis, 459 Phillips Sci Hall, Eau Claire, WI 54702. **E-Mail:** fking@uwec.edu

KING, GARY MICHAEL, MICROBIAL PHYSIOLOGICAL ECOLOGY, BIOGEOCHEMISTRY. **Personal Data:** b Ft Walton Beach, Fla, October 30, 1953; m 1979, Kathleen; c

Amanda, Andrew & Meredith. **Education:** Univ Ga, BS (hons), 1974, PhD (microbiol), 1978. **Professional Experience:** PROF OCENOG, UNIV MAINE, as of 2005; PROF MICROBIOL, OCEANOG & MARINE STUDIES, UNIV MAINE, 1992-; panelist, Div Environ Biol, NSF, 1991-1994; lektor, Aarhus Univ, Denmark, 1988-1990; Fulbright res scholar, Aarhus Univ, Denmark, 1988-1989; prin investr, NSF, NASA & Nat Oceanic & Atmospheric Admin, 1982-; from asst prof to assoc prof, Univ Maine, 1984-1992; vis asst prof, Mich State Univ, 1981-1982; res assoc, Mich State Univ, 1978-1981. **Memberships:** Am Soc Microbiol; Am Chem Soc; Am Soc Limnol & Oceanog. **Research Statement & Publications:** Microbiology, ecology and marine science, especially those related to biogeochemical transformations of carbon, nitrogen and sulfur at regional and global scales. **Mailing Address:** Darling Marine Ctr, Univ Maine, Walpole, ME 04573. **Fax:** 207-563-3119. **E-Mail:** gking@maine.maine.edu

KING, GAYLE NATHANIEL, PHYSICAL CHEMISTRY. **Personal Data:** b Paulding, Ohio, July 17, 1948; m 1971, Helen; c Daniel & Tisha. **Education:** Heidelberg Col, BS, 1970; Univ Pac, PhD (phys chem), 1977. **Honors & Awards:** Emmon's Prize, Asn Asphal & Paving Technol. **Professional Experience:** MGR CUSTOMER TECHNICAL SERVICE, KOCH PAVEMENT SOLUTIONS, as of 2003; chief chemist, koch mat, beginning 1981; consult, Bituminous Mat Inc, beginning 1978; asst prof chem, Rose Hulman Inst Technol, 1977-1981; Instr statist, USAF, 1970-1974. **Memberships:** Am Chem Soc; Sigma Xi; Asn Asphalt Paving Technol. **Research Statement & Publications:** Modified asphalt; asphalt and oil emulsions. **Mailing Address:** Koch Pavement Solutions, PO Box 1875, Wichita, KS 67201. **Fax:** 316-828-7385. **E-Mail:** kingg@kochind.com

KING, GENERAL TYE, MEAT SCIENCE. **Personal Data:** b King, Ky, April 7, 1920; m 1940. **Education:** Union Col, Ky, BS, 1948; Univ Ky, BS, 1950, MS, 1951; Tex A&M Univ, PhD (meats), 1958. **Professional Experience:** PROF EMER ANIMAL SCI, TEX A&M UNIV, 1989-; prof animal sci, Tex A&M Univ, 1976-1989; asst head dept, Tex A&M Univ, 1969-1989; assoc prof animal sci, Tex A&M Univ, 1969-1976; assoc prof meats, Tex A&M Univ, 1960-1969; from instr to asst prof meats, Tex A&M Univ, 1953-1960; Asst animal husbandman, SDak State Col, 1951-1953. **Memberships:** Am Meat Sci Asn; Am Soc Animal Sci; Inst Food Technol. **Research Statement & Publications:** Animal science; nutrition. **Mailing Address:** 1011 Walton Dr, College Station, TX 77840-2310.

KING, GEORGE III, EXPERIMENTAL NUCLEAR PHYSICS. **Personal Data:** b Tampa, Fla, November 12, 1946; m 1968, c 2. **Education:** Talladega Col, BA, 1968; Stanford Univ, MS, 1974, PhD (nuclear physics), 1977. **Professional Experience:** PROF & CHMN, DEPT PHYSICS, MARY WASH COL, as of 2003; mem prof staff, dept nuclear, Schlumberger Doll Res, beginning 1979; res assoc nuclear physics, Lawrence Berkeley Lab, 1977-1979; Xerox Corp fel, 1974-1977; res asst nuclear physics, Stanford Univ, 1973-1977; instr physics, Albany State Col, 1969-1971 & Col Notre Dame, 1972-1973. **Memberships:** Am Phys Soc. **Research Statement & Publications:** Giant resonance excitation for light nuclei; relativistic heavy ion central collisions. **Mailing Address:** Depr Physics & Astron, Mary Wash Col, 1301 Col Ave, Fredricksburg, VA 22401. **Fax:** 540-654-1081. **E-Mail:** gking@mwc.edu

KING, GERALD WILFRID, CHEMICAL PHYSICS. **Personal Data:** b Eng, January 22, 1928; m Gwyneth; c Richard J, Juliette M, Jennifer W & Gillian C. **Education:** Univ London, BSc, 1949, PhD (chem), 1952. **Honorary Degrees:** DSc, Univ London, 1970. **Honors & Awards:** Gerhard Herzberg Award, Spectros Soc Can, 1981. **Professional Experience:** PROF EMER CHEM, MCMASTER UNIV, 1989-; bd gov, McMaster Univ, 1985-1988; chmn, dept chem, McMaster Univ, 1979-1982; ed, Can J Chem, 1974-1979; hon res assoc, Univ Col, London, 1965; from asst prof to prof, Mcmaster Univ, 1957-1989; lectr, Univ Col, London, 1956-1957; Asst lectr, Univ Col, London, 1954-1956. **Memberships:** Fel Chem InstCan; Optical Soc Am; fel Royal Soc Chem; fel Royal Soc Can. **Research Statement & Publications:** Electronic states and structures of molecules; multi-photon laser spectroscopy; optical-optical double resonance; high resolution electronic molecular spectroscopy. **Mailing Address:** 674 Northland Ave, Burlington, ON L7T 3J7, Can. **Fax:** 905-522-2509. **E-Mail:** kingw@mcmaster.ca

KING, GORDON JAMES, REPRODUCTIVE PHYSIOLOGY, ENDOCRINOLOGY. **Personal Data:** b Toronto, Ont, June 8, 1932; m 1957, c 2. **Education:** Univ Toronto, DVM, 1959; Univ Guelph, MS, 1966, PhD (reproduction physiol), 1968. **Professional Experience:** UNIV PROF EMER, UNIV GUELPH, as of 2002; Nat Res Coun Can res grant, beginning 1976; Can Dept Agr res grant, 1976-1978; prof, Animal & Poultry Sci, Univ Guelph, beginning 1975; assoc prof, Univ Guelph, 1970-1975; asst prof, Univ Guelph, 1968-1970; tech mgr, Hamilton Dist Cattle Breeding Asn, 1962-1965; field vet, Hamilton Dist Cattle Breeding Asn, 1960-1962; pvt pract vet med, 1959-1960; consult, Food & Agr Asn, Can Int Develop Agency, Int Agr Exchange Asn, IFS. **Memberships:** Am Soc Animal Sci; Soc Study Reprod; Soc Study Fertil; fel Inst Biol. **Research Statement & Publications:** Reproductive biology. **Mailing Address:** Dept Animal & Poultry Sci, Univ Guelph, Guelph, ON N1G 2W1, Can. **Fax:** 519-767-0573. **E-Mail:** gking@uoguelph.ca

KING, GREGORY L, NEUROSCIENCE, PHYSIOLOGY. **Personal Data:** b Plainsview, Tex, March 1, 1948. **Education:** Univ Houston, MA, 1971; Baylor Col Med, PhD (physiol), 1980. **Honors & Awards:** Minoru Susuki Award, 1980. **Professional Experience:** RES PHYSIOLOGIST, ARMED FORCES RADIOBIOL RES INST, 1984-; fel physiol, Univ NC, Chapel Hill, 1980-1984. **Memberships:** Soc Neuroscience; Am Physiol Soc. **Mailing Address:** Dept Radiation Pathophysiol & Toxicol, Armed Forces Radiobiol Res Inst, Bethesda, MD 20889-5603. **Fax:** 301-295-0313. **E-Mail:** king@afrri.usuhs.mil

KING, HAROLD, SURGERY. **Personal Data:** b Bedford, Ind, August 12, 1922; m 1952, c 2. **Education:** Yale Univ, MD, 1946. **Professional Experience:** EMER PROF SURG, MED CTR, IND UNIV, INDIANAPOLIS, as of 2006; DIR DIV THORACIC & CARDIOVASC SURG, IND UNIV, INDIANAPOLIS, 1972-; prof surg, med ctr, Ind Univ, Indianapolis, beginning 1964; from instr to assoc prof, Ind Univ, Indianapolis, 1955-1964; mem staff, Vet Admin Hosp & Indianapolis Gen Hosp. **Memberships:** Soc Vascular Surg; Soc Univ Surg; Am Col Surg; Soc Thoracic Surg; Am Surg Asn. **Research Statement & Publications:** Cardiovascular surgery. **Mailing Address:** Cardiothoracic Surg Inc, 545 Barnhill Dr, Indianapolis, IN 46202-5112.

KING, HARRISS THORNTON, NUCLEAR PHYSICS. **Personal Data:** b Ames, Iowa, June 15, 1947; m 1976. **Education:** Iowa State Univ, BS, 1969; Stanford Univ, MS, 1970, PhD (physics), 1975. **Professional Experience:** MEM STAFF, MEASUREX CORP, 1980-; asst prof physics, Stanford Univ, 1977-1980; Res assoc physics, Rutgers Univ, 1974-1977. **Memberships:** Sigma Xi; Am Phys Soc. **Research Statement & Publications:** Hyperfine interactions; nuclear electromagnetic moments; polarization phenomena. **Mailing Address:** 11171 Bobb Rd, Cupertino, CA 95014.

KING, HARTLEY H(UGHES), AERONAUTICAL SCIENCES, MECHANICAL ENGINEERING. **Personal Data:** b Fresno, Calif, April 21, 1936; m 1962, c 2. **Education:** Univ Calif, Berkeley, BS, 1957, MS, 1959, PhD (mech eng), 1963. **Professional Experience:** SR RES ENGR, EFFECTS TECHNOL INC, 1975-; sr res engr, Gen Res Corp, 1968-1975; sr res engr, AC Electronics Defense Res Labs, Gen Motors Corp, 1965-1968; Sr engr, Electrooptical Systs, 1962-1965. **Memberships:** Am Inst Aeronaut & Astronaut; Inst Elec & Electronics Engrs. **Research Statement & Publications:** Compressible fluid mechanics; wakes and separated flows; re-entry aerodynamics; flight mechanics. **Mailing Address:** Gen Res Corp, 5383 Hollister Ave PO Box 6770, Santa Barbara, CA 93111.

KING, H(ENRY) E(UGENE), PSYCHOLOGY. **Personal Data:** b Wilmington, Va, September 24, 1922; m 1948, c 2. **Education:** Univ Richmond, BA, 1942; Columbia Univ, MA, 1943, PhD, 1948. **Professional Experience:** PROF EMER PSYCHOL, WASH & LEE UNIV, 1990-; prof psychol, Wash & Lee Univ, 1980-1990; prof psychol, Sch Med & Chief Serv, Western Psychiat Inst, Univ Pittsburgh, 1960-1980; vis scientist, Charity Hosp, New Orleans, 1949-1960; assoc prof psychiat & neurol, Sch Med, Tulane Univ, 1949-1960; sr res scientist, NY State Brain Res Proj, 1948-1949; lectr, Columbia Univ, 1946-1949; asst psychologist, NY State Psychiat Inst, 1942-1943 & 1946-1948. **Memberships:** fel AAAS; Am Physiol Soc; Soc Exp Biol & Med; fel Am Psychol Asn; Am Psychopath Asn. **Research Statement & Publications:** Psychophysiology; experimental psychopathology; motor response systems; central nervous system stimulation and ablation. **Mailing Address:** Dept Psychol, Wash & Lee Univ, Lexington, VA 24450. **Fax:** 540-463-8945.

KING, HENRY LEE, ORGANIC CHEMISTRY, POLYMER CHEMISTRY. **Personal Data:** b Muleshoe, Tex, April 12, 1921; m 1948, c 4. **Education:** Tex Tech Col, BS, 1952, MS, 1954. **Professional Experience:** RETIRED; sr res specialist, Chemstrand Res Ctr, Inc, Monsanto Co, 1976-1981; res specialist, Chemstrand Res Ctr, Inc, Monsanto Co, 1970-1976; sr res chemist, Chemstrand Res Ctr, Inc, Monsanto Co, 1965-1970; res chemist, Chemstrand Res Ctr, Inc, Monsanto Co, 1954-1965. **Memberships:** Am Chem Soc. **Research Statement & Publications:** Synthetic polymers and fibers; polymer processes; polymer modification for specific end uses; intermediate synthesis; condensation polymers, especially polyesters. **Mailing Address:** 102 Bogue Ct, Cary, NC 27511-5427.

KING, HERMAN (LEE), ACADEMIC ADMINISTRATION. **Personal Data:** b Grand Ledge, Mich, February 24, 1915; m 1939, Alice Williams; c Judith & Margaret. **Education:** Mich State Univ, BS, 1939; Pa State Univ, MS, 1941, PhD (biochem), 1942. **Professional Experience:** RETIRED; dir acad serv, Mich st univ, 1974-1981; asst provost, Mich st univ, 1963-1974; asst dean, Col Natural Sci, 1962-1963; dir, Div Biol Sci, 1960-1962; prof & asst dean, Col Arts & Sci, 1959-1962; from asst prof to assoc prof entom, Mich State Univ, 1946-1959; exten entomologist, Mich State Univ, 1945-1946; orchard mgr, Mich, 1944; instr agr & biol chem, Pa State Univ, 1943; Res fel, Reilly Tar & Chem Corp, Ind, 1939-1942. **Research Statement & Publications:** University administration. **Mailing Address:** 2700 Burcham Dr Rm 536, East Lansing, MI 48823-3895.

KING, HOWARD E, ELECTRICAL ENGINEERING. **Personal Data:** b Seattle, Wash, October 16, 1924; m 1950, c 5. **Education:** Wash Univ, BS, 1946; Univ Ill, MS, 1955. **Professional Experience:** HEAD, ANTENNAS & PROPAGATION DEPT, AEROSPACE CORP, 1970-; mgr electromagnetics sect, Antennas & Propagation Dept, Aerospace Corp, 1962-1970; Lectr, Univ Calif, Los Angeles, 1962-1964; mem tech staff, Antennas & Propagation Dept, Aerospace Corp, 1961-1962; mem tech staff, Ramo-Wooldridge Corp, Calif, 1955-1958 & Space Tech Labs Inc, 1958-1961; res asst electromagnetics, Univ Ill, Urbana, 1953-1955; Engr, RCA Victor Div, NJ, 1946-1952 & Andrew Corp, Ill, 1952-1953. **Memberships:** Inst Elecs & Electronics Engrs. **Research Statement & Publications:** Frequency modulation and television transmitters, antennas and diplexers; antennas for aircraft, reentry vehicles, spacecraft and ground installations; millimeter wavelength research in antennas and components; radar cross section measurements and analysis. **Mailing Address:** Aerospace Corp, 2350 E El Segundo Blvd, El Segundo, CA 90245.

KING, HUBERT E, POLYMER PHYSICS, HIGH PRESSURE PHYSICS, ROCK PHYSICS. **Personal Data:** b Covington, Ky, October 11, 1949; m Linda; c Elizabeth. **Education:** State Univ NY, Stony Brook, PhD (crystallog), 1979; Univ Ky, BS, 1971. **Honors & Awards:** Exxon Golden Tiger Res Award, Exxon, 1990, 1995. **Professional Experience:** Advan res assoc, ExxonMobil, 1999-current; from staff to sr staff physicist, Exxon, 1994-1999; Fel Am Phys Soc 1994; sr physicist, Exxon, 1986-1994; res physicist, Exxon, 1982-1986. **Memberships:** Am Phys Soc fel; Am Geophys Soc; Am Crystallographic Asn. **Research Statement & Publications:** Structure, thermodynamics and kinetics of complex systems such as polymers; studing the influence of pressure on these properties; studies of crystals, liquids, and glasses. **Mailing Address:** ExxonMobil Res & Eng Co, 1545 Rte 22 E, Annandale, NJ 08801. **E-Mail:** hubert.e.king@exxonmobil.com

KING, HUBERT WYLAM, MATERIALS SCIENCE, ENGINEERING PHYSICS. **Personal Data:** b Cardiff, Wales, January 20, 1930; Canadian citizen; m 1957, c 4. **Education:** Univ Birmingham, BSc, 1954, PhD (metall), 1956; Imp Col, London, DIC(metall), 1971. **Professional Experience:** PROF, DEPT MECH ENG, UNIV VICTORIA, as of 2004; Nat Sci Eng Res Coun grant, Univ Western Ont, beginning 1991; PROF MAT ENG, UNIV WESTERN ONT, 1991-; bd coun fed, Inf Space Univ, 1987; head, Eng Physics Dept, 1986-1991; prof eng physics, Tech Univ, NS, 1983-1991; nat sci eng res coun grant, Tech Univ NS, 1983-1991; prof eng physics, Dalhousie Univ, 1971-1983; nat Res Coun Can grant, Dalhousie Univ, 1971-1983; reader phys metall, Imp Col, Univ London, 1967-1970; consult, US AEC, 1967-1969; vis prof metall, Univ Calif, Berkeley, 1967; co-ed comn struct reports, Int Union Crystallog, 1966-; sr lectr, Imp Col, Univ London, 1965-1967; UK Atomic Energy Authority & Sci Res Coun grant, Imp Col, Univ London, 1962-1970; lectr phys metall, Imp Col, Univ London, 1962-1965; US AEC grant metal physics, Mellon Inst, 1959-1962; fel metall, Univ Birmingham, 1956-1958; mem, Asn Prof Engrs NS. **Memberships:** Fel Brit Inst Metall; fel Brit Inst Physics; Can Inst Min Metall; Can Ceramic Soc; Am Ceramic Soc. **Research Statement & Publications:** Structure and stability of oxide ceramic phases; effect of phase transformations on superconducting transition magnetic and ferroelectric properties of stainless steels; electronic properties of ceramics. **Mailing Address:** Dept Mech Eng, Univ Victoria, PO Box 3055, MS 8895, Victoria, BC N6A 5B9, Can.

KING, IRENA B, NUTRITION, MOLECULAR BIOLOGY. **Personal Data:** b Poland, June 22, 1948. **Education:** Univ Wash, BA, 1976, MS, 1981, PhD (molecular biol), 1985. **Professional Experience:** SR STAFF SCIENTIST BIOCHEM, FRED HUTCHINSON CANCER RES CTR, as of 2006; MGR, BIOMARKER LAB, FRED HUTCHINSON CANCER RES CTR, as of 2004; staff scientist Biochem, Fred Hutchinson Cancer Res Ctr, beginning 1992; res fel nutrit, 1988-1992; fel nutrit, 1985-1988. **Memberships:** AAAS; Am Inst Nutrit; Am Asn Cancer Res. **Mailing Address:** Fred Hutchinson Cancer Res Ctr, PO Box 19024 1100 Fairview Ave N, Seattle, WA 98109.

KING, IVAN ROBERT, ASTRONOMY. **Personal Data:** b Far Rockaway, NY, June 25, 1927; m 2002, Judith; c David, Lucy, Adam & Jane. **Education:** Hamilton Col, AB, 1946; Harvard Univ, AM, 1947, PhD (astron), 1952. **Honorary Degrees:** Laurea, Univ Padua, 2002; DSc, Hamilton Col, 2005. **Honors & Awards:** George Darwin Lecturer, Royal Astronomical Society, 1979. **Professional Experience:** Res prof, Univ Wash, 2002-;

EMER PROF ASTRON, UNIV CALIF, BERKELEY, 1993-; from assoc prof to prof, Univ Calif, Berkeley, 1964-1993; from asst prof to assoc prof, Univ Ill, 1956-1964; methods analyst, US Dept of Defense, 1954-1956; instr astron, Harvard Univ, 1951-1952. **Memberships:** Nat Acad Sci; Am Astron Soc (pres, 1978-1980); Int Astron Union; Am Acad Arts & Sci; Am Asn Adv Sci (fel); Astr Soc Pacific. **Research Statement & Publications:** Structure of stellar systems; populations in globular clusters. **Mailing Address:** Dept Astron, Univ Wash, Seattle, WA 98195-1580. **Fax:** 206-685-0403. **E-Mail:** king@astro.washington.edu

KING, JAMES JR, PHYSICAL CHEMISTRY, PHYSICS. **Personal Data:** b Columbus, Ga, April 23, 1933; div, c 2. **Education:** Morehouse Col, BS, 1953; Calif Inst Technol, MS, 1955, PhD (chem, physics), 1958. **Professional Experience:** ASST LAB DIR, JET PROPULSION LAB, CALIF INST TECHNOL, 1993-; dept asst lab dir, Jet Propulsion Lab, Calif Inst Technol, 1988-1993; mgr space sci & appln, Jet Propulsion Lab, Calif Inst Technol, 1981-1987; mgr space physics, Jet Propulsion Lab, Calif Inst Technol, 1979-1980; mgr, User Prog Develop Off, Jet Propulsion Lab, Calif Inst Technol, 1976-1978; dir, Upper Atmospheric Sci Prog, 1975-1976; dir, Space Shuttle Environ Effects, Space Shuttle Prog, NASA, Wash, DC, 1974-1975; sect mgr physics, Jet Propulsion Lab, Calif Inst Technol, 1969-1974; sr scientist, Jet Propulsion Lab, Calif Inst Technol, 1961-1969; sr scientist, Electro-Optical Systs, Inc, 1960-1961; sr res engr thermal properties, Atomics Int Div, NAm Aviation, Inc, 1958-1960; res engr electrochem, Jet Propulsion Lab, Calif Inst Technol, 1956. **Memberships:** Am Chem Soc; Am Phys Soc; Sigma Xi; AAAS; Am Geophys Union. **Research Statement & Publications:** Nuclear and electron resonance; radiation chemistry. **Mailing Address:** Calif Inst Technol, 500 Semira St Sw, Atlanta, GA 30331.

KING, JAMES CLAUDE, LOW TEMPERATURE PHYSICS, SOLID STATE PHYSICS. **Personal Data:** b St Joseph, Mo, October 2, 1924; m 1949, Martha H Dawson; c Elizabeth, Kathleen, Helen & Robert. **Education:** Amherst Col, BA, 1949; Yale Univ, MS, 1950, PhD (physics), 1953. **Honors & Awards:** C B Sawyer Award, Sawyer Res Prod, Inc, 1973. **Professional Experience:** RETIRED; dir mats process eng & fabrication, Sandia Labs, 1983-1989; dir weapons elec subsysts, Sandia Labs, 1977-1983; dir electrochem components & measurement systs, Sandia Labs, 1971-1977; dir appl res, Sandia Labs, 1968-1971; mgr radiation physics dept, Sandia Labs, 1965-1968; mgr thin film & acoust device dept, Bell Tel Labs, Inc, 1962-1965; mem tech staff, Bell Tel Labs, Inc, 1953-1965; asst, Yale Univ, 1950-1953; Instr physics, Yale Univ, 1950. **Memberships:** Fel Am Phys Soc; Sigma Xi. **Research Statement & Publications:** Solid state physics; acoustic wave interactions with lattice defects; effects of radiation on the acoustic properties of alpha-quartz. **Mailing Address:** 7832 Academy Trail NE, Albuquerque, NM 87185.

KING, JAMES EDWARD, PALYNOLOGY. **Personal Data:** b Escanaba, Mich, July 23, 1940; m 1973, Fronces Bartos; c Scott. **Education:** Alma Col, BS, 1962, DSc, 2002; Univ NMex, MS, 1964; Univ Ariz, PhD (geosci), 1972. **Professional Experience:** CONSULT, MUS & ORGN, 2001-; dir, Cleveland Mus Natural History, 1996-2000; adj prof geol, Univ Pittsburgh, 1988-1996; res assoc, Hunt Bot Inst, Carnegie-Mellon Univ, Pittsburgh, beginning 1988; ADJ RES SCIENTIST, HUNT INST BOT DOCUMENTATION, CARNEGIE MELLON UNIV, 1988-; dir, Carnegie Mus, 1987-1996; asst dir sci, Ill State Mus, Springfield, 1985-1987; adj assoc prof geol, Univ Ill-Urbana, 1978-1988; head sci sect, Ill State Mus, Springfield, 1978-1985; cur paleobot, Ill State Mus, Springfield, 1972-1978; NSF res grants, 1972, 1974, 1976 & 1981; res assoc geochronol, Univ Ariz, 1971-1972. **Memberships:** AAAS; Am Quaternary Asn (former treas); Am Asn Stratigraphic Palynologists; Ecol Soc Am; Asn Sci Mus Dirs (pres 1993-); Am Asn Mus. **Research Statement & Publications:** Quaternary palynology, biogeography and paleoenvironments of North America; the ecology and extinction of the Pleistocene megafauna and the interaction of early man to his environments. **Mailing Address:** Hunt Inst Bot Doc, Carnegie Mellon Univ, 4909 Frew St, Pittsburgh, PA 15213-3890.

KING, JAMES FREDERICK, ORGANIC CHEMISTRY. **Personal Data:** b Moncton, NB, April 6, 1934; m 1965, Diane; c Sarah, Peter & Thomas. **Education:** Univ NB, BSc, 1954, PhD (org chem), 1957. **Honors & Awards:** Merck, Sharp & Dohme Lectr Award, 1976. **Professional Experience:** PROF EMER, UNIV WESTERN ONT, as of 2001; prof chem, Univ Western Ont, beginning 1967; Alfred P Sloan res fel, 1966-1968; from asst prof to assoc prof, Univ Western Ont, 1959-1967; res fel chem, Harvard Univ, 1958-1959; Beaverbrook overseas scholar, Imp Col, London, 1957-1958. **Memberships:** Am Chem Soc; Chem Inst Can; Royal Soc Chem. **Research Statement & Publications:** Organic sulfur chemistry; reaction mechanisms; stereochemistry; organic reactions in water. **Mailing Address:** Dept Chem, Univ Western Ont, London, ON N6A 5B7, Can. **Fax:** 519-661-3022. **E-Mail:** scijfk@uwo.ca

KING, JAMES P, PHYSICAL INORGANIC CHEMISTRY. **Personal Data:** b Kiangsu, China, November 11, 1933. **Education:** Newberry Col, BS, 1953; Loyola Univ, Ill, MS, 1956; Purdue Univ, PhD (chem), 1960. **Honors & Awards:** Edmond E Bisson Award, Soc of Tribologists & Lubrication Eng, 2002. **Professional Experience:** PRES, DESILUBE TECHNOL INC, 1989-; proj leader, Pennwalt Chem Corp, beginning 1959. **Memberships:** Am Chem Soc; Am Soc Lubrication Eng. **Research Statement & Publications:** Lubrication products on high temperature application; Thermochemistry of rhenium compounds; heats of formation of various rhenium compounds determined by solution calorimetry and electrochemical cell measurements; synthesis and characterization of coordination compounds and inorganic polymers. **Mailing Address:** 904 Breezewood Lane, Lansdale, PA 19446-5210. **Fax:** 610-948-0744.

KING, JANET CARLSON, NUTRITION. **Personal Data:** b Red Oak, Iowa, October 3, 1941; m 1967, Charles; c Matthew & Samuel. **Education:** Iowa State Univ, BS, 1963; Univ Calif, Berkeley, PhD (nutrit), 1972. **Honors & Awards:** Frances Fischer Mem Lectr, 1985; Lederle Award Human Nutrit, 1989; Agnes Higgins Award, Maternal Nutrit, 1993; Int Award Human Nutrit, 1996. **Professional Experience:** WESTERN HUMAN NUTRIT RES CTR, UNIV CALIF, BERKELEY, 1995-; chmn, Food & Nutrit Bd, Inst Med, Nat Acad Sci, beginning 1994; Food & Nutrit Bd, Inst Med-Nat Acad Sci, 1991-1993; chmn, Dept Nutrit Sci, 1988-1994; mem, Comt Nutrit Status During Pregnancy & Lactation, Nat Res Coun, Nat Acad Sci, 1988-1992; Comt Mil Nutrit Res, Nat Acad Sci, Nat Res Coun, 1985-1990; PROF NUTRIT, UNIV CALIF, BERKELEY, beginning 1983; Nutrit Study Sect, NIH, 1981-1985; consult, NIH, 1979-1980; mem, Comt Nutrit Mother & Presch Child, Nat Acad Sci, Nat Res Coun, 1974-1980; from asst prof to assoc prof, Univ Calif, Berkeley, 1972-1983; fel, Univ Calif, Berkeley, 1972; dietitian, Fitzsimons Gen Hosp, Denver, 1964-1967. **Memberships:** Inst Med Nat Acad Sci; Am Dietetic Asn; Sigma Xi; Soc Nutrit Educ; Am Inst Nutrit; AAAS; Am Soc Clin Nutrit. **Research Statement & Publications:** Study of the nutritional requirements for protein, energy; calcium and zinc during pregnancy; zinc metabolism. **Mailing Address:** Nutri Sci & Toxicol, USDA western Human Nutrit Res Ctr, 119 Morgan, San Francisco, CA 94720. **E-Mail:** jking@nature.berkeley.edu

KING, JERRY PORTER, MATHEMATICS. **Personal Data:** b Dyersburg, Tenn, July 9, 1935; m 1962, c 2. **Education:** Univ Ky, BSEE, 1958, MS, 1959, PhD (math), 1962. **Professional Experience:** PROF EMER MATH, LEHIGH UNIV, as of 1996; dean grad sch, Lehigh Univ, 1981-1987; assoc dean arts & sci, Lehigh Univ, 1979-1981; prof math, Lehigh Univ, beginning 1968; Asst prof, Lehigh Univ, 1962-1968. **Memberships:** Math Asn Am; Am Math Soc. **Research Statement & Publications:** Complex variables, summability. **Mailing Address:** Math Dept, Lehigh Univ, 14 E, Packer Ave, Bethlehem, PA 18015. **E-Mail:** jpk2@lehigh.edu

KING, JERRY W, ANALYTICAL CHEMISTRY. **Professional Experience:** PROG MGR & SR SCIENTIST, SUPERCRITICAL FLUID FACIL, LOS ALAMOS NAT LAB, as of 2004; adj prof chem eng & food sci, Univ Ark, as of 2004. **Mailing Address:** Los Alamos Nat Lab, PO Box 1663, Los Alamos, NM 87545. **Fax:** 505-667-6561. **E-Mail:** kingjw@lanl.gov

KING, JOAN C, BIOLOGY. **Education:** Tulane Univ, PhD (neurosciences & psychol). **Professional Experience:** PROF EMER, TUFTS UNIV SCH MED, as of 2001. **Memberships:** Nat Sci Found. **Mailing Address:** Tufts Univ Sch Med, 42 Garrison Rd Suite 2, Brookline, MA 02445-4437. **Fax:** 617-232-6938. **E-Mail:** joanking@concentric.net

KING, JOE MACK, PHYCOLOGY. **Personal Data:** b Conroe, Tex, July 25, 1944; m 1967, c 1. **Education:** Sam Houston State Univ, BS, 1967, MA, 1968; Univ Tex, Austin, PhD (bot), 1971. **Professional Experience:** DEAN, COL SCI, UNIV NEW ORLEANS, 1992-; from asst prof to prof biol, Murray State Univ, 1978-1992; res assoc aquatic ecol, Rice Univ, 1973-1978; Consult, Exxon Corp, Baytown, Tex, 1973-1974; asst prof biol, Univ Wis, La Crosse, 1971-1973; Res scientist aquatic ecol, Univ Tex, Austin, 1968-1970. **Memberships:** Am Soc Limnol & Oceanog; Phycol Soc Am; Int Phycol Soc; Am Inst Biol Sci. **Research Statement & Publications:** Phytoplankton ecology; impact of nutrient enrichment on aquatic ecosystems; aquatic phytotoxicity; algal taxonomy. **Mailing Address:** Col Sci, Univ New Orleans, Orleans, LA 70148.

KING, JOHN, PLANT PHYSIOLOGY, PLANT METABOLISM. **Personal Data:** b Darlington, Eng, November 4, 1938; m Myrna; c Kate, Marie & Vicki. **Education:** Univ Durham, BSc (Hons, Class 1), 1960; Univ Man, MSc, 1962, PhD, 1966. **Honors & Awards:** Gold Medal, Can Soc Plant Physiol, 2001. **Professional Experience:** Professor Emeritus of Biology, 2003-; D S RAWSON PROF OF BIOL, UNIV SASK, 1999-2002; Acting Head Chem, Univ Sask, 1988-1989; Head Biol, Univ Sask, 1981-1987; PROF BIOL, UNIV SASK, 1977-; assoc prof Biol, Univ Sask, 1971-1977; asst prof biol, Univ Sask, 1967-1971; asst prof biol, Bishop's Univ, 1965-1967; lectr biol, Bishop's Univ, 1964-1965. **Memberships:** Am Soc Plant Biol (Emeritus member); Can Soc Plant Physiol (Emeritus member; Pres, 1983-1984). **Research Statement & Publications:** Genetic transformation of plant cells; isolation and use of resistance mutants in cell culture; isolation and use of Arabidopsis metabolic mutants; 1-carbon metabolism in higher plants. **Mailing Address:** Dept Biol, Univ Sask 112 Sci Pl, Saskatoon, SK S7N 5E2, Can. **Fax:** 306-966-4461. **E-Mail:** john.king@usask.ca

KING, JOHN A(LBERT), RESEARCH ADMINISTRATION, NEW PRODUCT LICENSING. **Personal Data:** b Columbus, Ind, September 6, 1916; m 1941, c 4. **Education:** Ind Univ, AB, 1938; Univ Minn, MS, 1940, PhD (org chem), 1942. **Professional Experience:** RETIRED; dir licensing agr prod, Agr Div, Am Cyanamid Co, 1978-1985; assoc dir agr & pharmaceut res, Agr Div, Am Cyanamid Co, 1970-1977; mgr res & develop, Agr Div, Am Cyanamid Co, 1960-1969; dir res & gen mgr res div, Armour & Co, 1957-1960; dir chem res, Warner Lambert Pharmaceut Co, NJ, 1946-1957; civilian, Off Sci Res & Develop, 1944; sr chemist, Winthrop Chem Co Div, Sterling Drug, 1943-1946; fel, Merck, 1942-1943; asst chem, Univ Minn, 1938-1941; asst chem, Ind Univ, 1937-1938. **Memberships:** AAAS (vpres, 1959-1960); Am Chem Soc; fel Inst Chem; Sigma Xi; Soc Chem Indust. **Research Statement & Publications:** Synthesized pharmacologically active organic compounds; mechanisms of chemical reactions; coordination of chemical research with evaluation of compounds produced; research management; research development and commercialization of pharmaceutical, nutritional and industrial chemical products; licensing of pharmaceutical and agricultural products. **Mailing Address:** 90 Battle Rd, Princeton, NJ 08540.

KING, JOHN ARTHUR, ZOOLOGY, ANIMAL BEHAVIOR. **Personal Data:** b Detroit, Mich, June 22, 1921; m 1949, Joan McGinty; c Christopher L & Andrea J. **Education:** Univ Mich, AB, 1943, MS, 1948, PhD, 1951. **Professional Experience:** EMER PROF ZOOL, MICH STATE UNIV, 1986-; Develop res career award, USPHS, 1964-1970; from assoc prof to prof, Mich State Univ, 1961-1986; Nat Acad Sci-Nat Res Coun fel, 1960-1961; staff scientist, Jackson Mem Lab, 1953-1960; USPHS fel, Jackson Mem Lab, 1951-1953; Asst genetics, Univ Mich, 1947-1951. **Memberships:** Am Soc Mammal; Animal Behav Soc (secy, 1962-1965, pres, 1970). **Research Statement & Publications:** Sociobiology; mammalian behavior; effects of early experience; behavioral evolution. **Mailing Address:** 4619 Frost Rd, Webberville, MI 48892. **E-Mail:** tamias@aol.com

KING, JOHN EDWARD, ANATOMY, HISTOLOGY. **Personal Data:** b Columbus, Ohio, November 16, 1939. **Education:** Ohio State Univ, BA, 1961, PhD (anat), 1965. **Professional Experience:** Asst dean, Ohio State Univ; RETIRED; assoc prof physiol optics, Col Optom, 1973-1991; from instr to assoc prof anat, Ohio State Univ, 1965-1973. **Memberships:** AAAS. **Research Statement & Publications:** Hematology. **Mailing Address:** Col Optom, Ohio State Univ 338 W Tenth Ave, Columbus, OH 43210.

KING, JOHN GORDON, ATOMIC PHYSICS. **Personal Data:** b London, Eng, August 13, 1925; American citizen; m 2001, Jane. **Education:** Mass Inst Technol, SB, 1950, PhD (physics), 1953. **Honorary Degrees:** ScD, Univ Hartford, 1972. **Honors & Awards:** Millikan Award, 1965; Harbison Award, 1971 Cersted Medal 2000. **Professional Experience:** FRANCIS FRIEDMAN PROF EMER PHYSICS, MASS INST TECHNOL, as of 2005; Francis L Friedman prof physics, Mass Inst Technol, 1974-1996; from instr to prof physics, Mass Inst Technol, 1953-1974. **Memberships:** Am Phys Soc fel; Am Asn Physics Teachers. **Research Statement & Publications:** Studies of biological surfaces; molecule microscopy; Fundamental null experiments. **Mailing Address:** Mass Inst Technol, Rm 26-169 / Rm 26-548, Cambridge, MA 02139. **E-Mail:** jgking@mit.edu

KING, JOHN MATHEWS, ORGANIC CHEMISTRY. **Personal Data:** b New York, NY, October 25, 1939; m 1962, c 2. **Education:** Cornell Univ, AB, 1961; Univ Mich, MS, 1963, PhD, 1965. **Professional Experience:** MGR, COM ADDITIVE PROCESS DIV, CHEVRON RES CO, STAND OIL CO CALIF, 1982-; mgr, Lubricating Oil Additives Div, 1979-1982; sr res assoc, Com Additive Process Div, Chevron Res CO, Stand Oil CO Calif, 1967-1979; univ fel, Calif Inst Technol, 1966-1967; NSF fel, Calif Inst Technol, 1965-1966. **Memberships:** Am Chem Soc. **Research Statement & Publications:** Synthesis of organic peroxides; organic photochemistry; radiation chemistry of organic compounds; lube oil additives; organic process development. **Mailing Address:** 1194 Idylberry Rd, San Rafael, CA 94903-1128.

KING, JOHN PAUL, SOLID STATE PHYSICS. **Personal Data:** b Zena, Okla, November 23, 1938; m 1961, c 3. **Education:** Cent State Col, Okla, BS, 1961; Okla State Univ, PhD (solid state physics), 1966. **Professional Experience:** PROF PHYSICS, CENT STATE UNIV, OKLA, 1977-; from asst prof to assoc prof, Univ Of Central Oklahma, 1968-1977; Eng sci specialist, Missiles & Space Div, LTV Aerospace Corp, 1966-1968. **Memberships:** Am Phys Soc; Sigma Xi; Okla Acad Of Sci. **Research Statement & Publications:** Study of basic optics associated with imaging and interference. **Mailing Address:** 3420 Baird Dr, Edmond, OK 73013-6327.

KING, JOHN STUART, GEOLOGY. **Personal Data:** b Buffalo, NY, November 12, 1927. **Education:** Univ Buffalo, BA, 1955, MA, 1957; Univ Wyo, PhD (geol), 1963. **Professional Experience:** PROF EMER GEOL, STATE UNIV NY, BUFFALO, as of 2005; assoc dean fac natural sci & math, State Univ Ny, Buffalo, beginning 1990; prof geol, State Univ Ny, Buffalo, beginning 1977; from actg chmn dept to chmn dept, State Univ NY, Buffalo, 1966-1971; consult electro minerals div, Carborundum Co, 1964-1966; from asst prof to assoc prof, State Univ NY, Buffalo, 1963-1977; res engr petrog, Res Div, Carborundum Co, 1957-1960. **Memberships:** Fel Geol Soc Am; Am Asn Petrol Geologists. **Research Statement & Publications:** Igneous and metamorphic petrology and structures; structural geology; field interpretations; planetology and analog studies. **Mailing Address:** State Univ NY, Dept Geol, PO Box 600001 876 Nat Sci Complex, Buffalo, NY 14260-0001. **Fax:** 716-645-3999. **E-Mail:** jking@pcom.net

KING, JOHN SWINTON, PHYSICS. **Personal Data:** b Detroit, Mich, October 31, 1920; m 1943, c 3. **Education:** Univ Mich, PhD (nuclear physics). **Professional Experience:** PROF EMER NUCLEAR ENG, UNIV MICH, ANN ARBOR, as of 2003; chmn dept nuclear eng, Univ Mich, Ann Arbor, beginning 1974; prof nuclear eng, Univ Mich, Ann Arbor, beginning 1962; assoc prof, Univ Mich, Ann Arbor, 1959-1962; mgr submarine adv reactor physics sub-sect, Knolls Atomic Power Lab, Gen Elec Co, 1956-1959; res assoc reactor physics, Knolls Atomic Power Lab, Gen Elec Co, 1953-1956; asst, appl physics lab, Johns Hopkins Univ, 1942-1945. **Memberships:** Am Nuclear Soc; Am Phys Soc. **Research Statement & Publications:** Neutron physics as applied to reactor design and neutron optics. **Mailing Address:** 2311 Vinewood, Ann Arbor, MI 48104. **E-Mail:** jsking@umich.edu

KING, JOHN WILLIAM, AGRONOMY, CROP SCIENCE. **Personal Data:** b Butler, Ind, March 31, 1938; div, c 3. **Education:** Purdue Univ, BS, 1963; Univ RI, MS, 1966; Mich State Univ, PhD (crop sci), 1970. **Professional Experience:** ASSOC PROF AGRON, UNIV ARK, FAYETTEVILLE, 1970-; machinist, Gen Elec Co, Ind, 1956-1960. **Memberships:** Am Soc Agron; Crop Sci Soc Am; Weed Sci Soc Am. **Research Statement & Publications:** Turf grass soils fertilization, species and variety adaptation, cultural systems, weed control, irrigation management; shade and allelopathy. **Mailing Address:** Dept Agron, Univ Ark, Fayetteville, AR 72701. **E-Mail:** jking@uark.edu

KING, JONATHAN ALAN, MOLECULAR BIOLOGY, BIOCHEMISTRY. **Personal Data:** b Brooklyn, NY, August 20, 1941; m 1976, c 2. **Education:** Yale Univ, BS, 1962; Calif Inst Technol, PhD (genetics), 1967. **Professional Experience:** Guggenheim fel, 1987; PROF MOLECULAR BIOL, MASS INST TECHNOL, 1978-; DIR BIOL ELECTRON MICROSCOPE FACIL, MASS INST TECHNOL, 1970-; from asst prof to assoc prof, Mass Inst Technol, 1970-1978; fel struct biol, Lab Molecular Biol, Brit Med Res Coun, 1969-1970; Childs Mem Fund Med Res res fel, 1968-1970; fel molecular biol, Purdue Univ, 1968-1969; assoc scientist microbial ecol, Jet Propulsion Lab, Calif Inst Technol, 1967-1968; counr, Am Soc Virol; chmn, Microbiol Physiol Study Sect & Genetic Based Dis Study Sect, NIH. **Memberships:** Genetics Soc Am; Am Soc Microbiol; Biophys Soc; fel AAAS; Am Soc Virol; Am Soc Biochem & Molecular Biol. **Research Statement & Publications:** Genetic control of morphogenesis; virus assembly; protein folding. **Mailing Address:** Dept Biol, Mass Inst Technol, 77 Mass Ave, Cambridge, MA 02139-4307. **Fax:** 617-252-1843. **E-Mail:** jaking@mit.edu

KING, JONATHAN STANTON, clinical chemistry; deceased, see previous edition for last biography

KING, JOSEPH HERBERT, SPACE PHYSICS. **Personal Data:** b Malden, Mass, November 16, 1939; m 1965, c 2. **Education:** Boston Col, PhD (physics), 1966. **Professional Experience:** RETIRED; head, Nat Space Sci Data Ctr, NASA, 1992-2003; head, Cent Data Serv Facil, NASA, 1984-1992; staff mem, Lab Extraterrestrial Physics, NASA, 1977-1983; proj scientist, Interplanetary Monitoring Platform Satellite, NASA, 1974-1997; staff mem, Nat Space Sci Data Ctr, NASA, 1969-1977; Nat Acad Sci assoc fel, Nat Space Sci Data Ctr, NASA, 1967-1969; staff scientist, Aerospace Corp, 1965-1967; lectr physics, Regis Col, Mass, 1963-1964. **Memberships:** Am Geophys Union. **Research Statement & Publications:** Spacecraft plasma and field data concerning the mass and energy coupling between the solar wind and the earth's magnetosphere. **Mailing Address:** Goddard Space Flight Ctr, NASA, Code 633, Greenbelt, MD 20771. **Fax:** 301-286-1771. **E-Mail:** joseph.h.king@gsfc.nasa.gov

KING, KATHERINE CHUNG-HO, PEDIATRICS, NEONATOLOGY. **Personal Data:** b Peiping, China, August 27, 1937; American citizen; m 1985, Louis. **Education:** Meredith Col, AB, 1957; Bowman Gray Sch Med, MD, 1962; Am Bd Pediat, dipl, 1968, dipl, Neonatal & Perinatal Med, 1977. **Professional Experience:** ASSOC PROF PEDIAT, ALBERT EINSTEIN SCH MED, 1989-; NEONATOLOGIST, SCHNEIDER CHILDREN'S HOSP, LONG ISLAND JEWISH HOSP, 1985-; assoc prof pediat, State Univ NY, Stony Brook, 1985-1989; dir, Newborn Serv, 1981-1984; assoc prof neonatology, dept Reproductive Biol, 1978-1985; actg dir, Newborn Serv, 1974-1975; from asst prof to assoc prof pediat, Sch Med, Case Western res Univ, 1971-1985; asst pediatrician, Cleveland Metrop Gen Hosp & co-dir, Perinatal Clin res Ctr, 1969-1985; sr instr, Case Western Reserve Univ, 1969-1971; Cleveland Diabetes Found grant, Cleveland Metrop Gen Hosp, 1969-1970; USPHS trainee, 1966-1968; from intern pediat to resident pediat metab, Cleveland Metrop Gen Hosp, 1962-1966. **Memberships:** Am Fedn Clin Res; Am Acad Pediat; fel Am Col Nutrit; Soc Pediat Res. **Research Statement & Publications:** Carbohydrate metabolism of human fetus and neonatal; metabolism. **Mailing Address:** Long Island Jewish-Hillside Med Ctr, Schneider Children's Hosp, New Hyde Park, NY 11042. **Fax:** 718-347-3850. **E-Mail:** kking@lij.edu

KING, KATHLEEN, NURSING. **Education:** State Univ NY, BSN, 1973; Univ Rochester, MS, 1976, PhD (nursing), 1984. **Professional Experience:** PROF, SCH NURSING, UNIV ROCHESTER, as of 2006. **Memberships:** Fel Am Acad Nursing; fel Am Heart Asn. **Mailing Address:** Sch Nursing, Univ Rochester, 601 Elmwood Ave HWH 2W307, Rochester, NY 14642. **Fax:** 585-756-8299. **E-Mail:** Kathleen_King@URMC.rochester.edu

KING, KENNETH JR, BIOGEOCHEMISTRY. **Personal Data:** b Philadelphia, Pa, December 27, 1930; m 1961, c 2. **Education:** Mass Inst Technol, SB, 1952, SM, 1960; Columbia Univ, PhD (geol), 1972. **Professional Experience:** RES ASSOC BIOGEOCHEM, LAMONT-DOHERTY GEOL OBSERV, COLUMBIA UNIV, 1972-; fel, Carnegie Inst Wash, 1972-1974; res asst, Columbia Univ, 1967-1972; dir res planning, Merck & Co, 1965-1967; indust res & develop, Merck & Co, 1955-1964. **Memberships:** Sigma Xi; AAAS; Am Chem Soc; Geol Soc Am; Geochem Soc. **Research Statement & Publications:** Proteins of modern and fossil mineralized tissues; amino acid racemization; mechanism of biomineralization. **Mailing Address:** 275 Jones Rd, Falmouth, MA 02540-3338.

KING, KEVIN F, MEDICAL IMAGING PHYSICS. **Professional Experience:** SR PHYSICIST, APPL SCI LAB, GE MED SYSTS, as of 2004. **Mailing Address:** Global Appl Sci Lab, GE Healthcare, Milwaukee, WI 53151.

KING, LAFAYETTE CARROLL, ORGANIC CHEMISTRY. **Personal Data:** b Marysvale, Utah, September 9, 1914; m 1937, c 5. **Education:** Utah State Col, BS, 1936; Mich State Col, MS, 1938, PhD (chem), 1942. **Honors & Awards:** Chem Educ Award, Am Chem Soc, 1969. **Professional Experience:** PROF EMER CHEM, NORTHWESTERN UNIV, 1985-; chmn org comt, Indo-US Binat Conf Chem Educ, 1969; US-Japan Conf Chem Educ, Berkeley, 1968 & First Int Am Conf Chem Educ, Buenos Aires, 1965; chmn adv coun col chem, 1966-; US-Japan Conf Chem Educ, Japan, 1964; indust consult, Food Chem, 1950-; from instr to prof chem, Northwestern Univ, 1942-1985; res assoc, Northwestern Univ, 1942; asst biol chem, Mich State Col, 1936-1942. **Memberships:** Fel AAAS; Am Chem Soc; Oil Chem Soc; Royal Soc Chem. **Research Statement & Publications:** Synthesis of quaternary salts, thiazoles and selenazoles; structures of sterols; mechanism of organic reactions. **Mailing Address:** Dept Chem, Northwestern Univ, Evanston, IL 60201.

KING, LARRY DEAN, SOIL SCIENCE. **Personal Data:** b Atlanta, Ga, March 10, 1939; div, c 2. **Education:** Ga Inst Technol, BS, 1962; Univ Ga, MS, 1968, PhD (agron), 1971. **Professional Experience:** EMER PROF, NC STATE UNIV, as of 2005; prof soil sci, NC state Univ, beginning 1988; from asst prof to assoc prof, NC State Univ, 1974-1988; agronomist agr develop, Tenn Valley Authority, 1973-1974; fel soil sci, Univ Guelph, Ont, 1971-1972; Aircraft engr comput prog, Lockheed Aircraft, 1962-1965. **Memberships:** Am Soc Agron. **Research Statement & Publications:** Alternative agricultural systems; land application of municipal and industrial wastes. **Mailing Address:** Dept Soil Sci, Col Agri & life Sci, NC State Univ, PO Box 7619, Raleigh, NC 27695-7619. **Fax:** 919-515-2167. **E-Mail:** larry_king@ncsu.edu

KING, LARRY GENE, IRRIGATION & DRAINAGE ENGINEERING, GROUNDWATER HYDROLOGY. **Personal Data:** b Prosser, Wash, June 24, 1936; m 1956, Shirley; c Steven J, James P, Jani L (Rima) & Robert J. **Education:** Wash State Univ, BS, 1958; Colo State Univ, MS, 1961, PhD (civil eng), 1965. **Professional Experience:** Westinghouse-Hanford Co, 1994-1995 & Off Atty Gen Wash, 1995-1996; Gary J Libey, atty, 1993-1994; Culp, Guterson & Grader, atty, 1993; Backman, Blumel & Reed, attys, 1991-1992; Velikanje, Moore & Shore Inc, atty, 1989-1992; PROF, BIOL SYSTS ENG DEPT, WASH STATE UNIV, 1987-2005; Paine, Wash State Dept Transp, 1987; Paine, Kenniwick Irrig Dist, 1984-1986; Paine, USAID, 1984, 1986-1990; chmn, Agr Eng Dept, 1979-1987; Paine, McCrosky Terr Trailer Park, 1979; Paine, Hamblin, Coffin, Brooke & Miller, atty, 1977; Ken Earl, atty, 1976; Paine, Wash State Dept Ecol, 1975-1981; consult, City Wash Terr, 1973-1975; assoc prof agr & irrig eng, Utah State Univ, 1969-1974; res assoc, Pac Northwest Labs, Battelle Mem Inst, 1968-1969; sr res engr, Pac Northwest Labs, Battelle Mem Inst, 1965-1968; res scientist, Pac Northwest Labs, Battelle Mem Inst, 1965; res engr hydrol, Gen Elec Co, 1962-1965; consult, Orchards Unlimited, 1962-1965; jr agr engr, Colo State Univ, 1962; asst civil eng, Colo State Univ, 1958-1962; mem, US Nat Comt, Int Comn Irrig & Drainage. **Memberships:** Am Soc Civil Engrs; Am Soc Agr Engrs. **Research Statement & Publications:** Irrigation; drainage; water quality; salinity control; hydrology; groundwater hydrology; soil and water use and conservation; soil water movement; erosion control; wells; on-farm water management; irrigation system management; computer modeling. **Mailing Address:** Dept Biol Syst Eng, Wash State Univ, Pullman, WA 99164-1620. **Fax:** 509-335-2722. **E-Mail:** king@wsu.edu

KING, LARRY MICHAEL, MATHEMATICS. **Personal Data:** b Brooklyn, NY, November 29, 1942; m 1968. **Education:** Brooklyn Col, BS, 1963; Univ Md, Col Park, MA, 1966, PhD (math), 1968. **Professional Experience:** ASSOC DEAN, COL ARTS & SCI, 1982-; ASSOC PROF MATH, UNIV MICH, FLINT, 1979-; asst prof, Col Arts & Sci, 1974-1979; asst prof math, Univ Mass, Amherst, 1968-1974. **Memberships:** Am Math Soc; Math Asn Am. **Research Statement & Publications:** Slices in transformation groups; topological dynamics and dynamical systems; R-isomorphisms of transformation groups; actions of non-compact semigroups; new ways of teaching calculus. **Mailing Address:** Dept Math, Univ Mich, Flint, MI 48502-2186. **Fax:** 810-766-6880. **E-Mail:** lmk@umflint.edu

KING, LEE CURTIS, FIBERGLASS COATINGS, TEST DEVELOPMENT. **Personal Data:** b Greenville, SC, October 20, 1954. **Education:** Univ SC, BS, 1976, MEd, 1980. **Professional Experience:** RES CHEMIST, CLARK-SCHWEBEL FIBER GLASS, 1984-; Real Estate Assocs, Anderson, SC, 1983-; instr chem, math, phys & astron, Tri Co Tech Col, 1983-1984; salesperson, Am Indust, Lumberton, NC, 1983; teacher chem, phys sci & math, N Greenville Col, 1982-1983; teacher chem, phys sci, Anderson Col, 1980-1982; teacher math, chem & phys, Midlands Tech Col, 1978-1980; technician, Cardinal Chem Co, 1976-1978. **Memberships:** Am Soc Mat. **Research Statement & Publications:** Development, evaluation, fiberglass coatings based on customer needs (market or applied orientation); polymer properties and processing characteristics; test development from size preparation to end product in many fields. **Mailing Address:** 2207 W N Ave, PO Box 27, Anderson, SC 29622.

KING, L(EE) ELLIS, TRANSPORTATION ENGINEERING, ERGONOMICS. **Personal Data:** b Jamestown, NC, August 21, 1939; m Rachel. **Education:** NC State Univ, BS, 1961, MSCE, 1963; Univ Calif, Berkeley, D.Eng, 1967. **Honors & Awards:** Walter L Huber Civil Engr Res Prize, Am Soc Civil Engrs, 1973. **Professional Experience:** PROF EMERITUS DEPT CIVIL ENG, UNIV NC, CHARLOTTE, 2002-; chmn & prof, Univ NC, Charlotte, 1976-1995; prof, Wayne State Univ, 1975-1976; assoc prof, Univ Colo, Denver Ctr, 1973-1975; from asst prof to assoc prof, WVa Univ, 1967-1973; consult, various pvt & pub agencies. **Memberships:** Am Soc Civil Engrs; Human Factors & Ergonomics Soc; Nat Soc Prof Engrs; Inst Transp Engrs. **Research Statement & Publications:** Traffic engineering problems; transportation planning; driver, vehicle and roadway interaction; driver behavior; reduced visibility performance; roadway lighting; roadway signing and marking; pedestrian behavior; traffic signals. **Mailing Address:** 389 Fairway Court, Blowing Rock, NC 28605-9330. **E-Mail:** ellisking@aol.com

KING, LEWIS H, MARINE GEOLOGY. **Personal Data:** b Lockeport, NS, November 10, 1924; m 1955, c 6. **Education:** Acadia Univ, BSc, 1949; Mass Inst Technol, PhD (geol), 1955. **Professional Experience:** Mem fac, Dalhousie Univ, 1968-; GEOLOGIST, BEDFORD INST, DEPT ENERGY, MINES & RESOURCES, 1963-; geochemist, Mines Br. Dept Mines & Tech Surv, Ont, 1956-1963; geologist, Geol Surv Can, NS, 1954-1956. **Memberships:** AAAS; fel Geol Soc Am; fel Geol Asn Can; Sigma Xi. **Research State-**

ment & Publications: Geological mapping of the sea floor across the Scotian Shelf, eastern Gulf of Maine and the Grand Banks. **Mailing Address:** 50 Swanton Dr, Dartmouth, NS B2W 2C5, Can.

KING, LLOYD ELIJAH, DERMATOLOGY, ANATOMY. **Personal Data:** b Mayfield, Ky, September 10, 1939; m 1968, c 3. **Education:** Vanderbilt Univ, BA, 1961; Univ Tenn, Memphis, MD, 1967, PhD (anat), 1970. **Professional Experience:** PROF MED & CHIEF DERMAT, VANDERBILT UNIV, 1977-; clin investr, Vet Admin Hosp, Nashville, Tenn, 1977-1980; vet admin trainee dermat, Vet Admin res & educ associateship, 1975-; asst prof dermat, Med Units, Univ Tenn, Memphis, 1975-1977; NIH spec fel, St Jude Children's Res Hosp, 1974-1976; instr med, Med Units, Univ Tenn, Memphis, 1973-1976; vet admin trainee dermat, Vet Admin Hosp, Memphis, 1972-1974; resident dermat, City Memphis Hosps, 1971-1974; instr anat, Med Units, Univ Tenn, Memphis, 1970-1974; resident internal med, City Memphis Hosps, 1970-1971; Intern med, City Memphis Hosps, 1969-1970; NIH fel anat, Med Units, Univ Tenn, Memphis, 1968-1969. **Memberships:** AAAS; Am Acad Dermat; fel Am Col Physicians; Am Fedn Clin Res; AMA. **Research Statement & Publications:** Skin diseases; cell membranes; growth factors; spider venom/bites. **Mailing Address:** Dept Med & Dermat Med Ctr Vanderbilt Univ, 3900 TVC Vanderbilt Clin Bldg, Nashville, TN 37212. **Fax:** 615-320-7055. **E-Mail:** lloyd.king@vanderbilt.edu

KING, LOWELL ALVIN, PHYSICAL PROPERTIES, ADA COMPUTER LANGUAGE. **Personal Data:** b Spencer, Iowa, June 16, 1932; m 1954, Mary; c 3. **Education:** Iowa State Univ, BS, 1953, PhD (inorg chem), 1963; Wash Univ, AM, 1955. **Honors & Awards:** Air Force Res & Develop Award, 1970; Sci Eng Award, Air Force Asn, 1971. **Professional Experience:** RETIRED; distinguished vis prof, USAF Acad, 1996-1967; lectr comput sci, Europ Div, Univ Md, 1984-1986; prof comput sci, Colo Tech Col, 1983-1996; prof phys sci, Europ Christian Univ, Vienna, Austria, 1981-1986; consult, F J Seiler Lab, Air Force Systs Command, USAF, 1981-1983; sr scientist, Chem Div, F J Seiler Lab, Air Force Systs Command, 1975-1980; dir, Chem Div, F J Seiler Lab, Air Force Systs Command, 1974-1975; prof chem, USAF Acad, 1971-1980; dir, Chem Div, F J Seiler Lab, Off Aerospace Res, 1966-1968; assoc prof chem, F J Seiler Lab, Off Aerospace Res, 1965-1971; res assoc, F J Seiler Lab, Off Aerospace Res, 1964-1965; assoc prof, USAF Acad, 1963-1964; asst prof chem, USAF Acad, 1963; res assoc, Ames Lab, Iowa State Univ, 1961-1963; instr chem, USAF Acad, 1959-1961; group leader, Mat Lab, USAF, 1956-1959. **Research Statement & Publications:** Electrochemistry; molten salt chemistry; measurement of physical and electrochemical properties of molten salt mixtures containing complex halo-anions. **Mailing Address:** 3945 Hill Cir, Colorado Springs, CO 80904.

KING, LOWELL RESTELL, UROLOGY, PEDIATRIC UROLOGY. **Personal Data:** b Salem, Ohio, February 28, 1932; div, c 2. **Education:** Johns Hopkins Univ, BA, 1952, MD, 1956. **Honors & Awards:** Cancer Achievement Award, Am Urol Asn, 1996; Medal Urol Sect, Am Acad Pediat. **Professional Experience:** PROF EMER SURG, DUKE UNIV, as of 1997; prof urol, Duke Univ, beginning 1981; head, Sect Pediat Urol, beginning 1981; mem, Am Bd Urol, 1975-1981; SURGEON-IN-CHIEF, CHILDREN'S MEM HOSP, 1974-; prof urol, Northwestern Univ, 1970-1981; chmn, Div Urol, 1970-1977; prof, Univ Ill, 1968-1970; chmn, Dept Urol, Presby-St Luke's Hosp, 1968-1970; from asst prof to assoc prof, Northwestern Univ, 1963-1968; asst prof urol, Med Sch, Johns Hopkins Univ, 1963; Am Cancer Soc fel, 1958-1959; resident, Johns Hopkins Hosp, 1957-1961; intern, Johns Hopkins Hosp, 1956-1957. **Memberships:** Am Urol Asn; fel Am Acad Pediat; fel Am Col Surgeons; Soc Pediat Urol; Am Asn Genito-Urinary Surgeons; Clin Soc Genito Urinary Surgeons. **Research Statement & Publications:** Pediatric urology; investigate causes/treatment of fetal/cogenital urinary obstruction; new types of treatment for high impalpable testis; new methods of continant urinary diversion. **Mailing Address:** Duke Univ Med Ctr, PO Box 3831, Durham, NC 27710. **Fax:** 919-684-4611.

KING, LUCY JANE, PSYCHIATRY, ADDICTION PSYCHIATRY. **Personal Data:** b Vandalia, Ill, December 23, 1932. **Education:** Wash Univ, AB, 1954, MD, 1958; Am Bd Psychiat & Neurol, dipl psychiat, 1966. **Professional Experience:** EMER PROF PSYCHIAT, IND UNIV, INDIANAPOLIS, as of 2004; assoc clin prof psychiat, Med Sch, Ind Univ, beginning 1992; PVT PRACT PSYCHIAT, ST VINCENT HOSP, INDIANAPOLIS, IND, 1991-; pvt pract psychiat, Prince William Hosp, Manassas, Va, 1982-1991; med officer, Food & Drug Admin, 1980-1981; prof psychiat & pharmacol, Med Col Va, Va Commonwealth Univ, 1974-1979; from instr to assoc prof, Sch Med, Wash Univ, 1970-1974; NIMH res career develop awards neuropharmacol, 1963-1973; chief resident, Renard Hosp, St Louis, Mo, 1962-1963; asst resident psychiat, Renard Hosp, St Louis, Mo, 1959-1962; intern, Butterworth Hosp, Grand Rapids, Mich, 1958-1959. **Memberships:** Fel Am Psychiat Asn; Sigma Xi; Am Soc Addiction Med; Am Acad Clin Psychiatrists; Am Acad Psychiatrist Alcoholism & Addiction. **Research Statement & Publications:** Clinical and social psychiatry; neuropharmacology. **Mailing Address:** Midtown Comm Mental Health Ctr, 1001 W 10th St, Indianapolis, IN 46202.

KING, LUNSFORD RICHARDSON, MATHEMATICS. **Personal Data:** b Greensboro, NC, July 22, 1937; m 1961, c 2. **Education:** Davidson Col, BS, 1959; Duke Univ, PhD (math), 1963. **Professional Experience:** RETIRED; prof math, Davidson Col, 1980-2002; vis scholar, Dartmouth Col, 1974-1975; from asst prof to assoc prof, Davidson Col, 1964-1980; res instr math, Univ Va, 1963-1964. **Memberships:** Math Asn Am; Am Math Soc. **Mailing Address:** Dept Math, Davidson Col, Rm 126-A Chambers Bldg 200 D Rd, Davidson, NC 28036-1719. **E-Mail:** riking@davidson.edu

KING, M, ANALYTICAL CHEMISTRY. **Personal Data:** b Seattle, Wash, June 5, 1935; m 1965, c 1. **Education:** Wash State Univ, BS, 1957; Calif Inst Technol, PhD (chem), 1963. **Professional Experience:** PROF ANAL CHEM, WESTERN WASH STATE UNIV, as of 2004; chmn dept, Western Wash State Col, beginning 1974; assoc prof chem, Western Wash State Col, beginning 1969; NSF res grant, 1968-1970; asst prof, Western Wash State Col, 1966-1969; chemist, Org Chem Div, E I du Pont Del Nemours & Co, 1964-1966; welsh fel, Univ Tex, 1963-1964; asst prof chem, Calif State Col Los Angeles, 1961-1963. **Memberships:** Am Chem Soc. **Research Statement & Publications:** Application of electroanalytical techniques to the study of reaction kinetics and mechanisms. **Mailing Address:** Dept Chem, Western Wash Univ, CB241, 516 High St, Bellingham, WA 98225-9150. **Fax:** 360-650-2826. **E-Mail:** king@chem.wwu.edu

KING, MALCOLM, MEDICINE, LUNG DISEASE. **Personal Data:** b January 24, 1947. **Education:** McMaster Univ, BSc, 1968; McGill Univ, PhD (polymer chem), 1973. **Professional Experience:** Lab Atmospheric Pollution, Univ Sao Paulo, Brazil, 1994; Univ Freiburg, Ger, 1991-1992; PROF, PULMONARY MED DIV, UNIV ALTA, EDMONTON, 1990-; guest prof, Robert Koch Clin, 1986-1987; CO-DIR, PULMONARY & CELL BIOL RES GROUP, 1985-; assoc prof, Pulmonary & Cell Biol Res Group, 1985-1990; asst prof, Meakins-Christie Labs, McGill Univ, 1979-1985; Centennial fel, Meakins-Christie Labs, McGill Univ, 1974-1978; prin investr, Med Res Coun, Can Cystic Fibrosis Found, Alta Lung Asn, Galephar SA, Glaxo Inc; fel, Weizmann Inst; guest prof, Dept Anat, Univ Bern, Switz. **Memberships:** Chem Inst Can; Can Soc Clin Invest; Can Thoracic Soc; Am Physiol Soc; Am Thoracic Soc; Am Col Chest Physicians. **Research Statement & Publications:** Epithelial defense mechanisms relating to lung disease involving mucociliary dysfunction; author of 36 publications. **Mailing Address:** Dept Med, Heritage Med Res Ctr, Univ Alta, 173, Edmonton, AB T6G 2B7, Can. **Fax:** 780-407-3340. **E-Mail:** king@gpu.srv.ualberta.ca

KING, MARVIN, OPTICAL SYSTEMS, ELECTRONIC SYSTEMS. **Personal Data:** b New York, NY, April 23, 1940; m 1961, Carole; c Sarah M. **Education:** City Col NY, BEE, 1961; Polytech Inst Brooklyn, MSEE, 1963; Columbia Univ, EngScD, 1966. **Professional Experience:** PRES, RIVERSIDE RES INST, 1990-; exec vpres, Riverside Res Inst, 1988-1990; vpres res, Riverside Res Inst, 1982-1988; exec dir prog develop, Riverside Res Inst, 1981-1982; res dir, Riverside Res Inst, 1977-1981; adj assoc prof, City Col NY 1972-1974; spec study sect optics, NIH, 1970; mgr optics lab, Riverside Res Inst, 1969-1976; Adv Optics Ctr, Radiation Inc, Mich, 1969; asst head electrooptics lab, Riverside Res Inst, 1968-1969; sr res engr, Riverside Res Inst, 1967-1968; consult, US Army Electronics Command, Ft Monmouth, NJ, 1967-1968; lectr, Columbia Univ Sci Honors Prog, 1966-1973; res engr, Electronics Res Labs, Columbia, 1966-1967; res asst, Electronics Res Labs, Columbia, 1964-1966; electrophysicist, ITT Fed Labs, 1963-1964; jr elec engr, ITT Fed Labs, 1962-1963. **Memberships:** Inst Elec & Electronics Engrs; Optical Soc Am; Am Inst Physics; Quantum Electronics Soc. **Research Statement & Publications:** Signal processing for radar and communications systems utilizing holography, photographic film, photonics and ultrasonics; atmospheric optics; optical oceanography; infrared holography; laser radar; laser signatures; infrared acquisition and tracking systems; image processing. **Mailing Address:** Riverside Res Inst, 330 W 42nd St, New York, NY 10036. **Fax:** 212-502-1729. **E-Mail:** king@rringc.org

KING, MARY MARGARET, DRUG METABOLISM, NUTRITION. **Personal Data:** b Oklahoma City, Okla, May 26, 1946. **Education:** Cent State Univ, BS, 1969; Univ Okla, Health Sci Center, PhD (med physiol & biophys), 1975; Okla City Univ, MBA, 1984; Okla State Univ, DVM, 1993. **Honors & Awards:** Young Investr Award, NIH, 1976; National Psi Kappan of the Year, 1996. **Professional Experience:** OWNER, PRES & PRIMARY VET, ACRE VIEW PET HOSP & LASER CTR EDMOND INC, 1993-; spec asst to pres, Lab Animal Resources Ctr, 1990-1993; adj assoc prof biochem & molecular biol, Lab Animal Resources Ctr, 1988-1993; assoc mem, Okla Med Res Found, 1986-1993; consult, Nat Cancer Inst, NIH, 1983-; grad fac, Univ Okla, Health Sci Ctr, 1983-; dir, Sci Support Serv, 1982-1990; dir, Lab Animal Resources Ctr, 1982-1990; res asst prof biochem & molecular biol, Univ Okla Health Sci Ctr, 1981-1988; Young Investr Award, NIH Nat Inst Environ Health Sci, 1978-1981; staff scientist, Okla Med Res Found, 1977-1980; res assoc biomembrane res, Okla Med Res Found, 1976-1977; fel, Okla Med Res Found, 1975-1976; instr, Okla City Pub Schs, 1969-1971; instr physiol, Cent State Univ, 1969. **Memberships:** NY Acad Sci; Am Asn Cancer Res; Am Inst Nutrit; Sigma Xi; Soc Exp Biol Med; Am Vet Med Asn; OK Vet Med Asn Central OK Vet Med Asn; Nat Laser Soc. **Research Statement & Publications:** Chemical carcinogens and dietary fat-antioxidant interactions as relates to mammary cancer; carcinogenesis; chemical carcinogens; dietary parameters; hormonal interactions in mammary gland, especially relating to the drug metabolizing system. **Mailing Address:** Acre View Pet Hosp Inc, 1900 S Bryant Ave, Edmond, OK 73013. **Fax:** 405-348-8955.

KING, MARY-CLAIRE, EPIDEMIOLOGY, HUMAN GENETICS. **Personal Data:** b Evanston, Ill, February 27, 1946; m 1973, c 1. **Education:** Carleton Col, BA, 1966; Univ Calif, Berkeley, PhD (genetics), 1973. **Honors & Awards:** Clowes Award Basic Res, Am Asn Cancer Res. **Professional Experience:** PROF GENOME SCI & MED, UNIV WASH, as of 2003; Am Cancer Soc Res prof, Dept Med & Genetics, Univ Wash, beginning 1995; assoc prof epidemiol, Univ Calif, San Francisco, beginning 1980; assoc prof epidemiol, Univ Calif, Berkeley, 1980-1995; prin investr, genetic epidemiol breast cancer families, NIH grant, 1979-; asst prof, Univ Calif, Berkeley, 1976-1980; asst prof genetics, Univ Calif, San Francisco, 1974-1980; vis prof, Univ Chile, Santiago, 1973. **Memberships:** Inst Med-Nat Acad Sci; Soc Epidemiol Res; Am Epidemiol Soc; Sigma Xi; fel AAAS. **Research Statement & Publications:** Genetics and epidemiology of breast cancer and other common chronic diseases, pedigree analysis, human and primate molecular evolution. **Mailing Address:** Dept Genome Sci, Univ Wash Sch Med, PO Box 357720, Seattle, WA 98195-7720. **Fax:** 206-616-4295. **E-Mail:** mcking@u.washington.edu

KING, MERRILL KENNETH, COMBUSTION SCIENCE. **Personal Data:** b Claymont, Del, November 15, 1938; m 1964, c 2. **Education:** Carnegie Inst Technol, BS, 1960, MS, 1962, PhD (chem eng), 1965. **Professional Experience:** ENTERPRISE SCIENTIST, MICROGRAVITY COMBUSTION SCI PROG, NASA HQ, as of 2003; MGR, COMBUSTION RES DEPT, ATLANTIC RES CORP, 1984-; chief scientist res & technol, Energy & Pollution Technol Sect, 1976-1984; chief kinetics & combustion group, Energy & Pollution Technol Sect, 1974-1976; head, Energy & Pollution Technol Sect, 1973-1974; staff scientist, Thermodyn & Combustion Sect, Atlantic Res Corp Div, Susquehanna Corp, 1972-1973; head, Thermodyn & Combustion Sect, Atlantic Res Corp Div, Susquehanna Corp, 1967-1972; sr res engr, 1964-1967. **Memberships:** Am Inst Aeronaut & Astronaut; Combustion Inst. **Research Statement & Publications:** Solid propellant combustion; metals combustion; graphite oxidation and erosion; air-breathing propulsion; chemical thermodynamics; chemical kinetics; vortex flow; combustion instability. **Mailing Address:** NASA Hq, Code UG, 300 E St SW, Washington, DC 20546. **Fax:** 202-358-3091. **E-Mail:** merrill.king@hq.nasa.gov

KING, MICHAEL DUMONT, ATMOSPHERIC RADIATION, REMOTE SENSING. **Personal Data:** b Kansas City, Mo, October 20, 1949; m 1972, Diana; c Jason & Hailey. **Education:** Colo Col, BA, 1971; Univ Ariz, MS, 1973, PhD (atmospheric sci), 1977. **Honorary Degrees:** DSc, Colo Col, 1995. **Honors & Awards:** Except Serv Medal, NASA, 1985; Except Sci Achievement Medal, NASA, 1992; Verner E Suomi Award, Am Meteorol Soc, 2000; William Nordberg Award, Earth Sci, Goddard Space Flight Center, 2001. **Professional Experience:** EARTH OBSERVING SYST SR PROJ SCIENTIST, GODDARD SPACE FLIGHT CTR, NASA, 1992-; assoc ed, J Atmospheric Sci, 1991-1993; prin investr, Moderate Resolution Imaging Spectroradiometer Sci Team, 1989-; mem, Clouds & Earth's Radiant Energy Syst Sci Team, 1989-2003; chmn, Comt Atmospheric Radiation, Am Meteorol Soc, 1986-1988; vis prof, Dept Atmospheric Sci, Univ Wash, 1986-1987; 1983-1992; Prin investr, Earth Radiation Budget Exp Sci Team, 1980-1992; atmospheric scientist, Goddard Space Flight Ctr, NASA, 1978-1992; adj prof, Dept Atmospheric and Oceanic Science, Univ Maryland, 2000-. **Memberships:** Fel Am Meteorol Soc; Am Geophys Union; Senior Mem IEEE. **Research Statement & Publications:** Multiple light scattering and radiative transfer in cloud free and cloudy atmospheres; application of inversion methods to determination of aerosol size distribution and absorption properties; determination of the optical thickness and effective particle radius of clouds from airborne and spaceborne measurements. **Mailing Address:** 14613 Peach Orchard Rd, Silver Spring, MD 20905-4437. **E-Mail:** michael.d.king@nasa.gov

KING, MICHAEL M, ORGANIC CHEMISTRY, ORGANIC SYNTHESIS. **Personal Data:** b Chicago, Ill, May 10, 1944; m 1970, Linda; c Jacob. **Education:** Ill Inst Technol, BS,

1966; Harvard Univ, AM, 1967, PhD (org chem), 1970. **Honors & Awards:** Trachtenberg Prize for University Service-George Washington University 2004. **Professional Experience:** CHAIR, DEPT CHEM, COLUMBIAN COL, GEORGE WASH UNIV, as of 1995; PROF CHEM, GEORGE Wash UNIV, 1984-; from asst prof to assoc prof, George Wash Univ, 1973-1984; Asst prof chem, NY Univ, 1970-1973. **Memberships:** Am Chem Soc. **Research Statement & Publications:** Biomolecules, enzyme model systems, imidazoles and pyrroles, organofluorides. **Mailing Address:** Dept Chem, George Wash Univ, 725 21st St NW, Rm 107a, Washington, DC 20052. **Fax:** 202-994-5873. **E-Mail:** kingm@gwu.edu

KING, MICHAEL STUART, GEOLOGICAL ENGINEERING, APPLIED GEOPHYSICS. **Personal Data:** b Brackley, Eng, June 2, 1931; m 1962, c 3. **Education:** Univ Glasgow, BSc, 1953; Univ Calif, Berkeley, MS, 1961, PhD (eng sci), 1964. **Professional Experience:** Staff scientist, Dept Mech Eng, Univ Calif, Berkeley, 1981-; prof geol sci, Univ Sask, 1966-1981; sr sci officer, Geotech Div, Ministry Technol, Eng, 1965-1966; lectr, Univ Calif, Berkeley, 1964-1965; teaching asst mineral technol, Univ Calif, Berkeley, 1959-1964; field engr, Iraq Petrol Co, Kirkuk, 1954-1959; design engr, John Brown & Co, Scotland, 1952-1954; MEM STAFF, DEPT ENG TECHNOL, CABOT INST ARTS & TECHNOL; mem Can Nat Comt Rock Mech. **Memberships:** Am Geophys Union; Soc Explor Geophys; Am Inst Mining Metall & Petrol Engrs; Brit Inst Mech Engrs; Can Inst Mining & Metall. **Research Statement & Publications:** Geological sciences; application of ultrasonics in geology; rock mechanics; fluid flow in porous media. **Mailing Address:** Dept Eng Technol, Cabot Inst Arts & Technol PO Box 1693, St John's, NL A1C 5P7, Can.

KING, NICHOLAS S P, NUCLEAR STRUCTURE, NUCLEAR INSTRUMENTATION. **Personal Data:** b Lafayette, Ind, December 3, 1940; m 1966, Sally; c Alison & Peter. **Education:** Dartmouth Col, BA, 1962; Univ NMex, MS, 1964; Univ Colo, PhD (physics), 1970. **Professional Experience:** LAB FEL, LOS ALAMOS NAT LAB, as of 2003; GROUP LEADER, LOS ALAMOS NAT LAB, 1984-1997; assoc group leader, Los Alamos Nat Lab, 1981-1984; staff physicist, Los Alamos Nat Lab, 1978-1980; Res physicist, Univ Calif, Davis, 1971-1977. **Memberships:** Am Phys Soc; Inst Elec & Electronics Engrs; Soc Photo-Optical Instrumentation Engrs. **Research Statement & Publications:** Investigation of the reaction mechanisms of nuclear particles; determination of material properties under dynamic shock conditions; development of nuclear detector systems. **Mailing Address:** Los Alamos Nat Lab, PO Box 1663, Los Alamos, NM 87545. **E-Mail:** nspk@lanl.gov

KING, NORVAL WILLIAM, VETERINARY PATHOLOGY, COMPARATIVE PATHOLOGY. **Personal Data:** b Salisbury, Md, April 29, 1938; m 1964, c 2. **Education:** Univ Ga, DVM, 1962. **Professional Experience:** Assoc dir, New Eng Regional Primate Res Ctr, 1980-1997; LECTR, SCH MED & VET MED, TUFTS UNIV, 1979-; ASSOC PROF, COMP PATH, HARVARD MED SCH, 1976-; dir, NIH Training grant, vet & comparative path, NIH, 1975-; consult, Pathobiology Inc, 1974-; prin assoc, Harvard Med Sch, 1972-1976; res Award, Am Asn Lab Animal Sci, 1969; res assoc, Harvard Med Sch, 1968-1972; res fel, Harvard Med Sch, 1965-1967. **Memberships:** Int Acad Path; Am Asn Pathologists; Am Col Vet Pathologists; Am Vet Med Asn; New Eng Soc Pathologists; AAAS. **Research Statement & Publications:** Ultrastructure of viruses and viral induced lesions; pathology of the reproductive tract; animal models for human diseases. **Mailing Address:** New Eng Regional Primate Res Ctr, Tufts Univ Sch Med, 136 Harrison Ave, Boston, MA 02111.

KING, PATRICIA ANN, ETHICS OF MEDICINE, BIOETHICS. **Personal Data:** b Norfolk, Va, June 12, 1942. **Education:** Wheaton Col, BA, 1963; Harvard Univ, JD, 1969. **Professional Experience:** CARMACK WATERHOUSE PROF LAW, MED, ETHICS, PUB POLICY, LAW CTR, GEORGETOWN UNIV, as of 2004; adj prof, Dept Health Policy & Mgt, Johns Hopkins Univ, as of 2004; prof law, 1973; dep dir, Civil Rights Off, HEW, 1971-1973; mem, Nat Res Coun Comt, Assessment Family Violence Interventions; dep asst atty gen, Civil Div Dept Justice; bd mem, Hospice Found, Womens Legal Defense Fund, Wheaton Col; adj prof, Dept Health Policy & Mgt, Sch Hyg & Pub Health, Johns Hopkins Univ. **Memberships:** Inst Med-Nat Acad Sci; Am Soc Law & Med; Am Law Inst. **Mailing Address:** Georgetown Law Ctr, Georgetown Univ, 1507 Isherwood St NE One 489 McDonough Hall, Washington, DC 20002-5564. **E-Mail:** kingp@law.georgetown.edu

KING, PAUL HARVEY, BIOMEDICAL ENGINEERING, MECHANICAL ENGINEERING. **Personal Data:** b Ft Wayne, Ind, September 4, 1941; m 1982, Betty; c Paul E, Kelsey, Sarah M & Elizabeth. **Education:** Case Inst Technol, BS, 1963, MS, 1965; Vanderbilt Univ, PhD (mech eng), 1968. **Honors & Awards:** Skylab Awards. **Professional Experience:** Assoc prof anethesiol dept, vanderbilt univ, beginning 1987; researcher, Oak Ridge Assoc Univ, Med & Health Sci Div, Radiopharmaceut Develop Group, 1978-1979; chmn biomed eng, Ortho & Rehab, 1975-1977; asst prof, Ortho & Rehab, 1973-1981; ASSOC PROF BIOMED & MECH ENG, VANDERBILT UNIV, 1972-; prog dir biomed eng, Vanderbilt Univ, 1972-1975; actg chmn dept biomed eng, Vanderbilt Univ, 1971-1972; asst prof eng, Vanderbilt Univ, 1968-1972; Sr teaching fel mech eng, Vanderbilt Univ, 1965-1968; Res asst eng, Case Inst Technol, 1963-1965. **Memberships:** Biomed Eng Soc; Am Soc Eng Educ; Sigma Xi; Int Anesthesia Res Soc; Asn Advan Med Instrumentation; Inst Elec & Electronics Engrs. **Research Statement & Publications:** Orthopedics research; computer analysis of electro-cardiograms; radioisotope scanning systems; biomedical data analysis; modelling and research; positron emission tomography; computer assisted monitoring in anesthesiology; instrumentation in anesthesiology. **Mailing Address:** Dept Biomed Engg, Vanderbilt Univ, 5819 Stevenson Ctr, Nashville, TN 37240. **Fax:** 615-343-7919. **E-Mail:** paul.h.king@vanderbilt.edu

KING, PETER FOSTER, PHYSICAL CHEMISTRY. **Personal Data:** b New York, NY, October 7, 1929; m 1954, Ellen; c Katherine, Kenneth & Karl. **Education:** Ind Univ, BS, 1951, MA, 1952. **Honorary Degrees:** DSc, Mass Inst Technol, 1957. **Professional Experience:** RETIRED; res scientist, Parker & Amchem, 1988-1991; sr res chemist, res & develop, 1980-1987; group leader, 1967-1980; chemist, Parker Chem Co, 1965-1967; res & develop engr, Dow Chem Co, 1957-1965. **Memberships:** Electrochem Soc; Am Chem Soc; Nat Asn Corrosion Eng. **Research Statement & Publications:** Electrochemistry; chemistry and electrochemistry of surfaces; corrosion, metal cleaning and conversion coating; cold forming lubricants. **Mailing Address:** 26500 Orchard Lake Rd, Farmington Hills, MI 48334.

KING, PETER RAMSAY, COMPUTER SCIENCE. **Personal Data:** b Blackpool, UK, November 22, 1943; m 1970, c 1. **Education:** Univ Nottingham, BSc, 1965, PhD (comput sci), 1969. **Professional Experience:** PROF COMPUT SCI, UNIV MAN, 1980-; assoc prof, Univ Man, 1977-1980; asst prof, Univ Man, 1969-1977; Nat Res Coun Can grants, 1969-1972; lectr math & comput sci, Univ Nottingham, 1967-1969. **Memberships:** Asn Comput Mach; Brit Comput Soc; Brit Inst Math & Appln. **Research Statement & Publications:** Compiler construction for high level languages, especially Algol 1968; spline interpolation; interactive problem solving. **Mailing Address:** Dept Comput Sci, Univ Man, Winnipeg, MB R3T 2N2, Can. **Fax:** 204-474-7609. **E-Mail:** prking@cs.umanitoba.ca

KING, RAY J(OHN), ELECTRICAL ENGINEERING, MATERIALS EVALUATION. **Personal Data:** b Montrose, Colo, January 1, 1933; m 1964, Diane; c Karl V & Kristin J. **Education:** Ind Inst Technol, BS, 1956 & 1957; Univ Colo, Boulder, MS, 1960, PhD (elec eng), 1965. **Professional Experience:** Admin comt mem, Antennas & Propagation Soc, 1989-1992; VPRES, KDC TECHNOL CORP, 1983-; staff res engr, Lawrence Livermore Labs, 1982-1989; Erskine fel, Univ Canterbury, Christchurch, NZ, 1977; Fulbright guest prof, Tech Univ Denmark, 1973-1974; mem US nat comt, Int Sci Radio Union, Comns A, B & F, beginning 1967; from assoc prof to prof elec eng, Univ Wis-Madison, 1965-1982; res assoc, Univ Ill, Urbana, 1965; vis lectr, Univ Colo, Boulder, 1964-1965; res assoc, Univ Colo, Boulder, 1962-1965; asst prof elec eng & assoc chmn dept, Ind Inst Technol, 1961-1962; asst prof electronic eng, Ind Inst Technol, 1960-1961; prin investr, NSF, Air Force Off Sci Res grants; contracts, Mat Technol Inst, Naval Surface Warfare Ctr, Dept Com, Dept Agr, Naval Air Eng Ctr, Wright-Patterson AFB. **Memberships:** Fel Inst Elec & Electronics Engrs; Fel Inst Elec & Electronics Engrs Soc Microwave Theory & Tech; Fel Inst Elec & Electronics Engrs Antennas & Propagation; fel Inst Elec & Electronics Engrs Instrumentation & Measurement; Forest Prods Soc; Mat Res Soc. **Research Statement & Publications:** Electromagnetic wave propagation over nonuniform surfaces; microwave surface and leaky wave antennas; microwave instrumentation and measurement systems; microwave nondestructive testing; environmental effects on antenna performance; high power microwave effects; microwave evaluation of materials; electromagnetism. **Mailing Address:** KDC Technol Corp, 2011 Res Dr, Livermore, CA 94550. **Fax:** 925-449-4121. **E-Mail:** kdc@ant-s.com

KING, RAYMOND LEROY, food science; deceased, see previous edition for last biography

KING, REATHA CLARK, INORGANIC CHEMISTRY, PHYSICAL CHEMISTRY. **Personal Data:** b Pavo, Ga, April 11, 1938; m 1961, c 2. **Education:** Clark Col, BS, 1958; Univ Chicago, MS, 1960, PhD (chem), 1963; Columbia Univ, MBA, 1977. **Professional Experience:** PRES, METROP STATE UNIV, ST PAULS, as of 2002; Pres & exec dir, Gen Mills Found, 1988-2003; vpres, Gen Mills Inc, 1988-2002; pres, Metrop State Univ, St Paul, 1977-1988; prof chem & assoc dean acad affairs, York Col, NY, 1974-1977; assoc prof chem & assoc dean div natural sci & math, 1970-1974; asst prof chem, 1968-1970; chemist, Nat Bur Standards, 1963-1968. **Memberships:** AAAS; Am Chem Soc; Nat Orgn Prof Advan Black Chemists & Black Engrs; Sigma Xi. **Research Statement & Publications:** Experimental study on thermochemical properties of alloys using tin solution calorimetry; heats of formation of refractory compounds; fluorine flame calorimetry at room temperature. **Mailing Address:** Metrop State Univ, 110 Bank St Se Apt 2005, Minneapolis, MN 55414.

KING, RICHARD ALLEN, MEDICINE, GENETICS. **Personal Data:** b Fresno, Calif, March 20, 1939; m 1963, c 2. **Education:** Pa State Univ, AB, 1961; Jefferson Med Col, MD, 1965; Univ Minn, PhD (genetics), 1975. **Honors & Awards:** Seiji Award, Pigment Cell Soc, 1996. **Professional Experience:** Assoc dir clin res, Dept Med & Pediat & Inst Human Genetics, beginning 1996; DIR, DIV GENETICS & METAB, DEPT MED & PEDIAT & INST HUMAN GENETICS, 1990-; dir, Genetics Div, 1985-1990; PROF MED & PEDIAT, UNIV MINN, MINNEAPOLIS, 1984-; from instr to assoc prof, Div Genetics & Metab, Dept Med & Pediat & Inst Human Genetics, 1971-1984; USPHS surgeon, Atomic Bomb Casualty Comn, Hiroshima, Japan, 1969-1971; resident, Univ Minn, 1966-1969; Intern med, Univ Minn, 1965-1966. **Memberships:** Am Soc Human Genetics; AAAS; Am Fedn Clin Res; fel Am Col Physicians; Pan Am Soc Pigment Cell (pres-elect); fel Am Col Med Genetics. **Research Statement & Publications:** Gene mapping in common complex disease, cancer, SLE, asthma, diabetes; genetic regulation of melanin metabolism. **Mailing Address:** Dept Med, Univ Minn, 516 Delaware St SE, Minneapolis, MN 55455. **Fax:** 612-624-6645. **E-Mail:** kingx002@maroon.tc.umn.edu

KING, RICHARD AUSTIN, PSYCHOPHYSIOLOGY, NEUROBIOLOGY. **Personal Data:** b Philadelphia, Pa, March 26, 1929; m 1956, Margy; c Richard, Gordon & Sarah. **Education:** Univ Cincinnati, AB, 1954, MA, 1955; Duke Univ, PhD (psychol), 1959. **Professional Experience:** PROF EMER, DEPT PSYCHOL, UNIV NC, CHAPEL HILL, as of 2004; assoc dir neurobiology, Univ NC, Chapel Hill, 1973-1990; prof psychol, Univ Nc, Chapel Hill, beginning 1971; vis prof psychol, Brown Univ, 1971; assoc prof, Univ NC, Chapel Hill, 1965-1971; fel physiol, Univ Wash, 1963-1965; from instr to asst prof psychol, Univ NC, Chapel Hill, 1958-1963. **Memberships:** Soc Neuroscience; Psychonomic Soc. **Research Statement & Publications:** Biology of memory. **Mailing Address:** Dept Psychol, Univ NC, Chapel Hill, NC 27599. **Fax:** 919-962-2537. **E-Mail:** kink@email.unc.edu

KING, RICHARD JOE, ANIMAL PHYSIOLOGY. **Personal Data:** b Kansas City, Mo, August 30, 1937; m 1963, Leslie; c Deborah A & David L. **Education:** Univ Mo, Columbia, BA, 1959; Univ Calif, Berkeley, PhD (biophys), 1970. **Professional Experience:** RETIRED; assoc ed, Am Rev Respiratory Dis, 1988-1989; prof physiol, Univ Tex Health Sci Ctr, San Antonio, 1980-2001; consult, Review Comt, NIH, 1975-1976, 1978-1979 & 1980-1981; from asst prof to assoc prof, Univ Tex Health Sci Ctr, San Antonio, 1974-1980; Asst res biophysicist, Univ Calif, San Francisco, 1971-1974. **Memberships:** Am Physiol Soc. **Research Statement & Publications:** Composition and properties of pulmonary surfactant; metabolism and isolation of its associated apoproteins; interaction of lipids and proteins in pulmonary surfactant; correlation of structure function relationships; effects of nitrogens on lung cells; alterations in surfactant in chronic lung injury. **Mailing Address:** 9203 Wagons W, San Antonio, TX 78255.

KING, RICHARD WARREN, ANALYTICAL CHEMISTRY, PHYSICAL CHEMISTRY. **Personal Data:** b Philadelphia, Pa, March 25, 1925; m 1947, June Weigand; c Linda B, Judith A, Andria J & Melissa B. **Education:** Kenyon Col, AB (chem), 1947; Univ Del, MS (organ chem), 1959. **Honors & Awards:** Award Merit, Am Soc Testing & Mat, 1981; Certi Apprec, Am Petrol Instit, 1980. **Professional Experience:** RETIRED; mgr res serv, Res & Develop Dept, 1969-1983; sect chief, Anal Sect, 1960-1969; res chemist, Res & Develop Dept, Sun Oil Co, 1947-1959. **Memberships:** Emer mem Am Chem Soc; fel Am Soc Testing & Mat. **Research Statement & Publications:** Catalytic reactions of hydrocarbons; application of physical separation techniques to the study of high-boiling fractions from petroleum; gas chromatography of petroleum fractions; toxicology of petroleum hydrocarbons. **Mailing Address:** 3031 Hermosa Lane, Havertown, PA 19083-1124.

KING, ROBBINS SYDNEY, EMBRYOLOGY. **Personal Data:** b San Diego, Calif, April 23, 1922; m 1947, c 4. **Education:** Stanford Univ, AB, 1947, PhD (biol), 1954. **Professional Experience:** PROF EMER, DEPT BIOL SCI, CALIF STATE UNIV, CHICO, as of 2005; prof biol sci, Calif State Univ, Chico, 1965-1989; chmn dept, Calif State Univ, Chico, 1965-1969; asst prof biol, Calif State Univ, Chico, 1956-1965; asst prof, Wabash Col, 1955-1956; asst prof biol, Univ, 1955; instr, Menlo Col, 1954-1955; res assoc, Hopkins Marine Sta, Stanford Univ, 1952-1954. **Memberships:** AAAS; Am Soc Mammal; Nat Sci Teachers Asn. **Research Statement & Publications:** Experimental embryology; regeneration. **Mailing Address:** Dept Biol Sci, Col Natural Sci, Calif State Univ, Holt Hall 279, Chico, CA 95926.

KING, ROBERT (BAINTON), NEUROSURGERY. **Personal Data:** b Pittsburgh, Pa, August 26, 1922; m 1951, Molly; c 3. **Education:** Rochester Univ, MD, 1946; Am Bd Neurol Surg, dipl, 1954. **Honors & Awards:** Lifetime Achievement Award, MD Anderson-univ TX, AOA, 2001; Chancellors Distinguished serv prof, SUNY, 1995; Robert B & Molly G endowed prof, SUNY, 1995; Distinguished serv Award, ABMS, 1990; Distinguished serv Award, Soc of neurol surgeons, 1988; Cushing Medal, Am Asn Neurol Surgeons, 1990. **Professional Experience:** Attend surg, Crouse-Irving mem Hosp, 1957 & State Univ Hosp, Syracuse, 1957-; PROF NEUROSURG, COL MED, STATE UNIV NY HEALTH SCI CTR, 1957-; chmn div & dept, Col Med, State Univ NY Health Sci Ctr, 1957-1988; consult, Vet Admin Hosp, 1957; from instr to asst prof neurosurg, Med Sch, Wash Univ, 1951-1957; Markle scholar, 1951-1956; asst chief, WalterReed Army Hosp, 1949-1951; asst neuroanat, Med Sch, Wash Univ, 1948; distinguished serv prof neurosurg, State Univ NY; MED DIR, STATE UNIV HOSP. **Memberships:** Neurosurg Soc Am; Am Asn Neurol Surg; Am Col Surgeons; Am Acad Neurol Surg; Soc Neurol Surg; Sigma Xi; Am Neurol Asn. **Research Statement & Publications:** Neurosurgery; neurophysiology/neur anatomy pain studies. **Mailing Address:** Dept Neurosurg, Univ Hosp 750 E Adams St, Syracuse, NY 13210-2306. **Fax:** 315-464-5520. **E-Mail:** kingr@upstate.edu

KING, ROBERT BRUCE, INORGANIC CHEMISTRY. **Personal Data:** b Rochester, NH, February 27, 1938; m 1960, Jane; c Robert B II & David S. **Education:** Oberlin Col, BA, 1957; Harvard Univ, PhD (inorg chem), 1961. **Honors & Awards:** Am Chem Soc Awards, 1971, 1991. **Professional Experience:** Consult, Westinghouse Savannah River Co, 1996-; fel, Japan Soc Promotion Sci, 1981; actg head chem, Univ Ga, 1980-1982; consult, Los Alamos Nat Lab, 1979-1983; REGENTS' PROF CHEM, UNIV GA, 1973-; res prof, Univ Ga, 1968-1973; Sloan Found fel, 1967-1969; res assoc prof chem, Univ Ga, 1966-1968; ed, J Organometallic Chem, 1964-1998; tech adv, Pressure Chem Co, Pa, 1964-1975; sr res fel, Mellon Inst, 1964-1966; Ed, Organometallic Syntheses, 1963-1994; res fel, Mellon Inst, 1962-1964; res chemist, Explosives Dept, E I du Pont de Nemours, Del, 1961-1962. **Memberships:** Am Chem Soc; Chem Soc London; Sigma Xi. **Research Statement & Publications:** Synthetic and spectroscopic studies on organometallic compounds of transition metals; molecular catalysis; organophosph or ous chemistry; chemical applications of topology and group theory; environmental inorganic chemistry. **Mailing Address:** Dept Chem, Univ Ga, Athens, GA 30602. **Fax:** 706-542-9454.

KING, ROBERT CHARLES, GENETICS. **Personal Data:** b New York, NY, June 3, 1928; m 1979, c 5. **Education:** Yale Univ, BS, 1948, PhD (zoology), 1952. **Professional Experience:** EMER PROF BIOL SCI, NWESTERN UNIV, 2001-; NSF sr fel, Han Yang Univ, 1979; NSF sr fel, Sericulture Exp Sta, Tokyo, 1970; prof biol sci, Nwestern Univ, 1964-2000; vis investr & fel, Rockefeller Inst, 1959; NSF sr fel, Univ Edinburgh, 1958; from asst prof to assoc prof, Nwestern Univ, 1956-1963; scientist, Brookhaven Nat Lab, 1951-1956. **Memberships:** Fel AAAS; Genetics Soc Am; Am Soc Zool; Entom Soc Am; Am Soc Cell Biol (treas 1972 1973 & 1974). **Research Statement & Publications:** Developmental genetics; genetic control of oogenesis in Drosophila; authored a dictionary of genetics. **Mailing Address:** 2890 Fredric Ct, Northbrook, IL 60062-7504. **E-Mail:** r.king@northwestern.edu

KING, ROBERT EDWARD, BIOLOGICAL CHEMISTRY, PHARMACEUTICAL CHEMISTRY. **Personal Data:** b Zanesville, Ohio, December 27, 1923; m 1950, Jane; c Susan, Timothy, Peter, Christina & Jonathan. **Education:** Ohio State Univ, BSc, 1944; Univ Minn, PhD (pharmaceut chem), 1948. **Professional Experience:** RETIRED; Ed, J Parenteral Drug Asn, 1964-1978; emer prof indust pharm, Philadelphia Col Pharm, 1961-1986; res assoc, Merck Sharp & Dohme Res Labs, 1948-1961. **Memberships:** Am Pharmaceut Asn; Parenteral Drug Asn. **Research Statement & Publications:** Pharmaceutical dosage forms. **Mailing Address:** 3475 Aqtng Rd, Carversville, PA 18913.

KING, ROBERT WILLIAM, MATHEMATICS. **Personal Data:** b Wesson, Miss, November 18, 1929; m 1959, c 2. **Education:** Univ Southern Miss, BS, 1951, MA, 1956; Fla State Univ, MS, 1965, PhD (math, educ), 1967. **Professional Experience:** ASSOC PROF MATH, UNIV SOUTHERN MISS, 1969-; asst prof, Univ Southern Miss, 1967-1969; asst prof, Miss Col, 1959-1964; Instr math, Copiah-Lincoln Jr Col, 1956-1957. **Memberships:** Math Asn Am; Nat Coun Teachers Math. **Research Statement & Publications:** Use of various modifications of programmed instruction to investigate the effects of selected social and psychological factors in the teaching and learning of mathematics. **Mailing Address:** 2857 Olive Dr, Cheyenne, WY 82001.

KING, ROBERT WILLIS, MOLECULAR BIOLOGY, MICROBIOLOGY. **Personal Data:** b Grand Haven, Mich, June 9, 1961; m 1992, Emily S Shen. **Education:** Mich State Univ, BS, 1983; Purdue Univ, PhD (microbiol), 1989. **Professional Experience:** RES DIR, AVID THERAPEUT INC, PHILADELPHIA, PA, 1994-; fel, DuPont Merck Pharmaceut Co, 1993-1994; res assoc, Univ Chicago, 1990-1992; instr med microbiol, Ind Univ, Sch Med, 1989; Instr microbiol, Purdue Univ, 1987-1988. **Memberships:** Am Soc Microbiol; AAAS. **Research Statement & Publications:** Designing infectivity and assay systems for the screening of potential therapeutic agents for antiviral activity. **Mailing Address:** Avid Therapeutics Inc, 3401 Market St Suite 300, Philadelphia, PA 19104.

KING, ROBERT WILSON, GEODESY. **Personal Data:** b Fayetteville, NC, February 8, 1947; m 1970, Mary; c Elizabeth R & Leslie W. **Education:** Davidson Col, BS, 1970; NC State Univ, BS, 1970; Mass Inst Technol, PhD (instrumentation), 1975. **Professional Experience:** PRIN RES SCIENTIST, DEPT EARTH, ATMOS & PLANETARY SCI, MASS INST TECHNOL, 1985-; res assoc, Dept Earth, Atmos & Planetary Sci, Mass Inst Technol, 1977-1985; res geodesist, Terrestrial Sci Div, Air Force Geophys Lab, 1974-1977. **Memberships:** Am Geophys Union. **Research Statement & Publications:** Use of precise extraterrestrial measurement techniques to monitor earth rotation, polar motion and crustal deformation. **Mailing Address:** Dept Earth, Atmospheric & Planetary Sci, Mass Inst Technol, Rm 54-620 77 Mass Ave, Cambridge, MA 02139. **Fax:** 617-253-1699. **E-Mail:** rwk@chandler.mit.edu

KING, ROGER HATTON, PEDOLOGY, SOIL GEOGRAPHY. **Personal Data:** b Barry, Wales, December 16, 1941; m 1965, c 2. **Education:** Univ Wales, BSc (geog), 1963; Univ Aberdeen, MSc (soil science), 1965; Univ Sask, PhD (geog), 1969. **Professional Experience:** CHAIR, DEPT GEOG, UNIV WESTERN ONT, 1996-2005; PROF GEOG, UNIV WESTERN ONT, 1988-; vis prof, Dept Geog, Univ Canterbury, NZ, 1985; Vis prof, Inst Archaeol, Oxford Univ, Eng, 1977-1978; from asst prof to assoc prof, Univ Western Ont, 1970-1988; Tutor geog, Univ Wales, 1969-1970. **Research Statement & Publications:** Persistence of chemical residues in archaeological soils and sediments; impact of environmental stress on soil development in arctic and alpine areas; palaeoenvironmental reconstruction in the Canadian Cordillera and the Canadian High Arctic; paleolimnology; archaeological pottery provenance; tephras; clay mineralogy and composition. **Mailing Address:** Dept Geog, Univ Western Ont, London, ON N6A 5C2, Can. **Fax:** 519-661-3750. **E-Mail:** king@uwo.ca

KING, RONALD PETER, MINERAL PROCESSING. **Personal Data:** b Springs, SAfrica, March 12, 1938; m 1961, Ellen; c Jeremy P, Andrew J & Janet M (Tyrrell-Ead). **Education:** Univ Witwatersrand, BSc, 1958, MSc, 1962; Univ Manchester, PhD (chem eng), 1963. **Honors & Awards:** Gold Medal, SAfrica Inst Mining & Metall, 1991. **Professional Experience:** PROF METALL ENG, UNIV UTAH, 1990-; vis prof, Univ Utah, 1987-1988; vis fel, Camborne Sch Mines, 1980; prof extractive metall eng, Univ Witwatersrand, 1974-1990; lectr, Univ Manchester, Eng, 1973-1974; chief scientist, Nat Inst Metall, SAfrica, 1968-1974; sr lectr, Univ Natal, SAfrica, 1966-1967; lectr chem eng, Univ Witwatersrand, 1963-1965. **Memberships:** SAfrican Inst Mining & Metall (pres); Soc Mining, Metall & Explor; Soc Indust & Appl Math. **Research Statement & Publications:** Modeling and simulation of complex processing systems. **Mailing Address:** 306 Browning Bldg, Salt Lake City, UT 84112. **Fax:** 801-581-8119. **E-Mail:** rpking@mines.utah.edu

KING, RONOLD (WYETH PERCIVAL), PHYSICS & BIOPHYSICS, ELECTRICAL ENGINEERING. **Personal Data:** b Williamstown, Mass, September 19, 1905; m 1991, Mary; c Christopher M. **Education:** Univ Rochester, AB, 1927, SM, 1929; Univ Wis, PhD (electrodyn), 1932. **Honorary Degrees:** AM, Harvard Univ, 1942. **Honors & Awards:** Centennial Medal, Inst Elec & Electronics Engrs, 1984; Distinguished Service Clation, Univ Wis, 1973 Distinguished Serv Award, Inst Elec & Electronics Engrs, Antennas & Propagation Soc, 1991 Pandar Award Univ Pa, 1986; Inst electronics Engs, Chan-To Tai Distinguished edu award, 2001. **Professional Experience:** Consult, Mitre Corp, 1990; IBM distinguished scholar, Northeastern Univ, 1985; consult, Raytheon Co, 1974-1975, 1987-1993; PROF EMER APPL PHYSICS, HARVARD UNIV, 1972-; Guggenheim Mem Found fel, 1958; from asst prof to prof, Harvard Univ, 1939-1972; fac instr physics & commun eng, Harvard Univ, 1938-1939; Guggenheim Mem Found fel, Berlin & Munich, 1937-1938; asst prof, Lafayette Col, 1935-1937; instr physics, Lafayette Col, 1934-1935; asst elec eng, Alumni Res Found fel, 1934; asst elec eng, Univ Wis, 1932-1934; asst physics, Univ Rochester, 1928-1929; mem comn B, Int Sci Radio Union. **Memberships:** AAAS; fel Inst Elec & Electronics Engrs; fel Am Phys Soc; fel Am Acad Arts & Sci; corresp mem Bavarian Acad Sci. **Research Statement & Publications:** Electromagnetic theory, radiation and antennas; transmission-line theory; microwave circuits; insulated antennas, crossed antennas, antennas in dessipative media near surface; subsurface communication; electromagnetic pulses; electromagnetic surface waves; resonant antenna arrays; bioelectromagnetics; microwave beacome. **Mailing Address:** Harvard Eng & Appl Sci, Gordon McKay Lab, 60 Oxford St 403, Cambridge, MA 02138. **Fax:** 617-496-4654.

KING, ROY WARBRICK, NUCLEAR MAGNETIC RESONANCE. **Personal Data:** b Liverpool, Eng, July 4, 1933; American citizen; m 1970. **Education:** Cambridge Univ, BA, 1954, MA & PhD (org chem), 1958. **Professional Experience:** RETIRED; asst res scientist, Univ Fla, beginning 1984; res assoc chem, Univ Fla, 1969-1984; asst prof chem, Iowa State Univ, 1966-1969; supvr instrument serv, Iowa State Univ, 1960-1966; univ fel, Iowa State Univ, 1958-1960; Norman fel org chem, Hickrill Chem Res Found, NY, 1958. **Memberships:** Am Chem Soc; Sigma Xi; Royal Soc Chem. **Research Statement & Publications:** Organic structure determination; organic analysis; applications of physical methods to organic chemistry. **Mailing Address:** Dept Chem, Univ Fla, PO Box 117200, Gainesville, FL 32611-7200. **E-Mail:** rwking@chem.ufl.edu

KING, S(ANFORD) MACCALLUM, SOIL FERTILITY, CROP MANAGEMENT. **Personal Data:** b St Catharines, Ont, May 21, 1926; American citizen; div, c Marilyn, Nancy, Gordon & Laura. **Education:** Ont Agr Col, BSA, 1948; Purdue Univ, MS, 1950; Univ Wis, PhD (soil fertil), 1956, Keller Grad Inst Mgt, MBA, 1981. **Professional Experience:** Instr mkt, Columbia Col, 1997-; consult, IMC Global, 1995-; sr adv, Pro-Crop, Inc, 1992-; instr mkt, Northern Ill Univ, 1990-; PRES, KING INT, 1990-; vpres, Seed-Prep Corp & sr vpres, Competitive Edge Inc, 1988-1990; Consult, 1980-1983; vpres, Taralan Corp, 1973-1987; dir agr, Develop & Resources Corp, 1971-1973; mkt & tech serv specialist fertilizer, Int Minerals & Chem Corp, 1962-1970; res asst, prof & sta supt, Mich State Univ, 1956-1961; proj asst soil fertil, Univ Wis, 1953-1956; Soil scientist, Stand Fruit & Steamship Co, 1951-1953; Agr proj develop & mkt tasks 18 countries, Potash Corp, Sask. **Memberships:** Am Soc Agron; Soil Sci Soc Am. **Research Statement & Publications:** Crop nutrition; crop management and production. **Mailing Address:** 36 Pine Ave, Lake Zurich, IL 60047-2326.

KING, SHELDON SELIG, MEDICAL ADMINISTRATION. **Personal Data:** b New York, NY, August 28, 1931. **Education:** NY Univ, AB, 1952; Yale Univ, MS, 1957. **Professional Experience:** PRES, SALICK HEALTH CARE, as of 2004; Coun 2000 Comn, Accreditation Coun Grad Med Educ, 1987-1990; Coun 2000 Comn, Am Podiatric Asn, 1985-1986; Exec vpres, Salick Health Care, beginning 1994; bd dirs, Nat Comt Qual Health Care & Vol Hosps Am, 1990-; Bd Health Sci Policy, inst Med & Health Leadership Coun, 1989-; pres, Cedars-Sinai Med Ctr, Los Angeles, 1989-1994; pres, exec vpres & dir, Stanford Univ Hosp, 1986-1989; chmn, Bd Adv, Am Bd Internal Med, 1985-1991; mem, Gov Coun, Sect Metrop Hosps, Am Hosp Asn, 1984-1989; assoc vpres med affairs, exec vpres & dir, Stanford Univ Hosp, 1981-1985; Pres, Hosp Coun San Diego & Imp Co, 1977; dir hosp & clin, Univ Hosp & assoc clin prof, Univ Calif, San Diego, 1972-1981; exec dir, Albert Einstein Col Med, Bronx Munic Hosp Ctr, 1968-1972; dir planning, Mt Sinai Hosp, 1966-1968; asst dir, Mt Sinai Hosp, 1960-1966. **Memberships:** Inst Med-Nat Acad Sci; fel Am Col Health Care Execs; fel Am Pub Health Asn; fel Royal Soc Health; Am Hosp Asn. **Mailing Address:** Salick Health Care, 111 8th Ave, Ste 1510, New York, NY 10011.

KING, STANLEY SHIH-TUNG, PHYSICAL CHEMISTRY, MOLECULAR SPECTROSCOPY. **Personal Data:** b Liau-Ning, China, November 12, 1934; m 1966, c 3. **Education:** Taiwan Normal Univ, BS, 1957; Drexel Univ, MS, 1962; Univ Minn, Minneapolis, PhD (phys chem), 1966. **Professional Experience:** ASSOC SCIENTIST, DOW CHEM USA, 1980-. **Memberships:** Am Chem Soc; Am Catalypis Soc. **Research Statement & Publications:** Vibrational spectroscopy; low temperature matrix isolation study; microsample analysis by vibrational spectroscopy; polymer analysis; chromatographic analysis; electromicroscopy; catalysis; analytical chemistry. **Mailing Address:** 1311 Kirkland Dr, Midland, MI 48640.

KING, STEPHEN MURRAY, MONOCLONAL ANTIBODIES, PROTEIN SUBSTANCES. **Education:** Univ London, Eng, PhD (cell biol), 1982. **Professional Experience:** ASSOC DIR, MOLECULAR BIOL & BIOCHEM PROG, UNIV CONN HEALTH CTR GRAD SCH, as of 2004; res assoc, Worcester Found Exp Biol, beginning 1983. **Mailing Address:** Dept Molecular Biol & Biochem, Univ Conn Health Ctr, 263, Farmington Ave, Farmington, CT 06032-3305. **Fax:** 860-679-1239. **E-Mail:** sking@nso2.uchc.edu

KING, TALMADGE EVERETT, INTERNAL MEDICINE, PULMONARY MEDICINE. **Personal Data:** b Sumter, SC, February 24, 1948; m 1968, Mozelle; c Consuelo & Malaika M. **Education:** Gustavus Adolphus Col, BA, 1970; Harvard Univ, MD, 1974. **Professional**

Experience: Vchmn, Health Sci Ctr, 1993; EXEC VPRES CLIN AFFAIRS, NAT JEWISH CTR IMMUNOL & RESPIRATORY MED, 1992-; Prof med, Univ Colo Sch Med, 1991; sr staff mem, Nat Jewish Ctr Immunol & Respiratory Med, 1990; Prin investr, Specialized Ctr Res, 1981-. **Memberships:** Am Thoracic Soc; Am Lung Asn; fel Am Col Chest Physicians; fel Am Col Physicians; Am Fedn Clin Res; Nat Med Asn. **Research Statement & Publications:** Pathogenesis, diagnosis and management of inflammatory and immunologic lung injury. **Mailing Address:** Nat Jewish Ctr Immunol & Respiratory Med, 1400 Jackson St, Denver, CO 80206. **Fax:** 303-398-1040. **E-Mail:** kingt@njc.org

KING, TE PIAO, IMMUNOLOGY. **Personal Data:** b Shanghai, China, August 21, 1930; c 2. **Education:** Univ Calif, AB, 1950, MS, 1951; Univ Mich, PhD, 1953. **Professional Experience:** ASSOC PROF EMER BIOCHEM, ROCKEFELLER UNIV, 1963-; asst prof, 1957-1963; res assoc biochem, 1953-1957. **Memberships:** Am Soc Biol Chemists; Am Acad Allergy. **Research Statement & Publications:** Peptides; proteins. **Mailing Address:** Dept Biochem, Rockefeller Univ, 1230 York Ave, New York, NY 10021. **Fax:** 212-327-7974. **E-Mail:** king@rockefeller.edu

KING, TERRY LEE, ANALYSIS OF DATA, LINEAR MODELS. **Personal Data:** b Akron, Iowa, February 24, 1945; m 1971, Carol; c Kevin, Shawn & Heather. **Education:** Westmar Col, BA, 1967; Univ Iowa, MS, 1969; Pa State Univ, PhD (statist), 1980. **Professional Experience:** Vis prof, Dept Statist, Pa State Univ, 1992; chair, Mo Sect, Math Asn Am, 1991-1992; vice chair, Mo Sect, Math Asn Am, 1990-1991; PROF MATH & STATIST, NW MO STATE UNIV, 1989-; chmn dept, Nw MO State Univ, 1988-1993; assoc prof, Nw MO State Univ, 1981-1988; instr, Dept Math, Frostburg State Col, 1979-1981; statistician, Desmatics, Inc, 1975-1979; instr math, Thiel Col, 1969-1971. **Memberships:** Am Statist Asn; Biometric Soc; Math Asn Am; Nat Coun Teachers Math. **Research Statement & Publications:** Sample size determination; linear models; data analysis. **Mailing Address:** Dept Math & Statist, NW Mo State Univ, Maryville, MO 64468. **Fax:** 660-562-1188. **E-Mail:** tlking@acad.nwmissouri.edu

KING, THEODORE OSCAR, TOXICOLOGY, PHARMACOLOGY. **Personal Data:** b Portsmouth, Ohio, May 29, 1922; m 1952, c Jeremy & Naomi. **Education:** Univ Mich, BS, 1943; Georgetown Univ, PhD (pharmacol), 1949; Univ Wyo, JD, 1960; Am Bd Toxicol, dipl, 1981. **Professional Experience:** Intra-Acad (NAS-HAS) Exchange Scientist, Hungary, 1985, 1988; ASSOC RES PROF, COL PHARMACOL, UNIV CONN, 1980-; sr dir safety eval, Pfizer, Inc, 1976-1992; dir, Pfizer, Inc, 1971-1976; vpres & dir res, Bio/Dynamics, Inc, 1965-1971; dir div pharmacol, Ortho Res Found, NJ, 1959-1965; lectr, Rutgers Univ, 1958-1965; sr pharmacologist, Johnson & Johnson Res Found, NJ, 1957-1959; Fulbright res fel, State Univ Ghent, 1955-1956; WHO pub health fel, UK, 1951; from assoc prof to prof pharmacol, Col Pharm, Univ Wyo, 1949-1958; anal chemist, Res Div, Colgate-Palmolive-Peet Co, NJ, 1946; Pharmaceut control chemist, Wm R Warner & Co, NY, 1943-1945. **Memberships:** Soc Toxicol; Am Soc Pharmacol & Exp Ther; Am Chem Soc, emer mem; NY Acad Sci; fel AAAS. **Research Statement & Publications:** Drug safety evaluation; physiology of reproduction; endocrine pharmacology. **Mailing Address:** 185 Old Norwich Rd, Quaker Hill, CT 06375-1223. **E-Mail:** tokstox@aol.com

KING, THOMAS CREIGHTON, THORACIC SURGERY, CRITICAL CARE. **Personal Data:** b Salt Lake City, Utah, April 10, 1928; m Joan; c 4. **Education:** Univ Utah, BS, 1950, MD, 1954; Univ Mo, Kansas City, MA, 1963. **Professional Experience:** JOSE M FERRER PROF SURG, COLUMBIA COLLEGE OF P&S 1973-; attend surg, New York Presby Med Ctr, 1973-1997; prof surg, New York Presby Med Ctr, beginning 1973; provost, Univ Utah, 1969-1973; chief thoracic surg, Salt Lake City Vet Admin Hosp, 1968-1973; acad vpres, Univ Utah, 1968-1969; staff surgeon, Med Ctr, Univ Utah, 1966-1973; from assoc prof to prof surg, Med Sch, Univ Utah, 1966-1973; assoc dean med sch, Med Sch, Univ Utah, 1966-1968; assoc prof surg & psychol & chief training, Ctr Study Med Educ, Univ Ill Med Ctr, 1964-1966; assoc chief staff & dir res, Kansas City Vet Admin Hosp, 1962-1964; staff surgeon, Kansas City Vet Admin Hosp, 1960-1964; asst prof med sch, Univ Kans, 1960-1964; assoc, Univ Kans, 1960; from asst resident to chief resident, Univ Utah Hosps, 1955-1959; fel surg, Univ Utah Hosps, 1959 & 1960; Intern, Columbia-Presby Med Ctr, 1954-1955. **Memberships:** AAAS; Am Fedn Clin Res; Asn Am Med Cols; Soc Univ Surg; Am Asn Thoracic Surg; Am Col Surgeons; Am Surg Asn; Soc Int Surgeons. **Research Statement & Publications:** Medical education and teacher training; surgical nutrition and metabolism; skin degerming and infection control; surgical intensive care. **Mailing Address:** Dept Surg, Columbia-Presby Med Ctr, Ste 6-S, 35 Claremont Ave, New York, NY 10027. **E-Mail:** tck1@columbia.edu

KING, THOMAS K C, PULMONARY PHYSIOLOGY, PULMONARY DISEASES. **Personal Data:** b Shanghai, China, June 1, 1934; American citizen; m 1959, Amy; c Susan & Caroline. **Education:** Univ Edinburgh, MB, ChB, 1959, MD, 1963; FRCP, 1980. **Honors & Awards:** Pulmonary Acad Award, Nat Heart & Lung Inst, 1972. **Professional Experience:** Nat Defense Med Ctr, Taiwan, 1987; vis prof, Univ Hong Kong, 1981; ASSOC PROF BIOPHYS, COL MED, CORNELL UNIV, 1975-; ASSOC PROF MED, COL MED, CORNELL UNIV, 1973-; asst prof, Col Med, Cornell Univ, 1970-1973; lectr med, Sch Med, Univ Hong Kong, 1967-1970; Eli Lilly Int fel, Polachek Found Cardiopulmonary Lab fel, 1966-1967; Eli Lilly Int fel, Bellevue Hosp, Columbia Univ, 1965-1966. **Memberships:** Med Res Soc UK; Am Fedn Clin Res; Am Physiol Soc; Am Thoracic Soc; Am Col Chest Physicians. **Research Statement & Publications:** The mechanism and quantitation of impaired blood gas exchange in the lungs in disease. **Mailing Address:** Col Med Cornell Univ, 1300 York Ave, New York, NY 10021. **Fax:** 212-746-8808.

KING, THOMAS MORGAN, PHYSICAL INORGANIC CHEMISTRY, POLYMER CHEMISTRY. **Personal Data:** b Morristown, Tenn, August 28, 1940; m 1962, Judith; c Carole & Ashley. **Education:** Carson-Newman Col, BS, 1962; Univ Tenn, PhD (chem), 1966. **Professional Experience:** TECH & MGT CONSULT, MONSANTO, 1996-; dir, Tech Plastics Div, 1992-1996; dir, Tech D&P Div, 1986-1992; dir bus develop, Monsanto, 1983-1985; dir results mgt & personnel planning, Monsanto, 1980-1982; com dir sorbates, Monsanto, 1977-1980; dir planning & control, Monsanto, 1977; com develop mgr, Monsanto, 1972-1976; res group leader, Monsanto, 1969-1972; res specialist, Monsanto, 1969; sr res chemist, Monsanto, 1968-1969; Res chemist, Monsanto, 1966-1968. **Memberships:** Am Chem Soc. **Research Statement & Publications:** Coordination chemistry of Cobalt-II and Nickel-II compounds; basic and applied research on phosphonate compounds; precipitation inhibition and corrosion inhibition. **Mailing Address:** 17 Muirfield Lane, St Louis, MO 63141.

KING, THOMAS SCOTT, REPRODUCTIVE NEUROENDOCRINOLOGY, FEMALE REPRODUCTIVE HEALTH. **Personal Data:** b Ft Campbell, Ky, May 13, 1953; m 1985, Rita; c Matthew G & David R. **Education:** Davidson Col, NC, BS, 1975; Med Univ SC, Charleston, PhD (anat-path), 1980. **Honors & Awards:** Presidential Award Excellence Teaching, 1997; Golden Apple Award, Med Class, 1998; Barbara Sanford-Gender Equity Award, Teaching Excellence, Am Med Womens Assoc & Upjohn Pharmaceut, 2002. **Professional Experience:** Univ Tex Health Sci Ctr, San Antonio Reproductive Health Ctr, 1993-; consult, West Brabant Polytech Inst, Ctr Med Biotechnol, Eiten-Leur, Neth, 1992-; prin investr, Nat Inst Drug Abuse, 1990-; ASSOC PROF, DEPT OBSTET-GYNEC & DEPT CELLULAR & STRUCT BIOL, 1990-; DIR NEUROENDOCRINE CORE, DEPT OBSTET-GYNEC, UNIV TEX HEALTH SCI CTR, SAN ANTONIO, 1985-; asst prof, Dept Cellular & Struct Biol, 1982-1990; fel, Dept Obstet-Gynec, 1980-1982. **Memberships:** Endocrine Soc; Soc Gynec Invest; Soc Neuroscience; Soc Neuroendocrinol; Soc Neurochem. **Research Statement & Publications:** Regulation of cyclic reproductive function in females and the adverse effects of drug abuse (cocaine, ethanol); human placental transport-metabolism of selected drugs of abuse and selected therapeutic drugs. **Mailing Address:** Dept Cell Struct Biol, Univ Tex Health Sci Ctr, 7703 Floyd Curl Dr, San Antonio, TX 78284-3900. **Fax:** 210-567-3803. **E-Mail:** kingt@uthscsa.edu

KING, WILLIAM CONNOR, RADAR SYSTEMS, COMMUNICATION SYSTEMS. **Personal Data:** b Newark, Ohio, March 10, 1927; m 1950, c 2. **Education:** Denison Univ, BA, 1949; Duke Univ, PhD (physics), 1953. **Professional Experience:** RETIRED; sr staff, Software Systs Lab, 1981-1989; mgr, Wayland Software Eng Dept, Raytheon Corp, 1978-1980; leader tradex programming, Missile & Surface Radar Div, 1974-1977; mgr, Hard Point Demonstration Array Radar Prog, RCA Corp, 1971-1974; data systs, Pa, 1967-1970; Commun Eng Spacecraft Dept, Pa, 1964-1967; mgr, Space Systs Anal Proj, 1962-1964; commun physicist, Space Sci Lab, Missile & Space Div, Gen Elec Co, 1956-1962; res assoc, Radiation Lab, Johns Hopkins Univ, 1953-1956; res assoc, Duke Univ, 1953; Asst physics, Duke Univ, 1949-1953. **Memberships:** Am Phys Soc; Asn Comput Mach; sr mem Inst Elec & Electronics Engrs; Am Inst Aeronaut & Astronaut. **Research Statement & Publications:** Microwave spectroscopy and wave propagation in ionized media; design and development of real-time computer programs for radar, missile and communication systems; communications applications of computers. **Mailing Address:** 2556 S Leilani Dr, Homosassa, FL 34448.

KING, WILLIAM DAVID, CLINICAL TOXICOLOGY, INJURY EPIDEMIOLOGY. **Personal Data:** b Owensboro, Ky, April 9, 1953; m 1978. **Education:** Samford Univ, BS, 1978; Univ Ala, Birmingham, MPH, 1987. **Honors & Awards:** Child Advocacy Award, Am Acad Pediat. **Professional Experience:** PROF PEDIAT, INJURY FREE COALITION KIDS, as of 2004; assoc prof pediat, Univ Ala, Birmingham, 1990; div dir, Southeast Child Safety Inst, 1987; DIR TOXICOL, POISON CONTROL CTR, CHILDREN'S HOSP ALA, 1983-; prin investr, Prescription Drug Ingestions Preschool Aged Children, US Consumer Prod Safety Comn, 1983-1984; ed, Poison Info Bull, Children's Hosp, beginning 1979; adj clin fac, Sch Pharm, Samford Univ, beginning 1979. **Memberships:** Am Asn Poison Control Ctrs; Am Acad Clin Toxicol. **Research Statement & Publications:** Childhood injury epidemiology; adolescent parasuicide by drug ingestion; epidemiology of poison exposures; development of a regional secondary prevention system for poison injuries. **Mailing Address:** Cent Ohio Poison Ctr, 1600 Seventh Ave S, Brimingham, AL 35233. **Fax:** 614-221-2672. **E-Mail:** Bking@peds.uab.edu

KING, WILLIAM EMMETT, CHEMICAL ENGINEERING. **Personal Data:** b Pittsburgh, Pa, July 27, 1943. **Education:** Univ Pittsburgh, BS, 1965; Carnegie-Mellon Univ, MS, 1968; Univ Pa, PhD (chem eng), 1976. **Professional Experience:** PROF CHEM ENG & BIOMED ENG, BUCKNELL UNIV, 1989-; CHMN, DEPT CHEM ENG, BUCKNELL UNIV, 1986-; assoc prof, Bucknell Univ, 1983-1989; sr res engr, Gulf Res & Develop Co, 1981-1983; asst prof chem eng, Univ Md, 1975-1980; engr mathematician, Cities Serv Res & Develop Co, 1968-1970; chem engr, Esso Res & Eng Co, 1966-1968. **Memberships:** Am Inst Chem Engrs; Am Chem Soc; Am Soc Eng Educ. **Research Statement & Publications:** Fluid-solid reactions; applied mathematics; biomedical engineering. **Mailing Address:** Dept Chem Eng, Bucknell Univ, Moore Ave, Lewisburg, PA 17837. **Fax:** 717-524-1141. **E-Mail:** wking@bucknell.edu

KING, WILLIAM MATTERN, APPLIED CHEMISTRY. **Personal Data:** b Cando, NDak, March 12, 1930; m 1989, Linda Mott; c Julie K (Smith). **Education:** NDak State Univ, BS, 1957, MS, 1958. **Professional Experience:** RETIRED; res dir, Spectrum Separations/Separex, 1979-1990; mgr develop membranes, Envirogenics Systs Co, 1960-1978; Chemist polymers, Hooker Chem Corp, 1958-1960. **Memberships:** Am Chem Soc. **Research Statement & Publications:** Asymmetric membranes for the separation of gases and organic liquids as well as the desalination of water by reverse osmosis. **Mailing Address:** 2830 Ithaca Dr, Prescott, AZ 86301.

KING, WILLIAM STANELY, APPLIED PHYSICS, ENGINEERING. **Personal Data:** b Monroe, La, June 16, 1935; m 1958, Velmo McGowan; c William Douglas & Vanessa Suzanne. **Education:** Univ Calif, Berkeley, BSME, 1957; Univ Calif, Los Angeles, MS, 1960, PhD (appl math, physics), 1966. **Professional Experience:** SYST ENGR, JPL, 1991-; instr eng, Calif State Univ, Northridge, 1985-; res scientist, Rocketdyne Div, Rockwell Int Corp, 1983-1991; instr eng, Univ Calif, Los Angeles, 1977-; Instr math, Santa Monica Col, 1973-; sr res scientist, Rand Corp, 1972-1983; staff scientist, Aerospace Corp, 1961-1972; Res engr, Rocket Div, Rockwell Int Corp, 1957-1961. **Memberships:** Assoc fel Am Inst Aeronaut & Astronaut; Sigma Xi. **Research Statement & Publications:** Fluid dynamics; numerical analysis; electromagnetic theory; laser physics; applied mathematics. **Mailing Address:** 4472 Don Milagro Dr, Los Angeles, CA 90008.

KING, WILLIS KWONGTSU, COMPUTER SCIENCE, ELECTRICAL ENGINEERING. **Personal Data:** b Shanghai, China, September 23, 1936; m 1970. **Education:** Darmstadt Tech Univ, Dipl Ing, 1963; Univ Pa, PhD (elec eng), 1969. **Professional Experience:** PROF COMPUT SCI, UNIV HOUSTON, as of 2002; chmn dept comput sci, Univ Houston, beginning 1979; assoc prof comput sci, Univ Houston, beginning 1973; asst prof comput sci, Univ Houston, 1969-1973; res engr comput design, IBM Labs, 1963-1965. **Memberships:** Asn Comput Mach; Sigma Xi; Inst Elec & Electronics Engrs. **Research Statement & Publications:** Computer architecture; distributed computing; microprogramming. **Mailing Address:** Dept Comput Sci, Univ Houston, 4800 Calhoun rd, Houston, TX 77204-3010. **Fax:** 713-743-3335. **E-Mail:** wkking@cs.uh.edu

KING, WILTON W(AYT), ENGINEERING MECHANICS. **Personal Data:** b Richmond, Va, August 11, 1937; m 1958, c 4. **Education:** Univ Va, BME, 1959, MME, 1961; Va Polytech Inst, PhD (eng mech), 1965. **Professional Experience:** PROF EMER CIVIL & ENVIRON ENG, GA INST TECHNOL, as of 2004; prof eng mech, Ga Inst Technol, beginning 1977; from asst prof to assoc prof, GA Inst Technol, 1964-1977; instr eng mech, Va Polytech Inst, 1961-1964. **Memberships:** Am Soc Mech Engrs; Sigma Xi. **Research Statement & Publications:** Vibrations; fracture mechanics. **Mailing Address:** Sch Civil & Environ Eng, Ga Inst Technol, 790 Atlantic Dr, Atlanta, GA 30332-0355. **Fax:** 404-894-2278.

KING, YAEMSIRI Y, APPLIED MATH, ALGEBRA, COMPLEX VARIABLE. **Personal Data:** b Bangkok, Thailand, August 26, 1957; m Dan. **Education:** Chulalonghorn Univ, BEd, 1979; NC State Univ, Med, 1982, MS, 1985, PhD (math), 1989. **Professional Experience:** CHAIR, MATH DEPT, PFEIFFER UNIV, 1998, as of 2005; PROF MATH, PFEIFFER UNIV, 1998-; assoc prof, Pfeiffer Univ, 1992-1998; asst prof, Pfeiffer Univ, 1989-1992. **Memberships:** NC Coun Teachers Math; Am Math Soc. **Research Statement &**

Publications: Lie algebras whose subalgebra lattice is complemented; the analogeous concept in group theory has been developed by several authors and many of the results carry over to the present setting. **Mailing Address:** Dept Math, Pfeiffer Univ, Harris 06B2, Charlotte, NC 28027. **Fax:** 704-463-1363. **E-Mail:** nyking@pfeiffer.edu

KINGAN, ROBERT J, MATHEMATICS. **Education:** La State Univ, BS, 1987, MS, PhD (math). **Professional Experience:** ASST PROF, DEPT MATH, CLAYTON STATE UNIV, as of 2006. **Mailing Address:** Dept Math, Clayton State Univ, 2000 Clayton State Blvd, Morrow, GA 48326. **Fax:** 678-466-4459. **E-Mail:** RobertKingan@clayton.edu

KINGAN, SANDRA M, MATHEMATICS. **Education:** Oakland Univ, PhD, 1990. **Professional Experience:** ASSOC PROF, DEPT MATHS, CLAYTON STATE UNIV, GA, as of 2006. **Mailing Address:** Clayton State Univ, 2000 Clayton State Blvd, Univ Ctr-426, Morrow, GA 30260. **Fax:** 678-466-4459. **E-Mail:** SandraKingan@mail.clayton.edu

KINGDON, HENRY SHANNON, BIOCHEMISTRY, HEMATOLOGY. **Personal Data:** b Puunene, Hawaii, July 2, 1934; m 1985, Jodi; c Holly, Cathy & Henry C. **Education:** Oberlin Col, AB, 1956; Western Res Univ, MD & PhD (biochem), 1963. **Professional Experience:** AT, BAXTER BIOTECH GROUP, as of 2006; vpres clinn & regullatory affairs, Gen Ther Unit, baxter Health Care, beginning 1993; vpres sci affairs & chief med officer, Blood Ther Group, 1991-1993; vpres & gen mgr, Hyland Biotechnol, Hayward, Calif, 1990-1991; vpres, Hyland Therapeut, Glendale, Calif, 1984-1990; med dir, Hyland Therapeut, Glendale, Calif, 1981-1990; prof med & biochem, Univ NC, Chapel Hill, 1973-1981; Guggenheim fel, 1972-1973; from asst prof to assoc prof med & biochem, Univ Chicago, 1967-1973; clin assoc, Nat Heart Inst, 1965-1967; intern & resident internal med, Univ Wash, 1963-1965. **Memberships:** Am Chem Soc; Am Fedn Clin Res; Int Soc Thrombosis & Haemostasis; Am Soc Hemat; Am Soc Biol Chem. **Research Statement & Publications:** Hematology; enzymology of blood coagulation; regulation of nitrogen metabolism in microorganisms; primary structure of regulatory and coagulation enzymes; human immunodeficiency virus inactivation of blood products. **Mailing Address:** Gene Ther Unit, Baxter Healthcare, Baxter Technol Park 1627 Lake Cook Rd, Deerfield, IL 60015. **Fax:** 847-940-6271.

KINGHORN, ALAN DOUGLAS, PHARMACOGNOSY, PHYTOCHEMISTRY. **Personal Data:** b Newcastle-upon-Tyne, UK, August 31, 1947; m 1976, Helen. **Education:** Univ Bradford, UK, BPharm, 1969; Univ Strathclyde, Glasgow, UK, MSc, 1970; Sch Pharm, Univ London, PhD (pharmacog), 1975, DSc, 1990. **Honors & Awards:** Platinum award, Div Agr & Food Chem, Am Chem Soc, 1996. **Professional Experience:** JACK L BEAL PROF & CHAIR, COL PHARM, OHIO STATE UNIV, 2004-; ed adv bd, Mini Reviews Organic Chem, 2004-; prestige lectr, Sch Pharm, Univ Bradford, 2000; consult, Smith-Kline Beecham Nutrit Healthcare Res Develop, 2000; consult, Ministry Sci Technol, Korean Sci Eng Found, 1996; vis prof, Univ Salerno italy, 1996; ASST HEAD, DEPT MED CHEM & PHARMACOG, 1995-; ed-in-chief, J Natural Prod, 1994; B Kenneth West Univ Scholar, Univ Ill, 1993-; mem, AIDS & Related Dis D Study Sect, NIH, 1993-1997; ASSOC DIR, PROG COLLAB RES PHARMACEUT SCI, UNIV ILL, CHICAGO, 1992-; guest prof pharmacog, ETH-Zentrum, Zurich, Switz, 1990; ed, Phytochem Anal, 1989-1993; PROF PHARMACOG, UNIV ILL, CHICAGO, 1986-; from asst prof to assoc prof, Dept Med Chem & Pharmacog, 1977-1986; res assoc, Dept Med Chem & Pharmacog, 1976-1977; postdoctoral pharmacog, Univ Miss, 1975-1976; teaching fel pharmacog, Sch Pharm, Univ London, UK, 1971-1975; anal chemist, Burroughs Wellcome Co, Dartford, UK, 1970-1971. **Memberships:** Am Chem Soc; Am Soc Pharmacog (pres, 1990-1991); fel Royal Pharmaceut Soc Gt Brit; Soc Econ Bot (pres, 1991-1992); fel Linean Soc London; fel Am Asn Pharmaceut Scientists. **Research Statement & Publications:** Isolation, structure elucidation, semi-synthesis, chemical analysis, and bioassay of plant secondary metabolites with interesting biological activities, especially compounds that exhibit antineoplastic, antiviral, bitter-tasting, cytotoxic, insecticidal mutagenic, skin-irritant, or sweet-tasting properties; published over 340 articles. **Mailing Address:** Dept Med Chem & Pharmacog Col Pharm Ohio State Univ, 500 W 12th Ave, Columbus, OH 43210-1291. **Fax:** 614-247-8081. **E-Mail:** kinghorn.4@osu.edu

KINGMAN, HARRY ELLIS, JR, veterinary medicine; deceased, see previous edition for last biography

KINGMAN, ROBERT EARL, PHYSICS. **Personal Data:** b Phoenix, Ariz, June 24, 1938; m 1959, c 4. **Education:** Walla Walla Col, BS, 1961; Univ Ariz, MS, 1967, PhD (physics), 1971. **Professional Experience:** PROF, ANDREWS UNIV, 1979-; CHAIR, PHYSICS DEPT, 1971-; from asst prof to assoc prof, Physics Dept, 1971-1979; instr physics, Univ Ariz, 1971; asst prof, Walla Walla Col, 1966-1967; Instr physics, Walla Walla Col, 1963-1966. **Memberships:** Am Phys Soc; Am Asn Physics Teachers; Sigma Xi; Coun Undergrad Res. **Research Statement & Publications:** Study of super clustering of galaxies; method of describing decay of unstable quatum states; study of cosmological models based on the Robertson-Walker metric. **Mailing Address:** Physics Dept, Andrews Univ, Berrien Springs, MI 49104-0001.

KINGREA, JAMES I, QUALITY ASSURANCE MANAGEMENT, SUPPLIER SOURCE ASSURANCE MANAGEMENT. **Personal Data:** b Philadelphia, Pa, March 10, 1928; m 1947, c James I III & Kathleen V. **Education:** Pa Mil Col, BSEE, 1950. **Professional Experience:** RETIRED; dir qual, Eng Systs Co, Div Datron, 1989-1994; mgr, Advan Develop & Eng Ctr, 1986-1989; weld inspector, Am Weld Soc, beginning 1982; qual consult, beginning 1970; mgr, Qual Systs & Serv, Steam Div, Westinghouse Elec Corp, 1969-1986. **Memberships:** Sr mem, Am Soc Qual Control; Am Soc Mech Engrs; Am Welding Soc. **Research Statement & Publications:** Quality discipline relating to surface texture and lay; mathematical definition of finishes; equipment used to measure different finishes; specification of surface finish requirements; generation of specific finishes. **Mailing Address:** 65 Worrell Dr, Springfield, PA 19064.

KINGSBURY, CHARLES ALVIN, ORGANIC CHEMISTRY. **Personal Data:** b Louisville, Ky, January 12, 1935; m 1958, c 5. **Education:** Iowa State Col, BS, 1956; Univ Calif, Los Angeles, PhD (org chem), 1960. **Professional Experience:** PROF ORG CHEM, UNIV NEBR, LINCOLN, 1972-; from asst prof to assoc prof, Univ Nebr, Lincoln, 1967-1972; instr org chem, Iowa State Univ, 1963-1967; NSF fel, Harvard Univ, 1962-1963. **Memberships:** Royal Soc Chem; Am Chem Soc. **Research Statement & Publications:** Stereochemistry; reaction mechanisms. **Mailing Address:** Dept Chem, Univ Nebr, Lincoln, NE 68506. **E-Mail:** ckingsbu@unlinfo.unl.edu

KINGSBURY, DAVID THOMAS, VIROLOGY, MICROBIOLOGY. **Personal Data:** b Seattle, Wash, October 24, 1940; m 1982. **Education:** Univ Wash, BS, 1962, MS, 1964; Univ Calif, San Diego, PhD (biol), 1971. **Professional Experience:** FOUNDER & SR CONSULT, DISCOVERY BIOSCIENCE CORP, 2000-; chief info officer, Johns Hopkins Univ, beginning 1997; dir, Div Biomed Info Sci, Welch Biomedical Library, beginning 1997; adj prof microbiol, George Wash Univ, beginning 1985; mem, bd regents, Nat Libr Med, 1984-; asst dir biol, behav & social sci, NSF, 1984-1988; prof med microbiol & virol, Berkeley, 1981-1986; dir, Naval Bioscience Lab, Oakland, 1981-1984; Am Cancer Soc Dernham fel oncol, Univ Calif, San Diego, 1971-1972 & 1977 & NIH, 1978-1979; vis scientist, Scripps Clin & Res Found, La Jolla, Calif, 1973-1980; from asst prof to assoc prof microbiol, Univ Calif, Irvine, 1972-1981; res fel microbiol, Am Inst Biol Sci, 1967-1968; Microbiologist, Naval Med Res Inst, 1964-1967. **Memberships:** Fel AAAS; Am Soc Microbiol; Am Soc Virol; Soc Genetic Microbiol. **Research Statement & Publications:** Oncogenic viruses; viral genetics; biochemistry of virus replication; techniques in diagnostic virology and microbiology; biochemistry and genetics of the unconventional viruses. **Mailing Address:** Discovery Bioscience Corp, 655 NE Northlake Way, Seattle, WA 98105. **Fax:** 206-675-1125. **E-Mail:** dkingsbury@discoverybio.com

KINGSBURY, DAVID WILSON, VIROLOGY, MOLECULAR BIOLOGY. **Personal Data:** b Jersey City, NJ, April 2, 1933; m 1957, c 7. **Education:** Manhattan Col, BS, 1955; Yale Univ, MD, 1959. **Honorary Degrees:** DSc, Manhattan Col, 1990. **Professional Experience:** RETIRED; sr sci officer, Howard Hughes Med Inst, 1988-1996; adj prof microbiol, Univ Tenn, Memphis, 1972-1985; mem div virol, St Jude Hosp, Memphis, 1969-1988; career develop award, Memphis, 1964-1973; from res fel to mem, 1963-1969; USPHS res fel, St Jude Hosp, Memphis, 1963-1964; USPHS res fel, Yale Univ, 1961-1963; asst resident, Yale Univ, 1960-1961; intern path, Yale Univ, 1959-1960. **Research Statement & Publications:** Negative strand RNA viruses. **Mailing Address:** 4000 Cathedral Ave NW, Washington, DC 20016.

KINGSBURY, HERBERT B, SOLID MECHANICS, BIOMECHANICS. **Personal Data:** b Pittsburgh, Pa, February 15, 1934; m 1990, Ellen; c 3. **Education:** Univ Conn, BS, 1958; Univ Pa, MS, 1961, PhD (eng mech), 1964. **Professional Experience:** RETIRED; prof mech eng, Univ Del, 1980-1996; adj assoc prof, Sch Vet Med, Univ Pa, 1978-1982; Eng consult, Scott Paper Co, beginning 1970; from asst prof to assoc prof aerospace eng, Univ Del, 1967-1980; asst prof aerospace eng, Pa State Univ, 1966-1967; engr, Missile & Space Div, Gen Elec Corp, 1964-1966; Scientist, Dyna/Struct Inc, 1961-1964. **Memberships:** Am Soc Mech Engrs; Am Soc Biomech; Nat Soc Prof Engrs; Am Acad Mech. **Research Statement & Publications:** Structural mechanics; mechanics of biological structures; mechanics of porous deformable solids; structural dynamics. **Mailing Address:** 40 Goodwin Rd, Gerrish Island, Kittery Point, ME 03905.

KINGSBURY, ROBERT FREEMAN, ATOMIC SPECTROSCOPY. **Personal Data:** b Ithaca, NY, June 26, 1912; wid, c Robert A, Martha K (Bate), Mary K (Clark) & Rita K (Cassellins). **Education:** Bowdoin Col, BS, 1934; Cornell Univ, MS, 1939; Univ Pa, PhD (physics), 1956. **Professional Experience:** PROF EMER PHYSICS, BATES COL, 1978-; prof, Bates Col, 1964-1978; from instr to assoc prof, Trinity Col, Conn, 1950-1964; bates Col, 1944; Univ Maine, 1944-1947; instr physics, Bowdoin Col, 1943; instr sci, Mass State Teachers Col, Westfield, 1942-1943. **Memberships:** AAAS; Am Phys Soc; Am Asn Physics Teachers; Am Optical Soc; Sigma Xi. **Research Statement & Publications:** Atomic spectra. **Mailing Address:** Dept Physics & Astron, Bates Col, Two Andrews Rd, Lewiston, ME 04240-6028.

KINGSBURY, WILLIAM DENNIS, ORGANIC CHEMISTRY, MEDICINAL CHEMISTRY. **Personal Data:** b Buffalo, NY, November 21, 1941; m 1967, c 3. **Education:** State Univ NY, Buffalo, BA, 1965; Wayne State Univ, PhD (chem), 1970. **Professional Experience:** AT DEPT PHYSICS & STRUCT CHEM, SMITH KLINE & BEECHAM PHARMACEUT, as of 2000; SR CHEMIST, SMITH KLINE & FRENCH LABS, 1971-; NIH fel, Univ Kans, 1970-1971; instr chem, Wayne State Univ, 1965-1967; Chemist, Electro Refractories & Abrasives, 1961-1962. **Memberships:** Am Chem Soc. **Research Statement & Publications:** Anthelmintics; animal nutrition; heterocyclic chemistry; organo sulfur chemistry; immunochemistry; antimicrobial chemotherapy. **Mailing Address:** SmithKline Beecham Pharmaceut, PO Box 1539, King of Prussia, PA 19406.

KINGSLAND, GRAYDON CHAPMAN, PLANT PATHOLOGY. **Personal Data:** b Burlington, Vt, August 28, 1928; m 1950, c 4. **Education:** Univ Vt, BA, 1952; Univ NH, MS, 1955; Pa State Univ, PhD (plant path), 1958. **Professional Experience:** PROF EMER PLANT PATH & PHYSIOL, CLEMSON UNIV, 1993-; Prof Plant Path & Physiol, Clemson Univ, 1984-1993; Plant pathologist, USAID/SECID Seych Is food crop improv proj, 1981-1982 & 1984; assoc prof, Clemson Univ, 1967-1984; asst prof bot & asst pathologist, Clemson Univ, 1960-1967; assoc pathologist, United Fruit Co, Honduras, 1958-1960; Res technician, Conn Tobacco Lab, 1952-1953. **Memberships:** Am Phytopath Soc; Sierra Club; Wilderness Soc; Nat Audubon Soc; Sigma Xi. **Research Statement & Publications:** Diseases of cereal grains; ecology of microflora of rhizospheres and seeds of cereal grains; chemical control of cereal grains diseases; teaching introductory and graduate phytopathology; tropical agriculture; mycology. **Mailing Address:** 209 Manley Dr, Clemson, SC 29631.

KINGSLEY, HENRY A(DELBERT), CHEMICAL ENGINEERING, PROCESS ENGINEERING. **Personal Data:** b Wakefield, RI, May 5, 1921; m 1943, Helen Polis; c John & Joyce. **Education:** Univ RI, BS, 1943; Yale Univ, DEng, 1949. **Professional Experience:** Pres, Comtech Consults Inc, 1984-1998; consult, 1982-2002; mgr support process eng, Shell Oil Co, 1974-1982; mgr chem process eng, Explor & Prod Res Ctr, Shell Develop Co, 1972-1974; mgr chem & chem eng dept, Explor & Prod Res Ctr, Shell Develop Co, 1970-1972; mgr proj develop, Plastics & Resins Div, NY, 1967-1970; dir res & develop lab, Indust Chem Div, Shell Chem Co, Tex, 1965-1967; dept head licensing & design eng, Shell Develop Co, Calif, 1964-1965; supvr process eng, Shell Develop Co, Calif, 1959-1963; Engr, Shell Develop Co, Calif, 1949-1959. **Memberships:** Am Inst Chem Engrs; Am Chem Soc; Sigma Xi. **Mailing Address:** 411 W Fair Harbor Lane, Houston, TX 77079-2515. **E-Mail:** consultengr@juno.com

KINGSLEY, JACK DEAN, SOLID STATE DEVICES, OPTOELECTRONICS. **Personal Data:** b Wonewoc, Wis, August 10, 1934; m 1962, Beverly; c Lawrence, Robert & Andrew. **Education:** Univ Wis, BSEE, 1956, MSEE, 1957; Univ Ill, MS, 1958, PhD (physics), 1960. **Professional Experience:** RETIRED; physicist, Gen Elec Res & Develop Ctr, beginning 1985; mgr, Display Br, 1983-1985; mgr, Electronic Mat Br, 1981-1983; mgr, Optoelectronics Br, 1972-1981; mgr, Light Emitting Diode Array Prog, 1971-1972; Physicist, Gen Elec Res & Develop Ctr, 1960-1971. **Memberships:** Am Phys Soc. **Research Statement & Publications:** Optical spectroscopy of solids; quantum electronics; luminescence; point defects in solids; imaging and display devices. **Mailing Address:** 460 Tiara Vista Dr, Grand Junction, CO 81503.

KINGSLEY, MICHAEL CHARLES STEPHEN, ECOLOGY, BIOMETRICS. **Personal Data:** b Harrow, UK, October 20, 1941; Canadian citizen. **Education:** Univ Cambridge, MA, 1966; Lancaster Univ, MA, 1968. **Professional Experience:** RES SCIENTIST, CAN DEPT FISHERIES & OCEANS, 1983-; biologist, Can Wildlife Serv, 1978-1983; statistician, Can Wildlife Serv, 1973-1978; statistician, Can Forestry Serv, 1971-1973. **Memberships:** Biomet Soc; Soc Marine Mammal; Arctic Inst NAm. **Research Statement & Publications:** Ecology of marine mammals; behavior, vocalizations, population dynamics, population estimation, growth. **Mailing Address:** Inst Maurice LaMontague, 850 Rte de la Mar PO Box 1000, Mont-Joli, PQ G5H 3Z4, Can.

KINGSOLVER, CHARLES H, PLANT PATHOLOGY. **Personal Data:** b Peru, Nebr, August 31, 1914; wid, c Carolyn (Purvis), John G, Joel G & Cynthia (Gittinger). **Education:** Nebr State Teachers Col, Peru, AB, 1935; Iowa State Univ, MS, 1939, PhD (plant path), 1943. **Professional Experience:** CONSULT PLANT DIS RES, 1979-; Adj prof plant path, Pa State Univ, 1972-; dir, Plant Dis Res Lab, Northeast Region, Sci & Educ Admin-Agr Res, USDA, 1971-1979; chief plant path div, Crops Div, US Army Biol Labs, 1968-1971; chief biol br, Crops Div, US Army Biol Labs, 1962-1968; agr adminr, Mkt Qual Res Div, Agr Mkt Serv, USDA, 1957-1962; sect chief, chief biol br II, 1955-1957; sect chief, Biol Br, Chem Corps, Biol Warfare Labs, Md, 1951-1955; Asst prof bot, Univ Mo, 1946-1951. **Memberships:** Sigma Xi; Am Phytopath Soc. **Research Statement & Publications:** Plant disease epidemiology; quantitation of disease increase and spread; predictive systems; threat potential of foreign plant disease; biological control of weeds with plant pathogens. **Mailing Address:** PO Box 337, Braddock Heights, MD 21714.

KINGSOLVER, JOEL G, BIOLOGY. **Education:** Duke Univ, BS, 1976; Univ Wis, MS, 1978; stanford Univ, PhD, 1981. **Professional Experience:** WILLIAM RAND KENAN, JR, PROF, DEPT BIOL, UNIV NC, 2000-. **Research Statement & Publications:** Interface of environmental physiology and functional morphology with population ecology and evolution, working primarily with insects and the organisms that they eat or that eat them; selection and evolution of morphological and physiological plasticity; nutritional physiology and evolutionary ecology of feeding and growth in caterpillars; patterns of phenotypic selection and fitness surfaces for quantitative traits in natural populations; functional morphology and evolutionary ecology of flight and predator escape in butterflies; physiological, ecological and evolutionary responses of insects to climate change. **Mailing Address:** Dept Biol, Univ NC, 334A Wilson Hall CB No 3280 Coker Hall, Chapel Hill, NC 27599-3280. **E-Mail:** jgking@bio.unc.edu

KINGSOLVER, JOHN MARK, ENTOMOLOGY, TAXONOMY SEED BEETLES BRUCLIDAE. **Personal Data:** b Selma, Ind, March 20, 1925; wid, c John M (deceased) & Rebecca D. **Education:** Purdue Univ, BS, 1951; Univ Ill, MS, 1956, PhD (entom), 1961. **Professional Experience:** RETIRED; res entomologist, Syst Entom Lab, USDA, 1962-1990; res assoc, Ill Natural Hist Surv, 1961-1962; res asst entom, Univ Ill, 1954-1961; res assoc, USDA & Fla State Dept Agr. **Memberships:** Am Entom Soc; Asn Trop Biol; Ctr Syst Entom; Coleop Soc. **Research Statement & Publications:** Taxonomy of seed-beetles (Bruchidae) of Western Hemisphere. **Mailing Address:** 3035 SW First Ave, Gainesville, FL 32607.

KINGSTON, CHARLES RICHARD, FORENSIC SCIENCE. **Personal Data:** b San Diego, Calif, April 11, 1931; m 1969, c 1. **Education:** Univ Calif, Berkeley, BS, 1959, MCriminol, 1961, Dr Criminol, 1964. **Professional Experience:** Prof emer, John Jay col, City univ, NY 1996- PROF CRIMINALISTICS, JOHN JAY COL, CITY UNIV NY, 1968- 1996; chief criminalistics res bur, NY State Identification & Intel Syst, 1966-1968; consult, NY State Identification & Intel Syst, 1965-1966; asst res criminalist, Criminalistics Lab, Sch Criminol, Univ Calif, Berkeley, 1964-1965; res criminalist, Criminalistics Lab, Sch Criminol, Univ Calif, Berkeley, 1963-1964; Lab technician, Criminalistics Lab, Sch Criminol, Univ Calif, Berkeley, 1958-1963. **Memberships:** Am Acad Forensic Sci. **Research Statement & Publications:** Application of probability and statistics in criminalistics; computer applications in criminology and criminalistics. **Mailing Address:** 6 Surray Close, White Plains, NY 10607.

KINGSTON, DAVID GEORGE IAN, NATURAL PRODUCTS CHEMISTRY. **Personal Data:** b London, Eng, November 9, 1938; American citizen; m 1966, Beverly; c Joy, Christy & Jonathan. **Education:** Cambridge Univ, BA, 1960, PhD (org chem), 1963; dipl theol, Univ London, 1962. **Honors & Awards:** Am Soc Pharmacoq Res Achievement Award 1999 & Va Sci of the Yr, 2002. **Professional Experience:** UNIV DISTINGUISHED PROF, VA POLYTECH INST & ST UNIV, 1999-; mem, Bioorganic & Natural Prod Chem IRG, NIH, 2000-2004; chmn, Div Cancer Treatment Contracts Rev Comt, NIH, 1989-1992; mem, Div Cancer Treatment Contracts Rev Comt, NIH, 1987-1992; mem, Div Cancer Treatment Contracts Rev Comm, NIH, 1987-1991; assoc ed, J Natural Prod, 1983-1998; mem, biomed sci study sect, NIH, 1979-1984; prof chem, VA Polytech Inst St Univ, 1977-1999; assoc prof, VA Polytech Inst & State Univ, 1971-1977; asst prof chem, State Univ NY Albany, 1966-1971; Res fel chem, NATO fel, 1964-1966; Res assoc, Mass Inst Technol, 1963-1964; Res fel chem, Queens' Col, Cambridge Univ, 1962-1966. **Memberships:** Am Chem Soc; Royal Soc Chem; Am Soc Pharmacog (vpres, 1987-1988, pres, 1988-1989). **Research Statement & Publications:** Natural products chemistry; structure and synthesis of biologically active natural products; chemistry of taxol and related tubulin polymerization agents. **Mailing Address:** Dept Chem M/C 0212, Va Polytech Inst & State Univ, Blacksburg, VA 24061. **Fax:** 540-231-3255. **E-Mail:** dkingston@vt.edu

KINGSTON, DAVID LYMAN, solid state physics, semiconductor material characterization; deceased, see previous edition for last biography

KINGSTON, GEORGE C, POLYMER PROCESS DESIGN & DEVELOPMENT. **Personal Data:** b New York, NY. **Education:** Manhattan Col, BS, 1970; Clarkson Col Tech, MS, 1972, PhD (chem eng), 1975. **Professional Experience:** RES & DEVELOP MGR, CHEM GROUP MONSANTO, 1996-; new prod develop process redesign leader, Monsanto Polymer Prod Co, 1994-1996; applications develop mgr, Monsanto Polymer Prod Co, 1993-1994; res & develop mgr, Monsanto Polymer Prod Co, 1989-1993; tech leader, Monsanto Polymer Prod Co, 1987-1989; res specialist, Monsanto Polymer Prod Co, 1982-1987; Univ Mass, Amherst, 1982; sr res engr, Monsanto Polymer Prod Co, 1979-1982; adj chem eng, Univ Dayton, 1978-1979; instr chem eng, Clarkson Col Tech, 1974-1975. **Memberships:** Am Inst Chem Engrs; Soc Plastics Engrs; Prod Develop Mgt Asn. **Research Statement & Publications:** Design and development of polymer processes; polymerization; process effects on polymer structure and properties; oxidative stability of polymers. **Mailing Address:** Monsanto, 730 Worcester St, Springfield, MA 01151. **E-Mail:** 72643.3640@compuserve.com

KINGSTON, H M, ANALYTICAL ENVIRONMENTAL CHEMISTRY, LABORATORY AUTOMATION. **Personal Data:** b Indiana, Pa, July 9, 1949; m 1976, Mary. **Education:** Indiana Univ Pa, BS, 1973, MS, 1975; Am Univ, PhD (anal chem), 1978. **Honors & Awards:** Research & Develop 100 Award, 1996. **Professional Experience:** PROF ANALYTICAL & ENVIRON CHEM, DUQUESNE UNIV, 1991-; proj mgr, Consortium Automated Lab Systs, 1989-1991; supvry res chemist & group leader, Nat Inst Stand & Technol, 1988-1991; res prof, Dept Chem, Am Univ, Wash, DC, 1985-1988; cong sci fel, US Cong, House Rep, 1984-1985; res chemist, Nat Inst Stand & Technol, 1976-1991; instr, Dept Chem, Am Univ, Wash, DC, 1975-1976. **Research Statement & Publications:** Fundamental research in separation science, speciation, chromatography and microwave energy application, methods and instrument development, standard reference materials development and certification, environmental test method development, and automation including robotics. **Mailing Address:** Dept Chem & Biochem, Duquesne Univ, 308 Mellon Hall Sci 600 Forbes Ave, Pittsburgh, PA 15229. **Fax:** 412-396-4013. **E-Mail:** kingston@duq.edu

KINGSTON, ROBERT HILDRETH, SOLID STATE DEVICES, OPTICS. **Personal Data:** b Somerville, Mass, February 13, 1928; m 1952, c 4. **Education:** Mass Inst Technol, BS, 1948, MS, 1948, PhD (physics), 1951. **Honors & Awards:** Centennial Medal, Inst Elec & Electronics Engrs, 1984. **Professional Experience:** RETIRED; sr lectr, Mass Inst Technol, beginning 1990; sr staff, Lincoln Lab, 1987-1990; adj prof, Mass Inst Technol, 1985-1990; assoc leader, Optical Communs Technol Group, 1984-1987; auth, Detection Optical & Infrared Radiation, 1978; sr staff, Infrared Radar Group, 1977-1984; leader, Infrared Radar Group, 1972-1977; head, Optics Div, 1969-1972; ed, J Quantum Electronics, Inst Elec & Electronics Engrs, 1965-1970; vis assoc prof, Stanford Univ, 1964-1965; leader, Optics & Infrared Group, 1961-1969; mem, Solid State Physics Group, Mass Inst Technol, 1952-1961; mem staff, Transistor Res & Develop, Bell Labs, 1951-1952. **Memberships:** Nat Acad Eng; fel Optical Soc Am; fel Inst Elec & Electronics Engrs; fel Am Phys Soc. **Research Statement & Publications:** Physical principles of semiconductor devices; physics of semiconductor surfaces; magnetic resonance; solid state maser, parametric amplifiers; optical masers; non-linear optics; tuneable semiconductor lasers; infrared detectors. **Mailing Address:** 4 Field Rd, Lexington, MA 02173.

KINI, ARAVINDA MATTAR, ORGANIC SOLID STATE CHEMISTRY& PHYSICS, ORGANIC SUPERCONDUCTORS. **Personal Data:** b Karkala, India, January 14, 1951; American citizen; m 1979, Mridula; c Rohini, Nutan, Seema & Ashvin. **Education:** Univ Mysore, India, BSc, 1970; Indian Inst Technol, Madras, MSc, 1971; Univ Hawaii, Manoa, PhD (chem), 1979. **Honors & Awards:** Outstanding Sci Accomplishment Award, Dept Energy, 1990. **Professional Experience:** PROG MGR, DIV MAT SCI & ENG, US DEPT ENERGY, 2002-; prin investr, NATO, 1995-1996; vis prof chem, Univ Angers, France, 1995; chemist, Argonne Nat Lab, beginning 1991; consult, Strem Chems Inc, 1988-1989; asst chemist, Argonne Nat Lab, 1986-1991; res scientist, LTV Aerospace & Defense Co, Dallas, 1984-1986; postdoctoral fel, Johns Hopkins Univ, Baltimore, 1980-1984; jr researcher, Univ Hawaii, 1979; lectr chem, Manipal Eng Col, India, 1971-1972. **Memberships:** Am Chem Soc; Am Phys Soc. **Research Statement & Publications:** Design and synthesis of organic electrical conductors and superconductors; conducting polymers; organic synthesis; electrochemistry; crystal growth; organic thin films; isotope effect and superconductivity. **Mailing Address:** Off Basic Energy Sci, Mat Sci & Eng Div, US Dept Energy, SC 13/G TN 1000 Independence Ave SW, Washington, DC 20585-1290. **Fax:** 301-903-9513. **E-Mail:** a.kini@Sci.doe.gov

KINKADE, JOSEPH M, BIOCHEMISTRY. **Education:** Princeton Univ, BA, 1959; Univ Calif, PhD, 1966. **Professional Experience:** PROF, DEPT BIOCHEM, EMORY UNIV SCH MED, as of 2005. **Mailing Address:** Dept Biochem, Emory Univ Sch Med, Atlanta, GA 30322-3050. **Fax:** 404-727-2738. **E-Mail:** joseph.kinkade@emory.edu

KINKEL, ARLYN WALTER, PHARMACY. **Personal Data:** b Fond du Lac, Wis, October 15, 1929; m 1955, c 3. **Education:** Univ Wis, BS, 1952, MS, 1957, PhD (pharm), 1958. **Professional Experience:** RETIRED; dir clin pharmacokinetics, Pharmacokinetic-Drug Metab Dept, 1981-1992; sect dir pharmaceut res & develop, Parke-Davis Res Div, Warner-Lambert Co, 1970-1980; from assoc res pharmacist to sr res pharmacist, Parke-Davis Res Div, Warner-Lambert Co, 1958-1970. **Memberships:** Am Pharmaceut Asn; fel Acad Pharmaceut Sci; Am Col Clin Pharmacol; fel Am Asn Pharmaceut Sci. **Research Statement & Publications:** Biopharmaceutics; assay of blood levels and drugs; pharmacokinetics. **Mailing Address:** 13966 N Buckingham Dr, Oro Valley, AZ 85737-5851.

KINLOCH, BOHUN BAKER, JR, GENETICS, PLANT PATHOLOGY. **Personal Data:** b Charleston, SC, July 21, 1934; m 1969, c 4. **Education:** Univ Va, BA, 1956; NC State Univ, BS, 1962, MS, 1965, PhD (genetics), 1968. **Professional Experience:** RES GENETICIST, US FOREST SERV, as of 2001; GENETICIST, PAC SOUTHWEST FOREST & RANGE EXP STA, US FOREST SERV, 1968-; Res asst forest genetics & path, NC State Univ, 1962-1968. **Memberships:** Am Phytopath Soc. **Research Statement & Publications:** Genetics of disease resistance in forest trees; population genetics of forest trees. **Mailing Address:** 2525 Hill Ct, Berkeley, CA 94708.

KINLOCH, ROBERT ARMSTRONG, NEMATOLOGY. **Personal Data:** b Dumbarton, Scotland, February 15, 1939; m 1963, c 3. **Education:** Glasgow Univ, BS, 1963; Univ Calif, Davis, PhD (entom, nematol), 1968. **Professional Experience:** ASSOC PROF AGRON, AGR EXP STA, UNIV FLA, 1980-; assoc nematologist, Agr Exp Sta, Univ Fla, 1968-1980; ed, Ann Appl Nematol. **Memberships:** Soc Nematol; Orgn Trop Am Nematol. **Research Statement & Publications:** Biology and host-parasite relationships of plant parasitic nematodes; economic control of plant parasitic nematodes affecting agronomic crops. **Mailing Address:** Dept Entomol & Nematol Agr Res Ctr Univ Fla, PO Box 110620, Gainesville, FL 32611-0620. **Fax:** 352-392-0190. **E-Mail:** rakh@gnv.ifas.ufl.edu

KINLOUGH-RATHBONE, ROELENE L, HEMATOLOGY, ATHEROSCLEROSIS. **Personal Data:** b Adelaide, South Australia, August 20, 1938. **Education:** Univ Adelaide, MB & BS, 1961, MD, 1967; McMaster Univ, PhD (med sci), 1971. **Professional Experience:** Assoc vpres fac health sci, McMaster Univ, 1992-; actg assoc dean educ, McMaster Univ, 1987-1988; PROF PATH, MCMASTER UNIV, 1982-; chmn grad prog med sci, McMaster Univ, 1981-1987; Sci Rev Comt, Ont Heart Found, 1981-1984; res assoc, Ont Heart Found, 1980-1983; mem, Sci Prog Comt, 8th Int Cong Haemostasis & Thrombosis, 1979-1981; consult, NIH, 1977-1979; sr res fel, Ont Heart Found, 1975-1980; prin investr, Med Res Coun, Can, 1974- & NATO res grant, 1984; from asst prof to assoc prof, Mcmaster Univ, 1973-1982; lectr, Mcmaster Univ, 1971-1973; fel, Med Res Coun Can, 1967-1971; res asst, Nat Heart Found, Australia, 1964-1967; Coun Thrombosis, Am Heart Asn. **Memberships:** Int Soc Thrombosis & Haemostasis; Am Heart Asn; AAAS; Can Soc Clin Invest; Am Soc Hemat; Am Soc Invest Path; Can Atherosal Soc; Sr Women's Acad Admin Can. **Research Statement & Publications:** Mechanisms influencing hemostasis, thrombosis and the development of atherosclerosis; cellular and biochemical mechanisms in platelet response to stimuli; factors governing the response of blood and vessels to injury. **Mailing Address:** Dept Path, McMaster Univ Med Ctr, 1200 Main St W Rm 2E5C, Hamilton, ON L8N 3Z5, Can. **Fax:** 905-546-0800.

KINMAN, RILEY NELSON, CIVIL & SANITARY ENGINEERING, ENVIRONMENTAL ENGINEERING. **Personal Data:** b Dry Ridge, Ky, January 25, 1936; m 1957, Barbara Brown; c Joe R & Kathy. **Education:** Univ Ky, BS, 1959; Univ Cincinnati, MS, 1962; Univ Fla, PhD (sanit eng), 1965. **Professional Experience:** PRES, RNK ENVIRON, INC, 1980-; PRES, PRISTINE, INC, 1974-; PROF CIVIL ENG, UNIV CINCINNATI, 1973-; assoc prof, Rnk Environ, Inc, 1968-1973; chief, Demonstration Grants Br, Fed Water Pollution Control Admin, 1967-1968; asst chief, Demonstration Grants Br, Fed Water Pollution Control Admin, 1966-1967; res assoc chem & sanit sci, Univ Fla, 1965-1966; Engr-in-training, Water Dept, City of Dayton, Ohio, 1959-1961, 1962. **Memberships:** Am Soc Civil

Engrs; Water Pollution Control Fedn; Am Water Works Asn; Am Chem Soc; Sigma Xi; Soc Prof Engrs. **Research Statement & Publications:** Treatment and ultimate disposal of hazardous wastes; research and development for control of water pollution, especially the physical, chemical, biological, physiological, economic and political aspects of water pollution; solid and hazardous waste management. **Mailing Address:** 415 Stevenson Rd, Erlanger, KY 41018-2472.

KINMAN, THOMAS DAVID, ASTRONOMY. **Personal Data:** b Rugby, Eng, August 10, 1928; m 1963, c 2. **Education:** Oxford Univ, BA, 1949, MA & DPhil(astron), 1953. **Professional Experience:** Astronr, 1969-; from asst astronr to astronr, Lick Observ, Univ Calif, Santa Cruz, 1960-1969; sr sci officer, Royal Observ, Cape Town, 1959-1960; mem comn, Int Astron Union, 1958; Radcliffe travelling fel astron, Univ Observ, Oxford Univ, 1954-1956 & Radcliffe Observ, Pretoria, 1956-1959; sci officer physics, Admirality Res Lab, Teddington, 1953-1954; dept demonstr, Univ Observ, Oxford Univ, 1949-1953; EMER ASTRONR, KITT PEAK NAT OBSERV. **Memberships:** Am Astron Soc. **Research Statement & Publications:** Large scale structure of our own and other galaxies, particularly constitution and dynamics of older stars and star clusters; quasistellar objects. **Mailing Address:** Kitt Peak Nat Observ, PO Box 26732, Tucson, AZ 85726.

KINN, DONALD NORMAN, ACAROLOGY, NEMATOLOGY. **Personal Data:** b Chicago, Ill. **Education:** Lawrence Col, BS, 1956; Univ Wyo, MS, 1962; Univ Calif, Berkeley, PhD (entom), 1969. **Professional Experience:** RETIRED; res entomologist acarol, Southern Forest Exp Sta, 1975; asst res entom, Div Biol Control, Univ Calif, 1971-1973; assoc specialist, Div Biol Control, Univ Calif, 1969-1970. **Memberships:** Entom Soc Am; Entom Soc Can; Int Orgn Biol Control; Acarol Soc Am; Soc Nematologists. **Research Statement & Publications:** Natural control of forest insects, especially bark beetles, by mites and nematodes; control of the pine wood nematode in wood products. **Mailing Address:** Southern Forest Exp Sta, 2500 Shreveport Hwy, Alexandria, LA 71360.

KINNAMON, KENNETH ELLIS, PHYSIOLOGY, RADIOBIOLOGY. **Personal Data:** b Denison, Tex, May 28, 1938; m 1957, c 3. **Education:** Okla State Univ, BS, 1956; Tex A&M Univ, DVM, 1959; Univ Rochester, MS, 1961; Univ Tenn, PhD (physiol), 1971. **Professional Experience:** PROF & DIR, CENTERS PREV MED & PUB HEALTH, UNIFORMED SERV UNIV HEALTH SCI, as of 2002; PROF PHYSIOL & ASSOC DEAN OPERS, UNIFORMED SERV UNIV HEALTH SCI, 1980-; assoc prof physiol & asst dean instrnl & res support, Uniformed Serv Univ Health Sci, 1975-1980; res investr biol, Med Dept, US Army Vet Sch, 1971-1975; chief dept surveillance inspection, Med Dept, US Army Vet Sch, 1965-1968; chief radioisotope lab, Army Nutrit Lab, Fitzsimons Gen Hosp, Colo, 1961-1965; res investr radiation chem, Walter Reed Army Inst Res, 1959-1960. **Memberships:** Radiation Res Soc; Am Physiol Soc; Health Physics Soc; Am Vet Med Asn; Soc Exp Hemat; Sigma Xi. **Research Statement & Publications:** Mineral metabolism; physiology of wound healing; bone marrow transplantation; secondary disease; immunology; cancer therapy; chemical radiation therapy; radiation injury therapy. **Mailing Address:** Ctr Prev Med & Pub Health, Uniformed Serv Univ Health Sci, 4301 Jones Bridge Rd, Bethesda, MD 20814. **E-Mail:** kkinnamon@usuhs.mil

KINNARD, MATTHEW ANDERSON, NEUROPHYSIOLOGY, DENTAL RESEARCH. **Personal Data:** b Nashville, Tenn, April 12, 1936; m 1962, c 2. **Education:** Tenn State Univ, BS, 1957, MA, 1960; Georgetown Univ, PhD (neurophysiol), 1970. **Professional Experience:** DIR, EXTRAMURAL ASSOC PROG, NAT INST CHILD HEALTH & HUMAN DEVELOP, NIH, as of 2004; physiologist, US Civil Serv Bd Examrs, beginning 1985; HEALTH SCI ADMINR, NAT INST DENT RES, NIH, BETHESDA, 1985-; adminr, health sci specialist, Cent Off, Vet Admin, 1979-1985; Physiol Dept, Howard Univ, 1979-1980; scientist, admin, Nat Inst Dent Res, NIH, Bethesda, 1972-1979; lectr, Univ DC, 1971-1979; asst prof physiol, DC Teachers Col, 1970-1971; consult, NIMH, 1968-1970; biologist, brain res, Nat Inst Dent Res, NIH, Bethesda, 1963-1967; biologist, virol res, Walter Reed Army Med Ctr, 1960-1962. **Memberships:** AAAS; Am Physiol Asn; Orgn Black Scientists; Int Asn Dent Res. **Research Statement & Publications:** Oral soft tissue diseases (oral cancer, herpes, and AIDS). **Mailing Address:** Nat Inst Child Health & Human Develop, NIH, 6100 Exec Blvd 5E03 MSC 7510, Rockville, MD 20892-7510. **Fax:** 301-480-0393. **E-Mail:** kinnardm@mail.nih.gov

KINNARD, WILLIAM J, HIGHER EDUCATION ADMINISTRATION. **Personal Data:** b Wilmington, Del, April 18, 1932; m 1959. **Education:** Univ Pittsburgh, BS, 1953, MS, 1955; Purdue Univ, PhD (pharmacol), 1957. **Honors & Awards:** Honor Achievement Award, Angiol Res Found, 1965. **Professional Experience:** RETIRED; actg assoc chancellor, Grad Sch, 1991-1997; actg pres, Grad Sch, 1990-1991; consult pharm, Surgeon Gen USAF, 1984-1990; dean, Grad Sch, 1976-1990; chmn bd trustees, US Pharmacopoeial Conv, 1974-1985; actg dean, Grad Sch, 1974-1976; prof pharmacol & dean, Sch Pharm, Univ Md, 1968-1990; from asst prof to prof pharmacol, Univ Pittsburgh, 1958-1968. **Memberships:** Inst Med-Nat Acad Sci; fel AAAS; Am Phys Soc; Am Pharmaceut Asn; Am Asn Pharmaceut Scientists; Am Asn Cols Pharm (pres, 1976-1977); Am Coun Pharm Educ (vpres, 1986-). **Research Statement & Publications:** Health care systems and education; higher education administration. **Mailing Address:** 4000 N Charles St, Baltimore, MD 21218.

KINNAVY, M(ARTIN) G(ERALD), MECHANICAL ENGINEERING, MECHANICS. **Personal Data:** b Chicago, Ill, November 20, 1921; m 1956, c 5. **Education:** Ill Inst Technol, BS, 1943, MS, 1952. **Professional Experience:** VPRES PROD DEVELOP, HERR-VOSS CORP, 1987-; VPRES ENG, HERR-VOSS CORP, 1976-; dir, Herr-voss Corp, 1970-1976; vpres, Herr Equip Corp, Ohio, 1968-1970; dir eng, Herr Equip Corp, Ohio, 1965-1968; assoc dir eng res dept, Continental Can Co, Inc, Ill, 1960-1965; assoc dir adv res dept, Sunbeam Corp, 1959-1960; supvr mechanisms anal & vibration eng, Ill Inst Technol Res Inst, 1952-1959; res engr, Ill Inst Technol Res Inst, 1950-1952; assoc engr, Ill Inst Technol Res Inst, 1949-1950; asst engr, Armour Res Found, Ill Inst Technol, 1948-1949; Proj engr, Fisher Body Detroit Div, Gen Motors Corp, 1943-1944. **Memberships:** Am Soc Mech Engrs; Am Soc Metals; Asn Iron & Steel Engrs. **Research Statement & Publications:** Dynamic behavior of mechanisms, linkages and structures; vibration analysis of artillery weapons; dynamics of space vehicles; methods of cam synthesis; mill equipment; tension leveling. **Mailing Address:** Herr-Voss Corp, Callery, PA 16024.

KINNEL, ROBIN BRYAN, ORGANIC CHEMISTRY. **Personal Data:** b Milwaukee, Wis, January 18, 1937; m 1960, Anne; c Timothy S & Geoffrey C. **Education:** Harvard Univ, AB, 1959; Mass Inst Technol, PhD (org chem), 1965. **Professional Experience:** Res assoc Univ Hawaii, 1999; vis prof, Univ Hawaii, 1990; SILAS D CHILDS PROF CHEM, HAMILTON COL, 1986-; chmn Dept, Hamilton Col, 1982-1998; res assoc, Univ Hawaii, 1981-1982, 1986, 1991-1992; vis prof, Univ Wis-Madison, 1979; res assoc, Cornell Univ, 1976-1977; assoc dean, Hamilton Col, 1973-1976; from asst prof to prof org chem, Hamilton Col, 1966-1978; res assoc org chem, Stanford Univ, 1964-1966; jr chemist, Merck, Sharp & Dohme, NJ, 1959-1960; asst chem, Hercules Powder Co, Del, 1956-1957. **Memberships:** Sigma Xi; AAAS; Am Chem Soc; Fedn Am Scientists; Union Concerned Scientists; Am Soc Pharmacog. **Research Statement & Publications:** Organic reaction mechanisms; medium ring chemistry; chemistry of marine natural products; synthetic organic and natural products chemistry. **Mailing Address:** Dept Chem, Hamilton Col, Chem 121 198 Col Hill Rd, Clinton, NY 13323. **Fax:** 315-859-4744. **E-Mail:** rkinnel@hamilton.edu

KINNEN, EDWIN, ELECTRICAL ENGINEERING. **Personal Data:** b Buffalo, NY, March 9, 1925; American citizen; m 1952, Ellen; c Susan, Janet, Peter & Andrew. **Education:** Univ Buffalo, BS, 1949; Yale Univ, ME, 1950; Purdue Univ, PhD, 1958. **Professional Experience:** Sr scientist, Univ Rochester, 1992-2000; PROF EMER ELEC ENG, UNIV ROCHESTER, 1992-; sci res fel, Paul Harris fel, 1990; chair, Univ Rochester, 1989-1992; sci res fel, Neth, 1978 & 1981; NIH spec fel, 1971; from assoc prof to prof, Univ Rochester, 1963-1992; asst prof elec eng, Purdue Univ, 1958-1959 & Univ Minn, 1959-1963; Westinghouse fel, 1955-1957; res engr, res lab, Westinghouse Elec Corp, 1950-1955; consult, Minneapolis-Honeywell, Wash Sci, Control Data Corp, Eastman Kodak. **Memberships:** Inst Elec & Electronics Engrs. **Research Statement & Publications:** Computer aided design for integrated circuits; pediatric orthoses; dynamics of blood flow; computer aided design for floorplanning, placement and routing of custom integrated circuits, based on methods of analytic optimizations; design and development of lower body orthoses for paraplegic children; Resonance, History of Electrical Engineering at the University of Rochester, 2003, Un of Rochester P. **Mailing Address:** Dept Elec Eng, Univ Rochester, Rochester, NY 14627. **Fax:** 585-275-2073. **E-Mail:** kinnen@ece.rochester.edu

KINNER, NANCY E, ENVIRONMENTAL ENGINEERING. **Education:** Univ NH, PhD, 1983. **Professional Experience:** PROF CIVIL ENG & ENVIRON ENG, UNIV NH, as of 2005; DIR, BEDROCK BIOREMEDIATION CTR, as of 2005; CO-DIR, COASTAL RESPONSE RES CTR, as of 2005. **Memberships:** Nat Acad Sci; Am Soc Civil Engrs; World Econ Forum; Asn Europ Econs Educ Description; Am Water Works Asn; Am Soc Metals; Asn Environ Eng & Sci Prof; Int Asn Water Qual. **Mailing Address:** Dept Civil Eng Univ NH, 236 Environ Technol Bldg 35 Coluvos Rd, Durham, NH 03824. **Fax:** 603-862-2364. **E-Mail:** nancy.kinner@unh.edu

KINNEY, ANTHONY JOHN, PROTEIN PURIFICATION, LIPIDOLOGY. **Personal Data:** b Ilkeston, Derbyshire, UK, September 9, 1958; m 1989, c Gabriel Isaak & Lukas Baldwin. **Education:** Sussex Univ, UK, BSc, 1980; Oxford Univ, UK, DPhil, 1985. **Professional Experience:** PRIN INVESTR, AGBIOTECH, DUPONT EXP STA, 1989-; res fel biochem & food sci, Rutgers Univ, 1987-1989; res assoc bot, La State Univ, 1983-1987; mem, Univ Col, Oxford, 1980-1983; res student, Agr & Food Res Coun, Letcombe Lab, 1980-1983. **Memberships:** Am Soc Biochem & Molecular Biol; Biochem Soc; NY Acad Sci; Sigma Xi. **Research Statement & Publications:** Biochemistry, molecular biology and genetics of membrane and storage lipid metabolism in plants and yeast; genetic engineering of crop plants; biotechnology of plant transformation. **Mailing Address:** Dupont Exp Sta, PO Box 80402, Wilmington, DE 19880-0402. **Fax:** 302-695-4296. **E-Mail:** anthony.kinney@usa.dupont.com

KINNEY, DOUGLAS MERRILL, geology, maps & illustrations; deceased, see previous edition for last biography

KINNEY, JOHN JAMES, SYMMETRIC FUNCTIONS IN STATISTICS, PROBABILITY. **Personal Data:** b Dansville, NY, August 2, 1932; m 1962, Cherry Carter; c Kaylyn. **Education:** St Lawrence Univ, BS, 1954; Harvard Univ, AMT, 1956; Univ Mich, MS, 1959; Iowa State Univ, PhD (statist), 1971. **Professional Experience:** PROF EMER OF MATH, ROSE-HULMAN INST TECH, 1999-; chair, Joint Comt on Curric in Probability & Statist, Am Statist Asn-Nat Coun Teachers Math, 1989-1991; dir, Ind Quant Literacy Proj, 1985-; prof math, Rose-Hulman Inst Technol, 1979-1999; assoc prof, Rose-Hulman Inst Technol, 1974-1979; asst prof, Univ Nebr, 1971-1974; Dupont fel, NSF Sci Fac, 1968; assoc prof, State Univ NY, Oneonta, 1964-1968; asst prof math, St Lawrence Univ, 1960-1964; Dupont fel, AmAsn Qual Control, 1958; Instr, St Lawrence Univ, 1955-1958; Dupont fel, Harvard Univ, 1954. **Memberships:** Am Statist Asn; Sigma Xi; Nat Counc Teachers Math; Am Soc Qual. **Research Statement & Publications:** Multivariate polykays; simulation in probability theory; author of one publication; Author, Probability-an introd with statist applications, John Wiley & Sons, 1997; author, statist for sci & eng, addison-Wesley, 2001. **Mailing Address:** 221 Highland Ct, Terre Haute, IN 47802-4957. **Fax:** 719-667-0270. **E-Mail:** skinney@attglobal.net

KINNEY, JOHN MARTIN, SURGERY. **Personal Data:** b Evanston, Ill, May 24, 1921; m 1944, c 3. **Education:** Denison Univ, AB, 1943; Harvard Univ, MD, 1946; Am Bd Surg, dipl; Am Bd Nutrit, dipl. **Honors & Awards:** New York Health Res Coun Career Scientist Award, 1965. **Professional Experience:** Vis prof, Rockfeller Univ, as of 2004; PROF EMER SURG, COLUMBIA UNIV, as of 1996; chmn comt shock, Comn Emergency Med Serv, Nat Res Coun, 1969; mem adv panel to comt on interplay eng with biol & med, Nat Acad Eng, 1968; prof surg, Col Physicians & Surgeons, Columbia Univ, beginning 1967; attend surgeon, Presby Hosp, beginning 1967; mem adv comt metabolism trauma, US Army Med Res & Develop Command, 1967; DIR SURG METAB, PRESBY HOSP, 1963-; assoc prof, 1963-1967; assoc attend surgeon, Presby Hosp, 1963-1967; jr assoc surgeon, Peter Bent Brigham Hosp, 1958-1963; Henry E Warren fel surg, Harvard Med Sch, 1958-1960 & 1962-1963; Mead Johnson scholar, Am Col Surgeons, 1956-1959; from asst resident surgeon to chief resident surgeon, Peter Bent Brigham Hosp, 1952-1957; AEC-Nat Res Coun fel, Med Sch, Univ Colo, 1949-1952; surg intern, Peter Bent Brigham Hosp, 1946-1947. **Memberships:** Am Burn Asn; Am Asn Surg Trauma; Soc Univ Surg; fel Am Col Surgeons; Am Surg Asn. **Research Statement & Publications:** Metabolic response to injury, burns, shock and peritonitis; gas exchange; calorimetry; energy balance; intensive care; patient monitoring; surgical nutrition. **Mailing Address:** Dept Surg, Columbia Univ, 41 Maple Ave Apt 3A, Hastings on Hudson, NY 10706. **Fax:** 914-478-5015. **E-Mail:** johnmkinney@aol.com

KINNEY, LARRY LEE, ELECTRICAL ENGINEERING. **Personal Data:** b Salem, Iowa, October 26, 1941; m 1962, c 2. **Education:** Univ Iowa, BS, 1964, MS, 1965, PhD (elec eng), 1968. **Professional Experience:** PROF ELEC & COMPUT ENG, UNIV MINN, MINNEAPOLIS, 1968-; asst prof elec eng, Univ Iowa, 1968. **Memberships:** Inst Elec & Electronics Engrs; Asn Comput Mach. **Research Statement & Publications:** Switching theory; computer systems. **Mailing Address:** Dept Elec Eng, Univ Minn 200 Union St SE, Minneapolis, MN 55455. **E-Mail:** kinney@ece.umn.edu

KINNEY, MICHAEL J, INTERNAL MEDICINE, NEPHROLOGY. **Personal Data:** b Chicago, Ill, July 9, 1937; m 1971, c 6. **Education:** Univ Chicago, BS, 1959, MD, 1963. **Professional Experience:** MED DIR, FLA MED CARE CLIN, 1989-; med dir, Nephrol Res & Educ Found, 1980-1982; assoc prof med & chief nephrology sect, Marshall Univ, Sch Med, 1978-1980; asst prof, State Univ NY, Downstate Med Ctr, 1977-1978; assoc chief, Renal Div Nephrol, US Pub Health Serv Hosp, 1969-1978. **Memberships:** Fel Am Col Physicians; fel Am Col Clin Pharmacol; Am Soc Nephrology; Soc Exp Biol & Med; Am

Physiol Soc. **Research Statement & Publications:** Hypertension; nuclear medicine. **Mailing Address:** Fla Med Care Clin, 333 S Tamiami Trail Ste 395, Venice, FL 34285.

KINNEY, RALPH A, ELECTRICAL ENGINEERING. **Personal Data:** b Frostproof, Fla, November 7, 1930; m 1960, c 3. **Education:** Univ Fla, BEE, 1956, MSE, 1958, PhD (elec eng), 1967. **Professional Experience:** JOHN E & BeEATRICE L. RITTER PROF EMER ELEC ENG, LA STATE UNIV, BATON ROUGE, as of 2001; prof elec eng, La State Univ, Baton Rouge, beginning 1976; assoc prof elec eng, LA State Univ, Baton Rouge, 1967-1976; asst res elec eng & aerospace, Univ Fla, 1964-1967; scientist, Northrop Space Labs, Calif, 1960-1962; Res asst elec eng, Univ Fla, 1957-1960. **Memberships:** Inst Elec & Electronics Engrs. **Research Statement & Publications:** Wave phenomena in homogeneous media; induction heating; computer applications; field theory. **Mailing Address:** Dept Elec Eng, La State Univ, Baton Rouge, LA 70803. **E-Mail:** kinney@ee.lsu.edu

KINNEY, ROBERT BRUCE, MECHANICAL ENGINEERING. **Personal Data:** b Joplin, Mo, July 20, 1937; m 1961, Carol; c Rodney M, David S & Linda G. **Education:** Univ Calif, Berkeley, BS, 1959, MS, 1961; Univ Minn, Minneapolis, PhD (mech eng), 1965. **Professional Experience:** PROF EMER AEROSPACE & MECH ENG, UNIV ARIZ, as of 2003; vis prof, US Mil Acad, West Point, NY, 1984; assoc head, Univ Ariz, 1981-1984; Alexander von Humboldt Found vis scientist, Ger, 1976; assoc tech ed, J Heat Transfer, Am Soc Mech Engrs, 1973-1976; from assoc prof to prof aerospace & mech eng, Univ Ariz, 1968-1987; sr res engr, United Aircraft Res Labs, 1965-1968. **Memberships:** Am Soc Mech Engrs. **Research Statement & Publications:** Energy transport in gases and liquids; dynamics of fluid flow, including unsteady viscous aerodynamics; fluid flow analogies and experimental methods. **Mailing Address:** 456 22nd Ave SE, St Petersburg, FL 33705.

KINNEY, TERRY B, POPULATION GENETICS. **Personal Data:** b Norfolk, Mass, September 12, 1925; m 1946, c 2. **Education:** Univ Mass, BS, 1955, MS, 1956; Univ Minn, PhD, 1963. **Professional Experience:** RETIRED; adminr, Sci & Educ Admin-Agr Res, 1980-1988; assoc adminr, NCent Region, 1978-1980; asst adminr livestock vet sci, NCent Region, 1974-1978; assoc dept adminr, NCent Region, 1972-1974; asst dir, Animal Sci Res Div, USDA, 1969-1972; res geneticist, Ind, 1965-1969; biometrician, USDA, Md, 1963-1965; instr poultry, Univ Minn, 1957-1962; geneticist, Hubbard Farms Inc, NH, 1956-1957; res asst poultry, Univ Mass, 1955-1956. **Memberships:** Poultry Sci Asn; Sigma Xi. **Research Statement & Publications:** Statistics; population genetic studies; administration of research relating to livestock and veterinary sciences. **Mailing Address:** 4480 Partridge Pl, York, SC 29745.

KINNIE, IRVIN GRAY, COMPUTER SYSTEM DESIGN. **Personal Data:** b Orlando, Fla, April 28, 1932; m 1968. **Education:** US Mil Acad, BS, 1953; Univ Ariz, MS, 1960. **Professional Experience:** COMPUT ARCHITECT, PC TECHNOL FORECASTING, IBM CORP, 1988-; comput architect, Entry Systs Div, 1986-1988; nationwide network design, Entry Systs Div, 1982-1986; engr, comput systs design, command & space systs, Fed Systs Div, 1981-1982; engr command, control & commun archit, 1980-1981; engr solar eng, IBM Corp, 1978-1980; engr mkt develop, IBM Corp, 1977-1978; engr software res, IBM Corp, 1976-1977; syst analyst & engr tech planning, IBM Corp, 1974-1976; dep dir res & develop, USArmy Comput Systs Command, 1973-1974; chief info sci, US Army Res & Develop Group, London, 1969-1973; chief plans & opers, US Army Regional Commun Group, Saigon, 1968-1969; standards specialist, Mallard Proj, Ft Monmouth, NJ, 1967-1968; EDP specialist info sci, Allied Mil Commun Electronics Agency, Paris, 1965-1967; asst prof eng & info sci, US Mil Acad, 1961-1965; area signal officer, Longlines Signal Battalion Pusan, Korea, 1960-1961; Res officer, E W Div, Army Proving Ground, Ariz, 1956-1958. **Memberships:** Asn Comput Mach; Inst Elec & Electronics Engrs; Armed Forces Comn Electronics Asn. **Research Statement & Publications:** Communications; electronics and information sciences; software engineering; computer systems architecture. **Mailing Address:** 10 Sugar Pine Lane, Hilton Head Island, SC 29926.

KINNISON, GERALD LEE, PHYSIOLOGY. **Personal Data:** b San Diego, Calif, July 16, 1931; m 1989, c Dana S, Susan K (Christiansen), Mark L & Leanne K (Peterson). **Education:** Univ Calif, Los Angeles, BS, 1958, MS, 1960, PhD (physics), 1963. **Honors & Awards:** Arthur S Fleming Award, 1968. **Professional Experience:** RETIRED; master ASW study group, Chief Naval Opers, beginning 1984; res physicist, Electronics Lab, Ocean Systs Ctr, USN, 1977-1995; Sonar adv panel, Navsea Explor Develop Panel, Passive Sonar, 1967-1986; res physicist, Undersea Ctr, 1967-1977; res physicist, Electronics Lab, Ocean Systs Ctr, USN, 1963-1967; postdoctoral fel physics, Univ London, 1963-1964. **Memberships:** Acoust Soc Am; Am Physics Teachers Soc. **Research Statement & Publications:** Passive sonar arrays design, instrumentation, beamforming that is conventional and optimal, signal processing, display and performance prediction in various environmental noises like predicted and measured; granted one patent. **Mailing Address:** 3274 Trumbull St, San Diego, CA 92106-2421.

KINNISON, ROBERT RAY, EXTREME VALUE & GEOGRAPHICAL STATISTICS, QUALITY ASSURANCE. **Personal Data:** b Los Angeles, Calif, September 10, 1934; m 1959, Karen; c 2. **Education:** Pomona Col, BA, 1956; Univ Calif Los Angeles, PhD (statist), 1971. **Professional Experience:** RETIRED; prin statistician, Bechtel Nev Corp, 1989-2002; mem, Desert Res Inst, 1985-1989; mem, Battelle Pac NW Lab, 1979-1985; assoc ed, J Simulation, beginning 1972; US Environ Protection Agency, Las Vegas, 1972-1979; statistician, Univ Calif San Francisco, 1971-1972; pharmacologist, Rexall Drug & Chem Co, 1960-1968. **Memberships:** Am Statist Asn; Biomet Soc; AAAS; Sigma Xi. **Research Statement & Publications:** Extreme value statistics; bioassay statistics; exposure-dose assessment statistics for environmental pollutants; spatial and geographic statistics; quality assurance statistics. **Mailing Address:** 846 E Pescados Dr, Las Vegas, NV 89123-1359.

KINNMARK, INGEMAR PER ERLAND, NUMERICAL METHODS OF DIFFERENTIAL EQUATIONS, SCIENTIFIC & TECHNICAL TRANSLATION. **Personal Data:** b Sundbyberg, Sweden, December 8, 1953; c Elizabeth Solvig. **Education:** Royal Inst Technol, MS, 1979; Princeton Univ, MA, 1982, PhD (water resources), 1984. **Professional Experience:** Asst prof hydraul & numerical methods, Univ Notre Dame, 1986-1989; FREELANCER, RES MATHEMATICIAN & SWEDISH SCI & TECHNICAL TRANSLR, 1984-; res assoc, Univ Notre Dome, 1984-1986; Wallace Mem Hon fel, Princeton Univ, 1983. **Memberships:** Sr mem Am Translatr Asn; sr mem Swedish Asn Prof Translr; sr mem Soc Indust & Appl Math. **Research Statement & Publications:** Mathematical modeling of flow in shallow seas, estuaries and rivers; design, analysis and application of numerical methods for the solution of ordinary and partial differential equations. **Mailing Address:** 107 High Ave Apt 207, Nyack, NY 10960. **Fax:** 530-323-9433.

KINO, GORDON STANLEY, ELECTRICAL ENGINEERING, ACOUSTICS. **Personal Data:** b Melbourne, Australia, June 15, 1928; American citizen; m 1957, c 1. **Education:** Univ London, BSc, 1948, MSc, 1950; Stanford Univ, PhD (elec eng), 1955. **Honors & Awards:** Centennial Medal, Inst Elec & Electronics Engrs, 1984, Sonics & Ultrasonics Group Achievement, 1984. **Professional Experience:** WM KECK FOUNDATION EMER PROF ELEC ENG, as of 2003; dir, Ginzton Lab, 1994-1996; assoc dean planning & facil, Elec Eng Dept, 1987-1992; assoc chmn, Elec Eng Dept, 1985-1988; EMER PROF APPL PHYSICS, STANFORD UNIV, 1976-; Guggenheim fel, 1967-1968; Wm keck prof elec eng, stanford Univ, 1965; assoc prof, Stanford Univ, 1961-1965; Consult, Varian, Tex Instruments, Lockheed Aircraft Corp & Advan Res Projs Agency, beginning 1957; res assoc, Stanford Univ, 1957-1961; mem tech staff, Bell Tel Labs, NJ, 1955-1957; res assoc, Microwave Lab, 1955; res asst, Electronics Res Lab, Stanford Univ, 1951-1955; jr scientist, Mullard Radio Valve Co, Eng, 1947-1951. **Memberships:** Nat Acad Eng; fel Inst Elec & Electronics Engrs; fel Am Phys Soc; fel AAAS. **Research Statement & Publications:** Electromagnetic theory; design of electron and ion guns; wave propagation in plasmas; microwave tubes; microwave acoustics; acoustic imaging; non-destructive testing; waves in solids; author of more than 460 technical publications; fiber optics, optical microscopy. **Mailing Address:** Ginzton Lab Rm 9, Stanford Univ, Stanford, CA 94305-4088. **E-Mail:** kino@ee.stanford.edu

KINOSHITA, FLORENCE KEIKO, TOXICOLOGY, PHARMACOLOGY. **Personal Data:** b Salem, Ore, August 6, 1941. **Education:** Univ Chicago, BS, 1963, MS, 1966, PhD (pharmacol), 1969; Am Bd Toxicol, dipl. **Professional Experience:** Mem, commt on Toxicol Nat Acad of Sci, 1997-2000; PRIN, TOXICOL SCI, HERCULES INC, 1997-; toxicol scientist, Hercules, Inc, 1991-1997; AFFIL ASST PROF, DEPT PHARMACOL & TOXICOL, MED COL VA, 1984-; mem, Toxicol Data Bank Peer Rev Comt, Nat Libr Med, 1983-1985; mem, Toxicol Study Sect, NIH, 1979-1983; sr toxicologist, Hercules, Inc, 1978-1991; tech mgr toxicol, Indust Bio-Test Labs, Inc, 1974-1977; toxicologist, Indust Bio-Test Labs, Inc, 1973-1974; consult, US Fed Drug Admin, 1972-1973; consult, US Environ Protection Agency, 1971-1972; from instr to asst prof pharmacol, Univ Chicago, 1969-1973. **Memberships:** Soc Toxicol; Am Indust Hyg Asn; Soc Exp Biol & Med; Am col of Toxicol soc of Environm Chem & Toxicol; soc of Sigma Xi. **Research Statement & Publications:** Interactions of drugs, pesticides and chemicals as inducers of hepatic microsomal enzyme systems; effects of organophosphorus compounds on cholinestrase and aliesterases; development of hepatic microsomal enzymes in fetal and neonatal animals. **Mailing Address:** Hercules Inc, 1313 N Market St, Wilmington, DE 19894.

KINOSHITA, JIN HAROLD, BIOLOGICAL CHEMISTRY, OPHTHALMIC RESEARCH. **Personal Data:** b San Francisco, Calif, July 21, 1922; m 1948. **Education:** Columbia Univ, AB, 1944; Harvard Univ, PhD, 1952. **Honorary Degrees:** ScD, Bard Col, 1967, Oakland Univ, 1980. **Honors & Awards:** Friedenwald Award, Asn Res Vision & Ophthal, 1965, Proctor Medal, 1974. **Professional Experience:** CLIN PROF OPHTHAL, UNIV CALIF, DAVIS, as of 2001; sci dir, Lab Vision Res, Nat Eye Inst, 1981-1990; chief, Lab Vision Res, Nat Eye Inst, 1971-1981; mem visual sci study sect, NIH, 1965-1969; from assoc prof to prof biochem ophthal, Harvard Med Sch, 1964-1973; Biochemist, Mass Eye & Ear Infirmary, 1955-1973; from instr to asst prof biochem, Harvard Med Sch, 1952-1964; Asst chem, Bard Col, 1944-1946. **Memberships:** AAAS; Am Chem Soc; Am Soc Biol Chemists; Asn Res Vision & Ophthal. **Research Statement & Publications:** Chemistry and metabolism of ocular tissues. **Mailing Address:** 44269 Clubhouse Dr, El Macero, CA 95618. **Fax:** 530-753-1656.

KINOSHITA, KAY, PHYSICS. **Personal Data:** b Princeton, NJ, July 17, 1954; m 1989, Alan. **Education:** Harvard Univ, AB & AM, 1976; Univ Calif, Berkeley, PhD (physics), 1981. **Professional Experience:** PROF PHYSICS, UNIV CINCINNATI, 1998-; prof, Va Polytechnic Inst & State Univ, 1993-1998; sci scholar, Mary Ingraham Bunting Inst, 1985-1987; from asst prof to assoc prof physics, Harvard Univ, 1984-1993; res assoc, Harvard Univ, 1982-1984. **Memberships:** Am Phys Soc; Asn Women Sci. **Research Statement & Publications:** Elementary particle physics; weak interactions of heavy quarks; exotic heavily ionizing particles. **Mailing Address:** Dept Physics, Univ Cincinnati, Rm 413, Cincinnati, OH 45221. **Fax:** 513-556-3425. **E-Mail:** kayk@physics.uc.edu

KINOSHITA, KIMIO, ELECTROCHEMISTRY. **Personal Data:** b Vancouver, BC, August 5, 1942; m 1965, c 2. **Education:** Univ Alta, BSc, 1964; Univ Calif, Berkeley, PhD (chem), 1969. **Professional Experience:** INVESTR, LAWRENCE BERKELEY NAT LAB, UNIV CALIF, as of 1996; MEM STAFF, SRI INT, 1979-; mem staff, Chem Eng Div, Argonne Nat Lab, 1976-1979; Sr res assoc phys chem, Mat Eng Res Lab, Pratt & Whitney Aircraft, 1969-1976. **Memberships:** Am Chem Soc; Electrochem Soc; Am Carbon Soc. **Research Statement & Publications:** Corrosion; electrochemistry; carbon chemistry; catalysis. **Mailing Address:** Lawrence Berkeley Nat Lab, Univ Calif, One Cyclotron Rd MS 90-1142, Berkeley, CA 94720. **E-Mail:** k_kinoshita@lbl.gov

KINOSHITA, SHIN'ICHI, TOPOLOGY. **Personal Data:** b Osaka, Japan, June 5, 1925; m 1954, c 4. **Education:** Osaka Univ, BS, 1948, PhD (math), 1958. **Professional Experience:** PROF, FAC SCI, KWANSEI GAKUIN UNIV, JAPAN; from assoc prof to prof, Fla State Univ, 1964-1984; asst prof, Univ Sask, 1962-1964; res assoc, Princeton Univ, 1961-1962; vis mem, Inst Advan Study, 1959-1961; lectr math, North Col, Osaka Univ, 1958-1959. **Memberships:** Am Math Soc; Math Soc Japan; Sigma Xi. **Research Statement & Publications:** Topological transformations; knot theory and its applications, fundamental group phenomena. **Mailing Address:** Kwansei Gakuin Univ, Nishinomiya 662, Japan.

KINOSHITA, TOICHIRO, THEORETICAL HIGH ENERGY PHYSICS. **Personal Data:** b Tokyo, Japan, January 23, 1925; American citizen; m 1951, Magsako; c Kay, June & Ray. **Education:** Univ Tokyo, BS, 1947, PhD (physics), 1952. **Honors & Awards:** J J Sakurai Prize, Am Phys Soc, 1990; SUN-AMCO Medal, Int Union Pure & Appl Physics, 1998. **Professional Experience:** GOLDWIN SMITH EMER PROF THEORET PHYSICS, CORNELL UNIV, 1995-; comt fundamental constants, Nat Res Coun, 1984-1986; tech adv panel univ progs, Dept Energy, 1982-1983; Guggenheim Found fel, 1973-1974; Ford fel, Europ Orgn Nuclear Res, Geneva, Switz, 1962-1963; from asst prof to prof, Cornell Univ, 1958-1995; res assoc, Cornell Univ, 1955-1958; fel theoret physics, Columbia Univ, 1954-1955; mem, Inst Adv Study, Princeton, NJ, 1952-1954. **Memberships:** Nat Acad Sci; fel AAAS; fel Am Phys Soc. **Research Statement & Publications:** Quantum field theory; quantum theory of atoms; elementary particles; symmetry law; high precision determinaton fundamental physical constants. **Mailing Address:** Cornell Univ, 310 Newman Lab, Ithaca, NY 14853-5001. **E-Mail:** tk@hepth.cornell.edu

KINRA, VIKRAM KUMAR, ENGINEERING MECHANICS, MATERIALS SCIENCE. **Personal Data:** b Lyallpur, India, April 3, 1946; m 1988, c 1. **Education:** Indian Inst Technol, Kanpur, BTech, 1967; Utah State Univ, MS, 1968; Brown Univ, PhD (eng mech), 1975. **Honors & Awards:** Dow Outstanding Young Fac Award, 1980; Ralph R Teeter Award, 1982. **Professional Experience:** DIRECTOR, CTR MECH COMPOSITES, TEX A&M UNIV, 1995-1999; GENERAL DYNAMICS PROF AEROSPACE ENG, TEX A&M UNIV, 1995-; consult, Martin-Marietta Corp, 1988; Halliburton prof, 1986; assoc prof, Ctr Mech Composites, Tex A&M Univ, 1982-1989; consult, Ponderosa Asn, Louisville, 1980; consult, Corning Glass, 1980; prin investr & proj dir, NSF grants, Univ Colo, Boulder, 1976-1981; consult, Willow Water Dist, Denver, 1976-1977; asst prof, Univ Colo, Boulder, 1975-1982;

asst & res assoc, Brown Univ, 1971-1975; proj engr mech eng, Ostgaard & Assocs, Inc, Gardena, 1970-1971; struct eng stress anal, Northrop Corp, Hawthorne, 1968-1970; prin investr & proj dir, Off Naval Res, Air Force Off Sci Res, Tex Adv Tech Prog grants, NASA grants, IBM grant & Martin-Marietta grant. **Memberships:** Soc Exp Mech; Am Acad Mech; Am Soc Eng Educ; Am Soc Mech Engrs; Sigma Xi; Acoust Soc Am. **Research Statement & Publications:** Damping; wave propagation; nondestructive testing and evaluation; composite materials; ultrasonics. **Mailing Address:** Dept Aerospace Eng, Tex A&M Univ, 739 H R Bright Bldg, College Station, TX 77843-3141. **Fax:** 979-845-6051. **E-Mail:** kinra@tamu.edu

KINRAIDE, THOMAS B, PLANT PHYSIOLOGY. **Education:** Univ Montana, PhD. **Professional Experience:** PLANT PHYSIOLOGIST, USDA, AGR RES SERV, 1981-; res assoc, Univ Vt, 1978-1981; asst prof, Colo Col, 1971-1978. **Mailing Address:** USDA Agr Res Serv, 1224 Airport Rd, Beaver, WV 25813-9423. **Fax:** 304-256-2921. **E-Mail:** tom.kinraide@ars.usda.gov

KINSBOURNE, MARCEL, PEDIATRIC NEUROLOGY, EXPERIMENTAL PSYCHOLOGY. **Personal Data:** b Vienna, Austria, November 3, 1931; m 1965, c David, Daniel, Jeremy & Emily. **Education:** Oxford Univ, BA, 1952, MD, 1955, MA, 1956, DM(neuropsychol), 1963. **Honors & Awards:** Queen Square Prize neurol, 1961; J Arthur lectr, 1974. **Professional Experience:** PROF PSYCHOL, NEW SCH UNIV, 1995-; res prof cognitive studies, Tufts Univ, beginning 1991; consult neurologist, Boston Vet Admin Med Ctr, 1989-; adj prof cognitive sci, Brandeis Univ, 1983-; lectr neurol, Harvard Med Sch, 1980-1991; dir, Behav Neurol Dept, Eunice Kennedy Shriver Ctr, 1980-1991; prof psychol, Univ Toronto, 1975-1980; sr staff physician, Hosp Sick Children, Toronto, 1974-1980; prof pediat, Univ Toronto, 1974-1980; prof psychol, Univ Waterloo, 1974-1979; assoc prof pediat & neurol & lectr psychol, Med Ctr, Duke Univ, 1967-1974; fel, New Col, Oxford Univ, 1965-1967; lectr psychol, Oxford Univ, 1964-1967. **Memberships:** Fel Am Psychol Asn; Am Neurol Asn; fel Geront Soc; Int Neuropsychol Soc; Psychonomic Soc; Child Neurol Soc. **Research Statement & Publications:** Human neuropsychology; developmental psychology; visual information processing; age-related changes in behavior. **Mailing Address:** Dept Psychol, New Sch Univ, Rm 342 65 Fifth Ave, New York, NY 10003. **Fax:** 212-989-0846. **E-Mail:** kinsboum@newschool.edu

KINSEL, JANE F, MICROBIOLOGY. **Education:** Univ Del, BS; Univ Kans, MS, PhD (pharmaceut chem); Wharton Sch, MBA. **Professional Experience:** DIR, OFF RES ADMIN BOSTON UNIV MED CAMPUS, as of 2006. **Mailing Address:** Boston Univ Med Campus, 715 Albany St 560-5th Floor, Boston, MA 02118.

KINSEL, NORMA ANN, MICROBIOLOGY. **Personal Data:** b Boston, Mass, February 26, 1929. **Education:** Univ Va, BS, 1949; Pittsburgh Univ, MS, 1952, PhD (bact), 1959. **Professional Experience:** SR MICROBIOLOGIST, ELI LILLY & CO, 1974-; res biologist, Gulf Res & Develop Co, 1969-1973; fel petrol, microbiol & micros sect, 1963-1969; USPHS res fel, Rutgers Univ, 1962-1963; assoc microbiologist, microbiol & micros sect, 1956-1962; asst, microbiol & micros sect, 1953-1956; Asst fel yeast chem, Mellon Inst, 1952-1953. **Memberships:** AAAS; Am Soc Microbiol; Soc Indust Microbiol. **Research Statement & Publications:** Autotrophic iron and sulfur bacteria; petroleum microbiology; antibiotic fermentation technology. **Mailing Address:** 5258 Whisperwood Lane, Indianapolis, IN 46226.

KINSELLA, B THERESE, MEDICAL RESEARCH. **Education:** Univ Col Cork, BSc, 1981, PhD (biochem), 1985. **Professional Experience:** ASSOC PROF BIOCHEM, UNIV COL DUBLIN, 2005-; SR LECTR, DEPT BIOCHEM, UNIV COL DUBLIN, as of 2005. **Mailing Address:** Univ Col Dublin Sch Biomolecular & Biomed Sci, Belfield, Ireland. **Fax:** 353-1-283-7211. **E-Mail:** therese.kinsella@ucd.ie

KINSELLA, JAMES L, PHARMACOLOGY. **Personal Data:** b Oneida, NY, March 9, 1950. **Education:** Alfred Univ, BS, 1972; Syracuse Univ, PhD (pharmacol), 1978. **Honors & Awards:** Res Develop Award, US Fed Govt, 1994. **Professional Experience:** Res chemist pharmacol, Geront Res Ctr, Nat Inst Aging, 1988-2003; sr staff fel, 1983-1988. **Memberships:** AAAS; NY Acad Sci; Am Soc Biochem & Molecular Biol. **Mailing Address:** Geront Res Ctr Nat Inst Aging, NIH 4940 Eastern Ave, Baltimore, MD 21224-2735. **Fax:** 410-558-8150.

KINSELLA, JOHN J, PHYSICS, SEMICONDUCTORS. **Personal Data:** b Seneca Falls, NY, October 15, 1926; m 1949, Lucille Taylor; c Susan, Daniel, Timothy, Thomas, Patricia, Elizabeth, James & Christopher. **Education:** Univ Tex, BA, 1949; Syracuse Univ, MS, 1953. **Professional Experience:** CONSULT, RAVEN CONSULT, 1986-; from physicist to sr physicist, strategic planning Corp Planning Consumables & Supplies, 1981-1986; mem res & eng tech staff, Xerox Corp, 1978-1981; mfg prog mgt, Xerox Corp, 1973-1978; mgr advan mfg eng, Xerox Corp, 1970-1973; mgr xerographic consumables mfg, Xerox Corp, 1968-1970; mgr photoreceptor technol, Xerox Corp, 1965-1968; res mgr, Xerox Corp, 1962-1965; Scientist, Xerox Corp, 1959-1962; from physicist to sr physicist, Xerox Corp, 1956-1959; Res physicist, Consol Vacuum Corp Div, Bell & Howell, 1951-1956. **Memberships:** Am Vacuum Soc; Inst Elec & Electronics Engrs; Optical Soc Am; Soc Photog Sci & Eng. **Research Statement & Publications:** Vacuum pump and gauge design development; thin film microcircuit, resistors and capacitors; evaporated silver bromide research; xerographic photoconductors. **Mailing Address:** 2846 St Paul Blvd, Rochester, NY 14617. **Fax:** 585-266-2142. **E-Mail:** jackk2846@aol.com

KINSELLA, RALPH A, JR, internal medicine; deceased, see previous edition for last biography

KINSER, DONALD LEROY, MATERIALS SCIENCE, ENGINEERING. **Personal Data:** b Loudon, Tenn, September 28, 1941; m 1961, Barbara; c Elizabeth & Cynthia. **Education:** Univ Fla, BS, 1964, PhD (mat sci), 1968. **Professional Experience:** PROF EMER, MECH ENG & MAT SCI ENG, VANDERBILT UNIV, as of 2003; Co-ed, J Non Crystalline Solids, beginning 1988; prof mat sci & mech eng, vanderbilt Univ, beginning 1975; from asst prof to assoc prof ceramic eng, Vanderbilt Univ, 1968-1975. **Memberships:** Am Ceramic Soc; Am Soc Metals; Am Inst Mining Metall & Petrol Engrs; Soc Glass Technol UK; Mat Res Soc; AAAS. **Research Statement & Publications:** Electrical behavior of two-phase alkali-silicate glasses; semiconducting glasses; mechanical properties of glasses; electrical behavior of glasses; radiation damage and mechanical properties of materials. **Mailing Address:** Dept Mech Eng, Vanderbilt Univ, Sch Eng, 610 Olin Hall VU Station B 351592, Nashville, TN 37235-1592. **Fax:** 615-343-8645. **E-Mail:** donald.l.kinser@vanderbilt.edu

KINSEY, BARRY A, CRIMINOLOGY, SOCIOLOGY. **Education:** Univ Nebr, PhD. **Professional Experience:** PROF EMER, UNIV TULSA, as of 2005. **Mailing Address:** Univ Tulsa, Chapman Hall 220, Tulsa, OK 74104. **Fax:** 918-631-2057. **E-Mail:** barry-kinsey@utulsa.edu

KINSEY, DAVID WEBSTER, MATHEMATICS. **Personal Data:** b Warsaw, Ind, March 11, 1939; m 1961, c 2. **Education:** Manchester Col, BA, 1961; Univ Ariz, MS, 1964; Ind Univ, PhD (math), 1972. **Professional Experience:** ASSOC PROF MATH, UNIV SOUTHERN IND, EVANSVILLE, 1972-; Instr math, Millikin Univ, 1964-1968; Instr math, Carthage Col, 1963-1964. **Memberships:** Math Asn Am; Nat Coun Teachers Math; Am Math Soc. **Mailing Address:** Dept Math, Univ Southern Ind, 8600 Univ Blvd SC 3261, Evansville, IN 47712-3596. **E-Mail:** dkinsey@usi.edu

KINSEY, JAMES HUMPHREYS, APPLIED PHYSICS. **Personal Data:** b Xenia, Ohio, June 6, 1932. **Education:** Princeton Univ, AB, 1960; Univ Md, Col Park, PhD (physics), 1970. **Professional Experience:** SR SCIENTIST, APPL RES CORP, 1988-; advan projs physicist, space telescope sci Inst, 1982-1988; asst prof biophys, 1979-1982; assoc consult, Mayo Clinic, 1976-1982; consult, Control Data Corp, 1974-1976; lectr, Princeton Univ, 1973-1974; mem res staff x-ray diffraction, Princeton Univ, 1971-1973; aerospace technologist, NASA, 1968-1971. **Memberships:** Am Phys Soc; Am Astron Soc; Am Geophys Union; Sigma Xi; Inst Elec & Electronics Engrs; Biomed Eng Soc; Optical Soc Am. **Research Statement & Publications:** Optical aurora; low energy cosmic rays and energetic solar particles; x-ray diffraction studies of large biological molecules; computer analysis of radiographs; x-ray and optical detector systems for biomedical imaging computer tomography; photo therapy of cancer; imaging instrumentation. **Mailing Address:** Appl Res Corp, 8201 Corporate Dr, Landover, MD 20785. **Fax:** 301-731-0765.

KINSEY, JAMES LLOYD, PHYSICAL CHEMISTRY. **Personal Data:** b Paris, Tex, October 15, 1934; m 1962, Berma; c 3. **Education:** Rice Univ, BA, 1956, PhD (chem), 1959. **Honors & Awards:** E O Lawrence Award, US Dept Energy, 1987; Nobel Laureate Signature Award, Am Chem Soc, 1990; Earle K Plyler Award, Am Phys Soc, 1995. **Professional Experience:** D R BULLARD WELCH FOUND PROF SCI & PROF CHEM, RICE UNIV, as of 2003; interim provost, Rice Univ, 1993-1994; dean nat sci, Rice Univ, 1988-1998; mem, Am Phys Soc, Div Chem, Phys Exec Comn, 1986-1989; chmn, Am Chem Soc, Div Physics & Chemistry, 1985; co-chmn, Bd Chem Sci & Technol, Nat Acad Sci-Nat Res Coun, 1982-1983; mem, Adv Comt, Army Res Off-Nat Res Coun, 1981-1986; assoc ed, J Chem Physics, 1981-1984; mem, Bd Chem Sci & Technol, Nat Acad Sci-Nat Res Coun, 1980-1983; chmn dept, Mass Inst Technol, 1977-1982; consult, Los Alamos Nat Lab, 1974-1992; prof chem, Mass Inst Technol, 1974-1984; Guggenheim fel, 1969-1970; vis assoc prof, Univ Wis, 1969-1970; Alfred P Sloan res fel, 1963-1967; from asst prof to assoc prof, Mass Inst Technol, 1962-1974; Miller res fel, Univ Calif, Berkeley, 1960-1962; NSF fel, Univ Uppsala, 1959-1960. **Memberships:** Nat Acad Sci; Am Chem Soc; Sigma Xi; fel Am Acad Arts & Sci; fel AAAS; fel Am Phys Soc. **Research Statement & Publications:** Chemical dynamics; spectroscopy; lasers; theoretical chemistry. **Mailing Address:** Dept Chem, Rice Univ, MS-600 PO Box 1892, Houston, TX 77251. **Fax:** 713-348-5401. **E-Mail:** jlkinsey@rice.edu

KINSEY, JOHN AARON, GENETICS. **Personal Data:** b Panama City, Fla, March 12, 1939; m 1962. **Education:** Fla State Univ, BS, 1961; Univ Tex, PhD (zoology), 1965. **Professional Experience:** PROF & DIR FUNGAL GENETIC STOCK CTR, MED CTR, UNIV KANS, as of 2006; from asst prof to assoc prof, microbiol, Univ kans, 1967-1980; NIH res fel genetics, Univ Wash, 1965-1967. **Memberships:** Genetics Soc Am. **Research Statement & Publications:** Biochemical aspects of Neurospora genetics. **Mailing Address:** Dept Microbiol, Molecular Genetics & Immunol, Univ Kans Sch Med, 3025 Wahl Hall W Mail Stop 3029, Kansas City, KS 66160. **Fax:** 913-588-7295. **E-Mail:** jkinsey@kumc.edu

KINSEY, KENNETH F, PHYSICS. **Personal Data:** b Providence, RI, September 14, 1933. **Education:** Brown Univ, AB, 1955; Univ Rochester, PhD (physics), 1961. **Professional Experience:** PROF EMER PHYSICS, COL GENESEO, STATE UNIV NY, as of 2003; prof physics, Col Geneseo, State Univ Ny, beginning 1966; asst prof, Univ Rochester, 1964-1966. **Memberships:** Am Phys Soc; Am Asn Physics Teachers. **Research Statement & Publications:** Medium energy particle physics. **Mailing Address:** Dept Physics & Astron, Col Geneseo, State Univ Ny, 1, Col Circle, Geneseo, NY 14454. **Fax:** 585-245-5288.

KINSEY, PHILIP A, PHYSICAL CHEMISTRY. **Personal Data:** b Warsaw, Ind, February 10, 1931; m Marjorie; c Robert, Caryl & James. **Education:** Manchester Col, AB, 1953; Purdue Univ, PhD (chem), 1957. **Professional Experience:** Univ Ill, Urbana, 1980-1981; Sabbatical, Univ Calif, Santa Barbara, 1969-1970; PROF CHEM, UNIV EVANSVILLE, 1956-. **Research Statement & Publications:** Uses of computers in chemical education. **Mailing Address:** 1612 Southeast Blvd, Evansville, IN 47714. **E-Mail:** pk2@evansville.edu

KINSEY, WILLIAM HENDERSON, REPRODUCTION & FERTILIZATION, CELL BIOLOGY. **Education:** Univ Wash, Seattle, PhD (anat & cell biol), 1976. **Professional Experience:** PROF ANAT & CELL BIOL, UNIV KANSAS MED CENTER, 1997-; assoc prof gross anat & cell biol, Sch Med, Univ Miami, 1985-1991. **Mailing Address:** Dept Anat & Cell Biol, Kans Med Ctr, 39th & Rainbow Blvd, Kansas City, KS 66103. **Fax:** 913-588-2710. **E-Mail:** wkinsey@kumc.edu

KINSINGER, JACK BURL, HOSPITAL ADMINISTRATION. **Personal Data:** b Akron, Ohio, June 23, 1925; m 1987, Addie; c Paul & Amy. **Education:** Hiram Col, BA, 1948; Cornell Univ, MSc, 1951; Univ Pa, PhD (phys chem), 1958. **Professional Experience:** PRES & CHIEF EXEC OFFICER, MIDWESTERN UNIV, 1993-; pres & chief exec officer, Chicago Osteop Health Syst, 1987-1993; mem bd, Kirksville Osteop Col, 1986-1987; mem bd, Ariz State Univ Res Park, 1984-1987; vpres acad affairs, Ariz State Univ, 1982-1987; asst vpres res, Mich State Univ, 1977-1982; assoc provost, Mich State Univ, 1977-1982; dir chem div, NSF, 1975-1977; prof chem, Mich State Univ, 1966-1975; from assoc chmn to chmn dept, Mich State Univ, 1965-1975; consult, Union Carbide Chem Co, 1958-1980; from asst prof to assoc prof phys chem, Mich State Univ, 1957-1966; group leader polymer chem, Rohm & Haas Co, 1951-1956. **Memberships:** Fel AAAS; Am Chem Soc; Am Phys Soc; Am Osteop Asn. **Research Statement & Publications:** Micro-structure of polymers; laser light scattering spectroscopy. **Mailing Address:** 680 N Lake Shore Dr, Chicago, IL 60611.

KINSINGER, JAMES A, ANALYTICAL CHEMISTRY, MASS SPECTROMETRY. **Personal Data:** b Ottumwa, Iowa, December 6, 1944; m 1966, c 3. **Education:** Wartburg Col, BA, 1967; Univ Wis, PhD (anal chem), 1972. **Professional Experience:** MANAGING DIR, INDUST LABS CO, 1988-; vpres mkt, Masstron, Inc, 1987; head, Appln & Training, Nicolet Instruments, 1981-1986; res scientist, Warf Inst, Raltech Sci Serv & Hazelton Labs, 1977-1982; res assoc, Univ Wis, 1976-1977; Head, Chem Dept, Tougaloo Col, 1974-1976; Asst prof chem, Tougaloo Col, 1972-1976. **Memberships:** Am Chem Soc; Am Soc Mass Spectrometry; Asn Off Anal Chemists; Inst Food Technologists; Am Oil Chemists Soc; Asn Off Racing Chemists. **Mailing Address:** 1680 Oak Ave, Boulder, CO 80304.

KINSINGER, RICHARD ESTYN, MEDICAL IMAGING PHYSICS. **Personal Data:** b Wilmington, Del, July 23, 1942; m 1964, Barbara; c Lara & W Mark. **Education:** Cornell Univ, BEngPhys, 1964, MEng, 1965, PhD (aerospace eng), 1969. **Professional Experience:** MGR, GLOBAL ADVAN TECHNOL, GEN ELEC MED SYSTS, 1996-; mgr, Appl Sci Lab, 1982-1996; mgr plasma technol progs, Res & Develop Ctr, 1981-1982; mgr arc interruption res, Res & Develop Ctr, 1976-1981; res physicist, Res & Develop Ctr, 1968-1976. **Research Statement & Publications:** Direct development of new concepts and technology for medical imaging. **Mailing Address:** W349 S4698 Kingdom Dr, Dousman, WI 53118-9725. **Fax:** 414-521-6599. **E-Mail:** kinsingr@execpc.com

KINSKY, STEPHEN CHARLES, BIOCHEMISTRY. **Personal Data:** b Berlin, Ger, February 9, 1932; American citizen; m 1959, c 2. **Education:** Univ Chicago, AB, 1951; Johns Hopkins Univ, PhD (biochem), 1957. **Professional Experience:** PROF BIOCHEM, NAT JEWISH HOSP, 1978-; res career develop awards, 1964-1970; from instr to prof, Sch Med, Wash Univ, 1959-1978; USPHS fel, 1957-1959. **Memberships:** Am Soc Biol Chem; Am Asn Immunol. **Research Statement & Publications:** Membrane biochemistry; immunology. **Mailing Address:** 5309 Oakbank Ct, Las Vegas, NV 89130.

KINSLAND, GARY LYNN, GEOPHYSICS, SEISMIC, POTENTIAL FIELDS. **Personal Data:** b Eugene, Ore, June 10, 1947; m 1997, Kellie; c Cynthia Lorraine, Mikaila Mary Estelle & Victoria Jamison. **Education:** Univ Rochester, BS (physics), 1969, MS (geol), 1971, PhD (geol), 1974. **Honors & Awards:** Pioneer Production Endowed Professorship in Geology and Petroleum Engineering, First place paper, GCAGS convention, 1998; A I Leversen Mem Award, Am Asn Petrol Geol, 1984. **Professional Experience:** PROF GEOL, UNIV LA LAFAYETTE, 1989-; assoc prof geol, Univ Southwestern La, 1980-1989; asst prof, Univ Southwestern LA, 1977-1980; vis asst prof, Ariz State Univ, 1976-1977; Res asst geol, Univ Rochester, 1974-1976. **Memberships:** Am asn pet geol; Geol soc am; Am Geophys Union; Soc Explor Geophysicists. **Research Statement & Publications:** High pressure-high temperature simulation and study of earth mantle properties; geopressure-geothermal energy prospects; high pressure materials science; high-resolution 3-d seismic surveys; continental crustal structure deduced from potential field data; minimal effort time lapse seismic studies, Chicxulub impact structure geophysics, Big Bend nat park geophysics. **Mailing Address:** Dept Geol Univ La at Lafayette, PO Box 44530, Lafayette, LA 70504-4530. **Fax:** 337-482-6688. **E-Mail:** glkinsland@louisiana.edu

KINSLAND, LESLIE N, CHEMICAL EDUCATION. **Education:** Univ Rochester, BS, 1971; Univ Southwestern La, MS, 1981. **Professional Experience:** RETIRED; instr chem, Univ La, Lafayette, ending 1999. **Mailing Address:** PO Box 44370, Lafayette, LA 70504-4370. **E-Mail:** lk65@cornell.edu

KINSLEY, HOMAN BENJAMIN, WET LAID NONWOVEN ENGINEERING, FIBER PHYSICS. **Personal Data:** b Baltimore, Md, December 31, 1940; m 1962, c 3. **Education:** Western Md Col, BA, 1963; Lawrence Univ, MS, 1964, PhD (chem), 1967. **Honors & Awards:** Nonwovens Tech Award, 2002. **Professional Experience:** VPRES, RES & DEVELOP, FIBERMARK INC, as of 2002; sr res fel, Custom Papers Group Inc, beginning 1991; sr res fel, James River Corp, 1986-1991; dir technol, James River Corp, 1982-1986; tech dir, James River Corp, 1978-1982; res assoc, James River Corp, 1975-1978; res chemist, Du Pont, 1974-1975; res assoc, Ethyl Corp, 1967-1974. **Memberships:** Am Chem Soc; Tech Asn Pulp & Paper Indust; AAAS; Filtration Soc. **Research Statement & Publications:** Wet laid nonwovens; forming techniques; fibers and binders; physical properties of the resulting web structures. **Mailing Address:** Fibermark Inc, 161 Wellington Rd, Brattleboro, VT 05302. **Fax:** 802-257-5900. **E-Mail:** hkinsley@fibermark.com

KINSMAN, DONALD VINCENT, ORGANIC CHEMISTRY. **Personal Data:** b Toledo, Ohio, July 16, 1943; m 1969, c 2. **Education:** Univ Cincinnati, BS, 1965; Pa State Univ, PhD (chem), 1969. **Professional Experience:** TECH DIR, HENKEL EMERY GROUP, 1987-; mgr, Emery Chem, 1979-1987; group leader oleo chem res, Emery Chem, 1974-1979; group leader develop, Lever Bros, 1971-1974; Develop chemist household prod, Lever Bros, 1969-1971. **Memberships:** Am Chem Soc; Am Oil Chemists Soc; Soc Automotive Engrs; Tech Asn Pulp & Paper Indust; Soc Tribologists & Lubrication Engrs. **Research Statement & Publications:** Develop and administration of applications for oleo chemicals, synthetic lubricants, fatty alcohols, azelaic and pelargonic acids. **Mailing Address:** Henkel Emery Group, 4900 Este Ave, Cincinnati, OH 45232-1491.

KINSON, GORDON A, PHYSIOLOGY, ENDOCRINOLOGY. **Personal Data:** b Wood End, Eng, September 21, 1935; m 1982, c 2. **Education:** Univ Aston, BS, 1957; Col Advan Technol, Birmingham, ARIC, 1961; Univ Ala, Birmingham, MS, 1962; Univ Birmingham, PhD (endocrinol), 1967. **Honorary Degrees:** FRSC (UK), London, 1973. **Professional Experience:** Comp Cancer Unit, UAB, USA, 1983; Consult, Europ Orgn for Control Circulatory Dis, 1982; PROF PHYSIOL, FAC MED, UNIV OTTAWA, 1979-; from asst prof to assoc prof, Fac Med, Univ Ottawa, 1968-1979; sr res assoc, Med Sch, Birmingham Univ, 1964-1968; Res asst endocrinol, Univ Ala, Birmingham, 1959-1963. **Memberships:** Brit Soc Endocrinol; Royal Soc Chem; Can Physiol Soc; Am Physiol Soc. **Research Statement & Publications:** Extrahepatic metabolism of androgen hormones; steroid hormone production by seminiferous tubules of the testis; chronic consequences of vasectomy; reninangiotensin and other factors influencing adrenocortical hormone secretion; pineal gland-adrenocortical hormone relationships; role of the pineal gland and indoles in testicular function and androgen biosynthesis; cardiac actions of anabolic androgens and estrogens; exercise and female reproductive function; steroids and Cyclosporin A in renal function. **Mailing Address:** Dept Physiol Univ Ottawa Fac Med, 451 Smyth Rd, Ottawa, ON K1H 8M5, Can. **Fax:** 613-787-6718.

KINSTLE, JAMES FRANCIS, POLYMER CHEMISTRY. **Personal Data:** b Lima, Ohio, November 23, 1938. **Education:** Bowling Green State Univ, BS, 1966, MA, 1967; Univ Akron, PhD (polymer sci), 1970. **Honors & Awards:** A K Doolittle Award, Am Chem Soc, 1977. **Professional Experience:** CHMN, CHEM TECH ADV BD, as of 2002; MGR CORP CHEM & POLYMER RES & DEVELOP, JAMES RIVER CORP, 1987-; sr res group leader, Polaroid, 1983-1987; Ed-in-chief, J Radiation Curing, Technol Mkt Corp, 1974-1979; consult, 1973-1983; from asst prof to assoc prof chem, Univ Tenn, Knoxville, 1972-1983; sr res scientist, Ford Motor Co Sci Res Labs, 1970-1972; res & develop chemist, Allied Mat Corp, 1963-1965; res & develop polymers, Wyandotte Chem Corp, 1960-1963. **Memberships:** Am Chem Soc (treas, 1985-1987); Soc Petrol Engrs; Soc Vacuum Coaters. **Research Statement & Publications:** Polymer synthesis and characterization; homogeneous and surface reactions on polymers; cellulose and paper chemistry; radiation chemistry in polymer sciences; polymer reuse and disposal. **Mailing Address:** James River Corp, One Better Way Rd, Milford, OH 45150-2741. **Fax:** 513-576-7107.

KINSTLE, THOMAS HERBERT, ORGANOFLUORINE CHEMISTRY, MASS SPECTROMETRY. **Personal Data:** b Lima, Ohio, December 18, 1936; m 1958. **Education:** Bowling Green State Univ, BA, 1958; Univ Ill, PhD (org chem), 1963. **Professional Experience:** PROF CHEM, BOWLING GREEN STATE UNIV, 1974-; assoc prof org chem, Bowling Green State Univ, 1970-1974; Res Corp grant, 1965-; Am Chem Soc-Petrol Res Found grant, 1964-; from instr to asst prof org chem, Iowa State Univ, 1964-1970; res assoc org chem, Univ Ill, 1963-1964. **Memberships:** Am Chem Soc; Am Acad Arts & Sci; Am Soc Mass Spectrometry. **Research Statement & Publications:** Applications of mass spectrometry to organic chemical problems; synthesis and reactions of strained ring systems; structure determination; synthesis and biosynthesis of natural products; organofluorine chemistry. **Mailing Address:** Dept Chem, Bowling Green State Univ, Bowling Green, OH 43402-2839. **E-Mail:** tkinstl@bgnet.bgsu.edu

KINTANAR, AGUSTIN, NUCLEAR MAGNETIC RESONANCE SPECTROSCOPY, MACROMOLECULAR STRUCTURE. **Personal Data:** b New Haven, Conn, April 28, 1958; m 1989, Karen A Smith; c Ryan & Dylan. **Education:** Univ Ill, Chicago, BS, 1979; Univ Ill, Urbana, PhD (phys chem), 1984. **Professional Experience:** ASST PROF, IOWA STATE UNIV, 1988-; postdoctoral, Univ Wash, 1985-1988; Postdoctoral mem tech staff, AT&T Bell Labs, 1984-1985. **Memberships:** Am Chem Soc. **Research Statement & Publications:** Nuclear magnetic resonance studies of protein and DNA structure and dynamics. **Mailing Address:** Dept Biochem & Biophys, Iowa State Univ, Ames, IA 50011-2010. **Fax:** 515-294-0453. **E-Mail:** kintanar@iastate.edu

KINTER, LEWIS BOARDMAN, VASOPRESSIN, WHOLE ANIMAL MODELS. **Personal Data:** b Exeter, NH, August 15, 1950; m 1973, c 3. **Education:** Union Col, BS, 1973; Harvard Univ, PhD (physiol), 1978. **Professional Experience:** Assoc dir toxicol, Smith Kline Beecham Pharmaceuticals, 1990-; asst dir toxicol, 1988-1990; asst dir pharmacol, 1984-1988; SCIENTIST, SMITH KLINE & FRENCH LABS, 1981-; adj asst prof physiol, Univ Pa. **Memberships:** Am Physiol Soc; Am Soc Nephrology; Inst Soc Nephrology. **Research Statement & Publications:** Homeostatic mechanisms involved in control of renal function and body fluid volume and body fluid composition. **Mailing Address:** Dept Biol Nycomed Inc, 466 Devon Park Dr Box 6630, Wayne, PA 19087-8630. **Fax:** 610-225-4416.

KINTNER, EDWIN E, ENGINEERING. **Personal Data:** c 4. **Education:** US Naval Acad, BS, 1942; Mass Inst Technol, MA, 1946, MA, 1950. **Professional Experience:** RETIRED; exec vpres, Gen Pub Utility, Nuclear Corp, 1983-1990; US rep, Int Fusion Res Coun; chmn, Re-conceptualize Utility Power Reactors Prog, Elec Power Res Inst Advan Light Water Reactors & Comt Environ Technol, Nat Res Coun; mem bd dir, Brit Nuclear Fuels Inc; asst dir reactor eng & dep dir, Reactors Develop Div, AEC. **Memberships:** Nat Acad Eng; Am Nuclear Soc; Elec Power Res Inst. **Research Statement & Publications:** Nuclear power. **Mailing Address:** Bradley Hill Rd, PO Box 682, Norwich, VT 05055.

KINTNER, ROBERT ROY, ORGANIC CHEMISTRY. **Personal Data:** b Weeping Water, Nebr, April 3, 1928; m 1952, Helen R Remmers; c Timothy R, Melinda R (Hooper) & Sue-Lynn R (Lautt). **Education:** Iowa State Univ, BS, 1953; Univ Wash, PhD (org chem), 1957. **Professional Experience:** Sr Mentor in chem (vol) Calif Lutheran Univ, 1994-2002; vis prof chem, Univ Calif, Santa Cruz, 1987-1988; vis lectr chem, Munich, Ger Campus, Univ Md, 1985-1987; vis prof chem, Univ Nebr, Lincoln, 1980-1981; prin investr, Sioux Falls Refuse Derived Fuel Proj, 1978-1980; NSF fac fel, Univ Calif, Santa Cruz, 1971-1972; Petrol res fund adv sci award, Univ Wash, Seattle, 1964-1965; chmn dept, Augustana Col, SDak, 1960-1965 & 1977-1985; From asst prof to prof chem, Augustana Col, SDak, 1957-1994. **Memberships:** Am Chem Soc (emer mem); sigma xi (emer mem). **Research Statement & Publications:** Physical-organic chemistry, especially in reaction mechanisms; structure; investigation of the mechanism of the formation of 2, 3, 7, 8-tetrachlorodibenzodioxin. **Mailing Address:** Chem Dept Calif Lutheran Univ, 60 W Olsen Rd, Thousand Oaks, CA 91360. **Fax:** 805-493-3392. **E-Mail:** kintner@clunet.edu

KINZEL, GARY LEE, COMPUTER-AIDED DESIGN, KINEMATICS. **Personal Data:** b Bremen, Ohio, January 18, 1944; m 1967, c 2. **Education:** Ohio State Univ, BME, 1968, MS, 1969; Purdue Univ, PhD (mech eng), 1973. **Professional Experience:** PROF, OHIO STATE UNIV, 1987-; from asst prof to assoc prof, Ohio State Univ, 1978-1987; res eng, Batelle Columbus Labs, 1968-1969; Researcher, Batelle Mem Inst, 1968-1969. **Memberships:** Sigma Xi; Am Soc Mech Engrs. **Research Statement & Publications:** Interactive computer graphics; machine element design; biomechanics; mechanism analysis and design; design and development of CAD software. **Mailing Address:** 216 Bldg 1, 650 Ackerman Rd, Columbus, OH 43202. **E-Mail:** kinzel.1@osu.edu

KINZEL, JERRY J, MICROBIAL PHYSIOLOGY, INTERMEDIATE METABOLISM. **Personal Data:** b Avon, Ohio, April 24, 1952; m 1981. **Education:** Cleveland State Univ, BS, 1976; Miami Univ, MS, 1978, PhD (microbiol), 1981. **Professional Experience:** SR ASSOC RES SCIENTIST, 1981-; SR RES SCIENTIST, INT MINERALS & CHEM CORP. **Memberships:** Sigma Xi; Am Soc Microbiol. **Research Statement & Publications:** Microbial physiology with special emphasis on genetics and enzymology. **Mailing Address:** 250 S 21st St, Terre Haute, IN 47803.

KINZER, EARL T, JR, THEORETICAL PHYSICS, SOLID STATE PHYSICS. **Personal Data:** b Beckley, WVa, April 7, 1931; m 1957, Mary J Smith; c Charles & Kathleen. **Education:** Auburn Univ, BEP, 1958, MS, 1960; Univ Va, PhD (physics), 1962. **Professional Experience:** ASSOC PROF EMER PHYSICS, AUBURN UNIV, 1993-; Adj assoc prof physics, LaGrange Col, 1993-; actg head, Physics Dept, 1986-1989; assoc prof, Auburn Univ, 1967-1993; From asst prof to assoc prof physics, Univ Ala, Tuscaloosa, 1961-1967. **Research Statement & Publications:** Operational solution of partial difference equations; foundations of electromagnetic theory. **Mailing Address:** 317 Kimberly Dr, Auburn, AL 36832. **E-Mail:** ekinzer@@auburn.campus.mci.net

KINZER, H GRANT, ENTOMOLOGY. **Personal Data:** b Grandfield, Okla, July 22, 1937; m 1981, c 5. **Education:** Okla State Univ, BS, 1959, MS, 1960, PhD (entom), 1962. **Professional Experience:** PROF & HEAD ENTOM, PLANT PATH, & WEED SCI, NMEX STATE UNIV, 1976-; from asst prof to assoc prof, Nmex state Univ, 1964-1976. **Memberships:** Entom Soc Am; Am Registery Prof Entomologists; Can Entom Soc; Am Mosquito Control Asn. **Research Statement & Publications:** Biology; physiology and control of livestock insects; biology and physiology of bark beetles. **Mailing Address:** Dept Entom, Plant Path & Weed Sci, Coll Agri & Home Econ, NMex State Univ, SK N141 Skeen Hall, Las Cruces, NM 88003. **Fax:** 505-646-8087. **E-Mail:** gkinzer@nmsu.edu

KINZER, ROBERT LEE, GAMMA RAY & X-RAY ASTRONOMY. **Personal Data:** b Grandfield, Okla, June 23, 1941; m 1967, c 2. **Education:** Univ Okla, BS, 1962, MS, 1966, PhD (elem particle physics), 1967. **Professional Experience:** RES PHYSICIST, US NAVAL RES LAB, 1969-; resident res fel cosmic ray physics, Nat Acad Sci, 1967-1969. **Memberships:** Am Phys Soc; AAAS; Sigma Xi; Am Astron Soc. **Research Statement & Publications:** Experimental elementary particle physics; experimental gamma-ray astronomy and x-ray astronomy. **Mailing Address:** Naval Res Lab C, Code 7653, Washington, DC 20375-0001. **E-Mail:** kinzer@osse.nrl.navy.mil

KINZEY, BERTRAM Y(ORK), ARCHITECTURAL ACOUSTICS. **Personal Data:** b Rutland, Mass, September 25, 1921; m 1944, c 2. **Education:** Va Polytech Inst, BS, 1942,

MS, 1943. **Professional Experience:** EMER PROF ARCHIT, UNIV FLA, 1985-; consult archit acoust, 1960-; from assoc prof to prof, Univ Fla, 1959-1985; chmn joint comt church archit & music, Nat Coun Churches, beginning 1956; mem comn archit, Nat Coun Churches, beginning 1954; Mem comt archit & acoust, Am Guild Organists, 1952-1956; from asst prof to assoc prof archit eng, Va Polytech Inst, 1947-1959; archit draftsman & struct engr, Baskervill & Son, Va, 1945-1947; Naval architect, Norfolk Navy Yard, 1943-1945. **Memberships:** Fel Acoust Soc Am; Am Inst Archit; Am Soc Heating, Refrig & Air-Conditioning Engrs; Nat Coun Acoust Consults. **Research Statement & Publications:** Heating, lighting, acoustics and sanitation; tests on wood box columns to determine formulas for design; thermal performance of ventilated building skins. **Mailing Address:** 212 SW 42nd St, Gainesville, FL 32607-2769. **Fax:** 352-378-1878.

KINZIE, JEANNIE JONES, RADIATION ONCOLOGY, RADIOLOGY & NUCLEAR MEDICINE. **Personal Data:** b Gt Falls, Mont, March 14, 1940; m 1991, Johnson; c Daniel. **Education:** Mont State Univ, BS, 1961; WashUniv, MD, 1965; Univ Phoenix, MBA, 1997. **Professional Experience:** ASST PROF, UNIV COLO, as of 2000; fel Nuclear Med, Univ Colo, beginning 1996; consult, Rose Med Ctr, Denver Gen Hosp & Denver Vet Hosp, 1985- & Food & Drug Admin, 1987; prof radiol, Univ Colo, 1985-1995; dir radiation oncol, Univ Colo, 1985-1991; assoc prof radiation oncol, Wayne State Univ, 1980-1985; Children's Hosp Mich, Detroit Receiving Hosp, Hutzel Hosp & Harper Grace Hosps, Detroit, 1980-1985; assoc prof, Univ Chicago, 1978-1980; asst prof, Univ Chicago, 1975-1978; asst prof, Med Col Wis, 1973-1974; Vet Hosp, Wood, Wis & West Allis Mem Hosps, 1973-1974; Am Cancer Soc advan clin fel, 1971-1974; instr radiol, Wash Univ, 1971-1973; consult radiol, Homer G Phillips Hosp, St Louis, 1971-1973; resident therapeut radiol, Wash Univ, 1968-1971; intern surg, Univ NC, 1965-1966. **Memberships:** Fel Am Col Radiol; AMA; Am Soc Therapeut Radiol & Oncol; Am Soc Clin Oncol; Wilderness Med Soc; Soc Head & Neck Surgeons; Sigma Xi. **Research Statement & Publications:** Patterns of care in Hodgkins disease and other cancers; combination treatment of head and neck cancer; combination radiation/chemotherapy studies for numerous types of cancer. **Mailing Address:** PO Box 2767, Health Sci Ctr, Denver, CO 80439. **Fax:** 303-372-6262. **E-Mail:** jeannie.kinzie@uchsc.edu

KINZIE, ROBERT ALLEN, III, ZOOLOGY. **Personal Data:** b Santa Cruz, Calif, June 7, 1941. **Education:** Univ Hawaii, MS, 1966; Yale Univ, PhD (biol), 1970. **Professional Experience:** PROF ZOOLOGY, UNIV HAWAII, as of 2005; chair, Ecol, Evolution & Conserv Biol, Univ Hawaii, as of 2003; from asst prof to assoc prof zoology, Univ Hawaii, 1971-1979; fel, Univ Ga, 1970-1971; consult, Upjohn Drug Co, beginning 1970. **Memberships:** Ecol Soc Am; Soc Study Evolution; Soc Syst Zool; Am Soc Limnol & Oceanog. **Research Statement & Publications:** Coral reef ecology; symbiosis. **Mailing Address:** Dept Zool, Univ Hawaii Manoa, Social Sci Res Inst, 2538 Mall 2424 Maile Way Ste 704, Honolulu, HI 96822. **Fax:** 808-956-2884. **E-Mail:** kinzie@hawaii.edu

KINZLER, KENNETH W, ONCOLOGY. **Personal Data:** b Philadelphia, Pa, January 30, 1962; m 1984, Jacquelyn; c Kathryn & William. **Education:** Philadelphia Col Parm & Sci, BS, 1983; Johns Hopkins Univ Sch Med, PhD, 1988. **Professional Experience:** ASSOC PROF ONCOL, JOHNS HOPKINS UNIV SCH MED, AS OF 2006; Assoc ed, Cancer Res, 1993; asst prof, Johns Hopkins Univ Sch Med, 1990-1994; Postdoctoral fel, Johns Hopkins Univ Sch Med, 1988-1990. **Mailing Address:** Johns Hopkins Oncol Ctr Res Lab, 424 N Bond St Rm 111, Baltimore, MD 21231-1001. **Fax:** 410-955-0548. **E-Mail:** kinzlke@welch.jhu.edu

KINZLY, ROBERT EDWARD, ELECTROOPTICS, OPTICAL ENGINEERING. **Personal Data:** b North Tonawanda, NY, July 4, 1939; m 1963, c 2. **Education:** Univ Buffalo, BA, 1961; Cornell Univ, MS, 1964. **Professional Experience:** PRES, SCIPAR INC, 1975-; sect head & br head, Calspan Corp, 1967-1975; physicist, Cornell Aeronaut Lab Inc, 1963-1967; mem, Am Stand Inst working group microdensity. **Memberships:** Optical Soc Am; Asn Old Crows. **Research Statement & Publications:** Camouflage; image evaluation; atmospheric optics; remote sensing; visual perception; planetology; computer science; electro-optical warfare; optical countermeasures; target acquisition; image processing. **Mailing Address:** SCIPAR Inc, 26 W Spring St, Buffalo, NY 14221.

KIPHART, KERRY, INORGANIC TREATMENT, HAZARDOUS WASTE MANAGEMENT. **Personal Data:** b South Haven, Mich, April 21, 1949; m Scott. **Education:** Ill Wesleyan Univ, BA, 1971; Univ Notre Dame, MS, 1980, PhD (environ eng), 1984. **Professional Experience:** ENVIRON ENGR, IBM CORP, POUGHKEEPSIE, NY, 1987-; Develop engr, Endicott, NY, 1983-1987. **Memberships:** Am Chem Soc. **Research Statement & Publications:** Physical and organizational structures ensuring responsible chemical and waste management; software development for chemical management data and product environmental assessment. **Mailing Address:** Int Bus Mach Corp, 522 S Rd, Poughkeepsie, NY 12601-5400. **Fax:** 845-432-9786. **E-Mail:** kiphart@vnet.ibm.com

KIPLING, ARLIN LLOYD, SURFACE SCIENCE, BIOSENSORS. **Personal Data:** b Melfort, Sask, December 15, 1936; m 1963, Joan; c Caroline, Diane & Arlene. **Education:** Univ Sask, BEng, 1958; McGill Univ, MSc, 1961; Univ Exeter, PhD (physics), 1967. **Professional Experience:** ADJ ASSOC PROF PHYSICS, CONCORDIA UNIV, as of 1999; physicist, Noranda Res Ctr, Que, 1963-1964; engr, Northern Elec Co, Que, 1958-1959. **Research Statement & Publications:** Sensing of biomolecules in a liquid using acoustic wave sensors, with applications in the medical field. **Mailing Address:** Dept Physics, Concordia Univ, Montreal, PQ H3G 1M8, Can. **Fax:** 514-848-2828.

KIPLINGER, GLENN FRANCIS, CLINICAL PHARMACOLOGY. **Personal Data:** b Indianapolis, Ind, September 29, 1930; m 1953, Martha Peterson; c Jeffrey, Jonathan, Jason & Jennifer. **Education:** Butler Univ, BS, 1953; Univ Mich, PhD (pharmacol), 1958; Univ Tex, Galveston, MD, 1967; Sietsow U, I, D Lan, 1995. **Professional Experience:** CONSULT, 1989-, TRUSTEE, BUTLER UNIV, INDIANAPOLIS, 1989-; vpres res & develop, Ortho Pharmaceut, Johnson & Johnson, 1980-1988 & R W Johnson Pharmaceut Res Inst, 1988-1989; managing dir, Lilly Res Ctr, UK, 1977-1980; vpres res, Eli Lilly & Co, Indianapolis, 1975-1977; dir toxicol, Eli Lilly & Co, Indianapolis, 1972-1975; clin pharmacologist, Eli Lilly & Co, Indianapolis, 1967-1972; asst pharmacol, Boston Univ Sch Med, 1958-1962 & Univ Tex, Galveston, 1962-1967. **Memberships:** Am Soc Pharmacol & Exp Therapeut; Am Soc Clin Pharmacol & Therapeut. **Research Statement & Publications:** Cardiovascular pharmacology; clinical pharmacology of analgesics and of marijuana; research and development management. **Mailing Address:** 1360 Tearose Pl, Sarasota, FL 34239. **Fax:** 941-373-9523.

KIPNIS, DAVID MORRIS, INTERNAL MEDICINE, ENDOCRINOLOGY. **Personal Data:** b Baltimore, Md, May 23, 1927; m 1953, c 3. **Education:** Johns Hopkins Univ, AB, 1945, MA, 1949; Univ Md, MD, 1951. **Honorary Degrees:** ScD, Univ Md. **Honors & Awards:** Oppenheimer Award, Endocrine Soc. **Professional Experience:** CHMN EMER, DEPT INTERNAL MED, SCH MED, WASH UNIV, as of 2002; PROF MOLECULAR BIOL & PHARMACOL, SCH MED, WASH UNIV, as of 2002; DISTINGUISHED UNIV PROF MED, SCH MED, WASH UNIV, 1993-; mem & chmn, Nat Diabetes Adv Bd, 1977-1981; Busch prof med & chmn dept, Clin Res Ctr, 1973-1992; from assoc prof to prof, Clin Res Ctr, 1962-1973; dir, Clin Res Ctr, 1960-1987; asst prof biochem, Wash Univ, 1957-1962; Markle scholar, 1956-1961; Am Col Physicians fel biochem, Sch Med, Wash Univ, 1955-1956; chief resident, Univ Md Hosp, 1954-1955; from jr asst resident to sr asst resident, Duke Univ Hosp, 1952-1954; intern med, Johns Hopkins Hosp, 1951-1952; mem, Nat Pituitary Agency; mem, Fel Comt Burroughs Wellcome Fund; mem sci adv bd, USAF; mem Endocrinol Study Sect, NIH. **Memberships:** Nat Acad Sci; Inst Med-Nat Acad Sci; Asn Am Physicians; Endocrine Soc; Biochem Soc; Am Soc Clin Invest; Am Acad Arts & Sci. **Research Statement & Publications:** Hormonal control of carbohydrate and protein metabolism. **Mailing Address:** Dept Med, Sch Med, Wash Univ, St Louis, MO 63110.

KIPOUROS, GEORGES JOHN, LIGHT, REFRACTORY & RARE EARTH METALS. **Personal Data:** b Patras, Greece, July 17, 1948; Canadian citizen; m 1982, Matina; c Yiannis & Athanasios. **Education:** Nat Tech Univ Athens, Dipl Eng, 1971; Univ Toronto, MASc, 1977, PhD (metall & mat sci), 1982. **Professional Experience:** DIR MINERALS ENG CTR, DALHOUSIE UNIV, 2000; asst dean, fac eng, Dalhousie Univ, 2000-2005; FAC CONSULT, MEHARAN UNIV ENG & TECHNOL, SINDH, PAKISTAN, 1998-; fac consult, Gen Motors Res & Develop Ctr, 1995-1996; vis prof, Norweg Inst Technol, 1993; Univ Patras, Greece, 1993, 1994 & 1996; assoc prof, Dept Mining & Metal Eng, Dalhousie Univ, 1989-1974; head, Dept Mining & Metall Eng, Dalhousie Univ, beginning 1989; sr res scientist, Gen Motors Res & Develop Ctr, 1985-1989; postdoctoral assoc, Mass Inst Technol, 1982-1985; actg head, permanent Comt Receiving Ammunition, Pyrkal, 1972-1974. **Memberships:** Electrochem Soc; Can Inst Mining & Metall; Inst Soc Electrochem; Minerals Metals & Mat Soc; Europ Rare Earth & Actinide Soc. **Research Statement & Publications:** Chemical process metallurgy, both in fundamental and engineering applications of light, refractory, and rare earth metals; value-added metallurgy; materials science and engineeering; transfer of technology from laboratory to plant; author of various articles. **Mailing Address:** Minerals Eng Ctr, Dalhousie Univ, Rm 212 Bldg G PO Box 1000 1360 Barrington St, Halifax, NS B3J 2X4, Can. **Fax:** 902-429-3506. **E-Mail:** georges.kipouros@dal.ca

KIPP, EGBERT MASON, RESEARCH ADMINISTRATION. **Personal Data:** b Angola, November 27, 1914; m 1935, c 3. **Education:** Iowa Wesleyan Col, BS, 1934; Boston Univ, MS, 1935; Pa State Univ, PhD (phys chem), 1939. **Honorary Degrees:** DSc, Iowa Wesleyan Col, 1961. **Professional Experience:** Plenary lectr, 3rd Int Conf Metal Working Lubricants, Esslingen, Ger, 1982; pres, 1975-1976; mem, Res Mgt Group Philadelphia, pres elect, 1974; consult, chem & metals indust, 1971-; INDEPENDENT CONSULT TECH MGT, 1970-; assoc dir res & develop, Sun Oil Co, 1962-1970; mgr basic res, Sun Oil Co, 1960-1962; asst prod develop, Sun Oil Co, 1959-1960; dir res & develop, Foote Mineral Co, 1957-1959; chief lubricants div, Aluminum Co Am, 1947-1957; exec secy oils & lubricants comt, Aluminum Co Am, 1946-1957; asst chief phys chem div, Aluminum Co Am, 1944-1947; res chemist, Aluminum Co Am, 1939-1944; asst chem, Pa State Univ, 1935-1939; eval agent, Off Energy Related Inventions, Nat Bur Stand; chmn, tech comt, Am Soc Test & Mat; vchmn, Pittsburgh Dist; chmn, Am Inst Chemists, Philadelphia; pres-elect, Pa Inst Chemists. **Memberships:** Am Chem Soc; fel Am Soc Lubrication Eng (pres, 1946); fel Am Inst Chemists (treas, 1970); Sigma Xi; Am Soc Testing & Mat. **Research Statement & Publications:** Lubrication engineering sciences; research and development management and organization; energy, market and commercial development; air, soil and water conservation; technology audits; author of one book and 16 publications; granted for 11 patents. **Mailing Address:** 745 Thomas St, State College, PA 16803.

KIPP, JAMES EDWIN, CHEMICAL KINETICS, PHARMACEUTICAL FORMULATIONS. **Personal Data:** b Detroit, Mich, June 15, 1953; m 1986, Patricia; c William R. **Education:** Albion Col, BA, 1975; Univ Mich, MS, PhD (chem), 1983. **Honors & Awards:** Cert Recognition, Nat Aeronaut & Space Admin, 1991. **Professional Experience:** SR RES SCIENTIST, BAXTER HEALTHCARE CORP, 1990-; res scientist, Baxter Healthcare Corp, 1985-1990; Sr res assoc, Baxter Travenol, 1983-1985. **Memberships:** Am Chem Soc; Am Asn Pharmaceut Scientist. **Research Statement & Publications:** Mathematical modeling of nonisothermal decomposition of drugs in pharmaceutical formulations; prediction of pharmaceutical shelf life; variable pH experiments for rapid preformulation screening; development of parenteral drug formulations; pulmonary drug delivery; computer modeling of chemical equilibria. **Mailing Address:** Baxter Healthcare Corp Pharmaceut Res & Develop, Rte 120 & Wilson Rd, Round Lake, IL 60073.

KIPPENBERGER, DONALD JUSTIN, PHYSICAL CHEMISTRY. **Personal Data:** b St Louis, Mo, February 25, 1947; m 1973, c 2. **Education:** Univ St Thomas, BS & BA, 1970; Sam Houston State Univ, MS, 1972; Tex A&M Univ, PhD (chem), 1982. **Professional Experience:** AT RES DYNAMICS INC, as of 2000; MEM STAFF, OFF ARMY SURGEON GEN, 1990-; mem staff, Weisbbaden Forensic Toxicol Drug Testing Lab, Ger, 1987-1990; chemist off chem readiness, Edgewood Arsenal, 1982-1987; chemist path residents, Gorgas Army Hosp, 1977-1980 & Tex A&M Univ, 1980-1982; consult chem, Commander XVIII Airborne Corp, 1974-1977 & Gov, Canal Zone, 1977-1980; asst prof, Canal Zone Col, 1977-1980; co-investr, Heart Enzyme Group, Walter Reed Army Inst, 1976-1977; Lectr, Fayetteville Univ, 1974-1977. **Memberships:** Am Inst Chemists. **Research Statement & Publications:** Membrane memitic chemistry: characterization of polymeric vesicles utilizing proton and carbon nuclear magnetic resonance, fluorescense and absorption techniques; surface chemistry: characterization of catalytically active inorganic complexes in zeolites and ambevlytes using electron spin resonance techniques. **Mailing Address:** Res Dynamics, Inc, 1355 Central Pkwy S, Suite 100, San Antonio, TX 78232.

KIPPENHAN, C(HARLES) J(ACOB), MECHANICAL ENGINEERING. **Personal Data:** b Middle Amana, Iowa, November 8, 1919; m 1941, Jane; c Kurt & Judith. **Education:** Univ Iowa, BSME, 1940, MSME, 1946, PhD (mech eng), 1948. **Professional Experience:** PROF EMER MECH ENG, UNIV WASH, SEATTLE, 1988-; prof, Univ Wash, Seattle, 1963-1988; chmn dept, Univ Wash, Seattle, 1963-1973; prof & head dept, Wash Univ, St Louis, 1954-1963; from asst prof to assoc prof, Wash Univ, St Louis, 1948-1954; instr mech eng, Univ Iowa, 1941-1942; jr mech engr, Stanley Eng Co, 1940; adj prof archit, Univ Wash, Seattle; mech eng consult. **Memberships:** Am Soc Heating Refrig & Air Conditioning Engrs; Am Soc Mech Engrs; Am Soc Eng Educ. **Research Statement & Publications:** Building energy systems analysis, simulation; energy conservation and management; convective and radiation heat transfer; thermal properties; transient techniques. **Mailing Address:** 3908 Northeast 38th St, Seattle, WA 98105.

KIPPS, THOMAS CHARLES, MATHEMATICS. **Personal Data:** b Eureka, Utah, February 28, 1923; m 1948, c 4. **Education:** Univ Calif, Berkeley, AB, 1949, MA, 1950, PhD (math), 1957. **Professional Experience:** PROF EMER MATH, CALIF STATE UNIV, FRESNO, as of 2000; chmn dept, Calif State Univ, Fresno, 1969; Prof Math, Calif State Univ, Fresno, beginning 1967; from instr to assoc prof, Calif State Univ, Fresno, 1956-1967; asst math, Univ Calif, Berkeley, 1955-1956; Instr math & physics, Univ Santa Clara, 1953-1955. **Memberships:** Am Math Soc; Math Asn Am; Sigma Xi. **Research Statement**

& Publications: Double integral problems in the calculus of variations; methods of linear algebra in numerical analysis. **Mailing Address:** Calif State Univ, 5241 N Maple Ave, Fresno, CA 93706.

KIPPS, THOMAS JAMES, HEMATOLOGY. **Education:** Harvard Univ, MD, PhD. **Honors & Awards:** Henry Ashbury Christian Award, Harvard Univ. **Professional Experience:** PROF MED & HEAD, DIV HEMATOL/ONCOL, UNIV CALIF, SAN DIEGO, as of 2005. **Mailing Address:** Dept Med, Univ Calif, San Diego, 9500 Gilman Dr, LaJolla, CA 92093-0663. **Fax:** 858-534-5620. **E-Mail:** tkipps@ucsd.edu

KIPROV, DOBRI D, IMMUNOLOGY. **Personal Data:** b Sofia, Bulgaria, May 1, 1949; American citizen; c 1. **Education:** Med Acad, Bulgaria, MD, 1974. **Professional Experience:** CHIEF, DIV IMMUNOL, CALIF PAC MED CTR, SAN FRANCISCO, as of 1999; dir plasmapheresis, dept cellular immunol, 1982-; clin res fel, dept cellular immunol, 1981-1982; clin res fel, Mass Gen Hosp, Harvard Med Sch, 1979-1981; resident, Mt Sinai Hosp, Case Western Res Univ, 1977-1979; instr path, Sackler Sch Med, Israel, 1974-1977; training & res awardee, Nat Inst Allergies & Infectious Dis. **Memberships:** AMA; Am Soc Clin Path; Am Col Pathologists; World Apheresis Asn; World Med Asn. **Research Statement & Publications:** Basic immunologic defects in autoimmune diseases, including renal diseases; evaluation of lymphocyte subsets from peripheral blood and tissues using moncolonal antibodies; effect of plasmapheresis, lymphocytapheresis and immunosuppressive therapy on the immunologic system of patients with autoimmune diseases; clinical correlation with immunologic assays. **Mailing Address:** Calif Pac Med Ctr, 2100 Webster St Ste 220, San Francisco, CA 94115. **E-Mail:** dkiprovcai@aol.com

KIRBER, MARIA WIENER, MICROBIOLOGY, VIROLOGY. **Personal Data:** b Prague, Czech, February 19, 1917; American citizen; m 1943, c Michael T & William M. **Education:** Univ Prague, MUC, 1938; Univ Pa, MS, 1941, PhD (bact), 1942; Am Bd Microbiol, dipl. **Honorary Degrees:** ScD, Med Col Pa, 1973. **Honors & Awards:** Christian R & Mary E Lindback Award, 1971. **Professional Experience:** EMER PROF VIROL & MICROBIOL, MED COL PA, 1972-; Nat Coun Combat Blindness grant, 1962-1963 & 1966-1967 & Nat Soc Prev Blindness grant, 1968-1970; prof microbiol, Med Col PA, 1962-1972; Nat Coun Combat Blindness grant, Med Col Pa, 1958-1959; mem res staff, Children's Hosp, Philadelphia, 1951-1952; from instr to prof, Med Col PA, 1943-1972; Asst bact, Med Col PA, 1941-1943. **Memberships:** Fel Am Acad Microbiol; Am Soc Microbiol. **Research Statement & Publications:** Antigenic structure of hemolytic streptococci; complement fixing antigens of influenza viruses; mouse brain tissue culture; experimental viral infections and auto-immune reactions of the eye; experimental mycobacterial eye infection. **Mailing Address:** Juniper Dr, Lakeville, CT 06039.

KIRBY, ALBERT CHARLES, PHYSIOLOGY. **Personal Data:** b Baton Rouge, La, March 31, 1941; m 1961, c 3. **Education:** La State Univ, Baton Rouge, BS, 1962, MS, 1963; Univ Ill, Urbana, PhD (physiol), 1967. **Professional Experience:** ASSOC DEAN, CASE WESTERN RES UNIV, 1984-; ASSOC PROF PHYSIOL, CASE WESTERN RES UNIV, 1975-; NIH res grants, Case Western Reserve Univ, beginning 1969; asst prof, Case Western Res Univ, 1969-1975; NIH sr fel physiol, Univ Wash, 1967-1969. **Memberships:** Soc Gen Physiol; Biophys Soc; Am Physiol Soc. **Research Statement & Publications:** Excitation-contraction coupling and contractile proteins in denervated mammalian muscle. **Mailing Address:** Sch Med, case western Univ, Rm T308, 10900 Euclid Ave, Cleveland, OH 44106-4920. **Fax:** 216-368-6011. **E-Mail:** ack@cwru.edu

KIRBY, ANDREW FULLER, SPECTROSCOPY, REMOTE SENSING. **Personal Data:** b Washington, DC, February 15, 1955; m 1981, Martha R Diaz; c Eleanor R & John R. **Education:** Col Holy Cross, AB, 1977; Duke Univ, PhD (phys chem), 1981. **Professional Experience:** SR PHYS SCIENTIST, INTEL TECHNOL & INNOVATION CTR, CIA, as of 2003; SR PROG CHIEF, OFF RES & DEVELOP, CIA, 1994-; div chief mat res, Off Sci & Weapons Res, CIA, 1991-1993; res scientist br chief, Off Sci & Weapons Res, CIA, 1987-1990; phys scientist, Off Sci & Weapons Res, CIA, 1985-1987; Fel assoc, Univ Va, 1981-1982. **Memberships:** Am Chem Soc; Sigma Xi. **Research Statement & Publications:** Detailed electronic and molecular structures of solid-state lanthanide complexes; advanced spectroscopic measurement techniques; remote sensing and geophysical techniques; technical research management. **Mailing Address:** Intel Technol & Innovation Cte, CIA, Oak Hill, VA 20171.

KIRBY, BRUCE JOHN, APPLIED MATHEMATICS. **Personal Data:** b Toronto, Ont, November 19, 1928; m 1958, c 2. **Education:** Univ Toronto, BA, 1950, MA, 1951; Univ London, PhD, 1967. **Professional Experience:** PROF EMER MATH, QUEEN'S UNIV, ONT, as of 2004; prof, Queen's Univ, Ont, 1969-; asst dir serv, Skidaway Inst Oceanog, 1967-1995; from asst prof to assoc prof, Queen's Univ, Ont, 1960-1969; lectr, Queen's Univ, Ont, 1954-1960; lectr, Univ Liverpool, 1953-1954; Teaching fel math, Univ Toronto, 1951-1953. **Memberships:** Soc Indust & Appl Math. **Research Statement & Publications:** Mathematics of control theory. **Mailing Address:** Dept Math & Statist, Queen's Univ, Rm 310, Jeffery Hall, Kingston, ON K7L 3N6, Can. **Fax:** 613-533-2964. **E-Mail:** kirbyb@post.queensu.ca

KIRBY, CONRAD JOSEPH, JR, ECOLOGY. **Personal Data:** b Opelousas, La, August 2, 1941; m 1968, c 2. **Education:** Univ Southwestern La, BS, 1964; La State Univ, MS, 1967, PhD (marine sci), 1971. **Professional Experience:** CHIEF, DIV ECOL RES, WATERWAYS EXP STA, as of 2004; SUPVRY ECOLOGIST, WATERWAYS EXP STA, 1974-; res ecologist, Waterways Exp Sta, 1972-1974; Asst prof biol, Univ Southeastern La, 1967-1972. **Memberships:** Ecol Soc Am; Nat Estuarine Res Fedn; Gulf Estuarine Res Fedn. **Research Statement & Publications:** Impacts and mitigation of construction activities in wetlands; development and management of wetlands and other ecosystems. **Mailing Address:** US Army Engr, Waterways Exp Sta, 3909 Halls Ferry Rd, Vicksburg, MS 39180-6199.

KIRBY, HILLIARD WALKER, INTEGRATED PEST MANAGEMENT. **Personal Data:** b Asheville, NC, June 12, 1949; m 1981. **Education:** Univ NC, BS, 1971; NC State Univ, MS, 1974, PhD (plant path), 1981. **Professional Experience:** TRAINING COORDR, SOYBEAN PROG, AGRIGROWTH, INC, as of 2003; assoc prof plant path, Col Agr, Univ Ill, as of 1997; asst prof plant path, Col Agr, Univ Ill, beginning 1981; Agr exten agent, NC Agr Exten Serv, 1974-1978. **Memberships:** Am Phytopath Soc. **Research Statement & Publications:** Effects of conservation tillage on plant disease development. **Mailing Address:** AgriGrowth Inc, Hollendale, MN 55102.

KIRBY, JAMES RAY, ANALYTICAL CHEMISTRY. **Personal Data:** b Goldsboro, NC, October 22, 1933; m 1962, c 3. **Education:** E Carolina Col, AB & BS, 1955; Duke Univ, MA, 1957, PhD (chem, physics), 1960. **Professional Experience:** VPRES, EDWARD R KIRBY & ASSOCIATES INC, 1987-; mgr, Chem Analysis, IBM, Res Triangle Park, beginning 1984; sr res specialist, Monsanto Co, beginning1973; res specialist, 1968-1973; from res chemist to sr res chemist, 1960-1968. **Memberships:** Am Chem Soc. **Research Statement & Publications:** Chelate chemistry; polymer characterization. **Mailing Address:** Edward R Kirby & Assoc, 783 N York Rd, Elmhurst, IL 60126. **Fax:** 630-941-1750. **E-Mail:** jkirby@kirbyinvestigations.com

KIRBY, JAMES T, MATHEMATICS. **Personal Data:** b December 25, 1952. **Education:** Brown Univ, BSc, 1975, MSc, 1976; Univ Del, PhD (civil eng), 1983. **Professional Experience:** EDWARD C DAVIS PROF, CIVIL & ENVIRON ENG, UNIV DEL, as of 2006. **Mailing Address:** Dept Civil Eng, Univ Del, Newark, DE 19716. **Fax:** 302-831-1228. **E-Mail:** kirby@udel.edu

KIRBY, KATE PAGE, ATOMIC & MOLECULAR PROCESSES IN ASTROPHYSICS, ATMOSPHERIC PHYSICS. **Personal Data:** b Washington, DC, December 5, 1945; m 1977, c 4. **Education:** Harvard, AB, 1967; Univ Chicago, MS, 1968, PhD (chem physics), 1972. **Professional Experience:** DIR, INST THEOR, ATOMIC & MOLECULAR PHYSICS, HARVARD-SMITHSONIAN CTR ASTROPHYS, 2001-; DEP DIR, INST THEOR ATOMIC & MOLECULAR PHYSICS, HARVARD-SMITHSONIAN CTR ASTROPHYS, ATOMIC & MOLECULAR PHYSICS DIV, 1989-; ASSOC DIR, HARVARD-SMITHSONIAN CTR ASTROPHYS, ATOMIC & MOLECULAR PHYSICS DIV, 1988-; mem, Comt Opportunities Physics, Am Phys Soc, 1987-1989; mem, Comt Atomic & Molecular Sci, Nat Acad Sci/Nat Res Coun, 1982-1985 & 1999-2003; RES PHYSICIST, SMITHSONIAN ASTROPHYS OBSERV, 1973-; lectr, Astron Dept, Harvard, 1973-1983 & 1984-1986; res fel astrophys, Harvard Col Observ, 1972-1973. **Memberships:** Fel Am Phys Soc; Int Astron Union; Am Astron Soc; Am Geophys Union; fel AAAS. **Research Statement & Publications:** Theoretical studies of atomic and molecular structure and processes; molecular excited states and transition probabilities; molecular photoionization; autoionization and photo dissociation; charge transfer; applications of atomic and molecular physics to astrophysics and atmospheric physics. **Mailing Address:** Harvard-Smithsonian Ctr Astrophys, Observ B-321 60 Garden St MS-14, Cambridge, MA 02138. **Fax:** 617-496-7668. **E-Mail:** kkirby@cfa.harvard.edu

KIRBY, MARGARET LOEWY, ANATOMY, PHARMACOLOGY. **Personal Data:** b Ft Smith, Ark, June 5, 1946; m 1971, c 2. **Education:** Manhattanville Col, AB, 1968; Univ Ark, PhD (anat), 1972. **Professional Experience:** PROF EMER, GRAD STUDIES, MED COL GA, as of 2005; PROF CELLULAR BIOL & ANAT, MED COL GA, as of 2005; regents prof anat, Med Col Ga, beginning 1988; Nat Heart, Lung & Blood Adv Coun, 1985-1991; NIH, 1981-1989; Nat Inst Drug Abuse, 1979-1981; Prin investr, Ga Heart Asn, 1978-1979; from asst prof to prof, Med Col GA, 1977-1988; asst prof gross anat, Cent Univ Ark, 1972-1974; Teaching asst anat, Univ Ark, 1969-1971. **Memberships:** Am Asn Anatomists; Sigma Xi; Soc Neuroscience; Soc Develop Biol. **Research Statement & Publications:** Effects of neurotransmitters on embryonic development; neural crest; heart development; molecular biology of development; pediatric cardiology. **Mailing Address:** Dept Cellular Biol & Anat, Med Col Ga, CA 4006, Augusta, GA 30912-2000. **Fax:** 706-721-6839. **E-Mail:** mkirby@mail.mcg.edu

KIRBY, PAUL EDWARD, CELL BIOLOGY. **Personal Data:** b Washington, DC, March 12, 1949; m 1971, c 4. **Education:** Mt St Mary's Col, Md, BS, 1971; Cath Univ Am, MS, 1974, PhD (cell biol), 1978. **Professional Experience:** CHMN, SITEK RES LAB, as of 1998; vpres, dir oper, sitek res lab, beginning 1984; dir oper, Microbiol Asn, 1982-1984; consult, 1980-; chief, Mammalian Mutagenesis Sect, 1980-1982; Res scientist vitro mutagenesis, EG&G Mason Res Inst, 1978-1980; Prin investr, Nat Cancer Inst. **Memberships:** AAAS; Environ Mutagen Soc; Tissue Cult Asn; Genetic Toxicol Asn; Genetic & Environ Mutagen Soc. **Research Statement & Publications:** In vitro carcinogenesis and mutagenesis in mammalian cells, especially the L5178Y mouse lymphoma mutagenesis assay as a tool for the screening of compounds for mutagenic potential; invitro toxicity test development. **Mailing Address:** Sitek Res Lab, 15235 Shady Grove Rd, Rockville, MD 20852. **Fax:** 301-926-8891.

KIRBY, RALPH C(LOUDSBERRY), EXTRACTIVE METALLURGY, MINERAL ENGINEERING. **Personal Data:** b Washington, DC, July 21, 1925; m 1950, Madge; c Charles. **Education:** Cath Univ Am, BChE, 1950. **Honors & Awards:** Gold Medal, Am Inst Chem, 1950; Invention Award, US Bur Mines; 1962, 1987 sr Exec service performance, 4, 200, 1980 Dept of the interior meritorios service award, 1978 Wash, DC, section, AIME, Herbert Hoover award, 1993. **Professional Experience:** CONSULT, NETWORK CONSULT, 1985-; chief engr, US Bur Mins, 1985; asst dir, Planning and Budget 1982-1984; dir, Min Resources Technol, 1979-1982; asst dir metall, 1976-1979; chief, Div Metall, 1972-1976; sr staff metallurgist, Div Metall, 1971-1972; staff metallurgist, Div Metall, 1966-1970; proj leader, US Bur Mines, 1959-1965; metall engr, US Bur Mines, 1955-1958; Chem engr, Metall Res Ctr, US Bur Mines 1950-1954. **Memberships:** Am Inst Mining, Metall & Petrol Engrs emer mem; Am Inst Chem Engrs emer mem; Sigma Xi emer mem; The Minerals, Metals & Metals soc. **Research Statement & Publications:** Metallurgical research; research and development management. **Mailing Address:** 15101 Interlachen Dr Apt 604, Silver Spring, MD 20906-5617.

KIRBY, RICHARD C(YRIL), ELECTRICAL ENGINEERING. **Personal Data:** b Galesburg, Ill, November 22, 1922; m 1944, c Richard C Jr, Kathleen A (Sullivan), Elizabeth, Andrew F, Eleanor C, Christine T (Bourguignon) & Michael J. **Education:** Univ Minn, BEE, 1951. **Honors & Awards:** US Dept Com, Gold Medal Award, 1956 & 1968; Award Int Commun, Inst Elec & Electronics Engrs. **Professional Experience:** DIR, RADIOCOMMUN BUR, 1993-; dir, Int Radio Consult Comt, Geneva, Switz, 1974-1993; assoc dir, Off Telecommun, 1971-1974; adj prof, Univ Denver, 1969-1974; chmn, Commun Technol Group, Inst Elec & Electronics Engrs, 1969-1971; dir, Inst Telecommun Sci, 1968-1971; dir, Ionospheric Telecommun Lab, US Dept Com, 1965-1968; US Dept Com fel sci & technol, 1965-1966; chief, Radio Systs Div, 1959-1965; mem, Interdept Radio Adv Comt, Exec Off Pres, 1959-1960; asst chief, Radio Propagation Physics Div, 1957-1959; chief, Ionospheric Res Sect, 1955-1957; res worker & proj leader radio propagation studies, Nat Bur Stand, 1948-1955; asst chief engr radio broadcast, KFEQ Inc, Mo, 1946-1948; Asst, Univ Minn, 1941-1942; telegrapher, West Union Tel Co, Minn, 1940-1942. **Memberships:** AAAS; Sigma Xi; fel Inst Elec & Electronics Engrs; Int Union Radio Sci; fel Radio Club Am. **Research Statement & Publications:** Telecommunications; radio wave propagation; antennas; information transmission; ionospheric studies; defined charcteristics of ionospheric scatter propagation and developed radio systems for application. **Mailing Address:** Int Radio Consult Comt, 2 Rue Varembe 1211, Geneva, 20, Switzerland.

KIRBY, ROBERT EMMET, ANALYTICAL CHEMISTRY. **Personal Data:** b Stowe Twp, Pa, February 27, 1921; m 1995, Etsu; c Kevin, Theresa, Margaret & Roger. **Education:** Univ Pittsburgh, BS, 1949; Carnegie Inst Technol, MS, 1952; Univ Ariz, PhD (anal chem), 1961. **Professional Experience:** RETIRED; from asst prof to assoc prof chem, Queens Col, NY, 1963-1983; sr res chemist, Colgate-Palmolive Co, 1962-1963; instr, Tex Col Arts & Indust, 1958-1959; salesman, William C Buchanan Co, 1957-1958; res chemist, Shell Chem Co, 1952-1957. **Memberships:** Am Chem Soc. **Research Statement & Publica-**

tions: Electroanalytical methods; chelate chemistry; photoelectron spectroscopy. **Mailing Address:** 5051 N Grey Mountain Trail, Tucson, AZ 85790. **E-Mail:** chikaro@theriver.com

KIRBY, ROBERT F, CARTOGRAPHY, REMOTE SENSING & PHOTOGRAMMETRY. **Personal Data:** b Norfold, Va, September 1, 1946; m Angela; c Pamela, Brian & Jennifer. **Education:** Univ Ill, BA, 1968; Purdue Univ, MS, 1974. **Professional Experience:** ACTG DIR, TOPOG ENG CTR, US ARMY, ALEXANDRIA, VA, 1996-; COMDR, US ARMY TOPOG ENG CTR, as of 1996; dir, Defense Mapping Agency, Dept Consumer Interface, 1995-1996; dir, Defense Mapping Agency Combat Support Ctr, Bethesda, Md, 1994-1995; asst dep dir oper req, Plans & Req Directorate, Hq, Defense Mapping Agency, 1992-1994; dir, Defense Mapping Agency, Hydrographic & Topog Ctr, Bethesda Md, 1991-1992; dir, Dept Topog Eng, Engr Sch, Ft Leonardwood, Mo, 1988-1991; battalion comdr, 29th Engr Battalion Topog, Ft Shafter, Hawaii, 1985-1988; topog prog officer, Off Asst Chief Staff Intel, Wash, DC, 1981-1985; sr prog officer & test & eval officer, Directorate Combat Develop, Engr Sch, 1979-1981; opers officer & exec officer, 30th Engr Battalion Topog Ft Belvoir, Va, 1977-1979; detachment opers officer, 227th Engr Detachment Topog, Hq, Ger, 1974-1977; instr, Dept Topog, Engr Sch, VA, engr intel officer, Long Binh, 1970; US Army, 1968-; comdr, 69th Engr Battalion Vietnam, theatre mapping officer. **Research Statement & Publications:** Geodetic science; topography. **Mailing Address:** US Army Topog Eng Ctr, 7701 Telegraph Rd, Alexandria, VA 22315-3864.

KIRBY, ROBION C, MATHEMATICS. **Personal Data:** b Chicago, Ill, February 25, 1938; m 1982, c 2. **Education:** Univ Chicago, BS, 1959, MS, 1960, PhD (math), 1965. **Honors & Awards:** Veblen Prize Geom, 1971. **Professional Experience:** Dep dir, Math Sci Res Inst, 1985-; PROF MATH, UNIV CALIF, BERKELEY, 1971-; asst prof, Univ Calif, Los Angeles, 1965-1969. **Memberships:** Am Math Soc. **Research Statement & Publications:** Topology, specifically topology of manifolds differential and combinatorial topology. **Mailing Address:** Dept Math, Univ Calif, Berkeley, CA 94720-3840. **Fax:** 510-642-8204. **E-Mail:** kirby@math.berkeley.edu

KIRBY, ROGER D, PHYSICS, SOLID STATE PHYSICS. **Personal Data:** b Lansing, Mich, June 1, 1942; m 1964, Suzanne; c Steven R. **Education:** Mich State Univ, BS, 1964; Cornell Univ, PhD (physics), 1969. **Professional Experience:** CHAIR, DEPT PHYSICS & ASTRON, 1995-; PROF PHYSICS, UNIV NEBR, LINCOLN, 1981-; from asst prof to assoc prof, Dept Physics & Astron, 1971-1981; res assoc physics, Cornell Univ, 1968-1969 & Univ Ill, 1969-1971. **Memberships:** Am Phys Soc; Am Asn Physics Teachers. **Research Statement & Publications:** Magnetic and magneto optic properties of solids; thin film magnetism. **Mailing Address:** Behlen Lab Physics, Univ Nebr, Lincoln, NE 68588. **Fax:** 402-472-2879. **E-Mail:** rkirby1@unl.edu

KIRBY, RONALD EUGENE, WILDLIFE BIOLOGY, GOVT RES POLICY. **Personal Data:** b Angola, Ind, November 26, 1947; m Dona J; c Peter Waye, Joshua M Brosten, Andrew J Brosten & Emily A Brosten. **Education:** Duke Univ, BS, 1969, Southern Ill Univ, MA, 1973; Univ Minn, PhD, 1976. **Professional Experience:** DIR, US GEOL SURVEY, FOREST AND RANGELAND ECOSYSTEM SCI CTR, 2001-; dir, US Nat Biol Serv, N Prairie Sci Ctr, Jamestown, 1993-2001; from asst dir to dir, N Prairie Wildlife Res Ctr, 1991-1993; leader, Info Transfer Sect, 1988-1990; regional assistance biologist, Off Info Transfer, Ft Collins, 1983-1988; res coordr, Nat Wildlife Refuge Syst, 1982-1983; pop mgt specialist, Div Refuge Mgt, Washington, 1980-1982; wildlife biologist, Patuxent Wildlife Res Ctr, US Fish & Wildlife Serv, Md, 1976-1980; res biologist, Antarctic Res Prog NSF, McMurdo Sta, 1974; grantee, AEC, 1972-1976; NIH res trainee, Dept Ecol & Behav Biol, Univ Minn, 1972-1976; Collaborating biologist, US Forest Serv, Minn, 1970-1972; Staff biologist, Coop Wildlife Res Lab, Southern Ill Univ, 1969-1972. **Memberships:** Wildlife Soc. **Research Statement & Publications:** Contributed to numerous professional publications, science journals and professional reports; waterfowl ecology and management, wetland management, census/survey techniques, large scale population research on birds, management of federal lands for wildlife. **Mailing Address:** US Geological Survey Forestland Rangeland Ecosystem Science Center, 3200 SW Jefferson Way, Corvallis, OR 97331. **Fax:** 541-758-7761. **E-Mail:** ronald.kirby@usgs.gov

KIRBY, STEPHEN, ROCK MECHANICS. **Personal Data:** b Ft Benning, Ga, May 5, 1945; m 1990, Lyle; c Adam & Ben. **Education:** Univ Ill, BS, 1967; Univ Calif, Los Angeles, PhD (geol), 1975. **Honors & Awards:** Richard Glen Award, Fuels Div, Am Chem Soc, 1997. **Professional Experience:** Mem, Sci Adv Comt, Geol Div, US Geol Surv, 1992-1995; chmn, Mineral Physics Comt, Am Geophys Union, 1991-1993; coordr, Nat Earthquake Hazard Reduction Prog, 1990-1993; Ocean Drilling Prog, Southwest Indian Ridge, 1987; mem, Int Comt Physics & Chem Ice, 1986-; co-prin investr, Planetary Geol & Geophysics Prog, NASA, 1982-; co-proj chief, China-US Coop Res, 1979-1985; RES GEOPHYSICIST, WESTERN EARTHQUAKE HAZARD TEAM, US GEOL SURV, 1968-; staff specialist, Leg 118. **Memberships:** Fel Am Geophys Union; fel Mineral Soc Am; Sigma Xi. **Research Statement & Publications:** Investigate the properties of Earth and planetary materials, including ordinary rock-forming minerals and planetary ices; physics of earthquake sources in relation to mineralogical phase changes. **Mailing Address:** Western Earthquake Hazard Team, US Geol Surv, 345 Middlefield Rd, MS 977, Rm 6-666, Menlo Park, CA 94025-3591. **Fax:** 650-329-5163. **E-Mail:** skirby@usgs.gov

KIRCH, DARRELL G, PSYCHIATRY. **Personal Data:** b Denver, Colo, May 3, 1949. **Education:** Univ Colo, BA, 1973, MD, 1977. **Honors & Awards:** Commendation Award, USPHS, 1989, Outstanding Serv Medal, 1992; Exemplary Psychiatrist Award, Nat Alliance Ment Illness, 1996. **Professional Experience:** CHIEF EXEC OFFICER, MILTON S HERSHEY MED CTR, PA STATE UNIV, 2000-; SR VPRES, HEALTH AFFAIRS, COL MED, PA STATE UNIV, 2000-; DEAN, COL MED, PA STATE UNIV, 2000-; Dean sch med & grad studies, Med Col Ga, beginning 1994. **Memberships:** AAAS; Am Col Psychiatrists; AMA; Am Soc Clin Psychiat Pharmacol; Am Psychiat Asn. **Mailing Address:** Milton S Hershey Med Ctr, Col Med, Pa State Univ, 500 Univ Dr, Hershey, PA 17033.

KIRCH, MURRAY R, PROGRAMMING METHODOLOGY. **Personal Data:** b Philadelphia, Pa, October 11, 1940; m 1965, c 2. **Education:** Temple Univ, AB, 1962; Lehigh Univ, MS, 1964, PhD (math), 1968. **Professional Experience:** Vis prof & chair comput sci, Ind Univ Coop Prog, Malaysia, 1990-1991; vis scientist, Software Eng Inst, Carnegie Mellon Univ, 1989; asst dir, Inst Retraining Comput Sci, Clarkson Univ, 1985-1988; PROF COMPUT SCI & MATH, STOCKTON COL NJ, 1984-; MacArthur distinguished vis prof arts & sci, New Col, Univ SFla, 1984-1985; assoc prof info sci & math, Stockton Col NJ, 1983-1984; assoc prof math, Stockton Col NJ, 1972-1983; asst prof, State Univ NY, Buffalo, 1968-1972; instr math, Lehigh Univ, 1965-1968; Opers analyst, Ctr Naval Anal, 1965. **Memberships:** Am Math Soc; Math Asn Am; Soc Indust & Appl Math; Am Statist Asn; Asn Comput Mach; Inst Elec & Electronics Engrs. **Research Statement & Publications:** Point-set topology; functional analysis; numerical methods for nonlinear systems; mathematical analysis of gambling and risk taking; algorithms and data structure; programming methodology; computer science theory; computer science education; artificial intelligence and expert systems; software engineering; computational science. **Mailing Address:** Dept Comput Sci, Stockton Col NJ, Jim Leeds Rd, Pomona, NJ 08240-9988. **Fax:** 609-652-4858. **E-Mail:** kirchm@stockton.edu

KIRCH, PATRICK VINTON, ARCHAEOLOGY, PALEOECOLOGY. **Personal Data:** b Honolulu, Hawaii, July 7, 1950; div. **Education:** Univ Pa, BA, 1971; Yale Univ, MPhil, 1974, PhD (anthrop), 1975. **Professional Experience:** Dir, P A Hearst Mus Anthrop, Berkeley, 1999; PROF ANTHROP, UNIV CALIF, BERKELEY, 1987-; from assoc prof to prof anthrop, Burke Mem Wash State Mus, Univ Wash, 1985-1989; dir, Burke Mem Wash State Mus, Univ Wash, 1985-1987; RES ASSOC, BERNICE P BISHOP MUS, HAWAII, 1984-; prin investr, NSF grants, Bernice P Bishop Mus, 1976-; head, Div Archaeol, 1983-1984; affil assoc prof, Univ Hawaii, 1982-1984; assoc anthropologist, Bernice P Bishop Mus, Hawaii, 1974-1975; anthropologist, Bernice P Bishop Mus, Hawaii, 1973-1985. **Memberships:** Nat Acad Sci; Sigma Xi; Asn Field Archaeol; Soc Am Archaeol; Am Anthrop Asn; Am Acad Arts & Sci; AAAS; Am Philos Soc. **Research Statement & Publications:** Archaeology, paleoecology and biogeography of the oceanic region. **Mailing Address:** Dept Anthrop, Univ Calif, Berkeley, CA 94720-0001. **Fax:** 510-643-9637. **E-Mail:** kirch@sscl.berkeley.edu

KIRCHBERGER, MADELEINE, PHYSIOLOGY. **Personal Data:** b Buffalo, NY. **Education:** Hunter Col, BA, 1960; Columbia Univ, MA, 1962, PhD (cell physiol), 1966. **Professional Experience:** ASSOC PROF PHYSIOL, BIOPHYS & MED, MT SINAI SCH MED, 1978-; asst prof, Biophys & Med, Mt Sinai Sch Med, 1974-1978; assoc, Biophys & Med, Mt Sinai Sch Med, 1971-1974; instr physiol, Biophys & Med, Mt Sinai Sch Med, 1970-1971; res fel med, Mass Gen Hosp & Sch Med, Harvard Univ, 1966-1969. **Memberships:** Am Physiol Soc; Biophys Soc; Am Soc Biol Chem; Int Soc Heart res. **Research Statement & Publications:** Regulation of cardiac contractility by catecholamines; calcium transport in biological membranes. **Mailing Address:** Dept Physiol & Biophys, Mount Sinai Sch Med, 1 Gustave L Levy Pl, New York, NY 10029. **Fax:** 212-860-3369. **E-Mail:** madeleine.kirchberger@mssm.edu

KIRCHER, JOHN FREDERICK, RADIATION CHEMISTRY, MATERIALS SCIENCES. **Personal Data:** b Athens, Ohio, January 31, 1929; m 1951, c 4. **Education:** Ohio Univ, BS, 1950, MS, 1951; Syracuse Univ, PhD (chem), 1956. **Professional Experience:** AT, BATTELLE MEM INST, as of 2004; PROG MGR, ENERGY SYSTS GROUP, BATTELLE MEM INST, 1989-; Syst Anal Dept Mgr, Off Nuclear Waste Isolation, 1982-1989; waste package dept mgr, Energy & Environ Technol Dept, 1980-1982; prog mgr, Energy & Environ Technol Dept, 1978-1980; sr chemist, Energy & Environ Technol Dept, 1976-1978; sr chemist, dept physics, 1973-1976; div chief chem physics res, Battelle Mem Inst, 1970-1973; fel chem physics res, Battelle Mem Inst, 1965-1970; assoc div chief chem physics res, Battelle Mem Inst, 1960-1965; proj leader, Battelle Mem Inst, 1957-1960; Design & develop engr, Radio Corp Am, 1955-1957. **Memberships:** AAAS; Am Chem Soc; fel Am Inst Chem; Sigma Xi. **Research Statement & Publications:** Radiation chemistry of inorganic gas phase reactions; polymers and other organic systems; radiation dosimetry; surface chemistry; vacuum techniques; gas kinetics and electrical discharges; flames; nuclear waste disposal. **Mailing Address:** 1174 Rockport Lane, Columbus, OH 43235.

KIRCHGESSNER, JOSEPH L, PHYSICS, ELECTRICAL ENGINEERING. **Personal Data:** b Wheeling, WVa, June 23, 1932; m 1956, c 3. **Education:** Le Moyne Col, NY, BS, 1954; Cornell Univ, MS, 1956. **Professional Experience:** RETIRED; res staff, Lab Elem Particles Physics, Dept Physics, Cornell Univ, as of 2001; consult, Princeton Pa Accelerator, 1971; ACCELERATOR PHYSICIST, CORNELL ELECTRON SYNCHROTRON, 1970-; Mass, 1967 & USSR, 1969; div head, Princeton Pa Accelerator, 1968-1970; mem prog comn, US Nat Particle Accelerator Conf, 1966 & 1967; sr tech staff, Princeton Pa Accelerator, 1965-1970; Del, Int Accelerator Conf, Italy, 1965; mem prof tech staff, Princeton Pa Accelerator, 1956-1965. **Memberships:** Am Phys Soc. **Research Statement & Publications:** Accelerator design and development. **Mailing Address:** Lab Elem Particle Physics, Dept Physics, Cornell Univ, 123 Newman Lab, Ithaca, NY 14853. **Fax:** 607-254-4552. **E-Mail:** jlk20@cornell.edu

KIRCHHEIMER, WALDEMAR FRANZ, microbiology; deceased, see previous edition for last biography

KIRCHHOFF, WILLIAM HAYES, PHYSICAL CHEMISTRY. **Personal Data:** b Chicago, Ill, November 27, 1936; m 1958, Ann; c Margaret A (Shearer), Daniel R, David P & Jennifer A. **Education:** Univ Ill, BS, 1958; Harvard Univ, MA, 1961, PhD (chem physics), 1963. **Honors & Awards:** Distinguished Career Service Award, Dir Off Sci. **Professional Experience:** RETIRED; dir, Chem Sci, US Dept Energy, 2002-2004; tech mgr chem physics, Div Chem Sci, Off Energy Res, US Dept Energy, beginning 1987; chief off environ measurements, Ctr Thermodyn & Molecular Sci, 1980-1982; dept dir, Ctr Thermodyn & Molecular Sci, 1978-1980; phys sci adminr off air & water measurement, Nat Bur Stand, 1972-1978; physicist, Nat Bur Stand, 1966-1972, 1983-1987; nat Res Coun res assoc chem physics, Nat Bur Stand, 1964-1966; NATO fel phys chem, Inorg Chem Lab, Oxford Univ, 1962-1963. **Memberships:** AAAS; Am Phys Soc; Am Chem Soc. **Research Statement & Publications:** Statistical analysis of physical chemistry data including spectroscopy and thermodynamics; computer modelling of physical chemical systems. **Mailing Address:** Chem Sci, GeoScis & BioScis Div, US Dept Energy, 1000 Independence Ave SW, Washington, DC 20585-1290. **Fax:** 301-903-4110. **E-Mail:** william.kirchhoff@Sci.doe.gov

KIRCHMEIER, ROBERT L, FLUORINE CHEMISTRY, SYNTHETIC CHEMISTRY. **Personal Data:** b Portland, Ore, April 25, 1942; m 1970, Nancy; c Benjamin R, Samuel & Katherine M. **Education:** Univ Mont, BS, 1968; Univ Idaho, PhD (chem), 1975. **Professional Experience:** RETIRED; exec comt, Fluorine Div, beginning 1993; assoc res prof chem, Univ Idaho, 1992-2000; vis RESAF fel, Japanese Agency Sci & Technol, 1992; assoc mem, Women Chem Comt, Am Chem Soc, 1991-1992; asst res prof, Univ Idaho, 1987-1992; pres & founder, W Analytical Lab, 1981-1987; chemist process develop, Parke-Davis Warner Lambert, 1979-1981; res scientist qual control, Charles Pfizer, Inc, 1975-1979; chemist, Univ Idaho, 1971-1975; chemist, US AEC, 1968-1971. **Memberships:** Am Chem Soc. **Research Statement & Publications:** Synthesis and physical and chemical characterization of fluorine containing inorganic and organic compounds. **Mailing Address:** Dept Chem, Univ Idaho, Moscow, ID 83844-2341. **Fax:** 208-885-6173. **E-Mail:** rlkirch@uidaho.edu

KIRCHNER, ERNST KARL, DESIGN & PRODUCTION OF BULK ACOUSTIC WAVE DEVICES. **Personal Data:** b San Francisco, Calif, June 18, 1937; m 1960, Ursula; c Mark, Christi & Steven. **Education:** Stanford Univ, BS, 1959, MS, 1960, PhD (elec eng), 1963. **Professional Experience:** DIR MICROWAVE COMPONENT PROD, TELEDYNE ELECTRONIC TECHNOLOGIES, MOUNTAIN VIEW, CALIF, 1993-; vpres, Delay Device Prod Line, 1990-1993; vpres bus develop, Teledyne Microwave, 1988-1993; dir eng, Mountain View Calif, 1987-1988; mgr eng, Mountain View Calif, 1984-1987; sr mgr, Mountain View Calif, 1983-1984; opers mgr, Mountain View Calif, 1982-1983; mgr,

Mountain View Calif, 1981-1982; staff engr, Teledyne MEC, Palo Alto, Calif, 1979-1981; proj engr, Teledyne MEC, Palo Alto, Calif, 1972-1979; mem tech staff, Teledyne MEC, Palo Alto, Calif, 1965-1972; teacher physics, Univ Ariz, 1963-1965; res physicist, US Army Res & Develop Activ, Ft Huachuca, Ariz, 1963-1965. **Memberships:** Inst Elec & Electronics Engrs; Am Phys Soc. **Research Statement & Publications:** Study of bulk acoustic waves in single crystals and their use as microwave delay devices and acousti-optic components. **Mailing Address:** 41 Ashfield Rd, Atherton, CA 94027. **Fax:** 650-962-6834. **E-Mail:** e.kirchner@mview.tet.com

KIRCHNER, FREDERICK KARL, ORGANIC CHEMISTRY, INFORMATION SCIENCE. **Personal Data:** b New YOrk, NY, May 10, 1911; m 1938, c 1. **Education:** Maryville Col, AB, 1934; Univ Tenn, MS, 1935; Ohio State Univ, PhD (org chem), 1938. **Professional Experience:** RETIRED; dir coord, Sterling Winthrop Res Inst, 1966-1976; sr res chemist & group leader, Sterling Winthrop Res Inst, 1945-1966; res chemist, Winthrop Chem Co, NY, 1943-1945; asst prof chem, Bridgewater Col, 1938-1943. **Memberships:** Am Chem Soc; fel NY Acad Sci; fel Am Inst Chem. **Research Statement & Publications:** Synthesis of pharmaceuticals; scientific information research. **Mailing Address:** 1714 Glen Echo Rd, Nashville, TN 37215.

KIRCHNER, H(ENRY) P(AUL), CERAMICS. **Personal Data:** b Buffalo, NY, September 9, 1923; m 1950, Elizabeth; c Peter D, James W & Robert L. **Education:** Cornell Univ, BME, 1947; Pa State Univ, PhD (ceramics), 1955. **Professional Experience:** RETIRED; consult, 1988-1993; pres, Ceramic Finishing Co, 1968-1988; vpres, Linden Labs, Inc, 1966-1968; tech dir, Linden Labs, Inc, 1963-1966; asst head, Mat Dept, 1960-1963; prin ceramic engr, Aeronaut Lab, Cornell Univ, 1957-1960; proj engr, Corning Glass Works, 1954-1957; prod engr, Carborundum Co, 1947-1951. **Memberships:** Fel Am Ceramic Soc; Nat Inst Ceramic Engrs. **Research Statement & Publications:** Physical and chemical properties of ceramic materials, especially refractories, abrasives and dielectrics; processes to improve strength; fractography; failure analysis; fracture mechanics. **Mailing Address:** 700 S Sparks St, State College, PA 16801.

KIRCHNER, JAMES GARY, IGNEOUS PETROLOGY, FIELD GEOLOGY. **Personal Data:** b Detroit, Mich, September 11, 1938; m 1976, Kathleen; c 5. **Education:** Wayne State Univ, BS, 1960, MS, 1962; Univ Iowa, PhD (geol), 1971. **Professional Experience:** RETIRED; prof geol, ILL state Univ, beginning 1969; Geologist petrol, Gulf Oil Corp, Libya & Nigeria, 1962-1966. **Memberships:** Geol Soc Am; Nat Asn Geol Teachers; Sigma Xi; Am Geophys Union. **Research Statement & Publications:** Igneous geology of the northern Black Hills in South Dakota. **Mailing Address:** Rural Route one, Carlock, IL 61725.

KIRCHNER, JOHN ALBERT, OTOLARYNGOLOGY. **Personal Data:** b Waynesboro, Pa, March 27, 1915; m 1947, Aline; c John C, Thomas L, Paul E, Marie C & Christine A. **Education:** Univ Va, MD, 1940. **Honorary Degrees:** MS, Yale Univ, 1952. **Honors & Awards:** Mosher Award, 1958; Casselbery Award, Am Laryngol Asn, 1966, Newcomb Award, 1969, DeRoaldes Medal, 1985; Semon lectr, Univ London, 1981. **Professional Experience:** PROF EMER, OTOLARYNGOL, SCH MED, YALE UNIV, as of 1999; Commonwealth Fund fel otolaryngol, Royal Col Surg, 1963-1964; mem, otolaryngol post-grad training comt, NIH, 1956-1959; assoc surgeon, Grace-New Haven Community Hosp, 1951-; from asst prof to prof, Sch Med, Yale Univ, 1951-1985; jr attend otolaryngologist, Children's, Deaconess, Christ & Good Samaritan Hosps, 1949-1950; resident, Johns Hopkins Hosp, 1949; instr otolaryngol, Johns Hopkins Hosp, 1948-1949. **Memberships:** Am Laryngol Asn (pres, 1979); Am Laryngol Rhinol & Otol Soc (pres, 1981-1982); Am Acad Ophthal & Otolaryngol; Am Soc Head & Neck Surg (pres, 1976); Ger Soc Otolaryngol; Ital Soc Otolaryngol. **Research Statement & Publications:** Physiology of the larynx and pharynx; pathology of laryngeal cancer. **Mailing Address:** Sect Otolaryngol, Sch Med, Yale Univ, 333 Cedar St, New Haven, CT 06510. **Fax:** 203-785-5269.

KIRCHNER, RICHARD MARTIN, INORGANIC CHEMISTRY, STRUCTURAL CHEMISTRY. **Personal Data:** b San Francisco, Calif, December 1, 1941; m 1994, A'gota. **Education:** Univ Calif, Berkeley, AB, 1964; Calif State Univ, San Jose, MS, 1966; Univ Wash, PhD (chem), 1971. **Professional Experience:** Consult, UOP LLP, 1993-; PROF CHEM, MANHATTAN COL, 1987-; res collabr chem, Brookhaven Nat Lab, 1975-1985; Consult, Tarrytown Tech Ctr, Union Carbide Corp, 1974-1993; from asst prof to assoc prof, Manhattan Col, 1973-1987; Fel chem, Northwestern Univ, 1971-1973. **Memberships:** Am Crystallog Asn; Am Chem Soc; Am Phys Soc; Sigma Xi; Int Zeolite Asn. **Research Statement & Publications:** Characterization of transition metal complexes with unusual ligands; x-ray crystallography; structural characterization of micro-crystaline molecular sieves. **Mailing Address:** Dept Chem, Manhattan Col, Bronx, NY 10471. **Fax:** 718-862-7814. **E-Mail:** richard.kirchner@manhattan.edu

KIRCHNER, ROBERT P, MECHANICAL ENGINEERING. **Personal Data:** b Orange, NJ, January 21, 1939; m 1962, c 2. **Education:** Newark Col Eng, BS, 1962, MS, 1964; Rutgers Univ, PhD (mech eng), 1968. **Professional Experience:** PROF EMER, MECH ENG, NJ INST TECHNOL, as of 2005; prof mech eng, NJ Inst techol, beginning 1976; from asst instr to assoc prof, Newark Col Eng, 1962-1976; consult, Solar Energy Syst Design. **Memberships:** Am Soc Mech Engrs; Int Solar Energy Soc. **Research Statement & Publications:** Thermodynamics; fluid mechanics; heat transfer; solar energy; energy conservation. **Mailing Address:** Dept Mech Eng, NJ Inst Technol, 323 King Blvd, Newark, NJ 07102. **E-Mail:** kirchner@admin.njit.edu

KIRCHOFF, WILLIAM F, MICROBIOLOGY. **Personal Data:** b New Rochelle, NY, April 28, 1929; m 1954, c 4. **Education:** Fordham Univ, BS, 1951; Purdue Univ, MS, 1957, PhD (microbiol), 1959; Seton Hall Univ, JD, 1972. **Professional Experience:** SR ATTY, WARNER-LAMBERT CO, 1979-; consult, Short Term Res & Develop, 1977-1979; asst dir, Short Term Res & Develop, 1974-1977; dir res, Drug Regulatory Affairs, Sandoz Inc, 1972-1974; tech coordr drug regulatory affairs, Hoffmann-La Roche, Inc, 1965-1972; res microbiologist biochem res & develop, Chas Pfizer & Co, 1960-1965; Sr microbiologist, Nuodex Prod Co Div, Tenneco Corp, 1959-1960. **Memberships:** Am Soc Microbiol; NY Acad Sci; Sigma Xi; Am Bar Asn. **Research Statement & Publications:** Microbial fermentation; antibiotics; enzymes. **Mailing Address:** 284 Roseland Ave, Essex Fells, NJ 07021.

KIRCZENOW, GEORGE, THEORY OF NANOSTRUCTURES. **Personal Data:** Australian citizen. **Education:** Univ Western Australia, BSc, 1970; Oxford Univ, DPhil(theoret physics), 1974. **Honors & Awards:** Sci and eng gold medal, sci council of british columbia canada, 1986. **Professional Experience:** PROF PHYSICS, SIMON FRASER UNIV, 1987-; US Dept Energy, 1983 & Natural Sci & Eng Res Coun, Can, 1984-; assoc prof, Simon Fraser Univ, 1983-1987; Prin investr, NSF grant, 1981-1983; Asst prof physics, Boston Univ, 1979-1983. **Memberships:** Fel Am Phys Soc; Can Asn Physicists. **Research Statement & Publications:** Theoretical solid state physics; semiconductor nanostructures; superconductors; intercalation compounds; surface physics including scanning tunneling microscopy theory; mesoscopic persistent currents; optical properties of fullereness; composite fermions. **Mailing Address:** Dept Physics, Simon Fraser Univ, Burnaby, BC V5A 1S6, Can. **Fax:** 604-291-3592. **E-Mail:** kirczeno@sfu.ca

KIRDANI, RASHAD Y, ORGANIC CHEMISTRY, BIOCHEMISTRY. **Personal Data:** b Cairo, Egypt, October 20, 1929; American citizen; m 1958, c 2. **Education:** Cairo Univ, BSc, 1950, MSc, 1955; Univ Buffalo, PhD (org chem), 1961. **Professional Experience:** Assoc res prof biochem, State Univ NY, Buffalo, 1986-; asst res prof chem, 1972-1986; PRIN CANCER RES SCIENTIST, ROSWELL PARK MEM INST, 1965-; staff scientist steroid chem & biochem, Worcester Found Exp Biol, 1962-1965; res assoc steroid chem, Worcester Found Exp Biol, 1961-1962; trainee steroid training prog, Worcester Found Exp Biol & Clark Univ, 1960-1961. **Memberships:** AAAS; Endocrine Soc; NY Acad Sci; Sigma Xi. **Research Statement & Publications:** Chemistry and biochemistry of steroid hormones and interferons. **Mailing Address:** Dept Genetic & Endocrinol Roswell Park Mem Inst, 666 Elm St, Buffalo, NY 14263-0001.

KIREMIDJIAN, ANNE SETIAN, EARTHQUAKE Engineering, Structural Health Monitoring, Wireless Sensing Systems. **Personal Data:** b Sofia, Bulgaria, August 11, 1949; American citizen; m 1972, Garo; c Seta N. **Education:** Columbia Univ, BS, 1972; Stanford Univ, MS, 1973, PhD (civil eng), 1977. **Honors & Awards:** School of Engineering Distinguished Advisor Award, Stanford University, June 1989; National Science Foundation Faculty Award for Women, 1991-1995; Society of Women Engineers Distinguished Educator Award, 1992; American Society of Civil Engineer, Technical Council on Lifeline Earthquake Engineering; Distinguished Service Award, August 11, 1995. **Professional Experience:** Visiting Lecturer, Dept. of Civil Engineering (1976-77); Postdoctoral Research Affiliate, Department of Civil Engineering (1976-78); Assistant Professor, Department of Civil Engineering (1978-85); Associate Professor (1985-91); Co-Director of the John A. Blume Earthquake Engineering Center (1987-94); Full Professor, Department of Civil and Environmental Engineering (1991-); Director of the John A. Blume Earthquake Engineering Center (1995-02); Committee on Undergraduate Admissions and Financial Aid (1982-86); Committee on Undergraduate Standards and Policy (2003-); Committee on Building and Land Development (1996-98, 2004-); Member, Editorial Board: International Journal of Soil Mechanics and Earthquake Engineering(1995-), International Journal of Structural Safety (1985-95), International Journal on Probabilistic Mechanics (1989-), Earthquake Spectra (1990-00), Journal of Earthquake Engineering (1998-), Journal of Earthquake Engineering and Engineering Seismology (2000-); Chairman of the Board, K2 Technologies, Inc. (1994-98); Chairman of the Board, Sensametrics. Inc. (2003-). **Memberships:** Am Soc Civil Engrs; Seismol Soc Am; Int Asn Struct Safety & Reliability; Earthquake Eng Res Inst; Structural Engineers Asn of California. **Research Statement & Publications:** Research Statement Earthquake occurrence modelings; earthquake ground motion characterization; damage estimation and forecasting modeling; application of stochastie processes to earthquake engineering; structural reliability analysis models; wireless sensorf for structural damage monitoring; damage detection algorithms; risk assessment of spatially distributed systems; More than 150 publications in refereed journals, conference proceedings and reports. **Mailing Address:** Dept Civil Eng, Stanford Univ, Rm 238, Terman Eng Ctr, Stanford, CA 94305-4020. **Fax:** 650-723-7514. **E-Mail:** ask@stanford.edu

KIRK, ALEXANDER DAVID, INORGANIC CHEMISTRY, PHYSICAL CHEMISTRY. **Personal Data:** b London, Eng, April 17, 1934; Canadian citizen; m 1980, Glenda; c Natalie S, Robin A & Madeleine R. **Education:** Univ Edinburgh, BSc, 1956, PhD (chem), 1959. **Professional Experience:** ADJ PROF CHEM, UNIV VICTORIA, BC, as of 2004; NSERC/Swiss Nat Res Found Int Sci Exchange Award, Univ Bern, Switz, 1991 & 1995; actg dir, Can Ctr Picosecond Laser Flash Photolysis, Concordia Univ, Montreal, 1983; res assoc, Univ Southern Calif, Los Angeles, 1980; vis prof, Sch Molecular Sci, Univ Sussex, 1975-1976; chmn dept, Univ Victoria, Bc, 1974-1979; prof chem, Univ Victoria, Bc, beginning 1971; Humbolt fel, 1968-1969; from asst prof to assoc prof, Univ Victoria, BC, 1961-1971; res fel chem, Univ BC, 1959-1961. **Research Statement & Publications:** retired. **Mailing Address:** Dept Chem, Univ Victoria, PO Box 3065, Victoria, BC V8W 3V6, Can. **Fax:** 250-721-7147. **E-Mail:** kirkad@uvic.ca

KIRK, BEN TRUETT, PLANT PATHOLOGY. **Personal Data:** b Natchitoches, La, October 1, 1942; m 1966. **Education:** La Polytech Inst, BS, 1964; La State Univ, MS, 1966, PhD (plant path), 1968. **Professional Experience:** EMER PROF BOT, 1989-; from asst prof to assoc prof, 1968-1987. **Memberships:** Am Phytopath Soc. **Research Statement & Publications:** Fungal ultrastructure; systemic fungicides. **Mailing Address:** 80407 Meadow Lark Loop, Bush, LA 70431.

KIRK, BILLY EDWARD, VIROLOGY. **Personal Data:** b Robinson, Ill, May 5, 1927; div, c 2. **Education:** Univ Ill, BS, 1949; Ohio State Univ, MSc, 1955, PhD (microbiol), 1957. **Professional Experience:** ASSOC PROF MICROBIOL, WVA UNIV, 1973-; asst prof, Wva Univ, 1964-1973; instr, Univ Mich, 1962-1964; Sr bacteriologist, Eli Lilly & Co, Ind, 1957-1962. **Memberships:** AAAS; Am Soc Microbiol; Brit Soc Gen Microbiol; Tissue Cult Asn; Sigma Xi. **Research Statement & Publications:** Virology; biology and pathogenic role of defective viruses; virus persistence. **Mailing Address:** 914 Guyasuta Lane, Pittsburgh, PA 15215-1650.

KIRK, DALE E(ARL), AGRICULTURAL ENGINEERING, FOOD PROCESSING. **Personal Data:** b Payette, Idaho, July 2, 1918; m 1939, Esther; c Janet E Laind, Stanley D, Carolyn V Johnson, Joyce L Jennings & Marvin D. **Education:** Ore State Univ, BS, 1942; Mich State Univ, MS, 1954. **Professional Experience:** EMER PROF, ORE STATE UNIV, 1983-; actg head dept, agr eng, Ore State Univ, 1970-1971 & 1980-1981; PROF AGR ENG & AGR ENGR, ORE STATE UNIV, 1963-; assoc prof agr eng, agr eng, Ore State Univ, 1954-1963; asst agr engr, agr eng, Ore State Univ, 1942-1944 & 1946-1954; Asst, agr eng, Ore State Univ, 1941-1942. **Memberships:** Fel Am Soc Agr Engrs; Sigma Xi. **Research Statement & Publications:** Food engineering; processing and handling agricultural products; agricultural machine design. **Mailing Address:** 8150 NW Mitchell Dr, Corvallis, OR 97330-2823.

KIRK, DANIEL EDDINS, BIOLOGY. **Personal Data:** b Rocky Mount, NC, February 19, 1924; m 1946, c 4. **Education:** Furman Univ, BS, 1948; Univ NC, MA, 1950; Emory Univ, PhD, 1957. **Professional Experience:** PROF EMER BIOL, CATAWBA COL, 1998-; prof biol, Catawba Col, 1957-1998; Asst prof biol, Furman Univ, 1950-1957. **Memberships:** Am Soc Parasitol; Am Micros Soc. **Research Statement & Publications:** Helminthology; reptilian blood flukes. **Mailing Address:** Dept Biol, Catawba Col, 2300 W Innes St, Salisbury, NC 28144.

KIRK, DAVID BLACKBURN, mathematics; deceased, see previous edition for last biography

KIRK, DAVID CLARK, PHYSICAL CHEMISTRY, PROTECTIVE COATINGS PIGMENT MANUFACTURING. **Personal Data:** b Newark, NJ, May 19, 1924; m 1953, Frances S Sutherland; c Winifred, Linda & Andrew. **Education:** Lehigh Univ, BS, 1944; Polytech Inst

New York, MS, 1951; Univ Iowa, PhD (chem), 1953; Furman Univ, MBA, 1979. **Professional Experience:** TECH DIR, TULIP GAP TECHNOL, 1989-; tech dir, Allied Paper Div, SCM Corp, 1976-1989; dir res & develop, Ecusta Paper Div, Olin Corp, 1969-1976; dir fundamental res, Ecusta Paper Div, Olin Corp, 1959-1969; res chemist, Hercules Powder Co, 1953-1959; chemist, Merck & Co, 1948-1950; Chem engr, Am Dyewood Co 1946-1948. **Memberships:** Am Chem Soc; Sigma Xi; Tech Asn Pulp & Paper Indust. **Research Statement & Publications:** Organic chemistry; kinetics, photo and surface chemistry of protective coatings; elastomers and papers. **Mailing Address:** 114 River Ridge Rd, Brevard, NC 28712-9530.

KIRK, DAVID LIVINGSTONE, DEVELOPMENTAL BIOLOGY, VOLVOCINE EVOLUTION. **Personal Data:** b Clinton, Mass, March 19, 1934; m 1958, Marilyn; c 1. **Education:** Northeastern Univ, AB, 1956; Univ Wis, MS, 1958, PhD (biochem), 1960. **Professional Experience:** PROF, DEPT BIOL, WASH UNIV, beginning 1979; Dean Grad Sch, Wash Univ, 1979; assoc prof, Biol, Wash Univ, 1969-1979; asst prof, Univ Chicago, 1965-1969; res assoc develop biol, Univ Chicago, 1962-1965; sr res chemist, Biol Res Labs, Colgate-Palmolive Co, 1960-1962; res asst biochem, Univ Wis, 1956-1960; res technician, Lovett Mem Lab, Mass Gen Hosp, Boston, 1952-1956. **Memberships:** Fel AAAS; Am Chem Soc; Soc Develop Biol; Am Soc Cell Biol; Sigma Xi. **Research Statement & Publications:** Developmental biochemistry and genetics; analysis of genetic, cytological and molecular basis of cell determination and cytodifferentiation in simple eukaryotes; evolution of multicellularity and germ/soma differentiation. **Mailing Address:** Dept Biol, Wash Univ, Campus Box 1137, St Louis, MO 63130. **Fax:** 314-935-5125. **E-Mail:** kirk@biodec.wustl.edu

KIRK, DONALD EVAN, ELECTRICAL ENGINEERING. **Personal Data:** b Baltimore, Md, April 4, 1937; m 1962, Judith Sand; c Kara, Valerie & Dana. **Education:** Worcester Polytech Inst, BS, 1959; Naval Postgrad Sch, MS, 1961; Univ Ill, PhD (elec eng), 1965. **Honors & Awards:** fel, IEEE, 1992; fel, ASEE, 1998. **Professional Experience:** DEAN ENG, SAN JOSE STATE UNIV, 1994-; prog officer, Div Undergrad Studies, NSF, 1993-1994; PROF ELEC ENG, SAN JOSE STATE UNIV, 1990-; assoc dean eng, San Jose State Univ, 1987-1990; Vis staff scientist, Lincoln Lab, Mass Inst Technol, 1981-1982; prof elec eng, Naval Postgrad Sch, 1976-1987; chmn dept, Naval Postgrad Sch, 1976-1983; from asst prof to assoc prof, Naval Postgrad Sch, 1965-1976; instr, Univ Ill, 1963-1964; teaching asst, Univ Ill, 1962-1963; Instr elec eng, Naval Postgrad Sch, 1959-1962. **Memberships:** Fel Inst Elec & Electronics Engrs; Am Soc Eng Educ; Sigma Xi; Soc Women Engrs. **Research Statement & Publications:** Signal processing. **Mailing Address:** Col Eng, San Jose State Univ, San Jose, CA 95192-0080. **Fax:** 408-924-3818. **E-Mail:** dkirk@email.sjsu.edu

KIRK, DONALD WAYNE, CIVIL ENGINEERING, RESEARCH ADMINISTRATION. **Personal Data:** b Carleton Place, Ont, August 18, 1934; m 1958, Diane; c Beth, Janice & David. **Education:** Queen's Univ, BSc, 1956, MSc, 1965, PhD (struct eng), 1969. **Honors & Awards:** Duggan Medal, Eng Inst Can, 1965. **Professional Experience:** DEAN, ACAD SERV, 1993-; dean, Can Forces Mil Col, 1984-1993; head, Dept Civil Eng, 1977-1984; PROF STRUCT, ROYAL MIL COL CAN, 1975-; from lectr to prof, Acad Serv, 1962-1975; officer, Royal Can Engrs, Can Forces, 1956-1965. **Memberships:** Am Concrete Inst; Eng Inst Can; Am Soc Eng Educ. **Research Statement & Publications:** Ultimate strength of reinforced concrete slab and girder systems; analysis and design of beams containing web openings; slab column connections. **Mailing Address:** Acad Serv, Royal Mil Col, Kingston, ON K7K 5L0, Can. **Fax:** 613-545-3481.

KIRK, HAROLD GLEN, HIGH ENERGY PHYSICS. **Personal Data:** b Konawa, Okla, December 18, 1941. **Education:** Univ Okla, BS, 1964, PhD (physics), 1972. **Professional Experience:** RES STAFF, BROOKHAVEN NAT LAB, as of 2003; STAFF SCIENTIST, BROOKHAVEN NAT LAB, 1979-. **Memberships:** Am Phys Soc. **Mailing Address:** Brookhaven Nat Lab, Bldg 901A PO Box 5000, Upton, NY 11973-5000. **Fax:** 631-344-3248. **E-Mail:** hkirk@bnl.gov

KIRK, IVAN WAYNE, COTTON PRODUCTION, COTTON PROCESSING & APPLICATION TECHNOLOGY. **Personal Data:** b Lark, Tex, January 25, 1937; m 1960, Latrelle; c Kimberly (Westbrook) & Kendal W. **Education:** Tex Tech Univ, BS, 1959; Clemson Univ, MS, 1961; Auburn Univ PhD (agr eng), 1968. **Honors & Awards:** Arthur S Fleming Award, 1975. **Professional Experience:** MEM, GRAD FAC, TEX A&M UNIV, 1994-; AGR ENGR, SOUTHERN PLAINS AGR RES CTR, AGR RES SERV, USDA, COLLEGE STATION, TEX, 1987-; dir, Southern Regional Res Ctr, 1982-1987; actg dir, New Orleans, 1980-1982; assoc dir, New Orleans, 1977-1980; lab dir, NMex, 1971-1977; Agr Res Serv, USDA, Lubbock, 1965-1967; instr & asst prof, dept agr eng, Tex Tech Univ, 1963-1965; res agr engr, Agr Res Serv, USDA, Lubbock, 1960-1965 & 1967-1971. **Memberships:** AAAS; Am Soc Agr Engrs; Coun Agr Sci & Technol; Am Stand Testing Mat; Ent Ecol Soc Am. **Research Statement & Publications:** New and improved methods, and machinery for cotton production, harvesting, and ginning; improved technology for aerial application of pesticides. **Mailing Address:** Agr Res Serv USDA, 2771 F & B Rd, College Station, TX 77845. **Fax:** 979-260-9386. **E-Mail:** i-kirk@tamu.edu

KIRK, JAMES CURTIS, ORGANIC CHEMISTRY. **Personal Data:** b Hubbard, Tex, May 10, 1921; m 1944, c 5. **Education:** Baylor Univ, BS, 1944; Ohio State Univ, PhD (chem), 1949. **Professional Experience:** VPRES RES & DEVELOP DEPT, CONOCO INC, 1975-; gen mgr, Environ Conserv, Res & Eng Dept, 1967-1975; dir, Environ Conserv, Res & Eng Dept, 1966-1967; dir, Petrochem Res Div, Res & Develop Dept, Conoco Inc, 1960-1966; dir res, Petrol Chem, Inc, 1957-1960; supvry res chemist, Continental Oil Co, 1955-1957; res group leader, Continental Oil Co, 1953-1955; from assoc res chemist to sr res chemist, Continental Oil Co, 1949-1953; asst chem, Ohio State Univ, 1946-1949; Analyst, Pan Am Ref Corp, 1944-1946. **Memberships:** Am Chem Soc; Soc Petrol Engrs. **Research Statement & Publications:** Hydrocarbon oxidation; lubricating oil additives; surface active agents; reaction mechanisms; polymerication; research administration. **Mailing Address:** 1308 Arronimink Circle, Austin, TX 78746-6303.

KIRK, JAMES ROBERT, FOOD SCIENCE & TECHNOL. **Personal Data:** b Du Bois, Pa, October 30, 1941; m 1985, Paulette; c Leanne, James J & John D. **Education:** Holy Cross Col, BS, 1964; Mich State Univ, MS, 1966, PhD (food sci & human nutrit), 1971. **Honors & Awards:** Future Leader Award, Nutrit Found, 1977; Babcock Hart Award, Inst Food Technol, 1983. **Professional Experience:** PRES, CAMPBELL INST RES & TECHNOL, 1988-; dir, DNA Plant Technol Corp, 1986-1990; SR VPRES RES & DEVELOP & QUALITY ASSURANCE, CAMPBELL SOUP CO, 1983-; dir, Nat Nutrit Consort, 1979-1983; prof, Mich State Univ, 1978; prof & chmn, Food Sci & Human Nutrit Dept, Univ Fla, 1978; from asst prof to assoc prof, Mich StateUniv, 1971-1978. **Memberships:** Joseph Stokes Jr Res Inst; Am Inst Nutrit; Nat Food Process Asn; Inst Food Technol; Int Life Sci Inst. **Research Statement & Publications:** Effects of food processing on the stability and bioavailability of nutrients in foods. **Mailing Address:** Res & Develop Campbell Soup Co, Campbell Pl, Camden, NJ 08103-1799. **Fax:** 856-342-6445.

KIRK, JOE ECKLEY, MATHEMATICS. **Personal Data:** b Houston, Tex, May 17, 1939; m 1967, c 3. **Education:** Sam Houston State Univ, BA, 1960; Univ Tex, Austin, MA, 1962, PhD (math), 1967. **Professional Experience:** PROF MATH, SAM HOUSTON STATE UNIV, 1988-; assoc prof math, Sam Houston State Univ, 1980-1988; assoc prof, Univ Tenn, Chattanooga, 1976-1980; asst prof math, Univ Tenn, Chattanooga, 1974-1976; asst prof math, Univ Wyo, 1969-1974; opers res analyst, US Arms Control & Disarmament Agency, 1967-1969. **Memberships:** Asn Comput Mach; Am Math Soc; Math Asn Am. **Research Statement & Publications:** Complex analysis; function theory. **Mailing Address:** Dept Math, Sam Houston State Univ, PO Box 2206 LDB 433, Huntsville, TX 77341-2206. **E-Mail:** mth_jek@shsu.edu

KIRK, JOHN GALLATIN, SOLAR PHYSICS, AEROSPACE SCIENCES. **Personal Data:** b Wilmington, Ohio, October 21, 1938. **Education:** Amherst Col, AB, 1960; Univ Mich, AM, 1962, PhD (astron), 1966. **Honors & Awards:** Tech Innovation Award, NASA, 1981. **Professional Experience:** MEM PROF STAFF, ILLGEN SIMULATION TECHNOL, INC, 1995-; mem prof staff, Geodynamics Corp, 1980-1995; sr analyst, Electronics Div, Gen Dynamics Corp, 1979-1980; staff scientist, Comput Sci Corp, 1974-1979; asst prof astron, Univ Toledo, 1969-1974; Jr astronr, Kitt Peak Nat Observ, 1966-1969. **Memberships:** Am Astron Soc; Sigma Xi; Am Geophys Union; Inst Navig. **Research Statement & Publications:** Physics of the solar atmosphere; physical geodesy; satellite orbit management. **Mailing Address:** 325 Palisades Dr, Santa Barbara, CA 93109.

KIRK, MARILYN M, DEVELOPMENTAL BIOLOGY. **Personal Data:** b Bridgeport, Nebr, May 8, 1927; m 1958, c 1. **Education:** Univ Nebr, BS, 1948; Univ Wis, MS, 1954, PhD (nutrit, biochem), 1956. **Professional Experience:** RETIRED; res assoc, Dept Biol, Wash Univ, 1969-1995; res assoc, Dept Biol, Univ Chicago, 1965-1969; res assoc, Am Meat Inst Found, Ill, 1963-1964; asst prof foods & nutrit, Sch Home Econ, Univ Wis, 1956-1960; asst nutrit, Univ Nebr, 1948-1952. **Research Statement & Publications:** Biochemical studies of development and cytodifferentiation in simple eukaryotes. **Mailing Address:** 1115 Cheshire Lane, St Louis, MO 63119. **Fax:** 314-935-4432.

KIRK, PAUL WHEELER, MYCOLOGY, BACTERIOLOGY. **Personal Data:** b Jacksonville, Fla, February 23, 1931; m 1958, c 2. **Education:** Univ Richmond, BS, 1957, MS, 1961; Duke Univ, PhD (bot), 1966. **Professional Experience:** RETIRED; prof biol, Old Dom Univ, 1977-1995; asst dean sci & health professions, Old Dom Univ, 1973-1978; assoc prof biol, Old Dom Univ, 1971-1977; asst prof bot, Va Polytech Inst, 1966-1970; asst prof biol, Western Carolina Col, 1965-1966; consult med microbiol & pre-health prof adv. **Memberships:** Mycol Soc Am; Sigma Xi; Nat Asn Adv Health Prof. **Research Statement & Publications:** Marine ascomycetes and deuteromycetes. **Mailing Address:** 1213 Kittery Dr, Virginia Beach, VA 23464.

KIRK, R(OBERT) S(TEWART), CHEMICAL ENGINEERING. **Personal Data:** b Chicago, Ill, November 2, 1922; m 1958, c 2. **Education:** Ill Inst Technol, BS & MS, 1943; Univ Wis, PhD (chem eng), 1948. **Professional Experience:** ASSOC PROF EMER CHEM ENG, UNIV MASS, AMHERST, 1989-; assoc prof chem eng, Univ Mass, Amherst, 1966-1989; sr res engr, Chevron Res Co, Standard Oil Co Calif, 1964-1966; group supvr thermal recovery, Calif Res Corp, 1958-1964; res engr, Calif Res Corp, 1955-1958; asst prof chem eng, Univ Wis, 1948-1955. **Memberships:** Am Chem Soc; Am Inst Chem Engrs. **Research Statement & Publications:** Process design and evaluation; chemical kinetics and reactor design; thermal methods of secondary recovery of crude oil. **Mailing Address:** Univ Mass, Dept Chem Eng, 159 Goessman Lab N Pleasant St, Amherst, MA 01003. **Fax:** 413-545-1647.

KIRK, ROBERT WARREN, VETERINARY MEDICINE. **Personal Data:** b Stamford, Conn, May 20, 1922; m 1949, c 3. **Education:** Univ Conn, BS, 1943; Cornell Univ, DVM, 1946; Am Col Vet Internal Med, dipl & cert internal med & dermat. **Honors & Awards:** Fido Award, Am Animal Hosp Asn, 1964; Gaines Medal, 1967. **Professional Experience:** EMER, NY State Col Veterinary Med, as of 2006; trustee, Seeing Eye Found, 1977-; vis prof, Sch Med Stanford Univ, 1975; pres, Am Col Vet Internal Med, 1974-1976; Evelyn Williams fel & vis scholar, Univ Sydney, Australia, 1974; mem Grants Adv Bd, Seeing Eye Found, NY, 1970-1973; chmn, Dept Small Animal Med & Surg & dir, Small Animal Hosp, 1969-1977; NSF sci fac fel, Sch Med Stanford Univ, 1967-1969; Fel, Sch Med, Univ Colo, 1960-1961; from asst prof to prof med, Vet Col, State Univ NY, Cornell Univ, 1952-1985; Pvt pract, 1946-1950; pres & chmn, Bd Regents, Am Col Vet Internal Med. **Memberships:** Am Vet Med Asn; Am Animal Hosp Asn; Am Col Vet Dermat (pres). **Research Statement & Publications:** Clinical medicine and dermatology therapeutics. **Mailing Address:** 440 Savage Farm Rd, Ithaca, NY 14850-6507.

KIRK, ROGER E, EXPERIMENTAL DESIGN. **Personal Data:** b Princeton, Ind, February 23, 1930; m 1983, Jane. **Education:** Ohio State Univ, BS, 1951, MA, 1952, PhD (psychol), 1955. **Honors & Awards:** Jacob Cohen Award for Distinguished Contributions to Teaching and Mentoring for 2005; Ohio State University Department of Psychology Distinguished Alumnus Award for 2001; Fellow of the American Psychology Assoc Divisions 1, 2, 5, 13; Distinguished Professor of Psychology and Statistics, title conferred by Baylor U 3/1995; President of the Southwestern Psychological Association, 1995-1996; Master Teacher, title conferred by Baylor University 6/1993; Outstanding Tenured Teacher in the College of Arts and Sciences, Baylor University, 1992-1993. **Professional Experience:** Distinguished prof of Psychology & Statistics, 1995-; dir, Inst Statist, 1991-2001; PRES, RES CONSULTS, 1982-; dir, Behav Statist Prog, Baylor Univ, 1976-; vis prof, Seinan Gaukin Univ, Fukuoka, Japan, 1973-1974; Postdoctoral statist, Univ Mich, 1971; prof psychol, Baylor Univ, 1964-; from asst prof to assoc prof, Baylor Univ, 1958-1964; Sr psychoacoust engr, Baldwin Piano & Organ Co, 1955-1958. **Memberships:** Fel Am Psychol Asn; Am Statist Asn; Psychometric Soc; Human Factors Soc; fel Am Psychol Soc. **Research Statement & Publications:** Statistical methodology; author of various publications; author of five textbooks on statistics and over 100 scientific papers. **Mailing Address:** Psychol Dept, Baylor Univ, Waco, TX 76798-7334. **E-Mail:** roger_kirk@baylor.edu

KIRK, T KENT, MICROBIAL BIOCHEMISTRY & OXIDATIVE PROCESSES, WOOD BIODETERIORATION. **Personal Data:** b Homer, Louisiana, October 13, 1940; wid Celeste; c Sharon, Katherine, Sandra & Kathryn. **Education:** La Polytech Inst, BS, 1962; NC State Univ, MS, 1964, PhD (biochem & plant path), 1968; postdoctoral org chem Chalmers Technical Univ, Sweden 1968-9. **Honors & Awards:** International Academy of Wood Science, 1972; USDA Award for Superior Service, 1978, 1982; Marcus Wallenberg Prize, Sweden, 1985; National Academy of Sciences, elected 1988; William H Aiken Prize, Tech Asn Pulp & Paper Indust, 1986; Marvin Johnson Award, Am Chem Soc, 1992. **Professional Experience:** PROF EMER, DEPT BACT, UNIV WIS-MADISON, as of 2004; Co-organizer, Int Conf Biotechnol Pulp & Paper Indust, 1989; dir, Inst Microbiol & Biochem Technol, 1985-1997 USDA Forest Service, Forest Products Laboratory; Prof Dept Bact, Univ Wis-Madison, beginning 1982; chmn, Gordon Res Conf Chem & Mat Natural Resources, 1982; supvry microbiologist, Forest Prod Lab, Forest Serv, USDA, 1980-1985; Vis prof, Kyoto Univ, Japan, 1979-1980; res microbiologist, Forest Prod Lab, Forest Serv,

USDA, 1970-1980; res assoc org chem, Chalmers Univ Technol, Sweden, 1968-1969; fel polymer chem, NC State Univ, 1967-1968; consult lignin biodegradation & applications bio-ligninolytic systs, industs, univs & res insts. **Memberships:** Nat Acad Sci; fel Int Acad Wood Sci (secy-treas 1985-1990; president 1990-1993); Am Soc Microbiol; Am Chem Soc; Am Soc Biochem & Molecular Biol; Tech Asn Pulp & Paper Indust. **Research Statement & Publications:** Biochemistry and physiology of wood decomposition by fungi, industrial application of fungi and enzymes; author of over 200 articles in scientific journals. **Mailing Address:** 3788 Lars Vale Rd, Deerfield, WI 53531. **Fax:** -. **E-Mail:** tkkirk@wisc.edu

KIRK, THOMAS BERNARD WALTER, HIGH ENERGY PHYSICS. **Personal Data:** b Denver, Colo, June 13, 1940; m 1974, c 2. **Education:** Univ Colo, Boulder, BS, 1962; Univ Wash, MS, 1964, PhD (physics), 1967. **Professional Experience:** ASSOC DIR HIGH ENERGY & NUCLEAR PHYSICS, BROOKHAVEN NAT LAB, 1994-; dir, Hep Div, Argonne Nat Lab, 1989-1994; consult, Dept Eng, Can Sci Coun, 1984-; Tev II proj mgr, physics res div head, 1981-1989; head, Neutrino Dept, Fermi Nat Accelerator Lab, 1976-1981; assoc prof physics, Univ Ill, Urbana, 1973-1976; Mem, Prog Adv Comt, Fermilab, 1970-1972; from asst prof to assoc prof, Harvard Univ, 1969-1973; fel physics, Harvard Univ, 1967-1969. **Memberships:** Fel Am Phys Soc. **Research Statement & Publications:** Experimental investigation of fundamental particle processes in strong; electromagnetic and weak interactions at high energies. **Mailing Address:** Brookhaven Nat Lab, Bldg 510F PO Box 5000, Upton, NY 11973-5000. **Fax:** 631-344-5820. **E-Mail:** tkirk@bnl.gov

KIRK, WILEY PRICE, CONDENSED MATTER PHYSICS, NANOSTRUCTURES, LOW TEMPERATURE & MESOSCOPIC PHYSICS & NANOELECTRONIC SYSTEMS & DEVICES. **Personal Data:** b Joplin, Mo, July 24, 1942; American citizen; m 1964, Sally; c Alexander P & Camille M. **Education:** Wash Univ, BA, 1964; State Univ NY, Stony Brook, MS, 1967, PhD (physics), 1970. **Professional Experience:** PROF ELEC ENG, UNIV TEX-ARLINGTON, 1999-; dir, Ctr Nanostruct Mat & Quantum Device Fabrication, 1990-2002; dir, Nano FAB Ctr, 1990-2002; prof physics & elec eng, Tex A&M Univ, 1985-1999; TEX INSTRUMENTS INC, 1983-; consult, Nalorac Cryog Corp, 1980-1984; from asst prof to prof physics, Tex A&M, 1975-1984; asst prof, Univ Fla, 1973-1975; interim asst prof, Univ Fla, 1971-1973; consult, Sci Instruments, Inc, 1970-1975; fel, Univ Fla, 1970-1971; instr, State Univ NY, Stony Brook, 1969-1970; tech collabr, Brookhaven Nat Lab, 1969-1970; jr res assoc physics, Brookhaven Nat Lab, 1967-1969; assoc ed, Superlattices & Microstruct. **Memberships:** AAAS; Am Phys Soc; Sigma Xi; Am Vacuum Soc; Mat Res Soc; Inst Elec & Electronics Engrs. **Research Statement & Publications:** 2-D charge transport and magnetoconduction; quantum Hall effect; nanostructures and electron-beam patterning; transport in mesoscopic systems and superlattics; molecular beam epitaxy; quantum effect devices; thermodynamic, magnetic and nuclear magnetic resonance properties of materials; quantum crystals of helium; methods of low temperature thermometry; cryogenic and superconducting devices; low temperature thermoelectric studies; millikelvin-thermocouple-thermometry; superconducting quantum interference detector and pulsed nuclear magnetic resonance techniques; high temperature superconductivity; magnetic surface effects. **Mailing Address:** Elec Eng Dept, Univ Tex, 416 Yates St PO Box 19016, Arlington, TX 76010. **Fax:** 817-272-7458. **E-Mail:** kirk@uta.edu

KIRK, WILLIAM ARTHUR, MATHEMATICS. **Personal Data:** b Montour Falls, NY, October 3, 1936. **Education:** DePauw Univ, AB, 1958; Univ Mo, MA, 1960, PhD (math), 1962. **Professional Experience:** Chmn dept, Univ Iowa, 1985-1991; PROF MATH, UNIV IOWA, 1970-; assoc prof, Univ Iowa, 1967-1970; asst prof math, Univ Calif, Riverside, 1962-1967. **Memberships:** Am Math Soc; Math Asn Am. **Research Statement & Publications:** Metric and geodesic geometry; functional analysis. **Mailing Address:** Dept Math, Univ Iowa, 14 MLH, Iowa City, IA 52242-1419. **Fax:** 319-335-0627. **E-Mail:** william-kirk@uiowa.edu

KIRK, WILLIAM LEROY, nuclear engineering; deceased, see previous edition for last biography

KIRKALDY, J(OHN) S(AMUEL), PHYSICAL METALLURGY. **Personal Data:** b Victoria, BC, May 13, 1926; m 1952, c 3. **Education:** Univ BC, BASc, 1949, MASc, 1951; McGill Univ, PhD (physics), 1953. **Professional Experience:** PROF EMER METALL, MCMASTER UNIV, as of 2004; STEEL CO CAN CHAIR METALL, MCMASTER UNIV, 1966-; prof metall, Mcmaster Univ, 1963-; chmn dept, Mcmaster Univ, 1962-1966; from asst prof to assoc prof metall, Mcmaster Univ, 1957-1963; asst prof metall eng, McGill Univ, 1954-1957; Res assoc physics, McGill Univ, 1953-1954. **Memberships:** Am Soc Metals; Am Inst Mining Metall & Petrol Engrs; Can Asn Physicists; Can Inst Mining & Metall; Sigma Xi. **Research Statement & Publications:** Application of thermodynamics of irreversible processes to metallurgy. **Mailing Address:** Dept Metallurgy & Mat Sci, McMaster Univ, 1280 Main St West, Hamilton, ON L8S 4L8, Can. **Fax:** 905-521-2773.

KIRKBRIDE, CLYDE ARNOLD, VETERINARY BACTERIOLOGY. **Personal Data:** b Los Angeles, Calif, March 14, 1924; m 1944, c 5. **Education:** Okla State Univ, DVM, 1953; SDak State Univ, MS, 1970. **Professional Experience:** Pres-elect, Western Vet Conf, 1988; PROF VET MED, ANIMAL DIS RES & DIAG LAB, SDAK STATE UNIV, 1982-; pres, Am Leptospirosis Res Conf, 1981; Vet investr officer, NZ Ministry Agr & Fisheries, 1974-1975; from instr to assoc prof, Animal Dis Res & Diag Lab, Sdak State Univ, 1967-1982; asst prof vet med, Col Vet Med, Kans State Univ, 1963-1967; vet practr, 1953-1963. **Memberships:** Am Vet Med Asn; Am Asn Vet Lab Diagnosticians; US Animal Health Asn. **Research Statement & Publications:** Water intoxication in cattle; relationship of milking machine function to mastitis in cattle; diseases affecting reproduction in animals; fetal serology in diagnosis of bovine abortion; swine tuberculosis; diagnosis of leptospirosis; nonclassified anaerobic bacterium that causes abortion in sheep. **Mailing Address:** 2015 Iowa St, Brookings, SD 57006.

KIRKBRIDE, JOSEPH HAROLD, TAXONOMIC BOTANY. **Personal Data:** b St Louis, Mo, February 4, 1943; m 1975, Maria; c Joseph III & Tatiana. **Education:** St Louis Univ, BA, 1966, MS, 1968; City Univ NY, PhD (biol), 1975. **Honors & Awards:** Outstanding Achievemt Biol Sci, Wash Aca Sci, 1994. **Professional Experience:** Mem bd adv, Int Ctr Trop Ecol, 1985-; BOTANIST, AGR RES SERV, USDA, 1984-; Consult, Interamer Inst Coop Agr, 1983; RES ASSOC, SMITHSONIAN INST, 1979-; Prof, Univ Brazil, 1979-1984; assoc cur bot, Agr Res Serv, USDA, 1975-1979. **Memberships:** Am Asn Plant Taxonomists; Int Asn Plant Taxon; Asn Trop Biol; Sigma Xi; Bot Soc Brasil. **Research Statement & Publications:** Taxonomic revision of plants cultivated on American farms; taxonomic revision of selected neotropical Rubiaceae. **Mailing Address:** USDA, Agr Res Serv, Syst Bot & Mycol Lab, Rm 304 Bldg 011A BARG W, Beltsville, MD 20705-2350. **Fax:** 301-504-5810. **E-Mail:** jkirkbri@asrr.arsusda.gov

KIRKBRIDE, L(OUIS) D(ALE), MEDICAL INSTRUMENTATION. **Personal Data:** b Morris, Ill, October 18, 1932; m 1957, c 3. **Education:** Carnegie Inst Technol, BS, 1954, MS & PhD (metall), 1957. **Professional Experience:** VPRES, MKT & VPRES, BIONETICS LAB PROD, ORGANON TEKNIKA CORP, 1985-; vpres & gen mgr, Lab Prod Div, Litton Bionetics, 1981-1985; gen mgr, Diag Div, J T Baker, 1974-1981; mgr nuclear diag, Med Systs Div, 1971-1974; mgr bus develop & strategic planning, Med Systs Bus Div, Gen Elec Co, 1970-1971; mgr clin equip develop, Med Develop Oper, 1968-1970; proj analyst, Gen Elec Res & Develop Ctr, Schenectady, 1966-1968; group leader power reactor mat, Los Alamos Sci Lab, 1961-1966; mgr core mat develop, Knolls Atomic Power Lab, Gen Elec Co, 1960-1961; Develop engr nuclear mat, Knolls Atomic Power Lab, Gen Elec Co, 1957-1960. **Memberships:** Am Nuclear Soc; Instrument Soc Am; fel Am Inst Chemists. **Research Statement & Publications:** Semiconductor materials; radioimmunoassay; clinical chemistry; hematology; immunology; enzyme immunoassay. **Mailing Address:** 12712 Waterman Dr, Raleigh, NC 27614.

KIRKENDALL, ERNEST OLIVER, diffusion in solid state metals; deceased, see previous edition for last biography

KIRKENDALL, THOMAS DODGE, AEROSPACE MATERIALS & DEVICES. **Personal Data:** b Columbus, Ohio, September 8, 1937; m Dorothy; c 3. **Education:** Colby Col, BA, 1961. **Honors & Awards:** NASA ATS-6 Propagation Exp Award, Commun Satellite Corp, 1974 & Centimeter Wave Beacon Award, 1976; Outstanding Mem of the Year, Soc Appl Spectros, 1980 Thirty six publications and three U S patents. **Professional Experience:** CONSULT, 1993-; mgr, Dept Semiconductor Reliability & Qual Assurance, 1989-1993; mgr, Dept Anal Chem & Failure Anal, 1981-1989; tech staff mem, Comsat Labs, 1969-1981; res scientist, Machlett Labs, Raytheon Co, 1962-1969; asst physics, Middlebury Col, 1961-1962; consult, Commun Satellite Corp, Intelsat, JPL. **Research Statement & Publications:** Physics and failure mechanisms of solid state devices; energy conversion and storage; surface analysis and characterization; satellite component reliability assurance. **Mailing Address:** 8610 Camille Dr, Potomac, MD 20854. **E-Mail:** tom@kirkendall.com

KIRKHAM, M B, SOIL-PLANT-WATER RELATIONSHIPS. **Personal Data:** b Cedar Rapids, Iowa. **Education:** Wellesley Col, BA; Univ Wis-Madison, MS, PhD (bot). **Honors & Awards:** Travel Award, Soil Sci Soc Am, 1990. **Professional Experience:** PROF, KANS STATE UNIV, MANHATTAN, as of 2006; vis scientist, environ & risk mgt group, Hortes, as of 2002; sabbatical, Crown Res Inst, Palmerston North, NZ, 1998; vis scientist, Landcare res, Crown res inst Canterbury agr & sci center, Lincoln, New Zealand, sabbatical, Jan-Mar, 1998; vis scientist, Dept Sci Indust Res, Palmerston North, NZ, 1991; vis scholar, Biol Labs, Harvard Univ, 1990; Vis lectr evapotranspiration, Italy, 1989; Vis lectr evapotranspiration, China, 1985; prin investr, NSF, USDA & Dept Energy; plant physiologist, US Environ Protection Agency, Cincinnati, Ohio; asst prof, Okla State Univ, Stillwater; asst prof, Univ Mass, Amherst; NSF fel, Inst Environ Studies, Univ Wis-Madison. **Memberships:** Am Soc Plant Physiol biologists; Am Meteorol Soc; fel Soil Sci Soc Am; fel Am Soc Agron; Bot Soc Am; fel AAAS; fel Crop Sci Soc Am. **Research Statement & Publications:** Plant-soil-water relationships; uptake of trace elements by plants; effect on plants of elevated levels of carbon dioxide. **Mailing Address:** Dept Agron Throckmorton Hall, Kans State Univ, Manhattan, KS 66506-5501. **Fax:** 785-532-6094, 785-539-1850. **E-Mail:** mbk@ksu.edu

KIRKIEN-RZESZOTARSKI, ALICJA M, CHEMICAL DYNAMICS. **Personal Data:** b Lodz, Poland, m 1973, Waclaw Janusz. **Education:** Polish Univ Col, London, MChEng, 1951; Univ London, PhD (phys org chem), 1955. **Professional Experience:** PROF EMER CHEM, TRINITY COL, WASH DC, 1992-; res assoc, George Wash Univ, 1984; Hon res fel, Univ Col, Univ London, 1971-1972; prof & chair, Trinity Col DC, 1969-1992; assoc prof, Trinity Col DC, 1965-1969; assoc prof, Univ West Indies, 1961-1965; From asst prof to assoc prof phys chem, Univ Col West Indies, 1956-1961. **Memberships:** Royal Chem Soc; Royal Inst Chem; Am Chem Soc; Polish Acad Arts & Sci. **Research Statement & Publications:** Physical organic chemistry; kinetics of reactions in solutions and in the gas-phase, kinetic isotope effects; organic mass spectrometry, effect of chemical structure on ionization potentials; fragmentation patterns; high performance liquid chromatography; history of science. **Mailing Address:** Dept Chem, Trinity Col, Millersville, MD 21108-1764. **Fax:** 531-671-2826.

KIRKLAND, JAMES B, NUTRITION. **Education:** Univ Guelph, BSc & PhD. **Professional Experience:** ASSOC PROF, DEPT HUMAN BIOL & NUTRIT SCI, UNIV GUELPH, as of 2004. **Research Statement & Publications:** Niacin is a B vitamin that is involved in energy metabolism, but it also plays key roles in DNA repair and in signal transduction; effect of niacin deficiency on poly(ADP-ribose) synthesis, DNA repair rates; apoptosis and the progression of leukemia in response to carcinogen exposure. **Mailing Address:** Dept Human Health & Nutrit Sci, Univ Guelph, Rm 335 Animal Sci/Nutrit Bldg, Guelph, ON N1G 2W1, Can. **E-Mail:** jkirklan@uoguelph.ca

KIRKLAND, JERRY J, MICROBIOLOGY. **Personal Data:** b Elk City, Okla, May 18, 1936; m 1957, c 4. **Education:** Northwestern State Col, Okla, BS, 1958; Okla State Univ, MS, 1961, PhD (microbiol), 1964. **Professional Experience:** SR RES SCIENTIST, SHARON WOODS BEAUTY CTR, 1993-; Microbial physiologist, Procter & Gamble, 1964-1993. **Memberships:** Am Soc Microbiol. **Research Statement & Publications:** Inducible enzyme formation in microorganisms and their role in dental plaque; microbiology of skin; etiology of acne; toxic shock syndrome; etiology of acne and development of anti-acne products; quality control of manufacture of acne product and etiology of acne; the organisms of dental plaque and dental plaque formation; co-author of numerous articles. **Mailing Address:** Sharon Woods Health & Beauty Tech Ctr, Procter & Gamble Co 11511 Reed Hartman Hwy, Cincinnati, OH 45241.

KIRKLAND, JOSEPH JACK, ANALYTICAL CHEMISTRY. **Personal Data:** b Winter Garden, Fla, May 24, 1925; m 1983, Karin; c Kent Gordon, Kerry Lynn, Celeste Ann, Mark Robert & Holly Anne. **Education:** Emory Univ, AB, 1948, MS, 1949; Univ Va, PhD (chem), 1953. **Honorary Degrees:** DSc, Emory Univ, 1974. **Honors & Awards:** Chromatography Award, Am Chem Soc, 1972; Stephen Dal Nogare Award in Chromatography, Chromatography Forum, 1973; Anachem Award, 1979; Torbern Bergman Medal, Anal Chem, Swed Chem Soc, 1982; Delaware Sect Award, Am Chem Soc, 1988; Eastern Analytical Symposium Award; Dupont Lavoisier Medal, 1997; AJP Martin Gold Medal, 1997. **Professional Experience:** RETIRED; Du Pont fel, E I Du Pont de Nemours & Co, Inc 1982-1992; adj prof chem, Univ Del, 1980, 1982; res fel, E I Du Pont de Nemours & Co, Inc, 1969-1982; res assoc, E I Du Pont de Nemours & Co, Inc, 1961-1969; from res chemist to sr res chemist, E I Du Pont de Nemours & Co, Inc, 1953-1961; chemist, Exp Sta, Hercules Powder Co, 1949-1951. **Memberships:** Am Chem Soc. **Research Statement & Publications:** Gas chromatography; Liquid chromatography; field flow fractionation; analytical separations. **Mailing Address:** 19 Kendall Ct, Wilmington, DE 19803.

KIRKLAND, LARRY V, NEURAL NETWORKS, NEW TECHNOLOGY. **Personal Data:** b Ogden, Utah, m Susan; c 3. **Education:** Weber State Univ, BS, 1976. **Honors & Awards:**

ATE Neural Network Usage Award, Inst Elec & Electronics Engrs, 1989, Walter E Peterson Award New Technol, 1992, ATE Future COncepts Award, 1994. **Professional Experience:** Co-chair, Interoperability Stand for KB Systs, beginning 1994; SR ELECTRONIC ENGR, OGDEN AIR LOGISTICS CTR, USAF, 1988-; chair, Artificial Intel Human Interface Group, Inst Elec & Electronics Engrs, 1988-1992; electronic engr, Ogden Air Logistics Ctr, USAF, 1981-1987; electronic technician, Ogden Air Logistics Ctr, USAF, 1966-1980. **Memberships:** Inst Elec & Electronics Engrs. **Research Statement & Publications:** Testing utilizing alternative software technolgoies to improve test performance, accuracy and reliability; artificial intelligence and its inclusion into test and diagnosis. **Mailing Address:** US Airforce Acad, Ctr Acad Dr, Hilltop, CO 80840.

KIRKLAND, WILLIS L, CANCER RESEARCH. **Personal Data:** b Galesburg, Ill, August 8, 1944; m Suzzane; c Steve & Marc. **Education:** Univ Kans, PhD (physiol & cell biol), 1973. **Professional Experience:** PROF BIOL, MT MERCY COL, AS OF 2006; From asst prof to assoc prof, 1980-1992. **Memberships:** Am Soc Cell Biol; Am Soc Col Sci Teachers. **Mailing Address:** Dept Biol, Mt Mercy Col, 1330 Elmhurst Dr NE, Cedar Rapids, IA 52402.

KIRKLIN, PERRY WILLIAM, PETROLEUM CHEMISTRY, SECONDARY & UNIVERSITY EDUCATION. **Personal Data:** b Ellwood City, Pa, February 28, 1935; m 1956, Betty; c 3. **Education:** Westminster Col, BS, 1957; Univ Minn, Minneapolis, PhD (phys chem), 1964. **Honors & Awards:** Westminster College Distinguished Alumni Lecturer, 1997. **Professional Experience:** RETIRED; adj prof chem, Cheyney Univ PA, 1996-1997; assoc prof Bloomfield Col, 1991-1995; mem, Aviation Fuels Res, Mobil Oil NJ, 1970-1991; group leader anal res, Rohm & Haas Co, Pa, 1964-1970. **Memberships:** Nat Orgn Black Chemists & Chem Engrs. **Research Statement & Publications:** My thesis was on ESR. I began my career doing NMR and pesticide analyses. I moved on to physico chemical catalyst characterization and from there to automobile emissions and finally aviation fuels. **Mailing Address:** 1860 Hillside Rd, Southampton, PA 18966.

KIRKMAN, HENRY NEIL, JR, MEDICINE, PEDIATRICS. **Personal Data:** b Jacksonville, Fla, September 14, 1927; m 1950, c 4. **Education:** Ga Inst Technol, BS, 1947; Emory Univ, MS, 1950; Johns Hopkins Univ, MD, 1952; Am Bd Pediat, dipl, 1960. **Honors & Awards:** Mead Johnson Award, 1967. **Professional Experience:** PROF EMER PEDIAT, UNIV NC, CHAPEL HILL, as of 2000; prof pediat, Sch Med, Univ Nc, Chapel Hill, beginning 1965; Markle scholar, 1961; asst prof pediat, Sch Med, Univ Okla, 1959-1965; res investr, Nat Inst Arthritis & Metab Dis, 1958-1959; Nat Inst Arthritis & Metab Dis fel metab enzymes, 1957-1958; resident, Vanderbilt Univ Hosp, 1955-1957; Intern pediat, Johns Hopkins Hosp, 1952-1953. **Memberships:** Am Pediat Soc; Am Soc Biol Chem. **Research Statement & Publications:** Metabolic and enzymatic disturbances in children; human biochemical genetics. **Mailing Address:** Dept Pediat, Univ NC Sch Med, Chapel Hill, NC 27599-7487.

KIRKMAN, KATHERINE, ENVIRONMENTAL SCIENCE. **Education:** Col William & Mary, BS, 1976; Univ Ga, Athens, MS, 1978, PhD (bot), 1992. **Professional Experience:** ASSOC SCIENTIST, JOSEPH W JONES ECOL RES CTR, 1999-; asst scientist, Joseph W Jones Ecol Res Ctr, 1995-1999; adj ecologist, Inst Ecol, Univ Ga, 1992-1995. **Mailing Address:** Joseph W Jones Ecol Res Ctr, Route Two Box 2324, Newton, GA 39870. **Fax:** 229-734-4707.

KIRKNER, DAVID J, MATHEMATICS. **Education:** Youngstown State Univ, BE, 1971; Case Western Reserve Univ, PhD (Maths), 1979. **Professional Experience:** ASSOC PROF, DEPT CIVIL ENG & GEOL SCI, UNIV NOTRE DAME, as of 2006. **Mailing Address:** Univ Notre Dame, Dept Civil Eng, Notre Dame, IN 46556. **Fax:** 574-631-9236. **E-Mail:** kirkner@nd.edu

KIRKPATRICK, CHARLES HARVEY, ALLERGY, IMMUNOLOGY. **Personal Data:** b Topeka, Kans, November 5, 1931; m 1959, Janice Fosha; c Heather, Michael & Brian. **Education:** Univ Kans, BA, 1954, MD, 1958. **Honors & Awards:** Richard Farr lectr, Aspen Allergy Conf, 1987; Stanislaus Jaros lectr, Am Col Allergy & Immunol, 1987; Robert Bolinger Citation for Academic Distinction, Univ Kans Med Ctr, 1993; Winona Campbell Award for Contrib to Med, Colo Med Soc, 1995. **Professional Experience:** VPRES, ITFS, as of 2001; CO-DIR, ADULT IMMUNE DEFICIENCY PROG, UNIV COLO, 1999-; pres, Innovative Therapeut, 1993-1996; PROF ALLERGY & CLINICAL IMMUNOL, DEPT MED, UNIV COLO, DENVER 1979-; dir, Div Allergy & Clinical Immunol, Dept Med, Nat Jewish Hosp, 1979-1993; sr investr & head, Sect Allergy & Hypersensitivity, Lab Clin Invest, Nat Inst Allergy & Infectious Dis, 1968-1979; assoc prof, Med Ctr, Univ Kans, 1968; asst prof, Med Ctr, Univ Kans, 1965-1968; instr, Med Ctr, Univ Colo, 1963-1965; Fel allergy & immunol, Univ Colo, 1962-1965; Asst med, Med Ctr, Univ Colo, 1962-1963. **Memberships:** AAAS; fel Am Acad Allergy; Am Soc Clin Invest; Am Asn Immunol; fel Am Col Physicians; Clin Immunol Soc; fel Molecular Med Soc. **Research Statement & Publications:** Mechanisms of cellular immunity and the role of cellular immunity to resistance to infectious diseases and neoplasia; methods of correcting diseases associated with abnormal cellular immunity. **Mailing Address:** 4200 E Ninth Ave, B164, Sch Med, Univ Colo, Denver, CO 80262. **Fax:** 303-333-9621. **E-Mail:** ckirkpat@eri.uchsc.edu

KIRKPATRICK, CHARLES MILTON, wildlife ecology; deceased, see previous edition for last biography

KIRKPATRICK, DIANA (RORABAUGH) M, QUALITY ASSURANCE AUDITING. **Personal Data:** b Washington, DC, March 24, 1944. **Education:** George Wash Univ, BS, 1967, PhD (phys chem), 1972. **Professional Experience:** CONSULT, 1988-; res assoc, Paffenbarger Res Ctr, Am Dent Asn, Nat Bur Stand, Gaithersburg, Md, 1985-1988; mgr, Prod Assurance Div Off Qual Assurance, Bur Engraving & Printing, Wash, DC, 1983-1985; prof leader thermal insulation & lab accreditation, Nat Bur Stand, 1977-1983; res analyst, Consumer Prod Safety Comn, 1974-1977; res analyst, Bur Alcohol, Tobacco & Firearms, 1973-1974; forensic scientist chem, Bur Alcohol, Tobacco & Firearms, 1972. **Research Statement & Publications:** Quality assurance testing programs; dental composites and bonding materials. **Mailing Address:** 18341 NW 142nd Ct Rd, Williston, FL 32696.

KIRKPATRICK, EDWARD SCOTT, SOLID STATE PHYSICS. **Personal Data:** b Wilmington, Del, December 12, 1941. **Education:** Princeton Univ, AB, 1963; Harvard Univ, PhD (physics), 1969. **Honors & Awards:** Am Phys Soc Prize Indust Appln Physics, 1987. **Professional Experience:** Vis prof, Racah Inst Physics & Ctr Neural Comput, Hebrew Univ, Jerusalem, Israel, 1993-1994; exchange prof, Ecole Normale Superieure, Paris, France, 1978-; vis assoc prof, State Univ NY, Stony Brook, 1977; STAFF MEM, RES DIV, IBM CORP, 1971-; Res assoc physics, James Franck Inst, Univ Chicago, 1969-1971; Argonne Nat Labs, AEC, 1969-1971; Consult, Lincoln Labs, Mass Inst Technol, 1965-1966. **Memberships:** Fel Am Phys Soc; Fel AAAS. **Research Statement & Publications:** Magnetic order and excitations in disordered materials, transport in low-mobility materials; optimization and pattern recognition using techniques of statistical physics, computer design and architecture for computers based around multimedia capabilities. **Mailing Address:** IBM Res Ctr, Yorktown Heights, NY 10598.

KIRKPATRICK, E(DWARD) T(HOMSON), MECHANICAL ENGINEERING. **Personal Data:** b Cranbrook, BC, January 15, 1925; American citizen; m 1948, Barbara J Kelsberg; c Allan, Karen, Ann & Keith. **Education:** Univ BC, BS, 1947; Carnegie Inst Technol, MS, 1956, PhD, 1958. **Professional Experience:** RETIRED; pres, Wentworth Inst Technol, 1971-1990; dean, Col Appl Sci, Rochester Inst Technol, 1964-1971; prof & chmn dept, Univ Toledo, 1959-1964; asst prof, Univ Pittsburgh, 1958-1959; from instr to asst prof mech eng, Carnegie Inst Technol, 1954-1958; sales mgr, F D Bolton, Ltd, 1953-1954; dist mgr, F D Bolton, Ltd, 1951-1953; sales engr, F D Bolton, Ltd, 1947-1951; test engr, Gen Elec Co, Can, 1947. **Memberships:** Fel Am Soc Eng Educ; Am Soc Mech Engrs; Sigma Xi. **Research Statement & Publications:** Conduction heat transfer; numerical analysis and digital computer technology. **Mailing Address:** 40 Radcliffe Rd, Weston, MA 02193.

KIRKPATRICK, FRANCIS HUBBARD, BIOTECHNOLOGY, SEPARATIONS TECHNOLOGY. **Personal Data:** b Laurel Hill, NC, November 7, 1943; m 1969, c 1. **Education:** Harvard Col, BA, 1964; Stanford Univ, PhD (biophys), 1970. **Professional Experience:** Consult, Juvenile Diabetes Res Found, as of 2003; ASSOC DIR, INTEL PROP, FOCAL INC, 1994-; SBIR study sect genetics, NIH, 1987-; tech dir, Bioprod Dept, Marine Colloids Div, FMC Corp, 1984-1994; lab mgr, Pall Corp, 1980-1984; asst prof biophys, Sch Med, Univ Rochester, 1974-1980; postdoctoral fel, Sch Med, Univ Rochester, 1972-1974; postdoctoral fel, Wash State Univ, 1969-1971. **Memberships:** Biophys Soc; Optical Soc Am; Am Soc Cell Biol; Am Chem Soc; Electrophoresis Soc; Am Soc Biochem & Molecular Biol. **Research Statement & Publications:** Development of innovative products for research and analysis in biotechnology, life sciences and medicine. **Mailing Address:** Focal Inc, One Kendall Sq, Bldg 600, Cambridge, MA 02139. **Fax:** 207-594-3426.

KIRKPATRICK, JAY FRANKLIN, ANIMAL PHYSIOLOGY. **Personal Data:** b Quakertown, Pa, February 24, 1940; m 1966. **Education:** EStroudsburg State Col, BS, 1962, MS, 1964; Cornell Univ, PhD (physiol), 1971. **Honors & Awards:** Burlington Northern Found Res Award, 1986. **Professional Experience:** Consult, human soc US, as of 2004; ASSOC ADJ PROF, SCH VET MED, UNIV CALIF, as of 2002; DIR, SCI & CONSERV BIOL, ANIMAL CUR, ZOOMONTANA, 1994-; assoc prof physiol, Sch Arts & Sci, 1985-1994; dean, Sch Arts & Sci, 1976-1985; fel, Col Vet Med, Univ Pa, 1973; assoc prof animal physiol, Eastern Mont Col, 1970-1976; asst prof & chmn dept, Bucks Co Community Col, 1965-1967; teacher biol, Pennsburg High Sch, Yardley, Pa, 1964-1965; teacher biol, Quakertown High Sch, Pa, 1962-1963. **Memberships:** Soc Study Reproduction; Soc Exp Biol & Med. **Research Statement & Publications:** Comparative mammalian reproduction; especially species indigenous to hostile environments; such as the pika and wild horses; chemical fertility control in wild and feral species. **Mailing Address:** ZooMont, 2100 S Shiloh Rd, Billings, MT 59106. **Fax:** 406-652-9281.

KIRKPATRICK, JOEL BRIAN, NEUROPATHOLOGY. **Personal Data:** b Odessa, Tex, February 19, 1936; m 1993, Elisabeth; c Susan C, Andrew L, Katherine F & Patti J. **Education:** Rice Univ, BA, 1958; Wash Univ, MD, 1962. **Professional Experience:** Mem, Study Sect Path A, 1987-1991; PROF PATH, BAYLOR COL MED, 1981-; prof, Univ Tex Health Sci Ctr, Dallas, 1978-1980; assoc prof path & neurol, Univ Tex Health Sci Ctr, Dallas, 1972-1978; staff, Vet Admin, NIH, beginnning 1971; assoc prof path, Univ Ariz, 1970-1972; Nat Inst Neurol Dis & Stroke grantee, 1970; asst prof pharmacol, Rutgers Univ, New Brunswick, 1968-1970; NIH spec fel, 1967-1968; instr path, Wash Univ, 1965-1967; Am Cancer Soc fel, 1964-1965. **Memberships:** Am Asn Neuropath. **Research Statement & Publications:** Video enhancement microscopy; quantitative analysis of cerebral cortex; dementia and trauma. **Mailing Address:** Dept Path, Baylor Col Med, One Baylor Plaza, Houston, TX 77030. **Fax:** 713-793-1473. **E-Mail:** joelk@bcm.tmc.edu

KIRKPATRICK, JOEL LEE, ORGANIC & PROCESS CHEMISTRY, PESTICIDE CHEMISTRY. **Personal Data:** b Abilene, Tex, June 21, 1936; m 1991, c 2. **Education:** Abilene Christian Col, BS, 1958; Univ Tex, MS, 1960; Univ Ill, PhD (org chem), 1969. **Professional Experience:** SR MGR, BASF, 1996-; sr mgr, Sardoz Agro Inc, 1989-1996; res mgr, Sardoz, Ltd, 1986-1989; sr scientist, Velsicol Chem Corp, 1981-1986; res assoc, Mobil Chem Co, 1979-1981; sr res chemist, Gulf Oil Chem Co, 1969-1979; Med chemist, Smith Kline & French Labs, 1961-1965. **Memberships:** AAAS; Am Chem Soc. **Research Statement & Publications:** Synthetic organic chemistry; nitrogen containing heterocycles; structure activity relationships, particularly pesticides; pheromones insect growth regulants; organophosphorus chemistry; process chemistry. **Mailing Address:** 4601 Sunken Ct, Port Arthur, TX 77642.

KIRKPATRICK, LARRY DALE, PHYSICS, PHYSICS EDUCATION. **Personal Data:** b 1941; American citizen. **Education:** Wash State Univ, BS, 1963, Mass Inst Technol, PhD (physics), 1968. **Honors & Awards:** Distinguished Serv Citation, Am Asn Physics Teachers, 1982. **Professional Experience:** PROF Emeritus, DEPT PHYSICS, MONT STATE UNIV, as of 2003; field ed physics, Quantum Mag, 1992-2001; coach, US Physics Team, 1988-1995; prof physics, Mont State Univ, 1985-2002; Vis assoc prof physics, Kans State Univ, 1983-1984; from asst prof to assoc prof, Mont State Univ, 1974-1985; asst prof, Univ Wash, 1969-1974; Res assoc physics, Mass Inst Technol, 1968-1969. **Memberships:** Am Asn Physics Teachers (pres 1997); pres elect 1998; pres 1999; past pres 2000); Nat Sci Teachers Asn; fel Am Phys Soc. **Research Statement & Publications:** Physics education; use of computers and personal response systems in physics education; textbook writing for general physics. **Mailing Address:** Dept Physics, Mont State Univ, Bozeman, MT 59717-3840. **Fax:** 406-994-4452. **E-Mail:** kirkpatrick@physics.montana.edu

KIRKPATRICK, MARK ADAMS, ZOOLOGY. **Personal Data:** b New York, NY, April 20, 1956. **Education:** Harvard Univ, BA, 1978; Univ Wash, PhD (zoology), 1983. **Professional Experience:** PROF INTEGRATIVE BIOL, SCH BIOL SCI, UNIV TEX, AUSTIN, as of 2005; asst prof zoology, Univ Tex, Austin, 1985-; Miller fel zoology, Miller Inst Basic Res Sci, Univ Calif, Berkeley, 1983-1985. **Memberships:** Soc Study Evolution; Am Soc Naturalists; Ecol Soc Am. **Research Statement & Publications:** Theoretical population genetics; evolution of mating systems; sexual selection; morphology; development. **Mailing Address:** Dept Zoology, Univ Tex, PAT 652, Austin, TX 78712-1026. **Fax:** 512-471-3878. **E-Mail:** kirkp@mail.utexas.edu

KIRKPATRICK, RALPH DONALD, WILDLIFE ECOLOGY. **Personal Data:** b Jonesboro, Ind, February 10, 1930; m 1967, Susan Clouse; c Maureen, Kathleen, Lindley S & Shane. **Education:** Ball State Univ, BS, 1953; Univ Ariz, MS, 1957; Okla State Univ, PhD (zool), 1964. **Professional Experience:** EMER PROF BIOL, BALL STATE UNIV, 1993-; Consult, Upper Wabash Resource Ctr, Huntington Col, Huntington, Ind, 1975-1985 & Consult, Aquatic Control, Inc, Seymour, Ind, 1971-; from asst prof to prof, Ball State Univ, 1967-1993; Consult, Pac Proj, Div Birds, Smithsonian Inst, 1965-; asst prof zool, Ind Univ, 1965-1967; res cur, Div Birds, Smithsonian Inst, 1964-1965; asst prof biol, Taylor Univ, 1959-1960; game res biologist, State Dept Conserv, Ind, 1956-1959; Game biologist,

State Dept Conserv, Ind, 1954-1955. **Memberships:** Wildlife Soc; Am Soc Mammal; Wilson Soc. **Research Statement & Publications:** Ecology of Indiana wildlife; population dynamics of mammals, including rodents and house cats on coral atolls; Pacific Ocean. **Mailing Address:** Osage Farm, 7552 S 350 E, Jonesboro, IN 46938. **E-Mail:** osagerok@comteck.com

KIRKPATRICK, ROBERT JAMES, MINERALOGY-PETROLOGY, GEOCHEMISTRY. **Personal Data:** b Schenectady, NY, December 31, 1946; m 1985, Carol; c Gregory R & Geoffry S. **Education:** Cornell Univ, AB, 1968; Univ Ill, PhD (geol), 1972. **Honors & Awards:** Brunauer Award, American Ceramic Society, 2000 Dana Medal, Mineralogical Society of America, 2004. **Professional Experience:** ASSOC DEAN, 1998-2006 & R. E. Grim PROF GEOL 2005-date, UNIV ILL, URBANA, Dept head, Univ Ill, Urbana, 1988-1997; prog chmn, Int Mineral Asn Meeting, 1986; fel, Churchill Col, Cambridge, Eng, 1985; prof geol, Univ Ill, Urbana, beginning 1983; US Rep Int Mineral Asn Crystal Growth Comn, 1981-; consult, 1978-; from asst prof to assoc prof, Univ Ill, Urbana, 1978-1983; NSF, DOE & other grants, 1977-; asst res scientist, Deep Sea Drilling Proj, Scripps Inst Oceanog, Univ Calif, San Diego, 1976-1978; res fel geophys, Harvard Univ, 1973-1976; sr res geologist, Exxon Prod Res Co, 1972-1973; ed, Deep Sea Drilling Proj Initial Reports Legs, 1946, 1955 & 1977-1978. **Memberships:** Am Geophys Union; fel Am Mineral Soc; AAAS; fel Am Ceramic Soc; fel Geol Soc Am. **Research Statement & Publications:** Geochemistry, mineralogy, materials chemistry, cement chemistry and mineralogy, nuclear magnetic resonance spectroscopy of solids, structure of amorphous materials, crystal physics and chemistry, rates and mechanisms of geologic processes, processes of crystallization of igneous rocks. **Mailing Address:** Dept Geol Univ Ill 254 Natural, Hist Bldg 1301 W Green St, Urbana, IL 61801. **Fax:** 217-244-4996. **E-Mail:** kirkpat@uiuc.edu

KIRKPATRICK, ROY LEE, NUTRITIONAL ECOLOGY, REPRODUCTIVE PHYSIOLOGY. **Personal Data:** b Fairview, WVa, April 16, 1940; m 1961, Thelma; c Tamra J (Kazmierczak) & Roy D II. **Education:** WVa Univ, BS, 1962; Univ Wis, MS, 1964, PhD (reproductive physiol, endocrinol), 1966. **Honors & Awards:** Wildlife Prof Award, Wildlife Soc, 1993. **Professional Experience:** ASSOC DEAN & T H JONES PROF FISHERIES & WILDLIFE, VA POLYTECH INST & STATE UNIV, 1989-; prof wildlife sci, Va Polytech Inst & State Univ, 1977-1989; from asst prof to assoc prof, Va Polytech Inst & State Univ, 1972-1977; asst prof animal sci, Univ Wis, 1969-1971; asst prof wildlife ecol, Va Polytech Inst & State Univ, 1966-1969; instr, Univ Wis, 1964-1966; res asst reproductive physiol, Univ Wis, 1962-1964. **Memberships:** emer mem Wildlife Soc. **Research Statement & Publications:** Environmental influences on reproduction and mortality of wildlife, particularly effects of nutrition. **Mailing Address:** Dept Fisheries & Wildlife Va Tech Univ, Blacksburg, VA 24061.

KIRKPATRICK, THEODORE ROSS, STATISTICAL MECHANICS, CONDENSED MATTER THEORY. **Personal Data:** b Kalispell, Mont, August 29, 1953. **Education:** Univ Calif, Los Angeles, BS, 1977; Rockefeller Univ, PhD (theoret physics), 1981. **Honors & Awards:** Pres Young Investr Award, NSF, 1984. **Professional Experience:** PROF THEORET STATIST MECH, INST PHYS SCI & TECHNOL, UNIV MD, COLLEGE PARK, 1991-; from asst prof to assoc prof, Inst Phys Sci & Technol, Univ Md, College Park, 1983-1991; res assoc, 1981-1983. **Memberships:** Am Phys Soc. **Research Statement & Publications:** Condensed matter theory and statistical mechanics; physics of disordered solids and liquids; Quantum Critical Behavior of Itinerant Ferromagnets; A Metal-Insulator Transition as a Quantum Glass Problem; author of various articles. **Mailing Address:** Inst Phys Sci & Technol, Univ Md, 1110 Technol bldg, College Park, MD 20742-4111. **E-Mail:** tk10@umail.umd.edu

KIRKSEY, AVANELLE, NUTRITION, BIOCHEMISTRY. **Personal Data:** b Mulberry, Ark, March 23, 1926. **Education:** Univ Ark, BS, 1947; Univ Tenn, MS, 1950; Pa State Univ, PhD (nutrit), 1961. **Honorary Degrees:** DSc, Purdue Univ, 1997. **Honors & Awards:** Borden Award, Am Soc Family & Consumer Sci, 1980; Lederle Award, Am Soc Nutrit Sci, 1994. **Professional Experience:** MEREDITH DISTINGUISHED PROF EMER NUTRIT, PURDUE UNIV, 1997-; meredith distinguished prof nutrit, Purdue Univ, beginning 1985; from assoc prof to prof, Purdue Univ, 1961-1985; res asst nutrit, Pa State Univ, 1956-1959; assoc prof home econ, Ark Polytech Col, 1950-1955; nutrit prog coordr, Indonesian Second Univ develop proj; prog dir, Nutrit Collab Res Support Prog, Egypt, Kenya & Mex. **Memberships:** Fel Am Inutrit Sci; NY Acad Sci; Am Dietetic Asn; Am Soc Family & Consumer SciAsn; Sigma Xi. **Research Statement & Publications:** Vitamin B-6 metabolism; nutrition in pregnancy and development; human lactation; international nutrition; human functional effects of mild-moderate malnutrition in Egypt. **Mailing Address:** Dept Food & Nutrit, Purdue Univ, West Lafayette, IN 47907. **Fax:** 765-494-0674.

KIRKSEY, DONNY FRANK, PHARMACOLOGY. **Personal Data:** b Aberdeen, Miss, April 13, 1948; m 1970. **Education:** Delta State Univ, BS, 1970; Univ Miss, PhD (pharmacol), 1976. **Professional Experience:** VPRES, BUS & CORP DEVELOP, ATHEROGENICS INC, as of 2005; dir licensing & worldwide alliances, Glaxo, Inc, beginning 1991; assoc dir clin res, Glaxo Inc, 1987-1991; pres, Clindar, Inc, Durham, NC, 1986-1987; clin res scientist, Burroughs Wellcome, 1980-1986; asst prof biomed sci, Ohio Univ, 1978-1980; NIH fel, Nat Inst Drug Abuse, 1978; grant, NC Heart Asn, 1977-1978; Neuroscience fel, NIMH, 1976-1978; fel, Duke Univ, 1976-1978. **Memberships:** Sigma Xi. **Research Statement & Publications:** Investigations of pre and postsynaptic neuronal mechanisms in the central monoaminergic systems and pharmacological manipulation of those systems by drugs of abuse. **Mailing Address:** AtheroGenics, Inc, 8995 Westside Pkwy, Alpharetta, GA 30004. **Fax:** 678-336-2501.

KIRKSEY, HOWARD GRADEN, SCIENCE EDUCATION. **Personal Data:** b Memphis, Tenn, June 19, 1940; c 3. **Education:** Mid Tenn State Univ, BS, 1961; Auburn Univ, PhD (phys chem), 1966. **Professional Experience:** Consult, Dermagenics Inc, as of 2003; chmn dept chem, Memphis State Univ, 1982-1991; PROF CHEM, MEMPHIS STATE UNIV, 1979-; staff scientist phys sci group, Boston Univ, 1970-1972; assoc prof, Memphis State Univ, 1969-1979. **Memberships:** AAAS; Am Chem Soc. **Research Statement & Publications:** Chemical education; especially development of text and laboratory teaching materials. **Mailing Address:** Dept Chem, Memphis State Univ, RM 105 213 Jm smith hall, Memphis, TN 38152-3050. **Fax:** 901-678-4444. **E-Mail:** hkirksey@memphis.edu

KIRKWOOD, BESSIE H, MATHEMATICS. **Education:** Univ Ark, BS, MS; Univ Va, PhD (math), 1995. **Professional Experience:** PROF, DEPT MATH SCI, SWEET BRIAR COL, as of 2006. **Mailing Address:** Dept Math Sci, Sweet Briar Col, PO Box 142, Sweet Briar, VA 24595. **Fax:** 434-381-6488. **E-Mail:** bkirk@sbc.edu

KIRKWOOD, CHARLES EDWARD, MATHEMATICAL SCIENCES. **Personal Data:** b Richmond, Va, October 10, 1913; m 1942, c 2. **Education:** Lynchburg Col, AB, 1935; Univ Ga, MS, 1937. **Professional Experience:** RETIRED; assoc prof comput sci & math sci, Clemson Univ, 1975-1979; mgr prog, Comput Ctr, Clemson Univ, 1970-1975; comput analyst, Comput Ctr, Clemson Univ, 1964-1970; assoc prof elec eng, Comput Ctr, Clemson Univ, 1951-1952; assoc prof math sci, Clemson Univ, 1948-1979; from instr to asst prof math, Clemson Univ, 1937-1942; teacher pub sch, Ga, 1936-1937. **Research Statement & Publications:** Dielectric properties of ceramic materials; electrical properties of cotton; thermoconductivity of felts. **Mailing Address:** Wren St, Clemson, SC 29631.

KIRKWOOD, JAMES BENJAMINE, ZOOLOGY, RADIATION BIOLOGY. **Personal Data:** b Beulah, Ky, January 22, 1924; m 1953, Ola. **Education:** West Ky State Col, 1948; Univ Louisville, MS, 1952, PhD (zoology), 1962. **Professional Experience:** RETIRED; coastal ecosysts activ leader, US Fish & Wildlife Serv, Region IV, 1975-1989; mgr, W F Clapp Labs, 1973-1975; tech coordr bio environ studies, Battelle, Columbus, 1968-1973; prog leader, 1964-1968; prog supvr invert biol, 1962-1964; US Bur Com Fisheries, 1957-1960; proj leader fishery biol, Ky Dept Fish & Wildlife Resources, 1952-1957. **Memberships:** AAAS; Am Fisheries Soc; Sigma Xi; Nat Shellfish Asn; Int Acad Fishery Scientists. **Research Statement & Publications:** Ecology and ichthyology of Kentucky teleost fishes; life history and ecology of Pacific salmon; biology and population dynamics of shellfish species in Gulf of Alaska and Bering Sea. **Mailing Address:** 34 N Country Club Dr, Crystal River, FL 34429.

KIRMSE, DALE WILLIAM, COMPUTER AIDED DESIGN, ENERGY SYSTEMS. **Personal Data:** b Alva, Okla, July 9, 1938; m 1979, Sue; c Kevin D, Karen H, Katherin M & Kristina J. **Education:** Okla State Univ, BS, 1960; Iowa State Univ, MS, 1963, PhD (chem eng), 1964. **Professional Experience:** PROF EMER CHEM ENG, UNIV FLA, as of 2005; Reynolds Smith & Hill, 1975-1976; mgr asst, Parma Tech Ctr, Union Carbide Corp, 1967-1969; from asst prof to assoc prof chem eng, Univ Fla, 1965-1980; res assoc chem eng, Univ Fla, 1964-1965. **Memberships:** Am Soc Qual Control; Am Inst Chem Engrs. **Research Statement & Publications:** Statistical process quality control and reliability; mathematical modeling and computer methods; stochastic systems and Monte Carlo techniques; knowledge base export systems; computer aided process design; energy systems analysis and design. **Mailing Address:** Dept Chem eng, Univ Fla, Rm 237 PO Box 116005 223 Chem Eng Bldg, Gainesville, FL 32605. **Fax:** 352-392-9513. **E-Mail:** kirmse@che.ufl.edu

KIRMSER, P(HILIP) G(EORGE), APPLIED MATHEMATICS, ENGINEERING. **Personal Data:** b St Paul, Minn, December 17, 1919; m 1942, Jeune E Blomquist; c Sandra & Lawrence. **Education:** Univ Minn, BChE, 1939, MS, 1944, PhD, 1958. **Professional Experience:** EMER PROF ENG & MATH, KANS STATE UNIV, 1990-; vis prof, Ecole Polytech Federale, Lausanne, Switz, 1978; prof, Kans State Univ, 1975-1990; vis lect, Soc Indust & Appl Math, 1974-1975; head dept, Kans State Univ, 1962; from assoc prof appl mech, Kans State Univ, 1954-1975; Instr, Univ Minn, 1949-1954; mech engr, US Naval Ord Lab, 1946-1948; Instr, Kans State Col, 1942-1944; Consult, Phillips Petrol Co, Bayer & McElrath & Boeing Co, Digital Equip Co. **Memberships:** Am Math Soc; Math Asn Am; Soc Indust & Appl Math; Neth Royal Inst Eng. **Research Statement & Publications:** Partial differential equations of engineering dealing with heat flow, vibrations and stresses; dynamics and motion of artificial satellites; analog computers; simulation; approximation; automatic controls; industrial processes; analysis of data; co-inventor of Chinese word-processing and typing system; decoupler to protect buildings from earthquakes; co-inventor of expansion joint assembly having load transfer capability. **Mailing Address:** Dept Elec & Comput Eng, Kans State Univ, Manhattan, KS 66506. **E-Mail:** kirmser@ksu.edu

KIRON, MA RAVI, CARDIOLOGY. **Education:** Indian Inst Sci, PhD. **Professional Experience:** EXEC DIR, ALZA CORP, as of 2006. **Mailing Address:** Alza Corp, 1950 Charleston Rd, Mtain View, CA 94043. **Fax:** 650-564-7070.

KIRON, RAVI, PROTEIN PURIFICATION, RECEPTOROLOGY. **Personal Data:** b Shimoga, Karnataka, India, March 4, 1959; m 1989. **Education:** Bombay Univ, India, BS, 1979, MS, 1981; Indian Inst Sci, Bangalore, India, PhD (biochem), 1986. **Professional Experience:** GLOBAL HEAD, STRATEGIC ANAL & KNOWLEDGE MANAGEMENT, PFIZER GLOBAL RES & DEVELOP, as of 2003; SR RES SCIENTIST, PFIZER CENT RES, 1991-; asst prof biochem, Cornell Univ Med Col, 1990-1991; asst prof med, Cornell Univ Med Col, 1989-1991; young investr award, Eastern Hypertension Soc, 1988; postdoctoral, Cornell Univ Med Col, 1986-1989; young leadership award, Am Biograph Inst, 1986; sr res fel, Indian Inst Sci, 1985-1986; res fel, Cornell Univ Med Col, 1982-1986; sr res fel, US Dept Agr, 1982-1985. **Memberships:** AAAS; Harvey Soc; Am Soc Hypertension. **Research Statement & Publications:** Biochemistry of renin angiotensin system; characterization of angiotensin II receptors; immunologic analysis and cloning of gene for receptor; renin and prorenin study and analysis. **Mailing Address:** Pfizer Cent Res, Eastern Pt Rd, Groton, CT 06340.

KIRPEKAR, ABHAY C, FERMENTATION-SCALE UP, OPTIMIZATION & DESIGN, MIXING-AGITATION. **Personal Data:** b Nagpur, India, June 9, 1956; m 1986, Sadhana Tikekar; c Pooja. **Education:** Indian Inst Technol, Bombay, BTech, 1978; Univ RI, MS, 1981; Univ Va, PhD (chem eng), 1985. **Professional Experience:** SR PROJ ENGR, MERCK & CO INC, as of 2004; FEL BIOCHEM ENGR, MERCK & CO INC, 1991-; sr engr, 1987-1991; staff engr, 1985-1987. **Memberships:** Am Inst Chem Engrs; Am Chem Soc. **Research Statement & Publications:** Fermentor design, scale-up, optimization, onlinemeasurements, novel control strategies, agitation and aeration, mass transfer (gas liquid). **Mailing Address:** Merck & Co, Inc, PO Box 100, One Merck Dri, Whitehouse Station, NJ 08889-0100.

KIRSCH, DONALD R, MOLECULAR BIOLOGY. **Personal Data:** b Newark, NJ, April 28, 1950. **Education:** Rutgers Col, BA, 1972; Princeton Univ, MA, 1974, PhD (biol), 1978. **Professional Experience:** DIR, WYETH RES, WYETH PHARMA, 1998-; dir, Agr Res Div, Am Cyanamid Co, 1997-1998; assoc dir, Am Cyanamid Co, 1995-1996; res mgr, Am Cyanamid Co, 1992-1995; res group leader, Am Cyanamid Co, 1989-1991; prin res scientist, Am Cyanamid Co, 1988-1989; res group leader, Squibb Inst Med Res, 1983-1988; sr res investr, Squibb Inst Med Res, 1982-1983; Adj asst prof, Rutgers Med Sch, 1982-1983; res investr molecular biol, Squibb Inst Med Res, 1981-1982; Instr pharmacol, Rutgers Med Sch, 1978-1981. **Memberships:** Genetics Soc Am; Am Soc Microbiol; SigmaXi. **Research Statement & Publications:** Design of mechanism based screening assays utilizing genetically engineered microorganisms. **Mailing Address:** 152 Terhune Rd, Princeton, NJ 08540. **Fax:** 732-274-4755. **E-Mail:** kirshd@wyeth.com

KIRSCH, EDWIN JOSEPH, microbiology; deceased, see previous edition for last biography

KIRSCH, FRANCIS WILLIAM, CHEMISTRY. **Personal Data:** b Wheeling, WVa, August 27, 1925; m 1961, c 2. **Education:** Univ Del, BChE, 1945, MChE, 1947; Univ Pa, PhD (chem), 1952. **Professional Experience:** Consult, World Bank, 1980; consult, NMex State Govt; consult, Gov Energy Coun Pa, 1979-; consult, Pa Pub Util Comn, 1977-1978; DIR & VPRES, CTR ENERGY MGT & ECON DEVELOP, UNIV CITY SCI CTR, PHILADELPHIA, 1973-; res assoc, Explor Res Div, 1967-1972; proj dir, Sun Oil Co, 1964-1967; proj dir, Houdry Process Corp, 1959-1964; assoc res chemist, Houdry Process

Corp, 1950-1959; instr inorg qual anal, Univ Pa, 1946-1950. **Memberships:** AAAS; Am Chem Soc. **Research Statement & Publications:** Catalysis, heterogeneous and homogeneous; basic and process research and development: petroleum, chemicals, edible oils; industrial energy conservation; offshore oil and gas production; science policy; economic analysis and evaluation of manufacturing processes. **Mailing Address:** Univ City Sci Ctr, 3624 Market St, Philadelphia, PA 19104.

KIRSCH, JACK FREDERICK, BIOCHEMISTRY. **Personal Data:** b Detroit, Mich, August 14, 1934; m 1962, c 2. **Education:** Univ Mich, BS, 1956; Rockefeller Inst, PhD (biochem, cytol), 1961. **Professional Experience:** PROF BIOCHEM & MOLECULAR BIOL, UNIV CALIF, BERKELEY, 1989-; vis prof, Univ Basel, 1979-1980; Guggenheim fel, Max Planck Inst Biophys Chem, 1971-1972; from asst prof to prof biochem, Univ Calif, Berkeley, 1964-1989; Helen Hay Whitney fel biophys, Weizmann Inst, 1963-1964; Jane Coffin Childs fel biochem, Brandeis Univ, 1961-1963. **Memberships:** Am Chem Soc; Fedn Am Socs Exp Biol; AAAS. **Research Statement & Publications:** Mechanism of enzyme action; genetic engineering. **Mailing Address:** Molecular & Cell Biol, Univ Calif, 142 LSA 3200, Berkeley, CA 94720-3206. **Fax:** 510-642-6368. **E-Mail:** jfkirsch@uclink.berkeley.edu

KIRSCH, JOSEPH LAWRENCE, PHYSICAL CHEMISTRY. **Personal Data:** b Indianapolis, Ind, August 20, 1942; m 1965, Linda; c Traci M (Berns) & Joseph L III. **Education:** Butler Univ, BS, 1964; Univ Ill, MS, 1966, PhD (phys chem), 1968. **Professional Experience:** Coordr, eng dual degree prog, Butler Univ, 1999-; JOHN HUME READE PROFESSORSHIP, BUTLER UNIV, 1993-; head dept chem, Butler Univ, 1988-1999; PROF PHYS CHEM, BUTLER UNIV, 1981-; from asst prof to assoc prof, Butler Univ, 1970-1981; asst prof, Butler Univ, 1970-1974; asst prof inorg chem, Fairleigh Dickinson Univ, 1968-1970. **Memberships:** Am Chem Soc; Sigma Xi. **Research Statement & Publications:** Study of chemical bonding in molecules through the use of chemical spectroscopy. **Mailing Address:** Dept Chem, Butler Univ, 4600 Sunset Gallahue Hall 347, Indianapolis, IN 46208. **Fax:** 317-283-9519. **E-Mail:** jkirsch@butler.edu

KIRSCH, LAWRENCE EDWARD, PHYSICS, COMPUTER SCIENCE. **Personal Data:** b Newark, NJ, February 24, 1938. **Education:** Columbia Univ, AB, 1960; Rutgers Univ, MS, 1962, PhD (physics), 1964. **Professional Experience:** Chair, dept physics, Brandeis Univ, 1987-1989; PROF PHYSICS, BRANDEIS UNIV, 1981-; dir comput ctr, Brandeis Univ, 1970-1985; from asst prof to assoc prof, Brandeis Univ, 1966-1981; res assoc physics, Nevis Labs, Columbia Univ, 1964-1966. **Memberships:** Am Phys Soc; Inst Elec & Electronics Engrs; Asn Comput Mach. **Research Statement & Publications:** High energy and particle physics. **Mailing Address:** Brandeis Univ, Dept Physics, Abelson-Bass-Yalem 221, Waltham, MA 02454-9110. **Fax:** 781-736-2915. **E-Mail:** kirsch@brandeis.edu

KIRSCH, NATHAN CARL, PHARMACEUTICAL MANUFACTURING, QUALITY ASSURANCE. **Personal Data:** b New Brunswick, NJ, October 27, 1918; m 1946, Ida Bass; c Kenneth & Phillip. **Education:** Rutgers Univ, BS, 1940; Univ Ill, MS, 1941. **Professional Experience:** VPRES & MEM BD DIRS, PARENTERAL DRUG ASN FOUND PHARMACEUT RES INC, 1980-; vpres qual control, Sterile Prods Dept, 1975-1983; dir domestic mfg, Sterile Prods Dept, 1973-1975; mgr pharmaceut prod, Sterile Prods Dept, 1968-1973; mgr, Sterile Prods Dept, 1953- 1968; actg mgr, Pharmaceut Develop Dept, 1951-1953; Supvr res & develop projs, Schering Plough Corp, 1942-1951. **Memberships:** AAAS; Am Chem Soc; Am Pharmaceut Asn; Pharmaceut Fedn; Royal Soc Health. **Research Statement & Publications:** Studied antibacterial action of oxidation products of adrenalin; methods of increasing yields of penecillin in submerged culture; selecting preservative for pharmaceutical products. **Mailing Address:** 93 Cedar St, Millburn, NJ 07041.

KIRSCH, WOLFF M, NEUROSURGERY, BIOCHEMISTRY. **Personal Data:** b St Louis, Mo, March 2, 1931; m 1955, c 4. **Education:** Wash Univ, BA, 1951, MD, 1955. **Professional Experience:** DIR, NEUROSURG CTR RES TRAINING & EDUC, MED CTR, LOMA LINDA UNIV, as of 2001; dir & chmn training prog & chmn div, Med Sch, Univ Colo, Denver, beginning 1971; consult, Fitzsimons Gen Hosp, Aurora, Colo, beginning 1969; assoc prof, Med Sch, Univ Colo, Denver, beginning 1968; attend, Vet Admin Hosp, Denver, beginning 1965; asst prof neurosurg, Med Sch, Univ Colo, Denver, 1965-1968; res fel neuro-pharmacol, Sch Med, Wash Univ, 1963 & 1965; fel neuroanat, Sch Med, Wash Univ, 1960; chief resident & instr, Barnes Hosp, Wash Univ, 1959-1960 & neurosurg, 1964; asst resident gen surg, Barnes Hosp, Wash Univ, 1959-1960 & neurosurg, 1961-1962; fel neurol med, NC Mem Hosp, Univ NC, 1956-1957; intern med, NC Mem Hosp, Univ NC, 1955-1956; at dept surg, Univ nmex, albuquerque. **Memberships:** Am Acad Neurol; Asn Acad Surg; Am Asn Neurol Surg; Int Soc Neurochem; Am Col Surg. **Research Statement & Publications:** Experimental biology of brain tumors. **Mailing Address:** Loma Linda Univ, Coleman Pavilion, Ste 11113, 11175 Campus St, Loma Linda, CA 92350. **Fax:** 909-558-0472. **E-Mail:** wkirsch@som.llu.edu

KIRSCHBAUM, H(ERBERT) S(PENCER), ELECTRICAL ENGINEERING. **Personal Data:** b Cleveland, Ohio, February 6, 1920; m 1946, c 4. **Education:** Cooper Union, BS, 1942; Univ Pittsburgh, MS, 1946; Carnegie Inst Technol, PhD (elec eng), 1953. **Professional Experience:** RETIRED; mgr systs eng, Info Systs Lab, Westinghouse Elec Co, 1969-1982; consult, Dept Eng Physics, 1959-1969; div consult, Systs Div, Battelle Mem Inst, 1957-1959; assoc prof elec eng, Ohio State Univ, 1947-1957; Engr, Westinghouse Elec Corp, 1942-1946. **Memberships:** Inst Elec & Electronics Engrs. **Research Statement & Publications:** Systems engineering; control systems; process control. **Mailing Address:** 257 Shope Creek Rd, Asheville, NC 28805.

KIRSCHBAUM, JOEL BRUCE, BIOTECHNOLOGY. **Personal Data:** b Palo Alto, Calif, August 29, 1945; m 1974, Felicity; c Morgan & Ethan. **Education:** Pomona Col, BA, (chem) 1967; Harvard Univ, PhD (molecular biol), 1972. **Professional Experience:** DIR, UNIV CALIF SAN FRANCISCO TECH. TRANSFER OFFICE, 1998-; Sr. licensing officer, Univ Calif San Francisco 1996-1998; interim vpres res develop, Megabios Corp, 1994; vpres res & develop, RiboGene, Inc, 1992-1993; actg vpres res & develop, Octamer, Inc, 1991; INDEPENDENT CONSULT, BIOTECHNOL RES DEVELOP, 1990-; dir res & develop, Codon, 1985-1990; supvr, Genetic Eng Div, Stauffer Chem Co, 1981-1985; prin investr, Am Cancer Soc, 1979-1981; res fel, Med Found Inc, 1978-1980; res assoc, Children's HospMed Ctr, 1977-1981; instr neuropath, Harvard Med Sch, 1977-1981; sr researcher, Univ Geneva, 1975-1977; Fel molecular biol, H H Whitney Found, 1973-1975; asst instr bact genetics, Cold Spring Harbor Lab, 1971; Teaching fel, Harvard Univ, 1969. **Research Statement & Publications:** Discovery and development of biopharmaceuticals, small molecule therapeutic drugs, vaccines, and gene therapies. **Mailing Address:** 21 Knickerbocker Lane, Orinda, CA 94563. **Fax:** 925-254-6180. **E-Mail:** joelkirs@aol.com

KIRSCHBAUM, JOEL JEROME, ANALYTICAL CHEMISTRY, BIOCHEMISTRY. **Personal Data:** b New York, NY, November 23, 1935; m 1960, Marilyn Johnson; c Amy & Fredric. **Education:** City Col New York, BS, 1957; Rutgers Univ, PhD (biochem), 1963. **Professional Experience:** RES LEADER, ANALYTIC RES & DEVELOP DIV, BRISTOL-MYERS SQUIBB PHARM RES INST, 1964-; mem, Dir Inst Motivated Behav, Belle Mead, NJ; Mem, Grants Comt, Am Found Scholarly Res. **Memberships:** Am Chem Soc; Am Soc Biochem & Molecular Biol; Am Asn Pharm Scientists. **Research Statement & Publications:** Analyses of drugs; lycanthropy; high pressure liquid chromatography; association and dissociation of proteins, enzymes and antibiotics. **Mailing Address:** Analytic Res & Develop Div, Bristol-Myers Squibb Pharm Res Inst 1 Squibb Dr, New Brunswick, NJ 08903-0191.

KIRSCHBAUM, THOMAS H, OBSTETRICS & GYNECOLOGY. **Personal Data:** b Minneapolis, Minn, April 22, 1929; m 1983, Ann; c Rachel Rebecca & Rex King. **Education:** Univ Minn, BA, 1950, BS, 1951, MD, 1953. **Professional Experience:** PROF OBSTET & GYNEC, ALBERT EINSTEIN COL MED, as of 1992; assoc ed, Yearbk Obstet-Gynec, 1987-; Nat & Child Health Res Comt, NIH, 1986-; prof obstet & gynec, Col Med, Univ Southern Calif, beginning 1985; spec expert, Nat Inst Child Health & Human Develop, 1983-1985; prof obstet, gynec & reproductive biol & chmn dept, Col Human Med, Mich State Univ, 1971-1983; assoc prof, Med Ctr, Univ Calif, Los Angeles, 1964-1971; consult, Rand Corp, Calif, 1964-1971; asst prof, Col Med, Univ Utah, 1959-1964; resident physician obstet & gynec, Univ Minn Hosps, 1956-1959. **Memberships:** AAAS; Perinatal Res Soc; Soc Gynec Invest; Am Gynec & Obstet Soc; Am Col Obstet-Gynec. **Research Statement & Publications:** Fetal physiology and maternal-fetal interrelationships. **Mailing Address:** Albert Einstein Col Med, Yeshiva Univ, 1300 Morris Park Ave, Bronx, NY 10461.

KIRSCHENBAUM, LOUIS JEAN, TRANSITION METAL SOLUTION CHEMISTRY, KINETICS & MECHANISMS. **Personal Data:** b Washington, DC, April 17, 1943; m 1964, Susan; c Jay & Cynthia. **Education:** Howard Univ, BS, 1965; Brandeis Univ, MS, 1967, PhD (chem), 1968. **Professional Experience:** PROF CHEM, UNIV RI, 1983-; vis scientist, Nat Cancer Inst, NIH, 1991-1992; vis prof, Ben Gurion Univ Negev, Israel, 1978-1979; asst prof to assoc prof, Univ RI, 1970-1983; Nat Res Coun fel, Naval Ord Lab, 1969-1970; Lectr chem, Brandeis Univ, 1968-1969; post doct, Naval Ordn Lab; 1969-1970. **Memberships:** Sigma Xi; Am Chem Soc. **Research Statement & Publications:** Transition metals in uncommon oxidation states; kinetics and mechanisms of metal ion oxidation-reduction and complexation reactions; rapid reaction techniques; kinetics of chemical analysis; sonochemistry; hair chemistry; free radicals. **Mailing Address:** Dept Chem, Univ RI, Kingston, RI 02881. **Fax:** 401-792-5072. **E-Mail:** kirschenbaum@chm.uri.edu

KIRSCHENBAUM, SUSAN S, ENGINEERING PSYCHOLOGY, HUMAN DECISION MAKING. **Personal Data:** b Washington, DC, September 15, 1943; m 1964, c 2. **Education:** George Wash Univ, BA, 1965; Univ RI, MA, 1975 & 1983, PhD (exp psychol), 1985. **Professional Experience:** Adj asst prof, Univ RI, 1985-; ENG PSYCHOLOGIST, NAVAL UNDERWATER SYSTS CTR, 1985-; personnel psychologist, Naval Underwater Systs Ctr, 1984-1985; spec instr psychol, Univ RI, 1981-1985; lectr eng as foreign lang, Ben Gurion Univ, Negev, 1978-1979; dir educ serv, S Co Community Action, 1977-1978; dir, S Kingstown Orgn Laymen Educ, 1974-1977; teacher, Boston Sch Dept, 1965-1967. **Memberships:** Am Psychol Asn; Asn Appl Exp & Eng Psychologists; Am Psychol Soc; Sigma Xi. **Research Statement & Publications:** Information management for submarine combat control; human information gathering and usage for situation understanding and decision making in complex environments; apply findings to design of command decision aids. **Mailing Address:** Naval Undersea Warfare Ctr Div, Bldg 1171-1 Code 2211 1176 Howell St, Newport, RI 02841. **E-Mail:** kirschenbaumsscsd.npt.nuwc.navy.mil

KIRSCHNER, DANIEL A, NEUROLOGY. **Education:** Harvard Univ, PhD. **Professional Experience:** PROF BIOL, BOSTON COL, as of 2006. **Mailing Address:** Dept Biol, Boston Col, 140 Commonwealth Ave, Chestnut Hill, MA 02467. **Fax:** 617-552-2011. **E-Mail:** daniel.kirschner@bc.edu

KIRSCHNER, LEONARD BURTON, PHYSIOLOGY. **Personal Data:** b Chicago, Ill, November 12, 1923; m 1950, c 4. **Education:** Univ Ill, BS, 1944, MS, 1947; Univ Wis, PhD (physiol), 1951. **Professional Experience:** PROF EMER ZOOL, WASH STATE UNIV, 1993-; from instr to prof, Wash State Univ, 1953-1993; Nat Found Infantile Paralysis res fel, Copenhagen Univ, 1951-1953. **Memberships:** Am Physiol Soc; Soc Gen Physiol; Am Soc Zoologists; Sigma Xi. **Research Statement & Publications:** Active transport of solutes and water; invertebrate excretory organs. **Mailing Address:** Dept Zool, Wash State Univ, Pullman, WA 99164-4236. **Fax:** 509-335-3184. **E-Mail:** kirscl@wsu.edu

KIRSCHNER, MARC WALLACE, BIOCHEMISTRY, CELL BIOLOGY. **Personal Data:** b Chicago, Ill, February 28, 1945; m 1968, c 3. **Education:** Northwestern Univ, BA, 1966; Univ Calif, Berkeley, PhD (biochem), 1971. **Honors & Awards:** J W Jenkinson Mem Lectr, Oxford Univ, 1986; Howard Taylor Ricketts Award Lectr, Univ Chicago, 1986; Harvey Lectr, 1987; Stetten Lectr, 1991; Richard Lounsberg Award, Nat Acad Sci, 1991. **Professional Experience:** PROF, DEPT SYST BIOL, HARVARD MED SCH, as of 2005; chmn, Dept Syst Biol, Harvard Med Sch, as of 2004; prof & chmn, Dept Cell Biol, Harvard Med Sch, beginning 1993; mem, Cell Biol Study Sect, 1980-1984; prof biochem & biophys, Univ Calif, San Francisco, 1978-1993; NIH res career develop award, 1975 & 1980; asst prof to assoc prof biochem sci, Princeton Univ, 1972-1978; NSF fel develop biol, Univ Calif, Berkeley, 1971-1972. **Memberships:** Nat Acad Sci; Am Soc Biol Chemists; Am Soc Cell Biol (pres-elect, 1989, pres, 1990-1991); Am Acad Arts & Sci. **Research Statement & Publications:** Mechanism of microtubule assembly, regulation of mitosis and regulation of cell division in amphibian eggs; biophysical studies of macromolecules; embryonic induction; granted one US patent. **Mailing Address:** Harvard Med Sch, Dept Syst Biol, 240 Longwood Ave, Boston, MA 02115. **Fax:** 617-432-0420. **E-Mail:** marc@hms.harvard.edu

KIRSCHNER, MARVIN ABRAHAM, INTERNAL MEDICINE, ENDOCRINOLOGY. **Personal Data:** b Brooklyn, NY, March 5, 1935; m 1957, Harriet Stock; c David, Lawrence & Kenneth. **Education:** Albert Einstein Col Med, MD, 1959. **Professional Experience:** DIR ENDOCRINOL, DIABETES & METAB, UNIV MED & DENT NJ, NJ MED SCH, as of 2004; prog proj comt, breast cancer task force-epidemiol, Nat Cancer Inst, 1980-1984; mem, breast cancer task force-epidemiol, Nat Cancer Inst, 1974-1978; PROF MED, UNIV MED & DENT NJ, NJ MED SCH, 1973-; vchmn med, Univ Med & Dent Nj, Nj Med Sch, beginning 1973; consult, res comt, East Orange Vet Admin Hosp, beginning 1971; assoc prof, Univ Med & Dent NJ, Nj Med Sch, 1969-1972; dir med, Newark Beth Israel Med Ctr, 1969; sr investr, Endocrinol Br, 1966-1969; fel reproductive endocrinol, Karolinska Inst, Stockholm, 1965-1966; resident med, Bronx Munic Hosp Ctr, 1964-1965; clin assoc endocrinol, Endocrine Br, Nat Cancer Inst, 1961-1964; asst resident, Bronx Munic Hosp Ctr, 1960-1961; med intern, Bronx Munic Hosp Ctr, 1959-1960. **Memberships:** Am Fedn Clin Res; Endocrine Soc; Am Asn Cancer Res; Am Diabetes Asn; Am Soc Clin Nutrit. **Research Statement & Publications:** Androgen and estrogen metabolism; hirsutism; endocrine tumors; breast cancer; obesity management. **Mailing Address:** Newark Beth Israel Med Ctr, Univ Hosp, 90 Bergen St, DOC 4400 & 4500, Newark, NJ 07103. **Fax:** 973-972-2510. **E-Mail:** njmedphysicians@umdnj.edu

KIRSCHNER, RONALD ALLEN, LASER-TISSUE INTERACTION, OPTICS & IMAGING. **Personal Data:** b New York, NY, January 18, 1942; m 1964, c 2. **Education:** NY Univ, BA, 1962; Philadelphia Col Osteopath Med, DO, 1966, MSc, 1972. **Professional Experience:** PROF OTOLARYNGOL, PHILADELPHIA COL OSTEOP MED, as of 2004; PHYSICIAN SURG, LANKENAU HOSP, as of 2004; chmn Head & Neck & Facial Surg, Philadelphia Col Osteopath Med, beginning 1990; pres, Kirschner Design Group Inc, beginning 1988; design consult, Sigma Dynamics, beginning 1987; contrib ed, Photonics Spectra, beginning 1987; clin prof, Kirschner Design Group Inc, 1985-1989; design consult, Inframed Corp, 1984-1987; exec vpres, Courtland Group Inc, 1984-1985; guest ed, Surg Clins NAm, 1984; chmn head & neck, Div Surg, 1983-1989; design consult, Pilling Corp, beginning 1981; exec dir, Inst Appl Laser Surg, beginning 1980; vpres, Courtland Group Inc, 1979-1984; chmn head & neck, Suburban Gen Hosp, beginning 1976; pres, Suburban Ear, Nose & Throat Group Ltd, beginning 1976; clin assoc prof head & neck, Kirschner Design Group Inc, 1975-1985; dir head & neck serv, Neurosensory Unit, 1973-1976; dir head & neck serv, Main Navy Dispensary, 1968-1970. **Memberships:** Laser Assoc Am; NY Acad Sci; Sigma Xi; Laser Inst Am; Am Soc Lasers Med Surv. **Research Statement & Publications:** Laboratory and clinical research regarding lasers of various wavelengths and their interaction with tissue, delivery systems, related imaging systems and development of new instruments. **Mailing Address:** Dept Otolaryngol, Philadelphia Col Osteop Med, 4170 City Ave, Philadelphia, PA 19131.

KIRSCHNER, STANLEY, INORGANIC CHEMISTRY. **Personal Data:** b Brooklyn, NY, December 17, 1927; m 1950, c 2. **Education:** Brooklyn Col, BS, 1950; Harvard Univ, AM, 1952; Univ Ill, PhD (chem), 1954. **Honors & Awards:** Fac Res Award, Sigma Xi, 1974; Heyrovsky Medal, Czech Acad Sci, 1978; Catalyst Award, Mfg Chem Asn, 1984. **Professional Experience:** PROF EMER, WAYNE UNIV, as of 2003; adv bd, Seaborg Ctr for Teaching & Learning Sci & Math, 1988-1997; ed, Inorg Synthesis, bd dirs, Am Chem Soc, 1988-1992; div chem educ, Am Chem Soc, 1986-; bd dirs, 1988-1992; Polytech Inst, Lisbon, & Univ Porto, Portugal, 1984; chmn, comt educ, 1981-1983; vis prof, Tohoku Univ, Sendai, Japan, Inst Chem, Cluj, Romania, 1978; vis prof, Univ Florence, Italy, 1976; Polytech Univ Timisoara, Romania, 1973; Univ Sao Paulo, Brazil, 1969; perm secy, Int Conf Coord Chem, 1966-1989; actg chmn, Wayne State Univ, 1964-1965; sr NSF fel, 1963-1964; Ford Found, 1969; Fulbright scholar, 1963-1964 & 1984; vis prof, Univ London, 1963-1964; NIH grant, 1962-1965; vchmn dept, Wayne State Univ, 1961-1964; prof chem, Wayne State Univ, beginning 1960; res fels, NSF, 1958, 1965-1967; res fels, Chattanooga Med Co, 1956; res fels, Res Corp, 1955-1957; from asst prof to assoc prof, Wayne State Univ, 1954-1960; res chemist inorg chem, Monsanto Chem Co, 1951. **Memberships:** fel AAAS; Am Chem Soc; fel NY Acad Sci; Chem Soc; Brazilian Acad Sci; fel Indian Chem Soc; fel Japan Soc Prom Sci; fel Chilean Chem Soc. **Research Statement & Publications:** Structure and stereochemistry of organosilicon and complex inorganic compounds; rotatory dispersion and circular dichroism of asymmetric coordination compounds; physiologically important complex inorganic compounds and their biological activity; application of computer techniques to the storage and retrieval of chemical literature references; optical properties of fast-racemizing complexes; the pfeiffer effect; chemistry education. **Mailing Address:** Dept Chem, Wayne State Univ, Detroit, MI 48202. **Fax:** 313-577-1377. **E-Mail:** skirsch@sun.Sci.wayne.edu

KIRSCHSTEIN, RUTH LILLIAN, PATHOLOGY. **Personal Data:** b Brooklyn, NY, October 12, 1926; m 1950, c 1. **Education:** Long Island Univ, AB, 1947; Tulane Univ, MD, 1951. **Honorary Degrees:** DSc, Mt Sinai Sch Med, 1984; LLD, Atlanta Univ, 1985; DSc, Med Col Ohio, 1986. **Professional Experience:** DEP DIR, NIH, 2003-; INDUCTEE, MD WOMEN'S HALL FAME, 2003-; actg dir, NIH, 2000-2002; PHS coord, Comt Women's Health Issues, 1985-; chmn, PHS Task Force Women's Health Issues, 1983-1984; chmn, NIH Grants Peer Rev Study Team, 1975-1976; dir, Nat Inst Gen Med Sci, 1974-1993; dep assoc comnr sci, Bur Biologics, Food & Drug Admin, 1973-1974; dep dir, Bur Biologics, Food & Drug Admin, 1972-1973; asst dir, Div Biologics Stand, 1971-1972; chief, Lab Path, 1965-1972; mem, expert comt poliomyelitis, WHO, 1965 & 1967 & 1971; asst chief, 1962-1965; chief, Sect Path, Lab Virol Immunol, 1960-1965; pathologist, Div Biologics Stand, NIH, 1957-1960. **Memberships:** Am Asn Pathologists; Am Asn Immunologists; Am Soc Microbiol. **Research Statement & Publications:** Pathology and pathogenesis of viral diseases; poliomyelitis, oncogenic viruses; viral vaccines; scientific peer review; scientific research administration; carcinogenesis. **Mailing Address:** NIH, 9000 Rockville Pike, Bethesda, MD 20892-0148. **Fax:** 301-402-2700.

KIRSHENBAUM, ABRAHAM DAVID, physical inorganic chemistry, explosives; deceased, see previous edition for last biography

KIRSHENBAUM, GERALD STEVEN, POLYMER CHEMISTRY, PLASTICS RESEARCH. **Personal Data:** b New York, NY, December 6, 1944; c Alan, Mark & Jeffrey. **Education:** Case Inst Technol, BS, 1966; Polytech Inst Brooklyn, MS, 1970, PhD (polymer chem), 1971. **Professional Experience:** MGR PROD STEWARDSHIP, HOECHST CELANESE, 1990-; develop assoc, supvr & mgr, Celanese Eng Resins Co, 1978-1989; sr chemist, Union Carbide Corp, Bound Brook, 1976-1978; ed, Polymer News, 1975-; sr res chemist, Soltex Polymer Corp, 1974-1975; Asst ed, Polymer News, 1972-1975; Res chemist, Celanese Plastics Co, 1971-1974. **Memberships:** Am Chem Soc; Soc Plastics Engrs. **Research Statement & Publications:** Polyolefins; high-density polyethylene; polyethylene catalysis; polyethylene terephthalate for container application and plastics for packaging; regulatory affairs; author of several books; engineering plastics; product safety. **Mailing Address:** 10 Byron Lane, Fanwood, NJ 07023.

KIRSHENBAUM, ISIDOR, CHEMISTRY. **Personal Data:** b New York, NY, June 22, 1917; m 1947, c 4. **Education:** City Col NY, BS, 1938; Columbia Univ, MA, 1939, PhD (chem), 1942. **Professional Experience:** RETIRED; pvt consult, 1986-1990; sci adv, Exxon Res & Eng Co, 1977-1985; sr res assoc, 1968-1977; consult, AEC, 1947-1955; res assoc, 1945-1968; res scientist, Columbia Univ, 1942-1945; asst instr phys chem, Columbia Univ, 1940-1942. **Memberships:** AAAS; Am Chem Soc. **Research Statement & Publications:** Oxidation reactions; patents and research analysis; polymer properties; petrochemical petroleum processes; heterogeneous catalysis; separation and physical properties of isotopes. **Mailing Address:** 260 Garth Rd, Scarsdale, NY 10583.

KIRSHNER, HOWARD STEPHEN, NEUROLOGY. **Personal Data:** b Bryn Mawr, Pa, July 11, 1946; m 1969, Carol; c Joshua D & Jodie A. **Education:** Williams Col, BA, 1968; Harvard Med Sch, MD, 1972. **Professional Experience:** VCHMN DEPT NEUROL, SCH MED, VANDERBILT UNIV, 1993-; DIR NEUROL, VANDERBILT STALLWORTH REHAB HOSP, 1993-; PROF NEUROL, SCH MED, VANDERBILT UNIV, 1987-; consult, Nashville Gen Hosp, beginning 1978; consult, Mid Tenn Ment Health Inst, beginning 1978; from asst prof to assoc prof, Vanderbilt Stallworth Rehab Hosp, 1978-1987; resident & clin instr, Mass Gen Hosp, 1975-1978; staff assoc lab perinatal physiol, Nat Inst Neurol & Commun Dis, 1973-1975; intern med, Mass Gen Hosp, 1972-1973; mem, Stroke Coun, Am Heart Asn. **Memberships:** Am Acad Neurol; Am Neurol Asn; Nat Aphasia Asn; Acad Aphasia; Am bil Neurorehab; fel Am Heart Asn. **Research Statement & Publications:** Aphasia; higher cortical functions; cerebrovascular disease; neurorehabilitation. **Mailing Address:** Dept Neurol, Vanderbilt Univ Sch Med, Nashville, TN 37232. **Fax:** 615-936-0223, 615-936-1286.

KIRSHNER, NORMAN, METABOLISM & CELL CULTURE PROTEIN SYNTHESIS. **Personal Data:** b Wilkes-Barre, Pa, September 21, 1923; m 1961, Anette; c Naomi, Susan & Amy. **Education:** Univ Scranton, BS, 1947; Pa State Univ, MS, 1951, PhD (biochem), 1952. **Professional Experience:** PROF EMER PHARMACOL, DUKE UNIV, 1993-; chmn, Neurol Sci Study Sect, 1985-1988; mem, Coun Sci Adv, 1979; ed, Molecular Pharmacol, 1978-1982; chmn, Dept Pharmacol, 1977-1987; mem, Prog Proj Rev Comt, Roche Inst Molecular Biol, 1975-1979; prof, Duke Univ, 1970-1993; career develop award, 1962-; from asst prof to assoc prof, Duke Univ, 1959-1970; USPHS sr res fel, 1959-1962; assoc biochem, Duke Univ, 1956-1959; res asst, Duke Univ, 1955-1957; res asst, Yale Univ, 1954; res asst physiol, Univ Rochester, 1952-1954. **Memberships:** Am Soc Biol Chem; Am Soc Pharmacol & Exp Therapeut; Am Soc Neurochem. **Research Statement & Publications:** Metabolism of Catecholamines; mechanism of storage and release of neurotransmitters. **Mailing Address:** Dept Pharmacol, Duke Univ Med Ctr, Durham, NC 27710-0001. **Fax:** 919-681-8609. **E-Mail:** nkirsh@acpub.duke.edu

KIRSHNER, ROBERT PAUL, ASTRONOMY. **Personal Data:** b Long Branch, NJ, August 15, 1949; m 1970, Lucy; c Rebecca & Matthew. **Education:** Harvard Col, AB, 1970; Calif Inst Technol, PhD (astron), 1975. **Honors & Awards:** Bowdoin Prize, Harvard Col, 1970; Russel Award, Univ Mich, 1980; Aaronson lectr, Univ Ariz, 1989. **Professional Experience:** Bd dirs, Asn Univ Res Astron, 1989-; vis comt, Space Telescope Sci Inst, 1988-1989; vis comt, Mt Wilson & Las Camponas Observ, 1987-1989; PROF ASTRON, HARVARD UNIV, 1985-; coun mem, Am Astron Soc, 1985-1987; chmn, NSF subcomt Large Optical-IR Telescopes, 1985-1986; vis comt mem, Asn Univ Res Astron, 1983-1986; sci adv comt, Nat New Technol Telescope, 1983-1984; comt, Space Astron & Astrophys, 1982-1985; dir, McGraw Hill Observ, 1980-1985; telescope allocation comt, Kitt Peak Nat Cerro-Tololo Inter Am Observ, 1980-1982; Alfred P Sloan fel, 1979-1982; users comt, Cerro-Tololo Inter-Am Observ, 1979-1982; users comt, Kitt Peak Nat Observ, 1978-1981; from asst prof to prof astron, Univ Mich, 1976-1985; res assoc astron, Kitt Peak Nat Observ, 1974-1976. **Memberships:** Am Astron Soc; Int Astron Union; Am Phys Soc; AAAS; fel Am Acad Arts & Sci. **Research Statement & Publications:** Extragalactic supernovae and galactic supernova remnants; extragalactic distance scale; large scale structure. **Mailing Address:** Dept Astron, Harvard Univ, 60 Garden St, Cambridge, MA 02138. **Fax:** 617-495-7467. **E-Mail:** rkirshner@cfa.harvard.edu

KIRSNER, JOSEPH BARNETT, INTERNAL MEDICINE, GASTROENTEROLOGY. **Personal Data:** b Boston, Mass, September 21, 1909; m 1934, c 1. **Education:** Tufts Col, MD, 1933; Univ Chicago, PhD (biol sci) & Am Bd Internal Med, dipl, 1942. **Honors & Awards:** Rudolph Schindler Award, Am Soc Gastrointestinal Endoscopy; Friedenwald Medal, Am Gastroenterol Asn; John Phillips Mem Award, Am Col Physicians; George Howell Coleman Medal, Inst Med, Chicago. **Professional Experience:** Chmn, Adv Group, Nat Comn Digestive Dis, 1978; LOUIS BLOCK DISTINGUISHED SERV PROF MED, UNIV CHICAGO, 1974-; dean med affairs & chief staff, Univ Hosp, 1971-1976; assoc ed, Advances Internal Med, 1970-; From asst prof to prof med, Univ Chicago, 1935-1974; mem nat adv coun, Nat Inst Arthritis & Metab Dis. **Memberships:** Am Soc Clin Invest; Am Soc Gastrointestinal Endoscopy (secy-treas Gastroscopic Soc 1942-1948 pres 1949-1950); fel AMA; Am Gastroenterol Asn (treas & pres 1965-1966); mastership Am Col Physicians. **Research Statement & Publications:** Gastroenterology, especially peptic ulcer, cancer, inflammatory diseases including regional enteritis and ulcerative colitis; protein metabolism; hepatic disease; immunological mechanisms in gastrointestinal disease. **Mailing Address:** Dept Med, Univ Chicago, 5841 S Maryland Ave MC 2100, Chicago, IL 60637-1470. **E-Mail:** jkirsner@medicine.bsd.uchicago.edu

KIRST, HERBERT ANDREW, ORGANIC CHEMISTRY. **Personal Data:** b St Paul, Minn, September 22, 1944; m 1990, Peggy A Hillman. **Education:** Univ Minn, BChem(chemistry) BS, 1966; Harvard Univ, PhD (org chem), 1971. **Professional Experience:** RES ADV, ELI LILLY & CO, 1992-; Ed, Antimicrobial Agents & Chemother, 1991-1996; sr res scientist, Eli Lilly & Co, 1984-1991; res scientist, Eli Lilly & Co, 1978-1983; sr chemist, Eli Lilly & Co, 1973-1977; Fel org chem, Calif Inst Technol, 1971-1973. **Memberships:** Am Chem Soc; AAAS; Am Soc Microbiol; NY Acad Sci Soc Indust Microbiol. **Research Statement & Publications:** Structure determination and chemical modification of new antibiotics and other fermentation products. **Mailing Address:** Elanco Animal Health Res & Develop, 2001 W Main St, Greenfield, IN 46140-0708. **Fax:** 317-277-4993. **E-Mail:** kirst_herbert_a@lilly.com

KIRSTEN, EDWARD BRUCE, NEUROPHARMACOLOGY, CLINICAL CARDIOLOGY. **Personal Data:** b New York, NY, January 28, 1942; m 1963, Miriam Medina; c Suzanne & Eric. **Education:** Fairleigh Dickinson Univ, BS, 1962; NY Univ, MS, 1966; City Univ New York, PhD (biol), 1969. **Professional Experience:** DIR CARDIO-RENAL, CNS & WOUND CARE, 1991-; adj asst prof pharmacol, Columbia Univ, 1977-; dir clin pharmacol, Knoll Pharmaceut Co, 1977-1992; res career develop award, Col Physicians & Surgeons, Columbia Univ, 1972-1977; asst prof pharmacol, Col Physicians & Surgeons, Columbia Univ, 1972-1977; Assoc, Col Physicians & Surgeons, Columbia Univ, 1971-1972; NIH fel pharmacol, Col Physicians & Surgeons, Columbia Univ, 1969-1971. **Memberships:** Am Soc Clin Pharmacol & Therapeut; Sigma Xi. **Research Statement & Publications:** Clinical development of new cardiovascular and CNS drugs including compounds for arrlythmias, hypertension and stroke; pharmacokinetics. **Mailing Address:** Knoll Pharmaceut Co, 3000 Continental Dr N, Mt Olive, NJ 07828-1234. **Fax:** 973-426-5593.

KIRTLEY, JOHN ROBERT, SUPERCONDUCTIVITY, MICROSCOPY. **Personal Data:** b Palo Alto, Calif, August 27, 1949; m 1973, Kathryn; c David Barr. **Education:** Univ Calif, Santa Barbara, BA, 1971, PhD (physics), 1976. **Honors & Awards:** Buckley Prize of APS -1998. **Professional Experience:** RES STAFF MEM, IBM RES DIV, 1978-; res asst prof, Univ Pa, 1977-1978; fel, Univ Pa, 1976-1977. **Memberships:** Fel Am Phys Soc; fel Am Acad Advan Sci; sr mem Inst Elec & Electronics Engrs. **Research Statement & Publications:** Solid state physics; collective phenomena such as superconductivity, quantum hall effect at low temperatures; scanning Squid Microscopy. **Mailing Address:** Int Bus Mach T J Watson Res Ctr, PO Box 218, Yorktown Heights, NY 10598. **Fax:** 914-945-4421.

KIRTLEY, MARY ELIZABETH, biochemistry; deceased, see previous edition for last biography

KIRTLEY, THOMAS L(LOYD), CHEMICAL ENGINEERING. **Personal Data:** b Salmon, Idaho, November 16, 1918. **Education:** San Jose State Col, AB(chem) & AB(physics & math), 1940; Calif Inst Technol, MS, 1942. **Professional Experience:** RETIRED; supt environ eng, Chem Cotton Prod, 1977-1982; supt eng develop, Chem Cotton Prod, 1975-1977; chem cotton supt, Chem Cotton Prod, 1969-1975; chem cotton tech coordr, Chem Cotton Prod, 1965-1969; chem supvr, Chem Cotton Prod, 1960-1965; asst chief chemist, Chem Cotton Prod, 1956-1960; serv supvr, Chem Cotton Prod, 1945-1956; shift supvr,

Rocket Powder Prod, 1944-1945; tech shift supvr, Ammonia Prod, Hercules Powder Co, Hercules Inc, 1942-1944. **Memberships:** Emer mem Am Chem Soc. **Research Statement & Publications:** Cellulose chemistry; chemical cotton; cellulose ethers. **Mailing Address:** 306 Sherwood Dr, Hopewell, VA 23860. **E-Mail:** tkirtey@erols.com

KIRTLEY, WILLIAM RAYMOND, CLINICAL MEDICINE. **Personal Data:** b Crawfordsville, Ind, May 30, 1914; m 1940, c 2. **Education:** Wabash Col, AB, 1936; Northwestern Univ, MB, 1940, MD, 1941. **Honors & Awards:** Banting Medal, Am Diabetes Asn, 1971. **Professional Experience:** RETIRED; assoc prof med, Sch Med, Ind Univ, 1973-1978; dir, Lilly Lab Clin Res, 1972-1978; dir, Med Res Div, 1965-1972; asst dir, Clin Res Div, 1963-1965; asst prof, Sch Med, Ind Univ, 1961-1973; head, Clin Med Dept, 1961-1965; sr physician, Diabetes Res Lab Clin Res, 1956-1961; physician in-chg, Diabetes Res Lab Clin Res, 1953-1970; chief, Diabetes Clin, 1953-1970; assoc med, Sch Med, Ind Univ, 1952-1961; abstr ed, Diabetes, Am Diabetes Asn, 1950-1968; assoc med, Wishard Mem Hosp, beginning 1949; staff physician, Eli Lilly & Co, 1947-1956. **Memberships:** Am Soc Clin Pharmacol & Therapeut; Endocrine Soc; AMA; Am Diabetes Asn. **Research Statement & Publications:** Insulin modifications; metabolism; diabetes mellitus; glucagon. **Mailing Address:** 33 Fairway Winds Pl, Hilton Head Island, SC 29928.

KIRTMAN, BERNARD, PHYSICAL CHEMISTRY. **Personal Data:** b New York, NY, March 30, 1935; m Tybie; c Ann M & Benjamin P. **Education:** Harvard Univ, PhD (phys chem), 1961. **Honors & Awards:** ICCMSE 2005 Prize for Theoretical and Computational Chemistry. **Professional Experience:** PROF THEORET PHYS CHEM, UNIV CALIF, SANTA BARBARA, 1972-; from asst prof to assoc prof chem, Santa Barbara, 1965-1968; asst prof chem, Univ Calif, Berkeley, 1962-1965; Fel chem, Univ Wash, 1960-1962. **Memberships:** Am Chem Soc; Am Phy Soc. **Research Statement & Publications:** Theoretical chemistry; application of quantum mechanics to electronic structure of atoms, molecules, polymers and surfaces; vibronic interactions; nonlinear optical properties. **Mailing Address:** Dept Chem, Univ Calif, Santa Barbara, CA 93106. **Fax:** 805-893-4120. **E-Mail:** kirtman@chem.ucsb.edu

KIRWAN, ALBERT DENNIS, PHYSICAL OCEANOGRAPHY. **Personal Data:** b Louisville, Ky, November 29, 1933; m 1956, c 3. **Education:** Princeton Univ, AB, 1956; Tex A&M Univ, PhD (phys oceanog), 1964. **Professional Experience:** PROF PHYS OCEAN SCI & ENG, as of 2005; MARY A S LIGHTHIPE CHAIR MARINE STUDIES, as of 2005; prog dir phys oceanog, Off Naval Res, 1970-1972; from asst prof to assoc prof, NY Univ, 1964-1970; res asst oceanog, Tex A&M Univ, 1959-1964. **Memberships:** AAAS; Am Meteorol Soc; Am Geophys Union. **Research Statement & Publications:** Air-sea interaction, general circulation of oceans; physics of fluids; engineering science. **Mailing Address:** Col Marine Studies, Univ Del, Paradee Ctr, Dover, DE 19901. **Fax:** 302-645-4007.

KIRWAN, WILLIAM ENGLISH, MATHEMATICAL ANALYSIS. **Personal Data:** b Louisville, Ky, April 14, 1938; m 1960, c 2. **Education:** Univ Ky, BA, 1960; Rutgers Univ, MS, 1962, PhD (math), 1964. **Professional Experience:** CHANCELLOR & CHIEF EXEC OFFICER, UNIV SYSTS MD, 2002-; pres & prof, Ohio State Univ, 1998-2002; pres, Univ Md Col Park, 1989-1998; actg pres, Univ MD, Col Park, 1988-1989; vchancellor acad affairs, Univ MD, Col Park, 1981-1988; chmn dept, Univ MD, Col Park, 1977-1981; prog dir, NSF, 1975-1976; prof math, Univ Md, Col Park, 1972-1998; vis lectr, Royal Holloway Col, Univ London, 1966-1967; from asst prof to assoc prof math, Univ MD, College Park, 1964-1972; Instr math, Rutgers Univ, 1963-1964. **Memberships:** Math Asn Am; Am Math Soc; Sigma Xi. **Research Statement & Publications:** Functions of one complex variable, particularly extremal properties of conformal and quasiconformal mappings of the unit disc. **Mailing Address:** Univ Systs Md, 3300 Metzerott Rd, Adelphi, MD 20783. **Fax:** 301-445-1931.

KIRWIN, GERALD JAMES, ELECTRICAL ENGINEERING, APPLIED MATHEMATICS. **Personal Data:** b Lowell, Mass, February 11, 1929; m 1955, c 2. **Education:** NE Univ, BSEE, 1952; Mass Inst Technol, MSEE, 1955; Syracuse Univ, PhD (elec eng), 1968. **Professional Experience:** RETIRED; prof elec eng, Sch Eng, Univ New Haven, 1973-1994; prof, Univ Maine, Portland-Gorham, 1968-1973; instr, Syracuse Univ, 1964-1968; assoc prof elec eng, Merrimack Col, 1956-1964; mem tech staff, Bell Tel Labs, 1955-1956. **Memberships:** Inst Elec & Electronics Engrs. **Research Statement & Publications:** Nonlinear systems; circuit theory and design; optimal network design, electrical engineering education. **Mailing Address:** 15 Aylesbury Circle, PO Box 1412, Madison, CT 06443.

KIRZ, JANOS, SYNCHROTRON RADIATION, X-RAY OPTICS. **Personal Data:** b Budapest, Hungary, August 11, 1937; American citizen; m 1988, Regina; c Steven. **Education:** Univ Calif, Berkeley, BA, 1959, PhD (physics), 1963. **Honors & Awards:** Compton Award, Advanced Photon Source, 2005. **Professional Experience:** Acting Director, Advanced Light Source, Lawrence Berkeley National Laboratory 2004-2006; DISTINGUISHED PROF PHYSICS, STATE UNIV NY, STONY BROOK, 1995-; chmn 1998-2001, Guggenheim fel, 1985-1986; assoc chmn, State Univ NY, Stony Brook, 1984-1985; prof, State Univ NY, Stony Brook, 1972-1995; visitor, Lab Molecular Biophys, Oxford Univ, 1972-1973; Sloan Found fel, 1970-1972; assoc prof, State Univ NY, Stony Brook, 1968-1972; Lectr, Univ Calif, Berkeley, 1967; physicist, Lawrence Radiation Lab, Univ Calif, 1964-1968; Nat Acad Sci-Nat Res Coun fel physics, Saclay Nuclear Res Ctr, France, 1963-1964. **Memberships:** Fel AAAS; fel Am Phys Soc; Optical Soc Am; Micros Soc Am. **Research Statement & Publications:** X-ray microscopy. **Mailing Address:** Dept Physics, State Univ NY, Stony Brook, NY 11794-3800. **Fax:** 516-632-8101. **E-Mail:** kirz@sbhep.physics.sunysb.edu

KISCHER, CLAYTON WARD, EMBRYOLOGY, CELL BIOLOGY IN SURGICAL RESEARCH. **Personal Data:** b Des Moines, Iowa, March 2, 1930; m 1964, Linda R Espejo; c Eric, Frank & Cynthia. **Education:** Univ Omaha, BS, 1953; Iowa State Univ, MS, 1960, PhD (embryol), 1962. **Professional Experience:** Lectr, Pima Community Col, 2001-2005; EMER ASSOC PROF ANAT, UNIV ARIZ COL MED, 1993-; assoc prof, Sem Lab, 1977-1993; dir, Sem Lab, 1977-1985; vis prof surg biol, Univ Ariz Col Med, 1976-1977; assoc prof, Univ Tex Med Br, 1970-1977; res consult to chief staff, Shriners Burns Inst, Galveston, 1970-1973; asst prof, Univ Tx Med Br, 1967-1970; chief sect electron micros, Southwest Found Res & Educ, 1966-1967; Fel biochem, Univ Tex M D Anderson Hosp, 1964-1966; asst prof zool, Iowa State Univ, 1963-1964; resident res assoc biol & med, Argonne Nat Lab, 1963; asst prof zool, Ill State Univ, 1962-1963; teacher high sch, Nebr, 1956-1958; cytologist, Col Med, Univ Nebr, 1953-1956. **Memberships:** sr mem Am Asn Anat; Tex, soc Microsc, sr mem. **Research Statement & Publications:** Ultrastructural changes during morphogenesis; electron microscopy; hypertrophic scarring and fibronectin; microvessels in wound healing; human embryology and public policy; analyses of public perception of human embryology through media sources; Adult stem cell research. **Mailing Address:** 6249 N Camino Miraval, Tucson, AZ 85718-3024. **Fax:** 520-626-2097. **E-Mail:** wkisch@netzero.net

KISER, KENNETH M(AYNARD), CHEMICAL ENGINEERING. **Personal Data:** b Detroit, Mich, November 28, 1929; m 1954, c 5. **Education:** Lawrence Tech Univ, BS, 1951; Univ Cincinnati, MS, 1952; Johns Hopkins Univ, DS(chem eng), 1956. **Professional Experience:** PROF EMER CHEM ENG, STATE UNIV NY, BUFFALO, 1997-; assoc dean eng, State Univ NY, Buffalo, 1978-1997; from asst prof to prof, State Univ NY, Buffalo, 1964-1997; adj staff, Rensselaer Polytech Inst, 1962-1964; res assoc, Chem dept, res lab, Gen Elec Co, 1956-1964; res assoc, Inst Coop res, Johns Hopkins Univ, 1952-1956; asst, Univ Cincinnati, 1951-1952; consult. **Memberships:** Am Inst Chem Engrs; Am Soc Eng Educ; Sigma Xi. **Research Statement & Publications:** Turbulent transport; non-Newtonian fluids; fluid mechanics in the human body; air and water pollution. **Mailing Address:** Dept Chem eng, State Univ NY, 307, Furnas Hall, Buffalo, NY 14260. **Fax:** 716-645-3822.

KISER, LOLA FRANCES, MATHEMATICS. **Personal Data:** b Selmer, Tenn, December 6, 1930. **Education:** Memphis State Univ, BS, 1952; Univ Ga, MA, 1954; Univ Ala, Tuscaloosa, PhD (math), 1971. **Professional Experience:** PROF EMER MATH, BIRMINGHAM-SOUTHERN COL, 1996-; from asst prof to prof, Birmingham-southern Col, 1955-1996; instr math, Univ Ga, 1954-1955. **Memberships:** Math Asn Am. **Research Statement & Publications:** Complex analysis; differential equations. **Mailing Address:** Dept Math, Birmingham-Southern Col, 900 Arkadelphia Rd, Birmingham, AL 35254.

KISER, ROBERT WAYNE, INORGANIC CHEMISTRY, MASS SPECTROMETRY. **Personal Data:** b Rock Island, Ill, April 26, 1932; m 1954, Barbara; c Mark D, Scott A & Ann M. **Education:** St Ambrose Univ, BA, 1953; Purdue Univ, MS, 1955, PhD, 1958. **Professional Experience:** PROF EMER CHEM, UNIV KY, as of 2003; dir gen chem, Mass Spectrometry Ctr, Univ Ky, 1988-1995; proj mgr, Student Info Syst, UK, 1985-1987; chmn chem dept, Mass Spectrometry Ctr, Univ Ky, 1968-1972; dir, Mass Spectrometry Ctr, Univ Ky, 1967-1996; prof chem, Univ Ky, 1967-1997; from asst prof to prof inorg chem, Kans State Univ, 1957-1967. **Memberships:** Am Soc Mass Spectrometry; Am Chem Soc. **Research Statement & Publications:** Excited states of negative ions; energetics and thermochemistry of ionic species; artificial intelligence in mass spectrometry; mass spectrometry and molecular structures; multiply-charged ionic species. **Mailing Address:** Dept Chem, Univ Ky, Lexington, KY 40506-0055. **Fax:** 606-323-1069. **E-Mail:** rwkiser@alltel.net

KISH, VALERIE MAYO, CELL BIOLOGY. **Personal Data:** b Paintsville, Ky, November 28, 1944. **Education:** Univ Ky, BS, 1965; Ind Univ, MA, 1966; Univ Mich, PhD (cell biol), 1973. **Professional Experience:** PROF DEPT BIOL, UNIV RICHMOND, VA, as of 2005; Chair dept biol, Univ richmond as of 2004; clarence E denoon prof sci, Univ richmond, VA, beginning 1993; prof biol, Hobart & William Smith Cols, 1976-1993; res assoc, Worcester Found Exp Biol, Shrewsbury, 1973-1976; res asst, Inst Cancer Res, Philadelphia, 1966-1969. **Memberships:** Am Soc Cell Biol; Am Soc Plant Physiol; Sigma Xi. **Research Statement & Publications:** Interaction of proteins with RNA in eukaryotic cells and the role these interactions play in the regulation of gene expression. **Mailing Address:** Dept Biol Univ Richmond, 28 Westhampton Way A-311 Gottwald Sci Bldg, Richmond, VA 23173. **Fax:** 315-781-3587. **E-Mail:** vkish@richmond.edu

KISHI, KEIJI, RESEARCH ADMINISTRATION & MANAGEMENT. **Personal Data:** b Tokyo, Japan, March 31, 1930; m 1963, c 2. **Education:** Keio Univ, BA, 1952, Dr(elec eng), 1969. **Professional Experience:** VPRES & GEN MGR, RES & DEVELOP CTR, TOSHIBA CERAMIC CO, 1987-; vpres & gen mgr, Silicon Div, 1987-1989; gen mgr planning, Res & Develop Ctr, Toshiba Ceramic CO, 1986-1987; Mem, Workshop Ministry State Sci & Technol, 1985-1988; gen mgr, Toshiba Corp, 1984-1986; dep dir, Toshiba Corp, 1979-1984; res fel, Toshiba Corp, 1973-1979; Sr researcher, Toshiba Corp, 1966-1973. **Memberships:** Fel Inst Elec & Electronics Engrs. **Research Statement & Publications:** Thyristor or converter for hvdc, power devices and their application; optoelectronics application for high voltage measurement. **Mailing Address:** Toshiba Ceramics Co Ltd, 26-2 Nishi-Shinjuku 1-Chrome Shinjuku-Ku, Tokyo 163, Japan.

KISHI, YOSHITO, MEDICINAL CHEMISTRY. **Personal Data:** b Nagoya, Japan, April 13, 1937; m 1963, c 2. **Education:** Nagoya Univ, BS, 1961; Harvard Univ, MA, 1974 PhD (chem), 1966. **Honors & Awards:** Japan Chem Soc Prize, 1967; Am Chem Soc Award Creative Work Synthetic Org Chem, 1980; Harrison Howe Award, 1981. **Professional Experience:** PROF EMER CHEM & CHEM BIOL, HARVARD UNIV, as of 2004; Javits Neuroscience invest award, 1988; Arthur C Cope scholar award, 1988; morris loeb prof chem, Harvard Univ, beginning 1982; prof, Harvard Univ, 1974-1982; vis prof, Harvard Univ, 1972-1973; assoc prof, Nagoya Univ, 1969-1974; Instr chem, Nagoya Univ, 1966-1969; fel, Harvard Univ, 1966-1968. **Memberships:** Am Chem Soc; Chem Soc Japan; Swiss Chem Soc; Am Acad Arts & Sci. **Research Statement & Publications:** Total synthesis of complex natural products typified by the completed works of neurotoxins, metabolites of microorganisms and polyether, ansamycin and antitumor antibiotics. **Mailing Address:** Dept Chem & Chem Biol, Harvard Univ, 12 Oxford St, Seven Divinity Ave, Cambridge, MA 02138. **Fax:** 617-495-5150. **E-Mail:** kishi@chemistry.harvard.edu

KISHIMOTO, TADAMITSU, PATHOLOGY IMMUNOLOGY. **Personal Data:** b Tondabayoshi, Japan, May 7, 1939; m 1967, Chizuko Tamura. **Education:** Osaka Univ, Md, 1964, PhD, 1969. **Honors & Awards:** Imperial Prize, Japan Acad, 1992; Sandoz Prize for Immunol, 1992. **Professional Experience:** DEAN, MED SCH, OSAKA UNIV, 1995-; PROF & CHMN MED, MED SCH, OSAKA UNIV, 1991-; prof immunol, Med Sch, Osaka Univ, 1983-1991; prof path, Med Sch, Osaka Univ, 1979-1983; Res fel & asst prof, Med Sch, Johns Hopkins Univ, 1970-1974. **Memberships:** Foreign assoc Nat Acad Sci; Japan Soc Immunbiol (pres, 1991-1992); Int Soc Immunopharmacol (pres, 1991-1994); foreign assoc Inst Med-Nat Acad Sci; hon mem Am Asn Immunologists; Japan Soc Immunobiol (pres, 1991-1992). **Research Statement & Publications:** Discovery in interleukin six. **Mailing Address:** 3-5-31 Nakanocho, Tonda Bayashi Osaka 584, Japan.

KISHIMOTO, YASUO, MOLECULAR BIOLOGY, GENETICS. **Personal Data:** b Osaka-Shi, Japan, April 11, 1925; m 1949, Miyoko; c 4. **Education:** Kyoto Univ, BS, 1948, PhD (pharmaceut chem), 1956. **Professional Experience:** RETIRED; adj prof, Dept Neuroscience Sch Med, Univ Calif, San Diego, 1988-1995; from assoc prof to prof, Sch Med, Johns Hopkins Univ, 1976-1988; dir biochem res, John F Kennedy Inst, 1976-1988; assoc biochemist neurol serv, Mass Gen Hosp, 1970-1976; sr investr, Eunice Kennedy Shriver Ctr Ment Retardation, 1969-1976; assoc neurol, Harvard Med Sch, 1969-1976; asst biochemist, Mass Gen Hosp, 1969-1970; mem staff, Div Chem Res, G D Searle & Co, Ill, 1967-1969; from asst to assoc res biochemist, Ment Health Res Inst, Univ Mich, Ann Arbor, 1962-1967; res asst biochem, Med Sch, Northwestern Univ, 1957-1959; asst prof, Shizuoka Col Pharm, 1954-1961; lectr pharm, Kyushu Univ, 1950-1954; res chemist, Osaka Gas Co, 1948-1950. **Memberships:** Am Soc Biochem & Molecular Biol; Int Soc Neurochem; AAAS; Am Soc Neurochem; Soc Glycobiol. **Research Statement & Publications:** Structures and metabolism of brain lipids; myelination, demyelination; role of saposins (sphingolipid activator proteins) in glycolipid metabolism; Biochemistry. **Mailing Address:** 13771, Royal Melbourne Sq, San Diego, CA 92128. **Fax:** 619-534-1383.

KISHK, AHMED A, APPLIED ELECTROMAGNETICS, NUMERICAL SOLUTIONS OF ELECROMAGNETIC PROBLEMS. **Personal Data:** b Ashmoun, Egypt, December 9, 1954; American citizen; m 1983, Iman; c Mohammad, Omayma, Yassev & Youssif. **Education:** Cairo Univ, Egypt, BS, 1977; Ain Shams Univ, Egypt, BS, 1980; Univ Man, Can, MS, 1983, PhD (elec engr), 1986. **Honors & Awards:** IEEE Microwave Theory & Technique, Microwave Prize, 2004. **Professional Experience:** Ed, Antennas & Propagation Mag, Inst Elec & Electronics Engrs, 1993-; PROF ELEC ENGR, UNIV MISS, 1995-; assoc prof, elec engr, Univ Miss, 1990-1995; asst prof, Univ Miss, 1986-1990; res assoc, Univ Man, Can, 1985-1986; teaching & res asst elec engr, Univ Man, Can, 1981-1985; teaching & res asst elec engr, Cairo Univ, 1977-1981; mem, Comn B, US Nat Comt Int Union Radio Sci. **Memberships:** Inst Elec & Electronics Engrs; Sigma Xi; Electromagnetic Acad; Phi Kappa Phi Soc. **Research Statement & Publications:** Numerical solutions of electromagnetic problems and antenna design, especially antenna feeds, microstrip antennas, ground station antennas and mobile satellite antennas; antenna design; dielectric antenna; phased array antennas artificial soft and hard surfaces. **Mailing Address:** Dept Elec Engr, Univ Miss, Univ, MS 38677. **Fax:** 662-915-7231. **E-Mail:** ahmed@okmiss.edu

KISHORE, GANESH M, PLANT GENETIC ENGINEERING, BIOCHEMISTRY. **Personal Data:** b Hunsur, India, September 26, 1953; American citizen; m 1976, c 2. **Education:** Univ Mysore, BS, 1970, MS, 1972; Indian Inst Sci, PhD (biochem), 1976. **Professional Experience:** CHIEF BIOTECHNOL OFFICER, DUPONT, as of 2005; VPRES SCI & TECHNOL, DUPONT, as of 2005; vpres, Technol, Dupont Agr & Nutrit, 2002-2005; pres, Nutrit Sector & Chief Biotechnologist, Monsanto Co, ending 2000; mgr, Monsanto Corp Res Labs, beginning 1990; res mgr, Monsanto Corp Res Labs, 1989-1990; assoc fel, Monsanto Corp Res Labs, 1987-1989; res specialist, Monsanto Corp Res Labs, 1982-1986; sr res biochem, Monsanto Corp Res Labs, 1980-1982. **Memberships:** Am Soc Biochem & Molecular Biol; Am Soc Plant Physiol. **Research Statement & Publications:** Plant biochemistry and plant genetics engineering; genetic engineering of herbicide tolerance, metabolism of herbicides and crop quality improvement. **Mailing Address:** DuPont Agr & Nutrit, 1007 Market St, Wilmington, DE 19898.

KISHORE, VIMAL, PHARMACOLOGY. **Education:** King Goerge's Med Col, Univ Lucknow, India, PhD (Med chem), 1976. **Professional Experience:** PROF, MED CHEM, DIV BASIC PHARMACEUT SCI, XAVIER UNIV LA COL PHARM, as of 2005. **Mailing Address:** Col Pharmaceut, Xavier Univ LA, 1 Drexel Dr, Rm 425C, New Orleans, LA 70125. **Fax:** 504-520-7954. **E-Mail:** vkishore@xula.edu

KISIEL, WALTER, PATHOLOGY. **Education:** Pa State Univ, BS, 1966; Ndak State Univ, MS, 1969, PhD (biochem), 1971. **Professional Experience:** PROF, DEPT PATHOL, UNIV NMEX SCH MED, as of 2006. **Mailing Address:** Dept Pathol, Univ NMex Sch Med, BRF337, Albuquerque, NM 87131-5301. **Fax:** 505-272-8084. **E-Mail:** wkisiel@salud.unm.edu

KISILEVSKY, ROBERT, BIOCHEMISTRY, PATHOLOGY. **Personal Data:** b Montreal, Que, December 19, 1937; Canadian citizen; m 1967, Barbara; c David, Alexandra & Sarah. **Education:** McGill Univ, BSc, 1958, MD, CM, 1962; Univ Pittsburgh, PhD (biochem), 1969; FRCP (C), 1972. **Honors & Awards:** Boyd lectr, Can Asn Pathologists, 1992; Claude P Beaubien Prize, Alzheimer Soc Can, 1996. **Professional Experience:** Mem, Nat Cancer Inst, 1988-1991; pathologist chief, Kingston Gen Hosp, 1986-1991; head, Queen's Univ, 1986-1991; PROF ANAT PATH, QUEEN'S UNIV, KINGSTON, 1979-; sci officer, Grant Comt, Med Res Coun, 1977-1983; mem, Grant Comt, Med Res Coun, 1974-1977; from asst prof to assoc prof biochem, Queen's Univ, 1971-1990; asst pathologist, Kingston Gen Hosp, 1970-1986; from asst prof to assoc prof, Queen's Univ, 1970-1979. **Memberships:** US-Can Acad Path; Am Soc Invest Path; Can Asn Pathologists; Can Biochem Soc. **Research Statement & Publications:** Pathogenetic mechanisms of Amyloidosis and its relationship to Alzheimer's disease; serum amyloid A and its role in cholesterol metabolism during inflammation. **Mailing Address:** Dept Path, Queen's Univ, Kingston, ON K7L 3N6, Can. **Fax:** 613-533-2907. **E-Mail:** kisilevsky@cliff.path.queensu.ca

KISKIS, JOSEPH EDWARD, THEORETICAL PHYSICS, HIGH ENERGY PHYSICS. **Personal Data:** b Lynwood, Calif, October 2, 1947. **Education:** Univ Calif, Davis, BS, 1969; Stanford Univ, MS, 1971, PhD (physics), 1974. **Professional Experience:** PROF PHYSICS, UNIV CALIF, DAVIS, as of 2001; Oppenheimer fel, Los Alamos Nat Lab, 1978-1980; mem, Inst Advan Study, 1977-1978; fel, Los Alamos Sci Lab, 1976-1977; fel, Mass Inst Technol, 1974-1976; VICE CHANCELLOR, DEPT PHYSICS. **Research Statement & Publications:** High energy physics; quantum field theory. **Mailing Address:** Dept Physics 443 Physics, Univ Calif, Davis, CA 95616. **E-Mail:** jekiskis@ecdavis.edu

KISLIUK, PAUL, PHYSICS. **Personal Data:** b Philadelphia, Pa, February 22, 1922; m 1950, c Amy, Margaret, Tom & Bill. **Education:** Queen's Col, NY, BA, 1943; Columbia Univ, MS, 1947, PhD (physics), 1952. **Professional Experience:** RETIRED; sr scientist, Aerospace Corp, 1966-1990; dept head, Aerospace Corp, 1962-1966; mem tech staff, Bell Tel Labs, 1952-1962. **Memberships:** Am Phys Soc. **Research Statement & Publications:** Microwave spectroscopy; contact physics; surface physics; lasers; solid state spectroscopy. **Mailing Address:** 2302 Veteran Ave, Los Angeles, CA 90064. **E-Mail:** pkisliuk@aol.com

KISLIUK, ROY LOUIS, BIOCHEMISTRY. **Personal Data:** b Philadelphia, Pa, August 4, 1928; m 1954, Ingrid; c Claudette (Beit-Aharon) & Michelle R. **Education:** Queen's Col, NY, BS, 1950; Yale Univ, MS, 1952; Western Reserve Univ, PhD (biochem), 1956. **Professional Experience:** PROF EMER BIOCHEM, SCH MED, TUFTS UNIV, as of 2005; prof pharmacol & exp therapeut, Sch Med, Tufts Univ, beginning 1992; prof biochem, Sch Med, Tufts Univ, beginning1972; prog dir biochem, NSF, Wash, DC, 1972-1973; assoc prof biochem, Sch Med, Tufts Univ, 1971-1972; from asst prof to assoc prof pharmacol, Sch Med, Tufts Univ, 1960-1971; vis scientist, Nat Inst Arthritis & Metab Dis, 1958-1960; Nat Found Infantile Paralysis fel biochem, Oxford Univ, 1956-1958. **Memberships:** Am Soc Biol Chem; Am Chem Soc; Am Soc Pharmacol & Exp Therapeut; Am Soc Microbiol; Am Soc Cancer Res; AAAS. **Research Statement & Publications:** Folate enzymes, coenzymes and antimetabolites. **Mailing Address:** Dept Biochem, Tufts Sch Grad Biomed Sci, 136 Harrison Ave, Boston, MA 02111-1800. **Fax:** 617-636-2409. **E-Mail:** roy.kisliuk@tufts.edu

KISMAN, KENNETH EDWIN, PETROLEUM ENGINEERING. **Personal Data:** b Sudbury, Ont, November 18, 1946; m 1970, c 2. **Education:** Queens Univ, BSc, 1968; Univ Toronto, MSc, 1970, PhD (molecular physics), 1974. **Professional Experience:** PRES & PRIN ENG, RANGEWEST RESOURCES, LTD, CALGARY, 1996-; prin reservoir engr, Kisman, 1984-1996; res supvr reservoir eng, Defence & Civil Inst Environ Med, Can, 1979-1984; res officer hyperbaric biophys, Defence & Civil Inst Environ Med, Can, 1974-1979; fel, Nat res council. **Memberships:** Soc Petrol Eng; Can Inst Mining & Metall; Asn prof engrs Geologists & Geo physicists AB. **Research Statement & Publications:** Engineering studies for heavy oil petroleum recovery processes; including field pilots; numerical simulation and direction of lab studies. **Mailing Address:** Rangewest Resources Ltd, 5760 Buckboard Rd NW, Calgary, AB T3A 4R6, Can. **Fax:** 403-247-8342. **E-Mail:** kkisman@rangewest.ca

KISPERT, LOWELL DONALD, SOLID STATE CHEMISTRY, RADIATION CHEMISTRY. **Personal Data:** b Faribault, Minn, June 9, 1940; m 1989, Doris; c David, Greg, Paul, Reggie, Lenny, Michael & Marisa Mulhern. **Education:** St Olaf Col, BA, 1962; Mich State Univ, PhD (chem), 1966. **Honors & Awards:** Burnum Award, 1988. **Professional Experience:** CHMN, CHEM DEPT, UNIV ALA, 1995-; RES PROF CHEM, UNIV ALA, 1980-; from asst prof to prof, Chem Dept, 1968-1980; radiation chem, Mellon Inst, 1968; fel, Carnegie Mellon Univ 1967-1968; fel electron spin resonance, Varian assocs Calif, 1966-1967. **Memberships:** Am Chem Soc; Am Phys Soc; Sigma Xi; Int Soc Magnet Resonance; Int EPR Soc. **Research Statement & Publications:** Free radicals as produced in irradiated organic single crystals by electron spin resonance; electron nuclear double resonance and electron-electron double resonance of paramagnetic single crystals; anions and cations in solution; radiation chemistry; conducting polymers; photosynthesis; solid-state photochemistry; polymer batteries; role of carotenoids in plant photosynthesis; coal porosity; materials for information technology. **Mailing Address:** Dept Chem, Univ Ala, PO Box 870336 113D Shelby Hall, Tuscaloosa, AL 35487-0336. **Fax:** 205-348-9104. **E-Mail:** lkispert@bama.ua.edu

KISS, HELEN G, PLANT PHYSIOLOGY. **Education:** Rutgers Univ, PhD, 1989. **Professional Experience:** ADJ ASST PROF, DEPT BOT, MIAMI UNIV, as of 2006. **Mailing Address:** Dept Bot, Miami Univ, 107 Roudebush Hall, Oxford, OH 45056. **E-Mail:** KissHG@muohio.edu

KISS, JOHN Z, PLANT DEVELOPMENT. **Education:** Rutgers Univ, PhD, 1987. **Professional Experience:** PROF, DEPT BOT, MIAMI UNIV, as of 2006. **Mailing Address:** Dept Bot, Miami Univ, 360 Pearson, Oxford, OH 45056. **E-Mail:** kissjz@muohio.edu

KISS, KLARA, PHYSICAL CHEMISTRY, POLYMER CHEMISTRY. **Personal Data:** b Budapest, Hungary, August 28, 1930; m 1951, c 2. **Education:** Budapest Tech Univ, dipl Chemiker, 1954, PhD, 1982. **Professional Experience:** SR RES SCIENTIST, AKZO CHEMICALS INC, 1987-; sr res assoc, Stauffer Chem Co, 1970-1987; res chemist, GAF Corp, 1967-1970; res assoc electron micros, Case Western Reserve Univ, 1965-1967; sr res assoc phys chem & polymer sci, Horizons, Inc, Ohio, 1961-1965; res chemist, Dom Dyeing & Printing Co, Can, 1957-1959; res & develop chemist, Filmfabrik AGFA, EGer, 1956; res chemist, Res Ctr Telecommun, 1955-1956; Jr chemist, Res Ctr Org & Polymer Chem, Budapest, 1949-1951. **Memberships:** Soc Appl Spectros; Asn Hungarian Chemists; Ger Chem Soc; Am Crystallog Asn; Microbeam Analysis Soc. **Research Statement & Publications:** Kinetics of redox bulk polymerization of acrylates; photopolymerization; controlled, ultrafine particle size ferroelectrics; epitaxial crystallization of polymers; identification of wairakite single crystals by electron diffraction; microbeam analysis; mechanical properties relationship in materials. **Mailing Address:** Akzo Chem Inc, Livingstone Ave, Dobbs Ferry, NY 10522. **Fax:** 914-693-5780.

KISS, LASZLO ISTVAN, HEAT TRANSFER, THERMOPHYSICAL PROPERTIES. **Personal Data:** b Rakoscsaba, Hungary, July 23, 1945; Canadian citizen; wid. **Education:** Hungarian Acad Sci, PhD, 1984. **Honors & Awards:** Krusper Mem Award, Sci Soc Measurement & Automation, 1988. **Professional Experience:** PROF, THERMODYN & HEAT TRANSFER, DEPT APPL SCI, UNIV QUE, 1989-; assoc prof, Inst Thermal & Syst Eng, 1983-1989; dir techn, 1981; head, Lab Thermal Physics, 1978-1989; lectr, Dept Energetics, Tech Univ Budapest, 1973-1983; asst lectr, Dept Energetics, Tech Univ Budapest, 1968-1973; consult, Alcan, Noranda, STAS, BLW. **Memberships:** Am Soc Mech Engrs; Instrument Soc Am. **Research Statement & Publications:** Physical and mathematical modeling of heat conduction and convection; two-phase flows; Theory and practice of thermophysical measurements; Heat and mass transfer in aluminum metallurgy; bubbles and droplets, nucleation and break-up; Optical diagnostics in heat-transfer and combustion. **Mailing Address:** Dept Appl Sci, Univ Que, Chicoutimi, PQ G7H 2B1, Can. **Fax:** 418-545-5012. **E-Mail:** lkiss@uqac.ca

KISSA, ERIK, COLLOID CHEMISTRY, TEXTILE CHEMISTRY. **Personal Data:** b Abja, Estonia, April 7, 1923; American citizen; m 1952, Selma; c Erik Harold & Karl Martin. **Education:** Karlsruhe Univ, dipl chem, 1951; Univ Del, PhD (chem), 1956. **Honors & Awards:** SDA Award, 1991. **Professional Experience:** CONSULT, 1994-; res fel, Du Pont Chem Dept, 1990-1993; sr res assoc, Du Pont Chem Dept, 1986-1990; UNIDO consult, Korea Res Inst Chem Technol, 1986-1988; Shanghai Dye Res Inst, China, 1982; UN Indust Develop Orgn consult, Atira Textile Res Inst, Ahmedabad, India, 1978 & 1979; res assoc, E I DuPont Del Nemours & Co, Inc, 1974-1986; sr res chemist, E I DuPont Del Nemours & Co, Inc, 1967-1974; res chemist, E I DuPont Del Nemours & Co, Inc, 1956-1967; analytical chemist, E I DuPont Del Nemours & Co, Inc, 1951-1956. **Memberships:** Am Chem Soc; fel Am Inst Chem; Int Asn Colloid & Interface Scientists; Am Oil Chem-.Soc. **Research Statement & Publications:** Author over 60 journal articles and book chapters. 11 US patents. Four books (listed above). **Mailing Address:** 1436 Fresno Rd, Wilmington, DE 19803-5122. **E-Mail:** ekissa@aol.com

KISSA, KARL MARTIN, INTEGRATED OPTICS & FIBEROPTICS, OPTICAL COMMUNICATIONS. **Personal Data:** b Wilmington, Del, June 5, 1961; m 2003, Wendy; c Emily Elisabeth Kissa. **Education:** Duke Univ, BS, 1982; Univ Del, MSEE, 1986, PhD (elec eng), 1989. **Professional Experience:** Prin electro-optic engr, JDSU, 1995- SR OPTICAL ENGR, UNIPHASE TELECOMMUN PROD, 1994- 1995; Tech staff, Clark Stark Draper Lab, 1989-1994. **Memberships:** Inst Elec & Electronics Engrs. **Research Statement & Publications:** Computer modelling and simulation techniques for integrated and fiber-optics; conduct experiments and collect empirical data to validate and refine models. **Mailing Address:** 1 Grant Estate Dr, West Simsbury, CT 06092. **Fax:** 860-243-6601. **E-Mail:** karl.kissa@jdsu.com

KISSANE, JOHN M, MEDICINE. **Personal Data:** b Oxford, Ohio, March 30, 1928; m 1951, c 5. **Education:** Univ Rochester, AB, 1948; Wash Univ, MD, 1952. **Professional Experience:** Med alumni scholar, Sch Med, Wash Univ, 1970-1971; PROF PATH & PROF PATH PEDIAT, SCH MED, WASH UNIV, beginning 1968; asst pathologist, Barnes & Assoc Hosps, 1958-; Nat Found Infantile Paralysis res fel, Sch Med, Wash Univ, 1954-1955 & 1957-1958; from instr to assoc prof, Sch Med, Wash Univ, 1953-1968; chief resident, Barnes Hosp, 1953-1954; intern, Barnes Hosp, 1952-1953; asst path, Sch Med, Wash Univ, 1952-1953; mem sect renal dis, Coun Circulation, Am Heart Asn. **Memberships:** AMA; Am Asn Path & Bact; Am Soc Exp Path; Histochem Soc; Int Acad Path. **Research Statement & Publications:** Pathology; pediatric pathology; quantitative histochemistry of nervous system; kidney. **Mailing Address:** Dept Path & Pediat, Wash Univ Sch Med, St Louis, MO 63110-1010. **Fax:** 414-259-0319.

KISSEBAH, AHMED H, ENDOCRINOLOGY. **Education:** Cairo Univ, MD, 1961; Univ London, PhD, 1973. **Professional Experience:** PROF MED, MED COL WIS, as of 2006. **Mailing Address:** Dept Med, Div Endocrin Med Col Wis, 9200 W Wisconsin Ave, Milwaukee, WI 53226-3522. **Fax:** 414-456-6210. **E-Mail:** kissebah@mcw.edu

KISSEL, CHARLES LOUIS, INDUSTRIAL ORGANIC CHEMISTRY. **Personal Data:** b Chicago, Ill, August 5, 1947; m 1970, c 2. **Education:** Univ Calif, Irvine, BA, 1969; Univ Calif, Santa Barbara, PhD (chem), 1973. **Professional Experience:** PRIN OWNER, CNC DEVELOP, 1990-; sr res chemist, Unocal Corp, 1985-1990; dir res, Magna Corp, 1984-1985; group leader chem res, 1973-1984. **Memberships:** Am Chem Soc; Sigma Xi; AAAS; Nat Asn Corrosion Engrs; Tech Asn Pulp & Paper Indust. **Research Statement & Publications:** Treating mechanisms and synthesis of industrial biocides, corrosion inhibitors, scale inhibitors, emulsion breakers and water clarifiers, zero formaldehyde textile binders for non-wovens, as well as specialty chemicals; special emphasis on acrolein chemistry; sol-gel chemistry; nonionic surfactants. **Mailing Address:** CNC Develop Inc, 2856 Skywood Circle, Anaheim, CA 92804-2061.

KISSEL, DAVID E, SOIL CHEMISTRY, SOIL FERTILITY. **Personal Data:** b Vanderburg Co, Ind, August 10, 1943; m 1966, Mary; c Eric, Laura & Anne. **Education:** Purdue Univ, BS, 1965; Univ Ky, MS, 1967, PhD (soil acidity), 1969. **Professional Experience:** PROF, DEPT CROP & SOIL SCI, UNIV GA, 1989-; head dept, Dept Crop & Soil Sci, Univ GA, 1989-1996; ed, Soil Sci Am J, 1988-1990; prof agron, Kans State Univ, 1978-1988; assoc prof & asst dir for res, Blackland Res Ctr, 1977-1978; assoc ed, J Environ Qual, 1975-1978; from asst prof to assoc prof soil chem, Tex A&M Univ, 1969-1977. **Memberships:** Fel Am Soc Agron; fel Soil Sci Soc Am (pres-elect, 1994, pres, 1995); Int Soc Soil Sci; fel AAAS; Soil & Water Conserv Soc. **Research Statement & Publications:** Plant nutrition; soil acidity; movement of water and nitrate in soils; nitrogen and phosphorus fertilizer use efficiency; ammonia volatilization; nitrogen mineralization. **Mailing Address:** Dept Crop & Soil Sci Univ Ga, 2400 Col Sta Rd, Athens, GA 30602-9105. **Fax:** 706-369-5734. **E-Mail:** dkissel@uga.edu

KISSEL, JOHN WALTER, PHARMACOLOGY. **Personal Data:** b St Louis, Mo, December 12, 1925; m 1953, Jeanette; c Carl, Catherine, Julia & John. **Education:** Wash Univ, AB, 1948; St Louis Col Pharm, BS, 1951; St Louis Univ, MS, 1955; Univ Mich, PhD (pharmacol), 1958. **Professional Experience:** RETIRED; sr clin res assoc, clin res dept, Lederle Labs, 1988-1991; clin res assoc, clin res dept, Lederle Labs, 1975-1988; clin res assoc med res dept, Cyanamid Int, 1973-1975; mgr drug eval, Am Cyanamid Co, 1971-1973; from pharmacologist to sr pharmacologist, 1969-1971; sect leader, Mead Johnson & Co, 1962-1969; group leader cent nerv syst pharmacol, Mead Johnson & Co, 1959-1962; assoc sr pharmacologist, Mead Johnson & Co, 1957-1959; asst prof pharmacog & pharmacol, Col Pharm, Univ Fla, 1956-1957. **Memberships:** Fel AAAS; Am Soc Pharmacol & Exp Therapeut; NY Acad Sci; Am Soc Clin Pharmacol Therapeut. **Research Statement & Publications:** Central nervous system pharmacology, especially opiate tolerance and addiction; spinal cord reflexes; muscle relaxants; effect of drugs on behavior; clinical evaluation of psychotherapeutic agents; antibiotics; anti-cancer therapy. **Mailing Address:** 115 Sherwood Dr, Ramsey, NJ 07446.

KISSEL, THOMAS ROBERT, ANALYTICAL CHEMISTRY, CLINICAL ANALYSIS. **Personal Data:** b Chicago, Ill, September 26, 1947; m 1972. **Education:** Univ Notre Dame, BS, 1969; Univ Wis, PhD (anal chem), 1974. **Professional Experience:** PROG LEADER, JOHNSON & JOHNSON CLIN DIAG, 1994-; Res Chemist, Eastman Kodak Co, 1974-1994. **Memberships:** Sigma Xi; Am Asn Clin Chem. **Research Statement & Publications:** Electrochemistry, specifically ion selective electrodes; immunol Assn; chemicuminescience; fluorescience; diagnostic systems design and performance. **Mailing Address:** 200 Willowood Dr, Rochester, NY 14612.

KISSEL, WILLIAM JOHN, POLYMER PROPERTIES. **Personal Data:** b New York, NY, March 12, 1941; m 1966, c 2. **Education:** City Col New York, BS, 1962; State Univ NY, Buffalo, PhD (org chem), 1968. **Professional Experience:** SR RES CHEMIST, AMOCO CHEM CO, 1967-. **Memberships:** Am Chem Soc; Am Soc Testing Mat. **Research Statement & Publications:** Polymer evaluation; polymer stability. **Mailing Address:** Amoco Polymers Inc, 4500 McGuinni's Ferry Rd, Alpharetta, GA 30005.

KISSELL, FRED N, MINE ENGINEERING. **Honors & Awards:** Howard N Eavenson Award, Soc Mining Metall & Explor, 1993. **Professional Experience:** MINING ENGR, US BUR MINES, PITTSBURGH. **Mailing Address:** Pittsburgh Res Ctr US Bur Mines, PO Box 18070, Pittsburgh, PA 15236.

KISSELL, KENNETH EUGENE, SPACE OBSERVATORIES, SPACE SURVEILLANCE. **Personal Data:** b Ohio, June 28, 1928; m 1988, Judith; c Kevin D & Bradley T. **Education:** Ohio State Univ, BSc, 1949, MSc, 1958, PhD, 1969. **Professional Experience:** Chief scientist, AMOS Observ, Rockwell Power Systs, 1990-1993; ASSOC RES PHYSICS, UNIV MD, 1987-1990, 1993-; staff mem, Automatic Photoelec Telescope Serv, Mt Hopkins, Ariz, 1985-; prin staff mem, Optical Astron, BDM Corp, 1983-1987; vis astronr, Kitt Peak Nat Observ, beginning 1981; staff scientist laser systs anal, Rocketdyne Div, Rockwell Int, 1980-1983; instr physics, Sinclair Community Col, beginning 1980; assoc dir, Aerospace Instrumentation Div, ISA, 1978-1983; sr scientist, Reconnaissance & Weapon Delivery Div, Air Force Avionics Lab, 1976-1980; br chief, Surveillance Br, Air Force Avionics Lab, 1972-1975; lectr, Wright State Univ, 1970-1971; vis prof, Arcetri Astrophys Observ, Italy, 1969; dir, Gen Physics Res Lab, Aerospace Res Labs, Off Aerospace Res, 1966-1972; ed measurement applns, Trans, Instrument Soc Am, 1962-1968; physicist, Gen Physics Res Lab, Aerospace Res Labs, Off Aerospace Res, 1961-1966; chief, Gen Physics Res Lab, Aerospace Res Labs, Off Aerospace Res, 1959-1961; physicist, Appl Math Lab, Aeronaut Res Lab, 1958-1959; solar eclipse experimenter, var expeds, 1954-1991; instrumentation physicist, Propulsion Br, Flight Res Lab, Wright-Patterson AFB, 1951-1957; Res assoc rocket res lab, Res Found, Ohio State Univ, 1948-1951; CHIEF SCIENTIST, KISSELL CONSULT, ANNANDALE, VA. **Memberships:** Am Astron Soc; Am Geophys Union; Am Inst Aeronaut & Astronaut; Int Astron Union; fel Royal Astron Soc; Optical Soc Am. **Research Statement & Publications:** Rocket exhaust temperature measurement; automated telescopes; satellite photometry; photoelectric imaging devices; stellar spectroscopy in near infrared; solar eclipse observation; optical scattering; super luminous stars; Cepheid variables; laser systems; space telescope optical systems and science instruments. **Mailing Address:** Univ Md, Dept Physics, 0113 Physics Bldg, College Park, MD 20742-4111. **Fax:** 301-314-9525. **E-Mail:** kissellk@umd.edu

KISSEN, ABBOTT THEODORE, PHYSIOLOGY. **Personal Data:** b New York, NY, November 24, 1922; m 1946, Bette; c Christine & David. **Education:** Brooklyn Col, BA, 1950; Ohio State Univ, MA, 1952, PhD (zoology), 1956. **Professional Experience:** RETIRED; res physiologist, Aerospace Med Res Lab, Wright-Patterson AFB, 1961-1979; asst prof, Ohio State Univ, 1959-1961; res assoc physiol, Ohio State Univ, 1957-1959; Am Heart Asn fel, 1957-1958. **Memberships:** Assoc fel Aerospace Med Asn; Am Physiol Soc; Sigma Xi. **Research Statement & Publications:** Physiological effects of acceleration stresses encountered or anticipated in aerospace flight. **Mailing Address:** 311 Passage Way, Osprey, FL 34229.

KISSICK, WILLIAM LEE, SCIENCE EDUCATION, MEDICINE. **Personal Data:** b Detroit, Mich, July 29, 1932; m 1956, Priscilla Harriet Dillingham; c William, Robert-John, Jonathan & Elizabeth. **Education:** Yale Univ, BA, 1953, MD, 1957, MPH, 1959, DrPH, 1961. **Professional Experience:** Dir, Health Policy, chmn bd govs Leonard Davis Inst Health Econ, 1989-; chmn comn on med affairs coun, fel Yale Corp, 1987-; mem, coun Col Physicians Pa, 1983-1988; coun med soc, Am Col Physicians, 1983-1988; DIR, CTR HEALTH POLICY, 1981-; mem, Mayor's Comn, 1981-1983; mem, Accrediting Comn on Educ for Health Serv Admin, 1980-1986; chmn comn on med affairs coun, Yale Univ, 1980-1986; PROF HEALTH POLICY & MGT, SCH NURSING, 1978-; vis prof, Inst European Health Serv Res, Leuven Univ, 1974-1975; PROF HEALTH CARE SYSTS, WHARTON SCH, 1971-; GEORGE S PEPPER PROF PUB HEALTH & PREVENT MED, SCH MED, UNIV PA, 1969-; prof & chmn dept community med, Ctr Health Policy, 1968-1971; exec dir nat adv comn health facil, White House, Wash, 1968; dir, Off Prog Planning Eval, Off Surgeon Gen, USPHS, 1966-1968; spec asst to asst secy health, US Dept HEW, 1964-1965; Div Community Health Serv, 1962-1963; resident, Montefiore Hosp & Med Ctr, New York City, 1961-1962; Intern, Yale-New Haven Med Ctr, 1957-1958; fel mem exec comt, Nat Ctr Health Care Mgt; cons, Nat Ctr Health Serv Res, Health Resources Admin, Benedum Found, WHO, Appalachian Regional Commun, Smith Kline-Beckman, Pew Mem Trust, Colonial Pa group, Ctr Disease Control; vis prof, community med, Guy's Hosp Med Sch, dept soc sci & admin, London Sch Econ & Polit Sci. **Memberships:** AAAS; Am Col Preventive Med; Am Pub Health Asn; Philadelphia Pa Col Physicians; Asn Health Serv Res; Asn Teachers Preventive Med; Am Col Physicians Exec; Physicians Soc Responsibility; Nat Asn Pub Health Policy. **Mailing Address:** 3400 Spruce St, Philadelphia, PA 19104.

KISSILEFF, HARRY R, PHYSIOLOGICAL PSYCHOLOGY, INGESTIVE BEHAVIOR. **Personal Data:** b Philadelphia, Pa, June 1, 1940; m 1963, Karen; c Beth P & Eliot I. **Education:** Univ Pa, BA, 1962, PhD (zoology), 1966. **Professional Experience:** ASSOC PROF CLIN PSYCHOL, PSYCHIAT & MED, COL PHYSICIANS & SURGEONS, COLUMBIA UNIV, 1988-; adj asst prof, NY Univ, 1977-1988; adj asst prof, Psychiat & Med, Col Physicians & Surgeons, Columbia Univ, 1976-1988; asst prof, Univ Pa, 1971-1976; asst prof, Rockefeller Univ, 1969-1971; guest investr, Rockefeller Univ, 1966-1969. **Memberships:** Soc Neuroscience; Soc Study Ingestive Behav (pres 1987-1989); Am Phys Soc. **Research Statement & Publications:** Physiological and physchological control of human food consumption; demonstrated that equienergetic foods differ in satiating effectiveness and that the naturally occuring hormone, cholecystokinin, reduces food intake in humans. **Mailing Address:** St Luke's-Roosevelt Hosp, 1111 Amsterdam Ave, New York, NY 10025. **Fax:** 212-523-4830. **E-Mail:** hrk2@columbia.edu

KISSIN, BENJAMIN, internal medicine; deceased, see previous edition for last biography

KISSIN, IGOR, ANESTHESIOLOGY. **Education:** MD, PhD. **Professional Experience:** PROF ANESTHESIOL, BRIGHAM & WOMEN'S HOSP, as of 2002. **Memberships:** Int Anesthesia Res Soc. **Mailing Address:** Brigham & Women's Hosp, 75 Francis St, Boston, MA 02115. **Fax:** 617-734-0682. **E-Mail:** kissin@zeus.bwh.harvard.edu

KISSIN, STEPHEN ALEXANDER, MINERALOGY, ECONOMIC GEOLOGY. **Personal Data:** b Ithaca, NY, April 11, 1942; m 1971, Margaret; c Saul & Alexandra. **Education:** Univ Wash, BS, 1964; Pa State Univ, MS, 1968; Univ Toronto, PhD (geol), 1974. **Professional Experience:** PROF GEOL, LAKEHEAD UNIV, 1987-; assoc, Comt Meteorites, Nat Res Coun Can, 1981-1991; vis Res prof, Dept Chem & Geol, Ariz State Univ, 1981-1982; from asst prof to assoc prof, Lakehead Univ, 1975-1987; Nat Res Coun fel, Dept Energy, Mines & Resources, Ottawa, 1974-1975; fel, McMaster Univ, Hamilton, 1973; engr, Siemens AG, WGer, 1969; Aerospace scientist, Goddard Space Flight Ctr, NASA, 1967-1968. **Memberships:** Geol Asn Can; Mineral Asn Can; Mineral Soc Am; Meteoritical Soc; Sigma Xi. **Research Statement & Publications:** Mineralogy and crystal chemistry of sulfides; genesis of ore deposits; meteoritics. **Mailing Address:** Dept Geol, Lakehead Univ, Off CB 4007 955 Oliver Rd, Thunder Bay, ON P7A 5G8, Can. **Fax:** 807-343-8023. **E-Mail:** stephen.kissin@lakeheadu.ca

KISSIN, YURY VIKTOR, POLYMER CHEMISTRY. **Personal Data:** b Moscow, USSR, February 17, 1937; American citizen; m 1960, Natalie; c Anna. **Education:** Lomonosov Inst Fine Chem Technol, MD, 1960; Semenov Inst Chem Physics, PhD (polymer chem), 1965. **Professional Experience:** RES ASSOC, EDISON RES LAB, MOBIL CHEM CO, 1985-; res assoc, Gulf Res & Develop Co, 1980-1985; Sr researcher, Semenov Inst Chem Physics, Russia, 1972-1980. **Research Statement & Publications:** Chemistry and kinetics of olefin homopolymerization and copolymerization reactions with transition metal-based catalysts (ziegler-natta and metallocene catalysts); chemistry and kinetics of alkane cracking over acidic catalysts; geochemistry: catagenesis of eight hydrocarbus in petroleum. **Mailing Address:** Edison Res Lab, Mobil Chem Co, PO Box 3029, Edison, NJ 08818-3029.

KISSINGER, CHARLES R, BIOCHEMISTRY. **Professional Experience:** AT PFIZER GLOBAL RES & DEVELOP, LA JOLLA, CALIF, as of 2001; at Agouron Pharmaceut, San Diego, Calif, as of 1999; at Dept Molecular Biol & Genetics, Johns Hopkins Univ Sch Med. **Mailing Address:** Pfizer Inc, 10350 N Torrey Pines Rd, San Diego, CA 92037. **E-Mail:** chuck_kissinger@stromix.com

KISSINGER, DAVID GEORGE, TAXONOMY, DATABASE SYSTEMS. **Personal Data:** b Reading, Pa, July 26, 1933; m 1955, c 2. **Education:** Columbia Union Col, BA, 1954; Univ Md, MS, 1955, PhD (entom), 1957; Univ Calif, MPH, 1958. **Professional Experience:** MGR DATABASE, LOMA LINDA UNIV, 1986-; NIH fel, 1974-1976; prof epidemiol, Loma Linda Univ, 1972-1983; prof biol & head dept, Atlantic Union Col, 1960-1972; prof biol & head dept, Oakwood Col, 1958-1960; Asst entom, Univ Md, 1955-1957; consult. **Research Statement & Publications:** Taxonomy of new world apionidae (coleoptera); application of computer techniques to taxonomic problems. **Mailing Address:** 24414 University Ave No 40, Loma Linda, CA 92354.

KISSINGER, HOMER EVERETT, METAL PHYSICS. **Personal Data:** b Ottawa, Kans, August 29, 1923; m 1948, Jane; c Alan, Donald, Charles & Brian. **Education:** Kans State Col, BS, 1949, MS, 1950. **Professional Experience:** RETIRED; sr res scientist, Battelle-Northwest, 1965-1987; sr scientist, Gen Elec Co, 1960-1965; physicist, Nat Bur Stand, 1950-1960; asst physics, Kans State Col, 1949-1950; phys sci aide, Nat Bur Stand, 1948. **Memberships:** Sigma Xi. **Research Statement & Publications:** Crystallography of radiation damage, phase transformations and x-ray diffraction methods; crystal chemistry of solid nuclear waste forms and containments. **Mailing Address:** 1733 Horn Ave, Richland, WA 99352. **E-Mail:** Hojak@juno.com

KISSINGER, JOHN CALVIN, MICROBIOLOGY. **Personal Data:** b Shamokin, Pa, June 8, 1925; m 1950, Nancey; c John A & George B. **Education:** Bucknell Univ, BS, 1949, MS, 1950. **Honors & Awards:** Medal, Fedn Sewage & Indust Wastes Asn, 1957 Cert Keris, Usda, 1969. **Professional Experience:** RETIRED; assoc, Nat Maple Strup Coun, 1967-1975; res microbiologist, Eastern Regional Res Ctr, USDA, 1957-1983; supvr fermentation, Grain Processing Corp, 1955-1956; asst mgr biol standards, Marcus, Sharp & Dohme, 1951-1955; chemist, Campbell Soup Co, 1950-1951. **Memberships:** Asn Off Anal Chem; Int Asn Milk, Food & Environ Sanit. **Research Statement & Publications:** Industrial waste treatment; food microbiology; meat and meat products; maple products. **Mailing Address:** 1018 S Tenth St, Emmaus, PA 18049.

KISSINGER, PETER THOMAS, CHEMISTRY, NEUROCHEMISTRY. **Personal Data:** b Staten Island, NY, December 19, 1944; m 1978, Candice; c William H & Samuel T. **Education:** Union Col, BS, 1966; Univ NC, PhD (chem), 1970. **Professional Experience:** CHMN & CEO, BIOANAL SYST INC, as of 2004; PROF BIOANAL CHEM, PURDUE UNIV, 1982-; from asst prof to assoc prof, Purdue Univ, 1975-1982; pres, Bioanal Systs Inc, 1974-; asst prof chem, Mich State Univ, 1972-1975; res assoc chem, Univ Kans, 1970-1972. **Memberships:** Am Chem Soc; Am Asn Clin Chemists; AAAS; Am Asn Mass Spectrometry; Sigma Xi; Soc Electronanal Chem (pres 1987-1989); Am Asn Pharm Scientists; Electrochem Soc. **Research Statement & Publications:** Trace organic analysis using chromatographic and electrochemical techniques; metabolic pathways of aromatic compounds; neurochemistry; organic redox reactions; chemical instrumentation; electrochemistry; pharmaceutical analysis. **Mailing Address:** Bioanal Systs, 2701 Kent Ave, West Lafayette, IN 47906-1350. **Fax:** 765-497-1102. **E-Mail:** pete@bioanalytical.com

KISSLING, DON LESTER, PALEOECOLOGY, SEDIMENTOLOGY. **Personal Data:** b St Louis, Mo, January 29, 1934; m 1959, c 2. **Education:** Mo Sch Mines, BS, 1958; Univ Wis, MS, 1960; Ind Univ, PhD (geol), 1967. **Professional Experience:** OWNER & PRES, JACKALOPE GEOLOGICAL LTD, 1984-; assoc prof geol, State Univ NY, Binghamton, 1974-1982; from instr to assoc prof paleont, State Univ NY, Binghamton, 1965-1974; Res geologist, Superior Oil Co, 1960-1962. **Memberships:** Geol Soc Am; Soc Econ Paleontologists & Mineralogists; Paleont Soc. **Research Statement & Publications:** Paleoecology of Paleozoic corals and biohermal fossil assemblages; ecology of modern corals; Paleozoic sedimentary environments and recent carbonate sediments. **Mailing Address:** Jackalope Geol Ltd, PO Box 115, Berthoud, CO 80513. **Fax:** 970-532-4146.

KISSLINGER, CARL, SEISMOLOGY. **Personal Data:** b St Louis, Mo, August 30, 1926; m Millicent; c Susan, Karen, Ellen, Pamela & Jerome. **Education:** St Louis Univ, BS, 1947, MS, 1949, PhD (geophys), 1952. **Honors & Awards:** Alexander von Humboldt Found US Sr Scientist Award, 1979; Commemorative Medal, USSR Acad Sci, 1985; John Wesley Powell Award, US Geol Surv, 1992. **Professional Experience:** RETIRED; EMER PROF GEOL SCI, UNIV COLO, BOULDER, 1994-; chmn, Panel Seismic Hazard Eval, Nat Res Coun, 1993-1996; mem, Gov Bd, Am Inst Physics, 1989-1995; mem comt scholarly communication with People's Repub China, chmn Subcomt on Earthquake Res, 1984-1988; vpres, US Nat Comt, Int Union Geod & Geophys, 1983-1991; mem comt adv, US Geol Surv, 1983-1988; chmn, US Geol Surv, 1981-1982; fel, Univ Colo, Boulder, 1979-; mem comt scholarly communication with People's Repub China, Nat Acad Sci, 1978-1981; mem earthquake studies adv panel, US Geol Surv, 1977-1982; mem earthquake hazards reduction adv group, Off Sci Technol Policy, 1977-1978; mem bur, US Nat Comt, Int Union Geod & Geophys, 1975-1983; chmn comt seismol, mem US Geodynamics Comt, 1975-1978; mem, US Nat Comt, Int Union Geod & Geophys, 1974-1992; prof geol sci, Univ Colo, Boulder, 1972-1994; dir, Coop Inst Res Environ Sci, 1972-1979 & 1993-1994; mem earth sci adv panel, NSF, 1971-1974; chmn comt seismol, Nat Acad Sci-Nat Res Coun, 1970-1972; consult, US Dept Energy, 1969-1978; UNESCO expert in seismol & chief tech adv, Int Inst Seismol & Earthquake Eng, Tokyo, 1966-1967; chmn dept earth & atmospheric sci, St Louis Univ, 1963-1972; From instr to prof geophys & geophys eng, St Louis Univ, 1949-1972. **Memberships:** Fel AAAS; emer mem, Soc Explor Geophys; emer mem, Seismol Soc Am (pres, 1972-1973); fel Am Geophys Union (foreign secy, 1974-1984); fel Geol Soc Am; corresp mem Austrian Acad Sci. **Research Statement & Publications:** Generation of seismic waves by explosions and earthquakes; earthquake source physics; eartquake aftershocks; earthquake prediction. **Mailing Address:** Coop Inst Res Environ Sci, Univ Colo Campus Box 216, Boulder, CO 80309-0216. **Fax:** 303-492-1149. **E-Mail:** kissling@cires.colorado.edu

KISSLINGER, FRED, METALLURGICAL ENGINEERING. **Personal Data:** b St Louis, Mo, November 19, 1919; m 1945, c 3. **Education:** Mo Sch Mines, BS, 1942; Univ Cincinnati, MS, 1945, PhD (metall eng), 1947. **Professional Experience:** PARTNER, ASKELAND, KISSLINGER & WOLF, METALL ENG CONSULTS, 1973-; prof Metall Eng, Univ MO-Rolla, 1969-; assoc prof, 1964-1969; From instr to assoc prof metall eng, Ill Inst Technol, 1947-1964. **Memberships:** Am Soc Metals; Am Inst Mining Metall & Petrol Engrs. **Research Statement & Publications:** Thermodynamics; heat treating. **Mailing Address:** 1108 Winchester Dr, Rolla, MO 65401.

KISSLINGER, LEONARD SOL, THEORETICAL PHYSICS. **Personal Data:** b St Louis, Mo, August 15, 1930; m 1956. **Education:** St Louis Univ, BS, 1951; Ind Univ, MS, 1952, PhD (physics), 1956. **Professional Experience:** Vis staff mem, Los Alamos Sci Lab, 1969-; PROF PHYSICS, CARNEGIE-MELLON UNIV, 1968-; res assoc, Mass Inst Technol, 1966-1967; res corp fel, Bohr Inst, Copenhagen, Denmark, 1958-1959; from instr to prof physics, Case Western Res Univ, 1956-1968. **Memberships:** Am Phys Soc; Sigma Xi. **Research Statement & Publications:** Nuclear models and structure; many-body problem; particle physics. **Mailing Address:** Dept Physics, Carnegie-Mellon Univ, Pittsburgh, PA 15213. **Fax:** 412-681-0648. **E-Mail:** kisslinger@kelvin.phys.cmu.edu

KISSMAN, HENRY MARCEL, ORGANIC CHEMISTRY, COMPUTER SCIENCES. **Personal Data:** b Graz, Austria, September 9, 1922; American citizen; m 1956, Elise; c 2. **Education:** Sterling Col, BS, 1944; Univ Cincinnati, MS, 1948; Univ Rochester, PhD (org chem), 1950. **Honors & Awards:** Super Serv Award, US Dept Health, Educ & Welfare, 1973; Dirs Award, NIH, 1985. **Professional Experience:** CONSULT, 1992-; retired, 1992-; chmn comt study environ qual info progs in fed govt, Off Sci & Technol; mem, Task Force, Environ Cancer & Heart & Lung Dis, 1989-1992; chmn, Sect Inform Comput & Commun, AAAS, 1980-1981; mem adv bd, Chem Abstr Serv, 1974-1977; chmn, Toxicol Info Subcomt, US Dept Health, Educ & Welfare, 1973-; assoc dir specialized info servs, US Nat Libr Med, 1970-1992; dir sci info facil, US Food & Drug Admin, DC, 1967-1970; dept head tech info, Lederle Labs Div, Am Cyanamid Co, 1962-1967; res chemist, Lederle Labs Div, Am Cyanamid Co, 1952-1962; sr asst scientist org chem, NIH, 1950-1952. **Memberships:** AAAS; Am Chem Soc; Soc Toxicol; hon mem Med Libr Asn. **Research Statement & Publications:** Ethylenimine chemistry; amino acids; carbohydrates; nucleosides; steroids; tetracyclines; chemical documentation; development and national operation of online databases in toxicology such as toxline, chemline, hazardous substances data bank; AIDS drugs, AIDS trials. **Mailing Address:** 14809 Pennfield Circle Apt 404, Silver Spring, MD 20906-1594. **E-Mail:** h.kissman@erols.com

KISSMEYER-NIELSEN, ERIK, FOOD SCIENCE, BOTANY. **Personal Data:** b Silkeborg, Denmark, October 22, 1922; m 1962, c 2. **Education:** Royal Vet & Agr Col, Copenhagen, BS, 1948; Cornell Univ, MS, 1960; Univ Wis, PhD (food sci), 1964. **Professional Experience:** Regional agr & food indust adv, Agr & Food Indust Adv Int, 1975-; regional agr & food indust adv, UN Econ Comn Africa, 1973-1975; agr & food indust adv, UN Indust Develop Orgn & World Bank, 1970-1973; INT ADV, AGR & FOOD INDUST, 1966-; asst prof biochem & food sci, Univ Del, 1963-1966; asst food sci, Univ Wis, 1960-1963; asst food sci, Cornell Univ, 1958-1960; asst mgr, Grimstrup Coop Starch & Dehydration Plant, Denmark, 1953-1958; inspector, R T French Co, NY, 1950-1953; trainee food technol, Am Scand Soc, 1948-1950. **Memberships:** Fel AAAS; Inst Food Technol. **Mailing Address:** 65 Crabtree Rd, Concord, MA 01742. **Fax:** 978-287-0181. **E-Mail:** kissmeyer@aol.com

KIST, JOSEPH EDMUND, MATHEMATICS, TOPOLOGICAL ALGEBRA. **Personal Data:** b Buffalo, NY, August 11, 1929; div, c 1. **Education:** Univ Buffalo, BA, 1952; Purdue Univ, MS, 1954, PhD (math), 1957. **Honors & Awards:** Sigma Xi; fel AAAS. **Professional Experience:** PROF EMER, NMEX STATE UNIV, 1994-; from assoc prof to prof math, NMex State Univ, 1966-1994; assoc prof, Pa State Univ, 1963-1966; vis assoc prof, Purdue Univ, 1962-1963; asst prof, Wayne State Univ, 1957-1959 & Pa State Univ, 1959-1962; Instr math, Purdue Univ, 1957. **Memberships:** Fel AAAS; Am Math Soc; Math Asn Am; Sigma Xi. **Research Statement & Publications:** Functional analysis; lattices; semigroups. **Mailing Address:** Dept Math, NMex State Univ, Las Cruces, NM 88003. **E-Mail:** jkist@juno.com

KISTER, JAMES MILTON, TOPOLOGY. **Personal Data:** b Cleveland, Ohio, June 29, 1930; m 1978, Jane; c Karen L. **Education:** Wooster Col, AB, 1952; Univ Wis, AM, 1956, PhD, 1959. **Professional Experience:** PROF EMER MATH, UNIV MICH, ANN ARBOR, as of 2003; hon res fel, Univ Col, London, 1993; managing ed, Mich Math J, 1978 & 1983-1988; vis fel Wolfson Col, Oxford Univ, Eng, 1977 & 1985-1986; ed, Mich Math J, 1976-1978; vis mem, Institut des Hautes Etudes, France, 1974; ed, Duke Math J, 1972-1975; chair dept, Univ Mich, Ann Arbor, 1971-1973; vis fel, Clare Hall, Cambridge Univ, Eng, 1970; vis prof, Univ Calif, Los Angeles, 1967; prof math, Univ Mich, Ann Arbor, beginning 1966; mem, inst Advan Study, 1962-1964; fel, Off Naval Res, Univ Va, 1960-1961; from instr to assoc prof, Univ Mich, Ann Arbor, 1959-1966; res asst, Los Alamos Sci Lab, 1953-1955. **Memberships:** Am Math Soc; Math Asn Am. **Research Statement & Publications:** Topology; isotopies; transformation groups; manifolds. **Mailing Address:** Dept Math, Univ Mich, Rm 4867, 2074 E Hall, Ann Arbor, MI 48109-1109. **Fax:** 734-763-0937. **E-Mail:** kister@umich.edu

KISTER, JANE E, MATHEMATICS. **Education:** Univ Oxford, PhD (math), 1972. **Professional Experience:** RETIRED; exec ed, Math Reviews, 1998-2004; assoc ed, Math Reviews, 1984-1998. **Memberships:** Am Math Soc. **Mailing Address:** Math Reviews, PO Box 8604, Ann Arbor, MI 48107.

KISTIAKOWSKY, VERA, ELEMENTARY PARTICLE PHYSICS. **Personal Data:** b Princeton, NJ, September 9, 1928; div, c Marc L & Karen M (Fischer). **Education:** Mt Holyoke Col, AB, 1948; Univ Calif, PhD (chem), 1952. **Honorary Degrees:** DSc, Mt Holyoke Col, 1978. **Professional Experience:** EMER PROF PHYSICS, MASS INST TECHNOL, 1994-; prof, Dept Physics, 1972-1994; sr res scientist, Dept Physics, 1969-1972; scientist, Lab Nuclear Sci, 1963-1969; from asst prof to adj assoc prof, Brandeis Univ, 1959-1963; instr, Columbia Univ, 1957-1959; res assoc, Columbia Univ, 1954-1957; Berliner fel physics, Radiation Lab, Univ Calif, 1953-1954; Scientist, USN Radiol Defense Lab, 1952-1953. **Memberships:** Fel AAAS; fel Am Phys Soc; Asn Women Sci (pres, 1982-1984). **Research Statement & Publications:** Observational astrophysics; experimental particle physics. **Mailing Address:** 134 Martin Steet, Rehoboth, MA 02769. **E-Mail:** verak@mit.edu

KISTLER, ALAN L(EE), FLUID DYNAMICS. **Personal Data:** b Laramie, Wyo, November 26, 1928; m 1955, c 3. **Education:** Johns Hopkins Univ, BE, 1950, MS, 1952, PhD (aeronaut), 1955. **Professional Experience:** PROF EMER, NORTHWESTERN UNIV, as of 2002; prof mech eng & astronaut, technol inst, Northwestern Univ, Evanston, beginning 1969; fluid physics sect mgr, Jet Propulsion Lab, Calif Inst Technol, 1965-1969; assoc prof, Yale Univ, 1961-1965; Res group supvr, Jet Propulsion Lab, Calif Inst Technol, 1957-1961. **Memberships:** Am Phys Soc; Am Soc Mech Engrs; AAAS. **Research Statement & Publications:** Diffusion in turbulent flow fields; turbulence in compressible media; mechanics of wakes and separated flows. **Mailing Address:** dept mech, Northwestern Univ, Evanston, IL 60201. **E-Mail:** a-kistler@northwestern.edu

KISTLER, ERNEST, AERONAUTICS. **Professional Experience:** STAFF, SPATIAL INFO MGT CO, as of 1998. **Memberships:** Am Soc Eng Mgt. **Mailing Address:** Spatial Info Mgt Co, 4125 Maryland Ave, Shreveport, LA 71106-1437. **Fax:** 318-868-6395. **E-Mail:** kistlere@asme.org

KISTLER, MALATHI K, CHEMISTRY. **Personal Data:** b India, October 29, 1944. **Education:** Indian Inst Sci, PhD (biochem), 1970. **Professional Experience:** RES ASSOC PROF, DEPT CHEM, UNIV SC, 1976-. **Memberships:** Endocrine Soc; Cell Biol Soc. **Mailing Address:** Dept Chem, Univ SC, GSRC 314, Columbia, SC 29208-0001. **Fax:** 803-777-9521. **E-Mail:** mkistler@mail.chem.sc.edu

KISTLER, ROBERT A, BIOLOGY. **Education:** George Fox Univ, BS; Prudue Univ, MS; Northern Ariz Univ, PhD (Ecol), 1985. **Professional Experience:** PROF BIOL & DIR ENVIRON STUDIES, BETHEL COL, as of 2005. **Mailing Address:** Dept Bio Sci, Bethel College, 3900 Bethel Dr, St Paul, MN 55112. **E-Mail:** r-kistler@homer.bethel.edu

KISTLER, RONALD WAYNE, GEOLOGY, ISOTOPE GEOCHEMSITRY. **Personal Data:** b Chicago, Ill, May 18, 1931; m 1957, Joyce; c Julie & Bryan. **Education:** Johns Hopkins Univ, BA, geol, 1953; Univ Calif, Berkeley, PhD, (geol), 1960. **Professional Experience:** Scientist emer, 1995-; Vis prof, Northwestern Univ, 1971; GEOLOGIST, US GEOL SURV, 1960-1995. **Memberships:** Geol Soc Am, sr mem; Am Geophys Union. **Research Statement & Publications:** Structural geology; geochronology; isotopegeology. **Mailing Address:** US Geol Surv, 345 Middlefield Rd MS 937, Menlo Park, CA 94025. **Fax:** 650-329-4664. **E-Mail:** rkistler@usgs.gov

KISTLER, WILSON STEPHEN, BIOCHEMISTRY, REPRODUCTIVE BIOLOGY. **Personal Data:** b Newport News, Va, March 1, 1942; m 1976, Malathi; c Mira & Lisa. **Education:** Princeton Univ, AB, 1964; Harvard Univ, PhD (biochem), 1970. **Professional Experience:** PROF CHEM, UNIV SC, 1986-; from asst prof to assoc prof, Univ SC, 1975-1986; Ben May Lab Cancer Res, Univ Chicago, 1971-1975; res assoc, Dept Microbiol & Molecular Genetics, Sch Med, Harvard Univ, 1970-1971. **Memberships:** Am Soc Biochem Mol Biol; Am Chem Soc; Soc Study Reprod. **Research Statement & Publications:** Study of changes in basic nuclear proteins accompanying mammalian spermatogenesis with focus on histone H1t and spermatid nuclear transition proteins (TP1, TP2); gene analysis using recombinant DNA. **Mailing Address:** Dept Chem, Univ SC, Columbia, SC 29208-0001. **Fax:** 803-777-9521. **E-Mail:** wskistler@sc.edu

KISTNER, CLIFFORD RICHARD, INORGANIC CHEMISTRY. **Personal Data:** b Cincinnati, Ohio, December 16, 1936; m 1961, Kathleen Shannow; c Amalia. **Education:** Carthage Col, AB, 1959; Univ Iowa, MS, 1962, PhD (chem), 1963. **Professional Experience:** PROF CHEM & CHMN DEPT, UNIV WIS, LA CROSSE, 1968-; from asst prof to assoc prof, Univ Wis, LA Crosse, 1964-1968; asst prof, Univ Iowa, 1963-1964; Instr chem, Univ Iowa, 1963. **Memberships:** AAAS; Am Chem Soc; Sigma Xi. **Research Statement & Publications:** Inorganic coordination chemistry. **Mailing Address:** N1596 Skyline Blvd, La Crosse, WI 54601-8439.

KISTNER, DAVID HAROLD, ENTOMOLOGY. **Personal Data:** b Cincinnati, Ohio, July 30, 1931; m 1957, c 2. **Education:** Univ Chicago, AB, 1952, SB, 1956, PhD (zoology), 1957. **Professional Experience:** PROF EMER BIOL, CALIF STATE UNIV, 1993-; dir, Shinner Inst Study Interrelated Insects, 1968-1972; hon res assoc, Div Insects, Field Mus Natural Hist, Chicago, 1967 & Atlantica Ecol Res Sta, Zimbabwe; Guggenheim mem found fel, 1965-1966; from asst prof to prof, Calif State Univ, 1960-1993; instr, Calif State Univ, 1959-1960; NSF grants, 1958-1959, 1960-1971 & 1972-1978; instr biol, Univ Rochester, 1957-1959; field zoologist comp anat & arthropods, Univ Chicago, 1956-1957; asst comp anat, Univ Chicago, 1955; asst termites, Univ Chicago, 1953-1954; consult developer, Dowtlanco, Indianapolis, Ind. **Memberships:** AAAS; Entom Soc Am; Soc Study Evolution; Soc Syst Zool; Am Soc Zool; fel Explorers Club. **Research Statement & Publications:** Systematics, evolution; zoogeography and behavior of myrmecophilous and termitophilous insects; systematics of staphylinidae. **Mailing Address:** Dept Biol, Calif State Univ, Chico, CA 95929-0515. **Fax:** 530-898-6804. **E-Mail:** dkistner@csuchico.edu

KISTNER, OTTMAR CASPER, PHOTO NUCLEAR PHYSICS, HEAVY ION NUCLEAR REACTIONS. **Personal Data:** b New York, NY, March 22, 1930. **Education:** Polytech Inst Brooklyn, BS, 1952; Columbia Univ, PhD (physics), 1959. **Professional Experience:** Guest physicist, Weizmann inst Sci, 1980; Guest physicist, Max Planck inst Nuclear Physics, 1969-1970; PHYSICIST, BROOKHAVEN NAT LAB, 1966-; assoc physicist, Brookhaven Nat lab, 1963-1966; asst physicist, Brookhaven Nat lab, 1959-1963. **Memberships:** Sigma Xi; fel Am Phys Soc. **Research Statement & Publications:** Experimental nuclear physics; nuclear structure and hyperfine interactions by beta and gamma ray spectroscopy; on line spectroscopy with heavy ion reactions; Mossbauer effect; medium energy (350 MeV) photonuclear research and facility development of Laser-Electron-Gamma-Source at BNL NSLS. **Mailing Address:** Physics Dept 510A, Brookhaven Nat Lab, Upton, NY 11973. **Fax:** 631-344-3181. **E-Mail:** kistner@bnl.gov

KISVARSANYI, EVA BOGNAR, GEOLOGY, PETROLOGY. **Personal Data:** b Budapest, Hungary, American citizen; m 1956, c 1. **Education:** Univ Mo, Rolla, BS, 1958, MS, 1960. **Professional Experience:** ASST DIR, MO DEPT NATURAL RES, GEOL SURV, 1989-; mem, Working Group Precambrian Correlation Cent Interior Region US, Int Union Geol Sci, 1976-1984; Res geologist, MO Dept Natural Res, Geol Surv, 1959-1989. **Memberships:** Mineral Soc Am; Geol Soc Am; Soc Econ Geologists. **Research Statement & Publications:** Precambrian geology of the St Francois Mountains and vicinity in southeast Missouri; geology and structure of buried Precambrian basement, midcontinent region; mineral resources of Missouri. **Mailing Address:** Geol Survey, Mo Dept Natural Resources, PO Box 250, Rolla, MO 65401.

KISVARSANYI, GEZA, ECONOMIC GEOLOGY, ORE DEPOSITS. **Personal Data:** b Tokay, Hungary, February 23, 1926; American citizen; m 1956, Eva Bognar; c Erika G. **Education:** Eotvos Lorand, Budapest, MS, 1952; Univ Mo, Rolla, PhD (geol), 1966. **Professional Experience:** EMER PROF GEOL, UNIV MO, ROLLA, 1992-; from instr to prof, Univ MO, Rolla, 1962-1992; explor geologist, Bear Creek Mining Co Div, Kennecott Copper Corp, 1957-1962; chief geologist, Ore Mining & Develop Co, Hungary, 1955-1956; Asst prof geol, Eotvos Lorand, Budapest, 1952-1955; consult, gold explor; mem, doctoral fac, Univ Mo, Rolla; Chmn, Int Geol Conf. **Memberships:** Geol Soc Am; Soc Econ Geol. **Research Statement & Publications:** Hydrothermal ore deposits; Mississippi Valley-type lead-zinc deposits; iron-titanium ore deposits; geotectonics of the midcontinent; remote sensing, radar, landsat, of geologic structures, precious and base metal deposits, prophyry copper and molybdenum deposits; author and editor of four books and over 160 papers and reports of investigations. **Mailing Address:** 2339 Cass St, Sarasota, FL 34231.

KISZENICK, WALTER, PHYSICS, ELECTRICAL ENGINEERING. **Personal Data:** b New York, NY, April 1, 1918; m 1943, c 2. **Education:** Brooklyn Col, BA, 1939; Polytech Inst Brooklyn, MS, 1947, PhD (physics), 1951. **Professional Experience:** PROF EMER PHYSICS, POLYTECH UNIV, as of 2004; assoc prof physics & nuclear eng, Polytech Inst NY, beginning 1962; from instr to asst prof physics, Polytech Inst NY, 1953-1964; physicist, Freed Radio Co, 1952-1953; res asst phosphors, Polytech Inst Brooklyn, 1946-1952; jr scientist, Los Alamos Sci Lab, 1944-1946; jr metallurgist, NY Naval Shipyard, 1941-1943. **Memberships:** Am Phys Soc; Electron Micros Soc Am; Sigma Xi. **Research Statement & Publications:** Dielectric properties of phosphors; physical properties of ice. **Mailing Address:** Dept Physics, Polytech Univ, Brooklyn, NY 11201. **Fax:** 718-260-3136.

KIT, SAUL, BIOCHEMISTRY, CANCER. **Personal Data:** b Passaic, NJ, November 25, 1920; m 1945, Dorothy; c Sally, Malon & Gordon. **Education:** Univ Calif, AB, 1948, PhD (biochem), 1951. **Honors & Awards:** Nat Inst Arthritis & Infectious Dis Res Career Award, 1963-1988. **Professional Experience:** HEAD & PROF ACAD, BAYLOR COL MED, as of 2004; PROF EMER BIOCHEM, BAYLOR COL MED, 1993-; chmn sci adv bd, Novagene, Inc, Houston, 1982-; distinguished vis prof, dept microbiol, La Trobe Univ, Australia, 1982; sci adv bd mem, Am Genetics Int, Inc, Denver, Colo, 1981-1984; chmn, Pathobiology Chem Study Sect, NIH, 1975-1979; Univ Bueonos Aires, Argentina, 1971 & Calouste Gulbenkian Found, Lisbon, Portugal, 1973; consult, USPHS, 1971-; vis prof, Inst Venezuela, Olano & Caracas, 1971; sci consult, molecular biol dept, Miles Lab, Elkhart, Ind, 1969-1972; mem deleg, US-USSR exchange virol, 1967; prof biochem & head, Div Biochem Virol, 1962-1993; vis prof virol, Baylor Col Med, 1962; mem cancer virol panel, USPHS, 1961-1962; mem Cancer Virol Panel, Nat Cancer Inst, USPHS, 1961-1962; assoc biochemist, biochemist & chief Sect Nucleoprotein Metab, 1961-1962; from asst prof to assoc prof, Post-Grad Sch Med, Univ Tex, 1957-1961; assoc biochemist, Univ Tex M D Anderson Hosp & Tumor Inst, 1957-1960; asst prof biochem, Col Med, Baylor Univ, 1956-1957; res biochemist, Univ Tex M D Anderson Hosp & Tumor Inst, 1953-1955; Nat Cancer Inst fel biochem, Nat Found Infantile Paralysis fel, 1952; Nat Cancer Inst fel biochem, Chicago, 1951-1952. **Memberships:** Am Soc Biol Chemists; Am Soc Cell Biol (treas, 1965-1967, pres, 1971); Am Chem Soc; Am Soc Virol; Am Soc Microbiol; Am Asn Cancer Res; corresp mem Arg Soc Virol. **Research Statement & Publications:** Molecular biology; biochemical virology; biochemistry of cancer; nucleic acids; genetically engineered vaccines; author of over 250 research publications; holder of 11 US patents and 13 foreign patents on vaccines. **Mailing Address:** Dept Acad, Baylor Col Med, One Baylor Plaza, Houston, TX 77030. **Fax:** 713-781-6078. **E-Mail:** skit@bcm.tmc.edu

KITABCHI, ABBAS E, INTERNAL MEDICINE, ENDOCRINOLOGY & DIABETES. **Personal Data:** b Tehran, Iran, August 28, 1933; American citizen; c 4. **Education:** Cornell Col, BA, 1954; Univ Okla, MS, 1956, PhD (med sci), 1958, MD, 1965. **Professional Experience:** Vis scientist, Va Mason Res Ctr & Univ Wash, Seattle, 1990-1991; assoc chief metab, Med Serv, beginning 1973; PROF MED & BIOCHEM, CTR HEALTH SCI, UNIV TENN, 1973-; CHIEF, DIV ENDOCRINOL & METAB & DIR, CLIN RES CTR, 1973-; from asst prof to assoc prof med, Div Endocrinol & Metab & Dir, Clin Res Ctr, 1968-1973; assoc prof biochem, Div Endocrinol & Metab & Dir, Clin Res Ctr, 1968-1973; assoc chief staff res & chief, Endocrinol & Metab Labs, Vet Admin Hosp, 1968-1973; instr med, Univ Wash, 1966-1968; NIH spec fel endocrinol, Univ Wash, 1966-1968; sr investr, Okla Med Res Found, 1965-1966; biochemist, Okla Med Res Found, 1961-1965; Res assoc biochem, Okla Med Res Found, 1960-1961; fel biochem, Okla Med Res Found, 1958-1960; chief endocrinol & consult, Baptist Hosp; attend physcian, Univ Tenn Hosp; chief, Diabetes & Endocrinol Clin, City Memphis Hosp. **Memberships:** Fel Am Col Physicians; Asn Am Physicians; Am Fedn Clin Res; Am Diabetes Asn; Endocrine Soc; Am Soc Biochem & Molecular Biol; Am Soc Clin Investrs; Am Inst Nutrit. **Research Statement & Publications:** Mechanism of action of steroids and pancreatic hormones at molecular level; pathogenesis and treatment of diabetes; clinical diabetes and its acute complications. **Mailing Address:** Dept Med, Univ Tenn, 920 Madison Ave Ste 300, Memphis, TN 38103-3472. **Fax:** 901-448-7579.

KITAHATA, LUKE MASAHIKO, ANESTHESIA, PAIN & NEUROSURGICAL ANESTHESIA. **Personal Data:** b January 12, 1925; c 3. **Education:** Tokyo Imperial Univ, Japan, MD, 1947. **Professional Experience:** PROF EMER ANESTHESIOL, SCH MED, YALE UNIV, as of 2004; prof anesthesiol, Sch Med, Yale Univ, beginning 1973; chmn, dept anesthesiol, Yale Univ, 1973-1982. **Memberships:** Sigma Xi; Am Assoc Neurol surg; Am Soc Anesthesiol. **Mailing Address:** Dept Anesthesiol, Sch Med, Yale Univ, 333 Cedar St, PO Box 208051, New Haven, CT 06520. **Fax:** 203-785-6664.

KITAI, REUVEN, ELECTRICAL ENGINEERING. **Personal Data:** b Johannesburg, SAfrica, October 4, 1924; m 1952, c 3. **Education:** Univ Witwatersrand, BSc, 1944, MSc, 1948, DSc(elec eng), 1962. **Professional Experience:** PROF EMER ELEC ENG, MCMASTER UNIV, 1988-; pres, Instrumentation & Measurement Soc, Inst Elec & Electronics Engrs, 1982; brown Boveri Co, Switz, 1977; from assoc prof to prof, Mcmaster Univ, 1965-1988; dept Elec Eng, Imp Col, Univ London, 1961-1962; vis res officer, Stand Telecommun Labs, Ltd, Eng, 1961; sr lectr, Univ Witwatersrand, 1955-1964; vis lectr, Eng Labs, Cambridge Univ, 1953-1954; lectr elec eng, Univ Witwatersrand, 1947-1955. **Memberships:** Sr mem Inst Elec & Electronics Engrs. **Research Statement & Publications:** Instrumentation. **Mailing Address:** Dept Elec Eng, McMaster Univ, 1280 Main St W, Hamilton, ON L8S 4L8, Can.

KITAIGORODSKII, SERGEI ALEXANDER, PHYSICAL OCEANOGRAPHY. **Personal Data:** b Moscow, USSR, September 13, 1934; m 1969, Sisko-Kiuru; c Marins & Katarina. **Education:** Inst Physics Atmosphere Acad Sci, USSR, PhD (geophys), 1960; Inst Oceanology Acad Sci, DSc, 1968. **Honorary Degrees:** DSc, Univ Liege, Belfium, 1994. **Honors & Awards:** Rosenstiel Gold Medal Award, 1973. **Professional Experience:** CHIEF SCIENTIST, INST OCEANOG, P P SHIRSOV, ACAD SCI, RUSSIA, 1994-; foreign stypend, Finnish Acad Sci, 1993; prof oceanog, Dept Earth & Planetary Sci, Johns Hopkins Univ, 1980-1992; lectr, Inst Phys Oceanog, Univ Copenhagen, 1979-1985; Head lab res, Inst Oceanog Acad Sci, USSR, 1968-1978. **Memberships:** Foreign mem Danish Royal Acad Sci & Lett; hon mem Finnish Geophys Soc. **Research Statement & Publications:** Oceanic turbulence and its modelling; physics of air-sea interaction; wave motions in the ocean; geophysical fluid dynamics; 120 papers in Russian and major western journals; 4 scientific monographs. **Mailing Address:** Krasikova St 23, Moscow 117218, Russia. **Fax:** 7-095-1245983.

KITANI, OSAMU, AGRICULTURE. **Personal Data:** b Tokyo, Japan, April 1, 1935; m 1964, Shigeko Tanaka; c Yukiko & Mariko. **Education:** Univ Tokyo, BAgr, 1959, MAgr, 1961, DAgr, 1964; Mich State Univ, PhD, 1966. **Professional Experience:** Mem, Farm Mechanization Coun, Ministry Agr Forestry & Fishery, 1993-; dir libr fac, Dept Agr Eng, 1991-1993; Sci Coun, Ministry Educ, Tokyo, 1979-1989 & Coun Sci & Tech Prime Ministers Off, 1981-; chmn, Dept Agr Eng, 1980-1988; PROF, UNIV TOKYO, 1978-; expert mem, Sci & Tech Agency, Tokyo, 1976-1987; guest prof, Tech Univ Munich, 1972-1973; Fel, Alexander von Humboldt Found, Ger, 1972; Assoc prof, Mie Univ, Japan, 1966-1978. **Memberships:** Japan Fedn Agr Eng (vpres, 1983-1984); Japan Agr Systs Soc (vpres, 1985-1988, pres, 1989-1991); Am Japan Soc; Int Comn Agr Eng (secy, 1990-, vpres, 1994-); Japan Soc Energy & Resources; Japanese Soc Agr Mach (pres, 1992-); Am Soc Agr Engrs; hon mem Ital Asn Agr Engrs. **Mailing Address:** Kataseyama 3-3-10, Kanagaw Fugisawa-shi 251, Japan.

KITANIDIS, PETER K, CIVIL ENGINEERING. **Education:** National Technical Univ Athens, Greece, CE dipl, 1974; Mass Inst Technol, MSc, 1976; Mass Inst Technol, PhD, 1978. **Honors & Awards:** Lorenz G Straub Award, 1978; Walter L Huber Civil Eng Res Prize, Am Soc Civil Engrs, 1994. **Professional Experience:** PROF CIVIL ENG, STANFORD UNIV, as of 2003; assoc prof civil eng, Stanford Univ, 1987-1990; assoc prof civil & mineral eng, Univ Minn, 1984-1987; from asst prof civil & environ eng & res engr to assoc prof civil & environ eng & res engr, Univ Iowa, Inst Hydraulic Res, 1979-1984; civil engr, Greek Army Corps Engrs, 1978-1979. **Memberships:** Am Soc Civil Engrs; Soc Industrial & Appl Math; Sigma Xi; Am Meteorol Soc; Asn Ground Water Scientists. **Mailing Address:** Dept Civil & Environ Eng, Stanford Univ, M 19 Terman Eng Ctr, Stanford, CA 94305-4020. **Fax:** 650-725-9720. **E-Mail:** peterk@stanford.edu

KITAY, JULIAN I, INTERNAL MEDICINE, ENDOCRINOLOGY. **Personal Data:** b Kearny, NJ, August 29, 1927; m 1973, c 2. **Education:** Princeton Univ, BA, 1949; Harvard Med Sch, MD, 1954. **Professional Experience:** ASSOC VPRES & SR ASSOC DEAN ACAD & STUDENT AFFAIRS, UNIV TEX MED BR, GALVESTON, TEX, 1992-; asst vpres & assoc dean acad affairs, Univ Tex Med Br, Galveston, Tex, 1984-1992; PROF INTERNAL MED, PHYSIOL & BIOPHYS, 1978-; assoc dean curricular affairs, Univ Tex Med Br, Galveston, Tex, 1978-1984; prof internal med & physiol, Sch Med, Univ Va, 1970-1978; head div endocrinol & metab, Dept Internal Med, 1970-1978; USPHS res career develop award, 1961-1970; from asst prof to assoc prof physiol, Sch Med, Univ Va, 1961-1970; attend physician, Univ Hosp, Univ Va, 1959-1978; from asst prof to assoc prof internal med, Sch Med, Univ Va, 1959-1970; instr, Col Physicians & Surgeons, Columbia Univ, 1958-1959; asst physician, Med Serv, Presby Hosp, NY, 1958-1959; Commonwealth Fund fel, Col Physicians & Surgeons, Columbia Univ, 1956-1958; asst resident, Beth Israel Hosp, Mass, 1955-1956; intern med, Grace-New Haven Hosp, Conn, 1954-1955; mem neuroendocrinol panel, Int Brain Res Orgn. **Memberships:** Endocrine Soc; Am Fedn Clin Res; Am Soc Clin Invest; Am Physiol Soc; Soc Exp Biol & Med. **Research Statement & Publications:** Endocrine physiology; clinical aspects of endocrine disease. **Mailing Address:** Off Dean Med, Univ Tex Med Br, Galveston, TX 77550.

KITAZAWA, GEORGE, CHEMISTRY, WOOD SCIENCE. **Personal Data:** b San Jose, Calif, May 2, 1917; m 1943, c 3. **Education:** Univ Calif, BS, 1940; State Univ NY, MS, 1944, PhD (wood technol), 1947. **Professional Experience:** CONSULT & TECH INTERPRETER, 1980-; forest prod res sect, Wood Sci Group, Koppers Co, 1978-1980; mgr, Wood Sci Group, Koppers Co, 1973-1978; lab head, Cent Res Lab, Borden Chem Co, Philadelphia, 1959-1973; asst lab head, Cent Res Lab, Borden Chem Co, Philadelphia, 1957-1959; group leader, Cent Res Lab, Borden Chem Co, Philadelphia, 1956-1957; res physicist, Gillette Safety Razor Co, 1953-1956; res assoc, State Univ NY Col Forestry, Syracuse, 1950-1953; wood technologist, Timber Eng Co, 1947-1950; res wood technologist, Casein Co Am, NY, 1947; indust res fel, State Univ NY Col Forestry, Syracuse, 1944-1947; technician, Guayule Rubber Res, War Relocation Auth, Calif, 1942-1943; industrial liaison hydrostatic& ultrasonic pipe testers & coke oven mach for steel indust. **Memberships:** AAAS; Am Chem Soc; Asn Asian Studies. **Research Statement & Publications:** Wood preservatives and fire retardants; polymer characterization; analytical chemistry; adhesives; instrumentation; sonic and ultrasonic nondestructive testing; surface chemistry and physics; wood physics; steel industry machinery. **Mailing Address:** 926 Harvard Rd, Monroeville, PA 15146.

KITCHELL, JAMES FREDERICK, AQUATIC ECOLOGY, BIOENERGETICS. **Personal Data:** b Gary, Ind, July 20, 1942; m 1977, c 2. **Education:** Ball State Teachers Col, BS, 1964; Univ Colo, PhD (biol), 1970. **Professional Experience:** ASSOC DIR & PROF ZOOL, UNIV WIS, MADISON, 1982-; assoc Prof Zool, Univ Wis, Madison, 1977-1982; asst prof, Inst Environ Studies, 1974-1977; vis scientist, Nat Marine Fisheries Serv, Honolulu, 1973-1978; Scientist, Smithsonian Inst Proj, Skadar Lake, Yugoslavia, 1972-1977; asst scientist, Inst Environ Studies, 1972-1974; Proj assoc ecol, Inst Environ Studies, 1970-1972. **Memberships:** Am Fisheries Soc; Ecol Soc Am; Int Soc Limnol; AAAS; Am Inst Biol Sci. **Research Statement & Publications:** Application of ecosystem models; predator-prey interactions; trophic ecology. **Mailing Address:** Ctr Limnology, Univ Wis, 680 N Park St, Madison, WI 53706. **Fax:** 608-265-2340. **E-Mail:** kitchell@macc.wisc.edu

KITCHELL, JENNIFER ANN, PALEOBIOLOGY, EVOLUTIONARY THEORY. **Personal Data:** b Zanesville, Ohio, May 25, 1945. **Education:** Univ Wis, BS, 1968, MS, 1971, PhD (geol), 1978. **Professional Experience:** ASST PROF GEOL SCI, UNIV MICH, ANN ARBOR, as of 2005; ASST CUR, MUS PALEONT, UNIV MICH, ANN ARBOR, as of 2005; asst scientist geol & zool, Univ Wis-Madison, 1980-; res assoc, Univ Wis-Madison, 1978-1980. **Memberships:** Sigma Xi; Soc Econ Paleontol & Mineralogists; Soc Oceanog & Limnol; Paleont Soc; Geol Soc Am. **Research Statement & Publications:** Paleobiology; coevolution; taxonomic diversification; predator-prey interactions; siliceous sedimentation; paleolimnological studies of predator-prey interactions. **Mailing Address:** Dept Geol Sci, Uinv Mich, 2534 C C Little Bldg 425 E Univ Ave, Ann Arbor, MI 48109. **Fax:** 734-763-4690.

KITCHEN, W J, VERY LARGE SCALE INTEGRATION-ULTRA LARGE SCALE INTEGRATION RESEARCH, DEVELOPMENT & APPLICATIONS, SEMICONDUCTOR MANUFACTURING TECHNOLOGY. **Personal Data:** b Colonial Heights, Va, March 20, 1942; m 1964, Maryellen; c Scott & Jeffrey. **Education:** Va Mil Inst, BS, 1964; Univ Va, MS, 1966, ScD, 1968; Indust Col Armed Forces, MBA, 1981. **Professional Experience:** CHMN & CHIEF EXEC OFFICER, AMERANTH WIRELESS, as of 2005; vpres dir technol & qual, Motorola Automotive, Energy & Controls Group, beginning 1993; vpres dir technol, Advan Tech Ctr, 1991-1993; vpres dir, Advan Tech Ctr, 1986-1991; dir, Semiconductor Res & Develop Labs, Semiconductor Prods Sector, 1982-1986; Tech mgr & sr technologist, Nat Security Agency, 1968-1982; mem, Sci Adv Bd, Motorola. **Memberships:** Fel Inst Elec & Electronics Engrs; Electrochem Soc; Sigma Xi. **Research Statement & Publications:** Semiconductor technology and ultra large scale intergration applications; cost effective semiconductor manufacturing facilities and factory of the future research; packaging and assembly. **Mailing Address:** Ameranth Wireless, 5375 Mira Sorrento Pl Ste 150, San Diego, CA 92121. **Fax:** 858-362-0151.

KITCHENS, CLARENCE WESLEY, ARMOR-ANTI-ARMOR MECHANICS, BLAST DYNAMICS. **Personal Data:** b Panama City, Fla, November 8, 1943; m 1966, c 2. **Education:** Va Polytech Inst & State Univ, BS, 1966, MS, 1968; NC State Univ, PhD (eng mech), 1970. **Honors & Awards:** Fire Power Award, Am Defense Preparedness Asn. **Professional Experience:** RETIRED; principal deputy for technol, US Army Materiel Command, as of 2000; chief, Terminal Ballistics Div, Ballistic Res Lab, Us Army, beginning 1986; actg chief, Penetration Mech Br, 1985-1986; chief, Penetration Mech Br, 1982-1985; chief, Blast Dynamics Br, 1980-1982; leader fluid dynamics anal team, Aberdeen Res & Develop Ctr, 1978-1980; asst to dir, Aberdeen Res & Develop Ctr, 1977-1978; aerospace engr, Aberdeen Res & Develop Ctr, 1972-1977; res engr, Aberdeen Res & Develop Ctr, 1970-1972; Eng asst, Atlantic Res Corp, Va, 1962-1965; fel US Army Lab Command; fel US Army Ballistic Res Lab. **Memberships:** Assoc Fel Am Inst Aeronaut & Astronaut; Am Defense Preparedness Asn; Asn US Army; Sr Execs Asn. **Research Statement & Publications:** Numerical computations in gas dynamics; experimental techniques in fluid dynamics; numerical analysis; computer applications in engineering; blast loading and response; flight mechanics; penetration mechanics; armor and anti-armor research. **Mailing Address:** 123 Duncannon Rd, Bel Air, MD 21014.

KITCHENS, THOMAS ADREN, CONDENSED MATTER PHYSICS. **Personal Data:** b Amarillo, Tex, October 31, 1935; m 1958, c 3. **Education:** Rice Inst, BA, 1958, Rice Univ, MA, 1960, PhD (physics), 1963. **Professional Experience:** PROG DIR, MATH INFO & COMPUTATIONAL SCI DIV, DEPT ENERGY, as of 2001; SCI COMPUT STAFF, DEPT ENERGY, 1982-; staff assoc, div mat res, NSF, 1980-1982; group leader physics, Los Alamos Sci Lab, 1978-1980; alternate group leader, Los Alamos Sci Lab, 1976-1980; liaison physicist, Off Naval Res, London, 1975-1976; sr res fel, Univ Sussex, Gr Brit, 1970-1971; physicist, Brookhaven Nat Lab, 1965-1975; staff mem physics, Los Alamos Sci Lab, 1963-1965. **Memberships:** Fel Inst Physics UK; fel Am Inst Physics; Asn Comput Mach; AAAS. **Research Statement & Publications:** Ultralow temperature physics and condensed matter research utilizing neutron and light scattering; high performance computing. **Mailing Address:** Math Info & Computational Sci Div, Off Adv Sci Comput Res, Dept Energy, OCTR/MICS SC-31 19901 Germantown Rd, Germantown, MD 20874-1290. **Fax:** 301-903-7774. **E-Mail:** kitchens@er.doe.gov

KITCHENS, WILEY M, WETLANDS ECOLOGY, ESTUARINE ECOLOGY. **Personal Data:** b Port Arthur, Tex, January 6, 1944; m 1970, c 3. **Education:** Lamar Univ, BS, 1966; Miami Univ, MA, 1970; NC State Univ, PhD (zoology), 1978. **Professional Experience:** COURTESY PROF RESTORATION ECOL, UNIV FLA, as of 2002; GRAD COORDR, UNIV FLA, as of 2002; DIR, BIOL RESOURCES DIV, FLA COOP FISH & WILDLIFE RES UNIT, UNIV FLA, as of 2000; RES ECOLOGIST, FLA COOP FISH & WILDLIFE RES UNIT, 1997-; act leader, S Fla Ecosyst Res Team, Fla Carribean Sci Ctr, 1995-1997; adj assoc prof, Univ Fla, 1985-; leader, Fla Coop Fish & Wildlife Res Unit, 1985-1995; adj asst prof, La State Univ, 1982-1985; ecologist, Nat Coastal Ecosysts Team, US Fish & Wildlife Serv, 1979-1985; res assoc salt marsh ecol, Univ SC, 1973-1979; fel coastal ecol, Univ SC, 1971-1973. **Memberships:** Ecological Soc Am; Wildlife Soc. **Research Statement & Publications:** Ecosystems approach to wetlands ecology; simulation modelling; use of geographic information systems and remote sensing technologies; landscape dynamics through coupling of simulation and GIS models; The Santee Swamp as nutrient "sink"; author of various articles. **Mailing Address:** Dept Wildlife Ecol & Conserv, Univ Fla, PO Box 10485 Bldg 810, Gainesville, FL 32611-2002. **Fax:** 352-846-0841. **E-Mail:** kitchensw@wec.ufl.edu

KITCHIN, JOHN FRANCIS, RELIABILITY & LIFE TESTING. **Personal Data:** b Greenwood, Miss, May 6, 1953. **Education:** Univ Southern Miss, BS, 1976; Fla State Univ, MS, 1978, PhD (statist), 1980. **Professional Experience:** RES SCIENTIST, DIGITAL EQUIP CORP, 1988-; tech mgr, Bell Commun Res, 1985-; mem tech staff, Commun Res, 1984-1985; mem tech staff, Bell Labs, 1981-1984; asst prof statist, Purdue Univ, 1980-1981. **Memberships:** Am Statist Asn; Inst Math Statist; Inst Elec & Electronics Engrs; Reliability Soc. **Research Statement & Publications:** Development and comparison of statistical estimators of reliability; development of methods of reliability prediction for complex systems. **Mailing Address:** Digital Equip Corp, 77 Reed Rd, Hudson, MA 01749.

KITCHIN, ROBERT WALTER, PHYSICAL CHEMISTRY, INSTRUMENTAL ANALYSIS. **Personal Data:** b Ft Sill, Okla, January 1, 1945; m 1971, Ann; c Jonathan W. **Education:** Miss State Univ, BS, 1968, PhD (phys chem), 1976. **Professional Experience:** PROF & CHMN, DEPT CHEM & PHYSICS, SOUTHWEST BAPTIST UNIV, 1984-; assoc prof, Graceland Col, 1982-1984; vis prof chem, Univ Southern Miss, 1980-1991; temp assoc prof chem & physics, Miss State Univ, 1979; inst math, chem & physics, Miss Power Co, 1977-1978; instr chem & physics, Holmes Jr Col, 1976-1982; assoc chemist, Miss State Chem Lab, 1970-1971; res assoc, Pratt & Whitney Aircraft, 1968-1970. **Memberships:** Nat Sci Teachers Asn. **Research Statement & Publications:** Basic chemistry, general physics, engineering physics and physical science. **Mailing Address:** Dept Chem & Physics, Southwest Baptist Univ, Bolivar, MO 65613-2597. **Fax:** 417-328-1658. **E-Mail:** bkitchin@SBUniv.edu

KITCHING, PETER, PARTICLE PHYSICS. **Personal Data:** b Leeds, Eng, April 4, 1938; m 1964, Josephine M Rodgers; c John E, Andrew J & Matthew S. **Education:** Oxford Univ, BA, 1960; Yale Univ, MSc, 1962, PhD, 1966. **Professional Experience:** PROF EMER, UNIV ALTA, EDMONTON, as of 2003; DIR, CTR SUBATOMIC RES, 1988-; assoc dir, Triumf Lab, Vancouver, 1983-1988; prof, Univ Alta, Edmonton, beginning 1982; from asst prof to assoc prof, Ctr Subatomic Res, 1971-1982; res assoc, Ctr Subatomic Res, 1969-1971; Res scientist, Nat Inst Res Nuclear Sci, Eng, 1966-1969. **Memberships:** Can Asn Physicists. **Research Statement & Publications:** Physics. **Mailing Address:** Dept Physics, P-412, Avadh Bhatia Physics Lab, Univ Alta, Edmonton, AB T6G 2J1, Can. **Fax:** 780-492-0714. **E-Mail:** trpk@phys.ualberta.ca

KITE, FRANCIS ERVIN, cereal chemistry; deceased, see previous edition for last biography

KITE, GEORGE FREDRICK, PHARMACEUTICAL DOSAGE FORM FORMULATION, PHARMACEUTICAL UNIT PROCESS. **Personal Data:** b Los Angeles, Calif, June 14, 1937; div, c George F, Mary A, Philip C, Linda J, Richard E, Barbara A & Karen C. **Education:** Calif State Univ, BA, 1959; Purdue Univ, MS, 1962; Carnegie Mellon Univ, PhD (org chem), 1974. **Professional Experience:** VPRES RES & DEVELOP, VESTA PHARMACEUT INC, 1997-; dir res & develop, Mfg Chemists, 1994-1997; dir mfg opers, Creative Lab Prods, 1978-1993; Chemist, Gulf Res & Develop, 1962-1965 & Philip Morris, 1972-1979. **Memberships:** Am Chem Soc. **Research Statement & Publications:** Synthetic organic research and development; free radicals, petrochemicals, nitrite oxides, polyimides, tobacco flavor precursors; formulation and manufacture cleaning and personal care products, clinical diagnostic reagents, pharmaceutical dosage forms. **Mailing Address:** Vesta Pharmaceut, Inc, 8768 E 33rd St, Indianapolis, IN 46226. **Fax:** 317-895-9340.

KITE, JOSEPH HIRAM, TUBERCULOSIS, AUTOIMMUNE DISEASE. **Personal Data:** b Decatur, Ga, November 11, 1926; m 1970, Jane. **Education:** Emory Univ, AB, 1948; Univ Tenn, MS, 1954; Univ Mich, PhD (bact), 1959. **Professional Experience:** RETIRED; PROF MICROBIOL, SCH MED, STATE UNIV NY, BUFFALO, beginning 1972; from instr to assoc prof, Sch Med, State Univ NY, Buffalo, 1959-1972; res assoc, Sch Med, State Univ NY, Buffalo, 1958-1959. **Memberships:** AAAS; Am Soc Microbiol; Tissue Cult Asn; Am Asn Immunol; NY Acad Sci. **Research Statement & Publications:** Protective immunity to mycobacterium tuberculosis; autoimmune regulation in thyroiditis. **Mailing Address:** Dept Microbiol, State Univ NY Sch Med, 5032 Donnington Rd, Buffalo, NY 14214-3078. **Fax:** 716-829-2158. **E-Mail:** jkite@ubmedb.buffalo.edu

KITHIER, KAREL, IMMUNOCHEMISTRY, COMPARATIVE PATHOLOGY. **Personal Data:** b Prague, Czech, December 6, 1930; American citizen; m 1961, Viktoria Svecova; c Karel. **Education:** Charles Univ, MD, 1962, PhD (biochem), 1967. **Professional Experience:** RETIRED; med dir, Special Chem, Damon Clin Lab, Detroit Med Ctr, beginning 1989; div head immunol, Div Clin Chem, Detroit Res Hosp & Univ Health Ctr, 1980-1988; staff pathologist immunol, Vet Admin Med Ctr, Allen Park, 1978-; assoc prof path, Dept Path, Sch Med, Wayne State Univ, Detroit, 1978-; assoc head, div clin chem, Detroit Res Hosp & Univ Health Ctr, 1974-1988; asst prof chem & immunochem, Special Chem, Damon Clin Lab, Detroit Med Ctr, 1974-1978; Mich Cancer Found, Detroit, 1972-1974; res assoc, Child Res Ctr Mich, 1968-1971; Res scientist immunochem, Res Inst Child Develop, Charles Univ, 1967-1968. **Memberships:** Am Asn Cancer Res; Am Asn Immunol; Am Asn Clin Chem; Nat Acad Clin Biochem; NY Acad Sci non mem retired. **Research Statement & Publications:** Proteins of blood and tissues in health and disease; proteins of fetuses and cancer patients; development and pathology of proteins and related substances. **Mailing Address:** Dept Path 9374 Scott Hall, Wayne State Univ, Detroit, MI 48201-1928. **Fax:** 313-577-0057.

KITOS, PAUL ALAN, BIOCHEMISTRY. **Personal Data:** b Saskatoon, Sask, May 31, 1927; m 1952, c 7. **Education:** Univ BC, BSA, 1950, MSA, 1952; Ore State Univ, PhD (chem), 1956. **Honors & Awards:** Amoco Award, 1974. **Professional Experience:** PROF EMER BIOCHEM, UNIV KANS, as of 2001; fogarty fel, Inst d'Embryologie, Nogent-Sur-Marne, France, 1983; sr scientist, Mid Am Cancer Ctr, 1975-1979; NIH fel, dept microbiol, Harvard Med Sch, 1971-1972; prof biochem, Univ Kans, beginning 1969; actg chmn dept, Univ Kans, 1969-1971; from asst prof to assoc prof comp biochem & physiol, Univ Kans, 1962-1969; asst prof biochem, Univ Kans, 1959-1962; chemist, E I du Pont Del Nemours & Co, 1956-1959. **Memberships:** AAAS; Am Chem Soc; Tissue Cult Asn; Am Soc Biol Chem & Mol Biol. **Research Statement & Publications:** Metabolism in animal cells; developmental biology; effects of organophosphorus insecticides on avian embryos; biochemical basis of some birth defects; teratogenesis. **Mailing Address:** Dept Biol Sci, Univ Kans, Lawrence, KS 66045. **Fax:** 785-864-5321. **E-Mail:** kitos@ukans.edu

KITRON, URIEL D, EPIDEMIOLOGY. **Education:** Hebrew Univ, BSc, 1976; Univ Calif, Santa Barbara, PhD (Parasitol), 1981; Univ Mich, Ann Arbor, MPH (Epidemiol), 1982. **Professional Experience:** PROF VET PATHOBIOL & CO-DIR CTR ZOONOSES RES, COL VET MED, UNIV ILL, URBANA, as of 2003; prof & chair, Div Epidemiol & Preventive Med, Col Vet Med, Univ Ill, Urbana, beginning, 1997; Lady Davis vis assoc prof, Hebrew Univm Isreal, 1996-1997; assoc prof, Dept Vet Pathobiol, 1992-1997; head, Dept Pest Surveillance & Control, Ministry Environ Jerusalem, 1991-1992; asst prof Epidemiol, Dept Vet Pathobiol, Col Vet Med, Univ Ill, 1986-1992; researcher, Kuvin Ctr Study Infectious & Trop Dis, Hebrew Univ, 1983-1985. **Research Statement & Publications:** Eco-epidemiology of infectious diseases, particularly those carried by insects and ticks (vector-borne), and the zoonoses (diseases that are common to humans and other animals); study of Lyme disease and ticks in the Midwest. **Mailing Address:** Dept Vet Pathobiol, Col Vet Med, Univ Ill, 3225 Vet Med Basic Sci Bldg 2001 S Lincoln Ave, Urbana, IL 61802. **Fax:** 217-244-7421. **E-Mail:** ukitron@uiuc.edu

KITSON, JOHN AIDAN, FOOD SCIENCE. **Personal Data:** b Victoria, BC, February 14, 1927; m 1954, c 2. **Education:** Univ BC, BA, 1949; Ore State Univ, MSc, 1954. **Honors & Awards:** Prix Industs Award, 1968 & 1970; W J Eva Award for Indust Serv, 1977. **Professional Experience:** Mem, Adv Comt Sci & Technol, BC Govt, 1989-1993; PRES & SR CONSULT, KITSON CONSULT LTD, 1982-; assoc dir, Res Sta, Agr Can, 1980-1983; head, Food Processing Sect, 1971-1980; food technologist prod &process develop, Can Dept Agr, 1965-1971; food technologist & vis scientist, Eng & Develop Lab, USDA, Calif, 1964-1965; food technologist prod & process develop, Can Dept Agr, 1950-1964; Food technologist, Sun Rype Prod Ltd, BC, 1949-1950. **Memberships:** Inst Food Technologists; Can Inst Food Technologists; fel Inst Food Sci & Technol. **Research Statement & Publications:** Research and development of processes, products and equipment for fruit and vegetable processing industry. **Mailing Address:** Kitson Consult Ltd, RR Four, Site 104, C3, Summerland, BC V0H 1Z0, Can. **Fax:** 250-494-5475. **E-Mail:** ijkitson@img.net

KITSON, ROBERT EDWARD, polymer chemistry; deceased, see previous edition for last biography

KITTAKA, ROBERT SHINNOSUKE, FOOD SCIENCE, MICROBIOLOGY. **Personal Data:** b Los Angeles, Calif, September 23, 1934; m 1962, c 3. **Education:** Univ Ill, BS, 1957, MS, 1959, PhD (food sci), 1964. **Professional Experience:** MICROBIOL & QUAL ASSURANCE DIR, FOOD RES, CENT SOYA CO, INC, 1971-; mgr microbiol, Food Res, Cent Soya CO, Inc, 1969-1971; Microbiologist, Swift & Co, 1964-1969. **Memberships:** Inst Food Technol; Am Soc Microbiol; Asn Milk Food & Environ Sanitarians; Soc Indust Microbiol; Brit Soc Appl Bact. **Research Statement & Publications:** Food microbiology; public health and spoilage microbiology as related to food products and processes; development, implementation and auditing of quality assurance programs in food processing systems to assure compliance with governmental regulations and corporate standards for cost efficient operations. **Mailing Address:** 5231 Chippewa Trail, Ft Wayne, IN 46804.

KITTEL, CHARLES, PHYSICS. **Personal Data:** b New York, NY, July 18, 1916; m 1938, Muriel; c Peter, Timothy & Ruth. **Education:** Cambridge Univ, BA, 1938, MA, 1993; Univ Wis, PhD (physics), 1941. **Honors & Awards:** Buckley Prize, 1957; Oersted Medal, 1979. **Professional Experience:** EMER PROF PHYSICS, UNIV CALIF, BERKELEY, 1978-; prof, Univ Calif, Berkeley, 1951-1978; vis assoc prof, Univ Calif, Berkeley, 1950; res physicist, Bell Tel Labs, 1947-1950; Guggenheim fel, 1946, 1957, 1964; res assoc physics, Mass Inst Technol, 1945-1946; opers analyst, US Fleet, 1943-1945; physicist, Naval Ord Lab, Wash, DC, 1940-1942. **Memberships:** Nat Acad Sci; Am Acad Arts & Sci. **Research Statement & Publications:** Solid state physics; theory of ferromagnetism; extraterrestrial biogenies. **Mailing Address:** Dept Physics, Univ Calif, 559 Birge, Berkeley, CA 94720-7300. **E-Mail:** kittel@berkeley.edu

KITTEL, J HOWARD, TECHNOLOGY TRANSFER. **Personal Data:** b Ritzville, Wash, October 9, 1919; m 1943, c 4. **Education:** Wash State Univ, BS, 1943. **Professional Experience:** RETIRED; technol transfer specialist, Argonne Nat Lab, 1989-1994; mgr nuclear waste res & develop, Argonne Nat Lab, 1979-1985; mgr adv fuels, Argonne Nat Lab, 1974-1979; sr metallurgist, Argonne Nat Lab, 1961-1994; US deleg, UN Geneva Conf, 1958-1964; mem, Mat Adv Bd, Nat Acad Sci, 1956-1958; metal engr, Argonne Nat Lab, 1951-1961; aeronaut res scientist, NASA, 1943-1951. **Memberships:** Fel Am Nuclear Soc; Sigma Xi; Scientists & Engrs Secure Energy. **Research Statement & Publications:** Technology transfer. **Mailing Address:** PO Box 2112, La Conner, WA 98257.

KITTEL, PETER, PHYSICS, CRYOGENICS. **Personal Data:** b Mt Vernon Dist, Va, March 23, 1945; m 1972, Mary; c Katherine. **Education:** Univ Calif, Berkeley, BS, 1967; Univ Calif, San Diego, MS, 1969; Univ Oxford, Eng, DPhil(physics), 1974. **Honors & Awards:** Medal for Except Eng Achievement, NASA, 1990. **Professional Experience:** Bd dir, int Cryogenic eng Conf 1998-; Ed, adv Cryogenic eng 1992-1998 bd dir, Int Cryocooler Conf, 1992 -; Bd dirs, Cryogenic Eng Conf, 1983-1989 & 1992-; RES SCIENTIST & TEAM LEADER, AMES RES CTR, NASA, 1980-; Nat Res Coun assoc cryog, Ames Res Ctr, NASA, 1978-1980; res assoc radiol, Stanford Univ, 1978; Res assoc & adj asst prof physics, Univ Ore, 1974-1978. **Memberships:** Am Phys Soc; AAAS; fel Cryogenic soc of Am. **Research Statement & Publications:** Low temperature physics; far infrared spectroscopy; stocastic processes and applications of cryogenics in space. **Mailing Address:** MS 244-10, NASA-Ames Res Ctr, Moffett Field, CA 94035-1000. **Fax:** 650-604-1094. **E-Mail:** pkittel@mail.arc.nasa.gov

KITTEL, TIMOTHY G F, ENVIRONMENTAL SCIENCES. **Education:** Univ Calif, Davis, BS, 1975, MS, 1978, PhD (ecol), 1986. **Professional Experience:** RES AFFILIATE INST ARCTIC & ALPINE RES, UNIV CO, BOULDER, 2002-. **Mailing Address:** Inst Arctic & Alpine Res, PO Box 450, Boulder, CO 80309-0450. **Fax:** 303-258-3790. **E-Mail:** kittel@colorado.edu

KITTELBERGER, JOHN STEPHEN, PHYSICAL CHEMISTRY. **Personal Data:** b Palmerton, Pa, March 14, 1939; m 1963. **Education:** Hamilton Col, AB, 1961; Princeton Univ, AM, 1963, PhD (phys chem), 1966. **Professional Experience:** CONSULT, as of 2003; mgr, xerox corp, beginning 1981; scientist, Xerox Corp, 1973-1981; asst prof, Amherst Col, 1968-1973; res assoc, Mass Inst Technol, 1966-1968; consult, surface sci & powder technol. **Memberships:** Am Phys Soc; Am Chem Soc; Tech Asn Pulp & PaperIndust. **Research Statement & Publications:** Structural chemistry; surface science; reprographic science; materials science; powder technology; deinking technology; reactive extrusion. **Mailing Address:** Consultant, 160 Penarrow Rd, Rochester, NY 14618. **E-Mail:** stevekit@frontiernet.net

KITTELSON, DAVID BURNELLE, ENGINE EMISSIONS, PARTICLE MEASUREMENTS. **Personal Data:** b Pelican Rapids, Minn, March 12, 1942; m 1970, Vesna; c Andrei Karl. **Education:** Univ Minn, Minneapolis, BSc, 1964, MSc, 1966; Cambridge Univ, PhD (chem eng), 1972. **Honors & Awards:** Teeter Award, Soc Automotive Engrs, 1973, Arch TColwell Merit Award, 1978, 1983, 1995. **Professional Experience:** CO-DIR, CTR DIESEL RES, UNIV MINN, as of 2003; DIV DIR POWER & PROPULSION, UNIV MINN, as of 2003; Overseas fel, Churchill Col, Cambridge Univ, Cambridge, England, 1985-1986; PROF MECH ENG, UNIV MINN, 1980-; from asst prof to assoc prof, Univ Minn, 1970-1980. **Memberships:** Sigma Xi; Am Chem Soc; Am Soc Mech Engrs; fel Soc Automotive Engrs. **Research Statement & Publications:** Engine combustion and emissions; particle sampling and characterization; engine sensors; diagnostics and control. **Mailing Address:** Dept Mech Eng, Univ Minn, 111 Church St SE, Minneapolis, MN 55455. **E-Mail:** kitte001@umn.edu

KITTING, CHRISTOPHER LEE, ECOLOGY OF MARINE POPULATIONS. **Personal Data:** b Monroe, Mich, May 23, 1953. **Education:** Univ Calif, Irvine, BS, 1974; Stanford Univ, PhD (biol sci), 1979. **Professional Experience:** PROF BIOL SCI, CALIF STATE UNIV, HAYWARD, as of 2004; asst prof, Marine Studies & Zoology, Port Aransas Marine Lab, Univ Tex, Austin, 1979-; res biologist, Marine Sci Inst, Univ Calif, Santa Barbara, 1979; res assoc, Stanford Med Sch, Hopkins Marine Sta, 1978-1979; teaching asst, dept biol sci, Hopkins Marine Sta, Stanford Univ, 1977; vis investr, Wis Lab, Fairleigh Dickinson Univ, 1976; vis teaching asst, Wis Lab, Fairleigh Dickinson Univ, 1975; fel, dept biol sci, Hopkins Marine Sta, Stanford Univ, 1974-1979. **Memberships:** Ecol Soc Am; Am Soc Limnol & Oceanog; Sigma Xi; NY Acad Sci. **Research Statement & Publications:** Advancing ecological theory using specialized natural history studies, especially marine invertebrates, algae, foraging and competition; field experiments using close-up listeningand visual records of activities on semi-isolated surfaces of shallow rocks, pilings, oyster reefs and seagrass blades. **Mailing Address:** Dept Biol Sci, Calif State Univ, SC N 302 25800 Carlos Bee Blvd, Hayward, CA 94542. **Fax:** 510-885-4747. **E-Mail:** ckitting@csuhayward.edu

KITTLE, CHARLES FREDERICK, SURGERY. **Personal Data:** b Athens, Ohio, October 24, 1921; m 1971, c 4. **Education:** Ohio Univ, BA, 1942; Univ Chicago, MD, 1945; Univ Kans, MS, 1950; Am Bd Surg, dipl; Am Bd Thoracic Surg, dipl. **Honorary Degrees:** LLD, Ohio Univ, 1967. **Professional Experience:** DIR, RUSH CANCER CTR, 1978-; PROF SURG & HEAD SECT THORACIC SURG, RUSH MED COL, 1973-; mem, Bd Thoracic Surg, 1966-1977; prof surg & chief sect throacic & cardiovasc surg, Univ Chicago, 1966-1973; Markle scholar, 1953-1958; Murdock fel, 1951; Consult, Oak Ridge Inst Nuclear Studies, 1950-1957 & Vet Admin Hosps, Kans & Mo, 1953-1966; from instr to assoc prof surg, Sch Med, Univ Kans, 1950-1966; Am Cancer Soc Clin fel, 1950-1952; chief lab serv, Brentwood Vet Admin Hosp, Los Angeles, 1947-1948. **Memberships:** Soc Univ Surg (pres 1966-1967); Am Col Surgeons; Soc Thoracic Surgeons; Am Asn Thoracic Surgeons; Int Cardiovasc Soc (secy 1965-1971); Am Surg Assoc; Soc Clin Surg. **Research Statement & Publications:** Cardiovascular hemodynamics; extracorporeal circulation; clinical trials. **Mailing Address:** 1725 W Harrison St, Chicago, IL 60612-3828.

KITTLITZ, RUDOLF GOTTLIEB, CHEMICAL ENGINEERING. **Personal Data:** b Waco, Tex, April 19, 1935; m 1966, Linda; c Lenell, Theresa, Liesel & Rolf. **Education:** Univ Miss, BSChemE, 1957. **Honors & Awards:** W G Hunter Award, Am Soc Qual Control, 1989. **Professional Experience:** CONSULT, RUDY KITTLITZ & ASSOC, as of 2002; CHMN US TECH ADV GROUP, TECH COMMITTEE, INT ORGN STAND, as of 2001; sr res assoc, Du Pont Co, beginnign 1992; dir at large, Am Soc Qual Control, 1991-1993; res assoc, Du Pont Co, 1987-1992; exec regional dir, Am Soc Qual Control, 1987-1991; regional dir, Am Soc Qual Control, 1986-1991; Adj prof, Univ Tenn, Chattanooga, 1980-1982; sr res engr, Du Pont Co, 1968-1987; res engr, Du Pont Co, 1962-1968; Engr, Du Pont Co, 1957-1962. **Memberships:** Fel Am Soc Qual Control; Am Statist Asn. **Mailing Address:** Rudy Kittlitz & Assoc, 2006 Ceredo Dr, Alpine, TX 79830-8501. **E-Mail:** e300@brooksdata.net

KITTO, GEORGE BARRIE, BIOCHEMISTRY. **Personal Data:** b Wellington, NZ, July 31, 1937; m 1962, Mary; c David, Robyn & John. **Education:** Victoria Univ, BSc, 1961, MSc, 1962; Brandeis Univ, PhD (biochem), 1966. **Professional Experience:** Vis prof, Duke Univ, 1986; vis prof, Univ Calif, Berkeley, 1978; PROF CHEM & DIR, CTR BIOTECHNOL, UNIV TEX, AUSTIN, 1971-; res scientist, Clayton Found Biochem Inst, beginning 1966; asst prof, Clayton Found Biochem Inst, 1966-1971; Biochemist, Wellington Pub Hosp, 1960-1961; consult, Am Cyanamid, Dell Corp, Aquanautics Corp, Whatman Inc. **Memberships:** AAAS; Am Chem Soc; Royal Soc Chem; NZ Inst Chem; Royal Soc NZ; Am Soc Biochem Molecular Biol. **Research Statement & Publications:** Enzyme structure and taxonomy; evolution of protein structure; multiple molecular forms of enzymes; immobilized enzymes. **Mailing Address:** Dept Chem & Biochem, Univ Tex, One Univ Station A5300 Welch 4 260C, Austin, TX 78712-0165. **Fax:** 512-471-8696. **E-Mail:** bkitto@mail.utexas.edu

KITTO, JOHN BUCK, MECHANICAL ENGINEERING. **Personal Data:** b Evanston, Ill, December 22, 1952; m 1974, Cecilia; c Christopher Daniel & Andrew Comstock. **Education:** Lehigh Univ, BSME, 1975; Univ Akron, MBA, 1980. **Honors & Awards:** George Westinghouse Silver Medal, Am Soc Mech Engrs, 1991, Prime Movers Award & Dedicated Serv Award, 1992. **Professional Experience:** BUS DEVELOP SPECIALIST, BABCOCK & WILCOX CO, OHIO, 1995-; prog mgr, Babcock & Wilcox Co, Ohio, 1981-1994; res engr, Babcock & Wilcox Co, Ohio, 1980-1981; sr engr, Babcock & Wilcox Co, Ohio, 1975-1980. **Memberships:** Fel Am Soc Mech Engrs (sr vpres 1995-); Am Inst Chem Engrs. **Research Statement & Publications:** Author and patentee in field. **Mailing Address:** Res & Develop Div Babcock & Wilcox Co, 1562 Beeson St NE, Alliance, OH 44601-2165.

KITTO, MICHAEL E, ATMOSPHERIC CHEMISTRY. **Education:** Univ Md, College Park, PhD, 1987. **Professional Experience:** RES SCIENTIST & ASST PROF, SCH PUB HEALTH, WADSWORTH CTR LAB & RES, as of 2003. **Mailing Address:** Wadsworth Ctr Labs & Res, PO Box 509, Albany, NY 12201-0509. **Fax:** 518-473-2895. **E-Mail:** kitto@wadsworth.org

KITTRELL, BENJAMIN UPCHURCH, TOBACCO, SOYBEANS. **Personal Data:** b Kittrell, NC, October 25, 1937; m 1958, c 2. **Education:** NC State Univ, BS, 1960, MEd, 1969, PhD (crop sci), 1975. **Professional Experience:** RETIRED; resident dir, pee dee res & educ ctr, 1987-2003; from assoc prof to prof agron, Clemson Univ, 1978-1987; asst prof agron, Univ Ga, 1975-1978; agronomist tobacco, res sta, NC State Univ, 1968-1975; supt, res sta, NC State Univ, 1965-1968; teacher voc agr, Vance Co, NC, 1960-1963; teacher voc agr, Wake Co, NC, 1963-1965. **Memberships:** Am Soc Agron. **Research Statement & Publications:** Tobacco production management including plant density, leaf area index, fertilization, sucker control, harvest, curing, disease control; soybean production management. **Mailing Address:** Pee Dee Res & Educ Ctr, 2200 Pocket Rd, Florence, SC 29506-9706. **Fax:** 843-661-5676.

KITTRELL, JAMES RAYMOND, POLYMER CHEMISTRY. **Personal Data:** b Akransas City, Kans, October 28, 1940; m 1960, c 4. **Education:** Okla State Univ, BS, 1962; Univ Wis, MS, 1963, PhD (chem eng), 1966. **Professional Experience:** PRES, KSE INC, 1980-; prof chem eng, Univ Mass, Amherst, 1970-1980; oper asst, Stand Oil Co Calif, 1969-1970; from res engr to sr res engr, Chevron Res Co, 1966-1969; NSF fel & instr,

Univ Wis, 1966. **Memberships:** Am Inst Chem Engrs; Am Chem Soc. **Research Statement & Publications:** Petroleum refining; polymers; reactor design and analysis; catalyst deactivation; environmental processes; bioengineering. **Mailing Address:** KSE Inc, PO Box 368, Amherst, MA 01004. **Fax:** 413-549-5788. **E-Mail:** kseinc@aol.com

KITTRICK, JAMES ALLEN, SOIL MINERALOGY. **Personal Data:** b Milwaukee, Wis, August 4, 1929; m 1953, c 2. **Education:** Univ Wis, BS, 1951, MS, 1953, PhD, 1955. **Honors & Awards:** Fel Am Soc Agron. **Professional Experience:** RETIRED; from asst prof to prof soils, Wash State Univ, 1955-1991. **Memberships:** Soil Sci Soc; Clay Minerals Soc. **Research Statement & Publications:** Mineral stability, weathering. **Mailing Address:** 160 Osborn Rd, Port Angeles, WA 98362.

KITTS, DAVID BURLINGAME, VERTEBRATE PALEONTOLOGY, GEOLOGY. **Personal Data:** b Oswego, NY, October 27, 1923; m 1945, c 2. **Education:** Univ Pa, AB, 1949; Columbia Univ, PhD (zoology), 1953. **Professional Experience:** RETIRED; staff mem, Dept Geol Physics, Univ Okla, Norman, 1980-1987; head cur, Dept Geol, Stoval Mus, 1968-1980; from asst prof to assoc prof geol, David Ross Boyd prof geol & hist sci, 1966-1980; vis fel, Princeton Univ, 1964-1965; assoc prof geol & hist sci, Univ Okla, 1962-1966; from asst prof to assoc prof geol, Univ Okla, 1954-1962; instr biol, Amherst Col, 1953-1954. **Memberships:** Soc Vert Paleontol; Philos Sci Asn. **Research Statement & Publications:** Historical geology; Cenozoic mammals and stratigraphy; philosophy of geology and evolutionary theory. **Mailing Address:** 3786 Apex Ct, Norman, OK 73072.

KITTSLEY, SCOTT LOREN, CHEMICAL THERMODYNAMICS. **Personal Data:** b Port Washington, Wis, February 17, 1921; m 1946, Helen Jung. **Education:** Univ Wis, BS, 1942; Case Western Reserve Univ, MS, 1944, PhD (phys chem), 1945. **Professional Experience:** EMER PROF CHEM, MARQUETTE UNIV, 1982-; chmn dept, Marquette Univ, 1957-1962; from instr to prof, Marquette Univ, 1945-1981; Asst chem, Case Western Reserve Univ, 1942-1945. **Memberships:** Sigma Xi; Am Chem Soc. **Research Statement & Publications:** Chemical thermodynamics; solutions of nonelectrolytes. **Mailing Address:** 3838 N Oakland Apt 169, Shorewood, WI 53211-2258.

KITZ, DENNIS, IMMUNOLOGY. **Education:** Univ Iowa, 1980. **Professional Experience:** PROF, DEPT BIOL SCI, SOUTHERN ILL UNIV, as of 2004; fac, Kirksville Col Osteop, 1982-1985; adj fac, Truman state Univ, 1982-1985. **Research Statement & Publications:** Host-pathogen interactions; effect of antibiotics and cytokines on host immune response. **Mailing Address:** Dept Biol Sci, Southern Ill Univ, POBox 1651, Edwardsville, IL 62026. **Fax:** 618-650-3174. **E-Mail:** dkitz@siue.edu

KITZ, RICHARD J, ANESTHESIOLOGY, ENZYMOLOGY. **Personal Data:** b Oshkosh, Wis, March 25, 1929; m 1954, c 1. **Education:** Marquette Univ, BS, 1951, MD, 1954; Harvard Univ, MA, 1969; Am Bd Anesthesiol, cert, 1962. **Honors & Awards:** Many named lectureships, 1969-; Golden Emblem Award, Finnish Soc Anesthesiologists, 1977. **Professional Experience:** HENRY ISAIAH DORR PROF RES & TEACHING ANAESTHESIA & ANAESTHETICS, DIV HEALTH SCI TECHNOL, HARVARD UNIV, as of 2006; fac dean clin affairs, Harvard Univ, Mass Inst technol, 1994-; ANESTHETIST, MASS GEN HOSP, BOSTON, MASS, 1994-; co-dir, Harvard-Mass Inst Technol Div Health Sci & Technol, 1985-1990; pres, Am Bd Anesthesiol, 1984-1985; PROF RES & TRAINING ANAESTHETICS & ANAESTHESIA, HARVARD UNIV-MASS INST TECHNOL, 1978-; dir, Am Bd Anesthesiol, 1974-; HENRY ISAIAH DORR PROF ANESTHESIA, HARVARD MED SCH, 1970-; Brigham & Women's Hosp & Beth Israel Hosp, Boston, 1970-1994; consult, Air Force Surg Gen, 1970-1980; consult anesthesiol, Dept Navy, 1969-1971 & Surgeon Gen, USAF, 1970-1979; anesthetist-in-chief, Mass Gen Hosp, 1969-1994; prof, Mass Gen Hosp, Boston, Mass, 1969-1970; NIH spec res fel, Karolinska Inst, Stockholm, 1968; NIH spec res fel, Columbia-Presby Med Ctr, 1961-1962 & Karolinska Inst, Stockholm, 1968; from asst prof to assoc prof anesthesiol, Columbia-Presby Med Ctr, 1962-1969; instr, Columbia-Presby Med Ctr, 1960-1961; resident anesthesiol, Columbia-Presby Med Ctr, 1958-1960; surg resident, Columbia-Presby Med Ctr, 1956-1957; Surg intern, Columbia-Presby Med Ctr, 1954-1955; ed-in-chief, J Clin Anesthesia. **Memberships:** Inst Med-Nat Acad Sci; AMA; Am Soc Anesthesiologists; fel Am Col Anesthesiol; NY Acad Med; Am Chem Soc; Am Soc Pharmacol & Exp Therapeut; AAAS; fel Royal Col Anaesthesists Eng. **Research Statement & Publications:** Basic sciences as related to anesthesiology with emphasis on uptake and distribution of anesthetic agents and enzymology; design, synthesis and testing of novel compounds used as molecular probes (active site investigations) and drugs (short-acting, non-depolarizing neuromuscular blocking agents, anticholinesterases); design, constructing and testing of new anesthesia delivery systems and monitoring devices for care of the critically ill patient in operating rooms and intensive care units; monitoring patient safety and standards of aestheticare; regulation and economics of medical care in the US; author of 2 books andnumerous publications; granted 5 patents. **Mailing Address:** Dept Anesthesia, Mass Gen Hosp, Fruit St, Boston, MA 02114. **Fax:** 617-726-4382. **E-Mail:** kitz@etherdume.mgh.harvard.edu

KITZEN, JAN MICHAEL, PHARMACOLOGY. **Personal Data:** b Philadelphia, Pa, December 23, 1949. **Education:** Temple Univ, BS, 1972; Univ Iowa, PhD (pharmacol), 1977. **Professional Experience:** SECT MGR, DEPT CARDIOVASC BIOL, RHONE-POULENC RORER, 1990-; res assoc pharmacol, 1980-1990. **Memberships:** AAAS; Med Adv Serv; Int Soc Heart Res; Am Heart Asn. **Mailing Address:** Dept Cardiovasc Biol, Rhone-Poulenc Rorer, 500 Arcola Rd, Collegeville, PA 19426.

KITZES, ARNOLD S(TANLEY), NUCLEAR ENGINEERING, CHEMICAL ENGINEERING. **Personal Data:** b Boston, Mass, September 21, 1917; m 1978, Helen L Knox; c Judith A & David H. **Education:** City Col New York, BChE, 1939; Univ Minn, MChE, 1941, PhD (chem eng), 1947. **Professional Experience:** RETIRED; adv engr, Nuclear Serv Div, 1972-1986; mgr test eng, Atomic Power Div, Westinghouse Elec Corp, 1957-1972; group leader, Oak Ridge Nat Lab, 1948-1957; res assoc, Univ Minn, 1945-1947; chief chemist, Sangamon Ord, Ill, 1942-1945; Instr chem eng, Univ Minn, 1941-1942. **Research Statement & Publications:** Reactor technology; environment; spray drying and explosives; design of high pressure equipment; heat transfer; fluid flow; waste management; decontamination; technical administration. **Mailing Address:** 9 Hearthstone Dr, Pittsburgh, PA 15235-4530.

KITZES, LEONARD MARTIN, NEUROPHYSIOLOGY. **Personal Data:** b New York, NY, April 10, 1941; m 1967, c 2. **Education:** Univ Calif, Los Angeles, BA, 1962; Univ Calif, Irvine, PhD (psychobiol), 1970. **Professional Experience:** INTERIM CHAIR, DEPT ANAT & NEUROBIOLOGY, UNIV CALIF, IRVINE, 2003-; Nat Inst Neurol Dis & Stroke res grant, 1978; prof neurophysiol, Dept Anat, Univ Calif, Irvine, 1977-2003; asst prof neurophysiol, Dept Anat, Univ Calif, Irvine, ending 1977; res neurophysiol neurol, Dept Anat, Univ Calif, Irvine, 1975-1977; res assoc, Univ Wis, 1973-1974; fel neurophysiol, Univ Wis, 1970-1974. **Memberships:** Soc Neuroscience; Acoustic Soc Am. **Research Statement & Publications:** Auditory neurophysiology with primary interests in responses of single inferior colliculus neurons to binaural stimulation and functional and structural development of the brainstem auditory system. **Mailing Address:** Dept Anat & Neurobiology, Univ Calif, 337 Med Surge II 1275, Irvine, CA 92697-1275. **Fax:** 949-824-8549. **E-Mail:** lmkitzes@uci.edu

KITZKE, EUGENE DAVID, ENVIRONMENTAL HEALTH, TECHNICAL MANAGEMENT. **Personal Data:** b Milwaukee, Wis, September 2, 1923; m 1946, Lorraine G Shummon; c Mary (Shummon), Paul, Patrice (Elacqua) & Jerome. **Education:** Marquette Univ, BS, 1945, MS, 1947. **Professional Experience:** OWNER, DANEL ENTERPRISES; PRES, OAK CRETE BLOCK CORP, 1982-; distinguished scholar, Marquette Univ, 1995; vpres corp res & develop, S C Johnson & Son, Inc, 1976-1981; asst clin prof environ med, Dept Environ Med, Med Col Wis, 1973-1982; res mgr biol, S C Johnson & Son, Inc, 1957-1976; Instr microbiol, St Mary's Nursing Sch, Grand Rapids, Mich, 1947-1951; From asst prof to assoc prof, St Thomas Aquinas Col, Grand Rapids, Mich, 1947-1951. **Memberships:** AAAS; Sigma Xi; Hist Sci Soc; Int Palm Soc, Past Pres. **Research Statement & Publications:** Developer of wind crest, an environmentally integrated residential subdivision with boundaries coordinated along river frontage floodplain wetlands, and dedicated Department Natural Resources preservation lands. **Mailing Address:** 616 Aspen St, South Milwaukee, WI 53172.

KITZMILLER, JAMES BLAINE, GENETICS, MEDICAL ENTOMOLOGY. **Personal Data:** b Toledo, Ohio, June 30, 1918; m 1974, Dorothy Meyer; c 4. **Education:** De Sales Col, BS, 1939; Univ Mich, MS, 1941, PhD (genetics), 1948. **Honors & Awards:** Meritorious Serv Award, Am Mosquito Control Asn, 1978; John Belkin Mem Award, 1986. **Professional Experience:** EMER PROF ZOOL, UNIV ILL, URBANA, 1974-; vis prof, Fla Med Entomol Lab, 1974-1986; NIH fel, Univ Cagliari, Italy & Johannes Gutenberg Univ, Ger, 1965-1966; consult, NIH, 1958-; consult, WHO & Pan Am Health Orgn, 1953-; Fulbright fel, Univ Pavia, Italy, 1953; from instr to prof, Univ Ill, Urbana, 1948-1974; asst zool, Univ Mich, 1941-1942; Entomologist, Toledo Mus Sci, 1939-1941. **Memberships:** AAAS; Genetics Soc Am; Soc Study Evolution; Am Entom Soc; Am Mosquito Control Asn. **Research Statement & Publications:** Genetics and cytogenetics of mosquitoes, especially Anophelines; evolutionary cytogenetics, polymorphism and cytotaxonomy. **Mailing Address:** Fla Med Entomol Lab, 200 Ninth St SE, Vero Beach, FL 32962.

KIUSALAAS, JAAN, MECHANICS. **Personal Data:** b Tartu, Estonia, June 23, 1931; m 1959, c 3. **Education:** Univ Adelaide, BE, 1956; Northwestern Univ, MS, 1959, PhD (mech), 1962. **Professional Experience:** PROF ENG MECH, PA STATE UNIV, 1974-; Sr resident res assoc, Marshall Space Flight Ctr, NASA, 1971-1972; from asst prof to assoc prof, PA State Univ, 1963-1974; res fel, Mat Res Ctr, Northwestern Univ, 1962-1963; prod develop engr, Eng Div, Chrysler Corp, 1959-1960; prod design & test engr, Chrysler Australia Ltd, 1957-1958; Plant design engr, Chrysler Australia Ltd, 1956-1957. **Memberships:** Am Soc Mech Engrs; Am Acad Mech. **Research Statement & Publications:** Finite elements; optimal structural design; structural stability. **Mailing Address:** Dept Mech Eng, Pa State Univ, Eberly College of Sci, State College, PA 16801.

KIVELSON, MARGARET GALLAND, SPACE PHYSICS. **Personal Data:** b New York, NY, October 21, 1928; m 1949, Daniel; c Steven & Valerie. **Education:** Radcliffe Col, AB, 1950, AM, 1951, PhD (physics), 1957. **Honors & Awards:** Group Achievement Awards, NASA. **Professional Experience:** Chmn, Dept Earth & Space Sci, 1984-1987; PROF, UNIV CALIF, LOS ANGELES, 1980-; overseer, Harvard Col, 1977-1983; prof geophys & space physics in residence, Inst Geophys & Planetary Physics, 1977-1980; assoc prof in residence, Inst Geophys & Planetary Physics, 1975-1977; fel, John Simon Guggenheim Mem Found, 1973-1974; adj assoc prof, Inst Geophys & Planetary Physics, 1972-1973; res geophysicist, Inst Geophys & Planetary Physics, 1967-1980; adj asst prof physics, Univ Calif, 1967-1972; scholar, Radcliffe Inst Independent Study, 1965-1966; consult, Rand Corp, 1955-1971. **Memberships:** Fel AAAS; fel Am Geophys Union; Am Phys Soc; Am Astron Soc; mem Int Acad Astronaut; Nat Acad Sci. **Research Statement & Publications:** Magnetospheric physics; plasma physics; particles and fields in the magnetospheres of Earth and Jupiter; interplanetary magnetic fields; magnetic fields of moons. **Mailing Address:** Inst Geophys & Planetary Physics, Univ Calif, Los Angeles, CA 90024-1567. **Fax:** 310-206-8042. **E-Mail:** mkivelson@igpp.ucla.edu

KIVENSON, GILBERT, ENGINEERING INSTRUMENTATION. **Personal Data:** b Pittsburgh, Pa, December 5, 1920. **Education:** Carnegie Inst Technol, BS, 1942; Univ Pittsburgh, MS, 1947. **Professional Experience:** J B Lansing, Northridge, Calif, 1980-1981; CONSULT & PATENT AGENT, 1975-, sr engr, Audio Instruments, C F Braun Co, Calif, 1973-1975; sr engr, Liquid Metals Eng Ctr, Atomics Int, Chatsworth, 1971-1973; sr engr, Electro-Optical Systs Div, Xerox Corp, 1968-1970; sr engr, Res & Develop Ctr, 1962-1968; chem engr, Atomic Power Dept, Westinghouse Elec Corp, 1955-1962; consult instrumentation, 1953-1955; chem engr, US Steel Co, 1951-1953; develop engr, Mellon Inst, 1950-1951; Rubber Reserve Co fel fract distillation, Mellon Inst, 1947-1950; Lectr, Pa Technol Inst & Northrop Inst Technol. **Memberships:** Am Chem Soc. **Research Statement & Publications:** Electronic instruments; stroboscopes; control systems; transducers; process control instrumentation. **Mailing Address:** 22030 Wyandotte St, Canoga Park, CA 91303.

KIVER, EUGENE P, GEOMORPHOLOGY. **Personal Data:** b Cleveland, Ohio, February 26, 1937; m 1964, c 3. **Education:** Case Western Res Univ, BA, 1964; Univ Wyo, PhD (glacial geol, geomorphol), 1968. **Professional Experience:** PROF GEOL, EASTERN WASH UNIV, 1977-; from asst prof to assoc prof, eastern wash Univ, 1971-1977; chmn dept, wash Univ, 1971-1974. **Memberships:** Am Quaternary Asn; Geol Soc Am; Nat Speleol Soc. **Research Statement & Publications:** Pleistocene and neoglacial history of alpine regions of western US; general geomorphology; volcanism in the Cascade Mountains; geology of the national parks; quaternary geology of NE Washington. **Mailing Address:** Dept Geol, Eastern Wash Univ, Mail Stop 70 130 Sci Bldg, Cheney, WA 99004. **Fax:** 509-359-4386.

KIVIAT, ERIK, WETLAND & HUMAN ECOLOGY. **Personal Data:** b New York, NY, June 9, 1947; m 1982, Elaine. **Education:** Bard Col, BS, 1976; State Univ NY, New Paltz, MA, 1979; Union Inst, PhD, 1991. **Professional Experience:** PROF ENVIRON STUDIES, BARD COL, as of 2003; assoc prof environ studies, Grad Sch Environ Studies, Bard Col, beginning 1991; EXEC DIR, HUDSONIA LTD, BARD COL, 1988-; asst prof environ studies, Field Sta, 1988-1991; ecologist, Hudsonia Ltd, 1981-; RES ASSOC ECOL, FIELD STA, 1978-; from instr to asst prof natural his, Bard Col, 1973-1978; dir, Field Sta, 1972-1978. **Memberships:** Torrey Bot Soc; Ecol Soc Am; Estuarine Res Fedn; Soc Conserv Biol; Soc Wetland Scientists; Soc Study Amphibians & Reptiles. **Research Statement & Publications:** Wetland ecology and management; vertebrates; insects vascular plants; vegetation change; habitat ecology; rare species conservation; introduced species ecology; cultural ecology. **Mailing Address:** Hudsonia Ltd, Bard Col, Field Sta, Annandale, NY 12504. **Fax:** 845-758-7033. **E-Mail:** kiviat@bard.edu

KIVIOJA, LASSI A, GEODESY. **Personal Data:** b Finland, March 29, 1927; American citizen; m 1964, c 2. **Education:** Univ Helsinki, BS, 1951, MS, 1952; Ohio State Univ,

PhD, 1963. **Professional Experience:** PROF EMER CIVIL ENG, PURDUE UNIV, 1990-; res scientist, Defense Mapping Agency, 1979-1980 & 1986-1987; geologist, US Coast & Geod Surv, 1970-1971; prof, Purdue Univ, 1964-1990; instr, Dept Geod Sci, Ohio State Univ, 1959-1962; res assoc geod gravity, Ohio State Univ, 1955-1963; res asst, Int Isostatic Inst, Helsinki, Finland, 1949-1952. **Memberships:** Am Geophys Union; Am Cong Surv & Mapping. **Research Statement & Publications:** Gravity anomalies isostasy; geodetic and astro-geodetic instruments; geodetic lines on the ellipsoid; the vertical mirror and its applications; mean sea level; mercury leveling instruments; hydrostatic leveling on land; precise astro-azimuths by mercury leveling of a theodolite. **Mailing Address:** Dept Civil Eng, Purdue Univ, Lafayette, IN 47907. **E-Mail:** lkivioja@earthlink.net

KIVISILD, HANS R(OBERT), CIVIL ENGINEERING & OCEAN ENGINEERING. **Personal Data:** b Tartu, Estonia, July 19, 1922; m 1947, Livia Martina; c Maria (Ogrydziak), Ann (Smith), Julia (Bailey) & Emma (Kivisild). **Education:** Royal Inst Technol, Swed, CE, 1946, DEng(hydraul eng), 1954. **Honors & Awards:** Eng Medal, Asn Prof Engrs Ont, 1976; Queen Elizabeth II Silver Jubilee Medal, 1977; Award Merit Innovation, Manning Awards, 1985; Alta Achievement Award For Excellence, 1987; Frank Spragins Award, Asn Prof Engrs Geol Geophys Alta, 1989. **Professional Experience:** PRIN, HRK CONSULT INC, CALGARY, 1987-; mem tech comt, code for fixed offshore structs, Can Stands Asn, 1983-1991; vpres, Lavalin Inc, Calgary, 1982-1987; mem cold regions res comt, Nat Res Coun Can, 1977-1979; vpres & mgr, western opers & dir, Fenco Consults Ltd, Calgary, 1975-1981; vpres, Toronto, 1973-1975; dir res & develop, Toronto, 1970-1973; mem snow & ice subcomt, Nat Res Coun Can, 1965-1975; chief civil engr, Toronto, 1965-1970; chief hydraul engr, Toronto, 1964-1965; Tech Assistance Opers, Food & Agr Orgn, 1964; Tech Assistance Opers, Spec Fund, 1963; Tech Assistance Opers, UN, 1961; dist engr, Vancouver, 1957-1963; Consult, Belg Govt, 1956; designing engr, Found Can Eng Corp Ltd, Montreal, 1954-1956; with Found Co Can, Ltd, Montreal, 1950-1953; engr, VBB, Stockholm, Swed, 1948-1950; engr, City Stockholm, Swed, 1946-1948; chmn working group design principles & safety considerations. **Memberships:** Fel Can Soc Civil Eng; Int Asn Hydraul Res; Marine Technol Soc; fel Eng Inst Can. **Research Statement & Publications:** storm surges in oceans and lakes; stratified flow; earthquake resistance of subaqueous structures; ice effects on northern marine structures and vessels; river ice jamming and resulting floods. **Mailing Address:** 1420 Premier Way SW, Calgary, AB T2T 1L9, Can. **Fax:** 403-244-0075.

KIVLIGHN, SALAH DEAN, DRUG DEVELOPMENT & DESIGN NOVEL THERAPEUTICS AGENTS. **Personal Data:** b Iowa City, Iowa, July 12, 1957; m 1989, Jane Kersh. **Education:** Iowa State Univ, BS, 1979; Univ Houston, PhD (cardiovasc pharmacol), 1989. **Professional Experience:** SR RES FEL, MERCK, SHARP & DOHME RES LABS, WEST POINT, PA, 1996-; res fel, Merck, Sharp & Dohme Res Labs, West Point, PA, 1993-1996; sr res pharmacologist, Merck, Sharp & Dohme Res Labs, West Point, PA, 1990-1993; Referee ed, Heart & Circulatory & Res & Integ, Am J Physiol, 1988-; instr, Univ Miss Med Ctr, Jackson, 1988-1990; Fel physiol, Univ Miss Med Ctr, Jackson, 1987-1988. **Memberships:** Am Soc Hypertension; Am Physiol Soc; Am Soc Nephrol. **Research Statement & Publications:** Design and development of novel therapeutic agents for the treatment of hypertension and heart failure. **Mailing Address:** Merck Sharp & Dohme Res Lab WP46-100, West Point, PA 19486.

KIVNICK, ARNOLD, chemical engineering, applied math; deceased, see previous edition for last biography

KIYASU, JOHN YUTAKA, BIOCHEMISTRY. **Personal Data:** b San Francisco, Calif, December 25, 1927; m 1954, c 4. **Education:** Univ Calif, Berkeley, BA, 1950, MA, 1951, PhD (physiol), 1955. **Professional Experience:** ASSOC CLIN PROF PATH, COL PHYSICIANS & SURGEONS, COLUMBIA UNIV, 1972-; dir div biochem & asst dir lab, dept path, Roosevelt Hosp, 1970-1984; dir lab systs, Div Biochem, Meadowbrook Hosp, East Meadow, NY, 1969-1970; res biochemist & mem staff, Dept Path & Labs, Div Biochem, Meadowbrook Hosp, East Meadow, NY, 1967-1969; from asst prof to assoc prof chem, Adelphi Univ, 1963-1970; asst prof biochem & asst res prof psychiat, Sch Med & Dent, Univ Rochester, 1960-1963; instr & res assoc, Univ Chicago, 1957-1960; Fel biochem, Univ Chicago, 1956-1957, USPHS fel, 1955-1957; NIH grant, Adelphi Univ. **Research Statement & Publications:** Biosynthesis of phospholipids and liponucleotides; lipid enzymology and control mechanisms. **Mailing Address:** 94 Meadow St, Garden City, NY 11530.

KIYONO, HIROSHI, DENTISTRY. **Personal Data:** b Nagone, Japan, March 17, 1953; m 1986, Momoyo; c Erika. **Education:** Univ Ala, PhD (immunopathology), 1983. **Professional Experience:** ADJ PROF ORAL BIOL, UNIV ALA, as of 2006; CO-DIR IMMUNOL CTR, UNIV ALA, 1992-; RES PROF, UNIV ALA, 1991-; SR SCIENTIST TO SCIENTIST, UNIV ALA, 1988-; vis sr scientist, May-Planick Inst, Ger, 1986; From asst prof to assoc prof, Univ Ala, 1984-1991; vis scientist, NIH, Tokyo, 1984-1985; clin instr, Nikon Univ, 1977. **Memberships:** Am Asn Immunologists; Soc Murosal Immunol; Int Asn Dent Res; Am Soc Investigative Path; Am Soc Microbiol. **Research Statement & Publications:** Mucosal immunology; development of mucosal vaccine. **Mailing Address:** Dept Oral Biol Univ Ala, 1530 Third Ave S BBRB 273C, Birmingham, AL 35294-2170. **Fax:** 205-975-4431. **E-Mail:** kiyono@uab.edu

KIZANIS, ANN, MATHEMATICS. **Education:** Wesleyan Univ, PhD (MATH), 1991. **Professional Experience:** ASSOC DEAN ARTS & SCI, PROF, MATH, WESTERN NEW ENG COL, as of 2005. **Mailing Address:** Western New Eng Col, 1215 Wilbraham Rd, Springfield, MA 01119-2654. **Fax:** 413-782-1746. **E-Mail:** akizanis@wnec.edu

KIZER, DONALD EARL, BIOCHEMISTRY. **Personal Data:** b Benton Co, Iowa, October 12, 1921; m 1942, c 6. **Education:** Upper Iowa Univ, BS, 1947; Purdue Univ, MS, 1950; Univ NC, PhD (bact), 1954. **Professional Experience:** RETIRED; res assoc, 1964-1960; head biochem pharmacol sect, Biomed Div, Samuel Roberts Noble Found, Inc, 1960-1985; asst animal indust, Univ NC, 1952-1954; asst dairy, Purdue Univ, 1948-1950. **Memberships:** AAAS; Am Chem Soc; Am Soc Microbiol; Soc Exp Biol & Med; Am Asn Cancer Res. **Research Statement & Publications:** Biochemistry of carcinogenesis; biochemical changes in pre-cancerous tissues. **Mailing Address:** 825 H St NW, Ardmore, OK 73401.

KIZER, JOHN STEPHEN, NEUROENDOCRINOLOGY. **Personal Data:** b Charleston, WVa, January 8, 1945; m 1970, c 6. **Education:** Princeton Univ, AB, 1966; Duke Univ, MD, 1970. **Professional Experience:** CHAR, DISTINGUISHED MED SCHOLARS COMT, UNIV NC, CHAPEL HILL, as of 2004; PROF DIV OD GERIATRIC MED, SCH MED, UNIV NC, CHAPEL HILL, 1986-; assoc dir, Biol Sci Res Ctr, 1985-; res sci career develop award, 1977-1988; from asst prof to assoc prof, Sch Med, Univ NC, Chapel Hill, 1975-1985; res assoc neuroendocrinol, Lab Clin Sci, NIMH, 1972-1975; resident, Johns Hopkins Hosp, Baltimore, 1971-1972; intern med, Johns Hopkins Hosp, Baltimore, 1970-1971. **Memberships:** Am Soc Clin Invest. **Research Statement & Publications:** Investigation of protein neurotransmitters; post-translational processing of protien neu-

rotransmitters. **Mailing Address:** Program on Aging, Sch Med Univ NC, 141 MacNider Bldg Campus Box 7550, Chapel Hill, NC 27599-7550. **E-Mail:** jskizer@med.unc.edu

KJAR, RAYMOND ARTHUR, ELECTRONICS ENGINEERING. **Personal Data:** b Farnam, Nebr, February 27, 1938; m 1967, c 1. **Education:** Univ Nebr, BSEE, 1960; Iowa State Univ, MS, 1962, PhD, 1964. **Professional Experience:** DIR ADVAN PROCESS TECHNOL, ROCKWELL DIGITAL COMMUN DIV, ROCKWELL INT, 1990-; mgr, Mil IC Prod, 1980-1990; supvr, Electronics Div, IC Tech, 1976-1980; res engr, R & E Div, Rockwell Int, 1968-1976; res engr, Naval Res Lab, Off Naval Res, 1964-1968. **Memberships:** Inst Elec & Electronics Engrs. **Research Statement & Publications:** Semiconductor devices; integrated circuits; reliability physics; semiconductor surfaces. **Mailing Address:** Rockwell Int, 4311 Jamboree Rd 501-109, Newport Beach, CA 92666.

KJELDAAS, TERJE JR, theoretical physics; deceased, see previous edition for last biography

KJELDGAARD, EDWIN ANDREAS, APPLIED CHEMISTRY, METROLOGY. **Personal Data:** b Brush, Colo, September 14, 1939; m 1965, c 2. **Education:** St Olaf Col, BA, 1961; Univ Colo, PhD (chem), 1966. **Professional Experience:** PROJECT MGR, SANDIA NAT LAB, 1993-; sr mem tech staff, sandia nat lab, beginning 1984; div supvr, sandia nat lab, 1970-1984; staff mem, sandia nat lab, 1966-1970. **Research Statement & Publications:** Organic fluorine chemistry; fluorinated cyclobutenes; explosive chemistry; coordination compounds; Risk analysis. **Mailing Address:** Sandia Nat Lab, MS 0718, Albuquerque, NM 87185-0718. **Fax:** 505-844-0244. **E-Mail:** eakjeld@sandia.gov

KJELDSEN, CHRIS KELVIN, PHYCOLOGY. **Personal Data:** b Stockton, Calif, April 26, 1939; m 1962, c 3. **Education:** Univ Pac, BA, 1960, MS, 1962; Ore State Univ, PhD (bot), 1966. **Honors & Awards:** Mosser Award, Ore State Univ, 1966. **Professional Experience:** PROF EMER DEPT BIOL, SONOMA UNIV, AS OF 2005; Sonoma Co Hazardous Mat Comn, beginning 1985; ipa assignment, us dept energy, educ progs, Wash, DC, 1978-1979; sabbatical leave, Univ NWales, 1976; sonoma co planning comn, 1974-1976; prof biol, Sonoma State Univ, beginning 1973; chmn dept, Sonoma State Univ, 1972-1975; NSF, DOE, grants sci educ, beginning 1969; from asst prof to assoc prof, Sonoma State Univ, 1966-1973; instr bot, Ore State Univ, 1962-1966. **Memberships:** Sigma Xi (vpres 1967). **Research Statement & Publications:** Marine algae; physiological ecology and taxonomy; Sacramento San Jouquin Delta habitar analysis. **Mailing Address:** Dept Biol, Sonoma State Univ, Darwin 121, 1801 E Cotati Ave, Rohnert Park, CA 94928-3613. **Fax:** 707-664-3012. **E-Mail:** chris.kjeldsen@sonoma.edu

KJELGAARD, WILLIAM L, AGRICULTURAL ENGINEERING. **Personal Data:** b Lindley, NY, August 27, 1920; m 1950, c 5. **Education:** Pa State Univ, BS, 1950, MS, 1953. **Professional Experience:** RETIRED; assoc prof agr eng, Pa State Univ, beginning 1960; from instr to asst prof, 1952-1960; instr agr eng, WVa Univ, 1951-1952. **Memberships:** Am Soc Agr Engrs. **Research Statement & Publications:** Mechanization and processing of forage crops. **Mailing Address:** 1311 Circleville Rd, State College, PA 16803.

KJELSBERG, MARCUS OLAF, BIOSTATISTICS. **Personal Data:** b Mayville, NDak, December 27, 1932; m 1962, c 2. **Education:** Concordia Col, Moorhead, Minn, BA, 1952; Univ Minn, MA, 1955, PhD (biostatist), 1962. **Professional Experience:** RETIRED; prof biostatist, sch pub health, Univ Minn, Minneapolis, beginning 1975; mem, US Nat Comt Vital & Health Statist, 1973-1977; prin investr, Mult Risk Factor Intervention Ctr, 1972-; div head biomed, Sch Pub Health, Univ Minn, Minneapolis, 1972-1987; assoc prof, Sch Pub Health, Univ Minn, Minneapolis, 1966-1975; asst prof biostatist & res assoc epidemiol, Sch Pub Health, Univ Mich, Ann Arbor, 1961-1966; instr biostatist, Sch Med, Tulane Univ, 1957-1960; assoc dean Admin, Univ Minn, Minneapolis. **Memberships:** Am Pub Health Asn; Am Statist Asn; Am Heart Asn; Biometric Soc; Pop Asn Am. **Research Statement & Publications:** Statistical epidemiology; health statistics; clinical trials methodology. **Mailing Address:** 135 Valley View Pl, Minneapolis, MN 55419. **E-Mail:** marc@umn.edu

KJONAAS, RICHARD A, ORGANIC CHEMISTRY. **Personal Data:** b Minot, NDak, March 20, 1949; m 1979, Deborah; c Michael & Tamara. **Education:** Valley City State Col, BS, 1971; Purdue Univ, PhD (chem), 1978. **Professional Experience:** PROF CHEM, IND STATE UNIV, 1991-; assoc prof, Ind State Univ, 1987-1991, asst prof, Ind State Univ, 1983-1987; asst prof, Ft Hays State Univ, 1979-1983; fel, Ohio State Univ, 1978-1979; Teacher high sch, NDak, 1971-1973. **Memberships:** Am Chem Soc; Sigma Xi; Coun Undergrad Res. **Research Statement & Publications:** Transition metals and carbanionic reagents in organic synthesis; identification of naturally occurring flavors and fragrances. **Mailing Address:** Dept Chem, Ind State Univ, Terre Haute, IN 47809. **Fax:** 812-237-2232. **E-Mail:** rkjonaas@indstate.edu

KLAAS, ERWIN EUGENE, RESTORATION ECOLOGY. **Personal Data:** b Batchtown, Ill, August 23, 1935; m 1969, Janet; c Zachary, Abigail & Benjamin. **Education:** Univ Mo, BS, 1956; Univ Kans, MA, 1963, PhD (zoology), 1970. **Honors & Awards:** Scroll of Honor, U S Geological Survey. **Professional Experience:** PROF EMER, ANIMAL ECOL, IOWA STATE UNIV, 2000-; leader, Iowa Coop Fish & Wildlife Res Unit, Biol Resources Div, US Geol Surv, 1996-2000; res biologist, Nat Biol Surv, 1993-1996; UNIT LEADER, US FISH & WILDLIFE SERV, 1992-; prof, Animal Ecology, Iowa State Univ, 1980-2000; asst unit leader, US Fish & Wildlife Serv, 1975-1992; assoc prof, Iowa State Univ, 1975-1980; Res biologist, US Fish & Wildlife Serv, 1971-1993; From asst prof to assoc prof biol, Rockhurst Col, 1965-1971. **Memberships:** Am Ornith Union; Wildlife Soc; Soc Restoration Ecol. **Research Statement & Publications:** Population ecology of birds; restoration of disturbed ecosystems; management of habitat for optimal utilization by game and non-game species; conservaton of biodiversity. **Mailing Address:** Natural Resources Ecol Mgt, Iowa State Univ, 124 Sci II, Ames, IA 50011. **Fax:** 515-294-5468. **E-Mail:** eklaas@iastate.edu

KLAAS, NICHOLAS PAUL, ORGANIC CHEMISTRY. **Personal Data:** b Kieler, Wis, June 25, 1925; m 1949, Ruth Barry; c Paul, Patricia, Kathleen & James. **Education:** Loras Col, BA, 1945; Univ Notre Dame, PhD (org chem), 1948. **Professional Experience:** Adj prof, San Diego State Univ, 1985-1998; PRES, KLAAS ASSOCS INC, 1984-; from exec vpres to pres, J T Baker Chem Co, 1977-1984; gen mgr, J T Baker Chem Co, 1977-1984; gen mgr spec chem div, Ga-Pac Corp, 1977; group vpres chem group, GAF Corp, 1974-1977; vpres com develop, GAF Corp, 1971-1974; chief operating officer, Wyomissing Corp, Reading, 1970-1971; dir, Wyomissing Corp, Reading, 1968-1971; exec vpres, Wyomissing Corp, Reading, 1965-1971; mgr res & develop, 3M Co, 1960-1965; mgr oil indust prod, 3M Co, 1953-1959; mkt specialist, 3M Co, 1952-1953; tech asst to sales develop mgr, 3M Co, 1952; actg prod mgr, Rohm and Haas Co, 1949-1951; Chemist, Rohm and Haas Co, 1948. **Memberships:** AAAS; Am Chem Soc. **Research Statement & Publications:** Organic chemical intermediates and polymers; chemicals derived from acetylene; surfactants; dyes; pigments; carbonyl iron powders; textile auxiliaries; felts; filters; electronic, laboratory and agricultural chemicals; ceramics; materials science; roofing granules; building, photographic and quarry products; abrasives and adhesives;

herbicides; ion exchange; soils and soil science; horticulture; natural products. **Mailing Address:** 51 Hoot Owl Terr, Kinnelon, NJ 07405-2409. **Fax:** 973-838-3426. **E-Mail:** npaulklaas@aol.com

KLAASEN, GENE ALLEN, MATHEMATICS. **Personal Data:** b Holland, Mich, February 3, 1941; m 1963, c 3. **Education:** Hope Col, BA, 1963; Univ Nebr, Lincoln, MA, 1965, PhD (math), 1968. **Professional Experience:** ASSOC PROF MATH, UNIV TENN, KNOXVILLE, 1974-; asst prof, Univ Tenn, Knoxville, 1969-1974; Asst prof math, Univ Nebr, Lincoln, 1968-1969. **Memberships:** Am Math Soc; Math Asn Am. **Research Statement & Publications:** Boundary value problems for ordinary differential equations. **Mailing Address:** Univ Dar es Salaam, PO Box 35062, Dar es Salaam, Tanzania.

KLAASSEN, CURTIS DEAN, PHARMACOLOGY, TOXICOLOGY. **Personal Data:** b Ft Dodge, Iowa, November 23, 1942; m 1964, c 2. **Education:** Wartburg Col, BA, 1964; Univ Iowa, MS, 1966, PhD (pharmacol), 1968. **Honors & Awards:** Achievement Award, Soc Toxicol, 1976. **Professional Experience:** CHMN, MED CTR, UNIV KANS, 2003-; UNIV DISTINGUISHED PROF, DEPT PHARMACOL, TOXICOL & THERAPEUT, MED CTR, UNIV KANS, 2002-; comt mem, Comt Storage & Disposal Chems Lab, 1993-; trustee, Health & Environ Sci Inst, Int Life Sci Inst, beginning 1989; interim dir, Environ Health & Occup Med Ctr, 1989-1991; Coun Dent Therapeut, Am Dent Asn, 1988-; comt mem, Comt Toxicol, 1988-1991; distinguished vis prof, Univ Toledo, 1987; assoc dir, Environ Health & Occup Med Ctr, 1986-1989; distinguished vis prof, NMex State Univ, 1985; prof molecular cytol, Inst Invest Cytol, Valencia, Spain, 1984-1995; mem, Int Workshop Manpower Develop & Training Toxicol & Chem Safety, WHO, 1983-1984; Burroughs Wellcome scholar toxicol, 1982-1987; assoc ed, Toxicol & Appl Pharmacol, 1980-1990; comt mem, Alkyl Benzenes, Nat Acad Sci, 1979-1981; vis scientist, Dept Toxicol, Inst Radiation & Environ Res, Munich, Ger, 1978; head, sec toxicol dept pharmacol, toxicol & therapeut, Med Ctr Univ Kans, 1977-2002; assoc ed, J Pharmacol & Toxicol Methods, 1977-; PROF PHARMACOL & TOXICOL, MED CTR, UNIV KANS, 1977-; mem comt, Toxicol Study Sect, NIH, 1976-1980; Guest prof clin pharmacol, Univ Bern, Swit, 1975; from asst prof to assoc prof, pharmacol & toxicol Med Ctr Univ Kans, 1970-1977; instr, pharmacol & toxicol Med Ctr Univ Kans, 1968-1970. **Memberships:** Soc Toxicol (vpres, 1989-1990, pres, 1990-1991); Am Soc Pharmacol & Exp Therapeut; Sigma Xi; AAAS; Am Asn Study Liver Dis; Soc Exp Biol & Med. **Research Statement & Publications:** Biliary excretion of drugs and toxicants. **Mailing Address:** Dept Pharmacol Toxicol & Therapeut, Med Ctr, Univ Kans Med ctr, MS1018 3901 Rainbow Blvd, Kansas City, KS 66160. **Fax:** 913-588-7501. **E-Mail:** cklaassen@kumc.edu

KLAASSEN, DWIGHT HOMER, BIOCHEMISTRY. **Personal Data:** b Weatherford, Okla, August 15, 1936; m 1957, c 3. **Education:** Tabor Col, BA, 1958; Kans State Univ, MS, 1961, PhD (biochem), 1965. **Professional Experience:** Asst chancellor, Univ Relations, 1984-; assoc dean, Student Affairs, 1981-1984; Coordr Coop Educ & Internships, 1977-1981; PROF CHEM, UNIV WIS-PLATTEVILLE, 1967-; assoc prof, Univ Wis-Platteville, 1964-1967; asst instr biochem, Kans State Univ, 1963-1964. **Memberships:** Am Sci Affil; Sigma Xi. **Research Statement & Publications:** Binding of sulfur-containing azo dyes related to dimethylaminoazobenzene to rat liver proteins; comparative study of mitochondrial proteins involving amino acid composition and solubility. **Mailing Address:** Dept Chem, Univ Wis, Platteville, WI 53818. **E-Mail:** klaassen@uwtlatt.edu

KLAASSEN, HAROLD EUGENE, ECOLOGY, FISH BIOLOGY. **Personal Data:** b Hillsboro, Kans, April 18, 1935; m 1956, c 2. **Education:** Tabor Col, BA, 1957; Kans State Univ, MS, 1959; Univ Wash, Seattle, PhD (aquatic ecol), 1967. **Professional Experience:** ASSOC PROF EMER, BIOL, KANS STATE UNIV, as of 2004; assoc prof biol, Kans State Univ, beginning 1967; fishery biologist, Univ Wash, Seattle, 1959. **Memberships:** Am Fisheries Soc; Sigma Xi. **Research Statement & Publications:** Fisheries management; fish distribution and production; aquaculture. **Mailing Address:** Div Biol, Kans State Univ 232 Ackert Hall, Manhattan, KS 66506-4901. **E-Mail:** heklaas@ksu.edu

KLABUNDE, KENNETH JOHN, ORGANIC CHEMISTRY, INORGANIC CHEMISTRY. **Personal Data:** b Madison, Wis, May 30, 1943; m 1967, c 3. **Education:** Augustana Col, BA, 1965; Univ Iowa, PhD (org chem), 1969. **Honors & Awards:** Sigma Xi Res Award, 1977, 1987. **Professional Experience:** UNIV DISTINGUISHED PROF CHEM, KANS STATE UNIV, as of 2003; grants, Naval Res Off, 1985-1988; grants, Army Res Off, 1984-1991; prof chem & head dept, Kans State Univ, beginning 1979; grants, Indust, 1979-1988; grants, US Dept Energy, 1974-1980; grants from NSF, 1972-1991; grants, Petrol Res Fund, 1971-1974 & 1979-1985; from asst prof to prof org chem, Univ NDak, 1970-1979; grants, Univ NDak, 1970-1972; grants, Res Corp, 1970-1972; res assoc org chem, Pa State Univ, 1969-1970. **Memberships:** Am Chem Soc; Sigma Xi. **Research Statement & Publications:** Organic-Inorganic: reactive intermediates such as metal atom chemistry, carbonmonosulfide chemistry, organometallic synthesis, thin film materials; metal oxide surface chemistry; use of metal vapors and other reactive species as synthetic reagents; adsorbents. **Mailing Address:** Dept Chem, Kans State Univ 111 Willard Hall, Manhattan, KS 66506-3701. **Fax:** 785-532-6666. **E-Mail:** kenjk@ksu.edu

KLABUNDE, RICHARD EDWIN, CARDIOVASCULAR PHYSIOLOGY, PHARMACOLOGY. **Personal Data:** b Pasadena, Calif, October 7, 1948; m 1968, c 4. **Education:** Pepperdine Univ, BS, 1970; Univ Ariz, PhD (physiol), 1975. **Professional Experience:** ASSOC PROF PHYSIOL, DEPT BIOMED SCI, OHIO UNIV COL OSTEOPATHIC MED, 1998-; dir & sr res scientist, Deborah Res Inst, Browns Mill, NJ, 1996-1998; assoc dir & sr res scientist, Deborah Res Inst, Browns Mill, NJ, 1993-1995; adj assoc prof, Dept Physiol, Chicago Med Sch, beginning 1989; vis assoc prof, Dept Biomed Sci, Univ Ill Col Med, Rockford, beginning 1986; sr group leader, Cardiovasc Pharmacol, Abbott Labs, 1985-1993; from asst prof to assoc prof, Dept Physiol, WVa Univ Med Ctr, 1978-1985; asst res physiologist, Pharmacol Div, 1977-1978; fel, Nat Heart Lung & Blood Inst, Univ Calif, San Diego, 1976; Am Heart Asn fel physiol, Univ Ariz, 1975-1976. **Memberships:** Am Physiol Soc; Microcirculatory Soc. **Research Statement & Publications:** Mechanisms of blood flow regulation, particularly in skeletal muscle during exercise and following short periods of ischemia; EDRF and blood flow regulation in vivo; Published over 20 articles. **Mailing Address:** Dept Biomed Sci, Ohio Univ Col Osteopathic Med, 304 Irvine Hall, Athens, OH 45701. **E-Mail:** klabunde@ohio.edu

KLACSMANN, JOHN ANTHONY, organic chemistry finishes, toxic waste clean-up; deceased, see previous edition for last biography

KLAFTER, RICHARD D(AVID), CONTROLS, ROBOTICS. **Personal Data:** b New York, NY, August 5, 1936; m 1959, Marcia; c Leslie & Melissa. **Education:** Mass Inst Technol, SB, 1958; Columbia Univ, MSEE, 1959, EE, 1963; City Univ NY, PhD (optimal control), 1969. **Professional Experience:** PROF EMER ELEC ENG, TEMPLE UNIV, as of 2003; prof elec eng, Temple Univ, beginning 1984; proj dir cardiac pacemakers, NSF, 1973-1975; assoc proj dir, NASA-Am Soc Eng Educ, 1971; from asst prof to assoc prof elec eng, Drexel Univ, 1967-1984; lectr elec eng, City Col NY, 1959-1964, 1965-1967. **Memberships:** Sigma Xi; Inst Elec & Electronics Engrs; Soc Mfg Engr; Robotics & Automation Soc (pres). **Research Statement & Publications:** Mobile robots, optimal trajectory control of robots, tactile sensing, sensored and nonsensored robot navigation; motion control. **Mailing Address:** Dept Elec & Comput Eng, Temple Univ, 607 Park Lane, Wyncote, PA 19095-1315. **Fax:** 215-204-6936. **E-Mail:** v5442e@vm.temple.edu

KLAGSBRUN, MICHAEL, CELL BIOLOGY, BIOMEDICAL RESEARCH. **Personal Data:** b Antwerp, Belg, January 16, 1939. **Education:** City Col NY, BS, 1960; Univ Wis, PhD (biochem), 1968. **Professional Experience:** SR ASSOC MED, CHILDREN'S HOSP, HARVARD MED SCH, as of 2005; PARTRICIA K DONAHOE PROF SURG, CHILDREN'S HOSP, HARVARD MED SCH, as of 2005; PROF, DEPT SURG, HARVARD MED SCH, 1993-; assoc prof med res, 1980-1993. **Memberships:** Am Soc Cell Biol; Am Soc Biol Chemists; NY Acad Sci. **Mailing Address:** Childrens Hosp Harvard Med Sch, Dept Surg, Enders 1061 300 Longwood Ave, Boston, MA 02115. **Fax:** 617-730-0233. **E-Mail:** michael.klagsbrun@tch.harvard.edu

KLAHR, CARL NATHAN, APPLIED PHYSICS. **Personal Data:** b Pittsburgh, Pa, July 3, 1927; m 1953, c 3. **Education:** Carnegie Inst Technol, BS & MS, 1948, MS & DSc(physics), 1950. **Professional Experience:** PRES, FUNDAMENTAL METHODS ASSOCS INC, 1967-; sr assoc, Fundamental Methodsassocs, Inc, 1961-1967; proj mgr & sr physicist, Tech Res Group, Inc, 1957-1961; lectr, Columbia Univ, 1953-1958; physicist & proj mgr, Nuclear Develop Corp Am, 1952-1957; physicist, Res Labs, Westinghouse Elec Corp, 1950-1952. **Memberships:** Am Phys Soc; Am Nuclear Soc; Opers Res Soc Am; Inst Mgt Sci; Inst Elec & Electronics Engrs. **Research Statement & Publications:** Hypervelocity physics; space vehicle technology; semiconductor device design and technology; solid state physics; operations research; electromagnetic radiation and quantum electronics. **Mailing Address:** Fundamental Methods Assoc Inc, 678 Cedar Lawn Ave, Lawrence, NY 11559.

KLAHR, PHILIP, COMPUTER SCIENCE. **Personal Data:** b March 7, 1946; American citizen. **Education:** Univ Mich, BS, 1967; Univ Wis, MS, 1969, PhD (comput sci), 1975. **Professional Experience:** CONSULT, 1999-; vpres prof serv, Inference Corp, beginning 1986; dir, Info Processing Systs Prog, Rand Corp, 1978-1986; Sr analyst, Syst Develop Corp, 1972-1978. **Memberships:** Asn Comput Mach; Cognitive Sci Soc; Am Asn Artificial Intel; Inst Elec & Electronics Engrs. **Research Statement & Publications:** Artificial intelligence research in knowledge-based systems; rule-based modeling, simulation, languages; explanation techniques, man-machine interfaces, deductive question-answering, problem solving, learning, planning; abstraction, data-base management and cognitive modeling. **Mailing Address:** 473 Live Oak Dr, Mill Valley, CA 94941.

KLAHR, SAULO, NEPHROLOGY. **Personal Data:** b Santander, Colombia, June 8, 1935; American citizen; m 1965, Carol; c James & Robert. **Education:** Col de Santa Librada, BS, 1954; Nat Univ Colombia, MD, 1959. **Honors & Awards:** David M Hume Mem Award, 1992; Thomas Addis Award, Int Soc Renal Nutrit & Metab, 1996, President's Award, NKF, 1997, John P Peters Award, ASN, 1998 Fellow, Royal College of Physicians (London) 1999, American Kidney Fund Nat Torchbearer Award, 2002 Edward N Gibbs Award, NY Acad of Medicine, 2002. **Professional Experience:** Ed, Kidney Int, 1997-2005; Sr. Ed, Kidney Int, 2006- SIMON PROF MED, SCH MED, WASH UNIV, 1991-; co-chmn, Dept Med, 1991-1997; ed, Am Kidney Dis, 1991-1996; pres, Nate Kidney Found, 1988-1990; mem fel comt, Nat Kidney Found, 1977-1981 & chmn, 1980-1981; assoc ed, J Clin Invest, 1977-1982; physician, Barnes-Jewish Hosp, St Louis, Mo, 1975-; Kidney Found Eastern Mo & Metro East, 1973-1974; prof med & dir renal div, Wash Univ, 1972-1991; assoc physician, Barnes Hosp, St Louis, Mo, 1972-1975; mem adv comt, Artificial Kidney, Chronic Uremia Prog, Nat Inst Arthritis & Metab Dis, 1970-1978; established investr, Am Heart Asn, 1968-1973; asst physician, Barnes Hosp, St Louis, Mo, 1966-1972; from instr to assoc prof, Wash Univ, 1963-1972; USPHS trainee, Wash Univ, 1961-1963; chmn med adv bd & mem bd dirs. **Memberships:** NY Acad Sci; Am Physiol Soc; Biophys Soc; Am Soc Clin Invest; Assn Am Physicians. **Research Statement & Publications:** Hormonal control of ion transport across isolated membranes; studies on the functional and metabolic alterations produced by kidney disease; intermediary metabolism of the kidney. **Mailing Address:** Barnes- Jewish Hosp, Sch Med, Wash Univ, Ste 4300, 216 S KingsHwy Blvd, St Louis, MO 63110. **Fax:** 314-454-5110. **E-Mail:** sklahr@im.wustl.edu

KLAIBER, FRED WAYNE, STRUCTURAL ENGINEERING. **Personal Data:** b Lafayette, Ind, October 7, 1940; m 1964, Karen; c Brent & Kimberly K (Farmer). **Education:** Purdue Univ, BSCE, 1962, MSCE, 1964, PhD (struct eng), 1968. **Honors & Awards:** Raymond C Reese Res Prize, 1978. **Professional Experience:** ANSON MARSTON DISTINGUISHED PROF, COL ENG, IOWA STATE UNIV, as of 2004; ASCE Fel, 2001; ACI fel, 1987; PROF CIVIL ENG, IOWA STATE UNIV, 1968-; assoc prof, Iowa State Univ, 1968-1980; res engr, Caterpillar Tractor Co, 1968. **Memberships:** Am Soc Civil Engrs; Am Railway Eng Asn; Am Concrete Inst; Can Soc Civil Eng. **Research Statement & Publications:** Bridge rehabilitation and strengthening; prestressed folded plate theory; study of bridges behavior. **Mailing Address:** Dept Civil & Construct Eng, Iowa State Univ, Ames, IA 50011.

KLAIBER, GEORGE STANLEY, PHYSICS. **Personal Data:** b Toledo, Ohio, November 20, 1916; m 1944, c 2. **Education:** Univ Buffalo, BA, 1938; Univ Ill, MA, 1941, PhD (physics), 1943. **Professional Experience:** RETIRED; independent consult physicist, beginning 1967; consult physicist, Wurlitzer Co, 1960-1967; from asst prof to assoc prof physics, Univ Buffalo, 1947-1960; res physicist, Gen Elec Co, 1944-1947; from asst to instr, Univ Ill, 1939-1944; asst physics, Univ Buffalo, 1938-1939. **Memberships:** Am Phys Soc. **Research Statement & Publications:** Acoustics and vibrations. **Mailing Address:** 2504 Colvin Blvd, Tonawanda, NY 14150.

KLAINER, ALBERT S, INTERNAL MEDICINE, INFECTIOUS DISEASES. **Personal Data:** b Chelsea, Mass, October 29, 1935; m 1957, Jo-Ann; c Peter, Lori & Traci. **Education:** Mass Inst Technol, BS, 1957; Tufts Univ, MD, 1961. **Honors & Awards:** Hull Award, AMA, 1971, Morrissey Award, 1972 & Bronze Medal, 1972. **Professional Experience:** PROF CLIN MED, MORRISTOWN MEM HOSP, 1980-; CHMN, DEPT MED, MORRISTOWN MEM HOSP, 1975-; prof prof med, Med Sch, Rutgers Univ, beginning 1975; prof med & infectious dis, Sch Med, WVa Univ, 1972-1975; assoc prof med, Col Med, Ohio State Univ, 1971-1972; grant infectious dis & internal med, New Eng Med Ctr Hosps, 1963-1964. **Memberships:** Infectious Dis Soc Am; fel Am Col Physicians; Am Fedn Clin Res. **Research Statement & Publications:** Scanning electron microscopy; infectious diseases, antibiotic pharmacology and AIDS research. **Mailing Address:** Dept Med, Morristown Meml Hosp, 315 W 70th St, New York, NY 10023.

KLAINER, STANLEY M, INSTRUMENTATION, PHYSICAL & ANALYTICAL CHEMISTRY. **Personal Data:** b Chelsea, Mass, April 11, 1930; m 1952, c 6. **Education:** Clark Univ, BA, 1952, MA, 1955, PhD, 1959. **Professional Experience:** RETIRED; vpres, FiberChem Inc, as of 1994; pres, ST&E, Inc, beginning 1982; group mgr, Lawrence Berkeley Lab, 1981-1982; tech consult laser spectroscopy, ST&E, Inc, beginning 1978; dep group leader Geoscience, Lawrence Berkeley Lab, 1978-1981; mgr anal systs dept, Block Eng, Inc, 1970-1978; staff chemist, Block Eng, Inc, 1967-1970; from res & develop mgr to res mgr, Tracerlab Div, Lab for Electronics, Inc, 1964-1967; spec projs mgr instruments, Tracerlab Div, Lab for Electronics, Inc, 1963-1964; sr chemist, Tracerlab Div, Lab for Electronics, Inc, 1961-1963; sr chemist, Nat Res Corp, 1960-1961; chemist, Res Labs, Bendix Corp, 1959-1960; res coordr qual control, Martin Div, Martin Marietta Corp, 1957-1959; Joseph F Donnelly fel, 1955. **Memberships:** Am Chem Soc; Soc Appl Spectros; Soc Photo-Optical Engrs; Combustion Inst. **Research Statement & Publications:** Development of optical, RF and microwave spectrometers and nuclear instruments; analysis of trace atmospheric constituents, ablation, encapsulation, special quality control analytical techniques and ultracentrifugation; interferometry; Raman, remote Raman, micro Raman and infrared spectroscopy; nuclear quadrupole resonance; micro particle analysis; chemical transport in natural systems; fiber optical chemical sensors for environmental and chemical measurements; medical, biological diagnostics and process control; surface chemistry and structure studies. **Mailing Address:** FiberChem Inc, 1181 Grier Dr # B, Las Vegas, NV 89119-3746.

KLAMKIN, MURRAY S, mathematics; deceased, see previous edition for last biography

KLAND, MATHILDE JUNE, ENVIRONMENTAL CHEMISTRY, FOSSIL FUEL CHEMISTRY. **Personal Data:** b Chicago, Ill, June 6, 1916; m 1950, c 2. **Education:** Univ Chicago, BS, 1939; Northwestern Univ, PhD (org chem), 1948. **Professional Experience:** Writer, environ chem-toxicol, 1986-; CONSULT, HEALTH EFFECTS CHEMS, 1982-; staff scientist, Lawrence Berkeley Lab, Univ Calif, 1958-1982; res assoc, Med Sch, Tufts Univ, 1954-1956; writer & abstractor, 1952-1954 & 1956-1958; res assoc, Boston Univ, 1951-1952; E I du Pont fel, Ohio State Univ, 1949-1951; Dupont fel, Ohio State Univ, 1949-1951; asst prof chem, Goucher Col, 1948-1949; Univ fel, Allied chem & dye fel, 1945-1946; Univ fel, Northwestern Univ, 1944-1945; sr chemist, Revere & La Ord Divs, 1941-1943; Sr chemist, Distillation Prods, Inc, NY, 1939-1941; environ consult, Environ Asn. **Memberships:** AAAS; Am Chem Soc; NY Acad Sci; Asn Women Sci. **Research Statement & Publications:** Reactions of styrene oxide; structure of styrene oxide dimers; molecular structure and spectra of organic compounds; abnormal bimolecular reactions of furfuryl chloride; grignard reactions; radiation chemistry of peptides; water pollution monitoring of bio-parameters and organics; toxic effects of pollutants, food additives, pesticides and drugs; use of structure-toxicity/carcinogenicity relationships in prediction of health effects chemical teratogens/pesticedes; fossil fuel chemistry; teratogenicity of pesticides and other environmental pollutants. **Mailing Address:** 3678 Hastings Ct, Lafayette, CA 94549-3020.

KLANDERMAN, BRUCE HOLMES, ORGANIC CHEMISTRY, ENVIRONMENTAL SCIENCES. **Personal Data:** b Grand Rapids, Mich, February 27, 1938; m 1960, Alice; c Thomas J, David B & Paul W. **Education:** Calvin Col, AB, 1959; Univ Ill, MS, 1961, PhD (org chem), 1963. **Professional Experience:** RETIRED; sr prog mgr, Radian Corp, 1992-1998; dir, Health Environ Labs, 1988-1992; dir, Occup Health Lab, 1987; dir, Environ Tech Serv, Kodak Park Div, 1981-1986; govt regulations coordr, Gen Mgt, 1978-1980; dept head, Synthetic Chem Div, 1976-1977; tech assoc, Synthetic Chem Div, 1975; res assoc, Eastman Kodak Co, 1968-1974; sr res chemist, Eastman Kodak Co, 1964-1968; res chemist, Eastman Kodak Co, 1963-1964. **Memberships:** Am Chem Soc. **Research Statement & Publications:** Benzyne chemistry; liquid crystals; organic semiconductors; aliphatic diazonium chemistry; anthracene and triptycene chemistry. **Mailing Address:** 31 Shadow Pines Dr, Penfield, NY 14526.

KLAPPER, DAVID G, MICROBIOLOGY, IMMUNOLOGY. **Personal Data:** b New York, NY, March 15, 1944. **Education:** Tulane Univ, BS, 1965; Univ Fla, PhD (microbiol & immunol), 1972. **Professional Experience:** PROF MICROBIOL & IMMUNOL, MED SCH, UNIV NC, as of 2002; prof microbiol & immunol, Rockefeller Univ, Univ Tex Southwestern Med Sch. **Mailing Address:** Dept Microbiol & Immunol, Med Sch Univ NC CB No 7290, Chapel Hill, NC 27599-7290. **Fax:** 919-962-8103. **E-Mail:** dgk501@med.unc.edu

KLAPPER, GILBERT, PALEONTOLOGY. **Personal Data:** b Wichita, Kans, September 29, 1934; m 2002, c 3. **Education:** Stanford Univ, BS, 1956; Univ Kans, MS, 1958; Univ Iowa, PhD (geol), 1962. **Professional Experience:** PROF EMER GEOL, UNIV IOWA, 1998-present; Vis prof, Univ of Chicago, 1989; Vis prof, Ore State Univ, 1978; PROF GEOL, UNIV IOWA, 1973-1998; assoc prof, Univ Iowa, 1968-1973; res paleontol, Res Ctr, Pan Am Petrol Corp, 1963-1968; NSF fel & res assoc, Ill State Geol Surv, 1962-1963; Paleontol, Shell Oil Co, La, 1958-1959. **Memberships:** Paleont Res Inst; Paleont Soc; Soc Econ Paleont & Mineral; Brit Paleont Asn. **Research Statement & Publications:** Micropaleontology, research in conodonts; biostratigraphy and taxonomy, primarily of Devonian age. **Mailing Address:** 1010 Eastwood Rd, Glencoe, IL 60022. **E-Mail:** g-klapper@northwestern.edu

KLAPPER, ISAAC, MATHEMATICS. **Education:** NY Univ, PhD (maths), 1991. **Professional Experience:** PROF, DEPT MATH, MONT STATE UNIV, as of 2005. **Memberships:** Am Math Asn. **Mailing Address:** Math Dept, Montana State Univ, Bozeman, MT 59717. **Fax:** 406-994-1789. **E-Mail:** klapper@math.montana.edu

KLAPPER, JACOB, COMMUNICATIONS SYSTEMS, PHASE-LOCKED LOOPS. **Personal Data:** b Ulanow, Poland, September 17, 1930; American citizen; m 1958, Molly Teicher; c Rachele H & Robert D. **Education:** City Col New York, BEE, 1956; Columbia Univ, MS, 1958; NY Univ, EngScD, 1965. **Honors & Awards:** Region One Award, Inst Elec & Electronics Engrs, 1986. **Professional Experience:** Chmn dept, Elec Eng Dept, NJ Inst Technol, Newark, 1986-1992; PROF, ELEC ENG DEPT, NJ INST TECHNOL, NEWARK, 1971-; assoc prof elec eng, Newark Col Eng, 1967-1971; sr proj mem tech staff, Adv Commun Labs, Radio Corp Am, 1965-1967; sr mem tech staff, Adv Commun Labs, Radio Corp Am, 1960-1965; proj engr, Fed Sci Corp, 1959-1960; lectr elec eng, City Col New York, 1956-1959; Elec engr, Columbia Broadcasting Syst, 1952-1956; consult, var orgn. **Memberships:** Sr mem Inst Elec & Electronics Engrs; Commun Soc; Eng Med & Biol Soc. **Research Statement & Publications:** Electrical communication; systems and techniques with emphasis on phase-locked loops and FM systems. **Mailing Address:** NJ InstTechnol, 323 King Blvd, Newark, NJ 07102. **Fax:** 973-596-5680. **E-Mail:** klapper@admin.njit.edu

KLAPPER, MICHAEL H, BIOCHEMISTRY, BIOPHYSICS. **Personal Data:** b Berlin, Ger, June 10, 1937; American citizen; m 1960, c 2. **Education:** Harvard Univ, AB, 1958; Univ Rochester, MS, 1959; Univ Calif, PhD (biochem), 1964. **Professional Experience:** PROF EMER CHEM, OHIO STATE UNIV, as of 2004; co-dir, Nat Ctr Sci Teaching & Learning, 1990; prof chem, Ohio State Univ, beginning 1986; from asst prof to assoc prof, Ohio State Univ, 1966-1986; fel chem, Northwestern Univ, 1964-1966. **Memberships:** Biophys Soc; Am Soc Biol Chemists; Protein Soc; Am Chem Soc; AAAS. **Research Statement & Publications:** Physical biochemistry of enzyme structure; theoretical and experimental studies of enzyme catalysis; long range electron transfer in polypeptides and proteins; fast radical reactions. **Mailing Address:** Chem Dept, Ohio State Univ, 120 W 18th Ave, Columbus, OH 43210-1328. **Fax:** 614-292-1585. **E-Mail:** klapper.1@osu.edu

KLAPPROTH, WILLIAM JACOB, POLYMER CHEMISTRY. **Personal Data:** b Springfield, Ohio, August 2, 1920; m 1945, c 2. **Education:** Wittenberg Col, AB, 1942; Univ Chicago, MS & PhD (org chem), 1949. **Professional Experience:** RETIRED; consult, 1981-1983; prin scientist, Arco Chem Co, 1979-1981; sr group mgr, Monroeville Res Ctr, Arco Polymers Inc, 1970-1978; sr proj scientist, Monroeville Res Ctr, Arco Polymers Inc, 1967-1970; tech dir, Bridgeville Plant, Koppers Co Inc, 1963-1967; mgr acids & miscellaneous chems develop, Bridgeville Plant, 1959-1963; group leader catalytic & gen process improv, Bridgeville Plant, 1957-1959; group leader, Warners Plant, 1954-1957; res chemist, Stamford Res Labs, Am Cyanamid Co, 1949-1954. **Memberships:** Am Chem Soc. **Research Statement & Publications:** Research and development in polymers, especially polystyrene, high pressure polyethylene and related copolymers. **Mailing Address:** 3576 Logans Ferry Rd, Murrysville, PA 15668.

KLARFELD, JOSEPH, THEORETICAL PHYSICS. **Personal Data:** b Poland, December 22, 1935; c 2. **Education:** Israel Inst Technol, BSc, 1959, MSc, 1962; Yeshiva Univ, PhD (physics), 1969. **Professional Experience:** ASSOC PROF, GRAD CTR, CITY UNIV NY, 1980-; res fel, City Univ New York, 1978-1979; vis assoc prof, Tel Aviv Univ, 1978-1979; dep chmn dept, Queen's Col, NY, 1976-1978; assoc prof physics, QueensCol, NY, 1974; asst chmn dept, Queen's Col, NY, 1969-1976; asst prof, Queen's Col, NY, 1969-1973; res assoc, Israel Atomic Energy Comn, 1961-1963; instr physics, Israel Inst Technol, 1958-1961. **Memberships:** Asn Math Physics; Am Phys Soc; NY Acad Sci; Int Soc Gen Relativity & Gravitation. **Research Statement & Publications:** Quantization of general relativity; foundations of quantum field theory; relativistic astrophysics. **Mailing Address:** Dept Physics, Queen's Col, 6530 Kissena Blvd, Flushing, NY 11367.

KLARMAN, HERBERT E, medical administration; deceased, see previous edition for last biography

KLARMAN, KARL J(OSEPH), ELECTRICAL ENGINEERING. **Personal Data:** b Scotia, NY, March 18, 1922; c Nancy L & James D. **Education:** Union Col, BS, 1944; Columbia Univ, MS, 1947. **Professional Experience:** CONSULT, 1974-; eng scientist, Govt & Com Div, RCA Corp, 1971-1974; eng scientist, Defense Electronic Prod Div, 1961-1974; chief prod engr, Precision Prod Dept, Northrop, 1959-1961; sect head, Sanders Assocs, 1957-1959; vpres, Electro Tec Corp, 1955-1957; dir eng, Electro Tec Corp, 1953-1955; plant mgr, Electro Tec Corp, 1951-1953; Eclipse-Pioneer Div, Bendix Aviation Corp, 1947-1951; proj engr, Avion Instrument Corp, 1946-1947; lectr elec eng, Union Univ, NY, 1945-1946; Jr engr, Carl L Norden, Inc, 1944. **Memberships:** Sigma Xi; Sr mem Inst Elec & Electronics Engrs. **Research Statement & Publications:** Gyroscopic instruments, design, development and production; design, development, test and production of inertial and other electro-mechanical instruments and systems; grantedtwo patents, gyroscopic devices. **Mailing Address:** 20 Kipling St, Nashua, NH 03062.

KLARMAN, WILLIAM L, RESEARCH ADMINISTRATION. **Personal Data:** b Moweaqua, Ill, September 21, 1935; m Virginia; c Caren, Steven & Douglas. **Education:** Eastern Ill Univ, BS, 1957; Univ Ill, MS, 1960, PhD (plant path), 1962. **Professional Experience:** ACAD COOD, CENTENNIAL CAMPUS, NC STATE UNIV, 1993-; interim vchancellor res, Centennial Campus, NC State Univ, 1990-1993; dept head plant path, Centennial Campus, NC State Univ, 1984-1990; dept head plant path, Okla State Univ, 1980-1984; plant path, USDA, 1980; counr, Am Phytopath Soc, 1976-1980; Fullbright prof, 1974-1975; from asst prof to prof plant path, Univ Md, 1962-1980. **Memberships:** Am Phytopath Soc; AAAS. **Mailing Address:** Holladay Hall Box 7003, NC State Univ, Raleigh, NC 27695-7003. **Fax:** 919-515-7745. **E-Mail:** wklarman@cals1.cals.ncsu.edu

KLARMANN, JOSEPH, PHYSICS. **Personal Data:** b Berlin, Ger, January 16, 1928; m 1957, Erika; c A Daniel & Peter R. **Education:** Hebrew Univ, Israel, MSc, 1954; Univ Rochester, PhD (physics), 1958. **Professional Experience:** PROF EMER PHYSICS, WASH UNIV, 1996-; from asst prof to prof, Wash Univ, 1961-1996; instr, Univ Rochester, 1958-1961; res assoc & instr, Univ Rochester, 1957-1958. **Memberships:** Int Astron Union; Am Phys Soc. **Research Statement & Publications:** Cosmic ray astrophysics. **Mailing Address:** Dept Physics, Wash Univ, PO Box 1105, One Brookings Dr, St Louis, MO 63130. **Fax:** 314-935-6219. **E-Mail:** jkl@wuphys.wustl.edu

KLARSTROM, DWAINE L, METALLURGY. **Professional Experience:** DIR, RES & DEVELOP, HAYNES INT INC, as of 2005. **Memberships:** Am Soc Metals. **Mailing Address:** Haynes Int Inc Tech Dept, PO Box 9013 1020 W Park Ave, Kokomo, IN 46904-9013. **E-Mail:** dlklarstrom@haynesintl.com

KLASINC, LEO, MOLECULAR SPECTROSCOPY, ATMOSPHERIC CHEMISTRY. **Personal Data:** b Zagreb, Croatia, May 20, 1937; m 1961, Darka Jerkovic; c Natasa & Anton-Jan. **Education:** Univ Zagreb, dipl chem, 1960, PhD (chem), 1963. **Honors & Awards:** Ruder Boskovic Prize, Repub Croatia, 1988. **Professional Experience:** PROF CHEM, RUDJER BOSKOVIC INST, as of 2004; VIS PROF, DEPT CHEM, LA STATE UNIV, as of 2001; PROF FAC SCI, UNIV ZAGREB, 1979-; sr scientist, Ruder Boskovic Inst, Zagreb, 1977-; sr res assoc, Ruder Boskovic Inst, Zagreb, 1972-1977; from asst prof to assoc prof, Univ Zagreb, 1971-1979; res assoc, Ruder Boskovic Inst, Zagreb, 1968-1972; fel theoret & radiation chem, Nuclear Res Ctr, Karlsruhe, 1966-1968; res asst phys chem, Ruder Boskovic Inst, Zagreb, 1964-1968 & 1961-1963; vis prof, Dept Chem, La State Univ. **Memberships:** Am Phys Soc; Int Soc Quantum Biol; World Asn Theoret Org Chemists; Am Chem Soc; Croatia Chem Soc; Croatia Acad Sci & Arts; NY Acad Sci. **Research Statement & Publications:** Electronically excited states of molecules and ions, spectroscopy, quantum chemistry, photochemistry and chemical kinetics; chemical processes in the atmosphere, photosmog and troposphere ozone formation. **Mailing Address:** Rudjer Boskovic Inst, PO Box 1016, Zagreb, HR, 10001 Croatia. **Fax:** 385-468-0967. **E-Mail:** klasinc@joker.irb.hr

KLASING, KIRK C, BIOLOGY. **Education:** Purdue Univ, BS, 1977, MS, 1979; Cornell Univ, PhD, 1982. **Professional Experience:** PROF, DEPT ANIMAL SCI, UNIV CALIF, as of 2006. **Mailing Address:** Dept Animal Sci, Univ Calif, Davis, CA 95616. **Fax:** 530-752-0175. **E-Mail:** kcklasing@ucdavis.edu

KLASNER, JOHN SAMUEL, STRUCTURAL GEOLOGY, APPLIED GEOPHYSICS. **Personal Data:** b Flint, Mich, June 22, 1935; m 1964, Gretchen; c Christopher J, Frederick L, Laura M & Paul H. **Education:** Mich State Univ, BS, 1957, MS, 1964; Mich Technol Univ, PhD (geol), 1972. **Professional Experience:** PROF EMER GEOL, WESTERN Ill UNIV, as of 2001; dir hons prog, Western Ill Univ, 1994-1998; geologist econgeol, US Geol Surv, beginning 1992; assoc dir hons prog, Western Ill Univ, 1990-1993; chmn dept, Western Ill Univ, 1974-1978; prof geol, Western Ill Univ, beginning 1972; from asst prof to assoc prof geol, Western Ill Univ, 1972-1979; geophysicist, Standard Oil Co Calif, 1964-1969; geophys engr, Geophys Serv Inc, 1957-1962. **Memberships:** Sigma Xi; fel Geol Soc Am; Soc Explor Geophysicists; fel Geol Asn Can; Am Geophys Union; Nat Asn Geol Teachers. **Research Statement & Publications:** Economic and Precambrian geology of Northern Michigan; structural geology and tectonics of Northern Michigan and Wisconsin; geophysical archeology; regional geophysics Northern Michigan, Wisconsin, North and South Dakota. **Mailing Address:** Dept Geol, Western Ill Univ, 900 W Adams St, Macomb, IL 61455-1396. **Fax:** 309-298-2400. **E-Mail:** js-klasner@wiu.edu

KLASS, DONALD LEROY, ORGANIC CHEMISTRY & EDUCATOR, ENERGY & ENVIRONMENTAL SCIENTIST & INVENTOR. **Personal Data:** b Waukegan, Ill, July 23, 1926; m 1949, Barbara; c Richard R, Janet J (Grubbs) & Roger R. **Education:** Univ Ill, BS, 1951; Harvard Univ, AM, 1952, PhD (org chem), 1955. **Honors & Awards:** Nat Lubricating Grease Inst Award, 1966; Mem Award, Foote Chem Co, 1966; Clarence E Earl Mem Award, 1966; Richard A Glenn Award, Bituminous Coal Res, Inc, 1976. **Professional Experience:** DIR RES, ENTECH INT INC, 1992-; pres biolmass energy res assoc, beginning 1985; vis prof, EChina Univ Chem Technol, 1988; bd mem, Biomass Energy Res Asn, beginning 1985; tech ed, J Solar Energy Eng, 1983-1989; vpres educ, Inst Gas Technol, Ill Inst Technol, 1980-1992; asst vpres, Inst Gas Technol, Ill Inst Technol, 1979-1980; dir eng & sci res, Inst Gas Technol, Ill Inst Technol, 1977-1979; dir basic res, Inst Gas Technol, Ill Inst Technol, 1976-1977; asst res dir, Inst Gas Technol, Ill Inst Technol, 1969-1976; adj prof chem, Ill Inst Technol, 1967-1972; asst dir basic res, Inst Gas Technol, Ill Inst Technol, 1965-1969; dir process & prod res div, Pure Oil Co, Ill, 1959-1965; res chemist, Stand Oil Co, Ind, 1954-1955 & Am Can Co, 1956-1959; consult energy & chem prod. **Memberships:** Am Chem Soc; Biomass Energy Res Asn; Am Inst Chem Eng. **Research Statement & Publications:** Research and education administration; gas processing; petrochemicals; refining; catalysis; fermentation; waste treatment; pollution control; gasification-liquefaction of wastes, biomass and fossil fuels; energy supplies; environmental sciences and engineering; author of over 170 technical papers and granted numerous US and foreign patents. **Mailing Address:** 25543 W Scott Rd, Barrington, IL 60010. **Fax:** 847-382-5595. **E-Mail:** entechinternational@excite.com

KLASS, MICHAEL J, MATHEMATICS. **Professional Experience:** PROF, DEPT MATH, UNIV CALIF, BERKELEY, as of 2002. **Mailing Address:** Dept Statist, Univ Calif, 970 Evans Hall, Berkeley, CA 94720-3840. **E-Mail:** klass@stat.berkeley.edu

KLASS, MICHAEL R, EXPERIMENTAL BIOLOGY, MOLECULAR BIOLOGY. **Personal Data:** b Green Bay, Wis, July 31, 1949; m 1992, Dori; c 4. **Education:** Univ Wis-Madison, BS, 1971; Univ Wyo, Laramie, PhD (cell biol), 1974. **Professional Experience:** INTERIM DIR, CORP MOLECULAR BIOL, ABBOTT LABS, 1990-; NEW BUS VENTURE, as of 2002; R&D dir, new business develop, diagnostics division, Abbott labs, 1999-2001; lab head biochem genetics, Corp Molecular Biol, Abbott Labs, 1986-1990; res career develop award, NIH, 1984; from asst prof to assoc prof biol, Univ Houston, 1979-1986; res assoc, Dept Molecular, Cellular & Develop Biol, Univ Colo, 1974-1979; postdoctoral fel develop genetics, Univ Colo, 1974-1979; res asst, Dept Zool, Univ Wyo, 1972-1974. **Research Statement & Publications:** Molecular biology of diagnostic methods for the detection of various disease states including; infectious diseases, cancer and spongiform encephalopathics, molecular biology of aging and development. **Mailing Address:** Dept Molecular Biol, Abbott Labs, 100D9RB RIB/NC Bldg AP 20 Abbott Park Rd, Abbott Park, IL 60064. **Fax:** 847-937-1219. **E-Mail:** michael.klass@abbott.com

KLASS, PHILIP J, electrical engineering; deceased, see previous edition for last biography

KLASSEN, DAVID MORRIS, INORGANIC CHEMISTRY, SPECTROSCOPY. **Personal Data:** b Clovis, NMex, June 15, 1939; m 1965, Jan; c Kenneth & Christine. **Education:** Univ Tex, El Paso, BS, 1961; Univ NMex, PhD (phys chem), 1967. **Professional Experience:** PROF CHEM, MCMURRY UNIV, 1977-; from asst prof to assoc prof, Mcmurry Univ, 1969-1977; res assoc, Univ NC, Chapel Hill, 1967-1969; NATO res fel, Inst Phys Chem, Frankfurt, WGer, 1966-1967; teaching asst, Univ NMex, 1961-1962. **Memberships:** Am Chem Soc; Sigma Xi Sci Res Soc Am. **Research Statement & Publications:** Synthesis, bonding and electronic structure of transition-metal complexes; luminescence of ruthenium and osmium complexes. **Mailing Address:** Dept Chem, McMurry Univ, PO Box 158 S 218 McMurry Sta, Abilene, TX 79697. **E-Mail:** dklassen@mcm.edu

KLASSEN, J(OHN), CHEMICAL ENGINEERING. **Personal Data:** b Waterloo, Ont, January 9, 1928; m 1950, c 4. **Education:** Queen's Univ, Ont, BSc, 1948, MSc, 1949; Univ Wis, PhD (chem eng), 1954. **Professional Experience:** SR ENG SPECIALIST, DU PONT CAN, 1975-; tech mgr, Cent Res Lab, Maitland, 1971-1975; mgr, Cent Res Lab, Maitland, 1969-1971; asst works mgr, Du Pont Can, 1966-1969; tech mgr, Du Pont Can, 1962-1966; tech supt, Du Pont Can, 1959-1962; res supvr, Du Pont Can, 1957-1959; res engr, Du Pont Can, 1955-1957; asst res officer, chem eng, Nat Res Coun Can, 1953-1955; Jr res officer, chem eng, Nat Res Coun Can, 1949-1953. **Memberships:** Can Soc Chem Engrs; fel Chem Inst Can. **Research Statement & Publications:** Commercial processing of industrial chemicals. **Mailing Address:** Champaign Reg Col, St Lawrence Campus 790 Neree-Tremblay St, Ste Foy, PQ G1V 4K2, Can.

KLASSEN, LYNELL W, RHEUMATOLOGY, TRANSPLANT IMMUNOLOGY. **Personal Data:** b Gossel, Kans, January 24, 1947; m 1967, c 4. **Education:** Tabor Col, Hillsboro, Kans, AB, 1969; Univ Kans, Kansas City, MD, 1973. **Professional Experience:** PROF & CHAIR, INTERNAL MED, UNIV OF NE MED CTR (UNMC) 2005 - PRESENT; PROF & VICE CHMN INTERNAL MED, UNMC, 1990-; mem, Educ Coun, Am Col Rheumatology, 1989-; chmn, Sci Rev Comt, Nat Inst Alchol Abuse, Alcoholism, 1989-; CHIEF, ARTHRITIS SERV RHEUMAT, OMAHA VET ADMIN, 1982-; assoc prof rheumat & immunol, Arthritis Serv Rheumat, Omaha Vet Admin, 1982-1990; asst prof, Univ Iowa Hosps & Clins, 1978-1982; chief resident internal med, Univ Iowa Hosps & Clins, 1977-1978; res assoc immunol, Arthritis & Rheumatism Br, NIH, 1975-1977; Resident internal med, Univ Iowa Hosps & Clins, 1973-1975. **Memberships:** Am Col Physicians; Am Asn Immunol. **Research Statement & Publications:** Mechanisms of hematopoietic allograft rejection; pathophysiology of graft-versus-host disease; use of cytotoxic therapy in non-malignant diseases. **Mailing Address:** Dept Internal Med, Univ Neb Med Ctr, 983332 Nebr Medical Center, Omaha, NE 68198-3332. **Fax:** 402-559-6114. **E-Mail:** lklassen@unmc.edu

KLASSEN, NORMAN VICTOR, RADIATION CHEMISTRY, DOSIMETRY. **Personal Data:** b Winnipeg, Man, November 6, 1933; m 1961, c 3. **Education:** McGill Univ, BSc, 1954, PhD (chem), 1957; Univ Col, London, PhD (chem), 1961. **Professional Experience:** SR RES OFFICER, INST FOR NATIONAL MEASUREMENT STAND, NAT RES COUN CAN, as of 2004; mem res staff, Inst Nat Measurement Stand, Nat Rescoun Can, beginning 1966; fel phys chem, Mellon Inst, 1963-1966; fel, Nat Res Coun Can, 1961-1963. **Memberships:** Fel Chem Inst Can; Radiation Res Soc. **Research Statement & Publications:** Radiation chemistry; radiation biology; dosimetry. **Mailing Address:** Int Nat Measurement Stand, Nat Res Coun Can, Rm X-34 Build M-35, 1200 Montreal Rd, Ottawa, ON K1A 0R6, Can. **Fax:** 613-952-9865. **E-Mail:** norman.klassen@nrc-cnrc.gc.ca

KLASSEN, RUDOLPH WALDEMAR, GEOLOGY. **Personal Data:** b Hanna, Alta, September 30, 1928; m 1967, Carmel Despins; c 4. **Education:** Univ Alta, BSc, 1959, MSc, 1960; Univ Sask, PhD (geol), 1965. **Professional Experience:** EMER RES SCIENTIST, GEOL SURV CAN, 1994-; Lectr, Univ Calgary, 1974-1986; Res scientist quaternary geol, Geol Surv Can, 1965-1994. **Memberships:** Geol Asn Can; Am Quaternary Asn; Can Quaternary Asn. **Research Statement & Publications:** Quaternary stratigraphy and geomorphology; reports and maps on Quaternary geology of Manitoba, Southern Saskatchewan, Northern Northwest Territories and Southern Yukon published mainly by Geological Survey of Canada; current studies of Tertiary and Quaternary geomorphology and stratigraphy of Cypress Lake and Wood Mountain areas Southwestern Saskatchewan. **Mailing Address:** Geol Surv Can, 3303 33rd St NW, Calgary, AB T2L 2A7, Can.

KLASSEN, VURYL J, MATHEMATICS. **Education:** Butler Univ, BA; Univ Ariz, MS, PhD. **Professional Experience:** PROF DEPT MATH, CALIF STATE UNIV, FULLERTON, as of 2001. **Mailing Address:** Dept Math, Calif State Univ, MH-182E McCarthy Hall 154, Fullerton, CA 92834. **E-Mail:** vjklassen@fullerton.edu

KLASSEN, VYRON M, MATHEMATICS. **Education:** Butler Univ, BA; Va Polytech Inst & State Univ, MS, PhD. **Professional Experience:** PROF EMER DEPT MATH, CALIF STATE UNIV, 2003-; adj prof, Dept Math, Calif State Univ, Fullerton, as of 2001. **Mailing Address:** Dept Math, Calif State Univ, McCarthy Hall 154, Fullerton, CA 92834. **E-Mail:** wleonard@fullerton.edu

KLASSEN, WALDEMAR, ENTOMOLOGY, GENETICS. **Personal Data:** b Vauxhall, Alta, December 28, 1935; American citizen; m 1964, c 1. **Education:** Univ Alta, BSc, 1957, MSc, 1959; Univ Western Ont, PhD (zool), 1963. **Honors & Awards:** Dipl & Medal, Int Cong Plant Protection, 1975. **Professional Experience:** STAFF SCIENTIST PEST MGT, AGR RES SERV, USDA, 1972-; asst to dep adminr plant sci & entom, Metab & Radiation Res Lab, Entom Res Div, 1970-1972; leader insect physiol & metab sect, Metab & Radiation Res Lab, Entom Res Div, 1967-1970; res geneticist, Metab & Radiation Res Lab, Entom Res Div, 1965-1967; USPHS res assoc zool, Univ Ill, 1963-1965. **Memberships:** AAAS; Entom Soc Am; Am Chem Soc; Genetics Soc Can; Sigma Xi. **Research Statement & Publications:** Dispersal of mosquitoes; inheritance of resistance to insecticides in mosquitoes; cytogenetics of mosquitoes; chemosterilization of insects; program planning in entomological research; insect population dynamics. **Mailing Address:** PO Box 200, 1220 Wagramerstr S, Vienna, A-1400, Austria.

KLATT, ARTHUR RAYMOND, PLANT BREEDING, GENETICS. **Personal Data:** b Hamilton, Tex, June 10, 1943; m 1980, c 5. **Education:** Tex Tech Univ, BS, 1966; Colo State Univ, MS, 1968, PhD (plant breeding & genetics), 1969. **Professional Experience:** PROF PLANT & SOIL SCI, OKLA STATE UNIV, 1999-; asst dean, int prog, Okla State Univ, 1988-1992; assoc dir, Wheat Prog Int Maize & Wheat Improv Ctr, 1979-1987; plant breeder, 1969-1979. **Memberships:** Am Soc Agron; Crop Sci Soc Am; Am Genetic Asn; AAAS; Weed Sci Soc Am. **Research Statement & Publications:** Genetics and environmental factors affecting drought tolerance; genetics and environmental influence on dormancy vernalization and winterhardiness; incorporation of horizontal resistance; breeding adapted high yielding winter and spring wheat varieties. **Mailing Address:** Dept Plant & Soil Sci, Okla State Univ, 368 Agr Hall, Stillwater, OK 74078-6028. **Fax:** 405-744-5269. **E-Mail:** aklatt@okstate.edu

KLATT, GARY BRANDT, MATHEMATICS. **Personal Data:** b Milwaukee, Wis, November 22, 1939; m 1964, c 2. **Education:** Case Western Res Univ, BS, 1961; Univ Wis, MS, 1962, PhD (math), 1969. **Professional Experience:** PROF EMER MATH & COMPUT SCI, UNIV WIS, WHITEWATER, 1999-; prof math, Univ wis, Whitewater, beginning 1975; from asst prof to assoc prof, Univ Wis, Whitewater, 1967-1975; Instr math, Marquette Univ, 1964-1965. **Memberships:** Math Asn Am; Nat Coun Teachers Math. **Research Statement & Publications:** Theory of rings and modules. **Mailing Address:** Dept Math & Comput Sci, Univ Wis, Baker Hall 331 800 W Main St, Whitewater, WI 53190. **Fax:** 262-472-1372. **E-Mail:** klattg@mail.uww.edu

KLATT, LEON NICHOLAS, CHEMICAL INSTRUMENTATION. **Personal Data:** b Underhill, Wis, August 28, 1940; m 1961, c 2. **Education:** Univ Wis, Oshkosh, BS, 1962; Univ Wis-Madison, PhD (anal chem), 1967. **Professional Experience:** SITE MGR, ORNL CAA PROG, as of 1998; LEADER, DIM, ORNL, as of 1998; RES STAFF MEM, OAK RIDGE NAT LAB, 1974-; asst prof chem, Southern Ill Univ, 1967-1969 & Univ Ga, 1969-1974; asst, Univ Wis-Madison, 1963-1966; Chemist, Dow Chem Co, Mich, 1962-1963. **Memberships:** Am Chem Soc; Sigma Xi; AAAS; SAS. **Research Statement & Publications:** Instrumentation for remote analyses; on-line control of instruments with small computers; multi variable data reduction systems; application of small computers to analytical problems; process monitor and control systems. **Mailing Address:** Oak Ridge Nat Lab CAA Prog, Oak Ridge, TN 37831.

KLATTE, EUGENE, RADIOLOGY. **Personal Data:** b Indianapolis, Ind, March 19, 1928; m 1950, c 4. **Education:** Ind Univ, BA, 1949, MD, 1952. **Professional Experience:** DISTINGUISHED PROF EMER, RADIOL DEPT, SCH MED, IND UNIV, INDIANAPOLIS, beginning 1980; prof, Sch Med, Ind Univ, Indianapolis, 1971-1980; clin prof, Meharry Med Col, 1964-1971; prof & chmn dept, Sch Med, Vanderbilt Univ, 1962-1971; consult, Vet Admin Hosp, Nashville, Tenn, 1962-1971; from instr to assoc prof, Sch Med, Ind Univ, 1958-1962; Picker res scholar, Sch Med, Ind Univ, 1957-1958; resident radiol, Univ Calif, 1955-1957. **Memberships:** Am Col Radiol; Asn Univ Radiol; Radiol Soc NAm; Soc Pediat Radiol; AMA. **Research Statement & Publications:** Diagnostic radiology, especially cardiovascular radiology. **Mailing Address:** Riley Hosp C, Ind Univ Med Ctr 1053 702 Barnhill Dr, Indianapolis, IN 46202-5202.

KLATZO, IGOR, NEUROPATHOLOGY. **Professional Experience:** HEAD CEREBROVASC PATHOPHYSIOL SECT, NAT INST NEUROL DISORDERS & STROKE, NIH, 1991-. **Mailing Address:** 10101 Grosvenor Pl No 1214, Rockville, MD 20852.

KLAUBER, MELVILLE ROBERTS, PUBLIC HEALTH & EPIDEMIOLOGY. **Personal Data:** b San Diego, Calif, August 9, 1933; m 1953, Sylvia; c 6. **Education:** Stanford Univ, AB, 1954, MS, 1956, PhD (statist), 1964. **Professional Experience:** ADJ PROF EMER FAMILY & PREVENTATIVE MED, SCH MED, UNIV CALIF, LA JOLLA, as of 2004; adj prof family & preventative med, Sch Med, Univ Calif, La Jolla, beginning 1981; prin statistician, Sch Med, Univ Calif, LA Jolla, 1978-1981; adj prof math, Univ Utah, 1976-1978; adj assoc prof math, Univ Utah, 1972-1976; from asst prof to prof family & community med & chief, Div Biostatist, Col Med, Univ Utah, 1967-1978. **Memberships:** Am Statist Asn; Biomet Soc. **Research Statement & Publications:** Biostatistics; statistical methods for the medical sciences, especially epidemiology. **Mailing Address:** Dept Family & Preventative Med, Sch Med, Univ Calif, La Jolla, CA 92093-0816. **E-Mail:** mklauber@ucsd.edu

KLAUBERT, DIETER HEINZ, MEDICINAL CHEMISTRY. **Personal Data:** b Ger, December 15, 1944; Canadian citizen; m 1969, c 2. **Education:** Univ Alta, BSc, 1967; Mass Inst Technol, PhD (org chem), 1971. **Professional Experience:** VPRES,

PROMEGA BIOSCIENCE INC, as of 2006; res chemist, Wyeth Labs Inc, Am Home Prod Corp, beginning 1973; fel org chem, Univ Calif, Berkeley, 1971-1973. **Memberships:** Am Chem Soc; The Chem Soc; Sigma Xi. **Research Statement & Publications:** Synthesis of novel compounds of pharmaceutical interest. **Mailing Address:** Promega BioScis Inc, 277 Granada Dr, San Luis Obispo, CA 93401. **Fax:** 805-543-1531.

KLAUDER, JOHN RIDER, THEORETICAL PHYSICS, APPLIED MATHEMATICS. **Personal Data:** b Reading, Pa, January 24, 1932; m 1980, c 5. **Education:** Univ Calif, Berkeley, BS, 1953; Stevens Inst Technol, MS, 1956; Princeton Univ, MA, 1957, PhD (physics), 1959. **Professional Experience:** PROF, DEPT PHYSICS & MATH, UNIV FLA, 1988-; vis prof, Imperial Col, 1988 & 1990; vis prof, Univ Trento, 1988; vis prof, Gakushuin Univ, 1982 & 1984; vis prof, Univ Bern, 1980; head solid state spectros dept, Bell Tel Labs, 1971-1976; prof, Syracuse Univ, 1967-1968; head theoret physics dept, Bell Tel Labs, 1966-1967 & 1969-1971; adj prof, Rutgers Univ, 1965; vis assoc prof, Univ Bern, 1961-1962; mem tech staff, Bell Tel Labs, 1953-1988. **Memberships:** fel Am Phys Soc; fel AAAS. **Research Statement & Publications:** Solid state physics; quantum optics; quantum field theory; fundamentals of quantum theory. **Mailing Address:** Dept Physics Univ Fla, Off 2142 NPB PO Box 118440, Gainesville, FL 32611. **Fax:** 352-392-0524. **E-Mail:** klauder@phys.ufl.edu

KLAUNIG, JAMES E, ENVIRONMENTAL TOXICOLOGY, CHEMICAL CARCINOGENESIS. **Personal Data:** b Newark, NJ, May 27, 1951. **Education:** Ursinus Col, BS, 1973; Montclair State Col, MA, 1976; Univ Md, PhD (path), 1980. **Professional Experience:** FAC MEM, GRAD PROG MED NEUROBIOLOGY, SCH MED, IND UNIV, 2000-; ADJ PROF, BEIJING UNIV, 1997-; DIR, STATE DEPT TOXICOL, STATE IND, 1996-; PROF & DIR DEPT PHARMACOL & TOXICOL, SCH MED, IND UNIV, 1991-; vis scientist, Chem Indust Inst Toxicol, Res Triangle Park, NC, 1990-1991; assoc prof, Dept Pharmacol, 1987-1991; assoc prof path, Dept Path, Med Col Ohio, Toledo, 1986-1991; prin investr on grants, US Environ Protection Agency, NIH & US Army, 1982-; mem grad fac, Med Col, Ohio Grad Sch, 1982-; adj fac mem, W Alton Jones Cell Sci Ctr, Lake Placid, NY, 1981; from instr to asst prof, Dept Path, Med Col Ohio, Toledo, 1980-1986; Lab scientist, dept path, Univ Md, Baltimore, 1976-1980; adj prof, Ctr Photochemical Sci, Dept Chem, Bowling Green State Univ, Ohio. **Memberships:** Am Asn Cancer Res; Soc Toxicol Pathologists; Soc Toxicol; Sigma Xi; Tissue Cult Asn; Am Col Toxicol. **Research Statement & Publications:** Environmental toxicology and carcinogenesis; liver tumor promotion; hepatic carcinogenesis; cell pathology; liver cell isolation and tissue culture; hepatotoxicology. **Mailing Address:** Dept Pharmacol & Toxicol, Sch Med, Ind Univ, Rm MS547, 635 Barnhill Dr, PO Box 547, Indianapolis, IN 46202. **Fax:** 317-274-7787. **E-Mail:** jklauni@iupui.edu

KLAUS, EWALD FRED, JR, ZOOLOGY, ENTOMOLOGY. **Personal Data:** b Needville, Tex, October 22, 1928; m 1964. **Education:** Univ Tex, BA, 1952, MA, 1958; Tex A&M Univ, PhD (entom), 1965. **Professional Experience:** PROF BIOL, ETEX STATE UNIV, 1974-; NSF fel, col sci Improv Prog, 1971-1972; fac res grant, 1967-1968; from asst prof to assoc prof, ETex State Univ, 1964-1974. **Research Statement & Publications:** Biology and taxonomy of mosquitoes; genetics of insecticide resistance in cotton insects; insecticide residue studies; food sanitation; aquatic ecology and water quality studies. **Mailing Address:** 1805 Jefferson St, Commerce, TX 75428.

KLAUS, RONALD LOUIS, CHEMICAL ENGINEERING. **Personal Data:** b Brooklyn, NY, April 23, 1940; m 1968, c 2. **Education:** Rensselaer Polytech Inst, BChE, 1960, PhD (chem eng), 1967. **Professional Experience:** WRITER, 1990-; minister, 1978-1989; asst prof chem eng, Univ Pa, 1970-1976; resident res assoc fel, Jet Propulsion Lab, 1968-1970; res engr combustion, Jet Propulsion Lab, 1963-1965, 1968-1970. **Memberships:** Am Inst Chem Engrs. **Research Statement & Publications:** Computer-aided design in chemical engineering; thermodynamics of liquid mixtures; computer-based estimation of thermodynamic properties; numerical methods; design and implementation of computer-based problem-oriented languages for engineering. **Mailing Address:** 607 S 48th St, Philadelphia, PA 19143.

KLAUSMEIER, ROBERT EDWARD, MICROBIOLOGY, CHEMISTRY. **Personal Data:** b Evansville, Ind, June 6, 1926; m 1951, c 4. **Education:** Univ Ind, AB, 1951, MA, 1953; La State Univ, PhD (bact), 1958. **Professional Experience:** RETIRED; chemist, Weapons Qual Eng Ctr, Naval Weapons Support Ctr, 1980-1989; microbiologist, Weapons Qual Eng Ctr, Naval Weapons Support Ctr, 1958-1980; asst, La State Univ, 1957-1958; asst prof bact, Southwestern La Inst, 1955-1957; res bacteriologist, Army Chem Corps, Ft Detrick, Md, 1953-1955; asst bact, Univ Ind, 1951-1953. **Memberships:** AAAS; Am Soc Microbiol; Soc Indust Microbiol. **Research Statement & Publications:** Microbial deterioration of materials, particularly explosives and synthetic polymers; microbial physiology; enzymology; economically and environmentally effective demilitarization of ammunition. **Mailing Address:** 4111 Gran Haven Dr, Bloomington, IN 47401.

KLAUSNER, JAMES FREDERICK, HEAT TRANSFER, FLUID MECHANICS. **Personal Data:** b Chicago, Ill, December 29, 1961; m 1987, Casey; c Alexander & Jordan. **Education:** US Merchant Marine Acad, BS, 1984; Univ Ill, MS, 1986, PhD (mech eng), 1989. **Honors & Awards:** Tech Transfer Award, NASA, 1992. **Professional Experience:** PROF, DEPT MECH & AEROSPACE ENG, UNIV FLA, 1998-; from asst prof to assoc prof, Univ Fla, 1989-1998; res asst, Univ Ill, 1984-1989. **Memberships:** Am Soc Mech Eng; Am Soc Eng Educ; Sigma Xi. **Research Statement & Publications:** Fundamental mechanisms of flow boiling heat transfer and two phase flow, innovative instrumentation for multiphase flow research, particle science and technology, energy storage using phase change materials and solar photocatalytic oxidation. **Mailing Address:** Dept Mech Eng, Univ Fla, 231 MAE-A PO Box 116250, Gainesville, FL 32611-6250. **Fax:** 352-392-1071. **E-Mail:** klaus@ufl.edu

KLAUSNER, RICHARD D, METABOLISM. **Personal Data:** b New York, NY, December 22, 1951; c 2. **Education:** Yale Univ, BS, 1973; Duke Med Sch, MD, 1976. **Honors & Awards:** Young Investr Award, Am Fedn Clin Res, 1988; William Castle Lectr, Harvard Univ, 1990 & Kroc Lectr, 1991; Shannon Lectr, Mass Gen Hosp, 1991; Marcel Piche Lectr, Univ Montreal, 1991; Lamport Lectr, Columbia Univ, 1991; 5th Abelson Lectr, Washington Univ, St Louis, 1992; Damashek Prize, Am Soc Hemat, 1992; Lederle Award, 1992; Whitemore Lectr, Am Urol Asn, 1997; 7th Nycomed Lectr, Norway. **Professional Experience:** EXEC DIR, GLOBAL HEALTH, BILL & MELINDA GATES FOUND, as of 2002; PRIN INVESTR, NAT CANCER INST, 2001-; Cartwright vis prof, Univ Utah, 1996; dir, Nat Cancer Inst, 1995-2001; chief cell biol & metab br, Nat Inst Child Health & Human Develop, NIH, 1984-1997; asst clin prof med, Dept Med, USUHS, 1983-1985; sr res investr, Nat Inst Arthritis, Diabetes & Digestive & Kidney Dis, 1983-1984; instr, Dept Med, USUHS, 1982-1983; Attend physician, Acute Med Clin, Nat Naval Med Ctr, 1981-1985; med officer, Nat Inst Arthritis, Diabetes & Digestive & Kidney Dis, 1981-1983; res assoc, Nat Cancer Inst, NIH, 1979-1981; clin fel, Mass Gen Hosp, 1978-1979; house officer internal med, Mass Gen Hosp, 1977-1978; fel internal med, Duke Med Ctr, 1976-1977. **Memberships:** Nat Acad Sci; Inst Med-Nat Acad Sci; Am Soc Clin Invest (pres-elect 1993 pres 1994); Am Fedn Clin Res; Am Soc Cell Biol; Am Soc Hemat; Sigma Xi; fel Am Acad Arts & Sci; Am Asn Physicians; Am Asn Cancer Res; Am Asn Clin Oncol; Am Soc Endocrinol. **Research Statement & Publications:** Molecular basis of normal and pathological states of iron metabolism in humans; mechanisms of post-transcriptional gene regulation; organelle cell biology; receptor biology; tumor suppressor genes. **Mailing Address:** Bill & Melinda Gates Found, Washington, DC 20005.

KLAUSTERMEYER, WILLIAM BERNER, ALLERGY, IMMUNOLOGY. **Personal Data:** b San Pedro, Calif, November 30, 1939; m 1962, c 3. **Education:** Univ Calif, Los Angeles, BA, 1962; Univ Cincinnati, MD, 1966. **Professional Experience:** DIR, ALLERGY & IMMUNOL CLIN, W LOS ANGELS VA MED CTR, UNIV CALIF, as of 2005; PROF MED, UNIV CALIF, LOS ANGELES, as of 2003; CHIEF ALLERGY & IMMUNOL, WADSWORTH VET ADMIN HOSP, LOS ANGELES, 1972-; allergist, USAF Med Ctr, Wright Patterson AFB, 1970-1972; fel allergy & immunol, Nat Jewish Hosp, 1969-1970; fel pulmonary, Wadsworth Vet Admin Hosp, 1968-1969; resident, Wadsworth Vet Admin Hosp, 1967-1968; Intern, Wadsworth Vet Admin Hosp, 1966-1967. **Memberships:** Fel Am Acad Allergy; Am Thoracic Soc; fel Am Col Allergy; Am Fedn Clin Res. **Research Statement & Publications:** Pharmacologic and immunologic aspects of allergic and respiratory disease; nasal and bronchial provocation testing; diagnostic and therapeutic approaches to patients with severe steroid dependent asthma; role of troleandomycin; gold salts and methotrexate in the prevention of corticosteroid complications. **Mailing Address:** Allergy & Immunol Clin, Univ Calif, W Los Angeles VA Med Ctr, 11301 Wilshire Blvd Bldg 500 111R, Los Angeles, CA 90073. **Fax:** 310-268-4912. **E-Mail:** william.klaustermeyer@med.va.gov

KLAVANO, PAUL ARTHUR, PHARMACOLOGY. **Personal Data:** b Valley, Wash, November 30, 1919; wid, c 4. **Education:** State Col Wash, BS, 1941, DVM, 1944. **Professional Experience:** RETIRED; chmn dept, Wash State Univ, 1952-1972; from asst prof to prof vet pharmacol, Wash State Univ, 1948-1983; vet physiol & pharmacol, Wash State Univ, 1945-1948; instr vet anat, Wash State Univ, 1944-1945; chemist, Wash Horse Racing Comn, 1942-1946. **Memberships:** Am Col Vet Pharmacol & Therapeut; Am Soc Vet Physiol & Pharmacol (secy, 1953-1954, pres, 1964-1965); NY Acad Sci; Am Soc Vet Anesthesiol; Am Vet Asn. **Research Statement & Publications:** Anesthesia of domestic animals. **Mailing Address:** 1125 SE Kamiaken St, Pullman, WA 99163.

KLAVERKAMP, JOHN FREDERICK, PHARMACOLOGY, TOXICOLOGY. **Personal Data:** b Sauk Rapids, Minn, August 6, 1941; m 1965, c 4. **Education:** Univ Minn, BS, 1964; Univ Wash, MS, 1970, PhD (pharmacol), 1972. **Professional Experience:** RES SCIENTIST, FISHERIES & MARINE SERV, FRESHWATER INST, 1978-; adj prof, Dept Zool, Univ Man, 1977-; res mgr, Fisheries & Marine Serv, Freshwater Inst, 1977-1978; Res scientist, Fisheries & Marine Serv, Freshwater Inst, 1973-1977; Fel, Wash State Univ, Toxicol Lab, 1972-1973. **Research Statement & Publications:** Acidification of freshwater; biochemical mechanisms of tolerance in fish; cadmium toxicology; cardiovascular-respiratory physiology of fish; embryology of fish; heavy metal toxicology; mercury toxicology; selenium toxicology; organophosphate insecticides. **Mailing Address:** Box 1 Group 9, RR 1, Dugald, MB R0E 0K0, Can.

KLAVINS, JANIS VILIBERTS, MEDICINE. **Personal Data:** b Latvia, May 6, 1921; m 1950, Ilga; c Ilze M, Lize K, Janis P & Filips K. **Education:** Univ Kiel, MD, 1948, PhD, 1959; Am Bd Path, cert anal path, 1957, cert clin path, 1959; Am Bd Nutrit, cert, 1968. **Honorary Degrees:** Hon Dr Biol Sci, Univ Latvia, 1991. **Honors & Awards:** Scientist of the Year, Asn Clin Scientists, 1983. **Professional Experience:** Ed-in-chief, J Tumor Marker Oncol, 1987-; prof path, Med Col, Cornell Univ, 1985-; pres, Int Acad Tumor Marker Oncol, 1984-; chmn dept path, Cath Med Ctr, 1977-1998; prof path, State Univ NY Downstate Med Ctr, 1977-1985; prof path, State Univ NY Stony Brook, 1971-1977; prof lectr, State Univ NY Downstate Med Ctr, 1971-1977; DIR DEPT PATH, LONG ISLAND JEWISH MED CTR, QUEENS HOSP CTR, 1970-; clin prof path, Col Physicians & Surgeons, Columbia Univ, 1969-; adj prof biol, Fac Grad Arts, Long Island Univ, 1968-; clin prof path, State Univ NY Downstate Med Ctr, 1965-1971; pathologist-in-chief, Brooklyn-Cumberland Med Ctr, 1965-1970; dir sch cytotech, Med Ctr, Duke Univ, 1963-1965; chief lab serv, Vet Admin Hosp, Durham, NC, 1961-1963; from assoc prof to prof, Med Ctr, Duke Univ, 1960-1965; asst prof, Sch Med, Western Res Univ, 1960; assoc pathologist, Cleveland Metrop Gen Hosp, 1958-1960; from instr to sr instr, Sch Med, Western Res Univ, 1955-1960; cytologist-in-chg, Cleveland Metrop Gen Hosp, 1955-1960; asst pathologist, Marymount Hosp, Garfield Heights, Ohio, 1955-1957; demonstr path, Sch Med, Western Res Univ, 1954-1955. **Memberships:** Fel AAAS; Am Soc Cytol; Am Asn Pathologists; Col Am Path emer; Asn Clin Scientists emer; Int Acad Path emer; Biochem Soc; Col Am Path; Am Inst Nutrit; AMA; Int Acad Tumor Marker Oncol emer; hon mem Egypt Soc Tumor Marker Oncol; hon mem Nat Acad Eng Latvia; Nat Acad Med Venezuela. **Research Statement & Publications:** Iron metabolism; pathology of iron excess; effects of antimetabolites, particularly entionine; embryonic and specific proteins in malignant neoplasms; pathology of amino acid excess; tumor markers. **Mailing Address:** Dept Path, Long Island Jewish Med Ctr, Scarsdale, NY 10583. **Fax:** 718-558-2166.

KLAWE, MARIA, INTERACTIVE MULTI-MEDIA, EDUCATIONAL TECHNOLOGY. **Personal Data:** b Toronto, Ont, July 5, 1951; m 1980, Nicholas Pippenger; c Janek & Sasha. **Education:** Univ Alta, BSc, 1973, PhD (math), 1977. **Professional Experience:** DEAN, SCH ENG & APPL SCI, PRINCETON UNIV, as of 2003; PROF COMPUT SCI, PRINCETON UNIV, as of 2003; vpres, student & acad serv, Univ BC, beginning 1995; ed, Electronic J Combinatorics, 1994-; trustee, Am Math Soc, 1992-1997; mem bd, Comput Res Asn, 1990-1996; prof & head, Student & Acad Serv, Univ Bc, 1988-1995; ed, Soc Indust & Appl Math J Discrete Math, 1987-1993; ed, Soc Indust & Appl Math J Computing, 1986-1993; ed, Combinatorica, 1985-; mem bd, Can Math Soc, 1985-1989; mgr, Discrete Math Group, 1984-1988; res staff mem, Almaden Res Ctr, IBM, 1980-1984; asst prof comput sci, Univ Toronto, 1979-1980; Asst prof math, Oakland Univ, 1977-1978. **Memberships:** Fel Asn Comput Math; Am Math Soc; Comput Res Asn; Soc Indust & Appl Math; Can Math Soc; Asn Women Math. **Research Statement & Publications:** Interactive multi-media for mathematical education; computational geometry; complexity; data structures; graph theory; matrix searching. **Mailing Address:** Sch Eng & Appl Sci, Princeton Univ, C-230, EQuad, Princeton, BC Can. **Fax:** 609-258-6744. **E-Mail:** klawe@princeton.edu

KLAWE, WITOLD L, FISH BIOLOGY. **Personal Data:** b Piotrkow Trybunalski, Poland, June 9, 1923; American citizen; m 1955, Barbara Hillsdon; c David M. **Education:** Univ Toronto, BA, 1953, MA, 1955. **Honorary Degrees:** Dr hon causa, Acad Agr, Szczecin, Poland, 1991. **Honors & Awards:** Gold Insignia of the Order of Merit Polish People's Repub, 1988. **Professional Experience:** SR SCIENTIST EMER, INTER-AMTROP TUNA COMN, SCRIPPS INST OCEANOG, as of 2002; mem working groups, Expert Panel Facilitation Tuna Res, Food & Agr Orgn, UN, beginning 1965; sr scientist, Inter-Amtrop

Tuna Comn, Scripps Inst Oceanog, beginning 1961; scientist, Inter-am Trop Tuna Comn, Scripps Inst Oceanog, 1956-1961; jr scientist, Inter-am Trop Tuna Comn, Scripps Inst Oceanog, 1955-1956; consult, Food & Agr Orgn, UN & SPacific Comn. **Memberships:** Am Inst Fishery Res Biol; AAAS. **Research Statement & Publications:** Early life history of scombroid fishes; general marine biology; fishery oceanography; statistics on global catches of tunas. **Mailing Address:** Inter-Am Trop Tuna Comn, Scripps Inst Oceanog, 8604 La Jolla Dr, La Jolla, CA 92038. **Fax:** 619-546-7133.

KLAY, ROBERT FRANK, ANIMAL NUTRITION. **Personal Data:** b Ft Benton, Mont, January 2, 1930; m 1959, c 3. **Education:** Mont State Univ, BS, 1952; Wash State Univ, MS, 1958; Univ Minn, Minneapolis, PhD (nutrit), 1964. **Professional Experience:** NUTRITIONIST, MOORMAN MFG CO, 1964-; asst prof, Wash State Univ, 1961-1964; res asst animal nutrit, Univ Minn, Minneapolis, 1959-1961; res fel animal genetics, Commonwealth Sci & Indust Res Orgn, Australia, 1958-1959; Asst animal sci, Wash State Univ, 1956-1958. **Memberships:** Am Soc Animal Sci; Sigma Xi; ARPAS. **Research Statement & Publications:** Protein and amino acid digestion and availability; ruminant and nonruminant nutrition. **Mailing Address:** 936 Cameron Rd, Sequim, WA 98382.

KLEBACHER, FRED, CHEMISTRY. **Education:** Univ Notre Dame, PhD (chem), 1963. **Professional Experience:** RETIRED; anal mgr, Acushnet Co, as of 2000. **Mailing Address:** 22 Casey St, Canton, MA 02021. **Fax:** 781-821-8714. **E-Mail:** fredgail400@cs.com

KLEBAN, MORTON H, SOCIAL GERONTOLOGY, STATISTICS & MEASUREMENT. **Personal Data:** b Brooklyn, NY, October 23, 1931; m 1955, c 3. **Education:** City Col NY, BBA, 1953; State Univ Iowa, MA, 1955; Univ NDak, PhD (exp psychol), 1960. **Professional Experience:** DIR PSYCHOMET, POLISHER RES INST, as of 2006; sr res psychologist, philadelphia geriat ctr, beginning 1966; MED RES SCIENTIST, NORRISTOWN STATE HOSP, 1966-; res psychologist, Off Ment Health, State Pa, 1964-1966; clin psychologist, Norristown State Hosp, Pa, 1960-1964. **Memberships:** Am Psychol Asn; Geront Soc. **Research Statement & Publications:** Design, statistical applications and computer technology in applied gerontological research. **Mailing Address:** Polisher Res Inst, 5301 Old York Rd PO Box 728, Jenkintown, PA 19046. **Fax:** 215-371-3015. **E-Mail:** mkleban@abramsoncenter.org

KLEBANOFF, SEYMOUR J, INFECTIOUS DISEASES, BIOCHEMISTRY. **Personal Data:** b Toronto, Ont, February 3, 1927; m 1951, Evelyn; c Carolyn & Mark. **Education:** Univ Toronto, MD, 1951; Univ London, PhD (biochem), 1954. **Honors & Awards:** Marie T Bonazinga Annual Res Award, Soc Leukocyte Biol, 1985; Mayo Soley Award, Western Soc Clin Invest, 1991; Bristol Award, Infectious Dis Soc Am, 1993; Bristol-Myers Squibb Award Distinguished Achievement Infectious Dis Res, 1995. **Professional Experience:** PROF EMER MED, SCH MED, UNIV WASH, 2000-; merit award, NIH, 1988-; head, Div Allergy & Infectious Dis, 1976-1994; prof, Sch Med, Univ Wash, 1968-1999; res career develop award, NIH, 1964-1968; assoc prof, Sch Med, Univ Wash, 1962-1968; asst prof, assoc physician & radiation protection officer, 1959-1962; res assoc, Rockefeller Univ, 1959; guest investr & asst physician, Rockefeller Univ, 1957-1959; lectr path chem, Univ Toronto, 1954-1957; intern, Toronto Gen Hosp, 1951-1952. **Memberships:** Nat Acad Sci; Inst Med-Nat Acad Sci; Infectious Dis Soc Am; Asn Am Physicians; Am Soc Biol Chem; Am Soc Clin Invest; Am Acad Arts & Sci. **Research Statement & Publications:** Role of granulocytes in host defense; role of enzyme peroxidase in biological processes; microbicidal activity of peroxidases. **Mailing Address:** Dept Med, Sch Med, Univ Wash, Box 357185 1959 NE Pacific St, Seattle, WA 98195. **Fax:** 206-685-8681. **E-Mail:** seym@u.washington.edu

KLEBANOV, IGOR ROMANOVICH, STRING THEORY, QUANTUM GRAVITY. **Personal Data:** b March 29, 1962; American citizen; m 1991, Pamela Kato; c Rachel & Sarah. **Education:** Mass Inst Technol, SB, 1982; Princeton Univ, PhD (physics), 1986. **Professional Experience:** Co-dir, Ann Int Ctr Thomas P Jones, Prof Math Phys, Princeton Univ, 2000-2001; PROF PHYSICS, PRINCETON UNIV, 1998-; assoc prof physics, Princeton Univ, 1995-1998; Theoret Physics Spring Sch, Trieste, Italy, 1992-1996; Presidential young investr, NSF, 1991-1997; Alfred P Sloan Res fel, 1991-1995; asst prof, Princeton Univ, 1989-1995; Res assoc, Linear Accelerator Ctr, Stanford Univ, 1986-1989. **Research Statement & Publications:** Theoretical high energy physics; quantum field theory; string theory and quantum gravity. **Mailing Address:** Dept Physics, Princeton Univ, Jadwin Hall, PO Box 708, Princeton, NJ 08544-0708. **Fax:** 609-258-6360. **E-Mail:** klebanov@puhep1.princeton.edu

KLEBBA, PHILLIP E, MONOCLONAL ANTIBODIES, MEMBRANE BIOLOGY. **Personal Data:** b Ypsilanti, Mich, December 27, 1951; m 2000, Salete; c 3. **Education:** Univ Notre Dame, BS, 1975; Univ Calif, Berkeley, PhD (biochem), 1981. **Professional Experience:** PROF, DEPT CHEM & BIOCHEM, UNIV OKLA, as of 2005; assoc prof chem, Dept Chem & Biochem, Univ Okla, 1995-1998; CNRS vis assoc prof, Inst Pasteur, Paris France, 1993-1995; Thymax Corp, 1990-; Ensys Inc, 1988-1990; asst prof microbiol, Med Col Wis, 1986-1993; Prin investr, USPHS, 1986-1990; consult, Chevron Chem Co, 1986-1989; asst prof microbiol, Univ Notre Dame, 1984-1988; fel microbiol & immunol, Univ Calif, Berkeley, 1982-1984; fel med microbiol, Sch Med, Stanford Univ, 1981-1982. **Memberships:** Sigma Xi; Am Soc Microbiol; AAAS. **Research Statement & Publications:** Bacterial pathogens shield themselves from the mammalian immune system by the barrier properties of molecules that reside in their outer membrane; structure of outer membrane proteins and lipopoly saccharide and the interactions of these two molecules with each other and the immune system. **Mailing Address:** Dept Chem & Biochem, Univ Okla, 620A Perrington Oval Ste 314, Norman, OK 73019-0430. **Fax:** 405-325-6111. **E-Mail:** klebba@necker.fr

KLEBE, ROBERT JOHN, CELL ADHESION PROTEINS, TISSUE ENGINEERING. **Personal Data:** b Philadelphia, Pa, October 26, 1943. **Education:** Johns Hopkins Univ, BA, 1965; Yale Univ, PhD (biol), 1970. **Professional Experience:** PROF ANAT, GRAD SCH BIOMED SCI, UNIV TEX HEALTH SCI CTR, 1986-; assoc prof, Grad Sch Biomed Sci, Univ Tex Health Sci Ctr, 1981-1986; From asst prof to assoc prof human genetics, Grad Sch Biomed Sci, Univ Tex Med Br, Galveston, 1976-1981; Jane Coffin Child Mem Fund fel, Salk Inst, 1970-1972. **Memberships:** Am Soc Human Genetics; Am Soc Cell Biol. **Research Statement & Publications:** Somatic cell genetics; biochemistry of cell adhesion; developmental genetics; biochemical mechanism of cell adhesion: the analysis of the binding offibronectin, laminim and other cell adhesion proteins to cell surface molecules. **Mailing Address:** Dept Cell & Struct Biol, Univ Tex Health Sci Ctr, San Antonio, TX 78229. **E-Mail:** klebe@uthscsa.edu

KLEBER, EUGENE VICTOR, CHEMISTRY, ENVIRONMENTAL PROGRAMS. **Personal Data:** b Cleveland, Ohio, July 7, 1920; m 1978, c 5. **Education:** Univ Calif, Los Angeles, AB, 1940, MA, 1941; Univ Wis, PhD (chem), 1943. **Professional Experience:** RETIRED; phys scientist, Fed Energy Regulatory Comn, Dept Energy, 1978-1985; staff asst, Atomics Int Div, Rockwell Int Corp, 1962-1978; gen mgr res chem div, Nuclear Corp Am, 1959-1962; res chemist, Coast Paint & Chem Co, 1947 & Lockheed Aircraft Corp, 1951-1956; pres, Res Chem, Inc, 1947-1959; Golden Bear Oil Co, Calif, 1945-1946 & Lockheed Aircraft Corp, 1946-1947; res chemist, Sharples Chem, Inc, Mich, 1943-1945. **Memberships:** Am Chem Soc. **Research Statement & Publications:** Nuclear fuels and materials; organic synthesis; fine chemical manufacturing; production and use of purified rare earth oxides and metals; energy and environmental programs. **Mailing Address:** 406 Upper Wood Way, Burnsville, MN 55337-5728.

KLEBER, HERBERT DAVID, PSYCHIATRY, DRUG ABUSE. **Personal Data:** b Pittsburgh, Pa, June 19, 1934; div, c 3. **Education:** Dartmouth Col, BA, 1956; Jefferson Med Col, MD, 1960. **Honorary Degrees:** MA, Yale Univ, 1975; PhD, NY Med Col, 1991. **Honors & Awards:** Gold Medal, Am Psychiat Asn, 1975; Nathan B Eddy Mem Award, 1995. **Professional Experience:** EXEC VPRES & MED DIR, NAT CTR ADDICTION & SUBSTANCE ABUSE, 1992-; PROF PSYCHIAT, SCH MED, COLUMBIA UNIV, 1991-; DIR, DIV SUBSTANCE ABUSE RES, NY STATE PSYCHIAT INST, 1991-; dep dir demand redction, Off Nat Drug Control Policy, Exec Off Pres, 1989-1991; fund prize res psychiat, Am Psychiat Asn, 1981; Consult, Nat Inst Drug Abuse, 1971- & Nat Acad Sci, 1973-; from asst prof to prof, psychiat, Sch Med, Yale Univ, 1966-1989; chief receiving serv, USPHS Hosp, Lexington, Ky, 1964-1966; resident psychiat, Sch Med, Yale Univ, 1961-1964. **Memberships:** Inst Med-Nat Acad Sci; fel Am Col Neuropsychopharmacol; fel Am Acad Psychiat Alcoholism & Addiction; fel Am Col Psychiat; fel Am Psychiat Asn; fel Col Prob Drug Dependence. **Research Statement & Publications:** Treatment of drug dependence; etiological aspects of drug abuse; policy research in substance abuse; published over 20 articles. **Mailing Address:** Div Substance Abuse Columbia Univ Col Physicians & Surgeons, NY State Psychiat Inst 1051 Riverside Dr, Unit 66, New York, NY 10032. **Fax:** 212-543-6018. **E-Mail:** hdk3@columbia.edu

KLEBER, JOHN WILLIAM, BIOPHARMACEUTICS. **Personal Data:** b Warsaw, Ill, January 1, 1923; m 1945, c 5. **Education:** Duquesne Univ, BS, 1943; Univ Minn, PhD (pharmaceut chem), 1949. **Professional Experience:** RETIRED; sr formulations chemist, Eli Lilly & Co, 1975-1981; sr anal chemist, Eli Lilly & Co, 1970-1975; sr biologist, Eli Lilly & Co, 1960-1970; USPHS trainee grant steroid biochem, Univ Utah, 1959-1960; assoc prof, Univ Buffalo, 1952-1960; asst prof pharm, Univ Buffalo, 1949-1952. **Memberships:** Am Chem Soc. **Research Statement & Publications:** Development of animal health care products. **Mailing Address:** 7338 Castleton Farms N Dr, Seymour, IN 46256.

KLECK, ROBERT E, PSYCHOLOGY, SOCIAL COMMUNICATION. **Personal Data:** b Archbold, Ohio, August 3, 1937; m Jan; c Jennifer & Leslie (Bugbee). **Education:** Denison Univ, AB, 1959; Stanford Univ, PhD (social psychol), 1963. **Honors & Awards:** Phi beta kappa, Denison Univ, 1958; Danforth fel, Stanford Univ, 1959; Third Century Prof in the soc Sci, 1985-1990, Dartmouth College. **Professional Experience:** CHMN DEPT, DARTMOUTH COL, 1993-1999; John Sloan Dickey Third Century prof soc sci, Dartmouth Col, 1985-1990; Vet Admin Stroke Proj, 1983-1988, Can Res Coun, NSF & USPHS; Abilities Inc, NY, 1979-1981; fel, USPHS, 1977-1978; PROF PSYCHOL, DARTMOUTH COL, 1975-; Bur Develop Disabilities, NH, 1975-1980; consult ed, J Personality & Social Psychol, 1974-1978; vis res prof, Boy's Town Ctr Study Youth Develop, Stanford Univ, 1974-1975; Consult, Disadvantaged Children NH, 1974; Consult, Crotchet Mountain Rehab Ctr, 1973; assoc ed, J Personality & Social Psychol, 1971-1972; from asst to assoc prof, Dartmouth Col, 1966-1975; asst prof, Williams Col, 1964-1966; Fel, Stanford Univ, 1963-1964. **Memberships:** Fel Am Psychol Soc; Int Soc Res Emotion; Soc Exp Social Psychol; Sigma Xi; Soc Personality Social Psychol. **Research Statement & Publications:** Social psychological processes; interpersonal communication; nonverbal aspects of communication; stigmatization processes; emotional communications; contributed articles to professional journals. **Mailing Address:** Dept Psychol, Dartmouth Col, Hanover, NH 03755. **Fax:** 603-646-1419. **E-Mail:** r.kleck@dartmouth.edu

KLECKA, MIROSLAV EZIDOR, CHEMICAL ENGINEERING. **Personal Data:** b Yoakum, Tex, November 9, 1921; m 1945. **Education:** Univ Tex, BS, 1943, MS, 1946, PhD (chem eng), 1948. **Professional Experience:** RETIRED; staff res engr, Shell Oil Co, Houston, 1977-1985; staff res engr, Shell Oil Co, Houston, 1966-1977; sr res engr, Shell Oil Co, Houston, 1947-1966; instr, Univ Tex, 1946-1947; res assoc, Univ Tex, 1946; res asst chem eng, Univ Tex, 1945-1946. **Memberships:** Am Inst Chem Engrs. **Research Statement & Publications:** Petroleum refining design and evaluation; phase equilibria and separation processes; operations research and computer calculations systems design; process control systems. **Mailing Address:** 3908 Walnut Clay Dr, Austin, TX 78731.

KLECKNER, NANCY E, GENETICS. **Personal Data:** b Santa Monica, Calif, October 16, 1947. **Education:** Harvard Univ, AB, 1968; Mass Inst Technol, PhD (biol), 1974. **Professional Experience:** Bd dirs, Genetics Soc Am, 1986-1988; HERCHEL SMITH PROF MOLECULAR & CELLULER BIOL, HARVARD UNIV, 1984-; mem sci adv bd, New Eng Biolabs, 1982-; from asst prof to assoc prof, Dept Biochem & Molecular Biol, Harvard Univ, 1977-1984; NIH fel biol, Mass Inst Technol, 1974-1975. **Memberships:** Nat Acad Sci Inst Med; fel AAAS; fel Am Acad Arts & Sci; fel Am Acad Microbiol. **Research Statement & Publications:** Numerous publications. **Mailing Address:** Dept Molecular & Cellular Biol, Harvard Univ, Rm 301 Fairchild Bldg 7 Divinity Ave, Cambridge, MA 02138. **Fax:** 617-495-0758. **E-Mail:** kleckner@fas.harvard.edu

KLEE, CLAUDE BLENC, CALMODULIN, PROTEIN-PROTEIN INTERACTION. **Education:** Univ Marsailles, France, MD, 1959. **Professional Experience:** CHIEF, LAB BIOCHEM, NAT CANCER INST, 1989-; actg chief, Lab Biochem, Nat Cancer Inst, 1987-1989; head macromolecular interactions, Nat Cancer Inst, 1974-1987. **Memberships:** Inst Med-Nat Acad Sci. **Mailing Address:** Lab Biochem, Nat Cancer Inst, Bldg 37, Rm 6106C, 37 Convent Dr, MSC 4255, Bethesda, MD 20892-4255. **Fax:** 301-402-3095. **E-Mail:** ckl@helix.nih.gov

KLEE, GERALD D'ARCY, PSYCHIATRY, MEDICINE. **Personal Data:** b New York, NY, January 29, 1927; m 1950, c 5. **Education:** Harvard Med Sch, MD, 1952; Am Bd Psychiat & Neurol, dipl, 1959. **Professional Experience:** LECTR EMER PSYCHIAT, SCH MED, JOHNS HOPKINS UNIV, as of 2001; lectr psychiat, Sch med, Johns Hopkins Univ, beginning 1976; pvt pract, psychiat, 1971-; prof psychiat, Sch Med, Temple Univ, 1967-1970; from asst prof to assoc prof, Sch Med, Univ Md, 1958-1967; dir div outpatient psychiat, Psychiat Inst, 1958-1967; res assoc psychiat, Sch Med, Univ Md, 1956-1958; sr asst surgeon, USPHS, 1953-1954; med dir, USPHS. **Memberships:** AMA; fel Am Psychiat Asn. **Research Statement & Publications:** Psychopharmacology; psychotherapy; community psychiatry; epidemiology. **Mailing Address:** Dept psychiat & behav Sci, Johns Hopkins Hosp, 600 N Wolfe St, Baltimore, MD 21287-7131.

KLEE, VICTOR LA RUE, MATHEMATICS. **Personal Data:** b San Francisco, Calif, September 18, 1925; m 1985, Joann; c Wendy, Barbara, Lisette & Heidi. **Education:** Pomona Col, BA, 1945, Univ Va, PhD (math), 1949. **Honorary Degrees:** DSc, Pomona Col, 1965; Dr, Univ Liege, 1984, Univ Trier, 1995. **Honors & Awards:** Pres & Visitor's Res Prize, Univ Va, 1952; L R Ford Award, 1972; C B Allendoerfer Award, Math Asn Am, 1980; Vollum Award, Reed Col, 1982; Barrows Award, Pomona Col, 1988. **Professional**

Experience: PROF EMER, UNIV WASH, as of 2005; Max Planck res prize, von Humboldt Found, 1992; Fulbright fel, Univ Trier, 1992; sr fel, Inst Math & Its Applns, 1987; mem, Math Sci Res Inst, 1985-1986; Guggenheim fel & Von Humboldt awardee, Univ Erlangen-Nurnberg, 1980-1981; vis assoc prof, Univ Calif, Los Angeles, 1955-1956 & Univ Western Australia, 1979; adj prof comput sci, Univ Wash, beginning 1976; IBM Corp, 1972 & W H Freeman, 1976-1996; prof appl math, Univ Wash, 1976-1984; fel, Ctr Advan Study Behav Sci, 1975-1976; vis prof, Univ Victoria, 1975; adj prof comput sci, Univ Wash, 1974-; trustee, Conf Bd Math Sci, 1972-1973; vis prof, Univ Colo, 1971; Sigma Xi nat lectr, 1969; E I du Pont Del Nemours & Co, Inc, 1968-1972; Holt, Rinehart & Winston, 1966-1976; consult, Rand Corp, 1966-1969; consult, Boeing Sci Res Labs, 1963-1969; NSF sr fel, Sloan res fel, 1959-1960; NSF sr fel, Copenhagen Univ, 1958-1959; Sloan res fel, Univ Wash, 1956-1958 & 1960-1961; from asst prof to assoc prof math, Univ Wash, 1953-1957; Nat Res Coun fel, Inst Advan Study, 1951-1952; asst prof, Univ Va, 1949-1953; Instr math, Univ Va, 1947-1948. **Memberships:** fel AAAS; Am Math Soc (assoc secy, 1955-1958); Math Asn Am (first vpres, 1968-1969, pres-elect, 1970, pres, 1971-1972); Soc Indust & Appl Math; Math Prog Soc; Asn Comput Mach. **Research Statement & Publications:** Convex sets; mathematical programming; combinatorial mathematics; design and analysis of algorithms; functional analysis; point-set topology. **Mailing Address:** Dept Math, Univ Wash, PO Box 4350, Seattle, WA 98195-4350. **Fax:** 206-543-1150. **E-Mail:** klee@math.washington.edu

KLEE, WERNER A, MOLECULAR BIOLOGY. **Personal Data:** b Ger, August 6, 1933. **Education:** Yale Univ, BS, 1954, PhD (biochem), 1958. **Professional Experience:** CHIEF & RES CHEMIST, MOLECULAR BIOL LAB, NIMH, NIH, 1992-; sect chief chem, Ment Health Dept, 1982-1992; res chemist, Ment Health Dept, 1962-1982. **Memberships:** Cell Biol Soc; Soc Biochem & Molecular Biol. **Mailing Address:** NIMH Bldg 36 Rm ID-08, Bethesda, MD 20892-0001.

KLEEMAN, CHARLES RICHARD, PHYSIOLOGY, METABOLISM. **Personal Data:** b Los Angeles, Calif, August 19, 1923; m 1945, c 3. **Education:** Univ Calif, BS, 1944, MD, 1947. **Professional Experience:** PROF EMER MED & NEPHROL, SCH MED, UNIV CALIF, LOS ANGELES, as of 2001; NEPHROLOGIST, WEST LOS ANGELES VET ADMIN MED CTR, 1993-; SCI DIR, RES INST, 1983-; dir, Ctr Health Enhancement, 1981-1986; from prof & chief to emer prof & emer chief, Div Nephrol, Sch Med, 1975-1994; dir, Div Nephrol, 1975-1981; prof med & chief dept, Hadassah Med Sch, Hebrew Univ, Israel, 1972-1975; dir, Ctr Health Enhancement Educ & Res, Cedar Sinai Med Ctr, 1971-1986; chmn, Internal Med Sect, Nat Bd Med Examr, 1971; vis prof, St Francis Hosp, Honolulu, 1969; vis prof, Beilinson Hosp, Tel-Aviv Univ & Med Sch, Hadassah-Hebrew Univ, 1968; consult artificial kidney, Chronic Uremia Prog & Kidney Dis Control Prog, NIH, 1967-1972; vis prof, Univ Queensland, 1966; prof, Sch Med & dir, Div Med, Cedars-Sinai Med Ctr, 1964-1974; consult, Vet Admin Hosp, Los Angeles, 1962-; dir, Div Med, Mt Sinai Hosp, Los Angeles, 1961-1978; Upjohn-Endocrine Soc scholar, Univ Col, Univ London, 1960-1961; from assoc clin prof to assoc prof, Sch Med, Univ Calif, Los Angeles, 1956-1964; chief metab sect, Vet Admin Hosp, Los Angeles, 1956-1960; from instr to asst prof, Metab Sect, Sch Med, Yale Univ, 1953-1956; fel metab, Newington Vet Admin Hosp, 1950-1951; from intermediate resident to sr resident med, Newington Vet Admin Hosp, 1949-1951; asst resident path, Mallory Inst, Boston City Hosp, 1948-1949; rotating internship, San Francisco City Hosp, 1947-1948; mem sci adv bd, Nat Kidney Dis Found. **Memberships:** Inst Med-Nat Acad Sci; AMA; Am Physiol Soc; Am Soc Clin Invest; Endocrine Soc. **Research Statement & Publications:** Renal physiology; electrolyte and water metabolism; nephrology. **Mailing Address:** Dept Med, Wadsworth VA Med Ctr, Los Angeles, CA 90095. **Fax:** 310-268-4653. **E-Mail:** ckleeman@ucla.edu

KLEEN, HAROLD J, geology, petroleum & minerals exploration; deceased, see previous edition for last biography

KLEGERMAN, MELVIN EARL, IMMUNOBIOLOGY & IMMUNOTHERAPY OF CANCER, BACTERIAL IMMUNOMODULATORS & VACCINES. **Personal Data:** b Chicago, Ill, August 30, 1945; div, c Melanie & Jessica. **Education:** Univ Ill, Chicago, BA, 1968; Loyola Univ Chicago, PhD (biochem), 1984. **Professional Experience:** PRES & CHIEF EXEC OFFICER, ECHO DYNAMICS INC, as of 2005; Mid-Atlantic biomed res lab, Inc, Silver Spring, Md, beginning 1996; asst prof pharmaceut, Inst Tuberculosis Res, Univ Ill, Chicago, 1988-1995; assoc dir, Inst Tuberculosis Res, Univ Ill, Chicago, 1987-1996; adj asst prof, Univ Ill, Chicago, 1987-1988; res assoc, Rush Presby-St Luke Med Ctr, 1986-1987; adj res assoc, Univ Chicago, 1985-1986 & 1995-; res investr, Michael Reese Hosp & Med Ctr, 1980-1986; res assoc, Evanston Hosp, 1979; res assoc, Loyola Univ Med Ctr, 1973-1978; asst ed, Encycl Britannica, 1970-1973. **Memberships:** Am Asn Pharmaceut Scientists. **Research Statement & Publications:** Identification, purification and formulation of bacterial immunomodulators for cancer treatment; development of technology for rapid evaluation of anti-cancer immunotherapeutic drugs; ultrasonic diagnosis of atherosclerosis. **Mailing Address:** Echo Dynamics, Inc, College Park, MD 20742.

KLEI, HERBERT EDWARD, CHEMICAL ENGINEERING. **Personal Data:** b Detroit, Mich, May 5, 1935; m 1959, c 5. **Education:** Mass Inst Technol, BS, 1957; Univ Mich, MS, 1958 & 1959; Univ Conn, PhD (chem eng), 1965. **Honors & Awards:** Ralph Teetor Award, Soc Automotive Engrs, 1978. **Professional Experience:** PROF EMER, INST MAT SCI, UNIV CONN, as of 2005; vis prof, US Mil Acad, 1985; from asst prof to prof chem eng, Univ Conn, 1965-1993, instr, Sch Eng, Univ Conn, 1964-1965; res engr, Chas Pfizer & Co, 1959-1963. **Memberships:** Am Inst Chem Eng; Am Chem Soc; Catalysis Soc NAm. **Research Statement & Publications:** Water pollution control, including biological kinetics and reactor design, membrane polarization and process control. **Mailing Address:** Inst Mat Sci, Univ Conn, 97 N Eagleville Rd, Storrs, CT 06269-3136. **Fax:** 860-486-4745.

KLEI, THOMAS RAY, PARASITOLOGY, IMMUNOLOGY. **Personal Data:** b Detroit, Mich, December 11, 1942; m 1965, c 1. **Education:** Northern Mich Univ, BS, 1965; Wayne State Univ, PhD (biol & parasitol), 1971. **Professional Experience:** BOYD PROF PARASITOL & ASSOC DEAN, SCH VET MED, LA STATE UNIV, BATON ROUGE, as of 2005; prof parasitol, Sch Vet Med, La State Univ, beginning 1982; prin investr, WHO & USDA Coop States Res Study grants, 1977-; from asst prof to assoc prof, Sch Vet Med, La State Univ, 1977-1982; asst prof biol & zoology, Millersville State Col, 1973-1975; NIH fel parasitol, Sch Vet Med, Univ Ga, 1971-1973; consult vet parasitol. **Memberships:** Am Soc Parasitologists; Am Soc Trop Med & Hyg; AAAS; Am Asn Vet Parasitol (pres, 1987); Wildlife Dis Asn. **Research Statement & Publications:** Immunologic and pathologic responses of vertebrate hosts to parasitic animals; parasitic diseases of horses. **Mailing Address:** Dept Pathobiological Sci, Sch Vet Med, La State Univ, Skip Bertman Dr River Rd, Baton Rouge, LA 70803. **Fax:** 225-578-9702. **E-Mail:** klei@vetmed.lsu.edu

KLEIER, DANIEL ANTHONY, PHYSICAL CHEMISTRY, THEORETICAL CHEMISTRY. **Personal Data:** b Louisville, Ky, August 19, 1945; m 1968, Catherine; c Heidi & Curt. **Education:** Bellarmine Col, Ky, BA, 1967; Univ Notre Dame, PhD (chem), 1971. **Honors & Awards:** Dupont Corp Protection Scientific Leadership Award, 1999. **Professional Experience:** RES FEL, DU PONT CO, 1986-; chemist, Shell Develop Co, 1981-1986; vis staff mem, Los Alamos Nat Lab, 1978-1979; asst prof chem, Williams Col, 1975-1981; NSF fel, Am Cancer Soc fel, 1974-1975; res fel, Harvard Univ, 1972-1975; NSF fel, Harvard Univ, 1972-1973; Woodrow Wilson teaching intern & asst prof chem, Va State Col, 1970-1972. **Memberships:** Am Chem Soc; Sigma Xi. **Research Statement & Publications:** Theoretical investigations of chemical bonding and potential energy surfaces; nuclear magnetic resonance studies of stereodynamic processes; computer aided design of crop protection chemicals. **Mailing Address:** 31 Johnston Dr, Elkton, MD 21921. **Fax:** 302-366-5738. **E-Mail:** daniel.a.kleier@usa.dupont.com

KLEIMAN, DEVRA GAIL, ETHOLOGY, REPRODUCTIVE & CONSERVATION BIOLOGY. **Personal Data:** b New York, NY, November 15, 1942; m 1988, Ian; c 2. **Education:** Univ Chicago, BS, 1964; Univ London, PhD (zoology), 1969. **Honors & Awards:** Ann Wise Award, NSF, 1987; Distinguished Achievement Award, Soc Conserve Biol, 1988. **Professional Experience:** ASST DIR RES, NAT ZOOL PARK, SMITHSONIAN INST, as of 2003; asst dir animal progs, Nat Zool Park, Smithsonian Inst, 1983-1984; adj prof, George Mason Univ, 1980- & Univ Md, 1982-; head zool res, Nat Zool Park, Smithsonian Inst, 1979-1983; adj assoc prof, George Wash Univ, 1973-1976 & Univ Md, 1979-1981; reproduction zoologist, Nat Zool Park, Smithsonian Inst, 1972-1979; res assoc, Smithsonian Inst, 1970-1972; adj asst prof psychol, Rutgers Univ, 1970-1971; NIH fel develop, Inst Animal Behav, Rutgers Univ, 1969-1971; res asst reproductive biol, Wellcome Inst Comp Physiol, Zool Soc London, 1965-1969; res asst biopsychol, Univ Chicago, 1964-1965; grantee, Nat Geog Soc, Smithsonian Inst, World Wildlife Fund, Friends Nat Zoo, NIMH, Wildlife Preserve Trust Int & Am Zoo & Aquarium Asn; coordr, Golden Lion Tamarin Conserv Prog, Brazil. **Memberships:** Fel Animal Behav Soc (secy, 1977-1981 & pres, 1981-1982); Am Asn Zool Parks & Aquariums; Am Soc Mammalogists; Sigma Xi; Am Inst Biol Sci; fel AAAS. **Research Statement & Publications:** Social behavior and social organization of mammals; mammalian reproductive strategies; conservation and reintroduction of endangered species in the wild and in zoos; application of behavior techniques to management and breeding of endangered species in captivity. **Mailing Address:** 7216 Delfield St, Chevy Chase, MD 20815. **E-Mail:** dgkleiman@aol.com

KLEIMAN, HERBERT, PHYSICS. **Personal Data:** b New York, NY, October 1, 1933; m 1960, c 1. **Education:** Mass Inst Technol, BS, 1954; Purdue Univ, MS, 1957, PhD (physics), 1961. **Professional Experience:** RETIRED; mem staff, Lincoln Lab, Mass Inst Technol, beginning 1966; asst prof, Univ Calif, Berkeley, 1963-1966; NSF fel physics, Univ Calif, Berkeley, 1961-1963. **Research Statement & Publications:** High resolution spectroscopy; atomic structure and atomic spectra; quantum optics and photon correlation studies; physical optics. **Mailing Address:** 16 Reed Lane, Bedford, MA 01730. **E-Mail:** kleiman@ll.mit.edu

KLEIMAN, HOWARD, ALGEBRA, NUMBER THEORY. **Personal Data:** b New York, NY, April 15, 1929; m 1956, Edna M Benjamin; c Michele, Jeffrey & Daniel. **Education:** NY Univ, BA, 1950, MS, 1961; Columbia Univ, MA, 1954; King's Col, Univ London, PhD (math), 1969. **Professional Experience:** PROF EMER MATH, QUEENSBOROUGH COMMUNITY COL, 1991-; from asst prof to prof, Queensborough Community Col, 1967-1991; Teacher, New York City Bd Educ, 1955-1956 & Bur Educ Physically Handicapped, 1956-1967. **Memberships:** Am Math Soc. **Research Statement & Publications:** Investigation of ordinary arithmetic function fields which contain non-trivial units; improvement of running times for algorithms used to obtain Hamilton cycles in random graphs. **Mailing Address:** Dept Math, Queensborough Community Col, Hollis, NY 11423. **Fax:** 718-776-8478. **E-Mail:** rorryroon@aol.com

KLEIN, ABEL, MATHEMATICAL PHYSICS. **Personal Data:** b Rio de Janeiro, Brazil, January 16, 1945; m 1983, c 2. **Education:** Univ Brazil, BS, 1967; Inst Pure & Appl Math, MS, 1968; Mass Inst Technol, PhD (math), 1971. **Professional Experience:** Chair, Dept Math, Univ Calif, Irvine, 1996-1999; PROF MATH, UNIV CALIF, IRVINE, 1982-; from asst prof to assoc prof, Univ Calif, Irvine, 1974-1982; instr, Princeton Univ, 1972-1974; actg asst prof, Univ Calif, Los Angeles, 1971-1972; teaching asst, Mass Inst Technol, 1968-1971; instr math, Inst Pure & Appl Math, 1967. **Memberships:** Am Math Soc; Int Asn Math Physics. **Research Statement & Publications:** mathematical physics; functional analysis. **Mailing Address:** Dept Math, Univ Calif, 241 Multipurpose Sci & Technol Bldg, Irvine, CA 92697-3875. **Fax:** 949-824-7993. **E-Mail:** aklein@uci.edu

KLEIN, ABRAHAM, theoretical physics; deceased, see previous edition for last biography

KLEIN, ALBERT JONATHAN, TOPOLOGY. **Personal Data:** b Dayton, Ohio, November 16, 1944; m 1965, c 3. **Education:** Ohio State Univ, BSc, 1966, MS, 1967, PhD (math), 1969. **Professional Experience:** PROF EMER MATH & COMPUT SCI, YOUNGSTOWN STATE UNIV, 1995-; prof math & comput sci, Youngstown State Univ, 1983-1995; assoc prof, Youngstown State Univ, 1980-1983; from asst prof to assoc prof math, Youngstown-State Univ, 1969-1980. **Memberships:** Math Asn Am; Asn Comput Mach; Sigma Xi. **Research Statement & Publications:** Fuzzy topology; digital topology. **Mailing Address:** Dept Math & Comput Sci, Youngstown State Univ, Youngstown, OH 44555-0001. **Fax:** 330-941-3170.

KLEIN, ANDREW JOHN, TRACE ORGANIC ANALYSIS, ENVIRONMENTAL ANALYSIS. **Personal Data:** b Wilkes-Barre, Pa, December 31, 1951; m 1978. **Education:** King's Col, BS, 1973; Univ Wis, PhD (chem), 1978. **Professional Experience:** TEAM LEADER DEPT FORMULATION DEVELOP, MONSANTO, as of 2003; MGR, REGULATORY AFFAIRS, MONSANTO CO, 1986-; sr group leader, Monsanto Co, 1985-1986; res group leader, Monsanto Co, 1982-1985; res specialist, Monsanto Co, 1982; sr res chemist, Monsanto Co, 1980-1982; res assoc, Univ Wis, 1978-1980. **Memberships:** Am Chem Soc; AAAS; Asn Ground Water Scientists & Engrs. **Research Statement & Publications:** Trace organic analysis in environmental matrices and natural water; analysis of xenobiotics in animal tissues. **Mailing Address:** Monsanto Co, 800 N Lindbergh Blvd, St Louis, MO 63137. **Fax:** 314-694-2120.

KLEIN, ATTILA OTTO, PLANT PHYSIOLOGY. **Personal Data:** b Subotica, Yugoslavia, July 10, 1930; American citizen; m 1952, c 3. **Education:** Brooklyn Col, BA, 1953; Ind Univ, PhD (plant physiol), 1959. **Professional Experience:** ADJ PROF & PROF EMER BIOL, BRANDEIS UNIV, as of 2005; chmn dept, Brandeis Univ, 1968-1970; assoc prof biol, Brandeis Univ, beginning 1967; asst prof, Brandeis Univ, 1962-1967; asst biochemist, Conn Agr Exp Sta, 1961-1962; USPHS fel biochem, Yale Univ, 1959-1961. **Research Statement & Publications:** Cellular and plant physiology; developmental biochemistry of leaves; light-induced metabolic oscillations. **Mailing Address:** Brandeis Univ, Dept Biol, 415 S St Kalman 124, Waltham, MA 02154-2700. **E-Mail:** aklein@brandeis.edu

KLEIN, AUGUST S, PHYSICS, CHEMISTRY. **Personal Data:** b Newton, Mass, August 31, 1924; m 1957, Abigail; c Susan, August Jr & Franklin. **Education:** Williams Col, BA, 1948; Harvard Univ, MS, 1950. **Professional Experience:** CONSULT, 1992-; pres, pres

Saval Circuits, 1990-1992; pres, Ion Implantation Corp, 1985-1990; pres, Nuclear Equip Corp, 1967-1984; gen mgr, spec prod div, Tech Measurement Corp, 1964-1967; west coast mgr, High Voltage Eng Corp, 1959-1964; physicist, Atomic Power Div, Westinghouse, 1950-1958; bd dir, Northern Calif Sect, Am Vacuum Soc; chmn, Greater Silicon Valley Implant Users Group. **Memberships:** Electron Micros Soc Am; Am Inst Mining Engrs, Am Vacuum Soc. **Research Statement & Publications:** Energy dispersive x-ray fluorescent analysis; x-ray crystallography; ion implantation. **Mailing Address:** 160 La Questa Way, Woodside, CA 94062. **Fax:** 650-529-1068. **E-Mail:** akleinsr@hotmail.com

KLEIN, BARBARA P, FOOD CHEMISTRY, NUTRITIONAL SCIENCE. **Personal Data:** b New York, NY, December 30, 1936; m 1956, Miles; c Cynthia (Banai) & Gail Isabel. **Education:** Cornell Univ, BS, 1957, MS, 1959; Univ Ill, PhD (foods & nutrit), 1974. **Honors & Awards:** Borden Award, Am Home Econ Asn, 1988. **Professional Experience:** RETIRED; prog emer food sci & human nutrit, col agr, consumer & environ sci, Univ Ill, urbana, beginning 1985; div chmn, Col Agr, Univ Ill, Urbana, 1985-1990; from asst prof to assoc prof, Col Agr, Univ Ill, Urbana, 1974-1985; teaching asst, Col Agr, Univ Ill, Urbana, 1969-1972; res asst, Col Agr, Univ Ill, Urbana, 1966-1968; res asst food chem, Col Home Econ, Cornell Univ, 1957-1958. **Memberships:** Inst Food Technologists; Am Soc Nutrit Sci; Am Chem Soc; Am Dietetics Asn; Am Asn Cereal Chemists; fel Inst Food Technologists. **Research Statement & Publications:** Nutritional and sensory alterations in food quality during processing; particularly vegetables and soy products. **Mailing Address:** Dept Food Sci & Human Nutrit, Col Agri, Consumer & Environ Sci, Univ Ill, 461 Bevier Hall MC 182, Urbana, IL 61801. **Fax:** 217-333-9368. **E-Mail:** bpklein@uiuc.edu

KLEIN, BARRY M, SOLID STATE PHYSICS. **Education:** NY UNIV, BS, 1962, MS, 1965, PhD, 1969. **Professional Experience:** VICE CHANCELLOR, RES, UNIV CALIF, as of 2005; PROF PHYS, UNIV CALIF, as of 2005. **Mailing Address:** Dept Physics, Univ CA, Davis, CA 95616-8677. **Fax:** 530-752-0602. **E-Mail:** bmklein@ucdavis.edu

KLEIN, BENJAMIN GARRETT, MATHEMATICAL ANALYSIS. **Personal Data:** b Durham, NC, January 24, 1942; m 1971, Rosemary; c David G & Peter R. **Education:** Univ Rochester, BA, 1963; Yale Univ, MA, 1965, PhD (Ergodic theory), 1968. **Honors & Awards:** Thomas Jefferson Award, 1990. **Professional Experience:** Col board advanced placement Calculus comt, 1999-; chair, Dept Math, 1994-1998; BEVERLY F DOLAN PROF MATH, DAVIDSON COL, 1992-; chair, Southeastern Sect, Math Asn, 1992-1996; vpres, Col Western Region NC, Coun Teachers Math, 1989-1990; Consult, NC Dept Public Instr 1981-; from asst prof to prof, Dept Math, 1971-1992; asst prof, NY Univ, 1969-1971; Lectr math, NY Univ, 1967-1968. **Memberships:** Am Math Soc; Math Asn Am; Nat Coun Teachers Math. **Research Statement & Publications:** General mathematics. **Mailing Address:** Dept Math, Davidson Col, PO Box 1719 Chambers Bldg Rm 130-A 200 D Rd, Davidson, NC 28036-1719. **Fax:** 704-894-2005. **E-Mail:** beklein@davidson.edu

KLEIN, BERNARD, ORGANIC CHEMISTRY. **Personal Data:** b New York, NY, September 16, 1914; m 1942, Rose Shweitzer; c David Andrew & Peter Alan. **Education:** Brooklyn Col, BS, 1934; Polytech Inst Brooklyn, PhD (chem), 1950. **Honors & Awards:** Van Slyke Award, Am Asn Clin Chemists, 1969, Ames Award, 1975. **Professional Experience:** EMER PROF, DEPT LAB MED, EINSTEIN COL MED, BRONX, NY, 1985-; prof, Dept Lab Med, Einstein Col Med, Bronx, NY, 1981-1985; asst dir, Dept Diag Res, 1971-1980; group chief clin chem, Res Div, Hoffmann-La Roche, Inc, 1967-1971; biochemist, Res Div, Hoffmann-La Roche, Inc, 1967; biochemist, US Vet Admin Hosp, Bronx, 1948-1967; res chemist, Warner Inst, NY, 1946-1948 & Harlem Hosp Cancer Found, 1948; biochemist, Jewish Sanitarium & Hosp Chronic Dis, 1941-1942; Chemist, Bethel Hosp, NY, 1936-1941; Consult chemist, Area Reference Lab. **Memberships:** Am Chem Soc; Am Asn Clin Chem. **Research Statement & Publications:** Pyrazine chemistry; automated biochemical analyses. **Mailing Address:** 129 Patton Blvd, New Hyde Park, NY 11040-1726.

KLEIN, CARL FREDERICK, MANUFACTURING RESEARCH, SENSORS ACTUATORS & DIAGNOSTIC SYSTEMS. **Personal Data:** b Milwaukee, Wi, m 1969, Mary; c Christine, Mathew, John & James. **Education:** Univ Wis, Madison, BS, 1965, MS, 1967. **Professional Experience:** MGR NEW TECHNOL, JOHNSON CONTROLS INC, 1992-; res group mgr, Johnson Controls Inc, 1980-1990; mgr tech forecasting, Johnson Controls Inc, 1977-1980; res scientist, Johnson Controls Inc, 1972-1977; res engr, Johnson Serv Co, 1967-1972; instr physics semiconductor devices, Marquette Univ, 1967-1972. **Memberships:** Inst Elec & Electronics Engrs; Soc Mfg Engrs; Soc Automotive Engrs; Am Welding Soc. **Research Statement & Publications:** Enhanced profitability of manufacturing plants by accelerating the integration of new technology onto the factory floors; author/co-author of sixteen technical papers; inventor/co-inventor of eighteen US patents. **Mailing Address:** 5740 S Lochleven Lane, New Berlin, WI 53146. **Fax:** 414-524-2828.

KLEIN, CATHERINE B, ENVIRONMENTAL MEDICINE. **Education:** State Univ NY, BS; George Wash Univ, MS, 1978; NY Univ, PhD, 1988. **Professional Experience:** ASST PROF, DEPT ENVIRON MED, NY UNIV SCH MED, NY, as of 2005. **Mailing Address:** Dept Environ Med A J Lanza Lab 201W, NY Univ 57 Old Forge Rd, Tuxedo, NY 10987. **Fax:** 845-351-2058. **E-Mail:** kleinc@env.med.nyu.edu

KLEIN, CERRY M, OPTIMIZATION, COMPUTER AIDED DESIGN & MANUFACTURING. **Personal Data:** b Kansas City, Mo, December 11, 1955; m 1980, Debra; c Corey, Jonathan, Trevor, Nicolas, Breanna & Zachary. **Education:** N W Mo State Univ, BS, 1977; Purdue Univ, MS, 1980, PhD (indust eng), 1983. **Honors & Awards:** Ralph R Teetor Award, 1989. **Professional Experience:** CHMN, DEPT INDUST & MANUFACTURING SYSTEMS ENG, UNIV MO, COLUMBIA, as of 2004; prin investr, NSF, 1996; vis prof, Monteray Technol Univ, 1994; DIR UNDERGRAD & GRAD STUDIES, UNIV MO, COLUMBIA, 1992-; prin investr, Eisenhower grant, 1992, 1994, 1995, 1996; prin investr, Soc Mech Engrs, 1989, 1990; prin investr, Off Naval Res, 1988; prin investr, McDonnell Douglas Corp, 1988; consult, McDonnell Douglas Corp, 1987; consult, 3M Co, 1986; PROF INDUST ENG, UNIV MO, COLUMBIA, 1984-; systs analyst, Nisus Corp, Indianapolis, Ind, 1980-1983; teacher math, Consol Sch, Kansas City, Mo, 1977-1978. **Memberships:** Inst Opers Res & Mgt Sci; Soc Indust & Appl Math; Math Prog Soc; Inst Indust Eng; Sigma Xi. **Research Statement & Publications:** Dynamic programming; combinatiorial optimization; design and analysis of heuristics; submodular functions; manufacturing processes; decision analysis; applications of operations research techniques and interior methods for mathematical programming; fuzzy set methodology. **Mailing Address:** Dept Indust & Mfg Syst Eng, Col Eng, Univ Mo, E3437H Eng Bldg E, Columbia, MO 65211. **Fax:** 573-882-2693. **E-Mail:** kleinc@missouri.edu

KLEIN, CHRISTOPHER FRANCIS, LASERS, ELECTRO-OPTICS. **Personal Data:** b Los Angeles, Calif, September 11, 1943; m 1973, c 2. **Education:** Calif State Univ, Long Beach, BS, 1967, MS, 1972. **Professional Experience:** Instr physics, El Camino Col, 1976-1977; RES LASER SPECTROSCOPY, LASER SYSTS DESIGN & ANALYSIS, AEROSPACE CORP, 1975-; mem res & develop staff laser design, Hughes Aircraft Co, 1972-1975; mem res & develop staff electro-optic design, Autonetics Div, NAm Rockwell, 1967-1972. **Memberships:** Soc Photo-Optical Instrumentation Engrs. **Research Statement & Publications:** Laser spectroscopy; laser design; laser damage to optical materials. **Mailing Address:** Aerospace Corp, MS M4-980 PO Box 92957, Los Angeles, CA 99009-2957.

KLEIN, CLAUDE A, PHYSICS. **Personal Data:** b Strasbourg, France, November 4, 1925; American citizen; m 1950, c 1. **Education:** Univ Paris, EE, 1951, PhD (physics), 1955. **Professional Experience:** CONSULT SCIENTIST, 1989-; Univ Paris, 1954-1956 & Univ Lowell, 1962-1963; prin scientist, Res Div, Raytheon Co, 1957-1988; Asst to mgr, Mil Dept, French AEC, 1955-1957; Vis lectr, Univ Lyons, 1953-1954. **Memberships:** Fel Am Phys Soc; Inst Elec & Electronics Engrs. **Research Statement & Publications:** Solid state physics; lasers and infrared; systems engineering. **Mailing Address:** 9 Churchill Lane, Lexington, MA 02173.

KLEIN, CORNELIS, MINERALOGY, PETROLOGY. **Personal Data:** b Haarlem, Holland, September 4, 1937; American citizen; wid, c Stephanie W (Peponis) & Marc A. **Education:** McGill Univ, BSc, 1958, MSc, 1960; Harvard Univ, PhD (geol), 1965. **Honors & Awards:** Carnegie Mineral Award Int Recognized Achievements Mineral, 1997. **Professional Experience:** PROF & PRESIDENTIAL TEACHING FEL, as of 2005; assoc ed, & Can Mineralogist, 1989-1991; PROF EARTH & PLANETARY SCI, UNIV NMEX, 1984-; chmn, Dept Geol, 1984-1986; assoc ed, Precambrian Res, 1983-; mem, Precambrian Paleobiol Res Group, Univ Calif Los Angeles, 1979-; John Simon Guggenheim fel, 1978; assoc ed, Am Mineralogist, 1977-1982; profmineral, Ind Univ, Bloomington, 1972-1984; assoc prof mineral, Harvard Univ, 1969-1972; Allston Burr sr tutor & asst dean, Harvard Col, 1966-1970; lectr, Harvard Univ, 1965-1969; res assoc geol, Harvard Univ, 1963-1965. **Memberships:** Fel Mineral Soc Am; fel Geol Soc Am; Mineral Asn Can; fel AAAS. **Research Statement & Publications:** Precambrian iron formation; chemical; optical and x-ray properties of amphiboles; minerals in meteorites; mineralogy and petrology of lunar rocks; electron probe analysis of minerals; natural dust and asbestos. **Mailing Address:** Dept Earth & Planetary Sci, Univ NMex, Northrop Hall Rm 212, Albuquerque, NM 87131. **E-Mail:** cklein@unm.edu

KLEIN, DALE EDWARD, NUCLEAR ENGINEERING. **Personal Data:** b Cooper Co, Mo, July 6, 1947; m 1971. **Education:** Univ Mo, Columbia, BS, 1970, MS, 1971, PhD (nuclear eng), 1977. **Professional Experience:** PROF, MECH ENG, UNIV TEX, AUSTIN, as of 2004; ASST SECY DEFENCE NUCLEAR & CHEM & BIOL DEFENCE PROG, 2001-; mem, NUCLEAR ENERY RES ADV COMT, 2000; vice chancellor, Univ Tex Syst, 1995-2001; dep dir, Ctr Energy Studies, 1986-; assoc prof mech eng, nuclear eng, teaching prog, Univ Tex, beginning 1982; dir, nuclear eng teaching prog, Univ Tex, Austin, beginning 1978; asst prof, Univ Tex Syst, 1977-1982; Engr, Gen Atomic Co, 1974; teaching & res asst nuclear eng, Univ Mo, Columbia, 1973-1977; design engr, Procter & Gamble Co, 1970-1972. **Memberships:** Am Soc Mech Engrs; Am Nuclear Soc; Nat Soc Prof Engrs. **Research Statement & Publications:** Thermal analysis of nuclear shipping containers; heat transfer augmentation for flow over rough surfaces; liquid metal flows through a packed bed under the influence of a transverse magnetic field. **Mailing Address:** 1203 Wilshire Blvd, Austin, TX 78722. **Fax:** 512-499-4710. **E-Mail:** dale_klein@mail.utexas.edu

KLEIN, DAVID C, NEUROENDOCRINOLOGY. **Personal Data:** b New York, NY, May 11, 1940. **Education:** Cornell Univ, AB, 1962; Rice Univ, PhD (biol), 1968. **Professional Experience:** CHIEF NEUROENDOCRINOL SECT, LAB DEVELOP NEUROBIOLOGY, NATINST CHILD HEALTH & HUMAN DEVELOP, NIH, 1977-; chmn, NIH Child Care Adv Comt, 1975-1976; pres, Nat Inst Child Health & Human Develop Assembly Scientists, 1974-1975; physiologist, Sect Physiol Controls, Lab Biomed Sci, 1973-1977; sr staff fel, Sect Physiol Controls, Lab Biomed Sci, 1971-1973; fel pharmacol, Univ Rochester Sch Med & Dent, 1967-1969; Nat Inst Dent Res trainee, 1965-1967; lab instr gen biol, endocrinol & radioisotope methodology, Rice Univ, 1964-1966; rice fel biol, 1964; res asst biophys cytol, Rockefeller Univ, 1962-1964; res asst, phys biol, 1962; res asst endocrinol, Cornell Univ, 1961. **Memberships:** AAAS; Sigma Xi; Tissue Cult Soc; Endocrine Soc; Am Soc Pharmacol & Exp Therapeut; Int Soc Neurochem; Am Soc Neurochem. **Research Statement & Publications:** Biochemical signal transduction, using pinealocyte as an experimental model; the neural regulation of gene expression; the molecular basis of the biochemical "AND" gate. **Mailing Address:** Lab Develop Neurobiology, Nat Inst Child Health & Human Develop, NIH, Rm A82 MSC4480 Bldg 49, Bethesda, MD 20892-4480. **Fax:** 301-480-3526. **E-Mail:** klein@helix.nih.gov

KLEIN, DAVID HENRY, ANALYTICAL METHODS DEVELOPMENT. **Personal Data:** b Milwaukee, Wis, May 28, 1933; m 1954, Nancy Knuth Klein; c Martin Philip & Peter Gordon. **Education:** Albion Col, BA, 1954; Case Western Res Univ, PhD, 1959. **Professional Experience:** SR VPRES, PHARMACEUT DEVELOP, ALLIANCE PHARMACEUT CORP, as of 2002; distinguished res fel, Alliance Pharmaceut Corp, beginning 1994; div dir, pharmaceut res & develop, 1990-1994; dir analytical chem, 1989-1990; proj scientist, Parke Davis Co, 1981-1985; vis scientist, Oak Ridge Nat Lab, 1973-1974; chmn dept, Hope Col, 1969-1973; NSF fel, Scripps Inst Onceanog, 1968-1969; from assoc prof to prof chem, Hope Col, 1964-1981; asst prof, Los Angeles State Col, 1960-1964; Instr chem, Calif Inst Technol, 1959-1960; analytical group leader, Adamantech Inc. **Memberships:** AAAS; Am Chem Soc. **Research Statement & Publications:** Kinetics of nucleation; precipitation and co-precipitation; mercury and other heavy metals in the environment; geochemistry and marine chemistry; analysis of pharmaceutical materials; analysis of perfluorocarbons particle size measurements; pharmacokinetics of perfluorocarbons. **Mailing Address:** Alliance Pharmaceut Corp, 3040 Science Park Rd, San Diego, CA 92121. **Fax:** 858-410-5201.

KLEIN, DAVID JOSEPH, radiological physics; deceased, see previous edition for last biography

KLEIN, DAVID L, GEOPHYSICS. **Education:** Case Western Res Univ, BS, 1973; Univ Ill, MS, 1975, PhD (physics), 1978. **Professional Experience:** PRIN SCIENTIST & OWNER, IMAGE TOOLS, 1989-; Res staff geophysicist, Cogniseis Develop, 1988-1989; VPRES, TECHNOL DEVELOP, IMAGE TOOLS; CONSULT. **Memberships:** Am Phys Soc. **Mailing Address:** Image Tools, 5814 Braesheather, Houston, TX 77096.

KLEIN, DAVID M, ENVIRONMENTAL ANALYSIS, ORGANIC CHEMISTRY. **Personal Data:** b Ft Worth, Tex, October 31, 1956. **Education:** Univ Tex, BS, 1978; Tex Christian Univ, MA, 1980; Univ Hawaii, PhD (chem), 1986. **Professional Experience:** LAB MGR, ENVIRON CONTAMINANTS LAB, TEX PARKS & WILDLIFE, as of 2003; adj fac, Southwest Tex State Univ, 1995; lab mgr, Dept Agr, Univ Hawaii, 1990-1993; chem instr, Kapiolani Community Col, 1988-1990; postdoctoral, Univ Hawaii, 1986-1988. **Memberships:** Am Chem Soc (pres-elect 1993); Asn Off Anal Chemists (pres-elect 1997-). **Research Statement & Publications:** Environmental analysis; tissue matrices for residue analysis. **Mailing Address:** Environ Contaminants Lab, Tex Parks & Wildlife, 505 Staples Rd, San Marcos, TX 78666. **Fax:** 512-353-7329. **E-Mail:** david.klein@tpwd.state.tx.us

KLEIN, DAVID ROBERT, MAMMALIAN ECOLOGY. **Personal Data:** b Fitchburg, Mass, May 18, 1927; m 1988, Lou; c 3. **Education:** Univ Conn, BS, 1951; Univ Alaska, MS, 1953; Univ BC, PhD (zoology), 1963. **Honors & Awards:** Spec Recognition Serv Award, Wildlife Soc, 1991; Meritorius Serv Honor Award, Dept Interior, 1992. **Professional Experience:** Sr scientist, Alaska Coop Fish & Wildlife Res Unit, 1992-1997; PROF EMER, DEPT BIOL & WILDLIFE, UNIV ALASKA, 1992-; vis prof, Univ Pretoria, beginning 1983; vis prof, Univ Oslo, 1971-1972; vis res biologist, Kalo Game Biol Sta, Denmark, beginning 1967; Bur Sport Fisheries & Wildlife grant, 1964-1965 & Bur Land Mgr, 1965-1967; NSF inst grant, 1963-1964; prof wildlife ecol, Univ Alaska, 1962-1992; res dir, Alaska Dept Fish & Game, 1961-1962; biologist, Alaska Dept Fish & Game, 1959-1961; biologist, US Fish & Wildlife Serv, 1955-1959. **Memberships:** AAAS; Wildlife Soc; Arctic Inst NAm; Soc Range Mgt; Am Soc Mammalogists. **Research Statement & Publications:** Foraging dynamics of arctic ungulates, artic herbivory; man's impact on the environment. **Mailing Address:** Dept Wildlife & Biol, Univ Alaska, PO Box 757000, Fairbanks, AK 99775. **E-Mail:** ffdrk@aurora.alaska.edu

KLEIN, DEBORAH W, GENETICS. **Education:** EdD. **Professional Experience:** ASSOC COMNR, MASS DEP PUB HEALTH, MASS, as of 2006. **Mailing Address:** Dept Soc Human Develop & Health, Kresge Bldg Sixth Floor 677 Huntington Ave, Boston, MA 02115. **E-Mail:** debbie.walker@state.ma.us

KLEIN, DIANE M, CIRCULATORY SHOCK. **Personal Data:** b Chicago, Ill, March 21, 1948. **Education:** Univ Ill, PhD (physiol), 1978. **Professional Experience:** ASSOC PROF PHYSIOL, NEIHOFF SCH NURSING, LOYOLA UNIV, 1983-; asst prof, Loyola Univ, 1978-1983. **Memberships:** Am Physiol Soc; Circulatory Shock Soc. **Mailing Address:** Marcella Neihoff Sch Nursing, Loyola Univ, 6525 N Sheridan Rd, Chicago, IL 60626-5311. **E-Mail:** dklein@luc.edu

KLEIN, DOLPH, CLINICAL MICROBIOLOGY. **Personal Data:** b New York, NY, May 2, 1928; m 1956, c 4. **Education:** City Col NY, BS, 1950; Rutgers Univ, PhD (microbiol), 1961; Am Bd Med Microbiol, dipl, 1977. **Professional Experience:** ASSOC PROF EMER MOLECULAR GENETICS & MICROBIOL, DUKE UNIV, as of 2003; vis prof, Univ Amsterdam, Neth, 1991; vis prof, Univ Groningen, Neth, 1982-1983; assoc prof microbiol, Med Ctr, Duke Univ, beginning 1974; dir, Clin Microbiol Lab, Dulce Hosp, 1974-1989; asst prof microbiol & asst dir, Diag Microbiol Lab, Med Ctr, 1972-1974; asst prof biochem, Univ Minn, Minneapolis, 1967-1971; res assoc biophys chem, Purdue Univ, 1963-1967; sr res microbiologist, Monsanto Res Corp, Mass, 1962-1963; res microbiologist, Monsanto Co, Mo, 1961-1962; res asst agr microbiol, Rutgers Univ, 1958-1961; res asst biophys, Sloan-Kettering Inst Cancer Res, 1957-1958; chief med technologist, Lakeside Hosp, Copiague, 1954-1957; bacteriologist, Beth Israel Hosp, NY, 1953-1954; lab asst microbiol, New York City Dept Health, 1951-1953; med technologist, Manhattan Gen Hosp, 1950-1951. **Memberships:** Am Soc Microbiol. **Research Statement & Publications:** Applications of biotechnology for rapid detection and identification of pathogenic bacteria; bacterial dissimilation of streptomycin; evaluation of antimicrobial agents and their modes of action; physicochemical basis of biological stability in structural proteins. **Mailing Address:** Dept Microbiol & Immunol, Duke Univ, Box 2929, Durham, NC 27710. **Fax:** 919-684-8671. **E-Mail:** kledolph@acpub.duke.edu

KLEIN, DONALD ALBERT, MICROBIOLOGY. **Personal Data:** b Bridgeport, Conn, September 11, 1935; m 1956, c 4. **Education:** Univ Vt, BS, 1957, MS, 1961; Pa State Univ, PhD (microbiol), 1966. **Professional Experience:** PROF MICROBIOL, COLO STATE UNIV, 1978-; vis prof, Univ Kiel, 1975 & Univ Copenhagen, 1978; from asst prof to assoc prof, Colo State Univ, 1970-1978; asst prof, Ore State Univ, 1967-1970; res asst microbiol, Pa State Univ, 1962-1966; instr food microbiol, Univ Vt, 1958-1961; Asst qual control, Nat Dairy Prod Corp, Vt, 1957-1958. **Memberships:** Am Soc Microbiol; Am Soc Agron. **Research Statement & Publications:** Mined land reclamation microbiology; rhizosphere microbiology; microbial transformation of hydrocarbons and pesticides; soil ecology. **Mailing Address:** Dept Microbiol & Immunol & Path, Colo State Univ, Off B209, Microbiol Bldg, Ft Collins, CO 80523-0001. **Fax:** 970-491-1815. **E-Mail:** dakspk@lamar.colostate.edu

KLEIN, DONALD FRANKLIN, PSYCHIATRY, PSYCHOPHARMACOLOGY. **Personal Data:** b New York, NY, September 4, 1928; m Rachel; c 5. **Education:** Colby Col, BA, 1947; State Univ NY, MD, 1952; Am Bd Psychiat & Neurol, dipl psychiat, 1959. **Honors & Awards:** A E Bennett Neuropsychiat Res Award, 1964; Res Award, Nat Asn Pvt Psychiat Hosps, 1965 & 1971; Samuel W Hamilton Award, Am Psychopath Asn, 1980; William R McAlpin Award, Res Achievement, 1988; Gold Medal Award, Soc Biol Psychiat, 1990; Paul Hoch Distinguished Serv Award, Am Col Nuclear Physicians, 1991; Thomas W Salmon Medal, Distinguished Serv Psychiat, NY Acad Med, 1993; society of biological psychiatry, lifetime award, 1996; Exemplary Psychiatrist Award 1997; Castillo De Pino Prize for Achievment in Psychiatry, 1999; citation commentary 50 years of dedication to medicine from the medical society of the state of new york, 2002; Natl Alliance for the Mentally Ill. **Professional Experience:** Mem, Bd Sci Counr, Nat Inst Alcohol Abuse & Alcoholism, 1996-; consult, Nat Inst Drug Admin, 1990-; sr sci adv, Alcohol Drug Abuse & Ment Health Admin, 1989-1990; chmn, Clin Comt, 1988-; consult, Alcohol Drug Abuse & Ment Health Admin, 1988-1989; mem, Sci Adv Bd, Nat Depressive & Manic Depressive Asn, 1986-; pres, Nat Found Depressive Illness, 1983-; chmn, Res Adv Coun, Tex Dept Ment Health & Ment Retardation, 1983-1985; PROF PSYCHIAT, COL PHYSICIANS & SURG, COLUMBIA UNIV, 1978-; DIR, MENT HEALTH CLIN RES CTR, 1978-; DIR RES & DEPT THERAPEUTICS, NY STATE PSYCHIAT INST, 1976-; consult, Comt Res & Pub, Long Island Jewish-Hillside Med Ctr, 1976-1985; lectr, Columbia Univ, 1976-1978; vis prof psychiat, Albert Einstein Col Med, 1976-1977; vis prof psychiat, Univ Auckland, NZ, 1975; full attend psychiatrist, Queen Hosp Ctr, 1972-1985; prof psychiat, Col Med, State Univ NY, Stony Brook, 1972-1976; dir, Dept Psychiat Res & Eval, Long Island Jewish-Hillside Med Ctr, 1972-1976; chmn, Comt Res & Pub, Long Island Jewish-Hillside Med Ctr, 1972-1975; mem, Hofheimer Prize Bd, Am Psychiat Asn, 1969-1975 & task force methadone & narcotic antagonist eval, 1971-1973; mem, Clin Pharmacol Study Sect, NIMH, 1971-1975 & Neuropharmacol Adv Comt, Food & Drug Admin, 1971; psychiatrist-in-chief, Queen Hosp Ctr, 1970-1971; med dir eval, Hillside Hosp, 1970-1971; adj prof psychol, Queens Col, City Univ New York, 1969-; dir res, Hillside Hosp, 1965-1970; sr staff psychiatrist, 1965; NIMH grants, 1961-; USPHS ment health career investr, 1961-1964; res assoc, Hillside Hosp, 1959-1964; cand, NY Psychoanal Inst, 1957-1961; res assoc psychiat, Creedmoor Inst Psychobiol Studies, 1957-1959; Pvt pract, 1956-; sr asst surg & staff psychiatrist, USPHS Hosp, Lexington, Ky, 1954-1956; resident, Creedmoor State Hosp, 1953-1954 & 1956-1958; Intern, USPHS Hosp, Staten Island, NY, 1952-1953. **Memberships:** Fel Am Col Neuropsychopharmacol (pres 1981); fel Am Psychiat Asn; Am Psychopath Asn (treas 1972 pres 1978); Int Neuropsychol Soc; fel Royal Col Psychiat; Am Soc Clin Psychopharmacol (pres). **Research Statement & Publications:** Diagnosis and drug treatment of psychiatric disorders; psychiatric case studies, treatment, drugs and outcome; age of onset of drug abuse in psychiatric inpatients; phobic anxiety syndrome complicated by drug dependence and addiction; physiologyof panic attack. **Mailing Address:** NY State Psychiat Inst, 1051 Riverside Dr Unit, 22, New York, NY 10032. **Fax:** 212-543-6945. **E-Mail:** donaldk737@aol.com

KLEIN, DONALD LEE, INORGANIC CHEMISTRY SEMICONDUCTOR MATERIALS & PROCESSING. **Personal Data:** b Brooklyn, NY, December 19, 1930; m 1952, Ruth; c Emilie H (Packer), Lynn M (Wiener), Sandra A (Worona), Jeffrey D, Robin D (Schwartz) & Gail B (Buiumsohn). **Education:** Polytech Inst Brooklyn, BSCh, 1952; Univ Conn, MS, 1956, PhD (chem), 1959. **Honors & Awards:** Jack A Morton Award, Inst Elec & Electronics Engrs, 1994 New Jersy Inventors Hall of Fame, 1994; IBM Invention Achievement Award, 1982. **Professional Experience:** Ctr Lifetime Study, Marist Col, 1994-; CONSULT, 1987-; Lectr, Dutches Comm Unity Col, 1987-1993; adj lectr, Rochester Inst Technol, 1987-1992; Adj prof, Rensselaer Polytech Inst, 1986; sr engr, Gen Technol Div, IBM Corp, 1967-1987; mem tech staff, Bell Tel Labs, Inc, 1958-1967; asst instr, Univ Conn, 1955-1958; asst, Univ Conn, 1954-1955; Engr, Sylvania Elec Prod, Inc, 1952-1954. **Memberships:** Am Chem Soc; Sigma Xi. **Research Statement & Publications:** Electrochemistry; photochemistry; semiconductor materials and processing. **Mailing Address:** 4 Carnelli Ct, Poughkeepsie, NY 12603. **E-Mail:** w2gkr@aol.com

KLEIN, DOUGLAS J, THEORETICAL CHEMISTRY, CHEMICAL PHYSICS. **Personal Data:** b Portland, Ore, November 8, 1942; m 1966, Janet; c 2. **Education:** Ore State Univ, BS, 1965; Univ Tex, Austin, MA, 1967, PhD (chem), 1969. **Professional Experience:** Fulbright fel, oxford univ, 1994; PROF CHEM, TEX A&M UNIV, GALVESTON, 1988-; vis sci officer, Off Naval Res, 1984; from asst prof to assoc prof, Tex A&M Univ Galveston, 1979-1987; vis asst prof, Rice Univ, Houston, 1979; asst prof physics, Univ Tex, Austin, 1971-1978; Air Force Off Sci Res-Nat Res Coun fel, Princeton Univ, 1969-1970; Instr chem, Univ Tex, Austin, 1969. **Memberships:** Am Chem Soc; Am Phys Soc; Math Asn Am; Am math soc. **Research Statement & Publications:** Theoretical models for molecules, polymers; and solids with special emphasis on correlation effects and Resonance theory chemistry appl of graph theory; combinatories; and group theory; eco-environmental modelling. **Mailing Address:** Dept Marine Sci, Tex A&M Univ, PO Box 1675, Galveston, TX 77553-1675. **Fax:** 409-740-4429. **E-Mail:** kleind@tamug.edu

KLEIN, EDWARD LAWRENCE, WOOD ENERGY, FOREST PRODUCTS. **Personal Data:** b Roscoe, Pa, February 17, 1936; m 1963, c Paul, John, Erin & Stephanie. **Education:** Pa State Univ, BS, 1958, MS, 1961; Baylor Univ, MBA, 1963; La State Univ, PhD (forestry mkt), 1968. **Professional Experience:** RETIRED; Dir timber oper, Uologda, Russia, 1996-1998; vpres, Capital Resources E, 1994-2005; dir timber opers, Brooke Int, 1991-1994; dir mkt, Enerco Assocs, Langhorne, PA, 1979-1986; proj leader wood energy, Div Forestry, Tenn Valley Auth, Norris, 1977-1979; staff asst to dir, Div Forestry, Tenn Valley Auth, Norris, 1975-1977; mfg mgr, Indust Wood & Pallet Co, 1973-1975; supvr econ sect, Tenn Valley Auth, 1969-1973; mkt analyst, US Forest Serv, Princeton, WVa, 1968-1969; instr in charge mkt res, La State Univ, 1965-1968; asst dist forester, Md Dept of Forestry, 1958-1960. **Memberships:** Soc Am Foresters; Forest Prod Res Soc. **Research Statement & Publications:** Economics of new plant sites and construction; production of saw mills and pallet plants; utilization of biomass as an energy source; development of saw mills in Russia and develop of Monrets in Japan.

KLEIN, ELENA BUIMOVICI, MICROBIOLOGY, INFECTIOUS DISEASES. **Personal Data:** b Bucharest, Romania, November 12, 1930; m 1962, c 1. **Education:** Univ Bucharest, MD, 1953. **Professional Experience:** CONSULT, VIROLOGY LAB, ROOSEVELT HOSP, 1994-; dir, Virus Lab, St Luke's-Roosevelt Hosp Ctr, 1980-1994; asst prof pediat, Roosevelt Hosp, Columbia Univ, beginning 1973; res scientist virol, Bellevue Hosp, NY Univ, 1972-1973; Sr res scientist microbiol, Cantacuzino Inst, Bucharest, 1953-1972. **Memberships:** Romanian Soc Infectious Path; Am Soc Microbiol; fel Soc Infectious Dis. **Research Statement & Publications:** Epidemiology of diptheria; genetics of enteroviruses; epidemiology of poliomyelities; congenital rubella; cell mediated immunity in viral infections; viral vaccines. **Mailing Address:** Dept Pediat, St Luke's-Roosevelt Hosp Ctr, New Rochelle, NY 10804.

KLEIN, ELIAS, PHYSICAL CHEMISTRY. **Personal Data:** b Leipzig, Ger, October 26, 1924; m 1948, c 3. **Education:** Tulane Univ, MS, 1952, PhD (phys chem), 1954. **Professional Experience:** PROF MED, SCH MED, UNIV LOUISVILLE, 1984-; ASSOC PROF ENG, SCH CHEM ENG, UNIV LOUISVILLE, 1982-; adj prof, Loyola Univ, La, 1969-; dir phys chem, dir Lake Pontchartrain Lab, 1967-1981; dir phys chem, Gulf Southern Res Inst, 1967; dir res & develop, Courtaulds, Inc, Ala, 1964-1967; mgr res dept, Courtaulds, Inc, Ala, 1962-1964; sect head, Courtaulds, Inc, Ala, 1960-1962; res chemist phys chem, Courtaulds, Inc, Ala, 1958-1960; invest head, Southern Regional Res Lab, USDA, 1955-1958; Res chemist, Southern Regional Res Lab, USDA, 1954-1955; Consult, Kalvar Corp, 1952-1955; founder & pres, NAm Membrane Soc. **Memberships:** Am Chem Soc; Sci Res Soc Am; Am Soc Artificial Internal Organs. **Research Statement & Publications:** Kinetics; cellulose and fiber chemistry; membrane transport; hemodialysis; reverse osmosis. **Mailing Address:** 5517 Hempstead Rd, Louisville, KY 40207-1207.

KLEIN, FRANCIS MICHAEL, MOLECULAR MODELING, REACTION MECHANISMS. **Personal Data:** b Wilkes Barre, Pa, November 1, 1941; m 1964, Janet; c Kathleen (Murray), Kristin (Pluhacek), Mark, Matthew & Rachel (Kolb). **Education:** King's Col, Pa, BS, 1963; Univ Notre Dame, PhD (org chem), 1967. **Professional Experience:** ASSOC DEAN, Creighton Coll of Arts & Sci, 2002-; chmn dept, Creighton Univ, 1987-1993; asst dean, Creighton Univ, 1978-1979; ASSOC PROF CHEM, CREIGHTON UNIV, 1973-; asst prof, Creighton Univ, 1968-1973; NIH fel, Iowa State Univ, 1967-1968. **Memberships:** Am Chem Soc. **Research Statement & Publications:** reaction mechanisms, especially stereochemical factors; molecular orbital calculations of reaction energetics. **Mailing Address:** Col Arts & Scis, Creighton Univ, Omaha, NE 68178. **Fax:** 402-280-3392. **E-Mail:** fklein@creighton.edu

KLEIN, GEORGE D, PETROLEUM GEOLOGY & SEQUENCE & SEISMIC STRATIGRAPHY, SEDIMENTOLOGY. **Personal Data:** b s' Gravenhage, Neth, January 21, 1933; American citizen; m 1994, Suyon; c Richard L & Roger N. **Education:** Wesleyan Univ, BA, 1954; Univ Kans, MA, 1957; Yale Univ, PhD (geol), 1960. **Honors & Awards:** Outstanding Paper Award, SEPM (Soc Sedimentary Research), 1972; Research Fellow, Japan Soc Promotion of Science, 1983; Senior Fulbright Research Fellow, Netherlands, 1989; Lawrence L Sloss Award, Geological Society of America, 2000. **Professional Experience:** PROF EMER GEOL, UNIV ILL, URBANA-CHAMPAIGN, as of 1993; CONSULT, SED-STRAT GEOSCIENCE CONSULT INC, as of 1996; PRES, NJ MARINE SCI CONSORTIUM, 1993-1996; sr Fulbright res fel, VrijeUniv, Amsterdam, 1989; vis prof oceanog, Univ Tokyo, 1983; sr res fel, Japan Soc Prom Sci, 1983; vis prof oceanog, Seoul Nat Univ, 1980; vis exchange prof geophys sci, Univ Chicago, 1979-1980; assoc, Ctr Adv Study, Univ Ill, 1974 & 1983; vis prof oceanog, Ore State Univ, 1974; prof, Univ Ill, Urbana, 1972-1993; assoc prof geol, Univ Ill, Urbana, 1970-1972; vis fel, Oxford Univ, 1969; from asst prof to assoc prof, Univ Pa, 1963-1969; asst prof geol, Univ Pittsburgh, 1961-1963; res geologist, Sinclair Res, Inc, 1960-1961; Part-time geologist, State Geol

Surv, Kans, 1955-1956; vis assoc prof geol & geophys, UnivCalif, Berkeley. **Memberships:** Geol Soc Am; Am Asn Petrol Geol; Soc Econ Paleontologists & Mineralogists; Soc of Indepndent Professional Earth Scientists. **Research Statement & Publications:** Petroleum geology, Petroleum Play Concepts, Recent sediments; sedimentary and sandstone petrology; basin analysis; turbidites; sedimentation on tidal flats; tidalites; deltas, fluvial systems, back arc and cratonic basins; petroleum sandstone reservoir prediction and diagenesis. **Mailing Address:** SED-STRAT Geosci Consult Inc, 17424 W Grand Pkwy; Ste 127, Sugar Land, TX 77479-2564. **Fax:** 281-937-9456. **E-Mail:** gdkgeo@earthlink.net

KLEIN, GERALD I(RWIN), ELECTRICAL ENGINEERING. **Personal Data:** b Brooklyn, NY, September 22, 1928; m 1948, c 4. **Education:** Cooper Union, BEE, 1948; Polytech Inst Brooklyn, MEE, 1953. **Professional Experience:** ADV ENGR, HERLEY INDUST, 1988-; adv engr, Westinghouse Elec Corp, 1970-1988; vpres eng & mfg, Solitron Microwave, 1968-1970; mgr microwave tech lab, Aerospace Div, Md, 1965-1968; mgr, Microwave Tubes Sect, Electronic Tube Div, Westinghouse Elec Corp, 1958-1965; chief, Oscillators & Amplifiers Sect, Evans Signal Lab, NJ, 1955-1958; Asst head, Radar & Microwave Electronics Sect, Naval Mat Lab, NY, 1948-1955. **Memberships:** Sr mem Inst Elec & Electronics Engrs. **Research Statement & Publications:** Microwave electronics; electromagnetic theory; microwave plasmas; electron tubes. **Mailing Address:** 3061 Industry Dr, Lancaster, PA 17603.

KLEIN, GORDON LESLIE, GASTROENTEROLOGY, PEDIATRICS. **Personal Data:** b New York, NY, August 26, 1946; m 1973, Joann; c Adrienne L. **Education:** Columbia Univ, BA, 1967; Albert Einstein Col Med, MD, 1971; Univ Calif, Los Angeles, MPH, 1980. **Professional Experience:** Am Soc Bone & Mineral Res, Dir Pediat Bone Initiative, 2001-2003; spec gov employee, Food & Drug Admin, 1998-2002; Am Soc Parenteral & Enteral Nutrit Tech Adv Group Parenteral Nutrit, 1990-1996; US Pharmacopeia Gen Comt Rev & exec comt rev, 1990-2000; nutrit prog fel, proj HOPE & Nicaraguan ministry health, 1992; NIH panels & comm, 1989-1990, 1996-1997, 2005; PROF PEDIAT & NUTRIT, UNIV TEX MED BR, GALVESTON, 1986-; CLI ASSOC PROF PEDIAT, SCH MED, UNIV SOUTHERN CALIF, 1984-; chief serv, Pediat Gastroenterol & Nutrit, City Hope Nat Med Ctr, 1984-1986; asst prof pediat, Med Ctr, & adj asst prof nutrit, Sch Pub Health, Tulane Univ, 1982-1984; adj asst prof pediat, Med Ctr, Univ Calif, Los Angeles, 1980-1982; res affil, Wadsworth Med Ctr, Vet Admin, Calif, 1980-1982; fel gastroenterol, Med Ctr, Univ Calif, Los Angeles, 1978-1980; fel nutrit, Sch Med, Johns Hopkins Univ, 1976-1978; intern & resident pediat, Stanford Univ Med Ctr, Calif, 1971-1974; postgrad stud investigative med, Univ Cambridge, UK, 1970-1971. **Memberships:** Am Soc Bone & Mineral Res; Am Soc Clin Nutrit; Am Gastroenterol Asn; Soc Pediat Res; Am Acad Pediat; Am pediat Soc. **Research Statement & Publications:** Investigation of abnormalities in calcium and bone metabolism; aluminum contamination of parenteral solution and toxicity to bone and other organs; characterization of metabolic bone disease and its consequences following burn injury. **Mailing Address:** Univ Tex Med Br, 301 Univ Blvd, Galveston, TX 77555-0352. **Fax:** 409-747-2213. **E-Mail:** gklein@utmb.edu

KLEIN, HAROLD GEORGE, VERTEBRATE ZOOLOGY. **Personal Data:** b Jersey City, NJ, March 14, 1929; m 1965. **Education:** Cornell Univ, BS, 1953, MS, 1954, PhD (vert zool), 1958. **Professional Experience:** PROF EMER BIOL, STATE UNIV NY COL PLATTSBURGH, 1993-; from asst prof to assoc prof, State Univ NY Col Plattsburgh, 1962-1991; asst prof zool, Pa State Univ, 1959-1962; instr biol, Swarthmore Col, 1957-1958. **Memberships:** Ecol Soc Am; Am Soc Mammal; Animal Behav Soc. **Research Statement & Publications:** Ecological research on vertebrate animals, particularly mammals. **Mailing Address:** 185 Stafford Dr, Plattsburgh, NY 12901.

KLEIN, HARVEY G, TRANSFUSION MEDICINE, HEMATOLOGY. **Personal Data:** b Boston, Mass, May 8, 1943. **Education:** Harvard Univ, AB, 1965; Johns Hopkins Univ, MD, 1969. **Honors & Awards:** Cohn Delavel Award, World Apheresis Assn, 1996 NIH Director's Award 1999 Secretary HHS Distinguished Service Award 2000; Morrison Award ASFA. **Professional Experience:** CHIEF, DEPT TRANSFUSION MED, WARREN GRANT MAGNUSON CLIN CTR, NIH, 1975-; Spec asst to dir, Blood Div, Nat Heart Lung Blood Inst, 1973-1975. **Memberships:** Am Asn Blood Bank; Am Soc Hemat; Int Soc Bld Transf. **Mailing Address:** Warren Grant Magnuson Clin Ctr, NIH, Bethesda, MD 20892-7511. **Fax:** 301-402-2984. **E-Mail:** hklein@mail.cc.nih.gov

KLEIN, HARVEY GERALD, PHARMACEUTICS, MEDICAL INSTRUMENTATION. **Personal Data:** b New York, NY, October 22, 1930; m 1983, Lesli; c Zoe. **Education:** City Col NY, BS, 1953; NY Univ, MS, 1957; Purdue Univ, PhD (chem), 1961. **Professional Experience:** PRES, KLEIN BIOMED CONSULTS, 1981-; pres, Klein Assocs, 1973-1980; Wertheim & Co, 1969-1970 & Andresen & Co, 1971-1972; drug & health care financial analyst, R W Pressprich & Co, 1967-1969; tech rep & liaison, Wash, DC, 1966-1967; sr mkt analyst, Com Develop Div, Wayne, NJ, 1963-1966; chemist plastic additives res, Cent Res Div, Am Cyanamid Co, Stamford, Conn, 1961-1963. **Memberships:** Am Chem Soc; Am Inst Ultrasound Med; Inst Elec & Electronics Engrs; Am Soc Echocardiography; Am Heart Asn. **Research Statement & Publications:** Medical diagnostic instrumentation and pharmaceutical development. **Mailing Address:** Klein Biomed Consults, New York, NY 10024.

KLEIN, HERBERT A, NUCLEAR MEDICINE. **Personal Data:** b Milwaukee, Wis, March 28, 1936; m 1973, Inara; c Benjamin & Alexandra. **Education:** Columbia Univ, AB, 1956, MD, 1960; Harvard Univ, MA, 1968, PhD (biochem), 1975; Am Bd Nuclear Med, cert, 1974. **Professional Experience:** Prog Leader, Nuclear Med, 2001-; Prog Leader, Nuclear Medicine Radiol & Radiation Ther, 1997-2001; INTERIM CHIEF, NUCLEAR MED & RADIOL SERV, 1996-; CHIEF NUCLEAR MED SERV, VET ADMIN MED CTR, PITTSBURGH, 1991-; dir, Nuclear Med Educ, 1984-1991; Prin investr, Wechsler Res Found Grant, 1984-1985; MEM, MED STAFF, PRESBY-UNIV HOSP, PITTSBURGH, 1980-; assoc dir, Div Nuclear Med, Dept Radiol, Sch Med, Univ Pittsburgh, 1980-1996. **Memberships:** Soc Nuclear Med. **Research Statement & Publications:** Computer analysis of radionuclide studies of esophageal function; use of radioiodine in the diagnosis andtreatment of thyroid carcinoma. **Mailing Address:** Nuclear Med Div, Univ Pittsburgh Med Ctr, 200 Lothrop St, Pittsburgh, PA 15213. **E-Mail:** kleinha@upmc.edu

KLEIN, HOWARD JOSEPH, METALLURGICAL ENGINEERING. **Personal Data:** b Kokomo, Ind, July 5, 1941; m 1964, c 5. **Education:** Purdue Univ, BS, 1963; Univ Ala, MS, 1965; Univ Tenn, PhD (metall eng), 1969. **Honors & Awards:** Von Karman Award, Theodore Von Karman Mem Found, 1974; IR 100, Indust Res, 1975 & 1977. **Professional Experience:** DIR, SATELLITE RES & DEVELOP, SCH MAT ENG, PURDUE UNIV, as of 2004; vpres, Haynes Int Inc, beginning 1987; dir, Metals Property Coun, 1987; chmn tech bd, Am Soc Metals, 1985-1987; dir & gen mgr technol, Cabot Corp, 1985-1986; dir opers, CWP Div, 1983-1985; dir inventory mgt & qual control, CWP Div, 1982-1983; oper mgr high technol, Haynes Stellite Div, Cabot Corp, 1979-1982; dir technol, Haynes Stellite Div, Cabot Corp, 1977-1979; mem comt review US-USSR Agreement Coop Fields Sci & Technol, Nat Acad Sci, 1977; Comt Joint Coop Electro Metall, US State Dept, beginning 1976; Comt Electroslag Remelting & Plasma Melting Technol, Nat Mat Adv Bd, 1974-1975; sect mgr, Haynes Stellite Div, Cabot Corp, 1975-1977; group leader process metall & ceramics, Haynes Stellite Div, Cabot Corp, 1973-1975; sr engr process metall, Haynes Stellite Div, Cabot Corp, 1972-1973; engr, Haynes Stellite Div, Cabot Corp, 1969-1971. **Memberships:** fel Am Soc Metals Int; Am Inst Mining Metall & Petrol Engrs; Am Vaccum Soc. **Research Statement & Publications:** Development and processing of nickel and cobolt base alloys for application in the aerospace corrosion and wear resistant areas; primary and secondary processing technologies. **Mailing Address:** Sch Mat Eng, Purdue Univ, 501 Northwestern Ave, West Lafayette, IN 47907-2044. **Fax:** 765-494-1204.

KLEIN, JACOB, PHYSICS OF MATERIALS. **Personal Data:** b Tel Aviv, Israel, August 20, 1949; m 1974, Michele Castle; c 4. **Education:** Univ Cambridge, Eng, BA, 1973, MA & PhD, 1977. **Honors & Awards:** Charles Vernon Boys Prize, Brit Inst Physics, 1984; High Polymer Physics Prize, Am Phys Soc, 1995. **Professional Experience:** Kao fel, Japan, 1994; PROF, WEIZMAN INST SCI, ISRAEL, 1987-; Staff, Univ Cambridge, 1980-1984. **Research Statement & Publications:** Contributed over 120 papers to scientific journals in areas of polymer physics. **Mailing Address:** Fac Chem Weizman Inst Sci, PO Box 26, Rehovot 76100, Israel.

KLEIN, JAN, BIOLOGY, IMMUNOGENETICS. **Personal Data:** b Opava, Czech, January 18, 1936; m 1969, Dagmar; c Norman A, Daniel K & Pavel J. **Education:** Charles Univ, Prague, BS, 1955, MS, 1958; Czech Acad Sci, PhD (genetics), 1964. **Honors & Awards:** Elisabeth Goldschmidt Mem lectr; Rabbi Schacknai Mem Prize, Transplantation Soc. **Professional Experience:** DISTINGUISHED RES PROF, DEPT MICROBIOL & IMMUNOL, SCHMED, UNIV MIAMI, FLA, 1987-; DIR DEPT IMMUNOGENETICS, MAX PLANCK INSTBIOL, 1978-; from assoc prof to prof microbiol, Univ Tex Health Sci Ctr, Dallas, 1974-1978; from asst prof to assoc prof, Univ Mich, Ann Arbor, 1969-1974; res assoc, Sch Med, Stanford Univ, 1968-1969; Res assoc genetics, Inst Exp Biol & Genetics, Prague, 1964-1965; mem, Immunobiol Study Sect, NIH; managing ed, Immunogenetics. **Memberships:** Am Asn Immunol; Transplantation Soc; Scand Soc Immunol; Fr Soc Immunol. **Research Statement & Publications:** Immunogenetics; cellular immunology; molecular biology. **Mailing Address:** Max-Planck Inst fuer Biol Dept Immunogenetics, Corrensstr 42, Tuebingen, 72076, Ger. **Fax:** 497-071-600437. **E-Mail:** klein@mpib_tuebingen.mpg.de

KLEIN, JERRY ALAN, CHEMICAL ENGINEERING. **Personal Data:** b Neenah, Wis, April 19, 1945; m 1966, c 2. **Education:** Univ Wis, BS, 1967; Princeton Univ, PhD (chem eng), 1972. **Professional Experience:** CHMN, ISOTOPE PROG, OAK RIDGE NAT LAB, as of 2003; PROG MGR ISOTOPE PROG, OAK RIDGE NAT LAB, 1997-; group leader environ control technol, Chem Technol Div, 1978-1996; develop engr, 1972-1978. **Research Statement & Publications:** Environmental control technology for coal conversion processes. **Mailing Address:** Isotope Prod & Distrib, Oak Ridge Nat Lab, Mail Stop 6182 P0 Box 2008, Oak Ridge, TN 37831-6182. **Fax:** 865-574-0638. **E-Mail:** kleinja@ornl.gov

KLEIN, JOHN PETER, SURVIVAL ANALYSIS. **Personal Data:** b Milwaukee, Wis, December 30, 1950. **Education:** Univ Wis, Milwaukee, BA, MS, 1975; Univ Mo, PhD (statist), 1980. **Professional Experience:** Statist dir, IBM, 1993-; PROF & HEAD BIOSTATIST, MED COL WIS, 1993-; biostatistician, Ohio State Comprehensive Cancer Ctr, 1981-1993; from asst prof to prof statist, Ohio State Univ, 1980-1993; Res, Oak Ridge Nat Labs, 1976-1977; statistitian, Univ Mo, 1975-1980; Asst math, Univ Wis-Milwaukee, 1974-1975. **Memberships:** Biomet Soc; Am Statist Asn; Inst Mat Statist; Soc Clin Trials; Int Statist Inst. **Research Statement & Publications:** Survival analysis. **Mailing Address:** Dept Biostatist, Med Col Wis, 8701 Watertown Plank Rd, Milwaukee, WI 53226. **Fax:** 414-266-8481. **E-Mail:** klein@hpi.mcw.edu

KLEIN, JOHN ROBERT, MUCOSAL IMMUNOLOGY, EXTRATHYMIC T CELL DEVELOPMENT. **Personal Data:** b Detroit, Mich, August 27, 1947. **Education:** Elmhurst Col, BA, 1971; Johns Hopkins Univ, PhD, 1980. **Professional Experience:** PROF DIAG SCI, DENT BR, UNIV TULSA, as of 2004; study sect mem, NIH, NSF & Am Cancer Soc, 1992-1993; assoc prof diag sci, Dent Br, Univ Tulsa, beginning 1989; asst prof, Dept Biol Sci, Univ Tulsa, 1987-1989; res career develop award, Crohiss & Coltis Found, 1986-1987; asst res immunologist, Univ Calif, San Diego, 1983-1987; Fel, Scripps Clin & Res Found, 1982-1983; Fel, Mass Inst Technol, 1981-1982; Fel, Univ Pa, 1980-1981. **Memberships:** Soc Mucosal Immunol. **Research Statement & Publications:** Studiesof T cell development within the intestine; extrathymic nature of intestinal T cells. **Mailing Address:** Dept Diag Sci, Univ Tulsa, Suite 3 094F, 6516 M D Anderson Blvd, Houston, TX 77030. **Fax:** 713-500-4416. **E-Mail:** john.r.klein@uth.tmc.edu

KLEIN, JOHN SHARPLESS, APPLIED MATHEMATICS. **Personal Data:** b Ossining, NY, September 9, 1922; m 1963, Nancy; c Jeffrey & Carolyn. **Education:** Haverford Col, BS, 1943; Mass Inst Technol, SM, 1949; Univ Mich, PhD, 1959. **Professional Experience:** PROF EMER MATH, HOBART & WILLIAM SMITH COLS, 1988-; prof math, Hobart & William Smith Cols, 1964-1988; head dept, Hobart & William Smith Cols, 1964-1974; Monmouth Col, NJ, 1963-1964; Wilson Col, 1960-1963; assoc prof, Lafayette Col, 1959-1960; asst prof, Wilson Col, 1959; asst prof, Univ RI, 1956-1958; Case Inst Technol, 1955-1956; Oberlin Col, 1954-1955; instr math, Williams Col, 1949-1951. **Memberships:** Math Asn Am. **Research Statement & Publications:** Integral transforms-convolution theorems for Hankel transforms. **Mailing Address:** Dept Math, Hobart & William Smith Cols, Geneva, NY 14456.

KLEIN, LARRY L, ORGANIC CONDUCTORS, CARBOHYDRATE CHEMISTRY. **Personal Data:** b Chicago, Ill, January 24, 1953. **Education:** Ill Inst Technol, BS, 1975; Mich State Univ, PhD (chem), 1980. **Professional Experience:** AT ABBOTT LABS, as of 1997; asst prof chem, Tex A&M Univ, beginning 1982; NIH fel chem, Harvard Univ, 1980-1982. **Memberships:** Am Chem Soc. **Research Statement & Publications:** Organic synthesis of natural products. **Mailing Address:** Abbott Labs Dept 47M AP9A, 100 Abbott Park Rd, Abbott Park, IL 60064-3500.

KLEIN, LAWRENCE ROBERT, ECONOMICS. **Personal Data:** b Omaha, Nebr, September 14, 1920; m 1947, SoniaAdelson; c Hannah, Rebecca, Rachel & Jonathan. **Education:** Univ Calif, Berkeley, BA, 1942; Mass Inst Technol, PhD, 1944. **Honorary Degrees:** Numerous from US & foreign univs. **Honors & Awards:** John Bates Clark Medal, Am Econ Asn, 1959; Nobel Prize in Econ, 1980. **Professional Experience:** Co-ordr, Jimmy Carter's Econ Task Force, 1976; Stanford Univ, 1968 & Univ Copenhagen, 1974; Ford vis prof, Univ Calif, Berkeley, 1968 & Inst Advan Sci, Vienna, 1970 & 1974; BENJAMIN FRANKLIN PROF, UNIV PA, 1968-; vis prof, Princeton Univ, 1966; assoc ed, Int Econ Rev, 1965-; univ prof, Univ Pa, 1964-1968; vis prof, Hebrew Univ, 1964; vis prof, City Univ NY, 1962-1963 & 1982; vis prof, Univ Colo, 1962; vis prof, Univ Osaka, Japan, 1960; ed, Int Econ Rev, 1959-1965; prof, Univ PA, 1958-1964; res assoc, Oxford Inst Statist, 1954-1958; res assoc, Surv res Ctr, 1949-1954; res assoc, Nat Bur Econ res,

1948-1950; consult numerous orgns, 1947-; fac, Univ Chicago, 1944-1947. **Memberships:** Nat Acad Sci; fel Econometric Soc; fel Am Acad Arts & Sci; Am Econ Asn; Am Philos Soc. **Mailing Address:** Univ Pa McNeil Bldg Rm 335, 3718 Locust Walk, Philadelphia, PA 19104-6297. **Fax:** 215-573-2057. **E-Mail:** lrk@econ.sas.upenn.edu

KLEIN, LEONARD C, CHEMISTRY. **Professional Experience:** SECY, AM MICROCHEM SOC; SR RES CHEMIST, ANALYTICAL DEPT, AGR CHEM GROUP, FORD MOTOR CO. **Memberships:** Am Microchem Soc. **Mailing Address:** c/o FMC Corp, PO Box 8, Princeton, NJ 08543.

KLEIN, LEROY, BIOCHEMISTRY, MEDICAL RESEARCH. **Personal Data:** b Newark, NJ, October 1, 1926; m 1958, c 3. **Education:** Syracuse Univ, BA, 1950; Boston Univ, MA, 1952, PhD (biochem), 1958; Case Western Res Univ, MD, 1965. **Professional Experience:** EMER PROF ORTHOP, CASE WESTERN RES UNIV, 1995-; PROF BIOCHEM & ORTHOP & MACROMOLECULAR SCI, CASE WESTERN RES UNIV, 1977-; assoc prof biochem, Case Western Res Univ, beginning 1971; from sr instr to asst prof biochem, Case Western Res Univ, 1965-1971; res grants, 1963-; from instr to assoc prof biochem orthop surg, Case Western Res Univ, 1963-1977; instr orthop surg, Case Western Res Univ, 1963-1965; Kappa Delta res award, 1963; res fel orthop, Case Western Res Univ, 1960-1963; Res fel biochem, Case Western Res Univ, 1958-1960. **Memberships:** Am Fedn Clin Res; Am Soc Biol Chem; Orthop Res Soc; Geront Soc; Am Soc Bone & Mineral Res; Sigma Xi. **Research Statement & Publications:** Connective tissue metabolism and diseases; collagen and mineral turnover in experimental and metabolic bone diseases, aging, wound healing. **Mailing Address:** Dept Orthop, Sch Med, Case Western Res Univ, 511 Wearn Bldg, 1100 Euclid Ave, Cleveland, OH 44106-5043. **Fax:** 216-844-5970.

KLEIN, LEWIS S, THEORETICAL PHYSICS. **Personal Data:** b Youngstown, Ohio, September 2, 1932; m 1960. **Education:** Union Col, NY, BS, 1954; Yale Univ, MS, 1955, PhD (physics), 1958. **Professional Experience:** PROF PHYSICS, HOWARD UNIV, 1970-; assoc prof, Howard Univ, 1965-1970; sr res staff, Nat Bur Stand, 1960-1965; instr physics, Northwestern Univ, 1959-1960; Fulbright fel & res physicist, Nat Ctr Sci Res, France, 1958-1959. **Memberships:** Am Phys Soc. **Research Statement & Publications:** Field theory; statistical mechanics; plasma physics. **Mailing Address:** Dept Physics & Astron, Howard Univ, Thirkield Hall 2355 Sixth St NW, Washington, DC 20059. **Fax:** 202-806-5830.

KLEIN, LUELLA, GYNECOLOGY, MATERNAL FETAL MEDICINE. **Personal Data:** b Walker, Iowa, 1924. **Education:** Univ Iowa Sch Med, MD, 1949. **Professional Experience:** CHAS HOWARD CHANDLER PROF GYNEC & OBSTET, EMORY UNIV, as of 2004; chmn, Emory Univ, 1986-1993; PROF GYNEC & OBSTET, EMORY UNIV, 1973-; assoc prof, Emory Univ, 1967-1973; staff, Piedmont Hosp, Ga Byst Hosp, Crawford Hosp, Atlanta, 1960-; consult, Ga Dept Pub Health, 1958-1962; clin instr, Emory Univ, 1956-1967; sr Fulbright Res Scholar, Univ London, 1956; instr, Western Residency, 1955; resident obstet-gynec, 1954-1955; asst resident obstet- gynec, 1952-1954; jr asst resident surg, 1951-1952; jr asst resident med, 1950-1951; rotating intern, 1949-1950. **Memberships:** Inst Med-Nat Acad Sci; AMA; Am Col Obstet & Gynecol; Am Med Women's Asn. **Mailing Address:** Dept Gynec & Obstet Emory Univ, 69 Butler St SE, Atlanta, GA 30303. **Fax:** 404-521-3589. **E-Mail:** lklein@emory.edu

KLEIN, MARSHALL S, OPHTHALMOLOGY. **Personal Data:** b New York, NY, March 19, 1926; m Barbara Janet Cohen; c Marcia Jill & Geoffrey Lee. **Education:** Fairleigh Dickinson Univ, BS, 1966, MBA, 1980. **Professional Experience:** AT INST OPHTHALMOL & VISUAL SCI, MED SCH, UNIV MED & DENTISTRY, NJ, as of 2004; adminr, Eye Inst Nj, Newark, beginning 1972; Owner & dir, Styertowne Youth Ctr, 1952-1972. **Memberships:** Eye Bank Asn Am. **Mailing Address:** Inst Ophthalmol & Visual Sci, Sch Med, Univ Med & Dentistry, Rm 6153, Doctors Off Ctr, 90 Bergen St, Newark, NJ 07103-2499.

KLEIN, MARTIN J(ESSE), HISTORY OF PHYSICS. **Personal Data:** b New York, NY, June 25, 1924. **Education:** Columbia Univ, AB, 1942, AM, 1944; Mass Inst Technol, PhD (physics), 1948. **Professional Experience:** PROF EMER, PHYS & HIST SCI, YALE UNIV, as of 2006; EUGENE HIGGINS PROF EMER PHYSICS & HIST SCI, YALE UNIV, as of 2000; vis prof, Harvard, 1989-1990; Rockefeller Univ, 1975; Van der Waals prof, Zeeman prof, Univ Amsterdam, 1974; eugene higgins prof physics & hist sci, Yale Univ, beginning 1973; mem, Inst Advan Study, 1972; prof, Yale Univ, 1967-1973; Guggenheim fel, Yale Univ, 1967-1968; Guggenheim fel, Inst Lorentz, Leiden, 1958-1959; Nat Res fel, Dublin Inst Advan Studies, 1952-1953; from instr to prof, Case Inst Technol, 1949-1967; res assoc physics, Mass Inst Technol, 1946-1949; mem, Opers Res Group, Wash, DC, 1945-1946; physicist, Underwater Sound Ref Lab, 1944-1945; asst physics, Columbia Univ, 1942-1944. **Memberships:** Nat Acad Sci; fel AAAS; fel Am Phys Soc; Hist Sci Soc; Acad Int Hist Sci; Am Acad Arts & Sci. **Research Statement & Publications:** History of modern physics; statistical mechanics. **Mailing Address:** Dept Physics, Yale Univ, PO Box 208120, New Haven, CT 06520-8120. **Fax:** 203-432-6175. **E-Mail:** martin.klein@yale.edu

KLEIN, MAX, CHEMICAL PHYSICS, THERMODYNAMICS. **Personal Data:** b New Bedford, Mass, February 5, 1925; m 1985, Suzette Aldon; c Nehemiah D, David N & Sara H (Glashofer). **Education:** Univ Mass, BS, 1948; Univ Md, PhD (physics), 1962. **Honors & Awards:** Dept Silver Medal, US Dept Com. **Professional Experience:** CONSULT, 1991-; sr scientist thermodyn, Gas Res Inst, 1981-1991; supvry physicist, Nat Bur Stand, 1977-1981; sect chief, Nat Bur Stand, 1967-1977; mem adv comt grad sch, Dept Agr, 1967-1972; Mem fac grad sch, NIH, 1966-1976; physicist thermodyn, Nat Bur Stand, 1965-1967; physicist chem physics, Weizmann Inst Sci, 1963-1965; physicist thermodyn, Nat Bur Stand, 1955-1963; Electronics engr comput memory, Nat Bur Stand, 1950-1955. **Memberships:** Am Phys Soc; Am Inst Chem Engrs; AAAS; Sigma Xi; Am Chem Soc; Am Ceramic Soc; Mat Res Soc. **Research Statement & Publications:** Theory brittle fracture in polyethyene; accelerated testing measurement andfatigue behavior of polyethylene; thermodynamic properties of fluids. **Mailing Address:** 900 24th St NW Unit No G, Washington, DC 20037.

KLEIN, MICHAEL GARDNER, BIOLOGICAL CONTROL, INSECT PATHOLOGY. **Personal Data:** b Rockford, Ill, January 14, 1941; m 1964, Pauline; c Mary R & Steven M. **Education:** Univ Wis-Madison, BS, 1963, MS, 1965, PhD (entom), 1972. **Professional Experience:** RES ENTOMOLOGIST & LEAD SCIENTIST, HORT INSECTS RES LAB, OHIO STATE UNIV, as of 2005; adj assoc prof entom, Ohio State Univ, 1973-; RES ENTOMOLOGIST, HORT INSECTS RES LAB, APPLN TECHNOL RES UNITS, AGR RES SERV, USDA, 1969-. **Memberships:** Entom Soc Am; Soc Invert Path; Soc Nematologists; Soil Ecology Soc; Int Oregn Biol Control. **Research Statement & Publications:** Biological control of turf and ornamental insect pests such as the Japanese Beetle; finding new pathogens; demonstrating their effectiveness; and developing application techniques. **Mailing Address:** USDA-ARS Hort Insects Res Lab, Ohio State Univ, 1680 Madison Ave, Wooster, OH 44691. **Fax:** 330-263-3696. **E-Mail:** klein.10@osu.edu

KLEIN, MICHAEL JOHN, RADIO ASTRONOMY. **Personal Data:** b Ames, Iowa, January 19, 1940; m 1962, c 3. **Education:** Iowa State Univ, BS, 1962; Univ Mich, MS, 1966, PhD (astron), 1968. **Professional Experience:** MGR, DEEP SPACE NETWORK SCI, JET PROPULSION LAB, NASA, as of 2005; PROJ MGR SEARCH EXTRA-TERRESTRIAL INTEL, SPACE SCI DIV, JET PROPULSION LAB, CALIF INST TECHNOL, 1981-; mem tech staff, space sci div, Jet Propulsion Lab, Calif Inst Technol, beginning 1973; sr scientist radio astron, Space Sci Div, 1969-1973; Nat Res Coun-NASA resident res assoc, Space Sci Div, Jet Propulsion Lab, Calif Inst Technol, 1968-1969; asst res engr, Radio Astron Lab, Univ Mich, 1963-1964. **Memberships:** Am Inst Elec & Electronics Engrs; Am Astron Soc; Int Astron Union; Int Union Radio Sci; Am Inst Aeronaut & Astronaut. **Research Statement & Publications:** Measuring and interpretating radio frequency emission of galactic and extragalactic radio sources and solar system planets and satellites; apply radio astronomy techniques to the Search for Extraterrestrial Intelligence (SETI). **Mailing Address:** Deep Space Network Sci, Jet Propulsion Lab, 4800 Oak Grove Dr, Pasadena, CA 91109. **Fax:** 818-354-6290. **E-Mail:** michael.j.klein@jpl.nasa.gov

KLEIN, MICHAEL LAWRENCE, BIOPHYSICS. **Personal Data:** b London, Eng, March 13, 1940; m 1962, c 2. **Education:** Bristol Univ, BSc, 1961, PhD (theoret chem), 1964. **Honors & Awards:** Rahman Prize Recipient 1999. **Professional Experience:** Miller prof, Univ Calif, Berkeley, 1997; Humboldt fel, 1996; DIR, CTR MOLECULAR MODELLING, 1995-; HEPBURN PROF PHYS SCI, UNIV PA, 1993-; DIR, LAB RES STRUCT MATTER, 1993-; prof, Univ Firenze, 1993; William Smith prof chem, Univ Pa, 1991-1993; Guggenheim fel, 1989-1990; Louis Neel prof, Ecole Normale Superierre, Lyon, France, 1988; prof chem, Univ Pa, 1987-1991; pr res off chem, Nat Res Coun Can, 1985-1987; Commoner Trinity Col, Cambridge, UK, 1985; fel, Japan Soc Prom Sci, 1982; prof chem, McMaster Univ, Hamilton, Ont, 1977; prof, Univ Paris, 1975; res off chem, Nat Res Coun Can, 1974-1985; fel World Trade, IBM, San Jose, 1970; assoc res off chem, Nat Res Coun Can, 1968-1974; res assoc physics, Rutgers Univ, 1967-1968; Imp Chem Industs fel theoret chem, Bristol Univ, 1965-1967; Ciba Found fel physics, Univ Genoa, 1964-1965. **Memberships:** Am Phys Soc; Royal Soc Chem; Can Inst Physics; fel Chem Inst Can; fel Royal Soc Can. **Research Statement & Publications:** Computer simulation studies in physical chemistry; solid state physics and biophysics. **Mailing Address:** Dept Chem, Univ Pa, 102 LRSM 231 S 34 St, Philadelphia, PA 19104-6323. **E-Mail:** klein@lrsm.upenn.edu

KLEIN, MICHAEL TULLY, MODELLING, APPLIED & INDUSTRIAL CHEMISTRY. **Personal Data:** b Wilmington, Del, March 15, 1955; m Elizabeth; c Jennifer, Michael & Lisa. **Education:** Univ Del, BChE, 1977; Mass Inst Technol, ScD, 1981. **Professional Experience:** PROF & DEAN, RUTGERS UNIV, 1998-; elizabeth Inez kelley prof, Ctr Catalytic Sci & Technol, Univ Del, beginning 1994; dept chair, Col Eng, Univ Del, 1990-1996; prof chem eng, Ctr Catalytic Scil & Technol, Univ Del, beginning 1989; dir, Ctr Catalytic Sci & Technol, Univ Del, beginning 1988; assoc dean, Col Eng, Univ Del, 1987-1988; prin young investr, Outstanding Young Men Am, NSF, 1985 & 1988; lectr, var univs & orgs, 1982-1991; from asst prof to assoc prof chem eng, Univ Del, 1981-1989; Instr chem eng, Mass Inst Technol, 1980; Consult, var oil & chem cos. **Memberships:** Am Inst Chem Engrs; Am Chem Soc. **Research Statement & Publications:** Chemical reaction engineering of complex mixtures, including resid upgrading, hydroprocessing, and applied catalysis; author of over 150 technical papers. **Mailing Address:** Rutgers Univ, 100 Clifton Ave, New Brunswick, NJ 08901. **Fax:** 732-445-5313. **E-Mail:** mtklein@email.eng.rutgers.edu

KLEIN, MICHAEL W, SOLID STATE PHYSICS, STATISTICAL MECHANICS. **Personal Data:** b Teglas, Hungary, March 29, 1931; American citizen; m 1955, Lida Rosenfeld; c Ira J & David H. **Education:** Univ Colo, BS, 1956; Cornell Univ, PhD (physics), 1962. **Professional Experience:** PROF EMER PHYSICS, WORCESTER POLYTECH INST, as of 1998; prof physics, Worcester Polytech Inst, beginning 1979; head dept, Worcester Polytech Inst, 1979-1984; vis prof, Physics Dept, Univ Ill, 1977-1979; assoc prof physics, Bar-Ilan Univ, Israel, 1971-1977; assoc prof physics, Wesleyan Univ, 1968-1971; vis assoc prof, Brandeis Univ, 1967-1968; res physicist, Lincoln Labs, Mass Inst Technol, 1961-1962 & Sperry Rand Res Ctr, Mass, 1962-1968; Asst physics, Cornell Univ, 1956-1961. **Memberships:** Am Phys Soc. **Research Statement & Publications:** Theory of magnetism; solid state physics; statistical mechanics; plasma physics; glassy and amorphous systems; superconductivity. **Mailing Address:** Dept Physics, Worcester Polytech Inst, Worcester, MA 01609. **E-Mail:** mwklein@wpi.edu

KLEIN, MILES VINCENT, RAMAN SCATTERING, OPTICAL PROPERTIES. **Personal Data:** b Cleveland, Ohio, March 9, 1933; m Barbara; c Cynthia Banai & Gail. **Education:** Northwestern Univ, BS, 1954; Cornell Univ, PhD (physics), 1961. **Honors & Awards:** Frank Isakson Prize, Am Phys Soc, 1990, fel Am Acad of Arts and Sci 1997; mem Nat Acad of Sci 1998. **Professional Experience:** RES PROF PHYS, UNIV ILL, URBANA, 2000-; dir, Sci & Technol Ctr Superconductivity, 1989-2000; prof physics, Univ Ill, Urbana, 1969-2000; from asst prof to assoc prof, Sci & Technol Ctr Superconductivity, 1962-1969; NSF fel physics, Stuttgart Tech Univ, 1961-1962. **Memberships:** Sr mem Inst Elec & Electronics Engrs; fel Am Phys Soc; fel AAAS. **Research Statement & Publications:** Raman scattering in solids; optical properties of solids. **Mailing Address:** Loomis Lab, Univ Ill 1110 W Green, Urbana, IL 61801. **Fax:** 217-244-8544. **E-Mail:** mvklein@uiuc.edu

KLEIN, MILTON M, FLUID DYNAMICS. **Personal Data:** b New York, NY, April 19, 1917; m 1951, c 1. **Education:** NY Univ, MS, 1950, PhD (physics), 1956. **Professional Experience:** RES PHYSICIST, AIR FORCE CAMBRIDGE RES LABS, BEDFORD, 1967-; plasma physics & hydrodyn, GCA Corp, 1964-1967; re-entry physics, Lincoln Lab, 1963-1964; physicist nuclear debris studies, Geophys Corp Am, 1961-1963; Lectr, Grad Sch, Univ Pa, 1957-1958; physicist, Gen Elec Co, 1955-1961; instr physics, NY Univ, 1950-1955; aeronaut res scientist, Nat Adv Comt Aeronaut, 1948-1950; Physicist aerodyn, Nat Adv Comt Aeronaut, 1942-1947. **Memberships:** Am Phys Soc. **Research Statement & Publications:** Fluid dynamics; diffusion; turbulence; heat transfer; interaction of buoyant turbulent jets with air; dissipation of fog by heat; cloud physics; meteorology. **Mailing Address:** 1200 Univ St Apt 701, Seattle, WA 98101.

KLEIN, NATHAN, PHYSICAL CHEMISTRY. **Personal Data:** b New York, NY, July 29, 1931; m 1952, c 5. **Education:** City Col New York, BS, 1951; Columbia Univ, MA, 1952; Univ Del, PhD (chem), 1967. **Professional Experience:** Group leader, US Army Ballistic Res Labs, 1974-1993; group leader radiation chem, US Army Nuclear Defense Lab, 1966-1974; chemist, Edgewood Arsenal, 1955-1966; Res asst biochem, Sloan-Kettering Inst Cancer Res, 1952; AT US ARMY RES LAB, ABERDEEN PROVING GROUND, MD. **Memberships:** Am Chem Soc; Sigma Xi; fel Am Inst Chem. **Research Statement & Publications:** Physical chemistry of aqueous solutions; reactions rates of high energy compounds; chemical kinetics of propellants and explosives; high temperature, high pressure reaction studies. **Mailing Address:** 6813 Fox Meadow Rd, Baltimore, MD 21207-5628. **Fax:** 410-278-6159. **E-Mail:** klein@arl.army.mil

KLEIN, NELSON HAROLD, PHYSICS. **Personal Data:** b New York, NY, March 6, 1942; m 1966, c 2. **Education:** Drexel Univ, BS, 1964, MS, 1968, PhD (physics), 1972. **Profes-**

sional Experience: PROF, ASTRON & PHYSICS, BUCKS COUNTY COMMUN COL, 1980-; chmn, Dept Sci, 1978-1985; assoc prof physics, 1972-1978. **Memberships:** Am Asn Physics Teachers. **Mailing Address:** Dept Sci, Bucks County Commun Col, Founders 149 Swamp Rd, Newtown, PA 18940. **E-Mail:** kleinn@bucks.edu

KLEIN, NORMAN W, REPRODUCTIVE TOXICOLOGY. **Personal Data:** b San Francisco, Calif, February 6, 1931. **Education:** Univ Calif, PhD (nutrit), 1960. **Professional Experience:** PROF EMER ANIMAL GENETICS & NUTRIT & MOLECULAR CELLBIOL, UNIV CONN, 1976-. **Mailing Address:** Ctr Environ Health, Univ Conn, Storrs, CT 06268. **Fax:** 860-486-5067. **E-Mail:** norman.klein@uconn.edu

KLEIN, PAUL ALVIN, VIROLOGY, IMMUNOLOGY. **Personal Data:** b Weehawken, NJ, February 1, 1941; m 1963, c 2. **Education:** Rutgers Univ, New Brunswick, BA, 1963; Univ Fla, PhD (med sci), 1967. **Professional Experience:** PROF EMER PATH, COL MED, UNIV FLA, 2004-; assoc prof path, Col Med, Univ Fla, 1975-1987; prof path, col med, Univ Fla, 1969-2004. **Memberships:** AAAS; Am Asn Immunol; Reticuloendothelial Soc; Sigma Xi. **Research Statement & Publications:** Viral immunology; autoimmunity; diabetes; cancer biology. **Mailing Address:** Dept Path & Immunol & Lab Med, Univ Fla Col Med, PO Box 100275, Gainesville, FL 32610-0275. **Fax:** 352-846-2781. **E-Mail:** paklein@ufl.edu

KLEIN, PHILIPP HILLEL, MATERIALS PURIFICATION & CRYSTAL GROWTH. **Personal Data:** b New York, NY, September 14, 1926; m 1953, Charlotte; c Joshua D, Daniel W & Jonathan H. **Education:** Syracuse Univ, BS, 1948, MS, 1951, PhD (phys chem), 1953. **Professional Experience:** CONSULT, PHILIPP KLEIN CONSULT, 1990-; res consult electronic mat, Crystals & Pure Mat Sect, USN Res Lab, 1987-1990; head, Dielec Mat Sect, 1973-1987; head, Crystals & Pure Mat Sect, USN Res Lab, 1970-1973; head dielec mat sect, Electronics Res Ctr, NASA, Mass, 1966-1970; mem sci staff, Sperry Rand Res Ctr, 1961-1966; phys chemist, Electronics Lab, 1956-1961; res assoc, Knolls Atomic Power Lab, Gen Elec Co, 1952-1956; res asst, Syracuse Univ, 1951-1952; Asst chem, Syracuse Univ, 1948-1949. **Memberships:** Fel Am Inst Chem; sr mem Sigma Xi; emer mem Inst Elec & Electronics Engrs; Mat Res Soc; Am Phys Soc; Am Asn Crystal Growth. **Research Statement & Publications:** Effects of nuclear radiation on gasesand dielectric solids; thermoelectricity; compound semiconductors; thermal properties of solids; electronically and optically active solids; crystal growth. **Mailing Address:** 2017 Hillyer Pl NW, Washington, DC 20009-1005. **Fax:** 202-462-4493. **E-Mail:** phklein@juno.com

KLEIN, RALPH, PHYSICAL CHEMISTRY. **Personal Data:** b Pittsburgh, Pa, January 24, 1918; wid, c 2. **Education:** Carnegie Inst Technol, BS, 1938; Univ Minn, MS, 1940; Univ Pittsburgh, PhD (chem), 1950. **Professional Experience:** RETIRED; Lady Davis Fel, Technion, Israel, 1985-1986; sr scientist, Nat Bur Standards, Washington, DC, 1974-1985; chief surface chem sect, Nat Bur Standards, Washington, DC, 1961-1974; Olin Mathieson Chem Corp, 1956-1960 & Melpar, Inc, 1960-1961; Phys chemist, US Bur Mines, 1946-1956; Phys chemist, Chem Warfare Serv, 1940-1941; Phys chemist, US Bur Mines, 1938-1939. **Memberships:** Am Chem Soc; Am Phys Soc; Sigma Xi. **Research Statement & Publications:** Low temperature chemistry; surface science. **Mailing Address:** 11 Moriah St No 4, Beer Sheva, 84506, Israel.

KLEIN, RICHARD, PUBLIC HEALTH & EPIDEMIOLOGY, HEALTH STATISTICS. **Personal Data:** b Baltimore, Md, August 26, 1948. **Education:** Univ Md, BA, 1986; Johns Hopkins Univ, MA, 1988. **Professional Experience:** CHIEF, DATA MONITORING & ANALYSIS BR, DIV HEALTH PROMOTIONS & STATIST, CTR DIS CONTROL, 1992-; statistician, Div Vital Statist, 1992. **Memberships:** Am Pub Health Asn. **Mailing Address:** Nat Ctr Health Statist, 6525 Belcrest Rd Rm 770, Hyattsville, MD 20782. **Fax:** 301-458-4036. **E-Mail:** rjk6@cdc.gov

KLEIN, RICHARD I, STAR FORMATION & INTERSTELLAR MEDIUM, COMPUTATIONAL ASTROPHYSICS. **Personal Data:** b New York, NY, September 16, 1944; m 1989, Janice. **Education:** Renssalaer Polytech Inst, BS, 1966; Brandeis Univ, PhD (theoret phys), 1973. **Professional Experience:** ASSOC PROG LEADER, LAWRENCE LIVERMORE NATL LAB, 2000-; adj prof astron, Univ Calif Berkeley Dept Astron, 1996-; adj assoc prof astron, Univ Calif Berkeley Dept Astron, 1987-1996; adj asst prof astron, Univ Calif Berkeley Dept Astron, 1984-1987; THEORET PHYSICIST, LAWRENCE LIVERMORE NATL LAB, 1982-; res assoc astron, Univ Calif Berkeley Dept Astron, 1980-1982; post-doctoral res astron, Kitt Peak Natl Observ, 1977-1980; post-doctoral res fel, Adv Study Prog, Natl Ctr Atmospheric Res, 1976-1977; post-doctoral res assoc, Joint Inst Lab Astrophys, 1974-1976. **Memberships:** affil Amer Astron Soc; affil Intl Astron Union; affil Amer Physical Soc. **Research Statement & Publications:** theory of high and low mass star formation; interstellar medium; computational astrophysics; x-ray pulsars; laboratory astrophysics experiments. **Mailing Address:** Lawrence Livermore Nat Lab, PO Box 808 L-23, Livermore, CA 94550. **E-Mail:** rklein@astron.berkeley.edu

KLEIN, RICHARD LESTER, PHARMACOLOGY, CELL PHYSIOLOGY. **Personal Data:** b Hempstead, NY, November 6, 1929; m 1953, c 2. **Education:** Hofstra Univ, BA, 1951, MA, 1952; Vanderbilt Univ, PhD (biol, chem), 1957. **Professional Experience:** PROF PHARMACOL & TOXICOL, MED CTR, UNIV MISS, 1981-; vis prof, Karolinska Inst, 1969-1970; prof pharmacol, Med Ctr, Univ Miss, 1966-1981; vis prof, Biophys Lab, Wenner-Gren Inst, 1963-1964; NIH career prog award, 1962-1972; from asst prof to assoc prof, Med Ctr, Univ Miss, 1959-1966; Instr pharmacol, Vanderbilt Univ, 1958-1959; Nat Heart Inst fel pharmacol, Vanderbilt Univ, 1957-1959. **Memberships:** Am Soc Pharmacol & Exp Therapeut; Electron Micros Soc Am; Soc Neuroscience; Sigma Xi. **Research Statement & Publications:** Sympathetic nerve and catecholamine storage visicles, including permeability, enzyme activity, composition, histochemistry and ultrastructure; human serum dopamine beta-hydroxylase and sympathetic homeostasis. **Mailing Address:** 706 Shore Dr, Destin, FL 32541-5276. **Fax:** 850-837-9041.

KLEIN, RICHARD M, INORGANIC CHEMISTRY, ORGANIC CHEMISTRY. **Personal Data:** b Philadelphia, Pa, November 10, 1937. **Education:** Williams Col, BA, 1959; Univ Ill, MS, 1962, PhD (polymer chem), 1963. **Professional Experience:** DIR, NASH ENG CO & MANNINGTON MILLS INC, as of 2004; PRES & CHIEF EXEC OFFICER, SYBRON CHEM INC, 1984-; group vpres chem, Sybron Chem Inc, 1978-1984; pres, Gamlen Chem Co NAm, 1975-1978; pres, Ionac Chem Co, 1970-1978; asst to pres int opers, Tanatex Chem Corp, NJ, 1969-1970; asst managing dir, Triton Chem SAfrica, 1968-1969; mgr int opers sales develop, Pa, 1966-1968; mgr sales develop, Pa, 1965-1966; mem staff sales develop spec prod, Rohm& Haas Co, 1963-1965. **Memberships:** Am Chem Soc. **Research Statement & Publications:** Chemical management and development. **Mailing Address:** Sybron Chem Inc, PO Box 66, Birmingham, NJ 08011. **Fax:** 609-893-2063.

KLEIN, RICHARD MORRIS, MATERIALS SCIENCE, GLASS SCIENCE. **Personal Data:** b Brooklyn, NY, April 26, 1942; m 1964, Ronnie Suchman; c Michael & Jennifer. **Education:** State Univ NY Col Ceramics, Alfred, BS, 1963, PhD (ceramic sci), 1967. **Professional Experience:** DIR, NETWORK TECH, GTE LABS, INC, 1988-; Mem Nat Bd Adv, Rose-Hulman Inst Technol, Terre-Haute, Ind, 1987-; DEPT MGR, Network Tech, Gte Labs, Inc, 1982-; actg res mgr, Network Tech, Gte Labs, Inc, 1981-1982; PRIN INVESTR, Network Tech, Gte Labs, Inc, 1975-; MEM TECH STAFF, Network Tech, Gte Labs, Inc, 1966-. **Memberships:** Am Ceramic Soc; Nat Inst Ceramic Engrs; Soc Glass Technol; Sigma Xi; Inst Elec & Electronics Engrs. **Research Statement & Publications:** Management of research and development on the physical elements that comprise communication networks. **Mailing Address:** GTE Labs Inc, 40 Sylvan Rd, Waltham, MA 02154-1120. **E-Mail:** rmk0@gte.com

KLEIN, ROBERT HERBERT, PHYSICS. **Personal Data:** b New York, NY, December 5, 1932; m 1961, c 3. **Education:** Columbia Univ, AB, 1953; Carnegie Inst Technol, PhD (physics), 1963. **Professional Experience:** ASSOC PROF EMER PHYSICS, CLEVELAND STATE UNIV, as of 2004; Dir First Col, Cleveland State Univ, 1975-1978, 1984-1990; assoc prof physics, Cleveland State Univ, beginning 1967; res assoc physics, Case Inst Technol, 1965-1967; res scientist, Courant Inst, NY Univ, 1963-1965; asst theoret physics, Carnegie Inst Technol, 1959-1963; solid state physicist, Electronic Res Directorate, Air Force Cambridge Res Ctr, Mass, 1957-1959; assoc scientist, Avco Res & Adv Develop Corp, 1956-1957; Asst physics, Carnegie Inst Technol, 1953-1955. **Memberships:** Am Phys Soc. **Research Statement & Publications:** Theoretical physics. **Mailing Address:** Dept Physics, Cleveland State Univ, Cleveland, OH 44115.

KLEIN, ROBERT L, PROCESS DEVELOPMENT & SCALE-UP, PRODUCT DEVELOPMENT. **Personal Data:** m 1977, Mary; c Andrew, Lawrence & William. **Education:** Case Western Res Univ, BS, 1975; Univ Wis, MS, 1979; Univ Minn, PhD (chem eng), 1983. **Professional Experience:** DIR RES & DEVELOP, CARGILL HEALTH & FOOD TECHNOL, as of 2004; BD DIRS, POS PILOT PLANT CORP, as of 2004; vpres res & develop, Angus Chem Co, beginning 1990; dir res & develop, Henkel Corp, 1988-1990; group leader, UOP, 1984-1988. **Memberships:** Am Inst Chem Engrs; Am Chem Soc. **Research Statement & Publications:** Product and process development of nitroparaffins and their derivatives. **Mailing Address:** POS Pilot Plant Corp, 118, Vet Rd, Saskatoon, SK S7N 2R4, Can. **Fax:** 306-975-3766.

KLEIN, ROBERT MELVIN, ANATOMY, CELL BIOLOGY. **Personal Data:** b New York, NY, December 17, 1949; m 1975, c 3. **Education:** Queens Col, City Univ NY, BA, 1970; NY Univ, MS, 1973, PhD (anat), 1974. **Professional Experience:** DIR MED EDUC, MED CTR, UNIV KANS, as of 2005; PROF ANAT, MED CTR, UNIV KANS, 1987-; chmn dept anat, med ctr, Univ Kans, beginning 1987; from asst prof to assoc prof, Med Ctr, Univ Kans, 1981-1986; prin investr grants, Am Heart Asn 1980-1982; prin investr grants, NIH, 1978-1988; assoc scientist, Mid-Am Cancer Ctr, beginning 1975; fel, Marquette Univ, 1974-1975. **Memberships:** Am Asn Anatomists; Cell Kinetics Soc; Soc Develop Biol; NY Acad Sci; Am Soc Cell Biol; Sigma Xi. **Research Statement & Publications:** Influence of growth factors on tooth eruption and development; influences of autonomic nervous system on growth and differentiation of neonatal digestive system. **Mailing Address:** Dept Anat & Cell Biol, Univ Kans Med Ctr, 2008 Wahl Hall E Mail Stop 3038 3901 Rainbow Blvd, Kansas City, KS 66160. **Fax:** 913-588-2710. **E-Mail:** rklein@kumc.edu

KLEIN, RONALD, OPHTHALMOLOGY. **Personal Data:** b New York, NY, July 25, 1943; m 1965, c 1. **Education:** Brooklyn Col, BS, 1965; NY Univ, MD, 1969; Univ NC, MPH, 1973. **Professional Experience:** PROF OPHTHAL, SCH MED, UNIV WIS, MADISON, 1985-; from asst prof to assoc prof, Sch Med, Univ Wis, Madison, 1978-1985. **Memberships:** Am Epidemiol Soc; Soc Epidemiol Res; Am Col Epidemiol; Asn Res Vision & Ophthal; AMA; Am Diabetes Asn. **Research Statement & Publications:** Epidemiological studies on ocular and systemic complications of diabetes mellitus; age-related ocular diseases, macular degeneration and cataract; publications more than fifteen incuding dissection of genomewide-scan data in extended families reveals a major locus and oligogenic susceptibility for age-related macular degeneration, variation associated with measurement of retinal vessel diameters at different points in the pulse cycle. **Mailing Address:** Dept Ophthal, Univ Wis, Rm 460 Warf Off Bldg 610 N Walnut St, Madison, WI 53705. **Fax:** 608-263-0280. **E-Mail:** kleinr@epi.ophth.wisc.edu

KLEIN, RONALD DON, BIOTECHNOLOGY, SCIENTIFIC EVIDENCE. **Personal Data:** b Mt Clemens, Mich, July 30, 1948; m 1998, Suzanne. **Education:** Western Mich Univ, BA, 1970, MA, 1971; Univ Wis-Madison, PhD (molecular biol), 1981; Thomas M Cooley Law sch, JD, 2003. **Professional Experience:** RETIRED; Mgr, Emerging tech, Intellectual property, Pharmacia corp, 1999-2002; consult, beginning 1984; sr sci, res & develop Upjohn Co (Pharmacia), 1984-1999; res scientist, Res & Develop Div, Phillips Petrol Co, 1982-1984; fel, Chem Dept, Mass Inst Technol, 1981-1982; res asst, Biochem Dept, Univ Wis-Madison, 1976-1981; grad res fel, Biochem Dept, Wayne State Univ, 1975-1976; instr, Western Mich Univ, 1970-1972; adj prof, Thomas M Cooley Sch Law. **Memberships:** AAAS; Am Soc Microbiol; Sigma Xi; Genetics soc Am; Am acad Forensic sci-Jurisprudence section; Soc Competitive Intelligence Professionals; Am Intellectual Property Law Asn; Am Bar Asn. **Research Statement & Publications:** Relationship of DNA sequence and structure, gene regulation, analysis of DNA/protein interactions; plasmid vectors for the expression of cloned genes; large scale isolation of gene products; consultant biotechno; jurisprudence and scientific issues; Published over 15 articles. **Mailing Address:** 9721 S Sixth St, Schoolcraft, MI 49087. **Fax:** 269-382-1568. **E-Mail:** rdklein@net-link.net

KLEIN, SANFORD A, MECHANICAL ENGINEERING. **Education:** Univ Ill, BS (Chem), 1972; Univ Wis, MS, 1973, PhD, 1976. **Honors & Awards:** Charles G Abbot Award, 1989. **Professional Experience:** OUWENEEL BASCOM PROF, DEPT MECH ENG, UNIV WIS-MADISON, as of 2002. **Mailing Address:** Dept Mech Eng, Univ Wis, 1343 Eng Res Bldg 1500 Eng Dr, Madison, WI 53706. **E-Mail:** klein@engr.wisc.edu

KLEIN, SHERWIN JARED, PSYCHOPHYSIOLOGY. **Personal Data:** b Toledo, Ohio, January 13, 1919; m 1943, c 2. **Education:** Western Reserve Univ, AB, 1940; Univ Pa, MA, 1947, PhD, 1951. **Professional Experience:** PROF EMER PSYCHOL, WRIGHT STATE UNIV, as of 2003; prof psychol, Wright State Univ, beginning 1965; coordr, Wright State Univ, 1965-1974; assoc & lectr, Grad Sch Educ, Univ Pa, 1959-1965; proj scientist, Air Crew Equip Lab, Naval Air Eng Ctr, 1951-1965; instr, Western Reserve Univ, 1946-1951; asst psychol, Western Reserve Univ, 1940-1941. **Memberships:** Fel AAAS; Am Psychol Asn; Psychonomic Soc; Soc Psychophysiol Res. **Research Statement & Publications:** Neurophysiology; biophysics; electrophysiological correlates of behavior, especially quantitative measures of stress; relationships of electrophysiological patterns to performance in mental and motor work. **Mailing Address:** Dept Psychol, Wright State Univ, 335 Fawcett Hall, 3640 Colonel Glenn Hwy, Dayton, OH 45435-0001. **Fax:** 937-775-3347.

KLEIN, SIGRID MARTA, MICROBIOLOGY, BIOCHEMISTRY. **Personal Data:** b Koenigsberg, Ger, May 1, 1932. **Education:** Univ Kiel, Staatsexamen, 1957; Brigham Young Univ, MS, 1961, PhD (microbiol), 1964. **Professional Experience:** TRANSLR, SCI MAT-GERMAN TO ENGLISH, SIGRID, 1994-; qual assusrance mgr, Murdock Int, Springville,

1987-1994; chemist, Becton Dickinson, 1982-1987; res assoc biochem, Brigham Young Univ, 1970-1981; fel, Charles F Kettering Labs, 1967-1970; res assoc microbiol, Brigham Young Univ, 1964-1967; Res asst biochem, Sloan-Kettering Lab, 1958-1959. **Memberships:** Am Soc Microbiol. **Research Statement & Publications:** Organization of photosynthetic membranes; intermediary metabolism in blue-green algae; immunodiagnostics. **Mailing Address:** 39 N Valley View Dr No 99, St George, UT 84770.

KLEIN, STEVEN L, BIOLOGY. **Professional Experience:** RES ASST PROF ANAT & CELL BIOL, UNIV VA, as of 2005. **Memberships:** NIH. **Mailing Address:** 1308 Wertland St, Charlottesville, VA 22903. **Fax:** 434-924-1712. **E-Mail:** kleins@exchange.nih.gov

KLEIN, TERRY ALLEN, MALARIA EPIDEMIOLOGY & VECTOR STUDIES, NEW REPELLENTS-REPELLENT FORMULATIONS. **Personal Data:** m 1967, Jacqueline; c Kevin D, Aaron R, Michelle R & Robert A. **Education:** Ore Col Educ, BS, 1968; Ore State Univ, MS, 1975; Univ Fla, PhD (entom), 1985. **Professional Experience:** CHIEF, VECTER ASSESSMENT BR, VIROL DIV, US ARMY MED RES INST INFECTIOUS DIS, 1995-; comdr, 5th Med detachment, ento, Korea, 1995; repellent sect, dept entom, div CD & I, 1993-1994; adj prof, Uniformed serv Univ health sci, 1990-; mgr, Malaria sect, walter reed army Inst res, 1990-1993; adj prof, Univ para, Belem, 1989-1990; chief, entom sect, US Army med res Unit, Brazil, 1986-1990; vis prof, Univ Brasilia, 1986-1988; entomologist & asst chief, US Army med component, Bangkok, 1978-1980; entomologist, US army environ hyg agency, 1976-1978, 1980; teacher biol & earth sci, cascade union high sch, 1968-1973. **Memberships:** Am Entom Soc; Am Mosquito Control Asn; Am Soc Trop Med & Hyg. **Research Statement & Publications:** Field and laboratory malaria vector studies in Thailand and Brazil; research ondengue and evaluated arthropod repellents and repellent formulations against biting flies; arbounus epidemiology studies in Peru. **Mailing Address:** Comdr US Army Med Res Inst Infectious Dis, MCMR-UIV-V LTC Terry Kein 1425 Porter St, Ft Detrick, MD 21702-5011. **Fax:** 301-619-2492. **E-Mail:** ltc_terry_klein@ftdetrck-ccmail.army.mil

KLEIN, THOMAS W, MEDICAL RESEARCH. **Education:** Creighton Univ, PhD, 1973. **Professional Experience:** PROF & INTERIM CHAIR, UNIV S FLA, as of 2005. **Memberships:** Am Soc Microbiol; Am Asn Immunologists. **Research Statement & Publications:** Contemporary Molecular Biology and cellular Immunology techniques. **Mailing Address:** Dept Med Microbiol & Immunol Univ S Fla Col Med, 12901 Bruce B Downs Blvd, Tampa, FL 33612-4742. **Fax:** 813-974-4151. **E-Mail:** tklein@com1.med.usf.edu

KLEIN, THOMAS W, MICROBIOLOGY. **Education:** Creighton Univ, PhD, 1973. **Professional Experience:** PROF & INTERIM CHAIR, MED MICROBIOL & IMMUNOL, UNIV S FLA, as of 2006. **Mailing Address:** Dept Microbiol/Immunol, Univ S Fla Col Med, 12901 Bruce B Downs Blvd, Tampa, FL 33612-4766. **Fax:** 813-974-4151. **E-Mail:** tklein@hsc.usf.edu

KLEIN, V(ERNON) A(LFRED), CHEMICAL ENGINEERING. **Personal Data:** b Marion, Tex, September 10, 1918; m 1950, c 2. **Education:** Univ Tex, BSChE, 1940, MSChE, 1942. **Professional Experience:** RETIRED; sr process specialist, Dow Chem Co, 1968-1981; systs specialist, Dow Chem Co, 1963-1968; consult, Dow Chem Co, 1960-1963; sr tech specialist, Dow Chem Co, 1956-1960; tech specialist, Dow Chem Co, 1951-1956; res & develop engr & group leader org res, Dow Chem Co, 1944-1951; asst supt org chem prod, Dow Chem Co, 1942-1944; instr chem eng, Univ Tex, 1941-1942. **Memberships:** Am Chem Soc; Am Inst Chem Engrs; Sigma Xi. **Research Statement & Publications:** High pressure vapor-liquid equilibrium; physical chemistry. **Mailing Address:** 63 Plantation Ct, Lake Jackson, TX 77566-5865.

KLEIN, VLADISLAV, ENGINEERING. **Education:** Cranfield Inst Technol, Eng, PhD, 1974. **Professional Experience:** PROF EMER ENG, GEORGE WASH UNIV, as of 2006. **Mailing Address:** George Wash Univ, M/S 489, 2121 Eye St NW, Washington, DC 20037. **Fax:** 202-994-0894.

KLEIN, WILLIAM, STATISTICAL MECHANICS. **Personal Data:** b Philadelphia, Pa, April 1, 1943; m 1967, c 2. **Education:** Temple Univ, BS, 1965, PhD (physics), 1972. **Professional Experience:** PROF PHYSICS, BOSTON UNIV, 1984-; from asst prof to assoc prof, Boston Univ, 1976-1984; res scientist physics, Univ Cologne, 1974-1976. **Research Statement & Publications:** Mathematics and physics of phase transitions. **Mailing Address:** Dept Physics, Boston Univ, 590 Commonwealth, Boston, MA 02215. **E-Mail:** klein@bu.edu

KLEIN, WILLIAM L, MEDICAL RESEARCH. **Education:** Univ Calif, Los Angeles, PhD. **Professional Experience:** FOUNDER, ACUMEN PHARMACEUT INC, as of 2005; PROF NEUROBIOL & PHYSIOL, NORTHWESTERN'S WEINBERG COL ARTS & SCI, as of 2005. **Mailing Address:** Dept Neurobiol & Physiol Northwestern Univ, Hogan 5-110 2145 Sheridan Rd, Evanston, IL 60208-0001. **Fax:** 847-491-5211. **E-Mail:** wklein@northwestern.edu

KLEINBERG, ISRAEL, ORAL BIOLOGY. **Personal Data:** b Toronto, Ont, May 1, 1930; m 1955, Constance; c Michael E, Brian D, Alan J & Rochelle L. **Education:** Univ Toronto, DDS, 1952; Univ Durham, PhD (physiol & biochem), 1958; Royal Co Dentists Can, FRCD(C), 1969. **Honorary Degrees:** DSc, Univ Man, 1983. **Honors & Awards:** Can CentennialMedal, Govt Can, 1967. **Professional Experience:** DISTINGUISHED PROF, DEPT ORAL BIOL & PATH, STATE UNIV NY, STONY BROOK, as of 2003; mem, NY State Health Res Coun, 1981-1987; consult, Nat Inst Dent Res, NIH, 1974-1981; PROF, DEPT ORAL BIOL & PATH, STATE UNIV NY, STONY BROOK, 1973-; CHMN, DEPT ORAL BIOL & PATH, STATE UNIV NY, STONY BROOK, 1973-; exec mem, Nat Res Coun Can, 1960-1965; Mem assoc comt dent res, Nat Res Coun Can, 1959-1960; from asst prof to prof biochem, Univ Man, 1958-1973; demonstr, Univ Durham, 1955-1958. **Memberships:** Int Asn Dent Res; Am Asn Dental Res; Am Soc Microbiol; Am Asn Oral Biol (pres 1991-1992). **Research Statement & Publications:** Metabolism of the dental bacterial plaque; plaque formation; peptide growth factors in plaque and other microbial flora control, saliva composition and its oral microbial effects; microchemical and oral diagnostic techniques; biomedical instrumentation development; gingival crevice fluid and its relation to oral and systemic disease. **Mailing Address:** State Univ NY, Dept Oral Biol & Path, 195 Westchester Hall, Stonybrook, NY 11794-8702. **Fax:** 516-632-7130. **E-Mail:** israel.kleinberg@stonybrook.edu

KLEINBERG, JACOB, inorganic chemistry; deceased, see previous edition for last biography

KLEINBERG, ROBERT LEONARD, GEOPHYSICAL INSTRUMENTATION, PHYSICS OF POROUS MEDIA. **Personal Data:** b San Francisco, Calif, August 3, 1949. **Education:** Univ Calif, Berkeley, BS, 1971; Univ Calif, San Diego, PhD (physics), 1978. **Professional Experience:** SR RES SCIENTIST, SCHLUMBERGER-DOLL RES, 1988-; prog leader electromagnetics, Schlumberger-doll Res, 1985-1988; res physicist, Schlumberger-doll Res, 1980-1985; postdoctoral fel, Exxon Res & Eng Co, 1978-1980. **Memberships:** Am Phys Soc. **Research Statement & Publications:** Ultrasonic, electromagnetic, nuclear magnetic resonance, and gravimetric instrumentation for in situ characterization of subsurface geologic formations; physics of porous media. **Mailing Address:** Schlumberger-Doll Res, Old Quarry Rd, Ridgefield, CT 06877. **E-Mail:** kleinberg@slb.com

KLEINER, ALEXANDER F, MATHEMATICS. **Personal Data:** b New York, NY, June 18, 1942; m 1965, c 2. **Education:** Univ St Thomas, Tex, BA, 1964; Tex A&M Univ, MS, 1966, PhD (math), 1969. **Professional Experience:** THOMAS SHEEHAN PROF, DEPT MATH, DRAKE UNIV, as of 2006; chmn, dept math & comput sci, Drake Univ, beginning 1984; prof math, Drake Univ, beginning 1979; from asst prof to assoc prof, dept Math & Comput Sci, 1969-1979; instr math, Tex A&M Univ, 1966-1969. **Memberships:** Math Asn Am; Am Math Soc; Asn Comput Mach. **Research Statement & Publications:** Summability theory; mathematics of political processes; graph theory. **Mailing Address:** Dept Math & Comput Sci, Drake Univ, 232 Howard Hall, Des Moines, IA 50311-4505. **E-Mail:** alexander.kleiner@drake.edu

KLEINER, ISRAEL, MATHEMATICS. **Education:** McGill Univ, PhD, 1967. **Professional Experience:** PROF, DEPT MATH & STATIST, YORK UNIV, as of 2005. **Mailing Address:** Dept Math & Statist, York Univ, North York, ON M3J 1P3, Can. **Fax:** 416-736-5757. **E-Mail:** kleiner@home.com

KLEINER, SUSAN MALA, SPORTS NUTRITION, CARDIOVASCULAR NUTRITION. **Personal Data:** b Cleveland, Ohio, October 17, 1957. **Education:** Hiram Col, BA, 1979; Case Western Res Univ, MS, 1982, PhD (nutrit), 1987. **Professional Experience:** SPORTS NUTRITIONIST, HIGH PERFORMANCE NUTRIT, as of 2004; OWNER & CONSULT, HIGH PERFORMANCE NUTRIT, as of 2004; CONSULT, SEATTLE SONICS, as of 2004; Affil Asst Prof, Dept Med Hist & Ethics, U Wash Sch Med, 2001-; sports nutrit consult, Cleveland Browns/Cleveland Cavaliers, 1991-; adj prof, Dept Nutrit, Sch Med, Case Western Res Univ, 1991-; columnist, Exec Health Report Newslett, 1989-; asst res prof nutrit, Dept Med, Div Nutrit, Prev Approach Cardiol & assoc dir, Sarah W Stedman Ctr Nutrit Studies, Dept Med, Duke Univ Med Ctr, 1988-1991; columnist, Physician & Sportsmed J, 1988-; Vis prof nutrit, Univ NC, Greensboro, 1987-1988; Young investr award, Am Col Nutrit, 1987. **Memberships:** Am Dietetic Asn; Am Col Sports Med; fel Am Col Nutrit; Nat Strength & Conditioning Asn. **Research Statement & Publications:** Nutritional requirements of strength training and muscle building and bodybuilding; writings on nutrition and health. **Mailing Address:** High Performance Nutrit, 7683, SE 27th St, PMB, Mercer Island, WA 98040. **Fax:** 206-236-2188. **E-Mail:** smkleiner@aol.com

KLEINER, WALTER BERNHARD, ELECTROCHEMISTRY. **Personal Data:** b Plainfield, NJ, March 1, 1918; m 1944, Emily Meek; c Paula (Vuckovich), Tim, Diana (Scocchio) & Kim. **Education:** Rutgers Univ, BS, 1939; Ohio State Univ, PhD (electrochem), 1946. **Professional Experience:** From asst prof to prof chem, Essex County Col, 1968-1985; res dir, View-Formall Co, BC, 1967; lectr chem, Newark Col Eng, 1966-1967; asst prof chem, Upsala Col, 1965-1966; res dir, Ionic Mach Co, 1963-1965; res dir, Electrochem Mach Div, 1961-1963; res electrochemists, Hanson-Van Winkle-Munning Co, 1958-1961; res dir, Spiral Glass Pipe Co, 1953-1955; RES DIR & CONSULT, KLEINER ELECTROCHEM CO, 1952-; Instr chem, Rutgers Univ, 1951-1952; res electrochemist, Am Smelting & Refining Co, 1947-1952; res & develop electrochemist, Manhattan Proj, Dayton, 1945; res engr, Battelle Mem Inst, 1944; asst chem, Ohio State Univ, 1940-1943; Anat & control chemist, Calco Chem Div, Am Cyanamid Co, NJ, 1939-1940; mem, Am Electroplaters Soc Res Comt, Nat Bur Stand. **Memberships:** AAAS; Am Chem Soc; Electrochem Soc; Am Electroplaters Soc; emer mem Am Soc Metals; Sigma Xi. **Research Statement & Publications:** Electrochemical machining; electroplating-electrodeposition. **Mailing Address:** 1845 First St, Dunellen, NJ 08812-1340.

KLEINFELD, A M, MEMBRANE BIOPHYSICS. **Personal Data:** b New York, NY, February 6, 1941. **Education:** Univ Wis, BA, 1963; Rutgers Univ, PhD (nuclear physics), 1968. **Professional Experience:** RES SCIENTIST, ALZHEIMERS & AGING RES CTR, 1998-; mem, Med Biol Inst, Calif, beginning 1987; assoc prof physiol & biophys, Harvard Univ, 1976-1987; consult physics, Yale Univ, 1972; consult physics, Weiman Inst, 1970; privat dozent physics, Univ Cologne, Ger, 1968-1976; consult, Lidak Pharmaceut, La Jolla, Calif. **Memberships:** Am Phys Soc; Biophys Soc; AAAS; Am Chem Soc. **Research Statement & Publications:** Research in fatty acids transport and interaction with immune cells. **Mailing Address:** Alzheimer's & Aging Res Ctr, 3550 Gen Atomics Ct Ste Two-140, San Diego, CA 92121. **Fax:** 858-455-3976. **E-Mail:** akleinfeld@alz-aging-research.org

KLEINFELD, ERWIN, ALGEBRA, COMBINATORICS & FINITE MATHEMATICS. **Personal Data:** b Vienna, Austria, April 19, 1927; American citizen; m 1968, Margarot. **Education:** City Col NY, BS, 1948; Univ Pa, MA, 1949; Univ Wis, PhD (math), 1951. **Professional Experience:** PROF EMER MATH, UNIV IOWA, as of 2006; visitor, Univ New Eng Armidale, Australia, 1992; prof, ITM/Mucia, Prog Malaysia, 1988-1989; mucia consult, Univ Indonesia, Jakarta, 1985-1986; vis prof, Emory Univ, 1976-1977; prof math, Univ Iowa, beginning 1968; vis prof, Univ Hawaii, 1967-1968; ed, J Algebra, 1964-; Inst Defense Anal, 1961-1962 & Agency Int Develop Educ, India, 1964-1965; consult ed, Charles E Merrill Publ Co, 1963-; prof, Syracuse Univ, 1962-1968; vis lectr, Stanford Univ, 1960; vis lectr, Univ Calif, Los Angeles, 1959; res assoc, Cornell Univ, 1958; partic conf algebra, Bowdoin Col, 1957; vis lectr, Yale Univ, 1956-1957; from asst prof to prof, Ohio State Univ, 1953-1962; instr math, Univ Chicago, 1951-1953. **Memberships:** Am Math Soc. **Research Statement & Publications:** Algebra and the foundations of projective geometry. **Mailing Address:** 1555 N Sierra St Apt 120, Reno, NV 89503-1719. **Fax:** 319-335-0627. **E-Mail:** kleinfld@math.uiowa.edu

KLEINFELD, IRA H, ENGINEERING ECONOMY. **Personal Data:** b New York, NY, April 5, 1947; m 1971, c 2. **Education:** Columbia Univ, BS, 1967, MS, 1969, Eng ScD(indust eng), 1974. **Professional Experience:** DEAN, GRAD SCH, UNIV NEW HAVEN, as of 2004; ASSOC PROVOST, UNIV NEW HAVEN, as of 2004; PROF, DEPT INDUST ENG, UNIV NEW HAVEN, 1983-; chmn, dept indust eng & comput sci, sch eng, Univ New Haven, beginning 1983; from asst prof to assoc prof, Dept Indust Eng & Comput Sci, Sch Eng, Univ New Haven, 1976-1983; from instr to asst prof quant methods, Sch Bus, Hofstra Univ, 1972-1976; instr math, John Jay Col Criminal Justice, City Univ New York, 1970-1972. **Memberships:** Inst Indust Engrs; Inst Mgt Sci; Soc Mfg Engrs; Am Soc Eng Educ. **Research Statement & Publications:** Engineering economy; use of computers in industrial engineering; published over 10 articles. **Mailing Address:** Dept Indust Eng, Univ New Haven, Maxcy Hall 213, West Haven, CT 06516. **Fax:** 203-932-7158. **E-Mail:** kleinfld@charger.newhaven.edu

KLEINFELD, MARGARET HUMM, MATHEMATICS, ALGEBRA. **Personal Data:** b St Louis, Mo, April 7, 1938; m 1968, Erwin; c Barbara (Kenny) & David. **Education:** Univ Rochester, BA, 1960; Syracuse Univ, MS, 1963, PhD (math), 1965. **Professional Experience:** Vis fel, Univ New Eng, Armidale, NSW Australia, 1992; consult MUCIA, Univ Indonesia, 1985-1986; ASSOC PROF MATH, UNIV IOWA, 1976-; asst prof, Univ Iowa, 1968-1975; Asst prof math, Syracuse Univ, 1965-1968; PROF EMER MATH, UNIV IOWA.

Memberships: Am Math Soc; Asn Women in Math. **Research Statement & Publications:** Non associative ring theory; algebra. **Mailing Address:** 1555 N Sierra St Apt 120, Reno, NV 89503-1719. **Fax:** 319-335-0627. **E-Mail:** mkleinf@math.uiowa.edu

KLEINFELD, RUTH GRAFMAN, CELL BIOLOGY, REPRODUCTIVE BIOLOGY. **Personal Data:** b New York, NY, February 9, 1928. **Education:** Brooklyn Col, BS, 1949; Univ Wis, MA, 1951; Univ Chicago, PhD (cell biol), 1953. **Professional Experience:** PROF EMER ANAT & REPRODUCTIVE BIOL, UNIV HAWAII, MANOA, as of 2003; chmn, Univ Hawaii, Manoa, 1980-1983; prof anat & reproductive biol, Univ Hawaii, Manoa, beginning 1972; assoc prof anat, Univ Hawaii, Manoa, 1970-1972; assoc prof pharmacol, State Univ NY Syracuse, 1962-1970; USPHS res career develop award pharmacol, State Univ NY Syracuse, 1962-1970; res assoc path, Ohio State Univ, 1957-1962; res assoc prev med, Yale Univ, 1956-1957; USPHS fel physiol, Mary S Muellhaupt scholar, 1955-1956; USPHS fel physiol, Ohio State Univ, 1953-1955; mem NIH Reproductive Biol Study Sect. **Memberships:** Am Soc Cell Biol; Am Asn Anat; Soc Develop Biol. **Research Statement & Publications:** cell replication and cytodifferentiation; decidualization and placentation in pregnancy; cytochemistry and cell-fine structure. **Mailing Address:** Dept Anat & Reproductive Biol, Univ Hawaii, 1960 EW Rd Aux 210, Honolulu, HI 96822-2319. **Fax:** 808-956-9481. **E-Mail:** rkleinfe@hawaii.edu

KLEINHOFS, ANDRIS, GENETICS, AGRONOMY. **Personal Data:** b Dobele, Latvia, December 25, 1937; American citizen; m 1965, Jolanta Smeils; c Laura & Anita. **Education:** Univ Nebr, Lincoln, BS, 1958, MS, 1964, PhD (genetics), 1967. **Professional Experience:** Chair, Genetics & Cell Biol, 1983-1987; PROF GENETICS, WASH STATE UNIV, 1977-; from asst prof to assoc prof, Wash State Univ, 1967-1977; Instr genetics, Univ Nebr, Lincoln, 1965-1967. **Memberships:** AAAS; Genetics Soc Am; Sigma Xi. **Research Statement & Publications:** Molecular genetics and gemomics of plants disease resistance genes, cloning, mechamism of action. **Mailing Address:** 605 NW Polaris St, Wash State Univ, Pullman, WA 99163. **Fax:** 509-335-8674. **E-Mail:** andyk@wsu.edu

KLEINKOPF, GALE EUGENE, PLANT PHYSIOLOGY, POTATO SCIENCE. **Personal Data:** b Twin Falls, Idaho, October 2, 1940; c 1. **Education:** Univ Idaho, BS, 1963; Univ Calif, Davis, PhD (plant physiol), 1970. **Professional Experience:** RES PROF EMER CROP PHYSIOL, UNIV IDAHO, as of 2003; prof crop physiol, Univ Idaho, beginning 1982; assoc prof, Univ Idaho, 1975-1982; asst prof plant ecol, Univ Calif, Los Angeles, 1972-1975; fel plant sci, Univ Calif, Davis, 1970-1972; res assoc agron, Univ Calif, Davis, 1964-1970; chemist, Aerojet Gen Corp, 1963-1964. **Memberships:** Potato Asn Am; Crop Sci Soc Am; Am Soc Plant Physiol. **Research Statement & Publications:** Carbon and nitrogen cycling in some crop species as affected by environmental stress. **Mailing Address:** Kimberly R & E Ctr, Univ Idaho, 3793 N 3600 E, Kimberly, ID 83341. **Fax:** 208-423-6559. **E-Mail:** kleinkop@kimberly.uidaho.edu

KLEINKOPF, MERLIN DEAN, GEOPHYSICS. **Personal Data:** b Macomb, Ill, February 1, 1926; div, c 4. **Education:** Monmouth Col, Ill, BS, 1949; Univ Mo-Rolla, BS, 1951; Columbia Univ, PhD (geol), 1955. **Professional Experience:** EMER, US GEOL SURV, as of 2006; res geophysicist, US Geol Surv, beginning 1972; leader, US Deleg Geophysicists to USSR, 1971; dep asst to chief geologist, Br Regional Geophys, 1970-1972; res geophysicist, Br Regional Geophys, 1966-1970; prof specialist gravity & magnetics, Standard Oil Co Calif, 1965-1966; dist explor geologist, Standard Oil Co Calif, 1962-1964; lead geophysicist gravity & magnetics, Standard Oil Co Calif, 1958-1962 & 1964-1965; geologist, Standard Oil Co Calif, 1957-1958; geologist-geophysicist, Standard Oil Co Calif, 1955-1957; Seismic comput geologist, Atlantic Refining Co, 1951-1952. **Memberships:** Geol Soc Am; Am Inst Mining Metall & Petrol Engrs; Soc Explor Geophysicists; Am Asn Petrol Geologists; Soc Econ Geologists; Sigma Xi. **Research Statement & Publications:** Gravity and magnetic model studies using electronic computer; regional geophysical studies of Belt Basin, Northwestern Montana; geophysical studies of porphyry copper, Sonora, Mexico; geophysical studies of Arabian Shield, Saudi Arabia; geophysical studies of the Idaho batholith and associated mineral deposits; geological survey of Bangladesh. **Mailing Address:** US Geol Surv, 520 N Park Ave, Tucson, AZ 85719-5035. **Fax:** 520-670-5571. **E-Mail:** dklnkpf@usgs.gov

KLEINMAN, ARTHUR MICHAEL, PSYCHIATRY, MEDICAL ANTHROPOLOGY. **Personal Data:** b New York, NY, March 11, 1941; m 1965, c 2. **Education:** Stanford Univ, AB, 1962, MD, 1967; Harvard Univ, MA, 1974. **Honors & Awards:** Wellcome Medal Med Anthrop, Royal Anthrop Inst, 1980. **Professional Experience:** Chmn, Dept Social Med, 1991-2000; Carnegie Corp grant, 1989-; NIMH training grant, 1984-; Rockefeller Found grant, 1983-1986; prin investr, NSF res grant, 1983-1986; MAUDE AND LILLIAN PRESLEY PROF MED ANTHROP & PSYCHIAT, MED SCH & FAC ARTS & SCI, HARVARD UNIV, 1982-; prof psychiat & adj prof anthrop, Univ Wash, 1979-1982; prin investr, NIMH res grant, Univ Wash, 1978-1979; ed-in-chief, Cult, Med & Psychiat, 1976-1986; assoc prof & adj assoc prof, Univ Wash, 1976-1979; clin instr psychiat, Mass Gen Hosp & Harvard Med Sch, 1975-1976; Dupont Warren fel, Harvard Med Sch, 1974-1975 & Milton Fund fel, 1975-1976; Found Fund Res Psychiat fel, 1974-1976; Lectr anthrop, Harvard Univ, 1974-1976; resident psychiat, Mass Gen Hosp, 1972-1975; intern med, Yale-New Haven Hosp, Yale Univ, 1967-1968. **Memberships:** Inst Med-Nat Acad Sci; fel AAAS; fel Am Anthrop Asn; Soc Med Anthrop; fel Am Psychiat Asn. **Research Statement & Publications:** Medical anthropology; depression; cross cultural psychiatry; pain and disability; therapeutic relationships and indigenous healing; anthropology of suffering. **Mailing Address:** Harvard Univ, 330 William James Hall, Cambridge, MA 02138. **Fax:** 617-432-2565. **E-Mail:** mcdonald@wjh.harvard.edu

KLEINMAN, CHEMIA JACOB, PHYSICS. **Personal Data:** b Sandomierz, Poland, February 1, 1932; m 1955, c 2. **Education:** Yeshiva Univ, BA, 1953; NY Univ, MS, 1956, PhD (physics), 1965. **Professional Experience:** CHMN DEPT PHYSICS, LONG ISLAND UNIV, 1980-; consult, NY Univ, 1971; assoc res scientist, NY Univ, 1969; NSF fel, Univ Colo, Boulder, 1967; NASA fel, Goddard Space Flight Ctr, 1966; res fel, NY Univ, 1965; PROF PHYSICS, LONG ISLAND UNIV, 1964-; lectr physics, City Col New York, 1960-1964; instr, YeshivaUniv, 1958-1960, 1954-1955; engr microwave res, Ford Instrument Co, 1957-1960; consult, Budd-Lewyt Corp, 1956-1957; physicist, mat lab, Brooklyn Naval Shipyard, 1956-1957. **Memberships:** Am Phys Soc. **Research Statement & Publications:** Atomic and electromagnetic scattering and bound state problems. **Mailing Address:** Dept Physics, Long Island Univ, Brooklyn, NY 11201.

KLEINMAN, DUSHANKA V, RESEARCH ADMINISTRATION. **Education:** Univ Wis, BS, 1969; Univ Ill, DDS, 1973; Boston Univ, MScD, 1976. **Professional Experience:** ASST DIR, ROADMAP COORD, NIH, MD, as of 2005; DEP DIR, NAT INST DENT & CRANIOFACIAL RES, NIH, MD, as of 2005. **Mailing Address:** Nat Inst Dental Res, 9000 Rockville Pk Rm 2C39 Bldg 31, Bethesda, MD 20892.

KLEINMAN, HYNDA KAREN, CELL BIOLOGY, CONNECTIVE TISSUE RESEARCH. **Personal Data:** b Boston, Mass, May 20, 1947; m 1968, c 2. **Education:** Simmons Col, BS, 1969; Mass Inst Technol, MS, 1971, PhD (nutrit biochem), 1973. **Honors & Awards:** Doren Kamp-Zbinden Award, 1987. **Professional Experience:** CHIEF, CELL BIOL SECT, NAT INST DENT RES, NIH, 1985-; res chemist, Nat Inst dent res, NIH, 1975-1985; res fel, Med Sch, Tufts Univ & Vet admin hosp, 1973-1975. **Memberships:** Soc Biol Chemists; AM Soc Cell Biol; Soc Complex Carbohydrates; Tissue Cult Asn; Am Asn Cancer res; Wound Healing Soc; AAAS; Asn Women Sci. **Research Statement & Publications:** Structure and function of extracellular matrices and their role in development and in diseases. **Mailing Address:** Nat Inst Dent Res, NIH, Rm 433 Bldg 30 30 Convent Dr MSC 4370, Bethesda, MD 20892-4370. **Fax:** 301-402-0897. **E-Mail:** hynda.kleinman@nih.gov

KLEINMAN, JACK G, ACID-BASE PHYSIOLOGY, RENAL DISEASES. **Personal Data:** b New York, NY, February 8, 1944; m 1966, c 2. **Education:** NY Univ, MD, 1968. **Professional Experience:** PROF MED, MED COL, UNIV WIS, 1989-; CHIEF, RENAL DIS SECT, ZABLOSKI VET ADMIN MED CTR, 1986-; assoc prof, Renal Dis Sect, Zabloski Vet Admin Med Ctr, 1980-1989; Asst chief, Renal Dis Sect, Zabloski Vet Admin Med Ctr, 1976-1986. **Memberships:** Am Physiol Soc; Am Fedn Clin Res; Am Soc Nephrology. **Research Statement & Publications:** Cell biology of kidney disease and acid-base transport; smooth muscle acid-base transport; pathophysiology of kidney stone disease. **Mailing Address:** Dept Internal Med, Med Col Wis, Vet Admin Med Ctr, 5000 W National Ave, Milwaukee, WI 53226-0001. **Fax:** 414-382-5319. **E-Mail:** Kleinman@mcw.edu

KLEINMAN, KENNETH MARTIN, PSYCHOPHYSIOLOGY, BIOPSYCHOLOGY. **Personal Data:** b Brooklyn, NY, August 10, 1941; m 1982, Sheila; c Seth M & Scott E. **Education:** Grinnell Col, BA, 1962; Wash Univ, St Louis, MA, 1964, PhD (psychol), 1967. **Professional Experience:** PROF EMER, DEPT PSYCHOL, SOUTHERN ILL UNIV, EDWARDSVILLE, as of 2006; chmn, dept psychol, Southern Ill Univ, Edwardsville, 1979-2001; prof psychol, Southern Ill Univ, Edwardsville, beginning 1978; res fel psychiat, Charing Cross Hosp Med Sch, London, Eng, 1977; res consult, St Louis Vet Admin Med Ctr, 1969-; from asst prof to assoc prof, Southern Ill Univ, Edwardsville, 1969-1978; instr, Dept Psychiat, Univ Mo Sch Med, 1967-1969; res fel, Dept Psychiat, Wash Univ Sch Med, 1962-1966. **Memberships:** Sigma Xi; Soc Psychophysiol Res; Am Psychol Soc. **Research Statement & Publications:** Brain-behavior relationships; behavioral med; effects of stress on physiology and behavior; research design and statistical analysis; program evaluation. **Mailing Address:** Southern Ill Univ, 30 Moonglow Dr, Belleville, IL 62221-4325. **Fax:** 618-624-3494. **E-Mail:** kkleinm@siue.edu

KLEINMAN, LEONARD, SOLID STATE PHYSICS. **Personal Data:** b New York, NY, July 25, 1933; m 1957, Faye; c Paul & Julie A (Martin). **Education:** Univ Calif, Los Angeles, BA, 1955, MS, 1956; Univ Calif, Berkeley, PhD (physics), 1960. **Professional Experience:** PROF PHYSICS, UNIV TEX, AUSTIN, 1967-; assoc prof, Univ Southern Calif, 1964-1967; asst prof, Univ Pa, 1961-1964; res assoc physics, Univ Chicago, 1960-1961. **Memberships:** fel Am Phys Soc. **Research Statement & Publications:** Energy band theory; pseudopotential and density functional theory; semiconductor superlattices; covalent bonding and theory of cohesive energies; electron gas theory; theory of metal surfaces. **Mailing Address:** Dept Physics, Univ Tex, Austin, TX 78712. **Fax:** 512-471-9637. **E-Mail:** kleinman@mail.utexas.edu

KLEINMAN, MICHAEL THOMAS, ENVIRONMENTAL & OCCUPATIONAL HEALTH, TOXICOLOGY EXPOSURE & RISK ASSESSMENT. **Personal Data:** b Brooklyn, NY, March 8, 1942; m 1965, c 2. **Education:** City Univ NY, BS, 1965; Polytech Inst Brooklyn, MS, 1971; NY Univ, PhD (environ health), 1977. **Professional Experience:** ADJ PROF COMMUNITY & ENVIRON MED, UNIV CALIF, IRVINE, 1982-; dir Aerosol Lab, Rancho Los Amigos Hosp, 1977-1982; asst res scientist, NY Univ Med Ctr, 1972-1977; phys scientist, US AEC, 1965-1972; Radiochemist, US AEC, 1963-1965; consult, environ health & toxicology. **Memberships:** Air Pollution Control Asn; AAAS; Sigma Xi; Am Asn Aerosol Res; NY Acad Sci. **Research Statement & Publications:** Health effects of pollutant aerosols and gases in humans and animals; chemical alterations of airborne pollutants; development of methods for the generation and characterizations of air pollutants; industrial hygiene toxicology. **Mailing Address:** 3492 Lotus St, Irvine, CA 92714. **Fax:** 949-824-2070. **E-Mail:** mtkleinm@uci.edu

KLEINMAN, ROBERT L P, GEOMICROBIOLOGY, BIOGEOCHEMISTRY. **Personal Data:** b New York, NY, December 22, 1951; m 1976, c 2. **Education:** Pa State Univ, BS, 1974; Princeton Univ, MA, 1976, PhD (water resources) 1979. **Honors & Awards:** Five Star Award, Pollution Eng Mag; Stewardship Award Sci & Technol, US Dept Interior. **Professional Experience:** AT FED ENERGY TECH CTR, US DEPT ENERGY, as of 1998; Chair, Eastern sect, Am Soc Surface Mining & Reclamation, 1988; RES SUPVR ENVIRON TECHNOL, BUR MINES, PITTSBURGH RES CTR, 1983-; group supvr environ eng, Bur Mines, 1979-1983. **Memberships:** Am Soc Surface Mining & Reclamation; Int Mine Water Asn. **Research Statement & Publications:** ameliorate the environmental impacts of mining activities; fires in abandoned mines and acid mine draininge. **Mailing Address:** Fed Energy Technol Ctr US Dept Energy, PO Box 10940 Cochrans Mill Rd, Pittsburgh, PA 15236-0940. **Fax:** 412-386-4579. **E-Mail:** robert.kleinman@netl.doe.gov

KLEINMAN, ROBERTA WILMA, ORGANIC CHEMISTRY, CONSERVATION CHEMISTRY. **Personal Data:** b New York, NY, October 10, 1942. **Education:** Barnard Col, Columbia Univ, AB, 1964; Rutgers Univ, NB, PhD (org chem), 1969. **Professional Experience:** PROF CHEM, LOCK HAVEN UNIV PA, as of 2003; CONSERV CHEMIST, PANHANDLE-PLAINS HIST MUS, TEX, 1982-; lectr, Ann Arbor, 1979-1982; Consult, Henry Ford Mus, Dearborn, 1979-1980; asst prof chem, Univ Mich, Dearborn, 1972-1979; fel, Rutgers Univ, NB, 1971-1972; instr, Rutgers Univ, NB, 1970-1971; NIH fel chem, Rutgers Univ, NB, 1969-1970. **Memberships:** Am Chem Soc; AAAS. **Research Statement & Publications:** Carbene additions to steroid analogues; micelle formation and catalysis; synthetic polynucleotides as catalysts of enzymatic ractions; nucleic acid interactions; identification of natural dyes on textiles; stability studies of natural dyes. **Mailing Address:** Dept Chem, Lock Haven Univ Pa, 404B Ulmer Hall, Lock Haven, PA 17745. **E-Mail:** rkleinma@lhup.edu

KLEINMANN, DOUGLAS ERWIN, ASTRONOMY, PHYSICS. **Personal Data:** b Chicago, Ill, July 11, 1942; m 1970, Susan; c 1. **Education:** Rice Univ, BA, 1964, PhD (space sci), 1969; Mass Inst Technol, SM, 1980 ADO Brandeis Univ Master's Software Engg 1999. **Professional Experience:** Vpres, Mitsubishi Elect Res Lab, 2000-2001; prog mgr, Loral Infrared & Imaging Systs, 1980-1998; res affil, Mass Inst Technol, 1973-1979; mem infrared instrument definition team, Space Telescope, NASA, 1973-1977; lectr, Harvard Col Observ, Harvard Univ, 1971-1979; astronr, Smithsonian Astrophys Observ, Smithsonian Inst, 1970-1979; fel astron, Rice Univ, 1968-1970. **Memberships:** Am Astron Soc; Int Astrophys Union; Am Optical Soc; fel Explorers Club. **Research Statement & Publications:** Infrared devices, infrared astronomy; instrumentation using infrared devices. **Mailing Address:** 15 Hastings Rd, Lexington, MA 02173. **E-Mail:** dek@kleinmann.com

KLEINROCK, LEONARD, COMPUTER NETWORKS & COMPUTER SCIENCE. **Personal Data:** b New York, NY, June 13, 1934; m 1971, Stella; c Martin C, Nancy S (Schneider), Robin (Schorr) & Lynn (Hirschberg). **Education:** City Col NY, BEE, 1957; Mass Inst Technol, SMEE, 1959, PhD (elec eng), 1963. **Honors & Awards:** Lanchester Prize, 1976; L M Ericsson Prize, 1982; Marconi Int Fel, 1986; Sigcomm Award, Asn Comput Mach, 1990; Harry H Goode Award, 1996. **Professional Experience:** PROF EMER COMPUT SCI, UNIV CALIF, LOS ANGELES, as of 2004; pres, Nomadix, LLC, beginning 1995; mem, sci adv comt, IBM, Comput Sci & Technol Bd, Nat Res Coun, 1986-1993; chief exec officer, Technol Transfer Inst, beginning 1976; guggenheim fel, 1971-1972; prof comput sci, Univ calif, Los Angeles, beginning 1970; prin investr, Advan Res Projs Agency, Dept Defense Contract, beginning 1969; pres, Linkabit Corp, 1968-1969; from asst prof to assoc prof, Univ Calif, Los Angeles, 1963-1970; staff mem, Lincoln Lab, 1963; res asst, Electronics Res Lab, 1958-1961; res asst, Servomechanism Lab, Mass Inst Technol, 1957-1958; asst engr, photobell co, NY, 1951-1957; mem adv counsci & eng, City Col New York. **Memberships:** Nat Acad Eng; Opers Res Soc Am; fel Inst Elec & Electronics Engrs. **Research Statement & Publications:** Design of advanced packet switching networks: wireless packet radio networks to fiber-based to gigabit networks; queueing theory; distributed systems; pioneer in nomadic computing. **Mailing Address:** Dept Comput Sci, Univ Calif, 3732 Boelter Hall, Los Angeles, CA 90095-1596. **Fax:** 310-825-7578. **E-Mail:** lk@cs.ucla.edu

KLEINROCK, MARTIN CHARLES, CRUSTAL GENERATION & DEFORMATION, MARINE GEOLOGY & GEOPHYSICS. **Personal Data:** b Boston, Mass, August 21, 1958; m 2001, Adele Kleinrock; c Jacob, Jennifer, Kate, Micah, Noah & Abram. **Education:** Univ Calif, Santa Barbara, BA, 1981; Univ Calif, San Diego, MS, 1984, PhD (earth sci), 1988. **Professional Experience:** ASST PROF OF GEOL, VANDERBILT UNIV, 1994-; asst scientist marine geol & geophys, Woods Hole Oceanog Inst, 1989-1994; investr, Woods Hole Oceanog Inst, 1988-1989; W M Keck scholar, 1988; asst geophysicist, Hawaii Inst Geophys, 1988; vis prof colleague marine geol & geophys, Hawaii Inst Geophys, 1986-1987; Earle C Anthony fel, Univ Calif, San Diego, 1985-1986; Teaching asst field geol & optical mineral, Scripps Inst Oceanog, 1982-1983; res asst marine geol & geophys, Scripps Inst Oceanog, 1981-1986. **Memberships:** Am Geophys Union; Geol Soc Am; Oceanog Soc; Sigma Xi. **Research Statement & Publications:** Plate tectonics; plate boundary processes; generation and deformation of lithosphere; mid-ocean ridge tectonics; evolution of seafloor morphology; hydrothermal processes; seafloor survey instruments; author of various publications. **Mailing Address:** Box 1805 Sta B, Vanderbilt Univ, Nashville, TN 37235. **E-Mail:** martykleinrock@yahoo.com

KLEINSCHMIDT, ALBERT WILLOUGHBY, ORGANIC CHEMISTRY. **Personal Data:** b Clinton, Iowa, March 20, 1913; m 1943, c 3. **Education:** Iowa State Univ, BS, 1935; Purdue Univ, PhD (org chem), 1941. **Professional Experience:** RETIRED; vpres, J R Short Milling Co, 1969-1979; tech dir, J R Short Milling Co, 1967-1969; lab mgr, J R Short Milling Co, 1963-1967; res chemist, J R Short Milling Co, 1958-1963; res chemist, Am Maize Prod Co Inc, 1947-1958; res chemist, Beatrice Foods Inc, Ill, 1944-1947; res chemist, Cent Soya Co Inc, 1940-1944. **Memberships:** Am Chem Soc; Am Oil Chem Soc; Am Asn Cereal Chem; Inst Food Technol; Am Soc Brewing Chem. **Research Statement & Publications:** Oil; fats; carbohydrates. **Mailing Address:** 452 King St, Oviedo, FL 32765-9711.

KLEINSCHMIDT, R STEVENS, CIVIL ENGINEERING, WATER POWER ENGINEERING. **Personal Data:** b Boston, Mass, October 8, 1925; wid, c 4. **Education:** Harvard Univ, AB, 1949, SM, 1951, ScD(civil eng), 1958. **Honorary Degrees:** Dr Community Develop, Unity Col, Maine, 1976. **Honors & Awards:** Herschel Prize, 1951. **Professional Experience:** VPRES, KLEINSCHMIDT ASSOCS, as of 2004; pres, Kleinschmidt & Dutting Consult Engrs, 1985-; chmn bd & sr vpres, Kleinschmidt & Dutting Consult Engrs, 1980-1985; partner, Kleinschmidt & Dutting Consult Engrs, 1970-1980; independent consult engr, 1966-1970; hydraul engr, Great Northern Paper Co, Maine, 1962-1966; asst prof hydraul & sanit eng, Northeastern Univ, 1959-1962; asst engr water supply & sewage disposal, Camp Dresser & McKee, Mass, 1958-1959; Res engr, Harvard Univ, 1950-1958. **Memberships:** Am Soc Civil Engrs; Am Consult Engrs Coun; Sigma Xi. **Research Statement & Publications:** Hydraulics as applied to sanitary engineering. **Mailing Address:** 202 Beckwith Woods RR 4, Ellsworth, ME 04605.

KLEINSCHMIDT, ROGER FREDERICK, ORGANIC CHEMISTRY, PETROLEUM TECHNOLOGY. **Personal Data:** b New York, NY, May 12, 1919; m 1945, c 3. **Education:** Lehigh Univ, BS, 1940; Columbia Univ, PhD (org chem), 1944. **Professional Experience:** RETIRED; mem staff corp planning, Norweg Indust Develop, 1981-1997; prog mgr tertiary recovery petrol, Energy Res & Develop Admin Phillips Petrol Co Proj, 1975-1997; planning consult natural resources, Phillips Petrol Co, 1974-1997; licensing rep, Phillips Petrol Co, 1971-1974; vpres res & develop, Phillips Sci Corp, 1968-1971; mgr, Hydrocarbon Chem Br, 1965-1968; sect mgr org chem synthesis, Phillips Petrol Co, 1959-1965; sr group supvr, Phillips Petrol Co, 1957-1959; instr, Exten, Okla State Univ, beginning 1953; group leader org chem, Phillips Petrol Co, 1952-1957; res chemist, Gen Aniline & Film Corp, 1946-1952; res chemist, Interchem Corp, NY, 1944; asst chem, Columbia Univ, 1941-1944. **Memberships:** Soc Petrol Engrs. **Research Statement & Publications:** Synthetic organic chemicals; acetylene chemistry; polymerization; pressure reactions; petrochemicals from olefins and diolefins; naphthenes; non-aromatic cyclics; organometallic catalysts and intermediates; industrial organic chemistry; enhanced recovery of oil; micellar/polymer recovery methods; exploration and production planning, economics and budgets. **Mailing Address:** 1827 S E Hampden Rd, Bartlesville, OK 74006.

KLEINSCHUSTER, JACOB JOHN, ORGANIC POLYMER CHEMISTRY. **Personal Data:** b Northampton, Pa, July 5, 1943; m 1970, c 3. **Education:** Va Mil Inst, BS, 1964; Pa State Univ, MS, 1966, PhD (chem), 1972. **Professional Experience:** TECH DIR, E I DU PONT Del NEMOURS & CO, INC, 1989-; worldwide tech mgr, E I du Pont Del Nemours & Co, Inc, 1985-1989; tech mgr, E I du Pont Del Nemours & Co, Inc, 1984-1985; mfg supt, E I du Pont Del Nemours & Co, Inc, 1983-1984; tech supt, E I du Pont Del Nemours & Co, Inc, 1982-1983; sr supvr, E I du Pont Del Nemours & Co, Inc, 1979-1982; supvr org polymer chem, E I du Pont Del Nemours & Co, Inc, 1975-1978; sr res chemist, E I du Pont Del Nemours & Co, Inc, 1974-1975; Res chemist, E I du Pont Del Nemours & Co, Inc, 1972-1974. **Memberships:** Am Chem Soc. **Research Statement & Publications:** High performance organic industrial fibers, and apparel and spandex fibers. **Mailing Address:** 6 Twin Turns Lane, Chadds Ford, PA 19317-9347.

KLEINSCHUSTER, STEPHEN J, III, DEVELOPMENTAL BIOLOGY, IMMUNOTHERAPY. **Personal Data:** b Bath, Pa, June 3, 1939; m 1966, c 2. **Education:** Colo State Univ, BS, 1963, MS, 1966; Ore State Univ, PhD (zool), 1970. **Professional Experience:** PROF MARINE & COASTAL SCI, RUTGERS UNIV, 1989-; dean agr & nat resources, Rutgers Univ, 1985-1989; prof & head, Animal, Dairy & Vet Sci Dept, 1981-1985; actg head, Utah State Univ, 1980-1981; surg oncol res group, LDS Hosp, Salt Lake City, Utah, 1979-; organizer & dir, Vet Sci Tissue Cult Facil, Utah State Univ, 1979-; dir, Animal Tumor Prog, Animal, Dairy & Vet Sci, 1977-1985; Impact Rev Group, Dept Agr, State Utah, 1977; chmn exec comt anat, Colo State Univ, 1976-1977; prin investr, NIH, Cancer Immunoprophylaxis Contracts, 1977-1981 & Immunother Procurement Contracts, 1975-1981; assoc prof anat, Colo State Univ, 1975-1977; affil prof bot & plant path, Colo State Univ, 1973; Consult, NASA, 1971-1977; asst prof biol, Metrop State Col, Denver, 1971-1973; Fel develop biol, Univ Chicago, 1971. **Memberships:** AAAS; Am Asn Anatomists; Am Asn Vet Anatomists; NY Acad Sci; Am Soc Animal Sci. **Research Statement & Publications:** Cancer biology; immunotherapy and immunoprophylaxis; molecular biology of development and morphogenesis. **Mailing Address:** Marine Sci, Rutgers Univ, New Brunswick, NJ 08903.

KLEINSMITH, LEWIS JOEL, CELL BIOLOGY, BIOCHEMISTRY. **Personal Data:** b Detroit, Mich, April 13, 1942; m 1964, Cynthia; c 2. **Education:** Univ Mich, BS, 1964; Rockefeller Univ, PhD (life sci), 1968. **Honors & Awards:** Henry Russel Award, 1971; Distinguished Serv Award, Univ of Michigan, 1971; Guggenheim Fel, 1974-1975; Ann arbor Pub Sch golden Apple Award, 1988; EDUCOM Higher Edu Sortware Award, 1998; Michigan Technol Council Sci Quest Award, 1990; LSA Excellence in Edu Award, 1997; NIH Plain Language Award, 2001; Who's Among Am Techers, 2002. **Professional Experience:** PROF EMER MOLECULAR CELL & DEVELOP BIOL, UNIV MICH, ANN ARBOR, as of 2005; prof mol, cell, & develop biol, Univ Mich, Ann Arbor, beginning 2001; Arthur Thurnau prof, 1988-1991; prof biol sci, Univ Mich, Ann Arbor, beginning 1975; Guggenheim fel, 1974-1975; vis prof biochem, Univ Fla, Gainesville, 1974-1975; from asst prof to assoc prof zool, Univ Mich, Ann Arbor, 1968-1974. **Memberships:** Am Soc Cell Biol; Am Soc Biol Chemists. **Research Statement & Publications:** Biochemistry of cell nucleus; role of nuclear proteins in regulating gene function; nucleoprotein chemistry and function; biochemical regulatory mechanisms; regulation of normal and malignant cell growth. **Mailing Address:** Univ Mich, Dept Molecular Cell & Develop Biol, 3065A Kraus Nat sci Bldg, Ann Arbor, MI 48109-1048. **E-Mail:** lewisk@umich.edu

KLEINSPEHN, GEORGE, ORGANIC CHEMISTRY. **Personal Data:** b Middlebury, Vt, March 27, 1924; div, c Valerie K Marks & Eric Kleinspehn (Deceased). **Education:** Colgate Univ, AB, 1944; Johns Hopkins Univ, AM, 1947, PhD (chem), 1951. **Professional Experience:** WHITAKER PROF EMER CHEM, HOOD COL, 1993-; fel, DuPont, 1950 & Beneficial-Hodson, 1984; Whitaker prof, Hood Col, 1983-1993; dept chmn, Hood Col, 1979-1982; consult, US Army Ballistic Res Labs, 1968; prof, Hood Col, 1967-1983; chief, Org Chem Sect, Chem Br, 1963-1967; chemist, US Army Ballistic Res Labs, 1960-1963; res assoc, Johns Hopkins Univ, 1960; sr res assoc & treas, Monadnock Res Inst, 1956-1959; res assoc & univ fel, Johns Hopkins Univ, 1951-1956; USPHS fel, NIH, 1951-1952; jr instr, Johns Hopkins Univ, 1946-1949; jr chemist, Clinton Eng Works-Tenn Eastman Corp, 1944-1946. **Memberships:** Am Chem Soc; Sigma Xi. **Research Statement & Publications:** Nitrogenous heterocyclic compounds, especially pyrroles and porphyrins; organic substances of high nitrogen content. **Mailing Address:** Dept Chem & Physics, Hood Col, 401 Rosemont Ave, Frederick, MD 21701-8575.

KLEINSTEUBER, TILMANN CHRISTOPH WERNER, PHYSICS, PHYSICAL CHEMISTRY. **Personal Data:** b Berlin, Ger, July 16, 1934. **Education:** Univ Hamburg, BSc, 1956; Univ Munich, PhD (phys chem), 1961. **Professional Experience:** RETIRED; assoc prof, King's Col, Pa, 1968-1996; from asst prof to prof physics & chmn, King's Col, Pa, 1965-1996; chmn dept, King's Col, Pa, 1965-1996; asst prof chem, Amherst Col, 1964-1965; res assoc, Amherst Col, 1963-1964; res assoc phys chem, Univ Munich, 1961-1963. **Memberships:** Am Asn Physics Teachers; Sigma Xi. **Research Statement & Publications:** Calorimetry at high and low temperatures; thermodynamics of metals and alloys; surface chemistry; gas chromatography. **Mailing Address:** King's Col, 1646 E 1185 N, Wilkes-Barre, PA 84341-3036.

KLEIS, JOHN DIEFFENBACH, ELECTRONIC GRADE BONDING WIRE, ELECTRICAL CONTACTS. **Personal Data:** b Hamburg, NY, February 1, 1912; m 1949, Marie; c Cheryl, Lynn & John. **Education:** Univ Buffalo, BA, 1932, MA, 1933; Yale Univ, PhD (physics), 1936; Harvard Bus Sch, AMP, 1957. **Professional Experience:** TECH DIR, POLYMETALL CORP, 1989-; electronics consult, beginning 1983; CONSULT, STERN METALS, 1983-; vpres & technol dir precious metals group, Cooper Div, 1978-1982; pres, Cooper Div, 1970-1978; vpres res elec contacts, Sterndent Corp, 1969-1970; vpres & gen mgr elec & electronic prod, Fansteel, Inc, 1963-1969; vpres res refractory metals, Fansteel, Inc, 1957-1963; physicist elec contacts, Fansteel, Inc, 1936-1957. **Memberships:** Soc Automotive Engrs; fel Am Soc Testing & Mat; Inst Elec & Electronics Engrs; Am Soc Qual Control. **Research Statement & Publications:** Solid state, areas relating to bonding procedures and bonding, interconnect materials; precious metals, metallurgy of Al and AliSi materials. **Mailing Address:** 1944 S Daytona Ave, Flagler Beach, FL 32136.

KLEIS, ROBERT W(ILLIAM), AGRICULTURAL ENGINEERING MATERIALS HANDLING, INT DEVELOP. **Personal Data:** b Martin, Mich, November 30, 1925; m 1949, Beatrice; c Cinthia Lee (Johnson) & Pamela Sue (Trimmer). **Education:** Mich State Univ, BS, 1949, MS, 1951, PhD (agr eng), 1957. **Honors & Awards:** Distinquished collab, us dept of agr sec, 1984; Distinguished serv Award, US dept of Commerce, 1984; Seconded as Exec Dir, Food & Agr, US Dept of st, Presidential appointment, 1985-1987. **Professional Experience:** RETIRED; exec dir, Bd Int Food & Agr, Wash, DC, 1985-1987; exec dean int affairs, 1984-1990; dir, Int Collab Res Support Prog, beginning 1978; dir, MidAM Int Agr Consortium, Inc, beginning 1976; dean int progs, Agr Exp Sta, 1976-1984; consult, Indust, beginning 1950; consult, Int Agr Develop, beginning 1975; assoc dir, Agr Exp Sta, 1967-1983; prof & chmn dept, Univ Nebr, Lincoln, 1966-1967; prof & head dept, Univ Mass, Amherst, 1957-1966; asst prof, Univ Ill, 1953-1956; instr, Univ Ill, 1951-1953; instr agr eng, Mich State Univ, 1949-1951; mem bd dir, Self Help Found. **Memberships:** Fel Am Soc Agr Engrs; Am Soc Eng Educ; Nat Asn Univ Dirs Int Progs (pres); Agr Exp Sta Dir Asn (pres); Sigma Xi; Soc Int Develop. **Research Statement & Publications:** Materials handling systems for agriculture; product processing; food and feed preservation; farm operations mechanization; international food production systems development. **Mailing Address:** 6325 O St, Apt 602, Lincoln, NE 68510.

KLEITMAN, DANIEL J, MATHEMATICS. **Personal Data:** b New York, NY, October 4, 1934; m 1964, c 3. **Education:** Cornell Univ, BA, 1954; Harvard Univ, MA, 1955, PhD, 1958. **Professional Experience:** Head dept, Mass Inst Technol, 1979-1984; managing ed, Soc Indust & Appl Math J Algebraic & Discrete Methods, 1975-1982; consult, Nuclear Regulatory Comn, Gen Acct Off, 1973-1981; PROF MATH, MASS INST TECHNOL, 1969-; assoc prof, Mass Inst Technol, 1966-1969; asst prof, Brandeis Univ, 1960-1966; NSF fel physics, Copenhagen Univ, 1958-1959 & Harvard Univ, 1959-1960; ed, J Networks. **Memberships:** Am Math Soc; Oper Res Soc Am; Soc Indust & Appl Math; Am Acad Arts & Sci; NY Acad Sci. **Research Statement & Publications:** Combinatorial mathematics; graph theory; numeration and optimization; applications to operations research. **Mailing Address:** Dept Math, Mass Inst Tech, 77 Mass Ave, Newton, MA 02159. **E-Mail:** djk@math.mit.edu

KLEITMAN, DAVID, solid state physics; deceased, see previous edition for last biography

KLEKOWSKI, EDWARD JOSEPH, BOTANY, GENETICS. **Personal Data:** b Brooklyn, NY, October 24, 1940. **Education:** NC State Univ, BS, 1962, MS, 1964; Univ Calif, Berkeley, PhD (bot), 1968. **Professional Experience:** PROF EMER, DEPT BIOL, UNIV MASS, AMHERST, as of 2004; assoc prof bot, Univ Mass, Amherst, beginning 1973; asst prof, Univ Mass, Amherst, 1968-1973. **Memberships:** Bot Soc Am. **Research Statement & Publications:** Pteridology; genetic and evolutionary studies of homosporous ferns. **Mailing Address:** Dept Biol, Univ Mass, Amherst, MA 01003-0002. **E-Mail:** edk@bio.umass.edu

KLEMA, ERNEST DONALD, NUCLEAR PHYSICS. **Personal Data:** b Wilson, Kans, October 4, 1920; m 1953, Virginia; c Donald & Catherine. **Education:** Univ Kans, BA, 1941, MA, 1942; Rice Univ, PhD (physics), 1951. **Professional Experience:** PROF EMER ENG SCI, TUFTS UNIV, 1988-; DEAN EMER, COL ENG, TUFTS UNIV, 1988-; adj prof int politics, Fletcher Sch Law & Diplomacy, 1973-1983; prof, Col Eng, 1968-1988; dean col eng, Col Eng, 1968-1973; chmn dept eng sci, Northwestern Univ, 1960-1967; prof nuclear & sci eng, Northwestern Univ, 1958-1968; assoc prof nuclear eng, Univ Mich, 1956-1958; sr physicist nuclear physics, Oak Ridge Nat Lab, 1950-1956; jr scientist, Los Alamos Sci Lab, 1943-1946. **Memberships:** Fel Am Phys Soc; fel Am Nuclear Soc; sr mem Inst Elec & Electronics Engrs. **Research Statement & Publications:** Angular correlations of gamma rays; fission cross sections; empirical nuclear models; semiconductor detectors; science and technology policy. **Mailing Address:** Col Eng, Tufts Univ, 105 Anderson Hall, Medford, MA 02155. **Fax:** 617-627-3819.

KLEMANN, LAWRENCE PAUL, LIPIDS TECHNOLOGY, EDIBLE OILS PROCESSING. **Personal Data:** b Cincinnati, Ohio, August 13, 1943; m 1963, Diane; c Eric & Lauren. **Education:** Univ Mass, BS, 1965, MS, 1968, PhD (org chem), 1969. **Professional Experience:** RES PRIN, KRAFT FOODS INC, as of 2006; SR PRIN SCIENTIST, NABISCO BRANDS INC, 1986-; res assoc, Exxon Res & Eng Co, 1969-1986. **Memberships:** Am Chem Soc. **Research Statement & Publications:** Organic and organometallic synthesis; lipid chemistry; reduced calorie fats and oils; catalysis; coordination chemistry; lithium organic electrolytes and batteries; separation science and surfactant chemistry; author of 30 publications; granted 45 US patents. **Mailing Address:** Kraft Foods Inc, Three Lakes Dr, Northfield, IL 60093. **Fax:** 847-646-6005.

KLEMARCZYK, PHILIP THADDEUS, ORGANIC & POLYMER CHEMISTRY. **Personal Data:** b Exeter, NH, October 10, 1951. **Education:** Holy Cross Col, BA, 1973; Brandeis Univ, PhD (chem), 1979. **Professional Experience:** SR SCIENTIST, HENKEL LOCTITE CORP, 1996-; scientist, Loctite Corp, 1987-1996; sr chemist, Loctite Corp, 1982-1987; res chemist, Int Flowers & Fragrances, 1979-1982. **Memberships:** Am Chem Soc; Sigma Xi. **Research Statement & Publications:** Synthesis and evaluation of new monomers and polymers for use in adhesives and sealants; investigation of new processes for existing materials; exploration of new technologies. **Mailing Address:** Loctite Corp, 1001 Trout Brook Crossing, Rocky Hill, CT 06067. **E-Mail:** phil.klemarczyk@loctite.com

KLEMAS, VICTOR V, REMOTE SENSING, MARINE STUDIES. **Personal Data:** American citizen; m, c 3. **Education:** Mass Inst Technol, BS/MS EE, 1959; Univ Braunschweig, PhD, EE/Optical Physics, 1965. **Honors & Awards:** Achievement Medal, Korean Advan Inst Sci; Sir William Hershel Award, AmAcad of Thermology; General Electric Inventors Award; Member, Seven Committees of National Academy of Science/NRC (1984-2001); Board of Trustees, CoastEduc&ResFoundtn; EditBoards; JourCoastRes; RemSensEnvir; EnvirManagement; Geocarto Int; NASA Center of Excellence Grant. **Professional Experience:** Professor, Marine Studies(1972-P); Professor, Geography & Electrical Eng; Director, Ctr. for Remote Sensing(1976-); Director, Appl.Ocean ScienceProg(1981-98); Mgr, Optical Phys, GE Space Ctr(1965-71); Consultant, NOAA, NASA, EPA, USGS, UNDP, USAID; P.I., 48 Coastal Remote Sensing Projects; Mgr, Nat.Sci.Found.SEED Program (1977-78); Lecturer, 23 Workshops in 14 Countries; 1st Lieut, US Army Signal Corps (1959-62). **Memberships:** Am Geophys Union; Am Soc Photogram; Inst of Elec & Electronics Engrs; NOAA/NASA Coastal Ocean Science & Applications Team; NOAA/NERRS Remote Sensing Advisory Panel; Fulbright Senior Specialist Program; American Soc of Thermography. **Research Statement & Publications:** Remote sensing of coastal ecosystems and environment, including wetland health, estuarine pollutants and coastal dynamics; Application of remote sensing and GIS to coastal management; Published 108 scientific articles in international refereed journals. **Mailing Address:** Col Marine Studies, Univ Del, 107A Robinson Hall, Newark, DE 19716. **Fax:** 302-831-6838. **E-Mail:** klemas@udel.edu

KLEMCHUK, PETER PAUL, ORGANIC CHEMISTRY, POLYMER CHEMISTRY. **Personal Data:** b Oakville, Conn, October 31, 1928; m 1949, Helen; c 5. **Education:** Mass Inst Technol, BS, 1950; Rutgers Univ, MS, 1956, PhD (org chem), 1957. **Professional Experience:** PLASTICS INDU CONSULT, 1993-; RES PROF, INST MAT SCI, UNIV CONN, 1993-2000; sr res fel, Ciba-Geigy Corp, 1960-1992; chemist, Stauffer Chem Co, 1959-1960; chemist, Esso Res & Eng Co, 1957-1959; chemist, Merck & Co Inc, 1950-1956. **Memberships:** Am Chem Soc; Soc Plastics Engrs. **Research Statement & Publications:** Polymer stabilization; polymer additives; polymer degradation; polymers recycling; photochemistry, Ni reaction mechanisms. **Mailing Address:** Inst Mat Sci, Univ Conn, 903 Buckingham St, Watertown, CT 06795-1630. **Fax:** 860-274-7561.

KLEMCKE, HAROLD G, ENDOCRINOLOGY. **Personal Data:** b San Antonio, Tex, October 10, 1945. **Education:** Univ Md, BS, 1967, MS, 1973, PhD (endocrinol), 1978. **Professional Experience:** RES PHYSIOLOGIST ENDOCRINOL, USDA, 1984-; res asst, Univ Tex Health Sci Ctr, 1982-1984; fel endocrinol, Univ Tex Health Sci Ctr, 1978-1982. **Memberships:** Am Soc Reprod; Am Endocrinol Soc; Am Physiol Soc; Am Soc Exp Biol & Med; Sigma Xi. **Mailing Address:** USDA Meat Animal Res Ctr, PO Box 166, Clay Center, NE 68933-0166. **Fax:** 402-762-4382. **E-Mail:** klemcke@email.marc.usda.gov

KLEMENS, PAUL GUSTAV, PHYSICS, THERMAL CONDUCTIVITY. **Personal Data:** b Vienna, Austria, May 24, 1925; American citizen; m 1950, Ruth Wiener; c Michael W & Susan M. **Education:** Univ Sydney, BSc, 1946, MSc, 1948; Oxford Univ, DPhil(theoret physics), 1950. **Honors & Awards:** Y S Touloukian Award, Am Soc Mech Engrs, 1988. **Professional Experience:** EMER PROF PHYSICS, UNIV CONN, 1991-; consult, Los Alamos Nat Lab, 1970-; prof physics, Univ Conn, 1967-1991; chmn dept, Univ Conn, 1967-1974; mgr transport properties, Solids Dept, 1964-1967; physicist, Westinghouse Res Labs, 1959-1964; prin res officer, Nat Standards Lab, Sydney, Australia, 1950-1959. **Memberships:** Mat Res Soc; fel, Am physical soc. **Research Statement & Publications:** Theoretical solid state and low temperature physics, particularly thermal conductivity of solids and other non-equilibrium and transport properties; ultrasonic attenuation, properties of composites; laser welding and surface modification; thermal conductivity of ceramics at high temperatures. **Mailing Address:** Dept Physics Univ Conn, 2152 Hillside, Storrs, CT 06269. **Fax:** 860-486-3346. **E-Mail:** klemens@rcn.com

KLEMENT, VACLAV, RADIATION ONCOLOGY, MICROBIOLOGY. **Personal Data:** b Pilsen, Czech, May 7, 1935; m 1967, c 2. **Education:** Charles Univ, Prague, MD, 1959; Czech Acad Sci, Prague, PhD (biol), 1964. **Professional Experience:** EMER, as of 2006; ASSOC PROF RADIATION ONCOL & MICROBIOL, SCH MED, UNIV SOUTHERN CALIF, 1979-; res fel pediat, Sch Med, Univ Southern Calif, 1968-1969; vis scientist viral oncol, Nat Inst Allergy & Infectious Dis, NIH, 1967-1968. **Memberships:** Am Endocuriether Soc; Am Soc Therapeut Radiol & Oncol. **Research Statement & Publications:** Viral carcinogensis and tumor biology; radiation oncology; oncogenes. **Mailing Address:** Sch Med LAC-Univ Southern Calif Med Ctr, Norric Cancer hosp, 1441 Eastlake Ave, Los Angeles, CA 90033. **Fax:** 323-226-5970. **E-Mail:** vklement@usc.edu

KLEMENT, WILLIAM JR, MATERIALS SCIENCE. **Personal Data:** b Chicago, Ill, September 30, 1937; m 1991, Susan M Colby. **Education:** Calif Inst Technol, BS, 1958, PhD (eng sci), 1962. **Honors & Awards:** co-recipient, Int Prize New Ma, 1980. **Professional Experience:** CONSULT, 1994-; Inorg Chem Lab, Oxford Univ, 1979; vis scientist, Nat Phys Res Lab, Pretoria, SAfrica, 1974-1976; Ford Found Prog, Univ Chile, 1973; Guggenheim Mem Found fel, Australian Nat Univ, 1968-1969; from asst prof to assoc prof eng, Univ Calif, Los Angeles, 1966-1994; Miller res fel physics, Univ Calif, Berkeley, 1964-1966; NATO fel, Royal Inst Technol, Sweden, 1963; Asst res geophysicist, Inst Geophys & Planetary Physics, Univ Calif, Los Angeles, 1962-1964. **Research Statement & Publications:** Phase transformations. **Mailing Address:** PO Box 5153, Vancouver, WA 98668.

KLEMER, ANDREW ROBERT, PHYSIOLOGICAL ECOLOGY, LIMNOLOGY. **Personal Data:** b St Clair, Pa, June 4, 1942; m 1963, c 4. **Education:** La Salle Col, BA, 1964; Univ Minn, PhD (ecol), 1973. **Professional Experience:** PROF BIOL, UNIV MINN, DULUTH, as of 2005; State Univ NY Res Found fac res fel, 1977, 1979; ASST PROF BIOL & ENVIRON SCI, STATE UNIV NY, PURCHASE, 1976-; vis scientist algal physiol, Cawthron Inst, 1974-1975; res fel, Nat Res Adv Coun NZ, 1973-1975; consult limnol, dept Sci & Indust res, NZ, 1973-1974. **Memberships:** Phycol Soc Am; Am Soc Limnol & Oceanog; Int Asn Theoret & Appl Limnol; AAAS; Sigma Xi. **Research Statement & Publications:** Factors that limit the distribution and affect the community structure of phytoplankton; physiological mechanisms involved in responses to those factors. **Mailing Address:** Dept Biol, Univ Minn, LSci 305 1035 Kirby Dr, Duluth, MN 55812-3004. **Fax:** 218-726-8142. **E-Mail:** aklemer@d.umn.edu

KLEMES, VIT, HYDROLOGY, WATER RESOURCES. **Personal Data:** b Podivin, Czech, April 30, 1932; m 1957, Marie; c Marek & Ivo. **Education:** Tech Univ-Brno, Czech, Dipl Eng; Tech Univ, Bratislava, Slovakia PhD (hydrol & water resources), 1964; Tech Univ-Prague, Czech, DrSc. **Honors & Awards:** Gold Medal, Slovak Acad Sci, 1993; Int Hydrol Prize, Int Asn Hydrol Sci, 1994; Ray K Linsley Award, Am Inst Hydrol, 1995. **Professional Experience:** RETIRED; vis prof, Nat Inst Sci Res-Eau, Univ Que, Ste-Foy, beginning 1994; chief scientist, Saskatoon, 1980-1989; res hydrologist, Nat Hydrol Res Inst, Ottawa, 1972-1980; assoc prof mech eng, Univ Toronto, 1968-1972. **Memberships:** Fel Am Geophys Union; Int Asn Hydrol Sci. **Research Statement & Publications:** Water resources; waste storage theory; stochastic hydrology. **Mailing Address:** 3460 Fulton Rd, Victoria, BC V9C 3N2, Can.

KLEMM, DONALD J, AQUATIC BIOLOGY, AQUATIC ECOLOGY & TOXICOLOGY. **Personal Data:** b Detroit, Mich, January 13, 1938. **Education:** Valley City State Col, BS, 1963; Eastern Mich Univ, MS & SpecS, 1970; Univ Mich, Ann Arbor, PhD (fisheries), 1974. **Professional Experience:** RES AQUATIC BIOLOGIST, ENVIRON MONITORING & SUPPORTLAB, US ENVIRON PROTECTION AGENCY, 1974-; Res assoc malacol, Mollusk Div, Mus Zool, Univ Mich, Ann Arbor, 1972-1974. **Memberships:** Soc Environ Toxicol & Chem; Int Asn Theoret & Appl Limnol; Am Soc Testing & Mat; NAm Benthol Soc; Brit Freshwater Biol Asn; Am Fisheries Soc. **Research Statement & Publications:** Stream and lake ecology; ecology of polluted waters; invertebrate and fish zoology; macroinvertebrates and fish methodology, parasitology and toxicology; systematics and ecology of freshwater fish, macroparasites, insects, mollusks, annelids, aquatic oligochaetes and Hirudinea of the world. **Mailing Address:** US EPA, NERL, EERD, ERB, MS-642, 26 W Martin Luther King Dr, Cincinnati, OH 45268-0001. **Fax:** 513-569-7609. **E-Mail:** klemm.donald@epa.gov

KLEMM, DWIGHT J, IMMUNOLOGY. **Education:** Univ Nmex, BS, 1981, PhD (biochem), 1986. **Professional Experience:** ASSOC PROF, CARDIOVASC PULMONARY RES LAB, UNIV COLO HEALTH SCI CTR, 2001-. **Mailing Address:** Cardiovasc Pulmonary Res Lab, Univ Colo Health Sci Ctr, 4200 E Ninth Ave, Denver, CO 80262. **Fax:** 303-270-2240. **E-Mail:** dwight.klemm@uchsc.edu

KLEMM, JAMES L, APPLIED MATHEMATICS, COMPUTER SCIENCE. **Personal Data:** b South Bend, Ind, October 30, 1939; m 1981, c 2. **Education:** Univ Chicago, BS, 1961; Purdue Univ, MS, 1963; Mich State Univ, PhD (eng mech), 1970. **Professional Experience:** RETIRED; consult eng, Qual Assurance, Ncr Corp, 1991-1993; consult analyst, NCR Corp, 1982-1991; sr systs analyst, NCR Corp, 1980-1982; sr publ, NCR Corp, 1977-1980; asst prof eng sci, Univ Cincinnati, 1970-1977; res assoc, Dept Metall, Mech, Mat Sci, Mich State Univ, 1970; asst, Dept Metall, Mech & Mat Sci, Mich State Univ, 1967-1969; partic, NSF Inst Appl Math & Mech, Mich State Univ, 1967; asst prof, Ind Univ Pa, 1965-1967; asst math, Purdue Univ, 1961-1965. **Memberships:** Sigma Xi; AAAS. **Research Statement & Publications:** St Venant boundary value problems in 2 and 3 dimensional theories of classical elasticity; computer applications in manufacturing. **Mailing Address:** 136 Wood Dale Dr, Lexington, SC 29072. **E-Mail:** jamdmklemm@juno.com

KLEMM, LEROY HENRY, organic chemistry synthesis, heterocyclic compounds; deceased, see previous edition for last biography

KLEMM, REBECCA JANE, STATISTICS, OPERATIONS RESEARCH. **Personal Data:** b Bloomington, Ind, February 21, 1950. **Education:** Miami Univ, BS, 1971, Iowa State Univ, MS, 1973, PhD (statist), 1976. **Professional Experience:** BD DIR, KLEMM ANAL GROUP INC, as of 2000; PRES, KLEMM ANAL GROUP INC, 1987-; mem fac statist, Sch Bus Admin, Georgetown Univ, 1980-; US Dept Energy fac fel, Sch Bus, Am Assembly Col, 1978-1979; asst prof statist, Temple Univ, 1976-1980. **Memberships:** Am Statist Asn; Opers Res Soc Am; Inst Mgt Sci. **Research Statement & Publications:** Statistical education; constrained least squares econometric model building. **Mailing Address:** Klemm Anal Group Inc, Ste 501 1785 Mass Ave NW, Washington, DC 20036. **Fax:** 202-667-5793. **E-Mail:** rjklemm@klemmanalysis.com

KLEMM, RICHARD ANDREW, THEORETICAL SOLID STATE PHYSICS, SUPERCONDUCTIVITY. **Personal Data:** b Bloomington, Ind, March 13, 1948; m 1980, Dwaraka; c Amitabh R & Siddhartha R. **Education:** Stanford Univ, BS, 1969; Harvard Univ, MA, 1972, PhD (physics), 1974. **Professional Experience:** RESIDENT ASSOC, ARGONNE NAT LAB, as of 2004; tech staff scientist, Argonne Nat Lab, beginning 1992; tech staff mem & vis scientist, Argonne Nat Lab, 1990-1992; vis scientist, Oak Ridge Nat Lab,

1989-1990; vis scientist, Argonne Nat Lab, 1989; vis scientist, Ames Lab, Iowa StateUniv, 1988-1989; vis scientist, Univ Hamburg, Ger, 1987, 1981, 1980; vis scientist, Univ Calif, La Jolla, 1986; vis prof physics, Univ Calif San Diego, La Jolla, 1986-1988; sr staff physicist, Exxon Res & Eng Co, 1984-1986; staff physicist, Exxon Res & Eng Co, 1982-1984; assoc prof, Ames Lab, Iowa State Univ, 1981; vis scientist, Simon Fraser Univ, 1979; vis scientist, Univ BC, 1978; asst prof physics, Ames Lab, Iowa StateUniv, 1976-1981; vis scientist, Univ Koln, Ger, 1976; vis scientist, AT & T Bell Labs, 1975-1976; fel, Stanford Univ, 1974-1976. **Memberships:** Fel Am Phys Soc. **Research Statement & Publications:** Theory of condensed matter involving superconductivity; p-wave superconductivity; lower dimensional conductors; charge-density waves and spin-glasses; high temperature superconductors. **Mailing Address:** Mat Sci Div, Argonne Nat Lab, 9700 S Cass Ave Bldg 223 Rm D-209, Argonne, IL 60439. **Fax:** 630-252-7777. **E-Mail:** klemm@anl.gov

KLEMM, ROBERT DAVID, VERTEBRATE MORPHOLOGY, WILDLIFE CONSERVATION. **Personal Data:** b Youngstown, Ohio, September 13, 1929; div, c 1. **Education:** Capital Univ, BS, 1957; Ohio Univ, MS, 1959; Southern Ill Univ, PhD (vert zool), 1964. **Professional Experience:** DIR, CONSERV & RES, SUNSET ZOO PARK, as of 1999; CO-ORDR, AM ASN ZOOS & AQUARIUMS, PARAGUAY FAUNA INTEREST GROUP, as of 1999; prof, Dept Anat & Physiol, Col Vet Med, Kans State Univ, 1979-1991; guest prof, Institut fur Anat u Cytobiol Der Justus-Liebig Univ Giessen, WGer, 1979-1980; assoc prof anat, Dept Anat & Physiol, Col Vet Med, Kans State Univ, 1972-1979; invests leader, Avian Anat Invests, USDA, 1970-1972; asst prof, Mich State Univ, 1970-1972; asst prof anat, Col Vet Med, Kans State Univ, 1967-1970; asst prof biol, Capital Univ, 1964-1967. **Memberships:** Am Asn Anatomists; Am Asn Vet Anatomists; emer mem Am Soc Zoologists; Am Zoo & Aquarium Asn. **Research Statement & Publications:** Gross, light and electron microscopy studies of vertebrate structure with special reference to normal and diseased lungs of domestic animals. **Mailing Address:** Kans & Paraguay Partners, 411 Timberwick Pl, Manhattan, KS 66503. **Fax:** 785-587-2730. **E-Mail:** klemm@ci.manhattan.ks.us

KLEMM, WALDEMAR ARTHUR, JR, SILICATE CHEMISTRY. **Personal Data:** b Elgin, Ill, July 10, 1934; m 1959, c 3. **Education:** Univ Calif, Riverside, BA, 1956; Ore State Univ, MS, 1967. **Professional Experience:** SR PRIN SCIENTIST & SR SCIENTIST, Mat RES GROUP, CONSTRUCT TECHNOL LABS, PORTLAND CEMENT ASN, 1993-; trustee, Cements Div, Am Ceramic Soc, 1987-1990; mgr, Cent Process Lab, Southdown, Inc, 1983-1993; sr scientist, Martin Marietta Labs, 1975-1983; vchmn solid-liquid interactions cement hydration, Gordon Res Conf, 1975-1976; sr res scientist, Gen Portland Inc, 1972-1975; assoc specialist geochem, Inst Geophys & Planetary Physics, Univ Calif, 1970-1972; group leader cement chem, Tech Ctr, Am Cement Corp, 1966-1970; Res chemist propellant chem, Lockheed Propulsion Co, 1959-1966. **Memberships:** Fel Am Ceramic Soc; Am Chem Soc. **Research Statement & Publications:** High-temperature silicate chemistry; cement clinkering reactions; admixture interactions; expansive cements; cement hydration. **Mailing Address:** Construct Technol Lab, Portland Cement Asn, 5420 Old Orchard Rd, Skokie, IL 60077-1083.

KLEMM, WILLIAM ROBERT, ANIMAL PHYSIOLOGY. **Personal Data:** b South Bend, Ind, July 24, 1934; m Doris; c Mark & Laura. **Education:** Auburn Univ, DVM, 1958; Univ Notre Dame, PhD (biol), 1963. **Professional Experience:** PROF, TEX A&M UNIV, 1970-; assoc prof, Tex A&M Univ, 1966-1970; assoc prof physiol & pharmacol, Iowa State Univ, 1963-1966; NIH fel, 1960-1963; Retired colonel, USAF, 1958-1988. **Memberships:** Sigma Xi; Soc Neuroscience; AAAS; NSTA. **Research Statement & Publications:** Animal hypnosis; theta rhythm; brain stem functions; animal electroencephalography; psychopharmacology; chemical senses; alcohol; science education. **Mailing Address:** Dept Vet Anat & Pub Health, Tex A&M Univ, College Station, TX 77843. **Fax:** 979-847-8981. **E-Mail:** wklemm@cvm.tamu.edu

KLEMMEDSON, JAMES OTTO, SOIL SCIENCE, FOREST & RANGE ECOLOGY. **Personal Data:** b Ft Collins, Colo, August 20, 1927; m 1952, c 4. **Education:** Univ Calif, Berkeley, BS, 1950, PhD (soil sci), 1959; Colo State Univ, MS, 1953. **Professional Experience:** PROF EMER RANGE & WATERSHED MGT, UNIV ARIZ, as of 1993; NATO/Hienemann Found grant, study vis chair soil sci, Univ Munich, Ger, 1983; Vis scientist, Swiss Fed Inst Forest, Snow & Landscape Res, Bermensdorf, Switz, 1982-1983 & 1989-1990; RES SCIENTIST, AGR EXP STA, 1980-; Charles Bullard forest res fel, Harvard Univ, 1974-1975; prof range & watershed mgt, Univ Ariz, beginning 1966; prof range & forestry, Agr Exp Sta, 1966-1988; range scientist, Int Forest & Range Exp Sta, USDA, 1959-1966; soils & plant nutrit, Univ Calif, Berkeley, 1956-1959; res asst forestry, Univ Calif, Berkeley, 1955-1956; instr, Mont State Univ, 1953-1955; res asst range mgt, Colo State Univ, 1952-1953; instr forestry, Colo State Univ, 1951-1952; soil conservationist, Soil Conserv Serv, USDA, 1950-1951. **Memberships:** Soc Am Foresters; Soc Range Mgt; Soil Sci Soc Am; Am Soc Agron. **Research Statement & Publications:** Soil-plant-nutrient relations in forest, range and shrub ecosystems; ecology of forest and range ecosystems. **Mailing Address:** Sch Renewable Natural Resources Univ Ariz, 302 Biol Sci E Bldg, Tucson, AZ 85721.

KLEMOLA, ARNOLD R, ASTRONOMY. **Personal Data:** b Pomfret, Conn, February 20, 1931. **Education:** Ind Univ, AB, 1953; Univ Calif, Berkeley, PhD (astron), 1962. **Professional Experience:** RES ASTRONR, LICK OBSERV, UNIV CALIF, SANTA CRUZ, 1984-; from asst res astronr to assoc res astronr, Lick Observ, Univ Calif, Santa Cruz, 1967-1984; res staff astronr, Yale Univ, 1963-1967; res asst astron, Yale Univ, 1961-1963. **Memberships:** Am Astron Soc; Int Astron Union; Astron Soc Pac. **Research Statement & Publications:** Photographic astrometry. **Mailing Address:** UCO/Lick Observ, Univ Calif, Santa Cruz, CA 95064. **E-Mail:** klemola@ucolick.org

KLEMOLA, TAPIO, MATHEMATICS. **Personal Data:** b Pori, Finland, July 20, 1934; m 1955, c 2. **Education:** Univ Helsinki, MS, 1956, PhD (math), 1959. **Professional Experience:** Swiss Govt grant, Swiss Fed Inst Technol, 1971-1972; ASSOC PROF MATH, UNIV MONTREAL, 1965-; vis prof, Univ Montreal, 1964-1965; lectr & res assoc, Johns Hopkins Univ, 1963-1964; NSF grant, Inst Advan Study, 1962-1963; asst prof, Univ Windsor, 1960-1962; actg asst prof, Univ Oulu, 1959-1960; Aaltonen Saatio & Govt Finland grant, Paris, 1959; Asst math, Univ Helsinki, 1956-1958. **Memberships:** Am Math Soc; Can Math Cong. **Research Statement & Publications:** Complex manifolds and spaces; differential operators on manifolds. **Mailing Address:** Dept Math, Univ Mont CP 6128 Sta A, Montreal, PQ H3C 3J7, Can.

KLEMPERER, FRIEDRICH W, RHEUMATOLOGY. **Education:** Harvard Univ, MD, 1937. **Professional Experience:** RETIRED; prof med, Sch Med, Syracuse Univ, 1965-1978. **Mailing Address:** 37 Minuteman Rd, Acton, MA 01720.

KLEMPERER, MARTIN R, HEMATOLOGY, ONCOLOGY. **Personal Data:** b New York, NY, June 26, 1931; m 1959, Helen R Mitlof; c John, Thomas & Sally. **Education:** Dartmouth Col, AB, 1953; NY Univ, MD, 1957. **Professional Experience:** PROF EMER, DEPT PEDIAT, COL MED, UNIV S FLA, 2002-; dir, Bone Marrow Transplant Serv, All Children's Hosp, St Petersburg, Fla, 1987-; prof, Dept Pediat, Col Med, Univ S Fla, beginning 1987; prof & chmn, Dept Pediat, Marshall Univ, 1981-1987; prof pediat & med, Sch Med, Univ Rochester, 1974-1981; pediatrician & physician, Strong Mem Hosp, Med Ctr, Univ Rochester, 1974-1981; prof med, Sch Med, Univ Rochester, 1971-1974; sr assoc pediatrician, Strong Mem Hosp, Med Ctr, Univ Rochester, 1970-1974; assoc prof pediat, Sch Med, Univ Rochester, 1970-1974; asst prof, Harvard Med Sch, 1969-1970; assoc med, immunol & hemat, 1968-1970; tutor med sci, Harvard Med Sch, 1967-1970; assoc, Harvard Med Sch, 1967-1969; res assoc immunol & hemat, Children's Hosp Med Ctr, Boston, Mass, 1966-1968; Instr pediat, Harvard Med Sch, 1965-1967; asst med, Children's Hosp Med Ctr, Boston, Mass, 1965-1966; fel hemat & med, Children's Hosp Med Ctr, Boston, Mass, 1963-1965; Res fel pediat, Harvard Med Sch, 1963-1965. **Memberships:** Soc Pediat Res; Am Soc Hemat; AmPediat Soc. **Research Statement & Publications:** Hereditary and acquired defects of the serum complement system; role of the complement system in inflammation; therapy of childhood malignancies; bone marrow transplantation. **Mailing Address:** All Children's Hosp, 801 Sixth St S, St Petersburg, FL 33701-4816. **Fax:** 727-892-8542. **E-Mail:** helmar9@msn.com

KLEMPERER, SIMON LOUIS, REFLECTION SEISMOLOGY. **Personal Data:** b London, Eng, February 24, 1958. **Education:** Cambridge Univ, BA, 1980; Cornell Univ, PhD (geophys), 1985. **Professional Experience:** PROFESSOR GEOPHYSICS, Stanford University, 1990-present; vis prof geol, Univ London, Royal Holloway, 1999-2000; Royal Soc res fel, Cambridge Univ, 1985-1990. **Memberships:** Fel Geol Soc Am; Am Geophys Union; Geol Soc Am; Soc Explor Geophysicists; Sigma Xi. **Research Statement & Publications:** Crustal structure of active tectonic areas-California, Tibet, Alaska; regional tectonics; precursors to earthquakes. **Mailing Address:** Dept Geophysics, Stanford Univ, 353 Mitchell Bldg, Stanford, CA 94305-2215. **Fax:** 650-725-7344. **E-Mail:** sklemp@stanford.edu

KLEMPERER, WALTER GEORGE, MATERIALS CHEMISTRY. **Personal Data:** b Saranac Lake, NY, April 2, 1947; m 1977, c 2. **Education:** Harvard Univ, BA, 1968; Mass Inst Technol, PhD (chem), 1973. **Professional Experience:** PROF EMER, CHEM, UNIV ILL, URBANA-CHAMPAIGN, as of 2005; prof, Chem, Univ Ill, Urbana-Champaign, 1981-2005; Guggenheim fel, 1980; Camille & Henry Dreyfus Found grant, 1978; Alfred P Sloan Found fel, 1976; from asst prof to prof chem, Columbia Univ, 1973-1981. **Memberships:** Am Chem Soc. **Research Statement & Publications:** Inorganic chemistry; materials chemistry of oxides; polyoxuanion chemistry; sul-gel chemistry; cement chemistry; zeolite chemistry. **Mailing Address:** Dept Chem, Univ Ill, 600 S Mathews Ave, Urbana, IL 61801-2325. **Fax:** 217-333-2685. **E-Mail:** wklemper@uiuc.edu

KLEMPERER, WILLIAM, PHYSICAL CHEMISTRY. **Personal Data:** b New York, NY, October 6, 1927; m 1949, Elizabeth; c Joyce Hillary, Paul & Wendy Judith. **Education:** Harvard Univ, AB, 1950; Univ Calif, PhD, 1954. **Honorary Degrees:** DSc, Univ Chicago, 1996. **Honors & Awards:** John Price Wetherill Medal, Franklin Inst, 1978; The Irving Langmuir Award in Chem Physics, Am Soc Phys, 1980; Evans lectr, Ohio State Univ, 1981; Pratt lectr, Univ Va, 1984; Flygare Mem lectr, Univ Ill, Urbana, 1985; Oesper lectr, Univ Cincinnati, 1987; Kolthoff lectr, Univ Minn, 1987; Mary E Kapp lectr, Va Commonwealth Univ, 1987; Linus Pauling Distinguished lectr, Ore State Univ, 1988; Harry Emmett Gunning lectr, Univ Alta, 1988; Hinshelwood lectr, Oxford Univ, Eng, 1989; Fritz London Mem lectr, Duke Univ, 1989; Bomem Michelson Award, Coblentz Soc, 1990; Neckers lectr, Southern Ill Univ, 1990; Rollefson lectr, Univ Calif, Berkeley. **Professional Experience:** Asst dir, NSF, 1979-1981; PROF CHEM, HARVARD UNIV, 1965-; from instr to assoc prof, Harvard Univ, 1954-1965; instr chem, Univ Calif, 1954. **Memberships:** Nat Acad Sci; fel Am Chem Soc; Am Acad Arts & Sci; Am Phys Soc. **Research Statement & Publications:** Molecular structure; molecular spectroscopy; energy transfer and intermolecular forces; modelling molecule formation and detection in the intersellar medium. **Mailing Address:** Dept Chem, Harvard Univ, Cambridge, MA 02138. **Fax:** 617-496-5175. **E-Mail:** billk@otto.harvard.edu

KLEMPNER, DANIEL, PHYSICAL POLYMER CHEMISTRY & ENGINEERING, ENVIRONMENTAL STUDIES. **Personal Data:** b Brooklyn, NY, June 4, 1943; m 1982, Lois; c Jessica, Stephanie & Rebecca. **Education:** Rensselaer Polytech Inst, BS, 1964; Williams Col, MS, 1968; State Univ NY, Albany, PhD (phys chem), 1970. **Professional Experience:** DIR, POLYMER TECHNOL INC & DIR, CTR EXCELLENCE ENVIRON ENG & SCI, as of 2003; RES PROF POLYMER CHEM & ENG, POLYMER INST, UNIV DETROIT MERCY, as of 2003; assoc dir, Polymer Technol, Inc & dir, Ctr Excellence Environ Eng & Sci, Univ Detroit Mercy, beginning 1992; prof polymer chem & eng, Polymer Inst, Univ Detroit Mercy, beginning 1974; int consult, 1973-; mem fac, Polymer Inst, Univ Detroit Mercy, beginning 1972; vis scientist, Univ Mass, Amherst, 1970-1972; engr, Sprague Elec Co, Mass, 1964-1968; prin investr numerous indust & govt sponsored res proj. **Memberships:** Am Chem Soc; Am Inst Chem; Soc Plastics Engrs; Fedn Coatings Socs; Nat Forensic Ctr. **Research Statement & Publications:** Electrical properties of materials; inter-penetrating polymer networks; high pressure effects on polymers; x-ray diffraction studies of polymers; morphological and viscoelastic studies on polymers; theories of fusion and blending of polymers; polyurethanes of all types; flammability; environmental studies; polymer recycling; hazardous waste treatment. **Mailing Address:** Ctr Excellence Environ Eng & Sci, Univ Detroit Mercy, PO Box 19900, Detroit, MI 48219-0900. **Fax:** 313-993-1112. **E-Mail:** klempndi@udmercy.edu

KLEMPNER, MARK STEVEN, INFECTIOUS DISEASES. **Personal Data:** b Utica, NY, January 18, 1949; m 1979, c 3. **Education:** Cornell Univ, MD, 1973. **Professional Experience:** LOUISA C ENDICOTT PROF MED, NEW ENG MED CTR, as of 1997; PROF MICROBIOL & MOLECULAR BIOL, NEW ENG MED CTR, as of 1997; prof med, New Eng Med Ctr, beginning 1989; mem, NIH study sect, Nat Inst Allergy & Infectious Dis study sect & sub-spec Bd, Am Bd Internal Med, 1988-; vis prof, Boston Univ, 1987; assoc prof med, New Eng Med Ctr, 1983-1988; prin investr, NIH, Nat Inst Allergy & Infectious Dis & US Army Res Command, 1979-; asst prof med, Tufts Univ, 1978-1982; clin assoc, NIH, 1975-1978; resident, Mass Gen Hosp, 1974-1975; intern med, Mass Gen Hosp, 1973-1974; vis lectr, Austria, Brazil, Denmark, Italy, Sweden, Switz, UK. **Memberships:** Am Fedn Clin Res; Am Soc Clin Invest; Infectious Dis Soc Am; AAAS. **Research Statement & Publications:** Interactions of infectious agents with host cells; cell activation for eradicating pathogens; author of various articles. **Mailing Address:** Dept Med, Tufts New Eng Med Ctr, PO Box 236 750 Wash St, Boston, MA 02111-1854. **Fax:** 617-636-7119. **E-Mail:** mark.klempner@es.nemc.org

KLEMS, GEORGE J, METALLURGY, SHEET STEEL FORMABILITY. **Personal Data:** b Brno, Czech, May 4, 1936; American citizen; m 1968, Judith; c G Kyle & Ryan R. **Education:** Harvard Univ, AB, 1958; Ill Inst Technol, MS, 1961; Case Western Res Univ, PhD (metall & mat sci), 1971. **Professional Experience:** MARKET DEVELOP ENGR, AUTOMOTIVE DEVELOP GROUP, LTVSTEEL CO, 1986-; staff metallurgist, Flat Rolled & Coated Prods, Prod Develop Div, Res Ctr, 1985-1986; div metallurgist, Flat Rolled Div,

1984-1985; prod metallurgist high strength steels, Steel Group, Flat Rolled Div, Repub Steel Corp, 1976-1984; mkt develop metallurgist, Molycorp, Inc, 1973-1976; res metallurgist, Res Ctr, Repub Steel Corp, 1964-1973; res asst solid state physics & mat sci, Ill Inst Technol, 1958-1961 & x-ray crystallog, 1961-1964. **Memberships:** Am Soc Metals Int; Metall Soc Am Inst Mining & Metall Engrs; Soc Automotive Engrs; Sigma Xi; Am Soc Testing & Mat; Am Welding Soc; Soc Mfg Engrs. **Research Statement & Publications:** Phase transformations; alloy development; sheet steel formability. **Mailing Address:** 1681 N Pima Ct, Tucson, AZ 85716. **Fax:** 440-248-9499. **E-Mail:** 70253.1064@compuserve.com

KLEMS, JOSEPH HENRY, ENERGY CONSERVATION. **Personal Data:** b Cincinnati, Ohio, July 14, 1942; m 1967, Jeanne; c Julia A & Steven J. **Education:** Univ Chicago, SB, 1964, SM, 1965, PhD (physics), 1970. **Professional Experience:** DEP GROUP LEADER, LAWRENCE BERKELEY LAB, UNIV CALIF, 1989-; staff scientist, Lawrence Berkeley Lab, Univ Calif, beginning 1978; asst res physicist, Univ Calif, Davis, 1973-1978; res assoc physics, Lab Nuclear Studies, Cornell Univ, 1970-1973. **Memberships:** Am Phys Soc; AAAS; Sigma Xi. **Research Statement & Publications:** Energy-efficient windows and lighting systems; solar energy; measurement of energy flows through architectural windows under realistic conditions; contrast mechanisms for X-ray microscopy; optical measurements. **Mailing Address:** Appl Sci Div, Lawrence Berkeley Lab Univ Calif, 90-3111 One Cyclotron Rd, Berkeley, CA 94720. **Fax:** 510-486-7957. **E-Mail:** jhklems@lbl.gov

KLEMSZ, MICHAEL J, IMMUNOLOGY. **Education:** Univ Colo, Boulder, BA, 1982; Univ Colo Health Sci Ctr & nat Jewish Ctr Immunol & Respiratory Med, PhD, 1987. **Professional Experience:** ASSOC PROF MICROBIOL & IMMUNOL & ASSOC MEM WALTHER ONCOL CTR, IND UNIV SCH MED, as of 2004. **Research Statement & Publications:** Chromatin structure regulates the expression of the PU.1 gene; chromatin immunoprecipitation; regulation of TAP gene expression in macrophages. **Mailing Address:** Dept Microbiol & Immunol, Ind Univ, 635 Barnhill Dr MS 5010, Indianapolis, IN 46202. **E-Mail:** mklemsz@iupui.edu

KLENIN, MARJORIE A, MECHANICS. **Personal Data:** b Lancaster, Pa. **Education:** Swarthmore Col, BA, 1965; Univ Pa, MS, 1966, PhD (physics), 1970. **Professional Experience:** Guest scientist, Max Plank Inst Solid State Physics Res, 1985-; ASSOC PROF SOLID STATE PHYSICS, NC STATE UNIV, 1980-; asst prof, NC State Univ, 1977-1980; sr res assoc reactor safety, Brookhaven Nat Lab, 1976-1977; guest scientist, Brookhaven Nat Lab, 1974-1976; Vis asst prof solid state physics, State Univ NY, Stony Brook, 1974-1976; res assoc solid state physics, Inst Max von Lane-Paul Langevin, 1970-1972 & Univ Saarlandes, 1972-1974. **Memberships:** Am Phys Soc; Sigma Xi. **Research Statement & Publications:** Structural modeling and growth dynamics of bond-directed disordered compounds; covalent semiconductors; equilibrium dynamic properties; complex orientational ordering as mediated by quadrupolar couplings. **Mailing Address:** Dept Physics, 210 Bureau Mines, NC State Univ Box 8202, Raleigh, NC 27695. **Fax:** 919-515-6538. **E-Mail:** m_klenin@ncsu.edu

KLENKNECHT, KENNETH S(AMUEL), AEROSPACE & AERONAUTICAL ENGINEERING, TECHNICAL MANAGEMENT. **Personal Data:** b Washington, DC, July 24, 1919; m 1947, Patricia; c Linda (May), Patricia A & Frederick W. **Education:** Purdue Univ, BS, 1942. **Honors & Awards:** John J Montgomery Award, Nat Soc Aerospace Prof, 1963; W Randolph Lovelace, II Award, Am Astronaut Soc, Inc, 1975. **Professional Experience:** RETIRED; dir, Zenith Star Proj, Laser Paylord Element, 1988-1990; dir, design-to-cost productivity, Space Sta Proj, 1984-1988; sr space transport syst tech adv, Martin Marietta Denver Aerospace, Colo, 1981-1984; asst mgr, Orbiter Proj & vehicle mgr, Orbiter 102, NASAJohnson Space Ctr, 1979-1981; dep assoc adminr space transp systs, Europ Opers, NASA HQ, Wash, DC, 1977-1979; asst mgr, Orbiter Proj, 1976-1977; dir flight opers, Skylab Prog, 1974-1976; mgr, Skylab Prog, 1970-1974; mgr, Command & Serv Modules, Apollo Spacecraft Prog, 1967-1970; dep mgr, Gemini Prog, 1963-1967; mgr, Proj Mercury, 1962-1963; tech asst to dir, NASA Johnson Space Ctr, 1961-1962; mem, Space Task Group, Langley Field, Va, 1959-1961; head opers eng sect & aeronaut res scientist, NASA Flight Res Ctr, Calif, 1951-1959; proj engr, NASA Lewis Res Ctr, 1942-1951. **Memberships:** Fel Am Astronaut Soc; Int Acad Astronaut; assoc fel Am Inst Aeronaut & Astronaut. **Research Statement & Publications:** Aircraft icing research during 1950's; development of the X-15 research aircraft and implementation of scientific and medical experiments on the Mercury, Gemini, Apollo and Skylab space flight programs. **Mailing Address:** 825 Front Range Rd, Littleton, CO 80120.

KLENS, PAUL FRANK, MICROBIOLOGY, GERMICIDES & FUNGICIDES. **Personal Data:** b Scranton, Pa, July 21, 1918; wid Shirley (Deceased); c 4. **Education:** Syracuse Univ, AB, 1940, MS, 1942, PhD (microbiol), 1951. **Professional Experience:** PROF EMER BIOL SCI, LOCK HAVEN UNIV, 1986-; dean arts & sci, Lock Haven Univ, 1966-1974; from assoc prof to prof, Lock Haven Univ, 1958-1986; chief microbiol lab, Nuodex Prods Co, NJ, 1954-1958; chief germicides unit, QM Res & Develop, US Dept Army, 1951-1953; instr bact & mycol, Syracuse Univ, 1945-1951; chemist & mat engr, Carrier Corp, NY, 1942-1945; asst bot, Syracuse Univ, 1940-1942. **Memberships:** Am Soc Microbiol; Soc Indust Microbiol. **Research Statement & Publications:** Physiology of fungi; microbiological deterioration; industrial microbiology; water pollution studies. **Mailing Address:** Dept Biol, Lockhaven Univ, 401 N Fairview St, Lock Haven, PA 17745.

KLENSIN, JOHN, COMPUTER SCIENCE. **Personal Data:** b Tucson, Ariz, February 1, 1945. **Education:** Mass Inst Technol, BS, 1967, PhD (comput appln & use polit sci), 1979. **Professional Experience:** CONSULT, as of 2004; dir, Int Network Foods Secretariat, Mass Inst Technol, beginning 1989; proj coor, Infoods, Mass Inst Technol, 1989-1994; chmn, Comt X3J1, Am Nat Stand, 1984-; lectr, Dept Polit Sci, Mass Inst Technol, 1980-; prin scientist archit, Mass INst technol, beginning 1978. **Memberships:** Asn Comput Mach; Inst Elec & Electronics Engrs Comput Soc; Am Statist Asn; Int Asn Statist Comput. **Mailing Address:** Cambridge, MA 02140.

KLEPCZYNSKI, WILLIAM J(OHN), ASTRONOMY. **Personal Data:** b Philadelphia, Pa, April 16, 1939; m 1961, c 2. **Education:** Univ Pa, AB, 1961; Georgetown Col, MA, 1964; Yale Univ, PhD (astron), 1969. **Professional Experience:** Exec fel, Inst Navigation Inc, 2003-2004; CONSULT, INNOVATIVE SOLUTIONS INT, INC, as of 1998; pres, Inst Navigation Inc, 1988-1989; astronr, Time Serv Div, US Naval Observ, beginning 1971; ed, Navigation, Inst Navigation Inc, 1971-1978; astronr, Nautical Almanac Off, 1961-1971. **Memberships:** AAAS; Am Astron Soc; Am Inst Navig; Int Astron Union. **Research Statement & Publications:** Planetary motion; masses of the planets; motion of minor planets; observations of minor planets; eclipsing variable stars. **Mailing Address:** Innovative Solutions Int, Inc, 1608 Spring Hill Dr, Suite 200, Vienna, VA 22182. **Fax:** 202-651-7699. **E-Mail:** wklepczy@aol.com

KLEPINGER, LINDA LEHMAN, BIOLOGICAL ANTHROPOLOGY. **Personal Data:** b Hammond, Ind, March 27, 1941. **Education:** Ind Univ, AB, 1963; Univ Kans, MPhil, 1971, PhD (anthrop), 1972. **Professional Experience:** RETIRED; prof anthrop, Univ Ill, Urbana, 1992-2003; from asst prof to assoc prof, Univ Ill, Urbana, 1972-1992. **Memberships:** Am Asn Phys Anthropologists; AAAS; Paleopath Asn; Am Acad Forensic Sci. **Research Statement & Publications:** Biological relationships of prehistoric populations; paleopathology of New and Old World populations; forensic anthropology; chemical analyses of archaeological bone; bone biology. **Mailing Address:** Dept Anthrop, Univ Ill, 607 S Matthews Ave, Urbana, IL 60801. **Fax:** 217-244-3490. **E-Mail:** klepinge@uiuc.edu

KLEPPA, OLE JAKOB, PHYSICAL CHEMISTRY, METAL SCIENCE. **Personal Data:** b Oslo, Norway, February 4, 1920; American citizen; m 1948, Joy Stodder; c Karen J & Abbie L. **Education:** Norwegian Tech Univ, ChE, 1946, Dr techn(chem), 1956. **Honors & Awards:** Huffman Mem Award, the Calorimetry Conference, 1982; Hume-Rothery Mem Award, the Minerals, Metals, Materials Soc, 94. **Professional Experience:** EMER PROF, UNIV CHICAGO, 1990-; consult, Argonne Nat Lab; dir, Mat Res Lab, 1984-1987; Alexander von Humboldt Award, 1983-1984; vis prof, Univ Paris, Orsay, 1977; vis prof, Japan Soc Prom Sci, 1975; dir, James Franck Inst, 1971-1977; prof, Dept Geophys Sci, 1968-1990; assoc dir, James Franck Inst, 1968-1971; chmn calorimetry conf, Inst Study Metals & Dept Chem, 1966-1967; prof, Dept Chem, 1962-1990; assoc prof, Inst Study Metals & Dept Chem, 1958-1962; asst prof chem, Inst Study Metals, Univ Chicago, 1952-1957; res supvr, Dept Chem & Metall, Norweg Defense Res Estab, 1950-1951; instr, Inst Study Metals, Univ Chicago, 1948 -1950. **Memberships:** Am Chem Soc; Am Inst Mining, Metall & Petrol Eng; Am Ceramic Soc; Norweg Chem Soc; fel AAAS; fel Am Soc Metals; Soc Norweg Engrs; Norweg Acad Tech Sci; Royal Norweg Soc Sci & Letters. **Research Statement & Publications:** Thermodynamics; thermochemistry; electrochemistry; chemical and physical metallurgy; solid state chemistry; fused salts; oxide melt solution calorimetry. **Mailing Address:** James Franck Inst, Univ Chicago 5640 Ellis Ave, Chicago, IL 60637-1433. **Fax:** 773-702-5863. **E-Mail:** kleppa@control.uchiago.edu

KLEPPER, DAVID LLOYD, ARCHITECTURAL ACOUSTICS, ELECTROACOUSTICS. **Personal Data:** b New York, NY, January 25, 1932. **Education:** Mass Inst Technol, BS, 1953, MS, 1957. **Honors & Awards:** Silver Medal, Audio Eng Soc, 1987. **Professional Experience:** PRES ACOUST, KLEPPER MARSHALL KING ASSOC LTD, 1971-; sr consult acoust, Bolt Beranek & Newman, Inc, 1957-1971. **Memberships:** Fel Acoust Soc Am; fel Audio Eng Soc; US inst Theatre Technol; inst Noise Control Eng. **Research Statement & Publications:** Continuing search for improving existing room acoustics and electroacoustics for the speech and music to be optimized in same room. **Mailing Address:** 142 E 16th St, New York, NY 10003.

KLEPPER, ELIZABETH LEE (BETTY), PLANT PHYSIOLOGY. **Personal Data:** b Memphis, Tenn, March 8, 1936. **Education:** Vanderbilt Univ, BA, 1958; Duke Univ, AM, 1963, PhD (bot), 1966. **Professional Experience:** RETIRED; ed, Crop Sci, beginning 1992; tech ed, Crop Sci, 1990-1992; adv ed, Irrig Sci, 1987-1992; res leader, Agr Res Serv, USDA, beginning 1985; mem staff & supvry plant physiologist, Agr Res Serv, USDA, 1976-1985; sr res scientist, Ecosysts Dept, 1974-1976; res scientist, Battelle Northwest Labs, 1972-1974; asst prof bot, Auburn Univ, 1968-1972; res scientist, Div Irrig Res, Commonwealth Sci & Indust Res Orgn Griffith, Australia, 1966-1968; teaching asst bot, Duke Univ, 1963-1964; Teacher high sch, Tenn, 1960-1961. **Memberships:** Fel AAAS; fel Soil Sci Soc Am; Bot Soc Am; Am Soc Plant Physiol; fel Am Soc Agron; Sigma Xi; fel Crop Sci Soc Am. **Research Statement & Publications:** Environmental plant physiology including water relations and stress; root growth and uptake of water; cereal developmental history and modelling of cereal yield. **Mailing Address:** 1454 SW 45th St, Pendleton, OR 98701.

KLEPPER, JOHN RICHARD, ULTRASONIC IMAGING, PATTERN RECOGNITION. **Personal Data:** b Dayton, Ohio, September 20, 1947; m 1969, c 1. **Education:** Univ Ohio State, BS, 1969; Univ Wash, MA, 1975, PhD (physics), 1980. **Professional Experience:** STAFF MEM, SIEMENS ULTRASOUND, 1995-; exec dir, Dept Phys Sci, 1987-1995; Affil asst prof elec eng, Univ Wash, 1982-1987; dir, Dept Phys Sci, 1981-1995; res bioengr, Inst Appl Physiol & Med, 1980-1981; Res asst, Biomed Comput Lab, Wash Univ, 1977-1980. **Memberships:** Inst Elec & Electronics Engrs; Eng Med & Biol Soc; Am Inst Ultrasound Med. **Research Statement & Publications:** Development of computer aided ultrasonic imaging systems for use in medical diagnosis; ultrasonic tissue characterization, through application of computed tomographic techniques; blood flow analysis, through Doppler shift measurements. **Mailing Address:** Siemens Ultrasound, PO Box 7002, Issaquah, WA 98027-7002.

KLEPPNER, ADAM, MATHEMATICAL ANALYSIS. **Personal Data:** b New York, NY, June 5, 1931; m 1958. **Education:** Yale Univ, BS, 1953; Univ Mich, MA, 1954; Harvard Univ, PhD (math), 1960. **Professional Experience:** PROF EMER MATH, UNIV MD, COL PARK, as of 2005; vis prof, Univ Colo, 1970-1971 & Univ Calif, Berkeley, 1975; prof math, Univ Md, Col Park, 1968-; from asst prof to assoc prof, Univ Md, Col Park, 1961-1968. **Memberships:** Am Math Soc. **Research Statement & Publications:** Group representations; functional analysis. **Mailing Address:** Univ Md, Dept Math, 3306 Math Bldg, College Park, MD 20742-4015. **E-Mail:** akleppner@surfglobal.net

KLEPPNER, DANIEL, PHYSICS. **Personal Data:** b New York, NY, December 16, 1932; m 1958, Beatrice; c Paul S, Sofie R & Andrew N. **Education:** Williams Col, BS, 1953; Cambridge Univ, BA, 1955; Harvard Univ, PhD (physics), 1959. **Honors & Awards:** Davisson-Germer Prize, Am Phys Soc, 1985, Julius Edgar Lilienfeld Prize, 1990; Morris Loeb Lectr Physics, Harvard Univ, 1987; Starley H Klosk Vis Lectr, NY Univ, 1990; William F Meggers Award, Optical Soc Am, 1991; Houston Lectr, Rice Univ, 1992; Russel Marker Lectr, Pa State Univ, 1992; Edwin Yunker Lectr, Ore State Univ, 1993; Kay Malmstron Lectr, Hamline Univ, 1994; Donald R Hamilton lectr, Princeton Univ, 1995; Dersted Medal, Am Asn Physics Teachers, 1997. **Professional Experience:** DIR, MASS INST TECHNOL & HARVARD CTR ULTRACOLD ATOMS, as of 2005; LESTER WOLFE PROF EMER PHYSICS, MASS INST TECHNOL, as of 2005; assoc dir, Res Lab Eletronics, beginning 1987; mem, Bd Physics & Astron, Nat Acad Sci, 1987-1990; Lester Wolfe prof, Mass Inst Technol, beginning 1985; chmn, Div Atomic, Molecular & Optical Physics, Am Phys Soc, 1983-1984; head, Dept Physics, Div Atomic, Plasma & Condensed Matter Physics, 1976-1979; prof physics, Mass Inst Technol, beginning 1974; mem, Comt Atomic, Molecular & Optical Physics, Nat Res Coun, 1973-1976 & 1980-1985; assoc prof, Res Lab Electronics, 1966-1973; Alfred P Sloan Found fel, 1962-1964; from instr to asst prof, Harvard Univ, 1960-1966; res fel physics, Harvard Univ, 1959-1960; chair, Physics Planning Comt, Am Phys Soc. **Memberships:** Nat Acad Sci; fel AAAS; fel Am Phys Soc; fel Am Acad Arts & Sci; Optical Soc Am; Int Union Pure & Appl Physics (secy, 1988-1990); Japan Asn Math Sci. **Research Statement & Publications:** Atomic physics; redetermination of the Rydberg constant; quantum chaos; studies of hydrogen in the millikelvin regime; ultra precise laser spectroscopy. **Mailing Address:** Dept Physics, Mass Inst Technol, Rm 26-237 77 Mass Ave, Cambridge, MA 02139-4307. **Fax:** 617-253-8554. **E-Mail:** kleppner@mit.edu

KLERLEIN, JOSEPH BALLARD, FINITE MATHEMATICS. **Personal Data:** b Baltimore, Md, December 16, 1948; m 1970, c 4. **Education:** Furman Univ, BS, 1970; Vanderbilt

Univ, PhD (math), 1975. **Professional Experience:** PROF COMPUT SCI, WESTERN CAROLINA UNIV, as of 2004; head, Dept Math, Western Carolina Univ, beginning 1990; PROF MATH, WESTERN CAROLINA UNIV, 1985-; from asst prof to assoc prof, Western Carolina Univ, 1975-1985, instr, Western Carolina Univ, 1974-1975. **Memberships:** Am Math Soc; Math Asn Am; Sigma Xi. **Research Statement & Publications:** Graph theory especially the study of traversability in cayley color graphs; line graphs for directed graphs. **Mailing Address:** Dept Math, Western Carolina Univ, 309 A Stillwell Belk 391, Sylvia, NC 28779-9803. **Fax:** 828-227-7240. **E-Mail:** Klerlein@email.wcu.edu

KLERMAN, LORRAINE VOGEL, MATERNAL & CHILD HEALTH. **Personal Data:** b New York, NY, July 10, 1929; div, c Jacob, Elizabeth, Karen & Daniel. **Education:** Cornell Univ, BA, 1950; Harvard Univ, MPH, 1953, DrPH, 1962. **Honors & Awards:** Martha May Eliot Award, Am Pub Health Asn, 1996. **Professional Experience:** PROF, THE HELLER SCH SOCIAL POLICY & MGT, BRANDEIS UNIV, MASS, 2003-; vis prof, Sch Nursing & Health Studies, Georgetown Univ, Wash, DC, 2002-; vis prof, Dartmouth Med Sch, Hanover, NH, 2001-; prof dept & chair, Birmingham Prof Pub Health, Univ Ala, 1993-1998; prof, Univ Ala, Birmingham, Sch Pub Health, Birmingham, 1992-2001; chair person, Dept Maternal & Child Health, Univ Ala, Birmingham, 1992-1998; sec appointment, Dept Pediat; sr scholar, Lister Hill Ctr Health Policy, sr scientist, Civitan Int Res Ctr, 1992-2001; scholar in residence, Carnegie Corp NY, Wash, DC, 1991-1992; mem, tech adv comt, Community Childhood Hunger Identification Proj, 1990-1995; mem ed adv comt, Family Planning Perspectives, 1990-1994; Prog Develop Bd, Am Pub Health Asn, 1990-; dir, Masters Prog, Sch Med, Yale Univ, 1990-1991; mem, Chairperson, New Haven Family Alliance, 1989-1991; mem, coun adv, Nat Ctr c Poverty, 1989-1991; Priority Expert Panel A Low Birthweight, Nat Ctr Health Res, 1988-1989; Health Serv Res Rev Subcomt, Nat Ctr Health Serv Res & Health Care Technol Assessment, 1986-1990; mem, Comt Study Outreach Prenatal Care, Inst Med, 1986-1988; Expert Panel Content Prenatal Care, Pub Health Serv, 1986-1989; chair person, Maternal & Child Health Sect, Am Pub Health Asn, 1986-1988; head, Div Health Services Admin, 1984-1987; prof pub health, Dept Epidemiol & Pub Health, Sch Med, Yale Univ, New Haven, Conn, 1984-1992; consult, Comt Study Prev Low Birthweight, Inst Med, 1983-1985; Dept Health, Educ & Welfare, Ctr Health Services Res, Wash, DC, 1978-1980; from assoc prof to prof pub health, Florence Heller Grad Sch Advan Studies Social Welfare, Brandeis Univ, 1973-1984; Nat Inst Alcohol Abuse & Alcoholism, 1973-1976; consult, Sch Med, Yale Univ, 1971-1973; Florence Heller Grad Sch Advan Studies Social Welfare, Brandeis Univ, Waltham, Mass, 1971-1973; lectr, Res Assoc, Sch Med, Yale Univ, 1970-1971; asst prof, Pub Health, Dept Epidemiol & Pub Health, Sch Med, Yale Univ, New Haven, Conn, 1965-1970; fac assoc res, Brandeis Univ, Florence Heller Grad Sch Advan Studies Social Welfare, Waltham, Mass, 1962-1965; mem, Res Rev Comt, mem, Sci adv panel & bd dirs, Alan Guttmacher Inst; adv comt, Primary Care Asst & Accountability Proj. **Memberships:** Fel Am Pub Health Asn. **Research Statement & Publications:** Maternal and child health; prenatal care; adolescent parenting. **Mailing Address:** The Heller Sch Social Policy & Mgt, Brandeis Univ, PO Box 5491 Mail Stop 035, Waltham, MA 02454-9110. **E-Mail:** klerman@brandeis.edu

KLESIUS, PHILLIP HARRY, IMMUNOLOGICAL RESEARCH. **Personal Data:** b Bryn Mawr, Pa, March 1, 1938; m 1970, c 2. **Education:** Fla Southern Col, BS, 1961; Northwestern State Univ, MS, 1963; Univ Tex, Austin, PhD (microbiol), 1966. **Professional Experience:** SUPVRY MICROBIOLOGIST, AQUATIC ANIMAL HEALTH RES LAB, AGR RES SERV, US DEPT AGR, as of 2006; comn mem patent biotech, Agr Res Serv, 1988-; assoc prof, Med Univ SC, 1976-; vis prof vet microbiol, Col Vet Med, Tuskegee Univ, 1974-; RES LEADER & MICROBIOLOGIST, AQUATIC ANIMAL HEALTH RES LAB, AGR RES SERV, US DEPT AGR, 1973-; adj prof, Dept Pathobiol, Col Vet Med, Auburn Univ, 1973-; asst chief, Ctr Dis Control, Ft Collins, Colo, 1972-1973; asst prof, microbiol, Univ Ariz, 1969-1972; asst prof, microbiol, Univ Tex, Austin, 1968-1969. **Memberships:** Am Asn Vet Immunologists (secy-treas, 1988-1991); Am Asn Immunologists; Am Soc Microbiologists; fel Am Acad Microbiol. **Research Statement & Publications:** Immunological and parasitological research on control of internal parasites of fish; immune system of cultured catfish; EFFICACY OF A STREPTOCOCCUS INIAE MODIFIED BACTERIN DELIVERED USING ORALJECT-+ TECHNOLOGY IN NILE TILAPIA (OREOCHROMIS NILOTICUS); SENSITIVE AND RAPID DETECTION OF FLAVOBACTERIUM COLUMNARE IN CHANNEL CATFISH ICTALURUS PUNCTATUS BY A LOOP-MEDIATED ISOTHERMAL AMPLIFICATION METHOD; author of various articles. **Mailing Address:** Fish Dis & Parasites Res Lab, USDA Agr Res Serv, 990 WIRE RD, Auburn, AL 36832. **Fax:** 334-887-2983. **E-Mail:** klesiph@vetmed.auburn.edu

KLESSIG, DANIEL FREDERICK, MOLECULAR BIOLOGY, BIOCHEMISTRY. **Personal Data:** b Fond du Lac, Wis, February 24, 1949; m Judith. **Education:** Univ Wis-Madison, BS, 1971; Univ Edinburgh, BSc (hons), 1973; Harvard Univ, PhD (molecular biol, biochem), 1978. **Honors & Awards:** Phi Kappa Phi, Alpha Zeta, Phi Lambda Upsilon and Gamma Sigma Delta Honorary Fraternities; Danforth Leadership Scholarship, 1968; Marshall Scholar to the United Kingdom, 1971-1973; Searle Scholar, 1982-1985; McKnight Scholar, 1983-1986; Faculty Research Award from American Cancer Society, 1984-1988; Japan Society for Promotion of Science Fellow, 1997; Fellow of the American Academy of Microbiology, 2001-Present. **Professional Experience:** Senior Scientist, 2004-present, Boyce Thompson Institute for Plant Research; Adjunct Professor, 2000-present, Department of Plant Pathology, Cornell University; President & CEO, 2000-2004, Boyce Thompson Institute for Plant Research; Prof Molecular Biol & Assoc Dir Waksman Inst. 1985-2000; McKnight scholar, 1983-1986; Searle scholar, 1982-1985; mem fac, Dept Cell & Molecular Biol, Univ Utah, 1980-1985; staff scientist tumor virol, Cold Spring Harbor Lab, 1979-1980; fel, Cold Spring Harbor Lab, 1978; Marshall scholar, 1971-1973. **Memberships:** Am Soc Plant Physiologist; Am Phytopath Soc; Am Soc Microbiologists; AAAS; Plant Molecular Biol Soc. **Research Statement & Publications:** Control of gene expression in plants and in animal cells and their viruses; molecular and cellular biology; virus research; salicylic acid signal transduction pathway. **Mailing Address:** Boyce Thompson Inst Plant Res, Cornell Univ, Tower Rd, Ithaca, NJ 14853-1801. **Fax:** 607-254-6779. **E-Mail:** dfk8@cornell.edu

KLESTADT, BERNARD, ELECTROMECHANICAL-ELECTRONIC DEVICES & SYSTEMS, MEDICAL ELECTRONICS. **Personal Data:** b Buren, Ger, January 31, 1925; American citizen; m 1956, Bernice; c Ralph H. **Education:** Columbia Univ, BS, 1949, MS, 1950; Univ Southern Calif, PhD (elec eng), 1958. **Professional Experience:** TECH CONSULT, 1990-; prog mgr, Automotive Controls Eng, 1988-1989; chief scientist, Control Systs Dept, 1987-1988; mgr, Control Systs Dept, 1981-1986; sr scientist, Missiles Systs Group, 1976-1981; sr scientist, Space & Commun Group, 1969-1976; mgr missile control systs dept, Systs Develop Labs, Hughes Aircraft Co, 1966-1969; asst mgr flight control systs dept, Systs Develop Labs, Hughes Aircraft Co, 1963-1966; sr scientist, Systs Develop Labs, Hughes Aircraft Co, 1962-1963; sr staff eng, Systs Develop Labs, Hughes Aircraft Co, 1958-1962; Lectr, Univ Southern Calif, 1956-1958; mem tech staff, Systs Develop Labs, Hughes Aircraft Co, 1950-1958; asst proj engr, Sperry Gyroscope Co, 1950; Elec engr, Aircraft Radiation Lab, Wright Air Develop Ctr, 1949. **Memberships:** Sigma Xi; Inst Elec & Electronics Engrs; NY Acad Sci. **Research Statement & Publications:** Servomechanisms; circuit theory; guidance and control systems; automatic computation; space flight development. **Mailing Address:** 56-845 Merion, La Quinta, CA 92253. **Fax:** 760-771-1304. **E-Mail:** bkeng@aol.com

KLETSKY, EARL J(USTIN), ELECTRICAL ENGINEERING. **Personal Data:** b Springfield, Mass, July 22, 1930; m 1958, c 1. **Education:** Mass Inst Technol, BS, 1951, MS, 1953; Syracuse Univ, PhD (elec eng), 1961. **Professional Experience:** PROF EMER, COL ENG, SYRACUSE UNIV, as of 1995; asst dean, Col Eng, Syracuse Univ, beginning 1982; admin dir, inst Sensory res, Syracuse Univ, 1974-1980; coordr Bioengineering prog, lab Sensory Commun, 1973-1982; asst dir, lab Sensory Commun, 1964-1974; from instr to prof elec eng, Col Eng, Syracuse Univ, 1957-1982; elec engr, Gen Electronics labs, 1956-1957; Torchiana fel & res engr elec eng, Univ Delft, 1955-1956. **Memberships:** Inst Elec & Electronics Engrs; Am Soc Eng Educ. **Research Statement & Publications:** Biosimulation; analog and digital simulation of sensory systems; modeling of sensory information processing. **Mailing Address:** Col Eng & Comput Sci, Syracuse Univ, 223 Link Hall, Syracuse, NY 13224.

KLETT, JAMES ELMER, LANDSCAPE HORTICULTURE, NURSERY PRODUCTION. **Personal Data:** b Cincinnati, Ohio, May 20, 1947. **Education:** Ohio State Univ, BS, 1969; Univ Ill, MS, 1971, PhD (hort), 1974. **Professional Experience:** PROF HORT, COLO STATE UNIV, as of 2003; assoc prof ornamental hort, Colo State Univ, beginning 1979; assoc prof, SDak State Univ, 1977-1979; Water Qual Inst grant, SDak State Univ, 1976; asst prof, ornamental hort, SDak State Univ, 1974-1977; teaching asst, Univ Ill, 1972-1974; Res asst ornamental hort, Univ Ill, 1969-1972; new chem prod grants; numerous nat& indust res grants, landscape hort. **Memberships:** Am Soc Hort Sci; Am Hort Soc; Int Plant Propagators Soc; Sigma Xi; Int Soc Arboriculture. **Research Statement & Publications:** Herbaceous and woody ornamental plant evaluation research; water utilization studies with landscape plants; herbicide research with container nursery crops and landscape management studies. **Mailing Address:** Dept Hort, Colo State Univ, Ft Collins, CO 80523-0001. **Fax:** 970-491-7745. **E-Mail:** jeklett@lamar.colostate.edu

KLETZIEN, ROLF FREDERICK, BIOCHEMISTRY. **Personal Data:** b Beloit, Wis, December 15, 1946; m 1969, c 2. **Education:** Univ Wis, BS, 1970, PhD (oncol), 1974. **Professional Experience:** DIR, UPJOHN CO, as of 2006; sr scientist, Upjohn Co, beginning 1989; assoc prof biochem, WVa Univ, 1977-1989; Fel biochem, Harvard Univ, 1975-1977; fel biochem, Princeton Univ, 1974-1975. **Memberships:** Am Soc Cellular Biol. **Research Statement & Publications:** Regulation of cellular function and metabolism. **Mailing Address:** Upjohn Co, 7250-126-327, Kalamazoo, MI 49001. **Fax:** 269-384-9763.

KLEVANS, EDWARD HARRIS, PLASMA PHYSICS, NUCLEAR ENGINEERING. **Personal Data:** b Roaring Spring, Pa, October 13, 1935; m 1959, Deborah; c Linda Manning & Jennifer Heitler-Klevans. **Education:** Pa State Univ, BS, 1957; Univ Mich, MS, 1958, PhD (nuclear eng), 1962. **Professional Experience:** PROF & DEPT HEAD EMER, PA STATE UNIV, 1998-; dept head, Pa State Univ, 1987-1998; physicist, Off Fusion Energy, US Dept Energy, 1984-1985; assoc dean res, Pa State Univ, 1980-1984; prof nuclear eng, Pa State Univ, 1976-1998; from asst prof to assoc prof, Pa State Univ, 1966-1976; sr scientist, Jet Propulsion Lab, Calif Inst Technol, 1962-1966. **Memberships:** Am Phys Soc; Am Nuclear Soc; fel AAAS. **Research Statement & Publications:** Plasma physics; thermonuclear engineering; radiationinstrumentation. **Mailing Address:** Dept Nuclear Eng, Pa State Univ, 138 Reber Bldg, Univ Park, PA 16802. **Fax:** 814-865-8499. **E-Mail:** ehknuc@engr.psu.edu

KLEVATT, PAUL L, AERONAUTICS. **Professional Experience:** X-33 PROGRAM MGR, MCDONNELL DOUGLAS AEROSPACE, as of 1995. **Memberships:** Fel Am Inst Aeronaut & Astronaut. **Mailing Address:** McDonnell Douglas Space Systs Co, 5301 Bolsa Ave, Huntington Beach, CA 92467-2048. **Fax:** 714-896-4618.

KLEVATT, STEVE, SOFTWARE SYSTEMS. **Education:** Univ Calif, Los Angeles, MBA, 1990. **Professional Experience:** MGR, PROD SOFTWARE, METROLIGHT STUDIOS, LOS ANGELES; staff mem, WavefrontTech; staff mem, Robert Abel & Assocs. **Mailing Address:** Metrolight Studios, 5724 W Third St Ste 400, Los Angeles, CA 90036-3078.

KLEVAY, LESLIE MICHAEL, NUTRITION MEDICAL & HEALTH SCIENCES, ENVIRONMENTAL & PUBLIC HEALTH & EPIDEMIOLOGY. **Personal Data:** b Chicago, Ill. **Education:** Univ Wis, Madison, BS, 1956, MD, 1960; Harvard Univ, MS, 1962. **Honorary Degrees:** DSo, Harvard Univ, 1965. **Professional Experience:** CHIEF & PROF, DEPT INTERN MED, UNIV NDAK, as of 2002; RES LEADER, AGR RES SERV, USDA, as of 2002; chmn, Spec Study Sect, USPH, NIH & DHHS, 1986; tech adv, Comt Sci &Educ Res Grants Prog, USDA, 1983; adv, Nutrit Comt, Am Acad Pediat, 1981; adv, Scientific Rev Comt, Human Nutrit Res Coun, Ont, 1980; mem, attending med staff, beginning 1976; Joseph Goldberger vis prof clin nutrit, 1976; consult, Nat Heart & Lung Inst, 1976; res med officer, Human Nutrit Res Ctr, Agr Res Serv, USDA, beginning 1972; assoc prof & prof internal med, Univ NDak, 1972; Nat Ctr Health Statist, 1970; Div Chronic Dis Progs, Health Serv & Ment Health Admin, 1969; consult, Ky Dept Health, 1968-1969; consult, Off Int Res, NIH, 1967; from instr to asst prof internal med, Col Med, Univ Cincinnati, 1965-1972; from asst prof to assoc prof environ health, Col Med, Univ Cincinnati, 1965-1972; intern med, St Louis City Hosp, Mo, 1960-1961; asst, Wash Univ, 1960-1961; teaching asst chem, Univ Wis-Madison, 1955-1957; mem Comt ClinIssues Health Dis, Am Soc Clin Nutrit. **Memberships:** AAAS; Am Fedn Clin Res; Soc Exp Biol & Med; Am Inst Nutrit; Am Soc Clin Nutrit. **Research Statement & Publications:** Experimental atherosclerosis; epidemiology of ischemic heart disease; metabolism of metallic trace elements; definition of nutritional requirement; interrelationships of nutrients; nutritional aspects of the human environment; mammalian metabolism of insecticides; nutritional problems of underdeveloped countries. **Mailing Address:** Human Nutrit Res Ctr, Agr Res Serv, USDA, 2420 2nd Ave, Grand Forks, ND 58202. **Fax:** 701-795-8220. **E-Mail:** lklevay@gfhnrc.ars.usda.gov

KLEVECZ, ROBERT RAYMOND, CELL BIOLOGY, MOLECULAR BIOLOGY. **Personal Data:** b Stratford, Conn, February 8, 1939; m 1961, c 2. **Education:** Ga Inst Technol, BS, 1962; Univ Tex, PhD (cell biol), 1966. **Professional Experience:** PROF, DIV BIOL, BECKMAN RES INST, CITY HOPE, DURATE, as of 2003; HEAD & SR RES SCIENTIST, CELL BIOL DEPT, BECKMAN RES INST, CITY HOPE, DURATE, 1972-; from res scientist to sr res scientist, Biol Dept, Beckman Res Inst, City Hope, Druate, 1967-1972; fel, Nat Cancer Inst res fel enzyme chem, 1966-1967; fel, Yale Univ, 1966. **Memberships:** AAAS; Am Soc Cell Biol. **Research Statement & Publications:** Cellular regulatory mechanisms; cellular clocks and oscillators; control of growth and division in mammalian cells in culture; periodic gene function and the temporal organization of RNA and enzyme synthesis. **Mailing Address:** Div Biol, Beckman Res Inst, 1500 E Duarte Rd, Duarte, CA 91010. **Fax:** 626-358-7703. **E-Mail:** rklevecz@coh.org

KLEVEN, STANLEY H, VETERINARY MICROBIOLOGY, AVIAN MEDICINE. **Personal Data:** b Dawson, Minn, June 24, 1940; m 1960, c 3. **Education:** Univ Minn, St Paul, BS, 1963, DVM, 1965, PhD (microbiol), 1970. **Honors & Awards:** Am Feed Indust Award, Am Vet Med Asn, 1985; Upjohn Achievement Award, Am Asn Avian Pathologists, 80. **Professional Experience:** REGENTS PROF, UNIV GA, as of 2001; DISTINGUISHED RES PROF, AVIAN MED & MICROBIOL, UNIV GA, as of 2001; PROF & HEAD, AVIAN MED & MED MICROBIOL, POULTRY DIS RES CTR, UNIV GA, 1978-; head dept Avian Med, Poultry Dis Res Ctr, Univ GA, 1973-1982; from asst prof to assoc prof med microbiol, Poultry Dis Res Ctr, Univ GA, 1970-1978; res fel, Univ Minn, 1967-1970; instr vet microbiol, Univ Minn, 1966-1967; pvt pract, 1965-1966. **Memberships:** AAAS; Am Vet Med Asn; Am Asn Avian Path; World Vet Poultry Asn; Poultry Sci Asn. **Research Statement & Publications:** Respiratory infections of poultry; avian mycoplasmosis. **Mailing Address:** Avian Med, Univ GA, Athens, GA 30605. **Fax:** 706-542-5630. **E-Mail:** skleven@arches.uga.edu

KLIBANOV, ALEXANDER M, APPLIED ENZYMOLOGY & BIOTECHNOLOGY, DRUG DELIVERY. **Personal Data:** b Moscow, USSR, July 15, 1949; American citizen; m 1972, Margarita; c Tatyana. **Education:** Moscow Univ, MS, 1971, PhD (chem enzym), 1974. **Honors & Awards:** Leo Friend Award, Am Chem Soc; Ipatieff Prize, Am Chem Soc; Marvin J Johnson Award, Am Chem Soc; Int Enzyme Eng Prize, Arthur C Cope Scholar Award, Am Chem Soc. **Professional Experience:** PROF CHEM, MASS INST TECHNOL, 1988-; PROF BIOENG, MASS INST TECHNOL, 2000-; from assoc prof to prof appl biochem, Mass Inst Technol, 1983-1988; asst prof appl biochem & Henry L Doherty prof, Mass Inst Technol, 1979-1983; res assoc, Univ Calif, San Diego, 1978-1979; Res chemist, Moscow Univ, 1974-1977. **Memberships:** Member, Nat Acad Sci; Member, Nat Acad Eng; Am Chem Soc; Am Soc Biochem & Molecular Biol; Fellow, Am Inst Med & Biol Eng. **Research Statement & Publications:** Biocatalysis; Non-aqueous enzymology; Microbicidal materials; Stability and delivery of biopharmaceuticals. **Mailing Address:** Bldg 56, Rm 579, Mass Inst Technol, Cambridge, MA 02139. **Fax:** 617-252-1609. **E-Mail:** klibanov@mit.edu

KLICH, MAREN ALICE, MYCOLOGY, MYCOTOXICOLOGY. **Personal Data:** b Chicago, Ill, April 12, 1952; m 1989, Edward; c Gwen K Mullaney. **Education:** St Olaf Col, BA, 1974; Iowa State Univ, MS, 1978, PhD (bot), 1980. **Honors & Awards:** Fellow, Mycological Society of America 2004. **Professional Experience:** AT FOOD & FEED SAFETY RES, US DEPT AGR, as of 2004; RES MICROBIOLOGIST, SOUTHERN REGIONAL RES CTR, AGR RES SERV, USDA, 1980-. **Memberships:** Mycol Soc Am; Am Soc Microbiol; Am Phytopath Soc. **Research Statement & Publications:** Ecology and taxanomy of hyphomycetous fungi with emphasis on mycotoxigenic fungi in Aspergillus and Penicillium. **Mailing Address:** S Regional Res Ctr, US Dept Agr, PO Box 19687, Rm 2122, New Orleans, LA 70179-0687. **Fax:** 504-286-4419. **E-Mail:** mklich@srrc.ars.usda.gov

KLICK, CLIFFORD C, SOLID STATE PHYSICS. **Personal Data:** b Strausstown, Pa, August 31, 1918; m 1947, c 6. **Education:** Muhlenberg Col, AB, 1939; Harvard Univ, MA, 1947; Carnegie Inst Technol, ScD(physics), 1949. **Professional Experience:** RETIRED; mem staff, Off Naval Res, London, 1977-1979; supt mat sci div, Naval Res Lab, 1967-1977; head luminescent mat sect, Naval Res Lab, 1953-1967; physicist, Naval Res Lab, 1949-1952; Consult, US Army, 1945; assoc physicist, Radiation Lab, Johns Hopkins Univ, 1942-1945; Asst elec eng, Mass Inst Technol, 1941-1942. **Memberships:** Fel Am Phys Soc; Sigma Xi. **Research Statement & Publications:** Color centers and luminescent centers in solids. **Mailing Address:** 7200 Third Ave C-059, Sykesville, MD 21784-5201.

KLICKA, JOHN KENNETH, COMPARATIVE ENDOCRINOLOGY. **Personal Data:** b Chicago, Ill, December 9, 1933; m 1954, c 7. **Education:** Northern Ill Univ, BS, 1957, MS, 1958; Univ Ill, Urbana, PhD (physiol & endocrinol), 1962. **Honors & Awards:** career develop award environ toxicol, Nat Inst Environ Health Sci, NIH, 1981-1984. **Professional Experience:** RETIRED; res assoc, Vet Admin Hosp, Univ Minn, 1979-1988; NIH training prog fel, Med Sch, Univ Minn, 1965-1967; from instr to prof physiol & biochem, Wis State Univ, Oshkosh, 1962-1979. **Memberships:** AAAS; Am Soc Zool; Am Physiol Soc; NY Acad Sci; Sigma Xi. **Research Statement & Publications:** Mechanism by which estrogens act to induce renal tumors in Syrian golden hamsters; chemical carcinogenesis. **Mailing Address:** 15017 Stevens Ave, Burnsville, MN 55306.

KLIEBENSTEIN, JAMES BERNARD, ECONOMICS OF LIVESTOCK PRODUCTION, ANIMAL HEALTH MANAGEMENT. **Personal Data:** b Dodgeville, Wis, June 1, 1947; m 1967, c 3. **Education:** Univ Wis-Platteville, BS, 1969; Univ Ill, MS, 1970, PhD (agr econ), 1972. **Honors & Awards:** Alpha Gamma Rho Honorary Member, 1999; Cardinal Key Honorary, ISU, 2000; Outstanding Faculty Member, ISU, 2004; Who's Who Among American Teachers, 8th Edition, 2004; ISU Foundation Award for Outstanding Achievement in Teaching-ISU, 2003; ISU Foundation Award for Academic Advising-ISU, 2003; College of Ag Team Research Award, 2002; Dr Kathleen MacKay Advisor Hall of Fame, 2001; College of Ag Outstanding Achievement in Teaching, 2003. **Professional Experience:** PROFAGR ECON, IOWA STATE UNIV, 1986-; Vis prof, Univ Wis-Madison, 1982-1983; from asst prof to prof, Univ Mo, 1974-1986; Asst prof, Northwest Mo State Univ, 1972-1974. **Memberships:** Am Agr Econ Asn; Am Soc Farm Managers & Rural Appraisers; Nat Asn Cols & Teachers Agri. **Research Statement & Publications:** Economics of livestock production; economics of animal health management and food safety, sustainable production systems, primary focus at the product production level. **Mailing Address:** Dept Economics, Iowa State Univ, 174C Heady Hall, Ames, IA 50011. **Fax:** 515-294-4545. **E-Mail:** jklieben@iastate.edu

KLIEFORTH, HAROLD ERNEST, METEOROLOGY. **Personal Data:** b San Francisco, Calif, July 6, 1927; m 1954, c 2. **Education:** Univ Calif, Los Angeles, BA, 1949, MA, 1951. **Honors & Awards:** Paul Tuntland Mem Res Award, Soaring Soc Am, 1954. **Professional Experience:** ASSOC RES PROF EMER ATMOSPHERIC SCI, DESERT RES INST, UNIV NEV, RENO, as of 2004; res prof atmospheric sci, Desert Res Inst, Univ Nev, Reno, beginning 1965; chief, Exp Meterol Br, 1961-1965; field dir flight group meteorol, Air Force Cambridge Res Labs, Edwards AFB, Calif, 1958-1961; res meteorologist, Univ Calif, Los Angeles, 1951-1956. **Memberships:** AAAS; Am Meteorol Soc; Royal Meteorol Soc; Sigma Xi. **Research Statement & Publications:** Mountain meteorology; air flow over mountains; mountain lee waves; meso-scale meteorology; synoptic meteorology and climatology; severe storms; snow water resources; macrophysics of clouds. **Mailing Address:** Desert Res Inst Lab Atmo, Univ Nev, PO Box 60220, Reno, NV 89506. **Fax:** 702-677-3157.

KLIEJUNAS, JOHN THOMAS, PLANT PATHOLOGY. **Personal Data:** b Sheboygan, Wis, May 4, 1943; m 1968, Barbara; c Trina & Mary. **Education:** Univ Wis-Stevens Point, BS, 1965; Univ Minn, MF, 1967; Univ Wis-Madison, PhD (plant path), 1971. **Professional Experience:** SUPVR PLANT PATHOLOGIST, PAC SOUTHWEST REGION, USDA FOREST SERV, 1987-; plant pathologist, Pac Southwest Region, US Forest Serv, 1979-1987; asst plant pathologist, Univ Hawaii, Hilo, 1975-1979; jr plant pathologist, Univ Hawaii, Hilo, 1972-1975; fel plant path, Univ Wis-Madison, 1971-1972. **Memberships:** Am Phytopath Soc. **Research Statement & Publications:** Epidemiology and control of forest nursery disease and other diseases of Californian forest trees. **Mailing Address:** Forest Pest Mgt, 630 Sansome St, San Francisco, CA 94111.

KLIEM, PETER O, ANALYTICAL CHEMISTRY, PHOTOGRAPHIC CHEMISTRY. **Personal Data:** b Berlin, Ger, May 13, 1938; American citizen; m 1962, c 3. **Education:** Bates Col, BS, 1960; Northeastern Univ, MS, 1965. **Professional Experience:** CHIEF EXEC OFFICER, SELECTX PHARMACEUT INC, as of 2006; vpres res, Polaroid Corp, 1980; asst corp vpres res, Polaroid Corp, 1977-1980; div vpres negative res & develop, Polaroid Corp, 1975-1977; dept mgr to sr develop mgr, Polaroid Corp, 1966-1975; asst scientist to sr scientist, Polaroid Corp, 1960-1966; sr vpres, Polaroid Corp. **Memberships:** Nat Acad Sci; Soc Photog Sci & Eng; Indust Res Inst; Am Chem Soc. **Research Statement & Publications:** Electronic imaging, medical diagnostic research and development; general management, photographic research and development. **Mailing Address:** SelectX Pharmaceut Inc, One Innovation Dr Three Biotech, Worcester, MA 01605. **Fax:** 508-798-0217. **E-Mail:** pok@selectxpharm.com

KLIER, KAMIL, PHYSICAL CHEMISTRY. **Personal Data:** b Prague, Czech, March 21, 1932; m 1961, c 2. **Education:** Charles Univ, Prague, dipl chem, 1954; Czech Acad Sci, CSc(phys chem), 1961. **Professional Experience:** UNIV DISTINGUISHED PROF CHEM, LEHIGH UNIV, 1982-; assoc dir, Ctr Surface Res, 1978-1983; DIR, CATALYSIS LAB, 1975-; prof chem, Lehigh Univ, 1973-1982; res assoc prof, Ctr Surface Res, 1968-1973; vis prof physics & chem solids & surfaces, Ctr Surface Res, 1967-1968; res scientist, Inst Phys Chem, Czech Acad Sci, 1961-1967; Int Atomic Energy Agency fel radiation chem surfaces, Wantage Res Labs, Eng, 1959-1960; asst, Inst Phys Chem, Czech Acad Sci, 1957-1961; res fel surface phys chem, Inst Phys Chem, Czech Acad Sci, 1954-1957; consult catalysis, spectros & separation processes. **Memberships:** Am Chem Soc; Sigma Xi. **Research Statement & Publications:** Physics and chemistry of solids; surface chemistry; chemisorption; catalysis. **Mailing Address:** Dept Chem, Lehigh Univ, Seeley G Mudd Bldg Rm 491, Bethlehem, PA 18015. **E-Mail:** kk04@lehigh.edu

KLIEWER, JOHN WALLACE, MEDICAL ENTOMOLOGY, ENVIRONMENTAL PROTECTION. **Personal Data:** b Lanigan, Sask, January 20, 1924; American citizen; m 1954, c 4. **Education:** Bethel Col, Kans, BA (biol), 1950; Univ Utah, MS (Invert Zool), 1952; Univ Kans, PhD (entom), 1962. **Honors & Awards:** Spec Achievement Awards, Environ Protection Agency, 1987 & 1988. **Professional Experience:** CONSULT, 1990-; consult, AID, 1983; adj prof prev med, Med Univ SC, 1974-1983; pesticides specialist, Pesticide Prog, Environ Protection Agency, 1972-1990; sr res entomologist, Malaria Prog, Ctr Dis Control, USPHS, 1969-1972; proj officer, Aedes Aegypti Eradication Prog, 1967-1969; consult, WHO, 1966-; sr vector control specialist & proj leader, Calif State Dept Pub Health, 1960-1967; asst prof biol sci, Bethel Col, Kans, 1953-1956. **Memberships:** Entom Soc Am; Am Mosquito Control Asn; Am Registry Prof Entomologists; Soc Vector Ecologists. **Research Statement & Publications:** Ecology and behavior of insects, mites and ticks; public health and agricultural uses of pesticides; environmental aspects of pest control. **Mailing Address:** 9805 Meadow Knoll Ct, Vienna, VA 22181.

KLIEWER, KENNETH L, THEORETICAL SOLID STATE PHYSICS, COMPUTATIONAL SCIENCE. **Personal Data:** b Mountain Lake, Minn, December 31, 1935; m 1959, Kathleen Kay Zimmermann; c Steven Anthony, Lisa Jo & Christopher Lee. **Education:** Univ Minn, BS, 1957, MSEE, 1959; Univ Ill, PhD (physics), 1964. **Professional Experience:** DIR, CTR COMPUT & SCI, OAK RIDGE NAT LAB, 1992-; asst vpres res, Sch Sci, Purdue Univ, 1991-1992; dean, Sch Sci, Purdue Univ, 1986-1991; assoc dir phys res, Argonne Nat Lab, 1981-1986; mem staff, Off Basic Eng Sci, Off Energy Res, 1979-1980; assoc dir sci & technol, Ames Lab, US Dept Energy, 1978-1981; vis scientist, Rockwell Int Sci Ctr, Thousand Oaks, Calif, 1976; Free Univ, Berlin, 1974 & Fritz-Haber Inst, Berlin, 1975; prog dir solid state physics, Ames Lab, US Dept Energy, 1974-1978; guest prof, Univ Hamburg, Ger, 1972-1973; prof physics, Iowa State Univ, 1969-1981; From assoc physicist to sr physicist, Ames Lab, US Dept Energy, 1963-1981; From asst prof to assoc prof, Iowa State Univ, 1963-1969. **Memberships:** Fel Am Phys Soc; AAAS; Sigma Xi. **Research Statement & Publications:** Optical properties of solids, particularly metals; lattice dynamics; surface physics; photoemission; optics; electro chemistry; data storage systems and strategies for high performance computing environments. **Mailing Address:** Ctr Comput Sci, Oak Ridge Nat Lab, PO Box 2008, Oak Ridge, TN 37831-6203. **Fax:** 615-241-2850. **E-Mail:** kliewer@ccs.ornl.gov

KLIEWER, WALTER MARK, BIOCHEMISTRY, PLANT PHYSIOLOGY. **Personal Data:** b Escondido, Calif, December 10, 1933; m 1962, Helga E Bedacht; c 1. **Education:** Calif State Polytech Col, BS, 1955; Cornell Univ, MS, 1958, PhD (agron), 1961. **Professional Experience:** PROF EMER BIOCHEM, UNIV CALIF, DAVIS, as of 2001; Pres, Am Soc Viticult & Enol, 1982; biochem, Univ Calif, Davis, 1974-; assoc biochemist, Univ Calif, Davis, 1968-1974; asst biochemist, Univ Calif, Davis, 1963-1968; fel, Ore State Univ, 1961-1963; Scientist, Soil Conserv Serv, USDA, 1955. **Memberships:** Am Soc Plant Physiol; Am Soc Enol; Am Soc Hort Sci; Sigma Xi. **Research Statement & Publications:** Effect of environment on fruit quality and growth and development of grapevines; organic acid, amino acid and carbohydrate metabolism of grapevines; translocation; photosynthesis; plant growth regulators; fruit coloration; mineral nutrition; vineyard canopy management. **Mailing Address:** 615 Coolidge St, Davis, CA 95616.

KLIG, LISA S, BIOLOGY. **Education:** Albert Einstein Col Med, PhD. **Professional Experience:** PROF, DEPT BIOL SCI, CALIF STATE UNIV, CA, as of 2005. **Mailing Address:** Dept Biol, Calif State Univ, Long Beach, CA 90840-3702. **Fax:** 562-985-5670. **E-Mail:** lsklig@csulb.edu

KLIGER, DAVID SAUL, PHYSICAL CHEMISTRY, BIOPHYSICS. **Personal Data:** b Newark, NJ, November 3, 1943; m Rachel. **Education:** Rutgers Univ, BS, 1965; Cornell Univ, PhD (phys chem), 1970. **Professional Experience:** DEAN NATURAL SCI, UNIV CALIF, SANTA CRUZ, 1990-; NSF res grant, 1976-; NIH res grant, 1973-; PROF CHEM, UNIV CALIF, SANTA CRUZ, 1971-; petro Res Fund-Am Chem Soc res grant, Univ Calif, Santa Cruz, 1971-1974; NIH res fel phys chem, Harvard Univ, 1970-1971. **Memberships:** Am Soc Photobiol; Biophys Soc; Am Chem Soc. **Research Statement & Publications:** Protein Function; Protein Folding. **Mailing Address:** Div Natural Sci, Univ Calif, Santa Cruz, CA 95064. **Fax:** 831-459-4161. **E-Mail:** dkliger@natsci.ucsc.edu

KLIGMAN, ALBERT MONTGOMERY, DERMATOLOGY. **Personal Data:** b Philadelphia, Pa, March 17, 1916; m 1942, c 3. **Education:** Pa State Univ, BS, 1939; Univ Pa, PhD (bot), 1942, MD, 1947; Am Bd Dermat & Syphilol, dipl, 1951. **Professional Experience:** PROF EMER DERMAT, SCH MED, UNIV PA, as of 2004; prof, Div Grad Med, Hosp Univ Pa, 1958-1972; prof dermat, Sch Med, Univ PA, beginning 1957; from instr to assoc prof, Div Grad Med, Hosp Univ Pa, 1948-1957; resident dermat, Univ Hosp, 1948-1951; intern, N Div, Albert Einstein Med Ctr, 1947-1948; dir res, J B Swayne Co, Pa, 1939-1944. **Memberships:** AAAS; Soc Invest Dermat; Soc Exp Biol & Med; AMA; Am Acad Dermat;

Sigma Xi. **Research Statement & Publications:** Medical mycology; dermatologic allergy. **Mailing Address:** Dept Dermat, Univ Pa, 3600 Spruce St, Philadelphia, PA 19104. **E-Mail:** akligman@mail.med.upenn.edu

KLIGMAN, RONALD LEE, STATISTICAL MECHANICS, ACOUSTICS. **Personal Data:** b Philadelphia, Pa, August 20, 1940; m 1968, c 2. **Education:** Temple Univ, BA, 1962; Am Univ, MS, 1967, PhD (physics), 1968. **Professional Experience:** RES PHYSICIST STATIST MECH & ACOUST, NAVAL SURFACEWEAPONS CTR, 1972-; asst prof physics, Robert Col, 1971-1972; physicist acoust, Naval Ship Res & Develop Ctr, 1969-1971; Asst prof physics, Sweetbriar Col, 1968-1969. **Memberships:** Am Phys Soc. **Research Statement & Publications:** Statistical mechanics applied to phase transitions in solids; transport theory in ionized media; wave propagation and scattering, acoustic and electromagnetic. **Mailing Address:** 1394 Canterbury Way, Rockville, MD 20854.

KLIJANOWICZ, JAMES EDWARD, ORGANIC CHEMISTRY. **Personal Data:** b Baltimore, Md, September 24, 1944; m 1975, c 1. **Education:** Loyola Col, Md, BS, 1966; Carnegie-Mellon Univ, MS, 1969, PhD (org chem), 1971. **Professional Experience:** RES LAB HEAD, PHOTOG MECHANISMS LAB, EASTMAN KODAK CO, 1981-, res lab head, Chemiphotog Systs Lab, 1978-1981, sr res chemist, 1970-1978. **Memberships:** AAAS; Am Chem Soc; Sigma Xi. **Research Statement & Publications:** Mechanisms of photographic chemical reactions. **Mailing Address:** 7 Millstone Ct, Pittsford, NY 14534-3238.

KLIMA, MARK S, FUEL TECHNOLOGY & MINING ENGINEERING. **Education:** Penn State Univ, PhD. **Professional Experience:** ASSOCE PROF MIN PROCESSING & GEO-ENVIRON ENG, PENN STATE UNIV, as of 2005. **Mailing Address:** Dept Energy & Geo-Environ Eng, Penn State Univ, 153 Hosler Bldg, University Park, PA 16802. **E-Mail:** msk4@psu.edu

KLIMAN, ALLAN, INTERNAL MEDICINE. **Personal Data:** b Boston, Mass, December 20, 1933; m 1956, c 2. **Education:** Harvard Univ, AB, 1954, MD, 1958. **Professional Experience:** Chief, Hemat-Oncol Dept, Spaulding Rehab Hosp, beginning 1974; ASST CLIN PROF MED, HARVARD MED SCH, 1971-; med dir, Mass Red Cross Blood Prog, 1964-1974; instr, Hemat-oncol Dept, Spaulding Rehab Hosp, 1961-1971; chief, Clin Ctr Blood Bank, NIH, 1959-1961; intern, Beth Israel Hosp, 1958-1959; res assoc endocrinol, Harvard Univ, 1955; res assoc org chem, Harvard Univ, 1953-1954; clin assoc med, Mass Gen Hosp. **Memberships:** Am Fedn Clin Res; Am Soc Hemat. **Research Statement & Publications:** Hematology; blood transfusion; serum hepatitis; automation of laboratory procedures; plasmapheresis; cancer chemotherapy; clinical pharmacology. **Mailing Address:** Harvard Med Sch, Spaulding Rehab Hosp, 125 Nashua St, Boston, MA 02114. **Fax:** 617-573-2889. **E-Mail:** kliman.alan@mgh.harvard.edu

KLIMAN, GERALD BURT, rotating & linear electric machines, incident failure diagnostics; deceased, see previous edition for last biography

KLIMAN, HARVEY LOUIS, PHYSICAL CHEMISTRY, POLYMER PHYSICS. **Personal Data:** b Boston, Mass, May 28, 1942; m 1966. **Education:** Boston Univ, AB, 1963; Princeton Univ, MA, 1966, PhD (phys chem), 1970. **Professional Experience:** SR RES CHEMIST POLYMER CHEM & PHYSICS, FIBERS DEPT, FIBERS & COMPOSITES DEVELOP CTRS, E I DU PONT Del NEMOURS & CO, INC, 1969-. **Memberships:** AAAS; Am Chem Soc; Sigma Xi. **Research Statement & Publications:** High pressure physical chemistry of solutions; hydrophobic interactions in biochemical macromolecules; physical chemistry and physics of fiber forming polymers; textile yarn process engineering; computer modelling; composites. **Mailing Address:** 48 H Webb Rd, Chadds Ford, PA 19317-9125.

KLIMAS-TAVANTZIS, DOROTHY J, CLINICAL NUTRITION. **Personal Data:** b Greece, November 19, 1952; American citizen. **Education:** Beaver Col, Pa, BA, 1974; Pa State Univ, MS, 1978, PhD (nutrit), 1982. **Professional Experience:** PROF CLIN NUTRIT, UNIV MAINE, 2003-; fulbright fel, 1995-1996; assoc prof clin nutrit, Univ Maine, beginning 1994; asst prof clin nutrit, Univ Maine, 1988-1994; vis scientist, Dept Physiol Chem & Dept Clin Chem, Univ Cologne, WGer, 1986-1987; asst prof sci, Husson Col, 1983-1985; instr, Univ Maine, 1981; res asst, Nutrit Prog, Pa State Univ, 1978-1980; res asst, Dept Physiol, NO11 Lab Human Performance, Pa State Univ, 1975-1977; Lab asst, Dept Biol, Beaver Col, 1973-1974. **Memberships:** Sigma Xi. **Research Statement & Publications:** Assessment and nutritional intervention in reducing cardiovascular risk factors in children and adolescents; lipid and lipoprotein metabolism as related to heart disease and diabetes; trace element metabolism and nutriture as related to atherosclerosis and osteoporosis; obesity and its effects on lipid metabolism. **Mailing Address:** Dept Food Sci & Human nutrit, Univ Maine, 5735 Hitchner Hall, Rm 107, Orono, ME 04469-5736. **Fax:** 207-581-1636. **E-Mail:** dorothyklimis@apollo.umenfa.ma

KLIMEK, JOSEPH JOHN, INFECTIOUS DISEASES, HOSPITAL EPIDEMIOLOGY. **Personal Data:** b Wilkes-Barre, Pa, September 14, 1946; m 1971, Jane; c Adam. **Education:** Princeton Univ, AB, 1968; Pa State Univ, MD, 1972. **Professional Experience:** VPRES, MED AFFAIRS, HARTFORD HOSP, as of 2006; PROF MED, DEPT MED, UNIV CONN SCH MED, 1990-; dir, Dept Med, Hartford Hosp, Conn, 1990-; ASSOC DIR, DEPT MED, UNIV CONN SCH MED, 1990-; assoc dir med, Hartford Hosp, 1988-1990; dir, Aids Prog, 1985-1990; med ed, Asepsis, Infection Control Forum, 1983-; sr ed, Am J Infection Control, 1982-; lectr, Merck Sharpe & Dohme Vaccine, 1982-; bd dir, Asn Practr Infection Control, 1978-1982; from asst prof to assoc prof med, Sch Med, Univ Conn, 1977-1990; chief epidemiol, Hartford Hosp, 1976-1988; assoc dir infectious dis & asst dir med, Hartford Hosp, 1976-1988; fel infectious dis, Hartford Hosp, 1974-1976; intern & resident med, Hartford Hosp, 1972-1974. **Memberships:** Fel Am Col Physicians; fel Infectious Dis Soc Am; Am Soc Microbiol; Soc Hosp Epidemiologists Am; Am Pub Health Asn; AAAS; Asn Practr Infection Control. **Research Statement & Publications:** Hospital epidemiology and infection control; antibiotic pharmacokinetics; acquired immuno deficiency syndrome; primary care practice. **Mailing Address:** Hartford Hosp, 80 Seymour St PO Box 5037, Hartford, CT 06102-5037. **Fax:** 860-545-5057. **E-Mail:** jklimek@harthosp.org

KLIMISCH, RICHARD L, CATALYSIS, ENVIRONMENTAL HEALTH. **Personal Data:** b Yankton, SDak, January 1, 1938; m 1962, c 2. **Education:** Loras Col, BS, 1960; Purdue Univ, PhD (org chem), 1964. **Professional Experience:** EXEC DIR, ENVIRON ACTIVITIES STAFF, GEN MOTOR CORP, as of 2004; VPRES, ENG AFFAIRS, AM AUTOMOBILE MFR ASSOC, as of 1998; DEPT HEAD, ENVIRON SCI DEPT, GEN MOTORS RES LABS, 1975-; asst dept head, Phys Chem Dept, 1973-1975; supvry res chemist, Fuels & Lubrication Dept, 1971-1973; sr res chemist, Environ Sci Dept, Gen Motors Res Labs, 1967-1971; Res chemist, Explosives Dept, ExpSta, E I du Pont Del Nemours & Co, Inc, 1964-1967. **Memberships:** Am Chem Soc; Sigma Xi. **Research Statement & Publications:** Catalysis; air pollution; surface chemistry; atmospheric chemistry. **Mailing Address:** Gen Motors Corp, 43 Fairford Rd, Grosse Pointe Shores, MI 48236-2617.

KLIMKIEWICZ, GEORGE C, SEISMOLOGY. **Education:** Boston Col, MS. **Professional Experience:** PRES & SR SEISMOLOGIST, WESTON GEOPHYS ENGRS, INC, as of 2004. **Mailing Address:** Weston Geophys Engrs, Inc, 325 W Main St, Northborough, MA 01532. **Fax:** 508-393-7674.

KLIMKO, EUGENE M, MATHEMATICS. **Personal Data:** b Youngstown, Ohio, March 13, 1939. **Education:** Ohio State Univ, BS, 1961, MS, 1964, PhD (math), 1967. **Professional Experience:** ASSOC PROF MATH, STATE UNIV NY, BINGHAMTON, as of 2005; mem fac math, State Univ NY, Binghamton, beginning 1973; asst prof math, 1967-1975; sr res eng, N Am Aviation, Inc, 1962-1965. **Memberships:** Am Math Soc; Inst Math Statist. **Research Statement & Publications:** Application of ratio ergodic theorems to Glivenko-Cantelli theorem and to convergence of information ratios. **Mailing Address:** State Univ NY, Dept Math Sci, Vestal Pkwy E, Binghamton, NY 13902-6000. **Fax:** 607-777-2450. **E-Mail:** gene@math.binghamton.edu

KLIMPEL, GARY RONALD, INTERFERON, CYTOTOXIC EFFECTOR CELLS. **Education:** Univ Ariz, PhD (microbiol), 1976. **Professional Experience:** PROF MICROBIOL & IMMUNOL, MED BR, UNIV TEX, as of 2003; assoc prof microbiol & immunol, Med Br, Univ Tex, beginning 1980. **Research Statement & Publications:** Host defenses against enteric bacterial infectionsl; cell-mediated immunity; cytokines. **Mailing Address:** Dept Microbiol, Univ Tex Med Br, Galveston, TX 77555-1070. **Fax:** 409-772-6869. **E-Mail:** gklimpel@utmb.edu

KLINCK, JOHN MICHAEL, PHYSICAL OCEANOGRAPHY. **Personal Data:** b Ft Monmouth, NJ, May 15, 1950; m 1979, Eileen; c Julian Michael. **Education:** Clemson Univ, BS, 1972; Univ NC, MS, 1975; NC State Univ, PhD (marine sci), 1980. **Professional Experience:** PROF OCEANOG, CTR COASTAL PHYS OCEANOG, OLD DOMINION-UNIV, 1996-; assoc prof, Ctr Coastal Phys Oceanog, Old Dominion Univ, 1989-1996; asst prof, Tex A&M Univ, 1983-1989; asst res scientist, Tex A&M Univ, 1981-1983; postdoctoral res assoc, Fla State Univ, 1979-1981. **Memberships:** Am Geophys Union; Am Meteorol Soc; Europ Geophys Soc; AAAS; Nat Shellfisheries Asn. **Research Statement & Publications:** Analytical and numerical modelling of physical and biological processes in oceanic, coastal and estuarine environments; analysis of marine observations. **Mailing Address:** Dept Oceanog, Old Dominion Univ, Crittenton Hall 768 W 52nd St, Norfolk, VA 23529. **E-Mail:** jklinck@odu.edu

KLINCK, ROSS EDWARD, PHYSICAL & ORGANIC CHEMISTRY. **Personal Data:** b Kitchener, Ont, December 1, 1938; American citizen. **Education:** Univ Western Ont, BSc, 1960, PhD (chem), 1965. **Professional Experience:** RETIRED; exec asst to pres, Sci Div, Adirondack Community Col, 1989-1994; asst dean, Adirondack Community Col, 1984-1986; PROF CHEM, ADIRONDACK COMMUNITY COL, 1979-2004; assoc prof & chmn, Sci Div, Adirondack Community Col, 1978-1983; coordr sci, Urbana Col, 1974-1976; vis researcher chem, Univ Western Ont, 1972-1977 & 1986-1987; assoc prof chem, Urbana Col, 1971-1976; asst prof chem, Univ Conn, 1966-1971; Res assoc physics, Duke Univ, 1964-1966. **Memberships:** Am Chem Soc; Chem Inst Can. **Research Statement & Publications:** High resolution nuclear magnetic resonance spectroscopy related to conformational studies and barriers to rotation; homoenolization of cyclic ketones; MNDO and molecular mechanics calculations. **Mailing Address:** 17 Jefferson St, Glens Falls, NY 12801. **E-Mail:** RJKLINCK@HORIZON.NET

KLINDT, THOMAS H, AGRICULTURE. **Education:** Univ Mo, BS, 1967, MS, 1969; Univ Ky, PhD (agr econ), 1971. **Professional Experience:** INTERIM DEAN, AGR EXP STA, UNIV TENN, as of 2006. **Memberships:** Am Agr Econ Asn. **Mailing Address:** Agr Exp Sta 103 Morgan Hall, Univ Tenn, Knoxville, TN 37996. **Fax:** 865-974-6479. **E-Mail:** tklindt@utk.edu

KLINE, BERRY JAMES, CHROMATOGRAPHY. **Personal Data:** b Mont Alto, Pa, January 9, 1941; m 1963, Darlene Baranowske; c Michele & Danielle. **Education:** Philadelphia Col Pharm, BS, 1962; Temple Univ, MS, 1965; Univ Wis, PhD (pharm), 1968. **Professional Experience:** DIR, ANALYTICAL RES & DEVELOP, BRISTOL-MYERS SQUIBB PHARM RES INST, 1990-; asst dir, Analytical Res & Develop, Bristol-Myers Squibb Pharm Res Inst, 1983-1990; assoc prof & dir, anal serv, Sch Pharm, Med Col Va, 1976-1983; sr staff scientist, CIBA-Geigy Pharmaceut, 1972-1976; Sr scientist, CIBA Pharmaceut Co, 1969-1972; Sr analyst, Vick Divisions Res, Richardson-Merrell, Inc, 1968-1969; Consult, NIH-Nat Cancer Inst. **Memberships:** Am Pharmaceut Asn; Am Asn Pharmaceut Scientists; Am Chem Soc; fel Am Found Pharmaceut Educ; Sigma Xi. **Research Statement & Publications:** Homogeneous solution kinetics; complexation interactions; pharmaceutical analysis, especially gas and high performance liquid chromatography. **Mailing Address:** Bristol-Myers Squibb, PO Box 191, New Brunswick, NJ 08903-0191.

KLINE, BRUCE CLAYTON, MOLECULAR BIOLOGY, MICROBIOLOGY. **Personal Data:** b Grand Rapids, Mich, June 22, 1937; m 1963, c 3. **Education:** Aquinas Col, BS, 1959; Mich State Univ, MS, 1966, PhD (microbiol), 1968. **Professional Experience:** PROF BIOCHEM & MOLECULAR BIOL, GRAD SCH MED, MAYO CLIN, ROCHESTER, MINN, 1987-; assoc prof microbiol, Grad Sch Med, Mayo Clin, Rochester, Minn, 1984-1987; assoc prof microbiol, Univ Minn, 1980-1984; CONSULT, GRAD SCH MED, MAYO CLIN, ROCHESTER, MINN, 1975-; asst prof biochem, Univ Tenn, Knoxville, 1971-1975; NIH fel, Univ Calif, San Diego, 1968-1970; instr microbial genetics, Mich State Univ, 1968; Microbiologist, Mich Dept Health, 1960-1963. **Memberships:** Am Soc Microbiol; fel Am Acad Microbiol. **Research Statement & Publications:** Mechanism and control of plasmid maintenance in procaryotic organisms; control DNA replication, Domain analysis in proteins. **Mailing Address:** Dept Molecular Biol & Med, Mayo Med Sch, 200 First St SW, Rochester, MN 55905-0001. **Fax:** 507-284-3383. **E-Mail:** kline.bruce@mayo.edu

KLINE, D EARL, INDUSTRIAL & MANUFACTURING ENGINEERING, AGRICULTURAL ENGINEERING. **Personal Data:** b Warrenton, Va, October 5, 1958; m 1985, Karen; c Brian & Christiana. **Education:** Va Tech, BS, 1982, MS, 1984; Tex A&M Univ, PhD (agr eng), 1987. **Professional Experience:** PROF WOOD SCI & FOREST PROD, VA TECH, 2001-; from asst to assoc prof, Va Tech, 1988-2001; res assoc, Tex A & M Univ, 1987-1988. **Memberships:** Forest Products Soc; Soc Wood Science & Technol 1988-; Am Soc Agr Engrs 1982-. **Research Statement & Publications:** Development and application of appropriate systems engineering and management technologies that will build and sustain world-class forest products operations for the future. **Mailing Address:** Brooks Forest Prod Ctr, Va Tech, Mail Code 0503 1650 Ramble Rd, Blacksburg, VA 24061-0503. **Fax:** 540-231-8868. **E-Mail:** kline@vt.edu

KLINE, DAVID G, NEUROSURGERY. **Personal Data:** b Philadelphia, Pa, October 13, 1934; m 1988, Helen; c 5. **Education:** Univ Pa, AB, 1956, MD, 1960. **Honors & Awards:** Frederick A Coller Award, Am Col Surgeons, 1967; Hon mem Corostine 1991; German(1994) & Assn Hard- Surg, 1987; Societies Boyd Proc(1995), LSU Syst. **Professional Experience:** PROG DIR, LOUISIANA STATE UNIV MED CTR, as of 2005; certified 1969; Am Bd Neurol Surg, Secy, 1978-1983, chmn, 1983-1984; PROF NEUROSURG

& CHMN DEPT, SCH MED, LA STATE UNIV, NEW ORLEANS, 1976-; prof, USPHS Hosp, 1971-; prof, Vet Admin Hosp, 1974; prof surg & neurosurg, La State Univ, New Orleans, 1973-1976; chmn div, La State Univ, New Orleans, 1971-1976; assoc prof neurosurg, La State Univ, New Orleans, 1971-1973; assoc prof surg & neurosurg, La State Univ, New Orleans, 1970-1971; consult, Keesler AFB, 1969-; asst prof neurosurg, La State Univ, New Orleans, 1968-1970; vis surgeon, Charity Hosp, New Orleans, 1967-; mem staff, Southern Baptist Hosp, Hotel Dieu, Touro Infirmary & Ochsner Clin & Found, 1967-; vis investr, Delta Regional Primate Ctr, beginning 1967; instr surg & neurosurg, La State Univ, New Orleans, 1967-1968; teaching assoc, Univ Mich & res investr, Kresge Neurosurg Labs, 1964-1967; res investr neurosurg, Walter Reed Gen Hosp & Inst Res, 1962-1964; from intern to resident surg, Univ Mich, Ann Arbor, 1960-1962. **Memberships:** Cong Neurol Surg; Asn Acad Surg; Am Asn Neurol Surg; Soc Univ Surgeons; Res Soc Neurosurgeons; Soc Neurol Surg (treas, 1987-1992); Am Bd Neurol Surg (secy, 1978-1983, chmn, 1983-1984); Southern Neurol Surg Soc (secy, 1975-1978, pres, 1985-1986) Soc Neurologic Surg, (VPres, 1993) (Pres Elect, 1994) (Pres, 1995). **Research Statement & Publications:** Peripheral nerve injuries and their repair; computer utilization for neurosurgical research; hepatic encephalopathy. **Mailing Address:** Dept Neurosurg, La State Univ Sch Med 1542 Tulane Ave, New Orleans, LA 70112-2865. **Fax:** 504-568-6127. **E-Mail:** dkline@lsumc.edu

KLINE, DONALD EDGAR, PHYSICS. **Personal Data:** b DuBois, Pa, August 28, 1928; m 1949, c 3. **Education:** Pa State Univ, BS, 1951, MS, 1953, PhD (physics), 1955. **Professional Experience:** Prof mat sci, Pa State Univ, 1968-; from assoc prof to prof nuclear eng, Pa State Univ, 1961-1968; staff res physicist, HRB-Singer Inc, 1957-1961; vis physicist, Nuclear Reactor Facil, 1956-1957; asst prof physics, Pa State Univ, 1955-1956; instr eng mech, Pa State Univ, 1954-1955; EMER PROF MAT SCI, PA STATE UNIV; consult, Jet Propulsion Lab, Calif Inst Technol, NASA, HRB-Singer Inc, Avco Corp, Pfaudler, Hershey Med Ctr & NETCO. **Memberships:** Am Phys Soc; Am Nuclear Soc; Am Soc Eng Educ. **Research Statement & Publications:** Radiation effects; dosimetry; polymer physics; polymer impregnated concrete, wood, biomaterials; composite polymer systems. **Mailing Address:** 1210 E Branch Rd, State College, PA 16801.

KLINE, FRANK MENEFEE, PSYCHIATRY. **Personal Data:** b Cumberland, Md, May 14, 1928; m 1953, c 2. **Education:** Univ Md, BS, 1950, MD, 1952. **Professional Experience:** EMER PROF, UNIV SOUTHERN CALIF, as of 2006; staff physician, Martin Luther King Hosp, 1992-; consult, Los Angeles Co Ment Health, 1992-; EMER CLIN PROF PSYCHIAT, UNIV CALIF, IRVINE, 1992-; prof psychiat & vchmn dept, Univ Calif, Irvine, 1978-1992; chief psychiat, Long Beach Vet Med Ctr, 1977-1992; assoc prof psychiat, Sch Med, Univ Southern Calif, 1974-1978; assoc dir, Psychiat Outpatient Dept, Los Angeles Co-Univ Southern Calif Med Ctr, 1968-1977; instr, Inst, 1967-1979; fac mem, Psychother Group, Los Angeles Ctr, 1967-1969; regional chief, W Cent Ment Health Serv, Los Angeles Co, 1967-1968; psychiat consult, Univ High Sch & Francis Blend Sch Blind, Los Angeles, 1966-1967; instr, Exten Div, Southern Calif Psychoanal Inst, 1964-1967; consult, E Los Angeles Probation Off, 1960-1963; Pvt pract, 1958-; psychiat resident, Brentwood Vet Admin Hosp, Los Angeles, 1955-1958; Intern med, Cincinnati Gen Hosp, 1952-1953; reviewer, JAPA & J Neuropsychiat. **Research Statement & Publications:** Evaluation of psychotropic drugs; training of psychiatric residents and evaluation of the best methods for accomplishing this; group psychotherapy, particularly as a device for maintaining competence in practicing psychotherapists; historical evolution of psychoanalytic and psychodynamic theory. **Mailing Address:** 24 Sorrel Lane, Rolling Hills, CA 90274-4226. **E-Mail:** frankkline@aol.com

KLINE, IRWIN KAVEN, MEDICINE, PATHOLOGY. **Personal Data:** b Canton, Ohio, March 18, 1931; m 1956, Tilde; c 4. **Education:** Columbia Univ, AB, 1953; Western Res Univ, MD, 1957; Am Bd Path, dipl, 1962. **Professional Experience:** PROF PATH, JEFFERSON MED COL, THOMAS JEFFERSON UNIV, PA, 1979-; CHMN & EMER, DEPT PATH, LANKENAU HOSP, 1969-; from clin assoc prof to clin prof path, Sch Med, Temple Univ, 1969-1979; asst pathologist, Mass Gen Hosp, 1968-1969; clin assoc path, Harvard Med Sch, 1966-1968; pathologist & chief anat path, Cambridge City Hosp, 1966-1968; asst prof & assoc pathologist, Sch Med, Boston Univ, 1964-1966; instr, Univ Ill Col Med, 1963-1964; resident path, 1960-1963; resident path, Michael Reese Hosp, Chicago, 1958-1963; intern, Mt Sinai Hosp, Cleveland, 1957-1958. **Memberships:** Int Soc Lymphology; fel Col Am Pathologists; Am Soc Clin Path; Am Asn Path; fel Am Col Cardiologists; AMA. **Research Statement & Publications:** Cardiac disease, principally infections and immunologic myocarditis and the effect of the obstructed cardiac lymphatics. **Mailing Address:** Dept Path, Lankenau Hosp, 100 E Lancaster Ave, Wynnewood, PA 19096-1419. **Fax:** 610-645-8456.

KLINE, JENNIE KATHERINE, EPIDEMIOLOGY. **Personal Data:** b Boston, Mass, January 15, 1950. **Education:** Univ Chicago, BA, 1972; Columbia Univ, MS, 1974, PhD (epidemiol), 1977. **Professional Experience:** Adj prof epidemiol, Mailman Sch Public Health & Sergievsky Ctr, Columbia Univ, as of 2005; adj assoc prof public health, Sch Pub Health & Sergievsky Ctr, Columbia Univ, beginning 1985; SR RES SCIENTIST, NY STATE PSYCHIAT INST, 1975-. **Memberships:** Soc Epidemiol Res; Int Epidemiol Asn; Am Pub Health Asn; Am Epidemiol Soc. **Research Statement & Publications:** Epidemiology of fetal defects and spontaneous abortions; mental retardation; prenatal HIV infection. **Mailing Address:** Dept Epidemiol, Mailman Sch Pub Health, Columbia Univ, 600 W 168th St, PH18-110, New York, NY 10032. **Fax:** 212-305-4653. **E-Mail:** jkk3@columbia.edu

KLINE, JERRY ROBERT, SOIL CHEMISTRY, ANALYTICAL CHEMISTRY. **Personal Data:** b Minneapolis, Minn, May 20, 1932; m 1954, c 5. **Education:** Univ Minn, BS, 1957, MS, 1960; Univ Minn, PhD (soil sci), 1964. **Professional Experience:** ADMIN JUDGE, ATOMIC SAFETY & LICENSING BD, US NUCLEAR REGULATORY COMN, 1980-; sect leader, US Nuclear Regulatory Comn, 1976-1980; sr land use analyst, US Nuclear Regulatory Comn, 1974-1976; Adj prof, Univ Ill, Chicago Circle, 1972-1976; ecologist, Radiol & Environ Res Div, Argonne Nat Lab, 1968-1974; dir terrestrial ecol proj, PR Nuclear Ctr, 1966-1968; assoc scientist, PR Nuclear Ctr, 1965-1966; Res assoc neutron activation appl to soils, Argonne Nat Lab, 1964-1965. **Memberships:** Sigma Xi; Nature Conservancy. **Research Statement & Publications:** Terrestrial ecology; trace elements in environmental systems; water relationships in soil-plant systems. **Mailing Address:** 13624 Middlevale Lane, Silver Spring, MD 20906.

KLINE, KENNETH A(LAN), ENGINEERING MECHANICS, MECHANICAL ENGINEERING. **Personal Data:** b Chicago, Ill, July 11, 1939; m 1960, c 4. **Education:** Univ Minn, BS, 1961, PhD (eng mech), 1965. **Professional Experience:** CHMN MECH ENG, WAYNE STATE UNIV, beginning 1986; prin investr, TACOM res grant, 1984-1986; prin investr, Ford res grants, 1984; prin investr, Glm res grant, 1980-1981; prin investr, NSF res grants, 1980-1982, 1967-1978; co-prin investr, dept energy res grant, 1977-1979; PROF MECH ENG, WAYNE STATE UNIV, beginning 1973; sr US scientist award, Alexandervon Humboldt-Stiftung, 1972-1973; assoc prof, Wayne State Univ, 1966-1973; sr res engr, esso prod res co, Stand Oil Co, NJ, 1965-1966. **Memberships:** Soc Rheology; Soc Automotive Engrs; Am Soc Mech Engrs; Sigma Xi; Am Inst Astronaut & Aeronaut. **Research Statement & Publications:** Computer-aided structural analysis; boundary integral method of structural analysis; optimal design; structural dynamics, system identification. **Mailing Address:** Dept Mech Eng, Wayne State Univ, 2105 eng, Detroit, MI 48202-4095. **Fax:** 313-578-5933. **E-Mail:** kline@eng.wayne.edu

KLINE, LARRY KEITH, MOLECULAR BIOLOGY. **Personal Data:** b Buffalo, NY, October 20, 1939; Canadian & Columbian citizen; m 1961, c 3. **Education:** Valparaiso Univ, BS, 1961; Pa State Univ, MS, 1965; State Univ NY, Buffalo, PhD (biochem), 1970. **Professional Experience:** ASSOC PROF EMER BIOL SCI, STATE UNIV NY, COL BROCKPORT, as of 2004; assoc Prof Biol Sci, State Univ NY, Col Brockport, beginning 1974; asst prof, State Univ NY Col Brockport, 1971-1974; NIH fel, Yale Univ, 1969-1971; asst cancer res scientist, Roswell Park Mem Inst, 1965-1967. **Memberships:** AAAS; Sigma Xi. **Research Statement & Publications:** Nucleic acid biosynthesis and function in mammalian cells. **Mailing Address:** Dept Biol Sci, State Univ NY, 350 New Campus Dr, Brockport, NY 14420-2915. **E-Mail:** lkline@brockport.edu

KLINE, LOREN W, NEUROPHYSICS. **Personal Data:** b Bethlehem, Pa, July 18, 1946. **Education:** Buena Vista Col, BS, 1968; Okla State Univ, MS, 1969; Univ Alta, PhD (neurophys), 1973. **Professional Experience:** PROF PHYSIOL, UNIV ALTA, 1983-; asst prof med, Univ Alta, 1973-1983. **Memberships:** Am Physiol Soc; Am Soc Zoologists; Can Physiol Soc; Am Endocrinol Soc. **Mailing Address:** Dept Physiol, Univ Alta, 7-55 Med Sci Bldg, Edmonton, AB T6G 2N8, Can. **E-Mail:** lkline@ualberta.ca

KLINE, RALPH WILLARD, food science; deceased, see previous edition for last biography

KLINE, RAYMOND MILTON, ELECTRICAL ENGINEERING. **Personal Data:** b St Louis, Mo, February 25, 1929; m 1951, c 4. **Education:** Univ Mo-Rolla, BS, 1951; Iowa State Univ, MS, 1954; Purdue Univ, PhD (elec eng), 1962. **Professional Experience:** PROF EMER ELEC ENG, WASH UNIV, as of 2003; prof elec eng, Wash Univ, beginning 1977; from asst prof to assoc prof, Wash Univ, 1962-1977; instr elec eng, Purdue Univ, 1959-1962; sr systs engr, Aircraft Div, McDonnell Aircraft Co, Mo, 1957-1959; systs engr, Sperry Gyroscope Co, NY, 1954-1957. **Memberships:** Inst Elec & Electronics Engrs; Am Soc Eng Educ; Asn Comput Mach; Sigma Xi. **Research Statement & Publications:** Design and application of information processing systems including digital computers, switching theory, especially areas in the field of artificial intelligence, pattern recognition and learning machines; image processing. **Mailing Address:** Dept Elec Eng, Wash Univ, 309 Bryan Hall, Bridgeton, MO 63044-1936. **E-Mail:** jcs@ee.wustl.edu

KLINE, RICHARD WILLIAM, POLYMER RHEOLOGY, ENERGY ENGINEERING. **Personal Data:** b Philadelphia, Pa, December 1942. **Education:** Mass Inst Technol, SB, 1964, SM, 1965, PhD (chem eng), 1970. **Professional Experience:** Batchelder-Blasius, City Landrum, 1980; Consult, Am Hoechst, 1978-1979; Batchelder-Blasius, Inc, 1977-1981; SR DEVELOP ENGR, CRYOVAC DIV, W R GRACE & CO, 1976-; group leader, Lockwood Greene Engrs, 1975-1976; Res engr, Milliken, Inc, 1970-1975. **Memberships:** Am Inst Chem Engrs; Soc Plastics Engrs; Sigma Xi. **Research Statement & Publications:** Simulation and modelling of plasticating extrusion, including extruder screws and dies; development of rheological theory. **Mailing Address:** 711 Stallion Dr, Auburn, PA 17922.

KLINE, ROBERT L, BIOLOGY. **Education:** Univ Mass, PhD. **Professional Experience:** PROF, DEPT PHYSIOL, UNIV WESTERN ONTARIO, as of 2006. **Mailing Address:** Dept Physiol, Univ Western Ontario, London, ON N6A 5C1, Can. **Fax:** 519- 661-3827.

KLINE, RONALD ALAN, ENGINEERING. **Personal Data:** b Wilkes-Barre, Pa, June 28, 1952. **Education:** Johns Hopkins Univ, BES, 1974, MSE, 1975, PhD (mech & mat sci), 1978. **Professional Experience:** DIR, DEPT MECH ENG, SAN DIEGO STATE UNIV, as of 2003; assoc prof mech eng, Univ Okla, beginning 1982; sr res engr, Gen Motors Res Labs, 1979-1982; sr res scientist, Gen Dynamics Corp, 1978-1979; res asst, Johns Hopkins Univ, 1972-1978. **Memberships:** Adhesion Soc Am; Am Soc Nondestructive Testing. **Research Statement & Publications:** Mechanical behavior of fiber reinforced composite materials and adhesively bonded composite joints. **Mailing Address:** Dept Mech Eng, San Deigo State Univ, 5500 Campanile Dr, San Diego, CA 92182-1323. **E-Mail:** kline@kahuna.sdsu.edu

KLINE, TONI BETH, NEUROSCIENCES, PHARMACY. **Personal Data:** b Los Angeles, Calif, August 23, 1950; m 1976. **Education:** Univ Calif, Berkeley, AB, 1973; Univ Calif, San Francisco, MS, 1976; Univ Ala, Birmingham, PhD (chem), 1980. **Professional Experience:** ASST PROF CHEM, DEPT PHARMACOL, MT SINAI MED SCH, 1982-; lectr org chem, Dept Chem, State Univ NY, 1981-1982; res assoc, Dept Chem, State Univ NY, 1980-1982; res assoc, Dept Chem, Ore State Univ, 1979-1980; teaching asst biochem, Dept Chem, Univ Ala, 1978; res asst, Dept Chem, Univ Ala, 1976-1979; teaching asst org chem, Dept Chem, Univ Ala, 1976-1978; Teaching asst org chem, Dept Pharmaceut Chem, Univ Calif, 1974-1976. **Memberships:** AAAS; Am Chem Soc. **Research Statement & Publications:** Use of organic chemistry in investigating chamsims of drug actions and natural product synthesis; biogenesis, pharmacognosy and ecology; structure activity relationships of all biologically active compounds. **Mailing Address:** Bristol Myers Squibb, 675 Col Rd E, Princeton, NJ 08543-6625.

KLINE, VIRGINIA MARCH, plant ecology, vegetation management; deceased, see previous edition for last biography

KLINEBERG, JOHN MICHAEL, AEROSPACE ENGINEERING. **Personal Data:** b New York, NY, October 16, 1938; m 1967, Anne-Marie; c Eric, Arnaud & Logan. **Education:** Princeton Univ, BS, 1960; Calif Inst Technol, MS, 1962, PhD, 1968. **Honors & Awards:** Meritorious Exec, US Gov, 1986. **Professional Experience:** RETIRED; pres & v pres, Space Systs/Loral, 1999-2001; bd govs, Nat Space Club, beginning 1987; actg dir, aeronaut & space technol, 1986-1987; dep dir, aeronaut & space technol, 1979-1986; dep assoc adminr, aeronaut & space technol, 1978-1979; Hq, Ames Res Ctr, NASA, 1974-1978; aerospace engr, Ames Res Ctr, NASA, 1970-1974; res engr, Calif Inst Technol, 1968-1970; engr, Douglas Aircraft Co, Santa Monica, 1960-1962. **Memberships:** Fel Am Inst Aeronaut & Astronaut; Nat Space Club; Sigma Xi. **Research Statement & Publications:** Aerospace engineering. **Mailing Address:** Space Systems Loral, 3825 Fabian Way, Palo Alto, CA 94303.

KLINEDINST, KEITH ALLEN, CHEMICAL VAPOR DEPOSITION, ELECTROCHEMISTRY. **Personal Data:** b York, Pa, November 8, 1944; m 1974, Barbara; c Bradford H & Craig A. **Education:** Franklin & Marshall Col, BA, 1966; Stanford Univ, MS, 1970, PhD (chem), 1972; Boston Univ, MS (Comp sci), 1987. **Honors & Awards:** GTE Corp Warner Award Osram Sylvania Star Award. **Professional Experience:** Mem tech staff mat sci lab, GTE Labs Inc, Gen Tel & Electronics Corp, 1976-1986; Res assoc, Advan Fuel Cell

Res Lab, Pratt & Whitney Aircraft, United Technol Corp, 1972-1976; Woodrow Wilson fel, 1966. **Memberships:** Sigma Xi; Am Chem Soc; Electrochem Soc. **Research Statement & Publications:** Fuel cell electrochemistry; lithium batteries; heterogeneous catalysis; porous electrode research and development; luminescence; chemical vapor deposition; environmental engineering. **Mailing Address:** 111 Brigham St Apt 26C, Hudson, MA 01749-2649. **E-Mail:** kklinedinst@hotmail.com

KLINEDINST, PAUL EDWARD, JR, ORGANIC CHEMISTRY. **Personal Data:** b York, Pa, December 29, 1933; American citizen; m Marilyn; c Helene (DeStefano) & Paul III. **Education:** Lehigh Univ, BS, 1955; Univ Calif, Los Angeles, PhD (chem), 1959. **Professional Experience:** PROF EMER CHEM, CALIF STATE UNIV, 1997-; dean, Col Sci & Math, Calif State Univ Northridge, 1995-1997; assoc dean sci & math, Calif State Univ, Northridge, 1988-1991; chmn chem, Calif State Univ, Northridge, 1983-1988; prof chem, Calif State Univ, Northridge, 1969-1997; from asst prof to assoc prof, Calif State Univ, Northridge, 1960-1969; NSF fel chem, Harvard Univ, 1959-1960. **Memberships:** Am Chem Soc; Sigma Xi. **Research Statement & Publications:** Organic reaction mechanisms; salt effects and ion pairs in solvolysis and related reactions. **Mailing Address:** Dept Chem, Calif State Univ, Northridge, CA 91330. **E-Mail:** paul.klinedinst@csun.edu

KLING, GERALD FAIRCHILD, SOIL SCIENCE. **Personal Data:** b Lewisburg, Pa, December 12, 1941; m 1964, c 1. **Education:** Purdue Univ, BS, 1968; Cornell Univ, MS, 1973, PhD (soil sci), 1974. **Professional Experience:** PROF EMER SOIL SCI, ORE STATE UNIV, as of 2004. **Memberships:** Am Soc Agron; Soil Sci Soc Am; Int Soc Soil Sci; Sigma Xi. **Research Statement & Publications:** Quantification of the dynamic soil system so that predictions can be made regarding the probable effects of various land use changes on the system. **Mailing Address:** Dept Crop Sci, Ore State Univ, 109 Crop Sci Bldg, Corvallis, OR 97331-3002. **Fax:** 541-737-5725.

KLING, LINDA, ANIMAL NUTRITION. **Education:** Univ Del, BS, 1974; Univ Md, MS, 1977, PhD, 1980. **Professional Experience:** ADJ FAC, DEPT VET, UNIV MAINE, as of 2004. **Mailing Address:** Dept Vet Tech, Univ Maine, Augusta, ME 04469.

KLING, O(ZRO) RAY, REPRODUCTIVE ENDOCRINOLOGY, BIOLOGY. **Personal Data:** b Peru, Ind, May 3, 1942; m 1966, c 2. **Education:** Butler Univ, BS, 1965; Ind Univ, Bloomington, PhD (zoology), 1969. **Professional Experience:** ADJ PROF BIOL PSYCHOL, UNIV OKLA HEALTH SCI CTR, as of 1998; VPROVOST ACAD AFFAIRS & DEAN, GRAD COL, HEALTH SCI CTR, UNIV OKLA, 1993-; dean, Grad Col, 1990-1995; assoc dean, Grad Col & vprovost acad affairs & grad prof, 1987-1990; PROF GYNEC & OBSTET, PHYSIOL & BIOPHYS & ZOOL, HEALTH SCI CTR, UNIV OKLA, 1984-; Ford Found res fel, Human Reproductive Endocrinol Res Unit, Karolinska Inst, Stockholm, 1974-1975; from asst prof to assoc prof gynec & obstet, Sci Med, Univ Okla, 1970-1984; from adj asst prof to adj assoc prof physiol & biophys, Sci Med, Univ Okla, 1970-1984; NIH fel, Div Steroid Res, Ohio State Univ, 1969-1970; DEAN GRAD COLL, UNIV OKLA HEALTH SCI CTR. **Memberships:** Endocrine Soc; Am Soc Primatologists; Soc Study Reproduction; Soc Gynec Invest; Am Soc Zool. **Research Statement & Publications:** Reproductive biology and physiology; factors regulating ovarian function; endocrine regulation of pregnancy and fetal development. **Mailing Address:** Univ Okla Health Sci Ctr, 1000 Stanton L Young Blvd, Oklahoma City, OK 73190. **Fax:** 405-271-1155. **E-Mail:** ray-kling@ouhsc.edu

KLINGBEIL, DELIA H, MATHEMATICS. **Education:** Univ Md Col Park, PhD, 1974. **Professional Experience:** TREAS, JAMESTOWN PHILOMENIAN LIBR, as of 2005. **Mailing Address:** 37 Langworthy Ave, Stonington, CT 06378. **Fax:** 401-423-7281.

KLINGBEIL, WERNER WALTER, APPLIED MECHANICS, APPLIED MATHEMATICS. **Personal Data:** b Onoway, Alta, June 19, 1932; m 1966, c 2. **Education:** Univ Alta, BSc, 1954; Col Aeronaut, Eng, dipl, 1956; Brown Univ, SM, 1964, PhD (appl math), 1966. **Professional Experience:** RES ASSOC, RES CTR, UNIROYAL, INC, 1982-; sr res scientist, Res Ctr, Uniroyal, Inc, 1971-1982; res scientist, Res Ctr, Uniroyal, Inc, 1966-1971; res engr, Allied Res Assocs, Inc, 1959-1961; Stress engr, Avro Aircraft Ltd, Can, 1956-1959. **Memberships:** Sigma Xi. **Research Statement & Publications:** Stress analysis and design of engineering structures; deformation and flow behavior of polymeric materials; finite elasticity; viscoelasticity; composite materials; tire mechanics. **Mailing Address:** 9744 Shenandoah Dr, Brecksville, OH 44141.

KLINGE, CAROLYN M, MOLECULAR ENDOCRINOLOGY, ESTROGEN RECEPTOR. **Personal Data:** b Utica, NY, May 20, 1957. **Education:** Keuka Col, BA, 1979; Pa State Univ, MS, 1981, PhD (pharmacol), 1984. **Honors & Awards:** Nichols Inst New Investr Award, Endocrine Soc, 1990. **Professional Experience:** PROF BIOCHEM, SCH MED, UNIV LOUISVILLE, as of 2005; assoc prof Biochem, Sch Med, Univ Louisville, beginning 2001; asst prof dept biochem, sch med, Univ Louisville, 1996-2001; assoc res prof, Dept Biochem & Cancer Ctr, Sch Med & Dent, Univ Rochester, 1996; asst res prof, Dept Biochem & Cancer Ctr, Sch Med & Dent, Univ Rochester, 1989-1995; Adj asst prof biol, Monroe Community Col, 1987-1988; Fel biochemn & oncol, Dept Biochem & Cancer Ctr, Sch Med & Dent, Univ Rochester, 1984-1989. **Memberships:** AAAS; Am Asn Cancer Res; NY Acad Sci; Endoc r ine Soc; Fedn Am Soc Exp Biol. **Research Statement & Publications:** Molecular mechanisms regulating the transcription of steroid hormone-responsive genes in target tissues; role of the ligand, hormone agonist or antagonist, on estrogen receptor DNA binding and transactivation. **Mailing Address:** Dept Biochem Molecular Bio, Univ Louisville Sch Med, Louisville, KY 40202. **Fax:** 502-852-6222. **E-Mail:** carolyn.klinge@louisville.edu

KLINGELE, HAROLD OTTO, INFORMATION SCIENCE, BIOCHEMISTRY. **Personal Data:** b Niagara Falls, NY, August 4, 1937. **Education:** Mass Inst Technol, BSc, 1959; Yale Univ, MS, 1961; Cornell Univ, PhD (org chem), 1965. **Professional Experience:** PRES, AURORA CONSULT SERVS, 1993-; lectr, Dept Chem, Ctr Environ Educ & Res, State Univ NY, Buffalo, 1991-1992; pres, Soap Factory Stores, Inc, 1980-1991; vis indust chemist, Chem Dept, Canisius Col, Buffalo, NY, 1980-1982; mgr, treas & chem consult, Peninsula Chem Anal Ltd, 1976-1978; sr res assoc, Dept Chem, Ctr Environ Educ & Res, State Univ NY, Buffalo, 1973-1975 & 1982-1990; pres, HOK Assocs, 1971-1992; chem consult & chem anal, HOK Assoc, 1971-1992; asst prof, Univ Louisville, 1966-1971; instr pharmacol, Univ Louisville, 1965-1966. **Memberships:** Am Chem Soc; Royal Soc Chem. **Research Statement & Publications:** Forensics; analytical method development; industrial problems involving chemistry; carcinogens; toxicology; environmental chemistry; organic synthesis; electronics-radiowave propagation; atmospheric chemical reactions; photo oxidation of organic pollutents. **Mailing Address:** 505 Meadowbrook Dr, Lewiston, NY 14092-1936.

KLINGEMAN, PETER C, HYDRAULIC ENGINEERING, HYDROLOGY. **Personal Data:** b Evanston, Ill, May 31, 1934; m 1957, c 2. **Education:** Northwestern Univ, BS, 1957, MS, 1959; Univ Calif, Berkeley, PhD (civil eng), 1965. **Honors & Awards:** Hilgard Hydraul Prize, Am Soc Civil Eng, 1983. **Professional Experience:** PROF EMER WATER RESOURCES ENG, ORE STATE UNIV, as of 2003; actg dept head civil eng, Ore Water Resources Res Inst, 1989-1991; PROF CIVIL ENG, ORE STATE UNIV, 1976-; dir, Ore Water Resources Res Inst, 1975-1989; from assoc prof to prof, Ore State Univ, 1968-1976; from asst prof to assoc prof, Ore State Univ, 1966-1968; Ford Found Prog vis prof hydraul eng, Cath Univ Chile, 1964-1966; res engr, Univ Calif, Berkeley, 1962-1964; asst prof civil eng, NDak State Univ, 1959. **Memberships:** Am Soc Civil Eng; Am Geophys Union; Int Asn Hydraul Res. **Research Statement & Publications:** Planning development and management of river basins and estuaries, including hydraulics, hydrology, sediment transport, problem analysis, impact assessment and related aspects of water resources development. **Mailing Address:** Civil, Constru & Env Engr, Ore State Univ, 202 Apperson Hall, Corvallis, OR 97331-2302. **Fax:** 541-737-3052. **E-Mail:** peter.klingeman@oregonstate.edu

KLINGEN, THEODORE JAMES, PHYSICAL INORGANIC CHEMISTRY. **Personal Data:** b St Louis, Mo, October 7, 1931; m Maura; c Joseph & Anne. **Education:** St Louis Univ, BS, 1953, MS, 1955; Fla State Univ, PhD (chem), 1962. **Professional Experience:** PROF Emeritus 1999-; DIR, DEPT HEALTH & SAFETY; 1985-1999; dir, Ctr Radiation Res, 1972-1974; PROF CHEM, UNIV MISS, 1970-1999; from asst prof to assoc prof, Univ Miss, 1964-1970; res scientist, Res Div, McDonnell Aircraft Corp, 1962-1964; asst, Fla State Univ, 1960-1962; fel, Fla State Univ, 1958-1960; analyst chem, McDonnell Aircraft Corp, 1957-1958; Nuclear res officer, Res Div, Spec Weapons Ctr, USAF, NMex, 1955-1957; Grants, US Dept Energy & NSF. **Memberships:** Am Chem Soc; Sigma Xi Res Soc. **Research Statement & Publications:** Radiation chemistry of plastic crystals; radiation induced polymerization of organo-substituted carboranes; environmental chemistry. **Mailing Address:** 117 Pine Crest Dr, Oxford, MS 38655-2616. **Fax:** 662-234-6079. **E-Mail:** gstjk@olemiss.edu

KLINGENBERG, DANIEL J, CHEMICAL ENGINEERING. **Education:** Univ Mo-Rolla, BS; Univ Ill, MS & PhD. **Professional Experience:** AASOC PROF, DEPT CHEM & BIOL ENG, UNIV WIS-MADISON, as of 2005. **Research Statement & Publications:** Colloid science; suspension rheology; electromagnetic phenomena in materials. **Mailing Address:** Dept Chem & Biol Eng, Univ Wis-Madison, 2006 Eng Hall 1415 Eng Dr, Madison, WI 53706-1691. **Fax:** 608-262-5434. **E-Mail:** klingen@engr.wisc.edu

KLINGENSMITH, GEORGE BRUCE, PHYSICAL & ORGANIC CHEMISTRY, POLYMER CHEMISTRY & ENGINEERING. **Personal Data:** b Pittsburgh, Pa, December 6, 1934; m 1960, c 2. **Education:** Univ Pittsburgh, BSc, 1957, PhD (phys-org chem), 1963. **Professional Experience:** DIR RES & DEVELOP, HUNTSMAN POLYPROPYLENE CORP, 1990-; sr staff res chemist, Shell Develop Co, 1974-1990; res supvr, Shell Chem Co Woodbury, 1966-1974; Fel phys & org chem, Pa State Univ, 1963-1964. **Memberships:** Am Chem Soc; Sigma Xi; Soc Advan Mat & Process Eng. **Research Statement & Publications:** Reactions and physical properties of aromatic systems; solvent effects; crystallization and crystal structure of polymers; nuclear magnetic resonance spectroscopy. **Mailing Address:** 1222 N Bay Shore Dr, Virginia Beach, VA 23451-3763.

KLINGENSMITH, MERLE JOSEPH, PLANT PHYSIOLOGY. **Personal Data:** b Grenora, NDak, March 27, 1932; m 1959, Maree McGauhey; c Wesley J & Peter G. **Education:** Wheaton Col, Ill, BS, 1954; Univ Mich, MS, 1956, PhD (bot), 1959. **Professional Experience:** PROF EMER BIOL, ROCHESTER INST TECHNOL, as of 2004; prof biol, Rochester Inst Technol, beginning 1976; from asst prof to assoc prof, Rochester Inst Technol, 1965-1976; asst prof bot, Colgate Univ, 1960-1965; vis asst prof bot & bact, Ohio Wesleyan Univ, 1959-1960; asst bot, Univ Mich, 1955-1956; lab asst bact, Fla State Univ, 1954-1955. **Memberships:** Fel AAAS; Sigma Xi; Am Sci Affiliation. **Research Statement & Publications:** Plant tissue culture; exogenous growth regulators; radiation effects on plant growth. **Mailing Address:** 2281 NorthRd, Scottsville, NY 14546. **E-Mail:** mjksbi@rit.edu

KLINGENSMITH, RAYMOND W, nuclear physics; deceased, see previous edition for last biography

KLINGER, ALLEN, PATTERN ANALYSIS, ELECTRICIAL ENGINEERING. **Personal Data:** b New York, NY, April 2, 1937; American citizen; m 1988, Dorothy; c Deborah Ann & Richard Leslie. **Education:** Cooper Union, BEE, 1957; Calif Inst Technol, MS, 1958; Univ Calif, Berkeley, PhD (elec eng), 1966. **Honors & Awards:** Tau Beta Pi, mem, 1955. **Professional Experience:** TBP District 16 dir, 2001-; Fulbright Fel, 1990-1991; res travel fel, USSR, Nat Acad Sci, 1982-1983 & 1985-1986; consult, Aerospace Corp, 1980-1987; consult, US Army Eng Topogr Labs, 1978-1980; consult, IBM Los Angeles Sci Ctr, 1978-1979; consult, Jet Propulsion Lab, 1978; consult, Radiol Dept, Long Beach Mem Hosp, 1977-1978; consult, Los Angeles Unified Sch Dist, 1976-1978; chmn, Conf Data Struct Pattern Recognition & Comput Graphics, 1974-1975; prin investr, NSF, 1968-1971 & Air Force Off Sci Res, 1970-1977; consult, sr radar systs specialist, Litton Industs, 1968-1969; PROF COMPUT SCI & ENG, UNIV CALIF, LOS ANGELES, 1967-; consult, Syst Develop Corp, 1967 & 1978; consult, Rand Corp, 1967-1969 & 1972-1973; researcher math, Rand Corp, 1965-1967; sr res engr electronics systs, Jet Propulsion Lab, 1964-1965; electronics systs engr comput systs, Syst Develop Corp, 1959-1962; electronics engr elec systs, ITT Labs, 1958-1959; Mem tech staff electronics, Hughes Aircraft Co, 1957; Tan Beta Pi (TBP), 1955-; SAIC chmn, Panel Soviet Image Pattern Recognition. **Memberships:** Fel Inst Elec & Electronics Engrs. **Research Statement & Publications:** Computer vision and neural networks; image data bases; human computer interaction; allocation of unreliable units; composite views from tomography; biomedical wave forms; data analysis. **Mailing Address:** Dept Comput Sci, Univ Calif, 4532-K Boelter Hall, Los Angeles, CA 90095-1596. **Fax:** 310-794-5057. **E-Mail:** klinger@cs.ucla.edu

KLINGER, HAROLD P, GENETICS. **Personal Data:** b Brooklyn, NY, July 20, 1929; m 1959. **Education:** Harvard Univ, BA, 1952; Univ Basel, MD, 1959, PhD, 1963. **Professional Experience:** ASST PROF, DEPT PEDIAT, ALBERT EINSTEIN COL MED, as of 2004; PROF GENETICS, ALBERT EINSTEIN COL MED, 1972-; mem adv comt, Pop Coun, Rockefeller Univ, 1971-; NIH career develop award, 1965-1974; from asst prof to assoc prof anat & genetics, Albert Einstein Col Med, 1963-1972; dir cytogenetics res unit, Univ Basel, 1961-1963; ed, Cytogenetics & Cell Genetics, 1960-; from second asst to first asst, Univ Basel, 1959-1961; Demonstr anat, Univ Basel, 1955-1957. **Memberships:** Genetics Soc Am; Am Soc Human Genetics; Am Asn Phys Anthrop; NY Acad Sci; Swiss Anat Soc. **Research Statement & Publications:** Cytogenetics; role of chromosomal aberrations in human development; somatic cell genetics; gene regulation and interaction in normal and malignant cells. **Mailing Address:** Dept Genetics, Albert Einstein Col Med, Rm 1217, Ullmann Bldg, Jack & Pearl Resnick Campus, 1300 Morris Park Ave, Bronx, NY 10461. **Fax:** 718-430-2454. **E-Mail:** hklinger@aecom.yu.edu

KLINGER, KATHERINE W, GENETICS. **Education:** Trinity Univ, BA; Univ Tex Health Sci Ctr, PhD (biochem). **Professional Experience:** SR VPRES, GENETICS & GENOMICS,

GENZYME CORP, MASS, as of 2003. **Mailing Address:** Genzyme Corp, One Mountain Rd, Framingham, MA 01701-3000. **Fax:** 508-820-9742. **E-Mail:** kklinger@world.std.com

KLINGER, LAWRENCE EDWARD, FOOD ENGINEERING. **Personal Data:** b Chicago, Ill, November 18, 1929; m 1953, Ellen Reidy; c Patricia, Therese, Robert & Edward. **Education:** Loyola Univ, Ill, BS, 1951; Ill Inst Technol, MS, 1953. **Professional Experience:** RETIRED; dir qual assurance/regulatory affairs, Swift-Eckrich, Inc, 1986-1989; vpres, Beatrice Meats Inc, 1985-1986; mgr qual & assurance/regulatory, BeatriceRefrig Foods, 1984-1985; dir qual assurance, Swift Chem Co, 1978-1984; Dir, Food Update, 1975-1979; steering comt, Nutrit Planning Conf, Food & Drug Admin, 1975-1976; dir pub responsibility, Swift Chem Co, 1971-1977; sr adminasst, Swift Chem Co, 1970-1971; plant mgr, Swift Chem Co, 1969-1970; dir planning & acquisitions, Swift Chem Co, 1968-1969; gen mgr new prod develop dept, Res Labs, 1962-1968; div head, Res Labs, 1961-1962; asst to vpres res, Res Labs, 1959-1961; div head, Res Labs, 1955-1959; asst to dir labs, Swift & Co, 1954-1955; Res chemist, Swift & Co, 1952-1954; mem, Coun Agr Sci & Technol. **Memberships:** Inst Food Technol (treas, 1957 & 1958); Am Soc Qual Control. **Research Statement & Publications:** New products development; nutrition education; food safety. **Mailing Address:** 15435 Cedarwood Ln Apt 302, Naples, FL 34110.

KLINGER, THOMAS SCOTT, MARINE BIOLOGY, PHYSIOLOGICAL ECOLOGY. **Personal Data:** b Kalamazoo, Mich, May 5, 1955; div, c Austin T & Pepin S. **Education:** Macalester Col, BA, 1975; Univ SFla, MA, 1979, PhD (biol), 1984. **Professional Experience:** PROF BIOL, BLOOMSBURG UNIV, 1996-; assoc prof, Bloomsburg Univ, 1990-1996; vpres acad affairs, Marine Sci Consortium, 1988-2002; DIR, MARINE SCI CONSORTIUM, 1986-; asst prof, Bloomsburg Univ, 1985-1990; adj prof biol, St Leo Col, 1984-1985; instr biol, Pasco-Hernando Community Col, 1984; adj lectr, Univ SFla, 1983-1984; teaching asst biol, Univ SFla, 1976-1983. **Memberships:** AAAS; Sigma Xi; Am Micros Soc; Soc Integrative & Comp Biol. **Research Statement & Publications:** Physiological ecology and nutritional physiology of marine invertebrate animals, primarily echinoderms; feeding, digestion, and energetics. **Mailing Address:** Dept Biol & Allied Health Sci Bloomsburg Univ, 400 E Second St, Bloomsburg, PA 17815-1301. **Fax:** 717-389-3028. **E-Mail:** tklinger@bloomu.edu

KLINGER, WILLIAM RUSSELL, MATHEMATICS. **Personal Data:** b Columbia City, Ind, February 9, 1939; m 1960, c 1. **Education:** Taylor Univ, BS in Ed, 1961; Ohio State Univ, MSc, 1967, PhD (math, educ), 1973. **Professional Experience:** PROF MATH, TAYLOR UNIV, as of 2006; INTERIM VPRES, TAYLOR UNIV, as of 2004; prof math, marion col, 1989-1994; from asst prof to assoc prof math, Marion Col, 1973-1989; mem assoc fac, Ind Univ, Kokomo, 1973-; head dept, Marion Col, beginning 1973; instr, Ohio State Univ, 1968-1973; teacher math, Marion Community Schs, Ind, 1961-1968. **Memberships:** Math Asn Am. **Research Statement & Publications:** Necessary and sufficient conditions for continuity in metric spaces and topological spaces. **Mailing Address:** Dept math, Taylor Univ, 236 W Reade Ave Nussbaum Sci Ctr 203, Upland, IN 46989-1001. **Fax:** 765-998-4650. **E-Mail:** wlklinger@tayloru.edu

KLINGHAMMER, ERICH, ETHOLOGY, PSYCHOLOGY. **Personal Data:** b Kassel, Ger, February 28, 1930; m 1958, c 1. **Education:** Univ Chicago, AB, 1958, PhD (psychol), 1962. **Professional Experience:** Pres, Nam Wildlife Park Found, beginning 1972; DIR & FOUNDER, WOLF PARK, 1972-; assoc prof, Purdue Univ, Lafayette, 1968-1995; from instr to asst prof psychol, Univ Chicago, 1963-1968; sci ed, Grzimek's Animal Life Encycl. **Memberships:** AAAS; Am Ornith Union; Animal Behav Soc. **Research Statement & Publications:** Ethology; imprinting; effects of early experience on adult behavior; behavior mechanisms in canids development and motivation; predator-prey interactions in wolves and bison; applied ethology. **Mailing Address:** Wolf Park, 4004 E 800 N, Battleground, IN 47920. **Fax:** 765-567-4299.

KLINGHOFFER, JUNE F, INTERNAL MEDICINE. **Personal Data:** b Philadelphia, Pa, February 12, 1921; m 1947, Sidney; c Robert Wenger. **Education:** Univ Pa, BA, 1941; Woman's Med Col Pa, MD, 1945; Am Bd Internal Med, cert, 1951; Spec Bd Rheumatology, cert, 1976. **Professional Experience:** HON BD, FOUND HIST WOMEN MED, as of 2006; Ethel Russell Morris prof med, Med Col Pa, 1987-; from instr to prof, Med Col Pa, 1950-1987; dir stud health serv, Med Col Pa, 1948-1951; clin asst med, Med Col Pa, 1948-1950; fel path, Med Col Pa, 1947-1948; resident internal med, Albert Einstein Med Ctr, 1945-1947; intern, Albert Einstein Med Ctr, 1945. **Memberships:** Am Med Women's Asn; Asn Women Sci; fel Am Col Physicians; AMA; Am Col Rheumatology; Asn Am Med Col. **Mailing Address:** Dept Med, Med Col Pa, 3300 Henry Ave, Philadelphia, PA 19129. **Fax:** 215-849-1525.

KLINGLER, EUGENE H(ERMAN), ELECTROMECHANICAL ENGINEERING. **Personal Data:** b Ft Wayne, Ind, September 3, 1932; m 1954, c 6. **Education:** Ind Inst Technol, BSEE, 1953; NMex State Univ, MSEE, 1957; Carnegie Inst Technol, PhD (elec eng), 1961. **Professional Experience:** PRES & CHMN BD, EUGENE KLINGLER INC, 1970-; prof & chmn dept, Univ Detroit, 1969-1970; chmn, Dept Elec Eng, Ind Inst Technol, 1965-1969; mgr eng res lab, NAm Aviation Inc, Okla, 1963-1965; sr mem tech staff, Northrop Space Labs, 1962-1963; chief electronics engr, Fairchild Camera & Instrument Corp, 1962; staff engr, Space Tech Labs, 1961-1962; Instr, Ind Inst Technol, 1958; proj engr, Carnegie Inst Technol, 1957-1961; instr, NMex State Univ, 1957; Servomech engr, Bell Aircraft Corp, 1953-1955. **Memberships:** Inst Elec & Electronics Engrs. **Research Statement & Publications:** Synthesis of artificial dielectric materials by means of control of electric and magnetic losses as a function of frequency. **Mailing Address:** 3650 Washburn Rd, Vassar, MI 48768.

KLINGMAN, DAYTON L, agronomy; deceased, see previous edition for last biography

KLINGMAN, JACK DENNIS, biochemistry, neurosciences; deceased, see previous edition for last biography

KLINGSBERG, CYRUS, SOLID STATE CHEMISTRY, CERAMICS. **Personal Data:** b Philadelphia, Pa, November 12, 1924; m 1950, Vera. **Education:** Univ Pa, BA, 1948; Bryn Mawr Col, MA, 1949; Pa State Univ, PhD (geo chem), 1958. **Professional Experience:** RETIRED; geologist, US Dept Energy, 1977-1987; sr res assoc, Arhco, 1976-1977; vis prof, Japan Soc Prom Sci, 1975; exec secy, Comt Radioactive Waste Mgt, Nat Acad Sci-Nat Res Coun, 1968-1975; ceramist, London, 1964-1966; liaison scientist ceramics, London, 1963-1964; ceramist, Off Naval Res, 1959-1963; res chemist, Corning Glass Works, NY, 1957-1959; asst geochem, Pa State Univ, 1954-1957; petrologist, Simonds Abrasive Co, 1951-1954; res mgr, G F Pettinos Inc, 1950-1951. **Memberships:** Fel Am Ceramic Soc; Mineral Soc Am; Sigma Xi; AAAS. **Research Statement & Publications:** Solid state chemistry of ceramics, minerals and ionic solids; synthesis and characterization of crystalline phases; management of radioactive wastes. **Mailing Address:** 1318 Deerfield Dr, State College, PA 16803-2208.

KLINK, JOEL RICHARD, ORGANIC CHEMISTRY. **Personal Data:** b Nevada, Ohio, June 28, 1935; m 1959, c 2. **Education:** Ohio State Univ, BS, 1957, PhD (chem), 1964. **Professional Experience:** PROF EMER CHEM, UNIV WIS, EAU CLAIRE, as of 2003; chmn dept, Univ Wis-EauClaire, 1978-1983, 1991; from asst prof to assoc prof, Univ Wis-Eau Claire, 1963-1971; instr chem, Ohio Northern Univ, 1961-1963. **Memberships:** Am Chem Soc. **Research Statement & Publications:** Reactions of diazoalkenes. **Mailing Address:** Dept Chem, Univ Wis, 215 Corydon Rd, Eau Claire, WI 54701. **E-Mail:** klinkjr@uwec.edu

KLINK, WILLIAM H, THEORETICAL PHYSICS. **Personal Data:** b Chicago, Ill, September 29, 1937; m 1959. **Education:** Univ Mich, BA, 1959; Johns Hopkins Univ, PhD (physics), 1964. **Professional Experience:** PROF PHYSICS & ASTRON, UNIV IOWA, 1977-; from asst prof to assoc prof, Univ Iowa, 1965-1977; Fulbright grant, Univ Heidelberg, 1964-1965. **Memberships:** Am Phys Soc. **Research Statement & Publications:** Elementary particle physics, primarily using group theory. **Mailing Address:** 1101 Harlocke St, Iowa City, IA 52246-5133. **E-Mail:** william-klink@uiowa.edu

KLINKE, DAVID J, ORGANIC CHEMISTRY. **Personal Data:** b Detroit, Mich, February 27, 1932; m 1964, c 3. **Education:** Mich State Univ, BS, 1954, PhD (org chem), 1963. **Professional Experience:** SR QUAL MGR, E I DU PONT DEL NEMOURS & CO, INC, 1986-; supt safety, Environment, Protection, 1980-1986; sr supvr mat distrib, Chambers Works, 1974-1980; prod supvr dyes, Chambers Works, 1971-1974; supvr mgt training & personnel develop, Chambers Works, 1968-1971; prod supvr miscellaneous org intermediates, Chambers Works, 1966-1968; res chemist petrol additives, Jackson Lab, E I du Pont Del Nemours & Co, Inc, 1963-1966; Teacher jr high sch, Mich, 1954-1955 & high sch, 1955-1959. **Memberships:** Am Chem Soc. **Research Statement & Publications:** Thiophene chemistry; organo-metallics. **Mailing Address:** 44 Laurel Lane, Woodstown, NJ 08098-9638.

KLINMAN, DENNIS M, MEDICAL RESEARCH. **Personal Data:** b Philadelphia, Pa, October 9, 1954. **Education:** St Joseph's Univ, BS, 1976; Univ Pa, MA & PhD, 1982. **Honors & Awards:** Regional & Sr Rheumatology Awards, Am Rheumatology Asn, 1987. **Professional Experience:** CHIEF, SECT RETROVIRAL RES, CTR BIOLOGICS EVAL & RES, US FOOD & DRUG ADMIN, 1993-; tenured sr invstr, div viral prod, 1991-1993; med officer, div virol, 1989-1991; fel, Arthritis found, 1985-1987; med & sr staff fel, NIADDK & NINDS, NIH, 1983-1989; med internship, Faulkner hosp, 1982-1983; vis scientist, Inst animal physiol, ARC, 1978-1979. **Memberships:** Am Soc Clin Invest; Am Soc Immunologists; AAAS; Am Rheumatology Asn. **Research Statement & Publications:** Radioiodination of monoclonal antibodies; dialyzable serum components support the growth of hybridoma cell lines in vitro; analysis of non-dominaur idio types during alloimmune responses; suppression of autoantibody production with anti-class II antibodies; idiotypy and autoimmunity. **Mailing Address:** Ctr Biologics Eval & Res, US Food & Drug Admin, 5600 Fishers Lane, Rockville, MD 20857-0001.

KLINMAN, JUDITH POLLOCK, BIOCHEMISTRY, PHYSICAL ORGANIC CHEMISTRY. **Personal Data:** b Philadelphia, Pa, April 17, 1941; div, c 2. **Education:** Univ Pa, AB, 1962, PhD (org chem), 1966. **Honorary Degrees:** PhD, Univ Upsalla, Sweden 2000. **Honors & Awards:** Repligen Award, Am Chem Soc, 1994. **Professional Experience:** Chair, Dept Chem, Univ Calif, Berkeley, 2000-2003; Guggenheim fel, 1988; CHANCELLORS PROF CHEM & MOLECULAR & CELL BIOL, UNIV CALIF, BERKELEY, 1982-; assoc prof, Univ Calif, Berkeley, 1978-1982; assoc mem, Inst Cancer Res, 1977-1978; asst prof med biophys, Univ Pa, 1974-1978; asst mem, Inst Cancer Res, 1972-1977; res assoc biochem, Inst Cancer Res, 1970-1972; res Scientist, Inst Cancer Res, Pa, 1968-1978; assoc, Inst Cancer Res, 1968-1970; fel phys org chem, Isotopes Dept, Weizmann Inst, 1966-1967. **Memberships:** Nat Acad Sci; Am Soc Biochem & Molecular Biol; Am Acad Arts & Sci; Am Chem Soc; Am Philos Soc. **Research Statement & Publications:** Mechanism and regulation of enzyme action. **Mailing Address:** Dept Chem, Univ Calif, 125 Lewis Rm 419 Latimer Hall, Berkeley, CA 94720-1460. **Fax:** 510-643-6232. **E-Mail:** klinman@berkeley.edu

KLINMAN, NORMAN RALPH, IMMUNOLOGY. **Personal Data:** b Philadelphia, Pa, March 23, 1937; m 1978, c 4. **Education:** Haverford Col, AB, 1958; Jefferson Med Col, MD, 1962; Univ Pa, PhD (microbiol), 1965. **Honors & Awards:** Parke-Davis Award for Experimental Pathology, 1976; NIH Merit Award, 1986; AAI Excellence in Mentoring Award, 2006. **Professional Experience:** Adj prof, Univ Calif, San Diego, 1979-1999; MEM STAFF, THE SCRIPPS RESEARCH INST., 1978-; prof path, Sch Med, Univ Pa, 1975-1978; from asst prof to assoc prof microbiol, Sch Med, Univ Pa, 1968-1975; Weizmann Inst, 1966-1967 & Nat Inst Med Res, London, 1967-1968; Am Cancer Soc res scholar, 1966-1968; Helen Hay Whitney Found res fel, 1963-1966; Fel immunol, Univ Pa, 1962-1966; NIH res fel, 1962-1963. **Memberships:** Am Asn Immunol; Am Asn Exp Pathologists. **Research Statement & Publications:** Structure, activity and synthesis of antibody. **Mailing Address:** Dept Immunol, The Scripps Research Inst, IMM-16, 10550 N Torrey Pines Rd, La Jolla, CA 92037-1092. **Fax:** 858-784-2691. **E-Mail:** nklinman@scripps.edu

KLINTWORTH, GORDON K, PATHOLOGY, ANATOMY. **Personal Data:** b Ft Victoria, Rhodesia, August 4, 1932; American citizen; m 1957, Felicity; c 3. **Education:** Univ Witwatersrand, BSc, 1954, MB, BCh, 1957, BSc (Hons), 1961, PhD (anat), 1966. **Honors & Awards:** Zimmerman Award; Alcon Res Award. **Professional Experience:** A C JOSEPH RES PROF OPHTHAL, MED CTR, DUKE UNIV, 1986-; PROF OPHTHAL, MED CTR, DUKE UNIV, 1981-; PROF PATH, MED CTR, DUKE UNIV, 1973-; Louis B Mayer scholar, 1972; from asst prof to assoc prof, Med Ctr, Duke Univ, 1966-1973; assoc, Med Ctr, Duke Univ, 1964-1966; registr, Neurol & Neurosurg, 1960-1961; sr house physician, psychiat, 1959-1960; intern med & surg, Johannesburg Hosp, 1958-1959; distinguished prof, Duke Univ. **Memberships:** AAAS; Am Asn Pathologists; Sigma Xi; Int Soc Neuropath; Tissue Cult Asn; NY Acad Sci; Int Acad Path; Am Acad Ophthal. **Research Statement & Publications:** Diseases of the eye and nervous system; infectious diseases; secondary effects of increased intracranial pressure; human genetics and diseases of the cornea. **Mailing Address:** Dept Path, Duke Univ Med Ctr, Box 3802, Durham, NC 27710-0001. **Fax:** 919-684-9225. **E-Mail:** klint001@mc.duke.edu

KLINZING, GEORGE ENGELBERT, CHEMICAL ENGINEERING. **Personal Data:** b Natrona Heights, Pa, March 22, 1938; m 1969, c 2. **Education:** Univ Pittsburgh, BS, 1959; Carnegie Inst Technol, MS, 1961, PhD (chem eng), 1963. **Professional Experience:** VICE PROVOST RES, UNIV PITTSBURGH, 1995-; assoc dean res, Univ Pittsburgh, beginning 1987; W K WHITEFORD PROF CHEM ENG, UNIV PITTSBURGH, 1981-; PROF CHEM & PETROL ENG, UNIV PITTSBURGH 1966-; hon prof, Cent Univ Ecuador, 1966; from asst prof to assoc prof, Univ Pittsburgh, 1963-1981; consult, Univ Develop Proj, Ecuador, 1963-1966; continuing edlectr, Prev Transp, Am Inst Chem Engrs. **Memberships:** Fel Am Inst Chem Engrs; Am Soc Eng Educ; Int Freight Pipeline Soc; Sigma Xi. **Research Statement & Publications:** Solid and gas flow systems; electrostatics; mass transfer in partially miscible systems; molecular hydrogen permeation; micrographic analysis of particles. **Mailing Address:** Office Provost, Univ Pittsburgh, 826 Cathedral Learning, Pittsburgh, PA 15213. **Fax:** 412-624-4618. **E-Mail:** klinzing@engrng.pitt.edu

KLIONSKY, BERNARD LEON, MEDICINE, PATHOLOGY. **Personal Data:** b Binghamton, NY, October 8, 1925; m 1950, c 4. **Education:** Harvard Univ, AB, 1947; Hahnemann Med Col, MD, 1952; Am Bd Path, dipl, 1957. **Professional Experience:** PROF EMER PATH, SCH MED, UNIV PITTSBURGH, as of 2004; prof path, Sch Med, Univ Pittsburgh, beginning 1971; assoc prof, Sch Med, Univ Pittsburgh, 1961-1970; from instr to assoc prof, Med Ctr, Univ Kans, 1956-1961; fel path, Med Ctr, Univ Kans, 1956-1957; Nat Cancer Inst trainee path, Am Cancer Soc clin fel, 1955-1957; Nat Cancer Inst trainee path, Med Ctr, Univ Kans, 1953-1955. **Memberships:** Am Cancer Soc. **Research Statement & Publications:** Intrauterine fetal growth retardation; yellow hyaline membranes. **Mailing Address:** Dept Path, Univ Pittsburgh, Rm A 543 Scaife, Pittsburgh, PA 15213-2582. **Fax:** 412-421-1252. **E-Mail:** klionsky@pitt.edu

KLIORE, ARVYDAS JOSEPH, PLANETARY SCIENCE, ATMOSPHERIC PHYSICS. **Personal Data:** b Kaunas, Lithuania, August 5, 1935; American citizen; m 1960, c 2. **Education:** Univ Ill, BS, 1956; Univ Mich, MS, 1957; Mich State Univ, PhD (elec eng), 1962. **Honors & Awards:** Except Sci Achievement Medal, NASA, 1972. **Professional Experience:** TEAM LEADER, JET PROPULSION LAB, CALIF INST TECHNOL, NASA, as of 2003; SR RES SCIENTIST, JET PROPULSION LAB, CALIF INST TECHNOL, NASA, 1987-; res scientist, Jet Propulsion Lab, Calif Inst Technol, NASA, 1966-1987; res specialist, Jet Propulsion Lab, Calif Inst Technol, NASA, 1964-1966; lectr, Univ Calif, Los Angeles, 1963-1964; sr res engr, Jet Propulsion Lab, Calif Inst Technol, NASA, 1962-1964; instr elec eng, Mich State Univ, 1961-1962; engr, Armour Res Found, Ill Inst Technol, 1957-1959. **Memberships:** AAAS; Am Astron Soc; Am Geophys Union; Comt Space Res; Int Astron Union. **Research Statement & Publications:** Space astronomy; radio propagation experiments to measure planetary atmospheres; spacecraft radio propagation experiments to study the atmospheres and ionospheres of planets and their satellites. **Mailing Address:** Jet Propulsion Lab, Calif Inst Technol, NASA, 4800 Oak Grove Dr MS 161-260 Off 161-239, Pasadena, CA 91109-8099. **Fax:** 818-393-4643. **E-Mail:** arvydas.kliore@jpl.nasa.gov

KLIOZE, OSCAR, PHARMACEUTICAL CHEMISTRY. **Personal Data:** b Baltimore, Md, January 2, 1919; m 1943, Olive; c Solomon S, Susanne B (Edelson) & Lawrence H. **Education:** George Wash Univ, BS, 1940; Va Polytech Inst, BS, 1944; Univ Md, PhD (pharmaceut chem), 1949. **Professional Experience:** RETIRED; vpres pharm res & anal serv, A H Robins Co Inc, 1958-1960 & prod develop & qual control, 1981-1984; lectr, Med Col Va, 1966-1975; dir, A H Robins Co Inc, 1958-1960 & prod develop & qual control, 1965-1981; dir prod develop, A H Robins Co Inc, 1958-1960 & prod develop & qual control, 1960-1964; res supvr, Chas Pfizer & Co Inc, 1954-1958; res chemist pharmaceut chem, Chas Pfizer & Co Inc, 1950-1954; res assoc biochem, Northwestern Univ, 1949-1950; jr biochemist, Manhattan Proj, US Army Engrs, 1944-1946; jr chemist, Baltimore Paint & Color Works Inc, 1940-1941 & Bur Plant Indust, USDA, 1941-1942 & 1946. **Memberships:** Am Chem Soc; Am Pharmaceut Asn; Am Inst Chem; Parenteral Drug Asn. **Research Statement & Publications:** Relationship of chemical structure to biological activity; pharmaceutical research and development; physiological effects of radiant energy; plant biochemistry; protein synthesis. **Mailing Address:** Two High Stepper Ct Apt 203, Baltimore, MD 21208.

KLIOZE, SOLOMON S, DIABETES & METABOLISM, ENDOCRINOLOGY. **Personal Data:** b Baltimore, Md, March 17, 1946; m 1969, Trudy; c Jason D. **Education:** Univ NC, BS, 1968; Columbia Univ, PhD (org chem), 1972. **Professional Experience:** Sr assoc dir, clinical development, Pfizer Global R&R, 1998-; ASSOC DIR CLIN RES, PFIZER CENT RES, 1992-; assoc dir, Hoechst-Roussel Pharmaceut, 1988-1992; asst dir clin res, Hoechst-Roussel Pharmaceut, 1985-1987; sr clin res assoc, Hoechst-Roussel Pharmaceut, 1984-1985; clin res assoc, Hoechst-Roussel Pharmaceut, 1982-1983; res assoc, Hoechst-Roussel Pharmaceut, 1979-1982; sr res chemist, Hoechst-Roussel Pharmaceut, 1973-1979; postdoctoral res fel, Yale Univ, 1972-1973. **Memberships:** Am Diabetes Asn; Endocrine Soc; Am Soc Microbiol; Am Chem Soc. **Research Statement & Publications:** Clinical trials of new drugs on humans, primarily in the areas of diabetes, diabetes complications and metabolism; oncology, reproductive endocrinology and infectious diseases. **Mailing Address:** Pfizer Global Res & Development, 50 Pequot Ave MS-6025-A4234, New London, CT 06320. **Fax:** 860-715-9189. **E-Mail:** solomon_s_klioze@groton.pfizer.com

KLIP, AMIRA, BIOLOGY. **Education:** Univ Mex, PhD, 1976. **Professional Experience:** PROF BIOCHEM, UNIV TORONTO, as of 2006. **Mailing Address:** Univ Toronto, One King's Col Cir Med Sci Bldg, Toronto, ON M5S 1A8, Can. **Fax:** 416-813-5028. **E-Mail:** amira@sickkids.ca

KLIP, DOROTHEA A, FUNCTIONAL ANALYSIS, APPLIED MATHEMATICS. **Personal Data:** b Hague, Neth, September 27, 1921; m 1955, c 4. **Education:** State Univ Utrecht, Dr(theoret physics), 1962. **Professional Experience:** PROF EMER PHYSIOL & BIOPHYS, UNIV ALA, BIRMINGHAM, as of 2004; assoc prof physiol & biophys, Univ Ala, Birmingham, beginning 1973; asst prof info sci, Univ Ala, Birmingham, beginning 1971; asst prof, physiol, Univ Ala, Birmingham, 1963-1973; reviewer, NSF, Inst Elec & Electronics Engrs & J ComputAppl Math. **Memberships:** AAAS; Asn Comput Mach; Sigma Xi; Soc Indust & Appl Math; Math Asn Am. **Research Statement & Publications:** Design and implementation of algorithms for the solution of nonlinear (polynomial) equations; symbolic algebraic manipulation by computer. **Mailing Address:** 3137 Dolly Ridge Dr, Birmingham, AL 35243-5705.

KLIP, WILLEM, BIOPHYSICS. **Personal Data:** b Rotterdam, Neth, November 26, 1917; American citizen; m 1955, c 4. **Education:** Univ Utrecht, MD, 1945, PhD (bact), 1951, PhD (theoret physics), 1955, DSc(physics), 1962. **Professional Experience:** Emer prof physics, Univ Ala, Birmingham, 1988-1998; prof med physics, Dept Physiol Med & Physics, 1958-1988; Staff mem Dr H C Burger, Dept Med Physics, Univ Utrecht, 1953-1958. **Research Statement & Publications:** Medical and theoretical physics. **Mailing Address:** 3137 Dolly Ridge Dr, Birmingham, AL 35243.

KLIPHARDT, RAYMOND A(DOLPH), ENGINEERING SCIENCES. **Personal Data:** b Chicago, Ill, March 18, 1917; m 1945, Rhoda Joan Anderson; c Janis (Emery), Judith (Ecklund), Jill (White), Joan (Quinn) & Jennifer (Miller). **Education:** Ill Inst Technol, BS, 1938, MS, 1948. **Professional Experience:** PROF EMER ENG SCI & APPL MATH, NORTHWESTERN UNIV, 1987-; chmn dept, Northwestern Univ, 1978-1987; prof, Northwestern Univ, 1970-1987; from assoc prof to prof eng sci, Northwestern Univ, 1958-1970; from asst prof to assoc prof eng graphics, Northwestern Univ, 1946-1958; asst civil eng, Northwestern Univ, 1945-1946; asst math, Ill Inst Technol, 1943-1944; Instr graphics & math, NPark Col, 1938-1943; campus coordr, Khartoum Proj, USAID; consult, Appl Math Div, Argonne Nat Lab. **Memberships:** AAAS; Am Soc Eng Educ; Asn Comput Mach; Am Acad Mech. **Research Statement & Publications:** Abstract geometry; computer automation. **Mailing Address:** Dept Eng Sci & Appl Math, Northwestern Univ, Evanston, IL 60208.

KLIPPEL, JOHN HOWARD, MEDICAL RESEARCH. **Personal Data:** b Warren, Ohio, October 15, 1944; m 1967, c 2. **Education:** Bowling Green State Univ, BA, 1966; Univ Cincinnati, MD, 1970; Am Bd Internal Med, cert, 1974. **Honors & Awards:** Borden res award, Univ Cincinnati, 1970. **Professional Experience:** PRES & CEO, ARTHRITIS FOUND, 2003-; clin dir, Nat Inst Arthritis & Musculoskeletal & Skin Dis, bethesda, beginning 1987; clin asst prof med, Med Ctr, Georgetown Univ, 1985-; sr investr, Arthritis & Rheumatism Br, 1976-1987. **Memberships:** Am Col Physicians; Am Col Rheumatology. **Research Statement & Publications:** Numerous publications; medicine. **Mailing Address:** Arthritis Found, PO Box 7669, Atlanta, GA 30357-0669.

KLIPPERT, JOHN C, MATHEMATICS. **Education:** Ohio State Univ, MS, PhD. **Professional Experience:** PROF, JAMES MADISON UNIV, VA, as of 2005. **Mailing Address:** Math Dept, James Madison Univ, Burruss Hall Rm 112 MSC 7803, Harrisonburg, VA 22807. **Fax:** 540-568-6857. **E-Mail:** klippejc@jmu.edu

KLIPSCH, PAUL W, ELECTRICAL ENGINEERING. **Personal Data:** b Elkhart, Ind. **Education:** NMex State Univ, BSEE, 1926. **Honorary Degrees:** LLD, NMex State Univ, 1981; DSc, Ark State Univ, 1995. **Professional Experience:** RETIRED; founder, Klipsch & Assocs, 1946-1988; geophysicist, 1934-1941. **Memberships:** Fel Inst Elec & Electronics Engrs; Acoust Soc Am. **Research Statement & Publications:** Patents on firearms, geophysics and audio loudspeakers; contributed articles to professional journals. **Mailing Address:** Klipsch & Assocs, PO Box 688, Hope, AR 71802.

KLIPSTEIN, DAVID HAMPTON, ENGINEERING MANAGEMENT, ALTERNATIVE ENERGY UTILIZATION. **Personal Data:** b New York, NY, July 25, 1930; m 1972, c 8. **Education:** Princeton Univ, BSE, 1952; Mass Inst Technol, SM, 1956, ScD, 1963. **Professional Experience:** PRES & CHIEF EXEC OFFICER, REACTION DESIGN INC, as of 2004; dir biphase energy systs, Res Cottrell Inc, 1980-; dir advan technol corp develop, Res Cottrell Inc, 1976-1980; vpres particulate opers, Air Pollution Control Group, 1974-1976; mem, Environ Adv Comt, Fed Energy Admin, 1974-1976; vpres planning & develop oper, Air Pollution Control Group, 1973-1974; bus develop mgr, Res Cottrell Inc, 1972-1973; mkt mgr, Trade Paint Intermediates, 1971-1972; prod mgr acrylate monomers & polymers, Develop Div, 1970-1971; mkt develop mgr, Develop Div, 1969-1970; mkt rep, Union Carbide Chem Corp, 1962-1969; dir, Bound Brook Sta, Sch Chem Eng Practice, Mass Inst Technol, 1958-1960; res engr, Am Cyanamid Corp, 1951-1954; vpres corp develop, Biosym Technol. **Memberships:** Am Chem Soc; Am Inst Chem Eng; Geothermal Resources Coun. **Research Statement & Publications:** Commercial development; optimization of combustion processes, precombustion fuel cleaning, high efficiency energy conversion systems, load leveling controls. **Mailing Address:** Reaction Design Inc, Ste D-209, 6440 Lusk Blvd, San Diego, CA 92121. **Fax:** 858-550-1925.

KLIR, GEORGE JIRI, HISTORY & PHILOSOPHY OF SCIENCE, MATHEMATICS GENERAL. **Personal Data:** b Prague, Czech, April 22, 1932; American citizen; m 1962, Milena; c John & Jane. **Education:** Tech Univ, Prague, MSEE, 1957; Czech Acad Sci, PhD (comput sci), 1964. **Honorary Degrees:** Dr, Univ Econs, Czech, 1994, Techn Univ Brno, Moravia, Czech Techn Univ, Prague. **Honors & Awards:** Advancing Gen Systs Res Award, Neth Soc Systs Res, 1976; Outstanding Contribution to Systs Res & Cybernet Award, Austrian Soc Cybernet Studies; Gold Medal of Bernard Bolzano, Czech Acad Sci, 1994; Lotfi A Zadeh Best Paper Award, 1994; Distinguished Leadership Award, Int Soc Syst, Sci, 1996; Suny Univ Award for Excellence in Res, 1996; Arnold Kaufmann's Gold Medal Prize for "excellence in uncertainty res", 2000; Soc Comp Anticipatory Syst Award for "Outstanding Sci Work on Anticipatory & Intelligent Syst". **Professional Experience:** DISTINGUISHED PROF, T J WATSON SCH, 1984-; CHMN DEPT, SCH ADVAN TECHNOL, STATE UNIV NY, BINGHAMTON, 1976-; Japan Soc Prom Sci fel, 1980; Neth Inst Advan Studies fel, 1975-1976, 1982-1983; ed-in-chief, Int J Gen Systs, 1974; from assoc prof to prof systs sci, T J Watson Sch, 1969-1984; IBM Systs Res Inst fel, 1969; assoc prof elec eng, Fairleigh Dickinson Univ, 1968-1969; lectr comput sci, Univ Calif, Los Angeles, 1966-1968; lectr elec eng, Univ Baghdad, 1964-1966; lectr, Charles Univ, 1962-1964; ed, Czech Acad Sci, Prague, 1962-1963; res asst, Res Inst Telecommun, Prague, 1951-1952. **Memberships:** Fel Inst Elec & Electronics Engrs; Soc Gen Systs Res (pres, 1981); Int Fed Systs Res (pres, 1980-1984); Am Fuzzy Info Processing Soc (pres, 1988-1991); fel Intern Fuzzy Syst Asn (pres, 1993-1995). **Research Statement & Publications:** Switching and automata theory; logical design of digital computers; general systems theory and methodology; computer architecture; discrete mathematics; generalized information theory; intelligent systems. **Mailing Address:** State Univ NY, Dept Systs Sci & Indust Eng, EB L16 TJ Watson Sch, Binghamton, NY 13902-6000. **Fax:** 607-777-2577. **E-Mail:** gklir@binghamton.edu

KLISSLINGER, LEONARD S, PHYSICS. **Education:** Indiana Univ, PhD. **Professional Experience:** PROF PHYS, CARNEGIE-MELLON UNIV, as of 2002. **Mailing Address:** Physics Dept, Carnegie-Mellon Univ, Pittsburgh, PA 15213. **Fax:** 412-681-0648. **E-Mail:** kisslinger@kelvin.phys.cmu.edu

KLITGAARD, HOWARD MAYNARD, PHYSIOLOGY, ENDOCRINOLOGY. **Personal Data:** b Harlan, Iowa, October 16, 1924; m 1945, Anna Plazova; c Andrew G, Margaret A, Patricia B, Michael L & Diana C. **Education:** Univ Iowa, BA, 1949, MS, 1950, PhD (physiol), 1953. **Professional Experience:** Emer prof, Marquette Univ Sch Dent, 1990-; ADJ PROF, MED COL WIS, 1978-; chmn basic sci, Marquette Univ Sch Dent, 1978-1990; vchmn dept, Med Col Wis, 1967-1978; asst chmn dept, Med Col Wis, 1961-1966; Consult, Vet Admin Hosp, Wood, Wis, 1957-1989; from instr to prof, Med Col Wis, 1953-1978; Instr physiol, Univ Iowa, 1951-1953. **Memberships:** AAAS; Endocrine Soc; Am Physiol Soc; Soc Exp Biol & Med; Int Asn Dent Res. **Research Statement & Publications:** Physiology and biochemistry of the thyroid hormone, endocrines and metabolism; radioisotope methodology. **Mailing Address:** 9073 N Silver Brook Lane, Milwaukee, WI 53223-2209.

KLITZ, WILLIAM, BIOLOGY. **Education:** PhD, 1972. **Professional Experience:** ASSOC RES SCIENTIST, CHILDRENS HOSP OAKLAND RES INST, CA, as of 2003. **Mailing Address:** Children's Hosp Oakland Res Inst, 5700 Martin Luther King Jr Way, Oakland, CA 94609.

KLITZMAN, BRUCE, MICROCIRCULATION, PLASTIC & RECONSTRUCTIVE SURGERY. **Personal Data:** b Dayton, Ohio, November 4, 1951; American citizen; m 1980, Hardee; c Rachel & Page. **Education:** Duke Univ, BS, 1974; Univ Va, PhD (physiol), 1979. **Honors & Awards:** First Prize Investr, Plastic Surg Educ Found, 1988. **Professional Experience:** SR DIR, KENAN PLASTIC SURG RES LABS, DUKE UNIV MED CTR, as of 2003; ASST RES PROF, PLASTIC & MAXILLOFACIAL SURG & BIOMED ENG, DUKE UNIV MED CTR, as of 2003; ASSOC PROF BIOCHEM ENG, PLASTIC

SURG RES LABS, 1993-; assoc ed, J Reconstructive Microsurg, 1988-; study sect reviewer, NIH, 1985-; dir, Plastic Surg Res Labs, beginning 1985; ASST MED RES PROF PLASTIC SURG & PHYSIOL(CELL BIOL), DUKE UNIV MED CTR, 1985-; vis scientist, Burroughs-Wellcome Found, 1985; vis prof, Univ Manchester, UK, 1985; mem, Mem Comt, Microcirculatory Soc, 1982-1985; from asst prof to assoc prof physiol, La State Univ Med Ctr, Shreveport, 1982-1985; young investr award, European Soc Microcirculation, 1980; res assoc microcirculation, Univ Ariz, 1979-1981. **Memberships:** Microcirculatory Soc (secy 1993-); Am Physiol Soc; Plastic Surg Res Coun; Am Heart Asn; European Soc Microcirculation; Soc Biomat. **Research Statement & Publications:** Regulation of microcirculation and oxygenation of tissue; adaptation of microcirculation to different environments; hyperbaric physiol; biomaterials; microvascular prostheses; soft tissue implants; pressure sore prevention. **Mailing Address:** Duke Univ Med Ctr, Box 3906 Rm 019 Res Park 4, Durham, NC 27710-3906. **Fax:** 919-681-2670. **E-Mail:** klitz@duke.edu

KLOBUCAR, WILLIAM DIRK, ORGANOPHOSPHORUS CHEMISTRY. **Personal Data:** b Highland Park, Mich, March 16, 1953; m 1975, Judith; c Megan S & Adam D. **Education:** Univ Detroit, BS, 1975; Ohio State Univ, PhD (chem), 1981. **Professional Experience:** SR RES & DEVELOP SPECIALIST, ALBEMARLE CORP, 1981-. **Memberships:** Am Chem Soc. **Research Statement & Publications:** Synthesis-organic, organometallic, organophosphorus, orthoalkylation of phenols and aromatic amines. **Mailing Address:** Almerable Corp, Baton Rouge, LA 70817.

KLOBUCHAR, RICHARD LOUIS, NAVAL ANALYSIS. **Personal Data:** b Chicago, Ill, October 15, 1948; m 1971. **Education:** Univ Ill, BS, 1970; Carnegie-Mellon Univ, MS, 1972, PhD (chem), 1975. **Professional Experience:** DIR ADV TECHNOL, INC, 1981-; mem prof staff, Ctr Naval Analyses, 1977-1981; Res assoc nuclear chem, Brookhaven Nat Lab, 1975-1977. **Memberships:** Am Chem Soc; Am Nuclear Soc; Am Phys Soc; Sigma Xi. **Research Statement & Publications:** Scientific analysis of naval weapons systems; analytical support of fleet activities; applications of positronium chemistry; high energy nuclear reactions. **Mailing Address:** 758 Suffolk Lane, Virginia Beach, VA 23452.

KLOBUKOWSKI, MARIUSZ ANDRZEJ, MOLECULAR STRUCTURES & PROPERTIES. **Personal Data:** b Wroclaw, Poland, March 6, 1948; Canadian citizen; m 1984, c Anna & Emily. **Education:** NCopernicus Univ, Torun, Poland, BSc, 1971, PhD (physics), 1978. **Professional Experience:** PROF CHEM, UNIV ALTA, 2000-; assoc prof chem, Univ Alta, 1994-2000; asst prof chem, Univ Alta, 1989-1994; programmer analyst comput sci, Univ Alta, 1988-1989; res assoc, Univ Alta, 1983-1988; I W Killam fel, Univ Alta, 1980-1983; asst prof chem, NCopernicus Univ, Poland, 1978-1981. **Memberships:** Chem Inst Can. **Research Statement & Publications:** Development of Gaussian basis sets for the studies of molecular structure and properties; calculations of the molecular structure and properties of molecules in their excited electronic states; and in confinement. **Mailing Address:** Dept Chem, Univ Alta, Edmonton, AB T6G 2G2, Can. **Fax:** 780-492-8231. **E-Mail:** mariusz.klobukowski@ualberta.ca

KLOCK, BENNY LEROY, DIGITAL MAPPING, RESEARCH ADMINISTRATION. **Personal Data:** b Washington, DC, October 29, 1934; m 1976, Millie; c Mark S, Lorri A & Brian L. **Education:** Cornell Univ, BA, 1956, MS, 1960; Georgetown Univ, PhD (astron), 1964. **Honors & Awards:** NSF int grant, 1974; Distinguished Civilian Serv Award, 1989. **Professional Experience:** SR CONSULT, ADV MAPPING CONCEPTS, 1989-; phys scientist, Defense Mapping Agency, 1985-1989; geodesist, Defense Mapping Agency, 1984-1985; chief instrumentation br, US Naval Observ, 1976-1984; dir, Northern Transit Circle Div, 1969-1976; tech asst dir six-inch transit circle div, 1960-1969. **Memberships:** Am Astron Soc; Int Astron Union. **Research Statement & Publications:** Design and development of transit circle instrumentation; microcomputer systems; determination of star positions; automation of telescopes; electro-optics system design; advanced weapon system requirements for digital mapping data; digital mapping. **Mailing Address:** 3977 Holleyberry Lane, Milton, FL 32583. **E-Mail:** blklock@mchsi.com

KLOCK, GLEN ORVAL, FOREST SOILS. **Personal Data:** b Portland, Ore, August 26, 1937; m 1958, c 4. **Education:** Ore State Univ, BS, 1959, PhD (soil physics), 1968, MBA, 2004; Iowa State Univ, MS, 1963. **Professional Experience:** FOUNDER & PRINCIPAL, AGBASE INC & WESTERN RESOURCES ANAL INC, as of 2005; PRIN SCIENTIST, WESTERN RESOURCES ANAL, 1982-; prin res soil scientist, Pac Northwest Forest & Range Exp Sta, USDA Forest Serv, 1968-1982; res assoc soil physics, Ore State Univ, 1964-1967; pres, Western Resources Anal Inc. **Memberships:** Am Soc Agron; Soil Sci Soc Am; Soil Conserv Soc Am; Int Soil Sci Soc; Am Forestry assoc. **Research Statement & Publications:** Water resource and plant nutrient management for maintaining and enhancing the productivity of forest ecosystems in the western United States; use of image processing for development of geographic information system data bases for natural resources management. **Mailing Address:** AgBASE Inc, Confluence Technol Ctr 133 285 Technol Ctr Way, Wenatchee, WA 98801. **Fax:** 509-662-7678.

KLOCK, HAROLD F(RANCIS), ELECTRICAL ENGINEERING. **Personal Data:** b Miami Beach, Fla, March 21, 1929; m 1955, c 3. **Education:** Northwestern Univ, BS, 1952, MS, 1954, PhD (elec eng), 1956. **Professional Experience:** PROF EMER ELEC ENG, OHIO UNIV, 1994-; prof elec eng, Ohio Univ, 1966-1994; systs engr, Bailey Meter Co, Ohio, 1964-1966; prof lectr, Case Western Res Univ, 1962-1964; asst prof, Case Western Res Univ, 1956-1962; Lectr elec eng, Northwestern Univ, 1956; consult, Nat Cash Register Co; consult, Curtiss-Wright Corp; consult, Reliance Elec & Mfg Co. **Memberships:** Inst Elec & Electronics Engrs; Asn Comput Mach; Soc Indust & Appl Math. **Research Statement & Publications:** Feedback control systems; switching theory. **Mailing Address:** Dept Elec & Comput Eng, Ohio Univ, Athens, OH 45701-2979.

KLOCK, JOHN W, SANITARY & CIVIL ENGINEERING. **Personal Data:** b Orange, NJ, November 12, 1928; m 1953, c 2. **Education:** Southern Calif Univ, BE, 1951; Univ Calif, Berkeley, MS, 1956, PhD (sanit eng), 1960. **Professional Experience:** PROF EMER ENG, ARIZ STATE UNIV, as of 2004; Off Surgeon Gen, 1961- & Honeywell Corp, 1980-1984; prof eng, Ariz State Univ, beginning 1960; Consult, Commun Dis Ctr, 1960-; Consult, Ariz Health Planning Authority, USPHS, 1951-1955. **Memberships:** Am Water Works Asn; Water Pollution Control Fedn. **Research Statement & Publications:** Communicable disease control; water pollution; waste water reclamation. **Mailing Address:** 2626 N 58th Pl, Scottsdale, AZ 85257-1010.

KLOCKE, FRANCIS J, CARDIOLOGY. **Education:** Manhatten Col (Biol), BS, 1956; State Univ New York Buffalo, MD, 1960. **Professional Experience:** DIR, FEINBERG CARDIOVASC RES INST & PROF MED, MED CTR, NORTHWESTERN UNIV, 1991-; albert & elizabeth rekate prof, Univ Buffalo, Med & Cardio Vasc Dis, 1983-1991; prof physiol, Univ Buffalo, 1978-1991; chief, Div Cardiol, Univ Buffalo, 1976-1991. **Mailing Address:** Northwestern Univ, 303 E Chicago Ave Tarry 12-703, Chicago, IL 60611-3008. **Fax:** 312-503-0137. **E-Mail:** f-klocke@northwestern.edu

KLOCKE, ROBERT ALBERT, PULMONARY DISEASES, PULMONARY PHYSIOLOGY. **Personal Data:** b Buffalo, NY, October 4, 1936; c 3. **Education:** Manhattan Col, BS, 1958; State Univ NY, Buffalo, MD, 1962. **Professional Experience:** CHMN, DEPT MED, STATE UNIV NY, BUFFALO, 1996-; PROF PHYSIOL, STATE UNIV NY, BUFFALO, 1981-; PROF MED, STATE UNIV NY, BUFFALO, 1978-; chief pulmonary div, dept med, 1977-1995; from asst prof to assoc prof physiol, State Univ NY, Buffalo, 1976-1981; from asst prof to assoc prof med, State Univ NY, Buffalo, 1971-1978; mem attend staff, E J Meyer Mem Hosp, Buffalo, 1970-; res asst prof med, State Univ NY, Buffalo, 1970-1971; Chief pulmonary lab, Walter Reed Gen Hosp, Wash, DC, 1963-1966. **Memberships:** Am Physiol Soc; Am Thoracic Soc. **Research Statement & Publications:** Pulmonary gas exchange; particularly the rates of chemical reactions of carbon dioxide and oxygen in blood. **Mailing Address:** Dept Med & Physiol, State Univ NY, 462 Grider St, Buffalo, NY 14215. **Fax:** 716-898-3024. **E-Mail:** rklocke@ams.ecmc.edu

KLOET, WILLEM M, NUCLEAR PHYSICS. **Personal Data:** b Neth. **Education:** Univ Utrecht, PhD (theoret physics), 1973. **Professional Experience:** PROF THEORET PHYSICS, RUTGERS UNIV, as of 1999; assoc prof theoret physics, Rutgers Univ, beginning 1982; asst prof, Rutgers Univ, 1977-1982; Univ Md, 1973-1975 & Los Alamos Sci Lab, 1975-1977; Res assoc theoret physics, Inst Fisica Teorica, Sao Paulo, 1968-1970. **Memberships:** Am Phys Soc; AAAS. **Research Statement & Publications:** Theoretical nuclear physics. **Mailing Address:** Dept Physics & Astron, Rutgers Univ, 136 Frelinghuysen Rd, Piscataway, NJ 08854. **Fax:** 732-445-4343. **E-Mail:** kloet@physics.rutgers.edu

KLOETZEL, JOHN ARTHUR, CELL BIOLOGY, PROTOZOOLOGY. **Personal Data:** b Cambridge, Mass, March 21, 1941; m 1962, Judith; c Jeffrey, Steven, Jennifer & Melanie. **Education:** Univ Southern Calif, BA, 1962; Johns Hopkins Univ, PhD (biol), 1967. **Professional Experience:** Mem exec comt, Soc Protozool, 1994-; vis assoc prof biochem, Johns Hopkins Univ Sch Med, 1987; pres, Chesapeake Soc Electron Micros, 1980-1981; fel, Alexander von Humboldt Found, WGer, 1978; ASSOC PROF BIOL, UNIV MD, BALTIMORE CO, 1975-; asst prof, Univ MD, Baltimore CO, 1970-1975; NIH fel biol, Univ Colo, 1967-1970. **Memberships:** Soc Protozool; Am Soc Cell Biol; Micros Soc Am. **Research Statement & Publications:** Fine-structural aspects of cellular function, development and differentiation; Morphogenesis and post-conjugant development in ciliated protozoans, form and function of the ciliate cytoskeleton. **Mailing Address:** Univ Md, Dept Biol Sci, Catonsville, MD 21228. **Fax:** 410-455-3875. **E-Mail:** kloetzel@umbc.edu

KLOETZEL, MILTON CARL, ORGANIC CHEMISTRY. **Personal Data:** b Detroit, Mich, August 28, 1913; m 1938, Elizabeth; c John, James, Paul & Mark. **Education:** Univ Mich, BS, 1934, PhD (org chem), 1937. **Professional Experience:** PROF EMER, DEPT LETT, ARTS & SCI, UNIV SOUTHERN CALIF, as of 2004; ACAD VPRES EMER, UNIV SOUTHERN CALIF, 1975-; acad vpres, 1970-1975; vpres res & grad affairs, dean, Grad Sch, 1967-1970; dean, Grad Sch, 1958-1968; from asst prof to prof, Univ Southern Calif, 1945-1958; from asst prof to assoc prof, DePauw Univ, 1941-1945; instr, Harvard Univ, 1938-1941; Du Pont fel chem, Univ Mich, 1937-1938. **Memberships:** Am Chem Soc. **Research Statement & Publications:** Chemistry of polycyclic and heterocyclic compounds; Diels-Alder reaction; chemistry of nitroparaffins. **Mailing Address:** Dept Lett, Arts & Sci, Univ Southern Calif, Los Angeles, CA 90089.

KLOHS, WAYNE D, BIOCHEMISTRY, CELL BIOLOGY. **Education:** Ind State Univ, PhD (cell biol), 1977. **Professional Experience:** SR SCIENTIST, WARNER-LAMBERT CO, 1983-. **Mailing Address:** Dept Cancer Res Warner-Lambert Co, 2800 Plymouth Rd, Ann Arbor, MI 48105-2430. **Fax:** 734-996-1480.

KLOKHOLM, ERIK, SOLID STATE PHYSICS. **Personal Data:** b Nykobing, Denmark, March 13, 1922; American citizen; m 1943. **Education:** Mass Inst Technol, BS, 1951; Temple Univ, PhD (physics), 1960. **Professional Experience:** RES PROJ MGR, MFR RES LABS, DATA SYSTS DIV, IBM CORP, 1973-; res staff mem, Thomas J Watson Res Ctr, 1962-1973; assoc prof physics, State Univ NY Col Ceramics, Alfred Univ, 1961-1962; res physicist, Moorehead Patterson Res Ctr, Am Mach & Foundry Co, 1959-1961; From res asst to head struct & metals br, Labs Res & Develop, Franklin Inst, 1951-1959. **Memberships:** NY Acad Sci. **Research Statement & Publications:** Structure and properties of solids, particularly thin metallic films; crystallographic aspects of solid state physics. **Mailing Address:** 64 Willard Terr, Stamford, CT 06903.

KLOMBERS, NORMAN, ADMINISTRATION. **Personal Data:** b New York, NY, January 28, 1923; m 1955, Gloria; c 2. **Education:** NY Col Podiat Med, DPM, 1944. **Professional Experience:** RETIRED; exec dir, Anxiety Dis Asn, 1991-1993; exec dir, Am Podiatric Med Asn, 1980-1990; dir div sci affairs, Am Podiatric Med Asn, 1978-1980; mem, Health Comt, CityLong Beach, NY, 1976; mem, adv comm Health & Hosp Corp, New York, 1970-1977; dir peer rev activ & dir prof serv, Podiatry Soc State NY, 1969-1978; Fac mem & clin instr, New York Col Podiat Med, 1944-1978; practr podiatric med, New York, NY, 1944-1968. **Memberships:** Am Col Foot Orthopedists; Am Bd Podiatric Orthopedics; Nat Acad Pract; Acad Podiatric Med. **Mailing Address:** 11213 Joshua Tree Pl, North Potomac, MD 20878.

KLOMP, EDWARD D, MECHANICAL ENGINEERING, FLUID MECHANICS. **Personal Data:** b Detroit, Mich, October 18, 1930; m 1959, Hildegard Schuchardt; c Eric, Kurt & Karl. **Education:** Wayne State Univ, BS, 1952, MS, 1953. **Professional Experience:** SR STAFF RES ENGR, RES LABS, GEN MOTORS CORP, WARREN, 1980-; staff res engr, Gen Motors Corp, 1977-1980; sr res engr, Gen Motors Corp, 1965-1977; assoc sr res engr, Gen Motors Corp, 1959-1965; Instr, Wayne State Univ, 1955-1965; Res engr, Gen Motors Corp, 1953-1959. **Memberships:** Am Soc Mech Engrs; Soc Automotive Engrs; Sigma Xi. **Research Statement & Publications:** Fluid mechanics relating to turbomachinery and internal combustion engines; author of 7 publications; 46 US patents. **Mailing Address:** 36237 Acton Dr, Clinton Township, MI 48035.

KLOMPARENS, KAREN L, PLANT SCIENCE, ELECTRON OPTICS. **Personal Data:** b East Lansing, Mich, September 17, 1950. **Education:** Mich State Univ, BS, 1972, MS, 1974, PhD (bot & electron optics), 1977. **Professional Experience:** DEAN, GRAD SCH, MICH STATE UNIV, as of 2006; fulbright fel, Cambridge Univ, 1994; PROF ELECTRON OPTICS, DEPTS BOT & PLANT PATH ENTOM, MICH STATE UNIV, 1985-; dir, Ctr Electron Optics, 1980-; asst prof, Ctr Electron Optics, 1980-1985. **Memberships:** Electron Micros Soc Am; Am Phytopath Soc; AAAS; Am Inst Biol Sci; Mycol Soc Am. **Research Statement & Publications:** Ultrastructural and analytical electron microscopy methods relevant to plant science; applications to plant host pathogen vector relationships, fungal morphology and spore development. **Mailing Address:** Dept Entomol, Mich State Univ, 118 Linton Hall, East Lansing, MI 48824-1044. **E-Mail:** kklompar@msu.edu

KLOMPEN, J S H, SYSTEMATICS, PARASITOLOGY. **Personal Data:** b Roggel, Neth, July 3, 1956; m 1989. **Education:** Cath Univ Nijmegen, Neth, Doctoral, 1980; Univ Mich, Ann Arbor, PhD (biol), 1990. **Professional Experience:** CUR, OHIO STATE UNIV ACAROLOGY COLLECTION, as of 2003; ASSOC PROF, DEPT ENTOMOL, OHIO STATE UNIV, 2002-; asst Prof Entomol, Ohio State Univ, 1996-2002; res assoc, Colo State Univ,

1994-1996; res assoc, Ga Southern Univ, 1990-1994. **Memberships:** Acarological Soc Am; Entom Soc Am; Soc Syst Biol. **Research Statement & Publications:** Phylogenetic systematics and the role of phylogeny in the evolution of ecological and life-history characteristics of parasitic mites and ticks. **Mailing Address:** Dept Entomol, Ohio State Univ, 1315 Kinnear Rd, Columbus, OH 43212-1192. **Fax:** 614-292-7774. **E-Mail:** klompen.1@osu.edu

KLONER, ROBERT A, CARDIOLOGY, HYPERTENSION. **Personal Data:** b Buffalo, NY, October 8, 1949; m 1977, Judith; c Alissa & Susan. **Education:** Northwestern Univ, BS, 1971, PhD (exp path), 1974, MD, 1975. **Honors & Awards:** Sheard-Sanford Award, Am Soc Clin Pathologists, 1976; Continuing Serv Award, Am Heart Asn, 1991. **Professional Experience:** Mem, Cardiovasc Study Sect A, NIH, 1995-; fel, Coun Clin Cardiol, 1991-; PROF MED, UNIV SOUTHERN CALIF, 1988-; DIR RES, HEART INST & HOSP GOOD SAMARITAN, 1988-; estab investr award, Am Heart Asn, 1986; prof med, Wayne State Univ Med Sch, 1985-1988; assoc physician, Brigham & Women's Hosp, 1982-1984; asst prof to assof prof, resident & cardiol fel, Brigham & Women's Hosp, Harvard Med Sch, 1979-1986; jr assoc physician, Brigham & Women's Hosp, 1979-1982; Medintern, resident & cardiol fel, Brigham & Women's Hosp, Harvard Med Sch, 1975-1979. **Memberships:** Am Heart Asn; Am Soc Clin Invest; fel Am Col Cardiol Established Investr Award, Am Heart Asn, 1981. **Research Statement & Publications:** Pathophysiology of heart during is chemial/reperfusion; studies of stunned myocardrion, no-reflow phenomenon, hibernating myocardium, preconditioning phenomenon; studies of gene therapy of the heart; clinical studies involving thrombolysis, hypertension and triggers of heart disease. **Mailing Address:** Heart Inst Good Samaritan Hosp, 1225 Wilshire Blvd, Los Angeles, CA 90017. **Fax:** 213-977-4107. **E-Mail:** rkloner@goodsam.org

KLONTZ, EVERETT EARL, PHYSICS. **Personal Data:** b Akron, Ohio, September 28, 1921; m 1942, c 3. **Education:** Kent State Univ, BS, 1942; Univ Ill, MS, 1943; Purdue Univ, PhD (physics), 1952. **Professional Experience:** PROF EMER PHYSICS, PURDUE UNIV, as of 2005; assoc prof physics, Purdue Univ, W Lafayette, 1962-1992; res assoc & asst prof, Purdue Univ, W Lafayette, 1952-1962; asst, Purdue Univ, W Lafayette, 1946-1952; instr, Bowling Green State Univ, 1944; asst physics, Univ Ill, 1942-1944. **Memberships:** Am Phys Soc; Am Asn Physics Teachers. **Research Statement & Publications:** Effects of high energy particle irradiations on physical properties of crystals. **Mailing Address:** Dept Physics, Purdue Univ, West Lafayette, IN 47907-1396.

KLOOS, WESLEY F, GENETICS. **Professional Experience:** PROF EMER, DEPT GENETICS, NC STATE UNIV, as of 2005. **Memberships:** Am Soc Microbiol. **Mailing Address:** Dept Genetics, Gardner Hall, NC State Univ, Raleigh, NC 27695-0001.

KLOOSTERMAN, PETER, MATHEMATICS. **Education:** Mich State Univ, BS, 1973; Univ Wis, MS, 1980, PhD, 1984. **Professional Experience:** EXEC ASSOC DEAN & PROF MATHS, SCH EDUC, IND UNIV, as of 2006. **Mailing Address:** Ind Univ Educ3058, WW Wright Educ Bldg Rm 4140, Bloomington, IN 47405. **Fax:** 812-856-8088. **E-Mail:** klooster@indiana.edu

KLOPATEK, JEFFREY MATTHEW, ECOSYSTEM ECOLOGY, LANDSCAPE ECOLOGY. **Personal Data:** b Milwaukee, Wis, December 5, 1944; m 1984, c 2. **Education:** Univ Wis, Milwaukee, BS, 1971, MS, 1974; Univ Okla, PhD (bot), 1978. **Professional Experience:** Fulbright scholar, 1990-1991; vis scientist, US Environ Protection assoc, 1990; Bd mem-prof cert, Ecol Soc Am, 1981-; PROF & RES ECOLOGIST, PLANT BIOL, ARIZ STATE UNIV, 1981-; Consult, Forest Serv, USDA, 1981-; lectr, Univ Tenn, 1980-1981; chmn, Munic Planning Comn, Farragut, Tenn, 1980-1981; res ecologist, Environ Sci Div, Oak Ridge Nat Lab, 1976-1981; Consult, Elec Power Res Inst, AEC-Energy Res & Develop Admin, 1973-1974; res assoc ecol, Okla Biol Surv, 1973-1976. **Memberships:** Ecol Soc Am; Int Asn Landscape Ecol; Am Inst Biol Sci; Sci; Soil Sci Soc Am; Int Soc Ecol Model. **Research Statement & Publications:** Biogeochemical cycling; ecosystem analysis; landscape ecology; microbial processes; succession and disturbance in arid environments; forest ecology; global changes. **Mailing Address:** Dept Plant Biol, Sch Life Sci, Ariz State Univ, PO Box 874501, Tempe, AZ 85287-4501. **Fax:** 480-965-6899. **E-Mail:** klopatek@asu.edu

KLOPFENSTEIN, KENNETH F, MATHEMATICS. **Personal Data:** b Mt Pleasant, Iowa, March 13, 1940; m 1961, c 3. **Education:** Iowa Wesleyan Col, BA, 1961; Colo State Univ, MS, 1963; Purdue Univ, PhD (math), 1967. **Professional Experience:** PROF, DEPT MATH, COLO STATE UNIV, as of 2006; assoc prof math, colo state univ, beginning 1973; asst prof, Colo State Univ, 1967-1973; Instr math, Wabash Col, 1966-1967. **Memberships:** Math Asn Am; Am Math Soc. **Research Statement & Publications:** Hilbert space; operator theory; mathematics education. **Mailing Address:** Dept Math, Colo State Univ, Rm 121 101 Weber Bldg, Ft Collins, CO 80523-1874. **Fax:** 970-491-2161. **E-Mail:** kenk@math.colostate.edu

KLOPFENSTEIN, WILLIAM ELMER, BIOCHEMISTRY. **Personal Data:** b Paris, Ohio, December 23, 1935; m 1959, c 3. **Education:** Pa State Univ, BS, 1958, MS, 1961, PhD (biochem), 1964. **Professional Experience:** PROF EMER BIOCHEM, WESTERN ILL UNIV, as of 2004; prof biochem & chmn chem dept, Western Ill Univ, beginning 1988; chmn, grad biochem group, 1977-1986; assoc biochemist, Agr Exp Sta, 1972-1988; from asst prof to prof biochem, Kans State Univ, 1964-1988; instr biochem, Pa State Univ, 1960-1964; asst technologist food res, Gen Foods Corp, 1958. **Memberships:** Sigma Xi; Am Soc Biol Chemists; Am Oil Chem Soc; Am Chem Soc. **Research Statement & Publications:** Structure and function of lipids; physical properties of lipids; binding of lipids to proteins; use of lipids as alternative fuels. **Mailing Address:** Dept Chem, Western Ill Univ, Macomb, IL 61455. **E-Mail:** w-klopfenstein@wiu.edu

KLOPFER, PETER HUBERT, ZOOLOGY & ANIMAL BEHAVIOR, ECOLOGY. **Personal Data:** b Berlin, Ger, August 9, 1930; m 1955, Martha; c 3. **Education:** Univ Calif, Los Angeles, AB, 1952; Yale Univ, PhD (zoology), 1957. **Honors & Awards:** NIMH Res Scientist Award, 1970; HumboldtPrize, Fed Repub Ger, 1979. **Professional Experience:** PROF EMER BIOL, DUKE UNIV, as of 2005; prof biol, Duke Univ, as of 2003; Alexander von Humboldt Prize, 1979-1980; dir, Field Sta Animal Behav, 1968-1981; NIMH career develop award, 1965; from asst prof to prof zool, Duke Univ, 1958-1981; USPHS fel, Cambridge Univ, 1957-1958; head, Sci Dept, Windsor Mountain Sch, Mass, 1952-1953 & 1955-1956. **Memberships:** Fel AAAS; Ecol Soc Am; fel Animal Behav Soc; Int Soc Res Aggression. **Research Statement & Publications:** Behavior and ecology, especially analysis of the development of species-specific behavior in birds and mammals; maternal-filial relations and aggression. **Mailing Address:** Dept Zool, Duke Univ, Box 90338, Durham, NC 27708-0325. **Fax:** 919-684-6168. **E-Mail:** phk@duke.edu

KLOPMAN, GILLES, CHEMISTRY. **Personal Data:** b Brussels, Belg, February 24, 1933; American citizen; m 1957, Malvina. **Education:** Free Univ Brussels, Lic es Sci, 1956, Dr es Sci, 1960. **Honors & Awards:** Stas-Spring Award, Belg Chem Soc; Morley Award, Am Chem Soc, 1993. **Professional Experience:** CHIEF EXEC OFFICER & PRES, MULTICASE, INC, 1996-; CHARLES S MABERY PROF RES, 1988-; chmn, Chem Dept, Case Western Res Univ, 1988-1996; dean, math & sci, 1986-1988; chmn, Chem Dept, Case Western Res Univ, 1981-1986; assoc prof chem, Case Western Res Univ, 1967-1969; Welch fel, Univ Tex, 1965-1966; Res assoc org chem, Cyanamid Europ Res Inst, 1960-1967; vpres, Biofor Inc. **Memberships:** Am Chem Soc; The Chem Soc; Swiss Chem Soc; Belg Chem Soc; Am Asn Univ Professors; Sigma Xi. **Research Statement & Publications:** Applied theoretical organic chemistry; chemical reactivity; nucleophilic reactivity; quantum mechanical calculation of large organic molecules; quantitative structure activity relationship of pharmacological and of carcinogenic molecules. **Mailing Address:** Dept Chem, Case Western Res Univ, Cleveland, OH 44106-7078.

KLOPOTEK, DAVID L, ORGANIC CHEMISTRY. **Personal Data:** b Green Bay, Wis, January 11, 1942; m 1963, c 2. **Education:** St Norbert Col, BA, 1964; Utah State Univ, PhD (chem), 1968. **Professional Experience:** PROF EMER CHEM, ST NORBERT COL, as of 2001; NASA grants, polyimide res, 1986-; summer fac fel, Lewis Res Ctr, Cleveland, Ohio, 1985, 1986 & 1992, NASA, Am Soc Environ Educ; prof chem, St Norbert Col, beginning 1983; vis prof, Dartmouth Univ, 1983; Res Corp grant, 1972-1974; NSF grant, 1971-1973; fromasst prof to assoc prof, St Norbert Col, 1968-1982; res assoc chem, E I du Pont Del Nemours &Co Inc, 1967-1968. **Memberships:** Am Chem Soc. **Research Statement & Publications:** Chemistry of compounds containing nitrogen-fluorine bonds; reactivity of fluoronitrene with nucleophiles; diamines for polyimide composites. **Mailing Address:** Dept Chem, St Norbert Col, 100 Grant St, De Pere, WI 54115-2099.

KLOPPEL, THOMAS MATHEW, CELL BIOLOGY. **Personal Data:** b Denver, Colo, October 27, 1950; m 1976, Myra Nugent; c Erika & Seth. **Education:** Colo State Univ, BS, 1972, MS, 1974; Purdue Univ, PhD (cell biol), 1979. **Professional Experience:** BIOANAL GROUP LEADER, CORTECH, INC, 1993-; sr res scientist, Cortech, Inc, 1988-1992; asst prof biochem, Univ Colo Sch Med, 1981-1988; Res biologist, Vet Admin Med Ctr, Denver, 1981-1988; Fel, Am Cancer Soc, 1980. **Memberships:** Am Soc Cell Biol. **Research Statement & Publications:** Examination of potential anti-inflammatory drugs for clinical use; role of membrane receptors in intracellular vesicle trafficking. **Mailing Address:** 6400 S Helena St, Aurora, CO 80016.

KLOS, WILLIAM ANTON, ELECTRICAL ENGINEERING. **Personal Data:** b Houston, Tex, February 14, 1936; m 1963, c 1. **Education:** Univ Houston, BS, 1963, 1964, PhD (elec eng), 1969. **Professional Experience:** STAFF MEM, VECTOR GRAPHICS INC, 1983-; head dept, Univ Southwestern La, 1970-1983; from assoc prof to prof, Univ Southwestern La, 1970-1983; prin engr, Lockheed Electronics Co, Tex, 1969-1970; res asst elec eng, Univ Houston, 1966-1969. **Memberships:** Nat Soc Prof Engrs; Acoust Soc Am; Am Soc Eng Educ; Am Geophys Union; Inst Elec & Electronics Engrs; Sigma Xi. **Research Statement & Publications:** Electromagnetic wave propagation; radar cross-section and radar systems. **Mailing Address:** Vector Graphics Inc, 410 Audubon Blvd Ste 101 A, Lafayette, LA 70503-2612.

KLOSE, JULES ZEISER, atomic physics, vacuum ultraviolet radiometry; deceased, see previous edition for last biography

KLOSE, KARL R, MATHEMATICS. **Education:** Bucknell Univ, BS, 1958; Univ Ala, MS, 1962, MA, 1967, PhD, 1970; Kans State Univ, MS, 1983. **Professional Experience:** ASSOC PROF EMER, DEPT MATH SCI, SUSQUEHANNA UNIV, as of 2005. **Mailing Address:** Math Sci Dept, Susquehanna Univ, Selins Grove, PA 17870. **Fax:** 570-372-4048.

KLOSE, THOMAS RICHARD, ORGANIC CHEMISTRY. **Personal Data:** b Adelaide, Australia, April 20, 1946; m 1974, c 2. **Education:** Univ Adelaide, BSc, 1967, Hons, 1968, PhD (org chem), 1972. **Professional Experience:** RES CHEMIST ORG CHEM, EASTMAN KODAK CO RES LABS, 1975-; Fel org chem, Res Inst Med & Chem, 1972-1974 & Mass Inst Technol, 1974-1975. **Memberships:** Am Chem Soc. **Research Statement & Publications:** Synthesis of novel dyes and pigments for use in non-silver imaging systems. **Mailing Address:** 19 Sandpiper Hill, Fairport, NY 14450-9306.

KLOSEK, RICHARD C, microbiology; deceased, see previous edition for last biography

KLOSNER, JEROME M, APPLIED MECHANICS, STRUCTURAL DYNAMICS. **Personal Data:** b New York, NY, March 23, 1928; m 1965, Naomi; c Michael, Lise & Marc. **Education:** City Col NY, BCE, 1948; Columbia Univ, MS, 1950; Polytech Inst Brooklyn, PhD (appl mech), 1959. **Professional Experience:** PROF EMER, DEPT MECH AEROSPACE, INDUST, MFG & MAT SCI ENG, POLYTECH UNIV, as of 2003; consult, Weidlinger Assoos, Consult Engrs, 1976-; mem comt onrecommendations US Army basic sci res, Nat Res Coun, 1976-1979, 1985-1988; prof appl mech, Polytech Inst NY, beginning 1967; from res assoc to assoc prof, Polytech Inst NY, 1956-1967; sr scientist appl mech, Res & Advan Develop Div, Avco Corp, 1956; sr stress analyst, Repub Aviation Corp, 1952-1956; consult, Res & Advan Develop Div, Avco Corp, Gen Appl Sci Labs, Fed TradeComn, Res Ctr, Hazeltine Corp, Ingersoll-Rand Corp & Technautics Corp. **Memberships:** Am Soc Mech Engrs; assoc fel Am Inst Aeronaut & Astronaut; Soc Rheol; fel Am Soc Civil Engrs. **Research Statement & Publications:** Structural dynamics; hydroelasticity; acoustic radiation; elastodynamics. **Mailing Address:** Dept Mech, Aeropsace, Indust Mfg & Mat Eng, Polytech Univ, FMA 207, Brooklyn, NY 11201. **Fax:** 718-260-3532. **E-Mail:** jklosner@duke.poly.edu

KLOSTERGAARD, JIM, BIOLOGY. **Education:** PhD, State Univ of NY, 1976. **Professional Experience:** PROF, UNIV TEX, as of 2002. **Mailing Address:** Univ TX MD Anderson Cancer Ctr, 1515 Holcomb Blvd PO BOX 108, Houston, TX 77030-4095. **Fax:** 713-745-1446. **E-Mail:** jkloster@mdanderson.org

KLOSTERMAN, ALBERT LEONARD, SOLID GEOMETRIC MODELING, PRODUCT DEFINITION DATA BASE. **Personal Data:** b Cincinnati, Ohio, October 22, 1942; m 1964, c Scott, Lance, Kimberly & Brad. **Education:** Univ Cincinnati, BS, 1965, MS, 1968, PhD (mech eng), 1971. **Professional Experience:** BD DIR, INT TECHNEGROUP, INC, as of 2004; sr vpres & chief scientist, Struct Dynamics Res Corp, beginning 1995; sr vpres, chief tech officer & gen mgr, 1983-1995; vpres & gen mgr, Stuct Dynamics Res Corp, 1978-1983; dir tech staff, Stuct Dynamics Res Corp, 1973-1978; Adj assoc prof, Univ Cincinnati, 1972-; mem tech staff, Stuct Dynamics Res Corp, 1972-1973; proj mgr, Stuct Dynamics Res Corp, 1970-1972; Instr mech eng, Univ Cincinnati, 1965-1970. **Memberships:** Am Soc Mech Engrs; Asn Comput Mach. **Research Statement & Publications:** System dynamics; experimental modal analysis; solid geometric modeling; product definition data base for mechanical design; mechanical computer aided engineering (MCAE) technology. **Mailing Address:** Int Technegroup Inc, 5303 Dupont Circle, Milford, OH 45150. **Fax:** 513-576-3994.

KLOSTERMAN, HAROLD J, BIOCHEMISTRY. **Personal Data:** b Mooreton, NDak, January 11, 1924; m 1946, Mary Ann; c 7. **Education:** NDak State Univ, BS, 1946, MS, 1949; Univ Minn, PhD (biochem), 1955. **Honorary Degrees:** DSc, NDak State Univ, 1990. **Professional Experience:** EMER PROF, NDAK STATE UNIV, 1988-, prof biochem &

chmn dept, 1957-1988, From asst to assoc chemist, 1946-1957. **Memberships:** Am Chem Soc. **Research Statement & Publications:** Isolation and characterization of natural products. **Mailing Address:** 1437 12th St N, 8K, Fargo, ND 58102-2529.

KLOSTERMEYER, EDWARD CHARLES, ENTOMOLOGY. **Personal Data:** b Omaha, Nebr, February 25, 1919; m 1941, c 2. **Education:** Univ Nebr, BSc, 1940, MSc, 1942; State Col Wash, PhD, 1952. **Professional Experience:** RETIRED; emer prof entom, wash state univ, beginning 1981; prof, Irrig Exp Sta, 1975-1981; entomologist, Irrig Exp Sta, 1962-1981; assoc entomologist, Irrig Exp Sta, 1958-1962; asst entomologist, Irrig Exp Sta, 1947-1958; asst, Univ Calif, 1946-1947; asst entom, Univ Nebr, 1940-1942. **Memberships:** Entom Soc Am. **Research Statement & Publications:** Field crop insect control; insect pollination; bee behavior. **Mailing Address:** 1915 Benson Ave, Prosser, WA 99350-1543.

KLOSTERMEYER, LYLE EDWARD, ENTOMOLOGY. **Personal Data:** b Oakland, Calif, December 4, 1944. **Education:** Wash State Univ, BS, 1968; NDak State Univ, MS, 1974; Univ Nebr, PhD (entom), 1978. **Professional Experience:** OWNER, LYLES PEST CONTROL & ENTOM SERV, 1985-; asst prof entom, Dept Entom & Plant Path, 1980-1985; asst prof entom, Dept Agr Biol, Univ Tenn, 1978-1980; res asst, Univ Nebr, 1973-1978; res asst, Dept Entom, NDak State Univ, 1970-1973. **Memberships:** Entom Soc Am; Sigma Xi. **Mailing Address:** Lyle's Pest Control, PO Box 1167, Prosser, WA 99350.

KLOTE, JOHN H, FIRE TECHNOLOGY. **Professional Experience:** CONSULT, JOHN H KLOTE INC, as of 2002. **Memberships:** Soc Fire Protection Engrs. **Mailing Address:** John H Klote Inc, 43262 Meadowood Ct, Leesburg, VA 20176. **Fax:** 360-658-1178. **E-Mail:** jklote1111@aol.com

KLOTMAN, PAUL, NEPHROLOGY, CARDIOLOGY. **Education:** Ind Univ, MD, 1976. **Professional Experience:** PROF MED, MOUNT SINAI SCH MED, as of 2004; asst prof nephrology & dir, Duke Hypertension Med Ctr, Duke Univ, beginning 1982. **Research Statement & Publications:** Renal transplantation; prostaglandin metabolism; hypertension. **Mailing Address:** Mt Sinai Sch Med, New York, NY 10029. **Fax:** 212-769-3916. **E-Mail:** paul.klotman@mssm.edu

KLOTS, CORNELIUS E, UNIMOLECULAR REACTIONS, VAN DER WAALS MOLECULES. **Personal Data:** b Rochester, NY, October 19, 1933; m 1959, c 4. **Education:** Haverford Col, BS, 1955; Harvard Univ, PhD (phys chem), 1959. **Professional Experience:** Vis prof, Univ Paris-Sud, 1981-1982; Ford Found prof, Physics Dept, Univ Tenn, 1966-1969; STAFF SCIENTIST CHEM PHYSICS, OAK RIDGE NAT LAB, 1964-; res assoc chem, Fla State Univ, 1961-1964. **Memberships:** Fel Am Phys Soc; Sigma Xi. **Research Statement & Publications:** Properties of reactions in small isolated aggregates of matter. **Mailing Address:** Oak Ridge Nat Lab, 1028 W Outer Dr, Oak Ridge, TN 37830. **E-Mail:** Klotsce@post.harvard.edu

KLOTZ, EDWARD SEYMOUR, LINEAR & INTEGER PROGRAMMING. **Education:** Oberlin Col, BA, 1982; Stanford Univ, MS, 1988, PhD (opers res), 1988. **Professional Experience:** MATH PROG SPECIALIST, CPLEX OPTIMIZATION INC, 1991-; assoc, Stanford Bus Software, 1990-1991; analyst, Ketron Mgt Sci, 1988-1990. **Memberships:** Soc Indust & Appl Math. **Mailing Address:** ILOG, Inc, 1080 Linda Vista Ave, Mtain View, CA 94043. **E-Mail:** ed@cplex.com

KLOTZ, EUGENE ARTHUR, MATHEMATICS. **Personal Data:** b Fredericksburg, Iowa, June 25, 1935; m 1957, c 2. **Education:** Antioch Col, BS, 1958; Yale Univ, PhD (math), 1965. **Professional Experience:** Prin investr, prog math educ using info technol, NSF-Nat Inst Educ, 1981-1982; PROF MATH, SWARTHMORE COL, 1977-; NSF sci fac fel, 1974; assoc prof, Swarthmore Col, 1969-1977; instr, Swarthmore Col, 1963-1969; Actg instr math, Yale Univ, 1962-1963. **Memberships:** Am Math Soc; Math Asn Am; Asn Comput Mach; Asn Develop Comput Based Instrnl Systs; Sigma Xi. **Research Statement & Publications:** Real-time microcomputer color graphics units for mathematics instruction, using video arcade technology; social science mathematics. **Mailing Address:** Dept Math & Statist, Swarthmore Col, 3/5 - 126, 500 Col Ave, Swarthmore, PA 19081. **Fax:** 610-690-6854. **E-Mail:** cgrood1@swarthmore.edu

KLOTZ, IRVING MYRON, physical biochemistry; deceased, see previous edition for last biography

KLOTZ, JEROME HAMILTON, BIOSTATISTICS. **Personal Data:** b Loma Linda, Calif, June 21, 1934; m 1956, c 2. **Education:** Univ Calif, Berkeley, AB, 1956, PhD (statist), 1960. **Professional Experience:** PROF EMER STATIST, UNIV WIS, MADISON, as of 2005; prof, Ohio State Univ, 1981-1982; prof statist, Wis Clin Cancer Ctr, beginning 1973 & Cent Oncol Group, beginning 1972; consult statistician clin oncol, Univ Wis, 1972-; assoc prof, Univ Wis-madison, 1965-1969; asst prof, Harvard Univ, 1962-1965; asst prof statist, Univ Calif, Berkeley, 1961-1962; lectr math & statist, McGill Univ, 1960-1961. **Memberships:** Fel Inst Math Statist; Am Statist Asn; Biomet Soc. **Research Statement & Publications:** Nonparametric methods; computer techniques; components of variance; biostatistical methods. **Mailing Address:** Dept Statist, Univ Wis, 1210 W Dayton St 1300 Univ Ave, Madison, WI 53706-1685. **Fax:** 608-262-0032. **E-Mail:** klotz@stat.wisc.edu

KLOTZ, LOUIS HERMAN, STRUCTURAL ENGINEERING, GEOTECHNICAL ENGINEERING. **Personal Data:** b Elizabeth, NJ, May 21, 1928; m 1966, c Emily L & Jennifer C. **Education:** Pa State Univ, BSCE, 1951; NY Univ, MCE, 1956; Rutgers Univ, NB, PhD (civil eng), 1967. **Professional Experience:** PRES, KLOTZ CONSULT GROUP INC 1994-; exec dir, New Eng States Earthquake Consortium, 1991-1994; EMER ASSOC PROF CIVIL ENG, UNIV NH, 1986-; spec proj dir, ASCE Hq, NY, 1986-1987; consult engr, 1985-; Univ NH, 1987-; pres, Durham Inst, 1980-1985; Ed, Energy Sources, Promises & Probs, 1980; chmn dept, Univ NH, 1971-1973; assoc prof, Univ NH, 1969-1986; actg chmn dept, Univ NH, 1969-1971; asst prof, Univ NH, 1965-1969; consult engr, Ohio, 1961-1965; res assoc civil eng, Univ Ill, Urbana, 1959-1961; construct proj engr defense electronic prod, Missile & Surface Radar Div, Radio Corp Am, NJ, 1958-1959; civil engr, Ebasco Int Corp, NY, 1956-1958; struct engr, firms, NY, 1951-1956. **Memberships:** AAAS; Am Soc Civil Engrs; Am Soc Eng Educ; NY Acad Sci. **Research Statement & Publications:** Applications of linear graph system; mathematical models and computer applications in structures, manufacturing processes and soil mechanics; seismic analysis, design and rehabilitation of structures and life-lines; forensic analysis of structural problems. **Mailing Address:** 90 Mainmast Circle, New Castle, NH 03854-0204. **E-Mail:** lhk@attbi.com

KLOTZ, LYNN CHARLES, PHYSICAL BIOCHEMISTRY. **Personal Data:** b Trenton, NJ, November 25, 1940; c 1. **Education:** Princeton Univ, AB, 1965; Univ Calif, San Diego, PhD (chem), 1971. **Professional Experience:** CONSULT, BIOTECHNOL STRATEGY, 1989-; staff mem, Biotechnica Int, 1981-1989; vis lectr, Princeton Univ, 1979-1981; assoc prof, Harvard Univ, 1974-1979; asst prof biochem, Harvard Univ, 1971-1974; res asst molecular biol, Princeton Univ, 1961-1962. **Memberships:** AAAS; Sigma Xi; Am Chem Soc. **Research Statement & Publications:** Physical studies of DNA and chromosomes; evolution of DNA and chromosomes; triplex physical chemistry. **Mailing Address:** 5 Duley St, Gloucester, MA 01930.

KLOTZ, RICHARD LAWRENCE, BIOLOGY. **Personal Data:** b Philadelphia, Pa, January 4, 1950; m 1975, Laurie; c Leidy, Carrie & Rick. **Education:** Denison Univ, BS, 1972; Univ Conn, MS, 1975, PhD (bot), 1979. **Honors & Awards:** Distinguished Teaching Professor, SUNY 2002. **Professional Experience:** Distinguished Teaching Professor (2002) and PROF BIOL, STATE UNIV NY, CORTLAND, 1989-; from asst prof to assoc prof, State Univ NY, Cortland, 1979-1989. **Memberships:** Am Soc Limnol & Oceanog; Soc for Conservation Biology. **Research Statement & Publications:** Phosphorus and Nitrogen influence on stream ecosystems. **Mailing Address:** Dept Biol Sci, State Univ NY, 359, Bowers Hall, Cortland, NY 13045. **E-Mail:** klotz@cortland.edu

KLOUDA, MARY ANN ABERLE, PHYSIOLOGY. **Personal Data:** b Peoria, Ill, January 8, 1937; m 1962, c 4. **Education:** Col Notre Dame, Calif, BA, 1958; Loyola Univ, Ill, PhD (physiol), 1964. **Professional Experience:** INSTR BIOL SCI, CALIF STATE UNIV, SACRAMENTO, 1987-; from asst prof to assoc prof biol, Col Our Lady Elms, 1979-1987; lectr, Col Our Lady Elms, 1974-1979; from instr to asst prof, Univ Mass, Amherst, 1965-1971; Res assoc physiol, Loyola Univ, Ill, 1964-1965. **Research Statement & Publications:** Cardiac response to sympathetic stimulation; effects of cardiac sympathectomy. **Mailing Address:** 8539 Story Ridge Way, Antelope, CA 95843-5321.

KLOWDEN, MARC JEFFREY, MEDICAL ENTOMOLOGY, INSECT PHYSIOLOGY. **Personal Data:** b Chicago, Ill, June 6, 1948; m 1970, Anne; c Daniel & Amanda. **Education:** Univ Ill, Chicago Circle, BS, 1970, MS, 1973, PhD (biol), 1976. **Honors & Awards:** Sigma Xi Res Awards, 1980, 1982, 1988. **Professional Experience:** PROF ENTOM, UNIV IDAHO, MOSCOW, 1981-; res assoc, Dept Entom, Univ Ga, 1976-1981; teaching asst biol, Univ Ill, Chicago Circle, 1973-1976; res asst biol, Univ Ill, Chicago Circle, 1970-1973. **Memberships:** AAAS; Entom Soc Am; Sigma Xi; Soc Vector Ecologists; Am Mosquito Control Asn; Am Soc Zoology; Soc Vector Ecolgy. **Research Statement & Publications:** Physiology of mosquito behavior. **Mailing Address:** Dept Plant, soil & Entom Sci, Col Agr & Life Sci, Univ Idaho, 233 Moscow Campus Ag Sci, Moscow, ID 83844-2339. **Fax:** 208-885-7760. **E-Mail:** mklowden@uidaho.edu

KLUBA, RICHARD MICHAEL, FOOD SCIENCE, ANALYTICAL CHEMISTRY. **Personal Data:** b Altoona, Pa, July 16, 1947; m 1981. **Education:** Pa State Univ, BS, 1969, MS, 1973; Cornell Univ, PhD (food sci), 1977. **Professional Experience:** DIR RES, TAYLOR WINE CO INC, 1980-; res assoc, Taylor Wine Co Inc, 1977-1980. **Memberships:** Inst Food Technol; Am Soc Enologists; Sigma Xi. **Research Statement & Publications:** Wine chemistry; analytical instrumentation. **Mailing Address:** 78 Edward Dr, Eureka, MO 63025.

KLUBEK, BRIAN PAUL, SOIL MICROBIOLOGY, MICROBIAL ECOLOGY. **Personal Data:** b Buffalo, NY, April 21, 1948. **Education:** Colo State Univ, BS, 1971; Ore State Univ, MS, 1974; Utah State Univ, PhD (microbiol ecol), 1977. **Honors & Awards:** Cited in the 57th (2003) and thev 58th (2004) Who's Who in America; Cited in AcademicKeys Who's Who in Agriculture Higher Education, 2003. **Professional Experience:** Department Chair, Department of Plant, Soil and Agricultural Systems, 2006-present; Interim Chair, Department of Plant, Soil and Agricultural Systems, May 2004-2005; Ill Groundwater Symp, Ill Coun Food & Agr Res, 1996-2003; assoc ed, J Arid Soil Rest Rehab, 1992-; PROF SOIL MICROBIOL, SOUTHERN ILL UNIV, CARBONDALE, 1991-; ASST CHMN, DEPT PLANT & SOIL SCI, 1991-2004; Ill Groundwater Symp, USDA, Nat Mineland Reclamation Ctr, US Bur Mines, 1990-1995; co-investr, Ctr Res on High Sulfur Coal, Ill Dept Energy & Natural Resources, 1986-1991; adv, Southern Ill Fertilizer & Pest Conf com, 1978-; from asst prof to assoc prof, Dept Plant & Soil Sci, 1978-1991; Res assoc microbiol, NC State Univ, 1977-1978. **Memberships:** Am Soc Microbiol; Am Soc Agron; Soil Sci Soc Am; Sigma Xi. **Research Statement & Publications:** Soybean co-inoculation and root colonization, nitrification activity in acidic soils; induced by N fertlizers, and S oxidation of organic S compounds. **Mailing Address:** Dept Plant & Soil & Agricultural Systems, Southern Ill Univ, Carbondale, IL 62901-4415. **Fax:** 618-453-7457. **E-Mail:** bklubek@siu.edu

KLUBES, PHILIP, PHARMACOLOGY. **Personal Data:** b Brooklyn, NY, June 23, 1935; m 1964, Jane; c Benjamin & David. **Education:** Queens Col, NY, BS, 1956; Univ Minn, MS, 1959, PhD (biochem), 1962. **Professional Experience:** PROF EMER PHARMACOL, MED CTR, GEORGE WASH UNIV, as of 2005; prof pharmacol, Med Ctr, George Wash Univ, beginning 1979; from asst prof to assoc prof, Med Ctr, George Wash Univ, 1970-1979; asst res prof, Med Ctr, George Wash Univ, 1965-1970; instr, Sch Med, Univ Southern Calif, 1964-1965; res assoc microbiol, Sch Med, Univ Southern Calif, 1963-1964; res fel, Bank Am-Giannini Med Found, 1963-1964 & USPHS, 1962-1963; res fel bact, Harvard Med Sch, 1962-1963. **Memberships:** Am Asn Cancer Res; Am Soc Pharmacol & Exp Therapeut; AAAS. **Research Statement & Publications:** Studies on the mechanism of action and metabolism of drugs. **Mailing Address:** Dept Pharmacol, George Wash Univ Med Ctr, Washington, DC 20037. **Fax:** 202-994-2870. **E-Mail:** klubes@gwis2.circ.gwu.edu

KLUEH, RONALD LLOYD, ALLOY DEVELOPMENT, MECHANICAL PROPERTIES STUDIES. **Personal Data:** b Ferdinand, Ind, October 23, 1936; m Helen; c Rona A & Kevin G. **Education:** Purdue Univ, BS, 1961; Carnegie-Mellon Univ, MS, 1964, PhD (metall), 1966. **Honors & Awards:** Fellow, ASM International, 1997; Significant Achievement Award, American Nuclear Society, November 2004. **Professional Experience:** SR RES STAFF, ALLOY DEVELOP, OAK RIDGE NAT LAB, 1980-; sr res staff mech properties, OAK RIDGE NAT LAB, 1971-1980; Res staff corrosion, OAK RIDGE NAT LAB, 1966-1971. **Memberships:** Fel Am Soc Metals; Mat Soc. **Research Statement & Publications:** New steels for fusion-reactor applications; published over 180 papers; 3 patents; published book "High-Chromium Ferritic and Martensitic Steels for Nuclear Applications" (2001); published a novel, "The Pittsburgh Stealers" (2002). **Mailing Address:** Oak Ridge Nat Lab, PO Box 2008 MS 6138, Oak Ridge, TN 37831-6138. **Fax:** 865-241-3650. **E-Mail:** ku2@ornl.gov

KLUENDER, HAROLD CLINTON, ORGANIC CHEMISTRY, MEDICINAL CHEMISTRY. **Personal Data:** b Baraboo, Wis, January 28, 1944; m 1969, c 2. **Education:** Univ Wis, Stevens Point, BS, 1966; Univ Wis-Madison, MS, 1968; Wesleyan Univ, PhD (org chem), 1971. **Professional Experience:** RES SCIENTIST & SUPVR MED CHEM, NATURAL PROD LAB, 1973-, MILES DELEG, MILES LABS, INC; Res assoc org chem, Pharmaceut Dept, Univ Wis, 1972-1973; NIH fel org chem, Harvard Univ, 1970-1972. **Memberships:** Am Chem Soc; AAAS. **Research Statement & Publications:** Prostanoids, chemistry and biological activity. **Mailing Address:** 27 Academy Rd, Trumbull, CT 06611-1401.

KLUENDER, KEITH R, SPEECH PERCEPTION. **Education:** Univ Tex, PhD, 1988. **Professional Experience:** PROF, DEPT PSYCHOL, UNIV WIS-MADISON, as of 2006.

Research Statement & Publications: Human and animal models of speech perception. **Mailing Address:** Dept Psychol, Univ Wis-Madison, 1202 W Johnson St, Madison, WI 53706-1696. **Fax:** 608-262-4029. **E-Mail:** krkluend@facstaff.wisc.edu

KLUEPFEL, DIETER, MICROBIOLOGY, BIOCHEMISTRY. **Personal Data:** b Zurich, Switz, October 7, 1930; Canadian & Swiss citizen; m 1959, c 2. **Education:** Swiss Fed Inst Technol, Dipl Sc nat, 1954, Dr Sc nat, 1956. **Professional Experience:** HON PROF, INST A FRAPPIER, UNIV QUE, MONTREAL, as of 2003; DIR, APPL MICROBIOL, RES CTR, 1989-; adj prof, Univ Concordia, Montreal, 1978-1987; RES PROF, INST A FRAPPIER, UNIV QUE, MONTREAL, 1975-; lectr, Univ Montreal, 1970-1978; res assoc, Ayerst Labs, 1970-1975; sr res scientist microbiol, Ayerst Labs, 1965-1970; head, Lab Biochem, 1961-1965; res scientist microbiol, Lepetit SPA, Milan, Italy, 1959-1961; Nat Res Coun Can postdoctoral fel, 1957-1958; res assoc biochem, Swiss Fed Inst Technol, 1956-1957; res asst microbiol, Swiss Fed Inst Technol, 1954-1956. **Memberships:** Soc Indust Microbiol; Am Soc Microbiol; Can Soc Microbiol. **Research Statement & Publications:** Microbial metabolism; biosynthesis of natural products; biodegradation and bioconversion; isolation of secondary metabolites and antibiotics; cellulases and hemicellulases from streptosrycetes; structure function of entyries; molecular biology of actinouycetes. **Mailing Address:** Inst A Frappier, Univ Que, 2314 Grand Blvd, Montreal, PQ H4B 2W9, Can. **Fax:** 514-686-5501. **E-Mail:** dieter_kluepfel@iaf.uquebec.ca

KLUESSENDORF, JOANNE, PALEONTOLOGY. **Personal Data:** b Milwaukee, Wis, April 8, 1949. **Education:** Univ Ill, Urbana-Champaign, BS, 1983, MS, 1986, PhD. **Professional Experience:** DIR & CUR, WIES EARTH SCI MUS, UNIV WIS, FOX VALLEY, as of 2004; RES ASSOC, DEPT GEOL, UNIV ILL, as of 2004; cur, Mus Natural Hist, 1990-1993; CUR, GREENE GEOL MUS, UNIV WIS-MILWAUKEE, 1984-; res asst & teaching asst, Dept Geol, Univ Ill, beginning 1983; sci consult, Milwaukee Pub Mus, 1980-1983. **Memberships:** Geol Soc Am; Paleont Soc; Sigma Xi; Soc Sedimentary Geol; Soc Preserv Natural Hist Cols. **Research Statement & Publications:** Preservation of lagerstatten; genesis of oolitic iron stones; evolution and depositional environment of Silurian reefs; gastropod and polyplacophoran systematics and paleoecology. **Mailing Address:** Dept Geol Univ Ill, 245 Nat Hist Bldg 1301 W Greene St, Urbana, IL 61801. **Fax:** 217-244-4996. **E-Mail:** jkluesse@uiuc.edu

KLUETZ, MICHAEL DAVID, BIOPHYSICAL CHEMISTRY. **Personal Data:** b Wausau, Wis, June 20, 1948. **Education:** Univ Wis-Madison, BS, 1971; Univ Ill, Urbana, PhD (phys chem), 1975. **Professional Experience:** Asst prof biochem, Univ Idaho, 1980-; asst prof chem, Univ Idaho, 1975-; MEM STAFF, CARGILL INC. **Memberships:** Am Chem Soc; Biophys Soc. **Research Statement & Publications:** Biophysical, particularly magnetic resonance, studies of enzyme systems which are responsible for the degradation of several physiologically important polyamines and histamine in both plant and animal systems. **Mailing Address:** 701 County Road 10 N, Watertown, MN 55388.

KLUG, AARON, BIOLOGICAL CHEMISTRY, STRUCTURAL BIOCHEMISTRY. **Personal Data:** b August 11, 1926; c 2. **Education:** Univ Wit Watersrand, Cape Town & Cambridge. **Honorary Degrees:** Numerous from US & foreign univs, 1978-1994. **Honors & Awards:** Nobel Prize Chem, 1982; Heineken Prize, Royal Neth Acad Sci, 1979; Copley Medal, Royal Soc, 1985; Harden Medal, Biochem Soc, 1985. **Professional Experience:** RETIRED; dir, Lab Molecular Biol, Med Res Coun, 1986-1996; dir studies, Peterhouse Col, Univ Cambridge, 1962-1986; Dir, Virus Struct Res Group, Birkbeck Col, 1958-1961. **Memberships:** Foreign assoc Nat Acad Sci; Am Acad Arts & Sci; fel AAAS; fel Royal Soc (pres, 1995-). **Research Statement & Publications:** Protein-nucleic acid interactions and proteins involved in gene regulation. **Mailing Address:** Lab Molecular Biol, Med Res Coun, Cambridge CB2 2QH, UK.

KLUG, DENNIS DWAYNE, PHYSICAL & THEORETICAL CHEMISTRY, SPECTROSCOPY. **Personal Data:** b Milwaukee, Wis, August 22, 1942; m 1962, Joan; c Christopher A. **Education:** Univ Wis-Milwaukee, BS, 1964; Univ Wis-Madison, PhD (phys chem), 1968. **Professional Experience:** RES OFFICER, STEACIE INST MOLECULAR SCI, NAT RES COUN CAN, as of 2004; res chemist, Nat Res Coun Can, beginning 1970; fel, Nat Res Coun Can, 1968-1970. **Memberships:** Sigma Xi; Am Phys Soc. **Research Statement & Publications:** Experimental and theoretical studies of phase transformations and structures of crystalline and disordered solids; raman and infrared spectroscopy high pressure techniques and instrumentation. **Mailing Address:** Steacie Inst Molecular Sci, Nat Res Coun, Rm 2007 100 Sussex Dr, Ottawa, ON K1A 0R6, Can. **Fax:** 613-954-5242. **E-Mail:** klug@ned1.sims.nrc.ca

KLUG, GARY A, MEDICAL RESEARCH. **Education:** Wis State Univ, BS, 1970, MS, 1973; Wash State Univ, PhD, 1980. **Professional Experience:** ASSOC PROF & HEAD, DEPT HUMAN PHYSIOL, UNIV ORE, as of 2005. **Memberships:** Am Physiol Soc. **Mailing Address:** Inst Neurosci Univ Ore, 160 Esslinger Hall, Eugene, OR 97403. **E-Mail:** gklug@oregon.unoregon.edu

KLUG, MICHAEL J, MICROBIOLOGY, ECOLOGY. **Personal Data:** b Milwaukee, Wis, March 7, 1941; m 1969. **Education:** SDak State Univ, BS, 1963; Univ Iowa, MS, 1966, PhD (microbiol), 1969. **Professional Experience:** PROF, W K KELLOGG BIOL STA, MICH STATE UNIV, as of 2004; assoc prof, W K Kellogg biol sta, Mich State Univ, beginning 1980; mem staff, W K Kellogg Biol Sta, Mich State Univ, 1970-1980; NIH res fel microbiol, Univ Ill, Urbana, 1969-1970. **Memberships:** AAAS; Am Chem Soc; Am Soc Microbiol; Am Inst Biol Sci. **Research Statement & Publications:** Ecology and metabolism of heterotrophic bacteria in natural waters and insects. **Mailing Address:** 3700 E Gull Lake Dr, Hickory Corners, MI 49060. **E-Mail:** klug@kbs.msu.edu

KLUG, WILLIAM STEPHEN, BIOLOGY, MOLECULAR BIOLOGY. **Personal Data:** b Parkersburg, WVa, September 2, 1941; div, c Cynthia, Braden & Dori. **Education:** Wabash Col, BA, 1963; Northwestern Univ, PhD (develop genetics), 1968. **Professional Experience:** Chmn dept, Trenton State Col, 1981-1993; PROF BIOL, TRENTON STATE COL, 1979-; assoc prof biol & chmn dept, Trenton State Col, 1973-1978; asst prof, Wabash Col, 1968-1973; Instr biol, Wabash Col, 1963-1965. **Memberships:** AAAS; Sigma Xi. **Research Statement & Publications:** Developmental genetics in the ovarian system of Drosophila melanogaster; co-author two books on genetics. **Mailing Address:** Dept Biol, Col NJ, PO Box 7718 Biol Bldg 239, Ewing, NJ 08650. **Fax:** 609-771-2674. **E-Mail:** klugstev@tcnj.edu

KLUGE, ARNOLD GIRARD, VERTEBRATE ZOOLOGY. **Personal Data:** b Glendale, Calif, July 27, 1935; m 1959, c 2. **Education:** Univ Southern Calif, BA, 1957, MS, 1960, PhD (biol), 1964. **Professional Experience:** PROF BIOL, UNIV MICH, ANN ARBOR, 1976-; assoc prof biol, Ann Arbor, 1974-1976; guggenheim fel, 1971-1972; am Philos Soc grant, 1969; UNIV MICH, ANN ARBOR, 1966-; asst prof comp anat & embryol, Ann Arbor, 1965-1966; asst prof comp anat, San Fernando Valley State Col, 1964-1965; lectr embryol, Univ Southern Calif, 1964; sigma Xi & Sci Res Soc Am fel, 1963; fulbright scholar, Australia, 1961-1962; USPHS grant, 1960-1961; NSF fel, 1960; NSF grants, 1959 & 1969-1971; res asst, Los Angeles Ment Health Asn grant, 1958. **Memberships:** AAAS; Am Soc Ichthyol & Herpet; Soc Study Evolution; Soc Syst Zool. **Research Statement & Publications:** Evolution; numerical taxonomy; herpetology. **Mailing Address:** 3140 Dolph Dr, Ann Arbor, MI 48103. **Fax:** 734-763-4080. **E-Mail:** akluge@umich.edu

KLUGE, JOHN PAUL, VETERINARY PATHOLOGY, COMPARATIVE PATHOLOGY. **Personal Data:** b St Louis, Mo, July 7, 1937; m 1958, Joan; c Paula M (Johnson), Janna Marie (Morrison), Thomas J & Erika J. **Education:** Univ Mo, BS & DVM, 1962; Iowa State Univ, MS, 1965; George Wash Univ, PhD (comp path), 1968; Am Col Vet Path, dipl, 1970. **Professional Experience:** PROF EMER, DEPT VET PATH, IOWA STATE UNIV, as of 2006; prof, Dept Vet Path, Iowa State Univ, beginning 1975; chmn dept, Iowa State Univ, 1975-1990; from assoc prof to prof path, Iowa State Univ, 1968-1975; res vet, Nat Animal Dis Lab, 1962-1968; mem bd dirs, Bethesda Lutheran Homes & Serv, Inc; consult, Agr Res Serv & Animal & Plant Health Inspection Serv, USDA. **Memberships:** Am Asn Vet Lab Diagnosticians; Am Vet Med Asn; US Animal Health Asn; Conf Res Workers Animal Dis; Am Col Vet Path. **Research Statement & Publications:** Comparative pathology of infectious diseases and neoplasms. **Mailing Address:** Col Vet Med, Iowa State Univ, Christensen Dr, Ames, IA 50011-1250. **Fax:** 515-294-5423. **E-Mail:** jkluge@iastate.edu

KLUGE, MARK D, CONDENSED MATTER THEORY. **Professional Experience:** AT COMPLEX SYSTS THEORY BR, NAVAL RES LAB, as of 1993. **Mailing Address:** Complex Systs Theory Br, Naval Res Lab, Washington, DC 20375-5000.

KLUGER, MATTHEW JAY, PHYSIOLOGY. **Personal Data:** b Brooklyn, NY, December 14, 1946; m 1967, c Sharon & Hilary. **Education:** Cornell Univ, BS, 1967; Univ Ill, MS, 1969, PhD (zoology), 1970. **Honors & Awards:** Napolean Cybulski's Medal, Polish Physiol Soc, 1993. **Professional Experience:** VPRES RES & DEAN GRAD STUDIES, MED COL GA, as of 2005; PROF PHYSIOL & GRAD STUDIES, MED COL GA, as of 2003; DIR & SR SCIENTIST, INST BASIC & APPL MED RES, LOVELACE INSTS, ALBUQUERQUE, NMex, 1993-; Paul Levy Mem lectr, Univ Witwatersrand, 1991; vis scientist, Cetus Immune Corp, Palo Alto, Calif, 1986-1987; vis prof med, St Thomas's Hosp Med Sch, London, Eng, 1979; from asst prof to prof physiol, Med Sch, Univ Mich, Ann Arbor, 1972-1993; NIH fel, Yale Univ & J B Pierce Found Lab, 1970-1972. **Memberships:** Am Physiol Soc; Am Soc Zoologists; Am Asn Immunologists; Int Soc Neuroimmunomodulation; Soc Neuroscience; Am Col Sports Med. **Research Statement & Publications:** Temperature regulation and bioenergetics; evolution and adaptive value of fever; host responses to infection; role of monokines and cytokines in regulation of body temperature and food intake. **Mailing Address:** Dept Physiol, Med Col Ga, 1120 15th St CJ 3317, Augusta, GA 30912. **Fax:** 706-721-7603. **E-Mail:** mkluger@mail.mcg.edu

KLUGER, RONALD H, ORGANIC CHEMISTRY, BIOCHEMISTRY. **Personal Data:** b Newark, NJ, December 22, 1943; m 1969, Ronna; c Melissa & Jennifer. **Education:** Columbia Univ, AB, 1965; Harvard Univ, AM, 1966, PhD (chem), 1969. **Honors & Awards:** Labatt Award, Can Soc Chem, 1990; Dales Award Med Res, Univ Toronto, 1993; Bader Award, 1996. **Professional Experience:** Syntex lectr, 1994; assoc chair, Univ Toronto, 1989-1992; PROF CHEM, UNIV TORONTO, 1981-; Merck Sharp & Dohme lectr, Chem Inst Can, 1983; from asst prof to assoc prof, Univ Toronto, 1974-1981; Sloan Found fel, 1973; asst prof chem, Univ Chicago, 1970-1974; NIH fel biochem, Brandeis Univ, 1969-1970. **Memberships:** Can Soc Chem; Am Chem Soc; fel AAAS. **Research Statement & Publications:** Mechanisms of biochemical catalysis and related organic reaction mechanisms; thiamin, biotin and enzymes; enzyme inhibitors based on mechanistic analysis; functional group interactions and reactive intermediates; drug design; blood substitutes; protein modification. **Mailing Address:** Dept Chem, Univ Toronto, Toronto, ON M5S 3H6, Can. **Fax:** 416-978-3482. **E-Mail:** rkluger@chem.utoronto.ca

KLUGHERZ, PETER D(AVID), CHEMICAL REACTION ENGINEERING, CATALYSIS. **Personal Data:** b Brooklyn, NY, February 25, 1942; m Joyce; c 4. **Education:** Cornell Univ, BChE, 1963, PhD (chem eng), 1969. **Professional Experience:** DISTINGUISHED SCIENTIST, ROHM AND HAAS CO, SPRING HOUSE, PA, 1968-2005; SR CHEMIST, RES LABS, ROHM AND HAAS CO, SPRING HOUSE, PA, 1968-2005. **Memberships:** Am Chem Soc; Catalysis Club of Philadelphia, Catalysis Soc. **Research Statement & Publications:** Heterogeneous catalytic oxidation; monomer process research. **Mailing Address:** 760 Killdeer Lane, Huntingdon Valley, PA 19006. **E-Mail:** pklugherz@rohmhaas.com

KLUIBER, RUDOLPH W, INORGANIC CHEMISTRY. **Personal Data:** b Chicago, Ill, February 20, 1930; m 1955. **Education:** Univ Ill, BS, 1950; Columbia Univ, AM, 1952; Univ Wis, PhD (chem), 1954. **Professional Experience:** PROF CHEM, RUTGERS UNIV, NEWARK, 1971-; from asst prof toassoc prof, Rutgers Univ, Newark, 1966-1971; res assoc, Princeton Univ, 1964-1966; Chemist, Plastics Div, Union Carbide Corp, 1954-1964. **Memberships:** Am Chem Soc. **Research Statement & Publications:** Metal chelate compounds. **Mailing Address:** Dept Chem, Rutgers Univ, 73 Warren St, Newark, NJ 07102-1897. **Fax:** 973-353-5329. **E-Mail:** kluiber@newark.rutgers.edu

KLUK, EDWARD, APPLICATION OF COMPUTERS IN TEACHING PHYSICS. **Personal Data:** b Warsaw, Poland, June 31, 1936; American citizen; m 1958, Herminia; c Dorota Kolinska. **Education:** Adam Mickiwicz Univ, Poland, MSc, 1958, DrSc, 1963; Jagiellonian Univ, Poland, Dr HabSc, 1978. **Honors & Awards:** Award of Polish Acad Sci, Polish Acad Sci, 1979. **Professional Experience:** PROF PHYSICS, DICKINSON STATE UNIV, 1984-; chmn, Dept Physics, Silesian Univ, Poland, 1979-1982; assoc prof, Dept Physics, Silesian Univ, Poland, 1968-1982; lectr, Dept Physics, Adam Mickiewicz Univ, Poland, 1963-1967. **Memberships:** Am Asn Physics Teachers. **Research Statement & Publications:** Molecular motion liquids; application of computers in teaching physics and physics labs on introductory level. **Mailing Address:** Campus Dr, Dickinson, ND 58601. **E-Mail:** edward_kluk@dsu.nodak.edu

KLUKSDAHL, HARRIS EUDELL, CHEMISTRY, HETEROGENEOUS CATALYSIS. **Personal Data:** b Bismarck, NDak, March 4, 1933; m 1989, Jacqueline Bailey; c James H, Scott N & Thomas R. **Education:** Western Wash Univ, BA, 1954; Univ Wash, PhD (inorg chem), 1958. **Professional Experience:** CONSULT SCIENTIST, CHEVRON RES & TECHNOL CO, 1992-; res scientist, Chevron Res Co, 1989-1991; sr res assoc, Chevron Res Co, 1970-1989; sr res chemist, Chevron Res Co, 1967-1970; res chemist, Chevron Res Co, 1960-1967; Res chemist, E I du Pont Del Nemours & Co, 1958-1960. **Memberships:** AAAS. **Research Statement & Publications:** Inventor of platinum- rhenium reforming catalyst; catalytic reforming; petroleum refining processes; bimetallic catalysts and processes; heterogeneous catalysts; extractive metallurgy of platinum group metals. **Mailing Address:** 871 Tamarack Dr, San Rafael, CA 94903.

KLUMPAR, DAVID MICHAEL, SPACE PHYSICS. **Personal Data:** b Jacksonville, Fla, April 14, 1943; m 1964, c 2. **Education:** Univ Iowa, BA, 1965, MS, 1968; Univ NH, PhD (physics), 1972. **Professional Experience:** CHMN, GEOSPACE MGT OPERS WORKING GROUP, NASA, as of 2004; RES PROF PHYSICS, MONT STATE UNIV, BOZEMAN,

2000-; DIR, SPACE SCI & ENG LAB, MONT STATE UNIV, BOZEMAN, 2000-; vis scientist, swedish inst space physics, 1993; staff scientist, Lockheed Martin Missiles & Space Co Inc, 1990-2000; res scientist, Ctr Space Sci, Lockheed Missiles & Space Co Inc, 1984-1990; res scientist, Ctr Space Sci, 1977-1984; res assoc space physics, Inst Phys Sci, Univ Tex, Dallas, 1974-1977; res assoc physics, Univ NH, 1972-1974; res physicist, Univ Iowa, 1968; proj asst, Univ NH, 1968-1972; res asst, Univ Iowa, 1965-1968; res aide, Univ Iowa, 1964-1965. **Memberships:** Am Geophys Union; Sigma Xi; Am Phys Soc; Int Union Radio Sci Comn. **Research Statement & Publications:** Investigations of the low energy charged particle environment in the earth's near magnetosphere and interactions between the magnetosphere and ionosphere especially at high latitudes in the auroral region. **Mailing Address:** Dept Physics, Space Sci & Eng Lab, Mont State Univ, PO Box 173840 Off 243 EPS, Bozeman, MT 59717-3840. **Fax:** 406-994-4452. **E-Mail:** klumpar@physics.montana.edu

KLUMPAR, IVAN V, FLUID MECHANICS. **Honors & Awards:** Lawrence K Cecil Award. **Professional Experience:** STAFF, AACE INT, as of 2005. **Memberships:** Ichthyologists Boston; Am Inst Chem Engrs. **Mailing Address:** AACE Int, 209 Prairie Ave Suite 100, Morgantown, WV 26501. **Fax:** 304-291-5728.

KLUN, JEROME ANTHONY, ENTOMOLOGY. **Personal Data:** b Ely, Minn, May 4, 1939; m 1993, Harriet; c Curt, Eric, Toinette, Karen & Greg. **Education:** Univ Minn, Duluth, BS, 1961; Iowa State Univ, PhD (entom), 1965. **Professional Experience:** RES ENTOMOLOGIST, AGR RES SERV, USDA, as of 2006; assoc prof entom, Iowa State Univ, 1969-1977; RES SCIENTIST, EDUC ADMIN & RES LEADER, INSECT CHEM ECOL LAB, AGR RES SERV, USDA, 1965-; res asst, Iowa State Univ, 1961-1965. **Memberships:** AAAS; Am Chem Soc; Entom Soc Am. **Research Statement & Publications:** Insect sex pheromone chemistry behavior biosynthesis and deertick kairomones and insect repellents. **Mailing Address:** USDA Agr Res Serv, 10300 Baltimore Ave Bldg 007 BARC-W, Beltsville, MD 20705-0000. **Fax:** 301-504-6580. **E-Mail:** klunj@ba.ars.usda.gov

KLUNDT, IRWIN LEE, ORGANIC CHEMISTRY. **Personal Data:** b Pasco, Wash, August 7, 1936; m 1959, c 3. **Education:** State Col Wash, BS, 1958; Mont State Univ, MS, 1959; Wayne State Univ, PhD (org chem), 1963. **Professional Experience:** ADJ & VIS PROF CHEM, FT LEWIS COL, DURANGO, COLO, 1991-; mem staff, Earth Technol Corp, 1990-1991; dir, Sigma Chem Co, 1978-1990; dir, Aldrich Chem Co Inc, 1978-1990; vpres, Sigma-Aldrich Corp, 1975-1983; vpres, Aldrich Chem Co Inc, 1974-1990; tech serv mgr, Aldrich Chem Co, 1973-1974; biochem tech mgr, Aldrich Chem Co, 1971-1973; group leader, Aldrich Chem Co, 1966-1971; proj leader, Aldrich Chem Co, 1966; sr res scientist, Pac Northwest Labs, Battelle Mem Inst, 1965-1966; Chemist, Detroit Inst Cancer Res, 1963. **Memberships:** Am Chem Soc; NY Acad Sci. **Research Statement & Publications:** Aliphatic and alicyclic chemistry; small ring compounds; carbohydrates. **Mailing Address:** 655 Radiant Dr, Loveland, CO 80538. **E-Mail:** klundt_i@fortlewis.edu

KLURFELD, DAVID MICHAEL, ATHEROSCLEROSIS, TUMOR PROMOTION. **Personal Data:** b New York, NY, February 22, 1951; m 1973, c 2. **Education:** Cornell Univ, BS, 1972; Med Col Va, MS, 1975, PhD (pathol), 1977. **Honors & Awards:** Nutrit Res Award, J Nutrit Res, 1982. **Professional Experience:** NATIONAL PROGRAM LEADER FOR HUMAN NUTRITION, AGRIC RES SERV, USDA, BELTSVILLE, MD, 1994-; Prof & Chmn, Dept Nutrit & Food Sci, Wayne State Univ, Detroit, 1992-1994; Univ Pa Sch Med, assoc prof, nutrit surg, 1989-; assoc prof, Wistar Inst Anat & Biol, 1987-1992; asst prof, Wistar Inst Anat & Biol, 1982-1987; res assoc, Wistar Inst Anat & Biol, 1979-1982; USPHS fel, 1977-1979; Res fel, Wistar Inst Anat & Biol, 1977-1979. **Memberships:** Fel Am Col Nutrit; Am Heart Asn; Am Soc Nutrit; NY Acad Sci; Soc Exp Biol & Med; Sigma Xi; Am Soc Invest Pathol. **Research Statement & Publications:** Relationship of atherosclerosis to immune system, macrophages and nutrition; nutrition and tumor promotion; dietary fiber; lipid metabolism. **Mailing Address:** USDA Agricultural Res Service, 5601 Sunnyside Ave, Beltsville, MD 20705. **Fax:** 301-504-5467. **E-Mail:** david.klurfeld@usda.gov

KLUS, JOHN P, NEW PRODUCT DEVELOPMENT. **Personal Data:** b Goodman, Wis, June 13, 1935; m 1961, c 4. **Education:** Mich Technol Univ, BS, 1957, MS, 1961; Univ Wis, PhD (civil eng), 1965. **Honors & Awards:** Leonardo da Vinci Medal, 1987. **Professional Experience:** Fulbright Researcher, Finland, 1985; PROF EMER, UNIV WIS, MADISON, 1980-; gen chmn, 1st World Conf Continuing Eng Educ, 1979; chmn, Working Group Continuing Educ Engrs, UNESCO, 1973-; chmn dept eng & prof struct, Univ Wis-madison, 1970-1980; Fulbright scholar, Finland, 1966-1967; from instr to assoc prof struct, Univ Wis-madison, 1962-1970; struct designer, Warzyn Eng Co, 1962; instr drawing, Univ Wis, 1961-1962; instr, Mich Technol Univ, 1960-1961; res engr designer, Eng & Res Develop Labs, Va, 1958-1959; appraiser, Am Appraisal Co, 1957-1958. **Memberships:** AAAS; Am Soc Civil Engrs; Am Soc Eng Educ; Nat Soc Prof Engrs. **Research Statement & Publications:** Continuing education research; new product development. **Mailing Address:** Dept Eng Prof Develop, Col Eng, Univ Wis, 729 Exten Bldg 432 N Lake St, Madison, WI 53706. **E-Mail:** klus@engr.wisc.edu

KLUSKENS, LARRY F, PATHOLOGY, CYTOPATHOLOGY. **Education:** Univ Chicago, PhD (path), 1975, MD, 1976, Am Bd Path, cert. **Professional Experience:** Pathologist, Rush-Presby-St Lukes Med Ctr, as of 2004; ASST PROF, MED CTR, RUSH UNIV, as of 2003; PATHOLOGIST, MED CTR, RUSH UNIV, as of 2003; DIR CYTOPATHOLOGY, MED CTR, RUSH UNIV, as of 2003; ASSOC ATTEND, RUSH UNIV, as of 2003; dir cytol, Univ Iowa; resident, Univ Chicago, dir, cellular immunol. **Memberships:** Fedn Am Soc Exp Biol; Am Soc Psychol. **Mailing Address:** Med Ctr, Rush Univ, Chicago, IL 60176. **Fax:** 847-942-4228.

KLUSMAN, RONALD WILLIAM, GEOCHEMISTRY. **Personal Data:** b Batesville, Ind, June 16, 1941; m 1964, c 2. **Education:** Ind Univ, Bloomington, BS, 1964, MS, 1967, PhD (geochem), 1969. **Professional Experience:** PROF CHEM, COLO SCH MINES, 1980-; PROF GEOCHEM, COLO SCH MINES, 1977-; assoc prof, Colo Sch Mines, 1972-1977; asst prof, Purdue Univ, 1969-1972; Instrumental analyst geochem, Ind Geol Surv, 1964-1967. **Memberships:** Geol Soc Am; Soc Environ Geochem & Health. **Research Statement & Publications:** Trace elements in geological and environmental systems; instrumental analysis; computer applications in geology. **Mailing Address:** Dept Chem & Geochem, Colo Sch Mines, 1500 Ill St Coolbaugh Hall 246 Rm 204, Golden, CO 80401. **Fax:** 303-273-3629. **E-Mail:** rklusman@mines.edu

KLUSS, BYRON CURTIS, CELL BIOLOGY. **Personal Data:** b Luzerne, Iowa, May 25, 1928. **Education:** Univ Iowa, BA, 1949, MS, 1955, PhD (zool), 1957. **Professional Experience:** PROF EMER ZOOL, CALIF STATE UNIV, LONG BEACH, 1991-; Prof Zool, Calif State Univ, Long Beach, beginning 1980; dir spec progs, Calif State Univ, Long Beach, 1970-1975; prof biol, Calif State Univ, Long Beach, 1966-1980; Fulbright fel, Assiut, 1965-1966; from asst prof to assoc prof biol, Calif State Univ, Long Beach, 1959-1966; Lalor Found fel, 1958; instr, Albion Col, 1957-1959; asst zool, Univ Iowa, 1953-1957. **Memberships:** Am Soc Zool; Am Soc Cell Biol; Electron Micros Soc Am. **Research Statement & Publications:** Cytology; bioluminescence; electron microscopy. **Mailing Address:** Calif State Univ, 1250 Bellflower Bldg, Long Beach, CA 90840.

KLUTCHKO, SYLVESTER, SYNTHETIC ORGANIC CHEMISTRY, MEDICINAL CHEMISTRY. **Personal Data:** b Wilkes-Barre, Pa, September 2, 1933; m 1962, Carolyn Balchus; c Mark, Carole L & Melissa A. **Education:** Pa State Univ, BS, 1955. **Honors & Awards:** Excellence Indust Chem Res Award, Am Chem Soc. **Professional Experience:** RETIRED; res assoc med chem, Warner-Lambert Co, Inc, Ann Arbor, beginning 1993; from asst scientist to sr scientist org chem, Warner-lambert Co, Inc, Ann Arbor, 1955-1999. **Memberships:** Am Chem Soc. **Research Statement & Publications:** Synthesis of agents that affect the renin-angiotensin system, that is, angiotensin converting enzyme (ACE) inhibitors and renin inhibitors; invention of marketed antihypertensive ACE inhibitor quinapril (accupril); preparation of antiallergy chromones by novel synthetic procedure; study of a general rearrangement of 3-substituted chromones; synthesis of nonpeptide endothelin antagonists; synthesis of tyrosine kinase inhibitors useful as anticancer agents. **Mailing Address:** 5143 Pratt Rd Scio Twp, Ann Arbor, MI 48103.

KLUTE, ARNOLD, AGRONOMY. **Personal Data:** b Galein, Mich, September 24, 1921; m 1948, c 4. **Education:** Mich State Col, BS, 1947, MS, 1948; Cornell Univ, PhD (soil physics), 1951. **Honors & Awards:** Soil Sci Award, Am Soc Agron, 1965. **Professional Experience:** RETIRED; res leader, Irrig & Soil-Plant-Water Rels, Agr Res Serv, USDA, Ft Collins, 1978-1982; prof soils, Colo State Univ, 1970-1987; soil scientist, Sci & Educ Admin-Agr Res, USDA, 1970-1978; US Salinity Lab, Riverside, Calif, 1960; from asst prof to prof agron, Univ Ill, 1953-1970; res engr, Schlumberger Well Surv Corp, 1951-1953. **Memberships:** Am Soc Agron; Soil Sci Soc Am; Am Geophys Union; Sigma Xi. **Research Statement & Publications:** Investigations of the transport of water, gases, heat, and solutes in soils. **Mailing Address:** 1804 Ptarmigan Triangle, Estes Park, CO 80517.

KLYCE, STEPHEN DOWNING, PHYSIOLOGY. **Personal Data:** b Arlington, Mass, October 30, 1942; m 1964, c 3. **Education:** Univ Mass, BS, 1964; Yale Univ, PhD (physiol), 1971. **Honors & Awards:** Recognition Award Ophthalmic Res, Alcon Res Inst, 1986; Broadhurst lectr, Eye Res Inst, Boston, 1989; Everett Kinsey lectr, Contact Lens Asn Ophthal, 1990; Lans lectr, Int Soc Refractive Keratoplasty, 1991; Spec Recognition Award, Asn Res Vision & Ophthal, 1991; Max Schapero Mem lectr, Am Acad Optometry, 1991; Honor Award, Am Acad Ophthal, 1992; Holland Guest lectr, Europ Contact Lens Asn Ophthalmologists, 1993. **Professional Experience:** Adj fac, Dept Anat, La State Univ Med Ctr Sch Med, Neworleans, 1992-; counr, Int Soc Eye Res, 1992-; exec ed, Exp Eye Res, 1991-; Ophthal & Visual Optics Organizing Comt, Optical Soc Am, 1991-1992; vpres, Int Soc Contact Lens Res, 1990-; dir, Training Prog Vision Res, 1990-; adj prof biomed eng, Tulane Univ, New Orleans, La, 1990-; prog comt, Tenth Int Cong Eye Res, 1990-1992; pres, Physiol & Pharmacol Sect, 1990; invited participant, Meeting Policy Issues, Vision Res Prog Planning Subcomt, Nat Adv Eye Counb, 1990; guest ed, Refractive & Corneal Surg, 1989; sr sci consult, Computed Anat Inc, New York, NY, 1988-; mem, Tech Adv Panel, La State Univ Technol Transfer Prog, 1988-; mem, NIH DRG Visual Sci A1 Study Sect, NIH DRG Spec Study Sections, NSF, 1988-1991; vpres, Physiol & Pharmacol Sect, 1988-1990; consult, Comt Vision Use Contact Lenses Adverse Conditions, Nat Res Coun, 1988; grad fac mem, Med Ctr Grad Coun, La State Univ, 1987-; mem coun, Int Soc Contact Lens Res, 1986-1990; trustee, Physiol & Pharmacol Sect, 1985-1990; ad hoc consult, Prospective Eval Radial Keratotomy Study, Nat Eye Inst, 1984-; prin investr, Nat Eye Inst Res Grant, 1980-; mem, Corneal Dis Panel, Nat Adv Eye Coun, 1980-1981, 1984-1985; prog chmn, Southern Sect Meeting, 1980; spec reviewer, NIH DRG Visual Sci A1 Study Sect, NIH DRG Spec Study Sections, NSF, 1979-; PROF OPHTHAL, LA STATE UNIV MED CTR SCH MED, NEW ORLEANS, 1979-; prog comt mem, Physiol & Pharmacol Sect, Asn Res Vision & Ophthal, 1976-1980; sr res assoc ocular physiol, Stanford Univ, 1975-1979; res assoc, Stanford Univ, 1972-1975; res assoc ocular physiol, Yale Univ, 1971-1972. **Memberships:** Asn Res Vision & Ophthal; Biophys Soc; Am Physiol Soc; Int Soc Eye Res; Int Soc Contact Lens Res; Contact Lens Asn Ophthalmologists. **Research Statement & Publications:** Physiology and biophysics of membrane transport and permeability in epithelial tissues; corneal retractive surgery research. **Mailing Address:** Dept Ophthal, Sch Med Eye Ctr, La State Univ, 2020 Gravier St Ste B, New Orleans, LA 70112.

KLYMENKO, VICTOR, ELECTRO-OPTICAL DISPLAY, SCIENTIFIC DATA VISUALIZATION. **Personal Data:** b New York, NY, November 4, 1951; m 1994, Mexi. **Education:** Univ Buffalo, PhD (cognitive psychol), 1984. **Professional Experience:** SR SCIENTIST, UES INC, US ARMY AEROMED RES LAB, 1991-; res asst prof radiol, Univ NC, Chapel Hill, 1987-1991; vis asst prof psychol, Univ Buffalo, 1984-1987. **Research Statement & Publications:** Visual perception and visual psychophysics; identifying and characterizing the optical invariants to which the human visual system is tuned to present visual information efficaciously. **Mailing Address:** 505 Briarwood Dr No J3, Enterprise, AL 36330-2289.

KLYMKOWSKY, MICHAEL W, CELL BIOLOGY, DEVELOPMENTAL BIOLOGY, SCIENCE EDUCATION ASSESSMENT & IMPROVEMENT. **Personal Data:** b Philadelphia, March 28, 1953; m 1983, Hillary; c Rebecca, Sara & Andrew. **Education:** Calif Inst Technol, PhD (biophys), 1980. **Honors & Awards:** Pew Biomed Scholar Award. **Professional Experience:** PROF, MOLECULAR, CELLULAR & DEVELOP BIOL, UNIV COLO, 1983-. **Memberships:** Society for Developmental Biology, National Science Teachers Association. **Research Statement & Publications:** Intermediate filaments; early xenopus development, regulatory networks associated with germ layer and neural crest specification, scientific literacy. **Mailing Address:** Molecular, Cellular & Developmental Biology, Univ Colo, Boulder UCB347, Boulder, CO 80309-0347. **Fax:** 303-492-7744. **E-Mail:** michael.klymkowsky@colorado.edu

KMETEC, EMIL PHILIP, EXTRACELLULAR BASEMENT MEMBRANES, KIDNEY COLLAGEN & GLYCOPROTEIN. **Personal Data:** b Carlinville, Ill, September 29, 1927; m 1955, Jean Maize; c 5. **Education:** Univ Chicago, MS, 1953; Univ Wis, PhD (plant physiol), 1957. **Professional Experience:** Adj biol, Self Health Sch Med Massage, 1996-; adj biol, Edison State Community Col, 1993-1996; St George's Univ, Sch Med, Grenada, 1989-1993; PROF EMER, DEPT BIOCHEM & MOLECULAR BIOL, WRIGHT STATE UNIV, 1988-; Vis prof, Okayama Univ Sci, Japan, 1984; asst vpres acad affairs, Wright State Univ, 1979-1984; prof, Wright State Univ, 1975-1988; from assoc prof to prof biol, Wright State Univ, 1964-1975; asst prof, Sch Med, Case-Western Res Univ, 1961-1964; sr instr biochem & pediat, Sch Med, Case-Western Res Univ, 1960-1961; res assoc biochem, Sch Med, La State Univ, 1957-1960; res assoc, Univ Wis, 1957; asst, Univ Wis, 1953-1957; asst plant physiol, Iowa State Univ, 1952-1953; Asst bot, Univ Chicago, 1950-1952. **Memberships:** AAAS; Am Chem Soc; Sigma Xi. **Research Statement & Publications:** RNA metabolism and protein synthesis; extracellular Matrix and basement membranes. **Mailing Address:** Dept Biochem & Molecular Biol, Sch Med, Wright State Univ, Rm 234, 3640 Colonel Glenn Hwy, Dayton, OH 45435. **Fax:** 937-775-3730. **E-Mail:** emil.p.kmetec@wright.edu

KMETZ, JOHN MICHAEL, HISTOLOGY, CYTOCHEMISTRY. **Personal Data:** b Johnstown, Pa, January 14, 1943; m 1966, c 3. **Education:** Pa State Univ, BS, 1964, PhD (physiol), 1968. **Professional Experience:** ASSOC DEAN, KEAN COL NJ, as of 2002; asst prof biol sci, Kean col NJ, beginning 1978; res dir, Sci Unlimited Res Found, 1973-1978; asst prof biol, Pa State Univ, 1968-1973. **Memberships:** NY Acad Sci; Am Inst Biol Sci. **Research Statement & Publications:** Quantitative histochemistry and cytophotometry. **Mailing Address:** Sch Natural Sci, Nursing, & Math, Kean Col NJ, 1000 Morris Ave, Union, NJ 07083. **E-Mail:** jkmetz@turbo.kean.edu

KMIECIK, JAMES EDWARD, ORGANIC CHEMISTRY. **Personal Data:** b New Waverly, Tex, February 11, 1936; m 1959, c 1. **Education:** St Edwards Univ, BS, 1956; Univ Tex, MA, 1960, PhD (chem), 1961. **Professional Experience:** BUS MGR, TEXACO CHEM CO, 1980-; mgr new prod develop, Mkt Dept, 1977-1980; mgr amine prod develop, Mkt Dept, 1970-1977; proj chemist, Com Develop Div, Jefferson Chem Co, 1968-1970; sr res chemist, Com Develop Div, Jefferson Chem Co, 1966-1968; sr res chemist, Columbia Carbon Co, 1964-1966; Res chemist, Cities Serv Res & Develop Co, 1961-1964. **Memberships:** Soc Aerospace Mat & Process Engrs; Am Chem Soc. **Research Statement & Publications:** Synthesis of organic nitrogen heterocyclic compounds; reactions of carbon monoxide with organic compounds; reactions of aliphatic and aromatic nitro compounds. **Mailing Address:** 5807 Boyce Springs Dr, Houston, TX 77066.

KNAAK, JAMES BRUCE, BIOCHEMISTRY, TOXICOLOGY. **Personal Data:** b Milwaukee, Wis, August 20, 1932; m 1958, Scinta; c James R, Julie A & Robert B. **Education:** Univ Wis, BS, 1954, MS, 1957, PhD (biochem, dairy husb), 1962. **Professional Experience:** PROD STEWARDSHIP SCIENTIST, OCCIDENTAL CHEM CORP, 1990-; Asst adj prof, Dept Molecular Bioscience, Sch Vet Med, Univ Calif, Davis, 1989-; staff toxicologist, Calif Dept Health Serv, 1986-1989; staff toxicologist, Calif Dept Food & Agr, 1973-1985; group leader agr chem, CIBA-Geigy Corp, 1971-1973; sr res chemist, Niagara Chem Div, FMC Corp, 1967-1971; sr fel, Union Carbide Indust, Mellon Inst, 1967; fel biochem, Union Carbide Indust, Mellon Inst, 1961-1966; Res asst dairy husb, biochem & entom, Univ Wis, 1956-1961. **Memberships:** AAAS; Am Chem Soc; Soc Toxicol; NY Acad Sci; fel Am Inst Chem. **Research Statement & Publications:** Toxicology and metabolism of organophosphate and carbamate insecticides; urea and s-triazine herbicides; metabolism of industrial chemicals; biochemical pharmacology; dermal dose response and dermal absorption studies; environmental monitoring; behavioral and biochemical pharmacology; risk assessment; PBPK modeling; agricultural field worker safety studies; indoor safety studies; inhalation neurotoxicology. **Mailing Address:** Occidental Chem Corp, 5005 LBJ Freeway, Dallas, TX 75244. **Fax:** 972-404-3287.

KNABE, GEORGE W, JR, PATHOLOGY. **Personal Data:** b Grand Rapids, Mich, June 29, 1924; m 1954, L Jeanette Moffit; c Katharine, Elizabeth, Ann & Dorothy. **Education:** Univ Md, MD, 1949. **Professional Experience:** Mem staff, Univ Med Ctr-Mesabi, Hibbing, Minn, 1986-; PROF PATH, SCH MED, UNIV MINN, DULUTH, 1972-; assoc dean clin affairs, Sch Med, Univ Minn, Duluth, 1972-1975; dean sch med, Sch Med, Univ SDak, 1967-1972; prof path & chmn dept, Sch Med, Univ SDak, 1960-1972; asst prof path & chief clin lab, Sch Med, PR, 1959-1960; med ed adv, Int Coop Admin, 1957-1959; chief lab serv, Vet Admin Ctr, Dayton, Ohio, 1955-1957; resident path, Henry Ford Hosp, Detroit, 1953-1954; Fel path, Cleveland Clin Found, 1950-1951. **Memberships:** AMA; Am Soc Clin Pathologists; Col Am Pathologists; Int Acad Pathologists. **Research Statement & Publications:** Infectious disease; insect vectors of disease. **Mailing Address:** UMD School of Medicine, Room 113 Med, D599, 10 Univ Dr, Duluth, MN 55812.

KNACKE, ROGER FRITZ, ASTROPHYSICS, ASTRONOMY. **Personal Data:** b Stuttgart, Ger, June 22, 1941; American citizen; m 1972, Nancy; c Zachary & Elizabeth. **Education:** Univ Calif, Berkeley, BA, 1963, PhD (physics), 1969. **Professional Experience:** DIR, BEHREND SCH SCI, PA STATE ERIE, as of 2005; PROF PHYSICS, PA STATE ERIE BEHREND COL, 1992-; HEAD, DIV SCI, PA STATE ERIE, 1992-; scientist, Marshall Space Flight Ctr, NASA, Huntsville, Ala, 1989-1990; vis scientist, Max Plank Inst Nuclear Physics, Heidelberg, Ger, 1978-1985; from asst prof to prof astron, Dept Earth Sci, State Univ NY, Stony Brook, 1971-1992; fel astron, Lick Observ, Univ Calif, 1970-1971. **Memberships:** Am Astron Soc; Int Astron Union. **Research Statement & Publications:** Interstellar matter; infrared astronomy; planetary atmospheres; comets. **Mailing Address:** Dept Physics & Astron, Sch Sci, Behrend Col, Pa State Erie, 139 Behrend Otto Behrend Sci Bldg 5091 Sta Rd, Erie, PA 16563. **Fax:** 814-898-6213. **E-Mail:** rfk2@psu.edu

KNAEBEL, KENT SCHOFIELD, CHEMICAL ENGINEERING. **Personal Data:** b Cincinnati, Ohio, August 20, 1951; m 1973, c 3. **Education:** Univ Ky, BSChE, 1973; Univ Del, MChE, 1978, PhD (chem eng), 1980. **Professional Experience:** FOUNDER & PRES, ADSORPTION RES INC, as of 2006; assoc prof chem eng, Ohio State Univ, beginning 1986; vis scientist, Sch Aerospace Med, 1984; vis scientist, Brookhaven Nat Lab, 1981; asst prof, Ohio State Univ, 1980-1986; instr chem eng, Univ Del, 1979-1980; chem engr, Tenn Eastman Co. **Memberships:** Am Chem Soc; Am Inst Chem Engrs. **Research Statement & Publications:** Separation process cyclic sorption, including both gas and liquid phase versions; granted 11 patents. **Mailing Address:** 6175 Shamrock Ct Ste D, Dublin, OH 43016. **Fax:** 614-798-9091. **E-Mail:** k.knaebel@adsorption.com

KNAFF, DAVID BARRY, PHOTOBIOLOGY. **Personal Data:** b New York, NY, June 5, 1941; m 1962, c 1. **Education:** Mass Inst Technol, BS, 1962; Yale Univ, MS, 1963, PhD (chem), 1966. **Professional Experience:** PAUL WHITFIELD HORN PROF CHEM, TEX TECH UNIV, as of 2005; CO-DIR, CTR BIOTECHNOLOGY & GENOMICS, TEX TECH UNIV, as of 2005; prof chem, Tex Tech Univ, beginning 1980; assoc prof chem, Tex Tech Univ, 1976-1980; Biochemist, Dept Cell Physiol, Univ Calif, Berkeley, 1966-1976; fel, Univ Calif, Berkeley, 1966-1968. **Memberships:** Biophys Soc; Am Soc Photobiol; Am Soc Plant Physiol; AAAS; Am Soc Biol Chemists; Sigma Xi. **Research Statement & Publications:** Electron transport in plants and photosynthetic bacteria with emphasis on the roles of cytochromes and iron-sulfur proteins. **Mailing Address:** Dept Chem & Biochem, Tex Tech Univ, PO Box 41061, Lubbock, TX 79409-1061. **Fax:** 806-742-1289. **E-Mail:** knaff@ttu.edu

KNAGGS, EDWARD ANDREW, ORGANIC CHEMISTRY, SULFONATION/SULFOTION TECHOLOGY. **Personal Data:** b Oak Park, Ill, July 28, 1922; m 1947, Pearl; c Kathlene L & Thomas E. **Education:** YMCA Col, BS, 1945; Ill Inst Technol, MS, 1953; Univ Chicago, cert advan mgt, 1965. **Professional Experience:** RETIRED; corp vpres & gen mgr, petrol prod dept, 1977-1987; corp dir com develop, Indust Chem Div, 1975-1976; tech dir, Indust Chem Div, 1969-1974; asst to gen mgr, Stepan Chem Co, 1965-1969; dir res & develop, Stepan Chem Co, 1962-1987; assoc tech dir, Stepan Chem Co, 1958-1962; chief chemist & plant engr, Ninol Labs, Inc, 1949-1958; res chemist, Ninol Labs, Inc, 1945-1949; asst chemist, Inst Gas Technol, 1942-1945; pilot plant technician, Glue Div, Swift & Co, 1942; consult tech auth lectr, Ctr Prof Advan. **Memberships:** AAAS; Am Chem Soc; Am Oil Chemists' Soc; Water Pollution Control Fedn; Am Water Works Asn. **Research Statement & Publications:** Organic synthesis; organic sulfur compounds; desulfurization of gas and petroleum; SO_3 sulfation and sulfonation; advanced oil recovery; surface-active agents; author of 33 technical articles; granted 46 US and foreign patents. **Mailing Address:** 715 Colwyn Terr, Deerfield, IL 60015-3111.

KNAKE, ELLERY LOUIS, WEED SCIENCE, AGRONOMY. **Personal Data:** b Gibson City, Ill, August 26, 1927; m 1951, Colleen; c Gary L & Kim P. **Education:** Univ Ill, BS, 1949, MS, 1950, PhD (agron), 1960. **Honors & Awards:** Crops & Soils Mag Award, Am Soc Agron, 1967; Exten Educ Award, 1978; Outstanding Exten Worker Award, Weed Sci Soc Am, 1972; Ciba Geigy Award Outstanding Contrib Agr, 1972; Educr Award, Midwest Agr Chem Asn, 1975; Sustained Excellence Award, Ill Coop Exten Serv, 1983; Super Serv Award, US Dept Agr, 1983. **Professional Experience:** PROF EMER, COL AGR CONSUMER & ENVIRON SCI, UNIV ILL, URBANA, CHAMPAIGNE, as of 2006; prof, Col Agr Consumer & Environ Sci, Univ Ill, Urbana, Champaigne, ending 1997; mem, First Int Weed Control Cong, Australia, 1992; task force, Ecol Impacts Fed Conserv & Cropland Reduction Progs, 1988-1990; mem bd dirs, Coun Agr Sci & Technol, beginning 1984; mem bd dirs, Coun Agr Sci & Technol, 1984-1993; weed sci rep, People People Prog, Peoples Rep China, 1983; mem, Comt Integrated Pest Mgt, Off Technol Assessment, 1979; ed, Weeds Today Mag, 1978-1982; assoc ed, Agron J, 1976-1978; partic, East West Center Confs, Honolulu, 1976-1977; UNDP consult Yugoslavia, 1976; bd dirs, Weed Sci Soc Am, 1972-1975, 1986-1989; pres, N Cent Weed Control Conf, 1971; prof weed sci agron, Univ Ill, Urbana, beginning 1969; bd dirs, N Cent Weed Control Conf, 1968-1972, 1985-1988; from asst prof to assoc prof agron, Voc Agr Serv, 1960-1964; instr plant sci, Voc Agr Serv, 1956-1960; teacher, High Sch, Barrington, Ill, 1950-1956. **Memberships:** Fel Weed Sci Soc Am (pres, 1974); fel Am Soc Agron; Crop Sci Soc Am; Int Weed Sci Soc. **Research Statement & Publications:** Competitive effects of giant foxtail; cultivation versus chemical weed control; herbicide incorporation; improving effectiveness of pre-emergence herbicides; site of herbicide uptake; weed control for conservation tillage and conservation acreage reserve; herbicide performance; effect of herbicides on crops. **Mailing Address:** Col Agr Consumer & Environ Sci, Univ Ill, 214 Mumford Hall MC 710, Urbana, IL 61801.

KNALL, CINDY, PEDIATRICS. **Education:** George Wash Univ, BA, 1985; Univ Colo Health Sci Ctr, PhD, 1994. **Professional Experience:** DIR, LOVELACE RESPIRATORY RES INST, 2002-. **Mailing Address:** Lovelace Respiratory Res Inst, 2425 Ridgecrest Dr SE, 2425 Ridgecrest Drive SE, NM 87108-5127. **Fax:** 505-348-8567. **E-Mail:** cknall@lrri.org

KNAP, JAMES E(LI), INVESTMENT RECOVERY, CHEMICAL ENGINEERING. **Personal Data:** b Denver, Colo, October 5, 1926; m 1949, c 6. **Education:** Univ Colo, BS, 1949; Univ Ill, MS, 1951, PhD (chem eng), 1953. **Honors & Awards:** Bronze Medal & Chromium Plating Award, Am Electroplaters Soc, 1967. **Professional Experience:** EMER PRES, 1987-; consult, Invest Recovery Asn, 1986-1992; pres, Invest Recovery Asn, 1983-1985; gen mgr, Invest Recovery Dept, 1974-1986; asst mgr, Invest Recovery Dept, 1968-1974; group leader, Res & Develop Dept, Union Carbide Chem Div, 1955-1968; chem engr, Process Develop Lab, Carbide & Carbon Chem Co, 1952-1955; asst chem eng, Ill, 1949-1950. **Memberships:** Am Chem Soc; Am Inst Chem Engrs; Am Electroplaters Soc; Nat Soc Prof Engrs. **Research Statement & Publications:** High pressure reactions; reaction kinetics; reactions of carbon monoxide; organometallic reactions; vapor plating; unit operations. **Mailing Address:** 120 Pine Cone Dr, Huddleston, VA 24104-2824.

KNAPCZYK, JEROME WALTER, ADHESION, COATINGS. **Personal Data:** b Chicago, Ill, September 3, 1938; m 1986, Satsuki; c Jason, Sarah & Jeremy. **Education:** Benedictine Col, BS, 1960; Univ Mass, PhD (chem), 1964. **Honors & Awards:** Roon Award, Fedn Socs Coatings Technol, 1987. **Professional Experience:** SCI FEL, MONSANTO CHEM CO, as of 1999; fel chem, Univ Mass, Amherst, 1979-1980; chmn, Div Sci & Math, 1974-1979; prof chem, Johnson State Col, 1974-1978; vis prof chem, Univ Mass, Amherst, 1974-1977; res assoc, Univ Mass, 1971 & 1972; res assoc, Duke Univ, 1970; res assoc, Univ NC, 1969. **Memberships:** Am Chem Soc; Sigma Xi; Mat Res Soc; Am Vacuum Soc. **Research Statement & Publications:** Design of transparent, infrared reflecting films for glazing applications; mechanism of corrosion and transmission loss in optical stacks containing silver; adhesion modification of plastic substrates; photochemistry of onium compounds; polymer material science; adhesion of polymers to various substrates. **Mailing Address:** Monsanto Co, 730 Worcester St, Springfield, MA 01151.

KNAPKA, JOSEPH J, PHYSIOLOGY. **Personal Data:** b Benton Pa, January 27, 1935. **Education:** Univ Tenn, PhD (animal sci), 1967. **Professional Experience:** SPEC ASST, VET RESOUCRES PROG, as of 2004; NUTRITIONIST, DIV RES SERV, NIH, 1967-. **Memberships:** Am Inst Nutrit; NY Acad Sci; Am Asn Lab Sci. **Research Statement & Publications:** Animal nutrition. **Mailing Address:** Nat Ctr Res Resources, NIH, 9000 Rockville Pike, Bethesda, MD 20892.

KNAPP, ALPHIA E, CIVIL ENGINEERING. **Professional Experience:** SPECIAL RES ASSOC, AMOCO PROD CO, as of 2003. **Memberships:** Am Soc Civil Engrs. **Mailing Address:** Amoco Prod Co, PO Box 3385, Tulsa, OK 74121. **Fax:** 918-660-3001.

KNAPP, ANTHONY WILLIAM, LIE GROUPS, REPRESENTATION THEORY. **Personal Data:** b Morristown, NJ, December 2, 1941; m 1963, c 2. **Education:** Dartmouth Col, BA, 1962; Princeton Univ, MA, 1964, PhD (math), 1965. **Honors & Awards:** Leroy P Steele Prize Math Expos, Am Math Soc, 1997. **Professional Experience:** PROF EMER MATH, STATE UNIV NY, STONY BROOK, 1997-; vis prof, Univ Montreal, 1990; vis prof, Univ NSW, Australia, 1989; foreignexpert, Hunan Normal Univ, Changsha, PR China, 1988; vis prof, Tata Inst, Bombay, India, 1988; prof invite, Univ Paris Seventh, 1987; Prof Math, State Univ NY, Stony Brook, 1986-1997; vis prof, Univ di Trento, Italy, 1984; John Simon Guggenheim mem fel, 1982-1983; prof assoc, Univ Paris Seventh, 1982; vis scholar, Univ Chicago, 1981, 1983; Prof, Cornell Univ, 1975-1990; invited address, Int Congress Math, 1974; vis assoc prof, Rice Univ, 1973; prof d'echange, Univ Del Paris-Sud, Orsay, 1972; res assoc, Princeton Univ, 1971; mem, Inst Advan Study, NJ, 1968-1969, 1975-1976, 1982-1983; from asst prof to prof math, Cornell Univ, 1967-1975; C L E Moore instr math, Mass Inst Technol, 1965-1967. **Memberships:** Am Math Soc. **Research Statement & Publications:** Representations of semi-simple Lie groups. **Mailing Address:** Dept Math, State Univ NY, Stony Brook, NY 11794-3651. **Fax:** 631-632-7631. **E-Mail:** aknapp@math.sunysb.edu

KNAPP, CHARLES FRANCIS, BIOENGINEERING. **Personal Data:** b Evansville, Ind, March 28, 1940; m 1968, Ann; c 3. **Education:** St Procopius Col, BA, 1962; Univ Notre Dame, BS, 1963, MS, 1965, PhD (aerospace eng), 1968. **Professional Experience:** Dir, Biomed Eng Ctr, Univ Ky, 1990-2003; interim dir, Ctr Biomed Eng, Univ Ky, 1989-1990; PROF, BIOMED ENG PROG, GRAD SCH, UNIV KY, 1988-; dir, Grad Studies, Ctr Biomed Eng, Univ Ky, 1987-1990; actg dir, Ctr Biomed Eng, Univ Ky, 1987-1988; assoc dir, Ctr Biomed Eng, Univ Ky, 1986-1988; prof, Mechanical Eng, Univ Ky, 1985; chairperson, Biomed Eng Coun, Univ Ky, 1973-1975; from asst prof to prof mech eng, Biomed Eng Ctr, Univ KY, 1968-1985; co-investr, NIH grants; prin investr grants, NIH, NASA, Air Force Off

Sci Res. **Memberships:** Inst Elec & Electronics Engrs; Biomed Eng Soc. **Research Statement & Publications:** Frequency response characteristics of cardiovascular regulation; cardiovascular changes during oscillatory lower-body negative pressure; custom designed surgical implants and aids from CT scans; blood rheology. **Mailing Address:** Ctr Biomed Eng, Univ Ky, 021 Wenner-Gren Res Lab 0070, Lexington, KY 40506-0070. **Fax:** 859-257-1856. **E-Mail:** knapp@uky.edu

KNAPP, CHARLES H, ELECTRICAL ENGINEERING. **Personal Data:** b New York, NY, June 8, 1931; m 1955, c 4. **Education:** Univ Conn, BS, 1953, PhD (elec eng), 1962; Yale Univ, MS, 1956. **Professional Experience:** Consult, US Navy Underwater Systs Ctr, 1984-; consult, Unimation Inc, 1980; PROF EMER ELEC ENG, UNIV CONN, 1974-; consult, Elec Boat Div, Gen Dynamics Corp, 1961-1978; from instr to assoc prof, Univ Conn, 1957-1974; assoc engr, Res Div, Int Bus Mach Corp, 1956-1957; eng trainee, RCA Victor Div, Radio Corp Am, 1953. **Memberships:** Inst Elec & Electronics Engrs. **Research Statement & Publications:** Automatic control; estimation and identification; communications and signal processing. **Mailing Address:** Dept Elec & Comput Eng, Univ Conn, 371 Fairfield Rd U-1157 ITE Bldg 347, Storrs, CT 06269-2157. **Fax:** 860-486-2447. **E-Mail:** knapp@neca.com

KNAPP, DANIEL ROGER, PROTEOMICS, MASS SPECTROMETRY. **Personal Data:** b Evansville, Ind, July 29, 1943; c 2. **Education:** Univ Evansville, BA, 1965; Ind Univ, Bloomington, PhD (org chem), 1969. **Professional Experience:** DIR, PROTEOMICS CENTER, MED UNIV SC, as of 2003; MUSC DIR, CLEMSON-MUSC BIOENGINEERING PROGRAM, MED UNIV SC, as of 2003; adj prof biooengineering, Clemson Univ, as of 2003; DISTINGUISHED UNIV PROF, MED UNIV SC, 2004-; from asst prof to assoc prof to prof, Med Univ SC, 1972-1984; asst prof exp med, Col Med, Univ Cincinnati, 1971-1972; NIH fel, Univ Calif, Berkeley, 1969-1970. **Memberships:** Am Chem Soc; Am Soc Mass Spectrometry; Am Soc Pharmacol & Exp Therapeut. **Research Statement & Publications:** microfluidic devices for proteomic analysis, mass spectrometry, protein structure. **Mailing Address:** Dept Cell & Pharmacol, Med Univ SC, Rm CRI312, 173 Ashley Ave, PO Box 250505, Charleston, SC 29425. **Fax:** 843-792-2475. **E-Mail:** knappdr@musc.edu

KNAPP, DAVID ALLAN, PHARMACY, DRUGS & PUBLIC POLICY. **Personal Data:** b Cleveland, Ohio, February 25, 1938; m 1962, Deanne; c Wendy K (Steagall). **Education:** Purdue Univ, BS, 1960, MS, 1962, PhD (pharm admin), 1965. **Honors & Awards:** E H Volwiler Res Award, Am Asn Col Pharm, 1986. **Professional Experience:** DEAN, SCH PHARM, UNIV MD, 1991-; dir, Ctr Drugs & Pub Policy, Grad Sch, 1987-1996; chmn pharm pract admin, Sch Pharm, Univ Md, 1987-1991; Schering-Plough scholar residence, Am Asn Col Pharm, 1986-1987; consult, Am Pharm Asn, 1984-1985; assoc dean, Sch Pharm, Univ Md, 1981-1983; dir grad studies, Sch Pharm, Univ Md, 1979-1981; researcher, Nat Ctr Health Serv Res, Dept Health & Human Serv, 1978; chmn, Sch Pharm, Univ Md, 1973-1979; PROF PHARM ADMIN, SCH PHARM, UNIV MD, 1972-; assoc prof, Sch Pharm, Univ Md, 1971-1972; vis scholar, Sch Pub Health, Univ Mich, 1970-1971; from asst prof to assoc prof pharm admin, Col Pharm, Ohio State Univ, 1964-1971. **Memberships:** Fel AAAS; fel Am Pharmaceut Asn; fel Am Pub Health Asn; Am Asn Col Pharm; Am Soc Hosp Pharm (pres elect, 1993-). **Research Statement & Publications:** Applications of the social and administrative sciences to the drug component of medical care; cost and quality control methods in third party drug programs; drugs and public policy. **Mailing Address:** Sch Pharm, Univ MD, Pharm Hall Rm 730, Baltimore, MD 21201-1180. **Fax:** 410-706-4012. **E-Mail:** dknapp@rx.umaryland.edu

KNAPP, DONA D, MEDICAL SCIENCES. **Education:** Univ S Dakota, PhD. **Professional Experience:** DIR, DIV HEALTH SCI SCH MED, SIOUX VALLEY HOSP, as of 2006. **Mailing Address:** Dept Lab Med, Sch Med, Univ Sdak, Vermillion, SD 57069. **Fax:** 605-677-6581. **E-Mail:** dknapp@usd.edu

KNAPP, EDWARD ALAN, PHYSICS. **Personal Data:** b Salem, Ore, March 7, 1932; m 1954, c Sandra K, David, Robert & Mary F (Parlange). **Education:** Pomona Col, BA, 1954; Univ Calif, PhD (physics), 1958. **Honorary Degrees:** DSc, Pomona Col, 1984, Bucknell Univ, 1984. **Honors & Awards:** Tiletson Physics Prize, Pomona Col, 1954; David Barrows Awards, Pomona Col, 1988. **Professional Experience:** Pres, Santa Fe Inst, 1991-1995; pres, Univs Res Asn, Wash, DC, 1985-1989; SR FEL, LOS ALMOS NAT LAB, 1982-; dir, NSF, Wash, DC, 1982-1984; div leader, Accelerator Technol Div, 1978-1982; alt div leader, Physics Div, 1976-1977; assoc div lab, Medium Engery Physics Div, 1972-1976; asst div leader, Los Alamos Sci Lab, Univ Calif, 1968-1972; group leader, Los Alamos Sci Lab, Univ Calif, 1959-1968; mem bd dir, ABC Inc, K/P Co Inc. **Memberships:** Fel AAAS; fel Am Phys Soc; Sigma Xi; Inst Elec & Electronics Engrs. **Research Statement & Publications:** Medical application of accelerators and accelerator produced particles to cancer therapy; application of particle accelerators; high energy nuclear physics; photomeson processes and pi meson interactions; high energy linear accelerators, microwave cavities and related electromagnetic phenomena; applied physics; scientific administration. **Mailing Address:** Santa Fe Inst, 1399 Hyde Park Rd, Sante Fe, NM 87501. **Fax:** 505-982-0565. **E-Mail:** eak@santafe.edu

KNAPP, FRANCIS MARION, CARDIOVASCULAR PHYSIOLOGY, NEUROPHYSIOLOGY. **Personal Data:** b Caldwell, Idaho, October 17, 1924; div, c 3. **Education:** Col Idaho, AB, 1949; Univ Southern Calif, MS, 1955, PhD (physiol), 1960. **Professional Experience:** PROF EMER BIOL, STETSON UNIV, as of 2005; prof biol, Stetson Univ, beginning 1991; chmn, Dept Biol, 1983-1991; dir acad affairs, Pa State Univ, New Kensington, 1978-1983; chmn, Dept Biol, Stetson Univ, 1970-1977; from asst prof to assoc prof physiol & biol, Duquesne Univ, 1964-1970; res assoc, Thudichum Lab, State Res Hosp, Galesburg, Ill, 1961-1964; NIH fel, Karolinska Inst, Sweden, 1960-1961; asst physiol, Sch Med, Univ Southern Calif, 1954-1959. **Memberships:** AAAS; Am Physiol Soc; Am Inst Biol Sci; Microcirc Soc; Am Soc Zool; Sigma Xi. **Research Statement & Publications:** Cerebro-vascular and peripheral blood flow problems; neurophysiology and central nervous system; behavioral studies and drug action. **Mailing Address:** 1001 Genter St Apt 8I, La Jolla, CA 92037-5526.

KNAPP, FRED WILLIAM, ENTOMOLOGY. **Personal Data:** b Princeton, Ill, October 14, 1928; m 1958, c 2. **Education:** Univ Ill, BS, 1956; Kans State Univ, MS, 1958, PhD (entom), 1961. **Honors & Awards:** Distinguished Med Vet Entomologist, 1986; C V Riley Award, Entom Soc Am. **Professional Experience:** PROF EMER ENTOM, UNIV KY, as of 2002; pres, Am Registry Prof Entomologist, 1987; consult pesticide indust, 1971-; prof entom, Univ Ky, beginning 1971; entom adv, Agr Ctr NE, Thailand, 1968-1970; consult, US-AID, pub health & indust, 1961-1985; from asst prof to assoc prof, Univ KY, 1961-1971; instr, Kans State Univ, 1960-1961; asst instr, Kans State Univ, 1958-1960; asst entom, Kans State Univ, 1956-1958; pres, Ky Vector Control Asn & NCent Br, Entom Soc Am. **Memberships:** Entom Soc Am; Am Mosquito Control Asn; Thailand Agr Soc; Sigma Xi pres Entomol soc of Am; pres Am registrs of phof entomologist; pres N cent Entomil soc Am; pres Am Mosq control ASN. **Research Statement & Publications:** Medical and veterinary entomology; insecticides; application methods and residues; pest management; integrated control of insects affecting man and animals; administratin past 10grams (assist dir, Agerp sta univ of Kg). **Mailing Address:** Dept Entom, Univ Ky, Lexington, KY 40506-0001. **E-Mail:** fkwzgp@ukg.edu

KNAPP, GAYLE, MOLECULAR BIOLOGY, BIOTECHNOLOGY. **Personal Data:** b Norwich, NY, July 31, 1949; m 1990, Bruce. **Education:** Barnard Col, AB, 1971; Univ Ill, PhD (biochem), 1977. **Professional Experience:** MKT DIR & RES SCIENTIST, CYBERSYM, 1995-; sr res scientist, Nat Ctr Design Molecular Function, 1993-1995; asst prof, Dept Chem & Biochem, Utah State Univ, 1988-1993; asst prof micro-molecular biol, Dept Microbiol, Univ Ala, Birmingham, 1981-1988; fel molecular biol, Dept Chem, Univ Calif, San Diego, 1977-1981. **Memberships:** Am Chem Soc; Sigma Xi; Am Soc Microbiol; NY Acad Sci; AAAS. **Research Statement & Publications:** Biosynthesis of eukaryotic (yeast) tRNA's, in particular those which arise through splicing of intron-containing RNA precursors; nucleic acid structure and how altering structure affects the biological activity of the nucleic acid. **Mailing Address:** CyberSym Technol, PO Box 127, Providence, UT 84332. **Fax:** 435-753-8384. **E-Mail:** gayle@cybersym.com

KNAPP, HOWARD R, PHARMACOLOGY. **Education:** Wash Univ, BA; Vanderbilt Univ, PhD (pharmacol). **Professional Experience:** EXEC DIR, DEACONESS BILLINGS CLIN RES CTR, BILLINGS, MONTANA, as of 2006. **Mailing Address:** Deaconess Billings Clin Res Ctr, 2800 10th Ave N PO Box 37000, Billings, MT 59107. **Fax:** 406-238-2871.

KNAPP, JOAN S, MICROBIOLOGY. **Personal Data:** b Dayleford, Victoria, Australia, April 12, 1946. **Education:** Univ Queenland, Brisbane, Australia, BA, 1970, PhD (microbiol), 1972. **Professional Experience:** CHIEF GONORRHEA DIV AIDS RES, NAT CTR INFECTIOUS DIS, 1987-; chief, Bact Res Br, Neisseria Res Lab, 1985-1987; res assoc prof, Dept Med, Univ Wash, 1973-1985. **Memberships:** Am Soc Microbiol; Int Soc Sexually Transmitted Dis Res. **Mailing Address:** Div AIDS Res, Nat Ctr Infectious Dis, G-39 Ctr, Atlanta, GA 30333. **Fax:** 404-639-3976. **E-Mail:** jska@cdc.gov

KNAPP, JOHN WILLIAMS, CIVIL & SANITARY ENGINEERING. **Personal Data:** b Huntington, WVa, December 9, 1932; m 1957, c 3. **Education:** Va Mil Inst, BS, 1954; Johns Hopkins Univ, MSE, 1962, PhD (sanit eng, water resources), 1965. **Professional Experience:** RETIRED; head dept, Va Mil Inst, 1966-1971; from asst prof to prof civil eng, Va Mil Inst, 1964-1995; res asst sanit eng, Johns Hopkins Univ, 1961-1964; instr civil eng, Va Mil Inst, 1959-1961; off engr, Concrete Pipe & Prod Co, 1958-1959; admin asst, Chesapeake & Potomac Tel Co, 1954. **Memberships:** Am Soc Civil Engrs; Am Water Works Asn; Water Pollution Control Fedn; Nat Soc Prof Engrs. **Research Statement & Publications:** Urban hydrology; economics and systems analysis; water supply and treatment; waste treatment and disposal; radioactive waste disposal. **Mailing Address:** 212 Barclay Lane, Lexington, VA 24450.

KNAPP, JOSEPH LEONCE, AGRICULTURAL CHEMISTRY, INTEGRATED PEST MANAGEMENT. **Personal Data:** b New Boston, Tex, November 6, 1937; m 1957, c 2. **Education:** Miss State Univ, BS, 1960, PhD (entom), 1965; Kans State Univ, MS, 1962. **Professional Experience:** PROF EMER ENTOM, UNIV FLA, as of 2002; prof entom & nematol, Univ Fla, beginning 1987; mem staff, Univ Fla, 1977-1980; plant scientist, Upjohn Co, 1970-1977; entomologist, Upjohn Co, 1969-1970; supvr field entom, Int Minerals & Chem Co, 1965; Scientist host plant resistance entom, USDA, 1962-1965; consult, IPM, Grenada, Honduras, Egypt, Israel. **Memberships:** Entom Soc Am; Am Registry Prof Entom. **Research Statement & Publications:** Field research and development of insecticides, fungicides, herbicides and plant growth regulators for use on a wide range of agronomic crops. **Mailing Address:** Dept Entom & Nematol, Univ Fla, PO Box 110620, Gainesville, FL 32611-0620. **Fax:** 352-392-0190. **E-Mail:** jlknapp@mail.ifas.ufl.edu

KNAPP, KENNETH T, ENVIRONMENTAL CHEMISTRY. **Personal Data:** b Jacksonville, Fla, June 9, 1930; m 1954, c 3. **Education:** Univ Fla, BS, 1954, PhD (chem), 1960. **Professional Experience:** CHIEF, MOBILE SOURCES EMISSIONS RES BR, ATMOSPHERIC RES& EXPOSURE ASSESSMENT LAB, US ENVIRON PROTECTION AGENCY, RESEARCHTRIANGLE PARK, NC, 1988-; chief, Stationary Sources Emissions Res Br, 1980-1988; chief, Particulate Emissions Res Sect, 1973-1980; chief non-metal sect, Div Atmos Surveillance, US Environ Protection Agency, 1971-1973; head anal sect, Vick Chem Co, Mt Vernon, NY, 1970-1971; chemist, Southern Res Inst, 1967-1970; chemist, Int Latex & Chem Corp, 1965-1967; chemist, Foods Div, 1963-1965; chemist, Res Div, Procter & Gamble Co, 1960-1963. **Memberships:** Am Chem Soc. **Research Statement & Publications:** Instrumental analysis, especially gas chromatography, x-ray analysis; infrared spectroscopy, ultraviolet and visible spectroscopy, isolation and identification of naturally occurring compounds; measurement and characterization of air pollutants from source emissions. **Mailing Address:** Off Res Develop, Environ Protection Agency, 1200 Pennsylvania Ave, N W, Washington, DC 20460.

KNAPP, LESLIE W, ICHTHYOLOGY. **Personal Data:** b Port Byron, NY, November 17, 1929; m 1957, Betty; c Leslie Jr & Glenn. **Education:** Cornell Univ, BS, 1952, PhD (vert zoology), 1964; Univ Mo, MA, 1958. **Professional Experience:** Emer, Marine Biologist, 1998-, dir, 1981-1988, dep dir, 1968-1972, SUPVR VERT, OCEANOG SORTING CTR, SMITHSONIAN INST, 1963-1998, 1972-1981 & 1988-. **Memberships:** Am Soc Ichthyol & Herpet; Soc Syst Zool; Biol, Soc, Washington; amer Soc, Zool. **Research Statement & Publications:** Systematic ichthyology, particularly the families Percidae and Platycephalidae. **Mailing Address:** Museum Support Center, 4210 Silver Hill Rd, Suitland, MD 20776-2863. **Fax:** 301-238-3798. **E-Mail:** knapp.leslie@nmnh.si.edu

KNAPP, MALCOLM HAMMOND, INDUSTRIAL ORGANIC CHEMISTRY. **Personal Data:** b Orange, NJ, September 20, 1939; m 1970, c 2. **Education:** Rutgers Univ, BS, 1961. **Professional Experience:** CONSULT, 1991-; mgr, Lubricants Res & Develop, Huls Am, 1985-1994; mgr lubricants, Res & Develop Dept, Tenneco Chem Inc, 1980-1982 & Nuodex Inc, 1983-1985; lab mgr, Nuodex Div, Tenneco Chem Inc, 1971-1980; sr chemist organometallics synthesis, Nuodex Div, Tenneco Chem Inc, 1967-1970; chemist electrochem, Nuodex Div, Heyden Newport Corp, 1964-1966. **Memberships:** Soc Automotive Engrs; Am Soc Testing & Mat; Soc Tribologists & Lubrication Engrs. **Research Statement & Publications:** Development of synthetic lubricants, novel base fluids, additives; test development. **Mailing Address:** 316 Raymond Ct, Bridgewater, NJ 08807. **Fax:** 732-981-5033.

KNAPP, RICHARD MAITLAND, HEALTH ADMINISTRATION. **Personal Data:** b Hartford, Conn, July 23, 1941; m 1969, Elizabeth; c Heather & Peter. **Education:** Marietta Col, Ohio, BA, 1963; Univ Iowa, MA, 1965, PhD (hosp & health admin), 1968. **Professional Experience:** EXEC VPRES, ASN AM MED COLS, WASH, 1994-; sr vpres, Dept Teaching Hosps, 1987-1993; bd dirs, Nat Asn Biomed Res & Hosp Fund Inc, beginning 1984; mem, Adv Comt Ambulatory Dent Servs Prog, Robert Wood Johnson Hosp, 1978-1983; dir, Dept Teaching Hosps, 1973-1987; dir, Div Teaching Hosps, 1969-1973; proj dir, Teaching Hosp Info Ctr, Coun Teaching Hosps, Asn Am Med Cols, 1968-1969; trainee,

USPHS, 1964-1965. **Memberships:** Inst Med-Nat Acad Sci; Am Hosp Asn. **Research Statement & Publications:** Contributed articles to professional journals. **Mailing Address:** Am Asn Med Cols, 1660 L St NW Ste 204, Washington, DC 20036. **Fax:** 202-862-6218. **E-Mail:** rmknapp@aamc.org

KNAPP, ROBERT C, MATHEMATICS. **Education:** NY Univ, PhD (maths), 1988. **Professional Experience:** PROF EMER, DEPT MATHS, UNIV WIS, as of 2004. **Mailing Address:** Univ Wis-Whitewater, Whitewater, WI 53190-1790. **Fax:** 262-472-1518.

KNAPP, ROBERT HAZARD, THEORETICAL PHYSICS, TECHNOLOGY STUDIES. **Personal Data:** b Boston, Mass, May 18, 1944; c 3. **Education:** Harvard Col, BA, 1965; Oxford Univ, PhD (theoret physics), 1968. **Honors & Awards:** Burlington Northern Award, 1986. **Professional Experience:** PROF PHYSICS, EVERGREEN STATE COL, as of 2005; mem, Nat Fac Humanities Arts & Sci, beginning 1987; CONSULT, 1980-; res asst, Univ Col, London, 1980; asst acad dean, Evergreen State Col, 1976-1979; mem fac physics, Evergreen State Col, 1972-; lectr, Calif State Polytech Col, 1970-1972; res physicist, Carnegie-Mellon Univ, 1968-1970. **Memberships:** Am Phys Soc; Soc Values Higher Educ; AAAS. **Research Statement & Publications:** Philosophy of education; energy and transportation; design of college-level interdisciplinary studies; physics and natural history. **Mailing Address:** Dept Physics, Evergreen State Col, 2700 Evergreen Parkway NW Library 3122, Olympia, WA 98505-0002. **Fax:** 360-866-6794. **E-Mail:** knappr@elwha.evergreen.edu

KNAPP, ROGER DALE, NUCLEAR MAGNETIC RESONANCE SPECTROSCOPY. **Personal Data:** b Natchez, Miss, September 6, 1943. **Education:** Miss State Univ, BS, 1965; Univ Houston, PhD (chem), 1974. **Professional Experience:** ASST PROF, BAYLOR COL MED, 1981-. **Memberships:** Am Soc Biochem & Molecular Biol. **Research Statement & Publications:** Biopolymer structure by nuclear magnetic resonance; computer, instrument interface. **Mailing Address:** Dept Med, Baylor Col Med 6535 Fannin A 601, Houston, TX 77030-2705. **Fax:** 713-798-4888.

KNAPP, ROY M, PETROLEUM RESERVOIR ENGINEERING, MATHEMATICAL SIMULATION OF PETROLEUM PRODUCTION PROCESSES. **Personal Data:** b Gridley, Kans, May 20, 1940; m 1962, Judith; c Charles F, Michael K & Richard W. **Education:** Univ Kans, BS, 1963, MS, 1969, DE, 1973. **Honors & Awards:** Kapitsa Gold medal, Russian Acad Natural Sci, 1997. **Professional Experience:** MEWBOURNE CHAIR PROF, UNIV OKLA, as of 2004; prof petrol engr, Univ Okla, beginning 1983; distinguished lectr, Soc Petrol Engrs, 1980-1981; dir, Sch Petrol & Geol Engr, 1979-1988; assoc prof, Univ Okla, 1979-1983; from asst prof to assoc prof petrol engr, Univ Tex, Austin, 1973-1978; res asst, Ctr for Res Inc, 1971-1973; dir opers res, Northern Nat Gas Co, 1964-1971. **Memberships:** Soc Petrol Inst; Am Soc Engr Educ; Am Petrol Inst; Am Gas Asn; Soc Hist Technol; Petrol Soc. **Research Statement & Publications:** Development and application of computer simulators for petroleum reservoirs and ground water hydrology; use of microorganisms for enhanced oil recovery. **Mailing Address:** Mewbourne Sch Petrol Geol Eng Univ Okla, T-301 Sarkeys Energy Ctr 100 E Boyd St, Norman, OK 73019-1003. **Fax:** 405-325-7477. **E-Mail:** knapp@ou.edu

KNAPP, STEVEN JOHN, CROP & SOIL SCIENCES. **Education:** Univ Nev, BS, 1978, MS, 1980; Univ Nebr, PhD, 1983. **Professional Experience:** EMINENT SCHOLAR, DEPT SOIL & CROP SCI, UNIV GA, as of 2006. **Mailing Address:** Ctr Appl Genetic Technol, 111 Riverbend Rd, Athens, GA 30602. **E-Mail:** sjknapp@uga.edu

KNAPP, WILLIAM ARNOLD, VETERINARY PHARMACOLOGY, TOXICOLOGY. **Personal Data:** b Atlanta, Ga, October 4, 1925; m 1950, c 3. **Education:** Univ Ga, DVM, 1951, MS, 1964. **Professional Experience:** CONSULT VET PHARMACEUT, AGRICHEM & RELATED INDUST, WASH KNAPP ASSOC, 1983-; vpres, Flow Labs Inc, McLean, Va, 1976-1983; dir, Animal Sci-Prod Div, Flow Labs Inc, Rockville, Md, 1971-1978; pres, Flow Res Animals Inc, 1971-1977; pres, Hazleton Res Animals, Inc, 1968-1971; assoc dir & res coordr, Toxicol Div, Hazleton Labs, Inc, 1965-1968; dir res, Morris Res Labs, Inc, 1962-1965; asst prof physiol & pharmacol, Sch Vet Med, Univ Ga, 1954-1962; pvt practice, 1952-1954; asst prof vet med & surg, Univ Ga, 1951-1952. **Memberships:** Am Soc Vet Physiol & Pharmacol; Vet Med Asn; Am Asn Lab Animal Sci; Indust Vet Asn (pres 1969-1970); Am Col Vet Toxicologists. **Research Statement & Publications:** Veterinary pharmacology; drug evaluations; toxicology; nutrition; research administration and general management. **Mailing Address:** 3212 Queens Rd, Raleigh, NC 27612.

KNAPPE, LAVERNE F, MECHANICAL ENGINEERING, APPLIED MECHANICS. **Personal Data:** b Ellsworth, Wis, January 8, 1922; m 1944, c 3. **Education:** Univ Minn, BME, 1944, MSME, 1947, PhD (mech eng), 1953. **Professional Experience:** SR ENGR, IBM CORP, 1970-; mgr mech analysis lab, IBM Corp, 1957-1970; consult, Booz, Allen & Hamilton, Inc, 1955-1957; res engr, Am Mach & Foundry Co, 1953-1955; Consult, Gen Mills, Inc, 1951-1953; instr mech eng, Univ Minn, 1950-1953; Mech engr, Barber Colman Co, 1947-1950. **Memberships:** Am Soc Mech Engrs; Soc Exp Stress Anal; NY Acad Sci. **Research Statement & Publications:** Research and development of computer-aided mechanical design systems, including engineer-computer communication, analytical design procedures, system modeling and design optimization. **Mailing Address:** 207 5th Ave Sw Apt 1008, Rochester, MN 55902.

KNAPPENBERGER, HERBERT ALLAN, INDUSTRIAL ENGINEERING, APPLIED STATISTICS. **Personal Data:** b Reading, Pa, May 24, 1932; m 1957, c 3. **Education:** Pa State Univ, BS, 1957, MS, 1960; NC State Univ, PhD (exp statist), 1966. **Professional Experience:** PROF EMER, DEPT INDUST ENG, WAYNE STATE UNIV, as of 2004; chmn opers res, Wayne State Univ, beginning 1981; mem staff, dept indust eng, Wayne State Univ, beginning 1977; from assoc prof to prof, Univ Mo-Columbia, 1968-1977; from instr to asst prof, NC State Univ, 1960-1968; instr indust eng, Pa State Univ, 1958-1960; apprentice draftsman, Textile Mach Works, Pa, 1950-1954; assoc dean, sch eng, Wayne State Univ; mem health serv res training comt, Nat Ctr Health Serv Res & Develop. **Memberships:** Am Inst Indust Engrs; Am Statist Asn; Opers Res Soc Am; Am Soc Eng Educ. **Research Statement & Publications:** Health care systems design; patient scheduling systems design; automated radiology systems design; resource allocation on large systems. **Mailing Address:** Dept Indust Mfg eng, Wayne State Univ, 5050 Anthony Wayne Dr, Detroit, MI 48202.

KNAPPENBERGER, JONATHAN C, MATHEMATICS. **Education:** Temple Univ, PhD (Maths), 1993. **Professional Experience:** ASST PROF, LA SALLE UNIV, as of 2003. **Mailing Address:** 134 Olney Hall, Philadelphia, PA 19114-2094. **Fax:** 215-824-2384. **E-Mail:** knappenb@lasalle.edu

KNAPPENBERGER, PAUL HENRY, SCIENCE ADMINISTRATION, ASTRONOMY. **Personal Data:** b Reading, Pa, September 5, 1942; m 1963, c 2. **Education:** Franklin & Marshall Col, AB, 1964; Univ Va, MA, 1966, PhD (astron), 1968. **Professional Experience:** PRES, ADLER PLANETARIUM & ASTRON MUSEUM, 1991-; pres, Asn Sci & Technol Ctrs, 1985; adj assoc prof, Univ Richmond, 1974-1981; asst prof, Va Commonwealth Univ, 1973-; dir, Sci Mus Va, 1973-1991; instr astron, Emory Univ & adj prof, Ga State Univ, 1970-1972; Chmn dept astron, Fernbank Sci Ctr, Atlanta, 1968-1972; councilman, Nat Mus Act. **Memberships:** Am Astron Soc; AAAS; Am Asn Mus; Int Coun Mus. **Research Statement & Publications:** Astronomical interferometry; astronomical applications of image converters and intensifiers; development of educational activities in astronomy; design and evaluation of interactive exhibits in science; education in science museums. **Mailing Address:** Adler Planetarium & Astron Museum, 1300 S Lake Shore Dr, Chicago, IL 60605. **Fax:** 312-583-0256.

KNASTER, TATYANA, DURABILITY OF CONCRETE, STRUCTURAL DESIGN. **Personal Data:** b Moscow, USSR, September 11, 1933; American citizen; m 1956, c 1. **Education:** Moscow Inst Transp Eng, BS, 1956, MS, 1958, PhD (civil eng), 1965. **Professional Experience:** CHMN CIVIL ENG, PA INST TECHNOL, 1979-; struct engr, struct design, Day & Zimmerman, Inc, 1978-1979; struct engr, struct design, Ruthroff & Englekirk, Co, 1977-1978; part-time lectr, Calif State Univ, 1977-1978; res assoc struct res, Univ Southern Calif, 1976-1977; sr res scientist concrete durability, Res Inst Concrete & Reinforced Concrete, Moscow, 1970-1976; prof civil eng, Moscow Inst Transp Eng, 1966-1970; part-time lectr, Moscow Inst Transp Eng, 1965-1966; struct engr, Design Inst, Moscow, 1956-1961. **Memberships:** Am Concrete Inst. **Research Statement & Publications:** Durability of building materials & structures, primarily concrete in severe weather conditions and in aggressive mediae. **Mailing Address:** Dept Civil Eng, Pa Inst Technol, 800 Manchester Ave, Media, PA 19063-4036.

KNATTERUD, GENELL LAVONNE, BIOSTATISTICS. **Personal Data:** b Minot, NDak. **Education:** Macalester Col, BA, 1952; Univ Minn, MS, 1959, PhD (biostatist), 1963. **Professional Experience:** CHMN BD & CHIEF EXEC OFFICER, MD MEDI RES INST, as of 2001; mem lipid metab adv comt, Nat Heart & Lung Inst, 1975-1983; vpres, Md Med Res Inst, 1974-; from assoc prof to prof, Inst Int Med, 1972-1984; mem Nat Cancer Adv Comt, Nat Bladder-Prostate Cancer Projs, 1972-1974; from asst prof to assoc prof, Inst Int Med, 1967-1972; asst prof epidemiol & biostatist, Pakistan Med Res Ctr, Univ Md, 1966-1967; anal statistician, Off Biomet, Consult Sect, NIMH, 1963-1964; instr, Sch Pub Health, 1960-1962; sr statistician, Biostatist Div, 1958-1960; statistician, Biostatist Div, 1956-1957; teaching asst anat, Univ Minn, 1954-1956; asst biochemist, Pillsbury Mills Res Labs, 1952-1953. **Memberships:** AAAS; Am Diabetes Asn; Am Pub Health Asn; Am Statist Asn; Biomet Soc. **Research Statement & Publications:** Design, methods and applications of clinical trials; epidemiology of cardiovascular disease and diabetes. **Mailing Address:** Md Med Res Inst, 600 Wyndhurst Ave, Baltimore, MD 21210. **Fax:** 410-323-8622. **E-Mail:** gknatterud@mmri.org

KNAUER, BRUCE RICHARD, PHYSICAL-ORGANIC CHEMISTRY. **Personal Data:** b New York, NY, November 24, 1942. **Education:** Cooper Union, BChE, 1963; Cornell Univ, MS, 1965, PhD (chem), 1969. **Professional Experience:** PROF ORG CHEM, STATE UNIV NY COL, ONEONTA, 1991-; chmn, Chem Dept, 1982-1985; from asst prof to assoc prof, State Univ NY Col, Oneonta, 1970-1991; USAF Off Aerospace Res fel, Univ Ga, 1968-1970. **Memberships:** Sr mem Am Chem Soc. **Research Statement & Publications:** Electron spin resonance; nitroxide free radicals; reaction mechanisms; solvent polarity. **Mailing Address:** Dept Chem, State Univ NY Col, Oneonta, NY 13820-4015. **Fax:** 607-436-2654. **E-Mail:** knauerbr@oneonta.edu

KNAUER, JAMES PHILIP, PLASMA PHYSICS X-RAY DIAGNOSTICS, HIGH TEMPERATURE HYDRODYNAMICS. **Personal Data:** b Sandusky, Ohio, May 12, 1950; m 1974, Susan. **Education:** Mass Inst Technol, BS, 1972; Univ Hawaii, MS, 1974, PhD, 1977. **Honors & Awards:** Excellence Plasma Physics Res Award, Am Phys Soc, 1995. **Professional Experience:** SCIENTIST MGR, LAB LASER ENERGETICS, UNIV ROCHESTER, NY, 1986-; MGR, NAT LASER USERS FACIL, ROCHESTER, 1986-; res Scientist, Lockheed Missiles & Space Co, 1979-1986; assoc res Scientist, Lockheed Missiles & Space Co, 1979-1986; jr researcher, Univ Hawaii, 1978-1979; res investr, Univ Pa, 1977-1978. **Memberships:** Am Phys Soc; Sigma Xi. **Research Statement & Publications:** Hydrodynamics of ionized plasmas; development of X-Ray radiographic instrumentation. **Mailing Address:** Lab Laser Energetics, Univ Rochester, 250 E River Rd, Rochester, NY 14623-1212.

KNAUER, THOMAS E, EXPERIMENTAL BIOLOGY. **Education:** Spring Hill Col, BS, 1968; Univ Nebraska, PhD (biochem), 1974; Col William & Mary, Marshall-Wythe Sch Law, JD, 1986. **Professional Experience:** ATTY REAL ESTATE & ENVIRON, MCGUIRE WOODS, as of 2004; shareholder, Williams Mullen, 1998-2003; prin, McSweeney, Burtch & Crump, 1990-1998; assoc, Hunton & Williams, 1986-1990. **Mailing Address:** McGuire Woods LLP, One James Ctr 901 E Cary St, Richmond, VA 23219-4030. **Fax:** 804-775-1061. **E-Mail:** tknauer@mcguirewoods.com

KNAUF, PHILIP A, BIOPHYSICS. **Personal Data:** b Rochester, NY, March 25, 1942. **Education:** Boston Col, BA, 1963; Univ Rochester, PhD (biophys), 1970. **Honors & Awards:** K S Collinswood Award, Biophys Soc, 1987. **Professional Experience:** PROF BIOPHYS & BIOCHEM, UNIV ROCHESTER, 1980-; prof biophys, Univ Toronto & Hosp Sick Children, 1972-1980. **Memberships:** Am Physiol Soc; Biophys Soc; Soc Gen Psychologists; Sigma Xi. **Research Statement & Publications:** Biophysics. **Mailing Address:** Dept Biophys, Univ Rochester Med Ctr, Box BPHYS 601 Elmwood Ave, Rochester, NY 14642. **Fax:** 585-275-6007. **E-Mail:** philip_knauf@urmc.rochester.edu

KNAUFF, RAYMOND EUGENE, ENDOCRINE BIOCHEMISTRY. **Personal Data:** b Venus, Pa, July 22, 1925; m 1949, Helen; c Patricia A. **Education:** Capital Univ, BS, 1947; Univ Mich, MS, 1949, PhD (biol chem), 1952. **Professional Experience:** EMER PROF & CHMN, PHILADELPHIA COL OSTEOP MED, 1989-; prof biochem & chmn dept, Philadelphia Col Osteop Med, 1974-1989; assoc prof biochem, Sch Med, Temple Univ, 1961-1974; dir res, Cystic Fibrosis Res Inst, 1961-1967; asst prof biochem, Univ Mich, 1957-1961; head bioanal dept, G D Searle Co, 1956-1957; endocrinologist, Upjohn Co, 1951-1955; asst biol chem, Med Sch, 1949-1950; biochemist, Univ Mich Hosp, 1947-1949; biochemist toxicol, Dow Chem Co, 1947; anal chemist, Dow Chem Co, 1946; org chemist, Dow Chem Co, 1945; chem technician, Barneby-Cheney Eng Co, 1944. **Memberships:** AAAS; Am Chem Soc; Am Inst Chemists; NY Acad Sci. **Research Statement & Publications:** Biological chemistry; endocrine biochemistry; bioanalytical chemistry; protein and amino acid chemistry and metabolism; cystic fibrosis; nutritional biochemistry; eicosanoid biochemistry. **Mailing Address:** 37 Meade Rd, Ambler, PA 19002-5122.

KNAUFT, DAVID A, PLANT BREEDING, FARMING SYSTEMS. **Personal Data:** b Evergreen Park, Ill, May 10, 1951; m 1978, c 1. **Education:** Univ Wis-Madison, BS, 1973; Cornell Univ, PhD (plant breeding), 1977. **Professional Experience:** ASSOC DEAN ACAD AFFAIRS, UNIV GA, as of 2004; PRIN INVESTR, SCI BEHIND OUR FOOD, UNIV GA, as of 2004; prof & head, dept crop sci, NC State Univ, beginning 1993; from asst prof to prof plant breeding & genetics, agron dept, Univ Fla, 1978-1993; vis instr genetics, agron & soils dept, Clemson Univ, 1977-1978. **Memberships:** Am Soc Agron; Am Genetic

Asn; Crop Sci Soc Am; AAAS. **Research Statement & Publications:** Genetic factors important in the improvement of cultivated peanuts, including genetic stability, response to stress environments, disease resistance and intercropping. **Mailing Address:** Off Acad Affairs, Col Agr & Environ Sci, Univ Ga, 102 Conner Hall, Athens, GA 30602. **Fax:** 706-542-2130. **E-Mail:** dknauft@uga.edu

KNAUS, EDWARD ELMER, MEDICINAL CHEMISTRY. **Personal Data:** b Leroy, Sask, January 7, 1943; m 1974, Alexis; c Valerie, Joanne & Gordon. **Education:** Univ Sask, BS, 1965, MS, 1967, PhD (pharmaceut chem), 1970. **Honors & Awards:** McNeill Res Award; McCall Prof Award; Janssen-Ortho Award; Killam Prof Award. **Professional Experience:** PROF PHARM, UNIV ALTA, 1980-; from asst prof to assoc prof pharm, Univ Alta, 1972-1980; Med Res Coun Can fel chem, Tex A&M Univ, 1970-1971 & Univ BC, 1971-1972. **Memberships:** Can Pharmaceut Asn; Chem Inst Can. **Research Statement & Publications:** Synthesis of new nitrogen heterocycles and diagnostic agents; structure-activity studies; drug design. **Mailing Address:** Fac Pharm & Pharmaceut Sci, Univ Alta, 2127 Dent/Pharm Ctr, Edmonton, AB T6G 2N8, Can. **Fax:** 403-492-1217. **E-Mail:** eknaus@pharmacy.ualberta.ca

KNAUS, RONALD MALLEN, RADIOECOLOGY, RADIOBIOLOGY. **Personal Data:** b San Jose, Calif, June 9, 1937; m 1960, Nancy Walsh; c Christopher & Scott. **Education:** San Jose State Univ, AB, 1960, MA, 1962; Ore State Univ, PhD (radiation biol), 1971. **Professional Experience:** Prin investr, Lake Restoration Proj, City Baton Rouge, 1977-, study marsh sediments, US Dept Interio; consult, Comp Planning Inst, Dallas, 1976- & City & Parish, East Baton Rouge, 1977-1981; PROF & RESEARCHER RADIOECOL & RADIOBIOL, LA STATEUNIV, 1975-; prof biol, Univ Tex, Arlington, 1971-1975; researcher biochem, Ore State Univ, 1968-1971; teacher, Fremont Union High Sch Dist, 1960-1965 & Fresno City Col, 1965-1968; southeast regional dir, Sigma Xi; neutron activation anal biol sci, US DeptEnergy. **Memberships:** AAAS; Sigma Xi. **Research Statement & Publications:** Investigation into the behavior of stable metal and rare earth tracers in the lotic environment; establish stable, activable tracers as soil horizon markers in fresh, brackish, and saltwater wetlands. **Mailing Address:** Nuclear Sci Ctr, La State Univ, Baton Rouge, LA 70803-0001. **Fax:** 504-388-2094.

KNAUS, ULLA G, IMMUNOLOGY. **Honors & Awards:** Katz Prize, 1992. **Professional Experience:** ASSOC PROF, DEPT IMMUNOL, SCRIPPS RES INST, as of 2006. **Mailing Address:** Dept Immunol, Scripps Res Inst, 10666 N Torrey Pines Rd IMM28, LaJolla, CA 92037. **Fax:** 858-784-9580. **E-Mail:** uknaus@scripps.edu

KNAUSENBERGER, WULF H, ELECTRONICS ENGINEERING. **Personal Data:** b Vienna, Austria, May 3, 1943; American citizen; m 1967, c 4. **Education:** Pa State Univ, BS, 1965, PhD (solid state sci), 1969. **Professional Experience:** RETIRED; assoc ed, chmn trans, Inst Elec & Electronics Engrs, beginning 1985; chmn, Comput Packaging Tech Comt, Inst Elec & Electronics Engrs, 1984-1985; tech supvr, Bell Labs, Lucent Technol, 1978-1999; mem tech staff, Bell Labs, 1970-1978; res assoc, Pa State Univ, 1969-1970. **Memberships:** Inst Elec & Electronics Engrs; Int Electronics Packaging Soc (pres, 1994). **Research Statement & Publications:** Analysis of electronic system design, electronic packaging and interconnection system design; history of computer packaging. **Mailing Address:** 88 Hainesburg River Rd, Columbia, NJ 07832.

KNAUSS, JOHN ATKINSON, OCEAN, CIRCULATION OCEAN POLICY. **Personal Data:** b Detroit, Mich, September 1, 1925; m 1954, Lynne; c Karl & William. **Education:** Mass Inst Technol, BS, 1946; Univ Mich, MA, 1949; Univ Calif, Los Angeles, PhD (oceanog), 1959. **Honorary Degrees:** DSc, Univ RI, 1992. **Honors & Awards:** Sea Grant Asn Award, 1974; Ocean Sci Award, Ocean Sci Sect, Am Geophys Union, 1988. **Professional Experience:** RES ASSOC, SCRIPPS INST OCEANOG, UNIV CALIF, SAN DIEGO, 1994-; first vchair, Int Oceanog Comm, 1991-1993; DEAN & EMER PROF, UNIV RI, 1990-; adminr, Nat Oceanic & Atmospheric Admin, US Dept Com, 1989-1993; vpres marine progs, Grad Sch Oceanog, 1982-1987; chmn, Univ Nat Oceanog Lab Syst, 1974-1975; chair, Ocean Policy Comt, 1973-1982; chmn, Ocean Policy Comt, 1972-1982; chmn, Ocean Sci Comt, 1971-1973; chair, comt Oceanog, Nat Res Coun, 1970-1973; provost marine affairs, Grad Sch Oceanog, 1969-1982; mem, Pres Comn Marine Sci, Eng & Resources, 1967-1968; Comt Oceanog, Nat Acad Sci, 1966-1970; prof oceanog, Univ RI, 1962-1990; dean, Grad Sch Oceanog, 1962-1987; oceanogr, Scripps Inst Oceanog, 1955-1962; res staff, Scripps Inst Oceanog, 1951-1952; oceanogr, Off Naval Res, 1950-1951 & 1953-1954; Physicist, Navy Electronics Lab, 1947-1948. **Memberships:** fel Am Geophys Union (pres 1998-2000); fel AAAS; fel Am Meteorol Soc; Sigma Xi; fel Marine Technol Soc; Oceanog Soc. **Research Statement & Publications:** Ocean circulation; law of the sea; marine affairs. **Mailing Address:** 2634 Ellentown Rd, La Jolla, CA 92037. **E-Mail:** jknauss@gso.uri.edu

KNAVEL, DEAN EDGAR, HORTICULTURE. **Personal Data:** b Windber, Pa, September 5, 1924; m 1947, c 3. **Education:** Pa State Univ, BS, 1954; Univ Del, MS, 1956; Mich State Univ, PhD (hort), 1959. **Professional Experience:** PROF EMER HORT, UNIV KY, as of 2004; prof hort, Univ Ky, beginning 1978; from asst prof to assoc prof, Univ Ky, 1959-1978. **Memberships:** Fel Am Soc Hort Sci. **Research Statement & Publications:** Breeding, nutrition and minimum tillage of vegetable crops. **Mailing Address:** 1112 Meridian Dr, Lexington, KY 40504.

KNAZEK, RICHARD ALLAN, MEDICINE, ENGINEERING. **Personal Data:** b Cleveland, Ohio, March 23, 1942; m 1967, c 2. **Education:** Case Inst Technol, BS, 1962; Lehigh Univ, MS, 1964; Ohio State Univ, MD, 1969; Am Bd Internal Med, dipl, 1974. **Professional Experience:** PhD thesis adv, Univ Del, 1976-1977; contract officer, Breast Cancer Task Force, Nat Cancer Inst, 1974-1980; vis lectr, Univ Toronto & Mass Gen Hosp, 1974; vis fac, W A Jones Cell Sci Ctr, 1973-1976; MED OFF, DIV CLIN RES, NAT CTR RES RESOURCES, NIH, 1971-; resident, Duke Hosp, 1970-1971; intern med, Duke Hosp, 1969-1970; engr plastics develop, E I du Pont Del Nemours & Co Inc, 1963-1965; engr cryogenic res, Air Prod & Chem, 1962-1963. **Memberships:** Endocrine Soc; Am Asn Cancer Res; Soc Exp Biol Med. **Research Statement & Publications:** Developer of artificial capillary cell culture technique to grow solid organs in vitro; study of the control of prolactin receptors in liver and mammary cancer. **Mailing Address:** Div Clin Res Resources, Nat Ctr Res Resources, NIH, One Democracy Plaza Rm 906 6701 Democracy Blvd MSC 4874, Bethesda, MD 20892-4874. **Fax:** 301-480-3661. **E-Mail:** KnazekR@mail.nih.gov

KNEALE, SAMUEL GEORGE, MATHEMATICS. **Personal Data:** b Tulsa, Okla, December 13, 1921; m 1945, Marian; c Andrew & Elizabeth. **Education:** Univ Kans, AB, 1947, MA, 1948; Harvard Univ, PhD (math), 1953. **Professional Experience:** RETIRED; prin scientist math, Opers Res Inc, 1961-1985; Avco Corp, Ohio, 1959-1961 & Gen Elec Co, 1956-1959; consult math, Philco Corp, Pa, 1951-1956. **Memberships:** Math Asn Am. **Research Statement & Publications:** Applied mathematics, including probability theory and statistics, game theory, systems analysis, and other aspects of operations research. **Mailing Address:** 4111 Cheney Pl, Wilmington, NC 28412.

KNEBEL, HARLEY JOHN, GEOLOGICAL OCEANOGRAPHY, MARINE GEOLOGY. **Personal Data:** b Iowa City, Iowa, November 10, 1941; m 1969, Carole; c Paula T & Ellen J. **Education:** Univ Iowa, BA, 1965; Univ Wash, MS, 1967, PhD (oceanog), 1972. **Professional Experience:** MARINE GEOLOGY CONSULT, VAR PVT CO, 2001-; supvr environ studies, Ctr Coastal & Marine Geol, US Geol Surv, 1996-2001; mem adv bd, Geol Dept, Univ Iowa, 1988-; assoc br chief, Ctr Coastal & Marine Geol, US Geol Surv, 1985-1993; OCEANOGR, CTR COASTAL & MARINE GEOL, US GEOL SURV, 1973-; Texaco fel oceanog, Univ Wash, 1971-1972; res assoc, Univ Wash, 1969-1973; oceanogr, Nat Oceanic & Atmospheric Admin, Atlantic Oceanog & Meteorol Labs, 1967-1969; res asst oceanog, Univ Wash, 1965-1967. **Memberships:** Am Geophys Union; fel Geol Soc Am; Sigma Xi. **Research Statement & Publications:** Sedimentology; estuarine, nearshore, and continental shelf sedimentary processes and stratigraphy; statistics applied to geological oceanography; mass movements of sediments on continental slopes; clay mineralogy; submarine canyon development; coastal environments. **Mailing Address:** 44 Cachalot Ln, Falmouth, MA 02540. **E-Mail:** hknebel@usgs.gov

KNECHT, CHARLES DANIEL, VETERINARY SURGERY, NEUROLOGY. **Personal Data:** b Halethorpe, Md, March 22, 1932; wid, c Charles M & Thomas R. **Education:** Univ Pa, VMD, 1956; Univ Md, Col Park, BS, 1960; Univ Ill, Urbana, MS, 1966; Am Col Vet Surgeons, dipl, 1968; Am Col Vet Internal Med, dipl & cert neurol, 1974. **Honors & Awards:** Norden Award, 1976; Gaines Award, 1982. **Professional Experience:** PROF EMER, SMALL ANIMAL SURG & MED, COL VET MED, AUBURN UNIV, 1997-; pres & chmn bd, Am Col Vet Surg, 1988-1990; assoc ed, Vet Med Report, 1987-1990; pres neurol specialty, Am Col Vet Internal Med, 1983-1986; mem grad fac, Auburn Univ, beginning 1980; prof & head, dept small animal surg & med, Col Vet Med, Auburn Univ, beginning 1979; abstractor, Auburn Univ, beginning 1979; prof & chief surg, Sch Vet Sci & Med, Purdue Univ, West Lafayette, 1972-1979; mem grad fac, Purdue Univ, 1972-1979; mem grad fac, Univ Ga, 1971-1972; prof med & surg, Col Vet Med, Univ Ga, 1970-1972; abstractor, J World & Europ Vet Surgeons, 1968-1972; mem grad fac, Univ Ill, Urbana, 1968-1970; assoc prof vet surg, Col Vet Med, Univ Ill, Urbana, 1968-1970; abstractor, Chirurgia Veterinaria, WGer, 1966-1968; from instr to asst prof vet med & surg, Col Vet Med, Univ Ill, Urbana, 1964-1968; assoc vet, Towson Vet Hosp, Md, 1959-1964; assoc vet, Wertz Memorial Animal Hosp, Pittsburgh, 1958-1959; assoc vet, Broad St Vet Hosp, Richmond, Va, 1956. **Memberships:** Am Vet Med Asn; Am Col Vet Surg (pres, 1988-1989); Am Asn Vet Neurol (pres, 1974-1975); Am Asn Vet Clinicians (pres, 1991-1992); Am Animal Hosp Asn; Am Col Vet Internal Med; Nat Acad Vet Pract. **Research Statement & Publications:** Orthopedic surgery; neurosurgery; electrodiagnostics. **Mailing Address:** Dept Small Animal Surg & Med, Col Vet Med Auburn Univ, Auburn, AL 36849-5523. **E-Mail:** knechcd@vetmed.auburn.edu

KNECHT, DAVID JORDAN, MAGNETOSPHERIC PHYSICS. **Personal Data:** b Elgin, Ill, June 2, 1930; m 1957, Dzidra; c Frederick Jordan. **Education:** Univ Ill, BS, 1951, MS, 1952; Univ Wis, PhD (physics), 1958. **Professional Experience:** SCI EMER, SPACE VEHICLES DIV, AIR FORCE RES LAB, HANSCOM, 1997-; physicist, Spacecraft Interactions Br, Phillips Lab, Mass, Hanscom AFB, 1991-1997; physicist, Space Physics Div, Geophys Lab, 1975-1991; res physicist, Space Physics Lab, Air Force Cambridge Res Labs, 1964-1975; sci dir, Space Physics Br, Air Force Weapons Lab, 1963-1964; res physicist spec proj div, Air Force Spec Weapons Ctr, 1961-1963; proj officer physics div, Air Force Spec Weapons Ctr, 1959-1961; Proj assoc nuclear physics, Univ Wis, 1958-1959. **Research Statement & Publications:** Magnetospheric substorms and other disturbances using magnetic measurements made by ground networks and spacecraft; interactions of orbiting vehicles with space plasmas using spectroscopic observations made on space shuttle. **Mailing Address:** 56 S Rd, Bedford, MA 01730. **E-Mail:** kewiki@mindspring.com

KNECHT, LAURANCE A, ANALYTICAL CHEMISTRY, PHYSICAL CHEMISTRY. **Personal Data:** b Elgin, Ill, March 16, 1932; m 1966, c 1. **Education:** Univ Ill, BS, 1953; Univ Minn, PhD (anal chem), 1959. **Professional Experience:** AT NC SCH SCI & MATH, 1985-; from assoc prof to prof chem, Marietta Col, 1968-1984; asst prof, Univ Cincinnati, 1963-1968; Instr chem, Iowa State Univ, 1960-1963. **Memberships:** AAAS; Am Chem Soc. **Research Statement & Publications:** Electroanalytical techniques. **Mailing Address:** 1303 Willow Dr, Chapel Hill, NC 27514-2607.

KNECHT, WILLIAM G, MECHANICAL ENGINEERING, NUCLEAR ENGINEERING. **Honors & Awards:** Bernard F Langer Nuclear Codes & Stand Award, Am Soc Mech Engrs, 1995. **Mailing Address:** 1330 Campbell St, Williamsport, PA 17701.

KNECHTLI, RONALD (C), PHYSICS. **Personal Data:** b Geneva, Switz, August 14, 1927; American citizen; m 1953, Diane; c Alain, Bernard & Daniel. **Education:** Swiss Fed Inst Technol, Dipl, 1950, PhD (elec eng), 1955. **Honors & Awards:** Outstanding Work Res Award, RCA Lab; L A Hyland Patent Award. **Professional Experience:** RETIRED; sr scientist, Res Labs, Hughes Aircraft Co, 1958-1986; res engr, Res Labs, Radio Corp Am, 1953-1958; res engr, Brown Boveri & Co, 1952-1953; asst, Mass Inst Technol, 1951-1952; res engr, Brown Boveri & Co, Switz, 1950-1951. **Memberships:** Am Inst Aeronaut & Astronaut; Am Phys Soc; Sigma Xi; Inst Elec & Electronics Engrs. **Research Statement & Publications:** Photovoltaic and electrochemical devices. **Mailing Address:** 22929 Ardwick St, Woodland Hills, CA 91364.

KNEE, DAVID ISAAC, TEACHING, TEACHER TRAINING. **Personal Data:** b New York, NY, July 13, 1934; m 1983, Myra; c Adam & Jonathan. **Education:** City Col NY, BS, 1956; Mass Inst Technol, PhD (math), 1962. **Professional Experience:** PROF EMER, DEPT MATH, HOFSTRA UNIV, 1999-; dir, teacher Training Inst, Hofstra Univ, 1986-1998; prof math, Hofstra Univ, 1989-1999; assoc prof math, Hofstra Univ, 1969-1989; asst prof, Hofstra Univ, 1965-1969; instr math, Columbia Univ, 1962-1965; mathematician, Arde Assocs, NJ, 1956. **Memberships:** Mem, Math Asn Am; Nat Coun Teachers Math. **Research Statement & Publications:** Algebra; mathematics education; representation theory; mathematical linguistics. **Mailing Address:** Dept Math, Hofstra Univ, Adams Hall Hempstead Turnpike, Hempstead, NY 11550-1090. **E-Mail:** matdzk@hofstra.edu

KNEE, TERENCE EDWARD CREASEY, SYNTHETIC TEXTILE FIBERS. **Personal Data:** b Brussels, Belg, April 20, 1932; m 1956, Martha; c Christine & Michael. **Education:** Trinity Col, Dublin, BASc, 1953; Mass Inst Technol, PhD (chem), 1956. **Professional Experience:** RETIRED; consult, 1985-1996; tech supt, Chattanooga Res & Develop Sect, 1976-1985; tech supt, E I Du Pont De Nemours & Co Inc, 1972-1976; sr supvr, E I Du Pont De Nemours & Co Inc, 1970-1972; res supvr, E I Du Pont De Nemours & Co Inc, 1960-1970; res chemist, Du Pont Co Can, 1957-1960; instr chem, Franklin Tech Inst, 1955-1956. **Memberships:** Am Chem Soc. **Research Statement & Publications:** Synthetic textile fibers; polymer chemistry; reaction mechanisms. **Mailing Address:** 228 Masters Rd, Hixson, TN 37343.

KNEEBONE, LEON RUSSELL, MYCOLOGY. **Personal Data:** b Bangor, Pa, May 28, 1920; m 1945, Elizabeth C Morgan; c Patricia A, Stephen B & Eileen E. **Education:** Pa

State Univ, BS, 1942, PhD (bot), 1950. **Professional Experience:** PROF EMER BOT & PLANT PATH, PA STATE UNIV, 1978-; founder & gen chmn, mushroom indust short course, Pa State Univ, 1956-1978; from asst prof to prof, PA State Univ, 1950-1978; Asst bot, PA State Univ, 1947-1950; Consult mushroom indust, int consult, nat govt Australia, Jamaica, Haiti & Dominician Repub. **Memberships:** AAAS; Bot Soc Am; Mycol Soc Am; Am Phytopath Soc; Am Inst Biol Sci; Am Mushroom Inst; Mushroom Grower Asn UK; Mushroom Grower Asn Can; Mushroom Grower Asn Australia; Int Soc Mushroom Sci; Sigma Xi. **Research Statement & Publications:** Mushroom culture, especially spawn and strain development, diseases; edible fungi. **Mailing Address:** Dept Bot & Plant Path, State Col, Pa State Univ, University Park, PA 16803.

KNEEBONE, WILLIAM ROBERT, AGRONOMY, PLANT BREEDING. **Personal Data:** b Eveleth, Minn, July 11, 1922; m 1948, c 3. **Education:** Univ Minn, BS, 1947, MS, 1950, PhD (plant genetics), 1951. **Professional Experience:** RETIRED; consult, revegetation & golf course maintenance; prof agron, Univ Ariz, beginning 1963; res agronomist, Okla Agr Exp Sta & Crop Res Div Agr Res Serv, USDA, 1951-1963; asst grass breeding, Univ Minn, 1947-1950. **Memberships:** Fel AAAS; Am Soc Agron; Coun Agr Sci & Technol; Soc Econ Bot; Sigma Xi. **Research Statement & Publications:** Breeding; genetics; seed production; factors involved in stand establishment, vigor and spread of forage and turf grasses; water use by grasses. **Mailing Address:** 2491 N Camino De Oeste, Tucson, AZ 85745.

KNEECE, ROLAND ROYCE, JR, MATHEMATICS, OPERATIONS RESEARCH. **Personal Data:** b Tifton, Ga, October 15, 1939; m 1963. **Education:** Ga Inst Technol, BS, 1961, MS, 1962; Univ Md, PhD (math), 1970. **Professional Experience:** MEM STAFF, ACQUISITION &LOGISTICS, OFF SECY DEFENSE, 1974-; prof lectr, Am Univ, 1969-; mem staff opers res, Inst Defense Anal, Arlington, 1967-1974; OPER RES ANALYST, DEFENSE DEPT. **Memberships:** Am Math Soc; Asn Comput Mach. **Research Statement & Publications:** Operator theory; functional analysis; strictly singular operators; computer technology. **Mailing Address:** 7406 Colshire Dr 3, McLean, VA 22102.

KNEIB, RONALD THOMAS, ECOLOGY. **Personal Data:** b Pittsburgh, Pa, January 29, 1951; m 1994, Jennifer. **Education:** Pa State Univ, BS, 1972; Univ NC, Chapel Hill, MA, 1976, PhD (ecol), 1980. **Professional Experience:** TEMP GRAD FAC, UNIV S CAROLINA, 2003-; SR RES SCIENTIST, UNIV GA MARINE INST, 1994-; adj assoc prof, Dept Marine Sci, Univ Ga, 1992-; GRAD FAC, UNIV GA, 1991-; adj assoc res scientist, Zool Dept, Univ Ga, 1986-; assoc res scientist, Univ Ga Marine Inst, 1986-1993; vis assoc prof, Col Marine Studies, Univ Del, 1986; adj asst prof, Zool Dept, Univ Ga, 1985-1986; asst res scientist, Univ Ga Marine Inst, 1984-1986; res assoc, Univ Ga Marine Inst, 1981-1983. **Memberships:** Ecol Soc Am; Am Fisheries Soc; Estuarine Res Fedn; Am Soc Zoologists; Am Soc Ichthyologists & Herpetologists; Sigma Xi; Soc Wetland Scientists. **Research Statement & Publications:** Ecological interactions within and between populations of estuarine fishes and invertebrates; laandscape ecology of coastal wetlands. **Mailing Address:** Univ Ga Marine Inst, Sapelo Island, GA 31327. **Fax:** 912-485-2182. **E-Mail:** rtkneib@uga.edu

KNEIP, THEODORE JOSEPH, ANALYTICAL CHEMISTRY, ENVIRONMENTAL CHEMISTRY. **Personal Data:** b St Paul, Minn, December 20, 1926; div, c 6. **Education:** Univ Minn, BCh, 1950; Univ Ill, MS, 1952, PhD, 1954. **Professional Experience:** RETIRED; mem, Intersoc Comt Methods Air Sampling & Anal, beginning 1987; consult, US NIH, US Environ Protection Agency, Off Tech Assessment-Cong, Nat Oceanic & Atmospheric Admin, State NY & NJ, NY City Dept Health & var industs; chmn & ed, CLSP Subcomt Biol Monitoring-Manual Method, Am Pub Health Asn, 1986-1988; mem, Environ Health Subcomt, NY Acad Med, beginning 1984; dir, Lab Environ Studies, NY Univ Med Ctr, 1984-1991; asst dir, Lab Environ Studies, NY Univ Med Ctr, 1971-1983; mgr, Lab Supply Res, 1963-1966; asst mgr, Uranium Div, Anal Lab, 1961-1963; head, Anal Res Lab, 1959-1961; chemist, Mallinckrodt Chem Works, 1954-1958. **Memberships:** Fel NY Acad Sci; AAAS; Inst Stand Orgn (secy, 1975-1983); Am Chem Soc; Am Pub Health Asn; Am Indust Hyg Asn; Sigma Xi. **Research Statement & Publications:** Analysis, wet and instrumental; sampling and evaluation of natural and polluted environmental systems, air, water, biota, hazardous wastes; toxicological studies in aquatic and mammalian species. **Mailing Address:** Rte One Box 1836, Manchester Center, VT 05255.

KNELLER, ROBERT WILLIAM, LAW BIOMEDICAL RESEARCH & TECHNOLOGY TRANSFER, JAPANESE BIOMEDICAL SCIENCE & SCIENCE POLICY. **Personal Data:** b Chicago, Ill, February 7, 1954; m 1991, Sachiko Shudo. **Education:** Swarthmore Col, BA, 1975; Harvard Univ, JD, 1980; Mayo Med Sch, MD, 1984; Johns Hopkins Univ, MPH, 1986. **Professional Experience:** Abe fel & guest res, Univ Tokyo, Res Ctr Advan Sci & Technol, 1997-1998; technol transfer & develop scientist, Technol Develop & Commercialization Branch, NCI, NIH, 1995-199; prog off japan, Fogarty Int Ctr, NIH, 1992-1995; resident physician, Occup Safety & Health Admin, 1992; med officer, WHO, 1991-1992; prev med resident, Johns Hopkins Univ, 1991-1992; disaster relief Turkey & China, Red Cross, 1991; cancer epidemiologist, Nat Cancer Inst, 1988-1991; physician & pub health teacher, China, 1986-1987; pediat resident, Univ Hawaii, 1984-1985. **Research Statement & Publications:** Epidemiology of stomach and other cancers; refugee health; protein engineering and environmental biotechnology in Japan. **Mailing Address:** Ctr Advan Sci & Technol, Univ Tokyo, 4-6-1 Komaba, Meguro-ku, 153-8904, Japan. **E-Mail:** kuukai@kneller.jp

KNEPPER, MARK A, ELECTROLYTE METABOLISM. **Personal Data:** b Toledo, Ohio, October 23, 1948. **Education:** Univ Mich, BSE, 1970; Case Western Res Univ, Phd, 1975 (biomed engineering), MD, 1976. **Professional Experience:** CHIEF, INTRAMURAL RES DIV, NAT HEART, LUNG & BLOOD INST, NIH, 2002-; cheif, Renal Mech Sect, Nat Heart Lung & Blood Inst, NIH, 1988. **Memberships:** Int Soc Nephrology; Am Soc Nephrology. **Research Statement & Publications:** Electrolyte metabolism. **Mailing Address:** Lab Kidney & Electrolyte Metab, Nat Heart Lung & Blood Inst, NIH, Rm 6N260 10 Ctr Dr Bldg 10 MSC 1603, Bethesda, MD 20892-1603. **Fax:** 301-402-1443. **E-Mail:** knepperm@mail.nih.gov

KNEPPER, SHEILA M, PHARMACOLOGY. **Personal Data:** b SDak, February 27, 1953. **Education:** Univ Nebr, BS, 1975; Univ Kans, MS, 1984, PhD (pharmacol), 1985. **Professional Experience:** SR RES PHARMACOLOGIST, ABBOTT LABS, 1988-; sr res pharmacologist, Monsanto Labs, 1985-1988. **Memberships:** Am Soc Cell Biol; Am Soc Pharmacol. **Research Statement & Publications:** Pharmacology. **Mailing Address:** 573 Pine Grove St, Gurnee, IL 60031.

KNERR, REINHARD H, MICROWAVES, LIGHTWAVE. **Personal Data:** b Pirmasens, Ger, February 18, 1939; m 1968, c 4. **Education:** Tech Univ Aachen, BS, 1960; Enseeht, Toulouse France, dipl eng, 1962; Lehigh Univ, MS, 1964, PhD (elec eng), 1968. **Professional Experience:** Lectr, Inst Elec & Electronics Engrs-Microwave Theory & Tech Soc, 1988-; pres, Inst Elec & Electronics Engrs-Microwave Theory & Tech Soc, 1986; supvr lightwave technol, supvr, Integrated Optics, 1981-1984; mem admin comt, Inst Elec & Electronics Engrs-Microwave Theory & Tech Soc, 1980-; supvr, At&T Bell Labs, beginning 1979; supvr fiber optic components, 1979-1981; mem tech staff, 1968-1979, AT&T Bell Labs. **Memberships:** Fel Inst Elec & Electronics Engrs. **Research Statement & Publications:** Fiber optics; lightwaves; microwave circulators; power amps; integrated optics; local area networks; data interfaces. **Mailing Address:** AT&T Bell Labs, 9999 Hamilton Blvd, Breinigsville, PA 18031-9359. **Fax:** 610-391-2236. **E-Mail:** rhknerr@aluxpo.att.com

KNESEL, JOHN ARTHUR, REPRODUCTIVE PHYSIOLOGY, CHELONIAN REPRODUCTION. **Personal Data:** b Ferriday, La, January 20, 1949; c Martha K atherine. **Education:** NE La Univ, BS, 1971, MS, 1974; Purdue Univ, PhD (reproductive physiol), 1983. **Professional Experience:** ASSOC PROF BIOL, UNIV LA MONROE, 1990-; asst prof, NE La Univ, 1985-1990; asst prof, Purdue Univ, 1984-1985; vis lectr biol, Purdue Univ, 1981-1984; Grad instr, David Ross fel, 1978-1981; Grad instr, Purdue Univ, 1975-1978. **Memberships:** Sigma Xi; Soc Study Reproduction; Soc Study Reptiles & Amphibians; Am Soc Animal Sci; Human Anat & Physiol Soc. **Research Statement & Publications:** Reproductive physiology in macroclemys temmincki and other turtles; physiology of the oviduct and the effects of elevated temperature on reproduction in the female. **Mailing Address:** Dept Biol, Univ La at Monroe, Monroe, LA 71209. **E-Mail:** biknesel@ulm.edu

KNEVEL, ADELBERT MICHAEL, MEDICINAL CHEMISTRY. **Personal Data:** b St Joseph, Minn, October 20, 1922; m 1950, c 5. **Education:** NDak State Univ, BS, 1952, MS, 1953; Purdue Univ, PhD (med chem), 1957. **Professional Experience:** Assoc dean, Sch Pharm & Pharm Sci, Purdue Univ, W Lafayette, beginning 1975; asst dean, Sch Pharm & Pharm Sci, 1968-1975; PROF EMER MED CHEM & MOLECULAR PHARMACOL, SCH PHARM & PHARM SCI, PURDUE UNIV, W LAFAYETTE, 1965-; from instr to assoc prof med chem, Sch Pharm & Pharm Sci, Purdue Univ, West Lafayette, 1954-1965; Instr pharmaceut chem, NDak State Univ, 1953-1954. **Memberships:** AAAS; Am Chem Soc; Am Asn Pharm Scientists; fel Am Asn Pharm Sci. **Research Statement & Publications:** Methods development for drugs; drug metabolites in biological systems; studies of mechanism of drug action. **Mailing Address:** Dept Med Chem & Molecular Pharmacol, Sch Pharm, Purdue Univ, Lafayette, IN 47907-9980.

KNEZOVICH, JOHN, ENVIRONMENTAL CHEMISTRY. **Education:** Univ Calif, Davis, MS 1980, PhD (Chem Ecol) 1983; Univ Pac, BS (biol) 1977. **Professional Experience:** ADJ PROF ENVRION TOXICOL, LAWRENCE LIVERMORE NAT LAB, UNIV CALIF, as of 2004. **Mailing Address:** Dept Envrion Toxicol, Lawrence Livermore Nat Lab, Univ Calif, PO Box 808 L-397, Livermore, CA 94550. **Fax:** 925-423-7884. **E-Mail:** knezovich1@llnl.gov

KNIAZZEH, ALFREDO G(IOVANNI) F(RANCESCO), MECHANICAL ENGINEERING, PHYSICAL CHEMISTRY. **Personal Data:** b New York, NY, July 31, 1938; m 1968, c 2. **Education:** Mass Inst Technol, BS, 1959, MS, 1961, PhD (mech eng), 1966. **Professional Experience:** DISTINGUISHED SCIENTISTS POLARID CARB, 2000-; prod develop mgr, Polaroid Corp, 1984-2000; asst lab mgr, Polaroid Corp, 1978-1984; from scientist to sr scientist, Polaroid Corp, 1970-1978; Physicist, Electronics Res Ctr, NASA, 1966-1970. **Memberships:** Am Phys Soc; Am Vacuum Soc; Electrochem Soc; Mat Res Soc. **Research Statement & Publications:** Thin films; physical electronics; mechanics of materials; photochemistry; chemical kinetics; thermodynamics; radiation transport; fluid mechanics; direct energy conversion; electrochemistry; optics; solid state physics; electronics engineering. **Mailing Address:** 1265 Main St W4 4H, Waltham, MA 02154.

KNICKLE, HAROLD NORMAN, CHEMICAL ENGINEERING. **Personal Data:** b Boston, Mass, January 6, 1936; m 1963, Sharon; c Kimberly & Norman. **Education:** Univ Mass, BSME, 1962; Rensselaer Polytech Inst, MS, 1965, PhD (nuclear eng), 1969. **Professional Experience:** PROF CHEM ENG, UNIV RI, as of 1982; Associate Dean Engr 1992-2004, Res prof, Pittsburgh Energy Technol Ctr, 1977-1980; assoc prof chem eng, Univ Ri, 1969-1982; Engr nuclear eng, Knolls Atomic Power Lab, Gen Elec Co, 1962-1966. **Memberships:** Am Inst Chem Engrs; Am Soc Eng Educ; Sigma Xi; Tau Beta Pi. **Research Statement & Publications:** Fuel Cells and Batteries, Mass transfer including azeotropic and extractive distillation, gas absorption, and leaching; heat transfer including single and two phase flow and insulation properties; design including mass transfer and heat transfer equipment; multiphase flow. **Mailing Address:** Dept Chem Eng, Univ Ri, Rm 122, Crawford Hall, Kingston, RI 02881. **Fax:** 401-874-4689. **E-Mail:** knickle@egr.uri.edu

KNICKMEYER, JOE W, MATHEMATICS. **Professional Experience:** INSTR MATH, FLA INST TECHNOL, VA, as of 2005. **Memberships:** Am Math Soc. **Mailing Address:** Fla Inst Technol, 206 Deauville Circle, Newport News, VA 23606-1526. **E-Mail:** jknickmeyer@cox.net

KNIEBES, DUANE VAN, ANALYTICAL CHEMISTRY, RESEARCH ADMINISTRATION. **Personal Data:** b Marquette, Mich, May 17, 1926; m 1950, c 3. **Education:** Mich State Univ, BS, 1948; Ill Inst Technol, MS, 1954. **Honors & Awards:** Merit Award, Am Soc Testing & Mat; Gold Merit Award, Am Gas Asn. **Professional Experience:** CONSULT, 1984-; asst vpres educ serv, Instrumental Anal Lab, Inst Gas Technol, 1975-1984; dir opers, Instrumental Anal Lab, Inst Gas Technol, 1969-1975; assoc dir, Instrumental Anal Lab, Inst Gas Technol, 1962-1969; asst res dir, Instrumental Anal Lab, Inst Gas Technol, 1957-1962; supvr, head Anal Div, 1954-1957; supvr, Instrumental Anal Lab, Inst Gas Technol, 1951-1954; asst chemist, Instrumental Anal Lab, Inst Gas Technol, 1949-1951. **Memberships:** Am Chem Soc; Am Soc Testing& Mat; Am Gas Asn. **Research Statement & Publications:** Odorization of natural and liquid propane gases; analysis of gaseous fuels; management of research and research facilities; design and operation of engineering education and technician training programs in natural gas technology. **Mailing Address:** 4612 Hampshire St, Boulder, CO 80301.

KNIEF, RONALD ALLEN, REACTOR & FUEL FACILITY SAFETY, EDUCATION & TRAINING & RISK MANAGEMENT. **Personal Data:** b Hinsdale, Ill, October 8, 1944; m 1983, Pamela; c Kyle A. **Education:** Albion Col, BA, 1967; Univ Ill, PhD (nuclear eng), 1972. **Honors & Awards:** Achievement Award, Am Nuclear Soc, Nuclear Criticality Safety Div, 1983. **Professional Experience:** PRIN CONSULT, OGDEN ENVIRON & ENERGY SERV CO, 1990-; consult, Babcock & Wilcox Naval Nuclear Fuel Div & Westinghouse Goco Nuclear Safety Comt, 1988-1993; staff consult, prog safety comn, 1987-1990; mgr corp training, prog safety comn, 1986-1987; co-chair, prog safety comn, 1985-1986; mgr educ develop, Three Mile Island, GPU Nuclear Corp, 1983-1985; adj prof, Univ NMex & Pa State Univ, 1980- & Pa State Univ, 1980-1993; mgr plant training, Three Mile Island, GPU Nuclear Corp, 1980-1983; consult, Sandia Nat Lab, 1974-1981; from asst to assoc prof nuclear eng, Univ NMex, 1974-1980; sr physicist, Combustion Eng, Inc, 1972-1974; adj prof, Univ Hartford, 1972-1974. **Memberships:** Am Nuclear Soc; Sigma Xi; Inst Nuclear Mat Mgt; AAAS. **Research Statement & Publications:** Nuclear reactor technology and safety; nuclear fuel facility safety and risk management; education and training development. **Mailing Address:** PO Box 90818, Albuquerque, NM 87199-0818. **Fax:** 505-881-9357.

KNIEVEL, DANIEL PAUL, CROP PHYSIOLOGY, STRESS PHYSIOLOGY. **Personal Data:** b West Point, Nebr, January 29, 1943; m 1965, c Jason & Ann. **Education:** Univ Nebr, Lincoln, BS, 1965; Univ Wis-Madison, MS, 1967, PhD (agron, biochem), 1968. **Professional Experience:** Topic mgr, Rev Panel, USDA-Small Bus Innovation Res Grant Prog, 1989; mem, Rev Panel, USDA- Small Bus Innovation Res Grant Prog, 1988; bd dirs, Coun Agr Sci & Technol, 1987-1990; crop sci adv, Postgrad Develop Proj Sri Lanka, 1985; vis scientist, Sea Educ Admin, USDA, 1980-1981; assoc ed, Agron J, 1978-1983; ASSOC PROF CROP PHYSIOL, PA STATE UNIV, UNIV PARK, 1975-2005; asst prof, PA State Univ, Univ Park, 1972-1975; crop sci adv, Pa State Univ-USAID, Grad Sch Develop Proj Arg, 1972-1974; NSF grant, 1969-1972; crop physiologist plant sci, Univ Wyo, 1968-1972. **Memberships:** Am Soc Agron; Crop Sci Soc Am; Am Soc Plant Physiol; Coun Agr Sci & Technol; Soil Sci Soc Am; Nat Asn Col Teachers Agr. **Research Statement & Publications:** Physiology of assimilate transport in plants; physiology of crop response to environmental stress; computer simulation of crop growth and development; phloem unloading and sink metabolism. **Mailing Address:** Dept Agron, Pa State Univ, 254 Agr Sci & Indust Bldg, Univ Park, PA 16802. **Fax:** 814-863-7043. **E-Mail:** dpk@psu.edu

KNIFFEN, DONALD AVERY, ASTROPHYSICS, GAMMA-RAY ASTRONOMY. **Personal Data:** b Kalamazoo, Mich, April 27, 1933; m 1952, Janis; c Karyol (Poole), Donald Jr & Kimberly. **Education:** La State Univ, BS, 1959; Wash Univ, St Louis, MA, 1960; Cath Univ Am, PhD, 1967. **Professional Experience:** Adj prof, Hampden-Sydney Col 2001-2002; DEP PROG SCIENTIST CHANDRA X-RAY OBSERV, NASA HQ, 1999-; WILLIAM W ELLIOTT PROF & CHMN, DEPT PHYSICS & ASTRON, HAMPTON-SYDNEY COL, 1992-; consult, Compton Observ, Goddard Space Flight Ctr, NASA, beginning 1991; astrophysicist & proj scientist, Compton Observ, Goddard Space Flight Ctr, NASA, 1960-1991. **Memberships:** Royal Astron Soc; Am Astron Soc; Am Phys Soc; Am Asn Univ Profs; Sigma Xi; Int Astro Union. **Research Statement & Publications:** Galactic and solar cosmic rays, including both charged particles and gamma rays; trapped radiation, pulsars; historic research includes pioneering work in the study of trapped radiation, Von Allen belts, galactic and solar cosmic rays and space instrumentation; gamma-ray astronomy; science program management. **Mailing Address:** Chandra X-Ray Observ, NASA, Harvard-Smithsonian Ctr Astropys, Cambridge, MA 02138. **Fax:** 202-358-3096, 617-495-7356. **E-Mail:** dkniffen@hq.nasa.gov

KNIGHT, ALAN, ENTOMOLOGY. **Professional Experience:** RES ENTOMOLOGIST, YAKIMA AGR RES LAB, AGR RES SERV, USDA, as of 2004. **Mailing Address:** Yakima Agr Res Lab, USDA, Agr Res Serv, 5230 Konnowac Pass Rd, Wapato, WA 98951. **Fax:** 509-454-5646. **E-Mail:** aknight@yarl.ars.usda.gov

KNIGHT, ALAN CAMPBELL, POLYMER SCIENCE. **Personal Data:** b Hartford, Conn, November 2, 1922; m 1948, c 2. **Education:** Ore State Col, BS, 1948; Univ Calif, Berkeley, PhD (chem), 1950. **Professional Experience:** RETIRED; res assoc, Polymer Prod Dept, Wash Lab, 1973-1986; res assoc, E I du Pont de Nemours & Co, Inc, Wilmington, 1967-1973; sr supvr res & develop, E I du Pont de Nemours & Co, Inc, Wilmington, 1958-1967; tech supt, E I du Pont de Nemours & Co, Inc, Wilmington, 1956-1958; asst tech supt mfg, E I du Pont de Nemours & Co, Inc, Wilmington, 1955-1956; chemist, E I du Pont de Nemours & Co, Inc, Wilmington, 1950-1955. **Memberships:** Am Chem Soc. **Research Statement & Publications:** Reaction kinetics and mechanisms; polymer synthesis; degradation mechanisms; stabilization; relation of structure to properties; manufacture of heavy organic chemicals; applied mathematics; computer applications; applied physical theory. **Mailing Address:** Rte One Box 231, Parkersburg, WV 26101.

KNIGHT, ALLEN WARNER, AQUATIC ECOLOGY, WATER POLLUTION. **Personal Data:** b Grand Rapids, Mich, February 7, 1932; m 1955, Barbara; c Valerie L, Kimberly S, Pamala A & Richard A. **Education:** Western Mich Univ, BS, 1959; Mich State Univ, MS, 1961; Univ Utah, PhD (zoology), 1965. **Professional Experience:** PROF EMER WATER SCI, UNIV CALIF, DAVIS, 1994-; from asst prof to prof hydrobiol, Univ Calif, Davis, 1968-1994; asst prof entom & zool, Mich State Univ, 1965-1968; consult, EBASCO Environ Inc. **Memberships:** AAAS; Ecol Soc Am; Am Soc Limnol & Oceanog; Inst Soc Limnol; Entom Soc Am. **Research Statement & Publications:** Pollution ecology; effect of environmental factors and pollutants on aquatic life; aquaculture, culture of freshwater organisms; growth metabolism studies of aquatic life; hydrobiology; trace element (Se) bioaccumulation and toxicity. **Mailing Address:** Dept Hydrol, Univ Calif, 113 Veihmeyer Hall, Davis, CA 95616. **Fax:** 530-752-1552.

KNIGHT, ARTHUR ROBERT, PHOTOCHEMISTRY. **Personal Data:** b St John's, Nfld, February 24, 1938; m 1986, c 8. **Education:** Mem Univ Nfld, BSc, 1958, MSc, 1960; Univ Alta, PhD (chem), 1962. **Professional Experience:** ACTG ASSOC VPRES ACAD, UNIV SASK, 1990-; dean, Col Arts & Sci, 1981-1990; PROF CHEM, UNIV SASK, 1976-; head dept, Univ Sask, 1976-1981; from asst prof to assoc prof, Univ Sask, 1964-1976; Fel chem, Univ Alta, 1962-1964. **Memberships:** Fel Can Inst Chem. **Research Statement & Publications:** Reactions of radicals produced in photolytic decompositions; primary process studies in photolyses; photochemistry and photophysics of sulfur containing compounds. **Mailing Address:** 354 Balfour St, Saskatoon, SK S7H 3Z5, Can.

KNIGHT, BRUCE L, CHEMICAL & PETROLEUM ENGINEERING. **Personal Data:** b Kansas City, Mo, January 4, 1942; m 1964, c 2. **Education:** Univ Kans, BS, 1964; Univ Colo, MS, 1965, PhD (chem eng), 1969. **Professional Experience:** SR RES ENGR, MARATHON OIL CO, 1981-; environ coordr, Denver Res Ctr, 1977-1981; sr petrol engr, Denver Res Ctr, 1975-1977; Res engr, Denver Res Ctr, 1969-1975. **Memberships:** Am Inst Chem Engrs; Soc Petrol Engrs; Am Petrol Inst; Sigma Xi. **Research Statement & Publications:** Cryogenic heat transfer through porous media; tertiary oil recovery processes; production logging. **Mailing Address:** Marathon Oil Co, PO Box 269, Littleton, CO 80160.

KNIGHT, BRUCE WINTON, BIOPHYSICS, APPLIED MATHEMATICS. **Personal Data:** b Milwaukee, Wis, December 4, 1930; m 1973, Catherine; c Bruce & Ian. **Education:** Dartmouth Col, BS, 1952. **Professional Experience:** PROF BIOPHYS, ROCKFELLER UNIV, 1961-; staff mem, Los Alamos Sci lab, 1955-1961. **Research Statement & Publications:** Neurophysiology of vision; applied theoretical physics. **Mailing Address:** Dept Biophys, Rockefeller Univ, 1230 York Ave, New York, NY 10021. **E-Mail:** knight@rockefeller.edu

KNIGHT, CHARLES ALFRED, CLOUD PHYSICS, ICE PHYSICS. **Personal Data:** b Chicago, Ill, March 28, 1936; m Nancy. **Education:** Univ Chicago, MS, 1957, PhD (geol), 1959. **Honors & Awards:** Publications Prize, Nat Ctr Atmospheric Res, 1970; Education Prize, 1992; Fellow, American Meteorological Society and AAAS. **Professional Experience:** Mem fac, Univ Wyo, 1977-& Univ Okla, 1995-; SR SCIENTIST, NAT CTR ATMOSPHERIC RES, 1976-; prog scientist cloud physics, Lab Atmospheric Sci, 1962-1974; Res scientist arctic ice, Univ Wash, 1959-1961. **Memberships:** Am Meteorol Soc; Am Geophys Union; Am Asn Crystal Growth; Soc Cryobiology; Glaciol Soc: Am Chem Soc. **Research Statement & Publications:** Structure of hail; formation of rain; biological antifreezes; ice crystal nucleation and growth. **Mailing Address:** Nat Ctr Atmospheric Res, P O Box 3000, Boulder, CO 80307. **Fax:** 303-497-8171. **E-Mail:** knightc@ucar.edu

KNIGHT, CLIFFORD BURNHAM, INSECT ECOLOGY. **Personal Data:** b Rockville, Conn, January 6, 1926; m 1980, c 2. **Education:** Univ Conn, BA, 1950, MA, 1952; Duke Univ, PhD (invert ecol), 1957. **Professional Experience:** RETIRED; dir undergrad studies biol, prof zool, E Carolina Univ, beginning 1989; dir grad studies biol, prof zool, E Carolina Univ, beginning 1964; from asst prof to assoc prof zool, E Carolina Univ, 1957-1964; instr biol, E Carolina Univ, 1956-1957. **Memberships:** Ecol Soc Am; Nat Audubon Soc; Am Inst Biol Sci; Nat Wildlife Fed; Am Entom Soc. **Research Statement & Publications:** Ecology of Collembola in forest communities of North Carolina; benthic invertebrate estuarine ecology. **Mailing Address:** Dept Biol, E Carolina Univ, 1000 W Fifth St, Greenville, NC 27834-3006. **E-Mail:** knightc@mail.ecu.edu

KNIGHT, DAVID BATES, ORGANIC CHEMISTRY. **Personal Data:** b Louisville, Ky, September 23, 1939; m 1965, c 2. **Education:** Univ Louisville, BS, 1961; Duke Univ, MA, 1963, PhD (org chem), 1966. **Professional Experience:** PROF CHEM, UNIV NC, GREENSBORO, 1982-; from asst prof to assoc prof, Univ NC, Greensboro, 1967-1982; vis res assoc chem, Ohio State Univ, 1966-1967, 1977-1978. **Memberships:** AAAS; Am Chem Soc. **Research Statement & Publications:** Protium-deuterium exchange in hydrocarbons; chemistry of fulvenes. **Mailing Address:** Dept Chem & Biochem, Univ NC, 435 New Sci Bldg PO Box 26170, Greensboro, NC 27402-6170. **Fax:** 336-334-5402. **E-Mail:** david_knight@uncg.edu

KNIGHT, DENNIS HAL, PLANT ECOLOGY, ECOSYSTEM ANALYSIS. **Personal Data:** b Clear Lake, SD, December 24, 1937; m 1967, Judith; c Christina L & Charles A. **Education:** Augustana Col, SDak, BA, 1959; Univ Wis-Madison, MS, 1961, PhD (bot), 1964. **Professional Experience:** PROF EMER, DEPT BOT, UNIV WYO, 2000-; prof bot, Univ Wyo, 1979-2000; from asst prof to assoc prof, Univ Wyo, 1966-1979; Instr bot, with Peace Corps, Loja, Ecuador, 1964-1966. **Memberships:** Ecol Soc Am. **Research Statement & Publications:** Ecology of Great Plains and Rocky Mountain Ecosystems; Impact of vegetation structure on ecosystem function. **Mailing Address:** Dept Bot, Univ Wyo, 3165 1000 E Univ Ave, Laramie, WY 82071. **Fax:** 307-766-2851. **E-Mail:** dhknight@uwyo.edu

KNIGHT, DOUGLAS MAITLAND, educational administration; deceased, see previous edition for last biography

KNIGHT, DOUGLAS WAYNE, COMPUTER SCIENCE, ASSEMBLER. **Personal Data:** b Batavia, NY, October 7, 1938; m 1961, c 3. **Education:** Ariz State Univ, BS, 1961, MS, 1969, PhD (elec eng), 1975. **Professional Experience:** PROF COMPUT INFO SYSTS, COLO STATE UNIV, PUEBLO, as of 2003; PROF, DEPT COMPUT ENG TECHNOL FAC, UNIV SOUTHERN COLO, 1993-; assoc prof, Comput Sci Technol Fac, 1991-1993; dept chmn, Dept Comput Eng Technol Fac, Univ Southern Colo, 1980-1990; prog mgr, Kentron Int, 1979; owner, Computerland, Colorado Springs, 1978-1981; prog supvr, Trans Test Ctr, Dynalectron Corp, 1974-1979; contractor, Govt ElectronicsDiv, Motorola, 1973-1974; Referee, Fed Info Processing Stand, 1973; fac assoc prog, Ariz State Univ, 1971-1973; Geophysicist seismol, Shell Oil Co, 1961-1967. **Memberships:** Data Processing Mgt Asn; Asn Comput Mach. **Research Statement & Publications:** Microprocessing operating systems; real-time dynamic structures; role playing simulations; gaming strategies. **Mailing Address:** Dept Comput Info Systs, Colo State Univ, T-234, Pueblo, CO 81001. **E-Mail:** douglas.knight@colostate-pueblo.edu

KNIGHT, DOYLE D, MECHANICAL ENGINEERING. **Education:** Calif Inst Tech, BS, 1971; Occidental Col, BA, 1971; Calif Inst Tech, MS, 1972, PhD (aeronaut), 1974. **Professional Experience:** MARY W RAISLER DISTINGUISHED TEACHING CHAIR, RUTGERS UNIV, 2004-. **Mailing Address:** Rutgers Univ, 98 Brett Rd, Piscataway, NJ 08854-8058. **Fax:** 732-445-3124. **E-Mail:** knight@soemail.rutgers.edu

KNIGHT, ERNEST, IMMUNOLOGY. **Education:** Penn State Univ, BS. **Professional Experience:** STAFF, CEPHALON INC, as of 2006. **Mailing Address:** Cephalon Inc, 145 Brandywine Pkwy, W Chester, PA 19380. **Fax:** 610-344-0065.

KNIGHT, FRANK B, MATHEMATICS & MATHEMATICAL STATISTICS, PREDICTION OF STOCHASTIC PROCESSES & LOCAL TIMES OF BROWNIAN MOTION. **Personal Data:** b Chicago, Ill, October 11, 1933; m 1970, Ingeberg; c Marion A, Marc A & Ellen D. **Education:** Cornell Univ, BA, 1955; Princeton Univ, PhD (math), 1959. **Professional Experience:** PROF EMER MATH & STATIST, UNIV ILL, URBANA, 1991-; prof, Univ Ill, Urbana, 1969-1991; from asst prof to assoc prof, Univ Ill, Urbana, 1963-1969; from instr to asst prof, Univ Minn, 1960-1963; res asst math, Univ Minn, 1959-1960. **Memberships:** Emer mem Am Math Soc; emer mem Inst Math Statist. **Research Statement & Publications:** Probability theory; continuous time stochastic processes. **Mailing Address:** Dept Math Univ Ill, 350 Altgeld Hall, Urbana, IL 61801. **E-Mail:** f-knight@math.uiuc.edu

KNIGHT, FRED BARROWS, FOREST ENTOMOLOGY. **Personal Data:** b Waterville, Maine, December 12, 1925; m 1945, c 3. **Education:** Univ Maine, BSF, 1949; Duke Univ, MF, 1950, DF(forest entom), 1956. **Professional Experience:** EMER PROF & DEAN, FOREST RESOURCES, UNIV MAINE, ORONO, 1991-; dean, Sch Forest Resources, Univ Maine, Orono, 1986-1990; assoc dean, Sch Forest Resources, Univ Maine, Orono, 1983-1986; assoc dir, Maine Agr Exp Sta, Univ Maine, Orono, 1976-1983 & 1986-1990; from vpres to pres, Forestry Res Orgn, Asn State Col & Univ, 1976-1980; prof, Sch Forest Resources, Univ Maine, Orono, 1972-1990; dir, Sch Forest Resources, Univ Maine, Orono, 1972-1983; Vis prof, Sch Forestry, Univ Canterbury, 1970; chmn dept, Univ Mich, 1966-1970; from assoc prof to prof forestry, Univ Mich, 1960-1972; entomologist, Forest Insect & Dis Lab, US Forest Serv, Colo, 1954-1960; Entomologist, Bur Entom & Plant Quarantine, NC, 1950-1951 & Colo, 1951-1954. **Memberships:** Fel AAAS; fel Soc Am Foresters; Entom Soc Am; Soil & Water Conserv Soc; Ecol Soc Am; Forestry Hist Soc. **Research Statement & Publications:** Forest insect population, biological and silvicultural control; silviculture; forest ecology. **Mailing Address:** 395 Main St, Orono, ME 04473-1322.

KNIGHT, GENEVIEVE M, MATHEMATICS. **Education:** Ft Valley State Univ, BS; Clark Atlanta Univ, MS; Univ Md, PhD. **Professional Experience:** PROF, DEPT MATHS & COMPUT SCI, COPPIN STATE UNIV, as of 2005. **Mailing Address:** Dept Math & Comput Sci, Coppin State Univ 2500 W N, Baltimore, MD 21216. **Fax:** 410-669-2861.

KNIGHT, GLENN B, MOLECULAR BIOLOGY. **Education:** Univ Mass, Amherst, BS, 1975; Ohio State Univ, MS, 1977; Boston Univ, PhD (biochem), 1985. **Professional Experience:** STAFF RESEARCHER, LAHEY CLIN MED CTR, 1988-; post doctoral fel, Dana Farber Cancer Inst, Harvard Med Sch, 1984-1988. **Memberships:** Am Soc Microbiol; Am Soc Biol & Molecular Biol. **Mailing Address:** Lahey Clin Med Ctr, Dept Immunol Res & Molecular Biol, 41 Mall Rd, Burlington, MA 01805-0001. **E-Mail:** glenn.knight@lahey.hitchcock.org

KNIGHT, JAMES ALBERT, RADIATION CHEMISTRY OF HYDROCARBONS, PYROLYSIS OF CELLULOSIC MATERIALS. **Personal Data:** b La Grange, Ga, October 16, 1920; m 1948, Marian; c Marcia (Orr), James K & John C. **Education:** Wofford Col, BS, 1942; Ga Inst Technol, MS, 1944; Pa State Univ, PhD (chem), 1950. **Professional Experience:** RETIRED; UNFAD, 1984-1985; Nat Bur Stand, 1980-1981; consult, Indust Firms, 1970-1990; from res assoc prof to res prof, Ga Tech Res Inst, Ga Inst Technol, 1958-1985; from assoc prof to assoc prof chem, Ga Tech Res Inst, Ga Inst Technol, 1950-1958. **Memberships:** AAAS; Am Chem Soc. **Research Statement & Publications:** Pyrolytic and carbon technologies utilizing agricultural and forestry materials; radiation chemistry of organic systems; synthetic organic chemistry; gas and liquid chromatography. **Mailing Address:** 2117 Kodiak Dr NE, Altanta, GA 30345-4149.

KNIGHT, JAMES MILTON, THEORETICAL PHYSICS. **Personal Data:** b Jacksonville, Fla, February 20, 1933; m 1967, c 2. **Education:** Spring Hill Col, BS, 1954; Univ Md, PhD (physics), 1960. **Professional Experience:** PROF PHYSICS & ASTRON, UNIV SC, 1977-; assoc prof physics, Univ SC, 1965-1977; res assoc, Duke Univ, 1963-1965; res assoc & instr physics, Univ Md, 1960-1961. **Memberships:** Am Phys Soc. **Research Statement & Publications:** Quantum optics; chaotic dynamics; symmetry properties; phase transitions. **Mailing Address:** Dept Physics, Univ SC, Columbia, SC 29208. **E-Mail:** knight@sc.edu

KNIGHT, JAMES WILLIAM, REPRODUCTIVE PHYSIOLOGY. **Personal Data:** b Alexandria, La, November 27, 1948. **Education:** Univ Southwestern La, BS, 1970; Univ Fla, MS, 1972, PhD (reprod physiol), 1975. **Professional Experience:** Sabbatical, Fed Repub Ger, 1988-1989; PROF REPROD PHYSIOL, VA POLYTECH INST & STATE UNIV, 1976-; fel reprod physiol, Univ Mo, 1975-1976. **Memberships:** Am Soc Animal Sci; Soc Study Reprod; AAAS. **Research Statement & Publications:** Conceptus-maternal interrelationships; uterine protein secretions; placental function; endocrinology of gestation. **Mailing Address:** Dept Animal & Poultry Sci, Col Agr & Life Sci, Va Tech, 3460 Litton-Reaves Hall, Blacksburg, VA 24061-0306. **Fax:** 540-231-3010. **E-Mail:** knight@vt.edu

KNIGHT, JERE DONALD, physical chemistry; deceased, see previous edition for last biography

KNIGHT, JOHN C (IAN), UNDERWATER ACOUSTICS, AOPERATIONS RESEARCH, ANTI-SUBMARINE WARFARE. **Personal Data:** b Musselburgh, Scotland, June 16, 1926; American citizen; wid Rita (Deceased). **Education:** Univ Edinburgh, BSc, 1950, PhD (physics), 1953. **Professional Experience:** RETIRED; asst tech dir oper, SSBN Security Prog, Off Chief Naval Opers, 1988-1993; consult, Saclant ASW Res Ctr, La Spezia, Italy, 1987; tactical analyst, Staff Comdr ASW Forces, Sixth Fleet, Naples, Italy, 1983-1987; mem prin staff, Summit Res Corp, 1980-1988; prin scientist, EG & G Wash Anal Serv Ctr, 1980; staff scientist, Comdr Oceanog Syst Atlantic, 1974-1977; head, Systs Anal Group, Acoust Div, Naval Res Lab, 1970-1980; sr staff & dep dir, John D Kettelle Corp, Va, 1968-1970; consult, Comt Undersea Warfare, Nat Acad Sci, 1967-1970; sr staff mem, Opers Res Inc, Md, 1965-1968; prin sci officer, Ministry of Defence, Eng, 1963-1965; sci asst to chief scientist, Royal Navy, 1963-1965; mem staff opers res, Saclant Anti-Submarine Warfare Res Ctr, Italy, 1959-1963; prin sci officer, Home Fleet, 1958-1959; sr sci officer, Admiralty, Eng, 1954-1958; asst physics, Univ Edinburgh, 1952-1954. **Memberships:** Sigma Xi. **Research Statement & Publications:** Beta and gamma ray spectroscopy; military operations research; analysis of naval system performance; naval tactics development and evaluation. **Mailing Address:** 3403 Fessenden St NW, Washington, DC 20008.

KNIGHT, JOSIAH D, MECHANICAL ENGINEERING. **Education:** Univ Va, BS (mech eng), 1980, MS (mech eng), 1982, PhD (mech eng), 1986. **Professional Experience:** ASSOC PROF, DEPT MECH ENG & MAT SCI, SCH ENG, DUKE UNIV, as of 2006. **Mailing Address:** Dept Mech Eng, Duke Univ, Durham, NC 27706. **Fax:** 919-660-8963. **E-Mail:** jknight@acpub.duke.edu

KNIGHT, KATHERINE LATHROP, BIOCHEMISTRY, IMMUNOLOGY. **Personal Data:** b Jackson, Mich, May 13, 1941. **Education:** Elmira Col, BA, 1962; Ind Univ, PhD (chem), 1966. **Professional Experience:** CHAIR MICROBIOL & IMMUNOL, UNIV ILL MED CTR, CHICAGO, as of 2005; PROF MICROBIOL & IMMUNOL, UNIV ILL MED CTR, CHICAGO, 1975-; NIH res career develop award, 1970-1975; from asst prof to assoc prof, Univ Ill Med Ctr, Chicago, 1968-1975; res assoc, Univ Ill Med Ctr, Chicago, 1966-1968. **Memberships:** AAAS; Am Chem Soc; Am Asn Immunologists. **Research Statement & Publications:** Immunochemistry; immunogenetics; protein chemistry. **Mailing Address:** Dept Microbiol & Immunol, Loyola Univ Chicago, Stritch Sch Med, 2160 S First Ave Bldg 105 Rm 3846, Maywood, IL 60153. **Fax:** 708-216-9574. **E-Mail:** kknight@lumc.edu

KNIGHT, KATHY B, TEACHING UNDERGRADUATE & GRADUATE NUTRITION & FOODS COURSES, CALCIUM & HYPERTENSION. **Personal Data:** b Memphis, Tenn, June 20, 1957; m 1979, Scott; c Bradley S & Anna B. **Education:** Univ Miss, BA, 1979; Miss State Univ, MS, 1981; Auburn Univ, PhD (nutrit), 1989. **Honors & Awards:** Miss Recognized Young Dietitian, Am Dietetic Asn, 1990. **Professional Experience:** ASSOC PROF DIETETICS, UNIV MISS, as of 2004; asst prof nutrit, Univ Miss, beginning 1989; actg asst prof, Univ Miss, 1985-1989; nutrit educ specialist, Miss State Dept Health, 1984-1985. **Memberships:** Am Dietetics Asn; Am Home Econ Asn. **Research Statement & Publications:** Calcium and hypertension, eating behavior in children and feeding children in a day care setting. **Mailing Address:** Dept Family & Consumer Sci, Univ Miss, Univ, MS 38677. **E-Mail:** kknight@olemiss.edu

KNIGHT, LARRY V, PHYSICS. **Personal Data:** b Pocatello, Idaho, March 13, 1935; m 1958, Jewel O; c 8. **Education:** Brigham Young Univ, BS, 1958, MS, 1959; Stanford Univ, PhD (physics), 1965. **Professional Experience:** Ed, J X-ray Sci & Technol, 1987-; DIR, X RAY IMAGING CTR, BRIGHAM YOUNG UNIV, 1987-; pres, Moxtek Corp, 1986-; PROF PHYSICS & ASTRON, BRIGHAM YOUNG UNIV, 1980-; consult, Lawrence Livermore Lab, 1975-; vpres, Holograf Corp, 1970-1972; from asst prof to assoc prof, Brigham Young Univ, 1969-1980; Res assoc physics, Stanford Univ, 1965-1969; Mem tech staff, Hewlett-Packard Co, 1964-1969. **Memberships:** Am Phys Soc. **Research Statement & Publications:** Low temperature physics; fundamental constants; magnetic resonance; electron spectroscopy; quantum electronics; holography; laser fusion; plasma and x-ray physics. **Mailing Address:** dept Physics & Astron, Provo, UT 84602. **Fax:** 801-378-2265. **E-Mail:** knight@physc1.byu.edu

KNIGHT, LEE H, MECHANICAL ENGINEERING. **Personal Data:** b Westville, Fla, July 8, 1928; m 1960, c 1. **Education:** Univ SC, BS, 1957; Ga Inst Technol, MS, 1962. **Professional Experience:** CONSULT, 1995-; asst dir serv, Skidaway Inst Oceanog, 1967-1995; br head mech eng, Ga Inst Technol, 1964-1967; sr engr, Lockheed Ga Co, 1962-1964; asst res engr, Ga Inst Technol, 1960-1962; res asst, Ga Inst Technol, 1957-1969. **Memberships:** Oceanog Soc. **Research Statement & Publications:** Heat and mass transfer; underwater propulsion systems; electromechanical equipment for oceanographic research. **Mailing Address:** Skidaway Inst Oceanog, Ten Ocean Sci Circle, Savannah, GA 31411.

KNIGHT, LEWIS E, MATHEMATICS. **Honors & Awards:** Richard H. Balomenos Award. **Professional Experience:** STAFF, STANFORD UNIV, as of 2004. **Mailing Address:** Stanford Univ, 9 Meserve Rd, Durham, NH 03824. **Fax:** 650-725-4066.

KNIGHT, LON BISHOP, PHYSICAL CHEMISTRY. **Personal Data:** b Milledgeville, Ga, April 24, 1944; m 1966, c 2. **Education:** Mercer Univ, BS, 1966; Univ Fla, PhD (chem), 1970. **Professional Experience:** CHARLES EZRA DANIEL PROF & CHAIR CHEM, FURMAN UNIV, as of 2004; assoc prof chem, Furman Univ, beginning 1975; asst prof, Furman Univ, 1971-1975; res assoc phys chem, Univ Fla, 1970-1971. **Memberships:** Am Chem Soc; Am Physical Soc. **Research Statement & Publications:** Study of reactions of metal atoms in the gas phase at low temperatures; metallic transport mechanisms; ESR matrix isolation of high temperature species. **Mailing Address:** Dept Chem, Furman Univ, 122 Plyler Hall, Greenville, SC 29613. **Fax:** 864-294-3559. **E-Mail:** lon.knight@furman.edu

KNIGHT, PATRICIA MARIE, MEDICAL DEVICE RESEARCH & DEVELOPMENT, BIOMATERIALS. **Personal Data:** b Schnectady, NY, January 25, 1952. **Education:** Ariz State Univ, BS, 1974, MS, 1976; Univ Utah, PhD (biomed eng), 1983. **Professional Experience:** VPRES RES & DEVELOP, ALLERGAN MED OPTICS, 1991-; dir res, Allergan Med Optics, 1988-1991; dir mat res, Allergan Med Optics, 1987-1988; mgr mat res, Am Med Optics, 1983-1987; res asst & PhD cand, Univ Utah, 1979-1983; proj engr, Am Med Optics, 1976-1977; teaching & res asst, Ariz State Univ, 1974-1976. **Memberships:** Soc Biomat; Asn Res in Vision & Ophthal; Am Chem Soc; Biomed Eng Soc; Soc Women Engrs. **Research Statement & Publications:** Lead R&D Organization in development of products for ophthalmic surgery including implants, surgical equipment and disposables; polymer research; optical and mechanical engineering; biological science. **Mailing Address:** Allergan Inc, 2525 Dupont Dr PO Box 19534, Irvine, CA 92713-9534. **Fax:** 714-246-2230.

KNIGHT, PAUL R, ANESTHESIOLOGY. **Personal Data:** b Mechanicsburg, Pa, June 27, 1947; c 2. **Education:** Pa State Univ, MD & PhD (med microbiol), 1973. **Professional Experience:** PROF ANESTHESIOL & MICROBIOL, STATE UNIV NY, 1992-; prof, Univ Mich Hosps, 1986-1992; assoc prof anesthesia, Univ Mich Hosps, 1982-1986. **Memberships:** Am Soc Microbiol; Asn Univ Anesthesiologists; Am Soc Anesthesiol. **Research Statement & Publications:** Anesthetic action and its effects and on cellular function and viral replication. **Mailing Address:** Dept Anesthesiol & Microbiol, State Univ NY, 245 Biomed Res Bldg, Buffalo, NY 14214. **E-Mail:** pknight@acsu.buffalo.edu

KNIGHT, STEPHEN, EXPERIMENTAL PHYSICS. **Personal Data:** b San Mateo, Calif, February 24, 1938; m 1959, c 3. **Education:** Beloit Col, BS, 1959; Yale Univ, MS, 1960, PhD (physics), 1964. **Professional Experience:** DIR, OFF MICROELEC PROG, ELEC & ELEC ENG LAB, NAT INST STANDARDS & TECHNOL, as of 2006; dir, Sematech Technol Transfer, AT & T Bell Labs, beginning 1990; dir, AT&T Bell Labs, Kelly Educ & Training Ctr, 1986-1990; pub chmn, Inst Elec & Electronics Engrs Trans Electron Devices, 1983-1986; div mgr, AT&T Corp Hq, 1983-1986; head electronics technol planning, Bell Tel Labs, 1981-1984; supvr technol options, Bell Tel Labs, 1980-1981; ed, Inst Elec & Electronics Engrs Trans Electron Devices, 1979-1983; supvr govt systs support, Bell Tel Labs, 1978-1980; supvr opto-isolators group, Bell Tel Labs, 1973-1978; supvr displays group, Bell Tel Labs, 1972-1973; supvr optical mat properties group, Bell Tel Labs, 1971-1972; assoc ed, Inst Elec & Electronics Engrs Trans Electron Devices, 1968-1979; supvr explor device tech group, Bell Tel Labs, 1968-1971; mem tech staff, Bell Tel Labs, 1964-1968. **Memberships:** Am Phys Soc; sr mem Inst Elec & Electronics Engrs; Electron Devices Soc. **Research Statement & Publications:** Low temperature physics, turbulent superfluid helium; semiconductor physics, bulk negative resistance; light emitting diodes; magnetic bubble materials; integrated circuit planning; high performance technology evaluation. **Mailing Address:** Off Microelec prog, Nat Inst Stand & Technol, Rm A317 Bldg 225 MS 8101 100 Bureau Dr, Gaithersburg, MD 20899. **Fax:** 301-975-6513. **E-Mail:** stephen.knight@nist.gov

KNIGHT, VERNON, MEDICINE. **Personal Data:** b Osceola, Mo, September 6, 1917; m 1946, c 4. **Education:** William Jewell Col, AB, 1939; Harvard Univ, MD, 1943; Am Bd Internal Med, dipl. **Honorary Degrees:** ScD, William Jewell Col. **Professional Experience:** DISTINGUISHED PROF MICROBIOL & IMMUNOL, BAYLOR COL MED, as of 2004; actg chmn, dept molecular physiol & biophys, Baylor Col Med, beginning 1995; prof med & chmn, dept microbiol & immunol, Baylor Col Med, beginning 1966; dir, Ctr biotechnol & prof biotechnol, med, microbiol & immunol, 1966-1995; clin dir, Nat Inst Allergy & Infectious Dis, Md, 1959-1966; assoc prof, Sch Med, Vanderbilt Univ, 1954-1959; asst prof med, Med Col, Cornell Univ, 1953-1954. **Memberships:** Soc Exp Biol & Med; Am Soc Clin Invest; Am Clin & Climat Asn; Am Col Physicians. **Research Statement & Publications:** Infectious disease and allergy. **Mailing Address:** Dept Physiol, Baylor Col Med, 1 Baylor Plaza, Houston, TX 77030. **Fax:** 713-798-3125. **E-Mail:** vknight@bcm.tmc.edu

KNIGHT, WALTER REA, PSYCHOBIOLOGY. **Personal Data:** b Cortland, Ohio, April 25, 1933; m 1954, c 3. **Education:** Baldwin-Wallace Col, AB, 1954; Pa State Univ, MS, 1956, PhD (psychol), 1961. **Professional Experience:** PROF EMER, HIRAM COL, as of 2005; prof physiol & biol, Hiram Col, beginning 1968; assoc prof, Hiram Col, 1965-1968; NIMH spec res training fel, Univ Fla, 1964-1966; asst prof, Hiram Col, 1957-1958, 1960-1965; instr psychol, Hiram Col, 1956-1957. **Memberships:** AAAS; Animal Behav Soc; Psychonomic Soc; Sigma Xi. **Research Statement & Publications:** Neural, hormonal and early experience factors in animal social behavior and social stress. **Mailing Address:** Hiram Col, PO Box 67, Hiram, OH 44234. **E-Mail:** knightwr@hiram.edu

KNIGHT, WILLIAM ALLEN, GASTROENTEROLOGY. **Personal Data:** b St Louis, Mo, October 5, 1914; m 1941, c 3. **Education:** Drury Col, AB, 1936; St Louis Univ, MD, 1940; Am Bd Int Med cert, 1951. **Professional Experience:** ASSOC PROF MED, DIV GASTROENTEROL, SCH MED, ST LOUIS UNIV, as of 2003; emer dir, Cancer Res & Treatment Ctr, beginning 1981; dir, Dept Internal Med, St Mary's Health Ctr, 1965-1980; Area consult int med, US Vet Admin, 1956-1960; dir int med, St Louis City Hosp, St Louis Univ Med Serv, 1948-1955 & Firmin Desloge Hosp, 1955-1958; DIR, DIV GASTROENTEROL, SCH MED, ST LOUIS UNIV, 1954-; asst prof med, St Louis Univ, 1951-1955; dir int med, Housestaff & Residency Training Prog, 1950-1959; sr instr, St Louis Univ, 1949-1951; instr, St Louis Univ, 1948-1949; asst int med, St Louis Univ, 1947-1948. **Memberships:** Am Col Gastroenterol; Am Soc Gastrointestinal Endoscopy; Am Gastroenterol Asn; Am Asn Study Liver Dis; fel Am Col Phys; Sigma Xi. **Research Statement & Publications:** Qualitative and quantitative analysis of pancreatic secretions, proteins and electrolytes in the normal and diseased pancreas to aid in the diagnosis of pancreatic disease. **Mailing Address:** Knight Int Inc, 1035 Bellevue Ste 503, St Louis, MO 63117-1854.

KNIGHT, WILLIAM GLENN, BIOGEOCHEMISTRY, RHIZOSPHERE CHEMISTRY-MYCORRHIZAE. **Personal Data:** b Greenville, SC, July 4, 1952; m 1985, Lorie Federman; c Elijah & Maya. **Education:** Utah State Univ, BS, 1974, MS, 1978, PhD (soil chem), 1987. **Professional Experience:** Co-prin investr, USDA-Coop State Res Serv, 1992-; SCI CHMN & ASSOC PROF CHEM, FRONT RANGE COMMUNITY COL, 1992-; co-dir, Ecol Sta, DESSED-Belize, 1991-; consult, Belize Citrus Growers Asn, 1990-; Dir & environ geochemist, Earth Sci Group, 1989-; res assoc soil biochem, USDA-Agr Res Serv, 1987-1989; res & teaching asst soil chem, Utah State Univ, 1984-1987; environ scientist, T W Mann & Co, 1982-1984; Sr soil scientist, Nerco, Inc, 1978-1982. **Research Statement & Publications:** Investigations of rhizosphere biochemistry of desert and rangeland plants including influence of mycorrhizae, exudates (oxalic acid and carbon dioxide) on mineral stability in soils; effects of elevated atmospheric carbon dioxide on biogeochemistry of soils. **Mailing Address:** Dept Sci, Front Range Community Col, PO Box 270490, Ft Collins, CO 80527-0490.

KNIGHT, WILSON BLAINE, PROTEIN CHEMISTRY, ENZYMOLOGY. **Personal Data:** b August 20, 1955. **Education:** Univ Va, BA; Univ Md, Col Park, PhD (biochem), 1983. **Professional Experience:** HEAD, DEPT ENZYM, GLAXO WELLCOME INC, as of 1998; DEPT BIOCHEM & BIOANAL CHEM, GLAXO WELLCOME, as of 1998; res fel, Merck Sharpe & Dohme Res Lab, beginning 1989; sr biochemist, Merck Sharpe & Dohme Res Lab, 1987-1989; res assoc, Univ Wis, 1983-1987. **Memberships:** AAAS; NY Acad Sci; Sigma Xi. **Research Statement & Publications:** Enzyme mechanisms; mechanism of inhibition of elastoses; mechanism of signal peptidase; enzyme inhibitors. **Mailing Address:** Dept Enzym, Glaxo Wellcome Inc, Bldg V248 5 Moore Dr, Research Triangle Park, NC 27709. **Fax:** 919-483-4320.

KNIGHTEN, JAMES LEO, ELECTROMAGNETICS, ELECTROMAGNETIC PULSE ENGINEERING. **Personal Data:** b Lafayette, La, April 1, 1943; m 1970, c 2. **Education:** La State Univ, BS, 1965, MS, 1968; Iowa State Univ, PhD (elec eng), 1976. **Professional Experience:** VPRES & MGR, DEFENSE ELECTRONICS, MAXWELL LABS, 1989-; mgr electromagnetics, IRT Corp, 1980-1989; staff engr, IRT Corp, 1977-1980; Asst prof electromagnetics, Iowa State Univ, Ames, 1976-1977. **Memberships:** Inst Elec & Electronics Engrs. **Research Statement & Publications:** Nuclear electromagnetic pulse effects on systems; numerical methods; nuclear electromagnetic pulse hardening of ground launched Cruise missile; assessment of electromagnetic pulse coupling to ground based command, control and communications facilities, tactical systems, aircraft and missiles. **Mailing Address:** 13248 Poway Hills Dr, Poway, CA 92064.

KNIGHTS, JOHN CHRISTOPHER, PHYSICS. **Personal Data:** b Felixstowe, Eng, July 2, 1947. **Education:** Univ Sussex, BSc, 1968; Univ Cambridge, MA & PhD (physics), 1972. **Professional Experience:** PRIN MARKET & TECHNOL, PALO ALTO RES CTR, XEROX CORP, as of 1999; RES SCIENTIST PHYSICS, PALO ALTO RES CTR, XEROX CORP, 1973-; res fel, Sidney Sussex Col, Cambridge, Eng, 1972-1973; Imp Chem Industs fel, Univ Cambridge, 1972-1973. **Memberships:** Am Phys Soc. **Research Statement & Publications:** Transport properties of amorphous and crystalline semiconductors. **Mailing Address:** Palo Alto Res Ctr, 3333 Coyote Hill Rd, Palo Alto, CA 94304.

KNIKER, WILLIAM THEODORE, ALLERGY, IMMUNOLOGY. **Personal Data:** b Seguin, Tex, August 30, 1929; div, c 4. **Education:** Univ Tex, BA, 1950, MD, 1953; Am Bd Pediat, dipl, 1959; Conjoint Bd Allergy & Immunol, dipl, 1974. **Honors & Awards:** Stanley Jaros Lectr, Am Asn Clin Immunol & Allergy, 1977; Bela Schick Award, Am Col Allergy & Immunol, 1984. **Professional Experience:** PROF PEDIAT, MICROBIOL & INTERNAL MED, UNIV TEX MED SCH, SAN ANTONIO, 1988-; lectr, Am Col Allergy & Immunol, 1984; mem bd regents, Am Col Allergy & Immunol, 1981-1984; dir sect immunol-allergy, Univ Ark Med Ctr, 1969-; from assoc prof to prof pediat & microbiol, Microbiol & Internal Med, Univ Tex Med Sch, San Antonio, 1969-1988; NIH res career develop award, 1968-1969; from asst prof to assoc prof pediat & path, Med Ctr, Univ Ark, 1965-1969; asst dir clin res unit, Univ Ark Med Ctr, 1965-1969; res fel, Div Exp Path, Scripps Clin & Res Found, Calif, 1962-1965; from instr to asst prof pediat, Med Ctr, Univ Ark, 1959-1962; res fel infectious dis, Am Thoracic Soc, 1959-1962; chief resident, Med Ctr, Univ Ark, 1958-1959; resident pediat, Univ Tex Med Br, 1956-1958; intern, Henry Ford Hosp, Detroit, 1953-1954. **Memberships:** Am Asn Path; Am Asn Immunologists; Am Col Allergy & Immunol; Am In Vitro Allergy & Immunol Soc (vpres); Am Acad Allergy & Immunol. **Research Statement & Publications:** Immunopathology, mechanisms of hypersensitivity and immunological diseases; immunochemistry of mycobacterial antigens; primate immunology; pediatrics. **Mailing Address:** Dept Pediat, Univ Tex Health Sci Ctr, 7703 Floyd Curl Dr, San Antonio, TX 78284-6200.

KNILL, RONALD JOHN, GEOMETRIC TOPOLOGY. **Personal Data:** b Chicago, Ill, February 20, 1935; m 1958, Barbara; c Joseph, David & Mary. **Education:** Marquette Univ, BS, 1956; Univ Notre Dame, MS, 1960, PhD (math), 1962. **Professional Experience:** PROF EMER MATH, TULANE UNIV, 1996-; vis prof, Col Holy Cross, 1985-1986; vis scholar, SpecolaVaticana, 1984; vis fel, Univ Warwick, 1978; res assoc, Col France, 1969-1970; from asst prof to prof, Tulane Univ, 1963-1996; NSF fel, Univ Calif, Berkeley, 1962-1963; vis scholar, Univ Md, Col Park. **Memberships:** Am Math Soc; Math Asn Am; Math Soc France; Sigma Xi. **Research Statement & Publications:** Low dimensional topology; knot theory and applications; fixed point theory. **Mailing Address:** Dept Math, Tulane Univ, New Orleans, LA 70118. **Fax:** 504-891-9273. **E-Mail:** knill@tulane.edu

KNIPE, DAVID MAHAN, VIROLOGY, CELL BIOLOGY. **Personal Data:** b Lancaster, Ohio, August 6, 1950; m 1973, Suzanne; c Rachel & Jennifer. **Education:** Case Western Res Univ, BA, 1972; Mass Inst Technol, PhD (cell biol), 1976. **Honorary Degrees:** MA, Harvard univ, 1990. **Honors & Awards:** Merit Award, NIMH. **Professional Experience:** MEM, VIROL STUDY SECT, 1990-; PROF VIROL, DEPT MICROBIOL & MOLECULAR GENETICS, HARVARD MED SCH, 1989-; mem, Clin Sci Study Sect, NIH, 1985-1989; fac res award, Am Cancer Soc, 1984; from asst prof to assoc prof, Dept Microbiol & Molecular Genetics, Harvard Med Sch, 1979-1989; fel, Univ Chicago, 1976-1979. **Memberships:** Am Soc Microbiol; Am Soc Virol; AAAS. **Research Statement & Publications:** How herpes simplex virus replicates in and interacts with its host cell; molecular biological and genetic approaches to study how viral and cellular proteins function within the cell nucleus; regulation of herpes simplex virus gene expression; mechanism of infection of the nervous system; host immune response, vaccines and vaccine vectors. **Mailing Address:** Dept Microbiol Molecular Genetics, Harvard Med Sch, 200 Longwood Ave, Boston, MA 02115. **Fax:** 617-432-0223. **E-Mail:** david_knipe@hms.harvard.edu

KNIPE, RICHARD HUBERT, CHEMICAL PHYSICS. **Personal Data:** b Salmon, Idaho, September 12, 1927; m 1957, Teresa; c Krina, Kevin & Kurt. **Education:** Calif Inst Technol, BS, 1950; Duke Univ, PhD (physics), 1954. **Professional Experience:** RETIRED; res physicist, Naval Weapons Ctr, 1962-1989; phys chemist, Naval Weapons Ctr, 1962; aeronaut power plant res engr, Naval Weapons Ctr, 1957-1962; physicist, Naval Weapons Ctr, 1954-1957. **Memberships:** Am Phys Soc; Am Chem Soc. **Research Statement & Publications:** Quantum theory of molecules; gas phase chemical kinetics and mechanism; performance analysis of flash lamps pumped dye lasers. **Mailing Address:** 1121 Lucille Ct, Ridgecrest, CA 93555-5901.

KNIPFEL, JERRY EARL, NUTRITION & BIOCHEMISTRY, RESEARCH ADMINISTRATION. **Personal Data:** b Calgary, Alta, June 30, 1941; m 1966, c 2. **Education:** Univ Sask, BSA, 1965, MSc, 1967; McGill Univ, PhD (nutrit), 1973. **Professional Experience:** CONSULT; lectr & dept chmn, Univ Regina, 1991; mem, Nat Res Coun, 1989-; sect head, Forage Prod & Utilization Sect, Res Sta, Agr Can, beginning 1989; chmn exec comt, Int Network Feed Info Ctr, 1988-; adj prof, Univ Sask, 1987-1992; dir & rep, Can Feed Info Ctr, 1986-; coordr, Forage Commodity Coord Directorate Agr Can, 1986; mgr, Res Br Prarie Region Contract Res & ERDA progs, 1985-1990; prog specialist, Forage Prod & Utilization Sect, 1984-1987; prog dir, Prairie Region Res Br, Forage Prod & Utilization Sect, 1984-1987; mem, Exp Comt Animal Nutrit, 1981-1991; asst prof biol, Univ Regina, 1981 & 1990; assoc ed, Can J Animal Sci, 1980-1983; prog rev comt, Agr Can Western Region, 1980; sci authority, Res Br, Agr Can, Contract Res Progs, 1979-; mem, Exp Comt, Forage Crops, 1979-1982; lectr, Dept Biol, Univ Regina, 1978; asst ed, Can J Animal Sci, 1977-1980; consult, Topline Feeds, Inc, Swift Current, 1974; RES SCIENTIST, FORAGE PROD & UTILIZATION SECT, RES STA, AGR CAN, 1973-1984, 1987-; res scientist, Health Protection Br, Nutrit Res Div, Health & Welfare Can, 1969-1973; chemist, Health Protection Br, Nutrit Res Div, Health & Welfare Can, 1967-1969. **Memberships:** Can Soc Animal Sci; Nutrit Soc Can; Can Asn Lab Animal Sci; Am Chem Soc; Inst Food Technologists; NY Acad Sci. **Research Statement & Publications:** Nutrition in relation to fetal development and post partum performance; nitrogen metabolism in ruminants; evaluation of nutritional quality and nutrient availability; improvement in nutritional value of roughage. **Mailing Address:** Forage Prod & Utilization Sect, Res Sta Agr Can, Swift Current, SK S9H 3X2, Can.

KNIPMEYER, HUBERT ELMER, ORGANIC CHEMISTRY, RESEARCH ADMINISTRATION. **Personal Data:** b Sharon, Conn, November 7, 1929; m 1952, c 4. **Education:** Mass Inst Technol, SB, 1951; Univ Ill, PhD (chem), 1957. **Professional Experience:** RETIRED; tech mgr, Polymers Prod Dept, 1985-1992; mgr membranes, Plastic Prod & Resins Dept & prog mgr corp automotive develop, Corp Plans Dept, 1983-1984; res mgr, Plastic Prod & Resins Dept, 1978-1982; prog mgr corp automotive develop, Corp Plans Dept, 1978-1982; lab supt, Film Dept, 1977; mgr mkt develop & customer serv, Film Dept, 1976; tech mgr, Film Dept, 1974-1975; prod mgr, Ohio, 1971-1974; res mgr, Ohio, 1969-1971; group mgr, Film Dept, 1965-1969; tech rep, Film Dept, 1964-1965; staff scientist, Film Dept, 1962-1963; res chemist, Film Dept, 1961-1962; tech investr, Film Dept, 1960-1961; res chemist, Cent Res Dept, E I Du Pont de Nemours & Co Inc, 1956-1960. **Memberships:** Am Chem Soc. **Research Statement & Publications:** Physical organic chemistry; organic synthesis; heterocyclic organic chemistry; polyimide, polyester and polyolefin chemistry; membranes. **Mailing Address:** Mitchell Rd RR 2 Box 201 F, Vineyard Haven, MA 02568.

KNIPP, ERNEST A, JR, COMPUTER SCIENCES, GENERAL. **Personal Data:** b Houston, Tex, October 10, 1929; m 1979. **Education:** Rice Univ, BS, 1950, MS, 1952; Yale Univ, PhD (chem eng), 1958. **Professional Experience:** CONSULT, 1971-; res specialist, Esso Res & Eng Co, 1968-1971; sr res chem engr, Esso Res & Eng Co, 1963-1965; res chem engr, Humble Oil & Ref Co, 1961-1963; Fel chem, Rice Univ, 1960; asst prof chem eng, Mich Col Mining & Technol, 1959; fel chem, Univ NC, 1957-1959. **Memberships:** Am Chem Soc; Am Inst Chem Engrs; Asn Comput Mach; Royal Soc Chem. **Research Statement & Publications:** Computer applications. **Mailing Address:** PO Box 3041, Houston, TX 77001.

KNIPPING, HANS D, PETROLEUM ENGINEERING. **Honors & Awards:** Michel T Halbouty Human Needs Award, Am Asn Petrol Geologists, 1990. **Mailing Address:** 40 Lafferty St, Etobicoke, ON M9C 5B6, Can.

KNIPPLE, DOUGLAS CHARLES, MOLECULAR BIOLOGY OF INSECTICIDE TARGET SITES, MOLECULAR BIOLOGY OF PHEROMONE BIOSYNTHESIS. **Personal Data:** b Johnstown, Pa, March 17, 1953. **Education:** Hobart Col, BS, 1976; Cornell Univ, PhD (genetics), 1983. **Professional Experience:** ASSOC PROF, DEPT ENTOMOL, CORNELL UNIV, 1991-; Europ Molecular Biol Orgn fel, NATO/NSF fel, 1984-1985; Europ Molecular Biol Orgn fel, Max-Planck Inst Evolutionary Biol, Tubingen, Ger, 1983-1984; asst prof, Dept Entomol, Cornell Univ, beginning 1983. **Memberships:** AAAS; Am Chem Soc; Genetics Soc Am; Entom Soc Am. **Research Statement & Publications:** Investigations of structure and function of key molecules mediating excitatory and inhibitory neurotransmission and sex pheromone biosynthesis of insects, which are current or potential targets for disruption in insect control strategies. **Mailing Address:** Dept Entomol, NY State Agr Exp Sta, Col Agr & Life Sci, Cornell Univ, PO Box 15 Kennedy, Geneva, NY 14456. **Fax:** 315-787-2326. **E-Mail:** dck2@cornell.edu

KNIPPLE, WARREN RUSSELL, INDUSTRIAL & PETROLEUM CHEMISTRY, REFRACTORY METALS. **Personal Data:** b Johnstown, Pa, May 28, 1934; m 1999, Barbara Ronay-knipple; c Warren R Jr & Eric john. **Education:** Univ Pittsburgh, BS, 1959; Case Western Reserve Univ, MS, 1961, PhD (chem), 1968. **Professional Experience:** REGIONAL SALES MGR, CLIMAX SPECIALTY METALS, 1986-; gen mgr, Cleveland Refractory Metals Div, 1972-1985; chem opers mgr, Chase Brass & Copper Co, Inc, 1970-1972; prod mgr chem, Chase Brass & Copper Co, Inc, 1969-1970; sr res chemist, Chase Brass & Copper Co, Inc, 1968-1969; Sr chemist, Res Dept, Standard Oil Co (Ohio), 1959-1968. **Memberships:** Am Chem Soc; AAAS; Am Mgt Asn. **Research Statement & Publications:** Organic synthesis; organometallic research; heterogeneous catalysis; peroxide chemistry; aromatic substitution; rhenium chemistry; ion exchange and solvent extraction technology; molybdenum; tungsten chemistry. **Mailing Address:** 872 Wellmon St, Bedford, OH 44146-3877.

KNISELY, JAMES, MATHEMATICS. **Education:** Clemson Univ, MS, PhD. **Honors & Awards:** Donaldson Award, 1986. **Professional Experience:** FAC, COMPUT SCI DEPT, BOB JONES UNIV, 1992-. **Mailing Address:** Math Dept Bob Jones Univ, 1700 Wade Hampton Blvd, Greenville, SC 29614. **Fax:** 864-770-1306.

KNISELY, WILLIAM HAGERMAN, anatomy; deceased, see previous edition for last biography

KNISKERN, VERNE BURTON, PARASITOLOGY. **Personal Data:** b Negaunee, Mich, October 16, 1921; m 1942, c 3. **Education:** Univ Mich, BS, 1947, MS, 1948, PhD (zoology), 1950. **Professional Experience:** EMER FAC; EASTERN ILL UNIV, 1986-; from assoc prof to prof, Eastern Ill Univ, 1950-1986. **Memberships:** Am Micros Soc; Am Soc Parasitol; Wildlife Dis Asn. **Research Statement & Publications:** Parasitology; protozoology; genetics; histology; malacology; medical biology. **Mailing Address:** 1531 Div St, Charleston, IL 61920.

KNISLEY, STEPHEN, ELECTROPHYSIOLOGY, BIOMEDICAL ENGINEERING. **Personal Data:** b Baltimore, Md, January 9, 1951; m 1978, Diane M McCarthy; c Matthew S & Samuel G. **Education:** Duke Univ, BS, 1973; Univ NC, PhD (biomed eng), 1988. **Professional Experience:** ASSOC PROF, UNIV NC, as of 2004; Vis scholar, Univ Technol, Sydney, 1992-1993; asst res prof, Duke Univ, beginning 1989; Res assoc, Univ NC, 1987-1989. **Memberships:** Biophys Soc; Am Heart Asn. **Research Statement & Publications:** Cardiac arrhythmias and electrical defibrillation. **Mailing Address:** Dept biomed eng, Univ NC, Chapel Hill, NC 27599-7575. **Fax:** 919-966-2963. **E-Mail:** knisley@bme.unc.edu

KNITTEL, MARTIN DEAN, MICROBIOLOGY. **Personal Data:** b Torrington, Wyo, December 19, 1932; m 1956, c 3. **Education:** Willamette Univ, BS, 1955; Ore State Univ, MS, 1962, PhD (microbiol), 1965. **Honors & Awards:** Gold Medal For Res, Environ Protection Agency, 1978. **Professional Experience:** RETIRED; res microbiologist, Western Fish Toxicol Sta, 1974-1988; res microbiologist, Pac Northwest Water Lab, Environ Protection Agency, 1971-1974; sr engr, Jet Propulsion Lab, 1969-1971; microbiologist, Pac Northwest Water Lab, Fed Water Pollution Control Admin, 1966-1969; sr res microbiologist, Norwich Pharmacal Co, 1965-1966; aquatic biologist, Ore Fish Comn, 1962-1963; med technologist, Doctors' Clin, 1958-1959; bacteriologist, Ore Agr Div, 1955-1956. **Memberships:** AAAS; Am Soc Microbiol. **Research Statement & Publications:** Physiology of the bacterium Sphaerotilus natans as is related to its growth in polluted streams; microbiology of waste treatment; detection of pathogenic organisms in wastewater; biochemistry of waste water treatment; effect of stress on disease in fish. **Mailing Address:** PO Box 1303, Florence, OR 97439.

KNIZE, RANDALL JAMES, LASER COOLING, OPTICAL COMPUTING. **Personal Data:** b Tacoma, Wash, February 4, 1953. **Education:** Univ Chicago, BA & MS, 1975; Harvard Univ, MA, 1976, PhD (physics), 1981. **Professional Experience:** DIR, DEPT PHYSICS, LASER & OPTICS RES CTR, US AIR FORCE ACAD, as of 2003; PROF, DEPT PHYSICS, LASER & OPTICS RES CTR, US AIR FORCE ACAD, as of 2003; asst prof, Univ Southern Calif, beginning 1988; res physicist, Princeton Univ, 1980-1988; res asst, Harvard Univ, 1976-1981. **Memberships:** Am Phys Soc; Am Vacuum Soc. **Research Statement & Publications:** Fundamental atomic physics; optical pumping. **Mailing Address:** Dept Physics, US Air Force Acad, Colorado Spring, CO 80840. **Fax:** 213-740-6653. **E-Mail:** randy.knize@usafa.af.mil

KNOBEL, LEROY LYLE, GROUND WATER, WATER-ROCK INTERACTION. **Personal Data:** b Valley City, NDak, July 10, 1945. **Education:** Univ Wash, BS, 1972; George Wash Univ, MS, 1979. **Honors & Awards:** Presidential Citation, Dominican Repub, 1975. **Professional Experience:** Chairperson, Group Saltwater Intrusion, Am Soc Testing & Mat, 1996-2001; chmn, Am Soc Testing & Mat, 1995-2001; HYDROLOGIST, US GEOL SURV, 1977-; hydrologist, Peace Corps, 1973-1975. **Memberships:** Geochem Soc; Am Geophys Union; Am Soc Testing & Math. **Research Statement & Publications:** Geochemical, microbial and physical processes controlling the carbon dioxide cycle and water-rock interactions in the Snake River Plain aquifer, Idaho. **Mailing Address:** US Geol Surv, PO Box 2230, Idaho Falls, ID 83403-2230. **Fax:** 208-526-6002. **E-Mail:** llknobel@usgs.gov

KNOBELOCH, F X CALVIN, SPEECH PATHOLOGY, AUDIOLOGY. **Personal Data:** b Tell City, Ind, August 5, 1925; m 1953, c 3. **Education:** Ind Univ, BSEd, 1949; Univ Fla, PhD (speech path, audiol), 1959. **Honors & Awards:** Hons, NC Speech-Hearing-Lang Asn, 1983. **Professional Experience:** ASSOC PROF, DIV SPEECH, HEARING & LANG, NC CENT UNIV, DURHAM, 1990-; clin prof, Inst Speech & Hearing Sci & Dept Pediat, Univ NC, Chapel Hill, 1985-1990; Clin assoc prof, 1977-1985; adj assoc prof, Speech, Lang & Auditory Path Prog, East Carolina Univ, 1972-1980; assoc prof, Shaw Univ, 1972-1979; co-dir interdisciplinary training & head, Commun Disorders Ctr Develop & Learning, 1969-1990; assoc dir, Biol Sci Res Ctr, Univ NC, Chapel Hill, 1969-1985; chief speech path & audiol, Winston-Salem, NC, 1962-1966 & Durham, NC, 1966-1969; asst chief speech path & audiol, Vet Admin Regional Off, Louisville, Ky, 1960-1962; assoc prof speech & dir, Speech & Hearing Clin, Univ Miss, 1959-1960. **Memberships:** Am Speech Language & Hearing Asn; fel Am Speech & Hearing Asn. **Research Statement & Publications:** Hearing and language development in high risk and normal infants. **Mailing Address:** 121 Larkspur Cir, Durham, NC 27713-2501.

KNOBLER, CAROLYN BERK, STRUCTURAL CHEMISTRY, INORGANIC CHEMISTRY. **Personal Data:** b New Brunswick, NJ, January 6, 1934; m Charles. **Education:** George Wash Univ, BS, 1955; Pa State Univ, PhD (inorg chem), 1959. **Professional Experience:** RES CHEMIST, DEPT CHEM & BIOCHEM, UNIV CALIF, LOS ANGELES, 1990-; res chemist, Pierre & Mario Curie Univ, 1983 1984 & 1987; res chemist, Univ Canterbury, 1978-1979; vis lectr dept chem, Univ Calif, Los Angeles, 1975; Res chemist, Univ Leiden, 1970-1971 & 1960-1961; from asst res chemist to assoc res chemist, Dept Chem & Biochem, 1964-1990; res asst geol, Calif Inst Technol, 1962-1964; Nat Sci Found fel chem, Univ Amsterdam, 1959-1960. **Memberships:** Am Crystallog Asn. **Research Statement & Publications:** Structural characterization (single crystal x-ray crystallography) of metal clusters, organometallic compounds and metallacarboranes; conformational changes in uncomplexed host and in host-guest complexes. **Mailing Address:** Dept Chem & Biochem, Univ Calif, 405 Hilgard Ave, Los Angeles, CA 90095. **Fax:** 310-825-5490. **E-Mail:** knoblerh@chem.ucla.edu

KNOBLER, CHARLES MARTIN, PHYSICAL CHEMISTRY. **Personal Data:** b Newark, NJ, June 1, 1934; m, c Daniel A & Michael D. **Education:** NY Univ, BA, 1955; Leiden Univ, Neth, PhD (molecular physics), 1961. **Honors & Awards:** Herbert Newby McCoy Award Dept Chem, UCLA, 1980; UCLA Alumni Teaching Award, 1983; UCLA Col of Letters & Sci Faculty Award, 1997; Kolthoff Lecturer, Univ of Minnesotam 2000; Am Chem Soc Award in Colloid Chem, 2002. **Professional Experience:** Sr Ed, Journal of physical chem; chmn, Univ Calif, Los Angeles, 1984-1987 & 1994-1997; PROF CHEM, UNIV CALIF, LOS ANGELES, 1977-; vchmn, Univ Calif, Los Angeles, 1975-1978; from asst prof to assoc prof, Univ Calif, Los Angeles, 1964-1977; fel chem eng, Calif Inst Technol, 1962-1964; Res assoc phys chem, Ohio State Univ, 1961-1962; Fulbright scholar; Alexander von Humboldt sr res award; 2005 assoc. dean physical sci. **Memberships:** Am Chem Soc; fel Am Phys Soc. **Research Statement & Publications:** Self-assembly and replication of viruses, monolayers, kinetics of phase transitions; statistical mechanics of complex fluids. **Mailing Address:** Dept Chem & Biochem, Univ Calif, Los Angeles, CA 90095-1569. **Fax:** 310-206-5381. **E-Mail:** knobler@chem.ucla.edu

KNOBLER, ROBERT LEONARD, NEUROIMMUNOLOGY, NEUROVIROLOGY. **Personal Data:** b New York, NY, November 10, 1948; m 1979, c Adam, Jonathan & Cory. **Education:** City Col NY, BS, 1969; State Univ NY, Brooklyn, MD & PhD (anat), 1975. **Honors & Awards:** Roland P Mackay Award, Am Acad Neurol. **Professional Experience:** PROF NEUROL, JEFFERSON MED COL, PHILADELPHIA, as of 2004; DIR, JEFFERSON MED COL, as of 1999; clin coordr, Mult Sclerosis Clin, Gen Clin Res Ctr, 1981-1984; fel, Immunopath, Scripps Clin & Res found, 1979-; resident neurol, Kings County Hosp Ctr, State Univ NY, 1976-1979; intern med & psychiat, Kings County Hosp Ctr, State Univ NY, 1975-1976; mem, Dept Neurol, Jefferson Med Col, Philadelphia; dir, Reflex Sympathetic Dystrophy Clin; co-dir, Mult Sclerosis Comprehensive Clin Ctr. **Memberships:** Am Acad Neurol; Am Asn Anatomists; Sigma Xi; Soc Neuroscience; Am Asn Neuropathologists. **Research Statement & Publications:** Viral and immune mechanisms of multiple sclerosis and reflex sympathetic dystrophy; ultrastructure of neurocellular relationships; clinical neurophysiology. **Mailing Address:** Dept Neurol Jefferson Med Col, 1025 Walnut St, Philadelphia, PA 19107-5083. **Fax:** 215-923-6792.

KNOBLOCH, EDGAR, STABILITY THEORY, NONLINEAR DYNAMICS. **Personal Data:** b Praha, Czech, March 30, 1953; British citizen; m 2000, Barbara. **Education:** Cambridge Univ, BA, 1974, ScD, 1994; Harvard Univ, AM, 1975, PhD (astron), 1978. **Honors & Awards:** Fel Am Physical Soc, 2001. **Professional Experience:** PROF PHYSICS, UNIV CALIF, BERKELEY, 1987-; Alfred P Sloan res fel, 1980-1984; from asst prof to assoc prof, Univ Calif, Berkeley, 1978-1987; Jr fel, Harvard Soc fels, 1978-1980; res asst astron, Harvard Univ, 1976-1978. **Memberships:** Am Phys Soc Siam Soc Industorial Applied Math. **Research Statement & Publications:** Astrophysical fluid dynamics; magnetohydrodynamics (dynamo theory); stochastic processes; stellar dynamics; bifurcation theory; nonlinear dynamics. **Mailing Address:** Dept Physics, Univ Calif, 457 Birge Hall, Berkeley, CA 94720. **Fax:** 510-643-8497. **E-Mail:** knobloch@tardis.berkeley.edu

KNOBLOCH, HILDA, PEDIATRICS, DEVELOPMENTAL DISABILITIES. **Personal Data:** b New York, NY, December 14, 1915; div. **Education:** Barnard Col, Columbia Univ, BA, 1936; NY Univ, MD, 1940; Johns Hopkins Univ, MPH, 1951, DrPH, 1955; Am Bd Pediat, dipl, 1947; Am Bd Prev Med, dipl, 1954. **Professional Experience:** RETIRED; emer prof pediat, Albany Med Col, 1982; prof, Albany Med Col, 1970-1982; med specialist, NY State Off Ment Retardation & Develop Disabilities, 1970-1981; prof, Mt Sinai Sch Med, 1967-1970; dir, Child Develop Div, Dept Pediat, Mt Sinai Hosp, NY, 1967-1970; prof pediat, Univ Ill Col Med, 1966-1967; dir div child develop, Children's Hosp, Colo, 1964-1966; asst prof psychiat, Col Med, Ohio State Univ, 1958-1966; dir clin child develop, Children's Hosp, Colo, 1956-1964; from assoc prof to prof pediat, Col Med, Ohio State Univ, 1955-1966; asst prof, Maternal & Child Health Div, Sch Hyg & Pub Health, Johns Hopkins Univ, 1955; res assoc, Maternal & Child Health Div, Sch Hyg & Pub Health, Johns Hopkins Univ, 1951-1955; pediat consult, Maternity & Newborn Div, New York City Health Dept, 1949-1950; clin asst child guid clin, Mt Sinai Hosp, NY, 1947-1949; asst clin vis pediatrician, Bellevue Hosp, NY, 1947-1949; Pvt pract, NY, 1947-1949; Asst clin child develop, Sch Med, Yale Univ, 1945-1946. **Memberships:** Fel Soc Res Child Develop; fel Am Acad Pediat; Am Pediat Soc; Am Acad Cerebral Palsy; Sigma Xi. **Research Statement & Publications:** Developmental assessment and infant neurology, especially etiologic factors in neuropsychiatric disabilities of childhood. **Mailing Address:** 230 E Oglethorpe Ave, Savannah, GA 31401.

KNOBLOCH, JAMES OTIS, ORGANIC CHEMISTRY. **Personal Data:** b Thibodaux, La, January 9, 1920; m 1950, Kathleen Breed; c John, Timothy & Susan. **Education:** La State Univ, BS, 1941; Univ Notre Dame, MS, 1947, PhD (chem), 1949. **Professional Experience:** CONSULT, 1982-; Adj prof, Ill Benedictine Col, 1982-1988; sr res chemist, Whiting Res Labs, Standard Oil Co, Ind, Amoco Chem Corp, 1970-1982; sr res scientist, Whiting Res Labs, Standard Oil Co, Ind, Amoco Chem Corp, 1959-1970; chemist, Whiting Res Labs, Standard Oil Co, Ind, Amoco Chem Corp, 1949-1959; chemist, Synthetic Rubber Plant, Firestone Tire & Rubber Co, 1944-1945; chem engr, Magnesium Plant, Mathieson Alkali Works, 1943-1944; shift supvr acid plant, Pa Ord Works, US Rubber Co, 1942-1943; Inspector, Radford Ord Works, 1941-1942. **Memberships:** Am Chem Soc. **Research Statement & Publications:** Structure of petroleum sulfonic acids; reactions of ozonides; synthesis of trifluoromethyl olefins; reduction of acetylenic glycols; oxidation studies; aromatic acid halogenations; polyanhydrides; fire retardants; catalytic hydrogenation of aromatic polycarboxylic acids. **Mailing Address:** 7s242 Green Acres Dr, Naperville, IL 60540.

KNOBLOCK, CRAIG, COMPUTER SCIENCE. **Education:** Syracuse Univ, BS, 1984; Carnegie Mellon Univ, BS, 1984, MS, 1988, PhD (comput sci), 1991. **Professional Experience:** SR PROJ LEADER, INFO SCI INST & RES ASSOC PROF COMPUT SCI, UNIV SOUTHERN CALIF, as of 2004; sr res scientist, Info Sci Inst & res asst prof comput sci, Univ So Calif, beginning 1991. **Research Statement & Publications:** Developing and applying planning, machine learning and knowledge representation techniques to the problem of providing access to distributed, heterogeneous information sources. **Mailing Address:** Info Sci Inst Univ Southern Calif, 4676 Admiralty Way, Marina del Ray, CA 90292. **Fax:** 310-822-0751. **E-Mail:** knoblock@isi.edu

KNOCHE, HERMAN WILLIAM, PHYTOPATHOLOGY. **Personal Data:** b Stafford, Kans, November 15, 1934; m 1955, c 2. **Education:** Kans State Univ, BS, 1959, PhD (biochem), 1963. **Professional Experience:** RETIRED; prof, dept biochem, Univ Nebr, 1973-2000; Consult, Smith Klein Beecham, 1973- & Vet Hosp, Lincoln Nebr, 1975-; hon res assoc & NIH fel, Harvard Univ, 1971-1972; Consult, Physicians Path Lab, Univ Nebr, 1966-1970; From instr to assoc prof biochem & nutrit, Dept Biochem, Univ Nebr, 1962-1973. **Memberships:** Sigma Xi; Am Chem Soc; Am Soc Biol Chemists. **Research Statement & Publications:** Biochemistry and structure of lipids; structures and activity of plant toxins; radioactive tracer methodology. **Mailing Address:** Dept Biochem, Univ Nebr, Lincoln, NE 68583-0664. **Fax:** 402-472-7842. **E-Mail:** hknoche1@unl.edu

KNOCKEMUS, WARD WILBUR, INORGANIC CHEMISTRY. **Personal Data:** b Des Plaines, Ill, January 29, 1934; m 1964, c 3. **Education:** Knox Col, BA, 1955; Pa State Univ, MS, 1958; Univ Nebr, PhD, 1969. **Professional Experience:** PROF EMER CHEM, HUNTINGDON COL, as of 2004; res consult, Wesley Indust Inc, Mobile Ala, beginning 1987; electrochem corrosion res, NASA, Marshall Space Flight Ctr, 1985, 1986; prof chem & chmn dept, Huntingdon Col, beginning 1974; consult, Great Lakes Res Inst, Pa, beginning 1970; asst prof chem, Behrend Campus, Pa State Univ, 1970-1974; from asst prof to assoc prof chem, Morningside Col, 1961-1970. **Memberships:** Am Chem Soc; Space Studies Inst. **Research Statement & Publications:** Chemistry of metal-organic chelates; hydrolysis of oxymolybdenum chelates; adduct type compounds of octamolybdic acid; elecrochemical corrosion studies. **Mailing Address:** 5749 Carriage Barn Lane, Montgomery, AL 36116-1535.

KNODEL, ELINOR LIVINGSTON, BIOCHEMISTRY, CELLCULTURE TECHNOLOGY. **Personal Data:** b New York, NY, January 25, 1947; m 1980, Peter; c Elinor & Steven Tuhy. **Education:** Columbia Univ, AB, 1969; Yale Univ, MS, 1972; Univ Conn, PhD (biochem), 1976. **Professional Experience:** KNOWLEDGE MANAGT CONSULT, 1998-; sr info designer, Clin Systs Div, E I Du Pont de Nemours & Co, 1990-1998; res & develop chemist, Clin Systs Div, E I Du Pont DE Nemours & Co, 1986-1990; process chemist, Clin Systs Div, E I Du Pont DE Nemours & Co, 1980-1985; res fel neurochem, Mayo Clin, 1978-1980; res fel neuroendocrinol, Rockefeller Univ, 1976-1977; res fel, Univ Conn, 1974-1976. **Memberships:** Am Chem Soc; Soc Tech Commun. **Research Statement &

Publications: Communications research into cognitive processes used in understanding online information; biochemistry of neural transmission in the brain and its regulation by hormones and drugs; automated clinical chemistry test development; cellculture technology; monoclonal antibody production. **Mailing Address:** 2518 Duncan Rd, Wilmington, DE 19808-4647. **E-Mail:** elinor.l.knodel@usa.dupont.com

KNODEL, RAYMOND WILLARD, MATHEMATICS EDUCATION. **Personal Data:** b Butte, NDak, June 10, 1932; m 1959, c 3. **Education:** Minot State Col, BS, 1955; Univ Northern Colo, MA, 1960, DEduc(math educ), 1970. **Professional Experience:** PROF EMER MATH, BEMIDJI STATE UNIV, 1992-; prof, Bemidji State Univ, 1961-1992; instr math, Anaconda Sr High Sch, Mont, 1960-1961; instr math, Mandan Sr High Sch, 1956-1959; instr sci, Ashley High Sch, NDak, 1955-1956. **Research Statement & Publications:** Team teaching mathematics and arithmetic methods to prospective elementary school teachers. **Mailing Address:** Dept Math, Bemidji State Univ, 1500 Birchmont Dr NE, Bemidji, MN 56601.

KNOEBEL, SUZANNE BUCKNER, INTERNAL MEDICINE, CARDIOLOGY. **Personal Data:** b Ft Wayne, Ind, December 13, 1926. **Education:** Goucher Col, BA, 1948; Ind Univ, Indianapolis, MD, 1960. **Honorary Degrees:** DSc, Goucher Col, 1988. **Professional Experience:** HERMAN C & ELLNORA D KRANNERT PROF MED, SCH MED, IND UNIV, INDIANAPOLIS, 1977-; assoc dir, Krannert Inst Cardiol, 1974-1990; from asst prof to prof, Ind Univ, Indianapolis, 1966-1977. **Memberships:** Fel Am Col Cardiol; Asn Univ Cardiologists; Am Fedn Clin Res; Am Heart Asn. **Research Statement & Publications:** Myocardial blood flow; arrhythmias in coronary artery disease; computer analysis of cardiovascular data. **Mailing Address:** Krannert Inst Med, Ind Univ, Rm E300D, 1800 N Capitol, Indianapolis, IN 46202-5305. **Fax:** 317-962-0065. **E-Mail:** sknoebel@iupui.edu

KNOECHEL, EDWIN LEWIS, PHARMACY. **Personal Data:** b Milwaukee, Wis, June 15, 1931; m 1953, c 2. **Education:** Univ Wis, BS, 1953, MS, 1955, PhD (pharm), 1958. **Professional Experience:** CONSULT, 1990-; head mat inspection, Control Div, 1965-1990; res assoc prod res & develop, Upjohn Co, 1958-1965. **Memberships:** Am Pharmaceut Asn; Am Acad Pharmaceut Scientists. **Research Statement & Publications:** Control activities associated with Food and Drug Administration, especially good manufacturing practices, self inspection, raw material evaluation, contract processor inspections, determination of mesh analysis, bulk volume, dissolution rates, surface area and particle size distributions, solids technology and in-process testing. **Mailing Address:** 12290 Pine Ridge Trl, Eastport, MI 49627.

KNOEDLER, ELMER L, CHEMICAL ENGINEERING. **Personal Data:** b Gloucester, NJ, February 12, 1912; m 1941. **Education:** Cornell Univ, ME, 1934; Columbia Univ, MS, 1936, PhD (chem eng), 1952. **Professional Experience:** SR PROJ ENGR & PARTNER, SHEPPARD T POWELL ASSOCS, 1958-; sr proj engr, Sheppad T Powell, 1941-1958; develop engr & supt iron powder prod, Metals Disintegrating Co, 1939-1941; asst supt, Davis Emergency Equip Co, NJ, 1936-1937; Mem tech staff, Atlantic Refining Co, Pa, 1934-1935. **Memberships:** Am Chem Soc; Am Soc Mech Eng; Inst Elec & Electronics Engrs; Am Inst Chemists; Am Inst Chem Eng. **Research Statement & Publications:** Industrial water; boiler feedwater; corrosion; industrial waste waters. **Mailing Address:** 513 Little John Hill, Sherwood Forest, MD 21405.

KNOERR, KENNETH RICHARD, FORESTRY. **Personal Data:** b Milwaukee, Wis, September 2, 1927; m 1952, c 3. **Education:** Univ Idaho, BSF, 1952; Yale Univ, MF, 1961, PhD, 1961. **Professional Experience:** PROF EMER ENVIRON METEOROL & HYDROLOGY & DIR GRAD STUDIES, SCH FORESTRY, DUKE UNIV, as of 2004; prof forestry & environ studies, Sch Forestry, Duke Univ, beginning 1981; assoc prof bot, Sch Forestry, Duke Univ, 1976-1981; prof forest meteorol, Sch Forestry, Duke Univ, 1972-1981; assoc prof biometeorol, Sch Forestry, Duke Univ, 1967-1981; assoc prof forest meteorol, Sch Forestry, Duke Univ, 1967-1972; mem, nat acad sci adv comt climat, US Weather Bur, beginning 1965; asst prof forest climat, Sch Forestry, Duke Univ, 1961-1967; proj leader forest microclimate studies, Cent States Forest Exp Sta, 1961; res forester meteorol & asst proj leader snow physics studies, Pac Southwest Forest & Range Exp Sta, US Forest Serv, 1956-1961. **Memberships:** AAAS; Soc Am Foresters; Am Meteorol Soc; Am Geophys Union; Int Asn Sci Hydrol; Sigma Xi. **Research Statement & Publications:** Micrometeorology and microclimatology of forests related to surface energy balance; evapotranspiration and watershed management. **Mailing Address:** Sch Forestry Duke Univ, A309A LSRC Box 90328, Durham, NC 27708. **Fax:** 919-684-8741. **E-Mail:** dknoer@duke.edu

KNOKE, JAMES DEAN, BIOSTATISTICS. **Personal Data:** b Des Moines, Iowa, March 22, 1941; m 1969, Bonnie; c Christine & Jeffrey. **Education:** Univ Iowa, BA, 1963; Stanford Univ, MS, 1965; Univ Calif, Los Angeles, PhD (biostatist), 1970. **Professional Experience:** Consult, as of 2002; SR STATISTICIAN, FORENSIC MED ADV SERV INC, 1993-; consult, 1992-1993; statistician, Emmes Corp, 1989-1992; res prof statist, George Wash Univ, 1987-1989; assoc prof biostatist, Univ NC, 1978-1987; asst prof biomet, Case Western Reserve Univ, 1971-1978; opers res analyst, autonetics div, NAm Rockwell Corp, 1965-1968. **Memberships:** Am Statist Asn; Biomet Soc; Soc Clin Trials. **Research Statement & Publications:** Statistical methodology and biomedical applications; clinical trials; health care evaluation. **Mailing Address:** One Peach Leaf Ct, North Potomac, MD 20878. **Fax:** 301-770-1423.

KNOKE, JOHN KEITH, VIROLOGY, EPIPHYTOLOGY. **Personal Data:** b Detroit, Mich, March 31, 1930; m 1956, c 2. **Education:** Univ Wis, BS, 1952, MS, 1959, PhD (entom), 1962. **Professional Experience:** RETIRED; adj assoc prof entom, Ohio Agr Res & Develop Ctr & Ohio State Univ, beginning 1967; res entomologist, Agr Res Serv, USDA, Ohio Agr Res & Develop Ctr, 1967-1989; asst prof, Univ Wis-Madison, 1963-1967; proj assoc, Univ Wis-Madison, 1963; entomologist, Cacao Entom, Inter-Am Inst Agr Sci, 1960-1963; collab, Univ Wis-Madison, 1960-1963. **Memberships:** Entom Soc Am; Am Phytopath Soc. **Research Statement & Publications:** Control of insects attacking vegetables, especially through the use of systemic insecticides; study of all phases of entomology relative to production of Theobroma cacao L; epidemiology of virus diseases of corn; vectors of maize viruses. **Mailing Address:** 550 Beechwood St, Wooster, OH 44691.

KNOLL, ALAN HOWARD, CIVIL ENGINEERING, SOFTWARE SYSTEMS. **Personal Data:** b St Joseph, Mich, April 16, 1931; m 1952, Ruth; c David A, Deborah A, Stephen R, Mark W, Rebecca M & Andrew A. **Education:** Univ Mich, BSc, 1952, MSc, 1956. **Professional Experience:** INDEPENDENT CONSULT, 1986-; vpres technol, REA Magnet Wire Co, 1982-1986; gen mgr, REA Magnet Wire Co, 1980-1982; mgr sci & bus systs, 1975-1977 & mgr elec prods div, 1977-1980; sect head, Alcoa Labs, 1970-1975; group leader, Alcoa Labs, 1967-1970; res engr, Alcoa Labs, 1956-1967; US Navy Civil Engr Corps, 1952-1955. **Memberships:** Sigma Xi; Am Soc Civil Engrs. **Research Statement & Publications:** Structural use of aluminum; application of digital computation to structural and other engineering problems; new products and test methods for overhead electrical transmission and magnet wire. **Mailing Address:** 15 Cambridge Dr, Frankenmuth, MI 48734-9779. **E-Mail:** alknoll@umich.edu

KNOLL, ANDREW HERBERT, PALEONTOLOGY, GEOLOGY. **Personal Data:** b West Reading, Pa, April 23, 1951; m 1974, c 2. **Education:** Lehigh Univ, BA, 1973; Harvard Univ, AM, 1974, PhD (geol), 1977. **Honorary Degrees:** PhD, Uppsala Univ, Sweden, 1996; DSc, Lehigh Univ, 1998. **Honors & Awards:** Walcott Medal, NAS, 1987; Schuchert Award, Paleontol Soc, 1987; Guggenheim Fellow, 1987; Fellow, Am Acad Arts Sci, 1987; Member, US Nat Acad Sci, 1991; Member, Am Phil Soc, 1997; Chang Ying-Chen Prize, Am Mus Nat Hist, 2001; Time/CNN America's Best Scientists, 2001; Honorary Fellow Eur Union Geosci, 2003; Phi Beta Kappa Book Award in Science, 2003; NASA Group Achiev Award, 2004; Bownocker Medal, Ohio St Uni, 2005; Moore Medal, Soc Sed Geol, 2005; Paleontological Society medal, 2005. **Professional Experience:** Science Team, NASA MER mission to Mars, 2004- Space Sci Bd Task Group, Major Directions Space Sci: 1985-1988; mem, Nat Bd US Nat Mus Natural Hist, 1992-1996; Nat Res Council, Bd Earth Sci & Resources, 1992-1994; CHMN, DEPT ORGANISMIC & EVOLUTIONARY BIOL, 1992-1998, 2004-2005; Visiting Fellow, Gonville & Caius Col, Cambridge, 1991-1992; chmn, Terminal Precambrian Syst, Int Stratig Comn Subcommission, 1988-2005; mem, NASA Exobiol Adv Comt, 1988-1996; vis scientist, Australian Bur Mineral Resources, 1987-; vis fel, Australian Nat Univ, 1987-; mem, Nat Res Coun Bd Earth Sci, 1987-1989; Guggenheim fel, 1987; FISHER PROF OF NAT HIST, HARVARD UNIV, 2000- PROF EARTH & PLANETARY SCI, HARVARD UNIV, 1985-; CUR BOT MUS, HARVARD UNIV, 1985-; assoc prof biol, Dept Organismic & Evolutionary Biol, 1982-1985; mem, Comt Planetary Biol & Chem Evolution, US Space Sci Bd, 1980-1988, 1997-; asst prof, Oberlin Col, 1977-1981. **Memberships:** Nat Acad. Sci., Bot Soc Am; Soc Econ Paleontologists & Mineralogists; Sigma Xi; Paleont Soc; fel Am Acad Arts & Sci; fel Geol Soc Am. **Research Statement & Publications:** Precambrian biological and environmental evolution; evolution of land plants; Geobiology; Astrobiology. **Mailing Address:** Dept organismic & Evolutionary Biology, Harvard Univ, Cambridge, MA 02138. **E-Mail:** aknoll@oeb.harvard.edu

KNOLL, CECILIA A, MATHEMATICS. **Education:** Univ Cent Fla, BA; Fla Inst Technol, MS, PhD, 1990 Associate Professor, Mathematical Sciences Ph.D. Cecilia A. Knoll Associate Professor, Mathematical Sciences Ph.D. Univ Central Fla, BA; Fla Inst Technol, MS & PhD. **Professional Experience:** ASSOC PROF, DEPT MATH SCI, FLA INST TECHNOL, as of 2005. **Mailing Address:** Dept Appl Math, Fla Inst Technol, 150 W Univ Blvd, Melbourne, FL 32901-6975. **Fax:** 321-674-7412. **E-Mail:** cknoll@fit.edu

KNOLL, GLENN F, NUCLEAR ENGINEERING. **Personal Data:** b St Joseph, Mich, August 3, 1935. **Education:** Case Western Res Univ, BS, 1957; Stanford Univ, MS, 1959; Univ Mich, PhD (nuclear eng), 1963. **Honors & Awards:** Glenn Murphy Award, Am Soc Eng Educ, 1979; Arthur Holly Compton Award, Am Nuclear Soc, 1991; Ann Merit Award, Inst Elec & Electronics Mgrs, 1996. **Professional Experience:** PROF EMER NUCLEAR ENG, UNIV MICH, ANN ARBOR, as of 2003; interim dean eng, Univ Mich, Ann Arbor, 1995-1996; consult to var indust orgn, 1982-; chmn dept, Univ Mich, Ann Arbor, 1979-1990; prof nuclear eng, Univ Mich, Ann Arbor, beginning 1972; fulbright travel grant & vis scientist, Nuclear Res Ctr, Karlsruhe, Ger, 1965-1966; from asst prof to assoc prof, Univ Mich, Ann Arbor, 1962-1972. **Memberships:** Fel Am Nuclear Soc; Am Phys Soc; fel Inst Elec & Electronics Engrs; Am Soc Eng Educ; fel Am Inst Med Biol Eng; Nat Acad Eng. **Research Statement & Publications:** Neutron spectroscopy; radiation detection and measurements; radioisotope imaging; medical instrumentation; neutron cross sections. **Mailing Address:** Dept Nuclear Eng, Univ Mich, Ann Arbor, MI 48105. **Fax:** 734-769-9049. **E-Mail:** gknoll@umich.edu

KNOLL, JACK, ANIMAL PHYSIOLOGY. **Personal Data:** b Ashland, Wis, February 17, 1924; m 1948, Ella Kripli; c Robert. **Education:** Mich State Univ, BS, 1950, MS, 1959, PhD (physiol), 1962. **Professional Experience:** EMER PROF BIOL, UNIV NEV, RENO, 1981-; prof, Univ Nev, Reno, 1976-1981; from asst prof to assoc prof, Univ Nev, Reno, 1962-1976; Asst physiol, Mich State Univ, 1957-1961. **Memberships:** emer mem AAAS; emer mem Sigma Xi. **Research Statement & Publications:** Ion transport across natural biological membranes; fish physiology. **Mailing Address:** 14015 Knolls Rd, Mason, WI 54856.

KNOLL, JOAN H M, GENETICS. **Education:** Univ Man, PhD, 1987. **Professional Experience:** DIR, CYTOGENETICS LAB, as of 2006; PROF PEDIAT, CHILDREN'S MERCY HOSP, as of 2006. **Mailing Address:** Cytogenetics Lab, 2401 Gillham Rd, Kansas City, MO 64108.

KNOLLENBERG, ROBERT GEORGE, INSTRUMENTATION. **Personal Data:** b Mattoon, Ill, August 28, 1939; m 1966, c 3. **Education:** Eastern Ill Univ, BS, 1961; Univ Wis-Madison, MS, 1964, PhD (cloud physics), 1967. **Professional Experience:** CHMN & CEO, RES ELECTRO-OPTICS INC, as of 2005; HEAD RES, RES ELECTRO-OPTICS INC, as of 2001; CHIEF RES EXEC, PARTICLE MEASURING SYSTS INC, 1976-; vis prof atmospheric sci, Colo State Univ, 1973-1975; pres, particle measuring systs Inc, beginning 1972; asst prof geophys sci, Univ Chicago, 1969-1972; scientist, NCAR Res Aviation, Colo, 1967-1969; res asst, Univ Wis-Madison, 1964-1966. **Memberships:** Am Meteorol Soc; Am Chem Soc; Am Inst Physics; Inst Elec & Electronics Engrs; Optical Soc Am. **Research Statement & Publications:** Particle physics research and instrumentation development applied to the development of particle size spectrometers. **Mailing Address:** Res Electro-Optics Inc, 5505 Airport Blvd, Boulder, CO 80301. **Fax:** 303-447-3279.

KNOLLMAN, GILBERT CARL, MATERIAL SCIENCE, ULTRASONICS. **Personal Data:** b Cleveland, Ohio, March 14, 1928; m 1959, Lorraine Gordon; c Katrina (Jaquette), Kristi (Barnes), Tom Jenkins & Scott Jenkins. **Education:** Ga Inst Technol, BS, 1949, MS, 1950, PhD (physics), 1961. **Professional Experience:** Consult, Analiytic Eng Co, 1990-; consult, Nat Res Coun Can, 1988-; consult, Air Force Astronaut Lab, 1986-; HEAD, LOCKHEED ACOUST IMAGING PROG, 1984-; head, Ultrasonics Lab, 1976-1984; staff, Lockheed Mat Sci, 1974-; consult, Naval Weapons Lab, 1973-; staff, Lockheed Eng Sci, 1972-1974; mem Lockheed Res Comt, 1970-1971, chmn, 1972-1973; dir, Adv Acoust Lab, 1971-1976; consult, Saratoga Systs, 1970-1976; SR MEM, LOCKHEED PALO ALTO RES LABS, 1966-; fel, Stanford Univ, 1965-1966; SR STAFF SCIENTIST, LOCKHEED PALO ALTO RES LABS, 1964-; head, Hydrospace Physics Lab, 1964-1970; consult, Ga Tech Res Inst, 1962-1965 & Lockheed Calif Co, 1964-1967; staff scientist, Hydrospace Physics Lab, 1963-1964; res scientist, Res Labs, Lockheed Missiles & Space Co, 1962-1963; NSF grant, 1960-1961; asst prof math, Inst, 1952-1960; res physicist, Eng Exp Sta, 1950-1962; Instr physics, Ga Inst Technol, 1949-1950. **Memberships:** Fel AAAS; fel Am Phys Soc; fel Am Inst Physics; fel NY Acad Sci; mem Res Soc Am; mem Acoust Soc Am; mem Sigma Xi. **Research Statement & Publications:** Quantum field theory; quantum and statistical mechanics; many-body theory; superconductivity and superfluidity; liquid state physics; theoretical acoustics and hydrodynamics; orbital and wave mechanics; electromagnetic theory; viscoelasticity; ultrasonics; underwater acoustics and electronics; material sciences; nondestructive test and evaluation; ocean science; granted one US patent. **Mailing Address:** 705 Charleston Ct, Palo Alto, CA 94303.

KNOLLMUELLER, KARL OTTO, INDUSTRIAL ORGANIC CHEMISTRY. **Personal Data:** b Regensburg, Ger, July 12, 1931; American citizen; m 1968, Ruth Nelson; c Linnea E & Marit R. **Education:** Univ Munich, MS, 1957, PhD (chem), 1960. **Professional Experience:** SR RES ASSOC, OLIN CORP, CONN, 1978-; res assoc, Olin Corp, Conn, 1974-1984; from res chemist to sr res chemist, Olin Corp, Conn, 1960-1974; Res chemist, Diversey Corp, Ill, 1960. **Memberships:** Am Chem Soc; AAAS; Sigma Xi. **Research Statement & Publications:** Inorganic and organic phosphorus compounds; sequestration agents; metal treatment chemicals; high temperature stable polymers; functional fluids; chemicals for electronics; photoresists; chlorine/hypochlorites; sulfur chemistry; hydrosulfite bleaching/reductions; pulp & paper chemistry; propellants. **Mailing Address:** 28 Apple Tree Lane, Hamden, CT 06518.

KNOOP, FLOYD C, INFECTIOUS DISEASES, MEDICAL MICROBIOLOGY & IMMUNOLOGY. **Personal Data:** b Troy, Ohio, November 11, 1944. **Education:** Defiance Col, BS, 1966; Univ Dayton, MS, 1969; Univ Tenn Med Ctr, PhD (medmicrobiol), 1974. **Professional Experience:** COMPONENT I DIR, CREIGHTON UNIV SCH MED, 1996-; PROF MED MICROBIOL, CREIGHTON UNIV SCH MED, 1993-; consult, Fermenta Animal Health, 1985-1990; consult, Norden Labs, 1982-1985; consult, Dellen Labs, 1980-1983; consult, Omaha-Douglas Co Health Dept, 1978-; consult, Burns-Biotec Labs, 1978-1982; numerous grants from private, state & nat orgns, 1976-; from asst prof to assoc prof, Creighton Univ Sch Med, 1975-1993; instr microbiol, Univ Tenn Med Ctr, 1974-1975; fel, Univ Tenn Med Ctr, 1974-1975. **Memberships:** Am Soc Microbiol; AAAS; NY Acad Sci; Sigma Xi; Am Soc Biochem & Molecular Biol; Int Ctr Diarrheal Dis; Col Am Pathologists; Int Soc Toxinology. **Research Statement & Publications:** Structure and biological function of microbial toxins; effects of pharmacologic agents on the secretory activity induced by bacterial enterotoxins; transmembrane receptor-mediated signalling; microbial vaccine production; monoclonal antibodies; technology assessment and transfer. **Mailing Address:** 208 Bellevue Blvd S, Bellevue, NE 68005. **Fax:** 402-280-1875.

KNOP, CHARLES M(ILTON), ELECTROMAGNETIC ENGINEERING, ELECTRICAL ENGINEERING. **Personal Data:** b Chicago, Ill, February 18, 1931; m 1977. **Education:** Ill Inst Technol, BSEE, 1954, MSEE, 1960, PhD (elec eng), 1963. **Professional Experience:** CHIEF SCIENTIST & DIR, ANTENNA RES, ANDREW CORP, 1980-; dir res & develop, Antenna Res, Andrew Corp, 1976-1980; mgr res & develop, Antenna Res, Andrew Corp, 1970-1976; independent consult electrodyn, 1968-1970; res consult, Andrew Corp, 1967-1968; Lectr, Dept Elec Eng, Ill Inst Technol, 1966-1972; assoc dir antenna design, Andrew Corp, 1965-1967; mem sr staff, Nat Eng Sci Co, Calif, 1964-1965; asst dir res & develop, Hallicrafters Co, 1961-1964; sr engr, Res Lab, Systs Div, Bendix Corp, 1960-1961; assoc engr, Armour Res Found, Ill, 1958-1960; asst engr, Armour Res Found, Ill, 1956-1958; res asst, Princeton Univ, 1955-1956; Mem tech staff antenna res, Hughes Aircraft Co, 1954-1955. **Memberships:** fel Inst Elec & Electronics Engrs; Life. **Research Statement & Publications:** Electromagnetic wave radiation, propagation, scattering and diffraction as related to antennas and communication systems; waveguiding systems. **Mailing Address:** Andrew Corp, 10500 W 153rd St, Orland Park, IL 60462.

KNOP, CHARLES PHILIP, INORGANIC CHEMISTRY. **Personal Data:** b Detroit, Mich, May 23, 1927; m 1952, c 9. **Education:** Aquinas Col, BS, 1952; Mich State Univ, PhD (chem), 1958. **Professional Experience:** PROF CHEM, GRAND VALLEY STATE COL, 1976-; chmn dept, Grand Valley State Col, beginning 1974; assoc prof, Grand Valley State Col, 1970-1976; chmn dept, Grand Valley State Col, 1969; res asst prof, Grand Valley State Col, 1965-1970; asst, Mich State Univ, 1953-1958; chemist, Haviland Prod Co, 1952-1953. **Memberships:** Am Chem Soc; Sigma Xi. **Research Statement & Publications:** Pollution abatement; plating wastes recovery. **Mailing Address:** Dept Chem, Grand Valley State Univ, Allendale, MI 49401.

KNOP, OSVALD, CRYSTALLOGRAPHY, SOLID STATE CHEMISTRY. **Personal Data:** b Kurim, Czech, July 11, 1922; Canadian citizen; m 1951, Helga Norregaard; c 1. **Education:** Masaryk Univ, Czech, BS, 1946; Laval Univ, DSc(phys chem), 1957. **Professional Experience:** PROF EMER CHEM, DALHOUSIE UNIV, 1990-; Harry Shirreff prof chem res, Dalhousie Univ, 1981-1990; from assoc prof to prof, Dalhousie Univ, 1964-1990; from asst prof to assoc prof chem, Dept Chem Eng, NS Tech Col, 1953-1964; lectr indust chem, Dept Chem Eng, NS Tech Col, 1950-1953; Asst, Calif Inst Technol, 1949. **Memberships:** Fel Chem Inst Can; Royal Soc Chem. **Research Statement & Publications:** Structural inorganic and solid state chemistry; computer-simulation methods; application of combinatorial analysis and graph theory to chemistry and physics; Structura; inorganic and solid-state chemistry; hydrogen bonding in solids; ab initio and semiempirical calculations. **Mailing Address:** Dept Chem, Dalhousie Univ, Halifax, NS B3H 4J3, Can. **Fax:** 902-494-1310. **E-Mail:** chemistry@dal.ca

KNOPF, FRITZ L, WILDLIFE ECOLOGY, ORNITHOLOGY. **Personal Data:** b Aurora, Ohio, June 6, 1945; c 3. **Education:** Hiram Col, Ohio, BA, 1967; Utah State Univ, MS, 1973, PhD (wildlife ecol), 1975. **Honors & Awards:** Douglas L Gilbert Award Outstanding Prof Achievement. **Professional Experience:** RES WILDLIFE BIOLOGIST, FT COLLINS SCI CTR, US GEOL SURV, as of 2005; SR SCIENTIST, US NAT BIOL SURV, 1996-; sect leader, US Fish & Wildlife Serv, 1993-1996; proj leader, US Nat Biol Surv, 1993-1996; ed, Wildlife Soc Bull, vols 11-13, 1983-1985; proj leader, US Fish & Wildlife Serv, 1982-1993; res wildlife biologist, US Fish & Wildlife Serv, 1980-1981; asst prof wildlife ecol, Okla State Univ, 1976-1979; Instr, Utah State Univ, 1975-1976. **Memberships:** Wildlife Soc; Cooper Ornith Union; Am Ornithologists Union; Wilson Ornith Soc; Soc Conserv Biol. **Research Statement & Publications:** Habitat preference and utilization by wild birds; landscape ecology, management of landscapes; conservation of biodiversity. **Mailing Address:** Ft Collins Sci Ctr, US Geol Surv, 2150 Ctr Ave Bldg C, Ft Collins, CO 80526-8118. **Fax:** 970-226-9230. **E-Mail:** fritz_knopf@usgs.gov

KNOPF, PAUL M, BIOLOGY. **Personal Data:** b Trenton, NJ, April 4, 1936; m Carol; c Jeffrey W, Steven H & Rachel A. **Education:** Mass Inst Technol, PhD (molecular biol), 1962. **Honorary Degrees:** Ad Eundem, Brown Univ, 1975. **Honors & Awards:** Fogarty fel, 1986-1987, London, UK Fulbright fel, 1978-1979, Melbourne, Australia NIH Post-doc fel, 1962-1964, Cambridge, UK. **Professional Experience:** CHARLES A. & HELEN B. STUART PROF. MED. SCI., emeritus, Brown U., 2003- chmn, Dept Molecular Microbiol. & Immunol., Brown U. 1994-1997; CHARLES A. & HELEN B. STUART PROF. MED. SCI., Brown U., 1977-2003; Assoc. prof. medical science, Brown U., 1972-1977; Res assoc, Salk Inst, 1964-1972; niv. **Memberships:** AAAS; Am Assn Immunol; Am Soc Trop Med & Hyg; Soc Neuroscience; Am Soc Microbiol. **Research Statement & Publications:** Development of vaccine against human schistosomiasis; central nervous system/immune system interactions; protein synthesis and secretion. **Mailing Address:** Div Biol & Med Brown Univ, PO Box G-B6, Providence, RI 02912. **Fax:** 401-863-1971. **E-Mail:** paul_knopf@brown.edu

KNOPF, RALPH FRED, INTERNAL MEDICINE. **Personal Data:** b Muskegon, Mich, March 26, 1926; m 1954, c 3. **Education:** Univ Mich, BS, 1951, MD, 1954; Am Bd Internal Med, dipl, 1963. **Professional Experience:** PROF EMER INTERNAL MED, MED CTR, UNIV MICH, ANN ARBOR, as of 2005; prof internal med, Med Ctr, Univ Mich, Ann Arbor, beginning 1973; from instr to assoc prof, Univ Mich, Ann Arbor, 1962-1973; fel internal med, Univ Mich, Ann Arbor, 1959-1962; resident ophthal, Univ Mich, Ann Arbor, 1958-1959; resident internal med, Univ Mich, Ann Arbor, 1956-1958; resident internal med, Va Mason Hosp, Seattle, Wash, 1955-1956; intern med, Va Mason Hosp, Seattle, Wash, 1954-1955. **Memberships:** Am Fedn Clin Res; Am Diabetes Asn; Endocrine Soc. **Research Statement & Publications:** Diabetes mellitus; inter-relationship between carbohydrate, protein and lipid metabolism and insulin glucagon and growth hormone secretion. **Mailing Address:** Univ Mich, Dept med, 3920 TC, Dearborn, MI 48128-0354. **E-Mail:** rknopf@umich.edu

KNOPF, ROBERT JOHN, ORGANIC CHEMISTRY, POLYMER CHEMISTRY. **Personal Data:** b West New York, NJ, April 18, 1932. **Education:** Gettysburg Col, BA, 1954; Princeton Univ, MA, 1956, PhD (org chem), 1957. **Professional Experience:** RETIRED; Consult alkoxylation chem, Union Carbide, 1986-1990; sr develop scientist, Ethylene Oxide-Glycol Div, 1975-1986; prod develop mgr, Union Carbide Corp, SCharleston, 1974-1976; res scientist, Union Carbide Corp, SCharleston, 1970-1975; group leader res & develop, Union Carbide Corp, SCharleston, 1966-1970; Chemist, Union Carbide Corp, SCharleston, 1957-1966. **Memberships:** Am Chem Soc. **Research Statement & Publications:** Flame retardants for plastics; chemistry of isocyanates; polyurethane foams, coatings and elastic fibers; aldol condensation chemistry; condensation polymerizations in solution; polyethers; hydrogel polymers; photocure coatings intermediates; surfactant intermediates; ethylene oxide derivatives; catalysis of ethoxylation reactions. **Mailing Address:** 2657 Lakeview Dr, St Albans, WV 25177.

KNOPKA, W N, FIBER TECHNOLOGY, WATER TREATMENT. **Personal Data:** b Buffalo, NY, December 1, 1938; m 1965, Carol; c 3. **Education:** Canisius Col, BS, 1961; Univ Seton Hall, MS, 1963, PhD (org chem), 1965. **Professional Experience:** VPRES, CORPORATE DEVELOP, OCTEL AM INC, 2001-; vpres, corporate develop, Hickson Corp, 1999-2000; pres, Quorum Assoc Inc, beginning 1990; pres, Interchem Develop Co, 1988-1990; vpres, corp develop, Interchem Inc, 1986-1988; dir, elastomer & chem res, Goodyear Tire & Rubber Co, 1979-1983; dir, fabric develop, Goodyear Tire & Rubber Co, 1977-1979; agr chem, Fiber Div, Pa, 1976-1977; prod mgr, Fiber Div, Pa, 1973-1976; group leader, Fiber Div, Pa, 1969-1973; sr res chemist, Cent Res & Develop, FMC Corp, NJ, 1965-1969. **Memberships:** Am Chem Soc; Com Develop Asn. **Research Statement & Publications:** Specialty organic chemical intermediates; fiber processing; wire process technology; condensation and addition polymers; synthetic rubbers; rubber chemicals; specialty monomers, coatings and adhesives radiation curable chemicals. **Mailing Address:** Octel Am Inc, Box 600 309 6300 Powers Ferry Rd, Atlanta, GA 30339. **Fax:** 770-952-4679. **E-Mail:** knopkaw@octel-corp.com

KNOPMAN, DEBRA SARA, HYDROLOGY & WATER RESOURCES, OPERATIONS RESEARCH. **Personal Data:** b Philadelphia, Pa, August 13, 1953; m 1985, Donald; c Leah & David. **Education:** Wellesley Col, BA, 1975; Mass Inst Technol, MSCE, 1978; Johns Hopkins Univ, PhD (hydrol), 1986. **Professional Experience:** DIR, CTR INNOVATION & ENVIRON, PROGRESSIVE FOUND, 1995-; dep asst secy water & sci, Dept Interior, 1993-1995; chief, Br Systs Anal, 1992-1993; chair, Pub Info Comt, Am Geophys Union, 1990-1992; hydrologist, Br Systs Anal, 1987-1992; res hydrologist, Nat Res Prog, 1986-1987; hydrologist, Off Groundwater, US Geol Surv, 1984-1986; teaching asst water resources systs design, Johns Hopkins Univ, 1983-1985; prof staff mem, US Sen Comt Environ & Pub Works, 1980-1983; luce scholar, Henry R Luce Found, 1978-1979; teaching asst hydrol & fluid dynamics, Dept Civil Eng, Mass Inst Technol, 1977-1978. **Memberships:** Am Geophys Union. **Research Statement & Publications:** Design of sampling strategies for model discrimination and parameter estimation in subsurface solute transport studies; use of water quality and other hydrologic information in the development of national water policy. **Mailing Address:** Progressive Policy Inst, 600 Pa Ave SE Ste 400, Washington, DC 20003. **Fax:** 202-544-5014. **E-Mail:** dknopman@pf.org

KNOPOFF, LEON, GEOPHYSICS, PHYSICS. **Personal Data:** b Los Angeles, Calif, July 1, 1925; m 1961, Joanne; c Katherine, Rachel & Michael. **Education:** Calif Inst Technol, BS, 1944, MS, 1946, PhD (physics), 1949. **Honors & Awards:** Harold Jeffreys Lectr, Royal Astron Soc, 1977; Emil Wiechert Medal, Ger Geophys Soc, 1978; Gold Medal, Royal Astron Soc, 1979; Sidney Chapman Mem Lectr, Univ Alaska, 1988; Medal, Seismol Soc Am, 1990. **Professional Experience:** PROF EMER PHYSICS & GEOPHYS, UNIV CALIF, LOS ANGELES, as of 2005; distinguished geophys lectr, Tex A&M Univ, 1990; mem, Educ Adv Bd, Guggenheim Found, 1989-; Guggenheim fel, 1976-1977; vis prof, Univ Chile, Santiago, 1973; vis prof, Harvard Univ, 1972; assoc dir, Inst Geophys & Planetary Physics, 1972-1986; chmn, Comt Math Geophys, Int Union Geophys & Geophysicists, 1971-1982; vis prof, Technische Hochschule, Karlsruhe, Ger, 1966; secy gen, Int Upper Mantle Comt & chmn, US Comt, 1963-1971; prof, Calif Inst Technol, 1962-1963; RES MUSICOLOGIST, UNIV CALIF, LOS ANGELES, 1961-; NSF sr fel, Cambridge Univ, 1960-1961; prof physics, Univ Calif, Los Angeles, beginning 1959; mem earth sci panel, NSF, 1959-1962; prof geophys, Univ Calif, Los Angeles, beginning 1957; assoc prof geophys, Inst Geophys, Univ Calif, Los Angeles, 1956-1957; from res assoc to assoc res geophysicist, Inst Geophys, Univ Calif, Los Angeles, 1950-1956; from asst prof to assoc prof physics, Miami Univ, 1948-1950; mem, US Nat Comt. **Memberships:** Nat Acad Sci; fel Am Acad Arts & Sci; Am Phys Soc; hon mem Seismol Soc Am; fel Am Geophys Union; fel AAAS; Royal Astron Soc; Am Philos Soc. **Research Statement & Publications:** Theory of earthquakes; self-organizing systems; acoustics of solids; physics and chemistry of deep interior of earth; elastic wave propagation; systematic musicology; author or co-author of over 300 scientific papers and publications; theoretical and observational seismology. **Mailing Address:** Inst Geophys & Planetary Physics, Univ Calif, Box 951567 595 Charles Young Dr E, Los Angeles, CA 90095-1567. **Fax:** 310-206-3051. **E-Mail:** knopoff@physics.ucla.edu

KNOPP, JAMES A, BIOPHYSICAL CHEMISTRY. **Personal Data:** b October 26, 1940; m 1962, c 2. **Education:** Carleton Col, BA, 1962; Univ Ill, PhD (biophys chem), 1967. **Professional Experience:** UNDERGRAD COORDR BIOCHEM, NC STATE UNIV, 1995-; ASSOC PROF BIOCHEM, NC STATE UNIV, 1974-; asst prof, NC State Univ, 1969-1974; biophysicist, Oak Ridge Nat Lab, 1967-1969; investr biol div, Oak Ridge Nat Lab, 1967-1969. **Memberships:** Am Soc Biol Chemists. **Research Statement & Publications:** Physical chemistry of proteins; fluorescence techniques in biochemistry; video image microscopy; plant pathogen interactions. **Mailing Address:** Dept Biochem NC State Univ, PO Box 7622, Raleigh, NC 27695-0001. **Fax:** 919-515-2047. **E-Mail:** jaknopp@ncsu.edu

KNOPP, MARVIN ISADORE, MODULAR FORMS, ANALYTIC NUMBER THEORY. **Personal Data:** b Chicago, Ill, January 4, 1933; m 1957, c Seth, Yudah, Abby & Elana. **Education:** Univ Ill, BS, 1954, AM, 1955, PhD (math), 1958. **Professional Experience:** Res grants, NASA, 1990-; prof, Bryn Mawr Col, 1988-1989; mem, Inst Advan Study, 1988; vis prof, Ohio State Univ, 1979; PROF MATH, TEMPLE UNIV, 1976-; visitor, Inst Advan Study, 1975, 1978; prof, Univ Ill, Chicago Circle, 1970-1976; vis prof, Math Inst, Univ Basel, Switz, 1968-1969; mathematician, Nat Bur Stand, 1963-1964; res grants, NSF, 1960-1989; from asst prof to prof, Univ Wis-Madison, 1960-1970; fel, NSF Inst Advan Study, 1959-1960; res mathematician, Space Tech Labs, 1958-1959; asst math, Univ Ill, 1954-1958. **Memberships:** Am Math Soc. **Research Statement & Publications:** Construction of automorphic forms; uniformization and Riemann surfaces; Eichler cohomology of automorphic forms; rational period functions of automorphic integrals and quadratic forms; Fourier coefficients of modular forms of small weight; Mellin transforms of modular integrals. **Mailing Address:** Dept Math, Temple Univ, Philadelphia, PA 19122-2585. **Fax:** 215-204-6433.

KNOPP, ROBERT H, MEDICINE. **Professional Experience:** PROF MED, SCH MED, UNIV WASH, 1982-; DIR, NORTHWEST LIPIDRES CLIN, 1978-. **Mailing Address:** Harborview Med Center, 325 Ninth Ave, Seattle, WA 98104-2499.

KNOPP, WALTER, PSYCHIATRY. **Personal Data:** b Ostrava, Czech, October 22, 1922; American citizen; m 1951, c 2. **Education:** Univ Heidelberg, MD, 1950; Am Bd Psychiat & Neurol, dipl, 1961. **Professional Experience:** PROF EMER PSYCHIAT, COL MED & PUB HEALTH, OHIO STATE UNIV, 1985-; from instr to prof, Col Med, Ohio State Univ, 1985; vet Admin Ment Hyg Clin, Columbus, 1965-1976 & Athens Ment Health Ctr, 1979-1985; premed educ, Ohio State Univ Hosps, 1973-1985; coordr preclin educ, Ohio State Univ Hosps, 1966-1985; asst prof phys med, Univ, 1966-1967; adv, Grad Sch, 1965-1985; dipl mem psychiat Pan-Am Med Asn, 1965-1975; asst prof, Sch Soc Work, 1964-1967; consult, Vet Admin Hosp, Chillicothe, Ohio, 1961-1985; attend staff physician, Ohio State Univ Hosps, 1960-1985; chief serv, Men's Group, 1958-1960; psychiat resident, Springfield State Hosp, Sykesville, Md, 1955-1958; intern, Glens Falls Hosp, NY, 1954-1955; toxicologist, Europ Lab, US Army Med Ctr, Ger, 1952-1954; resident pediat, Univ Heidelberg Hosp, 1951; intern med, Univ Heidelberg Hosp, 1950. **Memberships:** Fel Am Psychiat Asn; Soc Neuroscience; NY Acad Sci; Int Col Neuropsychopharmacol. **Research Statement & Publications:** Bridging the gaps between neuro-sciences, human behavior and patient oriented therapeutic research and between behavioral sciences, biological sciences and educational technology and research. **Mailing Address:** Col Med & Pub Health, Ohio State Univ, 370 W ninth Ave, Columbus, OH 43210.

KNOPPERS, ANTONIE THEODOOR, pharmacology; deceased, see previous edition for last biography

KNORR, DIETRICH W, FOOD TECHNOLOGY. **Personal Data:** b Waidhofen, Austria, July 3, 1944; m 1968, c 3. **Education:** Univ Agr, Austria, dipling, 1971, Dr, 1974. **Professional Experience:** Vis prof food sci, Asn Biotechnol Res, Braunschweig, Fed Repub Ger, 1985-1986; PROF FOOD PROCESSING & BIOTECHNOL, UNIV DEL, 1984-; assoc prof food processing, Univ Del, 1978-1984; Vis prof food sci, Western Regional Res Ctr-USDA, 1976-1977 & Cornell Univ, 1978; Asst prof, Dept Food Technol, Univ Agr, Vienna, 1974-1978; ed, J Food Biotechnol. **Memberships:** Am Chem Soc; Inst Food Technologist; Am Acad Appl Sci; NY Acad Sci; AsnAustrian Food & Biotechnologists. **Research Statement & Publications:** Food processing; biopolymers; plant cell culture, immobilization, enzyme technology; food technology. **Mailing Address:** Konigen Luise Str 22, 14195 Berlin, Ger.

KNORR, GEORGE E, PLASMA PHYSICS. **Personal Data:** b Munich, Ger, January 29, 1929; American citizen; m 1960, Christiane Bliersbach; c Berud(deceased), Stefau, Uerich & Edward. **Education:** Munich Tech Univ, Vordiplom, 1951, dipl, 1954; Univ Munich, PhD (physics), 1963. **Professional Experience:** Prof physics, Univ Iowa, 1974-1997; assoc prof physics & astron, Univ Iowa, 1967-1974; asst prof & res assoc physics, Univ Calif, Los Angeles, 1966-1967; res assoc, Inst Plasma Physics, Garching, Ger, 1965-1966; res fel plasma physics, Princeton Univ, 1963-1964; res asst, Max Planck Inst Physics, 1958-1965; Physicist, Philips Corp, C H F Mueller AG, 1955-1958. **Memberships:** Am Phys Soc. **Research Statement & Publications:** Radiation from plasmas; confinement and instabilities of plasmas; wave propagation, non-linear effects, numerical methods and computer simulation of plasmas; turbulence in fluids. **Mailing Address:** 330 Kimball Rd, Iowa City, IA 52242. **Fax:** 319-351-2952. **E-Mail:** geoknorr@mchsi.com

KNORR, PHILIP NOEL, FOREST ECONOMICS, RESOURCE MANAGEMENT. **Personal Data:** b Mitchell, Nebr, April 9, 1916; m 1964. **Education:** Univ Calif, BS, 1938; Duke Univ, MF, 1940; Univ Minn, PhD (forest econ), 1963. **Honors & Awards:** Ford-Bartlett Award, Am Soc Photogram, 1966. **Professional Experience:** PROF EMER FORESTRY, UNIV ARIZ, as of 2005; prof forestry, Univ Ariz, as of 2004; RES SCIENTIST, AGR RES STA, 1976-; prof forestry, Univ Ariz, beginning 1966; assoc prof forestry, Agr Res Sta, 1959-1966; from asst to instr forest mgt, Univ Minn, 1954-1959; asst prof forest mgt, Ore State Univ, 1948-1951; asst res forester, Weyerhaeuser Co, 1946-1948; jr forester, Southern Forest Exp Sta, New Orleans, 1941; timber supvr & mapper, US Forest Serv, 1938-1939. **Memberships:** Fel AAAS; Soc Am Foresters; Am Econ Asn; Am Agr Econ Asn; Am SocPhotogram; Sigma Xi. **Research Statement & Publications:** Decision making in forest management; remote sensing, including photo-interpretation; decision making in renewable resources policy. **Mailing Address:** Sch Natual Resources Univ Ariz, Rm 325 Biol Sci E, Tucson, AZ 85718-1184. **Fax:** 520-621-8801.

KNORR, THOMAS GEORGE, SOLID STATE PHYSICS. **Personal Data:** b Buffalo, NY, April 14, 1932; m 1956, c 5. **Education:** Canisius Col, BS, 1953; Case Inst Technol, MS, 1955, PhD (physics), 1958; UnivDetroit, MA, 1978. **Professional Experience:** PROF EMER PHYSICS, WHEELING COL, 1977-; assoc prof, WheelingCol, 1965-1977; sr physicist, Battelle Mem Inst, 1960-1965; from instr to asst prof physics, UnivDayton, 1958-1960; Asst, Case Inst Technol, 1953-1958. **Memberships:** Am Phys Soc; Am Inst Physics; Am Asn Physics Teachers. **Research Statement & Publications:** Thin films; defect properties and structure; radiation damage; linguistics; surface structures. **Mailing Address:** Dept Physics, Wheeling Col, Wheeling, WV 26003.

KNOSPE, WILLIAM H, HEMATOLOGY. **Personal Data:** b Oak Park, Ill, May 26, 1929; m 1954, Adris. **Education:** Univ Ill, Urbana, AB, 1951, BS, 1952; Univ Ill Med Ctr, MD, 1954; Univ Rochester, MS, 1962. **Professional Experience:** THE ELODIA KEHM PROF EMER HEMAT, RUSH MED COL, as of 2002; vis prof, Cancer Ctr, Univ NMex, 1992-1993; vis prof med, McGill Cancer Ctr, McGill Univ, Montreal, 1987; elodia kehn prog & dir hemat, Rush Presby St Luke's Med Ctr, 1986-1993; vis prof med, Nat Tiawan Univ Sch Med, Taipei, Taiwan, 1985; vis prof med, Free Univ Berlin, WGer, 1981; vis prof med, Dept Hematol, Univ Basel, Switz, 1980-1981; prin investr, Polycythemia Vera Study Group, 1978-; prof med, Rush Med Col, beginning 1974; dir clin hemat sect, Presby-St Luke's Hosp, 1974-1982; prin investr, Southeastern Cancer Study Group, 1969-1980; assoc prof med, Univ Ill Col Med, 1969-1972; asst prof med, Col Med, Univ Ill, 1967-1969 & assoc prof med, Rush Med Col, 1971-1974; attend staff & attend physician, Presby-St Luke's Hosp, 1967-; assoc dir hemat sect & chief radio hemat lab, Presby-St Luke's Hosp, 1967-1974; asst chief hemat serv, Walter Reed Gen Hosp, Wash, DC, 1964-1966; attend physician, Walter Reed Gen Hosp, Wash, DC, 1963-1964; Investr radiation biol, Walter Reed Army Inst Res, Wash, DC, 1962-1964 & investr hemat, 1964-1966; Chief med serv, US Army Hosp, Berlin, Ger, 1958-1961. **Memberships:** Fel Am Col Physicians; Am Soc Hemat; Am Fedn Clin Res; Radiation Res Soc; Sigma Xi; Int Soc Exp Hemat. **Research Statement & Publications:** Radiation effects upon bone marrow; role of sinusoidal microcirculation in aplastic anemias; regulation of hematopoietic stem cells; clinical investigation of leukemia and lymphomas; role of hematopoietic stroma in hematopoieisis. **Mailing Address:** Dept Hemat, Rush Med Col, Albuquerque, NM 87122.

KNOTEK, MICHAEL LOUIS, SOLID STATE PHYSICS, SURFACE PHYSICS. **Personal Data:** b Norfolk, Nebr, November 23, 1943; m 1969, c 3. **Education:** Iowa State Univ, BS, 1966; Univ Calif, Riverside, MS, 1969, PhD (physics), 1972. **Honors & Awards:** Distinguished Assoc Award, Dept Energy, 1993. **Professional Experience:** SR SCI DIR, PAC NORTHWEST LABS, 1989-; DIR, MOLECULAR SCIRES CTR & ENVIRON & MOLECULAR SCI LAB, 1989-; chmn, Nat Synchrotron LightSource, Brookhaven Nat Lab, 1985-1989; supvr, Surface Physics Div, 1979-1985; mem techstaff superionic conductors & surface physics, Sandia Lab, 1973-1985; Physicist amorphous semiconductors, Naval Weapons Ctr, 1970-1972; Consult, Bourns Inc, 1970. **Memberships:** Am Vacuum Soc; Sigma Xi; Am Phys Soc; Am Chem Soc; Coun Chem Res. **Research Statement & Publications:** Transport properties of amorphous and disordered semiconductors; transport properties of superionic conductors, especially related to surface and interface properties; surface studies of photocatalytic properties of rutile and related materials; surface science; electron and photon stimulated desorption. **Mailing Address:** US Dept Energy, 1000 Independence Ave, SW, Washington, DC 20585-1000. **Fax:** 202-586-7210. **E-Mail:** michael.knotek@hq.doe.gov

KNOTH, WALTER HENRY, HETEROPOLYANIONS, BORON HYDRIDES. **Personal Data:** b New York, NY, February 18, 1930; m Hedvika; c Bruce & Audrey. **Education:** Syracuse Univ, BS, 1950; Pa State Univ, PhD (chem), 1954. **Honors & Awards:** Belgian Chem Soc, 1960. **Professional Experience:** RETIRED; res chemist, E I du Pont de Nemours & Co, Inc, 1953-1985. **Memberships:** Sigma Xi. **Research Statement & Publications:** Organo-silicon and organoboron chem; boron hydrides; nitrogen complexes; transition metal chem; some 40 pubs and 40 patents in above fields. **Mailing Address:** PO Box 6, Burrows Run Rd, Mendenhall, PA 19357.

KNOTT, ALBERT W, FAILURE ANALYSIS. **Education:** Univ Colo, BS. **Professional Experience:** Founder & chmn bd, Knott Lab, beginning 1982. **Mailing Address:** 7185 S Tucson Way, Centennial, CO 80112. **Fax:** 303-925-1901. **E-Mail:** albertknott@aknott.com

KNOTT, DOUGLAS RONALD, CYTOLOGY. **Personal Data:** b New Westminster, BC, November 10, 1927; m Joan; c Holly A, Heather, Ronald & Douglas (deceased). **Education:** Univ BC, BSA, 1948; Univ Wis, MS, 1949, PhD, 1952. **Honors & Awards:** Order of Canada, Govt of Canada Fellow, Agricultural Institute of Canada Fellow, American Society of Agronomy Fellow, Crop Science Society of America. **Professional Experience:** PROF EMER, DEPT PLANT SCI, UNIV SASK, 1993-; assoc dean res, Univ Sask, 1988-1993; res Adv, Zambia-Can Wheat Proj, 1986-1991; prof, Univ Sask, 1975-1988; prof & head dept, Univ Sask, 1965-1975; From asst prof to assoc prof, Univ Sask, 1952-1965. **Memberships:** Am Soc Agron; Genetics Soc Can; Agr Inst Can; Can Soc Agron; Crop Sci Soc Am. **Research Statement & Publications:** Genetics and cytogenetics of rust resistance in wheat; transfer of resistance to wheat from its relatives; wheat breeding. **Mailing Address:** Dept Plant Sci, Univ Sask, Rm 4D74, Agr Bldg, Saskatoon, SK S7N 5A8, Can. **Fax:** 306-966-5015. **E-Mail:** dougknott@shaw.ca

KNOTT, FRED NELSON, ANIMAL NUTRITION. **Personal Data:** b Oxford, NC, July 18, 1933; m 1955, c 4. **Education:** NC State Col, BS, 1955; NC State Univ, MS, 1962; Va Polytech Inst, PhD (animalnutrit), 1968. **Professional Experience:** RETIRED; specialist in chg exten dairy husb, NC State Univ, 1982; Mem, Exten Serv Team, VI, 1978; from assoc prof to prof, NC State Univ, 1972-1992; exten dairyspecialist dairy husb, NC State Univ, 1967-1992; exten dairy specialist, NC State Univ, 1957-1965; agr exten agent, NC State Univ, 1956-1967; Res asst, NC State Univ, 1955-1956. **Memberships:** Am Dairy Sci Asn; Sigma Xi. **Research Statement & Publications:** Utilization of urea by dairy cattle as a supplement to protein nutrition. **Mailing Address:** 2132 US Hwy 158, Oxford, NC 27565.

KNOTT, GARY DON, MATHEMATICAL & STATISTICAL MODELING SOFTWARE. **Personal Data:** b Colfax, Wash, August 5, 1940. **Education:** Am Univ, BA, 1965; Calif Inst Technol, MS, 1969; Stanford Univ, PhD (comput sci), 1975. **Professional Experience:** FOUNDER, CIVILIZED SOFTWARE INC, 1985-; assoc prof comput sci, Univ Md, 1985-1989; res comput scientist, NIH, 1961-1985. **Research Statement & Publications:** Mathematical and statistical modeling software. **Mailing Address:** Civilized Software, Inc, 12109 Heritage Park Circle, Silver Spring, MD 20906. **Fax:** 301-962-3712. **E-Mail:** knott@civilized.com

KNOUS, TED R, FUNGAL PHYSIOLOGY & TOXINS, PLANT TISSUE CULTURE. **Personal Data:** b Ely, Nev, May 11, 1949; m 1969, c Taryn & Kristae. **Education:** Univ Nev, BS, 1972, MS, 1974; Univ Minn, PhD (plant path), 1979. **Professional Experience:** EXE DIR, UNIV KANSAS MED CTR, RES INSTIT, as of 2005; ASSOC VICE CHANCELLOR RES ADMIN, UNIV KANSAS MED CTR, as of 2005; ASSOC VPROST TECH TRANSFER & RES ADMIN, UNIV KANSAS STATE UNIV, beginning 2001; assoc dean Res & Gradstudies, Univ Wis-Stout, 1993-2000; asst dean res, Res Promo Serv, 1989-1993; dir, Grants & Sponsored Progs, Winona State Univ, 1988-1989; mem, Admin Comt, Nat Plant Pest Surv & Detection Prog, 1983-1988; mem, Dis & Pathogen Physiol Comt, Am Phytopath Soc, 1984-1987; assoced, Plant Dis, Am Phytopath Soc, 1984-1987; consult, Sierra Biotechnol, 1982-; asst prof disphysiol, Dept Plant Sci, Univ Nev, 1979-1988; teaching fel plant path, Univ Minn, 1979; mem, Nat Coun Univ Res Admin. **Memberships:** Am Phytopath Soc; Am Soc Plant Physiologists; AAAS; Sigma Xi. **Research Statement & Publications:** Plant disease physiology. **Mailing Address:** Kans State Univ, 102 Fairchild Hall, Manhattan, KS 66506. **Fax:** 785-532-2983. **E-Mail:** tknous@ksu.edu

KNOWLES, AILEEN FOUNG, BIOCHEMISTRY. **Personal Data:** b China, August 9, 1942; American citizen; m 1969, c 2. **Education:** Nat Taiwan Univ, BS, 1963; Univ Calif, Riverside, PhD (biochem), 1968. **Professional Experience:** ADJ PROF BIOCHEM, SAN DIEGO STATE UNIV, as of 2005; assoc prof biol, Northeastern Univ, beginning 1987; from res biochemist to assoc prof biochem, Cancer Ctr, Univ Calif, 1977-1987; res assoc, Cornell Univ, 1972-1977; scientist, Pub Health Res Inst, New York, 1970-1972; fel biochem, Cornell Univ, 1968-1970. **Memberships:** Am Soc Biochem & Molecular Biol. **Research Statement & Publications:** Biophysics and biochemsitry of membrane-bound enzymes; Adenosine triphosphate hydrolyzing enzymes of tumor membranes. **Mailing**

Address: Dept Chem, San Diego State Univ, GMCS 213B PO Box 22129 225 CSL, San Diego, CA 92192. **Fax:** 619-594-4634. **E-Mail:** aknowles@chemistry.sdsu.edu

KNOWLES, BARBARA B, GENETICS, EARLY MAMMALIAN DEVELOPMENT. **Personal Data:** b New York, NY, February 27, 1937; div, c Amanda (Gay-Lord) & Jared Applet o n. **Education:** Middlebury Col, AB, 1958; Ariz State Univ, MS, 1963, PhD (zoology), 1965. **Professional Experience:** PROF, UNIV MAINE, 1999-; ASSOC DIR, DIR RES & SR STAFF SCIENTIST, JACKSON LAB, BAR HARBOR, MAINE, 1993-; vis sr scientist, Cold Spring Harbor Lab, 1987-1988; Wistar prof path, Lab Med & Microbiol, 1984-; prof, Wistar Inst Anat & Biol, 1983-; mem, Can Res Manpower Review Bd, 1980-1983; mem, Univ Pa Immunol Grad Group, beginning 1977-; assoc prof, Univ Pa, 1977-1983; Career develop award, Nat Inst Allergy & Infectious Dis, 1975; from res asst to res assoc, Univ Pa, 1967-1976; res fel genetics, Univ Calif, Berkeley, 1965-1966; res asst drosophila genetics, Ariz State Univ, 1962-1965. **Memberships:** Am Soc Human Genetics; Genetics Soc Am; Am Soc Immunol; Human Genome Org, Soc Study Reproduction. **Research Statement & Publications:** Murine immune response genes to tumor specific antigens; cell surface molecules of preimplantation stage mouse embryos; molecular control of preimplantation embryogenesis, translational control of material MRNAS and definition of new genes and molecules that control the activation of the embryonic genome; development biology. **Mailing Address:** Jackson Lab, 600 Main St, Bar Harbor, ME 04609. **Fax:** 207-288-6071. **E-Mail:** bbk@jax.org

KNOWLES, CHARLES ERNEST, PHYSICAL OCEANOGRAPHY. **Personal Data:** b Ogden, Utah, March 7, 1937; m 1976, c 6. **Education:** Univ Utah, BS, 1960; Tex A&M Univ, MS, 1967, PhD (phys oceanog), 1970. **Professional Experience:** ALUMNI DISTINGUISHED UNDERGRAD PROF & EMER ASSOC PROF PHYSICAL OCEANOG, NC STATE UNIV, as of 2006; assoc prof phys oceanog, NC State Univ, beginning 1976; Consult, NUC Corp, 1975; asst prof, NC State Univ, 1970-1976; res scientist phys oceanog, Tex A&M Univ, 1969-1970. **Memberships:** Am Geophys Union. **Research Statement & Publications:** Wind wave generation and dissipation in deep and finite depth water; wave current interaction; non-ideal wind wave generation and parameterga-tion of directional wave spectrum; tributary esturarine circulation dynamics. **Mailing Address:** Dept Marine Earth & Atmospheric Sci, NC State Univ, PO Box 8208 1142 Jordan Hall, Raleigh, NC 27695-8208. **Fax:** 919-515-7802. **E-Mail:** ernie_knowles@ncsu.edu

KNOWLES, CHARLES OTIS, ENTOMOLOGY, PESTICIDE TOXICOLOGY. **Personal Data:** b Tallassee, Ala, February 1, 1938; m 1959, Marie; c Kathy K (Dowd), Lauri K (Hamilton) & Jeffrey C. **Education:** Auburn Univ, BS, 1960, MS, 1962; Univ Wis, PhD (entom), 1965. **Professional Experience:** RETIRED; prof entom, Univ Mo, Columbia, 1974-1998; vis sr scientist, Commonwealth Sci & Indust Res Orgn, Long Pocket Labs, Brisbane, Australia, 1972; from asst prof to prof, Univ Mo, Columbia, 1965-1974. **Memberships:** Entom Soc Am; Am Chem Soc. **Research Statement & Publications:** Toxicology of insecticides; comparative insect and mite biochemistry; mode of action and metabolism of acaricides; environmental impact of pesticides. **Mailing Address:** 3809 Wakefield Dr, Columbia, MO 65203. **E-Mail:** agcknowl@muccmail.missouri.edu

KNOWLES, DANIEL M, HEMATOPATHOLOGY, IMMUNOPATHOLOGY. **Personal Data:** b Brooklyn, NY, August 21, 1947; m 1980, Marian; c Tyler. **Education:** Univ Bridgeport, BA, 1969; Univ Chicago, MD, 1973. **Honors & Awards:** Arthur Purdy Stout Prize, 1987. **Professional Experience:** Adj prof path, Col Physicians & Surgeons, Columbia Univ, New York, 1995-1996; pathologist chief, NY Hosp, 1994-; DAVID D THOMPSON PROF PATH, CORNELL UNIV, 1994-; CHMN PATH, NY HOSP-CORNELL MED CTR, 1994-; prof, ColPhysicians & Surgeons, Columbia Univ, New York, 1987-1993; dir, Div Surg Path, 1987-1993; attend pathologist, Lymphocyte Marker Lab, Columbia Presby Med Ctr, 1987-1993; dir, Immunopath Lab, NY Univ Med Ctr, 1983-1987; assoc prof path, Sch Med, NY Univ, 1983-1987; assoc atten pathologist, Univ Hosp, 1983-1987; assoc prof, Col Physicians &Surgeons, Columbia Univ, New York, 1982-1983; assoc atten pathologist, Presby Hosp, 1982-1983; dir, Lymphocyte Marker Lab, Columbia Presby Med Ctr, 1981-1983; asst prof path, Col Physicians & Surgeons, Columbia Univ, New York, 1978-1981; Asst attend pathologist, Presby Hosp, 1978-1981; USPHS fel, 1976-1977. **Memberships:** Am Asn Pathologists; Am Soc Clin Pathologists; Asn Res Vision & Opthal. **Research Statement & Publications:** Correlative, clinical, morphologic, immunologic and molecular analysis of lymphoproliferative disorders to gain understanding of the clinical and biological aspects of lymphomagenesis; molecular biological analysis of the kaposis sarcoma associated herpesvirus. **Mailing Address:** Cornell Univ Med Col, 1300 York Ave, New York, NY 10021.

KNOWLES, DAVID M, GEOLOGY. **Personal Data:** b Saginaw, Mich, July 22, 1927; m 1945, c 2. **Education:** Mich Technol Univ, BS, 1954, MS, 1955; Columbia Univ, PhD (geol), 1967. **Professional Experience:** PROF EMER, LAKE SUPERIOR STATE COL, as of 2006; assoc prof geol, Lake Superior State Col, beginning 1969; Chief geologist, Can Javelin Ltd, 1954-1969. **Memberships:** Geol Soc Am; Geol Asn Can; Can Inst Mining & Metall; Sigma Xi. **Research Statement & Publications:** Structural geology of Labrador Trough formations near Wabush Lake; superposed folds, Hudsonian events and Grenville Province events. **Mailing Address:** Dept Geol & Physics, Lake Superior State Col, 650 W Easterday Ave, Sault Ste Marie, MI 49783. **Fax:** 906-635-2266.

KNOWLES, FRANCIS CHARLES, BIOPHYSICAL CHEMISTRY. **Personal Data:** b Akron, Ohio, September 11, 1941; m 1969, c 2. **Education:** Univ Southern Calif, BA, 1963; Univ Calif, Riverside, PhD (biochem), 1968. **Professional Experience:** ASST PROF CHEM, NICHOLLS STATE UNIV, as of 2000; SCIENTIST BIOCHEM, SCRIPPS INST OCEANOG, 1977-; res fel biochem, Cornell Univ, 1972-1977; lectr physiol & biochem, Mt Sinai Sch Med, New York, 1968-1972. **Memberships:** Am Soc Plant Physiol; Am Chem Soc; Scand Soc Plant Physiol. **Research Statement & Publications:** Biophysical chemistry; evolution of cooperative mechanisms of dioxygen transport proteins; arsenic biochemistry and mechanisms of arsenic toxicity; regulation of photosynthetic carbon dioxide fixation; pathways of photorespiration. **Mailing Address:** Dept Phys Sci, Col Arts & Sci, Nicholls State Univ, 127 Peltier Hall, Thibodaux, LA 70310. **Fax:** 985-448-4927.

KNOWLES, HAROLD LORAINE, PHYSICS. **Personal Data:** b Chicago, Ill, August 21, 1905; wid, c Carolyn (Eubank). **Education:** Phillips Univ, BA, 1926; Univ Kans, PhD (physics), 1931. **Professional Experience:** EMER PROF PHYS SCI, UNIV FLA, 1972-; prof phys sci, Univ Fla, 1954-1972; head dept, Univ Fla, 1954-1967; Supvr sig corps contract proj, War Res Lab, Fla Eng& Indust Exp Sta, 1944-1945; from instr to prof physics, Univ Fla, 1931-1954; Asst instrphysics, Univ Kans, 1927-1931. **Memberships:** Am Phys Soc; Am Asn Physics Teachers. **Research Statement & Publications:** Dielectric constant measurements; direction finder for atmospherics; physical sciences in general education. **Mailing Address:** 2805 NW 83rd St Apt C-104, Gainesville, FL 32606.

KNOWLES, HARROLD B, DESIGN RADIATION SHIELDING, ACCELERATOR HEALTH PHYSICS. **Personal Data:** b Berkeley, Calif, July 28, 1925; m 1949, Geraldine; c William B & Laura E. **Education:** Univ Calif, Berkeley, AB, 1947, MA, 1951, PhD (physics), 1957. **Professional Experience:** Consult, Johns Hopkins Univ, 1996-1997; consult, Mass Gen Hosp, 1995; consult, Univ Calif Los Angeles, 1992; consult, Dept Energy, 1992; PHYSICS CONSULT, 1990-; mem tech staff VI, Rocketdyne, 1984-1990; consult, Rensselaer Polytech Inst, 1983-1985; consult, Los Alamos Sci Lab, 1983-1985; consult, BDM Corp, 1983-1984; prin staffmem, BDM Corp, 1980-1983; res assoc, Air Force Weapon Lab, 1980; consult, LawrenceBerkeley Lab, 1978 & 1992-1993; vis staff mem, Los Alamos Sci Lab, 1974-1980; vis scientist, Los Alamos Sci Lab, 1973-1974; from assoc prof to prof physics, Wash State Univ, 1964-1980; res assoc, Yale Univ, 1961-1964; sr exp physicist, Lawrence Radiation Lab, Univ Calif, Livermore, 1957-1961; res asst physics, Univ Calif, Berkeley, 1951-1957; res asst oceanog, Univ Wash, 1948-1950. **Memberships:** Am Phys Soc; Health Phys Soc. **Research Statement & Publications:** Nuclear physics; accelerator physics; radiation protection; radiological physics; charged particle optics; dosimetry. **Mailing Address:** 4030 Hillcrest Rd, El Sobrante, CA 94803. **Fax:** 510-758-5508. **E-Mail:** hbknowls@ix.netcom.com

KNOWLES, JAMES KENYON, APPLIED MATHEMATICS & MECHANICS. **Personal Data:** b Cleveland, Ohio, April 14, 1931; m 1952, Jacqueline; c John, Jeffrey & James. **Education:** Mass Inst Technol, SB, 1952, PhD (math), 1957. **Honorary Degrees:** DSc, Nat Univ Ireland, 1985. **Honors & Awards:** Eringen Medal, Soc Eng Sci 1991 Koiter Medal Amer soc mech eng 2002. **Professional Experience:** EMER PROF APPL MECH, CALIF INST TECHNOL, 1996-; from asst prof to W M R Kenan prof, Calif Inst Technol, 1958-1996; instr math, Mass Inst Technol, 1957-1958. **Memberships:** Fel Am Soc Mech Engrs; fel Am Acad Mech; Soc Indust & Appl Math; fel AAAS. **Research Statement & Publications:** Mathematical problems in continuum mechanics. **Mailing Address:** 522 N Michillinda, Sierra Madre, CA 91024.

KNOWLES, JEREMY RANDALL, CHEMISTRY, BIOCHEMISTY. **Personal Data:** b Rugby, UK, April 28, 1935; m 1960, c Sebastian, Julis & Timothy. **Education:** Balliol col oxford, BA 1959; Christ chucm, Oxford, MA, Dphil, 1961. **Honorary Degrees:** Dr, Univ Edinburgh, 1992; Dr Eidgemossme technische hochs chule, Zurich, 2001. **Honors & Awards:** Charmian Medal, Royal Soc Chem, 1981; Prelog Medal, 1989; Alfred Bader Award, Am Chem Soc, 1989, Arthur Cope Scholar Award, 1989; Davy Medal, Royal Soc, 1991; Repligen Award, 1993; Nakanish prize, Am chem soc, 1999; robert a welch award, 1995. **Professional Experience:** Dean, Fac Arts & Sci, 1991-2002; Newton-Abraham vis prof, Oxford Univ, 1983-1984; AMORY HOUGHTON PROF CHEM & BIOCHEM, HARVARD UNIV, 1979-; Sloan vis prof, Harvard Univ, 1973; Vis prof, Yale Univ, 1969, 1971; lectr chem, Univ Oxford, 1966-1974; fel & tutor, Wadham Col, Oxford, 1962-1974; Res assoc, Calif Inst Technol, 1961-1962. **Memberships:** Foreign assoc Nat Acad Sci; fel Am Acad Arts & Sci; Am Philos Soc; fel Royal soc, London; fel Royal Soc Chem. **Research Statement & Publications:** Biorganic chemistry. **Mailing Address:** Dept Chem Harvard Univ, 12 Oxford St, Cambridge, MA 02138. **E-Mail:** jeremy_knowles@harvard.edu

KNOWLES, JOHN APPLETON, III, DRUG METABOLISM. **Personal Data:** b Portchester, NY, November 20, 1935; m 1984, c 2. **Education:** Middlebury Col, AB, 1958; Ariz State Univ, PhD (anal chem), 1966. **Professional Experience:** MGR DRUG KINETICS SECT, WYETH LABS, AM HOME PROD CORP, 1978-; res scientist, Wyeth Labs, Am Home Prod Corp, 1968-1978; Res chemist, Orchem Dept, Chambers Works, E I du Pont Del Nemours & Co, 1966-1968. **Memberships:** AAAS; Am Chem Soc. **Research Statement & Publications:** Analysis of drugs and their metabolites. **Mailing Address:** 402 Herritage Dr, Harleysville, PA 19438-3958.

KNOWLES, JOHN E, ANIMAL SCIENCE. **Education:** Colo State Univ, BS, 1987, DVM, 1991 & MS, 1993. **Professional Experience:** ASST PROF, DEPT ANIMAL SCI, BRIGHMAN YOUNG UNIV, as of 1998. **Mailing Address:** Dept Animal Sci, Brigham Young Univ, 380 WIDB POBox 25189, Provo, UT 84602. **Fax:** 801-422-0008.

KNOWLES, JOHN WARWICK, NUCLEAR PHYSICS. **Personal Data:** b Toronto, Ont, December 9, 1920; m 1943, c 5. **Education:** Univ Toronto, BA, 1943; McGill Univ, PhD (physics), 1947. **Professional Experience:** RETIRED; sr res officer nuclear physics, Atomic Energy Can Ltd, 1958-1985; from asst res officer to assoc res officer gen physics, Atomic Energy Can Ltd, 1947-1958; res physicist nuclear physics, Nat Res Coun, 1943-1945. **Memberships:** Fel Am Phys Soc; Can Asn Physicists. **Research Statement & Publications:** Low energy nuclear physics, crystal diffraction of neutron capture x-rays; precision measurements of reference x-rays; photo fission and related photo nuclear reactions. **Mailing Address:** 2 Alexander Pl, Box 736, Deep River, ON K0J 1P0, Can.

KNOWLES, RICHARD JAMES ROBERT, BIOPHYSICS. **Personal Data:** b McPherson, Kans, August 2, 1943; m 1970, Stephanie; c Guenevere R. **Education:** St Louis Univ, HBS, 1965; Cornell Univ, MS, 1969; Polytechnic Univ, PhD (physics), 1979. **Professional Experience:** ASSOC PROF PHYSICS RADIOL, CORNELL UNIV MED COL, 1989-; SR MED PHYSICIST, NY HOSP, CORNELL MED CTR, 1982-; asst prof, NY Hosp, cornell Med Ctr, 1982-1989; adj asst prof physics, Dept Natural Sci, York Col, City Univ NY, 1982; dir, Radiation Physics Lab, Downstate Med Ctr, 1981-1982; clin asst prof radiol, Col Med, State Univ NY Downstate Med Ctr, 1980-1982; chief med physicist, Long Island Col Hosp, 1977-1981. **Memberships:** Am Phys Soc; Soc Nuclear Med; Health Physics Soc; Am Asn Physicists Med; Soc Magnetic Resonance Med; Soc Photo-Optical Instrumentation Engrs. **Research Statement & Publications:** Medical image formation including radioisotopes, and ultrasound; computerized image processing and analysis; data processing including artificial intelligence; data communications including. **Mailing Address:** Dept Radio, Cornell Med Ctr, NY Hosp, 525 E 68th St, New York, NY 10021.

KNOWLES, RICHARD N, ORGANIC CHEMISTRY & MANUFACTURING, COMMUNICATING WITH THE PUBLIC ABOUT THE INDUSTRY & SAFETY MANAGEMENT & LEADERSHIP. **Personal Data:** b Wilmington, Del, August 8, 1935; m 1988, Claire; c Elizabeth, Dorothy, Cynthia & Christine (Stoelting). **Education:** Oberlin Col, BA, 1957; Univ Rochester, PhD (chem), 1960. **Honors & Awards:** Crystal Award, DuPont Agr Prods, 1991; Chemical Emergency Planning and Preparedness Award, EPA, 1995. **Professional Experience:** Retired: CONSULT, RICHARD N KNOWLES & ASSOC, INC, 1996-; director of Community Outreach and Emergency Preparedness 1995-1996, E I Du Pont De Nemours & Co, Inc, plant mgr, Belle, WVa, 1987-1995; Niagara, Indust Chem-Dept, 1983-1987; asst plant mgr, Indust Chem Dept, 1980-1983; mfg mgr, Indust Chem Dept, 1978-1980; prod supt, Indust Chem Dept, 1976-1977; tech supt, Indust Chem Dept, 1975; develop supvr, Indust Chem Dept, 1973-1975; res supvr, E I Dupont De Nemours & Co, 1973; res chemist, E I Dupont De Nemours & Co, 1960-1973; Bd mem, Nat Inst Chem Studies & WVa Manufacturer's Asn., Partner, The SOLiance Group, USA, Founder and Director, The Center for Self-Organizing Leadership. **Memberships:** Am Chem Soc; Nature Conserv:. **Research Statement & Publications:** Herbicides, fungicides, insecticides, pharmaceutical agents, azo catalysts and flame retardants; colloidal silica; production of organic and inorganic chemicals in volumes ranging from lab scale to bulk commodities; granted 40 US patents; Engaging the Natural Tendency of Self-Organization www.centerforselforganizingleadership.com. **Mailing Address:** Richard N Knowles & Assoc, Inc, Niagara Falls, NY 14304. **Fax:** 716-731-2822. **E-Mail:** rnknowles@aol.com

KNOWLES, ROGER, MICROBIOLOGY. **Personal Data:** b Halifax, Eng, July 7, 1929; m 1963, c 2. **Education:** Univ Birmingham, BSc, 1953; Univ London, PhD, 1957. **Honorary Degrees:** DSc, Univ London, 1986. **Honors & Awards:** Can Soc Microbiol Award, 1982. **Professional Experience:** PROF EMER NATURAL RESOURCE SCI, MACDONALD COL, MCGILL UNIV, as of 2000; prof microbiol, macdonald col, mcgill univ, beginning 1971; dept chmn, Macdonald Col, McGill Univ, 1970-1974 & 1979-1987; from asst prof to prof, Macdonald Col, Mcgill Univ, 1957-1971. **Memberships:** Soil Sci Soc Am; Am Soc Microbiol; Can Soc Microbiol; fel Royal Soc Can. **Research Statement & Publications:** Soil and aquatic microbiology; forest soils; nitrogen fixation; denitrification; nitrification; methane metabolism. **Mailing Address:** Dept Natural Resource Sci, Macdonald Campus, McGill Univ, 21111 Lakeshore Rd St Anne de Bellevue, Quebec, PQ H9X 3V9, Can. **Fax:** 514-398-7990. **E-Mail:** knowles@nrs.mcgill.ca

KNOWLES, STEPHEN H, IONOSPHERIC PHYSICS, RADIO ASTRONOMY. **Personal Data:** b New York, NY, February 28, 1940; m 1965, c 2. **Education:** Amherst Col, BA, 1961; Yale Univ, PhD (astron), 1968. **Professional Experience:** TECH ADV, NAVAL SPACE COMMAND, as of 2003; ASTRONOMER, US NAVAL RES LAB, 1961-; Astronr, US Naval Observ, 1961. **Memberships:** AAAS; Int Union Radio Sci; Am Astron Soc; Int Astron Union; Am GeophysUnion. **Research Statement & Publications:** Radar astronomy; celestial mechanics; radio spectroscopy; very long baseline interferometry; ionospheric physics. **Mailing Address:** 9455 Deramus Farm Ct, Vienna, VA 22182. **E-Mail:** sknowles@ssd5.nrl.navy.mil

KNOWLTON, DAVID A, CHEMISTRY. **Personal Data:** b Washington, DC, June 20, 1938; m 1983, c 2. **Education:** Capital Univ, BS, 1961; Ohio State Univ, MSc, 1967, PhD (biochem), 1969. **Professional Experience:** MGR RES & DEVELOP, QUIGLEY CO, INC, 1984-; dir new prof develop, Gunning Refractories Inv, 1982-1983; res chemist, Gunning Refractories Inv, 1977-1981; researcher, Battelle Mem Inst, 1973-1976; asst prof, Ohio State Univ, 1971-1973; Consult, CentLabs, State Ohio & Consolidated Biomed Labs, 1971-1973; Instr, Ohio State Univ, 1970-1971. **Memberships:** Sigma Xi; Am Chem Soc; Am Ceramic Soc. **Research Statement & Publications:** Development of carbon-bonded refractory, especially products for use in the manufacture of iron and steel. **Mailing Address:** PO Box 392, Bettsville, OH 44815.

KNOWLTON, FLOYD MARION, CHEMICAL ENGINEERING. **Personal Data:** b Milan, Ind, January 18, 1918; m Dorthea. **Education:** Purdue Univ, 1939, BchE 1939. **Professional Experience:** RETIRED; dir develop spec projs, Indust Div, 1975-1981; dir develop, Chem Develop Pilot Plant, 1967-1975; mgr chem develop, Chem Develop Pilot Plant, 1958-1967; dept head, Chem Develop Pilot Plant, 1950-1958; develop engr, Bristol Labs Div, Bristol-Myers Co, 1945-1950; develop engr, Naugatuck Chem Div, US Rubber Co, 1943-1945; supvr, Chem Control Div, Pa Ord Works, 1942-1943; from process operator to res chemist, Joseph E Seagram & Sons Inc, 1939-1942. **Memberships:** Am Chem Soc; Am Inst Chem Engrs. **Research Statement & Publications:** Industrial fermentations; recovery processes; organic syntheses. **Mailing Address:** 2857 Ptarmigan Dr, Walnut Creek, CA 94595.

KNOWLTON, FREDERICK FRANK, WILDLIFE RESEARCH. **Personal Data:** b Springville, NY, November 24, 1934; c 4. **Education:** Cornell Univ, BS, 1957; Mont Stat Col, MS, 1959; Purdue Univ, PhD (ecol, physiol), 1964. **Professional Experience:** RES PROF, DEPT FOREST & RANG & WILDLIFE SCI, UTAH STATE, as of 2004; BIOLOGIST, ANIMAL & PLANT HEALTH INSPECTION SERV, USDA, DENVER WILDLIFE RES CTR, as of 2002; assoc prof wildlife sci, Utah State Univ, beginning 1972; vis assoc prof, Cornell Univ, 1971; WILDLIFE BIOLOGIST, US FISH & WILDLIFE SERV, 1964-; lectr biol, Univ Mo, Kansas City, 1964; proj biologist, Mont Fish & Game Dept, 1959. **Memberships:** Wildlife Soc; Am Soc Mammal; Wildlife Dis Asn; Nat Audubon Soc. **Research Statement & Publications:** Dynamics and mechanisms of natural vertebrate populations; especially mammalian physiology and phenomenoon of predation; ungulates; larger carnivores. **Mailing Address:** Col Natural Resources, Utah State Univ, Logan, UT 84322-5230. **Fax:** 435-797-0288. **E-Mail:** knowlton@cc.usu.edu

KNOWLTON, GREGORY DEAN, CHEMISTRY OF PROPELLANTS, PYROTECHNICS & EXPLOSIVES. **Personal Data:** b Santa Barbara, Calif, January 6, 1946; m 1983, Wlatka; c Ryan. **Education:** San Jose State Univ, BS, 1974, MS, 1976; Ariz State Univ, PhD (chem), 1982. **Professional Experience:** Mgr pyrotechnics & explosives, Tally Defense Systs, 1994; sr chemist & prin investr, 1980-1983; anal lab mgr, Commerce Metal Refiners, 1979-1980; instr chem, Phoenix Col, 1978-1980; res assoc, Ariz State Univ, 1976-1979; res geochemist, Lawrence Livermore Nat Lab, 1975 & 1976. **Memberships:** Am Chem Soc; fel Am Inst Chemists; Int Pyrotechnics Soc; Sigma Xi; Am Defense Preparedness Asn; Soc Automotive Engrs. **Research Statement & Publications:** Pyrolysis of complex salts and organometallics; adsorption and desorption of gases and liquids inzeolites; determination of light elements in refractory materials; inorganic azide research; development, analysis and testing of propellants, pyrotechnics and explosives. **Mailing Address:** 615 W Summit Circle, Chandler, AZ 85236. **Fax:** 602-898-2402. **E-Mail:** gknowlton@talleyds.com

KNOWLTON, ROBERT CHARLES, CHEMICAL ENGINEERING. **Personal Data:** b Gardner, Mass, August 3, 1929; m 1952, Edith Lind; c Alison. **Education:** Northeastern Univ, BS, 1952; Newark Col Eng, MS, 1958. **Professional Experience:** CONSULT, 1988-; sr res assoc, Textile Fibers Dept, 1975-1987; sr res engr, Textile Fibers Dept, 1965-1975; res engr, Textile Fibers Dept, 1958-1965; serv engr, Eng Dept, El du Pont Del Nemours & Co, Inc, 1955-1958; Appl Engr, Worthington Corp, 1952-1955. **Memberships:** Am Inst Chem Engrs; Textured Yarn Asn Am. **Research Statement & Publications:** Synthetic fibers; spinning, drawing, and processing of polyester fibers; texturing of continuous filament yarns. **Mailing Address:** 1940 Hampton Rd, Kinston, NC 28504.

KNOWLTON, ROBERT EARLE, INVERTEBRATE ZOOLOGY, MARINE BIOLOGY. **Personal Data:** b Summit, NJ, October 14, 1939; m 1963, Dorothy Smith; c Julia & Kathryn. **Education:** Bowdoin Col, AB, 1960; Univ NC, Chapel Hill, PhD (zoology), 1970. **Professional Experience:** Asst dean, George Washington Univ, 1980-1985; PROF BIOL, GEORGE WASHINGTON UNIV, 1975-; vis lectr biol, Univ Southern Maine, 1972-1980; asst prof, George Washington Univ, 1972-1975; from instr to asst prof biol, Bowdoin Col, 1965-1972; res asst fisheries, Inst Marine Sci, 1964-1965; Teaching fel zool, Univ NC, Chapel Hill, 1962-1963; asst, Dept Zoology, Univ NC, Chapel Hill, 1960-1964. **Memberships:** AAAS; Am Inst Biol Sci; Sigma Xi; Soc Integrative & Comp Biol; Am Microscopal Soc Crustacean Soc. **Research Statement & Publications:** Autecology of decapod larvae; effects of eyestalk extirpation on snapping shrimp larvae; distribution, life history, and behavior of grass shrimp. **Mailing Address:** Dept Biol Sci, George Washington Univ, Washington, DC 20052. **Fax:** 202-994-6100. **E-Mail:** knowlton@gwu.edu

KNOWLTON, TED M, FLUID MECHANICS. **Honors & Awards:** Thiele Award, Dept Chem & Environ Eng, 2004. **Professional Experience:** TECH DIR, PARTICULATE SOLID RES INC, CHICAGO, as of 2005; adj prof Chem Eng, Ill Inst Technol, as of 2004. **Mailing Address:** Particulate Solid Res Inc, 4201 W 36th St, Chicago, IL 60632. **Fax:** 773-523-7367. **E-Mail:** ted.knowlton@psrichicago.com

KNOX, BRUCE E, MATERIALS SCIENCE, SCIENCE TECHNOLOGY & SOCIETY. **Personal Data:** b Binghamton, NY, August 4, 1931; m 1953, Susan; c Mark A, Kathern A & John M. **Education:** Rensselaer Polytech Inst, BS, 1953; Syracuse Univ, MS, 1958; Pa State Univ, PhD (fuel technol), 1963. **Professional Experience:** RETIRED; adj assoc prof sci, technol & soc, beginning 1992; vis prof, Pohang Inst Sci & Eng, Pohang, Korea, 1988; asst dir, Mat Res Lab, 1975-1991; assoc prof mat sci, 1967-1968; mat sci, 1968-1969; solid state sci, 1967-1968; asst prof solid state technol, Pa State Univ, 1963-1967; instr geochem, Pa State Univ, 1963; res asst shock tube chem, Pa State Univ, 1957-1959, 1960-1962; res asst, Syracuse Univ, 1956-1957. **Memberships:** AAAS; fel Am Inst Chemists; Am Chem Soc; Am Soc Eng Educ; Am Phys Soc; Am Vacuum Soc; NY Acad Sci; Sigma Xi; Nat Asn Sci; Technol & Soc. **Research Statement & Publications:** Mass spectrometry; vapor species of solid materials; laser-solid interaction; thin films; characterization of materials; chemical kinetics; trace elements in disease; materials science and engineering education; auger electron spectrometry; ion scattering spectrometry. **Mailing Address:** W Crestview Ave, Boalsburg, PA 16827.

KNOX, BURNAL RAY, FLUVIAL GEOMORPHOLOGY, SPELEOLOGY. **Personal Data:** b Pineville, Mo, March 29, 1931; m 1955, c 3. **Education:** Univ Ark, BS, 1953, MS, 1957; Univ Iowa, PhD (geol), 1966. **Professional Experience:** PROF EMER GEOSCIENCES, SOUTHEAST MO UNIV, as of 2004; prof geol sci, Southeast Mo Univ, 1976-1996; from asst prof to assoc prof, Southeast MO Univ, 1965-1976; teacher high sch, Kans, 1959-1962; explor geologist, Gulf Oil Corp, 1956-1958. **Memberships:** Geol Soc Am; Nat Asn Geol Teachers; Am Sci Affil; Sigma Xi. **Research Statement & Publications:** Geomorphic evolution of Ozarks and Mississippi-Ohio rivers confluence area; Karst geomorphology and speleology of southeast Missouri; correlation of landforms with quaternary events, particularly climatic changes as controls of landscape evolution. **Mailing Address:** Dept GeoSci, SE Mo State Univ, Rhodes Hall 107 One Univ Plaza, Cape Girardeau, MO 63701.

KNOX, CHARLES KENNETH, NEUROPHYSIOLOGY, ENGINEERING. **Personal Data:** b Minneapolis, Minn, November 19, 1938. **Education:** Univ Minn, Minneapolis, BS, 1961, MS, 1962, PhD (physiol), 1969. **Professional Experience:** ASSOC PROF PHYSIOL, UNIV MINN, MINNEAPOLIS, 1976-; NIH res grant, 1973-1976, 1976-1979; asst prof, Univ Minn, Minneapolis, 1969-1976; NIH res fel, Nobel Inst Neurophysiol, Stockholm, 1969-1970. **Memberships:** Am Physiol Soc; Soc Neuroscience; NY Acad Sci. **Research Statement & Publications:** Neural control of respiration. **Mailing Address:** 1000 Ingerson Rd, St Paul, MN 55126.

KNOX, DAVID LALONDE, NEURO-MEDICAL OPHTHALMOLOGY, OCULAR INFLAMMATION. **Personal Data:** b Chicago, Ill, September 3, 1930; m 1958, c 3. **Education:** Baylor Univ, MD, 1955. **Professional Experience:** Asst dean admis, Sch med, Johns Hopkins Univ, 1976-; ASSOC PROF OPHTHAL, SCH MED, JOHNS HOPKINS UNIV, 1967-; hon consult, moorfields eye hosp, London, 1965; sr lectr, dept opthal, inst opthal, Univ London, 1965; asst prof, sch med, Johns Hopkins Univ, 1963; instr, dept Ophthal, Sch med, Johns Hopkins Univ 1962-1963. **Research Statement & Publications:** Neuromedical ophthalmology; ocular inflammation; clinical investigations identifying etiologic factors especially gastrointestinal food and allergies. **Mailing Address:** Wilmer Ophthal Inst, Johns Hopkins Univ, 600 N Wolfe St Wilmer 110, Baltimore, MD 21287-9217. **Fax:** 410-955-2542. **E-Mail:** dknox@jhmi.edu

KNOX, ELLIS GILBERT, NEW CROP INTRODUCTION. **Personal Data:** b Sterling, Ill, March 25, 1928; m 1948, c 2. **Education:** Univ Ill, BS, 1949, MS, 1950; Cornell Univ, PhD (soils), 1954. **Professional Experience:** RETIRED; soil scientist, Soil Conserv Serv, USDA, 1985-1996; exec officer, Soil & Land Use Technol, Inc, 1975-1985; pedologist, Aero Serv Corp, Bogota, Colombia, 1973-1975; tech officer, Food & Agr Orgn UN, Turrialba, Costa Rica, 1969-1970; consult, InterAm Inst Agr Sci, Turrialba, Costa Rica, 1966; soil scientist, Soil Conserv Serv, USDA, 1962-1963; from asst prof to prof soils, Ore State Univ, 1954-1973. **Memberships:** AAAS; Soil Sci Soc Am; Sigma Xi; Soil & Water Conserv Soc; Am Soc Agron. **Research Statement & Publications:** Soil classification and mapping; soil survey interpretations; land resource and land use evaluation; analysis of crop production-marketing-consumption systems; biomass crops; development of crop systems. **Mailing Address:** 7011 Lincolnshire Rd, Lincoln, NE 68506.

KNOX, ERIC, BOTANY. **Honors & Awards:** George R Cooley Award, Am Soc Plant Taxonomists, 1992. **Professional Experience:** PROF, DEPT BOT, UNIV MICH, ANN ARBOR, as of 2002. **Mailing Address:** Univ Mich, Dept Bot, Ann Arbor, MI 48108.

KNOX, ERICK H, RESEARCH & DEVELOPMENT PROSTHETIC DEVICES, IMPACT BIOMECHANICS. **Personal Data:** b Oak Park, Ill, May 10, 1965. **Education:** Marquette Univ, BS, 1987; Northwestern Univ, MS, 1990, PhD (biomed eng), 1996. **Professional Experience:** MGR, ENG SYSTS INC, as of 2006; staff engr, Eng Systs Inc, beginning 1996. **Memberships:** Am Soc Mech Engrs; Inst Elec & Electronics Engrs; Eng Med & Biol; Am SocBiomech; Soc Automotive Engrs. **Research Statement & Publications:** Analysis of human locomotion, particularly as it relates to persons with disabilities; design and development of prosthetic and orthotic devices; human factors, impact biomechanics and injury causation related to workplace and motor vehicle accidents. **Mailing Address:** Eng Systs Inc, 3851 Exchange Ave, Aurora, IL 60504. **Fax:** 630-851-4870.

KNOX, FRANCIS STRATTON, III, PHYSIOLOGY, BIOMEDICAL ENGINEERING. **Personal Data:** b Wilmington, Del, January 28, 1941; m 1965, Carol; c 2. **Education:** Brown Univ, BA, 1963; Iowa State Univ, MS, 1966; Univ Ill, PhD (physiol & biomed eng), 1971. **Professional Experience:** AT WRIGHT-PATTERSON AIR FORCE BASE, as of 2003; PRIN BIOMED ENGR, USAF RES LAB, 1999-; fel, Aerospace Medicine Asn, 1998; chief, Escape & Impact Protection Br, USAF, Armstrong Lab, 1989-1999; supvry res physiologist & chief crew, spec proj, 1988-1989; supvry res physiologist, spec proj, 1987-1988; fel, US Army, Secretary Army, 1986-1987; res physiologist & chief crew biotechnol br, Biomed Appln Res Div, Aeromed Res Lab, 1980-1986; assoc prof physiol & biophys, Med Ctr, La State Univ, Shreveport, 1976-1980; AFFIL ASST PROF Bioengineering, LA TECH UNIV, 1975-; asst prof, mem Grad Fac, 1974-1980; consult physiol & Bioengineering, US Army Aeromed Res Lab, Ft Rucker, Ala, 1973-1980; asst prof, Med Ctr, La State Univ, Shreveport, 1973-1976; chief bioinstrumentation br, US Army Aeromed Res Lab, 1970-1973; USPHS trainee biomed eng, Med Ctr, Univ Ill, 1966-1970; Grad teaching asst zool, Iowa State Univ, 1963-1966; assoc prof, Community Med Dept, Wright State Sch Med. **Memberships:** Sigma Xi; Am Burn Asn; Inst Elec & Electronics Engrs; Soc Neurosci; Aerospace Med Asn; assoc fel Aerospace Med Asn. **Research Statement & Publications:** Quantitative physiology; systems analysis of physiological systems; use of biomedical instrumentation and computers to study physiological systems and to create economical, comprehensive diagnostic and patient monitoring systems; physiological effects of protective clothing under operational conditions. **Mailing Address:** Aeronaut Systs Ctr, Write Patterson Air Force Base, 150 Gracewood Dr, Centerville, OH 45458. **Fax:** 937-255-3343. **E-Mail:** ted.knox@wpafb.af.mil

KNOX, FRANKLYN G, RENAL PHYSIOLOGY. **Personal Data:** b Rochester, NY, December 20, 1937; m 1960, Anne; c Michael, Sally, David & Susan. **Education:** State Univ NY, Buffalo, MD & PhD (physiol), 1965. **Honorary Degrees:** DSc, State Univ NY, 1997. **Honors & Awards:** Daggs Award, Am Physiol Soc, 1996; Berliner Award, 1997. **Professional Experience:** CHAIR, STRATEGIC ALLIANCES & HEAD, NEPHROLOGY RES UNIT, as of 2002; PROF PHYSIOL & MED, MAYO CLIN COL MED, as of 1997; distinguished investr, Mayo found, 1992-; dean, Mayo Med Sch, 1982-1990; chair, Dept Physiol & Biophys, Mayo Clinc, 1974-1983; assoc prof physiol, Univ MO, beginning 1970-1971. **Memberships:** Am Physiol Soc (pres, 1986-1987); Am Soc Nephrol; Am Heart Asn; Am Asn Physicians; Am Soc Clin Invest; Am Fedn Clin Res; AAAS. **Research Statement & Publications:** Regulation of renal sodium and phosphate transport; publications above two hundered. **Mailing Address:** Dept Med & Physiol, Mayo Med Sch, 200 First St S W, Rochester, MN 55905. **Fax:** 507-266-4710. **E-Mail:** knox.franklyn@mayo.edu

KNOX, GAYLORD SHEARER, MEDICINE, RADIOLOGY. **Personal Data:** b Bangkok, Thailand, October 18, 1923; American citizen; m 1946, c 3. **Education:** Tulane Univ, MD, 1951; Am Bd Radiol, cert, 1958. **Professional Experience:** RADIOLOGIST, GREATER LAUREL BELTSVILLE HOSP, 1979-; Chesapeake Casualty Ins Co, Denver, 1974-1978; pres, Chesapeake Physicians, 1973-1978; active consult, Sinai Hosp Baltimore, 1966-; asst prof, Sch Med, Johns Hopkins Univ, 1965-; assoc prof, Sch Med, Univ Md, Baltimore City, 1965-; Consult, Vet Admin Hosp, Oklahoma City, 1961-1965 & Perry Point, Md, 1965-; chief, Dept Radiol, Baltimore City Hosps, 1965-1979; assoc prof radiol, Univ Okla, 1961-1965; chief radiol serv, Hosp, Bad Canstatt, Ger, 1958-1961; resident radiol, Walter Reed Army Hosp, 1955-1958; physician, US Army, Ft Bliss, Tex, 1953-1955; pvt pract, La, 1952-1953; Intern gen med, Charity Hosp, New Orleans, 1951-1952. **Memberships:** Radiol Soc NAm; fel Am Col Radiol; AMA; Soc Nuclear Med; Am Inst Ultrasound Med. **Research Statement & Publications:** Clinical radiology, particularlyskeletal and visceral changes in the aging process and vascular changes in aging. **Mailing Address:** 12340 Shadetree Lane, Laurel, MD 20708.

KNOX, JAMES CLARENCE, GEOMORPHOLOGY, PHYSICAL GEOGRAPHY. **Personal Data:** b Platteville, Wis, November 29, 1941; m 1964, Kathleen; c Lezlie S & Sara E. **Education:** Univ Wis, Platteville, BS, 1963; Univ Iowa, PhD (geog), 1970. **Honors & Awards:** Honors Award, Asn Am Geogr, 1990; G K Gilbert Award, Asn Am Geogr, 1996; M G Marcus Distinguished Career Award, Geomorphol Group, Asn Am Geogr, 2001. **Professional Experience:** RES ASSOC, WIS GEOL & NATURAL HIST SURV, as of 2005; EVJUE-BASCOM PROF GEOG & ENVIRON STUDIES, UNIV WIS-MADISON, 1997-; adj res assoc, Wis Geol & Nat Hist Surv, 1995-; assoc ed, Geog Annals, 1993-1996; assoc ed, Geol Soc Am Bull, 1991-; Geog & Regional Sci Panel, Continental Hydrol Panel, 1991-1993; Geog & Regional Sci Panel, NSF, 1988-1990; secy, US Nat Comt Int Quaternary Union, 1986-1991; US deleg & corresp mem, Int Geomorphol assoc, 1986-1990; vchmn & chmn, Quaternary Geol & Geomorphol Div, Geol Soc Am, 1985-1988; chmn dept, Univ Wis-Madison, 1983-1986; mem, US Nat Comt Int Quaternary Union, 1982-1991; assoc ed, Geog Annals, 1978-1981; prof geog, Univ Wis-Madison, 1977-1997; assoc ed, Coun Am Quaternary Asn, 1976-1980; dir, Ctr Geol Anal, Inst Environ Studies, 1973-1978; from asst prof to assoc prof geog, Univ Wis-Madison, 1968-1976. **Memberships:** Am Quaternary Asn; fel AAAS; fel Geol Soc Am; Soil Conserv Soc Am; Asn Am Geogr; Am Geophys Union. **Research Statement & Publications:** Fluvial geomorphology; paleoclimatology and paleohydrology of the Quaternary; effects of present-day climate variation and land use on stream flow characteristics and sedimentation problems; Quaternary landscape evolution of upper Miss Valley; erosion transportation and storage of sediment in river systems; hydrology and water resources. **Mailing Address:** Dept Geog, Univ Wis, 234 Sci Hall 550 N Park St, Madison, WI 53706-1404. **Fax:** 608-265-3991. **E-Mail:** knox@geography.wisc.edu

KNOX, JAMES L(ESTER), ELECTROMAGNETICS, INSTRUMENTATION. **Personal Data:** b Youngstown, Ohio, July 30, 1919; m 1946, c 5. **Education:** Univ Tenn, BS, 1942; Univ Mich, MSE, 1954; Ohio State Univ, PhD (elec eng), 1962. **Professional Experience:** RETIRED; prof elec eng, Univ Petrol & Minerals, Dhahran, Saudi Arabia, 1973-1975 & 1976-1978; prof, Mont State Univ, 1969-; assoc prof, Mont State Univ, 1965-1969; prof & dean, Cent Philippine Univ, 1962-1965; res assoc, Res Found, 1961-1962; instr elec eng, Ohio State Univ, 1960-1961; assoc prof, Cent Philippine Univ, 1051-1050; tech dir eng, Radio Sta DYSR, 1950-1951; asst prof eng, Cent Philippine Univ, 1948-1950; Am Baptist Mission Soc Missionary instr physics, Univ Shanghai, 1947-1948; engr, Gen Elec Co, 1943-1946; instr elec eng, Univ Tenn, 1942-1943; staff mem, Dept Elec Eng, Univ Petrol & Minerals, Saudi Arabia. **Memberships:** Inst Elec & Electronics Engrs; Instrument Soc; Am Soc Eng Educ; Sigma Xi. **Research Statement & Publications:** Electromagnetics; electric power; instrumentation; community acoustics; remote sensing. **Mailing Address:** 1331 Robin Lane, Bozeman, MT 59715.

KNOX, JAMES M, COMPUTER SCIENCE. **Education:** Univ Tex, BSEE, 1969, MA, 1971, PhD, 1978. **Professional Experience:** OWNER & COMPUT SCIENTIST, TRISOFT/CYBERSEARCH, as of 2005. **Mailing Address:** TriSoft/CyberSearch, 1300 W Koenig Ln Suite 200, Austin, TX 78756. **Fax:** 512-371-5716. **E-Mail:** jknox@trisoft.com

KNOX, JAMES RUSSELL, PHYSICAL BIOCHEMISTRY, X-RAY CRYSTALLOGRAPHY. **Personal Data:** b Bonne Terre, Mo, May 28, 1941; m 1965, Jane; c Craig P & Clara R. **Education:** Univ Mo, Rolla, BS, 1963; Boston Univ, PhD (phys chem), 1967. **Honors & Awards:** Author Award, Am Chem Soc, 1982 1984, univ conn distinguished fac res award; conn acad arts & sci, 1994-. **Professional Experience:** PROF, DEPT MOLECULAR & CELL BIOL, INST OF MATERIALS SCI, UNIV CONN, STORRS, CONN, as of 2002; consult, PanTherix, 2001-; sci comt, int B-lactamase Congress, Italy, 1999; NIH special reviewer BBCB, 1995; prog committee, soc indust microbiol, int con Antibiotic resistance, 1993-1994; advi committee, foundn che res, univ, MO Rolla, 1991-1999; consul, Eli Lilly Co, 1988-1991; adv committee, NSF facility for macromolecular computing, Purdue univ, 1988-1990; NIH study sections SSS-1-B, 1987-1989; consult, HOffmann-LaRoche inc, 1983-1987; invited prof, universidad de concepcion, Chile, 1981, 1986; NIH special reviewer BBCA, 1978; visiting prof, Harvard Univ biol lab, 1977; post-doctoral fel, molecular biophysics & biochem, Yale univ 1969-1970; NIH post-doctoral fel, chem crystallography lab, Oxford univ, 1966-1968. **Memberships:** AAAS; Am Chem Soc; Am Crystallog Asn (secy-treas, 1992-1994); Sigma Xi; Biophys Soc; Protein Soc. **Research Statement & Publications:** Enzyme structure and function by means of x-ray analysis; penicillin-binding proteins; beta-lactamases and bacterial cell-wall synthesizing enzymes; molecular modelling, energetics and dynamics; bacterial resistance to beta-lactams and vancomycin. **Mailing Address:** Molecular & Cell Biol Dept, Univ Conn, U-125, Storrs, CT 06269. **Fax:** 860-486-4745. **E-Mail:** knox@uconnvm.uconn.edu

KNOX, JOHN MACMURRAY, PHYSICS, ION BEAM ANALYSIS. **Personal Data:** b Sheboygan, Wis, November 21, 1946; m 1969, c 2. **Education:** Gustavus Adolphus Col, BA, 1968; Univ WYO, MS, 1976, PhD (physics), 1981. **Professional Experience:** PROF & CHAIR PHYSICS, IDAHO STATE UNIV, as of 2004; chair, dept physics, Idaho State Univ, 1997-2002; prof physics, Idaho State Univ, 1992-1997; vis researcher, dept nuclear physics, Lund Univ, Lund, Sweden, 1991-1992; actg chair, dept physics, Idaho State Univ, 1990; dir, Idaho State Univ Health Physics Program, 1987-1991; dir, Particle Beam Lab, 1985-; from asst prof to assoc prof physics, Idaho State Univ, 1985-1992; res fel & asst prof, Inst Paper Chem, 1981-1984. **Memberships:** Am Phys Soc; Am Asn Physics Teachers. **Research Statement & Publications:** Interaction of 2 Mev ion beams with materials, analysis, primarily using particle induced x-ray emission and backscattered ion. **Mailing Address:** Dept Physics, Idaho State Univ, PO Box 8106 785 S 8th Ave, Pocatello, ID 83209. **Fax:** 208-282-4649. **E-Mail:** knox@physics.isu.edu

KNOX, KENNETH L, CHEMICAL ENGINEERING. **Personal Data:** b Winnipeg, Man, September 18, 1920; American citizen; m 1951, Margaret; c 3. **Education:** Univ Saskatchewan, BE, 1942, MSc, 1946; Columbia Univ, PhD (chem eng), 1949. **Professional Experience:** RETIRED; res assoc, Circleville Res & Develop Lab, 1963-1982; tech supt, Cellophane Lab, Kans, 1960-1963; develop supvr, Cellophane Plants, NY, Iowa & Kans, 1952-1960; res engr, Yerkes Res & Develop Lab, E I Du Pont de Nemours & Co Inc, NY, 1948-1952. **Memberships:** Am Chem Soc; Am Inst Chem Engrs; Soc Plastics Engrs. **Research Statement & Publications:** Industrial research on polyester film. **Mailing Address:** 3580 Shaw Ave Apt 427, Cincinnati, OH 45208.

KNOX, KERRO, INORGANIC CHEMISTRY. **Personal Data:** b Philadelphia, Pa, June 17, 1924; m 1949, c 4. **Education:** Yale Univ, BS, 1945, PhD (phys chem), 1950; Cambridge Univ, PhD (phys chem), 1952. **Professional Experience:** PROF EMER CHEM, CLEVELAND STATE UNIV, OHIO, as of 2004; Vis prof, Univ, Mass, beginning 1989; prof chem, Cleveland State Univ, 1969-1985; assoc prof chem, Case Western Reserve Univ, 1963-1969; mem tech staff, Bell TelLabs, 1956-1963; From instr to assoc prof chem, Univ NC, 1951-1956. **Memberships:** Am Crystallog Asn. **Research Statement & Publications:** X-ray crystallography. **Mailing Address:** 11 Wildwood Lane, Amherst, MA 01002.

KNOX, KIRVIN L, NUTRITION. **Personal Data:** b Sayre, Okla, August 9, 1936; m 1958, c 3. **Education:** Fresno State Col, BS, 1958; Colo State Univ, MS, 1960; Univ Calif, PhD (physiol, nutrit), 1964. **Professional Experience:** RETIRED; vice Provost Agr & Natural Resources, Colo State Univ, ending 2000; dean emer agr & natural resources, Univ conn, beginning 1999; sabbatical leave, Univ Calif, Berkeley, 1978-1979; prof nutrit sci & dept head, Univ Conn, beginning 1972; prin investr, 1966-1969; Am Cancer Soc res grant, 1966-1968; from asst prof to assoc prof animal sci & physiol, ColoState Univ, 1965-1972; dir metab lab, Colo State Univ, 1965-1972; co-investr, NIH res grant, 1965-1968; asst prof animal sci, ColoState Univ, 1964-1965; lab supt, Escalon Packers Inc, 1960. **Memberships:** Am Dairy Sci Asn; Am Soc Animal Sci; Am Inst Nutrit; NY Acad Sci; AAAS. **Research Statement & Publications:** Comparative nutrition as related to energy and vitamin metabolism; behavioral response to nutrition. **Mailing Address:** Provost Off, Colo State Univ, 108 Admin Bldg, Ft Collins, CO 80523. **Fax:** 970-491-0215. **E-Mail:** kknox@vines.colostate.edu

KNOX, LARRY WILLIAM, PALEONTOLOGY, MICROPALEONTOLOGY. **Personal Data:** b Mishawaka, Ind, November 10, 1942; m 1964, Carol; c Christopher & Jennifer. **Education:** Ind Univ, AB, 1965, AM, 1971, PhD (geol), 1974. **Professional Experience:** CHAIR, TENN TECHNOL UNIV, 1995-; PROF GEOL, TENN TECHNOL UNIV, 1983-; from asst prof to assoc prof, Tenn Technol Univ, 1974-1983. **Memberships:** Paleont Soc; Paleont Asn; Soc Econ Paleontologists & Mineralogists; Intr Paleont Union; Micropaleont Soc. **Research Statement & Publications:** Paleoecology and biostratigraphy of paleozoic ostracodes. **Mailing Address:** Dept Earth Sci, Tenn Technol Univ, 815 Quadrangle Dr, Cookeville, TN 38505. **Fax:** 931-372-3363. **E-Mail:** lknox@tntech.edu

KNOX, ROBERT ARTHUR, PHYSICAL OCEANOGRAPHY. **Personal Data:** b Washington, DC, January 15, 1943; m 1966, c 2. **Education:** Amherst Col, AB, 1964; Mass Inst Technol-Woods Hole Oceanog Inst, PhD (oceanog), 1971. **Professional Experience:** CHMN, UNIV NAT OCEANO LAB SYST, UNIV CALIF, as of 2002; ASSOC DIR, SCRIPPS INST OCEANOG, 1992-; RES OCEANOGR, SCRIPPS INST OCEANOG, 1986-; assoc res oceanogr, Scripps Inst Oceanog, 1981-1986; acadadminr, Scripps Inst Oceanog, 1980-1990; res asst oceanogr, Scripps Inst Oceanog, 1973-1981; res assoc, Mass Inst Technol, 1971-1973. **Memberships:** Sigma Xi; Am Meteorol Soc; Am Geophys Union; Oceanog Soc. **Research Statement & Publications:** Equatorial ocean dynamics and circulation; structure and dynamics of oceanic mixed layer; acoustic sensing of ocean circulation. **Mailing Address:** Scripps Inst Oceanog, Univ Calif, La Jolla, CA 92093-0230.

KNOX, ROBERT GAYLORD, QUANTITATIVE FOREST ECOLOGY, ECOLOGICAL MODELING. **Personal Data:** b Washington, DC, October 24, 1956; m 1978, Julie. **Education:** Princeton Univ, AB, 1978; Univ NC, PhD (bot), 1987. **Professional Experience:** RES SCIENTIST FOREST ECOL, BIOSPHERIC SCI BR, GODDARD SPACE FLIGHT CTR, NASA, 1992-; sr res assoc, Rice Univ, 1990-1997; res scientist, Univ Space Res Asn, 1991-1992; vis lectr, Dept Ecol & Evolutionary Biol, Rice Univ, 1990; Huxley res instr evolution, Dept Biol, Rice Univ, 1987-1990; comput programmer cancer epidemiol, Syst Cancer Ctr, Univ Tex, 1978-1982. **Memberships:** Ecol Soc Am; Int Asn Veg Sci; Am Geophys Union; Sigma Xi; Torrey Bot Soc. **Research Statement & Publications:** Remote sensing of ecosystem structure and dynamics; plant community structure and distribution; methods of vegetation analysis; physiological ecology of resource capture and limitation; computer modeling of individuals, communities and ecosystems; remote sensing technology. **Mailing Address:** Biospheric Sci Branch, Code 6144, Goddard Space Flight Ctr, NASA, Greenbelt, MD 20771. **Fax:** 301-614-6695. **E-Mail:** Robert.G.Knox@nasa.gov

KNOX, ROBERT SEIPLE, BIOL PHYSICS, CHEM PHYSICS. **Personal Data:** b Franklin, NJ, July 13, 1931; m 1954, Myrta; c Bruce, Wayne & Lee. **Education:** Lehigh Univ, BS, 1953; Univ Rochester, PhD (physics, optics), 1958. **Honors & Awards:** Biol Physics Prize, Am Phys Soc, 1994. **Professional Experience:** PROF PHYSICS EMER, UNIV ROCHESTER, 1997-; UK Fulbright scholar, 1993; dean, Univ Col, Univ Rochester, 1982-1985; fel, Japanese Soc Prom Sci, Kyoto, Japan, 1979; chmn dept, Univ Rochester, 1969-1974; prof physics, Univ Rochester, 1968-1997; NSF sr fel, Univ Leiden, 1967-1968; Consult, Naval Res Lab, 1960-1970; from asst prof to assoc prof, Univ Rochester, 1960-1968; Consult, Solid State Sci Div, Argonne Nat Lab, 1959-1969; res asst prof, Univ Ill, 1959-1960; Res assoc physics, Univ Ill, 1958-1959. **Memberships:** Fel Am Phys Soc; emer & charter mem Am Soc Photobiol; emer mem Am Asn Physics Teachers; emer mem Biophys Socl; emer mem Intl Soc Photosyn. **Research Statement & Publications:** Optical and electrical properties of ionic and molecular crystals; theory of photosynthesis, picosecond spectroscopy. **Mailing Address:** Dept Physics & Astron, Univ Rochester, Rochester, NY 14627-0171. **Fax:** 585-242-0851. **E-Mail:** rsk@pas.rochester.edu

KNOX, WALTER ROBERT, organic chemistry, petrochemistry; deceased, see previous edition for last biography

KNOX, WAYNE H, ATOMIC & MOLECULAR PHYSICS. **Personal Data:** b November 8, 1957. **Education:** Univ Rochester, BS, 1979, PhD (physics), 1983. **Professional Experience:** RES SCIENTIST, AT&T BELL LABS, 1984-. **Memberships:** Am Phys Soc. **Mailing Address:** AT&T Bell Labs, 413-415 Crawfords Corner Rd, Holmdel, NJ 07733.

KNOX, WILLIAM JORDAN, NUCLEAR PHYSICS. **Personal Data:** b Pomona, Calif, March 21, 1921; m 1948, c 4. **Education:** Univ Calif, BS, 1942, PhD (physics), 1951. **Professional Experience:** PROF EMER PHYSICS, UNIV CALIF, DAVIS, as of 2004; vis scientist, Lawrence Berkeley Lab, 1981-1986; sr Fulbright Hayes Prog resfel France, Comt Int Exchange Persons, 1973-1974; vis scientist, Europ Ctr Nuclear Res, 1973-1974; chmn dept, Univ Calif, Davis, 1971-1975, 1980-1983; Vis sci, Cambridge Univ, 1967-1968; prof physics, Univ Calif, Davis, beginning 1966; actg dir Crocker Nuclear Lab, 1966-1967, 1978-1979; chmn dept, Univ Calif, Davis, 1963-1966; assoc prof physics, Univ Calif, Davis, 1960-1966; asst prof physics, Yale Univ, 1955-1959; consult, AEC, Wash, DC, 1955-1956; physicist, AEC, Wash, DC, 1953-1955; asst prof physics, Yale Univ, 1951-1953; physicist, Radiation Lab, UnivCalif, 1947-1951; chemist, Radiation Lab, Univ Calif, 1946; jr technologist, Hanford Eng Works, 1944-1945; from jr chemist to chemist, Clinton Labs, Oak Ridge, 1943-1946; asst chem, MetallLab, Univ Chicago, 1942-1943. **Memberships:** Fel Am Phys Soc; Am Asn Physics Teachers. **Research Statement & Publications:** Nuclear reactions; nuclear structure; plutonium and fission product chemistry; particle production. **Mailing Address:** Dept Physics, Univ Calif, Davis, CA 95616. **E-Mail:** knox@physics.ucdavis.edu

KNUDSEN, DENNIS RALPH, PHYSICAL CHEMISTRY. **Personal Data:** b Warren, Minn, July 22, 1943; m 1965, Bonita Peterson; c Sara & Rachel. **Education:** NDak State Univ, BS, 1965, PhD (phys chem) 1970. **Professional Experience:** PHYS SCIENTIST, US NAVAL SURFACE WARFARE CTR, 1986-; Res chemist, 1970-1986. **Research Statement & Publications:** Thermodynamics of solutions; determination of chemical compounds in air; chemical instrument development, combustion; fiber optics in adverse environments. **Mailing Address:** US Naval Surface Warfare Ctr, Dahlgren, VA 22448-5000.

KNUDSEN, ERIC INGVALD, NEUROSCIENCE, BIOLOGY. **Personal Data:** b Palo Alto, Calif, October 7, 1949; m 1975. **Education:** Univ Calif, Santa Barbara, BA, 1971, MA, 1973; Univ Calif, San Diego, PhD (neurosci), 1976. **Professional Experience:** CHMN, DEPT NEUROBIOLOGY, STANFORD UNIV SCH MED, as of 2004; EDWARD C & AMY H SEWALL PROF NEUROBIOLOGY, STANFORD UNIV, as of 2003; MEM FAC, DEPT NEUROSCIENCE, STANFORD SCH MED, 1980-; res fel neuroscience, Calif Inst Technol, 1976-1980. **Memberships:** Acoust Soc Am; AAAS; Soc Neuroscience; Sigma Xi; Nat Acad Sci. **Research Statement & Publications:** Neurophysiology, anatomy and ethology related to the evolution of the auditory system, specifically encoding of space by the auditory system. **Mailing Address:** Dept Neurobiology, Sch Med, Stanford Univ, Fairchild D204, Stanford, CA 94305-5125. **Fax:** 650-725-3958. **E-Mail:** eknudsen@leland.stanford.edu

KNUDSEN, HAROLD KNUD, ELECTRICAL ENGINEERING. **Personal Data:** b San Francisco, Calif, August 6, 1936; m 1958, c 2. **Education:** Univ Calif, Berkeley, BS, 1958, MS, 1960, PhD (elec eng), 1962. **Professional Experience:** PROF EMER COMPUT SCI, UNIV NMEX, as of 2005; prof, Univ NMex, beginning 1974; assoc prof, Univ NMex, 1966-1974; Staff mem data systs anal, Lincoln Lab, Mass Inst Technol, 1962-1966. **Memberships:** Inst Elec & Electronics Engrs; Sigma Xi. **Research Statement & Publications:** Data systems analysis; system theory especially the application of theories of optimization. **Mailing Address:** Dept Comput Sci, Univ NMex, Rm 313 Mail stop MSC01 1130 One Univ NMex, Albuquerque, NM 87131-0001. **Fax:** 505-277-6927. **E-Mail:** knudsen@cs.unm.edu

KNUDSEN, J(AMES) G(EORGE), CHEMICAL ENGINEERING. **Personal Data:** b Youngstown, Alta, March 27, 1920; American citizen; m 1947, c 2. **Education:** Univ Alta, BS, 1943, MS, 1944; Univ Mich, PhD (chem eng), 1950. **Honors & Awards:** Founders Award, Am Inst Chem Engrs, 1977. **Professional Experience:** PROF EMER, DEPT CHEM ENG, ORESTATE UNIV, as of 2002; Assoc dean, Ore State Univ, 1971-1981; Nat Sci sr fel, Cambridge Univ, 1961-1962; asst dean, Ore State Univ, 1959-1971; prof, Dept Chem Eng, Ore state Univ, beginning 1957; from asst prof to assoc prof, Ore State Univ, 1949-1957; eng consult. **Memberships:** Am Inst Chem Engrs (pres 1981); Am Chem Soc; Sigma Xi. **Research Statement & Publications:** Fluid mechanics; heat transfer; relationship between these processes; applied mathematics. **Mailing Address:** Dept Chem Eng, Col Eng, Ore State Univ, 102 Gleeson Hall, Corvallis, OR 97331-2409.

KNUDSEN, JOHN R, APPLIED MATHEMATICS. **Personal Data:** b Brooklyn, NY, July 12, 1916; m 1942, Ruth; c John K & Thomas P. **Education:** NY Univ, BS, 1937, PhD (math), 1951. **Professional Experience:** RETIRED; mem tech staff, Educ Ctr, Bell Tel Labs, 1972-1983; 1983-1987 & Univ Bangalore, India, 1968; asst dean & budget officer, NY Univ, 1966-1972; consult, Bell Tel Labs, NJ, 1957-1972; from asst prof to prof, NY Univ, 1951-1972; instr math, NY Univ, 1939-1951. **Memberships:** Am Math Soc; Math Asn Am; NY Acad Sci. **Research Statement & Publications:** Self-study instructional techniques. **Mailing Address:** 10105 Jupiter Hills Dr, Austin, TX 78747-1322.

KNUDSEN, KAREN ANN, CELL ADHESION, MYOGENESIS. **Personal Data:** b June 30, 1943; c 1. **Education:** Univ Pa, PhD (biochem), 1977. **Professional Experience:** PROF & DIR SCI ADMIN, LANKENAU INST MED RES, as of 2004; sr scientist, Lankenau Inst Med Res, beginning 1985. **Memberships:** AAAS; Am Women sci; Am Soc Cell Biol. **Mailing Address:** Dept Cell Biol, Lankenau Inst Med Res, Rm 234 100 Lancaster Ave NEB, Wynnewood, PA 19096. **Fax:** 610-645-2205. **E-Mail:** knudsenk@mlhs.org

KNUDSON, ALFRED GEORGE, JR, MEDICINE, GENETICS. **Personal Data:** b Los Angeles, Calif, August 9, 1922; m 1976, Anna Taback; c Linda (Butler), Nancy & Dorene. **Education:** Calif Inst Technol, BS, 1944, PhD (biochem, genetics), 1956; Columbia Univ, MD, 1947. **Honorary Degrees:** DSc, Thomas Jefferson Univ, 1993. **Honors & Awards:** Mott Prize, Gen Motors Cancer Res Found, 1988; Medal of Hon, Am CancerSoc, 1989; William Allan Award, Am Soc Human Genetics, 1991. **Professional Experience:** SR ADV, FOX CHASE CANCER CTR, 1992-; SR MEM, SCI RES STAFF, INST CANCER RES, FOX CHASE CANCER CTR, 1976-; dir, Inst Cancer Res, Fox Chase Cancer Ctr, 1976-1983; prof med genetics & dean, Grad Sch BiomedSci, 1970-1976; prof biol & pediat & assoc dir educ, M D Anderson Hosp & Tumor Inst, UnivTex, Houston, 1969-1970; prof pediat & assoc dean, Health Sci Ctr, State Univ NY, StonyBrook, 1966-1969; chmn, Dept Biol, 1962-1966; Chmn, Dept Pediat, City Hope Med Ctr, Calif, 1956-1962. **Memberships:** Nat Acad Sci; fel AAAS; Am Asn Cancer Res; Am Pediat Soc; Am Soc HumanGenetics (pres 1978); Asn Am Physicians; Int Soc Pediat Oncol; Am Philos Soc; Am Acad Arts& Sci. **Research Statement & Publications:** Cancer genetics; medical genetics; tumor suppressor genes. **Mailing Address:** Cancer Res Inst, Fox Chase Cancer Ctr, Rm P3035, 7701 Burholme Ave, Philadelphia, PA 19111. **Fax:** 215-214-1623. **E-Mail:** agknudson@fccc.edu

KNUDSON, ALVIN RICHARD, RADIATION EFFECTS. **Personal Data:** b Minneapolis, Minn, August 17, 1934; m 1960, Christine; c Joann M, Cynthia E (Estienne) & Patricia R. **Education:** Cath Univ, AB, 1954; Johns Hopkins Univ, PhD (physics), 1960. **Professional Experience:** CONSULT, 1993-; RES PHYSICIST, US NAVAL RES LAB, as of 1990; head, Van Del Graaff Applns Sect, 1988-1992; head, Radiation Effects Sect, 1985-1988; head, Mat Anal Sect, 1970-1985; head, Charged Particle Reactions Sect, 1967-1970; res physicist, US Naval Res Lab, 1960-1967. **Memberships:** Am Phys Soc. **Research Statement & Publications:** Study of charged particle radiation effects in microelectronics; use of high energy ion beams for materials analysis. **Mailing Address:** US Naval Res Lab, Code 6613, Washington, DC 20375-5000. **E-Mail:** knudson@radef.nvl.navy.mil

KNUDSON, DOUGLAS MARVIN, FOREST RECREATION, TROPICAL SILVICULTURE. **Personal Data:** b Anoka, Minn, June 11, 1936; m 1957, Deloris; c Cynthia J & Scott D. **Education:** Colo State Univ, BS, 1959, MS, 1960; Purdue Univ, PhD (forest econ), 1965. **Professional Experience:** PROF EMER FORESTRY, PURDUE UNIV, WESTLAFAYETTE, as of 2005; vis scientist, Bogor Agr Univ, Indonesia, 1988; resident adv, Fuelwood ResProg, Dominican Repub, 1983-1987; prof forestry, Purdue Univ, Westlafayette, beginning 1982-1999; consult corp engrs, US Forest Serv, 1980-1981; res assoc, US Forest Serv, 1979; wilderness planner, Nat Park Serv, 1970; assoc prof, Purdue Univ, West Lafayette, 1969-1982; hon prof, Fed Univ Vicosa, Brazil, 1968; asst prof forestry, Purdue Univ-Agr UnivBrazil, 1965-1967; forester, Purdue Univ-Agr Univ Brazil, 1960-1962. **Memberships:** Soc Am Foresters; Int Asn Torch Clubs (pres 1978-1979); Nat Asn Interpretation. **Research Statement & Publications:** Outdoor recreation economics and planning, including interpretive services evaluation. **Mailing Address:** Dept Forestry & Natural Resources, Purdue Univ, Forestry bldg, Lafayette, IN 47901. **Fax:** 765-496-2422.

KNUDSON, RONALD JOEL, pulmonary physiology; deceased, see previous edition for last biography

KNUDSON, VERNIE ANTON, LIMNOLOGY. **Personal Data:** b Olsburg, Kans, September 18, 1932; m 1954, c 3. **Education:** Bethany Col, BS, 1954; Ft Hays Kans State Col, MS, 1959; Okla State Univ, PhD (zool), 1970. **Professional Experience:** ASSOC PROF NATURAL RESOURCES TECHNOL, LAKE SUPERIORSTATE COL, 1980-; asst prof, Lake Superior State Col, 1977-1980; asst prof biol sci, LakeSuperior State Col, 1971-1977; asst prof fisheries & wildlife, Mich State Univ, 1966-1969; partic, Acad Yr Inst, Univ Ore, 1964-1965; instr, Dodge City Col, 1960-1963; Instr biol, BethanyCol, 1959-1960. **Memberships:** Am Inst Biol Sci; Am Chem Soc. **Research Statement & Publications:** Water quality; eutrophication; nutrient removal by algae. **Mailing Address:** 2017 Marvonne Rd, Lawrence, KS 66047.

KNUDSON, WARREN, MEDICAL RESEARCH. **Education:** Univ Ill, PhD (biochem), 1981. **Professional Experience:** PROF BIOCHEM, RUSH MED COL, as of 2005. **Mailing Address:** Dept Biochem Rush-Presbyterian-St Luke's Med Ctr Rush Med Col, 1653 W Congress Pkwy, Chicago, IL 60612-3864. **E-Mail:** wknudson@rush.edu

KNUDTSON, JOHN THOMAS, PHYSICAL CHEMISTRY. **Personal Data:** b Charleston, SC, July 3, 1945; m 1984, c 2. **Education:** Colo Col, BS, 1967; Columbia Univ, MS, 1969, PhD (chem), 1972. **Professional Experience:** MEM TECH STAFF, AEROSPACE CORP, 1985-; from asst prof to assocprof chem, Northern Ill Univ, 1975-1985; Res assoc chem, Univ Utah, 1972-1974 & Univ Wis, 1974-1975. **Memberships:** Am Phys Soc; Am Chem Soc. **Research Statement & Publications:** Laser spectroscopy; spectral radiometery. **Mailing Address:** Aerospace Corp M5/747, PO Box 92957, Los Angeles, CA 90009-2957.

KNUEPPEL, NICHOLAS, MATHEMATICS. **Education:** PhD (Math). **Professional Experience:** PROF, DEPT MATH, LOS MEDANOS COL, as of 2004. **Memberships:** Math Soc Am. **Mailing Address:** Los Medanos Col, 3403 Cassena Dr, Walnut Creek, CA 94598. **Fax:** 925-439-8797.

KNULL, HARVEY ROBERT, BIOCHEMISTRY. **Personal Data:** b Thorsby, Alta, September 15, 1941; m 1965, Diane Zessin; c Tania & Tami. **Education:** Univ Alta, BSc, 1963; Univ Nebr, MS, 1965; Pa State Univ, PhD (biochem), 1970. **Professional Experience:** DEAN, GRAD SCH, 1990-; PROF BIOCHEM, UNIV NDAK, 1987-; assoc prof, Grad Sch, 1980-1987; assoc prof, Univ Man, 1978-1980; asst prof oral biol, Univ Man, 1973-1978; Fel neurochem, Dept Biochem, Mich State Univ, 1970-1973. **Memberships:** Int Soc Neurochem; Am Soc Neurochem; Soc Complex Carbohydrates; Can Biochem Soc; Can Fedn Biol Sci; Am Soc Biol Chemists; Sigma Xi. **Research Statement & Publications:** Neurochemistry; axonal transport; brain energy metabolism; compartmentation of glycolytic enzymes; carbohydrate metabolism, tubulin, microtubules, actin and cytoskeleton. **Mailing Address:** Dept Biochem, Sch Med, Univ NDak, Grand Forks, ND 58202. **Fax:** 701-777-3916. **E-Mail:** hknull@mail.med.und.nokak.edu

KNUTH, DONALD ERVIN, ALGORITHMS, DIGITAL TYPOGRAPHY. **Personal Data:** b Milwaukee, Wis, January 10, 1938; m 1961, Jill; c John & Jennifer. **Education:** Case Inst Technol, BS & MS, 1960; Calif Inst Technol, PhD (math), 1963. **Honorary Degrees:** Numerous from US & foreign univs, 1980- 2002 25. **Honors & Awards:** G M Hopper Award, 1971; A M Turing Award, Asn Comput Mach, 1974, Software Systs Award, 1986; Nat Medal of Sci, 1979; W McDowell Award, Inst Elec & Electronics Engrs, 1980, Comput Pioneer Award, 1982, John von Neumann Medal, 1995; J B Priestley Award, 1981; Steele Prize, Am Math Soc, 1986; NY Acad of Sci Award, 1987; Franklin Medal, 1988; J D Warnier Prize, 1989; Adelskold Medal, Swed Acad Sci, 1994; Harvey Prize, Technion, 1995; Kyoto Prize, Inamori Found, 1996. **Professional Experience:** EMER PROF ART COMPUT PROG, STANFORD UNIV, 1993-; prof, Stanford Univ, 1990-1992; Fletcher Jones prof comput sci & elec eng, Stanford Univ, 1977-1991; Guggenheim Found fel, 1972; prof, Stanford Univ, 1968-1977; staff mathematician, Commun Res Div, Inst Defense Anal, 1968-1969; from asst prof to prof math, Calif Inst Technol, 1963-1968; consult, Burroughs Corp, 1960-1968. **Memberships:** Nat Acad Sci; Nat Acad Eng; assoc Norweg Acad Sci; fel Asn Comput Mach; hon mem Inst Elec & Electronics Engrs; assoc Fr Acad Sci. **Research Statement & Publications:** Analysis of algorithms; combinatorial theory; programming languages; history of computer science; typography. **Mailing Address:** Comput Sci Dept, Stanford Univ, Stanford, CA 94305-9045.

KNUTH, ELDON L(UVERNE), MOLECULAR DYNAMICS, COMBUSTION. **Personal Data:** b Luana, Iowa, May 10, 1925; m 1973, Margaret; c Stephen, Dale, Margot &

Lynette. **Education:** Purdue Univ, BS, 1949, MS, 1950; Calif Inst Technol, PhD (aeronaut eng), 1953. **Honors & Awards:** Award, Am InstAeronaut & Astronaut, 1950; Alexander von Humboldt Found Award, 1975. **Professional Experience:** EMER PROF, UNIV CALIF, LOS ANGELES, 1991-; consult, TRW Inc, 1979-1984; consult, Jet Propulsion Lab, 1979-1981; chmn, Dept Energy & Kinetics, 1969-1975; prof eng, Dept Energy & Kinetics, 1965-1991; head, Chem, Nuclear & Thermal Div, 1963-1965; head molecular-beam lab, Heat Transfer & Fluid Mech Inst, 1961-1988; assoc prof, Univ Calif, 1959-1965; gen chmn, 1959; consult, Marquadt Aircraft Corp, 1958-1960; assoc res engr, Univ Calif, 1956-1968; group leader aerothermodyn, Aerophys Develop Corp, 1953-1956. **Memberships:** Am Phys Soc; Am Inst Aeronaut & Astronaut; Int Advisory Comt, Int Symposium Rarefied Gas Dynamics. **Research Statement & Publications:** Combustion; thermodynamics and statistical mechanics; transport phenomena and properties; free-molecule flows and molecular beams. **Mailing Address:** Dept Chem Eng, Univ Calif, 5531 Boelter Hall, Los Angeles, CA 90024. **E-Mail:** elknuth@ucla.edu

KNUTSON, CARROLL FIELD, GEOSCIENCES SCIENCE. **Personal Data:** b Santa Monica, Calif, March 14, 1924; m 1948, c 4. **Education:** Stanford Univ, BS, 1950, MS, 1951; Univ Calif, Los Angeles, PhD (geol), 1959. **Professional Experience:** SR SCIENTIST, EG & G IDAHO, INC, as of 2002; vpres, C K Geoenergy, 1976; PRES & BD DIRS, C K M RESOURCES, 1975-; Environ dir, Western Oil Shale Corp, 1975-1976; consult geologist, C F Knutson & Assocs, 1974-1976; chief geologist, CerGeonuclear Corp, 1967-1974; res assoc, Continental Oil Co, 1966-1967; res group leader, Continental Oil Co, 1961-1966; sr res engr, Continental Oil Co, 1958-1961; from prod engr to srprod engr, Continental Oil Co, 1954-1958; Reservoir engr, Continental Oil Co, 1951-1954. **Memberships:** Geol Soc Am; Am Asn Petrol Geol; Soc Petrol Engrs; Am Geophys Union; SocIndependent Prof Earth Scientists; Sigma Xi. **Research Statement & Publications:** Formation evaluation; rock mechanics; subsurface nuclear engineering geology; hydrology, environmental geology; development of energy with minimum adverse environmental impact. **Mailing Address:** Dept Geol, Univ Idaho, PO Box 443022, Moscow, ID 83844-3022. **Fax:** 208-885-5724.

KNUTSON, CLARENCE ARTHUR, ORGANIC CHEMISTRY, CARBOHYDRATE ANALYSIS. **Personal Data:** b Minot, NDak, June 18, 1937; m 1959, Lois; c Debra & David. **Education:** Concordia Col, Moorhead, Minn, BA, 1959; NDak State Univ, MS, 1961. **Professional Experience:** Assoc ed, Cereal Chem, 1989-1993; consult dir, Mericon Industs, 1978-1996; RES CHEMIST, NORTHERN REGIONAL RES CTR, AGR RES SERV, USDA, 1961-. **Memberships:** Am Chem Soc; Am Asn Cereal Chemists. **Research Statement & Publications:** Carbohydrate chemistry; composition structure and properties of cereal polysaccharides; quantitative analytical methods; starch-hydrolyzing enzymes. **Mailing Address:** 5927 Tampico Dr, Peoria, IL 61614-3861. **Fax:** 309-681-6685. **E-Mail:** knutsoca@ncaur1.ncaur.gov

KNUTSON, DAVID W, NEPHROLOGY. **Personal Data:** b Minneapolis, Minn, February 12, 1941; c 4. **Education:** Univ Minn, MD, 1967. **Professional Experience:** PROF MED, PA STATE UNIV, 1985-; chief, Milton S Hersheu Med Ctr, Pa State Univ, beginning 1985. **Memberships:** Am Soc Nephrology; Int Soc Nephrology; Nat Kidney Found; Am Asn Immunol. **Research Statement & Publications:** Immunology. **Mailing Address:** Dept Med, Pa State Univ, PO Box 850, PA 17033-0850. **Fax:** 717-531-6776. **E-Mail:** dknutson@psu.edu

KNUTSON, JAY R, BIOLOGY. **Education:** Minn Univ, Phd, 1978. **Professional Experience:** INVESTR, NAT HEART, LUNG, & BLOOD INST, as of 2004. **Mailing Address:** Nat Heart, Lung & Blood Inst, Bldg 10 Rm 5-D-10, Bethesda, MD 20892-0010. **Fax:** 301-480-6964. **E-Mail:** jaysan@helix.nih.gov

KNUTSON, KENNETH WAYNE, PLANT PATHOLOGY, POTATO CROP MANAGEMENT. **Personal Data:** b Williams, Minn, February 11, 1932; m 1957, Audrey; c 2. **Education:** Univ Minn, BS, 1954, MS, 1956, PhD (plant path), 1960. **Professional Experience:** RETIRED; exten assoc prof, Colo State Univ, 1964-1993; mgr, Colo PotatoCert Serv, 1964-1989; asst plant pathologist, Univ Idaho, 1960-1964. **Memberships:** Potato Asn Am; Sigma Xi. **Research Statement & Publications:** Potato diseases and other cultural problems; soil-borne fungi; viruses; seed potato improvement; potato variety development; growth analysis. **Mailing Address:** 817 E Elizabeth St, Ft Collins, CO 80524.

KNUTSON, LLOYD VERNON, BIOLOGICAL CONTROL, TAXONOMY. **Personal Data:** b Ottawa, Ill, July 4, 1934; m 1957, c David S Kari. **Education:** Macalester Col, BA, 1957; Cornell Univ, MS, 1959, PhD (limnol), 1963. **Professional Experience:** DIR, EUROP BIOL CONTROL LAB, as of 2002; spec asst, biosyst & biocontrol, PlantSci Inst, Agr Res Ctr, Agr Res Serv, beginning 1988; dir, Systematic Biol Prog, NSF, 1983-1984; dir, Biosystematics & Beneficial Insects Inst, 1973-1988; resident ecologist, Smithsonian Inst, 1971-1972; res entomologist, USDA, Beltsville, Syst Entom Lab, USDA, Beltsville, 1968-1973; SCI COOPERATOR, ROYAL INST NATURAL SCI, BELG, 1965-; Res assoc entom, Cornell Univ, 1963-1968. **Memberships:** Hon mem, Entom Soc Am (pres, 1988); Int Orgn Biol Control (vpres, 1996-); SocSyst Zool (treas, 1971-1974); AAAS; Am Registry Prof Entomologist (pres, 1987); hon memRussian Entomol Soc. **Research Statement & Publications:** Taxonomy and biology of Diptera, especially malacophagous and entomophagous groups; phylogeny of Sciomyzoidea; biological control of pest molluscs; taxonomic services; immigrant anthropods; computer applications to taxonomy and biocontrol. **Mailing Address:** Europ Biol Control Lab USDA ARS Parc Sci Agropolis, II, Montpellier Cedex 34397, France. **Fax:** 334-670-45620. **E-Mail:** ebch@cirad.fr

KNUTSON, LYNN D, POLARIZATION PHENOMENA IN NUCLEAR REACTIONS, FEW-BODY SYSTEMS. **Personal Data:** b Red Wing, Minn, August 22, 1946; m 1968. **Education:** St Olaf Col, BA, 1968; Univ Wis-Madison, MA, 1970, PhD (physics), 1973. **Professional Experience:** PROF PHYSICS, UNIV WIS-MADISON, 1985-; from asst prof to assoc prof, Univ Wis-Madison, 1977-1985. **Memberships:** Fel Am Phys Soc. **Research Statement & Publications:** Polarization effects in nuclear reactions and scattering at low and intermediate energies with emphasis on few-body systems; wave functions of A-2 and 3 nuclei; tests of charge symmetry; production of polarized beams and targets. **Mailing Address:** Dept Phy, Univ Wis-Madison, 1516 Sterling Hall, Madison, WI 53706. **E-Mail:** knutson@silphium.physics.wisc.edu

KNUTSON, ROGER M, BOTANY, PLANT LIFE HISTORIES & THERMOGENESIS. **Personal Data:** b Montevideo, Minn, January 3, 1933. **Education:** St Olaf Col, BA, 1957; Mich State Univ, MS, 1961, PhD (plant path), 1965. **Professional Experience:** RETIRED; vis researcher, Selby Bot Gardens, Sarasota, Fla, 1992; prof biol, Luther Col, Iowa, 1974; NSF sci fac fel, Univ Ga, 1971-1972; from asst prof to assoc prof, Luther Col, Iowa, 1964-1974. **Memberships:** Sr mem AAAS; sr mem Am Inst Biol Sci. **Research Statement & Publications:** Plant thermoregulation in members of the araceae, especially symplocarpus foetidus; forest litter decomposition. **Mailing Address:** 408 Burns St, Charlevoix, MN 49720.

KNUTSON, VICTORIA P, BIOCHEMISTRY, ENDOCRINOLOGY. **Education:** Univ Minn, BS, 1975, PhD (biochem), 1980. **Professional Experience:** ASST DEAN ADMIS, GRAD SCH BIOMED SCI, 2001-; ASSOC PROF INTEGRATIVE BIOL & PHARMACOL, SCH MED, HEALTH & SCI CTR, UNIV TEX, 1991-; asst prof pharmacol, Sch Med, Health & Sci Ctr, Univ Tex, 1983-1991. **Research Statement & Publications:** Insulin receptor; signal transduction; tyrosine kinase; breast cancer. **Mailing Address:** Dept Pharmacol, Univ Tex Med Sch, 6431 Fannin, Houston, TX 77030-1501. **E-Mail:** victoria.p.knutson@uth.tmc.edu

KNUTTGEN, HOWARD G, APPLIED PHYSIOLOGY. **Personal Data:** b Yonkers, NY, May 5, 1931; m 1961, c 2. **Education:** Springfield Col, BS, 1952; Pa State Univ, MS, 1953; Ohio State Univ, PhD (physeduc), 1959. **Professional Experience:** Chmn, Dept Health Sci, beginning 1980; assoc dean, Boston Univ, 1975-1980; Ed-in-chief, Med & Sci Sports, 1974-; PROF EMER PHYSIOL, COL ALLIED HEALTHPROFESSIONS, BOSTON UNIV, 1971-; Prof Physiol, Col Allied Healthprofessions, Boston Univ, beginning 1971; assoc prof physiol, Boston Univ, 1965-1971; asst profanat & physiol, Boston Univ, 1961-1965; Instr phys educ, Ohio State Univ, 1954-1959. **Memberships:** AAAS; Am Col Sports Med; Am Physiol Soc. **Research Statement & Publications:** Human performance; exercise physiology; muscle metabolism. **Mailing Address:** Ctr Sports Med, Pa State Univ 146 Rec Bldg, University Park, PA 16802-0001.

KNYCH, EDWARD THOMAS, PHARMACOLOGY. **Personal Data:** b Chicago, Ill, October 8, 1942; m 1965, c 3. **Education:** Loyola Univ, Chicago, BS, 1964; Creighton Univ, MS, 1966; WVa Univ, PhD (pharmacol), 1970. **Professional Experience:** ASSOC PROF PHARMACOL, SCH MED, UNIV MINN, 1979-; asst prof pharmacol, Univ Minn, 1972-1979; fel pharmacol, Univ Wis, 1970-1972. **Memberships:** AAAS; Sigma Xi. **Research Statement & Publications:** Mechanism of polypeptide hormone action and effect of drugs of abuse on hormone release. **Mailing Address:** Dept Pharmacol, Univ Minn Sch Med, Duluth, MN 55812-2403. **Fax:** 218-726-6235. **E-Mail:** eknych@d.umn.edu

KNYSTAUTAS, EMILE J, ATOMIC PHYSICS, MATERIALS SCIENCE. **Personal Data:** Canadian citizen. **Education:** Univ Montreal, BS, 1965; Univ Conn, MS, 1967, PhD (physics), 1969. **Professional Experience:** PROF PHYSICS, LAVAL UNIV, 1982-; foreign guest worker, Nat Bur Stand, Wash, DC, 1978-1979; from asst prof to assoc prof, Laval Univ, 1971-1982. **Memberships:** Can Asn Physicists; Mat Res Soc. **Research Statement & Publications:** Atomic spectroscopy; ion implantation; accelerator technology; advanced materials. **Mailing Address:** Dept Physics, Laval Univ, House Alexandre-Vachon, Quebec, PQ G1K 7P4, Can. **Fax:** 418-656-2040. **E-Mail:** ejknyst@phy.ulaval.ca

KO, CHE MING, THEORETICAL NUCLEAR PHYSICS. **Personal Data:** b Szechuan, China, January 7, 1943; American citizen; m 1973, Shiao-Yen; c Kevin & Shan-Wei. **Education:** Tunghai Univ, Taiwan, BSc, 1965; McMaster Univ, Can, MSc, 1968; State Univ NY, Stony Brook, PhD (physics), 1973. **Honors & Awards:** Humboldt Sr Scientist Res Award 1995; Tex A&M Univ Distinguished Res Award, 2004. **Professional Experience:** PROF PHYSICS, TEX A&M UNIV, 1988-; Vis scientist, Oak Ridge Nat Lab, 1984-1985; from asst prof to assoc prof, Tex A&M Univ, 1980-1988; staff physicist, Lawrence Berkeley Lab, 1978-1980; res assoc, Mich State Univ, 1977-1978; vis scientist, Max Planck Inst, 1974-1977; Res assoc, McMaster Univ, 1973-1974. **Memberships:** Fel Am Phys Soc. **Research Statement & Publications:** My research activities cover many areas of theoretical nuclear physics, including nuclear structure, hadronic interactions, and heavy ion collisions. In particular, I have developed a transport model for studying the properties of the hot dense matter produced in relativistic heavy ion collisions. **Mailing Address:** Physic Dept, Tex A&M Univ, Col Sta, TX 77843-3366. **Fax:** 979-845-1899. **E-Mail:** ko@comp.tamu.edu

KO, CHIEN-PING, DEVELOPMENTAL NEUROBIOLOGY. **Personal Data:** b Taipei, Taiwan, July 5, 1948; American citizen; m 1975, Jan; c Anthony L & Emily A. **Education:** Nat Taiwan Univ, BS, 1970; Wash Univ, PhD (physiol & biophys), 1975. **Honors & Awards:** Res Career Develop Award, NIH, 1983-1987. **Professional Experience:** PROF DEPT BIOL SCI, UNIV SOUTHERN CALIF, 1996-; assoc prof, dept biol sci, univ southern calif, beginning 1987; asst prof, Dept Biol Sci, Univ Southern Calif, 1981-1987; Nat Inst Neurol & Commun Dis & Stroke, NIH, 1978-1981; res fel, dept anat, Univ Colo, 1975-1978. **Memberships:** Soc Neuroscience; Am Soc Cell Biol. **Research Statement & Publications:** Membrane structure and function of synapses; development and plasticity of synaptic connections; freeze-fracture electron microscopy; The role of Glial cells in synaptic structone, function, formation and maint at the neuro Muscular Junction. **Mailing Address:** Dept Biol Sci, Univ Southern Calif, Los Angeles, CA 90089-2520. **E-Mail:** cko@mizar.usc.edu

KO, EDMOND INQ-MING, CHEMICAL CATALYSIS, SOLID STATE CHEMISTY. **Personal Data:** b Hong Kong, July 8, 1952. **Education:** Univ Wis-Madison, BS, 1974; Stanford Univ, MS, 1975, PhD (chem eng), 1980. **Honors & Awards:** Award Catalysis, Pittsburgh-Cleveland Catalysis Soc, 1992; Nat CatalystAward, Chem Manufacturers Asn, 1992. **Professional Experience:** CHAIR PROF, VPRES (EDUC), CITY UNIV HONG KONG, as of 2002 VICE PROVOST EDUC, CARNEGIE-MELLON UNIV, 1996-; vis prof, Hong Kong Univ Sci& Technol, 1995 & Calif Inst Technol, 1996; PROF CHEM ENG, CARNEGIE-MELLON UNIV, 1988-; Vis assoc prof, Univ Calif, Berkeley, 1987-1988; From asst prof to assoc prof, Carnegie-mellon Univ, 1980-1988. **Memberships:** AAAS; Am Inst Chem Engrs; Am Chem Soc; Sigma Xi; Am Soc Eng Educ; AmAsn Higher Educ; Mat Res Soc; Catalysis Soc. **Research Statement & Publications:** Synthesis and characterization of sol-gel catalytic materials; solid acids. **Mailing Address:** City Univ Hong Kong, 83 Tat Chee Ave, Kowloon, Hong Kong. **E-Mail:** edko@cityu.edu.hk

KO, FRANK K, TEXTILE MATERIALS ENGINEERING, TEXTILE STRUCTURAL COMPOSITES. **Personal Data:** b Canton, China, August 5, 1947; c 2. **Education:** Philadelphia Col Textiles & Sci, BS, 1970; Ga Inst Technol, MS, 1971, PhD (textileengr), 1977. **Honors & Awards:** Distinguished Achievement Award, Fiber Soc. **Professional Experience:** PROF MAT ENG, DREXEL UNIV, 1990-; mem, sci bd Am Composites Technol Inc, beginning 1988; comt mem, Soc Advan Mat & Process Eng, beginning 1988; advan compositesroadmap team mem, Aerospace Indust Asn, 1988; FAC, GEOSYNTHETIC RES INST, 1987-; chmn, student chapters comt, Soc Advan Mat & Processing Eng, beginning 1985; DIR FIBROUS MAT RES LAB, DREXEL UNIV, 1984-; assoc prof, Drexel Univ, 1984-1990; adj prof, Temple Univ, 1980; CONSULT, 1977-; from asst prof to assoc prof textile eng, Philadelphia Col Textile & Sci, 1976-1984; asst res engr, textile engr, Ga Inst Technol, 1972-1973. **Memberships:** Fel Soc Advan Mat & Process Eng; Am Ceramic Soc; AAAS; Am Soc Mech Eng; Sigma Xi; Fiber Soc; Am Soc Eng Educators; Soc Biomaterials Res. **Research Statement & Publications:** Fibrous materials ranging from textile surgical implants to textile structural composites; textile structural mechanics; 3-D composites; Nonlinear Viscoelasticity of Polyamide Fibers; Factors Affecting the Tuftability of Jute Carpet Backings; author of various articles. **Mailing Address:** Dept Mat Sci & Eng, Drexel Univ, 3141 Chestnut St, Philadelphia, PA 19104. **Fax:** 215-895-6684. **E-Mail:** fko@coe.drexel.edu

KO, HON-CHUNG, ATOMIC ABSORPTION SPECTROSCOPY, ELEMENTAL ANALYSIS. **Personal Data:** b Canton, China, June 27, 1937; m 1968, Erh-Mei; c Benjamin. **Education:** Chung Chi Col, BS, 1959; Univ Va, MS, 1962; Carnegie Inst Technol, PhD (phys chem), 1964. **Professional Experience:** RES CHEMIST, ALBANY RES CTR, DEPT ENERGY, 1996-; Albany Res Ctr, Bur Mines, 1974-1996; Univ Lethbridge, 1972-1974; Univ Pittsburgh, 1970-1972; res assoc chem, Univ Chicago, 1969-1970; res chemist, Space Sci Inc, 1967-1968; res chemist, res chemist, Rocket Power Res Lab, Maremont Corp, 1963-1967. **Memberships:** Sigma Xi; Am Chem Soc. **Research Statement & Publications:** Thermochemistry; thermodynamics; calorimetry; molten salts; solvent effects; high temperature chemistry; low-temperature heat capacities; chlorination of metals; vapor-liquid equilibria; instrumental analysis. **Mailing Address:** Dept Energy, Albany Res Ctr, Albany, OR 97321-3554.

KO, HON-YIM, SOIL & ROCK MECHANICS. **Personal Data:** b Hong Kong, China, January 18, 1940; m 1964, c 2. **Education:** Univ Hong Kong, BSc, 1962; Calif Inst Technol, MS, 1963, PhD (civil eng), 1966. **Honors & Awards:** Huber Res Prize, Am Soc Civil Engrs, 1979. **Professional Experience:** CHMN, DEPT CIVIL ENG, UNIV COLO, BOULDER, 1998-; consult, Earth Technol Corp, beginning 1984; dept chmn, Univ Colo, Boulder, 1983-1990; consult, Exxon Prod Res, 1981-; consult, Sandia Corp, 1979-1981; PROF CIVIL ENG, UNIV COLO, BOULDER, 1975-; consult, Martin Marietta Corp, 1970-; prin investr, NSF, Air Force Off Sci Res, US Bur Reclamation & US Bur Mines res grants, 1967-; from asstprof to assoc prof, Univ Colo, Boulder, 1967-1975; consult, Jet Propulsion Lab, Calif InstTechnol, 1967-1969; res fel eng, Calif Inst Technol, 1966-1967. **Memberships:** Am Soc Civil Engrs; Am Soc Eng Educ; Soc Exp Stress Anal. **Research Statement & Publications:** Fundamental mechanical properties of soil, rock and other geological materials, and the analysis of engineering problems in geotechnics; centrifugal modeling of geotechnical structures; geotechnical engineering. **Mailing Address:** Dept Civil & Environ Eng, Univ Colo Campus, PO Box 458, Boulder, CO 80309-0428. **Fax:** 303-492-7317. **E-Mail:** ko@colorado.edu

KO, H(SIEN) C(HING), ELECTRICAL ENGINEERING, RADIO ASTRONOMY. **Personal Data:** b Formosa, April 28, 1928; m 1955, c 3. **Education:** Nat Taiwan Univ, BS, 1951; Ohio State Univ, MSc, 1953, PhD (elec eng), 1955. **Professional Experience:** EMER CHMN, OHIO STATE UNIV, as of 1998; chmn, Dept Elec Eng, 1977-1989; PROF ELEC ENG & ASTRON, OHIO STATE UNIV, 1963-; asst dir, RadioObserv, 1957-1966; from instr to assoc prof elec eng, Radio Observ, Ohio State Univ, 1955-1963; res asst, Radio Observ, Ohio State Univ, 1952-1955; Asst, Radio Wave Res Labs, Formosa, 1951-1952. **Memberships:** Int Union Radio Sci; fel Inst Elec & Electronics Engrs; Am Asn Eng Educ. **Research Statement & Publications:** Space physics; electromagnetic theory and antennas; electronics and communications. **Mailing Address:** Dept Elec Eng, Ohio State Univ 2024 Neil Ave, Columbus, OH 43210. **E-Mail:** ko.3@osu.edu

KO, LI-WEN, EXPERIMENTAL BIOLOGY. **Personal Data:** b Taipei, Taiwan, January 31, 1949. **Education:** Taiwan Univ, Vet Med; Univ Wash, MS; Ohio State Univ, PhD (exp path). **Professional Experience:** ASST PROF NEUROSCIENCE, MAYO CLIN COL MED, as of 2003; ASST PROF PHARMACOL, MAYO CLIN COL MED, as of 2003; assoc prof, Nat Yeng-Ming Med, Taipei; vis scientist, Univ Miss, Kans City. **Memberships:** Am Soc Path Biol; Soc Exp Biol & Med. **Mailing Address:** Dept NeuroSci, Mayo Clin Col Med, Birdsall Bldg Rm 357 4500 San Pablo Rd, Jacksonville, FL 32224. **Fax:** 904-953-7117. **E-Mail:** ko.li-wen@mayo.edu

KO, PAK LIM, TRIBOLOGY. **Personal Data:** b Hong Kong, March 4, 1937; Canadian citizen; m 1964, c 2. **Education:** Univ Strathclyde, BSc, 1963; Univ BC, MASc, 1965, PhD (tribology), 1970. **Professional Experience:** SR RES OFFICER, INST FUEL CELL INNOVATION, NAT RES COUN CAN, as of 2004; RES ENGR, NAT RES COUN CAN, 1984-; adj prof, dept mech eng, UnivBC, 1984-; res engr, Chalk River Nuclear Labs, Atomic Energy Can Ltd, 1970-1984; fel mecheng, Univ BC, 1969-1970. **Memberships:** Inst Mech Engrs Eng; Inst Mech Engrs; Am Soc Mech Eng. **Research Statement & Publications:** Friction and friction-induced vibration mechanisms; impact and fretting wear studies; flow-induced vibration and tube fretting wear in steam generators and heat exchangers. **Mailing Address:** Inst Fuel Cell Innovation, Nat Res Coun Can, 3250 E Mall, Vancouver, BC V6T 1W5, Can. **Fax:** 604-221-3088. **E-Mail:** pak.ko@nrc-cnrc.gc.ca

KO, WEN HSIUNG, BIONICS, IMPLANT INSTRUMENTATIONS. **Personal Data:** b Fukien, China, April 12, 1923; American citizen; m 1957, Christina; c Kathleen, Janet, Linda & Alexander. **Education:** Nat Amoy Univ, BS, 1946; Case Inst Technol, MS, 1956, PhD (elec eng), 1959. **Honors & Awards:** Cecon Award, Electronics Rep Asn, 1970; Achievement Award, Inst ChineseAm Elec Engrs, 1977. **Professional Experience:** PROF EMER, DEPT ELEC BIOCHEM ENG, CASE WESTERN RES UNIV, 1993-; dir, Electronics Design Ctr, 1971-1983; mem oviduct panel, Contraceptive Develop Br, Ctr Pop Res, 1971; actg dir, Eng Design Ctr, 1970-1971; mem, NASA Life Sci Prog Space Sci Bd, Nat Acad Sci, 1969-1970; prof, Electronics Design Ctr, 1967-1993; NIH fel, SchMed, Stanford Univ, 1967-1968; mem biomed eng training comt, NIH, 1966-1970; assoc prof surg, Sch Med, 1964-1970; from asst prof to assoc prof elec eng, Case Western Res Univ, 1959-1967; engr, Taiwan Telecommun Admin, 1946-1954; reviewer, NIH, NASA, NSF & Inst Elec & Electronics Engrs; pres, Transducer Res Found. **Memberships:** fel Inst Elec & Electronics Engrs; Electronics & Biol Eng; Int Soc Biotelemetry; Biomed Eng Soc; Int Soc Hybrid Microelectronics; fel Int Asn Med & Biol Environ. **Research Statement & Publications:** Microelectronic instrumentation and technology; medical instrumentation; implant electronic transducers, telemetry and stimulators; solid state sensors and actuators; bulk and surface micromachining technol; micro sensors and actuators; micro-electro mechanical systems. **Mailing Address:** Dept Elec Eng & Comput Sci, Case Western Res Univ, 10900 Euclid Ave, 413 Olin Bldg LC-7071, Cleveland, OH 44106. **Fax:** 216-368-2801. **E-Mail:** whk@cwru.edu

KO, WEN-HSIUNG, PLANT PATHOLOGY, SOIL MICROBIOLOGY. **Personal Data:** b Chao Chow, Taiwan, May 14, 1939; m 1968, Sachi Su; c Subo & Supin. **Education:** Nat Taiwan Univ, BS, 1962; Mich State Univ, PhD (plant path), 1966. **Honors & Awards:** Ruth Allen Award, Am Phytopath Soc, 1984; fel, Am Phytopath Soc, 1990. **Professional Experience:** PROF PLANT PATH, UNIV HAWAII MANOA, HILO, 1976-; From res assoc to assoc prof, Univ Hawaii Manoa, Hilo, 1966-1976. **Memberships:** Am Phytopath Soc; Mycol Soc Am; Phytopathol Soc Japan. **Research Statement & Publications:** Ecology of soil-borne diseases; general soil microbiology; fungal physiology. **Mailing Address:** Beaumont Agr res Center, univ of Hawai at Manoa, 461 W Lanikaula st, Hilo, HI 96720.

KO, WINSTON TAI-KAN, HIGH ENERGY PHYSICS. **Personal Data:** b Shanghai, China, April 5, 1943; m 1970, Katy; c 2. **Education:** Carnegie Inst Technol, BS, 1965; Univ Pa, MS, 1966, PhD (physics), 1971. **Professional Experience:** DEAN PHYSICS, UNIV CALIF, DAVIS, as of 2005; Fulbright sr fel (Ger), 1992-1993; assoc, Europ Coun Nuclear Res, 1985-1986; PROF PHYSICS, UNIV CALIF, DAVIS, 1982-; from asst prof to assoc prof, UnivCalif, Davis, 1972-1982; asst res physicist, Univ Calif, Davis, 1970-1972. **Memberships:** Am Phys Soc. **Research Statement & Publications:** Experimental high energy physics; elementary particle physics; computer application to physics experiments. **Mailing Address:** Dept Physics, Univ Calif, Davis, CA 95616. **E-Mail:** wtko@ucdavis.edu

KOBALLA, THOMAS RAYMOND, ATTITUDE CHANGE. **Personal Data:** b Manchester, NH, June 28, 1954. **Education:** East Carolina Univ, BS, 1976, MA, 1978; Pa State Univ, PhD, 1981. **Professional Experience:** HEAD DEPT SCI EDUC, UNIV GA, 1997-; PROF DEPT SCI EDUC, 1994-; HEAD DEPT SCI EDUC, UNIV TEX, 1990-; prof dept Currie & Inst, Univ Tex, 1982-1990; asst prof, Pikeville Col, 1981-1982. **Research Statement & Publications:** Systematic design of attitude change paradigms in changing attitudes toward science. **Mailing Address:** Dept Sci Educ, Univ Ga, Aderhold Hall, Athens, GA 30602-7126. **Fax:** 706-542-1212. **E-Mail:** tkoballa@coe.uga.edu

KOBATA, AKIRA, SYNTHETIC ORGANIC & NATURAL PRODUCTS CHEMISTRY, MEDICAL SCIENCE. **Personal Data:** b Nemuro, Japan, March 17, 1933; m 1960, c 3. **Education:** Univ Tokyo, BS, 1956, MS, 1958, PhD (biochem), 1962. **Professional Experience:** DIR MGT, INST MED SCI, UNIV TOKYO, 1990-; dir, Japanese Soc ProteinEng, 1988- & Japanese biochem Soc, 1989-; nat rep, Int Glycoconjugata Asn, 1987-; Fogartyscholar-in-residence, Fogarty Int Ctr, 1985-1987; PROF, INST MED SCI, UNIV TOKYO, 1982-; prof, Kobe Univ Sch Med, 1971-1983; vis scientist, Nat Inst Arthritis & Metab Dis, NIH, 1969-1971; Vis assoc, Nat Inst Arthritis & Metab Dis, NIH, 1967-1969; Staff mem, Res Inst, Takeda Chem Indust Co, 1958-1967. **Memberships:** Am Soc Biol Chemists; AAAS. **Research Statement & Publications:** Structure and function of the sugar chains of glycoprotein; clinical application of glycoconjugate research. **Mailing Address:** Tokyo Metro Inst Geront, 35-2 Sakae-cho Itabashi-ku, Tokyo 173, Japan. **Fax:** 813-357-94776.

KOBAYASHI, ALBERT S(ATOSHI), SOLID MECHANICS. **Personal Data:** b Chicago, Ill, December 9, m Elizabeth; c Dori K (Ogami), Tina & Laura. **Education:** Univ Tokyo, BS, 1947; Univ Wash, MSME, 1952; Ill Inst Technol, PhD (mech eng), 1958. **Honors & Awards:** F G Tatnall Award, Soc Exp Stress Anal, 1973, B J Lazan Award, 1981, R E Peterson Award & William Murray Medal, 1983; Mech & Mat Div Award, Japan Soc Mech Engrs, 1991; M M Frocht Award, 1995 Genral elec sr res Award, Am soc eng educ 1995; the order of the rising sun, gold rays with neck ribbon, emperor of Japan, 1997; distinguish alumini, Award, univ student club, univ wash, 1997. **Professional Experience:** RES FEL, JAPAN SOC PROM SCI, 1996-; Boeing Pennell prof struct analysis, Univ Wash, 1988-1995; honoree, Int Conf Dynamic Fracture Mech, San Antonio, Tex, 1984; assoc ed, J Appl Mech, 1977-1984; ASSOC ED, TRANS JAPAN SOC COMPOSITE MATS, 1974-; from asst prof to prof, Univ Wash, 1958-1988; Mem staff, Boeing Co, Wash, 1958-1975; res engr exp stress anal, Armour Res Found, Ill Inst Technol, 1955-1958; design engr, Ill Tool Works, 1953-1955; Tool engr, Konishiroku Photo Indust, Japan, 1947-1950. **Memberships:** Nat Acad Eng; fel Am Soc Mech Engrs; fel Soc Exp Mech; hon mem, Soc Exp Mech; Japan Soc Mech Engrs; hon fel Int'l Congress of Fracture. **Research Statement & Publications:** Fracture mechanics; experimental stress analysis; theories of elasticity; theory of structures and dynamic response of structures; author of over 460 publications. **Mailing Address:** Dept Mech Eng, Box 352600, Univ Wash, Seattle, WA 98195-2600. **Fax:** 206-685-8047. **E-Mail:** ask@u.washington.edu

KOBAYASHI, FRANCIS MASAO, ENGINEERING MECHANICS. **Personal Data:** b Seattle, Wash, November 19, 1925; m 1963, Monique; c John F, Yvonne M & Robert F. **Education:** Univ Notre Dame, BS, 1947, MS, 1948, ScD(eng mech), 1953. **Professional Experience:** PROF EMER AEROSPACE & MECH ENG, COL ENG, UNIV NOTRE DAME, as of 2003; asst vpres advan studies res, Univ Notre Dame, 1971-1995; prof eng sci, Univ Notre Dame, beginning 1964; asst dir eng sci prog, NSF, 1959-1960; assoc prof eng sci, UnivNotre Dame, 1958-1964; asst prof eng mech, Univ Notre Dame, 1948-1958. **Research Statement & Publications:** Fluid mechanics; wave resistance; systems engineering; operations research. **Mailing Address:** Dept Aerospace & Mech Eng, Col Eng, Univ Notre Dame, 365 Fitzpatrick Hall, Notre Dame, IN 46556-5637. **Fax:** 574-631-8341. **E-Mail:** francis.m.kobayashi.1@nd.edu

KOBAYASHI, GEORGE S, mycology, biochemistry; deceased, see previous edition for last biography

KOBAYASHI, HISASHI, RESEARCH & UNIVERSITY EDUCATION. **Personal Data:** b Tokyo, Japan, June 13, 1938; m 1963, Masae. **Education:** Univ Tokyo, BS, 1961, MS, 1963; Princeton Univ, MA, 1966, PhD (elec eng) 1967. **Honors & Awards:** Humboldt Prize, 1979; Silver Core, Int Fed Info Processing, 1980. **Professional Experience:** Visiting prof, Univ Tokyo, 1991-1992; SHERMAN FAIRCHILD PROF ELEC ENG & COMPUT SCI, PRINCETON UNIV, 1986-; dean eng & appl sci, Princeton Univ, 1986-1991; dir, IBM Japan Sci Inst, 1982-1986; dept mgr, VLSI design, 1981-1982; vis prof, Technische Hochschule Darmstadt, WGer, 1979-1980; vis prof, int prof comput sci, Free Univ Brussells, Belgium, beginning 1980; consult prof, elec eng dept Stanford Univ, 1976; vis prof, Info Sci Dept, Univ Hawaii, 1975; sr mgr systs anal, IBM T J Watson Res Ctr, 1975-1975; sr mgr systs anal, IBM T J Watson Res Ctr, 1977-1979; consult, ALOHA systs proj, 1975; mgr syst measurement-modeling, IBM T J Watson Res Ctr, 1971-1973; vis asst prof, Syst Sci Dept, Univ Calif, Los Angeles, 1969-1970; res staff mem, IBM T J Watson Res Ctr, 1967-1971; radar system desing, Toshiba corp, 1963-1965. **Memberships:** fel, IEEE Eng Acad Japan. **Research Statement & Publications:** Radar signal design; detection and estimation theory; data transmission theory; seismic signal processing; image date compression; magnetic recording theory; optical networks; high-speed networks; queueing theory; author of various articles. **Mailing Address:** Dept Elect Eng, Princeton Univ, Eng Quadrangle Olden St, Princeton, NJ 08544. **Fax:** 609-258-3745. **E-Mail:** hisashi@princeton.edu

KOBAYASHI, KAZUMI, PHARMACEUTICAL SCIENCE. **Personal Data:** b Fukuyama City, Japan, February 16, 1952. **Education:** Kyoto Univ, Japan, BS, 1974, MS, PhD (pharmaceut sci), 1983. **Professional Experience:** PROCESS SCIENTIST II, BIOGEN, CAMBRIDGE, 1993-; prin investr, NIH, 1988-1989 & 1990-1992; staff scientist II & group leader protein chem, Cambridge Neuroscience, Inc, 1987-1993; res fel, Dept Molecular Biol, Mass Gen Hosp & Dept Genetics, Med Sch, Harvard Univ, 1985-1987; assoc, Dept Chem, Mass Inst Technol, 1983-1985; asst lectr & instr, Dept Biochem, Niigata Col Pharm, Japan, 1979-1983. **Memberships:** Am Soc Biochem & Molecular Biol; Am Chem Soc; Protein Soc; AAAS. **Research Statement & Publications:** Isolation of novel neuroactive compounds from natural products; author of 11 technical publications. **Mailing Address:** BioGen Inc, 14 Cambridge Ctr, Cambridge, MA 02142. **Fax:** 617-679-2617.

KOBAYASHI, NOBUHISA, COASTAL ENGINEERING, HYDRODYNAMICS. **Personal Data:** b Osaka, Japan, May 4, 1950; American citizen; m Yoko; c Sachi C & Orion A. **Education:** Kyoto Univ, Japan, BCE, 1974, MCE, 1976; Mass Inst Technol, PhD (civil engr), 1979. **Professional Experience:** DIR, CTR APPL COASTAL RES, 2001-; PROF, DEPT CIVIL & ENVIRON ENG, UNIV DEL, 2001-; mem, Waterway, Port, Coastal & Ocean Engr Exec comt, 1995-1999; mem, Coastal Engr Res Coun, 1995-1999; ed, J Waterway, Port, Coastal & Ocean Engr, Am Soc Civil Engrs, 1992-1994; prof coastal eng,

Univ Del, beginning 1991; assoc dir, Ctr Appl Coastal Res, Univ Del, 1989-2001; mem, Waves & Wave Forces Comt, Am Soc Civil Engrs, 1987-1999; chmn, Task Comt Sea Level Rise & Its Effects, 1987-1990; chmn, Tidal Hydraul Comt, Am Soc Civil Engr, 1986-1987; from asst prof to assoc prof, Univ Del, 1981-1991; sr ocean engr, Brian Watt Assocs, Inc, Houston, 1979-1981; res asst coastal engr, Mass Inst Technol, 1978-1979. **Memberships:** Am Soc Civil Engrs; Am Geophys Union; founding mem coasts, Oceans & rivers inst(copri). **Research Statement & Publications:** Interaction of wind waves with coastal structures; wave mechanics in surf and swash zones; sediment transport mechanics in nearshore region; transport and mixing processes; numerical prediction of tsunami run-up. **Mailing Address:** Ctr Appl Coastal Res Ocean Engr Lab, Univ Del, Newark, DE 19716. **Fax:** 302-831-1228. **E-Mail:** nk@coastal.udel.edu

KOBAYASHI, RIKI, CHEMICAL PHYSICS. **Personal Data:** b Webster, Tex, May 13, 1924; m Lee; c James B, Alec S, Anne W & Susan W. **Education:** Rice Inst, BS, 1944; Univ Mich, MSE, 1947, PhD (chem eng), 1951. **Honors & Awards:** Katz Lectr, Univ Mich, 1975; Katz Award, Gas Processor Asn, 1985. **Professional Experience:** PROF EMER CHEM ENG, RICE UNIV, as of 2003; louis calder prof chem eng, Rice Univ, beginning 1967; consult, appl thermodyn, gas transmission & gas processing, 1952; from asst prof to prof, Rice Univ, 1951-1967; res engr, Continental Oil Co, Okla. **Memberships:** Nat Acad Eng; fel Am Inst Chemists; Am Inst Physics; Am Chem Soc; Am InstMining & Metal Engrs; hon mem Inst Chem Engrs Japan; fel Japan Soc Prom Sci; fel Am InstChem Engrs. **Research Statement & Publications:** Thermodynamic and transport properties of fluids and solids, particularly at advanced pressures; cryogenic temperatures to moderately high temperatures; kinetics; phase and volumetric behavior of mixtures at high pressures and low temperatures; approx 200 papers in learned journals. **Mailing Address:** Dept Chem Eng, Rice Univ, PO Box 1892, Houston, TX 77251-1892. **Fax:** 713-348-5478.

KOBAYASHI, ROGER HIDEO, PEDIATRIC IMMUNOLOGY & ALLERGY, PEDIATRIC RHEUMATOLOGY. **Personal Data:** b Honolulu, Hawaii, May 21, 1947; m 1974, Ai; c Lisa & Timothy. **Education:** Univ Nebr, Lincoln, BA, 1969, MD, 1975; Univ Hawaii, MS, 1975; Am Bd Pediat, cert pediat, 1980; Am Bd Allergy & Immunol, cert allergy & immunol, 1981. **Professional Experience:** PHYSICIAN, ALLERGY, ASTHMA & IMMUNOL ASSOC, as of 2006; Expert Panel Blood Safety, 1998-; Expert Consult, Immune Deficiency Found, 1997-; Rare Antibody Inc, Bayer Pharm, 1996-; Rare Antibody Inc, Shanghai China, 1992-; Consult, Quantum Inc, 1991-1992; Lee Hill Prof, Iowa, 1991; gen partner, Allergy Asthma & Immunol Assoc PC Omaha, 1990-; assoc clin prof, Univ Calif, Los Angeles Ctr Health Sci, 1990-1995; Vis prof, Univ Kansas, 1990; Tripler Army Hosp, Hawaii, 1990; CLIN PROF PEDIAT, UNIV CALIF, LOS ANGELES CTR HEALTH SCI, 1988-; Assoc prof, Univ Calif, Los Angeles Ctr Health Sci, 1988-1990; assoc prof pediat, path & microbiol, 1984-1988; Vis prof, Univ Hawaii, 1982; asst prof pediat & microbiol, Univ Nebr Med Ctr, 1980-1984; res fel immunol, Sch Med, Univ Calif, Los Angeles, 1978-1980; clin fel pediat immunol, Sch Med, Univ Calif, Los Angeles, 1977-1978; Resident pediat, Sch Med, Univ Southern Calif, 1975-1977. **Memberships:** Am Soc Microbiol; Am Fedn Clin Res; Am Acad Pediat; Am Acad Allergy & Immunol; Clin Immunol Soc. **Research Statement & Publications:** Antimicrobiol treatment of respiratory infections adverse effects on viral infections of neutrophil function; treatment of asthma in infants and young children; use of intravenous gammaglobulin in children. **Mailing Address:** 2808 S 80th St Ste 210, Omaha, NE 68124. **Fax:** 402-391-1563. **E-Mail:** rhkobaya@unmc.edu

KOBAYASHI, SHOSHICHI, MATHEMATICS. **Personal Data:** b Kofu, Japan, January 4, 1932; m 1957, c 2. **Education:** Univ Tokyo, BS, 1953; Univ Wash, PhD (math), 1956. **Honors & Awards:** Geom Prize, Math Soc Japan, 1987. **Professional Experience:** PROF EMER MATH, UNIV CALIF, BERKELEY as of 2004; ed, Int J Math, 1990-; vis prof, Univ Tokyo, 1981; chmn dept, Univ Calif, Berkeley, 1978-1981; Guggenheim fel, 1977-1978; ed, J Differential Geometry, 1973-1985; assoc ed, Duke J Math, 1970-1980; Univ Bonn, 1969 & 1978 & Mass Inst Technol, 1970; prof math, Univ Calif, Berkeley, beginning 1966; vis prof, Univ Mainz, 1966; lectr, Univ Tokyo, 1965; A P Sloan fel, 1964-1966; from asst prof to assoc prof, Univ Calif, Berkeley, 1962-1966; asst prof, Univ BC, 1960-1962; res assoc math, Mass Inst Technol, 1958-1960; mem staff, Inst Advan Study, 1956-1958. **Memberships:** Am Math Soc; Math Soc Japan; Math Soc France; Swiss Math Soc. **Research Statement & Publications:** Differential geometry and functions of several complex variables. **Mailing Address:** Dept Math, Univ Calif, 707 Evans Hall, Berkeley, CA 94720-3840.

KOBAYASHI, YUTAKA, BIOCHEMISTRY. **Personal Data:** b San Francisco, Calif, March 11, 1924; m 1982, Maureen; c Andrew Y, David H & Thomas S. **Education:** Iowa State Col, BS, 1946, MS, 1950; Univ Iowa, PhD (biochem), 1953. **Professional Experience:** RETIRED; consult biotechnol, 1985-; staff mem, DuPont, 1982-1985; mgr, Appln Lab, New Eng Nuclear Corp, 1974-1982; sr scientist, Worcester Found Exp Biol, Inc, 1957-1974; res assoc, Rheumatic Fever Res Inst, Chicago, Ill, 1953-1957. **Memberships:** Am Chem Soc; Am Soc Pharmacol & Exp Therapeut; Am Soc Biol Chemists; Sigma Xi. **Research Statement & Publications:** Intermediary metabolism of amino acids and biogenic amines; amine oxidases. **Mailing Address:** 60 Audubon Rd, Wellesley, MA 02181.

KOBE, DONALD HOLM, QUANTUM PHYSICS. **Personal Data:** b Seattle, Wash, January 13, 1934; m 1992, Sonia Maria Couri. **Education:** Univ Tex, Austin, BS, 1956; Univ Minn, Minneapolis, MS, 1959, PhD (physics), 1961. **Professional Experience:** Fulbright lectr/researcher, Instituto Del Fisica Teorica, Sao Paulo, Brazil, 1988-1989; PROF PHYSICS, UNIV N TEX, 1975-; assoc prof, 1968-1975; vis asst prof physics, H C Oersted Inst, Copenhagen Univ, 1966-1967 & Northeastern Univ, 1967-1968; vis scientist, Quantum Chem Inst, Univ Uppsala, 1964-1966; Fulbright lectr, Nat Taiwan Univ & Taiwan Norm Univ, 1963-1964; Vis asst prof physics, Ohio State Univ, 1961-1963. **Memberships:** AAAS; Am Phys Soc; fel Am Sci Affil; Am Asn Physics Teachers; Sigma Xi. **Research Statement & Publications:** Quantum theory of many-particle systems; applications to superfluid helium; quantum theory of radiation; interaction of electromagnetic radiation and matter; geometrical phase in quantum theory; geometrical angle in classical mechanics. **Mailing Address:** Dept Physics, Univ N Tex, PO Box 311427, Denton, TX 76203. **E-Mail:** kobe@unt.edu

KOBERNICK, SIDNEY D, PATHOLOGY. **Personal Data:** b Montreal, Que, May 7, 1919; American citizen; m 1941, Gail; c Allan, Michael K & Joan. **Education:** McGill Univ, BSc, 1941, MD, CM, 1943, MSc, 1949, PhD (exp path), 1951; Am BdPath, cert path anat, 1953, cert clin path, 1959. **Professional Experience:** RETIRED; clin prof path, Wayne State Univ, 1953-1982; adj prof med technol, Wayne State Univ, 1953-1982; dir labs, Sinai Hosp, Detroit, 1952-1982; asst prof path, McGill Univ, 1951-1952. **Memberships:** Soc Exp Biol & Med; Am Asn Path & Bact; fel Am Soc Clin Path; fel Col AmPathologists; Electron Micros Soc Am; Sigma Xi. **Research Statement & Publications:** Experimental atherosclerosis; tissue hypersensitivity; morphological pathology. **Mailing Address:** 5627 County Lakes Dr, Sarasota, FL 34243. **Fax:** 941-355-9221.

KOBERSTEIN, JEFFREY THOMAS, POLYMER CHEMISTRY, CHEMICAL ENGINEERING. **Personal Data:** b Milwaukee, Wis, September 27, 1952; m 1975, c 2. **Education:** Univ Wis, BS, 1974; Univ Mass, PhD (chem eng), 1979. **Honors & Awards:** Doolittle Award, Am Chem Soc, 1984. **Professional Experience:** PROF & CHMN, DEPT CHEM ENG, COLUMBIA UNIV, as of 2002; prog Chem eng, Univ Conn, beginning 1989; assoc prof, Univ Conn, 1986-1989; vis res scientist, IBM, 1985; vis asst prof, Univ Wis, 1981; asst prof chem eng, Princeton Univ, 1980-1986; fel, Ctr ResMacromolecules, 1979-1980. **Memberships:** Am Chem Soc; Am Phys Soc; NAm Thermal Anal Soc; Soc Plastics Engrs. **Research Statement & Publications:** Polymer morphology; structure property relationships in block copolymers; polymer-polymer interfaces; microphase separation; small angle x-ray, neutron and light scattering; polymer blends; compatibility. **Mailing Address:** Dept Chem Eng, Columbia Univ, 500 W 120th St, New York, NY 10027. **Fax:** 212-854-3054. **E-Mail:** jk1191@columbia.edu

KOBILINSKY, LAWRENCE, BIOCHEMISTRY, MOLECULAR BIOLOGY. **Personal Data:** b New York, NY, November 7, 1946; m 1971, Estelle; c Hayley. **Education:** City Univ NY, BS, 1969, MA, 1971, PhD (biol), 1977. **Honors & Awards:** Honorary Prof, Univ of Mogi Das, 1996. **Professional Experience:** ASSOC PROVOST, JOHN JAY COL, 1995-; prof biol & immunol, John Jay Col, 1989-1995; res fel immunol, Sloan Kettering Inst Cancer Res, 1977-1980; John Jay Col Criminal Justice, 1975-1977; Hunter Col, 1974-1975; lectr biol, Brooklyn Col, 1972-1974; lectr biol, City Univ NY, 1970-1971; res asst biophys, Columbia Presby Med Ctr, 1969-1970; mem, Doctoral Fac Biochem Grad Ctr, City Univ NY. **Memberships:** Sigma Xi; AAAS; NY Acad Sci; Am Chem Soc; Am Acad Forensic Sci; Am Col Forensic Examrs. **Research Statement & Publications:** Indentification of individuals by DNA profiling analysis. **Mailing Address:** Dept Forensic Sci, John Jay Col Criminal Justice, 445 W 59th St, New York, NY 10019. **Fax:** 212-237-8957. **E-Mail:** lkobilins@aol.com

KOBISKE, RONALD ALBERT, ADMINISTRATION, PHYSICS LABORATORY DEVELOPMENT IN NUCLEAR SPECTROSCOPY. **Personal Data:** b New London, Wis, February 2, 1938; m 1958, Ann; c Bret R, Mark D & Suzanne. **Education:** Ind Inst Technol, BS (physics) & BS (math), 1962; Highlands Univ, MS, 1964; UnivWis Milwaukee, PhD (physics), 1976. **Professional Experience:** PROF EMER, DEPT PHYSICS & CHEM, MILWAUKEE SCH ENG, as of 2004; prof & chmn, Dept Physics, Milwaukee Sch Eng, beginning 1963. **Memberships:** Am Asn Physics Teachers. **Research Statement & Publications:** General relativity; teaching and laboratory development efforts. **Mailing Address:** Dept Physics & Chem, Milwaukee Sch Eng, PO Box 644, Milwaukee, WI 53201-0644. **Fax:** 414-277-2878.

KOBLICK, DANIEL CECIL, PHYSIOLOGY. **Personal Data:** b San Francisco, Calif, May 13, 1922; m 1960, c 2. **Education:** Univ Calif, AB, 1944; Univ Ore, PhD (biol), 1957. **Professional Experience:** ASSOC PROF PHYSIOL, ILL INST TECHNOL, 1963-; asst resphysiologist, 1960-1963; lectr physiol, Univ Calif, 1960-1961; USPHS fel, Univ Calif, Berkeley, 1959-1960; asst prof zool, Univ Mo, 1958-1959; instr biol, Univ Ore, 1957-1958. **Memberships:** Fel AAAS; Am Physiol Soc; Biophys Soc; Soc Gen Physiol; Sigma Xi. **Research Statement & Publications:** Ion transport; bioelectricity; invertebrate physiology. **Mailing Address:** Dept Biol, Ill Inst Technol, 3300 S Federal St, Chicago, IL 60616-3793.

KOBLICK, IAN, DIVING TECHNOLOGY, UNDERSEA LIVING TECHNOLOGY. **Personal Data:** b San Francisco, Calif, July 12, 1939; m 1962, Tonya; c Tav & Toren. **Education:** Calif State Univ, BA, 1964. **Honors & Awards:** Lowell Thomas Award, Underwater Explor, 1986. **Professional Experience:** MEM, SMITHSONIAN INST COMT, 2003-; CONSULT, FOREC, 1995-; CONSULT, CONSULTEX, 1990-; developer & co-owner, Jules Undersea Lodge, 1986-1994; captain & mgr, Marine Resources Develop Found, 1981-1983; port Everglades Environ consults, 1979-1980; consult, US Dept Com, 1979; PRES, KOBLICK MARINE CTR, 1976-; dir, Lead Agency Atty, 1974-1979; PRES & FOUNDER, MARINE RESOURCES DEVELOP FOUND, 1971-; developer & mgr, Puerto Rico Int Undersea Lab, 1971-1976; spec asst, Govt VI, 1969-1971; spec asst, Gov VI Undersea Prog, 1969-1971; coordr, Field Studies, Col VI Ecol Res Sta, 1966-1969; pres, VI Cruises, Inc, 1965-1972; developer & co-owner Brazen Onager, Inc, 1959-1965; bd dir, Int Defense Equip Exhibitors Asn. **Research Statement & Publications:** Undersea living, man-in-sea technology and diving physiology; natural resource management; environmental education; Living and Working in the Sea; author of various articles. **Mailing Address:** Marine Resources Develop Found, PO Box 787, Key Largo, FL 33037. **Fax:** 305-451-3909.

KOBLINSKY, CHESTER JOHN, SATELLITE REMOTE SENSING, OCEANOGRAPHY. **Personal Data:** b Hartford, Conn, March 25, 1948; m 1977, c 1. **Education:** Reed Col, BA, 1971; Ore State Univ, PhD (oceanog), 1979. **Honors & Awards:** Spec Achievement Award, NASA, 1985, Except Sci Achievement Medal, 1990. **Professional Experience:** HEAD, OCEANS & ICE BR, NASA, 1991-; Adj assoc prof, Univ Colo, 1987-; oceanogr, Goddard Space Flight Ctr, 1983-1991; asst res oceanogr, Scripps Inst Oceanog, 1982-1983; res fel, Scripps Inst Oceanog, 1979-1981; res assoc, Ore State Univ, 1979; Oceanogr, US Environ Protection Agency, 1975-1976. **Memberships:** Am Geophys Union; Inst Elec & Electronics Engrs; Am Meteorol Soc; OceanogSoc. **Research Statement & Publications:** Physical oceanography: general ocean circulation, models, observations; satellite remote sensing; airborne remote sensing. **Mailing Address:** Goddard Space Flight Ctr, NASA, 971 Greenbelt Rd, Greenbelt, MD 20771. **Fax:** 301-286-1761. **E-Mail:** chet@neptune.gstc.nasa.gov

KOBLITZ, NEAL I, MATHEMATICS. **Professional Experience:** PROF MATH, UNIV WASH, as of 2003; adj prof, Ctr Appl Cryptographic Res, Univ Waterloo, as of 2003. **Mailing Address:** Dept Math, Univ Wash, C 335 Padelford Hall Box 354350, Seattle, WA 98195-4350. **Fax:** 206-543-0397. **E-Mail:** koblitz@math.washington.edu

KOBRIN, ROBERT JAY, CHEMICAL INSTRUMENTATION. **Personal Data:** b New York, NY, November 4, 1937; m 1969, Eileen; c Michael, David & Daniel. **Education:** City Col NY, BS, 1960; Univ Del, PhD (phys chem), 1969. **Honors & Awards:** IR 100 Award, Indust Res Mag, 1976. **Professional Experience:** RES CONSULT, ADV AUTOMATION & DATA SYSTS, MOBIL RES & DEVELOP CORP, 1984-; res assoc, Adv Automation & Data Systs, Mobil Res & Develop Corp, 1974-1984; sr chem, Adv Automation & Data Systs, Mobil Res & Develop Corp, 1961-1973; jr chemist anal chem, Sonneborn Chem & Refining Co, 1960-1961. **Memberships:** Asn Comput Mach; Sigma Xi; Am Chem Soc. **Research Statement & Publications:** Laboratory automation; information systems and computer networks; analytical instrumentation. **Mailing Address:** 71 William Feather Dr, Voorhees, NJ 08043. **E-Mail:** 70252.3014@compuserve.com

KOBRINE, ARTHUR I, NEUROSURGERY. **Personal Data:** b Chicago, Ill, October 9, 1943; m 1969, Cynthia; c Steven & Nicole. **Education:** Northwestern Univ, BS, 1964, MD, 1968; George Wash Univ, PhD (physiol), 1979. **Professional Experience:** PARTNER, PROF TEAM PHYSICIANS INC, as of 2004; CLIN PROF, GEORGETOWN UNIV, as of 2004; prof neurosurg, George Wash Univ, beginning 1979; from asst prof to assoc prof,

George Wash Univ, 1975-1979; asst chief, Walter Reed Hosp, 1973-1975; resident neurosurg, Walter Reed Hosp, 1970-1973. **Memberships:** Soc Neurol Surgeons; Am Phys Soc; Am Bd Neurol Surg. **Mailing Address:** Prof Team Physicians Inc, 2440 M St NW Ste 315, Washington, DC 20037. **Fax:** 202-293-1857.

KOBSA, HENRY, physical chemistry; deceased, see previous edition for last biography

KOBYLARZ, ERIK J, NEUROLOGY. **Professional Experience:** NEUROLOGIST, WALTER REED ARMY MED CTR, 1991-. **Research Statement & Publications:** Neurology. **Mailing Address:** Dept Neurol, Walter Reed Army Med Ctr, 6900 George Ave NW, Washington, DC 20307.

KOBYLNYK, RONALD WILLIAM, LASER ENTOMOLOGY. **Personal Data:** b Calgary, Alta, August 19, 1942. **Education:** Univ Calgary, BSc, 1963; Univ Guelph, Ont, MSc, 1967, PhD (entom), 1972. **Professional Experience:** CONSULT, PESTICIDE MGT SECT, MINISTRY ENVIRON, VICTORIA, as of 2002; mem staff, pesticide mgt sect, ministry environ, victoria, beginning 1980; Eval officer insecticides, Agr Can, 1970-1980. **Memberships:** Entom Soc Can. **Research Statement & Publications:** Effects of laser radiation on insects. **Mailing Address:** 1699 BROUSSON DR, Victoria, BC V8N 5N2, Can. **Fax:** 250-472-3550. **E-Mail:** kobylnyk(at)island.net

KOCAN, KATHERINE M, TICK BORNE DISEASES OF CATTLE, VECTOR-BORNE HEMOPARASITES OF DOMESTIC & WILD ANIMALS. **Personal Data:** b Cleveland, Ohio, March 27, 1946; m 2003, Edmnour; c Jonathan M & Andrew J. **Education:** Hiram Col, BA, 1968; Univ NC, Chapel Hill, 1971; Okla State Univ, PhD (vetparasitol), 1979. **Honors & Awards:** Phizer Res Award, 1986 & 1996; Distinguished Alumni Award, Hiram College, May 1984; Women to Watch Award, Oklahoma State University, 1990; Patent Recognition Award, OSU, 2000; Innovator of the Year, "On the Brink Award", The Journal Record, Oklahoma City, 2001; OSU Regents Distinguished Research Award, 2003; Honored at Higher Education Day, Oklahoma State Capital, March 2004. **Professional Experience:** Adj prof, Dept Physiol Sci, Col Vet Med, Okla State Univ, as of 2000; ENDOWED CHMN, FOOD ANIMAL RES, COL VET MED, OKLA STATE UNIV, 1996-; OSU REGENTS PROF PATHOBIOLOGY, COL VET MED, OKLA STATE UNIV, 1993-; vet res inst, Onderstepoort, Repub S Africa, beginning 1986; visscientist, Int Lab Res Animal Dis, Kenya, 1984-1985; from asst prof to assoc prof path, OklaState Univ, 1983-1993; adj asst prof, Okla State Univ, 1980-1983; res assoc & mgr electronmicros, Okla State Univ, 1975-1980. **Memberships:** Sigma Xi (treas, 1988-1990, pres elect, 1995-1996, pres, 1996-1997); Soc Trop Vet Med(pres-elect, 1991-1993, pres, 1993-1995); Soc Vector Ecologists; Electron Micros Am; Am Soc Parasitol; Am Soc Mircobiology; Am Soc for Rickettsiology and Rickettsial Diseases; OSU Regents Professors (chair, 2004-2005). **Research Statement & Publications:** Tick-borne diseases of cattle; Anaplasma marginale in ticks; Tick-borne diseases of animals and humans. **Mailing Address:** Dept Pathobiology, Okla State Univ, 250 McElroy Hall, Stillwater, OK 74078. **Fax:** 405-744-5275. **E-Mail:** Katherine.Kocan@okstate.edu

KOCAOGLU, DUNDAR, ENGINEERING. **Education:** Robert Col, BS, 1960; Lehigh Univ, MS, 1962; Univ Pittsburgh, MS, 1972, PhD (oper res), 1976. **Professional Experience:** PROF & CHMN, ENG MGT & ENG COMPUT SCI, PORTLAND STATE UNIV, as of 2006. **Mailing Address:** Eng Mgt, Eng & Comput Sci, Portland State Univ, PO Box 751, Portland, OR 97207-0751. **Fax:** 503-725-4667. **E-Mail:** kocaoglu@etm.pdx.edu

KOCAOGLU, DUNDAR F, ENGINEERING MANAGEMENT, MULTICRITERIA DECISION MAKING. **Personal Data:** b Turkey, June 1, 1939; American citizen; m 1968, Alev; c Timur. **Education:** Robert Col, Turkey, BS, 1960; Lehigh Univ, MS, 1962; Univ Pittsburgh, MS, 1972, PhD (opers res), 1976. **Honors & Awards:** Centennial Medal, Inst Elec & Electronics Engrs, 1984. **Professional Experience:** PRES & CHIEF EXEC OFFICER, PORTLANT INT CONF MGT ENG & TECHNOL, as of 2003; PRES, PORTLANT INT CONF MGT ENG & TECHNOL, 1990-; PROF & CHMN, DEPT ENG & TECHNOL MGT, PORTLAND STATE UNIV, 1987-; ed-in-chief, Trans Eng Mgt, 1985-; publ dir, Eng Mgt Soc, Inst Elec & Electronics Engrs, 1982-1985; pres, Col Eng Mgt, Inst Mgt Sci, 1979-1981; consult, Tokten Prog, UN, 1979-1980, 1987; assoc prof opers res & dir eng mgt proj, Indust Eng & Eng mgt, 1976-1987; vis asst prof mgt, Univ Pittsburgh, 1974-1976; PRES, TECHNOL MGT ASSOCS, 1973-; res asst indust eng, Univ Pittsburgh, 1971-1974; consult proj engr, United Engrs & Constructors, 1969-1971; partner, Tekser Consult Co, 1966-1969; proj engr, United Engrs & Constructors, 1963-1966; struct engr, Modjeski & Masters, 1962-1963. **Memberships:** Am Soc Eng Educ; fel Inst Elec & Electronics Engrs; Am Soc Civil Engrs; Am Soc Eng Mgt; Inst Opers Res & Mgt Sci; hon mem Soc Turkish Scientists Engrs & Architects. **Research Statement & Publications:** Engineering management; hierarchical decision modeling; multicriteria decisions, project management, strategic planning, manpower analysis and strategic management; operations research; resource optimization; quantification of expert judgments; technological innovations; risk assessment; technology management; conflict resolution. **Mailing Address:** Dept Eng & Technol Mgt, Portland State Univ, PO Box 751, Portland, OR 97207-0751. **Fax:** 503-725-4667. **E-Mail:** kocaoglu@emp.pdx.edu

KOCAREK, THOMAS, BIOLOGY. **Education:** PhD. **Professional Experience:** ASSOC PROF, INST CHEM TOXICOL, WAYNE STATE UNIV, as of 2006. **Memberships:** Inst Elec & Electronic Engrs. **Mailing Address:** Inst Chem Toxicol Wayne State Univ, 2727 2nd Ave Rm 4000, Detroit, MI 48201-2654. **Fax:** 313-577-0082. **E-Mail:** t.kocarek@wayne.edu

KOCATAS, BABUR M(EHMET), CHEMICAL ENGINEERING. **Personal Data:** b Istanbul, Turkey, April 7, 1927; m 1955, Semra Ozsoydan; c Reha. **Education:** Robert Col, Istanbul, BS, 1947; Univ Tex, MS, 1953, PhD (chem eng), 1962. **Professional Experience:** CONSULT, 1985-; sr res group leader, Monsanto Co, 1976-1985; sr resengr, Monsanto Co, 1962-1976; lectr math, Univ Tex, 1957-1962; Design engr, Union CarbideChem Co, 1956-1957. **Memberships:** Am Chem Soc; Am Inst Chem Engrs; Sigma Xi. **Research Statement & Publications:** Process design and development; micro pilot planting; distillation; fuel cells; mathematical modeling; systems engineering; air pollution control. **Mailing Address:** Dilhayat Sok 22 13, Camlik Etiler, Istanbul, Turkey. **Fax:** 902-122-933082.

KOCH, ALISA ERIKA, IMMUNOLOGY. **Personal Data:** b Jerusalem, Israel, February 26, 1956; American citizen; m 1988, Howard; c Joshua W Stein. **Education:** Northwestern Univ, BS, 1978, MD, 1980. **Honors & Awards:** Henry Christian Award, Am Fedn Clin Res, 1992, Am Asn Clin Invest, 1994, Asb Am Phys, 2000. **Professional Experience:** GALLAGHER RES PROF MED, NWESTERN UNIV MED SCH, as of 2003; PROF RHEUMATOLOGY, RHEUMATOLOGY, as of 2003; PROF RHEUMATOLOGY, SECT RHEUMATOLOGY, VET ADMIN LAKESIDE MED CTR, 1995-; prin investr, Spec Study Sect 7, NIH, 1992-; assoc prof rheumatology, Sect Rheumatology, Vet Admin Lakeside Med Ctr, 1992-1995; CHIEF, SECT RHEUMATOLOGY, VET ADMIN LAKESIDE MED CTR, 1991-; mem, Spec Study Sect 7, NIH, 1991; vis scholar, Univ Mich, Ann Arbor, 1990-1991; staff physician, Vet Admin Lakeside Med Ctr, 1989-; consult physician, Rehab Inst Chicago, 1988-; staff physician, Nwestern Mem Hosp, 1986-; asst prof med, Sect Arthritis Connective Tissue Dis, 1986-1992; assoc investr, Vet Admin Lakeside Med Ctr, 1986-1989; Clin instr, Nwestern Univ Med Sch, 1983-1986. **Memberships:** Am Fedn Clin Res; Am Soc Clin Invest; fel Am Col Physicians; Am Col Rheumatology; Am Asn Immunologists; Sigma Xi. **Research Statement & Publications:** Immunopathogenesis of rheumatoid arthritis as regards to macrophage and endothelial interactions; macrophage production of cytokines and angiogenic factors. **Mailing Address:** Ward 3-315, 303 E Chicago Ave, Chicago, IL 60611. **Fax:** 312-503-0994. **E-Mail:** ae_koch@northwestern.edu

KOCH, ARTHUR LOUIS, THEORETICAL BIOLOGY, BACTERIAL PHYSIOLOGY. **Personal Data:** b St Paul, Minn, October 25, 1925; m 1983, c 2. **Education:** Calif Inst Technol, BS, 1948; Univ Chicago, PhD (biochem), 1951. **Professional Experience:** PROF MICROBIOL, IND UNIV, BLOOMINGTON, 1967-; prof biochem & microbiol, Col Med, Univ Fla, 1963-1967; Guggenheim fel, 1960-1961 & 1981-1982; from asst prof to assoc prof biochem, Col Med, Univ Fla, 1956-1963; assoc scientist, Argonne Nat Lab, 1952-1956; res assoc & instr, Univ Chicago, 1951-1952 & 1953-1956. **Memberships:** Am Soc Microbiol; Am Soc Biol Chemists. **Research Statement & Publications:** Enzyme and haploid evolution; active transport systems; microbial growth physiology; microbial response to toxic and antibiotic substances. **Mailing Address:** Dept Biol, Ind Univ, Bloomington, IN 47405-6801. **Fax:** 812-855-6705. **E-Mail:** koch@indiana.edu

KOCH, BRUCE D, NEUROPHARMACOLOGY. **Personal Data:** b Dayton, Ohio, November 27, 1957. **Education:** Bates Col, BS, 1979; Harvard Univ, PhD (cell & develop biol), 1986. **Professional Experience:** STAFF RESEARCHER, SYNTEX DISCOVERY RES, 1991-; sr fel, CalifAm Cancer Soc, 1989-1991; fel, Univ Calif Berkeley, 1986-1991; fel, Jane Coffin Childs MemFund Med Res, 1986-1989; res asst, Tufts New Eng Med Ctr, 1979-1980. **Memberships:** Soc Neuroscience; Am Soc Cell Biol. **Research Statement & Publications:** Neuropharmacology of pain; intracellular calcium homeostasis. **Mailing Address:** Roche BioSci, 3401 Hillview Ave, Palo Alto, CA 94304. **Fax:** 650-354-7400. **E-Mail:** bruce.koch@syntex.com

KOCH, CARL CONRAD, MECHANICAL ATTRITION, NANOSTRUCTURED MATERIALS. **Personal Data:** b Cleveland, Ohio, October 19, 1937; m 1965, Evelyn; c Paul & Alexander. **Education:** Case Inst Technol, BS, 1959, MS, 1961, PhD (metall), 1964. **Honors & Awards:** Metall & Ceramics Award, US Dept Energy, 1980; IR 100 Award, Indus Res & Develop Mag, 1983; Award for Spec Creativity, NSF, 1990-1992, RJReynolds Tobacco Co Award for Excellence in Teaching, Research, and Extension, 2003. **Professional Experience:** PROF MAT SCI & ENG, NC STATE UNIV, 1983-; chmn, Alloy-phases Comt, Metall Soc, 1983-1985; secy, Alloy-phases Comt, Metall Soc, 1981-1983; Vis scientist, AERE, Harwell, Eng, 1971-1972; lectr, Univ Tenn, Knoxville, 1971; group leader, Oak Ridge Nat Lab, 1970-1983; staff scientist superconducting mat, Oak Ridge Nat Lab, 1965-1970; NSF fel metall, Univ Birmingham, Eng, 1964-1965. **Memberships:** Fel Am Phys Soc; fel AAAS; Mat Res Soc(secy, 1994-1995); fel Am Soc Metals Int; fel Minerals, Metals & Materials Soc (TMS). **Research Statement & Publications:** Materials science; rare earth alloy behavior; superconducting materials; fluxoid pinning; amorphous superconductors; non-equilibrium processing; rapid solidification; vapor deposition; mechanical alloying; intermetallic compounds; solid state amorphization; nanocrystalline materials. **Mailing Address:** 1713 Lookout Point Ct, Raleigh, NC 27612-1754. **Fax:** 919-515-7724. **E-Mail:** carl_koch@ncsu.edu

KOCH, CARL FRED, PALEOECOLOGY, BIOSTRATIGRAPHY. **Personal Data:** b Washington, DC, July 13, 1932; m 1988, Joyce; c Carla. **Education:** Univ Md, BS, 1957, MS, 1961; George Wash Univ, PhD (geol), 1977. **Professional Experience:** PROF EMER GEOL SCI, OLD DOM UNIV, as of 1999; prof geol, Old Dom Univ, beginning 1989; res assoc, Smithsonian Inst, 1981-; from asst prof to assoc prof, Old Dom Univ, 1978-1989; geologist, US Geol Surv, 1977-1992; Rixon Electronics Inc, 1962-1967 & Seismic Data Anal Ctr, 1968-1977; engr, Appl Physics Lab, Johns Hopkins Univ, 1958-1961. **Memberships:** Geol Soc Am; Paleont Soc; Int Paleont Inst. **Research Statement & Publications:** Geologic data for restricted time intervals of large geographic extent; biosphere history; quantitative paleoecology and biostatigraphy using upper cretareous molluscs. **Mailing Address:** Dept Geol Sci, Old Dom Univ, 5215 Hampton Blvd, Norfolk, VA 23508.

KOCH, CARL MARK, SLUDGE MANAGEMENT, WASTEWATER TREATMENT. **Personal Data:** b Orefield, Pa, April 29, 1944; m 1966, Nancy; c Carcy, Roger & Janine. **Education:** Univ Del, BSCE, 1966; Univ Pa, MSCE, 1967, PhD (water resources), 1972. **Honors & Awards:** Outstanding Service Award, Water Environment Federation, Ocotber 2005 for CoChair of Bioogilcal Nutrient Removal Manual. **Professional Experience:** ASSOC, GREELEY & HANSEN, 1980-; ENVIRON ENGR, GREELEY & HANSEN, 1976-; PRIN & PROCESS ENGR, GREELEY & HANSEN, 1975-; consult, Engrs Energy & Environ, 1974-1977; consult engr, United Engrs & Constructors, 1974-1976; lectr water resources, Univ Del, 1973 & 1992; chmn, Gen Elec Corp Int-Div Panel Waste Disposal & Pollution Control, 1973-1974; nviron engr, Reentry & Environ Syst Div, Gen Elec Corp, 1970-1974; Hydraul engr, US Army CEngr, 1966; co-chair, Sludge Comt, Am Soc Civil Engrs. **Memberships:** Water Pollution Control Fedn; Am Soc Civil Engrs; Am Acad Environ Engrs. **Research Statement & Publications:** Biological treatment of municipal and industrial wastewaters and sludge residues; water resources, hydrological investigations and water quality modeling; environmental assessment and impact evaluations; sludge processing and management. **Mailing Address:** Greeley & Hansen LLC, 110 S Poplar St, Wilmington, DE 19801. **Fax:** 302-428-9533. **E-Mail:** ckoch@greeley-hansen.com

KOCH, CHARLES FREDERICK, MATHEMATICS. **Personal Data:** b Tarrytown, NY, March 23, 1932. **Education:** Union Col, BS, 1953; Univ Ill, MS, 1957, PhD (math), 1961. **Professional Experience:** RETIRED; asst prof math, Southern Ill Univ, Carbondale, 1966-1991; asst prof math, Kans State Univ, 1964-1966; instr math, Univ Minn, 1961-1964. **Memberships:** Am Math Soc; Math Asn Am; Sigma Xi. **Research Statement & Publications:** Summability of sequences and series. **Mailing Address:** RR1 PO Box 125, Grand Forks, ND 58201.

KOCH, DAVID GILBERT, INFRARED ASTRONOMY, EXTRA-SOLAR PLANET DETECTION. **Personal Data:** b Milwaukee, Wis, August 6, 1945; m 1974, c 3. **Education:** Univ Wis-Madison, BS, 1967; Cornell Univ, MS, 1971, PhD (physics), 1972. **Professional Experience:** Astrophysicist, planet detection, NASA Ames Research Center, 1988-; astrophysicist, IR astronomy, Smithsonian Astrophys Observ, 1977-1989; Associate, Harvard Col Observ, 1977-1989; staff scientist, Amer Sci & Eng, 1976-1977; Sr Scientist x-ray astron, Amer Sci & Eng, 1972-1976. **Memberships:** AAAS; Am Astron Soc; Int Astron Union. **Research Statement & Publications:** Search for other planetary systems using photometry; infrared, x-ray and gamma-ray astrophysics with particular emphasis on spaceborne instrumentation and computer aided data reduction. **Mailing Address:** NASA Ames Res Ctr, MS 244-30, Moffett Field, CA 94035. **E-Mail:** D.Koch@NASA.gov

KOCH, DAVID WILLIAM, AGRONOMY. **Personal Data:** b Frankfort, Kans, November 22, 1942; m 1966. **Education:** Kans State Univ, BS, 1964, MS, 1966; Colo State Univ, PhD (agron), 1971. **Professional Experience:** PROF EMER CROP PHYSIOL, UNIV WYO, 2005-; prof, crop physiol, Univ Wyo, 1985-2005; assoc prof crop physiol, Univ NH, 1977-1985; Asst prof, Univ NH, 1971-1977. **Memberships:** Am Soc Agron. **Research Statement & Publications:** Minimum tillage establishment of forage crops; forage crop management; methods of forage conservation. **Mailing Address:** Dept Plant Sci, Univ Wyo, PO Box 3354, Laramie, WY 82071-3354. **Fax:** 307-766-5549. **E-Mail:** dwkoch@uwyo.edu

KOCH, DONALD LEROY, STRATIGRAPHY, GROUNDWATER GEOLOGY. **Personal Data:** b Dubuque, Iowa, June 3, 1937; m 1962, C Jean Swede; c Kyle, Amy & Nathan. **Education:** State Univ Iowa, BS, 1959, MS, 1967. **Professional Experience:** STATE GEOLOGIST & BUR CHIEF, GEOL SURV BUR, 1986-; stategeologist & dir, Iowa Geol Surv, 1980-1986; asst state geologist, Geol Surv Bur, 1975-1980; chief subsurface geol, Geol Surv Bur, 1971-1975; res geologist, Geol Surv Bur, 1959-1971. **Memberships:** Sigma Xi. **Research Statement & Publications:** Carbonate petrology and carbonate hydrology, defining the relationship of primary and secondary porosity to parameters of water availability and water quality. **Mailing Address:** Dept Natural Resources109 Trowbridge Hall, 109 Trowbridge Hall, Iowa City, IA 52242-1319. **Fax:** 319-335-2754. **E-Mail:** dkoch@igsb.uiowa.edu

KOCH, ELIZABETH ANNE, BIOCHEMICAL GENETICS, ELECTRON MICROSCOPY. **Personal Data:** b Toronto, Ohio, October 8, 1936; m 1973. **Education:** Mt Union Col, BS, 1958; Northwestern Univ, PhD (genetics), 1964. **Professional Experience:** ASSOC PROF BIOCHEM & GENETICS, CHICAGO MED SCH, as of 2005; asst prof, Chicago Med Sch, 1969-1974; lectr, Eve Div, Nwestern Univ, 1965-1972; res assocelectron microscopy & genetics, Nwestern Univ, 1964-1969; fel, Cancer Inst, NIH, 1964-1966; instr gen biol & genetics, Hope Col, 1963-1964; teacher gen sci & eng, Ely Jr HighSch, Elyria, Ohio, 1958-1959. **Memberships:** Am Soc Cell Biol; Genetics Soc Am; AAAS; Sigma Xi; Am Asn Univ Prof. **Research Statement & Publications:** Ultrastructural localization of proteins using immune chemical methods; oogenesis. **Mailing Address:** Dept Biol Chem Chicago Med Sch, 3333 Greenbay Rd, North Chicago, IL 60064-3095. **Fax:** 847-578-3240.

KOCH, FREDERICK BAYARD, PHYSICAL METALLURGY. **Personal Data:** b St Paul, Minn, August 15, 1935; m 1963, c 3. **Education:** Carleton Col, BA, 1957; Univ Minn, Minneapolis, MS, 1962; Northwestern Univ, PhD (mat sci), 1967. **Professional Experience:** RETIRED; mem tech staff, Bellcore, 1997; mem tech staff, Bell Tel Labs, 1967-1990; Mem staff, Sci Lab, Ford Motor Co, 1960-1962. **Memberships:** Am Inst Metall Engrs; Electrochem Soc. **Research Statement & Publications:** Discrete wiring methods for circuit board development. **Mailing Address:** 92 Highland Ave, Highlands, NJ 07732.

KOCH, GARY MARLIN, ORNAMENTAL HORTICULTURE. **Personal Data:** b Pottsville, Pa, November 7, 1941. **Education:** Pa State Univ, BS, 1963, MS, 1965, PhD (hort), 1970. **Professional Experience:** PROF EMER PLANT SCI, CALIF STATE UNIV, FRESNO, as of 2006; prof Plant Sci Calif State Univ, Fresno, beginning 1977; assoc prof plant sci, Calif State Univ, Fresno, 1970-1977; asst prof ornamental hort, Univ Calif State Univ, 1970. **Memberships:** Am Soc Hort Sci. **Research Statement & Publications:** Plant materials and usage; commercial floriculture; floral design; turfgrass production. **Mailing Address:** Dept Plant Sci, Calif State Univ 2415 E San Ramon, Fresno, CA 93740-8033. **Fax:** 559-278-7413.

KOCH, GEORGE SCHNEIDER, ECONOMIC GEOLOGY, STATISTICS. **Personal Data:** b Washington, DC, October 30, 1926; m Ruth. **Education:** Harvard Univ, BS, 1948, PhD (econ geol), 1955; Johns Hopkins Univ, MA, 1949. **Professional Experience:** PROF EMER, DEPT GEOL, UNIV GA, as of 1999; res geologist, US Bur Mines, 1962-1971; asst prof geol, Ore State Univ, 1956-1962; chief geologist, Minera Frisco, SA, Mex, 1952-1956; geologist, US Geol Surv, 1948-1952; consult, firms mineral indust & US govt. **Memberships:** Soc Econ Geol; Am Inst Mining Metall & Petrol Eng; Int Asn Math Geol. **Research Statement & Publications:** Statistical analysis of geological data; exploration for and evaluation of mineral deposits; precious and nonferrous metal and uranium deposits. **Mailing Address:** Dept Geol Univ Ga, 210 Field St, Athens, GA 30602. **E-Mail:** geoskoch@mindspring.com

KOCH, HEINZ FRANK, PHYSICAL ORGANIC CHEMISTRY, FLUORINE CHEMISTRY. **Personal Data:** b Berlin, Ger, June 21, 1932; American citizen; m 1958, c 2. **Education:** Haverford Col, BS, 1954, MS, 1956; Cornell Univ, PhD (org chem), 1960. **Professional Experience:** Vis prof, Univ Grenoble, France, 1979 & Univ Auckland, NZ, 1979-1980; div Fluorine Chem, Dept Chem, 1977; vis prof, Univ Calif, Berkeley, 1972-1973; NSF fac fel, UnivCalif, Berkeley, 1971-1972; PROF ORG CHEM, ITHACA COL, 1970-; chmn, Dept Chem, 1967-1979; from asst prof to assoc prof, Ithace Col, 1965-1970; res chemist, Plastics Dept, E IDu Pont Del Nemours & Co, Inc, 1962-1965; res chemist, Univ Calif, Berkeley, 1960-1962. **Memberships:** Am Chem Soc (secy-treas Div Fluorine Chem, 1974-1975); Royal Chem Soc; NYAcad Sci; Sigma Xi. **Research Statement & Publications:** Physical organic studies of reaction mechanisms, particularly fluorohalocarbon chemistry; studies of 1, 2 elimination reactions, carbanions and isotope effects. **Mailing Address:** Dept Chem, Ithaca Col, CNS-356, Ithaca, NY 14850. **E-Mail:** heinz@ithaca.edu

KOCH, HENRY GEORGE, MEDICAL ENTOMOLOGY. **Personal Data:** b Mt Holly, NJ, May 22, 1948; m 1968, c 2. **Education:** Okla State Univ, BS, 1971, MS, 1974; NC State Univ, PhD (entom), 1977. **Professional Experience:** ENTOMOLOGIST, FOOD & DRUG ADMIN, NY, 1989-; Adj assoc profentom, Okla State Univ, 1978-; Res Entomologist, Lone Star Tick Res Lab, Sci & Educ Admin-Agr Res, USDA, 1977-1989. **Memberships:** Entom Soc Am; Coun Agr Sci & Technol; Am Registry Prof Entomologists. **Research Statement & Publications:** Acarology, tick ecology and biology; host suitability; acarid susceptibility. **Mailing Address:** 850 Third Ave, Brooklyn, NY 11232.

KOCH, HERMAN WILLIAM, PHYSICS. **Personal Data:** b New York, NY, September 28, 1920; m 1945, c 5. **Education:** Queens Col, NY, BS, 1941; Univ Ill, MS & PhD (physics), 1944. **Professional Experience:** RETIRED; dir, Am Inst Physics, 1966-1967; chief, Radiation Physics Div, 1962-1966; physicist, High Energy Radiation Sect, Nat Bur Stand, 1949-1962; asst prof res nuclear physics, Univ Ill, 1946-1949; res physicist, Univ Ill, 1944-1945 & Clinton Labs, Oak Ridge, 1945-1946; past-pres, Nat Fedn Abstracting & Indexing Serv; chmn, US Nat Comt, Comt Data Sci & Technol, past-chmn, Copy Clearance Ctr. **Memberships:** Fel Am Phys Soc; fel Optical Soc Am; Am Asn Physics Teachers; fel AAAS; Acoust Soc Am. **Research Statement & Publications:** Nuclear physics research on 20 million electron volt, 50 million electron volt and 180 million electron volt electron accelerator; development of high-energy x-ray spectrometer; Bremsstrahlung production; radiation physics research from 50 kiloelectron volts to 180 million electron volts; studies of science information flow. **Mailing Address:** 2105 Ambassador Dr 106, Colorado Springs, CO 30921.

KOCH, HOWARD A(LEXANDER), CHEMICAL ENGINEERING. **Personal Data:** b Evanston, Ill, June 15, 1922; m 1943, c 2. **Education:** Northwestern Univ, BS, 1943, MS, 1946, PhD (chem eng), 1949. **Professional Experience:** RETIRED; vpres eng, Arco Oil & Gas Co, 1973-1984; res eng mgr, Atlantic Richfield Co, 1969-1973; dist mgr, Rocky Mt-Mid Continent Dist, 1967-1969; mgr, Block 31Unit Opers, 1963-1967; div reservoir engr, Reservoir Mechs, Atlantic Refining Co, 1961-1963; sr reservoir engr, Reservoir Mechs, Atlantic Refining Co, 1959-1961; proj leader, ReservoirMechs, Atlantic Refining Co, 1949-1959; res supvr, Northwestern Univ, 1946-1949; asst chem engr, Northwestern Univ, 1946. **Memberships:** Am Inst Chem Engrs; Am Inst Mining, Metall & Petrol Engrs. **Research Statement & Publications:** Unit operations; gas absorption; reservoir mechanics; fluid flow and mass transfer. **Mailing Address:** 4529 Crooked Lane, Dallas, TX 75229.

KOCH, J FREDERICK, SEMICONDUCTOR PHYSICS. **Personal Data:** b Berlin, Ger, June 1, 1937; American citizen; m 1985, c 4. **Education:** NY Univ, BA, 1958; Univ Calif, Berkeley, PhD (physics), 1962. **Professional Experience:** PROF PHYSICS, TECH UNIV MUNCHEN, 1973-; from asst prof to profphysics, Univ Md, College Park, 1963-1973; Asst prof physics, Univ Calif, Berkeley, 1962-1963. **Memberships:** Fel Am Phys Soc; Deutsche Phys Gesellschaft. **Mailing Address:** Dept Physics, Tech Univ Munchen, 85747 Garching, Ger.

KOCH, KAY FRANCES, ORGANIC CHEMISTRY. **Personal Data:** b Tremont, Ill, June 18, 1936; m 1971. **Education:** Univ Ill, BS, 1958; Univ Calif, Berkeley, PhD (org chem), 1962. **Professional Experience:** RETIRED; mgr sci info serv, Res Labs, Eli Lilly Co, 1988-1993; head phys chem res, Res Labs, Eli Lilly Co, 1980-1988; head microbiol & fermentation res, Res Labs, EliLilly Co, 1977-1980; sr org chemist, Res Labs, Eli Lilly Co, 1966-1977; Nat Inst Gen Med Sci spec fel, 1964-1965; asst prof, Wellesley Col, 1963-1966; instr chem, Wellesley Col, 1961-1963. **Memberships:** Am Chem Soc. **Research Statement & Publications:** Photochemistry of highly conjugated cyclic organic and other organic compounds; biosynthesis of quinones in insects and study of defensive secretions of insects; fermentation products chemistry; antibiotics, especially amino glycosides. **Mailing Address:** 8518 Hughes Rd, North Salem, IN 46165.

KOCH, LEONARD JOHN, NUCLEAR POWER. **Personal Data:** b Chicago, Ill, March 30, 1920; m 1942, Rosemarie; c William. **Education:** Ill Inst Technol, BS, 1943; Univ Chicago, MBA, 1968. **Professional Experience:** RETIRED; vpres, Ill Power Co, 1976-1983; mgr nuclear projs, Ill Power Co, 1972-1976; var mgt positions, Argonne Nat Lab, 1948-1972. **Memberships:** Nat Acad Eng; fel Am Nuclear Soc. **Research Statement & Publications:** Nuclear power for generation of electricity. **Mailing Address:** 1 E Desert Sky Rd No 16, Tucson, AZ 85737.

KOCH, MELVIN VERNON, PHARMACEUTICAL CHEMISTRY. **Personal Data:** b Chicago, Ill, June 12, 1940. **Education:** St Olaf Col, BA, 1962; Univ Iowa, MS, 1964, PhD (med chem), 1967. **Professional Experience:** DIR, CTR PROCESS ANAL CHEM, UNIV WASH, as of 2005; group leader pharmaceut chem, Dow Chem US, beginning 1974; group leader, Dow Chem US, 1971-1974; proj leader fine organics, Dow Chem US, 1969-1971; res chemist, Dow Chem US, 1967-1969. **Memberships:** Am Chem Soc; Sigma Xi. **Mailing Address:** Ctr Process Anal Chem, Univ Wash, PO Box 351700, Seattle, WA 98195-1700. **Fax:** 206-543-6506. **E-Mail:** mel@cpac.washington.edu

KOCH, PETER M, ATOMIC PHYSICS, quantum chaos. **Personal Data:** b Washington, DC, February 11, 1945; m 1980, Nancy; c Amanda & Nathan. **Education:** US Naval Academy 1963-1965; Univ Mich, BS, 1966; Yale Univ, MP, 1969, PhD (physics), 1974. **Honors & Awards:** Alexander von Humboldt Foundation Senior US Scientist Award, 1989-1990; (Life) Fellow of the American Physical Society, 1992-. **Professional Experience:** Chair, Department of Physics and Astronomy, State Univ. of NY, Stony Brook, as of 2005; Associate DEAN, COL ARTS & SCI, STATE UNIV NY, STONY BROOK, 2003-5; PROF PHYSICS, STATE UNIV NY, STONY BROOK, 1989-; Visiting Professor, Ludwig-Maximillians University, Munich, 1989-1990; from Asst Prof to Assoc Prof, State Univ NY, Stony Brook, 1982-1989; A P Sloan Found fel, 1978-1982; from Asst Prof to Assoc Prof of Physics, Yale Univ, 1976-1982; Charge de Recherche, CNRS, Paris, 1980-1981. **Memberships:** (Life) Fellow, Am Phys Soc; Am Inst Physics. **Research Statement & Publications:** Quantum chaos and control experiments with highly excited atoms in intense electromagnetic fields; experimental and theoretical study of microwave resonators and networks as analogs for quantum billiards; ray-splitting phenomena. **Mailing Address:** Dept Physics & Astron, State Univ NY, Stony Brook, NY 11794-3800. **E-Mail:** peter.koch@stonybrook.edu

KOCH, RICHARD, PEDIATRICS, PHENYLKETONMIA. **Personal Data:** b NDak, November 24, 1921; m 1943, K Jean; c Jill, Thomas, Christine, Martin & Leslie. **Education:** Univ Rochester, MD, 1951; Univ Calif, AB, 1958. **Honors & Awards:** Distinguished Service Award, Cs Hosp Los Angeles, 1974; Res Award, Calif Asn Retardedk, 1985. **Professional Experience:** PROF EMER, UNIV SOUTHERN CALIF, 2002-; DIR, MATERNAL PKU NAT COL LAB STUDY, 1984-; actg head, Div Med Genetics, 1980-1986; prin Investr, Maternal PKU Proj, 1984-2002; prof clin pediat, Sch Med, Univ Southern Calif, 1976-2002; mem, Div Med Genetics, 1976-2002; dep dir chg ment health, develop, disabilities & drug abuse, Calif State Dept Health, 1975-1976; head, Div Child Develop, 1965-1975; from instr to prof pediat, Maternal Pku Nat Col Lab Study, 1955-1975; dir, Child Develop Clin, Los Angeles Cs Hosp, 1955-1975; prin Investr, PKU Collab Study, 1966-1984. Actg Head, Div. Med Gentics, 1981-1986. prof Clin Pediats, Univ Southern Calif Sch Med, 1969-2002; dir, Regional Ctr Develop. **Memberships:** Acad Pediat; Am Asn Ment Deficiency; Soc Inherited Metab Dis. **Research Statement & Publications:** Mental retardation in children; metabolic diseases; clinical genetics. **Mailing Address:** Cs Hosp, 4614 Sunset Blvd, Los Angeles, CA 90027. **Fax:** 323-664-0673. **E-Mail:** rkoch8@earthlink.net

KOCH, RICHARD CARL, MEDICINAL CHEMISTRY. **Personal Data:** b Pittsburgh, Pa, August 10, 1930; m 1947, c 4. **Education:** Cornell Univ, BA, 1952; Yale Univ, PhD (org chem), 1957. **Professional Experience:** DIR, CENT RES DIV, PFIZER, INC, 1976-; asst dir, Pfizer Inc, 1972-1976; sect mgr, Pfizer Inc, 1968-1972; proj leader, Pfizer Inc, 1966-1968; chemist, Pfizer Inc, 1959-1966; Res chemist, Res & Eng Div, Monsanto Chem Co, 1957-1959. **Memberships:** Am Chem Soc; Sigma Xi; Soc Environ Toxicol & Chem. **Research Statement & Publications:** Discovery and development of animal health drugs. **Mailing Address:** 22 Laurel Hill Dr S, Niantic, CT 06357-1508.

KOCH, RICHARD MONCRIEF, GEOMETRY. **Personal Data:** b Hutchinson, Kans, January 29, 1939. **Education:** Harvard Univ, AB, 1961; Princeton Univ, PhD (math), 1964. **Professional Experience:** PROF EMER MATH, UNIV ORE, as of 2004; prof math, Univ Ore, beginning 1984; from asst prof to assoc prof, Univ Ore, 1966-1984; Instr math, Univ Pa, 1964-1966. **Memberships:** Am Math Soc; Math Asn Am. **Research Statement & Publications:** Differential geometry, particularly pseudogroups. **Mailing Address:** Dept Math, Univ Ore, Eugene, OR 97403-1222. **E-Mail:** koch@math.uoregon.edu

KOCH, ROBERT HARRY, ASTRONOMY. **Personal Data:** b York, Pa, December 19, 1929; m 1959, c 4. **Education:** Univ Pa, AB, 1951, MA, 1955 & PhD (astron), 1959. **Professional Experience:** PROF EMER ASTRON, UNIV PA, as of 2004; prof Astron, Univ PA, beginning 1996; prof, Univ Pa, 1969-1996; actgchmn dept, Univ Pa, 1968-1973; assoc prof, Univ Pa, 1967-1969; assoc prof astron, Univ NMex, 1966-1967; from asst prof to assoc prof, Joint dept Astron, Amherst, Mt Holyoke & Smith Cols& Univ Mass, 1960-1966; instr astron, Amherst & Mt Holyoke Cols, 1959-1960. **Memberships:** AAAS; Am Astron Soc; Int Astron Union. **Research Statement & Publications:** Photoelectric photometry, polarimetry, visible band and ultraviolet spectroscopy and evolution of eclipsing variable stars. **Mailing Address:** Dept Physics & Astron, Univ Pa, 209 S 33rd St, Philadelphia, PA 19104-6394. **E-Mail:** rhkoch@sas.upenn.edu

KOCH, ROBERT MICHAEL, STRUCTURAL DYNAMICS & ACOUSTICS OF ADVANCED MARINE VEHICLES, STATE-OF-THE-ART FINITE ELEMENT ANALYSIS & UNDERWATER SHOCK ANALYSIS. **Personal Data:** b Mineola, NY, April 19, 1964; m 1991, Laureen; c 2. **Education:** Polytech Univ, BS, 1986, MS, 1988, PhD (appl mech), 1991. **Honors & Awards:** Winner, 2005 NSPE National Federal Engineer of the Year Award Top Ten Finalist, 2004 NSPE National Federal Engineer of the Year Award. **Professional Experience:** SR RES SCIENTIST, NAVAL UNDERSEA WARFARE CTR, as of 2004; Adj prof eng, Roger Williams Univ, 1993-; RES SCIENTIST APPL MECH, NAVAL UNDERSEA WARFARE CTR, 1991-; Consult, Beltran Inc, 1988-1991; teaching fel, Polytech Univ, 1986-1991; Engr, Vernitron Corp, 1983-1985. **Memberships:** Am Soc Mech Engrs; Am Inst Aeronaut & Astronaut; Acoust Soc Am, Sigma Xi. **Research Statement & Publications:** Underwater shock and structural acoustics; adaptive procedures in h-, p- and hp-version finite element analysis; rapid prototyping with stereolithography; probabilistic structural mechanics; ultrasonic wave propagation in elastic solids. **Mailing Address:** Naval Undersea Warfare Ctr, Bldg 1302, Newport, RI 02841-1708. **Fax:** 401-832-6202. **E-Mail:** kochrm@npt.nuwc.navy.mil

KOCH, ROBERT MILTON, ANIMAL BREEDING. **Personal Data:** b Sioux City, Iowa, May 15, 1924; wid Mary Jane; c William, James & Richard. **Education:** Mont State Univ, BS, 1948; Iowa State Univ, MS, 1950, PhD (animal breeding, genetics), 1953. **Honors & Awards:** Animal Breeding & Genetics Award, Am Soc Animal Sci, 1976; Pioneer Award, Beef Improvement Fed, 1979. **Professional Experience:** PROF ANIMAL SCI, UNIV NEBR, 1959-; chmn dept, Univ Nebr, 1959-1966; Supt, Ft Robinson Beef Cattle Res Sta, 1954-1957; From asst prof to assoc prof animal husb, Univ Nebr, 1950-1959. **Memberships:** Fel AAAS; fel Am Soc Animal Sci. **Research Statement & Publications:** Beef cattle breeding; population genetics. **Mailing Address:** Animal Sci Dept, Lincoln, NE 68583-0908.

KOCH, ROGER, PHYSICS. **Education:** Univ Calif, PhD (physics). **Professional Experience:** STAFF, INT BUS MACHINES T J WATSON RES CTR, as of 2004. **Mailing Address:** Int Bus Machines T J Watson Res Ctr, PO Box 218, Yorktown Heights, NY 10598. **Fax:** 914-945-2394. **E-Mail:** rhkoch@us.ibm.com

KOCH, RONALD JOSEPH, PHYSICS, MATERIALS SCIENCE. **Personal Data:** b Cincinnati, Ohio, June 30, 1939; m 1961, c 4. **Education:** Xavier Univ, Ohio, BS, 1961; Johns Hopkins Univ, PhD (physics), 1969. **Professional Experience:** MGR, SUPPORTING TECHNOL, ALASKA STEEL RES CTR, MIDDLETOWN, as of 2003; SR STAFF PHYSICIST, ARMCO INC, 1983-; RADIATION SAFETY OFFICER, ARMCO INC, 1978-; sr res physicist, Armco Inc, 1978-1983; sr res chemist, Armco Inc, 1975-1978; From res spectrochemistto sr res spectrochemist, Armco Inc, 1969-1975. **Memberships:** Am Iron & Steel Inst; Am Soc for Testing & Mat. **Research Statement & Publications:** X-ray physics and diffraction; auger spectroscopy; surface analysis; radiation safety. **Mailing Address:** AK Steel Res Ctr, 705 Curtis St, Middletown, OH 45044.

KOCH, RONALD N, FLOW MEASUREMENT. **Personal Data:** b Pittsburgh, Pa, August 19, 1941; m 1963, c 3. **Education:** Carnegie-Mellon Univ, BS, 1963; Univ Pittsburgh, MBA, 1983. **Honors & Awards:** Indust Prod Award, Soc Petrol Engrs, 1984. **Professional Experience:** OWNER, RONCOKE ASSOC, beginning 1989; CONSULT, beginning 1989; dir technol, Rockwell Int, 1985-1989; mgr eng, Rockwell Int, 1976-1985; develop engr, Rockwell Int, 1963-1976. **Memberships:** Am Water Works Asn; Am Soc Sanit Engrs; Asn Mech Engrs; Int Water Supply Asn. **Research Statement & Publications:** New product development activities for equipment in the field of flow measurement. **Mailing Address:** 112 Deer Valley Dr, Sewickley, PA 15143. **E-Mail:** RonCoke@aol.com

KOCH, STEPHEN ANDREW, INORGANIC CHEMISTRY. **Personal Data:** b Jamaica, NY, November 19, 1948; m 1975, Michelle. **Education:** Fordham Univ, BS, 1970; Mass Inst Technol, PhD (chem), 1975. **Professional Experience:** PROF CHEM, STATE UNIV NY, STONY BROOK, beginning 1993; from asst prof to assoc prof, StateUniv NY, 1978-1993; Assoc inorg chem, Tex A&M Univ, 1975-1977 & Cornell Univ, 1978. **Memberships:** Am Chem Soc. **Research Statement & Publications:** Structural, electronic and reactivity properties of transition metal compound; bioinorganic chemistry; catalysis. **Mailing Address:** Dept Chem, State Univ NY, Stony Brook, NY 11794-3400. **Fax:** 631-632-7960. **E-Mail:** stephen.koch@sunysb.edu

KOCH, STEPHEN DOUGLAS, PLANT TAXONOMY. **Personal Data:** b New York, NY, December 16, 1940; m 1968, Carol A Patrick; c Nicholas & Oliver. **Education:** Swarthmore Col, BA, 1962; Univ Mich, MS, 1964, PhD (plant taxon), 1969. **Honors & Awards:** Sistema Nacional de Investigadores, 1984-. **Professional Experience:** PROF-INVESTR BOT, POSTGRAD COL, CHAPINGO, MEX, 1973-; asstprof, NC State Univ, 1968-1973; Instr bot, Duke Univ, 1967-1968. **Memberships:** Fel AAAS; Am Soc Plant Taxonomists; Int Asn Plant Taxonomists; Mex BotSoc; Sigma Xi; Torrey Bot Club. **Research Statement & Publications:** Grass systematics. **Mailing Address:** Centro Botanica, Colegio de Postgraduados, Chapingo Edo, 56230, Mex. **Fax:** 525-454-5077.

KOCH, TAD H, ORGANIC CHEMISTRY. **Personal Data:** b Mt Vernon, Ohio, January 1, 1943; m 1976, Carol. **Education:** Ohio State Univ, BS, 1964, Iowa State Univ, PhD (org photochem), 1968. **Professional Experience:** Grants, Army Med Command, 1998-2001, 2001-2004; grants, Coun Tobacco res, 1992-2000; grants, Nat Heart Lung Blood Inst, 1987-1989; grants, NSF, 1986-1991; chair, Univ Colo, Boulder, 1983-1986; PROF ORG CHEM, UNIV COLO, BOULDER, 1980-; grants, Army res Off, 1980-1988; grants, Nat Cancer Inst, 1978-1991, 1993-1996, 1998-2001, 2001-2004; grants, Gen Med Sci Inst, 1971-1977; grants, Res Corp, 1969-1970; from asst prof to assoc prof, Univ Colo, Boulder, 1968-1980; grants, Petrol Res Fund, 1968-1972. **Memberships:** Am Chem Soc; Am Asn Cancer Res. **Research Statement & Publications:** Mechanistic and synthetic photochemistry; free radical chemistry; bio-organic chemistry; lasers; medicinal chemistry. **Mailing Address:** Dept Chem & Biochem, Univ Colo, Campus Box 215 Cristol Chem 159, Boulder, CO 80309-0215. **Fax:** 303-492-5894. **E-Mail:** kocht@Colorado.edu

KOCH, THEODORE AUGUR, PHYSICAL CHEMISTRY, CATALYSIS. **Personal Data:** b Schenectady, NY, October 21, 1925; m 1952, c 5. **Education:** St Michael's Col, BS, 1946, MS, 1947; Univ Pa, PhD (chem), 1952. **Professional Experience:** RETIRED; chemist, Petrochem Dept, E I Du Pont Del Nemours & Co Inc, beginning 1952; instr chem, Drexel Inst, 1947-1951; instr chem, Univ Vt, 1946. **Mailing Address:** Du Pont De Nemours & Co, 600 Cheltenham Rd, Wilmington, DE 19808.

KOCH, THOMAS L, OPTOELECTRONICS, OPTICAL FIBER COMMUNICATIONS. **Personal Data:** b Boston, Mass, July 13, 1955; m 1979, c 2. **Education:** Princeton Univ, AB, 1977; Calif Inst Technol, PhD (appl physics), 1982. **Professional Experience:** HEAD, LIGHTWAVE DEVICES RES, BELL LABS, as of 1999; CHIEF TECH OFFICER, OPTO-ELECTRONICS PROD, BELL LABS, as of 1999; Mem bd gov, Laser & Electroptics Soc, Inst Elec & Electronics Engrs, 1991-1993; distinguished lectr award, Laser & Electroptics Soc, Inst Elec & Electronics Engrs, 1990; HEAD, OPTOELECTRONICS RES DEPT, AT&T BELL LABS, 1989-; supvr, PhotonicCircuits Res Dept, 1987-1989; Mem prog comts for numerous int & nat conf, 1985-; Memtech staff, Electronic Device Res Dept, 1982-1987. **Memberships:** Sr mem Inst Elec & Electronics Engrs Laser & Electroptics Soc; fel Optical SocAm. **Research Statement & Publications:** Semiconductor lasers and optical fiber communications; single-frequency and tunable lasers; device fabrication, dynamic characteristics for high speed transmission; integration of semiconductor guided-wave optoelectronic components to form photonic integrated circuits. **Mailing Address:** Lucent Technol, Bell Labs, 600 Mountain Ave, Murray Hill, NJ 07974-0636. **Fax:** 908-949-8988. **E-Mail:** tlkoch@lucent.com

KOCH, THOMAS RICHARD, CLINICAL CHEMISTRY, ANALYTICAL CHEMISTRY. **Personal Data:** b Strasburg, Pa, October 9, 1944; m 1968, c 3. **Education:** Lebanon Valley Col, BS, 1966; Univ Md, PhD (anal chem), 1970. **Professional Experience:** LAB DIR, MD MED LAB, 1992-; assoc prof path & dir clin chem, Sch Med, Univ Md, 1982-1992; Consult, Vet Admin Hosp, 1976-1980 & Food & Drug Admin, USPHS, 1977-; asst prof path & assoc dir clin chem, Sch Med, Univ Md, 1975-1982; clin chemist, St JosephHosp, 1972-1975; Trainee clin chem, State Univ NY, Buffalo, 1970-1972. **Memberships:** Am Asn Clin Chem. **Research Statement & Publications:** Trace elements in human disease; bilirubin measurement. **Mailing Address:** 1117 Chatterleigh Circle, Baltimore, MD 21204.

KOCH, WALTER THEODORE, ORGANIC CHEMISTRY. **Personal Data:** b Orwigsburg, Pa, January 4, 1923; m 1946, c 3. **Education:** Albright Col, BS, 1944; Rutgers Univ, MS, 1950, PhD (org chem), 1951. **Professional Experience:** RETIRED; sect leader, FMC Corp, 1966-1978; res chemist, 1963-1966; res chemist, Am Viscose Corp, 1953-1963; res chemist, Merck & Co Inc, 1951-1953; asst gen chem, Rutgers Univ, 1947-1950. **Memberships:** Am Chem Soc. **Research Statement & Publications:** High polymers; cellophane, coatings; thermoplastic films. **Mailing Address:** 411 N Middletown Rd, Media, PA 19063.

KOCH, WILLIAM EDWARD, ANATOMY. **Personal Data:** b York, Pa, November 22, 1933; m 1961, c 2. **Education:** Univ Pa, AB, 1956, AM, 1959; Stanford Univ, PhD (biol), 1962. **Professional Experience:** ADJ PROF ZOOL, SCH MED, UNIV NC, CHAPEL HILL, 1977-; PROFANAT, SCH MED, UNIV NC, CHAPEL HILL, 1968-; assoc prof, Sch Med, Univ NC, ChapelHill, 1968-1975; From instr to asst prof anat, Sch Med, Yale Univ, 1962-1968. **Memberships:** AAAS; Am Soc Zoologists; Am Asn Anatomists; Soc Develop Biol. **Research Statement & Publications:** Study of embryonic tissue interacting and differentiating in vitro. **Mailing Address:** Cell Biol & Anat, Univ NC 108 Taylor Bldg CB 7090, ChapelHill, NC 27599.

KOCH, WILLIAM FREDERICK, INTERNATIONAL STANDARDS, CLINICAL DIAGNOSTICS. **Personal Data:** b March 11, 1950; m 1975, c 2. **Education:** Loyola Univ, Chicago, BS, 1972; Iowa State Univ, MS, 1974, PhD (anal chem), 1975. **Honors & Awards:** R&R 100 Award 1988 Nat acad of clinical biochem fel, 2000-. **Professional Experience:** DEP DIR, CHEM SCI & TECHNOL LAB, 1995-; DIV CHIEF, INORG ANALYTICAL RES DIV, NAT INST STAND & TECHNOL, 1994; bd dirs, Nat Comt Clin Lab Stand, 1990-2002; Gov Bd, council for chem res, 1997-2000, dep div chief, Nat Inst Stand & Technol, 1988-1993; Lectr chem, Montgomery Col, Rockville, Md, 1983-1988; group leader, Nat Inst Stand & Technol, 1979-1988; res chemist, Nat Inst Stand & Technol, 1977-1979; Res fel, Nat Inst Stand & Technol, 1975-1977. **Memberships:** Am Chem Soc; Soc Electroanal Chem; Sigma Xi; Am Soc Testing & Mat; Nat Comt Clin Lab Stand (Pres, 1998-2000); Am Asn Clin Chem; Council for Chem Res. **Research Statement & Publications:** Responsible for the nation's reference standards, measurements and data for chemistry, chemical engineering and biochemical science; ion chromatography; pH; coulometry; standard reference materials; clinical chemistry; electolytic conductivity. **Mailing Address:** National Inst Stand & Technol, 100 Bureau Dr, Stop 8300, Gaithersburg, MD 20899-8300. **Fax:** 301-975-3845. **E-Mail:** william.koch@nist.gov

KOCH, WILLIAM GEORGE, PHYSICAL CHEMISTRY. **Personal Data:** b Forsyth, Mont, May 16, 1924; m 1951, c 1. **Education:** Univ Notre Dame, BS, 1947; Mont State Univ, MA, 1953. **Professional Experience:** PROF EMER CHEM, UNIV NORTHERN COLO, 1984-; chmn dept, Univ Northern Colo, 1974-1977; prof chem, Univ Northern Colo, 1959-1984; from asst prof to assoc prof, Univ Northern Colo, 1955-1959; Asstchemist, Great Western Sugar Co, Colo, 1954-1955. **Memberships:** AAAS; Am Chem Soc. **Research Statement & Publications:** Carbon isotope effects in decarboxylation reactions; effect of deuterium on carbon isotope effects; kinetics in the reaction between organolithium compounds and ether. **Mailing Address:** Dept Chem, Univ Northern Colo, Greeley, CO 80631-8204.

KOCH, WILLIAM JULIAN, MYCOLOGY. **Personal Data:** b Durham, NC, May 17, 1924; m 1947, c 4. **Education:** Univ NC, MA, 1950, PhD (bot, plant physiol, zool), 1955. **Professional Experience:** RETIRED; 1958 & Int Bot Cong, Can, 1959; vis investr, Highlands Biol Sta, 1957; vis investr, Mich Biol Sta, 1956; from asst to prof bot, Univ NC, Chapel Hill, 1947-1986. **Memberships:** AAAS; Bot Soc Am; Mycol Soc Am; Am Soc Plant Taxon; Electron Micros SocAm. **Research Statement & Publications:** Culture, comparative morphology, sexuality and mobility of fungus of reproductive cells; fungi parasitic on algae. **Mailing Address:** 4402 W Creedance Blvd, Glendale, AZ 85310.

KOCHAN, IVAN, IMMUNOLOGY, BACTERIAL PATHOGENESIS, DELAYED HYPERSENSITIVITY. **Personal Data:** b Ukraine, August 20, 1923; American citizen; m 1949, Jean; c Andrew & Mark. **Education:** Univ Man, BSc, 1953, MSc, 1955; Stanford Univ, PhD (med microbiol), 1958; AmBd Med Microbiol, dipl. **Professional Experience:** PROF EMER MICROBIOL, MIAMI UNIV, 1989-; prof Microbiol, Sch Med, Wright State Univ, 1974-1977; prof Microbiol, Miami Univ, 1967-1989; prof & chmn dept, Baylor Univ, 1961-1967; assoc Prof Microbiol, Baylor Univ, 1959-1961; res Assoc, Stanford Univ, 1958-1959. **Memberships:** AAAS; Am Asn Immunologists; Reticuloendothelial Soc; Am Soc Microbiol; AmThoracic Soc; fel Am Trudeau Soc; Am Acad Microbiol. **Research Statement & Publications:** Study of transferrin-iron-mycobactin interplay in host-parasite relationship; nutritional immunity; role of fatty acids in cellular immunity and immunological diseases; mechanism og pathogenicity in bacteria. **Mailing Address:** Dept Microbiol, Miami Univ, Oxford, OH 45056.

KOCHAN, ROBERT GEORGE, EXERCISE PHYSIOLOGY, BIOCHEMISTRY. **Personal Data:** b Prince Albert, Sask, October 25, 1949; m 1972, c 4. **Education:** Univ Sask, BA, 1971; Univ Toledo, PhD (exercise physiol), 1978. **Professional Experience:** Asst prof exercise physiol, Univ Wis-Madison, 1980-1987; res assoc, Med ColOhio, 1979-1980; fel biochem, Med Col Ohio, 1977-1979; Res fel, Juvenile Diabetes Found, 1977-1979; Teaching asst, Univ Sask, 1971-1973 & Univ Toledo, 1973-1977. **Memberships:** Am Col Sports Med. **Research Statement & Publications:** Exercise metabolism; glycogen synthesis; insulin action mechanism; diabetes control. **Mailing Address:** 814 Lewis Ct, Madison, WI 53711.

KOCHAN, WALTER J, PLANT PHYSIOLOGY. **Personal Data:** b Plainfield, NJ, July 15, 1922; m 1948, c 1. **Education:** Utah State Univ, BS, 1950, MS, 1952; Rutgers Univ, PhD (plant physiol), 1955. **Professional Experience:** PROF EMER PHYSIOL, UNIV IDAHO, 1987-; res prof hort, Exp Sta, 1970-1987; fromasst horticulturist to assoc horticulturist, Univ Idaho, 1957-1970; asst plant biochemist, DivIndust Res, Wash State Univ, 1957; Asst horticulturist, Univ Idaho, 1955-1957. **Memberships:** Am Soc Plant Physiologists; Sigma Xi. **Research Statement & Publications:** Mineral nutrition of plants; post-harvest physiology of tree fruits. **Mailing Address:** Dept Physiol, Univ Idaho, Moscow, ID 83843.

KOCHANOWSKI, BARBARA ANN, EXPERIMENTAL BIOLOGY. **Personal Data:** b Beaver, Pa, 1957. **Education:** Pa State Univ, BS, 1979; Univ Ill, Champaign, MS, 1981, PhD (nutrit), 1984. **Professional Experience:** ASSOC DIR, PERSONAL HEALTH CARE, PROCTER & GAMBLE CO, as of 2004; sect head, Health Care, Procter & Gamble Co, beginning 1991; res scientist health care, 1985-1990. **Memberships:** Am Inst Nutrit. **Mailing Address:** Procter & Gamble Co, PO Box 8006, Mason, OH 45040-8006.

KOCHANSKI, GREGORY P, TECHNICAL STAFF ADMINISTRATION. **Professional Experience:** RES FEL, PHONETICS LAB, OXFORD UNIV, 2003-; mem tech staff, Bell Lab/Lucent Technologies, 1987-2002. **Mailing Address:** Oxford Univ Phonetics Lab, 41 Wellington Sq, Oxford, UK. **E-Mail:** kochanski@phon.ox.ac.uk

KOCHANSKY, JAN PETER, INSECT PHEROMONES & HORMONES, PESTICIDE SYNTHESIS. **Personal Data:** b New York, NY, June 21, 1944; m 1969, Mary; c Amanda & Justina. **Education:** Harvard Col, AB, 1966; Stanford Univ, MS, 1967; Univ Colo, PhD (chem), 1971. **Professional Experience:** Retired April 2006 RES CHEMIST, BRL, AGR RES SERV, USDA, 1976-2006; Res assoc, NY Agr Exp Sta, 1972-1976. **Memberships:** Am Chem Soc; Entom Soc Am; Int Soc Chem Ecol; Sigma Xi. **Research Statement & Publications:** Biology and control of diseases and pests or bees; insect neurohomones, phermones and their analogs; pesticide synthesis and structure-activity studies. **Mailing Address:** BRL, ARS, USDA, 10300 Baltimore Ave, Bldg 476, Barc- E, Beltsville, MD 20705-2350. **Fax:** 301-504-8736. **E-Mail:** kochansj@ba.ars.usda.gov

KOCHAR, HARVINDER K, MUSCLE DISEASES. **Personal Data:** b Punjab, India, January 15, 1953. **Education:** Punjab Univ, BS, 1974, MSc, 1975. **Professional Experience:** SR RES TECHNOLOGIST, RES DEPT, MED CTR, NORTHWESTERN UNIV, 1980-; res technologist, 1977-1980. **Memberships:** Histochem Soc Am; Int Histochem Soc. **Mailing Address:** 9325A Jamison Ave, Philadelphia, PA 19115.

KOCHEL, R CRAIG, GEOLOGY. **Education:** Franklin & Marshall Col, BA 1975; Southern Ill Univ, MS 1977; Univ Tex, Austin, PhD 1980. **Professional Experience:** PROF GEOL, BUCKNELL UNIV, as of 2004. **Mailing Address:** Dept Geol, Bucknell Univ, Lewisburg, PA 17837. **E-Mail:** kochel@bucknell.edu

KOCHEN, SIMON BERNARD, MATHEMATICS. **Personal Data:** b Antwerp, Belg, August 14, 1934; American citizen. **Education:** McGill Univ, BSc, 1954, MSc, 1955; Princeton Univ, MA, 1956, PhD (math). 1958. **Honors & Awards:** Cole Prize, Am Math Soc, 1967. **Professional Experience:** HENRY BURCHARD FINE PROF MATH, PRINCETON UNIV, as of 2003; prof math, Princeton Univ, beginning 1967; mem, Inst Advan Study, 1966-1967; Guggenheim fel, 1962-1963; from asst prof to prof, Cornell Univ, 1959-1967; NatRes Coun Can res assoc & asst prof, Univ Montreal, 1958-1959; Asst lectr math, Princeton Univ, 1957-1958. **Memberships:** Am Math Soc; Asn Symbolic Logic. **Research Statement & Publications:** Mathematical logic. **Mailing Address:** Dept Math, Princeton Univ, Fine Hall Washington Rd, Princeton, NJ 08544-1000. **E-Mail:** kochen@math.princeton.edu

KOCHER, BRYAN S, COMPUTER SCIENCE. **Personal Data:** b Easton, Pa, July 3, 1948; m 1971, Sandra; c Dana & Whitney. **Education:** Moravian Col, BA, 1970; Univ Mass, MS, 1975; Wang Inst, PhD, 1981. **Professional Experience:** PRES, G&E SYSTS, 1992-; consult proj mgr, Consults Mgt Decisions, Inc, 1986-1992; dept mgr, Data Resources Inc, 1985-1986; prod mgr, Interactive Data Corp, 1982-1985; regional vpres, Boston Chap, Asn Comput Mach, 1980-1988; sr software eng, Cullinane, 1980-1982; chmn, Boston Chap, Asn Comput Mach, 1978-1980; syst mgr, Raytheon Data Systs, 1977-1980; proj leader, Com Union, 1975-1977. **Memberships:** Asn Comput Mach (pres, 1988-1990, past pres, 1990-1992). **Mailing Address:** G&E Systs, 250 Edge Hill Rd, Sharon, MA 02067. **Fax:** 781-784-1737.

KOCHER, CARL A, EXPERIMENTAL ATOMIC PHYSICS. **Personal Data:** b Seattle, Wash, February 14, 1942; m 1968, Marilyn; c Suzanne, Paul & Scott. **Education:** Univ Calif, Berkeley, AB, 1963, PhD (physics), 1967. **Professional Experience:** PROF PHYSICS, ORE STATE UNIV, 1973-; lectr, Columbia Univ, 1969-1973; vis scientist, Mass Inst Technol, 1968-1969; fel, NSF, 1967-1969; fel, Oxford Univ, 1967-1968. **Memberships:** Am Phys Soc; Am Asn Physics Teachers; Fedn Am Scientists; Union Concerned Scientists. **Research Statement & Publications:** Atomic collisions; radiative and autoionization processes; high Rydberg states; surface physics; analytical and computer instrumentation. **Mailing Address:** Dept Physics, Ore State Univ, Corvallis, OR 97331-6507. **Fax:** 541-737-1683. **E-Mail:** kocher@physics.orst.edu

KOCHER, CHARLES WILLIAM, NUCLEAR PHYSICS. **Personal Data:** b Johnson City, NY, May 16, 1932; m 1954, c 3. **Education:** Harpur Col, BA, 1954; NC State Col, MS, 1956; Ind Univ, PhD (nuclear physics), 1961. **Professional Experience:** SR RES PHYSICIST, ANALYSIS LAB, DOW CHEM USA, 1967-; scientist, Analysis Lab, Dow Chem USA, 1965-1967; sr staff scientist, Phys Res Lab, Budd Co, 1962-1965; Res assoc physics, Solid State Physics Group, Brookhaven Nat Lab, 1960-1962. **Memberships:** AAAS; Am Chem Soc; Am Phys Soc; Sigma Xi. **Research Statement & Publications:** Nuclear research reactors and decay schemes; Mossbauer effect; solid state physics, corrosion testing; metalorganic chemistry. **Mailing Address:** Dow Chemical Co, 47 Bldg, Midland, MI 48667. **Fax:** 989-638-7238.

KOCHER, DAVID CHARLES, HUMAN HEALTH RISK ASSESSMENT & ENVIRONMENTAL LAWS, REGULATIONS & PUBLIC POLICY. **Personal Data:** b Washington, DC, November 9, 1941; m 1977. **Education:** Univ Md, BS, 1963; Univ Wis-Madison, MS, 1965, PhD (physics), 1970. **Honors & Awards:** Health and Safety Research Division, Oak Ridge National Laboratory, Excellence in Research Award, 1992; Health Physics Society Fellow, 2005. **Professional Experience:** SCI STAFF, SENES OAK RIDGE, INC, 2000-; res scientist physics & environ sci, Oak Ridge Nat Lab, 1976-2000; res assoc, Oak Ridge Nat Lab, 1971-1976; Res assoc physics, Univ Birmingham, 1970-1971. **Memberships:** Health Physics Soc, Soc Risk Analysis. **Research Statement & Publications:** Development of models and databases for the assessment of health and safety impacts on man from energy production technologies; analyses of environmental laws and regulations. **Mailing Address:** SENES Oak Ridge Inc, 102 Donner Dr, Oak Ridge, TN 37830. **Fax:** 865-481-0060. **E-Mail:** dck@senes.com

KOCHER, HARIBHAJAN S(INGH), FLUID MECHANICS. **Personal Data:** b Faisalabad, Pakistan, September 29, 1934; American citizen; m 1963, Ranjit K; c Dr Mininder S & Rubinder. **Education:** Okla State Univ, BS, 1957; Purdue Univ, MS, 1959; Mich State Univ, PhD (fluid mech), 1963. **Honors & Awards:** pres Award Nominee, Xerox Corporation, 1982. **Professional Experience:** SR RES ASSOC, EASTMAN KODAK CO, ROCHESTER, NY, 1982-; Adj asst prof, Univ Rochester, 1976-; scientist, Xerox Corp, 1966-1982; sr res physicist, Delco Prod Div, Gen Motors Corp, NY, 1964-1966; develop engr, Civilian Atomic Power Dept, Can Gen Elec Co, 1963-1964; Lectr mech eng, Indian Inst Technol, New Delhi, 1962-1963. **Memberships:** Am Soc Mech Engrs; Inst Elec & Electronics Engrs. **Research Statement & Publications:** Thermal properties of metals; heat transfer in nuclear reactors and electrical motors; boundary layer studies; fluid flow instability; air bearing technology; heat transfer in xerographic systems; photographic film process fluid mechanics. **Mailing Address:** 56 Leonard Crest, Penfield, NY 14526. **E-Mail:** hskocher@aol.com

KOCHERLAKOTA, KATHLEEN, STATISTICS. **Personal Data:** b Pittsburgh, Pa, March 31, 1938; m 1962, Subrahmaniam; c 2. **Education:** Muskingum Col, BS, 1960; Johns Hopkins Univ, MS, 1963, DSc (statist), 1969. **Professional Experience:** PROF, UNIV MAN, 1987-; from asst prof to assoc prof, Univ Man, 1969-1987; sessional lectr statist, Univ Man, 1967-1969; consult statist, Dept Community Med, Univ Western Ont, 1965-1970; Lectr math, Muskingum Col, 1962-1963. **Memberships:** Biomet Soc; Am Statist Asn. **Research Statement & Publications:** Applied multivariate analysis and analysis of discrete data. **Mailing Address:** Dept Statist, Univ Man, Winnipeg, MB R3T 2N2, Can. **Fax:** 204-275-5011. **E-Mail:** kocherl@ccu.umanitoba.ca

KOCHERLAKOTA, SUBRAHMANIAM, MATHEMATICAL STATISTICS. **Personal Data:** b Bangalore, India, February 3, 1935; m 1962, Kathleen Jackson; c 2. **Education:** Univ Col Sci, Benares, India, BSc, 1954, MSc, 1957; Inst Agr Res Statist, dipl, 1963; ScD, Johns Hopkins, 1964. **Professional Experience:** PROF STATIST, UNIV MAN, 1970-; Nat Res Coun operating grants pure &appl math, 1966-; assoc prof, Univ Man, 1966-1970; asst prof math, Univ Western Ont, 1964-1966; investr, Rockefeller Found, India, 1959-1960; sr res fel, Inst Agr Res Statist, 1958-1959; Jr res fel statist, Inst Agr Res Statist, 1957-1958. **Memberships:** Inst Math Statist; Am Statist Asn; fel Royal Statist Soc; Int Statist Inst. **Research Statement & Publications:** Multivariate analysis; distribution theory; statistical tests of significance; applied probability theory; non-normality. **Mailing Address:** Dept Statist, Univ Man, Winnipeg, MB R3T 2N2, Can. **Fax:** 204-275-5011. **E-Mail:** kocherl@cc.umanitoba.ca

KOCHERT, GARY DEAN, BOTANY. **Personal Data:** b Louisville, Ky, October 12, 1939; m 1963, c 2. **Education:** Ind Univ, BA, 1963, PhD (microbiol), 1967. **Professional Experience:** RETIRED; prof bot, Univ Ga, beginning 1978; chmn dept bot, Univ Ga, beginning 1978; from asst prof to assoc prof, Univ GA, 1967-1978. **Research Statement & Publications:** Molecular genetics and systematics of rice, peanuts, and bamboo. **Mailing Address:** Dept Bot, Univ Ga, Rm 4512 Plant Sci Blvd, Athens, GA 30602.

KOCHHAR, DEVENDRA M, ANATOMY, EMBRYOLOGY. **Personal Data:** b Sailkot, India, March 10, 1938; wid, c Vineet S & Romeen. **Education:** Punjab Univ, India, BSc, 1958, MSc, 1959; Univ Fla, PhD (anat), 1964. **Honors & Awards:** Warkany Award, 1990. **Professional Experience:** PROF EMER, THOMAS JEFFERSON UNIV, PHILADELPHIA, 2005-; vis prof, Univ Louisville, Ky, 2004-; prof anat, Jefferson Med Col, 1976-2005; from assoc prof to prof, Univ Va, 1971-1976; from asst prof to assoc prof anat, Univ Iowa, 1968-1971; guest investr, Rockefeller Univ, 1967-1968; vis scientist, Strangeways Res Lab, Cambridge, 1966-1967; vis scientist, Karolinska & Wenner-Grens Insts, Stockholm, Sweden, 1965-1966; Instr anat, Univ Fla, 1964-1965; consult pharmaceut indust, Environ Protection Agency & Food & Drug Admin. **Memberships:** Am Soc Cell Biol; Am Asn Anatomists; Teratology Soc (pres, 1982-1983); SocDevelop Biol. **Research Statement & Publications:** Experimental teratology; development of skeletal system; congenital abnormalities of limb; collagen genes in development; retinoids in health and disease. **Mailing Address:** Dept Path, Anat & Cell Biol, Jefferson Col Med, Thomas Jefferson Univ, 1020 Locust St, Philadelphia, PA 19107-6799. **Fax:** 215-923-3808. **E-Mail:** devendra.kochhar@mail.tju.edu

KOCHHAR, MAN MOHAN, MEDICINAL CHEMISTRY, BIOCHEMICAL TOXICOLOGY. **Personal Data:** b Lahore, Pakistan, September 14, 1932; American citizen; m 1954, c 3. **Education:** Punjab Univ, India, BS, 1953; Univ Tex, Austin, MS, 1961, PhD (med chem), 1964. **Professional Experience:** RES SCI, OFF STAND-FDA, 1983-; prof pharmacol & toxicol, Auburn Univ, 1981-1983; prof toxicol, Auburn Univ, 1975-1981; Dept Ment Health award, State Ala, 1974; dir, Drug Screening Training Prog, Auburn Univ & Drug Anal Lab, 1973-; Nat Inst Drug Abuse award, 1973; grant-in-aid, Auburn Univ, 1965-1968; from asst prof to assoc prof pharm & pharmaceut chem, Auburn Univ, 1964-1975; Lederle fac awards, 1964 & 1965; spec instr, Col Pharm, 1963-1964; asst med chem, Univ Tex, Austin, 1959-1963; med rep, Geigy Pharmaceut, India, 1955-1958; Chief chemist, Dr Nayer Chem Works, India, 1954-1955. **Memberships:** Am Acad Clin Toxicol; Am Asn Clin Chem; Am Pub Health Asn; Can Acad Clin Anal Toxicol. **Research Statement & Publications:** Structure-activity relationships among psychotropic and antineoplastic agents; biochemical approach to toxicology including analytical toxicology. **Mailing Address:** 9458 Macomber Lane, Columbia, MD 21045.

KOCHHAR, RAJINDAR KUMAR, POLYMER CHEMISTRY. **Personal Data:** b Nurmahal, India, August 1, 1922; American citizen; m 1954, c 2. **Education:** Panjab Univ, India, BS, 1945; Univ Delhi, MS, 1948; Univ Tex, Austin, PhD (physorg chem), 1965; Univ Mo-Kansas City, MBA, 1969. **Professional Experience:** CHEM CONSULT, 1983-; dir process chem, plastics div, 1981-1983; mgrpolymerization res, Gulf Res & Develop Co, 1977-1981; sr res chemist, Gulf Res & Develop Co, 1968-1977; res chemist, Gulf Res & Develop Co, 1964-1968; Asst med res, Lady Hardinge MedCol, Delhi, 1955-1958. **Research Statement & Publications:** Color and chemical constitution; dyes for nylon; research on medicinal plants; fixed oils; polymer synthesis and characterization; polyolefin development; polypropylene catalysts. **Mailing Address:** 610 Brenwick Ct, Katy, TX 77450.

KOCHI, JAY KAZUO, ORGANIC CHEMISTRY. **Personal Data:** b Los Angeles, Calif, May 17, 1927; m 1959, c Sims, Ariel & Julia. **Education:** Univ Calif, Los Angeles, BS, 1949; Iowa State Univ, PhD (chem), 1952. **Honors & Awards:** James Flack Norris

Award, Am Chem Soc, 1981; A V Humboldt Sr Scientist Award, 1987; A C Cope Scholar Award, Am Chem Soc, 1988. **Professional Experience:** ROBERT A WELCH PROF CHEM, UNIV HOUSTON, 1984-; prof chem, Earl Blough prof chem, 1974-1984; prof chem, Ind Univ, Bloomington, 1969-1974; from assoc prof to prof chem, Case Western Res Univ, 1962-1969; chemist, Shell Develop Co, 1957-1962; vis asst prof, Iowa State Univ, 1956; NIH fel, Cambridge Univ, 1955-1956; instr org chem, Harvard Univ, 1952-1955. **Memberships:** Nat Acad Sci; Am Chem Soc; Royal Soc Chem. **Research Statement & Publications:** Mechanisms of organic reactions catalyzed by metal complexes; application of metal complexes to organic synthesis; electron-transfer and charge-transfer processes in organic chemistry; photochemistry of organometallic compounds; application of electron spin resonance spectroscopy to organic and organometallic free radicals and to the mechanism of homolytic reactions; time-resolved spectroscopy of inactive intermediates. **Mailing Address:** Dept Chem, Univ Houston, 136 Fleming Bldg, Houston, TX 77204-5003. **Fax:** 713-743-2709. **E-Mail:** jkochi@mail.uh.edu

KOCHMAN, RONALD LAWRENCE, DRUG SURVEILLANCE & LABELING, CLINICAL RESEARCH. **Personal Data:** b Rome, NY, April 7, 1946; m 1968, c 2. **Education:** Pa State Univ, BS, 1968; Northeastern Univ, MS, 1974. **Professional Experience:** DIR LABELING & OPERS, WORLDWIDE SAFETY & LABELING, G DSEARLE & CO, SUBSID MONSANTO CO, 1993-; from asst dir to assoc dir, G D Searle & Co, 1988-1993; sr res assoc, G D Searle & Co, 1986-1988; res investr, G D Searle & Co, 1982-1986; res assoc, G D Searle & Co, 1979-1982; Res biologist, G D Searle & Co, 1975-1979. **Memberships:** Drug Info Asn; Am Soc Pharmacol & Exp Therapeut; Am Soc Neurochem. **Research Statement & Publications:** Clinical trails of anti-ulcer, analgesic and anxiolytic medications; neurochemistry of memory and learning; neuro-transmitters and drug receptors. **Mailing Address:** G D Searle & Co, 4901 Searle Pkwy, Skokie, IL 60077. **Fax:** 847-982-7715. **E-Mail:** rlkoch@searle.monsanto.com

KOCHMAN, STANLEY OSCAR, ALGEBRAIC TOPOLOGY. **Personal Data:** b New York, NY, July 18, 1946; m 1969, Ann; c Shoshanah, Leah, Sarah, Israel Zvi, Ruchama, Yehuda Leib & Chaim Ezra. **Education:** Kenyon Col, AB, 1966; Univ Chicago, MS, 1967, PhD (math), 1970. **Professional Experience:** Ed-in-chief, Can Math Bulletin, 1989-1995; PROF MATH, YORK UNIV, 1985-; from asst prof to assoc prof, Univ Western Ont, 1977-1985; lectr, Mass Inst Technol, 1973-1974; asst prof, Purdue Univ, West Lafayette, 1972-1977; Gibbs instr math, Yale Univ, 1970-1972. **Memberships:** Am Math Soc; Can Math Soc; Math Asn Am. **Research Statement & Publications:** Algebraic topology, especially homology operations, Cobordism theory and stable homology. **Mailing Address:** Dept Math & Stat, York Univ, 4700 Keele St, Toronto, ON M3J 1P3, Can. **E-Mail:** kochman@mathstat.yorku.ca

KOCHTANEK, THOMAS RICHARD, INFORMATION STORAGE & RETRIEVAL, INFORMATION SYSTEMS. **Personal Data:** b Cleveland, Ohio, January 21, 1951; m 1979, Barbara Brandt; c Jeffrey T & Kyle B. **Education:** Case Inst Technol, BS, 1973; Case Western Res Univ, PhD (info sci), 1978. **Professional Experience:** ASSOC PROF, SCH INFO SCI & LEARNING TECHNOL, UNIV MO, as of 2003; VIS PROF, SCH INFO & LIBR SCI, UNIV NC, CHAPEL HILL, 1989-; co-prininvestr, Nat Libr Med, 1984-1986; fel, Med Informatics, Univ Mo, Columbia, 1984; chmn, Dept Info Sci, Univ Mo, Columbia, 1984-1996; Fel, Nat Libr Med, 1983-1984; from asstprof to assoc prof, Dept Info Sci, Univ MO, Columbia, 1977-1983. **Memberships:** Am Soc Info Sci; Asn Libr & Info Sci Educators. **Research Statement & Publications:** Information storage and retrieval systems focusing on text-based information sources; address both the information technology component of open systems design and the end user/evaluative portion of applied information systems. **Mailing Address:** Sch Info Sci & Learning Technol, Univ Mo, 221 F Townsend Hall, Columbia, MO 65211. **E-Mail:** kochtanekt@missouri.edu

KOCH-WESER, DIETER, EXPERIMENTAL PATHOLOGY, PREVENTIVE MEDICINE. **Personal Data:** b Kassel, Ger, July 13, 1916; American citizen; m 1950, c 2. **Education:** Univ Sao Paulo, MD, 1943; Northwestern Univ, MS, 1950, PhD, 1956. **Honors & Awards:** Couto Prize, Acad Med, Brazil, 1945. **Professional Experience:** RETIRED; prof prev & social med, Med Sch, 1971-1984; assoc dean int progs, Sch Pub Health, Harvard Univ, 1967-1984; assoc prof, Sch Pub Health, Harvard Univ, 1964-1971; chief, Latin-Am Off, NIH, Brazil, 1962-1964; assoc prof, Sch Med, Western ResUniv, 1957-1962; from instr to asst prof med, Grad Sch Med, Univ Chicago, 1951-1956; asst path, Hektoen Inst Med Res, Cook Co Hosp, Chicago, 1949-1951; asst med, Hosps & Clin, SaoPaulo, Brazil, 1944-1947. **Memberships:** Am Soc Clin Invest; Am Thoracic Soc; AMA; Am Col Chest Physicians; SigmaXi. **Research Statement & Publications:** Isotope and biochemical studies in tuberculosis, hypersensitivity and liver diseases. **Mailing Address:** 19 Standish Rd, Wellesley, MA 02181.

KOCH-WESER, JAN, INTERNAL MEDICINE, CLINICAL PHARMACOLOGY. **Personal Data:** b Berlin, Ger, October 30, 1930; American citizen. **Education:** Univ Chicago, AB, 1950; Harvard Med Sch, MD, 1954. **Professional Experience:** F HOFFMANN LA ROCHE & CO, SWITZ, as of 2002: dir res ctr & vpres res, Merrell Int, beginning 1976; assoc dir res ctr & chief med res, Merrell Int, 1975-1976; Assoc physician & chief hypertension & clin pharmacol unit, Mass Gen Hosp, 1966-1975; USPHS res fel pharmacol, Burroughs Wellcome scholar clin pharmacol, 1966-1971; USPHS spec res fel, 1962 & grant, 1964-1975; from instr to assoc prof pharmacol, Harvard MedSch, 1962-1975; USPHS res fel pharmacol, Harvard Med Sch, 1960-1961; resident, Mass GenHosp, 1959; asst resident, Mass Gen Hosp, 1955-1956; Intern med, Mass Gen Hosp, 1954-1955; mem pharmacol-toxicol rev comt & prog comt, Nat Inst Gen Med Sci; mem sci adv bd, Pan Am Health Orgn; mem med adv bd, Coun High Blood Pressure Res, AmHeart Asn; mem bd trustees, US Pharmacopeial Coun. **Memberships:** Am Col Cardiol; Am Fedn Clin Res; Am Soc Clin Pharmacol & Therapeut; AmSoc Pharmacol & Exp Therapeut; Cardiac Muscle Soc. **Research Statement & Publications:** Cardiovascular physiology and pharmacology; clinical pharmacology and human therapeutics; adverse drug reactions; drug metabolism and pharmacokinetics; antiarrhythmic, antihypertensive and anticoagulant drugs. **Mailing Address:** 699 Kahiau Loop, Honolulu, HI 96821. **Fax:** 416-169-19391.

KOCIBA, RICHARD JOSEPH, VETERINARY PATHOLOGY, TOXICOLOGY. **Personal Data:** b Harbor Beach, Mich, April 8, 1939; m 1966, c 2. **Education:** Mich State Univ, BS, 1964, DVM, 1966, MS, 1969, PhD (path). 1970. **Professional Experience:** Adj asst prof path, Mich State Univ, beginning 1981; SR ASSOC SCIENTIST, TOXICOL RES LAB, DOW CHEM CO, 1980-; res pathologist, Toxicol Res Lab, Dow ChemCo, 1970-1980; instr anat, NIH fel path, 1968-1970; instr anat, Mich State Univ, 1967-1968; practr, Milford VetClin, 1966-1967. **Memberships:** Am Vet Med Asn; Am Col Vet Pathologists; Soc Toxicol; Soc Pharmacol &Environ Pathologists; Am Bd Toxicol. **Research Statement & Publications:** Design, conduction, evaluation and interpretation of research in the area of acute and chronic toxicity, with special emphasis on carcinogenesis and pathology. **Mailing Address:** Toxicol Res Lab 1803 Bldg, Dow Chem Co, Midland, MI 48640. **Fax:** 989-636-1875. **E-Mail:** rkociba@dow.com

KOCKS, U(LRICH) FRED, MATERIALS SCIENCE. **Personal Data:** b Dusseldorf, Ger, November 25, 1929; American citizen; m 1954, c 4. **Education:** Univ Gottingen, dipl physics, 1954; Harvard Univ, PhD (appl physics), 1959. **Honorary Degrees:** DrTech, Tampere Univ Tech, 1982. **Honors & Awards:** Japan Soc Promotion Sci Sr Award, 1985. **Professional Experience:** RETIRED; fel, Los Alamos Nat Lab, beginning 1986; tech staff mem, Los Alamos Nat Lab, beginning 1983; Humboldt award, Fed Repub Ger, 1979; Aachen Tech Univ, 1971-1972 & McMaster Univ, 1978; sr scientist, Argonne Nat Lab, 1965-1983; Vis prof, Munich Tech Univ, 1964; asst prof, Harvard Univ, 1961-1965; Lectr & res fel, Harvard Univ, 1959-1961. **Memberships:** The Metall Soc; Am Soc Mat; Int Soc Mat; fel Am Inst Mining Eng. **Research Statement & Publications:** Mechanics and thermodynamics of solids; defects in crystals; strengthening mechanisms; kinetics of plasticity and creep; textures, constitutive relations. **Mailing Address:** Los Alamos Nat Lab, Los Alamos, NM 87501. **Fax:** 505-667-8021.

KOCLOLEK, PATRICK, DIATOMS. **Education:** St Mary's Col, Maryland, BS, 1980; Bowling Green State Univ, MS, 1982; Univ Mich, PhD, 1988. **Professional Experience:** EXEC DIR, CALIF ACAD SCI, 1998-. **Mailing Address:** Calif Acad Sci, Golden Gate Park, San Francisco, CA 94118. **E-Mail:** kociolek@CAS.calacademy.org

KOCOL, HENRY, HEALTH PHYSICS. **Personal Data:** b Chicago, Ill, July 16, 1937; m 1971, Cleo; c Henry. **Education:** Loyola Univ, Chicago, BS, 1958; Purdue Univ, Lafayette, MS, 1961. **Professional Experience:** HEALTH PHYSICIST, RADIOL HEALTH BR, CALIF DEPT HEALTH SERVS, as of 2004; assoc health physicist, Radiol Health Br, Calif Dept Health Serv, beginning 1990; fed state liaison, Philadelphia, 1982-1990; mgr x-ray control & regulation, Wash State Dept Social & Health Serv, Seattle, 1979-1982; regional radiol health rep, Philadelphia, 1977-1979; regional radiation control, Philadelphia, 1973-1977; res chemist, Food & Drug Admin, Rockville, Md, 1971-1973; radiochemist, US Pub Health Serv, 1964-1971; radiochemist, Nat Bur Stand, 1961-1964. **Memberships:** Health Physics Soc. **Research Statement & Publications:** The explanation of scientific concepts and facts, especially in the field of radiation safety, to lay audiences, to enable societal decisions to be based on fact rather than hype. **Mailing Address:** Radiol Health Br, Calif Dept Health Servs, PO Box 942732, Sacramento, CA 94234. **Fax:** 916-324-3610. **E-Mail:** ckocol@ix.netcom.com

KOCON, RICHARD WILLIAM, CLINICAL CHEMISTRY, MEDICAL LABORATORY SCIENCE. **Personal Data:** b Fall River, Mass, April 18, 1942; m 1968, c 2. **Education:** Southeastern Mass Univ, BS, 1970; Providence Col, PhD (chem), 1973. **Professional Experience:** LAB DIR, DAMON MED LAB, INC, 1979-; org Chem, Rhode Island Hosp, 1974-1977. **Memberships:** Am Asn Clin Chem. **Research Statement & Publications:** Clinical chemistry, specifically clinical application of radioimmunoassay procedures and enzyme-linked immunosorbent blocking assay techniques. **Mailing Address:** 408 Oakland Pkwy, Franklin, MA 02038.

KOCSIS, JAMES JOSEPH, PHARMACOLOGY, TOXICOLOGY. **Personal Data:** b Barberton, Ohio, August 13, 1920; m 1952, Grace Herzog; c Rosemary, Elizabeth & Joan. **Education:** Ohio State Univ, BA, 1943; Univ Chicago, MS, 1952, PhD (pharmacol), 1956. **Professional Experience:** PROF PHARMACOL, JEFFERSON MED COL, 1974-; From instr to assocprof, Jefferson Med Col, 1956-1974. **Memberships:** Am Chem Soc; Am Soc Pharmacol & Exp Therapeut; Soc Toxicol; Sigma Xi. **Research Statement & Publications:** Bioassay; drug metabolism. **Mailing Address:** Jefferson Med Col, Thomas Jefferson Univ, 1020 Locust St, Philadelphia, Pa 19107-6731. **Fax:** 215-923-7144. **E-Mail:** james.kocsis@mail.tju.edu

KOCUREK, MICHAEL JOSEPH, PAPER SCIENCE, ENGINEERING. **Personal Data:** b New York, NY, January 6, 1943; m 1967, c 2. **Education:** State Univ NY, BS, 1964, MS, 1967; Syracuse Univ, PhD (paper sci & eng), 1971. **Professional Experience:** PROF & HEAD, DEPT WOOD & PAPER SCI, NC UNIV, as of 2001; DIR, NC UNIV, as of 2001; DIR, HEARTY FOUND, 1986-; prof paper sci & eng, Univ Wis-StevensPoint, 1980-1986; Mem acad adv coun, mem US-Can joint textbook comt, 1978-; mem profdevelop oper coun, Tech Asn Pulp & Paper Indust, 1976-; chmn continuing educ div, Tech AsnPulp & Paper Indust, 1976-1978; instr intro to pulp & paper tech, Tech Asn Pulp & Paper Indust, 1975-; Mem acad adv coun, Tech Asn Pulp & Paper Indust, 1971-; chmn dept, Univ Wis-StevensPoint, 1970-1986; Assoc prof paper sci, Univ Wis-Stevens Point, 1970-1980. **Memberships:** Tech Asn Pulp & Paper Indust. **Research Statement & Publications:** Wood and pulping chemistry; paper and fiber physics. **Mailing Address:** Dept Wood & Paper Sci, NC State Univ, Box 8005, Raleigh, NC 27695. **Fax:** 919-515-6302. **E-Mail:** mike_kocurek@ncsu.edu

KOCURKO, MICHAEL JOHN, GEOLOGY, SEDIMENTOLOGY. **Personal Data:** b Orange, Calif, January 28, 1945; m 1988, Debra. **Education:** Midwestern Univ (Geol), BS, 1966; Univ Wis-Milwaukee (Geol), MS, 1968; Tex Tech Univ, PhD (geol), 1972. **Professional Experience:** PROF EMER GEOL, MIDWESTERN STATE UNIV, WICHITA FALLS, TEX, as of 2005; prof geol, Midwestern State Univ, Wichita Falls, Tex, beginning 1979; asst prof geol, Tulane Univ, 1975-1979; explor geologist, Union Oil Co Calif, 1968-1969 & 1972-1975; chmn, Geol Dept, Midwestern State; Charles & Elizabeth Prothro distinguished prof geol sci. **Memberships:** Soc Econ Paleontologists & Mineralogists; Geol Soc Am; Paleont Soc. **Research Statement & Publications:** Application of modern carbonate depositional environments and post-depositional history to the paragenesis of carbonate rocks; taxonomy of fossil Octocorallia. **Mailing Address:** Dept Geol, Midwestern State Univ, Wichita Falls, TX 76308. **Fax:** 940-397-4893. **E-Mail:** john.kocurko@mwsu.edu

KODALI, DHARMA RAO, NEW & VALUE ADDED PRODUCT DEVELOPMENT, SYNTHESIS & PHYSICAL PROPERTIES PROCESS IMPROVEMENTS BY-PRODUCT UTILIZATION OF FATS & OILS. **Personal Data:** b Gudavalli, India, July 31, 1951; m 1982, Suseela; c Harsha S & Sithara. **Education:** Andhra Univ, India, BSc, 1973; Kurukshetra Univ, MSc, 1976, PhD (synthetic medchem), 1980. **Professional Experience:** CORP SR PRIN SCIENTIST, GENERAL MILLS INC, as of 2003; Tech chair indust uses fats & oils, Ind, 1995; circuit speaker, Fedn Socs CoatingTechnol, 1995; tech chair indust uses fats & oils, Ann Meeting, Am Oil Chemists Soc, Tex, 1994; lectr phys chem fats & oils applns to prod develop, Ill, 1993; staff scientist, Centres, Cargill Inc, beginning1991; lectr phys chem fats & oils applns to prod develop, Am OilChemists Soc, Calif, 1991; asst prof, Biophys Dept, 1990-1991; instr biophys, Biophys Inst, SchMed, Boston Univ, 1989-1990; Whitaker res grant, Whitaker Health Sci Fund, Mass, 1989-1990; Invited lectr, Nara Workshop Functional Fats & Lipids, Japan, 1988; res scientist, Biophys Inst, Sch Med, Boston Univ, 1984-1988; res assoc, Biophys Inst, Sch Med, Boston Univ, 1981-1984; Postdoctoral fel, Chem Dept, Polytech Inst NY, 1980-1981. **Memberships:** Am Oil Chemists Soc; fel Am Inst Chemists; Am Chem Soc; Indian Sci CongAsn; Fedn Soc Coatings Technol. **Research Statement & Publications:** Development of new and value added products from agricultural raw materials, fats, oils and their byproducts for industrial and food uses; investigation of lipid oxidation, technical problem solving and process improvement. **Mailing Address:** GBDT Riverside Tech Ctr, General Mills Inc, 330 Univ Ave SE, Minneapolis, MN 55414. **E-Mail:** dharma.kodali@genmills.com

KODALI, V PRASAD, RADAR, AEROSPACE ELECTRONICS & ELECTROMAGNETIC COMPATIBILITY. **Personal Data:** b Guntar, India, November 1, 1939; m 1987, Arati; c Mitul & Tara. **Education:** Univ Madras, BE, 1961; Case Inst Technol, MS, 1963; Univ Leeds, PhD (elec eng), 1967. **Honors & Awards:** Centennial Medal, Inst Elec & Electronics Engrs, 1984; Vasvik Res Award forElectronics, 1989. **Professional Experience:** Distinguished visitor, Univ Victoria, 1991-1992; nat proj dir, UN DevelopProg, UNIndust Develop Orgn, 1989-1993; ADV, DEPT ELEC, GOVT INDIA, 1986-; dir elec& instrumentation, Defense Res & Develop Org, 1984-1986; Vis scholar, Case Western ResUniv, 1983; from dir to sr dir, Dept Elec, Govt India, 1973-1984; Res scientist, Tata InstFundamental Res, 1968-1973. **Memberships:** Fel Inst Engrs; fel Inst Elec & Telecommun Engrs; fel Inst Elec & ElectronicsEngrs. **Research Statement & Publications:** Research and technology planning in radar and navigational aids; research in electromagnetic compatibility; author of two books on electromagnetic compatability. **Mailing Address:** Govt India Dept Elec Electronics Niketan, 6 CGO Complex Lodi Rd, New Delhi 110 003, India. **Fax:** 911-143-63079. **E-Mail:** kodalivp@xm.doe.ernet.in

KODAMA, ARTHUR MASAYOSHI, INDUSTRIAL HYGIENE. **Personal Data:** b Honolulu, Hawaii, December 17, 1931; m 1959, Laura; c Sharon & Richard. **Education:** Wash Univ, BA, 1954; Univ Calif, Berkeley, PhD (physiol), 1963, MPH, 1978. **Professional Experience:** PROF, ENVIRON & OCCUP HEALTH PROG, PUB HEALTH SCI DEPT, SCH PUB HEALTH, UNIV HAWAII, 1990-; from asst prof to assoc prof, Environ & Occup Health Prog, Pub Health Sci Dept, Sch Pub Health, Univ Hawaii, 1978-1989; res physiologist, Univ Calif, Berkeley, 1963-1977. **Memberships:** AAAS; Am Physiol Soc; Am Pub Health Asn; Am Indust Hyg Asn. **Research Statement & Publications:** Environmental physiology; environmental toxicology; occupational health and safety. **Mailing Address:** Dept Pub Health Sci Sch Pub Health, Univ Hawaii 1960 E-W Rd, Honolulu, HI 96822. **Fax:** 808-956-4585. **E-Mail:** akodama@uhunix.uhcc.hawaii.edu

KODAMA, GOJI, BORON HYDRIDE CHEMISTRY, METALLABORANE CHEMISTRY. **Personal Data:** b Sakai City, Japan, December 2, 1927; m 1957, c 2. **Education:** Tokyo Inst Technol, BE, 1951; Univ Mich, Ann Arbor, MS, 1952, PhD (chem), 1958. **Professional Experience:** RETIRED; res prof chem, Univ Utah, 1980-1996; assoc res prof, Univ Utah, 1969-1980; prof chem, Univ Utah, 1969-1996; from asst prof to prof, Tokyo Sci Univ, 1961-1969; res fel, Harvard Univ, 1960-1961; from res assoc to instr chem, Univ Mich, 1958-1960. **Memberships:** Am Chem Soc. **Research Statement & Publications:** Reactions of boron hydrides with various bases; transition metal-boron hydride complexes. **Mailing Address:** 1386 Laird Ave, Salt Lake City, UT 84105.

KODAMA, HIDEOMI, CRYSTAL CHEMISTRY, STRUCTURAL CHEMISTRY. **Personal Data:** b Tokyo, Japan, October 9, 1931; Canadian citizen; m 1959, Tomoko Maekawa; c Sakie F, Tohru M & Jun M. **Education:** Tokyo Univ Educ, BSc, 1956, MSc, 1958, DSc(mineral), 1961. **Professional Experience:** HON RES ASSOC, CTR LAND& BIOL RESOURCES RES, AGR CAN, 1997-; sr res scientist & study leader, Land ResourceRes Ctr, 1991-1997; consult ed, Soil Sci, 1990-1996; assoc ed, Clay Minerals Soc, 1986-1992; res scientist & proj leader, Land Resource Res Ctr, 1986-1990; vis res fel, Japan Soc Prom Sci, 1984; assoc ed, Mineral Asn Can, 1983-1986; sr res scientist, Chem & Biol Res Inst & head, Mineral Anal Serv, 1978-1986; Vis scientist, Nat Ctr Sci Res, Orleans, France, 1969-1970; resscientist, Soil Res Inst, Can Dept Agr, Agr Can, 1964-1977; Nat Res Coun Can fel, 1962-1964; Japan Soc Promoting Sci fel & lectr, Int Christian Univ, Tokyo, 1961-1962; vis prof, Grad Sch Sci & Eng Kanazawa. **Memberships:** Mineral Soc Am; Clay Minerals Soc; fel Can Soc Soil Sci; Int Asn Study Clay(treas 1978-1985); Mineral Soc Japan; Mineral Soc UK; fel Am Soc Soil Sci; Clay Sci Soc Japan. **Research Statement & Publications:** Structure and genesis of interstratified clay minerals; fine structure analysis of layer silicates; crystal chemistry of silicate minerals; interactions between clay minerals and soil organic matter; intercalations of clay materials; characterization of non-crystalline inorganic soil components; non-crystalline inorganic soil components. **Mailing Address:** 1251 Southwood Dr, Ottawa, ON K2C 3C4, Can. **Fax:** 613-759-1926. **E-Mail:** kodama@ncccot.agr.ca

KODAMA, JIRO KENNETH, PHARMACOLOGY, TOXICOLOGY. **Personal Data:** b Reedley, Calif, March 4, 1951; m 1951, c 5. **Education:** Univ Calif, AB, 1951, MS, 1955, PhD (pharmacol), 1957. **Professional Experience:** TECH LIAISON REP, CHEVRON CORP, CALIF, 1981-; staff toxicologist, Chevron Corp, Calif, 1977-1980; staff toxicologist, Agr Div, Shell Chem Co, 1970-1977; vis Shell scientist, Tunstall Lab, Shell Res Ltd, Eng, 1969-1970; supvr pharmacol dept, ShellDevelop Co, 1966-1968; pharmacologist, Shell Develop Co, 1963-1966; from asst dept chieftoxicol & pharmacol to sr pharmacologist, Hazleton Labs, Inc, 1959-1963; instr pharmacol, MedSch & toxicol, Sch Pub Health, Univ Calif, 1957-1959. **Memberships:** AAAS; Am Soc Pharmacol & Exp Therapeut; Soc Toxicol. **Research Statement & Publications:** Drug research and development; pharmacotoxic characterization of chemical warfare agents; mechanisms of toxic actions of organophosphorus chemicals and cytotoxic alkylating agents; toxicology and safety evaluation of industrial and agricultural chemicals; preclinical evaluation of pharmaceuticals; forensic toxicology; technical management. **Mailing Address:** 3 Corwin Dr, Alamo, CA 94507-2103.

KODAMA, KENNETH PHILIP, PALEOMAGNETISM, ROCK MAGNETISM. **Personal Data:** b New Brunsuick, NJ, July 31, 1951; m 1980, Anna; c Emily, Alice & Peterson. **Education:** Univ Pa, BA, 1973; Stanford Univ, MS & PhD (geophysics), 1977. **Honors & Awards:** fel Geological Soc of Am, 1996. **Professional Experience:** CHMN DEPT, LEHIGH UNIV, 1991-; assoc ed, J Geophys Res, Am Geophys Union, 1990-1993; PROF EARTH & ENVIRON SCI, LEHIGH UNIV, 1988-; from asst prof to assoc prof geol, Lehigh Univ, 1978-1988; secy, Geomagnatism & Paleomagnatism Sect. **Memberships:** Am Geophys Union; Geol Soc Am; Sigma Xi. **Research Statement & Publications:** Effects of rock or sediment deformation on the accuracy of the paleomagnetic; direction & intensity, Mineral magnetic records of environ change in recent lake sediments. **Mailing Address:** Lehigh Univ Dept of Earth & Env. Sci, 31 Williams Drive, Bethelem, PA 18015-3188.

KODAMA, ROBERT MAKOTO, CELL PHYSIOLOGY. **Personal Data:** b Kauai, Hawaii, May 30, 1932; m 1964, c 2. **Education:** Univ Hawaii, BA, 1955; Univ Ill, PhD (physiol), 1967. **Professional Experience:** PROF EMER BIOL, DRAKE UNIV, as of 2003; prof biol, Drake Univ, beginning 1976; from asst prof to assoc prof, Drake Univ, 1967-1976; physiol, Med Ctr, Univ Ill, 1966-1967; asst cell physiol, Med Ctr, Univ Ill, 1960-1962; med technologist, Mt Sinai Hosp, Chicago, Ill, 1959; Phys sci aide, US Fish &Wildlife Serv, 1955-1956. **Memberships:** Sigma Xi. **Research Statement & Publications:** Biological transport; endocrinology; electron microscopy. **Mailing Address:** Dept Biol, Drake Univ, Des Moines, IA 50310-4231.

KODAVANTI, PRASADA RAO S, TOXICOLOGY, NEUROSCIENCES. **Personal Data:** b Dharmavaram, AP, India, August 1, 1954; American citizen; m 1987, Urmila; c Preeti & Pooja. **Education:** Andhra Univ, India, BS, 1974, MS, 1976; SV Univ, India, PhD (toxicol), 1981. **Honors & Awards:** US EPA's Sci & Technol Achievement Award, 1996 & 1999. **Professional Experience:** TOXICOLOGIST, NEUROTOXICOL, NAT HEALTH EFFECTS RES LAB, US ENVIRON PROTECTION AGENCY, NC, 1991-; res asst prof, Dept Neurol, 1989-1991; res assoc, Dept Pharmacol & Toxicol, 1984-1989; fel, Dept Neurol, Univ Miss Med Ctr, Jackson, 1983-1984; scientist off, Dept Zoology, SV Univ PG Ctr, India, 1982-1983. **Memberships:** Sigma Xi; Soc Toxicol; Soc Toxicol. **Research Statement & Publications:** Neuro, hepato and pulmonary toxicity by chemicals and drugs. **Mailing Address:** Neurotox Div, Nat Health & Environ Effects Res Lab, US EPA Mail Drop 74B, Durham, NC 27711-0001. **Fax:** 919-541-4849. **E-Mail:** kodavanti.prasada@epa.gov

KODAVANTI, URMILA P, MOLECULAR BIOLOGY OF LUNG DISEASES, ENVIRONMENTAL AIR POLLUTANTS & LUNG TOXICITY. **Personal Data:** b Malpara, Gujarat, India, January 26, 1956; m Prasada Rao; c Preeti & Pooja. **Education:** Saurashtra Univ, India, BSc, 1977; MS Univ Baroda, India, MSci, 1979, PhD (toxicol), 1983. **Professional Experience:** RES BIOLOGIST, US ENVIRON PROTECTION AGENCY, 2002-; res biologist, US Environ Protection Agency, 1995-2002; res fel toxicol, Univ NC, 1992-1994; res fel, Univ Miss Med Ctr, 1985-1991; res fel, dept pharmacol & toxicol, Mich State Univ, 1984-1985; lectr, dept foods & nutrit, 1983-1984; teaching asst, dept zool, Miss Univ Baroda, India, 1982-1983. **Research Statement & Publications:** Cell and molecular biology of cardiopulmonary diseases. **Mailing Address:** MD 82 Health Effects Res Lab, US Environ Protection Agency, Research Triangle Park, NC 27711. **Fax:** 919-541-0026. **E-Mail:** kodavanti.urmila@epa.gov

KODIRA, UMESH CHENGAPPA, NEMATOLOGY. **Personal Data:** m 1988, Kaveramma; c Chengappa U. **Education:** Univ Agr Sci, India, BSc, 1984, MSc, 1986; Univ Calif, Davis, PhD (plant path), 1993. **Professional Experience:** PROG SUPVR, NURSERY SEED & COTTON PROG, UNIV CALIF, as of 2004; RESEARCHER, UNIV CALIF, DAVIS, 1993-; res asst, Univ Calif, Davis, 1988-1993; res assoc, Int Crops Res Inst Semi-Arid Tropics, 1987-1988; Jrmerit teaching fel plant path, Univ Agr Sci India, 1987. **Memberships:** Am Phytopath Soc; Soc Nematal. **Research Statement & Publications:** Interactions between plant parasitic nematodes, population biology and nematode management; epidemiology of viruses affecting melons in California; developing DNA-based detection methods for pathogenic bacteria on carrots and lettuce. **Mailing Address:** Dept Food & Agr, State Calif, 1220 N St Rm A-372, Sacramento, CA 95814. **Fax:** 916-654-0986. **E-Mail:** ukodira@cdfa.ca.gov

KODRICH, WILLIAM RALPH, ECOLOGY. **Personal Data:** b Cooperstown, NY, August 26, 1933; m 1960. **Education:** Hartwick Col, BA, 1955; Univ Pittsburgh, PhD (biol), 1967. **Professional Experience:** PROF BIOL, CLARION STATE COL, 1974-; assoc prof, Clarion State Col, 1967-1974. **Memberships:** Ecol Soc Am; Am Soc Mammalogists. **Research Statement & Publications:** Physiological rates of small mammals living freely in their natural environments; relative thyroid release rates of 131-I of mammals living at different altitudes; bioenergetics of mammals in natural environments. **Mailing Address:** Dept Biol, Clarion Univ Pa, Clarion, PA 16214.

KOE, B KENNETH, NEUROCHEMISTRY. **Personal Data:** b Astoria, Ore, April 15, 1925; wid. **Education:** Reed Col, BA, 1945; Univ Wash, MS, 1948; Calif Inst Technol, PhD (chem), 1952. **Professional Experience:** RETIRED; res adv, Pfizer Inc, 1979-1995; sr res investr, Pfizer Inc, 1974-1979; res chemist, Pfizer Inc, 1955-1974; assoc org chemist, Southwest Res Inst, 1954-1955; res fel chem, Calif Inst Technol, 1952-1954. **Memberships:** Am Soc Pharmacol & Exp Therapeut; Soc Neuroscience; Am Col Neuropsychopharmacol. **Research Statement & Publications:** Discovery of new psychotherapeutic drugs antidepressants, antipsychotics, anxiolytics; psychopharmacology; neurotransmitters; receptor binding. **Mailing Address:** 41 Woodridge Circle, Gales Ferry, CT 06335-1137.

KOEDERITZ, LEONARD FREDERICK, RESERVOIR SIMULATION & EVALUATION, TRANSIENT PRESSURE ANALYSIS. **Personal Data:** b St Louis, Mo, August 21, 1946; m 1968, Cheryl; c 3. **Education:** Univ Mo, BS, 1968, MS, 1969, PhD (petrol eng), 1970. **Professional Experience:** DISTINGUISHED TEACHING PROF EMER, UNIV MO-ROLLA, as of 2005; distinguished teaching prof, Univ Mo-Rolla, 1992-2002; head petrol eng dept, Univ Mo, Rolla, 1989-1994; dept chmn, Univ Mo, Rolla, 1980-1981; from assoc prof to prof petrol eng, Univ Mo-Rolla, 1975-1992; proj leader, Atlantic Richfield Prod Res Lab, 1974-1975; sr engr, Atlantic Richfield Co, 1970-1974. **Memberships:** Soc Petrol Engrs. **Research Statement & Publications:** Reservoir simulation; transient pressure analysis; advanced reservoir applications in petroleum engineering; reservoir valuation. **Mailing Address:** Univ Mo-Rollo 1870 Miner Circle, 129 McNutt Hall, Rolla, MO 65409-0420. **Fax:** 573-341-6935. **E-Mail:** koe@umvvmb.umr.edu

KOEGLE, JOHN S(TUART), CHEMICAL ENGINEERING. **Personal Data:** b Rochester, Pa, January 8, 1926; m 1950, c 5. **Education:** Purdue Univ, BChE, 1948; Kans State Col, MS, 1949; Ohio State Univ, PhD (chem eng), 1951. **Professional Experience:** SR PROCESS ENG & PROJ MGR, PEDCO, 1980-; dir process eng, Velsicol, 1977-1980; sr process eng, Pedco, 1974-1977; dir eng, Technol, Res & Develop, Inc, 1971-1974; dir develop marine colloids, Maine, 1970-1971; dir eng marine colloids, Monsanto Co, 1968-1970; pilot plant dir marine colloids, Monsanto Co, 1963-1968; res group leader, Monsanto Co, 1961-1963; res design engr, Monsanto Co, 1956-1961; Res chem engr, Monsanto Co, 1951-1956. **Memberships:** Am Chem Soc; Am Inst Chem Engrs. **Research Statement & Publications:** Plant design, process and product development. **Mailing Address:** 9302 Gregg Dr, West Chester, OH 45069.

KOEHL, WILLIAM JOHN, JR, FUEL SCIENCE, AIR POLLUTION. **Personal Data:** b Newport, Ky, July 27, 1935. **Education:** Xavier Univ, Ohio, BS, 1955, MS, 1957; Univ Ill, PhD (org chem), 1960. **Professional Experience:** RETIRED; res scientist, Mobil Res & Develop Corp, 1992-1996; scientist, Mobil Res & Develop Corp, beginning in 1988; sr res assoc, Prod Res & Technol Serv Di, 1983-1988; supv chemist, Mobil Res & Develop Corp, 1976-1983; sr res chemist, Mobil Res & Develop Corp, 1968-1976; Sr res chemist, Cent Res Div Lab, Socony Mobil Oil Co Inc, NJ, 1960-1968. **Memberships:** Am Chem Soc; Soc Automotive Engrs; Air & Waste Mgt Asn. **Research Statement & Publications:** Automotive fuels and exhaust emissions. **Mailing Address:** 6 Mimosa Lane, Woodstown, NJ 08098.

KOEHLER, ANDREAS MARTIN, MEDICAL PHYSICS, ACCELERATOR PHYSICS. **Personal Data:** b Weimar, Ger, January 21, 1930; American citizen; m 1952, c 3. **Education:** Harvard Univ, BS, 1950. **Professional Experience:** DIR ACCELERATOR MED PHYSICS, CYCLOTRON LAB, HARVARD UNIV, 1977-; asst dir, Cyclotron Lab, Harvard Univ, 1961-1977; tech assoc accelerator physics, Cyclotron Lab, Harvard Univ, 1953-1961; proj engr mech design, Hesse-Eastern Corp, 1951-1953. **Research Statement & Publications:** Radiation therapy using beams of charged particles; radiation physics and dosimetry of protons; radiography using protons and alpha particles; proton activation analysis; accelerator designs for medical applications. **Mailing Address:** Cyclotrons, Harvard Univ, 306 Beacon St, Somerville, MA 02143.

KOEHLER, ANNE B, MATHEMATICS. **Education:** IND UNIV, PhD (math), 1968. **Professional Experience:** PROF, DEPT SCI & GEORGE & MILDRED PANUSKA, MIAMI UNIV, as of 2006. **Mailing Address:** Miami Univ, Dept Sci, Oxford, OH 45056. **Fax:** 513-529-9689. **E-Mail:** koehleab@muohio.edu

KOEHLER, DALE ROLAND, RADIATION EFFECTS ON QUARTZ. **Personal Data:** b Milwaukee, Wis, October 13, 1932; m 1955, c 4. **Education:** Auburn Univ, BS, 1954, MS, 1955; Univ Ala, PhD (physics), 1964. **Professional Experience:** RETIRED; physicist, Sandia Labs, 1977-1997; mgr, Advan Res Lab, BulovaWatch Co, 1967-1977; chief, Radiation Physics Br, 1964-1967; physicist, Phys Sci Lab, ArmyMissile Command, 1958-1964; Physicist, Signal Eng Labs, NJ, 1955 & Army BallisticMissileAgency, Ala, 1957-1958. **Research Statement & Publications:** Ionizing radiation effects on quartz crystal resonators, primarily on frequency and acoustic loss changes; development of quartz purification and radiation hardness assurance technologies; quartz transducer development. **Mailing Address:** 1516 La Charles NE, Albuquerque, NM 87112.

KOEHLER, DON EDWARD, PLANT PHYSIOLOGY. **Personal Data:** b Urbana, Ill, May 10, 1942. **Education:** Univ Ill, BS, 1964; Purdue Univ, MS, 1967; Mich State Univ, PhD (biochem), 1972. **Professional Experience:** PLANT PHYSIOLOGIST, DEPT PESTICIDE REGULATION, CALIF ENVIRON PROTECTION AGENCY, 1982-; asst prof plant sci, Tex A&M Univ, 1977-1982; fel plant physiol, Univ Calif, Riverside, 1974-1977; Fel develop biol, Univ Chicago, 1972-1974. **Memberships:** Am Soc Plant Physiologists; AAAS; Western Soc Weed Sci; Western PlantGrowth Regulator Soc. **Research Statement & Publications:** Hormonal control of enzyme induction and developmental processes in plants. **Mailing Address:** Dept Pesticide Regulation, Calif Environ Protection Agency 1020 N St Rm 332, Sacramento, CA 95814. **E-Mail:** dkoehler@cdpr.ca.gov

KOEHLER, FRED EUGENE, SOIL FERTILITY. **Personal Data:** b Naylor, Mo, January 25, 1923; m 1947, Helen; c Carolyn, Mary Ruth (Schaumberg), Jane E & Kristin. **Education:** Univ Mo, BS, 1943, MS, 1950, PhD (soils), 1951. **Professional Experience:** RETIRED; prof emer soils, Wash State Univ, beginning 1988; prof Soils, Wash State Univ, beginning 1988; soil scientist & prof, Wash State Univ, 1966-1988; assoc soil scientist, Wash State Univ, 1958-1966; soil scientist & asst agronomist, Univ Nebr, 1951-1957. **Memberships:** Am Soc Agron; Soil Sci Soc Am; Sigma Xi. **Research Statement & Publications:** Soil fertility and soil chemistry. **Mailing Address:** 1140 S E Spring St, Pullman, WA 99163.

KOEHLER, JAMES K, CELL BIOLOGY. **Personal Data:** b Darmstadt, Ger, June 7, 1933; American citizen; m 1994, Alberta; c 5. **Education:** Univ Ill, BS, 1955; Univ Calif, Berkeley, MS, 1958, PhD (biophys), 1961. **Professional Experience:** PROF EMER BIOL STRUCT, UNIV WASH, as of 2005; mem exec coun, Electron Micros Soc Am, 1991-1993; prof biol struct, Univ Wash, beginning 1975; vis lectr, Dept Anat, Univ Malaya, 1971-1972; from asst prof to assoc prof, Univ Wash, 1963-1975; asst prof physics, NMex Highlands Univ, 1962-1963; NIH fel, Swiss Fed Inst Technol, 1961-1962. **Memberships:** Electron Micros Soc Am; Am Asn Anat; Am Soc Cell Biologists; Am Soc Study Reproduction. **Research Statement & Publications:** Fine structure of cells and tissues; cryobiology; gamete biology. **Mailing Address:** Dept Biol Struct, Univ Wash, Seattle, WA 98195. **Fax:** 206-543-1524. **E-Mail:** jkoehler@u.washington.edu

KOEHLER, JAMES STARK, PHYSICS. **Personal Data:** b Oshkosh, Wis, November 10, 1914; m 1940, c 2. **Education:** Wis State Teachers Col, BEd, 1935; Univ Mich, PhD, 1940. **Honors & Awards:** Fellow, American Physical Society, 1957. **Professional Experience:** PROF EMER, UNIV ILL, URBANA, as of 2004; Guggenheim fel, 1957; prof phys, Univ Ill, Urbana, beginning 1953; assoc prof, Univ Ill, Urbana, 1950-1953; assocprof, Carnegie Inst Technol, 1946-1950; instr physics, Carnegie Inst Technol, 1942-1946; Rackham fel, Westinghouse res fel, 1941-1942; Rackham fel, Univ Mich, 1940-1941; mem solid state adv comt, Oak Ridge Nat Lab. **Memberships:** Fel Am Phys Soc. **Research Statement & Publications:** Effects of internal rotation on molecular spectra; plastic deformation of solids; radiation damage; point defects produced by quenching, irradiation and ion bombardment. **Mailing Address:** 101 W Winsdor Rd, Urbana, IL 61801.

KOEHLER, KATHLEEN M, BIOLOGY. **Education:** Seton Hall Univ, BS, 1967; Univ Ill-Urbana, MS, 1972, PhD, 1976; Harvard Sch Pub health, MPH, 1998. **Professional Experience:** SCI POLICY ANALYST, OFF ASST SECY PLANNING & EVAL, DEPT HEALTH & HUMAN SERV, WASH, DC, 2005-. **Mailing Address:** Dept Health & Human Serv, Washington, DC 20001. **Fax:** 202-260-0794.

KOEHLER, KENNETH JOSEPH, APPLICATIONS OF SURVIVAL ANALYSIS & STATISTICAL MODELING IN ECOLOGY & HUMAN HEALTH RESEARCH. **Personal Data:** b USA, July 25, 1950; m 1978, Susan; c Kristine, John, Robert & Sarah. **Education:** Univ Wis, BS, 1972; Univ Minn, PhD (statist), 1977. **Professional Experience:** CHMN, DEPT STATIST, IOWA STATE UNIV, 2003-; PROF STATIST, IOWA STATE UNIV, 1977-. **Memberships:** Fel Am Statist Asn; Royal Statist Soc; Biomet Soc; Inst Math Statist. **Research Statement & Publications:** Development of statistical methods and models for the analysis of data from studies of ecology, the environment, and human and animal health and nutrition. **Mailing Address:** Iowa State Univ, 102 Snedecor Hall, Ames, IA 50011-1210. **Fax:** 515-294-4040. **E-Mail:** kkoehler@iastate.edu

KOEHLER, LAWRENCE D, DEVELOPMENTAL BIOLOGY, CELL BIOLOGY. **Personal Data:** b Grand Rapids, Mich, February 19, 1932; m 1960, Evelyn; c Daniel L, David L & Deborah L (Conner). **Education:** Otterbein Col, BS, 1954; Mich State Univ, PhD (zoology), 1960. **Professional Experience:** Vis researcher, Univ Queensland, Brisbane, Australia, 1992; vis scientist, Statzione Zoologica, Napoli, Italy, 1985; chmn dept, Cent Mich Univ, 1975-1993; PROF BIOL, CENT MICH UNIV, 1968-; NIH spec res fel, Inst Molecular Evolution, Univ Miami, 1968-1969; from asst prof to assoc prof, Cent Mich Univ, 1960-1968. **Memberships:** Soc Develop Biol; Am Soc Cell Biologists; Int Soc Develop Biol. **Research Statement & Publications:** Gametogenesis and fertilization, including ultrastructural changes in gametes and early zygotes. **Mailing Address:** Dept Biol, Cent Mich Univ, 217 Brooks Hall, Mt Pleasant, MI 48859. **Fax:** 989-774-3462. **E-Mail:** l.koehler@cmich.edu

KOEHLER, MARK E, INSTRUMENTATION. **Personal Data:** b Dayton, Ohio, July 6, 1949; m 1970, c 1. **Education:** Univ Dayton, BS, 1971; Wright State Univ, MS, 1973; Case Western Res Univ, PhD (chem), 1978. **Professional Experience:** ASST DIR, MAURICE MORTON INST POLYMER SCI, UNIV AKRON, as of 2004; Sect leader, Glidden Coatings & Resins, Div SCM Corp, 1980-1983; GROUPLEADER, GLIDDEN CO-ICI, 1977-; Chemist, Glidden Coatings & Resins, Div SCM Corp, 1977-1980. **Memberships:** Am Chem Soc. **Research Statement & Publications:** Development and computer interfacing of laboratory instrumentation; areas of computer applications in chemistry; scientific computing and analog and digital electronics. **Mailing Address:** Maurice Morton Inst Polymer Sci, Univ Akron, Akron, OH 44325-3909. **Fax:** 330-972-5290. **E-Mail:** koehler@uakron.edu

KOEHLER, P RUBEN, RADIOLOGY. **Personal Data:** b Berlin, Ger, April 29, 1931; American citizen; c 2. **Education:** Univ Bern, MD, 1956. **Professional Experience:** DOCTOR MED, UNIV BERNE, SWITZ, as of 2004; ADJ PROF RADIOL, COL MED, UNIV UTAH, beginning 2000; med dir, dept radiol, mercy hosp, 1994-1999; chief, Div Diag Radiol, 1980-1983; prof radiol, Col Med, Univ Utah, 1970-1983; from asst prof to prof, Sch Med, Wash Univ, 1964-1970; instr, Sch Med, Temple Univ, 1962-1964; assoc radiol, Albert Einstein Med Ctr, Philadelphia, Pa, 1961-1962. **Memberships:** Am Col Radiol; Am Roentgen Ray Soc; Radiol Soc NAm; Asn UnivRadiologists; Int Soc Lymphology. **Research Statement & Publications:** Lymphology; visceral arteriography. **Mailing Address:** Univ Utah, 2413 13th Ct N, Arlington, VA 22201. **E-Mail:** rkoehler@hsc.utah.edu

KOEHLER, PETER F M, PHYSICS. **Education:** Univ Rochester, PhD, 1967. **Professional Experience:** PROF, DEPT PHYSICS ASTRON, UNIV PITTSBURG, as of 2005. **Mailing Address:** Univ Pittsburgh, 200D Allen Hall, Pittsburgh, PA 15260. **Fax:** 412-624-9163. **E-Mail:** koehler+@pitt.edu

KOEHLER, PHILIP EDWARD, FOOD SCIENCE. **Personal Data:** b Kansas City, Mo, March 30, 1943; m 1966, Linda; c Brian & Warren. **Education:** Emporia Kans State Col, BS, 1965; Okla State Univ, PhD (biochem), 1969. **Professional Experience:** Prof food sci, Univ Ga, 1980-2005; from asst prof to assoc prof, 1969-1980. **Memberships:** Am Chem Soc; Inst Food Technologists; Sigma Xi. **Research Statement & Publications:** Food safety and toxicology; food colorants; flavor chemistry. **Mailing Address:** Dept Food Sci, Univ Ga, Athens, GA 30601. **Fax:** 706-542-1050. **E-Mail:** pkoehler@uga.cc.uga.edu

KOEHLER, PHILIP GENE, URBAN ENTOMOLOGY, HOUSEHOLD INSECTS. **Personal Data:** b Doylestown, Pa, July 21, 1947; m 1974. **Education:** Catawba Col, AB, 1969; Cornell Univ, PhD (entom), 1972. **Honors & Awards:** Award for Technol Transfer, Fed Lab Consortium, 1989; DistinguishedAchievement Award in Exten, Entom Soc Am, 1993. **Professional Experience:** PROF ENTOM, UNIV FLA, 1984-; from asst prof to assoc prof exten entom, Univ Fla, 1975-1984; proj leader, USDA Household Insect Res Proj. **Memberships:** Entom Soc Am; Sigma Xi. **Research Statement & Publications:** Cockroach and flea research; household and structural pest management. **Mailing Address:** Dept Entomol & Nematol Univ Fla, Bldg 970 PO Box 110620, Gainesville, FL 32611. **Fax:** 352-846-1500. **E-Mail:** pgk@ifas.ufl.edu

KOEHLER, RAYMOND CHARLES, BRAIN BLOOD FLOW. **Education:** State Univ NY, Buffalo, PhD (physiol), 1978. **Professional Experience:** PROF PHYSIOL, JOHNS HOPKINS HOSP, as of 2005; asst prof anesthesiol, Johns hopkins hosp, 1980-. **Mailing Address:** Dept Environ Health Scis, Johns Hopkins Hosp, Blalock 1404, Baltimore, MD 21205-2179. **Fax:** 410-955-7165. **E-Mail:** rkoehler@welchlink.welch.jhu.edu

KOEHLER, RICHARD FREDERICK, JR, PHYSICS, ELECTRICAL ENGINEERING. **Personal Data:** b New York, NY, March 27, 1945; m 1969, c 2. **Education:** Mass Inst Technol, BS, 1967; Stanford Univ, MS, 1968, PhD (elec eng), 1972. **Professional Experience:** AREA MGR, XEROX CORP, 1980-; sr scientist, Xerox Corp, 1978-1980; scientist, Xerox Corp, 1975-1978; Assoc scientist, Xerox Corp, 1972-1975. **Memberships:** Soc Photog Scientists & Engrs. **Research Statement & Publications:** Physics and materials of the xerographic system. **Mailing Address:** 15 Woodrose Dr, Webster, NY 14580.

KOEHLER, THOMAS RICHARD, PHYSICS. **Personal Data:** b Toledo, Ohio, August 8, 1932; m 1961. **Education:** Seattle Univ, BS, 1954; Calif Inst Technol, PhD (physics), 1960. **Professional Experience:** IBM EMER, IBM CORP, as of 1999; staff physicist, San Jose Res Lab, IBM Corp, beginning 1960; Physicist, Aeronutronic Div, Ford Motor Co, 1959-1960. **Memberships:** Am Phys Soc. **Research Statement & Publications:** Theoretical solid state and low temperature physics. **Mailing Address:** IBM Corp, 1133 Westchester Ave, White Plains, NY 10604.

KOEHLER, TRUMAN L, STATISTICS. **Personal Data:** b Allentown, Pa, April 9, 1931; m 1954, c 3. **Education:** Muhlenberg Col, BS, 1952; Rutgers Univ, MS, 1957. **Professional Experience:** CHIEF EXEC OFFICER, MASTER BUILDERS INC, as of 2004; dir, Master Builders Inc, beginning 1996; group vpres chem, Sandoz Corp, 1987-1996; pres & chief exec officer, Sandoz Corp, 1984-1987; exec vpres & chief oper officer, SodyecoDiv, Martin Marietta Chem, 1981-1984; gen mgr, Spec Prods Dept, 1979-1980; dir planning, Pigments Div, 1977-1979; mgr titanium dioxide dept, Pigments Div, 1970-1977; dir mkt, Pigments Div, 1968-1970; mfg mgr, Org Pigments Dept, 1966-1968; partic, NSF TV Prog, Pursuit Perfection, beginning 1965; mgr systs anal, Org Chem Div, 1962-1966; lectr, Rutgers Univ, beginning 1957; head qual control sect, Org Chem Div, 1957-1962; statistician, Am Cyanamid Co, 1957; engr qual control, Sylvania Elec Prod Inc, 1952-1957. **Memberships:** fel Am Soc Qual Control; Am Statist Asn; Am Inst Chem Engrs; Nat Asn Mfrs; Chem Mfrs Asn. **Research Statement & Publications:** Design and analysis of experimental programs; numerical analysis and computing. **Mailing Address:** Master Builders Inc, 5222 Winding Brook Rd, Charlotte, NC 28226.

KOEHLER, WILLIAM HENRY, INORGANIC CHEMISTRY. **Personal Data:** b Houston, Tex, February 17, 1939. **Education:** Southern Methodist Univ, BS, 1960, MS, 1962; Univ Tex, Austin, PhD (chem), 1969. **Professional Experience:** RETIRED; vice chancellor acad affairs, Tex Christian Univ, 1980-2004; actg dean grad sch, Tex Christian Univ, beginning 1978; assoc prof chem, Tex Christian Univ, beginning 1974; asst prof, Tex Christian Univ, 1969-1974; res scientist, Tracor, Inc, Tex, 1968-1969; instr chem, Southern Methodist Univ, 1961-1963; vpres, Tex Christian Univ Res Found. **Memberships:** Nat Coun Univ Res Adminr; Am Chem Soc. **Research Statement & Publications:** Raman spectroscopy; reflection and transmission spectroscopy; characterization of metal-ammonia solutions; synthesis and reaction mechanisms in nonaqueous solvents. **Mailing Address:** Tex Christian Univ, 2800 S Univ Dr, Ft Worth, TX 76129.

KOEHMSTEDT, PAUL LEON, INJECTION ELECTRICAL GROUNDING, CHEMICAL AGENT DECONTAMINATION. **Personal Data:** b Seattle, Wash, September 21, 1923; m 1956, c 3. **Education:** Ore State Univ, BS, 1949, MS, 1951. **Professional Experience:** RETIRED; res scientist mat, Battelle Pac Northwest Labs, 1967-1993; res engrmat, Boeing Airplane Co, 1953-1967; chemist, Gen Elec Co, 1950-1953. **Memberships:** Am Chem Soc; Nat Asn Corrosion Engrs. **Research Statement & Publications:** Innovative applications towards solving material and methods problems involving chemical processes, corrosion, chemical and radiochemical decontamination, preparation and testing. **Mailing Address:** 24410 Mt Wash View Lane NW, Poulsbo, WA 98370.

KOEHN, ENNO, PROJECT MANAGEMENT SYSTEMS, OPTIMAL PRODUCTIVITY & COST FACTORS. **Personal Data:** b Flushing, NY, April 29, 1936; m 1967, Carol; c William & James. **Education:** City Univ NY, BCE, 1958; Columbia Univ, MS, 1960; NY Univ,

MCE, 1965; Wayne State Univ, PhD (civil eng), 1975. **Honors & Awards:** Pres citation, Am Soc Civil Engrs, 1983 Certificate of appreciation Award, Am Soc Civil Engrs, 1987, 1996; Res Award, Undergrad Res Org (URO), 1998, 1999. **Professional Experience:** CHAIR, DEPT CIVIL ENG, LAMAR UNIV, 1984-; Prin investr, US Army Construct Eng Res Lab, 1983-1988; chmn, Social & Environ Concerns Comt, Am Soc Civil Engrs, 1979-1987; assoc prof, Purdue Univ, 1979-1984; sr civil engr, Bechtel Corp, 1978-1981; NASA-Am Soc Eng Educ & Stanford Univ Inst, 1977; Pa State Univ, Dept Energy Sem, 1976; fel, Univ Mich/NSF Construct Res Sem, 1972 & 1982; fel, Mass Inst Technol, 1972; prin investr, NSF grants, 1970-1972; from assoc prof to prof civil eng, Ohio Northern Univ, 1967-1979; educ specialist continuing educ, IBM, 1966-1967; prin investr, Stanford Univ/NSF grants, 1964-1966; asst prof eng, Long Island Univ, 1960-1966; res engr struct eng, NAm Rockwell, 1958-1959. **Memberships:** Fel Am Soc Civil Engrs; Sigma Xi; Am Asn Cost Engrs; Nat Soc Prof Engrs; Am Soc Eng Educ. **Research Statement & Publications:** International productivity in design and constructionsystems; probabilistic and pre-design cost estimating; optimal productivity and project management systems; weather related productivity factors in construction; national infrastructure/rehabilitation costs; engineering education, ethics and professionalism. **Mailing Address:** Civil Eng Dept, Lamar Univ PO Box 10024, Beaumont, TX 77710. **Fax:** 409-880-8121. **E-Mail:** koehneu@hal.lamar.edu

KOEHN, PAUL V, BIOCHEMISTRY. **Personal Data:** b Bristol, Conn, January 10, 1931; m 1963, c 3. **Education:** Bates Col, BS, 1952; Cent Mo State Col, MSEd, 1958; Univ Conn, PhD (biochem), 1964. **Professional Experience:** Fac grants, State Univ NY, 1974 & 1977; fac res grant, State Univ NY, Oneonta, 1971; chmn dept, State Univ NY, Oneonta, 1970-1982; PROF BIOCHEM, STATEUNIV NY, ONEONTA, 1969-; head dept, State Univ NY, Oneonta, 1969-1970; NY state res found grant, 1968-1970; assoc prof biochem, State Univ NY, Oneonta, 1967-1970; instrbiochem, Univ Conn, 1963-1964; instr gen chem, Cent Mo State Col, 1956-1958; jr chemist, Am Cyanamid Co, 1952-1955. **Memberships:** Am Chem Soc; Sigma Xi; NY Acad Sci. **Research Statement & Publications:** Synthesis of phosphopeptides and structural studies of proteins. **Mailing Address:** Dept Chem, State Univ NY, Oneonta, NY 13820.

KOEHN, RICHARD KARL, POPULATION GENETICS, RESEARCH MANAGEMENT AND BIOTECHNOLOGY. **Personal Data:** b Niles, Mich, August 25, 1940; m 1983, Sheryl A Scott; c Rachel, Christopher & Kathryn. **Education:** Western Mich Univ, BA, 1963; Ariz State Univ, PhD (genetics), 1967. **Honors & Awards:** Dist Alum, clas, Ariz st univ, 2001; Gold Aurora, producer, Learning through discovery, KUED-TV; fel, AAAS, 2001; entrepreneur of the yr, Ernst & young, merrill lynch, inc magazine, 1991; fel, guggenheim, 1988-1989; career devel fel, USPHS, 1971-1976; Stoye Prize, Am Soc Ichthyol & Herpet, 1965. **Professional Experience:** Pres & CEO, salus therapeutics inc, 2001-; chr bd dirs, Asn western univs, 1998-2000; bd dir, Utah life sci Asn, 1995-2000; huntsman cancer fd, 1996-2000; bd dir, energ geosci inst, 1994-2000; Governors adv coun sci tech, 1993-2000; bd dir, utah res inst, 1992-2000; vpres res, univ utah, 1992-2001; prof biol univ utah 1992-2001; bd dirs, LIHTI, 1989-1992; PRES, RES FOUND & RES INST, 1992-; bd dirs, Asn Biotechnol Co, 1991-1990; chmn, Coun Biotechnol Ctrs, 1989-1991; bd dirs, Boyce Thompson Inst Plant Res, 1988-1993; bd dir Orgn Trop Studies, 1982-1992; bd dirs, Long Island Forum Technol, 1988-1992; assoc ed, Molecular Biol Evolution, 1983-1992 & J Exp Marine Biol Ecol, 1984-1992; dir, Ctr Biotechnol, 1983-1992; prof ecol & evolution, State Univ NY, Stony Brook, 1978-1992; dean biol sci, State Univ NY, Stony Brook, 1978-1988; ed, Marine Biol Lett, 1978-1985; George C Marshall fel, Denmark, 1976-1977; assoc ed, J Soc Study Evolution, 1975-1977; NATO sr sci fel, 1975; assoc prof ecol & evolution & provost biol sci, State Univ NY, Stony Brook, 1971-1980; vis scientist genetics, Aarhus Univ, 1970-1971 & 1976-1977; asst prof zool, Univ Kans, 1967-1970; Trainee immunol, Univ Kans, 1967; NSF & NIH grants. **Memberships:** AAAS; Genetics Soc Am; Soc Study Evolution (vpres, 1983-1984, pres, 1985). **Research Statement & Publications:** Evolutionary genetics and physiological energetics of natural populations, particularly marine invertebrates; protein function, structure and adaptation. **Mailing Address:** Salus Therapeutics, Inc, 615 Arapeen Dr, Suite 102, Salt Lake City, UT 84108. **Fax:** 801-983-0342. **E-Mail:** rkoehn@salustherapeutics.com

KOEHN, UWE, STATISTICAL CONSULTING EXPERIMENTAL DESIGN & ANALYSIS. **Personal Data:** b Brooklyn, NY, March 25, 1940; m 1996, Helen; c John & Eric. **Education:** Queens Col, BS, 1961; Univ Ill, MS, 1962, PhD (statist), 1968. **Professional Experience:** PROF, DEPT STATIST, UNIV CONN, 1984-; from asst prof to assoc prof, Dept Statist, Univ Conn, 1968-1983; statist consult, 1966-; asst prof, Butler Univ, 1966-1968. **Memberships:** Am Statist Asn; Am Soc Qual. **Research Statement & Publications:** Application of statistics to industrial problems, biology, legal problems, employment and development of pay equity research designs. **Mailing Address:** 1 Eastwood Rd, Storrs, CT 06268-2401. **Fax:** 860-486-4113. **E-Mail:** uwe.koehn@uconn.edu

KOELLA, WERNER PAUL, NEUROPHYSIOLOGY. **Personal Data:** b Zurich, Switz, April 13, 1917; American citizen; m 1955, c 3. **Education:** Univ Zurich, MD, 1942. **Professional Experience:** RETIRED; sr mem staff, Lab Neurophysiol, Ciba-Geigy Ltd, 1970-1982; Boston Univ, 1959 & Univ Berne, 1970; chmn dept pharmacol & med, Robapharm Ag, 1968-1970; Prof affil, Clark Univ, 1957-; mem staff, Worcester Found Exp Biol, 1957-1968; assoc prof, Univ Minn, 1952-1955; res assoc neurophysiol, Univ Minn, 1951-1952; head asst dept, UnivZurich, 1948-1951; resident physiol, Univ Zurich, 1945-1948; Resident neurosurg, Univ Zurich, 1943-1945. **Memberships:** AAAS; Am Physiol Soc; Am Soc Pharmacol & Exp Therapeut; fel Am ColNeuropsychopharmacol; NY Acad Sci. **Research Statement & Publications:** Cerebellum; vestibular apparatus; subcortical-cortical relationships; sleep; organization of autonomic functions; neuropharmacology. **Mailing Address:** Buchenstrasse 1 CH-4104, Oberwil, CH4104, Switzerland.

KOELLE, WINIFRED ANGENENT, ESSENTIAL HYPERTENSION, CARDIAC DRUGS. **Personal Data:** b Soerakarta, Indonesia, March 26, 1926; m 1954, c 3. **Education:** Wellesley Col, BA, 1948; Columbia Univ, MD, 1952; Am Bd Internal Med, cert, 1979. **Professional Experience:** Vis prof, St George's Univ, St Vincent, Wis, 1984; deleg, US Pharmacopeia, Univ Pa, 1980-1985; vis prof, Mahidol Univ, Bangkok, Thailand, 1978; vis prof, Sch Med, Free Fac, Lille, France, 1976-; ASST PROF MED, SCH MED, UNIV PA, 1976-; co-chief & chief, med clin, Philadelphia Gen Hosp, Univ Pa Serv, 1973-1977; ASST PROF PHARMACOL, SCH MED, UNIV PA, 1972-; teaching assoc med, Sch Med, 1970-1976; asst prof pharmacol, Pahlavi Univ, Shiraz, Iran, 1969-1970; Chief, Intensive Care Unit, Taylor Hosp, Ridley Park, Pa, 1967-1969; teaching assoc pharmacol, Grad Sch Med & Sch Med, 1956-1972. **Memberships:** Am Soc Pharmacol & Exp Therapeut; fel Am Col Clin Pharmacol; Sigma Xi. **Research Statement & Publications:** Metabolism of catecholamines by ocular tissue; histochemistry and life cycles of cholinesterases; anti-cholinesterase agents; mechanisms of release of acetylcholine; neurotrophic factors. **Mailing Address:** Dept Pharmacol & Med Univ Pa Sch Med, 114 Med Labs G3, Philadelphia, PA 19104.

KOELLER, RALPH CARL, MECHANICAL ENGINEERING, CONTINUUM MECHANICS. **Personal Data:** b Chicago, Ill, August 9, 1933; div, c 3. **Education:** Ill Inst Technol, BS, 1957, MS, 1959, PhD (mech), 1963. **Professional Experience:** PRES, MECH DESIGN GROUP, 1989-; prof mech eng, Univ Wis, 1984-1989; consult, Ponderosa Assoc, 1978-1988; vis asst prof, Cornell Univ, 1976-1977; resident fac fel, Am Soc Eng Educrs, 1974-1975; Hewlett-Packard Co, 1974; Dieterich Stand Corp, 1973; consult, Dow Chem Co, 1970-1971; consult, Colo Instruments Inc, 1969; Univ Colo Fac fel, Univ Calif, Berkeley, 1965-1966; from instr to prof, Univ Colo, 1962-1984; res & teaching asst mech eng, Ill Inst Technol, 1959-1962. **Memberships:** Am Soc Mech Engrs; Sigma Xi. **Research Statement & Publications:** Engineering consulting; design analysis; scale models; product liability. **Mailing Address:** 960 Stonebridge No Six, Platteville, WI 53818-2078.

KOELLING, DALE DEAN, COMPUTATIONAL MATERIALS PHYSICS SOLID STATE SCIENCE, ELECTRONIC STRUCTURE CALCULATIONS. **Personal Data:** b Great Bend, Kans, May 8, 1941; m 1968, Maria; c Melinda & Alexia. **Education:** Kans State Univ, BS, 1963; Mass Inst Technol, PhD (physics), 1968. **Professional Experience:** PROG MANAGER, DIV MAT SCI, OFF BASIC ENERGY SCI, OFF ENERGY RES, DEPT ENERGY, GERMANTOWN, MD, 2000-; full admin training, Div Mat Sci, Off Basic Energy Sci, Off Energy Res, Dept Energy, Germantown, Md, 1994-1996; sr physicist mat sci div, Argonne Nat Lab, 1987-2000; vis prof, Northern Ill Univ, 1985-1987; physicist, Argonne Nat Lab, 1972-1987; res assoc, Northwestern Univ, 1968-1972. **Memberships:** Fel Am Phys Soc; Mat Res Soc; Soc Indust & Appl Math. **Research Statement & Publications:** Electronic structure and resulting properties primarily in metallic or semiconducting actinide, rare-earth, or transition element materials. **Mailing Address:** US Dept Energy, 19901 Germantown Rd, Germantown, MD 20874-1290. **Fax:** 301-903-9513. **E-Mail:** dale.koelling@Sci.doe.gov

KOELLING, MELVIN R, FORESTRY. **Personal Data:** b Sullivan, Mo, July 18, 1937; m 1959. **Education:** Univ Mo, BS, 1959, MS, 1961, PhD (bot), 1964. **Professional Experience:** PROF FORESTRY & EXTEN SPECIALIST, MICH STATE UNIV, 1977-; from asst prof to assoc prof, Mich State Univ, 1967-1977; assoc plant physiol, Northeast Forest Exp Sta, USDA, 1964-1967. **Memberships:** AAAS; Am Inst Biol Sci; Ecol Soc Am; Soc Am Foresters. **Research Statement & Publications:** Botany; improvement of sugar maple with respect to sap production; maple sap physiology. **Mailing Address:** Nat Resources Forestry, Mich State Univ, 126, East Lansing, MI 48824-1222. **Fax:** 517-432-1143. **E-Mail:** koelling@msu.edu

KOELTZOW, DONALD EARL, BIOCHEMISTRY, ORGANIC CHEMISTRY. **Personal Data:** b Clovis, NMex, May 9, 1944; m 1965, c 3. **Education:** NMex Inst Mining & Technol, BS, 1966; Univ Ill, MS, 1968, PhD (biochem), 1970. **Professional Experience:** DIR, AGR RES SERV, GRAIN MARKETING & PROD RES CTR, as of 2004; chmn dept, Luther Col, 1978-1988; assoc prof chem, Luther Col, beginning 1977; assoc res scientist pharmacol, Univ Iowa, 1977-1978; US Army med res grant, 1973-1975; asst prof, Luther Col, 1971-1977; fel med microbiol, Stanford Univ, 1970-1971. **Memberships:** Am Chem Soc; Am Soc Microbiol; AAAS; Midwest Asn Chem Teachers LibArts Cols. **Research Statement & Publications:** Structure and function of membrane components, particularly carbohydrates and lipids. **Mailing Address:** US Dept Agr, Agr Res Ser, GMPRC, 1515 Col Ave, Manhattan, KS 66502. **Fax:** 785-776-2789. **E-Mail:** dek@gmprc.ksu.edu

KOEMTZOPOULOS, C ROBERT, DIAMOND FILM TECHNOLOGY. **Personal Data:** b New York, NY, December 20, 1967. **Education:** Johns Hopkins Univ, BSc, 1989; Univ Houston, PhD, 1994. **Professional Experience:** RES ASST, CHEM ENG DEPT, UNIV HOUSTON, 1989-. **Memberships:** Am Inst Chem Engrs; Electrochem Soc. **Research Statement & Publications:** Designed and used two experimental configurations of a microwave plasma CVD reactor to produce diamond films; developed mathematical models to simulate a hydrogen glow discharge and determine the gas phase composition in a remote plasma CVD reactor for diamond film growth. **Mailing Address:** 25200 Carlos Bee Blvd Apt 553, Hayward, CA 94542. **Fax:** 713-743-4323. **E-Mail:** chee1la@jetson.uh.edu

KOEN, BILLY VAUGHN, NUCLEAR REACTOR RELIABILITY & SAFETY. **Personal Data:** b Graham, Tex, May 2, 1938; American citizen; m Deanne; c Kent & Douglas. **Education:** Univ Tex, Austin, BA, 1960, BS, 1961; Mass Inst Technol, MS, 1962; Saclay Nuclear Res Ctr, France, dipl eng, 1963. **Honorary Degrees:** DSc (nuclear eng), Mass Inst Technol, 1968. **Honors & Awards:** Chester F Carlson Award, Am Soc Eng Educ, 1980, W Leighton Collins Award, 1992 & Centennial Medallion Award, 1993. **Professional Experience:** Prof, Tokyo Inst Tech, 1994, summer, 1998-1999, 2001, summer; mem Acad Educ Develop, Tunisian Technol Transfer Proj, 1984; PROF MECH ENG, UNIV TEX, AUSTIN, 1982-; foreign collabr, Fr Atomic Energy Comn, 1971-1972 & 1976-1977; from asst prof to assoc prof, Univ Tex, Austin, 1968-1982. **Memberships:** fel Am Nuclear Soc; fel vpres, 1987-1993; Am Soc Eng Educ; Am Soc Mech Engrs. **Research Statement & Publications:** Discussion of the method. **Mailing Address:** Dept Mech Eng, Univ Tex, ETC 5160, Austin, TX 78712-1063. **E-Mail:** koen@uts.cc.utexas.edu

KOENEMAN, JAMES BRYANT, NEURO-REHABILITATION, ORTHOPEDIC BIOMECHANICS. **Personal Data:** b Minnesota, November 24, 1936; m 1964, Maryann; c Edward, Paul & Brian. **Education:** Univ Minn, BSME, 1959; Case Western Res Univ, MS, 1966, PhD (mech eng), 1969. **Honors & Awards:** Engineer of the Year, Erie Engineering Society Council 1982; Clemson Award Society for Biomaterials 1997; Fellow of SAMPE International 1992; International Fellow of Biomaterials Science and Engineering 1999. **Professional Experience:** Prog chmn, Soc Biomat, 1987; adj prof Bioengineering, Ariz State Univ, 1984-; President Kinetic Muscles, Inc. 1998-Pres; VP Engineering Orthologic Corp, 1994-1998; DIR BIOENGINEERING, HARRINGTON ARTHRITIS RES CTR, 1984-1994; pres, Paulson Med Devices, 1981-1983; adj fac, Case Western Res Univ, 1981-1983; dir res, Shrine Hosp, Erie, 1977-1982; sect chmn, Am Soc Mech Engrs, 1977-1979; instr biomech & biomat, Orthop Res Prog, Erie, 1975-1981; dir, Bioengineering Div, Lord Corp, 1974-1981; mem tech staff, Bell Tel Labs, 1970-1974; reactor engr, US AEC, 1960-1964; Reactor engr, Argonne Nat Labs, 1959-1960. **Memberships:** Am Soc Mech Engrs; Am Stroke Association. **Research Statement & Publications:** Development of medical devices; neuro-rehabilitation; evaluation of implant materials including composites, characterization of stress related bone changes, and the study of human and animal biomechanics. **Mailing Address:** Kinetic Muscles, Inc, 2103 E Cedar St, #3, Tempe, AZ 85281-7432. **Fax:** 480-557-0449. **E-Mail:** jkoeneman@kineticmuscles.com

KOENG, FRED R, ORGANIC CHEMISTRY. **Personal Data:** b Wilmington, Del, August 6, 1941; m 1963, c 1. **Education:** Franklin & Marshall Col, AB, 1963; Northwestern Univ, PhD (org chem), 1970. **Professional Experience:** RES ASSOC, EASTMAN KODAK CO, 1980-; sr res chemist, EastmanKodak CO, 1970-1980; Chemist, Rohm and Haas Co, 1965-1967. **Memberships:** AAAS; Soc Photog Scientists & Engrs; Sigma Xi. **Research Statement & Publications:** Photographic systems research. **Mailing Address:** 93 Damsen Rd, Rochester, NY 14612-3637.

KOENIG, CHARLES LOUIS, PHYSICAL CHEMISTRY. **Personal Data:** b Yonkers, NY, October 11, 1911; m 1952, Jamie; c Charlou, Arthur Shofner, Friederich & Olivia Ann.

Education: NY Univ, BS, 1932, PhD (chem), 1936. **Professional Experience:** RETIRED; adv, Advan Waste Treatment Prog, USPHS, 1960-1963; owner, Louis Koenig Res, 1956-; adv, Saline Water Conservation Prog, Secy Interior, 1952-1956; vpres, Southwest Res Inst, 1951-1956; asst dir res, Stanford Res Inst, 1950-1951; sect ed, Chem Abstr, beginning 1949; chmn dept chem & chem eng res, Armour Res Found, 1947-1949; chief res br, AEC, 1946-1947; res chemist, Lithaloys Corp, 1945-1946; sr chemist, Solvay Process Co, NY, 1936-1945. **Memberships:** Sigma Xi; Am Chem Soc. **Research Statement & Publications:** Phase relations of aqueous systems; water resources; waste disposal; cost engineering; market research; economics. **Mailing Address:** 26890 Sherwood Forest, San Antonio, TX 78258.

KOENIG, DANIEL RENE, NUCLEAR ENGINEERING, COMPUTER GRAPHICS. **Personal Data:** b Rouen, France, October 6, 1936; American citizen; div, c Christian & Mark. **Education:** Univ Calif, Berkeley, BS, 1959, MS, 1965, PhD (eng sci), 1966. **Honors & Awards:** Teller Award, Am Nuclear Soc, 1966. **Professional Experience:** SOFTWARE ENG, TIME ARTS, INC, SANTA ROSA, CALIF, 1986-; Visphysicist, Saclay, 1979-1980; physicist, Los Alamos Sci Lab, Univ Calif, 1969-1985; Visphysicist, Ctr Nuclear Studies, France, 1967-1968; Physicist, Defense Atomic Support Agency, 1965-1967. **Memberships:** Am Nuclear Soc. **Research Statement & Publications:** Surface physics phenomena such as thermionic emission and surface ionization; detection and theoretical transport of neutron, gamma and x-ray radiations; application of heat pipes to solar energy; design of fast-spectrum nuclear reactors for space applications; design of small solar thermodynamic engines; design and implementation of a comprehensive, object-oriented (C ++); computer graphics class library to facilitate the development of sophisticated graphics software on personal computers and work stations. **Mailing Address:** Time Arts Inc, 1425 Corporate Center Pkwy, Santa Rosa, CA 95407. **Fax:** 707-576-7731.

KOENIG, EDWARD, NEUROBIOLOGY, NEUROCHEMISTRY. **Personal Data:** b New York, NY, November 10, 1928; m 1953, c 3. **Education:** Franklin & Marshall Col, BA, 1956; Univ Pa, PhD (physiol), 1961. **Professional Experience:** PROF PHYSIOL & BIOPHYS, SCH MED, UNIV BUFFALO, 1975-; res career progaward, Nat inst Neurol Dis & Stroke, 1968-1973; from asst prof to assoc prof, State Univ NYBuffalo, 1963-1975. **Memberships:** AAAS; Am Physiol Soc; Am Soc Neurochem; Int Soc Neurochem; Soc Neuroscience. **Research Statement & Publications:** Cellular biology of the neuron as related to central and local regulation of synthesis of axonal proteins and structure, function and organizational regulation of axonal cytoskeleton; microchemistry; microanalysis. **Mailing Address:** Dept Physiol & Biophys, State Univ NY, 215 Sherman Hall, Buffalo, NY 14214-3078. **Fax:** 716-829-2569. **E-Mail:** ekoenig@acsu.buffalo.edu

KOENIG, ELDO C(LYDE), ELECTRICAL ENGINEERING. **Personal Data:** b Randolph Co, Ill, October 17, 1919; m 1950, Gloria; c Lloyd W, Evan F, Eva L & Beth E. **Education:** Wash Univ, St Louis, BS, 1943; Ill Inst Technol, MS, 1949; Univ Wis, MS, 1951, PhD, 1956. **Honors & Awards:** Alfred Nobel Prize. **Professional Experience:** RETIRED; fac, Univ Wis-Madison, 1962-1983; engr in chg eng anal, Allis-Chalmers Mfg Co, 1957-1962; supvr comput lab, Allis-Chalmers Mfg Co, 1954-1957; engr, Allis-Chalmers Mfg Co, 1946-1952; engr, Manhattan Proj, 1944-1946. **Memberships:** Fel AAAS; Asn Comput Mach; sr mem Inst Elec & Electronics Engrs. **Research Statement & Publications:** Engineering and mathematical analysis and research for computers; systems and design; intelligent properties of systems. **Mailing Address:** 35005 W Fairview Rd, Oconomowoc, WI 53066.

KOENIG, HEIDI M, NEUROANESTHESIOLOGY, NEUROSCIENCE RESEARCH-CEREBRAL VASCULAR REACTIVITY & BRAIN PROTECTION. **Personal Data:** b Newman Grove, Nebr, April 1958; m 1993, William. **Education:** Wayne State Col, BS, 1981; Univ Nebr, MD, 1993. **Professional Experience:** ASSOC PROF, UNIV ILL, as of 2005; asst prof anesthesiol, UNIV ILL, beginning 1993. **Memberships:** Am Soc Anesthesiol; Int Anesthesia Res Soc. **Research Statement & Publications:** Cerebrovascular reactivity in rat cranial window model to anesthetic agents carbon dioxide and hypoxia on health and disease; brain protection in transient focal cerebral ischemia in the rat. **Mailing Address:** Dept Anesthesiol, Univ Ill, 3200W MC 515, Chicago, IL 60612. **Fax:** 312-556-8943. **E-Mail:** hmkoenig@uic.edu

KOENIG, HERMAN E, ELECTRICAL ENGINEERING. **Personal Data:** b Marissa, Ill, December 12, 1924; m 1949, c 3. **Education:** Univ Ill, BS, 1947, MS, 1949, PhD (elec eng), 1953. **Professional Experience:** Asst vpres indust asst, Mich State Univ, 1985; PROF ELEC & COMP ENG, MICH STATE UNIV, 1985-; Off Vpres Res & Grad Studies, Mich State Univ, 1980-1985; Dir Ctr Environ Qual, Mich State Univ, 1975-1980; chmn dept elec eng & systs sci, Mich State Univ, 1969-1975; Dir Systs Sci Prog, Mich State Univ, 1967-1975; Prof Elec Eng, Mich State Univ, 1959-1967; assoc prof, Mich State Univ, 1956-1959; asst prof elec eng, Univ Ill, 1953-1954 & 1955-1956 & Mass Inst Technol, 1954-1955; Consult, Reliance Elec & Eng Co, Ohio, 1951-1954 & Lear Siegler, Inc, Mich, 1963-1965. **Memberships:** Am Soc Eng Educ; Soc Eng Sci; Inst Elec & Electronics Engrs. **Research Statement & Publications:** Theory of electrical networks and other physical systems; transportation, business and other socio-economic systems; operations research; industrialized ecosystem design and management; energy and energy resources. **Mailing Address:** Mich State Univ, 228 Admin Bldg 4733 Mohican Lane, East Lansing, MI 48824. **Fax:** 517-353-1980.

KOENIG, JACK L, POLYMER CHEMISTRY, PHYSICAL CHEMISTRY. **Personal Data:** b Cody, Nebr, February 12, 1933; m 1953, c 4. **Education:** Yankton Col, BA, 1956; Univ Nebr, MS, 1958, PhD (chem), 1960. **Honors & Awards:** Pittsburgh Soc Spectros Award, 1986; Soc Plastics Engrs Res award, 1991; Gold Medal, Eastern Anal Soc, 1992; Bomem-Michelson Award, 1993; ACS Phillips Award, Appl Polymer Sci, 1997; Res Award, Sigma Xi. **Professional Experience:** PROF MACROMOLECULAR SCI, CASE WESTERN RES UNIV, 1970-; NSF, US Army, US Navy res grants, 1965-1988; from asst prof to assoc prof chem, CaseWestern Res Univ, 1963-1970; Mem staff, Plastics Dept, E I du Pont Del Nemours & Co, 1959-1963; Consult, El Tech, Charden, Ohio & 3M Co, 1959-1963. **Memberships:** Am Chem Soc; Am Phys Soc; Soc Appl Spectros. **Research Statement & Publications:** Spectroscopy of polymeric materials. **Mailing Address:** Dept Macromolecular Sci, Case Western Res Univ, Rm 212, Kent Hale Smith Bldg, 10900 Euclid Ave, Cleveland, OH 44106-7202. **Fax:** 216-368-4171. **E-Mail:** jlk6@po.cwru.edu

KOENIG, JAMES BENNETT, STRUCTURAL GEOLOGY. **Personal Data:** b New York, NY, November 25, 1932; c 3. **Education:** Brooklyn Col, BS, 1954; Ind Univ, MA, 1956; USN Postgrad Sch, dipl meteorol, 1958. **Professional Experience:** SR ADV, GEOTHERMEX INC, as of 2003; pres-elect, Geothermal Resource Coun, 1987; mem int working group, Int Geothermal Asn, beginning 1986; mem bd dir, Geothermal Resource Coun, beginning 1975; pres, Geothermex, Inc, 1973-1995; consult, Weyerhaeuser Co & Pac Power & Light Co, 1971-1972; consult, UN Geothermal Explor, Ethiopia & El Salvador, 1971; instr geol, Univ Calif, Berkeley, 1968-1970; supvry geologist, Calif Div Mines, San Francisco, 1965-1972; supvry geologist, Calif Div Mines & Geol, 1965-1972; student geol & seismol, Univ Nev, 1963-1965; asst geologist, Calif Div Mines, San Francisco, 1960-1963; asst geologist, Calif Div Mines & Geol, 1960-1963; instr econ geog, Col William & Mary, 1959-1960; ensign & lt, USN Postgrad Sch, Monterey & USN Weather Res Facil, Norfolk, 1957-1960; jr mining geologist, Calif Div Mines, San Francisco, 1956-1957; ground water geologist, US Geol Surv, St Paul, Minn, 1955-1956. **Memberships:** fel Geol Soc Am; Am Geophys Union; Int Asn Volcanology. **Research Statement & Publications:** Exploration, drilling and development of geothermal resources as energy source, on behalf of electric utilities, international lender and donor agencies, major and independent oil/gas/mining companies, landowners, turbine manufacturers, government agencies in US and abroad (Japan, Costa Rica, Kenya, Philippines, etc); exploration for geothermal energy; feasibility assessments of energy resources. **Mailing Address:** Geothermex Inc, 5221 Central Ave, Ste 201, Richmond, CA 94804. **Fax:** 510-527-8164.

KOENIG, JAMES J(ACOB), CHEMICAL ENGINEERING. **Personal Data:** b Le Mars, Iowa, September 4, 1918; m 1951, Eva M Sprakties; c James G, Eva J, Donald M & Kenneth B. **Education:** Iowa State Col, BS, 1939. **Professional Experience:** RETIRED; mem staff, James J Koenig consult, Inc, 1981-; sr res engr, Aluminum Co Am, 1967-1977; res engr, Aluminum Co Am, 1956-1967; chief, Fla Field Off, 1952-1956; asst area mgr, Mo, 1947-1952; asst dir prod div, NY Opers Off, USAEC, 1946-1947; gen foreman & tech supvr, Tenn, 1941-1944; Foreman, Procter & Gamble Mfg Co, Kans, 1940-1941. **Memberships:** Sigma Xi. **Research Statement & Publications:** Explosives loading; uranium extraction and metallurgy; alumina chemicals. **Mailing Address:** 129 Country Club Acres, Belleville, IL 62223-3609.

KOENIG, JANE QUINN, RESPIRATORY PHYSIOLOGY. **Personal Data:** b Seattle, Wash, September 16, 1935; c 2. **Education:** Univ Wash, BS, 1959, MS, 1961, PhD (physiol psychol), 1963. **Professional Experience:** PROF, DEPT ENVIRON & OCCUP HEALTH SCI, SCH PUB HEALTH & COMMUNITY MED, UNIV WASH, as of 2003; DIR, PARTICULATE AIR POLLUTION & HEALTH CTR, UNIV WASH, as of 2003; assoc prof, Dept Environ & Occup Health, Sch Pub Health & Community Med, Univ Wash, beginning 1974; actg asst prof physiol, Dept Zoology, 1972-1973; vis scientist, Med Sch, Univ Wash, 1970-1971; asst prof, Med Sch, Univ Wash, 1966-1970; fel neurophysiol, Med Sch, Stanford Univ, 1963-1965; consult, Clear Air Sci Adv Comt, Environ Protection Agency. **Memberships:** AAAS; Fedn Am Scientists; Union Concerned Scientists; Am Thoracic Soc; Air Pollution Control Asn; Am Pub Health Asn. **Research Statement & Publications:** Effects of acute exposures to air pollutants upon respiratory physiology in human volunteers especially susceptible individuals. **Mailing Address:** Dept Environ & Occup Health Sci, Univ Wash, Health Sci Bldg F-561A Box 357234, Seattle, WA 98195-7234. **Fax:** 206-685-3990. **E-Mail:** jkoenig@washington.edu

KOENIG, JOHN WALDO, INVERTEBRATE. **Personal Data:** b Newark, NJ, July 19, 1920; m 1950, Paula; c Karl E. **Education:** Columbia Univ, BS, 1947; Univ Kans, MS, 1951. **Professional Experience:** RETIRED; lectr art, Univ Mo-Rolla, 1974-1980; tech ed, Univ Mo, Rolla, 1967-1985; Mo Geol Surv, 1966-1967; Continental Oil Co, 1965-1966; geologist, Mo Geol Surv & Water Resources, 1954-1965; geol engr, Phillips Petrol Co, 1951-1954; sci illusr, Kans State Geol Surv, 1947-1951. **Memberships:** Asn Earth Sci Ed. **Research Statement & Publications:** Invertebrate paleontology; Bryozoa and Crinoidea; Mississippian stratigraphy. **Mailing Address:** 1700 E Tenth St, Rolla, MO 65401.

KOENIG, KARL E, AMINO ACID SYNTHESIS, NEW PRODUCT DEVELOPMENT. **Personal Data:** b Washington, DC, December 27, 1947; American citizen; m Jo. **Education:** Univ Tex, Austin, BS, 1970; Univ Southern Calif, PhD (chem), 1974. **Professional Experience:** PRES, TECH CONSULT, 2000-; dir, New Prod Div, Pharm, 1995-2000; mgr process develop, New Prod Div, Monsanto Agr Group, 1989-1995; res group leader, Monsanto Agr Group, 1986-1989; sr res specialist, Nutrit Chem Div, Monsanto Agr Group, 1981-1986; res specialist, Corp Res & Develop Biomed Prog, Monsanto Agr Group, 1979-1981; sr res chemist asymmetric catalysis, Monsanto Corp Res Labs, 1976-1979; fel chem, Univ Calif, Los Angeles, 1974-1976. **Memberships:** Am Chem Soc; AAAS; Org Reactions Catalysis Soc; Am Inst Chemists. **Research Statement & Publications:** Homogeneous catalysis; drugs based on low molecular weight polyelectrolytes; asymmetric synthesis; nutritional chemicals; selective complexation of transition metals; organosilicon chemistry; growth promotants; weed control agents; strategic planning for product development. **Mailing Address:** 22260 White Peaks Dr, Bend, OR 97702. **E-Mail:** grantsexpress@earthlink.net

KOENIG, KARL JOSEPH, GEOLOGY. **Personal Data:** b Milwaukee, Wis, January 9, 1920; m 1959, c 1. **Education:** Univ Ill, BS, 1941, MS, 1946, PhD, 1949. **Professional Experience:** PROF EMER GEOL, TEX A&M UNIV, as of 2004; assoc prof geol, Tex A&M Univ, 1955-; Stratigrapher, Shell Oil Co, Tex, 1949-1955. **Memberships:** Soc Econ Paleont & Mineral; Geol Soc Am; Am Asn Petrol Geol. **Research Statement & Publications:** Miocene stratigraphy and paleontology; sedimentation and clay mineralogy. **Mailing Address:** Dept Geol, Tex A&M Univ, College Station, TX 77843-0100.

KOENIG, LLOYD RANDALL, METEOROLOGY. **Personal Data:** b St Louis, Mo, July 17, 1929; m 1955, c 2. **Education:** Washington Univ, BSChE, 1950; Univ Chicago, MS, 1959, PhD (meteorol), 1962. **Professional Experience:** SR SCI OFFICER, WORLD METEOROL ORG, GENEVA, SWITZ, 1980-; assoc prog dir meteorol, NSF, 1979-1980; phys scientist, Rand Corp, Santa Monica, 1966-1979; chief atmospheric sci br, Missile & Space Systs Div, Douglas Aircraft Co, 1962-1966; res assoc, Univ Chicago, 1960-1962; res asst meteorol, Univ Chicago, 1957-1959; Instr chem eng, USNPostgrad Sch, 1950-1953. **Memberships:** Am Geophys Union; Am Meteorol Soc; Sigma Xi. **Research Statement & Publications:** Cloud physics, including natural and artificial precipitation mechanisms, scavenging, effects of atmospheric processes on the atmosphere. **Mailing Address:** 258 Notteargenta Rd, Pacific Palisades, CA 90272-3110.

KOENIG, MICHAEL EDWARD DAVISON, INFORMATION MANAGEMENT. **Personal Data:** b Rochester, NY, November 1, 1941; m 1980, Luciana; c Christopher & Davison. **Education:** Yale Univ, BA, 1963; Univ Chicago, MS, 1968, MBA, 1970; Drexel Univ, PhD (infosci), 1982. **Honors & Awards:** Jason Farradane Award 2005. **Professional Experience:** Prof. CICS, College of Information and Computer Science, Long Island Univ., 2005 -Dean & Prof. CICS, 1999-2005. Dean & Prof grad schlibr & info sci & prof grad sch bus, Rosary Col, 1988-1995; vpres info mgt, Tradenet Inc, 1985-1988; Adj fac, Sch Libr Serv, 1985-1988; Adj fac, Grad Sch Bus, Columbia Univ, 1983-1988; assoc prof info systs, Sch Libr Serv, Columbia Univ, 1980-1985; vpres opers, SwetsNAm, Berwyn, Pa, 1978-1980; dir develop, Inst Sci Info, Philadelphia, Pa, 1977-1978; dir prodopers, Inst Sci Info, Philadelphia, Pa, 1974-1977; Mgr info serv, Pfizer, Inc, Groton, Conn, 1970-1974. **Memberships:** Am Soc Info Sci; Asn Comput Mach; AAAS; Spec Libr Asn; Int Soc Scientometrics & Informetrics (pres 1995-1997), Grolier Club, Elizabethan Club. **Research Statement & Publications:** Bibliometrics and scientometrics; relationship between information technology and productivity; research productivity and the information environment. **Mailing Address:** Col Information & Comput Sci, 720 Northern Blvd, Brookville, NY 11548. **E-Mail:** michael.koenig@liu.edu

KOENIG, MILTON G, THERMODYNAMICS, MECHANICAL ENGG DESIGN. **Personal Data:** b Moberly, Mo, August 23, 1927; m 1956, c 3. **Education:** Wayne State Univ, BSME, 1956, MSME, 1957. **Professional Experience:** Eng Consult, 2002-; EMER PROF MECH ENG, WAYNE STATE UNIV, 1989-; From instr to assoc prof, Wayne State Univ, 1956-1989. **Memberships:** Soc Automotive Eng. **Research Statement & Publications:** Thermodynamics and its applications; automotive design; vehicle dynamics and handling. **Mailing Address:** 46266 Pickford St, Northville, MI 48167. **E-Mail:** mgkoenig@bignet.com

KOENIG, PAUL EDWARD, ORGANIC CHEMISTRY. **Personal Data:** b Gallup, NM, May 30, 1929; m 1950, Norma Putnam; c Michael, Lawrence, Karen, Thomas, Paula, Thecla, Gretchen, Monica. **Education:** Univ Ariz, BS, 1950, MS, 1952; Univ Iowa, PhD (chem), 1955. **Professional Experience:** DEAN, RUNNELS SCH, BATON ROUGE, 1984-; CONSULT CHEMIST, RUNNELS SCH, BATON ROUGE, 1983-; vchancellor acad affairs, La State Univ, 1970-1981; assoc dean grad sch, La State Univ, 1967-1970; asst head dept, La State Univ, 1963-1967; from asst prof to prof chem, La State Univ, 1958-1983; Chemist, Ethyl Corp, 1955-1958. **Memberships:** Am Chem Soc. **Research Statement & Publications:** Organic reaction mechanisms; physical organic chemistry; organic synthesis; reactions of metal nitrides with organic compounds; structure of tertiary amides. **Mailing Address:** 2006 Cherrydale Ave, Baton Rouge, LA 70808-2817.

KOENIG, SEYMOUR HILLEL, BIOPHYSICS. **Personal Data:** b Manchester, NH, July 16, 1927; m 1947, c 2. **Education:** Columbia Univ, BS, 1949, MA, 1950, PhD, 1952. **Professional Experience:** PRES, RELAXOMETRY INC, 1993-; staff mem, Phys Sci dept, 1971-1993; lectr, dept Art Hist & Archeol, 1970-1976; mem gov coun, Am Phys Soc, 1970-1974; dir gensci, res Ctr, 1970-1971; from asst dir to dir, Watson res lab, IBM Corp, 1964-1970; consult, Physics div, Los Alamos Sci lab, 1959-; from adj asst prof to adj prof, dept ElecEng, Columbia Univ, 1957-1968; mem staff, Watson res lab, IBM Corp, 1952-1964; Asstphysics, Columbia Univ, 1949-1951. **Memberships:** Fel Am Phys Soc; Biophys Soc; Sigma Xi; Am Soc Biol Chemists; NY Acad Sci. **Research Statement & Publications:** Low temperature electrical transport in semiconductors and semi-metals; inelastic neutron scattering by solids; biophysics of proteins; nuclear magnetic relaxation in protein solutions; protein-water interactions; laser light scattering from macromolecule and virus solutions. **Mailing Address:** 457 N Lake Blvd, Mahopac, NY 10541.

KOENIG, THOMAS W, ORGANIC CHEMISTRY. **Personal Data:** b Kansas City, Mo, February 11, 1938; m 1961, c 2. **Education:** Southern Methodist Univ, BS, 1959; Univ Ill, MS, 1961, PhD (chem), 1963. **Professional Experience:** RETIRED; prof chem, Univ Ore, 1974-1992; from asst prof to assoc prof, Univ Ore, 1963-1974. **Memberships:** Am Chem Soc. **Research Statement & Publications:** Mechanisms of organic reactions. **Mailing Address:** 739 Edgemont Way, Springfield, OR 97403.

KOENIG, WALTER D, ORNITHOLOGY. **Education:** Stanford Univ, BS, 1972; Univ Calif, Berkeley, PhD (zoology), 1978. **Professional Experience:** RES ZOOLOGIST, MUS VERT ZOOLOGY, UNIV CALIF, BERKELEY, 1995-; ADJ PROF, DEPT INTEGRATIVE BIOLOGY, UNIV CALIF, BERKELEY, 1995-. **Mailing Address:** Dept Integrative Biol Univ Calif, 3060 Valley Life Scis Bldg Suite 3140, Berkeley, CA 93924. **Fax:** 831-643-6264. **E-Mail:** wicker@uclink.berkeley.edu

KOENIG, WALTER R, ENGINEERING. **Education:** Univ Mo, Rolla, PhD (elec eng), 1968. **Professional Experience:** Elec engr, Harris Corp, beginning 1977. **Memberships:** Inst Elect & Electronics Engrs. **Mailing Address:** Air Traffic Control Div, Harris Corp, 3925 Reka Dr, Anchorage, AK 99508-3517. **Fax:** 907-746-8009.

KOENIGSBERG, ERNEST, OPERATIONS RESEARCH, MANAGEMENT SCIENCE. **Personal Data:** b New York, NY, April 15, 1923; m 1955, c 2. **Education:** NY Univ, BA, 1948; Iowa State Univ, PhD (theoret physics), 1953. **Professional Experience:** PROF EMER, UNIV CALIF, 1993-; mem comt futureport develop, Maritime Transp Res Bd, Nat Acad Eng, 1974-1975; sr lectr, Schs Bus Admin, Univ Calif, Berkeley, 1972-1993; sr vpres & tech dir, Manalytics Inc, 1969-1972; lectr, Univ Calif, Berkeley, 1966-1972; vpres, Matson Res Corp, 1965-1969; prof indust, Univ Pa, 1964-1965; grad sch bus admin, Univ Calif, Berkeley, 1963-1964; mgr tech serv, CEIR Inc, 1961-1964; vis lectr, Univ Calif, Berkeley, 1961-1963; vis lectr, Stanford Univ, 1960; mgr mgtserv, Touche, Ross, Bailey & Smart, 1958-1961; sect head opers res, Midwest Res Inst, 1957-1958; group leader, EMI Eng Develop, 1955-1957; sr physicist, Midwest Res Inst, 1953-1955. **Memberships:** Fel Royal Statist Soc; Opers Res Soc; Inst Mgt Sci (vpres, 1961-1965). **Research Statement & Publications:** Application of operations research to business, commercial and non-military government problems; queue theory; inventory theory; linear programming; transportation, distribution and energy development. **Mailing Address:** Univ Calif, Berkeley, CA 94115. **E-Mail:** koenigsb@haas.berkeley.edu

KOEPF, ERNEST HENRY, CHEMICAL ENGINEERING. **Personal Data:** b Bruceville, Tex, January 23, 1912; m 1938, c 2. **Education:** Univ Tex, BS, 1934, MS, 1936, PhD (chem eng), 1939. **Professional Experience:** RETIRED; consult, 1982-1990; Syndrill Carbide Diamond Co, 1980-1982; PVT Inc, 1975-1978; vpres res & develop, Francore Lab, 1978-1982; Ecol Audits Inc, 1972-1978; pres, Ocean Pollution Control Inc, 1971-1972; vpres res & tech servs, Francore Lab, 1968-1978; gen mgr, Francore Lab, 1965-1968; mgr res & tech servs, Core Labs Inc, 1955-1965; admin coordr, Crude Oil Producing Dept, Atlantic Refining Co, 1954-1955; vpres & gen mgr, Tex City Chem, Inc, 1952-1954; chem engr, Atlantic Refining Co, 1939-1952; engr, AAAS, Interstate Oil Compact Comn Res Comt & Am Petrol Inst. **Memberships:** Am Chem Soc; Am Inst Mining, Metall & Petrol Engrs; Soc Independent Prof Earth Scientists. **Research Statement & Publications:** High pressure phase behavior of hydrocarbons; petroleum reservoir operation; physical properties of oil reservoir rock and their contained fluids; distribution and flow of hydrocarbons in porous media; environmental protection. **Mailing Address:** 3607 Greenbrier Dr, Dallas, TX 75225.

KOEPFINGER, J L, ELECTRICAL ENGINEERING. **Personal Data:** b Sewickley, Pa, May 6, 1925; m Genevieve; c 6. **Education:** Univ Pittsburgh, BS, 1949, MS, 1953. **Honors & Awards:** Steinmetz Award Excellent in Power Engineer Distribution Award. **Professional Experience:** Principle J.L. KOEPFINGER P.E. CONSULTING as of 2002 beginning 1985; dir, Commun & Protective Relaying, 1964-1985; Dir, Maglev Inc & Mehtu Tech, Inc. **Memberships:** Fel Inst Elec & Electronics Engrs Member of International Electrotechnical Commission Sector Board 1. **Research Statement & Publications:** Development of technology for operation of electronic utility. **Mailing Address:** J L Koepfinger PE Consulting, Coraopolsi, PA 15108-2945. **E-Mail:** joseph_l_koepfinger@email.msn.com

KOEPFLI, JOSEPH B, ORGANIC CHEMISTRY. **Personal Data:** b Los Angeles, Calif, February 5, 1904; m 1935, c 2. **Education:** Stanford Univ, BA, 1924, MA, 1925; Oxford Univ, DPhil(chem), 1928. **Professional Experience:** EMER SR RES ASSOC, CALIF INST TECHNOL, PASADENA, 1972-; res assoc chem, Calif Inst Technol, Pasadena, 1932-1972; Instr pharmacol, Sch Med, Johns Hopkins Univ, 1930-1932. **Research Statement & Publications:** Alkaloids; phytohormones; antimalarials. **Mailing Address:** 580 Freehaven Dr, Santa Barbara, CA 93108.

KOEPKE, BARRY GEORGE, CERAMICS, METALLURGY. **Personal Data:** b Detroit, Mich, October 27, 1937. **Education:** Univ Ill, BS, 1960, MS, 1962; Iowa State Univ, PhD (metall), 1968. **Honors & Awards:** fel, Am Ceramics Soc. **Professional Experience:** MKT MGR, DESPATCH INDUST. 1995-; environ eng mgr, Alliant Tech Systs, 1993-1995; opers mgr & components, Ceramics Ctr, 1988-1993; opers mgr, Ceramics Ctr, 1985-1988; res & develop, Ceramics Ctr, 1983-1985; prog mgr, syst & Res Ctr, 1981-1983; dir Ceramics Prog Div Mat Res, NSF, 1980-1981; ceramics prog dir, NSF, 1979-1981; Adj prof mat sci, Univ Minn, 1976-; scientist, Honeywell Corp Res Ctr, Honeywell Inc, 1964-1979; Res engr metall, Rocketdyne Div, NAm Aviation, 1962-1964. **Memberships:** fel Am Ceramic Soc; Am Soc Metals; Sigma Xi. **Research Statement & Publications:** Studies of the mechanical properties and fracture behavior of ceramic materials, the nature and extent of surface damage introduced into dielectrics by machining and polishing; piezo electric ceramics; production of ceramics with tailored microstructures by unique processing techniques. **Mailing Address:** 2122 Noble Lane, Mound, MN 55364.

KOEPKE, GEORGE HENRY, MEDICINE, ELECTRODIAGNOSTIC MEDICINE. **Personal Data:** b Toledo, Ohio, January 1, 1916; m 1940, Helen K; c Susan (Healy) & Sandra (Bunting). **Education:** Univ Toledo, BS, 1945; Univ Cincinnati, MD, 1949; Am Bd Phys Med & Rehab, dipl, 1955 AM BD ELECTRODIAGNOSTIC MED. **Professional Experience:** Honary staff blanchard, Valley Regional Health Ctr, findlay, 1985-; mem staff, Saginaw Community Hosp, StMary's Hosp, Saginaw Gen Hosp & St Luke's Hosp, 1976-1985; emer mem prof adv coun, United Cerebral Palsy Asn; RETIRED; Am Bd Electrodiag Med, 1990; chmn, Am Bd Phys Med & Rehab, 1976; Lapeer State Home & Training Sch, 1964-& Mary Free Bed Hosp, Grand Rapids, 1971-1976; Consult, Vet Admin Hosp, Ann Arbor, 1955-1975; from asst prof to prof phys med & rehab, Med Ctr, Univ Mich, Ann Arbor, 1954-1976; pvt pract, 1953-1954; instr phys med & rehab, Med Sch, 1952-1953; resident, Univ Mich Hosp, 1950-1952; Intern, Toledo Hosp, 1949-1950. **Memberships:** Fel Am Acad Phys Med & Rehab; Am Asn Electromyog & Electrodiag; Am Acad Orthop Surg; Am Cong Rehab Med; AMA. **Research Statement & Publications:** Retired Physical medicine and rehabilitation; electromyography and prosthetics. **Mailing Address:** 2222 S Main St, Findlay, OH 45840.

KOEPKE, JOHN ARTHUR, CLINICAL PATHOLOGY, HEMATOLOGY. **Personal Data:** b Milwaukee, Wis, March 25, 1929; m 1955, Evelyn; c Mary, John, Mark & James. **Education:** Valparaiso Univ, BA, 1951; Univ Wis, MD, 1956; Marquette Univ, MS, 1964. **Professional Experience:** PROF EMER PATH, MED CTR, DUKE UNIV, 1994-; prof & med dir, ClinHemat Labs, 1980-1994; vis colleague, Royal Postgrad Med Sch, London, Eng, 1978; attend pathologist, Univ Iowa Hosp & Clins, 1972-; prof path & vchmn dept, Col Med, Univ Iowa, 1972-1979; chief lab serv, Vet Admin Hosp, Iowa City, 1972-1978; dir lab, Lexington Clin, 1971-1972; assoc clin prof med technol, Col Med, Univ Iowa, 1970-1971; vis scientist, Karolinska Inst, Sweden, 1967-1968; attend pathologist, Vet Admin Hosp & consult, USPHS, 1963-1971; from asst pathologist to assoc pathologist, Univ Ky Hosp, 1961-1971; from asst prof to assoc prof, Univ Ky, 1961-1970; Instr path, Marquette Univ, 1958-1960. **Memberships:** Col Am Path; Am Soc Clin Path; AMA. **Research Statement & Publications:** Blood coagulation; flow cytometry; hematology instrumentation; quality assurance systems. **Mailing Address:** Dept Path, Duke Univ Med Ctr, PO Box 3712, Durham, NC 27710-2929. **E-Mail:** nckoepke@mindspring.com

KOEPKE, MARK E, EXPERIMENTAL, WAVES & INSTABILITIES. **Personal Data:** b Camp Pendleton, Calif, May 13, 1956. **Education:** Univ Md, BA, 1978, MS, 1980, PhD (physics), 1984. **Honors & Awards:** Distinguished Lecturer in Plasma Physics, Am Phys Soc, 2001; Benedum Distinguished Scholar, WV Univ, 2001. **Professional Experience:** PROF PHYSICS, WVA UNIV, 2000-; vis scientist Univ Greifswald, Ger, 1999, 2000; Guest prof, 1994, Univ Innsbruck, Austria, 1996; assoc prof., WVa Univ, 1993-2000; vis scientist, Univ Kiev, Ger, 1993; asst prof, WVa Univ, 1987-1993; Young investr award, Off Naval Res, 1987; res asst prof, Univ Wash, Seattle, 1986-1987; Res assoc, Univ Wash, Seattle, 1984-1986. **Memberships:** Am Phys Soc; Am Geophys Union. **Research Statement & Publications:** Laboratory investigation of plasma waves and instabilities in a laboratory device known as a Q machine; both linear and nonlinear phenomena are investigated, the results are applicable to space plasmas. **Mailing Address:** Dept Physics, Univ WV, Hodges Hall, Rm 138, MS 6315, Morgantown, WV 26506-6315. **Fax:** 304-293-5732. **E-Mail:** mkoepke@wvu.edu

KOEPNICK, RICHARD BORLAND, SEDIMENTARY PETROLOGY. **Personal Data:** b Dayton, Ohio, February 5, 1944. **Education:** Univ Colo, BA, 1967; Univ Kans, MS, 1969, PhD (geol), 1976. **Professional Experience:** SR GEOL RES ADV, EXPLOR & PRODUCING TECH CTR, MOBIL RES DEVELOP CORP, 1992-; res assoc geol, Dallas Res Lab, 1986-1992; assoc geol res, Mobil Field Res Lab, 1985-1986; res geologist, Mobil Field Res Lab, 1977-1984; asst prof, Dept Geol, Williams Col, 1975-1977. **Memberships:** Soc Econ Paleontologists & Mineralogists; Am Asn Petrol Geologists; Sigma Xi. **Research Statement & Publications:** Application of strontium isotope analysis to stratigraphicand diagenetic studies; diagenesis of carbonate rocks and sandstones; temporal controls on carbonate reservoir development; carbonate reservoir characterization. **Mailing Address:** Mobil Res & Develop Corp, Dallas, TX 75244.

KOEPP, LEILA H, SCIENCE EDUCATION. **Personal Data:** b Haifa, Israel, July 7, 1945; American citizen; m 1969, c 2. **Education:** Messiah Col, BA, 1968; NTex State Univ, MS, 1970; Univ Med & Dent NJ, PhD (microbiol), 1982. **Professional Experience:** PROF BIOL, BLOOMFIELD COL, NJ, as of 2004; assoc prof biol, Bloomfield Col, NJ, beginning 1981; asst med microbiol & researcher microbiol, Univ Med & Dent NJ, 1978-1981; instr biol, anat & physiol, Fairleigh Dickson Univ, Madison, 1976-1977; bacteriologist clin microbiol, genetics, immunol & gen biol, Overlook Hosp, Summit, NJ, 1975-1981; instr microbiol, Montclair State Col, 1974-1976. **Memberships:** Am Soc Microbiol. **Research Statement & Publications:** Molecular basis for the biological activity of the slime glycolipoprotein of Pseudomonas aeruginosa; isolation and identification of fungi from stone monuments of the New York metropolitan art museum. **Mailing Address:** Dept Math & Natural Sci, Bloomfield Col, 467 Franklin St, Bloomfield, NJ 07003. **Fax:** 973-743-3998. **E-Mail:** leila_koepp@bloomfield.edu

KOEPP, STEPHEN JOHN, ZOOLOGY, CYTOPATHOLOGY. **Personal Data:** b Los Angeles, Calif, April 24, 1946; m 1969, c 2. **Education:** Messiah Col, BA, 1968; NTex State Univ, MS, 1970, PhD (biol), 1973. **Professional Experience:** PROF BIOL, COL SCI & MATH, MONTCLAIR STATE UNIV, 1985-; from asst prof to assoc prof biol, Montclair State Col, 1973-1985; environ consult. **Memberships:** Electron Micros Soc Am; Am Col Toxicol. **Research Statement & Publications:** Histopathologicand cytopathologic response of aquatic fauna following toxic exposure to heavy metals; electron microscopy.

Mailing Address: Dept Biol & Molecular Biol, Col Sci & Math, Monclair State Univ, One Normal Ave, Montclair, NJ 07043. **E-Mail:** koepps@mail.montclair.edu

KOEPPE, MARY KOLEAN, ENVIRONMENTAL TOXICOLOGY, HERBICIDE METABOLISM IN PLANTS. **Personal Data:** b Holland, Mich, July 7, 1955; m 1978, John. **Education:** Hope Col, BA, 1977; Univ Wis, Madison, MS, 1979, PhD (entomol), 1983. **Professional Experience:** DUPONT CO, as of 2005; res assoc, E I Dupont Denemours & Co Inc, 1983-2002. **Memberships:** Am Chem Soc; Weed Sci Soc. **Research Statement & Publications:** Optimization of herbicide lead areas via a biokinetic approach; understanding rates of metabolism in plants as well as a high throughput screening approach. **Mailing Address:** Agr Dept Crop Protection, Dupont Stine-Haskell PO Box 30, Newark, DE 19714. **Fax:** 302-451-4602. **E-Mail:** mary.k.koeppe@usa.dupont.com

KOEPPE, OWEN JOHN, BIOCHEMISTRY. **Personal Data:** b Cedar Grove, Wis, May 29, 1926; m 1950, c 3. **Education:** Hope Col, AB, 1949; Univ Ill, MS, 1951, PhD (biochem), 1953. **Professional Experience:** PROF EMER BIOCHEM, UNIV MO, COLUMBIA, as of 2004; prof biochem, Kans State Univ, 1980-1990; provost, Kans State Univ, 1980-1988; provost, Sch Med, Univ Mo, Columbia, 1979-1980; provost acad affairs, Sch Med, Univ Mo, Columbia, 1973-1979; chmn dept, Sch Med, Univ Mo, Columbia, 1968-1973; prof, Sch Med, Univ Mo, Columbia, beginning 1961; from asst prof to assoc prof biochem, Sch Med, Univ Mo, Columbia, 1955-1961; USPHS res fel, UnivMinn, 1953-1955; asst biochem, Univ Ill, 1951-1952; asst chem, Univ Ill, 1949-1951. **Memberships:** Am Chem Soc; Am Soc Biochem & Molecular Biol. **Research Statement & Publications:** Mechanism of enzyme action; peptide bond synthesis. **Mailing Address:** Dept Biochem, Univ Mo, Columbia, MO 65211.

KOEPPE, ROGER E, II, CHEMISTRY, BIOCHEMISTRY, PIOPHYSICS. **Personal Data:** b Champaign, Ill, July 1, 1949; m 1971, Jessie; c Matthew, Julia, Franklin, Jason & Joshua. **Education:** Haverford Col, BA, 1971; Calif Inst Technol, PhD (chem & biochem), 1976. **Honors & Awards:** Harold Lamport Lectr, Cornell Univ, 1987. **Professional Experience:** UNIV PROF, DEPT CHEM & BIOCHEM, UNIV ARK, 1996-; vis prof, Univ Utrecht, Neth, 1992; vis assoc, Calif Inst Technol, 1985-1986; guest asst scientist, Brookhaven Nat Lab, 1980-1986; from asst prof to prof, Dept Chem & Biochem, Univ Ark, 1979-1996; NIH postdoctoral fel struct biol, Sch Med, Stanford Univ, 1976-1979. **Memberships:** Fedn Am Socs Exp Biol; Biophys Soc; Am Chem Soc; Sigma Xi; Fulbright Asn. **Research Statement & Publications:** Mechanism of ion transport through membrane channels; folding of mem proteins; author of 90 technical publications. **Mailing Address:** Dept Chem & Biochem, Univ Ark, CHEM 103 Chem Bldg, Fayetteville, AR 72701. **Fax:** 479-575-4049. **E-Mail:** rk2@uark.edu

KOEPPE, ROGER ERDMAN, BIOCHEMISTRY. **Personal Data:** b Amoy, China, May 2, 1922; m 1947, Norma Lemmer; c Roger III, Mary, Sarah, Edwin & Peter. **Education:** Hope Col, AB, 1944; Univ Ill, MS, 1947, PhD (biochem), 1950. **Professional Experience:** PROF EMER & HEAD BIOCHEM, OKLA STATE UNIV, 1990-; Sigma Xi lectr, 1974; NIH sr fel, Univ Pa, 1966-1967; head dept, Okla State Univ, 1963-1990; from assoc prof to prof, Okla State Univ, 1959-1990; from instr to assoc prof chem, Univ Tenn, 1952-1959; res assoc, Univ Tenn, 1951-1952; Asst, Univ Ill, 1946-1948 & 1950-1951. **Memberships:** AAAS; Am Chem Soc; Am Soc Biol Chemists; Brit Biochem Soc. **Research Statement & Publications:** Metabolism, including enzymology, of acetate, mannose, pyruvate and glutamate in mammalian brain and liver. **Mailing Address:** Dept Biochem & Molecular Biol, Okla State Univ, 246 Nat Res Coun, Stillwater, OK 74078.

KOEPPEN, BRUCE MICHAEL, ELECTROPHYSIOLOGY, ION TRANSPORT. **Personal Data:** b October 7, 1951; c 2. **Education:** Univ Chicago, MD, 1977; Univ Ill, PhD (physiol), 1980. **Professional Experience:** PROF MED & PHYSIOL, HEALTH CTR, UNIV CONN, as of 2003; DEAN ACAD AFFAIRS & EDUC, HEALTH CTR, UNIV CONN, as of 2003; ALBERT & WILDA VAN DUSEN PROF, ACAD MED, UNIV CONN, as of 2000; assoc prof med & physiol, health ctr, Univ Conn, beginning 1982. **Memberships:** Am Soc Nephrology; Am Physiol Soc; Am Biophys Soc; Int Soc Nephrol; Soc Gen Physiol. **Mailing Address:** Dept Med, Sch Med, Health Ctr, Univ Conn, MC 1920, Farmington, CT 06030-0001. **E-Mail:** koeppen@nso.uchc.edu

KOEPPL, GERALD WALTER, CHEMICAL PHYSICS, CHEMICAL REACTION DYNAMICS. **Personal Data:** b Chicago, Ill, December 4, 1942; m 1978, Karen; c Jacob & Rebecca. **Education:** Ill Inst Technol, BSc, 1965, PhD (chem), 1969. **Professional Experience:** Exec off, PhD prog in Chem, City Univ of NY, 1998-; Dir of hons in math & natural sci, Queens Col, 1994-2000; PROF CHEM, QUEENS COL, NY, 1989-; vis assoc prof, Harvard Univ, 1975 & Univ Vt, 1978; Sloan Found fel, 1975-1979; Proj dir res grant, Res Found City Univ New York, 1971-1997; from instr to assoc prof, Queens Col, NY, 1971-1988; res fel, Harvard Univ, 1970; NIH res fel chem, Harvard Univ, 1969-1970. **Memberships:** Am Chem Soc; Sigma Xi; Am Phys Soc. **Research Statement & Publications:** Classical mechanical trajectory studies of the statistical theories of chemical reaction dynamics; variational formulations of the transition state theory of reaction rates. **Mailing Address:** PhD Program in Chem, Cuny Graduate Center, 365 Fifth Ave, New York, NY 10016. **Fax:** 212-817-1507. **E-Mail:** gkoeppl@gc.cuny.edu

KOEPSEL, WELLINGTON WESLEY, ELECTRICAL ENGINEERING, MICROWAVE MEASUREMENTS ELECTROMAGNETIC SYSTEMS. **Personal Data:** b McQueeney, Tex, December 5, m Dorothy; c Kirsten, Gretchen & Lief. **Education:** Univ Tex, BS, 1944, MS, 1951; Okla State Univ, PhD (elec eng), 1960. **Honors & Awards:** Professional member Eta Kappa Nu. **Professional Experience:** Retired, 2005 Adjunct Professor, University of Texas at Austin, 1995-2002 Chief engineer and owner, Mutronic Systems, 1984-2005, Professor of Electrical Engineering, Kansas State University, Manhattan, Kansas, 1964-1984, Associate Professor of Electrical Engineering, Duke University, Durham, NC, 1963-1964, Associate Provessor of Electrical Engineering, University of New Mexico, 1960-1963. **Memberships:** Sr mem Inst Elec & Electronics Engrs; Sigma Xi. **Research Statement & Publications:** Magnetic field measurements to locate unexploded ordnance, Feedback control systems; microcomputer and digital control systems; electromagnetic techniques to measure fuel consumption in zero gravity environment; electromagnetic techniques to determine ice thickness on fuel tanks. **Mailing Address:** Mutronic Systems, Box 26806, Austin, TX 78755. **E-Mail:** wkoepsel@ieee.org

KOERBER, GEORGE G(REGORY), PROPAGATING DISTURBANCES, PIEZO ELECT SURFACE WAVES. **Personal Data:** b Akron, Ohio, August 30, 1924; m 1951, Barbara; c Anne (Koerber-Schwab), Laura Koerber & Gregory. **Education:** Hiram Col, BA, 1948; Purdue Univ, MS, 1950, PhD (phys chem), 1952. **Professional Experience:** PROF EMER ELEC & COMPUT ENG, IOWA STATE UNIV, as of 2004; from assoc prof to prof elec eng, Iowa State Univ, 1961-1984; assoc prof theoret & appl mech, Iowa State Univ, 1960-1961; assoc prof eng mech, Mich Col Mining & Technol, 1958-1959; assoc prof mech, Rensselaer Polytech Inst, 1956-1958; mem tech staff component develop, Bell Tel Labs Inc, 1952-1956. **Memberships:** Inst Elec & Electronics Engrs. **Research Statement & Publications:** Applied mathematics; properties of solids; propagating disturbances, particularly piezo electric surface waves. **Mailing Address:** Dept Elec & Comput Eng, Iowa State Univ, Ames, IA 50010. **E-Mail:** ggk@olypen.com

KOERBER, STEVEN C, BIOLOGY. **Education:** Univ Calif, BS, PhD, 1981. **Professional Experience:** STAFF, FOLEY & LARDNER LLP, 2003-. **Memberships:** Am Soc Biochem & Molecular Biol. **Mailing Address:** Foley & Lardner LLP, 11250 El Camino Real Ste 200, San Diego, CA 92130. **E-Mail:** skoerber@foley.com

KOERING, MARILYN JEAN, ANATOMY, REPRODUCTIVE BIOLOGY. **Personal Data:** b Brainerd, Minn, January 7, 1938. **Education:** Col St Scholastica, BA, 1960; Univ Wis-Madison, MS, 1963, PhD (anat), 1967. **Professional Experience:** PROF EMER DEPT ANAT & CELL BIOL, GEORGE WASH UNIV SCH MED & HEALTH CARE SCI, as of 2005; dir Neuroscience prog, med ctr, George Wash Univ, 1990-1993; Jones Inst Reproductive Med, E Va Med Sch, Norfolk, 1985-1992; DIR MICROS ANAT, MED CTR, GEORGE WASH UNIV, 1982-; prof anat, med ctr, george Wash univ, beginning 1979; mem primate res adv bd, NIH, 1978-1982; guest worker, Pregnancy Res Br, Nat Inst Child Health & Human Develop, 1977-1985; vis scientist, div biol, Calif Inst Technol, 1976; Consult, Primate Res Ctr, Univ Wis, 1975-1978; from asst prof to assoc prof, Med Ctr, George Wash Univ, 1969-1979; proj assoc, Univ Wis-Madison, 1968-1969; NIH fel, Primate Res Ctr, 1967-1968; res trainee reproductive physiol, Ore Primate Res Ctr, 1966-1967; instr anat, Univ Wis, 1963-1964; res asst chem, Col St Scholastica, 1960-1961. **Memberships:** AAAS; Am Asn Anatomists; Soc Study Reproduction. **Research Statement & Publications:** Cyclic changes in ovarian morphology as observed in light and electron microscopy; correlation of reproductive morphology with physiology. **Mailing Address:** Dept Anat, George Wash Univ, Ross Hall Ste 423, Washington, DC 20037. **Fax:** 202-994-8885. **E-Mail:** koering@gwis2.circ.gwu.edu

KOERKER, DONNA J, ENDOCRINOLOGY. **Education:** Howard Huges Med Ctr, PhD, 1981. **Professional Experience:** INSTR, UNIV WASH, as of 2006. **Mailing Address:** Harborview Med Ctr Univ Wash, Div Endocrin ZA-24 325 Ninth Ave, Seattle, WA 98104-2499. **Fax:** 206-287-8522.

KOERKER, FREDERICK WILLIAM, inorganic chemistry; deceased, see previous edition for last biography

KOERKER, ROBERT LELAND, PHARMACOLOGY. **Personal Data:** b Saginaw, Mich, January 10, 1943. **Education:** Kalamazoo Col, BA, 1965; Emory Univ, PhD (pharmacol), 1970. **Professional Experience:** DIR ACAD PROGAMS & IN-CHG EDUC PROGAMS, MED SCH, WRIGHT STATE UNIV, as of 2005; chair person, dept pharmacol & toxicol, Wright State Univ, 1990-1997; ASSOC PROF PHARMACOL, MED SCH, WRIGHT STATE UNIV, 1980-; asst prof pharmacol, La State Univ Med Ctr, 1974-1980; USPHS res fel, Emory Univ, 1973-1974; NIH res fel pharmacol, Univ Colo Med Ctr, 1970-1973; asst chemist, Dept ChemRes Lab, 1965; asst biologist microbiol, Biochem Res Lab, Dow Chem Co, 1963-1964. **Memberships:** Sigma Xi; AAAS; Am Soc Pharmacol & Exp Therapeut; Soc Toxicol. **Research Statement & Publications:** Toxicity of aldehydes, alcohols, organo-mercurials and other agents in cultured mouse neuroblastoma cells; characterization of uptake and storage mechanisms in cultured mouse neuroblastoma cells. **Mailing Address:** Dept Pharmacol & Toxicol, Wright State Univ, 232D Frederick A White Health Ctr, Dayton, OH 45401-0927. **Fax:** 937-775-2842. **E-Mail:** robert.koerker@wright.edu

KOERNER, E(RNEST) L(EE), CHEMICAL ENGINEERING. **Personal Data:** b Cleveland, Ohio, March 17, 1931; m 1953, c 6. **Education:** Univ Dayton, BChE, 1953; Iowa State Col, MS, 1955, PhD (chem eng), 1956. **Professional Experience:** PRES, TECHRAD INC, 1983-; pres, Technol Res & Develop Inc, 1970-1983; sr res group leader, Kerr-McGee Corp, 1967-1970; sr res specialist, Kerr-McGee Corp, 1967; res specialist, Monsanto Co, 1959-1967; res engr & sect leader extractive processes, Union CarbideMetals Co, 1957-1959; Asst chem eng, Ames Lab, AEC, Iowa State Col, 1953-1956. **Memberships:** Am Inst Chem Engrs; Am Inst Mining Metall & Petrol Engrs; Nat Soc Prof Engrs. **Research Statement & Publications:** Extractive metallurgical processes; liquid-liquid extraction; hazard wastes treatment; energy recovery from solid wastes; biological and enzyme treatment of waste waters. **Mailing Address:** 12721 St Andrews Terr, Oklahoma City, OK 73120-8807.

KOERNER, JAMES FREDERICK, BIOCHEMISTRY, NEUROSCIENCE. **Personal Data:** b Charles City, Iowa, June 30, 1929; m 1958, c 2. **Education:** Iowa State Col, BS, 1950, PhD (biochem), 1956. **Professional Experience:** PROF EMER, DEPT BIOCHEM, MOLECULAR BIOL & BIOPHYS, SCH MED, UNIV MINN, MINNEAPOLIS, as of 2003; prof biochem, sch med, Univ Minn, Minneapolis, beginning 1972; from asst prof to assoc prof, Sch Med, Univ Minn, Minneapolis, 1961-1972; res assoc, Mass InstTechnol, 1958-1961; USPHS fel, Mass Inst Technol, 1956-1958; asst, Iowa State Col, 1952-1956; res assoc biochem, Iowa State Col, 1950-1952. **Memberships:** AAAS; Am Soc Biol Chemists; Soc Neuroscience; Am Soc Neurochem. **Research Statement & Publications:** Neurochemistry; acidic amino acids as excitatory neurotransmitters; glutamate metabolism. **Mailing Address:** Dept Biochem, Molecular Biol & Biophys, Sch Med, Univ Minn, 2-236 BSBE, 435 Del St S E, Minneapolis, MN 55455. **Fax:** 612-625-5780. **E-Mail:** koern003@maroon.tc.umn.edu

KOERNER, JOHN E, PHARMACOLOGY. **Education:** Stanford Univ, PhD. **Professional Experience:** SR PHARMACOL, DIV CARDIOVASC & RENAL PROD, OFF NEW DRUGS, CDER, FDA, as of 2002. **Mailing Address:** Div Cardiorenal Drug Prod FDA, 5600 Fishers Ln HFD-110, Rockville, MD 20857. **Fax:** 301-480-5777.

KOERNER, ROBERT M, SOIL MECHANICS. **Personal Data:** b Philadelphia, Pa, December 2, 1933; m 1959, c 3. **Education:** Drexel Inst Technol, BSCE, 1956, MSCE, 1963; Duke Univ, PhD (soil mech), 1968. **Professional Experience:** PROF EMER CIVIL ENG, DREXEL UNIV, as of 2003; prof civil eng, Drexel Univ, beginning 1976; from asst prof to assoc prof, Drexel Univ, 1968-1976; instr, part-time, 1967-1968; NSF teaching intern, Duke Univ, 1965-1967; instr, Pa Mil Col, 1964-1965; engr & supt, J J Skelly, Inc, 1962-1963; engr analyst, Dames & Moore, 1960-1962; Engr & supt, Conduit & Found Corp, 1956-1960. **Memberships:** Am Soc Civil Engrs; Am Soc Eng Educ. **Research Statement & Publications:** Foundation engineering; particle mechanics; powder metallurgy. **Mailing Address:** Dept Civil Eng, Drexel Univ, Springfield, PA 19064. **Fax:** 215-895-1363. **E-Mail:** robert.koerner@coe.drexel.edu

KOERNER, T J, FACILITATE PEER REVIEW. **Personal Data:** b Rochester, NY, June 15, 1954; m 1978, c 3. **Education:** Univ Toronto, Ont, Can, BSc, 1976; Univ Cincinnati, PhD (develop biol), 1985. **Professional Experience:** SCI PROG DIR, AM CANCER SOC, 1988-; asst med res prof, Duke Univ Med Ctr, 1985-1988; Postdoctoral researcher, Columbia Univ, New York, 1982-1985. **Memberships:** Am Soc Biochem & Molecular Biol; Genetics Soc Am; Am Asn Cancer Res; Am Soc Microbiol; AAAS. **Research Statement & Publications:** Facilitate collaboration to advance health research and administration of the peer review of applications and oversight of awards in the areas of molecular biology, immunology, and virology. **Mailing Address:** Res Dept, Am Cancer Soc 1599 Clifton Rd NE, Atlanta, GA 30329-4251. **Fax:** 404-321-4669. **E-Mail:** tj.koerner@cancer.org

KOERNER, THEODORE ALFRED WILLIAM, BLOOD TRANSFUSION MEDICINE, CELL MEMBRANE BIOCHEMISTRY. **Personal Data:** b Waco, Tex, July 30, 1947; m 1971, c 2. **Education:** La State Univ, BS, 1970, PhD (biochem), 1975; Tulane Univ, MD, 1978. **Professional Experience:** ASSOC PROF BIOCHEM, UNIV IOWA COL MED, 1990-; legal expert, blood-borne acquired immune deficiency syndrome, Law Off Meis & Waite, San Francisco, 1989-; assoc med dir, DeGowin Blood Ctr, Univ Iowa Hosp & Clins, 1988-; ASSOC PROF PATH, UNIV IOWA COL MED, 1988-; asst prof, Univ Iowa Col Med, 1986-1988; asst med dir, DeGowin Blood Ctr, Univ Iowa Hosp & Clins, 1986-1988; asst prof path, Tulane Univ Sch Med, 1982-1986; adj asst prof, Dept Biochem, Tulane Univ Sch Med & med dir, Blood Ctr &Apheresis Serv, Tulane Univ Hosp, 1982-1986; Acad Clin Lab Physicians & Scientists younginvestr award, 1982; fel lab med, Yale Univ Sch Med, 1981-1982; resident physician, Yale-New Haven Hosp, 1979-1981; Intern path, Yale-New Haven Hosp, 1978-1979. **Memberships:** Am Chem Soc; Am Asn Blood Banks; Am Soc Biochem & Molecular Biol; AmAsn Pathologists; Am Soc Hemat; Am Soc Apheresis. **Research Statement & Publications:** Structure, function, immunology and pathophysiology of blood platelet membrane glycoproteins, glycolipids and phospholipids; oligosaccharide and lipid chemistry; high pressure liquid chromatography and multidimensional nuclear magnetic resonance spectroscopy; transfusion medicine; storage and survival of platelets; transfusion-transmitted acquired immune deficiency syndrome and other infectious diseases. **Mailing Address:** Dept Path Med Res Ctr 143, Univ Iowa Col Med, Iowa City, IA 52242-1087. **Fax:** 319-335-8348.

KOERNER, WILLIAM ELMER, PHYSICAL CHEMISTRY, ANALYTICAL CHEMISTRY. **Personal Data:** b Neenah, Wis, November 3, 1923; m 1947, Anita; c Pamela & Janet. **Education:** Univ Wis, BS, 1946, PhD (phys chem), 1949. **Professional Experience:** RETIRED; fel prog coordr, Phys Sci Ctr, 1986-1995; dual tech ladder consult & coordr, 1980-1995; dir phys sci, Phys Sci Ctr, 1980-1986; mgr, Phys Sci Ctr, 1964-1980; group leader phys chem, Monsanto Co, 1954-1964; res phys chemist, Monsanto Co, 1949-1954. **Memberships:** AAAS; Soc Appl Spectros; Am Chem Soc; Sigma Xi. **Research Statement & Publications:** Chemical reaction kinetics; thermochemistry; physical analytical chemistry. **Mailing Address:** 5642 Murdoch Ave, St Louis, MO 63109-2867.

KOERTING, LOLA ELISABETH, GENETICS, CYTOLOGY. **Personal Data:** b Munich, Ger, January 31, 1924; American citizen; m 1953, c 2. **Education:** Munich Tech Univ, BS, 1947, MS, 1949, PhD (biol, agr), 1953. **Professional Experience:** CONSULT GENETICIST, KITCHAWAN RES LAB, BROOKLYN BOT GARDEN, NY, 1975-; res fel cytogenetics, New Eng Inst Med Res, 1965-1973; res assoc forestgenetics, Sch Forestry, Yale Univ, 1955-1958; chief histol & ultrasonics, New Eng Inst Med Res, 1954-1955; res asst plant genetics, Munich Tech Univ, 1948-1953. **Memberships:** AAAS; Environ Mutagen Soc; Bot Soc Am; Sigma Xi; Tissue Cult Asn. **Research Statement & Publications:** Cytogenetics; induced chromosome abnormalities and mutations; tissue culture. **Mailing Address:** Kitchawan Res Lab, Brooklyn Bot Garden, Ossining, NY 6877.

KOESTEL, MARK ALFRED, FIELD GEOLOGY & GEOCHEMISTRY. **Personal Data:** b Cleveland, Ohio, January 1, 1951; c Bonnie & Jennifer. **Education:** Univ Ariz, BS, 1978. **Professional Experience:** GEOLOGIST & PHOTOGRAPHER, 1990-; proj mgr-sr geologist, ApplGeosysts, 1988-1990; mgr geol serv-hydrogeologist, Harmsworth Assocs, 1986-1988; NMexstate rep, Minerals Explor Coalition, 1982; sr geologist-proj mgr, Union Oil Calif, 1978-1986; Field geologist, Falconbridge Nickel Mines/Superior Oil Co, 1977. **Memberships:** Am Inst Prof Geologists; Geol Soc Am; Nat Geog Soc; Soc Mining Engrs. **Research Statement & Publications:** Environmental, economic and general education geology; base, precious and strategic metal exploration; subsurface investigation and interpretation; geochemistry. **Mailing Address:** 45 Brownfield Lane, Phillips Ranch, CA 91766.

KOESTER, CHARLES JOHN, OPHTHALMIC OPTICS, MICROSCOPY. **Personal Data:** b Niagara Falls, NY, January 26, 1929; m 1953, c 4. **Education:** Carnegie Inst Technol, BS, 1950; Univ Rochester, PhD (physics, optics), 1955. **Professional Experience:** RETIRED; assoc prof clin biophys ophthal, Columbia Univ Col Physicians & Surgeons, 1984-1991; asst prof biophys ophthal, Columbia Univ, Col Physicians & Surgeons, 1978-1984; dir res, Sci Instrument Div, 1975-1977; indust rep, Food & Drug Admin Ophthalmic Device Classification Panel, 1974-1978; mem bd dirs, Optical Soc Am, 1974-1976; lectrophthal, Columbia Univ, beginning 1970; appl res mgr, Am Optical Corp, 1965-1975; physicist, Am Optical Corp, 1959-1965; res assoc, Nat Bur Stand, 1958-1959; physicist, Am Optical Co, 1955-1958; asst, Univ Rochester, 1950-1955. **Memberships:** Optical Soc Am; Asn Res Vision & Ophthal; Am Acad Ophthal; Am Soc Cataract Refractive Surg; Am Acad Optom. **Research Statement & Publications:** Ophthalmic instruments and microscopes; interference, polarizing, and confocalmicroscopes; image enhancement in fiber optics; laser photocoagulation; microscopy of the cornea; intraocular lenses. **Mailing Address:** 60 Kent Rd, Glen Rock, NJ 07452.

KOESTER, JOHN D, BEHAVIOR, BIOPHYSIOLOGY. **Education:** Columbia Univ, PhD (physiol), 1971. **Professional Experience:** PROF NEUROBIOLOGY & BEHAV LEARNING, SCH MED, COLUMBIA UNIV, as of 2004; ACTG DIR, CTR NEUROBIOLOGY & BEHAV, SCH MED, COLUMBIA UNIV, 1974-. **Research Statement & Publications:** The cellular and network properties of those neurons in the abdominal ganglion that mediate control and coordination of the circulatory, respiratory, and renal systems; published over 20 articles. **Mailing Address:** Dept Neurobiology, Col Physicians & Surgeons, Columbia Univ, 722 W 168th St, New York, NY 10032-2695. **Fax:** 212-543-5410. **E-Mail:** jdk3@columbia.edu

KOESTER, MARTHA K, PULP & PAPER INCLUDING ADDITIVES, BIOCHEMISTRY OF SOFTWOOD EMBRYOLOGY. **Personal Data:** b Chicago, Ill, November 24, 1946; m 1970, Kurt. **Education:** Knox Col, BA, 1968; Univ Calif, PhD (biochem), 1979. **Professional Experience:** SCIENTIST, WEYERHAEUSER CO, 1988-; sci writer, 1982-1988; Postdoctoral assoc, Boston Biomed Res, 1980-1982. **Memberships:** Am Chem Soc; Asn Women Sci. **Research Statement & Publications:** Proprietary research in pulp and paper process characterization; biochemical characterization of softwood embryos. **Mailing Address:** WTC 2F25, Tacoma, WA 98477. **Fax:** 253-924-6654.

KOESTLER, ROBERT CHARLES, PESTICIDE CHEMISTRY. **Personal Data:** b Elizabeth, NJ, October 31, 1932; m Sally; c Jane, Julia & David. **Education:** Cornell Univ, BA, 1954; Univ NC, Chapel Hill, PhD (org chem), 1961. **Professional Experience:** RETIRED; sr res scientist, Atochem, 1986-1995; res scientist, Pennwalt Corp, 1983-1986; proj leader, Pennwalt Corp, 1977-1983; sr res chemist, Pennwalt Corp, 1965-1977; Res chemist, Am Viscose Div, FMC Corp, 1961-1965; Financial mgr, Controlled Release Soc. **Memberships:** Am Chem Soc; Int Controlled Release Soc. **Research Statement & Publications:** Organometallics; films and coatings; organic synthesis; microencapsulation and controlled release technology. **Mailing Address:** 2004 Pebblestone Ct, College Station, TX 77845. **E-Mail:** k3psw@aol.com

KOESTNER, ADALBERT, VETERINARY PATHOLOGY. **Personal Data:** b Hatzfeld, Rumania, September 10, 1920; American citizen; m 1951, c 2. **Education:** Univ Munich, DMV, 1951; Ohio State Univ, MSc, 1957, PhD, 1959. **Professional Experience:** PROF EMER, OHIO STATE UNIV, 1991-; chmn path, Mich State Univ, 1981-1991; chmn, Dept Vet Pathobiology, Ohio State Univ, 1972-1981; prof, Dept Vet Pathobiology, Ohio State Univ, 1964-1971; from instr to assoc prof, Vet Path, Ohio State Univ, 1955-1964; res assoc bact, Vet Col, Univ Munich, 1951-1952. **Memberships:** AAAS; Am Asn Pathologists; Soc Neuroscience; Am Vet Med Asn; Am Asn CancerRes; Am Asn Neuropath; Am Col Vet Path. **Research Statement & Publications:** Comparative neuropathology; comparative and experimental oncology. **Mailing Address:** Dept Pathobiology, Ohio State Univ, 1925 Coffey Rd, Columbus, OH 43210. **Fax:** 614-292-6473.

KOETHE, SUSAN M, IMMUNOLOGY. **Personal Data:** b San Diego, Calif, September 4, 1945; m 1968, c 1. **Education:** San Diego State Col, BS, 1967; Univ Harvard, PhD (immunol), 1974. **Professional Experience:** PROF PATH, MED COL WIS, as of 2003; assoc prof path, Med Col Wis, beginning 1981; chmn, Milwaukee Immunol Group, 1978-1982; asst prof, Med Col Wis, 1976-1981; NIH fel, Med Col Wis, 1974-1976. **Memberships:** Am Asn Immunol. **Research Statement & Publications:** Immunoregulation in myasthenia gravis and multiple sclerosis. **Mailing Address:** Dept Path Med Col Wis, 9200 W Wis Ave, Milwaukee, WI 53226. **Fax:** 414-805-6337.

KOETKE, DONALD D, NUCLEAR STRUCTURE. **Personal Data:** b Chicago, Ill, December 12, 1937; m 1959, c 3. **Education:** Concordia Col, Ill, BS, 1959; Northwestern Univ, Ill, MS, 1963, PhD (physics), 1968. **Professional Experience:** CHMN PHYSICS, VALPARAISO UNIV, as of 2003; vis scientist, Los Alamos Nat Lab, beginning 1982; consult, Int Atomic Energy Agency, beginning 1980; PROF PHYSICS, VALPARAISO UNIV, 1977-; vis scientist, Argonne Nat Lab, 1969 &1971-1982; assoc prof physics, Concordia Col, Ill, 1967-1977. **Memberships:** Am Phys Soc; Am Asn Physics Teachers; Sigma Xi. **Research Statement & Publications:** Experiments in muon and neutrino physics done at Los Alamos; low energy nuclear cross-section measurements relative to solar neutrino production. **Mailing Address:** Dept Physics & Astron, Valparaiso Univ, Neils Sci Ctr 139, Valparaiso, IN 46383. **Fax:** 219-464-5489. **E-Mail:** donald.koetke@valpo.edu

KOETZLE, THOMAS F, CHEMICAL CRYSTALLOGRAPHY, NEUTRON AND X-RAY DIFFRACTION. **Personal Data:** b New York, NY, October 15, 1943; American citizen; m 1967, Carole E Peltz; c Laura E & John H. **Education:** Harvard Univ, BA, 1964, MA, 1965, PhD (chem), 1970. **Professional Experience:** Pres, Pittsburgh Diffraction Soc, 2006; mem, Macromolecular Neutron Diffractometer Inst Develop Team, Spallation Neutron Source, 2003-; mem exec comn, Single Crystal Diffraction Inst Develop Team, Spallation Neutron Source, 2002-; STA SR SCI, ARGONNE NAT LAB, 2001-; chair, Synchrotron Radiation Spec Interest Group, Am Crystallog Asn, 1999; guest scientist, Argonne Nat Lab, 1999-2001; mem, US Nat Comt Codata, 1992-1994; mem ed bd, J Phys Chem Ref Data, 1991-1993; sr chemist, Brookhaven Nat Lab, 1989-1998; ed, Molecular Struct Biol, 1988-1992; mem, US Nat Comt Crystallog, 1988-1990; mem, Task Force Sci Numerical Data, Am Chem Soc, 1987-1994; mem, US Nat Comt Crystallog, 1984-1986; chmn, Neutron Scattering Spec Interest Group, Am Crystallog Asn, 1983-1984; mem, Int Union Crystallog Comn, Crystallog Data, 1981-1993; chemist, Brookhaven Nat Lab, 1975-1989; prin investr, Protein Data Bank, 1973-1993; assoc chemist, Brookhaven Nat Lab, 1973-1975; NIH fel, 1971-1973; res assoc chem, Brookhaven Nat Lab, 1970-1973; AEC fel, 1970-1971. **Memberships:** AAAS; NY Acad Sci; Am Chem Soc; Am Crystallog Asn; Mats Res Soc; Neutron Scattering Soc Am; Pittsburgh Diffraction Soc. **Research Statement & Publications:** Applications of neutron and x-ray diffraction to the analysis of molecular structure and chemical bonding; transition metal hydride and molecular hydrogen complexes and related organometallic systems important in catalysis site-specific isotope labeling. **Mailing Address:** IPNS Div, Argonne Nat Lab, Bldg 360, Argonne, IL 60439. **Fax:** 630-252-4163. **E-Mail:** tkoetzle@anl.gov

KOEVENIG, JAMES L, BOTANY, BIOLOGY. **Personal Data:** b Postville, Iowa, March 18, 1931; wid, c Kimberly K & Kurt L. **Education:** Univ Iowa, BA, 1955, PhD (sci educ & bot), 1961; State Col Iowa, MA, 1957. **Professional Experience:** PROF EMER BIOL, UNIV CENT FLA, as of 2005; fac res partic, Savannah River Ecol Lab, 1978; prof biol, Univ Cent Fla, 1972-1995; NSF sci fac fel, Princeton Univ, 1967-1968; mem eval panel, Comn Undergrad Educ in Biol, 1965; from assoc prof to prof bot & biol, Univ Kans, 1964-1972; United Nations Educ Sci & Cult Orgn Panel on Short Biol Films, 1964; vis lectr, Univ Colo, 1963-1964; res consult, Biol Sci Curric Study, Univ Colo, 1962-1964; asst prof zool, San Diego State Col, 1961-1962; res assoc, Univ Iowa, 1961; elem sch teacher, 1955-1956. **Memberships:** AAAS; Bot Soc Am; Nat Asn Biol Teachers; Am Inst Biol Sci; Sigma Xi. **Research Statement & Publications:** Myxomycete taxonomy; plant growth and development; science visual aid and evaluation. **Mailing Address:** Dept Biol, Univ Cent Fla, PO Box 25000, Orlando, FL 32816.

KOFF, BERNARD LOUIS, MILITARY & COMMERCIAL AIRCRAFT & ROCKET PROPULSION. **Personal Data:** b Huntington, NY, March 24, 1927. **Education:** Clarkson Univ, BS, 1951; NY Univ, MS, 1958. **Honorary Degrees:** DSc, Clarkson Univ, 1993. **Honors & Awards:** Air Breathing Propulsion Award, Am Indust Arts Asn, 1984; Theodore vonKarman Award, Air Force Asn, 1988; R Tom Sawyer Award, Am Soc Mech Engr, 1988; George Mead Medal, United Technologies Corp, 1988; Reed Aeronaut Award, 1990; DanielGuggenheim Award, Am Indust Arts Asn, Am Soc Mech Engrs, Soc Automotive Engrs, 1992; Franklin W Kolk Award, Soc Automotive Engrs, 1993. **Professional Experience:** RETIRED; exec vpres eng & technol, Govt Eng Bus, 1990-1997; exec vpres eng & technol, 1983-1987; mem, Space Div Adv Bd, beginning 1988; mem, Govt Eng Bus, 1987-1990; mem, Eng Div, 1983-1987; mem, Sci Adv Bd, USAF, 1986-1990; sr vpres, Govt Prod Div, Pratt & Whitney, 1980-1983; chief engr, Gen Elec, 1975-1980; mgr to gen mgr, Gen Elec, 1965-1975; sr engr, Gen Elec, 1962-1964; design engr, Gen Elec, 1958-1962; design engr, Curtis Wright, 1956-1958; design engr, Fairchild, 1952-1956; test engr, Gen Elec, 1951-1952. **Memberships:** Nat Acad Eng; Am Soc Mech Engrs; fel Am Inst Aeronaut & Astronaut; fel SocAutomotive Engrs. **Research Statement & Publications:** Aircraft and spacecraft engine industry; author of 16 technical publications; awarded 13 patents. **Mailing Address:** 8 Cambria Rd E, Palm Beach Gardens, FL 33418. **Fax:** 561-626-9434. **E-Mail:** benlkoff@worldnet.att.net

KOFF, RAYMOND STEVEN, INTERNAL MEDICINE, GASTROENTEROLOGY. **Personal Data:** b Brooklyn, NY, June 11, 1939; m 1960, c 2. **Education:** Adelphi Col, BA, 1958; Albert Einstein Col Med, MD, 1962; Am Bd Internal Med, dipl. **Professional Experience:** PROF, SCH MED, UNIV MASS, 1991-; dir, clin Hepathology res, Univ Mass; chmn med, Columbia MetroWest Med Ctr, 1986-; chief hepatology sect, Vet Admin, 1973-1986; from asst prof to prof, Sch Med, Boston Univ, 1969-1991; clin investr, Vet Admin, 1969-1972; res fel, Mass Gen Hosp, Harvard Med Sch, 1968-1969; NIH trainee gastroenterol, Mass Gen Hosp, 1966-1969; clin & res fel, Mass Gen Hosp, Harvard Med Sch, 1966-1968; res fel, Tufts Univ & Lemuel Shattuck Hosp, 1965-1966; teaching fel, Tufts Univ & Lemuel Shattuck Hosp, 1964-1965; asst resident, Barnes Hosp, Wash Univ, 1963-1964; intern med, Barnes Hosp, Wash Univ, 1962-1963. **Memberships:** Soc Epidemiol Res; Am Asn Study Liver Dis; fel Am Col Physicians; Am Gastroenterol Asn; Int Asn Study Liver; fel Am Col Gastroenterol. **Research Statement & Publications:** Viral hepatitis; drug hepatotoxicity; chronic hepatitis. **Mailing Address:** Univ Mass Memorial Health Cen, 55 Lake Ave, North Worcester, MA 01655.

KOFF, WAYNE C, BIOLOGY. **Education:** Wash Univ, BA; Baylor Col of Med, Phd. **Professional Experience:** SR VPRES, UNITED BIOMED INC, as of 1998. **Mailing Address:** United Biomed Inc, 25 Davids Dr, Hauppauge, NY 11788. **Fax:** 516-273-1717.

KOFFLER, HENRY, MICROBIOLOGY. **Personal Data:** b Vienna, Austria, September 17, 1922; American citizen; m 1946. **Education:** Univ Ariz, BS, 1943; Univ Wis, MS, 1944, PhD (bact), 1947. **Honors & Awards:** Eli Lilly & Co Award, 1957. **Professional Experience:** RETIRED; PROF BIOCHEM & MICROBIOL & PRESIDENT, UNIV ARIZ, 1982-; prof biochem & microbiol, Univ Mass, Amherst, 1979-1982; prof biochem & microbiol& vpres acad affairs, Univ Minn, Minneapolis, 1975-1979; From asst prof to assoc prof bact, F LHovde Distinguished prof, 1974-1975; mem, Purdue Res Found, 1967-; consult-examr, NCentAsn Cols, 1967-; chmn, Comn Undergrad Educ in Biol Sci, 1967-1969; mem, Comn UndergradEduc in Biol Sci, 1966-1969; vchmn, Comn Undergrad Educ in Biol Sci, 1966-1967; head deptbiol sci, Purdue Univ, West Lafayette, 1959-1975; asst dean, Purdue Univ, West Lafayette, 1959-1960; asst to dean grad sch, Purdue Univ, West Lafayette, 1957-1959; Guggenheim fel, Sch Med, Case Western Reserve Univ, 1953-1954; prof biol, Purdue Univ, West Lafayette, 1952-1974; coordr res, Purdue Univ, West Lafayette, 1949-1959; From asst prof to assoc profbact, Purdue Univ, West Lafayette, 1947-1952; mem, 5th Int Cong ElectronMicros, Philadelphia, 16th Int Zool Cong, Washington, DC, 4th Int Cong Chemother, Washington, DC, 24th Int Cong Physiol Sci, 1st Int Cong Bact, Jerusalem & 1st Int Cong Int AsnMicrobiol Soc, Tokyo; mem, 2nd-7th Int Cong Biochem, Paris, Brussels, Vienna, Moscow & Tokyo; mem, 1st-3rd Int Biophys Cong, Stockholm, Vienna & Boston; mem, 9th & 11th Int Bot Cong, Montreal & Seattle; mem, 6th-8th & 10th Int Cong Microbiol, Rome, Stockholm, Montreal & Mexico City. **Memberships:** Am Soc Biol Chemists; Biophys Soc; Am Soc Microbiol; fel Am Acad Microbiol; Am Soc Cell Biologists. **Research Statement & Publications:** Biosynthesis of carbohydrates; chemistry, biosynthesis and mechanism of action of antibiological peptides; structure and biosynthesis of flagellin and bacterial flagella; self-assembly of macromolecular structures; molecular bases for biological stability. **Mailing Address:** Dept Bio-Chem Henry Koffler Bldg, 1340 E Univ Blvd, Tucson, AZ 85721-0001. **Fax:** 520-626-7800.

KOFFMAN, ELLIOT B, COMPUTER SCIENCE EDUCATION, ARTIFICIAL INTELLIGENCE. **Personal Data:** b Boston, Mass, May 7, 1942; m 1963, Caryn; c Richard, Deborah & Robin. **Education:** Mass Inst Technol, SBEE & SMEE, 1964, PhD (eng), 1967. **Professional Experience:** PROF COMPUT & INFO SCI, TEMPLE UNIV, 1977-; assoc prof, Temple Univ, 1974-1977. **Memberships:** Asn Comput Mach. **Mailing Address:** Dept Comput & Info Sci, Temple Univ, Rm 311 Wachman Hall, Philadelphia, PA 19122-2585. **E-Mail:** koffman@temple.edu

KOFFOLT, JOSEPH H, CHEMISTRY. **Honorary Degrees:** DSc, Ohio State Univ, 1972. **Professional Experience:** PROF EMER, OHIO STATE UNIV, as of 2005. **Mailing Address:** Ohio State Univ, 100 W 18th Ave, Columbus, OH 06906. **Fax:** 614-292-1685.

KOFFYBERG, FRANCOIS PIERRE, solid state science; deceased, see previous edition for last biography

KOFLER, RICHARD ROBERT, PHYSICS. **Personal Data:** b Milwaukee, Wis, July 4, 1935; m 1959, c 3. **Education:** Marquette Univ, BS, 1958; Univ Wis, MS, 1960, PhD (elem particle physics), 1964. **Professional Experience:** PROF EMER PHYSICS, UNIV MASS, AMHERST, 2001-; LAWRENCE BERKELEY LAB, as of 2002; assoc prof physics, Univ Mass, Amherst, beginning 1969; asst prof, Univ Mass, Amherst, 1965-1969; res assoc physics, Univ Wis, 1964-1965. **Memberships:** Am Inst Physics; Am Phys Soc. **Research Statement & Publications:** High energy elementary particle physics. **Mailing Address:** MS67 SLAC, Stanford Univ PO Box 4349, Stanford, CA 94309. **Fax:** 413-545-0648. **E-Mail:** kofler@physics.umass.edu

KOFORD, JAMES SHINGLE, VLSI COMPUTER AIDED DESIGN. **Personal Data:** b Cheyenne, Wyo, July 26, 1938. **Education:** Stanford Univ, BS, 1959, MS, 1960, PhD (elec eng), 1964. **Professional Experience:** PRES & CEO, MONTEREY DESIGN SYST, as of 2006; vpres comput aided design, Lsi Logic Inc, beginning 1981; mgr, Network Develop Lab, Boeing Comput Servs, 1975-1981; vpres develop, Packet Commun, Inc, 1973-1975; sr mem tech staff, Fairchild Semiconductor Corp, 1969-1973; mem tech staff, Fairchild Semiconductor Corp, 1966-1969; proj engr, IBM Components Div, 1964-1966; res asst mem tech staff, Stanford Electronics Lab, 1960-1964. **Memberships:** Inst Elec & Electronics Engrs. **Research Statement & Publications:** Adaptive pattern-recognition systems speech recognition; threshold elements adaptation algorithms; computer-aided design for microelectronic circuits logic simulation graphic data processing. **Mailing Address:** Monterey Design Syst, 2171 Landings Dr, Mtain View, CA 94043. **Fax:** 650-919-0411.

KOFRON, JAMES THOMAS, PHOTOGRAPHIC CHEMISTRY. **Personal Data:** b Petersburg, Va, March 11, 1928; m 1960, c 4. **Education:** Univ Notre Dame, BS, 1952; Mass Inst Technol, PhD (org chem), 1956. **Honors & Awards:** Progress Medal, Photog Soc Am, 1988. **Professional Experience:** RETIRED; res assoc chem, Res Labs, Eastman Kodak Co, 1976-1975; sr res assoc, Res Labs, Eastman Kodak Co, 1975-1992. **Memberships:** AAAS; Am Chem Soc. **Research Statement & Publications:** Reaction mechanisms in chemistry of photographic processes. **Mailing Address:** 123 El Mar Dr, Rochester, NY 14616.

KOFRON, WILLIAM G, ORGANIC CHEMISTRY. **Personal Data:** b Petersburg, Va, August 9, 1934. **Education:** Univ Notre Dame, BS, 1956; Univ Rochester, PhD (chem), 1961. **Professional Experience:** PROF EMER CHEM, UNIV AKRON, 1996-; from asst prof to prof, Univ Akron, 1965-1996; sr chemist, Med Chem Dept, Geigy Res Labs, NY, 1963-1965; fel, Columbia Univ, 1962-1963; Res assoc chem, Duke Univ, 1960-1962. **Memberships:** Am Chem Soc. **Research Statement & Publications:** Chemistry of carbanions; heterocyclic chemistry. **Mailing Address:** Dept Chem, Univ Akron, 190 E Buchtel Commons, Akron, OH 44325-3601. **E-Mail:** wgk@uakron.edu

KOFSKY, IRVING LOUIS, PHYSICS. **Personal Data:** b New York, NY, 1925; m 1969, c 3. **Education:** Syracuse Univ, BA, 1945, PhD (physics), 1952. **Professional Experience:** PRES & TECH DIR, PHOTOMETRICS INC, 1968-; physicist, Tech Opers, Inc, 1957-1968; asst prof, Smith Col, 1952-1956; instr physics, Syracuse Univ, 1947-1951. **Memberships:** Am Phys Soc; Am Asn Physics Teachers. **Research Statement & Publications:** Extensive showers in cosmic radiation; weapons effects; gaseous electronics; atmospheric optics; photometry, image analysis and scanning theory. **Mailing Address:** PhotoMetrics Inc, 4 Arrow Dr, Woburn, MA 01801. **Fax:** 781-935-0747.

KOFT, BERNARD WALDEMAR, BACTERIOLOGY. **Personal Data:** b Hammonton, NJ, November 21, 1921; m 1944, Betty J Ward; c Susan, Helen, David, Daniel & Paul. **Education:** Rutgers Univ, BS, 1943; Univ Pa, MS, 1947, PhD (bact), 1950. **Professional Experience:** PROF EMER MICROBIOL, RUTGERS UNIV, 1987-; from asst prof to prof, Rutgers Univ, 1957-1987; From instr to asst prof bact, Jefferson Med Col, 1950-1957. **Memberships:** Am Soc Microbiol; fel NY Acad Sci; Sigma Xi. **Research Statement & Publications:** Bacterial nutrition; metabolism; vitamin synthesis; cellulose degradation. **Mailing Address:** Div Life Sci, Rochester Univ, Rochester, NJ 08816.

KOGA, PHILIP G, CYTOKINES, BIOSENSORS. **Personal Data:** b Fresno, Calif, August 15, 1950; m 1994, Lori. **Education:** Univ Calif, BS, 1972, PhD (molecular biol), 1978. **Professional Experience:** ASSOC DIR SPECIAL PROG US ARMY EDGEWOOD CHEM BIOL CTR, 2004-; dir, Cel-Sci Corp, ending 2001; consult, biogerontronix corp, Sci applns intCorp, 1992-; team leader, indust adv group biosensors, NATO, 1992; mem, tech adv comt, Univ Wash, 1989-1990; prog mgr & prin engr, allied signal, 1987-1994; int deleg biodefense, 1985; group leader, US army chem & eng ctr, 1984-1987; sr scientist, becton-Dickinson, 1983-1984; NIH fel immunochem, Johns hopkins sch med, 1980-1983; post-doctoral biochem, State Univ NY Upstate Med Ctr, 1979. **Memberships:** Am Chem Soc; AAAS; Sigma Xi; Am Soc Microbiol. **Research Statement & Publications:** Application of cytokine mixtures to stimulate immune response in test subjects for treatment of various forms of cancer and AIDS. **Mailing Address:** Edgewood Chem Biol Ctr, AMSRD-ECB-AP-B/Michel E3330 5183 Black Hawk RD, Edgewood, MD 21010-5424. **Fax:** 410-436-2014.

KOGA, ROKUTARO, SPACE RADIATION, ASTROPHYSICS. **Personal Data:** b Nagoya, Japan, August 18, 1942; American citizen; m 1981, Cordula; c Even A & Nicole A. **Education:** Univ Calif, Berkeley, BA, 1966; Univ Calif, Riverside, PhD (physics), 1974. **Professional Experience:** DISTINGUISHED SCIENTIST, SPACE SCI APPLN LAB, AEROSPACE CORP, as of 2003; RES PHYSICIST SPACE & ASTROPHYS, AEROSPACE CORP, 1981-; asst prof physics, Case Western Reserve Univ, 1979-1980; sr res assoc astrophys, Case Western Reserve Univ, 1977-1978; res assoc astrophys, Case Western Reserve Univ, 1974-1976; fel, Univ Calif, Riverside, 1974; physicist, Berkeley Sci Labs, 1966-1969. **Memberships:** Am Phys Soc; Sigma Xi; NY Acad Sci; Am Geophys Union. **Research Statement & Publications:** The effects of cosmic rays on microcircuits in space; measurements of heary ions in space using satellite based sensors; gamma-ray astronomy. **Mailing Address:** Aerospace Corp, PO Box 92957 Mail Stop M2-259, Los Angeles, CA 90009-2957. **Fax:** 310-336-1636. **E-Mail:** rocky.koga@aero.org

KOGA, TOYOKI, FOUNDATIONS OF QUANTUM PHYSICS. **Personal Data:** b Japan, April 1, 1912; div, c Rokutaro & Akiya. **Education:** Univ Tokyo, MS, 1937. **Honorary Degrees:** DSc, Univ Tokyo, 1948. **Professional Experience:** RES & WRITING, 1969-; mem prof staff, TRW Systs, Inc, 1967-1969; visprof, Univ Calif, 1956-1959 & Grad Ctr, Polytech Inst Brooklyn, 1964-1967; prof mech eng, UnivNC, 1963-1964; res scientist, Eng Ctr, Univ Southern Calif, 1959-1963; Fulbright sr res fel, CalifInst Technol, 1955-1956; prof mech eng & appl physics, Nagoya Univ, 1948-1959; Asst profaeronaut, Nagoya Univ, 1940-1948. **Memberships:** Am Phys Soc. **Research Statement & Publications:** Gas dynamics; kinetic theory of gases; plasma physics; kinetic theory of quantum mechanical systems; revision of quantum mechanics; theory of elementary particles; superconductivity. **Mailing Address:** 3061 Ewing Ave, Altadena, CA 91001.

KOGAN, MARCOS, ENTOMOLOGY, ECOLOGY. **Personal Data:** b Rio de Janeiro, Brazil, June 9, 1933; m 1953, c 2. **Education:** Univ Rural do Rio de Janeiro, BS, 1961; Univ Calif, Riverside, PhD (entom), 1969. **Honors & Awards:** ASA/ICI-Am Soybean Res Award, 1986. **Professional Experience:** PROF EMER ENTOM & DIR, INTEGRATED PLANT PROTECTION CTR, ORE STATE UNIV, as of 2004; prof entom & dir, Integrated Plant Protection Ctr, Orestate Univ, Corvallis, beginning 1991; ed comt, Thomas Say Pub Entom Soc Am, 1988-1991; edcomt, Entomologia Experimentalis et Applicata, 1985-1990; ed comt, Ann Rev Entom, 1984-1988; mem sci deleg Repub China, 1981; prof entom & agr entom, Univ Ill, Urbana, 1977-1990; entomologist, Ill Natural Hist Surv, Urbana, 1976-1990; consult soybean entom Brazil, 1974-1978, Korea, 1978-1979; assoc prof agr entom, Univ Ill, Urbana, 1973-1977; assoc entomologist res, Ill Natural Hist Surv, Urbana, 1969-1976; res assoc, Univ Calif, Riverside, 1969; res fel entom, Univ Calif, Riverside, 1966-1969; biologist res, Inst Oswaldo Cruz, Rio deJaneiro, 1963-1966; Entomologist res, SCent Inst Agr Res, Rio Del Janeiro, 1961-1963. **Memberships:** Entom Soc Am; Brazilian Entom Soc; Sigma Xi; Am Chem Soc. **Research Statement & Publications:** Management of soybean insect pests; soybean resistance to insects; insect plant interactions; nutrition of phytophagous insects; bionomics of Strepsiptera; international cooperation in soybean entomology and crop protection; chemical ecology. **Mailing Address:** Dept Entom, Ore State Univ, 2034 Cordley Rm, 126 Strand Agr Hall, Corvallis, OR 97330-2212. **E-Mail:** koganm@Sci.oregonstate.edu

KOGELMAN, STANLEY, MATHEMATICS. **Education:** Rensselaer Polytech Inst, BS, MS, PhD (math). **Professional Experience:** DIR RES, SALOMON BRO, as of 2006; PRES, DELFT STRATEGIC ADV LLC, as of 2006. **Mailing Address:** Salomon Bro, Seven World Trade Ctr, 41st Floor, New York, NY 10048. **Fax:** 212-783-3833.

KOGELNIK, H W, LASERS, COMMUNICATIONS. **Personal Data:** b Graz, Austria, June 2, 1932; m 1964, c 3. **Education:** Vienna Tech Univ, Dipl Ing, 1955, Dr Tech, 1958; Oxford Univ, DPhil(electromagnetic theory), 1960. **Honors & Awards:** Frederic Ives Medal, Optical Soc, 1984; David Sarnoff Award, Inst Elec &Electronics Engrs, 1989; Quantum Electronics Award, Lasers & Electro Optics Soc, 1991. **Professional Experience:** ADJ PHOTONICS SYSTS RES LAB, LUCENT TECHNOLS, as of 2001; DIR, PHOTONICS SYSTS RES LAB, LUCENT TECHNOLS, 1983-; dir, Electronics Res Lab, 1976-1983; head coherent optics, Res Dept, 1967-1976; mem staffelectronics res, Bell Labs, 1961-1967; Brit Coun scholar, Oxford Univ, 1958-1960; Asst profelectronics, Inst High Frequency Electronics, Vienna, Austria, 1955-1958. **Memberships:** Nat Acad Sci; Nat Acad Eng; fel Inst Elec & Electronics Engrs; fel Optical SocAm; AAAS; Am Phys Soc. **Research Statement & Publications:** Lasers; integrated optics; optical communication. **Mailing Address:** Lucent Technols, 791 Holmdel Keyport Rd, Holmdel, NJ 07733. **Fax:** 732-888-7013. **E-Mail:** herwig@bell.labs.com

KOGER, JOHN W, PHYSICAL METALLURGY. **Personal Data:** b Florence, Ala, August 20, 1940. **Education:** Ga Tech, BChE, 1963, MS, 1965; Univ Fla, PhD (metall & mat), 1967. **Professional Experience:** Adj prof, Dept Eng, Univ Tenn, as of 2006; PROG MGR, LOCKHEEN MARTIN ENERGY SYST, 1993-; Prog Mgr Waste Minimalization, Martin

Marietta Energy Systs Inc, 1990-1993. **Mailing Address:** Y-12 Manufacturing Tech Serv, Lockheed Martin Energy Syst, 9203A MS 8084, Oak Ridge, TN 37831-8084. **Fax:** 423-576-5925. **E-Mail:** kogerjw@ornl.gov

KOGGE, PETER MICHAEL, COMPUTER ARCHITECTURE. **Personal Data:** b Washington, DC, December 3, 1946; m 1971, Mary; c Peter M, Mary E & Timothy M. **Education:** Univ Notre Dame, BSEE, 1968; Syracuse Univ, MS, 1970; Stanford Univ, PhD (eleceng), 1973. **Honors & Awards:** IBM Informal Award, Space Shuttle Computer, 1973; IBM Outstanding Innovation Award for AI Parallel Processor, 1990. **Professional Experience:** CONCURRENT PROF ELEC ENG, UNIV NOTRE DAME, 2003-; ASSOC DEAN RES, UNIV NOTRE DAME, 2001-; distinguished vis scientist, Jet Propulsion Lab, 1997; TEDH MCCOURTNEY PROF COMPUT SCI, UNIV NOTRE DAME, 1994-; mem sr tech staff, IBM, 1981-1993; adj prof comput sci, State Univ NY, Binghamton, 1977-1994; from jr engr to srengr, IBM, 1968-1981; fel, IBM. **Memberships:** Fel Inst Elec & Electronics Engrs; Asn Comput Mach; Am Asn Artificial Intel. **Research Statement & Publications:** Massively parallel computing using integrated memory and logic very large scale integration. **Mailing Address:** Dept Comput Sci & Eng, Univ Notre Dame, 384 Fitzpatrick Hall, Notre Dame, IN 46556. **Fax:** 219-631-9260. **E-Mail:** kogge@cse.nd.edu

KOGON, IRVING CHARLES, polymer chemistry; deceased, see previous edition for last biography

KOGOS, L(AURENCE), CHEMICAL ENGINEERING. **Personal Data:** b Boston, Mass, July 24, 1929; m 1951, Rae; c Michael & Leslie. **Education:** Northeastern Univ, BS, 1951. **Professional Experience:** CONSULT, 1990-; chief exec officer, Ouimet group, Brockton, Mass, 1984-1990; TLB Plastics, Brewster, NY, 1982-1984; vpres & gen mgr, Roper Plastics, Inc, NY, 1980-1982; pres, Plastics Div, W R Grace & Co, 1973-1979; pres, Polymeric Fabricants Div, Whittaker Corp, 1972-1973; dir opers, Plymouth Rubber Co, Inc, 1970-1972; gen mgr, Dynamic Coaters, Inc, 1963-1970; exec vpres, Farrington Texol Corp, 1959-1963; gen mgr, Sawyer-Tower, Inc, 1958-1959; tech dir, Sawyer-Tower, Inc, 1956-1958; dir tech sales, Sawyer-Tower, Inc, 1955; chief res engr, Sawyer-Tower, Inc, 1952-1953; Chem engr, Sawyer-Tower, Inc, 1951-1952. **Memberships:** Am Soc Plastics Engrs; Am Inst Chem Engrs emer mem. **Research Statement & Publications:** Application of protective and decorative coatings to fabrics; plastics molding, extrusion and forming. **Mailing Address:** 9 Pioneer Circle, Sharon, MA 02067. **E-Mail:** lrko@attbi.com

KOGUT, JOHN BENJAMIN, THEORETICAL PHYSICS. **Personal Data:** b Brooklyn, NY, March 6, 1945; m 1985, c 1. **Education:** Princeton Univ, BA, 1967; Stanford Univ, MS, 1968, PhD (physics), 1971. **Professional Experience:** Guggenheim fel, 1988-1989; PROF PHYSICS, UNIV ILL, URBANA-CHAMPAIGN 1978-; NSFgrant, Univ Ill, 1978-; Sloan Found fel & NSF grant, Cornell Univ, 1976-1978; from asst prof toassoc prof, Cornell Univ, 1974-1978; res assoc, Cornell Univ, 1973-1974; assoc physics, Inst Advan Study, 1971-1973 & Tel Aviv Univ, 1973. **Memberships:** Fel Am Phys Soc; Comt Concerned Scientists. **Research Statement & Publications:** Theory of elementary particles; field theory and statistical mechanics. **Mailing Address:** Dept Physics Univ Ill, 263 Loomis Lab 1110 W Green St, Urbana, IL 61801-3080. **Fax:** 217-333-9819. **E-Mail:** kogut@hp1.physics.uiuc.edu

KOGUT, MAURICE D, PEDIATRICS, ENDOCRINOLOGY. **Personal Data:** b Brooklyn, NY, July 7, 1930; m 1959, c 3. **Education:** NY Univ, BA, 1951, MD, 1955. **Professional Experience:** PROF EMER DEPT PEDIAT, WRIGHT STATE UNIV, DAYTON, OHIO; clin prof med, Sch Med, Univ Southern Calif, 1980-; assoc head dept, Sch Med, Univ Southern Calif, 1975-1980; prof pediat, Sch Med, Univ Southern Calif, 1973-1980; head div endocrinol & metab & prog dir, Clin Res Ctr, Children's Hosp, 1971-; from instr to assoc prof, Sch Med, Univ Southern Calif, 1962-1973; chief resident, USPHS fel endocrinol, 1960-1962; chief resident, Children's Hosp, Los Angeles, 1959-1960; resident, Bellevue Hosp, NY, 1956-1957; Intern pediat, Bellevue Hosp, NY, 1955-1956. **Memberships:** Endocrine Soc; Am Diabetes Asn; Am Acad Pediat; Soc Pediat Res; Am Pediat Soc. **Research Statement & Publications:** Carbohydrate metabolism in idiopathic hypoglycemia; growth hormone and insulin metabolism in hypopituitarism; the role of circulating insulin and glucagon in children with genetic predisposition to diabetes mellitus; uric acid metabolism. **Mailing Address:** Wright State Univ, One Childrens Plaza, Dayton, OH 45404-1815.

KOH, EUNSOOK TAK, NUTRITIONAL SCIENCE. **Personal Data:** b Seoul, Korea, May 3, 1936; American citizen; m 1961, c Kyung-Ho, Kyung-Run & Lucy. **Education:** Seoul Nat Univ, Korea, BS, 1958; Univ Md, MS, 1970, PhD (nutrit sci), 1973. **Professional Experience:** PROF EMER, DEPT NUTRIT SCI, COL ALLIED HEALTH, UNIV OKLA, OKLAHOMA CITY, as of 1994; prof, Dept Nutrit Sci, Col Allied Health, Univ Okla, Oklahoma City, beginning 1989; USDA, Agr Res Serv, Nutrit Inst, Beltsville, 1987-1988; vis prof, Hallym Univ, Kangwon Do, Korea, 1987; USDA, Agr Res Serv, Nutrit Inst, 1987-1988 & HallymUniv, 1987; Prin investr, Univ Okla, 1981-1991; prof, Univ Okla, Norman, 1981-1989; assocprof, Alcorn State Univ, Miss, 1974-1981; Prin investr, Alcorn State Univ, 1974-1981; res assoc, Agr Res Serv, Nutrit Inst, USDA, 1973-1974; res asst, Agr Res Serv, Nutrit Inst, USDA, 1970-1973; Res asst, Univ Md, College Park, 1968-1970. **Memberships:** Am Inst Nutrit; Am Dietetic Asn; Nutrit Educ Soc; Am Col Nutrit; Sigma Xi. **Research Statement & Publications:** Nutrition survey; carbohydrates and lipid metabolism; copper and fructose interaction; interaction of fructose, magnesium deficiency and sex hormone on nephrocalcinosis; mechanism of the interaction on nephrocalcinosis; fructose, Magnesium and bone. **Mailing Address:** Dept Nutrit Sci Col Allied Health Rm 465 Univ Okla, PO Box 26901, Oklahoma City, OK 73104. **Fax:** 405-271-3120. **E-Mail:** eunsook-koh@uokhsc.edu

KOH, EUSEBIO LEGARDA, DISTRIBUTION THEORY, INTEGRAL TRANSFORMATIONS & OPERATIONAL CALCULUS. **Personal Data:** b Manila, Philippines, October 4, 1931; Canadian citizen; m 1958, Donelita; c Monette, Elizabeth, Ethel & Denise. **Education:** Univ Philippines, BS, 1954; Purdue Univ, Ind, MS, 1956; Univ Birmingham, UK, MSc, 1961; State Univ NY, Stony Brook, PhD (appl math), 1967. **Professional Experience:** PROF EMER, UNIV REGINA, AS OF 1999; prof, Univ Petrol & Minerals, Saudi Arabia, 1979-1982; dept head, Univ Regina, 1977-1979; prof math & statist, Univ Regina, 1975-1999; travel fel, Nat Sci Eng Res Coun, Ger, 1975-1976; guest prof, Technische Hochschule Dermstadt, Ger, 1975-1976; NAT SCI ENG RES COUN RES GRANT, CAN, 1971-; assoc prof, Univ Regina, 1970-1975; asst prof math, Univ Sask, 1968-1970; asst prof math, Univ SC, 1967-1968; dept head mech eng, Univ Philippines, 1963-1964; dir, DCCD Eng Corp, Philippines, 1962-1964; asst prof, Univ Phillipines, 1959-1964; res engr, Int Harvester Co, Ill, 1956-1957. **Memberships:** Am Math Soc; Math Asn Am; Soc Indust & Appl Math; Can Math Soc; Can Appl Math Soc. **Research Statement & Publications:** Extension of integral transformations to generalized functions; development of operational calculus by algebraic approach; association of variables technique; functional equations in distributions. **Mailing Address:** Dept Math & Statist, Univ Regina, Regina, SK S4S 0A2, Can. **Fax:** 306-585-4020. **E-Mail:** elkoh@math.uregina.ca

KOH, JOHN TZE-TZUN, BIOORGANIC CHEMISTRY, PROTEIN-LIGAND & PROTEIN DNA INTERACTIONS. **Personal Data:** b St Louis, Mo, April 3, 1967. **Education:** West Chester Univ, Pa, Bs, 1989; Columbia Univ, MS, 1990, MPhil, 1993, PhD (orgchem), 1994. **Professional Experience:** ASSOC PROF ORG CHEM, UNIV DEL, as of 2003; asst prof chem & biochem, Univ Del, beginning 1996; Am Cancer Soc postdoctoral fel, Univ Calif, Berkeley, 1994-1996. **Memberships:** Am Chem Soc. **Mailing Address:** Dept Chem & Biochem, Univ Del, 273 Brown Labs, Newark, DE 19716. **Fax:** 302-831-1738. **E-Mail:** johnkoh@udel.edu

KOH, KWANGIL, MATHEMATICS, MATHEMATICAL PHYSICS. **Personal Data:** b Seoul, Korea, July 8, 1931; m 1958, Toni L; c Debra, James & Patricia. **Education:** Auburn Univ, BS, 1959, MS, 1960; Univ NC, PhD (math), 1964. **Professional Experience:** PROF MATH, NC STATE UNIV, 1968-; From instr to assoc prof, NC State Univ, 1964-1968. **Memberships:** Am Math Soc; Math Asn Am. **Research Statement & Publications:** Algebra; theory of rings. **Mailing Address:** Dept Math, Box 8205, Nc State Univ, Raleigh, NC 27695-8205. **Fax:** 919-515-3798. **E-Mail:** kwangil@math.ncsu.edu

KOH, ROBERT CY, FLUID MECHANICS, APPLIED MATHEMATICS. **Personal Data:** b Shanghai, China, May 23, 1938; m 1961, c 1. **Education:** Calif Inst Technol, BS, 1960, MS, 1961, PhD (appl mech, math), 1964. **Professional Experience:** MEM STAFF, CALIF INST TECH, 1972-; sr scientist, Tetra Tech Inc, 1966-1972; mem tech staff, Nat Eng Sci Co, 1965-1966; Res fel eng, Calif Inst Technol, 1964-1965. **Memberships:** Int Asn Hydraul Res. **Research Statement & Publications:** Fluid mechanics; applied mathematics. **Mailing Address:** 212 S Marengo Ave, Pasadena, CA 91101.

KOH, SEVERINO LEGARDA, theoretical & applied mechanics, composite materials; deceased, see previous edition for last biography

KOH, SUNG-CHEOL, XENOBIOTICS DEGRADATION BY METHANOTROPHS, INDUSTRIAL ENZYME PRODUCTION & UTILIZATION. **Personal Data:** b Taego City, Korea, August 13, 1956; m Hea-Ok; c Jung-Hyun & Shana. **Education:** Seoul Nat Univ, Korea, BS, 1980, MS, 1983; Univ Tenn, Knoxville, PhD (microbialecol), 1994. **Professional Experience:** ASST PROF, ENVIRON MICRO BIOL & ECOL, KOREA MARITIME UNIV, as of 2004; RES ASST, CTR ENVIRON BIOTECHNOL, UNIV TENN, 1988-; Resscientist, Res & Technol Inst Pac Chem Co Ltd, Korea, 1983-1987. **Memberships:** Am Soc Microbiol. **Research Statement & Publications:** Characterization of a type I methanotroph that can produce soluble methane mono-oxygenase and degrade trichloroethylene as a hazardous waste chemical; molecular analysis of two-species competition of methanotrophs. **E-Mail:** skoh@mail.hhu.ac.kr

KOHAN, MELVIN IRA, POLYMER CHEMISTRY & ENGINEERING. **Personal Data:** b Boston, Mass, March 11, 1921; m 1943, Beatrice; c Stanford P, Allen M, Donald E & James M. **Education:** Harvard Univ, AB, 1942; Univ Ill, PhD (chem), 1950. **Professional Experience:** RETIRED; consult, Eng Thermoplastics, beginning 1983; adj prof, Drexel Univ, 1983-1985; res assoc, Polymer Products Dept, Exp Sta, 1980-1982; res assoc, Dept Plastics, 1974-1980; sr res chemist, Dept Plastics, 1962-1974; chemist, Dept Plastics, 1950-1962; chemist, Dept Electrochem, E I Du Pont de Nemours & Co Inc, 1942-1944 & 1946-1947. **Memberships:** Am Chem Soc; Soc Plastic Engrs; Sigma Xi. **Research Statement & Publications:** Polymer chemistry; plastics engineering; nylon plastics technology; publications, patents and books. **Mailing Address:** 1913 Longcome Dr, Wilmington, DE 19810-3864.

KOHANE, THEODORE, PHYSICS. **Personal Data:** b New York, NY, April 20, 1923; m 1955, c 2. **Education:** City Col New York, BS, 1944; Rutgers Univ, PhD (physics), 1953. **Professional Experience:** RETIRED; mem res staff, Raytheon Res Div, 1953-1989; asst & fel, RutgersUniv, 1948-1953; asst physics & instr, NY Univ, 1946-1948; Physicist, Nat Adv Comt Aeronaut, 1944-1946. **Memberships:** Am Phys Soc; Optical Soc Am. **Research Statement & Publications:** Nuclear magnetic resonance; magnetic andelectrical properties of ferrites; microwaves; optical properties of solids. **Mailing Address:** 8277 Springtree Rd, Boca Raton, FL 33496.

KOHEL, RUSSELL JAMES, CROP GERMPLASM RESEARCH. **Personal Data:** b Omaha, Nebr, November 30, 1934; m, c 3. **Education:** Iowa State Univ, BS, 1956; Purdue Univ, MS, 1958, PhD (plant breeding), 1959. **Professional Experience:** RES GENETICIST COTTON, AGR RES SERV, USDA, 1959-. **Memberships:** Am Soc Plant Physiologists; fel Am Soc Agron; Am Genetic Asn; Genetics Soc Am. **Research Statement & Publications:** Qualitative and quantitative genetics and genomics of the cotton plant. **Mailing Address:** Agri Res Serv, USDA, Rm 180, 2881 F & B Rd, College Station, TX 77845. **Fax:** 979-260-9333. **E-Mail:** kohel@qutun.tamu.edu

KOHIN, BARBARA CASTLE, MOLECULAR PHYSICS. **Personal Data:** b Providence, RI, December 11, 1932; m 1959, Roger P; c 3. **Education:** Col William & Mary, BS, 1953; Univ Md, MS, 1956, PhD (physics), 1960. **Professional Experience:** Exec dir, Accord, 1993-1995; actg dir, Off Spec Studies, Col of the Holy Cross, 1985-1986; assoc dir, Off Spec Studies, Col of the Holy Cross, 1978-1985 & 1986-1987; Res assoc, Mass Inst Technol, 1973-1974; asst prof physics, Clark Univ, 1967-1968; instr physics, Mass State Col Worcester, 1964-1967; physicist theoret physics, Inst Battelle, Geneva, Switz, 1961-1962; Res assoc molecular physics, Cath Univ Am, 1959-1961; Boyle Found Fel, Van Dir Waals Faboratorium, Amsterdam, 1956-1957. **Research Statement & Publications:** Quantum chemistry; solid state physics; elementary and atomic physics. **Mailing Address:** 11 Berwick St, Worcester, MA 01602.

KOHIN, ROGER P(ATRICK), PHYSICS. **Personal Data:** b Chicago, Ill, March 2, 1931; m 1959, Barbara; c Margaret (Nitschelm), Judith A & Suzanne. **Education:** Univ Notre Dame, BS, 1953; Univ Md, PhD (physics), 1961. **Professional Experience:** EMER ASSOC PROF, CLARK UNIV, 1994-; vis prof, Univ Nairobi, Kenya, 1987-1988; Indo-Am fel, Indian Inst Tech-Kanpur, 1976-1977; chmn dept, Clark Univ, 1974-1976 & 1985-1987; vis scientist, Inst J Stefan, Ljubljana, Yugoslavia, 1968-1969; assoc prof physics, Clark Univ, 1967-1994; asst prof, Clark Univ, 1962-1967; scientist physics, Battelle Mem Inst, Geneva, Switz, 1961-1962. **Memberships:** Am Phys Soc. **Research Statement & Publications:** Electron-spin resonance spectroscopy; radiation damage of solids; experimental ferroelectric materials; organic and inorganic free radicals; computer simulation. **Mailing Address:** Dept Physics, Clark Univ, Worcester, MA 01610. **E-Mail:** rkohin@clarku.edu

KOHL, A(RTHUR) L(IONEL), GAS PURIFICATION, NUCLEAR ENGINEERING. **Personal Data:** b Ont, August 21, 1919; American citizen; m 1943, Evelyn Belinsky; c Jeffrey Martin & Donald. **Education:** Univ Southern Calif, BE, 1943, MS, 1947. **Honors Awards:** Outstanding Achievement Award, Am Inst Chem Engrs, 1966; Tech Achievement Award, Engrs Joint Coun, 1967. **Professional Experience:** CONSULT ENGR, 1989-; prog mgr fossil energy, Rocketdyne Div, Rockwell Int, 1978-1989; proj engr & proj mgr advan develop, Atomics Int, 1968-1978; group leader process develop, Atomics Int, 1960-1968; chief chem eng res, Fluor Corp Ltd, 1947-1960; Res engr, Turco Prod, Inc,

1946-1947; Res engr, Turco Prod, Inc, 1942-1944. **Memberships:** Am Inst Chem Engrs. **Research Statement & Publications:** Gas purification; process equipment; saline water conversion; chemical process development; nuclear reactor fuels and materials; nuclear reactor component development; coal conversion; paper mill black liquor gasification; 35 U.S. patents. **Mailing Address:** 22555 Tiara St, Woodland Hills, CA 91367. **E-Mail:** akohlpe@aol.com

KOHL, DANIEL HOWARD, PLANT PHYSIOLOGY. **Personal Data:** b Cleveland, Ohio, July 30, 1928; m 1950, c 4. **Education:** Univ Calif, Berkeley, BS, 1960; Wash Univ, PhD (molecular biol), 1965. **Professional Experience:** RETIRED; prof biol, Wash Univ, beginning 1979; sr fel, Ctr Biol Natural Systs, 1971-1981; from asst prof to assoc prof bot, Wash Univ, 1965-1979. **Memberships:** Am Soc Plant Physiol; Soil Sci Soc Am. **Research Statement & Publications:** N isotope distribution in various components of N cycle; N fixation biochemistry. **Mailing Address:** Dept Biol, Wash Univ, Rebstock 206, St Louis, MO 63130-4862. **E-Mail:** kohl@biology.wustl.edu

KOHL, FRED JOHN, PHYSICAL CHEMISTRY. **Personal Data:** b Cleveland, Ohio, January 1, 1942. **Education:** Case Inst Technol, BS, 1963; Case Western Reserve Univ, PhD (chem), 1968. **Professional Experience:** PHYSICIST, NASA GLENN RES CTR, as of 2003; res chemist & mgr, Mat Sci Space Proj, Lewisres Ctr, NASA, beginning 1968; br chief. **Memberships:** Am Chem Soc; Am Soc Mass Spectrometry. **Research Statement & Publications:** Hot corrosion of superalloys; oxidation of metals; high temperature vaporization and thermodynamics; mass spectrometry; oxidation and vaporization processes; high temperature chemistry; vaporization of refractories; materials science experiments in space; combustion process related to corrosion; microgravity science and applications. **Mailing Address:** NASA Glenn Res Ctr, Microgravity Sci Div 21000 Brookpark Rd Mail Stop MS 77-4, Cleveland, OH 44135. **Fax:** 216-433-8050. **E-Mail:** fred.kohl@grc.nasa.gov

KOHL, JEROME, MANAGEMENT & MINIMIZATION OF HAZARDOUS WASTES. **Personal Data:** b Montreal, Que, March 13, 1918; American citizen; m 1945, Freeke von Novhuys; c Joyce E & Adelle P. **Education:** Calif Inst Technol, BS, 1940; NC State Univ, MS, 1975. **Professional Experience:** EMER NUCLEAR ENG SPECIALIST & LECTR, NC STATE UNIV, 1988-; sr nucleareng exten specialist & lectr nuclear eng, NC State Univ, 1969-1988; mkt mgr, Oak Ridge TechEnterprises, 1965-1969; coordr spec prod, Gen Atomic Div, Gen Dynamics Corp, 1960-1964; mgr eng & develop, Mobile Radiochem Lab, 1958-1960; lectr, Univ Delft, 1956 & int lectr on waste reduction, mgt & minimization hazardous waste, NC State Univ; chief engr, Mobile Radiochem Lab, 1953-1958; sect leader, Mobile Radiochem Lab, 1951-1953; chem engr, Tracerlab, Inc, 1948-1951; Instr & lectr, Univ Calif, Berkeley & San Diego, 1947-1964; asstsupt, Avon Refinery, Tidewater Assoc Oil Co, Calif, 1946-1948; Chem & proj engr, AvonRefinery, Tidewater Assoc Oil Co, Calif, 1943-1946. **Memberships:** Am Nuclear Soc; Am Inst Chem Engrs; Soc Photog Educ. **Research Statement & Publications:** Radiation monitoring instrumentation; industrial applications of radioisotopes; measurement of nuclear radiations; energy conservation; co-generation; management and minimization of hazardous waste. **Mailing Address:** Dept Nuclear Eng, NC State Univ Box 7909, Raleigh, NC 27695-7909. **Fax:** 919-515-5115.

KOHL, JOHN LESLIE, SOLAR PHYSICS, LABORATORY ASTROPHYSICS. **Personal Data:** b Zanesville, Ohio, April 27, 1941; m 1965, c 2. **Education:** Muskingum Col, BS, 1963; Univ Toledo, MS, 1966, PhD (physics), 1969. **Honors & Awards:** Fellow of the American Physical Society, 1995; 4 NASA/GSFC Group Achievement Awards for contributions to Spartan 201 missions; European Space Agency Award for contributions to SOHO mission; European Space Agency Award for contributions to SOHO Recovery. **Professional Experience:** SENIOR ASTROPHYSICIST, SMITHSONIAN Astrophysical Observatory, 1995-; ASTROPHYSICIST. SMITHSONIAN ASTROPHYSICAL BSERVATORY, 1976-; LECTR ASTRON, HARVARD UNIV, 1977-2003; ASSOC HARVARD COL OBSERV, HARVARD UNIV, 1977-. **Memberships:** Am Phys Soc; Am Astron Soc; Int Astron Union; Am Geophys Union. **Research Statement & Publications:** ULTRAVIOLET SPECTROSCOPY OF THE EXTENDED SOLAR CORONA FROM SPACE PLATFORMS; LABORATORY ASTROPHYSICS MEASUREMENTS OF THE CROSS SECTIONS AND COLLISION RATES THAT GOVERN ELECTRON IMPACT EXCITATION OF ASTROPHYSICALLY SIGNIFICANT IONS. **Mailing Address:** 60 Garden St, Mail Stop 50, Cambridge, MA 02138. **Fax:** 617-495-7455. **E-Mail:** jkohl@cfa.harvard.edu

KOHL, PAUL ALBERT, ELECTROCHEMISTRY, PHYSICAL CHEMISTRY. **Personal Data:** b Buffalo, NY, August 6, 1952; m 1974, c 2. **Education:** Bethany Col, BS, 1974; Univ Tex, PhD (chem), 1978. **Honors & Awards:** Weston Award, Electrochem Soc, 1977; Ayres Award, Univ Tex, 1978. **Professional Experience:** REGENTS PROF CHEM & BIOMOLECULAR ENG, GA INST TECHNOL, as of 2004; CHEMIST, AT&T BELL LABS, 1978-; Chemist, Nuclear Radiation Develop, 1974. **Memberships:** Am Chem Soc; Electrochem Soc. **Research Statement & Publications:** Chemical and electrochemical reactions involved in the processing of semiconductor materials for the development of microelectronic devices. **Mailing Address:** Sch Chem & Biomolecular Eng, GA Inst Tech, 311 Ferst Dr NW, Atlanta, GA 30332-0100. **Fax:** 404-894-2866. **E-Mail:** paul.kohl@che.gatech.edu

KOHL, ROBERT A, SOIL PHYSICS, IRRIGATION. **Personal Data:** b Harvey, Ill, January 22, 1936; m 1957, c 4. **Education:** Purdue Univ, BS, 1958; Utah State Univ, MS, 1960, PhD (soils, irrig), 1963. **Professional Experience:** RETIRED; prof plant sci, Sdak State Univ, 1987-2005; assoc prof, Sdak State Univ, 1975-1987; res soil scientist, Snake River Conserv Res Ctr, Agr Res Serv, USDA, Idaho, 1967-1974; Agr missionary, Lutheran Mission, Nigeria, 1963-1966. **Memberships:** Soil Sci Soc Am; Am Soc Agron. **Research Statement & Publications:** Water management; sprinkler irrigation. **Mailing Address:** Dept Plant Sci, SDak State Univ PO Box 2207a, Brookings, SD 57007-0001. **E-Mail:** robert_kohl@sdstate.edu

KOHLAND, WILLIAM FRANCIS, petrology, atmospheric science; deceased, see previous edition for last biography

KOHLBRENNER, PHILIP JOHN, INTL REGULATORY AFFAIRS. **Personal Data:** b South Bend, Ind, November 17, 1931; m 1957, Ann; c Michael, Kathleen, Matthew, Linda, Andrew & Elizab. **Education:** Purdue Univ, BS, 1953; State Univ NY Col Forestry, Syracuse Univ, PhD (org chem), 1958. **Professional Experience:** RETIRED; sr dir, Int Regulatory Affairs, 1990-1993; dir, Regulatory Affairs Int, 1989-1990; dir, Regulatory Affairs-Global Tech Support, Med Res Div, 1987-1989; assoc dir, Lederle Labs Div, 1980-1987; dept head basic pharmaceut, Lederle Labs Div, 1976-1980; group leader synthetic org chem, Am Cyanamid, 1964-1976; res chemist, Am Cyanamid, 1958-1964; res chemist synthetic org chem, Cowles Chem Co, 1957-1958. **Memberships:** Am Chem Soc; Am Asn Pharm Scientists. **Research Statement & Publications:** Synthetic organic chemistry. **Mailing Address:** Outlet Rd, Piseco, NY 12139.

KOHLER, CARL, MARINE BIOLOGY, ICHTHYOPLANKTON. **Personal Data:** b Hamilton, Ont, June 24, 1930; m 1950, Claire; c Michael, Brian, Christopher & Erik. **Education:** McMaster Univ, BA, 1953; McGill Univ, MSc, 1956, PhD (zoology), 1960. **Professional Experience:** RETIRED; prof hunting, fishing guide & outfitter, beginning 1986; technician, Kohler Guiding, 1986-1997; head fishery biol sect, Biol Sta, Fisheries Res Bd Can, 1973-1985; head groundfish prog, Biol Sta, Fisheries Res Bd Can, 1967-1973; sr scientist, BiolSta, Fisheries Res Bd Can, 1956-1967; demonstr, McGill Univ, 1955-1956; 1958-1959; technician to technician, Biol Sta, Fisheries Res Bd Can, 1953-1956; asst conservationist, Royal Bot Gardens, Ont, 1951-1953. **Memberships:** Am Fisheries Soc. **Research Statement & Publications:** Fishery biology and biostatistics; fishery management; wildlife biology. **Mailing Address:** 316 Prince Wales, St Andrews, NB E0G 2X0, Can.

KOHLER, CONSTANCE ANNE, PHARMACOLOGY, BIOCHEMISTRY. **Personal Data:** b Flushing, NY, January 9, 1943; m 1980, c 2. **Education:** St John's Univ, NY, BS, 1965; Univ Calif, San Francisco, PhD (pharmacol), 1973. **Professional Experience:** SR RES SCIENTIST, LEDERLE LABS, DIV AM CYANAMID, NY, 1980-; res pharmacologist, Lederle Labs, Div Am Cyanamid, NY, 1974-1980; Fel pharmacol, RocheInst Molecular Biol, NJ, 1972-1974. **Memberships:** AAAS; Am Heart Asn; Am Chem Soc; NY Acad Sci; Sigma Xi; Soc Exp Biol &Med. **Research Statement & Publications:** Allergy and asthma; platelet biochemistry; phospholipid, platelet-activating factor, arachidonic acid metabolism and pharmacology; mammalian cell culture; growth factors; hormones, drugs and signal transduction. **Mailing Address:** Wyeth Ayerst, 401 N Middletown Rd Bldg 200, Pearl River, NY 10965.

KOHLER, DONALD ALVIN, X-RAY PHYSICS, PLASMA PHYSICS. **Personal Data:** b Rainier, Ore, October 29, 1928; m 1959, c 2. **Education:** Univ Ore, BS, 1951, MS, 1952; Calif Inst Technol, PhD (physics), 1959. **Professional Experience:** SR STAFF SCIENTIST, LOCKHEED PALO ALTO RES LAB, 1979-; staff scientist, Lockheed Palo Alto Res Lab, 1973-1979; res scientist, Lockheed Palo Alto Res Lab, 1965-1973; lectr, Stanford Univ, 1962-1965; res assoc, Stanford Univ, 1962-1963; res assoc nuclear physics, Stanford Univ, 1959-1962. **Memberships:** AAAS; Am Phys Soc; Inst Elec & Electronics Engrs. **Research Statement & Publications:** X-ray physics and instrumentation; laser-plasma interaction; experimental low-energy nuclear physics, particularly of the light nuclei; cosmology and astrophysics; elementary particle physics; weak interactions. **Mailing Address:** 10481 Baywood Dr, Cupertino, CA 95014.

KOHLER, ERWIN MILLER, VETERINARY MICROBIOLOGY. **Personal Data:** b Cincinnati, Ohio, June 24, 1930; m 1954, c 2. **Education:** Ohio State Univ, DVM, 1955, MS, 1963, PhD (microbiol, immunol), 1965. **Professional Experience:** AT OHIO AFR RES & DEVELOP CTR, as of 2006; chmn dept, vet sci dept, Ohio Agr Res & Develop Ctr, beginning 1976; prof infectious dis domestic animals, vet sci dept, Ohio Agr Res &Develop Ctr, beginning 1973; from asst prof to assoc prof, Vet Sci Dept, Ohio Agr Res & DevelopCtr, 1965-1973; vet, Winchester Animal Hosp, Va, 1955-1962. **Memberships:** Am Vet Med Asn; Am Soc Microbiol; Conf Res Workers Animal Diseases; AmAsn Swine Practitioners. **Research Statement & Publications:** Studies of colibacillosis of gnotobiotic and conventional swine; studies of the oral immunization of sows as an aid in the prevention of neonatal enteric colibacillosis of pigs. **Mailing Address:** Ohio Agr Res & Develop Ctr, Wooster, OH 44691.

KOHLER, GEORGE OSCAR, BIOCHEMISTRY, PROCESS ENGINEERING. **Personal Data:** b Milwaukee, Wis, April 9, 1913; m 1940, Christie; c Cynthia (Castner), William M & Sylvia (Luftig). **Education:** Univ Wis, BS, 1934, MS, 1936, PhD (biochem), 1938. **Professional Experience:** Sr exec serv, USDA, 1979-1982; OWNER, G O KOHLER & ASSOC, 1972-; sr exec serv res leader, Western Regional Res Ctr, Sci & Educ Admin-AgrRes, USDA, 1956-1981; pres, Cerophyl Labs, Inc, 1955-1956; dir res, Alfalfa Dehydration &Milling Co, 1954-1955; vpres & dir res, Cerophyl Labs, Inc, 1950-1954; assoc dir res, CerophylLabs, Inc, 1939-1950; asst, Cerophyl Labs grant, 1938-1939; asst, Univ Wis, 1934-1939. **Memberships:** Am Inst Nutrit; Am Chem Soc; Inst Food Technologists; Am Asn CerealChemists; Poultry Sci Asn. **Research Statement & Publications:** Chicken and guinea pig nutrition; hormone assay and synthesis; vitamin assay; isolation of compounds from natural materials; process development; amino acid analysis; protein isolates from leaves and oilseeds for foods and feeds. **Mailing Address:** 12700 Sir Francs Drke Blvd, Inverness, CA 94937. **Fax:** 415-669-7147. **E-Mail:** gkohl@aol.com

KOHLER, HEINZ, PROTEIN CHEMISTRY, IMMUNOLOGY. **Personal Data:** b Duisburg, Ger, September 11, 1939; m 1965, c 2. **Education:** Univ Munich, MD, 1965. **Professional Experience:** PROF, DEPT MICROBIOL & IMMUNOL, UNIV KY, 1993-; DIR RES, LUCILLE PMARKEY CANCER CTR, 1993-; adj mem, San Diego Regional Cancer Ctr, La Jolla, 1990-; sr sci fel, Idec Pharmaceut Corp, La Jolla, Calif, 1989-1993; adj prof, Dept Path, Univ Calif, SanDiego, 1987-1990; dir res, Idec Pharmaceut Corp, La Jolla, Calif, 1987-1989; Dept Molecular Immunol, Roswell Park Mem Inst, Buffalo, NY, 1981-1987; assoc prof, depts path & biochem, Univ Chicago, 1974-1981; res career develop award, USPHS, 1973; asst prof, Dept Path, 1970-1974; res assoc, Div Biol Sci, Ind Univ, 1967-1970; res fel, Max Planck Inst Biochem, 1965-1967. **Memberships:** Fedn Am Soc Exp Biol. **Research Statement & Publications:** Relationship of function and structure of proteins; regulation of immune response. **Mailing Address:** Dept Microbiol, Univ Ky Med, 800 Rose St 205 Combs Res Bldg, Lexington, KY 40536-0096. **Fax:** 859-257-8941. **E-Mail:** hkohl00@uky.edu

KOHLER, MAX A, HYDROLOGY, GEOPHYSICS. **Personal Data:** b Lincolnville, Kans, September 6, 1915; m 1939, Estella; c Donna, Max II & Kathryn. **Education:** Univ NMex, BS, 1939. **Honors & Awards:** Hydrol Prize, Int Am Hydrol Sci, 1986. **Professional Experience:** RETIRED; World Met Orgn, NY, Geneva, Switz, 1974-1975; coun mem, Am-Meteorol Soc, 1972-1975; assoc dir, Nat Weather Serv, 1971-1973; consult, EAfrica, 1962 &1972; pres, Comn Hydrol, World Meteorol Orgn, 1960-1968; consult, UN, Yugoslavia, 1953; chief hydrologist, Nat Weather Serv, 1951-1971; hydrologist, Nat Weather Serv, 1941-1951. **Memberships:** Nat Acad Eng; fel Am Geophys Union; fel Am Meteorol Soc; Am Soc ChemEngrs. **Mailing Address:** 3530 Twin Branches Dr, Silver Spring, MD 20906.

KOHLER, PETER, ENDOCRINOLOGY, CELL CULTURE. **Personal Data:** b Brooklyn, NY, July 18, 1938; m 1959, c 4. **Education:** Univ Va, Charlottesville, BA, 1959; Duke Univ, MD, 1963. **Professional Experience:** PRES, ORE HEALTH SCI UNIV, 1988-; mem, Bd Sci Counrs, Nat Inst ChildHealth & Develop, beginning 1986; dean, Sch Med, Health Sci Ctr, Univ Tex, 1986-1988; interim dean, Col Med, beginning 1986; chmn, NIH Endocrinol Study Sect, 1984-1985; mem, Endocrinol Bd, Am BdInternal Med, beginning 1983; mem, NIH Endocrinol Study Sect, 1981-1985; prof & chmn med, UnivArk, Little Rock, 1977-1986; prof med & cell biol & chief endocrinol, Baylor Col Med, 1973-1977; prof med & cell biol & chief endocrinol, Baylor Col Med, 1973-1977; headendocrinol serv, Nat Inst Child Health & Develop, NIH, 1972-1973; sr investr, Nat Inst ChildHealth & Develop, 1968-1973; clin assoc, Nat Cancer Inst, NIH, 1965-1967; fel endocrinol, Duke

Hosp, 1964-1965; intern med, Duke Hosp, 1963-1964. **Memberships:** Inst Med-Nat Acad Sci; Am Soc Clin Invest; Asn Am Physicians; Am DiabetesAsn; Endocrine Soc; Sigma Xi; Am Soc Cell Biol; Am Fedn Clin Res. **Research Statement & Publications:** Regulation of cell function and pituitary pathophysiology. **Mailing Address:** Ore Health Sci Univ, 3181 SW Sam Jackson Park Rd, Portland, OR 97201-3098.

KOHLER, PETER FRANCIS, immunology; deceased, see previous edition for last biography

KOHLER, ROBERT HENRY, PHYSICS. **Personal Data:** b Philadelphia, Pa, April 25, 1933. **Education:** Mass Inst Technol, BS, 1955, PhD (physics), 1960. **Professional Experience:** PROF EMER PHYSICS, STATE UNIV NY COL BUFFALO, as of 2005; prof physics, state univ ny col buffalo, beginning 1966; vis asst prof, Rutgers Univ, 1965-1966; asst prof physics, NY Univ, 1963-1965; res assoc exp physics, Columbia Univ, 1960-1963. **Memberships:** Am Phys Soc; Am Asn Physics Teachers. **Research Statement & Publications:** Lasers and quantum electronics; optical pumping. **Mailing Address:** Dept Physics, State Univ Col Buffalo 1300 Elmwood Ave, Buffalo, NY 14222.

KOHLER, SIGURD H, NUCLEAR PHYSICS. **Personal Data:** b Uppsala, Sweden, December 1, 1928; wid. **Education:** Univ Uppsala, Fil Kand, 1951, Fil Mag, 1952, Fil Lic, 1956, Fil Dr(theoret physics), 1959. **Professional Experience:** PROF PHYSICS, UNIV ARIZ, 1968-; vis assoc prof physics, Rice Univ, 1965-1968; asst res physicist, Univ Calif, San Diego, 1963-1965; spec res, AEC Sweden, Uppsala, 1961-1963; asst res physicist, Univ Calif, Los Angeles, 1960-1961; res assoc, Cornell Univ, 1959-1960; fel theoret physics, Cern, Geneva, Switz, 1957-1959; asst, Inst Meteorol, Univ Uppsala, 1950-1953 & Inst Theoret Physics, 1953-1957. **Memberships:** Am Phys Soc. **Research Statement & Publications:** Nuclear theory; many body problems; properties of nuclear matter. **Mailing Address:** Dept Physics Univ Ariz, 1600 E U Bl, Tucson, AZ 85721-0001. **Fax:** 520-621-4721. **E-Mail:** kohler@physics.arizona.edu

KOHLHAAS, ANN, BIOLOGY. **Education:** Univ Colo, PhD. **Professional Experience:** PROF & CHAIR, DEPT BIOL SCI, CALIF STATE UNIV, STANISLAUS, as of 2006. **Research Statement & Publications:** Ecology; behavior; and conservation of vertebrates; especially primates; other mammals and birds; vertebrate zoology. **Mailing Address:** Dept Biol Sci, Calif State Univ Stanislaus, Turlock, CA 95382. **Fax:** 209-667-3694. **E-Mail:** kohlhaas@athena.csustan.edu

KOHLHAW, GUNTER B, BIOCHEMISTRY. **Personal Data:** b Elbing, Ger, May 5, 1931; m 1959, Ellen. **Education:** Univ Freiburg, MS, 1959, PhD (biochem), 1962. **Professional Experience:** PROF EMER BIOCHEM, PURDUE UNIV, as of 2005; prof biochem, Purdue Univ, West Lafayette, 1973; from asst prof to assoc prof, Purdue Univ, West Lafayette, 1966-1973; NATO felintracellular regulation, Purdue Univ, West Lafayette, 1964-1966; res asst gen biochem, UnivFreiburg, 1962-1964. **Memberships:** Genetics Soc Am; Am Soc Biol Chemists; Ger Soc Biol Chem. **Research Statement & Publications:** Gene structure function; metabolic regulation; analysis of the structure-function relationship of structural and regulatory genes in yeast; with special attention to the regulation of gene expression by upstream elements. **Mailing Address:** Dept Biochem, Purdue Univ, West Lafayette, IN 47907. **Fax:** 765-494-7897. **E-Mail:** kohlhaw@purdue.edu

KOHLHEPP, SUE JOANNE, ANALYTICAL BIOCHEMISTRY. **Personal Data:** b Kittanning, Pa, July 15, 1939. **Education:** WVa Wesleyan Col, BS, 1961; Pa State Univ, MS, 1963, PhD (biophys), 1969. **Professional Experience:** RES ASSOC, EARLE A CHILES RES INST, PROVIDENCE MED CTR, PORTLAND, 1977-; res assoc biochem, Ore State Univ, 1975-1977; assoc prof biochem, Catherine Spalding Col, 1971; res assoc clin chem, St Anthony Hosp, Louisville, Ky, 1969-1974; teacher physics & phys sci, Marple-Newtown Sch Dist, Pa, 1963-1966. **Memberships:** AAAS; Biophys Soc; Am Soc Microbiol; NY Acad Sci. **Research Statement & Publications:** Identification and quantitation of metabolic products of the anti-tumor agent 1-2-chloroethyl-3-cyclohexyl-1-nitrosourea in rats, monkeys and humans as a means of deducing the mechanisms of action of the drug and decreasing its toxicity; infectious diseases such as molecular mechanism of aminoglycoside renal toxicity and subcellular distribution of gentamicin in renal cortical tissue; mechanism of action of toxins from Clostridium difficila. **Mailing Address:** Earle A Chiles Res Inst, Providence Portland Med Ctr, 4805 NE Glisan, Portland, OR 97213. **Fax:** 503-215-6052. **E-Mail:** sue_kohlhepp@phsor.org

KOHLMAN, DAVID L(ESLIE), AERODYNAMICS, AIRCRAFT DESIGN. **Personal Data:** b Houston, Tex, October 13, 1937; m 1959, Linda; c Bradley D & Jeffrey A. **Education:** Univ Kans, BS, 1959, MS, 1960; Mass Inst Technol, PhD (aeronaut, astronaut), 1963. **Honors & Awards:** Univ of Kans Aerospace eng Alumni hon Roll, 1997. **Professional Experience:** PRIN ENGR EMER, ENG SYST INC, 1996-; vpres & dir aeronaut eng, eng syst Inc 1993-1996; chmn bd, Kohlman Syst Res Inc, 1988-; pres, Kohlman Syst Res Inc, 1982-1988; Piaggio, 1978 & Singer-Link, 1981-1988; mem, Flight Mech Panel, NAtlantic Treat Org-Adv Group Aeronaut Res & Develop, 1981-1985; dir, flight res lab, 1981-1982; consult, Gates Learjet, 1978-; PRES, KOHLMAN AVIATION CORP, 1977-; distinguished vis prof, USAF Acad, 1976-1977; consult, NASA, 1975-1977; consult, Cessna Aircraft Co, 1974 & 1978-; prof aerospace eng, Univ Kans, 1970-1981; consult, Bell Helicopter Co, 1970; consult, Beech Aircraft Corp, 1969-1970; chmn dept, Univ Kans, 1967-1972; consult, Centron Corp, 1966-1975; from asst prof to assoc prof, Univ Kans, 1964-1970; res engr, Boeing Co, 1963-1964. **Memberships:** fel Am Inst Aeronaut & Astronaut; Soc Automotive Engrs. **Research Statement & Publications:** Aerodynamic design of aircraft; aircraft stability and control; flight simulation; aircraft ice protection systems; flight testing; accident invest. **Mailing Address:** 4775 Centennial Blvd Ste 106, Colorado Springs, CO 80919. **Fax:** 719-535-0402.

KOHLMAYR, GERHARD FRANZ, MATHEMATICAL PHYSICS, APPLIED MATHEMATICS. **Personal Data:** b Klagenfurt, Austria, November 30, 1930; m 1963. **Education:** Graz Tech Univ, BS, 1951, PhD (theoret physics), 1959. **Professional Experience:** FOUNDER, MATHMODEL PRESS, 1979-; FOUNDER, MATHMODELCONSULT BUR, 1974-; sr appl mathematician, Pratt & Whitney Aircraft, 1971-1974; staffscientist, Mathmodel Press, 1961-1971; Adj asst prof, Rensselaer Polytech Inst, 1961-1966; fel, Von Humboldt Found, 1960-1961; Sci asst, Darmstadt Tech Univ, 1959-1960. **Memberships:** Am Math Soc. **Research Statement & Publications:** Acoustical duct lining theory; inconsistency of Zermelo-Fraenkel set theory; neutron transport theory; mathematical foundation of electrodynamic theory; elementary particle theory; negative solution of Hilbert's second problem; absolute invalidity of Hilbert's program; transient heat transfer; numerical operational calculus; generalized functions. **Mailing Address:** 80 Founders Rd, Glastonbury, CT 06033.

KOHLMEIER, LENORE A, EPIDEMIOLOGY. **Education:** PhD. **Professional Experience:** PROF NUTRIT & EPIDEMIOL, UNIV NC, CHAPEI HILL, 1999-. **Memberships:** Am Cancer Soc. **Mailing Address:** Dept Epidemiol & Nutrit, Univ NC, CB 7400 McGavran-Greenberg Hl 2105E, Chapel Hill, NC 27599-7400. **Fax:** 919-966-2089. **E-Mail:** LenoreA@unc.edu

KOHLMEIER, RONALD HAROLD, VETERINARY PHYSIOLOGY, NUTRITIONAL PHYSIOLOGY. **Personal Data:** b Craig, Nebr, October 16, 1936; c Debora L (Crull), Pamela & Douglas (deceased). **Education:** Univ Nebr, BS, 1959; Iowa State Univ, PhD (ruminant nutrit), 1966, DVM, 1968. **Professional Experience:** Int animal nutrit consult, 1992-; Tech dir animal nutrit, Soybean Asn, 1988-1992; technical sales mgr, Nutrius Inc, 1984-1987; mgr feed sci servs, The Andersons, 1980-1984; mgr tech serv processing group, 1975-1980; res ruminant nutrit & vet, Agr Res Serv, USDA; assoc prof animal sci, Univ Nebr, 1973-1975; assoc prof nutrit & physiol, Iowa State Univ, 1970-1973; Nutrit consult, Dr Richard Hubbard, Gowrie Vet Serv, 1968-1973; asst prof, Iowa State Univ, 1968-1970; res assoc nutrit & physiol, Iowa State Univ, 1966-1968; asst nutritionist, Iowa State Univ, 1960-1966; eng change notice coordr, RCA Missile Div, 1960; Active Duty US Army Artillery, 1959-1960; Farmed with parents 1936-1959. **Memberships:** Am Soc Animal Sci; Am Vet Med Asn; Sigma Xi; Am reg of professional animal sci; Nebraska veterinary medical assoc (life); amer assn of indust veterinarians. **Research Statement & Publications:** Animal nutrition and usage of feed additives; animal nutrition and disease interrelationships. **Mailing Address:** 15622 Century Lake Dr, Chesterfield, MO 63017-4912. **Fax:** 636-537-2086. **E-Mail:** rhk15622@aol.com

KOHLMEYER, JAN JUSTUS, MYCOLOGY. **Personal Data:** b Berlin, Ger, March 15, 1928; American citizen; m Brigitte. **Education:** Free Univ Berlin, Phd, 1955. **Professional Experience:** EMER PROF; UNIV NC, AS OF 2006; prof inst marine sci, Univ Nc, 1974-2001; assoc prof, Univ NC, 1969-1974; asst prof, Inst Fisheries Res, 1964-1969; res assoc, Duke Univ, 1963-1964; res asst mycol, Bot Mus, 1960-1964; res assoc, Univ Wash, 1959-1960; res asst mycol, Fed Inst Mat Testing, Berlin-Dahlem, Ger, 1956-1959. **Memberships:** Mycol Soc Am; hon mem Brit Mycol Soc; Am Inst Biol Sci; Sigma Xi. **Research Statement & Publications:** Marine mycology; taxonomy of fungi; animal-fungus relationships; phytopathology. **Mailing Address:** Inst Marine Sci, Univ NC, Morehead City, NC 28557. **Fax:** 252-726-2426. **E-Mail:** bjkohlm@email.unc.edu

KOHLS, CARL WILLIAM, DISCRETE APPLIED MATHEMATICS. **Personal Data:** b Rochester, NY, March 14, 1931. **Education:** Univ Rochester, AB, 1953; Purdue Univ, MS, 1955, PhD (math), 1957. **Professional Experience:** PROF EMER MATH, SYRACUSE UNIV, 1991-; translr, Am Math SocRussian Transl Proj, 1988-1991; from asst prof to prof, Syracuse Univ, 1961-1991; res assoc &vis asst prof, Univ Rochester, 1960-1961; asst prof, Univ Ill, 1958-1961; instr, Columbia Univ, 1957-1958; Res asst math, Purdue Univ, 1957. **Memberships:** Am Math Soc; Math Asn Am. **Research Statement & Publications:** The study of regulatory systems using Boolean methods. **Mailing Address:** Dept Math, Syracuse Univ, Syracuse, NY 13244.

KOHLS, DONALD W, EXPLORATION GEOLOGY. **Personal Data:** b Minneapolis, Minn, October 21, 1934; m 1962, c 2. **Education:** Carleton Col, BA, 1956; Univ Minn, MS, 1958, PhD (geol), 1961. **Professional Experience:** DIR, MADISON ENTERPRISES CORP, as of 2004; PRES, KOHLS EXPLORATION LTD, 1991-; vpres explor, Mem Bd Dirs, 1979-1989; vpres explor, Golf Fields Mining Corp, 1976-1991; gen mgr & asst to pres, NJ ZincExplor Co, 1974-1976; res scientist, NJ Zinc Co, 1964-1974. **Memberships:** Am Asn Petrol Geologists; Am Inst Mining Metall & Petrol Engrs; Geol SocAm; Soc Econ Paleont & Mineral; Soc Econ Geologists. **Research Statement & Publications:** Economic geology; petrology; mineralogy; geochemistry; field mapping. **Mailing Address:** Madison Enterprises Corp, 1055 W Hastings St, Ste 2000, Vancouver, BC V6E 2E9, Can. **Fax:** 604-331-8773.

KOHLS, ROBERT E, VETERINARY PARASITOLOGY, ENTOMOLOGY. **Personal Data:** b Portage, Wis, March 15, 1931; m 1954, Patricia; c 4. **Education:** Univ Wis, BS, 1953, MS, 1955, PhD, 1958. **Professional Experience:** ANIMAL HEALTH CONSULT, 1985-; consult & pres animal health, Grey Fox Ltd, 1985-; prod mgr, Bristol Labs, 1984-1985; chief parasitol, W Agro Chem Inc, 1977-1984; chief feed additives, Norwich Pharmacol Co, 1975-1977; chief avian prod develop, Norwich Pharmacol Co, 1973-1975; chief parasitol, Norwich Pharmacol Co, 1968-1973; vet parasitologist, Upjohn Co, 1959-1968; dir res, Specifide, Inc, Ind, 1958-1959; proj asst, Dept Vet Sci, Univ Wis, 1958. **Memberships:** Am Soc Parasitol. **Research Statement & Publications:** Insect taxonomy; Diptera and Coleoptera; prophylactic worm control in cattle and sheep using phenothiazine; internal parasite control, especially prophylaxis. **Mailing Address:** 1627 County Rd 36, Norwich, NY 13815.

KOHLSTEDT, DAVID L, GEOLOGIC & CERAMIC MATERIALS. **Personal Data:** m 1966, Sally Gregory; c Kristian Gregory & Kurt Frederick. **Education:** Valparaiso Univ, BS, 1965; Univ Ill, MS, 1967, PhD (physics), 1970. **Professional Experience:** I T DISTINGUISHED, PROF GEOL & GEOPHYS, UNIV MINN, as of 2003; Alexander von Humboldt award, 1993-1994; bayerisches geoinst, UnivBayreuth, 1993-1994; prof geol & geophys, Univ Minn, beginning 1989; vis scientist, Hannover Univ Physics, 1984; vis scientist, Australian Nat Univ, 1983; vis scientist, dept earthsci, Mich Technol Univ, 1982; from asst prof to prof, Dept Mat Sci & Eng, Cornell Univ, 1975-1989; dept earth & planetary sci, Mich Technol Univ, 1971-1975; res assoc, CavendishLab, Cambridge Univ, 1970-1971. **Memberships:** Fel Am Geophys Union; Am Ceramic Soc; Mat Res Soc. **Research Statement & Publications:** Physical and chemical properties of rocks and minerals; high temperature, high pressure experimental research kinetics of solid state reactions; role of water on kinetic properties of silicates; effects of small amount of melt on strength of rocks. **Mailing Address:** Dept Geol & Geophys, Univ Minn, 22 Pills H, 310 Pillsbury Dr, SE, Minneapolis, MN 55455. **Fax:** 612-625-3819. **E-Mail:** dlkohl@umn.edu

KOHLSTEDT, SALLY GREGORY, HISTORY OF SCIENCE. **Personal Data:** b Ypsilanti, Mich, January 30, 1943; m 1966, David; c Kris & Kurt. **Education:** Valparaiso Univ, BA, 1965; Mich State Univ, MA, 1966; Univ Ill, PhD (Am hist), 1972. **Honors & Awards:** Valparaiso Univ; Hist Sci Soc Plenary Lectr, 1988. **Professional Experience:** Serv ed, sci biography, cambridge univ press, 1998-; DIR, CTR ADVAN FEMINIST STUDIES, 1997-1999; Am-Inst, Univ Munich, 1997; PROF HIST SCI, UNIV MINN, 1989-; assoc ed, Am Nat Biog, 1989-1998; assoc dean acad affairs, Ctr Advan Feminist Studies, 1989-1995; vis prof, Cornell Univ, 1989; Smithsonian Inst Sr Fel, 1987; consult, NY Acad Sci, 1986-; chair, Sect L, AAAS, 1986-1987; res fel, Woodrow Wilson Int Ctr, 1986; NASA Hist Adv Comt, 1984-1987; Fulbright vis prof, Univ Melbourne, Australia, 1983; mem, Adv Comt, US Nat Archive Records Serv, 1979-1981; mem, US Nat Comt Int Union Hist & Philos Sci, 1978-1981; from asst prof to prof hist, Syracuse Univ, 1975-1989; asst prof hist, Simmons Col, 1971-1975; fel, Smithsonian Inst, 1970-1971. **Memberships:** Hist Sci Soc (secy, 1978-1981, vpres, 1990-1991, pres, 1992-1993); AAAS; Orgn Am Historians; Am Hist Asn; Am Asn Advan Sci (bd dirs, 1998-2002); Brit Soci Hist Sci. **Research Statement & Publications:** History of the institutional development of scientific activity in the United States; professional origins of scientific societies; inclusion of women in scientific organizations; role of museums in connecting science and the public; published over 100 articles. **Mailing Address:** Univ Minn, 123 Pillsbury Hall, Minneapolis, MN 55455. **Fax:** 612-625-3819. **E-Mail:** sgk@mailbox.mail.umn.edu

KOHMAN, TRUMAN PAUL, ASTRONOMY. **Personal Data:** b Champaign, Ill, March 8, 1916; m 1945, Jane Sievers; c Leslie, Paulette & Steven. **Education:** Harvard Univ, AB, 1938; Univ Wis, PhD (inorg & anal chem), 1943. **Honors & Awards:** Am Chem Soc Award, in nuclear chem 1962. **Professional Experience:** EMER PROF CHEM, CARNEGIE-MELLON UNIV, 1981-; vis prof, Indian Inst Technol, Kanpur, 1962-1963; NSF fel, Max-Planck Inst Chem, 1957-1958; from asst prof to prof, Carnegie-mellon Univ, 1948-1981; fel chem, Inst Nuclear Studies, Univ Chicago, 1946-1948; res assoc, Argonne Nat Lab, 1946; chemist, Hanford Eng Works, Wash, 1944-1945; res assoc metall lab, Univ Chicago, 1942-1944 & 1945-1946; Asst chem, Univ Wis, 1938-1942. **Memberships:** Fel AAAS; Am Chem Soc; fel Am Phys Soc; Am Astron Soc; Meteoritical Soc. **Research Statement & Publications:** Artificial and natural radioactivity; nuclear reactions; geochronometry; meteorites; high-energy astronomy instrumenutation. **Mailing Address:** Dept Chem, Carnegie-Mellon Univ Schenley Park, Pittsburgh, PA 15213. **Fax:** 412-681-0648. **E-Mail:** tk11@andrew.cmu.edu

KOHN, ALAN JACOBS, ZOOLOGY. **Personal Data:** b New Haven, Conn, July 15, 1931; m Marian; c 4. **Education:** Princeton Univ, AB, 1953; Yale Univ, PhD (zoology), 1957. **Professional Experience:** PROF EMER, UNIV WASH, AS OF 1998; Sr post-doctorial fel, Smithsonian Inst, 1990; RES ASSOC, SMITHSONIAN INST, 1985-; prog officer, NSF, 1985-1986; adj prof, Inst Environ Studies, Quaternary Res Inst, 1978-1995; Guggenheim Found fel, 1974; ADJ CUR MALACOL, THOMAS BURKE MEM WASH STATE MUS, 1971-; vis prof, Univ Hawaii, 1968; prof zool, Univ Wash, 1967-1998; sr vis res assoc, Smithsonian Inst, 1967; partic, Int Indian Ocean Exped, 1963; from asst prof to assoc prof, Univ Wash, 1961-1967; asst prof zool, Fla State Univ, 1958-1961; Anderson fel, Bingham Oceanog Lab, Yale Univ, 1958; Biologist, Yale Exped to Seychelles Islands, 1957-1958; Res assoc zool, Marine Lab, Univ Hawaii, 1954-1956; Vis Investigator, Univ Ryukyns, 1981-1982; Participant, Intl Marine Biological workshops (Australia), 1991, 1994, 2000, 2003. **Memberships:** Fel AAAS; fel linnean soc of londn; council for int exchange opf scholars, 1986-1990 (mem executive comt 1988-1989); Am Soc Zool (treas, 1971-1973); soc for intgrative and comparative biology (pres, 1997-1998); Am malacological union (pres, 1983); inst of malacology (vpres 2001-); Am Malacological Union (pres, 1983); Int Soc Reef Studies tropical marine mollusc prog univ aarhus, 1996-2001. **Research Statement & Publications:** Ecology, systematics and paleobiology of marine mollusks; coral reefs. **Mailing Address:** Dept Zool Box 351800, Univ Wash 3900 Seventh Ave NE, Seattle, WA 98195-1800. **E-Mail:** kohn@u.washington.edu

KOHN, DAVID H, BIOMECHANICS, BIOMATERIALS. **Personal Data:** b September 9, 1961; m 1996, Lisa. **Education:** Tulane Univ, BSE, 1983; Univ Pa, MSE, 1985, PhD (bioeng), 1989. **Honors & Awards:** Res Initiation Award, NSF, 1994. **Professional Experience:** PROF, BIOMEDICAL ENG, UNIV MICH, as of 2006; assoc prof biol & mat sci, Sch Dent & Biomed Col, Eng, 1996-; co-investr, NSF & Whitaker Found, 1994-; fac mem & adv, Oral Heakth Sci, Univ Wash, 1993-; prin invest, Delta Dent Fund, 1991-1992; co-investr, NIH, 1991-1992; co-investr, Nat Inst Dent Res, 1990-; grad prog Bioengineering, HoraceRackham Sch Grad Studies, 1990-1996; prin invest, Univ Mich, 1990-1992, 1990-1992, 1991-1992 & 1993; mem, Study Sect & Reviewer, NIH, 1989-; asst prof, Dept Biol & Mat Sci, Sch Dent, Univ Mich, 1989-1996; consult, Med Device Co, Labs & Individuals, 1988-; health sci specialist, VetAdmin, Pa, 1987-1989; Lectr, Dept Bioengineering, Univ Pa, 1986; res fel, Dept Bioengineering, Univ Pa, 1984-1989; teaching asst, Dept Bioengineering, Univ Pa, 1983; Res asst, Hosp Spec Surg, 1983; Resasst, Biomech Lab, Tulane Univ, 1982-1983. **Memberships:** Am Soc Testing & Mat; Biomed Eng Soc; Int Asn Dent Res; Soc Biomat; SigmaXi; Mat Res Soc; Am Soc Mech Engrs; Am Asn Dent Res. **Research Statement & Publications:** Biomechanics and biomaterials for hand tissue replacement and regeneration; smart materials bioninetics structure function relations in tissue; contributed over 100 papers, chapters, articles; granted 1 patent. **Mailing Address:** Dept Biol & Mat Sci Univ Mich, 1011 N Univ Ave, Ann Arbor, MI 48109-1078. **Fax:** 734-764-2110. **E-Mail:** dhkohn@umich.edu

KOHN, ERWIN, PHYSICAL CHEMISTRY, POLYMER CHEMISTRY, SIZE EXCLUSION CHROMATOGRAPHY. **Personal Data:** b Vienna, Austria, August 23, 1923; American citizen; m 1949, Henrietta; c Joseph H, Michael D, Daniel R, Benjamin, Samuel L & Susan M (Shay). **Education:** Univ Ill, BS, 1948; Univ Notre Dame, MS, 1950; Univ Tex, PhD (chem), 1956. **Professional Experience:** PRES, HAPPY FINS INC, as of 2005; consult, Los Alamos Nat Lab, 1998-2002; sr proj scientist, Appl Technol Div, Mason & Hanger Co, 1972-1997; dir NSF prog, NDak State Univ, 1971-1972; assoc prof polymer chem, NDak State Univ, 1968-1972; assoc prof chem, Southwestern Okla State Univ, 1966-1968; res specialist, Monsanto Co, Tex, 1962-1966. **Memberships:** Emer mem Am Chem Soc; emer mem Am Phys Soc. **Research Statement & Publications:** Kinetic isotope effects; physical and physical-organic chemistry; analytical chemistry; liquid and gel permeation chromatography; explosives analysis; kinetics and mechanisms; Ziegler-Natta polymerization; structure of polyolefins; polymer characterization; organometallic chemistry. **Mailing Address:** 3613 Nebr St, Amarillo, TX 79109. **Fax:** 806-351-2303. **E-Mail:** hapyfins@arn.net

KOHN, FRANK S, ORGANIZATIONAL BEHAVIOR SCIENCES. **Personal Data:** b Bristol, Pa, June 21, 1942; m 1982, Marge; c Frank A & David G. **Education:** NJ State Col Trenton, BA, 1969; Drexel Univ, Philadelphia, Pa, MS, 1972; UnivWis-Madison, PDD, 1979. **Honors & Awards:** H Burrows Award, Franklin Sch Sci, 1961. **Professional Experience:** Adj prof, Campbell Univ, 1995; instr clearing validation & barrier technol, Inst ApplPharmaceut Sci, 1992-; DIR MFG, WYETH-LEDERLE VACCINES & PEDIAT, WYETH-AYERST LABS, 1992-; dir mfg pharm, Sanofi AnimalHealth, Sanofi Inc, 1986-1991; instr org behavior, Iowa Cent Community Col, 1982-1987; dir mfg pharm & biol, Am HomeProd, Ft Dodge Labs, 1982-1986; dir oper pharm & biol, Schering Plough Corp, 1978-1982; scientist, Schering Plough Corp, 1976-1978; from asst microbiologist to assoc microbiologistpharmaceut, Schering Plough Corp, 1969-1972; Virologist, NJ Dept Health, 1963-1969; consult org development, Mussic & Assoc; Consult, Bristol Sanitation Co. **Memberships:** Am Soc Microbiologists; Parenteral Drug Asn; Am Soc Pharmaceut Engrs; AAAS; Am Acad Microbiol. **Research Statement & Publications:** Pharmaceutical microbiology; environmental microbiology in clean rooms; infectious diseases; leptospirosis lab methods development; management to technical staff; interpersonal relationship; value engineering as applied to the pharmaceutical industry. **Mailing Address:** 113 Cumberland Greens Dr, Cary, NC 27513.

KOHN, FRED R, EXPERIMENTAL BIOLOGY. **Professional Experience:** AT, XOMA CORP, as of 1995; PHARMACOLOGIST, XOMA CORP, 1989-. **Mailing Address:** Xoma Corp, 2910 Seventh St, Berkeley, CA 94710-2743. **Fax:** 510-841-7805.

KOHN, GUSTAVE K, CHEMISTRY. **Personal Data:** b Syracuse, NY, February 12, 1910; m 1950, c 3. **Education:** NY Univ, BS, 1930. **Professional Experience:** RETIRED; mgr licensing & technol, Sandor Corp, 1984-1990; Coun, Am Chem Soc, 1979-, immediate past chmn, agrochem div; sr scientist, Zoecon Corp, 1979-1990; resdir, Zoecon Corp, 1976-1978; pesticide prod adv to govt India, UN Indust Develop Orgn, NewDelhi, 1975-1976; sr res scientist, Ortho Div, Chevron Chem Co, Standard Oil Co, Calif, 1970-1975; mgr cent res labs, Ortho Div, Chevron Chem Co, Standard Oil Co, Calif, 1962-1970; chief res chemist, Ortho Div, Chevron Chem Co, Standard Oil Co, Calif, 1956-1962; groupleader org synthesis, Ortho Div, Chevron Chem Co, Standard Oil Co, Calif, 1954-1956; reschemist, Ortho Div, Chevron Chem Co, Standard Oil Co, Calif, 1951-1954; Control chemist, Ortho Div, Chevron Chem Co, Standard Oil Co, Calif, 1946-1951. **Memberships:** AAAS; Am Chem Soc; Entom Soc Am; Am Inst Biol Sci; Sigma Xi. **Research Statement & Publications:** Synthesis of biologically active and agriculturally useful compounds; organophosphate insecticides; halo-organic fungicides; plant and insect growth regulators. **Mailing Address:** 101 Alma St Apt 405, Palo Alto, CA 94301.

KOHN, HAROLD LEWIS, MECHANISM OF DRUG ACTION, SYNTHETIC METHODS. **Personal Data:** b New York, NY, April 1, 1945; m 1991, Carol; c Jeffrey S & Nicholas W. **Education:** Univ Mich, BS, 1966; Pa State Univ, PhD (chem), 1971. **Professional Experience:** KENAN PROF & CHMN, DIV MED CHEM & NAT PROD, SCH PHARM, UNIV NC, as of 2005; sloanscholar, A P Sloan Found, 1977; dreyfus scholar, Dreyfus Found, 1977; prof Chem, Univ Houston, 1973-1999. **Memberships:** Am Chem Soc; Sigma Xi. **Research Statement & Publications:** Determining the mechanism of drug action and the elucidation of the site of drug function. **Mailing Address:** Div Med Chem & Nat Prod, Sch Pharm, Univ NC, CB 7360 328A Beard Hall, Chapel Hill, NC 27599-7360. **Fax:** 919-843-7835. **E-Mail:** harold_kohn@unc.edu

KOHN, HAROLD WILLIAM, ENVIRONMENTAL SCIENCE. **Personal Data:** b Newark, NJ, November 9, 1920; m 1957, Janet Mitchell; c Frederick J, Marilyn L, Andrew D & Matthew J. **Education:** Univ Mich, Ann Arbor, BS, 1943; Syracuse Univ, PhD (chem), 1953. **Professional Experience:** RETIRED; staff scientist environ, Ohio Environ Protection Agency, 1973-1986; vis prof, Dickinson Col, 1971-1972; Vis lectr, Univ Calif, Berkeley, 1963-1964; res engr, Battelle Mem Inst, 1952-1953; asst chem, Syracuse Univ, 1948-1953; Chemist, Oak Ridge Nat Labs, 1947-1948 & 1954-1973. **Memberships:** Am Int Doulsle Reed Soc. **Research Statement & Publications:** Effects of ionizing radiations on heterogeneous catalysts; radiation chemistry of surfaces; molten salt chemistry; power plant siting and productivity; environmental impacts. **Mailing Address:** 147 Chatham Rd, Columbus, OH 43214.

KOHN, HERBERT MYRON, NEUROPSYCHOLOGY, ELECTROENCEPHALOGRAPHY. **Personal Data:** b Chicago, Ill, February 24, 1935; m 1957, c 2. **Education:** Univ Ill, BA, 1958; Roosevelt Univ, MA, 1960; Ill Inst Technol, PhD (psychol), 1965. **Professional Experience:** Adj assoc prof, Grad Sch Appl & Prof Psychol, Rutgers Univ, 1976-; ASSOC PROF PSYCHIAT, RUTGERS MED SCH, COL MED & DENT NJ, 1975-; CHIEF NEURODIAG LAB, RUTGERS MED SCH, COL MED & DENT NJ, 1972-; assoc psychobiol, Grad Fac, Rutgers Univ, 1972-1978; asst prof, Rutgers Med Sch, Col Med & Dent NJ, 1972-1975; lectr, Northeastern Ill State Univ, 1970-1972 & Univ Ill, Chicago Circle, 1972; res scientist, Ill State Pediat Inst, 1971-1972; asst prof, Ill Inst Technol, 1967-1972 & Abraham Lincoln Sch Med, Univ Ill, 1968-1972; dir, Darrow Mem Lab, Inst Juv Res, 1968-1970; Lectr, Roosevelt Univ, 1965-1972; Med res assoc, Ill State Psychiat Inst, 1960-1967. **Memberships:** Am Psychol Asn; Psychonomic Soc; Int Neuropsychol Soc. **Research Statement & Publications:** Neural bases of human behavior; primate behavior; vision and effects of early brain damage. **Mailing Address:** Dept Psychiat, Univ Med & Dent Robert Wood Johnson Sch 675 Hoes Lane, Piscataway, NJ 08854-5635.

KOHN, JACK ARNOLD, MATERIALS RESEARCH, CRYSTALLOGRAPHY. **Personal Data:** b Trenton, NJ, July 17, 1925; m 1951, Norma Bialy; c Steven B & Martha (Wurzel). **Education:** Univ Mich, BS, 1947, MS, 48, PhD (mineral), 1950. **Honors & Awards:** Prize, Army Sci Conf, 1959, 1962 & 1970. **Professional Experience:** Dir electronic mat res, Electronics Technol & Devices Lab, 1974-1985; dep dir technol, US Army Electronics Res & Develop Command, Ft Monmouth, 1971-1973; dep dir inst explor res, US Army Electronics Res & Develop Command, Ft Monmouth, 1969-1971; physicist & dep dir solid state sci div, US Army Electronics Res & Develop Command, Ft Monmouth, 1955-1969; mineralogist, Electrotech Lab, US Bur Mines, 1951-1955; res assoc, Univ Mich, 1950-1951; Consult mineralogist, US Bur Mines, 1950-1951; Asst mineral, Univ Mich, 1948-1950. **Memberships:** Fel AAAS; fel Mineral Soc Am; Am Crystallog Asn. **Research Statement & Publications:** Crystallography of electronic and magnetic materials; twinning; polymorphism; polytypism; general x-ray crystallography. **Mailing Address:** 65 Wigwam Rd, Locust, NJ 07760.

KOHN, JOSEPH JOHN, MATHEMATICS. **Personal Data:** b Prague, Czech, May 18, 1932; American citizen; m 1966, c 3. **Education:** Mass Inst Technol, BS, 1953; Princeton Univ, MA, 1954, PhD (math), 1956. **Honors & Awards:** Steele Prize, Am Math Soc, 1979; Czech Math & Physics Union Award, 1990& 1993. **Professional Experience:** Chmn dept, Princeton Univ, 1973-1976 & 1993-1996; PROF MATH, PRINCETON UNIV, 1968-; from asst prof to prof math, Brandeis Univ, 1958-1968; mem, Inst Advan Study, 1957-1958; Instr math, Princeton Univ, 1956-1957; Ed, Transactions Am Math Soc, Advances Math & Annals Math. **Memberships:** Nat Acad Sci; Am Acad Arts & Sci; Am Math Soc. **Research Statement & Publications:** Several complex variables; partial differential equations. **Mailing Address:** Dept Math, Princeton Univ, Fine Hall Washington RD, Princeton, NJ 08544. **Fax:** 609-258-1367. **E-Mail:** kohn@princeton.edu

KOHN, KURT WILLIAM, CHEMICAL PHARMACOLOGY. **Personal Data:** b Austria, September 14, 1930; American citizen; m 1956, c 2. **Education:** Harvard Univ, AB, 1952, PhD (biochem), 1965; Columbia Univ, MD, 1956. **Professional Experience:** PRIN INVESTR, LAB MOLECULAR PHARMACOL, NAT CANCER INST, as of 2004; CHIEF LAB MOLECULAR PHARMACOL, NAT CANCER INST, 1968-; sr investr, Nat cancer inst, beginning 1959; clin assoc, Nat cancer inst, 1957-1959. **Memberships:** Am Chem Soc; Am Asn Cancer res; Am Asn Biol Chemists. **Research Statement & Publications:** Effects of chemotherapeutic agents on structure and function of deoxyribonucleic acid. **Mailing Address:** Nat Cancer Inst, NIH Bldg 37 Rm 5D02, Bethesda, MD 20892. **Fax:** 301-402-0752. **E-Mail:** kohnk@dc37a.nic.nih.gov

KOHN, LEONARD DAVID, BIOCHEMICAL PHARMACOLOGY. **Personal Data:** b New York, NY, August 1, 1935; m 1962, c 2. **Education:** Columbia Univ, BA, 1957, MD, 1961. **Professional Experience:** PROF BIOMED SCI & J O WATSON D O ENDOWED RES CHMN, KONNEKER RES CTR, OHIO UNIV, as of 2003; PRIN INVESTR, KONNEKER RES LAB, OHIO UNIV, as of 2003; distinguished sr res scientist, Edison Biotechnol Inst, Ohio Univ, beginning 2000; chief, bell regulation sect, metab dis br, Nat Instarthritis, Metab & Digestive Dis, 1995-2000; chief, Sect Biochem Cell Regulation, LabBiochem Pharmacol, 1974-1995; Vis prof, Dept Med, Univ Liege, Belg, 1970-1971; med resofficer, Lab Biochem Pharmacol, 1966-1974; res assoc, Lab Biochem & Metab, Nat InstArthritis, Metab & Digestive Dis, 1964-1966; sr resident, Columbia Presby Med Ctr, 1963-1964;

asst resident, Columbia Presby Med Ctr, 1962-1963; Intern med, Columbia Presby Med Ctr, 1961-1962. **Memberships:** Am Soc Biol Chemists; Am Endocrinol Soc; Am Thyroid Asn. **Research Statement & Publications:** Mechanism by which hormones interact with membrane components to elicit functional responses and growth; enzymatic conversion of precursors of collagen to collagen; enzymes concerned with solute transport across membranes; autoimmunity. **Mailing Address:** Dept Biomed Sci, Konneker Res Ctr, Ohio Univ, Athens, OH 45701-2979. **Fax:** 740-593-4795. **E-Mail:** kohnl@ohio.edu

KOHN, MICHAEL, BIOMEDICAL ENGINEERING, NEUROPHYSIOLOGY. **Personal Data:** b Budapest, Hungary, June 18, 1934; American citizen; m 1955, c 1. **Education:** City Univ NY, BEE, 1960, MEE, 1968; NY Univ, PhD (elec eng), 1974. **Professional Experience:** DIR, Bioengineering DEPT, ROCKLAND RES INST, 1968-; consult, Mnemotron Corp, 1961-1962; res engr, Bioengineering dept, Rockland res inst, 1957-1968. **Research Statement & Publications:** Development of biomedical instrumentation; analysis of electrophysiological data. **Mailing Address:** Nathan Kline Inst, 140 Old Orangeburg Rd, Orangeburg, NY 10962.

KOHN, MICHAEL CHARLES, BIOMATHEMATICS, BIOCHEMISTRY. **Personal Data:** b Brooklyn, NY, July 29, 1941; m 1971, Lynn. **Education:** Mass Inst Technol, BS, 1964; Univ SC, PhD (chem), 1970. **Professional Experience:** STAFF SCIENTIST, NAT INST ENVIRON SCI, RES TRIANGLE PARK, NC, 1996-; expert, Nat Inst Environ Sci, Res Triangle Park, NC, 1991-1996; assoc med res prof, Depts Physiol & Cell Biol, Duke Med Ctr, 1984-1991; sr res investr & adj assoc prof, Univ, Pa, 1974-1984; chemist, Naval Undersea Res & Develop Ctr, 1971-1973; Nat Res Coun fel, Naval Undersea Res & Develop Ctr, 1971-1973; fel, Univ Tex, Austin, 1969-1971; consult, BB Chem Co, 1962-1963; technician chem, Gen Latex & Chem Co, 1962. **Memberships:** AAAS; Sigma Xi; Soc Comput Simulation; Soc Math Biol. **Research Statement & Publications:** Valence force field calculations of strain energy; molecular orbital theory; statistical mechanics of polymer solutions; biomedical computer models; sensitivity analysis; graph-theoretical analysis of metabolic networks; computer modeling of responses to toxins. **Mailing Address:** Lab Computational Biol & Risk Anal, Nat Inst Environ Health Sci, PO Box 12233 Mail Drop A3-06, Research Triangle Park, NC 27709-2233. **Fax:** 919-541-1479. **E-Mail:** kohn.at.niehs.nih.gov

KOHN, PETER H, GENETICS. **Education:** Pa State Univ, BS; Boston Univ, PhD (pop &d ecol genetics). **Professional Experience:** DIR, CLIN GENETICS & RES LAB, NEOGENOMICS INC, as of 2002. **Mailing Address:** NeoGenomics Inc, 840 111th Ave N, Naples, FL 34108. **E-Mail:** pkohn@ameripath.com

KOHN, SAMUEL, MATHEMATICS. **Education:** Yeshiva Univ, BA, MA, MS, & PhD. **Professional Experience:** ASST PROF, HEALTH SCI, TOURO UNIV INT, as of 2002. **Mailing Address:** Touro Univ, Dept Health Sci, 5665 Plaza Dr Third Floor, Cypress, CA 90630. **Fax:** 714-816-0367.

KOHN, WALTER, THEORETICAL PHYSICS. **Personal Data:** b Vienna, Austria, March 9, 1923; American citizen; m 1978, c J Marilyn, Ingrid E (Katz) & E Rosalind. **Education:** Univ Toronto, BA, 1945, MA, 1946; Harvard Univ, PhD (physics), 1948. **Honorary Degrees:** LLD, Univ Toronto, 1967; DSC, Univ Paris, 1980, Brandeis Univ, 1981; DPhil, Hebrew Univ, Jerusalem, 1981; DSc, Queens Univ, Can, 1986, Tech Univ Vienna, 1996; DNat Sci, Fed Inst Technol, Zurich, 1994; Drerum naturalium, Univ Wuerzburg, Ger, 1995. **Honors & Awards:** Nobel Prize in Physics, 1967; Oliver E Buckley Prize, 1960; Davisson Germer Prize, 1977; Nat Medal Sci, Pres US, 1988; Feenberg Medal, 1991. **Professional Experience:** PROF EMER PHYSICS, UNIV CALIF, SANTA BARBARA, 1991-; prof, Inst Theoret Physics, Santa Barbara, 1984-1991; dir, Inst Theoret Physics, Santa Barbara, 1979-1984; consult, Int Bus Mach, 1978; Battelle distinguished vis prof, Univ Wash, 1974; vis prof, Superior Normal School, Paris, 1963-1964 & Hebrew Univ, Jerusalem, 1970; NSF sr fel, Univ Paris, 1967; Guggenheim fel, 1963; chmn dept, San Diego, 1961-1963; prof, Univ Calif, 1960-1979; consult, Gen Atomic, 1960-1972; vis scholar, Univ Pa, Univ Mich, Univ Wash, Seattle, Univ Paris, Univ Copenhaagen, Univ Jerusalem, Imp Col, London, ETH, Zurich, 1958-1985; sr NSF fel, Imp Col, 1958; consult, Bell Tel Labs, 1953-1966; consult, Westinghouse Res Lab, 1953-1957; Nat Res Coun fel, Oersted fel, 1951-1952; prof, Carnegie-Mellon Inst, Pittsburgh Pa, 1950-1960; Nat Res Coun fel, Copenhaagen, 1950-1951; instr physics, Harvard Univ, Cambridge, Mass, 1948-1950; mem, Brookhaven Nat Labs, Argonne Nat Labs, Oak Ridge Nat Labs, Int Adv Comt Strongly Interacting Plasmas; mem solid state sci panel, Nat Acad Sci; ed, J Non-Metals & J Physics & Chem Solids. **Memberships:** Nat Acad Sci; fel Am Acad Arts & Sci; fel Am Phys Soc; Int Acad Quantum Molecular Sci. **Research Statement & Publications:** Theory of solids; surface physics; collision theory; theory of surfaces, chemisorption, physisorption, electron theory of metals, density functional theory. **Mailing Address:** Dept Physics, Univ Calif, Santa Barbara, CA 93106. **Fax:** 805-893-5816. **E-Mail:** kohn@physics.ucsb.edu

KOHNHORST, EARL EUGENE, MANUFACTURING RESEARCH DEVELOPMENT & ENGINEERING, PURCHASING & LOGISTICS. **Personal Data:** b Louisville, Ky, April 15, 1947; m 1972, Mary L Pierce; c 1. **Education:** Univ Louisville, BChE, 1970, MSChE, 1971. **Professional Experience:** OPERS DIR, BRIT AM TOBACCO HOLDINGS LTD, 1995-; exec vpres & chief operating officer, Batus, 1993-1995; exec vpres, Batus, 1989-1993; vpres planning, Batus, 1987-1989; dir mfg planning & eng, Develop Ctr, 1980-1987; mgr, Develop Ctr, 1976-1979; Process engr, Brown & WilliamsonTobacco Corp, 1971-1976; Bd mem, Coop Ctr Sci Res Rel Tobacco. **Memberships:** Am Inst Chem Engrs. **Research Statement & Publications:** Catalytic conversion of nitric oxides using rare earth catalysts; determining mechanisms and kinetic rate equations. **Mailing Address:** Brit Am Tobacco Holdings Ltd, Millbank Knowle Green, Staines Middlesex TW18 1DY, UK.

KOHONEN, TEUVO KALEVI, NEURAL NETWORKS. **Personal Data:** b Lauritsala, Finland, July 11, 1934; m 1959, Elvi A Trast; c Virpi, Eevi, Jussi & Jukka. **Education:** Helsinki Univ Technol, dipl, 1957, licentiate tech, 1960, DEng(physics), 1962. **Honorary Degrees:** PhD, Univ York, Eng, 1992, Abo Acad, Finland, 1993, D Eng, Dortmund, Germany, 1997. **Honors & Awards:** Academician, 2000; Knight First Class, White Rose of Finland, 1976; Comdr, Lion of Finland, 1987; Emil Aaltonen Prize, 1983; Cultural Prize of the Commercial Television, 1984; Medal of the City of Espoo, 1988; Trend-setter of the year, assoc, for Data Processing, 1988; Neural Networks Pioneer Award, Inst Elec & Electronics Engrs, 1991; INNS Lifetime Achievement Award, 1992; Prize of the Finnish Cultural Foundation, 1994; Medal of Lappeenranta univ, of Technology, 1995; Tech Achievement Award, Inst Elec & Electronics Engrs Signal Processing Soc, 1995; Centennial Prize, Finnish Asn Grad Engrs, 1996; King Sun Fu Prize, 1996 Medal of the Finnish Acad, fo Enginnering Sciences, 1997; SEFI Leonardo da Vinci Medal, European soc for Engineering Education, 1998; Jubilee Prize of the Finnish Foundation of Technology, 1999; Italgaz Prize, 1999; E R Caianiello International Award, 2000; IEEEE Third Millennium Medal, 2000. **Professional Experience:** RES PROF, ACAD FINLAND, 1980-; res prof, Acad Finland, 1975-1978; Vis prof, Univ Wash, 1968-1969; prof tech physics, Helsinki Univ Technol, 1965-1993; asst prof, Helsinki Univ Technol, 1963-1965; res assoc, Finnish Atomic Energy Comn, 1959-1962; Teaching asst physics, Helsinki Univ Technol, 1957-1959. **Memberships:** Fel Inst Elec & Electronics Engrs; Europ Neural Network Soc (pres, 1991-1992); Int Asn Pattern Recognition; Int Neural Network Soc; Europ Acad Sci; Finnish Acad Sci; Finnish Acad Eng Sci; hon mem Pattern Recognition Soc Finland; Finnish Soc Med Physics & Med Eng; Brain Res Soc Finland. **Research Statement & Publications:** Inventor of several neural-network algorithms, including the Self-Organizing map; Five monography books, three edited books, and over 300 original scientific publications. **Mailing Address:** Neural Networks Research Centre, Helsinki, Konemiehentie 2, Espoo FIN- 02015 HUT, Finland.

KOHOUT, FREDERICK CHARLES, III, LUBRICATION SCIENCE, ENVIRONMENTAL SCIENCE. **Personal Data:** b Flint, Mich, June 19, 1940; m 1961, Mary Lou; c Karen, Kevin & Christopher. **Education:** Mich State Univ, BS, 1962; Pa State Univ, PhD (phys chem), 1966. **Professional Experience:** RES CONSULT, CONSTAR CONSULTS, PARK CITY, UT 1996-; res consult, Res Ser Div, Mobil Res & Develop, Paulsboro Lab, 1988-1996; mgr, Res Ser Div, 1988-1993; mgr comp res & environ serv, Prod Res Div, 1981-1988; mem staff, Prod Res Div, 1973-1981; Mem staff, Mobil Res & Develop, Cent Res Div, 1966-1973. **Memberships:** Sr mem Am Chem Soc; Am Soc Lubrication Engrs. **Research Statement & Publications:** Development of marine diesel lubricants, gear lubricants and greases; analytical chemistry of petroleum streams and products; environmental science; groundwater protection; Consulting petroleum products. **Mailing Address:** 305 Seneca Dr, Wenonah, NJ 08090. **E-Mail:** fckohout@aol.com

KOHRMAN, ARTHUR FISHER, PEDIATRICS. **Personal Data:** b Cleveland, Ohio, December 19, 1934; m 1955, Claire; c Deborah, Benjamin, Ellen & Rachel. **Education:** Univ Chicago, BA & BS, 1955; Western Res Univ, MD, 1959. **Professional Experience:** PROF PEDIAT, CHILDREN'S MEM HOSP, NORTHWESTERN UNIV, 1997-; Prof biol sci, Col Div, Univ Chicago, 1985-1997; prof & assoc chmn, Dept Pediat, Pritzker Sch Med, Univ Chicago, 1981-1996; pres, La Rabida Children's Hosp & Res Ctr, 1981- 1996; assoc dean educ prog & prof med educ res & develop, Col Human Med, Mich State Univ, 1977-1980; from asst prof to prof, Col Human Med, Mich State Univ, 1968- 1981; NIH trainee & spec fel pediat, Stanford Univ, 1965-1968. **Memberships:** Lawson Wilkins Pediat Endocrinol Soc; Am Acad Pediat; Am Pediat Soc; Soc Pediat Res.; Health and Med Policy Res Group. **Research Statement & Publications:** Childhood chronic disease and health policy; developmental endocrinology and biochemistry; effects of environmental agents on human development. **Mailing Address:** Children's Mem Hosp, 2300 Childrens Plaza, Chicago, IL 60614. **Fax:** 773-665-7934. **E-Mail:** okohrman@northwestern.edu

KOHRT, CARL FREDRICK, SURFACE SCIENCE, PHOTOGRAPHIC IMAGING SCIENCES. **Personal Data:** b Normal, Ill, December 18, 1943; m 1962, Lynne; c Kristopher, Brian & Jason. **Education:** Furman Univ, BS, 1965; Univ Chicago, PhD (phys chem), 1971; Mass Inst Technol, MS, 1991. **Professional Experience:** PRES & CHIEF EXEC OFFICER, BATTELLE MEM INST, 2001-; vpres & gen mgr, health sci div, Eastman Kodak Co, 1991-2000; Sloan fel, Sloan Sch Mgt, Mass Inst Technol, 1990-1991; group lab dir, Photog Res Labs, 1987-1990; div dir, Hybrid Imaging Systs Div, 1985-1987; asst exec vpres, Corp Staff, 1984-1985; analyst, Corp Strategic Planning Off, 1983; asst div dir, Instant Photog Res Div, 1982-1983; lab head, Color-Photog Res Div, 1976-1982; sr scientist, Res Labs, Eastman KodakCo, 1971-1976; Fel, James Frank Inst, Univ Chicago, 1970-1971. **Research Statement & Publications:** Focus on heterogeneous catalysis or thermal catalysis to generate dyes or other photographically useful species; developed photographic quality sublimationthermal imaging systems and other digital imaging systems. **Mailing Address:** Battelle Mem Inst, 505 King Ave, Colombus, OH 43201.

KOHUT, ROBERT JOHN, POLLUTION EFFECTS ON VEGETATION, VEGETATION STRESS. **Personal Data:** b Cannonsburg, Pa, November 19, 1943. **Education:** Pa State Univ, BS, 1965, MS, 1972, PhD (plant path), 1975. **Professional Experience:** SCIENTIST, BOYCE THOMPSON INST, CORNELL UNIV, 1995-; assoc scientist, Boyce Thompson Inst, Cornell Univ, 1988-1995; asst scientist, Boyce Thompson Inst, Cornell Univ, 1986-1988; Toxic Substances Subcomt, Environ Protection Agency Sci Adv Bd, 1980-; res assoc, Boyce Thompson Inst, Cornell Univ, 1980-1986; comt mem, Colo Gov AirPollution Tech Working Comt, 1979-1980; affil fac, dept plant path, Colo State Univ, 1978-1980; plant pathologist, Environ Res & Technol, 1977-1980; res fel, dept plant path, UnivMinn, 1975-1977. **Memberships:** Am Phytopath Soc; Air Pollution Control Asn; Sigma Xi. **Research Statement & Publications:** Field and laboratory research evaluating the effects of air pollutants on growth and yield of agricultural crops, trees and on native plants and plant communities. **Mailing Address:** Boyce Thompson Inst Plant Res, Cornell Univ, Rm 131 214 Eastern Heights Dr, Ithaca, NY 14850-6304. **E-Mail:** rjk9@cornell.edu

KOIDE, FRANK T, BIOMEDICAL & ELECTRONICS ENGINEERING. **Personal Data:** b Honolulu, Hawaii, December 25, 1935; c Julie & Cheryl. **Education:** Univ Ill, BSEE, 1958; Clarkson Univ, MS, 1961; Univ Iowa, PhD (physiol), 1966. **Professional Experience:** External examr, Chinese Univ Hong Kong, 1977-; consult, Shared Clin EngServs Hawaii & Acupuncture Asn Hawaii, 1974-; PROF ELEC ENG & PHYSIOL, UNIVHAWAII, 1974-; assoc prof physiol, Univ Hawaii, 1972-1974; assoc prof elec eng, Univ Hawaii, 1969-1974; prin res scientist, Life Sci Div, Technol Inc, Tex, 1968-1969; NASA-Am Soc EngEduc fac fel, 1967; asst prof elec eng, physiol & biomed eng, Iowa State Univ, 1966-1968; consult, Collins Radio Co, 1961-1963; instr, Cedar Rapids Adult Educ, 1960-1961; engr res div, Collins Radio Co, 1959-1961. **Memberships:** Inst Elec & Electronics Engrs; Sigma Xi. **Research Statement & Publications:** Application of engineering techniques in solutionof biomedical problems; membrane physiology; electrophysiology; nerve; bioinstrumentation; operational amplifiers; electronic circuits. **Mailing Address:** Dept Elec Eng Univ Hawaii, 2540 Dole St, Honolulu, HI 96822. **Fax:** 808-956-3427. **E-Mail:** koide@spectra.eng.hawaii.edu

KOIDE, ROGER TAI, PLANT PHYSIOLOGICAL ECOLOGY, SOIL MICROBIOLOGY. **Personal Data:** b Berkeley, Calif, December 14, 1957; m 1979, c 3. **Education:** Pomona Col, BA (biol), 1980; Univ Calif, Berkeley, PhD (bot), 1984. **Honors & Awards:** NSF presidential young investr award, 1987. **Professional Experience:** PROF PLANT ECOL, PA STATE UNIV, AS OF 2006; from asst prof to assoc prof, PA State Univ, 1986-1996; Postdoctoral res affil plant ecol, Stanford Univ, 1984-1986; Fulbright sr scholar. **Research Statement & Publications:** Plant ecology; mycorrhizal symbiosis. **Mailing Address:** Dept Hort, Pa State Univ, Univ Park, PA 16802. **Fax:** 814-863-6139. **E-Mail:** rxk13@psu.edu

KOIDE, SAMUEL SABURO, BIOCHEMISTRY, INTERNAL MEDICINE. **Personal Data:** b Honolulu, Hawaii, October 6, 1923; m 1960, c 3. **Education:** Univ Hawaii, BS, 1945; Northwestern Univ, MD, 1953, MS, 1954, PhD (biochem), 1960. **Honors & Awards:** Joseph A Capps Prize Med Res, 1958. **Professional Experience:** ASSOC DIR & SR SCIENTIST, CTR FOR BIOMED RES, POP COUN, ROCKEFELLER UNIV, 1970-; asst dir biomed div, Ctr For Biomed res, Pop Coun, RockefellerUniv, 1965-1970; asst prof biochem, Sloan-Kettering inst, 1964-1965; nat inst Arthritis &Metab Dis career develop award, 1963-1965; asst prof, Cornell Univ, 1961-1965; assoc, Sloan-Kettering inst, 1960-1965. **Memberships:** Biochem Soc; Endocrine Soc; Am Col Physicians; Am Soc Biol Chemists; SocExp Biol & Med. **Research Statement & Publications:** Signal transduction system in genetics; immunobiology of sperm; causation of unexplained infertility; reproductive biology. **Mailing Address:** Biomed Div, Pop Coun, Rockefeller Univ, 1230 York Ave, New York, NY 10021-6399.

KOIKE, HIDEO, PHYTOPATHOLOGY, SUGARCANE DISEASES. **Personal Data:** b March 10, 1921. **Education:** Univ Hawaii, BA, 1944; Kans State Univ, MS, 1951, PhD (bact), 1956. **Professional Experience:** CONSULT, SUGARCANE PATH, 1984-; res plant pathologist, US Sugarcane Field Lab, USDA, 1969-1983; Sugar Crops Res Br, Crops Res Div, Agr Res Serv, Univ PR, Gurabo, 1966-1969; assoc pathologist, Exp Sta, Hawaiian Sugar Planters Asn, 1957-1966; asst, Kans State Univ, 1954-1956; asst pathologist, Exp Sta, Hawaiian Sugar Planters Asn, 1952-1954; Asst, Kans State Univ, 1949-1951; res microbiologist sugarcane & sweet sorghum invest, Tobacco. **Memberships:** Fel AAAS; Am Phytopath Soc; Int Soc Plant Path; Sigma Xi; Int Soc Sugarcane Technol. **Research Statement & Publications:** Effects of diseases on yields of sugureane varieties. **Mailing Address:** 180 Alamo Dr, Houma, LA 70360.

KOIKE, THOMAS ISAO, PHYSIOLOGY. **Personal Data:** b Watsonville, Calif, July 27, 1927; m 1955, c 2. **Education:** Univ Calif, Berkeley, AB, 1951, PhD (physiol), 1958. **Professional Experience:** PROF PHYSIOL & BIOPHYSICS, MED CTR, UNIV ARK, LITTLE ROCK, 1978-; NIH grant, 1966-1972; from asst prof to assoc prof, Med Ctr, Univ Ark, Little Rock, 1965-1978; asst res physiologist, Univ Calif, Davis, 1964-1965; co-prin investr grants, Nat Inst Arthritis & Metab Dis, 1963-1965; asst specialist physiol, Univ Calif, Davis, 1963-1964; USPHS fel animal physiol, Univ Calif, Davis, 1961-1963; jr res physiologist, Univ Calif, Berkeley, 1958-1961. **Memberships:** AAAS; Am Physiol Soc; Soc Exp Biol & Med; NY Acad Sci; Am Asn UnivProfessors; Sigma Xi. **Research Statement & Publications:** Regulation of body fluids. **Mailing Address:** Dept Physiol Biophys Univ Ark Med Ctr, 4301 W Markham Slot 505, Little Rock, AR 72205-7101.

KOIRTYOHANN, SAMUEL ROY, ANALYTICAL CHEMISTRY. **Personal Data:** b Washington, Mo, September 11, 1930; m 1952, c 3. **Education:** Univ Mo, BS, 1953, MS, 1958, PhD (agr chem), 1966. **Professional Experience:** Chmn chem dept, Univ Mo, Columbia, 1984-1990; PROF EMER CHEM, UNIV MO, COLUMBIA, 1980-; assoc prof agr chem, Univ Mo, Columbia, 1970-1980; from instr to asst prof, Univ Mo, Columbia, 1963-1970; Chemist, Oak Ridge Nat Lab, 1959-1963. **Memberships:** Am Chem Soc; hon mem Soc Appl Spectros. **Research Statement & Publications:** Determination of trace elements in biological and agricultural materials using spectroscopic and other instrumental methods. **Mailing Address:** Dept Chem, Univ Mo, 601 S Col Ave, Columbia, MO 65211. **Fax:** 573-882-2754.

KOISTINEN, DONALD PETER, METAL PHYSICS. **Personal Data:** b Lake Norden, SDak, November 19, 1927; m 1959, c 3. **Education:** Univ Mich, BS, 1952; Wayne State Univ, MS, 1958. **Professional Experience:** RETIRED; sr staff res scientist, Res Labs, 1982-1989; supvry res physicist metal physics, Res Labs, Gen Motors Corp, 1969-1982; sr res physicist, Res Labs, Gen Motors Corp, 1958-1969; res physicist, Res Labs, Gen Motors Corp, 1952-1958. **Memberships:** Am Phys Soc; Sigma Xi; Metall Soc; Am Inst Mining, Metall & Petrol Engrs. **Research Statement & Publications:** Mechanics of large-scale plasticity in metals; strain hardening; precipitation; crystalline deformation mechanisms and transformations; fatigue in metals; surface hardening techniques. **Mailing Address:** 441 Sandehurst Dr, Grand Blanc, MI 48439.

KOIVO, ANTTI J, ELECTRICAL ENGINEERING, ROBOTICS BIOENGINEERING. **Personal Data:** b Vaasa, Finland, April 9, 1932; div, c Lilli S & Allan T. **Education:** Inst Technol, Finland, dipl eng, 1956; Indiana Univ, MS; Cornell Univ, PhD (elec eng), 1963. **Professional Experience:** Wright lab, Tyndall AFB, Tyndall, Fla, 1995; Armstrong lab, Wright-Patterson AFB, Ohio, 1992-1996; MEL, Ministry Int Trade & Indust, Tsukuba, Japan, 1991; PROF ELEC ENG, PURDUE UNIV, WEST LAFAYETTE, 1978-; Sr researcher, Finnish Acad Sci & Technol, 1973-1974; from asst prof to assoc prof, Purdue Univ, West Lafayette, 1964-1978; Design engr, Oy Stroemberg Ab, Finland, 1957-1959. **Memberships:** Fel Inst Elec & Electronics Engrs; Sigma Xi. **Research Statement & Publications:** Robotics, control ofsensor-based robots, multiple robotic manipulators, fuzzy systems, artificial neural network; application of system theory and pattern recognition to biomedical problems. **Mailing Address:** Elec & Comput Eng, Purdue Univ, West Lafayette, IN 47907. **Fax:** 765-494-0880. **E-Mail:** koivo@ecn.purdue.edu

KOIVULA, JOHN I, GEMOLOGY. **Professional Experience:** CHIEF RES GEMOLOGIST, GEM TRADE LAB, GEMOLOGICAL INST AM, as of 2003. **Mailing Address:** Gem Trade Lab, Gemological Inst Am, 1660 Stewart St, Santa Monica, CA 90404.

KOIZUMI, CARL JAN, NUCLEAR GEOPHYSICS, ENVIRONMENTAL SCIENCES. **Personal Data:** b Reno, Nev, January 7, 1943; m 1968, Jean; c Emi M. **Education:** Univ Nev, Reno, BS, 1965, MS, 1973, PhD (physics), 1977; Ariz State Univ, MS, 1967. **Professional Experience:** PRIN SCIENTIST, RUST GEOTECH, 1993-; prin scientist, Westinghouse Hanford, 1987-1993; staff scientist, Rockwell Hanford, 1986-1987; mem, Spectral Gamma-RayCalibration Comt, Am Petrol Inst, 1982-1990; res physicist, Austin Res Ctr, Gearhart Indust, 1982-1986; Mem, Borehole Sensors Task Group, Am Soc Testing & Mat, 1979-1986; res geophysicist, Bendix Field Eng Corp, 1977-1981. **Memberships:** Am Phys Soc; Soc Prof Well Log Analysts; Minerals & Geotech Logging Soc. **Research Statement & Publications:** Calibration of devices used for uranium detection; gamma-ray logging theory; neutron logging theory; Mossbauer spectroscopic studies of hydrides of intermetallic compounds; modeling responses of nuclear logging tools with radiation transport calculations; characterization of nuclear waste disposal sites by nuclear logging; radiation measurements to characterize contaminated sites. **Mailing Address:** 3954 N Seville Circle, Grand Junction, CO 81506.

KOIZUMI, KIYOMI, AUTONOMIC NERVOUS SYSTEM, NEUROENDOCRINOLOGY. **Personal Data:** b Kobe, Japan, September 4, 1924; m 1954, Morimichi; c Tsugumichi. **Education:** Tokyo Women's Med Col, MD, 1947; Wayne State Univ, MS, 1951; Kobe Univ Med Col, PhD (physiol), 1957. **Honors & Awards:** Medal Hon, Semmelweis Med Univ, Hungary, 1979 hon mem; Japanese Physiolo soc; 1998-; hon mem, Japa Soc of Neurovegatative Res 2001-; fel NY acad of sci 1966-. **Professional Experience:** DISTINGUISHED PROF PHYSIOL & PHARMACOL DEPT, STATE UNIV NY, BROOKLYN, as of 2005; interim chair, Dept Physiol, 1990-1998; mem, Comt Antonomic Nerv Syst, Int Union Physiol Soc, 1991-1996; vis prof, Univ Occup Health, Japan, 1984, 1989-1990, 1991, 2002; assoc ed, J Autonomic Nerv Syst, 1979-1999; vis prof, Semmelweis Med Univ, Hungary, 1979-1980; sr int fel, Fogarty Ctr, NIH, 1979-1980; vis scientist, Tokyo Metrop Inst Geront, 1976; NSF & NIH grants, 1955-1990; vis scientist, Univ Heidelberg, from instr to asst prof, State Univ NY, Downstate Med Ctr, 1952-1960; fel physiol, State Univ NY, Downstate Med Ctr, 1951-1952. **Memberships:** Soc Neuroscience; Int Brain Res Orgn; Am Physiol Soc; Harvey Soc; fel NY Acad Sci; Sigma Xi; Int Behav Neuroscience Soc Japanese physiolo soc, Japan soc of Neurovegetative res. **Research Statement & Publications:** Neurophysiology; neuroendocrinology. **Mailing Address:** State Univ NY, Health Sci Ctr, Dept Physiol, 450 Clarkson Ave PO Box 31, Brooklyn, NY 11203. **Fax:** 718-270-3103. **E-Mail:** kiyomi.koizumi@downstate.edu

KOJIMA, HARUO, LOW TEMPERATURE PHYSICS. **Personal Data:** b Japan, May 18, 1945; m 1970, c 2. **Education:** Univ Calif, Los Angeles, BS, 1968, MS, 1970, PhD (physics), 1972. **Professional Experience:** PROF, DEPT PHYSICS & ASTRON, RUTGERS, STATE UNIV NJ, 1987-; from asst prof to assoc prof, Rutgers, state Univ NJ, 1975-1987; res assoc, Univ Calif, San Diego, 1973-1975; adj asst prof, Univ Calif, Los Angeles, 1972-1973. **Memberships:** Am Phys Soc. **Research Statement & Publications:** Experimental investigation of superfluid phases of helium at ultra low temperatures. **Mailing Address:** Dept Physics & Astron, Rutgers, State Univ NJ, 136 Frelinghuysen Rd Serin W120, Piscataway, NJ 08854-8019. **Fax:** 732-445-4343. **E-Mail:** kojima@physics.rutgers.edu

KOK, LOKE-TUCK, ENTOMOLOGY, BIOLOGICAL CONTROL. **Personal Data:** b Ipoh, Malaysia, November 10, 1939; American citizen; m Victoria; c Leon. **Education:** Univ Malaya, BAgrSc Hons, 1963, MAgrSc, 1965; Univ Wis-Madison, PhD (entom), 1971. **Honors & Awards:** Nat Agr Recognition Award, Outstanding Contrib Agr, Entom Soc Am, 1988; L O Howard Distinguished Achievement Award, Ent Soc Am Eastern br, 2005. **Professional Experience:** HEAD, DEPT ENTOM, VA POLTECH INST & STATE UNIV, as of 2005; PROF ENTOM, VA POLYTECH INST & STATE UNIV, 1982-; from asst prof to assoc prof, VA Polytech Inst & State Univ, 1978-1982; from res asst to res assoc, Univ Wis-Madison, 1968-1971; from asst lectr to lectr, Univ Malaya, 1965-1971; res scholar, Int Rice Res Inst, Philippines, 1964; Tutor, Univ Malaya, 1963-1965. **Memberships:** Entom Soc Can; fel Entom Soc Am; Weed Sci Soc Am; Int Orgn Biol Control. **Research Statement & Publications:** Biological control of insect and weed pests of forage and field crops in Virginia, with special emphasis on the control of Carduus thistles using introduced beneficial insects; pest management of cruciferous crop pests; Published more than 125 articles. **Mailing Address:** Dept Entom, Va Polytech Inst & State Univ, 216 Price Hall, Blacksburg, VA 24061. **Fax:** 540-231-9131. **E-Mail:** ltkok@vt.edu

KOKA, MOHAN, PATHOLOGY. **Personal Data:** b India, October 16, 1938. **Education:** Madias Univ, India, BVM, 1960; RI Univ, MS, 1963; Ohio State Univ, PhD (microbiol), 1967. **Professional Experience:** SR SCIENTIST PATH, HAZLETON LABS AM INC, 1978-; researcher pharmacol, Searle Labs, 1974-1978. **Memberships:** Int Soc Vet Path. **Mailing Address:** Dept Path, Hazleton Wash Inc, 9200 Leesburg Turnpike, Vienna, VA 22182-1699. **Fax:** 703-759-6947.

KOKALIS, SOTER GEORGE, INORGANIC CHEMISTRY. **Personal Data:** b East Chicago, Ind, January 29, 1936. **Education:** Purdue Univ, BSc, 1958; Univ Ill, MSc, 1960, PhD (inorg chem), 1962. **Professional Experience:** RETIRED; assoc prof inorg chem, William Rainey Harper Col, 1969-1991; from asst prof to assoc prof, Chicago State Col, 1964-1969; asst prof, Wash Univ, 1962-1964; asst org chem, Univ Ill, 1959-1962; Consult, Col Bd Advan Placement Chem Exam, Income Tax Planning. **Memberships:** AAAS; Am Chem Soc; Royal Soc Chem; Am Col Sports Med. **Research Statement & Publications:** Synthesis and chemical properties of inorganic ring structures; analysis of electron delocalization in heterocyclic compounds; phosphonitrilic compounds and their applications. **Mailing Address:** 1476 Dennison Rd, Hoffman East, IL 60195.

KOKAME, GLENN MEGUMI, SURGERY, THORACIC SURGERY. **Personal Data:** b Waimea, Hawaii, July 7, 1926; m 1953, c 2. **Education:** Univ Hawaii, BA, 1950; Tulane Univ, BS, 1952, MD, 1955; Am Bd Surg, dipl, 1962; Am Bd Thoracic Surg, dipl, 1963. **Professional Experience:** ASSOC PROF SURG, SCH MED, UNIV HAWAII, 1971-; asst prof, SchMed, Univ Hawaii, 1967-1971; Am Cancer Soc adv clin fel, 1964-1966; from instr to asstprof surg, Sch Med, Tulane Univ, 1955-1967. **Memberships:** Fel Am Col Surgeons; AMA; Am Asn Cancer Res; Am Soc Clin Oncol. **Research Statement & Publications:** Regional chemotherapy of cancer; hyperbaric oxygenation in medicine; immunology of cancer; vascular surgery; heterotransplantation of human cancer and tissue culture; transplantation of organs. **Mailing Address:** 321 Kuakini St Suite 307, Honolulu, HI 96817-2360.

KOKAR, MIECZYSLAW M, COMPUTER SCIENCE. **Professional Experience:** ASSOC PROF, DEPT ELEC & COMPUT ENG, NORTHEASTERN UNIV, as of 2006. **Memberships:** Inst Elec & Electronics Engrs. **Mailing Address:** Dept Elec & Comput Eng, Northeastern Univ, 360 Huntington Ave, Boston, MA 02115. **Fax:** 617-373-8970. **E-Mail:** mkokar@ece.neu.edu

KOKATNUR, MOHAN GUNDO, CLINICAL BIOCHEMISTRY, NUTRITION. **Personal Data:** b Belgaum, India, March 19, 1930; American citizen; m 1963, Saroj; c Sharmila & Vinita. **Education:** Univ Poona, BS, 1951; Univ Nagpur, BS, 1953; Univ Ill, Urbana, PhD (food sci, biochem, nutrit), 1959. **Professional Experience:** DIR, CLIN CHEM LAB, CHARITY HOSP, NEW ORLEANS, 1995-; PROF PATH, LA STATE UNIV MED CTR, NEW ORLEANS, 1993-; mem, Coun Arteriosclerosis, Am Heart Asn, 1968; La Heart Asn sr res grant-in-aid, 1967-1969; from asst to assoc prof, Clin Chem Lab, Charity Hosp, New Orleans, 1966-1993; res assoc nutrit biochem, Univ Ill, Urbana, 1963-1966; Coun Sci & Indust Res Pool fel biochem & nutrit, Cent Food Res Inst, Mysore, India, 1961-1963; res assoc food sci & lipids, Univ Ill, Urbana, 1959-1961. **Memberships:** Am Soc Clin Nutrit; Am Inst Nutrit; Am Asn Clin Chemists; Soc Exp Biol Med. **Research Statement & Publications:** Lipid chemistry, biochemistry and metabolism; importance of lipids and nutrition in atherosclerosis; lipids and atherosclerosis; clinical chemistry methodology; vitamin E deficiency and fat oxidation; prostate lipids; prostate specific antigen; cardiac disease markers. **Mailing Address:** Dept Path, La State Univ Med Ctr, New Orleans, LA 70112. **Fax:** 504-568-6037.

KOKE, JOSEPH R, CYTOSKELETON, MOLECULAR BIOLOGY & CARDIOVASCULAR PHYSIOLOGY. **Education:** Univ Ore, BS, 1966, MS, 1968; Univ Alta, PhD (cell biol), 1971. **Honors & Awards:** Am Physiol Soc; Am Soc Cell Biol. **Professional Experience:** Vis prof med, Univ Wis, 1989-; PROF BIOL, SOUTHWEST TEX STATE UNIV, 1988-; from asst prof to assoc prof biol, Univ Wis, 1978-1988; instr med, Univ Wis, 1974-1978; fel med, Univ Wis, 1972-1974; Fel biol, Univ Alta, 1971-1972. **Research Statement & Publications:** Cytoskeleton in muscle and nervous system disorders; cardiac renin-angiotensin system as an autocrine system that regulates left ventricular growth; mechanism by which striated myocytes take up naked DNA from their immediate environment; mechanism of nerve growth. **Mailing Address:** Dept Biol, SW Tex State Univ, San Marcos, TX 78666.

KOKENGE, BERNARD RUSSELL, INORGANIC CHEMISTRY. **Personal Data:** b Dayton, Ohio, December 7, 1939; m 1959, Joy C Grooms; c Dawn J & Todd R. **Education:** Univ

Dayton, BS, 1961; Ohio Univ, PhD (inorg chem), 1966. **Professional Experience:** PRES, TECH & MGT CONSULT, BRK ASSOCS, INC, 1990-; CONSULT, EG&G ROCKY FLATS, INC, 1990-; chmn, Dept Energy Mgt Team for Galileo & Ulysses RTG space mission progs; Achievement Awards, Significant Overall Prog Contrib, Dept Energy; vpres, Strategic Planning & Prog Develop, 1988-1990; chmn, Gen Studies Dept, Ky Christian Col, Grayson, Ky, 1986-1988; assoc dir & mound dir, Advan Devices Dept, 1985-1986; dir, Nuclear Oper Dept, 1982-1985; mgr nuclear technol, Mound Lab, Monsanto Res Corp, Miamisburg, Ohio, 1977-1982; plutonium processing mgr, Mound Lab, Monsanto Res Corp, Miamisburg, Ohio, 1972-1977; group leader inorg chem & isotopic fuels, Mound Lab, Monsanto Res Corp, Miamisburg, Ohio, 1966-1972; sr res chemist, Mound Lab, Monsanto Res Corp, Miamisburg, Ohio, 1965-1966; lab technician, Wright-Patterson AFB, 1960 & 1961. **Memberships:** Am Chem Soc. **Research Statement & Publications:** Synthesis of various compounds of plutonium for use as isotopic fuels; high temperature vapor pressure of various plutonium-oxide compounds; management of plutonium fuel fabrication and nuclear waste treatment facilities; patent on plutonium-238 isotopic fuels. **Mailing Address:** 5233 S Clayton Rd, Farmersville, OH 45325-9211. **Fax:** 937-696-2939.

KOKESH, FRITZ CARL, POLYMER CHARACTERIZATION, ORGANIC CHEMISTRY. **Personal Data:** b Minneapolis, Minn, January 12, 1943; m 1969, Judith Hanna; c Timothy & Christine. **Education:** Lewis Univ, BSc, 1965; Ohio State Univ, PhD (org chem), 1969. **Professional Experience:** CONTRACT RES, PHILLIPS PETROL CO, 1996-; technol transfer, Phillips Petrol Co, 1992-1996; technol planner, Phillips Petrol Co, 1990-1992; supvr, Phillips Petrol Co, 1986-1990; res chemist, Phillips Petrol Co, 1977-1986; asst prof biochem, Univ Guelph, 1972-1977; NIH fel, Harvard Univ, 1969-1971. **Memberships:** Am Chem Soc; Asn Univ Technol Managers. **Research Statement & Publications:** Collaborations with universities, federal laboratories and other companies; coordination of work-for-others. **Mailing Address:** Res Ctr, Phillips Petrol Co, Bartlesville, OK 74004.

KOKINI, JOZEF L, FOOD SCIENCE. **Education:** Bogazici Univ, BS, 1972; Carnegie-Mellon Univ, MS, 1974 & PhD (Chem Eng), 1977. **Honors & Awards:** Samuel Cate Prescott Award, Inst Food Technologists Excellence Res, 1986George W Scott Blair Award, Am Asn Cereal Chem Rheology Div, 1996; Harold Macy Foos Sci & Technol Award, Inst Food Technologists Minn Div, 2001; CW Barbender Award, Am Asn Cereal Chemists, 2002; Marcel Loncin prize Res Foos Engr, Inst Food Technologists, 2002. **Professional Experience:** MEM, NB FAC COUN, VICE CHAIR (2005-2006) & CHAIR (2006-2007); SENATOR, RUTGURS UNIV SENATE, 2001-2007; CHAIR, DEPT FOOD SCI, RUTGURS UNIV, 2000-; DIR, CAFT, RUTGURS UNIV, 2000-; PROF II, DEPT FOOD SCI, RUTGURS UNIV, 1994-; prof I, Dept Food Sci, Rutgers Univ, 1987-1994; assoc dir, CAFT, Rutgers Univ, 1992-2000; dir, Basic Res Prog, CAFT, Rutgers Univ, 1990-2000; COORD, FOOD MATS SCI, CAFT, RUTGERS UNIV, 1985-; from asst to asso prof, Dept Food Sci, Rutgers Univ, 1980-1987; lectr, Carnegie-Mellon Univ, 1979-1980; fel, Carnegie-Mellon Univ, 1979-1980; Yasar Foreign Trade Co & Aysu Holding inc, Turkey, 1977-1979. **Mailing Address:** Dept Food Sci, Cook Col, Rutgers Univ, 65 Dudley Rd, New Brunswick, NJ 08903. **Fax:** 732-932-6776. **E-Mail:** kokini@aesop.rutgers.edu

KOKJER, KENNETH JORDAN, ELECTRICAL ENGINEERING, COMPUTER SCIENCE. **Personal Data:** b Beatrice, Nebr, February 27, 1941. **Education:** Nebr Wesleyan Univ, B A, 1963; Univ Ill, Urbana-Champaign, MS, 1967, PhD (biophys), 1970. **Professional Experience:** ALASKA TEM LEADER, AUTOMATED FLIGHT FOLLOWING, BUR LAND MGT, as of 2004; Tech Syst Planner, Alaska Fire Serv Bur Land mgt 1998-; TECH SYSTS BR CHIEF, ALASKA FIRE SERV, BUR LAND MGT, 1991-; comput consult, Cognitech, 1988-1990; vis scientist, Tohoku Univ, Sendai, Japan, 1981; from asst prof to assoc prof elec eng, Univ Alaska, Fairbanks, 1970-1987. **Memberships:** Inst Elec & Electronics Engrs; Communication Soc. **Research Statement & Publications:** Applications of computers to real time support of biological research laboratories; computer based instrumentation. **Mailing Address:** Automated Flight Following, Bur Land Mgt, US Dept Interior, PO Box 80907, Fairbanks, AK 99708-0907. **E-Mail:** ken_kokjer@ak.blm.gov

KOKKINAKIS, DEMETRIUS MICHAEL, CARCINOGENESIS, DNA REPAIR & DAMAGE. **Personal Data:** b Heraklion, Crete, March 5, 1950; c 2. **Education:** Nat Univ Athens, BS, 1973; Pa State Univ, MS, 1975; WVa Univ, PhD (biochem), 1977. **Professional Experience:** ASST PROF NEUROL, Southwest MED CTR, UNIV TEX, 1993-; CHMN, IACUC, 1990-; res asst prof, Med Sch, Northwestern Univ, 1985-1993; assoc path, Med Sch, Northwestern Univ, 1981-1985; fel, Med Sch, Northwestern Univ, 1980-1981; fel med biochem, Sch Med, Tex Tech Univ, 1978-1980. **Memberships:** Am Asn Cancer Res; NY Acad Sci; AAAS. **Research Statement & Publications:** Chemistry of carcinogens; metabolism of carcinogens by target organs; carcinogen mediated DNA damage and cellular mechanisms of its repair. **Mailing Address:** 5320 Harry Hines Blvd, Dallas, TX 75235.

KOKKO, JUHA PEKKA, NEPHROLOGY. **Personal Data:** b March 26, 1937; m 1961, Nancy; c Ken & Karl. **Education:** Emory Univ, MD & PhD (phys chem), 1964. **Honors & Awards:** Berliner Award, Am Physiol Soc. **Professional Experience:** PROF EMER, DEPT MED, EMORY UNIV SCH MED, ATLANTA, GA, as of 2005; G Candler prof & chmn, dept med, Emory Univ Sch Med, Atlanta, Ga, beginning 1986; chief nephrol, Southwestern Med Ctr, Univ Tex, Dallas; assoc dean of clin res, Emory Univ. **Memberships:** Am Soc Clin Invest; Am Asn Physicians; Am Fedn Clin Res; Am Soc Nephrol (pres 1984); Am Physiol Soc; Asn Prof Med. **Research Statement & Publications:** Salt, water and acid-base homeostasis as examined by in vitro perfusion of isolated kidney tubules. **Mailing Address:** Dept Med, Emory Univ, 1364 Clifton Rd NE Ste F410, Atlanta, GA 30322-0001. **Fax:** 404-712-5567.

KOKNAT, FRIEDRICH WILHELM, INORGANIC ANALYSIS, X-RAY CRYSTALLOGRAPHY. **Personal Data:** b Muenster, Ger, February 19, 1938; m 1964, c 2. **Education:** Univ Giessen, BS, 1959; MS, 1963; PhD (chem), 1965. **Professional Experience:** PROF CHEM, YOUNGSTOWN STATE UNIV, 1980-; assoc prof, Youngstown State Univ, 1974-1980; asst prof, Youngstown StateUniv, 1969-1974; instr, Boone Jr Col, 1968-1969; fel, Iowa State Univ, 1966-1969; Instr chem, Univ Giessen, 1964-1966. **Memberships:** Am Chem Soc; Am Crystallog Asn; Sigma Xi. **Research Statement & Publications:** Structural inorganic chemistry; transition metal cluster compounds; phase relationships and stabilization of low oxidation states by formation of complexes and double salts. **Mailing Address:** Dept Chem, Youngstown State Univ, Youngstown, OH 44555-0001. **Fax:** 330-941-1579. **E-Mail:** fwkoknat@cc.ysu.edu

KOKOSKI, CHARLES JOSEPH, PHARMACY. **Personal Data:** b Chicopee Falls, Mass, June 2, 1927; m 1952, Catherine; c Mary F, Charles L & John D. **Education:** Univ Md, BS, 1951, MS, 1953, PhD (pharm), 1956. **Professional Experience:** RETIRED; chief, Div Toxicol, Stand & Monitoring Br, 1977-1992; biochemist, Dept Health & Human Serv, Food & Drug Admin, Wash, DC, 1964-1977; from asst prof to assoc prof pharm, George Wash Univ, 1956-1964. **Memberships:** AAAS; Am Pharmaceut Asn; Soc Toxicol; Sigma Xi. **Research Statement & Publications:** Toxicology; pharmaceutical and cosmetic product development; food additive and contaminants toxicology and safety assessment. **Mailing Address:** 4504 Maple Ave, Halethorpe, MD 21227.

KOKOSZKA, GERALD FRANCIS, PHYSICAL INORGANIC CHEMISTRY. **Personal Data:** b Meriden, Conn, September 26, 1938; m 1961, c 3. **Education:** Univ Conn, BA, 1960; Univ Md, MS, 1964, PhD (chem physics), 1967. **Professional Experience:** Bd dirs, State Univ NY, res found, 1984-1991; PROF CHEM, STATE UNIV NY, COL PLATTSBURGH, 1973-; Petrol res found grants, 1970, 1971-1973 & 1974-1990; res Corp grant, 1969; from asst prof to assoc prof, State Univ NY Col Plattsburgh, 1968-1973; State Univ NY res found grants, 1968 & 1970; res scientist, Inorg Chem Sect, Nat Bur Stand, 1961-1968. **Memberships:** Am Chem Soc; Am Phys Soc; Royal Chem Soc. **Research Statement & Publications:** Electron spin resonance of metal complexes, free radicals, minerals, low-dimensional systems and biochemical systems. **Mailing Address:** Dept Chem, State Univ NY, 0319B Hudson Hall, Plattsburgh, NY 12901. **E-Mail:** kokoszgf@plattsburgh.edu

KOKOTAILO, GEORGE T, SOLID STATE PHYSICS. **Personal Data:** b Willingdon, Alta, June 21, 1919; American citizen; m 1953, c 2. **Education:** Univ Alta, BSc, 1941, MSc, 1948; Temple Univ, PhD (physics), 1955. **Honors & Awards:** Sci Award, Am Chem Soc, 1976; Alexander von Humboldt Sr US ScientistAward, 1985. **Professional Experience:** VIS PROF PHYSICS, UNIV GUELPH, 1983-; res assoc, Mobil Res &Develop Corp, 1960-1982; Adj prof physics, Drexel Inst Technol, 1958-; sr res physicist, SoconyMobil Oil Co, 1948-1960; physicist, Nat Res Coun Can, 1944-1945; Physicist, Ont Res Found, 1941-1942 & Defense Indust Ltd, 1942-1944. **Memberships:** FelAm Phys Soc; Am Chem Soc; Electron Micros Soc Am; Am Crystallog Asn; AAAS. **Research Statement & Publications:** Radiowave propagation; cloud chamber physics; rubber physics; x-ray spectroscopy; x-ray absorption fine structure; crystal structure; anomolous transmission of x-rays and electrons; chemistry and structure of zeolites; solid state nuclear magnetic resonance. **Mailing Address:** 98 N American St, Woodbury, NJ 08096.

KOKOTOVIC, PETAR V, ELECTRICAL & COMPUTER ENGINEERING. **Education:** Univ Belgrade, BS, 1958, MS, 1963; USSR Acad Sci, PhD, 1965. **Honors & Awards:** Quazza Medal Highest Triennial Award, Int FednAutomatic Control, 1990; Bode Prize Lectr, Inst Elec & Electronic Engrs, 1991, Outstanding TransactionsAward, 1993, Control Systs Field Award, 1995. **Professional Experience:** PROF & DIR, CTR CONTROL ENG & COMPUT, UNIV CALIF, SANTA BARBARA, as of 2004; prof, dept elec & comput eng, Univ Calif, Santa Barbara, beginning 1991; dir, Ctr Control Eng & Comput, 1991-1995; co-dir, Ctr Control Eng & Comput, 1991-1995; assoc ed, Int J Adaptive Control &Signal Processing, 1987- & Math Control, Signals & Systs, 1990-; Univ Southern Calif, Los Angeles, 1989 & Univ Calif, Santa Barbara, 1988-1989; Univ Calif, Berkeley, 1988; distinguished lectr, Inst Elec & Electronic Engrs Control Systs Soc, 1987; Res Sch Physics, Univ Rome TorVegata, 1987; Res Sch Physics, Australian Nat Univ, 1985; Swiss Fed Inst Technol, Univ Notre Dame, 1984; lectr, Nat Ctr Sci Res, Paris, 1982; Swiss Fed Inst Technol, Zurich & Inst Nat Info & Automation, Paris, 1981; Stanford Univ & Systems Control Inc, Palo Alto, 1978; SystsControl Inc, Palo Alto, Calif, Eused & Gen Elec Co, NY, 1977-1986; vis prof, Swiss Fed InstTechnol, Zurich & Univ Brazil, Rio & San Paolo Campus, 1973; consult, Ford Motor Co, 1970-; prof, Dept Elec & Comput Eng, res prof coordr sci libr, 1970-1991; vis assoc prof, Dept ElecEng, vis res assoc & prof coordr sci lab, Univ Ill, 1966-1969; head process analysis & control sect, M Pupin Inst, Yugoslavia, 1962-1966; asst, Dept Elec Eng, Univ Belgrade, Yugoslavia, 1960-1964; res engr, Nuclear Sci Inst, Yugoslavia, 1958-1962. **Memberships:** Nat Acad Eng; fel Inst Elec & Electronics Engrs; Int Fedn Automatic Control. **Mailing Address:** Dept Elec & Comput Eng, Univ Calif, Santa Barbara, CA 93106-9560. **Fax:** 805-893-3262. **E-Mail:** petar@ece.ucsb.edu

KOKTA, BOHUSLAV VACLAV, COMPOSITES OF THERMOPLASTICS, EXPLOSION PULPING. **Personal Data:** b Brno, Czech, April 15, 1940. **Education:** Univ Chem Technol, Pardubice, BS, 1960, MSc, 1962, Acad Sci, Prague, PhD, 1967. **Honors & Awards:** Bates Prizes, Can Pulp & Paper Asn, 1983 & 1988. **Professional Experience:** CHMN CHEM ENG, QUE UNIV, as of 2004; PROF, WOOD CHEM, QUE UNIV, 1972-; res assoc, polymers, 1971-1972; sr res chemist, wood fibers, polymers, Consolidated Bathhurst Ltd, Grand Mere, Que, 1969-1971; fel, reverse osmosis, Syracuse Univ, 1967-1971; sr res chemist, res Inst Macromolecular Chem, Brand, Czech, 1962-1967. **Memberships:** Can Inst Can; Am Chem Soc; Can Pulp & Paper Asn. **Research Statement & Publications:** Composites of thermoplastics reinforced with wood fibers; grafting of thermoplastics with lignocellulosic materials; explosion pulping (ultra high yield pulp for paper); bleaching of ultra-high yield pulps. **Mailing Address:** Dept Chem Eng, Univ Que, CP 500, Trois Rivieres, PQ G9A 5H7, Can. **Fax:** 819-376-5148. **E-Mail:** kokta@uqtr.ca

KOKTA, MILAN RASTISLAV, SOLID STATE CHEMISTRY. **Personal Data:** b Brno, Czech, March 22, 1941; m 1970, Elena Tauc; c Robert & Theresa. **Education:** Inst Chem Technol, Pardubice, MS, 1968; Newark Col Eng, DESc, 1972. **Professional Experience:** STAFF SCIENTIST, UNION CARBIDE CORP, 1977-; staff chemist res, Allied Chem Corp, 1973-1977; mem tech staff, Bell Labs, 1972-1973; Staff chemist inorg chemres, Lachema, Czech, 1965-1968. **Memberships:** Am Chem Soc; Sigma Xi; Am Asn Crystal Growth; Am Optical Soc; Int SocOptical Eng. **Research Statement & Publications:** Liquid phase epitaxy; crystal chemistry of oxide and chalcogenide compounds; relation between structure and physical properties; magnetism; phase relations in oxide systems with respect to crystal growth; crystal growth of electro-optical materials. **Mailing Address:** 1906 SE 331st Ave, Washougal, WA 98671-9777. **Fax:** 253-835-8792.

KOLADE, ALABI E, SPECTROSCOPY, LABORATORY AUTOMATION. **Personal Data:** b Nigeria, February 1952; m 1977, Christianah; c 3. **Education:** Univ Nebr, BS, 1976, MS, 1981, PhD (soil sci agron), 1983. **Professional Experience:** TEAM MEM/SR PHARMACEUT ANALYST, NOVARTIS CONSUMERHEALTH INC, 1997-; managing dir, Ataba Inc, 1988-1992; sr scientist A, Sandoz Pharmaceuts, 1987-1996; youth leader, Cent States Conf, 1987-1990; chemist, scientist A, 1979-1983; chemist, Dorsey Labs, 1977-1978; human servs instr II, Region V, Lancaster Co, 1976-1978; technician, MidAm Webpress Inc, 1974-1976. **Memberships:** Am Chem Soc; Sigma Xi. **Research Statement & Publications:** Instrument design; automate, validate and evaluate automation technologies for data acquisitions and processing in a pharmaceutical quality control laboratory; laboratory electronic troubleshooting; team design member. **Mailing Address:** Novartis Consumer Health Inc, 10401 Hwy 6, Lincoln, NE 68517.

KOLAIAN, JACK H, colloid chemistry, coal gasification; deceased, see previous edition for last biography

KOLAKOWSKI, DONALD LOUIS, PSYCHOMETRICS, HUMAN QUANTITATIVE GENETICS. **Personal Data:** b Chicago, Ill, January 7, 1944. **Education:** Knox Col, BA, 1966; Univ Chicago, MA, 1967, PhD (measurement & statist), 1970. **Honors & Awards:** Res Career Develop Award, Nat Inst Dental Res, 1975-1980. **Professional Experience:** Asst prof behav sci, Univ Conn Health Ctr, 1974-1982; Prin investr, NIH & NIMH grants, Univ

Conn, 1973-1982; Asst prof biobehav sci, Univ Conn Health Ctr, 1970-1974. **Memberships:** Am Soc Human Genetics; Behav Genetics Asn; Psychometric Soc; Soc for Study Social Biol; Am Educ Res Asn. **Research Statement & Publications:** Inheritance of mental traits, cranio-facial structures, disease susceptibility, and their measurement in diverse human populations; human behavioral genetics; dental anthropology. **Mailing Address:** 15 Prentiss St, Cambridge, MA 02140.

KOLAR, JOHN JOSEPH, PLANT BREEDING. **Personal Data:** b Raynesford, Mont, June 14, 1922; m 1955, c 2. **Education:** Mont State Col, BS, 1950, MS, 1952; Iowa State Col, PhD (plant breeding), 1955. **Professional Experience:** RES PROF EMER AGRON, UNIV IDAHO, 1986-; res prof, Univ Idaho, 1977-1986; assoc prof agron & assoc agronomist, Univ Idaho, 1969-1977; Asst agronomist, UnivIdaho, 1956-1969. **Memberships:** Crop Sci Soc Am; Am Soc Agron; Sigma Xi; Coun Agr Sci & Technol. **Research Statement & Publications:** Bean breeding and production. **Mailing Address:** Dept Agron, Univ Idaho, Twin Falls, ID 83301.

KOLAR, JOSEPH ROBERT, VETERINARY VIROLOGY. **Personal Data:** b Chicago, Ill, September 26, 1938; m 1972, Carol; c Christina R. **Education:** Southern Ill Univ, Carbondale, BA, 1965, MA, 1968, PhD (microbiol), 1972. **Professional Experience:** CONSULT, VET VIROL, 1996-; virus prod mgr, Schering Plough Animal Health, 1995; virus res mgr, Biocor Inc, 1991-1995; virus res mgr, Fermenta Animal Health, 1987-1991; virus prod mgr, Biologics Corp, 1986-1987; virus group leader, Beecham Labs, 1984-1985; Consult com poultry oper, Maple Leaf Farms 1984; res dir, Fromm Labs Inc, Salisbury Labs, 1977-1984; res scientist vet virol, Fromm Lab Inc, Sacsbary Labs 1974-1977; prod mgr virus, Armour-Baldwin Labs, 1973-1974; res assoc dent med, Dent Res Ctr, Univ NC, 1972-1973. **Memberships:** Am Tissue Cult Asn; US Animal Health Asn. **Research Statement & Publications:** Applied in development of veterinary viral vaccines for domestic and international sales. **Mailing Address:** 5642 Blackwell Dr, Omaha, NE 68137-2471.

KOLAR, MICHAEL JOSEPH, DESIGN, MANUFACTURING. **Personal Data:** b Cleveland, Ohio, April 8, 1939; m 1961, Anne; c Marguerite, Michael, Joseph, David & Timothy. **Education:** John Carroll Univ, BS, 1961, MS, 1963; Case Western Res Univ, PhD (Mech & Nuclear Eng), 1968. **Professional Experience:** FAC MEM, ASIAN STUDIES PROG, as of 2004; PROF, DEPT MECH ENG, UNIV PITTSBURGH, 1987-; chmn, dept mech eng, Univ pittsburgh, beginning 1987; asst vpres, Sci Applns Int Corp, 1984-1987; radiation protection & shielding div, Am Nuclear Soc, 1982; sr prog mgr, Elect Power res Inst, 1978-1984; mgr eng analysis, Gilbert & Commonwealth, 1973-1978; chmn, math div, Am Soc Eng Educ, 1971; asst prof math, Cleveland State Univ, 1969-1973; aerospace engr, NASA, 1962-1969; res engr thermal sci, Am Gas Asn, 1961-1962. **Memberships:** Am Nuclear Soc; Am Soc Eng Educ; Am Soc Mech Engrs. **Research Statement & Publications:** Relation between culture and success in manufacturing; new product development and commercialization; design education. **Mailing Address:** Dept Mech Eng, Univ Pittsburgh, 640 Benedum Hall 3700 O'Hara St, Pittsburgh, PA 15232. **Fax:** 412-624-4846. **E-Mail:** majak@pitt.edu

KOLAR, OSCAR CLINTON, NUCLEAR CRITICALITY SAFETY. **Personal Data:** b Los Angeles, Calif, September 26, 1928; m 1982, Ingeborg; c Elizabeth L, John C & Walter M. **Education:** Univ Calif, Los Angeles, BA, 1949; Univ Calif, PhD (physics), 1955. **Professional Experience:** RETIRED; COURTESY PROF, ORE STATE UNIV, as of 2002; priv consult, US Dept Energy, 1987-1992; sr physicist, Lawrence Livermore Lab, Univ Calif, 1955-1987. **Memberships:** Emer mem Am Phys Soc; emer mem Sigma Xi; emer mem Am Nuclear Soc; emer mem Am Asn Physics Teachers; emer mem Am Soc Safety Engrs. **Research Statement & Publications:** Nuclear physics, especially nuclear reactions; reactor physics, including criticality hazards evaluation; geophysics; seismology. **Mailing Address:** 7595 NW McDonald Pl, Corvallis, OR 97330.

KOLASA, KATHRYN MARIANNE, NUTRITION, ANTHROPOLOGY. **Personal Data:** b Detroit, Mich, July 26, 1949; m 1983, Patrick Kelly. **Education:** Mich State Univ, BS, 1970; Univ Tenn, Knoxville, PhD (food sci), 1974. **Honors & Awards:** Career Achievement, Soc Nutrit Educ, 1995. **Professional Experience:** SECT HEAD RESIDENT EDUC, NUTRIT EDUC & SERV SECT, DEPTFAMILY MED, SCH MED, E CAROLINA UNIV, 1995-; PROF & SECT HEAD, NUTRITEDUC & SERV SECT, DEPT FAMILY MED, SCH MED, E CAROLINA UNIV, 1986-; kellogg Nat Leadership fel, 1985-1988; prof & chairperson food & nutrit, Nutrit Educ & ServSect, Dept Family Med, Sch Med, E Carolina Univ, 1983-1986; from asst prof to assoc profcommunity nutrit, Mich State Univ, 1980-1982; res assoc, Home Learning Ctr Res Proj, OffEduc, 1974-1975; Test kitchen home economist, Kellogg Co, 1971. **Memberships:** Am Inst Nutrit; Soc Nutrit Educ (pres 1984-1985); Am Dietetic Asn; Soc TeachersFamily Med; Am Soc Clin Nutrit. **Research Statement & Publications:** Interactions of nutrition and culture upon the health of the individual and family in the US and the developing world; nutrition in medicine; methods to teach nutrition to medical students, residents especially multimedia. **Mailing Address:** Dept Family Med, Brody Sch Med, E Carolina Univ, Greenville, NC 27858-4354. **Fax:** 252-816-4614. **E-Mail:** kolasa@brody.med.ecu.edu

KOLASSA, JOHN E, BIOSTATISTICS. **Education:** Unvi Chicago, BS & PhD (Stat), 1989; Cert, Cambridge Univ. **Professional Experience:** ASSOC PROF STATS, RUTGERS UNIV, 1999-; asst prof, Dept Stats, Univ Rochester, 1992-1999; vis asst prof, Dept Biostats, NWestern Univ, 1995-1996; fel, Dept Biostats, Univ Rocheater; fel, Math Sci Dept, TJ Watson Res Ctr, IBM corp, 1990-1991. **Memberships:** Inst Math Stats, 1998-; Am Stat Asn, 1990-. **Mailing Address:** Dept Biostats, Rutgers Univ, 467 Hill Ctr, Piscataway, NY 08854-8019. **E-Mail:** kolassa@stat.rutgers.edu

KOLAT, ROBERT S, ANALYTICAL CHEMISTRY. **Personal Data:** b Bay City, Mich, May 8, 1931; m 1954, c 4. **Education:** Mich State Univ, BS, 1958; Iowa State Univ, PhD (phys chem), 1961. **Professional Experience:** RES MGR, DOW CHEM CO, MIDLAND, 1973-; res chemist, Dow ChemCO, Midland, 1965-1973; Res chemist, Am Cyanamid Co, 1961-1965. **Memberships:** AAAS; Am Chem Soc. **Research Statement & Publications:** Chelation; bomb calorimetry; aerosol research. **Mailing Address:** 3370 Pkwy Dr, Bay City, MI 48706-3338.

KOLATA, ALAN L, ANTHROPOLOGY. **Education:** Harvard Univ, PhD, 1978. **Professional Experience:** NEUKOM FAMILY DISTINGUISHED SERV PROF ANTHROP & SOC SCI, UNIV CHICAGO, as of 2005. **Research Statement & Publications:** Human-environment interactions over the past 3000 years in the Lake Titicaca basin of Bolivia; on the north coast of Peru and most recently in Thailand and Cambodia; comparative work on agroecological systems; human-environment interactions; the human dimension of global change; agricultural and rural development; and archaeology and ethnohistory; particularly in the Andean region. **Mailing Address:** Dept Anthrop, Univ Chicago, 1126 E 59 St, Chicago, IL 60637. **Fax:** 773-702-4503. **E-Mail:** a-kolata@uchicago.edu

KOLATA, DENNIS ROBERT, STRATIGRAPHY, INVERTEBRATE PALEONTOLOGY. **Personal Data:** b Rockford, Ill, June 9, 1942; m 1963, c 2. **Education:** Northern Ill Univ, BS, 1968, MS, 1970; Univ Ill, PhD (geol), 1973. **Professional Experience:** SR GEOLOGIST & HEAD, EARTH RESOURCES CTR, ILL STATE GEOL SURV, as of 2003; ADJ FAC, DEPT GEOL, UNIV ILL, URBANA-CHAMPAIGN, as of 2003; geologist, Ill State Geol Surv, beginning 1980; assoc geologist, Ill StateGeol Surv, 1974-1980; geologist explor & develop, Texaco Inc, 1973-1974. **Memberships:** Paleontol Soc; Paleont Asn; Geol Soc Am. **Research Statement & Publications:** Stratigraphy and paleontology of Paleozoic rocks in the Eastern Interior of North America. **Mailing Address:** Dept Geol Univ Ill, 211 Natural Resources Bldg 615 E Peabody Dr, Champaign, IL 61820. **Fax:** 217-333-2830. **E-Mail:** kolata@isgs.uiuc.edu

KOLATA, JAMES JOHN, HEAVY-ION REACTION MECHANISMS. **Personal Data:** b Milwaukee, Wis, December 26, 1942; m 1967, Ann; c David & Kathryn. **Education:** Marquette Univ, BS, 1964; Mich State Univ, MS, 1966, PhD (physics), 1969. **Professional Experience:** Prog adv comt, Oak Ridge Nat Lab Radioactive Nuclear Beam Facil, 1992-1993; steering comt, Nat Superconducting Cyclotron Facil, Mich State Univ, 1990-1991; vis scientist, User's Group Exec Comt, Atlas facil, 1986-1987; PROF PHYSICS, UNIV NOTRE DAME, 1984-; vis scientist, Argonne Nat Lab, 1983-1984; steering comt, Nat Superconducting Cyclotron Facil, Mich State Univ, 1978-1979; vis prof, Ctr Nuclear Res, Strasbourg, France, 1978; assoc prof, Univ Notre Dame, 1977-1984; physicist, Brookhaven Nat Lab, 1976-1977; from asst to assoc physicist, Brookhaven Nat Lab, 1972-1976; res assoc physics, US Naval Res Lab, 1970-1972 & Univ Pittsburgh, 1969-1970. **Memberships:** fel Am Phys Soc; Sigma Xi. **Research Statement & Publications:** Nuclear reaction mechanisms; nuclear fusion of heavy ions; reactions with exotic nuclear beams. **Mailing Address:** Dept Physics, Univ Notre Dame, Nieuwland Sci Hall 217, Notre Dame, IN 46556-0338. **Fax:** 574-631-5952. **E-Mail:** james.j.kolata.1@nd.edu

KOLATTUKUDY, P E, GENE EXPRESSION, RESEARCH ADMINISTRATION. **Personal Data:** b Kerala, India, August 27, 1937; American citizen; m 1982, Marie; c Sunny. **Education:** Univ Madras, BSc, 1957; Univ Kerala, BEd, 1959; Ore State Univ, PhD (biochem), 1964. **Professional Experience:** PROF & CHAIR, DEPT MOLECULAR BIOL & MICROBIOL, UNIV CENT FLA, as of 2004; prof biochem & molecular & cellular, Ohio State Univ, 1995-2003; dir & prof, Ohio State Biotechnol Ctr, Ohio State Univ, 1986-1994; mem, Physiol Chem Study Sect, NIH, 1984-1988; dir, fel & prof, Inst Biochem, 1980-1986; from assoc prof to prof biochem, Wash State Univ, 1969-1980; asst biochemist, Conn Agr Exp Sta, 1964-1969. **Memberships:** Am Soc Plant Physiologists; Am Soc Biochem & Molecular Biol; Am Soc Advan Sci; Nat Heart Lung & Blood Inst. **Research Statement & Publications:** Structure and function of genes and enzymes involved in lipid metabolism; gene expression in fungal interaction with plant and animal hosts; molecular cordouasenlar lrology, kulberenlosie, mollular mecuobiology. **Mailing Address:** Dept Molecular Biol & Microbiol, Univ Cent Fla, Biomolecular Sci Ctr 136C, Orlando, FL 43210-1002. **E-Mail:** pkolattu@mail.ucf.edu

KOLB, ALAN CHARLES, PHYSICS. **Personal Data:** b Hoboken, NJ, December 14, 1928. **Education:** Ga Inst Technol, BS, 1949; Univ Mich, MS, 1950, PhD (theoret physics), 1955. **Professional Experience:** CHMN & CHIEF EXEC OFFICER, MAXWELL LABS INC, 1978-; pres &chief exec officer, Naval Res Lab, 1970-1978; adj prof, Univ Md, College Park, 1968-1970; vis prof, Cath Univ Am, 1965-1968; vis prof, Supt plasma physics div, Naval Res Lab, 1955-1970. **Memberships:** Fel Am Phys Soc; NY Acad Sci. **Research Statement & Publications:** Plasma physics and controlled thermonuclear research; theoretical and experimental spectroscopy; hydrodynamics and very high Mach number shock waves; electron beam research; high voltage engineering; laser development. **Mailing Address:** 9244 Balboa Ave, San Diego, CA 92123.

KOLB, BRYAN EDWARD, NEUROPSYCHOLOGY, BEHAVIORAL NEUROSCIENCE. **Personal Data:** b Calgary, Alta, November 10, 1947. **Education:** Univ Calgary, BSc, 1968, MSc, 1970; Pa State Univ, PhD (psychol), 1973. **Professional Experience:** Dept chair, Univ Lethbridge, 1987-1990; prof psychol, Univ Lethbridge, beginning 1983-; from asst prof to assoc prof, Univ Lethbridge, 1976-1983; med res councel, Montreal Neurol Inst, 1975-1976; fel psychol, Univ Western Ont, 1973-1975. **Memberships:** Soc Neuroscience; fel Am Psychol Asn; fel Can Psychol Asn; Am Psychol Soc. **Research Statement & Publications:** Frontal lobe function in mammals; recovery of function following brain damage. **Mailing Address:** Dept Psychol, Univ Lethbridge, Lethbridge, AB T1K 3M4, Can. **Fax:** 403-329-2555. **E-Mail:** kolb@uleth.ca

KOLB, CHARLES EUGENE, CHEMICAL KINETICS, ATMOSPHERIC CHEMISTRY. **Personal Data:** b Cumberland, Md, May 21, 1945; m 1965, Susan; c Craig, Eugene & Amy (Noyes). **Education:** Mass Inst Technol, SB, 1967; Princeton Univ, MS, 1968, PhD (phys chem), 1971. **Honors & Awards:** Award Creative Adv Environ Sci & Technol, Am Chem Soc, 1997. **Professional Experience:** CHMN, NAT ACAD SCI, RES COMN EVAL CHEM EVENTS ARMY DISPOSAL FACIL as of 2006; vice chair, Nat Acad Sci-Nat Res Comn, 1998-2000; ed, Geophys res Lett, 1996-1999; mem, Comt Res Opportunities & Priorities Environ Protection Agency, 1995-1997; trustee, Northeastern Sect, Am Chem Soc, 1994-1996; PRES & CHIEF EXEC OFFICER, AERODYNE RES INC, 1994-; mem, Nat Acad Sci-Nat Res Comn, 1993-1998; chair, Disposal Chem Weapons Stockpile, 1993-; res affil, Dept Aeronaut & Astronaut, 1993; chair, Northeastern Sect, Am Chem Soc, 1991; mem, Nat Acad Sci Res Comn Bd Atmosphere, Sci & Climate, 1990-1993, 1997-2000; chair, Nat Acad Sci-Nat Res Coun Comt, Atmospheric Chem, 1990-1993; chmn-elect, Northeastern Sect, Am Chem Soc, 1990; mem, Nat Res Coun Comt Tropospheric Ozone Formation Measures, Nat Acad Sci, 1989-1991; mem, Nat Acad Sci-Nat Res Coun Comt, Atmospheric Chem, 1987-1989; res affil, Spectros Lab, Mass Inst Technol, 1981-1992; vpres & dir, Appl Sci Div, 1981-1985; tech dir, Appl Sci Div, 1980-1981; dir, Ctr Chem & Environ Physics, 1977-1980; hon res fel atmospheric chem, Ctr Earth & Planetary Physics, Harvard Univ, 1976-1985; PRIN RES SCIENTIST, AERODYNE RES INC, 1975-; sr res scientist, Aerodyne Res Inc, 1971-1975. **Memberships:** Combustion Inst; Am Chem Soc; fel Am Phys Soc; fel Optical Soc Am; fel Am Geophys Union; fel AAAS. **Research Statement & Publications:** Experimental and theoretical studies of inelastic energy exchange in hyperthermal molecular collisions; chemistry and physics of trace atmospheric species; chemical kinetics and spectroscopy of combustion and gas lasers; laser and spectroscopic trace gas and aerosol particle sensors for environmental and industrial applications; published over 150 articles. **Mailing Address:** Aerodyne Res Inc, 45 Manning Rd, Billerica, MA 01821-39761. **Fax:** 978-663-4918. **E-Mail:** kolb@aerodyne.com

KOLB, DAVID A, BIOLOGY. **Education:** Knox Col, AB, 1961; Harvard Univ, MA, 1964, PhD, 1967. **Professional Experience:** PROF, CASE WESTERN RESERVE UNIV, as of 2006. **Mailing Address:** Case Western Reserve Univ, Cleveland, OH 44106. **Fax:** 216-368-4785. **E-Mail:** David.Kolb@case.edu

KOLB, DORIS KASEY, organic chemistry, chemical education; deceased, see previous edition for last biography

KOLB, EDWARD WILLIAM, COSMOLOGY. **Personal Data:** b New Orleans, La, October 2, 1951; m 1972, Adrienne; c Christine, Jeffrey & Karen. **Education:** Univ New Orleans, BS, 1973; Univ Tex, PhD (physics), 1978. **Honors & Awards:** Oorsted Medal, 2003; Quantrell Award, 1993; Am Acad Arts & Sci. **Professional Experience:** PROF, DEPT ASTRON & ASTROPHYS, ENRICO FREMI INST, UNIV CHICAGO, 1983-; FERMILAB ASTROPHYS, 1983-; mem staff astrophys, Los Alamos Nat Lab, 1980-1982; J Robert Opphenheimer res fel, Los Alamos Nat Lab, 1980-1981; fel astrophys, Calif Inst Technol, 1978-1980. **Memberships:** fel Am Phys Soc; Am Astron Soc; Int Astron Union. **Research Statement & Publications:** Application of particle physics to the study of the early universe; cosmology; neutrino processes in supernovae; weak interactions. **Mailing Address:** Theoret Astrophys, Fermilab, MS 209 PO Box 500, Batavia, IL 60510-0500. **Fax:** 630-840-8231. **E-Mail:** rocky@fnal.gov

KOLB, FELIX OSCAR, MEDICINE, ENDOCRINOLOGY. **Personal Data:** b Vienna, Austria, November 12, 1921; American citizen; m 1968, Susan Goldberger; c Lisa & Marc. **Education:** Univ Calif, AB, 1941, MD, 1943; Am Bd Internal Med, 1952, cert endocrinol &metab, 1973. **Professional Experience:** CLIN PROF MED, SCH MED, UNIV CALIF, SAN FRANCISCO, 1968-; assoc clin prof & assoc res physician, Univ Calif, 1959-1968; resphysician, Metab Unit, 1953-1959 & 1968-1981; from clin instr to asst clin prof, Univ Calif, 1952-1959; asst, Univ Calif, 1951-1953; asst, Mass Gen Hosp, 1950-1951; Asst med, Univ Calif, 1946-1949; assoc chief med, Mt Zion Univ Calif Med Ctr, San Francisco; Consultendocrinol, Calif Pac Med Ctr, San Francisco. **Memberships:** Endocrine Soc; AMA; Am Diabetes Asn; fel Am Col Physicians; Am Fedn ClinRes; Am Soc Bone & Mineral Res. **Research Statement & Publications:** Metabolic bone disease; renal tubular disorders and renal stones, including cystinuria. **Mailing Address:** 9 Starboard Ct, Mill Valley, CA 94941.

KOLB, FREDERICK J(OHN), RECORDING MEDIA, IMAGE & DATA RECORDING & REPRODUCTION. **Personal Data:** b Rochester, NY, May 7, 1917; m 1942, Priscilla; c Carolyn K (Grafton-Pearson), Katharine K (Zwemke), Frederick J III & Merribeth K (Advocate). **Education:** Mass Inst Technol, SB, 1938, SM, 1939, ScD (chem eng), 1947. **Honors & Awards:** Samuel L Warner Medal, Soc Motion Picture & TV Engrs, 1988; Tech Achievement Award, Acad Motion Picture Arts & Sci, 1991, Technicolor/Herbert T Kalmus GoldMedal, 1995. **Professional Experience:** RETIRED; res assoc, Eastman Kodak Co, 1982-1986; proj coordr, Eastman Kodak Co, 1973-1982; tech assoc, Eastman Kodak Co, 1967-1974; mem, Comt TC36, Deleg Int Stand Orgn, 1958-1987; sr sect supvr, Eastman Kodak Co, 1954-1967; instr, Univ Rochester, 1945; chem engr, Eastman Kodak Co, 1942-1950. **Memberships:** AAAS; Am Chem Soc; fel Soc Motion Picture & TV Engrs; Am Inst Chem Engrs; sr mem Inst Elec & Electronics Engrs; Soc Photog Scientists & Eng; Brit Kinematograph Sound & TV Soc; Sigma Xi. **Research Statement & Publications:** Physical and chemical properties of photographic and magnetic media; theory and practice of magnetic and photographic recording systems, especially from the viewpoint of information theory; production of cellulose ester and polyester films; cine film manufacture and applications; effects of radiation on motion-picture films; development, manufacture and applications of magnetic recording media; storage and retrieval of audio and visual information; international standardization; image recording and processing in film and video systems. **Mailing Address:** 211 Oakridge Dr, Rochester, NY 14617-2511.

KOLB, JAMES A, ENVIRONMENT, MARINE SCIENCE. **Personal Data:** b Berkeley, Calif, May 31, 1947; c 2. **Education:** Univ Calif, Berkeley, BA (zool) & BA (biosci), 1970, MS, 1972. **Honors & Awards:** nat Marine educator of the yr, 2000, nat marine educator assoc. **Professional Experience:** EXEC DIR, FOR SEA INST OF MARINE SCI, 1997-; exec dir, Marine Sci Soc Pac NW, Poulsbo, Wash, 1992-1997; consult, Hood Canal Wetlands Proj, Hoodsport, Wash, 1990; mem, Puget Sound Water Qual Authority Educ & Pub Involvement, 1987-1991; mem, Marine Plastics Debris Task Force, 1987; MEM, WASH STATE ENVIRON EDUC TASK FORCE, OLYMPIA, 1986-; dir, Marine Sci Ctr, Poulsbo, Wash, 1981-1992; Proj dir, Marine Sci Proj Sea, 1978-1981; teaching secondary sci, Hayward Unified Sch Dist, Calif, 1972-1977; res assoc, Air Pollution Resource Ctr, 1971; teaching asst, Dept Wildlife & Fisheries, 1970-1971; Res asst, Sagehen Creek Res Sta, Univ Calif, Berkeley, 1970. **Memberships:** Nat Sci Teachers Asn; Asn Supvr & Curric Develop; Int Reading Asn; Nat Marine Educr(pres); Wildlife Soc. **Research Statement & Publications:** Marine science. **Mailing Address:** PO Box 188, Indianola, WA 98342.

KOLB, KENNETH EMIL, ORGANIC CHEMISTRY. **Personal Data:** b Louisville, Ky, January 21, 1928; m 1948, c 3. **Education:** Univ Louisville, BS, 1948; Ohio State Univ, PhD (chem), 1953. **Professional Experience:** PROF EMER, BRADLEY UNIV, as of 1998; chemist, Bradley Univ, beginning 1965; Stand Oil Co, Ind, 1953-1958 & Corning Glass Works, 1958-1965; chemist, Nat Distillers, 1948. **Memberships:** Am Chem Soc; Soc Plastics Eng; Royal Soc Chem. **Research Statement & Publications:** Electro-organic chemistry; electrophilic bromination and aklylation; iodine organic complexes; furan chemistry. **Mailing Address:** 7309 N Edgewild Dr, Bradley Univ, Peoria, IL 61614-2113. **E-Mail:** dkkolb@bradley.edu

KOLB, LAWRENCE COLEMAN, PSYCHIATRY. **Personal Data:** b Baltimore, Md, June 16, 1911; wid, c Pamela, Mary (Clarke) & Richards J. **Education:** Trinity Col, Dublin, BA, 1932; Johns Hopkins Univ, MD, 1934; Am Bd Psychiat & Neurol, dipl, 1942. **Honors & Awards:** Joan Plehn Award Humane Serv, MentHealth Asn New York & Bronx Counties, 1972; Distinguished Serv Award, Am Psychiat Asn, 1983; Pioneer Award, Int Soc Traumatic Stress, 1991; Henry Wisner Miller Mem Award. **Professional Experience:** PROF PSYCHIAT, ALBANY MED COL, 1978-; distinguished physician, US Vet Admin, 1978-1990; PROF EMER PSYCHIAT, COL PHYSICIANS &SURGEONS, COLUMBIA UNIV, 1976-; comnr, NY State Dept Ment Hyg, 1975-1977; presadv bd, PR Inst Psychiat, 1972; ed, Yearbk Psychiat & Appl Ment Health, 1971-; trustee, PresbyHosp, New York, 1971-1973; assoc comnr res, NY State Dept Ment Hyg, 1968-1969; pres, AmBd Psychiat & Neurol, 1968; pres med bd, Presby Hosp, New York, 1962-1964; pres & chmn bd, Res Fedn Ment Hyg Inc, 1960-1975; dir, Am Bd Psychiat & Neurol, 1960-1968; mem comt, Navy Med Res, Nat Res Coun, 1956-1959; prof, Albany Med Col, 1954-1975; dir & mem bddirs, Res Fedn Ment Hyg Inc, 1954-1975; dir, NY State Psychiat Inst, New York, 1954-1974; chmn dept psychiat & dir psychiat serv, Presby Hosp, New York, 1954-1974; consult, USPHS, 1954-1962 & NIMH; consult, Mayo Clin, 1949-1954; assoc prof, Univ Minn, 1949-1953; res assoc, WashSch Psychiat, 1947-1949; dir res, Div Ment Hyg, USPHS, 1946-1949; consult, USN, Wash, DC, 1946-1949; resident psychiatrist, Milwaukee Sanitarium, 1941-1942; instrneurol, Sch Med, Johns Hopkins Univ, 1939-1941; Markle Found fel, Nat Hosp, London, 1938; asst dispensary neurologist, Sch Med, Johns Hopkins Univ, 1936-1938; Fel, Sch Med, JohnsHopkins Univ, 1936-1938; intern surg, Strong Mem Hosp, NY, 1935-1936; Intern med, StrongMem Hosp, NY, 1934-1935. **Memberships:** Am Psychoanal Asn; Am Neurol Asn; hon fel Royal Col Psychiat; Asn Res Nerv& Ment Dis (pres, 1959; Am Psychiat Asn (pres, 1968). **Research Statement & Publications:** Psychiatry and psychoanalysis; neurology; post traumatic stress. **Mailing Address:** PO Box 31187, Sea Island, GA 31561. **E-Mail:** lck1@columbia.edu

KOLB, VERA, ORGANIC CHEMISTRY, MEDICINAL CHEMISTRY. **Personal Data:** b Belgrade, Yugoslavia, February 5, 1948; div. **Education:** Univ Belgrade, BS, 1971, MS, 1973; Southern Ill Univ, Carbondale, PhD (org chem), 1976. **Honors & Awards:** Higher Educ Award, 2002-2005; Spec Initiatives Award, 2002-2003. **Professional Experience:** Vis scientist, NWestern Univ, 2002-2003; chmn, Dept Chem, Univ Wis, Parkside, 1995-1997; vis scientist, Salk Inst, San Diego, Calif, 1992-1994; vis scholar, Univ Calif, San Diego, 1992-1994; PROF CHEM, UNIV WIS, PARKSIDE, 1990-; assoc prof, Univ Wis, Parkside, 1985-1990; NIH/Nat Inst Drug Abuse grant, 1984-1985; adj asst prof, Southern IllUniv, Carbondale, 1981-1985; mem, task force occup safety & health, Am Chem Soc, 1980-; tour speaker, Am Chem Soc, 1980; res assoc & instr chem, Southern Ill Univ, Carbondale, 1978-1981; Fel, Univ Res Found, La Jolla, Calif, 1977-1978; Fulbright travel grant, 1973-1976. **Memberships:** Mem Am Chem Soc; Sigma Xi; Serbian Chem Soc; fel Am Soc Biochem & MolecularBiol; Int Soc Study Origins of Life. **Research Statement & Publications:** Reaction mechanisms; steroid chemistry; carbanion chemistry; electron transfer reactions; conformational analysis; mechanism of action of morphine agonists and antagonists; intra-red frequencies of semicarbazones; urazole based RNA precursors; polymerization reactions under prebiotic conditions. **Mailing Address:** Dept Chem, Univ Wis-Parkside, Greenquist 327, Kenosha, WI 53141. **Fax:** 262-595-2056. **E-Mail:** vera.kolb@uwp.edu

KOLBE, LLOYD J, ADOLESCENT HEALTH. **Education:** Towson State Univ, BS, 1973; Univ Toledo, MS, 1975, PhD (health educ), 1978. **Honors & Awards:** Presidential Citation, Asn Advan Health Educ, 1988; Milton J E Senn MemAward, Am Acad Pediat, 1992; Freedom Award, Nat Sch Health Educ Coalition, 1994; WilliamA Howe Award, Am Sch Health Asn, 1995. **Professional Experience:** PROF, DEPT APPL HEALTH SCI, INDIANA UNIV, as of 2004; US sr biomed res serv, beginning 1996; adj prof behav sci & health educ, Emory Univ Sch Pub Health & Ctr Int Health, beginning 1992; dir, CollaboratingCtr Health Educ & Prom Sch-Age Children & Youth, WHO, 1991-; assoc ed, AIDS Educ & Prev, beginning 1988; DIR, DIV ADOLESCENT & SCH HEALTH, NAT CTR CHRONIC DIS PREV &HEALTH PROM, CTR DIS CONTROL & PREV, 1988-; assoc ed, Prev Pediat, 1988-1990; chmn, Task Force AIDS Educ, Int Union Health Prom & Educ, 1987-1990; chmn, USPHS Liaison Comt, Nat Acad Sci & Comt AIDS Res & Behav, Soc & Statist Sci, 1987-1989; assoc ed, J Appl Social Res, 1986-1989; chief, Off Sch Health & Spec Proj, CtrHealth Prom & Educ, 1986-1987; assoc ed, J Sch Health, 1984-1985; assoc dir, Ctr Health Prom Res & Develop & assoc prof behav sci & health educ, Sch Pub Health, Univ Tex Health Sci Ctr, Houston, 1983-1985; chief, Eval Sect, US Off Dis Prev & Health Prom, Off Asst Secy Health, Wash, DC, 1982; dir, Sch Health Educ Proj, Nat Ctr Health Educ, San Francisco, 1981; dir eval, Sch Health Educ Proj, NatCtr Health Educ, San Francisco, 1979-1980; asst prof health sci, Univ Northern Colo, 1977-1978; res coun, Am Sch Health Asn, beginning 1973; health educ instr, Towson State Univ, Md, 1973; Health educ teacher, Mt Airy High Sch, Sheppard-Pratt Ment Hosp, Towson, Md, 1973. **Memberships:** fel Am Public Health Asn; Am Sch Health Asn (vpres 1988 pres elect 1989 pres 1990); Asn Advan Health Educ; Soc Adolescent Med; Int Union Health Prom & Educ; SocPub Health Educ. **Research Statement & Publications:** health behavior; school health programs; adolescent health; published more than 120 scientific articles and book chapters. **Mailing Address:** Div Adolescent & Sch Health, Nat Ctr Chronic Dis Prev & Health Prom, US Ctr Dis Control & Prev, k32 4770 Buford Hwy NE, Atlanta, GA 30341-3724.

KOLBECK, RALPH CARL, PHYSIOLOGY, BIOPHYSICS. **Personal Data:** b Wausau, Wis, September 2, 1944; m 1966, Donna; c Lisa Jean & John Carl. **Education:** Univ Minn, BA, 1966, PhD (physiol, biochem), 1970. **Honors & Awards:** Am Heart Asn Investigatorship Award, 1987; Professor of the Year Award, 2000, 2002. **Professional Experience:** ASSOC PROF PHYSIOL, MED COL GA, 1973-; Am Lung Asn grant, 1982-1983, 1987-1991 & 1994-1997; ASSOC PROF MED & DIR PULMONARY RES, MED COL GA, 1980-; lectr physiol, Med Col Ga, 1977-1989; Ga Heart Asn investr, 1977-1981; asst prof med & asst dir hemodynamic res, Med Col Ga, 1977-1980; Am Heart Asn grant, 1976-1978, 1977-1982 & 1987-1988; NIH grant, 1975-1978, 1987-1990 & 1993-1997; Gen Res Support grant, 1974-1976, 1980-1982, 1984-1985, 1988-1989 & 1993-1994; Ga Heart Asn grant, 1974-1976; instr med, Med Col Ga, 1973-1977; NIH Res fel cardiac physiol, Univ Minn, Minneapolis, 1970-1973; Fel, NIH, 1970-1973. **Memberships:** Am Physiol Soc; International Asn of Medical Science Educators. **Research Statement & Publications:** Fatigue of skeletal muscle; fatigue of diaphragm; calcium uptake by mammalian myocardium; subcellular calcium localization in mammalian myocardium; smooth muscle contractility; Medical Education. **Mailing Address:** Med Col Ga, CA-3143, Augusta, GA 30912. **Fax:** 706-721-7299. **E-Mail:** rkolbeck@mail.mcg.edu

KOLBER, HARRY JOHN, CHEMISTRY. **Personal Data:** b Buffalo, NY, June 5, 1918; c 2. **Education:** Hamilton Col, BS, 1940; Haverford Col, MS, 1941; Northwestern Univ, PhD (chem), 1943. **Professional Experience:** TECH SERV MGR, E I DU PONT DEL NEMOURS & CO, INC, 1966-; res supvr, Del, 1950-1966; res chemist, NY, 1945-1950; Proj engr, Naval Res Lab, Wash, DC, 1943-1944; Mem body armour comt, Nat Res Coun. **Memberships:** Sigma Xi. **Research Statement & Publications:** Thermodynamics of dehydration of alcohols; crystallography; corrosion chemistry; polymer chemistry; textile research. **Mailing Address:** 807 W 22nd St, Wilmington, DE 19802.

KOLBEZEN, MARTIN (JOSEPH), PESTICIDE CHEMISTRY, GAS DIFFUSION IN SOILS & PLASTICS. **Personal Data:** b Pueblo, Colo, April 16, 1914; m 1953, Fredrica. **Education:** Colo State Univ, BS, 1939; Univ Utah, MS, 1941, PhD (org chem), 1950. **Professional Experience:** CHEMIST EMER PLANT PATH, CITRUS EXP STA, UNIV CALIF, RIVERSIDE, 1981-; chemist & lectr, Univ Calif, Riverside, 1964-1981; from asst chemist to assoc chemist plant path, Univ Calif, Riverside, 1956-1964; asst insect toxicologist, Univ Calif, Riverside, 1950-1956; anal chemist, US Bur Mines, Utah, 1942-1944; Nat Defense Res Coun fel, Iowa State Univ, 1941-1942; asst, Univ Utah, 1939-1941, 1947-1948. **Memberships:** Am Chem Soc; Am Phytopath Soc. **Research Statement & Publications:** Chemistry and mode of action of pesticides; residue analysis and development of methods of analysis; climatic and biological breakdown of pesticides; soil fumigation measurements and techniques. **Mailing Address:** Dept Plant Path, Univ Calif, 2317 Webber Hall, Riverside, CA 92521.

KOLC, JAROSLAV JERRY F, REACTIVE MACROMOLECULES, APPLIED MACROMOLECULAR CHEMISTRY. **Personal Data:** b Hradec Kralove, Czech, April 27, 1937; American citizen; c Mark. **Education:** Charles Univ, Prague, BS, 1961; Czech Acad Sci, Prague, PhD (org chem), 1966. **Honors & Awards:** Czechoslovakian Acad Sci Award, 1967. **Professional Experience:** RES SCIENTIST, PERFORMANCE ADDITIVES, ALLIED SIGNAL INC, 1994-; res scientist res & technol, Allied Signal Inc, 1989-1993; sr res chemist, Allied Signal Inc, 1985-1989; res chemist, Allied Signal Inc, 1977-1985; res chemist, Vertac, Inc, 1976-1977; res fel, Chem Dept, Univ Calif, Los Angeles, 1975; vis scholar, Dept Chem, Univ Geneva, Switz, 1974; fac intern, Univ Utah, 1970-1973; fel, Univ Houston, 1969-1970; Res scientist, Inst Org Chem & Biochem, Czech Acad Sci, Prague, 1966-1968. **Memberships:** Am Chem Soc; Int Union Pure & Appl Chem.

Research Statement & Publications: Broad-based industrial research involving synthetic organic chemistry, in particular of carboxy, amino, amido, ester and similar functionalities, biological molecules and macromolecules, intermolecular interactions, separation science, and performance materials; published 40 publications and granted 14 patents. **Mailing Address:** Allied Signal Inc, TPL Bldg, Morristown, NJ 07962-1039. **Fax:** 973-455-2551. **E-Mail:** jerry.kole@alliedsignal.com

KOLDER, HANSJOERG E, OPHTHALMOLOGY, PHYSIOLOGY. **Personal Data:** b Vienna, Austria, November 29, 1926; c 3. **Education:** Univ Vienna, MD, 1950. **Professional Experience:** PROF EMER OPHTHAL, UNIV IOWA, as of 2004; prof ophthal, Univ Iowa, 1973-; assoc prof, Univ Iowa, 1968-1973; assoc prof, Emory Univ, 1963-1968; Europ Coun res fel aviation med, Karolinska Inst, Sweden, 1961; vis asst prof, Emory Univ, 1959-1963; docent, Univ Vienna, 1959; Europ Coun res fel aviation med, Karolinska Inst, Sweden, 1958; asstphysiol, Univ Vienna, 1951-1959. **Memberships:** AAAS; Am Acad Ophthal & Otolaryngol; Am Physiol Soc. **Research Statement & Publications:** Aviation and sensory physiology; ophthalmic electrodiagnosis; cataract management. **Mailing Address:** Dept Ophthal, Univ Iowa, Iowa City, IA 52242-0001. **E-Mail:** hekolder@lcom.net

KOLDEWYN, WILLIAM A, SYSTEM DESIGN MANAGEMENT, PRECISION MEASUREMENTS. **Personal Data:** b Ogden, Utah, April 23, 1942; m 1967, Katherine; c Kennis & Kami. **Education:** Weber State Univ, BS, 1967; Wesleyan Univ, PhD (physics), 1976. **Professional Experience:** STAFF CONSULT & PROG MGR, BALL CORP, 1991-; SR SYST MGR, BALL CORP, 1988-; dir eng, Scientech Inc, 1983-1987; consult syst design, 1982-; prin memstaff, Ball Aerospace Div, 1980-1983; staff physicist, Off Prod Div, IBM, 1978-1980; sr memtech staff, Ball Aerospace Div, 1975-1978; Electro-mech engr, Xytex Corp, 1974-1975. **Memberships:** Am Phys Soc; Laser Inst Am. **Research Statement & Publications:** Remote sensing; high precision control systems; high accuracy measurements of physical constants; laser power and energy measurements. **Mailing Address:** 933 Columbia Pl, Boulder, CO 80303. **E-Mail:** wkoldewy@ball.com

KOLE, HEMANTA KUMAR, INSULIN RESISTANT TYPE II DIABETES, CANCER BIOLOGY. **Personal Data:** b Calcutta, India, January 1, 1955; m 1983, Sutapa; c Abhisake & Ayeeshik. **Education:** Calcutta Univ, BA, 1974, MS, 1976, PhD (biochem), 1985. **Professional Experience:** STAFF DIABETES, NIA, NIH, as of 2004; SR STAFF FEL, NAT INST AGING, NIH, 1992-; ASST PROF, JOHNS HOPKINS UNIV, 1992-; res assoc, Univ Med & Dent NJ, Robert Wood Johnson Med Sch, 1988-1992; assoc, Cornell Univ, 1985-1988; Indian Coun Med Res fel award, 1983-1985. **Memberships:** Am Soc Cell Biol; AAAS. **Research Statement & Publications:** Insulin resistant type II diabetes is common for older people; studying to design a drug which can inhibit tyrogene phosphatase, as a result insulin-receptor will stay active for a longer period and cure type II diabetes. **Mailing Address:** Nat Inst Aging, NIH, 31 Ctr Dr, Baltimore, MD 20892.

KOLEGA, JOHN PATRICK, BIOLOGICAL IMAGING, CELL MOTILITY & CYTOSKELETON. **Personal Data:** b Manchester, Conn, February 23, 1957; m Wendy; c Kinsey & Hayley. **Education:** Mass Inst Technol, BS (chem) & BS (life sci), 1978; Yale Univ, MPhil, 1981, PhD (biol), 1984. **Professional Experience:** Prin investi AHA, 2000-2002; ASSOC PROF, SCH MED & BIOMED SCI STATE UNIV NY, BUFFALO, 2001-; prin investr, NSF, 1995-1998; asst prof, Sch Med & Biomed Sci, State Univ NY, Buffalo, 1993-2001; spec res fac, Carnegie Mellon Univ, 1992-1993; postdoctoral res fel, Carnegie Mellon Univ, 1989-1992; postdoctoral res fel, NY Univ Med Ctr, 1985-1989; postdoctoral res fel, NIH, 1984-1985. **Memberships:** AAAS; Am Soc Cell Biol; Am Soc Develop Biol; Union Concerned Scientists. **Research Statement & Publications:** Cytoskeletal mechanisms underlying cell migration, particularly the movements of endothelial cells during wound healing and angiogenesis; regulation and intracellular dynamics of actin-myosin interactions in non-muscle cells. **Mailing Address:** State Univ NY, Dept Anat & Cell Biol Sch Med, 3435 Main St, Buffalo, NY 14214. **Fax:** 716-829-2911. **E-Mail:** kolega@buffalo.edu

KOLEK, ROBERT LOUIS, PLASTICS TECHNOLOGY, MATERIALS SCIENCE. **Personal Data:** b Pittsburgh, Pa, February 5, 1936; m 1968, Gloria; c Robert A & Patrick L. **Education:** Univ Pittsburgh, BS, 1958, MS, 1961. **Professional Experience:** ADV SCIENTIST, WESTINGHOUSE ELEC CO, 1981-; fel scientist plastics, Westinghouse Elec CO, 1968-1981; Chemist fiber glass, PPG Industs, 1961-1968. **Memberships:** Soc Plastics Engrs; Am Chem Soc; Am Asn Testile Technol. **Research Statement & Publications:** Reinforced plastics; composite material; textile technology. **Mailing Address:** 401 E Hendy Ave, Sunnyvale, CA 94088-3499.

KOLENBRANDER, HAROLD MARK, METABOLISM, ENZYMOLOGY. **Personal Data:** b Sibley, Iowa, October 7, 1938; m 1958, c 3. **Education:** Cent Col, Iowa, BA, 1960; Univ Iowa, PhD (biochem), 1964. **Professional Experience:** SR CONSULT, CONSULT ACAD SEARCH, as of 2006; pres, Mt Union Col, 1986-2000; prof chem, provost & dean, Cent Col, Iowa, 1975-1986; dean, Col Planning, 1972-1975; asst to pres, Grand Valley State Col, 1971-1972; vis scientist, Case Western Reserve Univ, 1970; spec fel, 1969-1970; USPHS grant amino acid metab, 1965-1968; from asst prof to prof chem, Cent Col, Iowa, 1964-1971; interim pres Alma Col. **Memberships:** Biochem Soc; Sigma Xi; Royal Soc Chem. **Research Statement & Publications:** Histidine metabolism and the associated enzymes. **Mailing Address:** Acad Search Consult Serv, 1717 K St NW Ste 210, Washington, DC 20006. **Fax:** 202-234-7640.

KOLENBRANDER, LAWRENCE GENE, GEOGRAPHIC INFORMATION SYSTEMS. **Personal Data:** b Holland, Mich, July 9, 1943. **Education:** Grand Valley State Univ, BS, 1973; Colo State Univ, MS, 1975, PhD (resourceplanning & admin), 1981. **Professional Experience:** HEAD, DEPT NATURAL RESOURCES MGT, WESTERN CAROLINA UNIV, as of 2005; ASSOC PROF, DEPT NATURAL RESOURCES MGT, WESTERN CAROLINA UNIV, 1985-; owner-mgr, Natural Resource Consults, 1981-1985. **Memberships:** Am Soc Photogram & Remote Sensing; Am Water Resources Asn. **Research Statement & Publications:** Applications of geographic information systems to problems in natural resources planning, management and administration. **Mailing Address:** Dept GeoSci & Natural Resources Mgt, Western Carolina Univ, Stillwell 349C, Cullowhee, NC 28723. **Fax:** 704-227-7647. **E-Mail:** lkolenb@wcu.edu

KOLER, ROBERT DONALD, MEDICAL GENETICS, HEMATOLOGY. **Personal Data:** b Casper, Wyo, February 14, 1924; m 1945, c 2. **Education:** Univ Ore, Md, 1947; Am Bd Internal Med, dipl, 1955. **Professional Experience:** ASSOC VPRES ACAD AFFAIRS, ORE HEALTH & SCI UNIV, 1988-; chmn deptmed genetics, Med Sch, Univ Ore, 1981-1987; head div med genetics, Med Sch, Univ Ore, 1967-1981; PROF EMER MOLECULAR & MED GENETICS, ORE HEALTH & SCI UNIV, 1964-; head div hemat & exp med, Med Sch, Univ Ore, 1964-1967; USPHS res fel & hon res asst, Univ Col, UnivLondon, 1960-1961; from asst prof to assoc prof, Med Sch, Univ Ore, 1956-1964; clin assoc med& hemat, Med Sch, Univ Ore, 1953-1956; resident med, Med Sch, Univ Ore, 1951-1953; chief-gen med, 181st Gen Hosp, 1950-1951; instr basic sci, Med Dept Res & Grad Sch, US Army, 1949-1950; resident hemat, Med Sch, Univ Ore, 1948-1949; intern, Med Sch, Univ Ore, 1947-1948. **Memberships:** Am Soc Hemat; Am Fedn Clin Res; fel Am Col Physicians; Am Soc HumanGenetics; Int Soc Hemat. **Research Statement & Publications:** Medical and human genetics; characterization of hemoglobin and red cell enzymes. **Mailing Address:** Dept Molecular & Med Genetics, Ore Health & Sci Univ, 3181 SW Sam Jackson Park Rd, Portland, OR 97239-3098.

KOLESAR, EDWARD S, MICROELECTRONICS, SOLID STATE PHYSICS. **Personal Data:** b Canton, Ohio, June 24, 1950; m 1976, Llinor; c Lauren M, Elizabeth A & Gregory E. **Education:** Univ Akron, BSEE, 1973; Midwestern Univ, MBA, 1976; Air Force Inst Technol, MS, 1978; Univ Tex, Austin, PhD (elec eng), 1985. **Honors & Awards:** H V Nobel Award, Inst Elec & Electronics Engrs, 1988; Res & DevelopAward, USAF, Chief Staff Res & Develop, Washington, DC, 1988; Charles A Stone Award, AirForce Asn, Wright Mem Chap, Dayton, Ohio, 1989; Outstanding Engr & Scientist Award, Eng & Sci Found, E W Kettering Ctr, Dayton, Ohio, 1990. **Professional Experience:** Technispan LLC, Lutherville, Md, 1995-; EG&G Mound Appl Technol Lab, Lockheed-Martin Corp, 1995; W A MONCRIEF PROF ENG, DEPT ENG, ELEC ENG LABS, TEX CHRISTIAN UNIV, FT WORTH, TEX, 1993-; EG&G Mound Appl Technol Lab, MatDiv, Miamisburgh, Ohio, 1988-; Foreign Technol Div, Wright-Patterson AFB, Ohio, 1986-; prof elec eng, Air Force Inst Tech, Wright Patterson AFB, 1985-1993; ardex Inc, Austin Tex, 1985; Johns Hopkins Univ, Sch Hyg & Pub Health, Baltimore, MD, 1983; consult, USAF SciAdv Bd, Wash, DC, 1981; elec engr, Sch Aerospace Med, Brooks AFB, Tex, 1978-1982; elec engr, USAF Elec Syst Div, Hanscom AFB, Mass, 1973-1977. **Memberships:** Sr mem Inst Elec & Electronics Engrs; Am Soc Eng Educ; Sigma Xi. **Research Statement & Publications:** Design and development of microelectronic sensors to detect environmentally sensitive chemical compounds and to facilitate robotics potential, such as sensors having a tactile sense; microelectromechanical systems. **Mailing Address:** Dept Eng, Tex Christian Univ, Box 298640, Ft Worth, TX 76129. **Fax:** 817-921-7704. **E-Mail:** e.kolesar@tcu.edu

KOLESAR, PETER JOHN, OPERATIONS RESEARCH, STATISTICAL ANALYSIS. **Personal Data:** b New York, NY, November 25, 1936; m Miriam; c Alex, Lara & Angelica. **Education:** Queens Col, NY, AB, 1959; Columbia Univ, BS, 1959, MS, 1961, PhD (opers res), 1964. **Honors & Awards:** Lanchester Prize, Opers Res Soc Am, 1975; NATO Syst Sci Prize, 1976. **Professional Experience:** Consult, Int Paper, 1984 & Alcoa, 1988 & Merck, 1990; Consult, Citibank, 1981-1984; consult, New York, 1980-1981; PROF MGT SCI, COLUMBIA UNIV, 1976-; assoc prof, Columbia Univ, 1975-1977; consult, Mt Sinai Hosp, 1975-1980; consult, NY State, beginning 1973; assoc prof comput sci, City Col New York, 1973-1976; consult, Rand Corp, beginning 1972; sr analyst, Rand Corp, 1971-1972; assoc prof, Univ Montreal, 1970-1971; asst prof, Columbia Univ, 1965-1972; lectr opers res, Imp Col, Univ London, 1964-1965; systs analyst appl statist, Procter & Gamble Co, 1959-1961. **Memberships:** Opers Res Soc Am; Inst Mgt Sci; fel AAAS; Am Statist Assoc; Am Soc Qual Control. **Research Statement & Publications:** Quality management and control application of operations researches; applied optimization; probability and statistics particularly in litigation, clinical trial and public systems analysis. **Mailing Address:** Grad Sch Bus, Columbia Univ, 3022 Broadway Ave, Rm 408, Uris Hall, New York, NY 10027-6902. **Fax:** 212-316-9180. **E-Mail:** pjk4@columbia.edu

KOLESAR, PETER THOMAS, GEOCHEMISTRY, PETROLOGY. **Personal Data:** m 1965, Mary; c Michael & Matthew. **Education:** Rensselaer Polytech Inst, BS, 1966, MS, 1968 (geol); Univ Calif, Riverside, PhD (geol), 1973. **Honors & Awards:** Phi Kappa Phi, May 2001. **Professional Experience:** Fel, US Geol Surv, Water Resources Div, 1983-1993; ASSOC PROF GEOL, UTAH STATE UNIV, 1980-; asst prof, Utah State Univ, 1974-1980; Fel isotope geochem, Inst Geophys & Planetary Physics, Univ Calif, Riverside, 1973-1974. **Memberships:** Sigma Xi; Soc for Sed. Geology; Geochem Soc; Nat Asn Geosci Teachers; Int Asn Geochem & Cosmochem. **Research Statement & Publications:** Deciphering carbonate rocks; their original depositional environments, the changes which they have undergone (diagenesis) and the chemistry of fluids responsible for those changes; investigation of groundwater resources. **Mailing Address:** Dept Geol, 4505 Old Main Hill, Logan, UT 84322-4505. **Fax:** 435-797-1588. **E-Mail:** petes@cc.usu.edu

KOLESARI, GARY LEE, TERATOLOGY. **Personal Data:** b Milwaukee, Wis, August 5, 1948; m 1973. **Education:** Univ Wis, Milwaukee, BS, 1971; Med Col Wis, MS, 1973, PhD (anat), 1976, MD, 1977. **Professional Experience:** PROF CELLULAR BIOL, ANAT, FAMILY & COMMUNITY MED, MED COL WIS, as of 2003; assoc prof cellular biol & family & community med, Med Col Wis, beginning 1986; asst adj prof, Dept Anat, Med Col Wis, 1981-1986; asst prof anat & teratology, Med Col Wis, 1978-1981. **Memberships:** Teratology Soc; AMA. **Research Statement & Publications:** Teratology; environmental and abuse drug related. **Mailing Address:** Family Med Primary Care Clin, 9200 W Wis Ave, Milwaukee, WI 53226. **Fax:** 414-456-6564. **E-Mail:** edkoles@mcw.edu

KOLESKE, JOSEPH VICTOR, POLYMER CHEMISTRY, RADIATION CHEMISTRY & MATERIAL SCIENCE. **Personal Data:** b Stratford, Wis, January 23, 1930; m 1951, Mary A Casey; c Robert C & Krista K. **Education:** Univ Wis, BS, 1958; Inst of Paper Chem, MS, 1960, PhD, 1963. **Honors & Awards:** Charles Dudley award, ASTM int, 2000; Award for sci achievement, Am chem soc, 1978; Intertab award, univ southern MIss, 1981. **Professional Experience:** CONSULT, CONSOL RES INC, 1988-; corp res fel, polymer sci, solvents & coatings mat, 1983-1988; res assoc, chemicals & plastics, 1977-1983; Sr res scientist, Union Carbide Corp, 1963-1977. **Memberships:** Am Chem Soc; Am Soc Testing & Mats; Fedn Soc Coating Technol. **Research Statement & Publications:** Polymer physical chemistry; high solids; polyurethane; powder; water-borne and cationic free radical radiation cure coatings. **Mailing Address:** 1513 Brentwood Rd, Charleston, WV 25314.

KOLFF, WILLEM JOHAN, EXPERIMENTAL MEDICINE, CLINICAL MEDICINE. **Personal Data:** b Leiden, Holland, February 14, 1911; American citizen; m 1937, Janke; c Jack, Adriana, Kees, Albert & Therus. **Education:** Univ Leiden, MD, 1938; Univ Groningen, PhD, 1946. **Honorary Degrees:** DSc, Allegheny Col, 1960, Tulane Univ, 1975, Univ L'Aquila, Italy, 1981, Temple Univ, 1983, Univ Utah, 1983, Univ Twente, Neth, 1986; MD, Univ Turin, 1969, Univ Rostock, 1975, Univ Bologna, 1977 & Univ Athens, 1988, Univ d'Aix-Marseille II, France, 1993. **Honors & Awards:** Landsteiner Silver Medal, Neth Red Cross, 1942; Frances Amory Award, AmAcad Arts & Sci, 1948; Addingham Gold Medal, Univ Leeds, 1962; K Award, Nat Kidney DisFound, 1963; Oliver Sharpey Prize, Royal Col Physicians, 1963; Cameron Prize, UnivEdinburgh, 1964; Gairdner Found Prize, Can, 1966; 1st Gold Medal, Neth Surg Soc, 1970; LeoHarvey Prize, 1972; Austrian Gewerbeverein's Wilhelm-Exner Award, 1980; Jean HamburgerAward, Int Soc Nephrol, 1987; Christopher Columbus Discovery Award for Biomed Res, 1991. **Professional Experience:** RETIRED; dir, Kolff's Lab, 1986-1997; hon mem, Europ Dialysis &Transplant Asn, Europ Renal Asn & Europ Soc Artificial Organs, 1986; distinguished prof med& surg & res prof, Col Med, 1967-1997; dir, Inst Biomed Eng & Dept Artifical Organs, UnivUtah, 1967-1986; mem, Surg Div & head, Dept Artificial Organs, 1958-1967; prof clin invest, Educ Found, Cleveland Clin Found, 1950-1967; mem staff, Res Div, 1950-1963; Pvt docent, Med Sch, State Univ Leiden, 1949-1951; head dept, Munic Hosp, Kampen, 1941-1950; asst med, State Univ Groningen, 1938-1941; Asst path anat, State Univ Leiden, 1934-

1936. **Memberships:** Nat Acad Eng; fel Am Col Physicians; Am Heart Asn; hon fel AMA; Am PhysiolSoc; hon mem Austrian Soc Nephrol; AAAS; Am Soc Artificial Internal Organs; European SocInternal Organs; Int Soc Internal Organs. **Research Statement & Publications:** Kidney transplantation; application of heart-lung machines; development of artificial heart inside the chest; avoidance of thrombiosis on plastics; development of blood oxygenators; new types of artificial kidneys and dialysis techniques; development of techniques for organ preservation for transplantation and visual prosthesis; development of artificial hearts, valves and cardiac assist devices. **Mailing Address:** Kolff's Lab Dept Bioeng 2460a Merrill Eng Bldg, Univ Utah, Salt Lake City, UT 84112.

KOLI, ANDREW KAITAN, ORGANIC CHEMISTRY. **Personal Data:** b Bombay, India, August 1, 1925; American citizen; m 1958, c 2. **Education:** Univ Bombay, BSc, 1955; Howard Univ, MS, 1964, PhD (chem), 1968. **Professional Experience:** PROF CHEM, SC STATE COL, 1968-; instr, Dept Pharm, 1967-1968; resassoc, Howard Univ, 1966-1967; res asst, Howard Univ, 1961-1966; Develop chemist res, DowChem Co, 1955-1961. **Memberships:** Am Chem Soc; Sigma Xi; Indian Chem Soc; Am Soc Microbiol. **Research Statement & Publications:** Organic synthesis and environmental pollution. **Mailing Address:** Dept Phys Sci, SC State Univ, Orangeburg, SC 29117-0001. **Fax:** 803-536-8436. **E-Mail:** akoli@scsu.edu

KOLINER, RALPH, CIVIL ENGINEERING. **Personal Data:** b New York, NY, March 20, 1917; m 1942, Selma; c Charles. **Education:** Cooper Union, BChE, 1939; Univ Pa, MS, 1948, PhD (civil eng), 1956. **Honorary Degrees:** DSc, Villanova Univ, 1985. **Professional Experience:** RETIRED; from assoc prof to prof civil eng, Villanova Univ, 1957-1983; lectr & coordr, Rutgers Univ, 1953-1967; consult, beginning 1946; instr & asst prof civil eng, Univ Pa, 1946-1957; instr mech eng, Drexel Inst, 1946; naval architect, Philadelphia Naval Shipyard, 1940-1946. **Memberships:** Am Soc Eng Educ; Am Soc Civil Engrs; Am Concrete Inst. **Research Statement & Publications:** Reinforced concrete; fluid and applied mechanics; engineering materials. **Mailing Address:** 1290 Boyce Rd Apt C-230, Pittsburgh, PA 15241-3912.

KOLINSKI, ANDRZEJ, MOLECULAR BIOLOGY & COMPUTER SCIENCE. **Personal Data:** b Wysokie Mazowieckie, Poland, June 25, 1951. **Education:** Univ Warsaw, Poland, MSc, 1974, PhD (Chem), 1979. **Honorary Degrees:** DSc, Univ Warsaw, Poland. **Professional Experience:** Prof, Ctr Excellence Bioinformatics, Buffalo, 2002-2003; HEAD THEORY BIOPOLYMERS LAB & FAC CHEM, WARSAW UNIV, POLAND, 1998-; assoc prof, Scripps Res Inst, dept molecular biol, Calif, 1993-1999. **Research Statement & Publications:** Theoretical chemistry; Statistical physics, theory of phase transitions; Theory of protein folding, structure and dynamics; Bioinformatics. **Mailing Address:** Univ Warsaw, ul Pasteura 1, 02-093, Poland. **E-Mail:** kolinski@chem.uw.edu.pl

KOLIS, STANLEY JOSEPH, DRUG METABOLISM. **Education:** St Peter's Col, BS, 1967; Rutgers Univ, MS, 1970. **Professional Experience:** RES LEADER, HOFFMAN-LA ROCHE INC, 1969-. **Memberships:** Am Chem Soc; Am Soc Pharmacol & Exp Therapeut; American Association of Pharmaceutical Scientists. **Research Statement & Publications:** Bioanalytical Chemistry and Drug Metabolism. **Mailing Address:** Hoffman-La Roche Inc, Rm 1321, Bldg 123, 340 Kingsland St, Nutley, NJ 07110-1150. **E-Mail:** stanley.kolis@roche.com

KOLIWAD, KRISHNA M, MICROELECTRONICS, SEMICONDUCTORS. **Personal Data:** b Byadgi, India, February 27, 1938; m 1967, c 2. **Education:** Karnatak Univ, India, BSc, 1958, MSc, 1960; Rensselaer Polytech Inst, MS, 1964; Cornell Univ, PhD (mat sci), 1967. **Professional Experience:** MGR, DIV AVIONICS SYSTEM & TECHNOL, JET PROPULSION LAB, LA, as of 2002; MEM TECH STAFF, JET PROPULSION LAB, CALIF INST TECHNOL, 1975-; mem tech staff semiconductor, Tex Instruments Inc, 1970-1975; res assoc mat sci, Cornell Univ, 1968-1970; res assoc solid state physics, Univ Md, Col Park, 1967-1968; res assoc mat sci, Cornell Univ, 1967. **Research Statement & Publications:** Development of low cost silicon crystal growth technology for terrestrial solar energy application; photovoltaic devices. **Mailing Address:** Jet Propulsion Lab, Calif Inst Technol, 4800 Oak Grive Dr, Pasadena, CA 91109.

KOLKA, MARGARET A, TEMPERATURE REGULATION. **Personal Data:** b Bay City, Mich, August 19, 1952. **Education:** Ind Univ, PhD (exercise physiol), 1980. **Professional Experience:** CHAIR, INST ENVIRON, US ARMY RES LABS, as of 2006; RES PHYSIOLOGIST, INST ENVIRON, US ARMY RES LABS, 1983-; fel physiol, Ind Univ, 1980-1983. **Memberships:** Am Physiol Soc; Sigma Xi; AAAS. **Research Statement & Publications:** Evaluation of environmental shessors on the physiological and biophysical properties of heat exchange in humans; skin blood flow; local sweating. **Mailing Address:** Dept Thermals & Altitude, US Army Res Inst Environ Med, Natick, MA 01760-5007. **Fax:** 508-233-5298. **E-Mail:** margaret.kolka@us.army.mil

KOLLAR, EDWARD JAMES, ORAL BIOLOGY, EMBRYOLOGY. **Personal Data:** b Forest City, Pa, March 3, 1934; m 1963, c 5. **Education:** Univ Scranton, BS, 1955; Syracuse Univ, MS, 1959, PhD (zool), 1963. **Honors & Awards:** Quantrell Teaching Award, Univ Chicago, 1968, Ryerson Fac Fel, 1969; Fogerty Int Fel, 1978, Nat Acad Sci Exchange Fel, 1978; Isaac Schour Mem Award, Int AsnDent Res, 1981; City Medal, Paris, 1986. **Professional Experience:** PROF EMER ORAL BIOL, SCH DENT MED, UNIV CONN, FARMINGTON, as of 2004; ASSOC DEAN ACAD AFFAIRS, SCH DENT MED, UNIV CONN, FARMINGTON, 1988-; actg head dept, Sch Dent Med, Univ Conn, Farmington, 1985-1986; vpres & prog dir, Craniofacial Group, Asn Dent Res, 1981-1982; ed-in-chief, Arch Oral Biol, 1980-1996; nat bd exam comt, Am Dent Asn, 1978-1983; bd dir, craniofacial group, Int AsnDent Res, 1978-1981; prof oral biol, sch dent med, Univ Conn, Farmington, beginning 1976; mem educ comt, Tissue Cult Asn, 1974-1978; assoc prof, Sch Dent Med, Univ Conn, Farmington, 1971-1975; Vis fac, W Alton Jones Cell Sci Ctr, Lake Placid, NY, 1971-1975; asstprof anat, Univ Chicago, 1967-1971; asst prof biol, Univ Chicago, 1966-1967; Instr zool, UnivChicago, 1963-1966. **Memberships:** Int Asn Develop Biol; Soc Develop Biol; Am Asn Anatomists; Int SocDifferentiation; Am Asn Dent Res. **Research Statement & Publications:** Experimental studies of tooth and skin development with special reference to the etiology of craniofacial defects. **Mailing Address:** Dept Bio Struct & Function, Univ Conn Health Ctr, 263 Farmington Ave, Farmington, CT 0603.

KOLLEN, WENDELL JAMES, SURFACE PHYSICS, POLYMER SCIENCE. **Personal Data:** b Adrian, Mich, February 22, 1935; m 1955, c 4. **Education:** Hope Col, AB, 1964; Clarkson Col Technol, MS, 1967, PhD (physics), 1969. **Professional Experience:** RES PROF CHEM ENG, UNIV TOLEDO, 1995-; adj res prof, Univ Toledo, 1987-1995; sr physicist, Tech Ctr, Owens-Ill, Inc, 1974-1987; Res physicist, 1969-1974. **Memberships:** Am Phys Soc; Am Vacuum Soc; Am Chem Soc; NY Acad Sci; Sigma Xi; SocAutomotive Eng. **Research Statement & Publications:** Vacuum ultramicrogravimetry; gas-solid interactions; chemical physics; high temperature corrosion; catalysis; gas and vapor transport in polymers; plastic barrier packaging, surface properties of plastics; solvent sorption and permeation of plastics. **Mailing Address:** Dept Chem Eng, Univ Toledo, Toledo, OH 43606-3390. **Fax:** 419-530-5019. **E-Mail:** wkollen@eng.utoledo.edu

KOLLER, CHARLES RICHARD, TEXTILE FIBERS, NONWOVEN FABRICS. **Personal Data:** b North Manchester, Ind, November 16, 1920; m 1944, Joan Lautzenhiger; c James, John, William, Robert & David. **Education:** Manchester Col, AB, 1943; Purdue Univ, MS, 1948, PhD (chem), 1950. **Professional Experience:** Consult, Int Exec Serv Corp, 1989; CONSULT, C R KOLLER ASSOC, 1982-; res assoc, E I du Pont de Nemours & Co, 1967-1982; res supvr, E I du Pont de Nemours & Co, 1962-1967; from res chemist to sr res chemist, E I du Pont de Nemours & Co, 1950-1962; Asst, Purdue Univ, 1946-1949. **Memberships:** Am Chem Soc; Sigma Xi; fel Am Inst Chem; Fiber Soc. **Research Statement & Publications:** Textile and inorganic fibers; nonwoven fabrics; condensation and vinyl polymerization; nitroparaffins; polymer and textile chemistry; fiber and textile engineering; fiber reinforced composites; engineered fabrics design and evaluation; biopolymers. **Mailing Address:** 317 Cecil St, North Manchester, IN 46962.

KOLLER, EARL LEONARD, PHYSICS. **Personal Data:** b Brooklyn, NY, December 8, 1931; m 1956, Noemie Koller; c Daniel and David. **Education:** Columbia Univ, AB, 1952, MA, 1958, PhD (physics), 1959. **Honorary Degrees:** MEng, Stevens Inst Technol, 1973. **Honors & Awards:** Ottens Res Award, 1963. **Professional Experience:** PROF EMER PHYSICS, STEVENS INST TECHNOL, 1998-; prof physics, Stevens Inst Technol, 1969-1998; from instr to assocprof, Stevens Inst Technol, 1959-1969; Asst physics, Columbia Univ, 1952-1959. **Memberships:** Am Phys Soc; Sigma Xi; Am Asn Univ Prof. **Research Statement & Publications:** High energy nuclear physics, especially particle physics; investigation of strange particle and pi meson properties; K meson decays; pi-p, K-p, p-p and p-d interactions using the Fermilab 30 inch bubble chamber hybrid system; neutronino interactions using bubble chamber techniques. **Mailing Address:** Stevens Inst Technol, Hoboken, NJ 07030. **Fax:** 201-216-5638. **E-Mail:** ekoller@stevens-tech.edu

KOLLER, GLENN R, GEOSTATISTICS. **Personal Data:** b Buffalo, NY, November 25, 1951; c 3. **Education:** State Univ NY, Buffalo, BA, 1973; Univ Syracuse, MS, 1976, PhD (geol), 1978. **Professional Experience:** MATH GEOLOGIST, AMOCO PROD RES, 1980-; geologist, Savannah River Lab, Dept Energy, 1978-1980. **Memberships:** Sigma Xi. **Research Statement & Publications:** Mathematical and statistical manipulation of geologic data in the area of petroleum exploration; numerous patents. **Mailing Address:** Amoco Prod Res, 6642 S 67 E Ave, Tulsa, OK 74133-1721. **E-Mail:** grk1000@aol.com

KOLLER, LOREN D, NUTRITION, VETERINARY MEDICINE. **Personal Data:** b Pomeroy, Wash, June 16, 1940; m 1963, Kathleen; c Susan E, Michael D & Christopher L. **Education:** Wash State Univ, DVM, 1965; Univ Wis, MS, 1969, PhD (path), 1971. **Professional Experience:** Pres, Vet Spec Sect, 1993-1995; ed, J Clin Toxicol, 1991; comt Toxicol, Nat Res Coun, 1990-1996; chmn, Animals Res, 1989-1991; mem, Subcomt Immunotoxicol, Nat Acad Sci, 1989-1990; Pew Found, 1988-1989; Warner Lambert Co, 1987; adv ed, Int J Immunopharmacol, 1987-1989; pres, Immunotoxicol Spec Sect, 1986; prof, Col Vet Med, Ore State Univ, Corvallis, beginning 1985; dean, Col Vet Med, Ore State Univ, Corvallis, 1985-1995; vpres, Immunotoxicol Spec Sect, 1985; mem, Prog Comt, 1984-1987; mem, Immunotoxicol Steering Comt, 1984-1985; ed, J Toxicol & Environ Health, 1984-1985; ed, Can J Comp Med, 1984-1985; Merck, Idaho Beef Coun, 1984-1985; adm adv, WRCC-46Ram Epididymitis Regional Res Prog, 1982-; ed, J Reticuloendothelial Soc, 1982-1985; assoc dean, Vet Med, Univ Idaho, 1981-1985; mem, Pub Relations & Stand, Soc Toxicol, 1981-1984; Merck, Sharp & Dohme, 1981-1982; ed, J Am Vet Med Asn, 1980-1981, 1984-1986; grants, Dow Chem, 1980-1981; from assoc prof to prof, Vet Med, Univ Idaho, 1978-1985; asst dean, Vet Med, Univ Idaho, 1978-1981; assoc prof, Sch Vet Med, Ore State Univ, 1976-1978; ed, Am J Vet Res, 1976, 1986, 1987, 1989; prin investr & co-investr numerous grants, NIH, Environ Protection Agency, Health, Educ &Welfare Dept, US Dept Agr, Food & Drug Admin, 1975-1990; res assoc, Sch Vet Med, Ore State Univ, 1972-1976; head diag & comt path, Animal Sci & Technol Br, Nat Inst Environ Health Sci, Res Triangle Park, NC, 1971-1972; res assoc path, Vet Sci Dept, UnivWis, 1968-1971; capt, US Army Med Univ, 1966-1968; pvt vet pract, 1965-1966. **Memberships:** Soc Toxicol; Soc Toxicol Pathologists; Am Vet Med Assoc; Am Asn VetImmunolgists; Acad Vet & Comp Toxicologists; Soc Risk Analysis; fel Acad Toxicol Sci. **Research Statement & Publications:** Effect of drugs and chemicals on immunity; toxicological, pathological and immunological studies of toxic substances; effect of environmental contaminants on tumor growth and immunity; development of immunopharmacology/toxicology procedures; selenium responsive diseases in livestock; Risk Assessment; pathology service; extensive publications. **Mailing Address:** Loren Koller & Assocs LLC, NE Mistletoe Cir, Corvallis, OR 97330-9429. **Fax:** 541-745-5131. **E-Mail:** kollerl@pacifier.com

KOLLER, NOEMIE, NUCLEAR PHYSICS, SOLID STATE PHYSICS. **Personal Data:** b Vienna, Austria, August 21, 1933; American citizen; m 1956, Earl L; c Daniel & David. **Education:** Columbia Univ, BA, 1953, MA, 1955, PhD (physics), 1958. **Professional Experience:** Chairperson, Div Nuclear Physics, Am Phys Soc, 1993-1994; assoc dean, Natural Sci, Fac Arts & Sci, 1992-1995; PROF PHYSICS, RUTGERS UNIV, NEW BRUNSWICK, 1970-; from asst prof to assoc prof, Natural Sci, Fac Arts & Scis, 1960-1970; Fel physics, Columbia Univ, 1958-1960. **Memberships:** Fel Am Phys Soc; fel AAAS. **Research Statement & Publications:** Study of hyperfine interactions at nuclei in ionized atoms or in solids; nuclear spectroscopy; nuclear magnetic moments. **Mailing Address:** Dept Physics, Rutgers Univ, New Brunswick, NJ 08903. **Fax:** 732-445-4343. **E-Mail:** nkoller@physics.rutgers.edu

KOLLER, ROBERT DENE, PHYSICAL CHEMISTRY, STATISTICS. **Personal Data:** b Sidney, Nebr, March 7, 1945; m 1966, c 1. **Education:** Univ Nebr, BS, 1967, PhD (theoret chem), 1972. **Professional Experience:** SR SCIENTIST CHEM, ROHM & HAAS CO, 1973-; fel theoret chem, Mellon Inst, Carnegie Mellon Univ, 1972-1973; Anal chemist, Com Solvents Corp, 1967 &1968. **Memberships:** Am Chem Soc; Soc Automotive Engrs. **Research Statement & Publications:** The application of computer and statistical techniques for analysis of chemical problems arising in industrial research; research and development of oil additives. **Mailing Address:** 668 Sourwood Dr, Hatfield, PA 19440-3548.

KOLLIG, HEINZ PHILIPP, ANALYTICAL & CLINICAL CHEMISTRY, ENVIRONMENTAL FATE DATA OF ORGANIC COMPOUNDS. **Personal Data:** b Bonn, Ger, May 19, 1928; American citizen; m 1951, Hannelore Giessen; c Monika & Frank. **Education:** Univ Bonn, Ger, BS, 1950; Fla Inst Technol, BS, 1969. **Professional Experience:** RETIRED; res chemist water, US Environ Protection Agency, 1971-; analchemist environ health, TWA Kennedy Space Ctr, Fla, 1968-1971; anal chemist microanal, Southern Res Inst, 1960-1968; res chemist, Univ Ala, 1959-1960; chemist power plant chem, City Bonn, Ger, 1957-1959; Chemist clin chem, Univ Bonn, Ger, 1951-1957. **Memberships:** Am Chem Soc. **Research Statement & Publications:** Ecology; experimental and computational rate and equilibrium constants for organic chemicals. **Mailing Address:** 1050 Dogwood Hill NW, Watkinsville, GA 30677. **Fax:** 706-546-3636.

KOLLMORGEN, G MARK, CELL BIOLOGY, IMMUNOLOGY. **Personal Data:** b Bancroft, Nebr, June 23, 1932; m 1954, c 4. **Education:** Univ Iowa, BA, 1957, MA, 1960, PhD (radiation biol), 1963. **Professional Experience:** CONSULT, as of 2004; MEM, OKLA MED RES FOUND, 1976-; PROF RADIOL, SCH MED, UNIV OKLA, 1974-; assoc mem, Okla Med Res Found, 1969-1976; from asst prof to assoc prof, OklaMed Res Found, 1966-1974; asst mem, Okla Med Res Found, 1966-1969; asst biologist, Argonne Nat Lab, 1965-1966; resident res assoc, Argonne Nat Lab, 1963-1965; instr radiationbiol, Univ Iowa, 1961-1963; instr biol sci, Univ Iowa, 1958-1960. **Memberships:** Am Asn Cancer Res; Am Soc Cell Biol; Soc Exp Biol & Med; Tissue Cult Asn; Sigma Xi. **Research Statement & Publications:** Effects of dietary fat on tumor incidence and immune responses; serum factors which inhibit immune responses; influence of prostaglandins on tumor growth and transplantability; effects of products derived from cyclooxygenase and lipoxygenase pathways on function of natural killer cells. **Mailing Address:** 6425 W Kensington Rd, Oklahoma City, OK 73132.

KOLLROS, JERRY JOHN, EMBRYOLOGY, CELL BIOLOGY. **Personal Data:** b Vienna, Austria, December 29, 1917; American citizen; m 1942, Catharine Lutherman; c James C & Peter R. **Education:** Univ Chicago, SB, 1938, PhD (zool), 1942. **Professional Experience:** EMER PROF ZOOL, UNIV IOWA, 1988-; Comn Undergrad Educ Biol Sci, 1967-1971, chmn, 1969-1971; Biol Sci Training Rev Comt, NIMH, 1966-1970; consult, Div Inst Progs, NSF, 1964-1966; Mem, Cell Biol Study Sect, NIH, 1960-1964; chmn dept, Univ Iowa, 1955-1977; actg chmn, Univ Iowa, 1954-1955; from asst prof to prof, Univ Iowa, 1947-1988; assoc, Univ Iowa, 1946-1947; instr zool, Col, 1945-1946; Asst zool, Toxicity Lab, 1945; neurosurg, Univ Chicago, 1943-1945; Asst zool, Univ Chicago, 1940-1942; Consult, Am Col Dict & Random House Dict of Eng Lang. **Memberships:** AAAS; Am Soc Cell Biol; Soc Develop Biol; Am Asn Anat; Am Soc Zool (treas, 1959-1962). **Research Statement & Publications:** Control of skin gland development and segregation of skin regions; development of behavior in Amphibia; experimental embryology of amphibian central nervous system; amphibian metamorphosis; regeneration of Amphibia; neuroscience. **Mailing Address:** Dept Biol Sci, Univ Iowa, Iowa City, IA 52242.

KOLM, HENRY HERBERT, MAGNETISM. **Personal Data:** b Vienna, Austria, September 10, 1924; American citizen; m 1953, Elizabeth Cushing; c Margaret, Juliet (Gibbs), Edna (Dripps) & Cornelia (Cesari). **Education:** Mass Inst Technol, SB, 1950, PhD (physics), 1955. **Honors & Awards:** Peter Mark Medal, Dept Defense, 1983 eng of year; AIAA, 1994. **Professional Experience:** VPRES, PARAMAG CORP, 1989-; PRES, MAGNEPLANE INT INC, 1989-; pres, Electromagnetic Launch Res Inc, 1982-1989; dir, Piezo Elec Prod Inc, 1981-1993; sr scientist & lectr, Dept Aeronaut & Astronaut, Nat Magnet Lab, 1960-1982; mem res staff, Lincoln Lab, 1954-1960; Asst low temperature physics, Mass Inst Technol, 1950-1954. **Memberships:** Am Phys Soc; Am Inst Aeronaut & Astronaut; Inst Elec & Electronics Engrs. **Research Statement & Publications:** Hydrodynamics of liquid helium; semiconductor surface physics; cyclotron resonance in solids; design of pulsed and continous high-field solenoid magnets; superconductivity; magnetic separation; magnetic levitation and propulsion of high speed vehicles; applications of magnetism; piezoelectricity; electromagnetic launch technology. **Mailing Address:** One Weir Meadow Path, Wayland, MA 01778.

KOLMAN, BERNARD, MATHEMATICS. **Personal Data:** b Havana, Cuba, July 4, 1932; American citizen; m 1986, c 2. **Education:** Brooklyn Col, BS, 1954; Brown Univ, ScM, 1956; Univ Pa, PhD (math), 1965. **Professional Experience:** PROF EMER MATH, DREXEL UNIV, as of 2003; prof math, Drexel Univ, beginning 1976; from asst prof to prof, Drexel Univ, 1964-1976; Prin mathematician, Univac Div, Sperry Rand Corp, 1957-1964. **Memberships:** Am Math Soc; Math Asn Am; Soc Indust & Appl Math; Asn Comput Mach. **Research Statement & Publications:** Lie algebras; operations research. **Mailing Address:** Dept Math, Drexel Univ, Philadelphia, PA 19104. **E-Mail:** bkolman@mcs.drexel.edu

KOLMEN, SAMUEL NORMAN, PHYSIOLOGY PATHOPHYSOLOGY, MICROCIRCULATION, LYMPHATIC DYNAMICS. **Personal Data:** b Brownsville, Tex, March 20, 1930; m 1954, Barbara; c Benita (Solomon) & Jean n ette (Rosato). **Education:** Univ Tex, BA, 1954, Univ Texas, PhD (physiol), 1957. **Professional Experience:** RETIRED; dir med educ & res, Mercy Hosp, Pittsburgh, 1989-1994; bd mem, audobaun Soc, Pittsburgh, North Hills, Art Ctr Pgh; consult, Nat Bd Med Examr, Philadelphia, 1989; prof physiol & assoc dean acad affairs, Sch Med, Hahnemann Univ, 1984-1989; mem, Coun Thrombosis, Am Heart Asn, Res & Rev Comt, Ohio Affil, 1981-1984; asst dean sci & eng med, Sch Med, Wright State Univ, 1980-1984; prof physiol & chmn dept, Sch Med, Wright State Univ, 1975-1984; res coordr, Div Physiol, Shriners Burns Inst, 1970-1975; head, Div Physiol, Shriners Burns Inst, 1968-1970; from asst prof to prof physiol, Univ Tex Med Br, Galveston, 1958-1975; Kempner fel med, London Hosp Med Col, Univ London, 1957-1958. **Memberships:** fel AAAS; Soc Exp Biol & Med; Am Physiol Soc; Brit Biochem Soc; Microcirculatory Soc; Sigma Xi. **Research Statement & Publications:** Adsorptive phenomena related to biological processes; fibrinogen metabolism, storage and distribution; lymphatic circulation; microcirculation; burn physiopathology. **Mailing Address:** 256 Sweet Gum Rd, Pittsburgh, PA 15238. **E-Mail:** skolmen@earthlink.net

KOLMES, STEVEN ALBERT, ERGONOMIC EFFICIENCY, BEHAVIORAL TOXICOLOGY, SALMON RECOVERY. **Personal Data:** b Poughkeepsie, NY, September 17, 1954; m 1987, Linda; c Sara K & Elijah J. **Education:** Ohio Univ, BS, 1976; Univ Wis, Madison, MS, 1978, PhD (zoology), 1984. **Professional Experience:** DIR, ENVIRON STUDIES PROG, UNIV PORTLAND, as of 2005; PROF BIOL, UNIV PORTLAND, as of 2004; REV JOHN MOLTER CSC CHAIR, SCI, UNIV PORTLAND, 1995-; consult, 1994-; Fulbright res scholar, Utrecht Univ, Neth, 1991; assoc prof biol, Hobart & William Smith Cols, 1989-1994; assoc ed, J Apicult Res, 1989-1991; vis scientist, Univ Col, Cardiff, UK, 1987; asst prof, Hobart & William Smith Cols, 1984-1989; lectr, Univ Wis-Madison, 1983-1984. **Memberships:** Animal Behav Soc; Entom Soc Am; Acarological Soc Am; Int Union Study Social Insects; AAAS. **Research Statement & Publications:** Ethology of invertebrates, specifically how ecological considerations have evolutionary shaped different aspects of behavior; concentrations are social insect division of labor, and behavioral aspects of pesticide resistance in spider mites; salmonid recovery related to water quality. **Mailing Address:** Dept Biol, Univ Portland, 201 Buckley 5000 N Willamette Blvd, Portland, OR 97203-5798. **Fax:** 315-943-8079. **E-Mail:** kolmes@up.edu

KOLODKIN, ALEX L, MOLECULAR BIOLOGY. **Education:** Wesleyan Univ, BA, 1980; Univ Ore, PhD (molecular biol & genetics), 1987. **Professional Experience:** PROF, DEPT NEUROSCIENCE, THE JOHNS HOPKINS UNIV SCH MED, as of 2005. **Mailing Address:** Dept Neuroscience The Johns Hopkins Univ Sch Med, Preclinical Teaching Bldg 1001 725 N Wolfe St, Baltimore, MD 21205. **Fax:** 410-955-3623. **E-Mail:** kolodkin@jhmi.edu

KOLODNER, PAUL R, NONLINEAR DYNAMICS & PATTERN FORMATION. **Personal Data:** b Morristown, NJ, December 16, 1953; m 1980, Joan. **Education:** Princeton Univ, AB, 1975; Harvard Univ, AM, 1977, PhD (physics), 1980. **Honors & Awards:** IR-100 Award, 1985. **Professional Experience:** DISTINGUISHED MEM TECH STAFF, BELL LABS, 2002-; mem tech staff, Bell Labs, 1980-2002. **Memberships:** Am Phys Soc. **Research Statement & Publications:** Heat transfer and thermal management of electronics. **Mailing Address:** Bell Lab, Lucent Technol Inc, 600 Mountain Ave, Murray Hill, NJ 07974-0636. **E-Mail:** prk@lucent.com

KOLODNER, RICHARD DAVID, MOLECULAR BIOLOGY. **Personal Data:** b Morristown, NJ, April 3, 1951. **Education:** Univ Calif, Irvine, BS, 1971, PhD (biol), 1975. **Honorary Degrees:** DSc, Harvard Univ, 1988. **Professional Experience:** PROF, SCH MED, UNIV CALIF SAN DIEGO, as of 2002; prof biochem & molecular pharamcol, Sch Med & Dana-Farber Cancer Inst, Harvard Univ, beginning 1988; fac res award, Am Cancer Soc, 1988-1989; jr fac res award, Am Cancer Soc, 1981-1983; from asst prof to assoc prof, Sch Med & Dana-farber Cancer Inst, Harvard Univ, 1979-1988; fel, Cystic Fibrosis Found, 1975-1976 & NIH, 1976-1978; res fel molecular biol, Sch Med & Dana-farber Cancer Inst, Harvard Univ, 1975-1978. **Memberships:** Am Soc Biol Chemists; Am Soc Microbiol; Genetics Soc Am. **Research Statement & Publications:** Enzymatic and molecular mechanism of genetic recombination in procaryotes and eucaryotes; DNA structure; cancer genetics. **Mailing Address:** Univ CA San Diego, Ludwig Inst Canc Res, 9500 Gilman Dr, La Jolla, CA 92093-0660. **Fax:** 858-534-7750. **E-Mail:** rkolodner@ucsd.edu

KOLODNY, GERALD MORDECAI, RADIOLOGY. **Personal Data:** b Brookline, Mass, April 22, 1937; m 1964, c 3. **Education:** Harvard Univ, AB, 1958; Northwestern Univ, Chicago, MD, 1962; Am Bd Radiol, dipl, 1967; Am Bd Nuclear Med, dipl, 1974. **Professional Experience:** CHIEF, DIV NUCLEAR MED, BETH ISRAEL HOSP, 1979-; ASSOC PROF RADIOL, HARVARD MED SCH, 1975-; assoc radiologist & dir, Radiol Res Lab, 1975-1979; assoc chmn curric, Div Med Sci, 1974-; from instr to asst prof, Div Nuclear Med, Beth IsraelHosp, 1969-1975; asst radiologist, Mass Gen Hosp, 1969-1975; Picker Found grant, 1969-1971; res assoc biochem, Huntington Labs, Harvard Univ, 1969-1970; fel dept biol, Mass Inst Technol, 1966-1969; resident radiol, Mass Gen Hosp, 1963-1966; Intern med, Stanford Univ Med Ctr, 1962-1963. **Memberships:** Am Soc Cell Biol; Tissue Cult Asn; Inst Elec & Electronics Engrs; Soc Nuclear Med; Radiol Soc NAm. **Research Statement & Publications:** Gene regulation; RNA biochemistry; cell to cell communication; contact inhibition; electronics and computers in medicine; nuclear medicine; cellular radiation biology. **Mailing Address:** Div Nuclear Med, Beth Israel Deaconess Med Ctr, Harvard Med Sch, 330 Brookline Ave, Boston, MA 02215. **Fax:** 617-667-2185. **E-Mail:** gkolodny@bidmc.harvard.edu

KOLODNY, NANCY HARRISON, PHYSICAL BIOCHEMISTRY. **Personal Data:** b Brooklyn, NY, March 30, 1944; m 1964, c 3. **Education:** Wellesley Col, BA, 1964; Mass Inst Technol, PhD (phys chem), 1969. **Professional Experience:** NELLIE ZUCKERMAN COHEN & ANNE COHEN HELLER PROF HEALTH SCI, WELLESLEY COL, as of 2005; dean, Wellesley Col, 1992-1999; PROF CHEM, WELLESLEY COL, 1985-; res assoc & lectr ophthal, Mass Eye & Ear Infirmary, Harvard Med Sch, Boston, 1984-; dean, Class 1976, 1972-1974; Wellesley Col; dir, Sci Ctr, 1974-1977; Wellesley Col, Wellesley Col, 1972-1974; res fel med, Mass Gen Hosp, Boston, 1971-1972; Radcliffe Inst fel, 1970-1972; from asst prof to assoc prof, Sci Ctr, 1969-1985. **Memberships:** Am Chem Soc; Sigma Xi; Am Soc Microbiol; Int Soc Magnetic Resonance Med. **Research Statement & Publications:** Electron spin resonance spectroscopy of charge transfer complexes in solution; nuclear magnetic resonance spectroscopy of protein-nucleic acid interactions; magnetic resonance imaging and spectroscopy of ocular disorders. **Mailing Address:** Dept Chem, Wellesley Col, Rm 155 258 SC 106 Central St, West Newton, MA 02165-2839. **E-Mail:** nkolodny@wellesley.edu

KOLODZIEJ, BRUNO J, MICROBIOLOGY, MICROBIAL PHYSIOLOGY. **Personal Data:** b Chicago, Ill, August 27, 1934; wid, c B Allen, John A & Joy A. **Education:** Northern Ill Univ, BSEd, 1958; Northwestern Univ, MS, 1960, PhD (biol), 1963. **Professional Experience:** CONSULT, 1993-; from asst prof to assoc prof microbiol, Ohio State Univ, 1966-1993; res assoc, Albert Einstein Med Ctr, Pa, 1965-1966; NIH fel microbial physiol, UnivChicago, 1963-1965. **Memberships:** AAAS; Am Soc Microbiol; Sigma Xi. **Research Statement & Publications:** Elucidation and characterization of bacterial cell surface components with emphasis on membrane binding-transport proteins associated with sugar and amino acid transport and structure and function of exocellular capsule material. **Mailing Address:** 3225 Atwood Ter, Columbus, OH 43224. **Fax:** 614-292-1538.

KOLODZIEJSKI, LESLIE ANN, ELECTRONIC MATERIALS, OPTOELECTRONIC DEVICES. **Personal Data:** b Ft Leonard Wood, Mo, July 31, 1958; m 1979. **Education:** Purdue Univ, BS, 1983, MS, 1984, PhD (elec eng), 1986. **Professional Experience:** PROF ELEC ENG, MASS INST TECHNOL, as of 2003; PRIN INVESTER MAT & FABRICATION RES LAB, MASS INST TECHNOL, as of 2003; ESTHER & HAROLD E EDGERTON PROF ELEC, MASS INST TECHNOL, as of 2003; assoc prof elec eng, Mass Inst Technol, beginning 1993; asst prof eleceng, Mass Inst Technol, 1988-1993; NSF presidential young investr & Off Naval Res young investr, 1987; asst prof elec eng, Purdue Univ, 1986-1988. **Memberships:** Am Phys Soc; Mat Res Soc; Optical Soc Am; Inst Elec & Electronics Engrs. **Research Statement & Publications:** Fabrication of thin film semiconductors, such as zine-selenium and gallium-arsenic, which are layered to form sophisticated heterostructures. **Mailing Address:** Dept Elec Eng Mass Inst Technol, Rm 13-3065 77 Mass Ave, Cambridge, MA 02139. **Fax:** 617-253-8509. **E-Mail:** leskolo@mit.edu

KOLODZY, PAUL JOHN, NEURAL NETWORKS, SMART SENSORS. **Personal Data:** b Akron, Ohio, 1959; m 1986, c 1. **Education:** Purdue Univ, BS, 1983; Case Western Res Univ, MS, 1984, PhD (chem eng), 1986. **Professional Experience:** DIR, WIRELESS NETWORK SEC CTR, STEVENS INST TECHNOL, 2002-; PROG MGR, DARPA, 1999-; Sr Spectrum Policy Advice, DARPA, 1999-2002; Dir, Spectrum Policy task Force, 1999-2002; ASST GROUP LEADER, NEURALNETWORKS, MASS INST TECHNOL LINCOLN LAB, 1989-; Co-chair, Simulation Panel, DARPA Neural Network Study, 1988-1989; Staff mem, opto-radar systs, 1986-1989. **Research Statement & Publications:** Develop and exploit neural network techniques for active and passive optical sensors; design and model optical sensor systems; advanced simulation technology. **Mailing Address:** Wireless Network Security Ctr, Stevens Inst Technol, Lieb Bldg, Castle Point, Hoboken, NJ 07030. **E-Mail:** pkolodzy@stevens.edu

KOLONEL, LAURENCE N, EPIDEMIOLOGY. **Education:** Harvard Univ; Univ Calif-Berkeley, MPH & PhD (Epidemiol). **Professional Experience:** CTR DEPUTY DIR & DIR EPIDEMOL PROG, CANCER RES CTR HAWAII, as of 2005; PROF, SCH PUB HEALTH, CANCER RES CTR HAWAII, as of 2005. **Research Statement & Publications:** Understanding the striking variations in cancer incidence and survival that are observed among the several different ethnic populations. **Mailing Address:** Cancer Res Ctr Hawaii, Univ Hawaii, 1236 Lauhala St, Honolulu, HI 96813. **Fax:** 808-586-2982. **E-Mail:** lkolonel@crch.hawaii.edu

KOLOPAJLO, LAWRENCE HUGH, PHYSICAL-ANALYTICAL CHEMISTRY, CHEMICAL KINETICS. **Personal Data:** b Steubenville, Ohio, December 27, 1950; m 1980, c 1. **Education:** Muskingum Col, BS, 1974; Pa State Univ, MS, 1978; Wester Mich Univ, PhD (chem), 1982. **Professional Experience:** STAFF MEM, ST MARY'S COL, ORCHARD LAKE, MICH, 1994-; supvr, Ohio mat, Environ Qual Labs, 1992-1994; team leader, Ohio mat, Environ Qual Labs, 1988-1992; asstprof phys & analytical chem, Marietta Col, 1985-1988; Instr, Univ SC, 1985; asst prof physchem, Claflin Col, 1984-1985; res assoc, State Univ NY, Buffalo, 1982-1984; qual control, Allied Paper Co, SCM, 1978-1980; chemist, Dow Chem Co, 1976-1977. **Memberships:** Am Chem Soc. **Research Statement & Publications:** Coordination chemistry; kinetics and mechanisms of complex formation and ligand exchange reactions carried out in solution. **Mailing Address:** Dept Chem, Eastern Mich Univ, Ypsilanti, MI 48197. **E-Mail:** larry.kolopajilo@emich.edu

KOLP, BERNARD J, AGRONOMY, PLANT BREEDING. **Personal Data:** b Caroll, Iowa, October 20, 1928; m 1952, c 3. **Education:** Iowa State Univ, BS, 1954; Kans State Univ, MS, 1955, PhD, 1958. **Professional Experience:** RETIRED; prof plant breeding, Univ Wyo, 1970-1986; asst prof agron, UnivWyo, 1957-1970. **Research Statement & Publications:** Drought resistance and emergence of wheat; nitrate content in oats; winter hardiness in wheat. **Mailing Address:** 1808 Ord St, Laramie, WY 82070.

KOLSKI, THADDEUS L(EONARD), INORGANIC CHEMISTRY PHYSICAL CHEMISTRY. **Personal Data:** b Chicago, Ill, November 29, 1928; m 1955, Ann; c Lynda & Patricia. **Education:** Ill Inst Technol, BS, 1950; St Louis Univ, MS, 1954, PhD (inorg chem), 1957. **Professional Experience:** RETIRED; ed, High-Solids Coatings, 1979-1981; res chemist, E I du Pont de Nemours Co, Inc, 1956-1985. **Research Statement & Publications:** Oxidation of niobium and niobium alloys; anodic characteristics of tantalum and niobium; electrolytic capacitators; surface and boron chemistry; white and colored pigments. **Mailing Address:** 1116 Graylyn Rd, Chatham, Wilmington, DE 19803.

KOLSKY, HARWOOD GEORGE, PHYSICS, COMPUTER ENGINEERING. **Personal Data:** b Portland, Ore, January 18, 1921; m 1942, Frances G Cilek; c Barbara, Franklin, Alan & Douglas. **Education:** Univ Kans, BS, 1943, MS, 1947; Harvard Univ, PhD (physics), 1950. **Professional Experience:** EMER PROF COMPUT ENG, UNIV CALIF, SANTA CRUZ, 1991-; prof, Univ Calif, Santa Cruz, 1985-1991; mgr, IBM fel, 1969-1986; mgr, atmospheric physics dept, 1966-1969; univ prog, Palo Alto, 1964-1966; spec proj, Adv Systs Develop Lab, 1962-1964; mgr, Systs Sci Res Lab, San Jose, 1961-1962; asst mgr, 438 L Proj, Omaha, 1959-1960; projcoordr stretch comput, IBM Sci Ctr, 1959; sr planning rep prod planning, IBM Sci Ctr, 1957-1959; assoc group leader, Hydrodyn Group, Theoret Div, 1952-1957; mem staff, WeaponsDiv & Theoret Div, Los Alamos Sci Lab, 1950-1952; Asst instr physics, Univ Kans, 1946-1947. **Memberships:** Am Phys Soc; Inst Elec & Electronics Engrs; Sigma Xi. **Research Statement & Publications:** Digital computer application and design; compressible fluid hydrodynamics; nuclear moments by molecular beam technique; numerical meteorology. **Mailing Address:** 18950 Lynbrook Ct, Saratoga, CA 95070.

KOLSRUD, GRETCHEN SCHABTACH, TECHNOLOGY ASSESSMENT, DEMOGRAPHY. **Personal Data:** b Schenectady, NY, January 9, 1939. **Education:** McGill Univ, BSc, 1960; Johns Hopkins Univ, MA, 1963, PhD (psychol), 1966. **Professional Experience:** INDEPENDENT CONSULT, 1994-; fel, Green Ctr Study Sci & Soc, 1994; bd trustees, Pop Ref Bur, 1992-; actg group mgr, Health Group, prog mgr, biol appl, 1979-1989; sr assoc, Off Technol Assessment, 1978-1994; asst to dir, New & Emerging Technol, 1976-1978; prog mgr, Transp Prog, US Cong, 1974-1976; prog mgr, NASA, 1973-1974; staff-scientist, BioTechnol Inc, 1971-1973; consult, Flight Mgt Systs, 1967 & Nat Hwy Traffic SafetyAdmin, 1971; sr syst scientist human factors eng, Serendipity Inc, 1967-1971; prin res scientist psychol, Systs & Res Ctr, Honeywell Inc, 1966-1967. **Memberships:** Fel AAAS; Human Factors Soc (secy & treas, 1974-1975); NY Acad Sci; Sigma Xi. **Research Statement & Publications:** Science policy; demography; relationships between society and technology. **Mailing Address:** 114 Roberts Ct, Alexandria, VA 22314.

KOLTUN, DANIEL S, THEORETICAL PHYSICS, NUCLEAR PHYSICS. **Personal Data:** b Brooklyn, NY, December 7, 1933; m 1956, Judeth; c 2. **Education:** Harvard Col, AB, 1955; Princeton Univ, PhD (physics), 1961. **Professional Experience:** PROF EMER PHYSICS, UNIV ROCHESTER, as of 2005; lady Davis vis prof, Hebrew Univ, 1985; vis scientist, Mass inst Technol, 1984; assoc ed, Phys Rev Letters, 1979-1981; assoc ed, Phys Rev C, 1978-1980; vis prof, Tel Aviv Univ, 1976-1977 & J S Guggenheim fel, 1976-1977; prof physics, univ rochester, beginning 1974; Alfred P Sloan res fel, 1969-1971; res assoc ctr theoret physics, Mass inst Technol, 1969-1970; from asst prof to assoc prof, Univ Rochester, 1963-1974; res assoc physics, Univ Rochester, 1962-1963; NSF vis fel nuclear physics, Weizmann inst, 1961-1962 & inst Theoret Phys, Copenhagen, 1962; res assoc physics, Princeton Univ, 1960-1961. **Memberships:** Fel Am Phys Soc. **Research Statement & Publications:** Theoretical nuclear spectroscopy; many-body theory; interaction of nuclei with mesons; scattering theory; quarks in nuclei. **Mailing Address:** Dept Physics & Astron, Univ Rochester, Rochester, NY 14627-0171. **Fax:** 585-273-3237. **E-Mail:** koltun@pas.rochester.edu

KOLTUN, STANLEY PHELPS, CHEMICAL ENGINEERING. **Personal Data:** b Bogalusa, La, March 5, 1925; wid, c Karen (Lovett), Ellen K & Patricia (Calamari). **Education:** La State Univ, BSChE, 1948. **Professional Experience:** RES LEADER, FOOD & FEED ENGR RES UNIT, SOUTHERNREGIONAL RES CTR, USDA, 1982-; actg res leader, Oilseed Prod Res, 1976-1982; res chemengr, Food Prod Invests, 1970-1976; proj leader, Food Prod Invests, 1963-1970; cost engr, Cost& Design Unit, 1959-1963; Chem engr, Proc Design Unit, USDA, 1956-1959. **Memberships:** Am Inst Chem Engrs; Nat Soc Prof Engrs; Am Oil Chemists' Soc; Sigma Xi; InstFood Technologists. **Research Statement & Publications:** Detoxification and inactivation of aflatoxin contaminated oilseeds; oilseed solvent extraction; food dehydration; utilization of oilseed proteins as human food; oilseed meals; cottonseed; peanuts; sweetpotatoes; human nutrition; food safety. **Mailing Address:** 5601 Avron Blvd, Metairie, LA 70003-1011.

KOLTUN, WALTER LANG, BIOPHYSICAL CHEMISTRY. **Personal Data:** b New York, NY, April 23, 1928; m 1962, c 2. **Education:** Mass Inst Technol, BS, 1948, PhD (biochem), 1952. **Professional Experience:** CONSULT, 1994-; asst dir resources, Harvard-Mass Int Technol Health Prog, 1970-1993; dir prog advan study, Bolt, Beranek & Newman, 1968-1970; spec asst, Off vpres & Secy & Inst Secy Found, Mass Inst Technol, 1965-1968; prog dir molecular biol, Sci Resources Planning Off, NSF, 1964-1965; staff mem, Sci Resources Planning Off, NSF, 1961-1964; consult biophys, Univ Calif, Berkeley, 1959-1961; res assoc, Med Col, Cornell Univ, 1956-1959; asst prof biochem, Sch Med, Univ Va, 1955-1956; res assoc, Mass Inst Technol, 1952-1953; asst biol, Mass Inst Technol, 1951-1952. **Memberships:** AAAS; Fedn Am Sci; Am Soc Biol Chem; Sigma Xi. **Research Statement & Publications:** Structure, function and interaction of macromolecules, particularly proteins. **Mailing Address:** 76 Goodnough Rd, Chestnut Hill, MA 02467.

KOLYER, JOHN M, ORGANIC CHEMISTRY, POLYMER CHEMISTRY. **Personal Data:** b East Williston, NY, June 30, 1933. **Education:** Hofstra Col, BA, 1955; Univ Pa, PhD (org chem), 1960. **Honors & Awards:** Engineer of the Year, Rockwell International Corp, 1989. **Professional Experience:** ENGINEER & SCI, BOEING CO, 1999-; sr eng specialist, Autonetics Div, Rockwell Int Corp, 1973-1999; tech supvr, Morristown, 1967-1971; Mem, Lepidoptera Found, 1965-1973; group leader, Plastics Div, Allied Chem Corp, 1965-1967; sr res chemist, Plastics Div, Allied Chem Corp, 1964-1965; Thompson Chem Co, Mass, 1962-1963; res chemist, FMC Corp, NJ, 1960-1962; Technician pesticides, Olin Mathieson Chem Corp, NY, 1955-1956. **Memberships:** Am Chem Soc; NY Acad Sci; EOS/ESD Asn. **Research Statement & Publications:** Preparation processes for plastics additives and monomers; polymerization processes and fabrication methods; polymer modifications; lepidopterological research; ESD (electrostatic discharge) control; author of one book and 70 technical publications; granted 16 patents; materials science engineering. **Mailing Address:** Being Co, 3370 Miraloma Ave, MC GE-22, Anaheim, CA 92803-3105. **Fax:** 714-762-3655.

KOMAI, HIROCHIKA, ANESTHESIOLOGY. **Education:** Univ Calif, Berkeley, PhD (biochem), 1967. **Professional Experience:** ASSOC SCIENTIST EMER, UNIV WIS, beginning 1980. **Mailing Address:** Dept Anesthesiol, Univ Wis Health Sci Ctr, 4619 Med Sci Ctr 1300 Univ Ave 600 Highland Ave, Madison, WI 53792-3272. **E-Mail:** hkomai@facstaff.wisc.edu

KOMANDURI, AYYANGAR M, PHYSICS. **Professional Experience:** CHIEF PHYSICIST, DEPT RADIATION ONCOL, MED CTR, UNIV NEBR, OMAHA, as of 2006. **Memberships:** Am Assn Physicists. **Mailing Address:** Univ Nebr, 104 Nebraska Hall, Lincoln, NE 43699-0008. **Fax:** 402-472-4608. **E-Mail:** akomanduri@gmail.com

KOMAR, ARTHUR BARAWAY, THEORETICAL PHYSICS. **Personal Data:** b Brooklyn, NY, March 26, 1931; m 1952, c 2. **Education:** Princeton Univ, AB, 1952, PhD (physics), 1956. **Professional Experience:** PROF EMER PHYSICS, SYRACUSE UNIV, as of 2004; adj prof physics, NY Univ, 1985-; chmn, divmat sci, 1983-1986; prog dir, gravitational physics, NSF, 1982-1983, 1986-1987 & 1991-1992; chmn, deptphysics, 1978-1982 & beginning 1992; dean, belfer grad sch sci, 1969-1978; prof physics, Yeshiva Univ, beginning 1966; assoc prof, Yeshiva Univ, 1963-1966; assoc prof, Syracuse Univ, 1960-1963; asst prof physics, Syracuse Univ, 1958-1960; fel, Scandinavian-Am Found, Inst Theoret Physics, Denmark, 1956-1957. **Research Statement & Publications:** General relativity and quantum field theory. **Mailing Address:** Dept Physics, Syracuse Univ, 201 Physics Bldg, Syracuse, NY 13244-1130. **Fax:** 315-443-9103. **E-Mail:** komar@physics.syr.edu

KOMAR, PAUL D, OCEANOGRAPHY, MARINE GEOLOGY. **Personal Data:** b Grand Rapids, Mich, December 2, 1939; m 1962, c 1. **Education:** Univ Mich, BA, 1961, MS, 1962, 1965; Univ Calif, San Diego, PhD (oceanog), 1969. **Professional Experience:** PROF EMER OCEANOG, ORE STATE UNIV, as of 2004; Kajima Found fel, Japan, 1987; prof oceanog, Ore State Univ, beginning 1978; from asst prof to assoc prof, Ore State Univ, 1970-1978; NATO fel, St Andrews Univ, Scotland, 1969-1970. **Memberships:** Soc Econ Paleont & Mineral; Am Geophys Union; Int Asn Sedimentologists. **Research Statement & Publications:** Coastal process of waves, currents, sediment transport and changes in the morphology of beaches; mechanics of sediment transport. **Mailing Address:** Col Oceanic & Atmospheric Sci, Ore State Univ, 104 Admin Bldg Wgr 543, Corvallis, OR 97331-5503. **Fax:** 541-737-2064. **E-Mail:** pkomar@coas.oregonstate.edu

KOMARKOVA, VERA, plant ecology; deceased, see previous edition for last biography

KOMARMY, JULIUS MICHAEL, PHYSICAL CHEMISTRY, ORGANIC CHEMISTRY. **Personal Data:** b Franklin, NJ, October 19, 1926; m 1952, c 4. **Education:** SW Mo State Col, BS, 1949; Univ Ark, MS, 1952, PhD, 1958. **Professional Experience:** CATALYTIC CONVERTER COLLETORS INC, 1987-; sr staff resscientist, Res Dept, AC Spark Plug Div, Gen Motors Corp, 1966-1986; Supvr chem, Supvr chemres, 1965-1966; Supvr chem, Res Dept, AC Spark Plug Div, Gen Motors Corp, 1961-1965; instr, Flint Jr Col, 1957-1961; instr, Univ Ark, 1952-1954, 1956-1967; Asst chem, Univ Ark, 1949-1952. **Memberships:** AAAS; Am Chem Soc; Soc Automotive Eng; Am Soc Testing & Mat; Soc InfoDisplays. **Research Statement & Publications:** Automotive applications of plastics and elastomers; fuels and lubricants and filtration processes; catalyst development for automotive exhaust environmental controls; materials development for fabrication of large liquid crystal displays. **Mailing Address:** 8521 Pepper Ridge Dr, Grand Blanc, Flint, MI 48439-7959.

KOMARNENI, SRIDHAR, MATERIALS RESEARCH, CLAY MINERALOGY. **Personal Data:** b Komarneni Varipalem, India, September 26, 1944; American citizen; m 1979, Sreedevi; c Jayanth. **Education:** Andhra Pradesh Agr Univ, India, BSc, 1968; Indian Agr Res Inst, MSc, 1970; Univ Wis-Madison, PhD (soils), 1973. **Honors & Awards:** Fedn Mat Soc Award, 1994; Fellow, Royal Soc Chem; Elec Mem, European Acad Sci; Highly Cited Researcher, Instit Scientific Info. **Professional Experience:** PROF CLAY MINERAL, PA STATE UNIV, 1987-; assoc prof, Pa State Univ, 1984-1987; sr res assoc, Pa State Univ, 1981-1984; res assoc, Pa State Univ, 1978-1981; proj assoc solid state sci, Pa State Univ, 1976-1978; proj assoc, Univ Wis-Madison, 1973-1976. **Memberships:** Fel AAAS; fel Am Soc Agron; fel Soil Sci Soc Am; Clay Minerals Soc; fel Am Ceramic Soc; Sigma Xi. **Research Statement & Publications:** Crystal chemistry of clay minerals and zeolites; new materials preparation and characterization; sol-gel chemistry; nuclear and hazardous waste disposal; nanocomposites; porous materials; A Microwave-Assisted Method for the Rapid Removal of Potassium from Phlogopite; author of various articles. **Mailing Address:** Pa State Univ, 205 Mat Res Lab, Univ Park, PA 16802. **Fax:** 814-865-2326. **E-Mail:** komarneni@psu.edu

KOMERATH, NARAYANAN M, AEROSPACE ENGINEERING. **Professional Experience:** PROF, SCH AERO ENG, GA INST TECH, as of 2006. **Memberships:** Am Inst Aeronaut & Astronaut. **Mailing Address:** Sch Aero Eng, Ga Inst Tech M/S 0150, Atlanta, GA 30332. **Fax:** 404-894-2760. **E-Mail:** narayanan.komerath@aerospace.gatech.edu

KOMERS, PETR E, BEHAVIORAL ECOLOGY. **Personal Data:** b Prague, Czech, April 29, 1960; Canadian & Swedish citizen; m 1986, Eva; c Tanysia & Larin. **Education:** Univ Berne, Switz, BSc, 1984; Univ Alta, Can, MSc, 1987; Univ Sask, Can, PhD (zoology), 1992. **Professional Experience:** ADJ ASSOC PROF, UNIV CALGARY, 1998-; fel, Univ Cambridge, 1993-1995; sessional lectr anat, Univ Sask, 1991-1992. **Memberships:** Animal Behav Soc. **Research Statement & Publications:** Vertebrate mating systems in relation to the ecology of species; mate choice in black-billed magpies; mating strategies of wood bison; evolution of monogamy in antelopes. **Mailing Address:** Dept Biol Sci, Univ Calgary, 207 Edgebrook Close NW, Calgary, AB T3A 4W5, Can. **Fax:** 403-241-8679. **E-Mail:** petr.komers@mses.ca

KOMIAK, JAMES JOSEPH, MMIC & MIC TECHNOLOGY-CIRCUIT DESIGN, T-R MODULE & SYSTEM ARCHITECTURES. **Personal Data:** b Chicago, Ill, October 16, 1953; c 1. **Education:** Cornell Univ, BS, 1974, MS, 1976, PhD (elec eng), 1978. **Professional Experience:** Instr, IBM Systs Eng Course, 1981 & GE Eng Course, 1989-; PRIN STAFF, MICRO/MM-WAVE TECHNOL, GE ELECTRONICS LAB, 1987-; sr engr, Micro/mm-waveTechnol, Ge Electronics lab, 1983-1987; adj prof elec eng, State Univ NY, Binghamton, 1983; develop engr & mgr, staff & adv eng, antenna/receiver develop, IBM Fed Systs, 1981-1983; Srassoc, staff & adv eng, antenna/receiver develop, IBM Fed Systs, 1978-1981. **Memberships:** Sr mem Inst Elec & Electronics Engrs. **Research Statement & Publications:** Technical; management; consulting in microwave; millimeter-wave technology; system architectures; T/R module/MMIC/MIC circuit design; design of mil-spec analog, digital, RF, microwave sub-systems; holder of 2 US patents; author of 32 publications. **Mailing Address:** Electronics Lab, GE Aerospace Ep-3 Rm 134, Syracuse, NY 13221.

KOMINEK, LEO ALOYSIUS, MICROBIOLOGY & BIOCHEMISTRY, PSYCHOLOGY. **Personal Data:** b Chicago, IL, April 11, 1937; m Anita; c Stephen, Laura, Mary & Leo. **Education:** St Joseph's Col, Ind, BS, 1959; Univ Ill, PhD (microbiol), 1964; Western Mich Univ, MA, 1995. **Professional Experience:** PSYCHOL THERAPIST, DELANO CLINIC, as of 2004; PSYCHOLOGIST, BORGESS BEHAV MED, 1995-; sr scientist, sr scientist microbiol, 1979-1995; res mgr, sr scientist microbiol, 1978-1979; Upjohn Co, sr scientist microbiol, 1972-1978; res assoc microbiol, 1964-1972. **Memberships:** Am Soc Microbiol; Am Chem Soc; Am Acad Microbiol; NY Acad Sci; Michigan Asn of Professional Psychologists; Cognitive Behavioral Therapy Association. **Research Statement & Publications:** Biochemical aspectsof bacterial sporulation; microbial metabolism; antibiotic biosynthesis; steroid and sterol bioconversions; Psychologial specialization in the treatment of anxiety disorders. **Mailing Address:** DeLano Clinic, 7895 Currier Dr, Portage, MI 49002. **Fax:** 269-321-7095. **E-Mail:** lkominek@chartermi.net

KOMINZ, DAVID RICHARD, PROTEIN CHEMISTRY. **Personal Data:** b Rochester, NY, April 2, 1924; m 1988, Phyllis Damon; c 3. **Education:** Univ Rochester, MD, 1947; Harvard Univ, BA, 1950. **Professional Experience:** RES PROF PHYSIOL, UNIV MASS MED SCH, 1978-; assoc dir, NatBladder Cancer Proj, 1976-1978; chief sect bioenergetics, Lab Biophys Chem, 1970-1976; meddir, Nat Inst Arthritis, Metab & Digestive Dis, 1968-1976; chief, NIH Pac Off, Tokyo, 1966-1968; from sr asst surgeon to med dir, Nat Inst Arthritis & Metab Dis, 1951-1965; res felphys chem lab, Harvard Univ, 1950-1951; Intern, Gorgas Hosp, CZ, 1947-1948. **Memberships:** AAAS; Am Chem Soc; Am Soc Biol Chem; Biophys Soc. **Research Statement & Publications:** Amino acid analysis; comparative biochemistry of muscle proteins; protein modifications; interactions of muscle proteins. **Mailing Address:** Dept Physiol Univ Mass Med Sch, 55 N Lake Ave, Worcester, MA 01655-0001. **Fax:** 781-235-6263.

KOMISARUK, BARRY RICHARD, PSYCHOBIOLOGY, NEUROPHYSIOLOGY. **Personal Data:** b New York, NY, April 4, 1941; wid Carolyn; c Adam C & Kevin M. **Education:** City Univ NY, BS, 1961; Rutgers Univ, PhD (neuroendocrinol), 1965. **Honors & Awards:** Hugo F Beigel Award Res, Soc Sci Study Sex, 1989. **Professional Experience:** NIH res grant, 1992-1995; Minority Biomed Res Support-NIH grant, 1987-2001; PROG DIR MORE DIV-NIMH-NIH & PROF PSYCHOL, RUTGERS UNIV, NEWARK, 1984-; NSF res grant, Rutgers Univ, Newark, beginning 1979; prof zool, Rutgers Univ, 1972-1984; NIMH res grant, NIMH Res Scientist Develop Award, 1969-1979; assoc prof, Rutgers Univ, 1968-1972; NIMH res grant, Rutgers Univ, Newark, 1966-1979; asst prof zool, Rutgers Univ, 1966-1968; NIMH fel neuroendocrinol, Univ Calif, Los Angeles, 1965-1966. **Memberships:** Int Behav Neuroscience Soc; Soc Neuroscience; Soc Sci Study Sex. **Research Statement & Publications:** Neurophysiological bases of species characteristic, hormonally influenced behavior, analgesic mechanisms; sexual response in laboratory species and humans; neural pathways and brain activity imaging in humans and lab species. **Mailing Address:** Dept Psychol, Rutgers Univ, 101 Warren St Smith Hall Rm, Newark, NJ 07102. **Fax:** 973-648-1171. **E-Mail:** brk@andromeda.rutgers.edu

KOMISKEY, HAROLD LOUIS, TOXICOLOGY. **Personal Data:** b October 21, 1948; m 1970, Judy; c 2. **Education:** Univ Wis, PhD (pharmacol), 1975; Am Bd Toxicol, dipl, 1981. **Professional Experience:** ASSOC PROF TOXICOL, COL PHARM, XAVIER UNIV, 1989-; asst prof pharmacol, Col Pharm, Wash State Univ, 1977-1983 & Col Med, Univ Ill, 1983-1989. **Memberships:** Soc Toxicol; Soc Neuroscience; Am Soc Pharmacol & Exp Therapeut. **Research Statement & Publications:** Isolation and characterization of the actions of an endogenous substance with a high affinity for benzodiazepine receptors; determination of the subchronic neurotoxicity of various zinc salts. **Mailing Address:** Dept Toxicol, Col Pharm, Xavier Univ, 1 Drexel Dr, New Orleans, LA 70125. **Fax:** 504-520-7930. **E-Mail:** hkomiske@xula.edu

KOMKOV, VADIM, OPTIMIZATION, CONTROL OF NONLINEAR SYSTEMS. **Personal Data:** b Moscow, USSR, August 18, 1919; American citizen; m 1946, c 5. **Education:** Warsaw Polytech Inst, dipl mech eng, 1948; Univ Utah, PhD (math), 1964. **Professional Experience:** RETIRED; vis prof, Mercer Univ, Macon, Ga, 1993-1996; Winthrop Col, 1983-1987; Air Force Inst Technol, 1987-1993; prof & head math, W Va Univ, 1980-1983; US Army Arm Com, 1972-1977; Univ Cincinnati, 1980-1982; vis prof, Polish Acad Sci, Warsaw, 1980; ed, Math Rev, 1977-1980; consult, Southwest Res Inst, 1970-1975; prof, Tex Tech, 1969-1977; assoc prof, Fla State, 1965-1969; vis assoc prof math, Med Res Coun, Univ Wis, 1964-1965; asst prof mech eng, Univ Utah, 1957-1964. **Memberships:** Soc Indust & Appl Math; Math Asn Am; Am Math Soc. **Research Statement & Publications:** Applied mathematics-variational methods; theoretical classical mechanics; continuum mechanics; engineering optimization; sensitivity of mechanical and structural systems to design changes. **Mailing Address:** PO Box 51204, Jaxville Beach, FL 32240.

KOMM, HORACE, MATHEMATICS. **Personal Data:** b Russia, December 30, 1916; American citizen; m 1947, c 3. **Education:** Univ Buffalo, BA, 1937; Univ Mich, MA, 1938, PhD (math), 1942. **Professional Experience:** PROF MATH, HOWARD UNIV, 1971-; chmn dept, Howard Univ, 1971-1977; assoc prof, Howard Univ, 1963-1971; asst prof, Rensselaer Polytech Inst, 1953-1962; assoc prof, Univ South, 1952-1953; asst prof, Univ Rochester, 1948-1952; instr math, Univ Rochester, 1946-1948; asst to chief mathematician, Res Lab, 1944-1946; Structures engr, Curtiss-Wright Corp, 1942-1944. **Memberships:** Am Math Soc; Math Asn Am. **Research Statement & Publications:** Dimension of partially ordered sets; general and algebraic topology. **Mailing Address:** 5130 Wickett Terr, Bethesda, MD 20814-5715.

KOMMA, DONALD JERRY, DROSOPHILA GENETICS, CHROMOSOME SEGREGATION. **Personal Data:** b August 14, 1934. **Education:** Univ Col, BA, 1957; Ind Univ, MA, 1959; Univ Mich, PhD (human genetics), 1964. **Professional Experience:** ASSOC MICROBIOL, DUKE UNIV, MED CTR, 1993-; res assoc, Duke Univ, Med Ctr, 1984-1993; res assoc, Columbia Univ, 1972-1984; fel, Univ Ill, 1967-1972; fel, Columbia Univ, 1965-1967. **Memberships:** Genetics Soc Am; Planetary Soc. **Research Statement & Publications:** Non-claret disjunctional motor protein in Drosophila, which plays a major role in chromosome disjunction during meiosis in females. **Mailing Address:** Dept Microbiol & Immunol, Duke Univ Med Ctr, 437 Jones Bldg Box 3020, Durham, NC 27710.

KOMMEDAHL, THOR, PLANT PATHOLOGY. **Personal Data:** b Minneapolis, Minn, April 1, 1920; m 1951, Faye Jensen; c Kris, Siri & Lori. **Education:** Univ Minn, BS, 1945, MS, 1947, PhD (plant path), 1951. **Honors & Awards:** Award of Excellence, Weed Sci SocAm, 1966; Distinguished Serv Award, Nat Am Phytopath Soc, 1984; E C Stakman Award, 1990; Distinguished Serv Award, Regional Am Phytopath Soc, 1993. **Professional Experience:** External assessor, Univ Pertanian, Malaysia, 1994-1997; consult, Sci Mus Minn, 1990-; PROF CONTINUING EDUC & EXTEN, UNIV MINN, ST PAUL, 1990-; EMER PROF PLANT PATH, UNIV MINN, ST PAUL, 1990-; secy gen & treas, Int Soc Plant Path, 1983-1988; consult ed, McGraw-Hill Co, 1972-1978; counr, Int Soc Plant Path, 1972-1978; Fulbright fel, Iceland, 1968; Guggenheim fel, Waite Agr Res Inst, Australia, 1961-1962; Consult botanist & taxonomist, Div Plant Indust, State Dept Agr, Dairy & Food, Minn, 1954-1960; from asst prof to prof, Univ Minn, St Paul, 1953-1990; asst prof, Agr Exp Sta, Ohio State Univ, 1951-1953; Instr, Agr Exp Sta, Univ Minn, 1946-1951. **Memberships:** Fel AAAS; Am Inst Biol Sci; fel Am Phytopath Soc (vpres, 1969; pres, 1971); Mycol Soc Am; Int Soc Plant Path (treas, 1983-1993); Bot Soc Am; NY Acad Sci; Weed Sci Soc Am; Coun Sci Ed. **Research Statement & Publications:** Flax and corn diseases; weed ecology; root diseases and ecology of root-infecting fungi; biological control root diseases; Fusarium species. **Mailing Address:** Dept Plant Path, 495 Borlaug Hall Univ Minn, St Paul, MN 55108-6030. **Fax:** 612-625-9728. **E-Mail:** thork@puccini.crl.umn.edu

KOMOREK, MICHAEL JOESPH, NUCLEAR MEDICINE, RADIATION SAFETY. **Personal Data:** b Buffalo, NY, July 14, 1952; m 1982, Linda; c Michael J Komorek III. **Education:** State Univ NY, Buffalo, BA, 1974, BS, 1977; MS, 1995. **Honors & Awards:** West Valley Nuclear Serv Co, Eagle Awd, Engr Excellence, 2002. **Professional Experience:** Radiation safety officer, Roswell Park Cancer Inst, 1988-2000; health physicist, bd dirs, Elma Nuclear Consults, 1984-; corp health physicist, Syncor Int Radiopharm, 1983-1984; health physicist/nuclear engr, West Valley Demonstration Proj, 1983; PRES & RADIATION SAFETY OFFICER, ALARA MGT CO, 1979-; asst health physicist, Nuclear Sci & Technol Ctr, State Univ NY, Buffalo, 1978-1982; res radioactive gases, Nuclear Sci & Technol Ctr, State Univ NY, Buffalo, 1972-1977. **Memberships:** Health Physics Soc; Am Asn Physicists in Med; Laser Inst Am; Soc Nuclear Med; Am Indust Hyg Asn. **Research Statement & Publications:** Nuclear medicine related research for new imaging compounds which may be used for imaging of diseases related to cancer. **Mailing Address:** Alara Mgt Co, Elm & Carlton St, Buffalo, NY 14263.

KOMORIYA, AKIRA, STRUCTURE-FUNCTION OF GROWTH FACTORS & THEIR RECEPTORS. **Personal Data:** m Beverly. **Education:** Duke Univ, PhD (phys chem), 1977. **Professional Experience:** CO-FOUNDER, ONCO IMMUNIN INC, 1994-; SR STAFF FEL, DIV CYTOKINE BIOL, FOOD & DRUG ADMIN, BETHESDA, MD, 1988-; prin investr, Biotechnol Res Ctr, Meloy Lab, Inc, 1984-1988. **Mailing Address:** Onco Immunin Inc, 207A Perry Pkwy Ste 6, Gaithersburg, MD 20877. **Fax:** 301-987-7882.

KOMORNICKI, ANDREW, THEORETICAL CHEMISTRY. **Personal Data:** b Louth, Eng, October 23, 1948; American citizen. **Education:** Univ Wis-Milwaukee, BS, 1970; State Univ NY Buffalo, PhD (theoret chem), 1974. **Professional Experience:** AMES RES CTR, NASA, MOFFETT FIELD, CALIF, as of 1994; mem, Bd Dir, Molecular Res Inst, Atherton, Calif, 1979-1982; DIR RES & PRES, POLYATOMICS RES INST, 1978-; Nat Res Coun assoc, Ames Res Ctr, NASA, Moffett Field, Calif, 1976-1978; res assoc, Univ Rochester, NY, 1974-1976; res assoc, Univ Tex, Austin, 1973-1974. **Memberships:** Am Chem Soc; Am Phys Soc; fel Nat Res Coun; fel Samuel B Silbert. **Research Statement & Publications:** Theoretical chemistry; molecular quantum mechanics; molecular spectroscopy, infrared and raman vibrational intensities; dynamics of chemical reactions; Published Over 40 articles. **Mailing Address:** Polyatomics Res Inst, 1101 San Antonio Rd Ste 420, Mtain View, CA 94043-1002.

KOMOROSKI, RICHARD ANDREW, ANALYTICAL CHEMISTRY, PSYCHIATRY. **Personal Data:** b St Louis, Mo, February 4, 1947; m 1979, Eva; c Elizabeth, Christopher & Laura. **Education:** St Louis Univ, BS, 1969; Ind Univ, PhD (phys chem), 1973. **Professional Experience:** Affil prof staff, Ark Children's Hosp, 1989-2000; PROF RADIO, PATH & PSYCHIAT & PROF BIOCHEM, UNIV ARK MED SCI, 1986-; sr res chemist, Diamond Shamrock Corp, 1976-1979; fel chem, Fla State Univ, 1973-1976. **Memberships:** Am Chem Soc; AAAS; Int Soc Magnetic Resonance Med; Soc Biol Psychiat. **Research Statement & Publications:** Nuclear magnetic resonance spectroscopy; nuclear magnetic resonance imaging; in vivo nuclear magnetic resonance spectroscopy; applications of nuclear magnetic resonance in psychiatry. **Mailing Address:** Dept Radiol, Univ Ark Med, slot 556 4301 W Markham, Little Rock, AR 72205-7199. **Fax:** 501-257-1811. **E-Mail:** komoroskiricharda@uams.edu

KOMOROWSKI, MARY ELLEN, MATHEMATICS. **Education:** W Va Univ, BS, MS, EdD. **Professional Experience:** PROF & CHAIR, DEPT MATH & COMPUT SCI, BETHANY COL, as of 2005. **Mailing Address:** Dept Math & Comput Sci, Bethany Col, 107 Richardson Hall, Bethany, WV 26032. **Fax:** 304-829-7742. **E-Mail:** mkomorowski@bethanywv.edu

KOMP, RICHARD JOSEPH, SOLAR ENERGY, ENERGY ENGINEERING. **Personal Data:** b Chicago, Ill, August 7, 1938; m 1983, Mirdza. **Education:** Loras Col, BS, 1960; Wayne State Univ, PhD (phys chem), 1964. **Professional Experience:** Vis prof Universidad National de Ingeniera Managua, Nicaragua, 1997-; adj prof physics & renewable energy, Col Atlantic, Bar Harbor, Maine, 1991, 1997-; pres, Maine Solar Energy Asn, 1989-1992, 1995-; PRES, SUNWATT CORP, 1988-; vpres res & develop, Sunwatt Corp, 1981-1988; NATO fel, Univ Louis Pasteur, Strasbourg, France, 1980; res assoc, Wayne State Univ, 1975-1981; Dir, Skyheat Asn, 1973-; vpres, Zip Serv, Educ Activ Inc, 1973-1975; assoc prof physics & astron, Western Ky Univ, 1968-1973; Sr scientist, Xerox Corp, Webster, NY, 1964-1968. **Memberships:** Int Solar Energy Soc; AAAS; Sigma Xi; Northeast Sustainable Energy Asn, board mem, Maine solar Energy asso, pres. **Research Statement & Publications:** Development of new photovoltaic cells and systems including hybrid systems that distill or heat while producing electricity; new thin film solar cells; Solar medical instrument sterilizer. **Mailing Address:** 17 Rockwell Rd SE, Jonesport, ME 04649. **E-Mail:** sunwatt@juno.com

KOMPALA, DHINAKAR S, BIOPROCESS ENGINEERING, RECOMBINANT MICROBIAL & MAMMALIAN CELL CULTURE. **Personal Data:** b Madras, India, November 20, 1958; American citizen; m 1983, Sushila; c Tejaswi D & Chytanya R. **Education:** Indian Inst Technol, Madras, BTech, 1979; Purdue Univ, MS, 1982, PhD (chem eng), 1984. **Professional Experience:** ASSOC PROF CHEM ENG, UNIV COLO, BOULDER, 1991-; vis assoc, Calif Inst Technol, 1991-1992; presidential young investr, NSF, 1988-1993; asst prof, UnivColo, Boulder, 1985-1991. **Memberships:** Am Inst Chem Engrs; Am Chem Soc; Am Soc Eng Educ; Soc Indust Microbiol; Int Soc Anal Cytometry. **Research Statement & Publications:** Development of optimal operating strategies and novel bioreactor designs for maximizing bioprocesses or heterologous protein expressions in recombinant microbial and mammalian cultures; metabolic modeling; recombinant DNA; biotechnology. **Mailing Address:** Dept Chem Eng, Univ Colo, Boulder, CO 80309-0424. **Fax:** 303-492-4341. **E-Mail:** dhinakar.kompala@colorado.edu

KOMUNIECKI, RICHARD, BIOLOGY. **Education:** Univ Mass, PhD, 1976. **Professional Experience:** DISTINGUISHED UNIV PROF, UNIV TOLEDO, as of 2004. **Mailing Address:** Dept Biol, Univ Toledo, 2801 W Bancroft St, Toledo, OH 43606-3390. **Fax:** 419-530-7737.

KOMZSIK, LOUIS, MATHEMATICS. **Honorary Degrees:** DSc, Tech Univ Budapest, Hungary. **Professional Experience:** CHIEF NUMERICAL ANALYST, MSC SOFTWARE CORP, as of 2004 ADJ MEM, FAC DEPT SCI & MATH, SANTA ANA COL, as of 1999. **Mailing Address:** 2975 Redhill Ave, Costa Mesa, CA 92626. **Fax:** 714-445-3533. **E-Mail:** louis.komzsik@mscsoftware.com

KON, MARK A, NEURAL NETWORKS, BIOINFORMATICS, MATHEMATICAL PHYSICS. **Education:** Cornell Univ, BA, 1974; Mass Inst Technol, PhD (math), 1979. **Professional Experience:** PROF MATH & STATISTICS, AFFILIATE, COGNITIVE AND NEURAL SCIENCES AND BIOINFORMATICS PROGRAMS, BOSTON UNIV, as of 2005; Fulbright fel, 1996-1997; Assoc Prof Math & Statistics, Boston Univ, beginning 1988; asst & assoc prof math & comput sci, Columbia Univ, 1985-1987 & 1989-1990. **Memberships:** Am Math Soc; Int Asn Math Physics; AAAS; Int Neural Network Soc; Math AsnAm; Am Statistical Society. **Research Statement & Publications:** Neural network theory, primarily in learning theory; bioinformatics, primarily in mathematical genomics; mathematical physics, primarily in quantum statistical mechanics; complexity of approximately solved problems; wavelet theory. **Mailing Address:** Dept Math, Boston Univ, 111Cummington St, Boston, MA 02215. **Fax:** 617-353-8100. **E-Mail:** mkon@bu.edu

KONARSKA, MARIA MAGDA, NUCLEIC ACID BIOCHEMISTRY, RNA PROCESSING & REPLICATION. **Personal Data:** b Bukowina, Tatrz, Poland, August 22, 1955. **Education:** Univ Warsaw, MSc, 1979; Polish Acad Sci, PhD (biochem), 1983. **Honors & Awards:** Jakub Karol Parnas Award, Polish Biochem Soc, 1985. **Professional Experience:** PROF & HEAD LAB, ROCKEFELLER UNIV, as of 2005; Prin investr, NIH, 1993-; career scientist award, Monique Weill-CaulierAward, 1992-; ASST PROF & HEAD LAB, ROCKEFELLER UNIV, 1989-; prin investr, Lucille P Markey Charitable Trust, 1987-; res assoc, Ctr Cancer Res, Mass Inst Technol, 1987-1989; fel, Ctr Cancer Res, Mass Inst Technol, 1984-1986; Fel, Jane Coffin Childs MemFund, 1983-1986; Inst Biochem, Univ Wuerzburg, 1981-1983; Res fel, Max-Planck InstBiochem, 1979. **Memberships:** Am Soc Microbiol; AAAS. **Research Statement & Publications:** Mechanism of MRNA splicing, assembly of snRNP particles into spliceosome complex; replication of RNA by DNA-dependent RNA polymerases, specifically replication of hepatitis delta virus by RNA polymerase II. **Mailing Address:** Rockefeller Univ, 1230 York Ave, 504 E 63rd St, New York, NY 10021. **Fax:** 212-327-7147. **E-Mail:** konarsk@mail.rockefeller.edu

KONAT, GREGORY W, GENE EXPRESSION, NEURAL DEGENERATION & REGENERATION. **Personal Data:** b March 6, 1947; Danish citizen. **Education:** Univ Warsaw, MSc, 1969; Univ Odense Med Sch, PhD (med sci/biochem), 1975. **Honors & Awards:** Gold Medal, Univ Odense Med Sch, 1976. **Professional Experience:** Adj prof neurosurg, Dept Pediat, Sch Med, Wva Univ, Morgantown, 1996-; adj prof molecular neurobiology, Dept Pediat, Sch Med, Wva Univ, Morgantown, 1990-; PROF MOLECULAR NEUROBIOLOGY, DEPT ANAT, SCH MED, WVA UNIV, MORGANTOWN, 1989-; assoc prof neurochem & molecular biol, dept neurol med, Univ SC, Charleston, 1987-1990; asst prof neurochem, dept neurol med, Univ SC, Charleston, 1984-1987; res scientist neurochem, Dept Neurobiology & Anat, Med Sch, Univ Tex, Houston, 1983-1984; res assoc profneurochem, Inst Med Physiol & Neuropath, Univ Copenhagen, 1981-1983; res scientist biochem-neurochem, Neurochem Inst, Copenhagen, 1971-1981; Res teaching asst biochem, Dept Neurochem, Med Res Ctr, Polish Acad Sci, Warsaw, 1969-1971. **Memberships:** Int Soc Neurochem; Int Soc Develop Neuroscience; Soc Complex Carbohydrates; AmSoc Neurochem; Am Soc Biochem & Molecular Biol; Fedn Europ Biochem Soc. **Research Statement & Publications:** Mechanisms of myelin gene expression; spinal cord degeneration and regeneration; chromatin structure and function. **Mailing Address:** Dept Anat Sch Med, WVa Univ, 4052 HSN PO Box 9128, Morgantown, WV 26506. **Fax:** 304-293-8159. **E-Mail:** gkonat@hsc.wvu.edu

KONDEPUDI, DILIP K, CHEMISTRY. **Education:** Madras Univ, BSc, 1971; Indian Inst Technol, Bombay, MSc, 1973; Univ Tex, Austin, PhD, 1979. **Professional Experience:** Reynolds Found Res Leave, 1993; res assoc, Ctr Studies Statist Mech, Univ Tex, Austin, 1980-1987; vis prof, Solvay Inst, Brussels, 1978, 1981, 1984, 1985. **Research Statement & Publications:** Ubiquitous asymmetry; asymmetry in spiral galaxies. **Mailing Address:** Dept Chem, Wake Forest Univ, Winston-Salem, NC 27109. **E-Mail:** dilip@wfu.edu

KONDO, EDWARD SHINICHI, FOREST PATHOLOGY. **Personal Data:** b Victoria, BC, September 5, 1939; m 1970, Jeanne; c Christine & Michelle. **Education:** Univ Toronto, BScF, 1964, MScF, 1966, PhD (plant path), 1970. **Professional Experience:** DIR GEN, FOREST PEST MGT INST, CAN FORESTRY SERV, 1990-; dir, Forest Insect & Dis Surv, 1983-1988 & Biorational Control Agents Prog, 1988-1990; Adj prof, Forestry Fac, Univ Toronto, 1972-1974; res scientist forest path, Can Forestry Serv, DeptEnviron, 1971-1982; Res officer, Can Forestry Serv, Dept Environ, 1969-1971. **Research Statement & Publications:** Vascular wilt tree diseases; Dutch elm disease; urban forestry; tree and fungus physiology, mycology, chemotherapy of tree diseases. **Mailing Address:** Can Forestry Serv Box 490, Sault Ste Marie, ON P6A 5M7, Can. **Fax:** 705-759-5714.

KONDO, NORMAN SHIGERU, ORGANIC CHEMISTRY. **Personal Data:** b Honolulu, Hawaii, October 30, 1941; m 1971, c 1. **Education:** Univ Hawaii, BA, 1963; Univ Calif, Riverside, PhD (chem), 1967. **Professional Experience:** PROF CHEM, UNIV DC, as of 2005; assoc prof chem, Univ DC, beginning 1977; NIH grant, fed city col, Univ DC, 1975-; asst prof chem, fed city col, 1973-1977; res assoc biophys, argonne nat lab, 1971-1973; NIH fel, 1969-1971; NIH fel, Johns Hopkins Univ, 1967-1969. **Memberships:** Am Chem Soc; Biophys Soc. **Research Statement & Publications:** Synthesis and conformational studies on nucleic acid constituents. **Mailing Address:** Dept Chem & Physics, Univ DC, 4200 Conn Ave NW Bldg 42 Rm 215, Washington, DC 20008. **Fax:** 202-274-7466. **E-Mail:** nkondo@udc.edu

KONDO, YOJI, ASTRONOMY, ASTROPHYSICS. **Personal Data:** b Hitachi, Japan, May 26, 1933; American citizen; m 1965, Ursula; c Beatrice, Cynthia & Angela. **Education:** Tokyo Univ Foreign Studies, BA, 1958; Univ Pa, MS, 1963, PhD (astron), 1965. **Honors & Awards:** Fed Design Achievement Award, 1988; Except Achievement Medal, NASA, 1990; Sci Award, Nat Space Club, 1995. **Professional Experience:** ASTROPHYSICIST, GODDARD SPACE FLIGHT CTR, NASA, as of 2004; PROF, CATH UNIV AM, 1996-; spec adv to adminr, 1995-2001; pres comt 44 astron from space, Int Astron Union, 1985-1988 & comt 42 close binary stars, 1991-1994; prof, George Mason Univ, 1989-; PROJ SCIENTIST, EXTREME ULTRAVIOLET EXPLORER, 1988-; vis prof, Inst Space & Astronaut Sci, Tokyo, 1983; proj scientist, Int Ultraviolet Explorer Satellite Observ, 1982-1997; consult, NASA Hq, 1981-1982; ed, Earth & Extraterrestrial Sci, 1974-1979 & Comments Astrophys, 1979-; adj prof, Univ Pa, beginning 1978; adj prof, Univ Houston, 1974-1977; from adj assoc prof to adj prof, Univ Okla, 1971-1977; chief, Astrophys Lab, Johnson Space Ctr, 1968-1977; Mem adj grad fac, Univ Houston, 1968-1977; Nat Acad Sci res assoc, Astron & Space Lab, Goddard Space Flight Ctr, NASA, 1965-1968. **Memberships:** AAAS; Am Astron Soc; Int Astron Union; Int Astron Union Div V (pres, 1994-1997). **Research Statement & Publications:** Astronomical observations from space; interacting close binary stars; interstellar medium; active galactic nuclei. **Mailing Address:** Lab Astron & Solar Physics Code 680, Goddard Space Flight Ctr, Greenbelt, MD 20771. **Fax:** 301-286-1753. **E-Mail:** kondo@iue.gsfc.nasa.gov

KONDRA, PETER ALEXANDER, POULTRY GENETICS. **Personal Data:** b Mikado, Sask, July 30, 1911; m 1939, c 3. **Education:** Univ Man, BSA, 1934, MSc, 1943; Univ Minn, PhD (poultry genetics), 1953. **Professional Experience:** PROF EMER ANIMAL SCI, UNIV MAN, 1980-; exchange scientist, Acad Sci, USSR, 1964, adv, Thailand 1968-1969, Brazil, 1974 & Costa Rica, 1978; Mem poultry breeding comt, Can Dept Agr, 1953-; from asst prof to prof, Univ Man, 1946-1978; asst poultry specialist, ManDept Agr, 1945-1946; mgr hatchery, Univ Man, 1944-1945; asst poultry, Univ Man, 1940-1943; Poultry inspector, Man Dept Agr, 1936-1940. **Memberships:** Poultry Sci Asn; World Poultry Sci Asn; Genetics Soc Can; Agr Inst Can. **Research Statement & Publications:** Poultry breeding biology; incubation; housing. **Mailing Address:** Univ Man, Winnipeg, MB R3T 2N2, Can.

KONDRASKE, GEORGE V, INSTRUMENTATION. **Education:** Univ Tex, BS, 1978, MS, 1980; Univ Rochester, PhD, 1982. **Professional Experience:** PROF ELEC & BIOMED ENG, UNIV TEX ARLINGTON, as of 2006. **Mailing Address:** Univ Tex Arlington, S Cooper St, Arlington, TX 76019. **Fax:** 817-272-2253. **E-Mail:** gvk@hpi.uta.edu

KONECKY, MILTON STUART, PETROCHEMISTRY, RESEARCH CONSULTATION. **Personal Data:** b Omaha, Nebr, July 29, 1922; m 1948, Naomi M Schipporeit; c Mark & Chad. **Education:** Creighton Univ, BS, 1944, MS, 1948; Univ Ill, PhD (chem), 1958. **Professional Experience:** PRES, KONECKY ASSOCS ENTERPRISES, BRIDGEWATER, NJ, 1991-; sr res assoc, Exxon Res & Eng Co, 1988-1991; sr staff adv, Exxon Res & Eng Co, 1969-1987; sect head, Exxon Res & Eng Co, 1963-1969; res assoc, Exxon Res & Eng Co, 1961-1963; sr chemist, Exxon Res & Eng Co, 1957-1960; chemist pesticide chem res br, Entom Res Div, USDA, Md, 1950-1954; Chemist, Omaha Grain Exchange Labs, Nebr, 1947-1950. **Memberships:** fel AAAS; emer mem Sigma Xi; emer mem Am Chem Soc; fel NY Acad Sci. **Research Statement & Publications:** Agricultural chemicals; petrochemicals; biodegradation methods for and synthesis of detergents; industrial, trade sales and specialty resins for surface coatings; heterogeneous catalysis; information research and analysis; consulting industrial research. **Mailing Address:** Konecky Assocs Enterprises, 41 Jefferson Ct, Bridgewater, NJ 08807-3050.

KONECNY, VACLAV, MATHEMATICS. **Honors & Awards:** Problemist Year, Crux Mathemicorum, 1997. **Professional Experience:** PROF EMER, MATH DEPT, FERRIS STATE UNIV, 2001-. **Mailing Address:** Math Dept, Ferris State Univ, Big Rapids, MI 49307. **Fax:** 517-482-1241.

KONEN, HARRY P, NUMERICAL ANALYSIS. **Personal Data:** b Dayton, Ky, September 18, 1940; m 1971, Ann; c 2. **Education:** St Thomas Univ, BA, 1962; Tex A&M Univ, MS, 1965, PhD (math), 1967. **Professional Experience:** PROF MATH, SAM HOUSTON STATE UNIV, 1983-; from asst prof to assoc prof, Sam Houston State Univ, 1969-1983; instr math, San Jacinto Col, 1966-1969. **Research Statement & Publications:** Fifth-order Runge-Kutta methods for the numerical solution of differential equations. **Mailing Address:** Dept Math & Statist, Sam Houston State Univ, Lee Drain Bldg 417C, Huntsville, TX 77341-2206. **Fax:** 936-294-1882. **E-Mail:** konen@shsu.edu

KONES, RICHARD, CARDIOLOGY. **Professional Experience:** AT MED DIAG CTR, PHILADELPHIA, as of 1998. **Mailing Address:** Second Floor, 1525 Locust St, Philadelphia, PA 19102.

KONG, ERIC SIU-WAI, MATERIALS SCIENCE, POLYMER PHYSICS. **Personal Data:** b Hong Kong, January 14, 1953; American citizen. **Education:** Univ Calif, Berkeley, BA, 1974; Rensselaer Polytech Inst, MSc, 1976, PhD (polymerchem), 1978. **Professional Experience:** ADJ ASSOC PROF CHEM, NAT UNIV SINGAPORE, as of 2005; consult, Elec Power Res Inst, Palo Alto, beginning 1991; sr res chemist, Becton Dickinson, 1991-1992; fac med chem, Univ Calif, SanFrancisco, 1989-1990; biomat tech adv, Mentor Corp, 1987-1989; sr res specialist, Swedlow Inc, 1986-1987; mem tech staff, Hewlett Packard Labs, 1984-1986; mem tech staff, Sandia Nat Labs, 1983-1984; chmn, San Francisco Chap, Soc Plastics Engrs, 1983-1984; res scientist, Ames Res Ctr, NASA, 1979-1983; res assoc, Va Polytech Inst, 1978-1979. **Memberships:** Fel Am Inst Chemists; fel NY Acad Sci; Am Chem Soc; Am Phys Soc; SocPolymer Sci Japan; Soc Biomat. **Research Statement & Publications:** Polymer chemistry research and development where there is a close tie between basic science and applied engineering. **Mailing Address:** Dept Chem, Nat Univ Singapore, 3 Sci Dr 3, 117543, Singapore. **Fax:** 65-6779-1691. **E-Mail:** eswkong@sjtu.edu.cn

KONG, JIN AU, ELECTRICAL ENGINEERING. **Personal Data:** b Kiangsu, China, December 27, 1942; American citizen; m 1970, c 2. **Education:** Nat Taiwan Univ, BS, 1962; Chiao Tung Univ, MS, 1965; Syracuse Univ, PhD (elec eng), 1968. **Honors & Awards:** S T Li Prize yr 2000; Distinguished Achievement Award, Inst Elec & Electronics Engrs Geosci & Remote Sensing Soc yr 2000; Inst Elec & Electronics Engrs, Electromagnetics Award yr 2004. **Professional Experience:** PRES, ELECTROMAGNETICS ACAD as of 2005; PROF ELEC ENG, MASS INST TECHNOL, 1980-; Raytheon Co, Lincoln Lab & Hughes Aircraft Co, 1980; consult remote sensing technol, Off Tech Coop, UN, 1977-1979; from asst prof to assoc prof, Mass Inst Technol, 1969-1980; Vinton Hayes fel eng, Mass Inst Technol, 1969-1971; res engr elec eng, Syracuse Univ, 1968-1969. **Memberships:** Inst Elec & Electronics Engrs; Am Phys Soc; Optical Soc Am; Am Geophys Union; Am Soc Eng Educ; Int Union Radio Sci; Sigma Xi. **Research Statement & Publications:** Electromagnetic Wave Theory; author of 35 books 250 refereed journal articles and 350 conference papers. **Mailing Address:** Dept Elec Eng, Mass Inst Technol, Rm 26-305 77 Mass Ave, Cambridge, MA 02139. **Fax:** 617-258-9344. **E-Mail:** email kong@emwave.org

KONG, SIOW-KEE, BIOCHEMISTRY, PHYSIOLOGY. **Personal Data:** b Singapore, February 8, 1953; Canadian citizen; m 1982, Peng-Suat; c Hai-Yin & Hai-Li. **Education:** Nanyang Univ, BSc, 1977; Univ Man, MSc, 1981, PhD (physiol), 1985. **Professional Experience:** VIS ASSOC & SCIENTIST, NIH, 1990-; res assoc med physiol & cell biol, Univ Man, 1988-1990; postdoctoral fel, Med Res Coun Can, 1986-1988; postdoctoral fel, UnivCalgary, 1985-1987; postdoctoral fel, Alta Heritage Found Med Res, 1985-1986. **Memberships:** Am Soc Biochem & Molecular Biol; NY Acad Sci. **Research Statement & Publications:** Protein phosphorylation and cell regulation; smooth muscle physiology and biochemistry. **Mailing Address:** NIH, Bldg 3 Rm 203, Bethesda, MD 20892-0001. **Fax:** 301-496-0599.

KONG, YI-CHI MEI, IMMUNOLOGY, MICROBIOLOGY. **Personal Data:** b Boston, Mass, February 2, 1934; c 2. **Education:** Wellesley Col, BA, 1955; Univ Mich, MS, 1957, PhD (microbiol), 1961. **Professional Experience:** PROF IMMUNOL & MICROBIOL, SCH MED, WAYNE STATE UNIV, as of 2005; bd govs distinguished fac fel, Clare Hall, 1990-1992; life mem, Clare Hall, 1990; vis fel, Cambridge Univ, Eng, 1988; Fogarty Int Sr Fel, NIH, 1988; ed, Clin Immunol &Immunopath, 1987-1998; found lectr, Am Soc Microbiol, 1987; mem immunol sci study sect, NIH, 1974-1977 & bacteriol mycol study sect, 1981-1984; ed, Infection & Immunity, 1978-1983; from asst profto assoc prof, Sch Med, Wayne State Univ, 1966-1977; asst res bacteriologist, Naval Biol Lab, Univ Calif, Berkeley, 1961-1966; res assoc, Univ Mich, 1960-1961. **Memberships:** AAAS; Transplantation Am Soc Microbiol; Am Asn Immunologists; Am ThyroidAsn. **Research Statement & Publications:** Mechanisms of immunologic tolerance; transplantation antigens and immunity; immunogenetic and cellular control of autoimmunity; effect of adjuvants. **Mailing Address:** Dept Immunol & Microbiol, Wayne State Univ Sch Med, 540 E Canfield Ave, Detroit, MI 48201-1908. **E-Mail:** ykong@med.wayne.edu

KONGSAMUT, SATHAPANA, REGULATION INTRACELLULAR CALCIUM, NEUROTRANSMITTER & RECEPTOR FUNCTION. **Personal Data:** b Saigon, Vietnam, July 6, 1956; Thai citizen; m 1985, Siribhan Singhaviroj; c Narissa & Tira W. **Education:** Univ Ottawa, BSc, 1979; Univ Ill, Chicago, MS, 1982; Univ Chicago, PhD (neuropharmacol), 1986. **Professional Experience:** HEAD, CNS DIS GROUP, AVENTIS PHARMACEUT, as of 2003; adj asst prof physiol, Univ Med & Dent NJ, 1993-; RES ASSOC, HOECHST-ROUSSEL PHARMACEUT, 1993-; assoc ed, Thai Jour Physiol Sci, 1991-; sr resbiochemist, Hoechst-roussel Pharmaceut, 1991-1993; assoc, Yale Univ, 1987-1991; Fel, Cornell Univ, 1986-1987. **Memberships:** AAAS; NY Acad Sci; Soc Neurosci. **Research Statement & Publications:** Regulation in neutrons by various mechanisms and its effects on neurotransmitter release; neurotransmitter receptors that can contribute to the treatment of schizophrenia. **Mailing Address:** Aventis Pharmaceut, Inc, 300 Somerset Corp Blvd, Bridgewater, NJ 08807. **E-Mail:** kongsam1@hrpi6.enet.hcc.com

KONHEIM, ALAN G, MATHEMATICS. **Personal Data:** b Brooklyn, NY, October 17, 1934; m 1957, c 2. **Education:** Polytech Inst Brooklyn, BEE, 1955, MS, 1957; Cornell Univ, PhD (math), 1960. **Professional Experience:** PROF COMPUT SCI, UNIV CALIF, SANTA BARBARA, 1982-; res staff mem, IBM Res Lab, Switz, 1970-1971; Res staff mem math, Thomas J Watson Res Lab, IBM Corp, 1960-1982. **Memberships:** Am Math Soc; Math Asn Am; Soc Indust & Appl Math; Asn Comput Mach. **Research Statement & Publications:** Probability theory; harmonic analysis. **Mailing Address:** 3735 Essex Dr, Santa Barbara, CA 93105. **E-Mail:** konheim@cs.ucsb.edu

KONIECZNY, STEPHEN FRANCIS, GENE EXPRESSION, DIFFERENTIATION. **Education:** Brown Univ, PhD (biol), 1982. **Professional Experience:** PROF BIOL, PURDUE UNIV, 1984-. **Mailing Address:** Dept Biol Sci, Purdue Univ, West Lafayette, IN 47907-1392. **E-Mail:** sfk@bilbo.bio.purdue.edu

KONIG, RONALD H, STRUCTURAL GEOLOGY, ECONOMIC GEOLOGY. **Personal Data:** b Albany, NY, August 12, 1932; m 1976, Janet; c Elizabeth & Mary. **Education:** St Lawrence Univ, BS, 1954; Cornell Univ, MS, 1956, PhD (geol), 1959. **Professional Experience:** PROF GEOL, UNIV ARK, FAYETTEVILLE, 1971-; chmn Dept Geol, 1971-1980; from asst prof to assoc prof, Univ Ark, Fayetteville, 1959-1971. **Memberships:** Geol Soc Am; Soc Econ Geol. **Research Statement & Publications:** Areal geologic mapping; geologic investigation of mineral deposits. **Mailing Address:** Dept Geol, Univ Ark, Fayetteville, AR 72701. **Fax:** 501-575-3846.

KONIGES, ALICE E, MATHEMATICS. **Education:** Princeton Univ, PhD (Appl & Numerical Math). **Professional Experience:** SR SCIENTIST, CTR ACCELERATED STRATEGIC COMPUT, LAWRENCE LIVERMORE NAT LAB, as of 2005. **Mailing Address:** Lawrence Livermore Nat Lab, L 561 PO Box 808, Livermore, CA 94551-0808. **Fax:** 925-423-2993. **E-Mail:** koniges1@llnl.gov

KONIGSBERG, ALVIN STUART, ATMOSPHERIC SCIENCE, BIOMETEOROLOGY. **Personal Data:** b New York, NY, April 28, 1943; m 1994, Kathleen McCue; c Laura & Amy. **Education:** City Col New York, BS, 1963; Syracuse Univ, MS, 1965, PhD (physics), 1969. **Professional Experience:** ASSOC PROF GEOL SCI, STATE UNIV NY COL NEW PALTZ, 1982-; dir innovative studies, State Univ NY Col, New Paltz, 1979-1982; chmn dept, State Univ NY Col, New Paltz, 1977-1979; Aeronaut & Space res fel, NASA & Am Asn Eng Educ, 1973, 1974; from asst prof to assoc prof physics, State Univ NY Col, New Paltz, 1968-1977; Res assoc physics, Atmospheric Sci Res Ctr, State Univ NY, Albany, 1965; teaching asst, Syracuse Univ, 1963-1968; NY State Col teaching fel. **Memberships:** AAAS; Am Water Resources Asn; Sigma Xi; Am Meteorol Soc. **Research Statement & Publications:** Oxidant pollution; condensation nuclei studies; light scattering instrumentation; alternate energy systems; environ impact assesment. **Mailing Address:** Dept Geol Sci, State Univ NY Col, New Paltz, NY 12561. **Fax:** 845-257-3755. **E-Mail:** konigsba@newpaltz.edu

KONIGSBERG, WILLIAM HENRY, BIOCHEMISTRY. **Personal Data:** b New York, NY, April 5, 1930; m 1956, c 1. **Education:** Rensselaer Polytech Inst, BSc, 1952; Columbia Univ, PhD (chem), 1956. **Professional Experience:** PROF MOLECULAR BIOPHYS & BIOCHEM & HUMAN GENETICS, YALE UNIV, as of 2006; assoc prof molecular biophys & biochem & human genetics, Yale Univ, 1974-1977; assoc prof biochem, Yale Univ, 1964-1974; asst prof biochem, Rockefeller Inst, 1958-1964. **Research Statement & Publications:** Protein chemistry; structure of hemoglobin; structure and function of proteins, peptides and natural products; antibodies; virus proteins; mechanism of T4 DNA replication. **Mailing Address:** Dept Biochem & Molecular Biophys C-113 Sterling Hall, Yale Univ Sch Med 333 Cedar St, New Haven, CT 06510-3219.

KONIJN, HENDRIK SALOMON, ECONOMICS. **Personal Data:** b Amsterdam, Neth, March 17, 1918; American citizen. **Education:** Columbia Univ, MA, 1942; Univ Calif, PhD (statist), 1954. **Professional Experience:** Vis prof statist, Univ Minn, 1962-1963 & Univ BC, 1988; PROF STATIST, TEL-AVIV UNIV, 1965-; prof, City Col New York, 1963-1965; Vis assoc prof, Cowles Found, Yale Univ, 1961-1962; sr lectr econ statist, Sydney, 1956-1961; lectr agr econ, Univ Calif, Berkeley, 1954-1956; statist consult econ res, Univ Calif, 1953-1954; Off Far Eastern Affairs, US Dept State, 1945-1947; res analyst, Off Strategic Servs, 1945; statistician, CombinedShipping Adj Bd, DC, 1942-1945; Jr staff mem, Nat Bur Econ Res, NY, 1941-1942. **Memberships:** Fel AAAS; fel Am Statist Asn; Am Econ Asn; Inst Math Statist; Royal Statist Soc. **Research Statement & Publications:** Statistical methodology; econometric studies. **Mailing Address:** Rehov Hahaganall Apt 12, Jerusalem 97851, Israel.

KONIKOW, LEONARD FRANKLIN, HYDROLOGY & GEOLOGY, GROUND-WATER MODELING. **Personal Data:** b Far Rockaway, NY, January 26, 1946; m 1966, c 2. **Education:** Hofstra Univ, BA, 1966; Pa State Univ, MS, 1969, PhD (geol), 1973. **Honors & Awards:** Sci Award, Nat Groundwater Asn, 1989. **Professional Experience:** Ed bd, Ground Water, 1993-1995; chmn, Hydrogeol Div, Geol Soc Am, 1993-1994; lectr, Univ Va, 1991-1992; Nat Resh Couns Comt, Groundwater Modeling Assessment, 1987-1989; chmn, hydrol prog, Am Geophys Union, 1984-1987; assoc ed, Water Resource Res, 1981-1984; HYDROLOGIST, US GEOL SURV, 1972-; instr geol, Hofstra Univ, 1966; geologist, Geraghty& Miller Inc, 1966. **Memberships:** Fel Geol Soc Am; Am Geophys Union; Int Asn Hydrogeol; Nat Groundwater Asn. **Research Statement & Publications:** Transport and dispersion of solutes in flowing ground water. **Mailing Address:** US Geol Surv, 12201 Sunrise Valley Dr MS 431, Reston, VA 20192. **Fax:** 703-648-5832. **E-Mail:** lkonikow@usgs.gov

KONING, ROSS E, PLANT GROWTH REGULATION, FLOWER PHYSIOLOGY. **Personal Data:** b Adrian, Mich, October 5, 1953; m 1981, Christine; c Hans, Katje & Kurt. **Education:** Univ Mich, BS, 1975, MS, 1976, PhD (bot), 1981. **Professional Experience:** PROF BOT, EASTERN CONN STATE UNIV, 1994-; from asst prof to assoc prof, Eastern Conn State Univ, 1987-1993; spec ed, Am Jour Bot, 1983-1986; asst prof bot, Rutgers Univ, 1981-1987. **Memberships:** Bot Soc Am; Am Soc Plant Biologist; Nat Asn Biol, Toadha. **Research Statement & Publications:** Developmental physiology of flowering, particularly growth of flower parts and hormonal and environmental cues involved in the timing mechanisms; author of various articles. **Mailing Address:** Dept Biol, Eastern Conn State Univ, Windham, Willimantic, CT 06226-2211. **Fax:** 860-465-5213. **E-Mail:** koning@easternct.edu

KONINGSTEIN, JOHANNES A, CHEMISTRY, CHEMICAL PHYSICS. **Personal Data:** b Velsen, Neth, November 30, 1933; Canadian citizen; m 1959, c 2. **Honorary Degrees:** Dr, Univ Amsterdam, 1959. **Professional Experience:** PROF EMER, CARLETON UNIV, as of 2001; Isac Walton Killam res fel, 1985-1987; vis prof, Nat Res CounCan, beginning 1969; from asst prof to prof chem, Carleton Univ, 1965-1995; mem res staff, Bell Tel Labs, 1962-1965; fel, Nat Res Coun Can, 1959-1961. **Memberships:** Am Physics Soc; Chem Inst Can. **Research Statement & Publications:** Molecular and atomic research; electronic Raman spectroscopy. **Mailing Address:** Dept Chem, Col Natural Sci, Carleton Univ, 2240 Herzberg Labs 1125 Colonel Dr, Ottawa, ON K1S 5B6, Can.

KONISHI, FRANK, NUTRITION. **Personal Data:** b Ft Lupton, Colo, December 2, 1928; m 1950, Gladys; c Gayle, Greg & Laura. **Education:** Colo State Univ, BS, 1950, MS, 1952; Cornell Univ, PhD (animal nutrit), 1958. **Professional Experience:** RETIRED; adj prof, Univ Colo, Boulder, beginning 1984; prof sch med, Southern IllUniv, Carbondale, 1974-1983; prof nutrit, Southern Ill Univ, Carbondale, 1966-1983; chmn dept, Southern Ill Univ, Carbondale, 1965-1977; assoc prof nutrit, Southern Ill Univ, Carbondale, 1961-1965; radiobiologist, US Naval Radiol Defense Lab, 1958-1961; asst, ColoState Univ, 1950-1952 & Cornell Univ, 1952-1954, 1957-1958. **Memberships:** Am Inst Nutrit; Am Dietetic Asn; NY Acad Sci; Sigma Xi. **Research Statement & Publications:** Nutritional dietary surveys; obesity; energy metabolism. **Mailing Address:** Univ Colo, 2736 Winding Trail Pl, Boulder, CO 80304-1412.

KONISHI, MASAKAZU, NEUROBIOLOGY. **Personal Data:** b Kyoto, Japan, February 17, 1933. **Education:** Hokkaido Univ, BS, 1956, MS, 1958; Univ Calif, Berkeley, PhD (zoology), 1963. **Honors & Awards:** Newcomb Cleveland Prize, AAAS, 1978; Elliot Couse Award, Am OrnitholUnion, 1983; F O Schmitt Prize, 1987; Int Prize, Biol, Japanese Asn Prom Sci, 1990. **Professional Experience:** BING PROF BEHAV BIOL, CALIF INST TECHNOL, 1980-; prof, Calif Inst Technol, 1975-1980; from asst prof to assoc prof biol, Princeton Univ, 1970-1975; asst prof zool, Univ Wis, 1965-1966; Int Brain Res Orgn-UNESCO fel, 1964-1965; Alexander von Humboldt Found fel, 1963-1964. **Memberships:** Nat Acad Sci; AAAS; Am Soc Zoologistss; Am Soc Naturalists; Acoust Soc Am; Soc Neuroscience; Am Acad Arts & Sci; Int Soc Neuroethology (pres, 1987-1989). **Research Statement & Publications:** Behavior and neurobiology. **Mailing Address:** Div Biol, Calif Inst Technol, 1200 E Calif Blvd, Pasadena, CA 91125. **Fax:** 626-449-0756. **E-Mail:** konishim@caltech.edu

KONISHI, YASUO, MEDICINAL CHEMISTRY & PROTEIN SCIENCE, PEPTIDE CHEMISTRY. **Personal Data:** m 1976, Mamiko; c Akira, Misato & Kyoko. **Education:** Shizuoka Univ, BSc, 1971; Tohoku Univ, MSc, 1973, PhD (chem), 1976. **Professional Experience:** Adj prof, McGill Univ, 1993-; SR RES OFFICER, NAT RES COUN CAN, 1989-; res specialist, Monsanto Co, 1984-1989; res assoc, Cornell Univ, 1981-1984; shorei-kenkyu-in, Kyoto Univ, 1980-1981; Postdoctoral assoc, Cornell Univ, 1976-1980. **Memberships:** Am Chem Soc; Am Peptide Soc; Protein Soc; Biophys Soc; Am Soc Mass Spectrometry. **Research Statement & Publications:** Drug development through drug repositioning and evolution strategy; drug development for diabetic retinopathy; characterization of natural products by mass spectrometry. **Mailing Address:** Biotechnol Res Inst, 6100 Royalmount Ave, Montreal, PQ H4P 2R2, Can. **Fax:** 514-496-5143. **E-Mail:** yasuo.konishi@nrc.ca

KONISKY, JORDAN, MICROBIAL PHYSIOLOGY. **Personal Data:** b Providence, RI, April 8, 1941; m 1967, c 2. **Education:** Providence Col, BA, 1963; Univ Wis, Madison, PhD (genetics), 1968. **Honors & Awards:** Career develop award, NIH, 1975. **Professional Experience:** VICE PROVOST RES & GRAD STUDIES, RICE UNIV, 1996-; PROF BIOCHEM & CELL BIOL, RICE UNIV, 1996-; dir, Sch life Sci, 1989-; head, Dept Microbiol, 1984-1989; prof microbiol, Univ Ill, Urbana, beginning 1981; from asst prof to assoc prof, Sch Life Sci, 1970-1981; NIH fel molecular biophys & biochem, Yale Univ, 1968-1970; res assoc genetics, Univ Wis, Madison, 1968. **Memberships:** Am Soc Microbiol; AAAS; fel AAAS; fel Am Acad Microbiol. **Research Statement & Publications:** regulation of gene expression in bacteria; functions of bacterial membrane; physiology and molecular biology of methanogenic bacteria. **Mailing Address:** Dept Biochem & Cell Biol, Rice Univ, 6100 Main St MS-140 314 Lovett Hall, Houston, TX 77251. **Fax:** 713-737-5759. **E-Mail:** konisky@rice.edu

KONIUK, ROMAN G, THEORCTICAL PHYSICS. **Education:** Univ Toronto, BSc, 1976, MSc, 1977; Univ Toronto/Oxford, PhD (theoretical physics), 1980. **Professional Experience:** PROF, DEPT PHYSICS & ASTRON, YORK UNIV, as of 2003. **Mailing Address:** Dept Physics, York Univ, 4700 Keele St N York, Toronto, ON M3J 1P3, Can. **E-Mail:** koniuk@yorku.ca

KONIZER, GEORGE BURR, PHYSICAL ORGANIC CHEMISTRY, SYNTHETIC FIBERS. **Personal Data:** b Wilmington, Del, December 24, 1942; m 1998, Deborah; c Christopher G & Eric D. **Education:** Univ Del, BA, 1964, MBA, 1976; Univ SC, PhD (chem), 1968. **Professional Experience:** RETIRED; strategic planning, Lycra, 1994-1996; tech group mgr, Lycra, 1983-1994; supvr res & develop nylon, Textile Res Lab, 1981-1983; supvr res & develop orlon, Textile Res Lab, 1978-1981; sr res chemist, Textile Res Lab, 1975-1978; Res chemist, Dacron Res Lab, E I Du Pont de Nemours & Co Inc, 1969-1971 & Textile Res Lab, 1971-1975; Fel, State Univ NY Col Forestry, Syracuse Univ, 1968-1969. **Research Statement & Publications:** Fiber research. **Mailing Address:** 1965 Frontier Crag Rd, Prescott, AZ 86305-2102. **E-Mail:** konizerg@commspeed.com

KONKEL, DAVID ANTHONY, MOLECULAR GENETICS, CELL BIOLOGY. **Personal Data:** b Washington, DC, February 20, 1948; m 1970. **Education:** Boston Col, BS, 1970; Mass Inst Technol, PhD (biochem), 1977. **Professional Experience:** ASSOC PROF, HUMAN BIOL CHEM & GENETICS, MED BR, UNIV TEX, GALVESTON, 1995-; NIH, 1982-1985; asst prof, cell biol, dept human genetics & cell biol, Univ Tex Med Br, Galveston, 1980-1995; prin investr grants, NSF, 1980-1983; staff fel, Lab Molecular Genetics, Nat Inst Child & Human Develop, 1977-1980; asst biochem, Dept Biol, Mass Inst Technol, 1970-1977. **Memberships:** AAAS; Sigma Xi; Am Soc Cell Biol; Tex Heart Asn. **Research Statement & Publications:** Recombinant DNA technology to study the structure and regulation of genes encoding mouse and chicken myoglobin; characterization of a new gene family related to ras oncogenes; Published over 10 articles. **Mailing Address:** Dept Human Biol Chem & Genetics Med Br Univ Tex, Rm 111B Rte 0643 301 Univ Blvd, Galveston, TX 77550-0643. **Fax:** 409-772-5102. **E-Mail:** dkonkel@utmb.edu

KONKOWSKI, DEBORAH ANN, GENERAL RELATIVITY THEORY, NATURE OF SINGULARITIES. **Personal Data:** b Akron, Ohio, March 3, 1955. **Education:** Harvey Mudd Col, BS, 1977; Univ Tex, Austin, PhD (physics), 1983. **Professional Experience:** Prin investr, NSF, 1989-; PROF MATH, US NAVAL ACAD, 1987-; Queen Mary Col, Univ London, 1985-1987; res fel, Univ Md, Col Park, 1983-1985. **Memberships:** Am Phys Soc; Soc Gen Relativity & Gravitation; Am Math Soc; Math Asn Am; AAAS. **Research Statement & Publications:** Mathematical physics and theoretical physics; general theory of relativity; nature and stability of space time singularities; mild quasiregular and non-scalar curvature singularities and cauchy horizons. **Mailing Address:** US Naval Acad, 514 Andrew Hill Ct, Arnold, MD 21012. **E-Mail:** dak@usna.edu

KONNERTH, KARL LOUIS, MEDICAL ELECTRONICS, BIO-MEDICAL ENGINEERING. **Personal Data:** b Mt Pleasant, Pa, August 15, 1932. **Education:** Carnegie Inst Technol, BS, 1954, MS, 1955, PhD (elec eng), 1961. **Honors & Awards:** Outstanding Innovation Award, IBM Corp, 1976. **Professional Experience:** DIR, TECH ARCHIT INCYTE GENOMICS INC, as of 2000; MGR ADVAN TECHNOL, IBM BIOMED SYSTS, IBM CORP, 1977-; mgr, I/O Systs, IBM Res Div, 1974-1977; staff res engr, Thomas J Watson Res Ctr, 1964-1974; asst prof elec eng, Carnegie Inst Technol, 1961-1964. **Memberships:** Sr mem Inst Elec & Electronics Engrs; Asn Advan Med Instrumentation. **Research Statement & Publications:** Investigation of new types of bio-medical instrumentation. **Mailing Address:** Incyte Genomics, Inc, 3160 Porter Dr, Palo Alto, CA 94304. **E-Mail:** konnerth@incyte.com

KONNO, ICHISHIRO, ASTRONOMY. **Education:** Miyagi Univ, Japan, BA; Bowling Green State Univ, MS; Ariz State Univ, PhD. **Professional Experience:** SR LECTR, DEPT PHYSICS & ASTRON, UNIV TEX, SAN ANTONIO, as of 2005. **Mailing Address:** Dept Phyics & Astron, Univ Tex, San Antonio, TX 78284. **E-Mail:** ikonno@utsa.edu

KONON, WALTER, CIVIL ENGINEERING. **Education:** City Col New York, BS, MS, 1970. **Professional Experience:** ACTG CHAIR & PROF, DEPT CIVIL & ENVIRON ENG, NJ INST TECHNOL, NJ, as of 2006. **Mailing Address:** Dept Civil & Environ Eng, NJ Inst Technol, 245 Colton Hall, Newark, NJ 07102-1982. **Fax:** 973-596-5790. **E-Mail:** konon@adm.njit.edu

KONOPINSKI, VIRGIL J, SAFETY, INDUSTRIAL HYGIENE. **Personal Data:** b Toledo, Ohio, July 11, 1935; m 1964, Joan M Wielinski; c Ann M, Carol S & Peter J. **Education:** Univ Toledo, BS, 1956; Pratt Inst, MS, 1960; Bowling Green State Univ, MBA, 1971. **Professional Experience:** HUMAN RESOURCE ANALYST-SAFETY, US POSTAL SERV, CHICAGO, 1993-; regional safety engr, US Postal Serv, Chicago, 1991-1993; sr consult, Occusafe, Wheeling, 1990-1991; consult pvt pract, Zionsville, 1989-1990; exec vpres, Asbestos Technol, Indianapolis, 1987-1989; Consult pvt pract, 1975-; dir IH & RH, Ind State Bd Health, Indianapolis, 1975-1987; staff specialist, Williams Brothers Waste Control, Tulsa, 1973-1975; chief exec officer, Midwest Environ Mgt, 1972-1973; Asst to dir environ control, Owens Corning Fiberglass, Toledo, 1967-1972. **Memberships:** Am Soc Safety Engrs; Am Indust Hyg Asn. **Research Statement & Publications:** Occupational health and safety; formaldehyde; carbon monoxide; carbon dioxide; pesticides; indoor air; mercury; sampling strategies and techniques; long range planning and forecasting; lead; herbicides. **Mailing Address:** 14 Fairfield Lane, Cary, IL 60013-1946.

KONOPKA, ALLAN EUGENE, MICROBIOLOGY. **Personal Data:** b Chicago, Ill, February 26, 1950; m 1973, c 3. **Education:** Univ Ill, Urbana, BS, 1971; Univ Wash, MS, 1973, PhD (microbiol), 1975. **Professional Experience:** Erskine vis Prof, Univ Canterbury, Christchurch, NZ, 2005; ACTG DEPT HEAD BIOL, PURDUE UNIV, as of 2004; chmn, microbiol ecol div, Am Soc Microbiol, 1994; PROF BIOL, PURDUE UNIV, 1992-; fogarty fel, 1992; fulbright fel, 1984; from asst prof to assoc prof, Purdue Univ, 1977-1983; res assoc microbiol, Univ Wis-Madison, 1975-1977. **Memberships:** Am Soc Microbiol; Sigma Xi. **Research Statement & Publications:** Microbial ecology; microbiological growth kinetics; microbiological biodegradation. **Mailing Address:** Dept Biol Sci, Purdue Univ, Col Sci, LILY B-228 915 W State St, West Lafayette, IN 47907. **Fax:** 765-494-0876. **E-Mail:** akonopka@bilbo.bio.purdue.edu

KONOPKA, RONALD J, NEUROGENETICS. **Personal Data:** b Cleveland, Ohio, October 19, 1947. **Education:** Univ Dayton, BS, 1967; Calif Inst Technol, PhD (biochem), 1972. **Professional Experience:** BIOTECHNOL CONSULT, 1990-; mem, Biol Sci Study Sect, NIH, 1990-1994; assoc prof biol, Clarkson Univ, 1983-1990; asst prof biol, Calif Inst Technol, 1974-1982; Helen Hay Whitney fel, 1973-1974; mem sci adv bd, Found Res Hereditary Dis, 1972-1981; fel biol, Stanford Univ, 1972-1974; NSF fel, 1972-1973. **Research Statement & Publications:** Circadian rhythm; behavior genetics of Drosophila; genetic engineering. **Mailing Address:** 430 S Santa Anita Ave, Pasadena, CA 91107.

KONOWALOW, DANIEL DIMITRI, THEORETICAL CHEMISTRY. **Personal Data:** b Cleveland, Ohio, April 28, 1929; m 1978, Marcy. **Education:** Ohio State Univ, BS, 1953; Univ Wis, PhD (chem), 1961. **Professional Experience:** RETIRED; sr scientist, Univ Dayton Res Inst, beginning 1987; sr res assoc, Nat Res Coun, Ballistics Res Lab, Aberdeen Proving Ground, Md, 1985-1986; vis scientist, Nat Bur Stand, Gaithersburg, Md, 1978-1979; vis prof, Uppsala Univ, Sweden, 1971-1972; from asst prof to assoc prof, State Univ NY, Binghamton, NY, 1965-1989; asst dir, Theoret Chem Inst, Univ Wis, 1962-1965; chemist, Plastics Dept, E I Du Pont De Nemours & Co, Del, 1960-1962. **Memberships:** Am Chem Soc; AAAS; Am Phys Soc. **Research Statement & Publications:** Calculation and correlation of physical properties of atoms and molecules by quantum-mechanical methods; intramolecular and intermolecular interactions; theoretical spectroscopy. **Mailing Address:** Morrow Creek Farm, 199 Algerine Rd, Lansing, NY 14882. **E-Mail:** dankonowalow@hotmail.com

KONRAD, DUSAN, ELECTROCHEMISTRY. **Personal Data:** b Brno, Czech, January 7, 1935; American citizen; m 1972, Yitka Svachova; c Peter & Martin. **Education:** Masaryk Univ, Czech, MS, 1957; Czech Acad Sci, PhD (chem), 1962. **Professional Experience:** MEM TECH STAFF, TEX INSTRUMENTS, INC, DALLAS, 1978-; sr scientist electrochem, Technol Ctr, ESB Inc, Yardley, Pa, 1971-1978; res felchem, Calif Inst Technol, 1970-1971; sr res fel, Rudjer Boskovic Inst, Yugoslavia, 1968-1969; res chemist, Govt Assay Off, Czech, 1967-1968; res scientist phys chem, J Heyrovsky Inst Polarography, Czech Acad Sci, 1963-1966; Instr inorg chem, Masaryk Univ, Czech, 1957-1962. **Memberships:** Electrochem Soc. **Research Statement & Publications:** Electrochemical instrumentation; automatized data taking and processing; electrode impedance in Laplace plane analysis; electrochemistry of lead-acid cell; non-stoichiometric oxide electrodes; porous electrodes; computer software systems. **Mailing Address:** 13450 Maham Rd No 932, Dallas, TX 75240. **E-Mail:** dusankonrad@juno.com

KONRAD, GERHARD T(HIES), ELECTRICAL ENGINEERING. **Personal Data:** b Konigsberg, Ger, February 23, 1935; American citizen; m 1964, Martha Kespohl; c Matthew Nathan. **Education:** Univ Mich, BSE, 1957, MSE, 1960, PhD (elec eng), 1969. **Professional Experience:** Consult, Konrad Tech Enterprise, Danville, Ca as of 2002; mgr, Physics/Microwave Eng, Siem E NS Med Systs, Concord, Calif, 1988-2002; Consult, Litton Indust, 1979-1989 & Valvo, Ger, 1978-1982 & Los Alamos Nat Lab, 1988-; head, Klystron Dept, 1977-1986; staff mem, Stanford Linear Accelerator Ctr, 1972-1977; staff mem, Lincoln Lab, Mass Inst Technol, 1969-1972; assoc res engr, Univ Mich, 1961-1969; Asst res engr, Univ Mich, 1960-1961. **Memberships:** Inst Elec & Electronics Engrs; Am Phys Soc; Amer assoc of Physicists in med Sigma Xi. **Research Statement & Publications:** Electron devices; microwave circuits; electron optics; high-voltage techniques; vacuum techniques; plasma physics; electromagnetic theory; medical physics. **Mailing Address:** 787 Kirkcrest Rd, Danville, CA 94526. **Fax:** 925-743-9718. **E-Mail:** gtkonrad@worldnet.att.net

KONRAD, JANUSZ, IMAGE ANALYSIS. **Education:** Tech Univ Szczecin, ME, 1980; McGill Univ, Montreal, PhD, 1989. **Professional Experience:** ASSOC PROF, DEPT ELEC & COMPUT ENG, BOSTON UNIV, as of 2006. **Mailing Address:** Dept Elec & Comput Eng, Boston Univ, Eight St. Mary's St, Boston, MA 02215. **Fax:** 617-353-6440. **E-Mail:** jkonrad@bu.edu

KONRAD, MICHAEL WARREN, PHYSICAL CHEMISTRY OF NUCLEIC ACIDS, SIMULATIONS OF MOLECULAR DYNAMICS. **Personal Data:** b San Diego, Calif, December 20, 1936; m 1984, Wanda; c Robin (Dederich), Hans & Michel. **Education:** Calif Inst Technol, BS, 1958; Univ Calif, Berkeley, PhD (biophys), 1964. **Professional Experience:** PRES, GENE VUE INC, 1993-; dir, Del Vlaminck Inst, 1990-1993; sr scientist, Cetus Corp, 1980-1990; assoc res scientist, Univ Calif, Berkeley, 1974-1980; asst prof chem, Univ Calif, Los Angeles, 1966-1974; NSF res fel biochem, Harvard Univ, 1964-1966. **Memberships:** AAAS; Am Soc Biochem & Molecular Biol. **Research Statement & Publications:** Development of DNA diagnostics; computer simulations of the response of macromolecules to distorting forces. **Mailing Address:** Gene Vue Inc, Sausalito, CA 94549. **Fax:** 415-339-9134. **E-Mail:** mkonrad@genevue.com

KONRAD, VICTOR A, ARCHAEOLOGY. **Education:** York Univ, BA, MA; McMaster Univ, PhD. **Professional Experience:** Adj res prof, Dept Geog & Environ Studies, Carleton Univ, as of 2006. **Memberships:** Can Asn Geogr. **Mailing Address:** Carleton Univ, 1125 Col Dr, Ottawa, ON K1S 5B6, Can. **Fax:** 613-520-4301. **E-Mail:** vkonrad@hotmail.com

KONSLER, THOMAS RHINEHART, HORTICULTURE. **Personal Data:** b Henderson, Ky, April 17, 1925; m 1954, c 9. **Education:** Univ Ky, BS, 1955; NC State Univ, MS, 1957, PhD (exp statist), 1961. **Professional Experience:** EMER PROF HORT SCI, MOUNTAIN HORT CROPS RES, NC STATE UNIV, 1988-; from asst prof to prof, NC State Univ, 1961-1988. **Memberships:** Am Soc Hort Sci. **Research Statement & Publications:** Cultural practices and plant breeding with vegetable crops and American Ginseng. **Mailing Address:** 805 Oakland St, Hendersonville, NC 28791.

KONSTAM, AARON HARRY, PROGRAMMING LANGUAGES, EXPERT SYSTEMS. **Personal Data:** b Bronx, NY, August 11, 1936; m 1961, Patricia; c David. **Education:** Polytech Inst Brooklyn, BS, 1957; Pa State Univ, PhD (phys org chem), 1961. **Professional Experience:** PROF EMER COMPUT SCI, TRININTY UNIV, as of 2005; prof comput sci, Trinity Univ, beginning 1986; vpres, vanguard systs corp, 1980-1983; treas, vanguard systs corp, 1977-1980; assoc prof, Trinity Univ, 1972-1986; dir comput ctr & assocprof math, Lindenwood Cols, 1969-1972; sr res chemist, Monsanto Res Corp, 1965-1969; fel & res assoc phys org chem, Israel Inst Technol, 1962-1964; instr chem, Brooklyn Col, 1961-1962. **Memberships:** Asn Comput Mach; Inst Elec & Electronics Engrs. **Research Statement & Publications:** Artificial intelligence, genetic algorithims and programming languages. **Mailing Address:** Dept Comput Sci, Trinity Univ, One Trinity Pl, San Antonio, TX 78212-7200. **Fax:** 210-999-7477. **E-Mail:** akonstam@trinity.edu

KONSTAN, JOSEPH A, COMPUTER SCIENCE. **Personal Data:** b New York, NY, May 10, 1966; m Ellen Kletzman; c Benjamin Irving Konstan. **Education:** Harvard Univ, AB, 1987; Univ Calif, Berkeley, MS, 1990, PhD (comput sci), 1993. **Honors & Awards:** ACM Lecturer, ACM, 1997-. **Professional Experience:** Assoc prof, Univ of Minn, 1999; Asst Prof, Univ of Minn, 1993-1999; Instructor, Univ of Minn, 1992-1993; lectr, Asn Comput Mach, 1997-1998; NSF grantee, 1994-; ASST PROF, UNIV MINN, 1993-; Instr, Univ Minn, 1992-1993. **Memberships:** ACM SIGCHI, Executive Committee, 1997-; ACM SIG-Multimedia, Executive committee, 1999-; Asn Comput Mach. **Research Statement & Publications:** Graphical user-interface toolkits and frameworks; human computer interaction; multimedia systems; collaborative filtering; internet tools and applications. **Mailing Address:** Dept Comput Sci & Eng, Univ Minn, Minneapolis, MN 55455. **E-Mail:** konstan@cs.umn.edu

KONSTANTOPOULOS, TAKIS, APPLIED PROBABILITY & STOCHASTIC NETWORKS, STATIONARY & ERGODIC STOCHASTIC PROCESSES & SYSTEMS. **Personal Data:** b Patras, Greece, May 29, 1961. **Education:** Nat Tech Univ Athens, dipl, 1983; Univ Calif, Berkeley, MS, 1985, PhD (elec eng), 1989. **Professional Experience:** ASSOC PROF, UNIV TEX, AUSTIN, 1997-; asst prof, Univ Tex, Austin, 1992-1996; vis prof, Cornell Univ, 1992; lectr, Univ Calif, Berkeley, 1991-1992; sr res, Nat Res Inst, France, 1989-1991. **Memberships:** Inst Math Statist; Inst Elec & Electronics Engrs; Math Asn Am. **Research Statement & Publications:** Stochastic networks in the presence of long-range dependent data; macroscopic approximations of complex stochastic systems; stationarity and stability of stochastic networks; stochastic control and optimization of telecommunication systems; performance analysis of high speed networks. **Mailing Address:** Dept Elec & Comput Eng, Univ Tex, One Univ Sta Stop C0803, Austin, TX 78712. **Fax:** 512-471-5532. **E-Mail:** takis@ece.utexas.edu

KONTNY, VINCENT L, MINING ENGINEERING. **Personal Data:** b Chappell, Nebr, July 19, 1937; m 1970, Joan D FitzGibbon; c Natascha M, Michael C & Amber B. **Education:** Univ Colo, BSCE, 1958. **Honorary Degrees:** DSc, Univ Colo, 1991. **Professional Experience:** RETIRED; ceo, Wash Group Int, 2000-2002; vchmn, Fluor Corp, 1994; pres, Fluor Corp, 1990-1994; pres, fluordaniel, beginning 1988; group pres, Fluor Daniel, 1987-1988;

pres & chief exec officer, Fluor Engrs, Inc, 1985-1987; group vpres, Fluor Engrs, Inc, 1982-1985; managing dir, Fluor Australia, Melbourne, 1979-1982; sr vpres, Holmes & Narver, Inc, 1973-1979; sr proj mgr, Fluor Utah, 1972-1973; proj mgr, Fluor Australia, Queensland, Australia, 1969-1972; Proj mgr, Utah Construct & Mining Co, Western Australia, 1965-1969; mem eng adv coun, Stanford Univ, 1959-1965; Mem eng develop coun, Univ Colo, 1959-1965. **Memberships:** Am Asn Cost Engrs; Australian Asn Engrs; Am Petrol Inst. **Research Statement & Publications:** Author of numerous articles. **Mailing Address:** Wash Group Int, PO Box 73, 720 Park Blvd, Boise, ID 83729.

KONTOS, HERMES A, MEDICINE, PHYSIOLOGY. **Personal Data:** b Lefka, Cyprus, December 13, 1933; American citizen; m 1960, c 2. **Education:** Nat Univ Athens, MD, 1958; Med Col Va, PhD (physiol), 1967; Am Col Physicians, dipl, 1969. **Professional Experience:** DEAN & CEO, VCU HEALTH SYST, 2001-; VP HEALTH SCI DEAN, 1998-; chmn div cardio pulmonary med, Med Col Va, beginnig 1981; prof med, Med Col Va, beginning 1972; markle scholar acad med, 1969-1974; USPHS res career develop award, 1967-1972; from instr to assoc prof, Med ColVA, 1964-1972. **Memberships:** Am Fedn Clin Res; Am Heart Asn; Am Physiol Soc; Am Soc Clin Invest; SigmaXi. **Research Statement & Publications:** Circulatory physiology and pathophysiology. **Mailing Address:** Dept Med, Med Col Va, Va Commonwealth Univ, 1101 E Marshall St, Richmond, VA 23298-0565. **Fax:** 804-828-7628.

KONTRAS, STELLA B, PEDIATRICS, GENETICS. **Personal Data:** b Newport News, Va, June 28, 1929; m 1947, c 3. **Education:** Ohio State Univ, BA, 1948, MA, 1949, MD, 1953. **Professional Experience:** PHYSICS PSYCH, OHI UNIV MED CTR, as of 2003; Vchmn, Dept Pediat, 1980; PROF PEDIAT, COL MED, OHIO STATE UNIV, 1969-; assoc prof pediat, Ohio State Univ, 1966-1969; dir, Med Genetics Ctr, Children's Hosp, Columbus, 1965-1971; NIH spec fel cancer, Ohio State Univ, 1963-1964; consult, Ohio DeptHealth, 1962-1970; asst prof pediat & anat, Ohio State Univ, 1960-1966; resident path, OhioState Univ, 1957-1958; Resident pediat, Ohio State Univ, 1955 & 1956; instr pediat, Ohio StateUniv, 1954-1960; Intern med, Ohio State Univ, 1954. **Memberships:** Soc Pediat Res; Am Soc Hemat; Am Soc Human Genetics. **Research Statement & Publications:** Hematology. **Mailing Address:** Children's Hosp, 1670 Upham Dr, Rm 460B, Columbus, OH 43205-2696.

KONVALINA, JOHN, MATHEMATICS. **Education:** State Univ New York, PhD, 1975. **Professional Experience:** PROF, DEPT MATH, UNIV NEBR-OMAHA, as of 2005. **Mailing Address:** Durham Sci Ctr Rm 222, Univ Nebr-Omaha, Omaha, NE 68182-0243. **Fax:** 402-554-2975. **E-Mail:** johnkon@unomaha.edu

KONYA, CALVIN JOSEPH, MINING ENGINEERING, BLASTING. **Personal Data:** b Cleveland, Ohio, June 23, 1943. **Education:** Mo Sch Mines, BS, 1966; Univ Mo-Rolla, MS, 1968 & 1970, PhD (mining eng), 1972. **Honorary Degrees:** Dr, Univ Miskolc, Hungary. **Professional Experience:** PRES, INTERCONTINENTAL DEVELOP CORP INC, as of 2000; adj prof, Ohio Univ, 1988-; adj prof, John Caroll Univ, 1988- & Univ Miskolc, 1988-; adj prof, Ohio Stateuniv, beginning 1988; pres, precision blasting syst, 1987; pres, hydrocarbon fuels, 1983-1987; profmining eng, Ohio State Univ, 1981-1988; chmn dept, Ohio State Univ, 1981-1985; assoc prof, Ohio State Univ, 1978-1981; exchange scientist, nat acad sci, 1975; mgr tech servs, precision basting servs, 1973-; FOUNDER, INTERCONTINENTAL DEVELOP CORP INC, 1973-; from asst prof to assoc prof mining eng, WVa Univ, 1971-1978; dir, ohio mining & mineral resources res inst. **Memberships:** Soc Explosives Engrs (pres, 1975-1977, exec dir, 1974-1987); Am Inst Mining Metall& Petrol Engrs. **Research Statement & Publications:** Rock mechanics; explosives engineering; definition of mechanisms of rock fragmentation by blasting both for production rounds and for controlled blasting techniques; development of practical equations for prediction of blast design variables in the field. **Mailing Address:** Intercontinental Develp Corp, Inc, PO Box 189, Montville, OH 44064. **Fax:** 440-968-3967. **E-Mail:** info@idc-pbs.com

KONZ, STEPHAN A, ERGONOMICS. **Personal Data:** b Milwaukee, Wis, November 25, 1933; m 1958, c 5. **Education:** Univ Mich, BS, 1956, MBA, 1956; Univ Iowa, MS, 1960; Univ Ill, PhD (indust eng), 1964. **Honors & Awards:** Fitts Award, Human Factors Soc. **Professional Experience:** PROF EMER INDUST ENG, KANS STATE UNIV, as of 2004; prof indust eng, Kans State Univ, beginning 1969; from asst prof to assoc prof, Kans State Univ, 1964-1969; instr mech & indust eng, Univ Ill, 1960-1964; industengr, Westinghouse Elec Corp, 1956-1957 & Collins Radio Co, 1958-1960. **Memberships:** Inst Indust Engrs; Human Factors Soc; Am Indust Hyg Asn; Am Soc Heat Refrig & Air-Conditioning Engrs. **Research Statement & Publications:** Ergonomics, especially design of industrial jobs; heat stress; Inspection; hand tools. **Mailing Address:** Dept Indust Eng, Kans State Univ Durland Hall Rm 237, Manhattan, KS 66502-5101. **E-Mail:** sk@ksu.edu

KONZAK, CALVIN FRANCIS, INDUCED MUTATIONS IN PLANTS, GENETICS. **Personal Data:** b Devils Lake, ND, October 17, 1924; div, c Kenneth & Gary James. **Education:** NDak Agr Col, BS, 1948; Cornell Univ, PhD, 1952. **Professional Experience:** PRES, NORTHWEST PLANT BREEDING CO, 1994-; SCIENTIST DIR, NORTHWEST PLANT BREEDING CO INC, 1994-; PROPRIETOR, NORTHWEST PLANT BREEDING CO INC, 1982-; sci adv, Plant Breeding & Genetics Sect, Jt Food & Agr Orgn-Int Atomic Energy Agency Div Atomic Energy Food & Agr, 1973-1974 & 1982-1983; food & agr consult, Crop Res & Introd Ctr, Izmir, Turkey, 1971; spec adv, Plant Breeding & Genetics Sect, Jt Food & Agr Orgn-Int Atomic Energy Agency Div Food & Agr, Vienna, 1965-1967; USPHS sr fel, 1965-1966; prof genetics, Wash State Univ, 1963-1994; from assoc prof to prof & assoc agronomist to agronomist, Wash State Univ, 1957-1963; assoc geneticist, Dept Biol, Brookhaven Nat Lab, 1952-1957. **Memberships:** Fel AAAS; Genetics Soc Am; fel Am Soc Agron; fel Crop Sci Soc Am. **Research Statement & Publications:** Breeding semidwarf, hard red and soft white spring wheat, durum wheat oats for improved yield, and improved quality; genetics of reduced height and other traits in wheat and oats; induction of useful mutations in wheat and oats; herbicide tolorance, genetic analyses. **Mailing Address:** Northwest Plant Breeding Co, 2001 Country Club Rd, Pullman, WA 99163. **Fax:** 509-334-5320.

KONZELMAN, LEROY MICHAEL, ORGANIC CHEMISTRY. **Personal Data:** b Jersey City, NJ, May 27, 1936; m 1960, Mercedes D Franz; c Michael L, Patricia A & Christine. **Education:** St Peter's Col, NJ, BSc, 1958; Seton Hall Univ, MSc, 1964, PhD (org chem), 1966. **Professional Experience:** DIR BUS DEVELOP, CHEM DYNAMICS CORP, SOUTH PLAINFIELD, NJ, 1984-; mgr, color res & develop, Inmont Corp, Hawthorne, NJ, 1982-1983; chief chemistpharmaceut mfg dept, Am Cyanamid Co, Bound Brook, 1979-1982; chief chemist dyes &intermediates mfg dept, Am Cyanamid Co, Bound Brook, 1974-1979; group leader dyes & intermediates dept, 1972-1974; reschemist, 1966-1972; Chemist, Schering Corp, NJ, 1960-1965. **Memberships:** Am Chem Soc; NY Acad Sci; Sigma Xi; AAAS. **Research Statement & Publications:** Process and product development of organic intermediates for pharmaceutical and agricultural products and a variety of specialty organic intermediates; marketing and product development for organic intermediates for use in the pharmaceutical, agricultural and specialty fields. **Mailing Address:** 61 Elm St, Madison, NJ 07940. **Fax:** 732-981-8282.

KOO, BENJAMIN, STRUCTURAL ENGINEERING, APPLIED MECHANICS. **Personal Data:** b Shanghai, China, April 4, 1920; American citizen; wid. **Education:** St John's Univ, BS, 1941; Cornell Univ, MS, 1942, PhD (struct eng), 1946. **Honors & Awards:** Outstanding Teachers Award, 1974, Univ of Toledo. **Professional Experience:** PROF EMER ENG, UNIV TOLEDO, 1990-; prof civil eng, Univ Toledo, 1965-1990; proj engr, Am Car & Foundry Div, ACF Industs, 1961-1965; engr concrete & found sect, M H Treadwell Co, 1956-1961; struct engr, 1942-1955; NSF, NASA & Dept Transp Res Awards. **Memberships:** Am Soc Civil Engrs; Am Soc Eng Educ; Am Concrete Inst; Sigma Xi Tau Beta Pi. **Research Statement & Publications:** Structural reliability in reinforced concrete members and frames; trailer train freight car patent; cushioned underframe system patent; structural stability; structural analysis and design; structural reliability. **Mailing Address:** Dept Civil Eng, Univ Toledo, Toledo, OH 43606.

KOO, DAVID CHIH-YUEN, OBSERVATIONAL COSMOLOGY, EVOLUTION OF GALAXIES. **Personal Data:** b Bangkok, Thailand, January 1, 1951; m 1981, Anna; c 2. **Education:** Cornell Univ, AB, 1972; Univ Calif, Berkeley, MA, 1974, PhD (astron), 1981. **Professional Experience:** Astronomer/Prof Astronomy & Astrophysics, Univ Calif Observatories/Lick, AS OF 2006; Associ Astronomer/Assoc Prof Astronomy & Astrophysics, Univ Calif Observatories/Lick, 1991-1995; NSF Presidential Young Investr award, 1988-1993; Ass Astronomer/Assi Prof Astronomy & Astrophysics, Univ Calif Observatories/Lick, Univ Calif, Santa Cruz, 1988-1991; Assis Astronomer, Space Telescope Sci Inst, 1986-1987; fel, Space Telescope Sci Inst, 1984-1986; sr res fel, Dept Terrestrial Magnetism, Carnegie Inst Wash, 1983-1984; vis fel, Sci & Eng Res Coun, UK, 1983; fel, Dept Terrestrial Magnetism, Carnegie Inst Wash, 1981-1983. **Memberships:** Int Astron Union; Am Astron Soc; Astron Soc Pac; Int Asn Pattern Recognition. **Research Statement & Publications:** Faint imaging and spectroscopic studies of the formation and evolution of faint galaxies and active galactic nuclei; measurements of the geometry of the universe; probes of the large-scale distributions of galaxies. **Mailing Address:** UCO/Lick Observatory, Univ Calif, 1156 High St, Santa Cruz, CA 95064. **E-Mail:** koo@ucolick.org

KOO, DELIA WEI, MATHEMATICS, STATISTICS. **Personal Data:** b Hankow, China, May 14, 1921; American citizen; m 1943, Anthony; c Victoria (Hitchins), Margery (Bussey) & Emily. **Education:** St Johns Univ, China, BA, 1941; Radcliffe Col, AM, 1942, PhD (eng philol), 1947; Mich State Univ, MA, 1954. **Professional Experience:** RETIRED; from asst prof to prof math, Eastern Mich Univ, 1965-1983; instr, Mich State Univ, 1957-1958; lectr, Douglass Col, Rutgers Univ, 1956-1957; instr math, MichState Univ, 1955-1956. **Memberships:** Math Asn Am; Inst Math Statist; Economet Soc. **Research Statement & Publications:** Author of 2 books. **Mailing Address:** 4554 Sequoia Trail, Okemos, MI 48864.

KOO, GLORIA C, IMMUNOLOGY, CELL BIOLOGY. **Personal Data:** b Chunking, China, November 22, 1944; American citizen. **Education:** Goshen Col, BA, 1965; Temple Sch Med, PhD (immunol), 1970. **Honors & Awards:** NIH award, 1974-1986; ACS faculty Res Award, 1978-1982. **Professional Experience:** DIST SR INVESTR, MERCK RES LAB, NJ, 2001-; sr investr, 1991-2001; mem, NIH Exp Immunol Study Sect, 1991-1994; spec reviewer, NIH Exp Immunol Study Sect, 1989-1990; vis assoc prof, Dept biol, Rutgers Univ, 1985-1988; sr res fel, Merck Res Labs, 1984-1991; vis investr, Univ Helsinki, Finland, 1977 & Univ Calif, San Francisco Med Ctr, 1983; asst mem, Sloan-Kettering Inst, 1981-1984; asst prof, Sloan-Kettering Div, Cornell Univ Med Col, 1975-1984; assoc, Sloan-Kettering Inst, NY, 1974-1981; res assoc, Sloan-Kettering Inst, NY, 1972-1974; fel, Sloan-Kettering Inst, NY, 1970-1972; fel, Dept Microbiol, Temple Univ Sch Med, Pa, 1967-1970; med technologist clin microbiol, Temple Univ Hosp, Pa, 1966-1967; Med technologist, Clin Microbiol, Rhode Island Hosp, 1965-1966. **Memberships:** Sigma Xi; Am Asn Immunologists. **Research Statement & Publications:** Immune modulation and transplantation. **Mailing Address:** Merck Res Lab, PO Box 2000, 80W-107, Rahway, NJ 07065-0900. **E-Mail:** gloria_koo@merck.com

KOO, KEE P, FIBER-OPTIC SENSORS, LASER PHYSICS. **Personal Data:** b Hong Kong, March 30, 1949; British citizen; m 1987. **Education:** Univ Ill, Chicago, BS, 1971; Case Western Res Univ, MS, 1975, PhD (elec eng), 1977. **Professional Experience:** RES PHYSICIST, NAVAL RES LAB, 1980-; Res assoc, Brookhaven Nat Lab, 1977-1978 & John Carroll Univ, 1978-1980. **Memberships:** Inst Elec & Electronics Engrs; Optical Soc Am. **Research Statement & Publications:** Fiber-optic sensors research with emphasis in interferometric sensors, especially in magnetic field sensing; fiber-optic magnetometer, gradiometer. **Mailing Address:** 6813 Melrose Dr, Mclean, VA 22101.

KOO, PETER H, CANCER IMMUNOLOGY & BIOLOGY, NEURO-IMMUNO-REGULATION BY ALPHA-TWO-MACROGLOBULIN. **Personal Data:** b Shanghai, China, American citizen; m 1967, S Alice; c David & Christopher. **Education:** Univ Wash, BA, 1964; Univ Md, PhD (biochem), 1970. **Honors & Awards:** Award winner as the chirmen to reprisent the professional edu committee of Am concer foc; Postage county to receive program achivement award for excellence, 1986; pres, annual volunteer recognition award for the role as chairman of prof edu comm of Am concer for, Portege country, 1986; hon citatein, as the acitvity dir ofr the Am concel soc Ohio division. **Professional Experience:** PROF IMMUNOL & MICROBIOL, COL MED, NORTHEASTERN OHIO UNIV, 1994-; vis sci, Wood-whelan res, fel, 1999; prin investr & grantee, Ric-Man Fund, 1993-1994; prin invester & grantee, Nat Cancer Inst, NIH, 1992-1996; prin investr & grantee, Oncol Fund Akron Gen Develop Fund, 1990-1993; vpres, Prof Educ Comt, 1987-1989; chmn, Prof Educ Comt, 1985-1989; prin investr & grantee, NSF, 1984-1987; prin investr & grantee, Mefcom Found Funds, 1982-; prin investr & grantee, United Way, 1982-1983 & 1989-1990; bd dirs, Portage Co, 1981-1989; prin investr, Nat Cancer Inst, NIH, 1978-1982; Prin investr & grantee, Am Cancer Soc, 1978-1979 & 1981-1982; prin investr & grantee, Cystic Fibrosis Care Fund & Pediat Akron, Inc, 1978-1979; from asst prof to assoc prof, Col Med, Northeastern Ohio Univ, 1977-1993; asst prof oncol, Johns Hopkins Univ, 1975-1977; staff fel, NIH, 1974-1975; Fel immunol, Johns Hopkins Univ, 1971-1974; grad fac, Neurosci Prog, Cellular & Molecular Biol Prog, Sch Biomed Sci, Kent State Univ, OH. **Memberships:** Soc Neurosc; NY Acad Sci; Am Asn Immunologist; Am Soc Biochem & Molecular Biol. **Research Statement & Publications:** our res investigates the role of alpha-2-macroglobulin in immuno-regulation & neuroregulation, with the primary focus on immune deviation in T-helper lymphocyte subsets, neurotrophin regulation, nerve regeneration, & mechanism of action. **Mailing Address:** Dept Microbiol & Immunol Col Med, Northeastern Ohio Univ 4209 St Rte 44 PO Box 95, Rootstown, OH 44272. **Fax:** 330-325-5914. **E-Mail:** pkoo@neoncom.edu

KOO, ROBERT CHUNG JEN, POMOLOGY. **Personal Data:** b Shanghai, China, March 20, 1921; American citizen; m 1949, c 3. **Education:** Cornell Univ, BS, 1944; Univ Fla, MS, 1950, PhD (fruit crops), 1953. **Honors & Awards:** Presidential Gold Medal Award, Fla State Horticult Soc, 1965; Res Award, Fla Fruit & Vegetable Asn, 1975. **Professional Experience:** EMER PROF, CITRUS RES & EDUC CTR, UNIV FLA, 1990-; prof &

horticulturist, Agr Res & Educ Ctr, 1969-1990; from asst horticulturist to assoc horticulturist, Citrus Exp Sta, Univ Fla, 1957-1968; Interim asst biochemist, Citrus Exp Sta, Univ Fla, 1953-1957. **Memberships:** Am Soc Hort Sci; Am Agron Soc. **Research Statement & Publications:** Plant nutrition of citrus; irrigation and water management. **Mailing Address:** 2223 12th St NW, Winter Haven, FL 33881.

KOO, SUNG IL, NUTRITION, LIPID BIOCHEMISTRY. **Education:** Clemson Univ, PhD (nutrit), 1976; Univ NH, MS, 1973; Kon-Kuk Univ, BS, 1970. **Professional Experience:** HEAD, DEPT NUTRIT, UNIV CONN, 2002-; asst dept head Human nutrit, Kans State Univ, 1999-2002; Grad prog Co-ord, Dept Human Nutrit, Kans State Univ, 1998-2002; PROF FOODS & NUTRIT, KANS STATE UNIV, 1990-; PROF BIOCHEM, ORAL ROBERTS UNIV, 1989-; assoc prof, Oral Roberts Univ, 1978-1988. **Memberships:** Am Soc Nutrit Sci; Am Diebetic Asn. **Mailing Address:** Dept Nutrit Sci, Univ Conn, Storrs, CT 06269. **Fax:** 860-486-3674. **E-Mail:** skoo@canr.uconn.edu

KOOB, ROBERT DUANE, PHYSICAL CHEMISTRY. **Personal Data:** b Graettinger, Iowa, October 14, 1941; m 1960, c 7. **Education:** Univ Northern Iowa, BA, 1962; Univ Kans, PhD (chem), 1967. **Professional Experience:** PRES, UNIV NORTHERN IOWA, as of 2002; vpres acad affairs & sr vpres, Calif Polytech Univ, beginning 1990; interim pres, Col Sci & Math, 1987-1988; vpres acad affairs, Col Sci & Math, 1985-1990; dean, Col Sci & Math, 1981-1984; dir, Water Resources Res Inst, 1974-1985; chmn dept, 1973-1977; from asst prof to prof chem, NDak State Univ, 1967-1990; res assoc chem, Univ Kans, 1967; instr high sch, Iowa, 1963-1964. **Memberships:** Am Chem Soc; Sigma Xi. **Research Statement & Publications:** Radiation chemistry; photochemistry; mass spectrometry. **Mailing Address:** Univ Northern Iowa, Seerley 20, Cedar Falls, IA 50613. **Fax:** 319-273-6494. **E-Mail:** bob.koob@uni.edu

KOOB, ROBERT PHILIP, PHOTOCHEMISTRY, PHYSICAL CHEMISTRY. **Personal Data:** b Philadelphia, Pa, January 3, 1922; m 1954, c 3. **Education:** Villanova Col, BS, 1943; Univ Pa, MS, 1947, PhD (chem), 1949. **Professional Experience:** PROF EMER CHEM, ST JOSEPH'S COL, PA, as of 2003; prof chem, St Joseph's Col, Pa, beginning 1959; res chemist, E I du Pont Del Nemours & Co, 1947 & Eastern Lab, Dept Agr, 1959; from asst prof to assoc prof, St Joseph's Col, PA, 1955-1959; asst prof, Rosemont Col, 1951-1952; asst prof chem, Villanova Col, 1949-1955; Asst instr, Univ Pa, 1943-1944. **Memberships:** Am Chem Soc; Sigma Xi. **Research Statement & Publications:** Phase and reaction rate studies; effects of solvent on reaction; extensions of the Fries Rearrangement; organic photochemistry. **Mailing Address:** Dept Chem, St Joseph's Col, Drexel Hill, PA 19026-2435.

KOOBS, DICK HERMAN, PATHOLOGY, BIOLOGICAL CHEMISTRY. **Personal Data:** b Hinsdale, Ill, July 22, 1928; m 1955, Ardyce. **Education:** Andrews Univ, BA, 1950; Loma Linda Univ, MD, 1955; Univ Calif, Los Angeles, PhD (biol chem), 1965; Am Bd Path, dipl, 1966. **Professional Experience:** EMER PROF, DEPT PATH, LOMA LINDA UNIV, as of 2005; ASSOC PROF PATH, SCH MED, LOMA LINDA UNIV, 1978-; asst prof, Sch Med, Loma Linda Univ, 1965-1978; resident physician path, White Mem Hosp, Los Angeles, 1956-1959; intern, Robert B Green Mem Hosp, San Antonio, Tex, 1955-1956. **Memberships:** Int Acad Path. **Research Statement & Publications:** Experimental and molecular pathology, related to genetically acquired defective enzymes. **Mailing Address:** Dept Path, Loma Linda Univ, Loma Linda, CA 92350.

KOOH, SANG WHAY, PEDIATRICS. **Personal Data:** b Seoul, Korea, October 5, 1930; m 1956, Rak-Hay Kim; c Nancy (Zipple), Pamela J (Burtzlaff) & Michael. **Education:** Yan-Sei Univ, MD, 1955; Univ Toronto, PhD (physiol), 1967; Am Acad Pediat, dipl, 1961; FRCP, 1968. **Professional Experience:** AT DIV ENDOCRINOL, DEPT PEDIAT, HOSP SICK CHILDREN, UNIV TORONTO, as of 1998; Sr staff physician, Hosp Sick Children, 1968-; ASSOC PROF, DEPT PHYSIOL & DEPT PEDIAT, UNIV TORONTO, 1968-; sr res fel, Res Inst, Hosp Sick Children, Toronto, 1962-1967; Fel pediat, Michael Reese Hosp & Med Ctr, 1960-1962. **Memberships:** Soc Pediat Res; Can Soc Clin Investigation; Am Soc Bone & Mineral Res. **Research Statement & Publications:** Metabolism bone diseases in children; metabolism of vitamin D in human and in experimental animals; regulation of bone mineralization. **Mailing Address:** Dept Pediat, Hosp Sick Children, Univ Toronto, 555 Univ Ave, Toronto, ON M5G 1X8, Can.

KOOHMARAIE, MOHAMMAD, BIOCHEMISTRY, MICROBIOLOGY, FOOD SCIENCE TECHNOLOGY. **Education:** Pahlavi Univ, BS, 1978; Tex A&I Univ, MS, 1980; Ore State Univ, PhD (muscle biol), 1984. **Honors & Awards:** Fedn Am Soc Exp Biol; Am Meat Asn; Am Soc Animal Sci; Sigma Xi. **Professional Experience:** SUPVRY RES PHYSIOLOGIST, USDA-AGR RES SERV, 1991-; res physiologist, Usda-Agr Res Serv, 1987-1991; res fel food sci & human nutrit, Mich State Univ, 1986-1987; res fel, Usda-Agr Res Serv, 1984-1986; res asst animal sci, Ore State Univ, 1980-1984. **Mailing Address:** US Meat Animal Res Ctr, Agr Res Serv, USDA, Spur 18D, Clay Center, NE 68933-0000. **Fax:** 402-762-4149. **E-Mail:** koohmaraie@email.marc.usda.gov

KOOIJ, THEO, ACOUSTIC SIGNAL PROCESSING, ELECTRONICS ENGINEERING. **Personal Data:** b Dordrecht, Neth, November 29, 1933; American citizen; m 1956, c 3. **Education:** Delft Univ Technol, BSc, 1958, MSc, 1961; Cath Univ Am, PhD (elec eng), 1977. **Honors & Awards:** Royal. **Professional Experience:** PROG MGR, ADVANCED TECHNOL OFF, DEFENSE ADVAN RES PROJS AGENCY, 1993-; tech dir, Acoust Res Ctr, 1976-1978; advan head, Target Physics Br, Ocean Sci Dept, Naval Underwater Systs Ctr, New London, Conn, 1974-1976; sci adv sonar interpretation, US Naval Ship Res & Develop Ctr, Washington, DC, 1968-1974; Lectr, Am Univ, 1968-1969; sr res scientist & teamleader underwater acoustics, Saclant ASW Res Ctr, La Spezia, Italy, 1965-1968; jr res scientist, Saclant ASW Res Ctr, La Spezia, Italy, 1961-1965. **Memberships:** Acoust Soc Am; Netherlands Royal Inst Eng; Inst Elec & Electronics Engrs, sr or life mem. **Research Statement & Publications:** Theoretical, model and computer simulated, and full scale experimental research in detection and classification of underwater targets; design and development of digital sonar signal processing systems. **Mailing Address:** 7103 Tyndale St, McLean, VA 22101-5075. **E-Mail:** tkooij@darpa.mil

KOOMEN, MARTIN J, SOLAR PHYSICS. **Personal Data:** b Bristol, NY, December 30, 1917; wid, c Stephen D (deceased) & William N. **Education:** Univ Rochester, BS, 1940, MS, 1943. **Professional Experience:** INVESTR, US NAVAL RES LAB, as of 2004; res physicist, Us Naval Res Lab & SFA Inc, beginning 1982; res physicist, US Naval Res Lab, 1946-1982; res physicist, Univ Rochester, 1942-1946; Instrument inspector, Bausch & Lomb Optical Co, 1941-1942. **Memberships:** Optical Soc Am; Am Astron Soc; Am Geophys Union; AAAS. **Research Statement & Publications:** Night vision; light emission from the upper atmosphere (night airglow); solar physics; design of rocket and satellite-borne instrumentation for study of the night airglow and the sun. **Mailing Address:** US Naval Res Lab, Code 4171 4555 Overlook Ave SW, Washington, DC 20375.

KOONCE, ANDREA LAVENDER, FOREST PATHOLOGY, TROPICAL FORESTRY. **Personal Data:** b Denver, Colo, December 31, 1951. **Professional Experience:** PRES, INT ASSOC WILDLAND FIRE, as of 2004; AT DEPT FORESTRY, UNIV WIS, STEVENS POINT, as of 2002; prof ecol, bot, path & head genetic res, Nat Sch Forestry sci, beginning 1981; Consult, Lew Roth Forest, 1980-1981; Researcher, US Forest Serv, 1978; res asst, Ore State Univ, 1975-1981; teacher pathol & ecol, Ore State Univ, 1975-1978. **Memberships:** Soc Am Foresters; Soc Trop Foresters. **Research Statement & Publications:** Tree improvement of tropical pines, hardwoods and legumes; tree disease-fire interactions; tree physiology. **Mailing Address:** Int Assoc Wildland Fire, PO Box 328, Fairfield, WA 99012.

KOONCE, KENNETH LOWELL, EXPERIMENTAL STATISTICS. **Personal Data:** b Lake Charles, La, September 6, 1939; m 1962, c 3. **Education:** Univ Southwestern La, BS, 1961; La State Univ, MS, 1963; NC State Univ, PhD (animal genetics), 1968. **Professional Experience:** DEAN, COL AGR, AGR EXP STA, LA STATE UNIV, BATON ROUGE, as of 2001; asst dir, Agr Exp Sta, beginning 1989; head dept, exp statist, 1982-1989; prof exp statist, La State Univ, Baton Rouge, beginning 1976; from asst prof to assoc prof, Agr Exp Sta, 1967-1976; Instr animal sci, NC State Univ, 1967. **Memberships:** Biomet Soc; Am Soc Animal Sci; Am Soc Info Sci; Am Statist Asn. **Mailing Address:** Col Agr, Agr Exp Sta, La State Univ, 104 Ag Admin Bldg, Baton Rouge, LA 70803-5055. **Fax:** 225-578-2526. **E-Mail:** kkoonce@lsu.edu

KOONCE, MICHAEL P, BIOLOGY. **Education:** Univ Calif, Berkeley, PhD, 1987. **Professional Experience:** RES SCIENTIST, CELLULAR REGULATION & ASST PROF, SCH PUB HEALTH, BIOMED SCI, WADSWORTH CTR, as of 2006. **Mailing Address:** Lab Cell Regulation Wadsworth Ctr, Empire State Plaza Box 509, Albany, NY 12201-0509. **Fax:** 518-474-7992. **E-Mail:** koonce@wadsworth.org

KOONG, LING-JUNG, EXPERIMENTAL BIOLOGY. **Education:** North Carolina State Univ, MS, 1968, PhD, 1973; North Taiwan Univ, BS, 1964. **Professional Experience:** PROF, DEPT ANIMAL SCI, COL AGR SCI, ORE STATE UNIV, as of 2002; ASSOC DEAN, COL AGR SCI, ORE STATE UNIV, 1994-; Dept head animal sci, Ore State Univ, 1991-1994. **Mailing Address:** Dept Animal Sci, Col Agr Sci, Ore State Univ, 308 Withycombe Hall, Corvallis, OR 97331. **Fax:** 541-737-4174. **E-Mail:** l.j.koong@orst.edu

KOONIN, STEVEN ELLIOT, THEORETICAL NUCLEAR PHYSICS. **Personal Data:** b Brooklyn, NY, December 12, 1951; m 1975, c 3. **Education:** Calif Inst Tech, BS, 1972; Mass Inst Technol, PhD (physics), 1975. **Honors & Awards:** Humboldt Sr Scientist Award, 1985. **Professional Experience:** PROVOST, CALIF INST TECHNOL, 1995-; vpres, Calif Inst Technol, 1995-2001; PROF THEORET PHYSICS, CALIF INST TECHNOL, 1981-; assoc prof physics, Calif Inst Technol, 1978-1981; consult, Lawrence Berkeley Lab, Lawrence Livermore Lab, Los Alamos Sci Lab & Oak Ridge Nat Lab, beginning 1977; Alfred P Sloan Found res fel, 1977-1979; res fel, Niels Bohr Inst, 1976-1977; asst prof theoret physics, Calif Inst Technol, 1975-1978. **Memberships:** Fel Am Phys Soc; fel AAAS. **Research Statement & Publications:** Nuclear reaction models; heavy ion physics. **Mailing Address:** Off Provost, Calif Inst Technol, 206 Parsons-Gates, Pasadena, CA 91125. **Fax:** 626-795-1898. **E-Mail:** koonin@caltech.edu

KOONS, CHARLES BRUCE, ORGANIC CHEMISTRY. **Personal Data:** b Oklahoma City, Okla, November 14, 1929; m 1956, Margaret C Suter; c Robert, David & Steven. **Education:** Southern Ill Univ, BS, 1951; Univ Minn, PhD (org chem), 1958. **Professional Experience:** CONSULT, 1989-; res adv, Jersey Prod Res Co, Div Standard Oil Co, NJ, Exxon Prod Res Co, 1983-1989; res assoc, Jersey Prod Res Co, Div Standard Oil Co, NJ, Exxon Prod Res Co, 1975-1983; sr res chemist, Jersey Prod Res Co, Div Standard Oil Co, NJ, Exxon Prod Res Co, 1964-1975; res chemist, Jersey Prod Res Co, Div Standard Oil Co, NJ, Exxon Prod Res Co, 1958-1964. **Memberships:** Am Chem Soc. **Research Statement & Publications:** Kinetics of aromatic substitution reactions; organic geochemistry, involving studies of the origin, migration and accumulation of petroleum; environmental chemistry, involving the fate of petroleum in the marine environment. **Mailing Address:** 10835 Saint Marys Lane, Houston, TX 77079-3619. **E-Mail:** brucekoons@aol.com

KOONS, DAVID SWARNER, CHEMICAL ENGINEERING, PETROLEUM ENGINEERING. **Personal Data:** b Fresno, Calif, June 17, 1930; div, c 2. **Education:** Calif Inst Technol, BS, 1952, MS, 1955; Univ Colo, PhD (chem eng), 1960. **Professional Experience:** RETIRED; staff engr, Mobil Corp, 1977-1986; sr res technologist, Mobil Oil Co Inc, 1960-1977; res asst, Exp Sta, Univ Colo, 1960; process engr, Texaco Inc, 1952-1954. **Memberships:** Am Chem Soc; Am Inst Chem Engrs; Am Inst Mining, Metall & Petrol Engrs. **Research Statement & Publications:** Simultaneous fluid flow; heat transfer and reaction kinetics of processes for recovering oil from underground reservoirs; pneumatic conveying of solids and petroleum refining. **Mailing Address:** 30343 Arena Dr, Evergreen, CO 80439.

KOONS, DONALDSON, GEOMORPHOLOGY. **Personal Data:** b Seoul, Korea, August 23, 1917; American citizen; m 1944, c 4. **Education:** Columbia Univ, AB, 1939, AM, 1941, PhD (geol), 1945. **Honorary Degrees:** DSc, Col of Wooster, 1974, Unity Col, 1976. **Honors & Awards:** Huddleston Medal. **Professional Experience:** RETIRED; from asst prof to prof geol, Dana prof, 1975-1982; Comnr, Maine Dept of Conserv, 1973-1975; head dept, Colby Col, 1947-1982; from asst prof to prof geol, Colby Col, 1947-1975; asst prof, WVa Univ, 1946-1947; lectr geol, Columbia Univ, 1946; Instr geol & geog, Carleton Col, 1942-1943. **Memberships:** Fel AAAS; fel Geol Soc Am. **Research Statement & Publications:** Areal geology; dynamic geomorphology; geology of Colorado Plateau; Pleistocene Glaciation of Maine. **Mailing Address:** Pond Rd, Augusta, ME 04330.

KOONS, STEPHEN J, BIOPHYSICS. **Personal Data:** b Washington, DC, October 26, 1951. **Education:** Brandeis Univ, BA, 1973; State Univ NY, Buffalo, PhD (biophysics), 1981. **Professional Experience:** SR BIOMED ENG, VISX, INC, 1990-; Develop mgr physics, Lacktos Sigmor Labs, 1986-1990. **Memberships:** Am Biophys Soc; Am Soc Cell Biol; AAAS. **Research Statement & Publications:** Biophysics. **Mailing Address:** VISX Inc, 3400 Central Expressway, Santa Clara, CA 95051-0703.

KOONTZ, JAMES L, RESEARCH ADMINISTRATION. **Personal Data:** b Dayton, Ohio, 1934. **Honors & Awards:** Gold Medal, Soc Mfg Engrs, 1990. **Professional Experience:** PRES & CHIEF EXEC OFFICER, KINGSBURY CORP, KEENE, NH, 1982-; pres, Kingsbury Corp, Keene, NH, beginning 1982; exec vpres, Kingsbury Corp, 1978-1982; group vpres, Ex-Cell-O Corp, 1969-1978; gen mgr, XLO Parker, subsid, Ex-Cell-O Corp, Div Mach Tools, Ex-Cell-O Corp, 1968; staff, Micromatic Inc, subsid, Ex-Cell-O Corp, Detroit, Mich, 1966-1968; staff mfg & eng, Gen Motors, Chrysler & Bendix Corp; emer chmn, Nat Ctr Mfg Sci. **Memberships:** Mfg Sci Bd Dept Defense; Nat Mach Builders Asn. **Mailing Address:** Kingsbury Corp, 80 Laurel St, Keene, NH 03431-4207. **Fax:** 603-352-8789.

KOONTZ, JOHN W, BIOCHEMISTRY. **Education:** Earlham Col, BA; Univ KY, PhD. **Professional Experience:** INTERIM DEAN & PROF, DIV BIOL, UNIV TENN, as of 2006.

Mailing Address: Biol Div, Univ Tenn, 1414 W Cumberland Ave, Knoxville, TN 37996-0840. **Fax:** 865-974-4057. **E-Mail:** jkoontz@utk.edu

KOONTZ, WARREN WOODSON, JR, UROLOGY. **Personal Data:** b Lynchburg, Va, June 10, 1932; m 1957, c 2. **Education:** Va Mil Inst, BA, 1953; Univ Va, MD, 1957. **Professional Experience:** MODERATOR & PROF EMER SURG, as of 2001; prof urol & chmn dept, Med Col Va, beginning 1970; consult, McGuire Vet Admin Hosp, beginning 1970 & Portsmouth Naval Hosp, beginning 1971; asst prof, Harvard Univ, 1969-1970; asst urologist, Mass Gen Hosp, 1969-1970; from instr to asst prof, Med Col Va, 1966-1969; resident urol, Ny Hosp, 1962-1966; from intern to resident surg, Ny Hosp, 1957-1962; AT DEPT SURG, VA COMMONWEALTH UNIV. **Memberships:** Am Col Surgeons; Am Urol Asn; Soc Pediat Urol; Soc Univ Urol. **Research Statement & Publications:** Pediatric urology; urinary tract cancer. **Mailing Address:** Dept Surg, Med Col Va, PO Box 118, Richmond, VA 23201-0118.

KOOP, CHARLES EVERETT, SURGERY. **Personal Data:** b Brooklyn, NY, October 14, 1916; m Elizabeth; c Allen, Norman & Elizabeth Thompson. **Education:** Dartmouth Col, BA, 1937; Cornell Univ, MD, 1941. **Honorary Degrees:** DSc (med), Univ Pa, 1947; LLD, Eastern Baptist Col, 1960; MD, Univ Liverpool, 1968; LHD, Wheaton Col, 1973. **Honors & Awards:** Denis Brown Gold Medal, Brit Asn Pediat Surgeons; William E Ladd Gold Medal, Am Acad Pediat. **Professional Experience:** SR SCHOLAR, C EVERETT KOOP INST, DARTMOUTH, 1991-; ELIZABETH DECAMP MCINERNY PROF SURG, 1991-; chmn, Nat Safe Kids Campaign, Wash, DC, 1989-; dir, Off Int Health, 1982; surg gen, 1981-1989; dep asst secy health, USPHS, 1981-1989; prof pediat, Univ Pa, 1971-1989; ed-in-chief, J Pediat, Surg, 1964-1976; consult, US Naval Hosp, beginning 1964; prof pediat surg, Univ Pa, 1959-1989; from asst prof to assoc prof, Univ Pa, 1949-1959; surgeon-in-chief, Children's Hosp, Philadelphia, 1948-1981; from asst instr to instr surg, Univ Pa, 1942-1947; chmn, Bd Trustees, Nat Mus Health & Med Found & Bd Int Health, Inst Med. **Memberships:** Inst Med-Nat Acad Sci; Am Surg Asn; fel Am Col Surgeons; Brit Asn Pediat Surg; Am Pediat Surg Asn; fel Am Acad Pediat; Royal Col Surgeons Eng; Soc Univ Surgeons. **Research Statement & Publications:** Pediatric surgical techniques; neonatalogy; childhood tumors. **Mailing Address:** C Everett Koop Inst, Dartmouth Col, 7025 Strasenburgh Hall, Hanover, NH 03755.

KOOP, DENNIS RAY, ENZYMOLOGY, METABOLISM. **Education:** Northwestern Univ, PhD (biochem), 1979; Bradley Univ, BS, 1974. **Professional Experience:** PROF, DEPT PHYSIOL & PHARMACOL, OREGON HEALTH SCI UNIV, as of 2004; assoc prof, Dept Physiol & Pharmacol, Oregon Health Sci Univ, beginning 1991; assoc prof, Environ Health Sci & Pharmacol Case West, 1986-1991; Asst prof biochem, Univ Mich, 1983-1986. **Mailing Address:** Dept Physiol & Pharmacol, Ore Health Sci Univ, 3181 SW Sam Jackson Park Rd, Portland, OR 97239-3098. **Fax:** 503-494-4352. **E-Mail:** koopd@ohsu.edu

KOOP, JOHN C, STATISTICS. **Personal Data:** b Myitkyina, Burma, March 6, 1919; American citizen; m 1943, Elsie E Ure; c Wilfred, Rachel, Elizabeth, Helen, Thomas, Paul, Arthur & George. **Education:** Univ Rangoon, BSc, 1942; NC State Univ, PhD (statist), 1958. **Professional Experience:** CONSULT, 1982-; sr group scientist, statist sci admin, Res Triangle Inst, 1970-1981; sr adv sampling agr & head res training, Dom Bur Statist, Can, 1966-1970; assoc prof, NC State Univ, 1965-1966; vis assoc prof, NC State Univ, 1961-1965; vis asst prof exp statist, NC State Univ, 1960-1961; mem, Int Labour Off, Switz, 1959-1960; Chief labor statist, Directorate Labour, Govt Burma, 1948-1958. **Memberships:** Fel Am Statist Asn; Royal Statist Soc; Burma Res Soc; Int Asn Survey Statisticians; Int Statist Inst. **Research Statement & Publications:** Sampling theory for finite universes derived on basis of axioms; theory of ratio estimation; unified theory of estimation for sample surveys taking into account response and measurement errors; statistical inference; demographic study of minority community in Burma. **Mailing Address:** 3201 Clark Ave, Raleigh, NC 27607.

KOOPMAN, RONALD P, APPLIED PHYSICS. **Personal Data:** b Grand Rapids, Mich, March 15, 1943. **Education:** Univ Mich, BS, 1965, MS, 1967; Univ Calif, PhD (appl physics), 1977. **Professional Experience:** PROJ MGR, BIO NAT SECURITY PROG, LAWRENCE LIVERMORE NAT LAB, as of 2003; prog leader, Lawrence Livermore Nat Lab, beginning 1968. **Memberships:** Am Phys Soc. **Mailing Address:** Lawrence Livermore Nat Lab, PO Box 808, L-467, Livermore, CA 94550. **Fax:** 925-423-6425. **E-Mail:** koopman1@llnl.gov

KOOPMAN, WILLIAM JAMES, IMMUNOLOGY. **Personal Data:** b Lafayette, Ind, August 19, 1945; m 1968, Lilliane; c Benjamin, Anna, Rebecca & Steven. **Education:** Wash & Jefferson Univ, BA, 1967; Harvard Univ, MD, 1972; Am Bd Internal Med, dipl. **Honors & Awards:** Carol Nachman Res Prize, Fed Repub Ger, 1982; Master, American College of Physicians; Distinguished Faculty Lecturer UAB 2004; President's Gold Medal for Achievement 2004; Distinguished Professor and Chair Emeritus 2005-. **Professional Experience:** CHMN, DEPT MED, 1995-2005; chmn bd sci counselors, Nat Inst Arthritis, Metab & Digestive Dis, 1991-1995; Howard L Holley prof med, Univ Ala, 1988-1995; Spencer Chair for Medical Science Leadership 1995-2005 Ed, Arthritis & Rheumatism J, 1985-1990; Ed Arthritis and Allied Conditions (12th-15th Editions); DIR MULTIPURPOSE ARTHRITIS CTR, PROF MED RHEUMATOLOGY & CLIN IMMUNOL, UNIV ALA, 1983-1995; from asst prof to assoc prof, PROF MED RHEUMATOLOGY & CLIN IMMUNOL, UNIV ALA, 1977-2005; res fel, NIH, 1974-1977; Intern/resident med, Mass Gen Hosp, 1972-1974. **Memberships:** Inst Med-Nat Acad Sci; fel Am Col Rheumatology (treas 1992-1994 pres elect 1995-1996 pres 1996-1997); Am Soc Clin Invest (pres 1990-1991); Asn Am Physicians; Am Asn Immunologists; fel Am Col Physicians. **Research Statement & Publications:** Contributed over 260 articles to professional journals. **Mailing Address:** Faculty Office TowerRm 802, 1530 3rd Ave S, Birmingham, AL 35294-3408. **Fax:** 205-934-4198. **E-Mail:** wkoopman@uab.edu

KOOPMANN, GARY HUGO, MECHANICAL ENGINEERING. **Personal Data:** b Howells, Nebr, May 8, 1939; m 1972, Barbara; c Hannah & Eve. **Education:** Univ Nebr, BS, 1962; Cath Univ, MS, 1966, PhD, 1969. **Professional Experience:** DISTINGUISHED PROF MECH ENG, PA STATE UNIV, as of 2006; DIR, CTR ACOUST & VIBRATIONS, PA STATE UNIV, 1988-; prof mech eng, Pa State Univ, beginning 1988; prof, Univ Houston, 1976-1987; fel, Univ lectr, 1970-1976; fel, Inst Sound & Vibration, Southampton, Eng, 1969-1970; res scientist, US Naval Res Lab, 1962-1966. **Memberships:** Fel Am Soc Mech Engrs; fel Acoust Soc Am. **Research Statement & Publications:** Noise reduction; granted several patents. **Mailing Address:** Mech & Nuclear Eng, Pa State Univ, 157 Hammond Bldg, Univ Park, State College, PA 16802. **Fax:** 814-863-4848. **E-Mail:** ghk@kirkof.psu.edu

KOOPMANS, HENRY SJOERD, NUTRITION, ENERGY BALANCE. **Personal Data:** b Washington, DC, January 28, 1944; m 1990, Jan; c Robert, Lisa & Mark. **Education:** Harvard Col, BA, 1966; Univ Calif, San Diego, PhD (physiol psychol), 1972. **Honors & Awards:** NIH career develop Award, 1975-1986; Future Leader Award, Nutrit Found. **Professional Experience:** ADJ PROF MED PHYSIOL, UNIV CALGARY, as of 2005; PROF MED PHYSIOL, UNIV CALGARY, 1986-; Alta Heritage med res scholar, 1983-1995; assoc prof, Univ Calgary, 1983-1986; vis colleague, Hammersmith Hosp, London, 1979-1981; adj prof, Rockefeller Univ, 1978-1979; from asst prof to assoc prof, Columbia Univ, 1973-1983; res assoc, Obesity Ctr, St Luke's-Roosevelt Hosp, 1973-1983; res prof psychol, Univ Calif, San Diego, 1972-1973. **Memberships:** Neuroscience Soc; Int Union Physiol Sci; NAm Asn Study Obesity; Soc Study Ingestive Behav; Inst Asn Study Obesity. **Research Statement & Publications:** Internal control of food intake, energy expenditure and body weight; obesity. **Mailing Address:** Dept Physiol & Biophys Univ Calgary, Rm 1755 Health Sci Ctr, Calgary, AB T2N 4N1, Can. **Fax:** 403-282-8249. **E-Mail:** koopmans@ucalgary.ca

KOOPMANS, LAMBERT HERMAN, MATHEMATICAL STATISTICS. **Personal Data:** b Chicago, Ill, July 23, 1930; m 1955, c 4. **Education:** San Diego State Col, AB, 1952; Univ Calif, PhD, 1958. **Professional Experience:** RETIRED; diabetes proj, 1978-1982 & Vet Admin Hosp, Albuquerque, 1978-1979; civil eng fac & dept path, Univ NMex, 1976-1977; vis prof statist, Princeton Univ, 1975; sabbatical leave fac math, Univ Calif, Santa Cruz, 1971-1972; chmn dept, Univ NMex, 1969-1974; prof math & statist, Univ NMex, 1968-1989; consult, Westinghouse Corp, 1965-1967; consult, Sandia Corp, 1964-1972; assoc prof, Univ NMex, 1964-1968; mem staff, Sandia Corp, 1958-1964; assoc biostatist, Univ Calif, 1957-1958; asst statist, Univ Calif, 1952-1956. **Memberships:** Fel Am Statist Asn; Biomet Soc; fel Inst Math Statist. **Research Statement & Publications:** Data analysis; time series analysis. **Mailing Address:** 7312 Marilyn Ave, Albuquerque, NM 87109.

KOOPOWITZ, HAROLD, NEUROPHYSIOLOGY, INVERTEBRATE ZOOLOGY, CONSERVATION BIOLOGY. **Personal Data:** b East London, SAfrica, September 10, 1940; m 1969, c 1. **Education:** Rhodes Univ, SAfrica, BSc, 1962, MSc, 1964; Univ Calif, Los Angeles, PhD (zoology), 1968. **Honors & Awards:** Herbert Medal, Int Bulb Soc, 2003. **Professional Experience:** PROF BIOL, UNIV CALIF, IRVINE, as of 2004; assoc prof biol, Univ Calif, Irvine, beginning 1975; asst prof, Univ Calif, Irvine, 1968-1975. **Memberships:** Brit Soc Exp Biol; Am Soc Zool; Soc Gen Physiol; Soc Neuroscience. **Research Statement & Publications:** Organization of flatworm nervous systems; electrophysiology of vision in insect eyes. **Mailing Address:** Dept Ecol & Evolutionary Biol, Univ Calif, 475, 446 Steinhaus Hall, Irvine, CA 92697-2525. **Fax:** 949-824-2181. **E-Mail:** hkoopowi@uci.edu

KOOSIS, PAUL JACOB, MATHEMATICAL ANALYSIS. **Personal Data:** b Los Angeles, Calif, April 20, 1929. **Education:** Univ Calif, Berkeley, BA, 1950, PhD (math), 1954. **Professional Experience:** EMER PROF MATH, MCGILL UNIV, AS OF 2006; prof math, Univ Calif, Los Angeles, beginning 1970; from asst prof to assoc prof, Univ Calif, Los Angeles, 1963-1970; from asst prof to assoc prof, Fordham Univ, 1962-1963; NSF fels, 1960-1961, asst instr math sci, NY Univ, 1959-1960; Fulbright fel to France, 1957-1958; asst instr math sci, NY Univ, 1955-1957; instr math, Univ Mich, 1954-1955. **Memberships:** Am Math Soc; Math Soc France. **Research Statement & Publications:** Classical harmonic analysis; complex variable theory; theory of approximation. **Mailing Address:** Dept Math & Statist, McGill Univ, 805 Sherbrooke St W, Montreal, PQ H3A 2K6, Can. **Fax:** 514-398-3899. **E-Mail:** koosis@math.mcgill.ca

KOOTSEY, JOSEPH MAILEN, COMPUTER SIMULATION. **Personal Data:** b Houston, Tex, September 3, 1939; m 1961, Lynne; c Brenden & Sean. **Education:** Pac Union Col, BA, 1960; Brown Univ, ScM, 1964, PhD (physics), 1966. **Professional Experience:** DIR, UNIV INFO SYST, LOMA LINDA UNIV, as of 2006; PROF & CHAIR PHYSIOL PHARMACOL, LOMA LINDA UNIV, 1998-; chief info officer, Andrew Univ, 1997-1998; vpres acad, Col Arts & Sci, 1994-1997; pres, Simulation Resources, Inc, 1991-; dean, Col Arts & Sci, 1991-1994; adj assoc prof cell biol & comput sci, Duke Univ, 1991-1993; assoc prof cell biol, Nat Biomed Simulation Resource, 1989-1991; dir, Nat Biomed Simulation Resource, 1983-1991; res assoc prof computsci, Duke Univ, 1982-1991; assoc prof physiol, Duke Univ, 1982-1989; res assoc prof physiol, Duke Univ, 1979-1984; prof biophys, Andrews Univ, 1976-1979; asst prof physiol & pharmacol, Duke Univ, 1971-1976; NIH spec fel, Duke Univ, 1969-1971; Asst prof physiol & biophys, Loma Linda Univ, 1967-1969; Bank Am-Giannini Found grant, Loma Linda Univ, 1965-1967. **Memberships:** AAAS; Am Physiol Soc; Biophys Soc; Asn Comput Mach; Sr mem Soc Comput Simulations; Inst Elec & Electronics Engrs; Am Asn Higher Educ; Am Physical Soc; NY Acad Sci; fel Am Heart Assn; Soc Math Biol. **Research Statement & Publications:** Cardiac electrophysiology; computer simulation in physiology; medical education; utilization of computer simulation to reassemble complex biological systems; ion regulation and electrical activity in cardiac muscle cells; computer software for simulations. **Mailing Address:** Dept Physiol / Pharmacol, Loma Linda Univ, Loma Linda, CA 92350. **Fax:** 909-558-7916.

KOOYMAN, GERALD LEE, NATIONAL HISTORY, POLAR BIOLOGY. **Personal Data:** b Salt Lake City, Utah, June 16, 1934; m 1962, Melba; c Carsten & Tory. **Education:** Univ Calif, Los Angeles, AB, 1957; Univ Ariz, PhD (zoology), 1966. **Honors & Awards:** Creative Scientist Award, NSF, 1991. **Professional Experience:** MEM CTR MARINE BIOTECHNOLOGY AND BIOMED, SCRIPPS INSTITUTION, as of 2006; prof, scripps inst oceanog, univ calif, san diego, 1991-1994; from asst res physiologist to res physiologist, Scripps Inst Oceanog, Univ Calif, San Diego, 1968-1991; res physiologist, Scripps Inst Oceanog, Univ Calif, San Diego, 1967-1968; NSF fel, Anat & Physiol of Marine Mammals, London Hosp Med Col, Eng, 1966-1967; res asst Antarctic seal studies, Univ Ariz, 1963-1966; Sci fel Zool Soc London. **Memberships:** AAAS; Am Soc Zool; Am Physiol Soc; Sigma Xi; Explorers Club. **Research Statement & Publications:** Behavior and physiology of diving in aquatic birds and mammals, especially pressure effects; comparative respiratory physiology and anatomy of vertebrates; conservation of marine birds and mammals. **Mailing Address:** Scripps Inst Oceanog, CMBB-0204, La Jolla, CA 92093. **Fax:** 858-534-1305. **E-Mail:** gkooyman@ucsd.edu

KOOZEKANAI, SAID H, ELECTRICAL ENGINEERING, BIOMEDICAL ENGINEERING. **Personal Data:** b Mash-had, Iran, March 15, 1933; m 1965. **Education:** Univ Tehran, Electro-Mech Eng, 1956; Brown Univ, PhD (elec eng), 1961; Univ Dayton, MS, 1969. **Professional Experience:** PROF EMER ELEC ENG, OHIO STATE UNIV, as of 2004; prof Elec Eng, Ohio State Univ, beginning 1976; from asst prof to assoc prof, Ohio State Univ, 1966-1976; sr res scientist, Raytheon Res Div, Mass, 1961-1965. **Memberships:** Am Inst Physics; Am Phys Soc; Inst Elec & Electronics Engrs. **Research Statement & Publications:** Quantum electronics; lasers; antennas and propagation. **Mailing Address:** 756 Dreese LAB, 2015 Neil AVE, Columbus, OH 43210. **E-Mail:** koozekanani.1@osu.edu

KOPANSKI, JOSEPH J, INTEGRATED CIRCUIT ENGINEERING, SCANNING PROBE MICROSCOPY. **Personal Data:** b Cleveland, Ohio, February 8, 1960. **Education:** Case Western Reserve Univ, BS, 1982, MS, 1985. **Professional Experience:** ELEC ENGR, NAT INST STAND & TECHNOL, 1985-. **Memberships:** Inst Elec & Electronics Engrs; Electrochem Soc Am physicial soc. **Research Statement & Publications:** Electrical characterization of semiconductor materials, processes and circuits; developing scanning probe microscope based methods for semiconductor characterization. **Mailing Address:** Nat Inst Stand & Technol, 100 Bureau Dr, Gaithersburg, MD 20899. **Fax:** 301-948-4081. **E-Mail:** jkopanski@nist.gov

KOPASKA-MERKEL, DAVID CRISPIN, GROUND WATER RESOURCES, EDUCATIONAL TECHNOLOGY TRANSFER. **Personal Data:** b Charlottesville, Va, January 11, 1957; m 1979, c 2. **Education:** Col William & Mary, BS, 1978; Univ Kans, PhD (geol), 1983. **Professional Experience:** Mem, K12 Earth Sci Educ Comt, Soc Sedimentary Res, 1994-; HEAD, GROUND WATER SECT, GEOL SURV ALA, 1994-; chair, Geol Sect, Ala Acad Sci, 1994-1996; corresp ed, J Sedimentary Res, 1993-1996; Ed, Ala Geol Soc Newslettt, 1992-1996; geologist, Ground Water Sect, Geol Surv Ala, 1989-1994; res assoc, Northeastern Sci Found, 1987-1989; post doctoral, Univ Toronto, 1986-1987; Petrol geologist, Shell Oil Co, 1982-1986. **Memberships:** Soc Sedimentary Geol. **Research Statement & Publications:** Responsible for preparing annual reports summarizing Alabama's water resources; write educational materials for all levels from Kindergarten through adult on earth science in Alabama; participate in diverse water-related research projects. **Mailing Address:** Geol Surv Ala, 420 Hackberry Lane, PO Box O, Tuscaloosa, AL 35486. **Fax:** 205-349-2861. **E-Mail:** davidkm@ogb.gsa.tuscaloosa.al.us

KOPCHICK, JOHN J, MOLECULAR BIOLOGY, ZOOLOGY. **Personal Data:** b Punxsutawney, Pa, November 2, 1950. **Education:** Ind Univ Pa, BS, 1972, MS, 1975; Univ Tex, PhD (virol-biomed sci), 1980. **Professional Experience:** ADJ PROF, DEPT CHEM, OHIO UNIV, as of 2003; PRIN INVESTR GROWTH, OBESITY & DIABETES GROUP, OHIO UNIV, as of 2003; Competitive ResGrants Prog, USDA, 1990-1991; Adv Comt Emerging Agr Technologies, Off Technol Assessment, 1989-1990; mem, Child Health & Human Develop Grant Rev Comt, NIH, 1988 & 1991; PROF, DEPT BIOMED SCI, KONNEKER RES CTR, COL OSTEOP MED, OHIO UNIV, 1987-; Milton & Lawrence H Goll eminent scholar endowed prof molecular & cellular biol, Ohio Univ, 1987-; DIR, MOLECULAR BIOL DEPT, EDISON ANIMAL BIOTECHNOL CTR, OHIO UNIV, 1987-; group leader molecular biol, Dept Animal Drug Discovery, 1985-1986; res fel, Dept Biochem Genetics, Merck Inst Therapeut Res, Merck Sharp & Dohme Res Labs, 1984-1985; sr res biochemist, Dept Biochem Genetics, Merck Inst Therapeut Res, Merck Sharp & Dohme Res Labs, 1982-1984; Am Cancer Soc postdoctoral fel, Roche Inst Molecular Biol, 1980-1982; med technologist, Bellaire Gen Hosp, 1976-1980; Teaching asst microbiol, genetics & gen biol, Ind Univ Pa, 1972-1975; sci adv, DNX, Princeton, NJ. **Memberships:** Sigma Xi; Am Soc Microbiol; AAAS; Am Soc Biochem & Molecular Biol. **Research Statement & Publications:** Molecular cloning of DNA molecules encoding wildtype and in vitro mutated growth hormones, growth hormone receptors, hypothalmic regulatory proteins and neuropeptides; cloning of efficient eucaryotic expression vectors for the production of proteins in cultured mammalian cells; structure-function studies of growth hormone employing transgenic animals; author of more than 60 publications. **Mailing Address:** Dept Biomed Sci, Konneker Res Lab, Col Osteo Med, Ohio Univ, Athens, OH 45701. **Fax:** 740-593-4795. **E-Mail:** jkopchick1@ohiou.edu

KOPCHIK, RICHARD MICHAEL, POLYMER PRODUCT & PROCESS DEVELOPMENT, POLYMER MORPHOLOGY & MICROSTRUCTURE & REACTIVE EXTRUSION. **Personal Data:** b Punxsutawney, Pa, April 29, 1941; m 1964, Joan; c David & Ann. **Education:** Carnegie Mellon Univ, BS, 1963; Univ Rochester, PhD (org chem), 1968. **Professional Experience:** Consultant, Polymer Products and Proceses 2003-; Sr Technologist, Forbo-Novilon 1997-2003; PROJ MGR, CATALYST GROUP, 1995-1997; Senior Research Associate, Rohm & Haas Co, 1989-1994; tech mgr, Rohm & Haas Co, 1986-1989; sr res assoc, Rohm & Haas Co, 1980-1986; Res chemist polymers, Rohm & Haas Co, 1969-1980. **Memberships:** Am Chem Soc; Sigma Xi; Soc Plastics Eng; NY Acad Sci; Tau Beta Pi. **Research Statement & Publications:** Organic chemistry; free radical reactions; chemical modification of polymers; continuous preparation and processing of polymers; polymer chemistry; polymeric sorbents; engineering plastics; elastomers; polymer morphology and microstructure. **Mailing Address:** 1335 Stephen Way, Southampton, PA 18966-4349. **Fax:** 215-322-5031. **E-Mail:** rkopchik@voicenet.com

KOPE, ROBERT GLENN, STOCK ASSESSMENT, OPTIMAL MANAGEMENT. **Personal Data:** b Reedley, Calif, August 5, 1953; m 1976, Mary; c Laura & Rachel. **Education:** Calif State Univ, BA, 1980; Univ Calif, Davis, PhD (ecol), 1987. **Professional Experience:** FISHERY BIOLOGIST, NAT MARINE FISHERIES SERV, 1989-; lectr, Univ Calif, Davis, 1989; postgrad researcher, Univ Calif, Davis, 1987-1989. **Memberships:** Resource Modeling Asn; Pac Fisher y Biologists. **Research Statement & Publications:** Optimal management of renewable resources; stock assessment; spatial population modeling. **Mailing Address:** NMFS, NW fishery Sci Ctr, 2725 Mountlake Blvd E, Seattle, WA 98112-2013.

KOPECEK, JINDRICH, POLYMERIC DRUG DELIVERY SYSTEMS, BIOCOMPATIBILITY OF POLYMERS. **Personal Data:** b Strakonice, Czech, January 27, 1940; m 1985, Pavla; c Jana. **Education:** Inst Chem Technol, Prague, MS, 1961; Czech Acad Sci, Prague, PhD (polymer chem), 1965, DSc, (chem) 1990. **Honors & Awards:** Sci Award, Chem Sect, Czech Chem Soc, 1972, 1975, 1977, 1978 & 1985; Sci Award, Presidiums Czech & USSR Acad Sci, 1977; Barre's Lectr, Univ Montreal, 1990; J Heller award for best paper J controlled releas, clemson award and on basic res soc, biomaterials 1995, Pres, Controlled Rel Society, 1995-1996, 1999 foundrs award controlled release 1999; Millennial pharm scientist award, millennial world congress pharm sci 8, 2000 paul dawson biotech award Am assn col pharmay 2001; J Heyrovsky Honorary Medalfor Merit in Chemical Sciences, Academy of Sciences of the Czech Republi c, 2003, Chair, NIH Biomaterials and Biointerfaces Study Section, 2003-, Chair, Gordon Conf on Drug Carriers in Medicine and Biology, 2004. **Professional Experience:** Distinguished prof, Bioeng & Pharmaceut, 2002-; dept Chmn Pharmaceutics, 1999-2004; PROF BIOENG & PHARMACEUT, UNIV UTAH, 1989-; co-dir, Ctr Controlled Chem Delivery, Univ Utah, 1986-; vis prof, Univ Paris-Nord, 1983 & 2000; Univ Utah, 1986-1988; Tokyo med women's U, 1999; mem, Comt New Polymers, Ministry Health, Czech, 1976-1986; head lab med polymers, Czech Acad Sci, Inst Macromolecular Chem, 1972-1988; Prin investr numerous grants, 1969-; fel chem eng, Nat Res Coun Can, 1967-1968; Res sci officer, Czech Acad Sci, Inst Macromolecular Chem, 1965-1972. **Memberships:** Am Chem Soc; Biomat Soc; AAAS; fel Am Asn Pharmaceut Scientists; Am Asn Cancer Res; Controlled Release Soc; fel Am Inst Med Biomed Eng. **Research Statement & Publications:** Biocompatibility and biodegradation of polymers; tailor-made synthesis of bioactive, biorecognizable polymers; targetable polymeric anticancer drug carriers; self-assembly of macromolecules; genetically engineered biomaterials. **Mailing Address:** Dept Bioeng BPRB Rm 205, Univ Utah, Salt Lake City, UT 84112. **Fax:** 801-581-7848. **E-Mail:** jindrich.kopecek@m.cc.utah.edu

KOPECKY, KARL RUDOLPH, ORGANIC CHEMISTRY. **Personal Data:** b Hradec Kralove, Czech, October 5, 1932; American citizen; m 1963, c 2. **Education:** Iowa State Col, BS, 1954; Univ Calif, Los Angeles, PhD, 1959. **Professional Experience:** PROF EMER CHEM, UNIV ALTA, as of 2003; prof chem, Univ Alta, beginning 1977; from asst prof to assoc prof, Univ Alta, 1961-1977; NIH fel, Calif Inst Technol, 1959-1961; Instr chem, Univ Calif, Los Angeles, 1959. **Memberships:** Am Chem Soc; Chem Inst Can. **Research Statement & Publications:** Thermal reactions of styrene; radicals from chiral sources; peroxide reactions; chemiluminescent compounds; reactions of stable radicals. **Mailing Address:** Dept Chem, Univ Alta, Edmonton, AB T6G 2R3, Can. **Fax:** 780-492-8231. **E-Mail:** karl.kopecky@ualberta.ca

KOPELL, NANCY J, DYNAMICAL SYSTEMS. **Personal Data:** b New York, NY, November 8, 1942. **Education:** Cornell Univ, BA, 1963; Univ Calif, Berkeley, MA, 1965, PhD (dynamical systs), 1967. **Honors & Awards:** R Bowen Mem lectr, Berkeley, 1986; Vollmer Fries Mem lectr, Rensselaer Polytech Inst, 1991; KAC Mem lectrs, Los Alamos Nat Lab, 1992; Emmy Noether lectr, Am Math Soc, Baltimore, 1992; Matthew Vassar lectr, Vassar Col, 1994. **Professional Experience:** CO DIR, CTR BIO DYNAMICS, as of 2003; Ordway vis prof, Univ Minn, 1992; John D & Catherine T MacArthur fel, 1990-1995; PROF MATH, BOSTON UNIV, 1986-; J S Guggenheim fel, 1984-1985; consult, Sci Systs Inc, 1980-1984; consult, Math Res Ctr, Madison, 1979; prof, Northeastern Univ, 1978-1986; vis scholar, Mass Inst Technol, 1976-1977; vis sr res scientist, Sci Res Coun, Eng, 1976; vis scholar, Calif Inst Technol, 1976; Alfred P Sloan fel, 1975-1977; vis assoc prof appl math, Mass Inst Technol, 1975; assoc prof, Northeastern Univ, 1972-1978; Fel, Nat Ctr Sci Res, 1970; asst prof, Northeastern Univ, 1969-1972; CLE Moore instr math, Mass Inst Technol, 1967-1969; from asst dir to dir, High Sch Students & Teachers Regional Prog, NSF, 1965-1967. **Memberships:** Nat Acad Sci; Am Acad Arts & Sci. **Research Statement & Publications:** Contributed over 60 articles to professional publications. **Mailing Address:** Dept Math & Statist, Boston Univ, 111 Cummington St, Boston, MA 02215. **E-Mail:** nk@bu.edu

KOPELMAN, JAY B, INTERNATIONAL ENERGY SCIENCES. **Personal Data:** b New York, NY, February 24, 1939; m 1990. **Education:** Rensselaer Polytech Inst, BS, 1960; Northwestern Univ, PhD (physics), 1965. **Professional Experience:** RETIRED; mgr int activities & exec asst vpres, Elec Power Res Inst, 1982-1994; mgr spec studies, Elec Power Res Inst, 1978-1982; mgr, Energy Modeling Prog, Stanford Res Inst, 1974-1978; asst dean grad sch, Univ Colo, Boulder, 1968-1974; asst prof, Univ Colo, Boulder, 1966-1974; Res assoc physics, Univ Colo, Boulder, 1964-1966. **Memberships:** AAAS; Am Phys Soc. **Research Statement & Publications:** Energy technology; energy economics; modelling. **Mailing Address:** Elec Power Res Inst, PO Box 10412, Palo Alto, CA 94303.

KOPELMAN, RAOUL, PHYSICAL CHEMISTRY, ANALYTICAL CHEMISTRY. **Personal Data:** b Vienna, Austria, October 21, 1933; American citizen; m 1955, Chava; c Orion, Leeron & Shirli. **Education:** Israel Inst Technol, BS, 1955, dipl eng, 1956, MSc, 1957; Columbia Univ, PhD (chem), 1960. **Honors & Awards:** Sokol Award; Creativity Award, NSF. **Professional Experience:** FAJANS PROF CHEM, PHYSICS & APPL PHYSICS, UNIV MICH, ANN ARBOR, 1994-; prof physics, Physics & Appl Physics, Univ Mich, Ann Arbor, 1991-1994; Fulbright fel, 1987-1988; nat res serv award, NIH, 1987-1988; spec res fel, Fogarty int fel, 1979; sr fel, NATO, 1976; spec res fel, NIH, 1972-1973; from asst prof to prof chem, Physics & Appl Physics, Univ Mich, Ann Arbor, 1966-1994; sr res fel, Calif inst Technol, 1965-1966; res fel, Calif inst Technol, 1964-1965; lectr, Israel Inst Technol, 1962-1964; res assoc chem, Harvard Univ, 1960-1962; Fulbright award, 1957. **Memberships:** Fel Am Phys Soc; Am Chem Soc; Biophys Soc; Mat Res Soc; fel AAAS. **Research Statement & Publications:** Excitation dynamics in molecular and biomimetic aggregates, excitons and phonons in disordered materials, membranes and photosynthetic units; 1.5 K time-resolved high-resolution tunable-laser microspectroscopy; supercomputer simulations of critical phenomena, transport and chemical kinetics; heterogeneous kinetics in low-dimensional and fractal domains; near-field optical microscopy and chemical nanosensors. **Mailing Address:** Dept Chem, Univ Mich, Ann Arbor, MI 48109-1055. **Fax:** 734-936-2778. **E-Mail:** kopelman@umich.edu

KOPELOVE, ALAN BRIAN, ANALYTICAL INSTRUMENTATION DESIGN & CUSTOM SENSOR RESEARCH & DEVELOPMENT, WATER QUALITY INSTRUMENTATION & BUSINESS DEVELOPMENT FOR TECHNICAL PRODUCTS. **Personal Data:** b Norfolk, Va, February 22, 1954; m 1975, Merry; c Katherine & Daniel. **Education:** Va Polytech Inst, BS, 1976; Colo State Univ, MS, 1981; Daniels Col Business, Univ Denver, MBA, 2001. **Honors & Awards:** Sun's Top Achievement Recognition Summit Award, 2002; Two Teaching Awards for Excellence, Colorado State University Award of Merit for Scholarly Articles from Society of Technical Communications. **Professional Experience:** Business Development Consultant, 2005 - present; Business Development Manager, Sun Microsystems, 2001 - 2005; Worldwide Marketing Manager, Denver Instrument Company, 1999 - 2000; Faculty, University of Colorado at Denver, Metro State College of Denver, Red Rocks Community College, Front Range Community College, 1999; President and Founder, Clear Creek Chemistry, 1996-2000; Product Manager, Electrochemistry Products, DENVER INSTRUMENT CO, 1993-1999; Res Asst, Colo State Univ, 1988-1992; Research Chemist, Hach Co, 1981-1988; adj instr, Hunter Col, 1979-1981; Grad res asst, Colo State Univ, 1976-1979. **Research Statement & Publications:** Development of new analytical methodologies and instrumentation using electroanalytical techniques; Research and development for improved pH, ion, conductivity and dissolved oxygen measurements; study of conducting polymers and small molecule analogs of the active site of metalloproteins. **Mailing Address:** 7024 Blue Creek Rd, Evergreen, CO 80439. **E-Mail:** akopelove@aol.com

KOPELOVICH, LEVY, ONCOLOGY, MEDICAL SCIENCES. **Personal Data:** b Vilna, Poland, August 13, 1934; American citizen; m 1975, Lenore; c Rachel, Jonathan & Sarah. **Education:** Hebrew Univ Jerusalem, BSc, 1958; Univ Calif, Berkeley, PhD (toxicol), 1962. **Honors & Awards:** Edith Wolfson cancer res award, 1966. **Professional Experience:** PROG DIR, DIV CANCER PREVENTION, NAT CANCER INST, NIH, as of 2004; French nat cancer Inst, Ville Juiff, 1988, 1990; charter mem, Tampa Bay Sci Consortium, 1987-; dir res & develop, Univ Sfla Col Med, 1986-1992; mem, molecular biol ctr, Univ SFla, 1984-; consult, sci panel comt Interagency radiation, Wash, 1984-; SR SCIENTIST, VET ADMIN MED CTR, BAY PINES, 1984-; PROF PATH & BIOCHEM, UNIV SFLA COL MED, 1984-; Norweg Nat Cancer Ctr, Oslo, 1981; vis prof, Ger Cancer Ctr, Heidelberg, 1978; assoc prof, Cornell Univ Grad Sch Med Sci, 1977-1983; assoc mem, Mem Sloan Kettering Cancer Ctr, 1977-1983; asst prof biochem, Cornell Univ Grad Sch Med Sci, 1969-1977; asst mem, mem sloan kettering cancer ctr, 1969-1977; distinguished scientist, ford found, 1967; asst prof biochem physiol & dir cancer res unit, Univ Tel-aviv med sch, 1966-1968; fel, dept biochem, Brandeis Univ, 1965-1966; fel physiol chem, Univ Calif, Berkeley, 1962-1965. **Memberships:** Sigma Xi; AAAS; Am Soc biol chem; Am Asn Cancer res; NY Acad Sci. **Research Statement & Publications:** Genetic determinants of cancer predisposition in humans; systemic effects biomarkers in cancer and the role of oncogenes in normaldifferentiation including potential therapy. **Mailing Address:** Div Cancer Prev, Nat Cancer Inst, Nat Inst Health, Bethesda, MD 20982. **Fax:** 813-398-9549. **E-Mail:** lk94c@nih.gov

KOPF, ALFRED WALTER, ONCOLOGY. **Personal Data:** b Buffalo, NY, June 21, 1926; m 1949, Dorothy; c Christopher J, Katherine A, Cynthia J & Timothy D. **Education:** Cornell Univ, BA, 1948, MD, 1951; NY Univ, MS, 1955; Am Bd Dermat, dipl, 1957. **Honors & Awards:** Wershaw Lectr Israel, Am Acad Dermat, 1971; Dohi Lectureship, Japan, 1979; Louis A Duhring Lectr, Penn Acad Dermat, 1992. **Professional Experience:** Chmn bd dirs, Int Found Dermat, 1987; CLIN PROF DERMAT, SCH MED, NY UNIV, 1983-; med adv bd, Skin Cancer Found, 1982; Rudolf L Baer Found Skin Dis, Am Dermat Asn, 1981; Rudolf L Baer Found Skin Dis Inc, 1976; assoc dir serv, Dept Dermat, 1968; mem bd dirs, Am Acad Dermat, 1966; ATTEND PHYSICIAN, UNIV HOSP, 1965-; mem bd dirs, Inst Dermat Commun & Educ, 1963-1987; from co-ed to sr ed, Yearbook Dermat, 1963-1970; assoc attend dermat, Oncol Sect, 1962-1965; from asst prof to prof, Post Grad Med Sch, NY Univ, 1961-1983; asst clin prof, Post Grad Med Sch, NY Univ, 1959-1961; asst attend med staff, Oncol Sect, 1958-1962; instr, Post Grad Med Sch, NY Univ, 1957-1959; Pvt pract dermat, Ny, 1955-; asst dermat, Post Grad Med Sch, NY Univ, 1954-1955; organizer, Oncol Sect, 1954; clin res dermat, Skin & Cancer Unit, Univ Hosp, NY Univ Med Ctr, 1953-1954; intern, Cleveland City Hosp, Ohio, 1951-1952. **Memberships:** AAAS; Soc Invest Dermat; Am Acad Dermat (pres, 1980); Am Dermat Asn (treas, 1972); AMA; NY Acad Sci; fel NY Acad Med; Int Soc Trop Dermat; Am Asn Cancer Surg; Am Soc Dermat Surg. **Research Statement & Publications:** Cutaneous oncology, especially neoplasms of the melanocyte including clinical studies on pigmented nevi and malignant melanoma. **Mailing Address:** Dept Dermo, NY Univ, 550 First Ave, New York, NY 10016.

KOPF, PETER W, PHYSICAL CHEMISTRY, POLYMER CHEMISTRY. **Personal Data:** b Philadelphia, Pa, April 23, 1944; m 1970, c 2. **Education:** Rutgers Col, AB, 1966; Univ Rochester, PhD (phys chem), 1970. **Professional Experience:** Vice-President TIAX, LLC, 2002- present DIR, ARTHUR D LITTLE INC, 1990- 2002; sr consult, Arthur D Little Inc, 1985-1989; Group leader & technol mgr, Res & Develop Dept, Union Carbide Corp, Bound Brook, 1970-1985. **Memberships:** Am Chem Soc; Sigma Xi; Soc Advan Mat & Process Eng. **Research Statement & Publications:** Polymer physical chemistry; polymer microstructural analysis; stable and transient free radicals; engineering thermoplastics; computer assisted calculations and simulations; polymer synthesis; thermoset reaction mechanisms; surface chemistry; dynamic mechanical analysis; polymers in coatings and adhesives applications; new specialty chemicals. **Mailing Address:** Arthur D Little Inc, Acorn Park, Cambridge, MA 02140. **Fax:** 617-498-7250. **E-Mail:** kopf.p@adlittle.com

KOPFLER, FREDERICK CHARLES, ENVIRONMENTAL CHEMISTRY. **Personal Data:** b New Orleans, La, August 14, 1938; m 1961, Eliska; c Eliska, Gretchen, Frederick III & John. **Education:** Southeastern La Col, BS, 1960; La State Univ, MS, 1962, PhD (food sci), 1964. **Professional Experience:** SR ENVIRON SCIENTIST, GULF MEX PROG, US ENVIRON PROTECTION AGENCY, 1989-; chief, Exposure Assessment & Pharmacokinetics Sect, Health Effects Res Lab, 1987-1989; chief, Chem & Statist Support Br, 1979-1987; supvry chemist, Water Supply Progs Div, US Environ Protection Agency, 1971-1979; adj asst prof, Univ Ala, 1968-1973; supvry chemist, Agr Res Serv, USDA, 1966-1971; res chemist milk proteins, Agr Res Serv, USDA, 1964-1966. **Memberships:** Sigma Xi; Estuarine Res Fedn; Soc Environ Toxicol & Chem. **Research Statement & Publications:** Bioassay directed isolation, fractionation and identification of mutagenic organic chemicals from water; effects of toxic substances on estuarine ecosystems. **Mailing Address:** Gulf Mex Prog, US Environ Protection Agency, Bldg 1103 Rm 203, Stennis Space Ctr, MS 39529-6000. **Fax:** 228-688-2709. **E-Mail:** kopfler.fred@epa.gov

KOPIA, GREGORY A, PHARMACOLOGY. **Personal Data:** b Montclair, NJ, February 16, 1949. **Education:** Gettysburg Col, BA, 1971; Univ Med & Dent NJ, PhD (pharmacol), 1980. **Professional Experience:** DIR PHARMACOL, ZYNAXIS CELL SCI INC, 1990-; dir cardiovasc pharmacol, 1986-1990. **Memberships:** Heart Res Inst; Am Heart Asn; NY Acad Sci; AAAS; Am Soc Pharmacol & Exp Therapeut. **Mailing Address:** Six Oakwood Lane, Phoenixville, PA 19460.

KOPIN, IRWIN J, INTERNAL MEDICINE, PHARMACOLOGY. **Personal Data:** b New York, NY, March 27, 1929; m 1952, c 3. **Education:** McGill Univ, BSc, 1951, MD, 1955. **Professional Experience:** SCIENTIST EMER CLIN NEUROCARDIOLOGY SEC, NAT INST NEUROL DIS & STROKE, NIH, as of 2005; dir, irp, nat inst neurol &commun dis & stroke, Nih, beginning 1983; assoc dir, clin res, NIMH, 1982-1983; chief, lab clin sci, 1969-1983; actg chief, lab clin sci, 1968-1969; chief, sect med, 1963-1983; actg chief, sect med, lab clin sci, NIH, 1961-1963; resident med, Columbia-Presby med ctr, 1960-1961; res assoc, NIH, 1957-1960; resident, Boston City Hosp, 1956-1957; intern med, Boston City Hosp, 1955-1956. **Memberships:** AAAS; asn Am physicians; Am soc biol chemists; Am soc clin invest; Am soc pharmacol & exp therapeut. **Research Statement & Publications:** Biochemical pharmacology. **Mailing Address:** Clin Neurocardiology Sec, Nat Inst Neurol Dis & Stroke, Nat Inst Health, 10 Ctr Dr Rm 6N252 Bldg 10 MSC 1620, Bethesda, MD 20892-1620. **Fax:** 301-402-0180. **E-Mail:** kopini@ninds.nih.gov

KOPITO, RON RIEGER, BIOCHEMISTRY, NEUROSCIENCES. **Personal Data:** b Haifa, Israel, December 21, 1954; American citizen; m 1987, c 2. **Education:** Bowdoin Col, AB, 1976; Mass Inst Technol, PhD (biochem), 1982. **Honors & Awards:** NSF presidential young investr award, 1989; Basil O'Connor starter scholar res award, 1989. **Professional Experience:** PROF BIOL SCI, STANFORD UNIV, as of 2005; assoc prof biol sci, Stanford Univ, as of 2003; asst prof, Dept Molecular & Cell Physiol, Stanford Univ Sch Med, 1991-; asst prof biol sci, Stanford Univ, beginning 1987; Lucille P Markey scholar biomed sci, 1985; NIH postdoctoral fel, Mass Inst Technol & Whitehead Inst, 1982-1986. **Memberships:** Soc Gen Physiologists; Am Soc Cell Biol; Sigma Xi. **Research Statement & Publications:** Molecular physiology; membrane transport; cytoskeleton-membrane interactions. **Mailing Address:** Dept Biol Sci Stanford Univ, Gilbert Rm 304A, Stanford, CA 94305-5020. **Fax:** 850-723-8475. **E-Mail:** kopito@stanford.edu

KOPLAN, JEFFREY P, HEALTH SCIENCES. **Personal Data:** b 1945. **Professional Experience:** DIR, CTR DIS CONTROL, 1998-. **Mailing Address:** Ctr Dis Control & Prev, 1600 Clifton Rd, Atlanta, GA 30333.

KOPLIK, BERNARD, MECHANICAL ENGINEERING. **Education:** City Col NY, BME; Columbia Univ, MS; Polytech Inst NY, PhD. **Honors & Awards:** Achievement Award, Am Soc Mech Engrs, 1998. **Professional Experience:** PROF, DEPT MECH ENG, NJ INST TECHNOL, as of 2006. **Memberships:** Am Soc Mech Engrs. **Mailing Address:** Dept Mech Eng, NJ Inst Technol, 302 MEC, Newark, NJ 07102. **Fax:** 973-596-3288. **E-Mail:** bernard.koplik@njit.edu

KOPLIK, JOEL, THEORETICAL PHYSICS, FLUID MECHANICS. **Personal Data:** b Brooklyn, NY, October 31, 1948. **Education:** Cooper Union, BS, 1969; Univ Calif Berkeley, PhD (physics), 1974. **Professional Experience:** PROF PHYSICS, CITY COL NY, 1989-; mem prof staff, Schlumberger-Doll Res, 1979-1988; researcher, Ecole Normal Sup, Paris, 1977-1978; mem, Inst Advan Study, 1976-1979; res assoc physics, Columbia Univ, 1974-1976; assoc ed, Physics Fluids. **Memberships:** Fel Am Phys Soc. **Research Statement & Publications:** physics of transport in random systems; interfacial phenomena; molecular fluid mechanics; superfluidity; published over 10 articles. **Mailing Address:** Levich Inst, City Col NY, Steinman Hall 1M 19 140th St Convent Ave, New York, NY 10031. **Fax:** 212-650-6835. **E-Mail:** koplik@sci.ccny.cuny.edu

KOPLON, RENEE, MATHEMATICS. **Education:** Rutgers Univ, PhD (math), 1994. **Professional Experience:** ASST PROF, DEPT MATH & STATIST, WRIGHT STATE UNIV, as of 2006. **Mailing Address:** Dept Math & Statist, Wright State Univ, Dayton, OH 45435. **Fax:** 513-873-2512. **E-Mail:** rkoplon@discover.wright.edu

KOPLOW, JANE, MICROBIOLOGY, MOLECULAR BIOLOGY. **Personal Data:** b Ulm, Ger, March 15, 1948; American citizen. **Education:** Univ Wis, BA, 1970; Univ Pa, MS, 1973, PhD (molecular biol), 1977. **Professional Experience:** CONSULT, 1984-; fel plasmids, Dept Biol, washington univ, 1982-1984; fel immunol & membranes, Sch Med, Washington Univ, 1979-1981; Fel virol, Sch Med, Washington Univ, 1978-1979. **Research Statement & Publications:** Synthesis of microbial membranes; defense mechanisms of pathogens. **Mailing Address:** 7146 Tulane St, University City, MO 63130. **Fax:** 314-727-8206.

KOPLOWITZ, JACK, PATTERN RECOGNITION, IMAGE ANALYSIS. **Personal Data:** b Lenger, Kazakstan, March 12, 1944; American citizen; m 1982, c Abraham. **Education:** City Col NY, BE, 1967; Stanford Univ, ME, 1968; Univ Colo, PhD (elec eng), 1973. **Professional Experience:** Assoc ed, Pattern Recognition, 1990-; consult, Teltech Inc, 1989-; assoc ed, Inst Elec & Electronics Engrs Trans Info Theory, 1983-1987; secy, Info Theory Group, Inst Elec & Electronics Engrs, 1981-1983; ASSOC PROF, DEPT ELEC & COMPUT ENG, CLARKSON UNIV, 1973-; mem tech staff Elec Eng, Bell Tele Labs, 1967-1970. **Memberships:** Sigma Xi; sr mem Inst Elec & Electronics Engrs. **Research Statement & Publications:** Pattern recognition; image analysis; graphics; information theory; digital encoding of bilevel images; subpixel reconstruction of image edge information; estimation of shape characteristics of digitized shapes. **Mailing Address:** Dept Elec & Comput Eng, Clarkson Univ, 141 Camp Bldg PO Box 5720, Potsdam, NY 13699-5720. **Fax:** 315-268-7600. **E-Mail:** koplowitz@clarkson.edu

KOPLYAY, JANOS BERNATH, APPLIED MATHEMATICS, COMPUTER SCIENCE. **Personal Data:** b Budapest, Hungary, June 24, 1924; American citizen; m 1958, c 4. **Education:** Royal Hungarian Air Force Acad, BS, 1943; Royal Hungarian Polytech Inst, PhD (elect & mech eng), 1949; Northwestern Univ, MA, 1964, PhD (math, statist), 1966. **Professional Experience:** RETIRED; prof math, San Antonio Col, beginning 1975; charter mem, USAF Tech Adv Bd, beginning 1975; consult, US Armed Serv & Friendly Allied Nations, beginning 1974; sci adv math & comput sci, Aerospace Med Div, USAF Systs Command, 1968-1989; asst prof math & comput sci, Northwestern Univ, 1965-1968; engr design, Rochester & Goodell Engrs Inc, 1956-1963; asst chief engr mech eng, Sociedade Paulista de Inst Gerais, Brazil, 1951-1955; chief engr electronic mech, Ygnis AG, Switz, 1949-1951; elec engr, Hungarian Utilities, Budapest, 1948-1949. **Memberships:** Math Asn Am; Mil Testing Asn; Am Statist Asn; Asn Comput Mach; AAAS. **Research Statement & Publications:** Mathematics; aerospace medicine; computer science. **Mailing Address:** San Antonio Col, 5406 Merkens Dr 1300 San Pedro Ave, San Antonio, TX 78229.

KOPP, EUGENE H(OWARD), ELECTRICAL ENGINEERING. **Personal Data:** b New York, NY, October 1, 1929; m 1950, c 3. **Education:** City Col NY, BEE, 1950, MEE, 1953; Univ Calif, Los Angeles, PhD (eng), 1965. **Honors & Awards:** Excellence in Eng Educ Award, Western Elec Co, Inc, 1967. **Professional Experience:** MGR RES & DEVELOP, HUGHES AIRCRAFT CO, 1985-; sr scientist, Hughes Aircraft CO, 1980-1985; adj fac, Univ Calif, Los Angeles, 1979-; vpres acad affairs, West Coast Univ, 1973-1979; dean sch eng, Calif State Col, Los Angeles, 1967-1973; res fel, Univ Leeds, 1966-1967; from asst prof to prof eng, Calif State Col, Los Angeles, 1958-1973; chief engr, Precision Radiation Instruments, Inc, 1956-1958; proj engr, Precision Radiation Instruments, Inc, 1954-1956; roj engr, Polarad Electronics Corp, 1950-1953 & Kaye-Halbert Corp, 1953-1954. **Memberships:** Sr mem Inst Elec & Electronics Engrs. **Research Statement & Publications:** Microwave components and antennas; satellite communications. **Mailing Address:** 483 W Ave 46, Los Angeles, CA 90019.

KOPP, JAY PATRICK, PHYSICS. **Personal Data:** b Buffalo Center, Iowa, 1938. **Education:** Loras Col, BS, 1959; Univ Wis, MS, 1961; Northwestern Univ, PhD (physics), 1968. **Professional Experience:** RETIRED; asst prof physics, Loras Col, beginning 1969; res assoc, Solid State Physics Lab, Swiss Fed Inst Technol, 1967-1969; instr physics, Loras Col, 1961-1964. **Memberships:** Am Phys Soc; Am Asn Physics Teachers; Swiss Phys Soc. **Research Statement & Publications:** Experimental solid state physics using nuclear magnetic resonance and magnetization measurements to study magnetic properties of rare earth systems, principally indirect exchange mechanisms. **Mailing Address:** Dept Physics & Eng, Loras Col, 236 Sci Hall, Dubuque, IA 52001. **E-Mail:** jpkopp@loras.edu

KOPP, MANFRED KURT, INSTRUMENTATION. **Personal Data:** b Koenigsberg, Ger, March 8, 1932; American citizen; m 1958, c 1. **Education:** Univ Buenos Aires, Arg, BSEE, 1962; Univ Tenn, BSEE, 1970, MSEE, 1975. **Professional Experience:** PRES, ORDELA INC, as of 2001; res engr instrumentation, Oak Ridge Nat Lab, 1967-; Develop engr nuclear instrumentation, Comision Nac Del Energia Atomica, Buenos Aires, Arg, 1956-1967. **Memberships:** Inst Elec & Electronics Engrs; Sigma Xi. **Research Statement & Publications:** Low noise electronics; position sensitive proportional counters; radiation detectors, and basic measurement science. **Mailing Address:** Ordela Inc, 1009 Alvin Weinberg Dr, Oak Ridge, TN 37830. **Fax:** 865-483-8404. **E-Mail:** mkopp@ordela.com

KOPP, OTTO CHARLES, geology; deceased, see previous edition for last biography

KOPP, RICHARD E, SYSTEMS ANALYSIS, CONTROL THEORY. **Personal Data:** b Brooklyn, NY, July 12, 1931; m 1953, c 4. **Education:** Polytech Inst Brooklyn, BEE, 1953, MEE, 1957, DEE(control theory), 1961. **Professional Experience:** CONSULT, 1991-; dir, sci adv bd, 1990-1991; dir syst sci, Corp Res Ctr, 1974-1990; sect head, Grumman Corp, 1963-1974; Adj prof, Polytech Inst Brooklyn, 1961-; group leader comput res, Grumman Corp, 1957-1963; Res engr comput, Grumman Aircraft Eng Corp, 1953-1957. **Memberships:** Inst Elec & Electronic Engrs; Am Inst Aeronaut & Astronaut. **Research Statement & Publications:** Electronics; control theory; astrodynamics; computing; marine sciences; mathematics; data processing; image processing; filtering; simulation. **Mailing Address:** Grumman Aerospace Corp, Five Oyster Bay Rd A08-35, Bethpage, NY 11714.

KOPP, ROGER ALAN, SOLAR PHYSICS, LASER FUSION. **Personal Data:** b Detroit, Mich, February 17, 1940; m 1962, Joyce E Schrage; c Gregory, Lori & Duane. **Education:** Univ Mich, BS, 1961; Harvard Univ, MA, 1963, PhD (astron), 1968. **Honors & Awards:** Award of Excellence, US Nuclear Weapons Prog, Dept Energy, 1993. **Professional Experience:** Lab Associate, Los Alamos Nat Lab, 2000-; Adjunct Prof, Fort Lewis

Col, 2000-; full astronomer, Astrophys Observ Catania, 1996; guest prof, Univ Florence, 1988; TECH STAFF MEM, LOS ALAMOS NAT LAB, 1976-; Vis scientist, Max Planck Inst Physics & Astrophys, 1971-1972, 1979-1980; Staff scientist, High Altitude Observ, Nat Ctr Atmospheric Res, 1966-1976. **Memberships:** Am Astron Soc; Am Geophys Union; Int Astron Union; Am Phys Soc. **Research Statement & Publications:** Heating of the solar corona; origin and dynamics of the solar wind; structure of the chromosphere-corona transition region; laser fusion target design and experiments; laser-plasma interactions. **Mailing Address:** Los Alamos Nat Lab MS B259, PO Box 31206, Santa Fe, NM 89594. **Fax:** 505-665-7725. **E-Mail:** rak@lanl.gov

KOPP, STEPHEN J, BIOLOGY. **Education:** Univ Notre Dame, BS, 1973; Univ Ill, PhD (physiol & biophys), 1976. **Professional Experience:** INST EDUC MGT, HARVARD INST HIGHER EDUC, HARVARD GRAD SCH EDUC, 2002-; founding Dean, Col Allied Health Professions, Midwestern Univ, 1992-1997. **Mailing Address:** 301 Irvine Hall, 7650 Rosemary Lane, Athens, OH 45701. **Fax:** 740-589-2553. **E-Mail:** kopp@ohio.edu

KOPPA, RODGER J, HUMAN FACTORS, REHABILITATIVE ENGINEERING. **Personal Data:** b Oak Park, Ill, June 23, 1936; m Patricia; c Virginia K (Tipton) & Cynthia A (Grimes). **Education:** Univ Tex, Austin, BA, 1958, MA, 1960; Tex A&M Univ, PhD (indust eng), 1979. **Honors & Awards:** Trinity industs/Charley V Wootan dir Career achievement award, Texas transp inst, 2000. **Professional Experience:** ASSOC PROF EMER INDUST ENG DEPT, TEX AM UNIV, as of 2001; mem, Adaptive Devices Stand Comt, Soc Automotive Engrs, 1988-; assoc prof indust eng, Dept Tex A&M Univ, 1982-2001; chair spec task force, Transp Vehicle Res, Transp Res Bd Nat Res Coun-Nat Acad Sci, 1980-1981; ASSOC RES ENGR, TEX TRANSP INST, 1979-; Lectr, Dept Indust Eng, Tex A&M Univ, 1979-1982; asst res psychologist, Tex Transp Inst, Tex A&M Univ, 1973-1979; specialist, Gen Elec Co, 1967-1972; Engr, LTV Aerospace Corp, 1961-1967. **Memberships:** Fel Human Factors and Ergonomics Soc; Soc Automotive Engrs. **Research Statement & Publications:** Design and evaluation of automotive adaptive equipment for disabled drivers; transportation human factors; highway safety; visibility and driver information presentation; job performance aid design. **Mailing Address:** 1214 N Ridgefield Circle, College Station, TX 77840. **Fax:** 979-847-9005. **E-Mail:** rkoppa@iemail.tamu.edu

KOPPEL, GARY ALLEN, ORGANIC CHEMISTRY, IMMUNOLOGY. **Personal Data:** b Cleveland, Ohio, August 8, 1943; m 1966, c 2. **Education:** Case Western Res Univ, 1965; Univ Pittsburgh, PhD (org chem), 1969. **Professional Experience:** RES ASSOC, ELI LILLY & CO, 1980-; res scientist org chem, Eli Lilly & CO, 1970-1980; Nat Cancer Inst fel, 1969-1970; NIH fel org chem, Columbia Univ, 1969-1970; Mobay fel, 1966-1968. **Memberships:** Sigma Xi; AAAS; Am Asn Immunologist; Am Chem Soc; NY Acad Sci; Clin Immunol Soc. **Research Statement & Publications:** Synthesis of natural products; development of new cephalosporins; new synthetic methods in the synthesis of penicillins and cephalosporins; biochemistry; molecular biology. **Mailing Address:** Eli Lilly & Co, 7823 Sunset Lane, Indianapolis, IN 46285.

KOPPEL, LOWELL B, CHEMICAL ENGINEERING. **Personal Data:** b Chicago, Ill, September 13, 1935; m 1957, c 2. **Education:** Northwestern Univ, BS, 1957, PhD (chem eng), 1960; Univ Mich, MSE, 1958. **Professional Experience:** DIR & SR CONSULT, SETPOINT INC, 1994-; dir & sr consult, 1985-; consult, Argonne Nat Lab, beginning 1962; from asst prof to prof, Purdue Univ, 1961-1985; instr chem eng, Calif Inst Technol, 1960-1961; VPRES, PROF MGT DIV, ASPEN TECH INC. **Memberships:** Am ChemSoc; Am Inst Chem Engrs. **Research Statement & Publications:** Process control; transport phenomena; applied mathematics; process simulation and optimization. **Mailing Address:** Setpoint Inc, Houston, TX 77079-2905.

KOPPELMAN, ELAINE, MATHEMATICS. **Personal Data:** b Brooklyn, NY, March 28, 1937; m 1970. **Education:** Brooklyn Col, BA, 1957; Yale Univ, MA, 1959; Johns Hopkins Univ, PhD (hist sci), 1969. **Professional Experience:** PROF EMER MATH, GOUCHER COL, as of 2004; prof Math, Goucher Col, ending 2001; assoc prof math, Goucher Col, beginning 1974; from instr to asst prof, 1961-1974. **Memberships:** Math Asn Am; Hist Sci Soc. **Research Statement & Publications:** History of modern mathematics, particularly the development of algebraduring the nineteenth and twentieth centuries. **Mailing Address:** Dept Math & Comput Sci, Goucher Col, 1021 Dulaney Valley Rd, Baltimore, MD 21204-2794.

KOPPELMAN, LEE EDWARD, ENVIRONMENTAL SCIENCE. **Personal Data:** b New York, NY, May 19, 1927; m 1948, c 4. **Education:** City Col, New York, BEE, 1950; Pratt Inst Grad Sch Architecture, IASP, 1964; NY Univ Grad Sch, DPA, 1970. **Honorary Degrees:** LD, Long Island Univ, 1978. **Professional Experience:** LEADING PROF & DIR, CTR REGIONAL POLICY STUDIES, 1988-; consult, UN Off Ocean Econ & Technol, 1981; adj prof, Grad Sch Environ Sci & Forestry, Syracuse Univ, 1975-; consult, US Dept Housing & Urban Develop, 1975-1978; Nat Shoreline Erosion Adv Panel, US Army, 1974-1981; appointee, Coastal Zone Mgt Adv Coun, Nat Oceanic & Atmospheric Admin, 1973-1975; PROF PLANNING & RESOURCE MGT, STATE UNIV NY, STONY BROOK, 1967-; exec dir regional planning, Long Island Regional Planning Bd, 1965-; Dir planning, Suffolk County Planning Comn, 1960-. **Memberships:** Am Planning Asn; Sigma Xi; Am Inst Architect. **Research Statement & Publications:** Integraton of coastal zone sciences and the regional planning process, including pollution studies of surface waters and the institutional management mechanisms required for coastal development. **Mailing Address:** Two Dune Ct, Setauket, NY 11733-1527.

KOPPENAAL, THEODORE J, METALLURGY. **Personal Data:** b Milwaukee, Wis, December 19, 1931; m 1954, c 3. **Education:** Univ Wis, BS, 1954; Univ Ill, MS, 1958; Northwestern Univ, PhD (metall), 1961. **Professional Experience:** PRES, KOPPENAAL & ASSOC, 1981-; OWNER, KOPPENAAL & ASSOC, 1981-; dir eng, Heavy Metals Div, Aerojet Ordnance Co, 1979-1981; supvr phys metall, Aeronutronic Div, Ford Aerospace & Commun Corp, 1967-1979; assoc metallurgist, Argonne Nat Lab, Ill, 1966-1967; asst metallurgist, Argonne Nat Lab, Ill, 1962-1966. **Memberships:** fel Am Soc Metals. **Research Statement & Publications:** Technical consultant; technical marketing for diversified programs related to materials science and engineering. **Mailing Address:** Koppenaal & Assoc, 8220 Cedar Mesa Ave, Las Vegas, NV 89129. **Fax:** 702-658-3443. **E-Mail:** tjkoppenal@aol.com

KOPPENHEFFER, THOMAS LYNN, COMPLEMENTOLOGY, ACUTE PHASE RESPONSE. **Personal Data:** b Harrisburg, Pa, May 23, 1942; m 1967, Julie; c Michael & Alex. **Education:** Bloomsburg State Col, BS, 1964; Williams Col, MA, 1966; Boston Univ, PhD (biol), 1970. **Professional Experience:** PROF BIOL, DEPT BIOL, TRINITY UNIV, 1988-; from asst prof to assoc prof, Dept Biol, Trinity Univ, 1979-1988; asst prof biol, Williams Col, 1973-1979; assoc surg, Harvard Med Sch, 1972-1973; Res fel surg, Harvard Med Sch, 1971-1972; Asst prof biol, Boston Univ, 1970-1971. **Memberships:** Am Asn Immunol; Int Complement Soc; Int Soc Develop & Comp Immunol. **Research Statement & Publications:** Biology of vertebrate complement systems; interplay between the complement system and acute-phase pr. **Mailing Address:** Dept Biol, Trinity Univ, One Trinity Pl, San Antonio, TX 78212-7200. **Fax:** 210-999-7229. **E-Mail:** tkoppenh@trinity.edu

KOPPERL, SHELDON JEROME, HISTORY OF SCIENCE. **Personal Data:** b Cleveland, Ohio, September 11, 1943; m 1967, Susan Levy; c Benjamin & Robert. **Education:** Case Inst Technol, BS, 1965; Univ Wis-Madison, PhD (chem, hist sci), 1970. **Professional Experience:** PROF, DEPT BIOMED SCI, GRAND VALLEY STATE UNIV, 1981-; assoc prof, Grand Valley State Univ, 1975-1981; coordr hist sci prog, Grand Valley State Univ, beginning 1973; asst prof health sci, Grand Valley State Univ, 1972-1975; Asst prof hist sci, Grand Valley State Univ, 1970-1972. **Memberships:** Am Chem Soc; Hist Sci Soc; Soc Hist Technol; Sigma Xi. **Research Statement & Publications:** Historical studies in inorganic, physical and organo-metallic chemistry and medicine, chiefly since 1800; studies in the history of art and science, chiefly Renaissance and Baroque. **Mailing Address:** Dept Biomed Sci, Grand Valley State Univ, 256 Padnos Hall, Allendale, MI 49401. **Fax:** 616-331-2090. **E-Mail:** kopperls@gvsu.edu

KOPPERMAN, RALPH DAVID, SET-THEORETIC TOPOLOGY, MATHEMATICAL LOGIC. **Personal Data:** b New York, NY, February 17, 1942; m Connie; c David, Leah, Amy, Gail & Susan. **Education:** Columbia Col, AB, 1962; Mass Inst Technol, PhD (math), 1965. **Professional Experience:** PROF, CITY COL NEW YORK, 1984-; from asst prof to assoc prof, City Col New York, 1967-1983; asst prof, Univ RI, 1965-1967; lectr math, Boston Univ, 1963-1965. **Memberships:** Am Math Soc; Asn Symbolic Logic; Math Asn Am. **Research Statement & Publications:** Generalized metric spaces and uniform spaces; general topology applied to computer graphics; spaces of ideals; asymmetric topology. **Mailing Address:** Dept Math, City Col New York, NAC 6/291 A, Convent Ave, 138th St, New York, NY 10031. **Fax:** 212-862-0004. **E-Mail:** rdkcc@cunyvm.cuny.edu

KOPPLE, KENNETH D(AVID), PEPTIDE CHEMISTRY, NUCLEAR MAGNETIC RESONANCE. **Personal Data:** b Philadelphia, Pa, October 21, 1930; m 1960. **Education:** Mass Inst Technol, SB, 1951, PhD (chem), 1954. **Professional Experience:** ADV COMT, CAMBRIDGE HEALTHTECH INST, as of 2006; consult, as of 2003; dir phys & struct chem, Smith Kline & French Labs, beginning 1985; chmn dept, Ill Inst Technol, 1982-1985; res guest, SNAM Progetti Lab Ricerche Base, Rome, Italy, 1974; from assoc prof to prof chem, Ill Inst Technol, 1965-1985; J S Guggenheim Found fel, Lab Chem Biodynamics, Univ Calif, Berkeley, 1964-1965; res chemist, Gen Elec Co Res Lab, 1962-1965; asst prof, Univ Chicago, 1956-1962; instr org chem, Univ Chicago, 1954-1956. **Memberships:** Am Chem Soc; fel AAAS; Am Soc Biochem & Molecular Biol; Royal Soc Chem. **Research Statement & Publications:** Peptide chemistry, synthesis and spectroscopic determination of conformation; nuclear magnetic resonance. **Mailing Address:** Cambridge Healthtech Inst, King of Prussia, PA 19406-0939. **Fax:** 610-270-6608.

KOPROWSKA, IRENA, PATHOLOGY, CYTOLOGY. **Personal Data:** b Warsaw, Poland, May 12, 1917; American citizen; m Hilary; c Claude & Christopher D. **Education:** Warsaw Med Sch, MD, 1939. **Honors & Awards:** Woman Physician of Year, Polish Am Med Asn, 1977; Papanicolaou Award, Am Soc Cytol, 1985. **Professional Experience:** RETIRED; prof path & dir cytol serv, Health Sci Ctr, Temple Univ, 1970-1987; consult, WHO, 1962-; Am Cancer Soc grant, 1958-1961; from assoc prof to prof, Hahnemann Med Col, 1957-1970; Runyon Mem Fund grant, 1955-1956; USPHS res grants, 1954-; asst prof path, State Univ NY Downstate Med Ctr, 1954-1957; lectr, France, Poland, India & Iran, 1952-; res fel & assoc anat, Med Col, Cornell Univ, 1949-1954; Res fel, Med Col, Cornell Univ, 1949-1954; asst pathologist, New York Infirmary, 1947-1949; res asst appl immunol, Pub Health Res Inst, City of New York, 1946-1947; res asst & asst pathologist, Med Col, Cornell Univ & New York Hosp, 1945-1946; asst pathologist, Rio de Janeiro City Hosps, 1942-1944; Intern med, Villejuif Lunatic Asylum, France, 1940. **Memberships:** AAAS; Am Soc Cytol; Am Asn Cancer Res; Am Soc Exp Path; Am Soc Clin Pathologists. **Research Statement & Publications:** Studies of progressive morphologic cellular changes, especially neoplastic progression in human beings, mice and in tissue culture systems. **Mailing Address:** 334 Fairhill Rd, Wynnewood, PA 19096. **Fax:** 610-649-3998.

KOPROWSKI, HILARY, BIOLOGY. **Personal Data:** b Warsaw, Poland, American citizen; m 1938, c 2. **Education:** Univ Warsaw, MD, 1939. **Honorary Degrees:** Numerous from US & foreign univs. **Honors & Awards:** Comdr, Order of Merit, 1959; Polish Millennium Award, Alfred Jurzykowski Found, 1966; Felix Wankel Tierschutz Prize, 1979; Nicolaus Copernicus Medal, Polish Acad Sci, 1989; John Scott Award, 1990; Chevalier, Order of the Royal Lion, Belg. **Professional Experience:** DIR, INST BIOTECH & CTR NEUROVIROL, THOMAS JEFFERSON UNIV, 1994-; PROF LAUREATE, WISTAR INST ANAT & BIOL, 1993-; PROF, DEPT MICROBIOL & IMMUNOL, THOMAS JEFFERSON UNIV, 1992-; PRES, BIOTECHNOL FOUND INC, PA, 1992-; chmn, Bd Sci Counrs, Div Cancer Etiology, Nat Cancer Inst, 1987-1990; Alexander von Humboldt Sr Scientist Award, Max Planck Inst, W Ger, 1974; Fulbright scholar, Max Planck Inst Physiol Behav, Ger, 1971-1972; co-ed, Methods Virol, Viruses & Immunity, Current Topics Microbiol & Immunol, 1965-; Consult, Nat Cancer Inst, NIH & USPHS, 1962-1970; WISTAR PROF RES MED & PROF MICROBIOL, FAC ARTS & SCI, UNIV PA, 1957-; inst prof, Ctr Neurovirol, 1957-1993; dir, Ctr Neurovirol, 1957-1991; asst dir, Sect Viral & Rickettsial Res, Lederle Labs, Am Cyanamid Co, 1946-1957; res assoc, Sect Viral & Rickettsial Res, Lederle Labs, Am Cyanamid Co, 1944-1946; res assoc, Yellow Fever Res Serv, Rockefeller Found & Ministry Educ, Rio Del Janeiro, Brazil, 1940-1944; mem, Expert Comt Rabies, WHO, Switz. **Memberships:** Nat Acad Sci; NY Acad Med; NY Acad Sci (pres, 1959); AAAS; Am Acad Arts & Sci; foreign mem Yugoslav Acad Arts & Sci; foreign mem Polish Acad Sci; foreign mem Russian Acad Med Sci; fel Polish Inst Arts & Sci Am; foreign mem Finnish Soc Sci & Letts. **Research Statement & Publications:** Cell biology, virology, and immunology; cancer; vaccine against poliomyelitis, hog cholera and rabies; authored over 800 publications. **Mailing Address:** Inst Biotech 7 Ctr Neuro Virol, Thomas Jefferson Univ, 725 W Lombard St, Baltimore, MD 21201.

KOPTUR, SUZANNE, BIOLOGICAL SCIENCE. **Education:** Univ Calif, Berkeley, PhD (bot), 1982. **Professional Experience:** PROF BIOL, FLA INT UNIV, 1999-. **Mailing Address:** Dept Bio Sci, Fla Intl Univ, Miami, FL 33199. **Fax:** 305-348-3103. **E-Mail:** kopturs@fiu.edu

KORACH, KENNETH STEVEN, STEROID HORMONE ACTION, STEROID RECEPTOR PROTEINS. **Personal Data:** b Buffalo, NY, November 26, 1946; m 1970, c 2. **Education:** Augusta Col, Ga, BA, 1969; Med Col Ga, PhD (endocrinol), 1974. **Professional Experience:** Adj prof, Dept Environ & Molecular Toxicol, Nc State Univ, as of 2004; CHIEF, LAB REPRODUCTIVE & DEVELOP & DEVELOPMENTAL TOXICOL, NAT INST ENVIRON HEALTH SCI, NIH, as of 2003; DIR, ENVIRON DIS & MED PROG, NAT INST ENVIRON HEALTH SCI, NIH, as of 2003; Consult, Glaxo Res Inst, 1990-; adj prof, Dept Biochem, NC State Univ, 1990-; arts Graphics Comt, 1987-; Res Assoc Prom Comt, 1990-; adj prof, pharmacol, 1989-; CHIEF, RECEPTOR BIOL SECT, 1987-; chmn, Radiation Safety Comt & Res Prod Subcomt, Nat Inst Environ Health Sci, 1985-; sr res endocrinologist, Nat Inst Environ Health Sci, beginning 1985; transatlantic lectr, Soc Toxicol, 1985; adj prof, lab reproductive biol, Univ NC Med Sch, 1981-; guest lectr, Dept Biochem, NC State Univ, 1981-; res endocrinologist, Nat Inst Environ Health Sci, 1980-1984; sr staff fel, Nat Inst Environ Health Sci, 1978-1980; staff fel, Nat Inst Environ Health Sci, 1976-1978; res fel endocrinol, Ford res fel, 1975-1976; res fel endocrinol, Sch Med, Harvard Univ, 1974-1975. **Memberships:** Endocrine Soc; Sigma Xi. **Research Statement & Publications:** Estrogen hormone action; investigations of estrogen receptor proteins, using a structure-activity approach; determination of intracellular sites of action; tissue responses in protein synthesis and DNA-RNA induction. **Mailing Address:** Lab Reproductive Develop Toxicol, Nat Inst Environl Health Sci, NIH, PO Box 12233, MD B2-03, Research Triangle Park, NC 27709. **Fax:** 919-541-0696. **E-Mail:** korach@niehs.nih.gov

KORACH, MALCOLM, ORGANIC CHEMISTRY. **Personal Data:** b New York, NY, April 25, 1922; m 1946, c 3. **Education:** Yale Univ, BS, 1942, PhD (chem), 1948. **Professional Experience:** MGR RES, CHEM DIV, PPG INDUSTS, 1974-; dir res, org group leader & asst dir res, 1970-1974; res chemist, org group leader & asst dir res, 1949-1970; Asst, Manhattan Proj, Columbia Univ, 1943 & Oak Ridge Inst Nuclear Studies, 1944-1946. **Memberships:** Am Chem Soc. **Research Statement & Publications:** Heavy organic chemicals; chlorinated organics; hydrogen peroxide and its utilization. **Mailing Address:** 280 N Revere Rd, Fairlawn, OH 44333.

KORAKIANITIS, THEODOSIOS, THERMODYNAMICS, POWER & PROPULSION SYSTEMS & COMPONENTS. **Personal Data:** b Athens, Greece, January 25, 1959; American citizen. **Education:** Newcastle Univ, UK, BSc, 1981; Mass Inst Technol, SM, 1982, SM, 1987, DSc(mech eng), 1987. **Honors & Awards:** Ralph R Teetor Educ Award, Soc Automotive Engrs, 1989; Young Prof Award, Am Inst Aeronaut & Astronaut, 1990. **Professional Experience:** JAMES WATT PROF & CHAIR, MECH ENG, UNIV GLASGOW, 2001-; DIR, CTR EMERGING TECHNOL THERMOFLUID SCI & POWER & PROPULSION LAB, UNIV GLASGOW, 2001-; from asst prof to assoc prof mech eng, Wash Univ, 1988-2001; consult, NREC, 1987-1988; marine engr & naval architect, John J McMullen Assocs, Inc, 1982-1983. **Memberships:** Am Soc Mech Engrs; Am Inst Aeronaut & Astronaut; Sigma Xi; Soc Automotive Engrs. **Research Statement & Publications:** Thermal fluid sciences and design; application to power and propulsion systems design; thermodynamics, turbomachinery, piston engines and design. **Mailing Address:** Dept Mech Eng, Ctr Emerging Technol Thermal & Fluid Sci, James Watt Bldg, Univ Glasgow, Glasgow, Scotland. **Fax:** 44-0-141-330-2480. **E-Mail:** t.alexander@mech.gla.ac.uk

KORAN, LORRIN MICHAEL, OBSESSIVE-COMPULSIVE DISORDERS, AFFECTIVE DISORDERS. **Personal Data:** b Los Angeles, Calif, April 4, 1940; m 1967, c 2. **Education:** Harvard Col, BA, 1962; Harvard Med Sch, MD, 1966; Am Bd Psychiat & Neurol, cert, 1973. **Professional Experience:** DIR, OBSESSIVE COMPULSIVE DIS CLIN, STANFORD MED CTR, 1988-; PROF PSYCHIAT, STANFORD UNIV, 1984-; med dir, Comprehensive Med Unit, Stanford Hosp, Calif, 1980-1988; assoc prof, Stanford Univ, 1979-1984; dir, residency training prog, Stanford Univ, Calif, 1979-1981; dir, med student educ psychiat, State Univ NY, Stony Brook, 1973-1977; from asst prof to assoc prof psychiat, State Univ NY, Stony Brook, 1972-1977. **Memberships:** Fel Am Psychiat Asn. **Research Statement & Publications:** Relationships between physical and mental disorders; treatment of obsessive-compulsive disorder; treatment of affective disorders; published over 20 articles. **Mailing Address:** Dept Psychiat Stanford Univ Med Ctr, 401 Quarry Rd, Stanford, CA 94305-5721. **Fax:** 650-725-0363. **E-Mail:** lkoran@stanford.edu

KORAN, ZOLTAN, FOREST PRODUCTS, PULP & PAPER SCIENCE & TECHNOLOGY. **Personal Data:** b Hungary, May 27, 1934; Canadian citizen; m 1968, c 4. **Education:** Univ BC, BSc, 1959, MF, 1961; Syracuse Univ, PhD (forestry), 1964. **Professional Experience:** PROF ENG, UNIV QUE, 1976-; res scientist, Que Indust Res Ctr, 1973-1976; asst prof forestry, Univ Toronto, 1968-1973; res scientist pulp & paper, Pulp & Paper Res Inst Can, 1965-1968; Asst prof forestry, Univ NH, 1963-1964. **Memberships:** Forest Prod Res Soc; Int Asn Wood Anat; Can Pulp & Paper Asn; Micros Soc Can; Tech Asn Pulp & Paper Indust. **Research Statement & Publications:** Anatomy and ultrastructure of wood, bark, fiber, pulp and paper; thermomechanical pulping; pulp and paper properties; forest products and utilization; composite boards; wood finishing and impregnation; x-ray, light and electron microscopic studies; material science engineering. **Mailing Address:** 3845 Limoges, Trois-Rivieres, PQ G8Y 4P9, Can.

KORANT, BRUCE DAVID, VIROLOGY, ENZYMOLOGY. **Personal Data:** b Brooklyn, NY, August 9, 1943; m 1969, Mary; c Deborah. **Education:** Brooklyn Col, BS, 1965; Pa State Univ, MS, 1967, PhD (microbiol), 1969. **Professional Experience:** Res fel, Dupont Merck Pharmaceut Co, beginning 1990; NATO fac, 1978, 1982, 1984; biochemist virol, Cent Res Dept, Exp Sta, E I Du Pont Del Nemours & Co Inc, 1969-1990. **Memberships:** Am Soc Microbiol; Am Soc Virol; Soc Interferon Res. **Research Statement & Publications:** Animal virology; bacteriophages; virus structure and replication; effects of viruses on cells; protein chemistry; proteolytic enzymes; interferon mechanism. **Mailing Address:** Dept Molecular Biol, DuPont Merck Co, Exp Sta 336 Rm 24 PO Box 80336, Wilmington, DE 19880-0336. **Fax:** 302-695-9420. **E-Mail:** korantbd@a1.lldmpc.umc.dupont.com

KORANYI, ADAM, HARMONIC ANALYSIS, LIE GROUPS & SYMMETRIC SPACES. **Personal Data:** b Szeged, Hungary, July 13, 1932; American citizen; m 1969, Anna. **Education:** Univ Szeged, dipl, 1954; Univ Chicago, PhD (math), 1959. **Honors & Awards:** Foreign mem, Hungarian Acad Sci, 2001-. **Professional Experience:** DISTINGUISHED PROF, CITY UNIV NY, 1985-; prof math, Wash Univ, 1979-1985; prof, Belfer Grad Sch, Yeshiva Univ, 1968-1979; assoc prof math, Belfer Grad Sch, Yeshiva Univ, 1965-1968; vis asst prof, Princeton Univ, 1964-1965; asst prof, Univ Calif, Berkeley, 1960-1964; Instr math, Harvard Univ, 1959-1960. **Memberships:** Am Math Soc. **Research Statement & Publications:** Functions of several complex variables; non-commutative harmonic anal. **Mailing Address:** Herbert H Lehman Col, City Univ New York, Bronx, NY 10468-1589.

KORC, MURRAY, ENDOCRINOLOGY. **Personal Data:** b Ger, April 3, 1947; c 3. **Education:** Albany Med Col, MD, 1974. **Professional Experience:** PROF & CHIEF, DIV ENDOCRINOL & METAB, UNIV CALIF, IRVINE, 1989-; assoc prof internal med & biochem, Dept Internal Med, Health Sci Ctr, Univ Ariz, 1987-1989; from asst prof to assoc prof, Dept Internal Med, Health Sci Ctr, Univ Ariz, 1981-1989. **Memberships:** AAAS; Am Col Physicians; Am Soc Cell Biol; Am Diabetes Asn; Endocrine Soc; Am Fedn Clin Res. **Mailing Address:** Dept Med, Div Endocrinol & Metab, Univ Calif, Gillespie NeuroSci Bldg, Irvine, CA 92697. **E-Mail:** mkorc@uci.edu

KORCEK, STEFAN, PHYSICAL ORGANIC CHEMISTRY, LUBRICANTS CHEMISTRY. **Personal Data:** b Trnava, Czech, May 28, 1934; m 1965, c 2. **Education:** Slovak Tech Univ, Bratislava, MS, 1957, PhD (chem, chem eng & fuel technol), 1967. **Honors & Awards:** F R McFarland Award, Soc Automotive Engrs, 1981. **Professional Experience:** STAFF SCIENTIST LUBRICANT CHEM & PHYS ORG CHEM, RES FUELS & LUBRICANTS DEPT, FORD MOTOR CO, DEARBORN, MICH, 1981-; prin res scientist assoc, Res Fuels & Lubricants Dept, Ford Motor CO, Dearborn, Mich, 1976-1981; sr res scientist, Res Fuels & Lubricants Dept, Ford Motor CO, Dearborn, Mich, 1971-1976; Vis res off, Div Chem, Nat Res Coun, Ottawa, Can, 1970-1971; fel phys org chem, Div Chem, Nat Res Coun, Ottawa, Can, 1968-1970; Assoc prof chem kinetics & reactors design, Dept Chem & Technol Petrol, Slovak Tech Univ, 1957-1968. **Memberships:** Am Chem Soc; Soc Automotive Engrs. **Research Statement & Publications:** Kinetics and mechanisms of autooxidation and inhibited oxidation of organic substrates in liquid phase at elevated temperatures; mechanism of action of antioxidants; automotive lubricants, their chemistry and degradation in service; reactions of lubricant antioxidant additives in engines; author or coauthor of over 40 publications. **Mailing Address:** Ford Motor Co, PO Box 6248, Dearborn, MI 48126.

KORCHAK, ERNEST I(AN), COATINGS & ADHESIVES TECHNOLOGY, TECHNICAL MANAGEMENT. **Personal Data:** b Opava, Czech, February 15, 1934; Australian citizen; m 1959, Helen; c 3. **Education:** Univ Melbourne, BChE, 1957; Mass Inst Technol, SM, 1961. **Honorary Degrees:** DSc (chem eng), Mass Inst Technol, 1964. **Professional Experience:** PRES, PERFORMANCE COATINGS CORP, 1990-; CHMN, CHEMTECH MGT LTD, 1986-; chmn, Riverside Polymer Systs Inc, 1986-1990; pres, Chem Indust Asn, 1984-1985; pres, Sci Design Co, 1981-1986; pres, Halcon Res & Develop Corp, 1975-1980; vpres & gen mgr, Halcon Catalyst Industs, 1971-1975; sales exec, Sci Design Co Inc, 1967-1971; chem engr, Halcon Int Inc, 1964-1967; res engr chem eng, Imp Chem Industs, Australia & NZ, 1958-1959. **Memberships:** Am Chem Soc; Am Inst Chem Engrs. **Research Statement & Publications:** Gas flow and turbulence, application to packed beds; process research and development of organic chemical processes, special emphasis on kinetics and separations; oxidation and carbonylation processes. **Mailing Address:** Performance Coating Corp, 1610 Manning Blvd, Levittown, PA 19057-4732. **Fax:** 215-945-9401. **E-Mail:** pcc1606@bellatlantic.net

KORCHAK, HELEN MARIE, PHOSPHOLIPID METABOLISM. **Education:** Tufts Univ, PhD (physiol), 1962. **Professional Experience:** RES PROF PEDIAT & BIOCHEM & BIOPHYS, UNIV PA SCH MED, as of 2006; assoc prof exp med & dir res, Div Rheumatology, NY Univ Med Ctr, beginning 1984. **Research Statement & Publications:** Neutrophil activation. **Mailing Address:** Dept Pediat, Univ Pa Sch Med, 1208 C Abramson Bldg, Philadelphia, PA 19104. **Fax:** 610-525-1190. **E-Mail:** korchak@email.chop.edu

KORCHEV, DMITRIY VENIAMINOVICH, MAPPING ALGORITHMS TO PARALLEL COMPUTER ARCHITECTURE, DIGITAL SIGNAL PROCESSING. **Personal Data:** b Zhitomir, March 11, 1960; m Inna; c Max. **Education:** Polytech Inst, Kiev, MS, 1985; Geushkov Cybernetics Inst, Kiev, PhD (comput sci), 1990. **Professional Experience:** MEM TECH STAFF, IMAGE & SIGNAL PROCESSING INC, 1993-; consult, Visual Comput Systs, 1992-1993; Tech Diag Lab, Kiev, 1990-1991; res engr, Digital Signal & Image Processing Labs, Kiev Polytech Inst, 1981-1990. **Memberships:** Armed Forces Commun & Electronics Asn; Inst Elec & Electronics Engrs. **Research Statement & Publications:** Developed a new systematic approach for mapping algorithms to parallel computer architecture, obtained new parallel structural schemes fororthoformal transforms; benchmarks for performance evaluation of digital signal processing systems; developed a new algorithm for systolic implementation of multidimensional FFTs. **Mailing Address:** Tech Staff Image & Signal Processing Inc, 1250 N Lakeview Ave Ste H, Anaheim, CA 92807-1831. **Fax:** 714-970-0121.

KORCHIN, LEO, ORAL & MAXILLOFACIAL SURGERY. **Personal Data:** b Brooklyn, NY, July 1, 1914; m Norma Cruz; c Gregory & Paul. **Education:** Cornell Univ, BS, 1936; NY Univ, DDS, 1941; Georgetown Univ, MS, 1954; Am Bd Oral & Maxillofacial Surg, dipl; FACD; FICD. **Honors & Awards:** Novice Award, Int Asn Dent Res, 1954. **Professional Experience:** Assoc dean, Univ PR, 1984-1986; asst dean for clin instr, Univ PR, 1979-1982; fel oral path, Armed Forces Inst Path, 1975-1976; PROF ORAL & MAXILLOFACIAL SURG, SCH DENT, UNIV PR, SAN JUAN, 1972-; dir dept surg sci, Univ PR, 1972-1975; assoc prof oral surg, Univ PR, 1967-1972; chief dent serv & oral surg & dir dent intern training prog, Martin Army Hosp, Ft Benning, Ga, 1965-1967; chief dent clin & oral surg sect, 97th Gen Hosp, Frankfurt, Ger, 1962-1965; chief oral surg br, Dent Detachment, Ft Devens, Mass, 1957-1962; chief oral surg sect, Rodriguez Army Hosp, PR, 1954-1957; instr oral surg & asst prof mil sci & tactics, Sch Dent, Georgetown Univ, 1952-1954; chief oral surg sect, Army Hosp, US Army, Ft Jay, NY, 1948-1952. **Memberships:** Am Soc Oral & Maxillofacial Surgeons; Am Acad Oral Path; Am Dent Asn; Int Asn Oral & Maxillofacial Surgeons. **Research Statement & Publications:** Effects of starch sponge implanted in bone; effect of isotretinoin and triamcinolone acetonide on human skin fibroblasts in vitro. **Mailing Address:** Univ PR Sch Dent, San Juan, PR 00936.

KORCHYNSKY, M(ICHAEL), PHYSICAL METALLURGY & MICRO ALLOYED STEELS, MATERIALS SCIENCE. **Personal Data:** b Kiev, Ukraine, April 11, 1918; American citizen; m 1951, Taisija; c Michael Jr, Marina & Roksana. **Education:** Tech Univ Lviv, Ukraine, Dipl Ing, 1942. **Professional Experience:** Consult metall, Strategic Minerals Corp, 1986-; PRIN, KORCHYNSKY & ASSOCS, CONSULTS METALL, 1986-; sr fel, Union Carbide Corp, 1979; dir alloy develop, Umetco Minerals Corp, Union Carbide Corp, 1973-1986; dir prod res, Graham Res Lab, 1970-1973; asst dir res new prod develop, Graham Res Lab, 1965-1970; res supvr alloy & high strength steels, Jones & Laughlin Steel Corp, 1961-1965; tech supvr, Tech Dept, 1960-1961; res metallurgist phys metall, Metals Res Labs, Union Carbide Metals Co, 1951-1960; chief engr, US Army, Ger, 1945-1950; asst metall, Tech Univ Lviv, 1942-1944. **Memberships:** Fel Am Soc Metals Int; Iron & Steel Soc; Soc Automotive Engrs; foreign mem Acad Eng Sci Ukraine. **Research Statement & Publications:** Physical metallurgy of steels; materials for high-temperature service; nuclear fuels; alloy design and development; technology and application of high-strength, low-alloy microalloyed steels; management of industrial research and product development; technological marketing. **Mailing Address:** 2770 Milford Dr, Bethel Park, PA 15102-1763. **Fax:** 412-787-5030.

KORDA, PETER E, ENGINEERING MECHANICS, STRUCTURAL ENGINEERING. **Personal Data:** b Budapest, Hungary, December 5, 1931; American citizen; m 1954, c 4. **Education:** Budapest Tech Univ, Dipl Eng, 1954; Ohio State Univ, PhD (eng mech), 1964. **Professional Experience:** CHIEF EXEC OFFICER, KORDA/NEMETH ENG, 1985-; pres, Korda Eng Co Consult Engrs, 1967-1985; from asst prof to prof, Sch Archit, Ohio State Univ, 1964-1981; consult engr, Miller & Korda, 1964-1967; res assoc & instr eng mech, Sch Archit, Ohio State Univ, 1961-1963; asst proj design, Sch Archit, Ohio State Univ, 1960-1961; Livesley & Henderson Eng, 1956-1957 & Dominion Bridge Co, Ltd, Can, 1957-1960; Struct designer, Indust Bldg Design Off, Hungary, 1954-1956. **Memberships:** Am Soc Civil Engrs; Concrete Inst Am; Int Asn Shell Struct; Nat Soc Prof Engrs; Am Soc Eng Educ. **Research Statement & Publications:** Shallow shell theory with computer applications; dynamic stability and structural damping. **Mailing Address:** Korda/Nemeth Eng Inc, 1650 Watermark Pl, Columbus, OH 43215. **Fax:** 614-487-8981.

KORDAN, HERBERT ALLEN, DEVELOPMENTAL PHYSIOLOGY, PLANT MORPHOGENETICS. **Personal Data:** b St Louis, Mo, April 10, 1926; m 1949, c 3. **Education:** Univ Calif, Los Angeles, BA, 1955, MS, 1958, PhD (plant sci), 1961. **Professional Experi-**

ence: UNIV LECTR BOT, UNIV BIRMINGHAM, 1968-; USPHS fel, Univ Leeds, 1967-1968; assoc prof, Gustavus Adolphus Col, 1966-1967; asst prof biol, Mt St Mary's Col, Calif, 1964-1966; asst res plant physiologist, Univ Calif, Los Angeles, 1963-1965; res staff mem plant physiol & consult, Stanford Res Inst, 1963; Fel tumorigenesis, Cedars of Lebanon Hosp, Los Angeles, 1961-1962. **Memberships:** Soc Exp Biol; fel Bot Soc Edinburgh; Sigma Xi. **Research Statement & Publications:** Comparative cytology; morphology and physiology of growing and non-growing plant cells; investigations on effects of organic and inorganic central nervous system depressant chemical agents on pollen and seed germination and subsequent developmental behavior. **Mailing Address:** Dept Plant Biol, Univ Birmingham PO Box 363, Birmingham B15 2TT, UK.

KORDAS, GEORGE, SPECTROSCOPY. **Professional Experience:** RES SCIENTIST, INST MAT SCI, NAR CTR SCI RES, DEMOKRITOS, 1990-; Univ Ill, Urbana-Champaing, 1986-1991. **Memberships:** Soc Glass Technol. **Mailing Address:** Inst Mat Sci, Nat Ctr Sci Res, 153 10 Aghia Paraskevi, Demokritos, Greece. **Fax:** 30 1 6519430. **E-Mail:** gkordas@ims.demokritos.gr

KORDESCH, KARL VICTOR, ELECTROCHEMISTRY, BATTERIES & FUEL CELLS. **Personal Data:** b Vienna, Austria, March 18, 1922; American citizen; m 1946, c 4. **Education:** Univ Vienna, PhD (chem), 1948. **Honorary Degrees:** Dr techn hc, Tech Univ Vienna, 1990. **Honors & Awards:** Nat Energy Award, Austria, 1981; Vittorio De Nora-Diamond Shamrock Award, Electrochem Soc, 1987; E Schroedinger Prize, Austrian Acad Sci, 1990-. **Professional Experience:** VPRES ADVAN RES, BATTERY TECHNOL INC, 1988-; secy gen, Int Electrochem Soc, 1981; dir, Inst Inorg Chem Technol, 1977-; Prof, Tech Univ Graz, Austria, 1977-; CONSULT ELECTROCHEM, Battery Technol Inc, 1977-; corp res fel, Battery Prod Div, 1974-1977; sr res assoc, Parma Res Lab, Union Carbide Corp, 1970-1974; res chemist & group leader, Develop Dept, 1955-1970; chem engr, Signal Corps Eng Labs, NJ, 1953-1955; asst prof, Chem Inst, Univ Vienna, 1948-1953; Asst & lectr chem, Chem Inst, Univ Vienna, 1946-1948. **Memberships:** Am Chem Soc; Electrochem Soc; Austrian Chem Soc; Int Electrochem Soc (vpres, 1986). **Research Statement & Publications:** Electrochemical systems; batteries, especially with alkaline electrolytes; hydrogen-oxygen fuel cells; carbon electrodes; test and control instruments; electronic circuitry; technical management. **Mailing Address:** Tech Univ Graz, Stremayrgasse 16, Graz, A-8010, Austria. **Fax:** 905-881-6043.

KORDOSKI, EDWARD WILLIAM, ORGANIC CHEMISTRY, SCIENCE ADMINISTRATION. **Personal Data:** b New Britain, Conn, August 15, 1954; m 1977, Donna. **Education:** King's Col, BS, 1977; Univ Md, PhD (org chem), 1982; Monmouth Col, MBA, 1986. **Professional Experience:** EXEC DIR, ASSOC MGT CTR, SYNTHETIC ORGANIC CHEM MFR ASSOC INC, as of 2000; mgr libr servs, Am Chem Soc, beginning 1995; bd gov, Univ Md, Col Park, 1995-; sr analyst, Prog & Develop Off Indust Relations, 1993-1995; qual assurance team leader, Textile Prod Div, St Gabriel, La, 1991-1992; chem develop res team leader, Textile Prod Div, St Gabriel, La, 1990-1991; tech proj asst, Textile Prod Div, St Gabriel, La, 1988-1990; prod chemist, Ciba-Geigy Ltd, Basel Switz, 1987-1988; sr process develop chemist, Dyestaffs & Chem Div, Ciba-Geigy Corp, Toms River, NJ, 1984-1987; process develop chemist, Dyestaffs & Chem Div, Ciba-Geigy Corp, Toms River, NJ, 1982-1984; teaching asst org chem, res asst, 1979-1982; teaching asst org chem, Univ Md, 1977-1979. **Memberships:** Am Chem Soc; AAAS. **Research Statement & Publications:** Expand the existing portfolio of programs, products and services for industrial chemical scientists; enhance the image and stature of chemical professionals; development of continuous small reactor technology and analytical monitoring and feedback control. **Mailing Address:** Assoc Mgt Ctr, Synthetic Organic Chem Mfr Assoc Inc, Suite700, 1850 M St NW, Washington, DC 20036-5810. **Fax:** 202-296-8120. **E-Mail:** kordoskie@socma.com

KORDOVA, NONNA, RICKETTSIAL DISEASES. **Personal Data:** b Krasnodar, USSR, Canadian citizen; m 1945. **Education:** Charles Univ, Prague, MD, 1945; Czech Acad Sci, PhD (med virol), 1960. **Honors & Awards:** Recognition Dipl, Czech Acad Sci, 1965. **Professional Experience:** RETIRED; prof, Med Col, Univ Man, 1977-1987; assoc prof, Med Col, Univ Man, 1970-1977; res assoc, Univ Kans, 1968-1969; chief lab, Inst Virol, Czech Acad Sci, 1966-1968; sr scientist, Inst Virol, Czech Acad Sci, 1960-1966; res assoc rickettsioses, Inst Virol, Czech Acad Sci, 1956-1960; asst prof, Children's Hosp, Komensky Univ, 1954-1956; res assoc pediat, Children's Hosp, Komensky Univ, 1945-1954. **Memberships:** Can Soc Microbiol; Am Soc Microbiol; Can Pub Health Asn. **Research Statement & Publications:** Pathogenesis of chlamydial diseases; parasite-host interactions at the cellular and subcellular level. **Mailing Address:** 501-71 Roslyn Rd, Winnipeg, MB R3L 0G2, Can.

KORECKY, BORIVOJ, MEDICAL PHYSIOLOGY. **Personal Data:** b Prague, Czech, September 9, 1929; c 2. **Education:** Charles Univ, Prague, MD, 1955; Czech Acad Sci, PhD, 1961. **Professional Experience:** ADJ PROF CELLULAR & MOLECULAR MED, UNIV OTTAWA, as of 2003; PROF PHYSIOL, UNIV OTTAWA, 1971-; assoc prof, Univ Ottawa, 1966-1971; Med Res Coun Can res fel, 1963-1964; from asst prof to assoc prof path physiol, Charles Univ, Prague, 1955-1966. **Memberships:** Can Physiol Soc; Am Physiol Soc. **Research Statement & Publications:** Cardiovascular and respiratory physiology. **Mailing Address:** Dept Cellular & Molecular Med, Univ Ottawa, Ottawa, ON K1H 8M5, Can. **Fax:** 613-562-5434. **E-Mail:** bkorecky@med.uottawa.ca

KOREIN, JULIUS, NEUROSCI, BEHAVIOR. **Personal Data:** b New York, NY, September 27, 1928; m 1957, c James, Jonathan & Beth. **Education:** NY Univ, BA, 1949, MD, 1953. **Honorary Degrees:** AOA, NY Univ, 1988. **Honors & Awards:** Bronze Award, Diag of Brain Death, Int Film & TV Fest, NY, 1983. **Professional Experience:** EMER PROF NEUROL, NY UNIV MED CTR, 1996-; chmn, Biomed Ethics Comt, Bellevue Hosp, 1985-1994; mem, Sci & Soc Comt, NY Acad Sci, 1984-1986; adv, President's Comn Study Ethical Problems Med, Biomed & Behav res, Wash DC, 1980-1981; MEM ADV BD, INT J NEUROSCI, 1979-; adv bd, Neurosci Info Ctr, Upjohn Co, 1978-1984; assoc ed, Am Soc Cybernet Forum, 1974-1980; consult, Vet Admin Hosp, Manhattan, 1973-1987; ATTEND, BELLEVUE HOSP, 1972-; prof neurol, Med Ctr, NY Univ, 1972-1996; consult, sensory feedback ther, Int Ctr Disabled res & Rehab Ctr, 1972-1984; ATTEND, NY UNIV HOSP, 1971-; Children's Bur, Nat inst Neurol Dis & Stroke, 1971-1974; proj dir & vchmn study cerebral death, Nat inst Neurol Dis & Stroke, 1971-1972; CHIEF, BELLEVUE HOSP, 1970-; Nat Ctr Health Serv res & Develop, 1966-1970 & Hoffmann-La Roche labs, 1969-1970; vis assoc, Bellevue Hosp, 1968-1972; assoc dir anal & comput methodology, dept Radiol, 1968-1972; various educ videopresentations, 1967-1996; Children's Bur, Int Info Processing, 1967-1970; career scientist award, New York City Health Res Coun, 1966-1972; Children's Bur, dept Health, Educ & Welfare, 1966-1971; proj dir, Health res Coun Grants, City of New York, 1963-1965 & Nat Cancer inst, 1966-1970; prin investr, Warner-Lambert inst, 1966-1967; consult, Gen Elec Corp, 1966-1967; co-investr, Nat inst Neurol Dis & Stroke, 1965-1967; prin investr, USV Pharmaceut Corp, 1963-1972; attend physician, Vet Admin Hosp, Manhattan, 1961-1973; from asst prof to assoc prof, Med Ctr, NY Univ, 1961-1972; asst attend, NY Univ Hosp, 1961-1972; vis asst, dir EEG, 1961-1970; spec trainee, Mt Sinai Hosp, 1960-1961; asst attend, Mt Sinai Hosp, 1959-1970; vis asst, Bellevue Hosp, 1959-1968; spec trainee, NY Univ-Bellevue Hosp Ctr, 1959-1960; asst & chief resident, NY Univ-Bellevue Hosp Ctr, 1955-1957; asst resident neurol, Mt Sinai Hosp, 1954-1955; Intern, Maimonides Hosp, Brooklyn, 1953-1954; fel, Mt Sinai Hosp, 1953-1954. **Memberships:** AAAS; Am Neurol Asn; Am Acad Neurol; Asn Res Nerv & Ment Dis; Am Electroencephalographic; NY Acad Sci. **Research Statement & Publications:** Computer applications in capture, storage, retrieval and analysis of narrative medical data for the purpose of patient care and clinical research; sensory feedback therapy in neuromuscular disorders; electroencephalography and behavior, including computer analysis of the electroencephalogram, effects of drugs on the electroencephalogram and behavior, diagnosis of brain death; pathophysiology and treatment of segmental torsion dystonia; models of neurophysiological structures; ontogenesis of cerebral function in the human fetus; aquatic medicine; electro physiological probes to analyse movement of cortical and subcortical origins. **Mailing Address:** 240 Central Park South, Ste 20 D, New York, NY 10019. **Fax:** 212-582-8986. **E-Mail:** jkorein@aol.com

KOREN, EUGEN, ENDOCRINOLOGY, CELL BIOLOGY. **Personal Data:** b Zagreb, Croatia, October 10, 1940. **Education:** Zagreb Univ, BA, 1965, PhD (biochem), 1972. **Honors & Awards:** Merrick Award, Biomed Found; Johan Blumenbach Award, Univ Gottingen. **Professional Experience:** AT GENENTECH INC, as of 2002; ASST MEM ENDOCRINOL RES, OKLA MED RES FOUND, 1990-; asst mem cell biol, 1985-1990. **Memberships:** Am Soc Biochem & Molecular Biol; Am Soc Cell Biol; Am Chem Soc; Am Asn Endocrinol; NY Acad Sci; AAAS. **Research Statement & Publications:** Endocrinology; cell biology. **Mailing Address:** Genentech Inc, 460 Point San Bruno Blvd, South San Francisco, CA 94080. **Fax:** 650-225-1998.

KOREN, HILLEL, BIOLOGY. **Education:** Tel Aviv Univ, Tel Aviv, Israel, MS, 1968; Univ Freiburg & Max Planck Inst Immunobiology, Freiburg, Ger, PhD, 1971. **Professional Experience:** ADJ RES PROF, CAROLINA ENVIRON PROG, UNIV NC, CHAPEL HILL, as of 2005. **Mailing Address:** Carol Environ Prog, CB 1105 208 Miller Hall, Chapel Hill, NC 27599-1105. **Fax:** 919-966-9920. **E-Mail:** koren@unc.edu

KOREN, ISRAEL, COMPUTER ENGINEERING. **Personal Data:** American citizen; m Zahava; c Yuval & Yaron. **Education:** Technion/Israel Inst Technol, BSc, 1967, MSc, 1970, DSc, 1975. **Honors & Awards:** IEEE Fellow. **Professional Experience:** Consult, IBM, beginning 1995; consult, Advan Micro Devices, Inc, 1994; consult, Intel, 1992; consult, Digital Equip Corp, 1991; PROF ELEC & COMPUT ENG, UNIV MASS, AMHERST, 1986-; consult, Tolerant Systs, 1986; head, VLSI Syst Res Ctr, 1985-1986; Vis prof, Univ Calif, Berkeley, 1982-1983; sr lectr, Technion/Israel Inst Technol, Haifa, 1979-1985; Asst prof elec & comput eng, Univ Southern Calif, 1978-1979; Asst prof elec & comput eng, Univ Calif, Santa Barbara, 1976-1978. **Memberships:** Fel Inst Elec & Electronics Engrs; fel Japan Soc Promotion Sci; Asn Comput Mach. **Research Statement & Publications:** Author of one book and co-author of one book; main research activities: Fault-tolerant systems, VLSI yield and reliability, and computer arithmetic. **Mailing Address:** Dept Elec & Comput Eng, Univ Mass, Amherst, MA 01003. **Fax:** 413-545-1993. **E-Mail:** koren@ecs.umass.edu

KORENBROT, JUAN IGAL, BIOPHYSICS. **Personal Data:** b Mexico City, Mex, November 29, 1947; m 1972, c 2. **Education:** Johns Hopkins Univ, MA, 1971, PhD (biophys), 1972. **Professional Experience:** PROF PHYSIOL, UNIV CALIF, SAN FRANCISCO, 1985-; from asst prof to assoc prof, Univ Calif, San Francisco, 1974-1985; lectr, Univ Calif, Los Angeles, 1973-1974; vis scientist biochem, Nat Polytech Inst, 1973; res assoc physiol, 1972-1973; res assoc biophys, Johns Hopkins Univ, 1971-1972. **Memberships:** Soc Neuroscience; Soc Gen Physiol. **Research Statement & Publications:** Molecular mechanisms of ion transport; mechanisms of function of Rhodopsins and phototransduction; photoreceptor development. **Mailing Address:** Univ Calif, 513 Parnassus HSW-858 PO Box 0444, San Francisco, CA 94143-0444. **E-Mail:** juan@itsa.ucsf.edu

KORENMAN, STANLEY G, ENDOCRINOLOGY, BIOCHEMISTRY. **Personal Data:** b New York, NY, January 21, 1933; m 1956, c 3. **Education:** Princeton Univ, AB, 1954; Columbia Univ, MD, 1958. **Professional Experience:** ASSOC DEAN, ETHICS & MED SCIENTIST TRAINING PROG, UNV CALIF, LOS ANGELS, 1992-; assoc dean, Educ Develop, Sch Med, Univ Calif, Los Angels, 1989-1991; DIR, MED SCIENTIST TRAINING PROG, UNV CALIF, LOS ANGELS, 1981-; prof med & chmn dept, Sch Med, 1974-1989; PROF MED, UNV CALIF, LOS ANGELS, 1974-; mem, Breast Cancer Task Force, 1972; prof med & biochem & chief endocrinol div, Sch Med, Univ Iowa, 1970-1974; mem, Reproductive Biol Study Sect, 1970-1973; dir clin res ctr, Dept Med, Harbor Gen Hosp, 1969-1970; coordr regional med prog, Dept Med, Harbor Gen Hosp, 1968-1970; from asst prof to assoc prof med, Sch Med, Univ Calif, 1966-1970; clin instr, Med Ctr, George Wash Univ, 1965-1966; Collab investr, Lab Chem Biol, Inst Arthritis & Metab Dis, 1964-1965; med officer & sr investr, Endocrinol Br, Nat Cancer Inst, 1963-1966; clin assoc, Endocrinol Br, Nat Cancer Inst, 1961-1963; intern, Second Div, Bellevue Hosp & Mem Hosp, NY, 1958-1959; asst resident med, Second Div, Bellevue Hosp & Mem Hosp, NY, 1950-1961; chief med, Vet Admin Med Ctr, Sepulveda; chmn dept med, San Fernando Valley Prog. **Memberships:** Am Soc Clin Invest; fel Am Col Physicians; Am Fedn Clin Res; Endocrine Soc; Asn Am Physicians. **Research Statement & Publications:** Molecular mechanisms of hormone action; clinical reproductive endocrinology and impotence. **Mailing Address:** Dept Med, Univ Calif, Bldg 52-242 CHS, Los Angeles, CA 91343. **E-Mail:** skorenman@mednet.ucla.edu

KORENMAN, VICTOR, THEORETICAL CONDENSED MATTER PHYSICS. **Personal Data:** b Brooklyn, NY, February 5, 1937; m 1968, Joan; c Edward. **Education:** Princeton Univ, AB, 1958; Harvard Univ, MA, 1959, PhD (physics), 1966. **Professional Experience:** Retired 2005; ASSOC PROVOST, UNIV MD, 2000-; ASST VPRES, UNIV MD, 1991-; assoc dean, Univ Md, 1990-1991; PROF PHYSICS, UNIV MD, 1979-; Fel, Alfred P Sloan Found, 1971; from asst prof to assoc prof, Univ Md, 1967-1979; Res assoc, Univ Md, 1965-1967. **Memberships:** AAAS; fel Am Phys Soc; Fedn Am Scientists. **Research Statement & Publications:** Theory of itinerant ferromagnetism. **Mailing Address:** 3406 Stonehall Dr, Beltsville, MD 20705. **Fax:** 301-405-8195. **E-Mail:** vkor@umd.edu

KORENSTEIN, RALPH, INORGANIC CHEMISTRY, SOLID STATE CHEMISTRY. **Personal Data:** b Havannah, Cuba, December 6, 1951; American citizen; m 1976. **Education:** Polytech Inst Brooklyn, BS, 1973; Brown Univ, PhD (chem), 1977. **Professional Experience:** Mem tech staff chem, Tex Instruments Inc, 1976-; AT RES DIV, RAYTHEON CO, LEXINGTON, MASS. **Memberships:** Am Chem Soc. **Research Statement & Publications:** Crystal growth of oxides by liquid phase epitaxy; synthesis of new inorganic compounds; thin film technology. **Mailing Address:** Res Div, Raytheon Co 131 Spring St, Lexington, MA 02173-7801.

KORETZ, JANE FAITH, IMAGE ANALYSIS, COMPUTER MODELING. **Personal Data:** b New York, NY, August 12, 1947. **Education:** Swarthmore Col, BA, 1969; Univ Chicago,

PhD (biophys), 1974. **Honors & Awards:** Henry Fukui Mem Travel Award, 1989. **Professional Experience:** Hon res assoc, Open Univ Oxford Res Unit, 1992-& Nuffield lab of ophtal, univ of Oxford, 1999-2004; head biochem & biophys prog, Ctr Biophys, 1992-1994; dir, Ctr Biophys, 1991-1994; vis prof, Open Univ Oxford, 1991; Fulbright scholar, Univ Oxford, 1991; PROF, DEPT BIOL, RENSSELAER POLYTECH INST, 1990-; mem, Vis Study Sect, NIH, 1989-1993 SSIR, AIIH, 1993-; study sec; adj assoc prof, Sch Pub Health, State Univ NY, Albany, 1988-; from asst prof to assoc prof, Rensselaer Polytech Inst, 1977-1990; Adj asst prof human physiol, Kean Col, NJ, 1977; res affil, Dept Physiol, NJ Med Sch, 1976-1977; Vis scientist, Cell Biophys Unit, Med Res Coun, London, 1974-1976. **Memberships:** Biophys Soc (coun, 1988-1991); Optical Soc Am; Sigma Xi; Asn Women Sci; Asn Res Vision & Ophthal; Am Soc Biochem & Molecular Biol; Int Soc Eyes Res. **Research Statement & Publications:** Characterization of native and reconstituted alpha-crystallin assemblies; computer-based modelling of human and rhesus monkey visual accommodation; etiology of presbyopia. **Mailing Address:** BioChem & Biophysics Program, Rensselaer Polytechnic Inst, 110 8th St, Troy, NY 12180-3590. **Fax:** 518-276-2344. **E-Mail:** koretj@rpi.edu

KOREVAAR, JACOB, MATHEMATICS. **Personal Data:** b Neth, January 25, 1923; American citizen; c 8. **Education:** Univ Leiden, PhD (math), 1949. **Honorary Degrees:** Dr, Univ Gothenburg, 1978. **Honors & Awards:** Reynolds Teaching Award, 1958. **Professional Experience:** DIR, MATH INST, UNIV AMSTERDAM, 1980-; PROF, MATH INST, UNIV AMSTERDAM, 1974-; vis prof math, Univ Amsterdam, 1974-1976; chmn dept, Univ Calif, San Diego, 1971-1973; prof math, Univ Calif, San Diego, 1964-1974; Mem Nat Sci Found fel comt, 1964-1966; from asst prof to prof, Univ Wis, 1953-1964; prof, Delft Univ Technol, 1951-1953; res assoc, Math Ctr, Univ Amsterdam, 1947-1949; Asst math, Delft Univ Technol, 1944-1946. **Memberships:** AAAS; Am Math Soc; London Math Soc; Math Asn Am; Soc Indust & Appl Math. **Research Statement & Publications:** Approximation; complex analysis; distributions; Fourier analysis; Tauberian theorems. **Mailing Address:** Univ Amsterdam, Plantage Muidergracut 24 10181V, Amsterdam, Netherlands.

KORF, BRUCE R, GENETICS. **Education:** Cornell Univ, MD; Rockefeller Univ, PhD. **Professional Experience:** CHMN, FOUND MED POLICY COMT, as of 2005; PROF & CHAIR, DEPT GENETICS, UNIV ALA, as of 2005. **Mailing Address:** Univ Ala, 1802 Sixth Ave S, Birmingham, AL 35294.

KORF, RICHARD E, ARTIFICIAL INTELLIGENCE, HEURISTIC SEARCH. **Personal Data:** b Geneva, Switz, December 7, 1956; American citizen; m 2001, Victoria Cortessis. **Education:** Mass Inst Technol, BS, 1977; Carnegie-Mellon Univ, MS, 1980, PhD (comput sci), 1983. **Honors & Awards:** Presidential Young Investr Award, NSF, 1986. **Professional Experience:** PROF COMPUT SCI, UNIV CALIF, LOS ANGELES, 1995-; fel Am Asn Artificial Intel, 1994; from asst prof to assoc prof, Univ Calif, Los Angeles, 1985-1995; asst prof comput sci, Columbia Univ, 1983-1985. **Research Statement & Publications:** Development and analysis of heuristic search algorithms for combinatorial problems in artificial intelligence. **Mailing Address:** Dept Comput Sci, Univ Calif, Los Angeles, CA 90095. **E-Mail:** korf@cs.ucla.edu

KORF, RICHARD PAUL, MYCOLOGY, TAXONOMY. **Personal Data:** b Bronxville, NY, May 28, 1925; m 1959, Kumiko; c Noni, Mia, Ian F & Mario T. **Education:** Cornell Univ, BSc, 1946, PhD (mycol), 1950. **Professional Experience:** EMER PROF MYCOL, CORNELL UNIV, 1992-; prof & chmn theatre arts, Cornell Univ, 1985-1986; prof bot, Cornell Univ, 1982-1992; adj prof, Copenhagen Univ, 1978; co-ed, Mycotaxon J, 1974-1991; chmn, Nomenclature Secretariat, Int Mycol Asn, 1972-1977; prof mycol, Cornell Univ, 1969-1992; Fulbright res prof & NSF sr fel, Yokohama Nat Univ, Japan, 1957-1958; from asst prof to assoc prof, Cornell Univ, 1951-1960; lectr, Glasgow Univ, 1950-1951; asst plant path, Cornell Univ, 1947-1950. **Memberships:** Mycol Soc Am (secy-treas, 1965-1968, vpres, 1968-1969, pres, 1970-1971); Brit Mycol Soc; Mycol Soc France; Mycol Soc Japan; Int Asn Plant Taxon. **Research Statement & Publications:** Taxonomic mycology; taxonomy of discomycetes; life histories and genetics of ascomycetes; botanical nomenclature; fungi of Asia, Neotropics and Macaronesia. **Mailing Address:** Plant Path Herbarium, Cornell Univ, Ithaca, NY 14853. **Fax:** 607-273-4357. **E-Mail:** rpk1@cornell.edu

KORFHAGEN, THOMAS R, BIOLOGY. **Education:** Univ Cincinnati, BA, 1972, PhD, 1976, MD, 1981. **Professional Experience:** PROF PEDIATS, UNIV CINCINNATI, as of 2005. **Mailing Address:** Div Pulm Biol Children's Med Ctr Cincinnati Children's Hosp Med Ctr, 3333 Burnett Ave, Cincinnati, OH 45229-3039. **Fax:** 513-636-7868. **E-Mail:** thomas.korfhagen@cchmc.org

KORFMACHER, WALTER AVERILL, MASS SPECTROMETRY, TRACE LEVEL ANALYSIS. **Personal Data:** b St Louis, Mo, November 6, 1951; m 1974, Madeleine M Deutsch; c Mary & Joseph. **Education:** St Louis Univ, BSCh, 1973; Univ Ill, Urbana, MS, 1975, PhD (anal chem), 1978. **Professional Experience:** DIR & GROUP LEADER, EXPLORATORY DRUG METABOLISM, SCHERING-PLOUGH RES INST, as of 2002; prin scientist, Schering-Plough Res Inst, beginning 1991; adj assoc prof, Dept Toxicol, 1991; adj assoc prof med chem, Col Pharm, Univ Tenn, Memphis, 1988-1991; res chemist, Nat Ctr Toxicol Res, Food & Drug Admin, 1983-1991; adj asst prof, Dept Chem, Univ Ark, Little Rock 1982-1991; chemist, Nat Ctr Toxicol Res, Food & Drug Admin, 1978-1983; Res asst, Chem Div, Colo State Univ, Ft Collins, 1976-1978. **Memberships:** Sigma Xi; Am Chem Soc; AAAS; Am Soc Mass Spectrometry; Soc Appl Spectros; NY Acad Sci. **Research Statement & Publications:** Analytical methods, particularly trace organic quantitative methods; development of capillary gas chromatography combined with atmospheric pressure ionization mass spectrometry, chemical ionization mass spectrometry and LC-MS; thermospray mass spectometry, atmospheric pressure chemical ionization and tandem mass spectrometry. **Mailing Address:** Schering Plough Res Inst, 2015 Galloping Hill Rd, Kenilworth, NJ 07033. **Fax:** 908-740-3966. **E-Mail:** walter.korfmacher@spcorp.com

KORGEN, BENJAMIN JEFFRY, PHYSICAL OCEANOGRAPHY. **Personal Data:** b Duluth, Minn, January 6, 1931; m 1959, Judith K Waggoner; c Susan K, Jeffry D & James M. **Education:** Univ Minn, BS, 1956; Univ Mich, MA, 1958; Ore State Univ, PhD (phys oceanog), 1969. **Professional Experience:** OCEANOGR, US NAVAL OCEANOG OFF, 1978-; Adj assoc prof, Tulane Univ, 1978-; writing & consult, 1974-1978; Asst prof phys oceanog, Univ NC Chapel Hill, 1969-1974. **Memberships:** AAAS; Am Geophys Union; Am Soc Limnol & Oceanog; Geol Soc Am; Oceangraphy Soc. **Research Statement & Publications:** Analysis of ocean currents; non-acoustical detection of submerged objects; physical properties of sea water; underwater acoustics; tidal phenomena; analysis of ocean currents; seichesand related phenomena. **Mailing Address:** 219 Loop Dr, Slidell, LA 70458. **Fax:** 228-688-4234.

KORIN, AMOS, MEMBRANE SCIENCE, SEPARATION TECHNOLOGY. **Personal Data:** b Rehovoth, Israel, September 11, 1944; m 1967, c 3. **Education:** Technion Israel Inst Technol, BSc, 1967; Weizmann Inst Sci, MSc, 1972, PhD (polymer chem), 1978. **Professional Experience:** PRES & FOUNDER, KORTECH INC, as of 1995; dir technol, W R Grace, beginning 1987; dir technol, Stan Ohio, 1985-1987; independent consult, 1983-1985; dir, membrane develop, Gelman Sci Inc, 1979-1983; dept head, water distillation, Mehorot Water Co, 1978-1979; consult, Amplast Co, Israel, 1978-1979; proj engr, Weizmann Inst Sci, 1973-1978; lectr, chem & physics, Col Eng, Tel Aviv, 1973-1977; sr proj mgr, Israel Atomic Energy Comn, 1967-1973. **Memberships:** Israel Inst Chem Eng; Am Chem Soc; Filtration Soc. **Research Statement & Publications:** Novel polymer systems; polymeric ultra filtration and microporous membranes; separation systems and their application in industrial and medical fields. **Mailing Address:** Kortech Inc, 16 Mountainview Dr, Weston, CT 06883. **Fax:** 203-454-5561.

KORIN, BASIL PETER, MATHEMATICAL STATISTICS. **Personal Data:** b Oxford, Conn, September 15, 1932; m 1959, c 1. **Education:** Univ Conn, BA, 1957; Stanford Univ, MS, 1960; George Wash Univ, PhD (statist), 1967. **Professional Experience:** PROF EMER STATIST, AM UNIV, as of 2004; prof math & statist, Am Univ, beginning 1974; from instr to assoc prof math & statist, Am Univ, 1961-1974; math statist, US Bur Census, 1960-1961; mathematician, lockheed missiles & space co, 1957-1960. **Memberships:** Inst Math Statist; Am Statist Asn; Biometric Soc. **Research Statement & Publications:** Statistics; multivariate analysis. **Mailing Address:** Dept Math & Statist, Am Univ, 4400 Mass Ave, Washington, DC 20016-8050. **Fax:** 202-885-3155. **E-Mail:** bkorin@msn.com

KORINEK, GEORGE JIRI, PHYSICAL CHEMISTRY. **Personal Data:** b Jicin, Czech, July 8, 1927; American citizen; m 1958, Gisela; c 2. **Education:** Univ BC, MSc, 1954, PhD (metall), 1956. **Honors & Awards:** Indust Award, 1987, Soc of cavbide Engrs; pres, Refractory/Metals Asn, 1987-1989. **Professional Experience:** RETIRED; pres, H C Starck Inc, 1974-1992; managing dir, H C Starck Inc, 1970-1974; mgr, Rare Metals Dept, Ciba Corp, 1965-1970; group leader, Rare Metals Div, Ciba Ltd, Switz, 1961-1965; proj leader, Metals Res Lab, Union Carbide Metals Co, 1957-1961; fel, Nat Res Coun Can, 1956-1957. **Memberships:** Am Chem Soc; Electrochem Soc; Am Soc Metals; Am Inst Mining, Metall & Petrol Eng. **Research Statement & Publications:** Physical chemistry of extractive metallurgy; catalysis; hydrometallurgy; refractory metals; Ta capacitors. **Mailing Address:** Navoo Rd, PO Box 847, Windham, NY 12496. **Fax:** 518-734-4072.

KORITALA, SANBASIVAROA, LIPID CHEMISTRY. **Personal Data:** b India, April 10, 1932; American citizen; m 1961, c 2. **Education:** Andhra Univ, India, BS, 1952; Nagpur Univ, BS, 1954; Ohio State Univ, MS, 1957, PhD (physiol chem), 1960. **Professional Experience:** Abstr ed, Am Oil Chemists' Soc, 1975-; RES CHEMIST, NORTHERN REGIONAL RES CTR, AGR RES SERV, USDA, 1963-; Res assoc & instr physiol chem, Ohio State Univ, 1961-1963. **Memberships:** Am Chem Soc; Am Oil Chemists' Soc. **Research Statement & Publications:** Selective hydrogenation of vegetable oils to improve their flavor stability and to modify their functional properties for application in margarines, cooking and other food uses; preparations of selective and active catalysts for hydrogenation of animal and vegetable oils. **Mailing Address:** 7015 N Willow Wood Dr, Peoria, IL 61614.

KORITNIK, DONALD RAY, PHARMACOLOGY, REPRODUCTIVE ENDOCRINOLOGY. **Personal Data:** b Rock Springs, Wyo, February 28, 1946; m 1980, Deana; c Megan & Amanda. **Education:** Univ Wyo, BS (zoology), 1968, MS (zoology & physiology), 1973, PhD (animal sci), 1977. **Professional Experience:** ASSOC PROF PHARMACOL, FT WAYNE CTR MED EDUC 1990-2005; asst prof comp med, Bowman Gray Sch Med, Wake Forest Univ, 1980-1990; Fellow, Reprod Endocrinol Prog, Univ Calif, San Francisco, 1977-1980. **Memberships:** Endocrine Soc; Soc Study Reprod. **Research Statement & Publications:** Regulation of lipid and carbohydrate metabolism by reproductive hormones. **Mailing Address:** Ctr for Medical Education, Ind Univ Sch Med, Rm 311, Classrm Med Bldg, Ft Wayne, IN 46805-1499. **E-Mail:** koritnik@ipfw.edu

KORITZ, GARY DUANE, VETERINARY MEDICINE, PHARMACOLOGY. **Personal Data:** b DeKalb, Ill, May 18, 1944; m 1968, Barbara; c Matthew & Laura. **Education:** Univ Ill, Urbana, BS, 1966, DVM, 1968, PhD (vet pharmacol), 1975. **Professional Experience:** RETIRED; prof vet biosciences, Col Vet Med, Univ Ill, Urbana, beginning 1985; from asst prof to assoc prof, Col Vet Med, Univ Ill, Urbana, 1975-1985; NIH fel, Univ Ill, Urbana, 1973-1974; clinician pvt pract, Dundee Animal Hosp, 1968-1970. **Memberships:** Am Vet Med Asn; Am Col Vet Toxicol; Am Acad Vet Pharmacol & Therapeut; Am Soc Vet Physiologists & Pharmacologists. **Research Statement & Publications:** Comparative pharmacology including therapeutics, pharmacokinetics and drug disposition. **Mailing Address:** Dept Vet BioScis, Univ Ill, 3619 Vet Basic Sci Bldg MC-002, Urbana, IL 61802. **Fax:** 217-333-4628. **E-Mail:** gkoritz@cvm.uiuc.edu

KORITZ, SEYMOUR BENJAMIN, BIOCHEMISTRY. **Personal Data:** b Boston, Mass, November 25, 1921; m 1951, c 4. **Education:** Univ Mass, BS, 1944; Univ Wis, PhD (biochem), 1951. **Professional Experience:** PROF EMER MOLECULAR & CELL DEVELOP BIOL, MT SINAI SCH MED, as of 2004; prof biochem, Mt Sinai Sch Med, beginning 1968; from asst prof to prof biochem, Sch Med, Univ Pittsburgh, 1959-1968; staff biochemist, Worcester Found Exp Biol, 1953-1959; res assoc, Ohio State Univ, 1952-1953; Am Cancer Soc fel, Brussels, 1951-1952. **Memberships:** Am Soc Biol Chemists. **Research Statement & Publications:** Mode of action of adrenocorticotropic hormone. **Mailing Address:** Dept Molecular, Cell & Develop Biol, Mt Sinai Med Ctr, One Gustave L Levy Pl Box 1020, New York, NY 10029.

KORKEGI, ROBERT HANI, AEROSPACE VEHICLES, SPACE SYSTEMS. **Personal Data:** b Milan, Italy, December 3, 1925; American citizen; m 1946, Michele Caratini; c Paulette & Danielle. **Education:** Lehigh Univ, BS, 1949; Calif Inst Technol, MS, 1950, PhD (aerospace), 1954. **Honors & Awards:** Pub Serv Medal, NASA, 1988. **Professional Experience:** Chmn, SrScientist & Engrs Washington Vol Org, AAAS, 1994-; consult, Aerospace Res & Develop, 1991; VIS PROF, UNIV MD, COLLEGE PARK, 1990-; dir, Aerospace Bd, Nat Res Coun, Nat Acad Sci, 1981-1990; vis prof teaching & res, George Washington Univ, 1979-1981; int res & develop, dir Adv Group Aerospace Res & Develop, NATO, 1976-1979; US mem, Fluid Dynamics Panel, AGARD/NATO, 1969-1976 & bd dir, von Karman Inst Fluid Dynamics, 1976-1979; Mem, Adv Subcomt Fluid Mech, NASA, 1967-1971; dir res & tech admin, Hypersonic Res Lab, USAF, 1964-1976; tech dir teaching & res, von Karman Inst Fluid Dynamics, 1957-1964; Res assoc, Eng Ctr, Univ Southern Calif, 1954-1957. **Memberships:** Fel Am Inst Aeronaut & Astronaut mem Am asn fr the Advart of eng (AAAS). **Research Statement & Publications:** Aerodynamics of supersonic and hypersonic flows including two-and three-dimensional shock interactions with viscous flows; supersonic and hypersonic ground test facilities; aerospace policy issues; author of 60 publications. **Mailing Address:** 4418 Springdale St NW, Washington, DC 20016.

KORMAN, N(ATHANIEL) I(RVING), ELECTRONICS, COMPUTER SCIENCE. **Personal Data:** b Providence, RI, February 23, 1916; m 1941, Ruth; c Michael & Robert. **Education:** Worcester Polytech Inst, BS, 1937; Mass Inst Technol, MS, 1938; Univ Pa, PhD (elec eng), 1958. **Professional Experience:** PRES, VENTURES RES & DEVELOP GROUP, 1969-; dir med electronics plans & progs, RCA Corp, 1966-1969; chief engr graphic systs div, RCA Corp, 1965-1966; dir tech progs, RCA Corp, 1963-1965; dir advan mil systs, RCA Corp, 1958-1963; chief systs, RCA Corp, 1957-1958; asst chief engr, RCA Corp, 1954-1956; mgr systs eng group, RCA Corp, 1954; mgr develop eng group, RCA Corp, 1952-1954; adminr radar systs activities, RCA Corp, 1950-1952; eng group supvr, RCA Corp, 1948-1950; eng group leader, RCA Corp, 1944-1948; develop engr, RCA Corp, 1940-1944; Student engr, RCA Corp, 1938-1940. **Memberships:** Fel Inst Elec & Electronics Engrs. **Research Statement & Publications:** Advanced development of frequency modulation transmitters; microwave and waveguide components for radar and television; development of microwave studio-to-transmitter link; fire control radar; frequency modulation techniques; waveguide techniques; systems engineering; color science; patentee in field.

KORMENDY, JOHN, ASTRONOMY. **Personal Data:** b Graz, Austria, June 13, 1948; Canadian citizen; m 1987, Mary. **Education:** Univ Toronto, BS, 1970; Calif Inst Technol, PhD (astron), 1976. **Honors & Awards:** Gold Medal, Royal Astron Soc Can, 1970; Muhlmann Prize, Astron Soc Pac, 1988. **Professional Experience:** CURTIS T VAUGHAN JR CENTENNIAL CHMN ASTRON, UNIV TEX, AUSTIN, 2000-; Humboldt res award, Alexander von Humboldt Found, Ger, 1995; prof astron, Inst Astron, Univ Hawaii, Honalulu, 1990-2000; staff mem, Dominion Astrophys Observ, 1980-1989; sr vis fel, Inst Astron, Cambridge, 1978 & 1980; fel astron, Kitt Peak Nat Observ, 1978-1979; Parisot fel astron, Univ Calif, Berkeley, 1976-1978. **Memberships:** Am Astron Soc; Int Astron Union; Astron Soc Pac; Royal Astron Soc. **Research Statement & Publications:** Extragalactic observational astronomy, with particular emphasis on the structure of normal and peculiar galaxies; theoretical dynamics of the structure of galaxies; astronomical image processing. **Mailing Address:** Dept Astron, Univ Tex, RLM 15 308, Austin, TX 78712. **Fax:** 512-471-6016. **E-Mail:** kormendy@astro.as.utexas.edu

KORN, ALFRED, STRUCTURAL & CIVIL ENGINEERING. **Personal Data:** b Long Island City, NY, July 19, 1930. **Education:** Purdue Univ, BS, 1952; Univ Ill, Urbana, MS, 1961; Wash Univ, ScD (appl mech, struct), 1967. **Professional Experience:** Affil prof civil engr, Wash Univ, St Louis, 1991-; PROF EMER CIVIL ENG, SOUTHERN ILL UNIV, EDWARDSVILLE, 1990-; from assoc prof to prof, Southern Ill Univ, Edwardsville, 1969-1990; asst prof civil eng, Univ Ky, 1967-1969; lectr, Wash Univ, 1963-1966; engr, Sverdrup & Parcel Eng Co, Mo, 1955-1959 & 1961-1963; designer, Bell Aircraft Corp, NY, 1952-1953. **Memberships:** Am Soc Civil Engrs. **Research Statement & Publications:** Structural mechanics; elastic and inelastic frame stability; plastic design; numerical and computer analysis of structures; structural optimization. **Mailing Address:** Dept Civil Eng, Sch Eng, Southern Ill Univ, Edwardsville, IL 62026.

KORN, DAVID, BIOMEDICAL RESEARCH POLICY & RESEARCH INTEGRITY, RESEARCH FUNDING & RESEARECH TRAINING & CAREER DEVELOPMENT. **Personal Data:** b Providence, RI, March 5, 1933; m 1997, Carol; c Michael P, Stephen J, Daniel C & Joanna M. **Education:** Harvard Univ, BS, 1954, MD, 1959. **Honors & Awards:** Member, Institute of Medicine Distinguished Young Scientist Award, MD Academy of Science, 1967 Fellow, AAAS Gold-Headed Cane Award, Am Soc of Investigative Path, 2003 Distinguished Service Award Assoc Path Chairmen, 1999 Commissioner's Special Citation and Harvey W Wiley Medal, US FDA, 1997. **Professional Experience:** Vpres med, Stanford Univ, 1986-1995; dean, Sch Med, Stanford Univ, 1984-1995; chmn, Nat Cancer Adv Bd, 1984-1991; prof path (1968-97) & chmn dept, (1968-84), Sch Med, Stanford Univ; & pathologist-in-chief (1968-84), stanford unversity hospital; staff pathologist, NIH, 1964-1968; staff mem, Nat Inst Arthritis & Metab Dis, 1963-1968; Res assoc biochem, Nat Inst Arthritis & Metab Dis, 1961-1963; Sr vpres Biomedl & Health Sci Res, AAMC, 1997 - present. **Memberships:** Inst Med-Nat Acad Sci; Am Soc Biochem & Molecular Biol; Am Soc of Invetigative Path; AAAS; AMA; Col Am Path. **Research Statement & Publications:** Biomedical Research Policy; Biomedical Science, Technology, and Law; research integrity; academic medicine; structure and function of medical schools, medical education, and biomedical research training. **Mailing Address:** Asn Am Med Col, 2450 N St NW, Washington, DC 20037. **Fax:** 202-828-1125. **E-Mail:** dkorn@aamc.org

KORN, DAVID G, AERONAUTICS. **Education:** NY Univ, PhD (Appl Maths), 1969. **Professional Experience:** RES, AT & T BELL LABS, NJ, as of 2005. **Mailing Address:** AT&T Bell Labs, 180 Park Ave, Florham Park, NJ 07932. **Fax:** 973-360-8077. **E-Mail:** dgk@research.att.com dgk@research.att.com dgk@research.att.com

KORN, EDWARD DAVID, BIOCHEMISTRY, CELL BIOLOGY. **Personal Data:** b Philadelphia, Pa, August 3, 1928; m 1950, Muriel; c Elizabeth G & Sarah H (Gilchrist). **Education:** Univ Pa, AB, 1949, PhD (biochem), 1954. **Honors & Awards:** Dir Award 2002 Super Serv Award, USPHS, 1980; Mider Lectr, 1985; Presidential Meritorious Exec Rank Award, 1987. **Professional Experience:** LAB CELL BIOL & HEAD, SECT CELLULAR BIOCHEM & ULTRASTRUCT, NAT HEART, LUNG & BLOOD INST, 1989-; mem, Educ Comt, 1989-1994; mem, H-1 Waiver Comt, 1989-1991; mem, Facil Planning Group, 1989-1991; mem, AIDS Loan Repayment Comt, 1989; actg sci dir, Lab Biochem, Sect Cellular Biochem & Ultrastruct, Nat Heart & Lung Inst, 1988-1989; mem, Centennial Comt, NIH, 1987; rep, Am Soc Biol Chemists to AAAS, 1984-1989; pres, Found Advan Educ Sci, 1984-1986; dep sci dir, Lab Biochem, Sect Cellular Biochem & Ultrastruct, Nat Heart & Lung Inst, 1982-1988; vpres, Found Advan Educ Sci, 1982-1984; treas, Found Advan Educ Sci, 1980-1982; assoc ed, J Biol Chem, 1977-1993; mem bd dirs, Found Advan Educ Sci, 1977-1992; CHIEF, LAB CELL BIOL & HEAD, SECT CELLULAR BIOCHEM & ULTRASTRUCT, NAT HEART, LUNG & BLOOD INST, 1974-; head, Lab Biochem, Sect Cellular Biochem & Ultrastruct, Nat Heart & Lung Inst, 1969-1974; vis scientist, Inst Animal Physiol, Cambridge, Eng, 1969-1970; prof, FAES Grad Prog, Johns Hopkins Univ, 1966-1977; fac, FAES Grad Prog, NIH, 1966-1976; Vis scientist, Biochem Dept, Cambridge Univ, Eng, 1958-1959; res chemist, Lab Cellular Physiol & Metab & Lab Biochem, Sect Cellular Physiol, 1956-1969; asst scientist & sr asst scientist, Nat Heart & Lung Inst, 1954-1956; Damon Runyon fel, Lab Cellular Physiol & Metab, Nat Heart Inst, 1953-1954; asst instr, Damon Runyon fel, 1952-1953; asst instr, Harrison fel, 1951-1952; asst instr, Dept Physiol Chem, Univ Pa, 1949-1951. **Memberships:** Nat Acad Sci; Am Soc Biochem & Molecular Biol; Biophys Soc; Am Soc Cell Biol. **Research Statement & Publications:** Cell motility; cytoplasmic actin and myosin; author of 10 books and author or co-author of over 270 publications. **Mailing Address:** Lab Cell Biol, Nat Heart Lung & Blood Inst, Bldg Rm 50, Bethesda, MD 20892. **E-Mail:** edk@nih.gov

KORN, GRANINO A(RTHUR), COMPUTER SCIENCE, ELECTRICAL ENGINEERING. **Personal Data:** b Berlin, Ger, May 7, 1922; American citizen; m 1948, c 2. **Education:** Brown Univ, BA, 1942, PhD (physics), 1948; Columbia Univ, MA, 1942. **Honors & Awards:** Sr Sci Award, Soc Comput Simulation, 1968; Humboldt Prize, Humboldt Found, WGer, 1976. **Professional Experience:** GA & TM KORN INDUSTRIAL CONSULTS, 1984-; mem, NIH-Nat Adv Res Coun, 1978-1979; Consult, Nat Acad Sci, Chile, 1961; prof elec eng, Univ Ariz, 1957-1983; staff engr, Lockheed Aircraft Co, 1949-1952; head anal group, Airplane Div, Curtiss-Wright Corp, 1948-1949; Proj engr, Sperry Gyroscope Co, 1947-1948. **Memberships:** Int Asn Math-Simulation; fel Inst Elec & Electronics Engrs; Soc Comput Simulation; Sigma Xi. **Research Statement & Publications:** Desire computer systems for simulation; microdare desire laboratory-automation software; mini-microcomputer system design; DESIRE simulation system; neural-network simulations. **Mailing Address:** RR1 Box 96C, Chelan, WA 98816.

KORN, ISRAEL, DIGITAL COMMUNICATIONS. **Personal Data:** b Zamosc, Poland, March 2, 1934; m 1961, Nurit R Better; c Yoram, Neer & Dana. **Education:** Technion Israel Inst Technol, BSc, 1962, MSc, 1964, DSc, 1968. **Professional Experience:** VIS PROF, UNIV NSW, 1995-; assoc prof, Univ Nsw, 1978-1995; assoc prof, Univ Beer Sheva, Israel, 1976-1978; sr lectr, Technion Israel Inst Technol, 1972-1976; res assoc, NASA, 1971-1972; vis asst prof, Mich State Univ, 1969-1971; Lectr, Technion Israel Inst Technol, 1968-1969. **Memberships:** Fel Inst Elec & Electronics Engrs. **Research Statement & Publications:** Various problems of digital communication, particularly in fading channels with application to mobile, wireless and personal communications. **Mailing Address:** Sch Elec Eng, Univ NSW, Sydney NSW 2052, Australia. **E-Mail:** ikorn@unsw.edu.au

KORN, JOSEPH HOWARD, RHEUMATOLOGY, CELL BIOLOGY. **Personal Data:** b Augsburg, Ger, January 31, 1947; American citizen; m 1971, c 4. **Education:** City Col NY, BS, 1968; Columbia Univ, MD, 1972. **Professional Experience:** PROF MED, DIR & SECT CHIEF, ARTHRITIS CTR, BOSTON UNIV SCH MED, as of 2003; assoc chief staff res & develop, Vet Admin Med Ctr, Newington, Conn, 1985-1994; vis prof, Weitzmann Inst Sci, Israel, 1985-1986; Sch Med, Univ Conn, 1978-1994; from asst prof to prof, 1978-1989; asst prof med & immunol, Med Univ SC, 1977-1978. **Memberships:** Am Asn Immunologists; Am Col Rheumatology; Am Soc Clin Invest; NY Acad Sci; AAAS. **Research Statement & Publications:** Immunobiology of connective tissue; pathogenesis of scleroderma; fibroblast biology. **Mailing Address:** Arthritis Ctr, Boston Univ Sch Med, 715 Albany St K5, Boston, MA 02118-2394. **E-Mail:** jkorn@bu.edu

KORN, ROY JOSEPH, MEDICAL ADMINISTRATION. **Personal Data:** b Chicago, Ill, July 25, 1920; m 1955, c 4. **Education:** Northwestern Univ, BS, 1942, MD, 1946. **Professional Experience:** Prof med, Abraham Lincoln Sch Med, Univ Ill, 1972-; CHIEF STAFF, VET ADMIN WEST SIDE HOSP, CHICAGO, 1972-; clin prof med, Sch Med, Ind Univ-Purdue Univ, Indianapolis, 1965-1972; chief staff, Vet Admin Hosp, Indianapolis, 1965-1972; prof, Chicago Med Sch, 1964-1965; adv & prof med, Chiengmai Med Sch, Thailand, 1962-1964; from asst prof to assoc prof, Col Med, Univ Ill, 1955-1964; from asst chief to chief med serv, West Side Vet Admin Hosp, Chicago, Ill, 1953-1962; staff physician, Vet Admin Hosp, Omaha, Nebr, 1952-1953; Instr, Univ Nebr, 1952-1953; resident internal med, Vet Admin Hosp, Hines, Ill, 1949-1952; Intern med, Wesley Mem Hosp, Chicago, Ill, 1945-1946. **Memberships:** Fel Am Col Physicians. **Research Statement & Publications:** Liver disease. **Mailing Address:** 516 N Lincoln, Hinsdale, IL 60521-3447.

KORNACKER, KARL, Microarray data analysis. **Personal Data:** b Chicago, Ill, October 14, 1937; div, c 2. **Education:** Mass Inst Technol, BS (Physics), 1958, PhD (neurophysiol), 1962. **Professional Experience:** Emeritus Prof, Ohio State Univ, 2004-; ASSOC PROF, OHIO STATE UNIV, 1969-2004; asst prof biophys, Ohio State Univ, 1968-1969; Res assoc biol, Mass Inst Technol, 1962-1968. **Research Statement & Publications:** Development and application of computer algorithims for discovering diagnostic and/or prognostic gene expression profiles. **Mailing Address:** Columbus, OH 43214. **Fax:** 614-262-3271. **E-Mail:** kkornack@columbus.rr.com

KORNBERG, ARTHUR, BIOCHEMISTRY. **Personal Data:** b Brooklyn, NY, March 3, 1918; m 1943, c 3. **Education:** City Col New York, BS, 1937; Univ Rochester, MD, 1941. **Honorary Degrees:** Several from US & foreign univs, 1960-. **Honors & Awards:** Paul-Lewis Award, Am Chem Soc, 1951; Nobel Prize inMed & Physiol, 1959; Nat Medal Sci, Royal Soc, 1979. **Professional Experience:** EMER PROF, DEPT BIOCHEM, SCH MED, STANFORD UNIV, 1988-; prof, Dept Biochem, Sch Med, Stanford Univ, 1959-1988; chmn dept, Dept Biochem, Sch Med, Stanford Univ, 1959-1969; prof microbiol & head dept, Sch Med, Wash Univ, 1953-1959; chief enzyme & metab sect, Nat Inst Arthritis & Metab Dis, NIH, 1947-1953; asst surgeon to med dir, Nat Inst Arthritis & Metab Dis, NIH, 1942-1953; Intern, Strong Mem Hosp, Univ Rochester, 1941-1942; Mem bd gov, Weizmann Inst; sci adv, Div Schering-Plough, Inc, DNAX Res Inst Molecular & Cellular Biol, Regeneron Pharmaceut; mem bd dirs, Xoma Corp. **Memberships:** Nat Acad Sci; Am Philos Soc; Am Soc Biol Chemists (pres 1965); foreign mem Royal Soc. **Research Statement & Publications:** Enzymatic studies of DNA replication, membrane biochemistry; author of 6 publications. **Mailing Address:** Dept Biochem Beckman Ctr 400, BECKMAN CTR 415, Stanford, CA 94305-5307. **E-Mail:** arthur.kornberg@stanford.edu

KORNBERG, FRED, ELECTRONICS ENGINEERING. **Personal Data:** b Lemberg, Poland, January 28, 1936; American citizen; m 1958, c 3. **Education:** NY Univ, BSEE, 1958, MSEE, 1959. **Professional Experience:** PRES & CHIEF EXEC OFFICER, COMTECH TELECOMMUN CORP, 1976-; exec vpres, Comtech Telecommun Corp, 1971-1976; vpres, Nardcom Corp, 1969-1971; vpres, Radio Eng Labs, Dynamics Corp Am, 1959-1969; staff scientist, Res Div, NY Univ, 1958-1959; teacher, Col Eng, NY Univ, 1958-1959. **Memberships:** Sr mem Inst Elec & Electronics Engrs; sr mem Armed Forces Commun Eng Asn. **Mailing Address:** Comtech Telecommunications Corp, 105 Baylis Rd, Melville, NY 11747. **Fax:** 631-777-8877. **E-Mail:** fkornberg@comtechtel.com

KORNBERG, HANS L, MICROBIAL METABOLISM. **Personal Data:** b Herford, Ger, January 14, 1928; British citizen; m 1991, Donna. **Education:** Univ Sheffied, UK, BS, 1949, PhD (biochem), 1953; Univ Oxford, DSc, 1961; Univ Cambridge, DSc (biochem), 1975. **Honors & Awards:** Colworth Medal, Biochem Soc, UK, 1963; Warburg Medal, Soc Biol Chem, Ger, 1973; Knight Bachelor, HM Queen Gt Brit, 1978. **Professional Experience:** UNIV PROF, BOSTON UNIV, as of 2005; dir, Univ Prof Prog, Boston Univ, as of 2004; UNIV PROF BIOL, BOSTON UNIV, 1995-; prof biochem, Univ Cambridge, UK, 1975-1995; master, Christ's Col, Univ Leicester, UK, 1960-1975; mem, MRC Cell Metab Res Unit, Univ Oxford, UK, 1955-1960. **Memberships:** fel Royal Soc UK; foreign mem Nat Acad Sci; Am Acad Arts & Sci; Am Philos Soc; Accademia Nazionale Dei Lincei Italy; Japanese Biochem Soc. **Research Statement & Publications:** Nature and control of carbohydrate utilization by microorganisms. **Mailing Address:** Dept Biol, Boston Univ, Cummington St, Boston, MA 02215. **Fax:** 617-353-5084. **E-Mail:** hlk@bu.edu

KORNBERG, LORI, BIOLOGY. **Education:** Va Tech, BS, 1985; Med Col Va, PhD (biochem), 1990. **Professional Experience:** ASST PROF, DEPT OTOLARYNGOL, UNIV FLA, 2002-. **Mailing Address:** Dep Otolaryngol, Col Med, Univ Fl, Box 100264, Gainesville, FL 32610. **Fax:** 352-392-6781. **E-Mail:** kornblj@ent.ufl.edu

KORNBERG, ROGER DAVID, BIOCHEMISTRY. **Personal Data:** b St Louis, Mo, April 24, 1947; m 1984, Yahli; c Guy Joseph, Maya Lorch & Gil Lorch. **Education:** Harvard Univ, BA, 1967; Stanford Univ, PhD (chem), 1971. **Honorary Degrees:** Dr Honoris Causa, Hebrew Univ Jerusalem, 2001; Dr Honoris Causa, Univ Umea, 2003. **Honors & Awards:** Eli Lilly Award, 1980; Passano Award, 1981; Harvey Prize, 1997; Gairdner Award, 2000;

Welch Award, 2001; ASBMB-Merck Award, 2002; Le Grand Prix Charles-Leopold Mayer, 2003; Pasarow Award, 2003; Massry Prize, 2003; General Motors Cancer Research Award, 2005. **Professional Experience:** Chmn, Sch Med, Stanford Univ, 1984-1992; PROF STRUCT BIOL, SCH MED, STANFORD UNIV, 1978-; asst prof biol chem, Harvard Med Sch, 1976-1978; Mem sci staff cell biol, Med Res Coun Lab Molecular Biol, Cambridge, Eng, 1974-1975. **Memberships:** Nat Acad Sci; Amer Acad Arts Sci; Foreign Associate, EMBO. **Research Statement & Publications:** Structure and transcription of chromosomes. **Mailing Address:** Dept Structural Biol Fairchild D123, Stanford Univ Sch Med, Stanford, CA 94305. **Fax:** 650-723-8464. **E-Mail:** kornberg@stanford.edu

KORNBERG, SIR HANS LEO, BIOCHEMISTRY, MICROBIAL GENETICS. **Personal Data:** b Herford, Ger, January 14, 1928; m 1991, Donna; c Julia M, Rachel E, Johnathan P & Simon A. **Education:** Univ Sheffield, BSc, 1949, PhD, 1953; Oxford Univ, MA, 1958, DSc, 1961; Cambridge Univ, ScD, 1975. **Honorary Degrees:** ScD, Univ Cincinnati, 1974; DSc, Warwick Univ, 1975, Univ Sheffield, 1979, Leicester Univ, 1979, Bath Univ, 1980, Strathclyde Univ, 1985, Univ South Bank, London, 1994, Univ Leeds, 1995; DU, Essex Univ, 1979; MD, Leipzig Univ, 1984; LLD, Univ Dundee, 1999. **Honors & Awards:** Colworth Medal, Biochem Soc, 1963; Otto Warburg Medal, Ger Biochem Soc, 1973; Weizmann Mem Lectr, Rehovot, 1975; hon fel, Worcester Col, Oxford, 1981; Brasenose Col, Oxford, 1982; Wolfson Col, Cambridge, 1990; honmem, Phi Beta Kappa, 1996. **Professional Experience:** UNIV PROF & PROF BIOL, BOSTON UNIV, 1995-; Commonwealth Fund fel, Yale Univ, Univ Calif, Berkeley, Pub Health Res Inst, NY, 1953-1955; mem sci staff, Cell Metab Res Unit, Oxford, Med Res Coun, 1955-1960; lectr, Worcester Col, Oxford, 1958-1960; prof biochem, Univ Leicester, 1960-1975; Sir William Dunn prof biochem, Cambridge Univ, 1975-1995; pres, Int Union Biochem & Molecular Biol, 1991-1994; pres, Asn Sci Educ, 1991-1992; pres, Biochem Soc UK, 1990-1995; pres.Brit.Assoc.Advan.Sci, 1985 (hon.mem., 2003); chmn, Adv Comt Genetic Modification, 1986-1995; mem, Priorities Bd Res & Develop Agr, 1984-1990; master, Christ's Col, 1982-1995; sci gov, Weizmann Inst Sci, Rehovot, Israel, 1981-1990 (emer gov 1990-); mem, Agr Res Coun, 1981-1984; chmn, Royal Comn Environ Pollution, 1976-1981; managing trustee, Nuffield Found, 1972-1993; UK rep, NATO-ASI Panel, 1970-1976 (chmn, 1974-1975); mem, Sci Res Coun, 1967-1972 (chmn sci bd, 1969-1972); mem, UGC Biol Sci Comn, 1967-1976; gov, Wellcome Trust, 1990-1995. **Memberships:** Fel.Royal Soc.; foreign assoc Nat Acad Sci, USA; foreign mem., Am Acad Arts & Sci; fel., Inst Biol (vpres 1970-1972; hon.fel 2000); Royal Soc Arts, Am Acad Microbiol; hon mem Am Soc Biochem & Molec.Biol; Ger Soc Biol Chemists; Japanese Biochem.Soc; Am Philos Soc; Accad.Naz.Lincei; mem. Amer.Soc.Microbiol; Acad.Europaea; Ger.Acad.Sci"Leopoldina". **Research Statement & Publications:** Nature and regulation of carbohydrate transport in, and utilization by, micro-organisms. **Mailing Address:** Dept Biol, Col Arts & Sci, Boston Univ, 5 Cummington St, Boston, MA 02215. **Fax:** 617-353-5084. **E-Mail:** hlk@bu.edu

KORNBERG, THOMAS B, MOLECULAR & DEVELOPMENTAL BIOLOGY, GENETICS. **Personal Data:** b Washington, DC, November 10, 1948. **Education:** Columbia Col, NY, BA, 1970; Columbia Univ, PhD (biochem), 1973. **Professional Experience:** Prof biochem & biophys, Univ Calif, San Francisco, 1978-; mem staff, Molecular Biol Inst, Univ Calif, Los Angeles, 1976-1977; res assoc develop biol, Med Res Coun Lab Molecular Biol, Cambridge Univ, UK, 1975-1976; res assoc biochem, Princeton Univ, 1973-1975. **Research Statement & Publications:** Genetic and biochemical description of the cellular events which govern determination in higher organisms. **Mailing Address:** Dept Biochem & Biophys, Univ Calif Med Sch 513 Parnassus Ave, San Francisco, CA 94122-2722.

KORNBLITH, CAROL LEE, PHYSIOLOGICAL PSYCHOLOGY, NEUROBIOLOGY. **Personal Data:** b Chicago, Ill, September 6, 1945. **Education:** Calif Inst Technol, PhD (biol), 1972; Univ Mich, AB, 1966, AM, 1968. **Professional Experience:** MED ED, SECT PUBLS, MAYO FOUND, 1984-; assoc prof psychol, Oberlin Col, 1983-1984; assoc prof psychol, Ill State Univ, 1981-1983; interdisciplinary fel Neuroscience, Univ NC, 1980-1981; asst prof, Univ NC, 1974-1980; fel psychol, Princeton Univ, 1972-1974. **Memberships:** Soc Neuroscience; Sigma Xi; AAAS. **Research Statement & Publications:** Development and function of sexually dimorphic brain regions in the rat as revealed by deoxyglucose autoradiography and the development of feeding behavior and its relation to reinforcement. **Mailing Address:** Mayo Clin Sci Press, 200 First St SW, Rochester, MN 55905. **Fax:** 507-284-2107.

KORNBLUM, RONALD NORMAN, PATHOLOGY. **Personal Data:** b Chicago, Ill, December 5, 1933. **Education:** Univ Calif, Los Angeles, BA, 1955, MD, 1959. **Professional Experience:** CHIEF MED EXAMR, LOS ANGELES, CALIF, as of 2004; MED EXAMR, VENTURA COUNTY, CALIF, 1973-; Lectr pub health admin, Johns Hopkins Univ, 1969-; asst med examr, state med exam off, Md, 1968-1973; fel forensic path, Md Postmortem Exam, 1967-1968; resident neuropath, Md Dept Ment Hyg, 1966-1967; Resident gen path, Santa Clara County Hosp, 1962-1966. **Memberships:** Am Acad Forensic Sci; Am Soc Clin Pathologists; Col Am Pathologists. **Research Statement & Publications:** Forensic pathology; investigation into causes of sudden death in infancy syndrome; investigation of craniocerebral injuries and shock in relation to cerebral anoria. **Mailing Address:** 1104 N Mission, Los Angeles, CA 90033-1017.

KORNBLUM, SAUL S, PHYSICAL PHARMACY, PHYSICAL CHEMISTRY. **Personal Data:** b Far Rockaway, NY, February 24, 1934; m 1958, Sondra L Gilner; c Leslie F & Peter M. **Education:** Brooklyn Col Pharm, BS, 1955; Columbia Univ, MS, 1957; Rutgers Univ, PhD (pharm, phys chem), 1963. **Honors & Awards:** Lunsford Richardson Award, 1963. **Professional Experience:** PRES, S S KORNBLUM ASSOCS, 1985-; assoc sect head prod develop & clin prod, Sandoz Inc, 1973-1985; mgr, Sandoz Pharmaceut, 1967-1973; sr scientist, Sandoz Pharmaceut, 1966-1967; asst prof phys pharm, Brooklyn Col Pharm, Long Island Univ, 1962-1966; CIBA res grant, 1961-1962; Instr chem, Newark Col Eng, 1959-1961. **Memberships:** Am Acad Pharmaceut Sci; NY Acad Sci; Parenteral Drug Asn. **Research Statement & Publications:** Solid state kinetics; dissolution of poorly water-soluble drugs; sustained-release dosage forms; pharmaceutical dosage form design and evaluation; preformulation stability evaluation for new drugs; troubleshooting and reformulation. **Mailing Address:** 144 Short Hills Ave, Springfield, NJ 07081.

KORNBLUTH, RICHARD SYD, IMMUNOLOGY. **Personal Data:** b Kansas City, Mo, September 14, 1948; m 1985, c 2. **Education:** Harvard Col, BA, 1970; NY Med Col, MD, 1975; Columbia Univ, PhD (path), 1983; Am Bd Internal Med, cert, 1978, cert pulmonary dis, 1980. **Professional Experience:** ASSOC PROF MED, DIV INFECTIOUS DIS, DEPT MED, SCH MED, UNIV CALIF, SAN DIEGO, 1995-; adj prof, Univ Calif, San Diego, 1990-1995; Am Found AIDS Res, 1990-1991 & USPHS, NIH, Nat Inst Allergy & Infectious Dis, 1991-1994; prin investr, USPHS, NIH, Nat Heart, Lung & Blood Inst, 1989-1994 & 1996-; asst clin prof, 1986-1989; res assoc, Dept Immunol, Res Inst Scripps Clin, La Jolla, Calif, 1983-1986; Clairemont Community Hosp, San Diego, 1983-1986; vis physician, Columbia-Presby Med Ctr, 1981-1983; instr clin med, Pulmonary Div, 1981-1983; attend physician, Emergency Dept, Elmhurst City Hosp, Queens, NY, 1981-1983; Parker B Francis Found fel, 1980-1983; res fel, Cardiopulmonary Res Lab, Col Physicians & Surgeons, Columbia Univ, 1978-1983; fel, Pulmonary Div, Dept Med, Col Physicians & Surgeons, Columbia Univ, 1978-1981; Am Lung Asn fel, 1978-1980; intern & resident, Dept Med, Mt Sinai Hosp, 1975-1978; res asst, Dept Surg, Children's Hosp, Boston, 1973-1974. **Memberships:** Am Thoracic Soc; Am Asn Pathologists; Am Asn Immunologists; AAAS; Soc Leukocyte Biol; Physicians Social Responsibility. **Research Statement & Publications:** Human immunodeficiency virus; acquired immunodeficiency syndrome; macrophage immunobiology; cytokines; apoptosis; effects of human immunodeficiency virus on macrophage functions including the ability of macrophage to participate in anti-tuberculous immunity and the clearance of apoptic debris; tuberculosis; author of more than 20 technical publications; immunological regulation of macrophages in HIV infection, TB, cancer, and blood coogulation. **Mailing Address:** Dept Med, Univ Calif San Diego, 9500 Gilman Dr Mail Code 0679, La Jolla, CA 92093-0679. **Fax:** 858-552-7445. **E-Mail:** rkornbluth@ucsd.edu

KORNBREKKE, RALPH ERIK, COLLOID & SURFACE SCIENCE. **Personal Data:** b Brooklyn, NY, November 22, 1951; m 1974, Annette. **Education:** Rensselaer Polytechnic Inst, BS, 1974, PhD (chem), 1981. **Professional Experience:** SR RES CHEMIST, THE LUBRIZOL CORP, as of 2002; prin res scientist, The Lubritol corp, 1998-; IV, The Lubrizol Corp, 1990-1991; res chemist III, The Lubrizol Corp, 1987-1990; proj leader, Stand Oil Ohio, 1984-1987; chmn, Interface Sci Chap, 3M Tech Forum, 1982-1984; sr res chemist, The 3m Corp, 1980-1984; J Willard Gibbs res fel, Rensselaer Polytechnic Inst, 1979-1980; staff mem, Nat Bur Stand, Molten Salts Data Ctr, 1975-1976; Chemist, Rensselaer Res Corp Int, 1975-1976; chemist, Petrol Action Inc, 1974-1975. **Memberships:** Sigma Xi; Am Chem Soc; AAAS; Int Asn Colloid & Interface Sci; fel Am Inst Chemists; Soc Automotive Engrs; STLE. **Research Statement & Publications:** Surfactant interactions at solid-liquid interfaces (effect on wetting, dispersion stability and material properties) and non-aqueous colloid properties applied to dispersions and lubrication; discovery of the stochastic nature of emulsion inversion; discovery of the complex nature of wetting near the critical point. **Mailing Address:** 8340 Tulip Lane, Chagrin Falls, OH 44023.

KORNEL, LUDWIG, ENDOCRINOLOGY, BIOCHEMISTRY. **Personal Data:** b Jaslo, Poland, February 27, 1923; m 1952, c Eziel Edward & Amiel Maark. **Education:** Wroclaw Univ, MD, 1950; Univ Birmingham, PhD (endocrinol, steroid biochem), 1958. **Honors & Awards:** Physicians Recognition Award, AMA, 1969, 1973, 1976 & 1981. **Professional Experience:** SR ENDOCRINOLOGIST, KUPOT HOLIN KLOLIT OUT-PATENT CLIN, JERUSALEM, ISRAEL, 1996-; EMER PROF INTERNAL MED & BIOCHEM, RUSH MED COL, 1993-; 1982 & 1988 & Inst Hypertension, Tel-Hashomer Med Ctr, Univ Tel Aviv, Israel, 1990; co-ed, Yearbook Endocrinol, 1985-1990; mem bd dirs, Nat Acad Clin Biochem, 1982-1986; nat corresp, Fedn Am Socs Exp Biol, 1975-; vis prof, Kanazawa Univ, Japan, 1973; sr attend physician & sr scientist, Rush-Presby-St Luke's Med Ctr, 1971-; prof med & biochem, Kupot Holin Klolit Out-patent Clin, Jerusalem, Israel, 1970-1993; dir, Steroid Unit, Rush-Presby-St Luke's Med Ctr, 1967-1993; prof med, Col Med, Univ Ill, 1967-1971; assoc prof biochem, Med Ctr, Univ Ala, 1965-1967; hon vis prof, Polish Acad Sci, Warsaw, 1965; dir steroid sect & consult endocrinol, Med Ctr, Univ Ala, 1963-1967; from asst prof to prof med, Med Ctr, Univ Ala, 1961-1967; USPHS trainee, Inst Steroid Biochem, Univ Utah, 1959-1961; res fel endocrinol & metab, Med Ctr, Univ Ala, Birmingham, 1958-1959; asst physician med & community health, Hadassah Univ Hosp & Community Health Ctr, Jerusalem, 1957-1958; lectr med, Univ Birmingham, 1956-1957; Brit Coun res scholar med & steroid chem, Univ Birmingham, 1955-1957; asst physician & instr, Hadassah Med Sch, Hebrew Univ, Israel, 1954-1955; Res fel hemat, Hosp Broussai, Univ Paris, 1951-1952; from intern to resident med, Hadassah Univ Hosp, Jerusalem, 1950-1954; Intern med, surg, gynec & pediat, Wroclaw Univ Hosp, 1949-1950. **Memberships:** AAAS; Am Fedn Clin Res; Endocrine Soc; Sigma Xi; Cent Soc Clin Res; Am Asn Univ Prof; fel Am Soc Clin Pharmacol & Therapeut; Am Physiol Soc; fel Royal Soc Health; fel Nat Acad Clin Biochem. **Research Statement & Publications:** Metabolism and mechanism of action of steroidal hormones, especially relation of corticosteroids to mechanism of arterial hypertension; mineralocorticoid receptors in arterial walls and hypertension; role of mineralocorticoids in mechanism of hypertension; control by steroids of transmembrene ionic fluxes in vascular smooth muscle; co-author of encyclopedia on human biology. **Mailing Address:** 9 Haportzim St, Jerusalem 93662, Israel.

KORNELUK, ROBERT G, GENETICS. **Education:** Univ Toronto, PhD. **Professional Experience:** PROF, DEPT PEDIAT & MICROBIOL & IMMUNOL, UNIV OTTAWA, as of 2006; DIR APOPTOSIS RES, CTR CHILDREN'S HOSP EASTERN ONT, as of 2006. **Mailing Address:** Dept Genetics Children's Hosp Eastern Ont, 401 Smyth Rd, Ottawa, ON K1H 8L1, Can. **Fax:** 613-738-4833. **E-Mail:** bob@mgcheo.med.uottawa.ca

KORNET, MILTON JOSEPH, PHARMACEUTICAL CHEMISTRY, ORGANIC CHEMISTRY. **Personal Data:** b East Chicago, Ind, December 31, 1935; m 1962, Leona; c Linda, John & Frank. **Education:** Purdue Univ, BS, 1957; Univ Ill, PhD (pharmaceut chem), 1963. **Professional Experience:** ASSOC PROF EMER, PHARMACEUT CHEM, UNIV KY, as of 2004; assoc prof, pharmaceut chem, Univ KY, beginning 1967; asst prof, Pharmaceut Chem, Univ KY, 1963-1967; res assoc org synthesis, Northwestern Univ, 1962-1963; chemist, Abbott Labs, 1957-1959. **Memberships:** Am Chem Soc. **Research Statement & Publications:** Heterocyclic organic chemistry; medicinal chemistry; chemistry of hydrazines. **Mailing Address:** Col Pharm, Univ Ky, Lexington, KY 40536-0082.

KORNETSKY, CONAN, PSYCHOLOGY, PSYCHOPHARMACOLOGY. **Personal Data:** b Portland, Maine, February 9, 1926; m 1949, Marcia; c David & Lisa. **Education:** Univ Maine, BA, 1948; Univ Ky, MS, 1951, PhD (psychol), 1952. **Professional Experience:** Mem, Neuroscience Rev Comt, Nat Inst Alcohol Abuse & Alcoholism, 1985-1989; pres, Psychopharmacol Div, Am Psychol Asn, 1985-1986; NIH sr res fel, Nat Inst Drug Abuse res scientist award, 1983-1988; mem biomed rev comt, Nat Inst Drug Abuse, 1980-1984; mem psychopharmacol agents adv comt, Food & Drug Admin, 1973-1977; mem merit rev bd neurobiology, Vet Admin, 1972-1976; mem panel behav modification drugs for hyperkinetic children, Dept Health, Educ & Welfare, 1971; NIH sr res fel, NIMH res scientist award, 1970-1978; mem clin psychopharmacol res rev comt, NIMH, 1967-1971; mem comt tobacco habituation, Am Cancer Soc, 1966-1970; PROF PSYCHIAT & PHARMACOL, SCH MED, BOSTON UNIV, 1962-; NIH sr res fel, NIH res scientist award, 1962-1970; mem psychopharmacol study sect, NIH, 1962-1967; assoc prof, Sch Med, Boston Univ, 1959-1962; NIH sr res fel, Boston Univ, 1959-1962; res scientist, NIMH, 1952-1959. **Memberships:** Am Soc Pharmacol & Exp Therapeut; Am Psychol Asn; Am Col Neuropsychopharmacol; Int Col Neuropsychopharmacol; Psychonomic Soc; Soc Neuroscience. **Research Statement & Publications:** Neurobehavioral buses for the rewarding effects of abused substances, pain and analgesia; behavioral and neuropsychological studies of the action of antipsychotic and analgesic drugs. **Mailing Address:** Boston Univ Sch Med, 715 Albany St L602, Boston, MA 02118-2394. **Fax:** 617-638-4329. **E-Mail:** ckornets@bu.edu

KORNFELD, EDMUND CARL, MEDICINAL CHEMISTRY. **Personal Data:** b Philadelphia, Pa, February 24, 1919; m 1945, Virginia; c Cheryl, Marjorie & Jeanne. **Education:**

Temple Univ, AB, 1940, AM, 1942; Harvard Univ, MA, 1944, PhD (org chem), 1946. **Honorary Degrees:** DSc, Temple Univ, 1964. **Professional Experience:** RETIRED; res adv, Eli Lilly & Co, 1965-1983; res chemist, 1946-1965; res chemist, Off Sci Res & Develop Contract, Harvard Univ, 1945. **Memberships:** Am Chem Soc; Am Sci Affil. **Research Statement & Publications:** Rubber chemistry; organic structural determination; synthetic organic medicinals; organic chemicals development; medicinal chemistry of indol derivatives and ergot alkaloids. **Mailing Address:** 3550 Bay Rd S Dr, Indianapolis, IN 46240.

KORNFELD, LOTTIE, IMMUNOBIOLOGY. **Personal Data:** b Vienna, Austria, February 8, 1925; American citizen. **Education:** Col Wooster, BA, 1945; Ohio State Univ, MS, 1947; Univ Chicago, PhD (microbiol), 1960. **Professional Experience:** RETIRED; coordr, Univ Wide Aids Res Prog, Univ Calif, Berkeley, 1985-1989; health scientist adminr, NIH, 1974-1985; microbiologist, Div Biomed & Environ Res, US Atomic Energy Comn, 1972-1974; res microbiologist, Letterman Army Inst Res, 1969-1972; res microbiologist, US Naval Radiol Defense Lab, 1963-1969; lectr, Dept Microbiol, San Francisco State Col, 1969-1971; res fel, Dept Exp Path, Scripps Clin & Res Found, Calif, 1961-1963; res assoc, Dept Med & Argonne Cancer Res Hosp, 1960-1961; res asst bact, Dept Med, Univ Chicago, 1955-1960; res asst bact, Univ Mich, 1954-1955; bacteriologist, Viral & Rickettsial Res Div, Lederle Labs, Am Cyanamid Co, 1947-1954; asst bact, Ohio State Univ, 1945-1947. **Memberships:** Am Soc Microbiol; Radiation Res Soc; Soc Leucocyte Biol; Am Asn Immunologists. **Research Statement & Publications:** Immunology; host resistance; effects of irradiation on host-parasite relationship; science administration. **Mailing Address:** 508 Tampico Dr, Walnut Creek, CA 94598.

KORNFELD, MARIO O, NEUROPATHOLOGY. **Personal Data:** b Zagreb, Yugoslavia, July 9, 1927; m 1956, c 1. **Education:** Univ Zagreb, MD, 1953, ScD, 1964. **Honors & Awards:** Matthew T Moore Award, Am Asn Neuropath; Weil Award, Am Asn Neuropath. **Professional Experience:** PROF EMER, UNIV NMEX, as of 2001; prof path, Sch Med, Univ Nmex, beginning 1980; staff pathologist, Bernalillo County Med Ctr, Albuquerque, beginning 1970; attend neuropathologist, Vet Admin Hosp, beginning 1970; assoc prof path & neuropath, Sch Med, Univ Nmex, 1970-1980; asst prof, Sch Med, Univ Nmex, 1968-1970; instr neuropath, Col Physicians & Surgeons, Columbia Univ, 1967-1968; trainee & fel, Col Physicians & Surgeons, Columbia Univ, 1964-1967; staff pathologist, Inst Path, Gen Hosp, Zagreb, 1959-1964. **Memberships:** Assoc Am Asn Neuropathologists; Am Asn Pathologists; Asn Res Neuropath Ment Dis. **Research Statement & Publications:** Histopathology of inner ear and temporal bone; ultrastructural aspects of neurolipidoses, peripheral nervous system diseases and astroglia in metabolic encephalopathies; morphometry of secretion in pituitary adenonomas. **Mailing Address:** Dept Path, Univ NMex Sch Med 915 Sanford NE, Albuquerque, NM 87131. **Fax:** 505-277-7224.

KORNFELD, ROSALIND HAUK, OLIGOSACCHARIDE STRUCTURE, GLYCOPROTEIN SYNTHESIS. **Personal Data:** b Dallas, Tex, August 2, 1935; m 1959, c 3. **Education:** George Wash Univ, BS, 1957; Wash Univ, St Louis, PhD (biochem), 1961. **Professional Experience:** PROF EMER, DEPT INTERNAL MED, WASH UNIV, ST LOUIS, as of 2004; coordr, Grad Training Prog, beginning 1984; prof, Dept Biol Chem, Wash Univ, beginning 1981; mem, & Physiol Chem Study Sect, 1980-1983; assoc prof biochem, div hematoncol & assoc prof, 1978-1981; mem, Comt Cancer Immunobiol, Nat Cancer Inst, NIH, 1975-1978; from res instr to res assoc prof, Grad Training Prog, 1965-1978; staff fel, Nat Inst Arthritis & Metab Dis, NIH, 1963-1965; prof biochem, Div Hemat-Oncol, Dept Med, Sch Med. **Memberships:** Am Soc Hemat; Am Soc Biochem & Molecular Biol. **Research Statement & Publications:** Biosynthesis and structural analysis of the oligosaccharides on glycoproteins and the role of mannosidases in oligosaccharide processing. **Mailing Address:** Dept Internal Med, Wash Univ, Clin Sci R 8832, PO Box 8125, St Louis, MO 63110-1093.

KORNFELD, STUART ARTHUR, HEMATOLOGY. **Personal Data:** b St Louis, Mo, October 4, 1936; m 1959, c 3. **Education:** Dartmouth Col, AB, 1958; Washington Univ, MD, 1962. **Honors & Awards:** Biochemistry Award, Am Acad Arts & Sci, 1959; Jubilee lectr & Harden Medallist, Biochem Soc, 1989; Passano Award, 1991; E Donnall Thomas lectr & Prize, 1992; Karl Meyer Award, Soc Glycobiology, 1999. **Professional Experience:** DAVID C & BETTY FARRELL DISTINGUISHED PROF MED, WASH UNIV SCH MED, 2000-; CO DIR, DIV HEMAT WASH UNIV SCH MED, 1993-; counr, Asn Am Physicians, beginning 1991 & Am Soc Clin Invest, 1972-1975; sci rev bd, Howard Hughes Med Inst, 1986- & bd sci adv, Jane Coffin Childs Mem Fund Res, 1987-; bd sci counselors, Nat Inst Arthritis, Diabetes & Digestive & Kidney Dis, 1983-1987; assoc ed, J Biol Chem, 1982-1987; ed, J Clin Invest, 1981-1982; assoc ed, J Clin Invest, 1977-1981; PROF BIOCHEM, DIV HEMAT & ONCOL, 1976-; co-dir, Div Hemat & Oncol, 1976-1992; mem, Cell Biol Study Sect, NIH, 1974-1977; dir, Div Oncol, 1973-1976; dir, Div Oncol, Wash Univ School of Medicine, PROF MED, SCH MED, WASHINGTON UNIV, 1972-; NIH res career develop award, 1971-1976; from asst prof to assoc prof biochem, Sch Med, Washington Univ, 1967-1972; fac res assoc, Am Cancer Soc, 1966-1971; from instr to asst prof med, Sch Med, Washington Univ, 1966-1970; asst resident ward med, Barnes Hosp, 1965-1966; res assoc, Nat Inst Arthritis & Metab Dis, NIH, 1963-1965; intern ward med, Barnes Hosp, 1962-1963; res ast, Biochem Dept, Washington Univ Sch Med, 1958-1962. **Memberships:** Nat Acad Sci; Inst Med-Nat Acad Sci; Am Soc Clin Invest; Am Soc Hemat; Am Soc Biol Chemists; Asn Am Physicians (secy, 1986-1991); fel Am Acad Arts & Sci; Am Chem Soc; Sigma Xi; Am Fedn Clin Res; fel AAAS. **Research Statement & Publications:** Studies of the structure, biosynthesis and function of glycoproteins, especially those which are found on the surface of normal and malignant cells; targeting of newly synthesized acid hydrol a ses to lysosomes; author of 215 publications. **Mailing Address:** Hemat Div, Sch Med, Wash Univ, 660 S Euclid Ave Campus Box 8103, St Louis, MO 63110. **Fax:** 314-362-8826. **E-Mail:** skornfeld@im.wustl.edu

KORNFIELD, IRVING LESLIE, EVOLUTIONARY BIOLOGY. **Personal Data:** b Jacksonville, NC, July 16, 1945; m 1968, Victoria Jean Porter; c Molly Rebecca & Emily Caroline Porter. **Education:** Syracuse Univ, AB, 1968; State Univ NY, Stony Brook, NY, 1972, PhD (ecol), 1974. **Honors & Awards:** fel, AAAS 2001; prof of the yr, Carnegie Foundation, 1998. **Professional Experience:** PROF ZOOL, UNIV MAINE, 1985-; Assoc, Danforth Found, 1980-; assoc prof zool, Univ Maine, 1977-1985; res collabr, Dept Genetics, Hebrew Univ, 1975-1976; Fel, Smithsonian Inst, 1974-1975. **Memberships:** Am Soc Ichthyologists & Herpetologists; Genetics Soc Am; Soc Study Evolution; Soc Molecular Biol & Evolution. **Research Statement & Publications:** Evolutionary genetics of fishes; molecular systematics. **Mailing Address:** Sch of Marine Sci, Univ Maine, Orono, ME 04469. **Fax:** 207-581-2537. **E-Mail:** irvk@maine.edu

KORNFIELD, JACK I, SATELLITE METEOROLOGY. **Personal Data:** b New York, NY. **Education:** City Col New York, BS, 1961; Northeastern Univ, MS, 1963; Univ Wis, PhD (meteorol), 1973. **Professional Experience:** CONSULT, 1989-; Freelance ed & publ, 1989; tech ed, Bull Am Meteorol Soc, 1983-1989; assoc prog dir meteorol, NSF, 1981-1983; mem advan prog staff, OAO Corp, 1979-1980; sr scientist, Systs & Appl Sci Corp, 1978-1979; sr colorimetrist, SCI, Inc, Tex, 1977-1978; sr scientist, Agr Res Inst Israel, 1976-1977; sr mathematician, GTE, 1974-1976; Sr analyst, Space Res Corp, 1973-1974. **Memberships:** Am Meteorol Soc; Am Geophys Union; Sigma Xi; AAAS; Am Soc of Geol Teachers. **Research Statement & Publications:** Remote sensing to extract parameters of the earth's land, ocean and atmosphere systems; climate and hydrological modeling; colorimetry applied to the display and analysis of information; balistic analysis; laser propagation through the atmosphere; general theory of remote sensing. **Mailing Address:** 194 Beach 109 St, Rockaway Park, NY 11694.

KORNFIELD, JULIA ANN, CHEMICAL ENGINEERING. **Personal Data:** b Oakland, Calif, July 2, 1962. **Education:** Calif Inst Technol, BS, 1983, MS, 1984; Stanford Univ, PhD (chem eng), 1988. **Honors & Awards:** Dillon Medal, Am Phys Soc. **Professional Experience:** PROF, CHEM ENG, CALIF INST TECHNOL, 2001-; from asst prof to assoc prof, Chem Eng, Calif Inst Technol, 1990-2001; NSF/NATO fel chem eng, Max Planck Inst, 1989; teaching asst, Stanford Univ, 1986 & 1987; res asst chem eng, Stanford Univ, 1984-1988; res asst, Calif Inst Technol, 1983-1984. **Memberships:** Am Inst Chem Engrs; Am Phys Soc; Am Chem Soc; Soc Rheology. **Research Statement & Publications:** Chemical engineering. **Mailing Address:** Chem Eng 210-41, Calif Inst Technol, Pasadena, CA 91125. **Fax:** 626-568-8743. **E-Mail:** jak@cheme.caltech.edu

KORNGOLD, ROBERT, GRAFT VS HOST DISEASE, BONE MARROW TRANSPLANTATION. **Education:** Univ Pa, PhD (immunol), 1979. **Professional Experience:** PROF MICROBIOL & IMMUNOL, KIMMEL CANCER INST, THOMAS JEFFERSON UNIV, as of 2004; assoc prof microbiol & immunol, Kimmel Cancer Inst, Thomas Jefferson Univ, beginning 1987; asst prof, Wistar Inst Anat & Biol, 1981-1987. **Mailing Address:** Dept Microbiol & Immunol, Kimmel Cancer Inst, Thomas Jefferson Cancer Inst, 730A BLSB 233 S Tenth St, Philadelphia, PA 19107. **E-Mail:** r.korngold@mail.jci.tju.edu

KORNGUTH, STEVEN E, BIOCHEMISTRY. **Personal Data:** b New York, NY, December 1, 1935; m 1958, c 2. **Education:** Columbia Univ, BA, 1957; Univ Wis, MA, 1959, PhD (biochem), 1961. **Professional Experience:** PROF EMER NEUROL & PHYSIOL CHEM, UNIV WIS, MADISON, as of 1999; prof neurol & physiol chem, Univ Wis, Madison, beginning 1972; from asst prof to assoc prof, Univ Wis-madison, 1963-1972; res scientist neurochem, NY State Psychiat Inst, 1961-1963. **Memberships:** Am Soc Biol Chemists. **Research Statement & Publications:** Magnetic resonance contrast agents; antigenic properties of such proteins; synaptic complexes, isolation and chemical properties; paraneoplastic disorders. **Mailing Address:** Dept Neurol & Biomolecular Chem, Univ Wis, Waisman Med Ctr 1500 Highland Ave, Madison, WI 53705. **Fax:** 608-265-4103. **E-Mail:** kornguth@waisman.wisc.edu

KORNHAUSER, ALAIN LUCIEN, ASTRODYNAMICS, TRANSPORTATION. **Personal Data:** b Beaurepaire, France, June 12, 1944; American citizen; m 1965. **Education:** Pa State Univ, BS, 1965, MS, 1967; Princeton Univ, MA, 1969, PhD (aerospace sci), 1971. **Honors & Awards:** R T Knapp & Melville Medal, Am Soc Mech Eng, 1970. **Professional Experience:** PROF, OPER RES & FINANCIAL ENG, PRINCETON UNIV, as of 2004; CO-DIR, NJ TIDE CTR, as of 2004; PROF, DEPT CIVIL ENG, PRINCETON UNIV, 1978-; assoc prof, Transportation Prog, 1977-1978; DIR, TRANSPORTATION PROG, 1976-; Consult, Princeton Univ 1971- & Optimal Data Co, 1971-; asst prof astrodyn, Univ Minn, Minneapolis, 1971-1977; Res asst cavitation, Ord Res Lab, 1967. **Memberships:** Am Soc Mech Eng; Am Inst Aeronaut & Astronaut; Am Astronaut Soc; Sigma Xi. **Research Statement & Publications:** Optimal space flight; cavitation; urban transportation; computer graphics; freight railroad operations and planning analysis. **Mailing Address:** Dept Oper & Financial Res, Princeton Univ, Rm E-407 Eng Quad, Princeton, NJ 08544. **Fax:** 609-258-1563. **E-Mail:** alaink@princeton.edu

KORNHAUSER, ANDRIJA, TOXICOLOGY, BASIC MEDICAL SCIENCES. **Personal Data:** b Zagreb, Yugoslavia, February 5, 1930; American citizen; m 1978. **Education:** Univ Zagreb, Yugoslavia, BSci, 1954, PhD (biochem), 1962. **Professional Experience:** CHIEF, DERMAL & OCULAR BR, DIV TOXICOL, CFSAN, FOOD & DRUG ADMIN, 1980-; adj assoc prof dermat, Sch Med, George Wash Univ, 1978-; lectr oral path, Sch Dermal Med, Harvard Univ, 1978-; res biologist, res & mgt, Div Toxicol, 1978-1980; mem fac, Sch Med, Harvard Univ & Sch Dent Med, 1970-1978; assoc prof, Rudjer BoskavicInst, Univ Zagreb, 1966-1970; res assoc, Sch Med, Univ Frankfurt, Ger, 1964-1966. **Memberships:** AAAS; Am Asn Photobiol; Soc Investigative Dermat Inc; NY Acad Sci; hon fel Skin Cancer Found. **Research Statement & Publications:** Cutaneous toxicol; phototoxicity; carcinogenesis; photocarcinogenesis; photomedicine; molecular toxicology; pharmacology; protection against phototoxicity and carcinogenesis by dietary antioxidants; development of animal models for clinical studies. **Mailing Address:** Cosmetics Toxicol Br, USFDA, 200 C St SW HFS-1 28, Washington, VA 20204. **Fax:** 202-205-5098.

KORNICKER, LOUIS SAMPSON, GEOLOGY. **Personal Data:** b Brooklyn, NY, May 23, 1919; m 1951, c 3. **Education:** Univ Ala, BS, 1941 & 1942; Columbia Univ, MA, 1954, PhD, 1958. **Professional Experience:** Adj prof biol, George Wash Univ, 1970-; RES ZOOLOGIST & CUR, DIV CRUSTACEA, NATURAL HIST MUS, SMITHSONIAN INST, 1967-; assoc cur, US Natural Hist Mus, Smithsonian Inst, 1964-1967; from assoc prof to prof oceanog, Tex A&M Univ, 1961-1964; geologist, Off Naval Res, Chicago, 1960-1961; asst dir, Inst Marine Sci, Univ Tex, 1957-1960; asst, Columbia Univ, 1954-1957; treas & plant supt, Uncle Sam Chem Co, Inc, 1947-1954; sr process engr & pilot plant supt, Cities Serv Ref Co, 1944-1947; Prod supvr trinitrotoluene, Tech Invest Group, Hercules Powder Co, 1942-1944. **Memberships:** Soc Syst Zool; Crustacean Soc. **Research Statement & Publications:** Marine geology; micropaleontology; paleoecology; ecology; ostracodes; coral reefs; ostracoda systematics and ecology. **Mailing Address:** Smithsonian Inst, Washington, DC 20013-7012. **E-Mail:** kornicker.louis@nmnh.si.edu

KORNICKER, WILLIAM ALAN, ROCK-WATER INTERACTIONS, GEOCHEMICAL MODELING. **Personal Data:** b New York, NY, July 24, 1956. **Education:** Old Dominion Univ, BS, 1978, MS, 1980; Tex A&M Univ, PhD (oceanog), 1988. **Professional Experience:** CONSULT, 1993-; res assoc & asst prof, Clemson Univ, 1991-1993; Fel chem & environ eng, McMaster Univ, 1988-1991. **Memberships:** AAAS; Am Chem Soc; Am Geophys Union; Am Soc Limnol & Oceanog; Geochem Soc; Sigma Xi. **Research Statement & Publications:** Thermodynamics and kinetic control of mineral formation, dissolution and solute transport in low temperature environments. **Mailing Address:** 10400 Lake Ridge Dr, Oakton, VA 22124-1511.

KORNMAN, BRENT D, ARTIFICIAL INTELLIGENCE. **Personal Data:** b Dothan, Ala, September 20, 1956; m 1981, c 2. **Education:** Univ Md, BS, 1978. **Professional Experience:** AT, ADVAN SIMULATION CTR, LOCKHEED MARTIN CORP, as of 2001; ADV PROGRAMMER, IBM CORP, 1982-; staff programmer, PAR Technol Corp, 1979-1982. **Memberships:** Am Asn Artificial Intel. **Research Statement & Publications:** Expert system applications; automated plan construction; knowledge representation languages; knowledge base design and development techniques; knowledge base verification. **Mailing Address:** Lockheed Martin Corp, 6801 Rockledge Dr, Bethesda, MD 20817.

KORNREICH, HELEN KASS, PEDIATRICS, RHEUMATOLOGY. **Personal Data:** b Newark, NJ, September 4, 1931; m 1965. **Education:** Rutgers Univ, BS, 1952; Hahnemann Med Col, MD, 1956. **Professional Experience:** ASSOC PROF PEDIAT, SCH MED, UNIV SOUTHERN CALIF, 1970-; From instr to asst prof, Sch Med, Univ Southern Calif, 1963-1970; Arthritis & Rheumatism Found fel pediat rheumatology, Childrens Hosp, Los Angeles, Calif, 1963-1965. **Memberships:** Am Rheumatism Asn; Am Acad Pediat. **Research Statement & Publications:** Connective tissue diseases of childhood; medical education. **Mailing Address:** 4650 Sunset Blvd, Los Angeles, CA 90027-6016.

KORNREICH, LAWRENCE D, INDUSTRIAL HYGIENE. **Professional Experience:** STAFF, ENVIRO-SCI INC, as of 2001. **Memberships:** Am Bd Indust Hygiene. **Mailing Address:** Enviro-Sci Inc, Mt Arlington, NJ 07856. **Fax:** 973-398-8037.

KORNREICH, PHILIPP G, OPTICAL FIBERS, FIBER LIGHT AMPLIFIERS. **Personal Data:** b Vienna, Austria, November 4, 1931; American citizen; m 1960, Sandra V; c Harry, David & Paul. **Education:** Carnegie Inst Tech, BS, 1962; Univ Pa, PhD (elec eng), 1967. **Professional Experience:** CONSULT, ELECTRONIC DEVICE RELIABILITY GROUP, RADC, ROME, NY, 1982-; vis prof, Technon Israel Inst Technol, 1980-1981; PROF ELEC ENG, SYRACUSE UNIV, 1978-; from asst prof to assoc prof, Syracuse Univ, 1967-1978; res assoc solid state physics res, Univ Pa, 1966-1967; sr res engr thin film technol res, Sperry Rand Univac, 1960-1966; res remote optical sensing & light frequency electronic devices optical comput, US Air Force Photoni; consult, Gen Elec Co; consult & co-founder, DEFT Labs. **Memberships:** Am Phys Soc; Inst Elec & Electronics Engrs; Sigma Xi; AAAS; Soc Photo-Optical Instrumentation Engrs; Int Soc Optical Eng. **Research Statement & Publications:** Phonon microwave oscillator; variable delay magnetic strip line; directional dependence of photoconductivity; direct electronic fourier transforms of images; systems with delay and memory; vibrational modes of superlattices; ultra high speed electron devices for both microwave and very high speed integrated circuits applica; three dimensional integrated circuits; light frequency devices for optical computing; the use of Semiconductor Cylinder Fiber Light Amplifiers to make True Image Light Amplifying plates. **Mailing Address:** Dept Elec Eng & Comput Sci, Syracuse Univ, Link Hall, Syracuse, NY 13244. **E-Mail:** pkornrei@syr.edu

KORNSTEIN, EDWARD, ELECTRO-OPTICS, ENGINEERING MANAGEMENT. **Personal Data:** b New York, NY, September 7, 1929; m Marion; c Sandra P & Martin R. **Education:** NY Univ, BA, 1951; Drexel Inst Technol, MS, 1954. **Professional Experience:** Retired, 2003-; CEO & COB, ORS Automation, Inc, 1990-2002; pres, ORS Automation, INC, 1987-1990; vpres & gen mgr, ORS Automation, Inc, 1986-1987; vpres, Object Recognition Systs, Inc, 1977-1986; pres, Kortron Consults, 1972-1980; vpres, Optel Corp, 1970-1972; physicist, Radio Corp Am, 1960-1970; consult optics, 1959-1960; Physicist optics, Radio Corp Am, 1951-1957 & Phys Res Lab, Boston Univ, 1958; Dir, Affiliated Mfrs, Inc 1990-. **Memberships:** Optical Soc Am; Inst Elec & Electronics Engrs; Soc Info Display. **Research Statement & Publications:** Infrared optical and detection systems; physical optics; laser devices and systems; electro-optical displays; electronic digital timepieces; pattern recognition; machine vision systems. **Mailing Address:** 10 Channing Way, Princeton Junction, NJ 08550. **Fax:** 609-799-2451. **E-Mail:** emkor@aol.com

KOROBKIN, IRVING, PHYSICS, SYSTEMS ANALYSIS. **Personal Data:** b New York, NY, October 18, 1925; m 1947, c 4. **Education:** City Col New York, BME, 1945; Columbia Univ, BS, 1948; Univ Md, PhD (physics), 1960. **Honors & Awards:** MeritoriousCivil Serv Award, Naval Ord Lab, 1957. **Professional Experience:** OPERS RES ANALYST MIL OPERS RES, NAVAL SURFACE WEAPON CTR, 1968-; sr systs analyst, IBM Corp, 1961-1968; assoc prof lectr, George Wash Univ, 1957-1966; Consult, Missile & Space Vehicle Dept, Gen Elec Co, 1956-1959; res scientist & adminr fluid dynamics, US Naval Ord Lab, 1951-1961; instr mech eng, Syracuse Univ, 1948-1951; Instr physics, City Col New York, 1947-1948. **Memberships:** Sigma Xi; assoc fel Am Inst Aeronaut & Astronaut; AAAS. **Research Statement & Publications:** High speed fluid dynamics; reentry physics; nuclear weapons effects; military systems analyst with emphasis on strategic warfare. **Mailing Address:** 8510 Hunter Creek Trail, Potomac, MD 20854-2561.

KOROL, BERNARD, PSYCHOPHARMACOLOGY. **Personal Data:** b Chicago, Ill, February 2, 1929; m 1952, c 3. **Education:** Roosevelt Col, BS, 1949; Univ Chicago, MS, 1952; McGill Univ, PhD (pharmacol), 1956. **Professional Experience:** RES ADMIN, ENQUAY PHARMACEUT ASSOCS, 1987-; assoc prof psychiat, Sch Med, St Louis Univ & supvr psychopharmacol, St Louis Vet Admin Hosp, 1969-1987; asst prof physiol & pharmacol & chief pharmacol sect, Sch Med, Univ Mo, St Louis, 1964-1969; group leader pharmacol, Geigy Res Labs, 1961-1964; Res pharmacologist, Smith Kline & French Labs, 1956-1958 & Chas Pfizer & Co, Inc, 1958-1961. **Research Statement & Publications:** Physiology and pharmacology of mental illness. **Mailing Address:** Enquay, 2840 NW Second Ave, Boca Raton, FL 33431.

KOROLENKO, KYRILL V, UNDERWATER OBJECT DETECTION TECHNOLOGY. **Personal Data:** b Kharkov, Russia, May 12, 1932; American citizen; m 1958, Svetlana; c George & Alexandra. **Education:** Syracuse Univ, BEE, 1959; State Univ NY, Buffalo, MS, 1967. **Honors & Awards:** David Bushnell Award, Am Defense Preparedness Asn, 1991. **Professional Experience:** ASSOC DIR SENSOR TECHNOL, OFF NAVAL RES, as of 2002; vis lectr, Surface Officer Sch Command, 1987-1994; vis lectr, US Anti Submarine Training Ctr, 1986-1991; vis lectr, US Naval War Col, 1985-1990; chief scientist, Sharem Prog, 1974-1986; PRIN ENGR, CONSULT & CHIEF SCIENTIST, NAVAL UNDERSEA WARFARE CTR, 1972-; consult, US Naval Activ Fleet Command, Prog Off, Pentagon, 1972-; sr engr, Submarine Signal Div, Raytheon Co, 1967-1972; feelance translr, Inst Elec & Electronics Engrs, 1965-1966; engr, Heavy Mil Div, Gen Elec Co, 1959-1965 & 1966-1967. **Memberships:** Sr mem Inst Elec & Electronics Engrs; Am Defense Preparedness Asn. **Research Statement & Publications:** Using state of the art technology and hardware to solve underwater detection problems; anti-submarine sonar systems; granted 2 patents covering critical technology of sonar systems. **Mailing Address:** Code 309, Naval Undersea Warfare Ctr, Newport, RI 02841-1708. **Fax:** 401-841-7478. **E-Mail:** korolenko@1.vsdec.npt.nuwc.navy.mil

KOROLY, MARY JO, CELL BIOLOGY. **Personal Data:** b Philadelphia, Pa, January 28, 1943; c 1. **Education:** Bryn Mawr Col, PhD (biochem), 1969. **Professional Experience:** ASSOC SCIENTIST, DEPT BIOCHEM & MOLECULAR BIOL, COL MED, UNIV FLA, as of 2004; ASST PROF CELL BIOL, UNIV FLA, 1979-; asst prof cell biol, Harvard Univ, 1977-1979; asst prof cell biol, Bryn Mawr Col, 1972-1977. **Memberships:** AAAS; Am Soc Cell Biol; Am Women Sci; Am Soc Protozool; Am Soc Biol Chemists; Sigma Xi. **Mailing Address:** Dept Biochem & Molecular Biol Univ Fla, PO Box 100245, Gainesville, FL 32611-7035. **Fax:** 352-392-2344. **E-Mail:** korolymj@ufl.edu

KOROPCHAK, JOHN, ATOMIC MOLECULAR & MASS SPECTROMETRY, CHROMATOGRAPHY. **Education:** Lafayette Col, BA, 1976; Univ Ga, PhD (chem), 1980. **Professional Experience:** VICE CHANCELLOR RES & GRAD DEAN, SOUTHERN ILL UNIV, 1999-; chmn dept chem & biochem, 1995-1998, SIVC prog chmn, fedn anal chem & Spectros Socs, 1994; PROF CHEM, SOUTHERN ILL UNIV, 1993-; from asst prof to assoc prof, Southern Ill Univ, 1984-1993; res chem, US Army Chem Res & Develop Ctr, 1980-1984. **Memberships:** Am Chem Soc; Soc Appl Spectros; Am Soc Mass Spectrometry; Fedn Chem Spectros Soc. **Research Statement & Publications:** Development of methods of chemical analysis capable of detecting smaller quantities of various chemical species; methods for trace element analysis, for example, heavy metals such as lead; techniques intended to be able to selectively detect single molecules. **Mailing Address:** Dept Chem & Biochem, Southern Ill Univ, Neckers 285, Carbondale, IL 62901-4409. **Fax:** 618-453-6408. **E-Mail:** koropchak@chem.siu.edu

KOROS, AURELIA M CARISSIMO, immunology, cell biology; deceased, see previous edition for last biography

KOROS, PETER J, METALLURGY, MATERIALS SCIENCE. **Personal Data:** b Berlin, Ger, July 14, 1932; American citizen; m 1957, Aurelia Carissimo; c 5. **Education:** Drexel Univ, BS, 1954; Mass Inst Technol, SM, 1955 & ScD, 1958. **Honors & Awards:** Toy Award, 1962 & McKune & Herty Mem Awards, 1963, Am Inst Mining, Metall & Petrol Engrs; Jalmet Award, Jones & Laughlin Steel Corp, 1963; Silver Medal, Am Iron & Steel Inst, 1969, Gold Medal, 1977; Design & Appln Award, Int Magnesium Asn, 1978. **Professional Experience:** Chmn, Task Force on Degalvanizing Scrap, 1989-1991 & adv panel, Argonne Lab Prog for Electrochem Dezinc Scrap, 1991-1996; chmn prog comt, 5th Int Iron & Steel Cong, Iron & Steel Soc, 1986; adv bd, NSF Ctr Iron & Steel Res, Carnegie-Mellon Univ, 1985-; mem, Steel Initative Task Force, Am Iron & Steel Inst, 1985-1995; SR RES CONSULT, LTV STEEL CORP, 1984-; mem, US Bur Mines, Generic Technol Res Ctr Pyrometall, 1982- & Chmn, 1984-1985; sr res assoc, Qual Control Div, 1982-1984; mgr process develop & qual control, Qual Control Div, 1980-1982; dir res spec projs, Qual Control Div, 1978-1980; dir process metall res, Qual Control Div, 1975-1978; bd dirs, Iron & Steel Div, Am Inst Mining, Metall & Petrol Engrs, 1974; Chmn, Iron & Steel Div, Am Inst Mining, Metall & Petrol Engrs, 1969-1970; chief process metallurgist, Qual Control Div, 1965-1975; res supvr steelmaking, Jones & Laughlin Steel Corp, 1963-1965; Res engr & sr res engr, Jones & Laughlin Steel Corp, 1958-1963. **Memberships:** Am Iron & Steel Inst; fel Iron & Steel Soc Am Inst Mining Metall & Petrol Engrs; fel Am Soc Metals Int. **Research Statement & Publications:** Process and quality control in steel production; physical chemistry of iron and steelmaking; applied research in steelmaking, steel waste recycling, direct iron/steelmaking. **Mailing Address:** 154 Maple Heights Rd, Pittsburgh, PA 15232. **Fax:** 216-642-7080.

KOROS, WILLIAM JOHN, POLYMER & MEMBRANE SCIENCE, ENGINEERING. **Personal Data:** b Omaha, Nebr, August 31, 1947; m 1970, Ann. **Education:** Univ Tex, Austin, BS, 1969, MS, 1975, PhD (chem eng), 1977. **Honors & Awards:** Fel, Am inst of chem Engrs; Nat Acad Eng, 2000; AiChE Inst Award, 1995; NSF pres Young Invest Award, 1984. **Professional Experience:** ROBERTO C GOIZUETA CHAIR IN CHEM ENG, GEORGIA INST OF TECHNOL, 2001-; chmn, dept chem eng, Univ Tex, Austin, 1993-1997; B F Goodrich prof in mat eng, Univ Tex, Austin, 1991-2001; Paul D and Betty Robertson Meek and Am Petrofina found prof, Univ Tex Austin, 1986-1990; PROF CHEM ENG, UNIV TEX, AUSTIN, 1984-; asst prof chem eng, NC State Univ, Raleigh, 1977-1980; chem engr Polymer processing develop group, E I Du Pont Co, Camden, SC, 1971-1973; chem engr Polymer processing group E I Du Pont Co, Wilmington, Del, 1969-1971. **Memberships:** Am Inst Chem Eng; Sigma Xi; Am Chem Soc. **Research Statement & Publications:** Sorption and transport of low molecular weight compounds such as gases, solvents, monomers and additives in the polymeric solid state; development of advanced membrane materials and structures; diffusion in polymers. **Mailing Address:** Sch Chem & Biomolecular Engineeriing, Ga Inst Technol, Atlanta, GA 30332. **E-Mail:** wjk@che.gatech.edu

KOROSTOFF, EDWARD, dental materials; deceased, see previous edition for last biography

KOROTEV, RANDALL LEE, LUNAR GEOCHEMISTRY. **Personal Data:** b Green Bay, Wis, May 15, 1949; m 1974. **Education:** Univ Wis-Madison, BS, 1971, PhD (chem), 1976. **Professional Experience:** RES ASSOC PROF GEOCHEM, WASH UNIV, 1991-; sr res scientist, Wash Univ, 1979-1991; Proj assoc soil sci, Univ Wis-Madison, 1976-1979. **Memberships:** Geochem Soc; Am Geophys Union; Sigma Xi; Meteoritical Soc. **Research Statement & Publications:** Geochemistry of lunar soils and rocks; chemical analysis by neutron activation. **Mailing Address:** Dept Earth & Planetary Sci, Campus Box 1169 Wash Univ, St Louis, MO 63130. **Fax:** 314-935-7361. **E-Mail:** rlk@levee.wustl.edu

KORPEL, ADRIANUS, OPTICS, ACOUSTICS. **Personal Data:** b Rotterdam, Neth, February 18, 1932; m 1956, c 1. **Education:** Delft Technol Univ, MSEE, 1956, PhD, 1969. **Honors & Awards:** Alexander von Humboldt Award, 1984. **Professional Experience:** PROF EMER ELEC ENG, UNIV IOWA, as of 2003; prof elec eng, Univ Iowa, 1977-2002; dir res eng physics, Zenith Radio Corp, 1973-1977; div chief laser appln, Zenith Radio Corp, 1960-1973; res engr commun, Postmaster Gen Dept, Melbourne, Australia, 1956-1960. **Memberships:** Acoust Soc Am; fel Inst Elec & Electronics Engrs; fel Optical Soc Am; Soc Photog Instrumentation Eng; foreign assoc mem Royal Acad Belg. **Research Statement & Publications:** Information and communication theory; microwaves; laser optics; acoustic holography and microscopy; acousto-optics; nonlinear waves; optical metrology and microscopy. **Mailing Address:** 1704 Glendale Rd, Iowa City, IA 52245. **E-Mail:** adriankorpel@uiowa.edu

KORPELA, SEPPO A, HEAT TRANSFER. **Education:** Univ Mich, Phd (mech eng), 1972. **Professional Experience:** PROF, MECH ENG, OHIO STATE UNIV, as of 2005. **Mailing Address:** Ohio State Univ, 650 Ackerman Rd, Columbus, OH 43210. **Fax:** 614-299-4222. **E-Mail:** korpela.1@osu.edu

KORPER, SAMUEL, AGING RESEARCH. **Professional Experience:** ACTING ASSOC DIR EPIDEMIOL, DEMOG, & BIOMET PROG, NIH, as of 2001; assoc dir, Planning Analysis & Int Activ, Nat Inst Aging, NIH, beginning 1987. **Mailing Address:** Nat Inst Aging, NIH, Rm 5C27 Bldg 31 31 Ctr Dr, Bethesda, MD 20892.

KORPMAN, RALPH ANDREW, HEMATALOGY, MEDICAL INFORMATION SCIENCE. **Personal Data:** b New York, NY, August 9, 1952. **Education:** Loma Linda Univ, BA, 1971, MD, 1974; Claremont Grad Sch, CEM, 1978. **Honors & Awards:** Sheard-Sanford Award, Am Soc Clin Pathologists, 1976. **Professional Experience:** PRES & CEO, HEALTH TRIO INC, as of 2004; PROF PATH & LAB MED, LOMA LINDA UNIV, 1987-; pres & chmn, Health Data Sci, 1983-; from asst prof to assoc prof hemat & path, Med Ctr, Loma Linda Univ, 1983-1987; sci adv, HBO & Co, 1981-1983; DIR LABS, LOMA LINDA UNIV, 1979-; mem, comput adv comt, finance comt & chmn, govt rels, Am Soc Clin Path, 1978-; consult, Technician Instruments Corp, 1978-1981; fel hemat, Med Ctr, Loma Linda Univ, 1978-1979; dir, Med Data Corp, 1976-1981; resident path, Med Ctr, Loma Linda Univ, 1975-1978; intern, Med Ctr, Loma Linda Univ, 1974-1975. **Memberships:** fel Col Am Pathologists; fel Am Soc Clin Path; NY Acad Sci; fel Am Col Physician Execs.

Research Statement & Publications: Characterization of cellular membranes, especially red blood cells, laboratory quality control, applications of computers to medical care and instrument design and evaluation. **Mailing Address:** HealthTrio, Inc, 102 Woodmont Blvd Ste 200, Nashville, TN 37205. **Fax:** 615-298-2591. **E-Mail:** ralph.korpman@healthtrio.com

KORR, IRVIN MORRIS, physiology, neurosciences; deceased, see previous edition for last biography

KORRINGA, JAN, THEORETICAL PHYSICS, GEOPHYSICS. **Personal Data:** b Heemstede, Neth, March 31, 1915; m 1943, Johanna; c Maarten, Wouter & Derk-Jan. **Education:** Delft Univ Technol, DSc, 1942. **Honorary Degrees:** DSc, Univ Besancon, France, 1963. **Professional Experience:** RETIRED; sr res assoc, Chevron Oil Field Res Co, 1980-1986; vis prof, Univ Besancon, 1963; Univ Paris, 1968; Guggenheim fel, 1963; consult, Chevron Oil Field Res Co, 1955-1980; Union Carbide Nuclear Co, 1957-1980; from assoc prof to prof physics, Ohio State Univ, 1953-1980; from lectr to sr lectr, Univ Leiden, 1946-1953; from asst to instr physics, Delft Univ Technol, 1941-1946. **Memberships:** Fel Am Phys Soc; Neth Phys Soc. **Research Statement & Publications:** Statistical physics; metals physics; theory of solids; theory of heterogeneous materials. **Mailing Address:** 620 Mystic Way, Laguna Beach, CA 92651.

KORSCH, BARBARA M, PEDIATRICS. **Personal Data:** b Jena, Germany, March 30, American citizen; wid, c Robert Ward. **Education:** Smith Col, BA, 1941; Johns Hopkins Univ, MD, 1944; Am Bd Pediat, cert, 1950. **Honors & Awards:** George Armstrong Lectr, Ambulatory Pediat Asn, 1973; Katherine D McCormick Distinguished Lectr, Standford Univ, 1977; Kathy Newman Mem Lectr, Tulane Univ, 1987; C Anderson Aldrich Award, Am Acad Pediat, 1988. **Professional Experience:** Chair, Coun Am Pediat Soc, 1989; staff, Div Gen Pediat, Children's Hosp Los Angeles, 1981-1991; hon staff mem, Dept Pediat, Cedars-Sinai Med Ctr, 1976-; consult, Introd Clin Med & Res & Training Rehab, Sch Med, Univ Southern Calif, 1974-; vis prof numerous US & foreign univs, 1973-1989; PROF PEDIAT, SCH MED, UNIV SOUTHERN CALIF, LOS ANGELES, 1969-; dir, Introd Clin Med & Res & Training Rehab, Sch Med, Univ Southern Calif, 1969-1974; Med Ctr, Univ Southern Calif, 1969-1974; assoc prof, Sch Med, Univ Southern Calif, Los Angeles, 1964-1969; assoc attend pediatrician, Cedars Lebanon Hosp, 1961-; Gen Pediat, Children's Hosp Los Angeles, 1961-1965; pediat dir, Observ Clin Children Los Angeles, 1961-1964; assoc clin prof prev med, Sch Med, Univ Calif, Los Angeles, 1961-1964; pediat consult, Hosp Spec Surg, 1955-1961; assoc attend pediatrician, Pediat Outpatient Dept, 1955-1961; coordr, Pediat Rehab Prog, Nat Found Infantile Paralysis, 1953-1961; from instr to assoc prof, Med Col, Cornell Univ, 1950-1961; clin dir, Pediat Outpatient Dept, 1950-1961; asst attend pediatrician, NY Hosp, 1950-1955; pediat consult, Dept Health, NY, 1949-1951; asst pediat, Med Col, Cornell Univ, 1949-1950; Asst outpatient pediatrician, NY Hosp, 1949-1950; fel, Inst Child Develop, NY Hosp, 1948-1949; Asst resident, NY Hosp, 1947; Asst resident, Mary Imogene Basset Hosp, 1946; Asst resident, Bellevue Hosp, 1945. **Memberships:** Inst Med-Nat Acad Sci; Am Acad Pediat; Sigma Xi; Am Pediat Soc; Soc Behav Pediat (pres 1985); Soc Pediat Res. **Research Statement & Publications:** Doctor-patient communication; health care delivery; psychosocial aspects of pediatrics including growth and development; medical education; comprehensive care of patients with chronic illness; high risk infants, transition from hospital to home; author of numerous technical publications. **Mailing Address:** Div Gen Pediat Childrens Hosp, 4650 Sunset Blvd MS 76, Los Angeles, CA 90027. **E-Mail:** bkorsch@chla.usc.edu

KORSCH, DIETRICH G, ASTRONOMY. **Personal Data:** b Waren-Mueritz, Ger, November 30, 1937; American citizen; m 1966, c 2. **Education:** Univ Tubingen, Germany, BS, 1963, MS, 1965, PhD, 1969. **Professional Experience:** OPTICAL SCI CONSULT, KORSCH OPTICS INC, 1981-; vpres sci, TAI Corp, 1977-1981; eng consult, Sperry Rand Support Serv, 1973-1976; staff engr optics, Bendix Aerospace Systs, 1970-1973; res asst appl optics, Univ Tubingen, 1968-1970; from asst to pres, Univ Tubingen, 1966-1968. **Memberships:** Optical Soc Am; Soc Optical Eng. **Research Statement & Publications:** Design and analysis of optical systems, primarily in the area of large space optics; development of design and optimization methods for all-reflective imaging systems from near-normal to grazing incidence. **Mailing Address:** Korsch Optics, Huntsville, AL 35803.

KORSH, JAMES F, COMPUTER SCIENCE, OPERATIONS RESEARCH. **Personal Data:** b Philadelphia, Pa, June 16, 1938; m, c 3. **Education:** Univ Pa, BS, 1960, PhD (comput sci), 1966; Univ Ill, MS, 1962. **Professional Experience:** PROF COMPUT SCI, TEMPLE UNIV, 1977-; chmn, Temple Univ, 1975-1978 & beginning 1989; chmn, cis Dept, Temple Univ, 1975-1978; assoc prof, Temple Univ, 1972-1976; sr res fel, Calif Inst Technol, 1971-1972; asst prof comput sci, Univ Pa, 1966-1971. **Research Statement & Publications:** Quantitative methods in computer systems; analysis of algorithms; data structures; loopless algorithms. **Mailing Address:** Dept Comput & Info Sci, Temple Univ, Rm 300A, Wachman Hall, Philadelphia, PA 19122. **Fax:** 215-204-5082. **E-Mail:** korsh@temple.edu

KORSLUND, MARY KATHERINE, THERAPEUTIC NUTRITION. **Education:** Univ Nebr, Lincoln, PhD (nutrit), 1972. **Professional Experience:** ASSOC PROF EMER HUMAN NUTRIT & FOOD, VA POLYTECH INST & STATE UNIV, 1995-. **Mailing Address:** NVa Grad Ctr Va Tech, 1013 Mourning Dove Dr, Blacksburg, VA 24060.

KORSMEYER, STANLEY JOEL, internal medicine, immunology; deceased, see previous edition for last biography

KORSON, ROY, PATHOLOGY. **Personal Data:** b Philadelphia, Pa, October 24, 1922; m 1946, Lorraine. **Education:** Univ Pa, AB, 1943; Jefferson Med Col, MD, 1947; Am Bd Path, dipl, 1956. **Professional Experience:** PROF EMER, UNIV VT, as of 2006; actg chmn dept, Col Med, Univ Vt, 1974; prof, Col Med, Univ Vt, 1967-1992; sr res fel, USPHS, 1958-1963; assoc prof, Col Med, Univ Vt, 1957-1967; asst prof path, Col Med, Univ Vt, 1951-1952, 1954-1957; resident, Mary Fletcher Hosp, Burlington, Vt, 1951-1952; asst, Col Med, Univ Vt, 1950-1951; res fel, Col Med, Univ Vt, 1949-1950; res fel, Columbia Univ, 1948-1949. **Memberships:** AAAS; Am Asn Pathologists; Col Am Pathologists; Int Acad Path; Sigma Xi; Am Soc Cytol. **Research Statement & Publications:** Cytology; histopathology; histochemistry. **Mailing Address:** Col Med, Univ Vt, Med Alumni Bldg, Burlington, VT 05405-0068. **E-Mail:** roy.korson@uvm.edu

KORSRUD, GARY OLAF, ANTIBIOTIC RESIDUE ANALYSIS. **Personal Data:** b Peterborough, Ont, March 23, 1942; m 1965, c 3. **Education:** Univ Sask, BSA, 1964, MSc, 1966; Univ Calif, Davis, PhD (nutrit), 1970. **Professional Experience:** RES SCIENTIST, AGR CAN, 1977-; res scientist, Health & Welfare Can, 1970-1977; res asst, Univ Calif, Davis, 1967-1970; teaching asst animal sci, Univ Calif, Davis, 1966-1967; Res asst, Univ Sask, 1964-1966. **Memberships:** Agr Inst Can; Can Soc Animal Sci; Can Soc Nutrit Sci; Soc Toxicol Can; Am Col Vet Toxicologists. **Research Statement & Publications:** Antibiotic residue analysis research; nutritional and biochemical aspects of veterinary toxicology; human carbohydrate nutrition research and advising; lipid nutrition; detection and assessment of chemically induced liver damage. **Mailing Address:** Health Animals Lab, Agr Can 116 Vet Rd, Saskatoon, SK S7N 2R3, Can. **Fax:** 306-975-5711. **E-Mail:** gkorsrud@inspection.gc.ca

KORST, HELMUT HANS, GAS DYNAMICS, PROPULSION. **Personal Data:** b Vienna, Austria, January 4, American citizen; m, c 4. **Education:** Vienna Tech Univ, Dipl Ing, 1941, Dr tech Sc, 1947. **Honors & Awards:** Honorary Member, American Society of Mechanical Engineers-International 2001 Golden Doctor Diplome, Technical University Vienns, 1997 Daniel Guggenheim Medal, ASME, AIAA, SAE 1994, Centennial Medallion, American Society of Engineering Education, 1993 Fellow American Society of Aeronautical and Astronautics, 1973 Fellow Americal Society of Mechanical Engineers, 1972 NSF Senior Postdoctoral Fellow 1957. **Professional Experience:** PROF EMER MECH & INDUST ENG, UNIV ILL, URBANA, 1984-; Ebaugh chair prof mech eng, Univ Fla, 1984; res chair naval air power, Navy Postgrad Sch, Monterey, Calif, 1979; consult, Adv Group Aeronaut Res & Develop, NATO, 1964 & US Army Missile Command, 1971-; head dept mech &indust eng, Univ Ill, Urbana, 1962-1974; propulsion specialist, Rocketdyne Div, NAm Aviation, 1960 & 1965-1968; consult, Gen Elec Co, 1959; sr fel, NSF, 1957; Va Polytech Inst, 1954 & Vienna Tech Univ, 1957; owner, H H Korst engrs consult, Urbana, Ill, 1956-; design specialist, Gen Dynamics Convair, Ft Worth, 1955; vis prof, Kans State Univ, 1950; from assoc prof to prof mech eng, Univ Ill, Urbana, 1949-1984; vis lectr gas dynamics, Univ Ill, Urbana, 1948-1949; asst prof mech eng, Vienna Tech Univ, 1945-1948; res engr, Maschinenfabrik Augsburg-Nurnberg AG, Ger, 1941-1945. **Memberships:** Fel Am Soc Mech Engrs; fel Am Inst Aeronaut & Astronaut; Am Soc Eng Educ; Sigma Xi. **Research Statement & Publications:** Internal and external aerodynamics; jet and rocket propulsion; heat transfer. **Mailing Address:** Dept Mech & Indust Eng, 140 Mech Eng Bldg, 1206 W Green St, Urbana, IL 61801. **Fax:** 217-333-1942. **E-Mail:** h-korst@uiuc.edu

KORST, JAMES JOSEPH, ORGANIC CHEMISTRY. **Personal Data:** b Joliet, Ill, November 24, 1931; m 1960, c 3. **Education:** Univ Ill, BS, 1953; Dartmouth Col, MA, 1955; Univ Wis, PhD (org chem), 1959. **Professional Experience:** OPERS MGR, QUALITY CONTROL, PFIZER INC, 1973-; mgr qual control, Chas Pfizer & Co, Inc, 1971-1973; supvr, Chas Pfizer & Co, Inc, 1970-1971; Chemist, Chas Pfizer & Co, Inc, 1959-1970. **Memberships:** Am Chem Soc. **Research Statement & Publications:** Structures of steroid intermediates; tetracycline chemistry; quality control aspects of organic chemicals and pharmaceuticals; quality control management. **Mailing Address:** 13 Meetinghouse Lane, Old Lyme, CT 06371.

KORST, WILLIAM LAWRENCE, INORGANIC CHEMISTRY, PHYSICAL CHEMISTRY. **Personal Data:** b Joliet, Ill, March 23, 1922; m 1954, Mary Coutts; c David W, Lisa M, Timothy J & Pamela T. **Education:** Univ Chicago, PhB, 1946, SB, 1947, SM, 1949; Univ Southern Calif, PhD, 1956; Calif state univ, Northridge, M A, 1998. **Professional Experience:** RETIRED; vis prof, Tech Univ Vienna, 1978; from instr to prof chem, W Los Angeles Col, 1970-1993; instr chem, Los Angeles City Col, 1969-1970; res specialist, Atomics Int Div, NAm Aviation, Inc, 1959-1967; sr res chemist, Atomics Int Div, NAm Aviation, Inc, 1958-1959; asst prof chem, Polytech Inst Brooklyn, 1957-1958; Asst res chemist, Univ Calif, 1956-1957; Fulbright scholar, Univ Amsterdam, 1954-1955; Fel US AEC, Univ Southern Calif, 1952-1953. **Memberships:** Am Chem Soc. **Research Statement & Publications:** X-ray diffraction and crystal structures; solid-state chemistry; heavy metal hydrides; high-vacuum and high-temperature techniques; atmospheric chemistry. **Mailing Address:** 7106 Quartz Ave, Canoga Park, CA 91306-3636.

KORSTAD, JOHN EDWARD, II, LIMNOLOGY, AQUACULTURE. **Personal Data:** b Woodland, Calif, July 4, 1949; m 1972, Sally; c 4. **Education:** Calif Lutheran Col, BA & BS, 1972; Calif State Univ, Hayward, MS, 1980; Univ Mich, Ann Arbor, MS, 1979, PhD (zoology), 1980. **Honors & Awards:** Post-doctoral Fellowship to Norway, 1987-1988; Fulbright Scholar to Norway, 1993-1994; Carnegie Fnd Prof of the Year for Okla, 1996. **Professional Experience:** Fulbright Scholar, Norway, 1993-1994; vis scientist, SINTEF Ctr Aquacult, Trondheim, Norway, 1987-1988 & 1993-1994; vis scientist, Sintef Ctr for Aquacult, Trondheim, Norway, 1987-1988; adj instr, Tulsa Community Col, 1985-1999; col acad dir, Okla Acad Sci, 1983-1986; PROF BIOL, ORAL ROBERTS UNIV 1980-; asst limnologist, Great Lakes Res Div, Univ Mich, Ann Arbor, 1975 & res asst, 1975 & 1980; Calif State Univ, Hayward, 1972-1974 & Univ Mich, Ann Arbor, 1975-1979; asst consult, Univ Calif, Davis, 1974; res asst, Calif State Univ, Hayward, 1973; asst geologist, Cities Serv Oil Co, Alaska, 1971; Teaching asst, Calif Lutheran Col, 1970-1971. **Memberships:** Great Plains Limnologist; Am Asn Zool Parks & Aquariums; Okla Acad of Science (College Acad Dir); Beta Beta Beta Biolog. Soc; Gamma Beta Phi; Nat Collegiate Hon Council; Great Plains Hon Council. **Research Statement & Publications:** Lake management; invasive species in lakes; phytoplankton-zooplankton-fish interactions; nutrient regeneration; Aquaculture; Feeding and life history of Brachionus plicatilis. **Mailing Address:** Dept Biol, Oral Roberts Univ, Tulsa, OK 74171. **Fax:** 918-495-6297. **E-Mail:** jkorstad@oru.edu

KORT, MARGARET ALEXANDER, HISTOLOGY, CELL BIOLOGY. **Personal Data:** b Jerusalem, Jordan, January 16, 1928; American citizen. **Education:** Georgetown Col, BS, 1958; Univ Louisville, MS, 1960; Univ Northern Colo, EdD, 1968. **Professional Experience:** PROF EMER BIOL, SOUTHWEST BAPTIST COL, AS OF 2005; prof biol, Southwest Baptist Col, 1967-1990; instr biol, Coe Col, 1961-1963. **Memberships:** AAAS; Nat Sci Teachers Asn. **Research Statement & Publications:** Acid phosphatase patterns in the involuting rat uterus. **Mailing Address:** 1623 Northwood St, Bolivar, MO 65613.

KORTANEK, KENNETH O, FINANCIAL ENGINEERING, OPERATIONS RESEARCH, SYSTEMS ANALYSIS. **Personal Data:** b Chicago, Ill, November 13, 1936; m Irene; c 1. **Education:** Northwestern Univ, BSBA, 1958, MA, 1959, PhD (engr sci), 1964. **Professional Experience:** PROF EMER, UNIV IOWA, 2002-; Murray res prof, Univ Iowa, 1986-2002; pres, Kwel Corp, 1981; mem, Int Symp Semi-Infinite Prog & Applns, 1981; Vis prof, Col Engr, Va Polytech Inst & State Univ, 1979 & Univ NC, 1981; prof math sci, Carnegie-mellon Univ, 1969-1986; assoc prof opers res, Cornell Univ, 1966-1969; Asst prof appl math & indust adminr, Univ Chicago, 1965-1966. **Memberships:** sr mem Soc Indust & Appl Math. **Research Statement & Publications:** Linear programming; duality theory in mathematical programming; applications to engineering plasticity design; equilibrium theory in economic systems; theory and applications of semi-infinite programming and design of telecommunications networks; The Wiley finance-London book, "Building & using dynamic interst rate models, Nov 01 defines a new financial engr focus after 40 years of engr res resulting in 130 publication. **Mailing Address:** Gateway Towers 21C, Pittsburgh, PA 15222. **E-Mail:** ken_kortanek@uiowa.edu

KORTE, CLARE A, CELL DIVISION INHIBITORS, CELL MUTATIONS. **Personal Data:** b Pocahontas, Ill, January 31, 1934. **Education:** Alverno Col, BA, 1950; St Marys Col, Minn, MS, 1967; Univ NDak, Grand Forks, DA, 1980. **Professional Experience:** CHAIR BIOL, ST MARYS UNIV MINN, 1984-; PROF BIOL, ST MARYS UNIV MINN, 1975-; teacher biol, Boylan High Sch, 1965-1975; teacher biol, Madonna High Sch, 1960-1965. **Memberships:** Nat Asn Biol Teachers. **Research Statement & Publications:** Investigations on viruses, tradescantia and chironomid larvae to determine mitotic errors after exposure to electromagnetic fields. **Mailing Address:** St Marys Univ Minn, 700 Terrace Heights, Winona, MN 55987-1321. **Fax:** 507-457-1633. **E-Mail:** ckorte@smumn.edu

KORTE, WILLIAM DAVID, ORGANIC CHEMISTRY, ORGANIC ANALYSIS. **Personal Data:** b Chicago, Ill, October 11, 1937; m 1964, Margaret; c Jennifer, Christopher & Alison. **Education:** Northwestern Univ, BA, 1960; Univ Mich, MS, 1962; Univ Calif, Davis, PhD (chem), 1966. **Professional Experience:** PROF EMER, CALIF STATE UNIV, CHICO, AS OF 2005; US Army res assoc, IPA, 1987-1989; NSF grant, 1983, 1987; chmn dept, Calif State Univ, Chico, 1977-1980; prof chem, Calif State Univ, Chico, beginning 1975; Am Chem Soc-Petrol Res Fund res grants, 1970-1972; from asst prof to assoc prof, Calif State Univ, Chico, 1966-1975. **Memberships:** AAAS; Am Chem Soc; Sigma Xi. **Research Statement & Publications:** Stereochemistry; organometallic reaction mechanisms; organic analysis. **Mailing Address:** Dept Chem, Calif State Univ, Chico, CA 95929-0210. **E-Mail:** wkorte@csuchico.edu

KORTELING, RALPH GARRET, NUCLEAR CHEMISTRY. **Personal Data:** b Madanapalle, India, January 2, 1937; American citizen; m 1961, c 2. **Education:** Hope Col, BA, 1958; Univ Calif, Berkeley, PhD (chem), 1963. **Professional Experience:** PROF EMER CHEM, SIMON FRASER UNIV, as of 2006; prof chem & chmn, Simon Fraser Univ, beginning 1981; from asst prof to assoc prof, Simon Fraser Univ, 1965-1981; asst prof, Carnegie Inst Technol, 1963-1965; fel chem, Carnegie Inst Technol, 1962-1963. **Memberships:** Am Phys Soc. **Research Statement & Publications:** High energy nuclear reactions. **Mailing Address:** Dept Chem, Simon Fraser Univ, Burnaby, BC V5A 1S6, Can. **E-Mail:** kortelin@sfu.ca

KORTH, GARY E, METALLURGY, MATERIALS SCIENCE. **Personal Data:** b Tremonton, Utah, February 27, 1938; m 1961, c 5. **Education:** Univ Utah, BS, 1963, PhD (metall), 1968. **Professional Experience:** MAT RES SCIENTIST, IDAHO NAT ENG LAB, 1968-; Test lab engr, Gen Dynamics-Convair, 1963-1964. **Memberships:** Am Soc Mat Int. **Research Statement & Publications:** Elevated temperature fatigue and creep fatigue; mechanical properties; neutron irradiation effects of metals; rapidly solidified metals technology; dynamic consolidation of rapidly solidified metal powders using explosives. **Mailing Address:** 5 S 645 W, Blackfoot, ID 83221.

KORTH, MICHAEL STEVEN, SUPERFLUID HELIUM, MANY-BODY QUANTUM MECHANICS. **Personal Data:** b Breckenridge, Minn, March 18, 1956; m 1982, Sandra Golembeck; c Andrew M, Rebecca A & Laura J. **Education:** Univ Minn, BA, 1978; Univ Md, MS, 1981, PhD (physics), 1984. **Professional Experience:** CHAIR, DIV SCI & MATH, 1991-; ASSOC PROF PHYSICS, UNIV MINN, MORRIS, 1990-; asst prof, Univ Minn, Morris, 1984-1990. **Memberships:** Am Phys Soc; Am Asn Physics Teachers. **Research Statement & Publications:** Superfluid helium dynamics via an approach which builds on the idea of correlated basis functions. **Mailing Address:** Div Sci & Math, Univ Minn, Morris, MN 56267. **E-Mail:** korthms@mrs.umn.edu

KORTHUIS, RONALD JOHN, ISCHEMIA & REPERFUSION, MICROVASCULAR DYSFUNCTION. **Personal Data:** b Grand Rapids, Mich, February 7, 1955; m 1998, Shari; c 6. **Education:** Mich State Univ, PhD (physiol), 1983. **Honors & Awards:** Travel Award, World Cong Microcirculation, 84 Europ Microcirculatory Soc, 1989; Established Investigatorship, Am Heart Asn. **Professional Experience:** PROF & CHMN; DEPT MED PHYSIOL PHARMACOL, UNIV MO, 2004-; asst dean grad studies, Med Ctr, La State Univ, 1992-1996; estab investr, Nat Heart Asn, 1988-1993; from asst prof to assoc prof, Dept Physiol, 1987-1994; Prin investr, NIH, 1985-; asst prof, Univ Mo, 1985-1987; instr, Univ SAla, 1984-1985; Fel, Univ SAla, 1983-1984. **Memberships:** Am Physiol Soc Prog Comt; Microcirculatory Soc Exec Council; Am Gastroenterol Soc; Am Soc Pharmacol & Therapeutics; fel Am Heart Asn; Am Physiol Soc Prog Comt. **Research Statement & Publications:** We are investigating the mechanisms whereby preconditioning tissues with mildly noxious stimuli induces the development of an anti-inflammatory phenotype in endothelial cells subsequently exposed to ischemia and reperfusion. **Mailing Address:** Dept Med Pharmacol & Physiol, Univ Mo, 1 Hosp Dr, Columbia, MO 65212-0001. **Fax:** 573-884-4278. **E-Mail:** korthuisr@health.missouri.edu

KORTRIGHT, JAMES MCDOUGALL, MEDICAL PHYSICS, RADIOLOGICAL PHYSICS. **Personal Data:** b Huntington, NY, April 3, 1927; m 1952, c 2. **Education:** Cornell Univ, AB, 1949; Purdue Univ, MS, 1953, PhD (physics), 1963. **Professional Experience:** RETIRED; med physicist, Radiation Calibration Co, beginning 1974; physicist, St Francis Hosp, Lynwood, Calif, 1973-1974; physicist, Radiol Sci Dept, Calif Col Med, Univ Calif, Irvine, 1972-1973; assoc prof physics, Rose-Hulman Inst Technol, 1966-1972; from instr to asst prof, Temple Univ, 1962-1966. **Memberships:** Am Asn Physicists Med. **Research Statement & Publications:** X-ray diffraction; radiation damage; semiconductor properties; gamma ray scattering; radiological and health physics. **Mailing Address:** 436 E Hoover Ave, Orange, CA 92667. **E-Mail:** jkortright@aol.com

KORUS, ROGER ALAN, BIOREMEDIATION FOR POLLUTANT DEGRADATION, FERMENTATION TECHNOLOGY. **Personal Data:** b Upper Darby, Pa, January 9, 1943; m 1971, Jean; c David D & Jeannine A. **Education:** Univ Wash, BS, 1965; Stanford Univ, MS, 1967; Univ Waterloo, PhD (chem eng), 1974. **Honors & Awards:** Cert Recognition, NASA, 1980. **Professional Experience:** PROF & DEPT CHAIR CHEM ENG, UNIV IDAHO, 1978-; res specialist, Ames Res Ctr, NASA, 1976-1978; res assoc, Western Regional Res Ctr, USDA, 1974-1976; Instr chem, Barber-Scotia Col, 1967-1968. **Memberships:** Am Inst Chem Engrs; Am Soc Microbiol; Am Soc Eng Educ. **Research Statement & Publications:** Developedprocesses for the biodegradation of chlorinated and nitrated aromatic compounds that are environmental pollutants; developed a process for the production of a diesel fuel substitute from vegetable oils. **Mailing Address:** 1038 Va, Moscow, ID 83843. **Fax:** 208-885-7462. **E-Mail:** rkorus@uidaho.edu

KORWIN-PAWLOWSKI, MICHAEL LECH, ELECTRICAL ENGINEERING. **Personal Data:** b Warsaw, Poland, April 10, 1941; American citizen; m 1974, Barbara; c Wendy. **Education:** Warsaw Tech Univ, MS, 1963; Univ Waterloo, Can, PhD (elec eng), 1974; Length Island Univ, MBA, 1993. **Professional Experience:** PROF, DEPT DATA PROCESSING & ENG, UNIV QUE, as of 2006; mgr eng, Gen Instrument, Ireland Macroom Co, Cork, Ireland, beginning 1994; mgr develop eng, Power Semiconductor Div, Gen Instrument Corp, Melville, NY, 1987-1994; dir eng, Gen Instrument Taiwan, 1982-1987; vpres & chief engr, Nat Semiconductors Ltd, 1978-1982; product line mgr rectifiers, Erie Technol Prod, Can, 1974-1978; res & teaching asst elec eng, Dept Elec Eng, Univ Waterloo, Can, 1969-1974; sr scientist elec eng, Inst Electron Technol, Polish Acad Sci, 1963-1969. **Research Statement & Publications:** Silicon rectifiers; transient voltage suppressors; semiconductor process technology; semiconductor devices. **Mailing Address:** Dept Data Processing & Eng, Univ Que, B-2008 Lucien-Brault House, Gatineau, PQ J8X 3X7, Can. **Fax:** 819-773-1638. **E-Mail:** michael.korwin-pawlowski@uqo.ca

KORY, MITCHELL, BIOLOGICAL SCIENCE, MEDICINE. **Personal Data:** b Brooklyn, NY, January 6, 1914; m 1943, c 2. **Education:** Univ Calif, Los Angeles, AB, 1942, PhD (physiol bact), 1953. **Professional Experience:** RETIRED; mgr med educ serv, Res Labs, Eli Lilly & Co, 1966-1983; mgr pub info, Res Labs, Eli Lilly & Co, 1963-1966; sr res biochemist, Res Labs, Eli Lilly & Co, 1953-1963; instr bact, Univ Kans, 1946-1951. **Memberships:** Am Soc Biol Chemists; Brit Biochem Soc. **Research Statement & Publications:** Intermediary metabolism. **Mailing Address:** 129 Willow Rd, Greenfield, IN 46140.

KORZICK, DONNA H, CARDIOLOGY. **Education:** Pa State Univ, PhD (Physiology), 1994. **Professional Experience:** ASST PROF PHYSIOLOGY & KINESIOLOGY, COL HEALTH & HUMAN DEVELOP, PA STATE UNIV PARK, as of 2006. **Mailing Address:** Col Health & Human Develop Pa State Univ PA, 106 Noll Laboratory, University Park, PA 21224. **Fax:** 814-865-4602. **E-Mail:** dhk102@psu.edu

KOS, EDWARD STANLEY, MICROBIOLOGY. **Personal Data:** b Chicago, Ill, August 10, 1928; m 1952, c 2. **Education:** Loyola Univ, Ill, BS, 1950; Marquette Univ, MS, 1952; Univ Ill, PhD (microbiol), 1958. **Professional Experience:** PROF EMER BIOL, ROCKHURST UNIV, as of 2003; prof biol, Rockhurst Univ, beginning 1969; assoc prof, Rockhurst Univ, 1961-1969; prof biol & chmn dept, Parsons Col, 1960-1961; instr microbiol, Col Med, Univ Ill, 1958-1960; actg instr life sci, Univ Calif, Riverside, 1957-1958. **Memberships:** Am Soc Microbiol; Sigma Xi. **Research Statement & Publications:** Nutrition and metabolism of bacteria; melanin pigmentation in azotobacter chrococcum. **Mailing Address:** Dept Biol, Rockhurst Univ, RIC 220I, 1100 Rockhurst Rd, Kansas City, MO 64110. **Fax:** 800-842-6776. **E-Mail:** edward.kos@rockhurst.edu

KOS, JOSEPH FRANK, SOLID STATE PHYSICS. **Personal Data:** b Montreal, Que. **Education:** Univ Waterloo, BSc, 1962; Univ Ottawa, PhD (physics), 1967. **Professional Experience:** PROF PHYSICS & ASTRON, UNIV REGINA, 1981-; assoc prof, Univ Regina, 1974-1981; assoc prof, Regina Campus, Univ Sask, 1971-1974; Asst prof physics & astron, Regina Campus, Univ Sask, 1967-1971. **Memberships:** Can Asn Physicists; Electrochem Soc Am; Solar Energy Soc Can Inc. **Research Statement & Publications:** Measurements of electron transport properties of metals; design and construction of gravitational antenna; photoelectrochemical conversion of solar energy to electricity or to production of hydrogen gas. **Mailing Address:** Dept Physics & Astron, Univ Regina, 3737 Wascana Pkwy, Regina, SK S4S 0A2, Can.

KOSAI, KENNETH, SEMICONDUCTOR DEVICE PHYSICS, INFRARED DETECTORS. **Personal Data:** b Spokane, Wash, July 27, 1944; m Carol; c Kim M. **Education:** Calif Inst Technol, BS, 1966; Univ Southern Calif, MSEE, 1968, PhD (elec eng), 1973. **Professional Experience:** MEM TECH STAFF, SANTA BARBARA RES CTR, 1981-; Vis scientist, Dept Solid State Physics, Univ Lund, Sweden, 1979; Mem tech staff, Philips Labs, Briarcliff Manor, NY, 1973-1981. **Memberships:** Inst Elec & Electronics Engrs; Am Phys Soc; assoc, Sigma Xi. **Research Statement & Publications:** Device physics of semiconductor heterojunctions and infrared detectors; semiconductor device modeling. **Mailing Address:** Raytheon Vision Systems, MS B3/8, 75 Coromar Dr, Goleta, CA 93117. **E-Mail:** kkosai@raytheon.com

KOSAK, ALVIN IRA, ORGANIC CHEMISTRY. **Personal Data:** b New York, NY, February 29, 1924; m 1958, Judith; c Deborah (Gussoff), Andrew & David. **Education:** City Col NY, BS, 1943; Ohio State Univ, PhD (org chem), 1948. **Professional Experience:** EMER PROF CHEM, NY UNIV, 1996-; dir grad study chem, All-Univ dept, 1984-1987; actg dean fac arts & sci, All-Univ dept, 1977-1978; head, All-Univ dept, 1965-1977; chmn dept, NY Univ, 1962-1965; USPHS spec fel, Univ Zurich, 1962; from assoc prof to prof chem, NY Univ, 1956-1995; asst prof indust med, NY Univ, 1952-1956; asst prof, Univ Cincinnati, 1949-1952; Jewett fel, Harvard Univ, 1948-1949; asst instr, Ohio State Univ, 1948; asst chem, Ohio State Univ, 1945-1946; res chemist, Socony-Vacuum Oil Co, 1943-1945. **Memberships:** Fel AAAS; Am Chem Soc; fel NY Acad Sci; Sigma Xi. **Research Statement & Publications:** Thiophene chemistry; natural products; polynuclear hydrocarbons. **Mailing Address:** Dept Chem Rm 1018, Main, 100 Wash Sq E, 1001-0, New York, NY 10003. **E-Mail:** kosak@152.nyu.edu

KOSAK, JOHN R, INDUSTRIAL ORGANIC CHEMISTRY. **Personal Data:** b Wilmington, Del, May 18, 1930; m 1957, c 3. **Education:** Univ Del, BS, 1951, MS, 1952; Mich State Univ, PhD (org chem), 1957. **Professional Experience:** CONSULT, 1993-; res assoc, E I Du Pont Del Nemours & Co, Inc, 1980-1993; sr chemist, E I Du Pont Del Nemours & CO, Inc, 1957-1980; instr org & gen chem, Ferris State Col, 1955-1956. **Memberships:** Am Chem Soc; Catalysis Soc. **Research Statement & Publications:** Catalysis; catalytic hydrogenation. **Mailing Address:** 103 Willowspring Rd, Wilmington, DE 19807-2433.

KOSAKA, MICHIKO, COMPUTER SCIENCE. **Education:** NY Univ, PhD. **Professional Experience:** ASSOC PROF, DEPT COMPUT SCI, MONMOUTH UNIV, as of 2004. **Research Statement & Publications:** Speech and natural language understanding. **Mailing Address:** Comput Sci Dept, Monmouth Univ, Rm B-23, Howard Hall, West Long Branch, NJ 07764. **Fax:** 732-571-3554. **E-Mail:** kosaka@monmouth.edu

KOSANOVICH, ROBERT JOSEPH, MATHEMATICS. **Personal Data:** b Monroe, Mich, September 27, 1938; m 1960, c 3. **Education:** Eastern Mich Univ, BS, 1960, MA, 1962; Univ Detroit, MA, 1963; Mich State Univ, PhD, 1972. **Professional Experience:** PROF EMER MATH, FERRIS STATE COL, as of 2004; head dept, Ferris State Col, beginning 1975; prof math, Ferris State Col, beginning 1965. **Mailing Address:** Technol Training Team, 717, Novak Lane, Big Rapids, MI 49307. **Fax:** 231-796-3138.

KOSARAJU, S RAO, COMPUTER THEORY. **Personal Data:** b andhra Pradesh, India, February 20, 1943. **Education:** Andhra Univ, India, BE, 1964; IIT, Kharagpur, India, MTech, 1966; Univ Pa, PhD (comput sci eng) 1969. **Professional Experience:** PROF, DEPT COMPUT SCI, JOHNS HOPKINS UNIV, 1977-. **Memberships:** Asn Comput Mach; Soc Int Appl Math; Instr Elec & Electronics Engrs. **Research Statement & Publications:** Design and analysis of parallel and sequential algorithms; algorithms for pattern matching, data structure simulations, universal graphs, DNA sequence assembly, n-body potentials, and paradigms for parallel data structures. **Mailing Address:** Dept Comput Sci, Johns Hopkins Univ, 224 New Eng Bldg, Baltimore, MD 21218. **Fax:** 410-516-6134. **E-Mail:** kosaraju@cs.jhu.edu

KOSARIC, NAIM, ENVIRONMENTAL BIOTECHNOLOGY, BIOSURFACTANTS FOR ENVIRONMENTAL & COSMETIC APPLICATIONS. **Personal Data:** b Sarajevo, Yugoslavia, September 27, 1928; Canadian citizen; m 1955, Zekija; c Senad & Alan. **Education:** Univ Zagreb, dipl, 1955; Univ Western Ont, PhD (biochem), 1969. **Professional Experience:** PRES & CHEIF EXEC OFFICER, KAYPLAN ENG CONSULTS, as of 2005; Inst Biochem Technol & Microbiol Tech Univ, Vienna, Austria, 1984; Fed Inst Biotechnol, Fed Repub Ger, 1984; Inst Fermentation & Biotechnol, Tech Univ, Ger, 1983; prof chem & biochem eng, Fac Eng & Sci, 1979-1996; expert, CIDA consult, Agr & Food Eng,

Unicamp, Compinas, Brazil, 1979, 1981, 1983; chmn, Univ Western Ont, 1977-1980 & 1984-1985; chmn chem & biochem eng, Univ Western Ont, 1977-1980 & 1984-1985; Inst Microbiol, Czech Acad Sci, Prague, 1975 & 1984; vis prof, Swiss Fed Inst Technol, Switz, 1975-1976; consult, Indust & Govt, beginning 1970; from asst prof to assoc prof, Univ Western Ont, 1969-1979; res asst, Dept Biochem, Univ Western Ont, 1966-1969; sr res eng, Bur Res & Partic Ministry, Rabat, Morocco, 1965-1966; vis engr, Nippon Kokan Chem, Tokyo-Kawasaki, Japan, 1962; sr process eng, petrochem, Organic Chem Indust, Zagreb, Yugoslavia, 1961-1965; Europ Nuclear Ctr, Mol, Belgium, 1960; process mgr, Pulp & Paper Indust, Maglay, 1959-1961; vis scientist, USSR Acad Sci, Moscow, 1957-1958; process engr & lab head, Iron, Coke Oven & Steelworks, Zenica, Yugoslavia, 1956-1959. **Memberships:** Am Inst Chem Engrs; NY Acad Sci; Am Oil Chemists Soc; AAAS; Int & Can Asn Water Pollution Res; Can Soc Chem Eng. **Research Statement & Publications:** Development of new processes and products in biochemical and food engineering; industrial wastewater treatment; biotechnology; microbial facts and oils; biosurfactants; fuel alcohol; anaerobic digestion of industrial pollutants; microbial detoxification; microbial proteins; economics in biotechnology. **Mailing Address:** 71 Sherwood Ave, London, ON N6A 5B9, Can. **Fax:** 519-649-1154.

KOSASKY, HAROLD JACK, GYNECOLOGY, INFERTILITY. **Personal Data:** b Winnipeg, Man, October 19, 1927; m 1955, Shirley; c Julia A, Leah E & Robert F. **Education:** Univ Man, BA, 1948, MD, 1953; FRCS, 1960; Am Bd Obstet & Gynec, dipl, 1964. **Professional Experience:** PROF, OBSTET & GYNEC, HARVARD MED SCH, as of 2005; active staff, Brigham & Women's Hosp, 1980-; consult, Jordan Hosp, 1969-; dir, Dept Obstet & Gynec, Cambridge Hosp, 1969-1970; instr obstet gynec, Harvard Med Sch, beginning 1966; obstetrician & gynecologist, Boston Hosp Women, 1966-1980; jr assoc surgeon, Peter Bent Brigham Hosp, 1966-1980; from asst prof to assoc prof, Sch Med, Univ Louisville, 1961-1965; exchange fel, Univ Durham, 1959-1960; sr res, Chicago Lying-In Hosp, Univ Chicago, 1958-1959; asst resident obstet & gynec, Chicago Lying-In Hosp, Univ Chicago, 1956-1958; resident psychiat, Warren State Hosp, Warren, Pa, 1955-1956; resident gen surg, Colonel Belcher Hosp, Calgary, 1953-1954; rotating intern, Deer Lodge Vet & Grace Hosps, Winnipeg, Can, 1952-1953; pres & chief res, Saltime Res Inc. **Memberships:** fel Am Col Surgeons. **Research Statement & Publications:** Endocrinology; gynecologic surgery; infertility. **Mailing Address:** Dept Obstet, Gynec & Reproductive Biol, Harvard Med Sch, 830 Boylston St Ste 207, Chestnut Hill, MA 02467. **Fax:** 617-566-6159.

KOSBAB, FREDERIC PAUL GUSTAV, PSYCHIATRY, INTERNAL MEDICINE. **Personal Data:** b Berlin, Ger, March 29, 1922; American citizen; m 1951. **Education:** Univ Berlin, MD, 1945; Am Bd Psychiat & Neurol, dipl, 1963; Okla State Univ, MA, 1989. **Professional Experience:** EMER PROF BIOL MED & PSYCHIAT & CHMN DEPT, SCH MED, ORAL ROBERTS UNIV, TULSA, 1987-; bd gov, City Faith Med & Res Ctr, 1982-; Med Pract Coun, Conf Med & Res Ctr, 1982-; prof psychiat & chmn dept, Sch Med, Oral Roberts Univ, Tulsa, 1982-1986; chief, Dept Behav Med & Psychiat, City Faith Med & Res Ctr, Tulsa, Okla, 1982-1986; prof, Dept Psychiat & Behav Sci, Eastern Va Med Sch, 1977-1982; chief psychiat servs, Hampton, Va Med Ctr, 1977-1982; med dir, E Plains Ment Health Ctr, 1974-1977; prof dir NIMH grant, 1969-1973; from actg chmn dept to assoc chmn dept, Med Col Va, Va Commonwealth Univ, 1969-1973; mem dean's comt, Richmond Vet Admin Hosp, 1969-1970; Residency Training Prog, East State Hosp, Williamsburg, Va, 1968-1973; chmn, Comt Postgrad Training Psychiat, 1967-1970; dir residency training psychiat, Med Col Va, Va Commonwealth Univ, 1966-1969; mem, Med Col Va Hosps, 1964-1973; from asst prof to prof psychiat, Med Col Va, Va Commonwealth Univ, 1964-1973; attend & consult, McGuire Vet Admin Hosp, Richmond, Va, 1964-1973; pvt pract psychiat, 1963-; clin instr psychiat, Med Sch, Univ Ore, 1962-1964; sr staff psychiatrist & unit med dir, Ore State Hosp, Salem, 1962-1963; Northern State Hosp, Sedro-Woolley, Wash, 1961-1962; resident psychiat, Sch Med, Univ Wash, 1960-1961; staff physician II, Psychiat Serv, Northern State Hosp, Sedro-Woolley, Wash, 1959-1960; resident psychiat, Col Med, Univ Nebr, 1958-1959; staff physician I, Psychiat Serv, Manteno State Hosp, Ill, 1957-1958; rotating intern, Swed Covenant Hosp, Chicago, Ill, 1956-1957; Consult, WGer Vet Admin, Landau, 1952-1956; pvt pract internal med, 1951-1955; Evangel Hosp, Goettingen-Weende, WGer, 1948-1951; resident internal med, Dist Hosp, Hannoversch Muenden, WGer, 1946-1948; Intern, Army Hosps & Refugee Infirmary, Friedland, WGer, 1945-1946. **Memberships:** Fel Am Psychiat Asn; hon fel Arbeitsgemeinschaft F Katathymes Bilderleben WGer; AMA. **Research Statement & Publications:** Contribution to the problem of superfetation and superfecundation in twins; camptocormia in the female; introduction of a buddy system for hospitalized geriatric patients; symbol formation; affective imagery and its didactic uses in psychiatry; teaching and learning in medical school. **Mailing Address:** PO Box 701677, Tulsa, OK 74170-1677.

KOSCH, PHILIP C, PHYSIOLOGY. **Education:** Ohio State Univ, MVM; Univ Calif, PhD (physiology). **Professional Experience:** RETIRED; dean, Cummings Sch Vet Med, Tufts Univ, as of 2005. **Mailing Address:** Dept Physiol Sci, Univ FLA, PO Box 100125, Gainesville, FL 32610. **Fax:** 904-392-6125.

KOSCHIER, FRANCIS JOSEPH, TOXICOLOGY, PHARMACY. **Personal Data:** b New York, NY, June 16, 1950. **Education:** Bard Col, AB, 1972; Univ Miss, PhD (pharmacol), 1976. **Professional Experience:** SR TOXICOL CONSULT, ARCO, 1989-; mgr toxicol, Ciba-Geigy Corp, 1983-1989; sr toxicologist, Am Cyanamid Corp, 1980-1983; sr toxicologist, Food & Drug Res Labs, 1979-1980; Res asst prof, State Univ NY, Buffalo, 1976-1979. **Memberships:** Soc Toxicol; Am Soc Pharmacol & Exp Therapeut; Soc Environ Toxicol & Anal Chem. **Research Statement & Publications:** Health and environmental risk assessment of petroleum products and synthetic chemicals. **Mailing Address:** ARCO AP 4151, 515 S Flower St, Los Angeles, CA 90071-2202.

KOSCO, JOHN C(ARROLL), METALLURGY, POWDER METALLURGY. **Personal Data:** b Du Bois, Pa, September 20, 1932; m 1956, Mary Mullaney; c Thomas, Mary Patricia, Anne, Ellen, Maurus & Joseph. **Education:** Univ Notre Dame, BS, 1954; Princeton Univ, MSE, 1956; Pa State Univ, PhD (metall), 1958. **Professional Experience:** DIR RES, KEYSTONE POWDERED METAL CO., 1972-; dir metall res, Stackpole Carbon Co, 1967-1971; chief engr metals, Stackpole Carbon Co, 1966-1967; Res metallurgist, Stackpole Carbon Co, 1958-1966. **Memberships:** Am Soc Metals; Am Powder Metal Inst; Am Chem Soc. **Research Statement & Publications:** Powder metallurgy of ferrous and nonferrous materials, high temperature materials and electrical contacts; electrical ceramics and thermoelectric materials; coatings and metal joining. **Mailing Address:** Keystone Powder Metal Co, 1933 State St, St Marys, PA 15857. **Fax:** 814-781-4280. **E-Mail:** jckosco@ncentral.com

KOSEL, PETER BOHDAN, MICROELECTRONIC DEVICES. **Personal Data:** b Northeim, Ger, August 20, 1946; Australian citizen; m 1973, c 2. **Education:** Univ Sydney, Australia, BSc, 1968; Univ NSW, Australia, PhD (elec eng), 1976. **Professional Experience:** PROF ELEC ENG, DEPT ELEC & COMPUT ENG & COMPUT SCI, UNIV CINCINNATI, 1989-; consult, Universal Energy Syst, Dayton, Ohio, 1988-; assoc prof, Univ Cincinnati, 1980-1989. **Memberships:** Inst Elec & Electronics Engrs; Sigma Xi; Electrochem Soc; Optical Soc Am; Soc Indust & Appl Math; Soc Photo-Optical Instrumentation Engrs. **Research Statement & Publications:** High speed charge-coupled devices in gallium arsenite and fabrication technology of compound semiconductor devices; computer aided design and simulation of signal processing devices and circuits; photonic devices and optical communications; fabrication process simulation; chalcopyrite semiconductors. **Mailing Address:** Dept Elec & Comput Eng & Comput Sci, Univ Cincinnati, 814 Rhodes Hall ML0030, Cincinnati, OH 45221-0030. **Fax:** 513-556-7326. **E-Mail:** peter.kosel@uc.edu

KOSERSKY, DONALD SAADIA, pharmacology; deceased, see previous edition for last biography

KOSH, JOSEPH WILLIAM, NEUROPHARMACOLOGY. **Personal Data:** b Hempstead, Tex, September 30, 1940; m 1978, Betsy; c 3. **Education:** Univ Tex, BS, 1964, MS, 1967; Univ Colo, PhD (pharmacol), 1971. **Professional Experience:** CHAIR & GRAD DIR, BASIC PHARMACEUT SCI COL OF PHARMACY, UNIV SC, 1998-; PROF BASIC PHARMACEUT SCI COL OF PHARMACY, UNIV SC, 1982-; assoc prof basic pharmaceut sci col of pharmacy, univ SC, 1976-1982; Asst prof basic pharmaceut sci col of pharmacy, univ SC, 1971-1976. **Memberships:** AAAS; Sigma Xi; ACS. **Research Statement & Publications:** Neuropharmacology-Cholinergic/Alzhoimers/Chocinesterase inhibitor toxicity. **Mailing Address:** Col Pharmacol, Univ SC, Columbia, SC 29208-0001.

KOSHEL, RICHARD DONALD, NUCLEAR PHYSICS. **Personal Data:** b Argo, Ill, February 1, 1936; m 1980, c 2. **Education:** Univ Ill, BS, 1958, MS, 1959; Univ Kans, PhD (theoret nuclear physics), 1963. **Professional Experience:** CO-DIR & DEAN, GRAD SCH, MISS STATE UNIV, as of 2003; PROF, DEPT PHYSICS & ASTRON, MISS STATE UNIV, as of 2003; PROF PHYSICS, Ill State Univ, 1985-; ASSOC PROVOST RES & DEAN GRAD STUDIES, ILL STATE UNIV, 1985-; assoc dean, Col Arts & Sci, Ohio Univ, 1980-1985; vis prof, Fla State Univ, 1969-1970 & Univ Md, 1978-1979; from asst prof to prof physics, 1963-1985. **Memberships:** Am Phys Soc; Am Asn Physics Teachers. **Research Statement & Publications:** Theoretical nuclear physics and numerical analysis; nuclear structure using many body techniques and nuclear reactions; non-linear system. **Mailing Address:** Miss State Univ, PO Drawer 5167, 141 Hilbun Hall, Mississippi, MS 39762. **Fax:** 662-325-8898. **E-Mail:** kosh@grad.msstate.edu

KOSHER, ROBERT ANDREW, DEVELOPMENTAL BIOLOGY. **Personal Data:** b Key West, Fla, March 1, 1945; m 1968, c 3. **Education:** Wilkes Col, BA, 1967; Temple Univ, PhD (biol), 1972. **Professional Experience:** PROF, DEPT BIOSTRUCTURE & FUNCTION, UNIV CONN, as of 2003; assoc prof anat, Sch Med, Univ Conn, beginning 1980; asst prof, Sch Med, Univ Conn, 1974-1980; NIH fel anat, Sch Med, Univ Pa, 1972-1974. **Memberships:** Soc Develop Biol; Am Soc Zoologists; Am Asn Anatomists. **Research Statement & Publications:** The role of extracellular matrix components in tissue interactions and other developmental processes; the control of somite chondrogenesis by extracellular matrix components produced by the embryonic notochord and spinal cord. **Mailing Address:** Dept Biostructure & Func, Univ Conn, Farmington, CT 06030-0001.

KOSHIGOE, SHOZO, MATHEMATICS. **Education:** Purdue Univ, PhD. **Professional Experience:** SR ACOUST SCIENTIST, VIBRO-ACOUSTIC SCI, as of 2006. **Mailing Address:** Vibro-Acoustic Sci Inc, 12555 High Bluff Dr, San Diego, CA 92130. **Fax:** 619-350-8328.

KOSHLAND, DANIEL EDWARD, BIOCHEMISTRY. **Personal Data:** b New York, NY, March 30, 1920; m 1945, Marian; c Ellen, Phyllis, James, Gail & Douglas. **Education:** Univ Calif, BS, 1941; Univ Chicago, PhD (biochem), 1949. **Honorary Degrees:** PhD, Weizman Inst Sci, 1984; DSc, Carnegie-Mellon Univ, 1985; LLD, Simon Fraser Univ, 1986, Univ Chicago, 1993; LHD, Mt Sinai Univ. **Honors & Awards:** T Duckett Jones Award, Helen Hay Whitney Found, 1977; Pauling Award & Edgar Fahs Smith Award, Am Chem Soc, 1979; Waterford Prize, Scripps Clin & Res Found, 1984; Rosentiel Award, Brandeis Univ, 1984; Nat Medal Sci, 1990; Merck Award, Am Soc Biochem & Molecular Biol, 1991. **Professional Experience:** Ed-in-chief, Sci Mag, 1985-; distinguished lectr, Soc Gen Physiol, 1978; vis fel, All Souls Col, Oxford, 1972-1973; fel, Guggenheim Found, 1972-1973; PROF BIOCHEM, UNIV CALIF, BERKELEY, 1965-; mem panel, USPHS, 1959-1964; affil, Rockefeller Univ, 1958-1965; sr biochemist, Brookhaven Nat Lab, 1956-1965; biochemist, Brookhaven Nat Lab, 1954-1956; assoc biochemist, Brookhaven Nat Lab, 1951-1954; fel, Harvard Univ, 1949-1951; group leader, Manhattan Proj, Univ Chicago, 1944-1946; asst, Manhattan Proj, Univ Chicago, 1942-1944; anal chemist, Shell Chem Co, 1941-1942. **Memberships:** Nat Acad Sci; AAAS; Am Chem Soc; Am Soc Biol Chemists (pres, 1973-1974); Japanese Biochem Soc; Royal Swed Acad Sci; Am Acad Arts & Sci; Am Philos Soc. **Research Statement & Publications:** General principles of enzymology and regulatory control; understanding of memory and sensory processes; correlation of protein structure and function. **Mailing Address:** Dept Molecular & Cell Biol, Univ Calif, 142 LSA, Berkeley, CA 94720. **Fax:** 510-643-6386. **E-Mail:** dek@uclink4.berkeley.edu

KOSHLAND, DOUGLAS E, GENETICS. **Personal Data:** b New York, NY, December 10, 1953. **Education:** Haverford Col, BA, 1976; Mass Inst Technol, PhD (biol), 1982. **Honors & Awards:** Helen Haynes Award; Lucy P Markell Award. **Professional Experience:** ASSOC INVESTR, HOWARD HUGHES MED INST, as of 2004; Adj prof biol, John Hopkins Univ, as of 2003; VIS ASSOC PROF GENETICS & MOLECULAR BIOL, SCH MED, JOHN HOPKINS UNIV, as of 2003; SR STAFF MEM GENETICS, CARNEGIE INST WASH, 1988-; res fel genetics, Univ Calif, San Francisco, 1984-1986. **Memberships:** Am Chem Soc; NY Acad Sci. **Research Statement & Publications:** Genetics. **Mailing Address:** Dept Embryol, Carnegie Inst Wash, 115 W Univ Pkwy, Baltimore, MD 21210-3399. **Fax:** 410-243-6311. **E-Mail:** koshland@ciwemb.edu

KOSHY, K THOMAS, PHARMACY, PHARMACEUTICAL CHEMISTRY. **Personal Data:** b Kerala, India, September 22, 1924; American citizen; m 1949, Accamma; c Elizabeth Ready, Thomas Isaac & Rachelle Shippy. **Education:** Kerala Univ, India, BSc, 1943; Benares Hindu Univ, BA, 1948; Univ Iowa, MS, 1958, PhD (pharm & pharmaceut chem), 1960. **Honors & Awards:** Am pharmaceut assn, acad of pharmaceut sci acad fel-awarded on 17th Nov 1982; fel of the Am asn of pharmaceut scientists on June 13, 1986. **Professional Experience:** RETIRED; sr res scientist, Upjohn Co, 1966-1989; sr res pharmacist, Miles Labs, Inc, 1961-1966; asst col pharm, Univ Iowa, 1960-1961; med serv rep, Parke Davis & Co, Ltd, 1951-1956; jr sci asst, Inspectorate of Gen Stores Lab, 1949-1951; mfg chemist, Sterling Pharmaceut, India, 1948-1949. **Memberships:** Acad fel Am Pharmaceut Asn; Am Chem Soc. **Research Statement & Publications:** Analytical methods development for drugs and pharmaceuticals; kinetic studies and stability testing of pharmaceuticals; residue analysis in plants and animals; metabolism in plants and animals; photolysis of pesticides and herbicides. **Mailing Address:** 723 Brandon Green Dr, Silver Spring, MD 20904.

KOSHY, THOMAS, DISCRETE MATHEMATICS, NUMBER THEORY. **Personal Data:** b Kozhancheri, Kerala, India, August 21, 1942; m 1967, Gracy; c Suresh & Sheeba. **Education:** Kerala Univ, BSc, 1962, MSc, 1964; Boston Univ, PhD (math), 1971. **Honors & Awards:** Marqui's Who's Who Registry of Outstanding Professionals. **Professional Experience:** Chmn math, Framingham State Col, beginning 1978; PROF MATH, FRAMINGHAM STATE COL, 1978-; from asst prof to assoc prof, Framingham State Col, 1970-1978; teaching fel, Boston Univ, 1967-1970; asst prof math, Kerala Univ, 1964-1967. **Memberships:** Math Asn Am; Nat Coun Teachers Math; Fibonacci Asn. **Research Statement & Publications:** Discrete mathematics; author of a number of publications; including six books. **Mailing Address:** Dept Math, Framingham State Col, 100 State St, PO Box 9101, Framingham, MA 01701-9101. **Fax:** 508-626-4003. **E-Mail:** tkoshy@frc.mass.edu

KOSIBA, WALTER LOUIS, PHYSICAL CHEMISTRY. **Personal Data:** b Braddock, Pa, February 13, 1921. **Education:** Canisius Col, BS, 1943; Ohio State Univ, MSc, 1949, PhD (chem), 1951. **Professional Experience:** SPECIALIST, LA JOLLA RADIOCARBON & TRITIUM LAB, UNIV CALIF, SAN DIEGO, 1971-; asst to dir, NAm Rockwell Sci Ctr, 1966-1970; sr scientist, Nuclear Dept, Douglas Aircraft Co, Inc, 1964-1966 & Aerospace Corp, 1966; consult, European Atomic Energy Community, Belgium, 1961-1963; Consult, Int Atomic Energy Agency, Austria, 1961; mem res staff, Gen Atomic Div, Gen Dynamics Corp, 1958-1961; assoc physicist, Brookhaven Nat Lab, 1953-1958; res chemist, Phys Chem Solids, Vitro Corp Am, 1951-1953; chemist, Phys Chem, Uranium, Tenn Eastman Corp, 1945-1946; Res assoc, S A M Labs, Columbia Univ, 1944-1945. **Memberships:** AAAS; Am Chem Soc; Sigma Xi. **Research Statement & Publications:** Materials sciences; radiation effects; solid state chemistry; radiocarbon dating. **Mailing Address:** 3920 Ingraham St Apt 118, San Diego, CA 92109-5915.

KOSIER, FRANK J, MATHEMATICS. **Personal Data:** b Lansing, Mich, July 2, 1934; m 1952, c 2. **Education:** Mich State Univ, BS, 1956, MS, 1957, PhD (math), 1960. **Professional Experience:** PROF EMER MATH, UNIV IOWA, as of 2000; Prof Math, Univ Iowa, beginning 1969; assoc prof, Univ Iowa, 1966-1969; asst prof, Syracuse Univ, 1963-1964 & Univ Wis-Madison, 1964-1966; Instr math, Univ Calif, Berkeley, 1960-1961 & Univ Wis, 1961-1963. **Memberships:** Am Math Soc; Math Asn Am. **Research Statement & Publications:** Non-associative rings. **Mailing Address:** Dept Math, Univ Iowa, Iowa City, IA 52240.

KOSIEWICZ, STANLEY TIMOTHY, NUCLEAR WASTE MANAGEMENT, RADIOLYSIS. **Personal Data:** b Chicago, Ill, July 21, 1944; m 1989, Amy E Anderson; c 1. **Education:** Univ Ill, BS, 1967; Univ Wis, MS, 1969, PhD (analytical chem), 1973. **Professional Experience:** TRANSURANIC WASTE MGT, LOS ALAMOS NAT LAB, UNIV CALIF, 1993-; technol interface, Environ Restoration, 1992-1993; staff scientist, Nuclear Waste Mgr, 1989-1992; independent consult, 1986-1989; staff mem analytical chem, Los Alamos Nat Lab, 1973-1986; Process engr chem eng, Olin Corp, 1968-1969. **Memberships:** Am Chem Soc; AAAS; Sigma Xi. **Research Statement & Publications:** Transuranium radioactive waste degradation; nuclear waste management; trace element geochemistry and archaeology; waste management and environmental restoration technology development. **Mailing Address:** Los Alamos Nat Lab, PO Box 1663, Los Alamos, NM 87545. **E-Mail:** stan@lanl.gov

KOSINSKI, ANTONI A, MATHEMATICS. **Personal Data:** b Warsaw, Poland, May 25, 1930; American citizen; div, c Marta. **Education:** Univ Warsaw, PhD, 1956. **Professional Experience:** PROF EMER MATH, RUTGERS UNIV, as of 2003; mem, Cont Profession, Am Math Soc, 1993-; dept chmn, Rutgers Univ, beginning 1993; vis prof, Univ Bonn, 1973-1974; prof math, Rutgers Univ, beginninig 1966; mem, Inst Advan Study, 1966-1967, 1985-1986 & 1996-1997; assoc prof math, Univ Calif, Berkeley, 1964-1966; mem, Inst Adv Study, 1962-1964; asst prof inst math, Polish Acad Sci, 1956-1959 & Univ Calif, Berkeley, 1959-1962. **Memberships:** Am Math Soc. **Research Statement & Publications:** Topology and differential topology; history & Math. **Mailing Address:** Dept Math, Rutgers Univ, New Brunswick, NJ 08854. **E-Mail:** kosinski@math.rutgers.edu

KOSINSKI, LESZEK ANTONI, GEOGRAPHY, DEMOGRAPHY. **Personal Data:** b Warszawa, Poland, June 13, 1929; Canadian citizen; m 1951, Maria L Bodakiewicz. **Education:** Cent Sch Planning & Statist, MA, 1951; Univ Warsaw, MA, 1954; Polish Acad Sci, PhD, 1958, Docent, 1963. **Honors & Awards:** Medal, SAfrican Geog Soc, 1987; Award for Serv to Prof Geog, Can Asn Geogrs, 1994. **Professional Experience:** SECY-GEN, INT SOCIAL SCI COUN, PARIS, 1994-; bd mem, Can Global Change Prog, 1991-; bd mem, Int Soc Sci Coun, 1986-1990; Univ Nat Autonoma de Mex, 1981 & Univ Guadalajara, 1985; Univ Liverpool, UK, 1981; chair, Comn Pop Geog, Int Geog Union, 1972-1980; Queen's Univ, Univ Wash, 1971; prof geog, Univ Alta, Can, 1969-1994; Vis prof, Pa State Univ, 1968; Vis prof, Northwestern Univ, 1968; Queen's Univ, Can, 1968; Vis prof, Univ Minn, 1967; Vis prof, Univ Calif, Berkeley, 1962; Vis prof, Ind Univ, 1962; sr researcher, Inst Geog, Polish Acad Sci, 1954-1968; Jr researcher, Inst Town Planning & Archit, Poland, 1950-1954. **Memberships:** Int Union Sci Study Pop; Europ Asn Pop Studies; Asn Pop Geogr India; Asn Am Geogr; Pop Asn Am Avocations; fel Royal Soc Can; Can Pop Soc (pres, 1984-1986); Int Geog Union (secy & treas, 1984-1992); hon mem Russ Geog Soc; hon mem Geog Soc France; hon mem Polish Geog Soc; corresp mem Geog Soc Italy. **Research Statement & Publications:** Human migration; human geography/demography. **Mailing Address:** ISSC Maison of UNESCO, 1 rue Miollis, Paris 75732 Cedex 15, France.

KOSINSKI, ROBERT JOSEPH, EDUCATIONAL USES OF SIMULATIONS, LIMNOLOGY. **Personal Data:** b Montclair, NJ, January 8, 1949; m 1989, Margaret; c Robert M & Joseph D. **Education:** Seton Hall Univ, BS, 1972; Rutgers Univ, PhD (ecol), 1977. **Professional Experience:** PROF, Biological Sciences, Clemson University, 1997-, Assoc Prof, Biol Prog, CLEMSON UNIV, 1986-1997; Asst Prof, Biol Prog, Clemson Univ, 1984-1986; Asst prof biol, Tex A&M Univ, 1977-1984; Grants, Environ Protection Agency, NSF & Dept Educ; software author, Worth Publ Co Benjamin/Cammings publ co, Freman publ co. **Memberships:** AAAS; Ecol Soc Am; Am Soc Limnol & Oceanog; Nat Asn Biol Teachers; Nat Sci Teachers Asn; Assoc for Biol Lab Edu(ABLE); vpres of ABLE 2000-2001. **Research Statement & Publications:** Stream ecology; primary productivity in streams; effects of pesticides in streams; computer modeling of antigenic variation of trypanosome infections; use of computers as teaching tools. **Mailing Address:** Biological Scis, Clemson Univ 132 Long Hall, Clemson, SC 29634-0314. **Fax:** 864-656-0435. **E-Mail:** rjksn@clemson.edu

KOSKI, RANDOLPH A, MARINE GEOLOGY. **Personal Data:** b Cloquet, Minn, June 22, 1946. **Education:** Univ Minn, BA, 1969; Stanford Univ, MS, 1974, PhD (geol), 1978. **Professional Experience:** CHIEF SCIENTIST, WESTERN REGION, MINERAL RESOURCES PROG, US GEOL SUPV, 1996-. **Memberships:** Fel Geol Soc Am; fel Soc Econ Geologists; Am Geophys Union. **Mailing Address:** US Geol Surv, 345 Middlefield Rd, Menlo Park, CA 94025. **Fax:** 650-329-5490. **E-Mail:** rkoski@usgs.gov

KOSKI, WALTER S, PHYSICAL CHEMISTRY. **Personal Data:** b Philadelphia, Pa, December 1, 1913; m 1940, Helen; c Carol L, Ann L, Nancy C & Phyllis. **Education:** Johns Hopkins Univ, PhD (phys chem), 1942. **Professional Experience:** BERNARD N BAKER PROF CHEM, JOHNS HOPKINS UNIV, 1974-; chmn dept, Johns Hopkins Univ, 1958-1969; PROF CHEM, JOHNS HOPKINS UNIV, 1955-; consult chem corps, US Army, 1949-; assoc prof phys chem, Johns Hopkins Univ, 1947-1955; physicist, Brookhaven Nat Lab, NY, 1947-1948; group leader, Los Alamos Sci Lab, 1944-1947; res chemist, Hercules Powder Co, 1942-1943. **Memberships:** Am Chem Soc; fel Am Phys Soc. **Research Statement & Publications:** Radioactive and stable isotopes as tracers; chemistry of boron hydrides; electron and nuclear magnetic resonance; mass spectroscopy; nuclear chemistry; ion-molecule reactions; reactive scattering of ions: mechanism of drug action. **Mailing Address:** Dept Chem, Johns Hopkins Univ, 3400 N Charles St, Baltimore, MD 21218. **Fax:** 410-516-8420. **E-Mail:** chm_wsk@jhuvms.hcf.jhu.edu

KOSKY, PHILIP GEORGE, ENGINEERING EDUCATION, CHEMICAL ENGINEERING RESEARCH. **Personal Data:** b London, Eng, March 25, 1939; m 1964, Mary; c Deirdre A & Nicole D. **Education:** Univ London, BSc, 1961; Univ Calif, Berkeley, MS, 1963, PhD (chem eng), 1966. **Professional Experience:** DISTINGUISHED GE RES PROF OF ENGINEERING, UNION COLLEGE, SCHENECTADY, NY, 2001 - present; Gen Elec Res & Develop Ctr, Staff Chemical Engineer, 1968/75 - 1977/2001 (Retired); sr sci officer, Harwell Nat Lab, England, 1966 - 1968; assoc prof mech eng & mechanics, Lehigh Univ, 1975 - 1977; Res asst, Univ Calif, Berkeley, 1961- 1965; adjunct assoc prof mech eng, Union Col, Schenectady, NY, 1970 - 1975. **Memberships:** Am Chem Soc; Am Soc for Engineering Education. **Research Statement & Publications:** Multiple research interests: Heat transfer, fuel chemistry, cryogenics, CVD, abrasive materials, applied polymer chemistry and engineering, nuclear engineering. **Mailing Address:** Union Col, Mechanical Eng Dept, 807 Union St, Schenectady, NY 12308. **E-Mail:** koskyp@union.edu

KOSLOW, JULIAN ANTHONY, BIOLOGICAL OCEANOGRAPHY. **Personal Data:** b Los Angeles, Calif, May 14, 1947; American & Australian citizen; div, c Ian Isaac & Ingrid. **Education:** Harvard Univ, BA, 1969; Univ Wash, BA, 1973; Univ Calif, San Diego, PhD (biol oceanog), 1980. **Honors & Awards:** E W Fager Award, Scripps Inst Oceanog, 1980; Chapman-Schaefer Award, Marine Technol Soc, 1975. **Professional Experience:** SR PRIN RES SCIENTIST, DIV MARINE RESEARCH COMMONWEALTH SCI & INDUST RES ORGN, 1997 -; sr res scientist, Div Fisheries, Commonwealth Sci & Indust Res Orgn, 1990- 1997; res assoc, Dept Fisheries & Oceans, Halifax, 1988-1989; Hon res assoc, Zool Dept, Univ West Indies, Jamaica, 1986; asst prof fisheries oceanog, Oceanog Dept, Dalhousie Univ, 1980-1988; Res asst biol oceanog, Scripps Inst Oceanog, Univ Calif, San Diego, 1974-1979. **Memberships:** Am soc for Limnology and Oceanography, Australian Marine Science Association. **Research Statement & Publications:** Deep water fisheries and ecology; biological; oceanography; the regulation between stock and recruitment in fish populations; interactions with biological and climatic change and larval ecology; effect of fisheries management on fishing communities; reef fish ecology and management. **Mailing Address:** Div Marine Res Commonwealth Sci & Ind Res Orgn, Marine Lab GPO Box 1538, Hobart, 7001 Australia. **Fax:** 613-623-25000. **E-Mail:** tony.koslow@csiro.au

KOSLOW, STEPHEN HUGH, NEUROSCIENCE, NEUROINFORMATICS. **Personal Data:** b New York, NY, October 14, 1940; m 1962, Diane; c Karin & James. **Education:** Columbia Univ, BS, 1962; Univ Chicago, PhD, 1967. **Honors & Awards:** Meritorious Achievement Award, Alcohol Drug Abuse & Ment Health Admin, 1979, 1985 & 1986, Pub Health Serv Spec Recognition Award, 1992; fel, Am Asn for the adven of sci; fel, Am col med Informatics; President Award, INt Neural Network soc, 2001. **Professional Experience:** Mem, White House Off Sci & Technol Deleg Orgn Econ Coop & Develop, Megascience Forum, Paris, beginning 1996; chair, Fed Interagency Coord Comt on Human Brain Proj, 1992; assoc dir, Dir Office Neuroinformation, NIHH, NIH, beginning 1999; DIR, DIV NEUROSCI & BEHAV SCI, NIMH, NIH, 1990-; dir, Div Basic Brain & Behav Sci, 1989-1990; chief, Neurosci Res Br, Div Basic Sci, 1985-1989; chief, Div Extramural Res, 1981-1985; Presidential Comn Mental Health, Special Asst Res Panel, 1978; dir, Clin Res Br Collab Prog Psychol Depression, NIMH, 1975-; chief, neurosci res, Biol Res Sect, Clin Res Br, 1975-1981; chief unit neurobiol & appl mass spectrometry, Lab Preclin Pharmacol, 1973-1975; staff fel, Lab Preclin Pharmacol, St Elizabeth's Hosp, NIMH, Wash, DC, 1970-1973; fel pharmacol, Karolinska Inst, Stockholm, Sweden, 1968-1969; med adv bd, Tourette Syndrome Asn. **Memberships:** Fel Am col med Informatics Am Soc Pharmacol & Exp Therapeut; Soc Neuroscience; fel Am Col Neuropsychopharmacol; Soc Biol Psychiat; fel Am Asn for the Advancement of sci. **Research Statement & Publications:** Neuropharmacology and psychopharmacology; depression and schizophrenia; neurotransmitters; metabolites and central nervous system function; neuroendocrinology; neuroscience; neuroscience databases. **Mailing Address:** NIH, NIHH, 6001 Exeutive Blvd, Rm 6167, Bethesda, MD 20892-9613. **Fax:** 330-144-31867. **E-Mail:** wiltchkoz@helix.nih.gov

KOSLOWSKY, VERNON THEODORE, NUCLEAR PHYSICS. **Personal Data:** b Leamington, Ont, December 15, 1953; m 1977. **Education:** Univ Waterloo, BSc 1977; Univ Toronto, MSc, 1978, PhD (physics), 1983. **Professional Experience:** ASST RES OFFICER, CHALK RIVER LABS, ONT, CAN, 1985-; res fel, GSI, Darmstadt, Fed Repub Ger, 1983-1984. **Memberships:** Can Asn Physicists. **Research Statement & Publications:** Experimental nuclear physics; use of accelerated heavy ions as probes of the nucleus; weak interaction and the nucleus; nuclei far from stability; accelerator mass spectrometry. **Mailing Address:** Chalk River Labs, Chalk River, ON K0J 1J0, Can.

KOSMAHL, HENRY G, ELECTRON PHYSICS. **Personal Data:** b Wartha, Ger, December 14, 1919; American citizen; m 1943, c 3. **Education:** Dresden Tech Univ, MS, 1943; Darmstadt Tech Univ, DS(electron physics), 1949. **Honors & Awards:** Sci Achievement Medal, NASA, 1974; Technol Adv Award, 1977, CECON Centennial Award, Inst Elec & Electronics Engrs, 1983. **Professional Experience:** CONSULT, ELECTRON DYNAMICS DIV, HUGHES AIRCRAFT, 1984-; Consult, Westinghouse Elec Defense Div, 1982-1983; head power amplifier, Lewis Res Ctr, NASA, 1962-1984; Consult, Aeronaut Systs & Space Div, USAF, Dayton, 1962-1984; head power amplifier, Electron Lab, US Army, 1956-1962; res physicist, AEG-Telefunken Res Ctr, Ger, 1952-1956; Asst prof physics, Darmstadt Tech Univ, 1949-1951. **Memberships:** Fel Inst Elec & Electronics Engrs. **Research Statement & Publications:** Interaction of charged particles with waves and matter. **Mailing Address:** 12700 Lake Ave Apt 606, Cleveland, OH 44107.

KOSMAN, DANIEL JACOB, BIOCHEMISTRY. **Personal Data:** b Chicago, Ill, November 29, 1941; m 1999, c 4. **Education:** Oberlin Col, BA, 1963; Univ Chicago, PhD (phys org chem), 1968. **Professional Experience:** PROF BIOCHEM, STATE UNIV NY, BUFFALO, 1981-; from asst prof to assoc prof, State Univ NY Buffalo, 1970-1981; Cornell Univ res assoc molecular biol, Dept Chem, Cambridge Univ & Med Res Coun Lab Molecular Biol, Cambridge, Eng, 1969-1970; Res assoc biophys, Univ Hawaii, 1968-1969. **Memberships:** AAAS; Am Chem Soc. **Research Statement & Publications:** Cell biology of metals; Metallobiochemistry; Bioinorganic chemistry; Iron metabolism. **Mailing Address:** Dept Biochem, State Univ NY, 140 Farber Hall, Buffalo, NY 14214. **Fax:** 716-833-2661. **E-Mail:** camkos@buffalo.edu

KOSMAN, WARREN MELVIN, CHEMICAL PHYSICS. **Personal Data:** b Chicago, Ill, March 23, 1946; m 1970, c 1. **Education:** Valparaiso Univ, BS, 1967; Univ Chicago, MS, 1969, PhD (chem physics), 1974. **Professional Experience:** CHMN, DEPT CHEM, VALPARAISO UNIV, as of 2004; PROF CHEM, VALPARAISO UNIV, 1989-; from asst prof to assoc prof, Valparaiso Univ, 1977-1989; asst prof chem, Ohio State Univ, 1974-1977; instr math, Valparaiso Univ, 1970-1971; instr chem, Valparaiso Univ, 1969-1970. **Memberships:** Am Chem Soc. **Research Statement & Publications:** Molecular spectroscopy and ab initio molecular orbital calculations of atoms and small molecules. **Mailing Address:** Dept Chem, Valparaiso Univ, Valparaiso, IN 46383-6493. **Fax:** 219-464-5489. **E-Mail:** warren.kosman@valpo.edu

KOSMATKA, JOHN BENEDICT, STRUCTURAL DYNAMICS, COMPOSITE MATERIALS. **Personal Data:** b Milwaukee, Wis, August 24, 1956; m 1988, Ellen; c Janell & Joel. **Education:** Univ Wis-Madison, BS, 1978; Univ Mich, MS, 1980; Univ Calif, Los Angeles, PhD (aerospace eng), 1986. **Honors & Awards:** Aerospace Struct & Mat Award, Am Soc Mech Engrs, 1991. **Professional Experience:** PROF APPL MECH, DEPT STRUCT ENG, JACOBS SCH ENG, UNIV CALIF, as of 2004; Newport News Shipbuilding, San Diego, Calif, 1990; assoc prof, Dept Struct Eng, Univ Calif, beginning 1989; Langley Res Ctr, Hampton, Va, 1989; fac fel, Ames Res Ctr, NASA, Moffettfield, Calif, 1988; asst prof mech eng, Va Polytech Inst, Blacksburg, 1986-1989; sr engr, TRW Corp, Redondo Beach, Calif, 1982-1986; engr, Aerospace Corp, El Segundo, Calif, 1980-1982. **Memberships:** Am Inst Aeronaut & Astronaut; Am Soc Mech Engrs; Am Helicopter Soc; Am Soc Engrs Educ. **Research Statement & Publications:** Structural dynamic and aeroelastic analysis of advanced composite helicopter, tilt-rotor, and turbo-propeller blades; hybrid composite materials that have reduced vibration behavior using passive and/or active techniques; author of various publications. **Mailing Address:** Dept Struct Eng, Jacobs Sch Eng, Univ Calif, 9500 Gilman Dr, La Jolla, CA 92093-0085. **Fax:** 858-822-2260. **E-Mail:** jkosmatka@ucsd.edu

KOSMICKI, JAMES JOSEPH, MATHEMATICS. **Professional Experience:** PROF, DEPT MATH, PASADENA CITY COL, as of 2006. **Mailing Address:** Pasadena City Col, 1570 E Colorado Blvd, Pasadena, CA 91106-2041. **Fax:** 626-585-7395. **E-Mail:** jjkosmicki@pasadena.edu

KOSNETT, VERDA DOGULU, INTERNET-BASED EMERGING TECHNOLOGIES, INTELLIGENT SYSTEMS. **Personal Data:** b Ankara, Turkey, January 30, 1960; American citizen; m 1985, Philip; c Alexander K & Nicole A. **Education:** Gazi Univ, BS, 1981; George Wash Univ, MS, 1989. **Professional Experience:** FOUNDER, VPC SOLUTIONS INC, 2000-; chief scientist, comput data systs inc, beginning 1996; instr bus applns & comput, Nanzan Univ, Japan, 1991-1992; Instr artificial intel, Trident Col, 1991-1992; instr comput sci, Cent Tex Col, 1990-1991; res scientist, Intellitek, 1988-1989. **Research Statement & Publications:** Development of advance search algorithms; design of internet-based security systems/transactions systems. **Mailing Address:** VPC Solutions, Inc, 1 Curie Ct, Rockville, MD 20850. **Fax:** 301-921-1004. **E-Mail:** verda.kosnett@cdsi.com

KOSOW, DAVID PHILLIP, ENZYMOLOGY, BLOOD COAGULATION. **Personal Data:** b Jersey City, NJ, March 15, 1936; m 1958, c 2. **Education:** Antioch Col, BS, 1958; Va Polytech Inst, MS, 1960, PhD (biochem & nutrit), 1962. **Professional Experience:** DIR TECH SERV, BAXTER HEALTHCARE, 1991-; coordr res & develop, Am Red Cross Blood Serv, 1985-1991; adj assoc prof, Dept Biol, Cath Univ Am, 1984-1987; asst dir, Am Red Cross Blood Serv, 1981-1984; fel, Fogarty Int Ctr, Oxford, UK, 1980-1981; sr res scientist, Am Red Cross Blood Serv, 1977-1981; res scientist, Am Red Cross Blood Serv, 1973-1977; sr res assoc, Inst Cancer Res, 1970-1973; res assoc, Inst Cancer Res, 1966-1970; neurochemist, Philadelphia Gen Hosp, 1965-1966; fel, Am Cancer Soc, Oak Ridge Nat Lab, 1963-1965; asst prof biochem, Va Polytech Inst, 1962-1963. **Memberships:** Am Soc Biol Chemists; Am Chem Soc; Sigma Xi; Int Soc Thrombosis & Haemostasis. **Research Statement & Publications:** Regulation and mechanism of plasma coagulation factors; development of blood plasma derivatives for clinical use; inactivation of viruses in plasma derivatives. **Mailing Address:** 525 N Canyon Blvd, Monrovia, CA 91016. **Fax:** 818-507-8635.

KOSOWER, EDWARD MALCOLM, BIOPHYSICAL ORGANIC CHEMISTRY. **Personal Data:** b Brooklyn, NY, February 2, 1929; m 1961, Nechama Sternschuss; c David A & Daria C. **Education:** Mass Inst Technol, SB, 1948; Univ Calif, Los Angeles, PhD (chem), 1952. **Honors & Awards:** Weizmann Prize, 1977; Kolthoff Award, 1984; Lemburg Lectr, Australian Acad Sci, 1991; Rothschild Prize, 1996. **Professional Experience:** PROF, DEPT CHEM, TEL-AVIV UNIV, ISRAEL, 1972-; adj prof, State Univ NY, Stony Brook, 1972-; Mass Inst Technol, 1983 & Bologna, Italy, 1987; Univ Calif, Berkeley, 1978; Kyoto, Japan, 1978; John Simon Guggenheim fel, 1977-1978; vis prof, Univ Calif, San Diego, 1977; NSF fel, Weizmann Inst Sci, Israel, 1968-1969; from assoc prof to prof chem, State Univ NY, Stony Brook, 1961-1972; Alfred P Sloan fel, 1960-1964; from instr to asst prof, Univ Wis, 1956-1961; asst prof chem, Lehigh Univ, 1954-1956; NIH res fel org chem, Univ Basel, 1952-1953 & Harvard Univ, 1953-1954. **Memberships:** Am Chem Soc; Royal Soc Chem; Am Soc Biochem; Soc Neurosci; Israel Chem Soc; fel AAAS. **Research Statement & Publications:** Charge-transfer spectra; pyridinium ion chemistry; solvent effects on spectra; stable free radicals; molecular medicine; neurophysiology; glutathione in chemistry, biochemistry, biology and medicine; fluorescence mechanisms; membrane mobility agents; mechanism of cell fusion; bimanes (diazabicyclo(3.3.0) octadienediones); sodium channel and acetylcholine receptor models; mechanism of fast intramolecular electron transfers; molecular basis learning and memory. **Mailing Address:** Dept Chem, Tel Aviv Univ, Ramat-Aviv Tel Aviv 69978, Israel. **Fax:** 972-364-09293. **E-Mail:** kosower@chemsq6.tau.a.il

KOSOWER, NECHAMA S, CELLULAR BIOCHEMISTRY, DIFFERENTIATION & AGING. **Personal Data:** b Tel Aviv, Israel, April 27, 1928; American & Israeli citizen; m 1961, Edward M; c David A & Daria (Inbar). **Education:** Univ Geneva, BS, 1952; Hebrew Univ, Jerusalem, MD, 1957. **Honors & Awards:** Weizmann Prize, Tel Aviv Munic, 1977; Career develop award, NIH, 1968-1973. **Professional Experience:** Prof emer (active), 1996-; The Igo Ornstein Chair for the study of Geriatrics, 1995-1998; chmn, Dept Human Genetics, 1986-1990; mem, Nat Bioethics Comt, Ministry Health, Israel, 1980-1983; PROF HUMAN GENETICS, SACKLER SCH MED, TEL AVIV UNIV, 1979-; vis Scientist (Dept of Med, Univ of Calif, San Diego; Harvard-MIT, Div, Health Sci & Technol; Molecular Plant Biology, Univ of Calif, Berkeley; Marine Sci Inst, Univ of Calif Santa Barbara; Dept of Anatomy and Reproductive Biology, Univ of Hawaii; Div of Hematology, Stanford univ School of Medicine) genetic counr, Inst Genetics, Tel-Hashomer, Israel, 1973-1977; assoc prof, Sackler Sch Med, Tel Aviv Univ, 1972-1979; assoc prof, Albert Einstein Col Med, NY, 1970-1972; Asst, assoc & attend physician, Bronx Munic Hosp Ctr, 1967-1972; asst prof, Albert Einstein Col Med, NY, 1967-1970. **Memberships:** Am Soc Clin Invest; Am Soc Hemat; Am Soc Human Genetics; Israeli Soc Cell Biol; Israeli Soc Hemat; Israeli Soc Biol Psychiat; Israeli Soc Biol Aging. **Research Statement & Publications:** Thiols in Biol; Bimane labeling; Cell differentiation and aging; genetics of schizophrenia; calpain-calpastatin system. **Mailing Address:** Sackler Sch Med, Tel Aviv Univ, Tel Aviv 69978, Israel. **Fax:** 972-640-9900. **E-Mail:** nkosower@post.tau.ac.il

KOSOWSKY, DAVID I, HEALTH SCIENCES, ELECTRONICS. **Personal Data:** b New York, NY, February 27, 1930; c 3. **Education:** City Col NY, BEE, 1951; Mass Inst Technol, SM, 1952, ScD(network theory), 1955. **Professional Experience:** CHMN EMER & CEO, DAMON CORP, as of 1996; chmn & chief exec officer, Damon Corp, beginning 1983; chmn, Childrens Hosp Med Ctr, 1983; vchmn, Childrens Hosp Med Ctr, 1976-1983; Trustee, New Eng Aquarium, 1968- & Univ Hosp Boston, 1970-; pres, Damon Corp, beginning 1961; vpres, Itek Electro-ProdCo, 1960-1961; dir crystal div, Hermes Electronics Co, 1955-1960; res asst & staff mem, Res Lab Electronics, Mass Inst Technol, 1951-1955. **Memberships:** Inst Elec & Electronics Engrs; Sigma Xi; AAAS; NY Acad Sci. **Research Statement & Publications:** Network theory; statistical theory of communication; crystal filters; voltage controlled crystal oscillators; spectrum analyzers; health service delivery systems; medical and electronic instrumentation. **Mailing Address:** Damon Corp, 52570 Gateway Dr, Elkhart, IN 46514.

KOSS, DONALD A, METALLURGY. **Personal Data:** b Dodge Co, Minn, m 1964, c 3. **Education:** Univ Minn, BS, 1960; Yale Univ, MS, 1962, PhD (metall), 1965. **Professional Experience:** PROF, DEPT METALS SCI & ENG, MAT RES INST, PA STATE UNIV, 1986-; chmn dept, Pa State Univ, beginning 1986; fel, Los Alamos Nat Lab, 1978-1979; from assoc prof to prof metall eng, Mich Technol Univ, 1970-1985; res assoc, Pratt & Whitney Aircraft, 1965-1970. **Memberships:** Am Soc Metals; Metall Soc; Mat Res Soc. **Research Statement & Publications:** Processing, deformation, and fracture of high performance alloys. **Mailing Address:** Dept Metals Sci & Eng, Mat Res Inst, Pa State Univ, 202A Steidle Bldg, Univ Park, PA 16802. **Fax:** 814-865-2917. **E-Mail:** koss@matse.psu.edu

KOSS, MICHAEL CAMPBELL, PHARMACOLOGY. **Personal Data:** b Ann Arbor, Mich, September 24, 1940. **Education:** NY Univ, BA, 1966; Columbia Univ, PhD (pharmacol), 1971. **Professional Experience:** PROF CELL BIOL, COL MED, UNIV OKLA, 1981-; from asst to assoc prof, 1971-1981. **Memberships:** Asn Res Vision & Ophthal; Soc Neurosci; Am Soc Pharmacol & Exp Therapeut; Sigma Xi. **Research Statement & Publications:** Neuropharmacology; neurophysiology; brain stem regulatory mechanisms; autonomic nervous system. **Mailing Address:** Dept Cell Biol, Univ Okla Health Sci Ctr, BMSB 724, Oklahoma City, OK 73190-0901. **E-Mail:** michael-koss@ouhsc.edu

KOSS, NEAL, MATHEMATICS. **Education:** Yale Univ, MD 1966, HS, 1974. **Professional Experience:** PVT PRACT COSMETIC SURGEON, as of 2002. **Mailing Address:** 3655 Lomita Blvd 215, Torrance, CA 90505-4802. **Fax:** 310-375-6685. **E-Mail:** nkoss@intl-informatics.com

KOSS, PETER, METALLURGY. **Personal Data:** b Vienna, Austria, March 21, 1932; m 1956, Elsa Vedra; c Michael, Christoph & Stephan. **Education:** Univ Vienna, PhD, 1958. **Honors & Awards:** Hon Merit Silver, Austrian Govt, 1969. **Professional Experience:** TECH SCI MANAGING DIR, AUSTRIAN RES CTR, 1981-; prof, Univ Vienna, 1981; head, Dept Metall, 1963-1981; Staff, Atomics Int, Calif, 1959; Res fel, Mass Inst Technol, 1959. **Memberships:** Austrian Phys Soc; Int Plansee Soc Power Metall; Chem Phys Soc. **Mailing Address:** Osterreiches Forschungszentruti Seibersdorf GmbH, 2444 Seibersdorf, Vienna Kramergasse 1 A-1010, Austria.

KOSS, VALERY ALEXANDER, MATHEMATICAL PHYSICS. **Personal Data:** b Dnepropetrovsk, USSR, August 4, 1941; American citizen; m 1967, c 1. **Education:** Leningrad Polytech Inst, USSR, MS, 1964; Phys Tech Inst, Leningrad, PhD (math physics), 1972. **Professional Experience:** PROGRAMMER ANALYST, INFOTECH RES INT INC, as of 2003; consult scientist, Tech Ctr, BOC Group, Inc, 1988-2002; Sr scientist, 1982-1988. **Research Statement & Publications:** Modeling of various phenomena pertaining to chemistry, vacuum technologies and optics. **Mailing Address:** Infotech Res Int Inc, 188 Route 10 W, Suite 202, E Hanover, NJ 07936. **Fax:** 973-463-1265.

KOSSIAKOFF, ALEXANDER, technical management, system engineering; deceased, see previous edition for last biography

KOSSLER, WILLIAM JOHN, PHYSICS. **Personal Data:** b Charleston, SC, March 26, 1937; m Margaret; c Neil, William & Paul. **Education:** Mass Inst Technol, BS, 1959; Princeton Univ, PhD (physics), 1964. **Honors & Awards:** fel, Am Phys Soc. **Professional Experience:** PROF PHYSICS, COL WILLIAM & MARY, 1978-; from asst prof to assoc prof, Col William & Mary, 1969-1978; asst prof physics, Mass Inst Technol, 1966-1969; Staff mem nuclear physics, Mass Inst Technol, 1964-1966. **Memberships:** Am Phys Soc AAAS. **Research Statement & Publications:** Experimental nuclear and solid state physics; use of muon spin rotation for the study of superconductors and magnetic systems. **Mailing Address:** Dept Physics, Col William & Mary, Williamsburg, VA 23187-8795. **Fax:** 757-221-3540. **E-Mail:** kossler@physics.wm.edu

KOSSOR, STEVEN ALBERT, CLINICAL PSYCHOLOGY, EDUCATIONAL RESTRUCTURING-REFORM. **Personal Data:** b Plainfield, NJ, November 29, 1954; m 1980, Kathleen Zampana; c Nicholas & Jaclyn. **Education:** Montclair State Col, BA, 1975; Fairleigh Dickinson Univ, MA, 1977. **Professional Experience:** EXEC DIR, INST BEHAV CHG, as of 2004; CLIN PSYCHOLOGIST, PVT PRACT, 1981- & STATE PA, 1992-; Clin psychologist, Devereuk Found, 1977-1992. **Memberships:** Am Psychol Asn. **Research Statement & Publications:** Exposing and stopping the illicit, inappropriate use of psychological methods in American public schools and the reform of the American education system to renew its commitment to focus on honest academic and vocational development. **Mailing Address:** 1850 E Lincoln Hwy, Coatesville, PA 19320. **Fax:** 610-383-1432. **E-Mail:** sakossor@voicenet.com

KOSSOVSKY, NIR, BIOTECHNOLOGY. **Education:** Univ Chicago, MD; Univ Southern Calif, MBA. **Professional Experience:** FOUNDER, PRES & CHIEF EXEC OFF, TECHNOL OPTION CAPITAL, LLC. **Research Statement & Publications:** Author of approximately 200 publications and 33 pending and issued patents. **Mailing Address:** Technol Option Capital LLC, 200 S Linden Ave Suite 300, Pittsburgh, PA 15208. **Fax:** 412-291-3155. **E-Mail:** nkossovsky@tocllc.com

KOSSOY, AARON DAVID, ORGANIC CHEMISTRY, ANALYTICAL CHEMISTRY. **Personal Data:** b New York, NY, August 19, 1936; m Joan-Lois. **Education:** City Col NY, BS, 1958; Polytech Inst Brooklyn, PhD (org chem), 1966; post doctoral fel & lecturer, Univ CA, Berkeley, 1996-1969. **Professional Experience:** RETIRED; res scientist, Eli Lilly Res Labs, beginning 1980; sr anal chemist, Eli Lilly Res Labs, 1969-1980; fel chem, Univ

Calif, Berkeley, 1966-1969; analytical chemist, Trubek Labs Inc, 1958-1961. **Memberships:** Am Chem Soc; Sigma Xi. **Research Statement & Publications:** Chemical and physical properties of organic compounds; spectroscopic characterization of organic compounds; organic structure determination; correlation of physical properties of organic compounds with biological activities. **Mailing Address:** 7627 Almaden Ct, Indianapolis, IN 46278.

KOSSUTH, SUSAN, PLANT PHYSIOLOGY, GENETICS. **Personal Data:** b Boston, Mass, April 28, 1946. **Education:** Colo State Univ, BS, 1968, MS, 1971; Yale Univ, MS, 1972, MPhil, 1973, PhD (tree physiol-genetics), 1974. **Professional Experience:** PROJ LEADER, US FOREST SERV, 1979-; co-prin investr, Fla Citrus Comn, 1977-1979; asst res scientist, Univ Fla, 1977-1978; asst prof tree physiol, Univ Ark, 1976-1977; prin investr, Weyerhaeuser Corp, Eli-Lilly Co, Ark Kraft Co, Southern Regional Educ Bd, 1976; Consult, Fla Citrus Comn, 1974-1976; adj asst prof, Univ Fla, 1974-1976. **Memberships:** Am Soc Plant Physiol; Sigma Xi; Soc Am Foresters; Am Forestry Asn; Plant Growth Regulator Soc Am. **Research Statement & Publications:** Reproductive physiology and breeding and improvement of Southern pines; vegetative propagation of pines; flowering in pines; early genetic testing of pines; effects of ultraviolet light on plants. **Mailing Address:** Dept Fruit Crops Univ Fla, 1119 HS-PP Bldg, Gainesville, FL 32611.

KOSTANT, BERTRAM, GEOMETRIC QUANTIZATION. **Personal Data:** b New York, NY, May 24, 1928; m 1968, c 5. **Education:** Purdue Univ, BS, 1950; Univ Chicago, MS, 1951, PhD (math), 1954. **Honorary Degrees:** DSc, Purdue Univ, 1997. **Professional Experience:** PROF EMER MATH, MASS INST TECHNOL, 1993-; prof, Oxford Univ, Tel Aviv Univ & Paris, France, 1974-1975, 1981-1982; prof, Mass Inst Technol, 1963-1993; Guggenheim fel, Paris, France, 1959-1960; mem, Miller Inst Basic Res, 1958-1959; from asst prof to prof math, Univ Calif, Berkeley, 1956-1963; Higgins lectr, Princeton Univ, 1955-1956; mem, Inst Advan Study, 1954-1956; NSF fel, Inst Advan Study, 1953-1954. **Memberships:** Nat Acad Sci; Am Acad Arts & Sci; Am Math Soc. **Research Statement & Publications:** Operator theory; Lie groups; representation theory; differential geometry; mathematical physics. **Mailing Address:** Mass Inst Technol, Dept Math, Rm 2-282, Cambridge, MA 02139. **E-Mail:** kostant@math.mit.edu

KOSTELECKY, V ALAN, THEORETICAL PHYSICS. **Education:** Yale Univ, PhD, 1982. **Professional Experience:** PROF, DEPT PHYSICS, IND UNIV, as of 2006. **Mailing Address:** Dept Physics, Ind Univ, 727 E Third St, Bloomington, IN 47405. **Fax:** 812-855-5533. **E-Mail:** kostelec@indiana.edu

KOSTELNICEK, RICHARD J, ELECTRICAL ENGINEERING. **Personal Data:** b Chicago, Ill, May 16, 1942; m 1967. **Education:** Univ Ill, Urbana, BS, 1964, MS, 1965, PhD (elec eng), 1969. **Professional Experience:** SR RES ASSOC, ESSO PROD RES CO, 1969-. **Memberships:** AAAS; Soc Explor Geophys; Inst Elec & Electronics Engrs. **Research Statement & Publications:** Antennas; plasma physics; wave propagation in inhomogeneous media; geoscience. **Mailing Address:** 609 Bayou Crest Dr, Dickinson, TX 77539.

KOSTENBAUDER, HARRY BARR, PHARMACY. **Personal Data:** b Danville, Pa, April 9, 1929. **Education:** Phila Col Pharm, BS, 1951; Temple Univ, MS, 1953; Univ Wis, PhD (pharm), 1956. **Professional Experience:** PROF EMER PHARM, COL PHARM, UNIV KY, as of 2000; prof pharm & assoc dean res, Col Pharm, Univ KY, beginning 1968; from asst prof to prof, Temple Univ, 1956-1968; asst pharm, Temple Univ, 1951-1953 & Univ Wis, 1955. **Memberships:** Am Chem Soc; Am Pharmaceut Asn; NY Acad Sci; fel Acad Pharmaceut Sci (pres, 1971-1972); fel Am Asn Pharmaceut Scientists. **Research Statement & Publications:** Drug binding by macromolecules; drug stability; pharmacokinetics. **Mailing Address:** Dept Pharmaceut Sci, Univ KY, Lexington, KY 40506.

KOSTER, DAVID F, PHYSICAL CHEMISTRY, SPECTROSCOPY. **Personal Data:** b Houston, Tex, November 3, 1936; m 1959, Dolores; c 5. **Education:** St Thomas Univ, BA, 1959; Tex A&M Univ, MS, 1963, PhD (chem), 1965. **Professional Experience:** PROF EMER CHEM, SOUTHERN ILL UNIV, CARBONDALE, as of 2006; prof chem, Southern Ill Univ, Carbondale, beginning 1981; from asst prof to assoc prof 1967-1981; res fel, Mellon Inst, 1964-1967; chemist, Diamond Alkali Co, 1959-1960; asst chmn, Dept Chem & Biochem, Southern Ill Univ, Carbondale. **Memberships:** Am Chem Soc; Sigma Xi; Nat Sci Teachers Asn. **Research Statement & Publications:** Chemistry. **Mailing Address:** Dept Chem, Southern Ill Univ, Carbondale, IL 62901. **Fax:** 618-453-6408. **E-Mail:** koster@chem.siu.edu

KOSTER, GEORGE FRED, PHYSICS. **Personal Data:** b New York, NY, April 9, 1927; m 1951, c 3. **Education:** Mass Inst Technol, SB, 1948, PhD (physics), 1951. **Professional Experience:** PROF EMER PHYSICS, MASS INST TECHNOL, 2001-; prof physics, Mass Inst Technol, 1964-2001; from asst prof to assoc prof, Mass Inst Technol, 1956-1964; Guggenheim fel, 1955-1956; Lincoln Lab, Mass Inst Technol, 1952-1955; res assoc, Mass Inst Technol, 1951-1952. **Memberships:** Am Phys Soc. **Research Statement & Publications:** Theoretical physics including theory of solids and molecular theory. **Mailing Address:** Mass Inst Technol, Dept Physics, Rm 4-334, Cambridge, MA 02139. **E-Mail:** phyjbm@mit.edu

KOSTER, JEAN NICOLAS, THERMOFLUID MECHANICS & SOLIDIFICATION OF METALLIC MELTS. **Education:** Univ Karlsruhe, Ger, Dr-Ing(fluid mech), 1980. **Professional Experience:** PROF, AERONAUT ENG SCI, UNIV COLO, as of 2003; assoc prof, Univ Colo, beginning 1994; asst prof, Univ Colo, 1985-1994; res asst, Univ Colo, 1985-1986; vis res scientist, Lewis Res Ctr, NASA, 1984-1985; res scientist, Nuclear Res Ctr, Karlsruhe, 1982-1984; Postdoctorate res asst, Univ Utah, 1980-1982. **Memberships:** APS Am Soc Mech Engrs ASM TMS MRS VDI; Assoc fel American Institute of Aeronaut. **Research Statement & Publications:** Visualization capabilities to study fluid mechanics and heat transfer-convective flow-in opaque metallic melts and alloys. **Mailing Address:** 872 Welsh Ct, Louisville, CO 80027. **Fax:** 303-492-7881. **E-Mail:** jean.koster@colorado.edu

KOSTER, ROBERT ALLEN, ORGANIC CHEMISTRY. **Personal Data:** b Grand Rapids, Mich, July 12, 1941; m 1963, Judith; c Kimberly & Tamara. **Education:** Hope Col, AB, 1963; Univ Mich, Ann Arbor, MS, 1965, PhD (chem), 1968. **Professional Experience:** FAC, CALVARY BAPTIST ACAD, 1999-; sr res assoc, 1988-1998; res assoc, Dow Chem USA, 1982-1988; res leader, Styrene Plastics, 1980-1982; proj leader, Org Chem Prod Res, 1970-1980; Res chemist, Dow Chem USA, 1968-1970. **Memberships:** Soc Plastics Engrs. **Research Statement & Publications:** Carbonium ion chemistry; reaction mechanisms via kinetic studies; process development on fine organic chemicals; chemistry of 2.2.1 bicyclic systems; polymer process development; materials science. **Mailing Address:** Calvary Baptist Acad, 6100 Perrine Rd, Midland, MI 48640. **E-Mail:** jarako@aol.com

KOSTER, WILLIAM HENRY, SYNTHETIC ORGANIC CHEMISTRY. **Personal Data:** b Teaneck, NJ, April 20, 1944; m 1968, c 1. **Education:** Colby Col, BA, 1966; Tufts Univ, PhD (chem), 1972. **Honors & Awards:** Thomas Alva Edison Award, 1992. **Professional Experience:** PRES & CHIEF EXEC OFFICER, NEUROGEN CORP, 2001-; vpres, Cardiovasc Drug Discovery, Bristol-Myers Squibb Pharm Res Inst, Princeton, Nj, beginning 1991; vpres, Div Chem, 1990-1991; exec dir, dept chem, Infectious & Metabolic Dis, 1987-1990; dir, dept chem, Infectious & Metabolic Dis, 1984-1987; sect head, Squibb Inst Med Res, 1983-1984; group leader synthetic antibact agents & nat prods, Squibb Inst Med Res, 1980-1983; sr res investr, Squibb Inst Med Res, 1977-1980; res investr, Squibb Inst Med Res, 1972-1977; fel, Squibb Inst Med Res, 1971-1972. **Memberships:** Am Chem Soc; Am Heart Asn; AAAS; NY Acad Sci; Fedn Am Soc Exp Biol. **Research Statement & Publications:** Synthetic organic chemistry; bioorganic chemistry; mechanism-based design of new antibacterials/antifungals; antiviral agents; cardiovascular agents and inhibitors of cholesterol biosynthesis; natural products isolation; structure elucidation; semi-synthetic modification; research administration. **Mailing Address:** Neurogen Corp, 35 NE Indust Rd, Branford, CT 06405. **Fax:** 203-481-8683.

KOSTER, WILLIAM PFEIFFER, METALLURGICAL ENGINEERING. **Personal Data:** b Fords, NJ, April 18, 1929; m 1954, Marcia; c Kenneth, Frank, Barrett & James. **Education:** Rutgers Univ, BS, 1950; Univ Cincinnati, MS, 1951, PhD (metall eng), 1953. **Honorary Degrees:** LHD, Cincinnati Tech Col, 1970. **Honors & Awards:** Gold Medal, Soc Mfg Engrs. **Professional Experience:** RETIRED; chmn, Metcut Res Assoc Inc, beginning 1992; pres, Metcut Res Assoc Inc, 1978-1992; dir, Metall Eng, Metcut Res Assoc Inc, beginning 1957; vpres, Metcut Res Assoc Inc, 1957-1978; staff mem, Metcut Res Assoc Inc, 1953-1957. **Memberships:** Fel Am Soc Metals; fel Soc Adv Mat & Process Eng; fel Soc Mfg Eng. **Research Statement & Publications:** Properties of materials surfaces. **Mailing Address:** 8005 S Clippinger Dr, Cincinnati, OH 45243.

KOSTER VAN GROOS, AUGUST FERDINAND, EXPERIMENTAL PETROLOGY, GEOCHEMISTRY. **Personal Data:** b Leeuwarden, Neth, January 9, 1938; m 1971, Elizabeth; c Sebastian & Paul. **Education:** Univ Leiden, BS, 1958, MS, 1962, PhD (exp petrol), 1966. **Professional Experience:** PROF EMER EARTH & ENVIRON SCI, UNIV ILL, 2001-; head, Dept Earth & Environ Sci, Univ Ill, 1991-2001; prof Earth & Environ Sci, Univ Ill, 1987-2001; assoc prof geol sci, Univ Ill, Chicago Circle, 1976-1987; asst prof geol sci, Univ Ill, Chicago Circle, 1970-1976; asst prof earch sci, State Univ Utrecht, Neth, 1968-1970; res assoc, Goddard Space Flight Center, NASA, 1966-1968. **Memberships:** AAAS; Mineral Soc Am. **Research Statement & Publications:** Genesis of carbonatite, H-P exp. systems containing CO2 and H2O; salt-silicate-water systems; liquid immiscibility in rocks; clay-H2O, clay-gas hydrates. **Mailing Address:** Dept Geol Sci Univ Ill, 845 W Taylor St, Chicago, IL 60612. **Fax:** 312-413-2279. **E-Mail:** kvg@uic.edu

KOSTIC, NENAD M, BIOINORGANIC CHEMISTRY, ORGANOMETALLIC CHEMISTRY. **Personal Data:** b Belgrade, Yugoslavia, November 18, 1952; American citizen; m 1976, Dragana; c Dimitrije N & Bogdan N. **Education:** Univ Belgrade, Yugoslavia, dipl, 1976; Univ Wis-Madison, PhD (inorg chem), 1982. **Honors & Awards:** Presidential Young Investr Award, NSF, 1988 Sloan res fel, A P Sloan Found, 1991; Karic Award for sci res, Karic found, 2001. **Professional Experience:** PROF CHEM & ADJ PROF BIOCHEM, IOWA STATE UNIV, 1994-; vis prof, Leiden Univ, Netherlands, beginning 1994; assoc prof chem & adj assoc prof biochem, Iowa State Univ, 1989-1994; asst prof chem, Iowa State Univ, 1984-1989; res fel chem, Calif Inst Technol, 1982-1984; teaching & res asst, Univ Wis-Mad, 1978-1982. **Memberships:** Am Chem Soc; Serbian Chem Soc. **Research Statement & Publications:** Bioinorganic electron-transfer reactions; Artificial enzymes for protein cleavage; reactions in sol-gel glasses. **Mailing Address:** Dept Chem, Iowa State Univ, 1605 Gilman Hall, Ames, IA 50011-3111. **Fax:** 151-529-40105. **E-Mail:** nenad@iastate.edu

KOSTISHACK, DANIEL F(RANK), ELECTRICAL ENGINEERING, SOLID STATE PHYSICS. **Personal Data:** b Pittsburgh, Pa, March 25, 1940; m 1966, c 2. **Education:** Carnegie Inst Technol, BS, 1963, MS, 1965; Carnegie-Mellon Univ, PhD (elec eng), 1968. **Professional Experience:** RETIRED; group leader, Lincoln Lab, Mass Inst Technol, beginning 1984; mem res staff, 1967-1981. **Research Statement & Publications:** Solid-state and high frequency devices and circuits; solid-state imaging devices and electro-optical systems. **Mailing Address:** Lincoln Lab, Mass Inst Technol, 244 Wood St, Lexington, MA 02173-9108.

KOSTIUK, THEODOR, SPACE PHYSICS. **Personal Data:** b Plauen, Ger, August 12, 1944; m 1970. **Education:** City Col NY, BS, 1966; Syracuse Univ, PhD (physics), 1973. **Professional Experience:** CHIEF SCIENTIST EXPLOR PROG, GODDARD SPACE FLIGHT CTR, NASA, as of 2002; SPACE SCI DIR, GODDARD SPACE FLIGHT CTR, NASA, as of 2002; ASTROPHYSICIST SPACE SCIENTIST, PLANETARY SYSTS BR, GODDARD SPACE FLIGHT CTR, NASA, 1985-; head Molecular Astrophys Sect, Infrared Astron Br, 1983-1984; space scientist, Infrared Astron Br, 1974-1983; Nat Acad Sci resident res assoc, Planetary Systs Br, Goddard Space Flight Ctr, NASA, 1973-1974; discipline leader, Auroral Discipline, Int Jupiter Watch. **Memberships:** Am Phys Soc; Optical Soc Am; Soc Photo-Optical Instrument Engrs; AAAS; Am Astron Soc Div Planetary Sci. **Research Statement & Publications:** Atmosphere of planets, comets, the sun, stars and the earth's stratosphere using ultra-high resolution infrared spectroscopy; infrared heterodyne spectroscopy; discovery of the first natural laser (carbon dioxide on Mars); molecular spectroscopy; hydrocarbon chemistry on outer planets; global circulation on Mars and Venus; dynamics and planetary oscillations on Jupiter; aurorae and infrared emission on Jupiter. **Mailing Address:** Goddard Space Flight Ctr, NASA, Code 693, Greenbelt, MD 20771. **Fax:** 301-286-1683. **E-Mail:** theodor.kostiuk@gsfc.nasa.gov

KOSTKOWSKI, HENRY JOHN, SPECTRORADIOMETRY. **Personal Data:** b Garwood, NJ, May 16, 1926; m 1976, c 3. **Education:** Johns Hopkins Univ, PhD (physics), 1954. **Honors & Awards:** Gold Medal Award, US Dept Com, Edward Bennett Rosa Award. **Professional Experience:** PROPRIETOR SPECTRORADIOMETRY CONSULT, 1981-; chief optical radiation sect, Nat Inst Stand & Technol, 1971-1981; chief radiation thermometry sect, Nat Inst Stand & Technol, 1965-1971; supvry physicist, Nat Inst Stand & Technol, 1958-1965; physicist high temperature, Nat Inst Stand & Technol, 1956-1958; 1955, 1957; molecular physicist, Nat Inst Stand & Technol, 1954-1956; consult, Inst Advan Study, 1954. **Memberships:** Fel Optical Soc Am. **Research Statement & Publications:** Spectroradiometry; optical pyrometry; spectral line intensity measurements; physical optics. **Mailing Address:** 1101 Cornwall Dr, La Plata, MD 20646.

KOSTOFF, MORRIS R, NUCLEAR PHYSICS, ACOUSTICS. **Personal Data:** b Jamestown, NDak, December 2, 1933; m 1955, Effie; c Sherrie, Terrie, Matthew, Kristine M & Mark A. **Education:** Pac Lutheran Univ, BS, 1962; Univ Tex, Austin, PhD (physics), 1967. **Honors & Awards:** Sen Warren G Magnuson Scholarship, 1960-1961. **Professional Experience:** RETIRED; dir acoust warfare prof, Anal & Appl Res Div, Appl Sci Group, 1982-1991; prin scientist, Anal & Appl Res Div, Appl Sci Group, 1979-1982; asst prof physics, Southwestern Univ, Tex, 1971-1974; sr scientist, Sci & Systs Div, Tracor Inc, 1970-1979; engr-scientist, Sci & Systs Div, Tracor Inc, 1966-1970; Nat Defense Educ Act fel, 1963-1966; res asst nuclear physics, Ctr Nuclear Studies, Univ Tex, Austin, 1963-1966. **Memberships:** Am Phys Soc. **Research Statement & Publications:** Spin polarization measurements for elastic and inelastic proton scattering; systems analysis and simulation of signal processors for sonar systems; propagation of acoustic waves in water medium; operator interactive; realtime computer simulation of state-of-the-art sonar systems for evaluating mission effectiveness in a countermeasure environment. **Mailing Address:** 11513 Juniper Ridge Dr, Austin, TX 78759-3845.

KOSTREVA, DAVID ROBERT, ANESTHESIOLOGY, CARDIOLOGY. **Personal Data:** b Milwaukee, Wis, August 14, 1945; m 1975, c 4. **Education:** Univ Wis, Milwaukee, Ba, 1972; Med Col Wis, MS, 1974, PhD (physiol), 1976. **Honors & Awards:** Young Cardiovasc Investr Award, NIH, 1979, Res Career Develop Award, 1982; Henry Pickering Bowditch Lectr, 1983. **Professional Experience:** SR SCIENTIST, PROCTER & GAMBLE PHARMACEUT, 1993-; from asst prof to assoc prof physiol & anesthesia, Med Col Wis, 1981-1993; Chmn, Ad Hoc Study Sect, NIMH, 1981; Fel, Am Heart Asn, 1976-1977 & Nat Heart, Lung & Blood Inst, NIH, 1977-1978. **Memberships:** Am Physiol Soc; Soc Neuroscience; Sigma Xi; Soc Exp Biol & Med; Int Soc Heart Res. **Research Statement & Publications:** Neural control of circulation and respiration in adult and fetal dogs, cats and monkeys, rabbits and chickens using afferent and efferent recording techniques and brain and heart mapping studies of visceral reflexes using the carbon-fourteen-deoxyglucose technique; antiarrhythmic and cardiotonic drug development. **Mailing Address:** Procter & Gamble Pharmaceut, 10200 Alliance Rd, Cincinnati, OH 45242. **Fax:** 513-626-6481.

KOSTREVA, MICHAEL MARTIN, MATHEMATICS. **Personal Data:** div. **Education:** Clarion State Col, BA, 1971; Rensselaer Polytech Inst, MS, 1973, PhD (math), 1976. **Professional Experience:** Consult, Gillette Res Inst, 1990-; pres, Systematica Inc, Clemson, 1989-; PROF MATH, CLEMSON UNIV, 1989-; Consult, Gen Motors Corp, 1987-; assoc prof, Clemson Univ, 1986-1989; mem tech staff, Alphatech, Inc, 1986; prin mem tech staff, GTE Labs, Inc, 1984-1986; res scientist, Gen Motors Res Labs, 1978-1984; Asst prof math, Univ Maine, Orono, 1976-1978. **Research Statement & Publications:** Complementarity theory of mathematical programming, multiple objective programming, game theory, lubrication theory, shift scheduling, circadian rhythms. **Mailing Address:** Dept Math Sci, Clemson Univ, O-307 Martin Hall, Clemson, SC 29634-1907. **Fax:** 864-656-5230. **E-Mail:** flstgla@clemson.edu

KOSTROUN, VACLAV O, ATOMIC PHYSICS. **Personal Data:** b Brasov, Rumania, December 30, 1938; American citizen; m 1963, c 2. **Education:** Univ Wash, BS, 1961, MS, 1963; Univ Ore, PhD (physics), 1968. **Professional Experience:** ASSOC PROF APPL & ENG PHYSICS, CORNELL UNIV, 1977-; asst prof, 1970-1977; res assoc & lectr, 1968-1970. **Memberships:** AAAS; Am Phys Soc. **Research Statement & Publications:** Interactions of highly charged ions with atoms at lee V energies; production of low energy, very highly charged ions; theoretical atomic physics. **Mailing Address:** Dept App & Eng Physics, Cornell Univ, 226 Clark, Ithaca, NY 14853. **E-Mail:** vok1@cornell.edu

KOSTRZEWA, RICHARD MICHAEL, DOPAMINE & SEROTONIN NEURAL SYSTEMS. **Personal Data:** b Trenton, NJ, July 22, 1943; m 1965, Florence Palmer; c Theresa, Richard, Joseph, Maria, Krystyna, Thomas J, John P, Frank, Roseanna & Monica. **Education:** Philadelphia Col Pharm & Sci, BS, 1965, MS, 1967; Univ Pa, PhD (pharmacol), 1971. **Professional Experience:** Vis prof, Silesian Med Acad, Poland, 1997-; res grant, John E Fogarty Int Ctr, 1990 & 1992; res grant, Scottish Rite Schizophrenia, 1989-1992; PROF PHARMACOL, E TENN STATE UNIV, 1984-; res award, E Tenn State Univ Found, 1981; assoc prof, E Tenn State Univ, 1978-1984; March Dimes grant, 1977-1979 & Am Parkinson's Dis Asn grant, 1977-1978; prin investr, NIH grant, 1975-1981, 1990-1994, 1998-2003; asst prof physiol, La State Univ Med Ctr, New Orleans, 1975-1978; Asst prof pharmacol, Tulane Univ Med Ctr, New Orleans, 1974-1975; Res pharmacologist, Vet Admin Hosp, New Orleans, 1971-1975. **Memberships:** Am Soc Pharmacol & Exp Therapeut; Neurosci Soc; Int Brain Res Orgn; Soc Neurosci; Fedn Am Socs Exp Therapeut. **Research Statement & Publications:** Development of monoaminergic neurons; dopamine receptors and behavior; Parkinson's disease; neurotoxins; psychopharmacology; schizophrenia; tardive dyseinesia; attention deficit hyperactivity disorder. **Mailing Address:** Col Med, East Tenn State Univ, Johnson City, TN 37614-0577. **Fax:** 423-439-8773. **E-Mail:** kostrzewa@etsv.edu

KOSTYNIAK, PAUL J, TOXICOLOGY. **Personal Data:** b Schenectady, NY, April 8, 1947; m 1970, c 3. **Education:** St John Fisher Col, BS, 1970; Univ Rochester, PhD (toxicol), 1976. **Professional Experience:** PROF PHARMACOL & TOXICOL, STATE UNIV NY, BUFFALO, as of 2003; CHAIR, DEPT CLIN LAB SCI, STATE UNIV NY, BUFFALO, as of 2003; speaker, Gordon Conf, 1987; DIR TOXICOL RES CTR, 1985-; assoc prof pharmacol, State Univ NY, Buffalo, beginning 1984; asst prof, State Univ NY, Buffalo, 1977-1984; fel radiation, biol & biophys, Univ Rochester, 1975-1977; dipl, Am Bd Toxicol; Reviewer, Toxicol & Appl Pharmacol, J Pharmacol & Exp Therapeut, J Appl Toxicol, Archives Biochem Biophys & Toxicol Letters. **Memberships:** Soc Toxicol; Sigma Xi; Am Chem Soc; AAAS; NY Acad Sci. **Research Statement & Publications:** Toxicology of heavy metals, antidote development and the metabolism and toxicity of organofluroic compounds; mechanisms of metal transport and disposition; role of endogenous thiols in the elimination of toxic metal pollutants; developing new in vitro models of nephrotoxicity and animal models of neurotoxicity; mechanisms of degradation of polymer films; author of various articles. **Mailing Address:** Pharmacol Dept, State Univ NY, 134 Cary Hall 24-26 Cary Hall, Buffalo, NY 14260. **Fax:** 716-829-2806. **E-Mail:** pjkost@buffalo.edu

KOSTYO, JACK LAWRENCE, PHYSIOLOGY, ENDOCRINOLOGY. **Personal Data:** b Elyria, Ohio, October 1, 1931; m, c 2. **Education:** Oberlin Col, AB, 1953; Cornell Univ, PhD (zoology), 1957. **Honorary Degrees:** MD, Univ Goteborg, 1978. **Honors & Awards:** Lederle Med fac award, 1961-1964; Ernst Oppenheimer Mem Award, Endocrine Soc, 1969. **Professional Experience:** DIR, GRANT PROGS, MICH DIABETES RES & TRAINING CTR, as of 1997; prof emeritus physiol, Med Sch, Univ Mich beginning 1995; Active prof emeritus in internal med, Med Sch, Univ Mich beginning 1995; mem international and cooperative projects study sect, NIH, 1992-1996; ed, Am Physiol Soc Handbook of Physiology, new sect on endocriology, Vol 5, 1992-1998; mem US med Licensure Exam Step 2 comt, 1990-1991; mem ed bd Growth Reg 1990-1997; chmn, Coun Endocrinol & Metabolism Sect, Am Physiol Soc, 1990-1991; mem comprehensive part II comt, Nat Bd Med Examr, 1986-1991 assoc dir, Mich Diabetes Res & Training Ctr, 1986-1997; mem ed bd Endocrine Rev, 1984-1988; mem admin bd Coun Acad Sci, Am Asn Med Col, 1983-1986; mem coun, Endocrine Soc, 1983-1985; sect ed, Endocrinol, Ann Rev Physiol, 1982-1986; mem sci adv comt, Searle Scholars Prog, 1982-1985; rep to coun Acad Socs, Asn Am Med Cols, 1981-1989; prof physiol, Med Sch, Univ Mich, 1979-1994; chmn dept, 1979-1985; mem coun, Am Physiol Soc, 1979-1982; pres, Asn Chmn Dept Physiol, 1979-1980; ed-in-chief, Endocrinology, 1978-1982; mem coun, Asn Chmn Dept Physiol, 1975-1978; mem physiol test comt, Nat Bd Med Examr, 1974-1977; mem ed bd, Proc Soc Exp Biol Med, 1973-1978; vis foreign scientist, Swed Med Res Coun, 1972; chmn educ comt, Am Physiol Soc, 1970-1976; prof physiol & chmn dept, Emory Univ, 1968-1979; mem endocrinol study sect, NIH, 1967-1971; asst prof to prof physiol, Duke Univ, 1959-1968; Nat Res Coun fel, Harvard Med Sch, 1957-1959. **Memberships:** Am Physiol Soc; Endocrine Soc; Sigma Xi; Am Diabetes Asn. **Research Statement & Publications:** Mechanism of action of pituitary growth hormone; relationship between structure and functions of growth hormone. **Mailing Address:** Mich Diabetes Res & Training Ctr, Univ Mich, Med Sch, 1331 E Ann St Bldg, Rm 5111, Box 0580, Ann Arbor, MI 48109. **Fax:** 734-647-2307. **E-Mail:** jkostyo@umich.edu

KOSTYRKO, GEORGE JURIJ, CIVIL ENGINEERING. **Personal Data:** b Ukraine, May 9, 1937; American citizen. **Education:** City Col New York, BChE, 1957; Univ Mich, Ann Arbor, MSE, 1958; Sacramento State Col, MS, 1963; Univ Calif, Davis, PhD (civil eng), 1969. **Professional Experience:** PROF, DEPT CIVIL ENG, CALIF STATE UNIV, as of 2003; HEAD PROG APPL MECH, SACRAMENTO STATE COL, 1971-; NSF grant, Sacramento State Col, 1971-1972; ASSOC PROF CIVIL ENG, SACRAMENTO STATE COL, 1968-; sr res engr, Calif, 1961-1968; Aerojet-Gen Corp, Calif, 1958-1961; Develop engr, Air Prod Inc, Pa, 1957. **Memberships:** Sigma Xi. **Research Statement & Publications:** Detection of static and dynamic stresses in solids and structures by means of acoustic wave propagation, holography and photoelasticity. **Mailing Address:** Dept Civil Eng, Calif State Univ, 1721 Cathay Way, Sacramento, CA 95864. **E-Mail:** kostyrko@ecs.csus.edu

KOSTYU, DONNA D, IMMUNOLOGY. **Personal Data:** b Ashtabula, Ohio, October 17, 1947; m 1970, Joel; c Jessica & Jennifer. **Education:** Duke Univ, PhD (microbiol & immunol), 1979; Heidelberg Col, B.S. 1969. **Professional Experience:** ASST DIR, ACAD ADVISING CTR & ADJ ASSOC PROF BIOL, DUKE UNIV, 2001-; asst res prof immunol, Sch Med, Duke Univ, 1986-2001; Res assoc, 1981-1986. **Memberships:** Am Asn Immunologists; Am Soc Histocompatibility & Immunogenetics. **Research Statement & Publications:** Research focuses on the immunogenetics of the HLA supergene, the human major histocompatibility complex. **Mailing Address:** Rm 116, Acad Advising Ctr, Durham, NC 27710-0001. **E-Mail:** donna.kostyu@duke.edu

KOSZALKA, THOMAS R, BIOCHEMISTRY. **Personal Data:** b Rochester, NY, January 25, 1927; m 1954, c 3. **Education:** Univ Rochester, BA, 1950, PhD, 1959. **Professional Experience:** PROF PEDIAT, JEFFERSON MED COL, 1987-; PROF BIOCHEM, JEFFERSON MED COL, 1975-; PROF RADIOL, JEFFERSON MED COL, 1970-; assoc prof biochem, Jefferson Med Col, 1967-1975; assoc dir, Eleanor Roosevelt Res Labs & dir, Harry Bock Labs, 1965-; assoc prof radiol, Jefferson Med Col, 1965-1970; from instr to asst prof biochem, Sch Med & Dent, Univ Rochester, 1959-1965. **Research Statement & Publications:** Developmental biochemistry; teratology. **Mailing Address:** 934 Irvin Rd, Huntingdon Valley, PA 19006.

KOSZIL, LOUIS A, ELECTRO-OPTICAL COMPONENTS. **Personal Data:** b Bethlehem, Pa, October 7, 1944; m 1970, Lorraine F; c Laura Lyn & Lacene Fay. **Education:** Moravian Col, BS, 1970. **Honors & Awards:** Eng Excellence Award, Optical Soc Am, 1992. **Professional Experience:** DISTINGUISHED MEM TECH STAFF, AT&T BELL LABS, 1988-; mem tech staff, AT&T Bell Labs, 1980-1988; assoc mem tech staff, AT&T Bell Labs, 1973-1980; sr tech aide, AT&T Bell Labs, 1970-1973. **Research Statement & Publications:** Electro-optical components; fabrication processes; fundamental semiconductor designs; applicable transmission systems; fundamental semiconductor designs; electro-optical components including fabrication processes; author of numerous articles; awarded 17 US and 5 European patents. **Mailing Address:** AT&T Bell Res Lab, 600 Mountain Ave, New Providence, NJ 07974-2008.

KOSZTARAB, MICHAEL, ENTOMOLOGY, INSECT TAXONOMY, SCALE INSECT BIOLOGY. **Personal Data:** b Bucharest, Romania, July 7, 1927; American citizen; m 1953, Matilda Pinter; c Eva. **Education:** Hungarian Univ Agr Sci, HortE, 1951; Ohio State Univ, PhD (entom), 1962. **Honorary Degrees:** Dr, Univ Horti, Budapest, 1994. **Honors & Awards:** L O Howard dist achievement award, entom soc am, 2001; Thomas Jefferson Medal, Va mus natural history found, 1998; External mem, Hungarian acad sci, 1995; Annual recognition award, asn syst collections, 1994. **Professional Experience:** EMER PROF ENTOM, VA POLYTECH INST & STATE UNIV, 1992-; pres, Va Natural History Soc, 1992-1993; FOUNDING DIR, VA MUS NATURAL HIST, VA TECH, 1990-; dir, Ctr Systs Collections, 1987-1991; chmn, Planning Comt, Nat Biol Surv Proj, 1984-1988; from assoc prof to prof entom, VA Mus Natural Hist, VA Tech, 1962-1992; asst dir res, Insect Control & Res Inc, Md, 1959-1960; consult entomologist, Insect Control & Res Inc, Md, 1957-1958; asst prof hort entom, Hungarian Univ Agr Sci, 1951-1956; Exten asst, Hungarian State Bur Plant Protection, 1947-1950. **Memberships:** Hon mem Entom Soc Am; hon mem Hungarian Entom Soc. **Research Statement & Publications:** Systematics and biology of scale insects (Homoptera Coccoidea) in North America and Europe; author of 171publications including 6 books and six res bulletins. **Mailing Address:** Dept Entom, Va Polytech Inst & State Univ, Blacksburg, VA 24061-0319. **E-Mail:** mkoszt@vt.edu

KOT, PETER ALOYSIUS, CARDIOVASCULAR PHYSIOLOGY. **Personal Data:** b Stanley, Wis, January 13, 1932; m 1958, c 6. **Education:** Marquette Univ, MS, 1956, MD, 1957. **Professional Experience:** PROF EMER PHYSIOL, MED SCH, GEORGETOWN UNIV, as of 2003; prof physiol, med sch, georgetown univ, beginning 1976; lectr, US Army Inst Dent Res, 1968-1971; lectr physiol, US Naval Dent Sch, Bethesda, Md, 1966-1971; from asst prof to assoc prof physiol, Med Ctr, Georgetown Univ, 1964-1976; investr, Am Heart Asn, 1964-1969; asst prof med, Med Ctr, Georgetown Univ, 1964-1969; instr med, Med Ctr, Georgetown Univ, 1963-1964; Fel coun circulation, Am Heart Asn, 1963; instr physiol, Med Ctr, Georgetown Univ, 1960-1964; resident, Med Ctr, Georgetown Univ, 1958-1960; intern med, Med Ctr, Georgetown Univ, 1957-1958. **Memberships:** AAAS; Am Fedn Clin Res; Am Physiol Soc; Soc Exp Biol & Med; Am Heart Asn. **Research Statement & Publications:** Cardiovascular physiology, especially hemodynamic effects of the prostaglandins and their precursors; radiation injury. **Mailing Address:** Dept Physiol/Biophys Georgetown Univ Med Sch, 3900 Reservoir Rd NW, Washington, DC 20007.

KOT, RICHARD ANTHONY, METALLURGY, MATERIALS SCIENCE. **Personal Data:** b Syracuse, NY, May 22, 1941; m 1961, c 3. **Education:** LeMoyne Col, BS, 1964; Syracuse Univ, MS, 1967, PhD (solid state sci), 1969. **Professional Experience:** MGR MAT TECH, RES & DEVELOP, WORTHINGTON INDUST, 1989-; dir res & develop, Touchstone Res Lab, 1986-1988; asst div head metall, Repub Steel Res Ctr, 1981-1986; sr res adv, 1980-1981; res adv, 1978-1980; sect chief, 1975-1978; supvr, 1974-1975; Res metallurgist, 1969-1974. **Memberships:** Am Soc Metals; Am Inst Mining Metall & Petrol Engrs; Sigma Xi; NY Acad Sci. **Research Statement & Publications:** Physical metallurgy; plastic deformation; recrystallization. **Mailing Address:** 4628 Bridle Path Lane, Dublin, OH 43017.

KOTAKE, YASHIGE, BIOLOGICAL CHEMISTRY. **Education:** Osaka Univ, BS 1967, MS 1969, PhD (Phys Chem) 1972. **Professional Experience:** ADJ ASSOC PROF PHARMA-

CEUT SCI, UNIV OKLA HEALTH SCI CTR, as of 2004. **Memberships:** Am Diabetes Assoc; Am Assoc Cancer Res. **Mailing Address:** Dept Pharmaceut Sci, Univ Okla Health Sci Ctr, 825 NE 13th St, Oklahoma City, OK 73104. **Fax:** 405-271-1795. **E-Mail:** yashige-kotake@omrf.ouhsc.edu

KOTANSKY, D(ONALD) R(ICHARD), FLUID MECHANICS, AERODYNAMICS. **Personal Data:** b Hinsdale, Ill, July 28, 1939; m 1962, c 3. **Education:** Gen Motors Inst, BME, 1962; Mass Inst Technol, SM, 1962, MechE, 1964, ScD(fluid mech), 1966. **Professional Experience:** BR CHIEF TECHNOL, AERODYN, MCDONNELL AIRCRAFT CO, MCDONNELL DOUGLAS CORP, 1980-; sect chief, McDonnel Douglas Res Lab, 1977-1980; sr scientist, McDonnel Douglas Res Lab, 1973-1977; sr group engr propulsion 1970-1973; sr & proj propulsion engr, Ft Worth Div, Gen Dynamics Corp, 1968-1970; consult, Allison Div, Gen Motors Corp, Ind, 1967-1968; Vis Caterpillar prof, Bradley Univ, 1966-1967; Asst prof mech eng, Purdue Univ, 1965-1968. **Memberships:** Assoc fel Am Inst Aeronaut & Astronaut; Am Soc Mech Engrs; Sigma Xi. **Research Statement & Publications:** Theoretical and experimental investigations of external and internal aerodynamics, including laminar and turbulent flows, boundary layers, rotational and secondary flows, jet and multiple jet dominated flows, unsteadiness, acoustics and shock boundary layer interaction. **Mailing Address:** 14575 Appalachian Tr, Chesterfield, MO 63017-1901.

KOTB, MALAK Y, BIOCHEMISTRY, IMMUNOLOGY. **Personal Data:** b Cairo, Egypt, July 20, 1953; m 1986. **Education:** Ain Shams Univ, Cairo, Egypt, BS, 1974; Univ Tenn, Memphis, PhD (biochem), 1982. **Professional Experience:** PROF, DEPT SURG & DIV ADV, SURG IMMUNOL, UNIV TENN, MEMPHIS, as of 2003; asst prof, dept surg & dir surg immunol, Univ Tenn, Memphis, beginning 1990; mem res serv, Va Med Ctr, Memphis, beginning 1986; asst prof, Div Infectious Dis, Dept Med, 1986-1990; res assoc, Duke Univ Med Ctr, 1982-1985; rotary Int Educ fel, 1977; instr, Aim Shams Univ, 1974; consult, Nat Inst Child Health & Develop. **Memberships:** Am Soc Biochemists & Molecular Biologists; Sigma Xi. **Research Statement & Publications:** Synthesis and metabolism of S-Adenosylmethonine; biochemical regulation of T lymphocyte differentiation; mechanism of pathogenesis of poststreptococcal autoimmune diseases; role of superantigenesis autoimmunity. **Mailing Address:** Dept Surg & Microbiol Univ Tenn, 956 Court Ave A-210, Memphis, TN 38163-2127. **Fax:** 901-448-7208. **E-Mail:** mkotb@utmem.edu

KOTCH, ALEX, SCIENCE & ACADEMIC ADMINISTRATION. **Personal Data:** b Edwardsville, Pa, August 18, 1926. **Education:** Pa State Col, BS, 1946, MS, 1947; Univ Ill, PhD (org chem), 1950. **Honors & Awards:** Evan Pugh Scholar, Pa State Col, 1946. **Professional Experience:** RETIRED; emer prof chem, Off Res & Develop, Univ NDak, 1991-2002; mem exec comt bd dir, Assoc Western Univ, 1988-1991; comnr-at-large, NCent Asn Cols & Schs, 1984-1988; prof & dir, Off Res & Develop, Univ NDak, 1982-1991; bd dir, Assoc Western Univ, 1982-1991; prog mgr, Univ Res & Storage Progs, 1981-1982; br chief, Acad & Univ Progs, 1978-1981; spec asst to dir, educ & int progs, Solar Energy Res Inst, 1978-1979; asst dir info, educ & int progs, Solar Energy Res Inst, 1977-1978; Consult-exam, NCent Asn Cols & Schs, 1969-1991; prof chem & assoc chmn dept, Univ Wis-Madison, 1967-1977; staff assoc, Sci Develop Eval Group, Div Instnl Progs, Nat Sci Found, 1966-1967; chief biosci div, Off Saline Water, US Dept Interior, 1965-1966; prog dir org chem, NSF, 1963-1965; assoc prog dir chem, NSF, 1959-1963; Org Chem Dept, Jackson Lab, 1954-1959; res chemist, Cent Res Dept, Exp Sta, E I du Pont de Nemours & Co, 1952-1954; Little fel, Mass Inst Tech, 1951-1952; Fulbright fel, Delft Tech Univ, 1950-1951; Asst org chem, Pa State Col, 1946-1947 & Univ Ill, 1947-1949. **Memberships:** Am Chem Soc. **Research Statement & Publications:** Synthetic organic chemistry; polymers; heterocyclics; fluorescent whitening agents; dyes; science research and academic administration. **Mailing Address:** 3030 Eldridge St, Golden, CO 80401-1407.

KOTCHOUBEY, ANDREW, COMPUTER SCIENCE, APPLIED MATHEMATICS. **Personal Data:** b Florence, Italy, March 31, 1938; American citizen; m 1968, c 5. **Education:** Stevens Inst Technol, ME, 1959; Columbia Univ, MA, 1961, PhD (appl math), 1966. **Professional Experience:** MGR, TRAIN SMITH COUNSEL, INC, 1983-; vpres, Automatech Graphics Corp, 1973-1983; pres, subsidiary I/W Data Systs, Inc, 1971-1973; dir info systs, Interway Corp, 1969-1971; adj asst prof, Columbia Univ, 1968-1969; Assoc grad facs math, Columbia Univ, 1967-1968; sr staff mem appl math & comput, Watson Lab, 1966-1969; res asst appl math, Watson Lab, 1962-1966; Supvr comput installation, Watson Sci Comput Lab, IBM Corp, 1960-1962. **Memberships:** AAAS; Asn Comput Mach; Sigma Xi; Soc Indust & Appl Math. **Research Statement & Publications:** Calculations in atomic and molecular physics; mathematical physics; numerical analysis. **Mailing Address:** 50 E 96th St, New York, NY 10128.

KOTCON, JAMES BERNARD, NEMATOLOGY, ENVIRONMENTAL IMPACTS OF PESTICIDES. **Personal Data:** b Neillsville, Wis, November 24, 1954; m Candice; c Sarah B & Rebekah J. **Education:** Univ Wis-Stevens Points, BS, 1976; Mich State Univ, MS, 1979; Univ Wis-Madison, PhD (plant path), 1983. **Professional Experience:** ASSOC PROF PLANT PATH, WVA UNIV, as of 2004; assoc ed, J Nematol, 1988-1989 & 1992-1993; prin investr several grants, beginning 1986; asst prof plant path, Wva Univ beginning 1985; res assoc, Cornell Univ, 1983-1985; chair, Ecol Comt, Soc Nematologists, beginning 1978; chair, Nematol Comt, Am Phytopath Soc, beginning 1978. **Memberships:** AAAS; Am Phytopath Soc; Ecol Soc Am; Orgn Nematologists Trop Am; Soc Nematologist; Union Concerned Scientists. **Research Statement & Publications:** Nematode ecology, population dynamics, yield loss and control; efficacy of pesticides and environmental impacts to groundwater and nontarget organisms; biologic control, integrated pest management and sustainable agriculture. **Mailing Address:** RR 12 PO Box 400, Morgantown, WV 26505. **Fax:** 304-293-2872.

KOTELES, EMIL STEVE, PHYSICS. **Professional Experience:** STAFF, INST MICROSTRUCTURAL SCI, NATL RES COUN CAN, as of 2006. **Memberships:** Am Phys Soc. **Mailing Address:** Inst for Microstructural Sci, Natl Res Council of Canada Bldg 23A Montreal Rd, Ottawa, ON K1A 0R6, Can. **Fax:** 613-952-6337.

KOTHEIMER, WILLIAM CONRAD, ELECTRICAL ENGINEERING. **Personal Data:** b Louisville, Ky, May 26, 1925; m 1960, Anne Sheila Collins; c William Conrad II. **Education:** Univ Louisville, BEE, 1951. **Professional Experience:** TECH DIR, ABB POWER T&D CO, CORAL SPRINGS, FLA, 1991-; dir eng, Allentown, Pa, 1986-1991; construct engr, Kotheimer Assocs, Lansdowne, Pa, 1983-1986; Malvern, Pa, 1982-1983; construct engr, Gen Elec Co, Phila, 1980-1982; mgr develop eng, Gen Elec Co, Phila, 1965-1980; Sr engr, Gen Elec Co, Phila, 1951-1965. **Memberships:** Fel Inst Elec & Electronics Engrs; Nat Soc Prof Engrs. **Research Statement & Publications:** Author numerous articles; awarded patents in field. **Mailing Address:** 5900 NW 99th Ave, Coral Springs, FL 33706-2566.

KOTHMANN, MARGRET F, MATHEMATICS. **Education:** Pa State Univ, PhD, 1977. **Professional Experience:** STAFF, UNIV WIS-STOUT, as of 2005. **Mailing Address:** Math Dept, Univ Wis-Stout, Menomonie, WI 54751. **Fax:** 715-232-1699.

KOTHMANN, MERWYN MORTIMER, RANGE SCIENCE, RANGE MANAGEMENT. **Personal Data:** b Castell, Tex, January 30, 1940. **Education:** Tex A&M Univ, BS, 1961, PhD (range sci), 1968; Utah State Univ, MS, 1963. **Professional Experience:** PROF RANGE SCI, TEX A&M UNIV, 1979-; from asst prof to assoc prof range mgt, Tex Agr Exp Sta, 1967-1979; res asst range nutrit, Tex A&M Univ, 1964-1967; res asst range nutrit, Utah State Univ, 1961-1964. **Memberships:** Soc Range Mgt; Am Soc Animal Sci; Am Forage & Grassland Coun. **Research Statement & Publications:** Simulation of natural vegetation and livestock responses to various grazing management systems; nutrition of range livestock and botanical and chemical characteristics of diets of grazing animals. **Mailing Address:** Dept Rangeland Ecol & Mgt, Tex A&M Univ, College Station, TX 77843-2126. **Fax:** 979-845-6430. **E-Mail:** m-kothmann@tamu.edu

KOTHNY, EVALDO LUIS, AIR POLLUTION. **Personal Data:** b Buenos Aires, Arg, October 6, 1925; American citizen; m 1960, Monica; c Cecilia (Person) & Lilian (McGlothlen). **Education:** Univ Buenos Aires, MS, 1955, PhD (chem), 1964. **Professional Experience:** RETIRED; chmn, Intersoc Comt, Am Pub Health Asn, 1971-1974; mem, Sub Comt No 3, 1971-1974, 1976-1979; mem, Intersoc Comt, Am Pub Health Asn, 1966-1986; mem Sub Comt No 3, 1966-1986; res chemist, Calif Dept Health Serv, 1964-1991; sr specialist, Gen Elec, Argentina, 1961-1964; asst specialist qual control, Monsanto, Argentina, 1960-1961; asst anal instrumentation, Univ Buenos Aires, 1957-1960 & 1961-1963; res chemist, Buenos Aires, 1956-1957; plant chemist, Coplan Br, US Rubber Co, Argentina, 1955-1956. **Memberships:** Am Chem Soc; Asn Explor Geochem. **Research Statement & Publications:** Industrial inorganic preparative chemistry; trace inorganic analysis; geochemistry; environmental chemistry; geochemistry of noble metals; nitrogen oxides analysis; geochemical cycle of mercury; platinum and palladium in the environment; exploration of noble metals; biogeochemistry of palladium. **Mailing Address:** 3016 Stinson Circle, Walnut Creek, CA 94598-3621.

KOTHS, JAY SANFORD, FLORICULTURE. **Personal Data:** b Taylor, Mich, July 22, 1926; m 1947, Margaret Edwards; c Kirston, Gwen & Kim. **Education:** Mich State Univ, BS, 1948; Purdue Univ, MS, 1950; Univ Mass, PhD, 1967. **Honors & Awards:** Extension Award A&A Fel, Am Soc Hort Sci. **Professional Experience:** PROF EMER PLANT SCI, UNIV CONN, 1987-; prof, Univ Conn, 1955-1986; gen mgr, A Weiler Greenhouse, Wis, 1954-1955; asst greenhouse mgr, A Washburn & Sons, Ill, 1953-1954; greenhouse mgr, Kemble-Smith Co, Iowa, 1950-1953; Instr floricult, Purdue Univ, 1948-1950; Consult greenhouse mgt. **Memberships:** Am Soc Agron; fel Am Soc Hort Sci; Soil Sci Soc Am; Int Soc Hort Sci; Am Hort Soc. **Research Statement & Publications:** Automation of greenhouse microclimate; greenhouse crop fertility control; biological control of soilborne diseases; pollution effects on soil nitrification. **Mailing Address:** Dept Plant Sci, Univ Conn, U-67, Storrs, CT 06269-4067.

KOTHS, KIRSTON EDWARD, PROTEIN ENGINEERING, PROTEIN CHEMISTRY OF PHARMACEUTICALS. **Personal Data:** b La Fayette, Ind, December 24, 1948; m 1985, Catherine. **Education:** Amherst Col, BA, 1971; Harvard Univ, PhD (biochem & molecular biol), 1979. **Professional Experience:** DIR BIOL THER RES, CHIRON CORP, 1991-; sr dir res, Cetus Corp, 1989-1991; sr scientist & dir protein chem, Cetus Corp, 1984-1991; mgr protein chem, Cetus Corp, 1982-1984; scientist, Cetus Corp, 1979-1984. **Memberships:** AAAS. **Research Statement & Publications:** Characterization of rare human proteins with therapeutic potential; development of cloned human proteins for clinical use; protein engineering; lectin-binding proteins; prohormone convertase inhibition; apoptosis; protease inhibitor screens. **Mailing Address:** Chiron Corp, 4560 Horton St, Emeryville, CA 94608-2916. **Fax:** 510-923-4115. **E-Mail:** kirston_koths@cc.chiron.com

KOTICK, MICHAEL PAUL, RECOMBINANT DNA, MEDICINAL CHEMISTRY. **Personal Data:** b Buffalo, NY, December 28, 1940; m 1965, c 2. **Education:** State Univ NY Buffalo, BS, 1962, PhD (med chem), 1968; Ind Univ, MS, BBA, 1981. **Professional Experience:** MGR, PROPRIETARY SERV, MILES PHARMACEUT DIV, MILES LABS, 1990-; supvr, recombinant DNA & prin staff scientist, Food Ingredients Div, 1988-1990; prin res scientist, biotechnol group, 1981-1988; sr res scientist, Chem Dept, 1975-1981; res scientist, Molecular Biol Dept, Miles Labs, 1969-1975; fel org chem, Walker Labs, Sloan-Kettering Inst Cancer Res, 1968-1969; res asst med chem, Sch Pharm, State Univ NY Buffalo, 1963-1968. **Memberships:** AAAS; Am Chem Soc. **Research Statement & Publications:** Chemistry of oligonucleotides, nucleosides, carbohydrates, narcotic drugs; medicinal chemistry; recombinant DNA technology; microbiology, molecular biology; research and resource management. **Mailing Address:** Miles Labs, Trumbull, CT 06611.

KOTIDIS, PETROS, ENGINEERING. **Professional Experience:** VPRES, BUS DEVELOP, AXSUN TECHNOLOGIES INC, as of 2004. **Mailing Address:** Axsun Technologies Inc, One Fortune Dr, Billerica, MA 01821. **Fax:** 978-262-0035.

KOTILA, PAUL MYRON, AQUATIC ECOLOGY, ENTOMOLOGY. **Personal Data:** b Hancock, Mich, October 14, 1950. **Education:** Mich Technol Univ, BS, 1972, MS, 1974; Univ Wis-Madison, PhD (entom), 1978. **Professional Experience:** PROF BIOL & ENVIRON SCI, FRANKLIN PIERCE COL, as of 2004; ACTG DEAN, ACAD AFFAIRS, DEPT BIOL & ENVIRON SCI, FRANKLIN PIERCE COL, as of 2002; FOUND, ENVIRON SCI PROG, FRANKLIN PIERCE COL, as of 2002; assoc prof biol, Franklin Pierce Col, beginning 1988; asst prof environ studies, St Lawrence Univ, 1986-1988; asst prof biol, Allegheny Col, 1978-. **Memberships:** AAAS; Am Fisheries Soc; Entom Soc Am; NAm Benthological Soc; Sigma Xi. **Research Statement & Publications:** Effects of impoundments, toxicants and other disturbances on stream insects; ecology of aquatic invertebrates. **Mailing Address:** Dept Biol & Environ Sci, Franklin Pierce Col, 105 Marcucella Hall 20 Col Rd, Rindge, NH 03461-0060. **Fax:** 603-899-6448. **E-Mail:** kotilapm@fpc.edu

KOTIN, PAUL, PATHOLOGY. **Personal Data:** b Chicago, Ill, August 13, 1916; m 1970, Pauline Stephan; c Joel & David. **Education:** Univ Ill, BS, 1937, MD, 1940; Am Bd Path, dipl, 1953. **Honors & Awards:** Sappington lectr, Am Occup Med Asn, 1980, Knudsen Award, 1981; Gehrmann lectr, Am Acad Occup Med, Nashville, 1981. **Professional Experience:** CONSULT PATHOLOGIST, 1981-; sr vpres health, safety & environ, Johns-Manville Corp, 1974-1981; prof path, vpres health sci & dean, Sch Med, Temple Univ, 1971-1974; dir, Inst, 1969-1971; dir, Div Environ Health Sci, Nat Inst Environ Health Sci, 1966-1969; sci dir etiology, Carcinogenesis Studies Br, Nat Cancer Inst, 1964-1966; chief, Carcinogenesis Studies Br, Nat Cancer Inst, 1962-1963; From instr to prof path, Paul Peirce prof, 1960-1962; Res fel path, NSF sr fel, 1959-1960; attend staff pathologist, Los Angeles Co Gen Hosp, 1951-1962; From instr to prof path, Univ Southern Calif, 1951-1960; med microbiologist, Los Angeles Co Gen Hosp, 1950-1951; Res fel path, Sch Med, Univ Southern Calif, 1949-1950. **Memberships:** Am Asn Cancer Res; Am Asn Pathologists & Bacteriologists; fel Col Am Pathologists; Sigma Xi; AAAS. **Research Statement & Publications:** Mechanisms of carcinogenesis; experimental cancer production; environmental factors in cancer; air pollution; teratogenesis. **Mailing Address:** 2304 E Sausalito Trail, Tucson, AZ 85737.

KOTLARSKI, IGNACY ICCHAK, MATHEMATICS. **Personal Data:** b Warsaw, Poland, July 29, 1923; American citizen. **Education:** Univ Warsaw, MA, 1952; Wroclaw Univ, PhD (math), 1961; Warsaw Tech Univ, Docent, 1967. **Professional Experience:** PROF EMER MATH & STATIST, OKLA STATE UNIV, as of 1998; prof math & statist, Okla State Univ, beginning 1969; vis prof, Rome Univ, 1968-1969 & Univ Md, College Park, 1969; lectr math, Warsaw Tech Univ, 1954-1968; lectr math, Army Tech Acad, Warsaw, 1953-1959; asst sampling inspection, Math Inst, Polish Acad Sci, 1953-1954; Mem staff sampling inspection, Polish Stand Comt, 1950-1953; Lectr math & statist, Planning & Statist Acad, Warsaw, 1950-1953. **Memberships:** Inst Math Statist. **Research Statement & Publications:** Characterization problems in probability; mathematical modeling. **Mailing Address:** Dept Math, Okla State Univ, Stillwater, OK 74074.

KOTLER, DONALD P, GASTROENTEROLOGY, CLINICAL NUTRITION, CLINICAL IMMUNOLOGY. **Personal Data:** b NewBrunswick, NJ, September 30, 1947; m 1973, Barbara; c Dana (Helice) & Aaron. **Education:** Rutgers Univ, BS, 1969; Albert Einstein Col Med, MD, 1973. **Honors & Awards:** Dsintinguished Alumnus, Albert Einstein College of Medicine 2006. **Professional Experience:** PROF MED, COL PHYSICIANS & SURGEONS, COLUMBIA UNIV, as of 2004; CHIEF, DIV GASTROENTEROL& LIVER DIS, ST LUKE'S-ROOSEVELT HOSP, as of 2004; VPRES, AIDS COMMUNITY RES INITIATIVE AM, as of 2004; Senior attending physician, St Lukes Roosevelt Hosp Ctr, 1979-; assoc prof Columbia Col 1987-1998; asst prof, Columbia Col, 1979-1987; asst prof med, Univ Pa, 1978-1979; fel gastroenterol, Hosp Univ Pa, 1976-1978; House officer internal med, Bronx Munic Hosp Ctr, 1973-1976. **Memberships:** AAAS; NY Acad Sci; Am Gastroenterol Asn; Int AIDS Soc; MIV Medical Association. **Research Statement & Publications:** Currently engaged in research to define, describe and control the gastrointestinal and nutritional complications of the acquired immunodeficiency syndrome. **Mailing Address:** St Lukes Roosevelt Hosp Ctr, 1111 Amsterdam Ave, New York, NY 10025-1708. **Fax:** 212-523-3678. **E-Mail:** dpkotler@aol.com

KOTLIAR, ABRAHAM MORRIS, PHYSICAL CHEMISTRY, POLYMER PHYSICS. **Personal Data:** b Brooklyn, NY, October 8, 1926; m 1955, c 4. **Education:** Adelphi Col, BA, 1949; Polytech Inst Brooklyn, PhD (chem), 1955. **Professional Experience:** ASSOC PROF, UNIV GA, 1988-; sr res assoc, Allied Chem Corp, 1969-1988; sr scientist, Allied Chem Corp, 1966-1969; group leader, Allied Chem Corp, 1964-1966; chemist polymer physics, Esso Res & Eng Co, 1960-1964; chemist radiation effects, US Naval Res Lab, 1956-1960; res assoc & fel chem, Duke Univ, 1955-1956. **Memberships:** Am Chem Soc; Am Phys Soc; Soc Rheology; Sigma Xi. **Research Statement & Publications:** Solution properties; molecular weight distributions; random processes; rheology and mechanical properties of plastics. **Mailing Address:** Ga Tech, Univ GA, Atlanta, GA 30332.

KOTLIAR, GABRIEL, CONDENSED MATTER THEORY. **Personal Data:** b February 26, 1957. **Education:** Hebrew Univ, BS, 1979, MS, 1980; Princeton Univ, PhD (physics), 1983. **Honors & Awards:** Grad Sch-New Brunswick Teaching Award, Rutgers Univ, 2002. **Professional Experience:** BD GOV PROF PHYSICS, RUTGERS UNIV, 2004-; John Simon Guggenheim Mem Found fel, 2003-2004; PROF II, DEPT PHYSICS & ASTRON, RUTGERS UNIV, 1996-; assoc ed, Phys Rev Lett, 1996-1997; Lady Davies fel, Hebrew Univ, 1994-1995; prof I, Dept Physics & Astron, Rutgers Univ, 1992-1996; consult, Los Alamos Nat Lab, 1991-1998; consult, AT&T Labs, 1988-1997; assoc prof, Rutgers Univ, 1988-1992; Presidential Young Investr Award, NSF, 1987-1992; Alfred P Sloan res fel, 1986-1988; asst prof, Mass Inst Technol, 1985-1988; postdoctoral fel, Inst Theoret Physics, Univ Calif, Santa Barbara, 1983-1985. **Memberships:** Fel Am Phys Soc. **Mailing Address:** Dept Physics & Astron, Serins Physics Lab, Rutgers Univ, Piscataway, NJ 08855-0849. **Fax:** 732-445-4400; 732-445-4343. **E-Mail:** kotliar@physics.rutgers.edu

KOTLYAKOV, VLADIMIR MICHAILOVICH, GEOGRAPHY, GLACIOLOGY. **Personal Data:** b Lobnya, Russia, November 6, 1931; m 1962, Valentina Bazanova; c Michail & Andrei. **Education:** Inst Geog, Russia, PhD (sci), 1967. **Honors & Awards:** Litke Gold Medal, Russian Geog Soc, 1985, Przhevalski Gold Medal, 1996. **Professional Experience:** Academician, Russian Acad Sci, 1991; people's dep, USSR Supreme Court, Moscow, 1989-1991; sci comt mem, Geosphere Biosphere Prog, Stockholm Int, 1987-1993; pres, Int Comn Snow & Ice, 1987-1991; World Atlas Snow & Ice Resources, 1976-& Izvestiya Acad Nauk, 1986-; DIR, INST GEOG, USSR ACAD SCI, 1986-; prof, Inst Geog, USSR Acad Sci, Moscow, 1971; head dept, Inst Geog, USSR Acad Sci, Moscow, 1968-1986; Ed, Data Glaciological Studies, 1961-; Researcher, Inst Geog, USSR Acad Sci, Moscow, 1954-1968. **Memberships:** Fel Am Geog Soc; Int Geog Union (vpres, 1988-1996); Int Glaciol Soc; Int Asn Hydrol Sci (vpres, 1983-1987); Mex Geog Soc; Ital Geog Soc; Acad Sci USSR; Georgian Acad Sci. **Research Statement & Publications:** Contribution to the study of the earth's snow cover, glaciers and ice sheets as well as to the synthesis of socio-economic and natural resource information on Russia and the world as a whole. **Mailing Address:** Inst Geog Russ Acad Sci, Staromonetny St 29, Moscow 109017, Russia. **Fax:** 709-595-90033. **E-Mail:** geography@glas.azc.org

KOTORYNSKI, WALTER P, MATHEMATICS. **Education:** Univ Toronto, PhD. **Professional Experience:** RETIRED; assoc prof, math & statist, Univ Victoria. **Mailing Address:** Math Dept, Univ Victoria, Victoria, BC V8W 3P4, Can. **Fax:** 250-721-8962. **E-Mail:** wkotory@math.uvic.ca

KOTOVYCH, GEORGE, BIOPHYSICAL CHEMISTRY, NMR SPECTROSCOPY. **Personal Data:** b January 3, 1941; Canadian citizen; m 1974, Halyna; c 4. **Education:** Univ Man, BSc, 1963, MSc, 1964, PhD (phys chem), 1968. **Professional Experience:** PROF CHEM, UNIV ALTA, 1989-; from asst prof to assoc prof, Univ Alta, 1970-1989; Nat Res Coun Can fel bio-phys chem, Lawrence Radiation Lab, Univ Calif, Berkeley, 1968-1969. **Memberships:** Chem Inst Can; Am Chem Soc. **Research Statement & Publications:** Application of nuclear magnetic resonance techniques to the study of biological systems; structure and conformation of polypeptides, bradykinin agonists and antagonists, receptor-antagonist interactions; neuropeptides F, AF, orexins, proadrenomedullin. **Mailing Address:** Dept Chem, Univ Alta, Edmonton, AB T6G 2G2, Can. **Fax:** 780-492-8231. **E-Mail:** george.kotovych@ualberta.ca

KOTT, EDWARD, ZOOLOGY. **Personal Data:** b Toronto, Ont, March 25, 1939. **Education:** Univ Toronto, BA, 1960, PhD (ecol), 1965. **Professional Experience:** PROF BIOL, WILFRID LAURIER UNIV, 1986-; asst prof biol, Waterloo Lutheran Univ, 1969-1986; assoc scientist fisheries res, Bedford Inst Oceanog, 1965-1969; lectr zool, lakehead col, 1963-1965. **Memberships:** Am Soc Mammalogists; Soc Syst Zool. **Research Statement & Publications:** Mammalian and fish population ecology. **Mailing Address:** Dept Biol, Wilfrid Laurier Univ, N3021 H, Sci Bldg, Waterloo, ON N2L 3C5, Can. **Fax:** 519-746-0677. **E-Mail:** ekott@wlu.ca

KOTTAS, JAMES ALAN, NEUTRAL NETWORKS & ADAPTIVE SYSTEMS, IMAGE PROCESSING & PATTERN RECOGNITION. **Personal Data:** b Buffalo, NY, February 8, 1961; m 1992, Cynthia; c Joel. **Education:** Carnegie-Mellon Univ, BS, 1983; Mass Inst Technol, SM, 1986, PhD (elec eng), 1991. **Professional Experience:** CHIEF SCIENTIST, MIROS INC, 1994-; res scientist, Symbus Technol Inc, 1991-1994; consult electronics, robotics & software, 1988-. **Memberships:** Sigma Xi; Inst Elec & Electronics Engrs; Int Neural Network Soc. **Research Statement & Publications:** Application of adaptive systems to intelligent pattern recognition; coinventor of the Trueface face recognition system and its associated family of products. **Mailing Address:** Miros Inc, 572 Wash St Ste 18, Wellesley, MA 02181. **Fax:** 781-235-0720. **E-Mail:** jimk@miros.com

KOTTAYIL, SANTOSH GEORGE, DRUG MANUFACTURING DEVELOPMENT, MEDICINAL CHEMISTRY. **Personal Data:** b Kerala, India, April 18, 1963; American citizen; m 1993, Anita George. **Education:** Univ Poona, BSc, 1983, MSc, 1985; Univ Ky, PhD (org chem), 1993. **Professional Experience:** DIR, PROD DEVELOP, UNIMED PHARMACEUT INC, as of 2004; MGR PHARMACEUT DEVELOP, UNIMED PHARMACEUT INC, 1993-; sr scientist, Oramed, 1992-1993; Res intern, Dupont Merck, 1991. **Memberships:** Am Chem Soc. **Research Statement & Publications:** Synthesis of novel and improved chemical entities for the efficient treatment of pain; chemical characterization, evaluation for pharmacological activity and study of the mechanism of action in animals and humans. **Mailing Address:** Unimed Pharmaceut Inc, 2150 E Lake Cook Rd, Buffalo Grove, IL 60089.

KOTTCAMP, EDWARD H, JR, METALLURGY & PHYSICAL METALLURGICAL ENGINEERING. **Personal Data:** b York, Pa, July 12, 1934; c 3. **Education:** Lehigh Univ, BS, 1956, MS, 1957, PhD (metall eng & mat sci), 1960. **Honors & Awards:** William Sparagan Award for Outstanding Res, 1973; William Eisenman Award, Am Soc Metals, 1988. **Professional Experience:** Chief exec officer, Newcomen Soc, beginning 1997; DIR, ELECTRON ENERGY CORP, 1995-; pres, ASM Int, 1992-1993; group vpres, SPS Technols, Inc, beginning 1987; exec vpres, Bethlehem Steel Corp, 1986-1987; sr vpres, Bethlehem Steel Corp, 1985-1986; Vpres res, Bethlehem Steel Corp, 1982-1985; prof, Lehigh Univ Col Eng. **Memberships:** Fel Am Soc Metals; Indust Res Inst; Am Iron & Steel Inst; Welding Res Coun. **Research Statement & Publications:** Cold extrusion of steels; pressure vessel design; research management and innovation; high-strength steels; pressure vessels; microstructure; fracutre; metal forming; author of numerous technical articles. **Mailing Address:** Electron Energy Corp, 924 Links Ave, Landisville, PA 17538. **Fax:** 717-898-0660.

KOTTER, FRED RALPH, ELECTRICAL MEASUREMENTS, HIGH VOLTAGE PHENOMENA. **Personal Data:** b Salt Lake City, Utah, December 8, 1915; m 1949, Lora; c Loralee, Wade, Nola, Shauna & Virginia. **Education:** Univ Utah, BSc, 1937; George Wash Univ, AM, 1940; Mass Inst Technol, ScD, 1955. **Professional Experience:** RETIRED; consult, beginning 1982; from instr to asst prof elec eng, Mass Inst Technol, 1947-1954; physicist, Nat Bur Stand, 1937-1947 & 1955-1981. **Memberships:** Inst Elec & Electronics Engrs. **Research Statement & Publications:** Precise electrical measurements; high voltage measurements. **Mailing Address:** 12921 Crisfield Rd, Silver Spring, MD 20906.

KOTTKE, BRUCE ALLEN, EXPERIMENTAL PATHOLOGY, INTERNAL MEDICINE. **Personal Data:** b Blue Earth, Minn, January 22, 1929; m 1979, c 2. **Education:** Hamline Univ, BS, 1951; Univ Minn, Minneapolis, MD, 1954, PhD, 1962. **Professional Experience:** PROF EMER MED, MAYO GRAD SCH MED, UNIV MINN, as of 2004; CONSULT, WATSON CLIN, LAKELAND, FLA, as of 2004; prof med, mayo grad sch med, Univ Minn, beginning 1976; from asst prof to assoc prof med, Mayo Found & Clin, 1962-1976; Consult, Mayo Found & Clin, 1962-1971; Fel int med, Mayo Found, 1957-1961. **Memberships:** Am Heart Asn; Am Fedn Clin Res; Sigma Xi Coun Arteriosclerosis Coun Thrombosis Fel Coun Circulation. **Research Statement & Publications:** Atherosclerosis; cholesterol metabolism; bile acid metabolism. **Mailing Address:** Mayo Clin, Rochester, MN 55905.

KOTTKE, FREDERIC JAMES, PHYSICAL MEDICINE & REHABILITATION. **Personal Data:** b Hayfield, Minn, May 26, 1917; m 1939, c 3. **Education:** Univ Minn, BS & MS, 1941, PhD (physiol), 1944, MD, 1945; Am Bd Phys Med & Rehab, dipl, 1949. **Honors & Awards:** Frank H Krusen Award, Am Acad Phys Med & Rehab, 1979; Sidney Licht lectr, Univ Pa, 1979 & Ohio State Univ, 1981; Lewis Leavitt Mem lectr, Baylor Univ Med Sch, 82. **Professional Experience:** PROF EMER PHYS MED & REHAB, UNIV MINN, MINNEAPOLIS, as of 2004; prof phys med & rehab, Univ Minn, Minneapolis, beginning 1986; Med Adv Comt, Social & Rehab Serv, 1968-1969 & Coun Cerebrovasc Dis & Coun Clin Cardiol, Am Heart Asn, 1970-1983; chmn, Am Bd Phys Med & Rehab, 1964-1970; mem, Minn State Bd Health, 1964-1967; secy & mem bd dirs & mem expert med comt, Am Rehab Found, 1964; mem Med Res Study Sect, Voc Rehab Admin, 1961-1963; mem med adv comt, Off Voc Rehab, 1960-1967; mem exec comt, prog chmn & vpres, Int Cong Phys Med, 1960; mem, Minn Gov Adv Comt Voc Rehab, 1956-1960; consult, Minneapolis Vet Admin Hosp, 1956; mem, Am Bd Phys Med & Rehab, 1955-1970; head dept, Univ Minn, Minneapolis, 1952-1982; dir div, Univ Minn, Minneapolis, 1949-1952; from asst prof to prof, Univ Minn, Minneapolis, 1947-1986; Baruch fel phys med, Univ Minn, Minneapolis, 1946-1947; Asst physiol, Univ Minn, 1941-1944. **Memberships:** Fel AMA; fel Am Cong Phys Med & Rehab (vpres 1954-1958 pres elect 1958-1959 pres 1959-1960); Am Acad Phys Med & Rehab (pres-elect 1977 pres 1978); Int Soc Rehab Disabled; hon mem Columbian Soc Phys Med & Rehab; hon mem Mex Acad Surg; hon mem Brazilian Acad Rehab Med; hon mem Venezuelan Soc Phys Med & Rehab; hon mem Neth Soc Phys Med & Rehab. **Research Statement & Publications:** Circulation; neuromuscular diseases; poliomyelitis; rehabilitation; work of the heart. **Mailing Address:** 2741 Drew Ave S, Minneapolis, MN 55416. **E-Mail:** kottk001@umn.edu

KOTTMAN, CLIFFORD ALFONS, MATHEMATICS. **Personal Data:** b San Diego, Calif, August 3, 1942; m 1966, c 3. **Education:** Loyola Univ, Los Angeles, BS, 1964; Univ Iowa, MS, 1966, PhD (math), 1969. **Professional Experience:** VPRES & CHIEF SCIENTIST, OPEN GIS CONSORTIUM, as of 2003; exec mgr, Iner Graph Corp, beginning 1990; mathematician, Defense Mapping Agency, 1977-1990; assoc prof, Ore State Univ, 1975-1977; asst prof math, Ore State Univ, 1970-1975; asst prof math, La State Univ, 1969-1970; consult non-destructive testing. **Memberships:** AAAS; Am Math Soc; Math Asn Am; Am Soc Photogram. **Research Statement & Publications:** Functional analysis; Banach spaces; photogrammetry. **Mailing Address:** Open GIS Consortium, 6614 Rockland Dr, Clifton, VA 20124-2414. **Fax:** 703-830-7096. **E-Mail:** ckottman@opengis.org

KOTTMEIER, PETER KLAUS, SURGERY. **Personal Data:** b Munich, Ger, February 1, 1928; m 1956, c 4. **Education:** Univ Munich, MD, 1951, Ohio State Univ, MMSc, 1960. **Professional Experience:** PROF SURG, STATE UNIV NY DOWNSTATE MED CTR, 1970-; DIR PEDIAT SURG SERV, UNIV HOSP, 1967-; from asst prof to assoc prof, Kings County Hosp, Brooklyn, 1967-1970; DIR PEDIAT SURG SERV, KINGS COUNTY HOSP, BROOKLYN, 1962-; instr, Ohio State Univ, 1960-1961; Asst instr surg, State Univ NY Downstate Med Ctr, 1957-1960. **Memberships:** Fel Am Acad Pediat; fel Am Col Surgeons; fel Am Pediat Surg Asn. **Research Statement & Publications:** Pediatric surgery. **Mailing Address:** 450 Clarkson Ave, Brooklyn, NY 11203-2012.

KOTULA, ANTHONY W, FOOD SCIENCE. **Personal Data:** b Holyoke, Mass, June 12, 1929; m 1957, Joan; c Kathryn & Valerie. **Education:** Univ Mass, BS, 1951, MS, 1954; Univ Md, PhD (food sci), 1964. **Honors & Awards:** Res Award, Poultry Sci Res Asn, 1967; Signal Serv Award, Am Meat Sci Asn, 1983, Distinguished Res Award; Meat Res Award, Am Soc Animal Sci, 1988. **Professional Experience:** RETIRED; prof residence, Univ Conn, beginning 1992; supvry res food technologists & chief, Meat Sci Res Lab, USDA, 1971-1992; invests leader, Animal Sci Inst, Agr Res Serv, USDA, 1967-1971; proj leader, Animal Sci Inst, Agr Res Serv, USDA, 1954-1967. **Memberships:** Poultry Sci Asn; Inst Food Technologists; World Poultry Sci Asn; Am Meat Sci Asn; fel Am Soc Animal Sci; Sigma Xi. **Research Statement & Publications:** Maintaining and improving quality of animal products; food safety. **Mailing Address:** 135 Maple Rd, Storrs, CT 06268.

KOTVAL, PESHO SOHRAB, MEDICAL ENGINEERING, MANAGEMENT SCIENCE. **Personal Data:** b Nagpur, India, August 31, 1942; American citizen; m 1965, c 2. **Education:** Univ Nagpur, BSc, 1960; Univ Sheffield, MMet, 1962, PhD (phys metall), 1965; Pace Univ, MBA, 1977; NY Med Col, MD, 1983; Nat Bd Med Examr, dipl, 1984; Am Bd Radiol, dipl, 1987. **Honors & Awards:** Coatings Award, Am Soc Metals, 1973. **Professional Experience:** ASSOC PROF SURG, NY MED COL, 1990-; ASSOC PROF RADIOL, NY MED COL, 1987-; res physician radiol, NY Med Col, 1983-1987; res mgr mat sci, Med Prod div, 1978-1980; adj prof mgt econ, Pace Univ, 1977-; sr group leader metals & ceramics, Corp res lab, Union Carbide Corp, 1971-1978; vis scientist metall, res inst Advan Studies, 1970-1971; adj prof physics, Ind Univ, 1967-1968; Scientist, res assoc & mgr superally metall, Stellite div, Union Carbide Corp, 1966-1970; fel, Sheffield Univ, 1965-1966. **Memberships:** Fel Am Soc Metals; Brit Inst Metallurgists; AMA; Radiol Soc NAm; Am Inst Ultrasound Med. **Research Statement & Publications:** Superalloys for high temperature gas turbines and corrosion resistance; powder metallurgy; crystal growth; process development; low cost solar cells; medical instruments; blood flow technology. **Mailing Address:** 280 Dobbs Ferry Rd Ste 103, White Plains, NY 10607-1910.

KOTVIS, PETER VAN DYKE, EXTREME PRESSURE TRIBOLOGY OF METALS, LUBRICANT APPLICATIONS & THEIR THERMODYNAMICS. **Education:** Univ Wis, BS, 1969, MS, 1971, PhD (surface phys chem), 1991. **Professional Experience:** RES DIR, BENZ OIL, INC, 1979-; res chemist, Vet Admin Med Ctr, 1975-1979; Instr, Univ Wis, 1971-1975. **Research Statement & Publications:** Application of thermodynamics, metallurgy, etc. to establish fundamental understanding of tribology, especially involving metals and lubricants. **Mailing Address:** Benz Oil Inc, 2724 W Hampton Ave, Milwaukee, WI 53209. **Fax:** 414-442-5244. **E-Mail:** pkotvis@benz.com

KOTYK, MICHAEL, METALLURGY, CERAMICS. **Personal Data:** b Ford City, Pa, March 10, 1929; m 1952, c 5. **Education:** Pa State Univ, BS, 1954, MS, 1956; NC State Univ, PhD (metall, ceramics), 1968. **Professional Experience:** RETIRED; technol coordr, prod technol, 1984-1992; div mgr tech serv, Basic Res Div, 1984-1992; div chief, Basic Res Div, 1982-1984; div chief sheet prod res, Appl Res Lab, US Steel Corp, 1973-1982; sect supvr, Appl Res Lab, US Steel Corp, 1968-1973; assoc dir metall & ceramics div, US Army Res Off, 1963-1968; sr technologist, US Steel Corp, 1956-1963; Instr metall, Pa State Univ, 1954-1956. **Memberships:** Am Soc Metals; Am Inst Mining, Metall & Petrol Engrs; fel Am Chem Soc; Iron & Steel Inst Japan. **Research Statement & Publications:** Formability of sheet steels; gases in metals; physical and mechanical properties of ferrous alloys; phase equilibria studies; productions sheet steel products. **Mailing Address:** 1017 Edgewood Rd, New Kensington, PA 15068.

KOTZ, ARTHUR RUDOLPH, SOLID STATE ELECTRONICS. **Personal Data:** b Eau Claire, Wis, February 21, 1933; m 1955, c 3. **Education:** Univ Minn, BA, 1955; Univ Wis, MS, 1962, PhD (solid state physics), 1966. **Professional Experience:** CORP SCIENTIST, 3M CO, 1973-; mgr electronic imaging group, 3M Co, 1970-1973; sr res specialist, 3M Co, 1968-1970; res specialist, 3M Co, 1966-1968; proj leader, 3M Co, 1960-1961; supvr phys res, 3M Co, 1958-1960; sr physicist, 3M Co, 1957-1958; Jr physicist, 3M Co, 1955-1957. **Memberships:** Am Phys Soc; Soc Photog Sci & Eng. **Research Statement & Publications:** Electrical transport properties of organic semiconductors; electron beam recording; gas discharge devices; photoeffects in solids, including photoconductivity, photovoltaic effect and photoemission; electrophotography; electronic imaging; electrography; reprography; electronic printing. **Mailing Address:** 5826 S Hobe Lane, St Paul, MN 55110.

KOTZ, JOHN CARL, INORGANIC & ORGANOMETALLIC CHEMISTRY, CHEMICAL EDUCATION. **Personal Data:** b Massillon, Ohio, June 27, 1937; m 1961, c 2. **Education:** Wash & Lee Univ, BS, 1959; Cornell Univ, PhD (inorg chem), 1964. **Honors & Awards:** Catalyst Award Chem Educ, Chem Mfr Asn, 1992. **Professional Experience:** DISTINGUISHED TEACHING PROF EMER CHEM, STATE UNIV NY, COL ONEONTA, as of 2005; distinguished teaching prof, Dept Chem, State Univ Ny, Col Oneonta, beginning 1987; Fulbright lectr & res scholar, Portugal, 1979; prof chem, Dept Chem, State Univ NY, Col Oneonta, 1970-1987; asst prof, Kans State Univ, 1965-1970; NIH fel chem, Manchester Col Sci & Technol, Eng, 1963-1964 & Ind Univ, 1964-1965. **Memberships:** Am Chem Soc. **Research Statement & Publications:** Synthetic organometallic chemistry; electrochemistry of organometallic compounds. **Mailing Address:** State Univ NY Col, Dept Chem, Oneonta, NY 13820-1381. **Fax:** 607-436-2654. **E-Mail:** kotzjc@oneonta.edu

KOTZ, SAMUEL, MATHEMATICAL STATISTICS, APPLIED PROBABILITY. **Personal Data:** b Harbin, China, August 28, 1930; American citizen; m 1963, Rosalie Greenwald; c Tamara, Harold David & Pauline. **Education:** Hebrew Univ, Israel, MSc, 1956; Cornell Univ, PhD (math statist), 1960 Harbin inst of technol, Harbin 1987. **Honorary Degrees:** DSc, Univ Athens, Greece, 1995, Bowling Green State Univ, Ohio, 1997. **Honors & Awards:** Wolfowitz Prize, 1983. **Professional Experience:** Vist prof univ of Salford 2000; vis prof, Univ Copenhagen, 1996; Univ Lulea, Sweden, 1994 & 1995; distinguished prof, Bowling Green State Univ, 1992 & 1994; distinguished vis prof, Guelph Univ, 1986; PROF STATIST, UNIV MD, 1979-; distinguished vis prof, Bucknell Univ, 1977; prof math, Temple Univ, 1967-1979; assoc prof, Univ Toronto, 1964-1967; sr res fel indust eng, 1963-1964; res assoc, Inst Statist, Univ NC, 1962-1963; lectr, Bar-Ilan Univ, Israel, 1960-1962; Instr math, 1956-1958; co-ed Encycl Statist Sci; adv prof, Harbin Polytech Inst; Assoc ed, J Am Statist Asn. **Memberships:** Am Math Soc; fel Am Statist Asn; fel Inst Math Statist; Intern Statist Inst; fel Royal Statist Soc. **Research Statement & Publications:** Information theory; statistical distribution theory and methodology; scientific terminology; probabilistic models with special applications to business and engineering; history of statistics in 20th century; encyclopedia of statistical sciences 10 volumes. **Mailing Address:** 619 Kenbrook Dr, Silver Spring, MD 20962. **Fax:** 202-994-0245. **E-Mail:** kotz@seas.guru.edu

KOTZEBUE, KENNETH LEE, ELECTRICAL ENGINEERING. **Personal Data:** b San Antonio, Tex, December 4, 1933; m 1954, c 3. **Education:** Univ Tex, BS, 1954; Univ Calif, Los Angeles, MS, 1956; Stanford Univ, PhD (elec eng), 1959. **Professional Experience:** RETIRED; from assoc prof to prof elec eng, Univ Calif, Santa Barbara, 1964-1992; dept head solid state devices res & develop, Watkins-Johnson Co, 1963-1964; mem tech staff elec eng, Watkins-Johnson Co, 1959-1963; sr engr, Tex Instruments Inc, 1958-1959. **Memberships:** Inst Elec & Electronics Engrs. **Research Statement & Publications:** Microwave solid-state device electronics. **Mailing Address:** 4737 Woodview Dr, Santa Rosa, CA 95405.

KOUBA, DELORE LOREN, CHEMICAL ENGINEERING, ORGANIC CHEMISTRY. **Personal Data:** b Lincoln, Nebr, April 18, 1919; m 1971. **Education:** Univ Nebr, BSc, 1941. **Professional Experience:** RETIRED; sr res chemist, Res & Develop Res Ctr, Hercules Inc, Del, 1979-1982; res chemist, Res & Develop Res Ctr, Del, 1950-1978; explosives chemist, Res & Develop Res Ctr, Del, 1946-1950; anal chemist, Res & Develop Res Ctr, Del, 1943-1946; chief chemist, Smokeless Powder Plant, Hercules Inc, NJ, 1942-1943; lab supvr, Smokeless Powder Plant, Hercules Inc, NJ, 1942; anal chemist, Smokeless Powder Plant, Hercules, Inc, NJ, 1941-1942. **Memberships:** Am Chem Soc. **Research Statement & Publications:** Smokeless powder testing; high explosives; semi-plant nitration; oxidation of aromatic compounds and hazardous chemicals evaluation; synthetic lubricants. **Mailing Address:** 1808 Windermere Ave, Wilmington, DE 19804-4025.

KOUBA, DUANE A, MATHEMATICS. **Education:** Colo State Univ, PhD, 1982. **Professional Experience:** LECTR, DEPT MATHS, UNIV CALIF, as of 2006. **Mailing Address:** One Shields Ave, Dept Math, Univ Calif, Davis, CA 95616. **Fax:** 530-752-6635. **E-Mail:** kouba@math.ucdavis.edu

KOUBEK, EDWARD, INORGANIC CHEMISTRY. **Personal Data:** b Bayshore, NY, July 25, 1937; m 1963, c 2. **Education:** State Univ NY Albany, BS, 1959; Brown Univ, PhD (chem), 1964. **Professional Experience:** PROF EMER CHEM, US NAVAL ACAD, as of 2004; Dartmouth Col, 1981 & Univ Canterbury, NZ, 1991; prof chem, US Naval Acad, beginning 1975; vis prof, Stanford Univ, 1971; from asst prof to assoc prof, US Naval Acad, 1967-1975; fel, Bell Tel Labs, NJ, 1963-1964. **Memberships:** Am Chem Soc. **Research Statement & Publications:** Kinetics and mechanisms of inorganic reactions. **Mailing Address:** Dept Chem, US Naval Acad, Annapolis, MD 21402-1398. **E-Mail:** koubek@artic.nadn.navy.mil

KOUCKY, FRANK LOUIS, JR, MINERALOGY, GEOCHEMISTRY ARCHEOGEOLGY. **Personal Data:** b Chicago, Ill, June 24, 1927; m 1949, Virginia Ruhl; c Frank III, David, Walter & Jonathan. **Education:** UnivChicago, MS, 1953, PhD (geol), 1956. **Honors & Awards:** Bucher Award, 1967. **Professional Experience:** EMER PROF GEOL, COL WOOSTER, 1992-; fel Nat Endowment Humanities, 1987; res assoc, Mass Inst Technol, 1978 & 1983-; prof, Col Wooster, 1971-1992; Assoc, Danforth Found, 1968; From asst prof to assoc prof, Univ Cincinnati, 1960-1971; asst prof & dir field camp, Univ Ill, 1957-1971; from instr to asst prof, Mont Sch Mines, 1955-1957; Instr phys sci, Navy Pier, Univ Ill, 1951-1955. **Memberships:** Am Mineral Soc; Geol Soc Am; Am Schs Oriental Res; Geochem Soc; Clay Mineral Soc; Soc Econ Geologists; Sigma Xi. **Research Statement & Publications:** X-ray crystallography; sulfide and sulfosalt minerals; geology of Wyoming and Montana; Precambrian geology; ancient technology related to mining and smelting; archaeological geology of Cyprus, Israel and Jordan; cryptoexplosion struct. **Mailing Address:** 122 W Easton Rd, Burbank, OH 44214. **E-Mail:** fandvkoucky@aol.com

KOUL, ASHOK KUMAR, SUPERALLOY TESTING & MICROSTRUCTURAL DESIGN, LIFE PREDICTION OF GAS TURBINE ENGINE COMPONENTS. **Personal Data:** m Anju; c Abhinav & Kalhan. **Education:** Banaras Hindu Univ, India, BSc, 1973; Coun Nat Acad Awards, PhD (metall), 1978. **Professional Experience:** PRES, LIFE PREDICTION TECHNOL INC, as of 2005; prof, Dept Mech Eng, Univ Ottawa, beginning 1993; GROUP LEADER HIGH TEMPERATURE METALL & GAS TURBINES, INST AEROSPACE RES, NAT RES COUN, 1990-; RES OFFICER, INST AEROSPACE RES, NAT RES COUN, 1980-; Res investr, Sheffield Labs, Brit Steel Corp, 1978-1980. **Memberships:** Am Soc Metals Int. **Research Statement & Publications:** Structure properties correlations in a wide variety of gas turbine engine materials; failure analysis and repair technologies. **Mailing Address:** Inst Aerospace Res, Nat Res Coun, 1500 Montreal Rd, Ottawa, ON K1A 0R6, Can. **Fax:** 613-990-7444. **E-Mail:** ashok.koul@nrc.ca

KOUL, HIRA LAL, MATHEMATICAL STATISTICS. **Personal Data:** b Srinagar, India, May 27, 1943. **Education:** Univ Jammu & Kashmir, India, BA, 1962, Univ Poona, MA, 1964; Univ Calif, Berkeley, PhD (math statist), 1967. **Professional Experience:** PROF STATIST & PROBABILITY, MICH STATE UNIV, 1977-; assoc prof, Mich State Univ, 1972-1977; asst prof statist, Mich State Univ, 1968-1972; asst, Univ Calif, Berkeley, 1965-1967. **Memberships:** Fel Inst Math Statist. **Research Statement & Publications:** Nonparametric statistics; inference on stochastic processes; reliability theory and survival analysis; author of numerous publications. **Mailing Address:** A435 Wells Hall, East Lansing, MI 48823. **Fax:** 517-432-1405. **E-Mail:** koul@stt.msu.edu

KOUL, MAHARAJ KISHEN, MATERIALS SCIENCE, METALLURGY. **Personal Data:** b Srinagar, Jammu Kashmir, India, September 10, 1941; m 1974, Sudha; c Keya & Yashomati. **Education:** Univ Jammu & Kashmir, BSc, 1959; Banaras Hindu Univ, BSc (Met Eng), 1963; Mass Inst Technol, PhD (mat sci), 1968. **Professional Experience:** Pres & COO, Atlantic Metals Corp, 1995-2000; vpres, Gen Mgr, Atlantic Metals Corp, Philadelphia, Pa 1990-1995; sr res scientist, Johnson & Johnson, 1980-1982; exec vpres, Div Indian Metals & Ferro Alloys Ltd, Newmont Mining Co, 1979-1980; mgr, Steel Res & Develop, Foote Mineral Co, 1976-1979; proj engr, New Prod Develop, 1970-1976; res scientist, Res & Develop, Mining & Metals Div, Union Carbide Corp, 1969-1970; fel, Mass Inst Technol, 1968-1969; res asst mat sci, Mass Inst Technol, 1965-1968; Metall asst, Union Carbide India Pvt Ltd, 1963-1965. **Memberships:** Am Inst Mining Metall & Petrol Engrs; Am Soc Metals; Iron & Steel Soc; Chair Scholarship Comm ISS. **Research Statement & Publications:** Electron microscopic investigation of phase transformation and deformation behavior in Beta-isomorphous titanium alloys; strengthening mechanisms and their application to the development of high strength-low alloy steels; dissolution kinetics of solids in liquid metals; thermodynamics and its application to metallurgical phenomenon; boron steel developments; deoxidation, desulfurization and sulfide modification in steel; dental alloy development; mold powders for casting of steel. **Mailing Address:** 136 E Delaware Ave, Pennington, NJ 08534. **Fax:** 609-737-7115. **E-Mail:** maharaj.koul@verizon.net

KOUL, OMANAND, NEUROCHEMISTRY, GLYCOCONJUGATES. **Personal Data:** b Kashmir, India, February 17, 1947; American citizen; m 1971, Prana; c Sidharth & Pamposh. **Education:** Jammu & Kashmir Univ, India, BSc, 1966; Banaras Hindu Univ, India, MSc, 1968, PhD (zoology), 1974. **Professional Experience:** RES ASSOC PROF, GRAD SCH NURSING, UNIV MASS MED SCH, as of 2005; grant, Stanley Res Found, 2002-2005; grant, Neurochemistry Autism, 2000-2001; grant, Nat Multiple Sclerosis Soc, 199-2000; Howard Hughes fel, Boston Univ, 1997; vis prof, Claude Bernard Univ, Lyon I, France, 1996; asst biochemist, Dept Neurol, beginning 1994; SCIENTIST, EUNICE KENNEDY SHRIVER CTR, MASS, 1987-; asst biochemist, Dept Neurol, 1986-1994; res assoc, Med Sch, Harvard Univ, 1984-1986 & 1988-; asst biochem, McLean Hosp, 1984-1986; res assoc, Eunice Kennedy Shriver Ctr Ment Retardation, 1976-1982; res fel, Dept Neurol, Mass Gen Hosp, 1976-1982; asst prof, genetics & biol, Govind Ballabh Pant Univ Agr & Technol, India, 1975-1976; lectr, physiol & biochem, Banaras Hindu Univ, India, 1970-1974; adj fac, Anat & Physiol, Bunker Hill Community Col. **Memberships:** Am Soc Neurochemistry; Soc Gerantol; Soc Glycobiol; Am Chem Soc; Nat Cancer Inst. **Research Statement & Publications:** Brain function in health and disease; enzymology of lipids; metabolism of glycolipids in animals and cell cultures; myelin biosynthesis during development; regulation of glycosylation in tissues; fetal alcohol; Published over 5 articles. **Mailing Address:** E K Shriver Center, Univ Mass, 200 Trapelo Rd, Waltham, MA 02452-6319. **E-Mail:** omanand.koul@umassmed.edu

KOULOURIDES, THEODORE I, DENTISTRY, ORAL BIOLOGY. **Personal Data:** b Preveza, Greece, September 11, 1925; American citizen; m 1956, c 3. **Education:** Nat Univ Athens, Dent Surgeon, 1950; Univ Rochester, MS, 1958; Univ Ala, DMD, 1960. **Honors & Awards:** USPHS res career develop award, 1963-1968. **Professional Experience:** RETIRED; sr scientist, Inst Dent Res, 1971-1991; prof dent, Med Ctr, 1969-; From asst prof to assoc prof, Med Ctr, Univ Ala, Birmingham, 1960-1969; fel, Eastman Dent Dispensary, Rochester, NY, 1955-1956; Fel pedodontics, Guggenheim Dent Clin, NY, 1955. **Memberships:** Am Dent Asn; Am Col Dent; Sigma Xi; Int Dent Fedn; Int Asn Dent Res. **Research Statement & Publications:** Biological mineralization, especially factors involved in dental caries and calculus formation. **Mailing Address:** 2228 Garland Dr, Birmingham, AL 35216.

KOUNOSU, SHIGERU, HIGH ENERGY PHYSICS, THEORETICAL PHYSICS. **Personal Data:** b Tokyo, Japan, August 23, 1928; m 1961, c 2. **Education:** Fukushima Univ, Japan, BEd, 1951; Univ Pa, MS, 1963, PhD (physics), 1965. **Professional Experience:** RETIRED; from asst prof to assoc prof physics, Univ Lethbridge, 1967-1990; res assoc physics, Princeton Univ, 1965-1967. **Memberships:** Am Phys Soc. **Research Statement & Publications:** Elementary particle physics. **Mailing Address:** 1054 Henderson Lake Blvd, Lethbridge, AB T1K 3B2, Can.

KOURANY, MIGUEL, MICROBIOLOGY, PUBLIC HEALTH. **Personal Data:** b Panama City, Panama, September 16, 1924; div, c 4. **Education:** Iowa State Col, BS, 1950; Loyola Univ, Chicago, MS, 1953; Univ Mich, Ann Arbor, MPH, 1954, PhD (epidemiol sci), 1963. **Honors & Awards:** Romulo Roux Medal, Ministry Health, 1997. **Professional Experience:** ASSOC INVESTR, GORGAS MEM LAB, MIN HEALTH, PANAMA, 1994-; dir, Gorgas Mem Lab & Tech Servs, 1983-1994; mem, Pan Am Health Org Sci Adv Comt to Zoonosis Ctr, Argentina, 1974 -; Consult, Pan Am Health Orgn Lab Serv var countries, 1971-; mem, Epert Adv Panel Health Lab Serv, WHO, 1967-1996; supv ad honoratium, Pub Health Lab Serv, Ministry Health, 1963-1983; chief, Bact Dept, 1963-1983; Dir, Pub Health Lab, Ministry Health, 1954-1963. **Memberships:** Am Soc Trop Med & Hyg; AAAS; Panamanian Soc Microbiol & Parasitol (pres, 1968, 1969 & 1978); Panamanian Acad Med & Surg. **Research Statement & Publications:** Intracellular infections; etiological agents of diarrheal disease; ecology of vibrio parahaemolyticus; zoonosis in Panama. **Mailing Address:** Gorgas Mem Lab, Ministry Health, Panama 1, Panama.

KOURI, DONALD JACK, THEORETICAL CHEMISTRY, CHEMICAL PHYSICS. **Personal Data:** b Hobart, Okla, July 25, 1938; m 1965, Shirley; c Lisa R & David M. **Education:** Okla Baptist Univ, BA, 1960; Univ Wis, MS, 1962, PhD (phys chem), 1965. **Honors & Awards:** US Sr Scientist Award, Alexander von Humboldt Found, 1973; Spec Creativity Award, NSF, 1992. **Professional Experience:** H R & L C CULLEN DISTINGUISHED UNIV PROF CHEM & PHYSICS, UNIV HOUSTON, 1996-; distinguished univ prof, Univ Houston, 1988-1996; J S Guggenheim fel, 1978-1979; fel Inst Advan Studies, Hebrew Univ, Jerusalem, 1978-1979; Weizmann Inst fel, 1973; Fel, A P Sloan Found, 1972-1974; from asst prof to prof, Univ Houston, 1967-1988; asst prof chem, Midwestern Univ, 1966-1967; res assoc physics & mem joint inst lab astrophys, Univ Colo, 1965-1966; Instr chem & physics, Okla Baptist Univ, 1962-1963. **Memberships:** Fel Am Phys Soc; Am Chem Soc; Am Asn Physics Teachers. **Research Statement & Publications:** Theoretical research on quantum mechanical scattering phenomena; reactive and nonreactive molecular collisions; approximations for inelastic and reactive collisions; accurate representation of multivariate functions and derivatives. **Mailing Address:** Dept Chem, Univ Houston, Houston, TX 77204-5641. **Fax:** 713-743-2709. **E-Mail:** kouri@uh.edu

KOUSHANPOUR, ESMAIL, PHYSIOLOGY, BIOPHYSICS. **Personal Data:** b Teheran, Iran, June 9, 1934; American citizen; m 1978, c 4. **Education:** Columbia Univ, AB, 1958; Mich State Univ, MS, 1961, PhD (physiol), 1963. **Professional Experience:** PROF EMER PHYSIOL, MED SCH, NORTHWESTERN UNIV, ILL, 1999-; sr Fulbright prof, 1983-1984; vis prof, Heidelberg Univ, WGer, 1983-1984; assoc prof anesthesia, 1982-1992; assoc prof physiol, med sch, Northwestern Univ, Ill, beginning 1968; Nat Heart Inst fel, 1965-; Asst prof, 1963-1968. **Memberships:** AAAS; Am Physiol Soc; NY Acad Sci; Am Heart Asn. **Research Statement & Publications:** Mathematical and experimental analyses of the cardiovascular and renal regulators; mechanism of the baroceptor process in the carotid sinus; role of carotid sinus in renal hypertension. **Mailing Address:** Dept Physiol, Northwestern Univ Med Sch, Chicago, IL 60611.

KOUSKOLEKAS, COSTAS ALEXANDER, ENTOMOLOGY. **Personal Data:** b Thessaloniki, Greece, May 10, 1927; m 1958, c 2. **Education:** Univ Thessaloniki, Dipl agr, 1951; Univ Mo-Columbia, MS, 1958; Univ Ill, Urbana, PhD (entom), 1964. **Professional Experience:** RETIRED; assoc prof entom, Auburn Univ, 1967-1993; sr res officer entom, Benaki Phytopath Inst, Athens, 1965-1967; consult, Doxiadis Assocs Int, Athens, Greece, 1964-1965; res assoc agr entom, Natural Hist Surv & Agr Exp Sta, Univ Ill, Urbana, 1962-1963; Teacher agron, Am Farm Sch, Thessaloniki, 1954-1956. **Memberships:** Entom Soc Am; Int Orgn Biol Control. **Research Statement & Publications:** Biology and control of insects of ornamentals and vegetables; integrated pest management. **Mailing Address:** 529 Sundilla Ct, Auburn, AL 36830.

KOUSKY, VERNON E, DYNAMIC METEOROLOGY, CLIMATE VARIABILITY. **Personal Data:** b Detroit, Mich, November 2, 1943; m 1973, Jamie; c Timothy, Jason & Justin. **Education:** Pa State Univ, BS, 1965, MS, 1967; Univ Wash, PhD (atmospheric sci), 1970. **Honors & Awards:** Silver Medal, Dept Com. **Professional Experience:** RES METEOROLOGIST, CLIMATE ANALYSIS CTR, 1984-; assoc researcher & researcher, Inst Space Res, Brazil, 1977-1983; prof collabr, Inst Astron & Geophys, Univ Sao Paulo, 1975-1977; asst prof meteorol, Univ Utah, 1970-1975. **Memberships:** Am Meteorol Soc. **Research Statement & Publications:** Synoptic meteorology; diagnostic study of wave motions in the tropical stratosphere; severe local storms; jetstream formation; tropopause deformation; atmospheric teleconnections; tropical meteorology; climate anomalies; weather and climate forecasting. **Mailing Address:** NOAA/National Weather Serv, 5200 Auth Rd Rm 605, Camp Springs, MD 20746. **E-Mail:** vernon.kousky@noaa.gov

KOUTCHER, JASON ARTHUR, NMR SPECTROSCOPY, METABOLIC STUDIES OF TUMORS. **Personal Data:** b Brooklyn, NY, February 18, 1950; m 1975, Sharon; c Lawrence, Stephanie & Sara. **Education:** Mass Inst Technol, BS, 1972; State Univ NY, MD, 1979, PhD (biophysics), 1979. **Professional Experience:** PROF, DEPT RADIOL & PHYSICS, SCH MED, CORNELL UNIV, as of 2005; CHIEF, DIAG IMAGING PHYSICS, MEM SLOAN KETTERING CANCER CTR, 1989-; assoc prof, Dept Radiol & Physics, Sch Med, Cornell Univ, beginning 1989; asst prof radiol & physics, Cornell Univ Sch Med, 1986-1989; assoc prof radiol & physics, Mem Sloan Kettering Cancer Ctr, beginning 1985; asst prof med, Harvard Med Sch, 1985; prin investr, NIH & Am Chem Soc, 1984-1997; instr med, Tufts Univ Sch Med, 1983-1985. **Memberships:** Radiation Res Soc; Soc Magnetic Resonance Med; Am Asn Cancer Res. **Research Statement & Publications:** Measuring changes in tumor metabolism that are caused by anti-cancer treatment, particularly chemotherapy and radiation, these studies include non-invasive measurements made on cells, animal tumors, and patients using nuclear magnetic resonance spectroscopy; long range goal to enhance the effectiveness of these agents. **Mailing Address:** Dept Radiol & Physics, Cornell Univ, New Rochelle, NY 10804. **Fax:** 212-717-3010. **E-Mail:** koutchej@mskcc.org

KOUTS, HERBERT JOHN CECIL, NUCLEAR ENERGY, NUCLEAR REACTOR SAFETY. **Personal Data:** b Bisbee, Ariz, December 18, 1919; m 1974, Barbara Stokes; c Anne (Golden) & Catherine. **Education:** La State Univ, BS, 1941, MS, 1946; Princeton Univ, PhD (physics), 1952. **Honors & Awards:** E O Lawrence Award, AEC, 1963 & Distinguished Serv Award, 1975; Distinguished Serv Award, US Nuclear Regulatory Comn, 1976; Theos Thompson Award, Am Nuclear Soc. **Professional Experience:** RETIRED; mem, Defense Nuclear Facil Safety Bd, US Govt, 1989-2000; mem, Int Nuclear Safety Adv Group, chmn, 1988-1991; sr scientist, Dept Nuclear Energy, Brookhaven Nat Lab, 1988-1989; chmn, Dept Nuclear Energy, Brookhaven Nat Lab, 1977-1987; dir, Off Nuclear Regulatory Res, US Nuclear Regulatory Comn, 1975-1976; dir, Div Reactor Safety Res, AEC, 1973-1975; prin adv reactor safety, NY State Atomic & Space Develop Authority, 1969-1973; mem, Mayor's Tech Adv Comt on Radiation, NY, 1969-1973; chmn, Nuclear Adv Comt, Hall Sci, NY, 1969-1973; mem, Europ-Am Comt Reactor Physics, Europ Nuclear Energy Agency, 1962-1968; sr scientist & assoc div head, Brookhaven Nat Lab, 1958-1973; group leader reactor physics, Brookhaven Nat Lab, 1952-1958; asst group leader, Brookhaven Nat Lab, 1951-1952; Assoc physicist, Brookhaven Nat Lab, 1950-1951. **Memberships:** Nat Acad Eng; fel Am Nuclear Soc; Int Atomic Energy Agency; Int Nuclear Safety Soc Group. **Research Statement & Publications:** Elementary particle physics; shielding and physics of nuclear reactors. **Mailing Address:** PO Box 560, Bellport, NY 11713.

KOUTSOPOULOS, HARIS, CIVIL ENGINEERING. **Education:** Nat Tech Univ Athens, Greece, BSc, 1980; Mass Inst Technol, MS, 1983 & PhD (Transp Syats), 1986. **Professional Experience:** ASSOC PROF, DEPT CIVIL & ENVIRON ENG, NWESTERN UNIV, as of 2004. **Research Statement & Publications:** Intelligent transportation systems; dynamic traffic management systems; large scale traffic simulation; driving behavior and safety; dynamic traffic assignment; automated data collection and analysis; machine learning applications to transportation problems; transportation network analysis. **Mailing Address:** Dept Civil Eng, NEastern Univ, 437 Snell Eng Ctr, Pittsburgh, PA 15213. **Fax:** 617-373 - 4419. **E-Mail:** haris@coe.neu.edu

KOUVEL, JAMES SPYROS, SOLID STATE PHYSICS, SUPERCONDUCTORS. **Personal Data:** b Jersey City, NJ, May 23, 1926; m 1953, Audrey; c Diana & Alexander. **Education:** Yale Univ, BS, 1946, PhD (phys & elec eng), 1951. **Professional Experience:** Eval panels, Nat Res Coun, 1981-1985; vis prof, Univ Paris, Orsay, 1981; mem, Mat Res Adv Comt, NSF, 1980-1982; vis scientist, Solid State Sci & Mat Sci Div, 1973-1974; PROF PHYSICS, UNIV ILL, CHICAGO, 1969-; consult, Argonne Nat Lab, 1969-1989; Guggenheim fel, 1967-1968; vis scientist, Atomic Energy Res Estab, Harwell, Eng, 1967-1968; physicist, Res & Develop Ctr, Gen Elec Co, 1955-1969; res fel solid state physics, Harvard Univ, 1953-1955; res fel physics, Univ Leeds, 1951-1953; res engr, Microwave Devices, Fed Telecommun Labs, NJ, 1947-1948. **Memberships:** Fel Am Phys Soc; fel AAAS. **Research Statement & Publications:** magnetic materials; critical phenomena; phase transitions; superconductors. **Mailing Address:** Dept Physics Univ Ill, 845 W Taylor St, Chicago, IL 60607-7059. **Fax:** 312-996-9016. **E-Mail:** kouvel@uic.edu

KOUYOUMJIAN, ROBERT G, ELECTROMAGNETICS, ANTENNAS. **Personal Data:** b Cleveland, Ohio, April 26, 1923. **Education:** Ohio State Univ, BS, 1948, PhD (physics), 1953. **Honors & Awards:** Centennial Medal Award, Inst Elec & Electronics Engrs, 1984, Tech Achievement Award, 1992. **Professional Experience:** PROF EMER, DEPT ELEC ENG, OHIO STATE UNIV, 1982-; distinguished lectr, Int Elec & Electronics Engr, 1973-1975; prof, 1962-1982; From asst to assoc prof, 1955-1962. **Memberships:** Nat Acad Eng; fel Inst Elec & Electronics Engrs. **Research Statement & Publications:** Application of electromagnetic theory to the analysis of antennas and scatterers; asymptotic high frequency methods and their ray optical interpretation; uniform geometrical theory of diffraction; contributed articles to professional journals. **Mailing Address:** Dept Elec Eng, Col Eng, Ohio State Univ, 2015 Neil Ave, 205 DL, Columbus, OH 43210-1275. **Fax:** 614-292-7596. **E-Mail:** kouyoumjian.1@osu.edu

KOUZES, RICHARD THOMAS, NUCLEAR PHYSICS, SCIENTIFIC INSTRUMENTATION. **Personal Data:** b Arlington, Va, July 8, 1947; m 1970, Jan M Costantino; c Ross & Emily. **Education:** Mich State Univ, BS, 1969; Princeton Univ, MA, 1972, PhD (physics), 1974. **Professional Experience:** SENIOR SCIENTIST, PAC NORTHWEST LAB, as of 2003; ADJ PROF PHYSICS, W VA UNIV, as of 2003; ADJ PROF PHYSICS, WASH STATE UNIV, as of 2003; staff scientist, Pac Northwest Lab, beginning 1987; sr res physicist & lectr, Princeton Univ, 1987; res staff & lectr, Princeton Univ, 1976-1987; res assoc nuclear physics, Cyclotron Facil, Ind Univ, Bloomington, 1975-1976; Sr systs analyst, Univ Comput Co, 1970-1971. **Memberships:** Am Phys Soc; Sigma Xi; Inst Elec & Electronics Engrs. **Research Statement & Publications:** Scientific Instrumentation devlopment for Molecular and Environmental Science. **Mailing Address:** Radiol & Chem Sci Group, Pac NW Nat Lab, PO Box 999, MS P8-20, Richland, WA 99352. **E-Mail:** richard.kouzes@pnl.gov

KOVAC, JEFFREY DEAN, PHYSICAL CHEMISTRY. **Personal Data:** b Cleveland, Ohio, May 29, 1948. **Education:** Reed Col, BA, 1970; Yale Univ, MPhil, 1972, PhD (chem), 1974. **Professional Experience:** DIR, TENN GOV'S SCH SCI, as of 2003; DIR UNDERGRAD STUDIES, UNIV TENN, as of 2000; ED BOOKS & REV, UNIV TENN, as of 2000; PROF CHEM, UNIV TENN, 1991-; Consult, Oak Ridge Nat Lab, 1984-1988; from asst prof to assoc prof, Univ Tenn, 1976-1991; Res assoc chem, Mass Inst Technol, 1974-1976; assoc, Univ Tenn Knoxville Ctr Appl & Prof Ethics. **Memberships:** AAAS; Am Phys Soc; Am Chem Soc. **Research Statement & Publications:** Statistical mechanics of polymers and simple fluids; equilibrium and non equilibrium thermodynamics; rubber elasticity; structure and formation of coal; computer simulation; scientific ethics; chemical education. **Mailing Address:** Dept Chem, Univ Tenn, Knoxville, TN 37996-1600. **Fax:** 423-974-3454. **E-Mail:** jkovac@utk.edu

KOVACH, ARISZTID G B, MEDICAL RESEARCH. **Education:** Pazmany Peter Univ, Budapest, MD, 1944; Karl Ruprecht Univ, Heiderberg, MS, 1942; Hungarian Acad Sci, Budapest, PhD, 1952. **Professional Experience:** RES PROF NEUROL, CVRC, DEPT NEUROL, UNIV PA, PHILADELPHIA, 1992-; SCI ADV, INST PHYSIOL, SCH MED, SEMMELWEIS UNIV, BUDAPEST, HUNGARY, 1991-; vpres, Int Union Physiol Sci, 1980-1983; chmn, Inst Physiol, 1979-1991; secy gen, Int Union Physiol Sci, 1974-1980; adj prof physiol, Dept Neurol, Univ Pa, 1970-1992; founder & head, Exp Res Dept, 1959-1991; from assoc prof to prof physiol, Dept Biochem, Semmelweis Univ Med Sch, Budapest, Hungary, 1950-1991; assoc prof, Dept Biochem, Semmelweis Univ Med Sch, Budapest, Hungary, 1949-1950; chief, Physiol Lab, Biol Res Inst, Hungarian Acad Sci, Tihany, Lake Balaton, 1945-1948. **Memberships:** Int Union Physiol Sci. **Research Statement & Publications:** Irreversibility of hemorrhagic shock, the role of regulatory and metabolic processes; control of heart and peripheral circulation; neuroendocrinology; cerebral blood flow and metabolism; the role of nitric oxide in cerebral blood flow metasbolism and function. **Mailing Address:** 429 Johnson Pavillion, 36th Hamilton Walk, Philadelphia, PA 19104-6063.

KOVACH, EUGENE GEORGE, ORGANIC CHEMISTRY, SCIENCE ADMINISTRATION. **Personal Data:** b Irvington, NJ, May 18, 1922; m 1950, Mary Eleauor; c George, Mary, Katherine, Christine & John. **Education:** Wayne State Univ, BS, 1943, MS, 1944; Harvard Univ, MA, 1948, PhD, 1950. **Professional Experience:** CONSULT, OFF ADVAN TECHNOL, US DEPT STATE, 1983-; dir, Off Technol Policy, 1980-1982; mem staff, Off Technol Policy, 1978-1980; with Div of Policy Res, NSF, 1976-1978; dep asst secy gen for sci affairs, NATO, 1970-1976; actg dir, Off Gen Sci Affairs, 1965-1970; asst sci adv, Int Sci & Tech Affairs, US Dept State, 1959-1965; chem prog, NSF, 1957-1959; sci adv, US Naval Forces, Ger, 1954-1957; asst prof, Univ Fla, 1951-1954; asst prof, Colgate Univ, 1950-1951; instr, Univ Fla, 1949-1950; Res tutor, Harvard, 1946-1949. **Memberships:** AAAS; Am Chem Soc; Ger Chem Soc; Sigma Xi; currently a mem. **Research Statement & Publications:** Structure of natural products; chelate compounds; theoretical organic chemistry; science education and administration; international relations. **Mailing Address:** 4118 Aspen St, Chevy Chase, MD 20815.

KOVACH, ILDIKO M, ORGANIC CHEMISTRY. **Personal Data:** b Hungary, June 22, 1939; American citizen; m 1958, Gyula; c Aolaw & Admenive. **Education:** Szemmelweisz Univ Med Sci, Budapest, Hungary, BS, 1964; Univ Kans, MS, 1973, PhD, 1974. **Honors & Awards:** Career develop award, NSF, 1990. **Professional Experience:** Mem, educ board, Bristol Biochem, 2000-; fel, NRC, 1996; PROF CHEM, CATH UNIV AM, 1995-; fel, NIH, 1991; assoc prof, Cath Univ Am, 1989-1995; sr scientist, Univ Kans, 1985-1989; fel, Am Inst Chemists, 1980; assoc scientist, Univ Kans, 1978-1985; res assoc chem, Univ Kans, 1974-1978. **Memberships:** Mem Am Chem Soc; mem Am Asn Univ Prof; mem AAAS; mem Am Women in Sci. **Research Statement & Publications:** Service hydrolases choliesterases methods; kineic satope effects, physical organic probes/ moleculer dynamic calculations and 1h-3lp-NMR. **Mailing Address:** Dept Chem, Cath Univ Am, Wheaon, MD 20902. **Fax:** 202-319-5381. **E-Mail:** kovach@cua.edu

KOVACH, JACK, GEOLOGY. **Personal Data:** b Rices Landing, Pa, March 23, 1940; m 1965, Frances Block; c Thomas & John. **Education:** Waynesburg Col, BSc, 1962; Ohio State Univ, MSc, 1967, PhD (geol), 1974. **Professional Experience:** PROF GEOL, MUSKINGUM COL, 1983-; Res assoc, Nat Res Coun, Nat Acad Sci, 1979-1980; From asst prof to assoc prof, Muskingum Col, 1968-1982; assoc, US Geol Surv, Denver. **Memberships:** Geochem Soc. **Research Statement & Publications:** Strontium isotope geochemistry and rubidium-strontium geochronology; biogeochemistry of nonmarine mollusk shells; composition of atmospheric precipitation; silurian stratigraphy and paleontology; biogeochemistry and isotopic composition of conodonts. **Mailing Address:** Dept Geol, Muskingum Col, New Concord, OH 43762. **E-Mail:** jkovach@muskingum.edu

KOVACHICH, GYULA BERTALAN, NEUROCHEMISTRY. **Personal Data:** b Budapest, Hungary, March 27, 1936; m 1990, Marilyn; c Jennifer & Stephen. **Education:** Haverford Col, BA, 1962; Univ Pa, PhD (pharmacol), 1975. **Professional Experience:** RES SCIENTIST, VET ADMIN MED CTR, 1985-; LECTR BIOCHEM & PHYSIOL, PA STATE UNIV, 1984-; asst prof, Dept Pharmacol, 1980-1985; res assoc, Sch Med, Univ Pa, 1977-1980; instr pharmacol, Sch Med, Univ Pa, 1975-1977; res asst neurochem, Ciba-Geigy Corp, 1964-1969. **Memberships:** Soc Neuroscience; Int Brain Res Orgn. **Research Statement & Publications:** Oxygen toxicity of the central nervous system; interaction of ascorbic acid with biological systems; mechanism of action of antidepressants. **Mailing Address:** Inst Environ Med, Univ Pa Sch Med, Philadelphia, PA 19104.

KOVACIC, GREGOR, APPLIED NONLINEAR DYNAMIC SYSTEMS, NEAR INTEGRABLE DYNAMIC SYSTEMS. **Personal Data:** b Koper, Slovenia, October 16, 1960; m 1990, Miriam. **Education:** Univ Ljub, BS, 1985; Calif Inst Technol, PhD (appl math), 1990. **Honors & Awards:** Career Award, NSF, 1995. **Professional Experience:** ASSOC PROF, DEPT MATH SCI, RENSSELAER POLYTECH INST, 1997-; res fel, A P Sloan Found, 1996; asst prof, Rensselaer Polytech Inst, 1991-1997; Director's funded postdoctoral fel, Los Alamos Nat Lab, 1989-1991. **Memberships:** Soc Indust & Appl Math; Am Phys Soc. **Research Statement & Publications:** Theory of nonlinear dynamical systems for ordinary and partial differential equations and its applications to laser and non-linear fiber optics, classical mechanics and fluid mechanics. **Mailing Address:** Dept Math Sci, Rensselaer Polytech Inst, Troy, NY 12180-3590. **Fax:** 518-276-4824. **E-Mail:** kovacg@rpi.edu

KOVACIC, JERALD J, MATHEMATHICS. **Education:** Stanford Univ, BS, 1962; Columbia Univ, MA, 1963, PhD, 1968. **Professional Experience:** VIS PROF, DEPT MATH, CITY UNIV NEW YORK, as of 2005. **Mailing Address:** City Univ New York, 29 E 10 St Second Floor, New York, NY 10003. **Fax:** 212-817-1614. **E-Mail:** jkovacic@verizon.net

KOVACIC, JOSEPH EDWARD, ORGANIC CHEMISTRY. **Personal Data:** b Youngstown, Ohio, April 4, 1930; div, c 5. **Education:** Univ Ohio, BS, 1952, MS, 1953. **Professional Experience:** SUPVR, CHEM & ANALYTIC SERV & POLYMER MAT LABS, UNISYS CORP, 1983-; prin chem engr & group supvr, Chem & Anal Serv Lab, 1969-1983; group supvr, Mat & Process Eng, Anal Serv Lab, 1968-1969; sr develop engr, Adv Tech Div, Sperry Corp, 1965-1968; actg head anal sect, Silicone Div, Stauffer Chem Co, 1963-1965; org chemist, Chem-Physics Res Lab, 1960-1963; res chemist, Resinous Prod Lab, Dow Chem Co, 1957-1960; teaching asst chem, Fla State Univ, 1956-1957; Chemist nylon res labs, E I Du Pont Del Nemours & Co, 1955-1956. **Memberships:** Fel Am Inst Chem. **Research Statement & Publications:** Infrared spectroscopy; infrared spectra of chelates; polymer chemistry; scanning electron microscopy; gas chromatography. **Mailing Address:** 1887 Silver Bell Rd No 314, St Paul, MN 55122.

KOVACIC, PETER, ORGANIC CHEMISTRY. **Personal Data:** b Wylandville, Pa, August 1, m, c 6. **Education:** Hanover Col, AB, 1943, DSc, 1964; Univ Ill, PhD (chem), 1946. **Professional Experience:** ADJ PROF, SAN DIEGO STATE UNIV, 1997-; prof chem, Univ Wis-Milwaukee, 1968-1987; from asst prof to prof chem, Case Inst Technol, 1955-1968; res chemist, E I du Pont Del Nemours & Co, 1948-1955; instr, Columbia Univ, 1947-1948; Asst org chem, Mass Inst Technol, 1946-1947. **Memberships:** Am Chem Soc. **Research Statement & Publications:** Charge transfer and oxy radicals in living systems; cell signaling; protein electron transfer, mechanism of drugs and toxins. **Mailing Address:** Dept Chem, San Diego State Univ, 5500 Campanile Dr, Milwaukee, WI 92182-1030. **Fax:** 619-594-4634. **E-Mail:** pkovacic@sundown.sdsu.edu

KOVACS, BELA A, PHARMACOLOGY, ALLERGY. **Personal Data:** b Nagykoros, Hungary, August 28, 1921; Canadian citizen; m 1952, c Eva Maria. **Education:** Med Univ Szeged, MD, 1946; Univ London, DrPhil(pharmacol), 1961. **Professional Experience:** SCI ADV, DEPT NAT HEALTH & WELFARE, FOOD & DRUG DIRECTORATE, 1969-; assoc prof exp med, McGill Univ, 1969-; assoc prof pharmacol & exp med, 1964-1969; asst prof, 1961-1964; lectr, Sch Pharm, Univ London, 1959-1961; res fel pharmacol, Nat Inst Med Res, London, 1957-1961; Res fel org chem, Univ Basel, 1956-1957; From asst prof to assoc prof pharmacol, Med Univ Szeged, 1949-1956. **Memberships:** Am Soc Pharmacol & Exp Therapeut; Pharmacol Soc Can; Brit Pharmacol Soc; Am Col Clin Pharmacol & Therapeut; Can Soc Immunol. **Research Statement & Publications:** Histamine and antihistaminics; inflammation; gastric secretion; pulmonary edema. **Mailing Address:** Dept Health & Welfare Can, 300 Driveway No 9D, Ottawa, ON K1S 3M6, Can.

KOVACS, CHARLES J, EXPERIMENTAL BIOLOGY. **Personal Data:** b Fairfield, Conn, April 7, 1941. **Education:** Siena Col, BS, 1963; St John's Univ, MS, 1965, PhD (microbiol & biochem, 1969. **Professional Experience:** PROF RADIATION ONCOL & DIR, DIV RADIATION THER, RADIATION ONCOL CTR, SCH MED, E CAROLINA UNIV, GREENVILLE, NC, 1985-; prin investr Ore co-prin investr grants, NIH, 1983-1986, 1984-1986 & 1990; assoc prof & dir, Radiation Oncol Labs, Dept Radiol, Sect Radiother, Bowman Gray Sch Med, Winston-Salem, NC, 1981-1985; assoc prof, Dept Radiol, Div Radiation Oncol, Col Med, Univ SAla, Mobile, 1980-1981; sr scientist, Cancer Res Labs, 1979-1980; assoc scientist, Cancer Res Unit, Div Radiation Oncol, Allegheny Gen Hosp, Pittsburgh, Pa, 1976-1979; asst prof, Dept Pediat, 1975-1976; instr, Div Radiobiol & Biophys, Sch Med, Univ Va, Charlottesville, 1972-1975; res instr, Dept Med, Hahnemann Med Col, Philadelphia, Pa, 1971-1972; Res assoc, Brookhaven Nat Lab, AEC, 1970-1971; USPHS fel, Nat Cancer Inst, NIH, 1969-1971; consult, NIH, Vet Admin, Mariculture, Inc, NC Biotechnol Ctr. **Memberships:** Sigma Xi; AAAS; Am Asn Cancer Res; Am Soc Cell Biol; Int Soc Exp Hemat; Am Soc Clin Immunol. **Mailing Address:** Dept Radiation Ther, Sch Med ECarolina Univ, Greenville, NC 27858. **Fax:** 252-744-3775. **E-Mail:** kovacsc@mail.ecu.edu

KOVACS, EVE MARIA, MEDICINE. **Personal Data:** b Budapest, Hungary, April 13, 1925; m 1952, A. **Education:** Univ Szeged, MD, 1952. **Professional Experience:** RETIRED; sci adv, Dept Nat Health & Welfare, Food Directorate, 1970-1992; asst prof pharmacol, McGill Univ, beginning 1964; lectr, McGill Univ, 1961-1964; Cancer res fel, Dept Pharmacol, Univ London, 1958-1961; pharmacologist, Geigy AG, Switz, 1957-1958; asst prof, Univ Clin, 1955-1956; lectr internal med, Univ Clin, 1954-1955; lectr pharmacol, Univ Szeged, 1952-1954. **Memberships:** Pharmacol Soc Can; Am Soc Pharmacol & Exp Therapeut; Int Soc Biochem Pharmacol; Can Med Asn. **Research Statement & Publications:** Cancer immunology; allergy; histamine; histamine metabolites; gastric secretion. **Mailing Address:** 300 Dr way No 9D, Ottawa, ON K1S 3M6, Can.

KOVACS, EVE VERONIKA, COMPUTER SCIENCE. **Personal Data:** b Melbourne, Australia, November 12, 1954. **Education:** Univ Melbourne, BS, 1976, PhD (physics), 1980, dipl comput sci, 1980. **Professional Experience:** RES STAFF, ARGONNE NAT LAB, as of 2002; Res assoc, Rockefeller Univ, 1981-; vis Scientist, Stanford Linear Accelerator Ctr, 1980-1981. **Memberships:** Am Phys Soc. **Research Statement & Publications:** Monte Carlo simulations of lattice guage theories with particular emphasis on finite size effects and the interquark potential. **Mailing Address:** Argonne Nat Lab, 9700 S Cass Ave, Argonne, IL 60439. **Fax:** 630-252-5047. **E-Mail:** kovacs@hep.anl.gov

KOVACS, GREGORY T A, ELECTRICAL ENGINEERING. **Education:** Univ BC, BASc, 1984; Univ Calif, Berkeley, MS, 1985; Stanford Univ, PhD (elec eng), 1990, MD, 1992. **Professional Experience:** ASSOC PROF ELEC ENG, STANFORD UNIV, as of 2006. **Mailing Address:** Elect Eng Dept, Stanford Univ, CISX-202, Stanford, CA 94305-4070. **Fax:** 650-725-5244. **E-Mail:** kovacs@cis.stanford.edu

KOVACS, JULIUS STEPHEN, THEORETICAL PHYSICS. **Personal Data:** b Trenton, NJ, August 20, 1928; m 1956, c 2. **Education:** Lehigh Univ, BS, 1950; Ind Univ, MS, 1952, PhD, 1955. **Professional Experience:** ASSOC CHMN DEPT, MICH STATE UNIV, 1977-; PROF PHYSICS, MICH STATE UNIV, 1968-; from asst prof to assoc prof, Mich State Univ, 1956-1968; res assoc, Ind Univ, 1955-1956; Asst prof physics, Univ Toledo, 1954-1955. **Research Statement & Publications:** Meson physics; elementary particles. **Mailing Address:** dept phy & astron, mich state univ, East Lansing, MI 48824-1116. **E-Mail:** kovacs@pa.msu.edu

KOVACS, KALMAN T, ENDOCRINOLOGY, ELECTRON MICROSCOPY. **Personal Data:** b Szeged, Hungary, July 11, 1926; Canadian citizen; m 1962, Eva. **Education:** Univ Szeged, Hungary, MD, 1950; Univ Liverpool, PhD (path), 1966; FCAP & FRCP (C), 1973; FRCPath, 1980, DSc 1966. **Honors & Awards:** Hungarian Acad Sci Award, 1968. **Professional Experience:** PROF PATH, ST MICHAELS HOSP, CANADA, as of 2004; PROF PATH, UNIV TORONTO, 1980-; asst prof, Univ Toronto, 1971-1980; vis scientist exp med, Univ Montreal, 1968-1971; res fel path, Docent Univ Szeged, 1960 & Crosby res fel, Univ Liverpool, 1964-1965; sr lectr, Dept Med, 1954-1968; demonstr & lectr, Dept Path, Univ Szeged, 1950-1954. **Memberships:** Int Acad Path; Am Path Soc; US Endocrine Soc; corresp mem Romanian Acad Sci. **Research Statement & Publications:** Morphologic study of endocrine glands, especially human pituitaries and pituitary adenomas; correlation of structural features with secretory activity. **Mailing Address:** Dept Lab Med & Pathobiology, Div Path, Second FISt Michaels Hosp, 30 Bond St, Toronto, ON M5B 1W8, Can. **Fax:** 416-864-5648. **E-Mail:** kovacsk@mail.smh.toronto.on.ca

KOVACS, KARL F, IV, BIOLOGY. **Education:** Gannon Univ, BS; Univ S Fla, PhD (biochem). **Professional Experience:** VPRES OPERATIONS, ORIGENE TECHNOLOGIES, as of 2006. **Mailing Address:** OriGene Technologies Inc, Six Taft Ct Suite 100, Rockville, MD 20850. **Fax:** 301-340-9254. **E-Mail:** kkovacs@Origene.com

KOVACS, KIT M, PARENTAL INVESTMENT STRATEGISTS, MATING SYSTEMS. **Personal Data:** b Iserloln, Ger, November 7, 1956; Canadian citizen; m 1981. **Education:** York Univ, Toronto, HBSC, 1979; Lakehead Univ, Thunder Bay, MSC, 1982; Univ Guelph, PhD (zoology), 1986. **Professional Experience:** PROF BIOL, UNIV WATERLOO, as of 1994; assoc prof biol, Univ Waterloo, beginning 1987; post doctorate fel zool, NSERC & NATO, 1986-1987; res assoc, La Vie Wildlife, Res Assoc Ltd, 1982-. **Memberships:** Marine Mammal Soc; Can Zool Soc; Am Ornith Union; Animal Behav Soc. **Research Statement & Publications:** Behavioral ecology, evolution, mating systems, parental investment, pinnipeds. **Mailing Address:** Biol Dept, Univ Waterloo, 200 Univ Ave W, Waterloo, ON N2L 3G1, Can.

KOVACS, MIKLOS I P, ANALYTICAL CHEMISTRY. **Personal Data:** b Budapest, Hungary, February 1, 1936; Canadian citizen; m 1961, c 2. **Education:** Univ Keszthely, Hungary, BS, 1960; Univ Budapest, BSc, 1964; Univ Guelph, MSc, 1969; Univ Man, PhD (biochem), 1974. **Professional Experience:** RES SCIENTIST GEN CHEM, AGR CAN RES INST, 1979-; res scientist marine lipids, fisheries & oceans res, 1975-1979; teaching fel biochem, Univ Sask, 1974-1975. **Memberships:** Am Asn Cereal Chemists. **Research Statement & Publications:** Wheat quality; interaction of protein, starch and lipids. **Mailing Address:** Agr & Agri Food Can, Cereal Res Ctr, 195 DaFoe Rd, Winnipeg, MB R3T 2M9, Can. **Fax:** 204-983-4604. **E-Mail:** mkovacs@agr.gc.ca

KOVACS, SANDOR J, CARDIOLOGY. **Personal Data:** b Budapest, Hungary, August 17, 1947; American citizen. **Education:** Univ Cornell, BS, 1969; Calif Inst Technol, MS, 1972, PhD (theoret physics), 1977; Univ Miami, MD, 1979. **Professional Experience:** ASSOC PROF, MED, SCH MED, UNIV WASH, as of 2006; assoc prof, Cell Biol, & Physiol, as of 2006; adj assoc prof physics, Univ Wash, 1996-; ADJ ASSOC PROF, BIOMED & BIOL ENG, SCH MED, UNIV WASH, 1996-; asst prof biomed eng, Univ Wash, 1993-1996; dir, Cardiovasc Biophys Lab, Barnes Jewis Hosp, Univ Wash, 1992-; asst prof med, Univ Wash, 1990-1996; dir, Cardiac Catheterization Lab Res, Barnes Jewis Hosp, Univ Wash, 1989-; instr med, dept Internal Med, Univ Wash, 1985-1986; res fel, dept Med, 1982-1985; med consult & lectr, Nat Asn Underwater Instrs, 1974-; res asst, theoret physics, Calif Inst Technol, 1971-1977. **Memberships:** Sigma Xi; Int Soc Gen Relativity & Gravitation; AAAS; Am Col Physicians; Am Col Cardiol; Am Bd Internal Med; Am Physiol Soc. **Research Statement & Publications:** Noninvasive cardiological diagnostic methods including cardiac electrophysiology, arrythmia detection and analysis; biophysics; Published over 6 articles. **Mailing Address:** Dept Med Wash Univ, 1107 Steinberg Bldg, St Louis, MO 63124-1730. **Fax:** 314-454-5265. **E-Mail:** sjk@howdy.wustl.edu

KOVACS (NAGY), HANNA, ORGANIC CHEMISTRY. **Personal Data:** b Szeged, Hungary, October 31, 1919; American citizen; m 1950, c 2. **Education:** Univ Szeged, PhD (org chem), 1945. **Professional Experience:** RETIRED; clin chemist, Mt Sinai Hosp, NY, 1970-1985; res chemist, Naval Appl Sci Lab, Brooklyn, 1963-1970; res assoc peptide chem, St John's Univ, NY, 1959-1963; res assoc bact, Univ Basel, 1957 & Detroit Inst Cancer Res, 1958-1959; res assoc org chem, Univ Budapest, 1950-1956; physiol, Univ Szeged, 1946-1950; Res assoc org chem, Univ Szeged, 1944-1946. **Memberships:** Nat Acad Clin Biochem; Am Chem Soc; NY Acad Sci; Sigma Xi; Am Asn Clin Chem. **Research Statement & Publications:** Author or coauthor of twenty-eight publications in the field of peptide, heterocyclic, polymer, medicinal and clinical chemistry. **Mailing Address:** 639 S Grand Ave, Pasadena, CA 91105-3322.

KOVAL, CARL ANTHONY, ELECTROCHEMISTRY, MEMBRANE SCIENCE. **Personal Data:** b York, Pa, June 28, 1952; m 1990, Christa; c Sara, Olivia & Kayla. **Education:** Juniata Col, BS, 1974; Calif Inst Technol, PhD (chem), 1979. **Professional Experience:** Fel, Coop Inst Res Environ Sci, as of 2005; PROF, DEPT CHEM & BIOCHEM, UNIV COLO, as of 2001; vis assoc prof, Calif Inst Technol, 1992-; assoc prof, Univ Colo, beginning 1987; asst prof chem, Univ Colo, 1980-1987; fel, Purdue Univ, 1978-1980. **Memberships:** Am Chem Soc; Electrochem Soc. **Research Statement & Publications:** Facilitated transport of molecules across liquid membranes; electrochemical processes for gas separations and for non-mechanical pumping of fluids; photoelectrochemistry; Published over 5 articles. **Mailing Address:** Dept Chem & Biochem Univ Colo, 215 UCB, Boulder, CO 80309-0215. **Fax:** 303-492-5894. **E-Mail:** carl.koval@colorado.edu

KOVAL, CHARLES FRANCIS, OUTREACH PROGRAMMING. **Personal Data:** b Ashland, Wis, May 10, 1938; m 1957, Patricia; c Michael, Daniel & Mary L. **Education:** Northland Col, BA, 1960; Univ Wis, MS, 1963, PhD (entom), 1966. **Professional Experience:** PROF EMER ENTOM, UNIV WIS, MADISON, 1995-; chmn dept, Wis Coop Exten Serv, 1988-1990; dean, Wis Coop Exten Serv, 1983-1987; dir, Univ Exp Farms, 1980-1983; from instr to prof, Univ Wis-Madison, 1965-1995; exten entomologist, Univ Wis-Madison, 1965-1980; res asst, Univ Wis-Madison, 1960-1965; village forester, Shorewood Hills. **Memberships:** Entom Soc Am; Inst Sci Anal; Acad Health Sci. **Research Statement & Publications:** Insect management on turf, landscape plants and greenhouse crops with emphasis on integrated pest management strategies; urban forestry; development of extension outreach programs. **Mailing Address:** Dept Entom, Univ Wis, 237 Russell Labs 1630 Linden Dr, Madison, WI 53706. **Fax:** 608-262-3322. **E-Mail:** koval@caishp.cals.wisc.edu

KOVAL, DON O, BIOLOGICAL ENGINEERING. **Personal Data:** b Pickle Crow, Ont, March 20, 1942. **Education:** Univ Saskatoon, Sask, BE, 1965, MSc, 1969, PhD, 1978. **Honors & Awards:** Commemorative Medal Honor, Am Biog Inst, 1991. **Professional Experience:** PROF ELEC ENG, UNIV ALTA, EDMONTON, 1980-; spec studies engr distrib, B C Hydro Power Authority, Can, 1967-1979; subtransmission design engr distrib, Sask Power Corp, Can, 1965-1966. **Memberships:** fel Inst Elec & Electronics Engrs; Int Asn Sci & Technol Develop; Int Inst Advan Studies Systs Res & Cybernetics; fel Am Biog Inst; fel Int Biog Asn. **Research Statement & Publications:** Reliability of Industrial, Commercial, and Utility Distribution Power Systems; Power Quality Characteristics of Industrial, Commercial, and Rural Power Systems. **Mailing Address:** Dept Elec Eng, Univ Alta, Edmonton, AB T6G 2G7, Can. **Fax:** 780-492-1811. **E-Mail:** donkoval@home.com

KOVAL, LESLIE R(OBERT), ENGINEERING MECHANICS, STRUCTURAL DYNAMICS, ACOUSTICS, SMART STRUCTURES. **Personal Data:** b Rochester, NY, January 12, 1933; m 1957, Barbara Glenn; c Marshall, Deborah & Jerald. **Education:** Univ Rochester, BS, 1955; Cornell Univ, MS, 1957, PhD (eng mech), 1961. **Honors & Awards:** Sigma Xi. **Professional Experience:** PROF EMER MECH & AEROSPACE ENG, UNIV MO, ROLLA, 2000-; assoc chmn mech eng, Univ Mo, Rolla, 1985-1998; consult, fed systs div, IBM Inc, 1959 & Lockheed-Calif Co, 1978-1985; prof mech & aerospace eng, Univ Mo, Rolla, 1976-2000; assoc prof mech eng, Univ MO, Rolla, 1971-1976; mem tech staff, Litton Ship Systs, Calif, 1971; US Agency Int Develop vis prof, Fed Univ Rio Del Janeiro, 1969-1970; staff engr, TRW Systs Inc, Calif, 1966-1969; lectr, Univ Southern Calif, 1962-1969; mem tech staff, TRW Systs Group, 1961-1966; instr eng mech, Cornell Univ, 1958-1961; mem tech staff, Ramo-Wooldridge Corp, 1957-1958; mcmullen fel, Cornell Univ, 1955-1956. **Memberships:** Am Soc Mech Engrs; Acoust Soc Am; Am Acad Mech; Am Inst Aeronaut & Astronaut. **Research Statement & Publications:** Vibrations and dynamic response of shell structures; liquid sloshing in rigid and flexible tanks; shimmy of aircraft landing gears; liquid behavior in low-gravity environments; acoustics; structure-borne noise propagation; smart structures; published more than 35 articles. **Mailing Address:** Dept Mech & Aeronaut Eng & Eng Mech, Univ Mo-Rolla, 1870 Miner Circle, Rolla, MO 65409-0257. **Fax:** 573-341-6899. **E-Mail:** lkoval@umr.edu

KOVAL, THOMAS MICHAEL, CELL BIOLOGY, RADIATION BIOLOGY. **Personal Data:** b Brownsville, Pa, November 20, 1950; m 1984, Amy Cvengros; c Thomas II, Matthew & Rachel. **Education:** Pa State Univ, BS, 1972; Ohio State Univ, MS, 1974, PhD (zool), 1976. **Professional Experience:** Consult, Zanvyl Kreiger sch arts & sci, 2000-; adj prof, Johns Hopkins Univ, 2000-; sr staff scientist, Nat Coun Radiation Protection & Measurement, 1993-2000; sr assoc consult, Div Radiation Oncol, Mayo Clin, 1988-1993; prof oncol, Div Radiation Oncol, Mayo Clin, 1988-1993; staff scientist, Nat Coun Radiation Protection & Measurements, 1987-1988; assoc res prof radiol, George Wash Univ Sch Med, 1982-1988; assoc staff scientist, Nat Coun Radiation Protection & Measurements, 1982-1986; from asst prof to assoc prof radiation ther & nuclear med, Hahnemann Med Col, 1979-1982; res assoc cancer res, Allegheny Gen Hosp, 1977-1979; Nat Res Serv award fel physiol & biophys, Univ Ill, 1976-1977. **Memberships:** Radiation Res Soc; Am Soc Cell Biol; Tissue Cult Asn; Sigma Xi; Am Soc Photobiol; Am Asn Cancer Res; AAAS. **Research Statement & Publications:** Stress-inducible processes in eukaryotic cells; cell and molecular biology; cell differentiation; radiation biology; mechanisms of radioresistance of cultured lepidopteran insect cells. **Mailing Address:** 4653 Cherry Valley Dr, Rockville, MD 20853.

KOVALAK, WILLIAM PAUL, AQUATIC BIOLOGY. **Personal Data:** b Detroit, Mich, April 12, 1946; m 1970, c 3. **Education:** Eastern Mich Univ, BS, 1967; Univ Mich, MS, 1969, PhD (fisheries), 1975. **Professional Experience:** LEC III BIOL, UNIV MICH, DEARBORN, as of 2005; biol systs scientist, Detroit Edison, beginning 1979; asst prof aquatic biol, Univ Mich, Dearborn, beginning 1978; asst prof biol, Allegheny Col, 1975-1978. **Memberships:** NAm Benthological Soc. **Research Statement & Publications:** Behavioral ecology of stream insects; ecology of Great Lakes fishes. **Mailing Address:** Univ Mich, Dept Nat Sci, 1125 CW, Dearborn, MI 48128-1491. **E-Mail:** kovalakw@detroitedison.com

KOVALICK, GAE E, BIOCHEMISTRY. **Education:** Univ NC, PhD, 1984. **Professional Experience:** ASSOC PROF BIOL, DEPT SCI & MATHS, THE UNIV TEX. PERMIAN BASIN, as of 2004. **Mailing Address:** Dept Sci & Math Univ Tex, 3140 Mesa Bldg, Odessa, TX 79762. **Fax:** 432-552-2265. **E-Mail:** kovalick_g@utpb.edu

KOVALY, JOHN J, RADAR, MISSILE SYSTEMS. **Personal Data:** b McKeesport, Pa, June 12, 1928; m 1957, c 2. **Education:** Muskingum Col, BS, 1950; Univ Ill, MS, 1953. **Professional Experience:** Lectr, UCLA, 1976-1986; CONSULT ENG, RAYTHEON CO, 1965-; adv res eng, Sylvana Electronics Corp, 1958-1965; lectr, Northeastern Univ, 1956-1958; Lieutenant, US Navy, 1956-1958; res eng, Control Systs Lab, 1951-1956; teaching asst, Physics Dept, Univ Ill, 1950-1951. **Memberships:** Fel Inst Elec & Electronics Engrs (pres, 1972). **Research Statement & Publications:** Synthetic aperture radar, a class of high resolution radar which obtains fine angular resolution by coherent processing of backscattered doppler histories; member of which did much of the original research and development on synthetic arrays, built the first flyable system and made first synthetic aperture radar map. **Mailing Address:** Raytheon Co, Missile Syst Div, Hartwell Rd, Bedford, MA 01730.

KOVAR, FREDERICK RICHARD, NUCLEAR PHYSICS, PLASMA PHYSICS & MECHANICS. **Personal Data:** b Cleveland, Ohio, September 20, 1933; m 1962, Margaret Wright; c Kathleen, Karen, Frederick Jr & Christine. **Education:** John Carroll Univ, BS, 1955; Washington Univ, St Louis, MA, 1957, PhD (physics), 1963. **Professional Experience:** INSTR PHYSICS, DIABLO VALLEY COL, 1994-; spec sci adv, Asst Secy Defense Atomic Energy, 1984-1986; sr physicist & proj mgr, Lawrence Livermore Lab, Univ Calif, 1963-1993; Consult, Bradford Components Co, NY, 1960; Instr physics, St Bonaventure Univ, 1959-1961. **Research Statement & Publications:** Hydrodynamics, strategic analysis, and nuclear energy. **Mailing Address:** 1078 Hacienda Dr, Walnut Creek, CA 94598.

KOVASH, MICHAEL, PHYSICS. **Education:** Ohio State Univ, BSc, 1973, PhD (Nuclear Physics), 1978. **Professional Experience:** PROF, DEPT PHYSICS & ASTRON, UNIV KY, as of 1999. **Research Statement & Publications:** Electromagnetic studies of the nucleon, two-nucleon system, and nuclei of special astrophysical. **Mailing Address:** Dept Physics & Astron, Univ Ky, 177 Chem Phys Bldg CP-371, Lexington, KY 40506-0055. **E-Mail:** kovash@pa.uky.edu

KOVATCH, GEORGE, ELECTRONICS & SYSTEMS ENGINEERING, TRANSPORTATION SYSTEMS. **Personal Data:** b Scranton, Pa, February 20, 1934; m 1968, c 4. **Education:** Princeton Univ, BSE, 1955; Cornell Univ, MS, 1960, PhD, 1962. **Honors & Awards:** Bronze Medal, US Dept Transp. **Professional Experience:** DIR, SMALL BUS INNOVATION RES PROG, 1984-; CHIEF, UNIV RES & TECHNOL INNOVATION OFF, TRANSP SYSTS CTR, US DEPT TRANSP, 1983-; chief, Indust Anal & Productivity Div, 1981-1983; chief, Transp Indust Anal Br, 1976-1981; proj mgr, US Dept Transp, 1970-1976; vis lectr, Brown Univ, 1968-1970; dept dir, Off Control Theory & Appln, 1967-1970; lab chief control & info systs, NASA, 1964-1967; vis lectr, Drexel Inst, 1963-1964; sr eng specialist control & guid systs, Martin Co, 1962-1964; mem vis sci staff, Res Inst Adv Studies, Md, 1962-1964; instr control eng, Cornell Univ, 1960-1962; commun officer, USAF, 1956-1957; engr electronics, Gen Elec Co, 1955-1960. **Memberships:** Sr mem Inst Elec & Electronics Engrs. **Research Statement & Publications:** Analysis and synthesis of automatic control and guidance systems utilizing modern control theory and techniques; analysis of intermodal transportation systems including new urban systems; automotive fuel economy studies; automotive industry analysis; university research and small business innovative research programs management; defense conversion small business; high technology research and development. **Mailing Address:** Volpe Nat Transp Syst Ctr, US Dept Transp, 55 Broadway Kendall Square, Cummaquid, MA 02142-1093. **Fax:** 617-494-2370. **E-Mail:** kovatch@volpe1.dot.gov

KOVELMAN, ROBERT, VIROLOGY, TRANSCRIPTIONAL REGULATION. **Personal Data:** b New York, NY, October 30, 1963. **Education:** Columbia Univ, AB, 1985; Rockefeller Univ, PhD (biochem & molecular biol), 1992. **Professional Experience:** SCIENTIST, SIGNAL PHARMACEUT LLC, 1994-; postdoctoral fel, Scripps Res Inst, 1992-1994. **Memberships:** AAAS. **Mailing Address:** Signal Pharmaceut LLC, 5555 Oberlin Dr, San Diego, CA 92121. **Fax:** 858-558-7513.

KOVES, WILLIAM JOHN, STRESS, THERMAL & DYNAMIC ANALYSIS OF PROCESS EQUIPMENT, COMPUTATIONAL FLUID MECHANICS FOR PROCESS EQUIPMENT. **Personal Data:** b Chicago, Ill, November 5, 1943; m 1977, Evelyn; c Brian & Melissa. **Education:** Univ Ill, BS, 1966, MS, 1967; Ill Inst Technol, PhD (mech eng), 1993. **Honors & Awards:** Dedicated Serv Award, Am Soc Mech Engrs, 2002; Certif Appreciation Meritorious Serv Profession, Chicago Sect, Am Soc Mech Engrs, 2002; Certif Recognition, Pressure Vessel & Piping Div, Am Soc Mech Engrs, 2002, 2004; Certif Excellence, Pressure Vessel Res Coun, 2003, 2005; Certif Commendation, Welding Res Coun, 2005; Certif Appreciation, Post Construct Stand Comt, Am Soc Mech Engrs, 2005. **Professional Experience:** Chmn, Am Soc Mech Engrs B31.3 Piping Code Comt, 2002-2005; VICE-CHMN, PRESSURE VESSEL RES COUN, 2000-; vice-chmn, Am Soc Mech Engrs B31.3 Piping Code Committee 1999-2002; mem, Comt Post Construct, Am Soc Mech Engrs, 1996-; chmn, Comt Flaw Eval, Am Soc Mech Engrs, 1996-1998; chmn Task Group Large Shell Intersections, 1993-; ENG FEL, UOP Llc, 1992-; chmn, Comt Elevated Temperature Design, Pressure Vessel Res Coun, Am Soc Mech Engrs, 1991-; tech mgr, UOP Llc.,

1987-1992; mem, Mech Design Comt, 1986-; mem, Subgroup Design Anal/External Pressure, 1980-; chmn, Subgroup High Pressure Piping, 1980-1984; mem, High Pressure Vessels, 1980-1982; eng staff, Uop, 1973-1987; sr engr, Aerojet Gen Corp, 1971-1973; engr & scientist, Douglas Aircraft, 1967-1971. **Memberships:** Fel Am Soc Mech Engrs. **Research Statement & Publications:** Stress analysis of pressure vessels and piping systems, specifically high temperature design, fatigue vibration, fracture mechanics and finite element analysis; fluid mechanics, multi-phase flow and granular solids as they apply to the performance of process equipment. **Mailing Address:** UOP Llc, 25E Algonquin Rd, Des Plaines, IL 60017-5017. **Fax:** 847-391-2758. **E-Mail:** bill.koves@uop.com

KOVESI-DOMOKOS, SUSAN, ELEMENTARY PARTICLE PHYSICS. **Personal Data:** b Budapest, Hungary, August 16, 1939; American citizen; m 1967. **Education:** Eotvos Lorand Univ, dipl physics, 1963. **Professional Experience:** PROF, DEPT PHYSICS, JOHNS HOPKINS UNIV, as of 2000; Univ Florence, Italy, 1983 & Stanford Linear Acceleration Ctr, 1984; prof theoret physics, Johns Hopkins Univ, beginning 1982; assoc prof physics, Johns Hopkins Univ, 1979-1982; vis sci staff mem, Deutsches Electronen-Synchrotron, Hamburg, Ger, 1976; vis scientist, Europ Orgn Nuclear Res, Switz, 1975-1976; asst prof theoret physics, Johns Hopkins Univ, 1974-1979; vis sci consult, Rutherford Lab, Eng, 1973; assoc res scientist, Johns Hopkins Univ, 1969-1974; res assoc, Cent Res Inst Physics, Budapest, 1963-1968; res asst theoret physics, Eotvos Lorand Univ, 1962-1963. **Memberships:** Ital Phys Soc; Europ Phys Soc; Am Math Soc. **Research Statement & Publications:** Strong interactions of elementary particles at high energy; critical phenomena. **Mailing Address:** Dept Physics & Astron, Johns Hopkins Univ, 3400 N Charles St, Baltimore, MD 21218-2686. **Fax:** 410-526-7239. **E-Mail:** skd@pha.jhu.edu

KOVITZ, ARTHUR A(BRAHAM), FLUID DYNAMICS. **Personal Data:** b Detroit, Mich, August 6, 1928; m 1957, Valerie; c Claudia R & Jordan A. **Education:** Univ Mich, BSE, 1950, MS, 1951; Princeton Univ, PhD (aeronaut eng), 1957. **Professional Experience:** PROF EMER MECH ENG, NORTHWESTERN UNIV, EVANSTON, 1969-; AFOSR, 1986-1987 & Visl e ase Corp, 1988-; consult, Universal Energy Systs, 1985; consult, Southern Conf Eng Educ, 1984; consult, Argonne Nat Labs, 1979-1980 & 1981-1982; actg chmn dept mech eng & astronaut sci, Northwestern Univ, Evanston, 1971-1973; consult, Am Mach & Foundry, 1962; consult, Bendix Aviation Corp, 1960; from asst prof to assoc prof, Northwestern Univ, Evanston, 1958-1969; res assoc, asst dir proj Squid, 1957-1958; consult, Aeronaut Res Assocs, Princeton, 1957-1958; res assoc, Princeton Univ, 1957; Rocket res engr, Bell Aircraft Corp, NY, 1951-1952. **Research Statement & Publications:** Heat transfer; fluid mechanics. **Mailing Address:** Dept Mech Eng, Technol Inst Northwestern Univ, Evanston, IL 60201-2970. **E-Mail:** akovitz@northwestern.edu

KOW, LEE-MING, HYPOTHALAMUS, NEUROPEPTIDES. **Education:** Calif Inst Technol, PhD (neurophysiol), 1972. **Professional Experience:** SR RES ASSOC, ROCKEFELLER UNIV, 1972-. **Mailing Address:** Dept Neurobiol, Rockfeller Univ, 1230 York Ave, New York, NY 10021-6399. **E-Mail:** kowl@rockefeller.edu

KOWAL, CHARLES THOMAS, ASTRONOMY. **Personal Data:** b Buffalo, NY, November 8, 1940; m 1968, c 1. **Education:** Univ Southern Calif, BS, 1963. **Honors & Awards:** James Craig Watson Medal, Nat Acad Sci, 1979. **Professional Experience:** STAFF SCIENTIST, COMPUT SCI CORP, SPACE TELESCOPE SCI INST, 1986-; mem prof staff, Calif Inst Technol, 1981-1985; scientist astron, Calif Inst Technol, 1978-1981; assoc scientist, Calif Inst Technol, 1976-1977; res asst, Calif Inst Technol, 1966-1975; res asst astron, Univ Hawaii, 1965-1966; res asst astron, Calif Inst Technol, 1963-1965. **Memberships:** Am Astron Soc; Int Astron Union. **Research Statement & Publications:** Supernovae; planetary satellites; asteroids; comets. **Mailing Address:** Space Telescope Sci Inst, 3700 San Martin Dr, Baltimore, MD 21218. **Fax:** 410-338-4579. **E-Mail:** kowal@stsci.edu

KOWAL, GEORGE M, NUCLEAR ENGINEERING, MECHANICAL ENGINEERING. **Personal Data:** b July 6, 1938; American citizen; m 1963, c 4. **Education:** Univ Detroit, BS, 1961; Pa State Univ, MS, 1964. **Professional Experience:** STAFF, APPL ANAL CORP, as of 2003; instr, Reading Area Community Col, beginning 1976; adj assoc prof, Drexel Univ, 1976-; dept mgr appl eng analysis, Gilbert Assocs Inc, beginning 1973; mem indust prof adv coun, Pa State Univ, 1973-1977; nuclear proj engr gen anal, 1967-1973; nuclear eng radiation protection, Elec Boat Div, Gen Dynamics Corp, 1964-1967. **Memberships:** Am Nuclear Soc. **Research Statement & Publications:** Analysts associated with nuclear power generation, especially nuclear safety, shielding, heaalth physics, fuel management, licensing, regulation and emergency core cooling systems. **Mailing Address:** Appl Anal Corp, PO Box 518, Shillington, PA 19607. **Fax:** 610-777-3718. **E-Mail:** gmkowal@applied-analysis.com

KOWAL, JEROME, INTERNAL MEDICINE & GERIATRICS, BIOCHEMISTRY. **Personal Data:** b New York, NY, March 16, 1931; m 1958, Martine; c Ann & Robert. **Education:** Tufts Univ, BS, 1952; Johns Hopkins Univ, MD, 1956. **Professional Experience:** CHEIF DIR OFF GERIATRIC MED & ASSOC DEAN GERIATRIC MED & AMASA B FORD MD PROF GERIATRIC MED, CASE WESTERN RES UNIV, as of 2003; assoc chief staff, geriatric extended care, Cleveland Va Med Ctr, beginning 1984; dir, Geriatrics Ctr Clin Assessment, Educ & Res, 1984; Div Geriatric Med, Case Western Res Univ, 1984; chief staff, Cleveland Vet Admin Med Ctr, 1977-1984; assoc dean vet affairs, Sch Med, Case Western Res Univ, 1977-1984; chief med serv, Cleveland Vet Admin Hosp, 1973-1977; assoc prof, Sch Med, Case Western Res Univ, 1970-1974; from asst prof to assoc prof med, Mt Sinai Sch Med, 1965-1970; fel molecular biol, Albert Einstein Col Med, 1963-1965; Steroid trainee, Worcester Found Exp Biol, 1962-1963; fel endocrinol, Mt Sinai Sch Med, 1960-1961. **Memberships:** Endocrine Soc; Am Soc Clin Invest; Am Soc Biol Chemists; Am Geriat Soc; Geront Soc Am. **Research Statement & Publications:** Mechanisms of hormone and enzyme action; biochemical regulation of adrenal cells; aging. **Mailing Address:** Dept Geriatric Med, Case Western Res Univ, 12200 Fairhill Rd, Cleveland, OH 44120. **Fax:** 216-844-7254. **E-Mail:** jxk9@po.cwru.edu

KOWAL, NORMAN EDWARD, WASTEWATER TREATMENT, COMPUTER SIMULATION. **Personal Data:** b Paterson, NJ, September 3, 1937; m 1962, c 3. **Education:** NY Univ, BA, 1958; Duke Univ, MA, 1960, PhD (plant ecol), 1966; WVa Univ, MD, 1977. **Professional Experience:** RES MED OFFICER, HEALTH EFFECTS RES LAB, US ENVIRON PROTECTION AGENCY, 1977-; asst prof biol, WVa Univ, 1969-1973; fel entom, Univ Ga, 1968-1969; fel systs ecol, Oak Ridge Nat Lab, 1967-1968; asst & assoc prof biol, Clark Col, 1965-1967; instr bot, Univ Philippines, 1963-1965. **Memberships:** AAAS; Soc Comput Simulation. **Research Statement & Publications:** Health effects of nonconventional municipal wastewater treatment, including land treatment, wastewater aquaculture, and land application of sludge; human exposure to and health effects of cadmium; computer simulation of pharmacokinetics; environmental exposure assessment. **Mailing Address:** Environ Criteria & Assessment Off, US Environ Protection Agency, Cincinnati, OH 45268.

KOWAL, ROBERT RAYMOND, SYSTEMATIC BOTANY, BIOMETRY. **Personal Data:** b Paterson, NJ, April 23, 1939. **Education:** Cornell Univ, BA, 1960, PhD (plant taxon & ecol), 1968. **Professional Experience:** PROF EMER BOT, UNIV WIS-MADISON, 1997-; prof bot, Univ Wis-Madison, 1994-1997; assoc prof bot, Univ Wis-Madison, 1976-1994; asst prof, Univ Wis-madison, 1971-1976; vis asst prof biol, Kans State Univ, 1969-1971; fel biomath, Dept Exp Statist, NC State Univ, 1967-1969. **Memberships:** AAAS; Bot Soc Am; Am Soc Plant Taxon; Int Asn Plan Taxon; Southern Appalachian Botanical Soc; New England Botanical Club. **Research Statement & Publications:** Systematics of Packera (Asteraceae); multivariate analysis, especially canonical analysis, as a tool in plant systematics; cytology of asteraceae tribe senecioneae. **Mailing Address:** Dept Bot, Univ Wis-Madison, 430 Lincoln Dr 238 Birge Hall, Madison, WI 53706. **Fax:** 608-262-7509. **E-Mail:** rrkowal@wisc.edu

KOWALAK, ALBERT DOUGLAS, PHYSICAL INORGANIC CHEMISTRY, BIOINORGANIC CHEMISTRY. **Personal Data:** b Portsmouth, Va, August 14, 1936; div, c 2. **Education:** Col William & Mary, BS, 1958; Va Polytech Inst, MS, 1963, PhD (chem), 1965. **Honors & Awards:** Fulbright lectr, Univ Repub, Montevideo, Uruguay. **Professional Experience:** PROF EMER CHEM, LOWELL TECHNOL INST, as of 2004; chmn dept, Lowell Technol Inst, beginning 1977; assoc prof chem, Lowell Technol Inst, beginning 1971; asst prof, Lowell Technol Inst, 1967-1971; instr inorg chem, Rose Polytech Inst, 1965-1967; res asst, Air Force Off Sci Res, 1963; teacher math high sch, Va, 1960-1961; rubber chemist, O'Sullivan Rubber Corp, 1960; teacher chem high sch, Va, 1958-1959. **Memberships:** Am Chem Soc. **Research Statement & Publications:** Kinetics of the arsenic-chromium reaction in various buffer solutions; synthesis coordination compounds. **Mailing Address:** Univ Lowell, Dept Chem, Rm 502b Olney Hall, Lowell, MA 01854-2881. **E-Mail:** kowalaka@woods.uml.edu

KOWALCZYK, JEANNE STUART, BIOCHEMISTRY. **Personal Data:** b Atlanta, Ga, December 22, 1942; m 1982, c 3. **Education:** Jacksonville State Univ, BS, 1965, MS, 1966; Auburn Univ, PhD (zoology), 1972. **Professional Experience:** PROF BIOL, UNIV SC, SPARTANBURG, as of 2004; ASSOC PROF BIOL, UNIV SC, SPARTANBURG, 1978-; asst prof biol & head dept, Belmont Abbey Col, 1973-1978; res assoc biochem, Auburn Univ, 1972-1973; teaching asst zool, Auburn Univ, 1968-1972; instr biol, Jacksonville State Univ, 1967-1968; Teacher French, Calhoun County Bd Educ, Ala, 1965-1967. **Memberships:** AAAS; Sigma Xi; Am Soc Parasitologists; Am Inst Biol Sci. **Research Statement & Publications:** Immunological phenomena associated with trichostrongylid parasitism and ecological factors in the distrubution of pathogenic Naegleria Fowleri. **Mailing Address:** Dept Math & Sci, Univ SC, 800 Univ Way, Spartanburg, SC 29303-4932. **Fax:** 864-503-5709. **E-Mail:** jkowalczyk@uscupstate.edu

KOWALCZYK, ROBERT E, MATHEMATICS. **Education:** Univ Mass, BA; Brown Univ, PhD. **Professional Experience:** PROF, DEPT MATHS, UNIV MASS, as of 2006. **Mailing Address:** Mass Univ, 323 Hixville Rd, North Dartmouth, MA 02747-2300. **Fax:** 508-910-6917. **E-Mail:** rkowalczyk@umassd.edu

KOWALCZYKOWSKI, STEPHEN C, MICROBIOLOGY. **Education:** Rensselaer Polytech Inst, BS, 1972; Georgetown Univ, PhD (biochem), 1976. **Professional Experience:** PROF, UNIV CA-DAVIS, as of 2005; DIR, CENTER GENETICS & DEVELOP, UNIV CA-DAVIS, as of 2005. **Mailing Address:** Univ CA-Davis, Davis, CA 95616-8665. **Fax:** 916-752-5939. **E-Mail:** sckowalczykowski@ucdavis.edu sckowalczykowski@ucdavis.edu

KOWALENKO, CHARLES GRANT, SOIL FERTILITY, SOIL BIOCHEMISTRY. **Personal Data:** b Saskatoon, Sask, May 14, 1946; m 1971, Joan; c Andrew Charles & Joanne Lynne. **Education:** Univ Sask, BSA, 1968, MSc, 1970; Univ BC, PhD (soil sci), 1974. **Professional Experience:** Ed, Can J Soil Sci, 1990-1993; Soils adv, Sri Lanka-Can Dry Zone Res & Develop Proj, Kandy, 1982-1983; Assoc ed, Can J Soil Sci, 1980-1982 & 1988-1989; RES SCIENTIST, SOIL BIOCHEM & FERTIL, AGR CAN RES STA, 1978-; res scientist, Soil Res Inst, 1974-1978. **Memberships:** Can Soc Soil Sci; Int Soc Soil Sci; Agron Soc Am; Soil Sci Soc Am; Agr Inst Can-BC Inst Agrologists. **Research Statement & Publications:** Studies on the nutrient requirements of a wide range of crops including forages, vegetables, and fruit; while minimizing environmental pollution with primary specialization in nitrogen and sulfur but also concerned with entire range of nutrients, both macro and micro. **Mailing Address:** Pac Agri-Food Res Ctr, Agr Can, PO Box 1000, Agassiz, BC V0M 1A0, Can. **Fax:** 604-796-0359. **E-Mail:** kowalenkog@agr.gc.ca

KOWALEWSKI, EDWARD JOSEPH, FAMILY MEDICINE. **Personal Data:** b Mt Carmel, Pa, April 21, 1920; m 1942, c 3. **Education:** Gettysburg Col, BS, 1942; George Washington Univ, MD, 1945. **Honors & Awards:** Clarence E Shaffner Award, 1971. **Professional Experience:** RETIRED; prof family med & chmn dept, Sch Med, Univ Md, Baltimore, 1972-1991; Pvt pract, 1933-1971. **Memberships:** Am Acad Family Physicians (pres, 1969-1970); Soc Teachers Family Med. **Research Statement & Publications:** Teaching of family medicine; core content of family medicine. **Mailing Address:** 1210 Buckingham Rd, Arnold, MD 21012.

KOWALIK, JANUSZ SZCZESNY, KNOWLEDGE-BASED SYSTEMS, HIGH PERFORMANCE COMPUTING. **Personal Data:** b Krzemieniec, Poland, February 28, 1934; American citizen; m 1959, Krystyna; c 1. **Education:** Gdansk Tech Univ, MSc, 1957; Polish Acad Sci, Dr Techn Sc, 1961. **Professional Experience:** AFFIL PROF COMPUT SCI, UNIV WASH, SEATTLE, 1985-; MGR, SCI COMPUT & ANALYSIS, BOEING CO, 1983-; dir systs & comput & prof comput sci, Wash State Univ, 1974-1983; mem fac, Dept Comput Sci, Sir George Williams Univ, 1973-1974; sr specialist & mgr math anal, Boeing Comput Serv, Inc, 1967-1973; res fel comput sci, Inst Advan Studies, Australian Nat Univ, 1966-1967; res fel, Royal Norweg Coun Sci & Indust Res, 1964-1966; Head comput ctr, Cent Shipbuilding Design Off, Poland, 1961-1964; vis prof, Univ Calabria, Italy; Consult. **Memberships:** Am Asn Artificial Intel; Asn Comput Mach; Inst Elec & Electronics Engrs. **Research Statement & Publications:** Parallel computation; artificial intelligence; knowledge based systems; coupling numerical and symbolic computation; supercomputing. **Mailing Address:** PO Box 24346 MS 7L-49, Seattle, WA 98124. **Fax:** 206-865-2966. **E-Mail:** kneves@atc.boeing.com

KOWALIK, VIRGIL CECIL, mathematics; deceased, see previous edition for last biography

KOWALSKI, BRUCE RICHARD, ANALYTICAL CHEMISTRY. **Personal Data:** b Chicago, Ill, March 7, 1942; m 1974, c 2. **Education:** Millikin Univ, BA, 1965; Univ Wash, PhD, 1969. **Honors & Awards:** Res Award, Eli Lilly Res Lab, 1976; Alexander von Humboldt Award, 1980; Coun Chem Res Award, 1987. **Professional Experience:** ENDOWED PROF, DEPT CHEM, UNIV WASH, as of 2004; DIR EMER, CTR PROCESS ANALYTICAL CHEM, as of 2004; distinguished prof analytical chem, Ctr Process Analytical Chem, beginning 1991; dir, Ctr Process Analytical Chem, beginning 1983; prof, Univ Wash, beginning 1978; from asst prof to assoc prof, Ctr Process Analytical Chem, 1975-1977; asst prof, Colo State Univ, 1972-1973; chemist, Lawrence Livermore Lab, Univ Calif, 1971-1972 & consult, 1972-; Houston, Tex, 1971-1972; chemist, Shell Develop Co, Emeryville, Calif, 1969-1971; mem, Dir Res Appln, NSF. **Memberships:** Pattern Recognition

Soc; Am Chem Soc; AAAS; NY Acad Sci; Chemometrics Soc. **Research Statement & Publications:** Chemometrics-the development of novel mathematical approaches for improving the measurement process; application of pattern recognition and other multivariant analysis methods to chemical data; process analytical chemistry including non invasive chemical analysis. **Mailing Address:** Dept Chem, Univ Wash, PO Box 351700, Seattle, WA 98195-1700. **Fax:** 206-685-8665. **E-Mail:** bruce@cpac.washington.edu

KOWALSKI, CHARLES JOSEPH, STATISTICS, BIOMETRICS. **Personal Data:** b Chicago, Ill, May 8, 1938; m 1962, c 3. **Education:** Roosevelt Univ, BS, 1962; Mich State Univ, MS, 1965; Univ Mich, Ann Arbor, PhD (biostatist), 1968. **Professional Experience:** PROF DENT BIOLOGIC & MAT SCI, SCH DENT, UNIV MICH, ANN ARBOR, as of 2005; asst dir statist res lab, sch dent, Univ Mich, Ann Arbor, beginning 1971; Nat Football League, 1969; Parke, Davis & Co, 1970; dir biomet lab, Dent Res Inst, beginning 1968; asst prof dent, Sch Dent, 1968-1974; consult, Statist Res Lab, 1968-1971. **Memberships:** Am Statist Asn; Biomet Soc; Inst Math Statist; Int Asn Dent Res; Am Asn Phys Anthrop. **Research Statement & Publications:** Multivariate statistical analysis, especially as applied to biomedical research; problems in growth and development; sequential and time series analysis. **Mailing Address:** Univ Mich, Sch Dent, Dept Biologic & Mat Sci, 3228 Dent, Ann Arbor, MI 48109-1078. **Fax:** 734-763-3453. **E-Mail:** chuckk@umich.edu

KOWALSKI, CONRAD JOHN, CARBANION CHEMISTRY, SYNTHETIC METHODOLOGY. **Personal Data:** b Chicago, Ill, July 9, 1947; m 1968, c 2. **Education:** Mass Inst Technol, SB, 1968; Calif Inst Technol, MS, 1971, PhD (chem), 1974. **Professional Experience:** GROUP DIR, SYNTHETIC CHEM, SMITH KLINE BEECHAM, 1988-; dir, Smith Kline Beecham, 1986-1988; assoc dir, Smith Kline Beecham, 1985-1986; asst dir, Smith Kline Beecham, 1982-1985; founder & ed, Synthetic Pathways J, 1981-1984; asst prof chem, Univ Notre Dame, 1976-1982; NIH fel, Columbia Univ, 1974-1976. **Memberships:** Am Chem Soc; AAAS; Sigma Xi. **Research Statement & Publications:** Development of new reactions and reactive intermediates for organic synthesis; devising syntheses of pharmaceutical products. **Mailing Address:** Dept Synthetic Chem, SmithKline Beecham Pharmaceut, 709 Swedeland Rd, PO Box 153, King of Prussia, PA 19406.

KOWALSKI, DAVID FRANCIS, DNA ENZYMOLOGY, DNA STRUCTURE. **Personal Data:** b Chester, Pa, February 20, 1947; m 1981, c 2. **Education:** LaSalle Col, BA, 1968; Purdue Univ, PhD (chem), 1974. **Professional Experience:** RES PROF, CANCER GENETICS DEPT, ROSEWELL PARK CANCER INST, as of 2004; res Scientist Biochem, Roswell park cancer inst, 1974-; asst, Purdue Univ, 1969-1973; Chemist, Eastern Regional lab, USDA, 1968. **Memberships:** Am Soc Biol Chemists. **Research Statement & Publications:** Structure, reactivity and functions of supercoiled DNA; occurrence, properties and functions of DNA topoisomerses; purification and characterization of mung bean nuclease. **Mailing Address:** Dept Molecular & Cell Biol, Roswell Park Cancer Inst, Buffalo, NY 14263-0001. **Fax:** 716-845-5906. **E-Mail:** david.kowalski@roswellpark.org

KOWALSKI, DONALD T, MYCOLOGY. **Personal Data:** b Dearborn, Mich, March 23, 1938; c 3. **Education:** Univ Mich, BS, 1960, MS, 1961, PhD (bot), 1964. **Professional Experience:** PROF EMER, CALIF STATE UNIV, CHICO, as of 2005; NSF res grants, 1965-1975; from asst prof to prof biol, Calif State Univ, Chico, 1964-1990. **Memberships:** Mycol Soc Am; Am Bryol & Lichenol Soc; Brit Mycol Soc; Sigma Xi. **Research Statement & Publications:** Developmental and cytological studies in the Ascomycetes and taxonomy of Myxo mycetes; biosystematics of Myxomycetes; lichen distribution. **Mailing Address:** Box 1415, Ft Bragg, CA 95437.

KOWALSKI, KENNETH L, SCATTERING THEORY, STRONG-INTERACTION & NONLINEAR OPTICS PHYSICS. **Personal Data:** b Chicago, Ill, July 24, 1932; m 1960, Audrey Bellin; c Claudia & Eric. **Education:** Ill Inst Technol, BS, 1954; Brown Univ, PhD (physics), 1963. **Professional Experience:** Scientist-in-residence, Argonne Nat Lab, 1986-1987; PROF PHYSICS, CASE WESTERN RES UNIV, 1973-; chmn dept, Dept Physics, 1971-1976; exec officer, Dept Physics, 1970-1971; Vis prof, Inst Theoret Physics, Univ Leuven, 1968-1969; from asst prof to assoc prof, Case Western Res Univ, 1963-1973; res assoc, Case Western Res Univ, 1962-1963; res assoc physics, Brown Univ, 1962; Aeronaut res scientist, Nat Adv Comt Aeronaut, 1954-1956. **Memberships:** Am Phys Soc. **Research Statement & Publications:** Properties of field theories and elementary particle interactions at high energies. **Mailing Address:** Dept Physics, Case Western Res Univ, Cleveland, OH 44106. **Fax:** 216-368-4671. **E-Mail:** klk3@po.cwru.edu

KOWALSKI, LUDWIK, NUCLEAR PHYSICS & NUCLEAR CHEMISTRY, COMPUTER SCIENCE. **Personal Data:** b Warsaw, Poland, October 24, 1931; m 1967, Ruth Linda; c Elaine Marcie. **Education:** Warsaw Tech Univ, ME, 1955; Univ Paris, MS, 1962, PhD (nuclear physics), 1963; Kean Col NJ, MA, 85. **Honors & Awards:** Distinguished Scholar-Montclair State coll 1992; Sokol fac fell Award-Montclair State univ 1995. **Professional Experience:** Teaching gifted children comput sci, 1990-; PROF PHYSICS, MONTCLAIR STATE COL, 1978-; assoc prof, Montclair State Col, 1969-1978; Res assoc nuclear chem, Columbia Univ, 1964-1969; Teaching & using VAX/VMS Comput Simulations. **Memberships:** Am Asn Physics Teachers. **Research Statement & Publications:** Experimental nuclear physics; high energy fission; nuclear reactions at low energies; heavy ion nuclear reactions; application of semiconductor detectors and mica track detectors for nuclear research. **Mailing Address:** Dept Physics & Earth Sci, Montclair State Col, Upper Montclair, NJ 07043.

KOWALSKI, RICHARD, MATHEMATICS. **Personal Data:** b Boston, Mass, April 8, 1940. **Education:** Northeastern Univ, BS, 1962; Case Inst Technol, MS, 1963, PhD (math), 1967. **Professional Experience:** Ed, Trans on Reliability, 1986-1987; mem, Reliability Soc Admin Comt, Inst Elec & Electronics Engrs, beginning 1984; sr proj leader, ARINC Res Corp, beginning 1981; group mgr, Arinc Res Corp, 1975-1981. **Memberships:** Armed Forces Commun & Electronics Asn; Math Asn Am; Sigma Xi; Inst Elec & Electronics Engrs (secy 1989-1990 treas 1991-). **Research Statement & Publications:** Software quality assurance and reliability. **Mailing Address:** ARINC Res Corp, 2551 Riva Rd, Annapolis, MD 21401.

KOWALSKI, STANLEY BENEDICT, NUCLEAR PHYSICS. **Personal Data:** b Wishart, Sask, February 23, 1935; m 1961, c 2. **Education:** Univ Sask, BS, 1957, MS, 1958; Mass Inst Technol, PhD (physics), 1963. **Professional Experience:** PROF PHYSICS, MASS INST TECHNOL, as of 2003; SR RES SCIENTIST, MASS INST TECHNOL, 1964-; asst prof physics, 1964-1977; res physicist, 1963-1964. **Memberships:** Am Phys Soc. **Research Statement & Publications:** Photonuclear reactions; accelerator physics. **Mailing Address:** Dept Physics, Mass Inst Technol, Rm 26-427 77 Mass Ave, Cambridge, MA 02139-4307. **Fax:** 617-253-8554. **E-Mail:** sk@mitlns.mit.edu

KOWALSKI, STEPHEN WESLEY, INORGANIC CHEMISTRY, SCIENCE EDUCATION. **Personal Data:** b Bayonne, NJ, June 24, 1931; m 1971, Barbara A Soffe; c Scott N, Brian A, Stephen E, Kristine E, Kathryn L & Lillian A. **Education:** Fairleigh Dickinson Univ, BS, 1953; NY Univ, MA, 1954, PhD (sci educ), 1964. **Professional Experience:** EMER PROF, MONTCLAIR STATE UNIV, 1995-; chmn, Physics-Geosci Dept, 1968-1972; coordr & supvr sci & math, MA in Teaching Prog, 1968-1969; coordr-supvr, Summer Sci Insts, AID, India, 1966 & 1967; consult, sr assoc, Danforth Found, 1962-; prof sci, Montclair State Univ, 1956-1995; res chemist, Hoffmann-La Roche, 1956-1967; guest lectr, Upsala Col, 1954-1965 & Fairleigh Dickinson Univ, 1955-1964; teacher high sch, NJ, 1955-1956; Instr, Upsala Col, 1953-1954 & NY Univ, 1954-1955; Res chemist & consult, Shulton, Inc, NJ, 1953-1956; consult, NSF & Memory Flavors, Inc. **Memberships:** AAAS; Am Chem Soc; Nat Sci Teachers Asn. **Research Statement & Publications:** Consumer testing; polyethylene permeability; synthetic flavor derivatives; chromatography; consumer science. **Mailing Address:** 23 Dwyer Rd, Wayne, NJ 07470.

KOWANKO, NICHOLAS, ORGANIC CHEMISTRY. **Personal Data:** b Charkov, Ukraine, June 7, 1934; div, c 2. **Education:** Univ Adelaide, BS, 1956, PhD (org chem), 1961. **Professional Experience:** PROF EMER, MINN STATE UNIV, MOORHEA, 1996-; prof chem, Minn State Univ, Moorhea, 1977-1996; chmn dept chem, Minn State Univ, Moorhea, 1969-1973; assoc prof, Minn State Univ, Moorhea, 1968-1977; sr chemist cent res labs, Minn Mining & Mfg Co, 1964-1968; Instr chem exten div, Univ Minn, 1962-1968; asst prof, Univ Minn, 1962-1964; fel, Univ Minn, 1961-1962; res assoc chem, Univ Calif, Berkeley, 1961; Fulbright travel grant to US, 1960; Teacher high sch, Australia, 1957. **Memberships:** Am Chem Soc; Royal Soc Chem; Royal Australian Chem Inst. **Research Statement & Publications:** Catalysis and desulfurization of organic compounds by metals; structure and synthesis of natural products, biosynthesis of natural products; direct fluorination studies. **Mailing Address:** Dept Chem, Minn State Univ, 1104 7th Ave S, 411 Hagen Hall, Moorhead, MN 56563. **Fax:** 218-477-2137.

KOWARSKI, A AVINOAM, PEDIATRICS, ENDOCRINOLOGY. **Personal Data:** b Tel-Aviv, Israel, December 30, 1927; m 1950, c 2. **Education:** Hebrew Univ, MD, 1955. **Professional Experience:** PROF & DIR, DIV PEDIAT ENDOCRINOL, SCH MED, UNIV MD, 1981-; assoc prof pediat, Sch Med, Johns Hopkins Univ, 1972-; from instr to asst prof, 1967-1972; chief physician, Hadassah Univ Hosp, Israel, 1965-1967; fel pediat endocrinol, Sch Med, Johns Hopkins Univ, 1962-1965; asst physician, Hadassah Univ Hosp, Israel, 1955-1962. **Memberships:** Endocrine Soc; Am Pediat Soc; Soc Pediat Res; Am Fedn Clin Res. **Research Statement & Publications:** Human metabolism of hormones in healthy and diseased children and adults; growth hormone; diabetes; hypoglycemia; hypertension. **Mailing Address:** Univ Md, Sch Med Pediat, 655 W Baltimore St, Baltimore, MD 21201-1559.

KOWARSKI, CHANA R, PHARMACEUTICS. **Personal Data:** b Kaunas, Lithuania, June 1, 1929; American citizen; m 1950, c 2. **Education:** Sch Pharm, Switz, BS, 1953; Sch Pharm, Israel, PhD (pharm chem), 62. **Honors & Awards:** Lederle Res Award, 1976. **Professional Experience:** PROF PHARM, TEMPLE UNIV, 1975-; assoc prof, vis prof, 1969-1975; Temple Univ, vis prof, 1967-1969; fel phys chem, Hebrew Univ, Jerusalem, 1966-1967; fel, Temple Univ, 1963-1965; teaching fel, Sch Pharm, Israel, 1957-1962; Chief pharmacist, RAFA Labs, Israel, 1953-1959. **Memberships:** Am Pharmaceut Asn; Am Pharmaceut Soc; Sigma Xi; Am Asn Cols Pharm. **Research Statement & Publications:** Absorption and bioavailability of drugs using the nonthrombogenic continuous withdrawal method; exemplary subjects include sulfamthiazole, sulfaethylthiadiazole, aspirin; insulin glucagon; novel delivery systems; nasal delivery, drugs and proteins (insulin, growth hormone). **Mailing Address:** Dept Pharmaceut Sci, Temple Univ Sch Pharm, 3307 N Broad St, Philadelphia, PA 19140-5101.

KOWEL, STEPHEN THOMAS, ELECTRICAL ENGINEERING, OPTOELECTRONICS. **Personal Data:** b Philadelphia, Pa, November 20, 1942; m 1970, Janis; c Ann, Eugene & Rose. **Education:** Univ Pa, BSEE, 1964, PhD (elec eng), 1968; Polytech Univ, MSEE, 1966. **Honors & Awards:** Centennial Medal 1984. **Professional Experience:** PROF ELEC ENG, 2004-, Geier Prof Eng Educ, and dean, 1999-2004, ENG COL, UNIV CINCINNATI; interim dean eng, 1997-1998, dir, phd prog optical sci & eng, 1992-1997; prof, 1990-1999 & chmn, 1990-1997, dept elec & comput eng, Univ Ala, Huntsville; dir, Organized Res Prog Polymeric Thin Film Systs, 1988-1990; vchmn, Dept Elec Eng & Comput Sci, Univ Calif, Davis, 1986-1990; prof, Dept Elec Eng & Comput Sci, Univ Calif, Davis, 1984-1990; vis prof, Nat Nanofabrication Facil, Sch Elec Eng, Cornell Univ, 1982-1983; prof elec eng, Syracuse Univ, 1979-1984; vpres, Deft Labs, Inc, 1976-1984; consult, Electronics Lab, Gen Elec Co, 1976-1984; grants & res contracts, NSF, US Army Night Vision & Electrooptics Lab, USAF Rome Air Develop Ctr, 1971-; from asst prof to assoc prof, Syracuse Univ, 1969-1979; assoc elec eng, Moore Sch, Univ Pa, 1968-1969; Prin investr, Syracuse Univ, UC Davis, Univ Ala, Huntsville. **Memberships:** Fel Inst Elec & Electronics Engrs; Sigma Xi; fel Optical Soc Am, Am Assoc Univ Profs. **Research Statement & Publications:** Acoustooptics and electrooptics; optical imaging with surface acoustic waves; optical and electronic applications of polymers, liquid crystals; three-dimensional autostereoscopic displays. **Mailing Address:** ECECS Dept, Col Eng, Univ Cincinnati, ML 0030, Cincinnati, OH 45221-0030. **E-Mail:** stephen.kowel@uc.edu

KOWERT, BRUCE ARTHUR, physical chemistry; deceased, see previous edition for last biography

KOWKABANY, GEORGE NORMAN, ORGANIC CHEMISTRY. **Personal Data:** b Jacksonville, Fla, September 16, 1923. **Education:** Univ Fla, BS, 1947; Yale Univ, MS, 1949, PhD (chem), 1951. **Professional Experience:** PROF EMER CHEM, CATH UNIV AM, as o f 1998; res chemist, USDA, Beltsville, Md, 1980-1981; vis assoc prof, Med Sch, Univ Miami, 1970-1971; NIH spec fel, Univ Ferrara, 1963-1964; assoc prof org chem, Cath Univ Am, 1960-1986; from instr to asst prof, 1953-1960; chemist, Nat Bur Standards, 1952-1953; fel carbohydrate res, Ohio State Univ, 1950-1952. **Memberships:** Fel AAAS; fel Am Inst Chemists; Am Chem Soc. **Research Statement & Publications:** Paper chromatography; separation of amino acids and carbohydrates; structures of polysaccharides; enzymology. **Mailing Address:** Cath Univ Am, 620 Mivh Ave N E, Washington, DC 20064.

KOWLES, RICHARD VINCENT, CELL BIO ANAL CYTOL. **Personal Data:** b Ivanhoe, Minn, May 9, 1932; m 1956, Rose; c 5. **Education:** Winona State Col, BS, 1954, MS, 1963; St Mary's Col Minn, MS, 1967; Univ Minn, St Paul, PhD (genetics), 1972. **Honors & Awards:** 1986 Prof with Distinction, St Marys Univ of Minn; 1984 Minn Sci Teacher of the yr, Minn Academy of Sci; 1979 Brother Charles Severin Award for Teacher of the year, St Mary's Univ of WHS inn; 2002 Winone State Univ, Alumnus with Distinction, Winona State Univ. **Professional Experience:** PROF BIOL WITH DISTINCTION, ST MARYS UNIV MINN, 1986-; vis res prof, Univ Minn, 1983-1984; from asst prof to prof, St Marys Univ Minn, 1972-1986; asst prof, Univ Wis, River Falls, 1971-1972; Teacher high schs, Minn, 1954-1968. **Memberships:** Genetics Soc Am; Am Genetic Asn; Soc Study Evolution; Radiation Res Asn; AAAS; Am Bot Soc. **Research Statement & Publications:** Chromosome aberrations; molecular cytogenetics of endosperm in maize; Chromosome non-disjunction. **Mailing Address:** Dept Biol, St Marys Univ Minn 700 Terrace Heights, Winona, MN 55987-1321. **Fax:** 507-494-6035. **E-Mail:** dkowles@smumn.edu

KOWLESSAR, O DHODANAND, MEDICINE. **Personal Data:** b India. **Education:** Univ Rochester, PhD (med), 1955. **Professional Experience:** PROF & ASSOC CHMN, DEPT MED, THOMAS JEFFERSON UNIV, 1987-; dir gastroneurol, Med Sch, Cornell Univ, dir med, 1966; asst prof, Med Sch, Cornell Univ, dir med, 1964; Resident internal med, Cornell Hosp, NY, fel. **Memberships:** Sigma Xi; Am Soc Clin Nutrit; Inst Nutrit. **Mailing Address:** Dept Med Jefferson Med Col Thomas Jefferson Univ, 1025 Walnut St, Philadelphia, PA 19107-5083. **Fax:** 215-955-2318.

KOWOLENKO, MICHAEL D, IMMUNOTOXICOLOGY. **Personal Data:** b July 23, 1955. **Education:** Northeastern Univ, BS, 1978, MS, 1981, PhD (med lab sci), 1986. **Professional Experience:** VPRES, GLOBAL QUALITY, BIOGEN INC, as of 2002; mgr immunotoxicol, Dept Investigative Toxicol, Bristol-Myers Squibb Pharmaceut Res Inst, 1989-1993; asst res prof, Dept Microbiol & Immunol & Dept Med, 1988-1989; Nat Inst Environ Health Sci fel, Albany Med Col, 1987-1988; teaching asst, Northeastern Univ, 1983-1985. **Memberships:** Am Asn Immunologists; Soc Toxicol. **Research Statement & Publications:** Investigative toxicology; author of more than 20 technical publications. **Mailing Address:** Biogen Idec Inc, 14 Cambridge Ctr, Cambridge, MA 02142. **Fax:** 617-679-2617.

KOYAMA, RICHARD Y, ELECTRICAL ENGINEERING. **Professional Experience:** STAFF, TRIQUINT SEMICONDUCTOR, as of 2000. **Memberships:** Advan Mat & Mfg. **Mailing Address:** TriQuint Semiconductor, PO Box 4935, Beaverton, OR 97076. **Fax:** 331-470-3333.

KOZA, JOHN R, MATHEMATICS. **Education:** Univ Mich, PhD (comput sci), 1972. **Professional Experience:** CONSULT PROF, DEPT ELEC ENG, SCH ENG, STANFORD UNIV, as of 2006. **Mailing Address:** Stanford Univ, PO Box K, Los Altos, CA 94023-1669. **Fax:** 650-941-9430. **E-Mail:** john@johnkoza.com

KOZAI, YOSHIHIDE, CELESTIAL MECHANICS, SATELLITE GEODESY. **Personal Data:** b Tokyo, Japan, April 1, 1928; m 1958, Mine Nagai; c Aya K & Kay O. **Education:** Univ Tokyo, MS, 1951; Ministry Educ, DSc, 1958. **Honors & Awards:** Acad & Imperial Prizes, Japan Acad, 1979; D Brouwer Award, Am Astron Soc, 1988. **Professional Experience:** DIR, NAT ASTRON OBSERV, 1988-; dir, Tokyo Astron Observ, 1981-1988; managing ed, Japanese Astron Soc, 1975-1982; from assoc prof to dir of nat Astronomical Obsevatory 1988-1994; prof astron, Univ Tokyo, 1963-1988; res assoc Harvard Col Observ, 1959-1962; astronr, Smithsonian Astrophys Observ, 1958-1962; Res asst, Univ Tokyo, 1952-1958. **Memberships:** Japanese Astron Soc (pres, 1982-1984); Int Astron Union (pres, 1988-1991); Astron Soc Japan; Royal Astron Soc London. **Research Statement & Publications:** Theoretical researches on motions of earth satellites, minor planets and others; investigation on gravitational fields of the earth by use of artificial satellites; dynamical theory of asteroid orbit gravitational wave detector. **Mailing Address:** 3-6-27 Suginami-Ku, Tokyo 168, Tokyo, Japan. **Fax:** 813-422-343690. **E-Mail:** kozai@wave.plala.or.jp

KOZAK, ANTAL, FOREST BIOMETRICS. **Personal Data:** b Tiszapuspoki, Hungary, May 22, 1936; Canadian citizen; m 1963, c 2. **Education:** Univ BC, BSF, 1959, MF, 1961, PhD (biomet), 1963. **Honorary Degrees:** DSc, Sopron, Hungary, 1989. **Professional Experience:** PROF EMER FAC FORESTRY, UNIV BC, as of 2004; assoc dean, Univ BC, beginning 1978; prof fac forestry, Univ Bc, beginning 1972; from asst prof to assoc prof, Univ Bc, 1965-1972; res off statist, Can Dept Forestry, 1963-1965; Vis lectr, Univ BC, 1963-1965; Res asst data processing, Univ BC, 1962-1963. **Memberships:** Am Statist Asn; Biomet Soc; Can Inst Forestry. **Research Statement & Publications:** Application of statistics for forestry problems; development of estimating systems for forest inventory; taper equations; biomass equations. **Mailing Address:** Fac Forestry, Forest Sci Ctr, Univ BC, Second Floor, 2045 - 2424 Main Mall, Vancouver, BC V6T 1Z4, Can. **Fax:** 604-822-9106. **E-Mail:** kozak@interchg.ubc.ca

KOZAK, GARY S, ANALYTICAL CHEMISTRY, PHYSICAL CHEMISTRY. **Personal Data:** b Pittsburgh, Pa, June 13, 1938; m 1996, Carole; c Scott L, Gretchen L & Troy S. **Education:** Ind Univ, BS, 1960; Univ Ariz, PhD (chem), 1963. **Professional Experience:** RETIRED; prog dir, Health & Environ Progs, CHQ/Armonk, 1993-1995; prog dir, Tech Interchange Prog, 1987-1993; prog dir tech personnel resources, IBM Europe, Paris, 1981-1986; dir spec univ prog, IBM Europe, Paris, 1978-1981; dir sci & contrib progs, IBM Europe, Paris, 1974-1978; mgr educ & sci rels, IBM World Trade Corp, 1971-1974; sr assoc chemist, mgr PhD recruitment progs, 1969-1971; proj mgr & develop chemist, IBM Corp, 1968-1969; proj chemist, IBM Corp, 1966-1968; staff chemist, IBM Corp, 1964-1966; sr assoc chemist, IBM Corp, 1963-1964. **Memberships:** AAAS; Am Chem Soc; World Wildlife Fund. **Research Statement & Publications:** Kinetic studies with electrogenerated halogens; photosensitive polymers; epoxy resins and laminates. **Mailing Address:** Fox Run Redcoat Rd, West Norwalk, CT 06850.

KOZAK, JOHN JOSEPH, CHEMICAL PHYSICS, BIOPHYSICAL CHEMISTRY. **Personal Data:** b Cleveland, Ohio, September 14, 1940; m 1969, c 3. **Education:** Case Inst Technol, BS, 1961; Princeton Univ, PhD (chem), 1965. **Professional Experience:** DEAN & PROF CHEM, FRANKLIN COL ARTS & SCI, UNIV GA, 1988-; vis prof, Ecole Polytechnique Federale Del Lausanne, 1978; from asst prof to prof chem, Univ Notre Dame, 1976-1988; vis prof, Free Univ Brussels, 1975; chmn, Prog Unified Sci, Univ Notre Dame, beginning 1970; res assoc, Univ Chicago, 1967-1968; NIH fel chem, Free Univ Brussels, 1965-1967. **Memberships:** Am Chem Soc; Sigma Xi. **Research Statement & Publications:** Interaction of radiation and matter; investigations of liquid dissolved state; theory of phase transitions; studies on nature of irreversibility; reaction-diffusion theory. **Mailing Address:** Dept Chem, Iowa State Univ, 1605 Gilman Hall, Ames, IA 50011-3111. **E-Mail:** kozak@iastate.edu

KOZAK, LESLIE P, BIOLOGY. **Personal Data:** b Dauphin, Man, October 28, 1940. **Education:** Univ Notre Dame, PhD (biochem), 1969. **Professional Experience:** PROF MOLECULAR GENETICS, PENNINGTON BIOMED RES CTR, LA STATE UNIV, as of 2004; SR STAFF SCIENTIST, JACKSON LAB, 1970-. **Research Statement & Publications:** Molecular genetics of mammals. **Mailing Address:** Dept Molecular Genetics, Pennington Biomed Res Ctr, La State Univ, Baton Rouge, LA 70808. **Fax:** 225-763-3030.

KOZAK, MARILYN SUE, BIOCHEMISTRY OF PROTEIN SYNTHESIS. **Education:** Johns Hopkins Univ, PhD (microbiol), 1972. **Professional Experience:** PROF BIOCHEM, JOHNSON MED SCH, 1990-; Prof biol, Univ Pittsburgh, 1985-1990. **Mailing Address:** Dept Biochem, Johnson Med Sch, Johns Hopkins Univ, Rm 153, 675 Hoes Lane, Piscataway, NJ 08854-5635. **Fax:** 732-235-5356. **E-Mail:** kozakma@umdnj.edu

KOZAK, WLODZIMIERZ M, VISUAL PHYSIOLOGY, PSYCHOPHYSICS. **Personal Data:** b Warsaw, Poland, May 7, 1927; m 1974, Eva; c J Ashot. **Education:** Univ Lodz, MS, 1951; Univ Sydney, PhD (visual electrophysiol), 1964. **Honorary Degrees:** DSc (visual electrophysiol), Polish Acad Sci, 1966. **Honors & Awards:** Sci Award, Div Natural Sci, Polish Acad Sci, 1955. **Professional Experience:** PROF EMER PHYSIOL & BIOENGINEERING, CARNEGIE-MELLON UNIV, 1995-; grant, NSF, Diabetes Res & Educ Found grant, 1989-1990; grant, Hewlett-Packard Inc, 1987; res scholar, Monash Univ, Australia, 1986; grant, Pfizer Inc, 1984; exchange scholar, Hungary, 1984; vis fel, Australian Nat Univ, Canberra, 1979; Sch Med, Johns Hopkins Univ, Chile, 1970; NSF, Japan, 1978; sr scientist dept med, Shadyside Hosp, Pittsburgh, 1975-; grant, Scaife Fund grant & Ford Found, Health Res & Serv Found grant, 1973-1975, 1988; grant, Scaife Fund grant & Ford Found, Carnegie-Mellon Univ, 1971-1972; from assoc prof to prof, Carnegie-mellon Univ, 1970-1995; vis assoc res prof visual physiol, State Univ NY, Buffalo, 1968-1970; fel, Wellcome Trust Inst Ophthal, Univ London, 1968; Lab Afferent Systs, 1967-1968; head, Lab Electrophysiol, 1964-1967; Kkarolinska Inst, Sweden, 1966; recipient habitation grant, Div Natural Sci, Po lish Acad Sci, 1965-1966; visitor, Brit Coun, Gt Brit, 1965; Polish Acad Sci & Acad Sci, USSR, 1965; Warsaw Tech Univ, 1965; lectr, Univ Lodz, 1952-1955; fel, Ophthalmic Res Inst Australia, Univ Sydney, 1960-1963; fel, Rockefeller Found, 1959-1960; assoc prof & sr scientist, Nencki Inst Exp Biol, Polish Acad Sci, Warsaw, 1956-1964; asst prof neurophysiol, Nencki Inst Exp Biol, Univ Lodz, 1946-1956. **Memberships:** Int Brain Res Orgn; Polish Inst Arts & Sci Am. **Research Statement & Publications:** Electrophysiology and conditioning of salivary secretion; plasticity and memory traces of spinal cord reflexes; eye optics; electrophysiology of retina and visual pathway; oscillatory components of electroretinograms and evoked potentials; electroretinograms in diabetic retinopathy; coding of brightness and color information in eye and brain; subjective color sensations; computer Fourier analysis; neurophysiology; aldose reductase inhibition in diabetes mellitus; nuclear magnetic resonance imaging of the eye; integrity of blood retinal barrier in diabetes mellitus. **Mailing Address:** Biomed Eng Prog, Carnegie-Mellon Univ, Doherty Hall 2313, Pittsburgh, PA 15213-3890. **Fax:** 412-268-1173. **E-Mail:** wk01@andrew.cmu.edu

KOZAM, GEORGE, ANATOMY, PATHOLOGY. **Personal Data:** b Union City, NJ, March 28, 1924; m 1953. **Education:** NY Univ, BA, 1945, MS, 1946, PhD (human anat), 1950, DDS, 1953. **Professional Experience:** PROF ANAT, COL MED & DENT NJ, 1971-; Vis asst prof path, Dent Col, Fairleigh Dickinson Univ, 1964-1965; from asst prof to assoc prof, Col Med & Dent NJ, 1958-1971; instr bact, Dent Col, 1953-1954; instr anat, Dent Col, 1947-1950; Asst biol, NY Univ, 1946-1947. **Memberships:** Am Dent Asn; fel Am Acad Oral Path; NY Acad Sci; Int Asn Dent Res. **Research Statement & Publications:** Capillary fragility; circulation in dental pulp; respiration of rat and rabbit dental pulp; effects of local anesthetics on the respiration of dental pulp; research on trigeminal nerve; effect of eugenol on nerve transmission and oral mucous membranes. **Mailing Address:** Dept Anat, Univ Med & Dent NJ Med Sch 185 S Orange Ave, Newark, NJ 07103-2714.

KOZARICH, JOHN WARREN, BIOLOGICAL CHEMISTRY, BIOCHEMISTRY. **Personal Data:** b Jersey City, NJ, June 20, 1949; m 1985, Marcia. **Education:** Boston Col, BS, 1971; Mass Inst Technol, PhD (biol chem), 1975. **Honors & Awards:** Pfizer Award in Enzyme Chem, Am Chem Soc, 1988. **Professional Experience:** CHMN & PRES, ACTIVX Inc, as of 2005; VPRES BIOCHEM, MERCK RES LABS, beginning 1993; Metallobiochem Study Sect, NIH, 1992-; vpres res & develop, Alkermes, Inc, Cambridge, Mass, 1989-1992; PROF, AGR BIOTECH CTR, MD BIOTECH INST, 1987-; PROF CHEM & BIOCHEM, UNIV MD, 1984-; Am Cancer Soc Fac Res Award, 1983-1988; Bioorg & Natural Prod Study Sect, NIH, 1983-1987; from asst prof to prof pharmacol, Yale Univ, 1977-1984; NIH fel biochem, Harvard Univ, 1974-1977. **Memberships:** Am Chem Soc; Sigma Xi; Am Soc Biochem & Molecular Biol. **Research Statement & Publications:** Design of enzyme inhibitors; mechanisms and stereochemistry of enzyme action; chemistry and biochemistry of modified nucleosides; mechanisms of drug induced DNA degradation. **Mailing Address:** ActivX BioScis Inc, 11025 N Torrey Pines Rd; Ste 120, La Jolla, CA 92037.

KOZEK, WIESLAW JOSEPH, IMMUNOLOGY, ULTRASTURCTURE. **Personal Data:** b Poniatowka, Poland, February 6, 1939; m 1971, Mireya; c Mark R, Laura W & Robert C. **Education:** Canisius Col, BS, 1961; Tulane Univ, MS, 1967, PhD (Parasitol), 1969. **Honors & Awards:** Diatome US Award, Micros Soc Am, 1998. **Professional Experience:** PROF, DEPT MICROBIOL & ZOOLOGY, UNIV PR SCH MED, as of 2003; prof, Dept Microbiol & Med, Med Sci Campus, Univ PR, 1996-2001; assoc prof, Dept Microbiol & Med Zool, Med Sci Campus, Univ Pr, 1984-1996; prin investr human filariasis, Int Collabr Infectious Dis Res Prog, Cali, Columbia, 1980-1984; adj assoc prof, Dept Trop Med, Tulane Sch Pub Health & Trop Med, 1980-1984; scientist, Int Collabr Infectious Dis Res Prog, Tulane Univ, Calif, Colombia, 1977-1984; asst res parasitologist, Calif Primate Res Ctr, Univ Calif, Davis, 1973-1977; Dept Immunol & Med Microbiol, Univ Fla, Gainesville, 1971-1972; fel, Dept Microbiol, Univ Chicago, 1969-1971. **Memberships:** Am Soc Trop Med & Hyg; Am Asn Vet Parasitologists; Am Soc Parasitologists; Sigma Xi; Wildlife Dis Asn; Am Soc Trop Vet Med. **Research Statement & Publications:** Medical helminthology; immunology, morphology, ultrastructure, animal models, and host-parasite relationship of filariae; epidemiology of human filariases in Columbia; culture of helminth cells; characterization of intracellular microorganisms of filarids; host-parasite relationships of Trichinella spiralis. **Mailing Address:** Dept Microbiol & Zoology, Univ PR Sch Med, PO Box 365067, San Juan, PR 00936-5067. **Fax:** 787-759-8257. **E-Mail:** wkozek@rcm.upr.edu

KOZEL, THOMAS RANDALL, MEDICAL MYCOLOGY, MEDICAL BACTERIOLOGY. **Personal Data:** b Ft Dodge, Iowa, January 31, 1946. **Education:** Univ Iowa, BA, 1967, MS, 1969, PhD (microbiol), 1971. **Professional Experience:** PROF & CHMN MICROBIOL, UNIV NEV, RENO, 1982-; vis assoc prof, Rockefeller Univ, 1980-1981; dir med admis, Univ Nev, Reno, 1972-1976; from asst prof to assoc prof, Univ Nev, Reno, 1971-1982; instr microbiol, Univ Iowa, 1969-1970. **Memberships:** Am Soc Microbiol; Harvey Soc; Sigma Xi. **Research Statement & Publications:** Cellular and molecular mechanisms of infection and resistance in systemic mycoses. **Mailing Address:** Dept Microbiol & Immunol, Sch Med, Univ Nev, 320, Reno, NV 89557-0046. **Fax:** 775-327-2332. **E-Mail:** trkozel@med.unr.edu

KOZIAR, JOSEPH CLEVELAND, POLYMER CHEMISTRY, ORGANIC CHEMISTRY. **Personal Data:** b Baltimore, Md, January 6, 1946; m 1968, c David. **Education:** Johns Hopkins Univ, BA, 1968, PhD (org chem), 1975. **Professional Experience:** TECH DIR, ABBEY COLOR, INC, 2000-; Lead chemist, Biosides Process Res, Rohm & Haas Co, 1992-2000; lead chemist, Emulsion Process Group, Rohm & Haas Co, 1990-1992; sr res chemist plastics & coatings, Emulsion Process Group, Rohm & Haas CO, 1975-1990; Res chemist process develop, Diamond Shamrock Corp, 1969-1971. **Memberships:** Am Chem Soc; AAAS. **Research Statement & Publications:** Polymer synthesis and characterization; monomer synthesis; organic photochemistry; polymer process research; organic process res. **Mailing Address:** 219 Liberty Dr, Langhorne, PA 19047. **E-Mail:** jckol@aol.com

KOZICKI, WILLIAM, THERMODYNAMICS. **Personal Data:** b Kenora, Ont, June 11, 1931; m 1963, c 1. **Education:** Univ Toronto, BASc, 1953, MASc, 1957; Calif Inst Technol, PhD (thermodyn), 1962. **Professional Experience:** PROF EMER CHEM ENG, UNIV

OTTAWA, 1996-; assoc dean eng, Univ Ottawa, 1976-1996; from asst prof to prof, Univ Ottawa, 1962-1996; res fel thermodyn, Calif Inst Technol, 1961-1962; Process engr, Textile Fibres Div, Du Pont Can, 1953-1955. **Memberships:** Sigma Xi. **Research Statement & Publications:** Transport phenomena: rheology and flow of complex systems with particular emphasis on characterization of polymer adsorption and its role in improved oil recovery, turbulent drag reduction and as filtration aid. **Mailing Address:** Dept Chem Eng, Univ Ottawa, Tabaret Hall, 75 Laurier Ave E, Ottawa, ON K1N 6N5, Can.

KOZICKY, EDWARD LOUIS, WILDLIFE MANAGEMENT. **Personal Data:** b Elberon, NJ, February 11, 1918; m 1941, Carolyn; c Frank, Sarah & Charles. **Education:** Univ Maine, BS, 1941; Pa State Col, MS, 1942, PhD (zoology), 1948. **Professional Experience:** CERITIFIED WILDLIFE BIOLOGIST & DOG TRAINER, GODFREY, ILL, as of 2004; dir conserv dept, Winchester-Western Div, Olin Corp, 1956-1982; leader, Wildlife Res Unit, Iowa State Col, 1948-1956; chief res, State Div Fish & Game, NJ, beginning 1948; dir, Wildlife Legis Fund. **Memberships:** Wildlife Soc (pres, 1969-1970); Am Forestry Asn. **Research Statement & Publications:** Life history, ecology and management of game birds and mammals; the development, evaluation and improvement of game animal census techniques; development and promotion of shooting preserves. **Mailing Address:** 817 Southmoor Pl, Godfrey, IL 62035. **E-Mail:** cozie@joiasanet.com

KOZIK, EUGENE, COMPUTER SCIENCE, OPERATIONS RESEARCH. **Personal Data:** b Duquesne, Pa, September 22, 1924; m 1956, c 2. **Education:** Univ Pittsburgh, BS, 1949, ML, 1950, PhD, 1960. **Professional Experience:** PRES, KOZIK & ASSOCS, 1970-; comput comt, Am Inst Planners, 1967- & urban info & measurement comt, Nat Acad Sci, 1968-; mgr info sci, Gen Elec Co, 1966-1970; Univ Rochester, 1961 & Pa State Univ, 1964-; mem, Int Comt Sci Mgt, Hist Eval Res Orgn, McLean, Va, 1962-; dir adv studies, Burroughs Corp, 1962-1966; prog mgr mgt sci, Opers Res, Inc, 1961-1962; mgr planning & controls, Gen Dynamics Corp, 1960-1961; Lectr, Duquesne Univ, 1960; mgt sci consult, Univ Pittsburgh, 1959-1960; tech adminstr res & develop, Wright Air Develop Ctr, 1953-1957; Engr, Gulf Oil Corp, 1948-1950. **Research Statement & Publications:** Management and information science; intergrated management system; data management; computer technology. **Mailing Address:** 38 Rabbit Run Rd, Malvern, PA 19355.

KOZIK, MARIUSZ M, INORGANIC CHEMISTRY. **Education:** Jagiellonian Univ, MSc, 1981; Georgetown Univ, PhD, 1987. **Professional Experience:** CHMN, DEPT CHEM, CANISIUS COL, BUFFALO, 2003-; PROF CHEM, CANISIUS COL, BUFFALO, 1999-; from asst to assoc prof, Dept Chem, Canisius Col, Buffalo, 1990-1998. **Memberships:** Sigma Xi; Royal Soc Chem. **Mailing Address:** Dept Chem, Canisius Col, Buffalo, NY 14208.

KOZIKOWSKI, ALAN PAUL, ORGANIC CHEMISTRY, NEUROCHEMISTRY. **Personal Data:** b Menominee, Mich, October 27, 1948; m 1975, c 2. **Education:** Univ Mich, BS, 1970; Univ Calif, Berkeley, PhD (org chem), 1974. **Honors & Awards:** Ciba-Geigy Award, 1982. **Professional Experience:** PROF & HEAD, DEPT MED CHEM & PHARMACOG, UNIV ILL, as of 2003; VPRES MED CHEM, TROPHIX PHARMACEUT, 1994-; dir chem, Mayo Clin, 1990-1994; prof behav Neurosci, 1988; prof chem, Univ Pittsburgh, 1984-1990; fel, Japan Soc for Promoting Sci, 1984; asst prof, assoc prof & Camille & Henry Dreyfus teacher scholar, 1980-1983; asst prof, Alfred P Sloan Fel Org Chem, 1976-1990; asst prof, Univ Pittsburgh, 1976-1980; NIH fel org chem, Harvard Univ, 1974-1976. **Memberships:** Am Chem Soc; Chem Soc; Sigma Xi; Soc Neuroscience. **Research Statement & Publications:** Synthetic organic chemistry; synthesis of alkaloids and carbohydrates; organometallics; neuroscience. **Mailing Address:** Dept Med Chem & Pharmacog Univ Ill, 539C Pharm, Chicago, IL 60607-7173. **Fax:** 312-996-7107. **E-Mail:** kozikowa@uic.edu

KOZIKOWSKI, BARBARA ANN, PHYSICAL CHEMISTRY. **Personal Data:** b Chicago, Ill, January 20, 1954. **Education:** Loyola Univ, BS, 1975; Univ Ill, Chicago Circle, MS, 1977, PhD (phys chem), 1981. **Professional Experience:** STAFF SCIENTIST, PROCTER & GAMBLE CO, 1981-. **Memberships:** Am Chem Soc; Soc Biomolecular Screening. **Research Statement & Publications:** Electronic structure of heavy transition metal complexes; developing high throughput assays for pharmaceutical drug development. **Mailing Address:** Procter & Gamble Co, Health Care Res Ctr, PO Box 8006, Mason, OH 45040. **Fax:** 513-983-9369.

KOZINSKI, ANDRZEI, BIOCHEMISTRY. **Personal Data:** b Poland, October 1, 1925; m 1949, c 1. **Education:** Univ Warsaw, MD, 1950, PhD (biochem), 1956. **Professional Experience:** PROF HUMAN GENETICS, UNIV PA, 1968-; assoc prof biochem, Univ PA, 1962-1968; NIH fel biochem, Johns Hopkins Univ, 1959-1962; asst prof, inst Microbiol, Rutgers Univ, 1958-1959; res assoc, Virus Lab, Univ Calif, 1957-1958; asst prof, inst Biochem, Polish Acad Sci, 1955-1957; res assoc, State Inst Health, Poland, 1950-1955. **Research Statement & Publications:** Biochemistry of DNA replication; structure of phage chromosome. **Mailing Address:** Dept Human Genetics, Univ Pa, Philadelphia, PA 19104.

KOZIOL, BRIAN JOSEPH, CLINICAL BIOCHEMISTRY, CLINICAL NUTRITION. **Personal Data:** b Gardner, Mass, August 24, 1951. **Education:** Univ Mass, Amherst, BS, 1973; Univ Calif, Los Angeles, MS, 1977, PhD (exp & clin nutrit), 1984. **Professional Experience:** Mem, Jonsson Comprehensive Cancer Ctr, 1985-; dir, Lipid-Hormone Lab, 1985-; res assoc, Lipid Metab, Div Nutrit, Sch Pub Health & Ctr Health Enhancement, 1984-; asst prof biochem & nutrit, dept med, Div Clin Nutrit, 1984-; ASSOC PROF BIOL, UNIV BRIDGEPORT, 1984-; Adj lectr biochem, dept chem & biochem & NIH scholar, Univ Calif, Sch Pub Health, Los Angeles, 1984; consult, Calif Museum Sci & Ind, 1983-; consult-lectr, Northrop Aircraft Div, 1982-; dir, Lipid Lab, Div Nutrit, Univ Calif, Sch Pub Health, Los Angeles, 1978-; res asst physiol, Dept Kinesiol, 1973-1978; Res asst biochem, Univ Mass, Amherst, 1969-1973. **Memberships:** Am Inst Nutrit; Am Soc Clin Nutrit; Sigma Xi; AAAS; Am Coun Sci & Health. **Research Statement & Publications:** Effect(s) of both the quantity and quality of dietary fat on the incidence of breast tumors in humans and experimental animals; possible link between dietary fat, the breast tissue hormonal milieu and breast cancer development. **Mailing Address:** 19116 Killoch Way 842 Northridge, 30401 Agoura Rd, Agoura Hills, CA 91326.

KOZIOL, DELORIS E, PATHOLOGY, CLINICAL EPIDEMIOLOGY. **Personal Data:** b Alexandria, Va, April 29, 1949. **Education:** Univ Del, BA, 1971; Johns Hopkins Univ, MPH, 1986, PhD (epidemiol), 1990. **Professional Experience:** Clin epidemiologist, Biostatistics & clin epidemiology, CLIN CTR, NIH, 1999-; DEPT CHIEF HOSP EPIDEMIOL SERV, CLIN CTR, NIH, 1983-; med technologist, Dept Transfusion Med, 1973-1983. **Memberships:** Soc Epidemiol Res; Am Pub Health Asn. **Research Statement & Publications:** Clin and infectious disease epidemiology. **Mailing Address:** Clin Ctr, NIH, Bldg 10 Rm 105246, Bethesda, MD 20892-1871. **E-Mail:** dkoziol@nih.gov

KOZLOFF, EUGENE NICHOLAS, ZOOLOGY. **Personal Data:** b Teheran, Iran, September 26, 1920; American citizen; m 1944, Anne Solomon; c Rae Annettte. **Education:** Univ Calif, AB, 1942, MA, 1946, PhD (zool, protozool), 1950. **Professional Experience:** PROF ZOOL, UNIV WASH, 1966-; resident assoc dir, Friday Harbor Labs, Univ Wash, 1966-1973; dir, NSF Inst Col Teachers, Univ Ore, 1964; vis prof, Pac Marine Sta, 1963; vis prof, Friday Harbor Labs, Univ Wash, 1961 & 1962; chmn dept, Lewis & Clark Col, 1960-1966; vis prof, Inst Marine Biol, Univ Ore, 1957-1960, 1994-1995, 1995-1996; Guggenheim fel, 1953-1954; from instr to prof biol, Lewis & Clark Col, 1945-1966; lectr micros tech, Univ Calif, 1945; Asst zool, Univ Calif, 1944. **Memberships:** Marine Biol Asn UK; Soc Protozoologists. **Research Statement & Publications:** Cytology, morphology and taxonomy of protozoa; commensal ostracodes; acoel and rhabdocoel Turbellaria; Orthonectida Mesozoa; development of kinorhynchs; Marine invertebrate Pacific NW. **Mailing Address:** Friday Harbor Lab, Friday Harbor, WA 98250.

KOZLOFF, LLOYD M, VIROLOGY, MOLECULAR BIOLOGY. **Personal Data:** b Chicago, Ill, October 15, 1923; m 1947, c 4. **Education:** Univ Chicago, BS, 1943, PhD (biochem), 1948. **Professional Experience:** PROF EMER MICROBIOL & DEAN, GRAD DIV, UNIV CALIF, SAN FRANCISCO, as of 2004; Prof Microbiol & Dean, Grad Div, Univ Calif, San Francisco, beginning 1981; assoc dean fac affairs, Univ Colo Med Ctr, Denver, 1976-1979; Found Microbiol lectr, 1975-1976; chmn, Virol Sect, Am Soc Microbiol, 1975-1976; vchmn, Virol Sect, Am Soc Microbiol, 1974-1975; chmn dept, Univ Colo Med Ctr, Denver, 1966-1976; ed, J Virol, 1966-1974; prof microbiol, Univ Colo Med Ctr, Denver, 1964-1980; Mem virol & rickettsiology study sect, NIH, 1963-1968; from asst prof to prof, Univ Chicago, 1952-1964; Res assoc biochem, Univ Chicago, 1949-1952. **Memberships:** Hon fel AAAS; Am Soc Microbiol; Am Soc Biol Chemists; Am Chem Soc. **Research Statement & Publications:** Virus structure, function and assembly; reactions during viral invasion. **Mailing Address:** PO Box 1877, Ft Bragg, CA 95437.

KOZLOSKI, RICHARD PETER, HPLC ANALYSIS OF PESTICIDES & EXPLOSIVES, GC ANALYSIS OF ENVIRONMENTAL STANDARDS. **Personal Data:** b Derby, Conn, June 25, 1946; m 1976, Elizabeth; c Allen & Paul. **Education:** Univ Conn, BA, 1968; Va Polytech Inst & State Univ, PhD (chem), 1977. **Professional Experience:** ANALYTICAL CHEMIST, ACCUSTANDARD INC, 1991-; sr scientist, Upjohn, Fine Chem Div, 1986-1990; scientist II, Cohn Agr Exp Sta, 1979-1985. **Memberships:** Am Chem Soc. **Research Statement & Publications:** Investigation of the chemistry of decompostions in environmental standard formulations and the anals of pesticides, pollvant, explosives and aflatoxins. **Mailing Address:** AccuStand Inc, 125 Mkt St, Newhaven, CT 06483. **Fax:** 203-786-5287.

KOZLOV, ALEKSEY A, EPOXY & POLYURETHANE ADHESIVES. **Personal Data:** b Kiev, Ukraine, January 2, 1957; m 1991, Olga Y Zakharova; c Gleb & Sofya. **Education:** Leningrad Technol Inst, PhD (radiation chem), 1986. **Professional Experience:** AT, A N FRUMKIN INST ELECTROCHEM, RUSSIAN ACAD SCI, as of 1998; RES & DEVELOP CHEMIST, ABATRON INC, 1997-; Head, Radiation Chem Lab, Inst Phys Chem, Kiev, 1989-1997. **Research Statement & Publications:** Epoxy and polyurethane adhesives and coatings for special applications. **Mailing Address:** A N Frumkin Inst Electrochem, Russian Acad Sci, Leninsky Prospect 31, Moscow, Russia. **E-Mail:** vanlab@glas.apc.org

KOZLOWSKI, ADRIENNE WICKENDEN, INORGANIC CHEMISTRY, CHEMICAL INFORMATION, CHEMICAL EDUCATION. **Personal Data:** b Hackensack, NJ, April 26, 1941; m 1977, John. **Education:** MacMurray Col, AB, 1962; Univ Conn, MS, 1964, PhD (chem), 1968. **Professional Experience:** RETIRED; vis educr, Chem Abstrs Serv, 1984-1985; prof chem, Cent Conn State Univ, 1982-1996; from asst prof to assoc prof, Cent Conn State Univ, 1970-1982; fel biol sci, Univ Conn, 1969-1970; lectr, Univ Copenhagen, 1969; res asst phys chem, Univ Conn, 1968. **Memberships:** Am Chem Soc; Sigma Xi. **Research Statement & Publications:** Coordination compounds; inorganic structural chemistry; information retrieval, computerized searching by inorganic structure. **Mailing Address:** Dept Chem, Cent Conn State Univ, 1615 Stanley St, New Britain, CT 06053-2439.

KOZLOWSKI, BETTY ANN, NUTRITION. **Personal Data:** b Dothan, Ala, December 14, 1943; m 1978, c 1. **Education:** Ala Col, BS, 1965; Univ Tenn, Knoxville, PhD (nutrit), 1970. **Professional Experience:** ASSOC PROF NUTRIT, DEPT HUMAN NUTRIT & FOOD MGT & CHIEF NUTRIT, NISONGER CTR MENTAL RETARDATION & DEVELOP DISABILITIES, OHIO STATE UNIV, 1974-; asst prof, Auburn Univ, 1970-1974; res asst nutrit, Univ Tenn, Knoxville, 1969-1970. **Memberships:** Sigma Xi. **Research Statement & Publications:** Nutritional needs, and ways of meeting them in persons with developmental disabilities. **Mailing Address:** 4360 Woodhill Rd, Columbus, OH 43220-4380.

KOZLOWSKI, DON ROBERT, AVIONICS. **Personal Data:** b St Louis, Mo, December 5, 1937; m 1960, c 3. **Education:** Univ St Louis, BS, 1959; Wash Univ, St Louis, MS, 1967. **Professional Experience:** RETIRED; sr vpres, Mcdonnell Aircraft Co, Mcdonnell Douglas Corp, as of 1997; chief prog engr advan eng, Mcdonnell Aircraft Co, Mcdonnell Douglas Corp, beginning 1980; dir & consult, USAF/Air Force Systs Command Offensive Air Support Mission Anal, 1974-1976; sr prog engr, Mcdonnell Aircraft CO, Mcdonnell Douglas Corp, 1972-1980; sect mgr advan reconnaissance systs, Mcdonnell Aircraft CO, Mcdonnell Douglas Corp, 1965-1972; vpres, Aerospace Systs Corp, 1964-1965; mgr prog develop, Electronic Specialty Co, 1962-1964; sr engr, McDonnell Aircraft Co, McDonnell Douglas Corp, 1959-1962. **Memberships:** Inst Elec & Electronics Engrs; Am Soc Photogram; Am Inst Aeronaut & Astronaut; Am Defense Preparedness Asn. **Research Statement & Publications:** Avionics, displays and data processing systems for reconnaissance and intelligence; communications and electronic warfare; aircraft systems design. **Mailing Address:** PO Box 516 64-2142, St Louis, MO 63136.

KOZLOWSKI, GERALD P, NEUROENDOCRINOLOGY. **Personal Data:** b Grand Rapids, Mich, December 24, 1942. **Education:** Aquinas Col, BS, 1964; Mich State Univ, MS, 1967; Univ Ill, Urbana-Champaign, PhD (anat), 1971. **Professional Experience:** ADJ ASSOC PROF, DEPT PHYSIOL, SOUTHWESTERN MED CTR, UNIVTEX, DALLAS, as of 2006; assoc prof, Dept Physiol, Southwestern Med Ctr, Univ Tex, Dallas, beginning 1980; assoc prof neurobiology & anat, Univ Tex Health Sci Ctr, Houston, 1978-1980; assoc prof, Col Vet Med & Biomed Sci, Colo State Univ, 1976-1978; NIH grant, 1974-1992; asst prof anat, Col Vet Med & Biomed Sci, Colo State Univ, 1973-1976; teaching fel, Sch Med & Dent, Univ Rochester, 1971-1973; instr, Univ Ill, Urbana-Champaign, 1968-1970; res assoc, Univ Mo-Columbia, 1967-1968; asst instr anat, Mich State Univ, 1965-1966; technician histopath, Mich State Univ, 1964-1965; ed, Histochem. **Memberships:** Am Asn Anatomists; Int Soc Neuroendocrinologists; Biol Stain Comn; Soc Neuroscience; Res Soc Alcoholism. **Research Statement & Publications:** Effects at alcohol on central nervous system; vasopressin and oxytocin; scanning and high-voltage electron microscopy of the median eminence; immunocytochemistry of HIV receptor; neuroimmunology; light and election microscopic immunocytochemistry for visualization of releasing-hormines and neuropeptides of the hypothalamus. **Mailing Address:** Dept Physiol, Univ Tex

Southwestern Med Ctr, 5323 Harry Hines Blvd, Dallas, TX 75235-9040. **Fax:** 214-648-8885. **E-Mail:** gerald.kozlowski@utsouthwestern.edu

KOZLOWSKI, LESTER JOSEPH, HIGH DENSITY INFRARED FOCAL PLANE ARRAYS DESIGN, ULTRA LOW NOISE FOCAL PLANE ARRAYS DESIGN & TEST. **Personal Data:** b Chicago, Ill, August 31, 1953; m 1983, Dawn; c Amanda & Daniel. **Education:** Univ Ill, Chicago, BSEE, 1975, MSEE, 1977. **Professional Experience:** CHIEF EXEC OFFICER, ALTESENS INC, 2003-; mem tech staff, Rockwell Int Sci Ctr, beginning 1987; sr scientist, Hughes Aircraft Missile Systs Group, 1978-1987; tech asst elec eng, Univ Ill, Chicago, 1975-1977. **Memberships:** Inst Elec & Electronics Engrs Electronic Devices Soc; Optical Soc Am; Soc Photo-Optical Instrumentation Engrs. **Research Statement & Publications:** Design, development and characterization of infrared focal plane arrays for a variety of applications including military and astronomy. **Mailing Address:** AltaSens Inc, 501 Marin St Ste 200, Thousand Oaks, CA 91360. **Fax:** 805-778-0771. **E-Mail:** lkozlowski@altasens.com

KOZLOWSKI, RICHARD WILLIAM HUGH, OBSERVATIONAL PLANETARY ASTRO-ATMOSPHERE & MINERALOGY REMOTE SENSE. **Personal Data:** b Ogden, Utah, October 10, 1953; m 1990. **Education:** Susquehanna Univ, BA, 1975; Univ Maine, MS, 1977, PhD (physics), 1982. **Professional Experience:** HEAD PHYSICS, SUSQUEHANNA UNIV, as of 2003; Vis prof, lunar & planetary lab, Univ Ariz, 1998-; PROF PHYSICS & ASTRON, SUSQUEHANNA UNIV, 1993-; chair physics, Susquehanna Univ, 1989-; Vis scientist, Lunar & Planetary Lab, Univ Ariz, 1986-; From asst prof to assoc prof, Dept Physics & Astron, Susquehanna Univ, 1983-1993. **Memberships:** Am Geophys Union; Am Astrological Soc Div Planetary Sci; Am Asn Physics Teachers. **Research Statement & Publications:** Observational planetary astronomy; sodium and potassium atmospheres of the planet Mercury and Earths moon-done with telescopes in Arizona; remote sensing of surface rock type Mercury, the moon, and asteroids with thermal infrared telescopes in Hawaii, Arizona and the Kuiper Airborne Observatory. **Mailing Address:** Dept Physics, Susquehanna Univ, Selinsgrove, PA 17870. **Fax:** 570-372-2751. **E-Mail:** kozlowsk@susqu.edu

KOZLOWSKI, ROBERT H, PETROLEUM CHEMISTRY. **Personal Data:** b Duquesne, Pa, May 17, 1928; div, c Michael & Nancy. **Education:** St Mary's Col Calif, BS, 1950; Northwestern Univ, PhD (chem), 1955. **Professional Experience:** MGR, ADMIN SUPPORT, LAW DEPT, CHEVRON CORP, 1988-; litigation support mgr, Secy's Dept, Stand Oil Co Calif, 1985-1988; litigation support mgr, Secy's Dept, Stand Oil Co Calif, 1978-1984; litigation support coordr, Secy's Dept, 1976-1977; Consult, Kenwood Vineyards, 1970-1986; sr res assoc, Petrol Process Res & Develop, Chevron Res Co Div, 1966-1976; supvry res chemist, Chevron Corp, 1964-1966; sr res chemist, Chevron Corp, 1960-1964; Res chemist, Chevron Corp, 1955-1960; Ipatieff fel. **Memberships:** Am Chem Soc; Am Soc Enol. **Research Statement & Publications:** Petroleum processing; hydrocarbon reactions and mechanisms. **Mailing Address:** 41 Sutter St 1300, San Francisco, CA 94104.

KOZLOWSKI, THEODORE R, PHYSICAL INORGANIC CHEMISTRY. **Personal Data:** b Niagara Falls, NY, December 21, 1937; m 1961, Ann; c Christopher M, Karen E (Kennedy), Maureen M (Schurman), David M & Natalie A. **Education:** Niagara Univ, BS, 1959; Rensselaer Polytech Inst, PhD (phys inorg chem), 1963; Harvard Univ, PMD, 1972. **Professional Experience:** RETIRED; dir develop & energy prod, Corning Inc, ending 1998; bus technol dir, Corning Ashahi Video, beginning 1994; dir tech prod develop, tech & elec prod, 1987-1994; develop mgr tech & elec prod, 1984-1987; develop mgr elec & electronic prod, 1982-1984; portfolio mgr, consumer prod, 1976-1982; mgr, Sunglass Proj, France, 1973-1976; mgr, Indust Prod Develop, 1970-1973; res chemist, Corning Glass Works, 1966-1970; researcher, Picatinnu Arsenal, US Army, 1964-1966; sr chemist, Corning Glass Works, 1963-1964. **Memberships:** AAAS; Am Chem Soc; Sigma Xi; Nat Geog Soc. **Research Statement & Publications:** Glass-molten salt interactions; high strength glasses and glass ceramics by ion exchange from molten salts; high strength materials; product development of photochromic ophthalmic and sunglass products; consumer tableware ovenware clear glass ceramics, hybrid PC boards; low dielectric materials, strong glass ceramics, epoxy products, specialty glasses, LCD display glasses, magnetic disk substrates, dental glass ceramics, sheet, pressing and tubing processes; granted seven patents. **Mailing Address:** 43 Reynolds Dr Ext, Horseheads, NY 14845. **Fax:** 607-974-2103. **E-Mail:** kozlowski_tr@corning.com

KOZLOWSKI, THEODORE THOMAS, PLANT PHYSIOLOGY, FOREST BIOLOGY. **Personal Data:** b Buffalo, NY, May 21, 1917; m 1954, Maude. **Education:** Syracuse Univ, BS, 1939; Duke Univ, MA, 1941, PhD (plant physiol), 1947. **Honorary Degrees:** DSc, Univ Louvain, Belg, 1978, State Univ NY, 1980, Agr Univ Poznan, Poland, 1992. **Honors & Awards:** Auth Award, Int Shade Tree Conf, 1971; Barrington Moore Res Award Biol Sci, Soc Am Foresters, 1974; George Lamb lectr, Univ Nebr, 1974; Arboriculture Res Award, Inst Soc Arboriculture, 1976; George S Long lectr, Univ Wash, 1978; Merit Award, Bot Soc Am, 1984; Merit Award, Int Soc Arboriculture, 1987; Gold Medal Forest Physiol Res, Asn Forestry Poland, 1990. **Professional Experience:** EMER PROF TREE PHYSIOLOGY, FORESTWISEDU, as of 2003; vis scholar, Dept Environ Sci, Policy & Mgt, Univ Calif, Berkeley, 1993-; trustee, Santa Barbara Bot Garden, 1992-1993; adj prof, Environ Studies Prog & Dept Biol Sci, Univ Calif, Santa Barbara, 1987-1993; distinguished prof, Wis Alumni Res Found, 1984-1987; dir biotron, Univ Wis-Madison, 1977-1987; prof, A J Riker prof forestry, 1972-1987; 1971-; assoc ed, Can J Forest Res, 1970-1976; Int Shade Tree Conf res fel, 1969, 1970, 1971; assoc ed, Am Midland Naturalist, 1965-1971; Fulbright sr res scholar & exchange lectr, Oxford Univ, 1964-1965; vis scientist, Soc Am Foresters, 1963, 1966, 1968, 1969, 1970; chmn dept, Univ Wis-Madison, 1961-1964; prof, Univ Wis-Madison, 1958-1972; vis prof, Univ Pa, 1954; head dept, Univ Mass, 1950-1958; from asst prof to prof bot, Univ Mass, 1947-1958; res collabr, US Forest Serv; external PhD thesis examr, Australian Nat Univ, Univ Western Australia, Univ Ibadan, Nigeria, Sri Venkateswara Univ, India & Univ Wis Found; consult, UN Food & Agr Orgn, Nat Park Serv, Oak Ridge Nat Lab, Stanford Res Inst, NSF, Fed Forest Res Sta, Brazil & Univ BC. **Memberships:** Soc Am Foresters; Am Soc Plant Physiol; Bot Soc Am; Ecol Soc Am; Am Inst Biol Sci; Sigma Xi; Scand Soc Plant Physiologists; Int Soc Arboriculture; hon mem Finnish Forestry Soc; hon mem Polish Bot Soc. **Research Statement & Publications:** Physiology of woody plants; plant water relations; physiological ecology; effects of environmental stresses on plant growth. **Mailing Address:** Dept Environ Sci Policy & Mgt, Univ Calif, 145 Mulford Hall, Berkeley, CA 94720. **Fax:** 510-643-5438.

KOZMA, ADAM, RADAR SYSTEMS, ELECTROOPTICS. **Personal Data:** b Cleveland, Ohio, February 2, 1928; m 1993, Rebecca Chelius; c Paul (deceased) & Peter. **Education:** Univ Mich, BSE, 1952, MSE, 1964; Wayne State Univ, MSEM, 1961; Univ London, PhD (elec eng), 1968 & dipl, Imp Col, 1969. **Honors & Awards:** Ord Medal, Avionics Sect, Am Defense Preparedness Asn. **Professional Experience:** CONSULT ENGR, 1993-; adj prof, Synthetic Aperture Radar Course, Col Eng, Univ Mich, Ann Arbor, 1992-; head, Advan Systs Dept, Mitre Corp, 1989-1993; vpres & dir, Defense Electronics Eng Div, Syracuse Res Corp, 1986-1988; vpres corp develop, Radar & Optics Div, 1985-1986; co-chmn & lectr, Synthetic Aperture Radar Intensive Course, Col Eng, Univ Mich, Ann Arbor, 1980-; vpres & dir, Radar & Optics Div, 1976-1985; mgr tech staff, Electromagnetics & Electronics Dept, Environ Res Inst, Mich, 1975-1976; consult phys sci directorate, USAMRDEL, MICOM, Redstone, Ala, 1974-1978; sr res engr & mgr, Electromagnetics & Electronics Dept, Environ Res Inst, Mich, 1973-1975; gen mgr, Electrooptics Ctr, Radiation Div, Harris, Inc, 1969-1973; UK Atomic Weapons Estab, 1967-1968 & Radiation Inc, Fla, 1968-1969; acad visitor & lectr, Imp Col, Univ London, 1967-1968; on leave, Imp Col, Univ London, 1966-1968; Consult, IBM Systs Develop Div, 1966-1967; res engr & asst head, Optics Group, Radar & Optics Lab, 1965-1969; Consult, Conductron Corp, 1965-1966; assoc res engr, Inst Sci & Technol, Univ Mich, Ann Arbor, 1963-1965; res assoc, Inst Sci & Technol, Univ Mich, Ann Arbor, 1961-1963; asst mech & electrooptical design, Inst Sci & Technol, Univ Mich, Ann Arbor, 1958-1961; sales engr, US Broach Co, Mich, 1956-1958; Design engr, US Broach Co, Mich, 1951-1956. **Memberships:** Fel Optical Soc Am; fel Inst Elec & Electronics Engrs; Am Defense Preparedness Asn; Sigma Xi; Soc Photog & Instrument Engrs. **Research Statement & Publications:** Coherent optics with application to signal processing and optical correlation; holography; speckle effects in coherent systems; radar instrumentation, synthetic aperture radar systems and applications. **Mailing Address:** 2996 Appleway, Ann Arbor, MI 48104.

KOZUB, RAYMOND LEE, NUCLEAR PHYSICS. **Personal Data:** b Ladysmith, Wis, June 16, 1940; m 1965, Sandra; c John & Racheall. **Education:** Univ Wis-River Falls, BS, 1962; Mich State Univ, MS, 1964, PhD (physics), 1967. **Professional Experience:** Dept chmn, Tenn Technol Univ, 1986-1996; PROF PHYSICS, TENN TECHNOL UNIV, 1980-; Prin investr sponsored res, Dept Energy, 1978-; assoc prof, Tenn Technol Univ, 1977-1980; asst prof physics, Queen's Univ, Kingston, Ont, 1974-1977; res assoc chem, Columbia Univ, 1972-1974; res scientist, Cyclotron Inst, 1971-1972; Asst prof physics, Tex A&M Univ, 1967-1971. **Memberships:** Am Phys Soc; Sigma Xi; Am Asn Phys Teachers. **Research Statement & Publications:** Nuclear structure studies; transfer reactions; stripping reactions to unbound final states; isobaric analog states; nuclear lifetime measurements; heavy ion reactions; neutron-rich nuclei; rare electron capture processes; Nuclear astrophysics; radioactive beam experiments. **Mailing Address:** Dept Physics, Tenn Technol Univ, Cookeville, TN 38505. **E-Mail:** rkozub@tntech.edu

KRA, IRWIN, MATHEMATICS, EDUCATION. **Personal Data:** b Poland, January 5, 1937; American citizen; m Eleanor; c Douglas, Bryna & Gabriel. **Education:** Polytech Inst Brooklyn, BS, 1960; Columbia Univ, MA, 1964, PhD (math), 1966. **Professional Experience:** EXECUTIVE DIRECTOR, MATH FOR AMERICA as of 2004; DISTINGUISHED SERVICE PROF EMERITUS MATH, STATE UNIV NY, as of 2004; DISTIGUISHED SERVICE PROFESSOR MATH 1997-2004; DEAN, DIV PHYS SCI & MATH, STATE UNIV NY, STONY BROOK, 1991-1996; chmn dept, Div Phys Sci & Math, 1975-1981; prof math, 1972-; actg provost, Div Math Sci, 1971-1972; Guggenheim Found fel, 1970-1971; actg chmn, Dept Math, State Univ NY Stony Brook, 1970-1971; from asst prof to assoc prof, Div Phys Sci & Math, 1968-1971; C L E Moore instr math, Mass Inst Technol, 1966-1968; vis, Israel, Chile, Eng, Japan; adv prof, Fudan Univ, Shargai, China. **Memberships:** Am Math Soc, Math Assoc of Am, Am Women in Math. **Research Statement & Publications:** One complex variable, particularly moduli of Riemann surfaces and Kleinian groups; Secondary school mathematics. **Mailing Address:** Dept Math, State Univ NY, Stony Brook, NY 11794-3651. **Fax:** 631-632-7631. **E-Mail:** irwin@math.sunysb.edu

KRAAKEVIK, JAMES HENRY, ATMOSPHERIC PHYSICS. **Personal Data:** b Chicago, Ill, February 18, 1928; m 1950, Marilyn Morrison; c Timothy, Thomas, John, Mark, Stephen & Joel. **Education:** Wheaton Col, Ill, BS, 1948; Univ Md, PhD (physics), 1957. **Professional Experience:** Dir, Billy Graham Ctr, Wheaton Col, Ill, 1984-1996; dir, res & ministry, 1981-1984; educ consult, Ministry Educ, Sudan, 1973-1976; educ consult, Sudan Interior Mission, 1970-; from asst prof to prof physics, Physics Dept, 1970-1984; educ secy, Sudan Interior Mission, 1969-1970; prin, Titcombe Col, Nigeria, 1966-1967; teacher, Titcombe Col, Nigeria, 1964-1966; Ill State Water Surv, 1961-1964 & Coronet Instr Films, 1962-1965; chair, Physics Dept, 1960-1964 & 1970-1981; consult, US Naval Res Lab, 1958-1973; res sect head, US Naval Res Lab, 1954-1958; Physicist, US Naval Res Lab, 1948-1954. **Memberships:** Am Asn Physics Teachers; AAAS; Am Meteorol Soc; Am Sci Affil. **Research Statement & Publications:** Electrical properties of atmosphere and relationship with meteorology; electrical characteristics of upper atmosphere and relationship with radiation; conduction of electricity through gases; characteristics of sub-micron particles in the atmosphere. **Mailing Address:** 26 W 509 Prairie Ct, Winfield, IL 60190. **Fax:** 630-752-5916.

KRAATZ, CHARLES PARRY, BOTULINUM TOXIX, MUSCLE POTENTIALS. **Education:** Univ Cincinnati, PhD (physiol), 1936. **Professional Experience:** CONSULT, 1972-; Prof pharmacol, Med Col, Jefferson Univ, 1947-1972. **Mailing Address:** 329 S Norwinden Dr, Springfield, PA 19064.

KRAAY, GERRIT JACOB, GENETICS. **Personal Data:** b Amsterdam, Neth, October 14, 1935; m 1963, c 4. **Education:** State Agr Univ Wageningen, BSc, 1960, MSc, 1963, PhD, 1967. **Professional Experience:** PROG LEADER, SASKATCHEWAN RES COUN, BOVA-CAN LAB, as of 2004; DIR GENETIC BR, ANIMAL DIS RES INST EAST, CAN DEPT AGR, 1997-; HEAD BLOOD TYPING SECT, ANIMAL DIS RES INST EAST, CAN DEPT AGR, 1972-; asst prof biomed sci, Univ Guelph, 1969-1972; asst prof vet bact, Univ Guelph, 1967-1969; res scientist, Dept Animal Sci, State Agr Univ Wageningen, 1964-1967; Res scientist, Found for Blood Group Res, Wageningen, Netherlands, 1963. **Memberships:** Royal Dutch Soc Agr Sci; Int Soc Animal Bloodgroup Res; Genetics Soc Can. **Research Statement & Publications:** Population genetics of blood groups and serum-protein polymorphisms in animals; immuno-reproduction. **Mailing Address:** Beva-Can Lab, Saskatchewan Res Coun, 15 Innovation Blvd, Saskatoon, SK S7N 2X8, Can. **Fax:** 306-933-5505.

KRABACHER, BERNARD, PHYSICAL ORGANIC CHEMISTRY. **Personal Data:** b Cincinnati, Ohio, December 25, 1925. **Education:** Univ Cincinnati, Chem Eng, 1949, PhD (phys org chem), 1961. **Professional Experience:** RETIRED; chmn dept, WVa State Col, 1976-1982; from assoc prof to prof chem, WVa State Col, 1963-1990; group leader, Ozone Res, Emery Industs Inc, 1961-1963; chemist, Emery Industs Inc, 1949-1957. **Memberships:** Am Chem Soc; fel Am Inst Chemists. **Research Statement & Publications:** Reactions of organic compounds with cobalt carbonyls and ozone; preparation of unusual compounds; reaction mechanisms. **Mailing Address:** 1982 Baltimore Ave, Cincinnati, OH 45225-1905.

KRABACHER, JAY E, PHYSICAL SCIENCE. **Personal Data:** b Denver, Colo, March 15, 1949; m 1973, Deborah; c Garth & Gamma-Rae. **Education:** Colo State Univ, BS, 1977. **Honorary Degrees:** PhD, Inst Metamorphysics, Eng, 1972. **Professional Experience:** TECH ED & WRITER, SCI APPLN INT CORP, 1987-; geophys engr, Bendix Field Eng, 1978-1987. **Memberships:** Soc Prof Well Log Analysts. **Research Statement & Publica-**

tions: Certification that contaminated hazardous waste properties are cleaned up in accord with the canonically conjugate variables as per Heisenberg uncertainty; proposed the Bulbyon particle in opposition to tachyons; proposed that bulbyons are absolutely fixed and motionless with respect to all frames of reference. **Mailing Address:** Sci Appln Int Corp, 2597 B 3/4 Rd, Grand Junction, CO 81503.

KRABBE, GREGERS LOUIS, MATHEMATICAL ANALYSIS. **Personal Data:** b Roskilde, Denmark, January 5, 1920; American citizen; m 1955, c 2. **Education:** Univ Calif, AB, 1949, MS, 1951, PhD, 1954. **Professional Experience:** PROF EMER, PURDUE UNIV, as of 2005; prof, Purdue Univ, 1968-1989; assoc prof math, Purdue Univ, 1962-1968; NATO fel, Univ Rennes, 1961-1962; assoc prof math, Yale Univ, 1960-1961; assoc prof math, Purdue Univ, 1954-1960. **Memberships:** Am Math Soc. **Research Statement & Publications:** Algebraic operational calculus, as applied to lumped systems; theory of linear operators; electrical engineering, linear networks, signal and system analysis. **Mailing Address:** Purdue Univ, West Lafayette, IN 47907.

KRABBENHOFT, HERMAN OTTO, ORGANIC CHEMISTRY. **Personal Data:** b Detroit, Mich, July 15, 1945; m 1976, c 2. **Education:** Wayne State Univ, BS, 1970; Univ Mich, MS, 1971, PhD (chem), 1974. **Professional Experience:** Staff chemist, Gen Elec Plastics, 1982-1987; STAFF CHEMIST, GEN ELEC CORP RES & DEVELOP CTR, 1976-1981, 1988-; NIH grant chem, Univ Calif, Berkeley, 1975-1976. **Memberships:** Am Chem Soc. **Research Statement & Publications:** Structure and mechanism in organic chemistry; organic synthesis. **Mailing Address:** Gen Elec Corp/Res & Develop, PO Box 8, Schenectady, NY 12301-0008.

KRABBENHOFT, KENNETH LOUIS, MICROBIOLOGY. **Personal Data:** b Page, NDak, February 24, 1931; m 1955, c 3. **Education:** Univ Valparaiso, BA, 1953; NDak State Univ, MS, 1956; Ore State Univ, PhD (microbiol), 1965. **Professional Experience:** RETIRED; mem fac, Wayne State Univ, Mich, 1991; prof, Mankato State Univ, 1970-; NSF res grant, 1969-1971; assoc prof, Mankato State Univ, 1967-1970; NASA res grant, 1965-1967; asst prof, NMex State Univ, 1965-1967; Instr biol, Mankato State Col, 1958-1962. **Memberships:** AAAS; Am Soc Microbiol; Inst Food Technologists; Sigma Xi. **Research Statement & Publications:** Mechanisms of radiation resistance in microorganisms. **Mailing Address:** 5050 Anthony Wayne Dr, Detroit, MI 48202.

KRACHER, ALFRED, X-RAY MICROANALYSIS, COSMOCHEMISTRY. **Personal Data:** b Vienna, Austria, September 21, 1945; m 1974, c 2. **Education:** Univ Vienna, PhD (chem), 1974. **Professional Experience:** Asst scientist & microprobe specialist, Ames Laboratory (USDOE), 2003-current; res asst prof, Ark Ctr Space & Planetary Sci, Univ Ark, 2001-2003; asst scientist & microprobe specialist, Iowa State Univ, 1984-2001; researcher earth sci, Inst Meteoritics, Univ NMex, 1981-1982; researcher chem, Inst Geophys, Univ Calif, Los Angeles, 1977-1978; staff scientist mineral & petrol, Mus Natural Hist, Vienna, 1976-1981; res asst petrol, Univ Vienna, 1974-1976; Res asst chem, Univ Vienna, 1972-1974. **Memberships:** Meteoritical Soc; Am Geophys Union; Geochem Soc. **Research Statement & Publications:** Materials analysis; petrology and composition of meteorites and impact rocks; theory of science. **Mailing Address:** Ames Lab (US Dept Energy), Iowa State Univ, Ames, IA 50010-3020. **Fax:** 515-294-4291. **E-Mail:** akracher@iastate.edu

KRACHMER, JAY, MEDICINE. **Personal Data:** b Cedar Rapids. **Education:** Tulane Univ, La, MD. **Professional Experience:** PROF & CHMN, DEPT OPHTHAL, UNIV MINN, 1992-. **Mailing Address:** Dept Ophthal Univ Minn, Hosp Ctr PO Box 420 420 Del St SE, Minneapolis, MN 54455. **Fax:** 612-625-7107. **E-Mail:** krach001@umn.edu

KRACKOV, MARK HARRY, ORGANIC & FLUORINE CHEMISTRY, ORGANIC PROCESS DEVELOPMENT. **Personal Data:** b Brooklyn, NY, June 2, 1932; m 1954, Julia Kennedy; c Laure n ce & Michael. **Education:** Univ Calif, Berkeley, BS, 1955; Ore State Univ, PhD (org chem), 1962. **Professional Experience:** CONSULT CHEM RES & DEVELOP, 1995-; adj prof math, Wilmington Col, 1994-1995; adj prof chem, Rosemont Col & Del Co Community Col, 1994-1995; sr res assoc, Chem & Pigments Dept, E I Du Pont, 1965-1993; USPHS fel org chem, Sch Med, Yale Univ, 1962-1965; Instr chem, Ore State Univ, 1961-1962. **Memberships:** Am Chem Soc; AAAS; Sigma Xi; Catalysis Soc. **Research Statement & Publications:** Synthesis and physical properties of heterocyclic nitrogen, sulfur and selenium compounds; chemical synthesis of polynucleotides; labelling compounds via neutron activation; photopolymerization; reverse osmosis membranes; organic chemical process development; catalysis; fluoroaromatic chemistry; anthraquinone chemistry. **Mailing Address:** 906 Brinton's Bridge Rd, West Chester, PA 19382. **E-Mail:** krackovmh@aol.com

KRAELING, ROBERT RUSSELL, ANIMAL SCIENCE, REPRODUCTIVE PHYSIOLOGY. **Personal Data:** b Pittsburgh, Pa, August 22, 1942; m 1962, Lois; c David, Williams, Michael, James & Margaret. **Education:** Univ Md, BS, 1964, MS, 1967; Iowa State Univ, PhD (animal sci physiol reprod), 1970. **Honors & Awards:** Animal Physiol & Endocrinol Res Award, Am Soc Animal Sci, 1990. **Professional Experience:** Sr scientist, SAtlantic Area, Agr Res Serv, USDA, 1993; mem, grad fac, dept Animal & Dairy Sci, Univ Ga, 1979-; SUPVR RES PHYSIOLOGIST, ANIMAL PHYSIOL RES UNIT, RUSSELL RES CTR, AGR RES SERV, USDA, 1977-; adj prof, dept Animal & Dairy Sci, Univ Ga, 1974-; Animal Prod Lab, Russell Agr Res Ctr, Athens, 1974-1977; res animal physiologist, Animal Physiol & Genetics Inst, Reproduction Lab, Md, 1970-1974; agr res scientist, Swine Res Br, Animal Husb Res Div, Agr Res Serv, USDA, 1967; res assoc, Iowa State Univ, 1967-1970; agr res technician, Swine Res Br, Animal Husb Res Div, Agr Res Serv, USDA, 1966-1967; res asst, Swine Res Br, Animal Husb Res Div, Agr Res Serv, USDA, 1964-1966. **Memberships:** Am Soc Animal Sci; Soc Study Reproduction; Sigma Xi; Polish Acad Sci. **Research Statement & Publications:** Determining the physiological and endocrinolgoical factors which control puberty, ovulation, corpus luteum function and the post-partum interval in swine and cattle and the effects of environment and management systems. **Mailing Address:** Richard B Russell Agr Res Ctr, USDA PO Box 5677, Athens, GA 30613. **Fax:** 706-542-0399. **E-Mail:** rkraelin@saa.ars.usda.gov

KRAEMER, DUANE CARL, REPRODUCTIVE PHYSIOLOGY, MEDICINE. **Personal Data:** b Willow, Wis, October 27, 1933; m 1960, c 2. **Education:** Univ Wis, BS, 1955; Tex A&M Univ, MS, 1960, BS, PhD (physiol reproduction) & DVM, 1966. **Professional Experience:** PROF VET PHYSIOL & PHARMACOL, COL VET MED, TEX A&M UNIV, 1977-; assoc prof, Col Vet Med, Tex A&M Univ, 1975-1977; asst scientist, Southwest Found Res & Educ, 1966-1975. **Memberships:** Soc Study Reproduction; Sigma Xi; Am Vet Med Asn; Am Soc Animal Sci; Am Asn Lab Animal Sci. **Research Statement & Publications:** Reproductive gamete physiology; contraceptive development and testing. **Mailing Address:** Dept Vet Physiol & Pharmacol, Univ Tex A&M, 1101 Foster Ave, Col Sta, TX 77845. **E-Mail:** dkraemer@cvm.tamu.edu

KRAEMER, HELENA CHMURA, BIOSTATISTICS. **Personal Data:** b Derby, Conn, July 10, 1937; m 1962, Arthur; c Stacey A & Karen Clowe. **Education:** Smith Col, BA, 1958; Stanford Univ, PhD (statist), 1963. **Professional Experience:** PROF PSYCHIAT & BEHAV SCI, SCH MED, STANFORD UNIV, 1986-; from asst prof to assoc prof, Stanford Univ, 1972-1986; Lectr, Div Biostatist, Dept Community & Prev Med, Stanford Univ, 1971-; res assoc, Stanford Univ, 1969-1972; Actg asst prof, Stanford Univ, 1964-1969. **Memberships:** Fel Am Statist Asn; Psychomet Soc. **Research Statement & Publications:** Development of statistical methods for use in clinical and behavioral research, with particular emphasis on correlational methods. **Mailing Address:** Dept Psychiat & Behav Sci C305, Sch Med Stanford Univ, Stanford, CA 94305-5717. **E-Mail:** hck@stanford.edu

KRAEMER, JOHN FRANCIS, ORGANIC CHEMISTRY, POLYMER CHEMISTRY. **Personal Data:** b St Louis, Mo, June 20, 1941. **Education:** St Louis Univ, BS, 1963; Loyola Univ, MS, 1965, PhD (org chem), 1968. **Professional Experience:** RETIRED; consult, 1986-2000; org chemist, Int Minerals & Chem Corp, 1968-1986. **Memberships:** Am Chem Soc. **Research Statement & Publications:** Organic synthesis; synthesis of biologically active compounds. **Mailing Address:** 6179 S State Rd 63, Terre Haute, IN 47802.

KRAEMER, KENNETH H, DNA REPAIR, CARCINOGENESIS. **Personal Data:** b Newark, NJ, June 22, 1943; m 1965, c 4. **Education:** Brown Univ, BS, 1965; Tufts Univ, MD, 1969, diplomat, Nat Bd Med Examiners, 1970; Am Bd Internal Med, 1973; Am Bd Dermat, 1976. **Professional Experience:** PRIN INVESTR, BASIC RES LAB, NAT CANCER INST, NIH, as of 2004; med dir, US Pub Health Serv, NIH, 1986-; res scientist, lab Molecular Carcinogenesis, NIH, beginning 1976; sr surgeon, US Pub Health Serv, NIH, 1974-1986; resident dermat, Univ Miami Sch Med, 1974-1976; clin assoc dermat, Dermat Br, NIH, 1971-1974; surgeon, US Pub Health Serv, NIH, 1971-1974; med intern & resident, Harlem Hosp Ctr, NY, 1969-1971. **Memberships:** Am Acad Dermat; Soc Invest Dermat; Am Soc Photobiol; Am Soc Clin Invest. **Research Statement & Publications:** Cancer-prone human genetic disease, xerodorma pigmentosum, familial malignant melanoma or displastic nevus syndrome, atoxin telangiectasia; DNA repair; photo carcinogenesis; The effect of donor age on the processing of UV- damaged DNA by cultured human cells: Reduced DNA repair capacity and increased DNA mutability; author of various articles. **Mailing Address:** Basic Res Lab, Nat Cancer Inst, NIH, Bldg 37, Rm 4002, Bethesda, MD 20892. **Fax:** 301-594-3409. **E-Mail:** kraemerk@nih.gov

KRAEMER, LOUISE MARGARET, PHYSICAL CHEMISTRY, BIOCHEMISTRY. **Personal Data:** b New York, NY, December 26, 1910. **Education:** Univ Pa, AB, 1943; Univ Chicago, PhD (chem), 1949. **Professional Experience:** EMER PROF, UNIV ARK, 1983-; emer prof, Univ Colo, Boulder, 1976-1983; prof phys sci, Univ Colo, Boulder, 1966-1976; prof chem, New Col, 1964-1965; assoc prof phys sci, Univ Chicago, 1959-1964; asst prof natural sci, Univ Chicago, 1953-1959; assoc chemist, Argonne Nat Lab, 1951-1953; res assoc med, Univ Minn, 1949-1951; asst chem, Univ Chicago, 1945-1949; asst engr, Brown Instrument Co, 1943-1945; Prof, Dept Biol Sci, Univ Ark. **Memberships:** AAAS; Am Chem Soc. **Research Statement & Publications:** Enzymes in wheat germ; porphyrin chemistry; color centers in alkali halides. **Mailing Address:** Dept Biol Sci, Univ Ark Sci Eng Bldg, Fayetteville, AR 72701.

KRAEMER, LOUISE RUSSERT, MALACOLOGY. **Personal Data:** b Milwaukee, Wis, December 17, 1923; m 1950, c 4. **Education:** Marquette Univ, BS, 1945; Univ Mich, Ann Arbor, MS, 1947, PhD (malacol), 1966. **Professional Experience:** PROF EMER BIOL SCI, UNIV ARK, FAYETTEVILLE, 1992-; prof zool, Univ Ark, Fayetteville, 1977-1992; from asst prof to assoc prof, Univ Ark, Fayetteville, 1966-1977; instr, Univ Ark, Fayetteville, 1956-1958 & 1959-1966; asst prof zool, Univ Ark, Fayetteville, 1948-1950; Asst zool & fisheries, Univ Mich, Ann Arbor, 1946-1948. **Memberships:** AAAS; Am Malacol Union (pres 1981-1982); Am Soc Zoologists; Sigma Xi; Animal Behav Soc. **Research Statement & Publications:** Functional morphology; behavior of freshwater mollusks; nervous systems and reproductive systems of Lampsilis and Corbicula; macrobenthic communities in lotic systems. **Mailing Address:** Dept Zool, Univ Ark, 632 Sci-Eng Bldg, Fayetteville, AR 72701. **E-Mail:** rkraemer@uark.edu

KRAEMER, PAUL MICHAEL, CELL BIOLOGY, VIROLOGY. **Personal Data:** b Philadelphia, Pa, March 19, 1930. **Education:** Univ Colo, BA, 1957; Tulane Univ, MPH, 1959, DrPH, 1961; Univ Pa, PhD (microbiol), 1964. **Professional Experience:** Cellular physiol study sect, Am Cancer Soc, 1987-1990; Group leader exp pathol, Los Alamos Nat Lab, 1979-1981; cellular physiol study sect, NIH, 1977-1981; staff mem cellular biol, Los Alamos Nat Lab, 1964-1996; Fel, Wistar Inst, 1961-1964; ed, J Cellular Physiol. **Research Statement & Publications:** Mammalian cell surface complex carbohydrates; chromosome changes in cancer; tumor biology; bioterrorism. **Mailing Address:** 191 Cascabel St, Los Alamos, NM 87544. **E-Mail:** pkraemer@newmexico.com

KRAEMER, ROBERT S, AERONAUTICS. **Education:** Univ Notre Dame, BS (Aerospace and Mech Eng), 1950; Caltech Univ, MS. **Professional Experience:** RETIRED; dir planetary exploration, Nat Aeronauts & Space Admin, as of 1978. **Mailing Address:** 3102 Landfall Ln, Annapolis, MD 21403-4312. **Fax:** 410-268-5033.

KRAEMER, ROBERT WALTER, EXPERIMENTAL HIGH ENERGY PHYSICS. **Personal Data:** b Philadelphia, Pa, January 27, 1935; m 1987, c 3. **Education:** La Salle Col, BA, 1957; Johns Hopkins Univ, PhD (physics), 1962. **Professional Experience:** PROF PHYSICS, CARNEGIE-MELLON UNIV, 1974-; from asst prof to assoc prof, Carnegie-mellon Univ, 1965-1974; res assoc, Carnegie-mellon Univ, 1964-1965; res assoc, Johns Hopkins Univ, 1962-1964; instr physics, Johns Hopkins Univ, 1961-1962. **Memberships:** Am Phys Soc. **Research Statement & Publications:** High energy experimental nuclear physics. **Mailing Address:** Dept Physics, Carnegie-Mellon Univ, Pittsburgh, PA 15213. **Fax:** 412-681-0648. **E-Mail:** kraemer@cmuhep2.phys.cmu.edu

KRAEUTER, JOHN NORMAN, BIOLOGICAL OCEANOGRAPHY, MARINE ECOLOGY. **Personal Data:** b Glen Gardner, NJ, March 26, 1942; m 1970, Carol Foster; c Kirtis & Kristopher. **Education:** Fla State Univ, BA, 1964; Col William & Mary, MA, 1966; Univ Del, PhD (biol sci), 1971. **Honors & Awards:** Wallace Award, National Shellfisheries Asn. **Professional Experience:** ASSOC DIR, FISHERIES & AQUACULT TECH CTR, RUTGERS UNIV, 1987-; Baltimore Gas & Elec, 1982-1987; assoc prof marine sci, Univ Va & Col William & Mary, 1981-1982; assoc marine scientist, Va Inst Marine Sci, 1981-1982; asst prof, Va Inst Marine Sci, 1974-1980; asst marine scientist, Va Inst Marine Sci, 1974-1980; res assoc, Skidaway Inst Oceanog, Ga, 1973-1974; Res fel biol sci, Marine Inst, Univ Ga, 1971-1973. **Memberships:** Atlantic Estuarine Res Soc (pres, 1977-1979); Estuarine Res Fedn (treas, 1982-1985, secy, 1987-1988); Malacol Soc London; AAAS; Am Malacol Union; Am Fisheries Soc; Nat Shellfisheries Asn (pres, 1993-1994). **Research Statement & Publications:** Systematics and ecology of scaphopod mollusks; zoogeography of the western Atlantic marine invertebrates; benthic infaunal ecology; aquaculture. **Mailing Address:** 722 Jonathan Hoffman Rd, Cape May, NJ 08204. **Fax:** 609-785-1544. **E-Mail:** kraeuter@hsrl.rutgers.edu

KRAFFT, GEOFFREY ARTHUR, ACCELERATOR PHYSICS. **Personal Data:** b Enid, Okla, May 14, 1958; m 1994, Alicia; c Athena M & Konrad J J. **Education:** Rutgers Univ,

BA, 1978; Univ Calif, Berkeley, MA, 1980, PhD (physics), 1986. **Professional Experience:** SR SCIENTIST, THOMAS JEFFERSON NAT ACCELERATOR FACIL, 2002-; interim dir, Ctr Advan Studies Accelerators, 2001-2002; accelerator performance group leader, Continuous Electron Beam Accelerator Facil, 1993-1997; beam diagnostics group leader, Continuous Electron Beam Accelerator Facil, 1992-1993; staff scientist, Continuous Electron Beam Accelerator Facil/Thomas Jefferson Nat Accelerator Facil, 1986-2002. **Memberships:** Fel Am Phys Soc. **Research Statement & Publications:** Theory of particle accelerators; collective effects in intense particle beams; beam diagnostic devices; recirculated and energy recovered linear accelerators; high energy electromagnetic radiation sources. **Mailing Address:** TJNAF MS-7A, 12000 Jefferson Ave, Newport News, VA 23606-1909. **Fax:** 757-269-5024. **E-Mail:** krafft@jlab.org

KRAFFT, GRANT A, ALZHEIMERS DRUG DISCOVERY, BIO-ORGANIC CHEMISTRY. **Personal Data:** b Milwaukee, Wis, February 6, 1954; m 1984, c 2. **Education:** Valparaiso Univ, BS, 1976; Univ Ill, Urbana, PhD (org chem), 1980. **Professional Experience:** SR GROUP LEADER, NIA ALZHEIMERS DRUG DISCOVERY, ABBOTT LABS, 1993-; PROG DIR, NIA ALZHEIMERS DRUG DISCOVERY, ABBOTT LABS, 1991-; Assoc res fel, Abbott Labs, 1991-; lab head, Abbott Diags Div, 1988-1991; res assoc prof, Syracuse Univ, 1988-1990; asst prof chem, Syracuse Univ, 1982-1988; NIH fel, Univ Wis, 1980-1982. **Memberships:** Soc Neurosci; Am Chem Soc; Biophys Soc; AAAS; NY Acad Sci; Sigma Xi. **Research Statement & Publications:** Therapeutic targets to prevent neurodegeneration in Alzheimer's disease; development of organic molecular probes to elucidate biochemical and cellular pathways; development of molecular diversity strategies to enhance new lead drug discovery. **Mailing Address:** Dept Molecular Pharmacol & Biol Chem, Univ Northwestern, 303 E Chicago Ave, Suite 215, Chicago, IL 60611-3008. **Fax:** 847-937-9195. **E-Mail:** krafft.grant@igate.abbott.com

KRAFFT, JOSEPH MARTIN, PHYSICS. **Personal Data:** b Alexandria, Va, January 13, 1923. **Education:** Cath Univ Am, Washington, DC, BME, 1943, PhD, 1951. **Professional Experience:** CONSULT, STRUCT INTEGRITY BR, NAVAL RES LAB, WASH, DC, 1981-; Tech ed, Trans, Am Soc Mech Engrs, J Eng Mat & Technol, 1978-1981; head, Mech Mat Br, 1970-1981; physicist res & develop terminal ballistics, dynamic plastic flow & fracture fatigue mech, 1948-1970; Various positions teaching, eng, patent search & writing, DC, 1941-1949. **Memberships:** Fel Am Soc Metals; fel Am Soc Testing & Mat; Am Soc Mech Engrs. **Mailing Address:** 1709 Oakcrest Dr, Alexandria, VA 22302.

KRAFFT, MARIE ELIZABETH, TOTAL SYNTHESIS OF NATURAL PRODUCTS, ORGANOMETALLIC CHEMISTRY. **Personal Data:** b Washington, DC, August 15, 1956; m 1984. **Education:** Va Polytech Inst & State Univ, BA, 1979, MS, 1980, PhD (org chem), 1983. **Professional Experience:** PROF CHEM, FLA STATE UNIV, as of 2001; asst prof, Fla State Univ, beginning 1986; NIH res fel, Columbia Univ, 1983-1985. **Memberships:** Am Chem Soc; Sigma Xi. **Research Statement & Publications:** Synthetic organic and organometallic chemistry; natural products synthesis; synthetic methodology; author of various articles. **Mailing Address:** Dept Chem, Fla State Univ, Tallahassee, FL 32306-4390. **Fax:** 850-644-8281. **E-Mail:** mek@chem.fsu.edu

KRAFSUR, ELLIOT SCOVILLE, ENTOMOLOGY. **Personal Data:** b Frederick, Md, May 15, 1939; m 1966, Helen; c Edwin P. **Education:** Univ Md, BS, 1961, MS, 1963; Univ London PhD (zoology), 1972. **Professional Experience:** Int Agr Exchange Asn/USDA, 1993; Food & Agr Orgn, 1991; consult, Commonwealth Sci & Indust Res Org, New Guinea & Australia, USDA, 1986-1987; PROF ENTOM, IOWA STATE UNIV, 1985-; from asst prof to assoc prof, Iowa State Univ, 1976-1985; res entomologist, Animal, Plant & Health Inspection Serv, USDA, 1974-1976; fel zoology, Oxford Univ, 1972-1973; fel zoology, US NSF, 1970-1972; prin investr, USN Med Res Unit, Ethiopia, 1967-1969; ens lt entomol, USN, 1964-1969; res med entomologist, USN, 1964-1969; prin investr, US Army Biol labs, 1964-1967; res asst entomol, Dept Entomol, Univ Md, 1962-1964. **Memberships:** Soc Study Evolution; fel Royal Entom Soc; Molecular Biol Evolution Soc; Am Genetic Asn; Genetics Soc Am. **Research Statement & Publications:** Population ecology and genetics of synanthropic flies with special reference to age, breeding structure and phenology; epidemiology of arthropod borne disease; population genetics of predacious coccinellid beetles; sterile insect technique. **Mailing Address:** Dept Entom, Iowa State Univ, Ames, IA 50011-3222. **Fax:** 515-295-5957. **E-Mail:** ekrafsur@iastate.edu

KRAFT, ALAN M, PSYCHIATRY. **Personal Data:** b Passaic, NJ, May 24, 1925; m 1951, c 2. **Education:** Chicago Med Sch, MD, 1951. **Professional Experience:** PROF EMER PSYCHIAT, ALBANY MED COL, as of 2004; consult, Vet Admin Hosp, Albany, NY, beginning 1971; prof psychiat & chmn dept, Albany Med Col, beginning 1967; dir, capital dist psychiat ctr, Albany, 1967-1979; dir, Ft Logan Ment Health Ctr, 1961-1967; chief psychiatrist, Ment Health Ctr Am, 1958-1961; staff psychiatrist, Vet Admin Hosp, Denver, Colo, 1955-1957; fel psychiat, Menninger Sch Psychiat, 1952-1955. **Memberships:** Am Psychiat Asn. **Research Statement & Publications:** Treatment of chronic schizophrenia; program evaluation. **Mailing Address:** Dept Psychiat, Albany Med Col, 43 New Scotland Ave, Albany, NY 12208-3412.

KRAFT, ALLEN ABRAHAM, FOOD TECHNOLOGY. **Personal Data:** b New York, NY, 1923; m 1947, c 2. **Education:** Cornell Univ, BS, 1947, MS, 1949; Iowa State Col, PhD (food technol), 1953. **Professional Experience:** PROF EMER MICROBIOL, IOWA STATE UNIV, as of 2004; PROF EMER FOOD TECHNOL, IOWA STATE UNIV, as of 2004; prof microbiol, Iowa State Univ, beginning 1981; prof food technol, Iowa State Univ, beginning 1972; from asst prof to assoc prof, Iowa State Univ, 1959-1972; asst poultry prod technologist, Animal & Poultry Husb Res Br, Agr Res Serv, USDA, 1953-1959; Asst food technol & bact, Iowa State Col, 1949-1953. **Memberships:** Fel AAAS; Poultry Sci Asn; Inst Food Technologists; Am Soc Microbiol; World Poultry Sci Asn. **Research Statement & Publications:** Microbiology and technology of meat and poultry products. **Mailing Address:** 3624 Ross Rd, Ames, IA 50014.

KRAFT, CHRISTOPHER COLUMBUS, JR, AEROSPACE ENGINEERING. **Personal Data:** b Phoebus, Va, February 28, 1924; m 1950, c 2. **Education:** Va Polytech Inst, BS, 1944. **Honorary Degrees:** DEng, Ind Inst Technol, 1966 & St Louis Univ, 1967. **Honors & Awards:** Arthur S Flemming Award, 1963; Louis W Hill Award, Am Inst Aeronaut & Astronaut, 1970, Space Flight Award, 1970, W Randolph Lovelace II Award, 1977; Von Karman lectr, Am Inst Aeronaut & Astronaut, 1977; Daniel & Florence Guggenheim Int Astronaut Award, 1978; Goddard Mem Trophy, Nat Space Club, 1979. **Professional Experience:** PVT CONSULT, 1993-; aerospace consult, Rockwell Int, Houston, 1982-1993; dir, Lyndon B Johnson Space Ctr, 1972-1982; dep dir ctr, NASA, 1969-1972; dir flight opers, NASA, 1963-1969; chief div, NASA, 1962-1963; asst chief flight opers div, NASA, 1961-1962; supvry aeronaut res engr, NASA, 1959-1961; space task group, NASA, 1958-1959; Aeronaut res engr, Langley Aeronaut Lab, Nat Adv Comt Aeronaut, Va, 1945-1948. **Memberships:** Nat Acad Eng; fel Am Inst Aeronaut & Astronaut; fel Am Astronaut Soc. **Mailing Address:** 14919 Village Elm St, Houston, TX 77062.

KRAFT, DAVID WERNER, THEORETICAL & EXPERIMENTAL PHYSICS, RESEARCH ADMINISTRATION. **Personal Data:** b Worms, Ger, April 21, 1933; American citizen; m 1958, c Arthur, Mark & Jill. **Education:** City Col NY, BS, 1954; Pa State Univ, PhD (physics), 1959. **Honors & Awards:** Harry Epstein Award, Am Asn Physics Teachers. **Professional Experience:** PROF ELEC ENG, UNIV BRIDGEPORT, as of 2004; PROF MATH & PHYSICS, UNIV BRIDGEPORT, 1996-; dir, Kardell Technol Corp, NY, beginning 1993; vis prof physics, US Mil Acad, West Point, NY, 1993-1994; corresp mem, UN Comn Disarmament & Arms Control, beginning 1992; chair, Physics & Astron Sect, NY Acad Sci, beginning 1992; fac fel, Goddard Inst Space Studies, NASA, 1992-1993; vpres, A&D Assoc, beginning 1989; prin investr, Conn Coop High Technol Grant, 1988-1990; am inst physics, 1977 & sl electrostatic technol, 1988-1990; prof elec eng, technol develop unit, 1985-1996; found pres & dir, conn venture group, 1985-1989; dir, technol develop unit, 1985-1988; dir, res corp, 1985; assoc dean grad studies & res, math dept, Univ Bridgeport, 1984-1986; chair, math dept, Univ Bridgeport, 1982-1983; dep exec secy, Am Phys Soc, 1979-1982; dir, manpower placement div, am inst physics, 1977-1979; vis prof opers res, grad sch bus admin, NY Univ, 1976-1977; consult, ny tel co, 1976-1977; vis scientist, NY Univ, 1972-1974 & philips labs div, nam philips co, 1975; adj prof, Statist & Oper Res, NY Univ, beginning 1969; vis scientist & consult, gen tel & electronics labs, 1969-1970; from assoc prof to prof physics, cooper union, 1968-1976; res scientist, hudson labs, Columbia, 1965-1968; sr res physicist, cent res div, Am Cyanamid Co, 1965; consult, electronic systs div, loral corp, 1965; electronics systs div, loral corp, 1964; sr physicist, philips labs div, nam philips co inc, 1960-1964; res physicist, Pa State Univ, 1959-1960. **Memberships:** Am Phys Soc; Am Asn Physics Teachers; NY Acad Sci. **Research Statement & Publications:** Ultrasonic absorption; scattering of elastic waves; solid state physics; nuclear fusion; astrophysics. **Mailing Address:** Div Sci & Math, Univ Bridgeport, Bridgeport, CT 06601.

KRAFT, DONALD HARRIS, INFORMATION RETRIEVAL, FUZZY SET THEORY. **Personal Data:** b Omaha, Nebr, December 21, 1943. **Education:** Purdue Univ, BS, 1965, MS, 1966, PhD (indust eng), 1971. **Honors & Awards:** K S Fu Award, NAm Fuzzy Info Processing Soc, 1986; Watson Davis Award, Am Soc Info Sci, 1995; Am Soc Info Sci & Tech Res Award, 1999. **Professional Experience:** Distinguished vis prof, Dept Comput Sci, 2005-2006; vis prof, Libr & Info Sci, Univ Calif, Los Angeles, 1994; mem, NAm Fuzzy Info Processing Soc Coun, 1990-1992; adj prof libr & info sci, La State Univ, beginning 1983; chmn, Comput Sci, La State Univ, 1985-1991; ADJ PROF, LIB & INFO SCI, LA STATE UNIV, 1983-; PROF, DEPT COMPUT SCI, LA STATE UNIV, 1982-; assoc prof, LA State Univ, 1976-1982; vis asst prof librarianship, Univ Calif, Berkeley, 1975-1976; asst prof libr & info serv, Univ Md, 1970-1975; ed, J Am Soc Info Sci. **Memberships:** Asn Comput Mach; Inst Elec & Electronics Engrs Computer Soc; Asn Libr & Info Sci Educ; Am Soc Info Sci (Pres 2001-2002); fel Inst Elec & Electronics Engrs. **Research Statement & Publications:** Use of fuzzy set theory to model generalized Boolean information retrieval mechanisms; use of operations research to model and evaluate ranked retrieval output; author of numerous articles. **Mailing Address:** Dept Comput Sci, La State Univ, 298 Coates Hall, Baton Rouge, LA 70803-4020. **Fax:** 225-578-1465. **E-Mail:** kraft@bit.csc.lsu.edu

KRAFT, DONALD J, PLANT PHYSIOLOGY. **Personal Data:** b Strasburg, NDak, November 9, 1936; m 1960, Beverly; c Terrence, Brian, Karen & Margaret. **Education:** NDak State Univ, BS, 1959, PhD (plant physiol), 1968. **Professional Experience:** PROF EMER BIOL, BEMIDJI STATE UNIV, 1998-; prof biol, Bemidji State Univ, 1979-1998; assoc prof, Bemidji State Univ, 1972-1979; prin investr grants, NIH, 1968-1969 & Minn State Col Bd, 1969-1970 & 1973-1974; asst prof, Bemidji State Univ, 1969-1972; asst prof biol, St Mary's Col Minn, 1968-1969; chmn dept sci, NDak, 1962-1963; teacher high sch, NDak, 1961-1962. **Memberships:** AAAS; Am Soc Plant Physiologists; Sigma Xi. **Research Statement & Publications:** Biochemistry of seed germination as a means to eliminate noxious weeds through natural components of seeds rather than through use of sprays. **Mailing Address:** Dept Biol, Bemidgi State Univ, 2520 Calihan Ave NE, Bemidji, MN 56601.

KRAFT, EDWARD MICHAEL, AERODYNAMICS, WIND TUNNEL TECHNOLOGY. **Personal Data:** b Cincinnati, Ohio, November 13, 1944; m 1971, c 1. **Education:** Univ Cincinnati, BS, 1968; Univ Tenn, MS, 1972, PhD (aerodyn eng), 1975. **Honors & Awards:** Spec Achievement Award, Am Inst Aeronaut & Aatronaut. **Professional Experience:** TECH ADV, ARNOLD ENG DEVELOP CTR, ARNOLD AIR FORCE BASE, TENN, as of 2001; vpres & chief technical off, Allied Aerospace Industs, Inc, Tullahoma, Tenn, 2000-2001; exec vpres & chief operating officer, Micro Craft, Inc, 1996-2000; vpres enterprise develop, Micro Craft, Inc, Tullahoma, Tenn, 1995-2006; gen mgr, Micro Craft Technol, Arnold Eng Develop Ctr Oper, Arnold Air Force Base, Tenn, 1994-1995; dir, technol & develop facil, Calspan Corp, Arnold Air Force Base, Tenn, 1992-1994; dep dir, Aerospace Syst Facil, Calspan Corp, Arnold Air Force Base, Tenn, 1991-1992; br mgr, Calspan Field Serv Inc, 1981-1995; engr supv, Sverdrup/Aro, Inc, 1978-1980; asst prof, Space Inst, Univ Tenn, beginning 1977; res engr, Sverdrup/Aro, Inc, 1972-1978; proj engr, Sverdrup/Aro, Inc, 1969-1972; res asst, Space Inst, Univ Tenn, 1968-1969. **Memberships:** Am Inst Aeronaut & Astronaut; Univ Cincinnati Aerospace Eng & Eng Mech Adv Coun; Nat Alumni Asn; Nat Mgt Asn. **Research Statement & Publications:** Wind tunnel wall interference, including subsonic, transonic and vertical/short take off and landing theories and development of the adaptive wall concept. **Mailing Address:** Arnol Air Force Base, 207 Big Springs Ave, Tullahoma, TN 37388.

KRAFT, GERALD F, entomology, science education; deceased, see previous edition for last biography

KRAFT, IRVIN ALAN, CHILD PSYCHIATRY, PSYCHOANALYSIS. **Personal Data:** b Huntington, WVa, November 20, 1921; m 1951, Sherry; c 4. **Education:** NY Univ, MD, 1949. **Professional Experience:** EMER PROF MENT HEALTH, UNIV TEX SCH PUB HEALTH, HOUSTON, 1991-; clin prof psychiat, Baylor Col Med, 1977-; prof, Univ Tex Sch Pub Health, Houston, 1975-1991; med dir, Tex Inst Family Psychiat, 1964-1979; assoc prof psychiat & pediat, Baylor Col Med, 1961-1977; asst prof pediat, Baylor Col Med, 1958-1961; asst prof psychiat, Baylor Col Med, 1957-1961. **Memberships:** Fel Am Psychiat Asn; fel Am Acad Psychoanal; fel Am Acad Child Psychiat; fel Am Orthopsychiat Asn. **Research Statement & Publications:** Child psychiatry; psychoanalysis. **Mailing Address:** 2423 Gramercy, Houston, TX 77030. **Fax:** 713-668-2555.

KRAFT, JOAN CREECH, RETINOIC ACID, DYSMORPHOGENESIS. **Personal Data:** b Washington, DC, June 8, 1943; c 3. **Education:** Univ Pa, BS, 1965; Free Univ Berlin, Ger, dipl biol, 1975, Dr rer nat (biol), 1977. **Professional Experience:** POST GRAD RES, VET ADMIN MED CTR, 1997-; sr res fel teratology, Dept Pharmacol, Univ Wash, 1990-1997; sr res scientist, Inst Toxicol & Embryopharmacol, Berlin, 1984-1988; teaching asst biol, Free Univ Berlin, 1979-1983; Postdoctoral res protein biosynthesis, Inst Biochem & Molecular Biol, Free Univ Berlin & Max Planck Inst Molecular Genetics, 1978-1979; lab asst molecular biol, Free Univ Berlin, 1976-1981. **Memberships:** Teratology Soc. **Re-**

search Statement & Publications: Teratology; pharmacokinetics, metabolism and placental transfer of the potent teratogen accutane. Mailing Address: Vet Admin Med Ctr, 4150 Clement St Rm 111 N, San Francisco, CA 94121.

KRAFT, JOHN CHRISTIAN, HOLOCENE GEOLOGY, ARCHAEOLOGICAL GEOLOGY. Personal Data: b Schwenksville, Pa, November 15, 1929; c Christine L, John F & Amanda L Schlick. Education: Pa State Univ, BS, 1951; Univ Minn, MS, 1952, PhD (micropaleont), 1955. Honors & Awards: Archaeol Geol Award, Geol Soc Am, 1987; John C Kraft Celebration, Coastal Sediments, Am Soc Civil Engrs & Soc Econ Paleontologists & Mineralogists, 1991; Francis alism prof, Univ pel 1988-; outstanding achievement Award, board of regents, Univ of minnesoto, 2001. Professional Experience: PROF GEOL, UNIV DEL, 1969-; chmn dept, Univ Del, 1969-1984; H FLETCHER BROWN PROF GEOL & MARINE STUDIES, UNIV DEL, 1964-; from asst prof to assoc prof, Univ Del, 1964-1969; div stratigr, Shell Can Ltd, 1961-1964; geologist, Shell Can Ltd, 1955-1961. Memberships: Fel AAAS; Am Asn Petrol Geologists; fel Geol Soc Am; Soc Econ Paleont & Mineral; Am Inst Prof Geologists; Archaeol Inst Am. Research Statement & Publications: Geology of coasts; Holocene sedimentary environments; Ordovician and Holocene Ostracoda; archaeological geology; Greece, Turkey, U S A. Mailing Address: Dept Geol, Univ Del, Newark, DE 19716. Fax: 302-831-4158. E-Mail: 00218@udel.edu

KRAFT, JOHN M, PLANT PATHOLOGY. Personal Data: b Gary, Ind, July 14, 1938; m 1964, c 2. Education: Ariz State Univ, BS, 1960; Univ Minn, St Paul, MS, 1962; Univ Calif, Riverside, PhD (plant path), 1966. Professional Experience: PRIN INVESTR, AGR RES SERV, US DEPT AGR, as of 2000; RES LEADER VEG & FORAGE CROP RES, CROP RES DIV, AGR RES SERV, US DEPT AGR, beginning 1995; RES PLANT PATHOLOGIST, CROP RES DIV, AGR RES SERV, US DEPT AGR, beginning 1966; res asst plant path, Univ Calif, Riverside, 1962-1966; res asst plant path, Univ Minn, St Paul, 1960-1962; Mem grad fac, Dept Plant Path, Wash State Univ & Dept Plant Sci, Univ Idaho. Memberships: Am Phytopath Soc; Am Soc Agron & Soil Sci; Pisum Genetics Asn; Sigma Xi; Nat Pea Improv Asn. Research Statement & Publications: Soil-borne diseases of peas and their etiology, biology of the fungi, their control and the nature and inheritance of resistance when found; control of soil-borne diseases of peas; breeding for root disease resistance in peas. Mailing Address: Agr Res Serv, US Dept Agr, 24106 N Bunn Rd, Prosser, WA 99350-8694. Fax: 509-786-9277. E-Mail: jkraft@tricity.wsu.edu

KRAFT, KENNETH J, INVERTEBRATE ECOLOGY. Personal Data: b Dows, Iowa, March 3, 1930; m 1968, c 1. Education: Bemidji State Col, BS, 1952; Univ NDak, MS, 1953; Univ Minn, PhD (entom), 1958. Professional Experience: ASSOC PROF EMER FORESTRY & WOOD PRODUCTS & BIOL SCI, MICH TECHNOL UNIV, as of 2004; assoc prof biol, Mich Technol Univ, beginning 1964; asst prof, Mich Technol Univ, 1961-1964; asst prof, Moorhead State Col, 1958-1959 & Bemidji State Col, 1959-1961; Instr biol, Univ Minn, 1956-1958. Memberships: Entom Soc Am. Research Statement & Publications: Ecology of aquatic insects. Mailing Address: Sch Forestry, Mich Technol Univ, 1400 Townsend Dr, Houghton, MI 49931.

KRAFT, PATRICIA LYNN, TOXICOLOGY. Personal Data: b Somerville, NJ. Education: Rutgers Col Agr & Environ Sci, BS, 1972; Mass Inst Technol, PhD (toxicol), 1979. Professional Experience: Chmn, Toxicol & Safety Evaluation Div, 1985-1986; group mgr, Life Sci, Pepsi Co, Valhalla, NY, beginning 1983; Sr toxicologist, Best Foods Res & Eng Ctr, CPC North Am, 1980-1983. Memberships: Am Inst Nutrit; Am Col Toxicol; Inst Food Technologists; Sigma Xi. Research Statement & Publications: Nutritional biochemical mechanisms of tumorigenesis; effect of diet on maintenance of health and progression of disease, hunger and satiety. Mailing Address: Pepsi Co, 100 Stevens Ave, Valhalla, NY 10595-1299. Fax: 914-742-4501.

KRAFT, ROBERT PAUL, ASTROPHYSICS. Personal Data: b Seattle, Wash, June 16, 1927; m 1949, Rosalie; c Kenneth & Kevin. Education: Univ Wash, BS, 1947, MS, 1949; Univ Calif, Berkeley, PhD (astron), 1955. Honorary Degrees: DSc, Ind Univ, 1995. Honors & Awards: Warner Prize lectr, Am Astron Soc, 1962, Henry Norris Russell Lectr, 1995. Professional Experience: PROF EMER, ASTRON & ASTROPHYS, UNIV CALIF, SANTA CRUZ, 1993-; Beatrice Tinsley vis prof, Univ Tex, 1991-1992; dir, Univ Calif Observ, 1988-1991; dir, Lick Observ, 1981-1991; Fairchild scholar, Cal Inst Technol, 1980; vis fel, Univ Colo, 1970; chmn bd studies astron & astrophys, Univ Calif, Santa Cruz, 1968-1970, 1978-1980; actg dir, Univ Calif, Santa Cruz, 1968-1970, 1971-1973, 1980-1981; prof astron & astronr, Lick Observ, 1967-1992; mem staff, Mt Wilson & Palomar Observs, 1960-1967; asst prof astron, Univ Chicago, 1958-1959; asst prof astron, Ind Univ, 1956-1958; NSF fel, Mt Wilson & Palomar Observs, 1955-1956; instr math & astron, Whittier Col, 1949-1951. Memberships: Nat Acad Sci; Am Astron Soc (pres, 1974-1976); Am Acad Arts & Sci; Int Astron Union (vpres, 1982-1988, pres-elect, 1994-2000); Foreign Assoc Royal Astr Soc 1996. Research Statement & Publications: Stellar spectroscopy; galactic structure; abundances of the chemical elements. Mailing Address: Univ Calif, Kerr 231A, Santa Cruz, CA 95003. Fax: 831-426-3115. E-Mail: kraft@ucolick.org

KRAFT, RUSSELL P, IMAGE ANALYSIS. Education: Rensselaer Polytech Inst, BS, 1976, ME, 1978, PhD, 1983. Professional Experience: SR PROJ MGR, CTR INTEGRATED ELECTRONICS & ELECTRONICS MFG, RENSSELAER POLYTECH INST, as of 2006. Mailing Address: Rensselaer Polytech Inst, 110 8th St, Troy, NY 12180. Fax: 518-276-4072. E-Mail: kraftr2@rpi.edu

KRAFT, SUMNER CHARLES, INTERNAL MEDICINE, GASTROENTEROLOGY. Personal Data: b Lynn, Mass, August 21, 1928; m 1963, Patricia P Pink; c Gary, Jennifer & Steven. Education: Tufts Col, BS, 1948; Boston Univ, AM, 1949; Univ Chicago, MD, 1955; Am Bd Internal Med, dipl, 1962, Am Bd Gastroenterol, dipl, 1965. Honors & Awards: William Beaumont Award, 1977. Professional Experience: Vis affil prof med, Uniformed Serv Univ Health Sci, Bethesda, 1979-1987; PROF MED, SCH MED, UNIV CHICAGO, 1974-; USPHS res career develop award, 1967-1971; res fel, Div Allergy, Immunol & Rheumatol, Scripps Clin & Res Found, La Jolla, Calif, 1964-1966; USPHS spec res fel, 1961-1966; From instr to assoc prof, Sch Med, Univ Chicago, 1959-1973. Memberships: AAAS; Am Asn Immunologists; Am Col Physicians; Am Fedn Clin Res; Am Gastroenterol Asn; Am Soc Gastrointestinal Endoscopy; Sigma Xi. Research Statement & Publications: Gastrointestinal immunolgy. Mailing Address: Dept Med, Univ Chicago MC 4076 5841 S Maryland Ave, Chicago, IL 60637-1463. E-Mail: sckraft@midway.uchicago.edu

KRAFT, TIMOTHY W, ELECTRICAL ENGINEERING. Education: Univ Minn, PhD, 1985. Professional Experience: ASSOC PROF PHYSIOL OPTICS, UNIV ALA SCH MED, as of 2004; ASSOC SCIENTIST, VISION SCI RES CTR, as of 2004. Mailing Address: Dept Physiol Optics Univ Ala Sch Med, 1530 3rd Ave S, Birmingham, AL 35294. E-Mail: twkraft@uab.edu

KRAFT, WALTER H, MARKETING, CIVIL & ENGINEERING. Personal Data: b Newark, NJ, December 31, 1938; m 1959, c Robin, Karen & Lynda. Education: Newark Col Eng, BS, 1962, MS, 1965; NJ Inst Technol, DEngSc, 1975. Honors & Awards: Robert Ridgward Award, Am Soc Civil Engrs, 1962, Frank Masters Award, 1982; Ivor S Wisepart Transp Eng Award & Distinguished Serv Award, Inst Transp Engrs, 1986. Professional Experience: INT LEADER, INTELLIGENT TRANSP SYST, as of 2004; SR VPRES, PB FARRADYNE INC, 1994-; Sino-Am-British Urban Transp Planning Sem, Beijing, Peoples Repub China, 1988; lectr, Carnegie-Mellon Univ, St Johns Univ, Int Conf Traffic Eng & Planning, Beijing, Peoples Repub China, 1987; Comt AIE03 Intermodal Transfer Facil, Nat Res Coun, Transp Res Bd, 1982-1985; mem, Comt A3A10 Hwy Capacity & Qual Serv, 1980-1985; chairperson, Nat Transp Policy Comt, 1980-1982; chairperson, Urban Transp Div, Am Soc Civil Engrs, 1977-1979; asst eng, Edwards & Kelcey, Inc, beginning 1962; PARSONS BRINCKERHOFF; Adj prof, NJ Inst Technol & Polytech Inst, NY. Memberships: Fel Inst Transp Engrs (pres 1987); Am Soc Civil Engrs. Research Statement & Publications: Civil engineering; traffic engineering and planning; author of numerous technical articles. Mailing Address: PB Farradyne Inc, Summit, NJ 07901. Fax: 973-994-4902.

KRAFT, WILLIAM GERALD, BACTERIAL PATHOGENESIS, MICROBIAL PHYSIOLOGY. Personal Data: b Evansville, Ind, July 15, 1944; m 1977, Barbara A Betz. Education: Purdue Univ, BS, 1966; Univ Wash, MS, 1972; Ind Univ, PhD (microbiol), 1977. Professional Experience: SECT HEAD, PROCTER & GAMBLE PHARMACEUT, 1984-; group leader, Procter & Gamble Pharmaceut, 1982-1984; sr res microbiologist, Procter & Gamble Pharmaceut, 1977-1982; Res eng chem, Dow Chem Co, 1966-1968. Memberships: Am Soc Microbiol. Research Statement & Publications: Physiology and pathogenesis of campylobacters; thermal resistance of aerobic bacilli spores and define sterilization cycles for pharmaceutical products; microbial ecology of natural and synthetic substances; develop novel antibacterials. Mailing Address: 8700 Mason-Montgomery Rd, Mason, OH 45040.

KRAG, SHARON S, BIOCHEMISTRY. Personal Data: b Wharton, Tex, August 11, 1947. Education: Tex Lutheran Col, BS, 1969; Johns Hopkins Univ, PhD (biochem), 1974. Professional Experience: ASSOC DEAN RES, SCH HYG & PUB HEALTH, JOHNS HOPKINS UNIV, 1994-; res career develop award, NIH, 1980, 1985; PROF BIOCHEM, SCH HYG & PUB HEALTH, JOHNS HOPKINS UNIV, 1976-; fel, cancer res Ctr, Mass Inst Technol, 1974-1976. Memberships: Fedn Am Socs Exp Biol; Am Cell Biol Soc; AAAS. Mailing Address: Dept Biochem Sch Hyg & Pub Health, Johns Hopkins Univ, 615 N Wolfe St W1033, Baltimore, MD 21205. Fax: 410-614-7871. E-Mail: skrag@jhsph.edu

KRAH, DAVID LEE, VIROLOGY, CELL BIOLOGY. Personal Data: b Ashland, Pa, January 23, 1956. Education: Pa State Univ, BS, 1977; Hahnemann Med Col, MS, 1980; Hahnemann Univ, PhD (microbiol & immunol), 1982. Professional Experience: SR RES FEL, MERCK RES LABS, MERCK & CO INC, 1995-; res fel, Merck Sharp & Dohme Res Labs, 1991-1995; sr res virologist, Merck Sharp & Dohme Res Labs, 1988-1991; sr res scientist, Schering Corp, 1986-1988; res assoc, Rockefeller Univ, 1985-1986; fel, Rockefeller Univ, 1982-1985. Memberships: AAAS; Am Soc Microbiol; Am Soc Virol; Soc Gen Microbiol; Tissue Cult Asn. Research Statement & Publications: Development and characterization of live virus vaccines; measurement of humoral immune responses following viral infection or vaccination; interactions of viruses with cell membrane receptors. Mailing Address: Dept Virus & Cell Biol, Merck Res Labs, West Point, PA 19486.

KRAHENBUHL, JAMES LEE, INFECTIOUS DISEASES, LEPROSY. Personal Data: b Appleton, Wis, October 7, 1942; m 1965, Betty; c Jeffrey Lee. Education: Univ Wis-Madison, BS, 1964, MS, 1967, PhD (med microbiol), 1970. Honors & Awards: Distinguished Serv Award Biomed Res, USPHS, 1990. Professional Experience: ADJ PROF, DEPT PATHOBIOLOGY SCI, LA STATE UNIV, as of 2004; CHIEF, LAB RES BR, G W LONG HANSEN'S DIS CTR, CARVILLE, LA, 1994-; prof vet microbiol, Sch Vet Med, La State Univ, Baton Rouge, 1985-; chief, immunol res, 1983-1994; chief, Leprosy Res Unit, USPHS Hosp, San Francisco, 1979-1983; USPHS res career develop award, Nat Inst Allergy & Infectious Dis, 1974-1979; sr res assoc immunol & infectious dis, Palo Alto Med Res Found, 1972-1979; res assoc, Med Ctr, Stanford Univ, 1972-1978; fel, Palo Alto Med Res Found, 1970-1971; fel med, Med Ctr, Stanford Univ, 1970-1971. Memberships: AAAS; Am Asn Immunologists; Soc Exp Biol & Med; Am Soc Microbiol; Int Leprosy Asn. Research Statement & Publications: Mechanisms of host resistance to leprosy, tuberculosis and toxoplasmosis. Mailing Address: Dept Pathobiology Sci, Sch Vet Med, La State Univ, Skip Bertman Dr River Rd, Baton Rouge, LA 70803. Fax: 225-578-9701. E-Mail: jkrahe1@lsu.edu

KRAHMER, ROBERT LEE, FOREST PRODUCTS. Personal Data: b Forest Grove, Ore, December 28, 1932; m 1957, c 2. Education: Ore State Univ, BS, 1958, MS, 1960; State Univ NY Col Forestry, Syracuse Univ, PhD (wood prod eng), 1962. Professional Experience: PROF EMER FOREST PROD, ORE STATE UNIV, as of 2004; prof forest prod, Ore State Univ, ending 1991; From instr forest prod, Ore State Univ, beginning 1961. Memberships: Forest Prod Res Soc; Soc Wood Sci & Technol; Int Asn Wood Anat. Research Statement & Publications: Light and electron microscope studies of fine structure of wood; variability of anatomical properties of wood. Mailing Address: Dept Forest Prod, Ore State Univ, Corvallis, OR 97331. Fax: 503-737-3385.

KRAHN, ROBERT CARL, ORGANIC CHEMISTRY. Personal Data: b Minneapolis, Minn, December 1, 1941; m 1978, c Megan Bliss & Tara Cole. Education: Univ Minn, BChE, 1963; Univ Wash, PhD (org chem), 1968. Professional Experience: HEALTH CONSULT, as of 2006; sr chemist, Chem, Dyes & Pigments Dept, Jackson Lab, 1978-1982; process chemist, Org Chem Dept, E I Du Pont Del Nemours & Co, Inc, 1973-1978; res chemist, Org Chem Dept, E I Du Pont Del Nemours & Co, Inc, 1968-1973; DIR, GOLDEN PATHWAYS HEALING CTR. Memberships: Am Chem Soc. Research Statement & Publications: Emulsion polymerization; monomer synthesis; flurochemicals; surfactant chemistry; ethoxylation; textile finishing. Mailing Address: 17 Polaris Dr, Newark, DE 19711. E-Mail: bobkrahn@msn.com

KRAHN, THOMAS RICHARD, HORTICULTURE. Personal Data: b Swiftcurrent, Sask, May 23, 1943; m 1967, c 2. Education: Univ Alta, BSc, 1967; Mich State Univ, MSc, 1973. Professional Experience: CHAIR, BROOKS HEALTH FOUND, PALLISER HEALTH REGION, as of 2002; DIR, ALTA HORT RES CTR, 1983-; head lab serv, 1972-1983; exten specialist, 1967-1972. Memberships: Agr Inst Can. Research Statement & Publications: Post harvest physiology, mainly storage and handling practices for vegetables, potatoes, and nursey crops. Mailing Address: Brooks & Dist Health Found, Bag 300, Brooks, AB T1R 1B3, Can. Fax: 403-362-6039.

KRAHNKE, HAROLD C, PHYSIOLOGICAL CHEMISTRY, PHARMACY. Personal Data: b Beloit, Wis, October 12, 1907; m 1931, c 2. Education: Univ Wis, BS, 1940, MS, 1941. Professional Experience: RETIRED; dir pharmaceut dept, Lakeside Labs Div, Colgate-Palmolive Co, 1962-1973; chief pharmaceut div, Lakeside Labs, Inc, 1952-1962; chief control chemist, Lakeside Labs, Inc, 1947-1952; res chemist, Lakeside Labs, Inc, 1941-1947; res asst physiol chem, Univ Wis, 1940-1941; Pharmacist, Retail Pharm, 1926-1936. Memberships: Am Chem Soc; Am Pharmaceut Asn; Acad Pharmaceut Sci. Research

Statement & Publications: Pharmaceutical research and product development; formulation and manufacturing procedures; synthesis of organic medicinal compounds; quality control of pharmaceuticals. **Mailing Address:** 6770 N Yates Rd, Milwaukee, WI 53217.

KRAHULA, JOSEPH L(OUIS), MECHANICS. **Personal Data:** b Czech, July 22, 1923; m 1959, c 2. **Education:** Rensselaer Polytech Inst, BME, 1946, MS, 1950; Univ Ill, PhD (mech), 1952. **Professional Experience:** PROF EMER MECH, HARTFORD GRAD CTR, RENSSELAER POLYTECH INST, as of 2003; adj prof mech, Rensselaer Polytech Inst, as of 2002; prof mech, Hartford Grad Ctr, Rensselaer Polytech Inst, beginnin 1967; from asst prof to assoc prof, Hartford Grad Ctr, Rensselaer Polytech Inst, 1952-1967; asst, Univ Ill, 1950-1952; instr mech, Rensselaer Polytech Inst, 1946-1950. **Memberships:** Assoc fel Am Inst Aeronaut & Astronaut; Int Asn Bridge & Struct Engrs. **Research Statement & Publications:** Vibrations and elasticity. **Mailing Address:** Dept Eng & Sci, Rensselaer Polytech Univ, 275 Windsor St, Hartford, CT 06120-2991.

KRAICER, JACOB, ENDOCRINOLOGY, NEUROENDOCRINOLOGY. **Personal Data:** b Toronto, Ont, October 28, 1931; m 1957, c 2. **Education:** Univ Toronto, BA, 1954, MD, 1958, PhD (physiol), 1962. **Honors & Awards:** Sarrazin Lectr, Can Physiol Soc, 1983. **Professional Experience:** PROF PHYSIOL, UNIV WESTERN ONT, 1984-; chmn physiol, Univ Western Ont, beginning 1984; ed, Can J Physiol & Pharmacol, beginning 1981; from asst prof to prof physiol, Queen's Univ, Ont, 1964-1984; med res coun can scholar, 1964-1966; animal morphol lab, Free Univ Brussels, 1963-1964; med Res Coun Can fel, Endocrinol Lab, Fac Med, Laval Univ, 1962-1963; res assoc physiol, Banting & Best Dept Med Res, Univ Toronto, 1961-1962; rotating intern med, Toronto Gen Hosp, 1958-1959. **Memberships:** Int Soc Neuroendocrinol; Am Physiol Soc; Endocrine Soc; Can Physiol Soc (pres, 1985-1986); Can Soc Endocrinol & Metab. **Research Statement & Publications:** Mechanism and related peptides and of regulation of corticotrophin and growth hormone secretion in the adenohypophysis. **Mailing Address:** Dept Physiol, Univ Toronto, Med Sci Bldg, Toronto, ON M5S 1A8, Can. **Fax:** 416-978-4940. **E-Mail:** j.kraicer@utoronto.ca

KRAICHNAN, ROBERT HARRY, STATISTICAL MECHANICS. **Personal Data:** b Philadelphia, Pa, January 15, 1928; m 1989, Judy; c John L. **Education:** Mass Inst Technol, BS, 1947, PhD, 1949. **Honors & Awards:** ADION medal, observatoire de Nice, 1993; Otto Laporte Award, Am Phys Soc, 1993; Lars Onsager Prize, 1997. **Professional Experience:** CONSULT, LOS ALAMOS NAT LAB, 1982-; INDEPENDENT CONSULT, Los Alamos Nat Lab, 1962-; consult, Naval Res Lab, 1957-1959 & NASA, 1961-; assoc physics, Woods Hole Oceanog Inst, 1960-; sr res scientist, NY Univ, 1959-1962; inst math sci, NY Univ, 1956-1959; res assoc, Electronics Res Lab, Columbia Univ, 1952-1956; mem tech staff, Bell Tel Labs, Inc, 1950-1952; mem, Inst Advan Study, 1949-1950. **Memberships:** Fel Am Phys Soc fel AAAS, mem NAS. **Research Statement & Publications:** Quantum and classical statistical mechanics; random processes; turbulence, quantum field and relativity theory. **Mailing Address:** 369 Montezuma No 108, Sante Fe, NM 87501.

KRAIG, ELLEN, MOLECULAR IMMUNOGENETICS. **Personal Data:** b Ft Worth, Tex, February 9, 1953; m 1978, c 1. **Education:** Univ Denver, BS, 1975; Brandeis Univ, PhD (biol), 1981. **Professional Experience:** PROF, DEPT CELL BIOL & STRUCT BIOL, HEALTH SCI CTR, UNIV TEX, as of 2004; asst prof cell biol, Health Sci Ctr, Univ Tex, beginning 1983; teaching fel biol, Calif Inst Technol, 1980-1983. **Memberships:** Am Asn Immunologists; Sigma Xi. **Research Statement & Publications:** Use of recombinant DNA approaches to elucidate the molecular bases of immune response regulation. **Mailing Address:** Dept Cell Biol, Health Sci Ctr, Univ Tex, MC 7762 7703 FloydCurl Dr, San Antonio, TX 78229-3900. **Fax:** 210-567-2345. **E-Mail:** kraig@uthscsa.edu

KRAIHANZEL, CHARLES S, INORGANIC CHEMISTRY. **Personal Data:** b New Bedford, Mass, September 6, 1935; m 1957, Pauline; c 5. **Education:** Brown Univ, ScB, 1957; Univ Wis, MS, 1959, PhD (chem), 1962. **Professional Experience:** PROF EMER CHEM, LEHIGH UNIV, 2001-; prof chem, Lehigh Univ, beginning 1970; from asst prof to assoc prof, Lehigh Univ, 1962-1970. **Memberships:** Am Chem Soc. **Research Statement & Publications:** Syntheses, reactions, nature of bonding and physical properties, of organosilicon, organophosphorous and transition metal compounds; molecular modeling of inorganic and organometallic compounds. **Mailing Address:** Dept Chem, Lehigh Univ, Seeley G Mudd Bldg, Bethlehem, PA 18015. **E-Mail:** csk1@lehigh.edu

KRAIMAN, EUGENE ALFRED, POLYMER CHEMISTRY. **Personal Data:** b Philadelphia, Pa, April 11, 1929; m 1956. **Education:** Univ Pa, BS, 1950; Univ Ill, MS, 1951, PhD (chem), 1953. **Professional Experience:** PRES, POLYMER SYSTS CORP, 1968-; res sect head, Sun Chem Corp, 1961-1968; supvr, Plastics Div, Nopco Chem Co, 1958-1961; Res chemist, Union Carbide Plastics Co, 1953-1956 & Hooker Chem Co, 1956-1958. **Memberships:** Am Chem Soc. **Research Statement & Publications:** Polyurethanes; organic chemicals; elastomers; coatings; adhesives; ultraviolet radiation cured systems. **Mailing Address:** 7922 Sandpoint Blvd, Orlando, FL 32819.

KRAINES, DAVID PAUL, TOPOLOGY. **Personal Data:** b Chicago, Ill, March 7, 1941; m 1964, c 2. **Education:** Oberlin Col, AB, 1961; Univ Calif, Berkeley, MA, 1963, PhD (math), 1965. **Professional Experience:** ASSOC PROF MATH, DUKE UNIV, 1973-; asst prof, Duke Univ, 1971-1973; guest prof, Aarhus Univ, 1970-1971; actg chmn, Haverford Col, 1968-1969; asst prof, Haverford Col, 1967-1970; instr math, Mass Inst Technol, 1965-1967. **Memberships:** Am Math Soc. **Research Statement & Publications:** Algebraic topology. **Mailing Address:** Dept Math, Duke Univ, 228B Physics Bldg, Durham, NC 27708. **Fax:** 919-660-2821. **E-Mail:** dkrain@math.duke.edu

KRAINES, VIVIAN Y, MATHEMATICS. **Education:** Oberlin Col, AB, 1961; Univ Calif, MA, 1963, PhD, 1965. **Professional Experience:** ASSOC PROF, DEPT MATHS, DUKE UNIV, as of 2005. **Mailing Address:** Math Dept, Duke Univ, Box 90320, Durham, NC 27708-0320. **Fax:** 919.660.2821. **E-Mail:** dkrain@math.duke.edu

KRAJCA, KENNETH EDWARD, ADHESIVES & ADHESION, COATINGS TECHNOLOGY. **Personal Data:** b Witchita Falls, Tex, April 1, 1944; m 1967, Sherry; c Larur L & Shannon D. **Education:** Midwestern State Univ, BS, 1967; Univ Fla, PhD (chem), 1972. **Professional Experience:** MGR TECH SERV, UNION CAMP CORP, 1992-; develop mgr, Chem Div, 1986-1992; group leader, Union Camp Corp, 1984-1986; tech mgr, SCM Corp, 1984; sect head, SCM Corp, 1980-1984; res chemist, SCM Corp, 1976-1980; res scientist, Union Camp Corp, 1972-1976. **Memberships:** Am Chem Soc; Adhesion Soc. **Research Statement & Publications:** Design and development of tall oil-based products for the adhesives industry from thermoplastic polyamides and epoxy curing agents to rosin-based tackifying resins. **Mailing Address:** Union Camp Corp, 110 N Cromwell Rd, Savannah, GA 31410.

KRAJCINOVIC, DUSAN, MICROMECHANICS, DAMAGE & FRACTURE MECHANICS. **Personal Data:** b Zaqreb, Yugoslavia, March 28, 1935; American citizen; m 1963, Tanya; c Ivana & Maya. **Education:** Univ Belgrade, Yugoslavia, BSc, 1958, MSc, 1966; Northwestern Univ, PhD (theoret appl mech), 1968. **Honorary Degrees:** Dr, Politecnico di Milano, Italy. **Honors & Awards:** October Award for Sci, Belgrade, 1991; Gold Award for sci & technol, China. **Professional Experience:** Mem, Inst Theoret Physics, Univ Calif, Santa Barbara, beginning 1992; Gabinete da Area de Sines, Allied Signal, beginning 1992; PROF MECH SOLIDS, ARIZ STATE UNIV, 1989-; vis prof, Univ de Paris VI, 1987-1988; Gabinete da Area de Sines, E Fermi Nat Lab, 1983-1987; Gabinete da Area de Sines, Portugal, 1980-1984; mem, USA Plasma Team, US Dept Energy, 1976-1980; prof mech, Univ Ill, Chicago, 1973-1989; consult, Argonne Nat Lab, 1973-1980; mem tech staff, Argonne Nat Lab, 1969-1973; mem tech staff, Ingersoll Rand Res, 1968-1969; res asst, Northwestern Univ, 1966-1968; teaching asst mech, Univ Belgrade, 1961-1966; proj engr, Energoprojekt, Belgrade, 1959-1961. **Memberships:** Life Fel Am Soc Mech Engrs; fel Am Acad Mech. **Research Statement & Publications:** Brittle deformation of solids with disordered microstructure; nondeterministic models of critical states in solids weakened by diffused microcracks; formulation of continuum damage theories based and inspired by micromechanics. **Mailing Address:** Mech & Aerospace Eng, Ariz State Univ, Tempe, AZ 85287-6106. **Fax:** 480-965-1384. **E-Mail:** dusan@asu.edu

KRAJEWSKI, JOHN J, SYNTHETIC ORGANIC CHEMISTRY, POLYMER CHEMISTRY. **Personal Data:** b Chicago, Ill, March 27, 1931; m Jacqueline; c Christopher & Carolyn. **Education:** Loyola Univ Ill, BS, 1953, MS, 1954; Carnegie Inst Technol, PhD (org chem), 1958. **Honors & Awards:** Co-founder, DSM-Desotech fiber optics business. **Professional Experience:** Retired, 1998; POLYMER & COATINGS CONSULT, 1995-1996; mgr new venture polymers, Allied Signal Corp, 1991-1994; Polymer chem instructor, DePaul Univ, 1990; mgr, New Venture Res, 1987-1989; mgr polymer develop, De Soto, Inc, 1979-1987; tech mgr, De Soto, Inc, 1973-1979; res chemist, De Soto, Inc, 1970-1973; synthetic org specialist, Int Minerals & Chem Corp, 1967-1970; res chemist, Int Minerals & Chem Corp, 1962-1967; div head, Swift & Co, 1960-1962; Res chemist, Swift & Co, 1958-1960; adv res proj selection & mgt, dir, Innovative Prob Solving Service. **Memberships:** Am Chem Soc. **Research Statement & Publications:** Organic synthesis; polymer chemistry; natural products; photopolymerization; organic photoconductors; chemical coatings; laser curing of resins; radiation curable coatings. **Mailing Address:** 932 Valley Stream Dr, Wheeling, IL 60090-3949. **E-Mail:** jjkrajewski@juno.com

KRAJEWSKI, LAWRENCE L, MATHEMATICS. **Education:** Univ Wis-Milwaukee, BS, MS, PhD, 1970. **Professional Experience:** PROF, DEPT MATHS, VITERBO UNIV, WIS, as of 2005. **Mailing Address:** Viterbo Univ, La Crosse, WI 54601. **Fax:** 608-796-3859.

KRAKAUER, HENRY, BIOMETRICS-BIOSTATISTICS. **Personal Data:** b Jaworzno, Poland, May 31, 1939; American citizen; m 1974, c 2. **Education:** Yeshiva Univ, BA, 1960, BHL, 1960; NY Univ, MD, 1964; Yale Univ, PhD (chem), 1968. **Honors & Awards:** Commendation Medal, USPHS, 1981, Outstanding Serv Medal, 1988, Meritorious Serv Medal, 1991; Distinguished Serv Award, Dept Health & Human Serv, 1989. **Professional Experience:** DIR, OFF PROG ASSESSMENT & INFO, HEALTH STANDARDS & QUAL BUR, HEALTH CARE FINANCING ADMIN, as of 2006; med adv, health standards & qual bur, Health Care financing admin, beginning 1991; dir, Off prog assessment & info, 1988-1991; res assoc prof, Sch Med, Univ Md, 1987-; med adv, Off med rev, Health Care financing admin, 1985-1988; chief, Genetics & transplantation biol Br, Nat Inst Allergy & Infectious dis, 1979-1983; from asst prof to assoc prof chem, Wash State Univ, 1968-1979. **Memberships:** Am Soc Biochem & Molecular Biol; Am Asn Immunologists; Biophys Soc; Am Chem Soc; Biomet Soc; Sigma Xi. **Research Statement & Publications:** Epidemiologic analysis of medical practice. **Mailing Address:** Health Care Financing Admin, 7500 Security Blvd, Baltimore, MD 21244-1850.

KRAKAUER, LAWRENCE J, COMPUTER SCIENCE. **Education:** Mass Inst Technol, BS, 1963, MS, PhD, 1970. **Professional Experience:** RETIRED; vpres res & develop, Kronos Inc, ending 2003. **Mailing Address:** 8447 Wilshire Blvd Suite 206, Beverly Hills, CA 90211-3207. **Fax:** 310-655-3527.

KRAKAUER, TERESA, BIOCHEMISTRY, CELL BIOLOGY. **Personal Data:** b China, American citizen. **Education:** Wash State Univ, BSc(chem) & BSc(biochem), 1971; Iowa State Univ, PhD (biochem), 1975. **Professional Experience:** NIH staff fel, 1980-; NIH staff fel biochem, Nat Inst Arthritis, Metab & Digestive Dis, Nat Inst Dent Res, 1978-1980; res assoc biochem, Wash State Univ, 1975-1978; MICROBIOLOGIST, DEPT PATHOGENESIS & IMMUNOL DIS ASSESSMENT DIV, US ARMY MED RES INST INFECTIOUS DIS. **Memberships:** Am Chem Soc; Sigma Xi; Biophys Soc. **Research Statement & Publications:** Molecular biology; cell surface proteins; molecular basis of immunogenicity; developmental biology; gene transfer. **Mailing Address:** Dept Immunol & Molecular Biol, USAMRIID, Ft Detrick, Frederick, MD 21702-5011. **E-Mail:** teresa.krakauer@det.amedd.army.mil

KRAKE, KEITH, ENGINEERING. **Professional Experience:** AT DRYDEN FLIGHT RES CTR, NASA, EDWARDS, as of 2003. **Mailing Address:** Dryden Flight Res Ctr, NASA, PO Box 273, Edwards, CA 93523.

KRAKOFF, IRWIN HAROLD, MEDICINE. **Personal Data:** b Columbus, Ohio, July 20, 1923; m 1984, c 3. **Education:** Ohio State Univ, BA, 1943, MD, 1947; Am Bd Internal Med, dipl. **Honors & Awards:** Sloan Cancer Res Award, 1965; Karnofsky Award, 1993. **Professional Experience:** CHMN, DEPT MED, HEALTH CARE INT, 1984-; prof med pharmacol & head, Div Med, Univ Tex M D Anderson Cancer Ctr, 1983-1984; prof med & pharmacol, Univ Vt, 1977-1983; dir, Vt Regional Cancer Ctr, 1976-1983; Mem Hosp for Cancer & Allied Dis, assoc chmn, Dept Med, attend physician & chief clin chemother serv, 1974-1976; head, Lab Clin Chemother & Pharmacol, 1973-1976; chief med oncol serv, Div Chemother Res, 1970-1974; chief, Div Chemother Res, 1970-1972; from asoc mem to mem, Sloan-Kettering Inst Cancer Res, 1969-1976; chief, Med Oncol Serv, 1969-1974; from asst prof to prof med, Med Col, Cornell Univ, 1958-1976; from asst attend physician to physician, Mem Hosp Cancer & Allied Dis, 1958-1976; res assoc, Med Col, Cornell Univ, 1955-1958; clin asst, Mem Hosp Cancer & Allied Dis, 1955-1958; from asst to assoc, Sloan-Kettering Inst Cancer Res, 1954-1961; Spec fel, Mem Hosp Cancer & Allied Dis, 1953-1955; Res fel, Sloan-Kettering Inst Cancer Res, 1953-1954. **Memberships:** Harvey Soc; Am Asn Cancer Res; Am Col Physicians; Am Soc Clin Oncol; Am Soc Pharmacol & Exp Therapeut. **Research Statement & Publications:** Cancer chemotherapy. **Mailing Address:** Health Care Int, Beardmore St, Clydebank G81 4DY, Scotland. **Fax:** 444-195-15000.

KRAKOW, BURTON, PHYSICAL CHEMISTRY, SPECTROSCOPY. **Personal Data:** b Brooklyn, NY, February 12, 1928. **Education:** City Col New York, BS, 1949; Brooklyn Col, MA, 1958; Mass Inst Technol, PhD (phys chem), 1962. **Professional Experience:** SR RES ASSOC, CLEAN ENERGY RES CTR, UNIV S FLA, as of 2004; proj mgr adv technol, NY State Energy Res & Develop Authority, beginning 1978; res engr, ARO Inc, 1973-1978; sr prin develop engr, Honeywell Inc, 1969-1973; sr phys chemist molecular spectros, Control Instrument Div, Warner & Swasey Co, 1962-1969; Jr engr extractive metall, Metall Lab, Sylvania Elec Prod, 1954-1957. **Memberships:** Am Chem Soc; Am Phys Soc;

Coblentz Soc. **Research Statement & Publications:** Infrared spectroscopy; radiant heat transfer; spectroscopic pyrometry; infrared instrumentation; solar energy conversion. **Mailing Address:** Clean Energy Res Ctr, Univ S Fla, 4202 E Fowler Ave, ENB118, Tampa, FL 33620-5350. **Fax:** 813-974-5250. **E-Mail:** krakow@eng.usf.edu

KRAKOW, JOSEPH S, BIOCHEMISTRY, MOLECULAR BIOLOGY. **Personal Data:** b New York, NY, December 23, 1929; m 1955, c 2. **Education:** Univ Mich, BS, 1955; Yale Univ, PhD (pharmacol), 1961. **Professional Experience:** PROF EMER MOLECULAR BIOL & BIOCHEM, GRAD CTR, CITY UNIV NY, as of 2004; chmn, NIH, 1978; biochem study sect, NIH, beginning 1975; prof biol sci, Hunter Col, beginning 1971; lectr, Dept Med Physics, 1964-1971; assoc res biochemist, Space Sci Lab, Univ Calif, Berkeley, 1963-1971; USPHS fel biochem, NY Univ, 1961-1963. **Memberships:** Am Chem Soc; Am Soc Biol Chem. **Research Statement & Publications:** Nucleic acids; enzymology. **Mailing Address:** Dept Molecular Bio & Biochem, Grad Ctr, City Univ NY, 365 Fifth Ave, New York, NY 10016-4309. **Fax:** 212-817-1504.

KRAKOWER, GLENN R, BIOLOGY. **Professional Experience:** DIR, CORE LAB, GEN CLIN RES CTR, as of 2006. **Memberships:** Am Callers Assoc. **Mailing Address:** Froedtert Mem Lutheran Hosp, 9200 W WI Ave Cln Res Ctr, Milwaukee, WI 53226-3522. **Fax:** 414-805-0429. **E-Mail:** gkrakowe@mail.mcw.edu

KRAKOWSKI, FRED, MATHEMATICS. **Personal Data:** b Zuoz, Switz, July 31, 1927; m 1958, c 1. **Education:** Swiss Fed Inst Technol, DSc(math), 1957. **Professional Experience:** PROF EMER MATH, CALIF STATE UNIV, SACRAMENTO, as of 2004; Prof Math, Calif State Univ, Sacramento, beginning 1970; assoc prof, Sacramento State Col, 1967-1970; From instr to asst prof math, Univ Calif, Davis, 1957-1967. **Memberships:** Am Math Soc. **Research Statement & Publications:** Algebra. **Mailing Address:** Dept Math, Calif State Univ, Brighton Hall 141, Sacramento, CA 95819. **Fax:** 916-278-5586.

KRAL, ROBERT, PLANT TAXONOMY. **Personal Data:** b Highland Park, Ill, February 28, 1926; m 1957, c 1. **Education:** NC State Col, BS, 1952; Fla State Univ, PhD (bot), 1959. **Professional Experience:** PROF EMER BIOL, VANDERBILT UNIV, 1998-; prof biol, vanderbilt univ, beginning 1972; from asst prof to assoc prof biol, Vanderbilt Univ, 1965-1972; assoc prof, LA Tech, 1962-1965; asst prof, Va Polytech Inst, 1959-1965; instr, Northeast La State Col, 1958-1959; Asst bot, Fla State Univ, 1955-1958. **Research Statement & Publications:** Vascular plant taxonomy; floristics of southeastern coastal plain; studies in Annonaceae, Cyperaceae and Xyridaceae; flora of Alabama and Tennessee; flora of North America. **Mailing Address:** Dept Biol Sci, Vanderbilt Univ, Station B, PO Box 351634, Nashville, TN 37235-1634. **Fax:** 615-343-6707.

KRALEWSKI, JOHN EDWARD, PHARMACY, HEALTH ADMINISTRATION. **Personal Data:** b Durand, Wis, May 20, 1932; m 1957, Marjorie Gustafson; c Judy, Ann & Sara. **Education:** Univ Minn, BS, 1956, MHA, 1962, PhD (Health Admn), 1969. **Professional Experience:** WILLIAM WALLACE DISTINGUISHED PROF HEALTH SERV, RES & POLICY, UNIV MINN, MINN, as of 2004; prof health serv, res & policy, Univ Minn, Minneapolis, beginning 1978; prof, Univ Colo, Denver, 1969-1978; asst prof, Univ Minn, Minneapolis, 1965-1969. **Memberships:** Am Pub Health Asn; Asn Health Servs Res. **Research Statement & Publications:** Health administration. **Mailing Address:** Dept Health Serv, Univ Minn, 15-255 PWB, 516 Del St SE, Minneapolis, MN 55455. **Fax:** 612-624-2196. **E-Mail:** krale001@umn.edu

KRALL, ALLAN M, MATHEMATICS. **Personal Data:** b Bellefonte, Pa, February 25, 1936; m 1958, c 4. **Education:** Pa State Univ, BS, 1958; Univ Va, MA, 1960, PhD (math), 1963. **Professional Experience:** PROF EMER MATH, PA STATE UNIV, 1999-; grants, USAF, 1977-1979; grants, NASA, 1965-1969; from asst prof to prof, PA State Univ, 1963-1999. **Memberships:** Math Asn Am; Am Math Soc. **Research Statement & Publications:** Differential operators. **Mailing Address:** Dept Math, Pa State Univ, Mc Allister Bldg, State College, PA 16801. **Fax:** 814-865-3735. **E-Mail:** a2k@psu.edu

KRALL, ELIZABETH A, NUTRITION. **Personal Data:** b Lebanon, Pa, November 22, 1951. **Education:** Pa State Univ, BS, 1973; Univ Pittsburgh, MS, 1980, PhD (epidemiol), 1984. **Honors & Awards:** Pub Health Award, Pittsburgh Univ, 1985. **Professional Experience:** DIR EPIDEMIOL DIV, SCH DENT MED, BOSTON UNIV, as of 2005; ASSOC PROF, SCH DENT MED, BOSTON UNIV, 1996-; SCIENTIST NUTRIT, USDA, TUFTS UNIV, 1992-; ASST PROF, SCH NUTRIT, TUFTS UNIV, 1992-; res assoc, Tufts Univ, 1987-1992; res fel nutrit, Tufts Univ, 1984-1987. **Memberships:** Am Inst Nutrit; Am Soc Mineral Res; Sigma Xi. **Research Statement & Publications:** Nutrition; risk factors for osteoporosis; associations between skeletal health and oral health, including tooth loss and periodontal disease. **Mailing Address:** boston Univ, Goldman Sch Dent Med, 715 Albany St B-324, Boston, MA 02118-2394.

KRALL, JOHN MORTON, BIOSTATISTICS, RESEARCH. **Personal Data:** b Bellefonte, Pa, July 28, 1938; div, c Philip & Andrew. **Education:** Pa State Univ, BA, 1960; Univ Iowa, MS, 1962, PhD (statist), 1969. **Professional Experience:** DIR RES, ST LUKES HOSP, 1992-; sr biostatistician, Am Col Radiol, Philadelphia, 1982-1992; from assoc prof to prof biostatist, WVa Univ, 1973-1982; asst prof pub health & prev med, WVa Univ, 1970-1973; asst prof biomet, Univ Tex MD Anderson Hosp & Tumor Inst Houston, 1969-1970; mathematician, Comput Br, NIH, 1962-1965. **Memberships:** Am Statist Asn. **Research Statement & Publications:** Development of methodology for medical statistical applications; study of factors affecting survival. **Mailing Address:** St Lukes Hosp Res Inst, 801 Ostrum St, Bethlehem, PA 18105. **Fax:** 610-954-4979.

KRALL, JONATHAN, PHYSICS. **Professional Experience:** STAFF, PLASMA PHYSICS DIV, NAVAL RES LAB, as of 2005. **Memberships:** Mem Am Phys Soc. **Mailing Address:** Code 6790 NRL, 4555 Overlook Ave SW, Washington, DC 20375. **Fax:** 202-767-0631. **E-Mail:** krall@ppdu.nrl.navy.mil

KRALL, NICHOLAS ANTHONY, PHYSICS. **Personal Data:** b Kansas City, Kans, February 16, 1932; m 1985, Diane; c 6. **Education:** Univ Notre Dame, BS, 1954; Cornell Univ, PhD (theoret physics), 1959. **Professional Experience:** VPRES, KRALL ASSOCS, as of 2001; CO-FOUNDER, KRALL ASSOCS, 1988-; chmn, Fusion Power Asn, 1982-1984; chmn, APS/DPP, 1981; vpres, Jaycor, San Diego, 1978-1987; vpres, Sci Applns Inc, 1977-1978; dir lab appl plasma studies, Sci Applns Inc, 1974-1978; Guggenheim Found fel, 1973-1974; vis res prof physics, Univ Calif, San Diego, 1973-1974; dir joint prog plasma physics, Naval Res Lab, Univ Md, 1971-1973; prof physics, Univ Md, College Park, 1967-1973; asst mgr theory, Gen Atomic Controlled Fusion Res Prog, 1967; mem res staff theoret physics, John Jay Hopkins Lab Pure & Appl Sci, Gen Atomic Div, Gen Dynamics Corp, 1959-1967; mem res staff solid state physics, RCA Labs, NJ, 1954. **Memberships:** Fel Am Phys Soc; Sigma Xi; AAAS. **Research Statement & Publications:** Controlled thermonuclear fusion; plasma physics; high energy nuclear physics; electron scattering; application of dispersion relation technique to atomic physics; magnetohydrodynamics; plasma stability theory; laser system modeling; Raman cell modeling. **Mailing Address:** Krall Assocs, 1070 Am Way, Del Mar, CA 92014. **Fax:** 619-481-7827.

KRAMAN, STEVE SETH, PULMONARY MEDICINE. **Personal Data:** b Chicago, Ill, August 30, 1944; div, c Theresa, Pilar, Laura & Seth. **Education:** Univ PR, BS, 1967, MD, 1973. **Professional Experience:** CHIEF OF STAFF, VET ADMIN MED CTR, LEXINGTON, KY, 1986-2003; Professor med, Univ KY, 1990-present; Assoc prof med, Univ KY, 1984-1990; Asst prof, Univ KY, 1978-1984. **Memberships:** Am Col Chest Physicians; Am Thoracic Soc; Inst Elec & Electronics Engrs; Acoust Soc Am; Am Physiol Soc. **Research Statement & Publications:** Determination of the acoustic properties of the respiratory system including lung sounds and transmitted sounds; Full disclosure to avoid litigation resulting from medical negligence. **Mailing Address:** Univ Ky, Ky Clinic L547, Lexington, KY 40536. **Fax:** 859-257-2418. **E-Mail:** sskram01@uky.edu

KRAMER, AARON R, MECHANICAL ENGINEERING, INSTRUMENTATION. **Personal Data:** b New York, NY, April 26, 1932; m 1960, c 3. **Education:** State Univ NY Maritime Col, BME, 1954; City Col NY, MME, 1963. **Professional Experience:** PROF ENG, STATE UNIV NY, MARITIME COL, 1971-; Maritime Admin, US dept Commerce res grant, 1969-1973; Inst Environ Sci res grant, 1968-1969; consult, Simulation Autodyn Inc, 1967- & Stone & Webster Eng Corp, 1973-; assoc prof eng, State Univ NY, Maritime Col, 1963-1971; Appl engr instr, Bailey Meter Co, 1956-1963; prof eng, NY, NJ. **Memberships:** Instrument Soc Am; Am Soc Mech Engrs; Am Soc Eng Educ. **Research Statement & Publications:** Automatic control design and analysis; simulation of mechanical, chemical processes and energy management techniques with analogue, digital and hybrid computers; instrumentation and data collection systems and analysis. **Mailing Address:** Dept Engr, State Univ NY Maritime Col 6 Tennyfield Ave, Bronx, NY 10465-4198. **Fax:** 718-409-7421. **E-Mail:** akramer@sunymaritime.edu

KRAMER, ALFRED WILLIAM, JR, MORPHOLOGICAL BIOLOGY, TEACHING. **Personal Data:** b Astoria, NY, January 19, 1930; m 1987, Elizabeth J Haight; c Adrienne & Corinne. **Education:** Fordham Univ, BS, 1956, MS, 1959. **Professional Experience:** ASST PROF, CITY UNIV NY, 1993-; asst prof, Bronx Community Col, 1972-; Instr, Bronx Community Col, 1961-1972; res biologist exp path, Lederle Labs, Am Cyanamid Co, 1959-1993; Jr pharmacologist cardiovasc physiol, Res Labs, Burroughs Wellcome & Co, 1956-1959. **Memberships:** Soc Toxicol Pathologists; Am Med Writers Asn. **Research Statement & Publications:** Cardiovascular pharmacology of anti-arhythmia compounds; normal and pathological morphology and technical data of laboratory animals; development of practical techniques for use in experimental pathology. **Mailing Address:** 135 Lake Rd, Valley Cottage, NY 10989.

KRAMER, BARNETT SHELDON, MEDICAL ONCOLOGY, CANCER PREVENTION-PUBLIC HEALTH. **Personal Data:** b Baltimore, Md, July 29, 1948; m 1972, c 1. **Education:** Univ Md, MD, 1973. **Professional Experience:** ED-IN-CHIEF, NAT CANCER INST, NIH, as of 2005; DEP DIR, DIV CANCER PREV & CONTROL, NAT CANCER INST, 1996-; prof, Uniformed Serv Univ Health Sci, 1989-; sr investr med oncol, Div Cancer Prev & Control, Nat Cancer Inst, 1986-1996; assoc prof, 1986-1989; from asst prof to assoc prof med oncol, Univ Fla, 1978-1986; clin assoc oncol, Nat Cancer Inst, 1975-1978; resident, Wash Univ, 1974-1975; intern, Wash Univ, 1973-1974. **Memberships:** Am Asn Cancer Res; Am Soc Clin Oncologists; Asn Clin Trials. **Research Statement & Publications:** Infections in febrile neutropenic cancer patients; lung cancer; new drug development; cancer prevention and control. **Mailing Address:** Nat Cancer Inst, Rm 2B03 6100 Exec Blvd, Bethesda, MD 20892-2082. **Fax:** 301-480-7660. **E-Mail:** bk76p@nih.gov

KRAMER, BERNARD, SOLID STATE PHYSICS. **Personal Data:** b New York, NY, November 12, 1922; m 1946, c 2. **Education:** City Col New York, BS, 1942; NY Univ, PhD (physics), 1952. **Professional Experience:** ADJ PROF, FAIRLEIGH DICKINSON UNIV, 1986-; vis scholar, Univ Del, 1981; sci collab, Brookhaven Nat Lab, 1980-1981; vis fel, Princeton Univ, 1973-1974; res scientist, NY Univ, 1965-1969; chmn dept physics & astron, Hunter Col, City Univ New York, 1960-1971; Vis prof, Munich Technol Univ, 1959-1960; from asst prof to prof physics, Hunter Col, City Univ New York, 1955-1986; lectr, Hunter Col, City Univ New York, 1953-1955; res assoc, NY Univ, 1952-1965; res asst, NY Univ, 1949-1952; instr, Brooklyn Col, 1947-1949; Physicist, Fed Tel & Radio Corp, 1942-1947. **Memberships:** Am Phys Soc. **Research Statement & Publications:** Luminescence; photoconductivity; photovoltaic effects. **Mailing Address:** 1 Pennforest Way, Rockville, MD 20853.

KRAMER, BRADLEY ALAN, PRODUCTION PLANNING & CONTROL, ARTIFICIAL INTELLIGENCE APPLICATIONS IN MANUFACTURING. **Personal Data:** b Manhattan, Kans, May 30, 1958; m 1978, c 3. **Education:** Kans State Univ, BS, 1980, MS, 1981, PhD (indust eng), 1985. **Professional Experience:** HEAD INDUST ENG, KANS STATE UNIV, as of 2003; ASSOC PROF INDUST ENG, KANS STATE UNIV, 1991-; Dow outstanding young fac award, Am Soc Eng Educ, 1990; assoc dir res, Ctr Res Comput Controlled Automation, 1988-1990; Asst prof, Kans State Univ, 1985-1991. **Memberships:** Soc Mfg Engrs; Am Soc Eng Educ; Inst Indust Engrs. **Research Statement & Publications:** Manufacturing engineering; integration of the production process from product design to manufacturing to assembly with focus in production planning, scheduling and control. **Mailing Address:** Dept Indust Eng, Kans State Univ, 237 Durland Hall, Manhattan, KS 66506-5101. **E-Mail:** bradleyk@ksu.edu

KRAMER, BRIAN DALE, PHYSICAL ORGANIC CHEMISTRY. **Personal Data:** b Pottsville, Pa, November 17, 1942; m 1967. **Education:** Pa State Univ, BS, 1964; Harvard Univ, PhD (chem), 1969. **Professional Experience:** RET; dir res, paper chemicals group, Hercules Inc, 1989-1995; dir labs, Hercules Inc, 1987-1989; res assoc, mat sci dir, Hercules Inc, 1982-1987; project leader, paper chemicals group, Hercules Inc, 1980-1987; res scientist, chem sci div & mat sci div, Hercules Inc, 1977-1982; res super, New enterprises div, Hercules Inc, 1976-1977; sr res chemist, Res Ctr Div, Hercules Inc, 1973-1976; res chemist, Res Ctr Div, Hercules Inc, 1968-1973. **Memberships:** Am Chem Soc; Tech Asn Pulp Paper Indust. **Research Statement & Publications:** Kinetics and mechanisms of 1, 2 cycloaddition reactions; photochemical generation of reactive intermediates; Ziegler polymerization of alpha-olefins; physical and chemical characterization of organic polymers; radiation chemistry; chemical additives for paper. **Mailing Address:** 3 Boysenberry Dr, Ramsey Ridge, Hockessin, DE 19707.

KRAMER, BRUCE MICHAEL, MECHANICAL ENGINEERING. **Personal Data:** b New York, NY, July 23, 1949; m Patricia; c Katherine & Andrew. **Education:** Mass InstTechnol, SB & SM, 1972, PhD (mech eng), 1979. **Honors & Awards:** Blackall Award, Am Soc Mech Eng, 1982; F W Taylor Medal, Int Inst Prod Eng Res, 1984; R F Bunshah Award, Int Conf Metal Coating, 1986. **Professional Experience:** DIV DIR, ENG EDUC CTR DIV, NSF, as of 2002; staff mem, NSF, beginning 1995; prof mech eng, George Wash Univ, 1985-1995; consult, 1979-; from asst prof to assoc prof mech eng, Mass Inst Technol, 1979-1985; chmn, Zoom Telephonics, Inc, Boston, 1976-1989. **Memberships:** Am Soc Mech Engrs; Am Soc Metals; Sigma Xi. **Research Statement & Publications:** Machining automation and tool material development; tribology and wear theory. **Mailing Address:** NSF, Ste 585 4201 Wilson Blvd, Arlington, VA 22230. **Fax:** 703-292-9051. **E-Mail:** bkramer@nsf.gov

KRAMER, CAROLYN MARGARET, HIGH TECHNOLOGY CERAMICS. **Personal Data:** b Chicago, Ill, March 12, 1953. **Education:** Univ Ill, Champaign, BS, 1974; Univ Calif, Berkeley, MS, 1975; Univ Calif, Davis, PhD (mat sci & eng), 1980. **Professional Experience:** DIR RES & DEVELOP, CERAMCO, INC, 1989-; mgr & group mgr mat res, Boston Res & Develop Lab, 1984-1989; mat scientist, Advan Technol Lab, Gillette, 1983-1984; ceramic engr, Naval Res Lab, 1982-1983; postdoctoral, Nat Acad Sci, Nat Res Coun, 1981-1982; Staff mem, Sandia Nat Lab, 1973-1981. **Memberships:** AAAS; Soc Women Engrs; corp mem Am Ceramic Soc; Int Asn Dent Res; Am Soc Metals. **Research Statement & Publications:** Uses of high technology ceramics. **Mailing Address:** 312 Highland Ave, Moorestown, NJ 08057.

KRAMER, CHARLES EDWIN, POLYMER CHEMISTRY. **Personal Data:** b Lancaster, Pa, April 1, 1947; m 1969, Elizabeth; c Christopher & Timothy. **Education:** Franklin & Marshall Col, BS, 1969; Northeastern Univ, MS, 1971, PhD (chem), 1975. **Professional Experience:** PRES & CHIEF EXEC OFF, CDM SERV GROUP, as of 2004; PRES, KRAMER GROUP, as of 2004; res dir, Albany Int Corp, beginning 1993; asst dir res, Albany Int Corp, 1981-1993; sr res assoc, Albany Int Corp, 1977-1981; res chemist, Celanese Corp, 1974-1977. **Memberships:** Am Chem Soc; Sigma Xi; Tech Asn Pulp & Paper Indust. **Research Statement & Publications:** Polymer chemistry; monomer and polymer synthesis; polymer flammability; membrane science; polymer blends; polymer structure-property relationships. **Mailing Address:** Cdm Serv Group Inc, 34522 N Scottsdale Rd, Suite D8-485, Scottsdale, AZ 85262. **Fax:** 480-575-5852.

KRAMER, CHARLES LAWRENCE, MYCOLOGY. **Personal Data:** b Leavenworth, Kans, April 4, 1928; m 1951, c 2. **Education:** Univ Kans, BA, 1950, MS, 1953, PhD (bot), 1957. **Professional Experience:** PROF BOT, KANS STATE UNIV, 1973-; grants, USPHS, 1958- & NSF, 1967-; from asst prof to assoc prof, Kans State Univ, 1958-1973; asst prof biol, Western Ill Univ, 1957-1958. **Memberships:** Am Mycol Soc; Int Asn Plant Taxon; Brit Mycol Soc. **Research Statement & Publications:** Kansas fungi, especially parasitic forms; taxonomy of Taphinales; aeromycology. **Mailing Address:** Dept Biochem, Kans State Univ 104 Wilard Hall, Manhattan, KS 66506-3702. **E-Mail:** kramerc@ksu.edu

KRAMER, DAVID BUCKLEY, MECHANICAL ENGINEERING, COMPUTER SCIENCE. **Personal Data:** b Turtle Creek, Pa, October 21, 1927; m 1976, c 2. **Education:** Univ Pittsburgh, BS, 1950; Carnegie-Mellon Univ, MS, 1953; Univ Md, PhD (mech eng), 1975. **Professional Experience:** RES ENGR OPERS RES, ORI, INC, 1961-; res engr process control, E I du Pont Del Nemours & Co, Inc, 1953-1961; Res engr analog comput, Westinghouse Elec Corp, 1950-1952. **Memberships:** Am Soc Mech Engrs; Opers Res Soc Am. **Research Statement & Publications:** Acoustical holography; nonlinear programming; nuclear weapons effects; inventories; scheduling. **Mailing Address:** 2111 Saranac St, Hyattsville, MD 20783.

KRAMER, EARL SIDNEY, MATHEMATICS. **Personal Data:** b Chippewa Falls, Wis, November 13, 1940. **Education:** Wis State Univ, Eau Claire, BS, 1962; Univ Mich, MS, 1964 & 1966, PhD (math), 1969. **Professional Experience:** PROF EMER MATH, UNIV NEBR, as of 2000; prof math, Univ Nebr, beginning 1982; from asst prof to assoc prof, Univ Nebr, 1970-1982; Temp lectr, Univ Birmingham, 1969-1970. **Memberships:** Am Math Soc; Math Asn Am. **Research Statement & Publications:** Existence of various combinatorial structures. **Mailing Address:** Dept Math, Univ Nebr, 929 Old Father Hall, Lincoln, NE 68588-0323. **E-Mail:** ekramer@math.unl.edu

KRAMER, EDWARD JOHN, MATERIALS SCIENCE. **Personal Data:** b Wilmington, Del, August 5, 1939; m 1963, Gail; c Eric W & Jeanne N. **Education:** Cornell Univ, BChE, 1962; Carnegie-Mellon Univ, PhD (metal & mat sci), 1967. **Honorary Degrees:** Dr Ecole Polytech Federale de Lausanne, 1995. **Honors & Awards:** High Polymer Physics Prize, Am Phys Soc, 1985; Swinburne Award, Inst Mat, 1996. **Professional Experience:** PROF, MAT & CHEM ENG, UNIV CALIF, SANTA BARBARA, 1997-; Samuel B Eckert prof mat sci & eng, Univ Calif, Santa Barbara, 1988-1997; vis prof, Polytech Sch Fed Lausanne, 1982 & Johannes Gutenberg Univ, Mainz, 1987-1988; Gauss prof, Acad Wissenschaften, Gottingen, 1979; Vis scientist, Argonne Nat Lab, 1974-1975; from asst prof to prof, Univ Calif, Santa Barbara, 1967-1988; NATO fel metall, Oxford Univ, 1966-1967. **Memberships:** Nat Acad Eng; Am Chem Soc; Mat Res Soc; Soc Plastic Engrs; AAAS; Am Phys Soc. **Research Statement & Publications:** Surfaces, interfaces, diffusion, deformation and fracture of polymeric materials. **Mailing Address:** Dept Mats, Univ Calif, Univ Calif, Santa Barbara, CA 93106-5121. **Fax:** 805-893-8486. **E-Mail:** edkramer@mrl.ucsb.edu

KRAMER, ELIZABETH, DIETETICS, BIOCHEMISTRY. **Personal Data:** b Milwaukee, Wis, June 7, 1918. **Education:** Alverno Col, BSE, 1943; De Paul Univ, MS, 1948; St Louis Univ, PhD (chem), 1954; Mt Mary Col, BS, 1981. **Professional Experience:** CONSULT DIETITIAN, VILLA CLEMENT NSG HOME, MILWAUKEE, 1985 -; dietitian, Vet Admin Med Ctr, Milwaukee, Wis, 1981-1985; prof chem, Alverno Col, 1969-1979; Fel biochem, Univ Iowa, 1969-1970; assoc prof chem & chmn dept, Alverno Col, 1954-1969; instr biol, Alverno Col, 1947-1949; Instr biol & math, high sch, Ill, 1943-1947; asst archivist, Sch Sister St Francis, Milwaukee, Wis. **Memberships:** Am Dietetic Asn; Sigma Xi; Soc Nutrit Educ. **Research Statement & Publications:** Studies of drug binding, especially aspirin, salicylates and D-tubocurarine to purified proteins of human blood as well as to serum and plasma using fluorometric and gel filtration techniques. **Mailing Address:** 1425 S 26th St, Milwaukee, WI 53204.

KRAMER, FRANKLIN, PROCESS & EQUIPMENT DEVELOPMENT & ENGINEERING. **Personal Data:** b Brooklyn, NY, March 6, 1923; m 1951, Barbara; c Nancy K (Ducharme) & Harold. **Education:** City Col NY, BChE, 1944; Polytech Inst Brooklyn, MChE, 1947. **Professional Experience:** MANAGING DIR, ZUCKEK, KRAMER ASSOC INC, 1990-; vis prof & adj fac mem, Ctr Advan Food Technol, Rutgers Univ, 1990-; PRES FREMARK CO, FOOD PROCESS CONSULTS, 1988-; Sr consult, Ctr Advan Food Technol, Rutgers Univ, 1988-1993; prin scientist process eng, Cent res div, Gen Foods Corp, 1975-1988; vpres mfg, Seapak div, W R Grace & Co, 1973-1975; vpres mfg & eng, La Touraine-Bickford's Foods Inc, 1968-1973; mgr equip & process develop, Kitchens Sarah Lee, 1965-1968; mgr res & develop, Walter Baker Chocolate Co, 1959-1962 & Cracker Jack Co Div, Borden Co, 1962-1965; tech supt, Atlantic Gelatin div, 1953-1959; res chem engr, Cent res labs, Gen Foods Corp, 1944-1953; eng consult; chmn, Tech Achievement Awards, Gen Foods Corp. **Memberships:** Sr mem Am Chem Soc; fel Am Inst Chem Engrs; Inst Food Technol. **Research Statement & Publications:** Development of food processes from lab bench scale through commercialization; technical management and teaching. **Mailing Address:** Fremark Co, 132 Holbrook Rd, Briarcliff Manor, NY 10510. **Fax:** 914-923-1609. **E-Mail:** frankbrk@aol.com

KRAMER, FRED RUSSELL, MOLECULAR BIOLOGY, BIOCHEMISTRY GENETICS & BIOTECHNOLOGY. **Personal Data:** b New York, NY, July 7, 1942; m 1965, c 2. **Education:** Univ Mich, BS, 1964; Rockefeller Univ, PhD (molecular biol), 1969. **Professional Experience:** ADJ PROF MICBIO, NY UNIV, as of 2005; RES PROF, DEPT MICROBIOL, NY UNIV MED SCH, 1987-; NSF grant, 1987-1990; mem & chmn, dept molecular genetics, Pub Health Res Inst, 1986-; adv panalist, Nat Sci Found Biochem, 1985; prin investr, Am Cancer Soc grant, 1984-1986, 1989; NIH grant, 1984-; from sr res assoc to res scientist, human genetics & develop, 1980-1986; asst prof, human genetics & develop, 1973-1980; from instr to res assoc molecular biol, Inst Cancer Res, Col Physicians & Surgeons, Columbia Univ, 1971-1973; fel, Inst Cancer Res, Col Physicians & Surgeons, Columbia Univ, 1969-1971; pres, Kramer Consult Inc. **Memberships:** NY Acad Sci; Am Soc Molecular Biol & Biol Chem; Am Soc; Corp Bermuda Biol Asn Microbiologists; Am Asn Univ Prof; Am Cancer Soc; Sigma Xi. **Research Statement & Publications:** Evolution and synthesis of nucleic acids in vitro; morphology, physiology, genetics and evolution of replictable nucleic acids; molecular beacons and binary probes for diagnostic clinical assays; published more than 50 articles. **Mailing Address:** Dept Molecular Genetics, Pub Health Res Inst, 550 First Ave, New York, NY 10016-9102. **Fax:** 973-854-3371. **E-Mail:** kramer@phri.org

KRAMER, GEORGE MORTIMER, PHYSICAL ORGANIC CHEMISTRY. **Personal Data:** b Brooklyn, NY, May 15, 1929; m Vivian; c 2. **Education:** Queen's Col NY, BS, 1951; Univ Pa, MS, 1955, PhD (phys chem), 1957. **Professional Experience:** RETIRED, Sr res assoc, Corp Res Lab, Exxon Res & Eng Co, NJ, 1978-1995; res assoc, Cent Basic Res Lab, 1969-1978; res assoc, Cent Basic Res Lab, 1966-1969; Baytown Res & Develop Div, Tex, 1965-1966; chemist, Process Res Div, Esso Res & Eng Co, 1957-1964; Chemist, Frankford Arsenal, Pa, 1951-1952. **Memberships:** Sigma Xi; Am Chem Soc. **Research Statement & Publications:** Pressure-volume-temperature behavior of gases; equation of state; surface chemistry; thermochemical data; acid catalyzed alkylation and isomerization; catalysis; hydride transfer reactions; free radical reactions; carbonium ion rearrangement mechanisms and acid characterization; uranium chemistry; coal decomposition. **Mailing Address:** 206 Stone Manor Dr, Somerset, NJ 08873. **E-Mail:** gmchess@aol.com

KRAMER, GISELA A, Protein Synthesis in yeast mitochondria. **Personal Data:** b November 29, 1936; wid. **Education:** Univ Kiel, Ger, PhD (biochem), 1967; Univ Hamburg, Ger, Habilitation, 1973. **Professional Experience:** LECTR, UNIV TEX, AUSTIN, 1992-2004; RES SCIENTIST, UNIV TEX, AUSTIN, 1974-; Res assoc, Univ Hamburg, Ger, 1969-1974. **Memberships:** Am Soc Biochem & Molecular Biol; Ger Soc Biol Chem. **Research Statement & Publications:** Cloning, expression and characterization of genes and gene products, respectively, involved in initiation of protein synthesis in yeast mitochondria. **Mailing Address:** Dept Chem & Biochem, Univ Tex, Austin, TX 78712. **Fax:** 512-471-8696. **E-Mail:** g.kramer@mail.utexas.edu

KRAMER, HENRY HERMAN, NUCLEAR MEDICINE, DIAGNOSTIC MEDICINE. **Personal Data:** b New York, NY, August 19, 1930; m 1959, Carol; c 3. **Education:** Columbia Univ, BA, 1952, MA, 1953; Univ Ind, PhD (phys chem), 1960. **Professional Experience:** EXEC DIR, COUN RADIONUCLIDES & RADIOPHARMACEUT INC, as of 2003; CONSULT, 1990-; vpres res & develop, Medi Physics Inc, 1978-1989; mgr, Sterling Forest Res Ctr, 1976-1978; sr group leader, Tarrytown Tech Ctr, 1973-1976; group leader, Nucleonics Res & Develop, 1966-1973; res chemist nuclear methods anal, Union Carbide Corp, Nuclear Res Ctr, 1960-1965. **Memberships:** Am Chem Soc; Am Nuclear Soc; Soc Nuclear Med; fel Am Col Nuclear Physicians. **Research Statement & Publications:** Radiochemicals; radiodiagnostics; nuclear methods of analysis; biomedical significance of trace elements; nucleonics in industry and ore body exploration; diagnostic medicine. **Mailing Address:** Coun Radionuclides & Radiopharmaceut Inc, 3911 Campolindo Dr, Moraga, CA 94556-1551. **Fax:** 925-283-1850.

KRAMER, J DAVID R, ELECTRICAL ENGINEERING. **Personal Data:** b Bayonne, NJ, October 29, 1935; m 1966, Lynda; c 3. **Education:** Univ Pa, BS, 1957; Mass Inst Technol, MS, 1958. **Honorary Degrees:** DSc, Mass Inst Technol, 1964. **Professional Experience:** CONSULT SCIENTIST, MITRE CORP, 1984-; assoc dept hed, Mitre Corp, 1979-1984; group leader, Mitre Corp, 1969-1979; lectr, Northeastern Univ, 1965-1968; mem tech staff, Mitre Corp, 1964-1969. **Memberships:** Inst Elec & Electronics Engrs. **Research Statement & Publications:** Systems optimization; signal design and processing; operations research. **Mailing Address:** One Strobel Lane, Chelmsford, MA 01824. **E-Mail:** dkramer@mitre.org

KRAMER, JAMES J, BIOLOGY. **Education:** Kean Col, BA, Biol; Univ Med & Dent NJ, PhD (biochem). **Professional Experience:** Vpres, Serologicals Corp, 2005-2006. **Mailing Address:** Serologicals Corp, 5655 Spalding Dr, Norcross, GA 30092. **Fax:** 678-728-2299.

KRAMER, JAMES M, MOLECULAR BIOLOGY. **Professional Experience:** PROF CELL MOLECULAR BIOL, UNIV ILL, URBANA, as of 2004; assoc prof lab molecular biol, Univ Ill, begining 1990. **Mailing Address:** Dept CMS Biol Ward 7-334 Northwestern Univ Med Sch, 303 E Chicago Ave, Chicago, IL 60611-3072. **E-Mail:** jkramer@northwestern.edu

KRAMER, JAMES R(ICHARD), AQUATIC CHEMISTRY & METAL SPECIATION, MOLECULAR MODELLING. **Personal Data:** b Marine City, Mich, October 27, 1931; m Miriam; c Judith, William, Michael & Stephen. **Education:** Mass Inst Technol, BS, 1953; Univ Mich, MS, 1954, PhD (geol), 1958. **Professional Experience:** Prof emeritus, 1995; Invited prof, Univ Que, 1982; PROF GEOCHEM, MCMASTER UNIV, 1972-; assoc prof, Mcmaster Univ, 1968-1971; from asst prof to assoc prof, Syracuse Univ, 1964-1968; res assoc, Univ Mich, 1963-1964; asst prof, Nat Res Coun Can, Western Ont Univ, 1961-1963; lectr, Nat Res Coun Can, Western Ont Univ, 1959-1961; fel, Nat Res Coun Can, Western Ont Univ, 1958-1959; instr geol, Univ Mich, 1957-1958; Asst, Res Lab, Carter Oil Co, 1954. **Memberships:** Geol Soc of Am; Mineral Soc Am; Geochem Soc; Soc. Environ. Toxicol. Chem.; Am Chem Soc. **Research Statement & Publications:** metal sulfide complexes, uncertainty analysis; global carbon modelling, metal toxicity; limnological investigation of the Great Lakes; aquatic chemistry of shield lakes. **Mailing Address:** Sch Earth Scis, McMaster Univ, Hamilton, ON L8S 4K1, Can. **E-Mail:** kramer@mcmaster.ca

KRAMER, JERRY MARTIN, CHEMICAL PHYSICS. **Personal Data:** b Bronx, NY, December 16, 1942; m 1970, Cynthia; c Rebecca & Daniel. **Education:** Univ Calif, Berkeley, BS, 1965; Univ Chicago, PhD (chem), 1971. **Professional Experience:** MEM TECH STAFF, PHILIPS RES, 1992-; mem tech staff, GTE Labs, 1972-1992; res assoc chem, Case Western Reserve Univ, 1971-1972. **Memberships:** Am Phys Soc; Am Chem Soc. **Research Statement & Publications:** Arc and discharge physics optogalvanic spectroscopy laser chemistry; low energy ion-electron excitation of inorganic phosphors; photodissociation of gaseous ions; chemical kinetics. **Mailing Address:** Philips Reserch, 345 Scarborough Rd, Briarcliff, NY 10510-2027. **E-Mail:** jerry.kramer@philips.com

KRAMER, JOHN HOWARD, VADOSE ZONE MONITORING. **Personal Data:** b Cleveland, Ohio, September 10, 1950; m 1983, Renae Eckert; c Russell, Natalie & Stephanie. **Education:** Amherst Col, BA, 1973; Pa State Univ, MS, 1976; Univ Calif, Santa Barbara, PhD (geol, geog & environ eng), 1994. **Professional Experience:** SR HYDROGEOLOGIST, CONDOR EARTH TECHNOL INC, 1994-; prin scientist, Geraghty & Mitler, Inc, 1992-1994; Proj hydrogeologist, Metcalf & Eddy, Inc, 1990-1992. **Memberships:** Am Geophys Union; Nat Groundwater Asn; Geol Soc Am; Am Soc Testing & Mat. **Research Statement & Publications:** Innovative strategies to monitor soils above the water table; combination of network optimization and development of sensor technology to enhance environmental monitoring. **Mailing Address:** Condor Earth Technol, 21663 Brian Lane, Sonora, CA 95251-3095. **Fax:** 209-532-0773. **E-Mail:** jkramer@condorearth.com

KRAMER, JOHN J(ACOB), PHYSICAL METALLURGY, MATERIAL SCIENCE. **Personal Data:** b Pittsburgh, Pa, July 9, 1931; m 1956, c 3. **Education:** Carnegie Inst Technol, BS, 1953, MS & PhD (metall), 1956. **Professional Experience:** PROF EMER ELEC & COMPUT ENG, UNIV DEL, as of 2006; prof elec eng, Univ Del, beginning 1969; assoc prof elec eng, Univ Del, 1965-1969; adv metallurgist, res lab, 1965; sect mgr, res lab, 1964-1965; supv metallurgist, res lab, 1963-1964; res metallurgist, res lab, 1960-1963; phys metallurgist, ballistics res lab, Aberdeen Proving Grounds, Md, 1957; sr engr, magnetic mat develop sect, Westinghouse Elec Corp, 1956-1960. **Memberships:** Am Soc Metals; Am Inst Mining Metall & Petrol Engrs; Sigma Xi. **Research Statement & Publications:** Application of thermodynamics; surfaces; grain and crystal growth; solid state reactions; magnetic and electrical properties of solids. **Mailing Address:** Dept Elec & Comput Eng, Univ Del, Col Eng, Dean's Off, Newark, DE 19711. **Fax:** 302-831-8179.

KRAMER, JOHN KARL GERHARD, BIOCHEMISTRY, ORGANIC CHEMISTRY. **Personal Data:** b Bololo, Zaire, October 6, 1939; Canadian citizen; m 1968, Ana-Maria; c David J. **Education:** Univ Man, BSc, 1963, MSc, 1965; Univ Minn, Minneapolis, PhD (biochem), 1968. **Honors & Awards:** Govt Can Merit Award, 1983; CSP Canola Res Award, 1984; Dutton Res Award, 1999. **Professional Experience:** ASSOC ED, LIPIDS 1988-; RES SCIENTIST, CTR FOOD ANIMAL RES BR, AGR CAN, OTTAWA, 1970-; head, CODEX Committee Fats Oils, 1984-1998; core mem, Agr Can group, 1979-1985; fel, Nat Res Coun Can, Univ Ottawa, 1970-1971; hormel fel, Hormel Inst, Univ Minn, Austin, 1968-1970; fel, Eastman Kodak, 1964. **Memberships:** Am Oil Chemists Soc; Nat Res Coun Fats & Oils; Nat Stands Bd Can; Canola Coun Can. **Research Statement & Publications:** Lipid chemistry, biochemistry and nutrition; pesticide metabolism in animals. **Mailing Address:** Ctr Food Animal Res, Res Br Agr Can, Ottawa, ON K1A 0C6, Can. **Fax:** 613-943-2353, 519-829-2600. **E-Mail:** kramerj@agr.gc.ca

KRAMER, JOHN MICHAEL, CONTINUUM MECHANICS, RHEOLOGY. **Personal Data:** b November 22, 1941; American citizen. **Education:** Univ Wis, BS, 1963, MS, 1964, PhD (eng mech), 1969. **Professional Experience:** MECH ENGR, ARGONNE NAT LAB, 1974-; guest worker, Nat Bur Stand, US Dept Com, 1973, 1974; res fel, Rheology Res Ctr, Univ Wis, 1971-1972; asst prof mech eng, Lamar Univ, 1969-1971; asst prof mech eng, Lamar Univ, 1972-1974. **Research Statement & Publications:** Engineering problems requiring an interdisciplinary approach in the general areas of continuum mechanics, materials behavior and heat transfer; behavior of materials and structures in hostile stress, temperature and irradiation environments. **Mailing Address:** Reactor Eng Div, Argonne Nat Lab, 9700 S Cass Ave Bldg 207, Argonne, IL 60439.

KRAMER, JOHN PAUL, INSECT PATHOLOGY. **Personal Data:** b Elgin, Ill, March 13, 1928; div, c 2. **Education:** Beloit Col, BS, 1950; Univ Mo, MS, 1952; Univ Ill, PhD (entom), 1958. **Professional Experience:** EMER PROF INSECT PATH & MICROBIOL, CORNELL UNIV, 1990-; vis prof entom, Ohio State Univ, Columbus, 1984; Col Biol Sci, Ohio State Univ, 1984; Dept Biol, State Univ NY, Cortland, 1983; Dept Biol, Ithaca Col, 1981; res grant, US Dept Agr, 1980-1981; res grant, WHO, 1979-1982; vis biologist, WHO res agreement, beginning 1978 & Arctic Health Res Ctr, Inst Arctic Biol, Alaska, 1972; NIH-Off Naval Res res grant microbiol, 1971-1974; mem, Eval Panel Life Sci, Nat Res Coun, 1969-; NSF, fel, 1967; NSF vis insect pathologist, Japan, 1967; mem trop med & parasitol study sect, NIH, 1966-1969; from assoc prof to prof, Cornell Univ, 1965-1990; 2nd Int Conf Protozool, London, 1965; dept biol sci, Northwestern Univ, 1964; consult, Environ Biol Unit, WHO, Geneva, 1962-; lectr, 8th Int Cong Microbiol, Montreal, 1962; NIH res grant, 1959-1972; assoc entomologist, Ill Natural Hist Surv, 1959-1965; asst entomologist econ entom, Ill Natural Hist Surv, 1959; asst res prof entom, NC State Col, 1958-1959. **Research Statement & Publications:** Infectious diseases of insects, especially those caused by microsporidians and entomophthorans; ecology of microsporidians; epidemiology of diseases of insects. **Mailing Address:** Dept Entom, 3142 Comstock Hall Cornell Univ, Ithaca, NY 14853.

KRAMER, JOHN WILLIAM, CLINICAL PATHOLOGY. **Personal Data:** b Dearborn, Mich, August 17, 1935; m 1959, c 2. **Education:** Mich State Univ, BSc, 1958, DVM, 1960, MSc, 1968; Univ Calif, Davis, PhD (comp path), 1972; Am Col Vet Pathologists, dipl & cert vet clin path. **Professional Experience:** PROF VET CLIN SURG & MED, COL VET MED, WASH STATE UNIV, 1977-; assoc prof, Col Vet Med, Wash State Univ, 1972-1977; trainee, Col Vet Med, Univ Calif, Davis, 1968-1972; asst instr, Univ, 1966-1968; adv clin path, Mich State Univ, Nsukka, Nigeria, 1964-1966; vet, NZ Dept Agr, 1960-1964. **Memberships:** Am Vet Med Asn; Am Soc Vet Clin Pathologists; Am Col Vet Pathologists; Am Asn Clin Chem. **Research Statement & Publications:** Pathophysiology of diabetes mellitus. **Mailing Address:** 1415 NW Douglas Dr, Pullman, WA 99163.

KRAMER, KARL JOSEPH, ENTOMOLOGY, BIOCHEMISTRY. **Personal Data:** b Evansville, Ind, August 20, 1942; m 1966, c 2. **Education:** Purdue Univ, BS, 1964; Univ Ariz, PhD (chem), 1971. **Professional Experience:** COLLABR, GRAIN MKT & PROD RES CTR, USDA, as of 2004; adj prof, Kans State Univ, 1982-2003; res chemist biochem, USDA, beginning 1974; from asst prof to assoc prof biochem, Kans State Univ, 1974-1982; res assoc biochem, Univ Chicago, 1971-1974; fel, NIH, 1971. **Memberships:** Am Soc Biol Chemists; Am Chem Soc; Entom Soc Am; Am Inst Biol Sci; AAAS. **Research Statement & Publications:** Insect biochemistry; endocrinology; physiology. **Mailing Address:** US Grain Mkt & Res Lab, USDA, 1515 Col Ave, Manhattan, KS 66502. **Fax:** 785-537-5584. **E-Mail:** karl.kramer@gmprc.ksu.edu

KRAMER, MARTIN A, HEAVY ION PHYSICS. **Personal Data:** b Ellenville, NY, October 20, 1941; m 1963, Caroline; c Scott & Karen. **Education:** Columbia Univ, BA, 1963, MA, 1964, PhD (physics), 1969. **Professional Experience:** PROF EMER PHYSICS, CITY COL NEW YORK, 1997-; prof physics, City Col New York, 1973-1997; physicist, Brookhaven Nat Lab, 1971-1973; res assoc physics, Enrico Fermi Inst, Univ Chicago, 1969-1971. **Memberships:** Am Phys Soc. **Research Statement & Publications:** Designing, building, running and analyzing experiments in high energy and heavy ion physics. **Mailing Address:** Dept Physics, City Col NY, Marshak Sci Bldg J-419 Convent Ave 138th St, New York, NY 10031. **Fax:** 212-650-6940.

KRAMER, MILTON, PSYCHIATRY, SLEEP. **Personal Data:** b Chicago, Ill, November 11, 1929; m Fradier; c Ruth, Dan, Mary & Sam. **Education:** Univ Ill, BS, 1950, BS, 1952, MD, 1954; Am Bd Psychiat & Neurol, dipl & cert psychiat, 1961.Sleep Boards. **Professional Experience:** CLIN PROF PSYCHIAT, SCH MED, NY UNIV, as of 2003; Albert Einstein Col Med as of 2003 PROF EMER PSYCHIAT, SCH MED, UNIV CINCINNATI, as of 2000; Amer Col Psychiat. dir, dream & sleep lab & Sleep Disorders Ctr, beginning 1980; prin investr, US Vet Admin, 1975-1984; prof psychiat, sch med, Univ Cincinnati, beginning 1972; Assoc dir res, Dept Psychiat, 1972-1980; mem, Ohio Ment Health & Ment Retardation Adv Bd, 1971-1975; res investr, Wm S Merrell Co, 1970-1972 & Upjohn, 1970-; mem, Therapeut Care Comt, Group Advan Psychiat, 1970-; Upjohn Co grant, 1970-1972; proj dir sonic boom res data anal, Fed Aviation Admin, 1970-1972; clinician psychiat, Outpatient Dept, Cincinnati Gen Hosp, 1961- & attend staff psychiatrist, 1965-; dir psychiat res, Vet Admin Hosp, Cincinnati, 1963- & asst chief, Dept Psychiat, 1964-1980; consult, Coun Drugs, AMA, 1962-; Pvt practr psychiat, Cincinnati, 1960-; mem staffs, Christian R Holmes Hosp, Jewish Hosp & Good Samaritan Hosp. **Memberships:** Fel Am Psychiat Asn; AMA; Asn Psychophysiol Study Sleep (mem exec comt 1971); sci assoc Am Acad Psychoanal; Am Col Psychiat; Sigma Xi, AOA PRES Ohio Psychiat.Assoc.1971-72Pres ASSOC.STUDY OF DREAMS 1986-1987.Pres Cincinnati Psychiatric Soc 1977-1978. **Research Statement & Publications:** Psychology and psychophysiology of dreaming; drugs and sleep. **Mailing Address:** Dept Psychiat, Maimonides Medical Center, 920 48th St, Brooklyn, NY 11219. **E-Mail:** milton1929@yahoo.com

KRAMER, NOAH HERBERT, ELECTRICAL ENGINEERING. **Personal Data:** b New York, NY, April 10, 1924; m 1954, c 3. **Education:** Mich State Univ, BS, 1947, MS, 1949, PhD (elec eng), 1951. **Professional Experience:** TECH MGR, LITTON DATA COMMAND SYSTS, 1980-; mem staff, Am Satellite Corp, 1979-1980; pres, N H Kramer & Assocs, 1978-1979; mgr transmission planning, Int Tel & Tel Corp, 1973-1978; engr, Int Bus Mach Corp, 1951-1957 & Stelma, Inc, 1957-1970; instr, Mich State Univ, 1949-1951; Asst, Mich State Univ, 1947-1949. **Memberships:** Inst Elec & Electronics Engrs. **Research Statement & Publications:** Communication systems and equipment; digital data transmission; digital techniques; solid state electronics; computer peripherals. **Mailing Address:** 24410 Victory Blvd No 1, Woodland Hills, CA 91367.

KRAMER, NORMAN CLIFFORD, INTERNAL MEDICINE, IMMUNOLOGY. **Personal Data:** b New York, NY, August 16, 1928; m 1954, Patricia; c M Virginia, John D, Bernard M, Peter A & Anne M. **Education:** The Citadel, BS, 1948; George Wash Univ, MS, 1950, MD, 1954; Am Bd Internal Med, dipl, 1963. **Honors & Awards:** USPHS res career develop award, 1961-1966. **Professional Experience:** Dir, Immunogenetics & Immunohemat, Md Med Lab, Baltimore, 1987-1995; PROF EMER INT MED, GEORGE WASH UNIV, 1985-; from instr to prof, George Wash Univ, 1960-1985; USPHS res fel, 1959-1960; consult biochem, Vet Admin Hosp, Martinsburg, WVa, 1950-1953; dir, Wash Regional Histocompatability Typing Lab; dir, Hemopheresis Serv, Med Ctr, George Wash Univ. **Memberships:** Fel Am Col Physicians; Am Soc Histocompatibility & Immunogenetics; Int Soc Forensic Heamogenetics; Am Asn Blood Banks; Am Soc Transplant Physicians. **Research Statement & Publications:** Pathophysiology and immunology of diseases of the kidney; transplantation immunogenetics and forensic immunogenetics; nephrology. **Mailing Address:** 14505 Hollyhock Way, Burtonsville, MD 20866-1717.

KRAMER, PATRICIA L, NEUROLOGY. **Education:** Univ NMex, PhD, 1979. **Professional Experience:** PROF MOLECULAR & MED GENETICS & NEUROL, ORE HEALTH & SCI UNIV, as of 2005. **Mailing Address:** Dept Neurol Ore Health Sci Ctr, 3181 SW Sam Jackson Park Rd L-226, Portland, OR 97201-3098. **Fax:** 503-494-7499. **E-Mail:** kramer@ohsu.edu

KRAMER, PAUL ALAN, PHYSICAL PHARMACY, BIOPHARMACEUTICS. **Personal Data:** b Hartford, Conn, July 22, 1942; m 1987, c 2. **Education:** Rensselaer Polytech Inst, BChE, 1964; Univ Wis, MS, 1966, PhD (pharm), 1968. **Professional Experience:** PROF EMER PHARM, UNIV CONN, as of 2003; asst prof pediat, Univ Conn, beginning 1986; prof pharm & assoc prof lab med, Univ Conn, beginning 1976; asst prof phys pharm, Purdue Univ, 1971-1976; res biochemist, Walter Reed Army Inst Res, 1968-1971. **Memberships:** Am Asn Pharm Scientists; Controlled Release Soc; Int Asn Dent Res. **Research Statement & Publications:** Pharmacokinetics of drugs in the elderly; drug dispositon in the neonate; drug delivery systems; dental pharmaceutics. **Mailing Address:** Sch Pharm, Univ Conn, 372 Fairfield Rd, Unit 2092, Storrs, CT 06269-2092. **Fax:** 860-486-4998. **E-Mail:** paul.kramer@uconn.edu

KRAMER, PAUL ROBERT, PHYSICS, INSTRUCTIONAL TECHNOLOGY. **Personal Data:** b Montclair, NJ, November 17, 1935; m 1964, c 2. **Education:** Cornell Univ, BA, 1957; Rutgers Univ, MS, 1959, PhD (physics), 1966. **Professional Experience:** Mem, Fac Access, Comput Technol Adv Comt, State Univ NY, 1989-; treas & sci mkt consult, Safety Corp Am, Huntington, NY, 1984-1987; dean acad serv, State Univ NY, 1981-1984; chmn, student comput access prog Adv Comt, State Univ, NY, 1981; chmn dept, State Univ NY, 1977-1981; PROF PHYSICS, STATE UNIV NY COL TECHNOL, FARMINGDALE, 1975-; assoc prof, State Univ NY, 1970-1975; proj coordr, instr resources Ctr, 1968-1969; dir, Comput assisted Instr, State Univ NY, Stony Brook, 1967-1968; asst prof, State Univ NY Stony Brook, 1966-1969; instrumentation specialist physics, State Univ NY Stony Brook, 1964-1966. **Research Statement & Publications:** Instructional technology using computers and other media; improvement of instruction in physics and other fields; elementary school science. **Mailing Address:** State Univ NY Col Technol, Farmingdale, NY 11735. **Fax:** 631-673-1095. **E-Mail:** kramerpr@farmingdale.edu

KRAMER, RAYMOND ARTHUR, ANALYTICAL CHEMISTRY. **Personal Data:** b Buffalo, NY, December 7, 1929; m 1955. **Education:** Canisius Col, BS, 1954; Rensselaer Polytech Inst, PhD (anal chem), 1959. **Professional Experience:** ANALYTICAL CHEMIST, ALCOA TECH CTR, ALUMINUM CO AM, 1967-; phys chemist, Alcoa Res Labs, 1958-1967; asst, Rensselaer Polytech Inst, 1954-1958; Technician, Aluminum Co Am, NY, 1948-1954. **Memberships:** Am Chem Soc; Soc Appl Spectros; Am Soc Testing & Mat. **Research Statement & Publications:** Neutron activation analysis; x-ray diffraction and fluorescence; characterization of ultra-pure aluminum and gallium; emission spectroscopy; aluminum in fusion reactors. **Mailing Address:** 4377 Frederick Dr, Lower Burrell, PA 15068-6857.

KRAMER, RAYMOND EDWARD, ELECTRICAL ENGINEERING, PHYSICS. **Personal Data:** b Warren, Ohio, February 2, 1919; m 1947, c 3. **Education:** Heidelberg Col, BSc, 1943; Case Inst Technol, MSc, 1950. **Professional Experience:** PROF ELEC ENG, YOUNGSTOWN STATE UNIV, 1978-; consult develop engr, Westinghouse Elec Corp, 1954 & 1955 & Ohio Bell Tel, 1961; chmn dept, Youngstown State Univ, 1954-1978; assoc prof, Youngstown State Univ, 1954-1978; Consult elec engr, US Steel Corp, 1951 & ARC Res Inc, 1951-1953; Asst prof, Youngstown State Univ, 1950-1954. **Memberships:** Inst Elec & Electronics Engrs; AAAS. **Research Statement & Publications:** Spark machining; ferromagnetic domains and computer cores; particle physics; electrical, kinetic and quantum properties of fundamental particles; gravity waves. **Mailing Address:** Dept Elec Eng, Youngstown State Univ 410 Wick Ave, Youngstown, OH 44555.

KRAMER, RICHARD ALLEN, DRUG DISCOVERY, STRATEGIC ALLIANCES. **Education:** Yale Univ, PhD (biochem), 1975. **Mailing Address:** Novartis Insts for Biomedicval Res, 250 Mass Ave, Cambridge, MA 02139. **Fax:** 617-871-7262. **E-Mail:** richard.kramer@novartis.com

KRAMER, RICHARD MELVYN, HERBICIDES, PLANT GROWTH REGULATORS. **Personal Data:** b Brooklyn, NY, December 20, 1935; m 1957, Elaine Feingold; c Roy, Eric & Ian. **Education:** Polytech Inst Brooklyn, BChE, 1957, MChE, 1960, PhD (chem eng), 1963; St Louis Univ, MBA, 1971. **Professional Experience:** SR FORMULATION CONSULT, MONSANTO CO, 1990-; res mgr opers, Monsanto Co, 1982-1990; res mgr, Monsanto Co, 1979-1982; sr res group leader, Monsanto Co, 1973-1979; sr res engr, Monsanto Co, 1966-1973; sr process engr, Bioferm Div, Int Minerals & Chem Co, 1965-1966; develop engr, Bioferm Div, Int Minerals & Chem Co, 1963-1965; Res assoc electrodialysis, Bioferm Div, Int Minerals & Chem Co, 1962-1963. **Memberships:** Am Chem Soc. **Research Statement & Publications:** Herbicide and plant growth regulator research and development; pesticide residue chemistry; pesticide formulation and environmental science. **Mailing Address:** Monsanto Res Ctr, 800 N Lindbergh Blvd, St Louis, MO 63167.

KRAMER, ROBERT ALLEN, ENERGY, ELECTRIC TRANSMISSION & GENERATION. **Personal Data:** b Gary, Ind, January 6, 1949. **Education:** Purdue Univ, BS, 1971, MS, 1973, MS, 1979, PhD (nuclear eng), 1985. **Professional Experience:** CHEIF SCIENTIST, NISOURCE ENERGY TECHNOL, as of 2004; DIR ELECTRIC SERVS, NORTHERN IND PUB SERV, 1992-; dir electric opers, Northern Ind Pub Serv, 1986-1991; dir electric eng, Northern Ind Pub Serv, 1983-1986; mgr appl res, Northern Ind Pub Serv, 1981-1983; Lectr physics, Purdue Univ, 1975-; Nuclear fuel engr, Northern Ind Pub Serv, 1973-1981. **Memberships:** Am Phys Soc; Inst Elec & Electronics Engrs; Am Nuclear Soc. **Research Statement & Publications:** Energy and energy related fields; engineering in development and management; energy research and competitive aspects of industry. **Mailing Address:** NiSource Energy Technol, Merrillville, IN 46410. **E-Mail:** rakramer@nisource.com

KRAMER, RUTH M, CARDIOLOGY. **Professional Experience:** STAFF, LILLY RES LAB, as of 2005. **Memberships:** Am Soc Biochem & Molecular Biol. **Mailing Address:** Cardiovasc Res Dept Lilly Res Labs, Lilly Corp Ctr, Indianapolis, IN 46258-1543. **Fax:** 317-277-2934. **E-Mail:** kramer_ruth_m@lilly.com

KRAMER, SHELDON J, CHEMICAL ENGINEERING. **Personal Data:** b Chicago, Ill, August 17, 1938; m 1962, c 3. **Education:** Univ Ill, Urbana, BSChE, 1960; Princeton Univ, MAChE, 1962, PhD (chem eng), 1966. **Professional Experience:** SR RES ENGR, AMOCO RES CTR, 1977-; sr proj chem engr, Res & Develop Dept, 1968-1977; Chem engr, Gul Res & Develop Co, 1965-1968. **Memberships:** Am Inst Chem Eng; Am Chem Soc; Sigma Xi. **Research Statement & Publications:** Petroleum refining. **Mailing Address:** Amoco Oil Co H-1, PO Box 3011, Naperville, IL 60566-7011.

KRAMER, SHERMAN FRANCIS, PHARMACY, PHARMACOLOGY. **Personal Data:** b Elcho, Wis, November 15, 1928; m 1959, c 4. **Education:** Univ Wis, BS, 1950, PhD (pharm), 1960. **Professional Experience:** RETIRED; sect head, Upjohn Co, 1966-1990; res assoc, Upjohn Co, 1960-1966. **Memberships:** Am Pharmaceut Asn; Acad Pharmaceut Sci. **Research Statement & Publications:** Pharmaceutical product research and development. **Mailing Address:** 9701 Oakview St, Kalamazoo, MI 49002.

KRAMER, STANLEY ZACHARY, NEUROPHARMACOLOGY, BRAIN & BEHAVIOR. **Personal Data:** b Philadelphia, Pa, September 10, 1921; m 1941, Selma; c Erich Jan. **Education:** Univ Pa, AB, 1952, PhD (physiol), 1958. **Professional Experience:** RETIRED; from assoc prof to prof biol, Seton Hall Univ, 1967-1986; asst prof physiol, NY Med Col, 1960-1967; instr, Vassar Col, 1958-1960; asst instr physiol, Univ Pa, 1953-1958. **Research Statement & Publications:** Effects of drugs on brain electrical activity and behavior; neurophysiology. **Mailing Address:** 1801 John F Kennedy Blvd, Philadelphia, PA 19103.

KRAMER, STEPHEN LEONARD, ACCELERATOR PHYSICS & ACCELERATOR DIAGNOSTICS, EXPERIMENTAL HIGH ENERGY PHYSICS. **Personal Data:** m Jean; c Robyn T & Keith O. **Education:** Drexel Inst Technol, BS, 1966; Purdue Univ, MS, 1967, PhD (physics), 1971. **Honors & Awards:** Lark Horovitz Award; George Tautfest Award. **Professional Experience:** PHYSICIST VUV RING MGR, 1991-; PHYSICIST, BROOKHAVEN NAT LAB, 1990-; physicist, Argonne Nat Lab, 1981-1990; asst physicist, Argonne Nat Lab, 1974-1981; Res asst high energy physics, Argonne Nat Lab, 1971-1974. **Memberships:** Am Phys Soc, Union of Concerned Scientists. **Research Statement & Publications:** Synchrotron radiation sources; accelerator physics; radiographic imaging; applications of particle accelerators to medical research; high energy accelerator system design and application; nuclear instrumentation. **Mailing Address:** Accelerator Div, Nat Synchrotron Light Source, Brookhaven Nat Lab, Bldg 725C, Upton, NY 11973-5000. **Fax:** 631-344-3029. **E-Mail:** skramer@bnl.gov

KRAMER, STEVEN DAVID, LASER PHYSICS, NONLINEAR OPTICS. **Personal Data:** b Lakewood, NJ, August 27, 1948; m Phyllis. **Education:** Cornell Univ, AB, 1970; Harvard Univ, AM, 1971, PhD (physics), 1976. **Professional Experience:** RES STAFF, INST DEFENSE ANALYSIS, 1987-; Consult, Atom sci inc, 1982-1985; res staff, Oak Ridge Nat Lab, 1976-1987; teaching fel, Harvard Univ, 1974-1975; res fel, Harvard Univ, 1972-1976. **Memberships:** Am Phys Soc; Optical Soc Am; Archeol Soc Am; AAAS; Inst Elec & Electronics Engrs. **Research Statement & Publications:** Optics; optical sensors; nonlinear optics; spectroscopy; trace analysis. **Mailing Address:** Inst Defense Analysis, 1801 N Beuregard St, Alexandria, VA 22311.

KRAMER, STEVEN N, ROBOTICS. **Education:** Rensselaer Polytech Inst, PhD, 1973. **Professional Experience:** PROF & UNDERGRAD PROG DIR, UNIV TOLEDO, as of 2006. **Mailing Address:** Univ Toledo, 2801 W Bancroft St, Toledo, OH 43606. **Fax:** 419-530-8206. **E-Mail:** skramer@eng.utoledo.edu

KRAMER, THEODORE TIVADAR, VETERINARY MICROBIOLOGY, IMMUNOLOGY. **Personal Data:** b Novi-Sad, Yugoslavia, January 4, 1928; American citizen; m 1957, c 3. **Education:** Nat Vet Sch, Alfort, France, DVM, 1952; Univ Strasbourg, dipl, 1953; Colo State Univ, MSc, 1963, PhD (microbiol), 1965; Am Col Vet Microbiol, dipl, 1970. **Professional Experience:** PROF EMER VET MICROBIOL & PREV MED, COL VET MED, IOWA STATE UNIV, as of 2003; prof vet microbiol & prev med, Col Vet Med, Iowa State Univ, beginning 1980; prof microbiol & head dept, Sch Vet Med, Auburn Univ, 1971-1980; assoc prof vet microbiol, Western Vet Col Med, Univ Sask, 1967-1970; asst prof microbiol, Univ Col, Nairobi, Kenya, 1965-1967; jr pathologist, Colo State Univ, 1960-1965; Res off microbiol, Can Dept Agr, 1957-1960. **Memberships:** Am Soc Microbiol; Am Asn Immunologists; Am Vet Med Asn. **Research Statement & Publications:** Experimental colibacillosis in piglets; immunoglobulins of bovine colostrum; vaccine against bovine vibriosis; maternal immunity and the newborn; cell-mediated immunity to infectious diseases of animals; salmonellosis. **Mailing Address:** VMRI, 1802 Elwood Dr, Ames, IA 50011-0001.

KRAMER, TIM R, MICROBIOLOGY. **Personal Data:** b Garden Plain, Kans, March 1, 1943. **Education:** Okla Univ, MA, PhD (med sci), 1973. **Professional Experience:** RES BIOLOGIST, NIH, 1979-; mem proj, Sch Med, St Louis Univ & Fai-Land Anemia & Malnutrit Ctr, Chiang-Mai Univ, 1976-1978; fel, Sloan Cancer Inst, NY, 1973-1976. **Memberships:** Soc Exp Biol; Inst Nutrit. **Mailing Address:** Beltsville Human Nutrit Res Ctr, Bldg 307 BARC-E, Beltsville, MD 20705-2350.

KRAMER, WILLIAM GEOFFREY, PHARMACY, PHARMACOKINETICS. **Personal Data:** b Pittsburgh, Pa, September 16, 1948; m 1973, Beverly. **Education:** Univ Pittsburgh, BS, 1971; Ohio State Univ, PhD, 1976. **Professional Experience:** SR TECH ADV, QUINTILES, 1996-; dir clin res, Boehringer Manheim Pharmaceut, 1992-1996; assoc dir clin res, Boehringer Manheim Pharmaceut, 1989-1992; mgr pharmacokinetics, Schering-Plough, 1986-1989; res assoc, Inst Cardiovasc Studies, Col Pharm, Univ Houston, 1977-1986; from asst prof to assoc prof pharmaceut, Col Pharm, Univ Houston, 1976-1986. **Memberships:** Am Asn Pharm Scientists; Drug Info Asn; Am Asn Clin Pharmacol; Am Soc Clin Pharmacol & Therapeut. **Research Statement & Publications:** Pharmacokinetics and pharmacodynamics as the pertain to drug development areas of specialty-cardiovascular, metabolic. **Mailing Address:** Quintiles, 15825 Shady Grove Rd Ste 90, Rockville, MD 20850-4008. **Fax:** 301-548-1548. **E-Mail:** wkramer@qrvl.quintiles.com

KRAMER, WILLIAM J, ORGANIC CHEMISTRY, ANALYTICAL CHEMISTRY. **Personal Data:** b Coldwater, Ohio, October 13, 1919. **Education:** Univ Fribourg, Lic es Sci, 1952, ScD(chem), 1953. **Honorary Degrees:** ScD, Univ Fribourg, 1953. **Professional Experience:** CHMN DEPT, ST JOSEPH'S COL IND, 1977-; PROF CHEM, ST JOSEPH'S COL IND, 1968-; From instr to assoc prof, 1953-1968. **Memberships:** Am Chem Soc. **Research Statement & Publications:** Reactivity of methyl groups in substituted benzene rings; history and philosophy of science. **Mailing Address:** Dept Chem, St Joseph's Col, Rensselaer, IN 47979.

KRAMER, WILLIAM S, DENTISTRY, PEDIATRIC DENTISTRY. **Personal Data:** b Butte, Nebr, January 10, 1922; m 1944, Mary; c Kathryn, Steven, David & Mark. **Education:** Univ Nebr, BSc, 1946, DDS, 1948, MSc, 1954; Am Bd Pedodont, dipl. **Honors & Awards:** Sigma XI; Omicron Kappa Upsilon; Pres, Supreme Chap, 1967; Exec Sec, Hall of Fame NE State Dental Assn, 1970-1986. **Professional Experience:** RETIRED; prof pedodont, pedodont, 1980-1987; past examr, Am Bd Pedodont, exec secy, 1974-; chem dept, pedodont, 1958-1980; prof operative dent, Univ Nebr, Lincoln, 1954-1958; instr operative dent, Univ Nebr, Lincoln, 1948-1952; private practice, 1948-1982; dir, Dent Asst Utilization Prog. **Memberships:** Am Acad Pedodont (pres, 1978-); Int Asn Dent Res; Diplomate Am Bd Pedodontics. **Research Statement & Publications:** Clinical studies on local anesthetic solutions; morphology of the primary dentition; physical properties of gold foil; ultrasonic sterilization; pedodontic failures. **Mailing Address:** 5124 Ventura Dr, Fremont, NE 68025.

KRAMERICH, GEORGE L, CONTROL & ELECTRICAL ENGINEERING. **Personal Data:** b Aliquippa, Pa, November 26, 1929; m 1954, c 3. **Education:** Fla State Univ, BS, 1963, MS, 1964; Case Western Res Univ, PhD (control eng), 1970. **Professional Experience:** Gould Instrument Div, 1977- & Ohio Legis Serv Comn, 1978-1979; PROF ELEC ENG, CLEVELAND STATE UNIV, 1977-; consult, Chemstress Consults, beginning 1977; consult, Gen Elec Lighting Res Lab, beginning 1970; from asst prof to assoc prof, Cleveland State Univ, 1969-1977; teaching asst elec eng, Case Western Res Univ, 1964-1969; teaching asst eng sci, Fla State Univ, 1963-1964. **Memberships:** Sr mem Instrument Soc Am; Inst Elec & Electronics Engrs; Am Soc Eng Educ. **Research Statement & Publications:** Economic and management decision making applied to the evaluation of advanced process control technology; computer simulation. **Mailing Address:** Dept Elec Eng, Cleveland State Univ, Cleveland, OH 44115-2425. **Fax:** 216-687-5405. **E-Mail:** g.kramerich@csuohio.edu

KRAMISH, ARNOLD, NUCLEAR PHYSICS, INTERNATIONAL RELATIONS. **Personal Data:** b Denver, Colo, June 6, 1923; m 1952, Vivan; c 2. **Education:** Univ Denver, BS, 1945; Harvard Univ, MA, 1947. **Professional Experience:** Sr fel & assoc, Global Bus Access Ltd, 1990-; Rockefeller scholar, Bellagio, Italy, 1984; fel, Woodrow Wilson Ctr, Smithsonian Inst, 1982-1983; TECHNOL CONSULT, 1981-; sr scientist, Res & Develop Assocs, Arlington, 1976-1981; counr sci & technol, US Mission, Orgn Econ Coop & Develop, 1974-1976; US sci liaison attache, UNESCO, 1970-1973; adj prof int studies, Univ Miami, 1969-1973; Guggenheim fel, 1966-1967; prof residence, Univ Calif, Los Angeles, 1965-1966; consult, NSF, 1959-1962; fel, Coun For Rels, 1958-1959; consult, Int Bank Reconstruct & Develop, 1958; staff, physics dept, Rand Corp, Calif, 1951-1969; staff physicist, AEC, 1947-1951; physicist, Los Alamos Sci Labs, 1945-1946; mass spectroscopist, Oak Ridge Nat Lab, 1944-1945. **Memberships:** Am Phys Soc. **Research Statement & Publications:** Fission physics; applied nuclear energy; political and economic implications of nuclear energy; research and development policy and planning; space and strategic defense systems; international energy policy; technology transfer; history. **Mailing Address:** 2065 Wethersfield Ct, Reston, VA 20191.

KRAMP, ROBERT CHARLES, RADIATION BIOLOGY, ENDOCRINOLOGY. **Personal Data:** b Alexandria, Va, August 2, 1942; m 1965, c 2. **Education:** Univ Md, BS, 1964; Univ Okla, MS, 1969; Univ Tenn, PhD (radiation biol), 1973. **Professional Experience:** RETIRED; asst prof biol, Va Polytech Inst & State Univ, 1978-1983; res instr, Vanderbilt Univ, 1975-1978; fel endocrinol, Inst Clin Biochem, 1973-1975. **Memberships:** Am Diabetes Asn; Europ Asn Study Diabetes. **Research Statement & Publications:** Diabetes; transplantation of pancreatic islet tissue in mice; experimental and genetic diabetes in rodents. **Mailing Address:** 654 Dobbins Farm Rd N E, Floyd, VA 24091.

KRAMS, SHERI M, IMMUNOLOGY. **Education:** Univ Calif, PhD. **Professional Experience:** ASSOC PROF, DEPT SURG, STANFORD UNIV, as of 2005. **Mailing Address:** Dept Surg Stanford Univ Sch Med, MSLS, 3rd Floor, MC, 5492, 1201 Welch Road, Stanford, CA 94305-5102. **Fax:** 650-498-6250. **E-Mail:** smkrams@stanford.edu

KRANBUEHL, DAVID EDWIN, PHYSICAL CHEMISTRY, POLYMER PHYSICS. **Personal Data:** b Madison, Wis, April 16, 1943; m 1966, c 2. **Education:** DePauw Univ, BA, 1965; Univ Wis, PhD (chem), 1969. **Professional Experience:** PROF CHEM, COL WILLIAM & MARY, 1970-; consult, Nat Bur Standards, 1970-; Nat Acad Sci fel, 1969-1970; res chemist polymers, Nat Bur Standards, 1969-1970; consult, Union Carbide, Gen Elec, US Steel Corp, McDonnell Douglas Corp. **Memberships:** Am Chem Soc. **Research Statement & Publications:** Physical properties of polymers; dielectric phenomena; molecular dynamics in the liquid and glassy state; materials science engineering. **Mailing Address:** Dept Chem, Col William & Mary, Williamsburg, VA 23187. **E-Mail:** dekran@chem1.chem.wm.edu

KRANC, GEORGE M(AXIMILIAN), ELECTRICAL ENGINEERING. **Personal Data:** b Lodz, Poland, February 1, 1920; American citizen; m 1960, Joanna. **Education:** St Andrews Univ, BSc, 1944; Columbia Univ, MS, 1953, DEng Sc(elec eng), 1956. **Professional Experience:** PROF ELEC ENG, CITY COL NEW YORK, 1971-; sci ed, Scripta Technica Inc, 1963-1971; assoc prof, City Col New York, 1963-1971; vis prof, Polytech Inst Brooklyn, 1962-1963; consult, Gen Appl Sci labs, 1957 & Norden labs, 1958-1959; from instr to assoc prof, Columbia Univ, 1953-1962; asst elec eng, Columbia Univ, 1951-1953; Radio engr, Jewel Radio Co, 1949-1951. **Memberships:** Inst Elec & Electronics Engrs; Sigma Xi. **Research Statement & Publications:** Control systems theory, particularly sampled data systems and optimal controls. **Mailing Address:** Dept Elec Eng, Sch Eng, City Univ NY, T-668, Convent Ave, 140th St, New York, NY 10031. **Fax:** 212-650-8249. **E-Mail:** kranc@ccny.cuny.edu

KRANC, STANLEY CHARLES, MECHANICAL ENGINEERING, CHEMICAL PHYSICS. **Personal Data:** b Peoria, Ill, September 29, 1942. **Education:** Northwestern Univ, BS, 1964, PhD (mech eng), 1968. **Professional Experience:** DIR ENG FACIL, COL ENG, UNIV SFLA, 1997-; PROF ENG, UNIV SFLA, 1978-; from asst prof to assoc prof, Univ SFla, 1971-1978; asst prof eng sci, Fla State Univ, 1967-1971. **Memberships:** Am Inst Aeronaut & Astronaut; Newcomen Soc; Am Soc Mech Engrs. **Research Statement & Publications:** Gas dynamics; plasma physics; combustion; two phase flow; experimental and theoretical fluid mechanics; numerical analysis; magnetofluidmechanics and electrohydrodynamics. **Mailing Address:** Dept Civil & Environ Eng, Univ SFla, 4202 E Fowler Ave ENB 118, Tampa, FL 33620-5350. **Fax:** 813-974-2957. **E-Mail:** kranc@eng.usf.edu

KRANE, KENNETH SAUL, EXPERIMENTAL NUCLEAR PHYSICS, PHYSICS EDUCATION. **Personal Data:** b Philadelphia, Pa, May 15, 1944; m 1966, c 1. **Education:** Univ Ariz, BS, 1965; Purdue Univ, MS, 1967, PhD (physics), 1970. **Honors & Awards:** Millikan Medal, Ame Asn Physics Teachers, 2004. **Professional Experience:** Prog dir physics, Div Undergraduate Edu, NSF, 1993-1994; PROF PHYSICS, ORE STATE UNIV, 1984-; from asst prof to assoc prof, Ore State Univ, 1974-1984; dept chair & dir eng physics prog, Ore State Univ, 1984-1988; staff mem, Physics Div, Los Alamos National Lab, 1980-1981; res assoc nuclear chem, Lawrence Berkeley Lab, 1972-1974; res assoc physics, Los Alamos Sci Lab, 1970-1972; NASA fel, 1966-1969; teaching & res asst, Dept Physics, Purdue Univ, 1965-1970; lab asst, Dept Physics, Univ Ariz, 1962-1965. **Memberships:** Fel Am Phys Soc; Am Asn Physics Teachers; Sigma Xi. **Research Statement & Publications:** Angular distributions and correlations of gamma rays; nuclear spectroscopy; nuclear physics at ultralow temperatures; beta decay. **Mailing Address:** Dept Physics, Ore State Univ, 301 Weniger Hall, Corvallis, OR 97331. **Fax:** 541-737-1683. **E-Mail:** kranek@physics.orst.edu

KRANE, STANLEY GARSON, CELL BIOLOGY, MOLECULAR BIOLOGY. **Personal Data:** b New York, NY, February 16, 1937. **Education:** City Col NY, BS, 1957; Mich State Univ, MS, 1958; Calif Inst Technol, PhD (biochem), 1966. **Professional Experience:** RETIRED; fac biol, Fitchburg State Col, as of 2006; assoc prof biol, Fitchburg State Col beginning 1980; asst prof, Fitchburg State Col, 1975-1980; asst prof biol, Univ Mass, Boston, 1968-1975; res fel biochem, Brandeis Univ, 1966-1967. **Memberships:** Assoc mem AAAS; Am Inst Biol Sci. **Research Statement & Publications:** Mutagenesis of microorganisms. **Mailing Address:** Dept Biol, Fitchburg State Col, 160 Pearl St, Fitchburg, MA 01420-2697. **E-Mail:** skrane@fsc.edu

KRANE, STEPHEN MARTIN, MEDICINE, BIOCHEMISTRY. **Personal Data:** b New York, NY, July 15, 1927; m 1952, c 4. **Education:** Columbia Col, BA, 1946; Columbia Univ, MD, 1951; Am Bd Internal Med, dipl, 1958. **Honorary Degrees:** MA, Harvard Univ, 1968; MD, Univ Geneva, Switz, 1989. **Honors & Awards:** Geigy Rheumatism Prize, 1977; Heberden Medal, London, 1980; Kleruperer Medal, 1990. **Professional Experience:** PERIS, CYROS & MARLOW B HARRISON PROF MED, HARWARD MED SCH, 1987-; Guggenheim fel, Oxford Univ, 1973-1974; PHYSICIAN, MASS GEN HOSP, 1969-; from asst prof to prof, Harvard Med Sch, 1963-1987; assoc, Harvard Med Sch, 1960-1963; instr, Harvard Med Sch, 1959-1960; fel, Sch Med, Wash Univ, 1956; asst, Harvard Med Sch, 1955-1959; fel med, Harvard Med Sch, 1953-1955. **Memberships:** Am Soc Clin Invest; Endocrine Soc; Asn Am Physicians; Am Col Rheumatology; Am Fedn Clin Res; fel AAAS; Am Soc Biol Chemists; Am Soc Bone & Mineral Res. **Research Statement & Publications:** Connective tissue biology and metabolism; internal medicine and rheumatology; transport mechanisms. **Mailing Address:** Arthritis Unit, Mass Gen Hosp, 55 Fruit St, Boston, MA 02114-2698. **Fax:** 617-726-2872. **E-Mail:** krane.stephen@mgh.harvard.edu

KRANER, HOBART WILSON, SEMICONDUCTOR RADIATION DETECTORS. **Personal Data:** b Louisville, Ky, January 15, 1934; m 1956, Carol; c Keith, Neil, Jeffrey & Jennifer. **Education:** Mass Inst Technol, SB, 1955, PhD (physics), 1960. **Professional Experience:** RETIRED; sr physicist, Brookhaven Nat Lab, 1980-1997; physicist, Brookhaven Nat Lab, 1971-1980; assoc physicist, Brookhaven Nat Lab, 1966-1971; res assoc, Mass Inst Technol, 1960-1966. **Memberships:** Inst Elec & Electronics Engrs. **Research Statement & Publications:** Development of semiconductor radiation detectors for application in high energy physics and x-ray spectroscopy; position sensitive silicon detectors using integrated circuit technology and study radiation effects on such devices; applications of nuclear and x-ray spectroscopy to analytical problems in fields such as medicine and material science. **Mailing Address:** PO Box 1642, Murrells Inlt, SC 29576.

KRANIAS, EVANGELIA GALANI, ION TRANSPORT, PHOSPHORYLATION REGULATION. **Education:** Northwestern Univ, PhD (biochem), 1974. **Professional Experience:** PROF & DIR CARDIOVASC BIOL, DEPT PHARMACOL & CELL BIOPHYS, COL MED, UNIV CINCINNATI, as of 1997; assoc prof phosphorylation, Col Med, Univ Cincinnati, beginning 1978. **Mailing Address:** Dept Pharmacol & Cell Biophys, Col Med, Univ Cincinnati, 231 Albert Sabin Way, Cincinnati, OH 45267-0575. **Fax:** 513-558-2269. **E-Mail:** Litsa.Kranias@uc.edu

KRANING, KENNETH K, PHYSIOLOGY. **Honors & Awards:** The Nat Academies, 1988. **Professional Experience:** RES PHYSIOL, USA RES INST ENVIRON MED, as of 1998. **Mailing Address:** Dept Biophys, US Army Med R&D Command, Kansas St, Natick, MA 01760. **Fax:** 508-651-4848. **E-Mail:** nffk28a@prodigy.com

KRANNICH, LARRY KENT, MAIN GROUP CHEMISTRY. **Personal Data:** b Pekin, Ill, September 5, 1942; m 1974, Beverley; c Emily, Louis, Laura & Rachel. **Education:** Ill State Univ, BS, 1963, MS, 1965; Univ Fla, PhD (inorg chem), 1968. **Professional Experience:** PROF EMER, DEPT CHEM, UNIV ALA, BIRMINGHAM, as of 2005; prof & chmn dept chem, Univ Ala, Birmingham, 1976; actg chmn dept, 1974-1975; from asst prof to assoc prof, 1969-1976; vis prof, Tech Univ Vienna, 1969; asst prof, Univ Miss, 1968-1969; res asst, Univ Fla, 1968; asst, Univ Fla, 1965-1968; asst chem, Ill State Univ, 1963-1965. **Memberships:** Am Chem Soc; Sigma Xi. **Research Statement & Publications:** Chemistry of the arsenic-nitrogen bond; reactivity of alanes and gallanes with amines, phosphines, arsines and stibines; reactivity of boranes with arsenic-nitrogen and phosphorus-nitrogen containing bases. **Mailing Address:** Dept Chem, Univ Ala, Rm 201 Chem Bldg 901 14th St S, Birmingham, AL 35294-1240. **Fax:** 205-934-2543. **E-Mail:** krannich@uab.edu

KRANTZ, ALLEN, BIOCHEMISTRY. **Personal Data:** b New York, NY, January 25, 1940; m 1979, c 3. **Education:** City Col NY, BS, 1961; Yale Univ, MS, 1962, PhD (chem), 1967. **Professional Experience:** ASST VICE CHANCELLOR, UNIV/INDUSTRY LIAISON; adj prof, dept chem, Univ Guelph & Univ Toronto, beginning 1985; res dir, SYNTEX Can Inc, beginning 1981; adj assoc prof, dept pharmacol sci, State Univ NY Stony Brook, 1977-; NIH grant, 1977-1981; sr fel, NATO, 1975; NSF grants, 1974, 1976, 1977; State Univ NY Res Found fac fel & grant aid, 1969-1970; Res Corp grant, 1968-; from asst prof to assoc prof org chem, 1968-1981; Petrol Res Fund grant, 1968-1971; fel, Univ Reading, 1967-1968. **Memberships:** Am Chem Soc; Royal Soc Chem; Chem Inst Can. **Research Statement & Publications:** Drug design; photochemistry of matrix isolated species; mechanism of reactions of heterocycles; bio-organic chemistry; design of enzyme inhibitors. **Mailing Address:** Inst BioChem, Univ S Fla, Tampa, FL 33620. **E-Mail:** akrantz@research.usf.edu

KRANTZ, DAVID S, MEDICAL PSYCHOLOGY, BEHAVIORAL MEDICINE & CARDIOVASCULAR DISORDERS. **Personal Data:** b New York, NY, February 9, 1949; m 1982, Marsha; c Michael Douma & Della Krantz. **Education:** City Col NY, BS, 1971; Univ Tex, Austin, PhD (psychol), 1975. **Honors & Awards:** Health Psychol Ann Award, Am Psychol Asn, 1981& 2001; Am Psychol Asn Early Career Sci Award, 1982. **Professional Experience:** ASSOC PROF, MED PSYCHOL, UNIFORMED SERV UNIV HEALTH SCI, MD, as of 2005; PROF & CHAIR, DEPT MED & CLIN PSYCHOL, UNIFORMED SERV UNIV SCH MED, MD, as of 2000; ADJ PROF, PSYCHIATRY & MED (CARDIOL) GEORGETOWN UNIV MED CTR, 1993-; ed-in-chief, Health Psychol, 1994-2000, 1991-1993; prof, Med Psychol, Uniformed Serv Univ, 1987-; from asst prof to assoc prof, Uniformed Serv Univ, 1978-1987; asst prof psychol, Univ Southern Calif, 1975-1978. **Memberships:** fel Am Psychol Asn (pres, 2005-2006); Am Psychosomatic Soc; fel Acad Behav Med Res (pres, 1994-1995); fel Soc Behav Med. **Research Statement & Publications:** Behavioral and psychophysiological factors in cardiovascular disorders; psychological stress; silent cardiac ischemia; triggers of sudden cardiac death; behavior and heart failure. **Mailing Address:** Dept Med & Clin Psychol Uniformed Serv, Univ Health Sci 4301 Jones Bridge Rd, Bethesda, MD 20814-4799. **Fax:** 301-295-3034. **E-Mail:** dskrantz@usuhs.mil

KRANTZ, GERALD WILLIAM, ACAROLOGY, FUNCTIONAL MORPHOLOGY & BEHAVIOR. **Personal Data:** b Pittsburgh, Pa, March 12, 1928; m 1955, Vida; c Wayne, Georgia & Valerie. **Education:** Univ Pittsburgh, BSc, 1951; Cornell Univ, PhD, 1955. **Honors & Awards:** Berlese Award, 1979; Associe du Museum d'Histoire Naturelle, Paris, 1984-; Gilfillan Award, 1987 keynote speaker int congress of Acarology 1994; res fellowship, int journal of Acarology, 1997. **Professional Experience:** Vis res prof Univ sao paulo (piracicaba) 2000-2001; EMER PROF ENTOM, ORE STATE UNIV, 1994-; chmn, Ore State Univ, 1991-1994; vis prof, Nat Mus Natural Hist, Paris, 1987; assoc, Nat Mus Natural Hist, Paris, beginning 1984; prog officer, Systematic Biol, NSF, Wash, DC, 1984-1985; exec comt, Int Cong Acarology, beginning 1982; sr res scientist, Commonwealth Sci & Ind Res Organ, Pretoria, SAfrica, 1979; chmn, Gov Bd, Acarology Soc Am, 1975-1976; mem, Gov Bd, Acarology Soc Am, 1971-1976; zoologist & dep leader, Exped II, 1968; microzoologist, Am Quintana Roo Exped, 1965; from asst prof to prof, Ore State Univ, 1955-1996. **Memberships:** Entom Soc Am; Acarology Soc Am (pres, 1995); Sigma Xi soc of systematic & appl Acarology. **Research Statement & Publications:** Systematics and behavior of Acari diversi; systematics, behavior, and functional morphology of mites (Acari), with emphasis on insect associates. **Mailing Address:** Dept Entom, Ore State Univ, Corvallis, OR 97331. **Fax:** 541-737-3643. **E-Mail:** krantzg@bcc.orst.edu

KRANTZ, KARL WALTER, ORGANIC CHEMISTRY, POLYMER CHEMISTRY. **Personal Data:** b Waterbury, Conn, May 9, 1918; m 1942, Elizabeth Durkee; c David W & Kathryn E. **Education:** Univ Conn, BS, 1939, MS, 1940; Stanford Univ, PhD (chem), 1951. **Professional Experience:** SPECIALIST SILICONE RES TECHNOL, SILICONE PROD DEPT, GEN ELEC CO, 1975-; res chemist, Silicone Prod Dept, Gen Elec CO, 1950-1975; res chemist, E I du Pont de Nemours & Co, 1945-1950; res fel, Purdue Univ, 1943-1945; instr, Univ Conn, 1942-1943; Asst chem, Stanford Univ, 1940-1941. **Memberships:** Am Chem Soc; fel Am Inst Chemists. **Research Statement & Publications:** Aliphatic diamines; local anesthetics; fluorocarbons; catalytic oxidation of hydrocarbons; silicones. **Mailing Address:** 1609 S Arlington Dr, Seneca, SC 29672.

KRANTZ, KERMIT EDWARD, MEDICINE, ANATOMY. **Personal Data:** b Oak Park, Ill, June 4, 1923; m 1946. **Education:** Northwestern Univ, BS, 1945, BM & MS, 1947, MD, 1948; Am Bd Obstet & Gynec, dipl. **Honorary Degrees:** DLitt, William Woods Col, 1971. **Honors & Awards:** Found Award, SAtlantic Asn Obstetricians, Gynecologists, 1950, Am Asn Obstetricians & Gynecologists, 1950; Leslie Arey Lectr, Northwestern Univ Sch Med, 1966, Thomas W McElin Lectr, 1986; Distinguished Serv Award, Am Col Obstetricians & Gyecologists, 1982; Edward Crown Mem Lectr, Columbus Hosp, Chicago, 1983. **Professional Experience:** PROF & CHMN EMER, UNIV KANS MED CTR, 1994-; PROF ANAT EMER, UNIV KANS MED CTR, 1994-; distinguished prof, Med Ctr, 1991-1994; adj prof obstet & gynec, Sch Med, Univ NDak, 1981; Charles Jones Newcomb vis prof obstet & gynec, Univ Ariz Health Sci Ctr, 1979; pres, Int Family Planning Res Asn Inc, 1975-1976; assoc to exec vchancellor facil develop, Med Ctr, 1974-1983; dean clin affairs, Dept Gynec & Obstet, Univ Kans Med Ctr, 1972-1974; civilian Nat Consult, Surgeon Gen, US Air Force, 1964-; prof anat, Dept Gynec & Obstet, Univ Kans Med Ctr, 1963-1992; prof & chmn, Dept Gynec & Obstet, Univ Kans Med Ctr, 1959-1991; Markle scholar, Sch Med, Univ Kans, 1957-1962; asst prof, Sch Med, Univ Ark, 1955-1959; from instr to asst prof, Univ Vt, 1951-1955; asst dir, Div Maternal & Child Health & Welfare, Vt State Dept Health, 1951-1955; res fel, Col Med, Univ Vt, 1950-1951; NY Acad Med Bowen-Brooks fel, New York Hosp, 1948-1950; intern obstet & gynec, New York Lying-In-Hosp, Cornell Univ, 1947-1948; asst resident, New York Lying-In-Hosp, Cornell Univ, 1947-1948; resident anat, Med Sch, 1944-1947; Asst zool, Northwestern Univ, 1943. **Memberships:** AAAS; Am Asn Anatomists; found fel Am Col Obstetricians & Gynecologists; Am Med Writers Asn; Soc Med Consults Armed Forces (pres, 1990-1991). **Research Statement & Publications:** Human placenta; anatomy and physiology; female anatomy, urethra, bladder, vagina, uterus, tubes and ovaries; renal function in pregnancy. **Mailing Address:** Dept Obstet & Gynec, Med Ctr, Univ Kans, 3901 Rainbow Blvd, Kansas City, KS 66160.

KRANTZ, SANFORD B, INTERNAL MEDICINE, HEMATOLOGY. **Personal Data:** b Chicago, Ill, February 6, 1934; m 1958, Sandra Rae Goldstein; c Michael, Marcy (Glisczinski), Alan & Sarah (Derks). **Education:** Univ Chicago, AB & BS, 1955, MD, 1959. **Honors & Awards:** Joseph A Capps Prize, Inst Med Chicago, 1964. **Professional Experience:** PROF MED, SCH MED, VANDERBILT UNIV, as of 2004; dir hemat, Sch Med, Vanderbilt Univ, 1975-; CHIEF HEMAT UNIT, VET ADMIN HOSP, NASHVILLE, 1970-; assoc prof, Sch Med, Vanderbilt Univ, 1970-1975; asst chief hemat serv, Clin Ctr, NIH, 1968-1970; Leukemia Soc scholar, 1965-1968; asst prof med, Univ Chicago Hosps & Argonne Cancer Res Hosp, 1965-1968; NATO fel biochem, Univ Glasgow, 1964-1965; res assoc, Univ Chicago Hosps, 1963-1964; USPHS fel, Univ Chicago Hosps, 1962-1964; asst resident, Univ Chicago Hosps, 1961-1962; Intern med, Univ Chicago Hosps, 1960-1961. **Memberships:** AAAS; Am Soc ClinInvest; Am Fedn Clin Res; Am Soc Hemat; Asn Am Physicians; Int Soc Exp Hematol. **Research Statement & Publications:** Erythropoietin; erythropoietic diseases; polycythemia vera and red cell aplasia; anemia of chronic disease. **Mailing Address:** Sch Med, Vanderbilt Univ, 2-A229 VAMC, 1310 24th Ave, S, Nashville, TN 37212. **Fax:** 615-321-6327. **E-Mail:** sanford.krantz@med.va.gov

KRANTZ, STEVEN GEORGE, SEVERAL COMPLEX VARIABLES. **Personal Data:** b San Francisco, Calif, February 3, 1951; m 1974, Randi. **Education:** Univ Calif, Santa Cruz, BA, 1971; Princeton Univ, PhD (math), 1974. **Honors & Awards:** Chauvenet Prize, 1992; Kemper Award, 1993; Beckenbach Prize, 1994; Nagle Memorial Lectr, Univ S Fla, 1998. **Professional Experience:** PROF MATH, WASH UNIV, ST LOUIS, MO, 1986-; Kemper Found Educ Grant, 1994; from assoc prof to prof, Pa State Univ, Univ Park, 1981-1987; res fel, NSF, 1975-; asst prof math, Univ Calif, Los Angeles, 1974-1981. **Memberships:** Am Math Soc; Math Asn Am; Text & Acad Authors Asn. **Research Statement & Publications:** Function theory on pseudoconvex domains in complex n-space; harmonic analysis of euclidean spaces, real function theory, differentiability of functions, partial differential equations, facial recognition and interpolation theory. **Mailing Address:** Dept Math Campus Wash Univ, PO Box 1146, St Louis, MO 63130. **Fax:** 314-935-6839. **E-Mail:** sk@math.wustl.edu

KRANTZ, WILLIAM BERNARD, MEMBRANE SCIENCE & TECHNOLOGY, GEOMORPHOLOGY. **Personal Data:** b Freeport, Ill, January 27, 1939; m 1968, June; c Brigette Elise. **Education:** St Joseph's Col, Ind, BA, 1961; Univ Ill, Urbana, BS, 1962; Univ Calif, Berkeley, PhD (chem eng), 1968. **Honors & Awards:** Spec Achievement & Outstanding Performance Awards, NSF, 1978; George Westinghouse Award, Am Soc Eng Educ, 1980; John Wesley Powell Mem Lectr, AAAS, 1995; Fellow, AAAS, 1985; Fellow, ASEE, 1999; Fellow, AIChE, 2005; Malcolm E Pruitt Award, Council for Chemical Research, 2004; Dow Lectureship Award, ASEE, 2003; Outstanding Teaching Award, ASEE, 1998. **Professional Experience:** Isaac M. Meyer Chair Professor, National University of Singapore, 2005-; Rieveschl Ohio Eminent Scholar, University of Cincinnati, 2000-2005; Presdident's Teaching Scholar, University of Colorado, 1990-; Visiting Faculty Fellow, Nanyang Technological University (Singapore), 2004; Visiting Research Fellow, Australian National University, 2004 & 2005; NSF GOALI FAC FEL, CHEVRON RES & TECHNOL CO, CALIF, 1996; 3M Co, Minn, 1996; vis fac researcher, Univ Twente, Neth, 1995; consult, Bend Res, 1990-; Guggenheim fel, Univ Oxford, Eng, 1988-1989; Nat res lectr, Sigma Xi, 1984-1986; Fulbright-Hayes sr res fel, Aachen Tech Univ, WGer, 1981-1982; prof chem eng, Univ Colo, Boulder, 1979-2002; consult, US Dept Com, 1979-1980; mem area adv comt, US Coun Int Exchange Scholar, Int Commun Agency, 1977-1980; assoc prof, Univ Colo, Boulder, 1977-1979; dir, Thermodyn & Mass Transfer Prog, NSF, 1977-1978; CONSULT, Laramie Energy Technol Ctr, Dept Energy, 1976-; NSF, NATO sr fel, Univ Essex, Eng, 1975; Fulbright-Hays lectr, Istanbul Tech Univ, 1974-1975; Consult, Dow Chem Co, Mich, 1969-1971; Asst prof, Univ Colo, Boulder, 1968-1977. **Memberships:** Fel AAAS; Fel Am Inst Chem Engrs; Fel Am Soc Eng Educ; Am Chem Soc; Sigma Xi; NAm Membrane Soc. **Research Statement & Publications:** Polymeric membrane morphology; self-organization in geophysical processing; materials science in low-gravity; global change in polar and sub polar regions. **Mailing Address:** Dept Chem & Biomolecular Eng, National Univ Singapore, Singapore, 117576, Singapore. **Fax:** 65-6779-1936. **E-Mail:** bkrantz@alpha.che.uc.edu

KRANTZBERG, GAIL, CONTAMINANT TOXICITY & BIOAVAILABILITY, ECOLOGICAL RESTORATION. **Personal Data:** b Montreal, Que, August 19, 1957; m Douglas. **Education:** McGill Univ, BS, 1979; Univ Toronto, MS, 1982, PhD (ecotoxicol), 1987. **Professional Experience:** DIR, GREAT LAKE OFF, INT JOINT COMMISSION, WINDSOR, ONT, as of 2003; fac, Restoration ecol, York Univ, 1996-; prin investr, Environ Can, 1991-; adj prof environ mgt & aquatic chem, Univ Toronto, 1990-; sediment specialist & remedial action plan coordr, Ont Ministry Environ & Energy, 1988-; ECOTOXICOLOGIST, ONT MINISTRY ENVIRON & ENERGY, 1988-; great Lakes Remedial Action Plan coordr, 1988-1994; fel, Univ Toronto, 1987-1988; consult sediment mgt, Ont Ministry Environ & Energy, 1982-1984; lectr, Univ Toronto, 1979-1984. **Memberships:** Int Asn Great Lakes Res; Soc Environ Toxicol & Chem; NAm Benthological Soc; Nature Conservancy; Can Wildlife Fedn. **Research Statement & Publications:** Bioavailability and toxicity of contaminants in sediment; remedial action plans to rehabilitate Great Lakes ecosystems; structural and functional indicators of aquatic ecosystem health, environmental sustainability. **Mailing Address:** Ministry Environment, 135 St, Clair Ave W, Toronto, ON M4V 1K6, Can. **Fax:** 416-314-3924. **E-Mail:** krantzga@epo.gov.on.ca

KRANZ, DAVID M, BIOCHEMISTRY. **Education:** Ill State Univ, BS, 1975; Univ Ill, Urbana-Champaign, PhD, 1982. **Professional Experience:** PROF BIOCHEM, UNIV ILL, URBANA-CHAMPAIGN, as of 2005. **Mailing Address:** Univ Ill, 600 S Mathews, Urbana, IL 61801-3731. **Fax:** 217-244-5858. **E-Mail:** d-kranz@uiuc.edu

KRANZ, EUGENE FRANCIS, AERONAUTICAL ENGINEERING. **Personal Data:** b Toledo, Ohio, August 17, 1933; c 6. **Education:** St Louis Univ, BS, 1954. **Honors & Awards:** Lawrence Sperry Award, Am Inst Aeronaut & Astronaut, 1967. **Professional Experience:** CONSULT, as of 2003; dir mission opers, Johnson Space Ctr, NASA, 1983-1994; flight opers dir shuttle prog, NASA, Johnson Space Ctr, 1980-1983; chief flight control div, Apollo & Skylab Missions, Manned Spacecraft Ctr, NASA, 1969-1994; flight dir gemini, Apollo & Skylab Missions, Manned Spacecraft Ctr, NASA, 1964-1994; supvr carrier flight test maintenance & checkout, Holloman AFB, NMex, 1958-1960; Flight test engr, McDonnell Aircraft Co, 1954-1955; Flight controller, Mercury Missions. **Memberships:** Fel Am Astronaut Soc. **Mailing Address:** 1108 Shady Oak Lane, Dickinson, TX 77539.

KRANZER, HERBERT C, APPLIED MATHEMATICS, CONSERVATION LAWS. **Personal Data:** b New York, NY, April 10, 1932; m, c 3. **Education:** NY Univ, BA, 1952, PhD (math), 1957. **Honors & Awards:** Putnam Awards, 1951 & 1952. **Professional Experience:** PROF EMERITUS MATH, ADELPHI UNIV, 1997-; prof, Adelphi Univ, 1963-1997; assoc prof, Adelphi Univ, 1959-1963; instr, NY Univ, 1958-1959; assoc res scientist, NY Univ, 1957-1958; Visting scientist, SUNY Stony Brook, 1995-1997; Consult, FONAR Corp, 1983-; vis scholar, Columbia Univ, 1976-1977; vis prof, Imp Col London, 1966-1967, NSF sr fel, 1966; Consult, Los Alamos Sci Lab, 1956-1968; Asst math, NY Univ, 1952-1957. **Memberships:** Am Math Soc; Soc Indust & Appl Math; Math Asn Am; AAAS. **Research Statement & Publications:** Magnetohydrodynamics; numerical analysis; Weiner-Hopf problems; conservation laws; magnetic resonance imaging. **Mailing Address:** Dept Math & Comput Sci, Adelphi Univ, Garden City, NY 11530-0701. **E-Mail:** kranzer@panther.adelphi.edu

KRANZLER, ALBERT WILLIAM, MATHEMATICS. **Personal Data:** b Bismarck, NDak, July 11, 1916; m 1939, c 2. **Education:** Univ NDak, BS, 1937; Univ Minn, MS, 1950. **Professional Experience:** RETIRED; actg head dept, SDak State Univ, 1961-1968; from assoc prof to prof math, SDak State Univ, 1945-1981; prin pub sch, Colo, 1943-1945; instr training div, Sioux Falls Army Air Force Sch, 1942-1943; teacher, SDak, 1941-1942; Prin pub sch, NDak, 1937-1941. **Memberships:** Math Asn Am; Am Math Soc. **Research Statement & Publications:** Reorganization of high school mathematics curriculum. **Mailing Address:** 808 Christine Ave No 206, Brookings, SD 57006.

KRAPCHO, ANDREW PAUL, ORGANIC CHEMISTRY. **Personal Data:** b Alden, Pa, March 6, 1932; m 1958, Arlene; c Karen J, Susan D & Douglas P. **Education:** Pa State Univ, BS, 1953; Harvard Univ, MA, 1957, PhD (chem), 1958. **Professional Experience:** PROF EMER CHEM, UNIV VT, as of 2004; Fulbright scholar, France, 1968-1969; prof chem, Univ Vt, beginning 1967; from asst prof to assoc prof, Univ Vt, 1960-1967; res fel, Pa State Univ, 1959-1960; instr chem, Smith Col, 1957-1959. **Memberships:** Am Chem Soc. **Research Statement & Publications:** Chemistry of thiones and photochemistry of cyclic ketones; physical-organic chemistry; metal-amine reductions; solvolytic studies of spirane systems; sesquiterpene syntheses; bivalent carbon species; synthesis of antitumor agents. **Mailing Address:** Dept Chem, Univ Vt, 82 Univ Pl, Burlington, VT 05405. **Fax:** 802-656-8705. **E-Mail:** a.paul.krapcho@uvm.edu

KRAPF, GEORGE, analytical chemistry; deceased, see previous edition for last biography

KRAPU, GARY LEE, WILDLIFE RESEARCH, ANIMAL ECOLOGY. **Personal Data:** b Oakes, ND, March 12, 1944; m 1985, Madeline; c Jeff, Amy, Anne & Chris. **Education:** NDak State Univ, BS, 1966; Iowa State Univ, MS, 1968, PhD (animal ecol), 1972. **Professional Experience:** PRIN INVESTR, NORTHERN PRAIRIE SCI CTR, as of 2004; RES WILDLIFE BIOLOGIST, NORTHERN PRAIRIE SCI CTR, USGS, 1970-. **Memberships:** Wildlife Soc; Am Ornithologist's Union; Wilson Soc. **Research Statement & Publications:** Ecological aspects of waterfowl reproduction; sandhill crane biology; feeding ecology and nutrition; reproductive physiology; lipid storage; bioenergetics; marsh ecology; role of midcontinent staging areas to arctic-nesting geese, shorebirds and sandhill cranes; The Platte River Ecology Study; The role of nutrient reserves in mallard reproduction; Feeding ecology of pintail hens during reproduction. **Mailing Address:** Northern Prairie Sci Ctr, 8711 37th St SE, Jamestown, ND 58401. **Fax:** 701-253-5553. **E-Mail:** gary_krapu@usgs.gov

KRASAVAGE, WALTER JOSEPH, INDUSTRIAL TOXICOLOGY. **Personal Data:** b Luzerne, Pa, March 12, 1933; m 1955, c 4. **Education:** King's Col, BS, 1955; Univ Rochester, MS, 1963. **Professional Experience:** SR TOXICOLOGIST INDUST TOXICOL, HEALTH SAFETY & HUMAN FACTORS LAB, EASTMAN KODAK CO, 1965-; MGR REPROD & DEVELOP TOXICOL, HEALTH & ENVIRON LABS, EASTMAN KODAK CO, 1965-; Instr biol, Rochester Inst Technol, 1963-1965; sr res assoc, Atomic Energy Proj, Dept Radiation Biol & Biophys, Sch Med & Dent, Univ Rochester, 1958-1965; Technician parasitol, Merck Inst Therapeut Res, 1955-1956. **Memberships:** Soc Toxicol; Teratol Soc; Environ Mutagen Soc. **Research Statement & Publications:** Subchronic and chronic toxicology of industrial chemicals, especially reproduction and embryo-fetotoxicity. **Mailing Address:** 288 Shorecliff Dr, Rochester, NY 14612.

KRASHES, DAVID, METALLURGY. **Personal Data:** b Brooklyn, NY, January 31, 1925; m 1956, c 1. **Education:** Rensselaer Polytech Inst, BS, 1949, MS, 1952, PhD (metall), 1958. **Professional Experience:** Pres, Mass Mat Res, Inc, 1981-1982; RETIRED, pres, Lehigh Testing labs, beginning 1972; consult, Wyman-Gordon Co, 1959- & Reed Rolled Thread Die Co, 1960-; assoc prof, Worcester Polytech Inst, 1957-1965; mem staff, Nuclear Metals, Inc, 1955-1957; res assoc metall, Rensselaer Polytech Inst, 1953-1954; dir, Richard D Brew Co; chief exec officer, Mass Mat Res, Inc. **Memberships:** Fel Am Soc Metals (treas, 1971-1973, vpres, 1980-1981, pres, 1981-1982); Am Inst Mining Metall & Petrol Engrs; Am Soc Testing & Mat; Am Foundry Soc. **Research Statement & Publications:** Failure analysis of metals and mechanical products; solving industrial manufacturing problems relating to materials; fabrication; microscopy; economic studies. **Mailing Address:** Rensselaer Polytech Inst, 110 8th St, Troy, NY 12180.

KRASHIN, BERNARD R(OBERT), METALS. **Personal Data:** b Buffalo, NY, November 9, 1918; m 1946, c 2. **Education:** Western Reserve Univ, BS, 1941. **Professional Experience:** RETIRED; vpres & gen Mgr, Macco Adhesives Group, SCM Corp, 1971-1986; vpres opers, Glidden-Durkee Div, 1967-1970; vpres & gen mgr, Macco Chem Co Div, Glidden Co, 1964-1967; pres, Macco Chem Co Div, Glidden Co, 1962-1964; pres, Colton Chem Co Div, Air Reduction Co, Inc, 1956-1962; vpres, Colton Chem Co Div, Air Reduction Co, Inc, 1950-1956; chief chemist & asst tech dir, Cosma Labs Co, 1945-1950; dir metals labs, Cosma Labs Co, 1943-1945; Chemist, Cosma Labs Co, 1941-1943. **Memberships:** Am Chem Soc; Am Ord Asn; Am Inst Chem. **Research Statement & Publications:** Fungicides; vinyl resins; emulsions, wax and synthetic resin; process for fusion of bronze to steel; fungicide for ropes, nets and twine; radiological physics; synthetic resins; analytic chemistry. **Mailing Address:** 22150 Shaker Blvd, Shaker Heights, OH 44122.

KRASKIN, KENNETH STANFORD, MICROBIOLOGY. **Personal Data:** b Kearny, NJ, December 28, 1929; m 1954, Barbara Adler; c Richard & Andrew. **Education:** Rutgers Univ, BS, 1951, MS, 1955, PhD (bact), 1957. **Professional Experience:** TECH CONSULT, 1988-; dir appl res, Personal Prod Co, Johnson & Johnson, 1977-1988; head microbiol, Personal Prod Co, Johnson & Johnson, 1971-1977; microbiologist, Rohm & Haas Co, 1957-1970; Lab instr bact, Rutgers Univ, 1954-1957. **Memberships:** Am Soc Microbiol; Sigma Xi; Soc Indust Microbiol. **Research Statement & Publications:** Antibiotics; enzyme fermentations; sterility; disinfectants; biodegradation; vaginal microbiology and physiology. **Mailing Address:** 14 N Garden Terr, Milltown, NJ 08850. **Fax:** 732-297-9522.

KRASNA, ALVIN ISAAC, BIOCHEMISTRY, MICROBIOLOGY. **Personal Data:** b New York, NY, June 23, 1929; m 1955, Elaine; c Susan, Gary & Allen. **Education:** Yeshiva Col, BA, 1950; Columbia Univ, PhD (biochem), 1955. **Professional Experience:** PROF EMER BIOCHEM, COLUMBIA UNIV, as of 2005; prof biochem, Columbia Univ, beginning 1970; Guggenheim Memorial Found fel, Univ Calif SD, 1962-1963; from instr to assoc prof, Columbia Univ, 1956-1970; res worker, Columbia Univ, 1954-1956. **Memberships:** AAAS; Am Chem Soc; Harvey Soc; Am Soc Biol Chemists; Am Soc Microbiol; Am Soc Photobiol. **Research Statement & Publications:** Bioconversion of solar energy; regulation of biosynthesis of enzymes. **Mailing Address:** Col Physicians & Surgeons, Columbia Univ, New York, NY 10032. **Fax:** 212-305-7932. **E-Mail:** aik3@columbia.edu

KRASNEGOR, NORMAN A, HUMAN LEARNING & BEHAVIOR. **Personal Data:** b Boston, Mass, November 17, 1939. **Education:** Boston Univ, BA, 1961; Columbia Univ, MA, 1963; Univ Md, PhD (exp psychol), 1970. **Honors & Awards:** Distinguished Serv Award, Am Psychol Asn, 1981; Distinguished Serv Award, Int Soc for Develop Psychol & Biol, 1995. **Professional Experience:** CHIEF, HUMAN LEARNING & BEHAV BR, CTR

RES MOTHERS & C, NAT INST CHILD HEALTH & HUMAN DEVELOP, NIH, 1980-; health sci adminr, Nat Inst Drug Abuse, 1972-1980; exp psychologist, Walter Rood Army Inst Res, 1966-1972. **Memberships:** Fel Am Psychol Asn; Am Psychol Soc. **Mailing Address:** Nat Inst Child Health & Human Develop, NIH, Rm 4805 6100 Bldg 9000 Rockville Pike, Bethesda, MD 20892. **Fax:** 301-480-7773.

KRASNER, JEROME L, MANAGEMENT. **Personal Data:** b St Louis, Mo, February 25, 1940; wid, c Randy, Brett, Jay, Rachael, Douglas & Peter. **Education:** Wash Univ, BS, 1961, MS, 1964; Boston Univ, PhD (medsci), 1969; Nichols Col, MBA, 1987. **Honors & Awards:** Cert of Commendation, NASA, 1969. **Professional Experience:** FOUNDER & PRIN ANANLYST, EMBEDDED MARKET FORECASTERS, as of 2004; vpres, Embedded Market Forecasters, as of 2004; vpres, Am Technol Int, as of 2004; dir, Int Ctr Biomed Technologies, Becker Hill Community Col, Boston, as of 2002; vis prof, Univ Los Palmas, Spain, as of 2002; dept head & prof, Dept Elec Eng Technol, Wenthworth Inst Technol, 1990-1992; vpres res & develop, Clin Develop Corp, 1983-1989; exec vpres, Plasmedics, Inc, 1981-1985; dir, Ctr Med Sci, Carnegie-Mellon Inst Res, 1977-1979 & Ctr Clin Eng, Wentworth Inst Technol; pres, Clinco, Inc, 1975-1981; Pres, Biocybernetics, Inc, 1969-1975; Chmn, Dept Biomed Eng & assoc prof health sci, physiol & biomed eng, Boston Univ, 1969-1974. **Memberships:** Inst Elec & Electronics Engrs; Asn Advan Med Instrumentation; Sigma Xi; NY Acad Sci; AAAS. **Research Statement & Publications:** Design, development and international marketing of clinical instrumentation and medical devices. **Mailing Address:** Embedded Market Forecasters, Ste 500 1257 Worcester Rd, Framingham, MA 01701.

KRASNER, JOSEPH, BIOCHEMISTRY. **Personal Data:** b Buffalo, NY, January 10, 1926; m 1953, c 2. **Education:** Univ Buffalo, BS, 1948, EdM, 1950, MA, 1963, PhD (biochem), 1965. **Professional Experience:** RES PROF EMER OBSTET & GYNEC, STATE UNIV NY, BUFFALO, as of 2005; asst res prof, Obstet & Gynec, State Univ Ny, Buffalo, beginning 1979; cancer res scientist II, Roswell Park Mem Inst, Buffalo, 1979-1992; assoc res prof pediat, State Univ Ny-buffalo, 1966 1979; dir core labs, Children's Hosp, NY, 1966-1972; res assoc, Children's Hosp, Buffalo, NY, 1965-1966; asst cancer res scientist, Roswell Park Mem Inst, 1951-1961; high sch teacher, 1950-1951. **Memberships:** AAAS; Am Chem Soc; NY Acad Sci; Am Asn Clin Chemists; Am Soc Pharmacol & Exp Therapeut; Sigma Xi; Am Soc Biochem & Molecular Biol. **Research Statement & Publications:** Biochemical changes during mammalian development and the effect of endogenous and exogenous compounds on development; drug-protein interactions during development and in pathological situations; physical biochemical techniques as used to study the antibody combining site. **Mailing Address:** State Univ NY Childern's Hosp, Dept Gynecol & Obstetics, Buffalo, NY 14150. **E-Mail:** jkrasner@buffalo.edu

KRASNER, ROBERT IRVING, MICROBIOLOGY. **Personal Data:** b Providence, RI, December 3, 1929; m 1964, c 2. **Education:** Providence Col, BS, 1951; Boston Univ, AM, 1952, PhD (biol), 1956; Harvard Univ, MPH, 1999. **Professional Experience:** Vis prof, Sch Med, Georgetown Univ, 1969-1971; Haddasah Med Sch, Hewbrew Univ, Jerusalem; PROF BIOL, PROVIDENCE COL, 1965-; adv coun clin labs, US Army Biol Labs, Ft Detrick, Md, 1965-1966; adv coun clin labs, RI Dept Health, beginning 1962; mem, La State Univ Sch Med Interim Training Prog Trop Med Cent Am, 1962; from instr to assoc prof, Providence Col, 1958-1965. **Memberships:** AAAS; Am Soc Microbiol; Nat Asn Biol Teachers; Nat Sci Teachers Asn. **Research Statement & Publications:** Medical bacteriology; host-parasite relationships. **Mailing Address:** Dept Biol, Providence Col, Sowa Hall 222, Providence, RI 02918. **Fax:** 401-865-1438. **E-Mail:** rkrasner@providence.edu

KRASNER, SOL H, PHYSICS. **Personal Data:** b St Louis, Mo, June 14, 1923; m 1958, c 4. **Education:** Univ Calif, Los Angeles, BA, 1957, MA, 1948; Univ Chicago, PhD (physics), 1955. **Professional Experience:** PROF EMER PHYSICS, UNIV CHICAGO, as of 2004; Asst to chmn & dept counselor, Univ Chicago, 1976-; assoc prof physics, Univ Chicago, beginning 1970; DEAN STUDENTS, DIV PHYS SCI, 1963-; prof lectr, Div Phys Sci, 1963-1971; nuclear physicist, Off Naval Res, 1955-1963; Jr physicist, Argonne Nat Lab, 1949-1953. **Memberships:** Am Phys Soc; Am Asn Physics Teachers. **Research Statement & Publications:** Nuclear reactor physics; scientific administration. **Mailing Address:** Dept Physics, Univ Chicago, 5720 S Ellis Ave, Chicago, IL 60637-1434. **Fax:** 773-702-2045.

KRASNEY, JOHN ANDREW, CARDIOVASCULAR PHYSIOLOGY. **Personal Data:** b Long Beach, Calif, November 29, 1940; m 1975, c 5. **Education:** Elmhurst Col, BS, 1962; Univ Wis-Madison, PhD (physiol), 1966. **Professional Experience:** PROF PHYSIOL & BIOPHY, STATE UNIV NY, BUFFALO, 1983-; animal care & experimentation comt, Am Physiol Soc, 1982-1985; assoc prof, State Univ NY, Buffalo, 1974-1983; from instr to assoc prof physiol, Albany Med Col, 1967-1974; fel, Nat Heart Inst, physiol, Univ Wis-Madison, 1966-1967. **Memberships:** Am Physiol Soc; Can Physiol Soc; Am Heart Asn; Undersea Med Soc; Coun Cardiopulmonary Dis & Coun Circulation, Am Heart Asn. **Research Statement & Publications:** Regulation of circulation; respiration; renal function and blood volume during environmental stresses including chronic hypoxia, water immersion and exercise; neuroendocrine and mechanisms in control of fluid and electrolyte balance; cerebral circulation in chronic hypoxia; mechanisms of high-altitude cerebral edema and acute mountain sickness; ethanol on cerebral blood flow; cardiac function and arterial blood pressure. **Mailing Address:** Dept Physiol & Biophysiol State Univ NY Sch Med, 124 Sherman Hall S Campus, Buffalo, NY 14214. **Fax:** 716-829-2344. **E-Mail:** krasney@buffalo.edu

KRASNOW, FRANCES, BIOCHEMISTRY. **Personal Data:** b New York, NY, October 16, 1894; m 1930, c 1. **Education:** Columbia Univ, BS & AM, 1917, PhD (bact, chem, biochem), 1922. **Honorary Degrees:** LHD, Jewish Theol Sem Am, 1974. **Professional Experience:** RETIRED; specialist clin chem, Am Bd Clin Chem, beginning 1953; res consult, 1952-1990; res dir, Universal Coatings, Inc, 1952-1972; dir res, Sch Dent Hyg, Guggenheim Dent Clin, 1944-1952; spec consult, NY Bur Dent Info, 1940; asst dir & head fundamental sci, Sch Dent Hyg, Guggenheim Dent Clin, 1932-1944; consult biochemist, NY State Labor Dept, 1929; fel, Lehn-Fink Res Fund, NJ, 1925-1926; consult biochemist, Dept Dermat, Skin & Cancer Unit, NY Postgrad Med Sch & Hosp, Columbia Univ, 1923-1944; instr, Col Physicians & Surgeons, Columbia Univ, 1922-1932; asst biochem, Rhein-Levy Res Fund fel, 1920-1928; asst biochem, Col Physicians & Surgeons, Columbia Univ, 1919-1922. **Memberships:** AAAS; Am Chem Soc; fel Am Inst Chemists; Int Asn Dent Res; assoc fel NY Acad Med; fel NY Acad Sci. **Research Statement & Publications:** Skin disease; syphilis; cholesterol; phospholipids; biochemistry of saliva; caries; place of nutrition in dentistry; correlation between metabolic inorganic-organic levels in blood, saliva, urine and tooth conditions. **Mailing Address:** 595 Columbus Ave, New York, NY 10024.

KRASNOW, MARVIN ELLMAN, physical chemistry, electrical engineering; deceased, see previous edition for last biography

KRASNY, HARVEY CHARLES, TECHNOLOGY LICENSING & PHARMACOKINETICS, CLINICAL & PRE-CLINICAL DRUG DEVELOPMENT & DRUG METABOLISM. **Personal Data:** b Highpoint, NC, July 27, 1945. **Education:** Lynchburg Col, BS (Chem), 1967; Univ NC, MS, 1969, PhD (Biochem), 1976. **Professional Experience:** Pres, 1999-, VPres Licensing/Bus Development, 1996-1998, CaroTech LLC; Sr Resch Scientist, Wellcome Res Labs, Burroughs Wellcome Co, 1969-1995. **Memberships:** Am Soc Clin Pharmacol & Therapeut; Am Soc Pharmacol & Exptl Therapeut; Soc Toxicol; Sigma Xi; Lic Exec Soc; Assoc Univ Tech Mgrs. **Research Statement & Publications:** Pre-clinical and clinical development of chemotherapeutic agents. **Mailing Address:** PO Box 13416, Research Trg Park, NC 27709-3416.

KRASS, ALLAN S(HALE), THEORETICAL PHYSICS, SCIENCE POLICY. **Personal Data:** b Milwaukee, Wis, May 16, 1935. **Education:** Cornell Univ, BE, 1958; Stanford Univ, PhD (theoret physics), 1963. **Professional Experience:** ADJ PROF, SCH FOREIGN SERV, GEORGETOWN UNIV, as of 2005; sr arms analyst, Union Concerned Scientists, 1985-1989; PROF PHYSICS & SCI POLICY, HAMPSHIRE COL, 1981-; vis researcher, Stockholm Instrnl Peace Res Inst, 1980-1981, 1983-1984; consult, Off Technol Assessment, US Cong, beginning 1976; NSF fac fel, 1976-1977; assoc prof, Hampshire Col, 1974-1979; vis lectr, Open Univ Gr Brit, 1973-1974; lectr, Princeton Univ, 1972-1973; asst prof, Univ Calif, Santa Barbara, 1965-1972; lectr, Univ Calif, Santa Barbara, 1964-1965; res assoc physics, Univ Iowa, 1962-1964. **Research Statement & Publications:** Elementary particle physics; theoretical high energy physics; science policy, especially arms control, energy and environmental. **Mailing Address:** Dept Sci Tech & Int Affairs, Sch Foreign Serv, Georgetown Univ, 37th & O St NW, Washington, DC 20057.

KRASSNER, JERRY, ASTRONOMY. **Education:** State Univ NY, Stony Brook, BS, 1974; Univ Rochester, MA, 1976, PhD (physics & astron), 1983. **Professional Experience:** SR PRIN SYST ENGR, INTEGRITY APPLN INC, 2003-. **Memberships:** Nat Defender Investr Asn. **Mailing Address:** Integrity Appln Inc, 5180 Parkstone Dr Ste 260, Chantilly, VA 20151. **Fax:** 703-378-8978.

KRASSNER, STUART M, PARASITOLOGY, COUNSELING THERAPY. **Personal Data:** b New York, NY, August 21, 1935; m 1986, Liza; c David, Sarah, Mark & Joey. **Education:** Brooklyn Col, BS, 1957 The Johns Hopkins Univ, Sc.D. Parasitology, 1961. **Professional Experience:** RETIRED Board Member Spectrum Pharmaceuticals, Fac Am Behav Studies Inst, 1996-2005; actg dean grad studies & res, 1977-1980 & grad studies & res, 1985-1989; biol sci, 1977-1980 & grad studies & res, 1984-1985; assoc dean grad div, Univ Calif, Irvine, 1974-1976; JOINT PROF DEVELOP & CELL BIOL & MED MICROBIOL, UNIV CALIF, IRVINE, 1973-; from vchmn to chmn dept, Univ Calif, Irvine, 1969-1984; assoc prof develop & cell biol, Univ Calif, Irvine, 1969-1973; asst prof organismic biol, Univ Calif, Irvine, 1965-1969; instr invert zool, Hunter Col, 1964-1965; guest investr & NIH res trainee, Rockefeller Univ, 1962-1965; NIH fel, int coop med res & training prog, Johns Hopkins Univ-Sch Trop Med, Univ Calcutta, 1961-1962. **Memberships:** AAAS; Am Soc Parasitol; Soc Protozool; Am Soc Trop Med Hyg; California Asn of Marriage & Family Therapists. **Research Statement & Publications:** Immune responses in hemoflagellate infections; control of transformation in parasitic hemoflagellates. **Mailing Address:** Dept Develop & Cell Biol, Univ Calif, Irvine, CA 92717. **Fax:** 714-824-4709. **E-Mail:** smkrassn@uci.edu

KRASSOWSKA, WANDA, ELECTROPHYSIOLOGY, MODELS OF CARDIAC MUSCLE IN ELECTRIC FIELD. **Personal Data:** b Warsaw, Poland, November 1, 1954. **Education:** Warsaw Tech Univ, MS, 1978; Duke Univ, PhD (biomed eng), 1987. **Professional Experience:** ASSOC PROF BIOMED ENG, DUKE UNIV, as of 2002; asst prof biomed eng, Duke Univ, beginning 1991; res assoc, Duke Univ, 1988-1991; res assoc, Inst Biocybernetics & Biomed Eng, 1978-1983. **Memberships:** Inst Elec & Electronics Engrs; Eng Med & Bio Soc. **Research Statement & Publications:** Electrophysiology of syncytial tissues; mechanisms of pacing and defibrillation of the heart. **Mailing Address:** Dept Biomed Eng, Duke Univ, Box 90281 424B Teer Eng Libr, Durham, NC 27708-0281. **Fax:** 919-684-4488. **E-Mail:** wanda.krassowska@duke.edu

KRATOCHVIL, BYRON, ANALYTICAL CHEMISTRY. **Personal Data:** b Osmond, Nebr, September 15, 1932; m Marianne; c Susan J, Daniel J, Jean M & John D. **Education:** Iowa State Univ, BS, 1957, MS, 1959, PhD (analytical chem), 1961. **Honors & Awards:** Fel AAAS; Fel Chem Inst Can; Fisher Scientific Award, Can Soc Chem. **Professional Experience:** PROF EMER, UNIV ALTA, AS OF 1998; sr advisor, vice pres res office, 1998-2001; assoc vice pres res, Univ Alta, 1996-1998; chair, dept chem, Univ Alta, 1989-1996; sr ed, Can J Chem, 1988-1993; anal ed, Can J Chem, 1985-1988; ed bd, Can J Chem, 1982-1985; guest worker, Nat Bur Stand, Washington, DC, 1980-1981; Bd dirs, Chem Inst Can, 1977-1980; prof chem, Univ Alta, 1971-1998; assoc prof, Univ Alta, 1967-1971; asst prof, Univ Wis-Madison, 1962-1967; instr chem, Univ Wis-Madison, 1961-1962. **Memberships:** AAAS; Am Chem Soc; Chem Inst Can. **Research Statement & Publications:** Sampling for chemical analysis. **Mailing Address:** Dept Chem, Univ Alta, Edmonton, AB T6G 2G2, Can. **E-Mail:** ron.kratochvil@ualberta.ca

KRATOCHVIL, CLYDE HARDING, PHYSIOLOGY, BIOCHEMISTRY. **Personal Data:** b Racine, Wis, August 3, 1923; m 1944, Janice S Meissner; c Joanne (Claney), Pamela (Tyson), Antoinette (Pax), Patricia & Simone (Vanbellinger). **Education:** Univ Wis, Madison, BS, 1950, MD, 1952, PhD (physiol, biochem), 1956. **Professional Experience:** FLIGHT SURGEON, USAF, as of 2002; ACTG MED DIR, FAMILY HEALTH CTR, KALAMAZOO, MICH, 1991-; int med dir, Europe, 1982-1988; dir clin res, Europe, 1974-1982; group mgr, Med Serv, Upjohn Co, 1970-1974; clin prof prev med, Ohio State Univ, 1969-1971; Aerospace Med Res Labs, Wright Patterson AFB, 1968-1970; comdr, Aeromed Res Lab, Holloman AFB, NMex, 1963-1968; consult, Manned Spacecraft Ctr, NASA, 1962-; chief, Bioscience Div, 1961-1963; Flight controller, Proj Mercury, 1959-1962; proj officer bioscience div, Europ Off, Off Aerospace Res, Brussels, Belg, 1959-1961; officer-in-chg, Dept Physiol & Biophys, Sch Aviation Med, Randolph AFB, 1955-1959; Intern, USAF, William Beaumont Army Hosp, Tex, 1952-1953. **Memberships:** AAAS; Am Physiol Soc; fel Aerospace Med Asn; Am Soc Clin Pharmacol & Therapeut; Int Acad Aviation & Space Med; fel Am Inst Chemists. **Research Statement & Publications:** Aerospace medical research; immunohematology; use of primates in medical research; protein chemistry; renal physiology; central nervous system function in high stress environments; circadian rhythms. **Mailing Address:** USAF, Kalamazoo, MI 49081-1805. **Fax:** 269-324-0771.

KRATOCHVIL, JIRI, ELECTROCHEMISTRY, BIOMEDICAL SCIENCES. **Personal Data:** b Prague, Czech, June 11, 1944; m 1972, c 1. **Education:** Southampton Univ, PhD (electrochem), 1972. **Professional Experience:** PRES, IE SENSORS INC, SALT LAKE CITY, UTAH, 1984-; mgr res & develop, Critikon Inc, Salt Lake City, 1979-1983; sr chemist electrochem, Beckman Instruments Inc, 1977-1979; res fel, Webb-Waring Lung Inst, Denver, 1975-1976; lectr physiol, St Thomas' Hosp Med Sch, London, 1973-1975; Fel electrochem, Univ Okla, 1972-1973. **Memberships:** Fel The Chem Soc; Am Chem Soc.

Research Statement & Publications: Ion-selective electrodes; electrochemistry of membranes; polarography; biomedical transducers; semiconductor technology; semiconductor packaging. **Mailing Address:** IE Sensors Inc, 247 W 3680 South, Salt Lake City, UT 84115.

KRATOHVIL, JOSIP, COLLOID CHEMISTRY, POLYMER PHYSICAL CHEMISTRY. **Personal Data:** b Morovic, Yugoslavia, February 26, 1928; m 1952, c 2. **Education:** Univ Zagreb, BS, 1952, PhD (chem), 1954. **Professional Experience:** PROF EMER CHEM, CLARKSON COL TECHNOL, as of 2005; CO-ED, JOUR COLLOID & INTERFACE SCI, as of 2004; DIR, INST COLLOID & SURFACE SCI, 1981-; prof chem, clarkson Col technol, beginning 1967; from asst prof to assoc prof, inst Colloid & Surface Sci, 1964-1967; res assoc, inst Colloid & Surface Sci, 1960-1964; res fel, Nat res Coun Can, 1959-1960; asst chem, Med Sch, Univ Zagreb, 1952-1959. **Memberships:** AAAS; Am Chem Soc; Fine Particle Soc; NY Acad Sci; Sigma Xi. **Research Statement & Publications:** Coagulation and stability of colloids; light scattering; physical biochemistry; polymer chemistry; micellar systems; bile salts; polyelectrolytes and macromolecules in solutions. **Mailing Address:** Dept Chem, Clarkson Univ, Box 5010, Potsdam, NY 13699-0001.

KRATZ, HOWARD RUSSEL, EXPERIMENTAL PHYSICS. **Personal Data:** b Mattoon, Wis, November 2, 1916; m 1942, Mary; c William H & Marilyn J (Locker). **Education:** Ripon Col, AB, 1938; Univ Wis, PhD (physics), 1942. **Professional Experience:** RETIRED; sr res scientist, S-Cubed, 1972-1979; Res Lab, Gen Atomic Co, 1959-1972; Res Lab, Gen Elec Co, 1946-1959; res assoc, Northwestern Univ, 1946; res assoc, Los Alamos Sci Lab, 1944-1946; res assoc, Metall Lab, Univ Chicago, 1942-1944; asst spectros, Princeton Univ, 1940-1942; asst physics, Univ Wis, 1938-1940. **Memberships:** Am Phys Soc; Sigma Xi. **Research Statement & Publications:** Ultraviolet and infrared spectroscopy; thermal conduction and transfer; plasma physics; explosion phenomena; accelerator development; nuclear weapons effects; instrumentation. **Mailing Address:** 2620 Kanuga Pines Dr, Hendersonville, NC 28739.

KRATZ, LAWRENCE J, MATHEMATICS. **Education:** Univ Utah, PhD, 1976. **Professional Experience:** PROF, DEPT MATHS, IDAHO STATE UNIV, as of 2005. **Mailing Address:** Math Dept, Idaho State Univ, Pocatello, ID 83209-8085. **Fax:** 208-282-2636. **E-Mail:** KRATLAWR@ISU.EDU

KRATZ, LISA, GENETICS. **Education:** Western Md Col, BA, 1985; Univ Md, PhD (human genetics), 1989. **Professional Experience:** ASSOC DIR CLIN MASS SPECTROMETRY LAB, KENNEDY KRIEGER INST, as of 2005; RES ASSOC PEDIAT, JOHNS HOPKINS SCH MED, as of 2005. **Mailing Address:** Dept Neurogenetics Kennedy Krieger Inst, 707 N Broadway, Baltimore, MD 21205. **Fax:** 443-923-2781. **E-Mail:** kratz@kennedykrieger.org

KRATZEL, ROBERT JEFFREY, TRANSFUSION-TRANSMITTED INFECTIOUS DISEASES, MICROBILOGY, IMMUNOHEMATOLOGY. **Personal Data:** b New York, NY, February 5, 1949; m 1975, c 2. **Education:** Hofstra Univ, BA, 1971; State Univ NY, Buffalo, MA, 1973, PhD (microbiol), 1977, MBA, 1990. **Professional Experience:** DIR REGULATORY AFFAIRS, AVENTIS BIO-SERV, 1999-; clin asst prof, Dept Microbiol, State Univ NY, Buffalo, 1981-; sci dir buffalo region, Am Red Cross Blood Serv, 1981-1995; dir tech serv, Am Red Cross Blood Serv, 1978-1981; clin instr, Dept Microbiol, State Univ NY, Buffalo, 1977-1981; trainee lab med, Erie Co Lab, E J Meyer Mem Hosp, Buffalo, 1977; mem bd dir, Blood Bank Asn NY State Inc. **Memberships:** Am Asn Blood Banks; Am Soc Microbiol; Regulatory Affairs Prof Soc. **Research Statement & Publications:** The chemical characterization and localization of blood group antigens on blood and tissue cells; transfusion-transmitted infectious diseases. **Mailing Address:** 1505 E Woodbank Way, West Chester, PA 19380. **Fax:** 610-878-4742. **E-Mail:** robert.kratzel@aventis.com

KRATZER, D DAL, ANIMAL BREEDING, STATISTICS. **Personal Data:** b Amazonia, Mo, December 16, 1937; m 1963, c 2. **Education:** Univ Mo, BS, 1959; Iowa State Univ, MS, 1964, PhD (animal breeding), 1965. **Professional Experience:** BIOSTATISTICIAN, UPJOHN CO, 1978-; from asst prof to prof animal sci & statist, Univ Ky, 1968-1977; asst prof animal sci & comput sci, Iowa State Univ, 1965-1968; res assoc animal breeding & comput sci, Iowa State Univ, 1962-1965; asst animal breeding, Iowa State Univ, 1959-1962. **Memberships:** Am Soc Animal Sci; Biomet Soc. **Research Statement & Publications:** Behavior of domestic animals. **Mailing Address:** Upjohn Co, 5300 N 28th St, Richland, MI 49083.

KRATZER, FRANK HOWARD, NUTRITION. **Personal Data:** b Baldwinsville, NY, January 24, 1918; m 1946, c 3. **Education:** Cornell Univ, BS, 1940; Univ Calif, PhD (animal nutrit), 1944. **Honors & Awards:** Nat Turkey Fedn Res Award, 1949; Am Feed Mfrs Res Award, 1960; CPC Res Award, 1973. **Professional Experience:** EMER PROF ANIMAL SCI, COL AGR & ENVIRON SCI, UNIV CALIF, DAVIS, as of 2001; mem, Fed Univ Rio Grande do Sol, Porto Alegre, Brasil, 1982; chmn dept, Col Agr & Environ Sci, 1976-1981; vis prof, Univ Sydney, 1975-1976; guest prof, Justus Liebig Univ, Giessen, Ger, 1968-1969; NSF fel, Nat Inst Res Dairying, Reading, Eng, 1959-1960; from assoc prof to prof poultry husb, Col Agr & Environ Sci, 1949-1983; asst prof, Col Agr & Environ Sci, 1945-1949; assoc prof, Colo Agr & Mech Col, 1944-1945; res assoc, Univ Calif, 1943-1944; asst poultry husb, Univ Calif, 1940-1943. **Memberships:** Am Chem Soc; Soc Exp Biol & Med; fel Am Inst Nutrit; fel Poultry Sci Asn; Biochem Soc; fel Am Asn Adv Sci. **Research Statement & Publications:** Nutrition of poultry amino acid requirements of chickens and turkeys; vitamin needs and function; minerals and mineral availability; growth inhibitors. **Mailing Address:** Dept Animal Sci, Univ Calif, Davis, CA 95616. **Fax:** 530-752-8960. **E-Mail:** fhkratzer@ucdavis.edu

KRATZER, REINHOLD, polymer chemistry; deceased, see previous edition for last biography

KRATZKE, THOMAS MARTIN, STATISTICS, COMPUTER SCIENCE. **Personal Data:** b Seattle, Wash, October 29, 1953; m 1979, c 3. **Education:** Pac Lutheran Univ, BS, 1975; Wash State Univ, MA, 1978; Univ Ill, Urbana-Champaign, PhD (math), 1988. **Professional Experience:** ANALYST, METRON INC, 1988-; teaching & res asst, Math Dept, Univ Ill, 1982-1988; statistician, Rockwell Hanford Opers, 1980-1982; adv mem tech staff, Boeing Computer Serv, 1978-1980. **Memberships:** Soc Indust & Appl Math; Discrete Math Activ Group. **Research Statement & Publications:** Bayesian updating algorithm for use in anti-submarine warfare on different computers. **Mailing Address:** 2373 Old Trail Dr, Reston, VA 20191. **E-Mail:** kratzke@ilog.com

KRAUEL, DAVID PAUL, TURBULENT DIFFUSION, WIND-WAVE MODELLING. **Personal Data:** b Kitchener, Ont, November 20, 1944; m 1969, c 2. **Education:** McMaster Univ, BSc, 1966; DalhousieUniv, MSc, 1969; Liverpool Univ, PhD (phys oceanog), 1972. **Professional Experience:** DIR, INFO SERV & RESOURCES, ROYAL ROAD UNIV, as of 2005; assoc prof phys oceanog, Royal Roads Mil Col, beginning 1988; head, physics dept, Royal Roads Mil Col, 1981-1988; asst prof, Physics Dept, 1981-1988; assoc prof phys oceanog, Royal Roads Mil Col, 1974-1979; dean grad studies, dept physics, Royal Roads Univ, 1981-1988; CONSULT, 1979-; assoc prof phys oceanog, Royal Roads Mil Col, beginning 1979; res scientist coastal oceanog, Bedford Inst Oceanog, 1966-1974. **Memberships:** Am Geophys Union; Can Meteorol & Oceanog Soc; Estuarine & Brackish-Water Sci Asn. **Research Statement & Publications:** Modelling turbulent diffusion in coastal waters and wind-wave hindcast modelling; estuarine circulation; the effects of flux of wave energy on coastlines and coastal structures. **Mailing Address:** Royal Rds Univ, 2005 Sooke Rd, Victoria, BC V9B 5Y2, Can. **Fax:** 250-391-2594. **E-Mail:** david.krauel@royalroads.ca

KRAUS, ALFRED PAUL, MEDICINE. **Personal Data:** b Vienna, Austria, June 24, 1916; American citizen; m 1944, c 2. **Education:** Univ Chicago, MD, 1941. **Professional Experience:** PROF EMER MED, COL MED, UNIV TENN, MEMPHIS, 1981-; investr natural hist sickle cell dis, beginning 1979; dir, Ctr Res & Serv Sickle Cell Dis, 1974-1979; chief sect hemat, Univ Tenn, Memphis, 1964-1981; vis asst prof, Univ Indonesia, 1955-1956; consult hematologist, Baptist Mem Hosp, beginning 1953, Le Bonheur Children's Hosp, Methodist Hosp & St Joseph's Hosp; from asst prof to prof, Univ Tenn, Memphis, 1953-1981; asst chief, Kennedy Vet Admin Hosp, Tenn, 1950-1952; chief hemat sect, Vet Admin Hosp, Ala, 1949; resident dept hemat res, Michael Reese Hosp, Ill, 1948; asst resident & resident internal med, Michael Reese Hosp, Ill, 1942-1944; intern, Michael Reese Hosp, Ill, 1941-1942. **Memberships:** AAAS; Am Soc Hemat; fel AMA; fel Am Col Physicians; Am Fedn Clin Res. **Research Statement & Publications:** Hematology; sickle cell disease; abnormal hemoglobins; hemorrhagic diseases; red cell enzymes. **Mailing Address:** Univ Tenn, 920 Madison Ave, Ste 300, Memphis, TN 38103-3472. **Fax:** 901-448-5513.

KRAUS, ARTHUR SAMUEL, EPIDEMIOLOGY. **Personal Data:** b New York, NY, August 2, 1925; m 1946, c 3. **Education:** City Col NY, BS, 1949; Columbia Univ, MS, 1953. **Honorary Degrees:** DSc (biostatist), Univ Pittsburgh, 1958. **Professional Experience:** RETIRED; prof & coordr grad studies, Dept Community Health & Epidemiol, Queen Univ Ont, 1985-1990; consult biostatist, Ont Dept Health, beginning 1966; prof biostatist, Dept Community Health & Epidemiol, Queen Univ Ont, 1966-1985; head dept biostatist, Montefiore Hosp & Med Ctr, Bronx, NY, 1965-1966; asst dir, Off Res, NY Dept Health, 1962-1965; chief, Div Statist, Res & Rec, Md State Dept Health, 1958-1962; biostatistician, NY State Dept Health, 1950-1957. **Memberships:** Fel Am Pub Health Asn; Am Heart Asn; Can Pub Health Asn; Soc Epidemiol Res. **Research Statement & Publications:** Epidemiologic and health care studies, particularly regarding the elderly and conditions which are disabling to them, such as stroke, dementia, incontinence, deafness and depression. **Mailing Address:** 163 Casterton Ave, Kingston, ON K7M 1R9, Can.

KRAUS, ERIC BRADSHAW, ATMOSPHERE-OCEAN INTERACTION. **Personal Data:** b Liberec, Czech, March 22, 1913; m 1942, Heather; c Nigel, Sibella & Deborah. **Education:** Charles Univ, Prague, PhD (geophysics), 1946. **Honorary Degrees:** ScD, Univ Liege, Belg, 1992. **Honors & Awards:** Mem prize, Royal Meteorol Soc; fel AAAS. **Professional Experience:** India Nat Inst Oceanog Soc, Indian, 1988; at Univ Liege, Belgium, 1987; monash Univ, Melbourne, Australia, 1983; PROF EMER METEOROL & PHYS OCEANOG, UNIV MIAMI, 1981-; sr res assoc, Coop Inst Res Environ Sci, 1981-1989; vis prof, Paris, France, 1981; dir NATO Atmospheric Res Inst, Bonas, France, 1981; dir, Coop Inst Marine & Atmospheric Studies, 1977-1981; dir, NATO Atmospheric Studies Inst, Urbino Italy 1975; trustee, Univ Corp Atmospheric Res, 1974-1980; div Atmospheric Sci, Univ Miami, 1969-1977; prof, Univ Miami, 1966-1977; sr scientist, Woods Hole Oceanog Inst, 1961-1966; adj prof, Yale Univ, 1961-1963; mem panel water resources develop, World Meteorol Orgn, 1955-1956; chief, UN tech assistance mission, Nairobi, Kenya, 1955-1956; authority meteorologist, Snowy Mt, Hydro-Elec Authority, 1952-1961; convener sub-comt oceanog, 1952-1955; mem, Australian Nat Comt Geophys & Geod, 1949-1955; lectr, Univ Sydney, 1947-1951; sr res officer, Div Radiophysics, Commonwealth Sci & Indust Res Orgn, Australia, 1946-1949. **Memberships:** Fel Am Meteorol Soc; Am Geophys Union; fel Royal Meteorol Soc; fel AAAS. **Research Statement & Publications:** Symmetry Breaks and resulting progressive growth of Organized Diversity; author of 200 papers and several books on Atmosphere-Ocean Interaction and Climate; coberent structures in fluids. **Mailing Address:** Dept Metrol, Miami Univ, 610 Orchard St, Ashland, OR 97520. **E-Mail:** ebkraus@cs.com

KRAUS, GEORGE ANDREW, ORGANIC CHEMISTRY. **Personal Data:** b Buffalo, NY, June 28, 1950; m 1985, c 2. **Education:** Univ Rochester, BS, 1972; Columbia Univ, PhD (chem), 1976. **Honors & Awards:** DuPont Young Faculty Award, 1976; 3M Young Faculty Award, 1981; Frasch Award, 1987. **Professional Experience:** CHMN DEPT, DEPT CHEM, IOWA STATE UNIV, 1993-; PROF, DEPT CHEM, IOWA STATE UNIV, 1986-; 3M Young Fac grant, 1981-1982; from asst prof to assoc prof, Dept Chem, Iowa State Univ, 1976-1986; DuPont young fac grant, 1976-1978. **Memberships:** AAAS; Am Chem Soc; fel The Chem Soc; fel Alfred P. Sloan Found. **Research Statement & Publications:** Active in the development of new synthetic methods and the application of these methods to the total synthesis of natural products; interests include kinetic anions, photochemistry and thermal chemistry; research on antiprotozoan diseases, suicide enzyme inhibitors and antiretroviral drugs; author of 147 publications. **Mailing Address:** Dept Chem, Iowa State Univ, 1605 Gilman Hall, Ames, IA 50011-3111. **Fax:** 515-294-0105. **E-Mail:** gakraus@iastate.edu

KRAUS, JAN P, PEDIATRICS. **Education:** Basel Univ, PhD, 1972. **Professional Experience:** PROF PEDIAT / CELL & DEVELOP BIOL, UNIV COLO HEALTH SCI CTR, as of 2005. **Mailing Address:** Dept Pediat Univ Colo Health Sci Ctr, RC1-N C-233 Rm 4128 PO Box 6511, Aurora, CO 80045. **E-Mail:** jan.kraus@uchsc.edu

KRAUS, JESS F, EPIDEMIOLOGY, ENVIRONMENTAL HEALTH. **Personal Data:** b Los Angeles, Calif, April 4, 1936; m 1957, c 5. **Education:** Sacramento State Col, BA, 1959, MS, 1963; Univ Calif, Berkeley, MPH (occuptional health) 1964; Univ Minn, Minneapolis, PhD (environ epidemiol), 1967. **Professional Experience:** PROF EPIDEMIOL, UNIV CALIF, LOS ANGELES, as of 2005; DIR, SOUTHERN CALIF INJURY PREV RES CTR, UNIV CALIF, LOS ANGELES, as of 2005; prof, Sch Med, Univ Calif, Davis, beginning 1980; from asst prof to assoc prof community health, Sch Med, Univ Calif, Davis, 1969-1980; epidemiologist, Bur Environ Mgt, 1969-1971; adj asst prof, Univ Cincinnati, 1968-1969; chief environ epidemiol, USPHS, 1968-1969; instr epidemiol & environ health, Univ Minn, 1967-1968. **Memberships:** fel coun epidemiol; Am Heart Asn; Am Pub Health Asn; Soc Epidemiol Res; Asn Teachers Prev Med. **Research Statement & Publications:** Design and execution of community and epidemiologic research involving the interrelationship of man with his physical environment. **Mailing Address:** Dept Epidemiol Univ Calif, 10911 Weyburn Ave Ste 200, Los Angeles, CA 90024-2884. **Fax:** 310-206-6039, 310-794-7989. **E-Mail:** jfkraus@ucla.edu

KRAUS, JOHN DANIEL, electrical engineering, astronomy; deceased, see previous edition for last biography

KRAUS, JOHN FRANKLYN, FOREST GENETICS. **Personal Data:** b Brooklyn, NY, November 12, 1929; m 1957, Jeanie A Bell; c John II, Brenda, Rachel, Erica & Kirstin. **Education:** Univ Mich, BSF, 1953, MF, 1956; Univ Minn, PhD (forestry), 1966. **Professional Experience:** RETIRED; plant geneticist, Ga Forestry Ctr, 1972-1986; plant geneticist, Southeastern Forest Exp Sta, US Forest Serv, 1964-1972; Res forester, Southeastern Forest Exp Sta, US Forest Serv, 1956-1964. **Memberships:** AAAS; Soc Am Foresters; Sigma Xi. **Research Statement & Publications:** Breeding improved strains of southern pines. **Mailing Address:** 1211 Timberlane Dr, Macon, GA 31210.

KRAUS, JON ERIC, FUNCTIONAL ANALYSIS, OPERATOR ALGEBRAS. **Personal Data:** b Cambridge, Mass, May 16, 1951; m 1977, Veronica; c Rebecca & Jeffrey. **Education:** Univ Calif, Santa Barbara, BA, 1972; Univ Calif, Berkeley, MA, 1975, PhD (math), 1977. **Professional Experience:** PROF MATH, STATE UNIV NY, BUFFALO, 1995-; from asst prof to assoc prof, 1979-1995; Hill res instr, 1977-1979. **Memberships:** Am Math Soc. **Research Statement & Publications:** Operator algebras including von Neumann, C-algebras and reflexive algebras. **Mailing Address:** Dept Math, State Univ NY, 244 Math Bldg, Buffalo, NY 14260-2900. **E-Mail:** mthjek@acsu.buffalo.edu

KRAUS, KENNETH WAYNE, ORGANIC CHEMISTRY. **Personal Data:** b Waterloo, Iowa, October 20, 1935; m 1956, c 4. **Education:** Loras Col, BS, 1957; Univ Calif, Berkeley, PhD (chem), 1960. **Professional Experience:** PROF EMER CHEM, LORAS COL, as of 2004; VPRES ACAD AFFAIRS, 1987-; prof chem, Loras Col, 1972-; lectr, Dept Chem, Calif State Col Long Beach, 1969-1970; chmn dept, Loras Col, 72- Vpres Acad Affairs, 1965-1969 & 1970-1971; NSF grant, 1964-1966; From asst prof to assoc prof, Loras Col, 72- Vpres Acad Affairs, 1960-1972. **Memberships:** Am Chem Soc. **Research Statement & Publications:** Mechanism and use of the reaction of organocadmium reagents with acid chlorides, dipole moments, syntheses and structure proof. **Mailing Address:** Dept Chem, Loras Col, Dubuque, IA 52001-4399. **E-Mail:** kenneth.kraus@loras.edu

KRAUS, LORRAINE MARQUARDT, biochemistry; deceased, see previous edition for last biography

KRAUS, SAMUEL, AEROTHERMODYNAMICS, FLUID MECHANICS. **Personal Data:** b Irvington, NJ, March 15, 1925; m 1954, Joan; c Barbara D, Edward O & Russell A. **Education:** Rensselaer Polytech Inst, BAeroEng, 1944, MAeroEng, 1949. **Professional Experience:** RETIRED; prin eng specialist, gas dynamics, shuttle aerodyn, aero sci, Space Transp Systs Div, Rockwell Int Corp, 1985-1990; mem tech staff, Shuttle Aerodynamic Loads, 1969-1985; lead engr, Shuttle Aerodynamic Loads, beginning 1969; lead engr, S-II aerothermodynamics, 1967-1969; res specialist, Space Div, 1962-1967; aeronaut res engr, Ames Res Ctr, NASA, 1949-1962; jr engr preliminary aeronaut design, Propeller Div, Curtiss-Wright Corp, 1946-1947. **Memberships:** Assoc fel Am Inst Aeronaut & Astronaut; Sigma Xi. **Research Statement & Publications:** Experimental and theoretical research in aerothermodynamics; planning, development and utilization of corporate experimental facilities; preflight prediction and postflight verification of aerospace vehicle environment; ignition overpressure; wake recirculation; venting; free molecular flow forces. **Mailing Address:** 6108 Monero Dr, Rancho Palos Verdes, CA 90275-3319.

KRAUS, SHIRLEY RUTH, CLINICAL PHARMACOLOGY. **Personal Data:** b New York, NY, December 24, 1919; m 1946, c 2. **Education:** Hunter Col, BA, 1940; Cornell Univ, MA, 1942; Univ Ill, PhD (physiol), 1946. **Honorary Degrees:** DSc, Arnold & Marie Schwartz Col Pharm & Health Sci, Long Island Univ, 1996. **Professional Experience:** DISTINGUISHED RESEARCHER, LONG ISLAND UNIV, as of 2002; vis prof physiol & pharmacol, NY Col Pediat Med, 1983-1984; prof pharmacol & physiol, Long Island Univ, as of 1982; mem, Instnl Rev Bd, Clin Drug Investr Inc, 1981; dir, Div Pharmacotherapeut & Health Sci, 1979-1982; vis fel clin pharmacol, Med Col, Cornell Univ, 1977-1978; prof pharmacol & physiol, Long Island Univ, prof, Brooklyn Col Pharm, 1975-1982; assoc prof, Downstate Med Ctr, State Univ NY, 1969-1970; assoc prof pharmacol, Long Island Univ, prof, Brooklyn Col Pharm, 1965-1975; instr pharmacol, Sch Med, Howard Univ, 1955-1956; pharmacologist, Cancer Res & Metab Unit, Mt Alto Hosp, Wash, DC, 1951-1953; lectr physiol, Col Dent, NY Univ, 1950-1951; biochemist, Cancer Res Found, Harlem Hosp, 1948-1950; physiologist, Gastroenterol Res Lab, Mt Sinai Hosp, 1947-1948; Instr, Eve Sch, Brooklyn Col, 1947-1948; high sch teacher, 1946-1947; asst, Dept Zool & Physiol, Univ Ill, 1943-1946; instr, Sch Nursing, 1943; asst biol & chem, Adelphi Col, 1942-1943; hematologist, Jewish Mem Hosp, 1941; Asst, Dept Exp Biol, Am Mus Natural Hist, NY, 1940-1941. **Memberships:** Soc Exp Biol & Med; Endocrine Soc; Am Physiol Soc; Am Soc Pharmacol & Exp Therapeut; Am Soc Clin Pharmacol & Therepeut; fel Am Col Clin Pharmacol. **Research Statement & Publications:** Alloxan diabetes-anaphylaxis and granuloma pouch formation; pituitary-adrenal stress response in alloxan diabetes; anti-estrogenic action of B glycyrrhetinic acid; hyperthermia on blood platelets in male rats; corticosterone and adrenocorticotropic hormone in alloxan diabetic rats. **Mailing Address:** 13901 Coolidge Ave, Jamaica, NY 11435. **Fax:** 718-261-9589.

KRAUSCHE, DOLORES SMOLENY, PHYSICS, ELECTRICAL ENGINEERING. **Personal Data:** b Cleveland, Ohio, January 27, 1942. **Education:** Univ Fla, BS, 1965, MS, 1967, BSEE, 1967, PhD (physics, astron), 1975. **Professional Experience:** PROG DIR, FLA CTR ENG EDUC, as of 2002; prin staff mem, Oper Res Inc, 1978-; RES PHYSICIST, UNIV FLA, 1978-; fel physics, Univ Fla, 1976-1977; interim engr, Electronic Commun Inc, 1967; res asst radioastron, Univ Fla, 1965-1975. **Memberships:** Am Astron Soc; Sigma Xi; Inst Atmospheric Optics & Remote Sensing. **Research Statement & Publications:** Electromagnetic phenomena relating to engineering problems and astronomical research. **Mailing Address:** Fla Ctr Eng Educ, PO Box 271, Gainesville, FL 32602-0271. **E-Mail:** dsk@atlantic.net

KRAUSE, BRIAN ROBERT, MEDICAL RESEARCH. **Personal Data:** b December 2, 1949; m 1976, Lisa; c Christopher, Matthew & Kara. **Education:** Univ Ill, BS, 1972; La State Univ Med Ctr, PhD, 1978. **Honors & Awards:** Am Soc Pharmacol & Exp Therapeut; Am Physiol Soc; Am Heart Asn Coun Aerteriosclerosis. **Professional Experience:** SR VPRES, PRECLIN RES & DISCOVERY, ESPERION THERAPEUT INC, 2003-; assoc res fel pharmacol, Warner Lambert/Parke-Davis, beginning 1990; sr res assoc, Warner Lambert/Parke-Davis, 1989-1990; res assoc, Warner Lambert/Parke-Davis, 1985-1989; sr scientist athero-pharmacol, Warner Lambert/Parke-Davis, 1982-1985; asst prof physiol, La State Univ Med Ctr, 1981-1982; res fel, NIH, 1979-1981; trainee physiol, La State Univ Med Ctr, 1976-1979; trainee pharmacol, Univ Ill Med Ctr, 1975-1976; teaching asst, Univ Ill Med Ctr, 1973-1975. **Research Statement & Publications:** Lipoprotein metabolism. **Mailing Address:** Esperion Therapeut Inc, Ann Arbor, MI 48103.

KRAUSE, DANIEL, CHEMICAL OCEANOGRAPHY. **Personal Data:** b Sudbury, Mass, February 21, 1945; m 1975. **Education:** Univ Mass, BS, 1966, PhD (physics), 1972. **Professional Experience:** RES ASSOC OCEANOG, AMHERST COL, 1972-. **Memberships:** Sigma Xi; Am Phys Soc; Am Geophys Union. **Research Statement & Publications:** Mass spectrometric and gasometric studies of gases dissolved in water. **Mailing Address:** 734 Bay Rd, Amherst, MA 01002-3544.

KRAUSE, DAVID WILFRED, ANATOMY. **Personal Data:** b Medicine Hat, Alta, February 15, 1950; m 1978, Susan; c Wyatt M & Tyler M. **Education:** Univ Alta, BSc, 1971, MSc, 1976; Univ Mich, PhD (geol), 1982. **Honors & Awards:** Anna M Jackson Award, Am Soc Mammalogists, 1981. **Professional Experience:** DISTINGUISHED SERV PROF, STONY BROOK UNIV, as of 2004; PROF ANAT, STATE UNIV NY, STONY BROOK, 1993-; Res assoc, Mus Rockies, Bozeman, Mont, 1985-; from asst prof to assoc prof, State Univ NY, Stony Brook, 1982-1993. **Memberships:** Am Soc Mammalogists; Paleont Soc; Sigma Xi; Soc Syst Zool; Soc Vert Paleont (vpres, 1992-1994, pres, 1994-1996); AAAS. **Research Statement & Publications:** Evolution of late Mesozoic and early Cenozoic vertebrates, particularly mammals, and the form and function of the mammalian dentition and postcranial skelton; biogeography of Madagascar fauna. **Mailing Address:** Dept Anat Sci, Stony Brook Univ Sch Med, 100 Nicholls Rd, Stony Brook, NY 11794-0001. **Fax:** 516-444-3947. **E-Mail:** david.krause@stonybrook.edu

KRAUSE, DUNCAN C, MICROBIOLOGY. **Education:** Auburn Univ, BS, 1978; Univ NC, PhD (Microbiol), 1982. **Professional Experience:** HEAD, DEPT MICROBIOL, UNIV GA, 2000-; PROF, DEPT MICROBIOL, UNIV GA, 1996-; from asst to assoc prof, Univ Ga, 1985-1991; Univ S Ala, 1983-1985; grad res asst, Univ Tex Health Sci Ctr, San Antonio, 1981-1982; grad res asst, Univ NC, 1978-1980. **Research Statement & Publications:** Molecular aspects of host - parasite interactions, focusing on mycoplasma pneumoniae; bacteriology; cell cycle; communicable diseases; cytoskeleton; gene cloning; gene regulation; infectious diseases or agents; microbiology; pathogenesis; proteins and macromolecules; respiratory diseases. **Mailing Address:** Dept Microbiol, Univ Ga, 523 Bioll Sci Bldg, Athens, GA 30602. **Fax:** 706-542-2674. **E-Mail:** dkrause@uga.edu

KRAUSE, ELIOT, POPULATION GENETICS, BIOSTATISTICS. **Personal Data:** b New York, NY, June 7, 1938; m 1959, c 3. **Education:** Cornell Univ, BS, 1960; Purdue Univ, MS, 1963, PhD (genetics), 1968. **Professional Experience:** Dept chmn, Seton Hall Univ, 1988-1989; grad biol adv, Seton Hall Univ, 1977-1988; ASST PROF BIOL, SETON HALL UNIV, 1968-; instr, Seton Hall Univ, 1965-1968; res asst pop genetics, Purdue Univ, 1960-1965. **Memberships:** AAAS; Genetics Soc Am; Biomet Soc; Am Genetic Asn; Sigma Xi. **Research Statement & Publications:** Cytogenetic research with various mutagens using human lymphocytes as detected by sister chromatic exchange; selection of quantitative traits in Tribolium castaneum using genotype-environment, nutrition, interactions; study of cannibalism and competitive factors which affect population size in Tribolium; study of fragile sites in cytogenetics. **Mailing Address:** Dept Biol, Seton Hall Univ, Rm 309c McNulty Hall, South Orange, NJ 07079. **E-Mail:** krauseel@shu.edu

KRAUSE, EUGENE FRANKLIN, MATHEMATICS. **Personal Data:** b Kenosha, Wis, April 7, 1937; m Jane; c Edward & Thomas. **Education:** Univ Wis, BS, 1959, MA, 1960, PhD (math), 1963. **Honors & Awards:** Fulbright Prof, 1993. **Professional Experience:** PROF EMER, MATH, UNIV MICH, ANN ARBOR, as of 2005; prof math, Univ Mich, Ann Arbor, 1976-2002; from instr to assoc prof, Univ Mich, 1963-1976. **Memberships:** Nat Coun Teachers Math. **Research Statement & Publications:** Mathematics education. **Mailing Address:** Dept Math, Univ Mich Main Campus, Ann Arbor, MI 48109. **E-Mail:** krause@umich.edu

KRAUSE, HELMUT G L, LOW DENSITY AERODYNAMICS, THERMODYNAMICS. **Personal Data:** b Koenigsberg, Ger, November 10, 1911; American citizen; m 1955, c 1. **Education:** Albertus Univ, Ger, PhD (astron), 1938. **Honors & Awards:** Ernst Heinckel Space Flight Award, 1951. **Professional Experience:** RETIRED; aerospace scientist, Marshall Space Flight Ctr, NASA, 1978-1989; mgr bur anal res, 1975-1978; sci adv to dir aero-astrodyn lab, Marshall Space Flight Ctr, NASA, 1965-1974; sci adv studies off, Marshall Space Flight Ctr, NASA, 1960-1965; spec asst space sci, Army Ballistic Missile Agency, Ala, 1957-1960; sr res scientist, Res Inst Physics Jet Propulsion, 1954-1957; dep chief, Astronaut Res Inst, Univ Stuttgart, 1951-1954; tech physicist, Glycerine & Aliphatic Acid Factory, 1949-1950; sci res asst, Hamburg Univ Observ, 1947-1948; sci res asst, Inst Theoret Physics, Univ Jena, 1947; res scientist, Carl Zeiss Optical Factory, 1945-1947; res scientist Inst Ballistics, Ger Air Force Acad, 1944-1945; sci res asst, Koenigsberg Univ Observ, 1937-1944. **Memberships:** Am Inst Aeronaut & Astronaut; Am Astronaut Soc; Am Astron Soc; fel Brit Interplanetary Soc; Ger Soc Rocket & Space Flight. **Research Statement & Publications:** Rocket ballistics, space mechanics and astronautical sciences; first-order perturbation theory used for Explorer; author and coauthor of 50 scientific publications. **Mailing Address:** 2718 Briarwood Dr, Huntsville, AL 35801.

KRAUSE, HERBERT FRANCIS, ATOMIC PHYSICS, CHEMICAL PHYSICS, LASER PHYSICS. **Personal Data:** b Woodbury, NJ, March 10, 1942; m 1970, Carolyn; c Stephen A & Diane E. **Education:** Drexel Univ, BS, 1965; Univ Pittsburgh, PhD (physics), 1971. **Professional Experience:** SR RES PHYSICIST, OAK RIDGE NAT LAB, 1971-; Pvt computer consult. **Memberships:** Am Phys Soc; Am Asn Physics Teachers; AAAS; Sigma Xi. **Research Statement & Publications:** Atomic and molecular beam research; thermal-high energies, laser spectroscopy; molecular dynamics studies involving inner and outer shell excited species; high energy and ultra-relativistic atomic physics and particle solid interactions; low-energy ion-surface interactions; computerized data acquisition and control. **Mailing Address:** Physics Div, Oak Ridge Nat Lab, Rm 208, Bldg 6000, MS 6372, Oak Ridge, TN 37830. **Fax:** 865-574-4211. **E-Mail:** krause@mail.phy.ornl.gov

KRAUSE, HORATIO HENRY, analytical chemistry; deceased, see previous edition for last biography

KRAUSE, IRVIN, MECHANICAL ENGINEERING. **Personal Data:** b New York, NY, July 18, 1932; m 1953, c 3. **Education:** City Col NY, BS, 1954; Columbia Univ, MS, 1955; NY Univ, DSc (mech eng), 1960. **Professional Experience:** RETIRED; managing partner, Ctr Mfg Technol, Coopers & Lybrand, beginning 1986; vpres, Meritus Consult Serv, Comput Integrated Mfg, 1985-1986; dir, Comput Integrated Mfg, 1985-1986; tech dir, Comput Integrated Mfg, 1981-1985; mgr, Mfg Technol, Arthur D Little, Inc, 1978-1981; dir eng, Acushnet Co, 1976-1978; mgr eng, Indust Prod Div, 1970-1976; chief res & develop, Diehl Div, Singer Co, 1966-1970; consult, Army Res Off NC, 1964-; assoc prof mech eng & dir mat labs, Fairleign Dickinson Univ, 1963-1966; res scientist, Res Div, Am-Standard Corp, 1960-1963; asst mech eng, NY Univ, 1959-1960; NSF fel, 1959; lectr graphics, City Col New York, 1954-1959. **Memberships:** AAAS; Am Soc Mech Engrs; Sigma Xi; Soc Mfg Engrs. **Research Statement & Publications:** Visco-elastic behavior of polymeric materials; fracture in brittle materials; kinematics and mechanism synthesis; tunnel diode accelerometers; laser system metrology; electric motors and controls; automated production systems; computerization and automation as applied to the design and manufacturing activities in industry; benchmarking research and development productivity. **Mailing Address:** One Seaward Lane, S Dartmouth, MA 02748.

KRAUSE, JOSEF GERALD, ORGANIC CHEMISTRY. **Personal Data:** b Kearny, NJ, March 21, 1942; m 1963, c 2. **Education:** Hobart Col, BS, 1963; Northeastern Univ, PhD (org chem), 1967. **Professional Experience:** PROF CHEM, NIAGARA UNIV, 1968-;

sigma xi res grant-in-aid, Niagara Univ, 1968-1969; NSF res fel org chem, Univ Mass, 1967-1968. **Memberships:** Am Chem Soc. **Research Statement & Publications:** Organic nitrogen compounds; organic synthesis; reaction mechanisms; bicyclic ring systems. **Mailing Address:** Dept Chem Niagara Univ, DePaul Hall Sci Bldg, Niagara Falls, NY 14109. **Fax:** 716-286-8254. **E-Mail:** jkrause@niagara.edu

KRAUSE, KURT L, BIOCHEMISTRY. **Education:** Trinity Univ, BA, 1977; Baylor Col Med, MD cum laude, 1980; Harvard Univ, MA, 1983, PhD (chem), 1986. **Professional Experience:** ASSOC PROF BIOCHEM & BIOPHYS SCI, UNIV HOUSTON, as of 2006; ASSOC DIR, INST MOLECULAR DESIGN, as of 1998; ASST PROF MED, SECT INFECTIOUS DIS, BAYLOR COL MED, as of 1998. **Mailing Address:** Dept Biochem Sci Univ Houston, HSC 466, Houston, TX 77204-5001. **E-Mail:** kkrause@uh.edu

KRAUSE, LLOYD O(SCAR), ELECTRICAL ENGINEERING. **Personal Data:** b Hamburg, Wis, October 23, 1918; m 1942, c 2. **Education:** Rose-Hulman Inst Technol, BS, 1940; Syracuse Univ, MEE, 1964, PhD (elec eng), 1966. **Honors & Awards:** Coffin Award, Gen Elec Co, 1953 engr of the year, 1987; Rockwell Int Life fel, IEEE 1994 Put latest first, and so on. **Professional Experience:** PRIN ENG SPECIALIST, SATELLITE SYSTS DIV, ROCKWELL INT CORP, 1984-; systs analyst, Space Div, 1976-1984; tech adv, Autonetics Div, NAm Rockwell Corp, 1967-1976; consult engr, Electronics Lab, 1963-1967; mgr elec eng, Gen Elec Co, 1953-1963; asst sect engr, Gen Elec Co, 1952-1953; proj engr, Gen Elec Co, 1947-1952; develop engr, Gen Elec Co, 1943-1947; prog engr, Gen Elec Co, 1941-1943; Test engr, Gen Elec Co, 1940-1941. **Memberships:** Sigma Xi; Electronic Industs Asn; Inst Elec & Electronics Engrs; Nat Soc Prof Engrs. **Research Statement & Publications:** Radio frequency and microwave radiators; antennas; transmission lines and networks; solid state microwave; paramagnetic amplifiers; phase shifters; switches; ferrites; ferroelectrics; ground screens; electronic systems; computer reliability; correlation loops; low angle radiation; satellite sensors; navigation error analysis; adaptive arrays and noise filtering; coding and data compression; probability estimation and system simulation. **Mailing Address:** 4015 Topside Lane, Corona Del Mar, CA 92625.

KRAUSE, LUCJAN, PHYSICS, ATOMIC & MOLECULAR COLLISIONS & SPECTROSCOPY. **Personal Data:** b Poznan, Poland, January 8, 1928; Canadian citizen; m 1950, c 6. **Education:** Univ London, BSc, 1951, DSc(physics), 1968; Univ Toronto, MA, 1953, PhD (physics), 1955. **Honorary Degrees:** DSc, Copernicus Univ, Torun, Poland, 1983. **Professional Experience:** PROF EMER PHYSICS, UNIV WINDSOR, 1993-; res fel, Japan Soc Promotion Sci, 1988; adj prof eng sci, Wayne State Univ, Detroit, 1972-1985; Hon res fel, Univ Col, Univ London, 1970-1971; prof, Univ Windsor, 1963-1993; head dept, Univ Windsor, 1959-1983; assoc prof physics, Mem Univ, 1955-1958 & Assumption Univ, 1958-1963; fel, Churchill Col, Cambridge. **Memberships:** Fel Am Phys Soc; Can Asn Physicists; fel Brit Inst Physics; Optical Soc Am. **Research Statement & Publications:** Laser spectroscopy of atoms and molecules; sensitized fluorescence and quenching, lifetimes of excited atomic and molecular states particularly metal excimers and exciplexes. **Mailing Address:** Dept Physics, Col Eng & Sci, Univ Windsor, Rm 288-3 Essex Hall N, Windsor, ON N9B 3P4, Can. **Fax:** 519-973-7075. **E-Mail:** f34@uwindsor.ca

KRAUSE, MANFRED OTTO, ATOMIC PHYSICS, CHEMICAL PHYSICS. **Personal Data:** b Stuttgart, Ger, March 11, 1931; American citizen; m 2001, C Denise Caldwell. **Education:** Univ Stuttgart, dipl phys, 1957; Max Planck Inst, Dr rer nat, 1960. **Honors & Awards:** Alexander Von Homboldt Prize, 1975. **Professional Experience:** EMER SCIENTIST ELECTRON SPECTROMETRY, OAK RIDGE NAT LAB, 1995-; Alexander von Humboldt awardee, Stiftung, Ger, 1975-1976; Exchange prof, Lab Curie, Paris France, 1975; sr scientist, Oak Ridge Nat Lab, 1963-1995; sr scientist mass spectrometry, William H Johnston Lab, Inc, Md, 1960-1963. **Memberships:** AAAS; Sigma Xi; fel Am Phys Soc. **Research Statement & Publications:** Transuranic chemistry; electron spectrometry; x-ray analysis; photoionization; atomic and molecular sci. **Mailing Address:** 125 Baltimore Dr, Oak Ridge, TN 37830. **E-Mail:** mok@ornl.gov

KRAUSE, MARGARIDA OLIVEIRA, CELL BIOLOGY, GENETICS. **Personal Data:** b Lisbon, Port, January 13, 1931; Canadian citizen; m 1956, Helmut; c Henry M, George A & Edward A. **Education:** Univ Lisbon, BSc, 1953; Univ Wis, MSc, 1957, PhD (cell biol), 1960. **Professional Experience:** Nat Sci & Eng Res Coun Can, 1978-1994 & Fed Centres Excellence Prog in Insect Biotech Network, 1990-1994; Res grants, Cancer Res Soc Inc, 1988-1990; co-chmn, Prog Comt Int Congress Cell Biol, 1988; exchange scientists, Int Prog, Nat Res Coun, 1984-1987; chmn, Can Nat Comt Int Union Biol Soc, 1983-1986; mem int sci & technol affairs, Can Nat Comt Int Union Biol Soc, 1981-1987; mem, Nat Sci & Eng Res Coun Can grant selection comts, 1980-1986; mem, Can Nat Comt Int Union Biol Soc, 1980-1983; PROF CELL BIOL, UNIV NB, 1976-; Res grants, Nat Cancer Inst Can, 1976-1979 & 1984-1987; assoc prof, Univ Nb, 1970-1976; Res grants, Nat Res Coun Can, 1967-1978; res assoc, Univ Nb, 1966-1970; Res grants, Banting Res Found, 1965 & 1967; Res grants, Med Res Coun Can, 1965-1966; Res assoc cell biol, Univ Wis, 1960-1961 & Univ Toronto, 1963-1966. **Memberships:** Biol Coun Can; Am Soc Cell Biol; Can Soc Cell Biol (pres, 1984-1986); Int Cell Cycle Soc. **Research Statement & Publications:** Role of chromosomal proteins and small nuclear RNA in gene expression; c-myc promoter utilization in transformation; baculovirus-based insecticides. **Mailing Address:** Dept Biol, Univ NB, Fredericton, NB E3B 6E1, Can. **Fax:** 506-453-3583. **E-Mail:** mkrause@unb.ca

KRAUSE, PAUL CARL, JR, ELECTRICAL ENGINEERING. **Personal Data:** b Reynolds, Nebr, January 27, 1932; m 1953, c 4. **Education:** Univ Nebr, BS, 1956 & 1957, MS, 1958; Univ Kans, PhD (elec eng), 1961. **Professional Experience:** Inst Elec & Electronics Engrs fel, 1977; PROF ELEC ENG, PURDUE UNIV, 1970-; vis prof, Univ Kans, 1967-1969; assoc prof, Univ Wis-Madison, 1965-1970; Consult, Allis-Chalmers Mfg Co, 1963-1966; asst prof elec eng, Univ Wis-Milwaukee, 1962-1965; res elec engr, Allis-Chalmers Mfg Co, 1961-1962; Instr elec eng, Univ Kans, 1958-1961. **Memberships:** Sr mem Inst Elec & Electronics Engrs; Am Soc Eng Educ. **Research Statement & Publications:** Electric machines, power systems and control systems; hybrid computer applications in analysis of systems. **Mailing Address:** Dept Elec Eng, Sch Elec & Comp Eng, Purdue Univ, West Lafayette, IN 47907-1285. **Fax:** 765-494-6640. **E-Mail:** krause@ecn.purdue.edu

KRAUSE, PAUL FREDERICK, PHYSICAL CHEMISTRY. **Personal Data:** b Racine, Wis, July 30, 1945; m 1970, c 1. **Education:** Dubuque Univ, BS, 1967; Univ Iowa, PhD (chem), 1972. **Professional Experience:** PROF CHEM, UNIV CENT ARK, as of 2005; from asst prof to assoc prof chem, Univ Cent Ark, 1977-1999; teaching fel & vis asst prof chem, Miami Univ, 1974-1977; instr, Miami Univ, 1974; res assoc, Miami Univ, 1973-1974; res assoc, Univ Pittsburgh, 1972-1973; res asst chem, Univ Iowa, 1968-1972. **Memberships:** Sigma Xil; Am Chem Soc. **Research Statement & Publications:** Molecular spectroscopy and its use for structural considerations, particularly in the solid state. **Mailing Address:** Dept Chem, Univ Cent Ark, Rm 201C, Laney Hall, Conway, AR 72035. **Fax:** 501-450-3623. **E-Mail:** paulk@uca.edu

KRAUSE, PETER JAMES, PEDIATRICS, PEDIATRIC INFECTIOUS DISEASES. **Personal Data:** b Denver, Colo, March 17, 1945; m, c 3. **Education:** Williams Col, BA, 1967; Tufts Univ Sch Med, MD, 1971. **Professional Experience:** DIR, PEDIAT INFECTIOUS DIS, CONN CHILDRENS MED CTR, SCH MED, UNIV CONN, 1998-; PROF PEDIAT, CONN CHILDRENS MED CTR, SCH MED, UNIV CONN, 1991-; chief pediat infectious dis, Hartford Hosp, Sch Med, Univ Conn, 1979- 1996; from asst prof to assocprof pediat, Hartford Hosp, Sch Med, Univ Conn, 1979-1991; res fel pediat infectious dis, Med Ctr, Univ Calif, Los Angeles, 1976-1979; physician pediat, US Army, Bad Kreuznach, WGer, 1974-1976; resident pediat, Med Ctr, Stanford Univ, 1973-1974; Intern/resident pediat, New Haven Hosp, Yale Univ, 1971-1973. **Memberships:** Am Soc Microbiol; fel Infectious Dis Soc Am; Am Fedn Clin Res; Sigma Xi; AAAS. **Research Statement & Publications:** Dr. Krause's research interests focus on the epidemiology, pathogenesis, and clinical outcome of Ixodes tick-borne infections. **Mailing Address:** Dept Pediat, Conn Childrens Med Ctr, Hartford, CT 06106. **Fax:** 860-545-9371. **E-Mail:** pkrause@ccmckids.org

KRAUSE, RALPH M, MATHEMATICS. **Personal Data:** b New York, NY, November 23, 1931; m 1960, Marianne Schuelein; c Peter & Steven. **Education:** Harvard Univ, BA, 1953, MA, 1954, PhD (math), 1959. **Professional Experience:** Prog dir, NSF, beginning 1962; asst prof math, Univ Ill, 1958-1960 & Ill Inst Technol, 1960-1962. **Memberships:** Am Math Soc; Math Asn Am. **Research Statement & Publications:** Topology. **Mailing Address:** Topology & Foundations NSF, 4201 Wilson Blvd, Arlington, VA 22230. **E-Mail:** rkrause@nsf.gov

KRAUSE, RICHARD MICHAEL, MICROBIOLOGY, IMMUNOLOGY. **Personal Data:** b Marietta, Ohio, January 4, 1925. **Education:** Marietta Col, AB, 1947; Case Western Res Univ, MD, 1952. **Honorary Degrees:** DSc, Marietta Col, 1978, Sch Med & Dent, Univ Rochester, 1979, Med Col Ohio, 1981, Hahnemann Med Col & Hosp, 1982; LLD, Thomas Jefferson Univ, 1982. **Honors & Awards:** Robert Koch Gold Medal, 1984; Humboldt Award, 1986. **Professional Experience:** SR SCI ADV, FOGARTY INT CTR, NIH, BETHESDA, MD, 1989-; chmn, Middle East Res Prog, Inst Med, 1989; Woodruff prof med & dean, Sch Med, Emory Univ, 1984-1989; chmn, Bd Int Health, Inst Med, Nat Acad Sci, 1984-1988; consult & mem, Coccal Expert Comt, WHO, 1967- & mem steering comt, Biomed Sci Working Group, 1978-1983; asst surgeon gen, Nat Inst Allergy & Infectious Dis, 1977-1984; adj prof, Univ Hosp, Rockefeller Univ, 1975-; dir, Nat Inst Allergy & Infectious Dis, 1975-1984; treas, Royal Soc Med Found, Inc, 1973-1975; mem bd dirs, Royal Soc Med Found, Inc, 1971-1977; mem, Infectious Dis Adv Comt, Nat Inst Allergy & Infectious Dis, 1970-1974; mem bd dirs, NY Heart Asn, 1967-1973; from assoc prof to prof microbiol & immunol & sr physician, Univ Hosp, Rockefeller Univ, 1966-1975; chmn, Allergy & Immunol A Study Sect, NIH, 1966-1970; mem, Comn Streptococcal & Staphylococcal Dis, Armed Forces Epidemiol Bd, 1963-1972; mem, Coun Rheumatic Fever & Congenital Heart Dis & mem, Coun Epidemiol, Am Heart Asn, mem, Res Comt, 1963-1966; from assoc prof to prof epidemiol, Sch Med, Wash Univ, 1962-1966; from asst prof to assoc prof, Rockefeller Inst, 1957-1962; asst, Rockefeller Inst, 1954-1957; asst resident, Barnes Hosp, 1953-1954; intern med, Barnes Hosp, 1952-1953. **Memberships:** Inst Med-Nat Acad Sci; Am Soc Clin Invest; Harvey Soc; Asn Am Physicians; Am Acad Allergy; Am Acad Microbiol; fel AAAS; Am Asn Immunologists; Am Epidemiol Soc; Am Col Allergists. **Research Statement & Publications:** Pathogenesis and epidemiology of streptococcal diseases; immunochemistry; immunogenetics; antibody structure and mechanisms that generate antibody diversity; studies on streptococcal antigens; genetic control of the immune response; author or co-author of over 150 publications and 3 books. **Mailing Address:** Fogarty Int Ctr, NIH, 16 Ctr Dr MSC6705, Bethesda, MD 20892. **Fax:** 301-496-8496. **E-Mail:** krauser@fic16.fic.nih.gov

KRAUSE, RONALD ALFRED, INORGANIC CHEMISTRY. **Personal Data:** b Boston, Mass, October 30, 1931; m 1977, Kirsten Nielsen; c 2. **Education:** Ohio State Univ, BSc, 1956, PhD (chem), 1959. **Professional Experience:** PROF EMER CHEM, UNIV CONN, 1991-; consult, Arco, 1978-1981; Guest prof, Univ Copenhagen, Denmark, 1968-1969, 1976, 1983 & 1990; from asst prof to prof, Univ Conn, 1967-1991; Res scientist, Am Cyanamid Co, Conn, 1959-1962. **Memberships:** Am Chem Soc. **Research Statement & Publications:** Synthesis, reactions, structure, spectra and photochemistry of coordination compounds. **Mailing Address:** Dept Chem, Univ Conn, Storrs, CT 06269. **E-Mail:** rkkrause@sover.net

KRAUSE, SONJA, PHYSICAL CHEMISTRY, POLYMER CHEMISTRY, BIOPHYSICAL CHEMISTRY. **Personal Data:** b St Gall, Switz, August 10, 1933; American citizen; m 1970, Walter. **Education:** Rensselaer Polytech Inst, 1954; Univ Calif, PhD (phys chem), 1957. **Professional Experience:** Mem, Naval Res Lab Polymers Panel, 1993-1994; mem, Polymer Sci & Technol Comt, 1991-1993; sabbatical leave, Inst Charles Sadron, Strasbourg, France, 1987; Mem coun, Gordon Res Conf, 1981-1984; PROF EMERITA, 2003-PROF CHEM, RENSSELAER POLYTECH INST, 1978-2003; from asst prof to assoc prof, Rensselaer Polytech Inst, 1967-1978; asst prof chem, Univ Southern Calif, 1966-1967; US Peace Corps vol, Lagos Univ, Nigeria, 1964-1965 & Gondar Health Col, Ethiopia, 1965-1966; Res chemist, Rohm & Haas Co, Pa, 1957-1964; Nat Res Coun. **Memberships:** AAAS; Am Chem Soc; fel Am Phys Soc. **Research Statement & Publications:** Dilute solution properties of polymers; block polymer compatibility; transient electric birefringence; biophysical chemistry; membranes; effects of electric fields on polymer alloys; interfaces between semicrystalline polymers. **Mailing Address:** Dept Chem, Rensselaer Polytech Inst, Troy, NY 12180-3590. **E-Mail:** krauss@rpi.edu

KRAUSE, STEPHEN MYRON, CARDIAC MUSCLE BIOCHEMISTRY, MYOCARDIAL ISCHEMIA. **Personal Data:** b Grand Rapids, Mich, April 4, 1954; m 1989, Jennifer Turpin; c 2. **Education:** Mich State Univ, BS, 1976; Med Col Va, MS, 1978, PhD (physiol), 1983. **Professional Experience:** AT, PHARMACOL, MERCK RES LAB, as of 2004; AT MERCK SHARP & DOHME RES LABS, WEST POINT, PA, 1991-; asst prof physiol, Jefferson Med Col, Thomas Jefferson Univ, 1986-1991; Fel cardiol, Johns Hopkins Med Inst, 1983-1986. **Memberships:** Am Physiol Soc; Int Soc Heart Res; Biophys Soc; Am Heart Asn. **Research Statement & Publications:** Understanding the subcellular alterations in calcium 2 regulation in the post-ischemic heart, focus is on sarcoplasmic reticulum function as well as contractile protein function; drug development for treatments for heart failure. **Mailing Address:** Merck Res Labs, WP46-200, West Point, PA 19486. **Fax:** 215-652-3811. **E-Mail:** stephen_krause@merck.com

KRAUSE, THOMAS OTTO, THEORETICAL PHYSICS, GALACTIC STRUCTURE. **Personal Data:** b Grand Rapids, Mich, May 5, 1944; m 1982, Mary; c Peter. **Education:** Mass Inst Technol, BS, 1966; Ohio State Univ, PhD (physics), 1973. **Professional Experience:** ASSOC PROF PHYSICS, Towson Univ, as of 2003; asst prof physics, Towson Univ, beginning 1976; vis asst prof, Dept Physics, Ohio State Univ, 1973-1976. **Memberships:** Am Phys Soc; Sigma Xi. **Research Statement & Publications:** Theoretical astrophysics. **Mailing Address:** Dept Physics, Towson Univ, 465 Smith Hall, Towson, MD 21252. **Fax:** 410-830-3511. **E-Mail:** tkrause@towson.edu

KRAUSE, WILLIAM JOHN, II, ANATOMY, HISTOLOGY. **Personal Data:** b Glasgow, Mont, March 24, 1942; m 1967, Winifred; c 2. **Education:** Augustana Col, BA, 1964; Univ Iowa, MS, 1966; Univ Mo, Columbia, PhD (anat), 1969. **Professional Experience:** PROF, PATH & ANAT SCI, UNIV MO, COLUMBIA, beginning 1983; vis prof, Univ Western Australia, Perth, 1991 & St George's Univ, Grenada, 1993; Burroughs Wellcome res travel grant, Univ Southampton, UK, 1992; from asst prof to assoc prof, Univ MO, Columbia, 1971-1983; lectr anat, Monash Univ, 1969-1971. **Memberships:** Am Asn Anatomists; Anat Soc Gt Brit & Ireland. **Research Statement & Publications:** Postnatal development of respiratory, urinary and digestive systems; biology of Brunner's glands; distribution of heat-stable enterotoxin guanylin receptors. **Mailing Address:** Dept Path & Anat Sci, Univ Mo, Columbia, MO 65212. **Fax:** 573-884-4123. **E-Mail:** krause@health.missouri.edu

KRAUS-FRIEDMANN, NAOMI, PHYSIOLOGY. **Personal Data:** b Budapest, Hungary, July 4, 1933; div, c Daphna. **Education:** Hebrew Univ, Jerusalem, MS, 1960, PhD (biochem), 1965. **Professional Experience:** PROF PHYSIOL, SCH MED, UNIV TEX, HOUSTON, 1986-; Vis prof, Eidgenossische Tech Hochschule, Zurich, 1981-1982; from asst prof to assoc prof, Sch Med, Univ Tex, Houston, 1974-1986; instr biochem, Sch Med, Univ Pa, 1968-1974; res assoc physiol, Vanderbilt Univ, Nashville, 1966-1968; res assoc, Columbia Univ, 1965-1966. **Memberships:** Am Soc Cell Biol. **Research Statement & Publications:** Hormonal regulation of gluconeogenesis; role of calcium and other ions in signal transduction and regulation of metabolic processes. **Mailing Address:** Sch Med Univ Tex, PO Box 20708, Houston, TX 77025. **Fax:** 713-794-1349.

KRAUSHAAR, JACK JOURDAN, NUCLEAR PHYSICS. **Personal Data:** b Newark, NJ, September 6, 1923; m 1951, Nancy W Curtis; c Jeffrey C, Steven L & Matthew J. **Education:** Lafayette Col, BS, 1944; Syracuse Univ, MS, 1948, PhD, 1952. **Professional Experience:** Mem, Rocky Flats citizen Adv Bd, 1993-1996; PROF EMER PHYSICS, UNIV COLO, BOULDER, 1988-; vis prof, Osaka Univ, 1985; fac fel, Tri-Univ MesonFacil, Univ BC, Vancouver, 1978-1979; Fulbright award, Free Univ, Amsterdam, 1967-1968; from asst prof to prof, Univ Colo, Boulder, 1956-1988; instr physics, Stanford Univ, 1953-1956; res assoc nuclear spectros, Brookhaven Nat Lab, 1951-1953; asst physics, Syracuse Univ, 1946-1950. **Memberships:** AAAS; fel Am Phys Soc; Fedn Am Sci. **Research Statement & Publications:** Nuclear reactions and spectroscopy; pi meson interactions and scattering; energy and environmental problems in the United States; author. **Mailing Address:** Dept Physics, Univ Colo Campus PO Box 390, Boulder, CO 80309-0390. **Fax:** 303-492-7486. **E-Mail:** kraushaar@spectr.colorado.edu

KRAUSHAAR, WILLIAM LESTER, PHYSICS. **Personal Data:** b Newark, NJ, April 1, 1920; m 1980, c 3. **Education:** Lafayette Col, BS, 1942; Cornell Univ, PhD (physics), 1949. **Professional Experience:** PROF EMER PHYSICS, UNIV WIS, MADISON, 1985-; Max Mason prof, Univ Wis-madison, 1980-1985; prof, Univ Wis-madison, 1965-1980; from asst prof to prof physics, Mass Inst Technol, 1951-1965; res assoc, Mass Inst Technol, 1949-1951; physicist, Nat Bur Stand, 1942-1945. **Memberships:** Nat Acad Sci; fel Am Acad Arts & Sci; fel Am Phys Soc. **Research Statement & Publications:** High energy astrophysics; space science; cosmic rays. **Mailing Address:** Dept Physics, Univ Wis, 6201 Chamberlin Hall Thomas C 1150 Univ Ave, Madison, WI 53706. **Fax:** 608-238-0886.

KRAUSKOPF, JOHN, PSYCHOPHYSIOLOGY. **Personal Data:** b New York, NY, March 30, 1928; m 1952, c 3. **Education:** Cornell Univ, AB, 1949; Univ Tex, PhD, 1953. **Professional Experience:** RES PROF, NY UNIV, 1986-; mem tech staff, Bell Labs, 1966-1985; res scientist, Inst Behav Res, 1964-1966; res assoc, Univ Md, 1962-1964; mem vision comt, Armed Forces-Nat Res Coun, 1960-; asst prof, Rutgers Univ, 1959-1962; vis asst prof, Bryn Mawr Col, 1959-1960; asst prof, Brown Univ, 1957-1959; USPHS fel, Brown Univ, 1956-1957; res assoc, Univ Tex, 1952-1953; asst, Univ Tex, 1950-1952; asst psychol, Cornell Univ, 1949-1950. **Memberships:** Optical Soc Am. **Research Statement & Publications:** Vision; visual perception. **Mailing Address:** Ctr Neural Sci, NY Univ Four Wash Pl Rm 809, New York, NY 10003. **Fax:** 212-995-4011. **E-Mail:** jkr@cns.nyu.edu

KRAUSMAN, JOHN A, ENGINEERING. **Professional Experience:** STAFF, TCOM LP, as of 2006. **Memberships:** Am Inst Aeronaut & Astronaut. **Mailing Address:** TCOM LP, 7115 Thomas Edison Dr, Columbia, MD 21046-2113. **Fax:** 410-312-2455. **E-Mail:** jkrausman@yahoo.com

KRAUSMAN, PAUL RICHARD, WILDLIFE ECOLOGY. **Personal Data:** b Washington, DC, November 17, 1946; m 1966, Carol; c Curtis Drew & Julie Elizabeth (Wegner). **Education:** Ohio State Univ, BS, 1968; NMex State Univ, MS, 1971; Univ Idaho, PhD (wildlife sci), 1976. **Professional Experience:** PROF & RES SCIENTIST WILDLIFE & FISHERIES PROG, UNIV ARIZ, as of 2003; assoc prof wildlife ecol, Univ Ariz, beginning 1981; asst prof wildlife ecol & asst res assoc, Univ Ariz, 1978-1981; asst prof wildlife ecol, Auburn Univ, 1976-1978; Welder wildlife fel ecol, 1972-1976; res asst, Environ Res Lab & Radiation Lab, Brooks AFB, Tex, 1971-1972; res asst environ alteration, Aeromed Res Lab, NMex, 1968-1971. **Memberships:** Wildlife Soc; Am Soc Mammalogists; Soc Range Mgt. **Research Statement & Publications:** Ungulate ecology. **Mailing Address:** Dept Wildlife & Fisheries, Sch Renewable Natural Resources, Univ Ariz, 325 Biol Sci E Bldg, Tucson, AZ 85721. **E-Mail:** krausman@ag.arizona.edu

KRAUSS, GEORGE, PHYSICAL METALLURGY, METALLURGICAL ENGINEERING. **Personal Data:** b Philadelphia, Pa, May 14, 1933; m 1960, c 4. **Education:** Lehigh Univ, BS, 1955; Mass Inst Technol, MS, 1958, ScD, 1961. **Honors & Awards:** Adolf Martens Medal, 1990. **Professional Experience:** PROF EMER PHYS METALL, COLO SCH MINES, 1997-; prof phys metall, Colo Sch Mines, 1990-1997; pres, Int Fedn Heat Treatment, 1988-1990; DIR, ADVAN STEEL PROCESSING & PROD RES CTR, 1984-; Ed, J Heat Treating, 1978-1982; prof engr, Pa & Co; Amax Found prof, Advan Steel Processing & Prod Res Ctr, 1975-1990; dir electron micros lab, Lehigh Univ, 1969-1975; from asst prof to prof metall, Lehigh Univ, 1963-1975; NSF fel, Max-Planck Inst Iron Res, 1962-1963; mem staff div sponsored res, Mass Inst Technol, 1961-1962. **Memberships:** Am Inst Mining Metall & Petrol Engrs; fel Am Soc Metals; Electron Micros Soc Am. **Research Statement & Publications:** Mechanical and fracture behavior of steels; microstructural characterization by light and electron microscopy; failure analysis; author of over 170 publications; principles of heat treatment of steel. **Mailing Address:** Dept Metall Eng, Colo Sch Mines, Golden, CO 80401. **Fax:** 303-273-3016. **E-Mail:** gkrauss@mines.edu

KRAUSS, HERBERT HARRIS, CLINICAL PSYCHOLOGY, REHABILITATION PSYCHOLOGY. **Personal Data:** b Philadelphia, Pa, June 13, 1940; m 1965, Beatrice; c Michael C & Daniel A. **Education:** Pa State Univ, BS, 1962, MS, 1963; Northwestern Univ, PhD (psychol), 1966. **Professional Experience:** PROF & CHAIR, DEPT PSYCHOL, PACE UNIV, 2001-; chair psychol, Hunter Col, City Univ Ny, 1993-2001; dir res, Int Ctr Disabled, 1983-; adj assoc prof psychol & psychiat, Cornell Med Sch, 1979-; adj assoc psychologist, Payne Whitney Clin, NY Hosp, beginning 1979; prof psychol, Hunter Col, City Univ Ny, 1971-2001; assoc prof psychol, Univ Ga, 1969-1971; asst prof psychiat & psychol, Univ Kans Med Ctr, 1966-1967 & Col Med, Ohio State, 1967-1969. **Memberships:** Int Orgn Study Group Tensions; Am Psychol Asn; NY Acad Sci; Am Coun Ger; Sigma Xi; Eastern Psychol Asn. **Research Statement & Publications:** Psycho-social etiology and treatment of behavioral abnormalities; social construction of reality. **Mailing Address:** Dept Psychol Pace Univ, One Pace Plaza, New York, NY 10038. **E-Mail:** hkrauss@pace.edu

KRAUSS, JONATHAN SETH, HEMATOLOGY, COAGULATION. **Personal Data:** b Brooklyn, NY, May 25, 1945; m 2002, Janis; c Timothy, Rachel, Amy & Laurie. **Education:** Cornell Univ, AB, 1966; Univ Fla, Gainesville, MD, 1970. **Professional Experience:** Dir, Flow Cytometry Lab, 1995-2001; prof path, Hemat & Hemostasis Lab, Med Col Ga, 1993-2001; dir, Ambulatory Care Lab, 1993-2001; dir, Hemat & Hemostasis Lab, Med Col Ga, 1978-2001; from asst prof to assoc prof, Flow Cytometry Lab, 1978-1993; fel path, Univ NC, Chapel Hill, 1975-1976; resident path, NC Mem Hosp, 1973-1978; gen med officer, US Naval Reserve, 1971-1973; intern med, Med Col Va, 1970-1971. **Memberships:** Am Col Physicians; Col Am Pathologists; Soc Hematopath; Am Soc Hematol; Asn Clin Scientists. **Research Statement & Publications:** Von Willebrand factor antigen in body fluids; glycosylated hemoglobin determination hemolysis; measurement of fetal hemoglobin; granulocytic fragments in sepsis; factor VII deficiency. **Mailing Address:** 3005 Vassar Dr, Augusta, GA 30909. **Fax:** 706-736-8528. **E-Mail:** jkrauss@mail.mcg.edu

KRAUSS, LAWRENCE MAXWELL, PARTICLE & COSMOLOGY/ASTROPHYSICS INTERFACE. **Personal Data:** b New York, NY, May 27, 1954; Canadian & American citizen; m 1980, Kate; c Lilli. **Education:** Carleton Univ, BSc Hons, Mathematics & Physics, 1977; Mass Inst Technol, PhD (physics), 1982. **Honorary Degrees:** DSc, Carleton Univ, Ottawa, Canada, 2003. **Honors & Awards:** First Prize Award, Gravity Res Found, 1984; Presidential Investigator Award, 1986; Glover Award for Distinction in Physics Achievement and Education, Dickenson College, PA, 1997; Amer Assoc for the Advan of Sce Awd for Public Understanding of Sci & Tech, 1999-2000; Andrew R Gemant Awd, Amer Inst of Phys, 2001; Julius Edgar Lillenfeld Prize, Amer Phys Soc, 2001; American Institute of Physics Science Writing Award 2003; Humanism Award, FINO 2003; Oersted Medal, American Association of Physics Teachers 2003; Fellow, American Physical Society; Fellow, American Association for the Advancement of Science; Joseph Burton Award, American Physical Society, 2005. **Professional Experience:** 2005, member Institute for Advanced Study; 2003, Perimeter Institute; 2002-DIR, CTR EDUC & RES COSMOLOGY AND ASTROPHYSICS, CWRU; Isasac Newton Institute, Cambridge, 1999, Institut des Hautes Etudes Scientifique 1997-8; sci assoc, Europ Orgn Nuclear Res, 1996-1997; distinguished vis scholar, Lawrence Berkeley Lab, Dept Energy, 1995; AMBROSE SWASEY PROF PHYSICS & ASTRON & CHMN, PHYSICS DEPT, CASE WESTERN RES UNIV, 1993-; nat lectr, Sigma Xi, 1991-; visiting Prof. University Chicago 1989; assoc prof physics & astron, Yale Univ, 1988-1993; assoc, Physics Dept, Harvard Univ, 1987-1988; asst prof, Yale Univ, 1985-1988; Vis scientist, Smithsonian Ctr Astrophys, Harvard Univ, 1985-1988; Vis scientist, Boston Univ, 1985-1986; Jr fel, Harvard Soc Fels, 1982-1985. **Memberships:** Am Phys Soc; AAAS. **Research Statement & Publications:** Elementary particle physics and cosmology, early universe, dark matter, stellar evolution, neutrino astrophysics, dark energy; general relativity and quantum gravity, fundamental parameters; all level science education. **Mailing Address:** Dept Physics, Case Western Res Univ, 10900 Euclid Ave, Cleveland, OH 44106. **Fax:** 216-368-4671. **E-Mail:** krauss@cwru.edu

KRAUSS, MORRIS, QUANTUM PHYSICS QUANTUM CHEMISTRY. **Personal Data:** b New Haven, Conn, April 9, 1932; m Joy. **Education:** City Col NY, BS, 1951; Univ Utah, PhD (physics), 1955. **Professional Experience:** STAFF SCIENTIST, CTR ADVAN RES BIOTECHNOL, 1993-; res scientist, Nat Inst Stand & Technol, 1956-1993. **Memberships:** Am Phys Soc; Am Chem Soc. **Research Statement & Publications:** Appl Quantum chemistry with recent Studies in enzyme mechamism. **Mailing Address:** Ctr Advan Res Biotechnol, 9600 Gudelsky Dr, Rockville, MD 20850. **E-Mail:** krauss@carb.nist.gov

KRAUSS, ROBERT WALLFAR, BIOCHEMISTRY, ECOLOGY. **Personal Data:** b Cleveland, Ohio, December 27, 1921; m 1947, c 2. **Education:** Oberlin Col, BA, 1947; Univ Hawaii, MS, 1949; Univ Md, Col Park, PhD (bot), 1951. **Honors & Awards:** Darbaker Award, Bot Soc Am, 1956; Presidents Leadership Award, Am Inst Biol Sci, 1974; Achievement Awards, NASA, 1976, 1989. **Professional Experience:** CONSULT, 1992-; vis sr scientist, Calif Inst Technol, JPL, 1990-1992; exec dir, fedn Am Soc Biol, 1979-1990; dean col sci, Ore State Univ, 1973-1980; mem bd dirs, Ed Projs Inc, 1969-; sr res affil, Chesapeake Biol Lab, 1968-1973; head dept bot, Univ Md, College Park, 1964-1973; mem, Nat Res Coun, 1959-1960; biologist, Coastal Studies Inst, La State Univ, 1958-1959; from asst prof to prof, Univ Md, College Park, 1955-1973; res assoc plant physiol, Univ Md, College Park, 1951-1955; res fel, Carnegie Inst, 1951-1955; asst bot, Univ Md, College Park, 1949-1951; asst bot, Univ Hawaii, 1947-1949; mem corp, Marine Biol Lab, Woods Hole, Mass; consult, US Air Force sch aviation med, NASA & NSF. **Memberships:** Phycol Soc Am (pres, 1964); Bot Soc Am; Am Soc Plant Physiol; Am Inst Biol Sci (secy-treas, 1963-1969, vpres, 1972, pres, 1973); Sigma Xi. **Research Statement & Publications:** Algal physiology and biochemistry; science policy. **Mailing Address:** Denton, MD 21629.

KRAUSS, RONALD M, LIPOPROTEIN METABOLISM. **Personal Data:** b New York, NY, May 12, 1943; m 1969, Sharon; c Daniel & Jeffrey. **Education:** Harvard Univ, BA, 1964, MD, 1968. **Honors & Awards:** Am Heart Assn sci councils distinguished achievement award; 2001; Am Heart Assn Special Recognition Award, 2001; AHA Robert Levy Endowed Lecture in Lipid Metabolism, 2004. **Professional Experience:** Sr. scientist DIRECTOR, ATHEROSCLEROSIS RESEARCH, Children's Hospital Oakland Research Institute, 2003-; Guest Sr. scientist, Genome Sciences Division, Lawrence Berkeley National Lab; Sr scientist HEAD, DEPT MOLECULAR MED, 1992-2003; head, Molecular Med Res Prog, Donner Lab, Lawrence Berkeley Lab, 1989-1992; Adjunct Prof Nutritional Sciences, University of California, Berkeley, 1995-; dir, Endocrine & Metab Serv, Alta Bates Hosp, 1986-1989; SR SCIENTIST, LAWRENCE BERKELEY LAB, 1984-; Assoc adj prof med, Univ Calif, San Francisco, 1982-; staff scientist, Dept Molecular Med, 1976-1984; asst clin prof med, Univ Calif, San Francisco, 1974-1982; sr investr, NIH, 1973-1974; clin assoc, NIH, 1970-1973; fel, Arteriosclerosis Coun, Am Heart Asn; Intern, Boston City Hosp, 1968-1970. **Memberships:** Am Fed Clin Res; Am Soc Clin Invest; Am Diabetes Assn; Am Inst Nutrit Am Heart Assn Council on Nutrition, Physical Activity & Metabolism chair 2000-2002. **Research Statement & Publications:** Genetic traits affecting lipoprotein metabolism and risk for cardiovascular disease; dietary and drug effects on atherogenic lipoprotein particles. **Mailing Address:** Children's hosp Oakland Res Inst, 5700 Martin Luther King, Jr Way, Berkeley, CA 94609. **Fax:** 510-450-7909. **E-Mail:** rkrauss@chori.org

KRAUSZ, ALEXANDER STEPHEN, MATERIALS SCIENCE, MECHANICAL ENGINEERING. **Personal Data:** b Budapest, Hungary, September 16, 1924; Canadian citizen; m 1949. **Education:** Budapest Tech Univ, BSc, 1951; Queens Univ, Ont, MSc, 1959; Univ

Toronto, PhD (metall), 1965. **Professional Experience:** PROF EMER MECH ENG, UNIV OTTAWA, 1990-; prof mech eng & dir, Eng Mgt Prog, 1981-1986; prof & chmn dept, Univ Ottawa, 1972-1981; assoc prof mech eng, Univ Ottawa, 1970-1972; res off plastic deformation, Nat Res Coun Can, 1959-1970; Mgr mfg, Gamma Instrument Co, Hungary, 1949-1952; regional ed, Int J Fracture; Assoc ed, J Eng Mat & Technol. **Memberships:** Am Soc Metals; Eng Inst Can; fel Can Soc Mech Eng. **Research Statement & Publications:** Fracture mechanics; deformation kinetics, thermally activated plastic flow and fracture and deformation processes in manufacturing; product design. **Mailing Address:** Dept Mech Eng, Univ Ottawa, Ottawa, ON K1N 6N5, Can.

KRAUSZ, STEPHEN, SCIENCE EDUCATION, ANIMAL PHYSIOLOGY. **Personal Data:** b Salford, Eng, August 4, 1950; American citizen; m 1972, Vicki; c Joseph, Dora, Elisheva, Nili, Raphael & Gavriella. **Education:** Brooklyn Col, City Univ NY, BSc, 1971; Hebrew Univ, Jerusalem, Israel, MSc, 1973, PhD (physiol), 1977. **Honors & Awards:** 2003 President's Award, National Down Syndrome Congress. **Professional Experience:** Asst Director, Jewish Children's Adoption Network, 1990-present; Adj prof human anat & physiol, Metrop State Col, 1992-1994; CONSULT, 1987-; lab coordr gen sci, Hillel Acad, Denver, Colo, 1983-1987; asst prof anat & physiol Howard Univ Med Sch, Washington, DC, 1978-1983; Res fel, Sch Med, Univ Calif, Los Angeles, 1977-1978. **Memberships:** Sigma Xi; Am Physiol Soc. **Research Statement & Publications:** Respiratory, cardiovascular and endocrinological responses of mammals to extremes of environment. **Mailing Address:** 1635 Osceola St, Denver, CO 80204. **Fax:** 303-893-1447. **E-Mail:** jcan@qwest.net

KRAUT, EDGAR A, PHYSICS. **Personal Data:** b Cleveland, Ohio, May 4, 1934; m 1980. **Education:** Univ Calif, Los Angeles, AB, 1956, MA, 1957, PhD (physics), 1962. **Professional Experience:** MEM TECH STAFF, SCI CTR, ROCKWELL INT CORP, 1967-. **Memberships:** AAAS; Am Phys Soc; Inst Elec & Electronics Engrs; Soc Indust Appl Math. **Research Statement & Publications:** Theoretical and mathematical physics; wave propagation; physics of semiconductor surfaces and interfaces; heterojunctions; energy bands; device modeling. **Mailing Address:** Rockwell Int Sci Ctr Rm 167, 1049 Camino Dos Rios, Thousand Oaks, CA 91360.

KRAUT, JOSEPH, PROTEIN CRYSTALLOGRAPHY. **Personal Data:** b New York, NY, December 5, 1926; m 1953, Jean; c Isabel, Samuel & Rachel. **Education:** Bucknell Univ, BS, 1950; Calif Inst Technol, PhD (phys chem), 1954. **Honors & Awards:** Keilin Medal, Brit Biochem Soc, 1980. **Professional Experience:** RES PROF & EMER PROF CHEM, UNIV CALIF, SAN DIEGO, 1995-; actg chmn dept, Univ Calif, San Diego, 1972-1973; from assoc prof to prof, Univ Calif, San Diego, 1962-1995; fel, Howard Hughes Med Inst, 1955-1960; from instr to asst prof biochem, Univ Wash, 1953-1962. **Memberships:** AAAS; Nat Acad Sci; Am Chem Soc; Am Crystallog Asn; Am Soc Biol Chem. **Research Statement & Publications:** Structure, function and evolution of biological macromolecules; x-ray diffraction crystallography. **Mailing Address:** Dept Chem & Biochem, Univ Calif, San Diego, CA 92093-0506. **Fax:** 858-822-0346. **E-Mail:** jkraut@ucsd.edu

KRAUTER, ALLAN IRVING, MECHANICAL ENGINEERING. **Personal Data:** b Newark, NJ, October 15, 1941; m 1968, c 3. **Education:** Stevens Inst Technol, ME, 1963; Stanford Univ, MS, 1964, PhD (mech eng), 1968. **Professional Experience:** RES & DEVELOP MGR, WELCH ALLYN, 1985-; prog mgr, mech systs, Carrier Corp, 1981-1985; sr consult engr & mgr, Technol Dept, Shaker Res Corp, 1975-1981; asst prof mech eng, Cornell Univ, 1968-1974. **Memberships:** Am Soc Mech Engrs; Soc Automotive Engrs. **Research Statement & Publications:** Vibrations and dynamics of mechanical systems; simulation of mechanical and economic system behavior. **Mailing Address:** Welch Allyn, Inc, PO Box 220 4341 State St Rd, Skaneateles, NY 13153. **Fax:** 315-685-2546.

KRAUTHAMER, GEORGE MICHAEL, NEUROSCIENCE. **Personal Data:** b Ger, September 14, 1926; American citizen; div, c 6. **Education:** City Col New York, BS, 1951, MA, 1952; NY Univ, PhD (psychol), 1959. **Professional Experience:** PROF NEUROSCIENCE AND CELL Biol, ROBERT WOOD JOHNSON MED SCH, UNIV MED & DENT NJ, 1979-; assoc prof, Robert Wood Johnson Med Sch, Univ Med & Dent NJ, 1969-1979; asst prof, Col Physicians & Surgeons, Columbia Univ, 1967-1969; asst to exec secy, Int Brain Res Orgn-UNESCO, 1965-1968; res assoc, Univ Paris, 1963-1966; USPHS res fel, Ctr Study Physiol Cent Nerv Syst, Univ Paris, 1960-1963; res assoc, Hillside Hosp, Glen Oak, NY, 1959-1960; instr psychol, Sch Med, NY Univ, 1959-1960; Lectr psychol, City Col NY, 1959-1960; Asst psychophysiol, Sch Med, NY Univ, 1957-1959. **Memberships:** AAAS; Soc Neurosci. **Research Statement & Publications:** Electrophysiology and neuroanatomy of brain; behavior correlates of brain function; effects of brain injury; perception and intersensory relationships; electroencephalography; drug effects; History of Neuroscience. **Mailing Address:** Dept Anat, Robert Wood Johnson Med Sch UMDNJ 675 Hoes Lane, Piscataway, NJ 08854-5635. **Fax:** 732-235-4029.

KRAUTZ, FRED GERHARD, FIBER GLASS REINFORCEMENTS, FIBER GLASS COMPOSITES. **Personal Data:** b Cottbus, Ger, American citizen; m 1962, c 2. **Education:** Univ Cincinnati, ChE, 1961, MS, 1966. **Professional Experience:** VPRES RES & DEVELOP, VETROTEX CERTAINTEED CORP, 1991-; dir res & develop, Certainteed Corp, 1990-1991; res & develop dir, Certainteed Corp, 1987-1990; tech support mgr, Owens-Corning Fiberglas Corp, 1983-1987; mgr composite prod, Owens-Corning Fiberglas Corp, 1981-1983; mgr reinforcement & tires, Owens-Corning Fiberglas Corp, 1978-1981; supvr reinforcements & Mat, Owens-Corning Fiberglas Corp, 1972-1978; sr engr, Owens-Corning Fiberglas Corp, 1965-1972; consult, Cincinnati Milacron, 1963-1965; Engr, Cincinnati Milacron, 1961-1963. **Memberships:** Soc Plastics Engrs; Am Inst Chem Engrs. **Research Statement & Publications:** Fiberglass products for all thermosetting and thermoplastic composites for Vetrotex Certainteed fiberglass reinforcements division. **Mailing Address:** Vetrotex Certainteed Corp, 4515 Allendale Rd, Wichita Falls, TX 76310. **Fax:** 940-696-3652.

KRAVITZ, EDWARD ARTHUR, BIOCHEMISTRY, NEUROBIOLOGY. **Personal Data:** b New York, NY, December 19, 1932; m 1958, c 2. **Education:** City Col NY, BS, 1954; Univ Mich, PhD (biochem), 1959. **Honors & Awards:** Flexner Lectr, Univ Pa, 1972; Krantz Lectr, Univ Md, 1975; Magnes Mem Lectr, Hebrew Univ Med Sch, Jerusalem, 1981; Lang Lectr, Marine Biol Lab, 1983; Snider Lectr, Univ Toronto, 1987; Von Humboldt Award, 1991; Schmitt Lectr, Univ Pa, 1991. **Professional Experience:** Mem, Governing Coun, Inst Med, 1991-1993; GEORGE PACKER BERRY PROF NEUROBIOLOGY, HARVARD MED SCH, 1986-; dir prog Neuroscience, Harvard Med Sch, 1982-1990; mem, Bd Trustees & Exec Comt, Marine Biol Lab, dir Neurobiology course, 1975-1979; prof Neurobiology, Harvard Med Sch, 1969-1986; career develop award, 1966-1971; from asst prof to assoc prof, Harvard Med Sch, 1966-1969; assoc, Harvard Med Sch, 1963-1966; USPHS spec fel, 1961-1964; instr neurophysiol & neuropharmacol, Harvard Med Sch, 1961-1963; Nat Inst Neurol Dis & Blindness res fel neurophysiol & neuropharmacol, Harvard Med Sch, 1960-1961; Nat Heart Inst fel biochem, 1959-1960; co-founder, Neurobiology Dis Teaching Workshops, Soc Neuroscience. **Memberships:** Inst Med-Nat Acad Sci; Soc Neuroscience; Am Acad Arts & Sci; Am Soc Biol Chemists; NY Acad Sci. **Research Statement & Publications:** Biochemical studies on single physiologically identified nerve cells; identification of gamma-aminobutyric acid and other neurotransmitters in the lobster nervous system; amines, peptides neurohormones and behavior in lobsters. **Mailing Address:** Harvard Med Sch, Dept Neurobiol, 220 Longwood Ave, Boston, MA 02115. **Fax:** 617-734-7557. **E-Mail:** edward_kravitz@hms.harvard.edu

KRAVITZ, JOSEPH HENRY, MARINE GEOTECHNIQUE & PROGRAM MANAGER, PROFESSIONAL LECTURER. **Personal Data:** b Nanticoke, Pa, August 14, 1935; m 1965, Prudence; c Joseph III & Jonathon. **Education:** Syracuse Univ, BS, 1957; George Wash Univ, MS, 1975, MPH, 1977, PhD (geol), 1983. **Professional Experience:** PROF LECTR, DEPT EARTH & ENVIRON SCI, GEORGE WASH UNIV, as of 2004; assoc prof lectr geol, George Wash Univ, beginning 1987; PROG MGR, MARINE GEOL & GEOPHYS PROG, OFF NAVAL RES, 1986-; sci off, Marine Geol & Geophys Prog, Off Naval Res, 1984-1986; sr oceanogr, prog develop & coord staff, Off Oceanic & Atmoshperic Res, Nat Oceanic & Atmospheric Admin, 1984; hq staff geologist, Ocean Assessment Div, 1982-1984; res assoc, Inst Artic & Alpine Res, 1981-1986; actg dir, Marine Ecosysts Anal Div, Off Marine Pollution Assessment, 1980-1982; sr geologist, outer continental shelf environ assessment, Nat Ocean & Atmospheric Admin, 1978-1980; actg head, marine geol & geophys br, 1978; head, Geol Lab, 1971-1978; oceanographer, US Naval Oceanog Off, 1965-1971; marine geologist, Lamont-Doherty Geol Observ, Columbia Univ, 1964-1965; res asst, Geol Dept, Yale Univ, 1961-1964. **Memberships:** Fel Geol Soc Am; fel Artic Inst NAm; fel Explor Club; Soc Econ Paleontologists & Mineralogists. **Research Statement & Publications:** Geotechnical analysis of sediments and its relation to depositional environments; geochemistry of high lattitude marine sediments. **Mailing Address:** Marine Geol & Geophys Prog, Off Naval Res, 800 N Qunicy St, Arlington, VA 22217-5660. **E-Mail:** kravitj@exchange.onr.navy.mil

KRAVITZ, LAWRENCE C, PHYSICS, ELECTRONICS. **Personal Data:** b New York, NY, July 27, 1932; m 1958, c 3. **Education:** Kans Univ, BS, 1954; Air Force Inst Technol, MS, 1955; Harvard Univ, PhD (physics), 1963. **Professional Experience:** CONSULT, as of 1998; vpres technol, corp res & technol, Allied Signal, Inc, ending 1996; dir res, Bendix Advan Technol Ctr, beginning 1981; dir, Air Force Off Sci Res, 1978-1981; dir electronics, 1973-1978; mgr display prog, Corp Res & Develop Ctr, Gen Elec Co, 1972-1973; Physicist solid state, Corp Res & Develop Ctr, Gen Elec Co, 1963-1971. **Memberships:** Inst Elec & Electronics Engrs. **Research Statement & Publications:** Solid state science. **Mailing Address:** 7128 Wolftree Lane, Rockville, MD 20852.

KRAWETZ, ARTHUR ALTSHULER, ANAL CHEM, PHYSICAL CHEM. **Personal Data:** b Chicago, Ill, October 30, 1932. **Education:** Northwestern Univ, BS, 1952; Univ Chicago, SM, 1953, PhD (chem), 1955. **Professional Experience:** PRES, PHOENIX CHEM LAB, INC, CHICAGO, 1974-; Vpres, Phoenix Chem Lab, Inc, Chicago, 1954-1974. **Memberships:** Am Chem Soc; Am Soc Testing & Mat; fel Am Inst Chem; fel Royal Soc Chem; Nat Fire Protection Asn. **Research Statement & Publications:** Fuel and lubricant technology; spontaneous ignition; flammability; forensic chem; solution chem; thermodynamics; molecular sprectroscopy; industrial hygiene; safety; hydraulic fluids; protective coatings; rubber and plastic. **Mailing Address:** Phoenix Chem Lab Inc, 3953 W Shakespeare Ave, Chicago, IL 60647-3497. **Fax:** 847-864-7356. **E-Mail:** pclinc@xnet.com

KRAWETZ, STEPHEN ANDREW, HUMAN GENOME INITIATIVE, MEDICAL GENETICS & BIOTECHNOLOGY. **Personal Data:** b Fort Frances, Ont, September 17, 1955; m 1977, Qorraine; c Rhochelle T & Alexandra R. **Education:** Univ Toronto, BSc, 1977, PhD (biochem), 1983. **Honors & Awards:** Intel Genetics Comput Appln Award, 1988. **Professional Experience:** DIR, WAYNE STATE UNIV BIOINFORMATICS NODE MICH LIFE SCI CORRIDOR, as of 2005; CHARLOTTE B FAILING PROF OB-GYN & MOLECULAR MED AND GENETIC & INST, SCI COMPUT, WAYNE STATE UNIV, Detroit, 2000-; ASSOC PROF DEPT OBSTETS & GYNEC, CTR MOLECULAR MED & GENETICS, WAYNE STATE UNIV, 1994-; asst prof, Dept Molecular Biol & Genetics, 1992-1994; asst prof, Dept Molecular Biol & Genetics, 1990-1992; asst prof res, Dept Molecular Biol & Genetics & Ctr Molecular Biol, Wayne State Univ, 1989-1990; cofounder & med res dir, Genetic Imaging Inc, 1987-1988; prin investr, Comput Video Expert Systs Biochem Appl, 1987; biotechnol consult, 1985-; Alta Heritage Found med res fel, 1984-1989; Brit Columbia Children's Hosp res fel, 1984; fel, Dept Med Biochem, Univ Calgary, 1983-1989; lab demonstr biochem, Univ Toronto, 1977-1981; occas teacher math, music & sci, Scarborough Bd Educ, 1976-1977. **Memberships:** AAAS; Am Soc Human Genetics; Int Soc Matrix Biol; Soc Study Reproduction. **Research Statement & Publications:** Control of development and differentiation of spermatogenic and elastic tissue genes; human genome initiative; computer assisted sequence analysis; molecular diagnostic probes; gene therapy targeted to the ameliozation of human disease. **Mailing Address:** 253 C S Mott Ctr, 275 E Hancock Ave, Detroit, MI 48201. **Fax:** 313-577-8534. **E-Mail:** steve@compbio.med.wayne.edu

KRAWIEC, STEVEN STACK, MOLECULAR BIOLOGY, MICROBIOLOGY. **Personal Data:** b Corvallis, Ore, November 4, 1941; m 1965, Margaret; c Matthew & Rebecca. **Education:** Brown Univ, AB, 1963; Yale Univ, PhD (microbiol), 1968. **Professional Experience:** PROF, LEHIGH UNIV, 1982-; vis scientist, Univ Edinburgh, 1992-1993; assoc dean, Col Arts & Sci, 1985-1987; sr int fel, Autonomous Univ Madrid, 1978-1979; sr int fel, John E Fogarty Int Ctr, 1978-1979; chmn, Dept Biol, Lehigh Univ, 1976-1978; from asst prof to assoc prof, Lehigh Univ, 1970-1982; trainee, Nat Inst Gen Med Sci fel, 1969-1970; trainee, Univ Wis, Madison, 1968-1969; NIH grant; Nat Sci Found grant. **Memberships:** Am Soc Microbiol; AAAS; Sigma Xi. **Research Statement & Publications:** Characterization of genome organization of bacteria; chromosome organization of bacteria; degradation of xenobiotics. **Mailing Address:** Dept Biol Sci, Lehigh Univ, 27 Memorial Dr W, Bethlehem, PA 18015-4732. **Fax:** 610-758-4004. **E-Mail:** sk08@lehigh.edu

KRAY, LOUIS ROBERT, PETROLEUM CHEMISTRY, FUELS. **Personal Data:** b San Bernardino, Calif, October 20, 1938; m 1987, Bettye; c Leonard L, Roger K, Robert B, Katherine M & Ann L. **Education:** Univ Calif, Riverside, BA, 1961, PhD (org chem), 1965. **Professional Experience:** RES CHEMIST ORG CHEM, CHEVRON RES & TECHNOL CO, STAND OIL CO CALIF, RICHMOND, 1967-, SR STAFF SCIENTIST; researcher, 1965-1967. **Memberships:** Am Chem Soc; Soc Tribelogists & Lubrication Engrs; Soc Mfg Engrs. **Research Statement & Publications:** Fuel additive synthesis and development; industrial oil formulator. **Mailing Address:** 700 Bamboo Terr, San Rafael, CA 94903. **Fax:** 510-242-3758.

KRAYBILL, EDWARD K(READY), electrical engineering; deceased, see previous edition for last biography

KRAYBILL, HENRY LAWRENCE, EXPERIMENTAL HIGH ENERGY PHYSICS. **Personal Data:** b Washington, DC, April 13, 1918; m 1944, Helen; c April & Robert. **Education:** Univ Chicago, SB, 1938, PhD (physics), 1949. **Professional Experience:** PROF EMER,

YALE UNIV, as of 2005; from instr to prof physics, Yale Univ, 1948-1984. **Memberships:** Am Phys Soc; Am Asn Physics Teachers. **Research Statement & Publications:** High energy particles; bubble chamber analysis of hadron interactions. **Mailing Address:** 960 Benham, Hamden, CT 06514.

KRAYBILL, HERMAN FINK, ENVIRONMENTAL CANCER, PESTICIDE TOXICOLOGY. **Personal Data:** b Marietta, Pa, June 27, 1914; m 1941, Dorothy; c Linda J (Asper), Cynthia K Voth & David R. **Education:** Franklin & Marshall Col, BS, 1936; Univ Md, MS, 1938, PhD (biochem), 1941. **Honors & Awards:** Merit Award, NIH, 1981; US Army Med Dept Award in Nutrit Res, 1954. **Professional Experience:** CONSULT BIOMED SCI, 1984-; sci coordr, environ cancer, Nat Cancer Inst, 1972-1984; adj prof community health, Mt Sinai Sch Med, 1968-1970; assoc dir biol sci, Food & Drug Admin, 1966-1972; chief pesticides prog, USPHS, 1962-1966; sr biochemist & scientist adminstr, Div Radiation Health, Nat Cancer Inst, 1960-1963; sr scientist, Curtiss Wright Corp, NJ, 1959-1960; Lectr biochem, Univ Colo, 1954-1958 & lectr nutrit, Univ Denver, 1955-1958; supvry biochemist & chief chem div, Army Med Nutrit Lab, 1953-1959; Bur Animal Indust, USDA, 1949-1953; res assoc, Nat Res Coun, DC, 1948-1949; res biochemist, Moorman Mfg Co, Ill, 1946 & Nat Dairy Res Labs, Md, 1946-1948; res chemist, Swift & Co, 1941-1943; instr chem, Univ Md, 1936-1939. **Memberships:** Pan Am Med Asn; Am Chem Soc; Am Soc Nutrit Sci; Soc Toxicol; NY Acad Sci; Sigma Xi. **Research Statement & Publications:** Food research; fat enzymes; animal and human nutrition; dairy products; meats and fishery products; allergy; cancer; toxicology of irradiated foods; pesticides; radiological health; environmental cancer. **Mailing Address:** 17708 Lafayette Dr, Olney, MD 20832.

KRAYCHY, STEPHEN, ORGANIC CHEMISTRY, NUCLEAR MEDICINE. **Personal Data:** b Redwater, Alta, February 18, 1928; American citizen; m 1954, c 3. **Education:** Univ Alta, BSc, 1950; Univ Wis, PhD (org chem), 1955. **Professional Experience:** GROUP LEADER CHEMICAL DEVELOP, NUTRASWEET CO, UNIV PARK, as of 2002; sr res scientist, G D Searle & Co, beginning 1978; mgr radiopharmaceut, Searle Labs, 1975-1978; asst dir drug metab-radiochem, G D Searle & Co, 1973-1975; asst dir biochem res, G D Searle & Co, 1971-1973; sr investr chem res, G D Searle & Co, 1956-1971; Asst mem, Sloan-Kettering Inst Cancer Res, 1954-1956; Searle Food Resources, Park Forest. **Memberships:** Am Chem Soc. **Research Statement & Publications:** Synthesis of steroids; steroid metabolism; microbiological transformations of steroids; drug metabolism; radiochemicals; research and development of radiopharmaceuticals; anti-infective agents; peptide synthesis. **Mailing Address:** 2301 S Millbend Dr, Spring, TX 77380.

KRAYNAK, MATTHEW EDWARD, NUTRITION. **Personal Data:** b Scranton, Pa, December 19, 1927; m 1968. **Education:** Scranton Univ, BS, 1950; Univ Tenn, MS, 1952, PhD (biochem), 1956. **Professional Experience:** RETIRED; from asst prof to prof chem & nutrit, Univ Okla, 1962-1990; asst prof, Univ Tenn, 1961-1962; asst prof biochem & vis chmn dept, Indonesia, 1956-1960; instr chem, Univ Tenn, 1953-1955; mem, Okla Nutrit Task Force. **Memberships:** AAAS; Am Chem Soc; Am Dietetic Asn. **Research Statement & Publications:** Nutritional availability of plant galactosides; biochemistry of galactosemia and lactose intolerance. **Mailing Address:** 717 Chautauqua, Norman, OK 73069-4605.

KRBECHEK, LEROY O, ORGANIC CHEMISTRY. **Personal Data:** b Thief River Falls, Minn, May 21, 1934; m 1960, c 3. **Education:** Univ NDak, BS, 1957; Univ Mich, MS & PhD, 1961. **Professional Experience:** SR RES CHEMIST, HENKEL INC, 1980-; sr res chemist, Gen Mills Chem Inc, 1972-1980; sr res chemist, James Ford Bell Res Ctr, Gen Mills, Inc, 1969-1972; Chemist, Aerospace Corp, 1961-1964 & Int Minerals & Chem Corp, 1964-1969. **Memberships:** Am Chem Soc. **Research Statement & Publications:** Organic azides and synthesis. **Mailing Address:** 1119 Humboldt St, Santa Rosa, CA 95404.

KRC, JOHN JR, chemical microscopy, crystallography; deceased, see previous edition for last biography

KREAM, BARBARA ELIZABETH, BIOCHEMISTRY, ENDOCRINOLOGY. **Personal Data:** b New York, NY, March 11, 1948; m 1980, c 2. **Education:** Mt Holyoke Col, BA, 1969; Yale Univ, PhD (molecular biophys, biochem), 1974. **Professional Experience:** PROF, DEPT MED & GENETICS & DEVELOP BIOL, UNIV CONN, as of 2005; assoc prof, dept med, div endocrinol & metab, Univ Conn Health Ctr, beginning 1985; staff mem, Proctor & Gamble Co, 1981; staff mem, NIH, 1981-; asst prof, Dept Med, Div Endocrinol & Metab, Univ Conn Health Ctr, 1979-1985; res grants, Juvenile Diabetes Found, 1979-1981; instr med & endocrinol, Dept Med, Div Endocrinol & Metab, Univ Conn Health Ctr, 1978-1979; res grants, Am Diabetes Asn, 1978-1979; res assoc, Dept Med, Div Endocrinol & Metab, Univ Conn Health Ctr, 1977-1978; NIH fel, Dept Biochem, Univ Wis, 1974-1977. **Memberships:** AAAS; Sigma Xi; Endocrine Soc; Am Soc Bone & Mineral Res; Am Soc Biol Chemists. **Research Statement & Publications:** Bone and calcium metabolism; mechanism of action of hormones; effect of insulin on collagen synthesis in bone; hormonal regulation of bone collagen synthesis. **Mailing Address:** Dept Genetics & Develop Biol, Univ Conn, 263 Farmington Ave, Farmington, CT 06030-3705. **Fax:** 860-679-1258. **E-Mail:** kream@nso1.uchc.edu

KREAM, JACOB, CLINICAL CHEMISTRY, HORMONE IMMUNOASSAY. **Personal Data:** b New York, NY, April 16, 1919; m 1942, Rhoda; c Richard, Barbara, Steven & Shelley. **Education:** City Col NY, BS, 1942; Columbia Univ, PhD (biochem), 1952; Nat Registry Clin Chem, dipl; Nat Acad Clin Biochem, dipl. **Professional Experience:** CONSULT CLIN CHEM & ENDOCRINOL/HORMONE ASSAY, 1986-; dir, Biochem Labs, Inst Chronobiol, NY Hosp-Cornell Med Ctr, Cornell Univ Med Col, 1982-1986; assoc prof biochem psychiat & clin biochem, assoc prof lab med, Albert Einstein Col Med, 1978-1982; consult clin radioimmuno assay, Union Carbide Corp, 1975-1979; chmn, Nat Comt, Am Asn Clin Chem, Radionuclides & Radio assay, 1974-1976; chmn, Nat Comt, 1970-1975; dir, Core Lab, Clin Res Ctr & sr investr, Steroid Inst, Montefiure Hosp & Med Ctr, 1965-1982; mem bd examr, Bur Labs, NY Dept Health, 1965-1967; chmn, NY Sect, Am Asn Clin Chem, 1959-1960 & 1978-1979; lectr-consult, US Naval Hosp, St Albans, NY, 1958-1962; chief, Dept Clin Chem, Hosp Joint Dis, 1954-1965; res assoc biochem, Columbia Univ, 1953-1954; lectr, Hunter Col, 1951-1965; biochemist, Inst Cancer Res, 1950-1952, US Vet Admin Hosp, NY, 1952-1953; asst biochem, William J Geis fel biol chem, 1948-1949; asst biochem, Columbia Univ, 1946-1949; Pyridium Corp, 1944-1946; chemist, Kellex Corp, 1943-1944; asst, Rockefeller Inst Med Res, 1943. **Memberships:** emer mem Am Chem Soc; emer mem Am Asn Clin Chem; emer mem Sigma Xi; emer mem Endocrine Soc. **Research Statement & Publications:** Enzymology; purine and pyrimidine metabolism; purine analogs and cancer; nucleic acid chemistry; polypeptide metabolism; clinical chemistry; automated clinical methods; steroid analysis; radioimmunoassay; competitive protein binding analysis; episodic secretion of pituitary hormones and corticosteroids; radioisotopes, endocrinology of cancer, hormonal studies of mentalillness. **Mailing Address:** 3 Milford Lane, Glen Cove, NY 11542.

KREAM, RICHARD M, BIOCHEMISTRY, NEUROSCIENCE. **Professional Experience:** ADJ PROF, DEPT BIOCHEM, STATE UNIV NY HEALTH SCI CTR, as of 2004. **Mailing Address:** Dept Biochem, State Univ NY Health Sci Ctr, 450 Clarkson Ave, Brooklyn, NY 11203. **E-Mail:** richard_kream@netmail.hscbklyn.edu

KREAR, HARRY ROBERT, ETHOLOGY, ECOLOGY. **Personal Data:** b Pittsburgh, Pa, April 13, 1922. **Education:** Pa State Univ, BSF, 1949; Univ Wyo, MS, 1953; Univ Colo, PhD (ecol, ethology), 1965. **Honors & Awards:** Sigma Xi Phi Sigma. **Professional Experience:** RETIRED; assoc prof biol sci, Mich Technol Univ, 1973-1984; chmn div sci & math, US Int Univ, Colo Alpine Campus, 1967-1973; asst prof, Mankato State Col, 1965-1966; instr biol, Univ Colo, 1960-1961; vis lectr zool, NSF Insts, Univ Colo, 1959-1964; explor & res, Arctic Wildlife Range Exped, 1956; biologist wildlife res, Mont Fish & Game Dept, 1953-1954; Sea Otter Res, Amchitka, Aleutian Islands, 1957; Fur Seal Res, Pribilor Islands, 1953. **Memberships:** Animal Behav Soc; Ecol Soc Am; Am Soc Mammalogists. **Research Statement & Publications:** Ecology of selected vertebrates of Ungava; reproduction of cow fur seals pribilots; Arctic wildlife range; ecology of muskrats; behavior and ecology of sea otters amchitka; ecology and ethology of pikas. **Mailing Address:** 944 Ramshorn Rd, Estes Park, CO 80517.

KREBILL, RICHARD G, FOREST PATHOLOGY. **Personal Data:** b Upland, Calif, March 9, 1936; m 1958, c 3. **Education:** Univ Calif, Berkeley, BS, 1958; Univ Wis, PhD (plant path), 1962. **Professional Experience:** ASST DIR, ROCKY MOUNTAIN FOREST & RANGE EXP STA, US FOREST SERV, 1979-; Plant pathologist, 1962-1976. **Memberships:** Am Phytopath Soc; Soc Am Foresters. **Research Statement & Publications:** Tree diseases; rust fungi; shrub diseases; research administration. **Mailing Address:** Rocky Mountain Res Sta, USDA Forest Serv, 6209 Woodland Dr, Ogden, UT 84403. **E-Mail:** rkrebill/rmrs_ogden@fs.fed.us

KREBS, CHARLES J, ZOOLOGY. **Education:** Univ Minn, BSc; Univ BC, MA, PhD. **Professional Experience:** PROF EMER, DEPT ZOOLOGY, UNIV BC, CAN, as of 2005. **Mailing Address:** Univ BC Dept Zool, 2075 Wesbrook Pl, Vancouver, BC V6T 1Z4, Can. **E-Mail:** krebs@zoology.ubc.ca

KREBS, EDWIN GERHARD, BIOCHEMISTRY. **Personal Data:** b Lansing, Iowa, June 6, m Virginia; c Sarah, Robert & Martha. **Education:** Univ Ill, AB, 1940; Wash Univ, MD, 1943. **Honorary Degrees:** DSc, Univ Geneva, 1979; Dr, Med Col Ohio, 1993; DSc, Univ Ind, 1993. **Honors & Awards:** Distinguished Lectureship Award, Int Soc Endcrinol, 1972; Gairdner Foundation Award, 1978; J J Berzelivs lectr, Karolinska Inst, 1982; George W Thorn Award Sci Excellence, 1983; Sir Frederick Hopkins Mem lectr, London, 1984; Res Achievement Award, Am Heart Asn, 1987; Life Sci Award, 3M, 1989; Albert Lasker Basic Med Res Award, 1989; Louisa Gross Horwitz Award, Columbia Univ, 1989; Nobel Prize, 1992; Kawi Found Award, 1996. **Professional Experience:** EMER SR INVESTR, HOWARD HUGHES MED INST, 1991-; Emer Prof, Dept Pharmacol & Biochem, Sch Med, Univ Wash, Seattle, 1988-; Passano found award, Baltimore, Md, 1988; sr investr, Howard Hughes Med Inst, 1980-1990; Gairdner found award, Toronto, Ont, 1978; prof pharmacol, Sch Med, Univ Wash, Seattle, 1977-1988; chmn dept, Sch Med, Univ Wash, Seattle, 1977-1984; investr, Sch Med, Univ Wash, Seattle, 1977-1980; assoc ed, J Biol Chem, 1972-1993; mem, Res Comt, Am Heart Asn, 1970-1974; prof biochem & chmn dept, Sch Med, Univ Calif, Davis, 1968-1976; mem, Biochem Test Comt, Nat Bd Med Examiners, 1968-1971; asst dean planning, Sch Med, 1966-1968; mem, Educ Affairs Comt, Am Soc Biol Chemists, 1965-1968; Guggenheim fel, 1959, 1966; from asst prof to prof biochem, Wash Univ, 1948-1968; NIH res fel, Wash Univ, 1946-1948; Intern & asst resident, Barnes Hosp, St Louis, 1944-1945. **Memberships:** Nat Acad Sci; Am Acad Arts & Sci; Am Soc Biochem & Molecular Biol (pres 1985-1986); Am Pharm Soc; Am Soc Pharm & Exp Theopeuts. **Research Statement & Publications:** Enzyme chemistry; regulation of carbohydrate metabolism; mechanism of action of cyclic amp and other second messages; protein phosphorylation reactions. **Mailing Address:** Box 357750, Univ Wash, Seattle, WA 98195. **Fax:** 206-685-9720. **E-Mail:** egkrebs@u.washington.edu

KREBS, JAMES J(OHN), EXPERIMENTAL SOLID STATE PHYSICS. **Personal Data:** b St Louis, Mo, February 28, 1932; m 1972, Catherine; c Christopher & Matthew. **Education:** St Louis Univ, BS, 1954, PhD (physics), 1959. **Professional Experience:** RETIRED; vis fel, Princeton Univ, 1975-1976; physicist magnetic resonance, US Naval Res Lab, 1958-; Nat Res Coun res assoc, 1958-1959. **Memberships:** Fel Am Phys Soc; Sigma Xi. **Research Statement & Publications:** Investigation of electron-nuclear interactions by means of magnetic double resonance; resonance and optical absorption in exchange coupled systems; deep impurity resonance in III-V semiconductors; properties of ultra-thin magnetic single crystals. **Mailing Address:** Code 6340, Naval Res Lab, Washington, DC 20375-5000. **Fax:** 202-767-1697.

KREBS, JAMES N, JET ENGINE DESIGN & DEVELOPMENT. **Personal Data:** b Sauk Center, Minn, April 20, 1924. **Education:** Northwestern Univ, BS, 1945. **Honors & Awards:** Reed Aeronaut Award, Am Inst Aeronaut & Astronaut, 1992. **Professional Experience:** RETIRED; Lynn Eng Opers, GE Aircraft Engines, 1982-1984; Technol & Mgt Assessment, Aircraft Eng Group, GE Aircraft Engines, 1984-1985; vpres, Mil Eng Progs, 1978-1982; design develop mgr & mkt mgr, Gen Elec Co, 1946-1978. **Memberships:** Nat Acad Eng; Am Inst Aeronaut & Astronaut. **Mailing Address:** 84 Harbor Ave, Marblehead, MA 01945.

KREBS, JULIA ELIZABETH, TEACHING, ORNITHOLOGY. **Personal Data:** b Baton Rouge, La, March 29, 1943; m 1980, Roger. **Education:** Oberlin Col, AB, 1965; Boston Col, MEd, 1969; Univ Ga, MSc, 1972, PhD (zoology), 1977. **Professional Experience:** CHAIR, DEPT BIOL, FRANCIS MARION UNIV, as of 2005; DISTINGUISHED PROF BIOL, FRANCIS MARION UNIV, 1977-. **Memberships:** Ecol Soc Am; Asn Biol Lab Educ. **Research Statement & Publications:** Nutrient cycling; effect of man on natural systems; bird populations. **Mailing Address:** Dept Biol, Francis Marion Univ, LSF 204C, Florence, SC 29501-0547. **Fax:** 843-661-4660. **E-Mail:** jkrebs@fmarion.edu

KREBS, MARTHA, ENERGY RESEARCH. **Education:** Cath Univ Am, PhD (theoret physics), 1966. **Professional Experience:** DIR, OFF ENERGY RES, DEPT ENERGY, 1993-; assoc dir planning & develop, Lawrence Berkeley Lab, 1983-1993; Staff dir, House Subcomt Energy Develop Applns, Wash, 1977-1983. **Mailing Address:** Off Energy Res, US Dept Energy, 1000 Independence Ave SW, Washington, DC 20585.

KREBS, ROBERT DIXON, SOIL MECHANICS, FOUNDATION ENGINEERING. **Personal Data:** b Gowanda, NY, March 12, 1931; m 1954, c 3. **Education:** Rutgers Univ, BS, 1952, PhD (soil sci), 1956; Purdue Univ, MSE, 1959. **Professional Experience:** RETIRED; asst head dept, Va Polytech Inst & State Univ, 1970-1991; assoc prof civil eng, Va Polytech Inst & State Univ, 1959-1991; instr eng geol, Purdue Univ, 1958-1959; From asst to assoc prof agron, Va Polytech Inst, 1955-1957; assoc, Hwy Res Bd, Nat Acad Sci-Nat Res Coun. **Memberships:** AAAS; Am Soc Civil Engrs; Am Soc Eng Educ. **Research Statement & Publications:** Soil mechanics, physics, mineralogy and chemistry; soils and geologic engineering; soil genesis and classification; soil stabilization; soil behavior. **Mailing Address:** 101 Alleghany St, Blacksburg, VA 24060.

KREBS, WILLIAM H, INDUSTRIAL HYGIENE, TOXICOLOGY. **Personal Data:** b Detroit, Mich, April 6, 1938; m 1983, Jane; c Elizabeth L & William T II. **Education:** Univ Mich, Ann Arbor, BS, 1960, MPH (IH), 1963, MS, 1965, PhD, 1970; Am Bd Indust Hyg, cert. **Professional Experience:** VPRES, INDUST HEALTH SCI INC, 1993-; pres yuma pac swest sect, Am Indust Hyg Asn, 2002-; pres, Int Occup Hyg Asn, 1992-1993; asst dir, Occup Safety & Health Sect, 1992-1993; pres elect, Int Occup Hyg Asn, 1991-1992; dir, Indust Hyg Activ, 1990-1992; vpres, Int Occup Hyg Asn, 1990-1991; pres, Am Indust Hyg Asn, 1988-1989; pres-elect, Am Indust Hyg Asn, 1987-1988; vpres, Am Indust Hyg Asn, 1986-1987; dir, Toxic Mat Control Activ, 1981-1990; pres, Mich Indust Hyg Soc, 1980-1981; mgr, Indust Hyg Dept, Gen Motors Corp, 1977-1981; Dir, Am Indust Hyg Asn, 1976-1979; indust hygienist, Indust Hyg Dept, Gen Motors Corp, 1970-1977; indust hygienist, Lumbermens Mutual Casualty Co, Chicago, Ill, 1963-1964; res asst indust health, Sch Pub Health, Univ Mich, Ann Arbor, 1962. **Memberships:** AAAS; NY Acad Sci; fel Am Indust Hyg Asn; Am Acad Indust Hyg; Brit Occup Hyg Soc; Am Pub Health Asn; hon mem Am Indust Hyg Asn; Int Comn Occup Health. **Research Statement & Publications:** Formation of ferruginous bodies. **Mailing Address:** Indust Health Sci Inc, 1014 Bishop Rd, Grosse Pointe Park, MI 48230. **Fax:** 313-885-3130. **E-Mail:** whkrebs@umich.edu

KREBS-SMITH, SUSAN M, NUTRITION. **Personal Data:** b St Louis, Mo, June 2, 1955. **Education:** Bradley Univ, BA, 1976; Univ Minn, MS, 1980; Pa State Univ, PhD (nutrit), 1985. **Professional Experience:** NUTRITIONIST, NAT CANCER INST, NIH, 1991-; br chief, USDA, 1990-1991; nutritionist, USDA, 1986-1991; Res assoc dietary monitoring, Pa State Univ, 1985-1986. **Memberships:** Sigma Xi; Am Dietary Asn; Am Inst Nutrit; Soc Clin Nutrit; Am Pub Health Asn. **Mailing Address:** Nat Cancer Inst, NIH, 9000 Rockville Pike, Bethesda, MD 20892.

KRECZNER, ROBERT J, MATHEMATICS. **Education:** Univ Wis-Milwaukee, PhD, 1988. **Professional Experience:** PROF, DEPT MATH & COMPUT, UNIV WIS-STEVENS POINT, as of 2005. **Mailing Address:** Dept Math & Comput, Univ Wis SCI D357, Stevens Point, WI 54481. **Fax:** 715-346-2720. **E-Mail:** rkreczne@uwspmail.uwsp.edu

KREDICH, NICHOLAS M, INTERNAL MEDICINE, RHEUMATIC DISEASES. **Personal Data:** b Chicago, Ill, September 23, 1935; m 1957, Deborah; c Kathryn, Matthew & Nathan. **Education:** Duke Univ, BA, 1957; Univ Mich, MA, 1960, MD, 1962. **Professional Experience:** PROF INTERNAL MED, MED CTR, DUKE UNIV, 1980-; investr, Howard Hughes Med Inst, 1973-1989; Nat Inst Arthritis & Metab Dis res grant, 1968-1981; from asst prof to assoc prof, Med Ctr, Duke Univ, 1968-1980; staff assoc, Nat Inst Arthritis & Metab Dis, 1966-1968; res assoc molecular biol, Nat Inst Arthritis & Metab Dis, 1964-1966; asst resident, Duke Hosp, Durham, NC, 1963-1964; intern internal med, Duke Hosp, Durham, NC, 1962-1963. **Research Statement & Publications:** Regulation of metabolic pathways, including feedback inhibition and repression and induction of enzymes; bacterial and human genetics; sulfur metabolism inbacteria; adenosine deaminase deficiency; immunodeficiency disease; genetics; molecular biology. **Mailing Address:** Dept Biochem, Duke Univ, 34227 Hosp S, Durham, NC 27710. **Fax:** 919-684-8135. **E-Mail:** kredi001@mc.duke.edu

KREEGER, RUSSELL LOWELL, CELLULOSICS, PERSONAL CARE POLYMERS. **Personal Data:** b Amherst, Ohio, January 24, 1946; m 1973, c 2. **Education:** Kent State Univ, BS, 1968; Ohio State Univ, Columbus, PhD (org chem), 1976. **Professional Experience:** SR RES SCIENTIST, SPECIALTY CHEM DIV, UNION CARBIDE CORP, 1976-. **Memberships:** Am Chem Soc; Sigma Xi. **Research Statement & Publications:** Research and development; natural polymer process research; cellulosic derivatives; personal care polymers; water-soluble polymers. **Mailing Address:** Union Carbide, PO Box 670, Bound Brook, NJ 08822-0670.

KREER, JOHN B(ELSHAW), ELECTRICAL ENGINEERING. **Personal Data:** b Brooklyn, NY, September 25, 1927; m 1957, Vivienne; c Carolyn K (Bratzel) & Kenneth J. **Education:** Iowa State Col, BS, 1951; Univ Ill, MS, 1954, PhD (elec eng), 1956. **Professional Experience:** EMER PROF ELEC ENG, MICH STATE UNIV, as of 2005; chmn, Dept Elec Eng & Systs Sci, 1977-1987; from assoc prof to prof, Mich State Univ, 1964-1992; from assoc prof to prof, Univ WVa, 1959-1964; from instr to asst prof elec eng, Univ Ill, 1955-1959. **Memberships:** Inst Elec & Electronics Engrs; Am Soc Eng Educ. **Mailing Address:** Dept Elec Eng, Mich State Univ, East Lansing, MI 48824-1226. **E-Mail:** kreer@egrmsu.edu, kreer@msu.edu

KREEVOY, MAURICE M, CHEMICAL KINETICS, MEMBRANE DYNAMICS. **Personal Data:** b Boston, Mass, August 28, 1928; wid, c Edith K (Pang) & William S. **Education:** Univ Calif, Los Angeles, BS, 1950; Mass Inst Technol, PhD, 1954. **Professional Experience:** PROF EMER CHEM, UNIV MINN, MINNEAPOLIS, as of 2004; prof chem, Univ Minn, Minneapolis, beginning 1994; consult, Medtronic Inc, 1988; consult, Honeywell Inc, 1985-1986; consult, Henckel Am Inc, 1978-1985; consult, Ventron Corp, 1975-1979; partic, US Acad Sci exchange prog with Coun Acad Socialist Fed Repub Yugoslavia, 1969-1970; NSF sr fel, OxfordUniv, 1962-1963; Sloan Found fel, 1960-1964; consult, Gen Mills Inc, 1959-1978; from asst prof to prof, Univ Minn, Minneapolis, 1956-1994; NSF fel, Univ Utah, 1955-1956; res assoc chem, Pa State Univ, 1953-1955. **Memberships:** Am Chem Soc; Croatian Chem Soc; Sigma Xi. **Research Statement & Publications:** Physical and theoretical organic chemistry; chemical kinetics and dynamics in solution; isotope effects; dynamics of membrane transport. **Mailing Address:** Dept Chem, Univ Minn, Minneapolis, MN 55455. **Fax:** 612-626-7541. **E-Mail:** kreevoy@chem.umn.edu

KREFT, ANTHONY FRANK, III, ORGANIC CHEMISTRY, MEDICINAL CHEMISTRY. **Personal Data:** b Detroit, Mich, May 28, 1948. **Education:** Univ Mich, BS, 1970; Columbia Univ, MPh, 1973, PhD (org chem), 1976. **Professional Experience:** PRIN RES SCIENTIST, WYETH LABS, 2002-; res fel, Wyeth-Ayerst Labs, 1991-2002; prin scientist, Wyeth Res Labs, 1988-1991; SUPVR MED CHEM, WYETH-AYERST LABS, 1987-; supvr, Wyeth Res Labs, 1978-1987; fel, Stanford Univ, 1976-1978. **Memberships:** Am Chem Soc; Inflammation Res Asn; NY Acad Sci. **Research Statement & Publications:** Design and synthesis of drugs of medicinal interest especially in the areas of inflammation, allergy, asthma, and diseases of the central nervous system; author of 70 publications and granted 67 patents. **Mailing Address:** Wyeth Labs, CN 8000, Princeton, NJ 08540. **Fax:** 732-274-4505. **E-Mail:** krefta@wyeth.com

KREH, DONALD WILLARD, ORGANIC CHEMISTRY. **Personal Data:** b Frederick, Md, March 17, 1937; m 1966, c 4. **Education:** Univ Richmond, BS, 1959, MS, 1961; Va Polytech Inst, PhD (org chem), 1966. **Professional Experience:** SR CHEMIST, TENN EASTMAN CO, 1969-; chemist, Tenn Eastman CO, 1967-1968; Chemist, Great Lakes Res Corp, 1966-1967. **Memberships:** Am Chem Soc. **Research Statement & Publications:** Reactions and synthesis of small ring sulfides, sulfoxides and sulfones; synthesis of photographic chemicals, antioxidants, stabilizers, and industrial chemical intermediates. **Mailing Address:** Eastman Chem Co, PO Box 511, Kingsport, TN 37622-5075.

KREH, E(DWARD) J(OSEPH), JR, ENGINEERING. **Personal Data:** b Pittsburgh, Pa, February 26, 1915; m 1938, c 3. **Education:** Carnegie Inst Technol, BS, 1937. **Professional Experience:** CONSULT ENGR, O'DONNELL & ASSOC, 1982-; consult engr, Westinghouse Pressurized Water Reactors Div, 1979-1982; Prod Assurance, Westinghouse Pressurized Water Reactors Div, 1972-1979; mgr opers, Bettis Plant, 1967-1972; mgr cent labs, Core Mat Dept, 1965-1967; mgr, Core Mat Dept, 1961-1965; mgr, Nuclear Core Dept, 1959-1961; div apparatus engr, Stress Corrosion & Hydraul Fields, Bettis Plant, 1958-1959; mem div mgr staff, Stress Corrosion & Hydraul Fields, Bettis Plant, 1956-1958; mgr equip develop, Westinghouse Elec Corp, 1951-1956; plant engr, Camillus Cutlery Co, 1946-1951; Design engr, Westinghouse Elec Corp, 1937-1942. **Memberships:** Am Soc Mech Engrs; Nat Asn Corrosion Engrs; Am Inst Mgt; Am Nuclear Soc; Am Soc Chem Engrs. **Research Statement & Publications:** Thermal, mechanical and electrical design; corrosion studies; development of fabrication processes for nuclear reactors; development and management of qualty assurance systems to assure reactor safety and reliability. **Mailing Address:** 624 Trotwood Circle, Pittsburgh, PA 15241.

KREH, RICHARD EDWARD, BIOLOGICAL SCIENCES. **Personal Data:** b Waterbury, Conn, December 22, 1941; m 1967, c 2. **Education:** Univ Conn, BS, 1969; Va Polytech Inst & State Univ, MS, 1974. **Professional Experience:** RETIRED; sr res assoc, Forest Biol, Va Polytech Inst & State Univ, ending 2002; supt, Reynolds Homestead Forest Resources Res Ctr, Va Tech Col Nat Resources, ending 2002; res assoc Forest Biol, Va Polytech Inst & State Univ, beginning 1969. **Memberships:** Soc Am Foresters. **Research Statement & Publications:** Silviculture research on site preparation; root growth analysis of forest tree nursery growth seedlings; nitrogen dynamics of mine spoil soils for forestry reclamation; hybrid performance of selected pine crosses. **Mailing Address:** Reynolds Homestead Res Ctr, Va Tech Col Nat Resource, Cheatham Hall, Blacksburg, VA 24061. **E-Mail:** oak@vtvm1.cc.vt.edu

KREIBICH, GERT, CELL BIOLOGY. **Personal Data:** b Komotau, Czech, November 14, 1939; German citizen; m 1966, c 1. **Education:** Univ Heidelberg, dipl chem, 1965, PhD, 1968. **Professional Experience:** PROF CELL BIOL, MED CTR, NY UNIV, 1982-; mem cell biol study sect, Irma Hirschl Award, 1982-1986; mem cell biol study sect, NIH, 1978-1982; NIH res career develop award, 1977-1982; from asst prof to assoc prof, Med Ctr, NY Univ, 1972-1982; res assoc cell biol, Rockefeller Univ, 1970-1972; res fel, Ger Res Soc, 1970-1972; fel chem carcinogenesis, Ger Cancer Res Ctr, Heidelberg, 1965-1970. **Memberships:** Ger Soc Biol Chem; NY Acad Sci; Am Soc Cell Biol; Am Soc Biol Chemists. **Research Statement & Publications:** Structure, function and targeting of subcellular membranes in eukaryotic cells; function of membrane bound polysomes in membrane biogenesis. **Mailing Address:** Dept Cell Biol, Sch Med NY Univ, 550 First Ave MSB 697, New York, NY 10016-6402. **Fax:** 212-263-8139. **E-Mail:** kreibg01@popmail.med.nyu.edu

KREIBICH, ROLAND, organic chemistry; deceased, see previous edition for last biography

KREIDER, DONALD LESTER, MATHEMATICAL LOGIC. **Personal Data:** b Lancaster, Pa, December 5, 1931; m 1952, c 3. **Education:** Lebanon Valley Col, BS, 1953; Mass Inst Technol, PhD (math), 1959. **Professional Experience:** PROF EMER MATH & COMPUT SCI, DARTMOUTH COL, as of 2004; prof math, Dartmouth Col, beginning 1968; from asst prof to assoc prof, Dartmouth Col, 1960-1968; instr math, Mass Inst Technol, 1955-1960; asst, Mass Inst Technol, 1953-1955; instr, Lebanon Valley Col, 1952-1953. **Memberships:** Am Math Soc; Asn Symbolic Logic; Math Asn Am; Soc Indust & Appl Math; Nat Asn Math; Asn Women Math. **Research Statement & Publications:** Recursive functions; automata theory. **Mailing Address:** Dept Math & Comput Sci, Dartmouth Col, Hanover, NH 03755. **E-Mail:** donald.l.kreider@dartmouth.edu

KREIDER, EUNICE S, INTERNATIONAL PRODUCT DEVELOPMENT, HEMATOLOGY & ONCOLOGY. **Personal Data:** b Ohio, June 5, 1941; m 1963. **Education:** Goshen Col, BA, 1963; Purdue Univ, PhD (chem), 1967; Northwestern Univ, MM, 1977. **Professional Experience:** CLIN RES DIR, EUROPE, RWJ PRI, ZURICH, SWITZ, 1993-; vpres, Int Prod Develop, 1989-1992; dir, Int Prod Develop, Ortho Pharmaceut Corp, 1981-1988; dir proj mgt, Preclin Res & Develop, 1980-1981; assoc dir, Prog Planning & Qual Assurance, 1978-1980; dir, Prog Planning & Qual Assurance, 1976-1978; group leader, G D Searle & Co, 1974-1976; From res investr to sr res investr, G D Searle & Co, 1967-1974. **Memberships:** Sigma Xi; Am Chem Soc; Drug Info Asn. **Research Statement & Publications:** Heterocyclic medicinal chemicals; drug safety testing and GLP'S; project management; clinical development and registrations. **Mailing Address:** Witikonerstrasse 248, CH 8053, Zurich, Switzerland.

KREIDER, HENRY ROYER, PHYSICAL CHEMISTRY, ORGANIC CHEMISTRY. **Personal Data:** b Baltimore, Md, December 31, 1911; m 1936, c 2. **Education:** Univ Toledo, BA, 1933; Ohio State Univ, MS, 1935, PhD (chem), 1936. **Professional Experience:** CONSULT DRUG COSMETIC INDUSTS, 1971-; dir prod develop, Cooper Labs Inc, 1968-1971; dir res, Sherman Labs, 1960-1968; exec vpres, Viobin Corp, 1959-1960; dir res, Chesebrough-Ponds Inc, 1956-1959; assoc dir res, William S Merrell Co, 1950-1956; exec asst to vpres, William S Merrell Co, 1945-1950; Chemist, Am Med Asn, Chicago, 1936-1942 & Mead Johnson & Co, Ind, 1942-1945. **Memberships:** AAAS; Am Chem Soc; Soc Cosmetic Chem; Am Pharmaceut Asn; Asn Res Dirs; Sigma Xi. **Research Statement & Publications:** Development of foods, drugs & cosmetics; vitamins; proteins; fats; micronutrients. **Mailing Address:** 830 N Shore Dr NE Apt 14A, St Petersburg, FL 33701. **E-Mail:** vhkreider@aol.com

KREIDER, JACK LEON, ANIMAL SCIENCE, EQUINE REPRODUCTIVE PHYSIOLOGY. **Personal Data:** b Afton, Okla, March 12, 1941; m 1967, c 3. **Education:** Okla State Univ, BS, 1968; Univ Ky, MS, 1970, PhD (animal sci), 1971. **Professional Experience:** PROF ANIMAL SCI & RESIDENT DIR, DEAN LEE RES STA, ALEXANDRIA, LA, 1985-; assoc prof animal sci, Tex A&M Univ, 1979-1984; from asst prof to assoc prof animal sci, La State Univ, Baton Rouge, 1973-1979; asst prof animal sci, Univ Mo, Columbia, 1972. **Memberships:** Am Soc Animal Sci; Am Registry Prof Animal Scientists; Mem, La Forage & Grasslands Coun & Grasslands Coun, Am Forage. **Research Statement & Publications:** Reproductive physiology and endocrinology of the mare as related to improving efficiency of production of horses, particularly the perparturient period; reproductive physiology of the stallion, particularly semen physiology; administration of research in beef cattle and and service management as well as agronomy and weed control. **Mailing Address:** Dean Lee Res Sta, La State Univ, 8105 E Campus Ave, Alexandria, LA 71302. **Fax:** 318-473-6535. **E-Mail:** jkreider@agctr.lsu.edu

KREIDER, JAN F, ENERGY ENGINEERING. **Education:** Case Inst Tech, BSME, 1964; Univ Colo, MSME, 1968; Univ Colo, PhD, 1973. **Professional Experience:** PROF, DEPT CIVIL, ENVIRON & ARCHIT ENG, UNIV COLO, as of 2006. **Mailing Address:** Dept Civil,

Environ & Archit Eng, Univ Colo, Campus Box 428, Boulder, CO 80309-0428. **Fax:** 303-492-7317. **E-Mail:** kreider@bechtel.colorado.edu

KREIDER, JOHN WESLEY, CANCER RES, TUMOR IMMUNOL. **Personal Data:** b Philadelphia, Pa, March 24, 1937; m 1963, c 2. **Education:** La Salle Col, AB, 1959; Univ Pa, MD, 1963. **Honors & Awards:** Borden Award, AOA; Career Develop Award, USPHS, 1969. **Professional Experience:** RETIRED; mem, Path B Study Sect, NIH, 1979-; MEM FAC PATH, HERSHEY MED CTR, 1968-; mem fac path, Med Sch, Univ Pa, 1967-1968. **Memberships:** Am Asn Pathologists; Am Asn Cancer Res; Am Asn Immunologist. **Research Statement & Publications:** Host regulation of tumor growth; neoplastic cell differentiation; papillomavirus transformation. **Mailing Address:** Dept Path Pa State Univ Col Med, PO Box 850, Hershey, PA 17033-0850.

KREIDER, KENNETH GRUBER, THIN FILMS, SENSORS. **Personal Data:** b Lancaster, Pa, May 21, 1937; m 1961, Carole; c Kenneth B, Cynthia L & Christopher L. **Education:** Mass Inst Technol, SB, 1959, SM, 1961, ScD, 1963. **Honors & Awards:** Bronze Medal, US Dept Com. **Professional Experience:** GROUP LEADER, THIN FILM THERMOCOUPLES & RAPID THERMAL PROCESSING, as of 2004; Mass Inst Technol, Electronic Package, 1990-1992; adv panel, UPA Ctr Chem Elec, 1983-1986; judge, Am Paper Inst Energy & Environ Awards, 1978-1990; div chief, & sr scientist, Nat Bur Stand, 1975-; res supvr, United Aircraft Res Labs, 1965-1973; chmn, Inst Elec & Electronics Engrs Tech Comt Sensor Stand. **Memberships:** Am Vacuum Soc; Am Soc Testing & Mat; Mat Res Soc; Am Soc Metals; Inst Elec & Electronics Engrs Instruments & Measurements Soc. **Research Statement & Publications:** Thin Film Sensors; instrumentation for harsh environments; metal matrix composites; infrared thermography; sputtering of thin films; thin film electronics. **Mailing Address:** Nat Inst Stand & Technol, Bldg 221 Rm A303, Gaithersburg, MD 20899. **Fax:** 301-548-0206. **E-Mail:** kenneth.kreider@nist.gov

KREIDER, KEVIN L, COMPUTATIONAL AEROACOUSTICS, FRACTURE MECHANICS. **Personal Data:** b Baltimore, Md, March 15, 1959; m 1995, Valerie; c Maxwell Bruce, Mikayla Grace. **Education:** Purdue Univ, MS, 1982, PhD (appl math), 1986; Wittenberg Univ, BA, 1981. **Professional Experience:** PROF APPL MATH, UNIV AKRON, 2000-; from asst to assoc prof math, Univ Akron, 1989-2000. **Memberships:** SIAM. **Research Statement & Publications:** Numerical techniques for time dependent inverse problems in wave propagation; numerical methods in computational aeroacoustics. **Mailing Address:** Dept of Theoretical and Appl Math, Univ Akron, CAS 273, Akron, OH 44325-4002. **Fax:** 330-374-8630. **E-Mail:** kreider@math.uakron.edu

KREIDL, TOBIAS JOACHIM, DIGITAL IMAGE PROCESSING. **Personal Data:** b Rochester, NY, May 6, 1954. **Education:** Univ Vienna, Austria, PhD (astron), 1979. **Professional Experience:** ADJ FAC, DEPT PHYSICS & ASTRON, NORTHERN ARIZ Univ, as of 2004; lectr comput sci, Northern Ariz Univ, 1981; astronr, Lowell Observ, beginning 1980; res assoc, Ruhr Univ, Bochum, WGer, 1979-1980. **Memberships:** Am Astron Soc; Sigma Xi. **Research Statement & Publications:** Digital image processing and image processing systems; photometry of peculiar A type stars; computer analysis of astronomical data of various nature. **Mailing Address:** Dept Physics & Astron, Northern Ariz Univ, NAU Box 6010, Flagstaff, AZ 86011-6010. **Fax:** 928-523-1371. **E-Mail:** Tobias.Kreidl@nau.edu

KREIDLER, ERIC RUSSELL, PHASE EQUILIBRIA, LUMINESCENCE. **Personal Data:** b Lock Haven, Pa, July 21, 1939; m 1968, c 2. **Education:** Pa State Univ, BS, 1961, MS, 1963, PhD (ceramic sci), 1967. **Honors & Awards:** Ralph L Boyer Award, Col Eng, 1983; W E Cramer Award, Cent Ohio Sec Am Ceramic Soc, 1988. **Professional Experience:** PROF EMER, OHIO STATE UNIV, as of 2006; assoc prof ceramic eng, Ohio State Univ beginning 1980; assoc ed, Journal Am ceramic Soc, 1988-1993; contrib ed, Communications Am Ceramic Soc, 1981-1983; contrib ed, Phase Diagrams Ceramists, 1981-1990; consult, Gen Elec Co, 1980-1982; ed subchairman, Journal Am Ceramic Soc, 1974-1979; res chemist, Gen Elec Co, 1966-1980. **Memberships:** Fel Am Ceramic Soc; Electrochem Soc; Math Res Soc. **Research Statement & Publications:** Determination of phase diagrams; crystal chemistry and luminescence of inorganic materials; phosphors and luminescence; glass-metal composites; high temperature ceramic superconductors; electronic ceramics; ceramic processing. **Mailing Address:** Dept Mat Sci & Eng, Ohio State univ, 2041 Col Rd, Columbus, OH 43210-1124. **E-Mail:** kreidler.1@osu.edu

KREIER, JULIUS PETER, PROTOZOOLOGY, IMMUNOLOGY. **Personal Data:** b Philadelphia, Pa, November 30, 1926; m 1955, Ruth; c Rachel & Jesse. **Education:** Univ Pa, VMD, 1953; Univ Ill, MS, 1959, PhD, 1962. **Professional Experience:** RETIRED; lectr, China Nat Ctr Prev Med, Inst Parasitol, 1985; vis prof, State Univ De Sao Paulo, Botucatu, Brazil, 1981; prof microbiol, Ohio State Univ, 1972-1989; from asst prof to assoc prof, Ohio State Univ, 1962-1972; instr vet physiol, fel, USPHS, 1961-1962; instr vet path & hyg, Univ Ill, 1959-1961; instr vet physiol, Univ Ill, 1956-1959; vet, Agr Res Serv, USDA, 1953-1956. **Memberships:** Am Soc Trop Med Hyg; Soc Protozoologists; Am Soc Parasitol; Am Asn Immunol; Am Soc Microbiol. **Research Statement & Publications:** Host-parasite interactions, primarily the blood inhabiting protozoa; malaria parasites, babesia and trypanosomes; procaryotic protists which parasitize the blood; Anaplasmataceae and Bartonellaceae; pathogenesis of the anaemic changes associated with infection and the mechanisms by which the host controls the parasite population; immunological and biochemical events associated with disease and recovery from disease; isolation and identification of parasites and parasite parts for use as antigens. **Mailing Address:** 2047 Iuka Ave, Columbus, OH 43201.

KREIFELDT, JOHN GENE, ENGINEERING DESIGN, ERGONOMICS & HUMAN FACTORS. **Personal Data:** b Manistee, Mich, October 7, 1934; m 1964, c 2. **Education:** Univ Calif, Los Angeles, BS, 1961; Mass Inst Tech, MS, 1964; Case Western Res Univ, PhD (biomed & human factors eng), 1969. **Professional Experience:** PROF ENG DESIGN, TUFTS UNIV, 1980-; Nat Res Coun associateship, NASA-Ames Res Ctr, 1973; USPHS grants, Tufts Univ & New Eng Med Ctr, 1971-1981; From asst prof to assoc prof, Tufts Univ, 1969-1980; Dept Health, Educ & Welfare grant; NASA grants; NSF grant. **Memberships:** Human Factors & Ergonomics. **Research Statement & Publications:** Electromyographic processing and control; man-machine system design; air traffic control studies; computers in automation of radiotherapy treatment; multidimensional scaling in design; mathematical models of human operators; consumer product design; safety design. **Mailing Address:** Tufts Univ, Dept Mech Eng, Anderson Hall Rm 219, Medford, MA 02155. **Fax:** 617-627-3058. **E-Mail:** jkreife01@tufts.edu

KREIGHBAUM, WILLIAM EUGENE, MEDICINAL CHEMISTRY, SCIENCE COMMUNICATIONS. **Personal Data:** b Elkhart, Ind, June 17, 1934; m 1961, Carolyn; c David & Carol. **Education:** Wabash Col, AB, 1956; Ind Univ, PhD (org chem), 1960. **Professional Experience:** SR INFO ANALYST, BRISTOL MYERS SQUIBB CO, WALLINGFORD, 1987-; prin investr, Mead Johnson Res Ctr, Mead Johnson & Co, 1974-1986; sr investr, 1970-1973; group leader, 1968-1969; sr res scientist, 1961-1967; Bristol Labs res fel org chem, Ind Univ, 1960-1961. **Memberships:** Am Chem Soc. **Research Statement & Publications:** Synthesis and pharmacological activity of organic sulfur compounds; heterocyclic compounds containing sulfur or nitrogen; chemistry of the sympathetic nervous system. **Mailing Address:** Sci Info Dept, Bristol Myers Squibb Co, Wallingford, CT 06492-7660. **Fax:** 203-284-6006. **E-Mail:** tnbd70a@prodigy.com

KREILICK, ROBERT W, PHYSICAL CHEMISTRY. **Personal Data:** b Kalamazoo, Mich, January 3, 1938; m 1959, c 2. **Education:** Wash Univ, AB, 1959, PhD (magnetic resonance), 1964. **Professional Experience:** FOUNDER, ADAPTABLE LAB SOFTWARE, 1983; PROF CHEM, UNIV ROCHESTER, 1971-; Alfred P Sloan fel, 1969-1971; from asst prof to assoc prof, Univ Rochester, 1964-1971; consult, NIH. **Memberships:** Am Chem Soc. **Research Statement & Publications:** Nuclear magnetic resonance and electron spin resonance; biophysical chemistry; study of biologically important metal complexes; computer software for chemistry. **Mailing Address:** Dept Chem, Univ Rochester, PO BOX 270216, Rochester, NY 14627-0216. **E-Mail:** kreilick@chem.rochester.edu

KREILING, DARYL, MATHEMATICS. **Personal Data:** b Minatare, Nebr, May 18, 1936; m 1956, c 3. **Education:** Chadron State Col, BS, 1961; Bowling Green State Univ, MA, 1963; Univ Wyo, PhD (math), 1969. **Professional Experience:** Prof math, Univ Tenn, beginning 1980; dean arts & sci, Univ Tenn, 1980-1987; asst dean, Western Ill Univ, 1974-1980; from asst prof to assoc prof math, Western Ill Univ, 1973-1980; Instr math, Univ Wyo, 1966-1969. **Memberships:** Am Math Soc; Math Asn Am. **Research Statement & Publications:** Associative and non-associative rings; radicals of rings and ring-like structures. **Mailing Address:** 428 Moody Ave, Martin, TN 38237.

KREIMER, HERBERT FREDERICK, RING THEORY. **Personal Data:** b Cincinnati, Ohio, February 19, 1936; m 1961, Sarah; c Caroline L & Herbert F III. **Education:** Yale Univ, BS, 1958, PhD (math), 1962. **Professional Experience:** PROF MATH, FLA STATE UNIV, 1977-; dept chair, Fla State Univ, 1990-1993; NSF grant, 1965-1966 & 1968-1971; vis assoc prof, Northwestern Univ, 1965-1966; Univ Res Coun grant, 1964 & 1967; from asst prof to assoc prof, Fla State Univ, 1962-1977. **Memberships:** Am Math Soc; Math Asn Am; Sigma Xi. **Research Statement & Publications:** Hopfalgebras; separable algebras; Galois theory and its generalizations for rings; Galois cohomology. **Mailing Address:** Dept Math, Fla State Univ, Tallahassee, FL 32306-3027. **E-Mail:** kreimer@gauss.math.fsu.edu

KREIN, PHILIP T, POWER ELECTRONICS, ELECTROSTATICS. **Personal Data:** b Orange, Calif, April 22, 1956. **Education:** Lafayette Col, BS, 1978, AB, 1978; Univ Ill, Urbana, MS, 1980, PhD (elec eng), 1982. **Professional Experience:** PROF, DEPT ELEC & COMPUT ENG, UNIV ILL, URBANA, as of 2004; vpres, Power Electronics Soc, InstElec & Electronics Engrs, beginning 1997; assoc prof elec eng, Univ Ill, Urbana, beginning 1992; asst prof, Univ Ill, Urbana, 1987-1992; physicist, Tektronix, Inc, Beaverton, Ore, 1984-1987; vis researcher, Sundstrand Corp, Rockford, Ill, 1983; vis asst prof, Univ Ill, Urbana, 1982-1984. **Memberships:** Inst Elec & Electronics Engrs; Electrostatics Soc Am. **Research Statement & Publications:** Large-signal and nonlinear control issues in power electronics; advanced switching power converters; electrohydrodynamics and other applications of electrostatics; electric machines and drive systems. **Mailing Address:** Dept Elec & Comput Eng, Univ Ill 1406 W Green, Urbana, IL 61801. **Fax:** 217-333-1162. **E-Mail:** krein@ece.uiuc.edu

KREIPKE, MERRILL VINCENT, GEOTECHNICAL ENGINEERING, CIVIL ENGINEERING. **Personal Data:** b Evansville, Ind, February 14, 1916; wid Dorothy (Deceased); c Karen J & Jane A. **Education:** Purdue Univ, BS, 1936. **Honors & Awards:** Meritorious Civilian Serv Medal, Dept Army, 1966. **Professional Experience:** CONSULT, 1975-; chief mil res & develop team, Chief Engrs, Dept Army, 1974-1975; US nat leader, NATO long-term sci study on Arctic opers, 1971-; exec mem & US leader, subgroup T-ground mobility, Tech Coop Prog, US, UK, Can & Australia, 1969-; US nat leader, NATO long-term sci study mobility interface, 1969-; chief geophys sci br, US Army Res Off, 1969-1974; proj officer for US, NATO long-term sci study land-based mobility, 1966-; engr, Off Chief Res & Develop, 1961-1969; Permanent secy, quadripartite standing working group ground mobility, Armies of US, UK, Can & Australia, 1959-1966; civil engr, 1951-1956 & Off Chief Engrs, US Dept Army, 1956-1961; engr, US Army Engrs Dist, Ky, 1946-1951; asst engr, US Army Engrs Dist, Ky, 1942-1944; jr engr, US Army Engrs Dist, Ky, 1941-1942; inspector, US Army Engrs Dist, Ky, 1939-1941; resident engr, Off City Engr, Evansville, Ind, 1936-1939. **Memberships:** Fel Am Soc Civil Engrs; Soc Am mem Mil Engrs; Nat mem Soc Prof Engrs; Int mem Soc Soil Mech & Found Eng; Systs. **Research Statement & Publications:** Soil mechanics; terrain-vehicle interaction; quantitative terrain evaluation; design and construction of earth and rockfill dams; rapid earthwork; soil stabilization; soil surfacings. **Mailing Address:** 12191 Clipper Dr No 403, Woodbridge, VA 22192. **Fax:** 703-643-9812. **E-Mail:** mukreipke@prodigy.net

KREIS, RONALD W, PHYSICAL CHEMISTRY. **Personal Data:** b Passaic, NJ, October 20, 1942; m 1969, c 2. **Education:** Ursinus Col, BS, 1964; Univ Del, PhD (chem), 1969. **Professional Experience:** ANAL CHEMIST, LIVE OAK ENVIRON CONSULT, as of 1995; DIR QUAL RHONE-POULENC, ALCOLAC INC, 1990-; vpres res, Alcolac Inc, 1977-1990; Res scientist chem, Uniroyal Inc, 1969-1977. **Memberships:** Am Chem Soc. **Research Statement & Publications:** Latex and colloid chemistry; adhesion of rubber; paper chemicals; surfactants. **Mailing Address:** Live Oak Environ Consult, 2714 Cypress Point, Missouri, TX 77459.

KREIS, WILLI, CLINICAL PHARMACOLOGY & CHEMOTHERAPY. **Personal Data:** b Ebnat, Switz, November 3, 1924; m 1962, c 4. **Education:** Univ Zurich, MD, 1954; Univ Basel, PhD (org chem), 1957. **Professional Experience:** Prof, dept med, Ny Univ Sch Med, as of 2004; serv leader, don monti div med oncol hematol, N Shore Univ Hosp, as of 2004; assoc attending res prof, North Shore Univ Hosp, Cornell Univ Med Col, beginning 1989; adj staff mem, Mem Sloan-Kettering Cancer Ctr, 1982-1987; Am Cancer Soc grants, 1976, 1978, 1979, 1980 & 1981; asst attend clin pharmacologist, DeptMed, Mem Hosp, beginning 1975; Nat Cancer Inst grant, 1975; chmn biochem unit, Sloan-Kettering Inst Cancer Res, Cornell Univ, 1974-1975; Damon Runyon grant, 1973; assoc prof, Sloan-Kettering Div, Grad Sch Med Sci, Cornell Univ, beginning 1972; assoc prof pharmacol & therapeut, Sloan-Kettering Div Grad Sch Med Sci, Cornell Univ, 1970-1980; assoc mem, Sloan-Kettering Inst Cancer Res, Cornell Univ, 1969-1981; asst prof, Sloan-Kettering Inst Cancer Res, Cornell Univ, 1967-1972; assoc, Sloan-Kettering Inst Cancer Res, 1964-1969; res assoc, Sloan-Kettering Inst Cancer Res, 1961-1964; res mem biochem pharmacol, Sandoz, Ltd, Basel, Switz, 1958-1961. **Memberships:** Swiss Med Soc; Swiss Chem Soc; Am Asn Cancer Res; NY Acad Sci; Am Soc Biol Chemists; Am Soc Clin Oncol. **Research Statement & Publications:** Biochemical pharmacology of anticancer drugs; experimental and clinical pharmacology of cancer; biochemistry of nucleic acids; phase I and II evaluation of new anticancer agents, especially prostate cancer. **Mailing Address:** Dept Med, NY Univ Sch Med, 550 First Ave, New York, NY 10016. **Fax:** 516-562-8950.

KREISBERG, JEFFREY I, PATHOLOGY. **Education:** State Univ NY, Albany, BS; Univ Md Sch Med, PhD (exp pathol), 1975. **Professional Experience:** PROF SURG ONCOL, UNIV TEX HEALTH SCI CTR, SAN ANTONIO, as of 2006. **Memberships:** AAAS; Am Physiol Soc; Am Soc Nephrology. **Mailing Address:** Univ Tex Health Sci Ctr, Rm 265A, San Antonio, TX 78284-0001. **Fax:** 210-567-4664. **E-Mail:** kreisberg@uthscsa.edu

KREISBERG, JEFFREY IRA, EXPERIMENTAL PATHOLOGY. **Personal Data:** b Far Rockaway, NY, July 7, 1949; m Suzanne; c Michelle, Allison, Anna, Denise & Elaine. **Education:** State Univ NY, Albany, BS, 1971; Univ Md, PhD (exp path), 1975. **Professional Experience:** PROF MED & PATH, HEALTH SCI CTR, UNIV TEX, SAN ANTONIO, 1989-; CAREER SCIENTIST, VET ADMIN, 1989-; prog comt, Am Soc Nephrology, 1988-1989; Nat Kidney Found fel, 1987-1988 & 1989-1990; prog chmn, Tissue Cell Cult, Am Soc Nephrology, 1987; Cystic Fibrosis Core Ctr, Case Western Univ, 1986-1991; Coun Kidney Cardiovasc Dis, Am Heart Asn, 1986; Spec Planning Comt, Path A Study Sect, 1985-1988; Spec Planning Comt, Nat Inst Arthritis & Diabetes & Digestive Kidney Dis, 1985; mem, Spec Study Sect, NIH, 1984 & 1987; assoc prof med, Vet Admin, 1983-1989; prin investr, NIH, 1981-1995; from asst prof to assoc prof path, Vet Admin, 1980-1989; asst biologist, Dept Med, Mass Gen Hosp, 1979-1980; consult path, Sch Med, Yale Univ, Kidney Dis Inst, NY Dept Health, 1979; lectr, var univs, socs & hosps, 1978-1991; from instr to asst prof, Dept Path, Med Sch, Harvard Univ, 1977-1980; res fel, Dept Path, Med Sch, Harvard Univ, 1976-1977; res assoc, Dept Path, Univ Ala Med Ctr, 1975-1976. **Memberships:** AAAS; Am Soc Nephrology; Am Asn Pathologists; Am Soc Cell Biol; Am Diabetes Asn; Tissue Cult Asn; Int Soc Nephrology; Am Heart Asn. **Research Statement & Publications:** Author of more than 50 technical publications. **Mailing Address:** Dept Surgy, Univ Tex, 7703 Floyd Curl Dr, San Antonio, TX 78229. **Fax:** 210-567-4664. **E-Mail:** kviesberg@uthscsa.edu

KREISER, RALPH R, INORGANIC CHEMISTRY, ANALYTICAL CHEMISTRY. **Personal Data:** b Lebanon, Pa, October 7, 1941; c 2. **Education:** Lebanon Valley Col, BS, 1963; Brown Univ, MS, 1966; Univ Conn, PhD (chem), 1969. **Professional Experience:** Mem comn math & sci, State RI, 1984-1985; PROF CHEM, COMMUNITY COL RI, 1972-; chmn dept, Community Col RI, beginning 1972; inst chem, Univ Conn, 1971-1972; asst solid state chem, Philips Nature Sci Lab, Eindhoven, Holland, 1969-1970. **Memberships:** Am Chem Soc; Sigma Xi. **Research Statement & Publications:** Interface of science and the arts in the areas of conservation and restoration. **Mailing Address:** Dept Chem Community Col RI, 400 E Ave, Warwick, RI 02886. **E-Mail:** rkreiser@cccri.cc.ri.us

KREISER, THOMAS H(ARRY), ANALYTICAL CHEMISTRY. **Personal Data:** b Ono, Pa, August 12, 1935; m 1979, Liese M Davis-Kreiser; c Daniel, Douglas & James. **Education:** Lebanon Valley Col, BS, 1958; Univ Nebr, MS, 1960, PhD (chem), 1965. **Honors & Awards:** ser Award, Astm, oct 2000. **Professional Experience:** PART-TIME, SEMI-RETIRED SR SCIENTIST, SERIM RESEARCH CORP, 2001-; sr scientist, Environ Test Systs, Inc, 1987-2001; Res biochemist, Miles Labs Inc, 1962-1986. **Memberships:** Sigma Xi. **Research Statement & Publications:** med Test Device R&D. **Mailing Address:** 30182 Blue Spruce Dr, Elkhart, IN 46514-9723.

KREISHMAN, GEORGE PAUL, BIOPHYSICAL CHEMISTRY. **Personal Data:** b Nurnberg, Ger, January 28, 1946; American citizen; m 1972, Ilze; c Mara & Peter. **Education:** Univ Wis-Milwaukee, BS, 1967; Calif Inst Technol, PhD (chem), 1972. **Professional Experience:** PROF EMER CHEM, MCMICKEN COL ART & SCI, as of 2003; prof chem, Univ Cincinnati, beginning 1990; from asst prof to assoc prof, Univ Cincinnati, 1975-1990; vis teaching asst chem, Mich Technol Univ, 1974-1975; fel biophys, Univ Pittsburgh, 1972-1974; fel chem, Int Chem Nuclear Corp, 1971-1972. **Memberships:** Am Chem Soc; Res Soc Alcoholism. **Research Statement & Publications:** Application of nuclear magnetic resonance spectroscopy and electrochemical techniques to the study of biologically important systems. **Mailing Address:** Dept Chem, Univ Cincinnati, 404 Crosley PO Box 210172, Cincinnati, OH 45221-0172. **Fax:** 513-556-9239. **E-Mail:** george.kreishman@uc.edu

KREISLE, LEONARDT F(ERDINAND), mechanical engineering; deceased, see previous edition for last biography

KREISLER, MICHAEL NORMAN, HIGH ENERGY PHYSICS. **Personal Data:** b Bronx, NY, October 30, 1940; m 1963, Barbara; c David, Michele & Jeffrey. **Education:** Princeton Univ, AB, 1962; Stanford Univ, MS, 1963, PhD (physics), 1966. **Honors & Awards:** Defense Progs Award Excellence, DOE-Nat Nuclear Secuity Admin, 1998. **Professional Experience:** TECH ADV, DIR OFF RES DEVELOP & SIMULATION, NAT NUCLEAR SECURITY ADMIN, 2001-; sci adv, Dir Off Defense Res, Wash, as of 2006; div leader, N Div, 1994-; sci assoc, Europ Orgn Nuclear Res, Geneva, 1978-1979; prof physics, Univ Mass, Amherst, 1976-; grad dean res, N Div, 1975-1977; assoc prof, N Div, 1972-1976; from instr to asst prof physics, Joseph Henry Labs, Princeton Univ, 1966-1972; consult, Lawrence Livermore Labs, Los Alamos Labs. **Memberships:** Am Phys Soc; Sigma Xi. **Research Statement & Publications:** Investigation of the strong interactions of neutrons and protons, especially cross sections; study of the decays of multi-pionic resonances such as the eta meson; search for rare phenomena in weak interactions, kaon decays, beta decay of Lambda hyperon; search for tachyons; polarization in inclusive reactions; charm searches; macron accelerators; hadronic production of particles with strange, charm, and bottom quarks; new approaches to ultra high speed computation; application of nuclear and particle physics to weapons physics problems. **Mailing Address:** Dept Energy, Nat Nuclear Security Admin, NA-113, 1000 Independence Ave SW Forrestal Bldg, Washington, DC 20585. **Fax:** 202-586-8005. **E-Mail:** kreisler1@llnl.gov

KREISMAN, NORMAN RICHARD, NEUROPHYSIOLOGY. **Personal Data:** b Chicago, Ill, June 26, 1943; m 1975, c 1. **Education:** Ariz State Univ, BA, 1965; Univ Mich, MS, 1968; Med Col Pa, PhD (physiol), 1971. **Professional Experience:** PROF PHYSIOL, SCH MED, TULANE UNIV, as of 2006, assoc prof physiol, Sch Med, Tulane Univ, beginning 1979; prof & vice chmn physiol, Sch Med, Tulane Univ, 1998; vis prof neurol, Case Western Res Univ Sch Med, 1993; asst prof, Sch Med, Tulane Univ, 1973-1979; instr, Sch Med, Tulane Univ, 1971-1973. **Memberships:** Int Soc Cerebral Blood Flow & Metab; Soc Neuroscience; Am Heart Asn; Am Physiol Soc. **Research Statement & Publications:** Electrophysiological and metabolic relationships in brain in physiological and pathophysiological states; epilepsy; hypoxia. **Mailing Address:** Sch Med Tulane Univ, Dept Physiol SL-39 Rm 4063, New Orleans, LA 70112-2699. **Fax:** 504-988-2675. **E-Mail:** nkreism@tulane.edu

KREISS, HEINZ-OTTO, MATHEMATICS. **Education:** Univ Hamburg, W Ger, Dipl, 1955. **Professional Experience:** PROF EMER, DEPT MATH, UNIV CALIF, LOS ANGELES, as of 2004. **Mailing Address:** Dept Math, Univ Calif, PO Box 951555, Los Angeles, CA 90095-1555. **E-Mail:** kreiss@math.ucla.edu

KREITH, FRANK, SOLAR ENGINEERING, THERMODYNAMICS. **Personal Data:** b Vienna, Austria, December 15, 1922; American citizen; m 1951, c 3. **Education:** Univ Calif, BS, 1945; Univ Calif, Los Angeles, MS, 1949; Univ Paris, Dr Univ Paris(sci), 1965. **Honors & Awards:** Worcester Award, 1980; Max Jakob Award, 1985; Charles Greeley Abbott Award, 1988; Washington Award, 1997; ASME Medal, 1998; Yerrott Award, 1999. **Professional Experience:** RETIRED; pres, Kreith Eng Inc, 1988-1994; consult engr, Solar Energy Res Inst, 1987-1988; sr res fel, Solar Energy Res Inst, 1984-1987; emer prof chem eng, Univ Colo, Boulder, 1978-; chief thermal conversion, Solar Energy Res Inst, 1977-1984; pres, Environ Consult Serv, 1975-1977; NATO sr fel, 1975; fac res assoc, Inst Behav Sci, 1971-1977; Beech Aircraft Co, 1959 & Nat Ctr Atmos Res, 1967-1969; fac res asst, Inst Arctic & Alpine Res, 1965-1971; mem, Nat Adv Group Aeronaut Res & Develop-NATO, 1964-1965; Fulbright grants & vis lectr, France, Israel & Spain, 1964-1965; mem staff, Nat Bur Standards, 1961-1963; prof mech & chem eng, 1959-1978; Air Prod, Metals Disintegrating Co, 1957-1969; Air Prod, Inc, 1955-1957; assoc prof, Lehigh Univ, 1953-1959; asst prof mech eng, Univ Calif, 1951-1953; Consult, Proj Squid, 1950; Res engr, Jet Propulsion Lab, Calif Inst Technol, 1945-1949. **Memberships:** FelAm Soc Mech Engrs; Am Inst Chem Engrs; Int Solar Energy Soc. **Research Statement & Publications:** Heat transfer; boundary layer theory; solar engineering; solar energy thermal conversion; heat transfer & energy conservation; design of energy conversion & cogeneration systems; author of books on heat transfer, waste management, renewable energy conversion & solar building design; technical editor. **Mailing Address:** 1485 Sierra Dr, Boulder, CO 80302-7846. **Fax:** 303-443-4341. **E-Mail:** FKREITH@AOL.COM

KREITH, KURT, MATHEMATICS. **Personal Data:** b Vienna, Austria, May 3, 1932; American citizen; m 1957. **Education:** Univ Calif, Berkeley, AB, 1953, MA, 1957, PhD (math), 1960. **Professional Experience:** PROF EMER MATH, UNIV CALIF, DAVIS, as of 2001; prof math, Univ Calif, Davis, beginning 1969; assoc prof, Univ Calif, Davis, 1965-1969; phys sci officer, US Arms Control & Disarmament Agency, 1963-1965; asst prof math, Univ Calif, Davis, 1960-1963. **Memberships:** Am Math Soc; Math Asn Am. **Research Statement & Publications:** Differential equations and differential operators in Hilbert space. **Mailing Address:** Dept Math, Univ Calif, Davis, CA 95616-8633. **Fax:** 530-752-6635. **E-Mail:** kkreith@ucdavis.edu

KREITMAN, MARTIN E, GENETICS. **Education:** State Univ NY, BS; Univ Fla, MS; Harvard Univ, PhD (pop genetics). **Professional Experience:** PROF, DEPT ECOL & EVOLUTION, UNIV CHICAGO, as of 2005. **Mailing Address:** Dept Ecol & Evolution Biol Univ Chicago, 1103 E 57th St, Chicago, IL 60637. **Fax:** 773-702-9740. **E-Mail:** mkre@midway.uchicago.edu

KREITZBERG, CARL WILLIAM, meteorology; deceased, see previous edition for last biography

KREITZER, MELVYN, OPTICAL DESIGNING. **Personal Data:** b Cape Town, SAfrica, October 21, 1945; m 1971, Sharon; c Jason & David. **Education:** Univ Cape Town, BS, 1964, BS (Hons), 1966; Rochester Inst Technol, MS, 1968; Univ Ariz, MS & PhD, 1976. **Honors & Awards:** Eng Excellence Award, Optical Soc Am, 1995. **Professional Experience:** PRIN, OPCON ASSOC, as of 2003; CONSULT, as of 2002. **Memberships:** Optical Soc Am. **Research Statement & Publications:** Granted patents in professional field. **Mailing Address:** Opcon Assoc, 3997 McMann Rd, Cincinnati, OH 45245-2307. **Fax:** 513-752-1325.

KREIZINGER, JEAN DOLLOFF, GENETICS. **Personal Data:** b Presque Isle, Maine, October 17, 1931; div, c Diane (Ross), Kary (Evans) & Tracy (Johnson). **Education:** Univ Maine, BS, 1953; Cornell Univ, MS, 1956, PhD (genetics), 1958; Univ Conn, MBA, 1981. **Professional Experience:** PROF EMER, WESTERN CONN STATE UNIV, as of 2004; chmn dep biol & environ sci, Western Conn State Univ, beginning 1994; chmn dep biol & environ sci, Univ Conn, 1991; Iowa State Univ, 1992; asst dean arts & sci, Western Conn State Univ, 1982-1984; vis prof, Cornell Univ, 1981 & 1986; prof biol, Western Conn State Univ, beginning 1979; assoc prof, Western Conn State Univ, 1970-1979; res assoc biol, Univ Tex, Houston, 1969-1970; NIH res fel human genetics, M D Anderson Hosp & Tumor Inst, Univ Tex, 1967-1969; asst prof biol, Danbury State Col, 1965-1967. **Memberships:** Sigma Xi; Bot Soc Am. **Research Statement & Publications:** Chemical mutagenesis; plant cytogenetics. **Mailing Address:** Dept Biol & Environ Sci, Western Conn State Univ, 181 White St, Danbury, CT 06810-6845.

KREJCI, ROBERT HENRY, SOLID ROCKET MOTORS, BALLISTIC MISSILES. **Personal Data:** b Shenandoah, Iowa, November 15, 1943; m 1968, Carolyn R Meyer; c Christopher & Ryan. **Education:** Iowa State Univ, BS, 1967, ME, 1971; Nat Defense Univ, dipl, 1991. **Professional Experience:** MGR SPEC PROJS, STRATEGIC DIV, THIOKOL CORP, 1986-; Aeronaut engr, USAF, Wright Lab, Propulsion & Power Div, 1985-1996; space motor progs, Strategic Div, 1984-1986; mgr advan technol, Wasatch Div, 1978-1984; Officer, Ballistic Missiles Off, 1975-1978; res assoc, Lawrence Livermore Lab, 1973-1975; Officer, USAF Space Div, 1969-1973. **Memberships:** Am Inst Aeronaut & Astronaut; Nat Planetary Soc; Nat Space Soc. **Research Statement & Publications:** Develop and produce test vehicles to advance rocket motor propulsion understanding, including ignition mechanisms and motor dynamics. **Mailing Address:** 885 N 300 E, Brigham City, UT 84302.

KREJSA, RICHARD JOSEPH, CONODONT PALEOBIOLOGY, CYCLOSTOME TOOTH DEVELOPMENT. **Personal Data:** b Cleveland, Ohio, April 4, 1933; m 1962, c 6. **Education:** Mich State Univ, BS, 1954; Univ Calif, Los Angeles, MA, 1958; Univ BC, PhD (zoology), 1965. **Honors & Awards:** Frederick H Stoye Award, Am Soc Ichthyologists & Herpetologists, 1963. **Professional Experience:** PROF EMER, CALIF POLYTECH STATE UNIV, SAN LUIS OBISPO, 1994-; prof polit sci, Calif Polytech State Univ, 1988-1994; vis scholar, Mus Comp Zool, Harvard Univ, Cambridge, Mass, 1982-1983; hon life mem, Red Wind Found, 1980; co-chmn & bd dirs, San Luis Obispo Environ Ctr & hon life mem, 1980; prof biol sci, Calif Polytech State Univ, 1978-1994; co-chmn, San Luis Obispo Co Bd Supvrs, 1976; chmn bd, San Luis Obispo Co Bd Supvrs, 1975; elected mem, San Luis Obispo Co Bd Supvrs, 1973-1980; from asst prof to assoc prof, Calif Polytech State Univ, 1968-1978; nat inst dent res trainee comp calcification, Col Physicians & Surgeons, Columbia Univ, 1966-1968; vis asst prof zool, Univ Hawaii, 1965-1966; NSF stipend, Summer Inst Animal Behav, Utah State Univ, 1965; instr gen zool & biol, Western Wash State Col, 1964-1965; asst cur fishes, Scripps Inst Oceanog, Univ Calif, 1958-1959. **Memberships:** Am Soc Zoologists; Am Soc Ichthyologists & Herpetologists; Europ Soc Comp Skin Biol; AAAS; Pander Soc; Am Fisheries Soc. **Research Statement & Publications:** Comparative morphology and embryology of vertebrate skin, teeth and scales; origin of craniata; paleobiology of conodonta; effects of gold mining and other historic natural resource exploitations on California salmonid fisheries. **Mailing Address:** Dept Biol Sci, Col Arts & Sci, Calif Polytech State Univ, San Luis Obispo, CA 93407-0001.

KREKELER, CARL HERMAN, ZOOLOGY, ENTOMOLOGY. **Personal Data:** b Levenworth, Kans, January 12, 1920; m 1944, c 2. **Education:** Concordia Sem, BA, 1941; Univ Chicago, PhD (zoology), 1955. **Professional Experience:** PROF EMER BIOL, VALPARAISO UNIV, 1987-; prof biol, Valparaiso Univ, 1947-1987; instr biol, Bethany Col,

1942-1944. **Memberships:** Ecol Soc Am; Soc Study Evolution; Soc Syst Zoologists; Nat Speleol Soc. **Research Statement & Publications:** Speciation pattern in cave beetles; systematic entomology. **Mailing Address:** Dept Biol, Valparaiso Univ, Neils Sci Ctr, Valparaiso, IN 46383. **Fax:** 219-464-5489.

KREKORIAN, CHARLES O'NEIL, ANIMAL BEHAVIOR. **Personal Data:** b Los Angeles, Calif, April 17, 1941; m 1967, Jane; c Karl & Quinn. **Education:** Calif State Col, Los Angeles, BA, 1963, MA, 1966; Univ Toronto, PhD (zoology), 1970. **Professional Experience:** PROF ZOOL, SAN DIEGO STATE UNIV, 1979-; from asst prof to assoc prof, San Diego State Univ, 1970-1979; res assoc behav res, Am Inst Res, 1964-1966. **Memberships:** AAAS; Animal Behav Soc; Herpet Soc. **Research Statement & Publications:** Ethology of fish and reptiles with emphasis on their agonistic and gamopractic behavior. **Mailing Address:** Biol Dept, San Diego State Univ, San Diego, CA 92182-0001.

KRELL, ROBERT DONALD, IMMUNOPHARMACOLOGY. **Personal Data:** b Toledo, Ohio, December 2, 1943; m 1966, c 2. **Education:** Univ Toledo, BS, 1966; Ohio State Univ, PhD (pharmacol), 1972. **Professional Experience:** ICI AM INC, as of 2002; CO OWNER & VPRES, IPS THERAPEUTIQUE, UNIV SHERBROOKE, QUE, CAN, as of 2001; FOUNDER, REROK INC, as of 2001; sr mgr, pulmonary pharmacol sect, Stuart Pharmaceut, beginning 1981; sr scientist pharmacol, Smith Kline Corp, 1973-1981; fel, Sch Hyg & Pub Health, Johns Hopkins Univ, 1972-1973. **Memberships:** Soc Neuroscience; AAAS; Am Acad Allergy; Am Soc Pharmacol & Exp Therapeut; Am Thoracic Soc; Sigma Xi. **Research Statement & Publications:** Biochemical, pharmacological, physiological and immunological investigation into the mechanisms of asthma, immediate-type hypersensitivity reactions and chronic obstructive pulmonary diseases. **Mailing Address:** PO Box 847, Pocono Pines, PA 18350.

KREMBS, G(EORGE) M(ICHAEL), COMPUTER SYSTEMS INTEGRATION. **Personal Data:** b Merrill, Wis, September 2, 1934; m 1957, Shirley; c 5. **Education:** Notre Dame Univ, BS, 1956; Stanford Univ, PhD, 1959. **Professional Experience:** OWNER, KREMBS ASSOC, 1998-; total systs strategist, IBM Corp, 1987-1998; Guest lectr, IBM Systs Res Inst, New York, 1980-1982; mgr adv display technol, Eng Dept Adv Systs Develop, 1979-1987; mgr adv display prod, Eng Dept Adv Systs Develop, 1978-1979; mgr display prod technol, Eng Dept Adv Systs Develop, 1977-1978; mgr, Eng Dept Adv Systs Develop, 1970-1977; mgr adv display systs, Systs Develop Div, IBM Corp, 1968-1970; mgr adv graphic technol, Systs Develop Div, IBM Corp, 1965-1968; staff engr, Systs Develop Div, IBM Corp, 1964-1965; sect mgr solid state mat, Ford-Philco Appl Res Labs, 1961-1964; group supvr solid state mat, Philco Res Labs, 1959-1961; Elec engr, Ampex Corp, 1957-1958. **Memberships:** mem-at-Large for Mid-Hudson section; sr mem Inst Elec & Electronics Engrs; IEEE computer soc. **Research Statement & Publications:** Computer displays; electronic scanning; graphic image processing; electro-optical systems; television engineering; broadband communications; electron tube devices; solid state device and materials technology; transistor circuit design; design and development of multi-vendor computer networks for IBM large systems used by engineers and scientists. **Mailing Address:** 123 Pleasant Ridge Dr, West Hurley, NY 12491. **Fax:** 845-679-3326. **E-Mail:** krembsg1@hotmail.com

KREMENAK, CHARLES ROBERT, MAXILLOFACIAL GROWTH & DEVELOPMENT. **Personal Data:** b Newell, Iowa, April 17, 1931; m 1954, Nellie; c Sarah M H (Meyers), Erica A, Martha V & Charles V. **Education:** Univ Iowa, DDS, 1955, MS, 1961. **Professional Experience:** EMER PROF ORTHODONT, UNIV IOWA, 1994-; pres, Craniofacial Biol Group, Int Asn Dent Res, 1987-1988; pres, Am Cleft Palate Asn, 1987-1988; prof orthodont, Univ Iowa, 1972-1994; prof otolaryngol head & neck surg, Univ Iowa, 1972-1984; co-prin investr, Univ Iowa, 1971-1991; prog dir, Univ Iowa, 1969-1994; assoc prof, Univ Iowa, 1969-1972; asst prof otolaryngol & maxillofacial surg, Univ Iowa, 1966-1969; Nat Inst Dent Res fel, Nat Inst Dent Res investr cleft palate prog proj, 1965-1971; Nat Inst Dent Res fel, Univ Iowa, 1963-1964; asst prof orthodont, Univ Iowa, 1961-1969; prog writer & consult, Encycl Britannica Films, Inc, 1961-1962; instr ped dent, Univ Iowa, 1959-1961; dent officer, USN, 1955-1958. **Memberships:** Int Asn Dent Res; AAAS; Am Cleft Palate Asn; Am Polar Soc. **Research Statement & Publications:** Maxillofacial growth, especially elucidation of maxillofacial growth control systems; cleft palate habilitation with emphasis on prevention of postsurgical growth aberration; role of postsurgical wound contraction in midfacial growth and development. **Mailing Address:** Univ Iowa, Oakdale Hall, Iowa City, IA 52240. **E-Mail:** kremenak@aol.com

KREMENTZ, EDWARD THOMAS, surgical oncology, clinical research; deceased, see previous edition for last biography

KREMER, JAMES NEVIN, BIOLOGICAL OCEANOGRAPHY, ECOLOGY. **Personal Data:** b Montclair, NJ, July 19, 1945; m 1969, c 2. **Education:** Princeton Univ, BA, 1967; Univ RI, PhD (oceanography), 1975. **Professional Experience:** PROF MARINE SCI, UNIV CONN, as of 2006; assoc prof biol sci, Univ Southern Calif, beginning 1983; asst prof, Univ Southern Calif, 1976-1983; fel, NATO, 1975-1976; res asst marine ecol, Grad Sch Oceanog, Univ RI, 1970-1975. **Memberships:** Am Soc Limnol & Oceanog; Estuarine Res Fedn; Am Geophys Union; Sigma Xi. **Research Statement & Publications:** Marine plankton ecology; systems ecology and computer simulation, especially physical processes and nutrient dynamics in planktonic systems. **Mailing Address:** Dept Marine Sci, Univ Conn, 1080 Shennecossett Rd, Groton, CT 06320. **Fax:** 860-405-9153. **E-Mail:** james.kremer@uconn.edu

KREMER, PATRICIA MCCARTHY, ZOOPLANKTON ECOLOGY. **Personal Data:** b San Francisco, Calif, April 24, 1947; m 1969, James; c Katherine & Joseph. **Education:** Stanford Univ, BA, 1969; Univ RI, PhD (oceanog), 1976. **Professional Experience:** ADJ PROF & RES, DEPT MARINE SCI, UNIV CONN, as of 1995; assoc res prof, Univ Southern Calif, beginning 1992; asst res prof, Univ Southern Calif, 1985-1992; mem, Am Soc Limnol & Oceanog, 1981-1984; Allen Hancock Found res fel, Univ Southern Calif, 1976-1987; res asst, Grad Sch Oceanog, Univ RI, 1973-1974. **Memberships:** Am Soc Limnol & Oceanog; Am Geophys Union; Sigma Xi. **Research Statement & Publications:** Zooplankton ecology, soft-bodied forms including atnophores, salps and medusae; Growth dynamics of a ctenophore Mnemiopsis in relation to variable food supply II: Carbon budgets and growth model; Patterns of abundance for Mnemiopsis in US coastal waters: a comparative overview; author of various articles. **Mailing Address:** Dept Marine Sci, Univ Conn, 1080 Shennecossett Rd, Groton, CT 06340. **Fax:** 860-405-9153. **E-Mail:** patricia.kremer@uconn.edu

KREMER, RUSSELL EUGENE, CRYSTAL GROWTH, SEMICONDUCTOR CHARACTERIZATION. **Personal Data:** b Milford, Nebr, May 10, 1954; m 1984, c 1. **Education:** Goshen Col, BA, 1975; Purdue Univ, MS, 1978, PhD (physics), 1983. **Professional Experience:** CO-CHAIR, CRYSTAL SPECIALTIES INT, as of 2005; Colo Univ, Colo Springs, 1990; STAFF SCIENTIST, CRYSTAL SPECIALTIES INT, 1987-; adj assoc prof, Ore Grad Ctr, 1987-1990; consult, United Epitaxial Technol, 1985-1986; from asst prof to assoc prof appl physics & elec eng, Ore Grad Ctr, 1983-1987. **Memberships:** Am Phys Soc; Mat Res Soc; Sigma Xi; Am Asn Crystal Growth. **Research Statement & Publications:** Growth and characterization of compound semiconductor single crystal material; development of a process to grow semi-insulating GaAs using a vertical bridgman technique. **Mailing Address:** Crystal Specialties Int, 2853 Janitell Rd, Colorado Springs, CO 80906. **Fax:** 719-540-0994.

KREMERS, HOWARD EARL, INDUSTRIAL CHEMISTRY. **Personal Data:** b Urbana, Ill, September 21, 1917; m 1940, c 3. **Education:** Western Reserve Univ, AB, 1939; Syracuse Univ, MS, 1941; Univ Ill, PhD (chem), 1944. **Professional Experience:** RETIRED; dir mkt serv, Kerr-McGee Chem Corp, 1972-1990; mgr mkt serv, Kerr-McGee Chem Corp, 1970-1971; mgr mkt res & develop, Kerr-McGee Chem Corp, 1969-1970; mgr mkt develop & tech serv, Lindsay Chem Div, Am Potash & Chem Corp, 1963-1969; dist mgr, Lindsay Chem Div, Am Potash & Chem Corp, 1960-1963; vpres mkt develop, Lindsay Chem Div, Am Potash & Chem Corp, 1959-1960; secy, Lindsay Chem Co, 1956-1958; dir res, Lindsay Chem Co, 1951-1956; dir res, Lindsay Light & Chem Co, 1946-1951; chemist, Lindsay Light & Chem Co, 1944-1946. **Memberships:** Am Chem Soc. **Research Statement & Publications:** Rare earths; thorium. **Mailing Address:** 2020 S Monroe St No 620, Denver, CO 80210-3755.

KREMKAU, FREDERICK WILLIAM, MEDICAL ULTRASOUND. **Personal Data:** b Mechanicsburg, Pa, April 30, 1940; m 1967, c 1. **Education:** Cornell Univ, BS, 1963; Univ Rochester, MS, 1969, PhD (elec eng), 1972. **Honors & Awards:** Am Inst Ultrasound Med's Presidential Recognition Award, 1981; Joseph H Holmes Basic Sci Pioneer Award, 1994. **Professional Experience:** PROF & DIR, CTR MED ULTRASOUND, WAKE FOREST UNIV SCH MED, as of 2006; dir, Ctr Med Med Ultrasound, Bowman Gray Sch Med, 1985-; assoc prof, Yale Univ, 1981-1985; res asst prof, Ctr Med Ultrasound, Bowman Gray Sch Med, 1974-1980; instr med, Ctr Med Ultrasound, Bowman Gray Sch Med, 1972-1974; res asst, Univ Rochester, 1969-1972; teaching asst elec eng, Univ Rochester, 1967-1969; assoc editor, Journal Ultrasound Med. **Memberships:** Inst Elec & Electronics Engrs; Am Inst Ultrasound Med; Acoust Soc Am; secr & vpres Am Inst Ultrasound Med. **Research Statement & Publications:** Safety of ultrasound; acoustic properties of biological material; sonographic and doppler ultrasound artifacts. **Mailing Address:** Ctr Med Ultrasound, Wake Forest Univ Sch Med, Winston-Salem, NC 27157-1039. **Fax:** 336-716-2447.

KREMPL, ERHARD, MECHANICS OF MATERIALS, METALS & POLYMERS. **Personal Data:** b Regensburg, Ger, March 5, 1934; wid, c 2. **Education:** Munich Tech Univ, Dipl Ing, 1956, Dr Ing(mech mat), 1962. **Honors & Awards:** Nadai Award, Am Soc Mech Engrs, 1987. **Professional Experience:** ROSALIND & JOHN J REDFERN JR PROF ENG, MECH MAT LAB, RENSSELAER POLYTECH INST, 1993-; Humboldt sr scientist, Ger, 1993-1994; head, dept Mech Eng, Aeronaut Eng & Mech, 1987-1996; Fulbright fel, Austria, 1985; DIR, MECH MAT LAB, RENSSELAER POLYTECH INST, 1975-; from assoc prof to prof mech, Mech Mat lab, Rensselaer Polytech inst, 1968-1993; mech of mat engr, Gen Elec Co, NY, 1964-1968; res proj engr, Munich Tech Univ, 1956-1964. **Memberships:** Fel Am Soc Mech Engrs; Am Soc Exp Stress Anal; Am Soc Testing & Mat; Soc Eng Sci; fel Am Acad Mech. **Research Statement & Publications:** Mechanics of deformation and fracture behavior of metals and composites; creep, fatigue, fracture; applications to power plant such as steam and gas turbines and nuclear reactors; constitutive equation theory to describe time-dependent material behavior; inelastic analysis. **Mailing Address:** Dept Mech Eng Aeronaut Eng & Mech, Rensselaer Polytech Inst, Troy, NY 12180-3590. **Fax:** 518-276-6025. **E-Mail:** krempe@rpi.edu

KREMSER, THURMAN RODNEY, PHYSICS. **Personal Data:** b Temple, Pa, August 29, 1932. **Education:** Lehigh Univ, BS, 1954, MS, 1956; Temple Univ, PhD (physics), 1968. **Professional Experience:** PROF EMER PHYSICS, ALBRIGHT COL, 1994-; Prof & chmn dept, 1956-1994. **Memberships:** Am Asn Physics Teachers. **Mailing Address:** Dept Physics, Albright Col, 13th & Bern St, PO Box 15234, Reading, PA 19612-5234.

KRENDEL, EZRA SIMON, HUMAN FACTORS ENGINEERING. **Personal Data:** b New York, NY, March 5, 1925; m 1992, Janet Allen; c David A, Jennifer J (Hall) & Tamara Krendel-Clark. **Education:** Brooklyn Col, BA, 1945; Mass Inst Technol, ScM, 1947; Harvard Univ, AM, 19 50. **Honorary Degrees:** MA, Univ Pa, 1971. **Honors & Awards:** Louis E Levy Gold Medal, Franklin Inst, 1960. **Professional Experience:** EMER PROF STATIST OPERS & RES, SCH ENG & APPL SCI, UNIV PA, 1990-; prin scientist, Systs Technol, Inc, 1987-1988; prof systs, Sch Eng & Appl Sci, Univ Pa, 1983; chmn bd adv, Ctr, 1969-1970; NATO vis guest lectr in univs & res insts, Greece, Turkey, Eng Italy, France & Ger, 1968-1971; Consult to indust, res, non-profit, local & fed govt orgn, 1967-; dir, Mgt Sci Ctr, Univ Pa, 1967-1969; prof statist & opers res, Ctr, 1966-1990; tech dir opers res, Res Labs, 1963-1966; From res engr to mgr engr, Psychol Lab, Labs Res & Develop, Franklin Inst, 1949-1963. **Memberships:** fel AAAS; fel Inst Elec & Electronics Engrs; fel Am Psychol Asn; fel Human Factors Soc; Ergonomics Soc; fel Am Psychol Soc. **Research Statement & Publications:** Human control dynamics, tracking, decision making, power output and human error; command control and man-machine systems design. **Mailing Address:** 211 Cornell Ave, Swarthmore, PA 19081-1933. **Fax:** 610-543-9107. **E-Mail:** krendel@wharton.upenn.edu

KRENER, ARTHUR JAMES, APPLIED MATHEMATICS, SYSTEMS THEORY. **Personal Data:** b Brooklyn, NY, October 8, 1942; c 3. **Education:** Col the Holy Cross, BS, 1964; Univ Calif, Berkeley, MA, 1967, PhD (math), 1971. **Professional Experience:** PROF MATH, UNIV CALIF, DAVIS, 1980-; vis sr res fel, Imperial Col, London, 1980-1981; Fullbright Hays fel, Univ Rome, 1979; assoc prof, Univ Calif, Davis, 1976-1980; res fel eng & appl physics, Harvard Univ, 1974-1975; asst prof, Univ Calif, Davis, 1971-1976. **Memberships:** Soc Indust & Appl Math; Am Math Soc; Inst Elec & Electronics Engrs; Sigma Xi. **Research Statement & Publications:** Nonlinear systems theory; stochastic processes. **Mailing Address:** Dept Math, Univ Calif, One Shields Ave, Davis, CA 95616-8633. **E-Mail:** ajkrener@ucdavis.edu

KRENITSKY, THOMAS ANTHONY, BIOCHEMISTRY. **Personal Data:** b Throop, Pa, September 13, 1938. **Education:** Scranton Univ, BS, 1959; Cornell Univ, PhD (biochem), 1963. **Honors & Awards:** Aaron Bendich Award, Sloan-Kettering Cancer Inst, 1987. **Professional Experience:** PRES & CHIEF EXEC OFFICER, KRENITSKY PHARMACEUT, as of 2006; dir, Wellcome Fund, 1990-1996; vpres, Wellcome Res labs, Burroughs wellcome Co, beginning 1989; head, Div Exp Ther, 1983-1989; adj assoc prof, Dept Biochem & Nutrit, Univ NC, Chapel Hill, beginning 1976; head enzym, Wellcome Res Labs, Burroughs Wellcome Co, 1968-1983; sr res biochemist, Wellcome Res Labs, Burroughs Wellcome Co, 1966-1968; res assoc, Yale Univ, 1964-1966; fel biochem, Sloan-Kettering Inst Cancer Res, 1963-1964. **Memberships:** Am Chem Soc; Am Soc Biol Chemists. **Research Statement & Publications:** Specificities, mechanisms and phylogenetic relationships of the enzymes involved in purine and pyrimidine metabolism; purine and pyrimidine hydroxylating enzymes, ribosyltransferases, phosphoribosyltransferases, nucleoside and nucleotide kinases, and nucleotide interconverting enzymes; nucleoside antiviral agents. **Mailing Address:** Krenitsky Pharmaceuticals Inc, 4 Univ Pl 4611 Univ Dr, Durham, NC 27707. **Fax:** 919-403-0456. **E-Mail:** kpi@kpi-pharma.com

KRENKEL, PETER ASHTON, WATER QUALITY MANAGEMENT, THERMAL POLLUTION. **Personal Data:** b San Francisco, Calif, January 3, 1930; m 1985, Jessica; c Joshua H, Kim H & Heather H. **Education:** Univ Calif, Berkeley, BS, 1956, MS, 1958, PhD (environ eng), 1960. **Honors & Awards:** Rudolf Hering Award, Am Soc Civil Engrs, 1963; Serv, Integrity, Responsibility Award, Asn Gen Contractors, 1984; Eminent Speaker, Inst Engr, Australia, 1986. **Professional Experience:** PROF EMER CIVIL ENG, UNIV NEV, RENO, 1996-; prof civil eng, Col Eng, 1988-1995; Gen Motors Corp, Monsanto Res Corp, Mead Corp, Stouffer Chem Corp, Inland container, Olin Corp, Korean Adv Inst Sci Tech, Ministry Water & Power, Repub China, 1986; dean, Col Eng, 1982-1987; consult, Environ Protection Agency, 1982-1984; exec dir, Water Resources Ctr, Desert Res Inst, Reno, Nev, 1978-1982; dir, Div Environ Planning, Tenn Valley Authority, 1974-1978; chmn thermal pollution, Nat Water Comn, 1972-1974; consult, WHO, 1968-; Lectr, Am Inst Chem Engrs, 1968-; chmn & prof, Dept Environ & Water Resources Eng, Vanderbilt Univ, 1960-1974; Instr, Col Eng, Univ Calif, Berkeley, 1958-1960. **Memberships:** Am Inst Chem Engrs; Am Soc Civil Engrs; Am Acad Environ Engrs; Am Water Works Asn; Int Asn Water Pollution Res; Water Environ Fedn. **Research Statement & Publications:** Water quality management; thermal pollution; gas absorption in water; turbulent diffusion and mixing analysis; mercury in the aquatic environment; water, waste water treatment. **Mailing Address:** 3500 Cashill Blvd, Reno, NV 89509. **Fax:** 702-784-4466.

KRENOS, JOHN ROBERT, CHEMICAL PHYSICS. **Personal Data:** b New Britain, Conn, September 4, 1945. **Education:** Univ Conn, BA, 1967; Yale Univ, MS, 1968, PhD (chem), 1972. **Professional Experience:** PROF CHEM, RUTGERS UNIV, as of 2006; assoc prof chem, Rutgers Univ, beginning 1978; asst prof, Rutgers Univ, 1973-1978; fel chem, Harvard Univ, 1972-1973. **Memberships:** Am Phys Soc; Am Chem Soc. **Research Statement & Publications:** Energy transfer in hyperthermal collisions and collisions involving electronically excited reactants; molecular beam chemiluminescence; model calculations of chemical reactions. **Mailing Address:** Dept Chem, Rutgers Univ, 610 Taylor Rd, Piscataway, NJ 08854. **Fax:** 732-445-5312. **E-Mail:** krenos@rutchem.rutgers.edu

KRENZ, GARY S, COMPUTER SCIENCE. **Education:** Moorhead State Univ, BS, 1978; Iowa State Univ, PhD (appl Math), 1984. **Professional Experience:** PROF, DEPT MATHS & COMPUT SCI, MARQUETTE UNIV, WIS, as of 2005. **Memberships:** Am Heart Sci Coun; Am Physiol Soc. **Mailing Address:** Dept Math Statist & Comput Sci Marquette Univ, Katharine Reed Cudahy Hall Rm 379, Milwaukee, WI 53233. **E-Mail:** gary.krenz@marquette.edu

KRENZ, JERROLD H(ENRY), ELECTRICAL ENGINEERING. **Personal Data:** b Buffalo, NY, April 24, 1934. **Education:** Univ Buffalo, BS, 1956; Stanford Univ, MS, 1958, PhD (elec eng), 1964. **Professional Experience:** PROF EMER ELEC ENG, UNIV COLO, BOULDER, as of 2002; prof elec eng, Univ Colo, Boulder, beginning 1981; assoc prof, Univ Colo, Boulder, 1977-1981; dir eng honors prog, Univ Colo, Boulder, 1969-1973; asst prof elec eng, Univ Colo, Boulder, 1963-1977; consult, Gen Elec Co, 1962; engr microwave tubes, Gen Elec Microwave Lab, 1958-1961; engr antennas, Lockheed Missile Systs, Lockheed Aircraft Corp, 1956-1957. **Memberships:** Inst Elec & Electronics Engrs; Int Solar Energy Soc; AAAS; Sigma Xi. **Research Statement & Publications:** Energy systems and policy; modeling; economic studies. **Mailing Address:** ECE-Eng-Elecl/Comp Admin, Univ Colo Box 425, Boulder, CO 80309-0425. **E-Mail:** jerrold.krenz@colorado.edu

KRENZELOK, EDWARD PAUL, TOXICOLOGY, PHARMACY. **Personal Data:** b Ladysmith, Wis, March 11, 1947. **Education:** Univ Wis, Madison, BS, 1971; Univ Minn, DPharm, 1974. **Professional Experience:** ADJ RES SCIENTIST, HUNT INST BOTANICAL DOC, CARNEGIE-MELLON UNIV, 1992-; ADJ PROF CLIN PHARM, SCH PHARM, DUQUESNE UNIV, 1989-; FAC, DIV EMERGENCY MED, UNIV PITTSBURGH, 1984-; PROF PHARM & MED & DIR, PITTSBURGH POISON CTR, 1983-; mem fac toxicol, Dept Emergency Med, 1978-1983; chmn, Dept Prof Educ, Nat Poison Ctr Network, Pittsburgh, 1978-1983; emergency med serv div, Metrop Coun, St Paul, 1978-1983; consult, Emergency Med Serv Div, Minn Dept Health, Minneapolis, 1978; private consult, Prof Prob Toxicol, 1978-; Minneapolis Community Health Serv grant poison prev prog children day care ctrs, 1977-1982; dir toxicol, Hennepin Poison Ctr, Hennepin Co Med Ctr, Minneapolis, 1976-1983; from asst prof to assoc prof pharm, Univ Minn, 1974-1983. **Memberships:** Am Asn Poison Ctr; Am Soc Hosp Pharm; Am Acad Clin Toxicol; Soc Acad Emergency Med; Am Bd Appl Toxicol. **Research Statement & Publications:** Gastric decontamination of victims suffering from poisoning emergencies; drug overdosage; drug abuse; malpractice; standards of toxicologic care. **Mailing Address:** Pittsburgh Poison Ctr, C Hosp Pittsburgh, 3705 Fifth Ave, Pittsburgh, PA 15213. **Fax:** 412-390-3311. **E-Mail:** edward.krenzelok@chp.edu

KREPINSKY, JIRI J, ORGANIC CHEMISTRY, MOLECULAR GENETICS. **Personal Data:** b Prague, Czech, July 15, 1934; Canadian citizen; m 1988, c 2. **Education:** Charles Univ, Prague, MSc, 1957, Dr rer nat, 1966; Czech Acad Sci, PhD (chem), 1961. **Professional Experience:** PROF, DEPT MED GENETICS, UNIV TORONTO, 1988-; prof med biophysics, Ludwig Inst Cancer Res, Toronto Br, 1988-1990; sr staff scientist, Ludwig Inst Cancer Res, Toronto Br, 1981-1988; assoc prof, Dept Med Genetics, Univ Toronto, 1980-1988; consult, Ont Cancer Inst, 1978-1981; sr res scientist, Dept Med Genetics, Univ Toronto, 1976-1980; dir, Chem ResLab Simes, Milan, 1972-1975; lectr, Univ NB, 1970-1972; fel synthesis natural prod, Univ NB, 1968-1970; vis scientist, Inst Org Chem, Univ Milan, 1966-1967; res assoc natural prod, Inst Org Chem & Biochem, Czech Acad Sci, 1961-1966 & 1967-1968; Mem bot exped, Soviet Cent Asia, 1961; Res asst org chem, Inst Org Chem & Biochem, Czech Acad Sci, 1957-1961. **Memberships:** Am Chem Soc; Royal Soc Chem; Chem Soc Can; NY Acad Sci. **Research Statement & Publications:** Determination of structures of biologically important compounds, particularly glycoproteins; roles of oligosaccharides moieties of glycoproteins and glycolipids development and malignancy, in particular colon cancer; organic chemistry and mass spectrometry of carbohydrates and glycopeptides; development of protocols for population cancer screening. **Mailing Address:** Dept Molecular Med Genetics Sci Bldg, Univ Toronto, Toronto, ON M5S 1A8, Can. **E-Mail:** george.krepinsky@utoronto.ca

KREPS, DAVID PAUL, MICROBIOLOGY, IMMUNOLOGY. **Personal Data:** b Pottstown, Pa, January 13, 1943; m 1965, c 2. **Education:** Manchester Col, BS, 1964; Ohio State Univ, MS, 1968; Chicago Med Sch, PhD (microbiol), 1976. **Professional Experience:** PROF & CHAIR, DEPT BIOL, MANCHESTER COL, as of 2006; dir, NSF Int Soc Educ Planners grant, Manchester Col, 1978-1981; res Corp Res grant, 1978-1979; res asst microbiol, Chicago Med Sch, 1974-1975; assoc prof biol, Manchester Col, beginning 1967; teaching asst microbiol, Ohio State Univ, 1965-1967. **Memberships:** Sigma Xi; Am Soc Microbiol. **Research Statement & Publications:** Immunological responses to salmonella typhimurium vaccines and cell fractions in inbred and outbred mice. **Mailing Address:** Dept Biol, Manchester Col, S-101 600 E Col Ave, North Manchester, IN 46962. **Fax:** 219-982-5043. **E-Mail:** dpkreps@manchester.edu

KREPS, JUANITA MORRIS, ECONOMICS, EDUCATION. **Personal Data:** b Lynch, Ky, January 11, 1921; m 1944, Clifton; c Sarah, Laura & Clifton III. **Education:** Berea Col, AB, 1942; Duke Univ, MA, 1944, PhD, 1948. **Honorary Degrees:** Numerous hon degrees from US univs, 1972-1993. **Honors & Awards:** Stephen Wise Award, 1978; Woman Yr Award, Ladies Home J, 1978; Achievement Award, Am Asn Univ Women, 1981; Dirs Choice Leadership Award, Nat Women's Econ Alliance Found, 1987. **Professional Experience:** Kenan Inst Pvt Enterprise, Univ NC, Chapel Hill, 1995-; Univ NC, Wilmington, 1993-; trustee, Coun Foreign Rels, 1983-1989; trustee, Nat Humanities Ctr, 1983-1986; trustee, HumRRO, 1980-1983; trustee, Duke Endowment, 1979-; EMER JAMES B DUKE PROF & EMER VICE PRES, DUKE UNIV, 1979-; mem, Pres Comn Nat Agenda 80's, 1979, Nat Manpower Policy Task Force; secy, US Dept Com, 1977-1979; vpres, Duke Univ, 1973-1977; trustee, Berea Col, 1972-1978 & 1980-; James B Duke prof, Duke Univ, 1972-1977; bd dirs, Am Coun Ger, Res Triangle Found, Educ Testing Serv, 1972-1977; asst provost, Duke Univ, 1969-1972; prof econ, Duke Univ, 1968-1977; assoc prof, Duke Univ, 1962-1968; mem fac, Duke Univ, 1955-1977; asst prof, Denison Univ, 1948-1950; instr econ, Denison Univ, 1945-1946. **Memberships:** Fel Gerontol Soc (vpres, 1971-1972); fel Am Acad Arts & Sci; Am Asn Univ Profs; Am Asn Univ Women; Am Econ Asn (vpres, 1983-1984); Indust Rels Res Asn. **Research Statement & Publications:** Contributed to numerous publications. **Mailing Address:** Duke Univ, 115 E Duke Bldg, Durham, NC 27708-0768. **Fax:** 919-684-8351.

KRESA, KENT, AERONAUTICS. **Personal Data:** b New York, NY, March 24, 1938. **Education:** Mass Inst Technol, BS, 1959, MS, 1961, EAA, 1966. **Honors & Awards:** Meritorious Civilian Serv Medal, Secy Defense, 1974; Meritorious pub Serv Citation, USN, 1975; Arthur D Flemming Award, US Govt, 1975; Decoration Except Civilian Serv, USAF, 1987; Bob Hope Distinguished Citizen Award, Nat Security Indust Asn, 1996. **Professional Experience:** RETIRED; chief exec officer & chmn, northrop gruman corp, beginning 1990; pres, northrop gruman corp, beginning 1987; sr vpres technol develop & planning, Advan Systs Div Aircraft Div, Ventura Div & Aircraft Sens Div, 1986-1987; vpres aircraft group, Advan Systs Div Aircraft Div, Ventura Div & Aircraft Sens Div, 1982-1986; vpres & gen mgr, Ventura Div, 1976-1982; vpres & mgr, Res & Technol Ctr, Northrop Gruman Corp, 1975-1976; dir tactical technol, Strategic Technol Off, Defense Advan Res Projs Agency, 1973-1975; spec asst to dir, Strategic Technol Off, Defense Advan Res Projs Agency, 1972-1973; dep dir, Strategic Technol Off, Defense Advan Res Projs Agency, 1968-1972; staff, Lincoln Lab, Mass Inst Technol, 1961-1968; Sr scientist, Res & Advan Develop Div, Avco, 1959-1961; bd trustees, Calif Inst Technol; bd govs, Los Angeles Music Ctr; Bd dir, Arco Corp, Chrysler Corp, John Tracy Clinic, W M Keck Found, Los Angeles World Affairs Coun. **Memberships:** Nat Acad Eng; fel Am Inst Aeronaut & Astronaut. **Research Statement & Publications:** Integration and manufacturing of military surveillance and combat aircraft defense electronics and systems, airspace management systems and information systems. **Mailing Address:** Los Angeles, CA 90067.

KRESCH, ALAN J, PHYSICAL CHEMISTRY, DATA PROCESSING. **Personal Data:** b New York, NY, June 25, 1931; m 1975, c 1. **Education:** Cornell Univ, AB, 1952; Rutgers Univ, PhD (solution kinetics), 1961. **Professional Experience:** STAFF RES ASSOC, APPLETON PAPERS INC, 1973-; Sr res chemist, Nat Cash Register Co, Ohio, 1960-1973. **Memberships:** AAAS; Am Chem Soc; Sigma Xi. **Research Statement & Publications:** Solution kinetics of inorganic polymers; reversible photochemical reactions in solution; color technology; laboratory computer. **Mailing Address:** 3214 S Poplar Lane, Appleton, WI 54915.

KRESGE, ALEXANDER JERRY, PHYSICAL ORGANIC CHEMISTRY. **Personal Data:** b Wilkes-Barre, Pa, July 17, 1926; m 1963, Yvonne; c Nell S, Peter B & Nicole. **Education:** Cornell Univ, BA, 1949; Univ Ill, PhD (chem), 1953. **Honors & Awards:** Mardi Gras Lectr, La State Univ, 1981; Mobay Lectr, Univ NH, 1982-; Nelson J Leonard Lectr, Univ Ill, 1986; Morley Medal, 1988; Sytnex Award, 1988; Richard & Doris Arnold Lectr, Univ Ill, 1989; Ingold Lectr, 1994. **Professional Experience:** EMER PROF CHEM, UNIV TORONTO, as of 2006; lectr, Frontier Chem, Wayne State Univ, 1992; Killam fel, 1984-1986; Yamada fel, 1985; Kyoto Univ, 1985; Fed Univ Santa Catarina, 1984; vis prof, Univ San Paulo, 1984; vis scientist, Fritz Haber Inst, 1981 & Univ Goteborg, 1983; vis prof, Tech Univ Denmark, 1982; vis prof, Univ Lausanne, 1981; vis prof, Univ Mich, 1979; prof chem, Scarborough Col, Univ Toronto, beginning 1974; chmn chem group, Scarborough Col, Univ Toronto, 1974-1978; vis prof, Univ Toronto, 1970-1971; chmn, Gordon Res Conf Physics & Chem Isotopes, 1968; vis prof, Oxford Univ, 1965; guest, Mass Inst Technol, 1965; NSF sr fel, 1964-1965; vis lectr, Bedford Col, London, 1964-1965; Guggenheim fel, 1964; from asst prof to prof chem, Ill Inst Technol, 1960-1974; assoc chemist, Brookhaven Nat Lab, 1957-1960; res assoc, Purdue Univ, 1954-1955 & Mass Inst Technol, 1955-1957; Fulbright scholar, Univ Col, Univ London, 1953-1954. **Memberships:** Am Chem Soc; fel Royal Soc Can; fel Chem Inst Can; Sigma Xi; AAAS; hon mem Argentinian Soc Org Chem. **Research Statement & Publications:** Reaction mechanisms; isotope effects; acid-base catalysis; kinetics. **Mailing Address:** Dept Chem, Univ Toronto, Toronto, ON M5S 3H6, Can. **Fax:** 416-978-7259. **E-Mail:** akresge@chem.utoronto.ca

KRESGE, EDWARD NATHAN, POLYMER CHEMISTRY. **Personal Data:** b Noxen, Pa, August 14, 1935; m 1963. **Education:** Univ Tampa, BS, 1957; Univ Fla, PhD (chem), 1961. **Honors & Awards:** Chmn Gordon Res Conf, Elastomers, 1987; ACS Rubber Division's Arnold Smith Award, 1993; Am Chem Society Melvin Mooney Tech Acheivement Award, 1995. **Professional Experience:** Consult, 1993-2000; sci area leader, Exxon Chem Res, 1989-1993; cheif Polymer scientist, Elastomers Technol Div, Exxon Chem Co, 1978-1993; head Elastomers Explor Res, Elastomers Technol Div, Exxon Chem Co, 1975-1993; proj leader elastomers, 1963-1975; Res chemist, 1961-1963. **Memberships:** AAAS; Am Chem Soc. **Research Statement & Publications:** Elastomer, morphology, polymer rheology and physics. **Mailing Address:** 68 Parlin Lane, Watchung, NJ 07060.

KRESH, J YASHA, ARTIFICIAL INTERNAL ORGANS, MODELING & SIMULATION. **Personal Data:** b L'vov, Russia, July 13, 1948; American citizen; m 1986, Myrna. **Education:** NJ Inst Technol, BS, 1971; Rutgers Univ, MS, 1973, PhD (biomed eng & cardiovasc physics), 1977. **Professional Experience:** PROF & DIR RES, DEPT CARDIOTHORACIC SURG, DREXEL UNIV COL MED, AS OF 2006; prof med & dir cardiovasc biophys & comput, Dept Med, Allegheny Univ, beginning 1986; prof & dir res, dept cardiothoracic surg, Allegheny Univ, beginning 1986; adj prof, Biomed Eng & Sci Inst, Drexel Univ, beginning 1986; dir, Likoff Cardiovasc Inst, Comput Ctr, Allegheny Univ, beginning 1986; fac, biomed grad studies, molecular biol & immunol prog, Alleghney Univ, beginning 1986; prof bioengineering, biomed eng & sci inst, Drexel Univ, beginning 1984; assoc prof pharmacol, Thomas Jefferson Univ, 1984-1986; res assoc prof pharmacol, Thomas Jefferson Univ, 1984-1986; assoc prof surg, Thomas Jefferson Univ, 1983-1986; assoc prof pharmacol, Thomas Jefferson Univ, 1983-1986; res mem, Ischemia Shock Res Inst, 1981-1986; res asst prof surg, Thomas Jefferson Univ, 1979-1983; dir res, Dept Surg, Div Cardiothoracic, Surg, Thomas Jefferson Univ, 1979-1986; res assoc, Dept Surg, Newark Beth Israel Med Ctr, 1976-1979; res intern comp-med, Mt Sinai-Rutgers Health Care Comp Lab, 1975-1977; res intern biomed eng, Rutgers Univ, 1971-1975. **Memberships:** Sr mem Inst Elec & Electronics Engrs; sr mem Biomed Eng Soc; Am Heart Asn; Cardiovasc Syst Dynamics Soc; fel Am Col Cardiol; fel Acad Surg Res; Sigma Xi; fel Am Inst Med & Biol Eng. **Research Statement & Publications:** Cardiovascular system dynamics; heart assist devices; computers and cardiology; patient monitoring systems; physiological and biophysical sensors; closed-loop physiological control; numerous scientific publications. **Mailing Address:** Dept Cardiothoracic Surg, Allegheny Univ, Broad & Vine St, Ms-110, Philadelphia, PA 19102. **Fax:** 215-762-5021. **E-Mail:** JYasha.Kresh@drexelmed.edu

KRESHECK, GORDON C, PHYSICAL BIOCHEMISTRY. **Personal Data:** b North Tonawanda, NY, September 3, 1933; m 1961, c 3. **Education:** Ohio State Univ, BS, 1955, MS, 1959, PhD (dairy technol), 1961. **Professional Experience:** ADJ PROF CHEM, UNIV COLO, COLO SPRINGS, 1997-; prof chem, ctr biochem & biophys studies, Northern Ill Univ, 1978-1997; dir, ctr biochem & biophys studies, Northern Ill Univ, 1975-1997; assoc ed, Bull Thermodynamics & Thermochem, 1971-1976; assoc prof, Ctr Biochem & Biophys Studies, Northern Ill Univ, 1968-1978; res assoc, Argonne Nat Lab, 1966; asst prof, Ctr Biochem & Biophys Studies, Northern Ill Univ, 1965-1968; NIH res fel chem, Cornell Univ, 1963-1965; vis scientist, Procter & Gamble Co, 1963; res asst biochem, Nobel Med Inst, Stockholm, Sweden, 1962-1963. **Memberships:** Am Chem Soc; Biophys Soc; Am Soc Biol Chemists; Sigma Xi. **Research Statement & Publications:** Protein chemistry; solution calorimetry; lipids. **Mailing Address:** Dept Chem, Univ Colo, Sci 132, Colo Springs, CO 80918. **E-Mail:** gkreshec@uccs.edu

KRESHOVER, SEYMOUR J, PATHOLOGY. **Personal Data:** b New York, NY, June 22, 1912; m 1946, c 4. **Education:** NY Univ, BA, 1934, MD, 1949; Univ Pa, DDS, 1938; Yale Univ, PhD (clin med, path), 1942; Am Bd Oral Med, dipl. **Honorary Degrees:** DSc, State Univ NY Buffalo, 1961, Univ Pa, 1967, Boston Univ, 1969, Univ Mich, 1975; DOdont, Gothenburg Univ, 1973. **Honors & Awards:** Pierre Fouchard Medal, 1972; Callahan Medal, 1972. **Professional Experience:** RETIRED; vis prof oral biol, State Univ NY, Buffalo, 1975-1980; dir, Nat Inst Dent Res, 1966-1975; chmn comn dent res, Int Dent Fedn, 1961-1967; Assoc trustee, Bd Med Educ & Res, Univ Pa, 1956-1966; prof oral path & dir dent res, Grad & Postgrad Study, Med Col Va, 1949-1956; instr, NY Univ, 1947; assoc dir, Nat Inst Dent Res, 1946-1966; teaching fel histoanat, NY Univ, 1946-1947; clin asst dent surg, Yale Univ, 1942-1943; Asst instr, Sch Med, Univ Ill, 1938-1939. **Memberships:** Am Dent Asn; Am Pub Health Asn; Am Acad Oral Path; Int Asn Dental Res (pres, 1962). **Research Statement & Publications:** Dental histology and embryology; dental pathology; prenatal factors in congenital defects. **Mailing Address:** 838 John Anderson Dr, Ormond Beach, FL 32176.

KRESIN, VLADIMIR Z, PHYSICS. **Professional Experience:** RETIRED; staff scientist, Lawrence Berkeley Nat Lab. **Mailing Address:** 582 Westfield Way, Oakland, CA 94619.

KRESINA, THOMAS FRANCIS, IMMUNE NETWORK INTERACTIONS, SOMATIC CELL HYBRIDIZATION. **Personal Data:** b Baltimore, Md, June 18, 1954; m 1978, c 3. **Education:** Cath Univ Am, BS, 1975; Univ Ala, Birmingham, PhD (biochem), 1979. **Professional Experience:** ASSOC PROF MED, PROG GEOG MED, MIRIAM HOSP & BROWN UNIV INT HEALTH INST, 1987-; Prin investr scientist, NIH RO-1 res grant, 1985-; asst prof environ health, Med Sch, 1985-1987; Prin investr scientist, Orthop Res & Educ Found grant, 1985-1986; asst prof rheumatology & path, Univ Hosp, 1983-1987; sr res assoc rheumatology, Case Western Reserve Univ, 1982-1983; res assoc immunol, NIH asst, 1981-1982; res assoc immunol, Brandeis Univ, 1980-1981; NIH asst felbiochem, Univ Ala, Birmingham, 1979-1980. **Memberships:** Am Asn Immunologists; NY Acad Sci; Orthop Res Soc; AAAS. **Research Statement & Publications:** Elucidation of immunoregulatory mechanisms which can have application in understanding human disease; generation and molecular characterization of T cells which can suppress the erythema and adema associated with arthritis; analysis of the immune network and its potential usage in vaccine formulation in schistosomiasis; analysis of granulomas inflammation and hepatic pathology in schistosomiasis. **Mailing Address:** 6443 St Phillips Rd, Linthicum Heights, MD 21090.

KRESPAN, CARL GEORGE, ORGANIC CHEMISTRY. **Personal Data:** b Erie, Pa, August 10, 1926; m 1949, c 3. **Education:** Univ Rochester, BS, 1948; Univ Minn, PhD (org chem), 1952. **Professional Experience:** RETIRED; res scientist, Cent Res Dept, E I DuPont de Nemours & Co, 1970-1993; res supvr org chem, E I DuPont de Nemours & Co, 1960-1970; res schemist, E I DuPont de Nemours & Co, 1952-1960. **Memberships:** Am Chem Soc. **Research Statement & Publications:** Organic fluorine chemistry; free radical, sulphur, cyanocarbon, macroheterocycle chemistry, and fluoropolymer. **Mailing Address:** Mozart Dr, Wilmington, DE 19801.

KRESS, DONNIE DUANE, GENETICS, ANIMAL BREEDING. **Personal Data:** b American Falls, Idaho, March 17, 1942; m 1970, Charlotte; c Ellen R & Benjamin D. **Education:** Univ Idaho, BS, 1964; Univ Wis, MS, 1966, PhD (genetics & animal sci), 1969. **Honors & Awards:** Rockefeller Prentice Mem Award, Am Soc Animal Sci, 1996. **Professional Experience:** PROF EMER, ANIMAL & RANGE SCI, MONT STATE UNIV, as of 2005; interim assoc dean, COA, Mont State Univ, beginning 1999; guest partic, Cong Vet Med & Animal Prod, Buenos Aires, Arg, 1985; prof genetics & animal breeding, Mont State Univ, 1980-1999; asst & assoc prof, Mont State Univ, 1970-1980; NIH fel quant genetics, Univ Minn, 1969-1970. **Memberships:** Am Soc Animal Sci; Sigma Xi. **Research Statement & Publications:** Quantitative genetics and animal breeding; selection, genetic by environment interaction; maternal ability of beef cattle of varying biological types and beef sire evaluation. **Mailing Address:** Dept Animal & Range Sci, Mont Sate Univ, PO Box 172900, Bozeman, MT 59717. **Fax:** 406-994-5589. **E-Mail:** dkress@montana.edu

KRESS, KENNETH A, BIOPHYSICS. **Personal Data:** b Pittsburgh, Pa, April 19, 1942. **Education:** Valparaiso Univ, BS, 1964; Mont State Univ, PhD (physics), 1969. **Professional Experience:** OWNER, K-TECH CO, 1984-. **Memberships:** Am Phys Soc. **Mailing Address:** K-Tech Co, 6666 Van Winkle Dr, Falls Church, VA 22044.

KRESS, LANCE WHITAKER, AIR POLLUTION. **Personal Data:** b Camp Lejeune, NC, September 2, 1945; m 1969, Diane; c Nicole, Kerri & Nathan. **Education:** Pa State Univ, BS, 1968, MS, 1972; Va Polytech Inst & State Univ, PhD (plant path), 1978. **Professional Experience:** BIOL SCIENTIST, FOREST SERV, USDA, 1986-; ecologist, Argonne Nat Lab, 1984-1986; asst ecologist, Argonne Nat Lab, 1980-1984; res assoc, Va Polytech Inst & State Univ, 1975-1980; Jr res aide, Pa State Univ, 1972-1973. **Memberships:** Sigma Xi. **Research Statement & Publications:** Evaluating the impacts of low concentrations of air pollutants and pollutant combinations on the growth of forest tree species; investigating the effects of elevated carbon dioxide. **Mailing Address:** USDA Forest Serv, PO Box 12254, Research Triangle Park, NC 27709-2254. **Fax:** 919-549-4047.

KRESS, LAWRENCE FRANCIS, BIOCHEMISTRY. **Personal Data:** b Milwaukee, Wis, October 5, 1936; div, c 4. **Education:** Marquette Univ, BS, 1959, MS, 1961, PhD (physiol), 1964. **Professional Experience:** Res cancer scientist v, Rosewell Park Ctr Inst, beginning 1980; res scientist IV, Roswell Park Cancer Inst, 1978-1980; adv res fel, Am Heart Asn, Roswell Park Cancer Inst, 1976-1968; sr res scientist, Roswell Park Cancer Inst, 1968-1978; NSF fel biochem, Med Sch, Dartmouth Univ, 1964-1966. **Memberships:** Am Soc Biochem & Molecular Biol; Int Soc Toxinol. **Research Statement & Publications:** Enzymology; proteolytic enzymes and their inhibitors; interactions between snake venom proteinases and plasma proteinase inhibitors. **Mailing Address:** 620 Youngs Rd, Williamsville, NY 14221.

KRESS, THOMAS JOSEPH, ORGANIC CHEMISTRY. **Personal Data:** b Indianapolis, Ind, October 31, 1940; m 1965, c 4. **Education:** Xavier Univ Ohio, BS, 1962, MS, 1964; Ohio Univ, PhD (org chem), 1967. **Professional Experience:** RES ASSOC, ELI LILLY & CO, 1980-; res scientist, Eli Lilly & CO, 1974-1980; sr org chemist, Eli Lilly & CO, 1968-1974; res assoc, Ohio Univ, 1967-1968. **Memberships:** Int Soc Heterocycle Chem; Am Chem Soc; Royal Soc Chem; Sigma Xi. **Research Statement & Publications:** The synthesis and reactions of nitrogen heterocycles. **Mailing Address:** Lilly Corp Ctr, Res Chem Bldg 110, Indianapolis, IN 46285.

KRESS, THOMAS SYLVESTER, NUCLEAR ENGINEERING, AEROSOL SCIENCE. **Personal Data:** b Kingsport, Tenn, December 5, 1933; m 1956, c 3. **Education:** Univ Tenn, BS, 1956, MS, 1965, PhD (eng sci), 1971. **Professional Experience:** RETIRED; head, Appl Sci Tech, Eng Tech Div, Oak Ridge Nat Lab, 1989-1994; mgr, Nuclear Res Coun, Union Carbide Corp, 1980-1989; prog mgr & group leader advan reactor syst, Nuclear Div, 1976-1980; engr reactor safety, Nuclear Res Coun, Union Carbide Corp, 1959-1976; engr aircraft nuclear propulsion, Pratt & Whitney Aircraft, 1956-1959. **Memberships:** AAAS; Am Soc Mech Engrs; Am Nuclear Soc; Nat Soc Prof Engrs; Nat Mgt Asn. **Research Statement & Publications:** Thermal sciences, heat ransfer, fluid transfer, fluid mechanics and thermodynamics; nuclear safety; aerosol science. **Mailing Address:** 102 Newridge Rd, Oak Ridge, TN 37830.

KRESSE, JEROME THOMAS, ORGANIC CHEMISTRY. **Personal Data:** b Buffalo, NY, December 29, 1931; m 1962, c 5. **Education:** Mich State Univ, BS, 1958; Univ Fla, PhD (org chem), 1965. **Professional Experience:** PROF CHEM, D'YOUVILLE COL, 1974-; chmn, Div Math & Natural Sci, 1974-1978; assoc prof chem & chmn dept chem & physics, D'Youville Col, 1969-1974; asst prof, D'Youville Col, 1966-1969; Asst prof chem, Muskingum Col, 1965-1966. **Memberships:** AAAS; Am Asn Univ Prof; Am Chem Soc. **Research Statement & Publications:** Studies of factors influencing the stereochemistry of the Wittig reaction; synthesis of amino acid antagonists. **Mailing Address:** 51 Harwood Rd, Buffalo, NY 14224-4231.

KRESSEL, HENRY, ELECTROOPTICS. **Personal Data:** b Vienna, Austria, January 24, 1934; American citizen; m 1956, Bertha; c Aron & Kim. **Education:** Yeshiva Col, BA, 1955; Harvard Univ, MS, 1956; Univ Pa, MBA, 1959, PhD (mat sci), 1965. **Honors & Awards:** Achievement Award, RCA Corp, 1962, 1968 & 1969; Centennial Medal, Inst Elec & Electronics Engrs, 1984, David Sarnoff Award, 1985; Distinguished Serv Award, Inst Elec & Electronics Engrs Lasers & Electro-Optics Soc. **Professional Experience:** SR MANAGING DIR, WARBURG PINCUS & CO, 2001-; CHMN, SARNOFF CORP BD DIR, 2001-; managing dir, Warburg Pincus & Co, 1983-2001; staff vpres, RCA labs, 1979-1983; lab dir, RCA labs, 1977-1979; group head, RCA labs, 1969-1977; mem tech staff, RCA labs, 1967-1969; group device physics, Tech Progs lab, 1965-1966; group head microwave device, Semiconductor div, Radio Corp Am, 1961-1963; Engr, Semiconductor div, Radio Corp Am, 1959-1961; mem, Adv Coun Eng, NSF; consult, dept Defense; Cofounder, J Lightwave Technol. **Memberships:** Nat Acad Eng; fel Am Phys Soc; fel Inst Elec & Electronics Engrs; inst Elec & Electronics Engrs Laser & Electrooptics Soc. **Research Statement & Publications:** New semiconductor devices, particularly in area of microwaves and optical devices; lasers; properties of defects in semiconductors; author of 120 technical publications; awarded 33 US patents. **Mailing Address:** Warburg Pincus & Co, 466 Lexington Ave, New York, NY 10017.

KRESSEL, HERBERT YEHUDE, RADIOLOGY, MAGNETIC RESONANCE IMAGING. **Personal Data:** b Brooklyn, NY, November 20, 1947; c 2. **Education:** Brandeis Univ, Waltham, Mass, BA, 1968; Univ Southern Calif, MD, 1972. **Honors & Awards:** Crues Kressel Award, Soc Magnetic Resonance Med, 1991; Sylvia Sorkin Greenfield Award, Am Asn Physicists Med, 1993. **Professional Experience:** PRES & CHIEF EXEC OFFICER, BETH ISRAEL DEACONESS MED CTR & MIRIAM H STONEMAN PROF RADIOL, HARVARD MED SCH, as of 2002; RADIOLOGIST-IN-CHIEF, BETH ISRAEL HOSP, BOSTON, MASS, 1994-; prof radiol, Harvard Med Sch, 1993; chmn, Joint Merger Eval Comt, Soc Magnetic Resonance Med, Soc Magnetic Resonance Int, 1992-1993; fel, Am Col Radiol, 1991; prog chair, Soc Magnetic Resonance Med, 1990; med dir, RI Magnetic Resonance Imaging Network, Providence, 1988-; mem, Comn Magnetic Resonance, Am Col Radiol, 1987-; chmn, Comt Magnetic Resonance Clin Appln, 1987-; trustee, Soc Magnetic Resonance Med, 1987; from asst prof to prof radiol, Univ Pa, Philadelphia, 1977-1993; Clin instr radiol, Univ Calif, San Francisco, 1976-1977; NIH fel radiol, Univ Calif, San Francisco, 1976. **Memberships:** Asn Univ Radiologists; Soc Gastrointestinal Radiologists; Am Col Radiol; Radiol Soc NAm; Soc Magnetic Resonance Med (pres-elect, 1989-1990, pres, 1990-1991). **Research Statement & Publications:** Improved magnetic resonance for the abdomen and pelvis; magnetic resonance imaging of the liver. **Mailing Address:** Dept Radiol, Beth Israel Deaconess Med Ctr, 330 Brookline Ave, Boston, MA 02115. **Fax:** 617-278-8212. **E-Mail:** hkressel@caregroup.harvard.edu

KRESTA, JIRI ERIK, polymer chemistry, chemical engineering; deceased, see previous edition for last biography

KRESTENSEN, ELROY R, ENTOMOLOGY. **Personal Data:** b New York, NY, September 6, 1921; m 1948, Netta; c 1. **Education:** Univ Fla, BSA, 1949, MS, 1951; Univ Md, PhD (entom), 1962. **Professional Experience:** RETIRED; consult, 1984-1986; from instr to assoc prof entom, Sharpsburg Res Ctr, Univ Md, 1955-1984; entomologist, Fla Bd Health, 1952-1954; interim instr, Univ Fla, 1951-1952; asst entom, Univ Fla, 1949-1951. **Memberships:** Entom Soc Am. **Research Statement & Publications:** Insect pests and control methods for fruit. **Mailing Address:** 1050 St Clair St, Hagerstown, MD 21742-3135.

KRETCHMER, RICHARD ALLAN, SYNTHETIC ORGANIC CHEMISTRY. **Personal Data:** b Tracy, Minn, December 12, 1940; m 1967, Karla; c Erich, Sarah & Jeffrey. **Education:** Univ Minn, BChem, 1962; Univ Wis, PhD (org chem), 1966; Chicago-Kent Col Law, JD, 1975. **Professional Experience:** Adj prof law, Chicago Kent Col Law, 1983-1984 & 1987-1989; gen patent atty, Law Dept, Amoco Corp, 1976-2001; assoc gen patent atty, Patents & Licensing Dept, 1976; law firm assoc, Johnston, Keil, Thompson & Shurtleff, Chicago, Ill, 1975-1976; from asst prof to assoc prof chem, Ill Inst Technol, 1968-1976; USPHS fel chem, Columbia Univ, 1966-1968. **Memberships:** Am Asn Advan Sci. **Research Statement & Publications:** Organic chemistry; structure and synthesis; chemistry of natural products; the organic chemistry of mercury. **Mailing Address:** 270 Walker Ave, Clarendon Hills, IL 60514. **E-Mail:** richard.a.kretchmer@worldnet.att.net

KRETSCH, MARY JOSEPHINE, NUTRITIONAL STATUS ASSESSMENT, DIETARY ASSESSMENT. **Personal Data:** American citizen. **Education:** Univ Minn, BS, 1969; Univ Calif, San Francisco, RD, 1970; Univ Calif, Davis, PhD (nutrit sci), 1975. **Professional Experience:** RES PHYSIOL, WESTERN HUMAN NUTRIT RES CTR, AGR RES SERV, USDA, as of 2003; ASSOC ADJ PROF NUTRIT, UNIV CALIF, DAVIS, as of 2000; Res leader, Ctr, 1983-1986; RES NUTRIT SCIENTIST, WESTERN HUMAN NUTRIT RES CTR, AGR RES SERV, USDA, 1980-; Dir, Human Metab Res Unit, Western Human Nutrit Res Ctr, 1980-1983; nutrit scientist, Dept Defense, Letterman Army Inst Res, 1977-1980; postdoctoral fel human nutrit, Univ Calif, Berkeley, 1975-1977; Teaching asst nutrit, Univ Calif, Berkeley, 1971-1973. **Memberships:** Am Inst Nutrit; Am Soc Clin Nutrit; Am Dietetic Asn. **Research Statement & Publications:** Nutritional status assessment with expertise in dietary assessment and biological markers of dietary exposure; vitamin B-6; nutrition & cognitive function; human metabolic research study techniques; nutrition surveys. **Mailing Address:** Western Human Nutrit Res Ctr, Arg Res Serv, USDA, One Shield Ave, Davis, CA 95616. **Fax:** 530-752-5271. **E-Mail:** mkretsch@whnrc.usda.gov

KRETSCHMER, ALBERT EMIL, TROPICAL AGROSTOLOGY. **Personal Data:** b New York, NY, November 15, 1925; m 1949, c 3. **Education:** Univ Fla, BA, 1949; Rutgers Univ, PhD (soil chem), 1952. **Professional Experience:** PROF EMER, IFAS UNIV FLA, as of 2004; chief, Univ Fla-AID Prog, Costa Rica, 1969-1970; Consult soil chemist, Univ Fla-AID Prog, Costa Rica, 1958-1960; agronomist, IFAS Indian River Res & Educ Ctr, Univ Fla, beginning 1955; soil chemist, Everglades Exp Sta, 1952-1955; pvt consult trop pastures, overseas. **Memberships:** Am Soc Agron; Sigma Xi. **Research Statement & Publications:** Evaluation of tropical pasture legumes and grasses; micro and macro nutrient requirements of forages; management of grass-legume mixtures. **Mailing Address:** IFAS Indian River Res & Educ Ctr Univ Fla, 2199 S Rock Rd PO Box 248, Ft Pierce, FL 34945-3138.

KRETSCHMER, FRANK FREDERICK, JR, RADAR SIGNAL PROCESSING. **Personal Data:** b Philadelphia, Pa, July 31, 1930; m 1958, Shirley J Bacon; c Frank F III, John, Diane, Linda & Thomas. **Education:** Pa State Univ, BSEE, 1957; Drexel Inst Tech, MSEE, 1961; Johns Hopkins Univ, PhD (elec eng), 1970. **Professional Experience:** CONSULT, NAVAL RES LAB, 1990-; supvry electronics engr, Naval Res Lab, 1987-1990; res electronics eng, Naval Res Lab, 1970-1987; res assoc, Johns Hopkins Univ, 1964-1970; proj engr, Bendix Radio Corp, 1958-1964; Asst develop engr, Burroughs Corp, 1957-1958. **Memberships:** Fel Inst Elec & Electronics Eng; Sigma Xi. **Research Statement & Publications:** Over 30 publications in journals, national and international conferences; co-author of one book; awarded over 20 patents. **Mailing Address:** 514 Pennyroyal Pl, Venice, FL 34293-7233.

KRETSINGER, ROBERT H, MOLECULAR BIOLOGY, BIOPHYSICS. **Personal Data:** b Denver, Colo, March 20, 1937. **Education:** Univ Colo, BA, 1958; Mass Inst Technol, PhD (biophys), 1964. **Professional Experience:** COMMONWEALTH PROF BIOL, UNIV VA, as of 2005; Chmn dept biol, Univ VA, 1979-1984; PROF BIOL, UNIV VA, 1975-; assoc prof, Univ VA, 1967-1975; fel, Inst Molecular Biol, Geneva, Switz, 1966-1967; Helen Hay Whitney Found fel, Med Res Coun Lab Molecular Biol, Cambridge Univ, Eng, 1964-1965. **Memberships:** Am Crystallog Asn. **Research Statement & Publications:** Protein structure determination by x-ray crystallography; function and evolution of calcium modulated proteins; role of calcium as cytosolic messenger. **Mailing Address:** Dept Biol, Univ Va, Chem 205 PO Box 400328, Charlottesville, VA 22904-4328. **E-Mail:** rhk5i@virginia.edu

KRETZ, RALPH, PETROLOGY, GEOCHEMISTRY. **Personal Data:** Canadian citizen. **Education:** Univ Chicago, PhD (geol), 1958. **Professional Experience:** Adj prof, Univ Ottawa, as of 2004; PROF GEOL, UNIV OTTAWA, 1971-; assoc prof, Univ Ottawa, 1967-1971; sr lectr geol, Univ Queensland, 1961-1965; geologist, Geol Surv Can, 1958-1961. **Memberships:** Geochem Soc; Mineral Asn Can. **Research Statement & Publications:** Chemical composition and texture of metamorphic rocks. **Mailing Address:** Dept Earth Sci, Univ Ottawa, Marion Hall, 140 Louis Pasteur, Ottawa, ON K1N 6N5, Can.

KRETZMER, ERNEST R(UDOLF), ELECTRONICS, COMMUNICATION. **Personal Data:** b Ger, December 24, 1924; American citizen; m 1983, Alisa; c 2. **Education:** Worcester Polytech Inst, BS, 1945; Mass Inst Technol, SM, 1946, ScD(elec eng), 1949. **Professional Experience:** RETIRED; dir, Bell Tel Labs, Inc, 1970-1983; dept head, Bell Tel Labs, Inc, 1965-1970; supvr, Bell Tel Labs, Inc, 1956-1965; mem tech staff, Bell Tel Labs, Inc, 1949-1956; res assoc, Mass Inst Technol, 1949; mem tech staff, Mass Inst Technol, 1945-1949. **Memberships:** Fel Inst Elec & Electronics Engrs. **Research Statement & Publications:** Pulse modulation; phase measurement; redundancy in television; coded facsimile; transistor applications; electronic telephone system development; data communication. **Mailing Address:** 118 N Polk Dr, Sarasota, FL 34236.

KREULEN, DAVID, PHYSIOLOGY. **Education:** Calvin Col, BS; Wayne State Univ, PhD, 1974. **Professional Experience:** PROF, DEPT PHYSIOLOGY & NEUROL OPHTHAL, MICH STATE UNIV, as of 2006. **Mailing Address:** Dept Physiol, Mich State Univ, B-340 Life Sci Bldg, East Lansing, MI 48824-1314. **Fax:** 517-432-0881. **E-Mail:** dkreulen@msu.edu

KREUTEL, RANDALL WILLIAM, JR, ANTENNAS, SATELLITECOMMUNICATIONS. **Personal Data:** b Norwood, Mass, May 3, 1934; m 1975, Alice J Guillory; c John, James, Karen, Robert, Jacqueline & Michael. **Education:** Northeastern Univ, BS, 1961, MS, 1964; George Washington Univ, DSc(electrophys), 1978. **Professional Experience:** TEAM LEADER, SATCOM DIV MOTOROLA, 1993-; prin engr, Electromagnetic Sci, 1989-1993; dir, Sci-Atlanta, 1987-1989; Bd dir, SPC Antenna Corp, 1986-1988; dir, System Planning Corp, 1984-1987; dir, div develop eng, Comsat Labs, 1981- 1984; dir optical commun, Antennas Dept, 1979-1981; sr staff scientist res & develop, Antennas Dept, 1977-1979; mgr, Antennas Dept, 1968-1977; mem tech staff, Communications Satellite Corp, 1966-1968; Res eng antennas, Sylvania Electron Syst, 1957-1966. **Memberships:** Inst Elec & Electronics Engrs; Int Sci Radio Union; Am Inst Aeronaut & Astronaut; Sigma Xi; NY Acad Sci. **Research Statement & Publications:** Antennas, microwave circuits, fiber optics and communications; satellite communications; electromagnetics. **Mailing Address:** Satcom Div Motorola, 2501 S Price Rd, Chandler, AZ 85248. **Fax:** 602-732-2332.

KREUTLER, PATRICIA A, NUTRITION. **Professional Experience:** STAFF, INST FOOD TECHNOLOGISTS, as of 1995. **Memberships:** Food Nutrit Sci Alliance. **Research Statement & Publications:** '. **Mailing Address:** Inst Food Technologists, PO Box 926, Lombard, IL 60148. **Fax:** 630-889-4140.

KREUTNER, WILLIAM, PHARMACOLOGY, BIOCHEMISTRY. **Personal Data:** b Brooklyn, NY, February 20, 1941; m 1963, c 2. **Education:** Brooklyn Col, BS, 1962; Univ Minn, PhD (pharmacol), 1967. **Professional Experience:** ASSOC DIR, SCHERING CORP, 1988-; sect leader, Schering Corp, 1978-1988; Adj asst prof biochem, Fairleigh Dickinson Univ, 1972-1979. **Memberships:** Am Acad Allergy & Immunol; NY Acad Sci; Am Soc Pharmacol Exp Ther; Am Thoracic Soc; Am Col Allergy & Immunol. **Research Statement & Publications:** Prostaglandins; leukotrienes; cyclic nucleotides; neuronal pathways and neuropeptides; antihistamines. **Mailing Address:** Schering-Plough Corp, 2015 Galloping Hill Rd MS 1660, Kenilworth, NJ 07033-0539. **Fax:** 908-298-7175.

KREUTZ-DELGADO, KENNETH KEITH, ROBOTICS, MACHINE INTELLIGENCE. **Personal Data:** b Aguadilla, PR. **Education:** Univ Calif, San Diego, BA, 1976, MS, 1978, PhD (systs sci), 1985. **Professional Experience:** PROF DEPT ELEC & COMPUT ENG, UNIV CALIF, SAN DIEGO, as of 2006; asst prof Dept Elec & Comput Eng, Univ Calif, San Diego, beginning 1991; tech ed, Inst Elec & Electronics Engrs J Robotics & Automation, 1991-1992; NSF presidential young investr, 1990; asst prof robotics, Dept Appl Mech & Eng Sci, 1989-1991; vis assoc mech eng, Calif Inst Technol, 1989-1990; mem tech staff, Mach Intel Systs Group, NASA Jet Propulsion Lab, Calif Inst Technol, 1985-1989; sci programmer, Dept Neuroscience, 1978-1980. **Memberships:** AAAS; Inst Elec & Electronics Engrs Robotics & Automation Soc; Inst Elec & Electronics Engrs Comput Soc; Inst Elec & Electronics Engrs Systs Man & Cybernet Soc; Inst Elec & Electronics Engrs Controls Soc. **Research Statement & Publications:** Sensor-based real-time robot planning and control; robotic manufacturing, servicing and assembly; kinematics and dynamics of multibody systems with time-varying interconnection topologies. **Mailing Address:** Dept Chem & Elec Comput, Univ Calif San Diego, 9500 Gilman Dr Mail Code 0407, La Jolla, CA 92093-0407. **Fax:** 858-534-1004. **E-Mail:** kreutz@ece.ucsd.edu

KREUTZER, RICHARD D, CYTOGENETICS, BIOCHEMISTRY OF LEISHMANIA. **Personal Data:** b Evergreen Park, Ill, June 23, 1936; m Patricia; c Kimberly & Tamara. **Education:** Univ Ill, BS, 1963, MS, 1965, PhD (zoology), 1968. **Professional Experience:** RETIRED; prof emer biol, Youngstown State Univ, 1996; prof biol, Youngstown State Univ, 1979-1996; chief vector, Biol Sect, Gorgas Mem Lab, 1977-1979; from asst prof to assoc prof, Youngstown State Univ, 1969-1979; instr zool, Univ Ill, Urbana, 1967-1969. **Memberships:** Am Soc Zoologists; Am Mosquito Control Asn; Genetics Soc Am; Entom Soc Am; Am Soc Trop Med Hyg. **Research Statement & Publications:** Genetics; invertebrates; parasitology; entomology; cytogenetics and evolution of anophelines; isozyme studies on insects and protozoan parasites. **Mailing Address:** Dept Biol, Youngstown State Univ 410 Wick Ave, Youngstown, OH 44555-0001. **Fax:** 330-742-1483.

KREUZ, BETTE, CHEMISTRY. **Education:** Univ Mich, PhD. **Professional Experience:** COORDR & SR LECTR CHEM, DEPT NATURAL SCI, UNIV MICH, as of 2004. **Mailing Address:** Dept Natural Sci, Univ Mich, 4901 Evergreen Rd, Dearborn, MI 48128. **Fax:** 313-593-4937. **E-Mail:** bkreuz@umd.umich.edu

KREUZ, JOHN ANTHONY, ORGANIC POLYMER CHEMISTRY. **Personal Data:** b Buffalo, NY, September 18, 1933; m 1996, Frances Patricia; c 6. **Education:** St Bonaventure Univ, BS, 1955; Univ Notre Dame, PhD (org chem), 1960. **Honors & Awards:** Lavosier award, 1988; Pedersen award, 1994. **Professional Experience:** FEL, E I DUPONT Del NEMOURS & CO, INC, 1995-; res fel, E I Du Pont Del Nemours & Co, Inc, 1988-1995; sr res assoc, E I Du Pont Del Nemours & Co, Inc, 1985-1988; res assoc, E I Du Pont Del Nemours & Co, Inc, 1977-1985; staff scientist, E I Du Pont Del Nemours & Co, Inc, 1965-1977; Res chemist, E I Du Pont Del Nemours & Co, Inc, 1959-1964. **Memberships:** Am Chem Soc. **Research Statement & Publications:** Alkaline decomposition of aliphatic disulfides; addition and condensation polymerizations; polyimides and other high temperature polymers; polymer surface chemistry, polyimide and other adhesives. **Mailing Address:** E I DuPont de Nemours, Circleville Res Lab, Circleville, OH 43113. **Fax:** 614-474-0244.

KREUZER, HANS JURGEN, SURFACE SCIENCE, NON-EQUILIBRIUM STATISTICAL MECHANICS. **Personal Data:** b Lahnstein, Ger, August 9, 1942; Canadian citizen; m 1986, Kim; c Sophia A. **Education:** Univ Bonn, dipl, 1966, Dr rer nat, 1967. **Honors & Awards:** Vis fel, Wolfson Col, Oxford, 1987; fel, Max-Planck Soc, Ger, 1987; Heinrich-Welcker Visiting Prof, Univ of Erlangen, 1992; Fellow of the Royal Soc of Can, 1993; Humboldt res Award, 1995. **Professional Experience:** AC FALES PROF THEORET PHYSICS, DALHOUSIE UNIV, 1996-; KILLAM PROF, DALHOUSIE UNIV, 1995-; prof physics, Dalhousie Univ, 1990-1995; external sci mem, Fritz-Haber Inst, Berlin, 1988-; Killam res prof, Dalhousie Univ, 1982-1990; Lady Davies prof, Technion, Haifa, Israel, 1977; from asst prof to prof physics, Theoret Physics Inst, Univ Alta, 1971-1985; postdoctoral fel theoret physics, Theoret Physics Inst, Univ Alta, 1969-1971; Asst theoret nuclear physics, Inst Theoret Nuclear Physics, Univ Bonn, 1967-1969; bd mem, Int Soc Theoret Chem Physics. **Memberships:** Can Asn Physicists; Chem Inst Can; Int Soc Theoret Chem Physics; fel Royal Soc Can. **Research Statement & Publications:** Theoretical surface science; transport processes at surfaces and interfaces; kinetics of adsorption, desorption, diffusion and reactions at surfaces; physics and chemistry in high electric fields; holography. **Mailing Address:** Dept Physics, Dalhousie Univ, Halifax, NS B3H 3J5, Can. **Fax:** 902-494-5191. **E-Mail:** kreuzer@is.dal.ca

KREUZER, KENNETH N, MICROBIOLOGY. **Education:** Univ Chicago, PhD, 1978. **Professional Experience:** PROF BIOCHEM, DUKE UNIV MED CTR, as of 2005. **Mailing Address:** Dept Microbiol & Immunol Duke Univ Med Ctr, Box 3020 Rm 157& 157B, Durham, NC 27710-0001. **Fax:** 919-684-6525. **E-Mail:** kenneth.kreuzer@duke.edu

KREUZER, LLOYD BARTON, MICROCOMPUTERS, MICROCOMPUTER OPERATING SYSTEMS. **Personal Data:** b Los Angeles, Calif, August 26, 1940. **Education:** Swarthmore Col, BA, 1962; Princeton Univ, PhD (physics), 1966. **Professional Experience:** PRES, KREUZER SOFTWARE CORP, 1986-; pres, Menlo Corp, 1983-1986; vpres adv develop, Dynabyte Inc, 1981-1982; pres eng, Dynabyte Inc, 1978-1981; mem tech staff, Hewlett-Packard Lab, 1974-1978; vpres, Diax Corp, Calif, 1973-1974; mem tech staff physics, Bell Tel Labs, NJ, 1966-1973. **Memberships:** Am Phys Soc; Inst Elec & Electronics Engrs. **Research Statement & Publications:** Nonlinear optics; optical parametric effects; experimental gravitation; air pollution detection by IR laser; optoacoustic spectroscopy; microcomputers and microcomputer software. **Mailing Address:** Acuson, 1220 Charleston Rd, Mtain View, CA 94043.

KREVANS, JULIUS RICHARD, HEMATOLOGY. **Personal Data:** b New York, NY, May 1, 1942; c 5. **Education:** NY Univ, BS, 1944, MD, 1946; Am Bd Internal Med, dipl, 1956. **Honorary Degrees:** LLD, Rush Univ, 1984. **Honors & Awards:** Abraham Flexner Award, 1983; Convocation Medal, Am Col Cardiol, 1984; Belkin Mem Lectr, Albert Einstein Col Med, 1986. **Professional Experience:** PROF EMER, DEPT MED ADMIN, UNIV CALIF, SAN FRANCISCO, as of 2006; chancellor emer, Univ Calif, San Francisco, beginning 2004; MED DIR, INT MED CARE, UNIV CALIF, SAN FRANCISCO, 1996-; consult, Sch Med, Univ Calif, San Francisco, 1993-1996; consult, Sch Med, Univ Wash, Univ Colo & Med Serv Found, 1986; chmn, Asn Am Med Cols, 1980-1981; chmn, Comt Humanistic

Qual Internist, Am Bd Internal Med, 1983; chancellor, Sch Med, Univ Calif, San Francisco, 1982-1993; prof med & dean, Sch Med, Univ Calif, San Francisco, 1971-1982; dean acad affairs, Sch Med, 1968-1971; physician-in-chief, Baltimore City Hosps, 1963-; asst dean, Sch Med, 1962-1963; from asst prof to prof med, Sch Med, 1960-1971; asst prof, Johns Hopkins Univ, 1955-1960; Vis hematologist, Baltimore City Hosps, 1953-1963; dir, Blood Bank, 1953-1962; resident, Johns Hopkins Univ, 1952-1963; asst resident, Johns Hopkins Univ, 1951-1952; fel hemat, Johns Hopkins Univ, 1950-1951; resident path, Flushing Hosp, 1947; Intern, Queens Gen Hosp, 1946-1947. **Memberships:** Inst Med-Nat Acad Sci; Am Soc Hemat; assoc Am Col Physicians; Am Fed Clin Res; Int Soc Hemat. **Mailing Address:** Med Dir, Int Med Care Univ Calif, San Francisco, CA 94143. **Fax:** 412-502-6696.

KREY, LEWIS CHARLES, NEUROENDOCRINOLOGY. **Personal Data:** b New York, NY, October 1, 1944; m 1967, c 3. **Education:** Brown Univ, AB, 1966; Duke Univ, PhD (physiol), 1971. **Professional Experience:** PROF OBSTET & GYNEC & CELL BIOL, NEW YORK UNIV, as of 2004; assoc prof, New York Univ, beginning 1991; Reproductive Endocrinol Study Sect, NIH, 1985-1988; assoc ed, Endocrinol, 1983-1988; from asst prof to assoc prof neuroendocrinol, Rockefeller Univ, 1981-1991; fel, Irma T Hirschl Found, 1980-1985; fel, Alfred P Sloan Found, 1978-1980; asst prof, Univ Pittsburgh Sch Med, 1973-1975; res assoc & fel physiol, Univ Pittsburgh Sch Med, 1971-1973. **Memberships:** Endocrine Soc; Sigma Xi; Int Soc Neuroendocrinol. **Research Statement & Publications:** Role of hypothalamic and hypophyseal steroid receptors in the neuroendocrine regulation of anterior pituitary gland function; in particular, the control of gonadotropin release in several mammalian species. **Mailing Address:** Dept Obstet & Gynec, Sch Med NY Univ, 660 First Ave, New York, NY 10016-6481. **Fax:** 212-263-7853, 212-263-0059. **E-Mail:** kreyl01@popmail.med.nyu.edu

KREY, PHILIP W, RADIOCHEMISTRY, ENVIRONMENTAL SCIENCE. **Personal Data:** b Brooklyn, NY, June 18, 1927; m 1952, Dolores; c Mary Jo, Philip, Michael, Kathleen & Patrick. **Education:** St Francis Col, BS, 1948; Duquesne Univ, MS, 1950. **Professional Experience:** SR SCIENTIST, EG & G TECH SERV, INC, 2000-; SR SCIENTIST, URS CORP, 1997-; Actg lab dir, Environ measurements lab, US dept energy, 1991-1997; actg dep lab dir, Environ Measurements Lab, US Dept Energy, 1988-1991; dir, Anal Chem Div, 1980-1988; MEM TASK GROUP ON C-14 WASTE DISPOSAL, NAT COUN RADIATION PROTECTION & MEASUREMENTS, 1975-; environ scientist, US Energy Res & Develop Admin & US Dept Energy, 1975-1980; dir stratospheric radioactivity prog, Health & Safety Lab, 1967-1975; dir radioactivity in surface air prog, US Dept Energy, 1965-1967; mgr radiochem div, Isotopes, Inc, 1957-1964; chief radiochem div, Nuclear Defense Lab, 1955-1957; Chemist, Nuclear Defense Lab, 1950-1955. **Memberships:** AAAS; NY Acad Sci. **Research Statement & Publications:** Behavior and transport of artificial and natural radioactivity; trace metal and gaseous pollutants in the environment, from both local and global sources of contamination; collection and analysis techniques for nuclear safeguards and nuclear non-proliferation activities. **Mailing Address:** 7 Bluefield Ct, Hillsdale, NJ 07642.

KREY, PHOEBE REGINA, RHEUMATOLOGY. **Personal Data:** b Ambridge, Pa, m 1960, c 3. **Education:** Northeastern Univ, BS, 1955; Boston Univ, MD, 1960. **Professional Experience:** ASSOC PROF MED, COL MED & DENT, NJ, 1977-; asst prof med & dir rheumatology, Col Med & Dent, NJ, 1975-1977; asst prof, Boston Univ Med Sch, 1974-1975; instr med, Boston Univ Med Sch, 1969-1974; clin fel rheumatology, Boston City Hosp & res fel, Univ Hosp, 1963-1969; Intern, Newton-Wellesley Hosp, 1960-1961. **Memberships:** Am Rheumatism Asn; Reticuloendothelial Soc; Electron Micros Soc Am. **Research Statement & Publications:** Rheumatoid arthritis, fine structure and culture of the synovial membrane; gout, systemic lupus erythematons; immune experimental arthritis in animals. **Mailing Address:** Rheumatology Div, UMD New Jersey Med Sch, 185 So Orange Ave, Newark, NJ 07103. **Fax:** 201-982-3353.

KREZOSKI, JOHN R, MARINE BIOGEOCHEMISTRY. **Personal Data:** b Kalamazoo, Mich, January 15, 1947; m 1972, Susan; c 2. **Education:** Kalamazoo Col, BA, 1969; Univ Mich, MS, 1976, PhD (natural resources), 1981. **Professional Experience:** DIR, DEPT ENVIRON HEALTH & SAFETY MGT, 1988-; ASSOC SCIENTIST, CTR GREAT LAKES STUDIES, UNIV WIS-MILWAUKEE, 1988-; asst scientist, Ctr Great Lakes Studies, Univ Wis-milwaukee, 1984-1988; proj assoc, Ctr Great Lakes Studies, Univ Wis-milwaukee, 1982-1984; guest fac, res partic, Argonne Nat Lab, 1982-1984; res scientist, Argonne Nat Lab, 1981-1982. **Memberships:** AAAS; Am Soc Limnol & Oceanog; Int Asn Great Lakes Res; Int Asn Theoret & Appl Limnol; NAm Benthological Soc; Am Chem Soc. **Research Statement & Publications:** Multiple radiotracer techniques to study benthic community structure, biogenic nutrient regeneration from sediments, and burial and redistribution of hazardous substances by aquatic and marine invertebrates. **Mailing Address:** Environ Health & Safety, Univ Wis-Milwaukee PO Box 413, Milwaukee, WI 53201. **Fax:** 414-229-6729. **E-Mail:** jrk@uwm.edu

KRIBEL, ROBERT EDWARD, PLASMA PHYSICS, MAGNETOHYDRODYNAMICS. **Personal Data:** b Pittsburgh, Pa, September 17, 1937; m 1959, c 4. **Education:** Univ Notre Dame, BS, 1959; Univ Calif, San Diego, MS, 1966, PhD (physics), 1968. **Professional Experience:** Vpres acad affairs, Jacksonville State Univ, 1988-1992; actg dean, Col Sci, 1986-1988; Los Alamos Nat Lab, 1983-; prof & head dept physics, Auburn Univ, 1978-1986; assoc prof & head, dept physics, James Madison Univ, 1974-1978; vis assoc prof elec eng, Cornell Univ, 1973-1974; consult, Cornell Univ, 1970-1971 & Los Alamos Nat Lab, 1983-; asst prof physics, Drake Univ, 1970-1973; staff assoc, Gulf Gen Atomic Inc, Gulf Oil Corp, 1968-1969; Lectr, Univ San Diego, 1967-1968; Res asst plasma physics, Gulf Gen Atomic Inc, Gulf Oil Corp, 1963-1965 & Univ Calif, San Diego, 1965-1968. **Memberships:** Am Phys Soc; AAAS; Sigma Xi. **Research Statement & Publications:** Plasma production; confinement and stability. **Mailing Address:** VPres Acad Affairs, Jacksonville State Univ, Jacksonville, FL 36265-1573.

KRICHER, JOHN C, ECOLOGY. **Personal Data:** b Philadelphia, Pa, February 7, 1944. **Education:** Temple Univ, BA, 1966; Rutgers Univ, NB, PhD (zoology), 1970. **Professional Experience:** PROF BIOL, WHEATON COL, MASS, 1980-; earthwatch grants, 1981-1983; cottrell sci grants, Res Corp, 1974 & 1975; from asst prof to assoc prof, Wheaton Col, Mass, 1970-1980. **Memberships:** Am Inst Biol Sci; Ecol Soc Am; Am Ornith Union; Cooper Ornith Soc; Sigma Xi; Asn Field Ornith (pres, 1984-1987); Soc Study Evol. **Research Statement & Publications:** Bird species diversity in relation to secondary succession; species diversity of intertidal communities; tropical bird species diversity; ecology of migrant birds in the tropics; range expansions of North American birds. **Mailing Address:** Biol Dept, Wheaton Col, Sci Ctr 156A, Norton, MA 02766. **E-Mail:** jkricher@wheatoncollege.edu

KRICHEVSKY, MICAH I, MICROBIOLOGY, BIOCHEMISTRY. **Personal Data:** b Chicago, Ill, May 4, 1931; m 1952, c 2. **Education:** Univ Conn, BA, 1952; Univ Ill, MS, 1955, PhD (dairy sci), 1958. **Professional Experience:** CHMN, BIONOMICS INT, as of 2004; CHIEF MICROBIAL SYSTEMATICS SECT, NAT INST DENT RES, 1974-; chief environ mechanisms sect, Nat Inst dent res, 1968-1974; biochemist, Nat Inst dent res, 1961-1968; biochemist, Nat Heart Inst, 1959-1961; biochemist, Nat Inst Allergy & Infectious dis, 1958-1959; asst dairy sci, Univ Ill, 1953-1957, 1958. **Memberships:** Am Soc Microbiol; Sigma Xi. **Research Statement & Publications:** Biochemical differentiation in slime molds; metabolic pathways in bacteria; automation and computer technology in biomedical research. **Mailing Address:** Bionomics Int, 12231 Parklawn Dr, Bethesda, MD 20852. **Fax:** 301-881-1625. **E-Mail:** micahk@bioint.org

KRICK, MERLYN STEWART, NUCLEAR SCIENCE. **Personal Data:** b Shillington, Pa, January 13, 1938; m 1968. **Education:** Albright Col, BS, 1959; Univ Pa, PhD (physics), 1966. **Professional Experience:** RETIRED; mem staff nuclear safeguards, Los Alamos Nat Lab, Univ Calif, beginning 1975; from asst prof to assoc prof nuclear eng, Kans State Univ, 1970-1975; res appointee, Los Alamos Sci Lab, 1968-1970; res assoc physics, Univ Rochester, 1966-1968. **Memberships:** Am Phys Soc; Am Nuclear Soc; Inst Elec & Electronics Engrs. **Research Statement & Publications:** Nuclear safeguards; nuclear instrumentation; delayed neutron physics. **Mailing Address:** Los Alamos Nat Lab MS-E540, PO Box 1663, Los Alamos, NM 87545. **Fax:** 505-665-4433. **E-Mail:** mkrick@lanl.gov

KRIDER, EDMUND PHILIP, ATMOSPHERIC ELECTRICITY, ATMOSPHERIC PHYSICS. **Personal Data:** b Chicago, Ill, March 22, 1940; div, c Ruth & Reed. **Education:** Carleton Col, BA, 1962; Univ Ariz, MS, 1964, PhD (physics), 1969. **Honors & Awards:** Outstanding Contrib Advan Appl Meteorol, Am Metrol Soc, 1985. **Professional Experience:** Pres, Int Comn Atmospheric Elec, 1992-; co-chief ed, J Atmos Sci, 1990-1992; HEAD & DIR, DEPT ATMOSPHERIC SCI & INST ATMOSPHERIC PHYSICS, UNIV ARIZ, 1986-; head & dir, Inst Atmospheric Physics, Univ Ariz, 1986; PROF, DEPT ATMOSPHERIC SCI & INST ATMOSPHERIC PHYSICS, UNIV ARIZ, 1980-; assoc ed, J Geophys Res, 1977-1979; mem, Lightning & Sferics Subcomn, Int Comn Atmospheric Elec, 1976-; adv, NASA, 1976; from asst prof to assoc prof, Inst Atmospheric Physics, Univ Ariz, 1973-1980; prin investr numerous res grants & contracts, 1971-; asst res prof, Inst Atmospheric Physics, Univ Ariz, 1971-1975; Nat Acad Sci resident res assoc, Manned Spacecraft Ctr, NASA, 1969-1971. **Memberships:** Sigma Xi; fel Am Meteorol Soc; Am Geophys Union; Am Asn Physics Teachers; Inst Elec & Electronics Engrs. **Research Statement & Publications:** Lightning and atmospheric electricity; lightning physics, protection and lightning detection and warning systems. **Mailing Address:** Inst Atmospheric Physics, Univ Ariz, Tucson, AZ 85721. **Fax:** 520-621-6833. **E-Mail:** krider@atmo.arizona.edu

KRIDER, JAKE LUTHER, animal nutrition; deceased, see previous edition for last biography

KRIEBEL, DAVID, EPIDEMIOLOGY. **Education:** Univ Wis, BSc, 1977; Harvard Sch Public Health, ScM, 1983; ScD, 1986. **Professional Experience:** PROF & CO-DIR, LOWELL CTR SUSTAINABLE PROD, as of 2005. **Mailing Address:** Dept Work Environ, Univ Mass Lowell, Lowell, MA 01854. **Fax:** 978-452-5711. **E-Mail:** David_Kriebel@uml.edu

KRIEBEL, HOWARD BURTT, forest genetics, molecular biology cell culture; deceased, see previous edition for last biography

KRIEBEL, MAHLON E, PHYSIOLOGY, NEUROMUSCULAR TRANSMITTER. **Personal Data:** b Garfield, Wash, November 18, 1936; m 1980, c 3. **Education:** Wash State Univ, BS, 1958; Univ Wash, MS, 1964, PhD (zoology), 1967. **Professional Experience:** PROF PHYSIOL, STATE UNIV NY UPSTATE MED CTR, 1969-; fel, Albert Einstein Col Med, 1967-1969; Alexander von Humboldt sr scientist award; vis prof, Univ Konstanz, Max-Plank-Gottingen & Univ Calif, Irvine; Mem, Marine Biol Lab, Woods Hole. **Memberships:** Am Soc Cell Biologists; Soc Neuroscience. **Research Statement & Publications:** Transmitter release at the n-m junction; physiology of tunicate heart; neurophysioloy of fish oculomotor neurons; degranulation of mast cells; squid chromatophore nerve-muscle studies. **Mailing Address:** Dept Neurosci, State Univ NY, Syracuse, NY 13210. **E-Mail:** kriebelm@upstate.edu

KRIEBEL, RICHARD MARVIN, NEUROANATOMY. **Personal Data:** b West Reading, Pa, April 12, 1947; m 1966, c 5. **Education:** Albright Col, BA, 1969; Temple Univ, PhD (anat), 1974. **Honors & Awards:** Lindback Found Award Distinguished Teaching, 1991; Stud Nat Medical Asn Mentor Award 1995. **Professional Experience:** CHMN, DEPT BIOMED SCI, PHILADELPHIA COL OSTEOP MED, as of 2001; SUPVR, DIV NEUROSCIENCE, PHARMACOL & PHYSIOL, PHILADELPHIA COL OSTEOP MED, as of 2001; ASSOC DEAN, CURRIC & RES, PHILADELPHIA COL OSTEOP MED, as of 2001; PROF ANAT, PHILADELPHIA COL OSTEOP MED, 1992-; assoc prof anat, Philadelphia Col Osteop Med, 1987-1992; from asst prof anat to assoc prof anat & neurobiology, Col Med, Univ Vt, 1980-1987; instr & asst prof anat, Med Col Va, Va Commonwealth Univ, 1973-1975. **Memberships:** Am Asn Anatomists; Soc Neuroscience. **Research Statement & Publications:** Neuroendocrine mechanisms synaptology of thalamic nuclei in mammals with specific interest in lateral geniculate; automatic control both central and peripheral cardiovascular system. **Mailing Address:** Dept Biomed Sci, Philadelphia Col Osteop Med, 4150 City Ave, Philadelphia, PA 19131. **E-Mail:** rickk@pcom.edu

KRIEBLE, JAMES G(ERHARD), CHEMICAL ENGINEERING. **Personal Data:** b NJ, October 23, 1920; m 1943, c 3. **Education:** Princeton Univ, BS, 1942, PhD (chem eng), 1949. **Professional Experience:** MGR ENG, REFRACTORY METAL POWDER & GAS OPER, GEN ELEC CO, 1968-; mgr powder prod eng, Refractory Metals Lab, 1961-1968; process engr, Refractory Metals Lab, 1957-1961; Res assoc chem process eng, Res Lab, Gen Elec Co, NY, 1949-1957; Fel, Textile Res Inst, 1949. **Memberships:** Am Chem Soc; Am Inst Chem Engrs; NY Acad Sci. **Research Statement & Publications:** Development and economic evaluation of processes for refractory metals and gases used in lamps. **Mailing Address:** 80 Lyme Rd Apt 314, Hanover, NH 03755.

KRIEG, ARTHUR F, PATHOLOGY. **Personal Data:** b East Orange, NJ, October 23, 1930; wid, c Arthur M, Eric A & Sandra L. **Education:** Yale Univ, AB, 1952; Tufts Univ, MD, 1956. **Professional Experience:** RETIRED; prof & dir clin labs, Hershey Med Ctr, 1971-1996; assoc prof path, Pa State Univ, 1968-1971; asst prof, State Univ NY Upstate Med Ctr, 1964-1968; resident, New Eng Deaconess Hosp, 1963-1964; resident path, Western Reserve Univ, 1957-1960; Rotating intern, Western Reserve Univ, 1956-1957. **Memberships:** Fel Acad Clin Lab Physicians & Scientists; fel Am Soc Clin Pathologists; fel Col Am Pathologists. **Research Statement & Publications:** Clinical pathology; clinical laboratory management, computer applications to medical care. **Mailing Address:** Pa State Univ, Hershey, PA 17033.

KRIEG, DANIEL R, PLANT PHYSIOLOGY, BIOCHEMISTRY. **Personal Data:** b Taylor, Tex, May 19, 1943; m 1965, c 2. **Education:** Tex A&M Univ, BS, 1965, PhD (plant physiol), 1970. **Professional Experience:** PROF PLANT PHYSIOL, TEX TECH UNIV, 1977-; from asst prof to assoc prof, Tex Tech Univ, 1970-1977; assoc ed, Agron J. **Memberships:** Am Soc Plant Physiologists; Crop Sci Soc Am; Am Soc Agron. **Research Statement &**

Publications: Sorghum and cotton, physiological responses to environmental stress; environmental effects on biochemical changes in germinating cotton seeds; drought tolerance and photosynthetic activity of sorghum; environmental effects on seed development of grain sorghum. **Mailing Address:** Dept Plant & Soil Sci, Tex Tech Univ, PO Box 42122, Lubbock, TX 79409-2122. **Fax:** 806-742-2836. **E-Mail:** d.krieg@ttu.edu

KRIEG, DAVID CHARLES, ANIMAL BEHAVIOR, VERTEBRATE ZOOLOGY. **Personal Data:** b Bradford, Pa, June 10, 1936; m 1958, c 3. **Education:** Mansfield State Col, BS, 1958; St Bonaventure Univ, MS, 1961, PhD (biol), 1964. **Honors & Awards:** Marcia Brady Tucker Award, Am Ornith Union, 1966. **Professional Experience:** RETIRED; assoc prof biol, State Univ NY, Col New Paltz, 1967-1992; Frank M Chapman grants, Am Mus Natural Hist, 1966, 1971, 1972, & 1973; grad asst, St Bonaventure Univ, 1964-1967; asst prof zool, State Univ NY, Col Cortland, 1962-1964; instr biol high sch, NY, 1959-1962. **Memberships:** AAAS; Am Ornith Union; Am Soc Zoologists; Animal Behav Soc; Am Soc Ichthyologists & Herpetologists. **Research Statement & Publications:** Comparative behavior of genus Sialia; hybridization of bluebirds in great plains. **Mailing Address:** 913 State Rte 213, High Falls, NY 12440.

KRIEG, NOEL ROGER, MICROBIOLOGY. **Personal Data:** b Waterbury, Conn, January 11, 1934. **Education:** Univ Conn, BA, 1955, MS, 1957; Univ Md, PhD (microbiol), 1960. **Honors & Awards:** US Fedn Culture Collections J Roger Porter Award, Am Soc Microbiol, 1996; Bergey Medal Bacterial Taxonomy, 2003. **Professional Experience:** ALUMNI DISTINGUISHED PROF MICROBIOL, VA POLYTECH INST & STATE UNIV, 1983-; chmn, Acad Teaching Excellence, Va Polytech Inst & State Univ, 1982-1983; Bergey's Manual Trust, 1971-1991, 1996-2003; from asst prof to prof, VA Polytech Inst & State Univ, 1960-1983; asst bact, Univ Conn, 1955-1957; asst microbiol, Univ Md, 1957-1960. **Memberships:** Am Soc Microbiol; Soc Gen Microbiol; Am Acad Microbiol; Sigma Xi. **Research Statement & Publications:** Bacterial systematics; microaerophily; physiology and taxonomy of microaerophilic bacteria including campylobacter, spirillum, and azospirillum. **Mailing Address:** 617 Broce Dr, Blacksburg, VA 24060-2801. **Fax:** 540-808-8247. **E-Mail:** nrk@vt.edu

KRIEG, RICHARD EDWARD, BACTERIOLOGY. **Personal Data:** b New York, NY, October 16, 1942; m 1966, c 3. **Education:** Rutgers Univ, New Brunswick, BS, 1964; Iowa State Univ, MS, 1966, PhD (bact), 1968. **Professional Experience:** US DIR, MINISTRY HEALTH CENT MED LAB, US EPIDEMIOL RES CTR, BELIZE CITY, BELIZE, 1991-; fac adv, Uniformed Serv Univ Health Sci, 1987-; assoc prof, Div Trop Pub Health, Dept Prev Med & Biomet, Uniformed Serv Univ Health Sci, Bethesda, Md, 1986-1991; med inspector, Biomed Sci Br, HQ Air Force Inspection & Safety Ctr, Norton AFB, Calif, 1984-1986; pres, Soc Armed Forces Med Lab Scientists, 1984; chief bact, Armed Forces Inst Path, 1984-1980; asst clin lab mgr, microbiol Serv, Dept path, 1983-1984; pres-elect, Soc Armed Forces Med Lab Scientists, 1983; bd dirs, Soc Armed Forces Med Lab Scientists, 1982-; prog dir, Sch Med Technol, Malcolm Grow USAF Med Ctr, Andrews AFB, Md, 1980-1984; chief, microbiol Serv, Dept path, 1980-1984; adj asst prof, Dept Preventative Med & Biomet, Uniformed Serv Univ Health Sci, 1980-1981; prog comt, Bact Taxon Comt, Soc Armed Forces Med Lab Scientists, 1980; tech adv, Univ Md, 1977-1984; exec secy, Soc Armed Forces Med Lab Scientists, 1977; chief, Bacteriol Br, Microbiol Div, 1974-1980; secy, Soc Armed Forces Med Lab Scientists, 1974; mycobact comt, Bact Taxon Comt, Soc Armed Forces Med Lab Scientists, 1974; chmn, Bact Taxon Comt, Soc Armed Forces Med Lab Scientists, 1974; instr bact, Univ Md, 1973-1984; res microbiologist, Geog Path Div, Armed Forces Inst Path, Wash, DC, 1973-1974; res microbiologist, Armed Forces Inst Path, 1973-1974; biomed analyst, Aerospace Med Div, 1970-1973; res microbiologist, Bioscience Div, USAF Sch Aerospace Med, Brooiks AFB, Tex, 1968-1979; res microbiologist, US Air Force Sch Aerospace Med, 1968-1970. **Memberships:** Am Soc Microbiol; AAAS; Sigma Xi; fel Am Acad Microbiol. **Research Statement & Publications:** Pathogenicity of mycobacterial skin infections; epidemiology and etiology of Legionnaires' disease; numerical taxonomy; deoxyribonucleic acid base ration analysis; tropical infectious diseases. **Mailing Address:** Anat Dept, Med Col Va MCV Sta, PO Box 906, Richmond, VA 23298.

KRIEG, RICHARD J, JR, BIOLOGY. **Education:** Univ San Francisco, BS, 1967; Univ Calif Davis, MS, 1969; Univ Calif Los Angeles, PhD (Anat), 1975. **Professional Experience:** PROF ANAT & NEUROBIOLOGY & PEDIAT, VA COMMONWEALTH UNIV, as of 2006. **Mailing Address:** Dept Anat & Neurobiology Va Commonwealth Univ, Box 980709, Richmond, VA 23298-0709. **Fax:** 804-828-9477. **E-Mail:** krieg@hsc.vcu.edu

KRIEGER, ALLEN STEPHEN, SOLAR PHYSICS, X-RAY OPTICS. **Personal Data:** b New York, NY, February 23, 1941; m 1966, Jeanne; c Sara & Ruth. **Education:** Mass Inst Technol, BS, 1962, PhD (physics), 1967. **Professional Experience:** PRES, RADIATION SCI INC, 1986-; sr vpres space sci, Am Sci & Eng Inc, 1984-1986; vpres space systs, Am Sci & Eng Inc, 1980-1983; dir solar res, Am Sci & Eng Inc, 1978-1979; sr staff scientist, Am Sci & Eng Inc, 1974-1977; staff scientist, Am Sci & Eng Inc, 1972-1973; sr scientist, Am Sci & Eng Inc, 1968-1971; Res assoc cosmic ray physics, Ctr Space Res, Mass Inst Technol, 1967-1968. **Memberships:** Fel Am Phys Soc; Am Astron Soc; Am Geophys Union; Int Soc Optical Eng. **Research Statement & Publications:** Applicaiton of x-ray optics to solar astronomy and plasma diagnostics. **Mailing Address:** Radiation Sci, Inc, PO Box 293, Belmont, MA 02178-0002.

KRIEGER, GARY LAWRENCE, HEALTH PHYSICS, RADIATION PROTECTION PHYSICS. **Personal Data:** b New York, NY, May 2, 1948; m 1974, c 2. **Education:** NY Inst Technol, BS, 1971; Univ Kans, MS, 1976. **Professional Experience:** MGR, EMERGENCY PREPAREDNESS, LONG ISLAND LIGHTING CO, as of 1996; EMERGENCY PLANNING SCIENTIST, LONG ISLAND LIGHTING CO, 1985-; proj health physicist, KLM Eng, 1984-1985; lead sr engr, Impell Corp, 1982-1984; assoc scientist, Brookhaven Nat Lab, 1979-1982; health physics supvr, Siemens Corp, 1976-1979. **Memberships:** Health Physics Soc; Am Nuclear Soc. **Research Statement & Publications:** Dose assessment modeling technique for accidental radiological releases to the environment; impact of this exposure on man. **Mailing Address:** Long Island Lighting Co, 175 E Old Country Rd, Hicksville, NY 11801.

KRIEGER, HENRY ALAN, PROBABILITY & MATHEMATICAL STATISTICS. **Personal Data:** b Denver, Colo, May 7, 1936; m, c 2. **Education:** Rensselaer Polytech Inst, BAE, 1957; Brown Univ, PhD (appl math), 1964. **Professional Experience:** AVERY PROF MATH, HARVEY MUDD COL, as of 2003; PROF MATH, HARVEY MUDD COL, 1983-; vis prof math, University of South Australia, 2000; vis prof math, United States Military Academy, 1996; vis prof statist, Tel Aviv University, 1988-1989; vis res scientist, Commonwealth Sci Res Orgn, Div Math Statist, 1982; vis prof statist, Australian Nat Univ, 1982; vis prof statist, Hebrew Univ Jeusalem, 1981; vis assoc prof statist, Israel Inst Technol, 1974-1975; from asst prof to assoc prof math, Harvey Mudd Col, 1968-1983; asst prof, Calif Inst Technol, 1965-1968; Bateman res fel math, Calif Inst Technol, 1964-1965; Fulbright Scholar, Univ Manchester, 1957-1958. **Memberships:** Am Math Soc; Math Asn Am; Soc Indust Appl Math; Assoc for Women in Math; Sigma Xi. **Research Statement & Publications:** Probability theory, particularly limit theorems; measure theory. **Mailing Address:** Dept Math, Harvey Mudd Col, 1250 N Dartmouth Ave, Claremont, CA 91711. **Fax:** 909-621-8366. **E-Mail:** hkrieger@hmc.edu

KRIEGER, IRVIN MITCHELL, RHEOLOGY COLLOID SCI. **Personal Data:** b Cleveland, Ohio, May 14, 1923; m 1965. **Education:** Case Inst Technol, BS, 1944, MS, 1948; Cornell Univ, PhD (phys chem), 1951. **Honors & Awards:** Bingham Medal, Soc Rheol, 1989. **Professional Experience:** PROF EMER CHEM, CASE WESTERN RESERVE UNIV, 1988-; Vis prof, Nat High Sch Chem, Mulhouse, 1987-; prof invite, Ecole Nationale Superieure Del Chimie Del Mulhouse, 1987; dir, Ctr Adhesives, Sealants & Coatings, 1982-1988; prof phys chem & macromolecular sci, Case Western Reserve Univ, 1968-1988; from asst prof to assoc prof phys chem, Case Western Reserve Univ, 1951-1968; instr chem, Case Western Reserve Univ, 1949-1951; Asst, Cornell Univ, 1947-1948; assoc dir res, Univ Louis Pasteur, Strasbourg. **Memberships:** Am Chem Soc Sr Mem; Soc Rheol (pres 1977-1979); Am Inst Chem Eng; Sigma Xi. **Research Statement & Publications:** Rheology and statistical mechanics of colloids and polymers. **Mailing Address:** 3460 Green Rd, Beachwood, OH 44122. **E-Mail:** imk@po.cwru.edu

KRIEGER, JEANNE KANN, PHYSICAL ORGANIC CHEMISTRY. **Personal Data:** b Hartford, Conn, April 16, 1944; m 1966, c 2. **Education:** Bryn Mawr Col, BA, 1966; Mass Inst Technol, PhD (org chem), 1971; Boston Col, MBA, 1984. **Professional Experience:** CHMN, BD SELECTMEN LEXINGTON, as of 2000; MGR RES PROD OPERS, DUPONT MED PRODS, 1987-; area supvr, Dupont Med Prods, 1983-1987; asst to dir mgr, New England Nuclear, 1981-1983; proj leader, 1978-1980; lectr, Mass Inst Technol, 1975-1978; instr, Mass Inst Technol, 1972-1975; res assoc chem, Mass Inst Technol, 1971-1972. **Memberships:** Am Chem Soc; AAAS; Am Nat Stand. **Research Statement & Publications:** Radioactive waste disposal; scintillation techniques. **Mailing Address:** 1625 Mass Ave, Lexington, MA 02420. **Fax:** 781-863-9468. **E-Mail:** selectmen@ci.lexington.ma.us

KRIEGER, JOHN NEWTON, UROLOGY, INFECTIOUS DISEASES. **Personal Data:** b Philadelphia, Pa, May 3, 1948; m 1972. **Education:** Princeton Univ, AB, 1970; Cornell Univ Med Col, MD, 1974. **Honors & Awards:** Cornell Award Excellence Surg, 1974. **Professional Experience:** PROF UROL, UNIV WASH, 1990-; consult urol, Vet Admin Hosp, Seattle, 1982-; Univ Hosp, Seattle, 1982-; Harborview Med Ctr, Seattle, 1982-; Harborvion Med Ctr, Children's Orthop Hosp, 1982-; from asst prof to assoc prof, Univ Wash, 1982-1990; instr urol, Univ Va, 1980-1982; attend surgeon, Univ Va Hosp, 1980-1982; scholar, Am Urol Asn, 1980-1982; urol, gen surg, New York Hosp-Cornell Med Ctr, 1976-1979; asst surgeon, New York Hosp-Cornell Med Ctr, 1974-1976; surgeon, New York Hosp-Cornell Med Ctr, 1970-1980. **Memberships:** Am Fedn Clin Res; Am Venereal Dis Asn; Am Urol Asn; Am Soc Microbiol; Infectious Dis Soc Am; Sigma Xi. **Research Statement & Publications:** Genitourinary tract infections; bacteriuria; sexually transmitted diseases; prostatis. **Mailing Address:** Dept Urol, Univ Wash, PO Box 356510, Seattle, WA 98195-6510. **Fax:** 206-543-3272. **E-Mail:** rburol@u.washington.edu

KRIEGER, JOSEPH BERNARD, THEORETICAL SOLID STATE PHYSICS, DENSITY FUNCTIONAL THEORY WITH APPLICATIONS TO ATOMS & MOLECULES & SOLIDS. **Personal Data:** b Brooklyn, NY, July 10, 1937; m 1964, Rose; c Stephen. **Education:** Columbia Univ, AB, 1959, PhD (physics), 1965. **Professional Experience:** PROF EMERITUS, BROOKLYN COL, 2005- ARO Reseach Grants, 1993-2001, Consultant to Battelle, 1981-2001, exec officer, Doctoral Prog Physics, City Univ NY, 1990-1997; acad assoc, Calif Inst Technol, 1979; chmn dept, Brooklyn Col, 1976-1980; PROF PHYSICS, BROOKLYN COL, 1974-2005; assoc prof, Brooklyn Col, 1972-1974; vis assoc prof, Brooklyn Col, 1971-1972; From asst prof to assoc prof physics, Polytech Inst Brooklyn, 1965-1972. **Memberships:** Fel Am Phys Soc; Sigma Xi. **Research Statement & Publications:** Transport theory in solids; density functional theory; density functional theory with applications to atoms, molecules and solids. **Mailing Address:** Dept Physics, Brooklyn Col, 1407b Ingersoll Hall, Brooklyn, NY 11210. **Fax:** 718-951-4407. **E-Mail:** jkrieger@brooklyn.cuny.edu

KRIEGER, MONTY, BIOLOGY. **Education:** Calif Inst Technol, PhD, 1976. **Professional Experience:** WHITEHEAD PROF, MASS INST TECHNOL, as of 2006; PROF MOLECULAR GENETICS, MASS INST TECHNOL, as of 2006. **Mailing Address:** Dept Biol, Mass Inst Technol, 31 Ames St Rm 68-483, Cambridge, MA 02139. **Fax:** 617-258-5851. **E-Mail:** krieger@mit.edu

KRIEGER, ROBERT J, AERONAUTICS. **Education:** Carnegie Inst Technol, BS; Carnegie Mellon Univ, MS, PhD (appl space sci). **Professional Experience:** PRES, BOEING PHANTOM WORKS, as of 2006. **Mailing Address:** Boeing Phantom Works, PO Box 2515, Seal Beach, CA 90740. **Fax:** 562-797-5975.

KRIEGER, ROGER B, MECHANICAL ENGINEERING. **Personal Data:** b Milwaukee, Wis, May 4, 1941; m 1979. **Education:** Univ Wis-Madison, BS, 1964, PhD (mech eng), 1968. **Professional Experience:** GROUP LEADER, GEN MOTORS RES & DEVELOP CTR, WARREN, MI as of 2000; sr staff res engr, Engine Res Dept, Gen Motors Res Labs, beginning 1969; res engr, Fr Inst Petrol, 1968-1969. **Memberships:** Soc Automotive Engrs; Am Soc Mech Engrs; Combustion Inst. **Research Statement & Publications:** Combustion; pollutant formation and destruction during combustion; combustion modelling and internal combustion engine simulation. **Mailing Address:** 636 Lakeview Ave, Birmingham, MI 48009.

KRIEGER, STEPHAN JACQUES, THEORETICAL PHYSICS. **Personal Data:** b San Francisco, Calif, August 2, 1937; m 1958, c 4. **Education:** Univ Calif, Berkeley, BS, 1959, PhD (physics), 1963. **Professional Experience:** STAFF SCIENTIST, LAWRENCE LIVERMORE NAT LAB, 1980-; prof, Univ Ill, Chicago Circle, 1978-1980; assoc prof physics, Univ Ill, Chicago Circle, 1971-1978; res physicist, Carnegie Inst Technol, 1963-1966. **Memberships:** Am Phys Soc. **Research Statement & Publications:** Nuclear structure; many body problem. **Mailing Address:** L-291 Lawrence Livermore Nat Lab, PO Box 808, Livermore, CA 94550. **Fax:** 510-422-9523. **E-Mail:** krieger@ocfkms.llnl.gov

KRIEGER-BROCKETT, BARBARA, CHEMICAL ENGINEERING, CHEMICAL PHYSICS. **Personal Data:** b Madison, Wis, January 27, 1947. **Education:** Univ Wis-Madison, BS, 1968; Wayne State Univ, MS, 1972, PhD (chem eng), 1975. **Professional Experience:** PROF EMER, CHEM ENG, UNIV WASH, as of 2006; adj prof, Oceanog, Univ Wash, as of 2005; assoc prof, Oceanog, Univ Wash, as of 2003; assoc prof, chem eng, Univ Wash, beginning 1980; Consult, Rocket Res Corp, 1977-; Hanford Energy Develop Lab, 1978- & Nat Acad Adv Bd, Environ Protection Agency, 1976-; asst prof, Univ Wash, 1975-1980; res asst, Wayne State Univ, 1971-1975; res technician auto emission control, Gen Motor Res Labs, 1970-1971; res engr, Inst Francais du Petrole, 1968-1969. **Memberships:** Am Inst Chem Engrs; Am Chem Soc; AAAS; Sigma Xi. **Research Statement & Publications:** Chemical kinetics, chemical physics and transport related to chemical reaction engineering as applied to high temperature-high energy phenomena such as combustion, pyrolysis, laser and plasma processing, air pollution and atmospheric chemistry. **Mailing Address:** 255 Benson, PO Box 351750, Seattle, WA 98195-1750. **Fax:** 206-543-3778. **E-Mail:** krieger-brockett@cheme.washington.edu

KRIEGH, JAMES DOUGLAS, CIVIL ENGINEERING. **Personal Data:** b Dodge City, Kans, December 29, 1928. **Education:** Univ Colo, BS, 1955, MS, 1958. **Professional Experience:** PROF EMER CIVIL ENG & ENG MECHANICS, UNIV ARIZ, as of 1999; prof eng mech, Univ Ariz, 1981-1986; comt chmn, Hwy Res Bd, Nat Acad Sci, Nat Res Coun, 1964-1970; NSF fac fel, Univ Colo, 1963-1964; from asst prof to prof civil eng, Univ Ariz, 1958-1986; instr civil eng, Eng Exp Sta, Univ Colo, 1955-1958; asst, Eng Exp Sta, Univ Colo, 1954-1955; asst, Cryogenics Lab, Nat Bur Standards, Colo, 1953-1954. **Memberships:** Am Soc Civil Engrs; Am Concrete Inst. **Research Statement & Publications:** Epoxy resins for concrete construction and structural adhesives. **Mailing Address:** Dept Civil Eng & Eng Mechanics, Univ Ariz, PO Box 210072 CE Bldg Rm 206, Tucson, AZ 85721.

KRIEGSMAN, HELEN, MATHEMATICS. **Personal Data:** b Pittsburg, Kans, February 27, 1924. **Education:** Kans State Teachers Col Pittsburg, BS, 1944, MS, 1947; Ohio State Univ, PhD (math educ), 1964. **Professional Experience:** RETIRED; prof math & chmn dept, Pittsburg State Univ, beginning 1967; from instr to assoc prof, Pittsburg State Univ, 1947-1967; teacher, High Sch, Kans, 1944-1947. **Memberships:** Math Asn Am; Am Math Soc; Nat Coun Teachers Math. **Research Statement & Publications:** Curriculum and methods of teaching mathematics on the secondary school and college levels. **Mailing Address:** Dept Math, Pittsburg State Univ, Wilkinson Alumni Ctr 401 E Ford, Pittsburg, KS 66762-9987.

KRIEGSMANN, GREGORY A, PHYSICAL MATHEMATICS & ACOUSTICS, ELECTROMAGNETISM. **Personal Data:** b Chicago, Ill, September 20, 1946; m 1969, c 2. **Education:** Marquette Univ, BS, 1969; Univ Calif Los Angeles, MS, 1970, PhD (appl math), 1974. **Professional Experience:** FOUN CHAIR, APPL MATH, as of 2003; PROF MATH, NJ INST TECHNOL, 1990-; from assoc prof to prof appl math, Northwestern Univ, 1980-1990; assoc prof, Univ Nebr, 1979-1980; asst prof math, Univ Nebr, 1977-1979; mem tech staff, Hughes Aircraft Co, 1976-1977; instr math, Courant Inst, NY Univ, 1974-1976. **Memberships:** Soc Indust Appl Math; Am Math Soc; Acoust Soc Am; Inst Math & Its Applns. **Research Statement & Publications:** Numerical and asymstotic analysis of wave propagation; bifurcation problems in the physical sciences; microwave processing of materials. **Mailing Address:** Dept Math, NJ Tech Inst Technol, Newark, NJ 07102-9938. **E-Mail:** grkrie@micro.njit.edu

KRIENKE, ORA KARL, ASTRONOMY. **Personal Data:** b Seattle, Wash, January 31, 1931; m 1960, c 2. **Education:** Seattle Pac Col, BA, 1953, MA, 1955; Univ Wash, MS, 1959 & 1969, PhD (astron), 1973. **Professional Experience:** RETIRED; dean, Sch Nat & Math Sci, 1980-1997; prof physics, math & philos, 1971-1997; vis lectr, Univ Wash, 1964 & 1968; assoc prof physics, math & philos, 1963-1971; asst prof physics & math, Seattle Pac Univ, 1959-1963; instr math, Seattle Pac Univ, 1953-1959. **Memberships:** AAAS; Am Asn Physics Teachers; Am Astron Soc. **Research Statement & Publications:** Structure of galaxies, especially irregular type II galaxies. **Mailing Address:** 9251 20th Ave NW, Seattle, WA 98117.

KRIENS, RICHARD DUANE, ORGANIC CHEMISTRY. **Personal Data:** b Belmond, Iowa, October 16, 1932; m 1967, Linda; c John, Heidi & Rebecca. **Education:** Iowa State Teachers Col, BA, 1956; Iowa State Univ, PhD (org chem), 1963. **Professional Experience:** RETIRED; prof chem, Ashland Univ, 1973-; assoc prof, Ashland Univ, 1965-1973; asst prof chem, Iowa Wesleyan Col, 1963-1965; teacher, High Sch, Iowa, 1957-1958. **Memberships:** Am Inst Chem; Royal Soc Chem; Am Chem Soc. **Research Statement & Publications:** Free radical organic chemistry; reaction mechanisms in organic chemistry. **Mailing Address:** Dept Chem, Ashland Univ, Ashland, OH 44805.

KRIER, CAROL ALNOTH, MATERIALS SCIENCE AND ENGINEERING, PRODUCTION ENGINEERING. **Personal Data:** b Bismarck, ND, July 22, 1928; m 1957, Carol A Wilt; c David A & Elizabeth A. **Education:** St Martin's Col, BS, 1950; Univ Pittsburgh, PhD (chem), 1955. **Honors & Awards:** NASA-Apollo Achievement Award, 1970; Apollo/Saturn V Roll of Honor, 1971; Apollo 11 Manned Flight Awareness Award, 1971. **Professional Experience:** RETIRED; Mgr opers tecnhol, Boeing Defense & Space, 1991-1993; mgr, prod eng, Boeing Aerospace & Electronics, 1987-1991; mat adv bd mem, Aerospace Industs Asn, 1986-1989; mgr mfg tech, Boeing Aerospace, 1984-1986; eng mgr, Boeing Aerospace, 1971-1983; mgr advan develop & spec studies, Boeing Co, 1970-1971; supvr mat stress & environ simulation, Boeing Co, 1967-1970; metals res specialist, Boeing Co, 1962-1967; mat adv bd mem, Nat Acad Sci, 1961-1969; consult, Defense Metals Info Ctr, 1959-1962; prin chemist, proj leader & sr scientist, Battelle Mem Inst, 1955-1962; asst phys chem, Univ Pittsburgh, 1951-1955; asst, Univ Pittsburgh, 1950-1951; asst instr chem, pvt sch, Wash, 1948-1950; lab asst fuel oils, State Labs Dept, ND, 1945-1946. **Memberships:** Am Chem Soc; Am Soc Metals; Sigma Xi. **Research Statement & Publications:** Thermodynamics; calorimetry; cryogenics; theory of metals and alloys; extractive metallurgy; refractory, structural and electronic materials; high temperature coatings for metals; oxidation of metals and alloys; alkali metals; platinum-group metals; high temperature corrosion; physical metallurgy; vapor deposition; manufacturing processes; automation; environmental engineering. **Mailing Address:** 2212 Via Mariposa E Unit C, Laguna Woods, CA 92653.

KRIER, HERMAN, MECHANICAL ENGINEERING. **Education:** Princeton Univ, MA (arts & sci), 1966; Univ Pittsburgh, BS, 1964; Princeton Univ, PhD (aerospace sci), 1968. **Professional Experience:** PROF, DEPT MECH & INDUST ENG, UNIV ILL, URBANA-CHAMPAIGN, as of 2006. **Mailing Address:** Univ Ill, 140 Mech Eng Bldg, 1206 W Green St, Urbana, IL 61801-2906. **Fax:** 217-244-6907. **E-Mail:** krier@uiuc.edu

KRIKORIAN, ABRAHAM D, PLANT PHYSIOLOGY, BIOCHEMISTRY. **Personal Data:** b Worcester, Mass, May 5, 1937. **Education:** Mass Col Pharm, BS, 1959; Cornell Univ, PhD (plant physiol), 1965. **Honors & Awards:** Cosmos Achievement Award, NASA, 1975 & 1981; Founder's Award, Am Soc Gravitational & Space Biol, 1992. **Professional Experience:** PROF BIOCHEM & CELL BIO, STATE UNIV NY, STONY BROOK, 1988-; gov bd, Am Soc Gravitational & Space Biol, 1985-1987; mem comt space res, Int Coun, Sci Union, 1984-; assoc prof biochem, State Univ NY, Stony Brook, 1981-1988; plant sci book rev consult, Quart Rev Biol, 1979-; Ed, Ann Bot, 1976-1982; from asst prof to assoc prof biol sci, State Univ NY, Stony Brook, 1966-1981; from instr to asst prof, Cornell Univ, 1963-1966; from teaching asst to teaching assoc plant physiol, Cornell Univ, 1960-1964. **Memberships:** AAAS; Am Soc Pharmacog; Int Soc Plant Morphologists; Int Asn Plant Tissue Cult; Soc Develop Biol; Tissue Cult Asn; Soc Econ Bot (vpres, 1981-1982, pres 1982-1983); Bot Soc Am; Am Soc Plant Physiologists; Scand Soc Plant Physiol; Am Soc Gravitational & Space Biol (pres, 1987-1988); Int Palm Soc; Plant Growth Regulator Soc Am. **Research Statement & Publications:** Physiological and morphological aspects of growth and development in flowering plants; morphogenesis and biochemical differentiation; nitrogen metabolism; production of secondary products and expression of biochemical potentialities by cells and tissues grown in culture; clonal stability; totipotency of higher plant cells in terms of morphogenesis and biochemical competence. **Mailing Address:** Dept Biochem & Cell Biol, State Univ NY, Life Sci Bldg, Stony Brook, NY 11794-5215. **E-Mail:** akrikor@asterix.bio.sunysb.edu

KRIKORIAN, JOHN SARKIS, ELECTRICAL ENGINEERING, APPLIED MATHEMATICS. **Personal Data:** b Providence, RI, September 18, 1941. **Education:** Univ RI, BS, 1963; Syracuse Univ, MS, 1967, PhD (elec eng), 1968. **Professional Experience:** Mem tech staff, Mitre Corp, 1983-1984; VPRES, SARKIS CORP, 1981-; adj prof, Brown Univ, 1980-1981; asst prof, Univ RI, 1973-1980; Lectr elec eng, Univ Conn, 1969; res specialist elec eng, Elec Boat Div, Gen Dynamics Corp, Groton, Conn, 1968-1973. **Memberships:** Sigma Xi. **Research Statement & Publications:** Electrical engineering and related interdisciplinary activities. **Mailing Address:** Five Thayer Pl, Warwick, RI 02888.

KRIKORIAN, OSCAR HAROLD, HIGH TEMPERATURE CHEMISTRY. **Personal Data:** b Fresno, Calif, November 22, 1930; m 1953, c 2. **Education:** Fresno State Col, BS, 1952; Univ Calif, PhD (chem), 1955. **Professional Experience:** RES CHEMIST, LAWRENCE LIVERMORE NAT LAB, 1955-. **Memberships:** Am Chem Soc. **Research Statement & Publications:** High temperature chemistry; thermodynamic properties of gaseous species that exist at high temperatures; molten metal containment studies, estimation of heat capacities and thermal expansivities of refractory materials. **Mailing Address:** 22 Rio Del Ct, Danville, CA 94526.

KRIKOS, GEORGE ALEXANDER, PATHOLOGY. **Personal Data:** b Old Phaleron, Greece, September 17, 1922; American citizen; m 1949, Aspasia Manoni; c Helen, Alexandra & Alexios. **Education:** Univ Pa, DDS, 1949; Univ Rochester, PhD (path), 1959. **Honorary Degrees:** Dr, Univ Athens, Greece, 1981. **Professional Experience:** EMER PROF ORAL BIOL, SCH DENT, UNIV COLO, 1991-; clin prof, Univ Colo, 1986-1991; vis prof, Sch Dent, Univ Athens, Greece, 1980-1981; prof 1975-1986, assoc dean oral biol affairs, Univ Colo, 1975-1976; prof pathobiol, Univ Colo, 1968-1975; chmn dept, Univ Colo, 1968-1973; chmn path, Sch Dent Med, Univ Pa, 1964-1968; Assoc prof oral path, Grad Sch Arts & Sci, Div Grad Educ, Sch Med, Univ Pa, 1962-1968; from asst prof to prof, Sch Dent Med, Univ Pa, 1958-1968; NIH res fel path, Univ Rochester, 1954-1958. **Memberships:** Int Asn Dent Res; Sigma Xi; Am soc investgative pathology. **Research Statement & Publications:** Histochemical studies in connective tissue. **Mailing Address:** 350 Ivy St, Denver, CO 80220-5855.

KRILL, ARTHUR MELVIN, MECHANICAL ENGINEERING, ENGINEERING GENERAL. **Personal Data:** b Burlington, Colo, October 17, 1921; m 1944, c 3. **Education:** Univ Colo, BS, 1943, MS, 1951; Indust Col Armed Forces, Dipl, 1952. **Professional Experience:** Mgr corp planning, Stearns Roger Corp, 1982-1983; PRES, ARTHUR M KRILL CONSULTS, 1979-; chmn, Ogden Develop Corn, 1976-1978; CHMN, OGDEN DEVELOP CORN, 1970-; pres, Ken R White Co, 1963-1976; pres, Falcon Res & Develop, 1962-1970; head mech div, Denver Res Inst, 1956-1962; dir opers anal unit, Denver Res Inst, 1955-1962; proj supvr, Col Eng, Univ Denver, 1951-1956; head admin eng, Col Eng, Univ Denver, 1951-1952; Consult, Bond Eng Co, 1950-1952; coord coop plan, Col Eng, Univ Denver, 1948-1956; from instr to assoc prof mech engr, Col Eng, Univ Denver, 1947-1962; exp test engr, Pratt-Whitney Aircraft Div, United Aircraft Corp, 1943-1947; Prod engr, Pratt-Whitney Aircraft Div, United Aircraft Corp, 1942; mem, Metrop Air Qual Coun; mem, Colo State Air Pollution Variance Bd. **Memberships:** Fel AAAS; Am Soc Mech Engrs; Am Soc Eng Educ; Nat Soc Prof Engrs; Am Inst Consult Engrs. **Research Statement & Publications:** Theoretical and applied mechanics; operations research; behavioral sciences; magnetohydrodynamics. **Mailing Address:** 450 Westwood Dr, Denver, CO 80206.

KRIM, JACQUELINE, PHYSICS. **Education:** Univ Mont, BA, 1978; Univ Wash, PhD (Physics), 1984. **Honors & Awards:** Presidential Young Investr Award, NSF. **Professional Experience:** Sigma Distinguished Lectr, 2001-2003; PROF, DEPT PHYSICS, NC STATE UNIV, 1998; from asst to assoc to prof, NEastern Univ, 1985-1998; NATO res fel, Univ Marseille, France, 1984-1985. **Memberships:** Fel, Am Physical Soc; Am Vaccum Soc. **Research Statement & Publications:** Nanoscale science and technology; solid-film growth processes and topologies at submicron length scales; nantribology (the study of friction; wear and lubrication at atomic length and time scales); liquid-film wetting phenomena. **Mailing Address:** Dept Physics, NC State Univ, Campus Box 8202, Raleigh, NC 27695-8202. **Fax:** 919-515-4496. **E-Mail:** jkrim@unity.ncsu.edu

KRIM, MATHILDE, CYTOGENETICS, VIROLOGY. **Personal Data:** b Como, Italy, July 9, 1926; American citizen; m 1958, c 1. **Education:** Geneva Univ, BS, 1948, PhD (cytogenetics), 1953. **Professional Experience:** FOUNDING CHMN, FOUND AIDS RES-AMFAR, 2006-; chmn bd, Am Found AIDS Res, 1988-2006; pres, comn study ethnical probs med, Biomed & Behav Res, beginning 1980; assoc & mem, Sloan-Kettering Inst Cancer Res, beginning 1975; trustee, Rockefeller Found, beginning 1971; co-chmn, Nat Comt to Save our Schs Health, beginning 1971; mem panel consult conquest cancer, Comt Labor & Pub Welfare, US Senate, 1971; consult spec virus cancer prog & mem adv comt, Nat Colorectal Cancer Prog, Nat Cancer Inst, 1971; mem, Comt 100 for Nat Health Ins, beginning 1969; mem, Nat Endowment for Humanities, 1969-1973; secy, Adv Comt Health Protection & Dis Prev, Dept Health, Educ & Welfare, 1969-1970; mem, Pres's Comt Ment Retardation, 1966-1969; assoc, Sloan-Kettering Inst Cancer Res, 1962-1975; res assoc virol, Div Virus Res, Med Col, Cornell Univ, 1959-1962; jr scientist & res assoc cancer res, Weizmann Inst, 1953-1959; mem bd trustees, Nat Biomed Res Found; mem bd dirs, Inst Soc, Ethics & Life Sci. **Memberships:** AAAS; Am Cancer Soc; Am Asn Ment Deficiency. **Research Statement & Publications:** Structure of chromosomes; prenatal determination of sex; aberrations in human sexual development; cell biology and mechanisms of oncogenic transformation; interferon research. **Mailing Address:** Found AIDS Res-amfar, 120 Wall St 13th Floor, New York, NY 10005-3908.

KRIMIGIS, STAMATIOS MIKE, HELIOSPHERIC PHYSICS, PLANETARY MAGNETO-SPHERES. **Personal Data:** b Chios, Greece, September 10, 1938; American citizen; m 1990, Maria; c Michael & John. **Education:** Univ Minn, BPhys, 1961; Univ Iowa, MS, 1963, PhD (physics), 1965. **Honors & Awards:** Except Sci Achievement Medal, NASA, 1981 & 1986; Basic Sci Award, Intern Acad Astronaut, 1994; COSPAR Space Sci Award, 2002; Acad Athens Chair Sci of Space, 2005; Lifetime Achvmnt Award, Johns Hopkins APL, 2005. **Professional Experience:** EMERITUS HEAD, SPACE DEPT, 2004-, DEPT HEAD, SPACE DEPT, APPL PHYSICS LAB, JOHNS HOPKINS UNIV, 1991-2004; prin investr, Cassini mission to Saturn, 1990-; prin investr Voyager 1, 2, 1971-; NASA Space & Earth Sci Adv Comt, 1987-1990; prin investr, Imaging Neutral Particle Detector, NASA Innovative Res Prog, 1985-1989; mem, Space Sci Bd, Nat Acad Sci, 1983-1986; chmn, Comt Solar & Space Physics, 1983-1986; chief scientist, Space Physics & Instrumentation Group, 1980-1990; Studies Solar & Magnetospheric Particles, NSF, 1977-1983; co-prin investr, Galileo Mission, Energetic Particle Detector Exp, 1977; co-investr, Ulysses

Spacecraft, LAN Exp, 1977; Light Ion Release Exp, Active Magnetospheric Particle Tracer Explorers, 1977; assoc ed, J Geophys Res, Space Physics, 1975-1977; head, Space Physics & Instrumentation Group, 1974-1981; Light Ion Release Exp, NASA, 1973; prin investr, Voyager Low Energy Charged Particle Exp, 1972; prin investr, Multiple-Charged Energetic Trapped Nucleiin Radiation Belt, NSF, 1971-1974; from sr staff scientist to supvr space physics, Johns Hopkins Univ, 1968-1974; prin investr, Interplanetary Monitoring Platform on 7 & 8, 1967; asst prof physics, Univ Iowa, 1966-1968; Orbiting Geophys Observ-4, Mariner V Venus, 1966; Res assoc space physics, Univ Iowa, 1965-1966; Orbiting Geophys Observ-4, Explorer 33 & 35 & Injun V, 1965; Co-investr, Mariner IV & Injun IV, 1963; mem, Space Sci Working Group, Asn Am Univs; mem var NASA adv comts on space invests. **Memberships:** fel Am Geophys Union; fel Am Phys Soc; fel Am Asn Adv Sci; assoc fel Am Inst Aeronaut & Astronautics; Athens Acad Greece; Int Acad Astronaut; Hel.A.S. **Research Statement & Publications:** Space plasma physics; solar and heliospheric physics; geomagnetically trapped radiation; planetary magnetospheres; cosmic rays; particle instrumentation; over 385 publications in journals and books. **Mailing Address:** Appl Physics Lab, Johns Hopkins Univ, Laurel, MD 20723-6099. **Fax:** 240-228-0386. **E-Mail:** tom.krimigis@jhuapl.edu

KRIMM, SAMUEL, SPECTROSCOPY, POLYMER PHYSICS, COMPUTER SIMULATIONS. **Personal Data:** b Morristown, NJ, October 19, 1925; m Marilyn; c David & Daniel. **Education:** Polytech Inst Brooklyn, BS, 1947; Princeton Univ, MA, 1949, PhD (phys chem), 1950. **Honors & Awards:** High Polymer Physics Prize, Am Phys Soc, 1977; Alexander von Humboldt Prize, 1983. **Professional Experience:** PROF EMER PHYSICS, UNIV MICH, ANN ARBOR, as of 2001; Invited prof, French Govt, 1991; Univ Mainz, 1983 & Univ Paris, 1991; mem, Coun Mat Sci, DOE, 1986-1989; dir prog protein struct & design, Col Lit Sci & Arts, 1985-1994; chmn, Mat Res Adv Comt, NSF, 1984-1985; mem, Mat Res Adv Comt, NSF, 1981-1986; chmn, Div Biol Physics, Am Phys Soc, 1979; vchmn, Div Biol Physics, Am Phys Soc, 1978; chmn biophysics res div, Col Lit Sci & Arts, 1976-1986; chmn, Nat Bur Standards Polymers Div Eval Panel, Nat Acad Sci/Nat Res Coun, 1975-1976; chmn biopolymers subgroup, Biophys Soc, 1974-1975; mem, Nat Bur Standards Polymers Div Eval Panel, Nat Acad Sci/Nat Res Coun, 1973-1976; assoc dean res, Col Lit Sci & Arts, 1972-1975; sr fel, Univ Mich, 1971-1976; vis prof, Weizmann Inst, 1970; chmn, Gordon Res Conf, 1968; prof physics, Univ Mich, Ann Arbor, beginning 1963; NSF sr fel, 1962-1963; from instr to assoc prof, Univ Mich, Ann Arbor, 1952-1963; Fel, Univ Mich, Ann Arbor, 1950-1952. **Memberships:** Fel AAAS; Am Chem Soc; Biophys Soc; fel Am Phys Soc. **Research Statement & Publications:** Infrared and Raman spectroscopy; high polymers; protein structure; potential functions - over 290 publications. **Mailing Address:** Biophysics Research Division, Univ Mich 3303 Chem, Ann Arbor, MI 48109. **E-Mail:** skrimm@umich.edu

KRIMMER, EDWARD CHARLES, PHARMACOLOGY, PSYCHOPHARMACOLOGY. **Personal Data:** b Youngstown, Ohio, December 31, 1933; m 1958, c 3. **Education:** Univ Pittsburgh, BS, 1968, PhD (pharmacol), 1974. **Professional Experience:** ASSOC PROF PHARMACOL, UNIV PITTSBURGH, 1981-; investr, Nat Inst Drug Abuse grant, 1979-1983; co-investr, NIMH grant, 1976-; asst prof, Univ Pittsburgh, 1976-1981; fel, Nat Inst Drug Abuse grant, 1974-1976; Fel pharmacol, Univ Pittsburgh, 1974-1976; Consult, ICI US, 1974-1975; co-investr, Nat Inst Alcohol Abuse. **Memberships:** AAAS; Behav Pharmacol Soc; Am Soc Pharmacol & Exp Therapeut; Soc Stimulus Properties Drugs (secy-treas 1978-1980); Soc Neurosci; Res Soc Alcoholism; Sigma Xi. **Research Statement & Publications:** Investigate the stimulus properties of various sedatives, axiolytics, narcotics and cannabinoids and the pharmacological antagonism or enhancement of these perceived effects. **Mailing Address:** 318 Elmwood Dr, Kent, OH 44240-2890.

KRINER, WILLIAM ARTHUR, INORGANIC CHEMISTRY. **Personal Data:** b Pottsville, Pa, February 8, 1931; m 1957, c 2. **Education:** West Chester State Col, BS, 1953; Univ Pa, PhD (inorg chem), 1959. **Professional Experience:** PROF EMER CHEM, ST JOSEPHS UNIV, PA, as of 2004; assoc prof chem, St Josephs Univ, Pa, beginning 1970; asst prof, St Josephs Univ, Pa, 1965-1970; lectr chem, Univ Pa, 1962-1965; res chemist, rohm & haas co, Pa, 1959-1961. **Memberships:** Am Chem Soc; Sigma Xi. **Research Statement & Publications:** Small ring heterocyclics of Group IV preparation and reactivity; organometallic polymers; synthesis of novel organosilicon compounds; silicon hydride chemistry; boron cyanides and siloxy aluminum compounds. **Mailing Address:** Dept Chem, St Josephs Univ, 5600 City Ave, Philadelphia, PA 19131.

KRINGS, JOHN E, AERONAUTICS. **Education:** La State Univ, BS, 1952. **Professional Experience:** RETIRED; dir oper test & evaluation, Dept Defense, as of 2002. **Mailing Address:** 1200 Crystal Dr Apt 1703, 1713, Arlington, VA 22202. **Fax:** 703-416-6541.

KRINITZSKY, E(LLIS) L(OUIS), ENGINEERING GEOLOGY. **Personal Data:** b Norfolk, Va, July 1, 1924; m 1952. **Education:** Va Polytech Inst, BS, 1945; Univ NC, MS, 1947; La State Univ, PhD (geol), 1950. **Honors & Awards:** Richard H Jahns Distinguished Lectr Eng Geol, 1991. **Professional Experience:** CHIEF GEOL RES, WATERWAYS EXP STA, ARMY CORPS ENGRS, 1963-; vis prof, Univ Houston, 1962-1963; sr geologist, Creole Petrol Corp, 1953-1961; geologist, Army Corps Engrs, 1948-1953; asst prof geol, Southwestern La Inst, 1946-1947. **Memberships:** Fel Geol Soc Am; Earthquake Eng Res Inst; Am Soc Civil Engrs; Int Soc Rock Mech; Seismol Soc Am; Asn Eng Geologists. **Research Statement & Publications:** Engineering geology; earthquake hazards, x-radiography. **Mailing Address:** 3309 Highland Dr, Vicksburg, MS 39180.

KRINSKY, EUNICE L, MATHEMATICS. **Education:** Case Western Res Univ, BA, 1962; Univ Calif, Los Angeles, PhD, 1987; Kent State Univ, MA, 1970. **Professional Experience:** PROF MATH, CALIF STATE UNIV, DOMINGUEZ HILLS, as of 2006; DIR, CTR MATH & SCI EDU, CALIF STATE UNIV, DOMINGUEZ HILLS, as of 2006. **Mailing Address:** Dept Math, Calif State Univ, NSM A124, 1000 E Victoria St, Carson, CA 90747. **Fax:** 310-516-4268.

KRINSKY, NORMAN IRVING, BIOCHEMISTRY. **Personal Data:** b Iron River, Mich, June 29, 1928; m, c 2. **Education:** Univ Southern Calif, BA, 1948, MS, 1950, PhD (biochem), 1953. **Honors & Awards:** Trevor Goodwin Award, Int Carotenoid Soc, 2005; James A Olson Lecturer, Carotenoid Res Interaction Grp, 2005; National Associate, Nat'l Acad Sci/Nat'l Res Council, 2001; Robert S Harris Lecturer, MIT, 2001; Lars Ernster lecturer, Oxygen Club of California, 1999; Dozor Visiting Professor, Ben Gurion Univ, Beer Sheva, Israel, 1998; Mordchai Avron Memorial Lecture, Gifu/Tokyo, Japan, 1997; Honorary Member, The Vitamin Society of Japan, 1993; Lotte Arnrich lectr, Iowa State Univ, 1990. **Professional Experience:** PROF EMER BIOCHEM, SCH MED, TUFTS UNIV, as of 2000; SCIENTIST HUMAN NUTRIT RES CTR AGING, TUFTS UNIV, 1993-; prof biochem, Sch Med, Tufts Univ, beginning1987; res assoc, Boston Vet Admin Med Ctr, 1981-1982; Vis prof, Univ Calif, Berkeley, 1973; prof biochem & pharmacol, Tufts Univ Sch Med, 1970-1987; from asst prof pharmacol to prof biochem, Tufts Univ Sch ed, 1960-1970; lectr, Harvard Univ, 1959-1960; instr biol, Harvard Univ, 1956-1959; Nat Coun to Combat Blindness fel, Harvard Univ, 1955-1956; USPHS fel, Harvard Univ, 1953-1955. **Memberships:** Fellow, AAAS; Am Chem Soc; Soc Free Rad Biol Med; NY Acad Sci; Am Soc Photobiol (secy-treas 1975-1981 pres 1982-1983); Am Soc Biochem & Molecular Biol. **Research Statement & Publications:** Function and metabolism of carotenoids. **Mailing Address:** DEPT BIOCHEM, TUFTS UNIV Sch Med, 136 Harrison Ave, Boston, MA 02111. **Fax:** 617-636-2409. **E-Mail:** norman.krinsky@tufts.edu

KRINSKY, SAMUEL, ACCELERATOR PHYSICS. **Personal Data:** b Brooklyn, NY, January 14, 1945; m 1972, Faith; c Benjamin & Sylvia. **Education:** Mass Inst Technol, BS, 1966; Yale Univ, PhD (physics), 1971. **Honors & Awards:** R&D 100 Award, 1989. **Professional Experience:** Dep chair, Nat Synchroton Light Source, 1985-2001; SR PHYSICIST, BROOKHAVEN NAT LAB, 1985-; physicist, Brookhaven Nat Lab, 1978-1985; assoc physicist, Brookhaven Nat Lab, 1975-1978; asst physicist, Brookhaven Nat Lab, 1973-1975; res assoc physics, Inst Theoret Physics, State Univ NY, Stony Brook, 1971-1973. **Memberships:** AAAS; fel Am Phys Soc. **Research Statement & Publications:** Particle beam dynamics in storage rings, undulators and wigglers as sources of synchrotron radiation; free electron lasers. **Mailing Address:** Nat Synchrotron Light Source, Brookhaven Nat Lab, Bldg 725B, Upton, NY 11973. **Fax:** 631-344-4745. **E-Mail:** krinsky@bnl.gov

KRINSKY, WILLIAM LEWIS, MEDICAL FORENSIC ENTOMOLOGY, BIOSYSTEMATICS. **Personal Data:** b Brooklyn, NY, January 10, 1947; m 1970, c 2. **Education:** Yale Univ, AB, 1967, MD, 1974; Cornell Univ, PhD (entom), 1974. **Professional Experience:** ASSOC CLIN PROF EPIDEMIOL, SCH MED, YALE UNIV, 1987-; fac affil entomol, Peabody Mus Natural Hist, Yale Univ, 1980-; from asst prof to assoc prof epidemiol, Sect Med Entom, Dept Epidemiol & Public Health, 1977-1987; res assoc med entom, Rocky Mountain Lab, Nat Inst Allergy & Infectious Dis, 1974-1977. **Memberships:** Entom Soc Am; Coleopterist Soc; Am Entom Soc. **Research Statement & Publications:** Forensic entomology; medical entomology, acarology and parasitology; coleoptera systematics. **Mailing Address:** Dept Epidemiol & Public Health, Yale Univ, Sch Med, 60 Col St PO Box 208034, New Haven, CT 06520-8034. **E-Mail:** william.krinsky@yale.edu

KRINSLEY, DANIEL B, NATURAL HAZARDS. **Personal Data:** b New York, NY, June 22, 1923. **Education:** Brooklyn Col, AB, 1944, Brown Univ, MSc, 1949, Univ Md, PhD (geomorphol), 1970. **Honors & Awards:** Distinguished Serv Award, Dept Interior, US Geol Survey, 1983. **Professional Experience:** US GEOL SURV, US DEPT INTERIOR, as of 2004; consult geologist, beginning 1980; chief, environ impact anal prog, US Geol Surv, Wash, DC, 1974-1980; field geologist, 1949-1973. **Memberships:** fel Geol Soc Am. **Research Statement & Publications:** Arctic-desert geomorphological research into permafrost and saline crusts in arid regions; siting of roads, airfields and large installations away from areas of natural hazards. **Mailing Address:** US Geol Surv, US Dept Interior, 2475 Va Ave NW, Washington, DC 20037.

KRINSLEY, DAVID, SEDIMENTOLOGY. **Personal Data:** b Chicago, Ill, January 9, 1927; m 1958, c 3. **Education:** Univ Chicago, PhB, 1948, SB & SM, 1950, PhD (geol), 1956. **Professional Experience:** PROF EMER GEOL, ARIZ STATE UNIV, as of 2004; prof geol, Ariz State Univ, beginning 1976; chmn dept, Ariz State Univ, 1976-1982; overseas fel, Churchill Col, Cambridge Univ, 1970-1971; actg dean fac, Queens Col, NY, 1970; assoc dean fac, Queens Col, NY, 1966-1970; chmn dept geol & geog, Queens Col, NY, 1962-1965; from instr to prof geol, Queens Col, NY, 1957-1976; micropaleontologist & geochemist oceanog & geochem, Lamont Geol Observ, Columbia Univ, 1956-1957; instr, Univ Ill, 1955-1956; Asst geol, Univ Ill, 1954-1955; Grants, Am Philos Soc, Petrol Res Fund, Am Chem Soc, NASA, NSF, NATO, Dept Energy. **Memberships:** Fel AAAS; Soc Econ Paleont & Mineral; Geol Soc Am; Sigma Xi. **Research Statement & Publications:** Backscattered electron microscopy of fine grained sedimentary rocks. **Mailing Address:** Dept Geol Sci, Ariz State Univ, Tempe, AZ 85287-1404.

KRIPALANI, KISHIN J, DRUG METABOLISM, BIOPHARMACEUTICS. **Personal Data:** b Karachi, Pakistan, October 3, 1937; m 1966, Shanti; c Anjali & Renu. **Education:** Univ Bombay, BSc Hons, 1957, BSc (tech), 1959; Univ Calif, PhD (pharmaceut chem), 1966. **Professional Experience:** DIR, BRISTOL-MYERS SQUIBB PHARMACEUT RES INST, as of 2004; assoc dir, squibb inst med res, e r squibb & sons, inc, beginning 1989; res group leader drug metab, Squibb Inst Med Res, E R Squibb & Sons, Inc, 1969-1989; staff scientist, NIH fel steroid biochem, 1968-1969; staff scientist, Worcester Found Exp Biol, Shrewsbury, Mass, 1967-1968. **Memberships:** Am Chem Soc; Am Soc Pharmacol Exp Therapeut; Int Soc Study Xenobiotics; Am Asn Pharmaceut Sci. **Research Statement & Publications:** Drug metabolism; drug-protein interactions; biotransformations, and biopharmaceutics of drugs in animal species and humans, mechanism of drug-induced drug-enzyme interactions. **Mailing Address:** Dept Drug Metab, Bristol-Myers Squibb Res Inst, PO Box 4000, Princeton, NJ 08543-4000. **Fax:** 609-252-6802. **E-Mail:** kripalani@bms.com

KRIPKE, BERNARD ROBERT, VISION, LEARNING DISABILITIES. **Personal Data:** b Washington, DC, August 25, 1939; m 1979, c 1. **Education:** Harvard Col, AB, 1959; Harvard Univ, AM, 1960, PhD (math), 1964. **Professional Experience:** RETIRED mgr, ppc adv syst corp, electronic data syst, 1991-1995; sr design consult, Gen Data Syst, 1988-1991; partner, WKCG Software Develop Corp, 1983-1986; vpres, Future Software Inc, 1982-1983; consult, Utah State Div Data Processing, 1981-1982; consult, Utah State Budget Off, 1980-1981; asst prof physiol, Univ Utah Sch Med, 1976-1982; res instr, Univ Utah Sch Med, 1972-1976; vis fel, biophys, Ohio State Univ, 1970-1972; vis lectr vision, Hadassah Hosp, Hebrew Univ, 1969-1970; asst prof, Univ Calif, Berkeley, 1964-1969; asst prof, Univ Tex, Austin, 1963-1964; staff mem math, Mass Inst Technol, 1962-1963. **Memberships:** AAAS; Soc Neuroscience. **Research Statement & Publications:** Effects of visual deprivation on cat striate cortex; hereditary learning disability; analytic functions of several complex variables; approximation in banach spaces. **Mailing Address:** 1530 N Key Blvd, Arlington, VA 22209.

KRIPKE, DANIEL FREDERICK, SLEEP DISORDERS, BIOLOGICAL RHYTHMS. **Personal Data:** b Washington, DC, October 12, 1941; m 1965, Drescher; c Gawain & Clarissa. **Education:** Harvard Col, BA, 1961; Col Physicians & Surgeons, Columbia Univ, MD, 1965. **Professional Experience:** PROF EMER, DEPT PSYCHIAT, UNIV CALIF, SAN DIEGO, 1982-; attend physician, Dept Psychiat, Univ Hosp, Univ Calif, San Diego, beginning 1971; resident psychiat, Albert Einstein Col Med, 1968-1971; intern, Bronx Munic Hosp Ctr, 1965-1966; adj prof, Scripps Res Inst. **Memberships:** AAAS; Sleep Res Soc; Int Soc Chronobiol. **Research Statement & Publications:** Bright light treatment of depression; preliminary studies examining how genetic variations in circadian clocks may influence clinical pathology; published over 10 articles. **Mailing Address:** Dept Psychiat, Univ Calif, 9500 Gilman Dr, La Jolla, CA 92093-0667. **Fax:** 858-534-7405. **E-Mail:** dkripke@ucsd.edu

KRIPKE, MARGARET LOUISE (COOK), CANCER. **Personal Data:** b Concord, Calif, July 21, 1943; m 1975, c 1. **Education:** Univ Calif, Berkeley, AB, 1965, MA, 1967, PhD (immunol), 1970. **Honors & Awards:** Edna Roe Mem lectr, Int Cong Photo Biol, 1980; Thomas P Infusino Lectr Cancer Causation Epidemiol, 1993; Lila Gruber Hon Award,

Cancer Res. **Professional Experience:** EXEC VPRES & CHIEF ACAD OFFICER, M D ANDERSON CANCER CTR, UNIV TEX, 2001-; PROF IMMUNOL, M D ANDERSON CANCER CTR, UNIV TEX, 1983-; chmn, Dept Immunol, M D Anderson Cancer Ctr, Univ Tex, beginning 1983; chancellors distinguished lectr, Univ Calif, Berkeley, 1980; dir, Cancer Biol Prog, 1979-1983; sr prin scientist cancer, Frederick Cancer Res Ctr, 1975-1979; asst prof path, Col Med, Univ Utah, 1972-1975; res assoc, Sch Med, Univ Louisville, 1972; res assoc, Ohio State Univ, Columbus, 1970-1972; teaching asst immunol, Univ Calif, Berkeley, 1965-1966. **Memberships:** Am Asn Cancer Res; Am Soc Photobiol; Soc Leukocyte Biol; AAAS; Soc Investigative Dermat; Am Asn Immunol. **Research Statement & Publications:** Mechanisms of immunologic responses to tumors; relationship between the immune system and carcinogenesis; nature and significance of tumor antigens using the system of experimental ultraviolet carcinogenesis; effects of ultraviolet radiation on immunologic processes. **Mailing Address:** Dept Immunol, M D Anderson Cancer Ctr, Univ Tex, 1515 Holcombe Blvd, PO Box 0113, Houston, TX 77030. **Fax:** 713-745-1812. **E-Mail:** mripke@mail.mdanderson.org

KRIPPNER, STANLEY CURTIS, CROSS-CULTURAL STUDIES, PSYCHOLOGY OF CONSCIOUSNESS. **Personal Data:** b Edgerton, Wis, October 4, 1932. **Education:** Univ Wis-Madison, BS, 1954; Northwestern Univ, MA, 1957; PhD (educ psychol), 1961. **Honorary Degrees:** LHD, Univ Humanistic Studies, 1982. **Honors & Awards:** Citation Merit, Nat Asn Creative Children & Adults, 1974; Cert Recognition, US Dept Health & Human Serv, 1976 Award for distinguished contr of prof hypnosis am phys assn 2002; re inter advanced of phy Apa 2002. **Professional Experience:** Acad Sci, Beijing, China, 1981; Inst Psychodrama, Caracas, 1975 & West Ga Col, Carrollton, Ga, 1976; Univ Life Sci, Bogota, 1974; PROF PSYCHOL, SAYBROOK GRAD SCH, SAN FRANCISCO, 1972-; vis prof, Sonoma State Univ, 1972-1973; vis prof, Univ PR, Santurce, 1972; Lectr, Acad Pedag Sci, Moscow, 1971; Dream Lab, Maimonides Med Ctr, Brooklyn, 1964-1973; Dir, Child Study Ctr, Kent State Univ, Ohio, 1961-1964. **Memberships:** Fel Am Psychol Asn; Asn Humanistic Psychol (pres 1974-1975); Parapsychol Asn (pres, 1983); fel Am Soc Clin Hypn; fel Soc Sci Study sexuality; fel Am Psychol Soc; asn story Dreams, pres, 1993-1994. **Research Statement & Publications:** Anomalous effects in dreams; indigenous healing systems; creative problem-solving in altered states of consciousness; the effects of "personal myths" on cognition and behavior; hypnotherapy and learning. **Mailing Address:** Saybrook Inst, 450 Pacific Ave No 300, San Francisco, CA 94133. **Fax:** 650-433-9271.

KRISANS, SKAIDRITE, BIOLOGY. **Education:** Univ Mich, PhD. **Professional Experience:** PROF BIOL SCI, UNIV CALIF SAN DIEGO, as of 2006. **Mailing Address:** Dept Biol Sci, Univ Calif San Diego, 9500 Gilman Dr, La Jolla, CA 92093. **Fax:** 858-534-4543. **E-Mail:** skrisans@sunstroke.sdsu.edu

KRISCH, ALAN DAVID, HIGH ENERGY PHYSICS. **Personal Data:** b Philadelphia, Pa, April 19, 1939; m Jean; c Kathleen S. **Education:** Univ Pa, BA, 1960; Cornell Univ, PhD (physics), 1964. **Honors & Awards:** Guggenheim fel, 1971-1972; fel Am Phys Soc. **Professional Experience:** Chmn, Int Comt for High Energy Spin Physics Symposia, 1977-1994; past chmn, 1995-; vis prof, Niels Bohr Inst, Copenhagen, 1975-1976; chmn, Argonne ZGS Users Group, 1974-1976 & 1978-1979; trustee, Argonne Univ Assoc, 1972-1973 & 1980-1983; PROF PHYSICS, UNIV MICH, ANN ARBOR, 1968-; from asst prof to assoc prof, Univ Mich, Ann Arbor, 1964-1968; Instr physics, Cornell Univ, 1964; chmn, Comt for conf on intersections of particle & Nuclear Physics, 1983-1987; chmn, IUCF Users Group, 1999-2002; trustee, Ann Arbor Hands on Museuom, 2000-2005; Spokesperson, SPIN@U-70 experiment at IHEP-Protvino, Russia, 2000-; Spokesperson SPIN@COSY experiment at ForschungsZentrum-Julich, Germany, 2002-. **Memberships:** AAAS; Am Phys Soc. **Research Statement & Publications:** Experiments on high energy elastic and inelastic scattering of strongly interacting particles; experiments on spin dependence of strong interactions; phenomenology of strong interactions; acceleration of polarized beams; development of polarized targets and jets. **Mailing Address:** Randall Lab Physics, Univ Mich, Ann Arbor, MI 48109. **Fax:** 734-936-0794. **E-Mail:** krisch@umich.edu

KRISCH, JEAN PECK, GRAVITATIONAL PHYSICS. **Personal Data:** b Washington, DC, May 23, 1939; m 1961, Alan; c Kathleen S. **Education:** Univ Md, BS, 1960; Cornell Univ, MS, 1962, PhD (physics), 1965. **Professional Experience:** PROF PHYSICS, UNIV MICH, as of 2001; assoc prof physics, Univ Mich, beginning 1989; lectr, Univ Mich, 1976-1989; res assoc, Univ Mich, 1965-1975; teaching asst physics, Cornell Univ, 1960-1965. **Memberships:** Am Asn Physics Teachers; Am Phys Soc. **Research Statement & Publications:** Study of exact solutions and of spin fluid solutions to the field equations; general relativity. **Mailing Address:** Dept Physics, Univ Mich, 2425 Randall, Ann Arbor, MI 48109. **E-Mail:** jkrisch@umich.edu

KRISCH, ROBERT EARLE, RADIATION BIOLOGY, BIOPHYSICS. **Personal Data:** b Philadelphia, Pa, January 29, 1937; m 1970, c 1. **Education:** Univ Pa, BA, 1956, MS, 1962, PhD (physics), 1964; Temple Univ, MD, 1960. **Professional Experience:** ACTING CHIEF, RADIATION ONCO DEPT, VA MED CTR, PHILADELPHIA, 1995-; CLIN STAFF, RADIATION ONCO DEPT, VA MED CTR, PHILADELPHIA, 1994-; CLIN STAFF, CONSUL DEPT OTORHINOLARGY & MED ONCO, WILMINGTON VET ADMIN MED CTR, 1983-; ASSOC PROF, DEPT RADIATION ONCOL, SCH MED, UNIV PA, 1980-; CLIN STAFF, RADIATION ONCO DEPT, HOSP UNIV PA, PHILADELPHIA, 1980-; spec fel, Dept Radiation Ther, Harvard Med Sch, 1977-1980; biophysicist, Div Biol & Med Res, 1972-1977; asst biophysicist, Argonne Nat Lab, 1965-1972; instr physics, Univ Pa, 1964-1965. **Memberships:** Radiation Res Soc; Am Soc Ther Radiol & Oncol; AAAS. **Research Statement & Publications:** Radiation biology; radiation damage to DNA and its modification by the chemical environment. **Mailing Address:** Dept Radiation Oncol, Univ Pa, 3400 Spruce St, 2 Donner Bldg, Philadelphia, PA 19104.

KRISCIOKAITIS-KRISST, RAYMOND JOHN, INDUSTRIAL & MANUFACTURING ENGINEERING, OPERATIONS RESEARCH. **Personal Data:** b Barcdai, Lithuania, May 29, 1937; div, c Rima, Abe & Lara. **Education:** Univ Conn, AB, 1958; Mich State Univ, PhD (physics), 1965. **Professional Experience:** RES SCHOLAR PHYSICS, UNIV CONN, as of 2006; lectr Physics, Univ Conn, 1998-2003; GUEST RES COLLABR, BROOKHAVEN NAT LAB, 1996-; consult & teacher, Univ Hartford, 1991-; adj prof mech eng & elec eng, Univ Hartford, 1985-; dir eng, Appl Ctr, 1985-1991; consult, Hartford Area Indust, 1984-; adj prof nuclear eng & numerical math, Univ Conn, 1983-1984; prin physicist, Nuclear Power Dept, Combustion Eng Inc, 1974-1985; vis scientist, German Electron-Synchrotron Inst, 1970-1974; adj fac atomic physics, Harvard Univ, 1967-1970; res fel, Harvard Univ & res affil, Mass Inst Technol, 1965-1970; Res asst physics, Mich State Univ, 1962-1965; Nuclear Weapons Effects, US Army, 1959. **Research Statement & Publications:** Nuclear, high-energy and accelerator physics; nuclear engineering; polarized electron beams; nuclear instrumentation. **Mailing Address:** 20 Woodmere Rd, West Hartford, CT 06119. **Fax:** 860-232-6652. **E-Mail:** krisrim@att.net

KRISCIUNAS, KEVIN L, REAL-TIME DATA ACQUISITION & ANALYSIS, ASTRONOMICAL PHOTOMETRY. **Personal Data:** b Chicago, Ill, September 12, 1953. **Education:** Univ Ill, Urbana-Champaign, BS, 1974; Univ Chicago, MA, 1976. **Professional Experience:** PROF, DEPT PHYSICS, NOTRE DAME, 2004-; consult, 1996-; programmer & pub rels person, Joint Astron Ctr, 1982-1996; astron lectr, WValley Col, Saratoga, Calif, 1978-1982; programmer & onboard operator, Kuiper Airborne Observ, Ames Res Ctr, NASA, 1977-1982. **Memberships:** Int Astron Union; Am Astron Soc; Astron Soc Pac. **Research Statement & Publications:** Photometry of variable stars; infrared photometry and spectroscopy; astronomical site evaluation; history of astronomy. **Mailing Address:** Dept Physics, Univ Notre Dame, 225 Nieuwland Sci Hall, Notre Dame, IN 46556. **E-Mail:** kkrisciu@nd.edu

KRISE, GEORGE MARTIN, PHYSIOLOGY. **Personal Data:** b San Antonio, Tex, May 12, 1919; m 1943, c 2. **Education:** Univ Tex, BS, 1946, MA, 1948, PhD (zool), 1952. **Professional Experience:** PROF EMER BIOL, TEX A&M UNIV, 1982-; admin officer, Dept Biol, 1969-1974; prof, Dept Biol, 1958-1982; res scientist physiol, Univ Tex, 1952-1958; From instr to asst prof biol, St Edward's Univ, 1949-1951. **Research Statement & Publications:** Microbial physiology; effects of ionizing radiations on various species. **Mailing Address:** Dept Biol, Tex A&M Univ, College Station, TX 77843-3258.

KRIS-ETHERTON, PENNY M, NUTRITION. **Education:** Univ Minn, PhD, 1978. **Professional Experience:** DISTINGUISHED PROF, DEPT NUTR SCI, PA STATE UNIV, as of 2005. **Mailing Address:** Dept Nutr, PA State Univ, 271 Henderson S Bldg, University Park, PA 16802-0001. **Fax:** 814-863-6103. **E-Mail:** pmk3@psu.edu

KRISHAMURTI, RUBY EBISUZAKI, OCEANOGRAPHY. **Education:** Univ Calif, Los Angeles, PhD (Physical Oceanog), 1967. **Professional Experience:** J STEWART TURNER PROF, DEPT OCEANOG, FLA STATE UNIV, as of 2004. **Research Statement & Publications:** Turbulent convection; double-diffusive instability. **Mailing Address:** Dept Oceanog, Fla State Univ, Rm 431 OSB W Call St, Tallahassee, FL 32306-4320. **Fax:** 850-644-2581. **E-Mail:** krishnamurti@ocean.fsu.edu

KRISHAN, AWTAR, CANCER RESEARCH & CHEMOTHERAPY. **Personal Data:** b Srinagar, India, October 11, 1937; m 1965, Sarla; c Aruna, Ameeta & Neal. **Education:** Univ Punjab, India, PhD (zoology), 1963; Univ Western Ont, PhD (anat), 1964. **Honors & Awards:** Collip Medal, Univ Western Ont, 1965. **Professional Experience:** PROF & CHIEF, DIV EXP THERAPEUT, DEPT RADIOL & ONCOL, UNIV MIAMI, 1996-; sci dir, Mich Cancer Found, Detroit, 1993-1996; sci dir, Div Cytokinetic, Comp Career Ctr, State Fla, 1981-; sci dir, Comp Cancer Ctr, 1979-1993; Chief, Div Cytokinetic, Comp Career Ctr, State Fla, 1977-; from assoc prof to prof oncol, Med Sch, Univ Miami, 1977-1993; chief cancer res, Div Exp Path & Lab Cytokinetics, 1972-1977; cytologist, Children's Cancer Res Found, Boston, 1966-1971; Res prof, cytogenetics, Univ Minn, St Paul, 1965-1966. **Memberships:** Am Asn Cancer Res; Cell Kinetics Soc Am; Electron Micros Soc (pres, 1975-1976). **Research Statement & Publications:** Tumor cell kinetics; effect of cancer chemotherapy on tumor growth; use of laser flow cytometry for monitoring drug uptake; Published over 100 articles. **Mailing Address:** Papanicolau Cancer Res Bldg 1556 NW Tenth Ste 100, PO Box 0169-60 R-71, Miami, FL 33101. **Fax:** 305-243-5555. **E-Mail:** akrishan@med.miami.edu

KRISHEN, ANOOP, TECHNICAL MANAGEMENT. **Personal Data:** b Ludhiana, India, August 7, 1927; wid, c 2. **Education:** Univ Panjab, India, BSc, 1948, MSc, 1949; Univ Pittsburgh, PhD, 1957. **Professional Experience:** SECT HEAD, RES DIV, GOODYEAR TIRE & RUBBER CO, 1983-; sr res chemist, Res Div, Goodyear Tire & Rubber CO, 1963-1983; chief chemist, Synthetics & Chem Ltd, India, 1962-1963; sr res chemist, B F Goodrich Co Res Ctr, 1957-1962; res asst anal chem, Nat Phys Lab, India, 1950-1952; lectr chem, Govt Col, Ludhiana, India, 1949-1950. **Memberships:** Am Chem Soc. **Research Statement & Publications:** Pyrolysis-gas chromatography; high speed liquid chromatography; instrumental analysis; gas chromatography; laboratory robotics; laboratory information management. **Mailing Address:** Goodyear Tire & Rubber Co, Res Div 142 Goodyear Blvd, Akron, OH 44305-0001. **Fax:** 330-796-3304. **E-Mail:** akrishen@goodyear.com

KRISHEN, KUMAR, ELECTRONICS, REMOTE SENSING. **Personal Data:** b Srinagar, India, June 22, 1939; American citizen; m 1961, Vijay; c Lovely, Sweetie & Anjala. **Education:** Univ Jammu & Kashmir, BA, 1959; Univ Calcutta, BTech, 1962, MTech, 1963; Kans State Univ, MS, 1966, PhD (electronics), 1968. **Honors & Awards:** Houston Leadership Award, 1992 World Congress Superconductivity Conf, Munich, Ger, 1993; Outstanding Technol Achievement Award Opportunity Symposium Series (BOSS) Conf Tes Asn Minority Bus Enterprises, Austin, Tex, 1997; IEEE Third Millennium Medal Inst Elec & Electronic Engr Inc 2000. **Professional Experience:** INDEPENDENT RES & DEVELOP LEAD, OFF TECHNOL TRANSFER, NASA, JOHNSON SPACE CTR, HOUSTON, TEX, as of 2006; intergovernamental personal act, vis prof & fel technol transfer, Va Tech, beginning 2001; mem Tex Board Licensure Prof Med Physicists, 1999; CHIEF TECHNOLOGIST, TECH TRANSFER & COMMERCIALIZATION, JOHNSON SPACE CTR, NASA, 1995-; adj prof, RiceUniv, 1990-1996; chief technologist, nio, 1990-1994; prog chmn, World Cong Superconductivity, 1989-; mem, Synthetic Aperture Radar Team, NASA, 1976-1980 & Coun Sci & Technol, 1988-; asst to dir tech & advan progs mission support, Tracking & Commun Div, 1988-1990; mgr advan progs, Tracking & Commun Div, 1982-1988; mgr advan microwave prog, Johnson Space Ctr, NASA, 1978-1982; lectr, Univ Houston, 1977-1979; chmn water resources panel, Microwave Remote Sensing Symp, 1977; proj mgr, earth resources microwave prog, Johnson Space Ctr, NASA, 1976-1978; mem agr panel earth resources, NASA active microwave workshops, 1976-1977; reviewer, Radio Sci, 1975-; mem, NASA active microwave workshops, 1974-1977; proj leader, Skylab Microwave Sensors Eval Team, 1973-1975; staff scientist & engr earth observ, Lockheed Electronics Co, 1969-1976; consult applns investr, NASA, 1969-1976; asst prof, Kans State Univ, 1968-1969; res asst & instr elec engr, Kans State Univ, 1965-1968; Res fel, Univ Calcutta, 1964-1965. **Memberships:** Sr mem Inst Elec & Electronics Engrs; assoc fel Am Inst Aeronaut & Astronaut; Radio Physics & Electronics Asn; Sigma Xi; fel Soc Design & Process Sci. **Research Statement & Publications:** Applications of optical, infrared and microwave sensors to the field of remote sensing of earth resources and ocean/weather phenomena and human health; developing specifications for space borne systems for earth resources, ocean and weather sensing and robotic vision. **Mailing Address:** NASA Johnson Space Ctr Intergovernamental Personal Act, Va Tech, Code HA, Houston, TX 77058. **Fax:** 281-244-8452. **E-Mail:** kristen@vt.edu

KRISHNA, C R, ENGINEERING, COMBUSTION. **Personal Data:** b Bangalore, India, May 31, 1939; m 1974, c 3. **Education:** Indian Inst Sci, ME, 1961; State Univ NY, Stony Brook, PhD (eng), 1974. **Professional Experience:** MECH ENGR, BROOKHAVEN NAT LAB, 1976-; res assoc, Brookhaven Nat Lab, 1974-1976; engr, Hindustan Aeronaut Ltd, India, 1961-1969. **Memberships:** Combustion Inst; Am Soc Mech Engrs. **Research Statement & Publications:** Fluidized beds; coal-slurries and liquid fuels. **Mailing Address:** Energy Sci & Technol Dept, Brookhaven Nat Lab, Bldg 526, Upton, NY 11973. **Fax:** 631-344-2359. **E-Mail:** krishna@bnl.gov

KRISHNA, GOPAL A, PHARMACOLOGY. **Education:** Quincy Coll, BS; Ark State Univ, MS, EdS. **Professional Experience:** SR FAC, DEPT BIOL SCI, MOBERLY AREA COMMUNITY COL, as of 2006. **Memberships:** Am Soc Clin Pathologists. **Mailing Address:** Moberly Area Community Coll, 101 College Ave, Moberly, MO 65270-1304. **Fax:** 660-263-6252.

KRISHNA, GOPALA, GENETIC TOXICOLOGY, CYTOGENETICS & MUTAGENESIS. **Personal Data:** b Kaiwara, Karnataka, India, February 14, 1956; American citizen; m 1986, Leela D Ramappa; c Kavya A. **Education:** Univ Agr Sci, Bangalore, India, BS, 1978, MS, 1980; WVa Univ, PhD (genetics), 1984; Eastern Mich Univ, Ypsilanti, MBA, 1992; Am Bd Toxicol, cert, 1991. **Professional Experience:** AT, PARKE-DAVIS PHARMACEUT RES, WARNER-LAMBERT CO, as of 2003; SR MGR & GROUP LEADER, PARKE-DAVIS PHARMACEUT RES, WARNER-LAMBERT CO, 1996-; Hope Col, Holland Mich, 1995-; mgr & res assoc, Parke-davis Pharmaceut Res, Warner-lambert CO, 96-Warner-lambert CO, 1991-1996; sr scientist, Parke-davis Pharmaceut Res, Warner-lambert CO, 96- Warner-lambert CO, 1986-1991; res assoc, Oak Ridge Nat Lab, 1986; guest lectr cytogenetics, WVa Univ, 1984- & genetic toxicol, Eastern Mich Univ, 1987-; scientist, Nat Res Coun, Nat Inst Occup Safety & Health, 1984-1986; res asst, WVa Univ, 1982-1984; Teaching asst genetics, Univ Agr Sci, India, 1978-1980. **Memberships:** Environ Mutagen Soc; Soc Toxicol; Int Environ Mutagen Soc; Sigma Xi. **Research Statement & Publications:** Induction of gene mutation in bacteria and chromosome damage in human cells by air particulate extract; in vivo and in vitro comparative bone marrow and spleen systems in animals for toxicology testing; antibodies to detect chromosome damage; genotoxicity of vitamin C, ethylene dibromide, dimethylnitrosamine, cyclophosphomide, mitomycin C, vinblastine, vincristine, methyl methanesulfonate, x-rays, acrylamide, chlorambucil, coaldust extract and azodyes, molecular toxicology, b53 gene expression, apoptosis; toxicological safety evaluation of a variety of pharmaceuticals; author of various publications. **Mailing Address:** Parke-Davis Pharmaceut Res, Warner-Lambert Co, 2800 Plymouth Rd, Ann Arbor, MI 48105. **Fax:** 734-996-5001. **E-Mail:** krishng@aa.wl.com

KRISHNA, J HARI, SURFACE WATER RESOURCES, CONSERVATION & MANAGEMENT. **Personal Data:** b Madras, India, May 13, 1948; m Laxmi. **Education:** Osmania Univ, BS, 1967; Kans State Univ, MS, 1971; Utah State Univ, PhD, 1979. **Honors & Awards:** Distinguished Alumnus Award, Utah State Univ, 1997. **Professional Experience:** SR HYDROL & TEAM LEADER, TEX WATER DEVELOP BD, as of 2000; SR ENGR, TEX WATER DEVELOP BD, as of 2005; team leader, Tex Natural Resource Conserv Comn, beginning 1993; bd dirs, Int Rainwater Catchment Systs Asn, 1989-; mem tech adv group, Consortium Caribbean Univs, 1989-1993; vpres, Am Inst Hydrol, Tex Sect, 1987-1988; res scientist hydrol, Tex A&M Univ, 1984-1988; asst prof water resources, Utah State Univ, 1982-1984; consult, Food & Agr Orgn, UN, 1981-1982; scientist soil & water eng, Int Crops Res Inst Semi-Arid Tropics, 1972-1981; assoc prof & dir, VI Water Resource Res Inst, Univ VI. **Memberships:** Am Rainwater Catchment Syst Asn (pres); Am Inst Hydrol; Int Rainwater Catchment Systs Asn; Int Water Resources Asn; World Asn Soil & Water Conserv; Am Water Works Asn. **Research Statement & Publications:** Conduct research/assessment in the areas of alternative water resources and water conservation; author and co-author of approximately 60 technical/scientific papers and publications. **Mailing Address:** Tex Water Develop Bd, 1700 N Congress Ave, PO Box 13231, Austin, TX 78711-3231. **Fax:** 512-835-5663. **E-Mail:** hari.krishna@twdb.state.tx.us

KRISHNA, KUMAR, ZOOLOGY, ENTOMOLOGY. **Personal Data:** b Dehradun, India, June 21, 1930; American citizen; m 1960. **Education:** Agra Univ, BS, 1950; Univ Lucknow, MS, 1952; Univ Chicago, PhD (zoology), 1961. **Professional Experience:** PROF EMER BIOL, CITY COL NY, as of 2003; prof biol, City Col NY, beginning 1974; NSF res grant, 1962-; res assoc, Am Mus Natural Hist, 1962-; from instr to assoc prof, City Col New York, 1962-1974; res assoc, Univ Chicago, 1960-1962; teaching asst biol, Univ Ill at Chicago Circle, 1958-1960; res asst, Forest res inst, India, 1952-1954. **Memberships:** Am Soc Zoologists; Soc Syst Zoologists; Int Union Study Soc Insects. **Research Statement & Publications:** Taxonomy, ecology, zoogeography and evolution of termites; general evolutionary theory. **Mailing Address:** Dept Biol, City Col NY, 138th St & Convent Ave, New York, NY 10031. **E-Mail:** krishn@amnh.org

KRISHNA, N RAMA, BIOPHYSICAL CHEMISTRY, STRUCTURAL BIOLOGY. **Personal Data:** b Masulipatam, India, American citizen. **Education:** India Inst Technol, Kampur, PhD (physics), 1972. **Professional Experience:** PROF BIOCHEM, UNIV ALA, as of 2002; DIR NUCLEAR MAGNETIC RESONANCE CORE FACIL, CANCER CTR, as of 2002; leukemia Soc Am Scholar, 1982-1987. **Memberships:** AAAS; Biophys Soc; Soc Biol Chemists. **Research Statement & Publications:** Nuclear magnetic resonance; biomolecular conformations. **Mailing Address:** Dept Biochem, Univ Ala, Birmingham, AL 35294.

KRISHNAKUMAR, KALMANJE S, INTELLIGENT CONTROL, FLIGHT SIMULATION. **Personal Data:** b Madras, India, February 25, 1960; m 1986, Sujatha; c Priya & Nithya. **Education:** Indian Inst Technol, BTech, 1982; Univ Ala, MS, 1985, PhD (aerospace & elec eng), 1988. **Professional Experience:** PROF AEROSPACE ENG, UNIV ALA, as of 1998; chmn, Tech Comt, Am Inst Aeronaut & Astronaut, 1996-; consult, Charles River Analytics, Inc, 1994-; prin investr, NSF & NASA, 1991-; assoc prof, Univ Ala, beginning 1988; prin scientist, Flexible Intelligence Group, Tuscaloosa, Ala. **Memberships:** Am Inst Aeronaut & Astronaut; Inst Elec & Electronics Engrs. **Research Statement & Publications:** Intelligent control applications to aerospace problems; flight dynamics and simulation. **Mailing Address:** Dept Aero Eng & Mech Univ Ala, PO Box 870280 239 Hardaway Hall, Tuscaloosa, AL 35487-0280. **Fax:** 205-348-7240. **E-Mail:** kkumar@coe.eng.ua.edu

KRISHNAMOORTHY, GOVINDARAJALU, STRUCTURAL MECHANICS, CIVIL ENGINEERING. **Personal Data:** b Thanjavur, India, January 1, 1931; m 1956, Kousalya; c Rama & Praba. **Education:** Col Eng, Guindy, India, BSCE, 1952; Ill Inst Technol, MSCE, 1960, PhD (struct), 1965. **Professional Experience:** SAI, La Jolla & Gen Elec, Calma, 1989-1990; PROF CIVIL ENG, SCH ENG, SAN DIEGO STATE UNIV, 1974-; Consult, Rohr Corp, 1969-1970; from asst prof to assoc prof, Sch Eng, San Diego State Univ, 1968-1974; Consult, Ill Inst Technol Res Inst, 1967-; from instr to asst prof civil eng, Ill Inst Technol, 1961-1968; Jr engr, Madras Hwy Dept, India, 1952-1957. **Memberships:** Am Soc Civil Engrs; Am Soc Eng Educ; Sigma Xi. **Research Statement & Publications:** Buckling of shells; computer applications in structures; analysis and design of ocean structures; reinforced concrete masonry structures; dynamic and thermal response of mountings on main cooling pipe of nuclear reactors; computer graphics; computer aided design. **Mailing Address:** 5439 Maisel Way, San Diego, CA 92115. **Fax:** 619-286-3430. **E-Mail:** krish@mail.sdsu.edu

KRISHNAMOORTHY, MUKKAI S, COMBINATORICS. **Personal Data:** b Nagercoil, India, January 20, 1948; American citizen; m 1986, Janaki; c Subrahmanya. **Education:** Coimbatore Inst Technol, India, BE, 1969; Indian Inst Technol, India, MTech, 1971, PhD (comput sci), 1976. **Professional Experience:** ASSOC PROF, RENSSELAER POLYTECH INST, 1985-; from vis asst prof to asst prof, Rensselaer Polytech Inst, 1979-1985. **Memberships:** Inst Elec & Electronics Engrs Comput Soc; Soc Photo-Optical Inst rumentation Engrs. **Research Statement & Publications:** Develop tools to make problem solving easier. **Mailing Address:** Dept Comput Sci, Rensselaer Polytech Inst, 305 Lally, Troy, NY 12180. **Fax:** 518-276-4033. **E-Mail:** moorthy@cs.rpi.edu

KRISHNAMURTHY, LAKSHMINARAYANAN, COMBUSTION THEORY, COMPUTATIONAL FLUID DYNAMICS. **Personal Data:** b Kumbakonam, Madras, India, October 23, 1941; American citizen. **Education:** Univ Madras, BEng, 1962; Indian Inst Sci, MEng, 1964; Univ Calif, San Diego, PhD (eng sci), 1972. **Professional Experience:** PROF, DIV ENG SCI, FLA INST TECHNOL, 1990-; mem propellants & combustion tech comt, Am Inst Aeronaut & Astronaut, 1984-1986; reviewer, Appl Mech Revs, 1973-1984 & Am Inst Aeronaut & Astronaut J, 1982-; sr res eng fluid mech, Univ Dayton Res Inst, 1982-1990; instr, Sch Eng, 1981-; prin investr, Res Inst, Univ Dayton, 1978-; res engr, Univ Dayton Res Inst, 1978-1982; res assoc propulsion, Purdue Univ, 1977-1978; res staff mem aerospace eng, Princeton Univ, 1975-1976; staff scientist propulsion, Duvvuri Res Assocs, Chula Vista, Calif, 1973-1974; res engr, Univ Calif, San Diego, 1972-1973; res assist, Univ Calif, San Diego, 1968-1971; res fel, Univ Calif, San Diego, 1967-1968; scientist power eng, Cent Mech Eng Res Inst, India, 1965-1967; Sr res fel, Cent Mech Eng Res Inst, Durgapur, India, 1964-1965. **Memberships:** Am Inst Aeronaut & Astronaut; Am Soc Mech Engrs; Am Acad Mech; Combustion Inst; Sigma Xi; Soc Indust & Appl Math; Planetary Soc; Union Concerned Scientists. **Research Statement & Publications:** Fluid mechanics and combustion; analytical and computational fluid dynamics of nonreacting and reacting gas flows. **Mailing Address:** Div Eng Sci Fla Inst Technol, 150 W Univ Blvd, Melbourne, FL 32901-6975. **Fax:** 407-674-8813. **E-Mail:** krishna@zach.fit.edu

KRISHNAMURTHY, RAMANATHAPUR GUNDACHAR, FOOD CHEMISTRY, BIOCHEMISTRY. **Personal Data:** b Mysore, India, May 8, 1931; m 1960, c 3. **Education:** Univ Mysore, BS, 1951; Rutgers Univ, MS, 1964, PhD (food sci), 1965. **Professional Experience:** RES PRIN, KRAFT, INC, as of 1992; TECHNOL MGR, RES & DEVELOP DIV, KRAFT, INC, 1987-; from group leader, to sr group leader edible oil prod, 1967-1987; res chemist, Best Foods Div, Corn Prod Co, 1966-1967; asst res prof, Rutgers Univ, 1965-1966; res fel, 1963-1965; res asst food sci, 1961-1963; sci asst food technol, Cent Food Technol Res Inst, Mysore, 1954-1961; Lab asst metall, Indian Inst Sci, India, 1951-1954. **Memberships:** Am Chem Soc; Am Oil Chemists Soc; Inst Food Technol. **Research Statement & Publications:** Autoxidation and thermal oxidation of fats and oils; investigation of flavors and flavor percursors in foods; chemistry and technology of oils and fats and products derived from them. **Mailing Address:** 3059 Crestwood Lane, Glenview, IL 60025.

KRISHNAMURTHY, SUNDARAM, ORGANIC CHEMISTRY. **Personal Data:** b Coimbatore, Madras, India, November 26, 1944; m 1975. **Education:** Univ Madras, BS, 1964, MS, 1966; Purdue Univ, PhD (chem), 1971. **Honors & Awards:** Team Achievement Award, 1991; Kodak Distinguished Inventors Award, 1996. **Professional Experience:** RES LAB HEAD, IMAGING RES & ADV DEVELOP, EASTMAN KODAK CO, as of 2004; MEM RES STAFF, RES LAB, EASTMAN KODAK CO, 1980-; sr res assoc chem, Purdue Univ, West Lafayette, 1971-1980. **Memberships:** Am Chem Soc. **Research Statement & Publications:** Synthesis and application of trialkylborohydrides in stereospecific and reguospecific organic synthesis; selective reductions; organometallics in organic synthesis. **Mailing Address:** 172 Hillrise Dr, Penfield, NY 14526.

KRISHNAMURTI, CUDDALORE RAJAGOPAL, ANIMAL PHYSIOLOGY, ANIMAL BIOCHEMISTRY. **Personal Data:** b Cuddalore, India, April 16, 1929; m 1953, c 2. **Education:** Univ Madras, BVSc, 1951, MVSc, 1961; Univ Alta, PhD (animal nutrit), 1966. **Professional Experience:** PROF EMER AGR, DEPT ANIMAL SCI, UNIV BC, as of 2006; prof agr, dept animal sci, fac com, Univ Bc, beginning 1975; ACTG HEAD, DEPT ANIMAL SCI, FAC COM, UNIV BC, 1975-; assoc prof, Dept Animal Sci, Fac Com, Univ Bc, 1967-1975; res assoc animal nutrit, Univ Alta, 1966-1967; bacteriologist, Inst Vet Prev Med, Ranipet, 1962; asst lectr physiol, parasitol & bact, Madras Vet Col, 1955-1959. **Memberships:** Agr Inst Can; Nutrit Soc Can; Can Soc Animal Sci. **Research Statement & Publications:** Biochemical investigations on rumen microorganisms; fetal physiology; digestion, absorption and metabolism of nutrients by the ruminant animal, especially metabolic disorders. **Mailing Address:** Dept Agr Fac Com Univ BC, Henry Angus Bldg 2053 Main Mall, Vancouver, BC V6T 2A2, Can. **E-Mail:** crkrishn@interchange.ubc.ca

KRISHNAMURTI, PULLABHOTLA V, VETERINARY MICROBIOLOGY. **Personal Data:** b Gudivada, India, March 1, 1923; m 1949, c 5. **Education:** Univ Madras, BVSc, 1949, DVP, 1958; Univ Wis-Madison, MS, 1961; Tex A&M Univ, PhD (vet microbiol), 1967. **Professional Experience:** RETIRED; prof biol, Savannah State Col, 1974-1992; assoc prof microbiol, Savannah State Col, 1969-1974; from asst prof to assoc prof, Sch Vet Med, Tuskegee Inst, 1966-1969; res asst vet microbiol, Tex A&M Univ, 1965-1966; researcher poultry dis, Hy-line Poultry Farms, Iowa, 1964-1965; res asst, Univ Wis-Madison, 1959-1963; asst lectr, Andhra Vet Col, 1957-1958; instr vet sci & exten vet, Exten Training Ctr, 1955-1956; state vet, Andhra Vet Serv, India, 1948-1954. **Memberships:** Am Vet Med Asn; Am Soc Parasitol; Poultry Sci Asn; Am Asn Avian Path. **Research Statement & Publications:** Parasites and parasitism; plasmodium in Wisconsin chickens; cultivation of Histomonas meleagridis free of bacteria and its demonstration in tissues and cell cultures using fluorescent labeled antibody techniques; therapeutic agents in canine distemper. **Mailing Address:** 6002 Fairview Ave, Savannah, GA 31406.

KRISHNAMURTI, RUBY EBISUZAKI, PHYSICS, FLUID MECHANICS. **Personal Data:** b Haney, BC, October 23, 1934; m 1960. **Education:** Univ Western Ont, BSc, 1957; Univ Chicago, MS, 1960; Univ Calif, Los Angeles, PhD (physics), 1967. **Professional Experience:** PROF OCEANOG, GEOPHYS FLUID DYNAMICS INST, FLA STATE UNIV, 1975-; assoc prof oceanog, Geophys Fluid Dynamics Inst, Fla State Univ, 1971-1975; Asst prof oceanog, Fla State Univ, 1968-1971; SR RES ASSOC, GEOPHYS FLUID DYNAMICS INST, FLA STATE UNIV, 1967-; Res assoc fluid mech, Stanford Univ, 1967. **Memberships:** Am Phys Soc; Am Meteorol Soc; Am Geophys Union. **Research Statement & Publications:** Geophysical fluid dynamics, particularly theoretical and experimental studies of convection and ocean circulation modelling. **Mailing Address:** Dept Oceanog, Rm 431 OSB West Call Street Fla State Univ, Tallahassee, FL 32306-4230. **Fax:** 850-644-2581. **E-Mail:** krishnamurti@ocean.fsu.edu

KRISHNAMURTI, TIRUVALAM N, METEOROLOGY, ATMOSPHERIC SCIENCE. **Personal Data:** b Madras, India, January 10, 1932; American citizen. **Education:** Univ Delhi, BS, 1951; Andhra Univ, India, MS, 1953; Univ Chicago, PhD (meteorol), 1959. **Honors & Awards:** Half-Century Award, Am Meteorol Soc, 1974, Rossby Award, 1985; Creativity Award, NSF, 1982. **Professional Experience:** Mem, Comt Atmospheric Sci, Nat Acad Sci, 1979-; chmn, US MONEX Panel, Nat Acad Sci, 1976-; mem, US Global Atmospheric Res Prog, 1975-; assoc ed, J Atmospheric Sci, 1975-; consult, MONEX Comt, World Meteorol Orgn, 1975-1976; vis lectr, Ctr Theoret Physics, Trieste, Italy, 1975; external examr, Univ Nairobi, Kenya, 1973-1976 & McGill Univ PhD students, 1974-1977; consult synoptic subprog, GATE, Nat Acad Sci, 1973-1974; mem, Adv Panel to Nat Oceanic & Atmospheric Admin on Nuclear Metal Conf, 1971-1973; PROF METEOROL, FLA STATE UNIV, 1970-; Mem, Global Atmospheric Res Prog working group on struct trop atmosphere, 1969-1971; assoc prof, Fla State Univ, 1967-1970; Prof meteorol, Univ Calif, Los Angeles, 1960-1967; mem, Working Group on Numerical Experimentation Global Atmospheric Res Prog, Joint Organizing Comt. **Memberships:** Fel Am Meteorol Soc; Am Geophys Union; fel Royal Meteorol Soc; Meteorol Soc Japan. **Research Statement & Publications:** Dynamic and synoptic meteorology, including diagnostic and prognostic studies of tropical and mid-latitude systems using real input data together with analyses of tropical weather systems using satellite and aircraft information in sparse conventional data areas; global tropical mapping of the subtropical jet of winter; semilagravgian advection; multilevel non-linear balances omega equation; tropical east-west circulation; physical initialization; prediction of a life cycle of super typhoon with a global model. **Mailing Address:** Fla State Univ, 3014 Southshore Circle, Tallahassee, FL 32312. **E-Mail:** tnk@io.met.fsu.edu

KRISHNAN, B RAJENDRA, GENE THERAPY, VACCINE DEVELOPMENT. **Personal Data:** b Pune, Maharashtra, India, August 25, 1961; m 1991, Lalitha. **Education:** Univ Madras, MS, 1983, MPhil, 1985, PhD (genetics), 1990; Carleton Univ, PhD (molecular biol), 1990. **Honors & Awards:** Pfizer Central Res Achievement Award, 2000; Can Commonwealth Scholarship, Asn Univ & Colleges, Can, 1986-1989. **Professional Experience:** MANAGER, BACTERIOLOGY DESIGN, VET MED BIOL DISCOVERY, PFIZER GLOBAL R&D, 2000-; Project Leader, 1999-2000; sr res investr, 1999; sr res scientist, Pfizer Cent Res, 1995-1999; Arthritis Found fel, Wash Univ Sch Med, 1993-1995; res instr med, Wash Univ Sch Med, 1992-1995; res assoc, Wash Univ Sch Med, 1990-1992; commonwealth res scholar biol, Carleton Univ, 1986-1989; res fel genetics, Univ Madras, 1982-1985. **Memberships:** AAAS. **Research Statement & Publications:** Plasmid-mediated gene therapy for the treatment of hematopoietic and arthritic disorders; molecular genetic parametersin heterlogous gene expression; development of vaccines for bacterial diseases; identification of novel vaccine targets by genome methods and immunoreactive cloning; trasportation technology; genetics of DNA replication. **Mailing Address:** Pfizer Global R & D, Eastern Point Rd, Mailstop 81180-2081, CT 06340. **Fax:** 860-715-7910. **E-Mail:** Krishnanr@groton.pfizer.com

KRISHNAN, ENGIL KOLAJ, RADIATION ONCOLOGY, TUMOR IMMUNOLOGY. **Personal Data:** b Bangalore, India, 1942; American citizen. **Education:** Univ Mysore, BSc (physics) & BSc (math), 1964, Univ Mo, MS, 1970, Cetec Univ, WI, MD, 1982. **Professional Experience:** Consult, VA Med Ctr, 1982-; ASST PROF SURG & DIR RES, MED CTR, UNIV KANS, 1982-; instr oncol, Med Ctr, Univ Kans, 1975-1982; teaching assoc, Med Ctr, Univ Kans, 1971-1975; supvr electronics, Elec Radar Develop Eng, 1965-1967. **Memberships:** Am Asn Cancer Res; Am Asn Physicians Med; Am Asn Pediat Oncol; Soc Clin Trials. **Research Statement & Publications:** Published approximately fifty journal articles in the areas of biophysics, immunology and oncology. **Mailing Address:** Dept Surg WHE, Univ Kans Med Ctr Col Health Sci Rainbow Blvd & 39th, Kansas City, KS 66103.

KRISHNAN, GOPAL, CANCER IMMUNOLOGY, TRANSPLANTATION IMMUNOLOGY. **Personal Data:** b Kancheepuram, India, March 15, 1935; American citizen; m 1967, Prema; c Madhavan & Deepa. **Education:** Annamala; Univ, India, MA, 1955, MSc, 1956; Univ Madras, PhD (chem), 1965. **Professional Experience:** DIR, TISSUE-TYPING LAB, OUR LADY LOURDES MED CTR, 1984-; dir, immunol res sect, mercy cath med ctr, 1982-; immunologist, St Vincent Med Ctr, 1977-1982; res assoc, Pa Col Podiatric Med, 1976-1977; asst prof biochem & res instr med, Jefferson Med Col, Philadelphia, 1974-1976; res assoc immunol, Univ Pa, 1967-1974; lectr, Univ Madras Cols, India, 1956-1961. **Memberships:** Am Asn Med Lab Immunologists; Am Soc Transplant Physicians; Am Asn Immunologists; NY Acad Sci; Am Asn Histocompatibility & Immunogenetics. **Research Statement & Publications:** Human cancer; transplantation immunology; transplant rejections and factors affecting the allograft survival. **Mailing Address:** Our Lady Lourdes Med Ctr, PO Box 269, Swarthmore, PA 19081-0269. **Fax:** 610-543-6298.

KRISHNAN, K RANGA RAMA, AFFECTIVE DISORDERS, CHRONIC PAIN. **Personal Data:** b Madras, India, April 22, 1956; m 1987. **Education:** Univ Madras, MBBS, 1978. **Honors & Awards:** Laughlin Award, Am Col Psychiat, 1984; Rafaelsen Award, Col Int Neuro-Psychopharmacol. **Professional Experience:** CHMN, DEPT PSYCHIAT & BEHAV SCI, DUKE UNIV, 1998-; mem, Clin Neuroscience Rev Comt, NIH, 1996-; PROF, DEPT PSYCHIAT & BEHAV SCI, DUKE UNIV, 1995-; HEAD, Div Biol Psychiat, Duke Univ Med Ctr, 1992-; Dir, Affective Dis Prog, Duke Univ Med Ctr, 1992-; med dir, Affective Dis Unit, Med Ctr, Duke Univ, Durham, CC, 1989-1992; assoc prof to assoc prof, Div Biol Psychiat, 1984-1995; fel neurobiology, Duke Univ, 1982-1984; chief resident, Duke Umstead Prog, 1982-1983; resident psychiat, John Umstead Prog, 1981-1983; sr house officer, Dept Emergency Med, Queen Elizabeth Hosp, Univ Wis, Barbados, 1980-1981. **Memberships:** Int Asn Study Pain; Soc Biol Psychiat; AAAS; NY Acad Sci; Int Soc Psychoneuroendocrinol; Am Col Neropsychopharmacol; Am Psychiat Asn. **Research Statement & Publications:** Understanding the physiology and pathophysiology of the hypothalamo pituitary adrenal function in affective disorders; drug trials for the treatment of affective disorders; brain imaging, Magnetic Resonance Imaging and PET in affective disorders and Alzheimers disease. **Mailing Address:** Med Ctr Duke Univ, PO Box 3950, Durham, NC 27710. **Fax:** 919-681-5489. **E-Mail:** krish001@mc.duke.edu

KRISHNAN, KAMALA SIVASUBRAMANIAM, OPTICAL PHYSICS, SOLID STATE SCIENCE. **Personal Data:** b Tiruchirappalli, India, November 12, 1937; American citizen; m 1958, Shantha; c Kamala Harsha, Murali Swathi & Kantha Rajyashree. **Education:** Univ Madras, MA, 1957; Indian Inst Sci, Bangalore, DIISc, 1960; Univ Fla, PhD (physics), 1966. **Professional Experience:** AT COMPUT DEVICES INT, 1997; SR ENG, COMPUT DEVICES INT, 1993-; sr staff engr, Lockheed Missiles & Space Co, 1985-1992; mgr optical signal processing, Litton Appl Technol, 1982-1985; mgr electro-optics, Systs Control Technol, Inc, 1977-1982; vis prof mat sci, San Jose State Univ, 1974-1984; sr res physicist, Stanford Res Inst, 1968-1977; res scientist solid state physics, Res Div, Am Standard Inc, 1965-1968. **Memberships:** Optical Soc Am; Soc Photo-Optical Instrumentation Engrs. **Research Statement & Publications:** Optical and infrared systems; laser physics and applications; nonlinear optics; applied statistics; remote sensing; oceanography; fiber-optics. **Mailing Address:** 180 Walter Hays Dr, Palo Alto, CA 94303.

KRISHNAN, MAHADEVAN, ASTRONOMY. **Professional Experience:** BUS OFF, ALAMEDA APPL SCI CORP, 1994-. **Memberships:** Inst Elec & Electronics Engrs. **Mailing Address:** Alameda Appl Sci Corp, 626 Whitney St, San Leandro, CA 94577. **Fax:** 510-483-8107. **E-Mail:** general@aasc.net

KRISHNAN, RAMAYYA, DECISION SUPPORT SYSTEMS, CONCEPTUAL MODELING. **Personal Data:** b Rajkot, India, February 20, 1960; m 1987, Rema; c Divya. **Education:** Indian Inst Technol, BTech, 1981; Univ Tex, Austin, MSE, 1983, PhD (mgt sci & info systs), 1987. **Professional Experience:** PROF MGT SCI & INFO SYSTS, CARNEGIE-MELLON UNIV, 1997-; assoc prof mgt sci & info systs, Carnegie-mellon Univ, 1994-1997; assoc ed, Decision Support Systs, Opers Res Soc Am J Comput, 1992-; asst prof, Carnegie-mellon Univ, 1987-1994. **Memberships:** Asn Comput Mach; Inst Mgt Sci; Inst Elec & Electronics Engrs. **Research Statement & Publications:** Development of relevant theory tools and techniques to facilitate decision making support through the use of reliable information systems and technology; internet, information networking and electronic commerce. **Mailing Address:** Heinz Sch, Carnegie-Mellon Univ, Pittsburgh, PA 15213. **Fax:** 412-268-7036. **E-Mail:** rk2x@andrew.cmu.edu

KRISHNAN, RAVI, ELECTRICAL ENGINEERING. **Education:** NC State Univ, PhD (comput eng). **Professional Experience:** PRES, SYMBIOTIC TECHNOLOGIES INC, as of 2006. **Mailing Address:** Symbiotic Technologies Inc, Three Bethesda Metro Ctr Ste 750, Bethesda, MD 20814. **Fax:** 301-779-2464.

KRISHNAN, V S, NUCLEAR ENGINEERING. **Education:** Madras Univ, BTech; Rochester Univ, MS, PhD. **Professional Experience:** ADJ PROF, MCMASTER UNIV, as of 2006. **Mailing Address:** Dept Eng Physics, McMaster Univ, Hamilton, ON L8S 4L8, Can. **Fax:** 905-822-0567. **E-Mail:** vskrishnan@mcmaster.ca

KRISHNAN, VAIDYANADHAN, CONTROL & SYSTEMS ENGINEERING. **Personal Data:** b Hyderabad, India, January 19, 1943. **Education:** Indian Inst Technol, BTech, 1964, MTech, 1966; Univ Calif, Berkeley, MS, 1967, PhD, 1972. **Professional Experience:** PROF MECH ENG, SCH ENG, SAN FRANCISCO STATE UNIV, 1982-; asst prof mech eng, San Francisco State Univ, beginning 1977; postdoctoral fel, Univ Calif, Berkeley, 1972-1974; Design engr, Charles Bailey Co, 1968-1970. **Memberships:** Inst Elec & Electronics Engrs; Am Soc Eng Educ; Am Soc Mech Engrs; Instrument Soc Am. **Research Statement & Publications:** Systems modeling; biological control systems. **Mailing Address:** Dept Mech Eng, Sch Eng, San Francisco State Univ, 1600 Holloway Ave, San Francisco, CA 94132. **Fax:** 415-338-0525. **E-Mail:** krishnan@sfsu.edu

KRISHNAN, VENKATARAMA, ELECTRICAL & SYSTEMS ENGINEERING, PROBABILITY & STOCHASTIC MODELING. **Personal Data:** b Madras, India, October 20, 1929; American citizen; m 1967, Kamala; c Gayathri & Hemalekha. **Education:** Univ Madras, BS, 1948; Banares Hindu Univ, BS, 1953; Princeton Univ, MS, 1959; Univ Pa, PhD (elec eng), 1963. **Professional Experience:** PROF EMER, DEPT ELEC ENG, UNIV MASS, LOWELL as of 2005; prof, Dept Elec & Comput Eng, Univ Mass, Lowell, as of 2002; CO-DIR, CTR ADVAN COMPUT & TELECOMMUN, 1993-; prof, Univ Mass, Lowell, beginning 1982; prof, Indian Inst of Sci, Bangalore, 1971-1982; assoc prof, Polytech Inst Brooklyn, 1966-1971; asst prof, Polytech Inst Brooklyn, 1964-1966; assoc, Moore Sch Elec Eng, Pa, 1961-1964; asst prof, Villanova Univ, 1958-1961; instr, Princeton Univ, 1957-1958; sr res asst elec eng, Indian Inst Sci Bangalore, 1953-1956; instr chem, Loyola Col, Madras Univ, 1948-1949. **Memberships:** sr mem Inst Elec & Electronics Engrs. **Research Statement & Publications:** Probabilistic and statistical modeling; tomographic studies; time series analysis; navigation and guidance; queueing theory. **Mailing Address:** Dept Elec & Comput Eng, Univ Mass, One Univ Ave, Lowell, MA 01854. **Fax:** 978-934-3027. **E-Mail:** krishnanv@woods.uml.edu

KRISHNAPPA, GOVINDAPPA, SOUND INTENSITY MEASUREMENTS, AEROACOUSTICS. **Personal Data:** b Mysore, India, June 2, 1936; Canadian citizen; m 1964, c 2. **Education:** Univ Mysore, India, BEng, 1958; Indian Inst Sci, MSc, 1964; Univ Waterloo, Can, PhD (aeroacoust), 1967. **Professional Experience:** AT, NAT RES COUN, CAN, as of 2002; MECH RES, NAT RES COUN CAN, 1990-; GROUP LEADER NOISE & VIBRATION, NAT RES COUN CAN, 1985-; mem working group sound intensity, Int Stand Orgn & Int Electrotech Comn, 1984-; SR RES OFFICER MACH NOISE, NAT RES COUN CAN, 1981-; Mem & secy, Assoc Comt Mach Noise, Can Nat Comt, 1981-; assoc res officer aeroacoust & mach noise, Nat Res Coun Can, 1973-1981; asst res officer aeroacoust, Nat Res Coun Can, 1967-1973. **Memberships:** Am Nat Stand Inst; fel Acoust Soc Am; Inst Noise Control Eng; Int Stand Orgn. **Research Statement & Publications:** Machinery noise and vibration; developing techniques and methods of noise and vibration analysis and reduction; sound intensity measurements; structural noise reduction; groundborne vibrations; wind turbine noise. **Mailing Address:** Nat Res Coun Can, Bldg M-58, 1200 Montreal Rd, Ottawa, ON K1A 0R6, Can. **Fax:** 613-952-9907.

KRISHNAPPAN, BOMMANNA GOUNDER, HYDRAULICS, FLUID MECHANICS. **Personal Data:** b Madras, India, January 15, 1943; Canadian citizen; m 1972, c 2. **Education:** Madras Univ, BE, 1966; Univ Calgary, MS, 1968; Queen's Univ, Ont, PhD (civil eng), 1972. **Professional Experience:** RES SCIENTIST HYDRAUL, NAT WATER RES INST, CAN CTR INLAND WATERS, ONT, 1978-; flow syst engr, Ont Hydro, 1977-1978; res scientist, Can Ctr Inland Waters, 1972-1977; asst, Nat Res Coun Can, 1966-1972. **Memberships:** Int Asn Hydraul Res. **Research Statement & Publications:** Sediment transport in open channel flows; dispersion of mass in open channels; mathematical models for river morphology; thermal models. **Mailing Address:** NAt Water Res Inst, Can Ctr Inland Waters, PO Box 5050, 867 Lakeshore Rd, Burlington, ON L7R 4A6, Can. **Fax:** 905-336-4420. **E-Mail:** krish.krishnappan@cciw.ca

KRISHNAPRASAD, PERINKULAM S, SYSTEM THEORY. **Personal Data:** b Bombay, India, May 15, 1949; m 1986, Cheryl. **Education:** Indian Inst Technol, BTech, 1972; Syracuse Univ, MS, 1973; Harvard Univ, PhD (eng), 1977. **Professional Experience:** PROF SYSTS ENG & NEURO SCI, UNIV MD, as of 2003; DISTINGUISHED FAC RES FEL, UNIV MD, as of 2003; PROF ELEC ENG, UNIV MD, 1987-; from asst prof to assoc prof, Univ MD, 1980-1987; asst prof systs eng, Case Inst Technol, 1977-1980. **Memberships:** fel Inst Elec & Electronics Engrs; Am Math Soc; Am Inst Aeronaut & Astronaut; Am Acad Mech; Soc Indust Appl Math. **Research Statement & Publications:** System theory and applications to modeling; geometric methods applied to problems in systems; control theory and nonlinear mechanics; robotics; real-time control; biologically-inspired control system architectures. **Mailing Address:** Inst Systs Res & Elec Comput Eng Dept, Univ Md, Rm 2233 A V Williams Bldg 115, Col Park Campus, MD 20742-3285. **Fax:** 301-314-9920. **E-Mail:** krishna@src.umd.edu

KRISHNASWAMI, PRAKASH, MECHANICAL ENGINEERING. **Education:** Indian Inst Technol, Madras, BTech, 1978; State Univ NY, Stony Brook, MS, 1979; Univ Iowa, PhD (Mech Eng), 1983. **Professional Experience:** PROF, DEPT MECH & NUCLEAR ENG, KANS STATE UNIV, 2000-; from asst to assoc prof, Dept mech & Nuclear Eng, Kans Sate Univ, 1984-2000. **Mailing Address:** Dept Mech & Nuclear Eng, Kans State Univ, 3002 Rathbone Hall, Manhattan, KS 66506-5205. **E-Mail:** prakash@mne.ksu.edu

KRISHNASWAMY, S V, THIN FILM DEPOSITION, MICROWAVE ACOUSTICS. **Personal Data:** b Villianallur, India, April 15, 1940; American citizen; m 1971, c 2. **Education:** N Wadia Col, BSc, 1959; Univ Poona, MSc, 1961; Indian Inst Technol, MTech, 1966; Pa State Univ, PhD (physics), 1974. **Professional Experience:** ADJ SCIENTIST, MAT RES

INST, PA STATE UNIV, as of 2005; FEL SCIENTIST, NORTHRUP GRUMMAN SCI & TECHNOL CTR, as of 2005; mem prog comt, Thin Film Div, Am Vacuum Soc, 1988-; Ultrasonics Div, Inst Elec & Electronics Engrs, 1988-; FEL SCIENTIST, WESTINGHOUSE RES & DEVELOP CTR, 1981-; sr res assoc, Pa State Univ, 1978-1981; asst prof physics, Pa State Univ, 1976-1978; res assoc, Pa State Univ, 1974-1976; res assoc, Indian Inst Technol, Bombay, 1964-1968; sr scientist, Armament Res & Develop, Kirkee, India, 1962-1964. **Memberships:** Am Phys Soc; Am Vacuum Soc; Indian Vacuum Soc. **Research Statement & Publications:** Preparation and characterization of thin films of wide range of materials, using ion beam deposition, magnetron sputtering and other novel techniques; microwave acoustics and magnetics; high temperature super conducting applications. **Mailing Address:** Dept Mat Sci, Penn State Univ, 265 Mat Res Lab Bldg, Univ Park, PA 16802. **Fax:** 412-256-1348. **E-Mail:** sv.krishnaswamy@ngc.com

KRISHTALKA, LEONARD, MAMMALIAN PALEONTOLOGY, RESEARCH ADMINISTRATION. **Personal Data:** b Montreal, Que, January 30, 1946; m 1986, Beth; c Molly & Zack. **Education:** Univ Alta, BS, 1969, MS, 1971; Tex Tech Univ, PhD (biol & vert paleont), 1975. **Professional Experience:** DIR, NAT HIST MUS & BIODIVERSITY RES CTR, UNIV KANS, as of 2004; PROF ECOL & EVOL BIOL, UNIV KANS, as of 2004; prog dir, Div Environ Biol, NSF, Wash, DC, 1992-1993; cur & asst dir sci, Carnegie Mus Natural Hist, beginning 1987; ed, sci publ, 1986-; adj assoc prof, Univ Pittsburgh, 1980-; assoc cur, Carnegie Mus Natural Hist, 1980-1987; asst cur, Carnegie Mus Natural Hist, 1977-1980; adj asst prof, Univ Pittsburgh, 1977-1980; res fel, Carnegie Mus Natural Hist, 1976-1977; adj lectr, Univ Pittsburgh, 1976-1977; fel, Carnegie Mus Natural Hist, 1975-1976. **Memberships:** Soc Vert Paleont; AAAS; Nat Sci Collections Alliance. **Research Statement & Publications:** Origin, evolution, relationships, paleocology and systematics of early Tertiary and Mesozoic mammals, especially primates, artiodactyls, insectivores and multituberculates; biodiversity informatics; science policy and administration. **Mailing Address:** Nat Hist Mus, Univ Kans, Dyche Hall, Lawrence, KS 66045-2454. **Fax:** 785-864-5335. **E-Mail:** krishtalka@ku.edu

KRISS, MICHAEL ALLEN, PHYSICS, COMPUTER SCIENCES. **Personal Data:** b San Diego, Calif, December 14, 1940; m 1963, Gretchen; c Deborah J, Aaron A & Rebecc L. **Education:** Univ Calif, Los Angeles, BA, 1962, MS, 1964, PhD (physics), 1969. **Professional Experience:** CONSULT, 1993-; mgr, Image Processing Lab, 1990-1992; mgr, External Res Prog, Electronic Imaging Res Labs, 1988-1990; mgr, Physics & Comput Sci Dept, Kodak, Japan, 1985-1988; res assoc, Physics Div, Res Lab, 1979-1990; lectr, Univ Col, Univ Rochester, 1976-; res assoc, Color Photog Div, Eastman Kodak, 1969-1979. **Memberships:** Soc Photog Scientists & Engrs; Sigma Xi; Soc Motion Picture & TV; NY Acad Sci. **Research Statement & Publications:** Photographic sciences; photographic research with emphasis on the mechanisms of color reproduction and image structure photographic film systems; development of methods to measure and evaluate the color reproduction and image structure of photographic and non-photographic systems; image processing by use of computers; electronic imaging systems. **Mailing Address:** 2250 N W Hood Dr, Camas, WA 98607. **E-Mail:** makris@comcast.net

KRIST, BETTY J, MATHEMATICS. **Education:** EdD, 1980. **Professional Experience:** PROF EMER, DEPT MATHS, UNIV BUFFALO GRAD SCH EDUC, as of 2005; DIR, GIFTED MATH PROG, UNIV BUFFALO GRAD SCH EDUC, as of 2005. **Memberships:** Nat Coun Teachers Math. **Mailing Address:** Univ Buffalo, 436 Baldy Hall, West Seneca, NY 14224-2747. **Fax:** 716-645-6841. **E-Mail:** krist@buffalo.edu

KRISTA, LAVERNE MATHEW, VETERINARY ANATOMY. **Personal Data:** b Webster, SDak, December 24, 1931; m 1964, c 3. **Education:** SDak State Univ, BS, 1958, MS, 1960; Univ Minn, PhD (poultry sci), 1966, DVM, 1969. **Professional Experience:** PROF EMER VET ANAT & HISTOL, AUBURN UNIV, as of 2003; prof Vet Anat & Histol, Auburn Univ, beginning 1981; assoc prof, Auburn Univ, 1973-1981; asst prof, Auburn Univ, 1969-1973; res asst poultry nutrit & phys, Univ Minn, 1960-1969; res asst, SDak State Univ, 1958-1960. **Memberships:** Sigma Xi; Am Asn Vet Anat; World Poultry Sci; Am Vet Med Asn. **Research Statement & Publications:** Nutrition; atherosclerosis; cardiovascular physiology. **Mailing Address:** 500 Ogletree Rd, Auburn, AL 36830.

KRISTAL, MARK BENNETT, BIOPSYCHOLOGY, BEHAVIOR-ETHOLOGY. **Personal Data:** b New York, NY, April 19, 1944; m 1967, Tova; c Morgan. **Education:** Rutgers Univ, BA, 1965; Kans State Univ, MS, 1970, PhD (psychol), 1971. **Honors & Awards:** elected Fellow, International Behavioral Neuroscience Society, 1999. **Professional Experience:** Interim dean, School Health Related Prof 1999-2001; dean, Fac Soc Sci, 1996- 1998; chmn, Dept Psychol, 1995-1996; PROF PSYCHOL, STATE UNIV NY, BUFFALO, beginning 1991; assoc dean, Fac Soc Sci, 1989-1990; interim assoc dean, Sch Related Health Professions, 1986-1988; Dir, Biopsychol Prog, Psychol Dept, State Univ NY, Buffalo, 1978-1986; from asst prof to assoc prof, State Univ NY, Buffalo, 1973-1991; Postdoc Trainee behav genetics & neuroendocrinol, Jackson Lab, 1971-1973; NSF, NIMH, Nat Inst Drug Abuse grants. **Memberships:** AAAS; Soc Neuroscience; Int Soc Behav Neuroscience; Soc Behav Neuroendo; Am Psychol Soc. **Research Statement & Publications:** Neural, endocrine, and genetic bases of maternal, ingestive and sexual behaviors; functions of the hypothalamus; limbic-hypothalamic function interactions; opiates and analgesia; endocrinology; pharmacology. **Mailing Address:** Psychol Dept, Univ at Buffalo, B71 Park Hall, Buffalo, NY 14260-1100. **Fax:** 716-645-3801. **E-Mail:** kristal@buffalo.edu

KRISTIANSEN, MAGNE, PULSED POWER TECHNOLOGY. **Personal Data:** b Elverum, Norway, April 14, 1932; American citizen; m 1957, Aud; c Sonja & Eric. **Education:** Univ Tex, BS, 1961, PhD (elec eng), 1967. **Honors & Awards:** Nuclear & Plasma Sci Soc Merit Award, Inst Elec & Electronic Engrs, 1991; Peter Haas Award, 1987. **Professional Experience:** C B THORNTON PROF ELEC ENG, TEX TECH UNIV, 1990-; P W HORN PROF ELEC ENG, TEX TECH UNIV, 1977-; consult, Asahi Chem, Japan, 2000; consult, Agency Defence Develop, S Korea, 2000; consult, Integrated Technol, Inc, 1998-; consult, Lockheed Martin Defense Systems, 1995-1996; consult, Hazeltine Ocean syst, 1994-1995; consult, Swedish Defense Res Inst, 1992-; consult, Physics int Co, 1992-1997; consult, Rocket res Co, 1992-1993; NASA, 1991- & BMDO, 1991-; vpres res & develop, Integrated Tech Inc, 1986-1990-1998; sci adv bd, US Air Force, 1981-1985; assoc ed, Trans Plasma Sci, Inst Elec & Electronics Engrs, 1979-1989; contractor, Sandia Labs, Lawrence Livermore Nat Lab, Los Alamos Nat Lab, Defense Nuclear Agency, Strategic Defense Initiative Off & US Navy, 1977-1987; US Army & Air Force grants, 1969-; NSF grants, 1967-1986 & US Atomic Energy Comn grant, 1967-1972; from asst prof to prof elec eng, Integrated Tech Inc, 1966-1977; res engr, Univ Tex, 1963-1966; vis staff mem, Los Alamos Nat Lab & Lawrence Livermore Nat Lab; consult to various industs. **Memberships:** AAAS; fel Inst Elec & Electronics Engrs; fel Am Phys Soc; Am Soc Eng Educ; Nat Soc Prof Eng; foreign mem Ural Br Russian Acad Sci. **Research Statement & Publications:** Plasma dynamics, pulsed power technology and physical electronics; high power switching and radio frequency wave propagation and technology; high power microwaves; author of 330 publications, co-author of two books, editor of series of books. **Mailing Address:** Dept Elec Eng, Tex Tech Univ, MS 3102, Lubbock, TX 79409-3102. **Fax:** 806-742-1281. **E-Mail:** m.kristiansen@coe.ttu.edu

KRISTMANSON, DANIEL D, CHEMICAL ENGINEERING. **Personal Data:** b Vancouver, BC, October 10, 1929; m 1956, c 2. **Education:** Univ BC, BASc, 1953; Univ London, PhD (chem eng), 1960. **Professional Experience:** Sr chem engr, Monenco Consult, 1984-1985; PROF CHEM ENG, UNIV NB, 1968-; from asst prof to assoc prof, Univ Nb, 1962-1968; fertilizer mfg, Consolidated Mining & Smelting Co Can, Ltd, 1960-1962; Develop engr, Consolidated Mining & Smelting Co Can, Ltd, 1953-1956. **Memberships:** Chem Inst Can; Air Pollution Control Asn. **Research Statement & Publications:** Mixing in reactors and natural streams; atomization of liquids; aerial spraying. **Mailing Address:** Dept Chem Eng, Univ NB Col Hill Box 4400, Fredericton, NB E3B 5A3, Can.

KRISTOFFERSEN, THORVALD, FOOD SCIENCE. **Personal Data:** b Denmark, May 6, 1919; American citizen; m 1948, c 1. **Education:** Royal Vet & Agr Col, Denmark, BS, 1944; Iowa State Univ, MS, 1948, PhD (dairy bact), 1954. **Honors & Awards:** Pfizer-Paul Lewis Award Cheese Res, 1965. **Professional Experience:** RETIRED; chmn dept, Ohio State Univ, 1972-1984; from asst prof to prof dairy technol, Ohio State Univ, 1956-1984; res assoc sanitizers, Ohio State Univ, 1955-1956; lab asst cheese, Iowa State Univ, 1946-1954; asst milk & milk prod, Govt Res Inst Denmark, 1944-1946. **Memberships:** Fel AAAS; Am Soc Microbiol; Am Dairy Sci Asn; Inst Food Technol. **Research Statement & Publications:** Mechanism of flavor development in cheese; enzyme system of milk, its function and purpose; butter and its physical structure; dairy sanitizers; analysis and evaluation of dairy products. **Mailing Address:** 1433 Clubview Blvd S, Worthington, OH 43235-1652.

KRISTOL, DAVID SOL, BIOENGINEERING. **Personal Data:** b Brooklyn, NY, June 4, 1938. **Education:** Brooklyn Col, BS, 1958; NY Univ, PhD (chem), 1969. **Professional Experience:** DIR, BIOMED ENG PROG, 1982-; PROF CHEM, NJ INST TECHNOL, 1981-; asst prof to assoc prof, Biomed Eng Prog, 1966-1981; res asst, Jewish Hosp Brooklyn, 1958-1962. **Memberships:** Am Chem Soc; Sigma Xi; Inst Elec & Electronics Engrs Eng & Med & Biol Soc; NY Acad Sci. **Research Statement & Publications:** Effect of structure upon reactivity of organic molecules; reaction of amines with chlorocarbons; modeling of the cardiovascular system; molecular modeling of the acetylcholinesterase. **Mailing Address:** Dept Biomed Eng, NJ Inst Technol, 336 Colton Hall, Newark, NJ 07102. **Fax:** 973-596-5222. **E-Mail:** kristol@njit.edu

KRITCHEVSKY, DAVID, LIPID METABOLISM, NUTRITION. **Personal Data:** b Kharkov, Russia, January 25, 1920; American citizen; m 1947, Evelyn; c Barbara, Janice & Stephen. **Education:** Univ Chicago, BS, 1939, MS, 1942; Northwestern Univ, PhD (chem), 1948. **Honorary Degrees:** DSc, Purdue Univ, 2001. **Honors & Awards:** Borden Award, Am Inst Nutrit, 1974; Am Col Nutrit Award, 1978; Herman Award, Am Soc Clin Nutrit, 1992; Spec Recognition Award, Am Heart Asn, 1993; Avenbrugger Medal, Univ Graz, Austria, 1994; Res Achievement Award, Am Inst Cancer Res, 1996; Supelco-Aocs Award, 1996; fel Am Oil Chem Soc, 2001. **Professional Experience:** Caspar Wistar Scholar, 1994-; INST PROF, WISTAR INST, UNIV PA, 1991-; PROF EMER BIOCHEM SURG, WISTAR INST, UNIV PA, beginning 1990; prof, Sch Vet Med, 1972-1990; chmn grad group molecular biol, Sch Vet Med, 1971-1984; Wistar prof biochem, Sch Vet Med, 1967-1972; prof, Sch Vet Med, 1965-1967; MEM, WISTAR INST, UNIV PA, 1957-; asst prof, Sch Med, Univ Pa, 1957-1965; res chemist, Lederle Labs Div, Am Cyanamid Co, 1952-1957; mem staff, Radiation Lab, Univ Calif, 1950-1952; Am Cancer Soc fel, Swiss Fed Inst Technol, 1948-1950; asst & quiz instr, Northwestern Univ, 1946-1948; chemist, Ninol Labs, 1942-1946; jr chemist, Ninol Labs, 1941-1942. **Memberships:** AAAS; Soc Exp Biol & Med; Am Soc Biol Chem; Am Chem Soc; Sigma Xi; pres Am Soc Nutrit Sci; pres Soc Exp Biol Med. **Research Statement & Publications:** Synthesis and metabolism of compounds labeled with isotopic carbon and hydrogen; experimental atherosclerosis; organic synthesis; steroids; biology of deuterium oxide; lipid metabolism; nutrition and cancer. **Mailing Address:** Wistar Inst, Univ Pa, 36th & Spruce Sts, Philadelphia, PA 19104-4268. **E-Mail:** kritchevsky@wistar.upenn.edu

KRITIKOS, HARALAMBOS N, ELECTRICAL ENGINEERING. **Personal Data:** b Tripolis, Greece, March 8, 1933; American citizen; m 1964, Suzanne; c Melissa. **Education:** Worcester Polytech Inst, BS, 1954, MS, 1956; Univ Pa, PhD (elec eng), 1961. **Professional Experience:** PROF EMER ELEC & SYST ENG, UNIV PA, as of 2005; prof elec eng, Moore Sch Elec Eng, Univ Pa, 1976-2000; exec ed, Inst Elec & Electronics Engrs Trans of Geosci Electronics, 1976-1980; Res fel, Calif Inst Technol, 1966; from asst instr to assoc prof, Moore Sch Elec Eng, Univ PA, 1956-1976; Res asst elec eng, Worcester Polytech Inst, 1954-1956. **Memberships:** Inst Elec & Electronics Engrs. **Research Statement & Publications:** Diffraction theory; antennas; propagation; microwave hazards; remote sensing; electromagnetic field theory. **Mailing Address:** Elec & Syst Eng, Univ Pa, 200 S 33rd St, Philadelphia, PA 19104.

KRITSKY, GENE RALPH, ETHNOENTOMOLOGY, CICADA EVOLUTION & BIOGEOGRAPHY OF CICINDELIDAE. **Personal Data:** b Minot, NDak, June 26, 1953. **Education:** Indiana Univ, BA, 1974; Univ Ill, MS, 1976, PhD (entom), 1977. **Professional Experience:** Adj curator, Cincinnati Mus Natural Hist, 1990-; PROF BIOL, COL MT ST JOSEPH, 1987-; CHMN BIOL, COL MT ST JOSEPH, 1985-; assoc prof, Col MT St Joseph, 1983-1987; Fulbright Award, Coun Int Exchange Scholars, 1981-1982; entomologist, Tri-State Agri-Res, 1979-1983; from asst prof to assoc prof biol, Tri-State Univ, 1977-1983. **Memberships:** Entom Soc Am; fel AAAS; Coleopterists Soc; Am Entom Soc. **Research Statement & Publications:** Insect evolution; insect systematics; history of biology especially Darwin and entomology; Coleoptera; fossil insects. **Mailing Address:** Dept Biol, Col Mt St Joseph, Cincinnati, OH 45233-1670. **Fax:** 513-244-4222. **E-Mail:** cdurwin@aol.com

KRITZ, ARNOLD H, PLASMA PHYSICS. **Personal Data:** b Providence, RI, January 6, 1935; m Barbara; c Ann-Sheryl, Barry & David. **Education:** Brown Univ, ScB, 1956; Yale Univ, MS, 1957, PhD (physics), 1961. **Professional Experience:** PROF, LEHIGH UNIV, 1991-; IPA Office of Fusion Energy Science, DOE, 2000-2004; CHMN, DEPT PHYSICS, 1991-1998; vis scientist, Lawrence Livermore Lab, beginning 1986; vis res fel, Princeton Univ, beginning 1977; sci adj, Ctr Plasma Physics Res, Ecole Polytech Lausanne, 1975-1976 & 1982-1983; consult, Oak Ridge Nat Lab, beginning 1974; chmn, dept physics & astron, 1971-1977; from asst prof to prof, Hunter Col, 1969-1996; sr staff physicist, Aeronaut Res Assocs Princeton, Inc, 1965-1969; staff scientist, Space Sci Lab, Gen Dynamics/Astronaut, 1963-1965; asst prof, San Diego State Col, 1963-1964; sr physicist, Space Sci Lab, Gen Dynamics/Astronaut, 1961-1963; lectr, New Haven Col, 1959-1960 & Southern Conn State Col, 1960-1961; Res asst, Yale Univ, 1957-1961. **Memberships:** Am Phys Soc; Am Asn Physics Teachers; Sigma Xi, University Fusion Association. **Research Statement & Publications:** Integrated modeling to predict the time evolution of plasma profiles in tokamaks; Study of the pedestal and Edge Localized Modes (ELMs) that form at the edge of high confinement tokamak discharges including the verification and validation of first principles simulations of pedestal and ELMs. **Mailing Address:** Dept Physics, Lehigh Univ, 16 Memorial Dr E, Bethlehem, PA 18015. **Fax:** 610-758-5730. **E-Mail:** ahk3@lehigh.edu

KRITZMAN, JULIUS, MEDICINE, HEMATOLOGY. **Personal Data:** b Lawrence, Mass, September 15, 1924; m 1950, Elinor; c Julia & Marjorie. **Education:** Harvard Univ, AB, 1947; Boston Univ, MD, 1951; Am Bd Internal Med, dipl, 1958, dipl hemat, 1974, dipl med oncol, 1975, dipl advan achievement internal med, 1987. **Honors & Awards:** Internist of the Year, Mass Capitol Am Col Physicians, 1990. **Professional Experience:** Mass lectureship, Am Col Physicians, 1990; assoc med, Beth Israel Hosp, 1967-; STAFF INTERNAL MED, NEW ENG MED CTR HOSPS, 1967-; instr, Harvard Med Sch, 1961-1970; asst vis physician, Beth Israel Hosp, 1961-1967; res assoc, Arthur G Rotch Lab, 1960-; attend physician, Boston Vet Admin Hosp, 1960-; physician, Med Clin, Boston Dispensary, 1958-; res fel hemat, New Eng Ctr Hosp, 1953-1954. **Memberships:** Am Soc Hemat; Am Col Physicians; Mass Med Soc. **Research Statement & Publications:** Synthesis and function of antibodies, especially the use of in vitro systems for study of antibody synthesis; medical oncology. **Mailing Address:** New Eng Med Ctr, Boston, MA 02108.

KRITZ-SILVERSTEIN, DONNA, WOMENS HEALTH, STATISTICS. **Personal Data:** b Brooklyn, NY, August 22, 1957; m 1986, Irvin; c Sarah & Sharona. **Education:** Brooklyn Col, BS, 1979; NY Univ, MA, 1981, PhD (social psychol), 1984. **Professional Experience:** ADJ PROF, DEPT FAMILY & PREV MED, UNIV CALIF, SAN DIEGO, as of 2005; assoc adj prof epidemiol, Dept family & prev Med, Univ Calif, San Diego, beginning 1996; asst adj prof, Univ Calif, San Diego, 1989-1996; res assoc, Univ Calif, San Diego, 1986-1989; adj prof personality psychol, San Diego State Univ, 1986-1987; asst prof, Components & Effective Fertil Regulation Study, Downstate Med Ctr, State Univ NY, 1984-1986; data processing supvr, Components & Effective Fertil Regulation Study, Downstate Med Ctr, State Univ NY, 1982-1984. **Memberships:** Am Psychol Asn; Western Psychol Asn; NAm Menopause Soc; Am Pub Health Asn. **Research Statement & Publications:** Women's health, specifically the long term effects of pregnancy on the risk for diabetes and other diseases; menopause; menstrual symptoms; osteoporosis; long term effects of hysterectomy; phytoestrogens, isoflavones, and health. **Mailing Address:** Dept Family & Prev Med, Univ Calif San Diego, 9500 Gilamn Dr 0631-C, La Jolla, CA 92093-0631. **E-Mail:** dsilverstein@ucsd.edu

KRIVAK, THOMAS GERALD, INORGANIC CHEMISTRY. **Personal Data:** b Johnstown, Pa, August 21, 1940; m 1963, c 3. **Education:** Univ Pittsburgh, BS, 1962, MEd, 1964; Univ Notre Dame, PhD (inorg chem), 1969. **Professional Experience:** SR RES ASSOC, INDUST CHEM DIV, PPG INDUSTS, 1969-; res asst chem, Radiation Labs, Mellon Inst, 1962-1964. **Memberships:** Am Chem Soc; Sigma Xi. **Research Statement & Publications:** Silica pigments for paint, paper, plastics and rubber applications. **Mailing Address:** Two Highview Circle, Irwin, PA 15642-1303.

KRIVAN, HOWARD C, MICROBIOLOGY, GLYCOBIOLOGY. **Personal Data:** b Swickley, Pa, August 24, 1954; m 1998, Gail; c 2. **Education:** Univ NMex, BS, 1980, MS, 1982; Va Polytech Inst & State Univ, PhD (microbiol), 1986. **Honors & Awards:** Intramural Res Training Award, NIH, 1987. **Professional Experience:** PRES & CHIEF SCI OFFICER, LEGERE PHARMACEUT LTD, 1995-; vpres res & develop, Lectin BioPharmaceut Inc, 1994-1995; assoc prof microbiol, Am Univ Caribbean, 1994; Consult, Lectin BioPharma Inc, 1994; exec vpres & chief sci officer, MicroCarb Inc, 1991-1993; pres, MicroCarb Inc, 1991; vpres, BioCarb, Inc, 1990-1991; dir microbiol & sr scientist, BioCarb, Inc, 1989-1990; Staff fel, NIH, 1987-1989. **Memberships:** AAAS; Am Soc Microbiol. **Research Statement & Publications:** Adhesin, receptor technology and infectious agents; botanical biopharmaceuticals to treat and prevent infectious diseases; lectins; complex carbohydrates; vaccines. **Mailing Address:** Legere Pharmaceut Ltd, 3123 Research Way Suite 215, Carson City, NV 89706. **Fax:** 775-841-2263. **E-Mail:** biotahoe@earthlink.net

KRIVANEK, NEIL DOUGLAS, TOXICOLOGY. **Personal Data:** b Milwaukee, Wis, June 11, 1944; m 1969. **Education:** Univ Wis, BS, 1966; Wayne State Univ, MS, 1968, PhD (physiol), 1972. **Professional Experience:** CONSULT, ROUNDTABLE TOXICOL CONSULT, 2003-; consult, Haskell Lab Toxicol & Indust Med, E I Du Pont Del Nemours &Co, Inc, 1986; staff toxicologist, Haskell Lab Toxicol & Indust Med, E I Du Pont Del Nemours &Co, Inc, beginning1975; res toxicologist, Haskell Lab Toxicol & Indust Med, E I Du Pont Del Nemours &Co, Inc, 1974; instr toxicol, Dept Occup & Environ Health, Col Med, Wayne State Univ, 1972-1974. **Memberships:** Am Chem Soc; Am Indust Hyg Asn; Am Bd Indust Hyg Asn; Sigma Xi; Am Bd Toxicol; Soc Toxicol. **Research Statement & Publications:** Biochemical mechanisms of industrial toxicology; methods development for measuring toxic effects. **Mailing Address:** 2103 State Rd, Oxford, PA 19363. **Fax:** 610-932-2441. **E-Mail:** nkrivanek@earlthlink.net

KRIVANEK, ONDREJ LADISLAV, ELECTRON MICROSCOPY, ELECTRON SPECTROSCOPY. **Personal Data:** b Prague, Czech, August 1, 1950; British citizen. **Education:** Univ Leeds, BSc, 1971; Univ Cambridge, PhD (physics), 1976. **Professional Experience:** CO FOUNDER, NION CO, WASH, 1997-; DIR RES, GATAN INC, 1985-; adj assoc prof physics, Ariz State Univ, 1985-1997; asst prof solid state sci, Ariz State Univ, 1981-1985; asst res engr mat sci, Univ Calif, Berkeley, 1977-1980; res consult electron micros, Bell Lab, 1976-1977; res fel physics, Cavendish Lab, Cambridge, 1975-1976. **Memberships:** Am Phys Soc; Electron Micros Soc Am; Brit Inst Physics. **Research Statement & Publications:** High resolution and analytical electron microscopy; electron optics; electron energy loss spectroscopy; UHV electron microscopy. **Mailing Address:** Gatan Inc, 6678 Owens Dr, Pleasanton, CA 94588. **Fax:** 510-463-0204.

KRIVI, GWEN GRABOWSKI, GROWTH FACTORS, INFLAMMATION. **Personal Data:** b Huntington, NY, February 11, 1950; c 1. **Education:** Bucknell Univ, BA, 1972; Mass Inst Technol, PhD (biochem), 1978; Wash Univ, MBA, 1990. **Professional Experience:** VPRES, PROJ MGT, ELI LILLY & CO, as of 2004; VPRES RES & DEVELOP, MONSANTO, CO, 1996-; adj prof, Wash Univ, 1991-; sr fel, Dept Biol Sci, 1989-1996; Mem, Comt Biotechnol, Agr Res Serv, USDA, 1986-; sci fel, Dept Biol Sci, 1986-1989; res group leader II, Dept Biol Sci, 1985-1986; res group leader I, Dept Biol Sci, 1984-1985; res specialist, Dept Molecular Biol, Monsanto Co, 1982-1984; Sr res chemist, Dept Molecular Biol, Monsanto Co, 1980-1982. **Memberships:** AAAS; Am Chem Soc; Endocrine Soc. **Research Statement & Publications:** Function relationships of growth proteins and their receptors; role of arachidonic acid metabolites in inflammation; animal cell engineering; immunoassay; cell biology; molecular genetics technologies in support of human pharmaceutical product development. **Mailing Address:** Eli Lilly & Co, Sannomiya Plaza Bldg, Chuo-ku Kobe, Japan. **Fax:** 8178-242-9502.

KRIVIT, WILLIAM, pediatrics, hematology; deceased, see previous edition for last biography

KRIZ, GEORGE JAMES, AGRICULTURAL ENGINEERING, SOIL SCIENCE. **Personal Data:** b Brainard, Nebr, September 20, 1936; m 1989, Rhoda; c Rosalie S, Richard P & Thomas G. **Education:** Iowa State Univ, BS, 1960, MS, 1962; Univ Calif, Davis, PhD (eng), 1965. **Professional Experience:** RETIRED; assoc dir, NC Agr Res Serv, ending 1999; bd dirs, Agr Res Inst, 1992-1996; educ & res dir, Am Soc Agr Engrs, 1983-1985; prof & dir res, NC Agr Exp Sta, beginning 1973; assoc head dept, NC State Univ, 1969-1973; consult, Int Basic Econ Corp & Indian Inst Technol, 1967; from asst prof to assoc prof biol & agr eng, NC State Univ, 1965-1973; lectr groundwater hydrol, Univ Calif, Davis, 1965; asst engr, Univ Calif, Davis, 1964-1965; teaching asst agr eng, Iowa State Univ, 1960-1962; bd trustees, Am Soc Agr Engrs Found. **Memberships:** fel Am Soc Agr Engrs; Coun Agr & Sci Technol; Agr Res Inst. **Research Statement & Publications:** Animal waste management; saturated flow in porous media, especially soil water relationships. **Mailing Address:** Col Agr & Life Sci, NC State Univ, 100 Patterson Hall, Raleigh, NC 27695-7643. **Fax:** 919-515-7745. **E-Mail:** george_kriz@ncsu.edu

KRIZ, GEORGE STANLEY, PHYSICAL ORGANIC CHEMISTRY. **Personal Data:** b Santa Cruz, Calif, October 20, 1939; m 1989, Carolyn; c Brian, Kenneth & Michelle. **Education:** Univ Calif, Berkeley, BS, 1961; Ind Univ, PhD (org chem), 1966. **Professional Experience:** Vis prof, Indiana Univ, 1984-1985; PROF CHEM, WESTERN WASH UNIV, beginning 1979; assoc prof, Western Wash Univ, 1977-1979; exec asst to dean arts & sci, Western Wash Univ, 1975-1977; asst prof, Western, Wash Univ, 1967-1972; vis res assoc, Ohio State Univ, 1966-1967; Foreign asst chem, Univ Montpellier, 1965-1966. **Memberships:** AAAS; Am Chem Soc; Royal Soc Chem. **Research Statement & Publications:** Deuterium kinetic isotope effects; mechanisms of organic reactions; nuclear magnetic resonance spectroscopy; linear free energy relationships. **Mailing Address:** Dept Chem, Western Wash Univ, 516 High St, Bellingham, WA 98255-9150. **Fax:** 360-650-2826. **E-Mail:** george.kriz@wwu.edu

KRIZEK, DONALD THOMAS, ENVIRONMENTAL PHYSIOLOGY, STRESS PHYSIOLOGY. **Personal Data:** b Cleveland, Ohio, June 25, 1935; m 1962, Betty; c Kathleen, Beth & Susan. **Education:** Western Reserve Univ, BA, 1957; Univ Chicago, MS, 1958, PhD (bot), 1964. **Professional Experience:** USDA grantee, 1998-2002; res pant physiol, Climate Stress Lab, USAD, 1989-2000; actg res leader, Climet Stress Lab, USDA, 1989-1990; mem NASA Controlled Ecol Life Support Systs Discipline Working Group, 1989-1994; res plant physiologist, Sustainable Agr Syst Lab, Beltsville Agr Res Ctr, Agr Res Serv, USDA, 1989-2000; chmn Comn Int Del l'Eclairage Tech Comt Action Spectra Plants, 1988-; chmn, Am Inst Biol Sci, Kennedy Space Ctr Biomass prod tech panel, 1987-1990; ADJ ASSOC PROF, DEPT HORT, UNIV MD, 1986-; consult, NASA, 1979-; mem Plant Phys Adv Group, Am Inst Biol Sci/NASA, 1979-1990; chmn, Environ Protection Agency Interagency Task Group, Biol (non human) Effects, 1976-1978; NCR-101 comt Controlled evriron tech & use, Growth Chamber Use, 1975-; chmn Inadvertent Modification Stratosphere subcomt, Biol & Climate Effects Res, 1975-1978; USDA rep, White House Task Force Inadvertent Modification Stratosphere, 1975-1978; res plant physiologist, Plant Stress Lab, 1972-1989; mem, Am Soc Hort Sci Working Group Controlled Environ, 1969-; mem, Am Soc Agr Eng Plant & Animal Physiol Adv Group, 1966-; res plant physiologist, Phyto-Eng Lab, USDA, 1966-1972; instr bot & biol, Univ Chicago, 1964-1966; instr, Montgomery Ctr, Univ Ala, 1959-1961; res & develop officer, Arctic, Desert, Tropic Info Ctr, Res Studies Inst, Air Univ, 1958-1962. **Memberships:** Am Soc Plant Physiol; fel Am Soc Hort Sci; Brit Soc Exp Biol; Japanese Soc Plant Physiol; Scand Soc Plant Physiol; Am Inst Biol Sci; Am Soc Photobiol; AAAS; Int Soc Hort Sci. **Research Statement & Publications:** Plant growth and development; senescence of vascular plants; photoperiodism and photomorphogenesis; plant growth regulators; controlled environments; environmental stress physiology; carbon dioxide enrichment; plant growth chambers; ultra-violet radiation effects; water stress; global climate change; sustainable agriculture. **Mailing Address:** Sustainable Agr Syst Labs, USDA, Bldg 001 Rm 140 BARC-W, Beltsville, MD 20705-2350. **Fax:** 301-504-6626. **E-Mail:** dkrizek@asrr.arsusda.gov

KRIZEK, RAYMOND JOHN, GEOTECHNICAL ENGINEERING, PROJECT MANAGEMENT. **Personal Data:** b Baltimore, Md, June 5, 1932; m 1964, Claudia; c Robert A & Kevin J. **Education:** Johns Hopkins Univ, BE, 1954; Univ Md, MS, 1961; Northwestern Univ, PhD (geotech eng), 1963. **Honors & Awards:** C A Hogentogler Award, Am Soc Testing & Mat, 1970; Walter L Huber Res Prize, Am Soc Civil Engrs, 1971; Palmes Academiques, French Govt, 1993; Terzaghi Award, Am Soc Civil Engrs, 1997. **Professional Experience:** STANLEY F PEPPER PROF CIVIL ENG, NORTHWESTERN UNIV, as of 2004; DIR, MASTER PROJ MGT PROG, 1994-; chmn dept, Master Proj Mgt Prog, 1980-1992; prof civil eng, Norwestern Univ, beginning 1970; consult, 1963-; from asst prof to assoc prof, Master Proj Mgt Prog, 1963-1970; lectr soil mech, Cath Univ, 1961; instr civil eng, Univ Md, 1957-1961; vpres, GeoInst, Am Soc Civil Engrs. **Memberships:** Am Soc Civil Engrs. **Research Statement & Publications:** Soil-structure interaction of buried conduits; use of dredgings for landfill; relationship between soil fabric and its engineering properties; constitutive relations for soils; flow through porous media; disposal of solid waste materials; soil stabilization by grouting. **Mailing Address:** Dept Civil Eng, Northwestern Univ, A114 Tech Inst 2145 Sheridan Rd, Evanston, IL 60208-3109. **Fax:** 847-491-4011. **E-Mail:** rjkrizek@northwestern.edu

KRIZEK, THOMAS JOSEPH, PLASTIC SURGERY, RECONSTRUCTIVE SURGERY. **Personal Data:** b Milwaukee, Wis, December 1, 1932; m 1959, c 3. **Education:** Marquette Univ, BS, 1954, MD, 1957. **Honorary Degrees:** MA, Yale Univ, 1974. **Professional Experience:** PROF RELIG & MED, UNIV S FLA, as of 2003; vice chmn, dept surg, Univ Chicago, beginning 1987; prof surg & chief plastic & reconstructive surg, dept surg, Univ Chicago, 1984-1987; prof surg, Univ Southern Calif & chief, Div Plastic Surg, Los Angeles County, Univ Southern Calif, Med Ctr, 1981-1984; prof surg, Col Physicians & Surgeons, Columbia Univ & Chief, Div Plastic & Reconstructive Surg, Columbia-Presby Med Ctr, 1978-1981; assoc dean grad & continuing educ, Sch Med, Yale Univ, 1975-1977; prof plastic surg, sch med, Yale Univ, 1973-1978; assoc prof, sch med, Yale Univ, 1968-1973; asst prof plastic surg, Johns Hopkins Univ & Univ Md, 1966-1968. **Memberships:** Am Asn Plastic Surgeons; Asn Hand Surg (pres 1980-1981); Am Asn Surg of Trauma; Am Burn Asn; Am Col Surgeons. **Research Statement & Publications:** Surgical infection, particularly as related to burns and other trauma; surgery and epidemiology of head and neck cancer; aging. **Mailing Address:** Dept Plastic & Reconstructive Surg, Univ SFla, 4 Columbia Dr No 730, Tampa, FL 33606.

KRNJEVIC, KRESIMIR, NEUROPHYSIOLOGY, NEUROPHARMACOLOGY. **Personal Data:** b Zagreb, Yugoslavia, September 7, 1927; m 1954, Jeanne; c Peter & Nicholas. **Education:** Univ Edinburgh, MB, ChB, 1949, BSc, 1951, PhD (physiol), 1953. **Honors & Awards:** Forbes lectr, 1978; Gairdner Award, 1984; Officer Order Can, 1987; kershman lectr, 1993; wilder penfield prize, 1997; brusina award, 2001. **Professional Experience:** PROF EMER PHYSIOL, MCGILL UNIV, 2001-; mem coun, Int Union Physiol Sci, 1983-1993; Drake prof physiol, McGill Univ, 1978-1999; Drake prof & chmn, Dept Physiol, 1978-1987; head, Dept Anesthesia Res, McGill Univ, 1965-1999; from prin sci officer to sr prin sci officer, ARC Inst Animal Physiol, Eng, 1959-1965; res assoc & asst prof, Univ Wash, 1954-1956; Beit Mem res fel, Univ Edinburgh, 1951-1954. **Memberships:** Can Physiol Soc; Int Soc Neurochem; Royal Soc Can; Physiol Soc UK; AAAS; Can Physiol Soc (Pres, 1979); Soc Neuroscience; Physiol Soc UK; fel royal soc Can; Croatian Acad Arts & Sci. **Research Statement & Publications:** Central synaptic mechanisms and disruptive effects of anoxia, hypoglycemia and anesthesia. **Mailing Address:** Anesthesia Res Unit McGill Univ McIntyre Ctr, 3655 Promenade Sir William Osler, Montreal, PQ H3G 1Y6, Can. **Fax:** 514-398-4376. **E-Mail:** krnjevic@med.mcgill.ca

KROCHMAL, JEROME J(ACOB), ORGANIZATION DEVELOPMENT, ORGANIZATIONAL EFFECTIVENESS. **Personal Data:** b New York, NY, December 17, 1930; m 1952, Regina; c Kenneth, Frances & Linda. **Education:** Ga Inst Technol, BCerE, 1952. **Professional Experience:** RETIRED; sr mgt analyst, Aeronaut Labs, 1975-1988; sr plans analyst, US Air Force Mat Lab, USAF, 1971-1975; Stanford-Sloan fel, 1969-1970; sr proj officer, US Air Force Mat Lab, USAF, 1960-1969; staff consult, Mat Adv Bd, Nat Acad Sci-Nat Res Coun, 1960-1961; staff mem, US Air Force Mat Lab, USAF, 1957-1960; staff mem ceramics & graphites, USAF Propulsion Lab, 1954-1957; staff mem ceramics, Battelle Mem Inst, 1952. **Research Statement & Publications:** Organization effectiveness; synergistic problem solving in advanced technology; fostering creativity and innovation; high temperature materials. **Mailing Address:** PO Box 567764, Atlanta, GA 31156.

KROCHTA, WILLIAM G, ANALYTICAL CHEMISTRY. **Personal Data:** b Piney Fork, Ohio, September 24, 1930; m 1954, c 3. **Education:** Mt Union Col, BS, 1952; Purdue Univ, MS, 1954, PhD (chem), 1957. **Professional Experience:** AT PPG INDUSTS, as of 1992; SR SUPVR, CHEM DIV, PPG INDUSTS, BARBERTON, 1962-; supvr, Columbia-Southern Chem Corp, 1959-1962; Sr res chemist, Columbia-Southern Chem Corp, 1956-1959. **Memberships:** Am Chem Soc; Am Indust Hyg Asn. **Research Statement & Publications:** Absorption spectroscopy; gas chromatography. **Mailing Address:** 237 Tanglewood Trail, Wadsworth, OH 44281-2354.

KROCK, HANS J, ENVIRONMENTAL WATER QUALITY, OCEAN ENGINEERING. **Personal Data:** b Cracow, Poland, August 30, 1942; American citizen. **Education:** Ariz State Univ, BS, 1965, MS, 1967; Univ Calif, Berkeley, PhD, 1972. **Professional Experience:** PROF & RES OCEAN ENG DEPT, UNIV HAWAII, MANOA, as of 2006; PRES OCEAN ENG & ENERGY SYST INT INC, HONOLULU, HAWAII, 1988-; mem nat comt on Ocean Energy, Am Soc Civil Engrs, beginning 1987; prin investr, Open Cycle Ocean Thermal Energy Conversion, beginning 1982; consult engr, beginning 1980; assoc prof ocean eng & dir, J K K Look Lab, Univ Hawaii, Manoa, beginning 1980; sr environ engr, M&E Pac Inc, Honolulu, Hawaii, 1972-1980; res assoc, Sanit Eng Res Lab, Univ Calif, Berkeley, 1970-1972; assoc engr hydraul, Alameda County Flood Dist, Calif, beginning 1969; res engr tertiary treat, Los Angeles County Sanit Dists, Calif, 1967-1968; pub health engr, Dept Health, State Ariz, 1965-1966. **Memberships:** Fel Am Inst Chemists; Am Soc Civil Engrs; Water Pollution Control Fedn; Marine Technol Soc; Am Soc Limnol & Oceanog; AAAS; Am Chem Soc. **Research Statement & Publications:** Physical, chemical and biological interactions in the oceans and estuaries; gas exchange characteristics in sea water related to ocean thermal energy conversion; water quality standards. **Mailing Address:** Dept Ocean Eng, Univ Hawaii, 2444 Dole St, Honolulu, HI 96822. **E-Mail:** hkrock@soest.hawaii.edu

KROCK, LARRY PAUL, STRESS PHYSIOLOGY, ENVIRONMENTAL PHYSIOLOGY. **Personal Data:** b Santa Monica, Calif, October 18, 1949; m Becky L Smith; c Melissa, Laura & Anastasia. **Education:** San Fernando Valley State Col, BA, 1972; Calif State Univ, MA, 1974; Tex A&M Univ, PhD (physiol), 1985. **Professional Experience:** CHIEF SCI, USAF SCH AEROSPACE MED, as of 2004; DIR RES, HYPERBARIC MED, ARMSTRONG LAB, USAF, as of 2002; sci Prog Rev Comt, Aerospace Med Asn, 1991; adj prof, Univ Tex, San Antonio, beginning 1990 & Tex Lutheran Col, 1991; adj prof, Sch Aero Med, USAF, 1990-; mem, Coun Circulation, Am Heart Asn, Basic Res Rev Bd, Naval Res & Develop Command, 1990; res physiologist acceleration effects function, Crew Technol Div, Sch Aerospace Med, USAF, 1987-1994; res physiologist environ physiol function, 1985-1987; res asst, Dept Med, Baylor Col Med, 1984-1985; res asst, Dept Physiol & Appl Physics Lab, Col Vet Med, Tex A&M Univ, 1983-1984; asst, Dept Health & Kinesiology, 1982-1985; asst prof, Sports Med Facil & Undergrad Curric Sports Med, 1979-1982; dir, Sports Med Facil & Undergrad Curric Sports Med, 1975-1982; lectr, Dept Phys Educ, Calif State Univ, 1975-1977; res asst, Dept Phys Educ, Calif State Univ, 1973-1974. **Memberships:** Fel Aerospace Med Asn; Aerospace Physiologists Soc; AAAS; fel Am Col Sports Med; Am Heart Asn; Am Physiol Soc; Inst Elec & Electronics Engrs; Sigma Xi; NY Acad Sci. **Research Statement & Publications:** Increase understanding about the interaction between elevated oxygen concentrations and increased ambient pressure on the structure and function of the cell; immune response maintaining homeostasis during exposure to stressful environmental conditions. **Mailing Address:** Hyperbaric Med Div, Armstrong Lab, Brooks AFB, TX 78235-5304. **Fax:** 210-536-2946. **E-Mail:** larry.p.krock@platinum.brooks.af.mil

KROEGER, PETER G, FLUID DYNAMICS, HEAT TRANSFER. **Personal Data:** b Swinoujscie, Poland, April 26, 1930; American citizen; m 1958, c 2. **Education:** Inst Technol, Aachen, WGer, ME, 1956; Case Western Reserve Univ, PhD (mech eng), 1972. **Professional Experience:** Res engr, Brookhaven Nat Lab, beginning 1974; res engr, Kennecott Copper Co, 1967-1972; res engr, Gen Elec Co, 1962-1967 & 1972-1974. **Memberships:** Am Soc Mech Engrs; Sigma Xi; Am Nuclear Soc. **Research Statement & Publications:** Analysis of thermal and fluid dynamics systems and processes; nuclear reactor thermohydraulics; phase change processes such as freezing and melting; dynamics of propulsion plants. **Mailing Address:** Brookhaven Nat Lab, PO Box 5000, Upton, NY 11973-5000.

KROEGER, RICHARD ALAN, GAMMA-RAY OBSERVATIONS, GAMMA-RAY DETECTOR DEVELOPMENT. **Personal Data:** b Waterloo, Iowa, May 28, 1955. **Education:** Univ Northern Iowa, BA, 1977; Univ Chicago, MS, 1979, PhD (physics), 1985. **Professional Experience:** EXP ASTROPHYSICIST, NAVAL RES LAB, 1989-; staff engr, Hughes Aircraft Corp, 1987-1989; vis scientist astrophys, Univ Space Res Asn, 1985-1987; res assoc astrophys, Enrico Fermi Inst, 1985. **Memberships:** Am Inst Physics; Am Astron Soc, Inst Elec & Electronics Engrs. **Research Statement & Publications:** High energy astrophysics; gamma ray observations; measurements of cosmic rays. **Mailing Address:** Naval Res Lab, 4555 Overlook Ave SW, Washington, DC 20375-5352. **E-Mail:** kroeger@osse.nrl.navy.mil

KROEKER, RICHARD MARK, ELECTRON TUNNELING. **Personal Data:** b Bakersfield, Calif, September 7, 1952; m 1978, c 2. **Education:** Washington Univ, St Louis, BA, 1974; Univ Calif, Santa Barbara, PhD (physics), 1979. **Professional Experience:** SR ENGR, GEN PROD DIV, IBM CORP, SAN JOSE, 1981-; fel, Gen Prod Div, IBM Corp, San Jose, 1980-1981; Fel, Physics Dept, Univ Calif, Santa Barbara, 1979-1980. **Memberships:** Am Phys Soc. **Research Statement & Publications:** Physical chemistry of surfaces, including monolayer spectroscopy, radiation chemistry of thin films and mechanisms of heterogeneous catalysis; tribology and wear. **Mailing Address:** 700 Spring Hill Dr, Morgan Hill, CA 95037.

KROEMER, HERBERT, SEMICONDUCTORS. **Personal Data:** b Weimar, Ger, August 25, 1928; m 1950, c 5. **Education:** Univ Gottingen, Ger, dipl, 1951, PhD (Theoretical Physics), 1952. **Honorary Degrees:** Dr, Tech Univ Aachen, Ger, 1984. **Honors & Awards:** Nobel Physics Laureate, 2000; J Ebers Award, Inst Elec & ELectronics Engrs, 1973, Sr Res Award, Am Soc Eng Educ, 1982; Heinrich Walker Medal, 1982; Jack A Morton Award, 1986. **Professional Experience:** Nat lectr, Inst Elec & Electronics Engrs Device Soc, 1983; PROF ELEC ENG, UNIV CALIF, SANTA BARBARA, 1976-; prof elec eng, Univ Colo, Boulder, 1968-1976; head, New Phenomena Sect, Semiconductor Res & Develop Lab, Fairchild, 1966-1968; sr scientist, Varian Assocs, 1959-1966; res group leader, Ger Philips Lab, 1957-1959; res scientist, labs, Radio Corp Am, 1954-1957; res scientist, Ger Post Off Lab, 1952-1954. **Memberships:** Foreign assoc Nat Acad Eng; fel Inst Elec & Electronics Engrs; fel Am Phys Soc. **Research Statement & Publications:** Semiconductor physics and exploratory research on new device principles; physics and technology of semiconductor materials and devices; heterojunctions; molecular beam epitaxy. **Mailing Address:** Dept Elec & Comput Eng & Mat Eng, Univ Calif, 2205A Eng Sci Bldg, Santa Barbara, CA 93106-9560. **Fax:** 805-893-7990. **E-Mail:** kroemer@ece.uscb.edu

KROENBERG, BERNDT, FOOD SCIENCE, NUTRITION. **Personal Data:** b Riga, Latvia, October 31, 1936; m 1959, c 1. **Education:** Inst Divi Thomae, MS, 1961, PhD (biochem), 1963. **Professional Experience:** RETIRED; staff vpres technol & develop, Bausch & Lomb Inc, 1984-1996; dir licensing, Ross Labs Div, Abbott Labs, Columbus, 1976-1984; dir prod develop res, Ross Labs Div, Abbott Labs, Columbus, 1969-1976; mgr emulsion develop, Celanese Coatings Co, 1966-1969; group leader leaf chem, Brown & Williamson Tobacco Corp, 1963-1966; instr, Xavier Univ, Ohio, 1962-1963; instr ger, Our Lady Cincinnati Col, 1961-1963. **Memberships:** AAAS; Am Chem Soc; Licencing Exec Soc. **Research Statement & Publications:** Isolation and identification of natural products of animal and plant origin; amino acids, alkaloids, sterols; medicinal use of natural products; infant and geriatric foods; pediatric and obstetrics and gynecology drugs; diagnostic kits; enteral feeding pumps; contact lenses, ophthalmic drugs. **Mailing Address:** 16046 Autumn Oaks Circle, Ballwin, MO 63021.

KROENING, JOHN LEO, PHYSICS. **Personal Data:** b Princeton, Minn, August 18, 1934; m 1956, c 4. **Education:** Univ Minn, Minneapolis, BS, 1956, MS, 1959, PhD (physics), 1962. **Professional Experience:** ASSOC PROF PHYSICS, UNIV MINN, DULUTH, 1968-; asst prof, Univ Minn, Minneapolis, 1965-1968; res assoc physics, Univ Minn, Minneapolis, 1962-1965. **Memberships:** Am Geophys Union. **Research Statement & Publications:** Atmospheric physics and electricity; small ion content; atmospheric ozone distribution; chemiluminescent detection; atmospheric aerosol-effect on ozone and small ion content; stratosphere-troposphere transport. **Mailing Address:** 1933 W Kent Rd, Duluth, MN 55812. **E-Mail:** jkroenin@d.umn.edu

KROENKE, LOREN WILLIAM, MARINE GEOLOGY. **Personal Data:** b Milwaukee, Wis, July 2, 1938. **Education:** Univ Wis-Madison, BS, 1960; Univ Hawaii, MS, 1968, PhD (geol), 1972. **Professional Experience:** GEOPHYSICIST, HAWAII INST GEOPHYS, UNIV HAWAII, 1986-; assoc geophysicist marine geol & geophys, Hawaii Inst Geophys, Univ Hawaii, 1975-1986; mem, Adv Panel Ocean Margin, joint Oceanog Inst Deep Earth Sampling-Int Prog Ocean Drilling, 1974-; marine geologist & regional adv, UN Develop Prog, 1974-1976; sci adv, US-Japan Coop Prog Marine Sea-Bottom Surv Panel, 1973-1974; asst geophysicist, Hawaii Inst Geophys, Univ Hawaii, 1972-1975; tech adv, Comt Coord, Joint Prospecting Mineral Resources SPac Offshore Areas, Econ Comn Asia& Far East, UN, 1972-1973; jr geophysicist, Hawaii Inst Geophys, Univ Hawaii, 1967-1972; asst geophys, Hawaii Inst Geophys, Univ Hawaii, 1963-1966; proj asst marine geol & geophys, Geophys & Polar Res Ctr, Univ Wis, 1961-1963. **Memberships:** Am Geophys Union; Seismol Soc Am; Geol Soc Am; AAAS; Sigma Xi. **Research Statement & Publications:** Marine geology and geodynamics of the Pacific Ocean Basin with particular reference to the formation and deformation of oceanic crust and continental margins in the southwest Pacific. **Mailing Address:** Hawaii Inst Geophys, Univ Hawaii Sch Ocean & Earth Sci & Technol, 1000 Pope Rd, Honolulu, HI 96822. **Fax:** 808-956-3188. **E-Mail:** kroenke@elepaio.soest.hawaii.edu

KROENKE, WILLIAM JOSEPH, MATERIALS SCIENCE, TECHNOLOGY TRANSFER. **Personal Data:** b Cleveland, Ohio, August 16, 1934; m 1961, c 2. **Education:** Case Inst Technol, BS, 1956, PhD (inorg chem), 1963. **Professional Experience:** RES PROF, DEPT CHEM & NUCLEAR ENG, UNIV NMEX, 1996-; Assoc dir, Ctr Micro-Eng Mat, 1995-; NSF evaluator, Ctr Micro-Eng Ceramics, 1994-1995; res & develop fel & mgr, Res Ctr, B F Goodrich Co, 1980-1994; sr res assoc, Res Ctr, B F Goodrich Co, 1974-1980; res assoc, Res Ctr, B F Goodrich Co, 1970-1974; sr res chemist, Res Ctr, B F Goodrich Co, 1965-1970; res chemist, Res Ctr, B F Goodrich Co, 1963-1965; Chemist, Nat Carbon Res Lab, Union Carbide Corp, 1956-1961. **Memberships:** Am Chem Soc. **Research Statement & Publications:** Inorganic and organometallic chemistry; goechemistry; smoke retarders; synthesis; coordination numbers; molecular and crystal structure; property-structure relationships; solid state chemistry; phase relationships; fire retardants; catalysis; polymers; high-temperature chemistry; carbon/carbon composites. **Mailing Address:** PO Box 14627, Albuquerque, NM 87191. **Fax:** 505-277-1024. **E-Mail:** yonder@unm.edu

KROES, ROGER L, SOLID STATE PHYSICS. **Personal Data:** b Racine, Wis, December 3, 1935; m 1964, c 2. **Education:** Marquette Univ, BS, 1957; Univ Mo-Columbia, PhD (physics), 1968. **Professional Experience:** PROJ SCIENTIST, MARSHALL SPACE FLIGHT CTR, NASA, as of 1995; PHYSICIST, MARSHALL SPACE FLIGHT CTR, NASA, 1968-. **Memberships:** Am Phys Soc. **Research Statement & Publications:** Color centers in alkaline earth oxides; optical properties of solids; crystal characterization; solution crystal growth. **Mailing Address:** Migrogravity Exp Proj, Marshall Space Flight Ctr, Mail Code JA81, Huntsville, AL 35812.

KROGDAHL, WASLEY SVEN, COSMOLOGY. **Personal Data:** b Springfield, Ill, January 17, 1919; m 1942, Margaret; c Matthew, John & Marthine. **Education:** Univ Chicago, BS, 1939, PhD (astron), 1942. **Professional Experience:** PROF EMER, DEPT PHYSICS & ASTRON, UNIV KY, 1986-; prof physics & astron, Univ Ky, 1965-1986; prof math & astron, Univ Ky, 1964-1965; assoc prof math & astron, Univ Ky, 1958-1964; asst prof astron & astrophys, Dearborn Observ, Northwestern Univ, Ill, 1946-1958; instr, Yerkes Observ, 1945-1946; assoc prof math & astron, Univ SC, 1944-1945; instr physics, Army Specialized Training Prog, Ripon Col, 1943-1944; jr physicist, Naval Ord Lab, 1942-1943. **Memberships:** Int Astron Union. **Research Statement & Publications:** Theoretical astrophysics; relativistic cosmology. **Mailing Address:** Dept Physics & Astron Univ Ky, 177 Chem Physics Bldg 600 Rose St, Lexington, KY 40506-0055. **Fax:** 859-323-2846.

KROGER, F(ERDINAND) A(NNE), PHYSICAL CHEMISTRY, THERMODYNAMICS. **Personal Data:** b Amsterdam, Neth, September 11, 1915; div, c 2. **Education:** Univ Amsterdam, BSc, 1934, Drs, 1937, PhD (phys chem), 1940. **Honors & Awards:** Chaudron Gold Medal, Fr Soc High Temperatures & Refractors. **Professional Experience:** PROF EMER MAT SCI, UNIV SOUTHERN CALIF, 1985-; corresp, Royal Dutch Acad Sci, 1978; David Packard prof elec eng, Univ Southern Calif, 1972-1985; prof mat sci & chem, Univ Southern Calif, 1964-1985; sci adv, Mullard Res Labs, Eng, 1958-1964; res group leader, Philips Res Labs, Netherlands, 1940-1958; res worker, Philips Res Labs, Netherlands, 1938-1940. **Research Statement & Publications:** Solid state luminescence; compound semiconductors; imperfection chemistry. **Mailing Address:** Dept Chem, Univ Southern Calif, Vivian Hall Eng 602, Los Angeles, CA 90089. **Fax:** 213-740-7797.

KROGER, HANNS H, INORGANIC CHEMISTRY, ELECTROCHEMISTRY. **Personal Data:** b Hamburg, Ger, September 25, 1926; American citizen; m 1959, c 2. **Education:** Univ Hamburg, Cand, 1953, Dipl, 1956, Dr rer nat (chem, mineral), 1958. **Professional Experience:** ELECTROCHEMIST, BATTERY BUS SECT, EVERREADY CO, FLA, 1965-; electrochemist, NY, 1962-1965; chemist, Accumulatorenfabrik AG, Ger, 1959-1961; Sci asst chem, Univ Hamburg, 1956-1959. **Memberships:** Am Chem Soc. **Research Statement & Publications:** Battery technology; analytical chemistry. **Mailing Address:** 3841 Second Ave, Gainesville, FL 32607.

KROGER, HARRY, SOLID STATE ELECTRONICS, EXPERIMENTAL SOLID STATE PHYSICS. **Personal Data:** b Brooklyn, NY, August 13, 1936; m 1958, c 3. **Education:** Univ Rochester, BS, 1957; Cornell Univ, PhD (physics), 1962. **Professional Experience:** BARTLE PROF, BINGHAMTON UNIV, beginning 2004; mgr, Advan Device Dept, 1975-1992; MCC Echelon, Austin, 1975-1992; mgr, Semiconductor Device Dept, 1969-1975; group leader microwave semiconductors, Sperry Res Ctr, 1968-1969; Mem res staff, Sperry Res Ctr, 1962-1968. **Memberships:** Inst Elec & Electronics Engrs; Am Phys Soc. **Research Statement & Publications:** Soft x-ray spectroscopy; semiconductor memories; conduction through thin insulators; microwave semiconductor devices; Josephson devices. **Mailing Address:** Dept Elec Eng Comput, Watson Sch, Binghampton Univ, ENGB-Q12, Binghampton, NY 13902. **E-Mail:** hkroger@binghamton.edu

KROGER, HELMUT KARL, COMPUTATIONAL PHYSICS, LATTICE GAUZE THEORY. **Personal Data:** b Kassel, Ger, March 12, 1949. **Education:** Univ Mainz, WGer, dipl, 1973; Univ Bonn, PhD (physics), 1977. **Professional Experience:** PROF & RES PHYSICS, UNIV LAVAL, QUE, 1984-; fel Natural Sci & Eng Res Coun Can, 1983-; res assoc, Univ Laval, Que, 1982-1984; res staff, KWU Siemens Co, Erlanger, WGer, 1981-1982; res vis, Oak Ridge Nat Lab, 1979-1980; fel Ger Acad Exchange Serv, N Atlantic Treaty Orgn, 1979-1980; res assoc, Univ Giessen, WGer, 1977-1979 & 1980. **Memberships:** Am Phys Soc; Can Phys Soc; Inst Particle Physics. **Research Statement & Publications:** Nuclear physics; qual control data; gauge theories. **Mailing Address:** Dept Physics, Physics Genius & Optics, Univ Laval, Quebec, PQ G1K 7P4, Can. **Fax:** 418-656-2040. **E-Mail:** hkroger@phy.ulaval.ca

KROGER, LARRY A, NUCLEAR PHYSICS, MEDICAL PHYSICS. **Personal Data:** b Hastings, Nebr, December 6, 1943; m 1968, c 2. **Education:** Hastings Col, BA, 1966; Univ Wyo, PhD (physics), 1972. **Professional Experience:** SR REGULATORY PROG MGR, GE HEALTHCARE TECHNOL, as of 2006; HEALTH PHYSICIST, MED SYST DIV, GEN ELEC CO, 1978-; sr physicist, Emergency Care Res Inst, 1975-1978; res assoc, Univ Pa, 1973-1975; res assoc physics & NSF-Nat Res Coun fel, Nat Reactor Testing Sta, 1971-1973; lectr energy. **Memberships:** AAAS; Am Inst Physics; Am Asn Physicist Med; Sigma Xi; Am Phys Soc. **Research Statement & Publications:** Medical applications of x and gamma rays and performance of radiology systems; study of radioactivity and nuclear decay schemes; radiation safety. **Mailing Address:** GE Healthcare Technol, 3000 N Grandview W 400, Waukesha, WI 53188. **Fax:** 262-548-4768. **E-Mail:** larry.kroger@med.ge.com

KROGER, MANFRED, FOOD SCIENCE, SCIENCE COMMUNICATIONS. **Personal Data:** b Bad Oeynhausen, Ger, May 19, 1933; Canadian & American citizen; m 1962, Goldie Laris; c Hans, Erika & Stefan. **Education:** Univ Man, BSA, 1961; Pa State Univ, MS, 1963, PhD (food chem), 1966. **Honors & Awards:** Res Award, Int Dairy Foods Asn, 1994. **Professional Experience:** PROF EMER FOOD SCI, PA STATE UNIV, 1999-; PROF SCI TECHNOL & SOC, PA STATE UNIV, 1978-; from instr to assoc prof, PA State Univ, University Park, 1966-1978; Asst dairy sci, PA State Univ, University Park, 1961-1963; Tech ed dairy & other food jour; consult food indust; assoc ed, J Food Sci; co-ed, Nutrit Forum; food sci communicator, Inst Food Technologists. **Memberships:** Am Chem Soc; Am Dairy Sci; fel Inst Food Technologists; World Future Soc; Ger Dairy Sci Asn. **Research Statement & Publications:** Food flavor chemistry; pesticide residue analysis; chemistry of food contaminants; food safety; food laws and regulations; instrumental analysis of fat and protein in foods; milk processing; dairy products manufacture; yogurt quality; fermented milk. **Mailing Address:** Dept Food Sci, Pa State Univ, 104 Borland Lab, University Park, PA 16802. **Fax:** 814-8636132. **E-Mail:** kv7@psu.edu

KROGH, LESTERCHRISTENSEN, ORGANIC CHEMISTRY. **Personal Data:** b Ruskin, Nebr, August 22, 1925; m 1946, c 2. **Education:** Univ Nebr, BS, 1945, MS, 1948; Univ Minn, PhD (chem), 1952. **Honorary Degrees:** DSc, Univ Minn, 1990. **Honors & Awards:** Maurice Holland Award, Indust Res Inst, 1989; E B Barnes Award, Am Chem Soc, 1991. **Professional Experience:** RETIRED; chmn, Minn High Technol Coun, 1990-1991; sr vpres, res & develop, 3M, 1988-1990; vpres res & develop, Minn Mining & Mfg Co, 1982-1988; vpres, res & develop, Indust & Consumer Sector, 1981-1982; vpres, Com Chem Div, 1973-1981; exec dir, Cent Res Labs, 1970-1973; gen mgr, New Bus Ventures Div, 1969-1970; corp tech planning & coordr, Chem Res Lab, Cent Res Lab, 1965-1969; dir, Chem Res Lab, Cent Res Lab, 1964-1965; tech dir, Cent Res Lab, Minn Mining & Mfg Co, 1962-1964; asst tech dir, Cent Res Lab, Minn Mining & Mfg Co & Mgr Res Group, Abr Lab, 1960-1962; mgr res & develop group, Cent Res Lab, Minn Mining & Mfg Co & Mgr Res Group, Abr Lab, 1959-1960; sr chemist, Cent Res Lab, Minn Mining & Mfg Co, 1955-1959; asst, Univ Minn, 1948-1951; asst, Univ Nebr, 1946-1948; trustee, Univ Nebr Found; mem bd dirs, Indust Res Inst Inc. **Memberships:** Nat Acad Eng; fel AAAS; Am Chem Soc; Am Inst Chem Engrs. **Research Statement & Publications:** Preparation and reaction of polymers; fluorocarbons and the Michael reactions; coated abrasives; analysis of research projects; technology transfer; innovation in a large corporation. **Mailing Address:** 3570 Village Ct, Woodbury, MN 55125.

KROGH, THOMAS EDVARD, U-PB ISOTOPIC DATING, CRUSTAL EVOLUTION. **Personal Data:** b Peterborough, Ont, January 12, 1936; m 1961, Kathleen; c Erik, Kari, Sara & Jason. **Education:** Queen's Univ, Ont, BS, 1959, MS, 1961; Mass Inst Technol, PhD (isotope geol), 1964. **Honorary Degrees:** DSc, Queens Univ, 1991. **Honors & Awards:** Logan Medal, Geol Asn Can, 1989; J Tuzo Wilson Medal, Can Geophys Union, 1991; Past President's Medal, Mineral Asn Can, 1996. **Professional Experience:** PROF EMER, DEPT GEOL, UNIV TORONTO, as of 2006; fac, Dept Geol, Univ Toronto, as of 2004; dir, Geochronol Lab, Geol Dept, Royal Ont Mus, beginning 1975; mem sci staff, Dept Terrestrial Magnetism, Carnegie Inst, 1966-1975; fel, Dept Terrestrial Magnetism, Carnegie Inst, 1964-1966; fel, Carnegie Inst Dept Terrestrial Magnetism, 1964-1966. **Memberships:** Geol Asn Can; fel Am Geophys Union; Norweg Acad Sci & Lett. **Research Statement & Publications:** Isotope geology; use of isotopic variation in nature as natural tracers in geological processes; geochronology and genesis of rock systems; uranium-lead dating of zircon and low level lead isotopic analyses. **Mailing Address:** Dept Geol, Univ Toronto, Earth Sci Ctr, 22 Russell St, Toronto, ON M5S 3B1, Can. **Fax:** 416-586-5814. **E-Mail:** tomk@rom.on.ca

KROGMANN, DAVID WILLIAM, BIOCHEMISTRY. **Personal Data:** b Washington, DC, October 21, 1931; m 1958, Loretta; c 3. **Education:** Cath Univ Am, AB, 1953; Johns Hopkins Univ, PhD (biochem), 1957. **Professional Experience:** PROF EMER BIOCHEM, PURDUE UNIV, WEST LAFAYETTE, 1997-; prof, Purdue Univ, West Lafayette, 1967-1997; from asst prof to prof, Wayne State Univ, 1960-1967; res assoc, Univ Chicago, 1958-1960; fel biochem, Johns Hopkins Univ, 1957-1958. **Memberships:** Am Soc Biol Chemists; Am Soc Plant Physiol. **Research Statement & Publications:** Biological chemistry; biochemistry of electron transport and phosphate metabolism in photosynthesis; understanding of the photosynthetic mechanism in green plants by studying the structures of individual proteins and the interaction of these proteins in the photosynthetic membrane. **Mailing Address:** Dept Biochem, Purdue Univ, West Lafayette, IN 47907. **E-Mail:** krogmann@purdue.edu

KROGSTAD, BLANCHARD ORLANDO, INSECT ECOLOGY, INVERTEBRATE ECOLOGY. **Personal Data:** b Winger, Minn, October 6, 1921; m 1946, c 3. **Education:** Bemidji State Col, BA, 1946; Univ Minn, MA, 1948, PhD, 1951. **Professional Experience:** PROF EMER BIOL, UNIV MINN, DULUTH, as of 2004; head dept biol, Univ Minn, Duluth, beginning 1978; researcher, Mexican Inst Coffee, Xalapa, 1970-1971; prof biol, Univ Minn, Duluth, beginning 1963; mem staff, Rockefeller Found, Chapingo, Mex, 1963-1964; from asst prof to assoc prof, Univ Minn, Duluth, 1954-1963; asst prof biol, St Olaf Col, 1951-1954. **Memberships:** Ecol Soc Am; Entom Soc Am; Sigma Xi; Am Inst Biol Sci. **Research Statement & Publications:** Ecology of insects and other invertebrates. **Mailing Address:** Dept Biol, Univ Minn, Life Sci 221 1110 Kirby Dr, Duluth, MN 55812-3003. **Fax:** 218-726-8142.

KROGSTAD, DONALD JOHN, MEDICINE, BIOLOGY. **Personal Data:** b New York, NY, February 18, 1943; m 1965, c 2. **Education:** Bowdoin Col, AB, 1965; Harvard Med Sch, MD, 1969. **Honors & Awards:** Burroughs-Wellcome New Initiatives, Malaria Research, Award, 1996-1998. **Professional Experience:** HENDERSON PROF CHAIR, TROPICAL MED TULANE SCH PUB HEALTH & TROP MED, as of 2006; DIR CTR INFECTIOUS DIS, TULANE UNIV, 1998-; HENDERSON PROF TROPICAL MED, TULANE UNIV, 1994-; CHMN TROPICAL MED, TULANE UNIV, 1992-; dir, Microbiol Lab, Barnes Hosp, St Louis, beginning 1978; consult, Jewish Hosp, St Louis, 1978-; asst prof med & path, Sch Med, Wash Univ, 1978; clin & res fel med, Mass Gen Hosp, Boston, 1976-1978; lectr physiol & med, Med Asst Training Sch, Lilongue, Malawi, 1973-1975; physician, Lilongue Gen Hosp, 1973-1975; epidemic intel serv officer, Parasitic Dis Div & Parasitic Dis Drug Serv, Ctr Dis Control, Ga, 1971-1973; from asst resident to sr resident, Mass Gen Hosp, Boston, 1970-1976; intern, Mass Gen Hosp, Boston, 1969-1970. **Memberships:** Am Soc Microbiol; Am Soc Trop Med & Hyg; Am Col Physicians; Am Asn Pathologists; Am Col Epidemiol; Sci Prog Chair; Am Soc Tropical Med & Hyg; Am Soc Tropical Med & Hyg, (counr, pres elect & pres, 1989-1992, secy, 2000-2006). **Research Statement & Publications:** Mechanisms of drug resistance; pathogenicity; epidemiology of nosocomial infection. **Mailing Address:** Dept Tropical Med, Tulane Univ Sch Pub Health & Tropical Med, 1440 Canal St Ste 2210, New Orleans, LA 70112. **Fax:** 504-988-6686. **E-Mail:** krogstad@tulane.edu

KROH, GLENN CLINTON, PLANT ECOLOGY. **Personal Data:** b Philadelphia, Pa, December 20, 1941; m 1967, c 1. **Education:** Pa State Univ, BS, 1966, MS, 1970; Mich State Univ, PhD (plant ecol), 1975. **Professional Experience:** ASSOC PROF BIOL, TEX CHRISTIAN UNIV, as of 2004; asst prof biol, Tex Christian Univ, beginning 1975. **Memberships:** Ecol Soc Am; Am Inst Biol Sci; AAAS. **Research Statement & Publications:** The effects of intra and interspecific competition on the strategies of annual herbs with regard to how they partition available resources into roots, shoots and reproductive tissue. **Mailing Address:** Dept Biol, Tex Christian Univ, TCU Box 298930, Ft Worth, TX 76129. **Fax:** 817-257-6177. **E-Mail:** g.kroh@tcu.edu

KROHN, BURTON JAY, MOLECULAR PHYSICS. **Personal Data:** b St Louis, Mo, February 25, 1941; m 1967, Susan; c 2. **Education:** Vanderbilt Univ, BA, 1964; Ohio State Univ, MS, 1966, PhD (physics), 1971. **Professional Experience:** STAFF MEM MOLECULAR PHYSICS, THEORET DIV, LOS ALAMOS NAT LAB, 1974-; res assoc infrared spectros, Fla State Univ, 1973-1974; fel chem physics, Battelle Mem Inst, 1971-1972. **Memberships:** Am Phys Soc. **Research Statement & Publications:** Quantum-mechanical theory; modeling and computations of energies and properties of vibrating, rotating polyatomic molecules; analysis of positions of absorption lines and band- and line-intensities in high-resolution infrared spectra. **Mailing Address:** Los Alamos Nat Lab, PO Box 1663, Los Alamos, NM 87544. **Fax:** 505-665-4251. **E-Mail:** krohn@lanl.gov

KROHN, JOHN LESLIE, INSTRUMENTAL NEUTRON ACTIVATION ANALYSIS, NEUTRON SPECTRAL CHARACTERIZATION. **Personal Data:** b Clarksville, Ark, December 7, 1958; c 2. **Education:** Univ Ark, BS, 1981, MS, 1983; Tex A&M Univ, PhD (nuclear eng), 1992. **Professional Experience:** CHMN & ASSOC PROF, DEPT MECH ENG, ARK TECH UNIV, 2001-; asst dir, Nuclear Sci Ctr, 1988-1991; RADIATION SAFETY OFFICER, AAE/BCS TRADERS INC, 1986-; mgr reactor opers, Tex A&M Univ, 1986-1988; eng res assoc, Nuclear Sci Ctr, Tex Eng Exp Sta, 1984-1986; grad asst basic nuclear eng, Mech Eng Dept, Univ Ark, 1981-1983. **Memberships:** Am Nuclear Soc; Am Soc Testing & Mat. **Research Statement & Publications:** Instrumental neutron activation analysis; prompt gamma neutron activation analysis; characterization of neutron energy spectra and damage to electronic components by fast neutrons. **Mailing Address:** Dept Mech Eng, Ark Tech Univ, CES 104, Russellville, AR 72801. **Fax:** 479-964-0882. **E-Mail:** john.krohn@mail.atu.edu

KROHN, KENNETH ALBERT, NUCLEAR CHEMISTRY, RADIOPHARMACEUTICALS POSTRON EMISSION TOMOGRAPHY. **Personal Data:** b Stevens Point, Wis, June 19, 1945; div, c 1. **Education:** Andrews Univ, BA, 1966; Univ Calif, Davis, PhD (chem), 1971. **Honors & Awards:** fel, AAAS, 1992; paul c aebersold award, soc nuclear med, 1996. **Professional Experience:** PROF RADIOL & RADIATION ONCOL, SCH MED, UNIV WASH, SEATTLE, 1985-; Adjunt prof chem, 1986-; affiliate investr and assoc program head, Fred Hutchinson Cancer Res Cen, 1997- assoc prof, Sch Med, Univ Wash, Seattle, 1981-1985; assoc dir, Crocker Nuclear Lab, 1978-1980; Mem comt radiopharmaceut & radioassay, Am Col Nuclear Physicians, 1975-1978; from asst prof to assoc prof radiol, Sch Med, Univ Calif, Davis, 1973-1981; Instr radiation sci, Washington Univ, 1971-1973.

Memberships: Am Chem Soc; Soc Nuclear Med; Radiation Res Soc; AAAS; fel, Sigma Xi, Am Assoc Cancer Res, Am Soc Clinical Oncology. **Research Statement & Publications:** Application of isotopes to biological problems; development of new cyclotron produced radiopharmaceuticals for diagnostic procedures for cancer and heart disease; halogen and technetium chemistry and chemical effects of nuclear transformations. **Mailing Address:** Univ Wash Medical Center, Box 356004, Seattle, WA 98195-6004. **Fax:** 206-598-4192. **E-Mail:** kkrohn@u.washington.edu

KROL, GEORGE J, PHYSICAL CHEMISTRY, ANALYTICAL CHEMISTRY. **Personal Data:** b Wilno, Poland, June 6, 1936; American citizen; m 1962, c 3. **Education:** Univ Rochester, BS, 1958; Rutgers Univ, PhD (phys anal chem), 1968. **Professional Experience:** STAFF SCIENTIST, BAYER CORP, 1984-; supvr, Bayer Corp, 1978-1984; sect head, Ayerst Labs Inc, 1975-1978; sr res chemist, 1967-1975; res asst phys chem, Rutgers Univ, 1963-1967; chemist, Hoffmann-La Roche Inc, 1960-1962; res technician, Med Sch, Univ Rochester, 1958-1959. **Memberships:** Am Chem Soc; Am Asn Pharmaceut Scientists. **Research Statement & Publications:** Biochemistry; radiochemistry and kinetics; analytical method development, especially chromatography; drug metabolism and pharmacokinetic analysis. **Mailing Address:** Bayer Corp, 400 Morgan Lane, West Haven, CT 06516-4134.

KROLAK, JOHN MICHAEL, CLINICAL LABORATORY MEDICINE. **Personal Data:** b Kenmore, NY, February 1, 1953; m 1999, Brenda; c Julia E, John M Jr & Joy E. **Education:** Va Commonwealth Univ, BS (Biology), 1975, MS (Physiology), 1977; Okla State Univ, PhD (insect biochem), 1981. **Honors & Awards:** US Dept of Health and Human Services - Secretary's Award for Distinguished Service CDC/PHPPO 2001 Group Honor Award - Health Alert Network EOC Staff (September 11 events) CDC/PHPPO 2002 Group Award Certificate of Appreciation Certificates of Appreciation and Special Service Award - CDC and Prevention '95 Certificate of Appreciation - PHPPO, - CDC and Prevention '96 Certificate of Recognition for Sept 11, 2001 - CDC and Prevention 2001 International Who's Who in Science and Engineering Who's Who in Science and Engineering -1996 through 1999 Who's Who of Rising Young Americans Most Admired Men and Women of the Year - 1995 Men and Women of Science - 1995 Outstanding Young Men of America - 1985 NIH Postdoctoral Research Fellowship Award - National Institute of Arthritis, Diabetes, Digestive and Kidney Diseases, Diabetes Research Training Grant- 1982-1985 Gordon Research Conference on Cancer Sigma Xi Membership/Grant - Oklahoma State University Chapter Outstanding Graduate Student, Oklahoma State University. **Professional Experience:** SUPVRY HEALTH SCIENTIST, CTRS DIS CONTROL & PREVENT, NAT INST OCCUP SAFETY & HEALTH, 1993-; health scientist, Ctrs Dis Control & Prevent, Nat Inst Occup Safety & Health, 2006- Instructor of Biology, Georgia Perimeter College, 1992-1993; dir clin chem, Epidemiol Res Div, 1989-1992; dir clin & forensic toxicol, Epidemiol Res Div, 1989-1992; adj fac, Dept Pathol, Uniformed Serv, Univ Health Sci, 1986-1988; res biochemist, Armed Forces Radiobiol Res Inst, USAF, 1985-1989; NIH res fel, Univ Tex Med Sch, 1981-1985. **Memberships:** Soc Toxicol; Sigma Xi; AAAS; Entom Soc Am; Am Soc Cell Biol. **Research Statement & Publications:** Evaluation of clinical and public health laboratory standards and practices; evaluate information contained in national databases with the objective of identifying and defining clinical and public health laboratory managerial and technical problems; evaluation of scientific data as it relates to performance and practices of clinical and public health laboratory systems; design and implementation of scientific studies to assess the quality of laboratory testing in the Nation's laboratories; develop intervention strategies for improving the quality of laboratory testing and develops technically and scientifically valid plans for evaluating the changes and improvements in clinical outcomes associated with implementing improvements in testing. **Mailing Address:** Div Public Health Partnerships, MS G-23, 4770 Buford Hwy NE, Atlanta, GA 30341. **Fax:** 770-488-8275. **E-Mail:** jyk8@cdc.gov

KROLAK, PATRICK D, MANUFACTURING TECHNOLOGY. **Education:** Univ Chicago, BS; Wash Univ, MA, DSc. **Professional Experience:** PROF EMER, DEPT COMPUT SCI, UNIV MASS, LOWELL, as of 2005. **Mailing Address:** Univ Mass Lowell, One Univ Ave, Lowell, MA 01854. **Fax:** 978-934-4085. **E-Mail:** pat@cpe.uml.edu

KROLEWSKI, ANDRZEJ, GENETICS. **Education:** Warsaw Med Univ, PhD. **Professional Experience:** INVESTR, JOSLIN DIABETES CTR, as of 2005; ASSOC PROF MED, HARVARD MED SCH, as of 2005; HEAD, GENETICS & EPIDEMIOL, JOSLIN DIABETES CTR, as of 2004. **Mailing Address:** Res Div Joslin Diabetes Ctr, One Joslin Pl, Boston, MA 02215. **Fax:** 617-732-2667. **E-Mail:** andrzej.krolewski@joslin.harvard.edu

KROLICK, KEITH A, IMMUNOLOGY. **Personal Data:** b Chicago, Ill, May 21, 1951. **Education:** Univ Calif, Los Angeles, PhD (microbiol). **Professional Experience:** PROF MICROBIOL & IMMUNOL, UNIV TEX, 1992-. **Research Statement & Publications:** Immunology. **Mailing Address:** Dept Microbiol, Univ Tex Health Sci Ctr, 7703 Floyd Curl Dr, San Antonio, TX 78284-7758. **Fax:** 210-567-6451. **E-Mail:** krolick@uthscsa.edu

KROLIK, JULIAN H, THEORETICAL ASTROPHYSICS. **Personal Data:** b Detroit, Mich, April 4, 1950; m 1983, Elaine; c Theodore & Abigail. **Education:** Mass Inst Technol, BS, 1971; Univ Calif, Berkeley, PhD (physics), 1977. **Professional Experience:** Sackler distinguished visiting astronr, Inst Astron, Cambridge Univ, 2004; PROF PHYSICS & ASTRON, JOHNS HOPKINS UNIV, 1991-; from asst prof to assoc prof, Johns Hopkins Univ, 1984-1991; vis prof, Col France, 1984; res assoc, Smithsonian Ctr Astrophys, Harvard Univ, 1981-1984; lectr, Dept Astron, Harvard Univ, 1981-1984; scientist, Ctr Theoret Physics & Space Res, Mass Inst Technol, 1979-1981; mem, Inst Advan Study, 1977-1979. **Memberships:** Am Astron Soc. **Research Statement & Publications:** Theory of active galactic nuclei and related topics in high-energy astrophysics. **Mailing Address:** Dept Physics & Astron, Johns Hopkins Univ, Baltimore, MD 21218. **Fax:** 410-516-5096. **E-Mail:** jhk@pha.jhu.edu

KROLL, BERNARD HILTON, statistics, systems science; deceased, see previous edition for last biography

KROLL, HARRY, ELECTROLESS GOLD DEPOSITION, BRIGHT TIN LEAD ELECTROPLATING. **Personal Data:** b Chicago, Ill, November 28, 1914; m 1945, c 3. **Education:** Univ Ill, BS, 1938, Univ Chicago, PhD (org chem), 1942. **Professional Experience:** SR SCIENTIST, TECHNIC INC, 1983-; Adj prof, Univ RI, 1974-1975; res dir & vpres, Philip A Hunt Chem Corp, 1964-1982; prin investr, US Atomic Energy Comt, 1958-1964; res dir, Geigy Chem Corp, 1951-1958; prin investr, Am Cancer Soc, Yale Univ, 1951-1958; Chemist, Alrose chem co, Cranston, RI, 1942-1949. **Memberships:** Am Chem Soc. **Research Statement & Publications:** Chelating afents, photo resist and metal deposition. **Mailing Address:** 945 Main St Apt 7c, E Greenwich, RI 02818.

KROLL, JOHN ERNEST, FLUID DYNAMICS, PHYSICAL OCEANOGRAPHY. **Personal Data:** b Los Angeles, Calif, August 15, 1940; m 1973, c 3. **Education:** Univ Calif, Los Angeles, BS, 1963, MS, 1966; Yale Univ, PhD (eng & appl sci), 1973. **Professional Experience:** Sr Res Assoc, Nat Res Coun Dept Oceanog, Naval Postgrad Sch, Monterey, Calif, 1985-1986; ASSOC PROF APPL MATH, OLD DOMINION UNIV, 1981-; asst prof, Old Dominion Univ, 1976-1980; instr, Mass Inst Technol, 1975-1976; Res fel phys oceanog, Nova Oceanog Lab, 1972-1975. **Memberships:** Soc Indust & Appl Math; Am Geophys Union; Am Sci Affil. **Research Statement & Publications:** Investigate simple paleoclimate models and other applied mathematical modeling. **Mailing Address:** Dept Math, Old Dominion Univ Bal 500 Hampton Blvd, Norfolk, VA 23529-0077. **E-Mail:** jkroll@odu.edu

KROLL, MARTIN HARRIS, CLINICAL CHEMISTRY, CLINICAL PATHOLOGY. **Personal Data:** b Washington, DC, June 19, 1952; m 1975, Ellen; c Allison, Jonathan & Lauren. **Education:** Univ Md, Col Park, BS, 1974; Univ Sch Med, MD, 1978. **Honors & Awards:** Young Investr, Acad Clin Lab Physicians & Scientists, 1983; Past Chmn Award, Capital Sect, Am Asn Clin Chem, 1990; Roe Award, Capital Sect, Am Asn Clin Chem, 1995. **Professional Experience:** DIR CLIN CHEM, VET AFFAIRS N TEX HEALTH CARE SYST, DALLAS, 1999-; PROF PATH, UNIV TEX S WESTERN MED CTR, DALLAS, 2005-; assoc prof, 1999-2005; assoc prof, dept path, sch med, Johns Hopkins Univ, 1994-1999; assoc dir, clin chem div, Johns Hopkins Hosp, 1994-1999; med staff, Clin Chem Serv, Clin Path Dept, 1984-1994; fel clin chem, NIH, 1982-1984; Resident, path, Univ Md Hosp, 1978-1982; Fel, NSF Summer Res, 1973. **Memberships:** Am Asn Clin Chem; Am Chem Soc; Col Am Pathologists; Soc Math Biol; Amer Soc Clin Pathology; Amer Assoc Adv Science. **Research Statement & Publications:** Clinical chemistry; clinical pathology of cardiovascular disease; dynamics of biological systems; systems biology and integrative systems; the study of complex systems; modeling post-analytical interpretations in clinical pathology. **Mailing Address:** Dept Path VA Med Ctr & UTSW, 4500 Lancaster Rd, 113, Dallas, TX 75216. **Fax:** 214-857-0739. **E-Mail:** martin.kroll@med.va.gov

KROLL, NORMAN MYLES, mathematical, theoretical, physics; deceased, see previous edition for last biography

KROM, MELVEN R, MATHEMATICS. **Personal Data:** b Hospers, Iowa, October 4, 1931; m 1953. **Education:** Univ Iowa, BA, 1954, MS, 1957; Univ Mich, PhD (math), 1963. **Professional Experience:** PORF EMER MATH, UNIV CALIF, DAVIS, as of 2001; assoc prof, Univ Calif, Davis, 1969-1976; asst prof, Univ Calif, Davis, 1963-1969. **Memberships:** Asn Symbolic Logic; Math Asn Am; Am Math Soc. **Research Statement & Publications:** Mathematical logic. **Mailing Address:** Dept Math, Univ Calif, Davis, CA 95616-5224.

KROMAN, RONALD AVRON, GENETICS. **Personal Data:** b Minneapolis, Minn, March 30, 1927; m 1962, c 3. **Education:** Univ Minn, PhD (zool), 1957. **Professional Experience:** PROF EMER, CALIF STATE UNIV, LONG BEACH, 1990-; Adj prof, Chapman Col, 1975-; from asst prof to prof, Calif State Univ, Long Beach, 1959-1990; statist consult, Arthritis Found, Mem Hosp, Long Beach, Calif; Consult revision jr high & high sch math curricula, Sch Math Study Group & Calif State Dept Educ. **Memberships:** Sigma Xi. **Research Statement & Publications:** Soc Study Evolution; Am Genetic Asn; Genetics Soc Am; Am Inst Biol Sci; Sigma Xi. Res: Drosophila genetics; tumors; melanin metabolism; eye pigmentation; symbiotic associations in the Acarina. **Mailing Address:** Dept Biol, Calif State Univ, Long Beach, CA 90840-0001.

KROMANN, PAUL ROGER, PHYSICAL CHEMISTRY. **Personal Data:** b Racine, Wis, November 15, 1929; m 1960. **Education:** Hope Col, AB, 1952; Univ Calif, PhD, 1957. **Professional Experience:** ASST PROF CHEM, FT VALLEY STATE COL, 1971-; chemist, Plastics Fundamental Res Lab, Dow Chem USA, Mich, 1957-1971; asst chem, Univ Calif, 1952-1955; Chemist org synthesis, Hope Col, 1952. **Memberships:** Am Chem Soc. **Research Statement & Publications:** Radiation chemistry; photochemistry; fluorescence lifetimes. **Mailing Address:** PO Box 6317, Warner Robins, GA 31095.

KROMANN, RODNEY P, animal nutrition, bioenergetics; deceased, see previous edition for last biography

KROMBEIN, KARL VON VORSE, entomology; deceased, see previous edition for last biography

KROMER, LAWRENCE FREDERICK, NEUROBIOLOGY, NEURAL REGENERATION. **Personal Data:** b Sandusky, Ohio, September 1, 1950. **Education:** Univ Chicago, BA, 1972, PhD (anat), 1977. **Professional Experience:** ASSOC PROF, NEUROSCIENCE, GEORGETOWN UNIV, as of 2003; Georgetown Univ, beginning 1985; asst prof, dept Anat & Neurobiology, Univ Vt, beginning 1981; fel, A P Sloan Found, 1980-1986; prin investr, pvt found res grants, NIH, beginning 1979; asst res neuroscientist, Univ Calif, San Diego, 1979-1981; fel, dept Histol, Univ Lung, Sweden, 1977-1979. **Memberships:** Soc Neuroscience; Int Soc Develop Neuroscience; Am Asn Anatomists; AAAS. **Research Statement & Publications:** Development and regeneration in the mammalian central nervous system by utilizing and intracephalic implantation technique which allows the transplantation of embryonic and neonatal neural tissue into the brain of neonatal and adult rodents. **Mailing Address:** Dept NeuroSci, Med Ctr, Georgetown Univ, 3900 Reservoir Rd NW, Washington, DC 20007-2197. **Fax:** 202-687-0617. **E-Mail:** kromerl@georgetown.edu

KROMHOUT, ROBERT ANDREW, CHEMICAL PHYSICS. **Personal Data:** b Elgin, Ill, October 23, 1923; m 1950, Ora; c Sharon, Bian & Ethan. **Education:** Kans State Univ, BS, 1947; Univ Ill, Urbana-Champaign, MS, 1948, PhD (physics), 1952. **Professional Experience:** EMER PROF PHYSICS, FLA STATE UNIV, 1992-; head dept, Fla State Univ, 1960-1962; from asst prof to prof, Fla State Univ, 1956-1992; asst prof physics, Univ Ill, 1952-1956. **Memberships:** Am Phys Soc; Am Asn Physics Teachers; Sigma Xi. **Research Statement & Publications:** Phase transitions; statistical mechanics; intermolecular forces; Van der Waal's interactions, phase transitions, statistical mechanisms. **Mailing Address:** Dept Physics Fla State Univ, Fla State Univ, Tallahassee, FL 32306-4350. **Fax:** 850-644-8630. **E-Mail:** nkromhou@mailer.fsu.edu

KROMM, DAVID ELWYN, WATER MANAGEMENT IN NORTH AMERICAN HIGH PLAINS. **Personal Data:** b Grosse Pointe, Mich, September 1, 1938; m 1960, Roberta; c David, Randall & Christopher. **Education:** Eastern Mich Univ, BS, 1960; Mich State Univ, MA, 1964, PhD (geog), 1967. **Honors & Awards:** John Frasser Hart Award for Res Excellence, Asn Am Geogr, 1997. **Professional Experience:** RETIRED; vis prof, Lethbridge Univ, 1990; Happold vis prof, Univ Nebr, 1983; prof geog, Kans State Univ, 1967-2002. **Memberships:** Nat Coun Geog Educ; Asn Am Geogrs; Am Water Resources Asn; Am Asn Advan Slavic Studies. **Research Statement & Publications:** Examine response to ogaliala aquifer depletion; Response to groundwater depletion in the Am high plains and water-use in semi-arid areas of North Am. **Mailing Address:** Geog Dept, Kans State Univ 201 Dickens Hall, Manhattan, KS 66506-0801. **Fax:** 785-532-7310. **E-Mail:** krommgeo@ksuvm.ksu.edu

KROMMINGA, ALBION JEROME, THEORETICAL PHYSICS. **Personal Data:** b Mille Lacs Co, Minn, June 20, 1933; div, c 2. **Education:** St Cloud State Col, BS, 1955; Univ

Minn, PhD (physics), 1961. **Professional Experience:** PROF EMER PHYSICS, CALVIN COL, as of 2004; prof physics, Calvin Col, beginning 1969; assoc prof, Calvin Col, 1965-1969; asst prof physics, Idaho State Univ, 1963-1965; asst prof physics, Iowa State Univ, 1961-1963. **Memberships:** Am Phys Soc; Sigma Xi; Am Sci Affil. **Research Statement & Publications:** Theory of electromagnetic, atomic, and nuclear reactions. **Mailing Address:** Dept Physics, Calvin Col, 3201 Burton SE, Grand Rapids, MI 49546.

KRON, GERALD EDWARD, ASTRONOMY. **Personal Data:** b Milwaukee, Wis, April 6, 1913; m 1946, c 5. **Education:** Univ Wis, BS, 1933, MS, 1934; Univ Calif, PhD (astrophys), 1938. **Professional Experience:** RETIRED; Pinecrest Observ, Hawaii, 1985-; astron res, Pinecrest Observ, Flagstaff, Ariz, 1976-1985; sr res fel, Australian Nat Univ, 1974-1976; dir, US Naval Observ, Flagstaff Sta, 1965-1973; astronr, Lick Observ, Univ Calif, 1952-1965; assoc astronr, Lick Observ, Univ Calif, 1947-1952; physicist, US Naval Ord Test Sta, Calif, 1945; asst astronr, Lick Observ, Univ Calif, 1942-1947; res assoc, Calif Inst Technol, 1942-1945; res assoc, Mass Inst Technol, 1940-1941; jr astronr, Lick Observ, Univ Calif, 1938-1942. **Memberships:** AAAS; Am Astron Soc; Int Astron Union; Royal Astron Soc. **Research Statement & Publications:** Electronic camera research and development; investigation of integrated properties of globular clusters; distribution of interstellar reddening. **Mailing Address:** 2929 Poni Moi Rd, Honolulu, HI 96815.

KRON, RICHARD G, ASTRONOMY. **Professional Experience:** PROF ASTRON & ASTROPHYS, UNIV CHICAGO, as of 2004; SCIENTIST, FERMI NAT ACCELERATOR LAB, as of 2003; DIR, SLOAN DIGITAL SKY SURVEY, as of 2003; dir, Yerkes Observ, as of 2002. **Research Statement & Publications:** Astrophysics; astronomy. **Mailing Address:** 415 Grand View Ave, Williams Bay, WI 53191.

KRONAUER, RICHARD ERNEST, MECHANICAL ENGINEERING, BIOMEDICAL PHYSICS. **Personal Data:** b Paterson, NJ, August 5, 1925; m 1948, Joanne Edwards; c 3. **Education:** Stevens Inst Technol, MechEng, 1947; Harvard Univ, SM, 1948, PhD, 1951. **Professional Experience:** Arthur D Little Co, Brigham & Women's Hosp, 1991-; Arthur D Little Co, 1960-1967 & Campbell-Kronauer Assoc, 1980-1995; NIH int fel, 1978; PROF MECH ENG, HARVARD UNIV, 1964-; NSF fel, 1964 & 1971; Consult, Baldwin-Lima-Hamilton Corp, 1956-1961; Consult, Flow Corp, 1953-1967; from instr to assoc prof, Harvard Univ, 1951-1964; Consult, Pratt & Whitney Aircraft Div, United Aircraft Corp, 1951-1958. **Memberships:** Am Soc Mech Engrs; AAAS; Sleep Res Soc; Sigma Xi. **Research Statement & Publications:** Fluid dynamics and turbulence; nonlinear oscillations; visual system information processing; human circadian oscillators. **Mailing Address:** 14 Chauncy St Unit 7, Cambridge, MA 02138. **Fax:** 781-995-9837. **E-Mail:** kronauer@deas.harvard.edu

KRONAUGE, JAMES F, RADIOLOGY. **Education:** Mass Inst Technol, PhD (inorg chem). **Professional Experience:** VPRES PROCESS CHEM, MOLECULAR INSIGHT PHARMACEUT, as of 2005. **Mailing Address:** Molecular Insight Pharmaceut Inc, 160 Second St, Cambridge, MA 02142.

KRONBERG, PHILIPP PAUL, RADIO ASTRONOMY, ASTROPHYSICS. **Personal Data:** b Toronto, Ont, September 16, 1939; m 1963, c 3. **Education:** Queen's Univ Kingston, BS, 1961, MSc, 1963; Univ Manchester, PhD (physics), 1967. **Honorary Degrees:** DSc, Univ Manchester, 1995. **Honors & Awards:** Humboldt Res Prize, 1990. **Professional Experience:** PROF EMER, PHYSICS & ASTRON, UNIV TORONTO, 1999-; Killam fel, 1993; Guggenheim fel, 1985; chmn, Nat Res Coun Millimetre Telescope Steering Comt, 1983-1984; vis comt, US Nat Radio Astron Observ, 1982; prof, phys sci & astron, Univ Toronto, 1978-1999; mem, Univ Toronto Res Bd, 1978-1982; mem & chmn, VLA Adv Comt, 1978-1982; Alexander von Humboldt sr res fel, Max-Planck-Inst fur Radioastronomie, Ger, 1975-1977 & 1990-1991; sr von Humboldt fel, 1975-1977; mem, grant selection comt, Univ Astron & Space Res Can, 1974-1978; ed, Assoc Comt Astron, Nat Res Coun Can, 1974; mem, Assoc Comt Astron, Nat Res Coun Can, 1971-1974; from asst prof to assoc prof, Univ Toronto, 1968-1978; lectr physics, Univ Manchester & Jodrell Bank, 1966-1968; chmn, Assoc Univ Inc. **Memberships:** Am Astron Soc; Int Astron Union; Can Astron Soc; Sigma Xi; Can Inst Int Affairs; Atlantic Coun Can. **Research Statement & Publications:** Measurement and analysis of magnetic fields in space; structure of our galaxy; extragalactic astrophysics; radioastronomy; high-energy processes in space. **Mailing Address:** Dept Astron, Univ Toronto, 60 St George St, Toronto, ON M5S 1A7, Can. **Fax:** 416-412-0201. **E-Mail:** kronberg@physics.utoronto.ca

KRONBERGER, KARLHEINZ, POLYMER CHEMISTRY, ORGANIC CHEMISTRY. **Personal Data:** b Vienna, Austria, January 24, 1940. **Education:** Vienna Tech Univ, Dipl Ing, 1964; Univ Nebr, PhD (org chem), 1967. **Professional Experience:** RES DEPT MGR, RES DIV, ROHM & HAAS CO, 1990-; res sect mgr, Res Div, Rohm & Haas CO, 1978-1990; sr res chemist, Res Div, Rohm & Haas CO, 1968-1978; res assoc, Mass Inst Technol, 1967-1968. **Memberships:** Am Chem Soc. **Research Statement & Publications:** Coatings and polymer research; aqueous polymers; acrylics. **Mailing Address:** Spring House Tech Ctr, Rohm & Haas Co, PO Box 904, Spring House, PA 19477. **Fax:** 215-641-7857.

KRONE, LESTER H(ERMAN), JR, MANAGEMENT SCIENCE. **Personal Data:** b St Louis, Mo, October 8, 1931; m 1953, c 3. **Education:** Wash Univ, BS, 1952, DSc(chem eng), 1955; Univ Ill, MS, 1953. **Professional Experience:** MGR PROD PLANNING & MKT, MCDONNELL-DOUGLAS AUTOMATION CO, 1973-; independent consult, 1968-1973; mgr oper anal, Monsanto Co, 1958-1968; mgr appl sci, Mo, 1957-1958; appl sci rep, Int Bus Mach Corp, 1956-1957; Group leader process develop dept, Uranium Div, Mallinckrodt Chem Works, 1955-1956; assoc prof, Southern Ill Univ; Lectr, Wash Univ. **Memberships:** Asn Comput Mach; Am Inst Chem Engrs; Opers Res Soc Am; Inst Mgt Sci. **Research Statement & Publications:** Applied mathematics; computer techniques; operations research; mathematical programming, statistics and simulation. **Mailing Address:** 749 Chatelet Woods Dr, St Louis, MO 63135.

KRONE, RALPH WERNER, NUCLEAR PHYSICS. **Personal Data:** b Berlin, Ger, May 18, 1919; American citizen; m 1942, c 3. **Education:** Antioch Col, BS, 1942; Univ Ill, MS, 1943; Johns Hopkins Univ, PhD, 1949. **Professional Experience:** PROF EMER, DEPT PHYSICS & ASTRON, UNIV KANS, as of 2005; prof physics & astron, Univ Kans, beginning 1982; actg chmn dept, Univ Kans, 1965-1966; prof physics, Univ Kans, 1961-1982; from asst prof to assoc prof, Univ Kans, 1948-1961. **Memberships:** Fel Am Phys Soc. **Research Statement & Publications:** Nuclear structure; spectroscopy of light and medium light nuclei. **Mailing Address:** Dept Physics & Astron, Univ Kans, 1251 Wescoe Hall Dr Rm 1082, Lawrence, KS 66045-7582.

KRONEBERGER, GERALD F, COMBUSTION & EMISSIONS, ENERGY EFFICIENCY. **Personal Data:** b Chicago, Ill, September 7, 1929; m 1957, Kathryn; c Diane, Cris & Kevin. **Education:** Ill Tech, BS, 1951; Pepperdine Univ, MBA, 1979. **Professional Experience:** Expert witness serv, AAA/CSI, 1985-; OWNER, AAA/CSI, 1984-; ed, Nat Symposia Ser, 1976; nat bd dirs & nat chmn, Environ Div, Am Inst Chem Eng, 1974-1976; tech dir, BSP/ENVIRTECH/LURGI, 1964-1984; regional mgr, GATX, 1953-1964; sci & prof, Personnel Prog, USA/CC, 1951-1953. **Memberships:** Fel Am Inst Chem Eng; Am Acad Environ Engrs; Water & Environ Fedn. **Research Statement & Publications:** Extensive publications in thermal and combustion processes as well as environmental and reclamation processes; energy recovery and storage system; forensic expert services; awarded US and foreign patents. **Mailing Address:** AAA CSI, PO Box 5067, Novato, CA 94948. **Fax:** 415-382-9241.

KRONENBERG, AMY, MOLECULAR BIOLOGY. **Education:** Harvard Sch Pub Health, DSc (Cancer Biol). **Professional Experience:** STAFF SCIENTIST, LIFE SCI DIV, LAWRENCE BERKELEY NAT LAB, as of 2006. **Research Statement & Publications:** Dissect genetic pathways that modify the carcinogenic process. **Mailing Address:** Life sci Div, Lawrence Berkeley Lab, One Cyclotron Rd Mailstop 70A 1118, Berkeley, CA 94720. **Fax:** 510-486-4475. **E-Mail:** A_Kronenberg@lbl.gov

KRONENBERG, FREDI, IMMUNOLOGY, NEUROBIOLOGY. **Education:** Cornell Univ, BS; Stanford Univ (physiol & behav), PhD. **Professional Experience:** PROF CLIN BIOL, COLUMBIA UNIV, as of 2006; DIR, THE RICHARD & HINDA ROSENTHAL CTR, as of 2006. **Mailing Address:** The Richard & Hinda Rosenthal Ctr, 630 W 168th St Box 75, New York, NY 10032. **Fax:** 212-342-0100. **E-Mail:** fk11@columbia.edu

KRONENBERG, RICHARD SAMUEL, MEDICINE, PHYSIOLOGY. **Personal Data:** b Chicago, Ill, August 7, 1938; m 1963, c 3. **Education:** Northwestern Univ, BA, 1960, MD, 1963. **Professional Experience:** PHYSICIAN PULMONARY, TRINITY CLINIC-DOUGLAS, as of 2006; exec vpres, Clin Affairs, Univ Tex Health Ctr, 1995-2002; exec assoc dir, Clin Affairs, Univ Tex Health Ctr, 1994-1995; prof & chmn, Dept Med, 1984-1995; prof med & head, Pulmonary Div, Univ Minn Hosp, 1978-1984; assoc prof, Pulmonary Div, Univ Minn Hosp, 1974-1978; consult, Vet Admin Hosp, Minneapolis, 1971-1984; asst prof, Pulmonary Div, Univ Minn Hosp, 1970-1974; USPHS res fel, Cardiovasc Res Inst, Med Ctr, Univ Calif, San Francisco, 1968-1970. **Memberships:** AAAS; Am Physiol Soc; fel Am Col Physicians; Am Fedn Clin Res; Am Thoracic Soc. **Research Statement & Publications:** Repiratory physiology; pulmonary disease. **Mailing Address:** Trinity Clin-Douglas, 520 E Douglas, Tyler, TX 75708-3154.

KRONENTHAL, RICHARD LEONARD, POLYMER CHEMISTRY, SURGICAL DEVICES. **Personal Data:** b New York, NY, October 6, 1928; m 1949, c 2. **Education:** Brooklyn Col, BS, 1951; Polytech Inst New York, PhD (chem). 1955. **Professional Experience:** PRES, KRONENTHAL ASSOCS, INC, 1989-; dir res & develop, Ethicon, Inc, Johnson & Johnson, 1984-1989; dir res, Ethicon, Inc, Johnson & Johnson, 1972-1984; assoc dir res, Ethicon, Inc, Johnson & Johnson, 1968-1972; Instr, Polytech Inst New York, 1958-1964; mgr dept org & polymer chem, Ethicon, Inc, Johnson & Johnson, 1957-1968; Sr proj chemist org chem, Colgate Palmolive Co, 1954-1957. **Memberships:** AAAS; Am Chem Soc; Am Soc Artificial Internal Organs; Am Inst Chem; Royal Soc Chem; Sigma Xi. **Research Statement & Publications:** Chemistry of proteins; surgical devices; biomaterials; biodegradable polymers. **Mailing Address:** Kronenthal Assoc Inc, 301 Rte 17 N Suite 800, Rutherford, NJ 07070.

KRONENWETT, FREDERICK RUDOLPH, BACTERIOLOGY. **Personal Data:** b Newark, NJ, July 29, 1923; m 1950, c 5. **Education:** Upsala Col, BSc, 1948; Rutgers Univ, MS, 1950, PhD (dairy bact), 1954. **Professional Experience:** Fel, Upsala Col, 1972-; expert adv, Int Atomic Energy Agency, Vienna, 1972; specialist microbiol, Am Soc Clin Pathologists, 1965; dir bioanal lab, NJ Bd Med Examr, 1959; consult, Bergen Pines Hosp, 1959; from instr to prof biol sci, Fairleigh Dickinson Univ, 1958-1989; Lectr, Upsala Col, 1958-1959; fel, Rutgers Univ, 1958; DIR, AM BIOL CONTROL LABS, 1957-; Dir qual control, Hohneker Dairy Co, 1954-1957; chmn Adv Panel Biol Indicators, US Pharmacopeia, mem, Steril Comt, US Pharmacopeia XVIII. **Memberships:** Am Soc Microbiol; Am Pub Health Asn; Inst Food Technologists; NY Acad Sci; Sigma Xi. **Research Statement & Publications:** Identification of thermophilic bacteria; thermal death time studies on Brucella abortus; food poisoning; general microbiology; sterilization and disinfection; irradiation microbiology and dosimetry; medical device development; water microbiology. **Mailing Address:** PO Box 505, Tenafly, NJ 07670.

KRONER, KLAUS E(RLENDUR), INDUSTRIAL ENGINEERING, ENGINEERING GRAPHICS. **Personal Data:** b Gottingen, Ger, July 19, 1926; American citizen; m 1959, c 2. **Education:** Col Wooster, BA, 1949; NY Univ, BEE, 1957; Am Int Col, MBA, 1962. **Honors & Awards:** Distinguished Serv Award, Graphics Div, Am Soc Eng Educ, 1985. **Professional Experience:** EMER PROF INDUST ENG & OPERS RES, UNIV MASS AMHERST, as of 2005; emer prof indust eng & opers res, Univ Mass Amherst, 1987; asst head, Univ Mass Amherst, 1981-1986; res scientist, indust develop div, Ga Inst Technol, 1971; assoc prof indust eng & opers res, Univ Mass Amherst, 1969-1988; from asst prof to assoc prof basic eng, Univ Mass Amherst, 1957-1969; instr eng graphics, Univ Maine, 1955-1957; instr eng drawing, NY Univ, 1950 & 1951-1955. **Memberships:** Am Soc Eng Educ. **Research Statement & Publications:** Computer graphics; engineering economy; plant location and layout; industrial development. **Mailing Address:** 30 Plumtree Rd, Leverett, MA 01054.

KRONFELD, DAVID SCHULTZ, NUTRITION, VETERINARY PHYSIOLOGY. **Personal Data:** b Auckland, NZ, November 5, 1928; m 1957, c 2. **Education:** Univ Queensland, BVSc, 1952, BSc, 1954, MVSc, 1957, DSc(biochem), 1972; Univ Calif, Davis, PhD (physiol), 1959; Am Col Vet Internal Med, dipl, 1973. **Honorary Degrees:** MA, Univ Pa, 1971. **Professional Experience:** PROF EMER NUTRIT, SCH VET MED, UNIV PA, as of 2002; PAUL MELLON DISTINGUISED PROF AGR & PROF VET MED, SCH VET MED, VA POLY TECH STATE UNIV, 1988-; chief sect nutrit, Sch Vet Med, Univ PA, 1981-1988; prof nutrit, Sch Vet Med, Univ PA, beginning 1967; from asst prof to assoc prof pharmacol, Sch Vet Med, Univ PA, 1960-1967; asst prof physiol, Univ Calif, Davis, 1959-1960; lectr vet med, Univ Calif, Davis, 1958-1959; lectr vet physiol, Univ Queensland, 1954-1957; demonstr physiol, Univ Queensland, 1953-1954. **Memberships:** Am Dairy Sci Asn; Am Physiol Soc; Am Vet Med Asn; Am Inst Nutrit. **Research Statement & Publications:** Nutrition and high performance of exercise, growth, pregnancy and lactation; metabolic disorders, ketosis, hypercholesterolemia, hypoglycemia, hypocalcemia, hypomagnesemia; tracer methodology, kinetic analysis, regulatory models; preventive medicine, health economics. **Mailing Address:** Dept Animal & Poultry Sci, Va Tech, 3460 Litton-Reaves Hall, Blacksburg, VA 24061-0306. **Fax:** 540-231-3010. **E-Mail:** kronfeld@vt.edu

KRONGELB, SOL, PHYSICS. **Personal Data:** b Jersey City, NJ, August 15, 1932; m 1953, Gladys; c Harold, Philip & Lisa. **Education:** NY Univ, BS, 1953; Mass Inst Technol, MS, 1955, PhD, 1958. **Professional Experience:** CONSULT, 1993-; mgr device fabrication & magnetics, Int Bus Mach Corp, 1986-1993; mem res staff, Int Bus Mach Corp, 1960-1993; assoc, Int Bus Mach Corp, 1958-1960; asst physics, res lab Electronics, Mass inst Technol, 1954-1958. **Memberships:** Am Vacuum Soc; Inst Elec & Electronics Engrs; Electrochem Soc. **Research Statement & Publications:** Microwave spectroscopy;

paramagnetic resonance; parametric devices; semiconductor technology; thin film adhesion; deposition and properties of magnetic and glass thin films; device fabrication technology. **Mailing Address:** Greenlawn Rd, Katonah, NY 10536.

KRONICK, PAUL LEONARD, SOLID-STATE PROPERTIES OF COLLAGEN, BIOMECHANICS OF SKIN. **Personal Data:** b North Adams, Mass, October 19, 1931. **Education:** Williams Col, AB, 1953; Yale Univ, PhD (chem), 1957. **Professional Experience:** LEAD SCIENTIST, AGR RES & ECONS SERV, USDA, 1982-; consult, FMC Corp, 1980-1982; prin investr, Benners Fund, 1978-1979; fel, EMBO, Norsk Hydro Inst Cancer Res, 1978; prin investr, Clamer Fund, 1977-1979; assoc med, Univ Pa, Med Sch, 1974-1979; prin investr, NIH, 1971-1981; vis lectr, Robert Wood Johnson Found, Univ Pa, 1971-1973; fel, NIH, 1971-1973; Fulbright res scholar, Norweg Radium Hosp, 1968-1969; prin scientist, Franklin Inst, 1960-1982; res chemist, E I Dupont Del Nemours Inc, 1958-1960. **Memberships:** emer mem Am Chem Soc; sr mem AAAS; sr mem Sigma Xi. **Research Statement & Publications:** Connective tissue biophysics and collagen-platelet interactions; applies basic biophysics to making useful products from animal connective tissue; magnetophoretic cell separation. **Mailing Address:** Eastern Regional Res Ctr, Arg Res Serv, USDA, 600 E Mermaid Lane, Wyndmoor, PA 19038-8598. **Fax:** 215-233-6749. **E-Mail:** pkronick@errc.ars.usda.gov

KRONK, HUDSON V, MATHEMATICS. **Personal Data:** b Port Jervis, NY, October 6, 1938; m 1959, c 3. **Education:** Rensselaer Polytech Inst, BS, 1959; Mich State Univ, MS, 1960, PhD (math), 1964. **Professional Experience:** ASSOC PROF EMER MATH, STATE UNIV NY, BINGHAMTON, as of 2004; assoc prof math, State Univ NY, Binghamton, beginning 1968; asst prof, State Univ NY, Binghamton, 1964-1968; lectr math, Kalamazoo Col, 1963. **Memberships:** Am Math Soc; Math Asn Am. **Research Statement & Publications:** Graph theory. **Mailing Address:** Dept Math, Binghamton Univ, PO Box 6000, Binghamton, NY 13902-6000. **Fax:** 607-777-2450. **E-Mail:** hud@math.binghamton.edu

KRONMAL, RICHARD AARON, BIOSTATISTICS. **Personal Data:** b Los Angeles, Calif, May 3, 1939; m 1960, c 3. **Education:** Univ Calif, Los Angeles, BA, 1961, PhD (biostatist), 1964. **Honors & Awards:** Career Develop Award, 1968-1973. **Professional Experience:** PROF BIOSTATIST, SCH PUB HEALTH, UNIV WASH, 1975-; chmn biomath group, Sch Pub Health, Univ Wash, 1973-1985; from instr to assoc prof, Sch Pub Health, Univ Wash, 1964-1975. **Memberships:** fel Am Statist Asn; Soc Study Human Biol; AAAS; Biomet Soc; Renal Cardiovasc Ad Comt, Food & Drug Admin; Epidemiol Study Sect, NIH. **Research Statement & Publications:** Mathematical statistics; statistical computing; public health and epidemiology. **Mailing Address:** Dept Biostatist, Univ Wash, PO Box 357232, Seattle, WA 98195. **E-Mail:** kronmal@biostat.washington.edu

KRONMAN, JOSEPH HENRY, ANATOMY, DENTISTRY. **Personal Data:** b New York, NY, April 4, 1931; m 1961, c 3. **Education:** NY Univ, BS, 1952, DDS, 1955; Columbia Univ, cert orthodont, 1959; Med Col Va, PhD (anat), 1962. **Professional Experience:** PROF ORTHODONT, SCH DENT MED, TUFTS UNIV, 1968-; dir growth & develop div, Sch Dent Med, 1968-1969; dir postdoctoral studies, Sch Dent Med, 1964-1970; asst to dean, Grad Sch Arts & Sci, 1964-1969; assoc prof orthodont, Sch Dent Med, Tufts Univ, 1962-1968; Instr anat, Med Col Va, 1961-1962. **Memberships:** Am Asn Orthodont; Am Asn Anatomists; Int Asn Dent Res; Int Soc Craniofacial Biol. **Research Statement & Publications:** Growth and development; caries; histochemistry; endocrinology; physiology of salivary glands. **Mailing Address:** Sch Dent Med, Tufts Univ, Boston, MA 02111.

KRONMAN, MARTIN JESSE, PHYSICAL CHEMISTRY. **Personal Data:** b New York, NY, September 30, 1927; m 1965, c 3. **Education:** Rutgers Univ, BS, 1950; Temple Univ, PhD, 1955. **Honors & Awards:** Chem of Milk Award, Am Chem Soc, 1968. **Professional Experience:** PROF BIOCHEM, STATE UNIV NY UPSTATE MED CTR, 1968-; head biochem lab, US Army Natick Labs, 1961-1968; phys chemist, Eastern Regional Res Lab, USDA, 1956-1961; Nat Heart Inst fel, Purdue Univ, 1955-1956. **Memberships:** AAAS; Am Chem Soc; Am Soc Biol Chemists. **Research Statement & Publications:** Physicochemical properties of proteins and nucleic acids; theory and technique of light scattering; optical rotation dispersion, absorption and emission spectra as applied to biological macromolecules; protein denaturation in enzyme action. **Mailing Address:** 100 Dewitt Rd, Syracuse, NY 13214-2005.

KRONQUIST, KATHRYN E, GENETICS. **Education:** Mich State Univ, PhD (biochem), 1975. **Professional Experience:** ASST PROF, CLIN PATH & LAB MED, UNIV COL HEALTH SCI CTR, as of 2005; TECH DIR, MOLECULAR DIAG LAB, UNIV COLO HOSP, as of 2005. **Mailing Address:** Clin Path & Lab Med Univ Colo Health Scis Ctr, 4200 E Ninth Ave Box A022, Denver, CO 80262. **Fax:** 303-372-0382. **E-Mail:** kathryn.kronquist@uchsc.edu

KRONSTEIN, KARL MARTIN, algebra; deceased, see previous edition for last biography

KRONTIRIS, THEODORE G, GENETICS. **Education:** Univ Chicago, SB, 1968; Albert Einstein Col Med, MD, PhD (cell biol), 1977. **Professional Experience:** DIR, CANCER CTR, CITY HOPE COMPREHENSIVE CANCER CTR, 2000-; EXEC VPRES, MED & SCI AFFAIRS, CITY HOPE COMPREHENSIVE CANCER CTR, 2000-; ASSOC DIR, PREV & CONTROL RES, CITY HOPE NAT MED CTR, 1999-; PROF MOLECULAR MED, BECKMAN RES INST, CITY HOPE NAT MED CTR, 1996-. **Mailing Address:** City Hope Nat Med Ctr & Beckman Res Inst, 1500 E Duarte Rd, Duarte, CA 91010-3000. **Fax:** 626-930-5394.

KRONTIRIS-LITOWITZ, JOHANNA KAYE, CARDIOVASCULAR FUNCTION, CARDIAC HYPERTROPHY. **Personal Data:** b Wheeling, WVa, June 7, 1952; m 1977, Harvey; c 3. **Education:** Case Western Res Univ, BS, 1974, MS, 1977; Cleveland State Univ, PhD (regulatory biol), 1983. **Honors & Awards:** Distinguished prof, Youngstown State Univ, 2002. **Professional Experience:** PROF, YOUNGSTOWN STATE UNIV, 2002-; assoc prof, Youngstown State Univ, 1993-2002; asst prof, Youngstown State Univ, 1988-1993; postdoctoral fel, Baylor Col Med, 1983-1985 & Univ Tex Med Ctr, Houston, 1985-1987. **Memberships:** Asn Women Sci; Am Physiol Soc. **Research Statement & Publications:** Regulation of cardiovascular function and stress-evoked humoral responses in molluses especially Aplysia Californica. **Mailing Address:** Dept Biol Sci, Youngstown State Univ, One Univ Plz Rm 3040, Youngstown, OH 44555-3601. **Fax:** 330-941-1483. **E-Mail:** jkrontirislitowitz@ysu.edu

KRONZON, ITZHAK, ECHOCARDIOGRAPHY, DOPPLER. **Personal Data:** b Haifa, Israel, September 14, 1939; American citizen; m 1960, c 3. **Education:** Hebrew Univ, MD, 1965; Am Col Physicians, dipl, 1979 & 1981. **Professional Experience:** PROF MED, NY UNIV, as of 2005; Hebrew Univ, Jerusalem, 1989-; vis prof, Tel Aviv Univ, 1987-; assoc prof, NY Univ, 1978-1983. **Memberships:** AMA; Am Heart Asn; Am Soc Echocardiography; fel Am Col Physicians; fel Am Col Cardiol; fel Am Col Chest Physicians. **Research Statement & Publications:** Clinical applications of computorized technologies in the non-invasive diagnosis and evaluation of heart diseases; hemodynamics; angiography; cardiac imaging; non-invasive cardiology. **Mailing Address:** NY Univ Med Ctr Two HW-228, 560 First Ave, New York, NY 10016. **Fax:** 212-263-8461. **E-Mail:** itzhak.kronzon@med.nyu.edu

KROODSMA, DONALD EUGENE, ANIMAL COMMUNICAION, BEHAVIORAL ECOLOGY. **Personal Data:** b Zeeland, Mich, July 7, 1946; m 1968, c 3. **Education:** Hope Col, BA, 1968; Ore State Univ, PhD (zoology), 1972. **Professional Experience:** PROF EMER ZOOLOGY, UNIV MASS, AMHERST, as of 2003; prof zoology, Univ Mass, Amherst, beginning 1987; assoc prof, Univ Mass, Amherst, 1980-1987; mem adv panel, psychobiol, NSF, 1980; prin investr, grants, 1976-; asst prof, animal behav, Rockefeller Univ, 1974-1980; fel, animal behav, Rockefeller Univ, 1972-1974. **Memberships:** Fel Am Ornithologists Union; fel Animal Behav Soc; Cooper Ornith Soc. **Research Statement & Publications:** Diversity of vocal behaviors among birds; development, evolution, and functions of these diverse vocal communication systems. **Mailing Address:** Dept Biol, Univ Mass, 221 Morrill Sci Ctr, Amherst, MA 01003. **Fax:** 413-545-3243. **E-Mail:** kroodsma@bio.umass.edu

KROODSMA, ROGER LEE, WILDLIFE ECOLOGY, ORNITHOLOGY. **Personal Data:** b Zeeland, Mich, January 23, 1944; div, c 3. **Education:** Hope Col, BA, 1966; ND State Univ, MS, 1968, PhD (zoology), 1970. **Professional Experience:** RETIRED; mem res staff, Environ Sci Div, Oak Ridge Nat Lab, beginning 1974; mgr environ impacts prog, Environ Sci Div, Oak Ridge Nat Lab, 1977-1979; res assoc ecol, Univ Ga, Athens, 1973-1974; asst prof biol, Union Univ, Jackson, Tenn, 1970-1973. **Memberships:** Wildlife Soc; Am Ornithologists Union. **Research Statement & Publications:** Community ecology of birds in man-affected habitats, such as transmission line rights-of-way and pine plantations; edge effect. **Mailing Address:** 700 White Oak Cir, Morristown, TN 37814.

KROOK, LENNART PER, VETERINARY PATHOLOGY. **Personal Data:** b Eksh-rad, Sweden, August 28, 1924; m 1958, c 2. **Education:** Royal Vet Col Sweden, DVM, 1953, PhD (vet path), 1957. **Professional Experience:** PROF EMER VET PATH, COL VET MED, CORNELL UNIV, as of 2005; assoc dean postdoctoral educ, Ny state Col Vet Med, Cornell Univ, beginning 1981; prof vet path, Ny state Col Vet Med, Cornell Univ, beginning 1965; assoc prof, NY State Col Vet Med, Cornell Univ, 1959-1965; assoc prof, Sch Vet Med, Kans State Univ, 1958-1959; assoc prof, Res Inst Nat Defense, Sundbyberg, 1958; from asst prof to assoc prof vet path, Royal Vet Col Sweden, 1951-1957. **Memberships:** Am Inst Nutrit; Int Acad Path; Sigma Xi. **Research Statement & Publications:** Nutritional pathology. **Mailing Address:** Dept Path, Cornell Univ, Ithaca, NY 14853-6401.

KROON, JAMES LEE, SCIENCE EDUCATION. **Personal Data:** b Grand Rapids, Mich, April 24, 1926; m 1952, c 3. **Education:** Calvin Col, AB, 1948; Purdue Univ, MS, 1951, PhD (chem), 1954. **Professional Experience:** PROF EMER CHEM, BETHEL COL, as of 2001; prof chem, Bethel Col, beginning 1979; assoc prof, Bethel Col, 1969-1979; proj leader, Dow Chem Co, 1958-1969; chemist, Dow Chem Co, 1953-1958; asst, Purdue Univ, 1948-1951. **Memberships:** Am Chem Soc; Sigma Xi; Am Sci Affiliation. **Research Statement & Publications:** Polarography; electrochemistry; aerosols. **Mailing Address:** Dept Chem, Bethel Col, 1001 W McKinley Ave, Mishawaka, IN 46545.

KROON, PAULUS ARIE, PHYSICAL BIOCHEMISTRY. **Personal Data:** b Rotterdam, Neth, June 1, 1945; American citizen; m 1968, Ferguson; c Lisa, Natasha & Joanna. **Education:** Univ Auckland, BS, 1967, MS, 1968; Calif Inst Technol, PhD (chem), 1975. **Professional Experience:** DIR, CTR PROTEIN STRUCT, FUNCTION & ENG, 1995-; ASSOC PROF BIOCHEM, UNIV QUEENSLAND, 1989-; sr res fel, Merck Res Lab, 1977-1989; Res assoc, Life Sci Dept, Univ Pittsburgh, 1975-1977; Res scientist, Biosci Div, Jet Propulsion Lab, 1970-1973. **Memberships:** Australian Soc Biochem & Molecular Biol; Am Soc Biochem & Molecular Biol; Am Heart Asn. **Research Statement & Publications:** Structure and function of lipoproteins and their receptors, protein engineering. **Mailing Address:** Dept Biochem, Univ Queensland, St Lucia Qld 4072, Australia. **Fax:** 617-336-54699. **E-Mail:** pkroon@biosci.uq.edu.au

KROONTJE, WYBE, agronomy; deceased, see previous edition for last biography

KROP, STEPHEN, pharmacology, toxicology; deceased, see previous edition for last biography

KROPA, JAMES C, MATHEMATICS. **Education:** Emory Univ, PhD. **Professional Experience:** PROF, DEPT MATH, SOUTHERN POLYTECH STATE UNIV, as of 2004. **Mailing Address:** Southern Polytech State Univ, D130, Marietta, GA 30060-2896. **Fax:** 678-915-7425. **E-Mail:** jkropa@spsu.edu

KROPF, ALLEN, BIOPHYSICAL CHEMISTRY. **Personal Data:** b Queens, NY, October 3, 1929; m 1950, Rita; c Noel, Julie & Aaron. **Education:** Queens Col, NY, BS, 1951; Univ Utah, PhD (chem), 1954. **Honorary Degrees:** MA, Amherst Col, 1969. **Professional Experience:** PROF EMER PHYS CHEM, AMHERST COL, as of 2003; vis scientist, Hebrew Univ, 1991; vis scientist, Membrane Sci, Weizmann Inst Sci, 1986-1987; Julian H Gibbs prof natural sci, Amherst Col, beginning 1985; vis scholar biol, Harvard Univ, 1982-1983; assoc chmn, Gordon Conf Visual Transduction, 1978, 1980; vis prof phys chem, Hebrew Univ, 1976; vis prof biophys, Kyoto Univ, 1975-1976; mem Visual Sci Sect, NIH, 1973-1977; prof chem, Amherst Col, beginning 1968; NIH spec res fel, Weizmann Inst Sci, 1968-1969; NSF sci fac fel, Univ Calif, Berkeley, 1962-1963; from instr to assoc prof, Amherst Col, 1958-1968; Am Cancer Soc res fel chem vision, Harvard Univ, 1956-1958; chemist, Appl Physics Lab, Johns Hopkins Univ, 1954-1956. **Research Statement & Publications:** Photochemistry of visual pigments; preparation and properties of visual figments; chemistry of olfaction. **Mailing Address:** Amherst Col, Dept Chem, 417 Merrill Sci Ctr, Amherst, MA 01002-5000. **Fax:** 413-542-2735. **E-Mail:** akropf@amherst.edu

KROPF, DONALD HARRIS, MEAT SCIENCE, ANIMAL HUSBANDRY. **Personal Data:** b Watertown, Wis, March 8, 1931; m 1962, Gwendolyn Slover; c Gregory, Bradley & Martha. **Education:** Univ Wis, BS, 1952, PhD (animal husb), 1957; Univ Fla, MS, 1953. **Professional Experience:** PROF ANIMAL SCI & MEAT RES SCI, KANS STATE UNIV, 1972-; assoc prof, Kans State Univ, 1962-1972; asst prof animal husb, Clemson Col, 1958-1962; res asst meat sci, Univ Fla, 1952-1953 & Univ Wis, 1953-1956. **Memberships:** Fel AAAS; Am Soc Animal Sci; Am Meat Sci Asn; Inst Food Technologists; Int Asn Milk Food Environ Sanit. **Research Statement & Publications:** Meat color; effect of freezing system and rate packaging, display temperature and lighting on color; muscle histochemistry; carcass and live animal evaluation; processing and quality control. **Mailing Address:** Dept Animal Sci & Indust, 247 Weber Hall, Manhattan, KS 66506. **Fax:** 785-532-7059. **E-Mail:** dkropf@oznet.ksu.edu

KROPINSKI, MARY CATHERINE A, MATHEMATICS. **Education:** Renssellaer Polytech Inst, PhD, 1993. **Professional Experience:** ASSOC PROF, SIMON FRASER UNIV, 2001. **Mailing Address:** Dept Math & Statist, Simon Fraser Univ, Burnaby, BC V5A 1S8, Can. **Fax:** 604-291-4947. **E-Mail:** mkropins@cs.sfu.ca

KROPP, JAMES EDWARD, ORGANIC CHEMISTRY. **Personal Data:** b Chicago, Ill, July 25, 1939; m 1961, c 4. **Education:** Wabash Col, BA, 1961; Univ Colo, PhD (org chem), 1965. **Professional Experience:** SR RES SPECIALIST, MINN MINING & MFG CO, 1967-; res chemist, Film Dept, E I du Pont Del Nemours Inc, 1965-1967. **Memberships:** Am Chem Soc. **Research Statement & Publications:** Organic synthesis, mechanisms, stereochemistry; polymer synthesis, mechanisms, morphology, solvent effects; rheology; adhesion; new product development, marketing and production. **Mailing Address:** 21414 N 124th Ave, Sun City West, AZ 85375.

KROPP, JOHN LEO, PHYSICAL CHEMISTRY, SPECTROSCOPY. **Personal Data:** b Salem, Ore, June 26, 1934; m 1959, Joann Laure; c David, Michael, Daniel & Rachel. **Education:** Univ Santa Clara, BS, 1956; Univ Notre Dame, PhD (phys chem), 1961. **Professional Experience:** CONSULT, 1992-; proj mgr, TRW Space & Technol Group, 1984-1992; sr proj engr, TRW Space & Technol Group, 1980-1984; mem tech staff, TRW Space & Technol Group, 1962-1980; Res assoc radiation lab, Univ Notre Dame, 1961-1962. **Memberships:** AAAS; Sigma Xi; Am Inst Aeronaut & Astronaut. **Research Statement & Publications:** Photochemistry of large organic molecules, especially fluorescence and phosphorescence of aromatic hydrocarbons; microgravity research experiment development; development of instrument systems especially space-orientedinstruments; cost modelling of space communication and sensor systems. **Mailing Address:** 315 Via San Sebastian, Redondo Beach, CA 90277-6659.

KROPP, PAUL JOSEPH, ORGANIC CHEMISTRY. **Personal Data:** b Springfield, Ohio, June 29, 1935; m 1963, Patricia; c David E & Sonia M. **Education:** Univ Notre Dame, BS, 1957; Univ Wis, PhD (org chem), 1962. **Professional Experience:** Univ Bordeaux, 1982 & Duke Univ, 1989-1990; chmn, Curric Appl Sci, 1984-1991; vis prof, Univ Calif, Los Angeles, 1977-1978; Alfred P Sloan Found res fel, 1972; PROF CHEM, UNIV NC, CHAPEL HILL, 1970-; res chemist, Procter & Gamble Co, 1961-1970. **Memberships:** Am Chem Soc affil Inter-Amer Photochemical Soc affil. **Research Statement & Publications:** Photochemistry; surface-meditated reactions; organic synthesis. **Mailing Address:** Dept Chem, Univ NC, Chapel Hill, NC 27599-3290. **Fax:** 919-962-2388. **E-Mail:** kropp@unc.edu

KROPP, WILLIAM RUDOLPH, COSMIC RAY PHYSICS, ELEMENTARY PARTICLE PHYSICS, ASTROPHYSICS. **Personal Data:** b Chicago, Ill, November 10, 1936; m Christa; c Marianne & Kathryn. **Education:** DePaul Univ, BS, 1958; Case Inst Technol, PhD (physics), 1964. **Honors & Awards:** Rossi Prize, Am Astrophys Soc, 1989 (co-Recipient). **Professional Experience:** RES PHYSICIST, UNIV CALIF, IRVINE, 1980-; assoc res physicist, Univ Calif, Irvine, 1973-1980; asst prof physics, Univ Calif, 1967-1973; asst res physicist, Univ Calif, 1966-1967; Res assoc, Case Inst Technol, 1964-1966. **Memberships:** Am Phys Soc. **Research Statement & Publications:** Low background detection systems; neutrino interactions; cosmic rays. **Mailing Address:** Dept Physics & Astron, Univ Calif, Irvine, CA 92697-4575. **E-Mail:** wkropp@uci.edu

KROPSCHOT, RICHARD H, CRYOGENICS, SOLID STATE PHYSICS. **Personal Data:** b Kalamazoo, Mich, May 25, 1927; m 1950, Claire; c Susan & Anne. **Education:** Mich State Univ, BS, 1948, MS, 1950, PhD (physics), 1959. **Honors & Awards:** Gold Medal Except Serv Award, US Dept Com. **Professional Experience:** RETIRED; liaison officer, Off Pres, Univ Calif, 1990-1996; assoc dir energy sci, Lawrence Berkeley Lab, 1985-1990; dir, Off Basic Energy Sci, US Dept Energy, 1979-1985; adj prof, Univ Colo, Boulder, 1969-1979; guest prof, ETH, Zurich, 1964-1965; physicist, Nat Bur Stand, Boulder, Colo, 1951-1979; res engr low temp res, NAm Aviation Co, 1950-1951. **Memberships:** Fel Am Phys Soc, Am Assn advan of sci (AAAS). **Research Statement & Publications:** Solid state research at low temperatures; cryogenic engineering; properties of liquid helium; superconductivity and superconducting magnets. **Mailing Address:** 929 Calle Arco, Santa Fe, NM 87501-1095.

KROSCHEWSKY, JULIUS RICHARD, BOTANY, PHYTOCHEMISTRY. **Personal Data:** b Taylor, Tex, December 14, 1924; m 1946, c 3. **Education:** Univ Tex, BA, 1947, MA, 1949, PhD (bot), 1967. **Professional Experience:** ASST DIR, EDWARD'S AQUIFER RES & DATA CTR, SOUTHWESTERN UNIV, 1988-; prof biol, Bloomsburg State Col, 1967-1987; assoc prof, St Edward's Univ, 1961-1967; Odessa Col, 1954-1959 & high sch, Calif, 1960-1961; Instr biol, Lee Col, Tex, 1949-1952. **Memberships:** AAAS; Phytochem Soc NAm. **Research Statement & Publications:** Determination of structures and taxonomic significances of flavonoid compounds of plants; plant tissue culture studies. **Mailing Address:** 2935 Philo St, San Marcos, TX 78666.

KROSS, ROBERT DAVID, POLYMER CHEMISTRY, ANALYTICAL CHEMISTRY. **Personal Data:** b Brooklyn, NY, April 25, 1931; m 1952, c 2. **Education:** Brooklyn Col, BS, 1952; Iowa State Col, PhD (phys chem), 1956. **Professional Experience:** Vpres & dir res, Alcide Corp, 1984-1991; PRES, KROSS-LINK LABS, 1981-; vpres, Mkt-Tech Indust Ltd, 1981-1983; vpres & dir res, Hydro Optics Inc, 1973-1980; dir, Kross Ref Lab, 1969-1980; res dir, Foster D Snell, 1966-1969; chief chemist, Food & Drug Res Labs, 1959-1966; Anal group leader, Rayonier Inc, 1957-1959. **Research Statement & Publications:** Consulting and analysis in nutrition, pharmaceuticals, cosmetics, plastics and polymers; life sciences; biochemistry; infrared spectroscopy; physical analytical chemistry; federal regulations pertaining to chemically-oriented products; environmental sciences; microbiocidal systems for pharmaceutical, food and environmental applications. **Mailing Address:** 2506 Florin Ct, Bellmore, NY 11710.

KROTH, ANYA M, MATHEMATICS. **Education:** Moscow State Univ, Dipl; Fla State Univ, MA; Univ Mich, PhD. **Professional Experience:** MATH INSTR, DEPT MATH, W VALLEY COL, as of 2006. **Mailing Address:** W Valley Col, 14000 Fruitvale Ave, Saratoga, CA 95070. **Fax:** 408-741-2581. **E-Mail:** anya_kroth@westvalley.edu

KROTHE, NOEL C, GEOLOGY. **Personal Data:** b Shickshinny, Pa, May 22, 1938. **Education:** Bloomsburg State Univ, BS, 1961; Ind Univ, MAT, 1969; Penn State Univ, MS, 1973, PhD (geol), 1976. **Professional Experience:** PROF GEOL SCI, IND UNIV, as of 2005; assoc prof geol, Ind Univ, beginning 1981; asst prof, Ind Univ, 1976-1981; teacher sci, Tarrytown, NY, 1961-1968; teacher sci, Baltimore, Md, 1961-1968. **Memberships:** Fel Geol Soc Am; Int Asn Hydrologists. **Research Statement & Publications:** Chemical aspects of hydrology; isotopes in ground water. **Mailing Address:** Dept Geol, Ind Univ, 611 N Walnut Grove, Bloomington, IN 47405-2208. **Fax:** 812-855-2862. **E-Mail:** krothen@indiana.edu

KROTKOV, ROBERT VLADIMIR, ATOMIC PHYSICS. **Personal Data:** b Toronto, Ont, July 17, 1929; m 1958, c 4. **Education:** Queen's Univ, Ont, BA, 1951, MA, 1952; Princeton Univ, PhD, 1958. **Professional Experience:** PROF EMER PHYSICS, UNIV MASS, AMHERST, 1997-; prof physics, Univ Mass, Amherst, 1973-1997; assoc prof, Univ Mass, Amherst, 1966-1973; from instr to asst prof, Yale Univ, 1960-1966; res asst, Palmer Lab, Princeton Univ, 1958-1960; Instr physics, Palmer Lab, Princeton Univ, 1956-1958. **Memberships:** Am Phys Soc; Sigma Xi. **Research Statement & Publications:** Relativity and gravitation. **Mailing Address:** Dept Physics, Univ Mass, Hasbrouck Lab, Amherst, MA 01003. **Fax:** 413-545-1691. **E-Mail:** krotkov@physics.umass.edu

KROTO, HAROLD WALTER, CHEMISTRY. **Personal Data:** b October 7, 1939; m 1963, Margaret H Hunter; c 2. **Honors & Awards:** Nobel Prize in Chem, 1996; Tilden Lectr, 1981-1982; Int New Mat Prize, Am Phys Soc, 1992; Italgas Prize Innovation Chem, 1992; Longstaff Medal, Royal Soc Chem, 1993. **Professional Experience:** ROYAL SOC RES PROF, UNIV SUSSEX, ENG, 1991-; prof chem, Univ Sussex, Eng, 1985-1991; reader, Univ Sussex, Eng, 1977-1985; lectr, Univ Sussex, Eng, 1968-1977; res scientist, Bell Tel Labs, NJ, 1966-1967; Postdoctoral fel, Nat Registry Clin Chem, 1964-1966. **Research Statement & Publications:** Contributed many articles to professional journals. **Mailing Address:** Sch Chem & Molecular Sci Falmer, Univ Sussex, Brighton Sussex BN1 9QJ, UK.

KROTOSKI, DANUTA MARIA, RESEARCH ADMINISTRATION. **Personal Data:** b Preston, Eng, American citizen. **Education:** Univ Calif, Los Angeles, BA, 1968; Emory Univ, MS, 1972; Tulane Univ, PhD (genetics), 1982. **Professional Experience:** CHIEF, BASIC REHAB RES BR, NAT CTR MED REHAB RES, NAT INST CHILD HEALTH & HUMAN DEVELOP, NIH, as of 2006; prog officer, Int Grants & Fels, Int Res & Awards Br, Fogarty Int Ctr, NIH, 1990-1992; prog dir develop neurobiology, Limb Develop & Teratology Br, Nat Inst Child Health & Human Develop, 1988-1990; res specialist, Develop Biol Ctr, Univ Calif, Irvine, 1986-1988; Vis scientist, Anatomisches Inst, Univ Freiburg, Ger, 1986; fel, Develop Biol Ctr, Univ Calif, 1983-1986; Am Heart Asn Libby fel, La State Univ Med Ctr, 1982-1983. **Memberships:** Am Soc Cell Biol; Soc Neuroscience; Soc Develop Biol; AAAS; Polish Am Health Asn (treas). **Research Statement & Publications:** Defining the scope of basic science for medical rehabilitation research; establishing a research grant and contract program. **Mailing Address:** Basic Rehab Med Res Br, Nat Ctr Med Rehab Res, Nat Inst Child Health, NIH, Rm 2A32, Bldg 31, MSC 2425, 31 Ctr Dr, Bethesda, MD 20892-2425. **Fax:** 301-496-7101.

KROUSE, HOWARD ROY, PHYSICS, CHEMISTRY. **Personal Data:** b Norfolk Co, Ont, January 8, 1935; m 1958, c 2. **Education:** McMaster Univ, BSc, 1956, PhD (physics), 1960. **Professional Experience:** PROF EMER PHYSICS, UNIV CALGARY, 1997-; prof physics & chmn dept, Univ Calgary, 1971-1997; vis scientist, Japan, 1971; asst chmn dept, Univ Alta, 1970-1971; exchange scientist, USSR, 1969; NATO fel & res assoc, Univ Calif, San Diego, 1966-1967; from asst prof to prof physics, Univ Alta, 1960-1971; res grants, Nat Res Coun Can, Defence Res Bd Can & Geol Surv Can. **Memberships:** AAAS; Am Geophys Union; Am Phys Soc; Geochem Soc; Can Asn Physicists; Sigma Xi. **Research Statement & Publications:** Isotope fractionation studies in physical, geological, chemical, biological and environmental processes; mass spectrometry. **Mailing Address:** Dept Physics, Univ Calgary, SB 605 2500 Univ Dr NW, Calgary, AB T2N 1N4, Can. **Fax:** 403-289-3331.

KROUSKOP, THOMAS ALAN, BIOENGINEERING, BIOMATERIALS. **Personal Data:** b Washington, DC, July 11, 1945; m 1968, Arlene; c Peter E, Barbara J & Mark A. **Education:** Carnegie Inst Technol, BS, 1967; Carnegie-Mellon Univ, MS, 1969, PhD (civil eng, biotechnol), 1971. **Honors & Awards:** BCM Res Achievement Award, 1987; Koziak Award, 1993, BCM Outstanding Teaching Award in Rehabilitation Technology, 1998; Distinguished Eagle Scout BSA, 2004. **Professional Experience:** Rice Univ, 1990- & Univ Tex Dent Sch, 1995-; PROF PHYS MED & REHAB, BAYLOR COL MED, 1987-; Adj prof, Tex Woman's Univ, 1987-; assoc prof, Baylor Col Med, 1978-1987; from asst to assoc prof Bioengineering, Tex A&M Univ, 1971-1978; Design engr, Gen Analytics Inc, 1968. **Memberships:** Sigma Xi. **Research Statement & Publications:** Design of prosthetic appliances; materials for use as medical implants; effects of mechanical stress on soft tissue metabolism; development of assistive devices for the physically handicapped; elastography. **Mailing Address:** Dept Phys Med & Rehab, Baylor Col Med, 1333 Moursund Ave, Houston, TX 77030. **E-Mail:** krouskop@bcm.tmc.edu

KROW, GRANT REESE, ORGANIC CHEMISTRY. **Personal Data:** b Reading, Pa, June 30, 1941; m 1970, c 2. **Education:** Albright Col, BA, 1963; Princeton Univ, MFA, 1964, PhD (chem), 1967; Temple Univ, JD, 1978. **Honors & Awards:** Golden Key Award, Nat Honor Soc. **Professional Experience:** Summer adj prof, Univ Wisc, Madison, 1997-2002; PROF CHEM, TEMPLE UNIV, 1980-; sci & legal consult, 1978-; from asst prof to assoc prof, Temple Univ, 1969-1980; Res assoc chem & fel, Ohio State Univ, 1967-1969. **Memberships:** Am Chem Soc; Sigma Xi. **Research Statement & Publications:** Stereochemistry; chemistry of small ring nitrogen heterocycles; synthetic methods applied to natural products; published over 10 articles. **Mailing Address:** Dept Chem, Temple Univ, Beury Hall 201 1901 N 13th St, Philadelphia, PA 19122. **Fax:** 215-204-1532. **E-Mail:** grkrow@temple.edu

KROWN, SUSAN E, AIDS-ASSOCIATED CANCERS, MELANOMA. **Personal Data:** b Bronx, NY, September 8, 1946; div, c Catherine Pitt. **Education:** Barnard Col, AB, 1967; State Univ NY Downstate Med Ctr, MD, 1971. **Honors & Awards:** Milstein Award, Intl Soc Interferon Cytokine Res, 1995. **Professional Experience:** ATTENDING PHYSICIAN/MEMBER, MEM SLOAN KETTERING CANCER CTR, 1994-; PROF MED, CORNELL UNIV, 1994-; PRIN INVEST, AIDS MALIG CONSORTIUM, 1995-; consult, Oncol Drugs Adv Comt, US Food & Drug Admin, 1990-1996; mem, AIDS Clin Drug Discovery Comt, NIH, 1990-1992; chair, Oncol Comt, AIDS Clin Trials Group, Nat Inst Allergy & Infectious Dis, NIH, 1990-1992; vchair, Oncol Comt, AIDS Clin Trials Group, Nat Inst Allergy & Infectious Dis, NIH, 1987-1989; mem, Oncol Drugs Adv Comt, US Food & Drug Admin, 1986-1990; bd dirs, Soc Biol Ther, 1986-1989; assoc mem med, Sloan Kettering Inst Cancer Res, 1984-1994; adv bd, Cancer Treat Reports, 1984-1987; assoc attend, Mem Hosp, 1982-; res assoc immunbiol, Sloan Kettering Inst Cancer Res, 1977-1984; Clin asst & asst attend physician med, Mem Hosp, 1977-1982; fel med oncol & clin immunol, Mem Sloan Kettering Cancer Ctr, 1974-1977; resident, Mt Sinai Hosp, NY, 1972-1974; Intern internal med, Mt Sinai Hosp, NY, 1971-1972; mem, Int Soc Interferon Res; mem ed bd, J Interferon Res. **Memberships:** Am Asn Cancer Res; Am Soc Clin Oncol; AAAS; Int Soc Interferon Cytokine Res. **Research Statement & Publications:** Clinical investigations of chemotherapeutic, biologicals and antiviral agents in the treatment of AIDS-associated cancer and melanoma; targeted therapy; identification of prognostic parameters. **Mailing Address:** Mem Sloan-Kettering Cancer Ctr, Rm H804, 1275 York Ave, New York, NY 10021. **E-Mail:** krowns@mskcc.org

KRSTENANSKY, JOHN LEONARD, MEDICINAL CHEMISTRY, PEPTIDE CHEMISTRY. **Personal Data:** b Chicago, Ill, September 8, 1955. **Education:** Loyola Univ, Chicago, AB & BS, 1977; Univ Ill, Chicago, PhD (med chem), 1983. **Professional Experience:** Lectr med chem peptides, Univ Calif, Berkeley Extension, 1994; RES SECT LEADER, SYNTEX, 1991-; sr res biochemist, Marion Merrell Dow, 1985-1991; Res assoc, Univ Ariz, 1983-1985. **Memberships:** Am Chem Soc; Sigma Xi; Am Peptide Soc; Europ Peptide Soc; NY Acad Sci; Philos Sci Asn. **Research Statement & Publications:** Design of peptides and peptide mimetics for therapeutic applications. **Mailing Address:** 3455 Rambow Dr, Palo Alto, CA 94306. **Fax:** 650-354-2442.

KRUBINER, ALAN MARTIN, ORGANIC CHEMISTRY. **Personal Data:** b New York, NY, April 6, 1941; m 1962, c 2. **Education:** Queens Col, BS, 1961; Univ Calif, Berkeley, PhD (org chem), 1965; Seton Hall Univ, JD, 1974. **Professional Experience:** VPRES, INTELLECTUAL PROPERTY LAW, SYNTEX CORP, 1983-; dir patent law & licensing, Intellectual Property Law, Syntex Corp, 1981-1983; asst patent coun, Intellectual Property Law, Syntex Corp, 1979-1981; supvry patent atty, Intellectual Property Law, Syntex Corp, 1977-1979; patent atty, Intellectual Property Law, Syntex Corp, 1974-1977; patent chemist, Hoffman-La Roche Inc, 1970-1974; Sr chemist, Hoffman-La Roche Inc, 1964-1970. **Memberships:** Am Chem Soc. **Research Statement & Publications:** Proprietary information, primarily in health care area. **Mailing Address:** Syntex Corp, Patent Dept, 3401 Hillview Ave Box 10850, Palo Alto, CA 94304. **Fax:** 650-855-5526.

KRUBSACK, ARNOLD J, BIOLOGICAL EDUCATION. **Professional Experience:** PHYSICIAN, WIS PHYSICIANS SERV, as of 2006. **Memberships:** Am Chem Soc. **Mailing Address:** 1601 Engel St, Box 1787, Madison, WI 53701. **Fax:** 608-223-3614.

KRUCK, THEO P A, NEUROSCIENCE. **Professional Experience:** RETIRED; assoc prof physiol, Univ Toronto, ending 1999. **Memberships:** Alzheimer Asn. **Mailing Address:** Dept Physiol, Univ Toronto, Tanz Neurosci Bldg 6 Queen's Park Circle, Toronto, ON M5S 1A1, Can. **Fax:** 416-287-7525. **E-Mail:** helpdesk@utsc.utoronto.ca

KRUCKEBERG, ARTHUR RICE, BOTANY. **Personal Data:** b Los Angeles, Calif, March 21, 1920; m 1953, c 5. **Education:** Occidental Col, AB, 1941; Univ Calif, Berkeley, PhD (bot), 1951. **Professional Experience:** CO-FOUNDER, KRUCKEBERG BOTANIC GARDEN, as of 2004; PROF EMER BOT, UNIV WASH, 1988-; chmn dept, Univ Wash, 1971-1977; prof, Univ Wash, 1964-1988; from instr to assoc prof, Univ Wash, 1951-1963; asst bot, Univ Calif, Berkeley, 1946-1951; instr, Occidental Col, 1946; asst biol, Stanford Univ, 1941-1942; field asst, Carnegie Inst, 1941; asst biol, Occidental Col, 1939-1941. **Memberships:** Am Soc Plant Taxon. **Research Statement & Publications:** Experimental plant taxonomy; edaphic ecology of serpentine soils. **Mailing Address:** Kruckeberg Botanic Garden Found, PO Box 60035, Shoreline, WA 98160-0035. **E-Mail:** kbgf@kruckeberg.org

KRUCZYNSKI, WILLIAM LEONARD, RESOURCE MANAGEMENT. **Personal Data:** b Buffalo, NY, July 18, 1943; m 1966, Mary; c Gregory C & Amy M. **Education:** Canisius Col, BS, 1965; Univ NC, Chapel Hill, PhD (marine biol), 1971. **Honors & Awards:** Bronze Medal, US Environ Protection Agency, 1986-1996. **Professional Experience:** PROG SCIENTIST, WATER QUAL PROTECTION PROG, FLA KEYS NAT MARINE SANCTUARY, US ENVIRON PROTECTION AGENCY, 1995-; wetlands specialist, Gulfbreeze, Fla, 1987-1995; chief, Wetlands Protection Sect, Region IV, 1985-1987; life scientist, US Environ Protection Agency, 1979-1985; conserv consult, Inc, 1977; Tex A & M Univ & Tex Instruments, Inc, 1978-1979; asst prof res, Fla A&M Univ, 1974-1979; res assoc, Fla State Univ, 1974-1977; vpres, Environ Systs Serv, Inc, 1974-1976; vis prof, Col Ctr Finger Lakes, 1973; consult, Environ Anal, Inc, 1972-1975; asst prof biol, Hartwick Col, 1970-1974. **Memberships:** Am Soc Zoologists; AAAS; Ecol Soc Am; Estuarine Res Fedn. **Research Statement & Publications:** Ecology of a crab symbiotic with mollusk hosts; systematics of marine isopod crustaceans; ecology of saline marshes; wetland restoration. **Mailing Address:** FL Keys Nat Marine Sanctuary Off, US Environ Protection Agency, PO Box 500368, Marathon, FL 33050. **Fax:** 305-743-3304. **E-Mail:** kruczynski.bill@epa.gov

KRUEGEL, ALICE VIRGINIA, ORGANIC CHEMISTRY, FORENSIC SCIENCE. **Personal Data:** b Louisville, Ky, May 29, 1939; m 1965, David; c Scott & Ann. **Education:** Spalding Col, Louisville, BA, 1961; Univ Ky, PhD (org chem), 1972. **Professional Experience:** LAB DIR, NORTHEAST LAB, DRUG ENFORCEMENT ADMIN, 1992-; prog mgr, Off Forensic Sci, 1988-1992; supvry chemist forensic drug chem, Western Field Lab, 1978-1988; res chemist, Spec Testing & Res Lab, Drug Enforcement Admin, 1970-1978. **Memberships:** Am Chem Soc; Am Acad Forensic Sci; Am Soc Crime Lab Dir. **Research Statement & Publications:** Forensic drug analysis; identification of impurities in illictly manufactured drugs. **Mailing Address:** 300 Rector Pl No 3E, New York, NY 10280.

KRUEGER, ANNE O, INTERNATIONAL ECONOMICS & DEVELOPMENT. **Personal Data:** b Endicott, NY, 1934; m 1981, James; c 1. **Education:** Oberlin Col, BA, 1953; Univ Wis, MS, 1956, PhD (econ), 1958. **Honorary Degrees:** Dr, Hacettepe Univ, 1990, Monash Univ, 1996; LHD, Georgetown Univ, 1993. **Honors & Awards:** Robertson Prize, Nat Acad Sci, 1984; Frank E Seidman Distinguished Award, 1993. **Professional Experience:** DISTINGUISHED FEL AM ECON ASSOC, as of 2006-; FIRST DEP MANAGING DIR INT MONETARY FUND, 2001-; Delhi Sch Econs, 1995 & Kiel Inst World Econs, 1996; sr fel, Hoover Inst, beginning 1993; Herald & Carolyn Ritch prof Humanities & Sci, Stanford Univ, beginning 1993; Monash Univ, Univ Warsaw, 1993; chair, Task Force Int Econ Res Related to Global Warming, 1991-1992; sr res fel, Inst Policy Reform, 1990-1992; mem, Task Force Struct Rev Biol, Behav & Social Sci Directorate, NSF, 1990-1991; trustee, Oberlin Col, 1987-1995; arts & sci prof econ, Duke Univ, 1987-1993; res assoc, Nat Bur Econ Res, 1986-; mem, Panel Technol & Employment, Nat Acad Sci, 1985-1987; Monash Univ, Univ Md, 1983; vpres econ & res, World Bank, 1982-1986; Monash Univ, Australia, 1981; vis prof, Univ Paris, 1980; vis prof, Univ Aarhus, 1979; vis prof, Australian Nat Univ, 1977; vis prof, Northwestern Univ, 1976; vis prof, Mass Inst Technol, 1973-1974; from asst prof to prof, Univ Minn, 1959-1982; instr econ, Univ Wis, 1958-1959. **Memberships:** Nat Acad Sci; Am Econ Asn (vpres, 1977-1978, pres-elect, 1995, pres, 1996-); fel Am Acad Arts & Sci; Royal Econ Soc; fel Economet Soc; Int Econ Asn (vpres, 1994-). **Research Statement & Publications:** Analysis of trade and exchange rate regemes and global systems with special reference to international economic organizations and developing countries. **Mailing Address:** INT MONETARY FUND, 700 19TH ST, NW, Washington, DC 20431. **Fax:** 202-623-6729. **E-Mail:** akrueger@leland.stanford.edu

KRUEGER, ARLIN JAMES, STRATOSPHERIC OZONE, REMOTE SENSING OF VOLCANIC ERUPTIONS. **Personal Data:** b Lamberton, Minn, October 22, 1933; wid Susan; c Sandra, Timothy & Terry. **Education:** Univ Minn, BA, 1955; Colo State Univ, PhD (atmospheric sci), 1984. **Honors & Awards:** Except Achievement Award, Goddard Space Flight Ctr, 1986; NASA Exceptional Scientific Achievement Medal, 1991; Elkins Professorship, Univ of Maryland, Baltimore County, 2000; NASA Exceptional Service Medal, 2001. **Professional Experience:** Res Prof, Dept Physics & Earth Syst Technol, beginning 2000; Instr scientist, Earth Probe/TOMS, beginning 1989; prin investr, ADEOS/TOMS, beginning 1988; instrument scientist, Meteor 3/TOMS, beginning 1988; sr scientist, Nimbus 7 Total Ozone Mapping Spectrometer, TOMS, 1973-1993; aerospace technologist & astrophysicist, Goddard Space Flight Ctr, Nasa, Greenbelt, Md, 1969-2000; Prin investr, ROCOZ rocket ozonesonde, 1960-1984; Physicist, Naval Weapons Ctr, China Lake, Calif, 1959-1969. **Memberships:** Am Geophys Union; Am Meteorol Soc; Sigma Xi; AAAS. **Research Statement & Publications:** Atmospheric chemistry; development of satellite and rocket instruments to measure ozone and sulfur dioxide; analysis of ozone variability and volcanic clouds; modelling of stratospheric chemistry; Mars atmosphere; remote sensing. **Mailing Address:** Joint Ctr for Earth Systems Technol/ UMBC, 1000 Hilltop Circle, Baltimore, MD 21250. **Fax:** 410-455-5868. **E-Mail:** akrueger@umbc.edu

KRUEGER, CHARLES ROBERT, FORAGE CROP MANAGEMENT, FORAGE CROP UTILIZATION. **Personal Data:** b Milwaukee, Wis, June 21, 1938; m 1965, c 2. **Education:** Univ Wis, Madison, BS, 1960, MS, 1963, PhD (agron), 1967. **Professional Experience:** EMER PROF AGRON, PA STATE UNIV, as of 2006; prof agron, Pa State Univ, as of 2004; asst Dir Admin, Ohio Agr Res & Develop Ctr, Ohio State Univ, Wooster, 1978; prof & head admin, res & teaching, 1973-1978; assoc prof res & teaching, Dept Plant Sci, SDak State Univ, 1970-1973; asst prof extension, Dept Agron, Univ Wis-Madison, 1967-1970. **Memberships:** Am Soc Agron; Crop Sci Soc Am; Coun Agr Sci & Technol; Am Dairy Sci Soc; Am Soc Animal Sci. **Research Statement & Publications:** Interdisciplinary research on forage crop production, management and utilization; determination of forage nutritive value by in vitro and in vivo methods; pasture and forage systems for beef cattle; establishment and use of warm season perennial grasses; interseeding of native rangeland to improve productivity. **Mailing Address:** Dept Crop & Soil Sci, Penn State Univ, 242 Agr Sci & Indust Bldg, Univ Park, PA 16802. **Fax:** 814-863-7043. **E-Mail:** ckrueger@psu.edu

KRUEGER, DAVID ALLEN, THEORETICAL PHYSICS. **Personal Data:** b Sidney, Mont, August 21, 1939; m 1961, Minnie; c Ray David, Robert Allen, Patricia Ann & Michael Thomas. **Education:** Mont State Univ, BS, 1961; Univ Wash, PhD (physics), 1967. **Professional Experience:** Chair, dept physics, colo state univ, beginning 2001; vis scientist, Marathon Oil Co Res Ctr, Littleton, Colo, 1985-1986; PROF PHYSICS, COLO STATE UNIV, 1980-; Dept Energy, Energy Technol Ctr, Bartlesville, Okla, 1980; mem tech staff, Sandia Lab, Albuquerque, 1978-1979; vis prof, Watson Res Lab, Int Bus Mach Corp, Yorktown Heights, NY, 1975; from asst prof to assoc prof, Colo State Univ, 1969-1980; res assoc physics; Wis Alumni Res Found, Univ Wis, Madison, 1967-1969. **Memberships:** AAAS; Am Phys Soc; Am Asn Phys Teachers. **Research Statement & Publications:** physics of middle atmosphere (80-105km); lidar measurements of temperature and wind speed, geophysical phenomena. **Mailing Address:** Dept Physics, Colo State Univ, Ft Collins, CO 80523-1875. **Fax:** 970-491-7947. **E-Mail:** krueger@lamar.colostate.edu

KRUEGER, EUGENE REX, MATHEMATICS, COMPUTER SCIENCES. **Personal Data:** b Grand Island, Nebr, March 30, 1935; m 1957, c 3. **Education:** Rensselaer Polytech Inst, BS, 1957, MS, 1960, PhD (appl math), 1962. **Professional Experience:** Vpres, William C Norry Inst, 1995-1996; PRES, KROEGER & ASSOCS, 1989-; exec dir, William C Norry Inst, 1989-1995; vpres, Control Data Corp, 1985-1989; gen mgr, Control Data Corp, 1982-1985; vchancellor educ syst, Ore State Syst Higher Educ, 1974-1982; prof comput sci, Ore State Univ, 1974-1982; from asst prof to prof math & comput sci, Comput Ctr, 1968-1974; dir, Comput Ctr, 1967-1974; asst prof math, Univ Colo, Boulder, 1963-1968; vis fel, Math Res Ctr, Univ Wis, 1962-1963; Physicist, Res Ctr, Int Bus Mach Corp, 1957-1958. **Memberships:** Am Soc Eng Educ. **Research Statement & Publications:** Fluid mechanics with emphasis on hydrodynamic stability; mathematical methods of physics; numerical analysis; interactive computer graphics. **Mailing Address:** 3205 NW Kidd Pl, Bend, OR 97701.

KRUEGER, GEORGE CORWIN, optics; deceased, see previous edition for last biography

KRUEGER, GERHARD R F, ANATOMIC PATHOLOGY, LABORATORY IMMUNOLOGY. **Personal Data:** b Berlin, Ger, November 21, 1936; m 1960, c 3. **Education:** Intern med rotating, Hosps Free Univ, 1962-1964. **Professional Experience:** PROF PATH, DEPT PATH LAB MED, UNIV TEX, HOUSTON, 1991-; vis prof, Dept Path Lab Med, Univ Tex, Houston, 1990-1991; Chmn, Int Inst Immunopath, Inc, Cologne-Washington, 1989-; prof path & head immunopath, Dept Path, Univ Cologne, Ger, 1974-1991; asst prof path, Dept Path, Univ Cologne, Ger, 1972-1974; pathologist, Lab Path, 1968-1972; resident path, Dept Path, Free Univ, Berlin, 1967-1968; res pathologist, Nat Cancer Inst, NIH, 1965-1967; resident path, City Hosp Spandau, Berlin, 1964-1965. **Memberships:** Am Asn Pathologists; Am Soc Microbiol; Hematopath Soc; Int Asn Res Leukemia Asn Dis. **Research Statement & Publications:** Relationships between reactivated herpesvirus infections to immune deficiency, autoimmunity and lymphoproliferative disorders; influence of virus infection on cell membrane function. **Mailing Address:** Dept Path, Univ Cologne Joseph-Stelzmann-Str 9, 50931 Cologne, 50924, Ger.

KRUEGER, JACK N, ELECTRICAL & AGRICULTURAL ENGINEERING. **Personal Data:** b St Paul, Minn, August 29, 1922; m 1958, c 2. **Education:** Univ Minn, BEE, 1944, MS, 1949. **Professional Experience:** RETIRED; from assoc prof to prof elec eng, Univ NDak, 1969-1988; assoc prof elec eng, SDak State Univ, 1958-1959; head, Electromech Develop Dept, Pillsbury Mills Inc, 1956-1958; assoc prof elec eng, Va Polytech Inst, 1955-1956; consult engr, 1951-1955; res prof agr eng, Univ Ky, 1949-1951; instr elec eng, Univ Minn, 1944-1949. **Memberships:** Inst Elec & Electronics Engrs. **Research Statement & Publications:** Electrical power and machinery; electrical instrumentation; biomedical and industrial electronics; environmental conditioning of production, processing and storage areas for agricultural products; forensic engineering; solar and wind energy systems. **Mailing Address:** 41776 200th St S W, East Grand Forks, MN 56721.

KRUEGER, JAMES ELWOOD, ORGANIC CHEMISTRY. **Personal Data:** b Marinette, Wis, April 2, 1926; m 1953, c 3. **Education:** Univ Wis, BS, 1949; Mass Inst Technol, PhD (org chem), 1954. **Professional Experience:** VPRES, QUAL ASSURANCE, IND MGT, 1990-; qual auditor, qual mgt, 1979-1990; chemist, Lederle Labs Div, Am Cyanamid Co, 1961-1979; chemist, Dow Chem Co, 1955-1961; Res fel chem, Harvard Med Sch, 1953-1955; Cert qual auditor, Am Soc Qual Control. **Memberships:** AAAS; Am Chem Soc; Sigma Xi; Acad Pharmaceut Sci; Am Soc Qual Control. **Research Statement & Publications:** Pharmaceutical science; research quality assurance; laboratory quality assurance. **Mailing Address:** 101 N Main St, Pearl River, NY 10965.

KRUEGER, JAMES HARRY, INORGANIC CHEMISTRY. **Personal Data:** b Milwaukee, Wis, May 18, 1936; m 1959, c 3. **Education:** Univ Wis-Madison, BS, 1958; Univ Calif, Berkeley, PhD (chem), 1961. **Professional Experience:** PROF EMER CHEM, ORE STATE UNIV 1997-; prof Chem, Ore State Univ, 1976-; from asst prof to assoc prof, Ore State Univ 1961-1976. **Memberships:** Am Chem Soc. **Research Statement & Publications:** Kinetics and mechanisms of inorganic reactions; synthesis and characterization of transition metal complexes containing thiolate amino acid ligands. **Mailing Address:** Dept Chem, Ore State Univ, 153 Gilbert Hall, Corvallis, OR 97331-4003. **E-Mail:** james.krueger@oregonstate.edu

KRUEGER, JAMES MARTIN, NEUROBIOLOGY. **Personal Data:** b New York, NY, September 8, 1944. **Education:** Univ Wis, BS, 1966; Univ Pa, PhD (physiol), 1974. **Professional Experience:** PROF, DEPT VET & COMPARATIVE ANAT, PHARMA &

PHYSIOL, COL VET MED, WASH STATE UNIV, as of 2000; PROF NEUROBIOLOGY, UNIV TENN, 1987-; assoc prof, Univ Tenn, 1985-1987; from asst prof to assoc prof neurobiology, Chicago Med Sch, 1981-1985; Res fel, Harvard Med Sch, 1974-1981. **Memberships:** Am Sleep Res Soc; Am Physiol Soc; Europ Sleep Res Soc. **Research Statement & Publications:** Biochemistry of sleep regulation. **Mailing Address:** Col Vet Med, Wash St Univ, Pullman, WA 99164-6520. **Fax:** 509-335-4650. **E-Mail:** krueger@vetmed.wsu.edu

KRUEGER, KARL E, BIOCHEMISTRY, DRUG RECEPTORS. **Personal Data:** b Poughkeepsie, NY, September 28, 1954. **Education:** Marist Col, BA, 1976; Vanderbilt Univ, PhD (biochem), 1981. **Professional Experience:** ASSOC PROF RES MICROBIOL & IMMUNOL, GEORGETOWN UNIV MED SCH, as of 2004; ASSOC PROF MED & NEUROBIOLOGY, GEORGETOWN UNIV MED SCH, 1992-; asst prof, Georgetown Univ Med Sch, 1986-1992. **Memberships:** Am Soc Biochem & Molecular Biol; Soc Neuroscience. **Mailing Address:** Dept Microbiol & Immunol, Sch Med, Georgetown Univ, Washington, DC 20057-0001. **E-Mail:** kkrueg01@georgetown.edu

KRUEGER, MYRON W, COMPUTER SCIENCE. **Education:** Univ Wis, PhD. **Professional Experience:** PROF, COMPUT SCI DEPT, UNIV CONN, 1978-. **Mailing Address:** Comput Sci Dept, Univ Conn, U-157, Storrs, CT 06268. **Fax:** 860-486-5896. **E-Mail:** krueger@yahooo.com

KRUEGER, PAUL CARLTON, INORGANIC CHEMISTRY, PHYSICAL CHEMISTRY. **Personal Data:** b Louisville, Ky, June 1, 1936; m 1965, c 2. **Education:** Marquette Univ, BS, 1958; Case Inst Technol, PhD (chem), 1963. **Professional Experience:** MGR ENVIRON AFFAIRS, AIRCO INC, 1987-; mat selection & performance, Indust Health Serv & Safety, 1984-1987; mgr environ affairs, Indust Health Serv & Safety, 1980-1984; supvr, Indust Health Serv & Safety, 1978-1980; sr res chemist, Cent Res Labs, 1965-1978; res chemist, Air Reduction Co, 1963-1965. **Memberships:** Am Chem Soc. **Research Statement & Publications:** Chelate, silicon and slag chemistry; coordination compounds; inorganic and high temperature polymers; ferroalloy production; cutting of metals; corrosion of stainless steel alloys; development of stainless steel alloys; industrial hygiene sampling and interpretation; failure analysis of equipment and compressed gas cylinders. **Mailing Address:** BOC Group Inc, 100 Mountain Ave, Murray Hill, NJ 07974-2064.

KRUEGER, PETER GEORGE, AVIONICS & NAVIGATION. **Personal Data:** b Lodz, Poland, May 20, 1940; American citizen; div, c 3. **Education:** Loma Linda Univ, La Sierra Campus, BA, 1962; Univ Calif, Riverside, MA, 1966, PhD (physics), 1970. **Professional Experience:** SR TECH ADV, DEFENSE MAPPING AGENCY HQ, FAIRFAX, VA, 1993-; staff scientist, secy defense, Wash, DC, 1986-1993; Naval Air Systs Command, Wash, DC, 1980-1986; physicist, Naval Weapons Ctr, 1962-1980. **Memberships:** Am Phys Soc; Inst Navig; US Naval Inst. **Research Statement & Publications:** Defense mapping; agency research, development and production programs. **Mailing Address:** Defense Mapping Agency, 8613 Lee Hwy, Fairfax, VA 22031-2139. **Fax:** 703-285-9396.

KRUEGER, PETER J, CONFORMATIONS OF ORGANIC MOLECULES, INFRARED & RAMAN SPECTROSCOPY. **Personal Data:** b Altona, Man, November 11, 1934; m Dorothy; c Kathryn, Vivian & Jonathan. **Education:** Univ Man, BSc, 1955, MSc, 1956; Oxford Univ, DPhil(infrared spectros), 1958. **Honors & Awards:** Coblentz Award Spectros, Coblentz Soc, 1967; Gerhard Herzberg Award, Spetros Soc Can, 1973; Alberta Achievement Award, Gov't of Alberta, 1974. **Professional Experience:** Nat coordr, Can Univ Stud Exchange-Consortium, 1992-1994; PROF EMER CHEM, UNIV CALGARY, 1991-; EDUCATIONAL CONSULTANT, 1991-; ACAD-IN-RESIDENCE, INT CTR, 1991-2000; acad vpres & provost, Univ Calgary, 1976-1990; mem bd govs, Univ Calgary, 1970-1973; vdean fac arts & sci, Univ Calgary, 1970-1972; prof chem, Univ Calgary, 1966-1991; head dept, Univ Calgary, 1966-1970; vis scientist, Nat Res Coun Can, Ottawa, 1966-1967; from asst prof to assoc prof chem, Univ Alta, 1959-1966; Fel, Org Spectrochem Sect, Div Pure Chem, Nat Res Coun Can, Ont, 1958-1959. **Memberships:** Fel Chem Inst Can; Spectros Soc Can; fel Royal Soc Chem. **Research Statement & Publications:** University governance and administration; organic spectrochemistry; infrared and Raman spectra of organic compounds; normal coordinate analysis of vibrational spectra; molecular structure determination; internationalization of university programs. **Mailing Address:** Dept Chem, Univ Calgary, 2500 Univ Dr NW, Calgary, AB T2N 1N4, Can. **Fax:** 403-289-9488. **E-Mail:** pkrueger@ucalgary.ca

KRUEGER, ROBERT A, organic chemistry; deceased, see previous edition for last biography

KRUEGER, ROBERT CARL, BIOCHEMISTRY. **Personal Data:** b Philadelphia, Pa, October 11, 1920; m 1947, c 2. **Education:** Univ Pa, BS, 1942; Columbia Univ, PhD (biochem), 1948. **Professional Experience:** NIH spec fel, 1966-1967; vis scientist, Univ Brussels, 1966-1967; res assoc, Brookhaven Nat Lab, 1959-1960; ASSOC PROF BIOL CHEM, COL MED, UNIV CINCINNATI, 1956-; asst prof, Col Med, Univ Cincinnati, 1950-1956; res assoc immunochem, Col Physicians & Surgeons, Columbia Univ, 1947-1950. **Memberships:** Am Soc Biol Chemists. **Research Statement & Publications:** RNA synthesis; deoxribonucleoprotein structure and function. **Mailing Address:** Dept Biol, Univ Cincinnati Col Med, 231 Bethesda Ave, Cincinnati, OH 45267-0001.

KRUEGER, ROBERT GEORGE, immunology, virology; deceased, see previous edition for last biography

KRUEGER, ROBERT HAROLD, PHYSICAL CHEMISTRY. **Personal Data:** b Sioux City, Iowa, January 25, 1926; m Astrid. **Education:** Morningside Col, BS, 1950; Northwestern Univ, MS, 1955; Loyola Univ, PhD (chem), 1967. **Professional Experience:** RETIRED; consult, beginning 2002; scientist, Birl Lab, Northwestern Univ 1990-2001; mgr phys chem, Roy C Ingersoll Res Ctr, Borg-Warner Corp, 1978-1989; group leader, Roy C Ingersoll Res Ctr, Borg-Warner Corp, 1970-1978; sr res chemist, Roy C Ingersoll Res Ctr, Borg-Warner Corp, 1962-1970; res chemist, Roy C Ingersoll Res Ctr, Borg-Warner Corp, 1956-1962; chemist, Diversey Corp, Ill, 1954-1956; chemist, Cent Com Co, 1951-1954. **Memberships:** Am Chem Soc. **Research Statement & Publications:** Development of coatings for fluxes brazing of aluminum products. **Mailing Address:** 11514 Mich Dr, Spring Grove, IL 60081-8129.

KRUEGER, ROBERT JOHN, PHARMACOGNOSY, PHARMACEUTICAL CHEMISTRY. **Personal Data:** b Milwaukee, Wis, April 15, 1948; m 1971, c 2. **Education:** Univ Conn, BS, 1971; Univ Iowa, PhD (pharm), 1975. **Professional Experience:** PROF PHARMACOG, FERRIS STATE UNIV, 1986-; pres, Sigma Xi, Grand Valley St Univ, 1986-1987; chmn, Am Chem Soc Western Mich Region, 1985; vis scientist, Abbott, 1983; from asst prof to assox prof, Ferris State Univ, 1975-1986; Eli Lilly & Co fel, 1974-1975, PMA; NDEA fel, 1971-1974. **Memberships:** AAAS; Am Soc Pharmacog; Am Chem Soc; Phytochem Soc NAm; Am Asn Col Pharm; Sigma Xi; ASP Found. **Research Statement & Publications:** Plant tissue culture; isolation and identification of natural products; xenobiotic metabolism by plant cell cultures; fungal ellicitor stimulation of plant cell culture. **Mailing Address:** Dept pharm, Col Pharm, Ferris State Univ, PHR 211, 220 S Ferris Dr, Big Rapids, MI 49307. **Fax:** 231-591-2253. **E-Mail:** kruegerr@ferris.edu

KRUEGER, ROBERT WILLIAM, PHYSICS. **Personal Data:** b Philadelphia, Pa, November 16, 1916; m 1941, Marjorie E Jones; c Arlene R (Pappan) & Diane L (Lane). **Education:** Univ Calif, Los Angeles, AB, 1937, MA, 1938, PhD (physics), 1942. **Professional Experience:** PRES, PROF SERV INT, 1973-; dir, Prof Serv Coun, 1971-; Presfounder, Prof Serv Coun, 1971-1974; pres, Planning Res Corp, 1954-1973; asst chief, Missiles Div, Rand Corp, 1947-1953; Res physicist, Douglas Aircraft Co, 1942-1946. **Memberships:** Am Phys Soc; Opers Res Soc Am. **Research Statement & Publications:** Operations research; systems engineering; aerodynamics; propulsion; quantum mechanics; spectroscopy. **Mailing Address:** 1016 Moraga Dr, Los Angeles, CA 90049.

KRUEGER, ROGER WARREN, AGRICULTURE, BIOTECHNOLOGY. **Personal Data:** b Manhassett, NY, November 8, 1953; m 1976, Ann S Schaumburg; c Van, Mara & Hanna. **Education:** Univ NH, BS, 1976; Univ RI, MS, 1979; Univ Mo-Columbia, PhD (biol), 1983. **Professional Experience:** VPRES GLOBAL SEED QUAL LEAD, MO AGR PROD UTILIZATION & INCUBATION CTR, UNIV MO, as of 2002; mgr technol, Global Prod Stewardship Monsanto-Life Sci, beginning 1996; mgr biotechnol, Am Cyanamid, 1995-1996; sr prod develop mgr, Am Cyanamid, 1994; mem biotech educ comt, Future Farmers Am, Biotech Indust Orgn, Maize Genetics Soc, 1993-; sr biologist, Am Cyanamid, 1991-1993; res scientist genetics, Biol Dept, Yale Univ, 1991; lectr biol, Conn Col, 1986-1991; sr res scientist, Dekalb Plant Genetics, DeKalb-Pfizer, 1985-1991; Res assoc biochem, Univ Mo, 1983-1985. **Memberships:** Am Soc Plant Physiologists; Int Soc Plant Molecular Biol; Future Farmers Am; Biotech Indust Orgn; Maize Genetics Soc. **Research Statement & Publications:** Molecular genetics to plant development; using transposable elements to gain a better understanding of genes controlling development; commercial application to modern agriculture. **Mailing Address:** MO Agr Prod Utilization & Incubation Ctr, Univ MO, 131 Mumford Hall, Columbia, MO 65211.

KRUEGER, SUSAN, BIOLOGY. **Education:** Univ Md, BS, 1982; Univ MS, 1985, PhD, 1987. **Professional Experience:** RES PHYSICIST, NAT INST STAND & TECHNOL, as of 2006. **Mailing Address:** Nat Stand & Technol Bldg, 100 Bur Dr Bldg 235 Stop 8562, Gaithersburg, MD 20899-8562. **Fax:** 301-921-9847. **E-Mail:** susan.krueger@.nist.gov

KRUEGER, WILLIAM ARTHUR, AGRONOMY. **Personal Data:** b Milford, Iowa, March 24, 1941. **Education:** Univ Minn, BS, 1963; Univ Ill, PhD (agron), 1968. **Professional Experience:** ASSOC PROF PLANT & SOIL SCI, UNIV TENN, KNOXVILLE, 1974-; asst prof agron, Univ Tenn, Knoxville, 1968-1974. **Memberships:** Plant Growth Regulator Soc; Weed Sci Soc Am. **Research Statement & Publications:** The effects that herbicides exert on the physiology of plants, particularly mode of action and basis of selectivity. **Mailing Address:** Canton Hollow Rd, Knoxville, TN 37922.

KRUEGER, WILLIAM CLEMENT, RANGE SCIENCE. **Personal Data:** b Medford, Ore, August 19, 1942; m 1965, c 2. **Education:** St Mary's Col, Calif, BS, 1964; Humboldt State Col, MS, 1967; Utah State Univ, PhD (range sci), 1970. **Professional Experience:** PROF & HEAD, DEPT RANGELAND RESOURCES, ORE STATE UNIV, 1981-; head, Dept Range Sci, Colo State Univ, 1980-1981; leader rangeland resources prog, Dept Rangeland Resources, Ore State Univ, 1975-1980; asst prof, Dept Rangeland Resources, Ore State Univ, 1971-1975; asst prof, Humboldt State Col, 1970-1971; res technician range sci, Intermountain Forest & Range Exp Sta, 1967-1970. **Memberships:** Soc Range Mgt; Sigma Xi. **Research Statement & Publications:** Range restoration; interaction of livestock grazing, wildlife and timber production through integration of management systems. **Mailing Address:** Dept Rangeland Resources, Ore State Univ, 200A Strand Agr Hall, Corvallis, OR 97331-2218. **Fax:** 541-737-0504. **E-Mail:** william.c.krueger@orst.edu

KRUEGER, WILLIAM E, ORGANIC CHEMISTRY. **Personal Data:** b St Louis, Mo, June 26, 1940. **Education:** Univ Notre Dame, BS, 1962; Univ NH, PhD (org chem), 1967. **Professional Experience:** PROF EMER CHEM, STATE UNIV NY COL PLATTSBURGH, 1999-; prof chem, State Univ NY Col Plattsburgh, 1985-1999; from asst prof to assoc prof, State Univ NY Col Plattsburgh, 1966-1985; res fel org chem, Univ Ill, Chicago Circle, 1966-1999. **Memberships:** Am Chem Soc. **Research Statement & Publications:** Partially reduced pyridines; nitrenes; phosphorus additions. **Mailing Address:** Dept Chem, State Univ NY, Colligan Point Rd, Plattsburgh, NY 12901-2698. **E-Mail:** kruegewe@plattsburgh.edu

KRUEGER, WILLIE FREDERICK, POULTRY HUSBANDRY, GENETICS. **Personal Data:** b Riesel, Tex, October 12, 1921; m 1946, Ruth; c 2. **Education:** Tex A&M Univ, BS, 1943, MS, 1949; Univ Mo, PhD (genetics, animal breeding), 1952. **Honors & Awards:** Assoc of Former Students of Assoc Purina Mills Teaching Award; Poultry Sci Assoc Fel; Texas Poultry fedn Golden feather Award; V Chancellor of Agri Award on Excellence; BLUE and Gold Award; Texas FFA Assoc. **Professional Experience:** Endowed prof, Tex A&M Univ, 1998-; Head dept, Tex A&M Univ, 1972-1982; Prof poultry sci, Tex A&M Univ, 1959-1998; from asst prof to assoc prof, Tex A&M Univ, 1953-1959; from instr to asst prof, Univ Mo, 1950-1953; asst, Univ Mo, 1949-1950; asst, Agr & Mech Col Tex, 1947-1949; instr poultry husb, Miss State Univ, 1946-1947; flock supvr, Tex Poultry Improv Asn, 1942-1943; Teacher & prin pub sch, Tex, 1941-1942. **Memberships:** Poultry Sci Asn; Am Genetic Asn; Sigma Xi fel Phi Rafpa Phi; fel Gamms Sigma Delta; fel Phi Delta Kappa. **Research Statement & Publications:** Application of the principles of population genetics to poultry; embryology; embryology and incubation of chicken and turkey eggs; environmental factors influencing chickens and turkeys. **Mailing Address:** Dept Poultry Sci, Tex A&M Univ, College Station, TX 77843-2472. **Fax:** 979-845-1921. **E-Mail:** wkrueger@poultry.tamu.edu

KRUER, WILLIAM LEO, PLASMA PHYSICS. **Personal Data:** b Louisville, Ky, April 20, 1942; m 1965, Elizabeth; c Judith, Margaret & Kathleen. **Education:** Univ Louisville, BS, 1964, MS, 1965; Princeton Univ, MA, 1967, PhD (astron), 1969. **Honors & Awards:** Maxwell Prize, Am Physical Soc, 1990. **Professional Experience:** CHIEF SCIENTIST, PLASMA PHYSICS, INERTIAL CONFINEMENT FUSION THEORY DIV, LAWRENCE LIVERMORE NAT LAB, as of 2004; CHAIR PROF PHYSICS, NAVAL POST GRAD SCH, LAWRENCE LIVERMORE NAT LAB, as of 2001; chief scientist laser plasma physics, Lawrence Livermore Lab, beginning 1993; affil mem Ctr Plas Physics & Fusion Eng, Univ Calif, Los Angeles, beginning 1976; lectr, Univ Calif, Davis/Livermore, beginning 1976; group leader laser plasma theory & simulation, Lawrence Livermore Lab, 1972-1993; mem res staff, Plasma Physics Lab, Princeton Univ, 1970-1972; res assoc, Plasma Physics Lab, Princeton Univ, 1969-1970. **Memberships:** Fel Am Phys Soc. **Research Statement & Publications:** Plasma theory; computer simulation of plasmas; nonlinear plasma waves; plasma heating; laser fusion. **Mailing Address:** Naval Postgraduate Sch, Lawrence Livermore Nat Lab, 4055 Suffolk Way, Pleasanton, CA 94566. **Fax:** 831-656-2834. **E-Mail:** kruer@physics.nps.navy.mil

KRUG, EDWARD CHARLES, ENVIRONMENTAL GEOCHEMISTRY. **Personal Data:** b New Brunswick, NJ, August 24, 1947. **Education:** Rutgers Univ, BSc, 1975, MSc, 1978,

PhD (environ geochem), 1981. **Professional Experience:** BIOGEOCHEMIST, ILL STATE WATER SURV, 2000-; environ consult, 1990-2000; assoc prof scientist, Ill State Water Surv, 1985-1990; asst soil scientist, Conn Agr Exp Sta, 1980-1985. **Memberships:** Soil Sci Soc Am; Am Geophys Union; AAAS; Int Soc Soil Sci. **Research Statement & Publications:** Reactions, weathering, and biogeochemical cycling of elements and materials in soil, water, and lake sediment; environmental policy making. **Mailing Address:** Ill State Water Surv, 2204 Griffith Dr, Champaign, IL 61820-7495. **Fax:** 217-333-4983. **E-Mail:** ekrug@uiuc.edu

KRUG, JOHN CHRISTIAN, mycology, lichenology; deceased, see previous edition for last biography

KRUG, MAURICE F, MECHANICAL ENGINEERING. **Personal Data:** b 1929. **Education:** Univ Dayton, Ohio, BS, 1955. **Professional Experience:** FOUNDER, CHMN & CHIEF EXEC OFFICER, KRUG INT CORP, 1959-; researcher, Univ Dayton, Ohio, 1955-1960. **Mailing Address:** Krug Int Corp, 6 N Main St Ste 1900, Dayton, OH 45402-1900.

KRUG, ROBERT M, MEDICAL RESEARCH. **Personal Data:** b Newark, NJ, August 27, 1939. **Education:** Harvard Univ, BA, 1961; Rockefeller Univ, PhD, 1966. **Professional Experience:** PROF, DEPT MOLECULAR GENETICS & MICROBIOL, UNIV TEX, AUSTIN, as of 2004; prof chmn, dept molecular biol & biochem, Rutgers Univ, beginning 1990; dir joint grad prog biochem, Univ Med & Dent, Robert Wood Johnson Med Sch, beginning 1990; Karl Meyer lectr, Univ Calif, San Francisco Med Ctr, 1986; chmn, Molecular Biol Prog, 1983-1986; prof, Cornell Univ Grad Sch Med, 1980-1990; mem, Lab Viral & Cellular Gene Expression, 1979-1990; head, Lab Viral & Cellular Gene Expression, 1978-1990; assoc mem, Mem Sloan-Kettering Cancer Ctr, NY, 1972-1979; from asst prof to assoc prof molecular biol, Cornell Univ Grad Sch Med, 1969-1979; asst mem, Mem Sloan-Kettering Cancer Ctr, NY, 1968-1971; res assoc, Mem Sloan-Kettering Cancer Ctr, NY, 1965-1968. **Memberships:** Am Soc Microbiol; Am Soc Virology; Am Soc Biochem & Molecular Biol. **Research Statement & Publications:** Molecular biology and biochemistry. **Mailing Address:** Inst Cellular & Molecular Biol, Univ Tex, One Univ Sta A4800, Austin, TX 78712. **Fax:** 512-232-5566. **E-Mail:** rkrug@icmb.utexas.edu

KRUG, SAMUEL EDWARD, PSYCHOLOGICAL & EDUCATIONAL MEASUREMENT, PERSONALITY ASSESSMENT. **Personal Data:** b Chicago, Ill, November 15, 1943; m 1968, Marion; c Mark, Michael, David & Timothy. **Education:** Col Holy Cross, AB, 1965; Univ Ill Urbana-Champaign, MA, 1968, PhD (psychol), 1971. **Professional Experience:** PRES, INDUST PSYCHOL INT, LTD, 1989-; adj prof, Univ Ill, Urbana-Champaign, 1987-; PRES, METRITECH INC, 1982-; managing dir, Inst Personality & Ability Testing, 1971-1982. **Memberships:** Fel Am Psychol Asn; fel Soc Personality Assessment; Nat Coun Measurement Educ; Am Educ Res Asn, Diplomate Am bd assessment psychology. **Research Statement & Publications:** Applied psychological and educational measurement, including test development and computer-based interpretation of test results. **Mailing Address:** Metritech Inc, 4106 Fieldstone, Champaign, IL 61820-8801. **Fax:** 217-398-5798. **E-Mail:** skrug@metritch.com

KRUGER, ALBERT AARON, SOLID STATE CHEMISTRY, MATERIALS SCIENCE. **Personal Data:** b Brooklyn, NY, October 3, 1952; c Evelyne & Nathaniel R. **Education:** Brooklyn Col, BS, 1974; Syracuse Univ, MS, 1978. **Honors & Awards:** Solvay seminar-1985; BSA District Award of Merit. **Professional Experience:** CONSULT, ORE GRAD INST, 1994-; site eval team mem, NSF, beginning 1993; prin scientist, Westinghouse Hanford, 1991-1997; sr res scientist, Batelle-Pac NW Labs, 1988-1990; adj, Dept Physics, Brooklyn Col, 1987-1988; supvr & confirmed res scientist, St Gobain Res, 1982-1987; team leader & sr chemist, 3M Cent Res Labs, 1978-1982; sr tech assoc, Bell Tel Labs, 1975-1978. **Memberships:** Fel Am Inst Chemists; Sigma Xi; Am Chem Soc; Mat Res Soc; Am Ceramic Soc; Int Union Pure & Appl Chem. **Research Statement & Publications:** Materials science and in particular the preparation and synthesis of solids with novel electrical properties; surface treatments and correlating their effects on bulk physical properties of materials. **Mailing Address:** 2175 Clearview Ave, Richland, WA 99352-1809. **Fax:** 509-375-1705. **E-Mail:** albert@wastren.com

KRUGER, CHARLES HERMAN, PHYSICAL GAS DYNAMICS, PARTIALLY IONIZED PLASMAS. **Personal Data:** b Oklahoma City, Okla, October 4, 1934; m 1977, Nora; c Saran, Charles III, Elizabeth & Ellen. **Education:** Mass Inst Technol, SB, 1956, PhD (mech eng), 1960; Univ London, dipl, Imp Col, 1957. **Honors & Awards:** Fluid & Plasmadynamics Award & Medal, Am Inst Aeronaut & Astronaut, 1979; Fel AAAS. **Professional Experience:** DEP CHAIR BIOX PROG, as of 2004; vice provost & dean res & grad policy, stanford univ, 1993-2003; sr assoc dean, Standord Univ, 1988-1992; chmn, Standord Univ, 1982-1988; adv coun, MAE Dept, Princeton Univ, 1981-1991; mem, Environ Studies Bd, Nat Acad Sci, 1980-1983; vis scientist, Norwegian Inst Technol, 1979; chmn, Steering Comt, Eng Aspects of Magnetohydrodyn, 1978-1981; vis prof, Harvard Univ, 1968-1969 & Princeton Univ, 1978-1979; PROF MECH ENG, STANFORD UNIV, 1970-; mem hearing bd, Bay Area Air Pollution Control Dist, 1970-1983; sr fel, Nat Sci Found, 1968-1969; from asst prof to assoc prof, Standord Univ, 1962-1970; res scientist, Res Labs, Lockheed Missiles & Space Co, Calif, 1960-1962; from instr to asst prof mech eng, Mass Inst Technol, 1959-1960. **Memberships:** Am Phys Soc; Am Soc Mech Engrs; Am Inst Aeronaut & Astronaut; fel amer Assoc Adv Sci. **Research Statement & Publications:** Physical gas dynamics; partially ionized plasmas; plasma chemistry; plasma diagnostics; diamond synthesis. **Mailing Address:** Bldg 10, Stanford Univ, Stanford, CA 94305. **E-Mail:** Charles.Kruger@Stanford.Edu

KRUGER, FRED W, MECHANICAL ENGINEERING. **Personal Data:** b Chicago, Ill, December 17, 1921; m 1947, Esther Foelber; c Paul W, John R & ThomasH. **Education:** Univ Purdue, BS, 1943, BS, 1947; Univ Notre Dame, MS, 1954. **Professional Experience:** EMER PROF, VALPARAISO UNIV, 1987-; mem city coun, City of Valparaiso, 1972-1996 & City Planning Comn, 1976-1985; vpres, Valparaiso Univ, 1974-1987; dean col eng, Valparaiso Univ, 1965-1972; chmn dept, Valparaiso Univ, 1955-1965; Instr mech eng, Valparaiso Univ, 1947-1955; Consult, McDonnell Aircraft Co, Caterpillar Tractor Co, Argonne Nat Lab, Northern Ill Gas Co; Ind State Bd Registr Prof Eng. **Memberships:** Am Soc Mech Engrs; Am Soc Eng Educ. **Research Statement & Publications:** Heat power systems. **Mailing Address:** Gellerson Eng Bldg, Valparaiso Univ, Valparaiso, IN 46383.

KRUGER, JAMES EDWARD, ENZYMOLOGY, CEREAL CHEMISTRY. **Personal Data:** b Winnipeg, Man, October 14, 1938; m 1960, c 1. **Education:** Univ Man, BSc, 1960, MSc, 1963; Univ Sask, PhD (phys org), 1965. **Professional Experience:** WHEAT ENZYME & ASIAN END PROD RES, GRAIN RES LAB, 1989-; RES SCIENTIST CHEM CEREAL, GRAIN RES LAB, 1966-. **Memberships:** Am Asn Cereal Chemists; Chem Inst Can; Am Asn Plant Physiologists. **Research Statement & Publications:** Wheat systems such as amylase, proteases, polyphenol, and oxidoases; high performance liquid chromatography of sugars and proteins; automation of analytical techniques in cereal chemistry; preharvest sprouting problems. **Mailing Address:** 303 Main St Rm 1404, Winnipeg, MB R3C 3G8, Can.

KRUGER, JEROME, CORROSION SCIENCE & ENGINEERING. **Personal Data:** b Atlanta, Ga, February 7, 1927; m 1955, Mollee; c Lennard & Joseph. **Education:** Ga Inst Technol, BS, 1948, MS, 1950; Univ Va, PhD, 1953. **Honors & Awards:** Silver Medal, Com Dept, 1962, Gold Medal, 1972; W R Whitney Award, Nat Asn Corrosion engrs, 1976; U R Evans Award, Brit Inst corrosion, 1991; Olin Palladium Medal, electrochem Soc 1995. **Professional Experience:** PROF EMER, JOHNS HOPKINS UNIV, 1999-; prof, Johns Hopkins Univ, 1984-1999; sect chief, Corrosion & Electrodeposition Nat, Bur Stds, 1966-1980; mem staff, Nat Bur Stand, Com dept, Wash, 1955-1983; mem staff, Naval Res Lab, Wash, 1952-1955; consult, argonne nat lab, Lockheed, Baltimore Gas & Elec, Teletech, Thompson, Dalton & DeRose & Mueller Brass. **Memberships:** Fel & hon mem Electrochem Soc (treas, 1982-1986); fel Nat Asn Corrosion Engrs; AAAS; fedn mat soc (pres, 1977); Sigma Xi; Chmn Int corrosion coun 1987, 1990. **Research Statement & Publications:** Material science and engineering; corrosion science and engineering electrochemistry electrodeposition passivity breakdown of passivity and localized corrosion x-ray absorption spectroscopy economics of corrosion; underground marine and atmospheric corrosion conservation (artistic and historical objects) science. **Mailing Address:** Johns Hopkins Univ, 619 Warfield Dr, Rockville, MD 20850-1921. **Fax:** 301-762-5291. **E-Mail:** jk2727@aol.com

KRUGER, LAWRENCE, NEUROANATOMY, NEUROPHYSIOLOGY. **Personal Data:** b New Brunswick, NJ, August 15, 1929; m 1961, Virginia; c Erika & Paula. **Education:** Wagner Col, BS, 1949; Yale Univ, PhD (physiol), 1954. **Professional Experience:** Wellcome vis prof, 1981; DISTINGUISHED PROF ANAT, UNIV CALIF, LOS ANGELES, 1966-; Lederle med fac award, 1961-1964; from asst prof to assoc prof, Univ Calif, Los Angeles, 1960-1966; USPHS sr res fel anat, Univ Calif, Los Angeles, 1959-1960; Nat Res Coun fel anat, Oxford Univ, 1958-1959; Nat Res Coun fel, Col France, 1958; USPHS fel physiol, Johns Hopkins Univ, 1955-1958; asst neurophysiol, Inst Living, Conn, 1953-1954; asst physiol, Yale Univ, 1950-1953; mem, Int Brain Res Orgn, UNESCO. **Memberships:** AAAS; Am Asn Anatomists; Am Physiol Soc; Soc Neuroscience. **Research Statement & Publications:** Cutaneous receptors and their central nervous system representation; organization of the visual system in vertebrates with particular reference to the midbrain; thalamo-cortical relations; electron microscopy of neural degeneration; pain. **Mailing Address:** Dept Neurobiol, Univ Calif, 73-235 Health Sci Ctr, Los Angeles, CA 90024. **Fax:** 310-825-2224. **E-Mail:** lkruger@neurobio.medsch.ucla.edu

KRUGER, OWEN L, CERAMICS, METALLURGY. **Personal Data:** b Oak Park, Ill, December 1, 1932; m 1954, c 4. **Professional Experience:** SR ENGR & COST ANALYST, EXXON NUCLEAR CO, INC, 1977-; assoc chief, Plutonium Technol & Mat, Thermodyn Div, Columbus Div, Battelle Mem Inst, 1969-1977; assoc metallurgist, Argonne Nat Lab, 1957-1969; metallurgist, Continental Foundry & Mach Co, 1954-1955; Metall engr, Ill Inst Technol, 1954. **Memberships:** Fel Am Ceramic Soc; Am Nuclear Soc. **Research Statement & Publications:** Light water reactor fuel fabrication; plutonium ceramics and metallurgy; fast reactor fuel development. **Mailing Address:** 2360 Harris Ave, Richland, WA 99352.

KRUGER, PAUL, NUCLEAR CIVIL ENGINEERING. **Personal Data:** b Jersey City, NJ, June 7, 1925; m 1972, Claudia Mathis; c Sharon, Kenneth & Louis. **Education:** Mass Inst Technol, BS, 1950; Univ Chicago, MS, 1952, PhD (nuclear chem), 1954. **Professional Experience:** PROF NUCLEAR CIVIL ENG, STANFORD UNIV, 1962-; mgr nuclear proj, Hazelton-Nuclear Sci Corp, 1960-1962; vpres & head, Dept Phys Sci, Nuclear Sci & Eng Corp, Pa, 1954-1960; res physicist, Res Labs Div, Gen Motors Corp, 1953-1954; Asst instr nuclear & phys chem, Univ Chicago, 1950-1953. **Memberships:** Fel Am Nuclear Soc; Am Soc Civil Engrs; Am Chem Soc. **Research Statement & Publications:** Nuclear methods in civil engineering and environmental sciences; environmental radioactivity; energy and environment. **Mailing Address:** Stanford, CA 94305. **Fax:** 650-493-5122. **E-Mail:** kruger@cive.stanford.edu

KRUGER, RICHARD PAUL, ELECTRICAL ENGINEERING. **Personal Data:** b Chicago, Ill, July 27, 1944; m 1969, c 2. **Education:** Purdue Univ, BS, 1967; Univ Mo, MS, 1968, PhD (elec eng), 1971; Univ NMex, MBA, 1979. **Professional Experience:** CHIEF SCIENTIST, SAIC, 1993-; group leader, Los Alamos Nat Lab, Univ Calif, 1989-1993; asst vpres, Sci Int Applns Inc, 1982-1989; Aerospace Corp, 1975 & Univ Southern Calif, 1976-1977; staff mem elec eng, Los Alamos Nat Lab, Univ Calif, 1975-1982; Consult, Rockwell Corp, 1973; Asst prof elec eng & radiol, Univ Southern Calif, 1971-1975. **Memberships:** Sr mem Inst Elec & Electronics Engrs; Sigma Xi. **Research Statement & Publications:** Computer image processing applied to biomedical and industrial images; industrial automation; pattern recognition; computed tomography. **Mailing Address:** SAIC, 1710 Goodridge Dr PO Box 1303, McLean, VA 22102.

KRUGH, THOMAS RICHARD, BIOPHYSICAL CHEMISTRY. **Personal Data:** b Pittsburgh, Pa, May 3, 1943; m 1970, Rosemary; c Bradley. **Education:** Univ Pittsburgh, BS, 1965; Pa State Univ, PhD (phys chem), 1969. **Professional Experience:** PROF CHEM, UNIV ROCHESTER, 1978-; from asst prof to assoc prof, Univ Rochester, 1970-1978; NIH fel, Stanford Univ, 1969-1970. **Memberships:** AAAS; Biophys Soc; Am Chem Soc; Am Asn Cancer Res. **Research Statement & Publications:** Biophysical chemistry; drug-nucleic acid complexes; carcinogen-nucleic acid complexes; structures of nucleic acids; nuclear magnetic resonance. **Mailing Address:** Dept Chem, Univ Rochester, Rochester, NY 14627-0216. **Fax:** 585-473-6889.

KRUGMAN, STANLEY LIEBERT, FOREST GENETICS, FOREST PHYSIOLOGY, CONSERVATION ECOLOGY. **Personal Data:** b St Louis, Mo, June 8, 1932; m 1958, Judith; c Jeffrey J & Mark B. **Education:** Univ Mo, BS, 1954; Univ Calif, MS, 1956, PhD (plant physiol), 1961. **Honors & Awards:** William Schlich Memorial Medal, Soc Am Foresters, 1990; Forestry Gold Medals, Czech Repub & Repub Poland. **Professional Experience:** FOREST CONSULT, 1995-; sr forest consult, World Bank, 1990-1998; dir, Forest Mgt Res, 1981-1995; biotechnol comt, Nat Genetics Resources Bd, 1978-1986; biotechnol comt, USDA, 1974-1987; res forest geneticist, Inst Forest Genetics, 1974-1981; chief br genetic & related res, Inst Forest Genetics, 1971-1974; proj leader genetics res proj, Inst Forest Genetics, 1966-1971; res assoc, Agr Exp Sta, Univ Calif, 1962-1971; plant physiologist forest genetics, Pac Southwest Forest Range & Exp Sta, US Forest Serv, 1962-1966; res specialist, Univ Calif, 1960-1962; res asst forestry, Univ Calif, 1958-1960; teaching asst, Univ Calif, 1956-1958; res specialist, Univ Mo, 1953-1955. **Memberships:** Fel Soc Am Foresters; Soc Plant Physiol; fel AAAS; Int Union Forestry Res Orgn. **Research Statement & Publications:** Pigments, hormones and reproductive physiology as related to trees; forest and tree improvement/diversity; international research, including forest restoration, ecology and genetic resource conservation; forest biology/diversity. **Mailing Address:** 6515 Dryden Dr, Mc Lean, VA 22101. **Fax:** 703-356-9145.

KRUH, DANIEL, RESEARCH & DEVELOPMENT, CHEMICAL CONSULTING. **Personal Data:** b Brooklyn, NY, May 22, 1934; m Sheila; c Andrew & Ira (deceased). **Education:** WVa Wesleyan Col, BS (chem), 1955; Rensselaer Polytech Inst, PhD (org chem), 1963.

Honors & Awards: Inventors Award, Gen Elec. **Professional Experience:** BD DIRS, NORTHEAST AM OIL CHEMISTS SOC, 1995-; PRES, POLY(CHEM TECH), 1994-; prin res chemist, Metuchen Analytical, Kendall Infrared, 1994-1996; sr res assoc new technol, Block Drug Co Inc, 1993-1994; mgr new technol, Block Drug Co Inc, 1992-1993, 1988-1989; mgr, licensing & acquisitions, Block Drug Co Inc, 1988-1992; mem bd dirs, Soc Plastics Eng, Med Plastics Div, 1987-1990; sr res assoc, Block Drug Co Inc, 1987-1988; proj mgr, Nat Patent Develop Corp, 1984-1987; sr chemist, Electro-Sci Labs Inc, 1983-1984; supvr polymer tech serv, Johnson & Johnson Dental Prod Co, 1976-1983; sr res scientist, Johnson & Johnson Dental Prod Co, 1975-1976; res assoc, Johnson & Johnson Dental Prods Co, 1972-1975; mgr wire enamel develop, Insulating Mat Dept, Gen Elec Co, 1970-1972; specialist adv develop composites bus oper, Insulating Mat Dept, Gen Elec Co, 1966-1970; res chemist, Hercules Powder Co, 1963-1966. **Memberships:** Am Chem Soc; Soc Plastics Eng; Asn Consult Chemists & Chem Engrs; Soc Cosmetic Chemists; Am Asn Pharmaceut Scientists. **Research Statement & Publications:** Antiradiation drugs; phthalocyanine pigments; polyimides; chemical and light cured professional dental materials and products; high performance polymers in coatings and composites; silicone gas permeable and tinted soft contact lenses; conductive polymer thick films; consumer products like health and beauty aids, dental, household; published 9 articles and granted 7 US patents; consulting in new technology, polymer applications and dental products. **Mailing Address:** Eight Braddock St, East Brunswick, NJ 08816-2702. **Fax:** 732-238-3182. **E-Mail:** dankruh@aol.com

KRUH, ROBERT FRANK, PHYSICAL CHEMISTRY. **Personal Data:** b St Louis, Mo, June 15, 1925; m 1948, c 2. **Education:** Washington Univ, AB, 1948, PhD (chem), 1951. **Professional Experience:** Vice Provose, 1990-1994; chmn, Grad Record Exam Bd, 1980-1981; chmn, Bd Dirs, 1978-1979; MEM, GRAD RECORD EXAM BD, 1977-; PRES, KANS STATE UNIV RES FOUND, 1970-; mem bd trustees, Argonne Univ Asn, 1970-1977; mem policy comt, Coun Grad Schs, US, 1969-1973; mem coun res policy and grad educ, Nat Asn State Univs & Land Grant Cols, 1968-1972; prof chem & dean grad sch, Kans State Univ, 1967-1990; Vis prof, Wash Univ, 1960-1961; from asst prof to prof chem & dean col arts & sci, Univ Ark, 1952-1967; Asst prof chem, DePauw Univ, 1951-1952. **Memberships:** Sigma Xi; AAAS; Am Chem Soc; fel Am Inst Chemists; Am Phys Soc. **Research Statement & Publications:** Crystallography; x-ray diffraction; structure of liquids. **Mailing Address:** 2155 Blue Hills Rd, Manhattan, KS 66502-4561.

KRUISBEEK, ADA M, DEVELOPMENTAL BIOLOGY. **Personal Data:** b Rotterdam, Neth, October 2, 1938. **Education:** Leiden Univ, BS, 1973, PhD (immunol), 1978. **Professional Experience:** SR INVESTR, NIH, 1986-; cancer expert, 1982-1986; Vis scientist, 1979-1982. **Memberships:** Am Asn Immunologists; Brit Soc Immunologists; Europ Soc Geront. **Mailing Address:** Netherlands Kanker Inst, Res Bldg H7 Plesmanlaan 121, Amsterdam 1066CX, Netherlands. **Fax:** 312-051-22057.

KRUK, PATRICIA ANN, GERONTOLOGY, PATHOLOGY. **Education:** Univ BC, PhD, 1992. **Professional Experience:** ASSOC PROF, DEPT PATHOL, UNIV S FLA, as of 2005. **Memberships:** Am Asn Cancer Res. **Mailing Address:** Dept Pathol, Univ S Fla, MDC 11 12901 Bruce B Downs Blvd, Tampa, FL 33612. **Fax:** 813-974-0538. **E-Mail:** pkruk@hsc.usf.edu

KRUKAR, RICHARD HAROLD, DISTRIBUTED INTELLIGENT CONTROL, OPTICAL METROLOGY. **Personal Data:** b Aurora, Colo, May 24, 1962. **Education:** Univ NMex, BUS, 1984, MSEE, 1987, PhD (elec eng), 1993. **Professional Experience:** DEVELOP ENGR, BIO-RAD LABS, 1997-; Control Systs Engr, Lam Res, 1996-1997; mem tech staff, Lucent Bell Labs, 1994-1996; Pres, Desert Sage, 1992-1994. **Research Statement & Publications:** Distributed controls, pattern recognition and statistical analysis; designing and building instrumentation and writing software. **Mailing Address:** Bio-Rad Laboratories, Accent Optical Tech, 3825 Acadamy Pkwy S NE, Albuquerque, NM 87109. **E-Mail:** krukar@ectopia.com

KRUKOWSKI, MARILYN, CELL BIOLOGY, DEVELOPMENTAL BIOLOGY. **Personal Data:** b New York, NY, May 3, 1932; American & Canadian citizen; m 1955, Lucian; c Samantha. **Education:** Brooklyn Col, BA, 1954; NY Univ, MA, 1962, PhD (biol), 1965. **Professional Experience:** PROF EMER BIOL, WASH UNIV, as of 2004; prof biol, wash Univ, beginning 1987; assoc prof, Wash Univ, 1975-1987; from res asst prof to asst prof, Wash Univ, 1969-1975; asst prof pharmacol & coinvestr endocrinol& exp cardiovasc dis, NY Med Col, Flower & Fifth Ave Hosps, 1966-1969; instr pharmacol, NY Med Col, Flower & Fifth Ave Hosps, 1964-1966; res assoc, NY Med Col, Flower & Fifth Ave Hosps, 1962-1966; res asst endocrinol exp cardiovasc dis, NY Med Col, Flower & Fifth Ave Hosps, 1956-1962. **Memberships:** AAAS; AmSoc Cell Biol; Am Soc Bone & Mineral Res; Sigma Xi; Orthop Res Soc. **Research Statement & Publications:** Bone development; origin, induction and cytodifferentiation of bone-resorbing cells; factors and materials that stimulate bone formation. **Mailing Address:** Dept Biol, Wash Univ, PO Box 1229, St Louis, MO 63130-4899. **E-Mail:** krukow@biology.wustl.edu

KRUL, ELAINE, CARDIOLOGY. **Education:** PhD. **Professional Experience:** RES SCIENTIST, GD SEARLE & CO, as of 2006. **Memberships:** Wash Univ Senate Coun. **Mailing Address:** GD Searle & Co, 800 N Lindbergh Blvd T2M, St Louis, MO 63167. **Fax:** 847-470-1480.

KRULICH, LADISLAV, neuro-endocrinology; deceased, see previous edition for last biography

KRULL, IRA STANLEY, ANALYTICAL CHEMISTRY. **Personal Data:** b New York, NY, October 21, 1940; m 1973, Erica; c Marc A. **Education:** City Col NY, BS, 1962; NY Univ, MS, 1966, PhD (org chem), 1968. **Honors & Awards:** Innovative Res Award Anal Chem, Barnett Inst, 1983; Bioanal Sci Recognition Outstanding Achievement Award, 1988; Recognition Award, Am Asn Pharmaceut Scientists, 1988. **Professional Experience:** PROF CHEM, NORTHEASTERN UNIV, BOSTON, MA, as of 2005; vis scholar, Bioanal Systs Inc & Purdue Univ, Ind, 1991; vis sabbatical prof, Anal Res Dept, Ciba-Geigy Corp, Switz, 1990; proposal reviewer, Am Chem Soc Petrol res fund, 1985-; ad hoc res review comt, res assoc prog, 1985-1991; assoc prof chem, Northeastern Univ, beginning 1984; proposal reviewer, NSF, 1983-; sci adv, res assoc prog, 1983-1987; NIH Small Bus Innovation Res Study Sect, 1983, 1984, 1986 & 1988; Spec Study Sect & site visit, Univ Wash, 1983; Boston Dist Sci Adv, Food & Drug Admin, 1980-; sr scientist & fac fel, Barnett Inst, 1979-1992; sr scientist chem, Thermo Electron Corp, 1977-1979; asst scientist, Boyce Thompson Inst Plant Res, 1973-1976; weizmann fel chem, Weizmann Inst Sci, 1970-1973; Union Carbide fel, 1968-1970. **Memberships:** Am Chem Soc; NY Acad Sci; AAAS; Soc Electroanal Chem; Sigma Xi. **Research Statement & Publications:** Analytical biotechnology; analytical biochemistry; trace organic analytical chemistry; analytical method development; instrumentation research and development; drug analysis; bioanalytical chemistry; author of numerous publications. **Mailing Address:** Dept Chem, Northeastern Univ, 102 Hurtig Hall 360 Huntington Ave, Boston, MA 02115. **Fax:** 617-373-8795. **E-Mail:** i.krull@neu.edu

KRULL, JOHN NORMAN, ECOLOGY, WILDLIFE BIOLOGY. **Personal Data:** b Albany, NY, July 31, 1939; m 1963, c 2. **Education:** State Univ NY Col Forestry, Syracuse, BS, 1961, MS, 1963, PhD (wetland ecol), 1967. **Professional Experience:** Prof wildlife biol & conserv, cent mich univ, beginning 1975; PROF EMER WILDLIFE BIOL & CONSERV, CENT MICH UNIV, 1975-; assoc prof, Cent Mich Univ, 1971-1975; asst prof, Southern Ill Univ, 1967-1971. **Memberships:** Soc Am Foresters; Conserv Educ Asn; Soil & Water Conserv Soc; Wildlife Soc. **Research Statement & Publications:** Wetland ecology, especially green-treereservoir ecology, waterfowl use and production from various wetland habitats, and aquatic plant-invertebrate associations; wildlife management investigations; conservation. **Mailing Address:** Dept Biol, Cent Mich Univ, 217 Brooks Hall, Mt Pleasant, MI 48859-0001. **Fax:** 989-774-3462.

KRULL, ULRICH JORG, BIOSENSORS, CHEMICALLY MODIFIED SURFACES. **Personal Data:** b Berlin, Ger, October 28, 1956; Canadian citizen; m 1980, Carol; c Jeffrey M & Justin U. **Education:** Univ Toronto, BSc, 1979, MSc, 1980, PhD (anal chem), 1983. **Honors & Awards:** Maxxam lect award, can soc chem, 2002, Lansdowne lect award, U victoria, can, 2001, faculty award, alumni assn, U Toronto, 2000, Astrazeneca Chmn in biotechnol, Astrazeneca, inc, 1998 McBryde Medal, Can Soc Chem, 1994. **Professional Experience:** Astrazeneca Chmn in biotech, univ totonto, 1998-; counr, Can Int Inst, 1995-; PROF ANAL CHEM, UNIV TORONTO, 1995-; counr, Royal Can Inst, 1994-; ASSOC DEAN SCI & VPRIN RES, UNIV TORONTO, ERINDALE CAMPUS, 1994-; sec vpres, Royal Can Inst, 1993-1994; res assoc, Ctr Plant Biotechnol, 1992-1995; chmn, Anal Chem Div, Chem Inst Can, 1992-1994; assoc prof anal chem, Univ Toronto, 1990-1995; asst Chmn chem, Univ Toronto, 1990-1992; res fac, Inst Environ Studies, 1989-; prin investr, Chem Sensors Group, Univ Toronto, 1985-; asst prof anal chem, Univ Toronto, 1985-1990. **Memberships:** Fel Chem InstCan; Royal Can Inst; Royal Astron Soc Can; Can Int Inst. **Research Statement & Publications:** Investigation of organized organic monolayers for biosensor development, this has involved the study of lipid membranes as electrochemical and flourescent transducers of selective binding interactions of proteins; development of analytical techniques such as photopyroelectric spectroscopy and immobilization of amphiphile/enzyme assemblies and single stranded DNA for preparation of fibre-optic biosensors. **Mailing Address:** Dept Chem Erindale Col, Univ Toronto, Mississauga, ON L5L 1C6, Can. **Fax:** 905-828-5425. **E-Mail:** ukrull@credit.erin.utoronto.ca

KRULWICH, TERRY ANN, BIOCHEMISTRY & BIOENERGETICS, MICROBIAL PHYSIOLOGY. **Personal Data:** b New York, NY, April 7, 1943; m 1973, c 3. **Education:** Goucher Col, BA, 1964; Univ Wis-Madison, MS, 1966, PhD (bact), 1968. **Honorary Degrees:** DSc, Goucher Col, 1987. **Professional Experience:** PROF PHARMACOL & BIOL CHEM, MT SINAI SCH MED, as of 2004; mem, Microbiol Physiol Genetics Study Sect, 1983-1987; prof biochem, Mt Sinai Sch Med, beginning 1981; dean grad sch, Mt Sinai Sch Med, beginning 1981; NIH, mem Cellular Molecular Basic Dis Comt, 1978-1982; NIH, Res Career Develop Award, 1975-1980; from asst prof to assoc prof, MT Sinai Sch Med, 1970-1981; fel, NSF postdoctoral, 1968-1970; postdoctoral fel molecular biol, Albert Einstein Col Med, 1968-1970; NIH trainee bact, Univ Wis, 1968; fel NSF predoctoral, 1964-1968. **Memberships:** AAAS; Am Soc Microbiol; Am Chem Soc; Am Soc Biol Chemists; NY Acad Sci; Biophys Soc; Sigma Xi. **Research Statement & Publications:** Microbial bioenergetics; alkalophilic and acidophilic bacteria; protonophore resistance. **Mailing Address:** Dept Pharmacol & Biol Chem, Mt Sinai Sch Med, One Gustave L Levy Pl, PO Box 1603, New York, NY 10029-6504. **Fax:** 212-996-7214. **E-Mail:** terry.krulwich@mssm.edu

KRUM, ALVIN A, PHYSIOLOGY. **Personal Data:** b Fresno, Calif, May 14, 1928; m 1954, c 2. **Education:** Univ Calif, AB, 1950, PhD (physiol), 1957. **Professional Experience:** RETIRED; prof physiol, Med Ctr, Univ Ark, Little Rock, beginning 1973; Lederle Med Fac Award, 1964-1967; from asst prof to assoc prof, Med Ctr, Univ Ark, Little Rock, 1961-1973; fel, Steroid Training Prog, Univ Utah, 1958-1959; res physiologist, Univ Calif, 1957-1962. **Memberships:** AAAS; Am Physiol Soc; Endocrine Soc; Soc Exp Biol & Med; Sigma Xi. **Research Statement & Publications:** Endocrinology; steroid biosynthesis; metabolism. **Mailing Address:** 1829 Whispering Oaks, Poplar Bluff, MO 63901-2069.

KRUM, JACK KERN, FOOD TECHNOLOGY. **Personal Data:** b Kansas City, Mo, March 17, 1922; m 1946, Miriam; c Meredith, Mark, Eric & Andrew. **Education:** Hope Col, AB, 1944; Mich State Univ, MS, 1948; Univ Mass, PhD (food tech), 1949. **Honors & Awards:** Fel, Inst Food Technol, 1983. **Professional Experience:** PRES, TECHNIQUES INC, 1980-; tech dir, ITT Paniplus Co, 1973-1979; vpres & dir res & develop, R T French Co, 1972-1973; dir res & develop, R T French Co, 1971-1972; White House Conf Food Nutrit & Health, 1969 & tech comt, Grocery Mfrs Am, 1970-1973; asst res dir, R T French Co, 1969-1970; chmn, Flavoring Extract Mfrs Asn US, 1967-1971; mem indust comt, Food Protection Comn, Nat Acad Sci, 1964-1966; mem food additive comt, Flavoring Extract Mfrs Asn US, 1961-1972; tech dir, Sterwin Chem Inc, 1961-1969; asst tech dir, Sterwin Chem Inc, 1956-1961; res chemist, Nat Biscuit Co, 1952-1956; food technologist charge prod control labs, Oscar Mayer & Co, 1950-1952; assoc prof food technol, Univ Tenn, 1949-1950. **Memberships:** Am Asn Cereal Chem; Inst Food Technol. **Research Statement & Publications:** Food additives; new product development; fermentation; nutrition; food processing; dry mixes; food additives; dehydration; food flavors; stabilizers, emulsifiers and enrichment; research administration. **Mailing Address:** Techniques Inc, 16705 W 327th St, Paola, KS 66071.

KRUMBEIN, SIMEON JOSEPH, ELECTROCHEMISTRY, SURFACE PHYSICS. **Personal Data:** b Brooklyn, NY, m 1957, c 3. **Education:** Brooklyn Col, BS, 1956; NY Univ, PhD (phys chem), 1961. **Honors & Awards:** Lowenheim Mem Award, Am Soc Testing & Mat, 1992. **Professional Experience:** MEM, AMP INC, as of 2004; SR MEM TECH STAFF, TECHNOL DIV, AMP, INC, 1991-; sr eng scientist, Res Div, 1977-1991; assoc prof chem, Stern Col, Yeshiva Univ, 1975-1979; consult, Res Div, AMP, Inc, 1973-1976; co-adj asst prof chem, Univ Col, Rutgers Univ, 1972-1974; Consult, US Army Electronic Components Lab, 1970; asst prof, Stern Col, Yeshiva Univ, 1969-1975; sr scientist, Res Div, Burndy Corp, 1964-1969; phys chemist, Fuel Cell Lab, Gen Elec Co, 1961-1964; Chemist, TRG, Inc, 1956-1957. **Memberships:** Am Chem Soc; Electrochem Soc; Am Soc Testing & Mat; Sigma Xi; Int Inst Connector & Interconnection Technol. **Research Statement & Publications:** Experimental methods in fuel cell research; electrical contact phenomena; metallic corrosion; experimental electrode kinetics; contact materials; environmental testing; electromigration; plating porosity. **Mailing Address:** AMP Inc MS 106-13, PO Box 3608, Harrisburg, PA 17105. **Fax:** 717-986-5218.

KRUMDIECK, CARLOS L, BIOCHEMISTRY, NUTRITION. **Personal Data:** b Lima, Peru, November 11, 1932; c 2. **Education:** San Marcos Univ, Lima, BMed & MD, 1958; Tulane Univ La, PhD (biochem), 1964. **Honors & Awards:** Bordeu Award in Nutrit, 1985. **Professional Experience:** PROF EMER NUTRIT SCI, UNIV ALA, BIRMINGHAM, as of 2005; prof biochem, Univ Ala, Birmingham, beginning 1977; assoc prof pediat, Univ Ala, Birmingham, beginning 1976; assoc dir nutrit prog, Univ Ala, Birmingham, 1976-1985; assoc prof biochem, Univ Ala, Birmingham, 1970-1981; asst prof biochem & med, Univ Ala, Birmingham, 1967-1970; prof biochem, Univ Cayetano Heredia, Peru, 1965-1970; Rockefeller Found fel biochem, USPHS fel, 1962-1963; Rockefeller Found fel biochem, Tulane Univ La, 1960-1962 & 1964; biochemist, Hektoen Inst Med Res, Chicago, Ill, 1959-1960; resident med, Hosp 2nd May, Lima, Peru, 1958-1959. **Memberships:** Am Soc Biol Chemists; Sigma Xi; Am Inst Nutrit; Am Soc Clin Nutrit; NY Acad Sci; AAAS; Physicians Social Responsibility. **Research Statement & Publications:** Biochemistry of folic acid polyglutamates; biochemical assessment of nutrient status; pathogenesis of atherosclerosis; nutrition and cancer. **Mailing Address:** Dept Nutrit Sci, Univ Med Ala 1675 Univ Blvd Rm 304, Birmingham, AL 35294-3360.

KRUMM, CHARLES FERDINAND, ELECTRICAL ENGINEERING. **Personal Data:** b Macomb, Ill, August 3, 1941; m 1967, Patricia; c Jennifer & Frederick. **Education:** Univ Mich, BSE, 1963, MSE, 1965, PhD (elec eng), 1970. **Professional Experience:** MICROELECTRONICS DIV MGR, HUGHES RADAR SYSTS, 1996-; gas prod line mgr, Micoelectronics Lab, 1996; prog mgr, Micoelectronics Lab, 1989-1996; mgr, Micoelectronics Lab, 1986-1989; from asst dept mgr to dept mgr, Hughes Res Lab, 1978-1986; sect head, Hughes Res Lab, 1977-1978; mem tech staff, Hughes Res Lab, 1976-1977; sr res scientist, Res Div, Raytheon Co, 1969-1976; res asst, Electron Physics Lab, Univ Mich, 1965-1969; Mem, Adv Group Electron Devices, Dept Defense. **Memberships:** Fel Inst Elec & Electronics Engrs. **Research Statement & Publications:** Design, fabrication and testing of Gallium Arsenide and Silicon integrated circuits including ion implantation; electron beam and optical lithography; high resolution dry processing and molecular beam epitaxy. **Mailing Address:** Hughes Aircraft Co Microelectronics Div, PO Box H, Newport Beach, CA 92658-2027. **Fax:** 714-759-7353. **E-Mail:** ckrumm@ccmail.hac.com

KRUMMEL, DEBRA A, NUTRITION, CELLULAR VASCULAR DISEASE PREVENTION. **Personal Data:** b Akron, Ohio, July 31, 1957; m 1982, Daniel W; c Connor Fox & Trevor Fox. **Education:** Kent State Univ, BS, 1978; Case Western Res Univ, MS, 1980; Pa State Univ, PhD (nutrit), 1986. **Honors & Awards:** Huddelson Award, Am Dietetic Asn, 1993. **Professional Experience:** CONSULT NUTRIT, 1994-; res Scientist, Hershey Foods Corp, 1990-1994; res fel internal med, Sinai Hosp, Detroit, 1989-1990; nutritionist, Catherine McCauley Health Ctr, Ann Arbor, 1988-1989; Asst prof nutrit, Oakland Community Col, 1986-1988; Asst prof nutrit, Kent State Univ, 1986-1988. **Memberships:** Am Inst Nutrit; Soc Nutrit Educ; Am Dietetic Asn; Sports & Cardiovasc Nutrit Group. **Research Statement & Publications:** Nutrition; cellular vascular disease prevention. **Mailing Address:** Community Med, WVa Univ PO Box 9 190, Morgantown, WV 26506-9 190. **Fax:** 304-293-6685. **E-Mail:** dkrummel@hsc.wvu.edu

KRUMMEL, WILLIAM MARION, BIOMEDICAL ENGINEERING, ELECTRICAL ENGINEERING. **Personal Data:** b New York, NY, August 15, 1928; m 1962, Regina; c Miriamne, Daniel & Joseph. **Education:** City Col NY, BEE, 1949; Columbia Univ, MS, 1963; NY Univ, PhD (biomed Eng), 1967. **Professional Experience:** RETIRED; pres, Bridgeport Eng Inst, 1986-1995; pres, Norwalk State Tech Col, 1980-1986; assoc dean, Westchester Community Col, 1973-1980; assoc prof math, Bronx Community Col, City Univ NY, 1971-1973; adj assoc prof, NY Univ, 1971-1973; adj assoc prof, Univ Conn, 1967-1969; asst prof elec eng, NY Univ, 1969-1971; asst prof elec eng, Univ Conn, 1967-1969; systs engr, Control Div, Gen Elec Co, 1956-1962; engr, Control Div, Gen Elec Co, 1949-1954. **Memberships:** AAAS; Inst Elec & Electronics Engrs; NY Acad Sci; Sigma Xi; Am Soc Eng Educ. **Research Statement & Publications:** Application of mathematical and engineering techniques to experimental and theoretical biomedical problems; application of electrical engineering techniques to industrial process control. **Mailing Address:** Little Fox Lane, Norwalk, CT 06850.

KRUMMENACHER, DANIEL, GEOLOGY, CHEMISTRY. **Personal Data:** b Geneva, Switz, March 14, 1925; m 1951. **Education:** Univ Geneva, dipl chem eng, 1952, PhD (geol), 1959. **Professional Experience:** RETIRED; from asst prof to prof geol, San Diego State Univ, 1968-1988; res assoc, Univ Calif, Berkeley, 1967-1968; assoc prof geochem, Univ Geneva, 1962-1968; Researcher mass spectros, Univ Calif, Berkeley, 1960-1961; Res scientist, Univ Geneva, 1959-1962. **Memberships:** Geol Soc Am. **Research Statement & Publications:** Isotope geology; geochronometry. **Mailing Address:** Box 168, Rancho Sante Fe, CA 92067.

KRUMREI, W(ILLIAM) C(LARENCE), process development, product development; deceased, see previous edition for last biography

KRUPA, SAGAR, PHYTOPATHOLOGY, AIR POLLUTION. **Personal Data:** b Madras, India, October 11, 1940; American citizen; m 1967. **Education:** Andhra Univ, BSc, 1959; Univ Wis, MS, 1968; Univ Uppsala, PhD (plant physiol), 1971. **Professional Experience:** PROF PLANT PATH & PLANT PHYSIOL, DEPT PLANT PATH, UNIV MINN, 1985-; ENVIRON PATHOLOGIST, UNIV MINN, ST PAUL, 1974-; from asst prof to assoc prof, Dept Microbiol, Univ Minn, St Paul, 1974-1985; Docent, Inst Physiol Bot, Univ Uppsala, 1973-; res fel plant path, Dept Microbiol, Univ Minn, St Paul, 1973-1974; res fel soil sci, Dept Microbiol, Univ Minn, St Paul, 1972-1973; Swed Nat Sci Res Coun res fel physiol bot, Inst Physiol Bot, Univ Uppsala, 1972. **Memberships:** Am Phytopath Soc; Air Pollution Control Asn; AAAS; fel Air & Waste Mgt Asn. **Research Statement & Publications:** Atmospheric chemistry and effects of air pollution on vegetation. **Mailing Address:** Dept Plant Path, Univ Minn, 1991 Upper Buford Cir 495 Borlaug Hall, St Paul, MN 55108. **Fax:** 612-625-9728. **E-Mail:** krupa001@umn.edu

KRUPKA, LAWRENCE RONALD, PLANT PATHOLOGY. **Personal Data:** b New York, NY, March 7, 1933; m 1958. **Education:** Cornell Univ, BS, 1954; Univ Del, MS, 1956; La State Univ, PhD, 1959. **Professional Experience:** CHMN, DEPT GREAT ISSUES & INTERDEPT COURSES, 1973-; PROF NATURAL SCI, MICH STATE UNIV, 1968-; from asst prof to assoc prof, Dept Great Issues & Interdept Courses, 1965-1968; asst prof biol, Philadelphia Col Pharm, 1963-1965; biologist, Rohm and Haas Chem Co, Pa, 1961-1963; USPHS fel, 1959-1960; asst pathologist, Univ Nebr, 1959-1960; Asst plant path, Univ Del, 1954-1956 & La State Univ, 1956-1958; co-dir, sci, technol human values, NSF. **Memberships:** Mycol Soc Am; Am Phytopath Soc; Soc Indust Microbiol; Sigma Xi. **Research Statement & Publications:** Host-parasite relationships of plant pathogens, especially rusts; respiration studies; enzyme and organic acid metabolism; drug toxicity; effects of science and technology upon society. **Mailing Address:** Dept Natural Sci, Mich State Univ 100 N Kedzie Hall, East Lansing, MI 48824-1031.

KRUPKA, MILTON CLIFFORD, HIGH TEMPERATURE & HIGH PRESSURE PHYSICAL CHEMISTRY, SYSTEMS ENGINEERING MATERIALS. **Personal Data:** b New York, NY, January 1, 1924; m 1954, Emilia; c Denise, John & Nilda. **Education:** City Univ NY, BA, 1944; Univ NMex, MS, 1958, PhD (phys chem), 1962. **Professional Experience:** RETIRED; consult, 1989-1991; syst analyst & prin investr, technol & environ assessment, New Energy Technol & Conversion Systs, 1978-1989; mem staff & prin investr, technol & environ assessment, New Energy Technol & Conversion Systs, 1976-1978; staff mem & asst mgr high temp chem, Los Alamos Nat Lab, Univ Calif, 1971-1975; mat scientist high temp chem, Los Alamos Nat Lab, Univ Calif, 1959-1971; proj engr weapons develop, Los Alamos Nat Lab, Univ Calif, 1950-1959; lab supvr explosives, Los Alamos Nat Lab, Univ Calif, 1946-1950; asst chemist, Los Alamos Nat Lab, Univ Calif, 1945-1946; jr chemist, SAM Labs, Columbia Univ, 1944-1945. **Memberships:** Fel Am Inst Chemists; Am Chem Soc; Sigma Xi; Sci Res Soc. **Research Statement & Publications:** Elucidation of high temperature thermodynamics and properties of various refractory materials; ultrahigh pressure and temperature research; preparation of new materials and new superconductors; corrosion research in natural silicate melts; technology assessment; systems analysis for advanced energy systems; physics. **Mailing Address:** 6401 Turnberry Lane NE, Albuquerque, NM 87111-5860.

KRUPKA, RICHARD M(ORLEY), BIOCHEMISTRY. **Personal Data:** b Winnipeg, Man, January 17, 1932; m 1958, c 2. **Education:** Univ Sask, BA, 1953, MA, 1955; McGill Univ, PhD (plant biochem), 1957. **Professional Experience:** RES SCIENTIST, CAN DEPT AGR, 1960-; Fel enzyme kinetics, Univ Ottawa, 1958-1960. **Memberships:** Can Fedn Biol Socs; Fedn Am Soc Exp Biol. **Research Statement & Publications:** Transport kinetics; enzyme kinetics. **Mailing Address:** Res Ctr Can Agr London Res Ctr, 1391 Sanford St, London, ON N5V 4T3, Can.

KRUPKE, WILLIAM F, SOLID STATE PHYSICS. **Personal Data:** b Springfield, Mass, January 30, 1937; m 1961. **Education:** Rensselaer Polytech Inst, BS, 1958; Univ Calif, Los Angeles, MA, 1960, PhD (spectros), 1966. **Professional Experience:** PRES, APPL LASERS INC, as of 2004; DIR, IPG PHOTONICS CORP, as of 2004; EXEC DIR, NOVALUX, as of 2002; mem staff, Lawrence Livermore Nat Lab, beginning 1974; staff physicist, Hughes Aircraft Co, Culver City, 1966-1974; mem tech staff solid state res, Aerospace Corp, 1962-1966; mem tech staff laser res, Minneapolis Regulator Co, 1961-1962. **Memberships:** Am Phys Soc. **Research Statement & Publications:** Spectroscopic research on solid and gaseous systems as related to the dynamics of lasers; electronic structure of rare earth elements in solids; transition intensities and energy transfer processes. **Mailing Address:** IPG Photonics Corp, 50 Old Webster Rd, Oxford, MA 01540. **Fax:** 508-373-1101. **E-Mail:** krupke3@aol.com

KRUPOVAGE, DANIEL J, AERONAUTICS. **Professional Experience:** STAFF, HOLLOMAN AFB, USAF, as of 2000. **Memberships:** Fel Am Inst Aeronaut & Astronaut. **Mailing Address:** USAF, 6585 Test Group/TKE, Holloman AFB, NM 88330. **Fax:** 505-679-2133.

KRUPP, DAVID ALAN, BIOCHEMISTRY OF CORAL MUCUS, CALORIMETRY OF TISSUES. **Personal Data:** b Blue Island, Ill, February 6, 1953; American citizen; m 1986, c 2. **Education:** Univ Calif, Los Angeles, BA, 1976; Univ Hawaii, PhD (zoology), 1982. **Professional Experience:** AFFIL FAC, HAWAII INST MARINE BIOL, UNIV HAWAII, MANOA, 1994-; lectr, summer advan res & training prog, Hawaii Inst Marine Biol, Univ Hawaii, Manoa, 1991-; chair, Natural Sci Dept, Windward Community Col, 1989-1993; vis researcher, Marine Lab, Univ Guam, 1989; co-prin investr, Marine Option Prog Sea Grant Projs, 1985-1991; prin investr, Summer Prog Enhancement Basic Educ Oceanog, 1985-1990; sci fac coordr, Math-Sci Dept, Windward Community Col, 1985-1989; ASSOC PROF BIOL & MARINE SCI, DEPT NATURAL SCI, WINDWARD COMMUNITY COL, 1985-; instr biol & marine sci, Windward Community Col, beginning 1984; fac coordr, Marine Option Prog, Windward Community Col, beginning 1984. **Memberships:** AAAS; Am Soc Zoologists. **Research Statement & Publications:** Aspects of the biology of reef corals: reproduction, production of mucus and its properties, diffusion barriers and carbon limitation, pollution effects on coral reefs; biochemistry of sea cucumber body walls. **Mailing Address:** Dept Natural Sci Windward Community Col, 45-720 Keaahala Rd, Kaneohe, HI 96744-3528. **Fax:** 808-247-5362. **E-Mail:** krupp@hawaii.edu

KRUPP, EDWIN CHARLES, ASTRONOMY. **Personal Data:** b Chicago, Ill, November 18, 1944; m 1968, Robin; c Ethan H. **Education:** Pomona Col, BA, 1966; Univ Calif, Los Angeles, MA, 1968, PhD (astron), 1972. **Honorary Degrees:** LHD, WCoast Univ, 1996. **Honors & Awards:** Am Inst Phys, Best Sci Writing, 1978 & 1985; Klumpke-Roberts Award Contrib Pub Understanding Astron, Astron Soc Pac, 1989; Westren Amateur Astronomers, G BRUCE BLAIR MEDAL, 1996. **Professional Experience:** DIR, GRIFFITH OBSERV, CITY LOS ANGELES, 1976-; lectr & course coord, Univ Calif Exten, 1975-; consult, Los Angeles County Supt Sch, Community Col Consortium, 1974-1982; actg dir, Griffith Observ, City Los Angeles, 1974-1976; inst, Univ Southern Calif, 1974-1975; cur, Griffith Observ, City Los Angeles, 1972-1974; inst, El Camino Col, 1969-1974. **Memberships:** Am Astron Soc; Sigma Xi; fel Explorer's Club; Int Astron Union; Astron Soc Pac. **Research Statement & Publications:** Archaeoastronomy; ethnoastronomy; public astronomy education; childrens books on science. **Mailing Address:** Griffith Observ, 2800 E Observatory Rd, Los Angeles, CA 90027. **Fax:** 323-663-4323. **E-Mail:** eckrupp@earthlink.net

KRUPP, IRIS M, PARASITOLOGY, ALLERGY. **Personal Data:** b New Orleans, La, May 1, 1928. **Education:** La State Univ, BS; Tulane Univ, MS, 1955, PhD (parasitol), 1958, MD, 1971. **Professional Experience:** RETIRED; pvt pract dermat, 1976-1995; resident dermat, Charity Hosp, New Orleans, 1973-1976; mem adv bd parasitic dis & consult to surgeon gen, Dept Army, 1973-1975; res fel, Vet Admin Hosp, New Orleans, 1972-1973; clin assoc prof med, Med Sch, Tulane Univ, 1971-1991; intern, USPHS Hosp, 1971-1972; assoc prof trop med & pub health, Med Sch, Tulane Univ, 1966-1981; consult, USPHS grant, 1960-1965; from instr to asst prof trop med & pub health, Med Sch, Tulane Univ, 1959-1966; observer res technol, London Sch Hyg & Trop Med, 1959-1960; asst, Med Sch, Tulane Univ, 1954-1958; instr vet parasitol, Mich State Col, 1953-1954; res asst, Sch Med, Tulane Univ, 1949-1953. **Memberships:** Am Soc Dermat Surg; Int Soc Dermat Surg; Am Acad Dermat. **Research Statement & Publications:** Immunology of parasitic infections; schizophrenia; dermatology. **Mailing Address:** 4357 Folse Dr, Metairie, LA 70002.

KRUPP, MARCUS ABRAHAM, MEDICINE, METABOLISM. **Personal Data:** b El Paso, Tex, February 12, 1913; m 1958, Donna; c Michael, David (deceased), Peter & Sara. **Education:** Stanford Univ, BA, 1934, MD, 1939; Am Bd Int Med, dipl, 1947. **Honors & Awards:** Albion Walter Hewlett, 1987. **Professional Experience:** RES CHAIR & CHMN, DEPT IMMUNOL & INFECTIOUS DIS RES INST, PALO ALTO MED FOUND, as of 2006; PROF EMER MED, SCH MED, STANFORD UNIV, as of 2006; dir emer, Palo Alto Med Res Found, beginning 1987; clin prof, Sch Med, Stanford Univ, beginning 1965; assoc clin prof, Sch Med, Stanford Univ, 1956-1965; dir, Palo Alto Med Clin Lab, 1950-1986; dir, Palo Alto Med Clin Lab, 1950-1980; asst clin prof, Sch Med, Stanford Univ, 1946-1956; dir clin path, Vet Admin Hosp, San Francisco, 1946-1950. **Memberships:** Am Col Physicians; Am Fedn Clin Res; AAAS. **Research Statement & Publications:** Renal physiology; water and electrolyte metabolism; author of several medical textbooks. **Mailing Address:** Palo Alto Med Found, Palo Alto, CA 94301.

KRUPP, PATRICIA POWERS, GROSS ANATOMY, EXPERIMENTAL MORPHOLOGY. **Personal Data:** b New York, NY. **Education:** Beaver Col, BA, 1964; Hahnemann Med Col, PhD (anat), 1970. **Professional Experience:** ASSOC PROF ANAT, COL MED, UNIV

VT, 1978-; asst prof, Hahnemann Med Col, 1971-1978; sr instr gross anat, Hahnemann Med Col, 1970-1971; asst instr nursing anat & physiol, Pa State Univ, Ogontz Campus, 1963-1966. **Memberships:** Am Asn Anatomists; AAAS; NY Acad Sci; Am Fedn Clin Res; Am Women Sci. **Research Statement & Publications:** Experimental modification of thyroid gland structure and function; effects of diet, drugs, spontaneous hypertension and chronic stimulation. **Mailing Address:** Dept Anat & Neurobiol Col Med, Univ Vt, Given Bldg, Burlington, VT 05401.

KRUSBERG, LORIN RONALD, PLANT PATHOLOGY. **Personal Data:** b July 18, 1932; c 3. **Education:** Univ Del, BS, 1954; NC State Col, MS, 1956, PhD (plant path), 1959. **Professional Experience:** PROF PLANT PATH, UNIV MD, COL PARK, 1970-; from asst prof to assoc prof, Univ Md, College Park, 1960-1970; fel, NSF, Rothamsted Exp Sta, Eng, 1959-1960. **Memberships:** Am Phytopath Soc; fel Soc Nematol; Sigma Xi. **Research Statement & Publications:** Biology and control of nematodes parasitic on corn, soybeans and vegetables. **Mailing Address:** Univ Md, Dept Bot, College Park, MD 20742-0001.

KRUSCHWITZ, WALTER HILLIS, PHYSICS. **Personal Data:** b Edgerton, Ohio, July 20, 1920; m 1947, Virginia; c Nancy & Sharon. **Education:** Taylor Univ, AB, 1942; Vanderbilt Univ, MA, 1948; Univ Mich, PhD (higher ed), 1961. **Professional Experience:** RETIRED; assoc prof physics, Univ SFla, beginning 1973; assoc prof phys sci & physics, Univ SFla, 1969-1972; assoc prof physics & educ, Univ SFla, 1967-1969; prof physics, Mobile Col, 1963-1967; prof & head physics dept, Union Univ, Tenn, 1961-1963; asst prof physics & math, Union Univ, Tenn, 1951-1960; assoc prof physics, Cumberland Univ, 1948-1950. **Memberships:** Am Asn Physics Teachers. **Research Statement & Publications:** Measurement of the velocity of a gas immediately before combustion; undergraduate college physics research and its sponsorship; science education. **Mailing Address:** 3307 Korina Lane, Tampa, FL 33618.

KRUSE, ARTHUR HERMAN, MATHEMATICS. **Personal Data:** b Easton, Kans, February 5, 1928; m 1954, c 2. **Education:** Univ Kans, BA, 1949, MA, 1951; Univ Chicago, PhD (math), 1956. **Professional Experience:** PROF EMER MATH, NMEX ST UNIV, as of 2004; res prof math sci, NMex St Univ, beginning 1960; from instr to asst prof, Univ Kans, 1954-1960; res assoc math, Univ Kans, 1954-1960. **Memberships:** Am Math Soc; Math Asn Am. **Research Statement & Publications:** Topology; axiomatic set theory; analysis. **Mailing Address:** Dept Math Scis, NMex State Univ, Campus Mail 3MB, PO Box 30001, Las Cruces, NM 88003-8001. **Fax:** 505-646-1064. **E-Mail:** akruse@nmsu.edu

KRUSE, CARL WILLIAM, COAL DESULFURIZATION, COAL ANALYSES. **Personal Data:** b Aline, Okla, June 2, 1927; m 1949, T Marie Halford; c 4. **Education:** Bethany-Nazarene Col, AB, 1950; Univ Kans, MS, 1952; Univ Ill, PhD (chem), 1958. **Professional Experience:** RETIRED; fac, China Univ Mining & Technol, 1997-1999; sr scientist, Ill State Geol Surv, 1984-1996; head minerals eng sect, Ill State Geol Surv, 1980-1984; chemist, Ill State Geol Surv, 1978-1980; Consult, Midwest Res Inst, 1968-1974 & Oak Ridge Nat Labs, Energy Res & Develop Admin, 1975; prof chem, Mid-Am Nazarene Col, 1974-1978; chmn div environ serv, Mid-Am Nazarene Col, 1968-1978; assoc prof, Mid-Am Nazarene Col, 1968-1974; sect mgr, Phillips Petrol Co, 1964-1968; group leader org chem, Phillips Petrol Co, 1957-1964; res chemist, Phillips Petrol Co, 1952-1954 & Ill State Geol Surv, 1954-1956. **Memberships:** Am Chem Soc. **Research Statement & Publications:** Aromatic and aliphatic halides; alkylation of aromatics; acetylenic and olefinic compounds; organoaluminum compounds; energy problems; low temperature carbonization of coal; beneficiation of coal and coal char; oxidized activated carbon as a catalyst. **Mailing Address:** 2015 Barberry Circle, Champaign, IL 66062-2273. **Fax:** 217-333-8566. **E-Mail:** KRUSE@geoserv.isgs.uiuc.edu

KRUSE, CAROL A, CANCER RESEARCH. **Education:** Univ Calif, PhD, 1980. **Professional Experience:** ASSOC PROF, DEPT IMMUNOL, UNIV COLO HEALTH SCI CTR, as of 2006. **Mailing Address:** Dept Immunol, Univ Colo Health Sci Ctr, C-305 4200 E Ninth Ave, Denver, CO 80262. **E-Mail:** carol.kruse@uchsc.edu

KRUSE, CONRAD EDWARD, BACTERIOLOGY. **Personal Data:** b Philadelphia, Pa, September 14, 1923; m 1949, c 2. **Education:** Philadelphia Col Pharm, BSc, 1949, DSc(bact), 1953; Univ Wis, MSc, 1951. **Professional Experience:** PROF ENVIRON ENG, TEMPLE UNIV, 1990-; assoc prof biol, Ursinus Col, 1967-1989; asst prof biol sci, Drexel Inst, 1960-1967; Col Dept, Lea & Febiger, 1957-1960; res assoc, Can Div, Crown Cork & Seal Co, Pa, 1956-1957; instr, Misericordia Hosp, Philadelphia, 1955-1956; dept supvr bact, Childrens Hosp, Philadelphia, 1953-1956; instr bact, Philadelphia Col Pharm, 1951-1956. **Memberships:** AAAS; Am Soc Microbiol; Am Pharmaceut Asn; Inst Food Technologists. **Research Statement & Publications:** Industrial and medical microbiology; biochemistry; food technology; development of pharmaceutical and food products; development of biochemical fuel cell. **Mailing Address:** Dept Environ Eng, Temple Univ, 1701 N Broad St, Philadelphia, PA 19122-2504.

KRUSE, DAVID H, TECHNOLOGY. **Professional Experience:** RETIRED; staff, Portland General Electric Co, ending 2003. **Memberships:** Sigma Xi. **Mailing Address:** Portland Gen Elec Co, 1215 Salem St, Portland, OR 97204. **Fax:** 503-228-6322. **E-Mail:** info@portlandgeneral.com

KRUSE, FERDINAND HOBERT, PHYSICAL CHEMISTRY. **Personal Data:** b Council Bluffs, Iowa, July 9, 1925; m 1947, c 3. **Education:** Iowa State Col, BSc, 1945; Univ NMex, MSc, 1951; Univ Calif, Los Angeles, PhD (phys chem), 1956. **Professional Experience:** RETIRED; consult, 1980-1990; sr chemist corp tech, Tech Ctr, Owens-Ill, Inc, 1968-1980; Fulbright lectr, Univ Alexandria, 1965-1966; mem staff, Los Alamos Sci Lab, 1957-1967; res chemist phys chem, Esso Res & Eng Co, 1956-1957; instr inorg chem, Iowa State Col, 1946-1948; chemist, Gen Elec Co, Mass, 1945-1946. **Memberships:** Am Crystallog Asn. **Research Statement & Publications:** X-ray crystallography; single crystal structure analysis; optical properties of crystalline compounds; inorganic chemistry of actinide elements; chemistry of tellurium and selenium; digital computer programming and applications; analytical chemistry; x-ray fluorescence spectroscopy. **Mailing Address:** 4716 Crest Ridge Rd, Sylvania, OH 43560.

KRUSE, JAMES ALEXANDER, CRITICAL CARE MEDICINE, CLINICAL RESEARCH. **Personal Data:** b Cleveland, Ohio, August 28, 1952. **Education:** Ohio State Univ, BA, 1975, MD, 1979. **Professional Experience:** PROF MED, SCH MED, WAYNE STATE UNIV, as of 2003; guest ed, Critical Care Clins, WB Saunders Co, Philadelphia, 1991-1992; assoc prof med, Sch Med, Wayne State Univ, beginning 1991; specialist site vis, Accreditation Coun Grad Med Educ, 1989-1990; consult, Food & Drug Admin Working Group, 1988-1993; vis prof, Univ Ill & Univ Mich, 1987-1993; asst prof med, Sch Med, Wayne State Univ, 1986-1991; dir, Respiratory Care Unit, Detroit Receiving Hosp, 1985-1993; instr internal med, Sch Med, Wayne State Univ, 1984-1986; fel critical care med, Mt Carmel Mercy Hosp, Detroit, 1982-1984; resident, Akron City Hosp, Northeastern Ohio Univ, Col Med, 1980-1981; intern med, Akron City Hosp, Northeastern Ohio Univ, Col Med, 1979-1980; chief med resident, Akron City Hosp, Northeastern Ohio Univ, Col Med. **Memberships:** Fel Am Col Critical Care Med. **Research Statement & Publications:** Clinical studies of investigational drugs and medical devices (eg, intravascular catheters) and clinical and laboratory studies involving sepsis, oxygen transport, lactate metabolism, lactic acidosis, acid-base and electrolyte disorders. **Mailing Address:** Dept Med, Wayne State Univ, 4201 St Antoine Blvd, Detroit, MI 48201.

KRUSE, KIPP COLBY, BEHAVIORAL ECOLOGY. **Personal Data:** b Norfolk, Nebr, November 21, 1949; m 1975, Linda; c Colby E & Hilary P. **Education:** Wayne State Col, BSE, 1971; Univ SDak, MA, 1973; Univ Nebr, PhD (Ecol), 1978. **Professional Experience:** PROF ZOOL, EASTERN ILL UNIV, 1987-; from asst prof to assoc prof, Eastern Ill Univ, 1979-1987; instr biol, Univ Nebr, 1978-1979. **Memberships:** Sigma Xi; Soc Study Amphibians & Reptiles; Herpetologists League; Animal Behav Soc; Wildlife Soc. **Research Statement & Publications:** Aspects of sexual selection in frogs, toads and waterbugs. **Mailing Address:** Dept Biol Sci, Eastern Ill Univ, 1044, Life Sci Bldg 600 Lincoln Ave, Charleston, IL 61920. **Fax:** 217-521-2122. **E-Mail:** cfkck@eiu.edu

KRUSE, LAWRENCE IVAN, PHARMACEUTICAL CHEMISTRY. **Personal Data:** b Springfield, Vt, December 21, 1958; m 1980. **Education:** Mass Inst Technol, BS, 1976, PhD (chem), 1979. **Professional Experience:** VPRES CHEM RES & DEVELOP, STERLING RES GROUP, 1989-; assoc sr investr med chem, Smith Kline & French Labs, 1979-1989. **Memberships:** Am Chem Soc. **Research Statement & Publications:** Design and synthesis of selective enzyme inhibitors; synthesis of unnatural amino acids and antitumor-antimetabolic agents of potential therapeutic ability; stereoelectronic effects in organic chemistry; indole and other heterocyclic chemistry. **Mailing Address:** Sterling Res Group, Nine Great Valley Pkwy, Malvern, PA 19355-1314.

KRUSE, OLAN ERNEST, physics; deceased, see previous edition for last biography

KRUSE, PAUL WALTERS, JR, INFRARED TECHNOLOGY. **Personal Data:** b Hibbing, Minn, November 24, 1927; m 1954, Margaret M; c Paul W II, Robert J, John M, Mary (Beane), Margaret A, Charles F, Thomas E, William D & Catherine M. **Education:** Univ Notre Dame, BS, 1951, MS, 1952, PhD (physics), 1954. **Honors & Awards:** Recipient, H W Sweatt Award, Honeywell, Inc, 1966; Alan Gordon Mem Award, Int Soc Optical Eng, 1981; Outstanding Civilian Service Award & Medal, Dept of the Army, 1983; Levinstein Award, Infrared Information Symposia, 1999. **Professional Experience:** CONSULT, INFRARED TECHNOL, 1994-; chief scientist, Infrared Solutions, Inc, 1994-1998; consult infrared technol, 1993-1994; mem, Sci & Technol Operating Comt, Am Electronics Asn, 1990-; chief res fel, Sensor & Syst Develop Ctr, Honeywell, Inc, 1983-1993; mem, Comt Biol & Chem Sensor Technol, Nat Res Coun, Nat Acad Sci, 1983-1984; prin res fel, Corp Technol Ctr, 1980-1983; NATO rev panel Pres's Sci Adv Comt & Vietnam Panel, 1971-1972 & US/USSR Tech Balance Assessment Study, US Naval Res Adv Comt, 1979-1980; mem, Army Sci Bd, 1978-1982, 1985-1990; prin staff scientist, Res Ctr, Minn-Honeywell Regulator Co, 1978-1980; mem, US Army Near-Millimeter Wave Technol Base Develop Study, 1976-1977; chmn, US Army ERADCOM Technol Panel, 1975-1976; comt mat for electromagnetic radiation detection devices, Nat Acad Sci, 1971-1973 & Army Countermine Adv Comt, 1971-1974; sr staff scientist, Res Ctr, Minn-Honeywell Regulator Co, 1970-1977; ground warfare panel, President's Sci Adv Comt, 1970-1972; mem planning comt, Third Int Photoconductivity Conf, 1969-1971; Mem comt phys sci, adv bd military personnel supplies, Nat Res Coun, Nat Acad Sci, 1969-1971; Mem, US Army Sci Adv Panel, 1965-1977; staff scientist, Res Ctr, Minn-Honeywell Regulator Co, 1960-1969; prin res scientist, Res Ctr, Minn-Honeywell Regulator Co, 1959-1960; sr res scientist, Res Ctr, Minn-Honeywell Regulator Co, 1956-1959; Physicist, Farnsworth Electronics Co, 1954-1956. **Memberships:** Fel Am Phys Soc; assoc fel Am Inst Aeronaut & Astronaut; fel Optical Soc Am; sr mem Inst Elec & Electronics Engrs. **Research Statement & Publications:** Electrooptical physics; nonlinear optics; infrared detectors; crystal growth; solid state devices; lasers; photoeffects in high temperature superconductors. **Mailing Address:** 6828 Oaklawn Ave, Edina, MN 55435. **Fax:** 952-422-0344.

KRUSE, ROBERT LEROY, DATA STRUCTURES, ALGORITHM ANALYSIS. **Personal Data:** b Jacksonville, Fla, January 7, 1941. **Education:** Pomona Col, BA, 1960; Calif Inst Technol, MS, 1962, PhD (math), 1964. **Professional Experience:** Fel, Erskine, Univ Canterbury, New Zealand, 1990; vis prof, Univ Alberta, 1982; PROF MATH & COMPUT SCI, ST MARY'S UNIV, HALIFAX, 1979-; chmn dept, St Mary's Univ, Halifax, 1976-1979; assoc prof math, Emory Univ, 1973-1976; Fulbright-Hays grant & vis reader, Univ Canterbury, NZ, 1970-1972; staff mem, Sandia Lab, 1964-1970. **Memberships:** Am Math Soc; Asn Comput Mach. **Research Statement & Publications:** Data structures; applications of computers in abstract algebra; finite ring. **Mailing Address:** Dept Math & Comput Sci, St Mary's Univ, Rm McNally N MN126, Halifax, NS B3H 3C3, Can. **Fax:** 902-420-5141. **E-Mail:** robert.kruse@stmarys.ca

KRUSE, ULRICH ERNST, PHYSICS. **Personal Data:** b Berlin, Ger, May 22, 1929; American citizen. **Education:** Harvard Univ, PhD (physics), 1954. **Professional Experience:** PROF EMER PHYSICS, UNIV ILL, URBANA, as of 2002; from asst prof to prof physics, Univ Ill, Urbana, beginning 1959; from instr to asst prof physics, Univ Chicago, 1954-1959. **Memberships:** Fel Am Phys Soc. **Research Statement & Publications:** Experimental nuclear physics. **Mailing Address:** Dept Physics Univ Ill, 6-143 esb, Urbana, IL 61801. **E-Mail:** uek@mail.physics.uiuc.edu

KRUSE, WALTER M, INORGANIC CHEMISTRY, PHYSICAL CHEMISTRY. **Personal Data:** b Heide, Ger, October 6, 1928; m 1960, Edith; c Elke & Lakota. **Education:** Univ Cologne, PhD, 1958. **Professional Experience:** CONSULT, 1990-; res info scientist, 1988-1991; sr res chemist, ICI Americas, Inc, 1979-1990; ICI United States Inc, 1974-1979; Atlas Chem Industs, Inc, 1971-1974; res chemist, Hercules Res Ctr, Del, 1964-1971; asst kinetics, Max Planck Inst Phys Chem, 1960-1964; fel, Univ Chicago, 1958-1960. **Memberships:** Am Chem Soc; Sigma Xi. **Research Statement & Publications:** Preparative inorganic chemistry; complex chemistry; oxidation of olefins; hydrogenation of carbohydrates; homogeneous catalysis. **Mailing Address:** 2401 Pa Ave, Wilmington, DE 19806.

KRUSEMEYER, MARK I, MATHEMATICS. **Education:** Univ Utrecht, Phd. **Professional Experience:** PROF MATH, CARLETON COL, MINN as of 2005. **Mailing Address:** Carleton Col, Northfield, MN 55057-4025. **Fax:** 507-646-5196. **E-Mail:** mkruseme@carleton.edu

KRUSEN, EDWARD MONTGOMERY, medicine; deceased, see previous edition for last biography

KRUSHENSKY, RICHARD D, GEOLOGY, VOLCANOLOGY. **Personal Data:** b Ferndale, Mich, June 3, 1932; m 1960, Arvene; c Kari L. **Education:** Wayne State Univ, BS, 1955, MS, 1957; Ohio State Univ, PhD (geol), 1960. **Professional Experience:** DEP CHIEF LATIN AM, ASSOC CHIEF & CHIEF EUROPE, OFF INT GEOL, US GEOL SURV, 1983-; geologist, Br Eastern Environ Geol, 1980-1983; actg chief, Off Environ Geol, 1979-1980; geologist, Br Eastern Environ Geol & dep chief, Off Environ Geol, 1974-1979; Br Mil Geol,

1963-1964 & Br Int Geol, 1964-1970; geologist, Br Spec Projs, US Geol Surv, 1962-1963; geologist, Orinoco Mining Co Div, US Steel Corp, 1960-1962. **Research Statement & Publications:** Mineral exploration and training of local personnel in Turkey; study of Irazu Volcano, Costa Rica and other active and inactive volcanoes in Central America; volcanic petrology and petrography; volcanology; mineral exploration; regional geology of volcanogenic and intrusive rocks in Puerto Rico. **Mailing Address:** US Geol Survey, 8106 Timber Valley Ct, Dunn Loring, VA 22027. **Fax:** 703-648-4227. **E-Mail:** rkrushen@usgs.gov

KRUSIC, PAUL JOSEPH, ELECTRON SPIN RESONANCE, FREE RADICAL CHEMISTRY. **Personal Data:** b Trieste, Italy, November 28, 1934; m 1956, c Paul Jr, Sonja & Mara. **Education:** Wesleyan Univ, BA, 1959; Univ Calif, Berkeley, PhD (chem), 1966. **Honors & Awards:** Delaware Sec Award, Am Chem Soc, 1974. **Professional Experience:** MEM, DUPONT, as of 2004; vis prof, Ecole Normale Superieure, Paris, 1987; vis scholar, Centre d'Etudes Nucleaires Del Grenoble, France, 1981-1982; RES CHEMIST, CENT RES DEPT, E I DU PONT Del NEMOURS & CO INC, 1966-; chemist, Cent Res Lab, Gen Elec Co, NY, 1959-1961. **Memberships:** Am Chem Soc. **Research Statement & Publications:** Microwave spectroscopy; electron spin resonance spectroscopy; free radical chemistry; organometallic reaction mechanisms; homogeneous catalysis; organometallic photochemistry; autoxidation of hydrocarbons; radical chemistry of fullerenes; gas-phase nuclear magnetic resonance; fluorine chemistry. **Mailing Address:** Cent Res Dept, E I du Pont de Nemours & Co Inc, Wilmington, DE 19880-0328. **E-Mail:** krusic@esvax.dnet.dupont.com

KRUSIN-ELBAUM, LIA, PHYSICS. **Education:** NY Univ, PhD, 1979, MS, 1976. **Professional Experience:** RES STAFF, PHYS SCI DEPT, INT BUS MACH T J WATSON RES CTR, 1989-. **Memberships:** Fel Am Phys Soc. **Mailing Address:** IBM T J Watson Research Ctr, PO Box 218, Yorktown Heights, NY 10598. **Fax:** 805-893-2431. **E-Mail:** krusin@us.ibm.com

KRUSKAL, BENJAMIN A, PHAGOCYTOSIS, MYCOBACTERIAL INFECTIONS. **Personal Data:** b Ann Arbor, Mich, May 15, 1959; m 1984, Maureen; c Meira, Shoshana & Adina. **Education:** Univ Pa, BA, 1981; NY Univ, MS, 1984, MD, 1988, PhD (pharmacol), 1988. **Professional Experience:** ASST PEDIATRICIAN, MASS GEN HOSP, 1996-; Charles Janeway fel child health res, Children's Hosp, 1994; ASST MED, INFECTIOUS DIS, CHILDREN'S HOSP, 1993-; fel, Cancer Res Inst, 1991-1994. **Memberships:** Am Soc Cell Biol; AAAS; Infectious Dis Soc Am; Pediat Infectious Dis Soc; Am Acad Pediat; Am Soc Microbiol. **Research Statement & Publications:** Cell biology of phagocytosis; phagosome-lysosome fusion and its inhibition by microbial pathogens; the macrophage mannose receptor. **Mailing Address:** Div Infectious Dis, The Children's Hosp, 300 Longwood Ave, Boston, MA 02115. **Fax:** 617-355-6575. **E-Mail:** kruskal@a1.tch.harvard.edu

KRUSKAL, JOSEPH BERNARD, COMBINATORICS, STATISTICS. **Personal Data:** b New York, NY, January 29, 1928; m 1953, Rachel; c Joyce & Benjamin. **Education:** Univ Chicago, PhB & BS, 1948, MS, 1949; Princeton Univ, PhD, 1954. **Professional Experience:** RETIRED; vis prof, Rutgers Univ, 1977; vis prof, Columbia Univ, 1976; assoc ed jour, Soc Indust & Appl Math, 1967-1970; vis prof, Yale Univ, 1966-1967; mem tech staff, Bell Labs, 1959-1993; asst prof, Univ Mich, 1958-1959; res instr, Univ Wis, 1956-1958; instr math, Princeton Univ, 1955. **Memberships:** Am Math Soc; Classification Soc NAm (pres, 1974-1977); fel AAAS; fel Am Statist Asn; Psychometric Soc (pres, 1974-1975). **Research Statement & Publications:** Statistics, psychometrics and statistical linguistics. **Mailing Address:** 42 Oakland Rd, Maplewood, NJ 07040. **E-Mail:** kruskal@research.bell-labs.com

KRUSKAL, MARTIN DAVID, MATHEMATICAL PHYSICS, APPLIED MATHEMATICS. **Personal Data:** b New York, NY, September 28, 1925; m 1950, c 3. **Education:** Univ Chicago, BS, 1945; NY Univ, MS, 1948, PhD (math), 1952. **Honors & Awards:** Fulbright lectr, Grenoble, France, 1959 & 1978; Gibbs lectr, Am Math Soc, 1979; Dannie-Helmman Prize Math Physics, 1983; Potts Gold Medal, Franklin Inst, 1986; Appl Math & Numerical Anal, Nat Acad Sci, 1989; Nat Med Sci, 1993. **Professional Experience:** DAVID AILBERT PROF MATH, RUTGERS UNIV, NEW BRUNSWICK, 1989-; mem bd dir, Soc Indust & Appl Math, 1985-; co dir, Inst Termenoild Physics, Santa Barbara, 1985; prof, Prog Appl Math, 1979-; emer prof math, Prog Appl Math, 1979-1989; fel, Japanese Soc Prom Sci, Nagoya Univ, 1979-1980; vis prof, Weizman Inst Sci, Israel, 1973-1974; dir, Prog Appl Math, 1968-1986; Radio Corp Am, 1960-1962 & IBM Corp, 1963-; prof astrophys sci, Plasma Physics Lab, Princeton Univ, 1961-1989; sr res assoc & lectr astron, Plasma Physics Lab, Princeton Univ, 1959-1961; NSF sr fel, Max Planck Inst Physics & Astrophysics, Ger, 1959-1960; assoc head, Theoret Div, Plasma Physics, Lab, Princeton Univ, 1956-1964; Radiation Lab, Oak Ridge Nat Lab, 1955-1958, 1963-; Radiation Lab, Univ Calif, 1954-1957; Consult, Los Alamos Sci Lab, 1953-1959; res scientist, Plasma Physics Lab, Princeton Univ, 1951-1959; Asst & instr math, NY Univ, 1946-1951. **Memberships:** Nat Acad Sci; Am Math Soc; Math Asn Am; Am Phys Soc; Soc Indust & Appl Math; Am Acad Arts & Sci. **Research Statement & Publications:** Plasma physics; general mathematics; asymptotic phenomena; logic; magnetohydrodynamics; controlled fusion; relativity; minimal surfaces. **Mailing Address:** Dept Math Hill Centre, Rutgers Univ, Busch Campus, New Brunswick, NJ 08903. **E-Mail:** kruskal@math.rutgers.edu

KRUSKAL, WILLIAM HENRY, statistics; deceased, see previous edition for last biography

KRUTAK, JAMES JOHN, CHEMISTRY OF FUNCTIONAL DYES, DESIGN OF NEAR-ULTRAVIOLET NEAR INFRARED & VISIBLE DYES. **Personal Data:** b Atlanta, Ga, April 5, 1942; m 1980, Elsa; c James, Kim, Kari, Juan, Jon, David & Khristopher. **Education:** La State Univ, BS, 1964; Univ NC, PhD (org chem), 1968. **Professional Experience:** SR SCIENTIST, FBI INVEST TECH DIV, as of 2004; SR RES ASSOC, TENN EASTMAN CO, EASTMAN KODAK CO, 1994-; functional dye consult, 1991-; lab head, Colorants Res Lab, 1986-1991; asst to chem res dir, Photog Chem Res Lab, Eastman Kodak, 1984-1985; res assoc, Tenn Eastman Co, Eastman Kodak Co, 1975-1993; coordr, Photog Chem Res Lab, Eastman Kodak, 1973-1983; sr res chemist, Tenn Eastman Co, Eastman Kodak Co, 1969-1975; res chemist, Tenn Eastman Co, Eastman Kodak Co, 1967-1969; mem sci adv comt, Cosmetic, Toiletry & Fragrance Asn. **Memberships:** Am Chem Soc; Int Soc Heterocyclic Chem; Am Asn Textile Chemists & Colorists; Tech Asn Pulp & Paper Indust; Soc Plastics Engrs; Soc Cosmetic Chemists. **Research Statement & Publications:** Synthesis of natural products; development of novel indole synthesis; study of mechanisms of indole forming reactions using stable and radioactive isotope tracer methodology; cycloaddition reactions; chemical uses of lasers; photographic dye and developer synthesis and related technology; functional dye design and synthesis for plastics, fibers, inks, coatings, personal and household care products, safe coloration and UV-screen systems for cosmetics, medical products, construction products, security and automation systems; synthetic paper compositions and advanced materials of construction from recyclable polymers; automation of plastics recycling near infrared dye design; granted over 40 patents. **Mailing Address:** FBI Invest Tech Div, Tiara Group, 530 W Ojai Ave, Ste 108, Ojai, CA 93023-2471. **Fax:** 805-659-1493.

KRUTAK, PAUL RUSSELL, PETROLEUM GEOLOGY, OSTRACODE ECOLOGY & SYSTEMATICS. **Personal Data:** b Pueblo, Colo, October 6, 1934; m 1955, Jerri; c Paul R Jr, Helen E, Krag F, Kurt M & Lars F. **Education:** La State Univ, BS, 1956, MS, 1960, PhD (struct geol), 1963. **Honors & Awards:** Silver Medal, Geol Inst, Univ Mex, 1980. **Professional Experience:** CHMN GEOSCIENCE, FT HAYS STATE UNIV, 1992-; lectr, Korea Ocean Res Develop Inst, 1997; co-convenor, Geol Soc Am, 1990; res dir, Basin Res Inst, 1988-1991; vchmn, Global Sedimentary Geol Prog, 1988; consult geologist, Terra-Mar Geoserv Int, 1986-1988; sr geologist, Arco Explor Co, Lafayette, La, 1982-1985; fulbright res award, Nuevo Leon, Mex, 1980-1981; asesor, Inst Geol, Univ Mex, 1980; vis prof geol, Univ Mex, 1979 & La State Univ, 1979; prof geol, Univ Nebr, Lincoln, 1970-1982; consult, Sunrise Explor Co, Phoenix, Ariz, 1968; field geologist, Idaho Bur Mines, 1967 & 1968; sigma Xi grant, 1967; assoc prof, Eastern NMex Univ, 1965-1970; geol soc am grand, 1965-1966; asst prof geol, Ball State Univ, 1963-1965; res asst, La State Univ, 1960-1963; micropaleontologist, Shell Oil Co, 1960; asst geol, La State Univ, 1958-1963; geologist, stanolin oil & gas co, Wyo, 1956-1958; mem, cushman found foraminiferal res. **Memberships:** Am Asn Petrol Geologists; fel Geol Soc Am. **Research Statement & Publications:** Regional structure and stratigraphy; mesozoic-cenozoic micropaleontology; petrography; seismic stratigraphy; copper porphry exploration. **Mailing Address:** Dept Geosci, Ft Hays State Univ, 600 Park St, Hays, KS 67601-4099. **Fax:** 913-628-4096. **E-Mail:** gspk@fhsuvm.fhsu.edu

KRUTCHEN, CHARLES M(ARION), CHEMICAL ENGINEERING. **Personal Data:** b Gadsen, Ala, September 7, 1934; m 1959, Mary A Metaxas; c Carolyn P, Anne E, James C & Melissa M. **Education:** Vanderbilt Univ, BE, 1956; Cornell Univ, PhD (chem eng), 1964. **Professional Experience:** RETIRED; sr res assoc, Macedon, NY, 1992-1995; sr res assoc, Plastics Div, 1990-1992; res supvr, Plastics Div, 1977-1990; eng assoc, Res & Develop Lab, Mobil Chem, Edison, NJ, 1976-1977; staff chem engr, Gen Elec Res & Develop Ctr, 1966-1976; sr res engr, Res Div, W R Grace & Co, 1964-1966; res engr, Fiber Dept, 1962-1964; Chem engr, Res Ctr, Hercules Powder Co, 1956-1958. **Memberships:** Am Inst Chem Engrs; Am Chem Soc; AAAS; Soc Plastics Engrs. **Research Statement & Publications:** Chemical process studies; polymer fiber, film and foam technology; polymer processing; morphology-physical property relationships in polymers; polymer recycling; granted 33 patents. **Mailing Address:** 30514 Laurel Ct, Daphne, AL 36527. **Fax:** 251-621-8328.

KRUTCHKOFF, DAVID JAMES, ORAL PATHOLOGY, DENTISTRY. **Personal Data:** b Eureka, Calif, June 7, 1938; m 1966, Sumiko; c Tamara, Todd & Laurel. **Education:** Univ Calif, Berkeley, BA, 1960; Wash Univ, DDS, 1964; Univ Mich, MS, 1970. **Professional Experience:** PROF EMER ORAL DIAGNOSIS-PATH, UNIV CONN, as of 2003; CONSULT, ORAL PATH BIOPSY SERV, UNIV CONN, 1996-; vis prof, Tohoku Univ, Sendai, Japan, 1987; prof oral diagnosis-path, Univ Conn, beginning 1973; asst prof oral path, Univ Louisville, 1970-1973; Nat Inst Dent Res fel & instr oral path, Univ Mich, 1968-1970; res asst path, Wash Univ, 1967-1968. **Memberships:** Int Asn Dent Res; Am Acad Oral Path; Eastern Soc Teachers Oral Path. **Research Statement & Publications:** Dental caries; clinical studies; dental enamel; infrared internal reflection spectroscopy; oral cancer; lichenoid dysplasia; forensic consultation. **Mailing Address:** Dept Oral Path, Health Ctr, Univ Conn, 263 Farmington Ave, Farmington, CT 06030. **Fax:** 860-679-4334.

KRUTCHKOFF, RICHARD GERALD, APPLIED STATISTICS. **Personal Data:** b Brooklyn, NY, December 23, 1933; m 1987, Debra; c Barbara, Robyn & Daniel. **Education:** Columbia Univ, AB, 1956, MA, 1958, PhD (math statist), 1964. **Professional Experience:** PROF EMER STATIST, VA POLYTECH INST & STATE UNIV, 1996-; ed, J Statist Comput & Simulation, 1972-; from asst prof to prof, VA Polytech Inst & State Univ, 1964-1996; lectr, Queens Col, NY, 1960-1964; instr physics, Wilkes Col, 1958-1960. **Memberships:** AAAS; fel Am Statist Asn. **Research Statement & Publications:** Statistical inference; empirical Bayes decision theory; water pollution statistics; simulation; chaos. **Mailing Address:** Dept Statist, Va Polytech Inst & State Univ, 410 A Hutcheson Hall, Blacksburg, VA 24061-0439. **E-Mail:** rgkrutch@vt.edu

KRUTER, MARY HARLEY, MATHEMATICS. **Professional Experience:** PROJ DIR, PBS MATHLINE, NC, as of 2005. **Memberships:** Sr fel Math Sci Edu Bd. **Mailing Address:** 202 Adams Way, Chapel Hill, NC 27516-8060. **Fax:** 323-937.7440. **E-Mail:** mhkruter@mathernet.com

KRUTZ, RONALD L, COMPUTER ENGINEERING. **Personal Data:** b McKeesport, Pa, August 27, 1938; m 1961, Hilda M Napolitano; c Sheri R & Lisa M. **Education:** Univ Pittsburgh, BSEE, 1960, MSEE, 1967, PhD (elec eng), 1972. **Professional Experience:** DIR, PRIVACY CORBETT TECHNOL, as of 2004; DIR & FOUNDER, COMPUT ENG CTR, 1978-; assoc dir, Carnegie-Mellon Res Inst, Pittsburgh, beginning 1978; fac mem, Dept Elec Eng, 1975-1978; mgr, Comput Sci Dept, Res & Develop Ctr, Singer Corp, 1974-1975; Proj engr, Gulf Res & Develop Co, 1964-1974; lead instr, CISSP CBK. **Memberships:** Sr mem Inst Elec & Electronics Engrs. **Research Statement & Publications:** Microprocessors and logic design; developed video tape course on microprocessors and software; contributed articles to professional journals; distributed computing; awarded seven patents for computer and digital systems. **Mailing Address:** Corbett Technologies, Inc, 1600 Duke St, Suite 600, Alexandria, VA 22314-3421.

KRUTZSCH, PHILIP HENRY, ANATOMY, ZOOLOGY, REPRODUCTIVE PHYS. **Personal Data:** b St Louis, Mo, July 12, 1919; m 1940, Dorothy; c Eric W & Lynda C. **Education:** San Diego State Col, BA, 1943; Univ Calif, MA, 1948; Univ Kans, PhD (zool, anat), 1953. **Professional Experience:** PROF EMER ANAT, COL MED, UNIV ARIZ, 1990-; prof, Col Med, Univ Ariz, 1964-1989; head dept, Col Med, Univ Ariz, 1964-1973; assoc prof, Sch Med, Univ Pittsburgh, 1957-1964; asst prof, Univ Tex Health Sci Ctr, Dallas, 1955-1956; instr anat, Sch Med, Univ Pittsburgh, 1953-1954; asst, Univ Kans, 1949; asst instr, Univ Kans, 1948-1952; asst, Univ Calif, 1947-1948. **Memberships:** Am Soc Mammal; Am Asn Anatomists; Am Soc Zoologists; Soc Study Reproduction. **Research Statement & Publications:** Physiology of reproduction; studies of brown adipose tissue, prolonged sperm longevity and male and felmale reproductive cycles and controlling mech. **Mailing Address:** Dept Cell Biol & Anat Univ Ariz Col Med, 1501 N Campbell, Tucson, AZ 85724. **Fax:** 520-626-2097. **E-Mail:** krutzsch@email.arizona.edu

KRUUS, JAAN, ELECTRICAL ENGINEERING, INSTRUMENTATION. **Personal Data:** b Kuimetsa, Estonia, July 23, 1936; Canadian citizen; m 1962, Reet; c Erik, Karin, Kaia & Robert. **Education:** Univ Toronto, BASc, 1959; Univ Ill, MS, 1961, PhD (elec eng), 1963. **Professional Experience:** PRES, COMM INSTRUMENTS & METHODS OBSERVATION, WORLD METEOROL ORGN, 1989-; vpres, Comm Instruments & Methods Observation, World Meteorol Orgn, 1981-1989; dir, Data Acquisition Serv Br, 1980-1991; planning analyst, Atmospheric Environ Serv, 1978-1980; coordr remote sensing, Off Sci Adv, 1974-1978; head, Instrumentation Sect, Hydrol Sci Div, Inland Waters Br, Environ

Can, 1969-1974; assoc prof, Univ Ottawa, 1965-1969; asst prof elec eng, Queen's Univ, Ont, 1963-1965; engr, Spruce Falls Power & Paper Co, Ont, 1959-1960. **Memberships:** Inst Elec & Electronics Engrs; Sigma Xi. **Research Statement & Publications:** Application of artificial intelligence for meteorological measurements. **Mailing Address:** 15 Mich Dr, Willowdale, ON M2M 3H9, Can.

KRUUS, PEETER, physical chemistry; deceased, see previous edition for last biography

KRUUV, JACK, CRYOBIOLOGY, RADIOBIOLOGY. **Personal Data:** b Tartu, Estonia, June 1, 1938; Canadian citizen; m 1960, Joan; c Cindy, Wendy & Sean. **Education:** Univ Waterloo, BASc, 1962, MSc, 1963; Univ Western Ont, PhD (biophys), 1966. **Professional Experience:** PROF EMER, DEPT PHYSICS, UNIV WATERLOO, as of 2006; vis prof, Univ Calif, 1993; prof physics & biol, Univ Waterloo, 1977-1996; vis prof biophysics, Pa State Univ, 1974-1975; from asst prof to assoc prof physics, Univ Waterloo, 1967-1977; fel, Argonne Nat Lab, 1966-1967; fel & lectr, Ont Cancer Found, Victoria Hosp, 1966. **Memberships:** Radiation Res Soc; Cryobiol Soc. **Research Statement & Publications:** Cancer research; radiation biophysics; research with synchronized tissue culture cells; effects of low oxygen atmospheres on cells; radiotherapy of cancer cells; repair of radiation and freeze-thaw damage; cryobiology; multi-cellular tissue culture systems; hypothermia; hyperthermia; mechanisms of freeze-thaw damage. **Mailing Address:** Dept Physics, Univ Waterloo, 200 Univ Ave W, Waterloo, ON N2L 3G1, Can. **Fax:** 519-746-8115. **E-Mail:** kruuv@sciborg.uwaterloo.ca

KRYDER, MARK HOWARD, MAGNETIC RECORDING, Data Storage Technology. **Personal Data:** b Portland, Ore, October 7, 1943; m 1965, Sandra; c Christa M & Matthew C. **Education:** Stanford Univ, BS, 1965; Calif Inst Technol, MS, 1966, PhD (elec eng, physics), 1970. **Honors & Awards:** IEEE Third Millenium Medal (2000), Reynold B Johnson Information Storage Award (2000), Magnetics Soc Achievement Award (1995), Inst Elec & Electronics Engrs. **Professional Experience:** CHIEF TECHNICAL OFFICER and SENIOR VICE PRESIDENT, RESEARCH, SEAGATE TECHNOLOGY, as of 2003, SENIOR VICE PRESIDENT RESEARCH, 1998-2003; UNIV PROF ELEC & COMPUT ENG, CARNEGIE-MELLON UNIV, as of 2003; DIR, DATA STORAGE SYSTS CTR, 1990-; distinguished lectr, Inst Elec & Electronics Engrs, 1985; dir, Magnetics Technol Ctr, 1982-1990; PROF ELEC & COMP ENG, CARNEGIE-MELLON UNIV, 1980-; assoc prof, Data Storage Systs Ctr, 1978-1980; mgr explor bubble devices, IBM Res Ctr, 1975-1978; res staff mem, IBM Res Ctr, 1973-1975; scientist solid state physics, Univ Regensburg, 1971-1973; NSF res fel, Calif Inst Technol, 1969-1971; consult, IBM, Gen Elec, Nat Semiconductor Corp, Motorola, & Alcoa. **Memberships:** Nat Acad Eng; Fellow, Inst Elec & Electronics Engrs; Fellow, Am Phys Soc. **Research Statement & Publications:** Applied magnetics; magneto-optical, and magnetic recording devices including materials, fabrication, device design and use in systems. **Mailing Address:** Seagate Technol, 1251 Waterfront Pl, Pittsburgh, PA 15222. **Fax:** 412-918-7011. **E-Mail:** Mark.Kryder@seagate.com

KRYGER, ROY GEORGE, PHYSICAL ORGANIC CHEMISTRY. **Personal Data:** b Brooklyn, NJ, June 7, 1936; m 1958, c 2. **Education:** Atlantic Union Col, AB, 1957; Stevens Inst Technol, MS, 1966; Boston Univ, PhD (org chem), 1973. **Professional Experience:** RETIRED; prof chem, La Sierra Univ, Riverside, Calif, 1984-2002; prof chem, Atlantic Union Col, 1981-1984; chmn dept, Atlantic Union Col, 1966-1984; anal methods develop & antibiotic res & develop chemist, Lederle Lab Div, Am Cyanamid Co, 1960-1966; chemist food analyst, US Army Med Res & Nutrit Lab, 1959-1960; Chemist qual control, Lederle Lab Div, Am Cyanamid Co, 1957-1958. **Memberships:** AAAS; Nat Sci Teachers Asn. **Research Statement & Publications:** Relative and absolute reactivities of free radicals and relation of structure of free radicals to their reactivity. **Mailing Address:** Dept Chem, La Sierra Univ, 4700 Pierce St, Riverside, CA 92515. **E-Mail:** rkryger@lasierra.edu

KRYNITSKY, JOHN ALEXANDER, PETROLEUM FUELS, CHEMISTRY. **Personal Data:** b Far Rockaway Beach, NY, June 15, 1918; m 1949, c 1. **Education:** Univ Md, BS, 1939; Univ NC, PhD (org chem), 1943. **Professional Experience:** CONSULT, FUELS & PETROL PROD, 1981-; dir tech opers, defense fuel supply ctr, 1967-1981; staff asst, Off dir defense res & eng, 1964-1967; chemist, Naval res lab, DC, 1943-1944, 1945-1964; asst chem, Univ NC, 1939-1943. **Memberships:** Am Chem Soc; Am Soc Testing & Mat. **Research Statement & Publications:** Fuels; lubricants; petroleum products; organic materials; synthetic organic chemistry; detection and identification of organic substances; preparations and properties of some highly chlorinated hydrocarbons; hydrazine; aircraft and rocket fuels. **Mailing Address:** 4904 Cumberland Ave, Chevy Chase, MD 20815.

KRYSAN, JAMES LOUIS, INSECT PHYSIOLOGY. **Personal Data:** b Calmar, Iowa, March 12, 1934; m 1960, c 3. **Education:** Iowa State Teachers Col, BA, 1961; Univ Ill, MS, 1964, PhD (entom), 1965. **Professional Experience:** USDA, BELTSVILLE, MD, 1992-; res leader, res entomologist, Yakima res lab, agr res Serv, 1984-1992; entomologist, northern Grain insects res lab, sci & Educ admin-agr res, USDA, 1968-1984; asst prof biol, St Mary's Col, Minn, 1965-1968. **Memberships:** Entom Soc Am; AAAS; Am Soc Nat; Coleopterists Soc. **Research Statement & Publications:** Management of insect pests of pear; biosystematics of Diabrotica; seasonality of insects. **Mailing Address:** 5802 Nicholson Lane, Rockville, MD 20852.

KRYSTEK, STANLEY R, JR, COMPUTATIONAL BIOCHEMISTRY, PROTEIN & PEPTIDE MODELING. **Personal Data:** b Ft Belvoir, Va, May 6, 1961. **Education:** State Univ NY, Albany, BS, 1983; Albany Med Col, MS, 1985, PhD (biochem), 1989. **Professional Experience:** RES INVESTR II, BRISTOL-MEYERS SQUIBB, 1992-; res investr I, 1990-1992; Res fel, 1989-1990. **Memberships:** Biophys Soc; Protein Soc; Am Peptide Soc; AAAS; Am Chem Soc. **Research Statement & Publications:** Computational biochemistry; protein and peptide modeling. **Mailing Address:** Bristol-Myers Squibb Res Inst, PO Box 4000, Princeton, NJ 08543-4000. **Fax:** 609-252-6030. **E-Mail:** krystek-at-bms.com

KRYTER, KARL DAVID, PSYCHOPHYSIOLOGY, PSYCHOACOUSTICS. **Personal Data:** b Indianapolis, Ind, October 13, 1914; m 1946, c 3. **Education:** Butler Univ, AB, 1939; Univ Rochester, PhD (psychol), 1943. **Honors & Awards:** Distinguished Award Sci, Am Speech & Hearing Asn; Franklin V Taylor Award in Eng Psychol. **Professional Experience:** STAFF SCIENTIST EMER, SRI INT, as of 1995; LECTR & ADJ PROF, SAN DIEGO STATE UNIV, 1991-; staff scientist, SRI Int, 1985-1991; dir, Sensory Res Ctr, Stanford Res Inst, 1965-1985; Int Orgn Standard & Int Electrotechnol Comn, 1962-; chmn exec coun, bioacoust & biomech, Nat Acad Sci-Nat Res Coun, 1961-1964; mem adv panel psychol & soc sci, Off Asst Secy Defense, 1958-1963; mem comt hearing, bioacoust & biomech, Nat Acad Sci-Nat Res Coun, 1957-; head psychoacoust dept, Bolt Beranek & Newman, Inc, 1957-1965; dir human factors oper res lab, USAF, 1948-1952 & oper appln lab, Cambridge Res Ctr, 1952-1957; asst prof psychol, Univ Wash, St Louis, 1946-1948; Fel psycho-acoust, Harvard Univ, 1942-1946; adv, President's Comt Sci & Technol; Pres, Acousis Co. **Memberships:** Fel AAAS; Soc Eng Psychol (pres 1966); Am Psychol Asn; Acoust Soc Am (pres 1971); Human Factors Soc. **Research Statement & Publications:** Audition; psychoacoustics; speech communication; electrophysiology. **Mailing Address:** SRI Int, 333 Ravenswood Ave, Menlo Park, CA 94025.

KRYWOLAP, GEORGE NICHOLAS, MICROBIAL ECOLOGY. **Personal Data:** b Ukraine, January 4, 1936; American citizen; m 1957, Olha; c George W. **Education:** Drexel Univ, BS, 1960; Pa State Univ, MS, 1962, PhD (microbiol), 1964. **Professional Experience:** Vis prof, Col Dent, Univ Fla, 1988-1989; PROF MICROBIOL, UNIV MD, 1977-; from asst prof to assoc prof microbiol, Schs Pharm & Dent, 1964-1977. **Memberships:** AAAS; pres Am Soc Microbiol; Int Asn Dent Res; Brit Soc Gen Microbiol. **Research Statement & Publications:** Antibiotics; production of antibiotics by mycorrhizal fungi; microbial ecology of the oral cavity; microbiology of the periodontum. **Mailing Address:** Dept Microbiol, Univ MD, Baltimore, MD 21228. **Fax:** 410-418-9402. **E-Mail:** gnkrywolap@hotmail.com

KRZANOWSKI, JOSEPH JOHN, PHARMACOLOGY, PHYSIOLOGY. **Personal Data:** b Hartford, Conn, February 4, 1940; m 1963, Patricia; c Karen M & Jenifer A. **Education:** Univ Conn, BS, 1962; Univ Tenn, MS, 1965, PhD (pharmacol, physiol), 1968; Barry Col, MA, 1987. **Professional Experience:** Assoc dean res & grad affairs, Col Med, Univ SFla, beginning 1991; co-chmn, Am Acad Allergy & Immunol Role & Care Animals Res, 1988-1993; PROF PHARMACOL, COL MED, UNIV SFLA, 1983-; VCHMN DEPT, COL MED, UNIV SFLA, 1981-; NIH pulmonary young investr award, 1974-1976; from asst prof to assoc prof, Col Med, Univ SFla, 1971-1983; fel pharmacol, Med Sch, Wash Univ, 1968-1971. **Memberships:** Am Soc Pharmacol & Exp Therapeut; NY Acad Sci; AAAS; Am Acad Allergy & Immunol; Am Col Clin Pharmacol. **Research Statement & Publications:** Autonomic pharmacology; smooth muscle pharmacology; pulmonary and cardiac cyclic nucleotides; prostaglandins; pulmonary and immunopharmacol; Red Tide Toxin. **Mailing Address:** Dept Pharmacol & Molecular Therapeut, Col Med, Univ SFla, 12901 Bruce B Downs Blvd, MDC Box 9, Tampa, FL 33612-4799. **Fax:** 813-974-3081, 813-974-2565. **E-Mail:** jkrzanow@hsc.usf.edu

KRZEMINSKI, STEPHEN F, PHYSICAL CHEMISTRY, ANALYTICAL CHEMISTRY. **Personal Data:** b Philadelphia, Pa, December 26, 1943; m 1966, c 3. **Education:** La Salle Col, BA, 1965; Univ Pittsburgh, PhD (phys chem), 1969. **Professional Experience:** DIR, ROHM AND HAAS CORP, as of 2002; MGR, GOVT RELS & PROD STAND, AGR CHEM-NORTH AM, ROHM AND HAAS CO, 1980-; mgr, Govt Regulatory Rels, 1977-1980; proj leader, Res Div, 1975-1977; Sr res chemist, Bristol Res Labs, 1969-1975. **Memberships:** Am Chem Soc. **Research Statement & Publications:** Transition metal chemistry; coordination compounds; Mossbauer spectroscopy; pesticide residues; metabolism and environmental fate of pesticides; drug delivery systems; pharmacokinetics. **Mailing Address:** Indpndnce Mall, Philadelphia, PA 19102.

KRZYCH, URSZULA, IMMUNOLOGY. **Personal Data:** b Lancut, Poland, July 23, 1949. **Education:** Rutgers Univ, BA, 1972, PhD (physiol), 1977. **Professional Experience:** RES SCIENTIST, CATH UNIV, 1986-; vis prof for women, NSF, 1986; PROF IMMUNOL, CATH UNIV, 1982-; fel immunol, Univ Calif, Los Angeles, 1977-1982. **Memberships:** Am Asn Immunologists. **Research Statement & Publications:** Immunology. **Mailing Address:** Dept Immunol, Walter Reed Army Inst Res, 503 Robert Grant Ave, Silver Spring, MD 20910. **E-Mail:** urszula.krzych@na.amedd.army.mil

KRZYZANOWSKI, PAUL, COMPILER DESIGN. **Personal Data:** b New York, NY, February 7, 1964. **Education:** NY Univ, BS, 1985; Cooper Union, BE, 1985; Columbia Univ, MS, 1987. **Professional Experience:** PRIN ENGR, LUCENT TECHNOL, as of 2004; MEM TECH STAFF, COMPUT SYSTS RES, AT&T BELL LABS, 1989-; Mem tech staff, UNIX Systs Lab, 1985-1989. **Memberships:** Inst Elec & Electronics Engrs. **Mailing Address:** Lucent Technol, 600 Mountain Ave, Murray Hill, NJ 07974. **E-Mail:** paul@pk.org

KSHIRSAGAR, ANANT MADHAV, STATISTICS. **Personal Data:** b Satara, India, August 16, 1931; m 1957, c 2. **Education:** Univ Bombay, MSc, 1951; Univ Manchester, PhD (statist), 1961. **Honorary Degrees:** DSc, Univ Manchester, 1976. **Professional Experience:** PROF BIOSTATIST, UNIV MICH, 1977-; prof statist, Tex A&M Univ, 1971-1977; assoc prof statist, Southern Methodist Univ, 1968-1971; sr sci officer, Defence Sci Lab, India, 1963-1968; lectr statist, Univ Bombay, 1951-1963. **Memberships:** Fel Am Statist Asn; fel Inst Math Statist; Int Inst Statist. **Research Statement & Publications:** Design of experiments; multivariant and discriminant analysis; renewal theory, especially Markovian renewal theory. **Mailing Address:** 1420 Washinton Heights M4360, Ann Arbor, MI 48103. **Fax:** 734-763-2215. **E-Mail:** kay@umich.edu

KSIENSKI, A(HARON), ELECTRICAL ENGINEERING. **Personal Data:** b Warsaw, Poland, June 23, 1924; American citizen; m 1954, c 2. **Education:** Univ Southern Calif, MS, 1952, PhD (elec eng), 1958. **Honors & Awards:** Lord Brabazon Award, Inst Radio & Electronic Engrs, London, 1967 & 1976. **Professional Experience:** EMER PROF ELEC ENG, OHIO STATE UNIV, 1987-; assoc ed, Antennas, Inst Elec & Electronics Engrs, 1970-1972; prof elec eng & tech dir commun systs, Electrosci Lab, 1967-1987; head res staff, Antenna Res Dept, Hughes Aircraft Co, 1960-1967; sr staff engr, Antenna Res Dept, Hughes Aircraft Co, 1960; staff engr, Antenna Res Dept, Hughes Aircraft Co, 1958-1960; Lectr, Univ Southern Calif, 1954-1957; staff engr, Wiancko Eng Co, 1953-1957; Consult engr, W L Schott Co, Calif, 1952-1953. **Memberships:** Fel Inst Elec & Electronics Engrs; Int Union Radio Sci. **Research Statement & Publications:** Antennas and antenna systems; information theory; data processing; radar detection and identification; target identification; signal processing arrays communication. **Mailing Address:** Dept Elec Eng Ohio State Univ, 1320 Kinnear Rd, Columbus, OH 43212.

KSIR, CHARLES JOSEPH, PSYCHOPHARMACOLOGY. **Personal Data:** b Albuquerque, NMex, May 19, 1945; m 1967, c 1. **Education:** Univ Tex, Austin, BA, 1967; Ind Univ, Bloomington, PhD (psychol), 1971. **Professional Experience:** Univ Cambridge, Eng, 1983; vis scientist, Salk Inst Biol Study, 1981; PROF PSYCHOL, UNIV WYO, 1980-; assoc prof, Univ Wyo, 1976-1980; asst prof, Univ Wyo, 1972-1976; fel neurobiology, Worcester Found Exp Biol, 1971-1972. **Memberships:** Behav Pharmacol Soc; Psychonomic Soc; AAAS; Sigma Xi; Soc Neuroscience; Am Psychol Asn. **Research Statement & Publications:** Behavioral pharmacology; neuropharmacology. **Mailing Address:** Dept Psychol, Univ Wyo, Box 3415, Laramie, WY 82071-3415. **Fax:** 307-766-2926. **E-Mail:** cksir@uwyo.edu

KSYCKI, MARY JOECILE, radiation chemistry; deceased, see previous edition for last biography

KU, ALBERT B, ENGINEERING MECHANICS, APPLIED MATHEMATICS. **Personal Data:** b Changsha, China, June 15, 1933; m 1965, Jane; c Natalie & Elizabeth. **Education:** Univ Taiwan, BSCE, 1956; Va Polytech Inst, MSCE, 1961; Ohio State Univ, PhD (soil mech), 1965. **Professional Experience:** Chmn dept civil eng, Univ Detroit, Mercy, 1982-1985; PROF CIVIL & ENVIRON ENG, UNIV DETROIT, MERCY, 1976-; Gen Motors, beginning 1972; burrough's corp, beginning 1970; consult, chrysler corp, beginning 1966; from asst prof to assoc prof, Univ Detroit, Mercy, 1964-1976; engr, Kai-Nan Eng

Corp, 1959-1960; jr engr, Mil Construct Comt, 1958-1959. **Memberships:** Am Acad Mech. **Research Statement & Publications:** Rheological properties of bituminous concrete; linear viscoelasticity; nonlinear mechanics; static and dynamic stability; finite element analysis; artificial intelligence; computer software. **Mailing Address:** Dept Civil & Environ eng, Univ Detroit, 4001 W McNichols Rd PO Box 19900, Detroit, MI 48219-0900. **Fax:** 313-993-1187. **E-Mail:** kuab@udmercy.edu

KU, AUDREY YEH, ORGANIC CHEMISTRY, POLYMER CHEMISTRY. **Personal Data:** b Taiwan. **Education:** Providence Col, Taiwan, BS, 1971; Eastern Ill Univ, MS, 1973; State Univ NY, Buffalo, PhD (chem), 1977. **Professional Experience:** SR RES CHEMIST, MONSANTO CO, 1980-; res chemist, Union Carbide Corp, 1978-1980; fel chem, Ohio State Univ, 1977-1978; Teaching & res asst chem, Eastern Ill Univ, 1972-1973 & State Univ NY, Buffalo, 1973-1977. **Memberships:** Am Chem Soc; Sigma Xi. **Mailing Address:** 800 N Linderbergh Blvd, U 2 I, St Louis, MO 63166.

KU, BERNARD SIU-MAN, NEXT GENERATION SWITCHING TECHNOLOGIES, ADVANCED SOFTWARE ENGINEERING RESEARCH & DEVELOPMENT. **Personal Data:** b Hong Kong. **Education:** Univ Hong Kong, BS, 1981; Univ Tex, MBA, 1983; Univ NTex, MS, 1985; Southern Methodist Univ, PhD (telecommun), 1991. **Professional Experience:** SR MGR, MCI WORLDCOM TELECOMMUNICATIONS CORP, as of 2001; distinguished tech mem, Dept Network Architect & Stand, Mci, as of 2000; ADJ PROF ELEC ENG, SOUTHERN METHODIST UNIV, 1993-; mem tech staff telecommun res & develop eng, Adv Switching Lab, Nec Am Inc, Irving, Tex, 1989-1991; vis prof comput sci, Richland Col, 1989; computer mgr, Southern Methodist Univ, Dallas, Tex, 1988-1989; teaching fel & res asst, Southern Methodist Univ, Dallas, Tex, 1988; chmn, Dept Comput Sci, Univ Mary Hardin-Baylor, Belton, Tex, 1985-1988. **Memberships:** Int Commun Asn; Inst Elec & Electronics Engrs; Asn Comput Mach. **Research Statement & Publications:** Advanced software technology for telecommunication switching software development, like software reuse, case tools and integrated software engineering environment; telecommunication industry trends and technology assessment. **Mailing Address:** Mci WorldCom Telecommunications Corp, 2400 N Glenville Dr, Richardson, TX 75082. **Fax:** 972-729-6038. **E-Mail:** bernard.ku@mci.com

KU, DAVID D, PHARMACOLOGY. **Education:** Whittier Col, BA, 1972; Mich State Univ, PhD (Pharmacol), 1976. **Honors & Awards:** Am Inst Chemists Award, 1972; Young Investr Res Award, NIH, 1978. **Professional Experience:** PROF PHARMACOL & TOXICOL, UNIV AL, as of 2005. **Memberships:** Fel Am Heart Asn; fel Am Physical Soc. **Mailing Address:** Dept Pharmacol, Univ Ala, 1670 Univ Blvd Volker Hall VH G133D, Birmingham, AL 35294-0019. **Fax:** 205-934-7370. **E-Mail:** davidku@uab.edu

KU, DAVID NELSON, BIOFLUID DYNAMICS, VASCULAR SURGERY. **Personal Data:** b St Louis, Mo, March 15, 1956; m 1980, c 3. **Education:** Harvard Univ, BA, 1978; Ga Inst Technol, MS, 1982, PhD (aerospace eng & biofluid dynamics), 1983; Emory Univ, MD, 1984. **Honors & Awards:** NSF Presidential Young Investrs Award, 1987; Y C Fung Young Investr Award, Am Soc Mech Engrs, 1989; Gustus A Larson Mem Award, 1996. **Professional Experience:** PROF BIOENG, GA INST TECHNOL, 1995-; ASSOC PROF & DIR CARDIOVASC LAB, EMORY UNIV, 1986-; from asst prof to assoc prof, Emory Univ, 1986-1995; fel cardiovasc path, Univ Chicago, 1985-1986; dir, Cardiovasc Lab, Hyde Park Community Hosp, 1985-1986; Fulbright Gast professor, Munich, Ger, 1985; surg resident, Univ Chicago, 1984-1985; mem, Coun Arteriosclerosis. **Memberships:** Am Soc Mech Engrs; Am Heart Asn; AMA; Am Col Angiol; Am Phys Soc. **Research Statement & Publications:** Biofluid dynamics research on the development, diagnosis, and treatment of arterial disease; mechanisms of atherogenesis and the thrombosis of athersclerotic arteries; magnetic resonance imaging. **Mailing Address:** Sch Mech Eng, Ga Inst Technol, Atlanta, GA 30332-0405. **Fax:** 404-894-2291. **E-Mail:** david.ku@me.gatech.edu

KU, EDMOND CHIU-CHOON, LIPID METABOLISM. **Personal Data:** b Canton, China, August 11, 1932; American citizen; m 1959, c 2. **Education:** Taiwan Prov Col, BS, 1956; Va Polytech Inst, PhD (biochem), 1962. **Professional Experience:** RETIRED; sr res fel, Ciba-Geigy Corp, 1985-1997; mgr, Ciba-Geigy Corp, 1980-1985; sr staff scientist, Ciba-Geigy Corp, 1970-1979; NIH spec res fel, Cornell Univ, 1967-1969; Res scientist biochem, Parke, Davis & Co, 1963-1967. **Memberships:** Am Chem Soc; Sigma Xi; NY Acad Sci; Inflammable Res Asn. **Research Statement & Publications:** Enzyme kinetics and its application to the study of drug action at molecular level; regulatory mechanism involved in the biosynthesis and degradation of prostaglandins at subcellular level; cholesterol and triglyceride biosynthesis regulation. **Mailing Address:** 4533 Grenadier Pl, Castro Valley, CA 94546.

KU, HAN SAN, PLANT PHYSIOLOGY, BIOCHEMISTRY. **Personal Data:** b Hsin-Chu, Taiwan, November 20, 1935; m 1965, Lily S; c 2. **Education:** Nat Taiwan Univ, BS, 1958; Osaka Univ, MS, 1963; Univ Calif, Davis, PhD (plant physiol), 1968. **Honors & Awards:** Japanese Food Sci Soc Award, 1966; Campbell Award, Am Inst Biol Sci, 1969. **Professional Experience:** VPRES, RICERCA INC, 1990-; SR RES ASSOC BIOCHEM, T R EVANS RES CTR, 1974-; plant biochemist, Mich State Univ, 1973-1974; biologist & res leader plant sci, Allied Chem Res Lab, 1972-1973; res biologist, Allied Chem Res Lab, 1970-1971; NSF fel ethylene physiol, Purdue Univ, 1968-1970; res asst, NIH fel ethylene biosynthesis, 1968; res asst, Univ Calif, Davis, 1964-1968; asst plant physiol, Nat Taiwan Univ, 1960-1961; Lectr agr, Taipei Agr Prof Sch, 1957-1958; vpres, Ricenca, Inc & ISK Interprise; Mgr, Biol Eval SDS Biotech & Agr Chem Biol Evaluation. **Memberships:** AAAS; Am Soc Plant Physiologists; Am Soc Agron; Japanese Biochem Soc; Soil Sci Soc Am; Am Chem Soc; Japanese Silver Chem Soc. **Research Statement & Publications:** Ethylene biogenesis and action in plant tissue; plant growth regulator; photorespiration; nitrogen fixation; crop production pesticide; pesticide metabolism; animal, plant metabolism; Environ Fate EPA; allochemical mode of pesticide. **Mailing Address:** 8060 Conestoga Trail, Mentor, OH 44060.

KU, HARRY HSIEN HSIANG, mathematical statistics, engineering; deceased, see previous edition for last biography

KU, HSU-TUNG, TOPOLOGY, GEOMETRY. **Personal Data:** b Taiwan, October 24, 1933; American citizen; m 1964, Mei-Chin; c 2. **Education:** Taiwan Prov Norm Univ, BSc, 1961; Tulane Univ, MSc, 1964, PhD (math), 1967. **Professional Experience:** PROF EMER MATH, UNIV MASS, AMHERST, 2001-; prof math, Univ Mass, Amherst, beginning 1979; vis mem math, Inst Adv Study, 1977; assoc prof, Univ Mass, Amherst, 1973-1979; asst prof, Univ Mass, Amherst, 1968-1973; mem math, Inst Adv Study, 1967-1968; 1984. **Memberships:** Am Math Soc. **Research Statement & Publications:** Transformation groups; algebraic topology. **Mailing Address:** Univ Mass, Seven Maple Wood Terrace, Hadley, MA 01003. **E-Mail:** htku@math.umass.edu

KU, JENTUNG, THERMODYNAMICS & FLUID MECHANICS, COMPUTER MODELING & SIMULATION. **Personal Data:** b Hsinchu, Taiwan, March 1950. **Education:** Nat Tsing Hua Univ, BS, 1972; Purdue Univ, MS, 1976, PhD (mech eng), 1980. **Professional Experience:** TECHNOL DEVELOP GROUP LEADER, THERMAL ENG, NASA, as of 2004; SR ENGR, NASA GODDARD SPACE FLIGHT CTR, 1991-; sect head & prog mgr, OAO Corp, 1983-1991; mem tech staff, advan technol ctr, Bendix corp, 1980-1983. **Memberships:** Am Soc Mech Engrs; Am Inst Aeronaut & Astronaut; Am Nuclear Soc. **Research Statement & Publications:** Two-phase heat transport and thermal control systems; capillary pumped loops for spacecraft thermal management. **Mailing Address:** NASA Goddard Space Flight Ctr, Code 724-2, Greenbelt, MD 20771. **Fax:** 301-286-1692. **E-Mail:** jentung.ku-1@nasa.gov

KU, MEI-CHIN HSIAO, TOPOLOGY, GEOMETRY. **Personal Data:** b Taiwan, November 1, 1937; American citizen; m 1964, Hsu-Tung; c 2. **Education:** Taiwan Norm Univ, BSc, 1961; Syracuse Univ, MS, 1964; Tulane Univ, La, PhD (math), 1967. **Professional Experience:** PROF MATH, UNIV MASS, AMHERST, 1982-; Vis mem, Inst Advan Study, 1977 & 1984; from asst prof to assoc prof, Univ Mass, Amherst, 1970-1982; Mathematician, Inst Advan Study, 1967-1968. **Memberships:** Math Asn Am. **Research Statement & Publications:** Transformation groups; geometry; PDE. **Mailing Address:** Dept Math & Statist, Univ Mass, Amherst, MA 01003. **Fax:** 413-545-1801. **E-Mail:** meiku@math.umass.edu

KU, PAO KWEN, ANIMAL NUTRITION. **Personal Data:** b Anhing, China, December 18, 1933. **Education:** Mich State Univ, PhD (animal nutrit), 1970. **Professional Experience:** RETIRED; res specialist, Dept Animal Sci, Mich State Univ, beginning 1973. **Research Statement & Publications:** Animal nutrition. **Mailing Address:** Dept Animal Sci Animal Nutrit Lab, Mich State Univ, E Lansing, MI 48824-0001.

KU, PEH SUN, ENVIRONMENTAL PHYSICS. **Personal Data:** b Shangtung, China, August 23, 1922; American citizen; m 1957, Hui Chen Sun; c John & George. **Education:** Nat Cent Univ, BS, 1947; Univ Rochester, MS, 1955; Yale Univ, DEng(chem eng), 1960. **Professional Experience:** RETIRED; sr environ engr, Environ Affairs, 1978-1992; sr engr, Consol Edison Co, NY, 1973-1978; chem engr air pollution control, Consol Edison Co, NY, 1970-1973; staff scientist, Reentry Systs Div, Gen Elec Co, 1969-1970; theoret physicist, Reentry Systs Div, Gen Elec Co, 1965-1969; res engr, Boeing Co, 1960-1965; res asst, Carnegie Inst Technol, 1954-1955; Chem engr, Chinese Petrol Corp, Taiwan, 1947-1954. **Memberships:** AAAS; Am Chem Soc; Am Phys Soc; Am Geophys Union. **Research Statement & Publications:** Acoustics; high temperature thermodynamics and transport properties of matter; physical properties of matter under high pressures; chemical kinetics; control and dispersion of air pollutants in the atmosphere and their removal from industrial processes; water pollution and hazerdous wastes; novel methods of energy conversion. **Mailing Address:** 244 Old State Rd, Berwyn, PA 19312.

KU, ROBERT TIEN-HUNG, FIBER OPTICS, LASER COMPONENT PACKAGING & LASER APPLICATIONS. **Personal Data:** b Shanghai, China, January 19, 1947; American citizen; m 1971, c 2. **Education:** Univ Ill, Urbana, BS, 1967, MS, 1968, PhD (elec eng), 1973. **Professional Experience:** DEPT HEAD, SUBMARINE DEVICE PACKAGING ENG & MFG, AT&T BELL LABS, 1995-; supvr, Lightwave Device Packaging Dept, 1988-1994; mem tech staff, Laser Develop Dept, 1981-1988; mem tech staff, Optics Div, Lincoln Lab, Mass Inst Technol, 1973-1981; Res asst, Gaseous Electronics Lab, Univ Ill, 1967-1973; Fel, NSF. **Memberships:** Am Phys Soc; Inst Elec & Electronics Engrs; Optical Soc Am; Sigma Xi. **Research Statement & Publications:** Laser and optical components for fiber communication systems; laser spectroscopy studies of pollutant gases; laser diagnostics of plasma and chemically excited media; laser radars; high power lasers. **Mailing Address:** PO Box 13396, Reading, PA 19612. **Fax:** 610-939-7648. **E-Mail:** rku@lucent.com

KU, TEH-LUNG, GEOCHEMISTRY, OCEANOLOGY. **Personal Data:** b Shanghai, China, August 30, 1937; m 1970, Theresa; c Pamela, Christina & Joanna. **Education:** Nat Taiwan Univ, BS, 1959; Columbia Univ, PhD (geochem), 1966. **Honors & Awards:** Kapitsa Gold Medal, Russian Academy of Natural Sciences (USA Branch), 2004. **Professional Experience:** Vis prof, Hartwell Lab, UK, 1983- & Nat Taiwan Univ, 1991-; fel, Japan Soc Prom Sci, 1991-; fulbright prof, Ctr Weak Radioactivity, Nat Ctr Sci Res, 1984-; guggenheim fel, 1983-; Fulbright Sr Scholar, 1983, 2004; WILFORD & DARIS ZINSMEYER PROFESSOR OF MARINE STUDIES, 1998-; PROF EARTH SCI, UNIV SOUTHERN CALIF, 1975-; assoc prof, Univ Southern Calif, 1969-1975; asst scientist, Woods Hole Oceanog Inst, 1967-1969; post-doctoral, Lamont Geol Observ, Columbia Univ, 1966-1967. **Memberships:** fel AAAS; fel Am Geophys Union; Geol Soc Am; Geochem Soc. **Research Statement & Publications:** Isotope geochemistry; chemical oceanography; geochronology; Pleistocene geology; climatology; hydrogeochemistry. **Mailing Address:** Dept Earth Sci, Univ Southern Calif, Los Angeles, CA 90089-0740. **E-Mail:** rku@usc.edu

KU, TIMOTHY TAO, FORESTRY. **Personal Data:** b Chaochow, China, March 26, 1926; m 1950, Victoria Feng; c 2. **Education:** Nanking Univ, BS, 1948; Mich State Univ, MF, 1950, PhD (forest ecol, silvicult), 1954. **Professional Experience:** PROF EMER FORESTRY, UNIV ARK, MONTICELLO, as of 2004; Fel, Soc Am Foresters, 1985; vis prof forestry, Nat Taiwan Univ, Taipei, 1983; prof forestry, Univ Ark, Monticello, beginning 1963; from asst prof to assoc prof, Univ Ark, Monticello, 1959-1963; Forester, T S Coile, Inc, Forest Land Consults, 1956-1958. **Memberships:** Soc Am Foresters; Soil Sci Soc Am. **Research Statement & Publications:** Silviculture; forest soils and ecology; biomass production and nutrient cycling in forest stands, site evaluation and classification, and applied silviculture. **Mailing Address:** Dept Forestry, Univ Ark, Monticello, AR 71656. **E-Mail:** ku@uamont.edu

KU, VICTORIA FENG, ORGANIC CHEMISTRY. **Personal Data:** b Peking, China, March 14, 1930; American citizen; m 1950, c 2. **Education:** Barat Col, BS, 1950; Univ Ark, MS, 1964, PhD (chem), 1976. **Professional Experience:** ASSOC PROF CHEM, UNIV ARK, MONTICELLO, beginning 1976; asst prof, Univ Ark, Monticello, 1969-1975; chemist, Hercules Powder Co, 1957-1959; chemist, Mich State Health Dept Lab, 1952-1956. **Memberships:** Am Chem Soc. **Mailing Address:** 236 Mason Hill, Monticello, AR 71655.

KU, YI-YIN, PROCESS RESEARCH ON SYNTHESIS OF PHARMACEUTICAL DRUG CANDIDATES. **Personal Data:** b Xian, China, May 15, 1959; m 1985, Yao-En Li; c Kory K Li & Katherine H Li. **Education:** Northwestern Univ, China, BS, 1982; Univ Ill, Chicago, MS, 1985, PhD (org chem), 1988. **Professional Experience:** SR GROUP LEADER & ASSOC RES FEL, ABBOTT LABS, as of 2003; SR RES SCIENTIST, ABBOTT LABS, 1992-; res scientist, Abbott Labs, 1989-1992; Res assoc, Univ Ill, Chicago, 1988-1989. **Memberships:** Am Chem Soc. **Research Statement & Publications:** Discovery of new and efficient synthetic methods for the pharmaceutical drug candidates; process research and development of commercial chemical processes for synthesis of pharmaceutical bulk drugs. **Mailing Address:** Abbott Lab, D-R450, R-13 Bldg, 1401 Sheridan Rd, North Chicago, IL 60064. **Fax:** 847-938-5932. **E-Mail:** yiyin.ku@abbott.com

KU, Y(U) H(SIU), electrical engineering, systems engineering; deceased, see previous edition for last biography

KUAN, SHIA SHIONG, DEVELOPMENT OF BIOSENSORS. **Personal Data:** b Canton, China, October 18, 1933; American citizen; m 1973, c 1. **Education:** Nat Chung Hsing Univ, BS, 1953; WVa Univ, MS, 1965, PhD (biochem), 1968. **Professional Experience:** Consult, Taiwan Sugar Res Inst, 1968- & W China Univ Med Sci, 1985-; adj prof chem, Univ New Orleans, 1981-; DIR, NATURAL TOXINS RES CTR, FOOD & DRUG ADMIN, 1980-; sr res assoc, Univ New Orleans, 1971-1980; res fel, La State Univ, New Orleans, 1968-1970; res asst, WVa Univ, 1963-1968; Dir, Nanchow Sugar Factory, 1958-1963. **Memberships:** Am Chem Soc; Sigma Xi; NY Acad Sci; AAAS; Asn Anal Chemists; Inst Food Technologists. **Research Statement & Publications:** Induction, isolation, purification and immobilization of enzymes and the application of immobilized enzymes to agricultural, chemical and clinical analyses; the isolation of naturally occuring toxins and the development of fast, simple and inexpensive procedures for the determination ofthese toxins. **Mailing Address:** 3020 Transcontinental Dr, Metairie, LA 70006.

KUAN, T S, PHYSICS. **Education:** Nat Taiwan Univ, BS, 1970; Cornell Univ, MS, 1973, PhD (mat sci), 1977. **Professional Experience:** PROF, DEPT PHYSICS, STATE UNIV NY, ALBANY, as of 2006. **Mailing Address:** Dept Physics, State Univ NY, Albany, 1400 Washington Ave, Albany, NY 12222. **Fax:** 518-442-4607. **E-Mail:** kuan@csc.albany.edu

KUAN, TUNG-SHENG, ELECTRON MICROSCOPY, ELECTRONIC MATERIALS. **Personal Data:** b Taiwan, December 13, 1947; American citizen; m 1977, c 2. **Education:** Nat Taiwan Univ, BS, 1970; Cornell Univ, MS, 1973, PhD (mat sci), 1977. **Professional Experience:** Vis Fac, IBM T J Watson Res Ctr, 2001-2002; PROF PHYSICS, STATE UNIV NY, ALBANY, 1995-; mgr, Interconnect Mat & Modeling, IBM T J Watson Res Ctr, 1991-1995; mgr, Mat Struct & Properties, IBM T J Watson Res Ctr, 1986-1991; res staff mem, IBM T J Watson Res Ctr, 1977-1995; Mem, Metal Soc, Am Inst Mech Engrs. **Memberships:** Fel Am Phys Soc; Mat Res Soc; Am Inst Mech Engrs; Electron Micros Soc Am. **Research Statement & Publications:** Structural, mechanical and electrical properties of electronic materials; electron microscopy of thin film materials and interfaces. **Mailing Address:** Dept Physics, State Univ NY, Physics 212 1400 Wash Ave, Albany, NY 12222. **Fax:** 518-442-4607. **E-Mail:** kuan@csc.albany.edu

KUANG, JIAN, BIOLOGY. **Education:** Univ Tex, PhD, 1990. **Professional Experience:** ASST PROF, DEPT CELLULAR ONCOL, MD ANDERSON CANCER CTR, as of 2006. **Mailing Address:** MD Anderson Cancer Ctr, 1515 Holcombe Blvd Box 19 Rm Y1 5609, Houston, TX 77030. **Fax:** 713-792-3754. **E-Mail:** jkuang@notes.mdacc.tmc.edu

KUANG, YUNAN, EXPERIMENTAL PHYSICS. **Personal Data:** b Wuhan, China, March 7, 1962; m 1991, Feng; c Guang Y & Amy M. **Education:** Wuhan Univ, BS, 1982; Yale Univ, PhD (physics), 1988. **Professional Experience:** ASST PROF, COL WILLIAM & MARY, 1993-; res assoc, 1988-1993. **Research Statement & Publications:** Studied the fundamental principles of physics using muonium; observed for the first time the formation of muonium negative ion in vacuum; experimental test of muon number conservation in rare kaon decay and muon decay. **Mailing Address:** Dept physics, Col William & Mary, Williamsburg, VA 23187-8795. **Fax:** 804-221-3540. **E-Mail:** kuang@wmheg.physics.wm.edu

KUBAN, KARL, NEUROLOGY & EPIDEMIOLOGY. **Education:** Harvard Sch Pub Health, MSc, 1989. **Professional Experience:** PROF PEDIAT NEUROL, BOSTON UNIV SCH MED, as of 2006; CHIEF, DIV PEDIAT NEUROL, BOSTON UNIV SCH MED, as of 2006. **Mailing Address:** One Boston Med Ctr Pl, Dowling Three S, Boston, MA 02118. **Fax:** 617-414-4502.

KUBAS, GREGORY JOSEPH, TRANSITION-METAL & SMALL MOLECULE CHEMISTRY. **Personal Data:** b Cleveland, Ohio, March 12, 1945; m 1973, Chrystal; c Sherry Lopez. **Education:** Case Inst Technol, BS, 1966; Northwestern Univ, PhD (inorg chem), 1970. **Honors & Awards:** Am Chem Soc Award in Inorg Chem, Am Chem Soc, 1993; EO Lawrence Award in Chemistry, 1994; Elected Fellow of AAAS, 2005. **Professional Experience:** LAB FEL, LOS ALAMOS NAT LAB, 1988-; mem staff chem, Los Alamos Nat Lab, 1972-1988; Fel chem, Princeton Univ, 1971-1972. **Memberships:** Am Chem Soc, AAAS. **Research Statement & Publications:** Coordination chemistry of dihydrogen and sulfur dioxide, structure and reactivity of transition metal SO2 complexes; synthesis, characterization and structure of organometallic small molecule complexes new materials for hydrogen storage. **Mailing Address:** Chem Division, Los Alamos Nat Lab, MS J514, Los Alamos, NM 87545. **Fax:** 505-667-9905. **E-Mail:** kubas@lanl.gov

KUBENA, KAREN SIDELL, COLLEGE ADMINISTRATOR. **Personal Data:** b Madison, Wis, October 1, 1945; m 1968, Leon F; c Lance & Angela. **Education:** Univ Wis-Madison, BS, 1967; Miss State Univ, MS, 1976; Tex A & M Univ, PhD (nutrit), 1982. **Honors & Awards:** Assoc of Former Stud, TAMU, Teach Awd. **Professional Experience:** PROF ANIMAL SCI & FOOD SCI TECHNOL & NUTRITIONAL SCI, COL ARG & LIFE SCI, as of 2004; ASSOC DEAN, COL ARG & LIFE SCI, 1995-; Assoc prof nutrit, Tex A&M Univ, 1988-1996; sect leader, Human Nutrit Sect, 1984-1995; Prog dir, undergrad prog dietetics, Tex A&M Univ, 1982-2000; dir dietetic internship, Tex A&M Univ, 1982-1990; asst prof, Tex A&M Univ, 1982-1988; lectr nutrit, Tex A&M Univ, 1979-1982; dir, Dietary Dept, Grimes Mem Hosp, Navasoto, Tex, 1977-1979; prog coordr & instr, Dietary Asst Course, Blinn Col, Brenham, Tex, 1976-1977; consult dietitian, nursing homes & hosps, Miss, 1970-1974; Therapeut dietitian, Vet Admin Ctr, Temple, Tex, 1968-1969. **Memberships:** Am Dietetic Asn; Am Soc Clin Nutrit; Am Soc Nutr Sci. **Research Statement & Publications:** Magnesium adequacy during reproduction in rats and humans with regard to immune function and mineral metabolism; lipid metabolism; nutrition and social support through life cycle. **Mailing Address:** Col Arg and Life Sci, Tex A&M Univ, 2402 TAMU, College Station, TX 77843-2402. **E-Mail:** k-kubena@tamu.edu

KUBENA, LEON FRANKLIN, NUTRITION, TOXICOLOGY. **Personal Data:** b Caldwell, Tex, July 6, 1940; m 1968, c 2. **Education:** Tex A&M Univ, BS, 1965, PhD (poultry sci), 1970. **Professional Experience:** PROF, ENVIRON TOXICOL & FOOD SAFETY, TEX A&M UNIV, as of 2004; mem fac, Tex A&M Univ, beginning 1980; RES ANIMAL SCIENTIST, BIOCHEM & NUTRIT, FOOD ANIMAL PROTECTION RES LAB, AGR RES SERV, USDA, COLLEGE STATION, TEX, 1976-; res nutritionist, S Cent Poultry Res Lab, Animal Sci Div, 1970-1975. **Memberships:** Poultry Sci Asn; Asn Off Anal Chemists; AAAS; World Poultry Sci Asn; US Animal Health Assoc; Coun Agr Sci & Technol. **Research Statement & Publications:** Interrelationships of environment and nutrition; toxicology of environmental toxicants in poultry with special emphasis on interaction of these toxicants; Published over 15 articles. **Mailing Address:** Dept Environ Toxicol & Food Safety, Tex A&M Univ, PO Box 4461, College Station, TX 77843-4461. **Fax:** 979-862-4929. **E-Mail:** kubena@ffsru.tamu.edu

KUBENDRAN, LAGUDUVA R, AERONAUTICS. **Education:** Ga Inst Technol, PhD. **Professional Experience:** VPRES, ANALYTICAL SVCS & MAT, as of 2006. **Mailing Address:** Analytical Svcs & Mat, 107 Res Dr, Hampton, VA 23666-1340. **Fax:** 804-865-7309. **E-Mail:** laguduva.kubendran@dfrc.nasa.gov

KUBERSKY, EDWARD SIDNEY, LIMNOLOGY, ECOLOGY. **Personal Data:** b Brooklyn, NY, February 25, 1947; m 1998, Malka. **Education:** Brooklyn Col, CUNY, BS, 1967; Ind Univ, MA, 1968, PhD (zoology), 1973. **Honors & Awards:** Danforth Associate, 1980-1986. **Professional Experience:** CHMN BIOL, FELICIAN COL, 1994-1997, 2003-2006; Prof. Biol. 2005-; Assoc Prof Biol, Felician Col, beginning 1993; Chmn & Assoc Prof Biol, St Francis Col, 1989-1993; Chmn Dept, Upsala Col, 1979-1984; from Instr to Assoc Prof Biol, Upsala Col, 1972-1989; proj dir, NSF grant, 1972-1974 & 1976-1977. **Memberships:** Int Asn Theoret & Appl Limnol; Freshwater Biol Asn; Am Soc Limnol & Oceanog; NAm Lake Mgt Soc. **Research Statement & Publications:** Ecology and taxonomy of cladocera; lake restoration. **Mailing Address:** Dept Biol, Felician Col, 262 S Main St, Lodi, NJ 07644. **E-Mail:** kuberskye@inet.felician.edu

KUBES, GEORGE JIRI, PULP CHEMISTRY. **Personal Data:** b Prague, Czech, February 14, 1934; Canadian citizen; m 1959, c 2. **Education:** Tech Univ, Prague, MSc, 1958; Tech Univ, Bratislava, PhD (pulp chem). **Professional Experience:** SR SCIENTIST, PULP & PAPER RES INST CAN, 1985-; PAPRICAN ADJ PROF, DEPT CHEM ENG, MCGILL UNIV, 1985-; head Chem Pulping & Bleaching Sect, Chem Eng Dept, Mcgill Univ, 1977-1985; res scientist pulping, Chem Eng Dept, Mcgill Univ, 1972-1977; sr res chemist, CIP Res Ltd, Can, 1969-1972; head pulping group, Pulp & Paper Res Inst Czech, 1968; mgr res pulping, papermaking & pollution, 1962-1967; lectr, Chem Eng Fac, Tech Univ, 1962-1967; indust consult, Chem Eng Designing Inst, Czech, 1958-1968; supvr res group, NBohemian Pulp & Paper Mill, Czech, 1958-1962. **Memberships:** Can Pulp & Paper Asn; Tech Asn Pulp & Paper Indust; Chem Inst Can. **Research Statement & Publications:** Pulping with an effort to develop a sulphur-free pulping and chlorine-free bleaching process; consultant services to pulp and paper manufacturing industry all over the world; improvements in existing processes, pulping of tropical wood species and annual plants; viscosity of pulp; reaction kinetics in cellulose degradation during alkaline deliquification which resulted in the development of G-factor; differential thermal analysis of black liquor quality; reaction engineering studies and chemical kinetics, also fundamental studies in fluidized bed technology. **Mailing Address:** Dept Chem Eng, McGill Univ, 3420 Univ St, Wong Bldg, Montreal, PQ H3A 2A7, Can. **E-Mail:** gkubes@po-box.mcgill.ca

KUBIAK, CLIFFORD P, INORGANIC & ORGANIC CHARGE TRANSFER, NANOSCIENCE & MOLECULAR ELECTRONICS. **Personal Data:** b Stamford, CT, July 16, 1953; m Pam. **Education:** Brown Univ, BS, 1975; Univ Rochester, PhD, 1980. **Professional Experience:** CHMN CHEM & BIOCHEM, UNIV CALIF, SAN DIEGO, 2002-2006; HAROLD C UREY PROF CHEM, UNIV CALIF, SAN DIEGO, 1998-; Ed. Advis. Brds., Accts. Chem. Res. and Inorg. Chem.; UC San Diego Foundation, 2004 - 2007; Consult, Dow Chem, 1996-; Prof Chem, Purdue Univ, 1990-1998; CHMN, Div Inorg Chem, Am Chem Soc, 2005; fel, Alfred P Sloan Found, 1987-1991; from asst prof to assoc prof, Purdue Univ, 1982-1990; fel, Mass Inst Technol, 1980-1981. **Memberships:** Am Chem Soc; Inter-Am Photochem Soc; Sigma Xi. **Research Statement & Publications:** Ultrafast intramolecular electron transfer and the coalescence of IR spectra. Electronic conduction of individual molecules. Chemical Field Effect and Chemical Resistor sensor devices. Chemical, electrochemical, and photochemical reduction of carbon dioxide. **Mailing Address:** Dept Chem & Biochem, Univ Calif, San Diego, 2040 Urey Hall Addn, 9500 Gilman Dr, MC 0358, La Jolla, CA 92093-0358. **Fax:** 858-534-5383. **E-Mail:** ckubiak@ucsd.edu

KUBICA, GEORGE P, MEDICAL BACTERIOLOGY, BIOSAFETY. **Personal Data:** b Little Falls, NY, June 18, 1929; m 1953, Beverly G Smith; c Scott P & Kimberly A (Jones). **Education:** Cornell Univ, BA, 1951; Univ Mich, MA, 1952; Univ Wis, PhD (med bact), 1955. **Honors & Awards:** Commendation Medal, Surg Gen, USPHS, 1968, Meritorious Serv Medal, 1988. **Professional Experience:** CONSULT, TUBERCULOSIS BACT & DIRECTIONAL AIR FLOW DYNAMICS, 1989-; chief, Mycobact Ctr Dis Control, 1987-1989; chmn, Mycobact Div, 1985-1986; adv/lectr, Int Tuberc Course, Japan, 1984-1990; secy, Comt on Bacteriol, Int Union Against Tuberc, 1976-1982; microbiologist consult, Mycobact Ctr Dis Control, 1974-1986; chmn, Assembly on Microbiol & Immunol, Am Thoracic Soc, 1973-1974; mem & head mycobact sect, Trudeau Inst, Inc, 1969-1974; assoc prof, Univ NC, 1964-1969; chief, Tuberc Unit, Commun Dis Ctr, USPHS, 1962-1969; Instr, Sch Med, Emory Univ, 1959-1969; Actg chief, Tuberc Unit, Commun Dis Ctr, USPHS, 1955-1962. **Memberships:** Am Thoracic Soc; Am Soc Microbiol; Int Union Against Tuberc; fel Am Acad Microbiol; Am Biol Safety Asn. **Research Statement & Publications:** Tuberculosis. **Mailing Address:** 2383 Welton Pl, Atlanta, GA 30338.

KUBICEK, JOHN D, MATHEMATICS. **Personal Data:** b Owatonna, Minn, February 1, 1943. **Education:** St Johns Univ, BA, 1965, MS, 1967; Univ Mo, PhD (math), 1975. **Professional Experience:** ASST DEPT HEAD MATH, MO STATE UNIV, as of 2003; ACTG DIR, MATH CTR, 1988-; PROF MATH, MO STATE UNIV, 1981-. **Memberships:** Am Math Soc. **Research Statement & Publications:** Developmental education in colleges. **Mailing Address:** Dept Math, Mo State Univ, Cheek Hall 57M, Springfield, MO 65804. **E-Mail:** jdk114f@smsu.edu

KUBIK, PETER W, ACCELERATOR MASS SPECTROMETRY. **Personal Data:** b Penzberg, Ger, December 31, 1949; m 1992, Sabine G Teichmann. **Education:** Tech Univ Munich, Ger, MSc, 1978, PhD (physics), 1983. **Professional Experience:** SR RES ASSOC, PAUL SCHERRER INST, 1991-; sr res assoc, NuclearStruct Res Lab, 1987-1991; res assoc, Univ Rochester, 1983-1987; Res fel, Inst Nuclear Physics, Tech Univ Munich, Ger, 1978-1983. **Memberships:** Am Phys Soc; Ger Phys Soc. **Research Statement & Publications:** Measurements of long-lived radioisotopes in natural samples like meteorites, glacial ice, ground water, ocean sediments, surface rocks, etc, using accelerator mass spectrometry. **Mailing Address:** Paul Scherrer Inst Particle Physics, c/o ETH Hohggerberg, Zurich CH-8093, Switzerland. **Fax:** 411-633-1067. **E-Mail:** kubik@particle.phys.ethz.ch

KUBIK, PHILIP ROMAN, SQUID MAGNETOMETRY, THIN FILM SUPERCONDUCTIVE ELECTRONICS. **Personal Data:** b London, Eng, January 4, 1953. **Education:** Univ BC, BS, 1974, MS, 1977, PhD (physics), 1984. **Professional Experience:** SR PHYSICIST, CTF SYSTS INC, 1984-. **Memberships:** Am Phys Soc; Can Asn Physicists. **Research Statement & Publications:** Used nuclear magnetic resonance at temperatures from 0.3K- 20K to discover orientational ordering phase transitions of hydrogen and D2 on graphite; established a thin film deposition and lithography facility for fabrication of niobium squids; participated in the development of commercial systems for squid magnetometry, especially magnetoencephalography. **Mailing Address:** VSM MedTech, 9 Burbidge St, Port Coquitlam, BC V3K 7B2, Can. **Fax:** 604-472-2301. **E-Mail:** pkubik@ctf.bc.ca

KUBIK, ROBERT N, COMPUTER SCIENCE, CONTROL SYSTEMS. **Personal Data:** b Honolulu, Hawaii, November 17, 1931; m 1955, c 4. **Education:** Univ Calif, Berkeley, AB, 1954. **Professional Experience:** CONSULT, 1979-; mgr advan control & exp physics lab, Lynchburg Res Ctr, 1976-1979; mgr indust systs, Lynchburg Res Ctr, 1972-1976; mgr process control, Lynchburg Res Ctr, 1971-1972; chief instrument develop, Res & Develop Div, 1969-1971; prin engr, Nuclear Power Generating Dept, Babcock & Wilcox Co, 1968-

1969; acct rep, IBM Corp, 1967; chief comput serv, Atomic Energy Div, Babcock & Wilcox Co, 1963-1966; prog supvr, Atomic Energy Div, Babcock & Wilcox Co, 1962-1963; sr programmer, Atomic Energy Div, Babcock & Wilcox Co, 1961-1962; Programmer, Atomic Energy Div, Babcock & Wilcox Co, 1957-1961. **Memberships:** Inst Elec & Electronics Engrs; Am Soc Nondestructive Testing; Am Nuclear Soc. **Research Statement & Publications:** methodology; nondestructive examination. **Mailing Address:** PO Box 503, Point Reyes Station, CA 94956.

KUBIN, ROSA, BIOCHEMISTRY, VETERINARY PATHOLOGY. **Personal Data:** b St Poelten, Austria, December 15, 1906; American citizen; m 1931. **Education:** St Poeltner Obergym, Austria, BS, 1925; Univ Vienna, MS, 1929, PhD (org chem), 1931. **Professional Experience:** RETIRED; teacher advan chem & molecular biol, Waltham High Sch, 1961-1973; Lectr, Wellesley Col, 1955-1957 & Concord Acad, 1957-1961; consult vet pathologist, 1951-1990; assoc prof biochem, New Eng Col Pharm, 1950-1951; asst prof chem, Univ Mass, 1947-1949; asst prof biochem & clin path, Med Sch, Middlesex Univ, 1941-1947; asst, Med Sch, Univ Ore, 1940-1941; AMA fel, Lilly fel, 1939-1940; AMA fel, Med Sch, Univ Ore, 1938; Asst, Austrian Chem Works, 1931-1935 & Syngala, Inc, Austria, 1935-1938. **Memberships:** Fel AAAS; Am Chem Soc; NY Acad Sci. **Research Statement & Publications:** Medical biochemistry; bleaching of textiles; hormone extraction; laboratory methods applied in veterinary clinical pathology; diseases in veterinary medicine. **Mailing Address:** 865 Central Ave N Hill, B301, Needham, MA 02192-1338.

KUBIS, JOSEPH J(OHN), NONLINEAR MECHANICS, COMPUTATIONAL FLUID DYNAMICS. **Personal Data:** b New York, NY, April 15, 1938; m 1984, Kathleen; c Joseph H & Anne M. **Education:** Mass Inst Technol, BS, 1959; Princeton Univ, MA, 1961, PhD (physics), 1964. **Honorary Degrees:** MA, Cambridge Univ, 1967. **Professional Experience:** SR RES ENGR, FORD MOTOR CO, 1985-; prog specialist, Software ServCorp, 1983-1985; mem tech staff, Theory & Comput Div, KMS Fusion, Inc, 1972-1982; asst profphysics, Mich State Univ, 1969-1971; consult, Brookhaven Nat Lab, 1967 & Los Alamos Sci Lab, 1968 & 1971; sr res physicist, Cavendish Lab & fel, Clare Hall, Cambridge Univ, 1967-1969; asst prof physics, Tex A&M Univ, 1964-1967. **Memberships:** Am Phys Soc; Asn Comput Mach; Inst Elec & Electronics Engrs Comput Soc; Sigma Xi; Soc Indust & Appl Math. **Research Statement & Publications:** Nonlinear crash mechanics; finite element methods; computational fluid dynamics; optical ray tracing; numerical analysis; scientific computing; software engineering. **Mailing Address:** 3489 Oak Dr, Ypsilanti, MI 48197-3747.

KUBISEN, STEVEN JOSEPH, PHYSICAL ORGANIC CHEMISTRY, ORGANIC CHEMISTRY. **Personal Data:** b Iowa City, Iowa, June 21, 1952; m 1977. **Education:** Cornell Univ, BA, 1974; Harvard Univ, MA, 1975, PhD (org chem), 1978. **Professional Experience:** VPRES, TECHNOL COMMERCIALZATION OFF, UTAH STATE UNIV, as of 2006; dir, Off Technol Mgt & Commercialization, Utah State univ, as of 2004; vpres, Werner-Gershan Assoc, 1994-; technol mgr, Electromat Dept, Gen Elec, 1987-1991; polymer lab dir, Akeo-Coatings Am, 1986-1987; group leader, Union Carbide Corp, 1984-1986; proj scientist, UnionCarbide Corp, 1981-1984; res chemist, Union Carbide Corp, 1978-1981; dir, Develop MKTS & Partnerships, Alcoa. **Memberships:** Am Chem Soc; Sigma Xi; Inst Paper Chem. **Research Statement & Publications:** Phosphate ester hydrolysis; process chemistry; epoxidation chemistry; natural oils chemistry; acrylic, urethane technology; radiation cure; epoxy resins. **Mailing Address:** Off Technol Mgt & Commercialization, Utah State Univ, 570 Res Park Way, Ste 101, N Logan, UT 84341-9730. **Fax:** 435-797-9612. **E-Mail:** steve.kubisen@usurf.usu.edu

KUBISKE, MARK E, FOREST TREE PHYSIOLOGICAL ECOLOGY, STRESS PHYSIOLOGY. **Personal Data:** b East Lansing, Mich, September 30, 1958; m 1982, Alice. **Education:** Univ Wis-Stevens Point, BS, 1988; Pa State, MS, 1990, PhD (forestry), 1993. **Professional Experience:** ADJ ASSOC PROF FORESTRY, MISS STATE UNIV, as of 2004; RES ASSOC, DEPT FORESTRY, MICH STATE UNIV, 1993-. **Memberships:** Soc Am Foresters; Ecol Soc Am. **Research Statement & Publications:** Responses of eastern deciduous tree species to climatic drought; response of above and below ground processes to elevated atmospheric carbon dioxide from a forest ecology perspective. **Mailing Address:** Dept Forestry, Miss state Univ PO Box 9681, Mississippi State, MS 39762-9681. **Fax:** 601-325-8726. **E-Mail:** mkubiske@cfr.msstate.edu

KUBITZ, WILLIAM JOHN, HARDWARE SYSTEMS, COMPUTER SCIENCE. **Personal Data:** b Freeport, Ill, December 27, 1938; m 1960, Carol; c Emily & James. **Education:** Univ Ill, Urbana-Champaign, BS, 1961, MS, 1962, PhD (elec eng), 1968. **Professional Experience:** PROF EMER COMPUT SCI, UNIV ILL, as of 2005; prof comput sci & assoc head dept, Univ Ill, beginning 1985; from asst prof to assoc prof, Univ Ill, 1970-1985; res asst prof, Univ Ill, 1968-1969; res asst comput sci, Univ Ill, 1965-1968; teaching asst elec eng, Univ Ill, 1964-1965; develop engr, Gen Elec, 1962-1964. **Memberships:** Inst Elec & Electronics Engrs; AAAS; Sigma Xi; Asn Comput Mach. **Research Statement & Publications:** Automated chip and module layout of digital circuits based on automatic generation from a topological data structure with size, shape and timing constraints; object oriented graphics for a networked workstation environment with application to user interfaces, design systems and visualization; computeer graphics. **Mailing Address:** Dept Comput Sci, Univ Ill, 4211 Siebel Ctr Mc 258 201 N Goodwin, Urbana, IL 61801. **E-Mail:** kubitz@cs.uiuc.edu

KUBLER, DONALD GENE, ORGANIC CHEMISTRY. **Personal Data:** b Easton, Md, April 4, 1923; m 1947, Rose; c Matthew, Robbie, John & William. **Education:** Univ SC, BS, 1947; Univ Md, PhD (chem), 1952. **Professional Experience:** Grinnell Col, 1986-1987 & King Col, 1988-1989; EMER PROF, FURMAN UNIV, 1985-; vis prof, Univ Sterling, 1982; NSF fac fel sci, Clemson Univ, 1975; chmn dept, Furman Univ, 1967-1972; from assoc prof to prof chem, Furman Univ, 1961-1985; asst prof chem, Univ SC, 1958-1959 & Hampden-Sydney Col, 1959-1961; chemist, Develop Dept, Union Carbon Chem Co, WVa, 1952-1958; Instr chem, Univ SC, 1947-1948. **Memberships:** Am Chem Soc; Sigma Xi. **Research Statement & Publications:** Structure and mechanism for acetal and carbohydrate hydrolysis; forensic chemistry. **Mailing Address:** 136 Conder Dr, Marietta, SC 29661-9786. **E-Mail:** dkubler@infi.net

KUBLER-ROSS, ELISABETH, medicine, psychiatry; deceased, see previous edition for last biography

KUBO, ISAO, CHEMISTRY. **Education:** Okasa City Univ, PhD (org chem), 1969. **Professional Experience:** PROF, UNIV CALIF, as of 2005. **Mailing Address:** Univ Calif CNR ESPM, 232A Hilgard Hall, Berkeley, CA 94720-3112. **Fax:** 510-643-0215. **E-Mail:** ikubo@uclink.berkeley.edu

KUBO, RALPH TERUO, MOLECULAR IMMUNOLOGY, IMMUNOCHEMISTRY. **Personal Data:** b Hilo, Hawaii, March 28, 1942; m 1967, June; c Todd J Y & Kelly Ann M. **Education:** Univ Calif, Los Angeles, BA, 1965; Univ Hawaii, MS, 1967, PhD (microbiol), 1970. **Professional Experience:** RES ADMN, DEPT ALLERGY & IMMUNOL, LA JOLLA INST, as of 2000; PRIN SCIENTIST, CYTEL CORP, 1991-; mem study sect, NIH, 1989-1993; sr fac mem, Nat Jewish Ctr Immunol, 1989-1991; Japan Soc for Prom Sci Fels, UnivTokyo, 1987; from assoc prof to prof, Dept Microbiol, Med Sch, Univ Colo, 1980-1991; assoced, J Immunol & Develop Comp Immunol, 1978-1982; asst prof, Med Sch, Univ Colo, 1975-1980; mem immunol, Nat Jewish Ctr Immunol Respiratory Med, 1973-1989; sr fel, NatJewish Ctr Immunol Respiratory Med, 1971-1973; asst prof microbiol, Univ Hawaii, Honolulu, 1970-1971. **Memberships:** Am Soc Microbiol; Sigma Xi; Am Asn Immunologists; NY Acad Sci; Am Soc CellBiol. **Research Statement & Publications:** Characterization of modified synthetic peptides by analytical methods to support manufacter of such products for vaccine development; monocloral antibody reactivity with peptide-mitc liquads. **Mailing Address:** Dept Allergy & Immunol, La Jolla Inst, 178 W, 13th St, Upland, CA 91786. **Fax:** 909-981-0757.

KUBODERA, KUNIHARU, NUCLEAR & HADRONIC PHYSICS, NUCLEAR ASTROPHYSICS. **Personal Data:** b Ichikawa, Chiba, Japan, October 28, 1943; m 1978, Barbara Ann. **Education:** Univ Tokyo, Japan, BS, 1966; Univ Tokyo, Japan, MS, 1968; Univ Tokyo, Japan, (nuclear physics), PhD, 1970. **Professional Experience:** PROF, DEPT PHYSICS & ASTRON, UNIV SC, 1989-; vis prof, State Univ NY, Stony Brook, 1986-1987; from assoc prof to prof, Sophia Univ, Tokyo, 1980-1989; vis scientist, Schweizerishe Inst Nuclear Res, Switzerland, 1978-1980; res fel, Univ Tokyo, Japan, 1973-1980; fel, Ctr d'Etudes Nucleaires Del Saclay, France, 1970-1973. **Memberships:** Fel Am Phys Soc. **Research Statement & Publications:** Nuclear many-body problem; testing of fundamental symmetries using nuclear systems; neutrino astrophysics; chiral perturbation theory; nuclear matter under extreme conditions. **Mailing Address:** Dept Physics & Astron, Univ SC, Columbia, SC 29208. **Fax:** 803-777-3065. **E-Mail:** kubodera@sc.edu

KUBOTA, MITSURU, INORGANIC CHEMISTRY. **Personal Data:** b Eleele, Hawaii, September 25, 1932; m 1956, Jane Taketa; c Lynne K & Keith N. **Education:** Univ Hawaii, BA, 1954; Univ Ill, MS, 1958, PhD, 1960. **Honors & Awards:** Award Res Undergrad Inst, Am Chem Soc, 1992. **Professional Experience:** Vis prof, Univ Venice, 1988 & Cambridge Univ, 1989; consult, Chevron Res, 1981-1982; NSF prof develop award, Univ Calif, Berkeley, 1981-1982; NIH spec fel, Calif Inst Technol, 1974-1975; Fulbright-Hays advan res fel, Univ Sussex, Eng, 1973-1974; PROF CHEM, HARVEY MUDD COL, 1971-; NSF fel, Univ NC, Chapel Hill, 1966-1967; From instr to assoc prof, Harvey Mudd Col, 1959-1971. **Memberships:** Fel AAAS; Am Chem Soc; Royal Soc Chem; Sigma Xi. **Research Statement & Publications:** Organometallic chemistry; homogeneous catalysis; inorganic synthesis. **Mailing Address:** Dept Chem, Harvey Mudd Col, Claremont, CA 91711.

KUBU, EDWARD THOMAS, PHYSICAL CHEMISTRY, POLYMER PHYSICS. **Personal Data:** b New York, NY, November 19, 1926; m 1951. **Education:** NY Univ, BA, 1949; Princeton Univ, MA, 1951, PhD (chem), 1952. **Professional Experience:** PVT CONSULT, 1986-; tech dir, mgr Govt & Indust Liaison, 1977-1986; dirtech opers, Fibers Div, 1973-1977; bd trustees exec comt, Textile Res Inst, 1971-1978; tech dir, Fibers Div, 1970-1973; dir res &develop, Fibers Div, asst to pres, 1968-1970; dir lab res, Cent Res Lab, Allied Corp, 1962-1963; asst dir lab res, Cent Res Lab, Allied Corp, 1961-1962; supvr characterization res, Cent Res Lab, Allied Corp, 1959-1961; sect leader, Textile physics sect, Res Ctr, B F Goodrich Co, 1952-1959; mem adv bd, Textile Res Inst Regulatory Tech Info Ctr. **Memberships:** Am Chem Soc; Sigma Xi. **Research Statement & Publications:** Physical, chemical and mechanical properties of high polymers; manufacture and use of synthetic fibers; impact of government regulations on synthetic fiber, plastics and chemical manufacture and use. **Mailing Address:** 4720 Southmoor Rd, Richmond, VA 23234.

KUC, JOSEPH, PLANT BIOCHEMISTRY, PLANT PHYSIOLOGY. **Personal Data:** b New York, NY, November 24, 1929; m 1991, Karola; c Paul, Rebecca & Miriam. **Education:** Purdue Univ, BS, 1951, MS, 1953, PhD (biochem), 1955. **Honors & Awards:** Campbell Award, Am Phytopath Soc, Sturgill Award; Medal, Int PlantProtection. **Professional Experience:** RETIRED; emer prof, Univ KY, beginning 1995; sr sci awards, 1980-1990; prof, Univ KY, 1974-1995; fel, BrazilianCoffee Inst, 1969, 1971; Fulbright fel, 1960 & 1966; from asst prof to prof, Purdue Univ, 1955-1974; asst biochem, Purdue Univ, 1951-1954; consult Alexander von Humboldt Found res prize; hon prof, Univ Repub, Montevideo, Uzuaquay, Shandone Agr, Univ China. **Memberships:** Am Chem Soc; fel Am Phytopath Soc; Am Soc Plant Physiol; Phytochem Soc; felAm Inst Chemists; Am Soc Biochem & Molecular Biol. **Research Statement & Publications:** Biochemistry of disease resistance in plants; synthesis of natural products; plant immunization; plant microbe interactions. **Mailing Address:** 5502 Lorna St, Torrance, CA 90503. **Fax:** 619-237-1224.

KUCERA, LOUIS STEPHEN, VIROLOGY, AIDS /HIV THERAPEUTIC DRUGS. **Personal Data:** b New Prague, Minn, June 23, 1935; m 1959, JoAnn; c Gregory, Gary, Stephen & Scott. **Education:** St John's Univ, Minn, BA, 1957; Creighton Univ, MS, 1959; Univ Mo, PhD (microbiol), 1964. **Honors & Awards:** Microbiol Distinguished Serv Award, Am Soc Microbiol. **Professional Experience:** Prin investr & vis scientist, German Cancer Res Ctr, Heidelberg, 1986; PROF MICROBIOL, BOWMAN GRAY, WAKE FOREST UNIV, SCH MED 1980-; from asst prof to assoc prof, Bowman Gray Sch Med, Wake Forest Univ, 1970-1980; staff mem, Virol Lab, St Jude Res Hosp, Memphis, Tenn, 1968-1970; asst prof, Dept Microbiol, Univ Tenn Med Units, Memphis, 1968-1970; res assoc, Virol Lab, St Jude Res Hosp, Memphis, Tenn, 1966-1968; res assoc, Sect Microbiol, Mayo Clin, 1965-1966; res asst virol, Sect Microbiol, Mayo Clin, 1964-1965; res bacteriologist, Radioisotope Serv, Vet Admin Hosp, Omaha, Nebr, 1960; 2001, Sr Vice Pres/Founder, Kucera Pharmaceuticals Co; site visit reviewer, NC Biotechnol Ctr; cancer res, proceedings, Nat Acad Sci; Reviewer, Human Cell Biol Prog, NSF; NIH grant; NC biotechnol grant. **Memberships:** Int AIDS Soc; Am Soc Microbiol; fel Am Acad Microbiol; Sigma Xi; Am Soc Virol; Int Soc Antiviral Res. **Research Statement & Publications:** tumor promoters; chemical carcinogens and herpes viruses; human immunodeficiency virus and herpes virus interactions; ether lipids and chemotherapy of HIV infections; New drug development for AIDS; drug resistant nuriants mechamism of action of synthetic phospholipils against viruses incl hepatitis and herpes. **Mailing Address:** Dept Microbiol & Immunol, Bowman Gray Sch Med, Winston-Salem, NC 27157-1064. **E-Mail:** lkucera@wfubme.edu

KUCERA, THOMAS J, ORGANIC CHEMISTRY. **Personal Data:** b Oak Park, Ill, February 22, 1925. **Education:** Loyola Univ, Ill, BS, 1945; Ill Inst Technol, MS, 1952; Purdue Univ, PhD, 1953. **Professional Experience:** COMT CHAIR, CHICAGO ACS COMTS, as of 2006; CONSULT, 1982-; vpres res & eng, Apeco Corp, 1964-1981; consult, 1961-1964; mgr chem res, Charles Bruning Co Inc, 1956-1961; asst to pres, Mid-West Labs, 1955-1956; res fel, Purdue Univ, 1954-1955; fulbright scholar, Univ Auckland, 1953-1954; Res chemist, Miner Labs, Mid-West Div, Arthur D Little, Inc, 1945-1950; fulbright scholar, New Zealand. **Memberships:** AAAS; Am Chem Soc; The Chem Soc; Soc Photog Sci & Eng. **Research Statement & Publications:** Photoreproduction; organic photoreactions; inorganic photoconductors; electrostatics; organic mechanisms. **Mailing Address:** 9310 Hamlin Ave, Evanston, IL 60203. **E-Mail:** tjkucera@interaccess.com

KUCESKI, VINCENT PAUL, ORGANIC CHEMISTRY. **Personal Data:** b Superior, Wis, April 1, 1920; m 1944, c 2. **Education:** Univ Wis, BS, 1942, MS, 1948, PhD (chem), 1950. **Professional Experience:** PRES, VINCENT ASSOCIATES, INC, as of 2000; VPRES RES & DEVELOP, C P HALL CO ILL, 1974-; vpres res, C P Hall Colll, 1971-1974; dir res, C P Hall Co Ill, 1959-1971; sr chemist, C P Hall Co Ill, 1952-1959; Re-schemist, Southern Cotton Oil Co, 1950-1952. **Memberships:** Am Chem Soc; Am Inst Chemists; Am Oil Chemists Soc. **Research Statement & Publications:** Oxidations of organic compounds; oils and fats; analytical organic chemistry. **Mailing Address:** Vincent Associates, Inc, 26 Lesmill Rd, Toronto, ON M3B 2T5, Can. **Fax:** 416-445-4504.

KUCHAR, NORMAN RUSSELL, MATERIALS PROCESSING, MANUFACTURING TECHNOLOGY. **Personal Data:** b Cleveland, Ohio, June 22, 1939; m 1967, Christine; c 2. **Education:** Case Inst Technol, BS, 1961, MS, 1965; Case Western Res Univ, PhD (eng), 1968. **Professional Experience:** RETIRED; mgr mfg tech lab, Gen Elec Co, 1993-2001; mfg, Process Physics Lab, 1990-1993; mgr, Process Technol Br, 1983-1990; mgr process physics prog, Environ Sci Lab, 1980-1982; mech engr, Environ Sci Lab, 1972-1980; group leader biofluid mech, Environ Sci Lab, 1969-1972; fluid dynamicist fluid physics, Space Sci Lab, Gen Elec Co, 1967-1969. **Memberships:** Am Soc Mech Engrs; Am Soc Mat; Sigma Xi. **Research Statement & Publications:** Intelligent processingof materials; process modeling; computer-aided engineering; process sensors; laser and quality technology. **Mailing Address:** 60 Fredericks Rd, Scotia, NY 12302.

KUCHARCZYK, NORBERT, BIOLOGY. **Education:** Princeton Univ, BS. **Professional Experience:** STAFF, SHS SYNTHESIS SOFTWARE, as of 2006. **Mailing Address:** SHS Synthesis Software, Szucha 2/4, Warsaw, 00-582, Poland. **Fax:** 012 6306360. **E-Mail:** shs@neostrada.pl

KUCHAREK, THOMAS ALBERT, PLANT PATHOLOGY. **Personal Data:** b Cleveland, Ohio, November 16, 1939; m 1963, c 2. **Education:** Kent State Univ, BS, 1962; Univ Minn, MS, 1965, PhD (plant path), 1969. **Honors & Awards:** Outstanding Plant Pathologist Award, 2004. **Professional Experience:** PROF EMER PLANT PATH, UNIV FLA, as of 2005; prof plant path, Univ Fla, beginning 1980; from asst to assoc prof, plant path, Univ Fla, 1970-1980; instr Univ Minn, 1969; instr, Okla State Univ, 1965-1968; asst plant path, Univ Minn, 1962-1965. **Memberships:** Am Phytopath Soc; Sigma Xi. **Research Statement & Publications:** Diagnosis andcontrol of diseases on field crops and vegetables. **Mailing Address:** Dept Plant Path, Univ Fla, PO Box 110680, Gainesville, FL 32611-0680. **Fax:** 352-392-6532. **E-Mail:** tak@gnv.ifas.ufl.edu

KUCHEL, OTTO GEORGE, NEPHROLOGY. **Personal Data:** b Spis Stara Ves, Czech, June 22, 1924; Canadian citizen; m 1953, Gabriel; c George, Erica & Marie. **Education:** Charles Univ, Prague, MD, 1950, PhD (endocrinol), 1956, ScD(nephrology), 1965. **Honors & Awards:** Res Award, Asn French Speaking Physicians Can, 1972. **Professional Experience:** PROF EMER, CLIN RES INST, UNIV DEL MONTREAL, as of 2001; CONSULT, 1996-; dir, Lab Sympathetic Nerv Syst, Inst, 1975-1996; mem, Hypertension Task Force, NIH, 1975-1979; prof nephrology, Clin Res Inst, Univ Montreal, 1968-1996; mem serv nephrology, Hotel-DieuHosp & Univ Montreal, 1968; prof, III Dept Med, Charles Univ, Prague, 1967-1968; instr, Vanderbilt Univ, 1966; asst prof, III Dept Med, Charles Univ, Prague, 1957-1965; instr int med, Safarik Univ, Kosice, 1956; mem, Coun High Blood Pressure Res, Cleveland. **Memberships:** Endocrine Soc; Royal Soc Med; Am Col Physicians; Royal Col Physicians &Surgeons Can. **Research Statement & Publications:** Clinical nephrology and endocrinology related to research of mechanisms of hypertension, particularly the role of the sympathetic nervous system, adrenals and the kidney. **Mailing Address:** Clin Res Inst Montreal, Univ Montreal, 110 Pine Ave W, Montreal, PQ H2W 1R7, Can. **Fax:** 514-987-5675.

KUCHENREUTHER, MARGARET, BIOLOGY & ECOLOGY. **Education:** Univ Wisc, PhD (botany), 1991. **Professional Experience:** ASSOC PROF BIOL, UNIV MINN, MORRIS. **Mailing Address:** Div Sci & Math, Biol Discipline, 2320 Sci, Univ Minn, Morris, MN 56267. **E-Mail:** kuchenma@morris.umn.edu

KUCHERLAPATI, RAJU SURYANARAYANA, HUMAN GENETICS. **Personal Data:** b Kakinada, India, January 18, 1943; c 1. **Education:** Andhra Univ, India, BSc, 1960, MSc, 1962; Univ Ill, Urbana, PhD (genetics), 1972. **Professional Experience:** SCI DIR, HARVARD MED SCH-PARTNERS HEALTHCARE CTR GENETICS & GENOMICS, 2001-; Saul & Lola Kramer prof, Albert Einstein Col Med, beginning 1989; chmn & prof genetics, Albetrt Einstein Col Med, beginning 1989; mem, mammaliangenetics study sect, NIH, 1985-1989; prof genetics, Univ Ill, 1982-1988; asst prof, Princeton Univ, 1975-1982; res fel, Damon Runyon Cancer Fund, NIH fel, 1974-1975; res fel, Damon RunyonCancer Fund, Yale Univ, 1973-1974; res fel human genetics, Yale Univ, 1972-1975. **Memberships:** AAAS; Genetics Soc Am; Am Soc Microbiol. **Research Statement & Publications:** Human gene mapping; study of regulation of gene action in human cells; gene transfer, gene therapy; homologous recombination. **Mailing Address:** Dept Genetics, Harvard-Partners Ctr Genetic & Genomics, 77 Ave Louis Pasteur, Ste 250, Boston, MA 02115. **Fax:** 617-525-4440. **E-Mail:** kucherla@aecom.yu.edu

KUCHINSKAS, EDWARD JOSEPH, BIOCHEMISTRY. **Personal Data:** b Maspeth, NY, February 11, 1927; wid, c 1. **Education:** Queen's Col, NY, BS, 1949; Cornell Univ, PhD, 1954. **Professional Experience:** Prof, State Univ NY Downstate Med Ctr, beginning 1967; from asst dean to assoc dean sch grad studies, State Univ NY Downstate Med Ctr, 1967-1973; from asst prof to assoc prof, State Univ NY Downstate Med Ctr, 1956-1967; instr biochem, MedCol, Cornell Univ, 1954-1956. **Memberships:** AAAS; Am Chem Soc; Soc Exp Biol Med; Harvey Soc; Am Soc Biol Chemists; NY Acad Sci. **Research Statement & Publications:** Metabolic effects of cysteine analogues, especially vitamin requirements and enzyme activation; catalase; semisynthetic penicillins; S-methyl group oxidations; peroxidative mechanisms; metabolism of penicillamine. **Mailing Address:** Dept Oby & Gyn, State Univ NY, Brooklyn, NY 11201.

KUCHLER, ROBERT JOSEPH, MICROBIOLOGY, VIROLOGY CELL BIOLOGY. **Personal Data:** b Pittsburgh, Pa, March 28, 1928; m 1958, Marth; c David, Thomas & Kathryn. **Education:** Univ Pittsburgh, BS, 1950, MS, 1952; Univ Mich, PhD, 1958. **Professional Experience:** Prof Emer Rutgers Univ, 1993- D ir coord grad prog microbiol, Rutgers Univ, 1978-1981; Chairman, Dept of Microgiology Rutgers Univ, 1976-1981 PROF MICROBIOL, RUTGERS UNIV, 1975-1993; from asst prof to prof bact, Rutgers Univ, 1962-1975; bacteriologist & head dept, William Singer Res Lab, Allegheny Gen Hosp, 1958-1962; Asst bact, WVa Univ, 1952-1954 & Univ Mich, 1954-1958. **Memberships:** Am Soc Microbiol; Tissue Cult Asn; Am Soc Cell Biol; Sigma Xi. **Research Statement & Publications:** Development of metazoan cell populations in tissue culture with emphasis on their permeability to small molecular species and on the organization of macromolecules within these cells; viral nucleic acids. **Mailing Address:** 11 Dogwood Ct, East Brunswick, NJ 08816.

KUCHMENT, P A, MATHEMATICS. **Education:** Voronezh State Univ, USSR, MS, 1971; Kharkov State Univ, USSR, PhD (math), 1973. **Professional Experience:** PROF, DEPT MATH & STATIST, TEX A&M UNIV, as of 2006. **Mailing Address:** Dept Math & Statist, Texas A&M Univ, College Station, TX 77843-3368. **Fax:** 979-862-4190. **E-Mail:** kuchment@math.tamu.edu

KUCHNIR, FRANCA TABLIABUE, MEDICAL PHYSICS, RADIOLOGICAL SCIENCE. **Personal Data:** b Russe, Bulgaria, July 18, 1935; American citizen; m 1960, Moyses; c Louis & Deborah. **Education:** Univ San Paulo, BS, 1958; Univ Ill, MS, 1962, PhD (physics), 1965. **Professional Experience:** PROF EMER, DIV PHYSICS, 2000-; dir, Sect Med Physics, 1980-1984; prog dir, Nat Res Serv Awards, Nat Cancer Inst, 1979-1988; assoc prof med physics, Univ Chicago, beginning 1974; asst prof, Univ Chicago, 1973-1974; trainee, Univ Chicago, 1971-1973; asst physicist, Argonne Nat Lab, 1970-1971; asst prof, Univ Ill, 1969-1970; fel, Argonne Nat Lab, 1966-1968; res asst physics, Univ Ill, 1960-1965. **Memberships:** Am Asn Physicists Med; Radiol Soc NAm; Am Col Radiol; Am Soc Ther RadiolOncol. **Research Statement & Publications:** Radiation physics and dosimetry specifically related to radiation therapy and diagnosis. **Mailing Address:** Dept Radiation Oncol, Univ Chicago 5758 S Md Ave MC9006, Chicago, IL 60637. **Fax:** 773-702-0610. **E-Mail:** franca@rover.uchicago.edu

KUCHNIR, MOYSES, LOW TEMPERATURE PHYSICS, SUPERCONDUCTIVITY APPLICATIONS. **Personal Data:** b Sao Paulo, Brazil, May 18, 1936; American citizen; m 1960, c 2. **Education:** Univ Sao Paulo, BS, 1957; Univ Ill, Urbana, MS, 1962, PhD (physics), 1966. **Professional Experience:** PHYSICIST & APPL SCIENTIST, FERMI NAT ACCELERATOR LAB, 1974-; prof physics, Univ Estadual Campinas, Brazil, 1974; proj assoc cryogenics, Univ Wis-Madison, 1973; asst physicist, Argonne Nat Lab, 1968-1973; Mem staff solid state physics, Argonne Nat Lab, 1966-1968. **Memberships:** AAAS; Am Phys Soc; Inst Elec & Electronics Engrs; Mat Res Soc. **Research Statement & Publications:** Properties of quantum fluids; magnetic properties of superconductors; cryogenic and superconducting equipment and techniques; superconducting magnets for accelerators; properties of materials at low temperatures. **Mailing Address:** 934 Parkside, Elmhurst, IL 60126.

KUCHROO, VIJAY K, NEUROLOGY. **Education:** Univ Queen sland, Brisbane, Australia, PhD, 1985. **Honors & Awards:** Fred Z Eager Research prize; Javits Neuroscience Award, NIH, 2002. **Professional Experience:** PRIN INVESTR, CTR NEUROL DIS, HARVARD MED SCH, as of 2006. **Mailing Address:** Ctr Neurol Dis Harvard Med Sch, 77 Ave Louis Pasteur HIM 785, Boston, MA 02115-5817. **Fax:** 617-525-5566. **E-Mail:** vkuchroo@rics.bwh.harvard.edu

KUCHTA, ROBERT D, BIOCHEMISTRY. **Education:** Brandies Univ, PhD, 1986. **Honors & Awards:** Nat Res Serv Award, 1987; Am Cancer Soc Jr Fac Res Award, 1991-1994. **Professional Experience:** ASSOC PROF, DEPT CHEM & BIOCHEM, UNIV COLO, BOULDER, as of 2004. **Research Statement & Publications:** Mechanistic enzymology; DNA replication; glycosylation. **Mailing Address:** Dept Chem & Biochem, Univ Colo Boulder, Cristol Chem 257 215, Boulder, CO 80309-0215. **Fax:** 303-492-5894. **E-Mail:** Robert.Kuchta@colorado.edu

KUCK, DAVID JEROME, COMPUTER SCIENCE, COMPUTER ENGINEERING. **Personal Data:** b Muskegon, Mich, October 3, 1937; m 1977, Sharon; c Julianne & Jonathen. **Education:** Univ Mich, Ann Arbor, BS, 1959; Northwestern Univ, MS, 1960, PhD (eng), 1963. **Honors & Awards:** Emanuel R Piore Award, Inst Elec & Electronics Engrs, 1987, Eckert Mauchiy Award. **Professional Experience:** PROF EMER COMPUT SCI, UNIV ILL, URBANA-CHAMPAIGN, 1993-; bd dirs, Supercomput Systs Inc, beginning 1988; mem, comput sci &technol bd, Nat Res Coun, Wash, DC, beginning 1986; dana group, Sunnyvale, Calif, beginning 1986; mem tech adv bd, Sequent Comput Systs, Portland, Ore, beginning 1985; mem tech adv bd, Sci Comput Systs, San Diego, Calif, beginning 1985; dir, ctr comput res & develop, 1984-1993; assoc ed, J Asn Comput Mach, beginning 1980; assoc ed, J Digital Systs, beginning 1980; assoc ed, Int J Comput & Info Sci, beginning 1977; assoc ed, AsnComput Mach Database Systs, beginning 1977; assoc ed, Inst Elec & Electronics Engrs Trans Comput, 1973-1975; consult, Burroughs Corp, 1972- & Los Alamos Nat Lab, beginning 1978; NSF res grant, beginning 1970; from asst to prof, Univ Ill, Urbana-champaign, 1965-1993; ford fel & asst prof elec eng, Mass Inst Technol, 1963-1965; CHMN, KUCK & ASSOCS INC; pres, Kuck & Assocs Inc. **Memberships:** Nat Acad Eng; fel Inst Elec & Electronics Engrs; fel AAAS; fel Asn ComputMatch. **Research Statement & Publications:** Parallel, pipeline and multiprocessor computation methods; interconnection networks; memory hierarchies; compilation of ordinary programs for such machines. **Mailing Address:** Kuck & Assocs Inc, 1906 Fox Dr Ste 8, Champaign, IL 61820. **Fax:** 217-356-5199. **E-Mail:** dkuck@kai.com

KUCK, JAMES CHESTER, agricultural biochemistry, organic chemistry; deceased, see previous edition for last biography

KUCK, JOHN FREDERICK READ, BIOCHEMISTRY. **Personal Data:** b Savannah, Ga, January 27, 1927; m 1949, c 5. **Education:** Va Polytech Inst, BS, 1939, MS, 1940; Univ NC, PhD (biochem), 1951. **Professional Experience:** PROF EMER, EMORY EYE CTR, 1993-; prof Emer Ophthal, Sch Medmed, Emory Univ, 1988; vis prof, Sch Chem, Ga Inst Technol, 1988-1993; adj prof, SchChem, Ga Inst Technol, 1987-1988; from asst prof to prof ophthal, Eye Res Lab, 1963-1988; asst prof biochem, Eye Res Lab, 1963-1988; res assoc, Kresge Eye Inst, 1957-1963; res assoc surg, Col Med, Wayne State Univ, 1951-1956; prof chem, St ProcopiusCol, 1950-1951; Chemist, NatAdv Comn Aeronaut, 1940-1946. **Memberships:** AAAS; Am Chem Soc; Asn Res Vision & Ophthal; Sigma Xi. **Research Statement & Publications:** Lens metabolism; diabetic and radiation cataracts; anti-cataractogenic drugs; Raman spectroscopy of lens. **Mailing Address:** Eye Res Lab, Emory Univ, Atlanta, GA 30322-4750. **Fax:** 404-778-4143.

KUCZENSKI, RONALD THOMAS, PSYCHOPHARMACOLOGY. **Personal Data:** b Detroit, Mich, July 27, 1944. **Education:** Univ Notre Dame, BS, 1966; Mich State Univ, PhD (biochem), 1970. **Professional Experience:** PROF PSYCHAITRY & NEUROSCI, UNIV CALIF, SAN DIEGO, as of 2006; asst prof biochem, Vanderbilt Univ, beginning 1980; asst prof pharmacol, Vanderbilt Univ, beginning 1974; asst prof, Univ Calif, San Diego, 1973-1974; res psychobiologist psychiat, Univ Calif, San Diego, 1970-1973. **Research Statement & Publications:** Regulation of biochemical events of central nervous system synaptic transmission and relationship to effects of pharmacological manipulations on behavioral parameters. **Mailing Address:** Dept Psychiatry & Neurosci, Univ Calif San Diego, 9500 Gilman Dr, Mail Code 0603, La Jolla, CA 92093-0603. **Fax:** 858-534-7653. **E-Mail:** rkuczenski@ucsd.edu

KUCZKOWSKI, JOSEPH EDWARD, ALGEBRA, MATHEMATICS EDUCATION. **Personal Data:** b Buffalo, NY, November 18, 1939; m 1965, Elizabeth; c Edward, Ann, James & Laura. **Education:** Canisius Col, BS, 1961; Purdue Univ, MS, 1963, PhD (math), 1968. **Professional Experience:** PROF EMER MATH, IND UNIV PURDUE UNIV INDIANAPOLIS, as of 2006; assoc dean & prof, Sch Sci, Ind Univ, Purdue, beginning 1987; asst dean, Sch Sci, Ind Univ, Purdue, 1984-1987; from assoc prof to prof math, Sch Sci, Ind

Univ, Purdue, 1971-1987; from instr to asst prof math, Purdue Univ, 1966-1971. **Memberships:** Math Asn Am; Nat Coun Teachers Math. **Research Statement & Publications:** Subsemigroups of groups, with emphasis on nilpotent groups; semigroups satisfying certain non-tautological laws. **Mailing Address:** Dept Math Sci, Ind Univ Purdue Univ, 402 N Blackford St, Indianapolis, IN 46202. **Fax:** 317-274-0628. **E-Mail:** jkuczkow@indyvax.iupui.edu

KUCZKOWSKI, ROBERT LOUIS, PHYSICAL INORGANIC CHEMISTRY. **Personal Data:** b Buffalo, NY, August 2, 1938; m, c 3. **Education:** Canisius Col, BS, 1960; Harvard Univ, MA, 1962, PhD (chem), 1964. **Professional Experience:** Chair chem dept, Univ Mich, Ann Arbor, 1991-1997; PROF EMERITUS-CHEM, UNIV MICH, ANN ARBOR, 2002-; from asst prof to prof, Univ Mich, Ann Arbor, 1966-2002; Nat Acad Sci res fel chem, Nat Bur Stand, 1964-1966; NSF chem prog officer 2002-2004. **Memberships:** Am Chem Soc; Am Phys Soc fel; AAAS fel. **Research Statement & Publications:** Microwave spectroscopy of inorganic compounds; weakly bound complexes; van der waals molecules. **Mailing Address:** Dept Chem, Univ Mich, Ann Arbor, MI 48109-1055. **E-Mail:** kuczkows@umich.edu

KUCZMARSKI, EDWARD R, CELL BIOLOGY. **Personal Data:** b Cleveland, Ohio, September 4, 1949. **Education:** Hiram Col, BS, 1971; Yale Univ, PhD (cell biol), 1977. **Professional Experience:** ASSOC PROF PHYSIOL, CHICAGO MED SCH, 1989-; asst prof cell biol, Northwestern Univ Med Sch, 1982-1989; Postdoctoral, Stanford Univ, 1977-1982. **Memberships:** AAAS; Am Soc Cell Biol; Am Physiol Soc; Am Soc Biochem & Molecular Biol. **Research Statement & Publications:** Mechanism and regulation of cell motility; cytoskeleton and signal transduction. **Mailing Address:** Dept Physiol, Chicago Med Sch, 3333 Green Bay Rd Ste 3274, North Chicago, IL 60064-3095.

KUCZMARSKI, FRED CRAIG, MATHEMATICS. **Education:** Univ Wash, PhD, 1995. **Professional Experience:** LECTR MATH, UNIV WASH, as of 2004. **Mailing Address:** Dept Math, Univ Wash, PDL C 36H, Seattle, WA 98195-0001. **E-Mail:** kuczmars@math.washington.edu

KUDENOV, JERRY DAVID, INVERTEBRATE ZOOLOGY, PHYLOGENETIC SYSTEMATICS OF POLYCHAETOUS ANNELIDS. **Personal Data:** b Lynwood, Calif, December 19, 1946; m 1969, Kathryn; c Peter A & Michael W. **Education:** Univ Calif, San Diego, BA, 1968; Univ Pac, MSc, 1970; Univ Ariz, PhD (zoology), 1974. **Professional Experience:** PROF BIOL SCI, UNIV ALASKA, ANCHORAGE, 1987-; chair, Dept Biol Sci, 1986-1990; from asst prof to assoc prof, Dept Biol Sci, Univ Alaska, Anchorage, 1980-1987; vis prof, Dept Biol Sci & cur polychaeta, Allan Hancock Found, Univ Southern Calif, 1979-1980; res scientist zoology & pollution biol, Marine Pollution Studies Group, Fisheries & Wildlife Div, Australia, 1974-1979. **Memberships:** Am Soc Zoologists; Sigma Xi; AAAS; Int Asn Polychaetology; Biol Soc Wash. **Research Statement & Publications:** Functional morphology of feeding, biometrics and phylogenetic systematics of polychaaetous annelids, especially of the order amphimomida. **Mailing Address:** Dept Biol Sci, Univ Alaska, 3211 Providence Dr, Anchorage, AK 99508. **Fax:** 907-786-4607. **E-Mail:** afjdk@uaa.alaska.edu

KUDER, JAMES EDGAR, ORGANIC CHEMISTRY. **Personal Data:** b Madang, New Guinea, December 28, 1939; American citizen; m 1962, c 2. **Education:** Capital Univ, BS, 1962; Ohio Univ, PhD (org chem), 1968. **Professional Experience:** RETIRED; res assoc, Celanese Res Co, beginning 1977; scientist, Res Labs, Xerox Corp, 1969-1977; res fel, Rensselaer Polytech Inst, 1968-1969; chemist water anal, US Geol Surv, Ohio, 1962-1963. **Memberships:** Am Chem Soc; The Chem Soc; Sigma Xi; Soc Photo-Optical Instrumentation Engrs. **Research Statement & Publications:** Electronic structure and properties of organic dyes; photochemical rearrangements; quantum chemistry; reactions and spectroscopic studies of heterocyclic compounds; organic electrochemistry; optical recording materials. **Mailing Address:** 91 Willoughby Rd, Fanwood, NJ 07023-1244.

KUDER, ROBERT CLARENCE, PLASTICS CHEMISTRY. **Personal Data:** b North Baltimore, Ohio, December 31, 1918; m 1942, Agnes; c Kathleen, Roberta, Suzanne, Thomas, Martin, James & David. **Education:** Ohio State Univ, AB, 1939; Northwestern Univ, PhD (org chem), 1942. **Professional Experience:** RETIRED; consult, beginning 1984; res chemist, Precision Cosmet Co, 1980-1983; tech dir, Minneapolis Coatings & Chem Div, 1977-1980; tech dir resins, Whittaker Corp, 1968-1977; res assoc, Gen Mills Inc, 1963-1968; dir res & develop, Mol Rez Div, Am Petrochem Corp, 1958-1963; tech dir, Bemis Bros Bag Co, 1957-1958; supvr polymer res, Barrett Div, Allied Chem Corp, 1957; asst supvr res, Barrett Div, Allied Chem Corp, 1952-1957; sr res chemist, Barrett Div, Allied Chem Corp, 1948-1952; asst prof chem, Univ Dayton, 1946-1948; res chemist, Stand Oil Co, Ind, 1942-1946; jr chemist, Ethyl Gasoline Corp, 1939. **Memberships:** Am Chem Soc. **Research Statement & Publications:** Polyesters; polyurethanes. **Mailing Address:** 222 W Eagle Lake Dr, Maple Grove, MN 55369-6149. **E-Mail:** rckuder@aol.com

KUDMAN, IRWIN, METALLURGY, PHYSICS. **Personal Data:** b Brooklyn, NY, February 20, 1936; m 1959, c 2. **Education:** NY Univ, BMetEng, 1958, MS, 1960. **Professional Experience:** PRES, GRASEBY-INFRARED ASSOCS INC, 1976-; vpres, Princeton Infrared Equip Inc, 1972-1976; mem tech staff Mat, Res Lab, RCA Corp, 1962-1972; assoc engr, RCA, 1960-1962. **Research Statement & Publications:** Optical, electrical and thermal properties of semiconductor materials and alloy systems. **Mailing Address:** Graseby-Infrared Assocs Inc, 12151 Res Pkwy, Orlando, FL 32826-3207. **Fax:** 407-273-9046.

KUDO, AKIRA, ENVIRONMENTAL SCIENCES, WATER CHEMISTRY, RADIOLOGICAL HEALTH ENGINEERING. **Personal Data:** b Japan, April 6, 1939; m 1974, Yumiko; c Hiroki & Satoshi. **Education:** Kyoto Univ, Japan, BSc, 1963, MSc, 1965; Univ Tex, Austin, PhD (environ healtheng), 1969; Kyoto Univ, Japan, DEng, 1979. **Professional Experience:** PROF, KYOTO UNIV, as of 2001; SR RES OFFICER, INST ENVIRON CHEM, 1990-; vis scientist, France, 1981, 1983, 1985 & 1990; assoc ed, J Environ Conserv Eng, 1980-; vis scientist, Japan, 1976, 1985, 1988 & 1990; vis prof, Univ Ottawa, Can, 1975-; sr res officer biol, Nat Res Coun Can, 1971-1990. **Memberships:** Int Asn Water Pollution Res; Am Soc Civil Eng; Am Water Pollution Control Fedn. **Research Statement & Publications:** Distribution, transport, transformation, and transfer of heavy metal pollutants, including radioactive materials (plutonium etc), in the aquatic systems such as rivers, lakes, and estuaries; anaerobic treatment of wastewater; Arctic ice core studies. **Mailing Address:** Inst Environ Chem, Rm 236/M-12 Nat Res Coun, Montreal Rd, Ottawa, ON K1A 0R6, Can.

KUDO, SHINICHI, MOLECULAR GENETICS. **Personal Data:** b Yubaryri, Japan, August 29, 1956. **Education:** Asahikawa Med Col, Japan, MD, 1982; Sapporo Med Sch, PhD (virol), 1986. **Professional Experience:** RES ASSOC MOLECULAR GENETICS, LA JOLLA CANCER RESFOUND, 1990-; res fel, La Jolla Cancer Res Found 1987-1990. **Memberships:** Am Soc Biochem & Molecular Biol; Am Soc Cell Biol. **Research Statement & Publications:** Molecular genetics. **Mailing Address:** Dept Virol, Hokaido Inst Pub Health Kita-19 Nishi-12 Kita-Ku, Sapporo 060, Japan. **Fax:** 811-173-69476.

KUDOLO, GEORGE B, CHEMISTRY. **Honors & Awards:** Osher Award. **Professional Experience:** ASSOC PROF, CLIN LAB SCI, as of 2005. **Mailing Address:** Dept Clin Lab Sci, UTHSC, 7410 John Smith Dr Suite 214, San Antonio, TX 78229. **Fax:** 210-567-8846. **E-Mail:** kudolo@uthscsa.edu

KUDYNSKA, JADWIGA, SOLID STATE PHYSICS, SPECTROSCOPY & SPECTROMETRY. **Personal Data:** b Kluczkowice, Poland, February 3, 1948; Polish & Canadian citizen; m 1972, Richard; c Kate & Adam. **Education:** Jagiellonian Univ, MSc, 1971; A Mickiewicz Univ, PhD (physics), 1980. **Professional Experience:** RES ASSOC PHYSICS, DEPT ELEC & COMPUT ENG, UNIV VICTORIA, 1993-; res assoc, Dept Physics & Astron, 1991-1993; consult, SPEC Instruments Ltd, Calgary, 1988- & ESSO, Calgary, 1990-; res fel physics, Univ Calgary, 1987-1990; res assoc, Dept Physics, A Mickiewicz, 1981-1987; Res fel physics, Dept Physics, A Mickiewicz, 1972-1980. **Memberships:** Can Asn Physicists. **Research Statement & Publications:** Magnetic resonance spectroscopy; dynamic in-situ CW-EPR studies of coal; spin-labelled oil and erythrocyte membrane spectroscopy; dehydratation mechanisms in clay minerals; isolator-metal phase transitions; magnetic transitions. **Mailing Address:** Elec & Comput Eng Univ Victoria, PO Box 3055, Victoria, BC V8W 3P6, Can. **Fax:** 250-721-6052. **E-Mail:** kudymska@ece.vvic.ca

KUDZIN, STANLEY FRANCIS, ORGANIC CHEMISTRY. **Personal Data:** b Jersey City, NJ, March 1, 1926; m 1950, c 3. **Education:** Fordham Univ, BS, 1947, MS, 1949, PhD (chem), 1951. **Professional Experience:** PROF CHEM, STATE UNIV NY, COL NEW PALTZ, 1970-; assoc prof, State Univ NY Col New Paltz, 1962-1970; ed, Acad Press, Inc, 1961-1962; assoc prof org chem, Clemson Col, 1960-1961; tech supvr, Ciba Co, Inc, 1956-1960; res & tech serv chemist, E I du Pont Del Nemours & Co, 1951-1956; consult, AcadPress, Inc. **Memberships:** AAAS; Am Chem Soc. **Research Statement & Publications:** Chemical education and literature. **Mailing Address:** Dept Chem, State Univ NY, New Paltz, NY 12561. **Fax:** 845-257-3791. **E-Mail:** kudzins@newpaltz.edu

KUEBLER, JOHN RALPH, INDUSTRIAL CHEMISTRY. **Personal Data:** b Indianapolis, Ind, October 22, 1924; m 1957, c 2. **Education:** Univ Wis, BS, 1948; Univ Ill, MS, 1949, PhD, 1951. **Professional Experience:** RETIRED; qual control mgr, Calsicat Div, 1970-1981; inorg res chemist, Mallinckrodt Chem Works, 1951-1985. **Memberships:** Am Chem Soc; Am Soc Qual Control. **Research Statement & Publications:** Inorganic stereochemistry; inorganic analytical methods development. **Mailing Address:** 3922 Sterrettania Rd, Erie, PA 16506-4266.

KUECKER, JOHN FRANK, PHYSICAL CHEMISTRY. **Personal Data:** b Webster, SDak, March 21, 1932; m 1958, c 4. **Education:** Northern State Col, BS, 1954; SDak Sch Mines & Technol, BS, 1958; Univ Nebr, MS, 1963, PhD (chem), 1965. **Professional Experience:** PROF EMER CHEM, KEARNEY STATE COL, UNIV NEBR KEARNEY as of 2005; prof chem, Kearney State Col, Univ Nebr Kearney, 1971-1995; head dept, Kearney State Col, 1969-1972; from asst prof to assoc prof, Kearney State Col, 1965-1971; asst prof chem, DoaneCol, 1963-1965; teacher high sch, SDak, 1954-1955 & 1956-1957. **Memberships:** AAAS; Am Chem Soc; Nat Sci Teachers Asn. **Research Statement & Publications:** Viscosity of aqueous salt solutions; ultracentrifugation of inorganic polymer solutions. **Mailing Address:** Dept Chem, Univ Nebr Kearney, 905 W, 25th S, Kearney, NE 68849-1150. **Fax:** 308-865-8399.

KUEHL, GUENTER HINRICH, CATALYSTS, ZEOLITES. **Personal Data:** b Geesthacht, Ger, January 2, 1928. **Education:** Brunswick Tech Univ, dipl, 1955, Dr rer nat(chem), 1957. **Professional Experience:** CONSULT & ADJ PROF, DEPT CHEM & BIOMOLEC ENG, UNIV PA, 1994-; sr res assoc, Chem Catalyst Div, 1991-1993; Counr, Am Chem Soc, 1984-1992; res assoc, Paulsboro Res Lab, Catalyst Res & Develop Sect, 1983-1991; assoc 1975-1983; sr res chemist, Process Res & Develop Serv Div, Mobil Res & Develop Corp, 1969-1975; sr res chemist, Cent Res Div, Socony Mobil Oil Co, 1962-1969; res chemist, Kali-Chemie AG, Ger, 1960-1961; USPHS fel, Ind Univ, 1957-1959; mem, Synthesis Comn, Int Zeolite Asn. **Memberships:** Soc Ger Chem; emer mem Am Chem Soc; Int Zeolite Asn; Catalysis Soc. **Research Statement & Publications:** Crystallization, modification, characterization, and chemistry of zeolites; catalyst research and development for application in petroleum and petrochemical industry; preparation and investigation of hydrogenphosphato-carbonato-apatites; phosphato complexes; preparation and properties of organo-metallic acetylene compounds. **Mailing Address:** 1956 Cardinal Lake Dr, Cherry Hill, NJ 08003-2904. **Fax:** 215-573-2093. **E-Mail:** kuehl@seas.upenn.edu

KUEHL, HANS H(ENRY), ELECTRICAL ENGINEERING. **Personal Data:** b Detroit, Mich, March 16, 1933; m 1965, Anna Meidinger; c Susan & Michael. **Education:** Princeton Univ, BSEE, 1955; Calif Inst Technol, MS, 1956, PhD (elec eng), 1959. **Professional Experience:** Assoc chair, Elec Eng & Electrophysics, Univ Southern Calif, 1998-; chmn, Elec Eng & Electrophysics, Univ Southern Calif 1987-1998; vis assoc, Calif Inst Technol, 1976; PROF ELEC ENG, UNIV SOUTHERN CALIF, 1972-; from asst prof to assoc prof, Eng Ctr, 1960-1972; res scientist plasmas, Eng Ctr, 1959-1960; Res fel, Calif Inst Technol, 1959-1960; Mem tech staff, Hughes Aircraft Co, 1958-1959. **Memberships:** Am Phys Soc; fel Inst Elec & Electronics Engrs; Int Sci Radio Union. **Research Statement & Publications:** Plasma physics; electromagnetic theory; antennas. **Mailing Address:** Dept Elec Eng PHE 604, Univ Southern Calif, Los Angeles, CA 90089-0271. **Fax:** 213-740-8677.

KUEHL, LEROY ROBERT, BIOCHEMISTRY. **Personal Data:** b Ketchikan, Alaska, August 15, 1931; m 1959, c 3. **Education:** Iowa State Univ, BS, 1953; Ore State Univ, MS, 1955; Univ Calif, Berkeley, PhD (comp biochem), 1961. **Professional Experience:** PROF BIOCHEM, UNIV UTAH, 1980-; from instr to assoc prof, Univ Utah, 1965-1980; NIH fel, Max Planck Inst Biol, Tubingen, Ger, 1962-1965. **Memberships:** Fedn Am Soc Exp Biol; Am Chem Soc; AAAS. **Research Statement & Publications:** Biochemistry of the cell nucleus; chromosomal proteins. **Mailing Address:** Dept Biochem, Sch Med Univ Utah 50 N Medical Dr, Salt Lake City, UT 84132-0001.

KUEHLER, CHRISTOPHER W, PETROLEUM ENGINEERING. **Education:** Stanford Univ, PhD. **Professional Experience:** STAFF, CHEVRON RES & TECH CO, as of 2006. **Mailing Address:** Chevron Res & Tech Co, PO Box 1627, Richmond, CA 94802. **Fax:** 510-242-7022. **E-Mail:** chkr@chevron.com

KUEHLER, JACK D, ELECTRON OPTICS. **Personal Data:** b Grand Island, NB, August 29, 1932; m Carmen. **Education:** Santa Clara Univ, BS & MS. **Honorary Degrees:** DSc, Clarkson Univ, Univ Santa Clara, 1989. **Professional Experience:** BD DIR, AETNA, 2000-; pres & mem exec comt, Gen Technol Div, 1989-1993; IBM vpres & pres, IBM vchmn bd, 1988-1989; exec vpres, Data Processing Prod Group, 1987; mem bd dir, Data Processing Prod Group, 1986; Asst group exec systs develop, mem corp Mgt bd & US mfg, 1985; sr vpres, Gen Technol Div, 1982; info systs & tech group exec, Data Processing Prod Group, 1981; IBM vpres & pres, Gen Technol Div, 1980-1981; pres, Syst Prod Div, 1978-1980; Asst group exec systs develop, Data Processing Prod Group, 1977-1978;

vpres develop, Gen Prod Div, 1974-1977; vpres, Gen Prod Div, 1972-1974; dir, San Jose & Menlo Park Develop Labs, 1970-1972; dir, Raleigh Commun Lab, NC, 1967-1970; Assoc engr, San Jose Res Lab, IBM Corp, 1958-1967; INDEPENDENT CONSULT; mem bd dir, Olin Corp & Nat Asn Mfrs. **Memberships:** Nat Acad Eng; fel Inst Elec & Electronics Engrs; fel Am Acad Arts & Sci. **Mailing Address:** 8210 Hwy 145, Telluride, CO 81435.

KUEHN, GLENN DEAN, BIOCHEMISTRY OF POLYAMINES, MOLECULAR BIOLOGY OF POLYAMINE CATABOLISM. **Personal Data:** b Terry, Mont, April 13, 1942; m 1965, Donna; c Tara L Lynn. **Education:** Concordia Col, BA (math), 1964; BA (chem), 1964; Wash State Univ, PhD (biochem), 1968. **Honors & Awards:** Am Cancer Soc res support award, 1971-1976 & 1981-1983; NSF res support award, 1973-1979; NIH res support award, 1974-1977; USDA res support award, 1986-1991 & 1992-1997; 1977-1980, 1980-1985, 1985-1989, 1990-1995, 1996; Nat Presidential Award Excellence, sci, math & eng mentoring, NSF, 2000. **Professional Experience:** PROG DIR, CTR DISEASE CONTROL & PREVENTION TRAINING PROG, NMEX STATE UNIV, 2000-; Dir ctr for disease control training program, 2000-2005; dir, Score Prog NIH, 2000-2004; res support, NIH 2000-2004; dir, Bridges Am Indians Community Col, 1992-1997, 2006; res support, USGS, 1987-1992; PROF BIOCHEM, NMEX STATE UNIV, 1980-; fel, Roche Found Univ Berne, Switz, 1979; dir, Minorities Biomed Res Support Group prog, 1975-1997, 2004; from asst prof to assoc prof, Nmex State Univ, 1970-1975; NIH fel, Univ Calif, Los Angeles, 1968-1970; trainee, Nat Aeronaut & Space Admin, Wash State Univ, 1964-1967. **Memberships:** AAAS; Am Chem Soc; Fedn Am Soc Exp Biol; Am Soc Microbiol; Soc Adv Chicanos & Nat Am Sci; Am soc of Plant Biologists. **Research Statement & Publications:** Biosynthesis and regulatory functions of polyamines; carbon dioxide fixation in autotrophs; regulatory enzymology; biochemical mechanisms of drought and heat tolerance in plants; Catobolism of polymines; role of polymine oxidase in the initiation of apoptosis; programmed cell death; anit-sense RNA methods for manipulating polymine levels in cells. **Mailing Address:** Dept Biochem, NMex State Univ, MSC 3C, Box 30001, Las Cruces, NM 88003-8001. **Fax:** 505-646-6846. **E-Mail:** gkuehn@nmsu.edu

KUEHN, JEROME H, FISH BIOLOGY, FISHERIES ADMINISTRATION. **Personal Data:** b Minneapolis, Minn, July 20, 1920; m 1945, c 3. **Education:** Univ Minn, BS, 1942, MS, 1949. **Professional Experience:** RETIRED; chief fisheries, Survs & Inventories Unit, 1979-1982; natural resource planning dir, Survs & Inventories Unit, 1966-1979; supvr, Survs & Inventories Unit, 1956-1966; asst wildlife projs coordr, State Natural Resources Dept, Minn, 1952-1956; aquatic biologist, State Natural Resources Dept, Minn, 1947-1952; aquatic biologist aide, State Natural Resources Dept, Minn, 1946. **Memberships:** Am Fisheries Soc. **Research Statement & Publications:** Techniques of fisheries survey procedures; development of fisheries management investigations; fish toxicants; natural resource planning; environmental impact review; water resources planning. **Mailing Address:** 3198 Manitou Dr, St Paul, MN 55110.

KUEHN, LORNE ALLAN, BIOPHYSICS. **Personal Data:** b Sault Saint Marie, Ont, January 28, 1943; c 2. **Education:** Univ Alta, BSc, 1963; York Univ, PhD (physics), 1968. **Professional Experience:** RETIRED; dir, sci & tech intel, 1986-1992; SAS exp mgr, Can Astronaut ProgOff, 1983-1986; dir, res & develop, human performance, Dept Nat Defense, 1982-1986; chmn, NAm Affairs Comt, Under Sea Med Soc, 1980-1981; Can observer, Human Biol Working Party, Sci Comt for Anarctic Res, 1975-; dir, Biosci Div, Defence & Civil Inst Environ Med, 1971-1982; tech secy, Adv Panel Arctic Med & Climatic Physiol, Defence Res Bd, 1971-1975; Mem, proj revgroup develop pneumatic decompression comput, Dept Indust, Trade & Com, 1971-1972; Defence serv sci officer physics, Defence Res Estab Toronto, 1966-1971. **Memberships:** Arctic Inst NAm; Can Physiol Soc; Can Asn Physicists; assoc fel Aerospace MedAsn; Undersea Med Soc; assoc fel Aerospace Med Soc. **Research Statement & Publications:** Development of decompression theories and operational computers; development of measuring techniques in environmental stress, particularly in extreme heat and extreme cold; diagnosis and treatment of accidental and occupational hypothermia; defense against biological and chemical warfare. **Mailing Address:** Waitangi Kaitune No 2 Rd, Christ Church, New Zealand.

KUEHN, THOMAS HOWARD, ENVIRONMENTAL SCIENCES. **Education:** Univ Minn, BS, 1971, MS, 1973, PhD, 1976. **Professional Experience:** PROF, DEPT MECH ENG, UNIV MINN, as of 2006. **Mailing Address:** Dept Mech Eng, Univ Minn, 111 Church St SE, Minneapolis, MN 55455-0111. **Fax:** 612-624-1398. **E-Mail:** kuehn001@umn.edu

KUEHNE, DONALD LEROY, CHEMICAL ENGINEERING. **Personal Data:** b Oak Park, Ill, January 24, 1952. **Education:** Cornell Univ, BS, 1973; Calif Inst Technol, MS, 1975, PhD (chem eng), 1979. **Professional Experience:** SR RES ENGR & SR DEVELOP ENGR, CHEVRON RES & TECHNOL, RICHMOND, CALIF, 1988-; res engr, Chevron Oil Field Res Co, Chevron Corp, 1978-1988. **Memberships:** Am Inst Chem Engrs; Soc Petrol Engrs. **Research Statement & Publications:** Development and reservoir applications of enhanced oil recovery chemicals; technology for improving sweep efficiency in oil production. **Mailing Address:** Chevron Res & Technol, 100 Chevron Way Bldg 10 Rm 2214, Richmond, CA 94806.

KUEHNE, MARTIN ERIC, ORGANIC CHEMISTRY. **Personal Data:** b Floral Park, NY, May 29, 1931; m 1953, c 1. **Education:** Columbia Univ, AB, 1952, PhD (chem), 1956; Harvard Univ, MA, 1953. **Professional Experience:** PROF EMER CHEM, UNIV VT, as of 2004; chmn dept, Univ Vt, 1976-1978; prof Chem, Univ Vt, beginning 1968; from asst prof to assoc prof & Sloan fel, Univ VT, 1961-1968; sr chemist, Chem Res Dept, Ciba Pharmaceut Prod Inc, 1955-1961. **Memberships:** Am Chem Soc. **Research Statement & Publications:** Synthetic and degrative problems in natural products; general organic chemistry; medicinal chemistry. **Mailing Address:** Dept Chem, Univ VT, 82 Univ Pl, Burlington, VT 05405. **Fax:** 802-656-8705. **E-Mail:** martin.kuehne@uvm.edu

KUEHNER, CALVIN CHARLES, MEDICAL MICROBIOLOGY, PUBLIC HEALTH. **Personal Data:** b Put-in-Bay, Ohio, December 12, 1922; m 1947, Bonnie; c Charles, Carol & Mary. **Education:** Ohio State Univ, BS, 1949, MS, 1950, PhD (mycol), 1953. **Professional Experience:** RETIRED; assoc ed, J Manipulative & Physiol Therapeut, beginning 1978; prof microbiol & pub health, Basic Sci Div, Nat Col Chiropractic, 1975-1993; dir, Basic Sci Div, Nat Col Chiropractic, 1975-1989; consult microbiol, Palos Med Labs, Palos Heights, Ill, 1974-1976; prof microbiol, Moraine Valley Community Col, 1969-1975; prof & chmn dept, St Dominic Col, 1967-1969; assoc prof biol, Univ Windsor, 1958-1967; asst prof microbiol, Univ Detroit, 1954-1958; zymologist, Fermentation Div, Northern Regional Res Lab, Peoria, Ill, 1951-1954. **Memberships:** Am Inst Biol Sci; Am Pub Health Asn. **Research Statement & Publications:** Teaching of general and medical micrbiology; community health problems. **Mailing Address:** 995 W River Pt Circle, Salt Lake City, UT 84123.

KUEHNER, JOHN ALAN, NUCLEAR PHYSICS. **Personal Data:** b Lennoxville, Que, October 8, 1931; div, c 3. **Education:** Bishop's Univ, BSc, 1951; Queen's Univ, Ont, MA, 1954; Univ Liverpool, PhD (physics), 1956. **Professional Experience:** PROF EMER PHYSICS, MCMASTER UNIV, as of 2004; prof Physics, Mcmaster Univ, 1966-; res officer, Chalk RiverNuclear Labs, 1956-1966. **Memberships:** Am Phys Soc; Can Asn Physicists; Royal Soc Can. **Research Statement & Publications:** Nuclear structure studies using reactions induced with accelerated ion beams. **Mailing Address:** Dept Physics, McMaster Univ, Hamilton, ON L8S 4M1, Can. **Fax:** 905-546-1252. **E-Mail:** jak@physics.mcmaster.ca

KUEHNERT, CHARLES CARROLL, plant morphogenesis; deceased, see previous edition for last biography

KUEKER, DAVID WILLIAM, LOGIC. **Personal Data:** b Denver, Colo, December 14, 1943; div. **Education:** Univ Calif, Los Angeles, BA, 1964, MA, 1966, PhD (math), 1967. **Professional Experience:** PROF & ASSOC DEAN, UNIV MD, COL PARK, as of 2006; prof math, Univ Md, Col Park, beginning 1984; assoc prof math, Univ Md, College Park, 1976-1984; asst prof, Univ Md, Col Park, 1973-1976; asst prof, Univ Mich, Ann Arbor, 1970-1973; res instr, Hildebrandt, Univ Mich, Ann Arbor, 1968-1970; actg asst prof math, Univ Calif, Los Angeles, 1967-1968. **Memberships:** Am Math Soc; Asn Symbolic Logic. **Research Statement & Publications:** Mathematical logic, especially model theory for finitary, infinitary and other non-classical languages. **Mailing Address:** Dept Math, Univ Md, MTH 1102, Col Park, MD 20742-0001. **E-Mail:** dwk@math.umd.edu

KUEMMEL, DONALD FRANCIS, ANALYTICAL CHEMISTRY. **Personal Data:** b Milwaukee, Wis, December 27, 1927; m 1949, Juanita; c Victoria, Jerome & Katherine. **Education:** Marquette Univ, BS, 1950, MS, 1952; Purdue Univ, PhD (anal chem), 1956. **Professional Experience:** RETIRED; res chemist, Procter & Gamble Co, 1955-1988; chemist, Allis-Chalmers Mfg Co, Wis, 1951-1953. **Memberships:** Am Chem Soc; Am Oil Chem Soc. **Research Statement & Publications:** Chromatography; separations. **Mailing Address:** 3367 Nandale Dr, Cincinnati, OH 45239-4013.

KUEMMERLE, NANCY BENTON STEVENS, MOLECULAR GENETICS, DNA REPAIR MECHANISMS. **Personal Data:** b Marshall, Minn, March 6, 1948; m 1971. **Education:** Univ Iowa, BS, 1970; Univ Tex, MS, 1975; Univ Tenn, PhD, 1987. **Professional Experience:** RES ASSOC, DEPT RADIOL ONCOL, MED COL, VA, 1992-2005; res assoc, Dept Biol, Tufts Univ, Medford, Mass, 1990-1992; res assoc fel, Dept Molecular Biol, Princeton Univ, 1987-1990; res assoc, Biol Div, Oak Ridge Nat Lab, 1976-1982; sr res asst, UnivTenn-ERDA Comp Animal Res Lab, Oak Ridge, 1974-1976; microbiol technol, Med Ctr, Peoria Sch Med, Univ Ill, 1973-1974; microbiol tech, Ill State Univ, 1972-1973. **Memberships:** Am Chem Soc; Am Soc Microbiol; AAAS; Asn Women Sci. **Research Statement & Publications:** Molecular genetics and biochemical dissection of mouse spermatogenesis; investigation of expression and the effects of genetic regions on fertility and sterility by cloning into yeast artificial chromosome-vectors and characterization by pulsed-field gel electrophoresis. **Mailing Address:** Dept Radiol Oncol, Med Col, Va Commonwealth Univ, 401 Col St, Richmond, VA 23204.

KUENHOLD, KENNETH ALAN, GENERAL PHYSICS, ENGINEERING PHYSICS. **Personal Data:** b Cleveland, Ohio. **Education:** Cornell Univ, BEP, 1964; Ohio State Univ, PhD (physics), 1973. **Professional Experience:** RETIRED; Kistler prof physics, Univ Tulsa, as of 2001; chmn eng physics, Univ Tulsa, beginning 1977; assoc prof physics, Univ Tulsa, beginning 1976; adj res partic, Oak Ridge Assoc Univs, 1973-1978; asst prof, Univ Tulsa, 1973-1976. **Memberships:** Am Phys Soc; Am Asn Physics Teachers; Sigma Xi. **Research Statement & Publications:** Two-phase oil and gas instrumentation and measurement. **Mailing Address:** Dept Physics, Univ Tulsa, Keplinger Hall, 600 S Col, Tulsa, OK 74104-3189. **E-Mail:** kuenhold@utulsa.edu

KUENZEL, WAYNE JOHN, Neuroanatomy, neuroendocrinology. **Personal Data:** b Philadelphia, Pa, January 22, 1942; m 1983, Kimberley; c Lauren M, Carolyn A & Jonathan P. **Education:** Bucknell Univ, BS (biol), 1964, MS (biol), 1966; Univ Ga, PhD (zoology), 1969. **Honors & Awards:** Award for Achievement in Poultry sci, Merck & Co, 1998; res award, SigmaXi; Contribution to Sci Award, Univ of Maryland, 2000. **Professional Experience:** PROF PHYSIOL, NEUROSCI, UNIV AR, FAYETTEVILLE, 2000-; prof physiol, Univ Md, College Park, 1984-2000; assoc prof physiol, Univ MD, College Park, 1978-1984; asst prof poultry sci, Univ MD, College Park, 1974-1978; res assoc, Cornell Univ, 1973-1974; NIH fel neurophysiol, Cornell Univ, 1971-1973; Sabbatical leave, Scotland, 1981; Fulbright Hays sr res fel award, Ger, 1988-1989; Fulbright Hays sr res fel award, Scotland, 1981-1982; Fulbright-Hays sr res fel award, Gt Brit. **Memberships:** AAAS; World's Poultry Sci Asn; Poultry Sci Asn (mem, bd of dir, 1999-2002); Am Ornithologists Union; Soc for Neuroscience; Sigma Xi. **Research Statement & Publications:** Avian neuroanatomy, neuroendocrine regulation of sexual maturation, regulation of food and water intake, stress biology and behavior, avian physiology, neurobiology. **Mailing Address:** 1200 Reed Valley Rd, Fayetteville, AR 72704. **Fax:** 479-575-7139. **E-Mail:** wkuenzel@uark.edu

KUENZI, NORBERT JAMES, MATHEMATICS. **Personal Data:** b Beaver Dam, Wis, August 5, 1935; m 1960, c 5. **Education:** Wis State Univ-Eau Claire, BS, 1959; Univ Ill, Urbana, MA, 1963; Univ Iowa, PhD (statist), 1969. **Professional Experience:** PROF EMER, DEPT MATH, UNIV WIS-OSHKOSH, as of 2001; prof math, Univ Wis-Oshkosh, beginning 1980; CHMN DEPT, UNIV WIS-OSHKOSH, 1976-; assoc prof, Univ Wis-Oshkosh, 1970-1980; asst prof, Univ Wis-Oshkosh, 1964-1966 & 1969-1970; teacher high sch, Wis, 1959-1962. **Memberships:** Inst Math Statist; Am Statist Asn; Math Asn Am. **Research Statement & Publications:** Probability theory; mathematical statistics. **Mailing Address:** Dept Math, Univ Wis, Swart 204, Oshkosh, WI 54901. **E-Mail:** kuenzi@uwosh.edu

KUEPER, THEODORE VINCENT, EXPERIMENTAL STATISTICS. **Personal Data:** b Dubuque, Iowa, August 13, 1941; m 1963, c 3. **Education:** Iowa State Univ, BS, 1963. **Professional Experience:** PRES, WIS DATA LAB, LTD, 1989-; consult & high sch chem teacher, 1987-1989; vpres qual assurance cheese, Beatrice Foods Co, 1984-1987; dir res & develop qual assurance cheese, Beatrice Foods Co, 1983-1984; dir res & develop qual assurance grocery foods, Beatrice Foods Co, 1981-1983; dir formulated food res, Beatrice Foods Co, 1978-1981; res mgr new prod develop, Beatrice Foods Co, 1974-1978; res mgr sci serv, Beatrice Foods Co, 1970-1974; head statist, Beatrice Foods Co, 1967-1970; statistician exp statist, Beatrice Foods Co, 1963-1967; scientist biochem, Beatrice Foods Co, 1963. **Research Statement & Publications:** New food products, both consumer and industrial; statistical analysis, experimental design and computer applications in regard to food research and development; prediction of food sensitivities for patients of health practitioners. **Mailing Address:** 415 Cymric Ct, Wales, WI 53183. **E-Mail:** wdl@execpc.com

KUESEL, THOMAS ROBERT, BRIDGES, TUNNELS. **Personal Data:** b Richmond Hill, NY, July 30, 1926; m 1959, Lucia; c Robert & William. **Education:** Yale Univ, BEng, 1946, MEng, 1947. **Honors & Awards:** Ernest E Howard Award, Am Soc Civil Eng, 1988. **Professional Experience:** CHMN EMER BD, PARSONS, BRINCKERHOFF, QUADE & DOUGLAS, NY, 1991-; consult engr, Parsons, Brinckerhoff, Quade & Douglas, Ny, beginning 1991; chmn, geotech bd, Nat Res Coun, beginning 1987; chmn bd, San Francisco,

1983-1991; mem, USNat Comt Tunneling Technol, 1972-1974; vchmn, OECD Tunneling Conf, Wash, DC, 1970; dir, San Francisco, 1968-1990; partner & sr vpres, San Francisco, 1968-1983; proj mgr, San Francisco, 1967-1968; asst mgr eng, Parsons Brinckerhoff-Tudor-Bechtel, San Francisco, 1963-1967; mem staff, Parsons, Brinckerhoff, Quade & Douglas, NY, 1947-1963. **Memberships:** Nat Acad Eng; fel Am Soc Civil Eng; Int Asn Bridge Struct Eng; Brit TunnelingSoc; Sigma Xi. **Research Statement & Publications:** Structural engineering; designer of 120 bridges and 135 tunnels world wide. **Mailing Address:** Quade & Douglas, Norwalk, CT 06850.

KUETTNER, KLAUS E, BIOCHEMISTRY. **Personal Data:** b Bunzlau, Ger, June 25, 1933; m 1990, Erzsebet. **Education:** Univ Freiburg, MS, 1958; Univ Berne, PhD (pharmaceut chem), 1961. **Honors & Awards:** Kappa Delta Award, Am Acad Orthop Surgeons & Orthop Res Soc, 1978; Carol Nachman, Mainz, Fed Repub Ger, 1987; Pauwels Mem Medal, Ger Soc Orthop &Traumatology, 1988. **Professional Experience:** Assoc dean basic sci & res, Rush Arthritis & Orthop Inst, 1994-2002; head, Collab Ctr Field Osteoarthritis/Rheumatol, WHO, beginning 1991; CO-DIR, RUSHARTHRITIS & ORTHOP INST, 1991-; consult ed, Europ J Exp Musculoskeletal Res, 1990-; co-chmn, Bat Sheva Seminar, Nof Ginosor, Israel, 1989; organizer & chmn, Int Workshop ConfArticular Cartilage Biochem, Wiesbaden, Fed Repub fo Ger, 1987 & 1991; chmn, Deptbiochem, Rush Arthritis & Orthop Inst, 1980-2000; SR BIOCHEMIST, DEPT ORTHOP SURG, 1979-; PROF, DEPTBIOCHEM & ORTHOP SURG, RUSH MED COL, RUSH PRESBY-ST LUKE'S CTR, 1977-; prof, Cook Co Grad Sch Med, 1977-1982; assoc prof, Dept Orthop Surg & Biochem, Rush ColHealth Sci & Rush Med Col, 1972-1977; asst prof, Dept Biochem, Rush Col Health, 1971-1972; assoc biochemist, Dept Biochem, Rush Col Health, 1966-1979; res assoc, Dept Osthop Surg, Presby St Luke's Hosp, 1964-1971; from instr to asst prof biol chem, Univ Ill Col Med, 1964-1965; fel, Div Biol & Med Res, Argonne Nat Lab, 1962-1964; res assoc biochem, CibaPharmaceut Co, Switz, 1961-1962. **Memberships:** Soc Complex Carbohydrates; Orthop Res Soc; Int Asn Dent Res; Am Soc BiolChemists; Am Soc Cell Biol; Am Chem Soc; Am Soc Biol Chemist; Am Rheumatism Asn; AmSoc Bone & Mineral Res; Am Asn Advan Sci; Soc Biol Chem; NY Acad Sci; Sigma Xi. **Research Statement & Publications:** Biochemistry of connective tissue; biochemical changes during cartilage calcification; bone formation and development of diseases especially osteoarthritis; cartilage calcification. **Mailing Address:** Dept Biochem, Rush Presby St Luke Med Ctr, 1653 W Congress Pkwy, Chicago, IL 60612. **Fax:** 312-942-3053. **E-Mail:** klaus_kuettner@rush.edu

KUFF, EDWARD LOUIS, MOLECULAR BIOLOGY, RETROVIRUSES. **Personal Data:** b Baltimore, Md, June 1, 1924; m 1947, Suzanne; c Karen. **Education:** Johns Hopkins Univ, AB, 1943, MD, 1947; Wash Univ, PhD (cytol), 1952. **Professional Experience:** PROF EMER, NAT CANCER INST, 1996-; dept chief, Lab Biochem, 1981-1996; vis scientist, Virol Sect, Weizmann Inst Sci, Rehovot, Israel, 1974-1975; actg chief, Lab Biochem, 1969-1973; head, Bio Synthesis Sect, 1968-1996; med officer, Nat Cancer Inst, 1952-1996; instr anat, Sch Med, 1948-1952; intern med, Barnes Hosp, Wash Univ, 1947-1948. **Memberships:** Am Soc Biol Chemists; Am Asn Cancer Res; AAAS. **Research Statement & Publications:** Biochemical basis of cell structure; protein and nucleic acid biosynthesis; molecular biology of endogenous retroviruses. **Mailing Address:** Lab Biochem, Nat Cancer Inst, NIH, Bethesda, MD 20892. **Fax:** 301-402-3095. **E-Mail:** ekuff@dc37.nci.nih.gov

KUFFEL, EDMUND, HIGH VOLTAGE ENGINEERING. **Personal Data:** b Poland, October 28, 1924; m 1952, Alicja; c Anna, John, Richard & Peter. **Education:** Univ Col, Dublin, BS, 1953, MS, 1954, PhD, 1959; Univ Manchester, Eng, DSc, 1967. **Professional Experience:** PROF & DEAN EMER, DEPT ELEC & COMPUT ENG, UNIV MAN, WINNIPEG, 1989-; consult prof, Xi'an JiaotongUniv, China, 1986-; dean eng, Univ Man, Winnipeg, 1979-1989; head, Univ Man, Winnipeg, 1978-1979; head elec eng, Univ Windsor, Ont, 1970-1978; prof elec engr, Univ Man, Winnipeg, 1968-1970; mem fac & elec engr, Univ Manchester Inst Sci & Technol, 1960-1968; res engr, Met Vickers Elec Co, 1954-1960; bd dirs, Manchester Hydro Elec Bd, Indust Appln Microelectronic Ctr. **Memberships:** Fel Inst Elec & Electronics Engrs; Can Acad Eng. **Research Statement & Publications:** Author or co-author of over 150 published technical papers on high voltage engineering. **Mailing Address:** Dept Elec & Comput Eng, Univ Man, 563 Eng Bldg, Winnipeg, MB R2G 2K7, Can. **Fax:** 204-474-7522. **E-Mail:** kuffel@ee.umanitoba.ca

KUFFLER, DAMIEN PAUL, NERVE REGENERATION, SYNAPTIC PHYSIOLOGY. **Personal Data:** b Chicago, Ill, January 13, 1947. **Education:** Univ Mass, Amherst, BS, 1969; Univ Calif, Los Angeles, PhD (neurobiology), 1974. **Professional Experience:** PROF, DEPT PHYSIOL, INST NEUROBIOLOGY, UNIV PR, as of 2000; assoc prof, Inst Neurobiology, Univ PR, beginning 1990; Asst prof, Univ Basel, Switz, 1983-1990. **Research Statement & Publications:** Examination of factors promoting and directing axon regeneration. **Mailing Address:** Dept Physiol, Inst Neurobiology, Univ PR, PO Box 192017, San Juan, PR 00901-2017. **Fax:** 787-725-3804. **E-Mail:** d_kuffler@rcmad.upr.clu.edu

KUFTINEC, MLADEN M, ORTHODONTICS, NUTRITION. **Personal Data:** b Zagreb, Yugoslavia, April 18, 1943; American citizen; m 2005, Tena; c Sandra & Adam. **Education:** Univ Sarajevo, Yugoslavia, DStom, 1965; Harvard Sch Dent Med, cert orthod, 1968, DMD, 1972; MIT, ScD, Nutritional Biochemistry, 1971. **Honors & Awards:** Edward H Hatton res prize, Int Soc Dental Res, San Francisco, 1968; Special Award Res, Award Health Res, Inst Nutrit Central Am & Panama. **Professional Experience:** DIR, DEPT ORTHOD, COL DENT, NY UNIV, as of 2003; chmn, Orthod, NY Univ, beginning 1990; PROF ORTHOD, COL DENT, NY UNIV, 1990-; chmn growth & spec care, Sch Dent, Univ Louisville, 1987-1990; J Dent Res, 1977-1980 & J Am Orthod, 1979-; consult, Nat Bd Dent Examr, 1977-1980 & CranioFacial Anomalies Team, Louisville, 1976-; prof & chmn orthod, Sch Dent, Univ Louisville, 1976-1987; reviewer, J Dent Educ, 1976-1981; assoc prof, Va Commonwealth Univ, 1972-1976; staff assoc orthod, Forsyth Dent Ctr, Boston, 1972; res assoc & instr, Mass Inst Technol, 1971-1972; instr nutrit & health, Cambridge Ctr Adult Educ, 1971. **Memberships:** Omicron Kappa Upsilon Soc. **Research Statement & Publications:** Prediction of severity of malocclusions, Anomalies in dental development, Characteristics of preadjusted orthodontic fixed appliances; published over 300 articles. **Mailing Address:** Dept Orthod, Col Dent, NY Univ, 345 E 24th St Rm W686, New York, NY 10010-9405. **Fax:** 212-995-4241. **E-Mail:** miki.kuftinec@nyu.edu

KUGEL, HENRY W, NUCLEAR FUSION RESEARCH. **Personal Data:** b 1940; American citizen. **Education:** Canisius Col, BS, 1962; Univ Notre Dame, PhD (physics), 1967. **Professional Experience:** PRIN RES PHYSICIST, PRINCETON PLASMA PHYSICS LAB, 1978-; asst prof atomic physics, Rutgers Univ, 1972-1978; res fel nuclear & atomic physics, Rutgers Univ &Bell Lab, 1970-1972; res assoc, Univ Wis, 1968-1970; Res assoc nuclear physics, Univ NotreDame, 1967. **Memberships:** Am Phys Soc; AAAS; Sigma Xi. **Research Statement & Publications:** Neutral beam operations; tokamak operation; neutral beam diagnostics; radiological studies; plasma surface interactions. **Mailing Address:** Princeton Plasma Physics Lab, PO Box 451, Princeton, NJ 08543-0451. **Fax:** 609-243-0000. **E-Mail:** hkugel@pppl.gov

KUGEL, ROBERT BENJAMIN, DEVEOPMENTAL PEDIATRICS, ACADEMIC ADMINISTRATION. **Personal Data:** b Chicago, Ill, May 2, 1923; m 1950, Dorothy; c Rebecca, Gretchen & Jennie. **Education:** Univ Mich, AB, 1945, MD, 1946. **Honorary Degrees:** Brown Univ, MS, 1964. **Honors & Awards:** Mildred Thomson Award, 1973. **Professional Experience:** RETIRED; med dir, Cardinal Cooke Heart Care Ctr, New York, 1981-1989; vpres, Community Health Plan, Georgetown Univ, Wash, DC, 1977-1980; exec vchancellor, Univ Kans Med Ctr, 1976-1977; prof pediat & vpres health sci, Univ NMex Health Sci Ctr, 1974-1976; chief admin officer, Bernalillo Co Med Ctr, Albuquerque, NMex, 1974-1976; prof pediat & dean Col Med, Univ Nebr, Omaha, 1969-1974; mem, President's Comn on Ment Retardation, 1966-1970; found prof pediat, 1966-1969; chmn dept pediat, 1966-1969; from prof med sci to prof child health, Brown Univ, 1963-1966; assoc prof, Col Med, Univ Iowa & dir, Child Develop Clin, Univ Hosp, 1956-1963; res assoc, Sch Hyg & Pub Health & asst prof pediat, Johns Hopkins Univ, 1955-1956; dir, Sch Health, Baltimore Health Dept, Md, 1955-1956; instr, Univ, 1952-1953; Commonwealth Fund fel, Child Study Ctr, Yale Univ, 1950-1952; resident pediat, Univ Hosp, Univ Mich, 1948-1950; intern, Univ Hosp, Univ Mich, 1947; consult, State Hosp & Sch, Woodward, Iowa; Ment Retardation Br, Div Hosp & Med Facilities, USPHS, Health Res Facilities Br, NIH & US Children's Bur. **Memberships:** Soc Res Child Develop; fel Am Asn Ment Retardation; fel Am Acad Pediat; Am Pediat Soc; Am Col Physicians; AMA. **Research Statement & Publications:** Child development; medical ecology; mental retardation. **Mailing Address:** 6016 Claiborne Dr, McLean, VA 22101-2401. **E-Mail:** rkugel@aol.com

KUGLER, GEORGE CHARLES, ANALYTICAL CHEMISTRY. **Personal Data:** b Philadelphia, Pa, October 26, 1941. **Education:** La Salle Univ, BA, 1963; Univ Pa, PhD (chem), 1967; Fla Atlantic Univ, MBA, 1978. **Professional Experience:** DIR RES & ENG, MINE SAFETY APPLIANCES CO, 1987-; res dir, Integrated Ionics, 1985-1986; prin scientist, Leeds & Northrup, 1984-1985; dir mkt, ESB-Exide, 1980-1984; Lab head, ESB-Exide, 1969-1980. **Memberships:** Electrochem Soc; Am Chem Soc; Instrument Soc Am. **Mailing Address:** 216 Woodcroft Rd, Baden, PA 15005-2436.

KUGLER, LAWRENCE DEAN, GENERAL MATHEMATICS. **Personal Data:** b Orange, Calif, February 18, 1941; m 1962, c 2. **Education:** Calif Inst Technol, BS, 1962; Univ Calif, Los Angeles, MA, 1965, PhD (math), 1966. **Professional Experience:** RETIRED; NSF grants, 1967-1971; prof math, Univ Mich, beginning 1966. **Memberships:** Am Math Soc; Math Asn Am. **Research Statement & Publications:** Application of nonstandard analysis to the theory of almost periodic functions; division algebra. **Mailing Address:** Dept Math, Univ Mich, Flint, MI 48502-2186.

KUH, ERNEST SHIU-JEN, ELECTRICAL ENGINEERING. **Personal Data:** b Peking, China, October 2, 1928; American citizen; m 1957, Bettine; c Anthony & Theodore. **Education:** Univ Mich, BS, 1949; Mass Inst Technol, SM, 1950; Stanford Univ, PhD, 1952. **Honors & Awards:** Guillemin-Cauer Award, Inst Elec & Electronics Engrs, 1973; Alexander von Humboldt Award, 1977; Lamme Award, Am Soc Eng Educ, 1981; Educ Medal, Inst Elec & Electronics Engrs, 1981, Centennial Medal, 1983; Circuits & Systs Soc Award, 1988; C & C Prize, Found C & C Promotion, Japan, 1996. **Professional Experience:** PROF EMER ELECT ENG & COMPUT SCI, COL ENG, UNIV CALIF, BERKELEY as of 2004; William S Floyd prof eng, Col Eng, Univ Calif, Berkeley, beginning 1990; hon prof, Tsinghua Univ, 1985 & Tianiin Univ, 1985; Brit Sci & Eng fel, 1981; mem adv panel eng, NSF, 1979-; hon prof, Shanghai Jiao Tong Univ, 1979; mem adv panel elec sci, NSF, 1976-1977, vis comt, Gen Motors Inst, Sci Adv Bd, MillsCol & Peer Rev Panel, Nat Bur Stand; chmn, Dept Elec Eng & Comput Sci, Univ Calif, Berkeley, 1968-1972; Miller res prof, Univ Calif, Berkeley, 1965-1966; dean, Col Eng, prof elec eng, Univ Calif, Berkeley, beginning 1962; NSF sr fel, 1962-1963; consult, Res Lab, IBM Corp, 1957-1962; assoc prof, Univ Calif, Berkeley, 1956-1962; mem tech staff, Bell Tel Labs, NJ, 1952-1956; adv coun, Elec Eng Dept, PrincetonUniv; bd counr, Sch Eng, USC; mem vis comt, Elec Eng & Comput Sci Dept, Mass Inst Technol. **Memberships:** Nat Acad Eng; fel Inst Elec & Electronics Engrs; Acad Sinica; fel AAAS. **Research Statement & Publications:** Network system theory and computer-aided design in microelectronics; electric circuit theory; computer-aided design of integrated circuits. **Mailing Address:** Dept Elect Eng Comput Sci, Univ Calif, 501 Cory Ste 1770, Berkeley, CA 94720. **Fax:** 510-642-2739. **E-Mail:** kuh@eecs.berkeley.edu

KUHAJEK, EUGENE JAMES, CRYSTALLIZATION, ION EXCHANGE. **Personal Data:** b Chicago, Ill, March 4, 1934; m 1970, Margaret; c Dan & Jeanne. **Education:** Loyola Univ, Chicago, BS, 1955; Univ Minn, PhD (inorg chem), 1962. **Professional Experience:** MGR RES & DEVELOP, MORTON SALT DIV, MORTON INT, 1978-; res chemist, Morton Thiokol, 1962-1978. **Memberships:** Am Chem Soc; Am Soc Animal Sci; Am Water Works Asn; Int Desalination Asn. **Research Statement & Publications:** Product development, product and process improvements relate to sodium chloride and potassium chloride. **Mailing Address:** 973 Amberwood Dr, Crystal Lake, IL 60014. **Fax:** 815-337-5390.

KUHAR, MICHAEL JOSEPH, NEUROPHARMACOLOGY, NEUROSCIENCE. **Personal Data:** b Scranton, Pa, March 10, 1944; m 1969, c 2. **Education:** Univ Scranton, BS, 1965; Johns Hopkins Univ, PhD (biophys, pharmacol), 1970. **Honors & Awards:** Daniel H Efron Award, 1981; Mathilde Solowey Award, 1985; Otto Krayer Award, 1992; Eminent Scholar Award from State of Georgia and Emoru University, 1996; Top 25 most cited Neuroscientists, 2000; President, College on Problems of Drug Dependence, 1999; NIH Study Section, 2004. **Professional Experience:** CHIEF Neuroscience, Yerkes, as of 1995; FAC, EMORY UNIV, 1995-; CHIEF Neuroscience BR, NAT INST DRUG ABUSE ADDN RES CTR, 1985-1995; Prof Neuroscience, pharmacol & psychiat, Sch Med, John Hopkins Univ, beginning 1981; from asst prof to assoc prof, Johns Hopkins Univ, 1972-1981; fel psychiat, SchMed, Yale Univ, 1970-1972. **Memberships:** AAAS; Soc Neuroscience; Int Brain Res Orgn; Am Soc Pharmacol & Exp Therapeut; Am Col Neuropsychopharmacol; Col Prob Drug Dep. **Research Statement & Publications:** Interaction of drugs with central nervous system neurotransmitters. **Mailing Address:** Yerkes National Primate Research Ctr Emory Univ, 954 Gatewood Rd NE, Atlanta, GA 30322. **Fax:** 404-727-3278. **E-Mail:** mkuhar@rmy.emory.edu

KUHI, LEONARD VELLO, ASTROPHYSICS. **Personal Data:** b Hamilton, Ont, October 22, 1936; American citizen; m 1989, Mary; c Alison & Christopher. **Education:** Univ Toronto, BASc, 1958; Univ Calif, Berkeley, PhD (astron), 1963. **Professional Experience:** Chmn dept Minnesota 1997-; PROF ASTRON, UNIV MINN, 1991-; sr vpres acad affairs & provost, Univ Minn, 1988-1991; dean, Col Lett & Sci, 1982-1989; sr scientist, Alexander von Humboldt US, 1980-1981; inst astrophysics Univ Heidelberg, Landessternwarte, 1978; dean phys sci, Berkeley, 1976-1982; chmn dept, Berkeley, 1975-1976; prof astron, Berkeley, 1974-1989; inst astrophysics, Paris, 1972-1973; foreign prof, Col France, Paris, 1972-1973; vis prof, Joint Inst Lab Astrophys, Boulder, 1969; from asst prof to assoc prof astron Univ Calif, Berkeley, 1965-1974; fel astron, Carnegie, Mt Wilson & Palomar Observs, 1963-1965. **Memberships:** Fel AAAS; Astron Soc Pac (pres, 1978-1980); Int Astron Union; Am Astron Soc (treas, 1996-); Sigma Xi. **Research Statement & Publica-**

tions: Pre-main sequence stellar evolution; extended stellar atmospheres and mass flow problems. **Mailing Address:** Astron Dept, Univ Minn, 116 Church St SE, Minneapolis, MN 55455-0110.

KUHL, DAVID EDMUND, NUCLEAR MEDICINE. **Personal Data:** b St Louis, Mo, October 27, 1929; m 1954, Eleanor; c David Stephen. **Education:** Temple Univ, AB, 1951; Univ Pa, MD, 1955. **Honorary Degrees:** LHD, Loyola Univ, Chicago, 1993. **Honors & Awards:** Nuclear Med Pioneer Citation, Soc Nuclear Med, 1976; numerous hon lect awards, 1977-; Ernst Jung Prize Med, Ernst Jung Found, Ger, 1981; William C Menninger Mem Award, Am Col Physicians, 1989; Javits Neuroscience Investr Award, NIH, 1989; Benedict Cassen Prize Res, Soc Nuclear Med, 1996; Outstanding Researcher Award, Radiol Soc NAm, 1996; charles f kettering prize, gm Cancer Res found, 2001. **Professional Experience:** PROF RADIOL, MED SCH, UNIV MICH, 1986-; chief, Div Nuclear Med, Med Sch, Univ Mich, beginning 1986; consult, Outstanding Investr Prog, Nat Cancer Inst, 1984-; bd trustees, James T Case Radiol Found, 1982-1986; fel, Coun Circulation, Am Heart Asn, 1978; vice chmn dept, Lab Biomed & Environ Sci & chief, Lab Nuclear Med, Univ Calif, LA, 1977-1986; prof radiol sci, Lab Biomed & Environ Sci & chief, Lab Nuclear Med, Univ Calif, Los Angeles, 1976-1986; chief, Div Nuclear Med, Dept Radiol Sci, Sch Med, Univ Calif, LA, 1976-1984; assoc dir, Lab Biomed & Environ Sci & chief, Lab Nuclear Med, Univ Calif, Los Angeles, 1976-1984; vice chmn, Dept Radiol, Univ Pa Hosp, 1975-1976; prof eng, Moore Sch Elec Eng, Univ Pa, 1974-1976; chmn, Diag Radiol Comt, Nat Cancer Inst, NIH, 1973-1977; Comt Radiol, Nat Acad Sci, 1967-1971; Radiation Study Sect, NIH, 1968-1973; mem, Adv Comt, med uses isotopes, US Atomic Energy Comn, Nat Res Coun, 1967-1979; chief, Nuclear Med Div, Univ Pa Hosp, 1963-1976; from instr to prof, Sch Med, Univ Pa, 1961-1976; asst instr radiol, Sch Med, Univ Pa, 1958-1961. **Memberships:** Inst Med-Nat Acad Sci; fel Am Col Radiol; Soc Nuclear Med; Am Neurol Asn; fel Am Col Nuclear Physicians; Asn Am Physicians. **Research Statement & Publications:** Measuring altered cerebral neurochemistry using radiotracers and emission tomography in early degenerative brain disease. **Mailing Address:** Univ Mich, Med Ctr, Dept Radiol, UH B1 H408, Ann Arbor, MI 48109-0028. **Fax:** 734-936-8182. **E-Mail:** dkuhl@umich.edu

KUHL, FRANK PETER, JR, ELECTRICAL ENGINEERING. **Personal Data:** b New York, NY, October 28, 1935; m 1964, C Maxine Barrett; c Ellen, Francie (DeBeer), Peter, Margaret & Raymond. **Education:** Columbia Univ, BSEE, 1957, MSEE, 1958; Yale Univ, MEng, 1961, DEng, 1963. **Honors & Awards:** Region I Award, Inst Elec & Electronics Engrs; R & D Achievement Award, US Army, 1983 & 1990. **Professional Experience:** Adj prof, Fla Inst Technol, 1982-1984; proj leader, US Army Armament Res & Develop Command, 1978- 1998; sr engr, Avionics Div, ITT, 1976-1978; eng specialist, Singer-Kearfott, 1974-1976; asst prof elec eng, Union Col, NY, 1965-1967 & US Naval Acad, 1968-1973; sr engr, Missile Systs Div, Digital Systs Dept, Raytheon Co, 1963-1965; Engr, Sperry Gyroscope Co, NY, 1962-1963. **Memberships:** Sr mem Inst Elec & Electronics Engrs. **Research Statement & Publications:** Pattern recognition using computers, specifically handprinted letters and numbers; polarized radar backscatter of solid objects in free space; video images of airplanes; lead-angle prediciton of maneuvering targets. **Mailing Address:** 64 E Shawnee Trail, Wharton, NJ 07885. **E-Mail:** maxikuhl@aya.yale.edu

KUHL, PATRICIA K, SPEECH & HEARING SCIENCE. **Personal Data:** b November 5, 1946; m Andrew; c Katherine. **Education:** St Cloud State Univ, BA, 1967; Univ Minn, MA, 1971, PhD (psychol, speech), 1973. **Professional Experience:** CO DIR, UNIV WASH INST LEARNING & BRAIN SCI, as of 2003; Neuroscience fel, G Edelmans Neuroscience Res Group, 1994-; bd trustees, NeurosciRes Found Inc, 1994-; bd dirs, Wash Technol Ctr, 1994-; Neuroscience Prog, Univ Wash, 1994-; bddirs, Am Inst Physics, 1994-1996; Va Merrill Bloedel scholar, Univ Wash, 1992-1994; Neuroscience, Univ Wash, 1989-; assoc ed, J Acoust Soc Am, 1988-1992; otolaryngol, Univ Wash, 1987-; ADJ PROF OTOLARYNGOL, UNIV WASH, 1987-; adj prof psychol, Univ Wash, 1985-; PROF, UNIV WASH, 1982-; from asst prof to assoc prof, Univ Wash, 1977-1982; postdoctoral fel, Cent Inst Deaf, 1973-1976. **Memberships:** Fel Acoust Soc Am (vpres, 1997-); fel Am Phychol Soc; fel AAAS. **Mailing Address:** Dept Speech & Hearing Scis, Univ Wash, 1417 Northeast 42nd St, Seattle, WA 98105-6246. **Fax:** 206-543-1093. **E-Mail:** pkkuhl@u.washington.edu

KUHLERS, DARYL LYNN, ANIMAL BREEDING. **Personal Data:** b Mason City, Iowa, November 12, 1945; m 1976, c 3. **Education:** Iowa State Univ, BS, 1967; Univ Wis, MS, 1970, PhD (animal sci & genetics), 1973. **Professional Experience:** Consult, 1985 & 1987 Thailand, 1986; PROF ANIMAL & DAIRY SCI, AUBURNUNIV, 1984-; consult, Am Soybean Asn, 1982; assoc prof, Auburn Univ, 1978-1984; consult, US Feed Grains Coun, 1977; asst prof animal sci, Iowa State Univ, 1974-1978; res assoc, Univ Wis, 1973-1974. **Memberships:** Am Soc Animal Sci; Coun Agr Tech. **Research Statement & Publications:** Swine breeding; genetics; selection and swine production. **Mailing Address:** Dept Animal Sci, Auburn Univ, 108 Upchurch Hall, Auburn, AL 36849-3501. **Fax:** 334-844-1519. **E-Mail:** dkuhlers@acesag.auburn.edu

KUHLMAN, ELMER GEORGE, PLANT PATHOLOGY. **Personal Data:** b Beaver Dam, Wis, December 15, 1934; m 1961, Linda; c Jennifer, Sara & Kathleen. **Education:** Univ Wis, BS, 1956; Ore State Univ, PhD (plant path), 1961. **Professional Experience:** SCIENTIST EMER, US FOREST SERV, as of 1997; prin plant pathologist & proj leader, Forestry Sci Lab, SEastern Forest & Range Exp Sta, 1990-1994; assoc ed, Southern JAppl Forestry, 1987-1990; adj prof plant path, Univ Ga, 1984-; assoc ed, Phytopath, 1983-1985; assoc ed, Plant Dis, 1978-1981 & 1993-1996; adj prof plant path, NC State Univ, 1975-1983; supvry plant pathologist, SEastern Forest & Range Exp Sta, US Forest Serv, 1971-1973; prin plant pathologist, SEastern Forest & Range Exp Sta, US Forest Serv, 1968-1971; plant pathologist, SEastern Forest & Range Exp Sta, US Forest Serv, 1961-1968. **Memberships:** Mycol Soc Am; Am Phytopath Soc; Soc Am Foresters. **Research Statement & Publications:** Ecological studies of soil organisms; epidemiology of pitch canker disease; effect of environment and mycoparasites on sporulation by Cronartium fusiforme; hyperparasites and hypovirulence; taxonomy of Gibberella fujikuroi and Mortierella; resistance to fusiform rust and variation in virulence. **Mailing Address:** Southern Res Sta, USDA Forest Serv, 320 Green St, Athens, GA 30602. **Fax:** 706-546-2454.

KUHLMAN, GAIL, BIOLOGY. **Education:** PhD. **Professional Experience:** STAFF, LAMS CO, as of 2006; staff, Pet Nutr Brands, as of 1999. **Memberships:** Inst Elec & Electronic Engrs. **Mailing Address:** Iams Co, 6571 State Rte 503 N, Lewisburg, OH 45338. **Fax:** 513-945-2017. **E-Mail:** kuhlman.g@pg.com

KUHLMAN, JOHN MICHAEL, EXPERIMENTAL FLUID MECHANICS & AERODYNAMICS. **Personal Data:** b Akron, Ohio, June 1, 1948; m 1970, Patricia; c Jennifer, Benjamin, Melissa & Emily. **Education:** Case Western Reserve Univ, BS, 1970, MS, 1973, PhD (eng), 1975. **Professional Experience:** Co-prin investr, Army Res Off, 1996-1999; prin investr, Off Sci Res, USAF, 1995-1997; prin investr, Air Force Wright Aeronaut Lab, 1989-1991; PROF MECH & AEROSPACE ENG, WVA UNIV, MORGANTOWN, 1987-; assoc prof, Wva Univ, Morgantown, 1985-1987; co-prin investr, Naval Surface Weapons Ctr, 1981-1984; NSF grant, 1978-1980, 1984-1985; prin investr, Naval Surface Weapons Ctr, 1975-1977, 1978-1983, 1985-1993; from asst prof to assoc prof mech eng, Dept Mech Eng & Mech, Old Dom Univ, 1974-1985; prin investr, Langley Res Ctr, NASA grants. **Memberships:** fel Am Soc Mech Engrs; Am Soc Eng Educ; assoc fel Am Inst Aeronaut & Astronaut; Sigma Xi. **Research Statement & Publications:** Experimental and theoretical fluid mechanics and aerodynamics; laser velocimetry. **Mailing Address:** Dept Mech & Aerospace Eng, WVa Univ, Eng Sci Bldg, Morgantown, WV 26506-6106. **Fax:** 304-293-6689. **E-Mail:** john.kuhlman@mail.wvu.edu

KUHLMANN, GEORGE EDWARD, ORGANIC CHEMISTRY, PHYSICAL CHEMISTRY. **Personal Data:** b Bronxville, NY, April 7, 1942. **Education:** City Col NY, BS, 1964; Syracuse Univ, MS, 1965, PhD (org chem), 1968. **Professional Experience:** ASSOC RES SCIENTIST, AMOCO CHEM CORP, 1992-; SR RES CHEMIST, AMOCO CHEM CORP, 1983-; staff res chemist, Amoco Chem Corp, 1978-1983; res chemist, Amoco Chem Corp, 1971-1978; proj chemist, Amoco Chem Corp, 1968-1971. **Memberships:** AAAS; Am Chem Soc. **Research Statement & Publications:** Sulfur chemistry; aromatic acids; hydrocarbon oxidation. **Mailing Address:** Amoco Chem Corp E-1, PO Box 3011, Naperville, IL 60566-7011.

KUHLMANN, KARL FREDERICK, BIOPHYSICAL CHEMISTRY, ANALYTICAL DATA SYSTEMS. **Personal Data:** b Ogden, Utah, February 3, 1937; m 1977, c 2. **Education:** Johns Hopkins Univ, BA, 1959; Univ Utah, PhD (chem), 1963. **Professional Experience:** SR DEVELOP ENGR, NELSON ANALYSTS INC, 1981-; phys chemist, Life Sci Div, Stanford Res Inst, 1973-1981; assoc prof, Stanford Univ, 1971-1973; asst prof, Dartmouth Col, 1965-1971; fel, Alumni Res Found, Univ Wis, 1964-1965; fel, Int Bus Mach, Comput Ctr, 1963-1964; res fel chem, Harvard Univ, 1962-1964. **Memberships:** Am Phys Soc. **Research Statement & Publications:** Magnetic resonance; structure and relaxation in liquids; drug design; binding of drugs to macromolecules. **Mailing Address:** 1115 Hermosa Way, Menlo Park, CA 94025.

KUHLMANN-WILSDORF, DORIS, TRIBOLOGY, SLIDING ELECTRICAL CONTACTS. **Personal Data:** b Bremen, Ger, February 15, 1922; American citizen; m 1950, Heinz; c Gabriele & Michael. **Education:** Gottingen Univ, BS, 1944, MS, 1946, PhD (mat sci), 1947. **Honorary Degrees:** DSc, Univ Witwatersrand, Johannesburg, SAfrica, 1954. **Honors & Awards:** Medal Excellence Res, Am Soc Eng Educ, 1965, 1966; Heyn Medal, Ger Soc Mat Sci, 1988; Achievement Award, Soc Women Engrs, 1989; Ragnar Helm Sci-Achievement Award, Inst Elec & Electronics Engrs, 1991. **Professional Experience:** PROF EMER, DEPT MAT SCI & ENG, SCH ENG & APPL SCI, UNIV VA, as of 2006; vis prof physics, Pretoria Univ, S Africa, 1982-1983; prof appl sci, Dept Physics & Mat Sci, Univ Va, Charlottesville, beginning 1966; prof eng physics, Dept Physics & Mat Sci, Univ VA, Charlottesville, 1963-1966; from assoc prof to prof metall, Univ Pa, Philadelphia, 1957-1963; lectr, Univ Witwatersrand, S Africa, 1950-1956; fel physics, BristolUniv, Eng, 1949-1950; fel mat sci, Univ Gottingen, Ger, 1947-1948. **Memberships:** Nat Acad Eng; fel Am Soc Metals; fel Am Phys Soc; Am Inst Mech Engrs; Am Asn Univ Professors; Soc Women Engrs. **Research Statement & Publications:** Publications in the areas of crystal defect theory; theory of workhardening and plastic deformation of metals, triboloby, electrical sliding contacts. **Mailing Address:** Dept Mat Sci & Eng, Sch Eng & Appl Sci, Univ Va, 116 Engrs Way PO Box 400745, Charlottesville, VA 22904-4745. **Fax:** 804-924-4576.

KUHLTHAU, ALDEN ROBERT, TRANSPORTATION, SYSTEMS ENGINEERING. **Personal Data:** b New Brunswick, NJ, April 29, 1921; m 1943, Gay; c Peyton, Richard & Linda. **Education:** Wake Forest Col, BS, 1942; Univ Va, MS, 1944, PhD (physics), 1948. **Professional Experience:** PROF EMER CIVIL ENG, UNIV VA, AS OF 2006; prof transp, Dept Civil Eng, 1977-1986; pres, Univ Space Res Asn, 1969-1975; assoc provost res, Sch Eng & Appl Sci, 1967-1971; prof aerospace eng, Sch Eng & Appl Sci, 1959-1977; assoc dean, Sch Eng & Appl Sci, 1959-1967; dir, Res Lab Eng Sci, 1954-1967; asst dir, Ord Res Lab, Univ Va, 1951-1954; asst prof, Univ NH, 1948-1951; asst physics, Wake Forest Col, 1941-1942; Off Sci Res & Develop & Naval Bur Ord Contracts, 1942-1948. **Research Statement & Publications:** Rarefied gas dynamics; human factors in transportation; air transportation systems. **Mailing Address:** 1817 Meadowbrook Heights Rd, Charlottesville, VA 22901.

KUHN, DAISY ANGELIKA, BACTERIOLOGY. **Personal Data:** b Heidelberg, Ger, August 3, 1930. **Education:** Univ Pa, AB, 1952; Univ Calif, PhD (microbiol), 1960. **Professional Experience:** PROF BIOL, CALIF STATE UNIV, NORTHRIDGE, 1971-; from instr toassoc prof microbiol, Calif State Univ, Northridge, 1959-1971; asst bact, Univ Calif, 1957-1959. **Memberships:** AAAS; Am Soc Microbiol; Brit Soc Gen Microbiol; Can Soc Microbiologists. **Research Statement & Publications:** Systematics of bacteria; microbial ecology. **Mailing Address:** Dept Biol, Calif State Univ, Northridge, CA 91330-8303. **Fax:** 818-677-2034. **E-Mail:** daisy.kuhn@csun.edu

KUHN, DAVID TRUMAN, GENETICS. **Personal Data:** b Tucson, Ariz, April 4, 1940; m 1968, Judy; c Christopher & Carrie. **Education:** Colo State Col, BA, 1963; Univ Utah, MS, 1965; Ariz State Univ, PhD (zoology), 1968. **Professional Experience:** Chair, Dept Biol; sabbatical, Ariz State Univ, Tempe, 1984; PROF BIOL, UNIV CENT FLA, 1979-; sabbatical, Univ Geneva, Switz, 1978; assoc prof, Univ Cent Fla, 1972-1979; asst prof, Univ Cent Fla, 1970-1972; asst prof biol, Creighton Univ, 1968-1970. **Memberships:** AAAS; Genetics Soc Am; Sigma Xi; Am Genetic Asn. **Research Statement & Publications:** Developmental and molecular genetics of Drosophila. **Mailing Address:** Dept Biol Sci, Univ Cent Fla, Orlando, FL 32816. **Fax:** 407-823-5769. **E-Mail:** dkuhn@mail.ucf.edu

KUHN, HANS HEINRICH, POLYMER CHEMISTRY, CONDUCTIVE POLYMERS. **Personal Data:** b St Gallen, Switz, January 12, 1924; American citizen; m 1954, Edith L Peyer; c Johann H & Barbara E. **Education:** Swiss Fed Inst Technol, ChemEng, 1949. **Honorary Degrees:** DSc, Swiss Fed Inst Technol, 1954. **Honors & Awards:** The Olney Medal, Am Ass of Textile chem & Colorists (AATCC) 1997; Seam Award (search for Electroactive Materials) Polymer res inst, Polytecnic Univ of NY 1997. **Professional Experience:** RETIRED; res fel, Milliken Res Co, 1996-2000; sr scientist, Milliken Res Co, 1979-1996; hon consul Switz for SC & NC, 1970-1995; mgr polymer res, Milliken Res Co, 1965-1979; sect leader, Milliken Res Co, 1961-1965; group leader textile chem, Milliken Res Co, 1960-1961; Res chemist, Dewey & Almy Div, W R Grace & Co, 1957-1960; Asst to Prof H Hopff, Swiss Fed Inst Technol, 1953-1957. **Memberships:** Am Chem Soc; Swiss Chem Soc; Am Ass of Textile chem & Colorist. **Research Statement & Publications:** Chemistry of epoxy steroids, aliphatic and aromatic epoxides; polymer chemistry, specifically oriented toward textile applications including electroactive polymers. **Mailing Address:** 176 W Park Dr, Spartanburg, SC 29306.

KUHN, HAROLD WILLIAM, MATHEMATICS. **Personal Data:** b Santa Monica, Calif, July 29, 1925; m Estelle; c Clifford, Nicholas & Jonathan. **Education:** Calif Inst Technol, BS, 1947; Princeton Univ, MA, 1948, PhD (math), 1950. **Honorary Degrees:** Laurea Economia e commercio, Univ Bergamo, 2000. **Honors & Awards:** John von Neumann Theory Prize, INFORMS, 1980 Harold W Kuhn Award, Naval Research Logistics, 2004. **Professional Experience:** Guggenheim fel, 1982-1983; NSF fel, Univ Rome, 1965-1966; prof math & econ, Princeton Univ, beginning 1963; mem adv comt, Army Res Off, 1962-1965 & div math, Nat Res Coun, 1963-1965 & 1969-1971; sr consult, Mathematica, Inc, 1961-1983; assoc prof, Princeton Univ, 1959-1963; NSF fel & vis mem, London Sch Econ, 1958-1959 & 1971-1972; Exec secy, div math, Nat Acad Sci-Nat Res Coun, 1957-1958 & 1959-1961; from asst prof to assoc prof, Bryn Mawr Col, 1952-1959; lectr, Princeton Univ, 1951-1952; Fulbright res scholar, dept sci, Univ Paris, 1950-1951; Fine instr math, Princeton Univ, 1949-1950. **Memberships:** Am Math Soc; Soc Indust & Appl Math (pres 1953-1954); fel Economet Soc; Math Asn Am; Math Prog Soc; fel Am Acad Arts & Scientists. **Research Statement & Publications:** Mathematical economics; mathematical programming; combinatorial problems. **Mailing Address:** Dept Math, Princeton Univ, Fine Hall, Wash Rd, Princeton, NJ 08544-1000. **Fax:** 609-258-1367. **E-Mail:** kuhn@math.princeton.edu

KUHN, HOWARD A, MANUFACTURING ENGINEERING, BUILDING SCIENCE. **Personal Data:** b Pittsburgh, Pa, December 6, 1940; m 1962, Beverly; c Amy, Jeffrey, David & Stephen. **Education:** Carnegie-Mellon Univ, BS, 1962, MS, 1963, PhD (mech eng), 1966. **Honors & Awards:** Zay Jeffries Award, Am Soc Metals, 1987; Edgar C Bain Award, Am Soc Metals, 2000. **Professional Experience:** VPRES & CHIEF TECH OFFICER, SCIENDA BLDG SCI, 2000-; vpres & chief tech officer, Concurrent Technol Corp, 1992-2000; adj prof metall eng & mech eng, Univ Pittsburgh, 1989-2000; tech vpres, Metalworking Technol Inc, 1989-1992; tech dir, Deformation Control Technol, Inc, 1980-1987; from assoc prof to prof mat eng & mech eng, Univ Pittsburgh, 1975-1989; from asst prof to assoc prof metall eng, Drexel Univ, 1966-1974; instr mech eng, Carnegie-Mellon Univ, 1965-1966. **Memberships:** fel Am Soc Metals; Am Soc Mech Engrs; Am Powder Metall Inst; Soc Mfg Engrs Light Gage Steel Engr Assoc. **Research Statement & Publications:** Powder metallurgy; metal flow analysis; process design; mechanical and metallurgical analysis of net-shape forming processes (powder consolidation, precision forging), fracture during forming, expert systems for metalworking processes; concurrent engineering, simulation-based design and manufacturing. **Mailing Address:** Scienda Bldg Sci, 1525 Charleston Hwy, Orangeburg, SC 29116. **Fax:** 803-268-6414. **E-Mail:** hkuhn@scienda.com

KUHN, JANICE OSETH, TOXICOLOGY. **Personal Data:** b Canacao, Philippines, June 29, 1940; American citizen; c 3. **Education:** Univ RI, BS, 1962, PhD (biochem), 1970. **Professional Experience:** SR TOXICOLOGIST, STILLMEADOW INC, 1990-; toxicologist, Stillmeadow Inc, 1988-1990; res asst prof, Dept Med, Baylor Col Med, 1983-1988; from asst prof to assoc prof chem, Univ SFla, 1973-1983; res assoc biochem, Univ SFla, 1972-1973; asst prof biol sci, Va Polytech Inst & State Univ, 1969-1972. **Memberships:** Am Chem Soc; AAAS; NY Acad Sci; Sigma Xi; Soc Toxicol. **Research Statement & Publications:** Role of intracellular calcium in cell injury and metabolic regulation; mechanisms of chemical injury. **Mailing Address:** Stillmeadow Inc, 12852 Park One Dr, Sugar Land, TX 77478. **Fax:** 281-240-8448.

KUHN, KLAUS, CELL MATRIX. **Personal Data:** b Breslau, May 1, 1927; German citizen; m 1956, Barbara Bleimund; c Thomas, Sabine & Gabriele. **Education:** Univ Munich, dipl, 1950 & 1952; Max Planck Inst EiweiB-u Lederforschung, PhD (biochem), 1955. **Honorary Degrees:** Dr, Univ Ouler, Finland, 1994. **Professional Experience:** Mem sci adv bd, Inst Environ Res, Neuherberg nr Munich, 1991-1993; co-chmn, Gordon Res Conf Struct Macromolecules, Collagen, 1991; chmn, Biol Med Sect, 1987-1990; mem sci adv bd, Int Inst Cellular & Molecular Path, Brussels, 1984-1991; mem sciadv bd, Inst Arteriosclerosis Res, Munster, 1981-1991; Fogarty scholar, Fogarty Intern Ctr, NIH, Bethesda, 1981-1982; exec dir, Max-Planck Inst Biochem, 1977-1980; dir, Dept ConnectiveTissue Res & exec dir, Max Planck Inst Biochem, 1977-1980; dir, connective tissue dept, 1973-1995; MEM SCI COUN, MAX PLANCK INST BIOCHEM, 1966-; sci mem, Max-PlanckInst Proteinchem, 1966-1972; assoc prof, Univ Heidelberg, 1960-1966; asst prof, Darmstadt, 1958-1960; Fel Deutsche Forschungsgemeinschaft Inst Technol, Darmstadt, 1956-1958. **Memberships:** Hon mem Am Soc Biol Chemists; Europ Molecular Biol Orgn. **Research Statement & Publications:** Structure and function of extracellular matrix constituents; cell matrix interaction; molecular biology of collagen genes and other extracellular matrix constituents. **Mailing Address:** Max-Planck Inst Biochem, 82152 Martinsried nr Munich, Ger. **Fax:** 498-985-782422.

KUHN, LESLIE A, CARDIOLOGY. **Personal Data:** b South Falls, NY, May 10, 1924; m 1950, c 2. **Education:** State Univ NY Downstate Med Ctr, MD, 1948. **Professional Experience:** Consult, Coronary Care Unit, Mt Sinai Hosp, New York, beginning 1981; CLIN PROF MED, MT SINAI SCH MED, 1975-; ATTEND CARDIOLOGIST, MT SINAI HOSP, NY, 1975-; DIR, CORONARY CARE UNIT, 1970-; consult cardiologist, US Vet Admin Hosp, Bronx, beginning 1969; assoc attend cardiologist, Hosp, 1966-1975; assoc prof med, Coronary Care Unit, 1966-1975; fel coun clin cardiol, Am Heart Asn, beginning 1965; prin investr, Nat Heart Inst res grant, 1960; sr asst ed, J Am Col Cardiol. **Memberships:** fel Am Col Cardiol; fel Am Col Physicians; Am Fedn Clin Res; Am Soc ArtificialInternal Organs; Am Col Chest Physicians. **Research Statement & Publications:** Hemodynamic and cardiac metabolic effects of pharmacological agents and methods of mechanical circulatory support in experimental and clinical acute myocardial infarction with shock. **Mailing Address:** Cardiol Div, Mt Sinai Sch Med, 1050 Fifth Ave, New York, NY 10028-0110.

KUHN, MARTIN CLIFFORD, METALLURGY. **Personal Data:** b Tucson, Ariz, April 4, 1940; m 1963, Priscilla; c Katherine E R (Salah), Fletcher T & Clifford S. **Education:** Colo Sch Mines, Met Eng, 1963, MS, 1967, PhD (metall), 1968. **Professional Experience:** PRES, MINING FOUND SOUTHWEST, TUSCON, as of 2004; dir, pres & chief exec officer, Western States Eng, beginning 1992; PRES, DIR & CHIEF EXEC OFFICER, KEN CON INC, 1987-; dir, Netwest Develop Corp, 1985-; dir, Mountain States Mineral Enterprises, 1984-1990; vpres & gen mgr, Minerals Separation Corp, 1979-1987; mgr, Tech Develop Ctr, Mineral Sci Div, UOP Inc, 1976-1979; proj mgr, Hazen Res, 1975-1976; mgr process technol, Anaconda Co, 1974-1975; supvr mineral processing, Anaconda Co, 1972-1974; sr res engr, Anaconda Co, 1968-1972; vpres new ventures, Mountain States Mineral Enterprises Inc. **Memberships:** Am Inst Mining Metall & Petrol Engrs; Soc Mining Engrs; Mining & Metallurgical Soc Am; Am Mining Congress; Mining Found Southwest. **Research Statement & Publications:** Mineral processing; froth flotation; hydrometallurgy; extractive metallurgy; heavy media and ultrasonics. **Mailing Address:** Mining Found SouthWest, PO Box 42317, Tucson, AZ 85733. **Fax:** 520-577-7073.

KUHN, MATTHEW, MICROELECTRONICS, TELECOMMUNICATIONS & COMPUTING. **Personal Data:** b Sacalaz, Rumania, March 19, 1936; American citizen; m 1966, Betty; c Andrea Suzanne & Andrew Jason. **Education:** Queen's Univ, Ont, BSc, 1962; Univ Waterloo, MASc, 1963, PhD (elec eng), 1967. **Honorary Degrees:** DEng, Univ Waterloo, Ont, Can, 1985. **Professional Experience:** FARM MGR, BETTER N BETTER FARM, as of 2006; adj prof eng, Duke Univ, beginning 2000; mgt, Sch Eng, Duke Univ, 1970-2000; pres, Econtech Consult Servs, 1994-2000; pres, Microelectronics Ctr NC, 1989-1993; asst vpres resource develop Univ rel, Tech Dept, Bell Tell Labs, 1984-1989; mem, Nat Sci & Eng Res Coun Can, (Commun & Comput), 1981-1984; mem, Queen's Univ Adv Coun on Eng, 1980-1986; pres, Electron Devices Soc, Inst Elec & Electronics Engr, 1980-1981; dir, Tech Dept, Bell Tell Labs, 1979-1984; mgr, Advan Technol Lab, Bell Tell Labs, 1976-1979; res mgr, Elec Mat & Process Dept, Bell Northern, Bell Tell Labs, 1973-1976; supvr electroluminescence device develop, device res & develop, Bell Tell Labs, 1970-1973; mem staff, device res & develop, Bell Tell Labs, 1968-1970; fel, advan Res Proj Agency, Div Eng, Brown Univ, 1967-1968; bd vis, Duke Fac Eng. **Memberships:** Fel Inst Elec & Electronics Engrs; AAAS. **Research Statement & Publications:** Solid state device physics; electroluminescence; semiconductor-insulator interface physics; solid state display development; silicon integrated circuit research; optoelectronics, fiber optics and telecommunications systems applications; management and administration of advanced technology research laboratory and telecommunications systems research programs; special experience in collaborative university-industry-government consortium research and development administration. **Mailing Address:** 618 Tremont St PO Box 712, Southern Pines, NC 27514. **E-Mail:** Matt@BetterNBetterFarm.com

KUHN, NICHOLAS J, MATHEMATICS. **Personal Data:** b February 15, 1955. **Education:** Princeton Univ, BA, 1976; Univ Chicago, MS, 1977, PhD (math), 1980. **Professional Experience:** Vis prof, Cambridge Univ, 2006; PROF, DEPT MATH, UNIV VA, 1991-; assoc prof, dept math, Univ Va, 1986-1991; vis fel, Cambridge Univ, Cambridge, Eng, 1986-1987; Sloan Found Fel, 1985-1987; asst prof, Princeton Univ, 1982-1986; vis scholar, Northwestern Univ, Evanston, Ill, 1983; vis fel, Dept Math, 1982-1983; fel, Am Math Asn, 1982-1983; actg asst prof, Dept Math, Univ Wash, Seattle, 1980-1982. **Memberships:** Am Math Soc; Math Asn Am. **Mailing Address:** Dept Math, Univ Va, PO Box 400137 318 Kerchof Hall, Charlottesville, VA 22904-4137. **E-Mail:** njk4x@virginia.edu

KUHN, PETER MOUAT, meteorology, atmospheric physics; deceased, see previous edition for last biography

KUHN, RAYMOND EUGENE, IMMUNOBIOLOGY, PARASITOLOGY. **Personal Data:** b Biloxi, Miss, September 6, 1942; m 1964. **Education:** Carson-Newman Col, BS, 1965; Univ Tenn, PhD (zoology), 1968. **Professional Experience:** WILLIAM L POTEAT PROF, DEPT BIOL, WAKE FOREST UNIV, as of 2003; PROF, DEPT BIOL, WAKE FOREST UNIV, 1980-; assoc prof, Wake Forest Univ, 1968-1980. **Memberships:** Am Soc Parasitologists; Am Asn Immunol; Am Soc Trop Med & Hyg. **Research Statement & Publications:** Immunology of parasitic diseases. **Mailing Address:** Dept Biol Wake Forest Univ, PO Box 7325, Winston-Salem, NC 27109-7325. **Fax:** 336-758-6008. **E-Mail:** kuhnray@wfu.edu

KUHN, ROBERT W, BIOCHEMISTRY. **Education:** Wash State Univ, BSc; Univ Wash, seatlle, PhD (Biochem). **Professional Experience:** SR VPRES & CHIEF TECHNOL OFFICER, AEROVANCE INC, as of 2005. **Mailing Address:** Aerovance Inc, 2929 7th St Suite 130, Berkeley, CA 94710. **Fax:** 510-549-5501.

KUHN, WILLIAM FREDERICK, ANALYTICAL CHEMISTRY, SPECTROCHEMISTRY. **Personal Data:** b Kittanning, Pa, April 1, 1930; m 1953, Norma; c Jeffrey, Timothy, Diane & Gregory. **Education:** St Vincent Col, BS, 1957; Univ Richmond, MS, 1962. **Honors & Awards:** William J Poehlman Award, Soc Appl Spectros, 1975; St Vincent Gold Medal(chem). **Professional Experience:** RETIRED; asst to vpres res & develop, Philip Morris USA, 1991-1993; dir appl res, res & develop support, 1987-1991; mgr anal res, Philip Morris Inc, 1981-1984; mgr biochem res, Philip Morris Inc, 1974-1981; proj leader smoke condensation, Philip Morris Inc, 1972-1974; chemist, facil leader Instrument Sect, 1969-1972; sr scientist mass spectros, Philip Morris Inc, 1964-1969; group leader tech info, Philip Morris Inc, 1962-1964; res chemist, Philip Morris Inc, 1959-1962; chemist, Philip Morris Inc, 1957-1959. **Memberships:** Soc Appl Spectros; AAAS; Am Chem Soc; Am Soc Mass Spectrometry; Sigma Xi. **Research Statement & Publications:** Spectroscopic methods; chromatographic techniques; computer applications; technical information; environmental pollution; tobacco and smoke composition; ionization phenomena; entomology. **Mailing Address:** 2140 Galloway Terr, Midlothian, VA 23113-6447.

KUHN, WILLIAM R, PALAEOCLIMATE, CLIMATE DYNAMICS. **Personal Data:** b Columbus, Ohio, May 7, 1938; m 1957, c 3. **Education:** Capital Univ, BS, 1961; Univ Colo, PhD (astro-geophys), 1966. **Professional Experience:** Dept chmn, Univ Mich, 1980-1990; PROF ATMOSPHERIC OCEANIC & SCI, UNIV MICH, ANN ARBOR, 1977-; assoc prof atmosphere & ocean sci, Univ Mich, 1972-1977; asst prof, Univ Mich, 1967-1971; fel astro-geophys, Univ Colo, 1966-1967. **Memberships:** Am Geophys Union; Am Astron Soc; AAAS. **Research Statement & Publications:** Radiation and photochemical studies applicable to planetary atmospheres and the prebiotic earth atmosphere; climatology; radiative transfer. **Mailing Address:** Dept Atmospheric, Oceanic & Space Sci, Univ Mich, 1521B Space Res Bldg, Ann Arbor, MI 48109-2143. **Fax:** 734-936-0503. **E-Mail:** wkuhn@umich.edu

KUHNEN, SYBIL MARIE, BOTANY. **Personal Data:** b Haledon, NJ, September 12, 1917. **Education:** Montclair State Col, BA, 1941; Columbia Univ, MA, 1946; NY Univ, PhD (sci educ), 1960. **Professional Experience:** CONSULT, 1955-; chmn dept, Montclair State Col, 1969-1976; prof biol, Montclair State Col, 1966-1987; from instr to assoc prof bact & bot, Montclair State Col, 1946-1966; asst bot, Columbia Univ, 1943-1946; Pub sch teacher, NJ, 1941-1943. **Memberships:** AAAS; Bot Soc Am; Nat Sci Teachers Asn. **Research Statement & Publications:** Plant ecology. **Mailing Address:** 5 Charles Ct, Clifton, NJ 07013.

KUHNERT, BETTY R, OBSTETRICAL ANESTHESIA. **Personal Data:** b New York, NY, December 16, 1944. **Education:** Kent State Univ, PhD (biol), 1972. **Professional Experience:** ASST VPRES, GLOBAL CLIN COMPLIANCE, EDUC & TRAINING, WYETH, as of 2004; assoc prof reproductive biol, Case Western Res Univ, beginning 1984; SR DIR CLINRES & DEVELOP, WYETH-AYERS RES, 1984-; Asst prof, Case Western Res Univ, 1975-1984. **Memberships:** Fedn Am Socs Exp Biol; Am Soc Pharmacol & Exp Therapeut; Perinatal Res Soc; Sigma Xi; Soc Obstet Anesthesia & Perinatology; Am Soc Clin Pharm & Therapeut. **Mailing Address:** Wyeth, 5 Giralda Farms, Madison, NJ 07940.

KUHNLEIN, HARRIET V, ECOLOGY, STUDY OF DIETS. **Personal Data:** b Sadsburyville, Pa, August 14, 1939; c 3. **Education:** Pa State Univ, BS, 1961; Ore State Univ, MS, 1969; Univ Calif, Berkeley, PhD (nutrit), 1976. **Professional Experience:** FOUND DIR, CTR INDIGENOUS PEOPLE'S NUTRIT & ENVIRON, MCGILL UNIV, as of 2003; ed, Ecol Food & Nutrit, 1989-; consult, PCB contamination nutrit diet, Health & Welfare, Can, 1986; PROF NUTRIT, SCH DIETETICS & HUMAN NUTRIT, MCGILL UNIV, 1985-; mem, Nutrit Working Group, Int Strategic Issues Health Prom, Med Serv Health & Welfare, Can, 1984; mem adv bd, Herb Res Found, 1983-; can rep, Comt NutritAnthrop, Int Union

Nutrit Sci, 1983-; assoc prof nutrit, Sch Family & Nutrit Sci, Univ BC, 1976-1985; NIH trainee nutrit sci, Univ Calif, Berkeley, 1973-1976; res asst, Inst Molecular Biol, Univ Ore, 1969-1972; res fel, Int Ctr Med Res & Training, Calif, Colombia; res fel, Tulane Univ, 1967. **Memberships:** Am Dietetic Asn; Can Dietetic Asn; Soc Ethnobiol; Can Soc Nutrit Sci; Am Inst Nutrit; Can Soc Circumpolar Health; Am Soc Nutrit Sci; Soc Nutri Educ. **Research Statement & Publications:** Cultural and ecological determinants of diets and human nutritional status; nutrient levels in foods of indigenous people; Nuxalk of British Columbia, Canadian and other indigenous people. **Mailing Address:** Ctr Indigenous Peoples Nutrit & Environ, McGill Univ, CINE Bldg Macdonald Campus 21 111 Lakeshore Rd, Ste Anne de Bellevue, PQ H9X 3V9, Can. **Fax:** 514-398-1020. **E-Mail:** kuhnlein@macdonald.mcgill.ca

KUHNLEY, LYLE CARLTON, MICROBIOLOGY. **Personal Data:** b Buffalo, Minn, December 23, 1925; m 1953, c 4. **Education:** Univ Minn, BA, 1949; Univ Tex, MA, 1955, PhD (bact), 1961. **Professional Experience:** RETIRED; from assoc to emer prof biol, Tex Tech Univ, 1959-1988; Bacteriologist, Ariz State Dept Health, 1949-1950 & 1953-1955. **Memberships:** AAAS; Am Soc Microbiol. **Research Statement & Publications:** Inducible enzyme formation; rumen microbiology; ecology of coliphage; geomicrobiological prospecting; resistance mechanisms. **Mailing Address:** Box 409, Monroe, OR 97456-0409.

KUHNS, ELLEN SWOMLEY, PHYSICS, RESEARCH ADMINISTRATION. **Personal Data:** b Chester, Pa, February 6, 1919; m 1974, Charles C; c James L Stewart. **Education:** Coe Col, BA, 1941; Johns Hopkins Univ, PhD (physics), 1946. **Professional Experience:** RETIRED; dep independent res & independent exp develop dir, Naval Ocean Systs Ctr, 1977-1982; tech prog mgt off, Optical Physics Div, 1974-1977; planning office, Optical Physics Div, 1970-1974; res mgr, Optical Physics Div, 1968-1970; head, Optical Physics Div, 1966-1968; physicist, Naval Electronics Lab Ctr, 1951-1966; asst prof, NJ Col for Women, Rutgers Univ, 1946-1951; instr physics, Conn Col, 1945-1946; Instr astron, Teachers Col, Johns Hopkins Univ, 1941-1945. **Memberships:** Fel Am Phys Soc. **Research Statement & Publications:** Ultrasonics; underwater acoustics. **Mailing Address:** 875 Albion St, San Diego, CA 92106-2933.

KUHNS, JOHN FARRELL, WATER CHEMISTRY, ICHTHYOLOGY. **Personal Data:** b Albuquerque, NMex, March 2, 1947; m 1967, c 1. **Education:** Univ Mo, Kansas City, BS, 1969. **Professional Experience:** PRES, EECHO SYSTS, 1989-; mgr, Aquatic Data Ctr, 1989-; ed, Drum & Croaker, 1989-; ed & compiler, Codex Fishery Chem, 1984-; asst syst oper, Aquaria-Fish Forum, 1984-; PRES, CORP SECY & RES DIR, AQUASCI RES GROUP INC, 1982-; vis prof, Tex A&M Col Sta, Aqua Med Prog, 1982-1983; PRES, AQUASCI RES GROUP INC, 1982-; ed, J Aquaricult & Aquatic Sci, 1979-; CO-OWNER, WRITTEN WORD, 1979-; Founder, chmn bd & pres, Friends Aquarium, Inc, 1977-; res dir, Gen Drug & Chem Corp, 1974-1982; vpres & pres, Montserrat Educ & Sci Co, 1970-1973; partner & pres, Mid-Continent Fish Ltd, 1970; Co-owner, Piscean Fantasy, 1969; co-owner, Fish Ltd, 1967-1969; reviewer, AAAS Books & Films. **Memberships:** AAAS; Am Chem Soc; Am Soc Ichthyologist & Herpetologist; Am Fisheries Soc; World Aquaculture Soc; Am Cichlid Asn; Int Asn Aquatic Animal Med. **Research Statement & Publications:** Development of products for aquaculture, aquariculture and sport fisheries designed to control water quality in closed systems. **Mailing Address:** AquaSci Res Group Inc, 1000 Gentry St, North Kansas City, MO 64116-4112. **Fax:** 816-474-5597. **E-Mail:** JFK@compuserve.com

KUHNS, WILLIAM JOSEPH, CHEMISTRY. **Personal Data:** b Allentown, Pa, September 2, 1918; m 1961, c 7. **Education:** Muhlenberg Col, BS, 1940; Lehigh Univ, MS, 1942; Johns Hopkins Univ, MD, 1948. **Professional Experience:** Summer res, Marine Biol Lab, Woods Hole, MA, 1988-1990; VIS INVESTR, HOSP SICK CHILDREN, TORONTO, 1984-; fel biochem, Res Inst, Hosp Sick Children, Toronto, 1984-1986; Res Prof Path, Univ NC, 1981-; prof, NC Mem Hosp, 1977-1981; dirtransfusion serv, NC Mem Hosp, 1977-1981; Biochem res, Lister Inst, Univ London, 1974-1975; assoc prof path, Sch Med, NY Univ, 1960-1977; assoc prof path, Sch Med, Univ Pittsburgh, 1954-1959; vis investr & asst physician, Hosp, Rockefeller Inst, 1951-1954; fel microbiol, ColMed, NY Univ, 1950-1951; intern med, Salt Lake County Gen Hosp, 1949-1950; Chemist, Lederle Labs Div, Am Cyanamid Corp, 1942-1944. **Memberships:** Am Soc Clin Invest; Soc Exp Biol & Med; Am Asn Immunologists; Am AsnPathologists; fel AAAS; fel Am Acad Microbiol; Am Soc Cell Biol; Soc Develop Biol; Am SocHematol. **Research Statement & Publications:** Glycosyltransferases of O-linked glycans, sulfotransferases; blood groups and their precursors on cultured cells; blood groups on cells on culture; blood groups in infrahuman species; blood groups and antibodies in transplantation and cancer. **Mailing Address:** Biochem Res Hosp Sick Children, 555 University Ave, Toronto, ON M5G 1X8, Can.

KUHR, RONALD JOHN, ENTOMOLOGY, INSECT TOXICOLOGY. **Personal Data:** b Appleton, Wis, December 29, 1939; m 1961, c 3. **Education:** Univ Wis, BS, 1963; Univ Calif, Berkeley, PhD (agr chem), 1966. **Professional Experience:** PROF EMER ENTOMOL & TOXICOL, NC STATE UNIV, as of 2004; prof, dept entomol & toxicol, nc state univ, 1992-; assoc dean &dir res, Col Agr Life Sci, 1987-1991; prof & head, Dept Entomol 1980-1986; prof entomol, assoc dir res & assoc dir, Agr Exp Sta, Cornell Univ, 1977-1980; from asst prof to assoc prof insect toxicol, NY State Agr Exp Sta, 1973-1977; fel, NIH, Pest Infestation Lab, Slough, Eng, 1966-1968. **Memberships:** Am Chem Soc; Entom Soc Am. **Research Statement & Publications:** Metabolism of carbamate insecticide chemicals in plants and insects; environmental degradation of pesticides. **Mailing Address:** Dept Entomol & Toxicol, NC State Univ, 4316 Gardner Hall, Raleigh, NC 27695-7613. **Fax:** 919-515-7746. **E-Mail:** ron_kuhr@ncsu.edu

KUIDA, HIROSHI, INTERNAL MEDICINE, PHYSIOLOGY. **Personal Data:** b Ogden, Utah, October 23, 1925; m 1951, c 4. **Education:** Univ Utah, BS, 1949, MD, 1951. **Professional Experience:** PROF MED & PHYSIOL, COL MED, UNIV UTAH, 1969-; assoc prof physiol, Univ Utah, 1965-1969; chief, Div Cardiol, Univ Utah, 1964-1983; assoc prof, Univ Utah, 1964-1969; asst res prof, Univ Utah, 1961-1964; instr, Univ Utah, 1958-1961; chief resident med, Univ Utah, 1957-1958; res fel physiol, Univ Minn, 1956-1957; res career develop award, Am Heart Asn res fel, 1955-1957; res fel, Harvard Med Sch & Peter Bent Brigham Hosp, 1954-1956; USPHS fel, 1953-1955; fel cardiol, Harvard Med Sch & Peter Bent Brigham Hosp, 1953-1954; asst resident, Salt Lake County Gen Hosp & Univ Utah, 1952-1953; intern med, Salt Lake County Gen Hosp& Univ Utah, 1951-1952. **Memberships:** Am Physiol Soc; Am Fedn Clin Res. **Research Statement & Publications:** Pulmonary vascular hemodynamics; hemodynamics of endotoxin shock; pathophysiology of pulmonary hypertensive heart disease in cattle. **Mailing Address:** Div Cardiol, Univ Utah, Magna, UT 84044.

KUIJT, JOB, PLANT ANATOMY, PLANT MORPHOLOGY. **Personal Data:** b Velsen, Holland, May 25, 1930; Canadian citizen; div, c Steven, Ian, David, Tony & Nicola. **Education:** Univ BC, BA, 1954; Univ Calif, MA, 1955, PhD (anat), 1958. **Professional Experience:** PROF EMER BIOL, UNIV LETHBRIDGE, as of 2006; adj prof, Univ Victoria, beginning 1989; prof biol, Univ Lethbridge, beginning 1970; assoc prof, Univ Lethbridge, 1968-1970; from instr to asst prof biol & bot, Univ BC, 1959-1968. **Memberships:** Bot Soc Am. **Research Statement & Publications:** Structure and taxonomy of parasitic angiosperms; systematics of mistletoes. **Mailing Address:** Dept Biol, Univ Victoria, PO Box 3020, STN CSC, Victoria, BC V8W 3N5, Can. **Fax:** 250-721-6611. **E-Mail:** jkuijt@uvic.ca

KUIKEN, KENNETH (ALFRED), BIOCHEMISTRY. **Personal Data:** b Chicago, Ill, October 14, 1918; m 1944, c 2. **Education:** Geneva Col, BS, 1939; Univ Pittsburgh, PhD (biochem), 1943. **Professional Experience:** RETIRED; sr res chemist, Buckeye Cellulose Corp, 1974-1983; mem staff, Cellulose & Specialties Tech Div, Procter & Gamble Co, 1950-1974; assoc nutritionist & assoc prof biochem & nutrit, Exp Sta, Agr & Mech Col Tex, 1943-1950. **Memberships:** AAAS; Tech Asn Pulp & Paper Indust; Am Chem Soc; Soc Exp Biol & Med; fel Am Oil Chemists Soc; Sigma Xi. **Research Statement & Publications:** Microbiological methods of amino acid analysis; cottonseed processing; nutritional requirements of laboratory and farm animals; manufacture and application of wood and cotton cellulose; analytical methods for cellulose. **Mailing Address:** 4796 Gwynne Rd, Memphis, TN 38117-3210.

KUIPER, LOGAN KEITH, GROUNDWATER HYDROLOGY, FLUIDS. **Personal Data:** b Oskaloosa, Iowa, September 12, 1940; m 1972, c 3. **Education:** Univ Iowa, BA, 1962, MS, 1965, PhD (physics), 1969; Calif Inst Technol, MS, 1963. **Professional Experience:** AFFIL, LOS ALAMOS NAT LAB, NMEX, 1994-; res hrdrologist, US Geol surv & guest scientist, Los Alamos Nat Lab, Nmex, 1990-1994; res hydrologist, US Geol Surv, Austin, Tex, 1982-1990; hydrologist, US Geol Surv, 1979-1982; res geologist, Iowa Geol Surv, 1972-1978; asst prof physics, SDak Sch Mines, 1970; trainee scholar NASA, Univ Iowa, 1964-1967; scholar, Appomattox Regional Libr Syst, Calif Inst Technol, 1962-1964. **Memberships:** Am Geophys Union; Soc Indust & Appl Math. **Research Statement & Publications:** Groundwater hydrology and particularly the mathematical modelling; applied mathematics. **Mailing Address:** Los Alamos Nat Lab, PO Box 1663 MS D446, Los Alamos, NM 87545.

KUIPER, THOMAS BERNARDUS HENRICUS, RADIOASTRONOMY. **Personal Data:** b Amersfoort, Neth, July 14, 1945; Canadian citizen; m 1970, Linda; c Elizabeth Virginia. **Education:** Loyola Col, Montreal, BSc, 1966; Univ Md, PhD (astron), 1973. **Professional Experience:** MEM TECH STAFF ASTRON, JET PROPULSION LAB, CALIF INST TECHNOL, 1977-; sr scientist, Jet Propulsion Lab, Calif Inst Technol, 1975-1977; resident res assoc, US Nat Res Coun & Jet Propulsion Lab, 1973-1975. **Memberships:** Am Astron Soc; Can Astron Soc; Int Astron Union; AAAS; Int Union Radio Sci. **Research Statement & Publications:** Spectroscopy observations with emphasis on instrumentation and techniques; very large baseline interferometer; solar physics; radio search for extraterrestrial intelligence and evolution of civilization in space. **Mailing Address:** Jet Propulsion Lab, Calif Inst Technol, 169-506 4800 Oak Grove Dr, Pasadena, CA 91109-8099.

KUIPER-GOODMAN, TINE, TOXICOLOGY RISK ASSESSMENT, ELECTRON MICROSCOPY. **Personal Data:** b Leeuwarden, Neth, September 11, 1937; div, c Margaret. **Education:** McMaster Univ, BSc, 1961, MSc, 1963; Nat Res Coun Can & Ont fels & PhD (histol, embryol), Univ Ottawa, 1967. **Professional Experience:** RES SCIENTIST CELL TOXICOL & TOXICOLOGIST, HEALTHPROTECTION BR, BUR CHEM SAFETY, HEALTH & WELFARE, CAN, 1966-. **Memberships:** Can Soc Cell Biol; Micros Soc Can; Soc Toxicol Can; Am Soc Toxicol. **Research Statement & Publications:** Effect of exogenous substances that may be present in food on cell organelles of animal tissues; risk assessment of mycotoxins and natural toxicants present in food; development of quantitative morphological methods. **Mailing Address:** Toxicol Eval Sect, Bur Chem Safety, Health Can, 960, Carling Ave, Ottawa, ON K1A 0C6, Can. **Fax:** 613-957-1688.

KUIPERS, BENJAMIN JACK, INTELLIGENT ROBOTICS, QUALITATIVE REASONING. **Personal Data:** b Grand Rapids, Mich, April 7, 1949; m 1975, Laura; c Anna, Rebecca & David. **Education:** Swarthmore Col, BA, 1970; Mass Inst Technol, PhD (math), 1977. **Professional Experience:** Endowed Prof, Computer Science, No 3, Univ Tex, Austin, 1997-; Dept chair, Univ Tex, Austin, 1997-2001; Bruton Centennial Prof Computer Science, Univ Tex, Austin, 1992-1997; Assoc Prof, Dept Comput Sci, Univ Tex, Austin, 1985-1992; Res Assoc, Lab Computer Science, Mass Inst Technol, 1984-1985; Asst Prof, Dept Math, Tufts Univ, 1978-1984; Res Assoc, Div Study Res Educ, Mass Inst Technol, 1977-1978; Syst Programmer, Psychol Dept, Harvard Univ, 1970-1972. **Memberships:** Fellow, Inst Elec & Electronics Engrs; Fellow, Am Assn Artificial Intel; AAAS; ACM; Cognitive Sci Soc; Comput Prof Soc Responsibility; Fellow, Soc Values Higher Educ. **Research Statement & Publications:** Artificial intelligence; qualitative simulation and modeling of physical systems; artificial intelligence in medicine; knowledge representation; spatial learning, exploration and problem solving; robotics and intelligent control. **Mailing Address:** Comput Sci Dept, Univ Tex, Austin, TX 78712. **E-Mail:** kuipers@cs.utexas.edu

KUIPERS, JACK, MATHEMATICS. **Personal Data:** b Grand Rapids, Mich, March 27, 1921; m 1948, c 5. **Education:** Calvin Col, AB, 1943; Univ Mich, BS, 1943, MSE, 1959, ICE, 1966. **Professional Experience:** PROF EMER, CALVIN COL, as of 2006; Polhemus Navigation Sci, Inc & Advan Technol Systs, Div Austin Co, Cleveland, Ohio, 1975-; Precision Prod Dept & Avionics Div, Lear Jet Industs, 1967-; prof math, Calvin Col, beginning 1967; consult, Precision Prod Dept, Nortronics Div, Northrop Corp, 1967-; CONSULT, MATH MODELS AEROSPACE TECHNOL, 1967-; assoc res engr, Univ, 1965-1967; lectr aerospace eng, Inst Sci & Technol, Univ Mich, 1962-1965; res engr, NASA Apollo Appln, Aerospace Eng, Navig & Inst Sci & Technol, Univ Mich, 1962-1967; lect, Horace B Rackham Sch Grad Studies, Univ Mich, 1962-1967; sr physicist, Cleveland Pneumatic Industs, 1959-1962; sr proj engr, Lear, Inc, 1954-1959; chief engr, R C Allen Bus Mach, Inc, 1953-1954; proj engr, Lear Inc, 1950-1953; asst to dir res, Elec Sorting Mach Co, 1946-1950; mil serv, 1st Lt, US Army Signal Corps, 1942-1946. **Memberships:** sr mem Inst Elec & Electronics Engrs; Math Asn Am; Sigma Xi. **Research Statement & Publications:** Automatic control; analog-digital computer simulation; special purpose computer design; navigation and guidance control and instrumentation; coordinate converters for gyroscope inertial reference systems; mathematical models and optimization. **Mailing Address:** Dept Math, Calvin col, Grand Rapids, MI 49546. **Fax:** 616-957-6501. **E-Mail:** kprs@calvin.edu

KUIVANIEMI, S HELENA, GENETICS INTRACRANIAL & AORTIC ANEURYSMS, DNA LINKAGE ANALYSIS. **Personal Data:** b Karsamaki, Finland, October 7, 1959; m 1987, Gerardus. **Education:** Univ Oulu, Finland, MD, 1984, PhD (med biochem), 1985, Docent, 1993. **Professional Experience:** PROF, WAYNE STATE UNIV, 2004-; ASSOC PROF, WAYNE STATE UNIV, 1995-2004; Univ Oulu, Finland, 1993; Vis scientist, MeiKai Univ, Japan, 1992; res asst prof biochem, Thomas Jefferson Univ, 1990-1995; instr, Thomas Jefferson Univ, 1986-1990; fel, Thomas Jefferson Univ, 1986; fel, Rutgers Med Sch, 1985-1986; Teaching asst med biochem, Univ Oulu, Finland, 1981-1987. **Memberships:** AAAS; Am Soc Human Genetics; NY Acad Sci; Am Genetic Asn. **Research Statement & Publications:** Genetic basis of connective tissue disorders, including familial aortic aneurysms, intracranial aneurysms, the Blau syndrome and Schyder's crystalline corneal dystrophy. **Mailing Address:** Ctr Molecular Med & Genetics Wayne State Univ, Eugene Applebaum Bldg, Rm 3125, 259 Mack Ave, Detroit, MI 48201. **Fax:** 313-577-5218. **E-Mail:** kuivan@sanger.med.wayne.edu

KUIVILA, HENRY GABRIEL, organic chemistry; deceased, see previous edition for last biography

KUJATH, MAREK RYSZARD, DYNAMICS OF MACHINES, MACHINE DESIGN. **Personal Data:** b Poznan, Poland, April 25, 1950; Canadian citizen. **Education:** Warsaw Tech Univ, MASc, 1974; Polish Acad Sci, PhD (mech eng), 1980. **Professional Experience:** PROF, DEPT MECH ENG, DALHOUSIE UNIV, as of 2002; vis prof, Can Space Agency, 1990-1991; assoc prof mech eng, Tech Univ Ns, beginning 1982; postdoctoral mech eng, Norweg Inst Technol, 1981-1982; proj mgr, Cent InstIndust Safety, Poland, 1978-1981. **Memberships:** Am Soc Mech Engrs. **Research Statement & Publications:** Machine dynamics; machine design; time varying systems; robotics, rotors and vibration; signal processing; space structures; space mechanics. **Mailing Address:** Dept Mech Eng, Dalhousie Univ, PO Box 1000, Halifax, NS B3J 2X4, Can. **Fax:** 902-494-6711. **E-Mail:** marek.kujath@dal.ca

KUKAL, GERALD COURTNEY, LOG ANALYSIS, PETROLEUM GEOLOGY. **Personal Data:** b St Louis, Mo, October 1, 1943; m 1963, c 4. **Education:** Southwest Mo Univ, BS, 1967; Purdue Univ, MS, 1973. **Professional Experience:** SR GEOLOGIST & FORMATION EVALUATION SPECIALIST, CORP EDUC RESOURCES INC, 1977-; field engr, Dresser Atlas, 1973-1977; teaching asst & instr geol, Purdue Univ, 1970-1973; teacher geol, Riverview Gardens Sch Dist, 1967-1970. **Memberships:** Soc Prof Well Log Analysts; Am Asn Petrol Geologists. **Research Statement & Publications:** Development of log interpretation systems for low-permeability gas reservoirs. **Mailing Address:** CER Corp, 1126 53rd ct, West Palm Beach, FL 33407. **Fax:** 561-841-0820.

KUKALOVA-PECK, JARMILA, EARTH SCIENCES. **Professional Experience:** PROF, DEPT EARTH SCI, CARLETON UNIV, CAN, as of 2006. **Memberships:** Fel Royal Soc Can. **Mailing Address:** Dept Earth Sci, Carleton Univ, Ottawa, ON K1S 5B6, Can.

KUKES, SIMON G, CATALYSIS IN PETROLEUM. **Personal Data:** b Moscow, USSR, American citizen; m 1980, c 2. **Education:** Moscow Inst Chem Technol, BS & MS, 1970; USSR Acad Sci, Moscow, PhD (chem), 1973. **Professional Experience:** PRES, TYUMEN OIL CO, as of 2003; CHMN & BD DIR, YUKOS, as of 2003; vpres, Mem Mgt Bd, YUKOS, 1996-1998; alt counr, Pet Div, Am Chem Soc, 1989-; res assoc catalysus Petrol, Amoco Oil Co, 1986-1996; res assoc catalysis petrol, Phillips Petrol, 1984-1987; srchemist, Phillips Petrol, 1982-1984; chemist, Phillips Petrol, 1979-1982; Res chemist, Metalo-OrgInst, USSR Acad Sci, 1973-1977; postdoctoral org & phys chem, Rice Univ, 1971-1982. **Research Statement & Publications:** Petroleum; catalysis; kinetics; author of over 30 publications; awarded 110 US patents. **Mailing Address:** Tyumen Oil Co, 18/2, Schipok St, Moscow, 115093, Russia.

KUKI, ATSUO, QUANTUM BIOPHYSICS, MULTI-COMPONENT ELECTRON TRANSFER SYSTEMS. **Personal Data:** b Chicago, Ill, c 1. **Education:** Yale Univ, BS, 1978; Stanford Univ, PhD (phys chem), 1985. **Professional Experience:** AT, ALANEX CORP, as of 1997; NSF presidential young investr, 1989; Camille & Henry Dreyfus Foundteacher-scholar, 1989; ASST PROF CHEM, CORNELL UNIV, 1986-; NIH-NRSA postdoctoralfel, Univ Ill, 1985-1986. **Memberships:** Am Phys Soc; Am Chem Soc; Biophys Soc. **Research Statement & Publications:** Chemical physics of electron transfer reactions; electronically active peptides of de novo design; quantum theory of electronic interactions; biophysics. **Mailing Address:** Alanex Corp, 40919 Encyclopedia Circle, Fremont, CA 94538. **Fax:** 510-897-4189.

KUKIN, IRA, ENVIRONMENTAL CHEMISTRY. **Personal Data:** b New York, NY, April 4, 1924; m 1954, c 3. **Education:** City Col New York, BS; Harvard Univ, MA, 1950, PhD (inorg chem), 1951. **Honorary Degrees:** Yeshiva Univ, 1986. **Professional Experience:** PRES & FOUNDER, APOLLO CHEM CORP, 1963-; res dir & scientist, res Sonneborn Chem & Ref Corp, Div Witco Corp, 1957-1963; groupleader, Gulf Res & Develop Co, 1951-1957; Instr chem, Sampson Col, 1946-1948; chmn, Apollo TechnolInt. **Memberships:** Am Chem Soc. **Research Statement & Publications:** Energy conservation; pollution control; consultant with government agencies on air pollution. **Mailing Address:** 45 Edgemont Rd, West Orange, NJ 07052-2037.

KUKKONEN, CARL ALLAN, RESEARCH & DEVELOP MANAGEMENT, SPACE MICROELECTRONICS. **Personal Data:** b Duluth, Minn, January 25, 1945; m 1968, c 2. **Education:** Univ Calif, Davis, BS, 1968; Cornell Univ, MS, 1971, PhD (physics), 1975. **Professional Experience:** CHMN, CHIEF EXEC OFFICER, CO-FOUNDER, VIASPACE TECHNOL, 1998; dir, Ctr Space Microelec Technol, Jet Propulsion Lab, Calif Inst Technol, 1984-1998; res staff, Ford Motor Co, 1977-1984; res assoc physics, Purdue Univ, 1975-1977. **Memberships:** Am Phys Soc. **Research Statement & Publications:** Theory of electrons in metals; direct injection diesel engines; design and development of small high speed direct injection diesel engines for passenger cars; technological assessment of hydrogen as an alternative automotive fuel; concurrent computing; neural networks; solid state devices; photonics; custom microcircuits; supercomputing and computer sciences; solid state and theoretical physics; electrical engineering. **Mailing Address:** Viaspace Technol, 2400 Lincoln Ave, Pasadena, CA 91001. **Fax:** 626-296-6311.

KUKLA, MICHAEL JOSEPH, PHARMACEUTICAL CHEMISTRY. **Personal Data:** b Frankfort, Ger, September 23, 1947; American citizen; m 1969, c 3. **Education:** Kalamazoo Col, BA, 1969; Ohio State Univ, PhD (org chem), 1974. **Professional Experience:** VIS FAC, DEPT CHEM, HAVERFORD COL, as of 2006; vis asst prof, Dept Chem, haverford Col, as of 2003; SR SCIENTIST, MCNEIL PHARMACEUT, 1978-; res investr chem, G DSearle & Co, 1974-1978. **Memberships:** Am Chem Soc. **Research Statement & Publications:** Synthesis of heterocyclic ring systems which may alter functions in the central nervous system. **Mailing Address:** Dept Chem, Haverford Col, 370 Lancaster Ave, Haverford, PA 19041-1392.

KUKOLICH, STEPHEN GEORGE, PHYSICAL CHEMISTRY, STRUCTURAL CHEMISTRY. **Personal Data:** b Appleton, Wis, February 3, 1940; m, c 3. **Education:** Mass Inst Technol, BS, 1962, DSc(physics), 1966. **Professional Experience:** Res Corp grant, 1988-1990; PROF CHEM, UNIV ARIZ, 1979-; Am Chem Soc Petrol Res Fund, 1977-1981, 1983-1986, 1989-1991, 1991-1994 & 1994-1996; assoc prof, Univ Ariz, 1974-1979; NSF res grants, 1970-1979, 1983-1986 & 1996-1999; asst prof chem, Mass Inst Technol, 1969-1974; asst prof chem, Univ Ill, 1968-1969; instr physics, Mass Inst Technol, 1966-1968; res asst physics, Mass Inst Technol, 1962-1966. **Memberships:** Am Phys Soc; Sigma Xi; Am Chem Soc. **Research Statement & Publications:** Structures of weakly bound complexes, high resolution microwave spectroscopy; microwave measurements of structures of transition metal complexes; quadrupole coupling measurements; electron paramagnetic resonance spectroscopy of biological molecules; molecular relaxation studies; published over 165 articles. **Mailing Address:** Dept Chem, Univ Ariz, Old Chem 316, Tucson, AZ 85721-0041. **Fax:** 520-621-8407. **E-Mail:** kukolich@u.arizona.edu

KUKSIS, ARNIS, BIOCHEMISTRY. **Personal Data:** b Valka, Latvia, December 3, 1927; Canadian citizen; m Inese; c Anda, Davis, Lauris & Inga. **Education:** Iowa State Col, BS, 1951, MS, 1953; Queen's Univ, Ont, PhD (biochem), 1956. **Honorary Degrees:** Dr (Hon) Causa, Univ Turku, Finland, 2000. **Honors & Awards:** Fel, Royal Soc of Canada, 1988; Foreign Member, Latvian Academy of Sci, 1996; fel, Am Oil Chemist Soc, 2000; Dutton Award, Am Oil Chemists Soc, 2001. **Professional Experience:** Vis prof, Ensbana, Dijon, France, 1992; vis prof, Japanese Soc Prom Sci, 1981; prof, Dept Biochem & Banting & Best Dept Med Res, C H Best Inst, Univ Toronto, 1974-1997; DIR, REGIONAL GAS CHROMATOGRAPHY/MASS SPECTROMETRY LAB, MED RES COUN CAN, 1972-; from asst prof to assoc prof, Banting & Best Dept Med Res, 1965-1974; career investr, Med Res Coun Can, 1960-1997; asst prof, Queen's Univ, Ont, 1960-1965; res assoc biochem, Queen's Univ, Ont, 1958-1959; res fel org chem, Royal Mil Col, Ont, 1956-1958; fel coun arteriosclerosis, Am Heart Asn. **Memberships:** Am Oil Chem Soc; Can Biochem Soc; Am Soc Biol Chemists; Am Inst Nutrit; fel Royal Soc Can; Can Soc Biochem & Molecular Biol; Am Soc Biochem & Molecular Biol. **Research Statement & Publications:** Composition of food fats; mechanics of lipid digestion and absorption; metabolism of triacylglycerols and phospholipids, sterols and bile acids; chromatographic separations and mass spectrometry of lipids. **Mailing Address:** Banting & Best Dept Med Res, C H Best Inst Univ Toronto, 112 Col St, Toronto, ON M5G 1L6, Can. **Fax:** 416-978-8528. **E-Mail:** arnis.kuksis@utoronto.ca

KULA, ERIC BERTIL, PHYSICAL METALLURGY. **Personal Data:** b New York, NY, July 4, 1929; m 1951, Gulli; c Judith C Walklet & Lara E. **Education:** Mass Inst Technol, BS, 1948, MS, 1952, ScD(metall), 1954. **Professional Experience:** RETIRED; div dir, US Army Mat Technol Lab, Watertown, Mass, 1988-1993; br chief, US Army Mat Technol Lab, Watertown, Mass, 1973-1993; supvry metallurgist, US Army Mat Technol Lab, Watertown, Mass, 1956-1993; asst, Mass Inst Technol, 1950-1954; asst, Royal Inst Technol, Sweden, 1949-1950; metallurgist, Downarvet's Steelworks, Sweden, 1948-1949. **Memberships:** Am Soc Metals; Am Inst Mining, Metall & Petrol Engrs. **Research Statement & Publications:** Mechanical behavior of metals; high strength steels; failure analysis. **Mailing Address:** 23 Mason St, Lexington, MA 02173. **E-Mail:** ekula@aol.com

KULACKI, FRANCIS ALFRED, MECHANICAL ENGINEERING, HEAT TRANSFER, ENERGY. **Personal Data:** b Baltimore, Md, May 21, 1942; m Jane; c Sarah A (Huff) & Nancy B. **Education:** Ill Inst Technol, BSME, 1963, MSGE, 1966; Univ Minn, PhD (mech eng), 1971. **Honors & Awards:** ASME Dedicated Service Award 2004, Int Tech George Taylor Distiguished Service Awd 2001. **Professional Experience:** PROF MECH ENG, UNIV MINN, 1993-; dean, Inst Technol, 1993-1995; dean, Col Eng, Colo State Univ, 1986-1993; prof & chmn, Dept Mech & Aerospace Eng, Univ Del, Newark, 1980-1985; from asst prof to assoc prof mech eng, Ohio State Univ, 1971-1980; Consult to indust, govt labs & litigation. **Memberships:** Sigma Xi; fel Am Soc Mech Engrs; fel AAAS. **Research Statement & Publications:** Heat and mass transfer; convective heat transfer; hydrodynamic stability; electrofluid mechanics; nuclear waste disposal and storage; technology-based education; engineering education; energy resources, technology and policy. **Mailing Address:** Dept Mech Eng, Univ Minn Inst Technol, Minneapolis, MN 55455. **Fax:** 612-624-5230. **E-Mail:** kulacki@me.umn.edu

KULAK, GEOFFREY LUTHER, STRUCTURAL ENGINEERING. **Personal Data:** b Edmonton, Alta, November 26, 1936; m, c 2. **Education:** Univ Alta, BS, 1958; Univ Ill, Urbana, MS, 1961; Lehigh Univ, PhD (civil eng), 1967. **Honors & Awards:** Moiseff Award, Am Soc Civil Engrs, 1985. **Professional Experience:** PROF EMER CIVIL ENG, UNIV ALTA, as of 2006; invited prof, Swiss Fed Inst Technol, 1984; prof civil eng, Univ Alta, beginning 1970; mem, Res Coun Struct Conn, 1967-; assoc prof, NS Tech Col, 1967-1970; res asst, Lehigh Univ, 1964-1967; asst prof, NS Tech Col, 1962-1964; instr civil eng, Univ Alta, 1961-1962; design engr, bridge br, Prov Alta Dept Hwy, 1958-1960. **Memberships:** Am Soc Civil Engrs; Can Stand Asn. **Research Statement & Publications:** Strength and behavior of steel structures; strength of high-strength bolts and welds; behavior of welded and bolted connections; fatigue strength of steel structures. **Mailing Address:** Dept Civil & Environ Eng, Univ Alta, 3-063 Markin/CNRL Natural Resources Eng Facil, Edmonton, AB T6G 2W2, Can. **Fax:** 780-492-0249. **E-Mail:** geoff.kulak@ualberta.ca

KULAKOWSKI, BOHDAN T, MECHANICAL ENGINEERING. **Education:** Warsaw Tech Univ, MS, 1966; Polish Acad Sci, PhD, 1972. **Professional Experience:** PROF MECH ENG, PA STATE UNIV, 1991-; assoc prof mech eng, Pa State Univ, 1982-1991. **Mailing Address:** Dept Mech Eng, Pa State Univ, 331 Reber Bldg, University Park, PA 16802. **Fax:** 814-865-3039. **E-Mail:** btk1@psu.edu

KULAKOWSKI, ELLIOTT C, SCIENCE ADMINISTRATION. **Personal Data:** b February 18, 1951; c 3. **Education:** Fairfield Univ, BS, 1972; Long Island Univ, MS, 1975; Lehigh Univ, PhD (biochem), 1980. **Professional Experience:** RES ADMIN & MGT, STRATEGY GROUP INC, as of 2006; DIR SPONSORED PROJECTS, UNIV UTAH, as of 2006; dir, Res & Technol Develop, Albert Einstein Healthcare Network, as of 1998; assoc vprovost health sci res develop, Sch Med, Temple Univ, beginning 1989; assoc prof biochem, Sch Med, Temple Univ, beginning 1989; sr sci adv, NatHeart, Lung & Blood Inst, 1986-1989; sci prog adminr Ischemic Heart Dis, Specialized Ctr Res, 1985-1986; sci prog adminr res grants, Cardiac Dis Br, Div Heart & Vascular Dis, Nat HeartLung & Blood Inst, 1984-1988; prog officer biochem, Cardiac Functions Br, 1983-1984; staff fel, Hypertension Endocrine Br, NIH, 1980-1983; res assoc & instr chem, Lehigh Univ, 1977-1980; clin chemist, Upjohn Co, 1974-1977; res & teaching asst, Mich State Univ, 1974; med technologist, Cent Gen Hosp, Plainview, NY, 1973. **Memberships:** Am Soc Pharmacol & Therapeut; Am Heart Asn; Nat Coun Univ Res Admin; Soc Res Admin. **Research Statement & Publications:** Cardiovascular pharmacology and metabolism; clinical biochemistry. **Mailing Address:** Univ Utah Off Sponsored Projects, Univ Utah, 1471 Federal Way, Salt Lake City, UT 84112. **E-Mail:** elliott.kulakowski@osp.utah.edu

KULANDER, BYRON RODNEY, ROCK FRACTURES, FORELAND FOLD BELTS. **Personal Data:** b Huntington, WVa, August 27, 1937; m 1968, c 1. **Education:** Kent State Univ, BS, 1962; WVa Univ, MS, 1964, PhD (geol), 1968. **Professional Experience:** PROF EMER, DEPT GEOL SCI, WRIGHT STATE UNIV, as of 2004; chmn geol, dept geol sci, Wright State Univ, beginning 1989; consult, Oryx Energy Co, 1989-1990; consult, Amoco Corp, 1986-1989; consult, BDM Corp, 1985-1988; consult, Terra Tek, 1983-1985; consult, Mound Labs, 1981-1982; prof geol, dept geolsci, Wright State Univ, 1979-; vis prof, Dept Geol, WVa, Univ, 1978; consult, Dept Energy, 1976-1978; coop res geologist, WVa Geol Surv, 1969-; from asst prof to assoc profgeol, Dept Geol, Alfred Univ, 1966-1979. **Memberships:** Am Asn Petrol Geologists; fel Geol Soc Am. **Research Statement & Publications:** Rock fractures-fractured reservoirs, including application of fractography to fractured core and outcrop rocks; structural geology of foreland fold belts; application of geophysics to detached sedimentary rocks and basement structures. **Mailing Address:** Dept Geol Sci, Wright State Univ, 260 Brehm Lab, Dayton, OH 45435-0001. **E-Mail:** bkulander@desire.wright.edu

KULANDER, KENNETH CHARLES, MOLECULAR COLLISIONS, MULTIPHOTON PROCESSES. **Personal Data:** b St Paul, Minn, November 26, 1943; m 1969, Monica. **Education:** Cornell Col, BS (math), 1965; Univ Minn, PhD (phys chem), 1972. **Professional Experience:** Mem, Tech Coun, Optical Soc Am, 1997-; chmn, Few Body Sci Topical Group, Am Phys Soc, 1996-1997; vis fel, Univ Colo, 1993-1994; GROUP LEADER, THEORETATOMIC & MOLECULAR PHYSICS GROUP, LAWRENCE LIVERMORE NAT LAB, 1986-; physicist, Physics Dept, 1985-1986; chemist, Chem Dept, 1982-1985; Vis scientist, MaxPlanck Inst Quantum Optics, Garching, Ger, 1982-1983; staff scientist, Laser Prog, LawrenceLivermore Nat Lab, 1978-1982; sr res assoc, Daresbury Lab, Sci Res Coun, Warrington, Eng, 1975-1978; Fel, Chem Dept, Univ Minn, 1972-1975. **Memberships:** Fel Am Phys Soc; Optical Soc Am. **Research Statement & Publications:** Atomic and molecular collision theory; multiphoton processes; laser interactions with atoms and molecules; development of computational methods for quantum dynamics. **Mailing Address:** Lawrence Livermore Nat Lab, PO Box 808, Livermore, CA 94551. **Fax:** 925-423-7228. **E-Mail:** kulander@llnl.gov

KULASH, DAMIAN J, MATERIALS SCIENCE. **Education:** Sloan Sch Mgt, Mass Inst Technol, BS, PhD. **Professional Experience:** RETIRED; pres & chief exec officer, Eno Transportation Foundation, 1995-2003. **Mailing Address:** Nat Res Coun, 2101 Constitution Ave NW, Washington, DC 20418. **Fax:** 202-334-1961.

KULAWIEC, ROBERT JOSEPH, HOMOGENEOUS CATALYSIS, ORGANOMETALLIC CHEMISTRY. **Personal Data:** b St Louis, Mo, August 1, 1962; m 1987, Suzanne. **Education:** Univ Calif, Berkeley, BS, 1984; Yale Univ, MS, 1986, PhD (chem), 1989. **Professional Experience:** ASST PROF CHEM, GEORGETOWN UNIV, 1992-; Dreyfus new fac award, Camille & Henry Dreyfus Found, 1992; NIH res fel, Dept Chem, Stanford Univ, 1989-1992. **Memberships:** Am Chem Soc; Sigma Xi. **Research Statement & Publications:** Synthetic organic and organometallic chemistry; application of transition metal complexes in selective synthesis. **Mailing Address:** Dept Chem, Georgetown Univ, Washington, DC 20057-1227. **Fax:** 202-687-6209.

KULCINSKI, GERALD LA VERN, NUCLEAR ENGINEERING, MATERIALS. **Personal Data:** b LaCrosse, Wis, October 27, 1939; m 1961, Janet; c 3. **Education:** Univ Wis, BS, (chem eng), 1961, MS, (nuclear eng), 1962, PhD (nuclear eng), 1965. **Honors & Awards:** Curtis McGraw Res Award, Am Soc Eng Educ, 1978; Outstanding Achievement Award, Am Nuclear Soc, 1980; Leadership Award, Fusion Power Assocs, 1992; NASA Pul Serv Medal, Nat Acad Eng, 1993. **Professional Experience:** ASSOC DEAN FOR RES, COL ENG, UNIV WI, 2001-; Bechtel, San Francisco, 1989 & 1995; Grainger chair nuclear engrs, 1984-; assoc ed, Nuclear Engr & Design, 1983-; vis scientist, Karlsruhe Nuclear Res Ctr, Ger, 1977; DIR FUSION TECHNOL INST, UNIV WIS, 1974-; PROF NUCLEAR ENG, UNIV WIS, 1972-; adj prof nuclear eng, Ctr Grad Study, Richland, 1968-1971; sr res scientist & group leader radiation damage reactor mats, Battelle Northwest Lab, 1965-1972; asst scientist nuclear rockets, Los Alamos Sci Lab, 1963. **Memberships:** Nat Acad Eng; fel Am Nuclear Soc; Am Inst Aeronaut & Astronaut. **Research Statement & Publications:** Fission reactors; fusion reactor design; materials; radiation damage; environmental effects; nuclear power. **Mailing Address:** Dept Eng Physics, Col Eng, Univ Wis, 2620 Eng Hall 1500 Eng Dr, Madison, WI 53706-1691. **Fax:** 608-263-4499, 608-262-6400. **E-Mail:** kulcinski@engr.wisc.edu

KULCZYCKI, ANTHONY, IMMUNOCHEMISTRY, ALLERGY. **Personal Data:** b Easton, Pa, December 17, 1944; m 1969, Judy; c Alexander & Amy-Elizabeth. **Education:** Princeton Univ, AB, 1966; Harvard Univ, MD, 1970. **Honors & Awards:** J D Lane Award, USPHS, 1974. **Professional Experience:** ASSOC PROF MOLECULAR MICROBIOL, WASH UNIV, 1985-; ASSOC PROF MED, DIV ALLERGY & IMMUNOL, SCH MED, WASH UNIV, 1982-; asst prof microbiol& immunol, Dept Med, Div Allergy & Immunol, Sch Med, Wash Univ, 1980-1985; attending physician, Dept Med, Barnes Hosp, St Louis, beginning 1977; Assoc investr, Howard Hughes Med Inst, Wash Univ, 1977-1984; from instr to asst prof med, Dept Med, Div Allergy & Immunol, SchMed, Wash Univ, 1976-1982; NIH res fel, Sch Med, Wash Univ, 1974-1976; resassoc, Nat Inst Arthritis, Metab & Digestive Dis, NIH, Bethesda, 1972-1974; med resident, StateUniv NY, Buffalo, 1971-1972; Intern med, Buffalo Gen Hosp, & E J Meyer Hosp, 1970-1971. **Memberships:** fel Am Acad Allergy & Immunol; Am Soc Clin Invest; Collegium Internationale Allergologicum. **Research Statement & Publications:** Chronic hives; infantile colic; allergic reactions to aspartame (NutraSweet). **Mailing Address:** Div Allergy & Immunol, Sch Med, Wash Univ, 660 S Euclid Ave; Campus Box 8122, St Louis, MO 63110. **Fax:** 314-454-5140. **E-Mail:** akulczyc@wustl.edu

KULCZYCKI, LUCAS LUKE, PEDIATRICS. **Personal Data:** b Jurjampol, Poland, August 19, 1911; American citizen; c 2. **Education:** Univ Lwow, BSc, 1934, DVM, 1936; Univ Edinburgh, MB BCh, 1944, MD, 1946; Univ London, dipl pub health, 1948; Royal Col Physicians & Surgeons Can, cert pediat, 1958. **Honors & Awards:** Physician's Recognition Award, AMA, 1969, 1981 & 1984. **Professional Experience:** Prof pediat, Med Sch, Georgetown Univ, 1978-; DIR, CYSTIC FIBROSISCTR, GEORGETOWN UNIV HOSP, 1977-; prof clin pediat, Med Sch, Georgetown Univ, 1973-1978; assoc prof, Georgetown Univ, 1967-1972; consult pediatrician, Children's Convalescent Hosp, Wash, DC, 1963-1975; dir, Cystic Fibrosis Ctr, Children's Hosp Nat Med Ctr, 1962-1977; guest worker, NIH, 1962-1968; consult pediatrician & co-worker, Children's Hosp, Boston, Mass, 1962-1968; clin assoc prof pediat, Georgetown Univ, 1962-1967; consult pediatrician, Dept Health Maine & Maine Med Ctr, Portland, 1958-1968; clin dir, Wrentham State Sch, 1957-1958; instr, Harvard Med Sch, 1956-1962; asst physician, Children's Hosp Med Ctr, Boston, 1955-1962; res fel, Children's Hosp Med Ctr, Boston, 1955-1961; residential training pediat, Children's Hosp Med Ctr, Boston, 1953-1955; med dir pub health, Local Health Unit, Dept Health, Winnipeg, Can, 1951-1953; asst physician, London Exec Coun, Eng, 1947-1950; resident physician med & surg, Raigmore Hosp, Dept Health, Scotland, 1946-1947. **Memberships:** Fel Am Acad Pediat; fel Am Col Chest Physicians; AMA; fel NY Acad Sci; honmem Polish Pediat Soc; fel Royal Soc Health; Lung & Thoracic Soc; Brit Med Asn; Can MedAsn; fel Am Pub Health Asn; fel Am Lung Asn. **Research Statement & Publications:** Cystic fibrosis in caucasians and negroes; cyctic fibrosis, tuberculosis and allergy; upper respiratory tract in cystic fibrosis; hearing and cystic fibrosis; bronchoscopy and bronchial lavage in cystic fibrosis; impact of cystic fibrosis on the patient and his parents; patient home care; mucus retention and over-inflation as a basic pulmonary complication in cystic fibrosis; use and abuse of antibiotics in management of cystic fibrosis. **Mailing Address:** Children's Hosp, Nat Med Ctr, Washington, DC 20009.

KULFINSKI, FRANK BENJAMIN, ecology, environmental studies; deceased, see previous edition for last biography

KULGEIN, NORMAN GERALD, ENGINEERING, APPLIED PHYSICS. **Personal Data:** b Bridgeport, Conn, March 6, 1934; m 1960, c 2. **Education:** Mass Inst Technol, BS, 1955, MS, 1956; Harvard Univ, PhD (eng, appl physics), 1960. **Professional Experience:** CONSULT SCIENTIST, LOCKHEED PALO ALTO RES LABS, 1991-; lectr, Stanford Univ, 1969-1970; staff scientist & mgr aerophys group, Aerospace Sci Lab, 1967-1991; lectr, Univ Santa Clara, 1963-; res scientist, Aerospace Sci Lab, 1960-1967. **Memberships:** Am Inst Aeronaut & Astronaut; Combustion Inst. **Research Statement & Publications:** High temperature viscous flows; radiation gas dynamics; hydrodynamics; reentry vehicle hardening technology; infrared systems analysis. **Mailing Address:** 711 Gailen Ave, PaloAlto, CA 94303.

KULHAWY, FRED HOWARD, GEOTECHNICAL ENGINEERING. **Personal Data:** b Topeka, Kans, September 8, 1943; m 1966, Gloria. **Education:** NJ Inst Technol, BSCE, 1964, MSCE, 1966; Univ Calif, Berkeley, PhD (civil eng), 1969. **Honors & Awards:** Edmund Friedman Young Eng Award, Am Soc Civil Eng, 1974; Walter L Huber Res Prize, Am Soc Civil Eng, 1982; Cross-Can lectr, Can Geotech Soc, 1988; Outstanding Service Award, ADSC, 1993; Ardaman Lectr, Univ Fla, 1995; Casagrande Lectr, Boston Soc Civil Engrs, 1996; Mueser Rutledge Lectr, ASCE Met Section, 1999; Miles Kersten Lectr, Minnesota Geotech Soc, 2001; Converse Ward Lectr, ASCE NJ Section, 2002; Martin Kapp Lectr, ASCE Met Section, 2004; George Sowers Lectr, ASCE Georgia Section, 2005; Stanley Wilson Lectr, Univ Washington, 2005; Honorary Member, Am Soc Civil Eng, 2005; Karl Terzaghi Award, Am Soc Civil Eng, 2005; Norman Medal, Am Soc Civil Eng, 2005. **Professional Experience:** Chung Biu fel, Univ Hong Kong, 2000; vis prof, Natl Univ Singapore, 1998; vis prof, Univ Hong Kong, Univ Queensland, 1993; Maunsell fel, Univ Hong Kong, 1993; vis prof, Univ Cambridge, Univ Sydney, Univ Hawaii, 1985-1986; Fulbright Scholar, Univ Cambridge, 1985; PROF CIVIL ENG, CORNELL UNIV, 1981-; assoc prof, Cornell Univ, 1976-1981; Numerous consults to govt agencies, indust firms, eng & archit consults & attys, 1969-; from asst prof to assoc prof, Syracuse Univ, 1969-1976; assoc, Raamot Assoc PC, 1969-1971; res asst & jr res specialist, Univ Calif, Berkeley, 1966-1969; soils engr, Storch Engrs, 1966; Asst inst civil eng, Newark Col Eng, 1964-1966. **Memberships:** Honorary Member Am Soc Civil Eng; fel Geol Soc Am; Int Soc Rock Mech; Int Soc Soil Mech & Geotechnical Eng; Int Asn Eng Geol; hon tech aff ADSC-Int Asn of Found Drilling. **Research Statement & Publications:** Numerical and reliability methods applications in geotechnical engineering; soil and rock stress-strain-strength behavior; model and full-scale behavior of geotechnical structures; foundation engineering. **Mailing Address:** Sch Civil & Environ Eng, Cornell Univ Hollister Hall, Ithaca, NY 14853-3501. **Fax:** 607-255-9004. **E-Mail:** fhk1@cornell.edu

KULICK, JEFFREY H, COMPUTER DESIGN. **Education:** Ny Univ, BSc, 1966; Univ Pa, MSC, 1970 & PhD (Elec Eng), 1972. **Professional Experience:** PROF, DEPT ELEC & COMPUT ENG, UNIV ALA, HUNTSVILLE, as of 2005. **Research Statement & Publications:** Development of real-time embedded systems. **Mailing Address:** Dept Elec & Comput Eng, Univ Ala-Huntsville, 301 Sparkman Dr, Huntsville, AL 35899. **E-Mail:** kulick@ece.uah.edu

KULIER, CHARLES PETER, SYNTHETIC ORGANIC CHEMISTRY, PHARMACEUTICAL CHEMISTRY. **Personal Data:** b Chicago, Ill, August 11, 1935; m 1959, Beatrice; c David & Nancy. **Education:** Ill Wesleyan Univ, BS, 1957; Univ Kans, PhD (org chem), 1962. **Honors & Awards:** F Spencer Mortimer, Chem Award. **Professional Experience:** RETIRED; sr info scientist, Pfizer Inc, 1993-2004; info serv, Warner-Lambert Co, 1990-1992; res assoc, Warner-Lambert Co, 1976-1989; sr scientist, Warner-Lambert Co, 1972-1975; sr res chemist, Warner-Lambert Co, 1970-1972; from assoc res chemist to res chemist, Warner-Lambert Co, 1963-1970; res assoc & fel org chem, Johns Hopkins Univ, 1962-1963; asst chem, Univ Kans, 1957-1961; asst chem, Ill Wesleyan Univ, 1956-1957. **Memberships:** Am Chem Soc. **Research Statement & Publications:** Organic synthesis of heterocyclic compounds and natural products; use of newer reaction methods for preparation of organic compounds of potential medicinal use; process research; information science and systems. **Mailing Address:** 1181 Oak Hampton Rd, Holland, MI 49424-2663. **Fax:** 616-392-8916. **E-Mail:** charles.kulier@pfizer.com

KULIK, MARTIN MICHAEL, PLANT PATHOLOGY. **Personal Data:** b Brooklyn, NY, April 20, 1932; m 1962, c 3. **Education:** Cornell Univ, BS, 1954; La State Univ, MS, 1956, PhD (plant path), 1959. **Professional Experience:** RETIRED; plant pathologist, soybean & alfalfa res lab, Agr Res Serv, 1990-1996; res plant pathologist, Germplasm Qual & Enhancement Lab, 1986-1990; res plant pathologist, Seed Res Lab, 1972-1985; res plant pathologist, Seed Qual Lab, 1963-1972; plant pathologist, Seed Br, USDA, 1961-1963. **Research Statement & Publications:** Diseases of seeds and forages. **Mailing Address:** 5100 Moorland Lane, Bethesda, MD 20814.

KULIKOWSKI, CASIMIR A, ARTIFICIAL INTELLIGENCE, BIOMEDICAL COMPUTING. **Personal Data:** b Hertford, Eng, May 4, 1944; m Christine; c Michael E & Victoria A. **Education:** Yale Univ, BE, 1965, MS, 1966; Univ Hawaii, PhD (elec eng), 1970. **Professional Experience:** BD GOV, RUTGERS UNIV, as of 2005; PROF, DEPT COMPUT SCI, RUTGERS UNIV, as of 2005; dir lab, Comput Sci Dept, Rutgers Univ, 1985-1996; chmn, Comput Sci Dept, Rutgers Univ, 1984-1990; from asst prof to prof, Comput Sci Dept, Rutgers Univ, 1970-1990. **Memberships:** Inst Med-Nat Acad Sci; fel Am Acad Med Informatics; AAAS; Am Asn Artificial Intel; fel Inst Elec & Electronics Engrs. **Research Statement & Publications:** Knowledge-based systems; biomedical imaging; pattern recognition and-machine learning; medical decision analysis; interpretation of DNA and protein structures; multimedia systems modeling and simulation. **Mailing Address:** Dept Comp Sci, Rutgers Univ, Piscataway, NJ 08854. **Fax:** 732-445-0537. **E-Mail:** kulikowsi@cs.rutgers.edu

KULKA, JOHANNES PETER, pathology, psychiatry; deceased, see previous edition for last biography

KULKARNI, ANAND K, ELECTRONIC MATERIALS, ELECTRONIC DEVICES. **Personal Data:** b Gokak, Karnatak, India, October 18, 1946; m 1971, c 1. **Education:** Karnatak Univ, Dharwad, India, BS, 1967, MS, 1970; Iowa State Univ, Ames, MS, 1975; Univ Nebr-Lincoln, PhD (eng), 1979. **Honors & Awards:** Ralph R Teetor Educ Award, Soc Automotive Engrs, Inc, 1986. **Professional Experience:** ASSOC PROF ELECTRONICS, MICH TECHNOL UNIV, as of 2005; proj dir, Elec Eng Dept, 1991-1993; dir grad prog, Mich State, 1991-1992; proj dir, Mich State, 1990-1991; co-investr, NSF, 1989-1992; co-investr, Ramtron Corp, 1987-1988; co-investr, Int Bus Mach, 1985-1986; Prin investr, NSF, 1983-1986; asst prof, Mich Technol Univ, 1980-1985; vis asst profelectronics, Mich Technol Univ, 1978-1980; res asst elec eng, Univ Nebr-Lincoln, 1976-1978; res& teaching asst physics, Iowa State Univ, 1973-1975; jr sci asst, govt orgn, 1971-1972; asst engr, Pvt Electronics Co, 1971. **Memberships:** Inst Elec & Electronics Engrs; Am Vacuum Soc; Int Soc Hybrid Microelectronics. **Research Statement & Publications:** Ohmic contacts and schottky contacts to gallium arsenide; ferroelectric thin film memory devices; solder joints and metal/ceramic contacts; diamond thin films and thin film sensors. **Mailing Address:** Dept Elec Eng, Mich Technol Univ, 1400 Townsend Dr, Houghton, MI 49931. **Fax:** 906-487-2949. **E-Mail:** akkulkar@mtu.edu

KULKARNI, ANANT SADASHIV, CLINICAL PHARMACOLOGY, IMMUNOLOGY. **Personal Data:** b Kolhapur, India, July 31, 1934; m 1960, c 2. **Education:** Podar Med Col, GFAM (MD), 1958; Univ Minn, PhD (pharmacol), 1966. **Professional Experience:** PRES, AM CTR CLIN RES, 1985-; dir clin res, gen med & neuropsychiat, 1978-1985; assoc dir, G D Searle & Co, 1975-1977; sect head neuropsychiat & assoc dir clin res, Abbott Lab, 1973-1975; clin monitor, Med Dept, Dow Chem Co, 1971-1973; clin asst prof, MedCtr, Ind Univ, Indianapolis, 1971-1973; Vis lectr, Med Ctr, Ind Univ, Indianapolis, 1968-1971; res pharmacologist, Dow Human Health Res Lab, 1967-1971; sr scientist, Mead Johnson Res Ctr, 1965-1967; res asst pharmacol, Univ Minn, 1962-1965; res asst pharmacol, Univ Wis, 1961-1962; surg resident, St Anthony's Hosp St Louis, 1960-1961; Intern med, Sisters Hosp, Buffalo, NY, 1959-1960. **Memberships:** Acad Psychosom Med; Am Soc Pharmacol & Exp Therapeut; Sigma Xi; AmPsychol Asn; Am Pharmaceut Asn. **Research Statement & Publications:** CNS pharmacology; clinical psychopharmacology; animal behavior; rheumatology; drug behavior interactions. **Mailing Address:** 608 Carter St, Libertyville, IL 60048.

KULKARNI, ASHOK BALKRISHNA, GENE KNOCKOUT MOUSE TECHNOLOGY, MOLECULAR ENDOCRINOLOGY. **Personal Data:** b Satara, India, November 5, 1947; American citizen; m 1975, Chhaya; c Monica, Deepti & Vandance. **Education:** MS Univ, Baroda, India, PhD (biochem), 1980. **Professional Experience:** SR STAFF FEL, NIH, 1987-; res scientist, Columbia Univ, NY, 1982-1987; sci officer, Haffkine Inst, Bombay, 1976-1982. **Memberships:** Fedn Am Socs Exp Biol; NY Acad Sci. **Research Statement & Publications:** Molecular biology. **Mailing Address:** NIDCR, NIH, Bldg 30 Rm 529 30 Convent Dr, Bethesda, MD 20892-4326. **Fax:** 301-435-2888. **E-Mail:** akulkarni@dir.nidcr.nih.gov

KULKARNI, BIDY, MATERNAL & CHILD HEALTH, ABNORMAL PREGNANCY. **Personal Data:** b Maharashtra, India, April 18, 1930; American citizen; m 1957, Suman Sane; c Neela & Bob. **Education:** Univ Poona, India, MS, 1956, PhD, 1962. **Honors & Awards:** Outstanding New Citizen of Year, 1973. **Professional Experience:** CONSULT RES & EDUC SERVS 1992-; assoc prof obstet & gynec, Chicago Med Sch, 1980-1993; Sr sci officer, Cook County Hosp, 1979-1993; dir, reproductive endocrinol, Cook County Hosp, Chicago, 1979-1919 9 3; consult, Gottlieb Mem Hosp, 1977-1981; assoc prof obstet &gynec & dir reproductive endocrinol, Stritch Sch Med, Loyola Univ Chicago, 1973-1979; dir perinatal ctr labs, Forster G McGaw Hosp, Maywood, 1973-1977; asst prof obstet & gynec, Pritzker Sch Med, Univ Chicago, 1970-1973; Dir labs, Sect Gynecic Endocrinol, Michael Reese Hosp & Med Ctr, 1970-1973; sect chief, Dept Endocrinol, Div Clin Sci, Southwest Found Res & Educ, 1967-1970; sr sci officer biochem, Nat Chem Lab, Poona, 1966-1967; fel org chem, Nat Res Coun Can, 1964-1966; fel steroid biochem, Clark Univ, and Worcester found for exp biol 1961-1964; sr sci asst steroid chem, Nat Chem Lab, Poona, India, 1956-1961; Jr sci asst biochem & steroid chem, Nat Chem Lab, Poona, India, 1952-1956. **Memberships:** fel Endocrine Soc; Soc Study Reproduction; Asn Clin Scientist; Nat Acad Clin Biochem; Chicago Gynec Soc; Am Fertil Soc; Int Fertil Soc; Am Soc Reproductive Med Life mem. **Research Statement & Publications:** Natural and contraceptive steroid hormone metabolism in man and nonhuman primates; methods in hormone assays involving competitive protein binding and radioimmunoassays; clinical endocrinology fetoplacental function population control research; steroid biochemistry; abnormal pregnancy; contraception; clinical chemistry. **Mailing Address:** Nine S 155 Nantucket, Darien, IL 60561. **Fax:** 630-963-4692. **E-Mail:** subidaykay@msn.com

KULKARNI, KISHOR M, METALLURGY. **Education:** Ill Inst Technol, PhD. **Professional Experience:** PRES, ADVAN METALWORKING PRACTICES INC, IND, as of 2006. **Mailing Address:** Advan Metalworking Practices Inc, 12227 Crestwood Dr, Carmel, IN 46033-4322. **E-Mail:** kulkarni@advancedmetalworking.com

KULKARNI, PADMAKAR VENKATRAO, NUCLEAR CHEMISTRY, RADIOPHARMACEUTICALS. **Personal Data:** b Inamhongal, India, November 1, 1942; m 1968, Suma; c Brinda, Vishwas & Moha. **Education:** Janata Col, BS, 1963; Rensselaer Polytech Inst, MS, 1972, PhD (chem), 1973. **Professional Experience:** PROF RADIOL, SOUTHWESTERN MED SCH, UNIV TEX, as of 2006; assoc prof, Southwestern Med Sch, Univ Tex, beginning 1984; Radiopharmaceut scientist, Parkland Mem Hosp, Dallas, Tex, 1976-; asst prof, SouthwesternMed Sch, Univ Tex, 1976-1984; isotope chemist, Abbott Diag Div, Abbot, Ill, 1973-1976; radiopharmaceut specialist, Cambridge Nuclear Radiopharm Corp, Mass, 1972-1973; sci officer, Bhabha Atomic Res Ctr, Bombay, 1964-1968; sci officer trainee radiochem, Bhabha Atomic Res Ctr, Bombay, 1963-1964. **Memberships:** Am Chem Soc; Soc Nuclear Med; AAAS; Soc Magnetic Resonance Med. **Research Statement & Publications:** Development of radioisotope labeled compounds as radiopharmaceuticals for diagnostic purposes; development of radioimmunoassay systesm; diagnostic nuclear cardiology; radioisotope tracer techniques in health sciences; contrast agents for magnetic resonance imaging. **Mailing Address:** Radiol Imaging Ctr, Univ Tex, 5323 Harry Hines Blvd, Dallas, TX 75235-9058. **Fax:** 214-648-4538. **E-Mail:** pkulka@mednet.swmed.edu

KULKARNI, PRASAD SHRIKRISHNA, PHARMACOLOGY, OPHTHALMOLOGY. **Personal Data:** b Karad, India, May 22, 1943; American citizen. **Education:** Downstate Med Sch, State Univ NY, NY, MS, 1971, PhD, 1974. **Professional Experience:** PROF DEPT OPHTHAL, UNIV LOUISVILLE, 1993-; assoc prof, DeptOphthal, Univ Louisville, 1987-1993; asst prof, dept ophthal, Columbia Univ, 1980-1987; resassoc, dept ophthal, Columbia Univ, 1978-1980; teaching fel, dept ophthal, Columbia Univ, 1976-1978; fel, Wash Univ, St Louis, Mo, 1974-1976. **Memberships:** Am Soc Pharmacol & Exp Therapeut; Int Soc Eye Res; Asn Res Vision &Ophthal; Brit Pharmacol Soc; Inflam Res Asn. **Research Statement & Publications:** Role of prostaglandins, leukotrienes and other arachidonic acid metabolites in ocular inflammation; mechanism of steroidal and nonsteroidal anti-inflammatory agents in ocular inflammation; retinal microcirculation physiology and pathology. **Mailing Address:** Dept Opthal, Univ Louisville, 301 E Muhammad Ali Blvd, Louisville, KY 40202. **E-Mail:** pskulk01@athena.louisville.edu

KULKARNI, SHRINIVAS R, RADIO ASTRONOMY. **Education:** Indian Inst Technol, New Delhi, MS, 1978; Univ Calif, Berkeley, PhD (astron), 1983. **Honors & Awards:** Alan T Waterman Award, NSF, 1992. **Professional Experience:** YOUNG & ACTIVE RES, ASSOC UNIVS INC, as of 2006; MCARTHUR PROF ASTRON & PLANETARY SCI, CALIF INST TECHNOL, 2001-; vis prof, Mass Inst Technol, 2000-2001; prof astron & planetary sci, Calif Inst Technol, 1996-2001; from asst prof astron to prof astron, Calif Inst Technol, 1987-1995; Robert A Millikan fel. **Memberships:** Nat Acad Sci. **Mailing Address:** Dept Astron & Planetary Sci, Calif Inst Technol, M/C 105-24, Pasadena, CA 91125. **E-Mail:** srk@astro.caltech.edu

KULKARNI, SUDHIR RAJARAM, CHRONIC FORMULATIONS, THICK FILM CONDUCTORS. **Personal Data:** b Bombay, India, November 11, 1951; American citizen; m 1980, Vandana; c Tyaj & Ruta. **Education:** MS Univ, Baroda, India, BE, 1974; Indian Inst Technol, Kanpur, MTech, 1976; OreGrad Ctr, PhD (mat sci), 1985. **Professional Experience:** DIR, PROD DEVELOP GROUP, AVX CORP, 1996-; mgr, Assembly & PkgLab, 1994-1996; sr mem, AVX Corp, 1990-1994; sr res scientist, Ceramated Inc, 1988-1989; mem tech staff, AVX Corp, 1987-1990; res scientist, Ceramated Inc, 1986-1988; sr res engr, Asia Brown Boveri, 1976-1980. **Memberships:** Am Ceramic Soc. **Research Statement & Publications:** Electronic ceramics; developing formulations for various applications; developed thick film conductors for various applications. **Mailing Address:** AVX Corp, PO Box 867 17th Ave S, Myrtle Beach, SC 29575.

KULKARNI, VITTHAL SHRINIWAS, LIPID BIOPHYSICAL CHEMISTRY, TRANSMISSION ELECTRON MICROSCOPY. **Personal Data:** b Hangandi, India, July 7, 1957; m 1985, Anuvadha; c Girindra, Prajacta & Chaitrali. **Education:** Shivaji Univ, India, BSc, 1977, MSc, 1979; Univ Pune, India, PhD (chem), 1984. **Professional Experience:** ASSOC RES SCIENTIST, YALE UNIV, 1997-; Vanderbilt Univ, 1990-1992; Univ Minn, 1992-1997; res assoc, Jeol Ltd, Tokyo, 1988-1990; res asst prof, Univ Provence, France, 1984-1985. **Memberships:** Am Chem Soc; Am Oil Chemists Soc; Micros Soc Am. **Research Statement & Publications:** Exploring microstructural self-assemblies of lipids and sufactants; exploring their formations and applications in biotechnology; physical chemistry of biliary lipids. **Mailing Address:** Brady Mem Lab B130 Dept Path, Sch Med Yale Univ, New Haven, CT 06520-8023. **Fax:** 203-737-1064. **E-Mail:** vitthal.kularni@yale.edu

KULKARNY, VIJAY ANAND, FLUID DYNAMICS, APPLIED PHYSICS. **Personal Data:** b Karwar, India, May 3, 1947. **Education:** Indian Inst Technol, Bombay, BTech, 1969; Calif Inst Technol, MS, 1970, PhD (aeronaut), 1975. **Professional Experience:** MEM TECH STAFF, ENG SCI LAB, TRW DEFENSE & SPACE SYSTSGROUP, 1978-; consult, TRW Defense & Space Systs Group, 1978; instr aeronaut, Calif Inst Technol, 1976-1977; from res fel to sr res fel aeronaut, Calif Inst Technol, 1975-1978. **Memberships:** Am Phys Soc; Sigma Xi. **Research Statement & Publications:** Gas dynamics; acoustics; shock waves and associated linear and nonlinear wave phenomena in multidimensions and inhomogeneous media; dynamics of vortex interactions and vorticity dominated flows; flow and acoustics of high energy pulsed gas lasers. **Mailing Address:** TRW Inc, Manley Ford, CA 90274-4449.

KULKE, BERNHARD, ELECTRON BEAMS, DIAGNOSTICS. **Personal Data:** b Freiburg, Ger, November 29, 1932; American citizen; m 1962, c 2. **Education:** Univ Colo, BS, 1955; Stanford Univ, MS, 1960, PhD (microwave electronics), 1965. **Professional Experience:** CONSULT, 3M & ELECTRON BEAM MODELING, proj engr, Beam ResProg, 1984-1993; group leader accelerator technol, Lawrence Livermore Nat Lab, Univ Calif, 1974-1984; chief radar beacon sect, Dept Transp, Cambridge Univ, 1970-1974; physicist, Electronics Res Ctr, NASA, 1967-1970; asst prof elec eng, Syracuse Univ, 1965-1967; mem techstaff, Bell Tel Labs Inc, 1955-1958. **Memberships:** Inst Elec & Electronics Engrs; Am Phys Soc. **Research Statement & Publications:** Design and construction of state-of-the-art, high current, induction linear accelerator; X-band, cyclotron resonance oscillator; experimental, 100 kilowatt, traveling wave klystron; electron beam diagnostics, antenna design, radar systems analysis and solid state device characterization; magnet design. **Mailing Address:** 518 Bavarian Ct, Lafayette, CA 94549. **Fax:** 510-299-1440.

KULKOSKY, PAUL JOSEPH, PHYSIOLOGICAL PSYCHOLOGY. **Personal Data:** b Newark, NJ, March 3, 1949; m 1978, Tanya. **Education:** ColumbiaCol, BA, 1971, MA, 1972; Univ Wash, PhD (psychol), 1975. **Professional Experience:** PROF PSYCHOL, COLO STATE UNIV, as of 2006; exec comt, Undergrad Psychol Prog, 1991-1994; coun, Undergrad Psychol Prog, 1990-; from vchair to chair, Psychol Sci Sect, Southwestern & Rocky Mountain Div, AAAS, 1990-1992; regional liaison, Rocky Mountain Area, 1990-1991; PROF PSYCHOL, UNIV SOUTHERN COLO, 1989-; consortium Aquariums, Univs & Zoos, 1989-; chair, Dept Psychol, 1988-1991; bd adv, Pueblo Zool Soc, 1988-1991; bd dir, Pueblo Zool Soc, 1985-1988; prin investr, NIH grant, 1984-; from asst prof to assoc prof, Univ Southern Colo, 1982-1989; from res assoc to instr, Cornell Univ Med Col, 1980-1982; affil prof psychol, Am Univ, 1977-1980; staff fel, Nat Inst Alcohol Abuse & Alcoholism, 1976-1980. **Memberships:** Psychonomic Soc; Soc Neuroscience; Int Soc Biomed Res Alcoholism; Sigma Xi; NY Acad Sci; Soc Ingestive Behav; Am Psychol Soc; AAAS; Int Brain Res Orgn. **Research Statement & Publications:** Regulatory behaviors in mammals, including the learned and physiological controls of ingestive behaviors. **Mailing Address:** Dept Psychol, Colo State Univ, Pueblo, CO 81001. **Fax:** 719-549-2705. **E-Mail:** paul.kulkosky@colostate-pueblo.edu

KULL, FREDERICK CHARLES, RESEARCH ADMINISTRATION. **Personal Data:** b Newark, NJ, April 10, 1919; m 1943, Marguerite; c 5. **Education:** Villanova Univ, BS, 1941; Ind Univ, MA, 1949; Univ Mich, PhD (bact), 1952; Am Bd Med Microbiol, dipl. **Professional Experience:** RETIRED; Glaxo Wellcome co, Res Triangle Park, NC, beginning 1995; vpres, Exec Serv Corp Carolinas, 1990-2001; consult, Glaxo Inc, 1986-1995; consult, Nat Serv Exec Corp, 1985-1990; dir admin, res, develop & med, Burroughs Wellcome Co, 1977-1985; adj prof, Sch Pharm, Univ NC, 1972-1992; dir sci info ctr, CIBA-Geigy Pharmaceut Co, 1961-1968; dir bact, CIBA-Geigy Pharmaceut Co, 1959-1961; dir virol, CIBA-Geigy Pharmaceut Co, 1958-1959; instr, Rutgers Univ, 1955-1958; sr bacteriologist, CIBA-Geigy Pharmaceut Co, 1952-1958; from asst to instr, Univ Mich, 1949-1951; asst bact, Ind Univ, 1947-1949; chemist, Sherwin-Williams Co, NJ, 1941-1943. **Memberships:** Am Acad Microbiol; Am Soc Microbiol; Sigma Xi; Drug Info Asn. **Research Statement & Publications:** Medical information; documentation; biological sciences; virology; enzymology. **Mailing Address:** 3804 St Marks Rd, Durham, NC 27707-5013.

KULL, FREDRICK J, ENZYMOLOGY. **Personal Data:** b March 9, 1935; m Barbara; c F Jon & Carrie L. **Education:** Kent State Univ, BS, 1960; Ohio State Univ, MS, 1962, Brandeis Univ, PhD (biochem), 1967. **Professional Experience:** ASSOC PROF EMER BIOL SCI, STATE UNIV NY, BINGHAMTON, 1991-; acad coordr, Off Campus Col, State Univ NY, 1985-1989, 1991; dir biochem, State Univ NY, 1975-1984; from asst to assoc prof biol sci, State Univ NY, 1969-1991; fel, Oak Ridge Nat Lab, Oak Ridge, 1967-1969; vis prof chem. **Memberships:** Am Chem Soc Biol Chem Div; AAAS; Sigma Xi; Fedn Am Soc Exp Biol; Am Soc Biochem & Molecular Biol. **Mailing Address:** State Univ NY, 260 Poverty Lane, Lebanon, NH 03766-1432.

KULL, LORENZ ANTHONY, NUCLEAR PHYSICS. **Personal Data:** b Chicago, Ill, December 25, 1937; m 1985, c 2. **Education:** Ill Inst Technol, BSc, 1963; Mich State Univ, PhD (physics), 1967. **Professional Experience:** CONSULT, 1996-; pres & chief oper officer, Sci Applns Int Corp, 1988-1996; mem, Air Force Studies Bd, 1984-1990; exec vpres, Sci Applns Int Corp, 1979-1988; vpres &mgr appl sci & technol group, Sci Applns Int Corp, 1975-1979; physicist, Sci Applns Int Corp, 1969-1975; Physicist, Gulf Gen Atomic, Inc, 1967-1969. **Memberships:** Am Phys Soc; Am Nuclear Soc; Inst Elec & Electronics Engrs. **Research Statement & Publications:** Development of nuclear materials assay instrumentation; experimental studies of direct particle transfer reactions with light nuclei; experimental studies of photoneutron cross-sections, threshold photoneutrons and photo fission; modeling and analysis of nuclear fuel cycle systems; design of military electronics, components and systems. **Mailing Address:** 2018 Demayo Rd, Del Mar, CA 92014.

KULLBACK, JOSEPH HENRY, MATHEMATICAL STATISTICS. **Personal Data:** b Washington, DC, July 16, 1933; m 1960, c 3. **Education:** George Wash Univ, BA, 1955; Stanford Univ, MS, 1957, PhD (math statist), 1960. **Professional Experience:** CHIEF STAFF SCIENTIST, GRUMMAN DATA SYSTS INC, 1981-; Proflectr, George Wash Univ, 1977-; math statistician, US Naval Res Lab, 1967-1981; Mathematician, Stanford Res Inst, 1960-1967. **Memberships:** Armed Forces Commun Electronics Asn. **Research Statement & Publications:** Operations research; simulation techniques. **Mailing Address:** Grumman Data Systs, 5201 Leesburg Pike Ste 701, Falls Church, VA 22041.

KULLBERG, RUSSELL GORDON, botany; deceased, see previous edition for last biography

KULLEN, MARK K, OPTICS, PHYSICS. **Education:** Wayne State Univ, BS, 1984, MS, 1987. **Professional Experience:** ENG SCIENTIST, GEN DYNAMICS, 1989-. **Memberships:** Am Phys Soc. **Mailing Address:** 36719 Bobrich, Livonia, MI 48152.

KULLER, ROBERT G, MATHEMATICS. **Personal Data:** b Baltimore, Md, November 29, 1926; m 1959, c 5. **Education:** Swarthmore Col, AB, 1948; Univ Mich, MS, 1949, PhD (math), 1955. **Professional Experience:** RETIRED; assoc prof math, Northern Ill Univ, beginning 1968; assoc prof, WayneState Univ, 1965-1968; asst prof, 1961-1962 & Univ Colo, 1962-1965; vis lectr, Nat Taiwan Univ, 1960-1961; asst prof, Dartmouth Col, 1959-1960; from instr to asst prof, Wayne State Univ, 1955-1959; instr math, Dartmouth Col, 1953-1955. **Memberships:** Am Math Soc; Math Asn Am; Soc Indust & Appl Math. **Research Statement & Publications:** Functional analysis; computers in undergraduate mathematics curriculum. **Mailing Address:** Univ Northern Ill Univ, Dekalb, IL 60115.

KULLGREN, THOMAS EDWARD, MECHANICAL ENGINEERING. **Personal Data:** b Grand Rapids, Mich, April 10, 1941; m 1989, Elizabeth; c Kristin, Erin, Jeffrey & Ian. **Education:** USAF Acad, BS, 1964; Stanford Univ, MS, 1972; Colo State Univ, PhD (mech eng), 1976. **Professional Experience:** Dir, Ctr Appl Technol Res, Saginaw Valley State Univ, 1985 & Bus & Indust Develop Inst, 1988-1990; DEAN, COL SCI, ENG & TECHNOL, SAGINAW VALLEY STATE UNIV, 1984-; PROF MECH ENG, SAGINAW VALLEY STATE UNIV, 1984-; prof & actg head, USAF Acad, 1982-1984; prin investr, Wind Energy Res Proj, 1977-1984; vis scientist, Air Force Mat Lab, 1977; from asst prof to assoc prof eng mech, USAF Acad, 1976-1982. **Memberships:** Am Soc Mech Engrs; Am Soc Engr Educ; Soc Mfg Engrs. **Research Statement & Publications:** Numerical solution of three-dimensional problems in fracture mechanics; international wind energy resource assessments and feasibility studies; technology transfer and economic development. **Mailing Address:** Col Sci, Eng & Technol, Saginaw Valley State Univ, 7400 Bay Rd, Univ Center, MI 48710-0001. **Fax:** 517-790-2717. **E-Mail:** kullgren@pardis.svsu.edu

KULLMAN, DAVID ELMER, MATHEMATICS EDUCATION, HISTORY OF MATHEMATICS. **Personal Data:** b Kenosha, Wis, May 27, 1940; m 1965, Karen; c Bradley & Kristen. **Education:** Northwestern Univ, BA, 1962; Cornell Univ, MA, 1963; Univ Kans, PhD (math), 1969. **Honors & Awards:** Meritorious Serv Award, Math Asn Am, 1999. **Professional Experience:** Dept chair, Miami Univ, 1993-1999; PROF MATH, MIAMI UNIV, 1981-; from asst prof to assoc prof, Miami Univ, 1969-1981; high sch teacher, Ill, 1963-1965. **Memberships:** Nat Coun Teachers Math; Math Asn Am; Can Soc Hist & Philos Math; Am Math Soc. **Research Statement & Publications:** History of mathematics; problem solving and applications in school mathematics. **Mailing Address:** Dept Math & Statist, Miami Univ, Oxford, OH 45056. **Fax:** 513-529-1493. **E-Mail:** kullmade@muohio.edu

KULLNIG, RUDOLPH K, PHYSICAL ORGANIC CHEMISTRY. **Personal Data:** b Kirchberg, Lower Austria, October 2, 1918; American citizen; m 1954, Charlotte. **Education:** Univ Ottawa, Can, PhD (chem), 1958. **Professional Experience:** RETIRED; sr fel, Rensselaer Polytech Inst, Troy, NY, 1990-1993; adj prof, Rensselaer Polytech Inst, Troy, NY, 1983-1993; sect head, Sterling Res Group, 1968-1990; res chemist & group leader, Sterling Res Group, 1964-1968; asst res chemist, Sterling Res Group, 1958-1964; chemist, Bell-Craig Ltd, Ont, 1952-1955. **Memberships:** Emer mem Am Chem Soc; emer mem Am Crystallog Asn. **Research Statement & Publications:** Nuclear magnetic resonance spectroscopy; indoles and other heterocyclic compounds; single cryst x-ray diffraction. **Mailing Address:** Mc Clellan Rd, Nassau, NY 12123-9743. **E-Mail:** kullnr@rpi.edu

KULM, LAVERNE DUANE, GEOLOGICAL OCEANOGRAPHY. **Personal Data:** b Mobridge, SDak, February 17, 1936; m 1962. **Education:** Monmouth Col, BA, 1959; Ore State Univ, PhD (oceanog), 1965. **Professional Experience:** PROF EMER OCEANOG, ORE STATE UNIV, as of 2004; prof oceanog, Ore State Univ, 1974-; Fel, Marathon Oil Co, 1971; From asst prof to assoc prof, Ore State Univ, 1964-1974. **Memberships:** AAAS; Soc Econ Paleontologists & Mineralogists; fel Geol Soc Am; Am GeophysUnion. **Research Statement & Publications:** Continental margin structure, tectonics, sedimentation; deep-sea sedimentation. **Mailing Address:** Col Oceanog, Ore State Univ, 104 Ocean Admin Bldg, Corvallis, OR 97331-5503. **Fax:** 541-737-2064. **E-Mail:** lkulm@oce.orst.edu

KULMAN, HERBERT MARVIN, ENTOMOLOGY. **Personal Data:** b Sayre, Pa, June 12, 1929; div, c 2. **Education:** Pa State Univ, BS, 1952; Duke Univ, MF, 1955; Univ Minn, PhD, 1960. **Professional Experience:** PROF EMER ENTOMOL, DEPT ENTOMOL, UNIV MINN, as of 2003; prof, Univ Minn, St Paul, 1972-1989; NSF res group, Korea &Taiwan; Latin Inst Forestry, Merida Vez, 1970; assoc prof entom, Univ Minn, St Paul, 1969-1972; from asst to assoc prof forest entom, Va Polytech Inst, 1962-1969; asst prof entom, WVa Univ, 1959-1962; entomologist, Southeastern Forest Exp Sta, USDA, 1956-1957. **Memberships:** Entom Soc Am. **Research Statement & Publications:** Forest entomology, especially biological control and damage evaluation. **Mailing Address:** 4071 Vt St, San Diego, CA 92103.

KULP, BERNARD ANDREW, PHYSICS. **Personal Data:** b Columbus, Ohio, August 3, 1923; m 1952, c 9. **Education:** Univ Minn, BEE, 1946; Ohio State Univ, MS, 1947, PhD (physics), 1955. **Professional Experience:** CHIEF SCIENTIST & DIR LABS, AIR FORCE SYSTS COMMAND, 1975-; chief scientist, Air Force Armament Lab, Eglin AFB, 1969-1975; physicist, Aerospace Res Lab, Wright-Patterson AFB, 1958-1969; physicist, Linde Co, 1955-1958; res engr, Battelle Mem Inst, 1948-1955; res metallurgist, Carnegie-Ill Steel Corp, 1947-1948; Asst, Ohio State Univ, 1946-1947. **Memberships:** Fel AAAS; Am Phys Soc; Am Defense Preparedness Asn. **Research Statement & Publications:** Solid state physics; radiation damage; electrooptics; ordnance engineering. **Mailing Address:** 13418 Queens Lane, Ft Washington, MD 20744.

KULPA, CHARLES FRANK, APPLIED MICROBIOLOGY IN ENVIRONMENTAL AREAS, GENE EXCHANGE IN MIXED CULTURES. **Personal Data:** b Jackson, Mich, January 1, 1944; m 1984, Loretta; c David, Andrew, Marlo & Edward. **Education:** Univ Mich, BS, 1966, MS, 1968, PhD (microbiol), 1970. **Professional Experience:** CHMN, DEPT BIOL SCI, UNIV NOTRE DAME, as of 2003; prin investr, Amoco Oil, beginning 1994; ASSOC DEAN, COL SCI, 1993-; prin investr, Chevron, beginning 1992; consult, Energy Biosysts, 1991-; PROF MICROBIOL, UNIV NOTRE DAME, 1991-; res assoc, Argonne Nat lab, beginning 1990; consult, Newmont Metall Serv, 1990-1993; consult, construct technol lab, 1989-; prin investr, Argonne Nat Lab, 1989-1994; consult, AmocoChem, 1981-1993; vis scientist, Kyoto Univ, 1981; from asst prof to assoc prof, Col Sci, 1972-1979; Staff fel, NIH, 1970-1972. **Memberships:** Am Soc Microbiol; Am Acad Microbiol; AAAS; Soc Indust Microbiol. **Research Statement & Publications:** Use of bacteria for waste remediation and biodesulfurization of petroleum distillates; investigation of genetic exchange within mixed cultures for the maintenance of biodegradative genes. **Mailing Address:** Dept Biol Sci, Univ Notre Dame, Notre Dame, IN 46556-0369. **E-Mail:** charles.f.kulpa.1@nd.edu

KULPA, JOHN E, JR, AERONAUTICS. **Personal Data:** b 1929. **Education:** Bloomfield High Sch, BS, 1946; Air Force Inst Technol, OH, MS. **Honors & Awards:** Gen Thomas D. White Space Trophy, 1980. **Professional Experience:** RETIRED; dir spec proj, Off Secy Air Force & dep comdr space oper, Space Div, Los Angeles Air Force Sta, Calif, 1973-1983. **Mailing Address:** 984 Via Rincon, Bloomfield, NJ 90274. **Fax:** 310-371-3175.

KULSKI, JULIAN E, ARCHITECTURE. **Professional Experience:** STAFF, JULIAN KULSKI ASSOCS, as of 2006. **Memberships:** fel Am Inst Architects. **Mailing Address:** Julian E Kulski Assocs, 5759 Varzara Rd, Marshall, VA 20115. **Fax:** 540-364-4700.

KULSRUD, RUSSELL MARION, PLASMA PHYSICS. **Personal Data:** b Lindsborg, Kans, April 10, 1928; m 1955, c 3. **Education:** Univ Md, BA, 1949; Univ Chicago, MS, 1952, PhD (physics), 1954. **Honorary Degrees:** MS, Yale Univ, 1966. **Professional Experience:** PROF EMER ASTROPHYS SCI, PRINCETON UNIV, as of 2004; prof astrophys sci, Princeton Univ, beginning 1967; prof appl sci & astron, Yale Univ, 1966-1967; head theoret sect, Plasma Physics Lab, 1964-1966; RCA Corp, 1960 & GenAtomic Div, Gen Dynamics Corp, 1960; sr res assoc, Proj Matterhorn, Princeton Univ, 1959-1964; Consult, Oak Ridge Nat Lab, 1955; Mem staff physics, Proj Matterhorn, PrincetonUniv, 1954-1959. **Memberships:** fel Am Phys Soc; Int Astron Union; Am Astron Soc. **Research Statement & Publications:** Plasma physics with application to controlled fusion reactor research; astrophysics. **Mailing Address:** Peyton Hall, Princeton Univ, Princeton, NJ 08544. **E-Mail:** rkulsrud@astro.princeton.edu

KULWICH, ROMAN, BIOCHEMISTRY. **Personal Data:** b New York, NY, October 18, 1925; m 1948, Lucile Warnock; c Mark R, Carol (Ladd) & Paul L. **Education:** Univ Fla, BS, 1949, PhD (animal nutrit), 1951. **Professional Experience:** CONSULT, 1978-; from asst to assoc dir extramural progs, Nat Inst Allergy & Infectious Dis, 1973-1978; asst for rev & eval, 1971-1973; health scientist adminr, Nat Ctr Health Serv Res & Develop, 1969-1971; endocrinol prog dir extramural prog, Nat Inst Arthritis & Metab Diseases, 1964-1969; scientist adminr, Nat Inst Child Health & Human Develop, 1963-1964; grants assoc, Div Res Grants, NIH, 1962-1963; biochemist & supvry chemist, Mkt Qual Res Div, Agr Mkt Serv, Plant Indust Sta, Beltsville, 1957-1962; Animal nutritionist & animal husbandman, Animal Husb Res Div, Agr Res Serv, USDA, 1951-1957. **Research Statement & Publications:** Nutritional and biochemical research on trace mineral and sulfur metabolism in laboratory and farm animals involving the use of radioactive tracers; body composition research involving 4-pi low level gamma ray measurements; biomedical science administration. **Mailing Address:** 9504 SE 107th Pl, Belleview, FL 34420.

KULWICKI, ANAHID, NURSING, MEDICINE. **Professional Experience:** PROF, SCH NURSING, OAKLAND UNIV, as of 2004; Fulbright grantee cardiovasc risk, Univ Jordan, Amman, Jordan, 1996. **Research Statement & Publications:** Cardiovascular risk assessment and risk reduction. **Mailing Address:** Sch Nursing, Oakland Univ, Rochester, MI 48309-4401. **Fax:** 248-370-4279. **E-Mail:** kulwicki@oakland.edu

KULWICKI, BERNARD MICHAEL, CHEMICAL ENGINEERING, MATERIALS SCIENCE. **Personal Data:** b Detroit, Mich, July 3, 1935. **Education:** Univ Detroit, BChE, 1958; Univ Mich, MSE, 1960, PhD (chem engr), 1963. **Professional Experience:** RETIRED; SR MEM TECH STAFF, ADVAN DEVELOP, TEX INSTRUMENTS INC, 1980-; distinguished mem tech staff, 1997-1998 Assoc ed, J Am Ceramic Soc, 1990-; br mgr active mat develop, Mat & Elec Prod Group, Mat & Controls Div, 1971-1979; sect leader, Tex Instruments Inc, 1969-1970; proj engr semiconductor mat res, Tex Instruments Inc, 1964-1969; res fel, Inst Solid State Physics, Czech Acad Sci, 1963-1964. **Memberships:** AAAS; Am Ceramic Soc; Mat Res Soc; fel Am ceram soc. **Research Statement & Publications:** Phase equilibria; thermodynamic and electrical properties of semiconducting materials; ferroelectric materials; thermistors; ceramic varistors; developed infrared dir materials for night vision apllications awarded 24 US patents(allareas). **Mailing Address:** PO Box 1407, North Attleboro, MA 02763-1407.

KUMAGAI, LINDY FUMIO, MEDICINE. **Personal Data:** b Rock Springs, Wyo, August 5, 1927; m 1952, c 3. **Education:** Univ Utah, BA, 1949, MS, 1950, MD, 1954. **Professional Experience:** EMER PROF INTERNAL MED, SCH MED, UNIV CALIF, DAVIS, as of 2000; mem, Endocrine Study Sect, Dept Health & Human Sci, NIH, beginning 1980; mem, Calif Bd Med Quality Assurance, beginning 1980; assoc ed, Endocrinol, 1973-1977; HEAD ENDOCRINE SECT, SCH MED, UNIV CALIF, DAVIS, 1969-; assoc prof, Sch Med, Univ Calif, Davis, 1969-1971; asst dean, Col Med, 1968-1969; chief radioisotope serv, 1961-1969; from instr to assoc prof, ColMed, 1958-1969; clin investr, Vet Admin Hosp, Salt Lake City, Utah, 1958-1961; asst residentmed, Univ Hosp, Utah, 1957-1958; USPHS res fel, Thorndyke Mem Lab, Boston City Hosp, Harvard Med Sch, 1955-1957; med intern, Mass Mem Hosp, 1954-1955; asst anat, Sch Med, Univ Utah, 1949-1954. **Memberships:** Endocrine Soc. **Research Statement & Publications:** Metabolism of adrenocortical and thyroidal hormones. **Mailing Address:** Dept Med-Endocrinol, Univ Calif Davis Med Ctr, 145A Med Sci IC, Sacramento, CA 95817-2201. **E-Mail:** lfkumagai@ucdavis.edu

KUMAI, MOTOI, CLOUD PHYSICS, EARTH SCIENCES. **Personal Data:** b Nagano, Japan, March 22, 1920; m 1948, Yamanouchi Mutsuko; c Keiko I & Etsuko (Azar). **Education:** Sci Univ Tokyo, BS, 1941; Hokkaido Univ, PhD (physics), 1957. **Professional Experience:** RES PHYSICIST, SCI & TECHNOL CORP, 1990-; res physicist atmosphericsci, US Army Cold Regions Res & Eng Lab, 1961-1990; res assoc cloud physics, Univ Chicago, 1958-1961; lectr, Hokkaido Univ, 1955-1958; Res assoc physics, Hokkaido Univ, 1942-1955. **Memberships:** Am Meteorol Soc; Sigma Xi; Japanese Soc Snow & Ice; Meteorol Soc Japan; ClayMinerals Soc. **Research Statement & Publications:** Physics of atmosphere, research on snow crystal nuclei, and ice fog nuclei; electron diffraction of ice and aerosols, and attenuation of infrared radiation; scanning electron microscopy and acid snow and rain. **Mailing Address:** 21 Marlyn Dr, Burnt Hills, NY 12027-9737.

KUMAMOTO, JUNJI, PHYSICAL ORGANIC CHEMISTRY. **Personal Data:** b Sacramento, Calif, May 9, 1924; m 1950, c 4. **Education:** Univ Calif, Los Angeles, BS, 1950; Univ Chicago, PhD (phys org chem), 1953. **Professional Experience:** EMER LECTR &

CHEMIST, UNIV CALIF, RIVERSIDE, 1966-; chemist, res lab, IBM Corp, 1960-1966; chemist, Shell Develop Co, 1955-1960; NSF grant, Harvard Univ, 1953-1955. **Memberships:** AAAS; Am Chem Soc; NY Acad Sci; Sigma Xi. **Research Statement & Publications:** Reaction mechanisms of phosphate ester hydrolysis; free radical-metal ion reactions; relationship between structure and spectra; thermodynamic basis for temperature breaks in arrhenius plots. **Mailing Address:** Dept Bot & Plant Sci, Univ Calif, Riverside, CA 92521-0001.

KUMAR, AJAY, FLUID MECHANICS. **Education:** Agra Univ BS, 1964; Univ Roorkee, BE, 1968; Indian Inst Sci, ME(aerodyn), 1970; Indian Inst Technol, Kanpur, India, PhD (aeronaut eng), 1974. **Professional Experience:** DIR, SYST ANAL & CONCEPTS DIRECTORATE, NASA LANGLEY RES CTR, as of 2006. **Memberships:** Am Inst Aeronaut & Astronaut. **Mailing Address:** Langley Res Ctr, NASA, Bldg 1209 Rm 131 PO Box 449, Hampton, VA 23681-2199. **Fax:** 757-864-1649. **E-Mail:** Ajay.Kumar-1@nasa.gov

KUMAR, AJIT, CELL BIOLOGY, MOLECULAR GENETICS. **Personal Data:** b Bihar, India, March 2, 1940; m 1971, c 1. **Education:** Univ Bihar, India, BSc, 1958, MSc, 1960; Univ Chicago, PhD (biol), 1968. **Professional Experience:** PROF, BIOCHEM & MOLECULAR BIOL, MED CTR, UNIV GEORGE WASH, as of 2004; guest res scientist, Lab Biochem, Nat Cancer Inst, NIH, beginning 1980; assoc prof genetics, Univ George Wash, beginning 1980; assoc prof biochem, Sch Med, Univ George Wash, beginning 1979; vis scientist, biochem, Univ Cambridge, 1977; asst prof, microbiol & molecular genetics, Harvard Med Sch, 1977; tutor, Biochem & Molecular Biol, Univ Harvard, 1977-1979; vis fel microbiol, Univ Uppsala, Sweden, 1971; res assoc, Harvard Med Sch, 1971-1975; fel biochem, Albert Einstein Col Med, 1968-1971. **Memberships:** Am Soc Cell Biol; Am Soc Biol Chemists. **Research Statement & Publications:** RNA protein complexes and their role in eukaryotic gene expression; published over 10 articles. **Mailing Address:** Dept Biochem & Molecular Biol Med Ctr George Wash Univ, Ross Hall 232, Washington, DC 20037. **Fax:** 202-994-8974. **E-Mail:** akumar@gwu.edu

KUMAR, ALOK, COMPUTER AIDED DESIGN. **Personal Data:** b Meerut, India, September 22, 1951; m 1980. **Education:** Indian Inst Technol, Kanpur, India, BTech, 1972, MTech, 1976; Univ Houston, PhD (mech eng), 1980. **Professional Experience:** ASST PROF MECH ENG, UNIV DEL, NEWARK, 1981-; asst prof mecheng, Univ Wis Platteville, 1979-1981; res & teaching fel, Univ Houston, 1976-1979; res & teaching asst, Indian Inst Technol, Kanpur, India, 1973-1976. **Memberships:** Am Soc Mech Engrs; Soc Mfg Engrs; Am Soc Eng Educ. **Research Statement & Publications:** Computer aided design; kinematics; robotics and mechanical manipulator characterization; design and control; mathematical modeling of manufacturing processes; biomechanics. **Mailing Address:** WVa Univ PO Box 4260, Morgantown, WV 26506.

KUMAR, ANAND, PSYCHIATRY. **Education:** Madras Med Col, MD, 1980. **Professional Experience:** PROF PSYCHIAT & DIR GERIAT AMBULATORY CARE PROGS, UNIV CALIF, LOS ANGELES, as of 2004. **Mailing Address:** Neuropsychiat Hosp, Univ Calif, 760 Westwood Plz, Los Angeles, CA 90095.

KUMAR, ANUP, COMPUTER SCIENCE. **Education:** Univ Allahabad, BE; Univ Man, MS, 1983; NC State Univ, PhD, 1989. **Professional Experience:** PROF, UNIV LOUISVILLE, as of 2006. **Mailing Address:** Univ Louisville, Louisville, KY 40292. **Fax:** 502-852-2594. **E-Mail:** a0kuma01@louisville.edu

KUMAR, ASHOK, MATHEMATICS. **Education:** Delhi Univ, India, BSc, MSc; Univ Houston, MS; Bowling Green State Univ, PhD (Maths). **Professional Experience:** PROF, DEPT MATHS & COMPUT SCI, VALDOSTA STATE UNIV, GA, as of 2006. **Mailing Address:** Dept Math & Comput Sci, Valdosta State Univ, Valdosta, GA 31698-0040. **Fax:** 229-219-1257. **E-Mail:** akumar@valdosta.edu

KUMAR, ASHOK, MATERIALS SCIENCE & ENGINEERING, ENVIRONMENTAL SCIENCE. **Personal Data:** m 1962, Rosetta Campbell; c Derek & Dana. **Education:** Bihar Univ, India, BS, 1958, Univ Calif, Berkeley, MS, 1962, PhD (eng), 1966. **Honors & Awards:** IR-100 Award, 1984. **Professional Experience:** Ed comt, J Thermal Spray, 1995-; SR SCIENTIST, CONSTRUCT ENG RESLAB, US ARMY CORPS ENGRS, 1993-; mem, pub affairs comt, Nat Assoc Corrosion Engrs, 1986-1989; Adj prof, Univ Ill, 1985-; BR CHIEF, CONSTRUCT ENG RES LAB, US ARMYCORPS ENGRS, 1973-; unit head, Martin Marietta Corp, 1968-1973; res engr, Gen MotorsCorp, 1966-1968; Teaching fel, Univ Calif, Berkeley, 1966-1968. **Memberships:** Fel Am Soc Metals; Am Ceramic Soc; Nat Asn Corrosion Engrs; Am Soc Testing&Mat. **Research Statement & Publications:** Materials science and engineering as applied to corrosion and coatings used in infrastructure; new technologies to remove lead based paint using thermal spray vitrification process from steel structures; ceramic coated anodes for corrosion protection. **Mailing Address:** US Army Corps of Engr, PO Box 9005, Champaign, IL 61826-9005. **Fax:** 217-373-7222. **E-Mail:** a-kumar@cecer.army.mil

KUMAR, BALASUBRAMANIAN SHIVA, HIGH ENERGY PHYSICS. **Personal Data:** b India. **Education:** India Univ, BS, 1977, MS, 1979; Yale Univ, MS, 1980, PhD (physics), 1986. **Professional Experience:** PROF PHYSICS, YALE UNIV, 1986-. **Memberships:** Am Phys Soc. **Research Statement & Publications:** High energy physics. **Mailing Address:** WNSL, Yale Univ 272 Whitney Ave, New Haven, CT 06520.

KUMAR, CIDAMBI KRISHNA, ASTROPHYSICS, ATOMIC PHYSICS. **Personal Data:** b Madras, India, September 24, 1937; m 1968, c 2. **Education:** Andhra Univ, India, BSc, 1957; Univ Wis, MS, 1965; Univ Mich, PhD (astron), 1969. **Professional Experience:** PROF PHYSICS & ASTRON, HOWARD UNIV, 1984-; res assoc, CarnegieInst Wash Dept Terrestrial Magnetism, 1973-; from asst prof to assoc prof, Howard Univ, 1972-1984; carnegie fel atomic physics & astrophys, Carnegie Inst Wash Dept TerrestrialMagnetism, 1970-1972; jr sci officer nuclear physics, AEC, India, 1958-1963. **Memberships:** Am Astron Soc; Sigma Xi. **Research Statement & Publications:** Spectrophotometry of galaxies and comets; beam-foil spectroscopy; radio astronomy. **Mailing Address:** Dept Physics & Astron, Howard Univ, Rm 213, 2355 Sixth St, Washington, DC 20059. **Fax:** 202-806-5830. **E-Mail:** ckumar@howard.edu

KUMAR, DAVID DEVRAJ, CHEMISTRY. **Honors & Awards:** Chem Pioneer Award, Am Inst Chemists, 2006. **Professional Experience:** PROF, FLA ATLANTIC UNIV, as of 2006. **Mailing Address:** Fla Atlantic Univ, 2912 Col Ave, Davie, FL 33314. **Fax:** 561-367-8971. **E-Mail:** david@fau.edu

KUMAR, DEVENDRA, LASER SPECTROSCOPY, OPTOGALVANIC & PHOTOACOUSTIC SPECTROSCOPY. **Personal Data:** b Delhi, India, September 14, 1944; m 1969, Usha; c Ajay. **Education:** Univ Delhi, India, BS, 1963, MS, 1965, PhD (physics), 1976. **Professional Experience:** Assoc prof chem, La State Univ, 1991-2000; asst prof, LA State Univ, 1986-1991; asst prof, Dept Physics, Southern Univ, Baton Rouge, 1986-1987; res assoc, LA State Univ, 1978-1985; lectr physics, Kirori Mal Col, Univ Delhi, 1968-1978; asst lectr, Kirori Mal Col, Univ Delhi, 1965-1968. **Memberships:** Inst Elec & Elecronics Engrs; Optical Soc Am; Am Chem Soc. **Research Statement & Publications:** Laser optogalvonic spectroscopy in dc and rf discharges; study of highly excited Rydberg states of atoms and simple molecules; laser photoacoustic spectroscopy. **Mailing Address:** Dept Chem, La State Univ, Baton Rouge, LA 70803.

KUMAR, GANESH N, POLYMER SCIENCE, CHEMICAL ENGINEERING. **Personal Data:** b Madras, India, October 4, 1948; m 1975, Prema; c Bharat & Ramya. **Education:** Univ Madras, BTech, 1970; Clarkson Col Technol, MS, 1972; Case Western ReserveUniv, PhD (polymer sci), 1975; MBA, 1988. **Honors & Awards:** Gold Medal, Univ Madras, 1970; Johnson Medal, Johnson & Johnson, 1992. **Professional Experience:** STAFF MEM, JOHNSON & JOHNSON MED KK, TOKYO, JAPAN; vpresres & develop, Vistakon Inc Jacksonville, Fla, 1987-; dir polymer sci & qual assurance, VistakonInc, Jacksonville, Fla, 1985-1987; dir polymer sci, Vistakon Inc, Jacksonville, Fla, 1983-1985; mgr polymer res, Johnson & Johnson Dent Prod Co, 1980-1981; sr res scientist, Johnson &Johnson Dent Prod Co, 1978-1980; assoc scientist, Xerox Corp, 1974-1978; res fel, CWRU, 1971-1974; res assistantship, Clarkson Univ, 1970-1971. **Memberships:** Am Chem Soc; Am Phys Soc; NAm Thermal Analysis Soc; Sigma Xi; AAAS. **Research Statement & Publications:** Polymer structure property relationships; polymer mechanical and rheological properties; polymer blends and composites. **Mailing Address:** Johnson & Johnson Med KK 3-2, Toyo 6-Chome, Kotoku Tokyo 135, Japan.

KUMAR, K RAVI, MANUFACTURING TECHNOLOGY. **Education:** Northwestern Univ, PhD. **Professional Experience:** PROF, DEPT INFO & OPER MGT, UNIV SC, 1986-; VICE DEAN, MARSHALL SCH BUS, UNIV SC, 1986-. **Mailing Address:** Dept Info & Oper Mgt, Marshall Sch Bus, Univ SC, Bridge Hall 401, Los Angeles, CA 90089-0809. **Fax:** 213-740-9273. **E-Mail:** ravi.kumar@marshall.usc.edu

KUMAR, K SHARVAN, HIGH TEMPERATURE STRUCTURAL MATERIALS & INTERMETALLICS, AEROSPACE LIGHTWEIGHT ALLOY DEVELOPMENT. **Personal Data:** b Hyderabad, India, October 12, 1956; m 1985, Seema. **Education:** Drexel Univ, Philadelphia, MS, 1981, PhD (mat eng), 1984. **Professional Experience:** PROF DIV ENG, BROWN UNIV, as of 2005; sr scientist, Martin Marietta Labs, beginning 1993; vis scientist, Wright-Patterson AFB, 1992; from scientist to sr scientist, Martin Marietta Labs, 1985-1992; fel mat, Drexel Univ, 1984-1985. **Memberships:** Mat Res Soc; Metals Soc; Minerals Metals & Mats Soc. **Research Statement & Publications:** Lightweight materials for aerospace applications, particularly hot structures including jet engine components, missile fins, leading edges of wings and nose cones for hypersonic transportation; fundamental mechanisms controlling the microstructure and mechanical properties of such materials; authorof 65 technical publications. **Mailing Address:** Brown Univ, Barus & Holley, 182 Hope St, Providence, RI 02912. **Fax:** 410-204-2100. **E-Mail:** sharvan_kumar@brown.edu

KUMAR, K S P, ELECTRICAL ENGINEERING. **Personal Data:** American citizen. **Education:** Purdue Univ, MS, 1961, PhD (elec eng), 1964. **Professional Experience:** PROF EMER ELEC & COMPUT ENG, UNIV MINN, as of 2006; prof elec & comput eng, Univ Minn, beginning 1964. **Memberships:** Inst Elec & Electronics Engrs; Am Soc Eng Educ. **Research Statement & Publications:** Adaptive control of processes; stochastic filtering algorithms; robotic control. **Mailing Address:** Dept Elec & Comput Eng, Univ Minn, Roseville, MN 55113. **E-Mail:** kumar@ee.umn.edu

KUMAR, KAPLESH, INERTIAL INSTRUMENTS. **Personal Data:** b Lucknow, India, November 9, 1947; m 1974, Savinder; c Priyadarshini & Ruchira. **Education:** Indian Inst Technol, Kanpur, BTech, 1969, Stevens Inst Technol, MS, 1971; MassInst Technol, ScD, 1975. **Honors & Awards:** Invention Disclosure Award, NASA. **Professional Experience:** FMA Technical Director/Task Leader 1998-; Mem, Int Mat Rev Comt, Am Soc Metals Int, 1992-; mem, Mat Tech Comt, PRIN MEM TECH STAFF, CHARLES STARKDRAPER LAB, INC, 1991-; Vis lectr, Am Soc Metals Int, 1989; chief, Mat Sci & Technol Sect, 1988-1991; chief, Mat Develop Sect, 1980-1988; Staff scientist, Charles Stark Draper Lab, Inc, 1975-1980. **Memberships:** Am Soc Metals Int; Am Inst Aeronaut & Astronaut. **Research Statement & Publications:** Samarium-transition-metal permanent magnets; metal matrix composites; ion implantation; chemical vapor deposition; dimensional stability; printed circuit board adhesion degradation; manganese-zinc ferrites; rotating electrical contacts; high Tc superconductors; interial instruments. **Mailing Address:** Charles Stark Draper Lab, 555 Technol Sq, Cambridge, MA 02139-3563. **E-Mail:** kkumar@draper.com

KUMAR, KRISHNA, NUCLEAR THEORY, COLLECTIVE MODELS, NUCLEAR FORCES. **Personal Data:** b Meerut, Uttar Pradesh, India, July 14, 1936; American citizen; m 1960, Katherine; c Jai Robert & Raj David. **Education:** Agra Univ, India, MS, 1955; Carnegie-Mellon Univ, MS, 1959, PhD (physics), 1964. **Professional Experience:** PROF EMER PHYSICS, TENN TECHNOL UNIV, 1999-; univ prof, Tenn Technol Univ, 1989-1999; prof, Tenn Technol Univ, 1980-1983; Nordito Prof, Univ Bergen, Norway, 1979-1980; scientist, AEC France, 1977-1979; assoc prof, Vanderbilt Univ, 1971-1977; physicist, Oak Ridge Nat Lab, 1969-1971; Onsted Fel, Niels Bohr Inst, Denmark, 1967-1967; res assoc, Mass Inst Technol, 1966-1967; Res assoc, Mich State Univ, 1963-1966. **Memberships:** Corresp mem Am Phys Soc; Planetary Soc; Sigma Xi. **Research Statement & Publications:** Unified theory of different aspects of nuclear structure; superheavy elements; nuclear and other fundamental forces; neutron stars. **Mailing Address:** Dept Physics, Tenn Technol Univ, Box 5051, Cookeville, TN 38505. **Fax:** 931-372-6351. **E-Mail:** kkaadmi_99@yahoo.com

KUMAR, MADHURENDU B, HYDROLOGY & WATER RESOURCES. **Personal Data:** b Khagaria, India, January 4, 1942; c 2. **Education:** Indian Sch Mines, Ranchi Univ, BS, 1961, MS, 1962, La State Univ, PhD (geol), 1972. **Honors & Awards:** Sir Henry Hayden Medal, Mining, Metal & Geol Inst India, 1978; PresidentialCert Merit Prof Dedication & Leadership, Am Inst Prof Geol, 1993. **Professional Experience:** VPRES, LA DEPT NATURAL RESOUCES, as of 2006; GEOLOGIST SUPVR, OIL & GAS DIV, OFF CONSERV, LA DEPT NATURAL RESOURCES, 1982-; vis prof, Univ Southwest La, 1979; vis prof, Southern Univ, 1978-1990; sr res assoc, La State Univ, 1978-1982; sr investr geohydrol, Inst Environ Studies, 1978-1982; vis prof, La State Univ, 1977-1978; res assoc geol, Inst Environ Studies, 1975; instrgeol & geography, City Univ New York, Hunter Col, 1974-1977; CONSULT, 1972-; sr exec oilgeologist, Oil India, Ltd, 1963-1969; sci officer, Atomic Mines & Minerals Div, Dept AtomicEnergy, Govt India, 1963; Instr, Indian Sch Mines, Minerol & Petrol, 1962-1963. **Memberships:** Am Asn Petrol Geologists; Am Inst Prof Geologists; fel Geol Soc Am. **Research Statement & Publications:** Subsurface of petroleum geology; salt domes; mine hydrology; petroleum resource conservation. **Mailing Address:** 5802 Highland Rd, Baton Rouge, LA 70808. **E-Mail:** mbkumar1@gmail.com

KUMAR, MAHESH C, VETERINARY MICROBIOLOGY, PUBLIC HEALTH. **Personal Data:** b Montgomery, West Pakistan, September 21, 1935; m 1985, Shashi; c Sanjai, Ashwin, Sheen & Salil. **Education:** Univ Bihar, BVSc & AH, 1958; Univ Minn, Minneapolis, MS, 1964, PhD (vetmicrobiol), 1967. **Professional Experience:** DIR VET SERV, E B OLSON FARMS, ATWATER, MINN, 1989-; dir, Koronis Mills, 1986-1989; dir, Mill Farms Co, Paynesville, Minn, 1984-1985; dir vet servs, MileHigh Turkey Hatchery, Longmont, Colo,

1976-1984; res assoc vet microbiol, Univ Minn, St Paul, 1967-1976; res fel, Univ Minn, St Paul, 1967; vet asst surg, Animal Husb Dept, Bihar, India, 1958-1961. **Memberships:** Am Vet Med Asn; Am Asn Avian Path; Poultry Sci Asn; Am Soc Microbiol. **Research Statement & Publications:** Poultry diseases; mycoplasma and salmonella infections in turkeys; elimination of salmonella from turkeys and their environment; prevention and treatment of diseases in turkeys. **Mailing Address:** E B Olson Farms, Atwater Lab, Div Jennie-O Foods Box 439, Atwater, MN 56209. **Fax:** 320-974-8499.

KUMAR, NIRJAN, MOLECULAR BIOLOGY. **Personal Data:** b Vijawada, India, May 18, 1961. **Education:** Andhra Univ, India, BSc, 1981; Iari Agr Res Inst, PhD (biochem), 1989. **Professional Experience:** RES SCIENTIST, DEPT MED, STATE UNIV NY, 1991-; fel, Dept Biophys, Univ Rochester, 1989-1990; fel, Dept Oral Biol, Univ Buffalo, 1990-1991. **Memberships:** Nat Acad Sci; Am Thoracic Soc; Am Asn Cell Biologists. **Mailing Address:** State Univ NY, Dept Med, Buffalo Gen Hosp 100 High St, Buffalo, NY 14203.

KUMAR, P VIJAY, COMMUNICATION ENGINEERING. **Education:** Univ Southern Calif, PhD, 1983. **Professional Experience:** PROF, DEPT ELEC ENG, UNIV SOUTHERN CALIF, as of 2004. **Research Statement & Publications:** Communications research; efficient representation; storage; transmission; routing and reception of information. **Mailing Address:** Dept Elec Eng, Univ Southern Calif, EEB 534 Hughes Aircraft Elec Eng Bldg 3740 McClintock Ave, Los Angeles, CA 90089-2565. **Fax:** 213-740-8729. **E-Mail:** vijayk@usc.edu

KUMAR, PANGANAMALA RAMANA, Control, Communications. **Personal Data:** b Nagpur, India, April 21, 1952; m 1982, Devarakonda; c Ashwin & Shilpa. **Education:** Indian Inst Technol, Madras, BTech, 1973; Wash Univ in St Louis, MS, 1975, DSc, 1977. **Honors & Awards:** IEEE Field Award for Control Systems, 2006; Donald P Eckman Award, American Automatic Control Council, 1985; Fellow of Institute of Electrical & Electronic Engineers, 1988. **Professional Experience:** Franklin W Woeltge Prof Elec & Computer Eng, Univ of Ill, Urbana-Champaign, 2000-; Professor of Electrical & Computer Engineering, University of Illinois, Urbana-Champaign, 1987-; Associate Professor, Univ of Illinois, Urbana-Champaign, 1985-1987; From Assistant Professor to Associate Professor, Department of Mathematics, University of Maryland Baltimore County, 1977-1984. **Memberships:** Fellow, Institute of Electrical & Electronic Engineers. **Research Statement & Publications:** Wireless Networks, Control, Sensor Networks, Communications, Scheduling of Wafer Fabrication Plants, Machine Learning, Manufacturing Systems, Stochastic Systems, Optimization, Adaptive Systems, Game Theory, Probability Theory and Stochastic Processes, Information Theory. **Mailing Address:** Univ Ill, CSL, 1308 W Main St, Urbana, IL 61801. **Fax:** 217-244-2352. **E-Mail:** prkumar@uiuc.edu

KUMAR, PRADEEP, NONLINEAR PHENOMENA, SUPERCONDUCTIVITY & MAGNETISM. **Personal Data:** b Allahabad, India, January 1, 1949; American citizen; m 1987, Diana; c Casey A, Vijay A & Ravi A. **Education:** Univ Lucknow, India, BSc, 1966; Indian Inst Technol, Kanpur, MSc, 1968; Univ Calif, San Diego, PhD (physics), 1973. **Professional Experience:** PROG DIR MAT THEORY, DIV MAT RES, NSF, 1995-; PROF PHYSICS, UNIV FLA, 1993, 1995-1997 & 1999-2000; CEA, France, 1989; vis scientist, Helsinki Univ Technol, 1984; from asst prof to assoc prof, UNIn FLA 1979-1993; guest prof, Nordita, Copenhagen, Denmark, 1978-1979; Nordita prof, Helsinki Univ Technol, Finland, 1978-1979; asst prof, Univ Southern Calif, 1977-1978; res assoc, Univ Southern Calif, 1975-1977; res assoc physics, Univ Wis-Milwaukee, 1973-1975. **Memberships:** Am Phys Soc. **Research Statement & Publications:** Research on unconventional superconductor, espec the consequences of competing symmetries Effects of high magnetic fields on Superconductivity, Magnetism due to magnetic ions in semiconductors (also called Dilute Magnetic Semiconductors), Heavy Ferusious and their magnetic and superconducting properties, Heta magnetism, Higher Order Phase Transitions, Nanoelasticity. **Mailing Address:** Phys Dept, Univ Fla, PO BOX 118440, Gainesville, FL 32611. **Fax:** 352-392-0524. **E-Mail:** pkumar@ufl.edu

KUMAR, RAVINDER, COMMUTATIVE ALGEBRA, INSTRUCTIONAL TECHNOLOGIES. **Personal Data:** b Gujranwala, January 31, 1945; Indian citizen; m Kanchan; c Preeti. **Education:** Delhi Univ, India, BA, 1964, MA, 1966, PhD (math), 1972. **Honors & Awards:** Key to the city of Vicksburg, 1997; bd of direct, United Way of West Central Miss. **Professional Experience:** PROF MATH, ALCORN STATE UNIV, 2001-; ed, Teaching Math Technol, Alcorn State Univ, beginning 1996; prin investr, Title III grant, Alcorn State Univ, 1996-1997; assoc prof math, Alcorn State Univ, beginning 1995; coordr, Coop Consortium Clark Atlanta Univ, 1994-1996; co-prin investr, USDA, 1993-1996; prin investr, Teacher Enhancement Projs, Miss Insts Higher Learning, 1993, 1995-1997; coordr, Title III grant, Alcorn State Univ, 1992-1994; consult, Clark Atlanta Univ, beginning 1991; asst prof, Alcorn State Univ, 1990-1995; vis res guest scholar math, Kyoto Univ, Japan, beginning 1988; mombusho postdoctoral fel, Kyoto Univ, Japan, 1979-1982; from asst prof to assoc prof math, Ramjas Col, Delhi Univ, India, 1966-1990; NSF Proj HBCU-Up; NSF Proj Welcome. **Memberships:** Am Math Soc; Math Asn Am; Nat Coun Teachers Math; gen secy Forum for Interdicip Math; life mem Indian Math Soc. **Research Statement & Publications:** Commutative rings in multiplicative ideal theory; local rings; instructional technologies in mathematics. **Mailing Address:** Dept Math, Alcorn State Univ, 1000 ASU Dr #30, Alcorn State, MS 39096. **Fax:** 601-877-6256. **E-Mail:** rkumar@lorman.alcorn.edu

KUMAR, ROMESH, ENERGY SYSTEMS DESIGN & ANALYSIS, FUEL CELL SYSTEMS. **Personal Data:** b Rajpura, India, October 18, 1944; American citizen; m 1976, Kumkum; c Rahul & Ritu. **Education:** Panjab Univ, BSc, 1965; Univ Calif, Berkeley, MS, 1968, PhD (chem eng), 1972. **Honors & Awards:** R&D-100 Awards. **Professional Experience:** MGR FUEL CELL DEPT, CHEM ENG DIV, ARGONNE NAT LAB, as of 2002; CHEM ENGR, ARGONNE NAT LAB, 1976-; asst chem engr, Argonne Nat Lab, 1974-1976; Post-Doc Appointee, Argonne Nat Lab, 1972-1974. **Research Statement & Publications:** Fuel cell and systems for transportation; fuel processing of hydrocarbon and alcohol fuels for use in fuel cell systems; granted ten patents. **Mailing Address:** Chem Eng Div, Argonne Nat Lab, Bldg 205, 9700 S Cass Ave, Argonne, IL 60439-4837. **Fax:** 630-252-4176. **E-Mail:** kumar@cmt.anl.gov

KUMAR, S, SOLID STATE PHYSICS. **Personal Data:** b Ernakulam, India, July 31, 1959. **Education:** Indian Inst Technol, MS, 1980; Pa State Univ, PhD (physics), 1986. **Professional Experience:** RES PHYSICIST, QUANTUM MAGNETICS INC, 1990-; asst prof, Northeast Mo State Univ, 1989-1990; researcher, Ohio State Univ, 1986-1989; grad asst, Pa State Univ, 1980-1986. **Memberships:** Am Phys Soc. **Research Statement & Publications:** Liquid helium and the design and construction of cryogenic apparatus; design, construction and testing of SQUID-based magnetometers. **Mailing Address:** Quantum Magnetics Inc, 7740 Kenamar Ct, San Diego, CA 92121-2425. **Fax:** 619-566-9388.

KUMAR, S ANAND, BIOCHEMISTRY. **Personal Data:** b Bangalore, India, March 12, 1936; m 1963. **Education:** Univ Mysore, BSc, 1954; Univ Poona, MSc, 1957; Indian Inst Sci, PhD (biochem), 1963. **Professional Experience:** Consult, Fine Chem Div, Astra-IDL, Ltd, 1985-; mem gov bd, Astra Res &Develop Ctr, Bangalore, India, 1984-; Adj prof, State Univ NY, 1980-; RES SCIENTIST CLINSCI, WADSWORTH CTR LABS & RES, NY STATE DEPT HEALTH, 1978-; vis asst profbiol, Hunter Col, City Univ NY, 1972-1977; guest scientist biochem, Roche Inst Molecular Biol, Nutley, NJ, 1971-1972; lectr biochem, Indian Inst Sci, Bangalore, 1966-1971; res assoc biochem, Scripps Clin & Res Found, La Jolla, Calif, 1965-1966; Fel biochem, Sch Med, Tufts Univ, Boston, Mass, 1963-1965. **Memberships:** Sigma Xi; Am Soc Biol Chemists; NY Acad Sci. **Research Statement & Publications:** Structure and mode action of enzymes; genetic transcriptions; bacterial RNA polymerase and its site-specific inhibitors; steroid hormone receptors-DNA interactions; steroid hormone controlled gene expression. **Mailing Address:** Astra Res Ctr, PO Box 359 Malleswaram, Bangalore 560003, India.

KUMAR, SATYENDRA, PHYSICS. **Education:** Univ Ill, Urbana, PhD (Solid-Stae Physics), 1981. **Professional Experience:** PROF & GRAD COORDR, DEPT PHYSICS, KENT STATE UNIV, as of 2004. **Research Statement & Publications:** Structure and phase transition studies using microcalorimetry; atomic force microscopy; X-ray diffraction; and small angle neutron scattering. **Mailing Address:** Dept Physics, Kent State Univ, Kent, OH 44242-0001. **Fax:** 330-672-2959. **E-Mail:** satyen@xray.kent.edu

KUMAR, SHIV SHARAN, ASTRONOMY, ASTROPHYSICS, COSMOGONY. **Personal Data:** b Bannu, India, March 15, 1939; American citizen; m 1964, Madhu; c Mona, Veena & Anita. **Education:** Univ Mich, PhD (astron), 1962. **Professional Experience:** PRES, THE GALILEO INST, 2000-; EMER FAC MEM, UNIV VA, 1998-; fac mem, Dept Astron, Univ VA, 1965-1998; staff mem, Phys Res Lab, India, 1963-1965; res assoc, Goddard Inst Space Studies, 1962-1963; astrophysicist, Smithsonian Astrophys Observ, 1960-1961; asst astron, Univ Observ, Univ Mich, 1957-1960. **Memberships:** Int Astron Union; Am Astron Soc; Astron Soc India. **Research Statement & Publications:** Stellar atmospheres; stellar structure and evolution; origin of the solar system; star and planet formation; origin and evolution of life in the universe. **Mailing Address:** The Galileo Inst, PO Box 6516, Charlottesville, VA 22906-6516.

KUMAR, SHRAWAN, MOLECULAR GENETICS. **Personal Data:** b Calcutta, India, February 28, 1953; m 1992, Lina. **Education:** Calcutta Univ, BS, 1972; Ranchi Univ, MS, 1976, PhD (serogenetics), 1984. **Professional Experience:** STAFF SCIENTIST, BOYS TOWN NAT RES HOSP, 1993-; ASST PROF GENETICS, CREIGHTON UNIV, MED CTR, 1993-; ASST PROF ANTHROP, UNIV NEBR, OMAHA, 1993-; res assoc, Boys Town Nat Res Hosp, 1989-1992; res assoc, Univ Nebr, Med Ctr, 1988-1989; sr fel, Anthrop Surg, India, 1982-1988; res fel, Bur Police Res & Develop, 1977-1982. **Memberships:** AAAS; India Soc Human Genetics; Indian Anthrop Soc; SAsian Anthropologists; Am SocHuman Genetics; Asn Res Otoleryngol. **Research Statement & Publications:** Localization of human genetic diseases to its specific location in the human genome; clone and characterize the disease gene. **Mailing Address:** Boys Town Nat Res Hosp, 555 N 30th St, Omaha, NE 68131. **Fax:** 402-498-6331. **E-Mail:** kumar@boystown.org

KUMAR, SHRAWAN, GEOMETRIC TECHNIQUE IN REPRESENTATION THEORY. **Personal Data:** b Ghazipur, UP, India, June 12, 1953; Indian & American citizen; m 1978, Shyama; c Neeraj & Niketa. **Education:** Gorakhpur Univ, BSc, 1973; Bombay Univ, MSc, 1975, PhD (math), 1986. **Professional Experience:** PROF MATH, UNIV NC, 1991-; RIMS, Kyto Univ, Kyoto, 1996; Ecole Norm Sub, Paris, 1994; vis prof, Max Planck Inst Math, 1993; prin investr, NSF, 1992-1995, 1996-2005; reader, Tata Inst Fund Res, India, 1989-1992; mem, Inst Advan Study, Princeton, NJ, 1988-1989; CLE Moore instr, Mass Inst Technol, 1984-1985; post-doctoral fel, Math Sci Res Inst, 1983-1984; mem, TataInst Fund Res, India, 1975-1989. **Memberships:** Am Math Soc. **Research Statement & Publications:** Topology and geometry of finite and infinite dimensional flag varieties and also use them in some problems of representation theory of finite dimensional semi-simple groups as well as Kac-Moody groups. **Mailing Address:** Dept Math, Univ NC, Chapel Hill, NC 27599-3250. **Fax:** 919-962-2568. **E-Mail:** shrawan@email.unc.edu

KUMAR, SHRAWAN, BIOMECHANICS, ERGONOMICS. **Personal Data:** b Allahabad, India, July 1, 1939; m 1965, Rita; c Rajesh & Sheela. **Education:** Univ Allahabad, BSc, 1959, MSc, 1962; Univ Surrey, PhD (physiol), 1971. **Honorary Degrees:** DSc, Univ Surrey, 1994. **Honors & Awards:** Sir Frederic Bartlett Medal. **Professional Experience:** PROF NEUROSCIENCE, UNIV ALTA, 1992-; PROF PHYS THER, UNIV ALTA, 1982-; from asst prof to assoc prof, Univ Alta, 1977-1982; res assoc rehab med, Univ Toronto, 1974-1977; pool officer orthop, All-India Inst Med Sci, 1973-1974; fel eng, Univ Dublin, 1971-1973; lectr zoology, Univ Allahabad, 1962-1966. **Memberships:** Am Soc Biomech; Orthop Res Soc; Human Factors Soc; Human Factors Soc Can; Ergonomics Soc; Int Soc Study Lumbar Spine. **Research Statement & Publications:** Work physiology; occupational biomechanics; tissue biomechanics. **Mailing Address:** Dept Phys Ther, Univ Alta, Edmonton, AB T6G 2G4, Can.

KUMAR, SOMA, BIOCHEMISTRY. **Personal Data:** b Lucknow, India, May 16, 1924; m 1955, c 3. **Education:** Univ Lucknow, BSc, 1944, MSc, 1945; Univ Md, PhD, 1953. **Professional Experience:** PROF EMER CHEM, GEORGETOWN UNIV, as of 2002; prof chem, georgetown univ, beginning 1972; from asst prof to assoc prof, Georgetown Univ, 1958-1972; asst prof, All-India Inst Med Sci, New Delhi, 1956-1958; lectr, biochem, Univ Lucknow, 1954-1956; res assoc, Univ Md, 1953-1954. **Memberships:** AAAS; Am Chem Soc; Am Soc Biol Chemists; Sigma Xi. **Research Statement & Publications:** Biosynthesis of fatty acids; phospholipase A2. **Mailing Address:** Dept Chem, Georgetown Univ, 37th & O St NW, Washington, DC 20057-0001. **Fax:** 202-687-6209. **E-Mail:** kumars@georgetown.edu

KUMAR, SUDHIR, RAILROAD ENGINEERING. **Personal Data:** b Saharanpur, India, October 31, 1933; m 1960, Jyotsna; c Nisha, Raj & Anita. **Education:** Agra Univ, BSc, 1950, MSc, 1952; Indian Inst Sci, Bangalore, AIISc, 1955; Pa StateUniv, PhD (eng mech), 1958. **Honors & Awards:** Octave Chanute Medal, Western Soc Engrs, 1986. **Professional Experience:** RES PROF, DEPT MECH MAT & AEROSPACE ENG, ILL INST TECHNOL, as of 2004; dir, Acad RR Eng & Transp Mgr, beginning 1991; CHMN & CHIEF EXEC OFFICER, TRANERGY CORP, 1986-; mem, Fac Adv Comn, Ill BdHigher Educ, 1985-1987; vis lectr, Acad Railway Sci, People's Repub China, 1983-1984; dir, rr eng lab, beginning 1978; prof mech & aerospace eng, Ill Inst Technol, beginning 1971; chmn, Acad Rr Eng & Transp Mgr, 1971-1978; vis assoc prof, 1962-1971 & NC State Univ, 1968-1971; assoc dir, Eng Sci Div, US Army Res Off-Durham, 1962-1971; chief, Eng Sci Div, Off Ord Res, US Army, 1959-1962; vis lectr, Duke Univ, 1958-1962; asst solid mech br, Eng SciDiv, Off Ord Res, US Army, 1958-1959; asst prof, Pa State Univ, 1958-1959; res assoc, Pa StateUniv, 1957-1958; res asst eng mech, Pa State Univ, 1955-1957; demonstr physics, Bareilly Col, Agra Univ, 1950-1951. **Memberships:** Am Inst Aeronaut & Astronaut; Indian Soc Theoret & Appl Mech; Assoc RailwayEngrs Am; Am Acad Mech; Am Soc Mech Engrs. **Research Statement & Publications:** Wheel and rail interaction; railroad engineering; materials; helicopters; performance and efficiency of trains depends very much on optimizing the wheel-rail contact conditions separately for the powered and the nonpowered units, this still has not been accomplished, understanding wheel rail interaction is the key to it. **Mailing Address:** Tranergy Corp, 726 Foster Ave, Bensenville, IL 60106. **Fax:** 630-238-9264.

KUMAR, SUDHIR, BIOCHEMISTRY, NEUROCHEMISTRY. **Personal Data:** b Anjhi, India, September 16, 1942; m 1968, Nilima; c Avanti & Anjali. **Education:** Univ Rajasthan, India, BS, 1959, MS, 1961; Univ Lucknow, India, PhD (biochem), 1966. **Professional Experience:** PROF BIOL, TRITON COL, ILL, 1993-; DIR & PROF, CLIN REGION LAB, RUSH UNIV, HAZEL CREST, ILL, 1988-; consult, Govt India & UNESCO Prog, 1987, 1989& 1991; PROF BIOCHEM & NEUROL SCI, MED SCH, RUSH UNIV, 1986-; dir & pres, Clin Diagnostics, Hazel Crest, Oak Forest, Ill, 1982-1988; dir pediat res, Christ Hosp, Oak Lawn, Ill, 1978-1981; from asst prof to assoc prof, Rush Univ, 1976-1986; consult scientist med res, Vet Admin Hosp, Hines, Ill, 1976-1979; dir perinatal res & lab, Christ Hosp, Oak Lawn, Ill, 1975-1981; res biochemist hematol, Vet Admin Hosp, Brooklyn, 1973-1975; fel, Dreyfus Med Found, 1971 & 1973; Int Brain Res Org res fel award, UNESCO & Govt France, 1971; chief biochemist pediat, Methodist Hosp, Brooklyn, 1969-1973; sr res scientist, NY State Res Inst Neurochem, Columbia Univ, 1968-1969; res assoc pharmacol, Baylor Col Med, 1967-1968. **Memberships:** fel NY Acad Sci; Am Soc Biol Chemists; Am Inst Nutrit; Am Soc Neurochem; Soc Exp Biol & Med; Am Soc Clin Nutrit; Soc Pediat Res; Am Soc Microbiol; Int Soc Neurochem; fel Nat Acad Clin Biochemists; fel Am Inst Chemists. **Research Statement & Publications:** Study of vitamin B12 metabolism; effect of malnutrition on brain development and its correlation to mental retardation; changes in levels of nucleic acids and enzymes of purine catabolism; changes in amino acid levels; developing brain and metabolic disorders in newborn; perinatal medicine and development of screening tests for metabolic disorders in newborn; development of serum-free culture media and its use in growing neural and amniotic fluid cells; development of rapid tests for use in clinical laboratory; alzheimer's disease; effects of drugs in controlling syndromes associated with HIV (AIDS etc). **Mailing Address:** 18901 Springfield, Flossmoor, IL 60422. **Fax:** 708-799-8713.

KUMAR, SURIENDER, ORGANIC CHEMISTRY, BIOCHEMISTRY. **Personal Data:** b Panjab, India, December 5, 1938; m 1965, c 4. **Education:** Univ Delhi, BSc, 1958, MSc, 1960; Boston Univ, PhD (org chem), 1967. **Professional Experience:** PROF BIOCHEM & MOLECULAR BIOL, MED SCH, UNIV MED & DENT NJ, 1981-; assoc prof, Col Med &Dent NJ, 1975-1981; asst prof biochem, Col Med & Dent NJ, 1971-1975; res chemist, VetAdmin Hosp, 1968-1970; fel, Univ Wis-Madison, 1968; fel, Cornell Univ, 1966-1968; lectr chem, Deshbandhu Col, Delhi, 1960-1962. **Memberships:** AAAS; Am Chem Soc; fel Am Inst Chemists; NY Acad Sci; Am Soc BiolChemists; Am Asn Cancer Res. **Research Statement & Publications:** Cancer research; proteolytic enzymes; all transformation. **Mailing Address:** Dept Biochem, Med Sch, Univ Med & Dent NJ, E639 MSB, Newark, NJ 07103. **Fax:** 973-972-5594. **E-Mail:** kumarsu@umdnj.edu

KUMAR, VIJAY, LABORATORY MEDICINE, IMMUNOLOGY. **Personal Data:** b Punjab, India, April 15, 1945; m 1973. **Education:** Panjab Univ, BS, 1966, MS, 1968; State Univ NY, Buffalo, PhD (biochem), 1973; Am Bd Med Microbiol, dipl; Am Bd Med Lab Immunol, dipl. **Professional Experience:** CEO, IMMCO DIAGNOSTICS INC, as of 2003; PRES, IMMCO DIAGNOSTICS INC, 1987-; RES ASSOC PROF, STATE UNIV NY, BUFFALO, 1987-; asst prof & asst dir, Dept Microbiol, If Testing Serv Buffalo, 1976-1987; felimmunol, Erie County Lab, E J Meyer Mem Hosp, 1974-1976; from clin instr to clin asst prof, Dept Microbiol, State Univ NY, Buffalo, 1974-1976; fel, E J Meyer Mem Hosp, 1973-1974; teaching asst biochem, State Univ NY, Buffalo, 1969-1973. **Memberships:** Am Soc Microbiol; Soc Investigative Dermat; Am Asn Clin Chem. **Research Statement & Publications:** Isolation of proteins, enzymes, autoimmunity, and immunochemistry; Sluten Sensince entoromail. **Mailing Address:** Immco Diagnostics, 60 PineView Dr, Amherst, NY 14228. **E-Mail:** vkumar@immcodiagnostics.com

KUMAR, VINAY, CANCER, IMMUNOLOGY. **Personal Data:** b Montgomery, India, December 24, 1944; m 1972, Raminder; c Rohit & Ambika. **Education:** Poona Univ, BSc, 1962; Punjab Univ, MBBS, 1967; All India Inst Med Sci, MD (path), 1972. **Professional Experience:** PROF & CHMN PATH, UNIV CHICAGO, as of 2003; Vernie A Stembridge chair path, Univ Tex, beginning 1994; Charles T Ashworth prof, Chair Path, 1986-1994; mem, Immunobiol Study Sect, NIH, 1984-1987; prof path, SouthWestern Med Ctr, Univ Tex, beginning 1983; assoc prof, Chair Path, 1982-1983; assoc prof path & microbiol, Sch Med, 1978-1982; Am Cancer Soc res scholar award, 1978; prin investr, Nat Cancer Inst, 1977-; fel, Med Found Inc, Boston, 1974-1976; from instr to asst prof, Boston Univ, 1972-1978; tutor path, All India Inst Med Sci, 1969-1972. **Memberships:** Am Asn Immunol; Sci Res Soc; Am Soc Invest Path (vpres, 1997-1998). **Research Statement & Publications:** Tumor immunology; virus induced cancer; bonemarrow transplantation; natural killer cells; hematopoiesis; coauthor of two publications. **Mailing Address:** Dept Path, Univ Chicago, 5841 S Md Ave, Dallas, IL 60637. **Fax:** 773-702-0495. **E-Mail:** kumerol@utsw.swmed.edu

KUMAR, VIPIN, PARALLEL COMPUTING, ARTIFICIAL INTELLIGENCE. **Personal Data:** b Muzaffarnagar, Uttar Prad, October 21, 1956; m 1982, c 2. **Education:** Univ Roorkee, Uttar Prad, India, BE, 1977; Philips Int Inst, Eindhoven, Neth, ME, 1979; Univ Md, Col Park, PhD (computer sci), 1982. **Professional Experience:** PROF & HEAD COMPUT SCI, UNIV MINN, as of 2003; assoc prof comput sci, Univ Minn, beginning 1989; asst prof, DeptComput Sci, Univ Tex, Austin, 1983-1989. **Memberships:** Inst Elec & Electronics Engrs; Asn Comput Mach; Am Asn Artificial Intel. **Research Statement & Publications:** Algorithms for solving various scientific and artificial intelligence problems on massively parallel computers. **Mailing Address:** Dept Comput Sci & Eng, Univ Minn, 4-192 Elec Eng & Comput Sci Bldg, Minneapolis, MN 55455. **Fax:** 612-6250572. **E-Mail:** kumar@cs.umn.edu

KUMARAN, A KRISHNA, DEVELOPMENTAL BIOLOGY, MOLECULAR ENDOCRINOLOGY OF INSECTS. **Personal Data:** b Govada, India, July 17, 1932; American citizen; m 1956, Jyoti; c Nanda K Alapati. **Education:** Univ Madras, BSc, 1950, MSc, 1955, PhD (zoology), 1959. **Professional Experience:** PROF EMER BIOL, MARQUETTE UNIV, as of 2004; wehr prof, Marquette Univ, beginning1993; vis scientist, Chinese Acad Sci, 1989; vis lectr, Univ Guam, 1988; USDA res grant, 1986-; vis scientist biol, Harvard Univ, 1983; vis scientist, Czech Acad Sci, 1978; NIH res grant, 1975-; prof biol, Marquette Univ, beginning 1973; NSF res grants, 1970-; assoc prof, Marquette Univ, 1969-1973; sr res assoc biol, CaseWestern Res Univ, 1968-1969; reader, Osmania Univ, India, 1965-1968; NIH trainee, WesternRes Univ, 1962-1965; lectr, Sri Venkateswara Univ, India, 1957-1962; Demonstr zool, SriVenkateswara Univ, India, 1955-1957. **Memberships:** Fel AAAS; Entom Soc Am; Am Soc Cell Biol; Am Soc Zoologists; Int SocDevelop Biol; Am Soc Develop Biol. **Research Statement & Publications:** Molecular entomology; role of hormones in control of insect development; hormonal control of specific gene expression during post embryonic development in insects. **Mailing Address:** Dept Biol, Marquette Univ, PO Box 1881, Milwaukee, WI 53201. **Fax:** 414-288-7357. **E-Mail:** kumaran@vms.csd.mu.edu

KUMARAN, MAVINKAL KIZHAKKEVEETTIL, INSULATION, TRANSPORT PROPERTIES. **Personal Data:** b Cannonore, Kerala, India, June 1, 1946; Canadian citizen; m 1971, Dakshayani; c Jyothi & Ranjith. **Education:** Univ Kerala, India, BS, 1965, MS, 1967; Univ London, PhD (chem thermodynamics), 1976. **Professional Experience:** GROUP LEADER, INST RES CONSTRUCTION, NAT RES COUN, CAN, as of 2003; fel, Japan Soc Prom Sci, 1992; PRIN RES OFFICER, NAT RES COUN, CAN, 1990-; res officer, Nat Res Coun, Can, 1984-1989; res assoc, Nat Res Coun, Can, 1981-1984; res fel thermodyn, Massey Univ, NZ, 1980-1981; commonwealth scholar, Univ London, 1973-1976; res fel, Calcut Univ, India, 1972-1973; lectr phys chem, Sree Narayana Col, India, 1967-1980. **Research Statement & Publications:** Experimental and theoretical investigations on properties of liquids and liquid mixtures, especially in the critical region; experimental and theoretical investigation on heat and moisture transport properties of building materials. **Mailing Address:** Inst Res Construction, Nat Res Coun Can, Bldg M-24 Montreal Rd, Ottawa, ON K1A 0R6, Can. **Fax:** 613-998-6802. **E-Mail:** kumar.kumaran@nrc-cnrc.gc.ca

KUMARI, DURGA, ORGANIC CHEMISTRY, ANALYTICAL CHEMISTRY. **Personal Data:** b New Delhi, India, April 27, 1951; American citizen. **Education:** Meerut Univ, India, BS, 1972, MS, 1974; Delhi Univ, India, PhD (chem), 1980. **Professional Experience:** Sr support sci 1992; at geneva pharmaceut RESEARCHER CHEM, MAT DIV, FED HWY ADMIN, 1987-1991; res assoc chem, Univ Minn, Bemidji State Univ, Fla A&M Univ & Okla State Univ, 1981-1987; postdoctoral fel chem, Okla State Univ, Fla A&M Univ, Bemidji State Univ, Univ Minn, 1981-1987; Scientist chem, Indian Inst Technol, 1979-1981; Fulbright scholar, Fulbright Off, Wash, DC, 1977-1978. **Memberships:** Am Chem Soc; Am Soc Mass Spectrometry; AAAS; Indian Women Sci Asn. **Research Statement & Publications:** Isolation, identification and synthesis of novel compounds using organic chemistry; material science chemistry; author of various publications. **Mailing Address:** 4006 Birchwood Ct, North Brunswick, NJ 08902.

KUMAROO, KUZIYILETHU KRISHNAN, BIOCHEMISTRY. **Personal Data:** b Kerala, India, April 6, 1931; m 1967, Vatsala; c Vnod & Manoj. **Education:** Kerala Univ, India, BSc, 1955; Univ NC, PhD (biochem), 1969. **Professional Experience:** RES BIOCHEMIST, DEPT HYPERBARIC MED, NAVAL MED RES INST, BETHESDA, MD, 1979-; asst prof biochem, Univ NC, Chapel Hill, 1971-1979; NIH trainee, Univ Mich Med Ctr, 1968-1971; res asst biochem, Univ NC, Chapel Hill, 1963-1968; petrolchemist, Kuwait Oil Co, Arabia, 1957-1963; clin chemist, Grant Med Col, Bombay, 1956-1957; chemist, Capsulation Serv, India, 1955-1956. **Memberships:** Sigma Xi; Am Soc Biochem & Molecular Biol; Oxygen Soc; Nat Asn RetardedCitizens; Undersea Soc Int; Planetary Soc Int. **Research Statement & Publications:** Biochemistry of circulating blood factors and cells that regulate pulmonary, cardiovascular and central nervous system functions in normal and pathological conditions; cerebral ischemia and thrombosis; biochemistry of decompression sickness; regulatory role of proteases; basic chromosomal proteins in differentiating cells; biochemistry of oxygen/hydrogen gases in diving; complements in decompression sickness. **Mailing Address:** 2614 Urbana Dr, Wheaton, MD 20906. **Fax:** 301-949-5330.

KUMBAR, MAHADEVAPPA M, PHYSICAL CHEMISTRY, BIOPHYSICS. **Personal Data:** b Tallur, India, November 15, 1939; c 2. **Education:** Karnatak Univ, India, BSc, 1961, MSc, 1963; Adelphi Univ, PhD (phys chem), 1969. **Professional Experience:** CHIEF, INFO MGT SYSTS, PILGRIM PSYCHOL CTR, 1987-; ADJ ASSOCPROF BIOPHYS, ADELPHI UNIV, 1979-; ADJ FAC, Nassau Community Col, 1971-; adj asstprof, Info Mgt Systs, Pilgrim Psychol Ctr, 1971-1979; res assoc biophys, Info Mgt Systs, PilgrimPsychol Ctr, 1969-1971; lectr, Parle Col, India, 1963-1965. **Memberships:** Am Chem Soc. **Research Statement & Publications:** Statistical mechanics of macromolecules; dynamic and mechanical properties, conformational changes and conformational studies. **Mailing Address:** 2 Essex Rd, Plainview, NY 11803-2704.

KUMBARACI-JONES, NURAN MELEK, TEACHING, BIOLOGICAL CHEMISTRY. **Personal Data:** b Istanbul, Turkey, April 3, 1944; m 1981, Francis; c Anne & Marian. **Education:** Robert Col, Istanbul, Turkey, BS, 1966; Columbia Univ, MS, 1973, MA, 1974, MPhil, 1975, PhD (physiol), 1977. **Professional Experience:** ASSOC PROF CHEM, ARTHUR E IMPERATORE SCH SCI & ARTS, STEVENS INST TECHNOL, 1984-; asst prof, Stevens Inst Technol, 1979-1984; fel, Dept Physiol, Col Physicians & Surgeons, ColumbiaUniv, 1977-1979; chemist res & develop, Eczacibasi Pharmaceut Co, 1966-1971. **Memberships:** Am Physiol Soc; Soc Neuroscience; NY Acad Sci; Sigma Xi; Nat Asn Adv Health Prof. **Research Statement & Publications:** Thrombogenesis on artificial surfaces; biochemistry and biophysics of skeletal muscle contraction; electrophysiological properties of excitable membranes and synaptic transmission; immune mechanisms activating the complement system and inflammatory processes. **Mailing Address:** Dept Chem & Chem Eng, Stevens Inst Technol, Rm 417 McLean Chem Sci Bldg, Hoboken, NJ 07030. **Fax:** 201-216-8240. **E-Mail:** nkumbara@stevens.edu

KUMINS, CHARLES ARTHUR, surface chemistry; deceased, see previous edition for last biography

KUMKUMIAN, CHARLES SIMON, MEDICINAL CHEMISTRY. **Personal Data:** b Meriden, Conn, June 17, 1920; m 1961, c 4. **Education:** Temple Univ, BS, 1944, MS, 1951; Univ Md, PhD (med chem), 1962. **Professional Experience:** CONSULT, 1997-; dir regulatory affairs, Otsuka Am Pharmaceut Inc, 1995-1997; asst dir chem, Off drug res & rev, 1972-1995; supvry chemist, Bur Drugs, 1968-1972; chemist, Bur med, US food & drug admin, 1964-1968; asst ed, chem abstr serv, 1962-1963; instr chem, Univ Md, 1957-1960; instr, Temple Univ, 1947-1951. **Memberships:** Am Chem Soc. **Research Statement & Publications:** Synthesis and biological activity of steroids; structure activity relationships; analytical chemistry. **Mailing Address:** 5919 Holland Rd, Rockville, MD 20851.

KUMLER, PHILIP L, ORGANIC & POLYMER CHEMISTRY, THERMAL ANALYSIS. **Personal Data:** b Columbus, Ohio, May 23, 1941; m 1999, Rosemary; c Mark Philip & Melissa. **Education:** Miami Univ, BA, 1962; Univ Rochester, PhD (chem), 1967. **Professional Experience:** Vis prof, Mich Molecular Inst, 1990; adj fac, State Univ NY, Buffalo, 1989-; vis prof, Mich Molecular Inst, 1988 & 1989; vis prof, Mich Molecular Inst, 1987; Vis res assoc macromolecular sci, Case Western Res Univ, 1981; PROF CHEM, STATE UNIV NY, FREDONIA, 1980-; assoc prof, State Univ NY, Fredonia, 1976-1980; from asst prof to assoc prof chem, Saginaw Valley State Col, 1970-1976; fel & res assoc, Univ Chicago, 1970; fel & res assoc, NIH fel, 1969-1970; fel & res assoc, Univ Chicago, 1968-1969; NATO fel, Univ Copenhagen, 1967-1968; fac asst chem, Wabash Col, 1964; summer staff, Indust Soap & Chem Prod, 1963 & 1964; Jr chemist indust res, Procter & Gamble Co, 1962. **Memberships:** AAAS; Am Chem Soc; Sigma Xi; NY Acad Sci; NAm Thermal Anal Soc. **Research Statement & Publications:** Polymer chemistry and physics; surface analysis of polymers; thermal analysis. **Mailing Address:** Dept Chem, State Univ NY, Fredonia, NY 14063. **Fax:** 716-673-3347. **E-Mail:** kumler@fredonia.edu

KUMLI, KARL F, ORGANIC CHEMISTRY. **Personal Data:** b Denver, Colo, October 9, 1927; m 1953, c 2. **Education:** Kans State Teachers Col, BA, 1955; Univ Kans, PhD (chem), 1959. **Professional Experience:** PROF EMER CHEM, CALIFSTATE UNIV, CHICO, as of 2003; CHMN DEPT, CALIF STATE UNIV, CHICO, 1975-; prof Chem, Calif-state Univ, Chico, beginning 1971; from asst prof to assoc prof, Calif State Univ, Chico, 1964-1971; res scientist, Weyerhaeuser Co, 1961-1964; Res chemist, Celanese Chem Corp, 1959-1961. **Memberships:** Am Chem Soc. **Research Statement & Publications:** Stereochemistry and mechanisms of reactions of the phosphorus atom; synthesis and characterization of polyoxymethylene, phenol-formaldehyde, epoxy. **Mailing Address:** Dept Chem, Calif State Univ, Chico, CA 95929.

KUMMER, MARTIN, MATHEMATICAL PHYSICS, APPLIED MATHEMATICS. **Personal Data:** b Glarus, Switz, June 11, 1936; m 1967, Regula; c Lukas. **Education:** Swiss Fed Inst Technol, predipl math, 1957, dipl math phyiscs, 1959, PhD (mathphysics), 1962. **Professional Experience:** RETIRED; vis prof, Univ NMex, 1993; Naval Res Lab, Summer, 1987 & 1988; res grant, Swiss Fed Inst Technol, 1981; sabbatical leave, Courant Inst, NY Univ, 1978; prof math, Univ Toledo, beginning 1975; from asst prof to assoc prof, Univ Toledo, 1966-1975; NSF res assoc, Univ Mich, 1964-1966; asst theoret physics, Swiss Fed Inst Technol, 1960-1964. **Memberships:** Am Phys Soc; Math Asn Am; Int Asn Math Physicists; Am Math Soc. **Research Statement & Publications:** Study of linear and nonlinear Hamiltonian systems; in particular, perturbations of integrable systems with applications to celestial and quantum mechanics. **Mailing Address:** 3411 Queenswood Blvd, Toledo, OH 43606. **Fax:** 419-530-4720. **E-Mail:** mkummer@uoft02.utoledo.edu

KUMMER, W(OLFGANG) H(ELMUT), ELECTRICAL ENGINEERING. **Personal Data:** b Stuttgart, Ger, October 10, 1925; American citizen; m 1956, c 4. **Education:** Univ Calif, BS, 1946, MS, 1947, PhD (elec eng), 1954. **Professional Experience:** CHIEF SCIENTIST, RADAR MICROWAVE LAB, HUGHES AIRCRAFTCO, CULVER CITY, 1976-; sr scientist, Antenna Dept, Hughes Aircraft Co, 1966-1976; head res sect, Antenna Dept, Hughes Aircraft Co, 1959-1966; mem tech staff, Bell Tel Labs, 1953-1959; lectr, Univ Calif, 1950-1953; asst elec eng, Univ Calif, 1946-1950; mem comns B & F, Int Sci Radio Union. **Memberships:** Fel Inst Elec & Electronics Engrs (pres Antennas & Propagation Soc 1974). **Research Statement & Publications:** Electromagnetic theory; signal processing and electronically scanned antennas and tropospheric propagation beyond the horizon; microwave field; slot radiators in wave-guides. **Mailing Address:** 1310 Sunset Ave, Santa Monica, CA 90405.

KUMMEROW, FRED AUGUST, FOOD SCIENCE. **Personal Data:** b Berlin, Ger, October 4, American citizen; m Amy; c Max, Jean & Kay. **Education:** Univ Wis, BS, 1939, MS, 1941, PhD (biochem), 1943. **Honors & Awards:** Fellow American Society for Nutritional Sciences. **Professional Experience:** PROF EMER FOOD SCI & HUMAN NUTRIT, UNIV ILL, URBANA, as of 2004; prof food chem, Univ Ill, Urbana, beginning 1959; assoc prof foodchem, Univ Ill, Urbana, 1950-1959; assoc prof chem, Kans State Col, 1945-1950; assocnutritionist, Clemson Col, 1943-1945; mem comnarteriosclerosis, Am Heart Asn; mem, Assocs Food & Container Inst, Chicago. **Memberships:** AAAS; Am Chem Soc; Sigma Xi; Fedn Am Socs Exp Biol; Am Soc Microbiol. **Research Statement & Publications:** Nutrition; biochemistry; fat and oil chemistry; 350 papers total, largely in field of nutrition and heart disease. **Mailing Address:** Dept Food Sci & Human Nutrit, Univ Ill, Rm 206 Burnsides Res Lab, 1208 W Pa St, Urbana, IL 61801. **Fax:** 217-333-7370. **E-Mail:** fkummero@uiuc.edu

KUMMLER, RALPH H, CHEMICAL ENGINEERING, ENVIRONMENTAL ENGINEERING. **Personal Data:** b Jersey City, NJ, November 1, 1940; m 1962, c 3. **Education:** Rensselaer Polytech Inst, BS, 1962; Johns Hopkins Univ, PhD (chem eng), 1966. **Honors & Awards:** Fluor Serv Soc Award, Am Inst Chem Engrs, 1981; Waste Mgt Award, Air & Waste Mgt Asn, 2002. **Professional Experience:** DEAN, COL ENG, WAYNE STATE UNIV, 2004-; PROF CHEM ENG, WAYNE STATE UNIV, as of 2004; interim dean, Col Eng, Wayne State Univ; PROJ DIR, HAZARDOUS WASTE MGT PROG, WAYNE STATE UNIV, as of 2004; interim dean, Col Eng, Wayne State Univ, 2001-2002; assoc dean res, 1997-2001; chmn & prof chem eng, Wayne State Univ, 1974-1993; assoc prof, Wayne State Univ, 1970-1974. **Memberships:** Am Inst Chem Engrs; Air & Waste Mgt Asn; Sigma Xi. **Research Statement & Publications:** Chemical kinetics; environmental chemistry and transport including computer simulation of natural and polluted air and aquatic environments; chemiluminescence and hydrocarbon reactivity; hazardous waste management. **Mailing Address:** Dept Chem Eng, Wayne State Univ, 1150 Eng Bldg, Detroit, MI 48202. **Fax:** 313-577-5300. **E-Mail:** rkummler@eng.wayne.edu

KUMPEL, PAUL GREMMINGER, TOPOLOGY. **Personal Data:** b Riverside, NJ, September 5, 1935; div, c 2. **Education:** Trenton State Col, BS, 1956; Brown Univ, PhD (math), 1964. **Professional Experience:** Vis scholar, 1978 & assoc chair, Wesleyan Univ, 1987; PROF MATH, STATE UNIV NY, STONY BROOK, 1984-; dir undergrad prog math, Univ Hull, 1976-1982; dir teacherprep, Div Math Sci, 1971-1974; sci res coun sr vis fel, Univ Hull, 1971; from asst prof to assocprof math, State Univ NY, Stony Brook, 1964-1984; instr, Brown Univ, 1963-1964; asst, BrownUniv, 1959-1963; instr math, Lafayette Col, 1956-1959. **Memberships:** Math Asn Am. **Research Statement & Publications:** Topology of H-spaces. **Mailing Address:** Dept Math, State Univ NY, Off 3-120, Stony Brook, NY 11794-3651. **Fax:** 631-632-7631. **E-Mail:** pkumpel@math.sunysb.edu

KUMTA, PRASHANT NAGESH, ELECTRONIC PACKAGING, ELECTROCHEMICAL SYSTEMS. **Personal Data:** b Madras, India, August 17, 1960. **Education:** Indian Inst Technol, BTech, 1984; Univ Ariz, MS, 1987, PhD (mat sci & eng), 1990. **Professional Experience:** PROF, CARNEGIE-MELLON UNIV, as of 2004; res initiation award, NSF, 1993; summer fac fel, USAF, 1993; assoc prof, carnegie-mellon univ, beginning 1990. **Memberships:** Am Ceramic Soc; Mat Res Soc; Mat Soc; Electrochem Soc. **Research Statement & Publications:** Chemical processing and structure property correlation of electronic and optical ceramics, glasses and composites. **Mailing Address:** Carnegie Mellon Univ, Pittsburgh, PA 15213. **Fax:** 412-268-7596. **E-Mail:** kumta@cmu.edu

KUN, ERNEST, BIOCHEMISTRY, PHARMACOLOGY. **Personal Data:** b Sopron, Hungary, October 22, 1919; American citizen. **Education:** Eotvos Lorand Univ, Budapest, MD, 1944. **Honors & Awards:** Res Award Hungarian Physiol Soc, 1941; Estab Investr Award Am Heart Assoc, 1956-1961; Res Career Award U S Pub Health Serv, 1962-1989; fel, Am Assoc Advan Sci, 1970-; Sr Sci Award, Humboldt Found, Bonn, Germany, 1973; fel, Royal Soc Med, London, UK, 1993-. **Professional Experience:** PROF EMER, DEPT CELLULAR & MOLECULAR PHARMACOL, UNIV CALIF SAN FRANCISCO, as of 2003; PROF BIOCHEM, ROMBERG CTR ENVIRON STUDIES, 1990-; HEAD SCIENTIST, OCTAMER INC, 1990-; from assoc prof to prof exp pharmacol, biochem & biophys & exp therapeut, 1960-1990; estab investr, Am Heart Asn, 1956-1961; lectr pharmacol, Med Ctr, Univ Calif, San Francisco, 1956-1960; fel, Inst Enzyme Res, Univ Wis, 1953-1956; asst prof med & pharmacol & lectr biochem, Tulane Univ, 1949-1953; res assoc, Univ Chicago, 1947-1949; asst, Univ Chicago, 1946-1947; asst prof pharmacol, Eotvos Lorand Univ, 1944-1946; asst physiol, Eotvos Lorand Univ, 1939-1943. **Memberships:** AAAS; Am Chem Soc; Am Soc Pharmacol & Exp Therapeut; Soc Exp Biol & Med; Am Soc Biol Chemists. **Research Statement & Publications:** Enzymology of dehydrogenases; enzymes of sulfur metabolism; metabolic regulation studies by F-containing substrate homologs; bioenergetics; molecular mechanisms of growth regulation in eukaryotic cells at the chromatin level (poly adenosine diphosphate R. **Mailing Address:** Univ Calif, San Francisco, PO Box 0450, San Francisco, CA 94143-0450. **E-Mail:** ernestkun@mac.com

KUN, KENNETH ALLAN, technical planning & implementation, short & long term planning & implementation; deceased, see previous edition for last biography

KUN, ZOLTAN KOKAI, CRYSTAL GROWTHS OF SOLID STATE MATERIALS. **Personal Data:** b Satoraljaujhely, Hungary, February 28, 1932; American citizen; m 1963, Joan L Kies; c John, Daniel & Zoe. **Education:** Univ Miskolc, Hungary, Dipl Ing, 1954. **Professional Experience:** CONSULT, CARNEGIE MELLON RES INST, 1996-; consult scientist, Westinghouse Info & Security Systs Div, 1991-1995; consult scientist, Sci & Technol Ctr, 1990-1991; adv engr, Westinghouse Res & Develop Ctr, 1985-1990; fel engr, Westinghouse Res & Develop Ctr, 1982-1985; sr engr, Westinghouse Res & Develop Ctr, 1978-1982; Metallurgist I, Zenith Radio Corp, 1960-1977. **Memberships:** Soc Info Display; Soc Imaging Sci & Technol. **Research Statement & Publications:** Electro-optical materials; light emitting diodes in wide bandgap II-VI compounds; high field electroluminescence in thin films; discovery of high output edge emission from thin film electroluminescent devices leading to a light array replacing lasers in electrophotographic printers. **Mailing Address:** 2604 Saybrook Dr, Pittsburgh, PA 15235.

KUNA, SAMUEL, PHARMACOLOGY. **Personal Data:** b Velke Levare, Czech, May 7, 1912; American citizen; m 1936, c 2. **Education:** NY Univ, BA, 1943, PhD (biol), 1956; Temple Univ, MA, 1949. **Professional Experience:** PROF EMER, RUTGERS UNIV, 1984-; prof & dir Toxicol Prog, Grad Sch, 1980-1984; dir biol res, Calgon Consumer Prod Co Div, Merck & Co, 1974-1980; dir pharmacol & toxicol, Calgon Consumer Prod Co Div, Merck & Co, 1967-1974; asst dir res & develop, Bristol-Myers Prod Div, Bristol-Myers Co, 1963-1967; head pharmacol dept, Bristol-Myers Prod Div, Bristol-Myers Co, 1957-1962; res assoc & head pharmacol res unit, Merck Inst Therapeut Res, 1950-1957; instr, Temple Univ, 1947-1950; head biol control dept, Merck Inst Therapeut Res, 1947-1950, 1953-1956; res asst to dir, Merck Inst Therapeut Res, 1943-1950; mem, Mercklnst Therapeut Res, 1934-1943. **Memberships:** Am Soc Pharmacol & Exp Therapeut; Soc Toxicol; NY Acad Sci. **Research Statement & Publications:** Action of chemical agents on interchange of tissue fluids; analgesics; physiology of the stomach; psychopharmacology; product development. **Mailing Address:** Dept Internal Med Plum Div, Univ Tex Med Br, Galveston, TX 77555-0561. **Fax:** 409-772-9539.

KUNAPULI, SATYA P, CARDIOVASCULAR BIOLOGY, MOLECULAR CARDIOLOGY. **Personal Data:** b Kakinada, India, August 12, 1954. **Education:** Andhra Univ, India, BSc, 1975, MSc, 1977; Indian Inst Sci, PhD (enzymol), 1984. **Professional Experience:** ASSOC PROF PHYSIOL, THROMBOSIS RES CTR, TEMPLE UNIV, 1999-; asst prof physiol, Thrombosis Res Ctr, Temple Univ, 1993-1999; scientist, Astra Res Ctr, Bangalore India, 1988-1990; instr physiol, Univ Tex Med Br, Galveston, 1986-1988; Fel molecular biol, Univ Tex Med Br, Galveston, 1984-1985. **Memberships:** Am Soc Biochem & Molecular Biol; Am Soc Cell Biol. **Research Statement & Publications:** Cardiovascular biology; molecular cardiology. **Mailing Address:** Dept Physiol, Temple Univ Med Sch, Rm 212, Med Res Bldg, Philadelphia, PA 19140. **Fax:** 215-707-4003. **E-Mail:** kunapuli@nimbus.ocis.temple.edu

KUNASZ, IHOR ANDREW, ECONOMIC GEOLOGY. **Personal Data:** b Montlucon, France, September 24, 1939; American citizen; m 1965, Zenovia Tarczanyn; c Markian & Marta. **Education:** Case Western Res Univ, BA, 1963; Pa State Univ, MS, 1968, PhD (geol), 1970. **Professional Experience:** PRES & DIR, NEWMOUNT UZBEKISTAN LTD, UZBEKISTAN, as of 1998; DIR PROJ DEVELOP, CYPRUS FOOTE MINERAL CO, 1993-; CONSULT, 1990-; mgr bus develop, Cyprus Minerals Co, 1990-1993; bd mem, Indust Minerals Div, SocMining Eng, Am Inst Mining Eng, 1989-; gen mgr, Cyprus Minera Chile, 1988-1990; Chmn, Indust Minerals Div, Soc Mining Eng, Am Inst Mining Eng, 1987; chief geologist, Foote MineralCo, 1972-1988; staff geologist, Foote Mineral Co, 1970-1972. **Memberships:** Soc Mining Eng Am Inst Mining Eng; Geol Soc Am; Geochem Soc; ShevchenkoSci Soc. **Research Statement & Publications:** Economic and exploration geology associated with industrial minerals, especially saline deposits and lithium deposits of the world, precious metals and non-ferrous metals development; project development in the CIS. **Mailing Address:** Newmount Uzbekistan Ltd, Uzbekistan.

KUNAU, ROBERT, EXPERIMENTAL BIOLOGY. **Professional Experience:** FELS DIR & CLIN PROF, NEPHROLOGY, 2000-; pvt pract, Nephrology, beginning 1989. **Mailing Address:** Univ Tex Health Sci Ctr, Dept Med Div Nephrology, 7703 Floyd Curl Dr MC-7882, San Antonio, TX 78229-3900. **Fax:** 210-567-4712. **E-Mail:** kunau@uthscsa.edu

KUNC, JOSEPH ANTHONY, NON-EQUILIBRIUM PHENOMENA IN HIGH-TEMPERATURE GASES, MOLECULAR INTERACTIONS. **Personal Data:** b Baranowicze, Poland, November 1, 1943; American citizen; m 1979, Mary; c Robert. **Education:** Warsaw Tech Univ, MS, 1970, PhD (plasma sci), 1974. **Professional Experience:** Chmn, Thermophysics Publ Comt, Am Inst Aeronaut & Astronaut, 1995-1997; Harvard/Smithsonian fel, 1991; consult, B P Wolfsdorf & Assocs, 1991; vis scholar, Inst Theoret Atomic & Molecular Physics, Harvard Univ, Cambridge, 1991; vis scholar, Dept High-Temp Plasma, Nat Inst Nuclear Studies, Warsaw, Poland, 1991; PROF AEROSPACE ENG, PHYSICS & ASTRON, UNIV SOUTHERN CALIF, LOS ANGELES, 1990-; consult, Phys Optics Corp, 1988-; assoc prof, Dept Aerospace Eng & Dept Physics, 1985-1989; mem, Comt Arcs & Flames, Nat Res Coun1985-1986; consult, Nat Tech Systs, Los Angeles, 1984-1986; prin investr numerous grants, 1983-; res affil, Jet Propulsion Lab, Calif Inst Technol, Pasadena, 1982-1983; res assoc prof, Dept Aerospace Eng & Dept Physics, Univ Southern Calif, Los Angeles, 1980-1985; vis scholar, Atomic & Plasma Radiation Div, Nat Bur Stand, 1979; assoc prof, Warsaw Tech Univ, 1974-1978; mem, Thermophys Comt, Am Inst Aeronaut & Astronaut. **Memberships:** Fel Am Phys Soc; assoc fel Am Inst Aeronaut & Astronaut; sr mem Inst Elec &Electronics Engrs. **Research Statement & Publications:** General nonlinear collisional-radiative models of non-equilibrium in partially-ionized plasmas; atomic and molecular interactions with transfer of electronic, rotational and vibrational energy; kinetic processes in supersonic and hypersonic flows, thyratrons, high-power light sources. **Mailing Address:** Dept Aerspace Eng, Univ Southern Calif, RRB-219, Univ Park, Los Angeles, CA 90089-1191. **Fax:** 213-740-7774. **E-Mail:** kunc@usc.edu

KUNCE, HENRY WARREN, COMPUTER SIMULATION, HUMAN-SOCIAL RELATIONS. **Personal Data:** b St Louis, Mo, April 18, 1925; m 1948, Avon; c Catherine, Nancy, Christopher, Cynthia & James. **Education:** Wash Univ, BA, 1946; McCormick Theol Sem, Chicago, BD & MDiv, 1949; Univ Miami, MSIE, 1971, PhD (statist), 1979. **Professional Experience:** CHIEF SCI OFFICER, SOCIOCYBERNETICS INC, 1995-; pres, Sociocybernet, Inc, South Miami, Fla; adj math fac, Univ Miami, Coral Gables, Fla, 1980-; chief mgr syst eng, Mgt Info Systs & Opers Res, Metro Dade Co Govt, Fla, 1972-1995; res scientist sociocybernet, Univ Miami, 1971-1972; systs analyst, Clin Campesina, Homestead, Fla, 1970-1971; planner-analyst parish develop, Bd Missions, United Presby Church, Mo & Fla, 1961-1970; clergyman, Ohio & Mo, 1949-1961. **Memberships:** Opers Res Soc Am; Am Inst Indust Engrs; Inst Mgt Sci; Soc Comput Simulation; AAAS; Sigma Xi. **Research Statement & Publications:** Sociocybernetics, the application of cybernetics to the dynamics of human interaction and social structures, using systems analysis and computer simulation of stochastic and deterministic mathematical models, a discrete system, finite state automata, and a continuous model analyzed by phase space analysis; applications made in management; counseling education; personnel problems. **Mailing Address:** 5025 SW 74th Terr, Miami, FL 33143. **E-Mail:** kunce@ibm.net

KUNDEL, HAROLD LOUIS, RADIOLOGY. **Personal Data:** b New York, NY, August 15, 1933; m 1958, Alice; c 3. **Education:** Columbia Univ, AB, 1955, MD, 1959; Temple Univ, MS, 1963. **Honorary Degrees:** MA, Univ Pa, 1980. **Honors & Awards:** Mem Award, Asn Univ Radiologists, 1963, Stauffer Award, 1982. **Professional Experience:** PROF EMER RADIOL, UNIV PA, as of 2004; Wilson prof res radiol, Univ PA, beginning 1980; attend radiologist, Hosp Univ Pa, 1980-; prof radiol, Univ Hosp, 1968-1980; attend radiologist, Univ Hosp, 1966-1980; James Picker Found advan acad fel physiol, Sch Med, Temple Univ, 1964-1966; resident radiobiol, Sch Aerospace Med, 1963-1964; resident radiol, Temple Univ Hosp, 1960-1963; intern med, Mary Imogene Bassett Hosp, Cooperstown, NY, 1959-1960. **Memberships:** AAAS; Am Col Radiol; Asn Univ Radiologists. **Research Statement & Publications:** Image information processing and analysis; visual perception; diagnostic decision making. **Mailing Address:** Dept Radiol, Hosp Univ Pa, Philadelphia, PA 19104. **E-Mail:** KundelH@uphs.upenn.edu

KUNDELL, FREDRICK AUSTIN, POLYMERIZATION OF VEGETABLE OIL. **Personal Data:** b Pulaski, NY, October 20, 1940; m Karen; c 3. **Education:** Univ Md, PhD (phys chem), 1966. **Professional Experience:** PROF SCI ADMIS COORDR, SALISBURY STATE UNIV, as of 2004; chmn, dept Chem, 1981-1995; sci specialist, US House reps, 1978; assoc dean col, Salisbury State Univ, 1972-1976; PROF CHEM, SALISBURY STATE UNIV, 1970-. **Memberships:** Am Chem Soc. **Research Statement & Publications:** Develop polymerization processes for corn and soybean oil. **Mailing Address:** Dept Chem, Henson Sch Sci & Technol, Salisbury Univ, Devilbiss Sci Hall 240 Chem HS 301, Salisbury, MD 21801. **Fax:** 410-548-3318. **E-Mail:** fakundell@ssu.edu

KUNDERT, ESAYAS G, ALGEBRA. **Personal Data:** b Ruti, Switz, May 7, 1918; American citizen; m 1954, c Berta (Garafalo), Antony & Diana (Blackburn). **Education:** Swiss Fed Inst Technol, dipl, 1945, Dr Math, 1950. **Professional Experience:** EMER PROF MATH, UNIV MASS, AMHERST, 1982-; prof, Univ Mass, Amherst, 1962-1982; US Army grant, 1952-1953; from asst prof to prof, La State Univ, 1951-1962; asst prof math, Univ Tenn, 1950-1951. **Research Statement & Publications:** Algebraic geometry and algebraic topology; elementary number theory. **Mailing Address:** 19 Van Meter Dr, Amherst, MA 01002.

KUNDIG, WERNER, BIOLOGY. **Personal Data:** b 1931. **Professional Experience:** PROF EMER BIOL, HOOD COL, FREDERICK, MD, 1988-. **Mailing Address:** Hood Col, 401 Rosemont Ave, Frederick, MD 21701-8575.

KUNDSIN, RUTH BLUMFELD, MEDICAL MICROBIOLOGY. **Personal Data:** b New York, NY, July 30, 1916; m 1935, Edwin; c Andrea K (Dupree) & Dennis E. **Education:** Hunter Col, BA, 1936; Boston Univ, MA, 1949; Harvard Univ, ScD(microbiol), 1958. **Honorary Degrees:** ScD, Univ Mass, 1975. **Professional Experience:** PRES, KUNDSIN LAB INC, 1981-; ASSOC PROF MICROBIOL &MOLECULAR GENETICS, HARVARD SCH MED, 1976-; epidemiologist, Brigham &Women's Hosp, Boston, Mass, 1970-; mem assoc staff, Peter Bent Brigham Hosp, 1964-1970; res assoc, Kundsin Lab Inc, 1961-1976; asst surg, Peter Bent Brigham Hosp, 1958-1964; resbacteriologist, Peter Bent Brigham Hosp, 1951-1958; Res bacteriologist, Sch Pub Health, Harvard Univ, 1936-1937 & Sch Med, Univ Pa, 1937-1938. **Memberships:** AAAS; Am Soc Microbiol; fel NY Acad Sci; Int Org Mycoplasmology; Am AcadMicrobiol. **Research Statement & Publications:** Dynamics of disinfection as applied to environmental bacteriology; sanitary bacteriology; maintenance of standards for a hygienic environment; epidemiology of staphylococcal disease; skin disinfection; mycoplasmas and reproductive failure in humans; chlamydia infections. **Mailing Address:** Brigham & Women's Hosp, 75 Francis St, Boston, MA 02115. **E-Mail:** rbkundsin@bics.bwh.harvard.edu

KUNDT, JOHN FRED, DENDROLOGY, FORESTRY EDUCATION. **Personal Data:** b Denver, Colo, December 21, 1926; m 1948, Delores; c Charles F & Carol A. **Education:** WVa Univ, BS, 1952; NC State Univ, PhD (forestry), 1972. **Professional Experience:** RETIRED; assoc prof & exten forestry specialist, Univ Md, 1974-1988; asst prof bot, genetics & plant taxon, State Univ NY, 1969-1973; fel dendrol, NC State Univ, 1964-1969; forest supvr prod, Union Camp Paper Corp, 1957-1964; mgt chief, Forest Mgt Serv, Div Forestry, Va, 1952-1957. **Memberships:** Soc Am Foresters. **Research Statement & Publications:** Effects of adding composted sewage sludge to newly planted Pinus Taeda and Pinus Virginiana; developing pine hybrids between Pinus Taeda and Pinus Rigida by selecting superior parental phenotypes, and producing experimental seed orchard; developing a Pinus Virginiana seed orchard to produce seed for Christmas tree production; development of Paulownia tomentosa in plantations, initial establishment and cold hardiness development. **Mailing Address:** 103 Fox Run, Laurel, DE 19956.

KUNDU, MUKUL RANJAN, RADIOPHYSICS, ELECTRONICS. **Personal Data:** b Calcutta, India, February 10, 1930; American citizen; m 1958, Ranu; c Krishna, Rina & Sanjit. **Education:** Univ Calcutta, BSc, 1949, MSc, 1951; Univ, Paris, DSc, 1957. **Honors & Awards:** Sr US Scientist Award, Alexander von Humboldt Found, 1978; fel am Physical soc. **Professional Experience:** PROF EMER PHYSICS & ASTRON, UNIV MD, COL PARK, as of 2005; vis prof, Nat Astron Observ, Japan, 1993 & 1999; vis prof, Inst Space Astronaut Studies, Japan, 1994; vis SK Mitra distinguished prof, 1993; dir astron, Univ MD, Col Park, 1980-1985; actg dir astron, Univ Md, Col Park, 1978-1979; prof physics & astron, Univ Md, Col Park, beginning 1968; sr res assoc, Nat Acad Sci-Nat Res Coun, 1967, 1974-1975 & 1986-1987; assoc prof astron, Cornell Univ, 1962-1965; Tata Inst Fundamental Res, Bombay, 1965-1968; res assoc solar radio astron, Observ, Univ Mich, 1959-1962; sr res fel, Nat Phys Lab, India, 1958-1959; asst, Nat Ctr Sci Res, Ministry Educ, France & Meudon Observ, 1956-1958; French Govt scholar radio astron, Ecole Normale Superieure & Meudon Observ, 1954-1956; asst, Coun Sci & Indust Res, Univ Calcutta, 1952-1954. **Memberships:** Int Astron Union; sr mem Inst Elec & Electronics Engrs; Am Astron Soc; Int Radio Sci Union; fel Royal Astron Soc; fel Am Phys Soc; Am Geophys Union. **Research Statement & Publications:** Solar, stellar and galactic radio astronomy. **Mailing Address:** Univ Md, Astron Dept, Space Sci Bldg, College Park, MD 20742. **Fax:** 301-314-9067. **E-Mail:** kundu@astro.umd.edu

KUNDU, PRASUN K, PHYSICS. **Education:** St. Xavier's Col, Univ Calcutta, BSc, 1973, Indian Inst Technol, MS, 1976, Univ Rochester, PhD (Theoretical Physics), 1981. **Professional Experience:** STAFF, CLIMATE & RADIATION BR, NASA GODDARD SPACE FLIGHT CTR, as of 2006. **Mailing Address:** Code 913 NASA Goddard Space Flight Ctr, Lab for Atmospheres, Greenbelt, MD 20771. **Fax:** 301-614-6307. **E-Mail:** kundu@climate.gsfc.nasa.gov

KUNDU, SAMAR K, EXPERIMENTAL BIOLOGY. **Professional Experience:** SR SCIENTIST, DIAG DEPT, ABBOTT LABS, 1983-. **Mailing Address:** Diag Div, Abbott Labs, 100 Abbott Park Rd, Abbott Park, IL 60064-3500. **Fax:** 847-937-1219.

KUNELIUS, HEIKKI TAPANI, PLANT SCIENCE, FORAGE MANAGEMENT. **Personal Data:** b Konginkangas, Finland, March 21, 1940; Canadian citizen; m 1971, c 2. **Education:** Univ Helsinki, BSA & MSc, 1966; Univ Man, PhD (plant sci), 1970. **Professional Experience:** Asst dir, Forage-Beef Sect, 1991-1993; head, Forage-Beef Sect, 1985-1991; mem, Expert Comt, Forage Breeding, Can, 1979-; study leave, NZ-Australia, 1979-1980; RES SCIENTIST, DEPT CROP & LIVESTOCK RES CTR, AGR AGRI-FOOD CAN, 1970-; fel plant sci, Univ Man, 1970; res asst plant path, Agr Res Ctr, 1966. **Memberships:** fel Can Soc Agron; Am Soc Agron; Agr Inst Can; Finnish Asn Agr Grad; Swed Seed Asn. **Research Statement & Publications:** Physiology and management of forage grasses and legumes; pasture management; minimum tillage for pasture renovation. **Mailing Address:** Crop Livestock Res Ctr, Agr & Agri-Food Can, 440 Univ Ave, Charlottetown, PE C1A 4N6, Can. **Fax:** 902-566-6821.

KUNESH, CHARLES JOSEPH, FINE PARTICLE TECHNOLOGY, PAPER SCIENCE. **Personal Data:** b Greensburg, Pa, October 18, 1948; m 1974, Mary Ellen; c 2. **Education:** Carnegie-Mellon Univ, BS, 1970; Univ Pittsburgh, PhD (phys chem), 1973. **Professional Experience:** TECH CONSULT, KUNESH TECHNICAL CONSULTING, 1998-; dir res, Minerals Technol, Inc, 1992-1998; dir res, Pfizer Inc, 1988-1992; res mgr, Pfizer Inc, 1982-1988; sr res scientist, Pfizer Inc, 1980-1982; sr res chemist, Pfizer Inc, 1977-1980; Res chemist, Pfizer Inc, 1973-1977. **Memberships:** Am Chem Soc; Tech Asn Pulp & Paper Indust; Mat Res Soc. **Research Statement & Publications:** Synthesis and crystal engineering of fine particle inorganic materials, especially precipitated calcium carbonate; application of inorganic fine particles in filled and-or coated paper and in polymer composites. **Mailing Address:** 3305 Altonah Rd, Bethlehem, PA 18017-1846. **Fax:** 610-954-7604. **E-Mail:** ckunesh@aol.com

KUNESH, JERRY PAUL, CLINICAL PHARMACOLOGY, MEDICINE. **Personal Data:** b Kewaunee, Wis, January 19, 1938; m 1961, c 3. **Education:** Iowa State Univ, DVM, 1961, MS, 1966, PhD (physiol), 1969. **Professional Experience:** RETIRED; prof emer Vet Med & Surg, Iowa State Univ, as of 2003; prof Vet Med & Surg, Iowa State Univ, beginning 1975; assoc prof pharmacol & med, Iowa State Univ, 1970-1975; asst prof physiol & pharmacol, Iowa State Univ, 1965-1970; NIH fel physiol, 1964-1965; instr vet med & surg, Iowa State Univ, 1961-1962. **Memberships:** Am Asn Swine Practitioners; Am Asn Bovine Practitioners; Am Vet Med Asn. **Research Statement & Publications:** Porcine hemorrhagic syndromes and clinical evaluation of antimicrobial agents as well as their mechanisms of action. **Mailing Address:** 2034 Jensen Ave, Ames, IA 50010.

KUNG, CHING, GENETICS, NEUROBIOLOGY. **Personal Data:** b Kwang Tung, China, April 28, 1939; American citizen; c 3. **Education:** Chung Chi Col, Chinese Univ Hong Kong, dipl, 1963; Univ Pa, PhD (biol), 1968. **Professional Experience:** Hilldale prof, Univ Wis-Madison, 1990; VILAS PROF MOLECULAR BIOL &GENETICS, UNIV WIS-, MADISON 1977-; assoc prof, Univ Wis-Madison, 1974-1977; fromasst prof to assoc prof molecular biol, Univ Calif, Santa Barbara, 1971-1974; fel electrophysiol, Univ Calif, Los Angeles, 1970-1971; fel genetics, Ind Univ, Bloomington, 1968-1970. **Memberships:** AAAS; Genetic Soc Am; Am Soc Cell Biol. **Research Statement & Publications:** Genetic dissection of sensory transductions in microbes; ion channels of paramecium, yeast, and e coli. **Mailing Address:** 305 Molecular Biol Univ Wis, 1525 Linden Dr, Madison, WI 53706-1596. **E-Mail:** ckung@wisc.edu

KUNG, ERNEST CHEN-TSUN, METEOROLOGY. **Personal Data:** b Ping-tung, Taiwan, China, January 1, 1931; m 1959, Susan; c Felicia, Denise & David. **Education:** Nat Univ Taiwan, BS, 1953; Univ Ariz, MS, 1959; Univ Wis, PhD (meteorol), 1963. **Honors & Awards:** Res Award, Sigma Xi, 1983. **Professional Experience:** PROF EMER ATMOSPHERIC SCI, UNIV MO, COLUMBIA, as of 2004; US dept interior, 1994-1999; chmn soil & atmospheric sci, Univ Mo, Columbia, beginning 1993; nat ctr atmospheric sci, 1992-1994; nat oceanic & atmospheric admin grant, 1983-1988; pres grad fac senate, Univ Mo-Columbia, 1977-1978; prof atmospheric sci, Univ Mo, Columbia, beginning 1970; assoc prof, Univ MO, Columbia, 1967-1970; NSF grants, 1967-1969, 1970-1975, 1976-1988; res meteorologist, Geophys Fluid Dynamics Lab, Environ Sci Serv Admin, 1963-1967; proj assoc meteorol, Univ Wis, 1963; specialist agron, Taiwan Prov Govt, 1954-1958. **Memberships:** Fel Am Meteorol Soc; fel Royal Meteorol Soc; Meteorol Soc Japan; Sigma Xi. **Research Statement & Publications:** Atmospheric general circulation; long-range forecasting; dynamic climatology. **Mailing Address:** Soil Environ Atmospheric Sci, Univ Mo, 302 Anheuser-Busch, Nat Res Bldg, Columbia, MO 65211-7250. **Fax:** 573884-5070.

KUNG, HAROLD HING CHUEN, CATALYSIS, KINETICS. **Personal Data:** b Hong Kong, October 12, 1949; m 1971. **Education:** Univ Wis-Madison, BS, 1971; Northwestern Univ, MS, 1972, PhD (chem), 1974. **Honors & Awards:** Paul H Emmett Award, Catalysis Soc, 1991. **Professional Experience:** Fel, Japanese Soc Promoton Sci, 1996; dir, Ctr catalysis & Surface sci, beginning 1993; chmn, Ctr Catalysis & Surface Sci, 1986-1992; Henske Lectr, Yale Univ, 1986; PROF CHEM ENG, NORTHWESTERN UNIV, 1984-; from asst prof to assoc prof, Ctr Catalysis & Surface Sci, 1976-1984; res chemist, E I du Pont Del Nemours & Co, Inc, 1974-1976. **Memberships:** Am Chem Soc; Am Inst Chem Engrs; Catalysis Soc. **Research Statement & Publications:** Surface chemistry and physics; catalysis; chemical reaction engineering. **Mailing Address:** Dept Chem & Biol Eng, Northwestern Univ, 2145 Sheridan Rd, Evanston, IL 60208-3120. **Fax:** 847-491-3728. **E-Mail:** hkung@nwu.edu

KUNG, HSIANG-FU, BIOCHEMICAL PHYSIOLOGY. **Personal Data:** b Chungking, China, September 4, 1942; American citizen; c 2. **Education:** Nat Chung-hsing Univ, BS, 1963; Vanderbilt Univ, PhD, 1969. **Professional Experience:** CHAIR PROF, INST MOLECULAR BIOL, UNIV HONK KONG, as of 2004; HON PROF, PEKING UNION MED COL, CHINA, as of 2004; Adj Prof, Dept Chemi Biol & Pharmacog, Col Phar, Rutgers Univ, as of 2004; chief, Lab Biochem Physiol, Nat Cancer Inst, DCT, Biol Respons Modifiers Prog, NIH, 1986-1999; res leader, Dept Molecular Oncol, 1982-1986; srres fel, Dept Molecular Genetics, Res Div, Hoffmann-La Roche Inc, 1981-1982; res fel, DeptMolecular Genetics, Res Div, Hoffmann-La Roche Inc, 1980-1981; adj prof, Dept Zool &Physiol, Rutgers State Univ, 1976-1978; asst mem, Dept Biochem, Roche Inst Molecular Biol, 1973-1980; vis asst prof, Dept Biochem, Col Med & Dent NJ, 1971-1973 & 1973-1976; res fel, Dept Biochem, Roche Inst Molecular Biol, 1971-1973; sci asst, Max-Planck Inst Biol, 1970-1971; fel, Lab Biochem, Sect Enzymes, NIH, 1969-1970. **Memberships:** Fedn Am Socs Exp

Biol; AAAS. **Research Statement & Publications:** Biochemical physiology. **Mailing Address:** Inst Molecular Biol, Univ Honk Kong, 21 Sassoon Rd, Pokfulam, Hong Kong. **E-Mail:** hkung@hkucc.hku.hk

KUNG, HSIANG-TSUNG, COMPUTER ARCHITECTURE & NETWORKS, PARALLEL COMPUTATION. **Personal Data:** b Shanghai, China, November 9, 1945; m 1970, Ling-Ling; c 2. **Education:** Nat Tsing Hua Univ, BS, 1968; Univ NMex, MA, 1970; Carnegie Mellon Univ, PhD (math), 1974. **Professional Experience:** GORDON MCKAY PROF ELEC ENG & COMPUT SCI, HARVARD UNIV, 1992-; Guggenheim fel, 1983-1984; archit consult, ESL, Inc, 1982; from asst prof to prof computsci, Carnegie Mellon Univ, 1974-1992; res assoc, Carnegie Mellon Univ, 1973-1974. **Memberships:** Nat Acad Eng; Inst Elec & Electronics Engrs; Asn Comput Mach. **Research Statement & Publications:** Computer algorithms; computational complexity; parallel computation; multiprocessors; very large scale integration; numerical analysis; computer architectures; supercomputers; computer and telecommunications networks. **Mailing Address:** Div Eng & Appl Sci, Harvard Univ, 225 Maxwell Dworkin 33 Oxford St, Cambridge, MA 02138. **Fax:** 617-496-5508. **E-Mail:** kung@harvard.edu

KUNG, MAYFAIR CHU, CHEMISTRY. **Education:** Univ Wis-Madison, BS, 1970; NWestern Univ, PhD, 1974. **Professional Experience:** RES ASSOC PROF, DEPT CHEM ENG, CTR CATALYSIS & SURFACE SCI, NWESTERN UNIV, as of 2006. **Research Statement & Publications:** Environmental catalysis; oxide catalysis; preparation and characterization of oxidic gels; generate controlled density of surface unsaturation sites via different synthesis methods. **Mailing Address:** Int Inst Nanotechnol, NWestern Univ, 2145 Sheridan Rd No K111, Evanston, IL 60208. **E-Mail:** m-kung@northwestern.edu

KUNG, PATRICK C, EXPERIMENTAL BIOLOGY. **Professional Experience:** VICE CHMN BD & CHIEF SCI OFFICER, T CELL SCI INC, 1989-. **Mailing Address:** T Cell Sci Inc, 119 Fourth Ave, Needham, MA 02194-2725.

KUNG, ROBERT T V, NONLINEAR OPTICS. **Education:** Cornell Univ, PhD (phys chem). **Professional Experience:** SR VPRES & CHIEF SCI OFFICER, ABIOMED INC, 1995-. **Mailing Address:** R & D Abiomed Inc, 24 Cherry Hill Dr, Danvers, MA 01923. **Fax:** 978-777-8411.

KUNG, SHAIN-DOW, MOLECULAR BIOLOGY. **Personal Data:** b Lini, China, March 14, 1935; American citizen; m 1964, c 3. **Education:** Chung Hsing Univ, Taiwan, BSc, 1958; Univ Guelph, MSc, 1965; Univ Toronto, PhD (bot), 1968. **Honors & Awards:** Philip Morris Award, 1979. **Professional Experience:** RETIRED; dir, Ctr Agr Biotechnol, Univ Md, College Park, 1988-1993; actg dir, Ctr Agr Biotechnol, Univ Md, College Park, 1986-1993; assoc dean, Univ Md, Baltimore County, 1985-1987; Fulbright Award, 1983; prof biol, Univ Md, Baltimore County, 1982-1986; actg chmn, Univ Md, Baltimore County, 1982-1984; from asst prof to assoc prof, Univ Md, Baltimore County, 1974-1982; res assoc biol, Univ Calif, Los Angeles, 1971-1974; res assocbiochem, Univ Toronto, 1968-1971; instr bot, Chung Hsing Univ, Taiwan, 1958-1962. **Memberships:** AAAS; Am Soc Plant Physiologists. **Research Statement & Publications:** Biochemistry and genetics of chloroplast protein; properties, function and evolution of chloroplast DNA; molecular biology of genetic tumors. **Mailing Address:** 14713 Harvest Lane, Silver Spring, MD 20905.

KUNG, SILAS, MAGNETIC SENSING TECHNOLOGY FOR INDUSTRIAL & BIOMEDICAL IMAGING APPLICATIONS, INTEGRATION OF WIRELESS NETWORKS WITH FIBER OPTIC NETWORKS. **Personal Data:** b Hong Kong, November 11, 1948. **Education:** Lanchow Univ, BSc, 1967, MSc, 1968; Columbia State Univ, PhD (appl physics &elec eng), 1997. **Honorary Degrees:** PhD, Dalian Inst Geront, 1988. **Professional Experience:** CHIEF SCIENTIST, ITRON INC, 1995-; vis scientist, Biomed ImagingResource Lab, Mayo Clin, 1995-1996; chief consult, SPI Inc, 1992-1994; potential staff, Superconductive Super Collider Lab, Tex, 1991; dir photonic device res, develop & mfg, PCOCorp, 1990-1991; prog mgr, Compaq Comput Corp, 1989-1990; sr prin consult, Unisys Corp, 1988-1989; prof physics, Dalian Inst Geront, 1988; group mgr, Unisys Corp, 1985-1988; mem, Pvt Indust Coun, City Sunnyvalle, Calif, 1984-1985; pres, AIMS Inc, 1982-1984; sr engmgr, Fairchild Corp, 1976-1982; asst pres, Bowmar Instrument Corp, 1972-1976; Opers mgr, Carter Semiconductor Inc, 1970-1971; supt, Fairchild Corp, 1966-1968. **Memberships:** Inst Elec & Electronics Engrs. **Research Statement & Publications:** Indium phosphide/silicon, giant magnetresistive/indium phosphide/silicon and high temperature superconductor/silicon materials systems and processing technologies to build low cost intelligent fiber optic links and low cost intelligent wireless to fiber optic links; superconductive quantum interference device based biomag physiological imaging system for non-invasive diagnostics for heart, brain and other organs preventive health care. **Mailing Address:** 712 First St N, Waterville, MN 56096-1042. **Fax:** 507-362-8090.

KUNG, TED TESHIH, ALLERGY, INFLAMMATION. **Personal Data:** b Beijing, China, January 17, 1936; American citizen; m Christina; c Victor H & Cary W. **Education:** Nat Taiwan Univ, BS, 1957; Fairleigh Dickinson Univ, MS, 1968; NY Univ, PhD (biol), 1978. **Professional Experience:** Adj prof human anat & physiol, Kean Col, NJ, 1990-; PRIN RES SCIENTIST, SCHERING-PLOUGH RES INST, 1990-; adj assoc prof endocrinol, Fairleigh Dickenson Univ, 1989-1990; Lectr human anat & physiol, Bloomfield Col, 1984-1990; sr res scientist, ScheringCorp, 1979-1989; assoc scientist, Schering Corp, 1971-1975; asst scientist, NY Univ Med Ctr, 1968-1971; Instr genetics, Nat Taiwan Univ, 1962-1964. **Memberships:** Soc Invest Dermat; Inflammation Res Asn; NY Acad Sci; Soc Leukocyte Biol; AmThoracic Soc. **Research Statement & Publications:** Pulmonary inflammation in allergic mice or other rodents; effects of various cytokines on the pathogenesis of eosinophilia; involvement of mast cells in the development of eosinophilia in allergic mice. **Mailing Address:** Schering Plough Res Inst, 2015 Galloping Hill Rd, Kenilworth, NJ 07003. **E-Mail:** ted.kung@spcorp.com

KUNHARDT, ERICH ENRIQUE, ELECTROKINETICS, COMPUTATIONAL PHYSICS & TRANSPORT PHENOMENA. **Personal Data:** b Montecristy, Dominican Rep, May 31, 1949; m 1976, Christine. **Education:** NY Univ, BS, 1969, MS, 1972; Polytechnic Univ, PhD (electrophys), 1976. **Honorary Degrees:** ME, Stevens Inst Technol, 1996. **Honors & Awards:** Halliburton Found Award, 1983. **Professional Experience:** DEAN, Arthur E IMPERATORE SCH SCI & ARTS, as of 2003; GEORGE MEADE BOND PROF PHYSICS & ENG PHYSICS, STEVENSINST TECHNOL, 1996-; GTE Labs, 1982-1985; Lawrence Livermore Labs, 1988-1991; dir, WeberRes Inst, 1986-1996; prof electrophysics, Polytech Univ, 1985-1992; adv bd, Transport Theory & Statist J, 1982-; consult, Los Alamos Nat Lab, 1979-1987; from asst prof to prof elec eng & physics, Tex Tech Univ, 1976-1985. **Memberships:** Am Phys Soc; Sigma Xi; Inst Elec & Electronics Engrs. **Research Statement & Publications:** Experimental, theoretical and computational investigations of the non-equilibrium behavior of quantum and classical electron assemblies in matter under the influence of place-time varying electric and magnetic fields. **Mailing Address:** Dept Physics & Eng Physics, Stevens Inst Technol, Castle Point Hudson, Hoboken, NJ 07030. **Fax:** 201-216-8196. **E-Mail:** ekunhard@stevens.edu

KUNIN, ARTHUR SAUL, MEDICINE, PHYSIOLOGICAL CHEMISTRY. **Personal Data:** b Brooklyn, NY, August 11, 1925; m 1959, c 4. **Education:** Columbia Univ, BA, 1948; Univ Vt, MD, 1952. **Professional Experience:** PROF EMER, COL MED, UNIV VT, as of 2004; prof, Col Med, Univ VT, beginning 1982; fel Dept Physiol, Harvard Med Sch, 1978-1979; vis prof, Inst Chem Med, Univ Bern, 1970-1971; Lederle Med fac award, Col Med, Univ Vt, 1965-1968; Am Col Physicians Willard Thompson traveling scholar, Univ Col Hosp Med Sch, London, 1964; NIH spec fel, Mass Gen Hosp & Harvard Med Sch, 1962-1964; from instr to assoc prof, Col Med, Univ VT, 1957-1982; sr asst resident, Peter Bent Brigham Hosp, Boston, Mass, 1956-1957; NIH fel, Med Sch, Boston Univ, 1954-1956; jr asst resident, Peter Bent Brigham Hosp, Boston, Mass, 1953-1954; intern med, Peter Bent Brigham Hosp, Boston, Mass, 1952-1954. **Memberships:** Am Col Physicians; Am Fedn Clin Res. **Research Statement & Publications:** Renal physiology; mitochondrial metabolism; nutrition in renal disease; nephrology; diseases of metabolism; metabolic bone diseases and the intermediary metabolism of epiphyseal cartilage. **Mailing Address:** Col Med, Univ VT, E-126 Given Bldg 89 Beaumont Ave, Burlington, VT 05405-0068. **Fax:** 802-656-8577.

KUNIN, CALVIN MURRY, INTERNAL MEDICINE, INFECTIOUS DISEASE. **Personal Data:** b Burlington, Vt, May 3, 1929; m 1976, Ilene; c 3. **Education:** Columbia Univ, AB, 1949; Cornell Univ, MD, 1953. **Professional Experience:** PROF EMER, OHIO STATE UNIV, 2001-; prof med, Col Med, Ohio State Univ, beginning 1983; prof &chmn dept, Col Med, Ohio State Univ, 1979-1984; prof med & assoc chmn dept, UnivWis-Madison, 1970-1979; chief med, Vet Admin Hosp, 1970-1970; from asst prof to assoc profmed & prev med, Sch Med, Univ Va, 1959-1970; res fel, Harvard Med Sch, 1957-1959; asstresident, Peter Bent Brigham Hosp, Boston, 1956-1957; sr asst surg, USPHS, 1954-1956; internmed, New York Hosp, 1953-1954. **Memberships:** Am Fedn Clin Res; Am Asn Immunologists; Am Assoc Physicians; Am Soc ClinInvest; Soc Exp Biol & Med; fel Infectious Dis Soc Am (past pres). **Research Statement & Publications:** Epidemiology; antibiotic therapy; urinary tract infections. **Mailing Address:** Dept Med, Ohio State Univ, 320 W 10th Ave, Columbus, OH 43210. **Fax:** 614-293-5627. **E-Mail:** ckunin@columbus.rr.com

KUNIN, ROBERT, PHYSICAL CHEMISTRY. **Personal Data:** b West New York, NJ, July 16, 1918; m 1942, c 2. **Education:** Rutgers Univ, BS, 1939, PhD (colloidal chem), 1942. **Honors & Awards:** Franklin Inst Gold Medal, 1966. **Professional Experience:** CONSULT, 1976-; sr staff assoc, Rohm & HaasCo, 1970-1976; res assoc, Rohm & Haas Co, 1959-1970; lab head chg res & develop ionexchange resins, Rohm & Haas Co, 1946-1959; Gulf fel, Mellon Inst, 1945-1946; sr chemist, Manhattan Proj, Columbia Univ, 1944-1945; assoc chemist, Tenn Valley Authority, 1942-1944; lectr, Univ Pa; lectr, Am Univ. **Memberships:** AAAS; Am Chem Soc; Am Inst Chem Engrs; Electrochem Soc; Israel Chem Soc; Sigma Xi. **Research Statement & Publications:** Desalination; adsorption; liquid extraction; theory and application of ion exchange; inorganic chemistryof phosphates, uranium fluorides; analytical chemistry of inorganic constituents; ion exchange in silicates; electrochemistry of membrane processes; catalysis; water treatment and purification. **Mailing Address:** 860 Lower Ferry Rd, Trenton, NJ 08628.

KUNISHI, HARRY MIKIO, SOIL CHEMISTRY. **Personal Data:** b Honolulu, Hawaii, August 30, 1932; m 1959. **Education:** Univ Hawaii, BS, 1955, MS, 1956; Univ Wash, BS, 1958; Univ Wis, PhD (soils), 1963. **Professional Experience:** RETIRED; soil scientist, Agr Res Serv, USDA, 1962-1990. **Memberships:** Int Soc Soil Sci; Am Soc Agron; Am Chem Soc; Sigma Xi. **Research Statement & Publications:** Chemistry and mineralogy of potassium in soils; adsorption and movement of radionuclides in soils; phosphate reactions in field and streams; rates of phosphate supplied to plants by acid soils of southeastern United States; phosphorus management under no-tillage; model of phosphorus transport from agricultural fields; soil-water-plant-phosphorus reactions in fresh water and brackish water systems. **Mailing Address:** 2288 W Valley, Westminster, MD 21158.

KUNISI, VENKATASUBBAN S, ORGANIC CHEMISTRY. **Personal Data:** b Kottayam, India, m 1974, Saraswathi; c Sharmila & Satish. **Education:** Univ Madras, India, BSc, MSc; Univ Kans, PhD (chem), 1975. **Professional Experience:** CHMN, DEPT NATURAL SCI, UNIV NFLA, 1994-; PROF CHEM, UNIV NFLA, 1989-; from asst prof to assoc prof, Univ Nfla, 1981-1989; assoc pharmacol, Univ Fla, 1979-1980; lectr, Tex A&M Univ, 1976-1979; fel, Emory Univ, 1974-1976. **Memberships:** Am Chem Soc. **Research Statement & Publications:** Bio-organic mechanisms; chemical and enzyme catalysis; organic reaction mechanisms; solution kinetics; istope effects; nuclear magnetic resonance studies of drugs using shift reagents. **Mailing Address:** Dept Natural Sci, Univ NFla, Bldg 3, Rm 2203, Jacksonville, FL 32224. **Fax:** 904-620-3885. **E-Mail:** venkat@unf.edu

KUNKEE, RALPH EDWARD, FERMENTATIONS, ENOLOGY. **Personal Data:** b San Fernando, Calif, July 30, 1927. **Education:** Univ Calif, AB, 1950, PhD (biochem), 1955. **Honors & Awards:** Hon Res Lect Asev, 1997; Prin en Oenologie, Oiv Paris, 1998. **Professional Experience:** Consult, UN Food & Agr Orgn, Bangalore, India, 1996; PROF EMER ENOL, UNIV CALIF, DAVIS, 1991; France fel, Montpellier, 1977-1978; Fulbright fel, Ger, 1970-1971; prof enol, Univ Calif, Davis, 1963-1991; asst res biochemist, Univ Calif, Davis, 1960-1963; res biochemist, E I du Pont Del Nemours & Co, 1955-1960; asst biochemist, Univ Calif, 1950-1953. **Memberships:** Fel AAAS; Am Soc Microbiol; Am Soc Enol Viticulture (secy-treas, 1981-1983). **Research Statement & Publications:** Intermediary metabolism and control; fermentation; microbiology; enology. **Mailing Address:** Dept Viticult & Enol, Univ Calif, One Shields Ave, Davis, CA 95616-8749. **Fax:** 530-752-0382. **E-Mail:** rekunkee@ucdavis.edu

KUNKEL, BARBARA NICOLE, PLANT DISEASE RESISTANCE, BACTERIAL PATHOGENICITY. **Personal Data:** b Berkeley, Calif, December 26, 1962. **Education:** Univ Calif, Davis, BS, 1984; Harvard Univ, PhD (molecular genetics), 1990. **Professional Experience:** ASSOC PROF BIOL, WASH UNIV, as of 2004; searle scholar, beginning 1996; packard fel, beginning 1996; asst prof biol, Wash Univ, beginning 1994; am chem soc postdoctoral fel, 1993-1994; postdoctoral fel, Univ Calif, Berkeley, 1990-1994; life sci res fel, 1990-1993. **Mailing Address:** Dept Biol, Washington Univ, Monsanto 319, St Louis, MO 63130. **Fax:** 314-935-4432. **E-Mail:** kunkel@biology.wustl.edu

KUNKEL, HARRIOTT ORREN, NUTRITION, PHILOSOPHY OF AGRICULTURAL SCIENCE. **Personal Data:** b Olney, Tex, July 3, 1922; m 1960, Beverly; c 2. **Education:** Tex A&M Univ, BS, 1943, MS, 1948; Cornell Univ, PhD (biochem), 1950. **Professional Experience:** PROF EMER ANIMAL SCI BIOCHEM & BIOPHYS, TEX A&M UNIV, 1998-; DEAN EMER AGR & LIFE SCI, TEX A&M UNIV, 1998-; dean agr & life sci, Tex A&M Univ, beginning 1991; dean agr, Col Agr & actg dir, Tex Agr Exp Sta, 1972-1988; dean, Col Agr & actg dir, Tex Agr Exp Sta, 1968-1972; assoc dir, Exp Sta, 1962-1968; prof animal sci biochem & biophys, Tex A&M Univ, beginning 1957; from asst prof to assoc prof animal sci & biochem, Tex A&M Univ, 1951-1957; instr biochem, Univ Wis, 1950-1951. **Memberships:** Am Chem Soc; Am Soc Animal Sci; Am Soc Biochem & Molecular Biol; Am InstNutrit; Soc Exp Biol & Med. **Research Statement & Publications:** Science administration;

philosophy of agricultural science; theory of higher education in agriculture and life sciences. **Mailing Address:** Dept Animal Sci, Tex A&M Univ, TAMU 2471, College Station, TX 77843-2471.

KUNKEL, JOSEPH GEORGE, DEVELOPMENTAL BIOLOGY, MARINE BIOLOGY. **Personal Data:** b Oceanside, NY, August 17, 1942; m 1964, Gerda; c David & Peter. **Education:** Columbia Col, AB, 1964; Case Western Res Univ, PhD (biol), 1968. **Professional Experience:** Vis Scientist, Ladwig Maximillions Univ, Munich, Germany, 2001-2002; vis scientist, Marine Biol Lab, Woods Hole, MA, 1993-1994; entom, Univ Mass, 1985-; PROF BIOL, UNIV MASS AMHERST, 1985-; adj prof molecular & cellular biol prog, Univ Mass, 1984-; vis scholar, Dept Biochem, Univ Calif, Berkeley, 1977-1978; from asst prof to assoc prof, Univ Mass, Amherst, 1970-1985; Instr biol, Yale Univ, 1969-1970; NIH trainee develop biol, Yale Univ, 1968-1970; trainee biomet, Case Western Res Univ, 1968; res asst, Columbia Univ, 1963-1964; res asst, Columbia Univ, 1962-1963. **Memberships:** AAAS; Am Soc Zoologists; Marine biol lab corp; Soc Integrative & Comparitive Biol. **Research Statement & Publications:** Reproductive physiology and development; chemistry and function of vitellogenin; evolution; biometry; effect of oligosaccharides on proteins; role of ions in early development of oocytes; pattern formation. **Mailing Address:** Dept Biol, Univ Mass Amherst, 426N Morrill Sci Ctr, Amherst, MA 01003-0002. **Fax:** 413-545-3243. **E-Mail:** joe@bio.umass.edu

KUNKEL, LOUIS M, MEDICINE. **Personal Data:** b New York, NY, October 13, 1949. **Education:** Gettysburg Col, BA, 1971; Johns Hopkins Univ, PhD, 1978. **Honors & Awards:** Duchenne-Erb-Preis, Ger Muscular Dystrophy Asn, 1986; Warren Alpert Found Prize, 1988; George Cotzias Mem Lectr, Am Acad Neurol, 1988; Royal Soc Wellcome Found Prize, Eng, 1988; Pruzansky Lectr, March of Dimes Birth Defects Found, 1989; Gairdner Found Int Award, 1989; Passano Found Young Scientist Award, 1989; Nat Med Res Award, Nat Health Coun, 1989; Silvio O Conte Decade of the Brain Award, 1991; E Mead Johnson Award, 1991. **Professional Experience:** DIR PROG GENOMICS, CHILDREN'S HOSP, HARVARD MED SCH, as of 2004; investr, Howard Hughes Med Inst, 1990-; PROF PEDIAT, CHILDREN'S HOSP, HARVARD MED SCH, 1990-; CHIEF, DIV GENETICS, CHILDREN'S HOSP, BOSTON, 1989-; assoc investr, Howard Hughes Med Inst, 1987-1990; tutor human genetics, Harvard Med Sch, 1987-1989; lectr neurobiology, Harvard Med Sch, 1983-1989; from instr to assoc prof, Div Genetics, Children's Hosp, Boston, 1982-1990; res fel pediat, Div Genetics, Children's Hosp, Boston, 1980-1982; George Meany postdoctoral fel, Muscular Dystrophy Asn, 1980-1982; res fel med, Children's Hosp Med Ctr, Boston, 1980; fel, Univ Calif, San Francisco, 1978-1980. **Memberships:** Nat Acad Sci; Muscular Dystrophy Asn (vpres, 1987-1989). **Research Statement & Publications:** Linkage of human genetic diseases with DNA markers; molecular genetics of Duchenne muscular dystrophy; differential gene expression during development; structural organization of mammalian DNA. **Mailing Address:** Dept Genetics, Childen's Hosp, Harvard Med Sch, 300 Longwood Ave Enders 5, Boston, MA 02115. **Fax:** 617/355-7588. **E-Mail:** kunkel@genetics.med.harvard.edu

KUNKEL, M ELIZABETH, BIOLOGY. **Education:** Univ Central Ark, BSE, 1975; Univ Tenn, Knoxville, MS 1976, Phd, 1979. **Professional Experience:** PROF & PRIN INVESTR, DEPT FOOD SCI & HUMAN NUTRIT, CLEMSON UNIV, 1981-. **Mailing Address:** Dept Food Sci & Human Nutrit, Clemson Univ, 214 Poole Ag Ctr Bldg, Clemson, SC 29634-0371. **Fax:** 864-656-0331. **E-Mail:** kunkel@clemson.edu

KUNKEL, STEVEN L, IMMUNOLOGY, REGULATION OF CYTOKINE GENE EXPRESSION. **Education:** NDak State Univ, BS, 1973, MS, 1974; Univ Kans, PhD (biochem & microbiol), 1978. **Honors & Awards:** Establ Investr, Am Heart Asn, 1985. **Professional Experience:** ENDOWED PROF PATH & IMMUNOL, UNIV MICH, as of 2005; CO-DIR, DEPT PATH, UNIV MICH, as of 2005; assoc dean, Grad Sch Admin, Univ Mich, as of 2004; prof, Path & Immunol, Univ Mich, beginning 1991; from asst prof to assoc prof, Univ Mich, 1982-1991; instr, Univ Mich, 1980-1982; fel, inflammation & immunol, Univ Conn, 1978-1980. **Memberships:** Am Soc Invest Path; Am Asn Immunol; Shock Soc; Am Thoracic Soc. **Research Statement & Publications:** Immunology; regulation of cytokine gene expression. **Mailing Address:** Univ Mich, Med Sch, Dept Path, 4071 BSRB 109 Zina Pitcher Pl, Ann Arbor, MI 48109-0602. **Fax:** 734-764-2397. **E-Mail:** slkunkel@umich.edu

KUNKEL, THOMAS A, DEVELOPMENTAL BIOLOGY. **Personal Data:** b Cincinnati, Ohio, August 8, 1949. **Education:** Thomas More Col, BA, 1971; Univ Cincinnati, MS, 1973, PhD (develop biol), 1977. **Professional Experience:** PRIN INVESTR, NAT INST ENVIRONI HEALTH SCI, as of 2003; RES GENETICIST, LAB MOLECULAR GENETICS, NAT INST ENVIRONHEALTH SERV, NIH, 1986-; Genetics, Univ Prog Genetics, Duke Univ, 1986-; Adj prof, DeptMicrobiol & Immunol, Univ NC, Chapel Hill, 1982-; sr staff fel, Lab Molecular Genetics, Nat InstEnviron Health Serv, NIH, 1982-1986; fel, Univ Wash, 1978-1982; fel, NIH, 1978-1981; Res assoc, Inst Cancer Res, Philadelphia, 1977-1978. **Memberships:** Am Soc Biochem & Molecular Biol; Am Asn Cancer Res. **Research Statement & Publications:** Developmental biology. **Mailing Address:** Lab Genetics, NIEHS, NIH, PO Box 12233, Research Triangle Park, NC 27709-2233. **Fax:** 919-541-7613. **E-Mail:** kunkel@niehs.nih.gov

KUNKEL, WILLIAM ECKART, ASTRONOMY. **Personal Data:** b Berlin, Ger, March 25, 1936; American citizen; m 1969, Carmen D Rivera; c Jose F & Liza S. **Education:** Univ Calif, Berkeley, BA, 1959; Univ Tex, Austin, PhD (astron), 1967. **Professional Experience:** At LAS CAMPANAS OBSERV; astronr, Max Planck Inst Astron, Ger, 1980-1983; mem staff, Brazilian Nat Observ, 1977-1979; assoc astronr, Interam Observ Cerro Tololo, 1970-1977; Jr astronr, Interam Observ Cerro Tololo, 1967-1970. **Memberships:** Am Astron Soc; Int Astron Union. **Research Statement & Publications:** Interacting galaxies; dwarf galaxies, photometry; flare stars: no tuore. **Mailing Address:** Las Campanas Observ, Casilla 60, La Serena, Chile.

KUNKEL, WULF BERNARD, PLASMA PHYSICS. **Personal Data:** b Eichenau, Ger, February 6, 1923; American citizen; m 1960, Erika; c Laurence O, Barbara N & Maya T. **Education:** Univ Calif, BA, 1948, PhD (physics), 1951. **Honors & Awards:** Alexander von Humboldt award, 1980. **Professional Experience:** EMER PROF PHYSICS, UNIV CALIF, BERKELEY, 1991-; group leader Magnetic Fushion Energy Res Proj, Lawrence Berkeley Lab, 1970-1991; ed, Plasma Physics, 1970-1980; prof physics, Lawrence Berkeley Lab, 1967-1991; consult, Aerospace Corp, 1961-1971; physicist, Lawrence Berkeley Lab, 1956-1970; Guggenheim fel, 1955-1956 & 1972-1973; assoc res eng, Univ Calif, Berkeley, 1954-1955; lectr, Univ Calif, Berkeley, 1953-1967; asst res engr aerodyn, Univ Calif, Berkeley, 1951-1954. **Memberships:** Fel Am Phys Soc; Sigma Xi. **Research Statement & Publications:** Physics of ionized gases; magnetohydrodynamics; controlled-fusion research; ion sources; electric discharge. **Mailing Address:** Lawrence Berkeley Nat Lab, Univ Calif, 4-230, Berkeley, CA 94720-0001. **Fax:** 510-486-5105. **E-Mail:** wbkunkel@lbl.gov

KUNKLE, DONALD EDWARD, PHYSICS, MATHEMATICS. **Personal Data:** b New Kensington, Pa, March 9, 1928; m 1950, c 3. **Education:** Lafayette Col, BS, 1950. **Professional Experience:** TECH CONSULT, ANALYTE CORP, 1991-; nuclear engr, Dept Navy, 1987-1990; mgr prod anal & test syst, qual control, Kaiser Aluminum & Chem Corp, 1980-1986; staff physicist process technol, Kaiser Aluminum & Chem Corp, 1970-1980; process control, Alcoa Res Lab, 1962-1970; group leader nondestructive testing, Alcoa Res Lab, 1955-1962; resphysicist spectros, Alcoa Res Lab, 1950-1955. **Memberships:** Am Soc Non-destructive Testing; Anal Chem Appl Spectros; Am Soc Testing &Mat. **Research Statement & Publications:** Applied emission spectroscopy; eddy current testing; new principles of radiation thickness gauging for non-ferrous rolling mills; closed loop process control systems; quality control in metals industry; nuclear instrumentation for submarine program. **Mailing Address:** 1419 Village Ctr Dr, Medford, OR 97504-4501. **E-Mail:** hrfj25a@prodigy.com

KUNKLE, GEORGE ROBERT, ENVIRONMENTAL GEOLOGY, HYDROLOGY. **Personal Data:** b Elyria, Ohio, March 27, 1934; m 1958, c 4. **Education:** Iowa State Univ, BS, 1956; Univ Mich, MS, 1958, PhD (geol), 1961. **Professional Experience:** RETIRED; pres & prin hydrogeologist, G R Kunkle & Assoc, Inc, 1986-1996; assoc & mgr, Neyer, Tiseo & Hindo, Ltd, 1980-1986; sr scientist, Jones & Henry Eng, Ltd, 1977-1980; pres & environ consult, Earthview, Inc, 1971-1977; asst prof geol, Univ Toledo, 1966-1971; geologist, Res Coun Alta, Can, 1960-1962 & US Geol Surv, 1962-1966. **Memberships:** Nat Water Well Asn; Am Inst Prof Geologists. **Research Statement & Publications:** Groundwater resources and environmental geology; influence of land use and natural processes on the quality and quantity of ground and surface waters. **Mailing Address:** 319 Bay Run, Newport, NC 28570.

KUNO, H JOHN, MICROWAVE & SOLID STATE ELECTRONICS. **Education:** Univ Calif, Los Angeles, BSEE, 1961, MSEE, 1963, PhD, 1966. **Professional Experience:** FOUNDER, QUINSTAR TECHNOL INC, 1993-; mem tech staff & asst div mgr, Hughes Aircraft Co, 1969-1993; mem tech staff, David Sarnoff Res Ctr, RCA, 1966-1969; res engr, Elec Div, NCR, 1961-1966. **Memberships:** Fel Inst Elec & Electronics Engrs. **Research Statement & Publications:** Contributed over 100 articles on microwave and solid state electronics to professional journals. **Mailing Address:** QuinStar Technol, Inc, 1725 Del Amo Blvd, Torrance, CA 90501. **Fax:** 310-320-9968. **E-Mail:** quinstar@quinstar.com

KUNOS, GEORGE, MOLECULAR PHARMACOLOGY, RECEPTOR RESEARCH. **Personal Data:** b Budapest, Hungary, May 14, 1942; American citizen; m 1967, Ildiko; c Anne-Marie & Doreen. **Education:** Budapest Med Sch, MD, 1966; McGill Univ, Montreal, PhD (pharmacol), 1973. **Honors & Awards:** Elected foreign mem, Hungarian Acad of Sci, 1995; Elected Fellow of the Amer Heart Assn, 1998; Mechoulam Award of Intl Cannabinoid Res Society, 2005. **Professional Experience:** SCI DIR, NATL INST ALCOHOL ABUSE & ALCOHOLISM, NIH, BETHESDA, MD, 2000-; prof & chmn, Dept Pharmacol & Toxicol, Med Col Va, Richmond, 1992-2000; lab chief physiol & pharmacol, Nat Inst Alcohol Abuse & Alcoholism, Bethesda, Md, 1987-1992; from assoc prof to prof pharmacol & med, McGill Univ, Montreal, 1979-1988; asst prof pharmacol, McGill Univ, Montreal, 1974-1979; fel, Coun High Blood Pressure Res, Am Heart Asn; SR INVSTR AND CHIEF, LAB PHYSIOL STUDIES, NIAAA. **Memberships:** Am Soc Pharmacol & Exp Therapeut; Am Soc Biochem & Moleuclar Biol; Int Soc Hypertension; Soc for Neuroscience; Intl Cannabinoid Res Soc; Intl Soc Biomed Res on Alcoholism. **Research Statement & Publications:** Pharmacology, molecular biology and physiological regulation of drug and hormone receptors; biology of endocannabinoids; mechanisms of blood pressure regulation; regulation of energy homeostasis; author of over 170 publications and four monographs. **Mailing Address:** Sect Neuroendocrinol, Lab Physiol Studies, NIAAA, 5625 Fishers Lane Rm 2S-24, MSC-9413, Bethesda, MD 20892-9413. **Fax:** 301-480-0257. **E-Mail:** gkunos@mail.nih.gov

KUNOV, HANS, PHYSIOLOGICAL ACOUSTICS, ACOUSTICAL COMMUNICATION PROCESSES. **Personal Data:** b Copenhagen, Denmark, March 14, 1938; Canadian citizen; m 1977, Clare; c Mads J & Niels P. **Education:** Tech Univ Denmark, MASc, 1963, PhD (elec eng), 1966. **Professional Experience:** Dir res & co-foundr, Paul Madsen Med Devices Ltd, 1992-1998; assoc ed, Inst Elec& Electronics Engrs Trans Biomed Eng, 1991-1993; mem, Grant Selection Comt Elec Eng, NaturalSci & Eng Res Coun Can, 1990-1993; dir, Elec Eng Consociates, 1990-1992; DIR, INST BIOMEDENG, 1989-1999; PROF EMER 2003 -, PROF BIOMED ENG, ELEC & COMPUT ENG & OTOLARYNGOL, UNIVTORONTO, 1982-2003; from asst prof to assoc prof, Inst Biomed Eng, 1967-1982; Fel biomed eng, Tech Univ Denmark, 1966-1967; Pres, Div 934533 Ont Inc, Artel Eng, 1975-. **Memberships:** Inst Elec & Electronics Engrs; Acoust Soc Am; AAAS; Can Med & Biol Eng Soc; Sigma Xi; Instrument Soc Am. **Research Statement & Publications:** Acoustics and hearing; acousto-mechanical models of the head; hearing assistive devices; signal processing by the ear; signal processing for amelioration of hearing deficit; advanced audiometric instrumentation. **Mailing Address:** Dept Elec & Comput Eng, Univ Toronto, IBBME, 164 Col St, Toronto, ON M5S 3G9, Can. **Fax:** 416-978-4317. **E-Mail:** h.kunov@utoronto.ca

KUNSELMAN, A(RTHUR) RAYMOND, NUCLEAR PHYSICS, PARTICLE PHYSICS. **Personal Data:** b Witchita Falls, Tex, February 22, 1942; m 1992, Donna. **Education:** Univ Calif, Berkeley, BA, 1964, MA, 1965, PhD (physics), 1969. **Professional Experience:** RETIRED; prof emer physics, Univ Wyo, beginning 1998; Consult, Rutherford Lab, Eng, 1975; fac mem physics, Univ Wyo, beginning 1969; physicist, Lawrence Berkeley Lab, 1969. **Memberships:** Am Asn Physics Teachers; Sigma Xi. **Research Statement & Publications:** Muonic and hadronic atoms; leptonic conservations; muonic hydrogen isotopes. **Mailing Address:** Dept Physics, Univ Wyo, PO Box 3905, Laramie, WY 82071. **E-Mail:** rk@uwyo.edu

KUNTZ, GARLAND PARKE PAUL, CORROSION, COMPUTER ASSISTED INSTRUCTION. **Personal Data:** b Ft Worth, Tex. **Education:** Fla State Univ, BS, 1966; Case Western Res Univ, MS, 1969, PhD (chem), 1972. **Professional Experience:** HEAD CHEM DEPT, CONCORDIA COL, EDMONTON, 1996-; ASSOCPROF PHYSICS & CHEM, CONCORDIA COL, EDMONTON, 1975-; res assoc, Univ Alta, 1973-1975; Fel, Dept Chem, Case Western Res Univ, 1972-1973. **Memberships:** Nat Asn Corrosion Engrs. **Research Statement & Publications:** Computer assisted instruction. **Mailing Address:** Dept Sci, Concordia Col 7128 Ada Blvd, Edmonton, AB T5B 4E4, Can. **Fax:** 403-474-1933.

KUNTZ, IRVING, POLYMER CHEMISTRY, ORGANIC CHEMISTRY. **Personal Data:** b New York, NY, February 16, 1925; m 1977, c 2. **Education:** City Col New York, BS, 1948; Polytech Inst Brooklyn, MS, 1950, PhD (chem), 1955. **Professional Experience:** SR RES ASSOC, EXXON CHEM CO, 1968-; res assoc, Esso Res & Eng Co, 1963-1968; from sr chemist to sect head, Esso Res & Eng Co, 1955-1963; Res chemist, SpragueElec

Co, Mass, 1950-1953. **Research Statement & Publications:** Organic reaction mechanisms; polymer chemistry; ionic polymerizations; kinetics. **Mailing Address:** 725 Haven Pl, Linden, NJ 07036-5820.

KUNTZ, IRWIN DOUGLAS, PHYSICAL CHEMISTRY. **Personal Data:** b Nashville, Tenn, August 31, 1939; m 1961, c 3. **Education:** Princeton Univ, AB, 1961; Univ Calif, Berkeley, PhD (chem), 1965. **Honors & Awards:** Volwiler Res Achievement Award. **Professional Experience:** Assoc dean res, Schl Pharma, Univ Calif San Francisco, 1998-2001; DIR, MOLECULAR DESIGN INST, UNIV CALIF, SAN FRANCISCO, 1993-; PROF CHEM, UNIV CALIF, SAN FRANCISCO, 1976-; assoc prof, Univ Calif, San Francisco, 1971-1976; asst prof chem, Princeton Univ, 1965-1971; co-inventor, Thuris Corp. **Memberships:** Fel AAAS; Sigma Xi; Am Chem Soc. **Research Statement & Publications:** Physical chemistry of liquid state; hydration of macromolecules; spectroscopic studies of biological materials and fast reactions in biological systems; design of ligands. **Mailing Address:** Dept Pharmaceut Chem, Univ Calif, 513 Parnassus Ave Box 0446, San Francisco, CA 94143-0446. **Fax:** 415-476-9124. **E-Mail:** kuntz@cgl.ucsf.edu

KUNTZ, MEL ANTON, PETROLOGY, VOLCANOLOGY. **Personal Data:** b Minneapolis, Minn, July 4, 1939; m 1993, Carmela; c David, Brian, Stacy, Robert & Jeffrey. **Education:** Carleton Col, BA, 1961; Northwestern Univ, MS, 1964; Stanford Univ, PhD (geol), 1968. **Professional Experience:** SCIENTIST EMER, US GEOL SURV, as of 2006; res geologist, US Geol Surv, beginning 1974; asst prof geol, Amherst Col, 1968-1974. **Memberships:** Mineral Soc Am; Geol Soc Am. **Research Statement & Publications:** Petrogenesis of epizonal and catazonal plutons; application of experimental studies to natural igneous and metamorphic rocks; petrogenesis of basalts; basalts of Snake River Plain, Idaho; geology of intermountain western United States; geology of the Idaho batholith; geology of Lake Mead area, Nevada and Arizona. **Mailing Address:** US Geol Surv, Mail Stop 913 Post Box 25046, Denver, CO 80225. **Fax:** 303-236-0214. **E-Mail:** mkuntz@usgs.gov

KUNTZ, RICHARD A, MATHEMATICS. **Personal Data:** b Lakewood, NJ, September 7, 1939; m 1960, c 2. **Education:** Monmouth Col, BS, 1964; Univ Md, MA, 1967, PhD (math), 1969. **Professional Experience:** PROF EMER MATH, MONMOUTH COL, NJ, 2004-; vpres & dean, Sch Info Sci, 1987-2004; vpres admin, Monmouth Col, NJ, 1980-1987; prof math, Monmouth Col, Nj, 1976-2004; dean grad sch, Monmouth Col, NJ, 1976-1980; chmn dept, Monmouth Col, NJ, 1974-1976; from asst prof to assoc prof, MonmouthCol, NJ, 1968-1976; teaching asst math, Univ Md, 1964-1968. **Memberships:** Am Math Soc; Math Asn Am. **Research Statement & Publications:** Abstract algebra; ideal theory in commutative rings. **Mailing Address:** Monmouth Univ, West Long Branch, NJ 07764-1898.

KUNTZ, ROBERT ELROY, parasitology, helminthology; deceased, see previous edition for last biography

KUNTZ, ROBERT ROY, PHYSICAL CHEMISTRY. **Personal Data:** b Barry, Ill, April 10, 1937; m 1959, c 2. **Education:** Culver-Stockton Col, BA, 1959; Carnegie Inst Technol, MS, 1962, PhD (chem), 1963. **Honors & Awards:** Culver-Stockton Col Outstanding Alumni Award, 1986. **Professional Experience:** PROF EMER, DEPT CHEM, UNIV MO, as of 2006; assoc chair, Univ MO, Columbia, 1979-1981; interim chmn, Univ MO, Columbia, 1978-1979; assoc prog dir chem dyanmics, NSF, 1973-1974; assoc chmn chem, Univ Mo, 1972-1973; PROF CHEM, UNIV MO, COLUMBIA, beginning 1971; from asst prof to assoc prof, Univ MO, Columbia, 1962-1971. **Memberships:** Am Soc Photobiol; Sigma Xi; Am Chem Soc; Am Phys Soc; Inter Am PhotochemSoc. **Research Statement & Publications:** Photolysis and radiolysis of organic compounds, free radical kinetics, radiation protection; flash photolysis; photobiology; photocatalysis. **Mailing Address:** Dept Chem, Univ Mo, Columbia, MO 65211-0001. **E-Mail:** kuntzr@missouri.edu

KUNTZMAN, RONALD GROVER, BIOCHEMISTRY, PHARMACOLOGY. **Personal Data:** b New York, NY, September 17, 1933; m 1955, c 2. **Education:** Brooklyn Col, BS, 1955; George Washington Univ, MS, 1957, PhD (biochem), 1962. **Honors & Awards:** John Jacob Abel Award, Am Soc Pharmacol & Exp Therapeut, 1969. **Professional Experience:** Res & developsteering comt, chmn subcomt on Adv Comt Systs, Comn Drugs for Rare Dis, Pharmaceut MfrsAsn, 1985-; VPRES RES & DEVELOP, HOFFMANN-LA ROCHE INC, NUTLEY, NJ, 1984-; vpres & dir Pharmaceut Res &Develop, Hoffmann-La Roche Inc, 1980-1984; asst vpres & dir therapeuts res, Hoffmann-LaRoche, Inc, 1973-1981; assoc dir biol res, Hoffmann-La Roche, Inc, 1972-1973; assoc dir deptbiochem & drug metab, Hoffmann-La Roche, Inc, 1970-1972; dep head biochem pharmacol dept, Wellcome Res Labs, Burroughs & Co, 1967-1970; sr biochemist, Wellcome Res Labs, Burroughs& Co, 1962-1970; Chmn, Drug Metab Div, Am Soc Pharmacol & Exp Therapeut; corp mem, Muscular Dystrophy Asn; mem Adv Bd, Univ Ariz Col Pharm Nat Adv Bd; mem AdvBd, Univ Pa Natural Sci Asn; res adv coun, Nat Orgn Rare Dis; chemist, NIH. **Memberships:** Am Soc Pharmacol & Exp Therapeut (secy-treas 1981-1983); Am Soc BiolChemists; Sigma Xi; Am Col Neuropsychopharmacol; Soc Toxicol; AAAS. **Research Statement & Publications:** Biochemical effects and metabolism of drugs and steroid hormones, induced enzyme syntheses; syntheses metabolism and storage of biogenic amines; preclinical development of new drugs; pharmacokinetics and efficacy studies on new therapeutics. **Mailing Address:** 16 Reunion Rd, Rye Brook, NY 10573. **Fax:** 973-235-7605.

KUNYOSYING, SUDA, MATHEMATICS. **Education:** New York Univ, PhD, 1978. **Professional Experience:** PROF & MATH SPECIALIZATION COORDR, DEPT COMPUT SCI & MATH, SHEPHERD UNIV, as of 2006. **Mailing Address:** PO Box 3210, Shepherd Univ, Shepherdstown, WV 25443-3210. **Fax:** 304-876-3101. **E-Mail:** skunyosy@shepherd.edu

KUNZ, ALBERT L, PHYSIOLOGY, CONTROL OF RESPIRATION. **Personal Data:** b Bloomington, Ind, October 3, 1933; m Faye. **Education:** Ind Univ, AB, 1956, MD, 1959; Ohio State Univ, MS, 1965. **Honors & Awards:** Perkin's Award, Am Physiol Soc, 1974. **Professional Experience:** Alexander Von Humboldt fel, 1974-1975; Nat Heart Inst fel, 1963-1965; from instr to assoc prof, 1962-1976, prof, 1976-1992; EMER PROF PHYSIOL, OHIO STATE UNIV. **Memberships:** Am Physiol Soc; Am Heart Asn; Am Asn Univ Professors. **Research Statement & Publications:** Respiratory control; anomalous viscosity of blood. **Mailing Address:** 110 Glenmont Ave, Columbus, OH 43214.

KUNZ, BERNARD ALEXANDER, DNA REPAIR, MUTAGENESIS. **Personal Data:** b Montreal, Que, March 5, 1952; m 1980, Donna M Criss; c 1. **Education:** McGill Univ, Que, BS, 1974; Brock Univ, Ont, MS, 1976; York Univ, PhD (molecular genetics), 1981. **Professional Experience:** PROF & CHAIR BIOL, SCH BIOL & CHEM SCI, DEAKIN UNIV, 1995-; prof, dept microbiol, Univ Man, 1992-1995; from asst prof to assoc prof, Univ Man, 1986-1992; asst prof, York Univ, 1984-1986; res assoc, York Univ, 1983-1984; Fogarty fel, NatInst Environ Health Sci, 1981-1983. **Memberships:** Genetics Soc Can; Environ Mutagen Soc. **Research Statement & Publications:** Analysis of molecular mechanisms of mutation using genetic and recombinant DNA technique; influence of DNA repair and DNA precursor metabolism on genetic stability; isolation and characterization of plant DNA repair genes. **Mailing Address:** Sch Biol & Chem Sci, Deakin Univ, Rm SA118, Sci Bldg, Waurn Ponds Campus, Geelong, Australia. **E-Mail:** bkunz@deakin.edu.au

KUNZ, DONALD L, AERONAUTICS. **Education:** Syracuse Univ, BS, 1971; Ga Inst Technol, MS, 1972, PhD (aerospace eng), 1976. **Professional Experience:** ASSOC PROF AEROSPACE ENG, DEPT AERONAUT & ASTRONAUT, AIRFORCE INST TECHNOL, 2003-. **Mailing Address:** Dept Aeronaut & Astronaut, Airforce Inst Technol, 2950 Hobson Way, Whriht Patterson AFB, OH 85215-9797. **Fax:** 602-891-8947. **E-Mail:** Donald.Kunz@afit.edu

KUNZ, HAROLD RUSSELL, THERMODYNAMICS, HEAT TRANSFER. **Personal Data:** b Troy, NY, October 3, 1931; wid Helen; c Daryl L (Gottier) & Roderick R. **Education:** Rensselaer Polytech Inst, BME, 1953, MS, 1958, PhD (heat transfer), 1966. **Honors & Awards:** Research Award of energy technology, div of eLectrochemical, 1998. **Professional Experience:** Dir res, Jonomem corp, 2001-; PROF IN RESIDENCE, UNIV CONN, 1994-; FUEL CELL CONSULT, 1992-; adj prof, Dept Chem Eng, 1992-1994; sr proj engr fuel cell res, Int Fuel Cells, 1985-1992; sr proj engr fuel cell res, Power Systs Div, 1975-1985; sr proj engr, Power Systs Div, 1975; adj assoc prof, Hartford Grad Ctr, 1970-1994; sr proj engr, Pratt & Whitney Aircraft Div, United Technologies Corp, 1968-1974; adj asst prof mech eng, Hartford Grad Ctr, 1966-1970; proj engr heat transfer & fuel cell res, Pratt & Whitney Aircraft Div, United Technologies Corp, 1963-1968; asst proj engr heat transfer res, Pratt & Whitney Aircraft Div, United Technologies Corp, 1960-1963; sr anal engr, Pratt & Whitney Aircraft Div, United Technologies Corp, 1957-1960; anal engr, Pratt & Whitney Aircraft Div, United Technologies Corp, 1954-1957; Jr anal engr heat transfer & fluid mech res, Pratt & Whitney Aircraft Div, United Technologies Corp, 1953-1954. **Memberships:** Electrochem Soc; Am Soc Mech Engrs. **Research Statement & Publications:** Electrochemistry; thermodynamics; electrocatalysis; single-phase and two-phase fluid mechanics and heat transfer. **Mailing Address:** Dept Chem Eng, Univ Conn, 191 Auditorium Rd U-222, Vernon, CT 06066. **Fax:** 860-486-2959.

KUNZ, HEINZ W, PATHOLOGY, IMMUNOGENETICS. **Personal Data:** b Zurich, Switz, February 2, 1938; Swiss & American citizen; m Nancy. **Education:** Univ Pittsburgh, PhD (immunogenetics), 1978. **Professional Experience:** PROF PATH, UNIV PITTSBURGH, as of 2003; consult, Nat Res Coun, 1990-; prof path, Univ Pittsburgh, beginning 1990; dirgrad prog, Div Exp Path, 1988-1991; asst dir, Div Exp Path, 1987-1990; assoc dir, Div Exp Path, 1987-1988; mem, Pittsburgh Cancer Inst, 1986-; assoc staff, Presby-Univ Hosp, 1984-; from res asst prof to assoc prof, Univ Pittsburgh, 1976-1990; clin asst staff, Presby-Univ Hosp, 1971-1984; assoc, Dept Path, Harvard Med Sch, Boston, 1970-1971; tech assoc, Dept Path, Harvard Med Sch, Boston, 1969-1970; sr res asst, Dept Path, Harvard Med Sch, Boston, 1965-1969; res asst, Dept Path, Harvard Med Sch, Boston, 1962-1965. **Memberships:** AAAS; Am Chem Soc; Genetics Soc Am; Transplantation Soc; Am Asn Pathologists; Am Asn Immunologists; Int Soc Immunol & Reprod; Am Soc Immunol & Reprod; Am Asn Cancer Res. **Research Statement & Publications:** Experimental pathology; reproduction immunology; immunogentics. **Mailing Address:** Dept Path, Sch Med, Univ Pittsburgh, 3550 Terrace St S 713, Pittsburgh, PA 15261-0001. **Fax:** 412-648-1916. **E-Mail:** hwk@med.pitt.edu

KUNZ, JOAN C, CHEMISTRY. **Honorary Degrees:** Univ Mo, St Louis, BS; Univ Wis-Madison, PhD. **Professional Experience:** ASSOC PROF CHEM, AUGSBURG COL, MINN, as of 2006. **Mailing Address:** Dept Chem, Augsburg Col, 2211 Riverside Ave S, Minneapolis, MN 55454. **E-Mail:** kunz@augsburg.edu

KUNZ, KAISER SCHOEN, THEORETICAL PHYSICS, COMPUTATIONS IN ELECTROMAGNETISM. **Personal Data:** b New Middletown, Ind, October 16, 1915; m 1944, Ruth; c Karl, Peter & Kevin. **Education:** Univ Ind, AB, 1936; Univ Cincinnati, AM, 1937, PhD (theoret physics), 1939. **Honors & Awards:** Distinguished Scientist of Yr, NMex Acad Sci, 1982. **Professional Experience:** EMER PROF PHYSICS, NMEX STATE UNIV, 1981-; res prof physics, Nmex State Univ, 1976-1987; res prof physics & elec eng, Nmex State Univ, 1960-1976; from res physicist to head interpretation res dept, Schlumberger Well Surv Corp, 1951-1960; assoc prof elec eng, Case Inst Technol, 1949-1951; lectr appl math, comput lab, 1947-1949; res fel, Cruft Lab, Harvard Univ, 1946-1947; res assoc, Cruft Lab, Harvard Univ, 1945-1946; instrelectronics, Cruft Lab, Harvard Univ, 1942-1945; instr math, Univ Cincinnati, 1939-1942. **Memberships:** Fel AAAS; Am Phys Soc; Inst Elec & Electronics Engrs; Am Math Soc; Am AsnPhysics Teachers; Sigma Xi. **Research Statement & Publications:** Propagation of electromagnetic waves in dynamic media; quantum electronics and lasers; electrodynamics; field theory; numerical analysis. **Mailing Address:** 2047 Crescent Dr, Las Cruces, NM 88005-3301. **E-Mail:** kkunz@nmsu.edu

KUNZ, PETER DALE, THEORETICAL NUCLEAR PHYSICS. **Personal Data:** b Hubbard, Ore, July 20, 1928. **Education:** Ore State Col, BS, 1950, MS, 1953; Univ Wash, PhD, 1959. **Professional Experience:** PROF EMER, UNIV COLO, as of 2005; from asst prof to prof, Univ Colo, 1962-1992; asst prof, Univ BC, 1961-1962; res assoc, Univ Calif, Los Angeles, 1960-1961; instr, Univ Wash, 1960. **Memberships:** Fel Am Phys Soc. **Research Statement & Publications:** Research nuclear structure; nuclear reaction theory and nuclear reaction codes. **Mailing Address:** Nuclear Physics Labs, Univ Colo, PO Box 446, Boulder, CO 80309. **E-Mail:** peter.kunz@colorado.edu

KUNZ, SIDNEY EDMUND, ENTOMOLOGY, ECOLOGY. **Personal Data:** b Fredericksburg, Tex, December 24, 1935; m 1960, c 3. **Education:** Tex A&M Univ, BS, 1958, MS, 1962; Okla State Univ, PhD (entom), 1967. **Professional Experience:** LAB DIR, AGR RES SERV, USDA, KERRVILLE, 1986-; USAID, Tanzania, IAEA, Somalia, 1982; res leader & res entomologist, sci & educ, 1977-1986; Entom consult, Food & Agr Orgn UN Develop Prog, Mauritius, 1973-1974; res entomologist, Col Sta, 1969-1977; res entomologist, Agr Res Serv, USDA, Kerrville, 1967-1969; exten entomologist, Okla State Univ, 1964-1967; Surv entomologist, Okla State Univ, 1961-1964. **Memberships:** Entom Soc Am; Am Registry Prof Entomologists; Sigma Xi. **Research Statement & Publications:** Biology, ecology and area integrated pest management control of biting flies of cattle, horn flies and stable flies. **Mailing Address:** HC 5, Aqua Vista Estates, Kerrville, TX 78028.

KUNZ, THOMAS HENRY, ANIMAL PHYSIOLOGY, BEHAVIOR-ETHOLOGY. **Personal Data:** b Kansas City, Mo, June 11, 1938; m 1962, Margaret; c Pamela L & David T. **Education:** Cent Mo State Univ, BS, 1961, MS, 1962; Drake Univ, MA, 1968; Univ Kans, PhD (ecol), 1971. **Honors & Awards:** Gerritt S Miller Award, 1984. **Professional Experience:** DIR, CTR ECOL & CONSERV BIOL, 1996-; DIR GRAD PROGS, ECOL & BEHAV EVOLUTION, BOSTON UNIV, 1983-; RES ASSOC, CARNEGIE MUS NATURAL HIST, 1978-; res assoc, Smithsonian Inst, 1994-; chmn, Boston Univ, 1985-1990; PROF BIOL, ECOL & BEHAV EVOLUTION, BOSTON UNIV, 1984-; prin investr, Nat Geog Soc, 1984-1985 & 1996-1997; Orgn Am Statesgrant, 1984-1985; assoc chmn, Boston Univ, 1981-1985; dirgrad studies, Boston Univ, 1978-1981; assoc ed, Am Midland Naturalist, 1978-

1980; prin investr, NSF, 1973-; from asst prof to assoc prof, Boston Univ, 1971-1984; teaching fel, Univ Kans, 1970-1971; res fel, Kans Nat Hist Surv, 1967-1970; instr biol, Shawnee Mission Schs, 1962-1967. **Memberships:** Fel AAAS; Am Soc Mammalogists; Ecol Soc Am; Am Soc Naturalists; Soc StudyEvolution. **Research Statement & Publications:** Behavioral and physiological ecology of bats, with emphasis on social behavior, energetics, reproductive biology and feeding ecology of temperate and tropical species. **Mailing Address:** Dept Biol, Boston Univ, 5 Cummington St, Boston, MA 02215. **Fax:** 617-353-5383. **E-Mail:** kunz@bu_bio.bu.edu

KUNZE, A(DOLF) W(ILHELM) GERHARD, GEOPHYSICS. **Personal Data:** b Philadelphia, Pa, August 23, 1936; m 1992, Diana; c Peter & Karl. **Education:** Pa State Univ, BS, 1963, PhD (geophys), 1973. **Honors & Awards:** Fulbright Sr Prof Teaching & Res Award, 1990. **Professional Experience:** PROF EMER GEOL, UNIV AKRON, 2000-; prof geol, Univ Akron, 1985-2000; vis prof, Inst Geophys, Kiel, Fed Repub Ger, 1982, 1990 & 1994; from asst prof to assoc prof, Univ Akron, 1974-1985; Nat Res Coun res assoc lunar geophys, Johnson Space Ctr, NASA, Houston, 1973-1974. **Memberships:** Am Geophys Union. **Research Statement & Publications:** Engineering geophysics: shallow subsurface investigations using gravity/magnetic, electrical resistivity and seismic refraction methods. **Mailing Address:** Dept Geol, Univ Akron, 62 Crouse Hall, Akron, OH 44325-4101. **Fax:** 330-972-7611. **E-Mail:** akunze@uakron.edu

KUNZE, DIANA LEE, MEDICAL PHYSIOLOGY. **Personal Data:** b Winthrop, Mass, December 19, 1939. **Education:** Stetson Univ, BS, 1961; Emory Univ, MS, 1966; Univ Utah, PhD (physiol), 1970. **Professional Experience:** PROF NEUROSCIENCE, CASE WESTERN RES UNIV, 1996-; SR RES SCIENTIST, RAMMELKAMP CTR EDU & RES, METROHEALTH SYST, CLEVELAND, OHIO, 1996-; ADJ STAFF, DEPT CELL BIOLOGY, CLEVELAND CLINIC FOUND, CLEVELAND, OHIO, 1995-; from assoc prof to prof, physiol & biophys, Baylor Col Med, Houston, Tex, 1985-1995; from asst prof to assoc prof, Dept physiol & biophysics, Univ Tex Med Br, Galveston, 1973-1985res assoc, Div Cardiol, Dept Med, Univ Utah, 1972-1973; res neurophysiol, Nat Ctr Sci Res, France, 1971-1972; instr, Dade Coounty, Fla, Pub Sch, 1961-1963. **Memberships:** Am Physiol Soc; AAAS; Am Heart Asn; Biophysical Soc; Soc Neuroscience. **Research Statement & Publications:** Studies of control mechanisms of cardiac rhythm by neural input and by local factors. **Mailing Address:** Dept Neurosci, Case Western Res Univ, 2500 MetroHealth Dr, Cleveland, OH 44109. **Fax:** 216-778-2090. **E-Mail:** dxk35@case.edu

KUNZE, ERIC, OCEANOGRAPHY. **Personal Data:** b Nelson, BC, June 13, 1956. **Education:** Univ BC, Vancouver, BS, 1979; Univ Wash, MS, 1982, PhD (oceanog), 1985. **Honors & Awards:** Father James B Macelwane Young Investr Medal, Am Geophys Union, 1992; Sverdrup lectr, 1992. **Professional Experience:** PRIN OCEANOGRAPHER, DEPT OCEAN PHYSICS, UNIV WASH, as of 2006; chmn, Dept Ocean Physics, Appl Physics Lab, Univ Wash, 2002; PROF, SCH OCEANOG, UNIV WASH, SEATTLE, as of 2002; assoc prof, Sch Oceanog, Univ Wash, Seattle, beginning 1993; asst ed, J Marine Res, 1987-; res asst prof, Sch Oceanog, Univ Wash, Seattle, 1987-1993; res scientist, Woods Hole Oceanog Inst, Mass, 1986-1987; res assoc, Woods Hole Oceanog Inst, Mass, 1985-1986; fel, Woods Hole Oceanog Inst, Mass, 1983; res asst, Sch Oceanog, Univ Wash, Seattle, 1979-1985. **Memberships:** Fel Am Geophys Union; Am Meteorol Soc; Nat Conserv; Can Meteorol & Oceanog Soc. **Research Statement & Publications:** Interactions of meso- to microscale oceanic phenomena including fronts, eddies, internat waves, turbulence, double diffusion, bottom topography and surface forcing and their effects, through mixing and water-mass modification on larger scales; demonstration that internal waves are sensitive to rotation in the ocean. **Mailing Address:** Dept Ocean Physics, Univ Wash, 501 Henderson Hall 1013 NE 40 th St Box 357940, Seattle, WA 98105-6698. **Fax:** 206-543-6785. **E-Mail:** kunze@apl.washington.edu

KUNZE, GEORGE WILLIAM, SOIL MINERALOGY. **Personal Data:** b Warda, Tex, September 16, 1922; m 1948, c 2. **Education:** Tex A&M Univ, BS, 1947, MS, 1950; Pa State Univ, PhD (soil mineral), 1952. **Professional Experience:** RETIRED; pres, Conf Southern Grad Schs, 1980-1981; vpres, Conf SouthernGrad Schs, 1979-1980; grad prog consult, Bangladesh Agr Univ, 1970 & Grad Sch Agr Sci, Castelar, Arg, 1972; from assoc dean to dean grad col, Tex A&M Univ, 1967-1984; prof soils &crop sci, Tex A&M Univ, 1960-1984; consult ed, Soil Sci, 1958-; from asst prof to assoc prof, Tex A&M Univ, 1952-1960. **Memberships:** Fel AAAS; fel Am Soc Agron; Soil Sci Soc Am; Clay Minerals Soc; fel MineralSoc Am. **Research Statement & Publications:** Soil chemistry. **Mailing Address:** 5100 S US Hwy 77, LaGrange, TX 78945.

KUNZE, JAY FREDERICK, ENERGY, MEDICAL PHYSICS. **Personal Data:** b Pittsburgh, Pa, February 24, 1933; m 1981, Kristine; c John, Richard & Robert. **Education:** Carnegie Inst Technol (now Carnegie Mellon Univ.), BS, 1954, MS, 1955, PhD (nuclear physics), 1959. **Honors & Awards:** Fellow of American Nuclear Society (1980) Fellow of American Society of Mechanical Engineers (1999). **Professional Experience:** DEAN & PROF, COL ENG, IDAHO STATE UNIV, 1995-; Dir. of Health and Medical Physics, Univ. of Missouri, 1993-1995; chmn nuclear eng, Univ Mo, 1983-1993; vpres & gen mgr, Energy Serv Inc, 1978-1983; mgr geothermal & adv technol, EG&G Idaho, Inc, 1974-1978; mgr reactor technol, 1970-1974; vis assoc prof, Univ Utah, 1969-1970; mgr oper & anal, Aerojet Nuclear Corp, 1969-1970; mgr nuclear technol, Idaho Test Sta, Gen Elec Co, 1965-1969; affil prof, Univ Idaho, 1959-1982; physicist, Idaho Test Sta, Gen Elec Co, 1958-1965; Proj physicist & asst, Carnegie Inst Technol, 1954-1958; Site leader, Air Force res. solar eclipse expeds, 1954-1955. **Memberships:** Am Nuclear Soc; Am Soc of Mechanical Engineers; Nat Soc Prof Engrs; Health Physics Soc; Am. Soc of Heating, Refrigeration and Air Conditioning Engineers; Sigma Xi. **Research Statement & Publications:** Nuclear fuel cycle; experimental reactor physics and reactor analysis; energy engineering and conservation; Laser Isotope Separation; Health Effects of Low Level Radiation; Geothermal energy. **Mailing Address:** Col Eng, Idaho State Univ, PO Box 8060, Pocatello, ID 83209. **Fax:** 208-282-4538. **E-Mail:** kunzejay@isu.edu

KUNZE, OTTO ROBERT, ENGINEERING, AGRICULTURE. **Personal Data:** b Warda, Tex, May 27, 1925; m 1951, Alice R Eifert; c Glenn, Allen, Charles & Karen. **Education:** Tex A&M Univ, BS, agr eng 1950; Iowa State Univ, MS, Agr Eng 1951; Mich State Univ, PhD (agr eng), 1964. **Honors & Awards:** "Outstanding Agri Eng Achievement of the 20th Century" for discovery and explanation of the "Rice Fissuring Mechanism, Am Soc of Agri Eng, 2000. **Professional Experience:** Lectr & consult, Thailand, 1995; lectr & consult, China, 1993; EMER PROF ELEC POWER & PROCESSING, TEX A&M UNIV, 1990-; lectr & consult, Taiwan, 1985, 1987, 1994; mem, Tex Air Control Bd, 1978-1990; Consult postharvest rice processing, India, 1975 & 1985; prof, Tex A&M Univ, 1969-1990; assoc prof elec power & processing, Tex A&M Univ, 1957-1961 & 1964-1969; Agr & indust engr, Cent Power & Light Co, 1951-1956. **Memberships:** Fel Am Soc Agr Engrs; Am Asn Cereal Chemists; Nat Soc Prof Engrs; Sigma Xi. **Research Statement & Publications:** Electric power and processing in agriculture; physical properties of agricultural products; hygroscopicity of rice and its effects on the grain; moisture readsorption-rice fissure phenomenon and, fissuring of the rice grain after rapid drying. **Mailing Address:** PO BOX 3, Warda, TX 789600003.

KUNZE, RAY ALDEN, MATHEMATICS. **Personal Data:** b Des Moines, Iowa, March 7, 1928; m 1951, c 5. **Education:** Univ Chicago, BS, 1950, MS, 1951, PhD (math), 1957. **Professional Experience:** PROF EMER, UNIV GA, as of 2004; prof math, Univ Calif, Irvine, beginning 1969; chmn dept, Univ Calif, Irvine, 1969-1974; from assoc prof to prof, Wash Univ, 1963-1969; consult, Prentice Hall & McGrawHill, 1961-; asst prof math, Brandeis Univ, 1960-1962; consult, Inst Defense Anal, 1954-. **Memberships:** Am Math Soc. **Research Statement & Publications:** Harmonic analysis; representations of Lie Groups. **Mailing Address:** Dept Math, Univ Ga, Athens, GA 30602-3024.

KUNZE, RAYMOND J, SOIL PHYSICS. **Personal Data:** b La Grange, Tex, October 25, 1928; m 1951, c 2. **Education:** Tex A&M Univ, BS, 1951, MS, 1956; Iowa State Univ, PhD (soil physics), 1960. **Professional Experience:** ASSOC CHMN, MICH STATE UNIV, 1980-; vis prof, Purdue Univ, 1974; PROF SOIL SCI, MICH STATE UNIV, 1970-; RES SOIL SCIENTIST, SCI & EDUCADMIN-AGR RES, USDA, 1965-; assoc prof soils, Mich State Univ, 1965-1970; soil scientist, Mich State Univ, 1962-1965; from asst to res assoc, NSF res fel & asst prof soil physics, 1960-1962; from asst to res assoc, Iowa State Univ, 1956-1960; asst, Tex A&M Univ, 1954-1956. **Memberships:** Am Soc Agron; Soil Sci Soc Am. **Research Statement & Publications:** Measurement of unsaturated flow of moisture in soils; predictions, by computer techniques and analysis, of water movement and distribution in the profile based on measured characteristics of the soil; expertise in operating double-gamma beam for simultaneous, nondestructive, two-component soil and water analysis. **Mailing Address:** 2670 Linden St, East Lansing, MI 48823.

KUNZELMAN, KARYN S, CARDIOTHORACIC SURGERY RESEARCH. **Education:** MD, PHD. **Professional Experience:** DIR, CENT MAINE MED CTR, CENT MAINE HEART & VASCULAR INST, MAINE, as of 2006. **Memberships:** Am Heart Asn. **Mailing Address:** Cent Maine Med Ctr, Cent Maine Heart & Vascular Inst, Lewiston, ME 04240. **E-Mail:** karynk@surgery.wisc.edu

KUNZLE, HANS-PETER, MATHEMATICAL PHYSICS, RELATIVITY. **Personal Data:** b Kreuzlingen, Switz, September 1, 1940; Canadian & Swiss citizen; m 1968, Nicole; c Frederick, Caroline, Cyril & Elisabeth. **Education:** ETH, dipl(Physics), 1964; Univ London, PhD (relativity), 1967. **Professional Experience:** Prof Math, univ Alta, 1980-; from asst prof to assoc prof, univ Alta, 1970-1980; lectr & asst res mathematician, Univ Calif, Berkeley, 1968-1970; res asst, Kings Col, Univ London, 1967-1968; vis prof univ de la Mediterranee, Luminy, France 1997; vis scientist Albert-Einstein-Inst, potsdam, Ger, 1996, Inst Theoret Physics, univ of Zurich, 1996, Max Planck Inst Astrophysics, Garching, 1982-1983, Centre Phys Theor Nat Inst Sci Res, Marseille, France, 1975-1976. **Memberships:** Int soc on general Relativity and Gravitation Am Math Soc; Am Phys Soc; Can Math Soc. **Research Statement & Publications:** Mathematical problems in general relativity; applications of differential geometry to physics, especially relativistic mechanics and field theories; solutions to Einstein-Yang-Mills field equations with large symmetry groups. **Mailing Address:** Dept Math & Stat Sci, Univ Alta, Edmonton, AB T6G 2G1, Can. **Fax:** 780-492-6826. **E-Mail:** hp.kunzle@ualberta.ca

KUNZLER, JOHN EUGENE, SOLID STATE DEVICES, SUPERCONDUCTIVITY. **Personal Data:** b Willard, Utah, April 25, 1923; m 1950, Lois McDonald; c Carol (Blaine), Marilyn (Barker), Bonnie & Kim (Tomeo). **Education:** Univ Utah, BS, 1945; Univ Calif, PhD (phys chem), 1950. **Honors & Awards:** John Price Wetherill Award, Franklin Inst, 1964; Int Prize New Mat, Am PhysSoc, 1979; Kamerlingh Onnes Medal, Neth Asn Refrig, 1979. **Professional Experience:** RETIRED; dir, Future Device Studies Ctr, 1985-1986; dir, Electronic Mat, Processes & Devices Lab, 1979-1985; dir, Electronic Mat & Device Lab, 1969-1979; head, MetalPhysics Res Dept, 1961-1969; mem tech staff, AT&T Bell Labs, 1952-1961; from asst to resassoc, Univ Calif, 1946-1952; Asst, Purdue Univ, 1945-1946. **Memberships:** Nat Acad Eng; Am ChemSoc; fel Am Phys Soc. **Research Statement & Publications:** Electrical, thermal and magnetic properties of solids at low temperatures; Fermi surface; galvanomagnetic and magnetothermal effects; high purity metals; high-field superconductivity; superconducting magnets; low temperature heat capacity and related thermal effects. **Mailing Address:** Rte 2, PO Box 130, Port Murray, NJ 07865.

KUO, ALBERT YI-SHUONG, PHYSICAL OCEANOGRAPHY, HYDRODYNAMICS. **Personal Data:** b Tayuan, Taiwan, November 4, 1939; m 1965, c 2. **Education:** Nat Taiwan Univ, BS, 1962; Univ Iowa, MS, 1965; Johns Hopkins Univ, PhD (fluid mech), 1970. **Professional Experience:** INVESTR, GODDARD SPACE FLIGHT CTR, NASA, as of 2006; PROF EMER PHYS SCI, VA INST MARINE SCI, as of 2005; dept chmn, VA Inst Marine Sci, 1993-1995; asst dir, VA Inst Marine Sci, 1991-1992; prof, Col William & Mary, beginning 1981; sr marine sci & head, Hydraulics Sect, 1978-1981; vis prof, Nat Taiwan Univ, 1977-1978; from asst prof to assoc prof, Univ VA & Col William & Mary, 1970-1980; assoc marine sci, Col William & Mary, 1970-1978; res assoc, Johns Hopkins Univ, 1970; jr instr fluid mech, Johns Hopkins Univ, 1967-1969. **Memberships:** Am Soc Civil Engrs; Estuarine Res Fedn; Int Asn Hydraul Res. **Research Statement & Publications:** Turbulence, diffusion, dispersion; estuarine mathematical model; estuarine hydrodynamics; sediment transport; coastal circulation. **Mailing Address:** Dept Phys Sci VA Inst Marine Sci, PO Box 1346, Gloucester Point, VA 23062. **E-Mail:** kuo@vims.edu

KUO, BENJAMIN CHUNG-I, ELECTRICAL ENGINEERING. **Personal Data:** b China, October 5, 1930; m 1954, c 1. **Education:** Univ NH, BS, 1954; Univ Ill, MS, 1956, PhD (elec eng), 1958. **Professional Experience:** PROF EMER ELEC ENG, UNIV ILL, URBANA, as of 2000; prof elec eng, Univ Ill, Urbana, beginning 1966; from asst prof to assoc prof, Univ Ill, Urbana, 1958-1966; asst, Univ Ill, Urbana, 1954-1957; plant engr, Laible Mfg Co, 1953-1954. **Memberships:** Inst Elec & Electronics Engrs. **Research Statement & Publications:** Feedback control systems; sampled-data systems. **Mailing Address:** Dept Elec & Comput Eng, Univ Ill, Champaign, IL 61821. **E-Mail:** b-kuo@uiuc.edu

KUO, CHAN-HWA, ORGANIC CHEMISTRY. **Personal Data:** b Shanghai, China, October 7, 1931; American citizen; m 1957, c 3. **Education:** Hartwick Col, BS, 1957; Rensselaer Polytech Inst, MS, 1958; Polytech Inst Brooklyn, PhD (org chem), 1975. **Professional Experience:** SR RES CHEMIST, MERCK & CO, INC, 1974-; res chemist, Merck & Co, Inc, 1958-1974. **Memberships:** Sigma Xi. **Research Statement & Publications:** Synthesis of griseofulvin, fluoro- and polychlorogriseofulvin, estrone, prostaglandin E1; synthesis and conformational analysis of pantetheine analogs; synthesis and relative configurational studies of the chiral lactone derived from thermozymocidin (myriocin). **Mailing Address:** 105 E Nassau Ave, South Plainfield, NJ 07080-5219.

KUO, CHAO-YING, CELLULAR TRANSPLANTATION. **Personal Data:** b Taiwan, April 27, 1940; m 1967, Grace; c Alice A & Bobby F. **Education:** Nat Taiwan Normal Univ, BS, 1964; Ind State Univ, MA, 1970; Univ Iowa, PhD (microbiol), 1974. **Professional Experience:** Vis res assoc prof, Nat Sci Coun, Repub China, 1993; vis assoc prof, DeptPediat, Nat Taiwan Univ, 1993; ASST PROF, DEPT PEDIAT, CTR HEALTH SCI, UNIV TENN, 1991-; grants, LeBonheur Diabetes Res Fund, 1991-1992; res assoc, Dent Res Ctr, 1988 & Dept Pediat, 1989-1990; pvt enterprise, 1984-1988; grants, Am Cancer Soc, 1981-

1982; res microbiologist, Res Serv, Vet Admin Med Ctr, Memphis, Tenn, 1981-1984; from instr to asst prof, Dept Med, Microbiol & Immunol, Univ Tenn, 1980-1984; instr, Div Allergy & Immunol, Dept Med, 1980-1981; grants, Nat Cancer Inst, NIH, 1979-1983; grants, Leukemia Res Found, Inc, 1978-1979; assoc mem, Barbara Kopp Geriat Res Ctr, Auburn, NY, 1977-1980; asst resscientist, Div Allergy & Immunol, Dept Med, 1974-1977; res assoc, Lady Davis Inst Med Res, Jewish Gen Hosp, Montreal, 1973-1974; asst immunol, Univ Iowa, 1970-1973; gen bot, HumanAnat & Physiol, Ind State Univ, 1968-1970; teaching asst, Lab Invert, Zool & Human Physiol, Taiwan Normal Univ, 1965-1967. **Memberships:** Am Asn Immunologists; Asn Am-Chinese Professionals. **Research Statement & Publications:** Allergy and tumor immunology; monoclonal antibody production; islet transplantation and islet gland equivalent development; aging and cancer; author of numerous scientific publications. **Mailing Address:** Dept Pediat Col Med Univ Tenn, WPT 301 50 N Dunlap, Memphis, TN 38103. **Fax:** 901-572-5036.

KUO, CHARLES C Y, MATERIALS & PROCESSES, MICROELECTRONICS. **Personal Data:** b Hubei, China, m 1949, Deborah; c Sze-Ping, Sze-Wen-Seot & Stanley. **Education:** Col Ord Eng, China, BS, 1945; Lehigh Univ, Bethlehem, Pa, MS, 1957, PhD (chem), 1961. **Honors & Awards:** John Wagnon Tech Achievement Award, Int Soc Hybrid MicroeLectronics, 1987. **Professional Experience:** Spec ed, Soc Functional Mat, beginning 1990; mem prog comt, Int Conf Electronic Components & Mat, beginning 1989; TECH DIR RES & DEVELOP MAT, CTS CORP, ELKHART, IND, 1977-; dept head, res & develop mat, Engelhard Industs, NJ, 1971-1977; eng specialist, res & develop mat, Res & Develop Lab, GTE, NY, 1967-1971; mem staff, res & develop mat, BellTel Lab, AT&T, Pa, 1961-1967; res fel chem eng, Lehigh Univ, Bethlehem, Pa, 1955-1961; asst prof chem eng, Col Ord Eng, Taiwan, China, 1949-1955. **Memberships:** Am Chem Soc; Am Ceramic Soc; Am Soc Metals; Int Soc Microelectronics; SocFunctional Mat. **Research Statement & Publications:** Materials and processes of hybrid microelectronics; thick and thin films; resistors; conductors; dielectrics; reliability; interconnection; packaging; author of more than 80 publications; granted 34 patents. **Mailing Address:** CTS Corp, 905 W Blvd N, Elkhart, IN 46514.

KUO, CHENG-YIH, POLYMER SCIENCE. **Personal Data:** b Tainan, Taiwan, April 2, 1942; American citizen; m 1978, c 1. **Education:** Nat Taiwan Univ, BS, 1966; Univ Akron, MS, 1969, PhD (polymer sci), 1973. **Professional Experience:** SCIENTIST MAT SCI, RES CTR, GLIDDEN CO, 1982-; assoc scientist, ResCtr, Glidden CO, 1980-1982; sr chemist, Res Ctr, Glidden CO, 1975-1980; fel, Inst Polymer Sci, Univ Akron, 1973-1975. **Memberships:** Am Chem Soc. **Research Statement & Publications:** Characterization of polymers and analysis of organic coatings. **Mailing Address:** Glidden Co, 16651 Sprague Rd, Strongsville, OH 44136-1757.

KUO, CHIANG-HAI, CHEMICAL, ENVIRONMENTAL & PETROLEUM ENGINEERING. **Personal Data:** b Tainan, Taiwan, February 10, 1936; m 1959, c 2. **Education:** Nat Taiwan Univ, BS, 1957; Univ Houston, MS, 1961, PhD (chem eng), 1964. **Honors & Awards:** Award, Am Inst Chem Engrs, 1964; Bronze Medal Award, US Environ Protection Agency, 1975. **Professional Experience:** PROF EMER CHEM ENG, MISS STATE UNIV, as of 2004; Hearin-Hess distinguished prof, Miss State Univ, 1990-1993; prof chem eng, Miss State Univ, beginning 1977; assoc prof, Miss State Univ, 1970-1977; res engr, Shell Develop Co, 1964-1970; engr, Shell Develop Co, 1962-1964; teaching asst, Nat Taiwan Univ, 1957-1959. **Memberships:** Am Inst Chem Engrs; Am Inst Mining Metall & Petrol Engrs. **Research Statement & Publications:** Mass transfer and chemical reactions; reaction kinetics; flow through porous media; heat transfer; petroleum recovery processes; air and water pollution control. **Mailing Address:** Dept Chem Eng, Miss State Univ, 310 Swalm Chem Eng Bldg, PO Box 9595, Mississippi State, MS 39762. **Fax:** 662-325-2482. **E-Mail:** kuo@che.msstate.edu

KUO, CHING-CHIANG, STRUCTURAL DYNAMICS, SYSTEM INTEGRATION. **Personal Data:** m Ju-pi; c Roger W & Lillian W. **Education:** Cheng Kung Univ, BS, 1965; Univ Iowa, MS, 1968; Mass Inst Technol, PhD (aeronaut & astronaut), 1972. **Professional Experience:** CHMN, SINO SWERINGEN AIRCRAFT CORP, 2005-; bd dir, Sino Sweringen Aircraft corp, 2000-2005; mgr struct dynamics, Boeing Nam, beginning 1996; spec adv, Mayor TaipeiRapid Transit Systs, Taipei Munic Govt, 1995-1996; Blue Ribbon Comn Rapid Transit Systs, Taipei Munic Govt, 1995; mgr struct dynamics, Rockwell Int, 1991-1995 & 1996; supvr vehicle& syst dynamics, Rockwell Int, 1987-1991; mem tech staff, Rockwell Int, 1973-1987. **Memberships:** Assoc fel Am Inst Aeronaut & Astronaut; Sigma Xi. **Research Statement & Publications:** Nonlinear panel flutter when subject to forcing function; past flutter of the panel with various forcing amplitudes and frequencies; unsteady aerodynamics on lifting body using bath sources and doublets. **Mailing Address:** 1770 SkyPl Blvd, San Antonio, TX 92708. **Fax:** 210-258-3973. **E-Mail:** ching.kuo@boeing.com

KUO, CHO-CHOU, MEDICAL MICROBIOLOGY. **Personal Data:** b Taiwan, September 12, 1934; m 1964, c 1. **Education:** Nat Taiwan Univ, MD, 1960; Univ Wash, PhD (prev med), 1970. **Professional Experience:** PROF PATHOBIOLOGY, UNIV WASH, 1980-; assoc prof, Univ Wash, 1976-1980; asst prof, Univ Wash, 1971-1976; fel, Univ Wash, 1967-1971. **Memberships:** Am Pub Health Asn; Am Col Prev Med; Am Soc Microbiol; Am Asn Immunologists; Am Sexually Transmitted Dis Asn. **Research Statement & Publications:** Microbiology and immunology of the Chlamydia Trachomatis organisms which cause eye and genital infection and chlamydia pneumonic which causes respiratory infection; development of diagnostic methods and prevention of the disease. **Mailing Address:** Dept Pathobiology, Univ Wash, PO Box 357238, Seattle, WA 98195-7238. **E-Mail:** cckuo@u.washington.edu

KUO, CHUNG-CHIEH, IMAGE PROCESSING. **Education:** Nat Taiwan Univ, BS, 1980; Mass Inst Technol, MS, 1985, PhD (elec eng & comput sci), 1987. **Professional Experience:** PROF ELEC ENG & MATH, UNIV SOUTHERN CALIF, 1999-; assoc prof elec eng & math, Univ Southern Calif, 1994-1998. **Mailing Address:** Dept Elec Eng, Univ Southern Calif, Los Angeles, CA 90089. **Fax:** 213-740-4651. **E-Mail:** cckuo@sipi.usc.edu

KUO, CHUNG-MING, CELLULOSE, PULP & PAPER SCIENCES. **Personal Data:** b Chang-Hwa, Taiwan, China, August 6, 1935; American citizen; m 1966, Freda Lai; c Michael & Susan. **Education:** Chung-Shing Univ, Taiwan, BS, 1958; Syracuse Univ, MS, 1964, PhD (org chem), 1969. **Professional Experience:** RES ASSOC, EASTMAN CHEM CO, 1981-; sr res chemist, Eastman ChemCo, 1971-1981; res chemist, Eastman Chem Co, 1968-1971. **Memberships:** Am Chem Soc. **Research Statement & Publications:** Chemistry and new and improved methods for the preparation of cellulose and its derivatives; modification of cellulose and cellulose derivatives for fibers, films and plastics end uses; new products based on cellulose and the related carbohydrate materials. **Mailing Address:** 2625 Brighton Ct, Kingsport, TN 37660. **Fax:** 423-229-4558.

KUO, ERIC YUNG-HUEI, ONCOLOGY, VETERINARY MEDICINE. **Personal Data:** b Chiayi, Taiwan, August 8, 1934; American citizen; m 1968, c 2. **Education:** Nat Taiwan Univ, BS, 1960; Univ Ill, Urbana, MS, 1966, PhD (vet med sci), 1970. **Professional Experience:** RES STAFF, USDA, 1980-; lectr, Grad Div, Anna Maria Col, Mass, 1976-; vetmed officer, USDA, 1976-1980; prin investr oncol, Mason Res Inst, 1975-1976; sr investr vet-endocrinol, Mason Res Inst, 1971-1974; res assoc endocrinol, Dept Physiol, Sch Med, BostonUniv, 1969-1971; res asst vet physiol, Col Vet Med, Univ Ill, Urbana, 1963-1969; Vet, SoutheastVet Hosp, Taiwan, 1961-1963; Asst vet parasitol, Dept Vet Med, Nat Taiwan Univ, 1961-1963. **Memberships:** AAAS; Endocrine Soc; Am Vet Med Asn. China. **Research Statement & Publications:** The roles of infection, infection hormonal imbalance, radiation and immunosuppression in mammary oncogenesis; the responses of hosts and tumors to surgery, radiation and chemotherapy. **Mailing Address:** 2455 Sedgefield Dr, Chapel Hill, NC 27514.

KUO, FRANKLIN F(A-KUN), ELECTRICAL ENGINEERING. **Personal Data:** b China, April 22, 1934; m 1958, c 2. **Education:** Univ Ill, BS, 1955, MS, 1956, PhD (elec eng), 1958. **Professional Experience:** EXEC DIR, SRI INT, MENLO PARK, CALIF, 1982-; dir info systs, Off Secy Defense, 1976-1977; liaisonscientist, US Off Naval Res, London, 1971-1972; prof elec eng, Univ Hawaii, 1966-1982; memCosine comt, Nat Acad Eng, 1965-1972; mem tech staff, Bell Tel Labs, Inc, 1960-1966; asst profelec eng, Polytech Inst Brooklyn, 1958-1960; coun mem, AsnComput Mach; consult ed, Prentice-Hall, Inc. **Memberships:** Fel Inst Elec & Electronics Engrs; Asn Comput Mach. **Research Statement & Publications:** Digital computers; information transmission; computer networks; data communications. **Mailing Address:** 824 La Mesa Dr, Portola Valley, CA 94028.

KUO, HARNG-SHEN, CHEMISTRY, BIOCHEMISTRY. **Personal Data:** b Hangchow, China, June 9, 1935; m 1967, c 3. **Education:** Cheng Kung Univ Taiwan, BS, 1959; La State Univ, New Orleans, MS, 1966; PaState Univ, PhD (chem), 1970. **Professional Experience:** SR STAFF SCIENTIST, CUTTER LABS, 1975-; radiation safety officer, Cutter Labs, 1972-1975; anal res chemist, Cutter Labs, 1971-1972; chemist & fel, Lawrence-Berkeley Lab, 1970-1971; engr, Taiwan Fertilizer Co, 1961-1964; Analyst cement, Taiwan ChiHsin Co, 1961. **Memberships:** Am Chem Soc. **Mailing Address:** 1012 Leland Dr, Lafayette, CA 94549.

KUO, HSIAO-LAN, DYNAMIC METEOROLOGY, FLUID DYNAMICS. **Personal Data:** b Mancheng, China, January 7, 1915; m 1949, c 3. **Education:** Tsing Hua Univ, BS, 1937; Univ Chicago, PhD (meteorol), 1948. **Professional Experience:** PROF EMER METEOROL, UNIV CHICAGO, 1985-; prof meteorol, Univ Chicago, 1962-1985; supvr res meteorol &hurricaneres proj, Mass Inst Technol, 1958-1962; vis assoc prof meteorol, Univ Chicago, 1957-1958; Fromres assoc meteorol to res meteorologist, Mass Inst Technol, 1949-1957. **Research Statement & Publications:** Dynamics of planetary atmospheres and atmospheric vortices; general circulation; atmospheric radiation; high atmosphere; climate change. **Mailing Address:** Univ Chicago, 5801 S Ellis Ave, Chicago, IL 60637.

KUO, HUI-HSIUNG, STOCHASTIC DIFFERENTIAL EQUATIONS, BROWNIAN FUNCTIONALS. **Personal Data:** b Ta-chia, Taichung, Taiwan, October 21, 1941; American citizen; m 1969, Fukuko; c Isaac J & Henry G. **Education:** Taiwan Univ, BA, 1965; Cornell Univ, MA, 1968, PhD (math), 1970. **Professional Experience:** Spec vis prof Hiroshima Univ, 2001; NICHOLSON PROF MATH, LA STATE UNIV, 2000-; Kyushu Univ, 1991; Meijo Univ, 1996; prin investr, ARO Res Grant, 1994-1997; prin investr, ARO Res Grant, 1994-1997; vis prof, Univ Bielefeld, 1986 & 1988; vis prof, Nagoya Univ, 1984; Ctr Stochastic Processes, Univ NC, 1984; mem, Comt Summer Inst, Am Math Soc, 1983-1986; PROF RES & TEACHING, LA STATE UNIV, 1982-; assoc prof, LA State Univ, 1977-1982; assoc prof res & teaching, Wayne State Univ, 1976-1977; vis asst prof res & teaching, State Univ NY, Buffalo, 1975-1976; asst prof res & teaching, Univ Va, 1971-1975; vis mem res, Courant Inst, NY Univ, 1970-1971. **Memberships:** Am Math Soc; Math Soc Japan; Korean Math Soc. **Research Statement & Publications:** White noise theory, stochastic anal, Stochastic differential equations, probability and harmonic analysis on infinite dimensional spaces, guantum probability, interacting fock spaces. **Mailing Address:** Dept Math, La State Univ, 318 Lockett Hall, Baton Rouge, LA 70803. **Fax:** 225-578-4276. **E-Mail:** kuo@math.lsu.edu

KUO, JOHN TSUNG-FEN, GEOPHYSICS. **Personal Data:** b Hangchow, China, April 1, 1922; m 1957, c 3. **Education:** Univ Redlands, BS, 1952; Calif Inst Technol, MS, 1954; Stanford Univ, PhD (geophys), 1958. **Honorary Degrees:** ScD, Univ Redlands, 1978. **Professional Experience:** EWING & WURZEL PROF EMER GEOPHYS, COLUMBIA UNIV, as of 2005; Technische Universitat Clausthal, WGer, 1987; distinguished US sr scientist, Alexander von Humboldt Award, 1986-1987; Ewing & Wurzel prof geophys, Lamont Geol Observ, Columbia Univ, beginning 1985; Vinton prof mining, Lamont Geol Observ, Columbia Univ, 1983-1985; vis prof, Cornell Univ, 1978; vis prof, Univ Tex, Austin, 1977; NSF sr fel, Cambridge Univ, 1970-1971; from assoc prof to prof mining, Lamont Geol Observ, Columbia Univ, 1964-1982; res scientist, Lamont Geol Observ, Columbia Univ, 1960-1964; res assoc, Stanford Univ, 1958-1960; from instr to asst prof geol & geophys, San Jose State Col, 1956-1960. **Memberships:** Seismol Soc Am; Am Geophys Union; Soc Explor Geophys; fel Geol Soc Am; fel Royal Astron Soc. **Research Statement & Publications:** Acoustic, elastical, EM wave scattering and diffractions; geophysical exploration; solid earth and ocean dynamics. **Mailing Address:** Dept Geophys, Columbia Univ-2960, New York, NY 10027-6902. **E-Mail:** jtk2@columbia.edu

KUO, JYH-FA, BIOCHEMISTRY, PHARMACOLOGY. **Personal Data:** b Kaoshiung, Taiwan, May 19, 1933; m 1965, Alexandra; c Calvin & Frances. **Education:** Nat Taiwan Univ, BS, 1957; S Dak State Univ, MS, 1961; Univ Ill, Urbana, PhD (biochem), 1964; Linkoping Univ, Sweden, MD, 1980. **Professional Experience:** RETIRED; vis lectr, Nat Sci Coun, Taiwan, 1993; Peking Univ, China, 1983; Max Planckl nst Biophys Chem, Ger, 1989; merit Award, NIH, 1986-1996; prof biochem, Sch Med, Emory Univ, 1985-1992; prof Pharmacol, Sch Med, Emory Univ, 1976; assoc prof, Sch Med, Emory Univ, 1972-1976; vis prof, Swedish Med Res Found, Linkoping Univ, Sweden, 1970; from asst prof to assoc prof pharmacol, Sch Med, Yale Univ, 1968-1972; res biochemist, Lederle Labs, Am Cyanamid Co, 1964-1968. **Memberships:** AAAS; Am Soc Biochem & Molecular Biol; Am Soc Pharmacol & Exp Therapeut. **Research Statement & Publications:** Protein kinase C and protein phosohorylation/dephosohorylation systems in signal transduction, cancer, and cardiac function and pathophysiology. **Mailing Address:** 1819 Cedar Canyon Dr NE, Atlanta, GA 30345.

KUO, KENNETH K, AERONAUTICS. **Education:** Nat Taiwan Univ, BS, 1961; Univ Calif, MS, 1964; Princeton Univ, PhD (aerospace & mech sci), 1971. **Professional Experience:** DISTINGUISHED PROF MECH ENG, PA STATE UNIV, 1990-; DIR HIGH PRESSURE COMBUSTION LAB, PA STATE UNIV, 1990-. **Mailing Address:** Dept Mech & Nuclear Eng, Col Eng, Pa State Univ, 140 Res Bldg E Bigler Rd, University Park, PA 16802-2320. **Fax:** 814-863-3203. **E-Mail:** kenkuo@psu.edu

KUO, KENNETH K, AERONAUTICAL & ASTRONAUTICAL ENGINEERING. **Honors & Awards:** Propellants & Combustion Award, Am Inst Aeronaut & Astronaut, 1995. **Professional Experience:** DISTINGUISHED ALUMNI PROF MECH ENG, PA STATE UNIV, as of 2003. **Mailing Address:** Dept Mech Eng, Pa State Univ, University Park, PA 16802.

KUO, LAWRENCE C, MOLECULAR ENZYMOLOGY, STRUCTURAL BIOLOGY. **Personal Data:** b Hong Kong, February 8, 1951; American citizen; m Michelle; c Iain Garrihan & Anna Sophie. **Education:** Cornell Univ, BS, 1974; Univ Chicago, PhD (biophys), 1981. **Honors & Awards:** Harold Lamport Award, Biophys Soc. **Professional Experience:** SR DIR, BIOL CHEM, DEPT INTIVIRAL RES, MERCK & CO; as of 2005; asst prof, Boston Univ, beginning 1985; res fel chem, Harvard Univ, 1981-1985; res fel, Jane Coffin Childs Fund Med Res, 1981-1984; NIH res career develop award; pewscholar. **Memberships:** Am Chem Soc; AAAS; Am Soc Biochem & Molecular Biol. **Research Statement & Publications:** Biologically related organic and inorganic chemistry; use of chemical methods and approaches to the solution of enzyme actions; the roles of metal ions in metalloenzymes; protein isomerization; anti-HIV therapy; virol proteins. **Mailing Address:** Merck & Co, PO Box 4 WP26 344 Broad St, West Point, PA 19486. **Fax:** 215-652-6452.

KUO, LIH, HEMODYNAMICS & CIRCULATORY PHYSIOLOGY, CORONARY MICRO-CIRCULATION. **Personal Data:** b Taipei, Taiwan, August 28, 1957; m 1989, Athena; c Enoch & Esther (Ning. **Education:** Tung-Hai Univ, BS, 1979; Nat Taiwan Univ, MS, 1983; Med Col Va, PhD (physiol), 1987. **Honors & Awards:** Grega-Zacharkow Young Investr Award, Microcirculatory Soc, 1980. **Professional Experience:** PROF, HEATH SCI CTR, TEX A&M UNIV, 2001-; assoc prof, Health Sci Ctr, Tex A&M Univ, 1998-2001; mem, Exp Cardiovasc Sci Study Sect, NIH, beginning 1994; mem, Cent Res Rev Comt, Am Heart Asn Tex, beginning 1992; asst prof, Health Sci Ctr, Tex A&M Univ, 1992-1998; grad fac, Tex A&M Univ, beginning 1990; asst res scientist, Tex A&M Univ, 1990-1991; res assoc, Tex A&M Univ, 1986-1989; World Cong Microcirculation Travel Award, Microcirculation Soc, 1981; res asst, Nat Defence Med Ctr, 1979-1981. **Memberships:** Fel Am Physiol Soc; Microcirculatory Soc; fel Am Heart Asn. **Research Statement & Publications:** Pathophysiological study of coronary microcirculation; investigating the mechanisms of local regulation of microvascular tone; studying the signal transduction in endothelial cells; studying the interaction of endothelium and vascular smooth muscle in the regulation of vascular resistance; author of numerous publications. **Mailing Address:** Dept Med Physiol, Tex A&M Univ, College Station, TX 77843-1114. **Fax:** 979-847-8635. **E-Mail:** lkuo@tamu.edu

KUO, LOUIS, BIO-ORGGANIC CHEMISTRY. **Education:** NWestern Univ, PhD, 1989. **Professional Experience:** ASSOC PROF, DEPT CHEM, LEWIS & CLARK COL, as of 2005. **Mailing Address:** Dept Chem, Lewis & Clark Col, 0615 S W Palatine Hill Rd Off 219 Olin Ctr, Portland, OR 97219. **E-Mail:** kuo@lclark.edu

KUO, M TIEN, PATHOLOGY. **Education:** Univ Tex, PhD, 1973. **Professional Experience:** STAFF, UNIV TEX MD ANDERSON CANCER CTR, as of 2006. **Mailing Address:** Univ TX MD Anderson Cancer Ctr, MDA 2SCR4.3025 MDA 2SCR4 3025 Unit 951, Houston, TX 77030. **Fax:** 713-792-8424. **E-Mail:** tkuo@mdanderson.org

KUO, MINGSHANG, SPECTROSCOPY, CHROMATOGRAPHY. **Personal Data:** b Kaohsiung, Taiwan, October 11, 1949; m 1974, Hwa M Lin; c Alexander & Michelle. **Education:** Nat Tsing-Hua Univ, Taiwan, BS, 1971; Mich State Univ, PhD (chem), 1979. **Professional Experience:** PROJ LEADER CHEM & BIOL SCREENING, UPJOHN LABS, 1992-; SRRES SCIENTIST, PHARMACIA & UPJOHNCO, 1989-; SCIENTIST ANALYTI-CALCHEMIST NATURAL PROD, PHARMACIA & UPJOHNCO, 1979-. **Memberships:** Am Chem Soc. **Research Statement & Publications:** Isolation and identification of fermentation products; natural products chemistry; pharmacokinetics drug metabolism research. **Mailing Address:** Upjohn Co, 7700 Portage Rd, Kalamazoo, MI 49001. **Fax:** 269-833-2225.

KUO, PAO-KUANG, THEORETICAL PHYSICS. **Personal Data:** b Hopei, China, February 23, 1935; m 1961, c 2. **Education:** Nat Taiwan Univ, BSc, 1957; Univ Minn, PhD (physics), 1964. **Professional Experience:** PROF PHYSICS, WAYNE STATE UNIV, as of 2003; assoc prof physics, Wayne State Univ, beginning 1971; asst prof, WayneState Univ, 1969-1971; vis lectr, Johns Hopkins Univ, 1968-1969; from res assoc to instr, MassInst Technol, 1966-1968; instr physics, Cornell Univ, 1964-1966. **Memberships:** Am Phys Soc. **Research Statement & Publications:** Quantum electrodynamics; theory of elementary particles and coherence phenomena. **Mailing Address:** Dept Physics & Astron, Wayne State Univ, Rm 235 Bldg 666 W Hancock, 5950 Case Ave, Detroit, MI 48202. **E-Mail:** pkkuo@physics.wayne.edu

KUO, PETER TE, CARDIOLOGY, INTERNAL MEDICINE. **Personal Data:** b Fukien, China, March 21, 1916; American citizen; m 1949, Nancy Huang; c Lawrence & Katherine. **Education:** St John's Univ, China, MD, 1939; Univ Pa, MMSc, 1949, DSc(med), 1950. **Honors & Awards:** Sci Award, Am Chinese Asn, 1977, 1988, 1992 & 1993. **Professional Experience:** PROF MED, BAYLOR COL MED, 1988-; DIR HYPERLIPIDEMIA PROG, HOUSTON VET ADMIN MED CTR, 1987-; clin prof med, Houston Vet Admin Med Ctr, 1987-1988; prof med & dir, John G Detwiler prof cardiol, 1982-1987; dir, Atherosclerosis Res, Univ Med & Dent, Robert Wood Johnson Med Sch, 1982-1987; hon prof, 2nd Med Col, Shanghai, China, 1981; consult, Med & Cardiol Med Ctr, Muhlenberg Hosp, St Peter's Med Ctr, 1973-1987; prof med & dir, Cardiovasc Div, Robert Wood Johnson Med Sch, Univ Med & Dent NJ, 1973-1982; USPHS career develop award, 1961-1966; estab investr, Arteriosclerosis Coun, 1958; estab investr, Am Heart Asn, 1955-1960; sr staff mem, Robineete Found Cardiovasc Res, Hosp Univ Pa, 1952-1973; from instr to prof, Sch Med, Univ Pa, 1950-1973; From asst to asst prof med, Med Sch, St John's Univ, China, 1940-1946; Consult cardiol & probs lipid metab; fel, Arteriosclerosis Coun, Am Heart Asn. **Memberships:** Fel Gerontol Soc; fel Am Col Physicians; fel Am Col Cardiol; Am Soc Clin Nutrit; Am Nutrit Inst; fel AAAS; Am Fedn Clin Res; Am Med Asn; Asn Univ Cardiologists; fel Am Col Chest Physicians. **Research Statement & Publications:** Blood and tissue lipids and their relationship to the problem of arteriosclerosis; circulatory hemodynamics; promote detection, prevention and treatment of dyslipidemias and coronary heart disease; role of lipoprotein (a), oxidized low-density lipoprotein on atherosclerosis and very low blood cholesterol of less than 160 mg/dL on high all-cause mortality. **Mailing Address:** 4215 Milton, Houston, TX 77005. **Fax:** 713-661-1912. **E-Mail:** nancy77005@yahoomail.com

KUO, SCOT CHARLES, CELL BIOPHYSICS. **Personal Data:** b July 4, 1961; American citizen; m 1992. **Education:** Harvard Univ, BA, 1982; Univ Calif Berkeley, PhD, 1988. **Professional Experience:** ASSOC PROF, DEPT BIOMED ENG, SCH MED & WHITING SCH ENG, JOHNS HOPKINS UNIV, as of 2006; fel, Jane Coffin Childs Mem Fund Med Res, 1989-1992; res fel, Dept Cell Biol, Duke Univ, 1988-1993; res asst, Dept Biochem, Univ Calif Berkeley, 1982-1988; technician, Dept Chem, Harvard Univ, 1981; res, Dept Biochem, Harvard Univ, 1979-1982. **Memberships:** Am Soc Cell Biol; Biophys Soc; Biomed Engineering Soc. **Research Statement & Publications:** Biophysics of microtubule-dependent motility; cellular cytoskeletal mechanics; optical tools for biophysics. **Mailing Address:** Dept Biomed Eng, Sch Med & Whiting Sch Eng, Johns Hopkins Univ, Rm 724, Ross Res Bldg, 720 Rutland Ave, Baltimore, MD 21205. **Fax:** 410-955-0549. **E-Mail:** skuo@bme.jhu.edu

KUO, SHAN SUN, APPLIED MATHEMATICS, COMPUTER SCIENCE. **Personal Data:** b Nanking, China, November 22, 1922; m 1958, c 1. **Education:** Nat Chung Cheng Univ, China, BEng, 1944; Ohio State Univ, MSc, 1948; Harvard Univ, MEng, 1954. **Honorary Degrees:** DEng, Yale Univ, 1958. **Professional Experience:** PROF EMER COMPUT SCI, UNIV NH, 1996-; prof comput sci, Univ NH, 1977-1996; dir, Comput Ctr, 1964-1996; prof math, Univ NH, 1964-1977; dir, Comput Ctr, 1961-1964; from asst prof to assoc prof civil eng, Tufts Univ, 1958-1964; engr, Fay Spofford & Thorndike, 1954-1955; engr, Carew Steel Prod Corp, 1952-1953; struct engr, Ohio State Univ, 1948-1952; lectr, Formosa Inst Technol, 1946-1947; instr, Nat Chung Cheng Univ, China, 1944-1946. **Memberships:** Am Math Soc; Asn Comput Mach; Am Soc Civil Engrs; Am Soc Mech Engrs; Am Soc Eng Educ. **Research Statement & Publications:** Numerical analysis; computer applications. **Mailing Address:** Dept Comput Sci, Univ NH, M207 Kingsbury Hall, Durham, NH 03824. **Fax:** 603-862-3493. **E-Mail:** ssk@cs.unh.edu

KUO, SHIOU, SOIL CHEMISTRY, PHYSICAL CHEMISTRY. **Personal Data:** b Ping-Tung, Taiwan, October 8, 1941; m 1969, c 3. **Education:** Chung-Hsing Univ, Taiwan, BS, 1966; Utah State Univ, MS, 1970; Univ Maine, Orono, PhD (soil chem), 1973. **Professional Experience:** SOIL SCIENTIST, PUYALLUP RES & EXTEN CTR, WASH STATE UNIV, as of 2003; asst soil scientist, Western Wash Res & Exten Ctr, Wash State Univ, beginning 1978; res assoc agron, Univ Calif, Davis, 1975-1978; res assoc soils, Iowa State Univ, 1974-1975. **Memberships:** Am Soc Agron; Soil Sci Soc Am; Chinese Agr Asn; Sigma Xi. **Research Statement & Publications:** Nitrogen transformations in soils and their relation to the nitrogen uptake by plant; cations and anions reactions with soil colloidal particles and the plant growth. **Mailing Address:** Puyallup Res & Exten Ctr, Wash State Univ, 7612 Pioneer Way E, Puyallup, WA 98371-4998. **E-Mail:** skuo@wsu.edu

KUO, THOMAS TZU SZU, THEORETICAL PHYSICS. **Personal Data:** b Peiping, China, July 31, 1932; m 1962, c 2. **Education:** Naval Col Eng, Taiwan, BS, 1954; Tsing Hua Univ, Taiwan, MS, 1959; Univ Pittsburgh, PhD (physics), 1964. **Honors & Awards:** Humboldt Award Sr Am Scientists, 1977. **Professional Experience:** Hon prof, Inst High Energy Physics, China, Jilin Univ & Fudan Univ, 1981; vis prof, Julich Nuclear Res Ctr, WGer, 1979; Nordita guest prof physics, Univ Oslo, 1974-1975, 1978, 1983; PROF PHYSICS, STATE UNIV NY, STONY BROOK, 1972-; assoc prof, StateUniv NY, Stony Brook, 1968-1972; vis scientist, Argonne Nat Lab, 1968 & 1969; from instr to asst prof physics, Princeton Univ, 1964-1968. **Memberships:** Fel Am Phys Soc. **Research Statement & Publications:** Theoretical nuclear physics; nuclear structure and the free nucleon nucleon interaction; nuclear matter phase transitions; finite temperature; many body problems. **Mailing Address:** State Univ NY, Dept Physics, C-137, Stony Brook, NY 11794. **E-Mail:** thomas.kuo@stonybrook.edu

KUO, TZEE-KE, HIGH ENERGY PHYSICS. **Personal Data:** b Peking, China, April 13, 1937; m 1961. **Education:** Nat Taiwan Univ, BS, 1957; Univ Chicago, MS, 1960; Cornell Univ, PhD (physics), 1963. **Professional Experience:** PROF PHYSICS, PURDUE UNIV, 1977-; vis prof, Univ Calif, Santa Barbara, 1981; assoc prof, Purdue Univ, 1968-1977; vis prof, Imperial Col, London, Eng, 1973; asst prof, Purdue Univ, West Lafayette, 1965-1968; res assoc physics, Brookhaven Nat Lab, 1963-1965; res assoc, Cornell Univ, 1963. **Memberships:** Am Phys Soc. **Research Statement & Publications:** Elementary particle physics. **Mailing Address:** Dept Physics, Purdue Univ, 525 NWestern Ave, West Lafayette, IN 47907-2036. **Fax:** 765-494-0706. **E-Mail:** tkkuo@physics.purdue.edu

KUO, WAY, QUALITY CONTROL. **Education:** Kans State Univ, PhD. **Professional Experience:** PROF INDUST ENG & ELEC ENG, TEX A&M UNIV, 1993-. **Memberships:** Inst Elec & Electronics Engrs; Am Soc Qual Control; Int Acad Qual. **Mailing Address:** Dept Indust Eng & Elec Eng, Tex A&M Univ, 236B Zachry, College Station, TX 77843-3131. **Fax:** 979-847-9005. **E-Mail:** way@tamu.edu

KUO, WAY, RELIABILITY ENGINEERING, APPLIED STATISTICS. **Personal Data:** b Taipei, Taiwan, January 5, 1951; m 1977, Suzanne Lee; c Tiffany & Wendy. **Education:** Nat Tsing-Hua, Taiwan, BS, 1972; Kans State Univ, MS, 1977, 1978, PhD (eng), 1980. **Professional Experience:** WISENBAKER CHMN, DEPT ENG, TEX A&M UNIV, as of 2003; PROF, DEPT INDUST ENG, TEX A&M UNIV, 1993-; HEAD, DEPT INDUST ENG, TEX A&M UNIV, 1993-; sr FulbrightScholar, 1991-1992; prof & chmn, indust mfg syst eng, 1989-1993; sr res assoc, Nat Res Coun, 1986; from asst prof to prof, Iowa State Univ, 1984-1988; vis sci, Oak Ridge Nat Lab, 1981; techstaff mem, Bell Labs, 1980-1983. **Memberships:** Fel Inst Elec & Electronics Eng; Am Soc Qual Control; Inst Indust Engrs. **Research Statement & Publications:** Modeling, evaluation and estimating quality and reliability of modern systems, with emphasis on optional system design. **Mailing Address:** Tex A&M Univ, 236B Zachry, 3131 TAMU, College Station, TX 77843-3131. **Fax:** 979-847-9005. **E-Mail:** way@tamu.edu

KUO, YEN-LONG, ELECTRICAL ENGINEERING. **Personal Data:** b Taipei, Taiwan, November 18, 1936; m 1966, c 1. **Education:** Taipei Inst Technol, Taiwan, Dipl, 1957; Okla State Univ, MS, 1961; Univ Calif, Berkeley, PhD (elec eng), 1966. **Professional Experience:** MEM TECH STAFF ELEC ENG, BELL TEL LABS INC, 1970-; asst prof, Purdue Univ, 1966-1970; actg asst prof elec eng, Univ Calif, Berkeley, 1966. **Memberships:** Inst Elec & Electronics Engrs. **Research Statement & Publications:** Computer-aided circuit analysis and synthesis; nonlinear distortion analysis; system theory. **Mailing Address:** Bell Labs, 11 Brentwood Circle, North Andover, MA 01810.

KUO, YING L, TELECOMMUNICATION FIELD DESIGN, COMPUTER QUALITY CONTROL PLANNING. **Personal Data:** b Taipei, Taiwan, August 19, 1958. **Education:** Van-Nam Inst Technol, BS, 1981; Calif Century Univ, BS, 1988, MS, 1989; CenturyUniv NMex, PhD (comput eng), 1991. **Professional Experience:** ENG STAFF, DIR, RES & DEVELOP DEPT, FOUNTAIN TECH INC, 1989-; mgr, Res & Develop Dept, Telemate Tech, Inc, 1986-1988; supvr, Res & Develop Dept, All Best Inc, 1984-1986; chief engr, Res & Develop Dept, Microtel Inc, 1982-1984. **Research Statement & Publications:** Microcomputer and microprocessor; hardware design and software design. **Mailing Address:** 25 Truman Dr S, Edison, NJ 08817.

KUO, YUE, THIN FILM TRANSISTORS & VLSI, THIN FILM MATERIALS & PLASMA PROCESSING. **Personal Data:** b Taipei, Taiwan, January 2, 1953; American citizen; m Kiyomi. **Education:** Nat Taiwan Univ, BS, 1974; Columbia Univ, MS, 1978, PhD (chem eng), 1979. **Honors & Awards:** Fellow, IEEE Electronic Devices Society; Fellow, Electrochemical Society; 80 Keynote, invited, speakers in internaitonal confereences, universities, industry R&D centers, etc. **Professional Experience:** DOW Professor, Chemical Engineering, Electrical Engineering, Materials Science and Engineering, Texas A&M University, 1998-; Research Staff Member, IBM TJ Watson Research Center, 1987-1998; Principal Process Engineer, Semiconductor Div, Data Gen Co, 1984-1987; Visiting Research Engineer, Univ Calif, Berkeley, 1982-1984; Pilot Lab Manager, Bayer AG, 1980-1982; Research Assistant, Columbia Univ, 1976-1979. **Memberships:** IEEE, Electrochemical Society, Am Vacuum Society. **Research Statement & Publications:** Published over 200 articles, 10 proceedings, 2 textbooks, 3 lecture books. **Mailing Address:** Thin Film

Nano & Microelectronics Research Lab, 3122 TAMU, College Station, TX 77843-3122. **Fax:** 979-458-8836. **E-Mail:** yuekuo@tamu.edu

KUPCHELLA, CHARLES E, CANCER BIOLOGY, ENVIRONMENTAL EDUCATION. **Personal Data:** b Nanty Glo, Pa, July 7, 1942; m 1963, Adele; c Richard, Michele & Jason. **Education:** Ind Univ Pa, BSEd, 1964; St Bonaventure, PhD (physiol), 1968. **Professional Experience:** PRES, UNIV NDAK, 1999-; NIH/NCI Sci Rev & Eval Comt, 1993-1997; provost, Southeast Mo State Univ, beginning 1993; mem, Inst Res Grants Sci Adv Comt, Am Cancer Soc, 1993-1996; dean, Ogden Col Sci Technol & Health, Western Ky Univ, 1985-1993; chmn biol, Murray State Univ, 1979-1985; assoc dir, Cancer Res Ctr & assoc prof oncol, Sch Med, Univ Louisville, 1973-1979; from asst prof to assoc prof, Bellarmine Col, 1968-1973; consult environ progs var insts. **Memberships:** Am Asn Cancer Educ (pres 1999-2000). **Research Statement & Publications:** Biology of cancer; biology of the glycosaminoglycans-involvement in metastasis and wound repair; diseases of the skin; environmental science. **Mailing Address:** Univ NDak, Centennial Dr Twamley Hall Rm 300, Grand Forks, ND 58606. **Fax:** 701-777-3866. **E-Mail:** c_kupchella@mail.und.nodak.edu

KUPCHIK, EUGENE JOHN, ORGANOMETALLIC CHEMISTRY, CHEMICAL GRAPH THEORY. **Personal Data:** b Wallington, NJ, August 26, 1929; m 1965, Barbara Smith. **Education:** Rutgers Univ, BS, 1951, PhD (org chem), 1959. **Professional Experience:** PROF EMER ORG CHEM, ST JOHN'S UNIV, NY, as of 2004; prof org chem, St John's Univ, NY, beginning 1968; from asst prof to assoc prof, St John's Univ, NY, 1960-1968; instr chem, Rutgers Univ, 1958-1960; teaching fel, DuPont, 1957; Alfred P Sloan res fel, 1956; res chemist, Union Carbide Plastics Co, 1954-1955; firstlt chemist, Wright-Patterson AFB, USAF, 1951-1952. **Memberships:** Am Chem Soc. **Research Statement & Publications:** Organometallic chemistry; organotin compounds; biological properties of organometallic compounds; chemical graph theory; quantitative structure: activity relationships in chemistry, biology and pharmacy. **Mailing Address:** Dept Chem, St John's Univ, Jamaica, NY 11439.

KUPCHIK, HERBERT Z, CANCER. **Personal Data:** b Brooklyn, NY, December 6, 1940; m 1964, c 2. **Education:** Bethany Col, BS, 1962; Wayne State Univ, MS, 1965, PhD (biochem), 1967. **Professional Experience:** PROF MICROBIOL, PATH & LAB MED, SCH MED, BOSTON UNIV, 1991-; mem staff, Hubert H Humphrey Cancer Res Ctr, 1980-; mem spec sci staff, Boston CityHosp & Mallory Inst Path, 1978-; from asst prof to assoc prof, Path & Lab Med, Sch Med, Boston Univ, 1976-1991; sr res assoc, Mallory Gastroenterol Lab, Boston City Hosp, 1974-1980; prin res assoc biochem, Harvard Med Sch, 1972-1978; res assoc, Sch Med, Boston Univ, 1971-1976; assoc biol chem, Harvard Med Sch, 1971-1972; res assoc, Mallory GastroenterolLab, Boston City Hosp, 1969-1974; clin assoc, Thorndike Mem Lab, 1969-1973; assoc med, Harvard Med Sch, 1969-1971; res fel enzym, Harvard Med Sch, 1968-1969; NIH fel enzym, Cancer Res Inst, New Eng Deaconess Hosp, Boston, 1967-1969; res asst biochem, Wayne StateUniv, 1964-1967; instr biochem & org chem, Marygrove Col, 1964-1965; asst chem, WayneState Univ, 1962-1963. **Memberships:** Am Asn Pathologists; Am Soc Microbiol; Am Asn Cancer Res; Am Fedn Clin Res; NY Acad Sci. **Research Statement & Publications:** Properties of invasive human tumors; in-vitro screening and evaluation of immunotherapeutic agents; development of monoclonal antibodies to human tumors; in-vitro transformation of human colonic adenomas to carcinomas. **Mailing Address:** Dept Microbiol, Boston Univ, Sch Med 80 E Concord St, Boston, MA 02118-2394. **E-Mail:** hkupchik@bu.edu

KUPERMAN, ALBERT SANFORD, PHARMACOLOGY, EDUCATIONAL ADMINISTRATION. **Personal Data:** b New York, NY, August 1, 1931; m 1956, Barbara; c Laura & Meredith. **Education:** NY Univ, AB, 1952; Cornell Univ, PhD (pharmacol), 1957. **Professional Experience:** ASSOC PROF MOLECULAR PHARMACOL, ALBERT EINSTEIN COLMED, 1989-; ASSOC DEAN EDUC AFFAIRS, ALBERT EINSTEIN COL MED, 1975-; Rockefeller Found vis prof & actg chmn dept pharmacol, Fac Med Sci, Mahidol Univ, Thailand, 1968-1975; prof biol sci, Hunter Col, 1968; assoc prof, Hunter Col, 1965-1968; asst prof, MedCol, Cornell Univ, 1961-1965; asst prof, Col Med, NY Univ, 1959-1961; instr, Med Col, CornellUniv, 1958-1959; USPHS fel, 1957-1959; res fel pharmacol, Med Col, Cornell Univ, 1957-1958. **Memberships:** Am Soc Pharmacol & Exp Therapeut; fel Am Col Clin Pharmacol. **Research Statement & Publications:** General pharmacology; physiology and pharmacology of excitable cells. **Mailing Address:** Off Educ, Albert Einstein Col Med, Belfer Bldg Rm 209 Jack & Pearl Resnick Campus 1300 Morris Park Ave, Bronx, NY 10461. **Fax:** 718-430-8255. **E-Mail:** kuperman@aecom.yu.edu

KUPERS, RUDOLF CARL, IMMUNOLOGY. **Personal Data:** b Los Angeles, Calif, January 21, 1945. **Education:** Calif State Univ, Northridge, BS, 1969, MS, 1976; Johns Hopkins Univ, PhD (microbiol), 1978. **Professional Experience:** SR SCIENTIST, SCI APPLNS INT CORP, 1993-; asst prof chem, Johns Hopkins Univ, 1983-1993; res fel mech cell mediated cytotoxicity, max planck Inst, 1980-1983. **Memberships:** Am Asn Immunologists. **Research Statement & Publications:** Autoimmune diseases. **Mailing Address:** Sci Applns Int Corp, 5340 Spectrum Dr Ste N, Frederick, MD 21703. **Fax:** 301-698-6188.

KUPFER, CARL, OPHTHALMOLOGY. **Personal Data:** b New York, NY, February 9, 1928. **Education:** Yale Univ, BA, 1948; Johns Hopkins Univ, MD, 1952. **Honorary Degrees:** DSc, Univ Pa, 1982. **Honors & Awards:** Pub Serv Award, Am Acad Opthal, 1977; Pisart Vision Award, 1995. **Professional Experience:** Actg dep dir intramural res, NIH, 1991-1992; mem, Bd Dirs, Helen Keller Int, Inc, beginning 1975; chmn, Proj & Priorities Comt, IntAgency Prevention Blindness, beginning 1975; mem, Sci Adv Comt, Fight for Sight, beginning 1971; mem, Sci AdvPanel, Res to Prevent Blindness, Inc, 1971-1975; clin assoc prof, Howard Univ, beginning 1970; DIR, NAT EYE INST, NIH, 1970-; mem, Adv Comt Basic & Clinical Res, Nat Soc Prev Blindness, beginning 1969; mem, Vision Res Training Comt, NIH, 1963-1964 & Neurol Prog Proj B, 1967-1969; prof & chmn, dept ophthal, Sch Med & res affil, Primate Ctr, Univ Wash, 1966-1970; prog dir ophthal training grant, Mass Eye & Ear Infirmary, 1962-1966; from instr to asst prof ophthal, Harvard Med Sch, 1960-1966; res fel, Harvard Med Sch, 1958-1960; res fel ophthal, Wilmer Eye Inst, 1957-1958; lab asst biostatist, Med Sch, Johns Hopkins Univ, 1953-1954 & 1957-1958; intern & asstresident, Wilmer Eye Inst, Johns Hopkins Hosp, 1952-1953. **Memberships:** Inst Med-Nat Acad Sci; Am Physiol Soc; Asn Res Vision & Ophthal; Am AcadOphthal; Am Ophthal Soc; Pan Am Ophthal Soc. **Research Statement & Publications:** Intraocular pressure and neurophysiology; glaucoma; neuroophthalmology. **Mailing Address:** Nat Eye Inst, NIH, Rm 6A03 MSC 2510 31 Ctr Dr, Bethesda, MD 20892-2510. **Fax:** 301-496-9970. **E-Mail:** cak@b31.nei.nih.gov

KUPFER, DAVID, BIOCHEMICAL PHARMACOLOGY, DRUG METABOLISM. **Personal Data:** b Warsaw, Poland, November 27, 1928; American citizen; m 1961, c 3. **Education:** Univ Calif, Los Angeles, BA, 1952, PhD (biochem), 1958. **Professional Experience:** AFFIL FAC, DEPT CHEM, CLARK UNIV, as of 2003; SR SCIENTIST, WORCESTER FOUND EXP BIOL, 1971-; res scientist, Lederle Labs, Am Cyanamid Co, 1962-1971; intermediate scientist & fel, Weizmann Inst Sci, 1961-1962; scientist, Worcester Found Exp Biol, 1958-1960. **Memberships:** Am Chem Soc; Am Soc Biol Chemists; Soc Pharmacol & Exp Therapeut. **Research Statement & Publications:** Drug-drug interactions; prostaglandin metabolism; hepatic monoxygenases; hormonal activity of environmental pollutants. **Mailing Address:** Clark Univ, Dept Chem, 950 Main St, Worcester, MA 01610. **E-Mail:** kupfer@sci.wfbr.edu

KUPFER, DAVID J, PSYCHIATRY. **Personal Data:** b New York, NY, February 14, 1941; m 1975, Ellen; c Andrea, Jeffrey, Deborah, Nancy, Erica & Tonia. **Education:** Yale Univ, MD, 1965, Yale Univ, BA, 1961, magna cum laude. **Professional Experience:** PROF & CHMN, DEPT PSYCHIAT, UNIV PITTSBURGH; DIR RES, WESTERN PSYCHIAT INST & CLIN; THOMAS DETRE PROF, DEPT PSYCHIAT, UNIV PITTSBURGH; MED DIR, Western Psychiat Inst & Clin. **Memberships:** Inst Med-Nat Acad Sci; Am Psychiat Assoc; Am Psychosom Soc. **Mailing Address:** Dept Psychiat, Western Psychiat Inst & Clin, 3811 O'Hara St, Pittsburgh, PA 15213. **E-Mail:** kupferdj@upmc.edu

KUPFER, DONALD HARRY, STRUCTURAL & SALT DOME GEOLOGY. **Personal Data:** b Los Angeles, Calif, October 4, 1918; m 1952, Romaine Littlefield; c Madeline (Van Epps) & John C. **Education:** Calif Inst Technol, BS, 1940; Univ Calif, Los Angeles, AM, 1942; Yale Univ, MS, 1951, PhD (geol), 1951. **Honors & Awards:** A I Levorsen Award, 1975; fel AAAS, 1982; Outstanding Educator, GCAGS, 1997. **Professional Experience:** EMER PROF GEOL, LA STATE UNIV, BATON ROUGE, 1981-; pres, Geol Res Indust Minerals Corp, 1977-1992; fel, Cent Treaty Orgn minerals mapping consult, Turkey, 1966 & Pakistan, 1967; prof, LA State Univ, Baton Rouge, 1966-1980; NSF sr fel, NZ, 1962-1963; from asst prof to assoc prof, LA State Univ, Baton Rouge, 1955-1966; Geologist, Gladding McBean & Co, 1941-1942 & US Geol Surv, 1942-1955; Indust mineral consult, 1958-; Salt Domes, Spain, USA, & Ger, 1969; Can, Mexico, Israel, 1979. **Memberships:** Fel AAAS; Am Asn Petrol Geologists. **Research Statement & Publications:** Earthquakes; faults; salt domes; nonmetal mining; tectonics; areal geology; Gulf Coast geology; salt mine safety; energy resources; history of geology. **Mailing Address:** 210 West Circle Dr, Canon City, CO 81212.

KUPFER, JOHN CARLTON, SYSTEMS PERFORMANCE ANALYSIS. **Personal Data:** b Los Angeles, Calif, February 12, 1955; m 1987, Joan. **Education:** Rice Univ, BA, 1977; Univ Ariz, MS, 1981, PhD (physics), 1985. **Professional Experience:** MEM TECH STAFF, BOEING NAM, 1996-; mem tech staff, Rockwell Int, 1985-1996. **Memberships:** Am Phys Soc; Mat Res Soc. **Research Statement & Publications:** Systems analysis; development and operation of system performance models for requirements definition; design tradestudies, error tree flowdown and impact of baseline changes. **Mailing Address:** PO Box 577, Atwood, CA 92811.

KUPFER, SHERMAN, internal medicine, physiology; deceased, see previous edition for last biography

KUPFERBERG, HARVEY J, PHARMACOLOGY. **Personal Data:** b New York, NY, January 4, 1933; m 1962, c 2. **Education:** Univ Calif, Los Angeles, BS, 1955; Univ Southern Calif, PharmD, 1959; Univ Calif, San Francisco, PhD (pharmacol), 1962. **Professional Experience:** RETIRED; pharmacologist, Epilepsy Br, Neurol Dis Prog, Nat Instneurol & Comm Dis & troke; res grant, USPHS, 1966-1969; from instr to asst prof, Univ Minn, Minneapolis, 1965-1971; staff fel, Nat Heart Inst, 1963-1965; fel pharmacol, Univ Calif, San Francisco, 1960-1962, 1962-1963. **Memberships:** AAAS; Am Pharmaceut Asn; Acad Pharmaceut Sci; Am Soc Pharmacol & ExpTherapeut; Soc Toxicol. **Research Statement & Publications:** Pharmacodynamics; metabolism of drugs; mechanism of action of anticonvulsant drugs. **Mailing Address:** NIH, Bethesda, MD 20892-0001.

KUPFERBERG, LENN C, MATERIALS ANALYSIS. **Personal Data:** b Flushing, NY, July 27, 1951; m 1976, Karen; c David & Beth. **Education:** Trinity Col, Conn, BS, 1973; Univ Rochester, NY, MA, 1975, PhD (physics), 1979. **Professional Experience:** PRIN PHYSICIST, RAYTHEON, 2001-; sr develop scientist & mgr, Mat Anal Lab, Electronic Systs Lab, Raytheon, 1987-2001; sr res sientist, Mat Analysis Lab, Electronic Systs Lab, Raytheon, 1984-1987; asst prof physics, Worcester Polytech Inst, 1980-1984; vis Scientist physics, Mass Inst Technol, 1980-1984; assoc fel physics, Mass Inst Technol, 1978-1980. **Memberships:** Am Phys Soc; Sigma Xi; Mat Res Soc; Micros Soc Am; SPIE. **Research Statement & Publications:** Materials anaylsis; characterization of IR-optical materials; Failure anal. **Mailing Address:** Raytheon Company, 350 Lowell St, Andover, MA 01810. **Fax:** 978-470-9006. **E-Mail:** lenn_c_kupferberg@raytheon.com

KUPFERMAN, ALLAN, pharmacology, ophthalmology; deceased, see previous edition for last biography

KUPFERMAN, STUART L, METROLOGY, PHYSICAL OCEANOGRAPHY. **Personal Data:** b New York, NY, June 30, 1937; m 1966, Virginia Sullivan; c Jocelyn S & Kimberly J. **Education:** Polytech Inst Brooklyn, BS, 1959; Harvard Univ, AM, 1964, PhD (physics), 1967. **Professional Experience:** CONSULT, SANDIA NAT LABS, as of 2006; chair, NCSL Int, as of 2002; distinguished mem tech staff, Sandia Nat Labs, beginning 1980; vis investr, WoodsHole Oceanog Inst, 1978-1980; grantee, Univ Del Res Found, 1971-1972; grantee, NSF, 1971-1978; asst prof phys oceanog, Univ Del, 1970-1978; res assoc phys oceanog, Univ RI, 1968-1970. **Memberships:** AAAS; Am Phys Soc. **Research Statement & Publications:** Automation of high accuracy calibration and measurement systems. **Mailing Address:** Sandia Nat Lab, MS0665, Albuquerque, NM 87185. **Fax:** 505-844-4372. **E-Mail:** slkupfe@sandia.gov

KUPIECKI, FLOYD PETER, BIOCHEMISTRY. **Personal Data:** b Bronson, Mich, May 1, 1926; m 1950, Rose Johnson; c Erik & Stephanie. **Education:** Western Mich Univ, BS, 1950; Univ Notre Dame, PhD (chem), 1953. **Professional Experience:** RES SCIENTIST, UPJOHN CO, 1960-; Fulbright fel, Biochem Inst, Helsinki, Finland, 1959-1960; from res assoc to instr biochem, Univ Mich, 1956-1959; res assoc org chem& biochem, Univ Pa, 1955-1956; Res chemist, Mich Chem Corp, 1953-1955. **Memberships:** Am Soc Biochem & Molecular Biol; Am Chem Soc; Sigma Xi. **Research Statement & Publications:** Diabetes research; lipid metabolism and adipose tissue enzymes; metabolism in islets of diabetic animals. **Mailing Address:** 5409 Circlewood Dr, Kalamazoo, MI 49001-5546.

KUPIEC-WEGLINSKI, JERZY W, TRANSPLANTATION IMMUNOBIOLOGY, CELLULAR IMMUNOLOGY. **Personal Data:** b Warsaw, Poland, July 11, 1951; American citizen; m 1992, Krystyna. **Education:** Warsaw Med Acad, MA, 1975; Polish Acad Sci, PhD (immunol), 1979. **Professional Experience:** PROF SURG, SCH MED, UNIV CALIF, LOS ANGELES, 1997-; mem, Sci Studies Comt, Am Soc Transplant Physicians, 1993-; prin investr, NIH grant, 1988-; assoc prof Surg, Harvard Med Sch, 1987-1997; prin investr, Am Heart Found, 1987-1989; fel, Oxford Univ, 1986; asst prof, Harvard Med Sch, 1985-1987; instr, Harvard Med Sch, 1982-1984; res fel med, Brigham Women's Hosp, 1980-1983; res fel, Harvard Med Sch, 1979-1981; asst surg res, Polish Acad Sci, 1976-1979; vis prof, over 30 univs & hosps, USA, Europe & Sam; consult pharmaceut, SmithKline Beecham,

Bayer Inst. **Memberships:** Fel Transplant Soc; fel Am Soc Transplant Physicians; fel Am Asn Immunologists; fel Am Fedn Clin Res; fel Europ Soc Surg Res. **Research Statement & Publications:** Dissection of the host immune response after organ transplantation; efficiency and therapeutic applicability of various modalities which may prove beneficial as immunosuppressive drugs in allograft recipients; testing intricate cellular, humoral and cytokine events in transplanted hosts. **Mailing Address:** Depr Surg, Univ Calif, 10833 Le-Conte Ste 77 120 CHS, Los Angeles, CA 90095-7054.

KUPKE, DONALD WALTER, biochemistry; deceased, see previous edition for last biography

KUPPENHEIMER, JOHN D, OPTICS, NON-IMAGING OPTICS. **Personal Data:** b Orange, NJ, September 15, 1941; div. **Education:** Lafayette Col, BS, 1963; Boston Univ, MA, 1965; Worcester Polytech Inst, PhD (physics), 1969. **Honors & Awards:** Tech Achievement Award, Sanders Assoc, 1984; Chmn's Award, Sanders Asn, 1986; Robert E Gross Award, Lockheed Corp, 1987. **Professional Experience:** Prof phsyics, Tufts Univ, beginning 1984; ENG FEL, LOCKHEED SANDERS, 1984-; sr prin physicist, Optical Metrology Lab, 1979-1984; adj prof physics, Univ Lowell, 1975-1987; dir, Optical Metrology Lab, 1973-1979; asst mgr, Diffraction Ltd, Div, Sanders Assocs, 1972-1973; scientist, Diffraction Ltd, Inc, 1971-1972; asst prof, Worcester Polytech Inst, 1970-1971; fel physics, Worcester Polytech Inst, 1969-1970. **Memberships:** Optical Soc Am; Sigma Xi. **Research Statement & Publications:** Quantum optics; photon count statistics; lasers; optical constants of semiconductors; atmospheric optics; optical guidance; optical counter measures; development of IR lasers; development of IR countermeasures; applications of non-imaging optics to laser pumping; IR countermeasures and illumination. **Mailing Address:** 100 Brookfield Rd, Tewksbury, MA 01876-2123.

KUPPERMAN, MORTON, MATHEMATICAL STATISTICS. **Personal Data:** b New York, NY, March 19, 1918; m 1946, Anita. **Education:** City Col NY, BS, 1938; George Wash Univ, MA, 1950, PhD (math statist), 1957. **Professional Experience:** RETIRED; sr lectr math statist, Univ Leicester, Eng, 1973-1978; prof lectr, George Wash Univ, 1957-1973; mathematician, Nat Security Agency, 1955-1973; statistician, Med Statist Div, Off Army Surgeon Gen, 1947-1955; statistician, Europ Cent Inland Transp Orgn, France, 1946; statistician, Gen Staff, US War Dept, 1940-1941. **Memberships:** Inst Math Statist; Royal Statist Soc; Math Asn Am; Am Statist Asn; Sigma Xi. **Research Statement & Publications:** Distribution theory; application of information theory to multivariate analysis and statistical inference; counterexamples in probability and statistics. **Mailing Address:** 5904 Mt Eagle Dr, Apt 214, Alexandria, VA 22303-2535.

KUPPERMAN, ROBERT HARRIS, APPLIED MATHEMATICS, OPERATIONS RESEARCH. **Personal Data:** b New York, NY, May 12, 1935; m 1967, Helen; c 1. **Education:** NY Univ, BA, 1956, PhD (appl math), 1962. **Honors & Awards:** Outstanding Serv Awards, Exec Off President, 1968-1971, Order of Paul ReverePatriot, 1970; Presidential Citations, 1971-1973. **Professional Experience:** Mem, Coun Foreign Relations, beginning 1984; SR ADV, CTR STRATEGIC & INT STUDIES, 1983-; sr lab fel, Los Alamos Nat Lab, beginning 1980; pres, Kupperman Assocs Inc, beginning1979; mem, Army Sci Bd, beginning 1979; exec dir, Sci Technol, 1979-1985; visprof govt & polit, Univ Md, 1974-1976; chief scientist, US Arms Control & Disarmament Agency, 1973-1979; asst dir, Pres Off Emergency Preparedness, 1971-1973; dep exec dir, Pres Property Rev Bd, 1970-1973; dep asst dir, Pres Off Emergency Preparedness, 1970-1971; asst dir, Natural Resource Anal Ctr, Exec Off Pres, 1967-1970; expert consult, Exec Off Pres, 1967-1968; consult, US Civil Serv Comn, 1965 & US Army Security Agency, Army Intel & Army Electronic Warfare Bd, 1966; lectr, Univ Md, 1965; mem sr staff, Inst Defense Anal, 1964-1967; exec adv opers res, Douglas Aircraft Co, Inc, 1962-1964; sr engr, Jet Propulsion Lab, Calif Inst Technol, 1960-1962; prin engr, Repub Aviation Corp, 1959-1960; instr math, NY Univ, Pratt Inst & Hunter Col, 1956-1960. **Memberships:** Fel NY Acad Sci; fel Opers Res Soc; Soc Indust & Appl Math; Int Inst StrategicStudies; Mil Opers Res Soc. **Research Statement & Publications:** Strategic analysis and arms race stability; conversational computer systems and crisis management; conventional arms transfers; terrorism. **Mailing Address:** Ctr Strategic & Int Studies, 1800 K St NW Ste 400, Washington, DC 20006. **Fax:** 202-775-3199.

KUPPERMANN, ARON, CHEMICAL PHYSICS. **Personal Data:** b Sao Paulo, Brazil, May 6, 1926; American citizen; m 1951, Roza; c Baruch, Miriam, Nathan & Sharon. **Education:** Univ Sao Paulo, Brazil, ChemE, 1948, CE, 1953; Univ Notre Dame, PhD (phys chem), 1956. **Honors & Awards:** Werner lectr, Univ Kans, 1968; Reilly Lectr, Univ Notre Dame, 1965; Kolthoff lectr, univ minn, 1984; Venable lectr, Univ NC, 1967; Boys-Rahman Royal soc chem lectr, London, 1999. **Professional Experience:** Forchheimes vis prof, Hebrew Univ, 1998; vis res assoc, Paris, Observ, Meudon, 1992; Foreign export, Chinese Ministry Edu, Shondong Univ, 1984; consult, World Bank, 1983-; Guggenheim fel Weizmann inst & Univ Sao Paulo, 1976-1977; chmn joint chem study group, Nat Acad Sci-Nat Res Coun, Brazil, 1973-1976; consult, TRW Systs Group, 1970-1977; NSF fel, 1968-1969; consult, Jet Propulsion Lab, 1965-1969; PROF CHEM PHYSICS, CALIF INST TECHNOL, 1963-; res assoc, Inst Atomic Energy, Sao Paulo, 1959-1960; res assoc, Argonne Nat Lab, 1957; from instr to assoc prof, Univ Ill, 1955-1963; res assoc phys chem, Radiation Proj, Univ Notre Dame, 1953-1955; head, Ajax Indust & Trade Co, 1952; asst prof chem, Inst Aeronaut Technol, 1950-1951; asst prof phys chem, Cath Univ Sao Paulo, 1949-1950. **Memberships:** fel Am Inst Chem; fel Am Phys Soc; Am Chem Soc; AAAS. **Research Statement & Publications:** Experimental and theoretical chemical dynamics; collisions in crossed molecular beams; laser spectroscopy and photochemistry; radiation chemistry; low energy electron impact phenomena, experiment and theory; variable angle photoelectron spectroscopy. **Mailing Address:** Dept Chem 127-72, Calif Inst Technol, Pasadena, CA 91125.

KUPPERS, JAMES RICHARD, PHYSICAL CHEMISTRY. **Personal Data:** b Newland, Ind, August 4, 1920; m 1944, Faith; c James F, Theresa (Lanning), Kathryn & Mary (Stewart). **Education:** Univ Fla, BS, 1943, PhD (chem), 1957; La State Univ, MS, 1947. **Professional Experience:** RETIRED; from assoc prof to prof chem, Univ NC, Charlotte, 1965-1986; assoc prof chem, Pfeiffer Col, 1960-1964; res chemist textile fibers dept, E I Du Pont de Nemours & Co, 1957-1960; assoc biochemist, United Fruit Co, 1949-1954; Food technologist, United Fruit Co, 1947-1949. **Memberships:** Am Chem Soc. **Research Statement & Publications:** Solution thermodynamics. **Mailing Address:** Dept Chem, Univ NC, Charlotte, NC 28223-0001.

KUPRAT, ANDREW P, MATHEMATICS. **Education:** Univ Calif, PhD, 1992. **Professional Experience:** STAFF, THEORET DIV LOS ALAMOS NAT LAB. **Mailing Address:** Los Alamos Nat Lab, 933 Capulin Rd, Los Alamos, NM 87544. **Fax:** 505 665 2676. **E-Mail:** kuprat@lanl.gov

KUPRIYANOV, VALERY V, BIOENERGETICS, ION TRANSPORT. **Personal Data:** b Zhukorka, USSR, January 28, 1947; m 1979, Smirnova Elena; c Nina & Mikhail. **Education:** Lomonosov Moscow State Univ, BSc, 1970, PhD (chem), 1975; USSR Cardiol ResCtr, Moscow, DSc, 1987. **Professional Experience:** ASST PROF BIOCHEM & MED GENETICS, UNIV MAN, as of 2004; adj prof, Dept Biochem, Univ Man, 1997-; RES OFFICER, INST BIODIAG, NAT RES COUN CAN, 1996-; assoc res officer, Inst Biodiag, Nat Res Coun Can, 1994-1996; vis res scientist, Inst Biodiag, Nat Res Coun Can, 1992-1994; prin investr, USSRCardiol Res Ctr, Moscow, 1988-1992; sr res scientist, USSR Cardiol Res Ctr, Moscow, 1981-1988; jr res scientist, USSR Cardiol Res Ctr, Moscow, 1976-1981; Jr res scientist, Lomonosov Moscow State Univ, 1972-1976. **Memberships:** Int Soc Heart Res; Int Soc Magnetic Resonance Med; Am Heart Asn; NY AcadSci. **Research Statement & Publications:** Studies of relationship between energetics and ion fluxes in normal and abnormal cardiac muscle, using nuclear magnetic resonance; development of new methods for drug testing and non-invasive diagnostics. **Mailing Address:** Inst Biodiag, Nat Res Coun, Rm 268, 435 Ellice Ave, Winnipeg, MB R3B 1Y6, Can. **Fax:** 204-984-7036. **E-Mail:** kupriyanov@ibd.nrc.ca

KUPSTAS, EDWARD EUGENE, ORGANIC CHEMISTRY. **Personal Data:** b Eynon, Pa, August 1, 1921; m 1957, c 5. **Education:** Fordham Col, BS, 1951, MS, 1953, PhD (chem), 1958. **Professional Experience:** RETIRED; res chemist, Textile Fibers Dept, E I du Pont de Nemours & Co, Inc, 1955-1988. **Memberships:** Am Chem Soc. **Research Statement & Publications:** Structure and synthesis of ichtiamin; dyes; polymers; polyesters. **Mailing Address:** 1614 Hardee Rd, Kinston, NC 28501-2018.

KURACHI, KOTOKU, HUMAN GENETICS, MOLECULAR BIOLOGY. **Personal Data:** b Amagi City, Japan, November 16, 1941; c 2. **Education:** Kyushu Univ, Japan, BS, 1965, MS, 1967, PhD, 1970. **Honors & Awards:** Int Prize, French Asn Hemophiliacs-World Fedn Hemophilia, 1983; Res Career Develop Award, NIH. **Professional Experience:** PROF EMER, DEPT HUMAN GENETICS & CELLULAR & MOLECULAR BIOL PROG, UNIV MICH, as of 2006; mem, Res Peer Rev Comt, Am Heart Asn, Mich, beginning 1989; assoc prof, Dept Human Genetics & Cellular & Molecular Biol Prog, Univ Mich, 1986-1990; vis lectr, Ctr Biochem & Biophys Sci & Med, Harvard Med Sch, 1983-1986; from sr res assoc to res assoc prof biochem, Dept Biochem, Univ Wash, Seattle, 1975-1986; sr fel, Dept Biol Struct, 1972-1974; sr fel, Dept Biochem, Univ Wash, Seattle, 1970-1972 & 1974-1975; res assoc, Dept Biochem, Kyushu Univ, Japan, 1970; consult. **Memberships:** Am Chem Soc; Am Soc Biol Chem & Molecular Biol; AAAS; Am Soc Human Genetics; Am Soc Hemat. **Research Statement & Publications:** Human genetics; author of numerous scientific publications; blood coagulation; protease; gene therapy. **Mailing Address:** Dept Human Genetics, Med Sch Univ Mich, 3712 Med Sci II Bldg, Ann Arbor, MI 48109-0618. **Fax:** 734-747-3158. **E-Mail:** kkurachi@umich.edu

KURAJIAN, GEORGE MASROB, MECHANICAL DESIGN, SOLID MECHANICS, STRUCTURAL ANAL. **Personal Data:** b Highland Park, Mich, October 28, 1926; m 1955, Victoria; c George, Matthew & Mary. **Education:** Univ Detroit, BME, 1948, ME, 1963; Univ Mich, MSE, 1953. **Honors & Awards:** fel, Am soc of mech engr. **Professional Experience:** RETIRED; chmn, Dept Mech Eng, Univ Mich, Dearborn, 1975-1988; from asst prof to prof mech eng, Univ Mich, Dearborn, 1964-1990; consult, indust & govt agencies, 1954-; from instr to asst prof eng mech, Univ Detroit, 1948-1964. **Memberships:** Am Soc Eng Educ; fel Am Soc Mech Engrs; Soc Exp Stress Anal; Indust Math Soc; Int Asn Vehicle Design; Int Asn Struct Mech Reactor Technol; Am soc of mech engr systs & design (vpres, 1989-1991). **Research Statement & Publications:** Design and stress analysis of structural shells; space frames; amphibious vehicles; chemical machinery; automotive components; automotive dynamometers and test cells; physical testing laboratory projects; mechanical design; finite element; solid mechanics; theories of failure; fatigue. **Mailing Address:** 6346 East Brooke Dr, West Bloomfield, MI 48322-1041. **E-Mail:** kurajian@yahoo.com

KURAMITSU, HOWARD KIKUO, BIOCHEMISTRY. **Personal Data:** b Los Angeles, Calif, October 18, 1936; m 1970, Kim; c Tracy & Kristine. **Education:** Univ Calif, Los Angeles, BS, 1957, PhD (biol chem), 1962. **Honors & Awards:** merit award, NIH, 1986-1996. **Professional Experience:** DISTINGUISHED PROF EMER, STATE UNIV NY, BUFFALO, 2002-; prof oral biol, State Univ NY, Buffalo, 1993-2002; prof pediat dent, Univ Tex Health & Sci Ctr, San Antonio, 1989-1993; NIH Oral Biol & Med Study Sect, 1984-1989; prof microbiol, Med Sch, Northwestern Univ, 1979-1989; from asst prof to assoc prof, Med Sch, Northwestern Univ, 1967-1979; res assoc microbiol, Sch Med, Univ Southern Calif, 1963-1967; res fel bact, Harvard Med Sch, 1962-1963; jr res biochemist, Sch Med, Univ Calif, Los Angeles, 1961-1962. **Memberships:** AAAS; Am Soc Biol Chemists; Am Soc Microbiol; Int Asn Dent Res. **Research Statement & Publications:** Regulation of carbohydrate metabolism in oral microorganisms; isolation and characterization of genes involved in pathogenic properties of oral microorganisms. **Mailing Address:** Dept Oral Biol, State Univ NY, 3435 Main St, Buffalo, NY 14214-3092. **Fax:** 716-829-3942. **E-Mail:** kuramits@buffalo.edu

KURATA, MAMORU, SEMICONDUCTOR DEVICE MODELING. **Personal Data:** b Nagoya, Japan, April 27, 1936. **Education:** Yokohama Nat Univ, Bachelor, 1961; Univ Tokyo, Dr(elec eng), 1973. **Professional Experience:** CHIEF RES SCIENTIST, RES & DEVELOP CTR, TOSHIBA CORP, 1986-; sr researcher, Res & Develop Ctr, 1982-1986; researcher, Res & Develop Ctr, 1967-1982; Guestresearcher semiconductors, Tech Univ Aachen, Ger, 1964- 1966; engr, Illum Div, Toshiba Corp, 1961-1964. **Memberships:** Fel Inst Elec & Electronics Engrs. **Research Statement & Publications:** Semiconductor device modeling with its application to high power devices; gate turn-off thyristors; high speed devices such as heterojunction bipolar transistors; author of several books. **Mailing Address:** Toshiba Res Corp, 1 Koukai Toshiba-Cho Saiwai-Ku, Kawasaki Kanagawa 210, Japan.

KURATH, DIETER, THEORETICAL NUCLEAR PHYSICS. **Personal Data:** b Evanston, Ill, October 17, 1921; m 1945, c 4. **Education:** Brown Univ, AB, 1942; Univ Chicago, PhD (physics), 1951. **Professional Experience:** POST-RETIREMENT RES PARTIC, ARGONNE NAT LAB, as of 2001; vis prof, Univ Melbourne, 1988; sr vis fel, Nuclear Physics Lab, Oxford Univ, 1973-1974; vis prof, State Univ NY Stony Brook, 1969-1970; vis prof, Univ Wash, 1961-1962; vis prof, Univ Maryland, 1960; sr physicist, Argonne Nat Lab, 1959-1985; Guggenheim fel, Neils Bohr Inst, 1957-1958; from physicist to sr physicist, Argonne Nat Lab, 1951-1985; asst, Univ Chicago, 1947-1951. **Memberships:** Am Phys Soc. **Research Statement & Publications:** Shell model of nuclear structure. **Mailing Address:** Dept Physics, Argonne Nat Lab, 9700 S Cass Ave, Argonne, IL 60439. **Fax:** 630-252-3903. **E-Mail:** kurath@anl.gov

KURATH, SHELDON FRANK, POLYMER CHEMISTRY, RHEOLOGY. **Personal Data:** b Moscow, Idaho, March 29, 1928; m 1954, c 3. **Education:** Univ Wis, BS, 1950, MS, 1951, PhD (chem), 1954. **Professional Experience:** EMER PROF CHEM, UNIV WIS, OSHKOSH, 1993-; prof chem, Univ Wis, Oshkosh, 1969-1993; asn prof phy chem, Univ Wis, Oshkosh, 1965-1969; Res aide, Inst Paper Chem, Lawrence Univ, 195 7 -1965. **Memberships:** Am Chem Soc; Soc Rheol; Tech Asn Pulp & Paper Indust. **Research Statement**

& Publications: Non-Newtonian flow of polymers and pigment suspensions; polymer viscoelasticity; colloid chemistry. **Mailing Address:** 2413 S Greenview, Appleton, WI 54915-4832.

KURCHACOVA, ELVA S, ORGANIC CHEMISTRY. **Personal Data:** b Oriente, Cuba, August 5, 1921; American citizen; m 1944, c 2. **Honorary Degrees:** DSc (physics, chem), Univ Havana, 1945. **Professional Experience:** RETIRED; sr assoc res scientist, Miles Labs Inc, 1978-1989; assoc res chemist, Miles Labs Inc, 1961-1978; pres & dir, Yelene Prod, 1953-1961; dir res, Linner Labs, Cuba, 1945-1961. **Memberships:** AAAS; Am Chem Soc; NY Acad Sci. **Research Statement & Publications:** Pharmaceuticals; organic synthesis; development of medicinal drugs. **Mailing Address:** 3355 Jaywood Terr No J112, Boca Raton, FL 33431-6567.

KURCZEWSKI, FRANK E, ENTOMOLOGY. **Personal Data:** b Erie, Pa, May 24, 1936; m 1959, c 4. **Education:** Allegheny Col, BS, 1958; Cornell Univ, MS, 1962, PhD (insect taxon), 1964. **Professional Experience:** PROF EMER ENVIRON & FOREST BIOL, COL ENVIRON SCI & FORESTRY, STATE UNIV NY, as of 2006; prof Env & Forest Biol, Col Environ Sci & Forestry, State Univ NY, beginning 1977; from asst prof to prof entom, Col Environ Sci & Forestry, State Univ NY, 1966-1977; vis asst prof, Univ Kans, 1966; NIH fel, 1965-1966; res assoc entom, Univ Kans, 1964-1966; NSF fel, 1964-1965. **Research Statement & Publications:** Comparative behavior and systematics of digger wasps; insect behavior. **Mailing Address:** Dept Environ & Forest Biol, State Univ NY Col Environ Sci, 133 Illick Hall, One Forestry Dr, Syracuse, NY 13210-2723.

KURCZYNSKI, THADDEUS WALTER, CLINICAL GENETICS, CHILD NEUROLOGY. **Personal Data:** b Hamtramck, Mich, October 31, 1940; m 1992, Margaret; c Peter L & Karen L. **Education:** Univ Mich, BS, 1962, MS, 1963; Case Western Reserve Univ, PhD (human genetics), 1969, MD, 1970. **Professional Experience:** CHIEF, DIV GENETICS, MED COL OHIO, as of 2004; PROF PEDIAT & PATH & DIR, GENETICS CTR NORTHWEST OHIO, MED COL OHIO, 1994-; assoc prof pediat & path, Med Col Ohio, 1981-1994; asst prof Pediat, Div Pediat Neurol, Dept Med, DivNeurol & Human Genetics & Genetics Ctr, Case Western Reserve Univ, 1976-1981; fel pediatneurol, Albert Einstein Col Med, 1974-1976; resident pediat, Children's Hosp Mich, 1973-1974; from intern to resident neurol, Univ Mich Hosps, 1970-1973. **Memberships:** Am Soc Human Genetics; Am Acad Neurol; Child Neurol Soc; Am Med Asn; Am Col Med Genetics; Am Bd Psychiat & Neurol. **Research Statement & Publications:** Clinical genetics; metabolic disorders of the nervous system. **Mailing Address:** Dept Pediat & Pathology, Med Col Ohio, PO Box 10008, 3000 Arlington Ave, Toledo, OH 43614. **Fax:** 419-251-7719. **E-Mail:** tkurczynski@gemini.mco.edu

KUREY, THOMAS JOHN, NUCLEAR PHYSICS, REACTOR PHYSICS. **Personal Data:** b Boston, Mass, February 21, 1937. **Education:** Boston Col, BS, 1958; Pa State Univ, MS, 1961, PhD (physics), 1963. **Professional Experience:** Physicist, Knolls Atomic Power Lab, Gen Elec Co, 1964-1980; MED SYST, GEN ELEC CO, MILWAUKEE. **Memberships:** Am Phys Soc; Am Nuclear Soc. **Research Statement & Publications:** Beta and gamma spectroscopy; applications of solid state nuclear detectors; electron spin resonance study of decay of unstable free radicals in gamma irradiated solids; reactor physics analytical methods; critical experiments. **Mailing Address:** 2130 La Rochelle Ct, Brookfield, WI 53045.

KURFESS, JAMES DANIEL, ASTROPHYSICS. **Personal Data:** b Perrysburg, Ohio, November 8, 1940; m 1997, Mary; c Victoria, Christopher & John. **Education:** Case Inst Technol, BS, 1962, MS, 1963, PhD (physics), 1967. **Honors & Awards:** Fellow, American Physical Society. **Professional Experience:** HEAD, High Energy Space 5; chmn, Div Astrophys, Am Phys Soc, 1991; vice chmn, DivAstrophysics, Am Phys Soc, 1990; mem, Comt Space Astron & Astrophys, Nat Acad Sci, 1983-1987; secy-treas, Div Astrophysics, Am Phys Soc, 1980-1984; mem data base group study uses sci balloons, Nat Acad Sci, 1975; ASTROPHYSICIST, E O HULBURT CTR SPACE RES, US NAVAL RES LAB, 1969-; resassoc Space Sci Department, Rice Univ, 1967-1969; prin investr, Oriented Scintillation Spectrometer Exp, Compton Gamma Ray Observ, NASA; mem, Sci Adv Panel Long DurationBalloon Develop Prog. **Memberships:** Am Phys Soc; Am Astron Soc; Int Astron Union, IEEE. **Research Statement & Publications:** Hard x-ray and gamma-ray observations of solar and extra-solar sources using balloons and satellite instrumentation; development of Compton imaging for Astrophysics, nuclear medicine and homeland defense. **Mailing Address:** Naval Research Lab, 4555 Overlook Ave, SW, Washington, DC 20375-5352. **Fax:** 202-767-6473. **E-Mail:** kurfess@nrl.navy.mil

KURFESS, THOMAS ROLAND, PRECISION ENGINEERING, QUALITY ASSURANCE. **Personal Data:** m 1988, Adriana D Praddaude. **Education:** Mass Inst Technol, SB, 1986, SM, 1987 & 1988, PhD (mech eng), 1989. **Honors & Awards:** Young Investr Award, NSF, 1992; George Tallman Ladd Award, Carnegie InstTechnol, 1992. **Professional Experience:** ASSOC PROF MECH ENG, GA INST TECH, as of 1999; Guest, Lawrence Livermore Nat Lab, 1992-; ASSOC PROF MECH ENG, CARNEGIE MELLON UNIV, 1989-; Draper fel, C S Draper Lab, 1985-1989. **Memberships:** Am Soc Mech Engrs; Soc Mfg Engrs; Inst Elec & Electronics Engrs; Am Soc EngEduc; Nat Soc Prof Engrs. **Research Statement & Publications:** Research and development in system dynamics and control with applications to CAD/CAM/CAE systems. **Mailing Address:** Ga Inst Tech, Athens, GA 30602.

KURIAKOSE, AREEKATTUTHAZHAYIL, MATERIAL SCIENCE, CERAMICS PROCESSING & CHARACTERIZATION. **Personal Data:** b Palai, India, August 20, 1933; Canadian citizen; m 1960, Alice; c Neena, Binny & Joseph. **Education:** Univ Madras, India, BSc, 1953, MA, 1955, PhD (chem), 1961. **Professional Experience:** Ed-in-chief, J Can Ceramic Soc, 1987-1989; RES SCIENTIST, NATURALRESOURCES CAN, GOVT CAN, 1981-; supvr mat res, Norton Res Corp Can Ltd, 1975-1981; sr res engr, Norton Res Corp Can Ltd, 1969-1975; res engr, Norton Res Corp Can Ltd, 1966-1969; lectr chem, St Thomas Col, Palai, India, 1955-1956. **Memberships:** Can Ceramic Soc; Am Ceramic Soc; Sigma Xi. **Research Statement & Publications:** High temperature chemistry; abrasive materials; ceramics microstructure and properties; solid electrolytes and energy storage and generating systems; hydrogen fuel cells and sensors; toughened ceramics; silicon carbide. **Mailing Address:** Natural Resources Can, 555 Booth St, Ottawa, ON K1A 0G1, Can. **E-Mail:** akuriaks@nrcan.gc.ca

KURIGER, WILLIAM LOUIS, ELECTRICAL ENGINEERING. **Personal Data:** b Waterloo, Iowa, August 7, 1933; m 1956, c 7. **Education:** Univ Iowa, BSEE, 1958; Iowa State Univ, ME, 1963, PhD (elec eng), 1966. **Professional Experience:** PROF EMER ELEC & COMPUT ENG, UNIV OKLA, as of 2003; prof elec eng, Univ Okla, beginning 1980; from asst prof, to assoc prof, 1966-1980; engr, Collins Radio Co, 1958-1964. **Memberships:** Inst Elec & Electronics Engrs; Optical Soc Am; Sigma Xi. **Research Statement & Publications:** Laser applications; electronics. **Mailing Address:** Dept Elec Eng & Comput Sci, Univ Okla, Norman, OK 73019. **E-Mail:** william.l.kuriger-1@ou.edu

KURIHARA, NORMAN HIROMU, ORGANIC CHEMISTRY. **Personal Data:** b Oxnard, Calif, March 23, 1938; m 1965. **Education:** Univ Calif, Santa Barbara, BA, 1961; Univ Calif, Davis, PhD (org chem), 1965. **Professional Experience:** RETIRED; res specialist, Agr Org Dept, Dow Chem Co, beginning 1966; res fel, UnivCalif, 1965-1966. **Memberships:** Am Chem Soc; Sigma Xi. **Research Statement & Publications:** Agricultural and pesticide chemistry. **Mailing Address:** 503 Rock Oak Rd, Walnut Creek, CA 94598.

KURIHARA, YOSHIO, METEOROLOGY. **Personal Data:** b Korea, October 24, 1930; Japanese citizen; m 1960, Michiko Ishihara; c Junko & Takao. **Education:** Univ Tokyo, BA, 1953, PhD (geophys), 1962. **Honors & Awards:** Meteorol Soc Japan Award, 1975; B Miller Award, Am Meteorol Soc, 1984, JCharney Award, 1996; Gold Medal Award, US Dept Com, 1993; Fujiwara Award, Meterol SocJapan, 1994. **Professional Experience:** PROF EMER GEOSCIENCE, PRINCETON UNIV, as of 2004; PRIN INVESTR, GEOPHYS FLUID DYNAMICS LAB, NAT OCEANIC &ATMOSPHERIC ADMIN, as of 1998; Lectr & prof, Princeton Univ, 1991-; Vis lectr, Princeton Univ, 1971-1986; RES METEOROLOGIST, GEOPHYS FLUID DYNAMICS LAB, NAT OCEANIC &ATMOSPHERIC ADMIN, 1970-; res meteorologist, Environ Sci Serv Admin, 1967-1970; resofficer, Meteorol Res Inst, 1965-1967; res meteorologist, Geophys Fluid Dynamics Lab, USWeather Bur, 1963-1965; res officer, Meteorol Res Inst, 1959-1963; Tech officer, JapanMeteorol Agency, 1953-1959. **Memberships:** Fel Am Meteorol Soc; Am Geophys Union; Meteorol Soc Japan. **Research Statement & Publications:** Construction of statistical-dynamical model of the atmosphere; simulation of the hurricane; prediction of tropical cyclones. **Mailing Address:** Geophys Fluid Dynamics Lab, Princeton Univ, PO Box 308, Princeton, NJ 08542. **E-Mail:** yk@gfdl.gov

KURIS, ARMAND MICHAEL, PARASITOLOGY, MARINE ECOLOGY. **Personal Data:** b New York, NY, May 16, 1942. **Education:** Tulane Univ, BS, 1963; Univ Calif, Berkeley, MA, 1966, PhD (zoology), 1971. **Professional Experience:** Prin investr, Marine Sci Inst, Univ Calif, Santa Barbara, 1978-; ASSOC PROF BIOL SCI, UNIV CALIF, SANTA BARBARA, 1975-; asst prof zool & marine sci, Univ NC, Chapel Hill, 1974-1975; asst prof zool, Univ Fla, 1973-1974; actg asst prof, Bodega Marine Lab, Univ Calif, Bodega Bay, 1973-1975; NIH fel, Dept Zool, Univ Mich, Ann Arbor, 1972-1973; NIH fel, G W Hooper Found, Univ Calif, San Francisco, 1971-1972. **Memberships:** Am Soc Ichthyol & Herpetol; AAAS; Ecol Soc Am; Soc Protozool; Am SocParasitol; Crustacean Soc. **Research Statement & Publications:** Parasite ecology; biological control; crustacean biology; molting physiology; nemertean biology; competition; parasitic castration; shrimp taxonomy; limb regeneration; population biology; prawn aquaculture. **Mailing Address:** Dept Biol Sci, Univ Calif, 552 Univ Ave, Santa Barbara, CA 93106-0002. **Fax:** 805-893-4724. **E-Mail:** kuris@lifesci.ucsb.edu

KURITZKES, ALEXANDER MARK, ORGANIC CHEMISTRY. **Personal Data:** b Leipzig, Ger, May 3, 1924; American citizen; wid, c Linda A & Michael S. **Education:** Univ Calif, BA, 1948; Univ Basel, PhD (chem), 1959. **Professional Experience:** RETIRED; res chemist, Mattin Labs, Mearl Corp, 1959-1992; res chemist, R J Strasenburgh Co, NY, 1949-1952. **Memberships:** Sigma Xi. **Research Statement & Publications:** Isolation and determination of structures of natural products; organic analytical chemistry; spectroscopy. **Mailing Address:** Six Murray Hill Sq No 203, New Providence, NJ 07974-1528.

KURIYAMA, KINYA, DRUG RECEPTOR, GAMA-AMINOBUTYRIC ACID. **Personal Data:** b Kyoto, Japan, July 11, 1932; m 1959, Chieko; c Takuya & Nagato. **Education:** Kyoto Prefectural Univ Med, MD, 1957, PhD (pharmacol), 1963. **Honors & Awards:** Sci Award, Japanese Med Asn, 1982. **Professional Experience:** Pres, Japanese Pharmacol Soc, 1993-; pres, 15th Cong Int Soc Neurochem, 1993; Japanese Soc Neuropsychopharmacol, 1987-1990 & Asian WPac Pharmacol Soc, 1988-; assoced, Alcohol & Alcoholism, 1985-; ed, Neurochem Int, 1982-; DIR, GRAD SCH, 1979-; Memcoun, Japanese Pharmacol Soc, 1978-; PROF PHARMACOL & CHMN DEPT, KYOTOPREFECTURAL UNIV MED, 1971-; prof neurochem, Sch Med, State Univ NY, 1970-1971; assoc prof pharmacol, Sch Med, Loma Linda Univ, 1967-1969; sr res scientist, City Hope NatMed Ctr, 1964-1967; Res assoc pharmacol, Johns Hopkins Univ Sch Med, 1963-1964; from instrto asst prof, Grad Sch, 1958-1963. **Memberships:** Int Soc Neurochem; Int Soc Biomed Res Alcoholism (pres, 1995-); Am SocPharmacol & Exp Therapeut; Japanese Med Soc Alcohol & Drug Studies (pres, 1987). **Research Statement & Publications:** Neurochemical and pharmacological studies on amino acid neurotransmitters, drug receptors, drug dependence and signal transductions in exitable cells. **Mailing Address:** 69-1 Iwagakakiuchi-cho, Kamigamo Kita-Ku, Kyoto 603, Japan. **Fax:** 810-752-515314.

KURIYAMA, MASAO, X-RAY PHYSICS, MATERIALS SCIENCE. **Personal Data:** b Tokyo, Japan, October 29, 1931; m 1958, c 1. **Education:** Tokyo Metrop Univ, BS, 1953; Univ Tokyo, MS, 1955, DSc(physics), 1958. **Honors & Awards:** Silver Medal, US Dept Com, 1974, IR-100, 1979. **Professional Experience:** CONSULT, 1990-; vis prof, Nat Lab High Energy Physics, Japan, 1986; supvryphysicist, Inst Mat Sci & Eng, Nat Bur Standards, 1980-1990; physicist, Inst Mat Sci & Eng, NatBur Standards, 1967-1980; assoc prof physics, Univ Tokyo, 1966-1967; sr scientist, Westinghouse Elec Corp, 1962-1966; res assoc x-ray physics, Inst Solid State Physics, 1959-1962; res assoc, Tokyo Metrop Univ, 1958-1959. **Memberships:** Am Crystallog Asn; Am Phys Soc; Phys Soc Japan. **Research Statement & Publications:** Magnetism; x-ray dynamical diffraction; crystal perfection; crystal growth; x-ray inelastic scattering; synchrotron radiation topography; x-ray microscopy; x-ray nondestructive evaluation; x-ray tomographic imaging. **Mailing Address:** 20337 Bickleton Pl, Gaithersburg, MD 20886.

KURIYAN, JOHN, MOLECULAR & CELL BIOLOGY. **Education:** Juniata Col, Chem, BS; Ma Inst Tech, PhD. **Professional Experience:** CHANCELLORS PROF, DEPT CHEM, UNIV CALIF, as of 2006; INVESTR HOWARD HUGHES MED INST, 2001-. **Mailing Address:** Univ Calif, 16 Barker Hall MC 3202, Berkeley, CA 94720-3202. **Fax:** 510-643-2352. **E-Mail:** kuriyan@berkeley.edu

KURKJIAN, CHARLES R(OBERT), CERAMICS. **Personal Data:** b Wanamassa, NJ, December 7, 1929; m 1955, Dorothy; c Karen, Lynne & Robert. **Education:** Rutgers Univ, BS, 1952; Mass Inst Technol, ScD(ceramics), 1955. **Honors & Awards:** Nate acad of engrs 1994. **Professional Experience:** Vis sci, Rutgers Univ, 1999-; vis res, Coll Aborator, Princeton, 1999-; mem tech staff, Bellcore, Telcordia, 1994-1999; SCIENTIST, BELL COMMUN RES, 1994-; mem tech staff inorg chem, Bell Tel Labs, 1959-1994; fel, Univ Sheffield, Eng, 1957-1959; Res assoc glass, Mass Inst Technol, 1955-1957. **Memberships:** Nat Acad Eng; fel Brit Soc Glass Technol; fel Am Ceramic Engrs; Acad Ceramics. **Research Statement & Publications:** Glass; ceramics; general high temperature inorganic chemistry; mech properties of glasses and lightguide fibers. **Mailing Address:** 82 Harrison Brook Dr, Basking Ridge, NJ 07920. **Fax:** 732-445-3258. **E-Mail:** ckurkjia@aol.com

KURKOV, VICTOR PETER, ORGANIC CHEMISTRY, CATALYSTS. **Personal Data:** b Zrenjanin, Yugoslavia, March 29, 1936; American citizen; m 1957, Sara; c Paul & Theodore. **Education:** NY Univ, BChE, 1963; Columbia Univ, MA, 1965, PhD (org chem), 1967. **Professional Experience:** CONSULT, 1996-; staff scientist, Chem Res Dept, 1991-1996; sr res assoc, Chem Res Dept, 1983-1991; sr res chemist, Chem Res Dept, 1974-1983; res chemist, ChevronRes Co, 1967-1974; res asst biochem, Col Med, NY Univ, 1958-1963. **Memberships:** Am Chem Soc. **Research Statement & Publications:** Free radical reactions; oxidation; homogeneous catalysis; new petrochemical processes; polymer chemistry; reactive extrusion. **Mailing Address:** 66 Dunfries Terr, San Rafael, CA 94901.

KURLAND, ALBERT A, PSYCHIATRY. **Personal Data:** b Wilkesbarre, Pa, June 29, 1914; m 1941, c 2. **Education:** Univ Md, BS, 1936, MD, 1940. **Professional Experience:** RES PROF PSYCHIAT, SCH MED, UNIV MD, 1979-; dir, Md Psychiat Res Ctr, 1969-1977; dir res, Dept Ment Hyg, 1960-1969; dir med res, Spring Grove State Hosp, State Md, 1953-1960; staff psychiatrist, Spring Grove State Hosp, State Md, 1949-1953. **Memberships:** AMA; Am Psychiat Asn. **Research Statement & Publications:** Chlorpromazine in the treatment of schizophrenia; clinical reaction and tolerance to lysergic acid diethylamine tartrate in chronic schizophrenia; the drug placebo and its psychodynamic and conditional reflex action; comparative effectiveness of eight phenothiazines; author of over 185 publications in clinical Psychopharmacology. **Mailing Address:** Dept Psychiat, Sch Med, Univ Md, 6317 Park Heights NE, Baltimore, MD 21215-2937.

KURLAND, JEFFREY ARNOLD, SOCIOBIOLOGY, PRIMATOLOGY. **Personal Data:** b New York, NY, November 19, 1943; m 1967, c 2. **Education:** Cornell Univ, BA, 1967; Harvard Univ, MA, 1972, PhD (anthrop), 1976. **Professional Experience:** Assoc head, Dept Anthrop, Pa State Univ, 1987-1991; assoc prof, Dept Human Develop & Family Studies, Pa State Univ, 1986; ASSOC PROF BIOL ANTHROP & HUMAN DEV, PA STATE UNIV, UNIV PARK, 1984-; asst prof, Pa State Univ, Univ Park, 1975-1984; instr anthrop, Harvard Univ, 1974-1975; res assoc primatol, primate res inst, Kyoto Univ, 1972-1973. **Memberships:** AAAS; Animal Behav Soc; Int Primatol Soc; Soc Study Evolution; Am Asn PhysAnthropologists; Sigma Xi. **Research Statement & Publications:** Primate sociobiology and behavioral ecology; crab-eating, rhesus, Japanese and barbary macaques; human sociobiology. **Mailing Address:** Dept Anthrop, Pa State Univ, 416 Carpenter Bldg, Univ Park, PA 16802-3404. **Fax:** 814-863-1474. **E-Mail:** jak@psu.edu

KURLAND, JONATHAN JOSHUA, PHYSICAL ORGANIC CHEMISTRY. **Personal Data:** b Boston, Mass, January 11, 1939; m 1964, Dorothy; c Brenda & Zelig. **Education:** Univ Pa, BA, 1960; Harvard Univ, MA, 1967, PhD (chem), 1968. **Professional Experience:** RES LEADER, DOW CHEM CO, 2001-; sr res sci, Union Carbide Corp, 1999-2001; res scientist, Union Carbide Chem & Plastics Co, Inc, 1984-1999; proj scientist, Union Carbide Chem & Plastics Co, Inc, 1975-1984; chemist, Union Carbide Chem & Plastics Co, Inc, 1968-1975; res assoc chem, Columbia Univ, 1967-1968. **Memberships:** Am Chem Soc. **Research Statement & Publications:** Oxidation and free-radical chemistry; Atmospheric chem; process safety technology. **Mailing Address:** 1617 Kirklee Rd, Charleston, MI 25314-2426. **E-Mail:** kurlanjj@dow.com

KURLAND, ROBERT JOHN, NUCLEAR MAGNETIC RESONANCE. **Personal Data:** b Denver, Colo, April 2, 1930; m 1964, c 5. **Education:** Calif Inst Technol, BS, 1951; Harvard Univ, MA, 1953, PhD (chem physics), 1955. **Professional Experience:** SR RESEARCHER, DEPT SPEC IMAGING-RADIOL, GEISINGER MEDCTR, 1985-; assoc prof chem, State Univ NY Buffalo, 1968-1985; from instr to assoc prof chem, Carnegie Mellon Univ, 1958-1968; Res assoc, Nat Bur Standards-Nat Res Coun, 1956-1958. **Memberships:** Am Asn Phys Med; Soc Magnetic Resonance Imaging. **Research Statement & Publications:** Magnetic imaging and spectroscopy. **Mailing Address:** Dept Radiol, Geisinger Clin, Danville, PA 17821.

KURLAND, SUSAN L, AVIATION LAW. **Education:** Brandeis Univ, BA, 1973; Boston Univ, JD, 1976. **Professional Experience:** ASSOC ADMINR AIRPORTS, FED AVIATION ADMIN, as of 1997; GEN COUN, CHICAGO-GARY REGIONAL AIRPORT AUTHORITY, 1995-; DEP CORP COUN, DEPT LAW, CITY CHICAGO, 1988-; chief asst corpcoun, Chicago-Gary Regional Airport Authority, 1987-1988; attorney, Ancal, Glink, Diamond, Murphy & Cope, PC, Chicago, 1982-1987; asst city solicitor, Law Dept, City Newton, Mass, 1976-1982; chmn, Infrastructure Comt, US Dept Transp. **Research Statement & Publications:** National airport planning, including safety standards, design and engineering. **Mailing Address:** Fed Aviation Admin, 800 Independence Ave SW, Washington, DC 20591.

KURMES, ERNEST A, FORESTRY. **Personal Data:** b Brooklyn, NY, January 19, 1931; m 1991, Patricia; c 2. **Education:** Lehigh Univ, BA, 1953; Yale Univ, MS, 1957, MF, 1958, PhD (forest ecol), 1961. **Professional Experience:** PROF EMER FORESTRY, NORTHERN ARIZ UNIV, as of 1996; prof forestry, Northern Ariz Univ, beginning 1980; assoc prof, NorthernAriz Univ, 1967-1980; Asst prof forestry, Southern Ill Univ, Carbondale, 1961-1967. **Memberships:** Fel AAAS; Fel Soc Am Foresters; Sigma Xi. **Research Statement & Publications:** Forest ecology; regeneration of forest tree species. **Mailing Address:** Northern Ariz Univ, PO Box 15108, Flagstaff, AZ 86011-0001. **E-Mail:** ernest.kurmes@nau.edu

KURNICK, JOHN EDMUND, HEMATOLOGY, ONCOLOGY. **Personal Data:** b New York, NY, February 9, 1942; m 1969, Luann; c David S & Katherine R. **Education:** Harvard Univ, BA, 1962; Univ Chicago, MD, 1966. **Professional Experience:** MEM, MED ONCOL ASN SOUTHERN CALIF, as of 2003; assoc clin prof med (hemat/oncol), Univ Calif, Irvine, beginning 1979; asst prof med, Univ Colo Med Ctr & chief, Hemat Serv, Denver Vet Admin Hosp, 1973-1978; fel hemat, Univ Colo Med Ctr 1968-1970; resident med, Stanford Univ Hosps, 1967-1968; intern, Univ Wash Hosps, 1966-1967. **Memberships:** Am Col Physicians; Am Fedn Clin Res; Am Soc Clin Oncol; Am Soc Hemat; Int Soc Exp Hemat. **Research Statement & Publications:** Hematopoietic cellular differentiation and control of granulopoiesis; erythropoiesis in anemias of chronic diseases and uremia; chemotherapy of malignant disorders. **Mailing Address:** 10720 Paramount Blvd, Downey, CA 90241. **Fax:** 562-862-4034.

KURNICK, NATHANIEL BERTRAND, BIOCHEMISTRY, MEDICINE. **Personal Data:** b Brooklyn, NY, November 8, 1917; m 1989, Sally A Kr e ger; c John E, Katherine J (deceased) & James T. **Education:** Harvard Univ, BA, 1936, MD, 1940; Am Bd Internal Med, dipl, 1951, cert oncol, 1973, cert hemat, 1974. **Professional Experience:** Dir oncol-hemat lab, Long Beach Community Hosp, 1981-; CLIN PROF MED, UNIV CALIF, IRVINE, 1968-; chmn div hemat, Univ Calif, Irvine, 1966-1971; chmn dept med, Long Beach Community Hosp, 1966-1967; vis physician, Los Angeles County Hosp, 1965-1968; assoc prof med in residence & assoc internist, Univ Calif, Irvine, 1965-1968; consult, Vet Admin Hosp, Long Beach, Calif, 1959-; consult, Harbor Gen Hosp, Torrance Calif, 1959-1966; assoc internist, Univ Calif, Los Angeles, 1959-1965; assoc clin prof med, Univ Calif, Los Angeles, 1954-1965; vis physician, Harbor Gen Hosp, Torrance Calif, 1954-1959; mem staff, Vet Admin Hosp, Long Beach, Calif, 1954-1959; Vis physician, Charity Hosp, New Orleans, La, 1949-1954 & Touro Infirmary, 1952-1954; consult, Charity Hosp, Pineville, La, 1949-1954; asst prof med & dir lab cell res, Med Sch, Tulane Univ, 1949-1954; Nat Res Coun & Am Cancer Soc res fel biochem & cytochem, Rockefeller Inst, 1947-1948 & Karolinska Nobel Inst, Stockholm, 1948-1949; resident med, Mt Sinai Hosp, NY, 1946-1947; intern, Mt Sinai Hosp, NY, 1941-1942; Workman fel med & biochem, Mass Gen Hosp, Harvard Univ, 1940-1941; staff mem var hosps. **Memberships:** Histochem Soc; Am Soc Hemat; Soc Exp Biol & Med; Int Soc Hemat; Int Soc Exp Hemat Am Soc Cell Biol, Sigma Xi, central Soc Clin res, Am Coll phys (fel). **Research Statement & Publications:** Nucleic acids; chemistry and metabolism; nucleolytic enzymes; cytochemistry; hematology; in vitro chemosensitivity, autologous bone marrow implantation research (oncology); radiation biology. **Mailing Address:** 16251 Tisbury Circle, Huntington Beach, CA 92649. **Fax:** 714-846-7302. **E-Mail:** nbkurnick@pol.net

KURNIT, DAVID MARTIN, GENETICS, MOLECULAR BIOLOGY. **Personal Data:** b Brooklyn, NY, December 24, 1947; m 1993, Kristine; c Heather (Spicer), Katherine & Jennifer. **Education:** Brooklyn Col, BA, 1968; Albert Einstein Col Med, PhD (cell biol), 1974, MD, 1975. **Professional Experience:** PROF PEDIAT & HUMAN GENETICS, MED SCH, UNIV MICH, 1986-; INVESTR, HOWARD HUGHES MED INST, 1986-; res career develop award, Nat inst ChildHealth & Human Develop, 1985-1990; clin investr award, Nat Inst Child Health & HumanDevelop, 1982-1985; from asst prof to assoc prof pediat, Harvard Med Sch, 1979-1986; Nat resServ award, NIH, 1977-1979. **Memberships:** Am Soc Human Genetics; Soc Pediat Res; Cytogenetics & Cell Genetics; Am SocBiochem & Molecular Biol; Sigma Xi. **Research Statement & Publications:** Molecular analysis of cardiogenesis and Down syndrome; sequence copy changes in cancer. **Mailing Address:** Univ Mich, 3520 MSRB I, Ann Arbor, MI 48109-0650. **Fax:** 734-936-9353. **E-Mail:** sesame@umich.edu

KURNOW, ERNEST, STATISTICS. **Personal Data:** b New York, NY, October 21, 1912. **Education:** City Col NY, BS, 1932, MS, 1933; NY Univ, PhD (econ), 1951. **Professional Experience:** PROF EMER STATIST, SCH BUS, NY UNIV, 1986-; dir, Careers Bus Prog, 1978-1986; chmn doctoral prog, Grad Sch Bus Admin, 1976-1985; consult, New York Temp Comn City Finances, 1975-1976 & Tri-State Regional Planning Comn, 1973-1975; finance Mass Transit, 1971-1972 & Gov Spec Comn, 1971-1972; Fulbright grant, Athens, Greece, 1966-1967; study dir, Tri-State Transp Comt, 1964-1966; prof statist, Grad Sch Bus Admin, 1962-1986; chmn quant anal area, Schs Bus, NY Univ, 1962-1976; Lincoln Found grant, 1958-1961; From instr to prof econ, Schs Bus, NY Univ, 1948-1962. **Memberships:** Fel Am Statist Asn; Int Statist Inst; Inst Mgt Sci; Am Econ Asn; Am Inst Decision Sci. **Research Statement & Publications:** Applications of statistics in fields of transportation and state and local government; design of sampling studies. **Mailing Address:** Dept Statist, NY Univ, K-MEC 8-64, 44 W Fourth St, New York, NY 10012. **Fax:** 212-995-4003. **E-Mail:** ekurnow@stern.nyu.edu

KUROHARA, SAMUEL S, RADIOBIOLOGY, RADIOTHERAPY. **Personal Data:** b Hilo, Hawaii, April 21, 1931; m 1956, c 3. **Education:** Wash Univ, BA, 1953, MD, 1957; Univ Rochester, PhD (radiobiol), 1964. **Professional Experience:** CLIN PROF RADIOL, SCH MED, UNIV SOUTHERN CALIF, 1975-; ASSOC RADIOTHERAPIST, WHITTIER ONCOL MED CLIN, 1975-; Whittier Oncol MedClin, 1971- & Alpha Omega Serv, 1973-; Good Samaritan Hosp, Los Angeles, 1969-1972; specialistphysician, Los Angeles County Univ Southern Calif Med Ctr, 1968-; clin consult, Roswell ParkMem Inst, NY, 1968-; prof radiol, Med Ctr, 1968-1974; asst dir radio ther, Med Ctr, 1968-1974; assoc dir radiother & assoc chief cancer res, Roswell Park Mem Inst, NY, 1966-1968; radiotherapist, US Naval Hosp, San Diego, 1964-1966; asst radiotherapist, Strong Mem Hosp, 1961-1964; Instr radiol, Sch Med, Univ Rochester, 1961-1964; consult, Tech Serv Corp, 1960-1971; res radiol, Strong Mem Hosp, 1958-1961; Intern gen med, Jewish Hosp, St Louis, 1957-1958. **Memberships:** Radiol Soc NAm; AMA; Am Soc Therapeut Radiol; Radiation Res Soc; Sigma Xi. **Research Statement & Publications:** Computer applications in the study of medical and biological data; computer application to automated system in radiotherapy; effects of ionizing radiation on normal tissues; mechanisms of tumor control with radiation. **Mailing Address:** 825 Oak Knoll Circle, Pasadena, CA 91106.

KUROKAWA, KANEYUKI, MICROWAVES, OPTICAL COMMUNICATIONS. **Personal Data:** b Tokyo, Japan, August 14, 1928; m 1957, Yasuko Nomura; c Michiko & Hiroko. **Education:** Univ Tokyo, Bachelor Eng, 1951, Dr Eng, 1958. **Honors & Awards:** Pioneer Award, Inst Elec & Electronics Engr, 1996; Distingished ContribAward, Inst Electronic Info & Commun Engrs, 1996. **Professional Experience:** FUJITSU FEL, FUJITSU LABS, 1994-; vpres, Fujitsu Labs, 1992-1994; Visprof, Inst Indust Sci, Univ Tokyo, 1986-1989; managing dir, Fujitsu Labs, 1985-1992; dir, FujitsuLabs, 1979-1985; dep dir, Fujitsu Labs, 1975-1979; supvr, Bell Labs, 1964-1975; mem tech staff, Bell Labs, 1963-1964; Asst prof, Univ Tokyo, 1957-1963. **Memberships:** Fel Inst Elec & Electronics Engrs; Asn Comput Mach; Inst Electronics, Info &Commun Engrs Japan. **Research Statement & Publications:** Microwave circuit theory; parametric amplifier; balanced transistor amplifier; solid state oscillators theory; solid state switches; analysis of head crash of hard discs; technical management; optical fiber communication. **Mailing Address:** Fujitsu Labs Ltd, 4-1-1 Kamiodanaka Nakaharaku, Kawasaki 211, Japan.

KUROKAWA, KIYOSHI, MEDICINE. **Personal Data:** b Tokyo, Japan, September 11, 1936. **Education:** Univ Tokyo, MD, 1962, DMS, 1967; Am Bd Internal Med, cert. **Professional Experience:** DEAN & PROF MED, SCH MED, TOKAI UNIV, 1996-; Chmn bd, JapaneseSoc Internal Med, 1990-1993; prof & chmn, Dept Med, Univ Tokyo, 1989-1996; assoc prof, Dept Med, Univ Tokyo, 1983-1989; from asst prof to prof med, Dept Med, 1977-1984; asst profmed, Dept Med, Univ Southern Calif, 1974-1977; sr res fel, Univ Calif, Los Angeles, 1971-1973; sr res fel, Cedars Sinai Med Ctr, 1971-1973; res assoc, Dept Med, Univ Pa, 1969-1971; Clintraining internal med & nephrol, Dept Med, Univ Tokyo, 1962-1969. **Memberships:** Foreign assoc Inst Med Nat Acad Sci; Japanese Soc Internal Med (pres, 1995-1996); Int Soc Nephrol (pres-elect, 1995-1997); Japanese Soc Nephrology (pres, 1993-1994); Am Soc ClinInvest; Asn Am Physicians. **Mailing Address:** Sch Med Tokai Univ, 143 Shimokasuya Isehara, Kanagawa 259 11, Japan.

KUROKI, GARY W, AGRICULTURAL BIOTECHNOLOGY, PROTEIN BIOCHEMISTRY. **Personal Data:** b January 16, 1956. **Education:** Ft Lewis Col, BS, 1979; Univ Iowa, MS, 1982, PhD (bot), 1985. **Professional Experience:** RES SCIENTIST, DNA PLANT TECHNOL CORP, 1990-; res scientist, Dept Bot & Plant Sci, Riverside, 1988-1990; scholar, Dept Biochem & Biophys, Univ Calif, Davis, 1986-1988; res fel, Dept Bot, Univ Iowa, 1980-1985. **Memberships:** Am Soc Biochem & Molecular Biol; Am Soc Plant Physiologists; Phytochem SocNAm. **Research Statement & Publications:** Purification and characterization of plant proteins; analysis of metabolic pathways and metabolite pools associated with primary and secondary plant metabolism; analysis of the kinetic characteristics of chorismate mutase 1 purified from Solanum tuberosum tubers; author of numerous scientific publications. **Mailing Address:** DNA Plant Technol Corp, 6701 San Pablo Ave, Oakland, CA 94608. **Fax:** 510-547-2817.

KUROSAKA, MITSURU, MECHANICAL ENGINEERING, AERONAUTICAL & ASTRONAUTICAL ENGINEERING. **Personal Data:** b Shenyang, China, March 26, 1935;

American citizen; m 1963, c 3. **Education:** Univ Tokyo, BS, 1959, MS, 1961; Calif Inst Technol, PhD (mech eng), 1968. **Honors & Awards:** Gen H H (Hap) Arnold Award, Am Inst Aeronaut & Astronaut, 1983. **Professional Experience:** PROF AERONAUT & ASTRONAUT, UNIV WASH, 1987-; vis prof, Mass Inst Technol, 1984-1985; from assoc prof to prof mech & aerospace eng, Univ Tenn Space Inst, 1977-1987; fluid mech engr, Gen Elec Res & Develop Ctr, 1969-1977; eng specialist, AiResearch Mfg Co, 1967-1969; grad res & teaching asst, Calif Inst Technol, 1963-1967; design engr, Hitachi Ltd, 1961-1963; consult, Gen Elec Co, ARO, Inc, AiResearch Mfg Co, Calspan, & Pratt & Whitney Can. **Memberships:** assoc fel Am Inst Aeronaut & Astronaut; fel Am Soc Mech Engrs; Sigma Xi. **Research Statement & Publications:** Aerothermodynamics of gas turbines; aeroacoustics; unsteady flow, aeroelasticity; thermodynamics and heat transfer; fluid dynamics. **Mailing Address:** Dept Aeronaut & Astronaut, Univ Wash, PO Box 352400, Seattle, WA 98195-2400. **Fax:** 206-543-0217. **E-Mail:** kurosaka@aa.washington.edu

KUROSE, GEORGE, CHEMICAL ENGINEERING. **Personal Data:** b Eatonville, Wash, June 13, 1924; m 1956, c 3. **Education:** Columbia Univ, BS, 1949, MS, 1950. **Professional Experience:** RETIRED; group leader, Am Cyanamid Co, beginning 1977; sr res chem engr, Am Cyanamid Co, 1962-1977; res chem engr, Am Cyanamid Co, 1955-1962; chem engr, Am Cyanamid Co, 1950-1955. **Memberships:** Am Chem Soc; Am Inst Chem Eng. **Research Statement & Publications:** Process development; process design; process and economic evaluation; synthetic fiber process development. **Mailing Address:** Ten Wayfaring Rd, Norwalk, CT 06851.

KUROSKI DE BOLD, MERCEDES LINA, IMMUNOCYTOCHEMISTRY. **Personal Data:** b Cordoba, Arg, September 23, 1942; Canadian citizen; m 1968, c 5. **Education:** Nat Univ, Cordoba, Argentina, BSc, 1968; Queen's Univ, Can, MSc, 1972, PhD (path), 1974. **Professional Experience:** PROF, DEPT BIOCHEM, MICROBIOL & IMMUNOL, UNIV OTTAWA, as of 2002; STAFF SCIENTIST, UNIV OTTAWA HEART INST, as of 2002; actg chair, beginning 1996; vchair, Animal CareComt, beginning 1995; tutor, GI Block, Second Yr Fac Med, Univ Ottawa, beginning 1992; ASST PROF PATH & LAB SCI, UNIV OTTAWA, 1986-; asst prof, Queen's Univ, Kingston, 1985-1986; res assoc, Queen's Univ, Kingston, 1977-1985; instr, Queen's Univ, Kingston, 1972-1974; res fel path, Queen's Univ, Kingston, 1968-1974; bd dirs, Can-Arg Inst; bd dirs, Child Life & Play Ottawa Liaison. **Memberships:** Soc Exp Biol & Med; Int Soc Heart Res; Can Cardiovasc Soc. **Research Statement & Publications:** Correlation between the structure and function of mammalian and non-mammalian cells; sequence cardionatrins; functional morphology of mammalian atrial cardiocytes; published over 25 articles. **Mailing Address:** Univ Ottawa Heart Inst, 40 Ruskin St, Ottawa, ON K1Y 4W7, Can. **Fax:** 613-761-1597. **E-Mail:** mercedes@uottawa.ca

KUROSKY, ALEXANDER, PROTEIN STRUCTURE, PROHORMONE PROCESSING. **Personal Data:** b Windsor, Ont, September 12, 1938; American citizen; m 1963, Anna; c Lisa K, Tanya K & Stepanie A. **Education:** Univ BC, BS, 1965; Univ Toronto, MS, 1969, PhD, 1972. **Honors & Awards:** John G Sinclair Award, Sigma Xi, 1988. **Professional Experience:** PROF HUMAN BIOL CHEM & GENETICS, MED BR, UNIV TEX, GALVESTON, 1982-; NIH & NSF res grants, Burkitt Found, 1976-; from asst prof to assoc prof, Med Br, Univ Tex, Galveston, 1975-1982; res & develop chemist, Can Breweries, Ltd, Toronto, 1965-1967; res technician, Dept Agr, Harrow, Ont & Vancouver, BC, Can, 1959-1964. **Memberships:** Am Soc Biochem & Molecular Biol; Am Chem Soc; Can Biochem Soc; AAAS; Sigma Xi; Am Inst Chem. **Research Statement & Publications:** Biochemistry; structure, function and genetics. **Mailing Address:** Dept Human Biol Chem & Genetics, Univ Tex Med Br, Galveston, TX 77555. **Fax:** 409-747-4753. **E-Mail:** akurosky@utmb.edu

KUROWSKI, GARY JOHN, NUMERICAL ANALYSIS. **Personal Data:** b Fargo, NDak, March 22, 1931; m 1963, c 3. **Education:** Univ Minn, BS, 1953, MS, 1954; Carnegie Inst Technol, PhD (math), 1959. **Professional Experience:** PROF EMER MATH, UNIV CALIF, DAVIS, as of 2001; dir comput ctr, Univ Calif, Davis, 1969-1971; from asst prof to assoc prof math, Univ Calif, Davis, 1963-1972; Res assocmath, Off Ord Res, Duke Univ, 1959-1963. **Memberships:** Am Math Soc; Asn Comput Mach; Soc Indust & Appl Math. **Research Statement & Publications:** Applied mathematics, especially discrete and semi-discrete analogues of the classic fields of analysis and their application to numerical analysis. **Mailing Address:** 1009 Vassar Dr, Davis, CA 95616. **E-Mail:** kurowski@math.ucdavis.edu

KUROYANAGI, NORIYOSHI, DIGITAL TELECOMMUNICATIONS SYSTEMS, HIGH SPEED DIGITAL TRANSMISSIONS. **Personal Data:** b Tokyo, Japan, February 7, 1930; m 1959, Emiyo; c Noriko, Chiyoko & Yuri. **Education:** Tokyo Inst Technol, Bachelor, 1954, DrEng(comput), 1962. **Honors & Awards:** Maejima Award, Asn Post & Telecommun, 1979; Sci & Technol MinisterAward, Japanese Govt, 1980; Donald W McLellan Meritorious SErv Award, Inst Elec &Electronics Engrs, Commun Soc, 1987. **Professional Experience:** PROF TELECOMMUN, TOKYO ENG UNIV, 1986-; head, Info NetworksDept, Tokyo Eng Univ; dir, Elec Commun Labs, 1981-1986; dep dir, Elec Commun Labs, 1978-1981; sr staff engr, Elec Commun Labs, 1974-1977; dept head, Elec Commun Labs, 1971-1974; staff engr, Elec Commun Labs, 1964-1971; Mem tech staff, Nippon Tel & Tel PubCorp, 1954-1964. **Memberships:** Inst Elec & Electronics Engrs Commun Soc; Inst Elec Inf & Commun Engrs; fellnst Elec & Electronics Engrs. **Research Statement & Publications:** High speed computer-arithmetic circuits; high speed digital transmission systems; synchronization techniques; enhanced digital communication networks; local area networks; spread spectrum communication systems; development of PCM-400 Mb/s coaxial transmission systems. **Mailing Address:** Tokyo Eng Univ, 1404-1 Katakura Hachiohji, Tokyo 192, Japan.

KURSHAN, JEROME, MATHEMATICS. **Personal Data:** b Brooklyn, NY, March 10, 1919. **Education:** Columbia Univ, AB, 1939; Cornell Univ, PhD (physics), 1943. **Professional Experience:** RETIRED; mgr admin proj, RCA Labs, 1983-1987; mgr admin serv, RCA Labs, 1973-1983; mgr mkt, RCA Labs, 1966-1973; mgr, RCA Labs, 1959-1966; mgr employ & training, RCA Labs, 1955-1959; instr, Rutgers Univ, 1944; res physicist, RCA Labs, 1943-1955; asst physics, Cornell Univ, 1939-1943; asst physics, Columbia Univ, 1939. **Memberships:** Sr mem, Inst Elec & Electronics Engrs; Princeton Soc (Chmn, 1953). **Research Statement & Publications:** Ion sources; gated amplifiers; frequency modulated magnetrons; automatic frequency control oscillators; transistors; semiconductors physics; materials analysis; computer applications; research management; research administration. **Mailing Address:** 73 Random Rd, Princeton, NJ 08540. **E-Mail:** pandj@aol.com

KURSS, HERBERT, MATHEMATICS. **Personal Data:** b Brooklyn, NY, March 30, 1924; m 1963, Rachel. **Education:** Cooper Union, BEE, 1943; Polytech Inst Brooklyn, MEE, 1952; NY Univ, PhD, 1957. **Professional Experience:** EMER PROF MATH, ADELPHI UNIV, 1990-; prof, AdelphiUniv, 1969-1990; assoc prof, Adelphi Univ, 1962-1969; res asst prof, Microwave Res Inst, Polytech Inst Brooklyn, 1959-1962; res assoc appl math, Microwave Res Inst, Polytech Inst Brooklyn, 1957-1959; res asst math, NY Univ, 1954-1957; res assoc appl math, Microwave Res Inst, Polytech Inst Brooklyn, 1948-1954; instr elec eng, US Merchant Marine Acad, 1947-1948; tech writer radar, Techlit Consult, Inc, 1947. **Memberships:** Am Math Soc; Math Asn Am; Sigma Xi; Soc Indust & Appl Math; Inst Elec &Electronics Engrs. **Research Statement & Publications:** Problems associated with ordinary differential equations and with electromagnetic theory. **Mailing Address:** Dept Math, Adelphi Univ, Garden City, NY 11530. **E-Mail:** kurss@panther.adelphi.edu

KURSTEDT, HAROLD ALBERT, NUCLEAR ENGINEERING. **Personal Data:** b Columbus, Ohio, September 15, 1939; m 1961, c 3. **Education:** Va Mil Inst, BS, 1961; Univ Ill, Urbana, MS, 1963, PhD (nuclear eng), 1968. **Professional Experience:** PROF EMER MECH & NUCLEAR ENG, VA POLYTECH INST & STATE UNIV, 2003-; founder & dir, Mgt Systs Labs, 1981-1994; assoc prof mech & nuclear eng, Va Polytech Inst & State Univ, beginning 1976; prog mgr, Fed Systs Div, Indust Nucleonics Corp, 1970-1976; asst prof nuclear eng, Col Eng, Ohio State Univ, 1968-1970; res & develop coordr, Ballistic Res Labs, Aberdeen Proving Ground, Md, 1966-1968; instr mech eng, Va Mil Inst, 1961-1962. **Memberships:** Am Soc Civil Eng; Am Soc Eng Educ; Am Nuclear Soc; Sigma Xi. **Research Statement & Publications:** Nuclear reactor kinetics and heat transfer, particularly experimental and analytical techniques in pulsed thermal and fast reactors; nuclear instrumentation and control; nondestructive inspection. **Mailing Address:** Dept Indust & Systs Eng, Va Tech, 212 Hancock Hall, Blacksburg, VA 24061-0118. **Fax:** 540-231-3322.

KURT, CARL EDWARD, CIVIL ENGINEERING, STRUCTURAL ENGINEERING. **Personal Data:** b Muskogee, Okla, June 3, 1943; m 1969, Judith; c David. **Education:** Okla State Univ, BS, 1965, MS, 1966, PhD (civil eng), 1969. **Professional Experience:** PROF, CIVIL ENVIRON & ARCHIT DEPT, UNIV KANS, 1982-; from asst prof to assoc prof, Dept Civil Eng, Auburn Univ, 1974-1982; sr engrstrength, McDonnell Douglas Astronaut Corp, 1969-1974; instr civil eng, Okla State Univ, 1969; prin investr, numerous proj; pres, EnGraph. **Memberships:** Am Soc Civil Engrs; Am Soc Testing & Mat; Am Inst Steel Construct. **Research Statement & Publications:** Geographical information systems; behavior of structural materials and structural steel design; structural analysis and stability; engineering properties of thermoplastic water well casings; computer aided design. **Mailing Address:** Civil Environ & Archit Eng Dept, Univ Kans, 1530 W 15th St 2150 Learned Hall, Lawrence, KS 66045-7609. **Fax:** 785-864-5631. **E-Mail:** ckurt@ku.edu

KURTA, ALLEN, BATS, ENDANGERED SPECIES. **Personal Data:** b Detroit, Mich, September 6, 1952. **Education:** Mich State Univ, BS, 1975, MS, 1975; Boston Univ, PhD (biol), 1986. **Professional Experience:** PROF BIOL, EASTERN MICH UNIV, 1997-; assoc prof, Eastern Mich Univ, 1991-1997, asst prof, Eastern Mich Univ, 1988-1991; res assoc, Boston Univ, 1986-1988; asst prof biol, Nazareth Col, 1985-1986; consult, 1980-. **Memberships:** Am Soc Mammalogists; The Wildlife soc. **Research Statement & Publications:** Physiology, ecology and natural history of bats and other mammals. **Mailing Address:** Dept Biol Eastern Mich Univ, 324 Mark Jefferson, Ypsilanti, MI 48197. **Fax:** 734-487-9235. **E-Mail:** allen.kurta@emich.edu

KURTENBACH, AELRED J(OSEPH), ELECTRICAL ENGINEERING. **Personal Data:** b Dimock, SDak, January 3, 1934; m 1960, c 5. **Education:** SDak Sch Mines & Technol, BS, 1961; Univ Nebr, MS, 1962; Purdue Univ, PhD (elec eng), 1968. **Professional Experience:** CHMN BD DIRS, DAKTRONICS INC, BROOKINGS, SDAK, as of 2006; pres, Daktronics, Inc, Brookings, SDak, beginning 1969; CO-FOUND, DAKTRONICS INC, BROOKINGS, SDAK, 1968-; assoc prof, SDak State Univ, 1969-1972; asst prof, SDak State Univ, 1965-1969; instr elec eng, Purdue Univ, 1965-1966; instr elec eng, SDak State Univ, 1962-1965. **Memberships:** Inst Elec & Electronics Engrs. **Research Statement & Publications:** Biomedical telemetry; pulse-code modulation telemetry. **Mailing Address:** Daktronics Inc, 331 32nd Ave, Brookings, SD 57006. **Fax:** 605-697-4700.

KURTH, JANICE H, HUMAN GENETICS, EVOLUTIONARY GENETICS. **Personal Data:** b December 26, 1963; m 1987, Matthias; c Carol M & Susan A. **Education:** Austin Col, BA, 1985; Stanford Univ, PhD (genetics), 1991; Univ Ariz, MD, 1995. **Honors & Awards:** Frances Kallman Award, Stanford Univ, 1991. **Professional Experience:** Physician, Ariz Physicians, 1996-; STAFF SCIENTIST, ST JOSEPHS HOSP &MED CTR, 1993-; res assoc, Tex Tech Univ, 1991-1993. **Memberships:** AAAS; AMA; Am Soc Human Genetics; Am Col Med Genetics. **Research Statement & Publications:** Defining genetic predisposition to Parkinson's disease through population genetic analysis; linkage projects also in progress to localize genes for cavernous malformations, Navajo neuropathy and others. **Mailing Address:** St Josephs Hosp & Med Ctr, 350 W Thomas Rd, Phoenix, AZ 85013-4496. **Fax:** 602-406-7172. **E-Mail:** jkurth@mha.chw.edu

KURT-JONES, EVELYN A, BIOLOGY. **Education:** PhD. **Professional Experience:** RES ASSOC PROF, UNIV MASS MED SCH, as of 2005. **Memberships:** Am Soc Microbiol. **Mailing Address:** Univ Mass Med Sch, LRB 226, Worcester, MA 01605. **Fax:** 508-856-6176. **E-Mail:** evelyn.kurt-jones@umassmed.edu

KURTTI, TIMOTHY JOHN, INSECT PATHOLOGY, INSECT PHYSIOLOGY. **Personal Data:** b Minneapolis, Minn, March 8, 1942; m 1985. **Education:** Univ Minn, BA, 1965, PhD (entom), 1974. **Professional Experience:** PROF ENTOM, UNIV MINN, as of 2004; assoc prof entom, Univ Minn, beginning 1989; asst prof entom, Univ Minn, 1986-1989; asst res prof microbiol, Waksman Inst Microbiol, Rutgers Univ, 1980-1985; scientist, Int Lab for Res on Animal Dis, Nairobi, Kenya, 1977-1980; res assoc insect microbiol, DeptEntom, Fisheries & Wildlife, Univ Minn, St Paul, 1973-1977; res fel, Dept Entom, Fisheries & Wildlife, Univ Minn, St Paul, 1970-1973; res asst, Dept Entom, Fisheries & Wildlife, Univ Minn, St Paul, 1969-1970; from jr scientist to asst scientist insect microbiol, Dept Entom, Fisheries & Wildlife, Univ Minn, St Paul, 1966-1969. **Memberships:** Soc Invert Path; Entom Soc Am; Sigma Xi; Am Soc Parasitol; Soc Protozool. **Research Statement & Publications:** Insect microbiology; bovine and tick tissue culture; development physiology of insects; insect nutrition; biological calorimetry; theileriosis; intracellular parasitism; microbial control; lyme disease. **Mailing Address:** Dept Entomol, Univ Minn, 219 Hodson Hall 1980 Folwell Ave, St Paul, MN 55108. **Fax:** 612-625-5299. **E-Mail:** kurtt001@umn.edu

KURTZ, A PETER, PESTICIDE CHEMISTRY, STRUCTURE-ACTIVITY RELATIONSHIPS. **Personal Data:** b Staten Island, NY, June 12, 1942; m 1964, Marie; c Christine & Catherine. **Education:** Fordham Univ, BS, 1963; Columbia Univ, MA, 1964, PhD (org chem), 1968. **Professional Experience:** SR MED COORDR, PEST DETECTION EMERGENCY PROJ, CALIF DEPT FOOD & AGR, as of 2004; MGR SCI INFO MGT & SYSTS, TECH CTR, RHONE-POULENC AGRCO, 1988-; sr group leader pesticide chem, Tech Ctr, Rhone-Poulenc Agr Co, 1985-1988; group leader pesticide chem, Tech Ctr, Rhone-Poulenc Agr Co, 1978-1985; res chemist, Tech Ctr, Rhone-Poulenc Agr Co, 1971-1978; res chemist, Letterman Army Inst Res, 1969-1971. **Memberships:** Am Chem Soc. **Research Statement & Publications:** Development of quantitative structure; activity relationships and application to the design of selectively toxic pesticide chemicals; computerized chemical/biological information storage and analysis systems. **Mailing Address:** Pest Detection Emergency Proj, Calif Dept Food & Agr, Sacramento, CA 95814.

KURTZ, ANTHONY DAVID, PHYSICAL METALLURGY. **Personal Data:** b New York, NY, May 3, 1929; m 1985, Nora Morcos; c Jennifer (Unger), John & Sandria. **Education:** Mass Inst Technol, SB, 1951, SM, 1952, ScD(phys metall), 1955. **Honors & Awards:** Si Fluor Technol Award, Instrument Soc Am, 1978. **Professional Experience:** PRES, KULITE SEMICONDUCTOR PROD, 1966-; dir res & develop, KuliteSemiconductor Prod, 1959-1966; supvr appl res, Semiconductor Div, Minneapolis-HoneywellRegulator Co, 1956-1959; sr engr, Transistor Prod, Inc Div, Clevelite Corp, 1956; staff mem, Lincoln Lab, 1954-1955; Res asst, Mass Inst Technol, 1951-1954. **Memberships:** Am Soc Metals; Am Phys Soc; Inst Elec & Electronics Engrs; Sigma Xi. **Research Statement & Publications:** Solid state physics and tranducer design; semiconductor devices and materials; diffusion in solids; imperfections in metals and semiconductors; experimental mechanics; stress analysis. **Mailing Address:** Kulite Semiconductor Prod, One Willow Tree Rd, Hackensack, NJ 07605.

KURTZ, CLARK N, OPTICS. **Personal Data:** b Stillwater, Minn, November 24, 1937; m 1965, c 2. **Education:** SDak Sch Mines & Technol, BS, 1959; Univ Ill, MS, 1963; Univ Rochester, PhD (elec eng), 1967. **Honors & Awards:** Charles Ives Award, Soc Photog Scientists & Engrs, 1972. **Professional Experience:** Dir, Info & Computer Tech Div, Res, Eastman Kodak Co, beginning 1989; sr tech asst to dir res, Photo Div, Eastman Kodak Co, 1988-1989; adv dev mgr mass mem, Photo Div, Eastman Kodak Co, 1985-1988; dir Optical Rec Prod, Photo Div, Eastman KodakCo, 1984-1985; lab head res labs, Eastman Kodak Co, 1979-1984; res assoc optics, EastmanKodak Co, 1972-1979; sr res physicist, Eastman Kodak Co, 1966-1972; design engr electronics, Eastman Kodak Co, 1959-1962; adv bd, Nat Ctr Supercomputing, Univ Ill, Cornell Theory Ctr. **Memberships:** Optical Soc Am; Am Inst Physics. **Research Statement & Publications:** Physics of forming images on paper in copying; theory of light propagation in waveguides; design of optical screens and diffusers; optical disk; light waves. **Mailing Address:** Eastman Kodak Co, 343 State St, Rochester, NY 14650. **Fax:** 585-724-0663.

KURTZ, DAVID ALLAN, PESTICIDE CHEMISTRY, CHEMOMETRICS. **Personal Data:** b Evanston, Ill, January 31, 1932. **Education:** Knox Col, AB, 1954; Pa State Univ, MS, 1958, PhD (org chem), 1960. **Professional Experience:** PA STATE UNIV, as of 1999; CONSULT, 1995-; sr res assoc & environ chemist, Environ Resource Res Inst, 1993-1995; co-leader, Coop Regional Proj, Pa Agr Exp Sta, 1978-1983; anal chemist, Pesticides Res Lab, Pa State Univ, 1971-1993; asst prof pesticides anal, Mat Res Lab, Pa State Univ, 1967-1971; res assoc appl chem, Mat Res Lab, Pa State Univ, 1962-1966; sr chemist, HRB-Singer Inc, 1960-1962; instr gen chem, Pa State Univ, 1959-1960. **Memberships:** Am Chem Soc; Chemometrics Soc; Soc Environ Toxicol & Chem; Asn Off Anal Chemists; Int Union Pure & Appl Chem; Int Asn Great Lakes Res. **Research Statement & Publications:** Methods of analysis for pesticides and herbicides; chemometric methods statistical calibration methods in trace residue analysis for pesticides and environmental compounds; pesticide analysis in marine and marine atmosphere environments; long range transport of pesticides; groundwater pathways of pesticide movement. **Mailing Address:** Pa State Univ, State College, PA 16801. **Fax:** 814-863-0845. **E-Mail:** d1k@psu.edu

KURTZ, DAVID WILLIAMS, PHOTOCHEMISTRY, EDUCATION. **Personal Data:** b Altoona, Pa, July 27, 1942; m 1972, Saddie; c Stella A, Kimberly C & Eleanor J. **Education:** Houghton Col, NY, BS, 1964; Syracuse Univ, PhD (chem), 1971. **Professional Experience:** CHMN CHEM, OHIO NORTHERN UNIV, 1995-; PROF ORG CHEM, OHIO NORTHERN UNIV, 1984-; fel Petrol Res Found, Iowa State Univ, 1983; from asst profto assoc prof, Ohio Northern Univ, 1973-1983; res assoc photochem, Univ Wis, 1971-1973. **Memberships:** Am Chem Soc; Sigma Xi. **Research Statement & Publications:** Torsional processes in photochemical transformations and other syntheitic applications in organic chemistry. **Mailing Address:** Dept Chem & Biochem, Ohio Northern Univ, Meyer Hall Sci 263, Ada, OH 45810. **Fax:** 419-772-2985. **E-Mail:** d-kurtz@onu.edu

KURTZ, DONALD M, CHEMISTRY. **Education:** Northwestern Univ, PhD, 1977. **Professional Experience:** DISTINGUISHED RES PROF CHEM & MOLECULAR BIOL, UNIV GA, as of 2005. **Mailing Address:** Dept Chem, Univ GA, Athens, GA 30602-2556. **Fax:** 706-542-9454. **E-Mail:** kurtz@chem.uga.edu

KURTZ, EDWIN BERNARD, JR, SCIENCE EDUCATION. **Personal Data:** b Wichita, Kans, August 11, 1926; m 1952, Lois Leecing; c Kathryn & Jane. **Education:** Univ Ariz, BS, 1948, MS, 1949; Calif Inst Technol, PhD, 1952. **Professional Experience:** EMER PROF, UNIV TEX PERMIAN BASIN, 1989-; prof life sci & chmn dept, Univ Tex Permian Basin, 1972-1989; prof biol & head dept, Kans State Teachers Col, 1968-1972; Asst dir educ, AAAS, Washington, DC, 1965-1967; actg head dept, Univ Ariz, 1954-1955; from asst prof to prof, Univ Ariz, 1951-1968; predoc fel, Nat Res Council-Atomic Energy Comn, 1949-1951; Instr bot, Univ Ariz, 1947. **Memberships:** AAAS. **Research Statement & Publications:** Plant physiology; biochemistry of fats and waxes; palynology, cacti; science education; teaching with behaviorial objectives. **Mailing Address:** 1620 N Kutch Dr, Flagstaff, AZ 86001.

KURTZ, GEORGE WILBUR, ANALYTICAL CHEMISTRY. **Personal Data:** b Harrisburg, Pa, December 8, 1928; m 1953, c 3. **Education:** Pa State Univ, BS, 1950, MS, 1952, PhD (dairy sci), 1954. **Professional Experience:** RETIRED; consult, Clearwater, 1989-1994; plant mgr, R P Scherer, Monroe, NC, 1979-1989; mgr qual control, R P Scherer, Monroe, NC, 1969-1979; chemist, DalareAssocs, 1962-1969; head, Flavor & Phys Chem Lab, Armed Forces Qm Food & Container Inst, Chicago, 1956-1962; Res chemist, Swift & Co, 1954. **Memberships:** Am Chem Soc; Inst Food Technol. **Research Statement & Publications:** Analytical chemistry; food technology. **Mailing Address:** 3029 Brookfield Lane, Clearwater, FL 34621.

KURTZ, HAROLD JOHN, VETERINARY PATHOLOGY. **Personal Data:** b Brookings, SDak, February 18, 1931; m 1953, c 3. **Education:** SDak State Univ, BS & MS, 1954; Univ Minn, DVM, 1958, PhD (vet path), 1966. **Professional Experience:** PROF PATH, COL VET MED, UNIV MINN, ST PAUL, 1974-; from asst prof to assoc prof, vet med, 1966-1974; fel, vet med, 1962-1966; instr vet med, 1961-1962; instr vet surg, 1960-1961; fel vet path, 1960-1961. **Memberships:** Am Vet Med Asn; Am Col Vet Path; Int Cad Path. **Research Statement & Publications:** Dissecting aortic rupture in turkeys; neuropathology and pathology of animal diseases; comparative pathology; edema disease of swine. **Mailing Address:** Univ Minn Col Vet Med, 236-E Vet Diag Lab, St Paul, MN 55108. **E-Mail:** kurtz003@umn.edu

KURTZ, LAWRENCE ALFRED, NUMERICAL ANALYSIS. **Personal Data:** b Providence, RI, December 29, 1940. **Education:** Univ RI, BS, 1962; Univ Conn, MS, 1965; Univ Tenn, Knoxville, PhD (math), 1969. **Professional Experience:** PROF MATH, UNIV MONTEVALLO, 1978-; statist comput analyst, Hollins Col, 1971; asst prof, Hollins Col, 1970-1977; instr, Univ Tenn, Knoxville, 1970; teaching asst, Univ Tenn, Knoxville, 1965; teaching asst math, Univ Conn, 1963-1965; engr, Eastman Kodak Co, 1962-1963. **Memberships:** Am Math Soc; Soc Indust & Appl Math. **Research Statement & Publications:** Computational fluid dynamics; numerical analysis of partial differential equations; mathematics education. **Mailing Address:** Dept Math & Phys, Univ Montevallo, Montevallo, AL 35115. **E-Mail:** kurt@montevallo.edu

KURTZ, LESTER TOUBY, AGRONOMY. **Personal Data:** b Howard Co, Ind, November 7, 1914; m 1940, c 2. **Education:** Purdue Univ, BS, 1938; Univ Ill, PhD (agron), 1943. **Professional Experience:** EMER PROF SOIL FERTIL, UNIV ILL, URBARA, BEGINNING 1953; Guggenheim fel, soils lab, Agr Res Serv, USDA, 1953-1954; prof soil fertil & fertilizers, Exp Sta, 1950-1982; from asst prof to assoc prof, Dept Agron, Univ Ill, Urbana, 1944-1950; asst soil chemist, instr US army spec training prog, 1943-1945; assoc, Dept Agron, Univ Ill, Urbana, 1943-1944; asst soil chemist, Dept Agron, Univ Ill, Urbana, 1938-1943. **Memberships:** AAAS; fel Am Soc Agron; Am Chem Soc; Soil Sci Soc Am. **Research Statement & Publications:** Soil chemistry and fertility; analytical chemistry; phosphate fixation in Illinois soils; fate of fertilizer nitrogen in soils as indicated by nitrogen 15; role of fertilizer in water pollution. **Mailing Address:** 101 W Windsor Rd 1212, Urbana, IL 61802.

KURTZ, MARK EDWARD, WEED SCIENCE, CROP ROTATION & FIBER RESEARCH. **Personal Data:** b Trenton, Mo, November 8, 1946; m 1971, c 2. **Education:** Mo Valley Col, BS, 1969; Miss State Univ, MS, 1977, PhD (weed sci), 1980. **Professional Experience:** PLANT PHYSIOLOGIST & WEED SCIENTIST, DELTA RES & EXTEN CTR, as of 2001; Adj assoc prof, Dept Plant Path & Weed Sci, Miss State Univ, 1981-. **Memberships:** Weed Sci Soc Am; Int Kenaf Asn. **Research Statement & Publications:** Soybean and rice cotton weed control, utilizing existing techniques and improvising new ideas to solve unanswered problems as they arise in varied cropping systems; evaluating herbicides in a soybean-rice rotation; herbicide tolerance in Kenaf Hibiscus Cannabinus. **Mailing Address:** Delta Res & Exten Ctr, Miss State Univ, 82 Stoneville Rd PO Box 197, Stoneville, MS 38776. **Fax:** 662-686-7336. **E-Mail:** mekurtz@drec.msstate.edu

KURTZ, MICHAEL E, MEDICINE, RESEARCH ADMINISTRATION. **Personal Data:** b St Louis, Mo, March 30, 1952; m 1983, Karen; c Brian, Alison & Brendan. **Education:** Univ Mo, St Louis, BA, 1976, MS, 80. **Professional Experience:** Mem lab adv comt, HLA Servs, 1992 & 1993; instr res methodology, HLAServs, 1990-; MGR & ASSOC DIR, SURG RES INST, ST LOUIS UNIV, 1990-; res assoc, Surg & Transplant Servs, 1989-1990; consult, HLA Servs, 1986-; mgr, Histocompatibility Lab, 1985-1989; res biologist, John Cochran Vet Admin Hosp, St Louis, 1981-1985; Sr res tech, Cancer Biolsect, Washinton Univ, St Louis, 1976-1981. **Memberships:** Soc Res Adminr; Asn Acad Surg Admin; Am Soc Histocompatibility &Immunogenetics; Am Asn Lab Animal Sci; Nat Coun Univ Res Adminr. **Research Statement & Publications:** Medical and health sciences. **Mailing Address:** Ctr Adv Dent Educ, St Louis Univ, 3320 Rutger St, St Louis, MO 63104. **Fax:** 314-268-5181. **E-Mail:** kurtzme@wpogate.slu.edu

KURTZ, MYRA BERMAN, MICROBIOLOGY, GENETICS. **Personal Data:** b New York, NY, July 20, 1945; m 1970, Stuart; c Rachel L. **Education:** Goucher Col, AB, 1966; Harvard Univ, PhD (microbiol), 1971. **Professional Experience:** SR DIR, DEPT INFECTIOUS DIS, MERCK RES LABS, RAHWAY, NJ, 1996-; dir, Merck Res Labs, Rahway, NJ, 1989-1996; sr res fel, Merck Res Labs, Rahway, NJ, 1988-1989; sr res scientist, Squibb Inst, Princeton, NJ, 1982-1987; asst res prof, Waksman Microbiol, 1976-1982; res assoc, Rutgers Univ, 1975-1976; assoc prof microbiol, Fed Univ Sao Carlos, Brazil, 1972-1974; Res assoc, State Univ NY, Albany, 1971-1972; Ed, Fungal Genetics & Biol. **Memberships:** Am Soc Microbiol; AAAS; Sigma Xi. **Research Statement & Publications:** Molecular genetics of the dimorphic human pathogenic fungus; Candida albicans; systemic fungal disease; fungal cell wall synthesis. **Mailing Address:** Dept Infectious Dis, Merck Res Labs, PO Box 2000, Rahway, NJ 07065-0900. **Fax:** 732-594-1399. **E-Mail:** myra_kurtz@merck.com

KURTZ, PETER JR, CERAMIC ENGINEERING, THERMODYNAMICS. **Personal Data:** b Chicago, Ill, May 12, 1927; m 1950. **Education:** Univ Mo, Rolla, BS, 1952, MS, 1953; Univ Calif, Los Angeles, PhD (eng), 1964. **Professional Experience:** RETIRED; prof physics, Div Sci, 1980-1992; chmn, Div Sci, 1971-1980; profeng, Biola Col, 1968-1980; asst prof, Univ Calif, Los Angeles, 1964-1968; actg asst prof, UnivCalif, Los Angeles, 1963-1964; asst res engr, Univ Calif, Los Angeles, 1957-1958; assoc eng, Univ Calif, Los Angeles, 1956-1962; jr res engr, Univ Calif, Los Angeles, 1955-1957; Grad resengr, Univ Calif, Los Angeles, 1953-1955. **Memberships:** Am Asn Physics Teachers; Sigma Xi. **Research Statement & Publications:** Mechanical properties of ceramic materials; thermodynamic properties of multicomponent polyphase systems. **Mailing Address:** 115 Copa De Oro Dr, Brea, CA 92621.

KURTZ, RICHARD LEIGH, SURFACE SCIENCE, SYNCHROTRON RADIATION. **Personal Data:** b Dubuque, Iowa, October 19, 1956; m 1987, Helene; c Brian Laura. **Education:** Brandeis Univ, BA, 1978; Yale Univ, MS, 1979, PhD (appl Physics), 1983. **Honors & Awards:** Harding Bliss Prize, 1983. **Professional Experience:** PROF PHYSICS, LA STATE UNIV, 1997-; assoc prof physics, La State Univ, 1990-1997; staff res physicist, Nat Inst Stand & Technol, 1983-1992; Nat Res Coun assoc, Nat Bur Stand, 1983-1985. **Memberships:** Am Phys Soc; Am Vacuum Soc; AAAS; Mat Res Soc, Phys Elect conference (treas). **Research Statement & Publications:** Synchrotron radiation applications in surface science; photoelectron spectroscopy; surface electronic structure; molecular adsorption; stimulated desorption; transition-metal oxides; high temperature superconductors; high Tc thin films; Microtomography. **Mailing Address:** Dept Physics & Astron La State Univ, 202 Nicholson Hall, Baton Rouge, LA 70803-4001. **Fax:** 504-578-5855. **E-Mail:** kurtz@rouge.phys.lsu.edu

KURTZ, RICHARD ROBERT, SYNTHETIC ORGANIC CHEMISTRY. **Personal Data:** b Moose Jaw, Sask, March 20, 1945; m 1970, c 2. **Education:** Univ Calgary, BSc, 1967; Mass Inst Technol, PhD (org chem), 1971. **Professional Experience:** ASSOC DIR, UPJOHN CO, 1984-; res mgr, Upjohn Co, 1983-1984; res head, Upjohn Co, 1980-1983; res, Upjohn Co, 1973-1980; assoc org chem, John C Sheehan Inst Res, 1971-1973. **Memberships:** Am Chem Soc; AAAS; NY Acad Sci. **Research Statement & Publications:** Pharmaceutical research and development; synthesis of heterocycles. **Mailing Address:** Chem Process Res & Develop, Upjohn Co Unit 1510-91-1, Kalamazoo, MI 49001-3298.

KURTZ, STANLEY MORTON, PATHOLOGY. **Personal Data:** b Philadelphia, Pa, May 11, 1926; m 1957, c 2. **Education:** George Washington Univ, BS, 1949, MS, 1950, PhD (anat), 1953; Univ Ala, MD, 1958. **Professional Experience:** PROF PATH, SOUTHWESTERN MED CTR, DALLAS & STAFF PATHOLOGIST, DALLAS VET ADMIN HOSP, 1985-; prof path, Med Univ SC, Charleston & staff pathologist, Charleston Vet Admin Hosp, 1976-1985; Nat Acad Sci-Nat Res Coun, 1972- & Nat Inst Drug Abuse, 1974-; dir dept toxicol, Res Labs, Parke Davis & Co, 1965-1976; assoc prof, Med Ctr, Duke Univ, 1961-1965; Consult, Vet Admin Hosps, 1961-1965; sr res fel path, Univ Pittsburgh, 1958-1961; instr anat, Med Sch, Univ Ala, 1954-1958; Instr anat, Bowman Gray Sch Med, Wake Forest Col, 1952-1954. **Memberships:** AAAS; Am Soc Path & Bact; Am Soc Exp Path; Soc Toxicol. **Research Statement & Publications:** Cytology; electron microscopy; development, structure and pathology of mammalian renal glomerulus. **Mailing Address:** Dept Anat & Cell Biol, Tex Col Osteo Med, 3500 Camp Bowie Blvd, Ft Worth, TX 76107-2699.

KURTZ, STEVEN ROSS, ELECTRONIC MATERIALS, PHOTODETECTOR DEVELOPMENT. **Personal Data:** b Washington, DC, October 3, 1953; m 1978. **Education:** Bucknell Univ, BS, 1975; Univ Ill, Urbana-Champaign, MS, 1977, PhD (physics), 1980. **Professional Experience:** SR MEM TECH STAFF, SANDIA NAT LAB, 1980-. **Memberships:** Am Phys Soc. **Research Statement & Publications:** Electronic materials, semiconductors and insulators; photoconductivity and transport in layered semiconductors and disordered materials; optical and electron paramagnetic resonance spectroscopies; photodetector development, novel infrared materials and photodetectors; diode lasers; infrared optoelectronics. **Mailing Address:** Sandia Nat Lab, PO Box 5800, Albuquerque, NM 87185. **Fax:** 505-844-8985. **E-Mail:** srkurtz@sandia.gov

KURTZ, STEWART K, ELECTROOPTICS. **Personal Data:** b Bryn Mawr, Pa, June 9, 1931; m 1951, Dora Grandinetti; c Philip, David, Timothy & John. **Education:** Ohio State Univ, BSc, 1956, MSc, 1957, PhD (physics), 1960. **Professional Experience:** Vchair & elec adminr, Mat Res Inst, Murata prof mat res, 1989-1993; PROF ELEC ENG, PA STATE UNIV, 1987-; vpres eng, vpres technol & sr scientist, Bristol Myers, Clairol Appliance Div, 1978-1987; group dir explor res, Philips Labs Div, NAm Philips Corp, 1969-1978; Staff scientist, Bell Tel Labs, Inc, 1960-1969. **Memberships:** Am Phys Soc; sr mem Inst Elec & Electronics Engrs; NY Acad Sci; Mat Res Soc; Am Ceramic Soc. **Research Statement & Publications:** Grain growth in polyrystaline materials; microstructural simulation; ferroelectrics, primarily optical and electrooptical properties; nonlinear optical materials; powder survey methods; second harmonic coefficients; Raman scattering; statistical topology; phase transitions; crystal chemistry. **Mailing Address:** Mat Res Inst, Pa State Univ 188 MRI Bldg, University Park, PA 16802-1013. **Fax:** 814-863-1465. **E-Mail:** skkl@psu.edu

KURTZ, THOMAS EUGENE, MATH STATISTICS, COMPUTER SYSTEMS. **Personal Data:** b Oak Park, Ill, February 22, 1928; m 1974, c 3. **Education:** Knox Col, BA, 1950; Princeton Univ, PhD (math), 1956. **Honorary Degrees:** DSc, Knox Col, 1985. **Honors & Awards:** Pioneer Award, Am Fed Info Processing Socs, 1974. **Professional Experience:** VCHMN, TRUE B ASIC INC, 1983-; vchmn & chm, Prog Comput Info Sci, 1980-1988; chmn bd, NERComP Inc, 1974-1978; chmn coun, EDUCOM, 1973-1974; assoc prof, math, 1966-1993; mem Pierce panel, Presidents Sci Adv Coun Comput in Higher Educ, 1965-1967; dir, Comput Ctr, 1959-1975; Dartmouth col 1956-1993; Consult, Vet Admin, White River Junction, Vt. **Memberships:** Am Statist Asn; Asn Comput Mach fel. **Research Statement & Publications:** Computer languages; computer systems and their applications; computer use in education; statistics applications. **Mailing Address:** 3 Lakeview, Hanover, NH 03755-3407.

KURTZ, THOMAS GORDON, STOCHASTIC PROCESSES. **Personal Data:** b Kansas City, Mo, July 14, 1941; m 1963, Carolyn; c 2. **Education:** Univ Mo, Columbia, BA, 1963; Stanford Univ, MS, 1965, PhD (math), 1967. **Professional Experience:** PAUL LEVY PROF MATHEMATICS & STATIST, UNIV WIS-MADISON, as of 2005; dir, Ctr Math Sci, Univ Wis-Madison, 1990-1996; dept chair, Univ Wis-Madison, 1985-1988; PROF MATH, UNIV WIS, MADISON, 1975-; from asst prof to assoc prof, Univ Wis-Madison, 1969-1975; vis lectr math, Univ Wis-Madison, 1967-1969. **Memberships:** Math Asn Am; Soc Indust & Appl Math; Am Math Soc; fel Inst Math Statist; Opers Res Soc Am; Int Statist Inst. **Research Statement & Publications:** Probability theory and stochastic processes; Markov processes; approximation for stochastic process; filtering; stochastic control; stochastic analysis, applications to gentics and networks. **Mailing Address:** Dept Math & Stat Univ Wis, 525 Van Vleck Hall 480 Lincoln Dr, Madison, WI 53706-1388. **Fax:** 608-263-8891. **E-Mail:** kurtz@math.wisc.edu

KURTZ, VINCENT E, STRATIGRAPHY, ENVIRONMENTAL GEOLOGY. **Personal Data:** b Duluth, Minn, April 12, 1926; m 1953, c 5. **Education:** Univ Minn, BA, 1946, MS, 1949; Univ Okla, PhD (geol), 1960. **Professional Experience:** CONSULT GEOL, 1991-; prof geol, Southwest Mo State Col, 1974-1991; from asst prof to assoc prof earth sci, Southwest Mo State Col, 1965-1974; consult geologist, Mich, 1960-1965; dist geologist, Kans, 1956-1958; geologist, Aurora Gasoline Co, Colo, 1952-1955. **Memberships:** Am Inst Prof Geologists. **Research Statement & Publications:** Late Cambrian and early Ordovician stratigraphy; paleontology and paleoecology of trilobites, inarticulate brachiopods and conodonts. **Mailing Address:** 1643 S Saint Charles Ave, Springfield, MO 65804.

KURTZ, WILLIAM BOYCE, FOREST RESOURCE ECONOMICS, SOCIAL FORESTRY. **Personal Data:** b Austin, Tex, July 15, 1941; m 1965, c 2. **Education:** NMex State Univ, BS, 1963, MS, 1966; Univ Ariz, PhD (natural resource econ), 1971. **Honors & Awards:** Walnut Coun Res Award, 1984. **Professional Experience:** PROF FORESTRY, UNIV MO-COLUMBIA, 1980-; assoc prof, Univ Mo-Columbia, 1975-1980; asst prof natural resources mgt, Calif PolytechState Univ, 1970-1975; sr economist, Voorhies, Trindle & Nelson, Orange County, 1969-1970; proj economist, Daniel Mann Johnson & Mendenhall, 1969; res assoc watershed mgt, Univ Ariz, 1968-1969; range conservationist, Soil Conserv Serv, USDA, 1963-1964. **Memberships:** Sigma Xi; Am Agri Econ Asn; Soil Conserv Soc Am; Soc Am Foresters. **Research Statement & Publications:** Social forestry; agroforestry economics; non-industrial forest owner decision making. **Mailing Address:** Dept Forest, Univ Mo, Natural Resources Bldg, Rm 130, Columbia, MO 65211-0001. **Fax:** 573-884-2636. **E-Mail:** kurtzw@missouri.edu

KURTZE, DOUGLAS ALAN, PATTERN FORMATION, STATISTICAL PHYSICS. **Personal Data:** b Mt Vernon, NY, October 15, 1954; m 1992, Elena; c Jocelyn B & Benedict Z. **Education:** Lehigh Univ, BA & BS, 1974; Cornell Univ, MS, 1978, PhD (physics), 1980. **Professional Experience:** PROF PHYSICS, NDAK STATE UNIV, 1990-; res physicist, Inst TheoretPhysics, 1987; resident vis, AT&T Bell Lab, 1983-1984; asst prof physics, Clarkson Univ, 1982-1990; res physicist, Carnegie-Mellon Univ, 1979-1982. **Memberships:** Am Phys Soc; Soc Indust & Appl Math; Am Asn Crystal Growth; Am Asn PhysicsTeachers. **Research Statement & Publications:** Instabilities and pattern formation in solidifying and crystallizing systems; analytical and numerical methods for moving boundary problems; zeros of partition functions. **Mailing Address:** Dept Physics, NDak State Univ, Fargo, ND 58105-5566. **Fax:** 701-237-7088. **E-Mail:** kurtze@plains.nodak.edu

KURTZIG, SANDRA L, MATHEMATICS, AERONAUTICAL ENGINEERING. **Personal Data:** b Chicago, Ill, October 21, 1946; c Andrew Paul & Kenneth Alan. **Education:** Univ Calif, Los Angeles, BS, 1968; Stanford Univ, MS, 1968. **Professional Experience:** CHMN, EBENEFITS, as of 2001; CHMN EMER, ASK GROUP INC, 1993-; chmn, pres & chief exec officer, 1989-1993; chmn bd, chief exec officer & pres, ASK Comput Systs, 1986-1989; FOUNDER, ASK GROUP INC, 1972-; chmn bd, chief exec officer & pres, ASK Comput Systs, 1972-1985; Mkt rep, Gen Elec Co, 1969-1972. **Mailing Address:** EBenefits, Inc, 135 Stillman St, San Francisco, CA 94107.

KURTZKE, JOHN F, SR, NEUROLOGY, EPIDEMIOLOGY. **Personal Data:** b Brooklyn, NY, September 14, 1926; m 1950, Margaret Nevin; c John F Jr, Catherine (Brown), Elizabeth (Siebert), Joan (Brennan), Robert N, James S & Christine (Hughes). **Education:** St John's Univ, NY, BS, 1948; Cornell Univ, MD, 1952; Am Bd Psychiat & Neurol, dipl neurol, 1958. **Honorary Degrees:** MD Honoris causa, Univ Ferrarg, Ferrqra Italy, 2000. **Honors & Awards:** Zimmerman lectr, Stanford Univ, 1980; Hope Chest Award, Nat Mult Sclerosis Soc, 1982; Gold Vicennial Medal, Georgetown Univ, 1982; Tarbox lectr, Tex Tech Univ Health Sci, 1989; Geigy lectr Mult Sclerosis, Univ Western Ont, 1989; US Legion Merit, 1986, 1995; John Jay Dystel Prize Mult Sclerosis Res, Nat Mult Sclerosis Soc & Am Acad Neurol, 1997; secretary's distinguished carrer award, dept veterans affairs, 1998; charcot award intd, fedn mult sclerosis soc, 1998. **Professional Experience:** Consult Neurol, Vet Affairs Med Ctr, 2000-; serv, Neurolepidemiol Sect, vet Affairs med ctr, Georgetown Univ, Wash, DC, 1995-; serv, Neurolepidemiol Sect, vet Affairs med ctr, Georgetown Univ, Wash, DC, 1995-; stroke coun, Am Heart Asn, 1992-; DISTINGUISHED PROF NEUROL, UNIFORMED SERV UNIV HEALTH SCI, SCH MED, GEORGETOWN UNIV, 1992-; Neurol Panel, Inst Med, 1990; mem, Inst Res Bd, Nat Inst Neurol Dis & Stroke, 1989-; established investr, Nat Mult Sclerosis Soc, 1987; vice chmn, Rev Comt Neurol, 1985-1986; mem, Manpower Comt, Soc Med Consult Armed Forces, 1984-; residency, Rev Comt Neurol, 1983-1988; liaison officer, USN Med Sch, 1979-1986; mem, Comt Nat Needs for Neurol, Am Acad Neurol, 1979-1985; comn neuroepidemiol, comn geog neurol, epidemiol & statist, World Fedn Neurol, 1977-; vice chmn, Dept Neurol, 1976-1995; mem, Working Group Design Clin Studies, Nat Mult Sclerosis Soc, 1976-1984; chmn work group, Epidemiol, Biostatist & Pop Genetics, Comn Control Huntington's Dis, 1976-1977; mem epilepsy adv comt, NIH, 1974-1977; consult ad hoc comt Spinal Cord Injury, Nat Inst Neurol Dis & Stroke, 1973-1976; mem, Work Group Epidemiol, Nat Mult Sclerosis Soc, 1973; mem, Int Med Adv Bd, Int Fedn Mult Sclerosis Soc, 1972-; mem, Task Force Neurol Serv, Joint Comn Neurol, 1971-1975; consult surgeon gen, Dept Navy, 1970; prof neurol, Community & Family Med, 1968-1995; mem, Comn Mult Sclerosis, 1967-1998; mem, Med Adv Bd, Nat Multiple Sclerosis Soc, 1966-; consult neurol, Nat Naval Med Ctr, Bethesda, 1966-2000; assoc prof, Sch Med, Georgetown Univ, 1965-1968; mem, World Fedn Neurol, comn geog neurol, Epidemiol & Statist, 1964-1976; Vet Admin rep, Neurol Study Sect, Div Res Grant, 1964-1972; mem, Exec Comt Coop Study Adrenocorticotropic Hormone Mult Sclerosis, Nat Inst Neurol Dis & Blindness, 1964-1971; chief Neurol Serv, Vet Affairs Med Ctr, Wash, DC, 1963-1995; clin assoc prof, Sch Med, Georgetown Univ, 1963-1965; asst prof, Col, 1963; examr, Am Bd Psychiat & Neurol, 1961-1996; assoc clin neurol, Col, 1961-1963; asst neurologist, Hosp & Clin, 1958-1963; instr neurol, Jefferson Med Col, 1958-1961; assoc chief staff res, Vet Admin Hosp, Coatesville, Pa, 1957-1962; chief neurol serv, Vet Admin Hosp, Coatesville, Pa, 1956-1963; resident, Vet Admin Hosp, Bronx, 1953-1956; intern, Kings County Hosp, 1952-1953; rear adm, Med Corps, USNR, 1944-1986. **Memberships:** Fel Am Col Epidemiol; Am Neurol Asn hon; fel Am Col Physicians; fel Am Acad Neurol; Am Epidemiol Soc; fel Am Col Prev Med; hon mem Danish Neurol Soc; hon foreign mem French Neurol Soc; hon corresp mem, Ger Soc Neurol. **Research Statement & Publications:** Multiple sclerosis & neuroepidemiology; published over 450 articles. **Mailing Address:** Dept Neurol, Uniformed Serv Univ Health Sci, 4301 Jones Bridge Rd Rm A1036, Bethesda, MD 20814. **Fax:** 301-295-0620.

KURTZMAN, CLETUS PAUL, YEAST TAXONOMY, MOLECULAR SYSTEMATICS OF YEASTS & OTHER FUNGI. **Personal Data:** b Mansfield, Ohio, July 19, 1938; m 1962, Mary; c Mary, Mark & Michael. **Education:** Ohio Univ, BS, 1960; Purdue Univ, MS, 1962; WVa Univ, PhD (mycol/microbiol), 1967. **Honors & Awards:** J Roger Porter Award, US Fedn Cult Col, Am Soc Microbiol, 1990. **Professional Experience:** RES LEADER, MICROBIOL PROPERTIES RES, NAT CTR AGR UTILIZATION RES, USDA, 1985-; US res, Int Mycol Asn, 1983-; ADJ PROF MYCOL, ILL STATE UNIV, 1978-; res leader, Agr Res Serv Cult Col, 1981-1985; US res, Int Comn Yeasts, 1980-; microbiologist & cur, Yeast Col, Northern Regional Res Ctr, USDA, 1970-1981; microbiologist, Northern RegionalRes Ctr, USDA, 1967-1970. **Memberships:** Int Comn Yeasts; fel Am Acad Microbiol; Am Soc Microbiol; Int Mycol Asn (secy, 1990-); US Fedn Cult Collections (vpres, 1977-1978, pres, 1978-1980); World Fedn Cult Collections. **Research Statement & Publications:** Molecular systematics of yeasts and yeastlike fungi with emphasis on correlation of molecular divergence with organismal evolution. **Mailing Address:** Microbial Properties Res, Agr Res Serv, USDA, 1815 N Univ St, Peoria, IL 61604-3999. **Fax:** 309-681-6686. **E-Mail:** kurtzman@mail.ncaur.usda.gov

KURTZMAN, RALPH HAROLD, BIOCHEMISTRY, MYCOLOGY. **Personal Data:** b Minneapolis, Minn, February 21, 1933; m 1955, Virginia; c Steven & Sue K (Anderson). **Education:** Univ Minn, BS, 1955; Univ Wis, MS, 1958, PhD (plant path biochem), 1959. **Professional Experience:** CONSULT, INT J MUSHROOM SCI, 1997-; ED, INT J MUSHROOM SCI, 1995-; consult mushroom growing, 1981; guest scientist, VTT Tech Res Ctr Finland, 1980; lectr, Pakistan & Thailand, 1974; lectr, Pakistan & India, 1978; lectr, Univ Helsinki, 1980; biochemist, WesternRegional Res Lab, USDA, 1965-1997; NASA contract res with A H Brown & A O Dahl, UnivMinn, 1963; asst prof biol, Univ Minn, 1962-1965; asst prof plant path, Univ RI, 1959-1962. **Memberships:** Mushroom Growers Asn Gt Brit; Mycol Soc Am; Am Mushroom Inst; World SocMushroom Biol & Mushroom Sci; Mycol Soc Japan. **Research Statement & Publications:** Physiology of plant diseases, particularly Dutch elm disease; alkaloid metabolism of fungi; fungal decomposition of cellulose and lignin; mushroom production from wastes; bureaucratic vasilation; mushroom physiology; ethanol fermentation. **Mailing Address:** 445 Vassar Ave, Berkeley, CA 94708. **Fax:** 510-526-2492. **E-Mail:** rhktzl@worldnet.att.net

KURUCZ, ROBERT LOUIS, ASTROPHYSICS. **Personal Data:** b Columbus, Miss, September 7, 1944. **Education:** Harvard Col, AB, 1966, PhD (astron), 1973. **Honors & Awards:** George van Biesbroeck Award, 1992. **Professional Experience:** PHYSICIST, SMITHSONIAN ASTROPHYS OBSERV, 1974-; res fel, Harvard Col Observ, 1973-1974. **Memberships:** Am Astron Soc; Int Astron Union. **Research Statement & Publications:** Stellar atmospheres; solar physics; radiative transfer; atomicand molecular physics. **Mailing Address:** Smithsonian Astrophys Observ, 60 Garden St, Cambridge, MA 02138. **Fax:** 617-495-7049. **E-Mail:** rkurucz@cfa.harvard.edu

KURUGANTY, SASTRY P, POWER SYSTEM RELIABILITY EVALUATION FOR PLANNING BULK POWER SYSTEM SECURITY ASSESSMENT. **Personal Data:** b Masulipatam, India, January 12, 1941; Canadian citizen; m 1962, Lakshmi Bhagaratula; c Sailaja, Padmaja & Saroja. **Education:** Andhra Univ, BSc, 1959, ME, 1967; Birla Inst, BE, 1964; Univ NB, MScE, 1974; Univ Sask, PhD (power syst reliability), 1979. **Professional Experience:** DEPT ENERGY SAMUEL MASSIE CHAIR EXCELLENCE, UNIV TURABO, 1995-; prof & chmn, Dept Elec Eng, Univ NDak, 1989-1995; Consult, Man HVDC Res Ctr, 1986-; reliability specialist, Man Hydro, 1980-1989; from res asst to res assoc, Univ Sask, 1975-1980; from res asst to res assoc elec eng, Univ NB, 1971-1975; Asst prof elec eng, J N Technol Univ, India, 1966-1971. **Memberships:** Sr mem Inst Elec & Electronics Engrs; Nat Soc Prof Engrs; Am Soc Eng Educ. **Research Statement & Publications:** Power system planning using probabilistic methods; generation planning, transmission, planning and distribution planning; development of methodology for reliability and risk evaluation of power systems; rotating machine dynamics. **Mailing Address:** Dept Elec Eng Univ Turabo, PO Box 3030 Univ Sta, Gurabo, PR 00778-3030. **Fax:** 787-744-5476. **E-Mail:** kuruganty@altavista.net

KURUP, PRADEEP UNNIKRISHNAN, GEOTECHNICAL ENGINEERING, GEOENVIRONMENTAL ENGINEERING. **Personal Data:** b North Parur, Kerala, India, May 5, 1963; m, c Deepika & Anjali. **Education:** Univ Kerala, India, BTech, 1985; Indian Inst Technol, Madras MTech, 1987; La State Univ, PhD (civil eng), 1993. **Honors & Awards:** Excellence in Teaching Award Career Award, National Sci Foundation, 1999; Cerf Award, Civil Engineering Research Fondation, ASCE, 1999. **Professional Experience:** PROFESSOR, UNIV MASS, LOWELL, as of 2005; mem, Transp Res Bd, 1997-; assoc prof, Univ Mass, Lowell, 2001-2005, asst prof, Univ Mass, Lowell, 1997-2001; affil mem, Grad Fac, LA State Univ, 1996-; prin investr, NSF, 1996-; res assoc IV, res assoc V, 1996-1997; prin investr, Nat Res Coun, 1996-1997; res assoc IV, La Transp Res Ctr, 1994-1996; postdoctoral researcher, La State Univ, 1993-1994. **Memberships:** Am Soc Civil Engrs; Am Soc Testing & Mat; Am Soc of Eng Ed, Int Asn Comput Methods & Advan Geomech. **Research Statement & Publications:** Data Fusion, Site characterization by in situ methods; advanced laboratory calibration chamber studies of piezocone penetrometers; development of novel test devices for highway applications; geoenvironmental screening tool; underground space. **Mailing Address:** Dept Civil Eng, Univ Mass, 1 Univ Ave, Lowell, MA 01854. **Fax:** 978-934-3052. **E-Mail:** pradeep_kurup@uml.edu

KURUP, VISWANATH PARAMESWAR, MEDICAL MYCOLOGY, IMMUNOLOGY. **Personal Data:** b Thattayil, India, January 20, 1936; American citizen; m 1962, Indira; c Mini, Manoj & Vinod. **Education:** Univ Poona, BS, 1957, MS, 1959; Univ Delhi, PhD (med mycol), 1967. **Professional Experience:** Consult, UN Develop Prog, 1990; PROF MED, MED COL WIS, 1986-; Fulbright fel, Finland, 1984; Vis prof, PR, 1981-; MICROBIOLOGIST MED MYCOL, VETADMIN MED CTR, 1973-; from asst prof to assoc prof, Vet Admin Med Ctr, 1973-1986; microbiologist, St Anthony Hosp, Columbus, Ohio, 1970-1973; Fel med mycol, Ohio State Univ, 1968-1970. **Memberships:** Fel Am Soc Microbiol; Am Asn Immunologists; Int Soc Human & Animal Mycol; fel Am Acad Allergy & Clin Immunol; Med Mycol Soc Am; fel Am Acad Microbiol. **Research Statement & Publications:** Isolation and purification of antigens and allergens associated with HP from pathogenic fungi; characterization of the antigens and development of immunological tests for the early diagnosis of hypersensitivity lung disease and immune regulation in HP. **Mailing Address:** Dept Pediat & Med, Med Col Wis, 5000 W Nat Ave, Milwaukee, WI 53295. **Fax:** 414-382-5374. **E-Mail:** vkurup@mcw.edu

KURYLA, WILLIAM C, ORGANIC CHEMISTRY. **Personal Data:** b Cuyahoga Falls, Ohio, September 3, 1934; m 1957, c 2. **Education:** Kent State Univ, BS, 1956; Univ Minn, MS, 1958, PhD (org chem), 1960. **Professional Experience:** PRES, KOKOPELLI CHEMISTS INC, as of 2004; corp mgr prod & distrib risk, indust hyg & environ anal, Union Carbide Corp, 1986-1987; dir prod safety CIPS group, indust hyg & environ anal, Union Carbide Corp, 1985-1986; corp mgr into resources & technol, indust hyg & environ anal, Union Carbide Corp, 1984-1985; asst dir prod safety, Union Carbide Corp, beginning 1980; corp mgr appl toxicology serv, indust hyg & environ anal, Union Carbide Corp, 1980-1984; sr group leader, indust hyg & environ anal, Union Carbide Corp, 1978-1980; technol mgr, OccupHealth, Res & Develop Dept, Tech Ctr, Union Carbide Corp, 1977-1980; mgr recruiting & univrels, Tech Ctr, Union Carbide Corp, 1973-1977; group leader, Tech Ctr, Union Carbide Corp, 1971-1973; res scientist, Tech Ctr, Union Carbide Corp, 1969-1971; res & develop chemist, Chem Div, Union Carbide Corp, 1960-1969; Microanalyst, Univ Minn, 1956-1959; adj prof, WVa StateCol. **Memberships:** Am Chem Soc; Am Inst Chem; Am Ind Hyg Asn; Sigma Xi; NY Acad Sci; Am ColToxicol. **Research Statement & Publications:** Polyurethane chemistry and technology; ketene acetals and indole chemistry; radiochemical studies with polymers; textile and fiber chemicals; flame retardants; health effects of chemicals. **Mailing Address:** Kokopelli Chemists, Inc, 200 Battenfarm Rd, Ripley, WV 25271. **Fax:** 304-372-9637. **E-Mail:** wckuryla@citynet.net

KURYLO, MICHAEL JOHN, III, ATMOSPHERIC KINETICS, PHOTOCHEMISTRY. **Personal Data:** b Meriden, Conn, July 20, 1945; m 1966, Mary; c Michelle M, Michael J IV, Melinda S & Meredith L. **Education:** Boston Col, BS, 1966; Cath Univ Am, PhD (phys chem), 1969. **Honors & Awards:** Bronze Medal, US Dept Com, 1983, Silver Medal US Dept COM, 1991. **Professional Experience:** Sci prog mgr, NASA, 1987-; sci asst to dir, Nat Measurement Lab, Nat Bur Stand, 1979-1980; mem, Panel Lab Measurement & Data Eval, NASA, 1978-; RES CHEMIST, NAT INST STAND & TECHNOL, 1971-; Nat Res Coun res assoc, Nat Inst Stand & Technol, 1969-1971. **Memberships:** Am Chem Soc; Am Phys Soc; Am Geophysical Union. **Research Statement & Publications:** Rates and mechanisms of gas phase reactions of importance to atmospheric chemistry and combustion processes; temperature and pressure effects in free radical reactions; role of anthropogenic emissions on stratospheric ozone. **Mailing Address:** Chem Sci & Technol Lab, Nat Inst Stand & Technol, 100 Bur Dr Mail Stop 8381, Gaithersburg, MD 20899-8381. **E-Mail:** michael.kurylo@nist.gov

KURYLO-BOROWSKA, ZOFIA, BIOPHYSICS OF THE ORIGIN OF LIFE. **Personal Data:** b Lublin, Poland, May 13, 1929; American citizen. **Education:** Polytech Univ, Poland, MSci, 1950, PhD (biochem), 1958. **Professional Experience:** ASSOC PROF, ROCKEFELLER UNIV, 1972-; asst prof, Rockefeller Univ, 1967-1972. **Memberships:** Am Chem Soc; Am Polish Inst Art & Sci. **Research Statement & Publications:** Biosynthesis of biological active peptides; origin of life. **Mailing Address:** Rockfeller Univ, 1230 York Ave, New York, NY 10021.

KURZ, DAVID W, POLYMER COMPOSITES, SOLID POLYMER ELECTROLYTES. **Personal Data:** b Evanston, Ill, September 13, 1952; m 1984, Soo; c Shelby S. **Education:** Univ Ill, Champaign, BS, 1979; Case Western Res Univ, MS, 1985; Univ Southern Miss, PhD (polymer sci), 1989. **Professional Experience:** TECH DIR, KEYSTONE INC, 2001-; tech dir, Symmooth Corp, 2000-2001; tech dir, Genl Polymer, 1999-2000; dir res, UV Coatings, 1997-1999; res staff scientist, Gould Electronics, Inc, 1989-1999; polymer scientist, Lawter, Inc, 1981-1982; polymer scientist, Esmark, Inc, 1980-1981. **Memberships:** Am Chem Soc; Soc Plastics Engrs; AAAS. **Research Statement & Publications:** Polymer electrolytes; water soluble polymers; synthetic polymers; composites; initiators. **Mailing Address:** 7886 Skyline View, Concord, OH 44060.

KURZ, JAMES ECKHARDT, PHYSICAL CHEMISTRY, POLYMER CHEMISTRY. **Personal Data:** b Louisville, Ky, October 8, 1934; m 1963, Ann; c James & Jeffrey. **Education:** Centre Col, AB, 1956; Duke Univ, MA, 1958, PhD (phys chem), 1961. **Professional Experience:** RETIRED; techmcal fel, bdeine co, 1999-2000, grp mander, bubnc co, 1996-1999; group mgr, McDonnell-Douglas corp, beginning 1993; prin tech specialist, Mcdonnell-douglas Corp, 1986-1993; mgr res & develop, Monsanto Co, 1984-1985; mgr res, Monsanto Co, 1982-1984; sr group leader, Monsanto Co, 1975-1982; sr res specialist, Monsanto Co, 1966-1975; sr res chemist, Monsanto Co, 1961-1966. **Memberships:** Am Chem Soc; Soc Advan Mat & Process Eng. **Research Statement & Publications:** Characterization of polymers by dilute solution methods; column fractionation of polymers and gel permeation chromatography; physical, mechanical and thermal characterization of polymers and polymer structure; membrane structure and use in industrial processes; structure, property and applications of polymers; structural composites; processing science of aerospace materials. **Mailing Address:** 14317 Aitken Hill, Chesterfield, MO 63017. **E-Mail:** kurzie@msn.com

KURZ, JOSEPH LOUIS, PHYSICAL ORGANIC CHEMISTRY. **Personal Data:** b St Louis, Mo, December 13, 1933. **Education:** Wash Univ, AB, 1955, PhD (chem), 1958. **Professional Experience:** Prof Emeritus, 1994-; PROF CHEM, WASH UNIV, 1973-; from asst prof to assoc prof, Wash Univ, 1964-1973; Vis prof, Wash Univ, 1963-1964; res chemist, Cent Basic Res Lab, Esso Res & Eng Co, 1960-1964; Res fel, Harvard Univ, 1958-1960. **Memberships:** Am Chem Soc; AAAS. **Research Statement & Publications:** Mechanisms, kinetics and thermodynamics of reactions in solution; mechanisms of homogeneous catalysis; transition state structure; kinetic and equilibrium isotope effects. **Mailing Address:** 3640 Yellow Dog Rd, Lonedell, MO 63060-1718.

KURZ, KENNETH D, THROMBOSIS. **Personal Data:** b Palmer, Nebr, October 14, 1948. **Education:** Univ Nebr, BS, 1972; Univ Ill, PhD (physiol), 1976. **Professional Experience:** RES SCIENTIST, ELI LILLY & CO, 1987-; sr scientist, Eli Lilly & Co, 1979-1987; res fel hypertension, Univ Mo, Columbia, 1977-1979; mem, Thrombosis Coun, AmHeart Asn. **Memberships:** Am Physiol Soc; Am Heart Asn. **Research Statement & Publications:** Thrombosis. **Mailing Address:** Dept Cardiovasc Pharmacol Eli Lilly & Co, Lilly Corp Ctr, Indianapolis, IN 46285. **Fax:** 317-277-0892. **E-Mail:** kurz_kenneth_d@lilly.com

KURZ, MICHAEL A, PHARMACOLOGY. **Education:** Univ Louisville, Phd, 1988. **Professional Experience:** CLIN INFO SCIENTIST, CENTOCOR INC, as of 1998. **Mailing Address:** Centocor Inc, 800/850 Ridgeview Dr, Horsham, PA 19044. **Fax:** 610-651-6100.

KURZ, MICHAEL E, ORGANIC CHEMISTRY. **Personal Data:** b Detroit, Mich, March 5, 1941; m 1964, c 4. **Education:** St Mary's Col, BA, 1963; Case Western Reserve Univ, PhD (chem), 1967. **Professional Experience:** RETIRED, as of 2005; prof emer Chem, Ill State Univ, 2003-2005; sabbatical res, Univ Ill, 1988; chmn dept, Ill State Univ, beginning 1987; NSFgrant, 1985, 1989; prof chem, Ill State Univ, 1976-2003; sabbatical res, La State Univ, 1976-1977; actg chmn dept, Ill State Univ, 1974-1975; petrol res fund res grant, 1969-1972 &1985-1987; from asst prof to assoc prof, Ill State Univ, 1968-1976; instr & res assoc chem, Columbia Univ, 1967-1968. **Memberships:** Am Chem Soc; Int Assoc Arson Investr. **Research Statement & Publications:** Free radical aromatic substitution utilizing oxidative and photolytic methods of radical generation; oxidative aromatic substitutions; trace residue analysis; fire debris. **Mailing Address:** Seven Mary Ellen Way, Bloomington, IL 61701. **E-Mail:** mkurz@ilstu.edu

KURZ, RICHARD J, SPACE RESEARCH, INSTRUMENTATION. **Personal Data:** b Springfield, Ill, October 10, 1935; m 1958. **Education:** Univ Ill, BS, 1957, MS, 1958; Univ Calif, Berkeley, PhD (physics), 1963. **Professional Experience:** GEMINI PROJ MGR, ASSOC UNIVS RES & ASTRON, 1994-; asst mgr, Advan Systs Dept, TRW Systs Group, 1972-1994; Chief Physics Br, Planetary & Earth Sci Div, Manned Spacecraft Ctr, Houston, 1967-1972; Nat Acad Sci res assoc, Goddard Space Flight Ctr, NASA, Md, 1966-1967; physicist, Lawrence Radiation Lab, Univ Calif, Berkeley, 1965-1966; NSF fel, LePrince-Ringuet Lab, Ecole Polytech, Paris, 1964-1965; physicist, Lawrence RadiationLab, Univ Calif, 1962-1964; Asst physics, Lawrence Radiation Lab, Univ Calif, 1959-1962. **Memberships:** Am Phys Soc. **Research Statement & Publications:** Space research instrumentation development. **Mailing Address:** 2138 E Camino el Ganado, Tucson, AZ 85718.

KURZ, RICHARD KARL, PHOTOGRAPHIC CHEMISTRY. **Personal Data:** b New York, NY, February 4, 1936; m 1960, Catharine; c Ann, Carolyn, Patricia, Mark & Karl. **Education:** St John Fisher Col, NY, BS, 1957; Univ Ill, Urbana-Champaign, PhD (org chem), 1961. **Professional Experience:** RETIRED; sr tech staff, Graphics Imaging Syst Div, 1989-1992; prod develop mgr, Graphics Imaging Syst Div, 1985-1989; sr lab head, Res Labs, Eastman Kodak Co, 1981-1985; lab head photog chem, Res Labs, Eastman Kodak Co, 1974-1981; res assoc, Res Labs, Eastman Kodak Co, 1969-1974; res chemist, Res Labs, Eastman Kodak Co, 1961-1969. **Research Statement & Publications:** Design and development of advanced photographic materials for use in radiography, graphic arts, micrographics and instrumentation recording applications; environmental conformance technology. **Mailing Address:** 40 True Hickory Dr, Rochester, NY 14615.

KURZ, WOLFGANG GEBHARD WALTER, MICROBIOLOGY, PLANT PHYSIOLOGY. **Personal Data:** b Innsbruck, Austria, June 9, 1933; m 1963, Monica Birgit Sjostedt; c Kristina (Malin), Barbara (Asa) & Ulrika (Ebba). **Education:** Univ Vienna, PhD (microbiol, biochem), 1958. **Honors & Awards:** Can Soc Microbiologists Award, 1979. **Professional Experience:** HEAD BIOTECHNOLOGY DEVELOP DEPT, PLANT BIOTECHNOLOGY INST, NAT RES COUN CAN, 1989-; INT PROJ COORDR, PLANT BIOTECHNOLOGY INST, NAT RES COUN CAN, 1985-; head plantprod technol, Biotechnology Sect, Nat Res Coun Can, 1983-1986; head, Biotechnol Sect, Nat ResCoun Can, 1981-1986; sr res officer Microbiol & Fermentation Technol, Prairie Regional Lab, Nat Res Coun Can, 1973-1987; assoc res officer microbiol & fermentation technol, Nat Res CounCan, 1967-1973; res scientist, Tech Res Coun Sweden, 1965-1967; fel, Prairie Regional Lab, Nat Res Coun Can, 1963-1965; res asst microbiol & biochem, Royal Inst Technol, Sweden, 1955-1963; adj prof, Dept Appl Microbiol, Univ Sask, Saskatoon, Can. **Memberships:** Fel Chem Inst Can; Can Soc Microbiologists; Int Asn Plant Tissue Cult. **Research Statement & Publications:** Biological dinitrogen fixation; continuous cultivation of microbes and plant cells; fermentation biology; enzymology; microbial physiology; process development; apparatus design; biosynthesis of secondary metabolites by microbes and plant cells. **Mailing Address:** Plant Biotechnology Inst, Nat Res Coun Can, 310 Gymnasium Pl, Saskatoon, SK S7N 0W9, Can. **Fax:** 306-975-4839. **E-Mail:** wkurz@pbi.nrc.ca

KURZHALS, PETER R, AERONAUTICS. **Honors & Awards:** Gold Knight Mgt. **Professional Experience:** DIR SYSTS ENG & SOFTWARE, BOEING NASA SYSTS HB, as of 2004. **Memberships:** Am Inst Aeronaut & Astronaut. **Mailing Address:** Boeing NASA Systs, M/S 13/2 5301 Bolsa Ave, Huntington Beach, CA 92647-2048. **Fax:** 714-896-4694. **E-Mail:** peter.r.kurzhals@boeing.com

KURZROCK, RAZELLE, LEUKEMIA, MEDICINE. **Personal Data:** b Toronto, Ont, September 29, 1954; m 1985. **Education:** Univ Toronto, BS, 1973, MD, 1978. **Professional Experience:** PROF MED, MD ANDERSON CANCER CTR, UNIV TEX, as of 2005; assoc prof med oncol & hemat, MD Anderson Cancer Ctr, Univ Tex, beginning 1989. **Memberships:** AMA; AAAS; Am Soc Hemat; Am Soc Clin Oncol; Am Asn Cancer Res. **Research Statement & Publications:** Elucidation of the molecular genetic mechanisms responsible for leukemia and the treatment of this disorder. **Mailing Ad-**

dress: Dept Bioimmunotherapy, Univ Tex MD Anderson Cancer Ctr, 1515 Holcombe Blvd Unit 422 Md PO Box 302, Houston, TX 77030. **Fax:** 713-745-2374. **E-Mail:** rkurzroc@mdanderson.org

KURZWEG, FRANK TURNER, SURGERY. **Personal Data:** b Plaquemine, La, August 7, 1917; m 1956, Harriet; c Frank Turner & Gretchen Elaine. **Education:** Harvard Univ, SB, 1938; Harvard Med Sch, MD, 1942; Univ Minn, MS, 1947. **Professional Experience:** RETIRED; prof, Surg Div, Sch Med, LA State Univ, Shreveport, 1968-1980; head dept & div, Surg Div, Sch Med, La State Univ, Shreveport, 1968-1976; from assoc prof to prof, Med Sch, Univ Miami, 1956-1968; instr surg, Med Sch, Tulane Univ, 1949-1956. **Memberships:** Am Col Surgeons. **Research Statement & Publications:** General, thoracic and vascular surgery. **Mailing Address:** 58 Star Lake Rd, Pensacola, FL 32507-3475.

KURZWEG, ULRICH H(ERMANN), FLUID MECHANICS, APPLIED MATHEMATICS. **Personal Data:** b Jena, Ger, September 16, 1936; American citizen; m 1963, Sophia; c Tina. **Education:** Univ Md, BS, 1958; Princeton Univ, MA, 1959, PhD (physics), 1961. **Honors & Awards:** NASA Certificate of Recognition 1984; Woodrose Wibo fel 1958-1959. **Professional Experience:** PROF EMER, MECH & AEROSPACE ENG DEPT, UNIV FLA, as of 2005; prof eng sci, Univ Fla, beginning 1976; assoc prof, Univ Fla, 1968-1976; sr theoret physicist, United Technol Res Labs, Conn, 1964-1968; adj asst & assoc prof, Hartford Grad Ctr, Rensselaer Polytech Inst, 1963-1968; res Scientist physics, United Technol Res Labs, Conn, 1962-1964; Fulbright res grant appl math, Univ Freiburg, 1961-1962. **Memberships:** AAAS; Am Phys Soc; Sigma Xi; NY Acad Sci. **Research Statement & Publications:** Hydrodynamic and hydromagnetic stability of rotating flows; thermal instability of electrically conducting fluids; two-phase magnetohydrodynamic flows; numerical solutions of partial differential equations; optics of solar concentrators; heat exchange and gas separation by high frequency oscillations; fluid mechanics of time-periodic compressisble flow; micro-fluid mechanics. **Mailing Address:** Dept Mech & Aerospace Eng, Univ Fla, MAE-A Bldg Rm219C, Gainesville, FL 32611. **Fax:** 352-392-7303. **E-Mail:** uhk@aero.ufl.edu

KUSALIK, PETER GERARD, COMPUTER SIMULATION, LIQUID STATE THEORY. **Personal Data:** b Taber, Alta, July 17, 1959; m 1984, c 2. **Education:** Univ Lethbridge, BSc, 1981; Univ BC, MSc, 1984, PhD (chem), 1987. **Professional Experience:** ASST PROF, DEPT CHEM, DALHOUSIE UNIV, 1989-; NSERC Univ res fel, Dept Chem, Dalhousie Univ, 1989-; postdoctoral fel, Res Sch Chem, 1989; Vis fel, Res Sch Chem, Australian Nat Univ, 1987-1989, 1993; NSERC postdoctoral fel, Australian Nat Univ, 1987-1989. **Memberships:** Chem Inst Can. **Research Statement & Publications:** Computer simulation and theoretical studies of polar solvents and electrolyte solutions; non-equilibrium molecular dynamics techniques; applied field simulations; dynamics of polar liquids and solutions; solvation. **Mailing Address:** Dept Chem, Dalhousie Univ, Halifax, NS B3H 4J3, Can. **Fax:** 902-494-1310. **E-Mail:** kusalik@ac.dal.ca

KUSANO, KIYOSHI, NEUROPHYSIOLOGY. **Personal Data:** b Nagasaki, Japan, February 1, 1933; m 1961. **Education:** Kumamoto Univ, BSc, 1956; Kyushu Univ, DSc, 1960. **Professional Experience:** Mem, Physiol Study Sect, NIH, 1979-; PROF BIOL, ILL INST TECHNOL, 1973-; USPHS res grant, Ill Inst Technol, 1971-; assoc prof, Ill Inst Technol, 1970-1973; USPHSres grant, NSF grant, 1968-1970; USPHS res grant, Med Sch, Ind Univ, 1967-1969; corp mem, Marine Biol Lab, 1967; from asst prof to assoc prof psychiat, Med Sch, Ind Univ, 1965-1970; asst prof physiol, Tokyo Med & Dent Univ, 1963-1965; res assoc neurol, Columbia Univ, 1961-1963; jr res zoologist, Univ Calif, Los Angeles, 1960-1961; instr physiol, Med Sch, Kumamoto Univ, 1956-1959 & Tokyo Med & Dent Univ, 1959-1960. **Memberships:** Am Physiol Soc; Soc Gen Physiol; Soc Neurosci; Biophys Soc. **Research Statement & Publications:** Synaptology; comparative neurophysiology. **Mailing Address:** Div Intramural Res, Nat Inst Neurol Disorders & Stroke, Bethesda, MD 20892. **E-Mail:** kusano@codon.nih.gov

KUSERK, FRANK THOMAS, MICROBIAL ECOLOGY, LIMNOLOGY. **Personal Data:** b Philadelphia, Pa, March 26, 1951; m 1975, Evelyn; c Claire & Laura. **Education:** Univ Notre Dame, BS, 1973; Univ Del, Newark, PhD (biol), 1978. **Professional Experience:** Director, Environmental Studies Program, Moravian College, Bethlehem, PA 2004-; Chair, Dept biol, Moravian col, Bethlehem, PA 2000-2004; dean asst info technol, Moravian Co, Bethlehem, (1994-2000); PROF BIOL, MORAVIAN CO, BETHLEHEM, PA, 1992-; dir, Acad Comput, 1988-1994; consult ecol, ITT Res Inst, Chicago, Ill, 1984-1990; res assoc, Acad Natural Sci Philadelphia, 1981-1982; Res fel, Marine Biol Lab, Woods Hole, Mass, 1979; From asst prof to assoc prof, Moravian CO, Bethlehem, PA, 1977-1992. **Memberships:** Am Soc for Microbiology; Ecol Soc Am; Sigma Xi; Nat Cent Sci Educ; Nat Asn Biol Teachers; Nat Sci Teachers Asn. **Research Statement & Publications:** Microbial ecology; population dynamics and community structure of the dictyostelid cellular slime molds; uptake and utilization of dissolved organic carbon by streambed micro-organisms; structure of benthic freshwater macro-invertebrate communities. **Mailing Address:** Dept Biol, Moravian Col 1200 Main St, Bethlehem, PA 18018-6650. **Fax:** 610-625-7918. **E-Mail:** kuserk@moravian.edu

KUSHICK, JOSEPH N, THEORETICAL BIOPHYSICAL CHEMISTRY. **Personal Data:** b New York, NY, July 18, 1948; m 1970, Marilyn; c Rafael & Maia Shoshana. **Education:** Columbia Col, BA, 1969; Columbia Univ, PhD (chem phys), 1975. **Honors & Awards:** L P Hammett Award, Columbia Univ, 1973. **Professional Experience:** CHAIR, DEPT PHYS CHEM, AMHERST COL, as of 2004; chmn, dept chem, 1992-1995; adj prof, Mt Sinai Sch Med, NY, beginning 1988; prof chem, Amherst Col, beginning 1988; adj assoc prof physiol & biophys, Mt Sinai Sch Med, NY, 1986-1988; Camille & Henry Dreyfus teacher scholar grant, 1980; vis scholar, Harvard Univ, 1979-1980; from asst prof to assoc prof, Amherst Col, 1976-1988; fel NSF, 1976-1978; res assoc chem, Univ Chicago, 1974-1976. **Memberships:** Am Chem Soc. **Research Statement & Publications:** Computer simulation of biological molecules; statistical mechanics. **Mailing Address:** Dept Chem, Merrill Sci Ctr, Amherst Col, 523, Amherst, MA 01002. **E-Mail:** jnkushick@amherst.edu

KUSHIDA, TOSHIMOTO, SOLID STATE PHYSICS. **Personal Data:** b Tokyo, Japan, February 13, 1920; m 1946, Mieko; c Hiroko, Makiko & Yayoi. **Education:** Hiroshima Univ, BS, 1944, ScD(physics), 1956; Harvard Univ, MS, 1956. **Professional Experience:** RES PROF, WAYNE STATE UNIV, 1987-; res scientist, Sci Lab, Ford Motor Co, 1961-1987; res fel, Harvard Univ, 1956-1958; from instr to prof, Hiroshima Univ, 1948-1961; asst physics, Hiroshima Univ, 1944-1948. **Memberships:** fel Am Phys Soc; Inst Elec & Electronics Engrs; Sigma Xi. **Research Statement & Publications:** Nuclear magnetic resonance; high pressure physics; the puli susceptibility of alkali metals as a functionof pressure; phase transitions in high temperature superconductors. **Mailing Address:** 22836 Nona, Dearborn, MI 48124.

KUSHINSKY, STANLEY, BIOANALYTICS, DRUG METABOLISM. **Personal Data:** b Brooklyn, NY, September 20, 1930; div. **Education:** City Col NY, BS, 1951; Columbia Univ, MA, 1952; Univ Boston, PhD (chem), 1955; Nat Registry Clin Chem, dipl, 1968. **Professional Experience:** RETIRED; dir bioanal & metab res, Inst Pharmacol & Metab, 1986-1993; dir bioanal chem & metab, Inst Pharmacol & Metab, 1984-1986; asst dir, Inst Pharmacol & Metab, 1984; sr scientist, Anal & Metab chem, 1982-1984; dept head, Anal & Metab chem, 1981-1986; prin scientist, Syntex Res, 1979-1981; adj prof chem, San Diego State Univ, 1973-1976; dir biochem res, Rees-Stealy Clin Res Found, 1970-1979; res career develop award, USPHS, 1965-1970; from assoc res biochemist to res biochemist, Dept Obstet & Gynec, Sch Med, UnivCalif, Los Angeles, 1965-1970; asst prof biochem, Dept Surg, Sch Med, Univ Southern Calif, 1964-1965; asst prof, Dept Surg, Sch Med, Univ Southern Calif, 1962-1964; adj asst prof surg & biochem, Dept Surg, Sch Med, Univ Southern Calif, 1958-1962; res assoc, Dept Surg, Sch Med, Univ Southern Calif, 1957-1958; steroid chemist, Dept Surg, Sch Med, Univ Southern Calif, 1955-1957; res asst, Worcester Found Exp Biol, 1952-1955. **Memberships:** Fel AAAS; Am Chem Soc; Am Asn Clin Chem; Nat Acad Clin Biochem; Endocrine Soc; Am Asn Pharmaceut Scientists. **Research Statement & Publications:** Synthesis, isolation and metabolism of steroid hormones; enzyme kinetics; betaglucuronidase; gas chromatographic and radioimmunologic determination of steroids in blood and tissues; high performance liquid chromatography; drug metabolism; bioavailability; pharmacokinetics. **Mailing Address:** 2449 Geranium St, San Diego, CA 92109-2338.

KUSHLAN, JAMES A, ORNITHOLOGY, WETLAND ECOLOGY. **Personal Data:** b Cleveland, Ohio, October 11, 1947; m Paula; c Kristin & Philip. **Education:** Univ Miami, BS, 1969, MS, 1972, PhD (biol), 1974. **Honorary Degrees:** DSc, Thiel Col, 1996. **Professional Experience:** Coun mem, Am Ornithologists Union, 1994-; DIR, PATUXENT ENVIRON RES CTR, US GEOL SERV, 1994-; assoc ed, Wetlands, 1993-1995; Sci & Math Task Force, Miss Pub Educ Forum, 1993; mem, Asn Miss Biol Chairs, 1988-; PROF BIOL, UNIV MISS, 1988-; chmn, Patuxent Wildlife Res Ctr, 1988-1994; CHMN, DEPT BOIL, UNIV MISS, 1988-; mem, Nat Riparian Coun, 1986-1987; mem, N Am PrairieConf Comt, 1986; from assoc prof to prof biol, E Tex State Univ, 1984-1988; mem, CrocodileSpecialist Group, 1981-; adj assoc prof biol, Univ Miami, 1980-1986; lectr, Nordic Inst Ecol, 1980; res assoc, Inst Trop Zoology, Cent Univ Venezuela, 1979-1983; mem, Fed Cape SableSparrow Recovery Team, 1979-1983; vis scientist, Darwin Res Sta, 1978; Supvry res biologist, US Dept Interior, 1975-1984; mem, Fed Am Crocodile Recovery Team, 1975-1983; mem, Fed Fla Panther Recovery Team, 1975-1982; biol technician, Nat Park Serv, 1973-1975; res fel, Univ Miami, 1972-1974; hydrol technician, US Geol Surv, 1972-1973; Maytag fel, Univ Miami, 1969-1972. **Memberships:** Fel Am Ornithologists Union; Soc Wetland Scientists; Colonial Waterbird Soc(pres-elect 1993- pres 1996-1998); Ecol Soc Am. **Research Statement & Publications:** Wetland ecology, especially the adaptation and accommodation of animal populations to fluctuating water conditions using waterbirds and fishes; population and community ecology, especially the influence of environmental fluctuations on population and community dynamics. **Mailing Address:** Patuxent Environ Res Ctr, US Geol Serv, Ste 4039 12100 Beech Forest Rd, Laurel, MD 20708-4039. **Fax:** 301-497-5505. **E-Mail:** james_kushlan@usgs.gov

KUSHMERICK, MARTIN JOSEPH, RADIOLOGY, BIOPHYSICS. **Personal Data:** b Pa, May 21, 1937; m 1962, c 4. **Education:** Univ Scranton, BS, 1958; Univ Pa, MD, 1963, PhD (molecular biol), 1966. **Honors & Awards:** Res Career Develop Awards, NIH, 1976-1981. **Professional Experience:** PROF RADIOL & PHYSIOL & BIOPHYS, DEPT BIOENGINEERING, UNIV WASH, as of 2006; assoc prof biol, Harvard Univ, beginning 1978; assoc prof physiol, Harvard Med Sch, beginning 1976; asst prof, Harvard Univ, 1970-1976; hon res assoc & Brit-Am exchange fel, Am Heart Asn, Univ Col, Univ London, 1969-1970; staff assoc, Lab Phys Biol, Nat Inst Arthritis & Metab Dis, NIH, 1967-1969; asst prof biochem, Univ Pa, 1966-1967. **Memberships:** Am Physiol Soc; AAAS; Biochem Soc Eng; Biophys Soc; Soc Gen Physiologists; Am Soc Biol Chem; Soc Mag Res Med. **Research Statement & Publications:** Muscle physiology; energetics, metabolism and their control; mechanism and control of contraction; nuclear magnetic resonance spectroscopy of tissues; published over 5 articles. **Mailing Address:** Dept BioEng, Univ Wash, PO Box 357115, Seattle, WA 98195-7962. **Fax:** 206-543-3495. **E-Mail:** kushmeri@u.washington.edu

KUSHNARYOV, VLADIMIR MICHAEL, ELECTRON MICROSCOPY. **Personal Data:** b Odessa, USSR, January 2, 1931; m 1954, c 1. **Education:** 1st Moscow Med Inst, MD, 1954; Acad Med Sci, USSR, PhD (microbiol), 1961, DSc, 1969. **Professional Experience:** Adj prof microbiol, Med Col Wis, as of 2004; prof microbiol, electron micros instnl fac, Med Col Wis, beginning 1989; DIR, ELECTRON MICROS INSTNL FAC, MED COL WIS, 1980-; from asst prof toassoc prof med microbiol, Electron Micros Instnl Fac, Med Col Wis, 1978-1980; chief & labprof, Moscow Inst Vaccines & Serim, 1975-1977; Lectr, Moscow Postgrad Med Sch, 1960-1977. **Memberships:** AAAS; Am Soc Microbiol; NY Acad Sci; Int Soc Interferon Res; Electron MicrosSoc Am. **Research Statement & Publications:** Interaction of biologically active ligands-diptheria toxin, staphycoccal toxic shock syndrome toxin, interferons with mammalian cells; analysis of internalization of ligands by cells, employing quantitative immunocytochemistry, electron microscopy and biochemical techniques. **Mailing Address:** Dept Microbiol, Med Col Wis, 8701 Watertown Plank, Milwaukee, WI 53226-3548.

KUSHNER, ARTHUR S, METAL FINISHING CONSULT, TRAING CONSULT-ELECTROPLATING. **Personal Data:** b New York, NY, May 9, 1940; m 1964, Roberta; c 2. **Education:** Univ Evansville, BA, 1962; Pa State Univ, PhD (org chem), 1966; Cleveland State Univ, MBA, 1978. **Professional Experience:** Dir opers, Biosys Inc, 1988-1990; vpres marketing & sales, Biosys Inc, 1984-1988; mkt mgr, Chromatix, 1981-1984; prod develop mgr, Woodhill Permatex Div, Loctite Corp, Cleveland, 1980-1981; sales mgr, Mogul Div, Dexter Corp, Chagrin Falls, 1979-1980; prod mgr, Mogul Div, Dexter Corp, Chagrin Falls, 1978-1979; DIR, KUSHNER ELECTROPLATING SCH, 1978-; group leader cooling water prod, Mogul Div, Dexter Corp, Chagrin Falls, 1976-1978; mgr tech support serv, Photohorizons Div, Horizons Res, Inc, Cleveland, 1975-1976; supvr film chem sect, Photohorizons Div, Horizons Res, Inc, Cleveland, 1974-1975; asst prof, Cleveland State Univ, 1968-1974; fel chem, Univ Chicago, 1966-1968. **Memberships:** Am Soc Metals; Am Electroplaters & Surface Finishers Soc; Am Chem Soc; Sigma Xi. **Research Statement & Publications:** Eleotroplating Methods; corrosion inhibition; treatment of cooling water; preparation of new corrosion inhibition materials; photochemistry of free-radical film systems; corrosion inhibition; metal finishing and electroplating; development of biological insect controls. **Mailing Address:** 732 Glencoe Ct, Sunnyvale, CA 94087. **Fax:** 408-749-0176. **E-Mail:** platingman@platingschool.com

KUSHNER, HAROLD J(OSEPH), STOCHASTIC SYSTEMS, OPERATIONS RESEARCH. **Personal Data:** b New York, NY, July 29, 1933; m 1960, Linda; c Diana & Nina. **Education:** City Col NY, BSc, 1955; Univ Wis, MSc, 1956, PhD (elec eng), 1958. **Honors & Awards:** Control Theory Field Award, Inst Elec & Electronics Engrs; Lewis Levy Medal, Franklin Inst. **Professional Experience:** PROF EMER APPL MATH, BROWN UNIV, as of 2005; chmn, Div Appl Math, 1988-1992; DIR, LEFSCLETZ CTR DYNAMICAL SYST, 1987-; PROF APPL MATH & ENG, BROWN UNIV, 1964-; Res Inst Advan Studies, Martin-Marietta Corp, Md, 1963-1964; staff mem, Lincoln Lab, Mass Inst Technol, 1958-1963. **Memberships:** Inst Math Statist; Soc Indust & Appl Math; Opers Res Soc Am; Inst Elec &

Electronics Engrs. **Research Statement & Publications:** Theoretical study of automatic control and communication systems, especially when random phenomenon are of some significance; applied probability; stochastic systems theory; stochastic systems theory and applications to control and commun systems and oper research; analytical and numerical methods. **Mailing Address:** Div Appl Math Brown Univ, 37 Manning St, Providence, RI 02912. **Fax:** 401-863-1355. **E-Mail:** hjk@dam.brown.edu

KUSHNER, HARVEY, MATHEMATICAL BIOMEDICAL STATISTICS. **Personal Data:** b Philadelphia, PA, November 2, 1950; m 1973, c 4. **Education:** Temple Univ, AB, 1972, MA, 1974, PhD (math), 1978. **Professional Experience:** Grad sch, Med Col PA, 1980-1981 & 1985-; adj assoc prof, dept math, Temple Univ, 1979-; 1986; PROF MATH & BIOSTATIST & CHMN, DEPT BIOMET, HAHNEMANN UNIV, 1978-; treas, Biomed Comput Res Inst. **Memberships:** Am Math Soc; Am Statist Asn. **Research Statement & Publications:** Time series analysis; categorical data analysis. **Mailing Address:** Dept Biomet, Hahnemann univ, Philadelphia, PA 19115.

KUSHNER, HARVEY D(AVID), OPERATIONS RESEARCH. **Personal Data:** b New York, NY, December 28, 1930; m 1951, c 3. **Education:** Johns Hopkins Univ, BE, 1951. **Professional Experience:** PRES, KUSHNER MANAGEMENT PLANNIG CORP, as of 2003; chmn & chief exec officer, Ori Group Inc, begining 1985; chmn &chief exec officer, ORI Inc, 1983-1985; pres, Disclosure, Inc, 1972-1977; vpres, Govt & IndustSysts Div, 1971-1977; pres, ORI Inc, 1969-1983; dir, Govt & Indust Systs Div, 1964-1968; vpres& dir, Phys Systs Div, 1963-1964; Consult, Appl Physics Lab, Johns Hopkins Univ, 1957-1958 & NatAcad Sci Comt Undersea Warfare, 1963-1964; exec vpres, Govt & Indust Systs Div, 1962-1969; vpres & dir, Eastern Div, 1961-1962; prog dir, Reliance Group Inc, 1959-1961; group leader, Reliance Group Inc, 1957-1959; res engr, Reliance Group Inc, 1955-1957; mem tech staff, FlightSimulator Dept, 1954-1955; mem tech staff, Cent Res Lab, Melpar, Inc Div, Westinghouse AirBrake Co, 1953-1954; Engr, Mach Evals Group, Bur Ships, US Navy Dept, 1951 & Performance& Sci Sect, 1952-1953. **Memberships:** Opers Res Soc Am; Inst Mgt Sci; Am Inst Aeronaut & Astronaut; sr mem InstElec & Electronics Engrs; Am Soc Mech Engrs; fel NY Acad Sci. **Research Statement & Publications:** Systems analysis; operations research. **Mailing Address:** 9743 Redd Rambler Rd, Philadelphia, PA 19115.

KUSHNER, IRVING, RHEUMATOLOGY, MEDICINE. **Personal Data:** b New York, NY, January 16, 1929; m 1955, Enid; c Ellen, Philip & David. **Education:** Columbia Univ, BA, 1950; Wash Univ, MD, 1954. **Honors & Awards:** Master American College Rheumatology. **Professional Experience:** Prof med, Sch Med, Case Western Res Univ, 1974-; prof, WVa Univ 1973-1974; from asst prof to assoc prof, Case Western Res Univ, 1964-1973; med dir, Metro Health Ctr Rehab, 1985-1991; sr int fel, Fogarty Ctr, NIH, 1976; PROF MED, SCH MED, CASE WESTERN RES UNIV, 1974-; prof, WVa Univ, 1973-1974; from asst prof to assoc prof, Case Western Res Univ, 1964-1973; foreign fel, Inst Sci Res Cancer, France, 1962-1963; sr instr, Case Western Res Univ, 1961-1964; instr, Case Western Res Univ, 1960-1961; Helen Hay Whitney Found res fel, 1959-1962; USPHS res fel, 1958-1959; demonstr med, Case Western Res Univ, 1958-1959; asst resident, 2 & 4 med serv, Boston City Hosp, 1957-1958; Intern med, New Haven Hosp, 1954-1955. **Memberships:** Am Col Physicians; fel Am Coll Rheumatol. **Research Statement & Publications:** Acute phase reaction; C-reactive protein; mechanisms which regulate the acute phase response to inflammatory stimuli with particular emphasis on induction of c-reaction protein by cytokines. **Mailing Address:** Dept Med, Metro Health Med Ctr, Cleveland, OH 44109. **Fax:** 216-778-8376. **E-Mail:** ikushner@metrohealth.org

KUSHNER, LAWRENCE MAURICE, MATERIALS SCIENCE, TOXIC & HAZARDOUS SUBSTANCE REGULATION. **Personal Data:** b New York, NY, September 20, 1924; m 1972, Shirley; c Robb & Leslie. **Education:** Queens Col, BS, 1945; Princeton Univ, AM, 1947, PhD, 1949. **Professional Experience:** RETIRED; consult scientist, Mitre Corp, 1985-1989; adj prof eng & pub policy, Carnegie-Mellon Univ, 1981-1992; sr staff scientist, Mitre Corp, 1980-1985; coordr policy develop, Nat Bur Stand, 1977-1980; comnr, Consumer Prod Safety Comn, 1973-1977; mem, Md Gov Sci Adv Coun, 1972-1975; actg dir, Bur, 1972-1973; dep dir, Bur, 1969-1973; dir, Inst Appl Technol, 1968-1969; dep dir, Inst Appl Tech, 1966-1968; fel, Sci & Technol Fel Prog, Dept Com, 1964-1965; chief, Metall Div, 1961-1966; chief, Metal Physics sect, 1956-1961; mem ad hoc int group metal physics, Org Econ Coop & Develop, 1961; lectr chem, Am Univ, 1952-1960; staff mem, Nat Bur Stand, 1948-1956; teaching asst, Princeton Univ, 1947-1948. **Memberships:** Fel AAAS; hon mem Am Soc Testing & Mat; Am Chem Soc; Am Phys Soc; Sigma Xi (pres, 1976). **Research Statement & Publications:** Physical chemistry of surface active agents; relationship between physical properties of materials and their molecular and crystal structures. **Mailing Address:** 20506 Beaver Ridge Rd, Montgomery Village, MD 20886.

KUSHNER, MARK JAY, COMPUTER SIMULATION, COMPUTER AIDED DESIGN. **Education:** Univ Calif Los Angeles, BA & BS, 1976; Calif Inst Technol, MS, 1977, PhD (appl physics), 1979. **Honors & Awards:** Techn Excellence Award, Semiconductor Res Corp, 1995; avs plasma sci and technol prize, 1999; IEEE plasma sci and appin award, 2000. **Professional Experience:** Editorial board, j vac sci tech a 1998-2000; editorial board, Plasma Sources Sci & Technol, 1993-; Assoc ed, Trans Plasma Sci, 1989-; editorial board, plasma chemistry and plasma processing, 2005-; assoc. editor, J. Phys. D, 2005-; Dean of Engineering, Iowa State University, 2005-; ELEC & COMPUT ENG, UNIV ILL, URBANA, 1986-2004; dir electron, atomic & molecular physics, Spectra Technol, 1983-1986; physicist, Lawrence Livermore Nat Labs, 1981-1983; physicist, Sandia Nat Labs, 1980-1981; Postdoctoral, Calif Inst Technol, 1979-1980. **Memberships:** Fel Inst Elec & Electronics Engrs; fel Am Phys Soc; fel Optical Soc Am; fel Am Vacuum Soc; fel Inst of Phys; Mat Res Soc; Am Soc Eng Educ. **Research Statement & Publications:** Low temperature plasmas for materials fabrication, lighting sources, plasma chemistry and lasers. **Mailing Address:** Iowa State Univ, 104 Marston Hall, Ames, IA 50011. **E-Mail:** mjk@iastate.edu

KUSHNER, SIDNEY RALPH, MOLECULAR GENETICS, ENZYMOLOGY. **Personal Data:** b New York, NY, December 14, 1943; m 1969, Deena; c Aaron & Ze'eva. **Education:** Oberlin Col, BA, 1965; Brandeis Univ, PhD (biochem), 1970. **Honors & Awards:** Univ Georgia Creative Res Medal. **Professional Experience:** Bd dirs, Am Type Cult Collection, 1988-1993; head dept, Univ GA, 1987-1995; PROF GENETICS, UNIV GA, 1982-; Microbiol Genetics Study Sect, NIH, 1981-1985; assoc ed, Gene, 1980-; assoc prof, Univ GA, 1980-1982; NIH res career develop award, 1975; from asst prof to assoc prof biochem, Med Sch, Stanford Univ, 1973-1980; NIH fel, Med Sch, Stanford Univ, 1971-1973; NIH fel molecular biol, Univ Calif, Berkeley, 1970-1971. **Memberships:** fel Am Soc Microbiol; fel AAAS; Am Soc Biol Chemists; Genetics Soc Am; RNA Soc. **Research Statement & Publications:** Posttranscriptional regulation of gene expression; a nalysis of messenger RNA degradation; genetic control and enzymology of recombination and DNA repair; functional expression of eukaryotic DNA in prokaryotes. **Mailing Address:** Dept Genetics, Univ Ga, Life Sci Bldg, Athens, GA 30602. **E-Mail:** skushner@arches.uga.edu

KUSHNICK, THEODORE, PEDIATRICS, MEDICAL GENETICS. **Personal Data:** b Brooklyn, NY, March 29, 1925; m 1949, c 3. **Education:** Ohio State Univ, BS, 1944, MS, 1947; Harvard Med Sch, MD, 1951. **Professional Experience:** PROF EMER, SCH MED, E CAROLINA UNIV, as of 2000; prof pediat & dir med genetics, Sch Med, East carolina Univ, beginning 1979; Sci Adv Comm, Nat Tay-Sachs & Allied Dis Asn, 1974-; Nat Found-March Dimes MedServ Prog Grants, 1974-1975 & 1976-1977; dir, div human genetics, 1961-1979; NIH res grant, 1961-1963; Mead-Johnson res grant, 1960-1962; from asst prof to prof, Col Med & DentNJ, Newark, 1959-1979; clin instr pediat, Col Med & Dent NJ, Newark, 1958-1959; pvt pract, NJ, 1956-1959; clin res asst, Boston Children's Cancer Res Found, 1955-1956; clin instr, HarvardMed Sch, 1955-1956; resident psychiat, Boston State Hosp, 1953-1954; jr physician, WrenthamState Sch, Mass, 1953; resident pediat, Boston Children's Med Ctr, 1952-1955; intern med, BostonCity Hosp, 1951-1952; genetic consult, Nat Found March DimesSpec Birth Defects Treatment Ctr, Babies Hosp, Newark. **Memberships:** AAAS; Am Asn Ment Deficiency; fel Am Acad Pediat; Am Soc Human Genetics; NY Acad Sci. **Research Statement & Publications:** Clinical pediatrics; clinical genetics mental retardation; cytogenetics; immunology. **Mailing Address:** Dept Pediat, E Carolina Univ Sch Med, E Fifth St, Greenville, NC 27858.

KUSHWAHA, RAMPRATAP S, LIPID METABOLISM. **Personal Data:** b India, July 11, 1943. **Education:** Wash State Univ, PhD (nutrit), 1973. **Professional Experience:** SCIENTIST, DEPT PHYSIOLOGY & MED, SOUTHWEST FOUND BIOMED RES, 1982-; Adj prof, dept path, Univ Tex Health Sci Ctr, 1982-. **Memberships:** Am Heart Asn; Am Soc of Nutrition. **Research Statement & Publications:** Metabolic and molecular basis of genetic dyslipoproteinemias in pedigreed baboons; metabolic and molecular mechanisms by whichdietary factors such as cholestrol and sex steroid hormones modulate lipoprotein metabolism in normal and dyslipoproteinemic subjects. **Mailing Address:** Dept Physiol & Med, SW Found Biomed Res, PO Box 760549, San Antonio, TX 78245-0549. **Fax:** 210-670-3323. **E-Mail:** kush@icarus.sfbr.org

KUSIAK, ANDREW, INTELLIGENT SYSTEMS & ENGINEERING DESIGN & MANUFACTURING, COMPUTATIONAL INTELLIGENCE & DATA MINING. **Personal Data:** Canadian citizen; m Ana; c 3. **Education:** Warsaw Tech Univ, BS, 1972, MS, 1974; Polish Acad Sci, PhD (oper res), 1979. **Honors & Awards:** Institute of Industial Engineers, Fellow, 2005. **Professional Experience:** Vis prof, Inst Adv Studies, Vienna, Austria, 1991; chmn, Int Conf Artificial Intel, 1990; PROF INDUST ENG, UNIV IOWA, 1988-; Ed, Appl Artificial Intel, 1988-; chair, Univ Iowa, 1988-1995; chmn, Int Conf Adv Prod, 1987; Ed, Artificial Intel Indust, 1986-; res award, Univ Man, 1986; assoc prof, indust eng, Univ Man, Can, 1985-1988; asst prof indust eng, Tech Univ, Nova Scotia, 1982-1985; Proj mgr, Dept Automation, Inst Mgt & Org, 1979-1981; hon prof, Huazong Univ Sci & Technol, China. **Memberships:** Sr mem Soc Mfg Engrs; INFORMS; sr mem Am Asn Artificial Intel; Inst Indust Engrs; Inst Electrical and Electronics Engrs; Int Fedn Automation & Control; Int Fedn Info Processing. **Research Statement & Publications:** Intelligent systems for design of products and manufacturing systems; process modeling; complexity managemet; mass cutomization; prodict development; design automation; design methodologies; data mining and knowledge discovery; medical informatics. **Mailing Address:** Dept Mechanical & Indust Eng, Univ Iowa, Iowa City, IA 52242. **Fax:** 319-335-5669. **E-Mail:** andrew-kusiak@uiowa.edu

KUSIC, GEORGE LARRY, CONTROL ENGINEERING, COMPUTER SCIENCE. **Personal Data:** b Aliquippa, Pa, August 26, 1935; m 1969, c 1. **Education:** Carnegie Inst Technol, BSEE, 1957, MSEE, 1966, PhDEE, 1968. **Professional Experience:** ASSOC PROF, DEPT ELEC ENG, SCH ENG, UNIV PITTSBURGH, 1977-; grad prog coordr, Univ Pittsburgh, beginning 1977; sr Fulbright-Hays lect grant, Univ Belgrade, 1970-1971; facres fel, NASA-Am Soc Eng Educ, 1969; consult, Westinghouse Res Lab, 1969-1970; consult, IBM Data Processing Div, 1968; consult, NSF-Agency Int Develop India Prog, 1968; asst prof, Univ Pittsburgh, 1967-1977; elec develop engr, TRW Corp, 1959-1963; res engr, Sikorsky Aircraft Co, 1957-1959. **Mailing Address:** Dept Elec & Comput Eng, Sch Eng, Univ Pittsburgh, BENDM 0443, Pittsburgh, PA 15217. **Fax:** 412-624-8003. **E-Mail:** kusic@ee.pitt.edu

KUSIK, CHARLES LEMBIT, WASTE MINIMIZATION, RECYCLING OF SCRAP-WASTES. **Personal Data:** b New York, NY, April 24, 1934. **Education:** Mass Inst Technol, BS, 1956; NY Univ, DSc (chem eng), 1961. **Honors & Awards:** Nat Sci Found fel, 1959-1961. **Professional Experience:** PRIN, ARTHUR D LITTLE INC, 1996-; dir technol & prod develop, Arthur D Little Inc, 1989-1996; MNR metals & energy mgt, Arthur D Little Inc, 19 1980-1988; prof staff, Arthur D little Inc 1964-1980 scientist gas dynamics, Avco Corp, 1963-1964; scientist opers res, Mass Inst Technol, 1961-1962. **Memberships:** Am Inst Chem Engrs; The Metallurgical Soc; Asn Iron & Steel Engrs. **Research Statement & Publications:** Energy assessments; recycling; process development; economics; commercial feasibility studies; pollution prevention. **Mailing Address:** Arthur D Little Inc, 209 Lincoln Rd, Lincoln, MA 01773.

KUSKA, HENRY (ANTON), PHYSICAL CHEMISTRY. **Personal Data:** b Chicago, Ill, July 28, 1937; m 1964, c 3. **Education:** Cornell Col, BA, 1959; Mich State Univ, PhD (phys chem), 1965. **Professional Experience:** RETIRED; assoc prof phys chem, Univ Akron, 1965-1993; res assoc & res felphys chem, Mich State Univ, 1964-1965. **Memberships:** Am Chem Soc. **Research Statement & Publications:** Spectroscopy; nuclear magnetic resonance; electron spin resonance; electron-nuclear double resonance; infrared; visible ultraviolet. **Mailing Address:** 7352 Ashburton Circle NW, Canton, OH 44720.

KUSKE, RACHEL A, MATHEMATICS. **Education:** Univ Wis, BS, 1987; Nortwestern Univ, PhD, 1992. **Professional Experience:** ASSOC PROF, DEPT MATHS, UNIV BC, 2002-. **Mailing Address:** Math Dept Univ BC, 121-1984 Math Rd., Vancouver, BC V6T 1Z2, Can. **Fax:** 604-822-6074. **E-Mail:** rachel@math.ubc.ca

KUSKO, ALEXANDER, ELECTRICAL ENGINEERING. **Personal Data:** b New York, NY, April 4, 1921; m 1941, c 2. **Education:** Purdue Univ, BS, 1942; Mass Inst Technol, SM, 1944, ScD, 1951. **Professional Experience:** CORP VPRES, FAILURE ANALYSIS ASSOC, 1994-; div dir, FailureAnalysis Assoc, 1988-1994; lectr, Mass Inst Technol, 1958-1988; pres, Alexander Kusko Inc, 1956-1988; from instr to assoc prof, Mass Inst Technol, 1946-1958; asst, Mass Inst Technol, 1942-1944. **Memberships:** Inst Elec & Electronics Engrs. **Research Statement & Publications:** Energy conversion and control. **Mailing Address:** Failure Analysis Assoc, 3 Cambridge Ctr, Cambridge, MA 02142.

KUSLAN, LOUIS ISAAC, HISTORY OF SCIENCE. **Personal Data:** b New Haven, Conn, February 14, 1922; m 1947, c 2. **Education:** Univ Conn, BS, 1943; Yale Univ, MA, 1949, PhD (sci educ), 1954. **Professional Experience:** RETIRED; prof chem, Southern Conn State Univ, 1978-1988; dean arts & sci, Southern Conn State Univ, 1966-1978; hist sci, Yale Univ, 1962-1963; prof chem & chmn dept sci, Southern Conn State Univ, 1960-1966; fel chem, Yale Univ, 1958-1959; assoc prof chem, Southern Conn State Univ, 1956-1960; from instr to asst prof sci, Southern Conn State Univ, 1950-1956; instr, Waterbur Br, 1947-1949; asst chem, Univ Conn, 1946-1947; instr high schs, Conn, 1943-1946. Member-

ships: Am Chem Soc; Hist Sci Soc. **Research Statement & Publications:** History of analytical and American chemistry; elementary science education; nineteenth century American chemistry. **Mailing Address:** 653 Gaylord Mountain Rd, Hamden, CT 06518.

KUSMIK, WILLIAM F, ANALYTICAL CHEMISTRY. **Personal Data:** b Hartford, Conn, June 7, 1942; m 1992, Elaine; c William Aldo & Alexa Rae. **Education:** Col Holy Cross, Mass, BA, 1965; Cent Conn State Univ, MA, 1976; Univ Conn, PhD (cell physiol), 1982. **Professional Experience:** MGR ASSAY DEVELOP, CREATIVE BIOMOLECULES, 1993-; mgr qual control, Creative Biomolecules, 1991-1993; mgr cell biol & immunol, Creative Biomolecules, 1987-1991; res scientist, Univ Miami Med Sch, 1986-1987; res scientist, Univ Conn Med Sch, 1985-1986; res fel steroid receptor biochem, Res Inst, Temple Univ, 1982-1985. **Memberships:** AAAS; Wound Healing Soc; Am Soc Cell Biol; Tissue Cult Asn; Parenteral Drug Asn; Regulatory Affiars Prof Soc. **Research Statement & Publications:** Development of biological immuniological and analytical assays for the testing of recombinant protein pharmaceuticals. **Mailing Address:** Dept Bioassay, Creative Biomolecules, 35 S St, Hopkinton, MA 01748. **Fax:** 508-435-0454.

KUSPA, ADAM, DEVELOPMENTAL BIOLOGY. **Personal Data:** wid. **Education:** Univ Calif, BA, 1982; Stanford Univ, CA, PhD, 1989. **Professional Experience:** PROF, DEPT BIOCHEM & MOLECULAR BIOL, BAYLOR COL MED, as of 2006. **Mailing Address:** Dept Biochem & Molecular Biol, Baylor Col Med, One Baylor Plaza T321, Houston, TX 77030. **Fax:** 713-798-9438. **E-Mail:** akuspa@bcm.tmc.edu

KUSPIRA, J, CYTOGENETICS. **Personal Data:** b Yorkton, Sask, November 20, 1928; m 1958, c 4. **Education:** Univ Sask, BSc, 1951, MSc, 1952; Univ Alta, PhD (genetics), 1955. **Professional Experience:** PROF EMER, UNIV ALTA, AS OF 2001; assoc dean sci, Univ Alta, 1972-1990; prof genetics, Univ Alta, 1970-1990; assoc prof, Univ Alta, 1962-1970; assoc res prof cytogenetics, Univ Alta, 1958-1962; asst cytogeneticist, Univ Alta, 1955-1957. **Memberships:** Am Genetic Asn; Genetics Soc Can. **Research Statement & Publications:** Cytogenetic analysis of tetraploid and hexaploid wheats. **Mailing Address:** 12416 47th Ave, Edmonton, AB T6H 0B4, Can.

KUSSE, BRUCE RAYMOND, PLASMA PHYSICS. **Personal Data:** b Rochester, NY, August 10, 1938. **Education:** Mass Inst Technol, SB, 1960, SM, 1964, PhD (elec eng), 1969. **Professional Experience:** PROF & ASSOC DIR APP & ENG PHYSICS, CORNELL UNIV, as of 2003; assoc prof plasma physics, Cornell Univ, beginning 1976; vis scientist, Ma Inst Technol, 1976; asst prof, LabPlasma Studies, 1971-1976; res assoc, Lab Plasma Studies, 1970-1971; res assoc plasma physics, Res Lab Electronics, Mass Inst Technol, 1970; sr scientist, Eastern Sci & Technol Div, EG&G, 1969-1970. **Memberships:** Sigma Xi; Am Phys Soc; Univ Fusion Assoc. **Research Statement & Publications:** Plasma physics-experimental studies of intense, relativistic beam-plasma interactions, particularly in toroidalgeometry. **Mailing Address:** Dept App & Eng Physics, Cornell Univ, 206 Clark Hall, Ithaca, NY 14853. **E-Mail:** kusse@lps.cornell.edu

KUSSEROW, SUZANNE K, MEDICAL SCIENCES. **Education:** Univ Conn, BS, 1954; Yale Univ, MS, 1959; Univ VT, PhD, 1992. **Professional Experience:** ADJ ASST PROF NURSING, UNIV VT, 1996-. **Mailing Address:** Univ VT, 85 S Prospect St, Burlington, VT 05401. **Fax:** 802-656-3370.

KUSSMAUL, KEITH LEE, DESIGN & ANALYSIS OF EXPERIMENTS, STATISTICAL PROCESS CONTROL. **Personal Data:** b Sterling, Ill, April 9, 1939; m 1965, Carol; c Clifton, Kimberly, Katherine & Craig. **Education:** Univ Mich, BS, 1960, MS, 1961; NC State Univ, PhD (statist), 1966. **Professional Experience:** STATIST CONSULT, 1993-; vis lect prog, Soc Indust Appl Math, 1977-1983; lectr indust eng, Univ Pittsburgh, 1967-1970; statistician, Westinghouse Elec Corp, 1966-1993; mathematician, Int Bus Mach Corp, 1961-1962. **Memberships:** Am Statist Asn; Biomet Soc; Am Soc Qual Control. **Research Statement & Publications:** Design and analysis of industrial experiments; statistical methods; general statistical consulting. **Mailing Address:** 9 Oakmore Dr, Round Rock, TX 78664-9612. **E-Mail:** oakmoore@aol.com

KUSSY, FRANK WERNER, ELECTRICAL DISTRIBUTION & CONTROL. **Personal Data:** b Dresden, Ger, October 13, 1910; m 1945. **Education:** Tech Univ Munich, MS, 1934; Tech Univ Vienna, Dr Technische Wissenschaften, 1936. **Professional Experience:** Vol, Int Exec Serv Corp, Egypt, Zimbabwe, 1987, 1990 & 1991; CONSULT, 1980-; dir prod develop, ITE, 1975-1980; adv develop engr, ITE, 1968-1975; res engr & engr mgr, ITE, 1959-1968; chief engr, Square D Co, 1958-1959; asst chief engr, Square D Co, 1956-1958; proj engr, Square D Co, 1954-1956; Pres, Rheastab-Habege GmbH, Dresden. **Memberships:** Fel Inst Elec & Electronics Engrs. **Research Statement & Publications:** Patents in field of electrical distribution and control; combination starters; author of several books. **Mailing Address:** 21394 Magnolia Ct, Farmington, MI 48336.

KUST, ROGER NAYLAND, INORGANIC CHEMISTRY, PHYSICAL CHEMISTRY. **Personal Data:** b Berwyn, Ill, April 20, 1935; m 1957, c 2. **Education:** Purdue Univ, BS, 1957; Iowa State Univ, PhD (fused salts), 1963. **Professional Experience:** MGR METALS RECOVERY, TETRA TECHNOL, INC, 1987-; mgr, Minerals Processing Res Div, 1981-1987; sect head, Exxon Minerals Co, 1980-1981; sr staffengr, Exxon Minerals Co, 1979-1980; sect head chem, Ledgemont Lab, Kennecott Copper Corp, 1978-1979; group leader chem, Ledgemont Lab, Kennecott Copper Corp, 1977-1978; sr inorgchemist, Ledgemont Lab, Kennecott Copper Corp, 1971-1977; Asst prof inorg chem, Tex A&MUniv, 1964-1965 & Univ Utah, 1965-1971. **Memberships:** AAAS; Am Chem Soc; Electrochem Soc; Am Acad Arts & Sci; Am Inst Chemists; Metall Soc. **Research Statement & Publications:** Acid-base reactions in fused salts; electrochemical investigations in nonaqueous media with emphasis on fused salts; chemistry of metallurgical processes. **Mailing Address:** Tetra Technologies, Inc, Spring, TX 77379.

KUSTIN, KENNETH, INORGANIC CHEMISTRY, PHYSICAL CHEMISTRY. **Personal Data:** b Bronx, NY, January 6, 1934; wid Myrna (Deceased); c Brenda, Michael & Franklin. **Education:** Queens Col, NY, BSc, 1955; Univ Minn, Minneapolis, PhD (inorg chem), 1959. **Professional Experience:** EMER PROF CHEM, BRANDEIS UNIV, 1997-; adj res sci, Res Develop & Eng Ctr, USArmy Natick, 1991; counsr, Am Chem Soc, 1983-1985; Fulbright lectr, 1978; prog dir, NSF, 1985-1986; Vis prof, Dept Pharmacol, Harvard Med Sch, 1977-1978; chmn dept, Brandeis Univ, 1974-1977; from asst prof to prof, Brandeis Univ, 1961-1997; USPHS fel, Max Planck Inst Phys Chem, 1959-1961; Editor: Fast Reactions, vol 16 of Methods in Enzymology, 1969; Board of Editors: Internat. Jour. Chem. Kinetics, 1983-1990, Inorg. Chem. 1993-1995. **Memberships:** Am Chem Soc; AAAS; Phi Beta Kappa. **Research Statement & Publications:** Inorganic biochemistry; oscillating reactions; fast reactions. **Mailing Address:** 5210 Fiore Terr Apt 111, San Diego, CA 92122-5686. **E-Mail:** kmkustin@ix.netcom.com

KUSTOM, ROBERT L, ION ACCELERATION & FOCUSING, POWER ELECTRONIC NETWORKS. **Personal Data:** b Chicago, Ill, July 11, 1934. **Education:** Ill Inst Technol, BSEE, 1956, MSEE, 1958; Univ Wis-Madison, PhD (elec eng), 1969. **Professional Experience:** Sr elec engr, Spallation Neutron Source Proj Accelerator Systs Div Dir, 1999-2001; SCIENTIST, ARGONNE NAT LAB, as of 1996; group leader, RF Group, Advan Photon Source, Argonne Nat Lab, 1990-1998; interim dir, Advan Photon Source Accelerator Syst Div, 1989-1990; adj prof, Elec & Comput Eng Dept, 1983-; sr elec engr, Seven Giga Electronvolt Storage Ring-Advan Photon Source Proj, 1983-1988; assoc proj dir electron accelerator, Plasma Support Syst, Tokamaks & Accelerator Exp Area, 1981-1983; consult, Superconductive Energy Storage Group, 1981; div dir accelerator res & develop, Plasma Support Syst, Tokamaks & Accelerator Exp Area, 1979-1981; vis prof, Elec & Comput Eng Dept, Univ Wis-Madison, 1978-1979, 1980-1981; mgr accelerator syst intense pulsed neutron source, Plasma Support Syst, Tokamaks & Accelerator Exp Area, 1978-1979; Tokamak Fusion Test Reactor eng rev comt, Princeton Plasma Physics Lab, 1975-1977; assoc div dir, Plasma Support Syst, Tokamaks & Accelerator Exp Area, 1973-1978; group leader zero gradient synchrotron oper, Accelerator Res Facil Div, Argonne Nat Lab, 1971-1973; vis scientist, Rutherford High Energy Lab, Didcot, UK, 1970-1971; elec engr radio frequency separators & microwave discharge chambers, Accelerator Res Facil Div, Argonne Nat Lab, 1969-1971; elec engr particle detect develop, Accelerator Res Facil Div, Argonne Nat Lab, 1958-1969. **Memberships:** Inst Elec & Electronics Engrs; Sigma Xi. **Research Statement & Publications:** Development of ion acceleration, focussing, and detection techniques, and the electrodynamic interactions between ions and electromagnetic fields; theoretical and experimental development of superconductive energy storage and transfer techniques using power electronic circuits and electronic circuits and electrodynamic devices; radio frequency systems and accelerating cavities. **Mailing Address:** Argonne Nat Lab, 9700 S Cass Ave, Argonne, IL 60439. **Fax:** 630-252-5291. **E-Mail:** rlk@aps.anl.gov

KUSTU, SYDNEY GOVONS, PLANT & MICROBIAL BIOLOGY, GENETICS & GENOMICS. **Personal Data:** b Baltimore, Md, March 18, 1943. **Education:** Harvard Univ, BA, 1963; Univ Calif, Davis, PhD (biochem), 1970. **Professional Experience:** PROF PLANT & MICROBIOL, UNIV CALIF, BERKELEY, 1987-; prof molecular cell biol, Univ Calif, Berkeley, beginning 1987; from asst prof to assoc prof bact, Univ Calif, Davis, 1974-1987. **Memberships:** Nat Acad Sci; Am Soc Microbiol; Am Soc Biol Chemists; Sigma Xi; AAAS. **Research Statement & Publications:** Regulation of bacterial nitrogen metabolism; published over 20 articles. **Mailing Address:** Plant & Microbiol, Univ Calif, 481A Koshland Hall, Berkeley, CA 94720-3102. **Fax:** 510-642-4995. **E-Mail:** kustu@nature.berkeley.edu

KUSWA, GLENN WESLEY, EXPERIMENTAL PHYSICS & TECHNOLOGY TRANSFER, NATIONAL DEFENSE & ENERGY SYSTEMS ANALYSIS. **Personal Data:** b Milwaukee, Wis, December 12, 1940; m 2000, Chris; c Kevin, Erika & step children, Tyler, Oakley. **Education:** Univ Wis-Madison, BS, 1962, MS, 1964, PhD (physics), 1970. **Honors & Awards:** ERDA Special Achievement Award, 1976. **Professional Experience:** Principle MemberTechnical Staff, Energy Systems Analysis, 2004 Mgr, Enhanced Surveillance and Data Dept., Sandia nat Laboratories, 1999; MGR, LAB ASSESSMENTS, SANDIA LABS, 1995; mgr environ health & safety, Technol Transfer Dept, 1991-1992; supr plasma diag, Technol Transfer Dept, 1988-1990 & 1991-1992; mgr, Technol Transfer Dept, 1986-1988; mgr future options planning, Sandia Labs, 1984-1985; tech adv asst secy defense progs, US Dept Energy, 1982-1983; mgr, Particle Beam Fusion Res Dept, Sandia Labs, 1976-1981; physicist, Laser & Isotope Separation Technol Off, US Energy Res & Develop Admin, 1974-1976; Physicist, Sandia Labs, 1970-1974; Bd pres, Maxwell Mus Anthropol Found. **Memberships:** Am Phys Soc; AAAS; Sigma Xi; New Mexico Academy of Science. **Research Statement & Publications:** I am a generalist with specialized experience in the conduct and managemnt of research, including inertial and magnetic fusion, technology transfer, nuclear weapons, energy systems analysis. A current interest producing fuels from atmospheric CO2 and nuclear or renewable energy-derived hydrogen. **Mailing Address:** 96 Juniper Hill Rd N E, Albuquerque, NM 87122. **E-Mail:** gwkuswa@sandia.gov

KUSY, ROBERT PETER, DENTAL RESEARCH, MEDICAL RESEARCH. **Personal Data:** b Worcester, Mass, October 19, 1947; m 1969, Gisela; c Kimberly & Kevin. **Education:** Worcester Polytech Inst, BS, 1969; Drexel Univ, MS, 1971, PhD (mech eng), 1973. **Honors & Awards:** Spec Dent Res Award, NIH, 1977-1981; B F Dewel Hon Res Award, Am Asn Orthod Found 1995; Am Soc Metals Int Award. **Professional Experience:** PROF CURRIC APPLN & MAT SCI, DENT RES CTR & BIOMED ENG, UNIV NC, 1996-; mem, Inst Nutrit, 1990-; adj prof appl sci curric, Sch Med, 1990-1996; PROF DEPT ORTHOD, DENT RES CTR & BIOMED ENG, UNIV NC, 1989-; co-investr, Duke-NC Eng Res Ctr, 1988-; assoc prof biomed eng, Med Sch, 1985-1989; assoc prof orthod & Dent Res Ctr, Dent Sch, 1979-1989; asst prof oral biol, Med Sch, Univ NC, 1974-1979; res assoc, Med Sch, Univ NC, 1972-1974; res asst mat, dept metall eng, Drexel Univ, 1969-1972. **Memberships:** Am Soc Metals; Am Chem Soc; Soc Plastics Engr; N Am Thermal Anal Soc; Int Asn Dent Res; Soc Biomat. **Research Statement & Publications:** Properties of dental and medical materials; fractography and fracture work energy of polymers; fabrication of high strength/high modulus fibers; laser scattering experiments; thermal analysis and radiation properties of polymers; biosensors; ion implantation of dental and medical materials; specialize in orthodontic materials; published over 5 articles. **Mailing Address:** Orthod Dent Res, Sch Dent, Univ NC, Campus Box 7450 112 Dent Res Ctr, Chapel Hill, NC 27599-7450. **Fax:** 919-966-3683. **E-Mail:** rkusy@bme.unc.edu

KUSYK, CHRISTINE JOHANNA, GENETICS. **Education:** Temple Univ, BA, MS; Univ NC, PhD, 1991. **Professional Experience:** ADJ ASST PROF MED GENETICS, UNIV S ALA, as of 2004. **Mailing Address:** Dept Med Genetics Univ S Ala, CCCB-214, Mobile, AL 36688.

KUSZAK, JEROME R, PATHOLOGY. **Personal Data:** b May 26, 1951. **Education:** Wayne State Univ, BS, 1972, MS, 1976, PhD (anat), 1980. **Honors & Awards:** Alcon Res Inst Award, 1990. **Professional Experience:** PROF OPHTHAL, MED COL, RUSH UNIV, as of 2004; assoc prof ophthal, Conjoint Appointment Anat, Rush Med Col, beginning 1990; assocprof path, Conjoint Appointment Anat, Rush Med Col, 1987-; DIR ELECTRON MICROS, DEPT PATH, RUSH-PRESBY, ST LUKE'S MED CTR, 1983-; asst prof path, ConjointAppointment Anat, 1983-1987; New investr award, Nat Eye Inst, NIH, 1983-1986; Instr anat, cell biol & path, Rush Med Col, 1980-1983. **Memberships:** Inst Soc Eye Res; Asn Res Vision & Ophthal; Am Soc Cell Biol. **Research Statement & Publications:** Pathology. **Mailing Address:** Dept Path, RushPresby St Luke Med Ctr, 1653 W Congress Pkwy, Chicago, IL 60612-3833. **Fax:** 312-942-4228. **E-Mail:** jkuszak@rush.edu

KUTAL, CHARLES RONALD, INORGANIC CHEMISTRY & PHOTOCHEMISTRY, MASS SPECTROMETRY & MATERIALS SCIENCE & NANOTECHNOLOGY. **Personal Data:** b Chicago, Ill, August 9, 1944; m 1973, Judy. **Education:** Knox Col, Ill, AB, 1965; Univ Ill Urbana-Champaign, MS, 1968, PhD (chem), 1970. **Honors & Awards:** Res Award, Sigma Xi, 1979. **Professional Experience:** ASSOC DEAN ARTS & SCI, UNIV GA, 2002-; head, Univ Ga, 1991-1996; vis scientist, IBM Res Labs, 1986; PROF CHEM, UNIV GA, 1985-; from instr to assoc prof, Univ Ga, 1973-1985; res fel, Nat Res Coun-Nat Acad Sci, 1972-1973; res assoc chem, Univ Southern Calif, 1970-1972. **Memberships:** Am

Chem Soc; AAAS. **Research Statement & Publications:** Photochemical and photophysical investigations of transition metal and organometallic complexes; photocatalysis; photolithography; published over 5 articles. **Mailing Address:** Dept Chem, Univ Ga, Athens, GA 30602. **Fax:** 706-542-9454. **E-Mail:** ckutal@chem.uga.edu

KUTAS, MARTA, PSYCHOLOGY, PSYCHOPHYSIOLOGY. **Personal Data:** b Hungary, September 2, 1949; American citizen. **Education:** Oberlin Col, BA, 1971; Univ Ill, Urbana-Champaign, MA, 1974, PhD (biol psychol), 1977. **Honors & Awards:** Early Career Contrib Psychol Award, Am Psychiat Asn. **Professional Experience:** ADJ PROF, DEPT NEUROSCIENCE, UNIV CALIF, as of 2001; adj prof, Dept Psychol, Univ Calif, San Diego, beginning 1997; PROF, DEPT COGNITIVE SCI, UNIV CALIF, SAN DIEGO, 1990-; adj assoc prof, Dept Cognitive Sci, Univ Calif, San Diego, 1988-1990; assoc res neuroscientist, Univ Calif, San Diego, 1985-; asst res neuroscientist, Univ Calif, San Diego, 1980-1984; res neuroscientist, Univ Calif, San Diego, 1978-1980; vis res assoc, Dept Psychol, Univ Ill, 1977-1978. **Memberships:** Soc Psychophyisol Res; Int Neuropsychol Soc; Women Neuroscience. **Research Statement & Publications:** Brain function, including recording and interpreting pattern of brain waves (event related potentials) from the scalp as humans try to comprehend the oral, written or pictorial world. **Mailing Address:** Dept Cognitive Sci, Univ Calif, La Jolla, CA 92093-0515. **Fax:** 858-534-1128.

KUTCHAI, HOWARD C, PHYSIOLOGY, BIOCHEMISTRY. **Personal Data:** b Detroit, Mich, February 21, 1942; m 1993, Elizabeth; c Joshua J. **Education:** Univ Mich, BS, 1963; Univ Calif, San Francisco, PhD (physiol), 1967. **Professional Experience:** PROF & ACTG CHAIR MOLECULAR PHYSIOL & BIOL PHYSICS, SCH MED, UNIV VA, as of 2006; assoc ed, Biophys J, 1988-1993; prof physiol, Sch Med, Univ Va, beginning 1981; from asst prof to assoc prof, Sch Med, Univ VA, 1972-1981; fel, Univ Olso, 1969-1970; fel, Johns Hopkins Univ, 1970-1972; NIH trainee, Univ Mich. **Memberships:** AAAS; Am Physiol Soc; Biophys Soc; Soc Gen Physiol. **Research Statement & Publications:** Function of the calcium-ATP ase of sarcoplasmic reticulum, diffusion boundary layers; oxygen transport in red blood cells; influence of membrane lipids on transport processes; biophysics; published over 15 articles. **Mailing Address:** Dept Molecular Physiol & Biol Physics, Univ VA, PO Box 800736 Health Sci 4-38 Jordan Hall, Charlottesville, VA 22908-0736. **Fax:** 434-982-1616. **E-Mail:** hck4p@virginia.edu

KUTCHER, STANLEY PAUL, ADOLESCENT AFFECTIVE DISORDERS, PSYCHOPHARMACOLOGY. **Personal Data:** b Toronto, Ont, December 16, 1951; c 3. **Education:** McMaster Univ, BA, 1974, MA, 1975, MD, 1979; FRCPS, 1983. **Honors & Awards:** R O Jones Award; Renger Award. **Professional Experience:** ASSOC DEAN INT MED DEVELOP & RES, DALHOUSIE UNIV, as of 2005; PROF PSYCHIAT SERV, DEPT PSYCHIAT, DALHOUSIE UNIV, as of 2005; head psychiat serv, Dept Psychiat, Dalhousie Univ, ending 2003; asst prof, Sch Grad Studies, Univ Toronto, 1987-1988; head, Div Adolescent Psychiat, Sunnybrook Med Ctr, 1986-1991; dir adolescent psychiat serv; assoc prof psychiat & phys rehab med, UnivToronto, 1986-1991; vis clin scientist psychiat, Med Res Coun Gt Brit, 1983-1984; sci prog chair, Can Acad Child Psychiat. **Memberships:** Am Psychiat Asn; Can Phys Asn; Can Col Neuropharmacol; Am Col Neuropsychopharmacol; Am Acad Child Adolescent Psychiat. **Research Statement & Publications:** Psychopharmacology of adolescent affective disorders; neuroendovirology. **Mailing Address:** Dept Psychiat, Med Sch, Dalhousie Univ, QE2 Health Sci Ctr 5909 Vet Mem Lane Rm 9209 Lane Bldg, Halifax, NS B3H 2E2, Can. **Fax:** 902-473-4887. **E-Mail:** kutcher@dal.ca

KUTIK, LEON, ORGANIC CHEMISTRY, TECHNICAL MANAGEMENT. **Personal Data:** b New York, NY, March 6, 1927; m 1963, c 3. **Education:** City Col New York, BS, 1949; Univ Chicago, MBA, 1973. **Honors & Awards:** Roy H Kienle Award, 1965. **Professional Experience:** MGR, COM APPLN LAB, W R GRACE & CO, DAVISON DIV TECH CTR, 1983-; mgr mfg & tech serv, Sherwin Williams Corp, 1980-1983; tech mgr construct coatings, Chem Coatings Div, 1977-1980; mgr indust res, Chem Coatings Div, 1973-1977; mgr resindevelop, Chem Coatings Div, 1970-1973; tech dir chem coatings, Del Soto Inc, 1968-1970; mgrgraphic sci, Cent Res Labs, Interchem Corp, 1967-1968; prog mgr, Cent Res Labs, InterchemCorp, 1963-1967; asst dept dir appl res finishes & adhesives, Cent Res Labs, Interchem Corp, 1959-1963; group leader, Cent Res Labs, Interchem Corp, 1959; sr chemist, Cent Res Labs, Interchem Corp, 1957-1959; chemist, Cent Res Labs, Interchem Corp, 1955-1957; Chemist, Clover Leaf Paint & Varnish Corp, 1951-1955. **Memberships:** Am Chem Soc; Soc Paint Technol; Nat Asn Corrosion Engrs. **Research Statement & Publications:** Organic coatings for metal, paper, fiberboard, plywood, wood and plastics; adhesives for packaging and structural applications; methods of application for industrial coatings; powder coatings; matting agents; corrosion inhibiting pigments. **Mailing Address:** 10732 Autumn Splendor Way, Columbia, MD 21044.

KUTILEK, MICHAEL JOSEPH, WILDLIFE ECOLOGY. **Personal Data:** b Baltimore, Md, July 1, 1943; m 1968, c 1. **Education:** San Diego State Univ, BS, 1966, MS, 1968; Mich State Univ, PhD (fisheries & wildlife), 1975. **Professional Experience:** PROF BIOL SCI, SAN JOSE STATE UNIV, as of 2006; assoc prof biol sci, San Jose State Univ, beginning 1980; asst prof, San Jose State Univ, 1975-1980; wildlife biologist, Kenya Nat Parks, US Peace Corps, 1969-1971; res technician biol, Calif Dept Fish & Game, 1965. **Memberships:** Wildlife Soc. **Research Statement & Publications:** Foraging strategies of herbivorous large mammals of Africa particularly, grazing and browsing ungulates; ecological and evolutionary aspects of plant-herbivore interactions; radio-telemetry using light aircraft; wildlife management of large mammals. **Mailing Address:** Dept Biol Sci, San Jose State Univ, One Wash Sq Duncan Hall Rm 555, San Jose, CA 95192-0100. **Fax:** 408-924-4840. **E-Mail:** mkutilek@email.sjsu.edu

KUTINA, JAN, CHEMISTRY. **Education:** Charles Univ, CSc. **Professional Experience:** CHMN, DEPT CHEM, AM UNIV, WASH, as of 2006. **Mailing Address:** Dept Chem Lab Global Tectonics, Am Univ, Washington, DC 20016. **Fax:** 202-885-1752. **E-Mail:** jkutina@american.edu

KUTKUHN, JOSEPH HENRY, ECOLOGY, FISHERIES. **Personal Data:** b Weehawken, NJ, March 28, 1927; m 1953, Farner; c Michael, Constance, Jacquelyn, Holly & Kenneth. **Education:** Colo State Univ, BS, 1953; Iowa State Univ, MS, 1954, PhD (fishery mgt), 1956. **Honors & Awards:** Outstanding Contribution River Mgt Award, 2003. **Professional Experience:** RETIRED; consult, 1987; assoc dir, Fishery Resources, Wash, DC, 1983-1987; asst lab dir, US Fish & Wildlife Serv, Mich, 1976-1982; asst lab dir, US Fish & Wildlife Serv, Mich, 1972-1975; Agr Orgn, Fishery Res & Develop Proj, Lima, Peru, 1970-1972; asst lab dir, NC, US Fish & Wildlife Serv, 1965-1969; asst lab dir, US Fish & Wildlife Serv, Dept Interior, Tex, 1958-1965; fishery biologist, Dept Fish & Game, Calif, 1956-1958; consult, UN develop prog, Food. **Memberships:** Nat Acad Sci; Am Fisheries Soc; Am Inst Fishery Res Biol; Sigma Xi; Int Asn Great Lakes Res. **Research Statement & Publications:** Dynamics of exploited fish and shellfish resources. **Mailing Address:** 476 Wesman Dr, Grayling, MI 49738.

KUTLER, BENTON, dentistry; deceased, see previous edition for last biography

KUTNER, ABRAHAM, ORGANIC POLYMER CHEMISTRY, PHOTOCHEMISTRY. **Personal Data:** b Lynn, Mass, March 28, 1919; m 1947, Dorothy; c Richard M, Robert S & Janet L. **Education:** Ohio State Univ, PhD (org chem), 1950. **Professional Experience:** RETIRED; vol teaching prog sci res scientist, Hercules, Inc, 1980-1985; sr reschemist, Hercules, Inc, 1973-1980; res chemist, Hercules, Inc, 1950-1973; res chemist, Schering Corp, 1946-1947. **Memberships:** Am Chem Soc. **Research Statement & Publications:** Organic synthesis; polymers; polymer additives; stabilization; polymer reactions; photochemistry applications. **Mailing Address:** 12971 Bucklard Ct, West Palm Beach, FL 33414-6229.

KUTNER, LEON JAY, MEDICAL MICROBIOLOGY. **Personal Data:** b Camden, NJ, March 25, 1928; c 2. **Education:** Temple Univ, AB, 1949; Pa State Univ, MS, 1950, PhD (bact), 1953; UnivPittsburgh, MD, 1963. **Professional Experience:** RETIRED; assoc clin prof path, Univ Calif, San Diego, beginning 1977; chief microbiol lab, Lab Serv, Vet Admin Hosp, San Diego, 1973-1992; asst prof path residence, Univ Calif, San Diego, 1973-1977; asst prof microbiol in surg, Med Col, Cornell Univ, 1964-1973; assoc scientist, Hosp Spec Surg, NY, 1964-1973; intern, Second Med Div, Bellevue Hosp, New York, 1963-1964; res assoc virol, Sloan-Kettering Inst Cancer Res, 1956-1959; asst, Pa State Univ, 1949-1953. **Memberships:** Am Soc Microbiol; NY Acad Sci. **Research Statement & Publications:** Resistance to infectious disease. **Mailing Address:** 6833 Via Estradad, La Jolla, CA 92037.

KUTNER, MICHAEL HENRY, LINEAR MODELS, VARIANCE COMPONENTS. **Personal Data:** b Hartford, Conn, September 24, 1937; m 1966, c 2. **Education:** Cent Conn State Col, BS, 1960; Va Polytech Inst, MS, 1962; Tex A&M Univ, PhD (statist), 1971. **Honors & Awards:** H O Hartley Award, Former Students Tex A&M Univ, 1984. **Professional Experience:** ASSOC DEAN ACAD AFFAIRS, EMORY UNIV, 1990-; consult, NorwichEaton Pharmaceut, 1989-1991; prog chmn, Summer Res Conf, 1989; vice chmn publ comt, Atlantic Chap, 1988-1990; dir biostatistics, Emory Univ, 1987-; assoc ed, Am Statistician, 1986-1988; pres, Atlantic Chap, 1984-1986; PROF BIOSTATIST, EMORY UNIV, 1981-; regional adv bd, Biomet Soc, 1981-1983; bd mem, Am Statist Asn, 1981-1983; lectr, Ctr Dis Control, 1980-; from asst prof to assoc prof, Emory Univ, 1971-1980; asst prof statist, Tex A&M Univ, 1970-1971; lectr, NASA, Langley AFB, 1963-1967; asst prof math & statist, Col William & Mary, 1962-1967. **Memberships:** Inst Math Statist; fel Am Statist Asn; Biomet Soc. **Research Statement & Publications:** Repeated measures on analysis of variance; coauthor of two textbooks. **Mailing Address:** 11 Downing Lane, Decatur, GA 30033. **E-Mail:** mkutner@sph.emory.edu

KUTNEY, JAMES PETER, ORGANIC CHEMISTRY, BIOTECHNOLOGY. **Personal Data:** b Lamont, Alta, May 2, 1932; m 1953, c 3. **Education:** Univ Alta, BSc, 1954; Univ Wis, MSc, 1956; Wayne State Univ, PhD (org chem), 1958. **Honors & Awards:** Merck, Sharp & Dohme Award, Chem Inst Can, 1968. **Professional Experience:** PROF EMER CHEM, UNIV BC, as of 1997; mem, adv panel Biotechnol, NSERC, 1982-1984; mem, Sci Coun BC, 1978-1981; bd dir, Canadian Patents & Develop Ltd, 1976-1981; vis prof, Japan Soc Prom Sci, 1975; consult, MacMillan Bloedel, 1968-1978; prof chem, Univ BC, beginning 1966; NATO scholar, Bonn, W Ger, 1965; from instr to assoc prof, Univ BC, 1959-1966; res fel org chem, Syntex Res Labs, Mex, 1958-1959. **Memberships:** Am Chem Soc; The Chem Soc; fel Chem Inst Can; Swiss Chem Soc. **Research Statement & Publications:** Chemistry, biosynthesis and biodegradation of natural products and related biologically active compounds, particularly synthesis, isolation and structure elucidation of alkaloids, steroids and terpenes; biotechnology, plant cell cultures; microbial transformations; pharmaceutical drug development. **Mailing Address:** Dept Chem, Univ BC, 2036 Main Mall, Vancouver, BC V6T 1Z1, Can. **Fax:** 604-822-2710.

KUTSCHA, NORMAN PAUL, FOREST PRODUCTS. **Personal Data:** b Irvington, NJ, September 24, 1937; m 1962, c 2. **Education:** State Univ NY Col Forestry, Syracuse Univ, BS, 1959, PhD (wood prod eng), 1967; Univ Wis-Madison, MS, 1961. **Professional Experience:** CHAIR, INT ASN WOOD PRODUCTS SOC, as of 2006; sci adv, weyerhaeuser Co, as of 2003; sr scientist, beginning 1977; partic, McIntire-Stennis Res Proj, Maine Agr Exp Sta, USDA, 1969-; from asst prof to assoc prof wood technol, Sch ForestResources, Univ Maine, Orono, 1968-1977; asst prof wood prod eng, State Univ NY ColForestry, Syracuse Univ, 1967-1968; Forest prod technologist, US Forest Prod Lab, 1959-1962. **Memberships:** Soc Wood Sci & Technol; Electron Micros Soc Am; Int Asn Wood Anat; Forest Prod Res Soc; Sigma Xi. **Research Statement & Publications:** Light and electron microscopic studies of wood as a developing tissue inthe growing tree and as a raw material for various products. **Mailing Address:** Forest Products Soc, 2801 Marshall Court, Madison, WI 53705. **Fax:** 253-924-6220. **E-Mail:** norm.kutscha@weyerhaeuser.com

KUTSHER, GEORGE SAMUEL, analytical chemistry; deceased, see previous edition for last biography

KUTSKY, ROMAN JOSEPH, BIOLOGY, CHEMISTRY. **Personal Data:** b Allentown, Pa, May 13, 1922; div, c 3. **Education:** Princeton Univ, AB, 1944; Univ Calif, MA, 1949, PhD (zool), 1953. **Professional Experience:** Supvr & staff chemist, Bonneville PowerAdmin, 1978-1986; chemist, Army Med Ctr, El Paso, 1977-1978; prof life sci, Bishop Col, 1973-1977; NASA res grant, 1973-1976; assoc prof biol, Tex Woman's Univ, 1967-1973; Consult, Microchem Specialties Co, 1959; res biochemist, Vet Admin Hosp, 1957-1967; res felbiochem, Donner Lab, 1953-1957; asst specialist plant path, Univ Calif, 1949-1951; asst zool, Univ Calif, 1946-1949; asst physics, Princeton Univ, 1944-1946; CONSULT NUTRIT & TOXICOL. **Memberships:** AAAS; Am Chem Soc; Tissue Cult Asn; NY Acad Sci. **Research Statement & Publications:** Biochemical extractions of biologically active materials; cellular biochemistry and physiology; physical biochemistry; tissue culture growth and form; vitamins and hormones; continuous flow preparative electrophoresis; effects of antioxidants; hormones and vitamins in tissue culture; aging; nutrition. **Mailing Address:** 5719 Ne Hazel Dell Ave, Vancouver, WA 98663.

KUTTAB, SIMON HANNA, MEDICINAL CHEMISTRY. **Personal Data:** b Jerusalem, Palestine, April 17, 1946; American citizen; m 1978, Eileen Rizek; c Rania, Johnny & Rani. **Education:** Am Univ Beirut, Lebanon, BSc, 1968; Univ Kans, PhD (med chem), 1974. **Professional Experience:** ASSOC PROF CHEM, BIR-ZEIT UNIV, WEST BANK, ISRAEL, 1981-; asst prof, Northeastern Univ, 1976-1981; Asst res pharmacologist med chem, Univ Calif, Davis, 1974-1975 & Univ Calif, San Francisco, 1975-1976; Dep dir, Ctr Environ & Occup Health Sci, Birqeik Univ, West Bank, Via Israel. **Memberships:** Am Chem Soc; AAAS; Sigma Xi; Acad Am Pharmaceut Asn. **Research Statement & Publications:** Design and synthesis of compounds of biological interest; breakdown of xenobiotics and specific absorption rate correlations using such advanced analytical techniques as gas chromatography, high performance liquid chromatography and gas chromatography-mass spectrometry. **Mailing Address:** Dept Chem, Bir-Zeit Univ Box 14, Bir-Zeit West Bank, Israel. **Fax:** 972-2-9982166. **E-Mail:** skuttab@ceohs.birzeit.edu

KUTTEH, WILLIAM HANNA, REPRODUCTIVE ENDOCRINOLOGY & IMMUNOLOGY. **Education:** Wake Forest Univ, BA, 1975; Univ Ala, Birmingham, PhD (immunol), 1981; BowmanGray Sch Med, MD, 1985. **Honors & Awards:** Res Award, Sigma Xi, 1980 & 1984; Distinguished Res Award, Am Fertil Soc. **Professional Experience:** PROF OBSTET & GYNEC, UNIV TENN, MEMPHIS, as of 2006; DIR, DIV REPRODUCTIVE ENDOCRINOL, INFERTILITY & GENETICS, UNIV FERTILITY ASSOCS, as of 2006; ASST PROF OBSTET & GYNEC & DIR REPRODUCTIVE IMMUNOL, SOUTHWESTERN MED CTR, UNIV TEX, 1991-1996; Instr Fel Reproduction Endocrinol, Southwestern Med Ctr, Univ Tex, 1989-1991; Chief resident obstet & gynec, Univ Ala, Birmingham, 1989; consult, dept microbiol, 1985-1989-; NIH fel, 1989-1991; res instr obstet & gynec, Univ Ala, Birmingham, 1985-1989; Postdoctoral fel biochem, Bowman Gray Sch Med, 1981-1985; predoctoral fel microbiol, Univ Ala, Birmingham, 1978-1981; res asst immunol, Duke Univ MedCtr, 1975-1978. **Memberships:** Am Asn Immunologists; Am Fertil Soc; Am Col Obstet & Gynec; Soc MucosalImmunol; NY Acad Sci; Am Asn Gynec Laparoscopists; Soc Gynec Invest; Endocrine Soc. **Research Statement & Publications:** Secretory immune system of the female reproductive tract; immune response to human ovarian cancer; recurrent pregnancy loss; antisperm antibody mediated in fertility; antiphospholipid antibody syndrome. **Mailing Address:** Dept Obstet & Gynec, Univ Tenn, 80 Humphreys Ctr SSte 307, Memphis, TN 38120-2363. **Fax:** 901-747-4446. **E-Mail:** wkutteh@utmem.edu

KUTTER, ELIZABETH MARTIN, MOLECULAR BIOLOGY, GENOMIC DATABASES. **Personal Data:** b Chicago, Ill, August 11, 1939; c Bernard & Eric. **Education:** Univ Wash, BS, 1962; Univ Rochester, PhD (biophys), 1968. **Professional Experience:** Nat Acad Sci exchange mem USSR, 1990; mem bd dir, John Bastyr Col, 1979-1992; mem, NSF Adv Comt Ethics & Values Sci & Technol, 1978-1980; vis scientist, Dept Biochem, Univ Calif, San Francisco, 1978-1979; teacher ethics & molecular biol, AAAS, Chataqua, 1977-1980; mem, NIH Dir Adv Comt Recombinant DNA, 1975-1979; res grants, NIH, 1973-1976; MEM FAC BIOPHYS, EVERGREEN STATE COL, 1972-; res grants, NSF, 1970-1972 & 1976-; res assoc biol, Univ Va, 1969-1972. **Memberships:** Biochem Soc; AAAS; Am Soc Microbiol; Genetics Soc; Protein Soc. **Research Statement & Publications:** Biochemical developments during bacteriophage T4 infection of Escherichia coli, especially regulation of transcription and events governing the transition from host to phage metabolism; integrated genomic data bases. **Mailing Address:** Dept Sci Technol & Health, Evergreen State Col, Lab One 2023, Olympia, WA 98505. **Fax:** 360-866-6754. **E-Mail:** kutterb@elwha.evergreen.edu

KUTTLER, JAMES ROBERT, DIFFERENTIAL EQUATIONS, EIGENVALUES. **Personal Data:** b Burlington, Iowa, August 8, 1941; m 1963, Evelyn Ridgley; c John, Robert & Laura. **Education:** Rice Univ, BA, 1962, Univ Md, MA, 1964, PhD (math), 1967. **Professional Experience:** Lectr, math, Johns Hopkins Univ, GWC Whiting Sch Eng, Continuing Prof Progs, 1981-; MATHEMATICIAN, APPLIED PHYSICS LAB, JOHNS HOPKINS UNIV, 1963-. **Research Statement & Publications:** Differential equations, electromagnetics, eigenvalues. **Mailing Address:** Appl Physics Lab, Johns Hopkins Univ, Laurel, MD 20723-6099.

KUTUZOVA, GALINA DMITRIEVNA, BIOLUMINESCENCE, ENZYMOLOGY. **Personal Data:** b Moscow, USSR, March 27, 1955; m 1979, Audrey; c Andrey A. **Education:** Moscow State Univ, BS, 1975, MS, 1976, PhD (enzyme), 1981. **Professional Experience:** SR SCIENTIST BIOCHEM, COL AGR & LIFE SCI, UNIV WIS MADISON, as of 2006; ASSOC SCIENTIST BIOCHEM, COL AGR & LIFE SCI, UNIV WIS MADISON, as of 2004; sr scientist res & develop, Promega Corp, beginning 1992; res scientist, Biochem & Biophys Dept, Tex A&M Univ, 1990-1992; group leader, Chem Enzym Dept, Moscow State Univ, Russia, 1986-1989; sr scientist, Chem Enzym Dept, Moscow State Univ, Russia, 1983-1986; scientist, Chem Enzym Dept, Moscow State Univ, Russia, 1976-1983. **Memberships:** Am Soc Biochem & Molecular Biol; Int Soc Bioluminescence &Chemiluminescence; AAAS; Protein Soc. **Research Statement & Publications:** Biochemistry of beetle luciferases, its kinetics, stability and mechanism of action; genetic engineering of beetle luciferases and its mutants; purification and applications; adenosin triphosphate-assays technology development. **Mailing Address:** Dept Biochem, Col Agr & Life Scis, Univ Wis, 275 Biochem Addn 433 Babcock Dr, Madison, WI 53706. **E-Mail:** gkutuzova@biochem.wisc.edu

KUTZ, FREDERICK WINFIELD, ECOLOGY, MEDICAL ENTOMOLOGY. **Personal Data:** b Wilmington, Del, September 29, 1939; m 1963, Arlene; c Mark D & Heather L. **Education:** Univ Del, BS, 1962, MS, 1964; Purdue Univ, PhD (entom), 1972. **Honors & Awards:** Cert Recognition, Nat Marine Fisheries Serv Environ Protection Agency Gold medal, 2000; Environ Protection Agency Silver Medals, 1976, 2002; Environ Protection Agency Bronze medals, 1998 & 1996. **Professional Experience:** Adj prof, Univ Miami Sch Med, 1980-; monitoring panel, Fed Working Group Pest Mgr, 1975-1977 & subcomt, Comt Environ Carcinogens, Nat Cancer Inst, 1976-; mem, sci adv panel, Onchocerciasis Control Prog, WHO, 1974-1980; ECOLOGIST, US ENVIRON PROTECTION AGENCY, 1972-; entomologist & parasitologist, Insect Control & Res Inc, 1969-1972; res asst & instr, Purdue Univ, 1966-1969; entomologist, Med Serv Corps Officer, US Army, 1964-1966; res fel & assoc entom, Univ Del, 1962-1964. **Memberships:** Entom Soc Am; Am Soc Trop Med & Hyg; Am Mosquito Control Asn; Sigma Xi. **Research Statement & Publications:** Arthropod-insect pest management, particularly of medical significance and chemical and biological monitoring in humans and environmental components; environmental processes and effects of chemicals and other stressors; landscape approaches to environmental and public health monitoring. **Mailing Address:** Environ Protection Agency, 701 Mapes Rd, Ft Meade, MD 20755-5350. **Fax:** 410-305-3095. **E-Mail:** kutz.rick@epa.gov

KUTZKO, PHILIP C, NUMBER THEORY. **Personal Data:** b Brooklyn, NY, November 24, 1946; m 1967, c 1. **Education:** City Col NY, BA, 1967; Univ Wis, MA, 1968, PhD (math), 1972. **Professional Experience:** PROF MATH, UNIV IOWA, 1980-; assoc prof, Univ Iowa, 1977-1980; asst prof, Univ Iowa, 1974-1977; instr, Princeton Univ, 1972-1974; instr, Rock County Ctr, 1969-1972; instr math, Univ Wis, Green Bay, 1968-1969. **Memberships:** Am Math Soc. **Research Statement & Publications:** Representation theory of p-adic linear groups and applications to non-abelian classfield theory. **Mailing Address:** 1610 Muscatine Ave, Iowa City, IA 52240. **E-Mail:** philip-kutzko@uiowa.edu

KUTZLER, FRANK WILLIAM, PHYSICS. **Personal Data:** b Pueblo, Colo, August 8, 1952. **Education:** Univ Southern Colo, BS, 1974; Stanford Univ, PhD (physics), 1981. **Professional Experience:** PROF CHEM, TENN TECHNOL UNIV, 1985-; res scientist, Naval Res Lab, 1984-1985. **Memberships:** Am Phys Soc. **Mailing Address:** Dept Chem, Tenn Technol Univ, PO Box 5055, Cookeville, TN 38505.

KUTZMAN, RAYMOND STANLEY, TOXICOLOGY. **Personal Data:** b St Cloud, Minn, April 16, 1949. **Education:** St Cloud State Col, BA, 1971; Univ Notre Dame, MS, 1974; NC State Univ, PhD (zool), 1977. **Professional Experience:** CHEM MGR, NAT TOXICOL PROG, NAT INST ENVIRON HEALTH SCI, 1985-; from asst scientist toassoc scientist, Med Dept, Brookhaven Nat Lab, 1979-1985; res assoc, Chem Dept, BrookhavenNat Lab, 1977-1979; dir, Toxic Hazard Res Unit, Armstrong Aerospace Res Lab, USAF. **Memberships:** AAAS; Soc Toxicol; Int Soc Study Xenobiotics; Soc Risk Anal; Am SocPharmacol & Exp Therapeut. **Research Statement & Publications:** Biodistribution of xenobiotic agents after inhalation exposure; risk assessment; genetic disposition as an underlying factor in biochemical and physiological aspects of toxicity. **Mailing Address:** Mitretek Syst, 13526 George Rd Suite 200, San Antonio, TX 78230.

KUUS-REICHEL, KRISTINE, IMMUNOLOGY. **Personal Data:** b New York, NY, August 8, 1953. **Education:** State Univ NY, Buffalo, BS, 1975; Med Col Va, PhD (immunol), 1983. **Professional Experience:** MGR, CELL & MOLECULAR BIOL, HYBRITECH INC, 1993-; adj profimmunol, Calif State Univ, San Marcos, 1992-; res scientist, Hybritech Inc, beginning 1986; res fel B cell activation, Scripps Inst, 1983-1986. **Memberships:** Am Asn Immunologists; NY Acad Sci; AAAS; Asn Women Sci. **Research Statement & Publications:** Immunology. **Mailing Address:** Hybritech Inc, PO Box 269006, San Diego, CA 92196. **Fax:** 619-453-4124.

KUWABARA, JAMES S, ECOLOGY. **Personal Data:** b Honolulu, Hawaii, April 26, 1953. **Education:** Univ Hawaii, Manoa, BS, 1975; Calif Inst Technol, MS, 1976, PhD (environ eng sci), 1980. **Professional Experience:** HYDROLOGIST, WATER RESOURCES DIV, US GEOL SURV, as of 2006; mem, Environ Chem Task Group, 1988-1992; mem, Task Group Biol & Microbiol, Water Resources Div, US Geol Surv, 1986-1989; HYDROLOGIST & PROJ CHIEF, NAT RES PROG, GEOL SURV, US DEPT INTERIOR, 1980-; res assoc, Nat Res Coun, 1980-1981; comput operator trainee, Castle & Cooke Inc, 1971. **Memberships:** Am Soc Civil Engrs; fel Am Inst Chemists; Am Soc Agr Engrs; Am GeophysUnion; Phycological Soc Am; Inst Elec & Electronics Engrs; Am Inst Biol Sci. **Research Statement & Publications:** Contributed numerous articles to professional publications. **Mailing Address:** Water Resources Div, US Geol Surv, 345 Middlefield Rd, Menlo Park, CA 94025. **E-Mail:** kuwabara@usgs.gov

KUWAHARA, STEVEN SADAO, BIOCHEMISTRY HEMOSTASIS, ANALYTICAL BIOCHEMISTRY. **Personal Data:** b Lahaina, Hawaii, July 20, 1940; m 1973, Rene; c Daniel T & Sara S. **Education:** Cornell Univ, BS, 1962; Univ Wis, MS, 1965, PhD (biochem), 1967. **Professional Experience:** PRES, GXP BIOTECHNOLOGY LLC, as of 2005; chief educ officer, Bioinsights, Inc, as of 2004; mgr qual assurance validations, Immunother Div, Baxter Healthcare, Duarte, beginning 1992; adv coun, Dept Chem & Biochem, Calif State Univ Long Beach, 1991-; mgr test technol, Qual Assurance Labs, 1990-1992; mgr, QualAssurance Labs, 1987-1990; mgr test technol, Hyland Therapeut, Los Angeles, 1982-1987; adjres assoc, Dept Med, Mich State Univ, 1981-1982; sect chief biochem & bioassay, Bur DisControl & Lab Serv, Mich Dept Pub Health, 1978-1982; sect chief prod anal, Bur Dis Control &Lab Serv, Mich Dept Pub Health, 1976-1978; biochemist & unit chief, Bur Dis Control & LabServ, Mich Dept Pub Health, 1973-1976; asst res biologist, Dept Develop & Cell Biol, Univ Calif, Irvine, 1971-1973; Spec res fel, NIH, 1971-1973; asst prof chem, Calif State Col, Long Beach, 1967-1971; res assoc biochem, Univ Wash, 1966-1967. **Memberships:** NY Acad Sci; Am Chem Soc; Soc Exp Biol & Med; Am Fedn Clin Res; Am Soc Microbiol; AAAS. **Research Statement & Publications:** Biochemistry of blood coagulation factors; biochemistry of plasma proteins; analytical biochemistry. **Mailing Address:** BioInsights Inc, 153 Dorchester Dr, East Windsor, NJ 08520. **Fax:** 609-426-4733. **E-Mail:** skuwahara@bioinsights.com

KUWANA, THEODORE, ANALYTICAL CHEMISTRY, ELECTROCHEMISTRY. **Personal Data:** b Idaho Falls, Idaho, August 3, 1931. **Education:** Antioch Col, BS, 1954; Cornell Univ, MS, 1956; Univ Kans, PhD (anal chem), 1959. **Professional Experience:** REGENTS DISTINGUISHED PROF EMER, UNIV KANS, as of 2002; prof chem, Ohio State Univ, beginning 1971; from assoc prof to prof, Case Western Reserve Univ, 1966-1971; chmn, Gordon Res Conf Anal Chem, 1964; asst prof anal chem, Univ Calif, Riverside, 1960-1966; fel, Calif Inst Technol, 1959-1960; res chemist, Aerojet-Gen Corp Div, Gen Tire & Rubber Co, 1959; AT CTR BIOANALYTICAL RES, KANS UNIV, LAWRENCE. **Memberships:** AAAS; Am Chem Soc; Royal Soc Chem. **Research Statement & Publications:** Organic electrode processes; photoelectrochemistry and electroluminescence. **Mailing Address:** Dept Chem, Univ Kans, 1251 Wescoe Hall Dr, 2010 Malott Hall, Lawrence, KS 66045-7582. **Fax:** 785-864-5396. **E-Mail:** tkuwana@eureka.chem.ukans.edu

KUYPER, LEE FREDERICK, ORGANIC CHEMISTRY, MEDICINAL CHEMISTRY. **Personal Data:** b Mitchell, SDak, February 28, 1949; c 1. **Education:** Ouachita Univ, BS, 1971; Univ Ark, PhD (org chem), 1977. **Professional Experience:** PRIN RES SCIENTIST, GLAXOWELLCOME INC, as of 2005; sr scientist, Burroughs Wellcome Co, beginning 1977; res assoc, Univ NC, 1976-1977. **Memberships:** Am Chem Soc. **Research Statement & Publications:** Molecular modeling; drug design and synthesis. **Mailing Address:** Burroughs Wellcome Co, PO Box 1887, Greenville, NC 27834.

KUZEL, NORBERT R, ANALYTICAL CHEMISTRY, INSTRUMENTATION. **Personal Data:** b Angus, Minn, May 23, 1923; m 1949. **Education:** N Dak State Univ, BS, 1948, MS, 1949. **Professional Experience:** RETIRED; res assoc, Eli Lilly & Co, 1973-1984; res scientist, Eli Lilly & Co, 1968-1973; sr anal chemist, Eli Lilly & Co, 1963-1967; dept head anal develop, Eli Lilly & Co, 1959-1963; anal chemist, Eli Lilly & Co, 1949-1959. **Memberships:** Am Chem Soc; Instrument Soc Am. **Research Statement & Publications:** Development of analytical methods; residue analysis; laboratory and process automation and computerization. **Mailing Address:** 4611 Berkshire Lane, Indianapolis, IN 46226-3137.

KUZMA, JAN WALDEMAR, BIOSTATISTICS. **Personal Data:** b Warsaw, Poland, April 24, 1936; American citizen; m 1963, c 3. **Education:** Andrews Univ, BA, 1959; Columbia Univ, MS, 1961; Univ Mich, PhD (biostatist), 1963. **Professional Experience:** PROF PREV MED, SCH PUB HEALTH, LOMA LINDA UNIV, as of 2001; prof biostatist & chmn dept biostatist & epidemiol, schpub health, Loma Linda Univ, beginning 1973; chmn dept biostatist, Sch Pub Health, LomaLinda Univ, 1967-1973; consult biostatistician, Loma Linda Univ, 1964-1967; lectr biostatist &dir clin trials unit, Univ Calif, Los Angeles, 1963-1967. **Memberships:** Am Statist Soc; Biomet Soc; Am Pub Health Asn; AAAS. **Research Statement & Publications:** Lifestyle and longevity; health care costs; general statistical methodology. **Mailing Address:** 1280 E San Bernardino Ave, Redlands, CA 92374.

KUZMAK, JOSEPH MILTON, PHYSICAL CHEMISTRY, PAPER COATINGS. **Personal Data:** b Man, March 7, 1922; m 1942, Lillian; c James J, Sylvia D & Paula J (Smith). **Education:** Univ Man, BSc, 1949, MSc, 1950; McGill Univ, PhD (phys chem), 1953. **Professional Experience:** RETIRED; sr scientist, Champion Int Corp, 1984-1986; sr res chemist, St Regis Paper Co, 1967-1984; res chemist, Am Viscose Corp, Pa, 1957-1967; res officer, Nat Res Coun Can, 1953-1957. **Memberships:** Am Chem Soc; Tech Asn Pulp & Paper Indust. **Research Statement & Publications:** Mechanism of moisture movement in porous materials; chemical modification of regenerated cellulose; chemical modification of pulp and paper; paper coatings and coating process. **Mailing Address:** 2203 Apple Rd, Fogelsville, PA 18051.

KUZNESOF, PAUL MARTIN, REGULATORY FOOD CHEMISTRY, FOOD ADDITIVE SAFETY EVALUATION. **Personal Data:** b Bronx, NY, August 13, 1941; div, c Adam. **Education:** Brown Univ, BS, 1963; Northwestern Univ, PhD, 1967. **Professional Experience:** Sr chemist, off food additive safety, ctr food safety& appl nutrit, USFDA, 2001-; Chair, working group specif, Codex comt food additives & contaminants, 1996-; invited expert, Joint FAO/WHO comt food additives, 1989, 1993-; ACTG DEP DIR, DIV PROD MANUFACTURE & USE, OFF PRE-MKT APPROVAL, CTR FOOD SAFETY & APPL NUTRIT, US FOOD & DRUG ADMIN, 1996-; chief, Chem Rev Br, 1992-1996; sect head, Food & Color Additives Rev Sect, 1987-1992; regulatory chemist, US Food & Drug Admin, 1984-1987; vis scholar, Northwestern Univ, 1982; grants, Res Corp, 1977 & NSF, 1981; assoc prof, Agnes Scott Col, Decatur, Ga, 1979-1983; mem staff, Chem Div, Naval Res Lab, 1978-1979; vis assoc prof, Trinity Col, Hartford, Conn, 1976-1978; vis lectr, Univ Mich, Ann Arbor, 1975-1976; Grant, FAPESP Res Found, Sao Paulo, 1971; prof chem, Univ Campinas, Brazil, 1970-1975; asst prof chem, San Francisco State Col, 1969-1970; fFel inorg mat res div, Lawrence Radiation Lab, Univ Calif, 1967-1969. **Memberships:** Am Chem Soc; AAAS; Inst Food Technologists. **Research Statement & Publications:** Regulatory aspects of food additive safety; exposure and risk assessment; specif of identity and purity; dosimetry for radiation processing of food. **Mailing Address:** HFS-205 Ctr Food Safety & Appl Nutrit, 5100 Paint Branch Parkway, Col Park, MD 20740-3835. **Fax:** 202-418-3030. **E-Mail:** paul.kuznesof@fda.hhs.gov

KVAAS, THORVALD ARTHUR, PHYSICS, ENGINEERING. **Personal Data:** b Des Moines, Iowa, January 8, 1919; m 1942, Rosemary; c Robert & Ronald. **Education:** Univ Calif, Los Angeles, BA, 1940, MA, 1942. **Professional Experience:** CONSULT ACOUST, 1980-; opers mgr, Cetec Broadcast Corp, 1978-1980; consult, Moseley Assocs, 1977; vpres & opers mgr, Moseley Assocs, 1974-1976; pres, ADCON Corp, 1970-1974; mgr tech environ studies, tempo, Ctr Advan Studies, 1963-1970; tech anal & appln oper, Synthesis Sect, Tech Mil Planning Oper, Gen Elec Co, 1962-1963; prof staff, Synthesis Sect, Tech Mil Planning Oper, Gen Elec Co, 1960-1962; rep, Am Rocket Soc, Cong Int Astronaut Fedn, Amsterdam, 1958; mgr, Synthesis Sect, Tech Mil Planning Oper, Gen Elec Co, 1957-1960; sect chief missiles adv design, Douglas Aircraft Co, 1952-1957; proj engr, Rand Corp, 1948-1952; phys sci res engr, phys scientist proj Rand, 1946-1948; mem comt, Am Stand Asn Comt Acoust Terminology, 1946-1948; phys sci res engr, Res Lab, Douglas Aircraft Co, 1942-1946. **Memberships:** Assoc fel Am Inst Aeronaut & Astronaut; Acoust Soc Am. **Research Statement & Publications:** Technological and environmental forecasting and planning with particular emphasis on future technologies, technical resources and their application to future human needs; corporate long range strategic business planning. **Mailing Address:** 933 Roble Lane, Santa Barbara, CA 93103.

KVALNES, KALLA L, BIOCHEMISTRY. **Personal Data:** b September 15, 1960; c 2. **Education:** Univ Cincinnati, BS, 1982; Hahnemann Univ, PhD (biochem), 1987. **Professional Experience:** STAFF SCIENTIST, PROCTER & GAMBLE, 1992-; fel, Univ NC, 1990-1992; NIH grants, 1988-1991 & 1989-1990; fel, Dept Biochem, Albert Einstein Col Med, 1987-1990. **Memberships:** Am Chem Soc; AAAS; Am Soc Biochem & Molecular Biol. **Research Statement & Publications:** Protein, native and mutant, purification; chemical modification of proteins. **Mailing Address:** Procter & Gamble Co, 11511 Reed Hartman Hwy, Cincinnati, OH 45241. **Fax:** 513-626-4399.

KVALSETH, TARALD ODDVAR, STATISTICS, MATHEMATICAL MODELING. **Personal Data:** b Brunkeberg, Norway, November 7, 1938; American citizen; m 1964, Amy; c Erik, Lisbet & Andrew. **Education:** Univ Durham, Eng, BSc, 1963; Univ Calif, Berkeley, MS, 1966, PhD (indust eng), 1971. **Professional Experience:** Co-prin investr, Nat Inst Occup Safety & Health, 1987-1991; head indust eng, Univ Minn, 1983-1992; PROF MECH ENG, UNIV MINN, 1982-; assoc prof mech eng, Univ Minn, 1979-1982; sr lectr, Norweg Inst Technol, 1974-1979; asst prof indust eng, Ga Inst Technol, 1971-1974. **Memberships:** Int Ergonomics Asn (vpres, 1982-1985); AAAS fel; Sigma Xi; Human Factors & Ergonomics Soc; Ergonomics Soc; Inst Indust Engrs. **Research Statement & Publications:** Human factors engineering with emphasis on human performance measures, quantitative models, statistical methods, industrial ergonomics and safety. **Mailing Address:** 4980 Shady Island Cir, Mound, MN 55364-9218. **Fax:** 612-624-1398.

KVAM, DONALD CLARENCE, PHARMACOLOGY. **Personal Data:** b Escanaba, Mich, October 20, 1932; m 1954, Suzanne Irving; c Donald, Mark & Amy. **Education:** Ferris State Col, BS, 1954; Univ Wis, PhD (pharmacol), 1960. **Professional Experience:** RETIRED; lectr, Col Med Sci, Univ Minn; assoc dir, 3M Pharmaceut, 1982-1993; mgr clin pharmacol, 3M Pharmaceut, 1978-1982; mgr pharmacol, 3M Pharmaceut, 1971-1978; mgr biol res, 3M Pharmaceut, 1967-1971; supvr biol res, 3M Pharmaceut, 1964-1967; group leader pharmacol, Mead Johnson & Co, 1963-1964; sr pharmacologist, Mead-Johnson & Co, 1960-1963. **Memberships:** AAAS; Am Soc Pharmacol & Exp Therapeut; Am Soc Clin Pharmacol &Therapeut; Soc Exp Biol Med. **Research Statement & Publications:** Clinical pharmacology, phase 1 and pharmacokinetics studies. **Mailing Address:** 4 North Oaks Rd, St Paul, MN 55127-6431.

KVATERNIK, RAYMOND G, AERONAUTICS. **Professional Experience:** RESEARCHER, AEROELASTICITY BR, NASA LANGLEY RES CTR, as of 2003. **Memberships:** Am Inst Aeronaut & Astronaut. **Mailing Address:** NASA Langley Res Ctr, M/S 340, Hampton, VA 23681. **Fax:** 804-864-7722. **E-Mail:** raymond.g.kvaternik@nasa.gov

KVEGLIS, ALBERT ANDREW, POLYMER CHEMISTRY, ORGANIC CHEMISTRY. **Personal Data:** b Brooklyn, NY, February 10, 1934; m 1961, Ann; c 3. **Education:** Queens Col, NY, BS, 1956; Stevens Inst Technol, MS, 1965. **Professional Experience:** MGR, INK VEHICLES, SUNCHEMICAL CORP, 1982-; group leader, Polymers & Vehicles, Inmont Corp, 1972-1982; methods develop, Biomed Sci, Inc, 1971-1972; res chemist polymers, Trimflex Div, Teleflex Corp, 1971; Sr res chemist polymers, Plastics Div, Allied Chem Corp, 1956-1971. **Memberships:** Am Chem Soc. **Research Statement & Publications:** Polymer synthesis and characterization, development of resins and vehicles for inks and coatings, synthesis of flame retardant monomers and additives for plastics, modification of polymers. **Mailing Address:** 6 Buckingham Circle, Pine Brook, NJ 07058-9712.

KVENVOLDEN, KEITH ARTHUR, ORGANIC GEOCHEMISTRY. **Personal Data:** b Cheyenne, Wyo, July 16, 1930; m 1959, Mary Ann Lawrence; c Joan A & Jon W. **Education:** Colo Sch Mines, GpE, 1952; Stanford Univ, MS, 1958, PhD (geol), 1961. **Honors & Awards:** Meritorious Serv Award, US Dept Interior, 1985, Distinguished Serv Award, 1996; Treibs Medal & Award, Org Geochem Div, Geochem Soc, 1995; Distinguished Achievement Medal, Colorado sch of Mines, 2002. **Professional Experience:** SR SCIENTIST, US GEOL SURV, 1992-; mem, US Sci Adv Comt, Ocean Drilling Prog, 1985-1986; chmn, US Nat Comt Geochem, 1984-1986; chmn, Gordon Res Conf Org Geochem, 1984; mem, US Nat Comt Geochem, 1980-1983; geologist, US Geol Surv, 1975-1992; chmn, Jodies Adv Panel Org Geochem, 1974-1980; chief, Planetary Biol Div, 1974-1975; consult prof, Stanford Univ, 1973-; chief, Chem Evol Br, 1971-1974; Consult assoc prof geol, Stanford Univ, 1967-1973; res scientist, Ames Res Ctr, NASA, Calif, 1966-1971; sr res technologist petrol geochem, Mobil Field Res Lab, Tex, 1961-1966; Jr geologist, Socony Mobil Oil Co, Venezuela, 1952-1954. **Memberships:** Am Asn Petrol Geol; fel Geol Soc Am; fel Geochem Soc; fel Am Geophys Union; fel AAAS; fel Explorers Club. **Research Statement & Publications:** Organic geochemistry of modern and ancient sediments; petroleum geochemistry; environmental geochemistry; organic chemistry of meteorites; origin and evolution of life; geochemistry of amino acids; geochemistry of hydrocarbon gases and gas hydrates. **Mailing Address:** 2433 Emerson St, Palo Alto, CA 94301. **E-Mail:** kkvenvoiden@usgs.gov

KVIETYS, PETER R, CARDIOVASCULAR PHYSIOLOGY. **Personal Data:** b Strasbourg, France, January 12, 1948. **Education:** Western Mich Univ, BS, 1972, MS, 1975; Mich State Univ, PhD (physiol), 1979. **Professional Experience:** PROF, DEPT PHYSIOL MED & BIOPHYS, UNIV WESTERN ONT, as of 2006; prof med physiol & cardiovasc physiol, La State Univ Med Ctr, beginning 1991; assoc prof, LA State Univ Med Ctr, 1986-1991; from asst prof to assoc prof med & cardiovasc physiol, Univ SAla, 1981-1986; fel cardiovasc physiol, Univ SAla, 1979-1980. **Memberships:** Am Gastroenterol Asn; fel Am Physiol Soc; Am Heart Asn; AAAS; Tissue Cult Asn. **Research Statement & Publications:** Cardiovascular physiology. **Mailing Address:** Victoria Hosp, 375 S St Rm C206, London, ON N6A 4G5, Can. **Fax:** 519-432-7367. **E-Mail:** pkvietys@uwo.ca

KVIST, TAGE NIELSEN, DEVELOPMENTAL ANOMALIES, TERATOLOGY. **Personal Data:** b Copenhagen, Denmark, January 17, 1942; American citizen; m 1965, c 3. **Education:** Univ BC, BS, 1966, MS, 1969; Univ Pa, Philadelphia, PhD (biol), 1973. **Honors & Awards:** Lindback Found Award, Christian R & Mary F Lindback Found, 1985. **Professional Experience:** Rep, Health Sci Libraries Consortium, beginning 1987; PROF & CHMN ANAT, PHILADELPHIA COL OSTEOP MED, 1987-; chmn animal care & utilization, Strategic Planning Task Force, 1987; dir, Sch Allied Health, 1986-; curric, Philadelphia Col Osteop Med, 1986-; comput asst instr, Philadelphia Col Osteop Med, 1986-; chmn animal care & utilization, Philadelphia Col Osteop Med, 1986-; asst dean basic sci, Philadelphia Col Osteop Med, 1986-1990; mem, Nat Comt Res Neurol Commun Dis, Spina Bifida Asn Am, 1985-; mem, Inst Self Study Task Force & ExecFac, Philadelphia Col Obsteop Med, 1985-; guest lectr, Sch Nursing, Univ Pa, 1982-1987; rev bdhuman res, Philadelphia Col Obstet Med, 1981-; consult, NIH Sci Rev Group, 1979-; from asst prof to assoc prof, Philadelphia Col Osteop Med, 1976-1987; sci res adv, Pa Gov Conf Handicapped Individuals, 1976; res assoc develop, Univ Pa, Philadelphia, 1973-1976; chief neuro surg res, congenital anoms, Joseph Stokes Jr Res Inst, 1973-1976; lectr comp embryol, Rosemont Col, Pa, 1972; teaching fel biol, Univ Pa, Philadelphia, 1969-1972; teaching asst develop, Univ BC, Vancouver, 1966-1967; reviewer, March Dimes Birth Defects Found Grant. **Memberships:** Soc Develop Biol; Teratol Soc; Am Asn Anatomists; Spina Bifida Asn Am; Am Asn Clin Anatomists; Sigma Xi; Humanity Gifts Registry Pa Anatomists. **Research Statement & Publications:** Birth defects involving the central nervous system; Spina Bifida Cystica; Anencephalus; Hydrocephalus; connective tissue macromolecule formation in developing embryos and in rheumatoid arthritis. **Mailing Address:** Dept Anat, Philadelphia Col Osteop Med, 4170 City Ave, Philadelphia, PA 19131. **E-Mail:** tagek@pcom.edu

KWAAN, HAU CHEONG, INTERNAL MEDICINE, HEMATOLOGY & ONCOLOGY. **Personal Data:** b Hong Kong, September 30, 1931; American citizen; m 1958, c 2. **Education:** Univ Hong Kong, MB & BS, 1952, MD, 1958; FRCP (E), 1967; Am Bd Internal Med, Cert Internal Med, 1969, Cert Hemat, 1974, Cert Med Oncol, 1979. **Professional Experience:** Sr Fulbright travel scholar, 1974; PROF MED, MED SCH, NORTHWESTERNUNIV CHICAGO, 1972-; attend physician, Northwestern Mem Hosp, Chicago, beginning 1969; chiefhemat-oncol sect, Vet Admin Lakeside Med Ctr, Chicago, beginning 1967; assoc prof, Med Sch, Northwestern Univ Chicago, 1966-1972; mem coun thrombosis, Am Heart Asn, beginning 1964; clin asstprof, Sch Med, Georgetown Univ, 1964-1965; sr investr physiol, James F Mitchell Found, DC, 1962-1965; lectr, Univ Hong Kong, 1959-1961; China Med Bd NY fel pharmacol, 1958-1959; vis res fel, Col Physicians & Surgeons, Columbia Univ, 1958-1959; asst lectr, Univ Hong Kong, 1956-1959; sr clin asst med, Univ Hong Kong, 1953-1955; house physician, Univ Med Unit, Queen Mary Hosp, 1952-1953. **Memberships:** Fel Am Col Physicians; AMA; Am Physiol Soc; Am Soc Hemat; Am Fedn ClinRes; Int Soc Thrombosis Hemostasis. **Research Statement & Publications:** Blood coagulation; fibrinolysis; thrombosis. **Mailing Address:** Dept Med 333 E Huron St, Vet Admin Med Ctr Northwestern Univ Med Sch, Chicago, IL 60611-3004. **Fax:** 312-908-5057.

KWAK, DOCHAN, AERONAUTICS. **Education:** Seoul Nat Univ, BS; Stanford Univ, PhD (aeronautics & astronautics). **Professional Experience:** CHIEF, APPLN BR, NASA ADV SUPERCOMPUTING DIV, as of 2002. **Mailing Address:** NASA Ames Res Ctr, M/S T27B-1, Moffett Field, CA 94035. **Fax:** 415-604-6743.

KWAK, JAN C T, POLYMER SCIENCE, COLLOID SCIENCE. **Personal Data:** b Schagen, Neth, May 6, 1942; m 1965, c 3. **Education:** Univ Amsterdam, MSc, 1964, PhD, 1967. **Professional Experience:** Chmn Dept Chem, Dalhousie Univ, beginning 1986; PROF CHEM, DALHOUSIE UNIV, 1983-; from asst prof to assoc prof, Dept Chem, 1970-1983; res chemist, Sea Water Conversion Lab, Univ Calif, Berkeley, 1968-1970; res assoc molten salts, Neth Orgn Advan Pure Res, 1964-1968. **Memberships:** Am Chem Soc; Chem Inst Can. **Research Statement & Publications:** Polymer solutions; surfactants; surfactant nuclear magnetic resonance; biophysical chemistry; flocculation studies; coal beneficiation; colloid chemistry. **Mailing Address:** Dept Chem, Dalhousie Univ, Halifax, NS B3H 4J3, Can. **Fax:** 902-494-1310. **E-Mail:** jan.kwak@dal.ca

KWAK, LARRY W, BIOLOGY. **Education:** NWestern Univ Med Sch, MD, 1982; NWestern Univ Grad Sch, PhD, 1984. **Professional Experience:** CHMN & PROF, DEPT LYMPHOMA & MYELOMA, as of 2005. **Mailing Address:** MD Anderson Cancer Ctr, Univ Tex, 1515 Holcombe Blvd, Houston, TX 77030. **Fax:** 713-745-1163. **E-Mail:** kwak@ncifcrf.gov

KWAK, NOWHAN, HIGH ENERGY PHYSICS. **Personal Data:** b Seoul, Korea, September 16, 1928; American citizen; m 1958, c 2. **Education:** Seoul Nat Univ, BS, 1952; Emory Univ, MS, 1956; Univ Rochester, MA, 1959; Tufts Univ, PhD (physics), 1962. **Professional Experience:** PROF EMER PHYSICS & ASTRON, UNIV KANS, as of 2006; Deutsches Elektronen-Synchrotron, WGer, 1980-1981; prof physics & astron, Univ Kans, beginning 1965; vis scientist, Cern, 1974-1976; sr fel, Austrian Acad Sci, 1973-1974; res assoc high energy physics, Tufts Univ, 1962-1965. **Memberships:** Am Phys Soc assoc of korea-Am physicists. **Research Statement & Publications:** Experimental high energy physics. **Mailing Address:** Dept Phys Univ Kans, Lawrence, KS 66045. **Fax:** 785-864-5262. **E-Mail:** kwak@ku.edu

KWAK, YUN SIK, EXPERIMENTAL BIOLOGY. **Personal Data:** b Taegu, Korea, August 21, 1937; m 1966, Pil; c Kyu, Sue & Ken. **Education:** Kyungpook Nat Univ, MD, 1961; Union Univ, Albany, PhD (molecular biol & path), 1972; Am Bd Path, cert analysis & clin, 1978, cert chempath, 1980. **Professional Experience:** PROF MED INFORMATICS & MED EDUC, KYUNGPOOK NAT UNIV SCH MED, DAEGU, KOREA, as of 2004; PROF & CHMN, DEPT CLIN PATH, SCH MED, AJOU UNIV, SUWON, KOREA, 1994-; spec asst to med ctr dir, I/C Med Info Mgt Sect, Vet Admin Med Ctr, 1989-1993; chief lab serv, Cleveland, beginning 1981; chief lab serv, Dayton, 1979-1981; assoc prof, Dept Path, Sch Med, Wright & State Univ, 1979-1981; mem numerous comts, Vet Admin Hosp, Albany, NY, 1977-; asst prof, Dept Path, Sch Med, Case Western Res Univ, 1977-1995; chiefclin path sect, Lab Serv, Cleveland, 1977-1979; staff pathologist-in-chg clin chem, Vet Admin Hosp, Albany, NY, 1975-1977; chief resident, Dept Path, Albany Med Ctr Hosp, 1973-1974; from res instr to asst prof, Dept Path, Albany Med Col, 1969-1978; from instr to asst prof, DeptBiochem, Sch Med, Kyungpook Univ, 1966-1969; teaching fel, Dept Biochem, Sch Med, Kyungpook Univ, 1964-1966. **Memberships:** Am Asn Clin Chem; fel Am Soc Clin Pathologists; Am Asn Pathologists; NY AcadSci; fel Nat Acad Clin Biochem; fel Col Am Pathologists; AMA. **Research Statement & Publications:** Biochemical aspects of atherogenesis; effective utilization of laboratory information in clinical medicine and laboratory management; author of numerous scientific publications. **Mailing Address:** Kyungpook Nat Univ Sch Med, Daegu, Korea, 1908 Halls Carriage, Westlake, OH 44145-2033. **Fax:** 823-312-195778. **E-Mail:** yskwak@madang.ajou.ac.kr

KWAN, JOHN YING-KUEN, ASTROPHYSICS. **Personal Data:** b Hong Kong, April 5, 1947; m 1973, c 2. **Education:** Utah State Univ, BS, 1969; Calif Inst Technol, PhD (physics), 1972. **Professional Experience:** PROF ASTRON, UNIV MASS, 1987-; assoc prof, Univ Mass, 1981-1987; mem tech staff, Bell Labs, 1976-1980; asst prof astrophys, State Univ NY Stony Brook, 1975-1976; res fel astrophys, Inst Advan Study, 1973-1974; res fel astrophys, Calif Inst Technol, 1973. **Memberships:** Am Astron Soc; Inst Elec & Electronics Engrs. **Research Statement & Publications:** Theoretical studies of astrophysical masers, interstellar molecular clouds, quasars, young stellar objects. **Mailing Address:** Dept Astron, Univ Mass, Amherst, MA 01003-0134. **E-Mail:** kwan@phast.umass.edu

KWAN, KING CHIU, DRUG METABOLISM, PHARMACOKINETICS. **Personal Data:** b Hong Kong, January 14, 1936. **Education:** Univ Mich, BS, 1956, MS, 1958, PhD (pharmaceut chem), 1962. **Professional Experience:** VPRES DRUG METAB, MERCK RES LABS, 1992-; exec dir drug metab, Merck Res Labs, 1981-1992; mem, Pharmacol Study Sect, NIH, 1980-1983; sr dirbiopharmaceut, Merck Res Labs, 1979-1981; sr invest, Merck Res Labs, 1976-1979; sr res fel, Merck Res Labs, 1970-1976; pharmacokinetic specialist, Merck Res Labs, 1969-1970; unit head, Merck Res Labs, 1966-1969; res assoc, Merck Res Labs, 1964-1966; lectr pharm, Univ Mich, 1963-1964; res chemist, R P Scherer Corp, 1962-1963. **Memberships:** Am Pharmaceut Asn; Am Asn Pharmaceut Scientists; Am Soc Pharmacol & ExpTherapeuts; Int Soc Study Xenobiotics; Sigma Xi; Controlled Release Soc. **Research Statement & Publications:** Pharmaceutical research and development; drug metabolism; pharmacokinetics; biopharmaceutics. **Mailing Address:** Merck Res Labs, West Point, PA 19486. **E-Mail:** kc_kwan@merck.com

KWAN, PAUL WING-LING, CANCER, CELL BIOLOGY. **Personal Data:** b Hong Kong, November 7, 1942; American citizen. **Education:** Univ Md, BS, 1966; Clark Univ, MA, 1971, PhD (biol), 1975. **Professional Experience:** RES ASST PROF, DEPT PATH, SCH MED, TUFTS UNIV, 1985-; res assoc, Dept Path, Sch Med, Tufts Univ, 1975-1985; teaching asst biol, Clark Univ, 1967-1973; supvr, spec procedures lab, Path Dept, New Eng Med Ctr. **Memberships:** Nat Soc Histotechnol; Soc Appl Immunohistochem. **Research Statement & Publications:** Application of immunohistochemistry to the study of tumor biology and clinical diagnosis; pathogenesis of benign prostatic hyperplasia and prostate cancer in animal models. **Mailing Address:** Dept Path Sch Med Tufts Univ, 136 Harrison Ave, Boston, MA 02111. **E-Mail:** paul.kwan@tufts.edu

KWANG, JIMMY, MOLECULAR VIROLOGY, GENE EXPRESSIONS. **Personal Data:** b China, August 24, 1949; American citizen; m 1977, Chiao-herng; c Kay & Joyce. **Education:** Taiwan Pingtang Inst Agr, DVM, 1973; Univ RI, MS, 1981; Univ Calif, Davis, PhD (molecular virol), 1987. **Professional Experience:** RES MICROBIOLOGIST, US MEAT ANIMAL RES CTR, 1989-; sr scientist, Viogene, 1988-1989; NIH fel, Sch Med, Univ Calif, San Diego, 1987-1988; dir res & develop, Schuyler Swine Serv, 1981-1984; lectr vet path & histol, Taiwan Pingtang Inst Agr, 1975-1979. **Memberships:** Am Soc Microbiol; US Animal Health Asn; Am Asn Vet Lab Diagnosticians. **Research Statement & Publications:** Pathogenic mechanism of animal viral diseases; characterize each disease at the molecular level and develop a specific, sensitive, rapid, and economic diagnostic procedure for each; develop effective disease control measures for each. **Mailing Address:** USDA-Agr Res Serv US-Meat Animal Res Ctr, Clay Center, NE 68933.

KWAN-GETT, CLIFFORD STANLEY, SURGERY. **Personal Data:** b Emmaville, NSW, October 14, 1934; m 1961, c 2. **Education:** Univ Sydney, BSc, 1954, BE, 1956, MD, 1963. **Professional Experience:** ASSOC RES PROF SURG, UNIV UTAH, 1970-; asst res prof, Univ Utah, 1968-1970; consult, Aerojet Gen Corp, Calif, 1966-1968; felmed, Cleveland Clin Found, 1966-1967; resident med off, Lanceston Gen Hosp, Tasmania, 1964-1966; engr, Australian Postmaster Gen Dept, 1960-1961; cardiol, thoracic & vascularsurgeon. **Memberships:** Am Soc Artificial Internal Organs; Biomed Eng Soc; AMA. **Research Statement & Publications:** Developing total replacement artificial hearts to replace the irreparable human heart; use of artificial heart assist devices; development and use of artificial kidneys, especially for home use by patients. **Mailing Address:** Western Cardiovasc Assoc, 1055 E 3900 S, Salt Lake City, UT 84112.

KWASNY, STAN C, COMPUTER SCIENCE. **Professional Experience:** AFFIL FAC, COMPUT SCI & ENG, WASH UNIV, ST LOUIS, as of 2004; ASSOC PROF COMPUT SCI, WASH UNIV, ST LOUIS. **Research Statement & Publications:** Language processing with neural networks; recursive auto-associative memory; language identification; neurocomputation. **Mailing Address:** Dept Comput Sci, Wash Univ, St Louis, Campus Box 1045, St Louis, MO 63130. **Fax:** 314-935-7302. **E-Mail:** sck@cs.wustl.edu

KWATNY, EUGENE MICHAEL, BIOMEDICAL ENGINEERING. **Personal Data:** b Philadelphia, Pa, October 25, 1943; m 1966, c 2. **Education:** Drexel Univ, BS, 1966, MS, 1968, PhD (biomed eng), 1971. **Professional Experience:** Adj asst prof visual sci & biomed eng, Pa Col Optom, 1974-; PRIN INVESTRVISUAL SYSTS & DIR COMPUT & INFO SCI, KRUSEN CTR RES & ENG & ASST PROFREHAB MED, SCH MED, TEMPLE UNIV, 1971-; biomed engr, Aerospace Crew EquipmentDept, US Naval Air Develop Ctr, 1966-1971. **Memberships:** Inst Elec & Electronics Engrs. **Research Statement & Publications:** Sensory aids for rehabilitation; bioelectric signal processing; computers in medicine and biology. **Mailing Address:** Comput Sci Dept 38-24, Temple Univ Bd & Montgomery St, Philadelphia, PA 19122.

KWATRA, SUBHASH CHANDER, DIGITAL SATELLITE COMMUNICATIONS. **Personal Data:** b India, November 12, 1941; m 1966, c 2. **Education:** Birla Inst Technol, BE, 1962, MS, 1970; Univ SFla, PhD (elec eng), 1975. **Professional Experience:** PROF EMER ELEC ENG, UNIV TOLEDO, as of 2004; DIR, COMMUN LAB, UNIV TOLEDO, as of 2004; prof elec eng, Univ Toledo, beginning 1986; prin investr, Lewis Res Ctr, NASA, 1979-; from asst prof to prof, Univ Toledo, 1977-1986; lectr eng, Birla Inst Technol & Sci, 1965-1970. **Memberships:** Inst Elec & Electronics Engrs. **Research Statement & Publications:** Digital signal processing; satellite communications. **Mailing Address:** Dept Elec Eng & Comput Eng, Univ Toledo, NI 2039, Toledo, OH 43606. **E-Mail:** skwatra@eng.utoledo.edu

KWEI, GLORIA Y, NUTRITIONAL BIOCHEMISTRY. **Personal Data:** b Taipei, Taiwan, March 17, 1960. **Education:** Univ Calif, Berkeley, BS, 1982, PhD (nutrit sci), 87. **Professional Experience:** DIR, PHARMACEUT RES & DEVELOP, MERCK RES LAB, 2000-; res fel, dept drug metab, Merck Res Lab, Rahway, NJ, 1995-2000; sr res chemist, pharmaceut res & develop, Merck Res Lab, 1991-1994; Res assoc nutrit & cancer, Rutgers Univ, 1987-1991. **Memberships:** Am Asn Pharmaceut Sci; Am Inst Nutrit; AAAS; Int Soc Study Xenobiotics. **Research Statement & Publications:** Nutritional biochemistry; drug metabolism. **Mailing Address:** Pharmaceut Res & Develop, Merck & Co Inc, PO Box 100, One Merck Dr, Whitehouse Station, NJ 08889-0100. **E-Mail:** kwei@merck.com

KWEI, TI-KANG, POLYMER CHEMISTRY, PHYSICAL CHEMISTRY. **Personal Data:** b Shanghai, China, March 19, 1929; m 1954, Shen; c Joseph, Carol & Richard. **Education:** Chiao Tung Univ, BS, 1949; Univ Toronto, MASc, 1954; Polytech Inst Brooklyn, PhD (chem), 1958. **Honors & Awards:** Life Achievement Award, North Jersy Sect, Am Chem-Soc; Achievement Award, Chinese Inst Eng, USA; Res Award, Sigma Xi; Achievement Award, Chinese Mat Soc. **Professional Experience:** PROF, POLYTECH UNIV, 1984-; vpres, Indust Technol Res Inst, Taiwan, 1981-1984; mem tech staff, Bell Labs, 1965-1981; group leader polymer chem, Interchem Corp, 1963-1965; sr chemist, Interchem Corp, 1961-1963; polymer chemist, Interchem Corp, 1959-1961; polymer chemist, Stand Oil Co, Ind, 1958-1959. **Memberships:** Am Chem Soc. **Research Statement & Publications:** Thermodynamics of polymer mixtures; viscoelasticity and surface chemistry of polymers; transport phenomena in polymers. **Mailing Address:** Dept Chem, Polytech Univ, 6 Metrotech Ctr, Brooklyn, NY 11201-2990. **Fax:** 718-260-3125.

KWENTUS, GERALD K(ENNETH), CHEMICAL ENGINEERING. **Personal Data:** b St Louis, Mo, January 10, 1937; m 1972, Carolyn; c Susanne & Karen. **Education:** Wash Univ, BS, 1960; Mass Inst Technol, PhD (chem eng), 1967. **Professional Experience:** Tech dir, Occidental Chem Corp, 1993-2000; mgr res & develop, Monsanto Chem Intermediates Co, 1982-1993; sr res group leader, Org Div, Monsanto Co, 1980-1982; sr res specialist, Org Div, Monsanto Co, 1975-1980; res specialist, Org Div, Monsanto Co, 1970-1975; sr res engr, Org Div, Monsanto Co, 1966-1970. **Memberships:** Am Inst Chem Engrs. **Research Statement & Publications:** Preparative chromatography; fractional distillation; chemical kinetics; heat transfer. **Mailing Address:** 274 Avalon Hills Dr, Fenton, MO 63026.

KWIATEK, JACK, INDUSTRIAL ORGANIC & POLYMER CHEMISTRY, HOMOGENEOUS CATALYTIC HYDROGENATION. **Personal Data:** b Kansas City, Mo, February 9, 1924; m 1948, Lottie; c Sandra (Simenhoz), Kim D & Sharon (Gadoth). **Education:** Univ Ill, BS, 1944; Cornell Univ, PhD (chem), 1950. **Honors & Awards:** Chemist of the Year, Cincinnati Sect, Am Chem Soc, 1974. **Professional Experience:** RETIRED; res scientist, USI Div, Quantum Chem Corp, 1988-1992; sr fel, Weizmann Inst Sci, 1968-1970; adj asst prof, Eve Col, Univ Cincinnati, 1961-1965; sr res assoc, Nat Distillers & Chem Corp, 1958-1988; res assoc, Gen Elec Co, 1954-1958; org res chemist, M W Kellogg Co, 1950-1954. **Memberships:** Am Chem Soc; Catalysis Soc. **Research Statement & Publications:** Homogeneous and heterogeneous catalysis; hydrogenation; syngas reactions; oxidation; carbonylation; coordination compounds; organometallics; free radical reactions; organophosphorus compounds; conductive polymers; biodegradable polymers. **Mailing Address:** 964 Fawn Lea Trl, Dayton, OH 45459.

KWIATKOWSKI, DAVID JOSEPH, BIOLOGY. **Education:** Mass Inst Technol, PhD (math), 1975; Columbia Univ, MD, 1979. **Professional Experience:** ASSOC PROF MED, HARVARD MED SCH, as of 2005; BRIGHAM & WOMEN'S HOSP, beginning 1991. **Memberships:** Am Soc Clin Invest. **Mailing Address:** 221 Longwood Ave LM 302, Boston, MA 02115. **Fax:** 617-734-2248. **E-Mail:** dk@rics.bwh.harvard.edu

KWIATOWSKI, DAVID J, GENETICS. **Education:** Mass Inst Technol, PhD (math), 1975; Columbia Univ, MD, 1979. **Professional Experience:** PROF, DEPT MED, HARVARD MED SCH, as of 2005; MED ONCOLOGIST, THORACIC ONCOL PROG, DANA-FARBER CANCER INST, as of 2005; PHYSICIAN, DIV HEMAT, BRIGHAM & WOMEN'S HOSP, as of 2005. **Mailing Address:** Div Exp Med Brigham & Women's Hosp, 221 Longwood Ave LM-302 LMRC, Boston, MA 02115. **Fax:** 617-355-9016. **E-Mail:** dk@rics.bwh.harvard.edu

KWIECINSKI, GARY GEORGE, REPRODUCTION & IMMUNOLOGY OF CHIROPTERA VITAMIN D REPRODUCTION FERTILITY & NUTRITIONAL PHYSIOLOGY OF MAMMALS. **Personal Data:** b Suffern, NY, August 15, 1952. **Education:** Cornell Univ, BS, 1975, PhD (zool), 1984; Rutgers Univ, MS, 1976. **Professional Experience:** Prin investr, NIH Nat Inst Child Health & Human Develop, 1992-; ASSOC PROF BIOL, UNIV SCRANTON, 1988-; res assoc biochem, Univ Wis, 1986-1988; res assoc & instr vet cell biol, Tufts Univ, 1983-1985; Instr vet anat, Cornell Univ, 1979-1983; teaching asst zool, Cornell Univ, 1977-1983; Teaching asst physiol, Rutgers Univ, 1975-1976. **Memberships:** Am Soc Mammalogists; Soc Study Reproduction; Endocrinol-Endocrine Soc. **Research Statement & Publications:** Investigate nutritional and physiological adaptation in mammals; endocrinological aspects of the reproductive, thyroidal and immunological perturbations of seasonal cycling that accentuate general principles. **Mailing Address:** Dept Biol Univ Scranton, Scranton, PA 18510-4625. **Fax:** 717-941-7572. **E-Mail:** ggk301@scranton.edu

KWIRAM, ALVIN L, PHYSICAL CHEMISTRY, CHEMICAL PHYSICS. **Personal Data:** b Man, April 28, 1937; American citizen; m 1964, Verla; c Andrew B & Sidney M. **Education:** Walla Walla Col, BS (chem) & BA (physics), 1958; Calif Inst Technol, PhD (chem), 1963. **Honorary Degrees:** PhD, Andrew Univ, 1995. **Honors & Awards:** Eastman-Kodak Sci Award, 1962; Alfred A Noyes Award, Caltech, 1962-1963; Guggenheim fel, 1977-1978; Sloan fel, 1968-1970; Univ-Indust Rel Award, Coun Chem Res, 1986. **Professional Experience:** Chair elect, chair, past chair, council res policy graduate educstion, NASULGC, 2001-2003; mem, Adv Bd Graduate Education, 2001-; mem, Pac NW Nat Lab, Lab Adv Comt, 2000-; mem, Div Review Comt, Am Chem Soc, 1998-2002; prof chem, Univ Wash mem, Sci Prog Comt, 1994-1999; chair elect, chair, past chair Chem Div, AAAS, 1991-1994; vprovost res, Univ Wash, 1990-2002; from vprovost to sr vprovost, Univ Wash, 1987-1990; counr & exec comt mem, Div Phys Chem, Am Chem Soc, 1986-; chmn, Coun Chem Res, 1982-1983; mem, founding comt & bd dirs, Coun Chem Res, 1980-1984; mem, bd of dir, Lumera Corp; chmn dept, Univ Wash, 1977-1987; mem, Exec

Comt & secy-treas, Div Phys Chem, Am Chem Soc, 1976-1986; PROF CHEM, UNIV WASH, 1975-; assoc prof, Univ Wash, 1970-1975; Alfred D Sloan fel, 1968-1970; lectr, Harvard Univ, 1967-1970; instr chem, Harvard Univ, 1964-1967; res assoc physics, Stanford Univ, 1963-1964; instr & res assoc chem, Calif Inst Technol, 1962-1963; Woodrow-Wilson fel, 1958. **Memberships:** Am Chem Soc; fel Am Phys Soc; Sigma Xi; fel AAAS. **Research Statement & Publications:** Magnetic resonance in solids and molecular crystals; electron-nuclear double resonance; optical detection of magnetic resonance; structure and dynamics in ground and excited states of molecules. **Mailing Address:** Dept Chem Box 351700, Univ Wash, Seattle, WA 98195-1700. **E-Mail:** kwiram@u.washington.edu

KWITEROVICH, PETER O, LIPOPROTEIN METABOLISM. **Personal Data:** b Danville, Pa, June 24, 1940; m 1965, c 3. **Education:** Holy Cross Col, AB, 1962; Dartmouth Med Sch, BMS, 1964; Johns Hopkins Univ, MD, 1966. **Honors & Awards:** Blakeslee Award, Am Heart Asn. **Professional Experience:** Mem nutrit study sect, NIH, 1987-; chmn, Dietary Intervention Study C, 1987; PROF PEDIAT & MED, JOHNS HOPKINS UNIV MED SCH, 1984-; chief lipidres, Athereosclerosis Unit, 1976; from asst prof to assoc prof, Johns Hopkins Univ Med Sch, 1972-1984; prin investr lipidres clin, Johns Hopkins Univ, 1971-; resident pediat, Johns Hopkins Hosp, 1970-1972; staff assoc lipoprotein res, Molecular Dis Br, NIH, 1967-1970; intern pediat, Children's Hosp Med Ctr, 1966-1967. **Memberships:** Soc Pediat Res; Am Soc Clin Invest. **Mailing Address:** Dept Pediat, Johns Hopkins Univ Med Sch, 550 Bldg Ste 308, Baltimore, MD 21205-2109. **Fax:** 410-955-6657. **E-Mail:** pkwitero@jhmi.edu

KWITOWSKI, PAUL THOMAS, INORGANIC CHEMISTRY. **Personal Data:** b Buffalo, NY, November 14, 1939; m 1963, c 4. **Education:** Canisius Col, BS, 1961; Univ Wis, PhD (inorg chem), 1967. **Professional Experience:** PROF CHEM, NIAGARA COMMUNITY COL, 1980-; chmn, dept phys sci, Niagara Community Col, beginning 1971; assoc prof, Dept Phys Sci, 1969-1980; res chemist, Airco-Speer Res Labs, NY, 1966-1969. **Memberships:** Am Chem Soc. **Research Statement & Publications:** Gas chromatography; catalysis of organic reactions; halocarbon and organometallic chemistry; spectroscopy; chemistry of refractive compounds; chemical vapor deposition. **Mailing Address:** Dept Chem, Niagara Community Col, Rm C-155, Buffalo, NY 14226. **E-Mail:** kwitowsk@niagaracc.suny.edu

KWITTER, KAREN BETH, GASEOUS NEBULAE, EVOLUTION OF LOW-MASS STARS. **Personal Data:** b Brooklyn, NY, March 20, 1951; m 1979, Steven; c Randall & Aaron. **Education:** Wellesley Col, BA, 1972; Univ Calif, Los Angeles, MA, 1974, PhD (astron), 1979. **Professional Experience:** EBENEZER FITCH PROF ASTRON, WILLIAMS COL, 1998-; PROF, ASTRON, WILLIAMS COL, 1991-; chmn, Dept Astron, Williams Col, 1988-1991, 1994-1996, 2001-2004; assoc prof astron, Williams Col, 1986-1991; vis asst prof astron, Univ Ill, 1983-1984; Harlow Shapley vis lectr, Am Astron Soc, 1981-; asst prof astron, Williams Col, 1979-1986. **Memberships:** Am Astron Soc; Sigma Xi; Int Astron Union; AAAS; Astron Soc Pac. **Research Statement & Publications:** Gaseous nebulae, their chemical compositions and physical conditions, including nebulae around Wolf-Rayet stars and planetary nebulae; stellar evolution from planetary nebulae nucleus to sub dwarf to white dwarf; chemistry evolution of galaxies; published over 15 articles. **Mailing Address:** Dept Astron, Williams Col 33 Lab Campus Dr, Williamstown, MA 01267-2693.

KWO, JUEINAI, CONDENSED MATTER PHYSICS. **Personal Data:** b Taipei, Taiwan, October 1, 1953. **Education:** Nat Taiwan Univ, BS, 1975; Stanford Univ, MS, 1977, PhD (appl physics), 1981. **Professional Experience:** RES SCIENTIST, AT&T BELL LABS, 1981-. **Memberships:** Am Phys Soc. **Mailing Address:** AT&T Bell Labs, 1D-232, Murray Hill, NJ 07974.

KWOCK, LESTER, BIOCHEMISTRY, RADIATION BIOCHEMISTRY. **Personal Data:** b San Francisco, Calif, June 21, 1942; m 1968, c 1. **Education:** San Jose State Univ, BS, 1965; San Diego State Univ, MS, 1968; Univ Calif, Santa Barbara, PhD (chem), 1973. **Professional Experience:** PROF RADIOL, UNIV NC, CHAPEL HILL, as of 2003; Nat Cancer Inst grant, Tufts-New England Med Ctr, 1976-; ASST PROF, SCH MED, TUFTS UNIV, 1976-; NIH fel, Sch Med, Tufts Univ & Tufts-New England Med Ctr, 1974-1976; instr radiation biol, Sch Med, Tufts Univ, 1973-1976. **Memberships:** Am Chem Soc; Radiation Res Soc; Sigma Xi; AAAS. **Research Statement & Publications:** Membrane transport; effects of ionizing radiation on biological systems; radioprotectors and radiosensitizers for normal and neoplastic cells. **Mailing Address:** Dept Radiol, Sch Med Univ NC, Chapel Hill, NC 27599-7510. **Fax:** 919-966-2859. **E-Mail:** kwock@med.unc.edu

KWOK, CLYDE CHI KAI, MECHANICAL ENGINEERING. **Personal Data:** b Shanghai, China, May 26, 1937; m 1962, c 1. **Education:** McGill Univ, BEng, 1961, MEng, 1962, PhD, 1967. **Professional Experience:** RETIRED; prof eng, Sir George Williams Campus, Concordia Univ, 1977-1996; assoc prof mech eng, Sir George Williams Campus, Concordia Univ, 1969-1977; prin scientist, Aviation Elec Ltd, 1964-1969; res asst mech eng, McGill Univ, 1961-1964. **Memberships:** Am Soc Mech Engrs; Am Inst Aeronaut & Astronaut. **Research Statement & Publications:** Research and development of basic fluidic devices particularly the design and analysis of vortex type devices; fluid control elements and systems. **Mailing Address:** Dept Mech Eng, 2600 Pierre DuPuy Ave Apt 232, Montreal, PQ H3Z 3R6, Can.

KWOK, HOI S, DISPLAY TECHNOLOGIES, MATERIALS. **Personal Data:** b Hong Kong, China, March 1, 1951; American citizen; m 1978, Ying Hung Tung; c 3. **Education:** Northwestern Univ, BS, 1973; Harvard Univ, MS, 1975, PhD (physics), 1978. **Honors & Awards:** Presidential Young Investr Award, 1984. **Professional Experience:** PROF ENG, HONG KONG UNIV SCI & TECHNOL, 1992-; sci adv, Photochem Res Assocs, 1982-1989 & Excel Technologies, 1987-1992; Prin investr grants, NSF, USDept Energy, 1981-1992; from asst prof to prof eng, State Univ NY, Buffalo, 1980-1992; Res felchem, Lawrence Berkeley Lab, Univ Calif, 1978-1980. **Memberships:** Am Phys Soc; sr mem Inst Elec & Electronics Engrs; Am Chem Soc; fel OpticalSoc Am. **Research Statement & Publications:** Laser spectroscopy of semiconductors and superconductors; display technologies. **Mailing Address:** Dept Elec Eng, Hong Kong Univ Sci & Technol, Clearwater Bay Kowloon Hong Kong, China.

KWOK, JOHNNY H, AERONAUTICS. **Honors & Awards:** Exceptional Eng Achievement Medal, NASA, 2005. **Professional Experience:** STAFF, JET PROPULSION LABS, as of 2005. **Mailing Address:** Jet Propulsion Labs, 4800 Oake Grove Dr M/S 301-140L, Pasadena, CA 91109-8001. **Fax:** 818-354-3437.

KWOK, MUNSON ARTHUR, ATOMIC & MOLECULAR PHYSICS, FLUIDS. **Personal Data:** b San Francisco, Calif, April 28, 1941; m 1977, Suellen. **Education:** Stanford Univ, BS, 1962, MS, 1963, PhD (aeronaut & astronaut), 1967. **Professional Experience:** SR SCIENTIST, AEROSPACE CORP, as of 2003; dept dir, Aerospace Corp, beginning 1987; mgr, Aerospace Corp, 1984-1987; res scientist, Aerospace Corp, 1977-1984; staff scientist, Aerospace Corp, 1976-1977; mem, tech staff, Aerospace Corp, 1968-1976; NSF fel, Stanford Univ, 1967-1968; chair, Plasmadynamics & Lasers Tech Comt, Am Inst Aeronaut & Astronaut. **Memberships:** Am Phys Soc; Soc Photo-Optical Instrumentation Engrs; sr mem Am Inst Aeronaut & Astronaut; Am Soc Mech Engrs; Optical Soc Am; Chinese Am Engrs & Scientists Asn (pres, 1998-). **Research Statement & Publications:** Fluid mechanics; thermophysics; gas lasers; chemical lasers; kinetic theory; plasmas; high temperature gasdynamics; propulsion; microelectromechanics. **Mailing Address:** Aerospace Corp, PO Box 92957 M2 272, Los Angeles, CA 90009-2957. **Fax:** 310-336-1636. **E-Mail:** mumson_kwok@qmailz.aero.org

KWOK, SUN, ASTRONOMY. **Personal Data:** b Hong Kong, September 15, 1949; Canadian citizen; m 1973, Emily; c Roberta Wing-Yue & Kelly Wing-Hang. **Education:** McMaster Univ, BS, 1970; Univ Minn, Minneapolis, MS, 1972, PhD (physics), 1974. **Professional Experience:** DISTINGUISHED RES FEL, INST ASTRON & ASTROPHYSICS, ACADEMIA SINICA, TAIWAN, 2003-; Killiam fel, Can Coun Arts, 2000-2002; vis fel, Joint Inst Lab Astrophys, Univ Colo, 1989-1990; prof astron, Univ Calgary, 1988-2005; from asst prof to assoc prof, Univ Calgary, 1983-1988; res assoc astron, Herzberg Inst Astrophys, 1978-1983; res assoc, Ctr Res Exp Space Sci, York Univ, 1977-1978; asst prof, Dept Physics, Univ Minn, Duluth, 1976-1977; fel astron, Dept Physics, Univ BC, 1974-1976. **Memberships:** Am Astron Soc; Can Astron Soc; Int Astron Union; Astron Soc Pac. **Research Statement & Publications:** Stellar mass loss; the late stages of stellar evolution; planetary nebulae; infrared astronomy. **Mailing Address:** Inst Astron & Astrophysics, Academia Sinica, PO Box 23-141, Taipei, 10617, Taiwan. **E-Mail:** kwok@asiaa.sinica.edu.tw

KWOK, THOMAS YU-KIU, ELECTRONICS MATERIALS, VLSI TECHNOLOGY, ELECTRONIC COMMERCE & TECHNOLOGY. **Personal Data:** b Hong Kong, February 16, 1951; m 1981, Lily; c Jennifer & Angela. **Education:** Mass Inst Technol, BS, 1976, MS, 1978, PhD (mat sci), 1982. **Professional Experience:** RES STAFF MEM, IBM RES DIV, THOMAS J WATSON RES CTR, 1981-. **Memberships:** Am Phys Soc; Inst Elec & Electronics Engrs; Mat Res Soc; ACM. **Research Statement & Publications:** Grain boundary structure and diffusion; microstructure of metallic thin films and submicron metal lines; electromigration, mechanical properties and reliability of multilevel interconnection; very-large-scale integration metallization; molecular dynamics and computer simulations; electronic commerce, electronic contracts, electronic document processing technology. **Mailing Address:** Int Bus Mach Corp, 19 Skyline Dr, Hawthorne, NY 10532. **Fax:** 914-784-7455. **E-Mail:** kwok@us.ibm.com

KWOK, WO KONG, ORGANIC CHEMISTRY, POLYMER CHEMISTRY. **Personal Data:** b Hong Kong, January 13, 1936; m 1963. **Education:** Nat Taiwan Univ, BS, 1958; ETenn State Univ, MS, 1963; Ill Inst Technol, PhD (phys & org chem), 1967. **Honors & Awards:** DuPont Mkt Excellence Award, 1996. **Professional Experience:** AT, MAT SCI DIV, ARGONNE NAT LAB, as of 2003; RES ASSOC, CHESTNUT RUN, E I DU PONT Del NEMOURS & CO INC, 1995-; sr res assoc, Kinston, 1991-1995; res assoc, Kinston, 1984-1990; SR RES CHEMIST, CHESTNUT RUN, E I DU PONT Del NEMOURS & CO INC, 1981-; sr res chemist, Kinston, 1976-1984; res chemist, Exp Sta, E I Du Pont Del Nemours & Co, 1966-1976; Ill Inst Technol Res Inst fel, 1965-1967; chemist, SChina Bleaching & Dyeing Factory, 1958-1961. **Memberships:** Am Chem Soc. **Research Statement & Publications:** Elimination reaction kinetics and mechanism; polymer degradation mechanism; nonwoven technology. **Mailing Address:** Mat Sci Div, Argonne Nat Lab, Argonne, IL 60439.

KWOLEK, STEPHANIE LOUISE, POLYMER CHEMISTRY & PROCESSING. **Personal Data:** b New Kensington, Pa, July 31, 1923. **Education:** Carnegie Inst Technol, BS, 1946. **Honorary Degrees:** DSc, Worcester Polytech Inst, 1981. **Honors & Awards:** Publ Award, Am Chem Soc, 1959, Creative Invention Award, 1980; Howard NPotts Medal, Franklin Inst, 1976; Mat Achievement Citation, Am Soc Metals, 1978; ChemPioneer Award, Am Inst Chemists, 1980; Eng/Technol Award, Soc Plastics Engrs, 1985; Harold-DeWitt Smith Mem Award, Am Soc Testing & Mat, 1988; George Lubin Mem Award, SocAdvan Mat & Process Engrs, 1991; Jack Kilby Award, Kilby Awards Found, 1994; Am InnovatorAward, Patent & Trademark Off, 1995; Nat Medal Technol, 1996; Perkin Medal, Soc ChemIndust, 1997. **Professional Experience:** RETIRED; consult; res assoc, E I du Pont de Nemours Co, Inc, 1974-1986; from res chemist to sr res chemist, E I du Pont de Nemours Co, Inc, 1959-1974; chemist, FibersDept, Pioneering Res Lab, Exp Sta, E I du Pont de Nemours Co, Inc, 1946-1959. **Memberships:** Am Chem Soc; Sigma Xi; Am Inst Chem. **Research Statement & Publications:** Condensation polymers; high temperature polymers; low temperature interfacial and solution polymerizations; high tenacity and high modulus fibers and films; liquid crystalline polymers, solutions and melts. **Mailing Address:** 312 Spalding Rd, Wilmington, DE 19803-2422.

KWON, BYOUNG SE, IMMUNE RESPONSES & DISEASE STATES. **Personal Data:** b Seoul, Korea, December 17, 1947; American citizen; m 1971, Myung; c David H, Ed E & Pat M. **Education:** Seoul Nat Univ, DDS, 1972; Med Col Ga, Augusta, PhD (microbiol), 1981. **Honors & Awards:** Nat Res Serv Award, NIH; Swebilius Cancer Res Award, Yale; Feasibility Grant Prog Award. **Professional Experience:** DIR, IMMUNOMODULATION RES CTR, ULSAN, 1999; scientist, Walther Oncol Ctr, Ind Univ Sch Med & prof, Dept Microbiol & Immunol, 1993; assoc prof, Walther Oncol Ctr, Ind Univ Sch Med, assoc prof, Dept Microbiol & Immunol, 1988-1993; young investr res award, NIH, 1985-1988; feasibility grant prog award, Am Diabetes Asn Inc, 1985-1987; assoc scientist, Guthrie Res Inst, 1984-1988; Swebilius cancer res award, Yale Univ, 1983-1984; assoc scientist, Dept Human Genetics, Yale Univ Sch Med, 1983-1984; nat res serv award, NIH 1982-1983. **Memberships:** Am Soc Microbiol; Sigma Xi; AAAS; Am Diabetes Asn; Am Asn Immunologists; Nat Orgn Albinism & Hypopigmentation; Int Soc Exp Hemat. **Research Statement & Publications:** Immune cell functions in normal immune responses and disease states; molecular genetic studies on human pigmentation and its disorders. **Mailing Address:** Immunomodulation Res Ctr, PO Box 18 Moo-Keo Dong Nam-Ku, Ulsan, 680-749, Korea. **Fax:** 052-259-2740. **E-Mail:** bskwon@uou.ulsan.ac.kr

KWON, JOON TAEK, process chemistry-catalysis, applied instrumental analysis; deceased, see previous edition for last biography

KWON, TAI HYUNG, SOLID STATE PHYSICS. **Personal Data:** b Yechon, Korea, September 15, 1932; m 1969, Young-Ju Choi; c Wade J. **Education:** Univ Ga, BS, 1963, MS, 1965, PhD (physics), 1967. **Professional Experience:** PROF EMER PHYSICS, UNIV MONTEVALLO, as of 2004; prof physics, Univ Montevallo, beginning 1990; Frederick Gardner CottrellRes Corp grant, 1971-; from asst prof to assoc prof, Univ Montevallo, 1969-1990; res fel, Ga InstTechnol, 1967-1969. **Memberships:** Am Phys Soc; Am Asn Physics Teachers. **Research Statement & Publications:** Statistical physics; spin dynamics; neutron scattering; Heisenberg system; magnetism; lattice dynamics; anharmonicity; thermoelastic properties of ionic crystals. **Mailing Address:** Dept Physics, Univ Montevallo, Physics Bldg, Montevallo, AL 35115. **Fax:** 205-665-9495. **E-Mail:** thkwon@aol.com

KWON-CHUNG, KYUNG JOO, MEDICAL MYCOLOGY. **Personal Data:** b Seoul, Korea, October 5, 1933; m 1957, c 3. **Education:** Ewha Womans Univ, Korea, BS, 1956, MS, 1958; Univ Wis, MS, 1963, PhD (bact), 1965. **Honors & Awards:** Director's Award, NIH, 1977; Award, Int SocHuman & Animal Mycol, 1982; Dir Award, NIH, 1996; Rhoda Benham Award, Med Mycol Soc Am, 1996. **Professional Experience:** HEAD, MOLECULAR MICROBIOL SECT, LCI, NAT INST ALLERGY &INFECTIOUS DIS, NIH, 1995-; consult, Armed Forces Inst Path, Wash, DC, 1976-1986; res microbiologist, Molecular Microbiol Sect, Lci, Nat Inst Allergy & Infectious Dis, NIH, 1968-1994; vis fel med mycol, NIH, 1966-1968; fel, Univ Wis, 1965; res asst bact, Univ Wis, 1961-1965; instr microbiol, Ewha Womans Univ, 1959-1961. **Memberships:** Mycol Soc Am; Am Soc Microbiol; Med Mycol Soc Am; Int Soc Human &Animal Mycol. **Research Statement & Publications:** Morphology, genetics, molecular biology and pathogenicity of fungi. **Mailing Address:** Molecular Biol Sect, NIH, Nat Inst Allergy & Infectious Diseases, Bldg 10, Rm 11N103, Bethesda, MD 20892. **Fax:** 301-402-1003. **E-Mail:** june_kwon-chung@nih.gov

KWONG, DIM-LEE D, ELECTRICAL ENGINEERING. **Education:** Natl Tsing Hua Univ, BS, 1977, MS, 1979; Rice Univ, PhD, 1982. **Professional Experience:** PROF, DEPT ELEC ENG, UNIV TEX, as of 2005. **Mailing Address:** Univ Tex Austin, 10100 Burnet Rd Bldg 160, Austin, TX 78758. **Fax:** 512-471-4345. **E-Mail:** dlkwong@mail.utexas.edu

KWONG, MAN KAM, MATHEMATICS. **Personal Data:** b Canton, China, February 2, 1947; m 1970, c 2. **Education:** Univ Hong Kong, BSc, 1968; Univ Chicago, MSc, 1970, PhD (math), 1973. **Professional Experience:** MEMBER TECH STAFF, LUCENT TECHNOL, as of 2002; adj prof, Sch Comput Sci, Telecommunications & Info Syst, Depaul Univ, beginning 2000; scientist, Argonne Nat Lab, beginning 1987; spec term appointment, Argonne Nat Lab, 1985-1987; resident scientist, Argonne Nat Lab, 1982-1983; from asst prof to prof math, Northern Ill Univ, 1977-1989; lectr math, Hong Kong Polytech, 1975-1977; lectr math, Hong Kong Baptist Col, 1973-1975. **Memberships:** Sigma Xi; Am Math Soc; Soc Indust & Appl Math. **Research Statement & Publications:** Ordinary differential equations; functional analysis; inequalities; image processing; scientific computation. **Mailing Address:** Sch Comput Sci, Telecommunications & Info Systs, DePauls Univ, 243 S Wabash Ave, Chicago, IL 60604. **E-Mail:** mkkwong@cs.depaul.edu

KWONG, YUI-HOI HARRIS, GRAPH THEORY, INTEGER SEQUENCES. **Personal Data:** b Hong Kong, October 10, 1957. **Education:** Univ Mich, BS, 1980, MS, 1981; Univ Pa, PhD (math), 1987. **Professional Experience:** PROF MATH & COMPUT SCI, STATE UNIV NY, FREDONIA, 1999-; assoc prof math & comput sci, State Univ NY, Fredonia, 1992-1999; asst prof, State Univ NY, Fredonia, 1987-1992. **Memberships:** Am Math Soc; Math Asn Am; Sigma Xi. **Research Statement & Publications:** Graph labeling; extremal graph theory; divisibility; congruences of integer sequences; combinatorial proof. **Mailing Address:** Dept Math & Comput Sci, State Univ NY Col Fredonia, Fredonia, NY 14063.

KWUN, KYUNG WHAN, MATHEMATICS. **Personal Data:** b Seoul, Korea, March 7, 1929; m 1957, c 3. **Education:** Seoul Nat Univ, BS, 1952; Univ Mich, MS, 1954, PhD (math), 1958. **Professional Experience:** PROF MATH, MICH STATE UNIV, 1966-; assoc prof, Mich State Univ, 1965-1966; mem, Inst Advan Study, 1964-1965; assoc prof, Fla State Univ, 1964-1965; vis lectr, Fla State Univ, 1962-1964; Vis lectr, Univ Wis, 1961-1962; from instr to asst prof, Seoul NatUniv, 1960-1962; vis assoc prof, Seoul Nat Univ, 1959-1960; res assoc, Tulane Univ, 1958-1959; Instr math, Univ Mich, 1957-1958. **Memberships:** Am Math Soc. **Research Statement & Publications:** Topology, particularly theory of manifolds. **Mailing Address:** Pohang Inst Sci Tech, PO Box 125, Pohang 790-600, South Korea.

KYAME, JOSEPH JOHN, MATHEMATICAL PHYSICS. **Personal Data:** b New Orleans, La, March 12, 1924; wid, c 1. **Education:** Tulane Univ, BS, 1944, MS, 1945; Mass Inst Technol, PhD (physics), 1948. **Professional Experience:** EMER PROF PHYSICS, TULANE UNIV, as of 2006; assoc prof, Tulane Univ, beginning 1958; asst prof, Tulane Univ, 1948-1958; asst & instr, Tulane Univ, 1944-1945. **Memberships:** Am Phys Soc; Sigma Xi. **Research Statement & Publications:** Electromagnetic theory; piezoelectricity; thermodynamics. **Mailing Address:** 32 Warbler St, New Orleans, LA 70124. **Fax:** 504-282-4518.

KYANKA, GEORGE HARRY, MECHANICAL ENGINEERING, WOOD SCIENCE. **Personal Data:** b Syracuse, NY, July 17, 1941; m 1966, c 2. **Education:** Syracuse Univ, BS, 1962, MS, 1966, PhD (mech eng), 1975. **Professional Experience:** DIR, RENEWABLE MAT INST, as of 2006; chmn dept, Col Environ Sci & Forestry, State Univ Ny, beginning 1985; PROF WOOD ENG, COL ENVIRON SCI & FORESTRY, STATE UNIV NY, 1980-; proj dir, Weyerhaeuser Corp, 1978-; dir, Educ Opportunity Prog Forestry, 1973-1976; consult engr, 1970-; adj prof, Onondaga Col Archit, 1970-; proj dir, NSF, 1970-1973, 1976-; from asst prof to assoc prof, Col Environ Sci & Forestry, State Univ NY, 1968-1980; asst prof mech tech, Onondaga Col, 1967-1968; NSF res fel, Syracuse Univ, 1967; res asst aero eng, Syracuse Univ, 1964-1966; res engr gas turbines, Caterpillar Tractor Co, 1962-1964. **Memberships:** Am Soc Mech Engrs; Am Soc Testing & Mat; Soc Exp Stress Analysis; Forest Prod Res Soc; Am Acad Mech; Soc Exp Mech. **Research Statement & Publications:** Mechanical properties of wood and wood products; testing and design of wood products; professional responsibility and products liability in product design; wood in architecture and art. **Mailing Address:** Col Environ Sci & Forestry, State Univ NY, 320 Bray Hall, One forest Dr, Syracuse, NY 13210-2778. **E-Mail:** ghkyanka@esf.edu

KYBA, EVAN PETER, ORGANIC CHEMISTRY, SYNTHETIC MEDICINAL CHEMISTRY. **Personal Data:** b Canora, Sask, June 27, 1940; m 1962, c 1. **Education:** Univ Sask, BA, 1962; Univ Ala, PhD (org chem), 1971. **Professional Experience:** VPRES PHARMA RES, ALCON LAB INC, as of 2006; sr dir med chem, Alcon Lab Inc, beginning 1990; dir, Alcon Lab Inc, 1988-1990; prof chem, Univ Tex, Austin, 1985-1987; from asst prof to assoc prof, Univ Tex, Austin, 1972-1985; Nat Res Coun Can fel, Univ Calif, Los Angeles, 1971-1972; teacher chem, Regina Col Inst, Sask, 1962-1965. **Memberships:** Am Chem Soc; Chem Soc. **Research Statement & Publications:** Reactive intermediates; organophosphorus chemistry; stereochemistry; synthesis of unusual small heterocycles and multiheteromacrocycles; homogeneous catalysis; organometallic chemistry; medicinal chemistry. **Mailing Address:** Alcon Labs Inc, 6201 S Freeway R2-33, Ft Worth, TX 76134-2001.

KYBETT, BRIAN DAVID, PHYSICAL CHEMISTRY. **Personal Data:** b Oxford, Eng, May 10, 1938; m 1963, Gaynor; c Gareth S. **Education:** Univ Wales, BSc, 1960, PhD (chem), 1963. **Professional Experience:** DIR, ENERGY RES UNIT, UNIV REGINA, REGINA, as of 2005; PROF DEPT CHEM & BIOCHEM, UNIV REGINA, as of 2000; prof chem & dir, energy res unit, Univ Regina, beginning 1981; from asst prof to assoc prof, Energy Res Unit, Univ Regina, 1965-1981; res assoc chem, Rice Univ, 1963-1965. **Memberships:** Chem Inst Can; Royal Soc Chem; Am Chem Soc; Solar Energy Soc Can Inc; IntSolar Energy Soc. **Research Statement & Publications:** Lattice energies; thermochemistry; reactivity of coal; surfactants; renewable energy; environmental chemistry. **Mailing Address:** Dept Chem & Biochem, Univ Regina, 3737 Wascana Pkwy, Regina, SK S4S 0A2, Can. **Fax:** 306-337-2409. **E-Mail:** kybettbd@cas.uregina.ca

KYBURG, HENRY, UNCERTAIN INFERENCE INDUCTIVE LOGIC. **Personal Data:** b New York, NY, October 9, 1928; m 1960, c 8. **Education:** Yale Univ, BA, 1948; Columbia Univ, MA, 1952, PhD (philos), 1955. **Professional Experience:** RES SCI, INST HUMAN & MACH INTEL, UNIV ROCHESTER, 2001-; prof comput sci, Univ Rochester, beginning 1986; prof philos, Univ Rochester, beginning 1963; res assoc, Rockefeller Univ, 1961-1962; asst prof math, Wesleyan Univ, 1958-1961. **Memberships:** Fel AAAS; Am Philos Asn; Am Math Soc; fel Am Asn Artificial Intel; Asn Comput Mach. **Research Statement & Publications:** Uncertain inference; inductive logic; representation of uncertainty; decision under uncertainty. **Mailing Address:** Inst Human & Mach Intel, Univ Rochester, Lyons, NY 14489.

KYDD, PAUL HARRIMAN, PHYSICAL CHEMISTRY, CHEMICAL ENGINEERING. **Personal Data:** b New Haven, Conn, November 25, 1930; m 1956, Priscilla Clisham; c David M & Andrew H. **Education:** Princeton Univ, AB, 1952; Harvard Univ, MA, 1953, PhD (phys chem), 1956. **Professional Experience:** PRES, PARTNERSHIPS LTD INC, 1983-; vpres technol, Hydrocarbon Res, Inc, 1975-1983; mgr chem processes, Gen Elec Res & Develop Ctr, 1966-1975; lectr, HarvardUniv, 1959-1960; phys chemist, Gen Elec Res Lab, 1957-1966; Fel phys chem, Harvard Univ, 1956-1957. **Memberships:** Am Chem Soc. **Research Statement & Publications:** Coal liquifaction, gasification; petroleum production and refining; gas turbines, power generation; renewable resources, chemical intermediates; microcomputer applications; technology assessment; technology information management; contract research management. **Mailing Address:** Partnerships Ltd Inc, PO Box 6042, Lawrenceville, NJ 08648. **Fax:** 609-252-1288.

KYDD, RONALD A, CHEMISTRY. **Education:** Univ BC, BSc, 1963 & PhD, 1969. **Professional Experience:** PROF EMER, DEPT CHEM, UNIV CALGARY, as of 2004. **Research Statement & Publications:** Prepare and characterize new catalytic materials; synthesis, characterization and testing of metal-oxide-based catalysts; spectroscopic techniques; surfaces. **Mailing Address:** Dept Chem, Univ Calgary, 2500 Univ Dr NW, Calgary, AB T2N 1N4, Can. **Fax:** 403-289-9488. **E-Mail:** kydd@ucalgary.ca

KYDES, ANDY STEVE, NUMERICAL ANALYSIS, ENERGY SYSTEMS ANALYSIS. **Personal Data:** b Spilia, Greece, January 21, 1945; American citizen; c 2. **Education:** Harvard Univ, AB, 1968; State Univ NY, Stony Brook, MS, 1973, PhD (numerical analysis), 1974. **Professional Experience:** SR MODELING ANALYST, ENERGY INFO ADMIN, US DEPT ENERGY, as of 1999; energy syst analyst, Dept Energy & Environ, Brookhaven Nat Lab, beginning 1976; asst prof math, State Univ NY, Stony Brook, 1974-1976; instr math & physics, Milton Acad, Mass, 1968-1971. **Memberships:** Oper Res Soc Am; Inst Mgt Sci. **Research Statement & Publications:** Energy systems analysis; multi-criteria analysis; optimization. **Mailing Address:** Energy Info Admin, US Dept Energy, 1000 Independence Ave, SW, Washington, DC 20585. **E-Mail:** andy.kydes@eia.doe.gov

KYDONIEFS, ANASTASIOS D, APPLIED MATHEMATICS, CONTINUUM MECHANICS. **Personal Data:** b Athens, Greece, March 6, 1928; m 1953, c 2. **Education:** Univ Nottingham, MSc, 1965, PhD (theoret mech), 1967. **Professional Experience:** ASSOC PROF MATH, LEHIGH UNIV, 1973-; asst prof math, Lehigh Univ, 1968-1973; Res fel theoret mech, Univ Nottingham, 1967-1969; sr res asst, Univ Nottingham, 1967-1968. **Research Statement & Publications:** Finite elasticity and its applications to biomechanics. **Mailing Address:** Dept Math & Physics, Aristotle Univ Thessalonike Sch Technol, Thessaloniki 54006, Greece.

KYHOS, DONALD WILLIAM, PLANT TAXONOMY, PLANT CYTOGENETICS. **Personal Data:** b Los Angeles, Calif, April 10, 1929; m 1961, c 3. **Education:** Whittier Col, AB, 1951, MS, 1956; Univ Calif, Los Angeles, PhD (bot), 1964. **Professional Experience:** PROF EMER BOT, UNIV CALIF, DAVIS, as of 2001; prof biot, Univ Calif, Davis, beginning 1974; Australian Res Grant Comt fel, 1972; from asst prof to assoc prof, Univ Calif, Davis, 1965-1974; NIH fel biol, Stanford Univ, 1964-1965. **Memberships:** Am Soc Plant Taxon; Bot Soc Am; Soc Study Evolution; Sigma Xi. **Research Statement & Publications:** Plant systematics and evolutionary cytogenetics. **Mailing Address:** 909 Fordham Dr, Davis, CA 95616. **E-Mail:** dwkyhos@ucdavis.edu

KYLE, BENJAMIN G(AYLE), CHEMICAL ENGINEERING. **Personal Data:** b Atlanta, Ga, December 4, 1927; m 1952, c 4. **Education:** Ga Inst Technol, BChE, 1950; Univ Fla, MSE, 1955, PhD (chem eng), 1958. **Professional Experience:** PROF EMER CHEM ENG, KANS STATE UNIV, as of 2004; prof chem eng, Kans State Univ, beginning 1964; from asst prof to assocprof, Kans State Univ, 1958-1964. **Memberships:** Am Chem Soc; Am Inst Chem Engrs. **Research Statement & Publications:** Thermodynamics; mass transfer. **Mailing Address:** Dept Chem Eng, Kans State Univ, Manhattan, KS 66506-5102. **E-Mail:** che@ksu.edu

KYLE, HERBERT LEE, EARTH RADIATION BUDGET, SOLAR PHYSICS. **Personal Data:** b Monmouth, Ill, June 28, 1930; m 1960, c 1. **Education:** Univ Ariz, BS, 1954; Univ NC, MS, 1959, PhD (atomic physics), 1964. **Professional Experience:** PRIN INVESTR, GODDARD SPACE FLIGHT CTR, as of 2001; SPACE PHYSICIST, GODDARD SPACE FLIGHT CTR, NASA, 1959-. **Memberships:** Am Phys Soc; Am Geophys Union. **Research Statement & Publications:** Remote sensing of the earth's radiation budget; remote sensing for the cloud properties and cloud cover; atmospheric radiatine transfer theory and numerical analysis; measurement of the solar constant and it's variations; application of computers to scientific problems; creation of satellite climate data sets with emphasis on long-term sensor calibration and numerical analysis. **Mailing Address:** Goddard Space Flight Ctr, NASA, Code 636, Greenbelt, MD 20771. **E-Mail:** lkyle@daac.gsfc.nasa.gov

KYLE, MARTIN LAWRENCE, CHEMICAL ENGINEERING. **Personal Data:** b Akron, Ohio, January 2, 1935; m 1957, Evelyn Sveda; c Martin, Karen, Joan. **Education:** Univ Notre Dame, BS, 1956; Purdue Univ, MS, 1961; Univ Chicago, MBA, 1971. **Professional Experience:** ASST LAB DIR, ARGONNE NAT LAB, 1978-; chem engr, Argonne Nat Lab, 1960-1978; Chem engr, E I DuPont Del Nemours & Co, 1956-1957. **Memberships:** Am Chem Soc. **Research Statement & Publications:** Battery development; solar energy; coal technology. **Mailing Address:** 1105 Delles Rd, Wheaton, IL 60187.

KYLE, PHILIP R, VOLCANOLOGY. **Personal Data:** b Wellington, NZ, December 3, 1947. **Education:** Victoria Univ, PhD (geol), 1976. **Professional Experience:** PROF GEOCHEM, NMEX INST MINING TECHNOL, 1981-. **Memberships:** Fel Geol Soc Am. **Mailing Address:** Dept Earth & Environ Sci, NMex Tech, NM Bureau Geol & Mineral Resources, Socorro, NM 87801. **E-Mail:** kyle@nmt.edu

KYLE, ROBERT ARTHUR, HEMATOLOGY, GAMMOPATHIES. **Personal Data:** b Bottineau, NDak, March 17, 1928; m 1954, Charlene Showalter; c John, Mary, Barbara & Jean. **Education:** Univ NDak, BS, 1948; Northwestern Univ Med Sch, MD, 1952; Univ

Minn, MS, 1958. **Honors & Awards:** Waldenstrom's Award Res Multiple Myeloma, Int Workshop Myeloma, Torino, Italy, 1991. **Professional Experience:** Consult, PDQ Info Bank, Nat Cancer Inst, 1984-; chmn, myeloma comn, Eastern Coopr Oncol Group, 1984-; William H Donner prof med & Lab Med, Mayo Med Sch, 1981-1987; PROF MED & LAB MED, MAYO MED SCH, 1975-; prin invest, Acute Leukemia Group B, 1971-1972; from asst prof to assoc prof, Mayo Med Sch, 1966-1975; CONSULT MED, MAYO MED SCH, 1961-; postdoctoral fel hemat, Nat Cancer Inst, 1960-1961; Clin asst hemat, Tufts Univ Sch Med, 1960-1961. **Memberships:** NY Acad Sci; Am Assoc Cancer Res; Am Soc Hemat; fel Am Col Physicians; Am Soc Clin Oncol; Cent Soc Clin Res. **Research Statement & Publications:** Monoclonal gammopathies; includes multiple myeloma, amyloidosis, macroglobulinemia, and related plasma cell proliferative process. **Mailing Address:** 1207 6Th St SW, Rochester, MN 55902. **Fax:** 507-266-4088.

KYLE, THOMAS GAIL, INFRARED STUDIES, METEOROLOGICAL TRACERS. **Personal Data:** b Crawford, Okla, September 12, 1936; m 1958, c 2. **Education:** Univ Okla, BS, 1960, MS, 1962; Univ Denver, PhD (physics), 1965. **Professional Experience:** RETIRED; vis prof, Okla State Univ, 1983-1984; vis prof, Denver Univ, 1982-1983; vis prof, Clemson Univ, 1981-1982; staff mem, Los Alamos Nat Lab, 1976-1992; scientist, Nat Ctr Atmospheric Res, 1971-1976; res physicist, Univ Denver, 1966-1971; res officer, Commonwealth Sci & Indust Res Orgn, Australia, 1965-1966. **Research Statement & Publications:** Computational physics; theoretical and experimental studies of infrared spectra; laser studies; studies of the composition and radiative properties of the atmosphere; weather modification; artificial intelligence; atmospheric modeling; image processing; Paranormal phenomena. **Mailing Address:** 2413 Regal Rd, Plano, TX 75075. **E-Mail:** abique@earthlink.com

KYLSTRA, JOHANNES ARNOLD, MEDICINE, PHYSIOLOGY. **Personal Data:** b Manado, Neth Elndies, November 30, 1925; m 1956, c 2. **Education:** Univ Leiden, MD, 1958. **Honors & Awards:** Lockheed Award, Marine Technol Soc, 1970. **Professional Experience:** RETIRED; prof pulmonary & allergy, Duke Univ, 1972-1989. **Memberships:** AAAS; Am Physiol Soc; Undersea Med Soc (pres, 1973-1974). **Research Statement & Publications:** Liquid breathing and lung lavage. **Mailing Address:** 3615 Ocean Dr, Crp Christi, TX 78411.

KYNCL, J JAROSLAV, HYPERTENSION, ADRENERGIC RECEPTORS. **Personal Data:** b Prague, Czech, August 16, 1936; American citizen; m 1961, c 2. **Education:** Masaryk Univ, Czech, MS, 1959; Komensky Univ, Czech, PhD (pharmacol), 1963; Czech Acad Sci, Prague, ScC, 1967. **Honors & Awards:** Pfizer Lectr, Clin Res Inst Montreal, 1980. **Professional Experience:** AT, ABBOTT LABS RES & DEVELOP, 1972-; res fel, Cleveland Clin Res Div, 1970-1972; A V Humboldt fel cardiovasc res, Univ Heidelberg, Ger, 1968-1972; sr res scientist, Res Inst Pharm & Biochem, Prague, Czech, 1963-1968; mem, Coun High Blood Pressure, Am Heart Asn. **Memberships:** Fel Am Heart Asn; Am Endocrine Soc; Am Soc Pharmacol & Exp Therapeut; Am Soc Hypertension; Int Soc Hypertension. **Research Statement & Publications:** Pathophysiology of cardiovascularand endocrine disorders; novel concepts and specific agents useful in therapy; author of numerous scientific publications and patents; codiscoverer of Terazosin (Hytrin). **Mailing Address:** 1401 Sheridan Rd, Lake Forest, IL 60064.

KYRALA, GEORGE AMINE, OPTICS & LASER FUSION & INTERACTIONS, X-RAY RADIOGRAPHY & ULTRA-HIGH SPEED IMAGING. **Personal Data:** b Bhamdoun, Lebanon, April 20, 1946; American citizen; m 1973, Trish; c Michaelene & Kamaal. **Education:** Am Univ Beirut, BS, 1967; Yale Univ, MPh, 1969, PhD (physics), 1974. **Honors & Awards:** Michael Chiha Prize in Philosophy, National Competition, Lebanon (1964), President, Space Sci Club, Am Univ of Beirut, Lebanon, (1966 & 1967) Officer, Physics Mathematics Soc, Am Univ of Beirut, Lebanon (1966 & 1967), Rockefeller Fellow, Am Univ of Beirut, Lebanon (1966-67, Academic Year) BS With Distinction, Am Univ of Beirut, Lebanon, (1967), Gibbs Fellowship, Yale Univ, (1967-1968) Member, Graduate Professional Student Senate, (1970-1972), Yale Univ, New Haven, Connecticut, USA Charter member & Board of Directors, Graduate Professional Student Center, (1971-1972), Yale Univ, New Haven, Connecticut, USA Recipient of a student travel grant Award from the International Conference on the Physics of ELectronic & Atomic Collisions, General Committee, to attend its eighth meeting at Belgrade, (1973) Charter member, Arab Physical Soc, (1974) Award to attend "The Physics of Quantum ELectronics, " Santa Fe, New Mexico, June-July 1974 Distinguished Performance Award 1991, Los Alamos National Laboratory LIDAR PROJECT Chairman of the High Speed Photography, Videography, & Photonics Working group of the International Soc for Optical Engineering (1991-1993) Nuclear Weapons Program Award of Excellence April 19, 1993, Department of Energy, LABS project Fellow of the SPIE (elected July 1995) Los Alamos Achievement Program 1996, Physics Division, LANL Photosonics Award, The International Soc for Optical Engineering (2000) & the International Congress on High-Speed Photography & Photonics Harold E Edgerton Award, The International Soc for Optical Engineering (2002) Editorial Board, Defense Res Review (2004) Program Chair, X-ray Systems & Technologies, The International Soc for Optical engineering (1997-1999, & 2004-) Program Chair, High Energy Density Laboratory Astrophysics (2005-now). **Professional Experience:** VIS FAC, UNIV NMEX, LOS ALAMOS, 1986-; Chief Scientist ICF& C4, PHYSICS DIV, LOS ALAMOS NAT LAB, 1979-; res fel lasers & spectros, Dept Physics, 1978-1979; res assoc optics & physics, Optical Sci Ctr & Dept Physics, Univ Ariz, 1976-1978; vis fac & consult, Ala-Hazen Res Ctr, Baghdad, 1975; lectr, Dept Physics, Univ Colo, 1975; fel physics, Joint Inst Lab Astrophys, Univ Colo, 1974-1976. **Memberships:** Am Phys Soc; Int Optical Eng Soc; fel Int Soc Photo-Optical Instrumentation Engrs. **Research Statement & Publications:** Charge transfer in atomic collision; electron scattering from excited atoms; laser construction and use in ultra high resolution spectroscopy; laser fusion experiments and optics; plasma x-ray spectroscopy; ultrafast diagnostics; high speed and high resolution x-ray imaging; middle eastern politics. **Mailing Address:** Los Alamos Nat Lab, Plasma Physics Goup P-24, Los Alamos, NM 87545. **Fax:** 505-665-4409. **E-Mail:** kyrala@lanl.gov

KYRIAKIS, JOHN M, MEDICINE. **Personal Data:** b New York, New York, United States, American citizen. **Education:** Cornell Univ, AB, 1981; Boston Univ, PhD, 1987. **Professional Experience:** PROF MED, SCH MED, TUFTS UNIV, as of 2005; DIR & INVES MOLECULAR CARDIOL RES INST, TUFTS NEW ENGLAND MED CTR, as of 2005; assoc prof med, Havard Med Sch, 1996-2002; asst biochem, Dept Med, Mass Genl Hosp, 1994-2002; asst prof med, Havard Med Sch, 1993-1996; instr med, Harvard Med Sch, 1991-1993; sr teaching fel, Boston Univ, 1984-1987; teaching fel, Introductory Biol Lab, Boston Univ, 1983-1987; RES FEL, MASS GEN HOSP, begininng 1987. **Memberships:** AAAS; Biochem Study Sect, NIH; Biochem Study Sect, Arthritis Found; Am Soc Cell Biol. **Mailing Address:** Molecular Cardiol Res Inst, Tufts-New England Med Ctr, 750 Washington St Box 8486, Boston, MA 02111. **Fax:** 617-636-5204. **E-Mail:** jkyriakis@tufts-nemc.org

KYRIAKOPOULOS, NICHOLAS, SYSTEMS THEORY & CONTROLS, DIGITAL SIGNAL PROCESSING. **Personal Data:** b Atalanti, Greece, November 14, 1937; m 1967, Irene; c Anastasia & Aris. **Education:** George Wash Univ, BS, 1960, MS, 1963, DSc, 1968. **Professional Experience:** Expert, US Dept State, 2001-; consult, Int Atomic Energy Agency, 1982-; PROF ENG, GEORGE WASH UNIV, 1980-; sr scientist, US Arms Control & Disarmament Agency, 1979-2000; with NIK Assocs, 1977-; summer fac fel, 1974-1976; vis prof, Nat Tech Univ, Athens, 1972-1973; consult, Howard Res Corp & RCA Serv Co, 1967-; NASA-Am Soc Eng Educ fac fel, Goddard Space Flight Ctr, NASA, 1967-1968; from asst prof to assoc prof elec eng & comput sci, George Wash Univ, 1966-1979; consult, Nat Biomed Res Found, 1966-1967; instr elec eng, George Wash Univ, 1964-1966; aerospace engr, Goddard Space Flight Ctr, NASA, 1962-1964; electronic engr, Harry Diamond Labs, Dept Army, 1960-1962. **Memberships:** Inst Elec & Electronics Engrs; Sigma Xi. **Research Statement & Publications:** Computer-aided analysis and design; performance evaluation of space communication systems; digital signal processing; monitoring and data collection systems; process automation and control; applications of technology to arms control; sensors and security systems; published over 15 articles. **Mailing Address:** Dept Elec Eng & Comput Sci, George Wash Univ, Rm 638 Phillips Hall, Washington, DC 20052. **Fax:** 202-994-0227. **E-Mail:** kyriak@gwu.edu

KYSER, DAVID SHELDON, EXPERIMENTAL SOLID STATE PHYSICS. **Personal Data:** b Houston, Tex, August 29, 1936; m 1959, c 3. **Education:** Univ Tex, BS, 1958 & 1960, MA, 1963, PhD (physics), 1965. **Professional Experience:** PHYSICIST, NAVAL WEAPONS CTR, 1966-; res assoc chem phys, Inst Study Metals, Univ Chicago, 1964-1966. **Memberships:** Am Phys Soc; Sigma Xi. **Research Statement & Publications:** Modulation of optical properties of semiconductors. **Mailing Address:** 1539 N China Lake Blvd, Ridgecrest, CA 93555-2606.

KYSER, T KURT, GEOCHEMISTRY. **Education:** BSc, MSc; Univ Calif, PhD, 1980. **Professional Experience:** PROF& RES CHAIR, DEPT GEOL SCI & GEOL ENG, QUEENS UNIV, CAN, as of 2006. **Mailing Address:** Queen's Univ, Dept Geol Sci, Miller 410A, Kingston, ON K7L 3N6, Can. **Fax:** 613-533-6592. **E-Mail:** kyser@geol.queensu.ca

KYTE, JACK ERNST, BIOCHEMISTRY. **Personal Data:** b Pasadena, Calif, May 21, 1947. **Education:** Carleton Col, BA, 1967; Harvard Univ, PhD (biochem), 1972. **Professional Experience:** PROF EMER BIOCHEM, UNIV CALIF, SAN DIEGO, as of 2005; asst prof biochem, Univ Calif, San Diego, beginning 1974; fel biochem, Damon Runyon Fund, 1972-1974; fel, NSF, 1967-1971. **Research Statement & Publications:** Molecular structure of proteins which catalyze the transport of matter across biological membranes. **Mailing Address:** Dept Chem 0506, Univ Calif San Diego, La Jolla, CA 92093. **Fax:** 858-534-4864. **E-Mail:** jkyte@ucsd.edu

KYTHE, PREM KISHORE, GEOMETRIC FUNCTION THEORY, CONFORMAL MAPPING. **Personal Data:** b India, January 29, 1930; American citizen; m 1955, c 2. **Education:** Agra Univ, BSc, 1950, MSc, 1955; Aligarh Muslim Univ, PhD (math), 1961. **Professional Experience:** PROF EMER MATH, UNIV NEW ORLEANS, LA, 2000-; prof math, Univ New Orleans, LA, 1974-1999; vis Prof Computer Sci, Univ Ill, Urbana-Champaign, 1986; vis prof, Math Dept, Imp Col, London, 1973; from vis assoc to assoc prof, Univ New Orleans, LA, 1967-1974; consult, Inst Human Learning, Univ Calif, Berkeley, 1964; fel, UNESCO, 1963; invited speaker, NATO, Advan Inst Automotive Transl Lang, Italy, 1962; from lectr to asst prof, Indian Inst Technol, Bombay, India, 1960-1967; lectr math, Aligarh Muslim Univ, India, 1958-1960. **Research Statement & Publications:** Univalent functions; boundary-value problems in continuum mechanics; laplace transforms; wave theory; wave structure in unsteady free convection flows in a rotating medium; geometric and coefficient problems in some subclasses of univalent functions; fundamental solutions. **Mailing Address:** Dept Math, Univ New Orleans-Lake Front, New Orleans, LA 70148. **Fax:** 504-280-5516. **E-Mail:** pkythe@uno.edu

KYUNG, JAI HO, ORGANIC CHEMISTRY. **Personal Data:** b Seoul, Korea, December 26, 1947; m 1973. **Education:** Seoul Nat Univ, BS, 1969; Brown Univ, PhD (org chem), 1975. **Professional Experience:** SR RES CHEMIST, ASHLAND CHEM CO, 1976-; res chemist, 1974-1976. **Memberships:** Am Chem Soc. **Research Statement & Publications:** Synthesis of organic ligands for recovery of metals for mining industry and commercial development of solvent extraction of hydrometallurgy; homogeneous and heterogeneous catalysis of petrochemicals and industrial intermediate chemicals. **Mailing Address:** 3525 Trillium Lane, Appleton, WI 54915.

L

LA, SUNG YUN, PHYSICS. **Personal Data:** b Seoul, Korea, September 24, 1936. **Education:** WVa Wesleyan Col, BS, 1959; Univ Conn, MS, 1962, PhD (physics), 1964. **Professional Experience:** PROF PHYSICS & EARTH SCI, WILLIAM PATERSON COL NJ, 1978-; assoc prof, William Paterson Col NJ, 1968-1978; Res assoc appl physics, Mat Res Lab, Pa State Univ, 1965-1968. **Memberships:** Am Phys Soc. **Research Statement & Publications:** Theoretical studies of ionic crystals; defects investigated byelectron spin resonance technique, cohesive energy and compressibility. **Mailing Address:** Dept Chem & Physics, William Paterson Univ, 300 Pompton Rd Rm Sci 531A, Wayne, NJ 07470-2103. **E-Mail:** las@wpunj.edu

LAAKSO, JOHN WILLIAM, BIOCHEMISTRY. **Personal Data:** b Minn, January 28, 1915; m 1941, c 4. **Education:** Winona State Col, BS, 1938; Mont State Col, MS, 1949; Univ Minn, PhD (biochem), 1956. **Professional Experience:** RETIRED; chmn dept, St Cloud State Univ, 1966-1973; prof chem, St Cloud State Univ, 1963-1980; from instr to assoc prof, St Cloud State Univ, 1948-1963; instr math, Mont State Col, 1946-1947; Teacher high schs, Minn, 1938-1942. **Memberships:** Am Chem Soc; Sigma Xi. **Research Statement & Publications:** Synthesis and biological assay of orotic acid analogs. **Mailing Address:** 3496 160th St, South Haven, MN 55382.

LAALE, HANS W, EXPERIMENTAL EMBRYOLOGY, TERATOLOGY. **Personal Data:** b Copenhagen, Denmark, April 20, 1935; Canadian citizen. **Education:** Bob Jones Univ, BSc, 1959; Univ Western Ont, MSc, 1961; Univ Toronto, PhD (zoology), 1966. **Professional Experience:** RETIRED; vis prof, Univ BC, beginning 1980; vis prof, Tunghai Univ, Taiwan, beginning 1973; from asst prof to prof zool, Univ Man, 1967-1996; lectr, Chinese Univ Hong Kong, 1966-1967; asst lectr biol, Hong Kong Baptist Col, 1961-1963. **Memberships:** Can Soc Zoologists; Sigma Xi. **Research Statement & Publications:** Teleost embryology and teratology; in vitro fish embryo culture: differentiation and organogenesis. **Mailing Address:** Dept Zool, Univ Man, Winnipeg, MB R3T 2N2, Can.

LAALI, KENNETH KHOSROW, STRUCTURAL & MECHANISTIC CHEMISTRY, ORGANIC & ORGANOMETALLIC CHEMISTRY. **Personal Data:** b Tehran, Iran, July 5, 1951; American citizen. **Education:** Univ Tehran, BS, 1973; Univ Manchester, PhD (org chem), 1977. **Professional Experience:** PROF CHEM, KENT STATE UNIV, 1996-; from asst prof to assoc prof, Kent State Univ, 1985-1996; res scientist, Hydrocarbon Res Inst, Univ Southern Calif, 1982-1985; res assoc, Swiss Fed Inst Technol, 1981-1982; instr, Univ Amsterdam, 1980-1981; Nat Ctr Sci res fel, Univ Strasbourg, 1979-1980; res fel, Sci Res, King's Col, Univ London, 1977-1979. **Memberships:** Am Chem Soc; Royal Soc Chem; Am Soc Mass Spectros. **Research Statement & Publications:** Physical organic, organometalic, fluorine and hydrocarbon chemistry; reactive intermediates; superacid chemistry; catalysis Friedel-crafts, multinuclear magnetic resonance and modern mass spectrometry; Persistent Carbocations from PAHs; author of various articles. **Mailing Address:** Dept Chem, Kent State Univ, 311A WMH, Kent, OH 44242. **Fax:** 330-672-3816. **E-Mail:** klaali@kent.edu

LAANANEN, DAVID H, AERONAUTICS. **Education:** Worcester Polytech Inst, BS, 1964; Northeastern Univ, MS, 1965, PhD, 1968. **Professional Experience:** PROF, DEPT MECH & AERO ENG, ARIZ STATE UNIV, as of 2004. **Mailing Address:** Dept Mech & Aerospace Eng, Ariz State Univ, PO Box 876106, Tempe, AZ 85287. **Fax:** 602-965-2412. **E-Mail:** david.laananen@asu.edu

LAANE, JAAN, PHYSICAL CHEMISTRY, SPECTROSCOPY. **Personal Data:** b Paide, Estonia, June 20, 1942; American citizen; m 1966, Tiiu; c Christina & Lisa. **Education:** Univ Ill, Urbana, BS, 1964; Mass Inst Technol, PhD (chem), 1967. **Honors & Awards:** Kendall Award, 1964; Kodak Award, 1967; Alexander von Humboldt US Sr Scientist Award, 1979. **Professional Experience:** Ed, J Molecular Struct, 1994-; ASSOC DEAN, COL SCI, 1994-; sr policy adv, Koriyama, Japan, 1990-1994; dir, Inst Pac Asia, 1987-1990; vis prof, Univ Bayreuth, WGer, 1979-1980, 1981, 1983; chmn, Div Phys & Nuclear Chem 1977-1987 & 1993-1994; PROF CHEM, TEX A&M UNIV, 1976-; from asst prof to assoc prof, Col Sci, 1968-1976; asst prof chem, Tufts Univ, 1967-1968; vis scientist, Los Alamos Sci Lab, NMex, 1964 & 1967-1968. **Memberships:** Am Chem Soc; fel Am Phys Soc; Soc Appl Spectros; Coblentz Soc (treas, 1985-); fel Am Inst Chem; AAAS. **Research Statement & Publications:** Far-infrared spectroscopy of small ring compounds; potential energy functions; organometallic syntheses; infrared and Raman spectroscopy; nitrogen-oxygen chemistry. **Mailing Address:** Dept Chem, Tex A&M Univ, Col Sta, TX 77843. **Fax:** 979-845-3154. **E-Mail:** laane@chemvx.tamu.edu

LAASPERE, THOMAS, RADIOPHYSICS. **Personal Data:** b Estonia, March 17, 1927; American citizen; m 1955, Suzanne; c Hans, Liisa & Jaan. **Education:** Univ Vt, BS, 1956; Cornell Univ, MS, 1958, PhD (commun eng), 1960. **Professional Experience:** PROF EMER ENG, THAYER SCH ENG, DARTMOUTH COL, 1989-; mem comn IV, US Nat Comt, Int Sci Radio Union, 1964-; from asst prof to prof, Thayer Sch Eng, Dartmouth Col, 1961-1989; res assoc radiophys, Cornell Univ, 1960-1961. **Memberships:** Inst Elec & Electronics Engrs. **Research Statement & Publications:** Scattering of radio waves in the troposphere and ionosphere; whistlers and other audio-frequency electromagnetic waves; space research; electric rates, load management. **Mailing Address:** Thayer Sch Eng, Dartmouth Col, 8000 Cummings Hall, Hanover, NH 03755-8000. **Fax:** 603-646-3856.

LAATSCH, RICHARD G, MATHEMATICAL ANALYSIS. **Personal Data:** b Fairmont, Minn, July 14, 1931; m 1966, c 5. **Education:** Cent Mo State Col, BS, 1953; Univ Mo, MA, 1957; Okla State Univ, PhD (math), 1962. **Professional Experience:** RETIRED; prof math & assoc chmn dept, Miami Univ, beginning 1970; from asst prof to assoc prof, Miami Univ, 1962-1970; asst prof, Okla State Univ, 1962; instr math, Univ Tulsa, 1957-1960. **Memberships:** Math Asn Am. **Research Statement & Publications:** Subadditive functions; topological vector spaces and cones of functions. **Mailing Address:** Dept Math, Miami Univ, 123 Bachelor Hall, Oxford, OH 45056.

LABANA, SANTOKH SINGH, ORGANIC CHEMISTRY, POLYMER SCIENCE. **Personal Data:** b Maritanda, India, November 15, 1936; m 1964. **Education:** Univ Punjab, India, BSc, 1957, MSc, 1959; Cornell Univ, PhD (org chem), 1963. **Professional Experience:** Chmn coatings & films, Gordon Res Conf, 1980 & Org Coatings & Plastics Chem Div, Am Chem Soc, 1981; MGR POLYMER SCI DEPT, FORD MOTOR CO, 1972-; staff scientist, Ford Motor Co, 1970-1972; prin scientist assoc, Ford Motor Co, 1967-1970; scientist, Xerox Corp, 1964-1967; res chemist, Univ Calif, Berkeley, 1963-1964; lectr chem, G H G Col, Sadhar, India, 1958-1960; mem adv bd, J Coatings & Technol. **Memberships:** Am Chem Soc. **Research Statement & Publications:** Synthetic organic chemistry; polymer syntheses; mechanism of organic reactions; physical and thermal properties of polymers with special reference to network polymers; radiation induced polymerizations, coating and composites. **Mailing Address:** PO Box 2037, Dearborn, MI 48123-2037.

LABANAUSKAS, CHARLES K, PLANT PHYSIOLOGY. **Personal Data:** b Upyna, Lithuania, January 3, 1928; American citizen. **Education:** Hohenheim Agr Univ, dipl, 1947 Stanford, Germany; Univ Ill, MS, 1953, PhD, 1954. **Professional Experience:** EMER PROF HORT SCI, COL NATURAL & AGR SCI, UNIV CALIF, RIVERSIDE, 1988-; prof hort sci, Citrus Res Ctr, 1968-1988; Lectr, Univ Calif, Riverside, 1965-1968; From asst horticulturist to horticulturist, Citrus Res Ctr, 1955-1988. **Memberships:** Am Soc Hort Sci. **Research Statement & Publications:** Mineral metabolism in plants. **Mailing Address:** 3682 15th St, Riverside, CA 92501.

LABANICK, GEORGE MICHAEL, ZOOLOGY, HERPETOLOGY. **Personal Data:** b Passaic, NJ, September 27, 1950; m 1979, c 2. **Education:** Col William & Mary, BS, 1972; Ind State Univ, MA, 1974; Southern Ill Univ, PhD (zoology), 1978. **Professional Experience:** Div chair, Univ SC, Spartanburg, 1990-2000; PROF BIOL, UNIV SC, SPARTANBURG, 1989-; from asst prof to assoc prof, Univ SC, Spartanburg, 1979-1989; asst prof biol, Emory & Henry Col, 1978-1979. **Memberships:** Sigma Xi; Am Soc Ichthyologists & Herpetologists; Herpetologist's League; Soc Study Amphibians & Reptiles. **Research Statement & Publications:** Mimicry and other defense mechanisms; salamander ecology and systematics. **Mailing Address:** Div Natural Sci & Eng, Univ SC, 800 Univ Way, Spartanburg, SC 29303-4932. **Fax:** 864-503-5366. **E-Mail:** glabanick@uscs.edu

LABAR, MARTIN, POPULATION BIOLOGY, BIOETHICS. **Personal Data:** b Radisson, Wis, May 15, 1938. **Education:** Wis State Univ, Superior, BA, 1958; Univ Wis, MS, 1963, PhD (genetics, zool), 1965. **Professional Experience:** RETIRED; prof sci, Southern Wesleyan Univ, 1966-2005; chmn div sci, Southern Wesleyan Univ, 1964-2003; assoc prof, Southern Wesleyan Univ, 1964-1966. **Memberships:** Am Sci Affil; Ecol Soc Am; Soc Study Evolution. **Research Statement & Publications:** relationships between Christian faith and science; ethics of genetics. **Mailing Address:** Div Sci, Southern Wesleyan Univ, 907 Wesleyan Dr, PO Box 1020, Central, SC 29630-1020. **E-Mail:** mlabar@swu.edu

LA BARBERA, ANDREW RICHARD, REPRODUCTIVE BIOLOGY, MOLECULAR ENDOCRINOLOGY. **Personal Data:** b Teaneck, NJ, October 6, 1948. **Education:** Iona Col, BS, 1970; Columbia Univ, MA & MPhil, 1974, PhD (physiol), 1975. **Honors & Awards:** Spirit of Cincinnati Achievement Award, Greater Cincinnati Convention and visitors Bureau, 2001. **Professional Experience:** Scientific Director, Am Soc Reprod Med, 2004-; Prof, dept molecular & cellular physiol, col med, univ cincinnati, 1998-; PROF OBSTET & GYNEC, DEPT MOLECULAR & CELLULAR PHYSIOL, COL MED, UNIV CINCINNATI, 1995-; dir, sexual health, col med univ cincinnati, 2001-; consult, NIH, 1990-; mem, NIH reproductive endocrinology study section, 1998-2002; dir, Andrology Lab, Univ Cincinnati Hosp, 1988-2000; ASSOC PROF, DEPT MOLECULAR & CELLULAR PHYSIOL, COL MED, UNIV CINCINNATI, 1988-1998; assoc prof, Dept Obstet & Gynec, 1988-1995; vchmn admin & res, Dept Obstet & Gynec, Col Med, Univ Cincinnati, 1988-1993; grantee, USDA, 1986-1992; from asst prof to assoc prof, Dept Obstet & Gynec, 1985-1988; dir, In-vitro Fertil Lab, Northwestern Mem Hosp, 1985-1988; grantee, NIH, 1982-1986 & 1994-; from asst prof to assoc prof, Dept Physiol, Northwestern Univ Med Sch, 1980-1988; Dir, Hormone Assay Lab, Ctr Endocrinol Metab Nutrit, Northwestern Univ Med Sch, 1980-1985; res fel, Dept Cell Biol, Mayo Grad Sch Med, 1977-1980; Staff assoc, Int Inst Study Human Reproduction, Columbia Univ, 1975-1977. **Memberships:** AAAS; Am Physiol Soc; Am Soc Reprod Med; Endocrine Soc; Am soc andrology; endocrine soc; sigma Xi; univ cincinnati chapter, pres, 1998-1999; Soc Exp Biol Med; gynecologic investigation; Soc Study Reproduction, Board of Directors, 2004-2007. **Research Statement & Publications:** Mechanisms of signal transduction in the gonads; molecular and cellular regulation of gonadotropin receptors; human sexuality and sexual health. **Mailing Address:** Dept OB/GYN Univ Cinn Col Med, PO Box 670526, Cincinnati, OH 45267-0526. **Fax:** 513-558-6138. **E-Mail:** andrew.labarbera@uc.edu

LABARGE, ROBERT GORDON, CHEMISTRY. **Personal Data:** b Buffalo, NY, July 11, 1940. **Education:** Univ Rochester, BS, 1962; Carnegie-Mellon Univ, PhD (chem), 1966; Cent Mich Univ, MBA, 1978. **Professional Experience:** INDEPENDANT CONSULT, 1993-; mgr, Opportunities Identification, 1983-1993; adj prof, Northwood Inst, 1982; mgr, New Prod Develop, 1978-1983; econ & mgt, Delta Col, 1978-1982; res specialist, Designed Prod Dept, 1975-1978; adj prof chem, Cent Mich Univ, 1974; dir acad educ, Consumer Prod Dept, Dow Chem Co, 1973-1975; res chemist, Consumer Prod Dept, Dow Chem Co, 1966-1973. **Memberships:** Am Chem Soc; Inst Food Technologists; Am Oil Chemists Soc; Sigma Xi. **Research Statement & Publications:** New product exploration and development. **Mailing Address:** 709 Sterling Dr, Midland, MI 48640-2764.

LABARRE, ANTHONY E, MATHEMATICS. **Personal Data:** b New Orleans, La, July 18, 1922; m 1977, c 2. **Education:** Tulane Univ, BE, 1943, MS, 1947; Univ Okla, PhD (math), 1957. **Professional Experience:** PROF EMER MATH, CALIF STATE UNIV, FRESNO, as of 2005; prof math, Calif State Univ, Fresno, 1961-1990; chmn dept, Calif State Univ, Fresno, 1961-1966; from asst prof to assoc prof, Univ Idaho, 1956-1961; instr, Univ Wyo, 1954-1956; instr, Univ Okla, 1950-1954; asst prof, Univ Idaho, 1948-1950; instr math, Tulane Univ, 1946-1948. **Memberships:** Math Asn Am; Am Math Asn Two Year Col. **Research Statement & Publications:** Functional analysis, differential geometry. **Mailing Address:** 2809 Mckelvy Ave, Clovis, CA 93612.

LABARTHE, DARWIN RAYMOND, EPIDEMIOLOGY. **Personal Data:** b Berkeley, Calif, August 5, 1939. **Education:** Princeton Univ, BA, 1961; Columbia Univ, MD, 1965; Univ Calif, Berkeley, Master Pub Health, 1967, PhD (epidemiol), 1975. **Professional Experience:** ASSOC DIR, CARDIOVASC HEALTH POLICY & RES, US DEPT HEALTH & HUMAN SERV, as of 2005; JAMES W ROCKWELL PROF EPIDEMIOL, SCH PUB HEALTH, UNIV TEX, as of 2003; DIR, EPIDEMIOL RES CTR, SCH PUB HEALTH, UNIV TEX, as of 2003; dir design & analysis, Baylor Col Med, 1977-; prof epidemiol, Sch Pub Health, Univ Tex, beginning 1977; chmn & dir, US Seminar Cardiovasc Epidemiol, Am Heart Asn, 1975-; consult, coord ctr, Hypertension Detection & Followup Prog, Nat Heart & Lung Inst, 1974-; co-investr & co-dir, Study Incidence & Natural Hist Genital Tract Anomalies & Cancer Offspring exposed Utero to synthetic Estrogens, Nat Cancer Inst, 1974-; consult epidemiol, dept med statist & epidemiol, Mayo Clin & Mayo Found, 1974-1977; consult, Task Force Automated Blood Pressure Devices, Nat Heart & Lung Inst, 1973-1974; dep dir, Coord Ctr, Hypertension Detection & Followup Prog, Nat Heart & Lung Inst, 1971-1973; from assoc res epidemiologist to assoc prof epidemiol, Sch Pub Health, Univ Tex Health Sci Ctr, Houston, 1970-1973; dep chief & sr epidemiologist, Epidemiol Field & Training Sta, USPHS Heart Dis & Stroke Control Prog, San Francisco, 1969-1970; epidemiologist, Com Corps, Heart Dis & Stroke Control Prog, San Francisco, 1967-1969; dep dir, Beta-Blocker Heart Attack Trial Coord Ctr. **Memberships:** Fel Am Heart Asn; fel Am Col Prev Med; Soc Epidemiol Res (pres, 1972-1973); Am Pub Health Asn; Int Soc Cardiol. **Research Statement & Publications:** Epidemiology and prevention, especially of cardiovascular and other chronic conditions; drugs; intra-individual variability of blood pressure and other personal characteristics. **Mailing Address:** Dept Epidemiol, Univ Tex, PO Box 20186, Houston, TX 77225.

LABAVITCH, JOHN MARCUS, PLANT PHYSIOLOGY, BIOCHEMISTRY. **Personal Data:** b Covington, Ky, October 15, 1943. **Education:** Wabash Col, AB, 1965; Stanford Univ, PhD (plant physiol), 1973. **Professional Experience:** PROF POMOL, UNIV CALIF, DAVIS, as of 2002; ASSOC POMOLOGIST, UNIV CALIF, DAVIS, 1980-; lectr Pomol, Univ Calif, Davis, Beginning 1976; asst pomologist, Univ Calif, Davis, 1976-1980; NIH fel biochem, Univ Colo, 1972-1976; instr biol, Wabash Col, 1965-1967. **Memberships:** Am Soc Plant Physiologists; AAAS. **Research Statement & Publications:** Cell wall metabolism of fruit. **Mailing Address:** Dept Pomol, Univ Calif, 2055 Wickson Hall Univ Calif Davis, Davis, CA 95616-5200. **E-Mail:** jmlabavitch@ucdavis.edu

L'ABBE, MARY ROBERTA, TRACE ELEMENT & MINERALS NUTRITION, NUTRITION & HEALTH. **Personal Data:** b Ottawa, Ont, March 4, 1952. **Education:** Carleton Univ, BSc, 1975; McGill Univ, MSc, 1983, PhD (nutrit), 1988. **Professional Experience:** PROJ MGR, BANTING RES CTR, HEALTH CAN, as of 1999; adj prof, Dept Food & Nutrit, Univ Man, 1995-; lectr, USDA, 1995; lectr, Univ Alta, 1995; lectr, Univ Man, 1994; lectr, Can Inst Food Sci, 1994; lectr, Univ Laval, 1993; lectr, Am Oil Chemists, 1992 & 1997; lectr, Mem Univ, 1992; HEAD, MICRO NUTRIENTS SECT, BANTING RES CTR, HEALTH CAN, 1991-; RES SCIENTIST, NUTRIT RES, BANTING RES CTR, HEALTH CAN, 1989-; chemist, Micro Nutrients Sect, 1976-1989. **Memberships:** Can Fedn Biol Socs; Can Soc Nutrit Sci (treas 1989-1992); Am Soc Nutrit Sci; Oxygen Soc; Int Soc Free Radical Res. **Research Statement & Publications:** Trace element nutrition; vitamins and minerals; review of Canandian food fortification policy. **Mailing Address:** Banting Res Ctr, Health Can, 2203C, Ross Ave, Ottawa, ON K1A 0L2, Can. **Fax:** 613-941-6636. **E-Mail:** mlabbe@hpb.hwc.ca

LABBE, ROBERT FERDINAND, CLINICAL CHEMISTRY, NUTRITION. **Personal Data:** b Portland, Ore, November 12, 1922; m 1955, c 3. **Education:** Univ Portland, BS, 1947; Ore State Col, MS, 1949, PhD (biochem), 1951. **Honors & Awards:** Ames Award, Am Asn Clin Chemists. **Professional Experience:** PROF EMER, LAB MED, UNIV WASH, SEATLE, as of 2004; head, clin chem div, beginning 1980; prof lab med, Med Sch, Univ Wash, beginning 1974; prof pediat, Univ Wash, 1968-1974; NIH spec fel, 1965 & career develop award, 1966-1970; vis researcher, Commonwealth Sci & Indust Res Orgn, Australia, 1965; res assoc prof pediat, Univ Wash, 1960-1968; res asst prof pediat & lectr biochem, Univ Wash, 1957-1960; Vis asst prof, Inst Enzyme Res, Univ Wis, 1956-1957; res asst prof, Med Sch, Univ Ore, 1955-1957; res instr, Med Sch, Univ Ore, 1953-1955; AEC fel med sci, Col Physicians & Surgeons, Columbia Univ, 1951-1953. **Memberships:**

Fel AAAS; Am Chem Soc; Am Soc Biol Chemists; Acad Clin Lab Physicians & Scientists; Am Asn Clin Chemists; Am Soc Clin Nutrit. **Research Statement & Publications:** Heme biosynthesis; iron metabolism; related metabolic diseases; clinical nutrition, ascorbic acid metabolism, low power lasers. **Mailing Address:** Dept Lab Med, Harborview Med Ctr Box 359743, Seattle, WA 98104-2499. **Fax:** 206-223-3930.

LABBE, RONALD GILBERT, MICROBIOLOGY. **Personal Data:** b Berlin, NH, July 16, 1946; m 1978, c 2. **Education:** Univ NH, BA, 1968; Univ Wis, MS, 1970, PhD (bact), 1976. **Professional Experience:** PROF FOOD MICROBIOL, DEPT FOOD SCI, UNIV MASS, AMHERST, CHENOWETH LAB, 1988-; from asst prof to assoc prof, Dept Food Sci, Univ Mass, Amherst, Chenoweth Lab, 1976-1987; Res assoc microbiol, Food Res Inst, Univ Wis, 1976; Adj prof, Sch Pub Health, Univ Mass. **Memberships:** Sigma Xi; Int Asn Milk Food & Environ Sanitarians; Am Soc Microbiol; Inst Food Technologists; fel Am Acad Microbiol. **Research Statement & Publications:** Clostridium perfringens food poisoning; germination and sporulation of bacterial spores; microbial food safety. **Mailing Address:** Dept Food Sci Univ Mass Amherst Chenoweth Lab, 100 Holdsworth way, Amherst, MA 01003-9282. **E-Mail:** rlabbe@foodsci.umass.edu

LABELLA, FRANK SEBASTIAN, BIOCHEMICAL & CELLULAR PHARMACOLOGY. **Personal Data:** b Middletown, Conn, September 23, 1931; m 1952, c 3. **Education:** Wesleyan Univ, BA, 1952, MA, 1954; Emory Univ, PhD (basic health sci), 1957. **Honors & Awards:** John J Abel Award, Am Soc Pharmacol & Exp Therapeut, 1967; E W R Steacie Prize in Natural Sci, Pharmacol Soc Can, 1969, Upjohn Award, 1982. **Professional Experience:** PROF PHARMACOL & THERAPEUT, FAC MED, UNIV MAN, 1967-; career investr, Med Res Coun Can, beginning 1966; estab investr, Am Heart Asn, 1961-1966; from asst prof to assoc prof, Fac Med, Univ Man, 1960-1967; Can Rheumatism & Arthritis Soc res fel, Univ Man, 1958-1961; lectr pharmacol, Fac Med, Univ Man, 1958-1960; instr physiol, Emory Univ, 1957-1958; Am Heart Asn fel, Emory Univ, 1957-1958; asst histol, Emory Univ, 1955-1957; asst physiol, Emory Univ, 1954-1955; asst biol, Wesleyan Univ, 1952-1954; mem, Man Environ Res Comt & Int Narcotics Res Conf; mem coun arteriosclerosis. **Memberships:** Can Biochem Soc; Endocrine Soc; AAAS; Can Asn Geront; Am Soc Pharmacol & Exp Therapeut; Pharmacol Soc Can. **Research Statement & Publications:** Cellular pharmacology and biochemistry; neurochemistry; aging; endocrine pharmacology; neuroendocrinology; published recntly 10 books. **Mailing Address:** Dept Pharmacol & Therapeut, Univ Man, A406 Chown Bldg 753 McDermot Ave, Winnipeg, MB R3E 0T6, Can. **Fax:** 204-789-3932. **E-Mail:** labellaf@ms.umanitoba.ca

LABELLA, MARC J, COMPUTER SCIENCE. **Education:** Fairleigh Dickinson Univ, BS, MS; Concordia Univ, PhD. **Professional Experience:** PROF, DEPT PSYCHOL, FELICIAN COL, as of 2005. **Mailing Address:** Felician Col, 262 S Main St, Lodi, NJ 07644. **Fax:** 201-559-6188. **E-Mail:** labellam@inet.felician.edu

LABELLE, EDWARD FRANCIS, EXPERIMENTAL BIOLOGY. **Personal Data:** b Worcester, Mass, August 11, 1948; m 1972, Constance; c Devon N & Ross E LaBelle. **Education:** Col Holy Cross, BA & MS, 1970; Univ Mich, Ann Arbor, PhD (biochem), 1974. **Professional Experience:** Adj assoc prof, dept Physiol, Univ Pa, Philadelphia, 1988-; RES SCIENTIST, GRAD HOSP, BOCKUS RES INST, PHILADELPHIA, PA, 1987-; co-investr, NIH, 1982-1991 & NSF, 1984-1985; biochem Grad Student Adv Comt, 1981-1987 & Biohazards Comt, 1983-1984; from asst prof to assoc prof, Div Biochem, Med Br, Univ Tex, Galveston, 1978-1987; mem, Cancer Ctr Rev Comt, Med Br, Univ Tex, 1978-1986; prin investr, Western Ill Univ, NIH, Am Diabetes Asn, Muscular Dystrophy Asn & Am Heart Asn, 1977-1989; asst prof chem, Western Ill Univ, 1976-1978; postdoctoral fel, Sect Biochem, Cornell Univ, 1974-1976; Grad teaching asst, dept Biol Chem, Univ Mich, 1970-1974. **Memberships:** Am Chem Soc; AAAS; Am Soc Biol Chemists; Soc Gen Physiologists. **Mailing Address:** Sch Vet Med, Univ Pa, 3800 Spruce St, Philadelphia, PA 19104. **Fax:** 215-893-4178. **E-Mail:** labelle@vet.upenn.edu

LABEN, ROBERT COCHRANE, genetics, animal husbandry; deceased, see previous edition for last biography

LABER, LARRY JACKSON, PLANT PHYSIOLOGY. **Personal Data:** b Lincoln, Vt, July 9, 1937; m 1963, Doris. **Education:** Univ Vt, BS, 1959, MS, 1961; Univ Chicago, PhD (bot), 1967. **Professional Experience:** PVT PRACT OUTPATIENT PSYCHOLOGIST, 1986-; assoc prof, Univ Maine, Orono, 1977-1983; asst prof bot, Univ Maine, Orono, 1970-1976; NIH trainee, Brandeis Univ, 1969-1970; NSF trainee, Univ Ga, 1967-1969; asst prof, Pa State Univ, 1965-1966. **Memberships:** AAAS; NASA. **Research Statement & Publications:** Choroplast development; photophosphorylation; carbon dioxide fixation. **Mailing Address:** 95 Dole Hill Rd, Holden, ME 04429-7549. **E-Mail:** ljlaber@aol.com

LABERGE, GENE L, GEOLOGY. **Personal Data:** b Ladysmith, Wis, March 15, 1932; m 1962, c 2. **Education:** Univ Wis, BS, 1958, MS, 1959, PhD (geol), 1963. **Professional Experience:** PROF EMER GEOL, UNIV WIS-OSHKOSH, as of 2005; prof geol, Univ Wis-Oshkosh, beginning 1974; mem staff, Wis Geol & Natural Hist Surv, 1972-; from asst prof to assoc prof, Univ Wis-oshkosh, 1965-1974; Nat Res Coun Can fel, Geol Surv Can, 1964-1965; Sponsored res officer, Commonwealth Sci & Indust Res Orgn, Melbourne, Australia, 1963-1964. **Memberships:** AAAS; Geol Soc Am; Soc Econ Geologists. **Research Statement & Publications:** Origin of Precambrian iron formations; Precambrian geology and mineral deposits of Wisconsin. **Mailing Address:** Dept Geol, Univ Wis, 800 Algoma Blvd, Oshkosh, WI 54901-3551. **E-Mail:** laberge@uwosh.edu

LABERGE, WALLACE E, ENTOMOLOGY. **Personal Data:** b Grafton, NDak, February 7, 1927; m 1958, Elizabeth; c Daniel, Lesle & Laura. **Education:** Univ NDak, BSc, 1949, MS, 1951; Univ Kans, PhD (entom), 1955. **Professional Experience:** PROF ENTOM, UNIV ILL, URBANA, 1970-; TAXONOMIST, ILL NATURAL HIST SURV, 1967-; assoc taxonomist, Univ Ill, Urbana, 1965-1967; assoc prof entom, Univ Nebr, 1959-1965; asst prof zool, Iowa State Univ, 1956-1959; asst prof, Snow Entom Mus & instr entom, Univ Kans, 1955-1956; asst cur, Snow Entom Mus & instr entom, Univ Kans, 1954-1955. **Memberships:** Entom Soc Am; Soc Study Evolution; Soc Syst Zool; Am Entom Soc; Sigma Xi. **Research Statement & Publications:** Systematics of Hymenoptera, Apoidea and Braconidae. **Mailing Address:** 2012 S Race St, Urbana, IL 61801.

LABERGE, WALTER B, astrophysics; deceased, see previous edition for last biography

LABES, MORTIMER MILTON, CHEMICAL PHYSICS. **Personal Data:** b Newton, Mass, September 9, 1929; m 1972, Dina; c 6. **Education:** Harvard Univ, AB, 1950; Mass Inst Technol, PhD, 1954. **Professional Experience:** PROF CHEM, TEMPLE UNIV, 1970-; prof chem, Drexel Inst, 1966-1970; tech dir chem div, Franklin Inst, 1961-1966; lab mgr, Franklin Inst, 1960-1961; sr staff chemist, Franklin Inst, 1959-1960; sr res chemist, Franklin Inst, 1957-1959; res chemist, Sprague Elec Co, 1954-1957; asst, Mass Inst Technol, 1951-1954. **Memberships:** Am Chem Soc; Am Phys Soc; Sigma Xi. **Research Statement & Publications:** Chemistry and physics of organic solid state; molecular complexes; liquid crystals; electronic properties of polymers; synthesis and properties of carbon fibers and carbon composites; preparation and properties of fullerenes. **Mailing Address:** Dept Chem, Temple Univ, Philadelphia, PA 19122. **Fax:** 215-204-1532. **E-Mail:** labes@materials.temple.edu

LABIANCA, DOMINICK A, ORGANIC CHEMISTRY, POLYMER CHEMISTRY. **Personal Data:** b Brooklyn, NY, February 4, 1943; m 1973, Carol; c Dominick K. **Education:** Polytech Inst Brooklyn, BS, 1965; Univ Mich, PhD (chem), 1969. **Honors & Awards:** Ohaus-Nat Sci Teachers Asn Award, Ohaus Scale Corp, 1979, 1982, 1985, 1993. **Professional Experience:** Consult, expert witness in driving while intoxicated & related cases, 1985-; PROF, DEPT CHEM, BROOKLYN COL, CITY UNIV NY, 1983-; assoc prof, New Sch Lib Arts, 1978-1980; asst prof to assoc prof, New Sch Lib Arts, 1972-1980; res chemist, Res & Develop, Bound Brook Tech Ctr, Union Carbide Corp, 1970-1972; NSF fel org photochem, Calif Inst Technol, 1969-1970. **Memberships:** NY Acad Sci; Sigma Xi; Am Chem Soc; Nat Sci Teachers Asn; AAAS. **Research Statement & Publications:** Chemical education; chemistry/humanities integration, curriculum development; chemistry of breath-alcohol testing; science education. **Mailing Address:** Dept Chem Brooklyn Col City Univ NY, 2900 Bedford Ave 1159 Ingersoll Hall, Brooklyn, NY 11210-2889. **Fax:** 718-951-4607. **E-Mail:** labianca@brooklyn.cuny.edu

LABIANCA, FRANK MICHAEL, UNDERWATER ACOUSTICS, ACOUSTIC SIGNAL PROCESSING. **Personal Data:** b Brooklyn, NY, August 17, 1939; m 1970, Ann; c Carla & Elena. **Education:** Polytech Inst Brooklyn, BEE, 1961, MS, 1963, PhD (elec eng), 1967. **Professional Experience:** TECH MGR, AT&T BELL LABS, 1993-; tech supvr, AT&T Bell Labs, 1985-1992; mem tech staff, AT&T Bell Labs, 1967-1985; Instr elec eng, Polytech Inst Brooklyn, 1961-1967; prin investr, Off Naval Res & other govt agencies. **Memberships:** Inst Elec & Electronics Engrs; Sigma Xi. **Research Statement & Publications:** Propagation in surface ducts and underwater channel, scattering of sound from the ocean surface, radiation from cavitating propellers and the origins of ambient noise; adaptive array processing for underwater acoustic detection of signals in noise; speech recognition; digital filter design; LMS techniques in algorithm design with application to active control of sound and vibration. **Mailing Address:** 2 Slope Dr, Cedar Knolls, NJ 07927-1516. **Fax:** 973-386-6616. **E-Mail:** hogpb]fmlab@hogpa.ho.att.com

LABINGER, JAY ALAN, CATALYSIS, ORGANOMETALLIC CHEMISTRY. **Personal Data:** b Los Angeles, Calif, July 6, 1947; m 1970, Andrea; c Barbara. **Education:** Harvey Mudd Col, BS, 1968; Harvard Univ, PhD (chem), 1974. **Professional Experience:** MEM PROF STAFF & ADMINR, BECKMAN INST, CALIF INST TECHNOL, 1986-; res adv, Arco, 1983-1986; sr res chemist, Occidental Res Corp, 1981-1983; assoc ed, Chem Revs, 1979-1981; asst prof chem, Univ Notre Dame, 1975-1981; instr, Princeton Univ, 1974-1975; res assoc chem, Princeton Univ, 1973-1974. **Memberships:** Am Chem Soc; Soc Lit, Sci Arts; AAAS; Soc Social Studies Sci. **Research Statement & Publications:** Synthetic and mechanistic organo-transition metal chemistry; homogeneous and heterogeneous catalysis; alkane activation; literary and cultural aspects of science. **Mailing Address:** Calif Inst Technol 139 74, Pasadena, CA 91125. **Fax:** 626-449-4159. **E-Mail:** jal@its.caltech.edu

LABISKY, RONALD FRANK, WILDLIFE BIOLOGY, FISHERIES SCIENCE. **Personal Data:** b Aberdeen, SDak, January 16, 1934; div, c Dawn A & Holly H. **Education:** SDak State Univ, BS, 1955; Univ Wis, MS, 1956, PhD (wildlife ecol-zool), 1968. **Honors & Awards:** Grad Fac Adv Award, Am Fisheries Soc, 1978; Spec Recognition Serv Award, Wildlife Soc, 1988; Spec Recognition Serv Award, Nat Asn State Univ & Land-Grant Cols, 1995. **Professional Experience:** Adv bd, Critical Rev Natural Resources Mgt, 1987-1988; PROF, DEPT WILDLIFE ECOL & CONSERV, UNIV FLA, 1984-; chmn, Fish & Wildlife Resources Sect, Nat Asn State Univ & Land Grant Col, 1984-1995; chair, Sch Forest Resources & Conserv, 1984-1987; assoc ed, J Wildlife Mgt, 1983-1986; Chmn, Nat Fish & Wildlife Resources Res Coun, 1978-; prof & wildlife coordr, Sch Forest Resources & Conserv, 1978-1984; actg dir & asst dir, Univ Fla, 1976-1978; wildlife specialist, Ill State Natural Hist Surv, 1972-1976; from asst wildlife specialist to assoc wildlife specialist, Ill State Natural Hist Surv, 1959-1972; from asst proj leader to proj leader, Ill State Natural Hist Surv, 1957-1959; field asst game bird res, Ill State Natural Hist Surv, 1956-1957. **Memberships:** Am Fisheries Soc; Wildlife Soc; Am Ornith Union; Wilson Ornith Soc; Am Soc Mammal. **Research Statement & Publications:** Ecology and physiology of gallinaceous game birds, doves and waterfowl; population ecology, social biology and spatial distribution of pheasants and white-tailed deer; ecological, ethological, physiological and nutritive factors influencing distribution and abundance of terrestrial and aquatic wildlife; biology and management of spiny lobsters and deep-water reef fishes; ecology and management of nongame and endangered wildlife, particularly red-cockaded woodpeckers; wildlife conservation. **Mailing Address:** Dept Wildlife Ecol & Conserv, Univ Fla, Gainesville, FL 32611-0430. **E-Mail:** rfla@gnv.ifas.ufl.edu

LABODA, HENRY M, EXPERIMENTAL BIOLOGY, LIPIDS. **Personal Data:** b Kingston, Pa, December 9, 1950; m Beverly A Lyman; c Alex & Elizabeth. **Education:** Wilkes Col, BS, 1972; Temple Univ, MS, 1976; Hahnemann Univ, PhD (biol chem), 1981. **Professional Experience:** Mem, Prog Comt, Am Chem Soc, 1990-1992; SR SCIENTIST, SCHERING-PLOUGH HEALTHCARE PROD, MEMPHIS, TENN, 1988-; fel, Biophys Inst, Boston Univ Med Ctr, 1986-1988; NIH postdoctoral trainee, Dept Physiol & Biochem, Med Col Pa, Philadelphia, 1983-1986; clin chemist, Cooper Hosp, Camden, NJ, 1982-1983; biochemist, EM Sci, Gibbstown, NJ, 1981-1982; Med technologist, Robert Packer Mem Hosp, Sayre, Pa, 1972-1974. **Memberships:** Am Soc Biochem & Molecular Biol; Am Chem Soc. **Research Statement & Publications:** Analytical and preparative chromatographic methods; enzyme assay development; peroutaneous penetration-topical drug delivery; spectrophotometric methods; enzyme-linked immunosorbent assay; surface chemistry techniques including lipid monolayers, force-area isotherms and enzymatic hydrolysis; analytical method development. **Mailing Address:** 8540 Nottingwood Dr, Cincinnati, OH 45255. **Fax:** 901-320-5526.

LA BONTE, ANTON EDWARD, MACHINE INTELLIGENCE, TECHNOLOGY TRANSFER. **Personal Data:** b Minneapolis, Minn, May 6, 1935; m 1959, Ana. **Education:** Univ Minn, Minneapolis, BS, 1957, MSEE, 1960, PhD (elec eng), 1966. **Professional Experience:** RETIRED; consult, 1989; sr tech consult, Corp Res & Eng, 1975-1989; mgr systs analysis, Control Data Corp, 1969-1975; sr scientist, Control Data Corp, 1966-1969; instr elec eng, Univ Minn, Minneapolis, 1963-1965; res fel micromagnetics, Univ Minn, Minneapolis, 1962-1963; instr elec eng, Univ Minn, Minneapolis, 1959-1962. **Memberships:** Inst Elec & Electronics Engrs; Cognitive Sci Soc; Am Asn Artificial Intel. **Research Statement & Publications:** Machine intelligence with emphasis on knowledge-based information and decision systems; technology transfer strategies and techniques. **Mailing Address:** 4729 30th Ave S, Minneapolis, MN 55406.

LABORDE, ALICE L, BIOCHEMISTRY, CELL BIOLOGY. **Personal Data:** b January 8, 1947. **Education:** La Col, BS, 1970; Univ Southwestern La, MS, 1972; Univ Tex, Austin, PhD (microbiol), 1979. **Professional Experience:** SR RES SCIENTIST, CHEM & BIOL

SCREENING, UPJOHN CO, 1986-; Sr res scientist, Infectious Dis Res, 1979-1986. **Memberships:** Am Soc Microbiol; Soc Indust Microbiol; Am Soc Biochem & Molecular Biol. **Research Statement & Publications:** Development of screening assays and systems to detect novel therapeutic agents from natural products and/or chemical libraries; development of robotic systems to automate screens to ensure that a high volume of samples can be rapidly and successfully processed. **Mailing Address:** Chem & Biol Screening, Upjohn Co 301 Henrietta St, Kalamazoo, MI 49007-4940. **Fax:** 269-385-5225.

LABOSKY, PETER, WOOD CHEMISTRY, PULP & PAPER. **Personal Data:** b Manville, NJ, January 9, 1937; m 1967, Maryann; c Kevin & MaryJo. **Education:** Rutgers Univ, BS, 1963; Va Polytech Inst, MS, 1967, PhD (wood technol), 1970. **Professional Experience:** PROF EMER WOOD SCI & TECHNOL, PA STATE UNIV, as of 2003; prof wood Chem, Pa State Univ, beginning 1985; assoc pulp & paper, PA State Univ, 1979-1985; assoc exten, Clemson Univ, 1974-1979; res engr, Westvaco Corp, 1970-1974. **Memberships:** Tech Asn Pulp & Paper Indust; Forest Prod Soc; Soc Wood Sci & Technol. **Research Statement & Publications:** Relationship of fiber properties to paper properties; biopulping; kraft pulping of hardwoods; bark chemistry; author of many publications; wood composites. **Mailing Address:** Dept Wood Sci & Technol, Pa State Univ, 309 FRL, Univ Park, PA 16802. **Fax:** 814-865-7193. **E-Mail:** p21@psu.edu

LABOUNTY, JAMES FRANCIS, SR, LIMNOLOGY, LAKE MANAGEMENT. **Personal Data:** b Minneapolis, Minn, December 14, 1942; m 1969, c 2. **Education:** Univ Nev, Las Vegas, BS & BA, 1967, MS, 1968; Ariz State Univ, Tempe, PhD (zool), 1974. **Professional Experience:** MGR, US BUR RECLAMATION RES & INVEST GROUP, as of 1997; HEAD, ENVIRON SCI SECT, ENG & RES CTR, US BUR RECLAMATION, DENVER, 1984-; tech specialist, Eng & Res Ctr, Denver, 1980-1984; lectr, Univ Colo, Denver, 1977-1978; Prin investr, US Bur Reclamation, Denver, 1974-1984; res biologist, Eng & Res Ctr, Denver, 1974-1980; environ specialist, Phoenix, Ariz, 1972-1974; Fish & wildlife biologist, US Bur Reclamation, Boulder City, Nev, 1969-1972; bd dir, NAm Lake Mgt Soc. **Memberships:** NAm Lake Mgt Soc; Am Fisheries Soc; Southwestern Asn Naturalists; Desert Fishes Coun; Am Soc Ichthyologists & Herpetologists. **Research Statement & Publications:** Performing applied investigations on the ecology of lakes, reservoir and streams and in particular the nature of eutrophication research program for the US Bureau of Reclamation. **Mailing Address:** 920 Bramblewood Dr, Castle Rock, CO 80104.

LABOV, JAY BRIAN, PRE-COLLEGE & UNDER GRADUATE SCIENCE EDUCATION. **Personal Data:** b Philadelphia, Pa, September 19, 1950; m 1975, Jeri; c Adam & Rachel. **Education:** Univ Miami, Fla, BS, 1972; Univ RI, MS, 1974, PhD (biol sci), 1979. **Honors & Awards:** AAAS Fellow in Education, 2005 W K Kellogg Found Nat Fel Prog, 1988-1991. **Professional Experience:** Senior Advisor for Education and Communications, National Academies, 2003- Assoc. Dir., NRC Center for Education 1999-2002; vis scientist, Monell Chem Senses Ctr, 1985-1986; assoc prof biol, Colby Col, 1984-1997; vis investr, Jackson Lab, 1981; asst prof, Colby Col, 1979-1984; instr biol, Wash & Lee Univ, 1978-1979. **Memberships:** AAAS; Nat Sci Teachers Asn; Sigma Xi; Natl Assn Biol Teach. **Research Statement & Publications:** Pre-college and undergraduate science education. **Mailing Address:** National Res Council, Keck 1161, 500 Fifth St, NW, Washington, DC 20001. **Fax:** 202-334-2210. **E-Mail:** jlabov@nas.edu

LABOWS, JOHN NORBERT, FRAGRANCE CHEMISTRY. **Personal Data:** b Wilkes-Barre, Pa, June 27, 1941; m 1964, Mary; c Steven, Christopher, Gregory & Jennifer. **Education:** Lafayette Col, BS, 1963; Cornell Univ, PhD (org chem), 1967. **Professional Experience:** DIRECTOR COLGATE-PALMOLIVE, 2000-2005; ASSOC DIR, COLGATE PALMOLIVE CO, 1990-; 1996; Sr Res Assoc, Colgate Palmolive Co, 1985-1990; Assoc Mem, Monell Chem Senses Ctr, 1976-1985; Assoc Prof, Wilkes Col, 1967-1976; Nat Cancer Inst Fel, Fels Res Inst, Temple Univ, 1970-1971. **Memberships:** Am Chem Soc; Sigma Xi; Asn Chemoreception Sci. **Research Statement & Publications:** Odor/fragrance analysis; physical chemistry of flavors and fragrances in consumer products; chemical communication - body odor. **Mailing Address:** 631 Colonial Dr, Horsham, PA 19044. **E-Mail:** johnlabows@comcast.net

LABRACK, BRUCE W, ANTHROPOLOGY. **Education:** Univ Ariz, BA, 1967 & MA, 1969; Syracuse Univ, MPhil, 1976 & PhD (InterDisciplinary Soc Sci), 1980. **Professional Experience:** DIR, INT STUDIES, 2004-; CHAIR, MAIR, SCH INT STUDIES, UNIV PAC, 2001-; fac, MA Prog InterCul Relations, Antioch Univ, 1993-2001; SR FAC, SUMMER INST INTERCUL COMM, PORTLAND, 1989-; PROF ANTROP, UNIV PAC, STOCKTON, 1986-; US Educ Comm, sr Fulbright Res, Japan, 1982-1983; vis prof anthrop, Kansai Univ Foreign Studies, Osaka, 1981; from asst to assoc prof, Dept Sociol Anthrop, Univ Pac, 1975-1980. **Research Statement & Publications:** Cultural anthropology; physical anthropology; sociology. **Mailing Address:** Dept Anthrop & Sociol, Univ Pac, 3601 Pac Ave, Stockton, CA 95211. **Fax:** 209-946-2318. **E-Mail:** blabrack@pacific.edu

LABRECQUE, DOUGLAS R, EXPERIMENTAL BIOLOGY. **Professional Experience:** PROF INTERNAL MED, UNIV IOWA, 1987-; chief GI, Iowa City Vet Admin Hosp, 1982-2001; dir liver serv, Univ Iowa, 1979. **Memberships:** Am Physiol Soc; Am Gastroenterol Asn. **Mailing Address:** Dept Internal Med, Univ Iowa, 4553-G JCP 200 Hawkins Dr, Iowa City, IA 52242. **Fax:** 319-356-7918. **E-Mail:** douglas-labrecque@uiowa.edu

LABREE, THEODORE ROBERT, BACTERIOLOGY, FOOD TECHNOLOGY. **Personal Data:** b Lafayette, Ind, June 25, 1931; m 1951, June; c Steven & Catherine. **Education:** Purdue Univ, BS, 1958, MS, 1960. **Professional Experience:** RETIRED; dir, tech r&d, qa Am rice (ARI) TECH DIR, CORP RES & DEVELOP QUAL ASSURANCE, ERLY JUICE INC, 1989-; coordr & mgr qual assurance, Trbesweet Co Inc, 1986-1989; tech dir regulatory affairs, Riviana Foods, Inc, 1973-1986; mgr med admin, Mead Johnson & Co, 1965-1973; scientist bact, Mead Johnson & Co, 1962-1965; assoc bacteriologist, Mead Johnson & Co, 1959-1962; res asst food technol, Purdue Univ, 1958-1959. **Memberships:** Am Soc Microbiol; Inst Food Technologists. **Research Statement & Publications:** Active oxygen method; spore destruction of food spoilage organisms; new methods development; microbiology; government regulations, processing, packaging, labeling; good manufacturing practices regulations; low acid; sanitation; food plant; warehouse evaluation; pesticides; fumigation. **Mailing Address:** 9839 Canoga Lane, Houston, TX 77080. **E-Mail:** junted@worldnet.att.net

LABRIE, DAVID ANDRE, microbiology, biochemical genetics; deceased, see previous edition for last biography

LABRIE, FERNAND, ENDOCRINOLOGY, HORMONE-SENSITIVE CANCER. **Personal Data:** b June 28, 1937; Canadian citizen; m 1963, Nicole; c Claude, Pierre, Danielle, Anne & Isabelle. **Education:** Laval Univ, BA, 1957, MD, 1962, PhD (endocrinol), 1967; FRCP, 1973. **Honorary Degrees:** DSc, Univ Caen, France, 1996. **Honors & Awards:** Order of Can, 1982; Nat Order of Que, 1991. **Professional Experience:** EMER SCIENTIST, MED RES COUN GROUP, 1996-; head, Dept Physiol, Univ Laval, 1990-2002; pres, Can Soc Endocrinol Metab, 1984; DIR, RES CTR, CTR HOSP UNIV LAVAL, 1982-; pres, Can Soc Clin Invest, 1982; dir molecular endocrinol, Med Res Coun Group, beginning 1973; assoc prof, Laval Univ, beginning 1973; prof physiol, Lab Molecular Endocrinol, Hosp Ctr, Laval Univ, beginning 1973; med Res Coun Can scholar, Laval Univ, beginning 1969; HEAD, LAB MOLECULAR ENDOCRINOL, HOSP CTR, LAVAL UNIV, 1969-; Univ Sussex, 1967-1968 & centennial fel, Lab Molecular Biol, Univ Cambridge, 1968-1969; from asst prof to assoc prof physiol, dept physiol, 1966-1973; Med Res Coun Can fels, Univ Cambridge, 1966-1967; Med Res Coun Can fels, Laval Univ, 1963-1966. **Memberships:** Am Soc Biol Chemists; Am Physiol Soc; Endocrine Soc; Can Physiol Soc; Can Biochem Soc; Am Soc Androl. **Research Statement & Publications:** Molecular biology and regulation of formation and action of androgens and estrogens with specical application in prostate and breast cancer. **Mailing Address:** Ctr Hosp Univ Laval, 2705 Blvd Laurier Rm T-367, Ste Foy, PQ G1V 4G2, Can. **Fax:** 418-654-2735. **E-Mail:** fernand.labrie@crchul.ulaval.ca

LABROPULU, FOTINI, MATHEMATICS. **Education:** Univ Windsor, PhD (Math). **Professional Experience:** ADJ PROF, DEPT APPL MATH, UNIV WESTERN ONT, as of 2006. **Mailing Address:** Dept Appl Math, Univ Western Ont, London, ON N6A 5B7, Can. **Fax:** 306-585-4493. **E-Mail:** fotini.labropulu@uregina.ca

LABUDA, DAMIAN, BIOCHEMISTRY OF NUCLEIC ACIDS, MOLECULAR HUMAN & MAMMALIAN GENETICS. **Personal Data:** b Poznan, Poland, September 25, 1949; Canadian citizen; m 1974, Malgorzata Kranz; c Marcin, Zuzanna & Aleksander. **Education:** Adam Mickiewicz Univ-Poznan, Poland, MS, 1971, PhD (biochem), 1976. **Professional Experience:** PROF PEDIAT, UNIV MONTREAL, 1994-; from asst prof to assoc prof, Dept Pediat, Univ Montreal, 1984-1994; from res assoc, Dept Pediat, Univ Montreal, 1982-1984; fel, Max-Planck Inst Biophys Chem, Gottingen, 1978-1982; asst adj biochem, Inst Biol, Adam Mickiewicz Univ, 1971-1982; fel, Inst Plant Physiol, Hungarian Acad Sci, Szeged, 1971-1972. **Memberships:** Genetic Soc Am; Can Genetic Soc; Soc Molecular Biol & Evolution; Am Soc Human Genetics; Int Soc Molecular Evolution; Human Genome Orgn. **Research Statement & Publications:** Structure and evolutionary history of the human genome; origins of human genomic diversity and the mechanism of mutations involved; medical applications of molecular genetics in diagnosis and mapping of hereditary disorders; after mechanism of mutations involved evolution of human populations, mammalian and primate evolution, genome mapping. **Mailing Address:** Dept Pediat, Ste-Justine Hosp, Univ Montreal, 3175 Ch Cote Suite Catherine, Montreal, PQ H3T 1C5, Can. **Fax:** 514-345-4801. **E-Mail:** labuda@medclin.umontreal.ca

LABUDA, MITCHELL JOSEPH, PROCESS ENGINEERING, THIN FILMS ENGINEERING. **Personal Data:** b Highland Park, Ill, October 16, 1967; m Ava. **Education:** Univ Ill, BS, 1990; Univ Wis-Madison, PhD (chem), 1996. **Professional Experience:** PROCESS ENGR, CRYSTAL TECHNOL INC, 1996-. **Memberships:** Am Chem Soc. **Research Statement & Publications:** Crystal technology; cleaning and thin film deposition processes. **Mailing Address:** 1040 E Meadow Circle, Palo Alto, CA 94303-4230.

LABUDDE, ROBERT ARTHUR, LASER ANNEALING, DIGITAL CODING. **Personal Data:** b Flint, Mich, May 28, 1947; m 1969, c 2. **Education:** Univ Mich, Ann Arbor, BS, 1969; Univ Wis-Madison, PhD (chem), 1973. **Professional Experience:** Mem bd dirs, Tech Express Inc, 1990; secy, ERB Leasing Co Inc, 1983-1986; exec vpres, Labudde Eng Corp, 1983-1986; Burroughs Corp, 1980-1982; Optical Coating Labs Inc, 1982-1983; PRES, LEAST COST FORMULATIONS LTD, 1979-; Res Ctr, Digital Design Labs, 1979; Res Ctr, Allied Tech Corp, 1977-1978; asst prof math & comput sci, Old Dom Univ, Norfolk, Va, 1976-1979; consult, Gen Systs Div, IBM, 1975-1978; instr appl math, Mass Inst Technol, 1974-1975; asst scientist, Math Res Ctr, 1973-1974; lectr comput sci, Univ Wis, 1973; res asst chem, Univ Wis, 1968-1973. **Memberships:** Soc Indust & Appl Math; Asn Comput Mach; Am Soc Testing & Mat; Am Soc Qual Control; Inst Indust Engrs; Inst Food Technologists; Sigma Xi. **Research Statement & Publications:** Theoretical modeling of laser based optical disk memory systems, including thermal, optical and thin-film properties; noise sources and kinetics of environmental degraddation; digital coding and communication. **Mailing Address:** Least Cost Formulations Ltd, 824 Timberlake Dr, Virginia Beach, VA 23464-3239. **Fax:** 757-467-2947. **E-Mail:** ral@lcfltd.com

LABUDDE, SAMUEL FREEMAN, ENVIRONMENTAL ACTIVIST. **Personal Data:** b Madison, Wis, July 3, 1956. **Education:** Ind Univ, BA, 1986. **Honors & Awards:** Goldman Award, NAm Goldman Found, 1991. **Professional Experience:** EXEC DIR, ENDANGERED SPECIES PROJ, as of 2004; EC marine policy consult, Humane Soc US, 1990-1993; field investr, Friends Animals, 1990; field biologist, Earthtrust, Honolulu, 1989-1990; STAFF BIOLOGIST, MARINE MAMMAL FUND, 1987-; staff biologist, Earth Island Inst, 1987-1994; fisheries biologist, Nat Marine Fisheries Serv, 1987. **Research Statement & Publications:** East Pacific dolphin slaughter by tuna industry; Asian driftnet fleets; illegal trade in tigers and other endangered species. **Mailing Address:** Endangered Species Proj, E-205 Ft Mason Ctr, San Francisco, CA 94123.

LABUTE, JOHN PAUL, MATHEMATICS. **Personal Data:** b Tecumseh, Ont, February 26, 1938; Canadian citizen; m 1961, c 3. **Education:** Univ Windsor, BSc, 1960; Harvard Univ, MA, 1961, PhD (math), 1965. **Professional Experience:** ASSOC CHAIR & PROF MATH, MCGILL UNIV, as of 2002; assoc prof math, mcgill univ, beginning 1970; asst prof, Mcgill Univ, 1967-1970; Nat Res Coun Can res fel, Col France, 1965-1967. **Memberships:** Can Math Cong; Am Math Soc. **Research Statement & Publications:** Algebra and number theory. **Mailing Address:** Dept Math, McGill Univ, Rm 1112, Burnside Hall, 805 Sherbrooke St W, Montreal, PQ H3A 2K6, Can. **Fax:** 514-398-3899. **E-Mail:** labute@math.mcgill.ca

LABUZA, THEODORE PETER, FOOD SCIENCE, PHYSICAL CHEMISTRY. **Personal Data:** b Perth Amboy, NJ, November 10, 1940; m 1985, Mary; c Theodore, Peter & Kathrine. **Education:** Mass Inst Technol, BS, 1962, PhD (food sci), 1965. **Honors & Awards:** Samuel Cate Precott Res Award, Inst Food Technologists, 1972; Cruess Award, 1973; Babcock Hart Award, 1988; Apport Award 1998; Marcel Loncin Prize; IFT College Award; McFarland Outstanding Teaching, 2001; ASAE, Food Engr Award, 1997; Listed in ISI Most highly sited scientists in agr-food sci field. **Professional Experience:** Assoc dean grad sch, 1993-1996; Howard lectr, Univ Ill, 1987; PROF FOOD TECHNOL, UNIV MINN, ST PAUL, 1972-; assoc prof, Univ Minn, St Paul, 1971-1972; from instr to assoc prof food eng, Mass Inst Technol, 1965-1971; Food processing consult. **Memberships:** fel Inst Food Technologists (pres, 1988-1989); Am Inst Chem Eng; Am Chem Soc; Am Asn Cereal Chemists; Asn Food & Drug Officials; Sigma Xi. **Research Statement & Publications:** Physical chemical factors involved in water in foods; reaction kinetics and prediction of food storage life; stability of intermediate moisture foods; nutrient degradation in processing; kinetics of microbial growth and death; plant tissue culture; edible films. **Mailing Address:** Dept Food Sci & Nutrit, Univ Minn, 1354 Eckles Ave, St Paul, MN 55108. **Fax:** 612-625-5272. **E-Mail:** tplabuza@umn.edu

LACASCE, ELROY OSBORNE, ACOUSTICS. **Personal Data:** b Fryeburg, Maine, January 17, 1923. **Education:** Bowdoin Col, AB, 1943; Harvard Univ, AM, 1951; Brown Univ,

PhD (physics), 1955. **Professional Experience:** EMER PROF PHYSICS, BOWDOIN COL, 1993-; chmn dept, Bowdoin Col, 1977-1988; guest investr, Woods Hole Oceanog Inst, 1975-1976, 1982-1983; vis investr, Woods Hole Oceanog Inst, 1968-1969; NSF fac fel, 1960-1961; res assoc, Yale Univ, 1960-1961; from instr to prof, Bowdoin Col, 1954-1993; instr math, Bowdoin Col, 1951; teacher, high sch, 1946-1947; foreign serv officer, US Dept State, 1945-1946; physicist, Naval Res Lab, 1944; instr physics, Bowdoin Col, 1943, 1947-1949. **Memberships:** Emer mem Acoust Soc Am. **Research Statement & Publications:** Ultrasonics and underwater sound. **Mailing Address:** Dept Physics & Astron, Bowdoin Col, 8800 Col Sta, Brunswick, ME 04011-8488. **Fax:** 207-725-3638.

LACEFIELD, GARRY DALE, FORAGE PRODUCTION & MANAGEMENT. **Personal Data:** b McHenry, Ky, August 22, 1945; m 1967, c 2. **Education:** Western Ky Univ, BS, 1970, MS, 1971; Univ Mo, PhD (agron & physiol), 1974. **Professional Experience:** EXTEN PROF AGRON, UNIV KY, 1982-; exten forage specialist, beginning 1974; from asst exten prof to assoc exten prof, 1974-1982; teaching asst, Univ Mo, 1971-1974; lab instr & instr plant sci, Western Ky Univ, 1969-1971. **Memberships:** Am Soc Agron; Am Forage & Grassland Coun. **Research Statement & Publications:** Development and implementation of improved practices in forage establishment, production and utilization. **Mailing Address:** Dept Agron, Univ Ky Res & Edu Ctr, 1205 Hopkinsville St PO Box 469, Princeton, KY 42445-0469. **E-Mail:** glacefie@uky.edu

LACELLE, PAUL (LOUIS), HEMATOLOGY, PHYSIOLOGY. **Personal Data:** b Syracuse, NY, July 4, 1929; m 1953, c 4. **Education:** Houghton Col, BA, 1951; Univ Rochester, MD, 1959. **Honors & Awards:** Sr Humboldt Award. **Professional Experience:** SR ASSOC DEAN ACAD AFFAIRS & RES, as of 2002; chmn dept, Sch Med, Univ Rochester, 1977; PROF BIOPHYS, SCH MED, UNIV ROCHESTER, 1974-; NIH res grant, 1970-; from sr instr to prof, Sch Med, Univ Rochester, 1967-1974; Buswell fel, Sch Med, Univ Rochester, 1966-1967; NIH Spec fel, Univ Saarland, 1965-1966; fel biophys, Atomic Energy Comn, 1962-1965; Intern & resident, Strong mem Hosp, Univ Rochester, 1959-1962. **Memberships:** Biophys Soc; Am Phys Soc; Am Soc Hemat; Am Fedn Clin Res; Biorheology Europ Microcirculation. **Research Statement & Publications:** Biophysical properties of blood cells; microcirculation. **Mailing Address:** Box 706, 601 Elmwood Ave, Rochester, NY 14642-8408. **Fax:** 585-256-1131. **E-Mail:** pllace@biophysics.rochester.edu

LACELLE, SERGE, SURFACE CHEMISTRY. **Education:** Iowa State Univ, PhD, 1984. **Professional Experience:** PROF, DEPT CHEM, UNIV SHERBROOKE, CAN, as of 2006. **Mailing Address:** Dept Chem, Univ Sherbrooke 2500 Blvd, Sherbrooke, PQ J1K 2R1, Can. **Fax:** 819-821-8017. **E-Mail:** Serge.Lacelle@USherbrooke.ca

LACERDA, ALEX HUGO, LOW TEMPERATURE PHYSICS, HIGH MAGNETIC FIELD PHYSICS. **Personal Data:** b Pernambuco, Brazil, January 2, 1962; m 1986, Andrea; c Hugo. **Education:** UFPE, Brazil, BS, 1985; Univ J Fourier, France, MS, 1987, PhD (physics), 1990. **Honors & Awards:** LANL Accomplishment award Japanese Society for the Promotion of Science. **Professional Experience:** NSF Co-PI of the NHMFL. **Memberships:** Am Phys Soc; Brazilian Phys Soc. **Research Statement & Publications:** Magnetic and transport properties of novel materials at extreme conditions of very high magnetic fields and low temperature. **Mailing Address:** NHMFL Los Alamos Nat Lab, MS E536, Los Alamos, NM 87455. **Fax:** 505-665-4311. **E-Mail:** lacerda@lanl.gov

LACEWELL, RONALD DALE, RESOURCE ECONOMICS, PRODUCTION ECONOMICS. **Personal Data:** b Plainview, Tex, April 15, 1940; m 1962, c 3. **Education:** Tex Tech Univ, BS, 1963, MS, 1967; Am Univ, BS (stat), 1964; Okla State Univ, PhD (agr econ), 1970. **Professional Experience:** ASST VICE CHANCELLOR, AGR & LIFE SCI, TEX A&M UNIV, COL STA, beginning 1996-; ASSOC DIR, TEX AGR EXP STA, TEX A&M UNIV, COL STA, begininning 1996-; PROF, AGR ECON, TEX A&M UNIV, COL STA, 1978-; from asst prof to assoc prof, Tex A&M Univ, 1970-1978; economist, Econ Res Serv, US Dept Agr, 1967-1970; instr, agr econ, Tex Tech Univ, 1965-1966; statistician, Bur Census, US Dept Com, 1963-1964; consult, Govt, Legal & Corp. **Memberships:** Am Agr Econ Asn; Sigma Xi; Western Agr Econ Asn (vpres); Tex Plant Protection Asn. **Research Statement & Publications:** Economics of water resources emphasizing agriculture; alternative energy sources and impacts of energy price adjustments; economics and environmental impacts of integrated pest management systems used for crop production; Published over 10 articles. **Mailing Address:** Agr & Life Sci, Tex A&M Univ, 113 Admin Bldg, College Station, TX 77843-2142. **Fax:** 979-845-9769. **E-Mail:** r-lacewell@tamu.edu

LACEY, ELIZABETH PATTERSON, PLANT ECOLOGY. **Personal Data:** b Cleveland, Ohio. **Education:** Univ Colo, BA, 1969; Univ Mich, MS, 1974, PhD (bot), 1978. **Professional Experience:** PROF BIOL, UNIV NC, GREENSBORO, as of 2004; asst prof bot, Univ Nc, Greensboro, beginning 1978. **Memberships:** Bot Soc Am; Brit Ecol Soc; Ecol Soc Am; Soc Study Evolution; Sigma Xi. **Research Statement & Publications:** Plant population biology; evolution of life history patterns. **Mailing Address:** Dept Biol, Univ NC, 434 Bruce M Eberhart Bldg, Greensboro, NC 27412-0001. **Fax:** 336-334-5839. **E-Mail:** eplacey@uncg.edu

LACEY, HOWARD ELTON, MATHEMATICS. **Personal Data:** b Leaky, Tex, February 9, 1937; m 1958, c 4. **Education:** Abilene Christian Col, BA, 1959, MA, 1961; NMex State Univ, PhD (math), 1963. **Professional Experience:** RETIRED; prof emer math, Univ Tex A&M, beginning 1992; assoc dean, Col Sci Univ Tex A&M, 1991-1992; dept head math, Col Sci, Univ Tex A&M, 1980-1991; vchmn dept, Univ Tex, Austin, 1975-1977; res assoc, Inst Math, Polish Acad Sci, Warsaw, 1972-1973; mem grad fac, Univ Tex, Austin, 1968-1980; from assoc prof to prof math, Univ Tex, Austin, 1968-1980; res assoc, NASA Manned Spacecraft Ctr, 1967-1968; asst prof math, Univ Tex, Austin, 1964-1967 & Abilene Christian Col, 1963-1964. **Memberships:** Am Math Soc; Math Asn Am. **Research Statement & Publications:** Functional analysis; classical Banach spaces. **Mailing Address:** Dept Math, Tex A&M Univ, Col Sta, TX 77843-3368.

LACEY, JOHN I, psychophysiology, neurophysiology; deceased, see previous edition for last biography

LACEY, RICHARD FREDERICK, MAGNETISM. **Personal Data:** b Vallejo, Calif, May 29, 1931; m 1971, Ruth. **Education:** Mass Inst Technol, SB, 1952, PhD (physics), 1959. **Professional Experience:** STAFF SCIENTIST, HEWLETT-PACKARD LABS, 1969-; physicist, Hewlett-packard Labs, 1967-1969; sr physicist, Varian Assocs, 1963-1967; sr scientist, Am Sci & Eng Co, 1962-1963; sr engr, Sylvania Lighting Prod Co, 1959-1962. **Memberships:** Inst Elec & Electronics Engrs; Am Phys Soc. **Research Statement & Publications:** Atomic structure; radio-frequency spectroscopy; physical and quantum electronics. **Mailing Address:** Hewlett-Packard Labs, PO Box 10350, Palo Alto, CA 94303-0867. **E-Mail:** lacey@hpl.hp.com

LACH, JOSEPH T, PHYSICS. **Personal Data:** b Chicago, Ill, May 12, 1934; m 1965. **Education:** Univ Chicago, AB, 1953, MS, 1956; Univ Calif, Berkeley, PhD (physics), 1963. **Professional Experience:** RES AFILIARE, ILL STATE GEOL SURV, 1987-; chmn, Fermi Lab Physics Dept, 1974-1975; mem staff, Fermi Nat Accelerator Lab, beginning 1969; asst prof, Yale Univ, 1966-1969; Res assoc physics, Yale Univ, 1963-1965; Joint res prog, Leningrad Nuclear Physics Inst (USSR). **Memberships:** Am Phys Soc. **Research Statement & Publications:** Elementary particle physics; physics electronic data processing. **Mailing Address:** 28 W 364 Indian Knoll Trail, West Chicago, IL 60185.

LACHAINE, ANDRE RAYMOND JOSEPH, OPTICS. **Personal Data:** b Ottawa, Ont, September 22, 1945; m 1968, c 3. **Education:** Univ Ottawa, BSc Hons, 1967, MSc, 1970, PhD (physics), 1976. **Professional Experience:** PROF PHYSICS, ROYAL MIL COL CAN, 1990-; investr contract, 1977-; from asst prof to assoc prof, Royal Mil Col Can, 1976-1990; instr physics, Univ NB, 1976. **Research Statement & Publications:** Photoacoustics and photothermal physics. **Mailing Address:** Dept Physics, Royal Mil Col Can, PO Box 17000 Sta Forces, Kingston, ON K7K 7B4, Can. **Fax:** 613-541-6040. **E-Mail:** lachaine-a@rmc.ca

LACHANCE, DENIS, FOREST PATHOLOGY, RESEARCH MANAGEMENT. **Personal Data:** b Quebec City, Que, February 2, 1939; m 1964, Ruth; c Simon, Vincent & Renee. **Education:** Laval Univ, BSc, 1962; Univ Wis-Madison, PhD (phytopath), 1966. **Professional Experience:** BIOLOGIST, GENETIC ENG FOREST TREES, CAN FORESTRY SER, as of 2004; RES PROJ LEADER, ENVIRON STRESS ON FORESTS, 1989-; HEAD, FOREST INSECT & DIS SURV SECT, CAN FORESTRY SERV, 1979-; res scientist forest path, Laurentian Forestry Ctr, 1966-1979. **Memberships:** Can Phytopath Soc (secy-treas, 1971-1973); Can Inst Forestry; Int Soc Plant Path. **Research Statement & Publications:** Hardwood cankers and conifer root rot; hardwood decline diseases (sugar maple) and impact of environmental stress on forest health. **Mailing Address:** Can Forestry Serv, PO Box 3800 1055 Rue De Peps, Ste-Foy, PQ G1V 4C7, Can. **Fax:** 418-648-5849. **E-Mail:** dlachance@cfl.forestry.ca

LA CHANCE, LEO EMERY, GENETICS. **Personal Data:** b Brunswick, Maine, March 1, 1931; m 1955, Joan faureau; c 3. **Education:** Univ Maine, AB, 1953; NC State Col, MS, 1955, PhD (genetics), 1958. **Professional Experience:** CONSULT, 1992-; Ed, Anal Entomol Soc Am J, 1992-1999; dep dir, Joint Food & Agr Org Inst Atomic Energy Agency, Austria, 1986-1992; supvr insect geneticist & nat tech adv, Metab & Radiation Res Lab, 1982-1986; dir, Insect Genetics & Radiation Biol Sect, Agr Res Serv, USDA, 1977-1982; proj leader, Insect Genetics & Radiation Biol Sect, Agr Res Serv, USDA, 1971-1977; sci officer & head, Insect Eradication & Pest Control Sect, Joint Food & Agr Orgn-Int Atomic Energy Agency, Austria, 1969-1971; proj leader, Insect Genetics & Radiation Biol Sect, Metab & Radiation Res Lab, Entom Res Div, Agr Res Serv, 1963-1969; insect geneticist, USDA, 1960-1963; Res assoc biol, Brookhaven Nat Lab, 1958-1960. **Memberships:** AAAS; Genetics Soc Am; Entom Soc Am. **Research Statement & Publications:** Insect genetics and radiation biology; population genetics of screwworms, mechanism of hybrid sterility in Heliothis species; insect cytology and cytogenetic effects of radiation; factors influencing chromosome aberrations and dominant lethal mutations induced by radiation and chemicals; insect reproduction. **Mailing Address:** PO Box 5771, Fargo, ND 58105.

LACHANCE, MARC-ANDRE, SYSTEMATICS OF YEASTS, EVOLUTION OF YEASTS, ECOLOGY OF YEASTS. **Personal Data:** b Nairobi, Kenya, October 20, 1952; m 1980, Jane. **Education:** Univ Montreal, BA, 1969, BSc, 1972; McGill Univ, MSc, 1973; Univ Calif, Davis, PhD (microbiol), 1977. **Honors & Awards:** UWO Excellence in Teaching 1987 UWO-Science Florence Buck Award 1995. **Professional Experience:** PROF Biology, UNIV WESTERN ONT, 1994-; assoc ed, Int J Syst Evol Microbiol, 2001-; managing ed, Antonie van Leeuwenhoak, 2003-; mem, Int Comn Yeasts, 1988-; consult, var insts, 1979-; from asst prof to assoc prof, Univ Western Ont, 1979-1994; Fel, Pasteur Inst, 1977-1978. **Memberships:** Can Soc Microbiologists; Am Soc Microbiol; Can Soc Evol Ecol; Soc Gen Microbiol. **Research Statement & Publications:** Evolutionary systematics and ecology of yeasts; natural fermentations; speciation in yeasts; yeast biodiversity. **Mailing Address:** Dept Biology, Univ Western Ont, 1151 Richmond St, London, ON N6A 5B7, Can. **Fax:** 519-661-3935. **E-Mail:** lachance@uwo.ca

LACHANCE, MURDOCK HENRY, ELECTRO OPTICS. **Personal Data:** b Detroit, Mich, December 12, 1920; wid, c 1. **Education:** Mich Technol Univ, BS, 1942, MS, 1947. **Professional Experience:** MAT & FAILURE ANALYSIS CONSULT, 1983-; sr scientist, Xerox Electro-Optical Systs, 1962-1983; sr res metallurgist, Whirlpool Res Labs, 1957-1962; Prin phys metallurgist, Battelle Mem Inst, 1947-1957; naval aviator, USNR, 1944-1955; Com pilot & flight instr, Purdue Aeronaut Corp, 1942-1944. **Memberships:** Sigma Xi. **Research Statement & Publications:** Corrosion of stainless steels; development of refractory alloys, controlled porosity tungsten for ion propulsion and semiconductors for Peltier cooling; failure mechanisms of electro-optical devices; author and patentee in foregoing areas. **Mailing Address:** 260 S Chester Ave, Pasadena, CA 91106.

LACHANCE, PAUL ALBERT, NUTRITION, FOOD SCIENCE. **Personal Data:** b St Johnsbury, Vt, June 5, 1933; m 1955, c 4. **Education:** St Michael's Col, Vt, BSc, 1955; Univ Ottawa, PhD (biol, nutrit), 1960. **Honorary Degrees:** DSc, St Michael's Col, 1982. **Honors & Awards:** Gemini Prog Achievement Award, NASA, 1966. **Professional Experience:** Chmn, Univ Senate & Fac Rep Bd Gov, Rutgers Univ, beginning 1990; actg chmn, Dept Food Sci, beginning 1990; dir, grad prog food sci, beginning 1987; PROF FOOD SCI, RUTGERS UNIV, 1972-; dir, Sch Feeding Effectiveness Res Proj, 1969-1972; assoc prof food sci, Grad Prog Food Sci, 1967-1972; coord flight food & nutrit, NASA Manned Spacecraft Ctr, 1963-1967; lectr, Univ Dayton, 1963; res biologist, Aerospace Med Res Lab, Wright-Patterson AFB, Ohio, 1960-1963. **Memberships:** Fel Inst Food Technologists; Am Soc Clin Nutrit; Am Pub Health Asn; NY Acad Sci; Am Dietetic Asn; fel Am Col Nutrit. **Research Statement & Publications:** Aerospace food and nutrition; nutritional toxicology; nutritional aspects of food processing; micronutrient nutrification. **Mailing Address:** Dept Food Sci, Rutgers Univ, Dudley Road, New Brunswick, NJ 08901. **Fax:** 732-932-6776. **E-Mail:** lachance@aesop.rutgers.edu

LACHAPELLE, RENE CHARLES, MEDICAL MICROBIOLOGY. **Personal Data:** b Joliette, Que, January 28, 1930; American citizen; m 1959, c 3. **Education:** Seminaire de Joliette, BA, 1950; Univ Montreal, BSc, 1953; Syracuse Univ, MS, 1957, PhD (microbiol), 1962. **Professional Experience:** PROF EMER, DEPT MED TECHNOL, as of 2004; dir, Sch Allied Health, 1977 & 1982; chair person, Dept Med Technol, Univ Vt, beginning 1974; assoc prof biol, Univ Dayton, 1966-1974; lab admin dir clin path, Syracuse Mem Hosp, 1962-1966. **Memberships:** Sigma Xi; AAAS; Am Soc Med Tech; Am Soc Microbiol; Can Soc Microbiol. **Research Statement & Publications:** Morphogenesis and serological properties of Candida albicans; monomine oxidase and serotonin in germfree animals; skin bacteria in long-term space flights; educational aspects of medical technology; coagglutination of streptococcal groups. **Mailing Address:** Dept Med Technol, Univ Vt, 302 Rowell Bldg, Burlington, VT 05401. **E-Mail:** rene.lachapelle@uvm.edu

LACHENBRUCH, ARTHUR HEROLD, HEAT & DEFORMATION IN THE EARTHS CRUST. **Personal Data:** b New Rochelle, NY, December 7, 1925; m 1950, Edith Bennett; c Roger, Charles& Barbara. **Education:** Johns Hopkins Univ, BA, 1950; Harvard Univ,

MA, 1954, PhD (geophys), 1958. **Honors & Awards:** Kirk Bryan Award, Geol Soc Am, 1963; Distinguished Serv Award, Dept Interior, 1978; Walter H Bucher Medal, Am Geophys Union, 1989. **Professional Experience:** EMER GEOPHYSICIST, US GEOL SURV, as of 2002; vis prof, Dartmouth Col, 1963; geophysicist, beginning 1951. **Memberships:** Nat Acad Sci; fel AAAS; fel Am Geophys Union; fel Royal Astron Asn; fel Arctic Inst NAm; fel Geol Soc Am. **Research Statement & Publications:** Solid earth geophysics; terrestrial heat flow; tectonophysics; permafrost. **Mailing Address:** Br Tectonophysics, US Geol Surv 345 Middlefield Rd, Menlo Park, CA 94025.

LACHENBRUCH, PETER ANTHONY, BIOSTATISTICS. **Personal Data:** b Los Angeles, Calif, February 5, 1937; m 1962, Ella; c Jerry. **Education:** Univ Calif, Los Angeles, BA, 1958, PhD (biostatist), 1965; Lehigh Univ, MS, 1961. **Honors & Awards:** Mortimer Spiegelman Gold Medal Award, Am Pub Health Asn, 1971. **Professional Experience:** BIOSTATOSTICS BR CHIEF, DIV BIOSTATISTICS & EPIDEMIOL CTR BIOL EVAL & RES, FOOD & DRUGS ADMIN, as of 2006; staff, Food & Drug admin, beginning 1994; prof, Sch Pub Health, Univ Calif, Los Angeles 1985-1994; prof prev med, Univ Iowa, 1976; Univ NC, Chapel Hill, 1975-1976; from asst prof to prof biostatist, 1965-1976; USPHS fel biostatist, Univ Calif, Los Angeles, 1962-1965; res scientist, Am Inst Res, 1961-1962; sr opers res analyst, Syst Develop Corp, 1960-1961; programmer, Douglas Aircraft Co, 1959-1960; asst math, Lehigh Univ, 1958-1959. **Memberships:** fel Am Statist Asn; Biomet Soc; Royal Statist Soc; fel Intl Stat Inst. **Research Statement & Publications:** Discriminant analysis; statistical epidemiology; computer analysis of data; survival analysis. **Mailing Address:** Ctr Biol Eval & Res Food & Drug Admin, 1401 Rockville Pike, Rockville, MD 20852. **Fax:** 301-827-5218. **E-Mail:** lachenbruch@cber.fda.gov

LACHER, ROBERT CHRISTOPHER, TOPOLOGY, APPLIED MATHEMATICS. **Personal Data:** b Atlanta, Ga, October 14, 1940. **Education:** Univ Ga, BS, 1962, MA, 1964, PhD (math), 1966. **Professional Experience:** PROF EMER COMPUT SCI, FLA STATE UNIV, AS OF 2006; COMPUT SCI FAC, FLA STATE UNIV, 2003-; dir distributed & distance learning, Fla State Univ, 1999-2002; chair dept comput sci, Fla State Univ, 1991-1998; prof comput sci, Fla State Univ, 1984-2003; prof math, Fla State Univ, 1975-2003; NSF res grants, 1972-; mem, Inst Advan Study, 1972; Alfred P Sloan fel, 1970-1972; from asst prof to assoc prof, Fla State Univ, 1968-1975; vis mem math, Inst Advan Study, 1967-1968; res instr & asst prof math, Univ Calif, Los Angeles, 1966-1967. **Memberships:** AAAS; Sigma Xi; Am Math Soc; Phi Beta Kappa; Phi Kappa Phi; Asn Comput Mach; Inst Electrical Electronic Engrs; Am Cheml Soc; Int Neural Networks Soc. **Research Statement & Publications:** Geometric topology; cell-like mappings and generalized manifolds; embedding problems; catastrophe theory; published over 100 articles and granted 2 US patents. **Mailing Address:** Dept Comput Sci, Fla State Univ, 4750 Col Dr, Panama City, FL 32405-1099. **Fax:** 850-872-7720. **E-Mail:** lacher@cs.fsu.edu

LACHER, THOMAS EDWARD, TROPICAL ECOLOGY, CONSERVATION BIOLOGY. **Personal Data:** b Pittsburgh, Pa, August 9, 1949; m 1978, Susana; c Iara L & Lais M. **Education:** Univ Pittsburgh, BS, 1972, PhD (biol sci), 1980. **Honors & Awards:** Caesar Kleberg Endowed Professorship, Wildlife Ecology, Texas A&M Univ, 1996. **Professional Experience:** Sr VP, Conservation Int, 2002-; PROF, DEPT WILDLIFE & FISHERIES SCI, TEX A&M UNIV, 1996-2004; Empresa Brazil Pesquisa Agropecuaria, 1988 & Kellogg Found, 1991; mem, Working Group Comt Nat Inst Environ, 1990-1992; mem, Species Survival Comm IUCN, 1989-; dir trop ecol & prof, Dept Aquacult, Fisheries & Wildlife & Dept Environ Toxicol, Clemson Univ, 1989-1996; consult, World Wildlife Fund, 1986; Vis prof, Univ Fed Minas Gerais, 1986; from asst prof to assoc prof environ studies, Western Wash Univ, 1981-1989; asst prof zool, Univ Brazil, 1979-1981; Teaching asst biol, Univ Pittsburgh, 1972-1979. **Memberships:** AAAS; Am Soc Mammalogists; Ecol Soc Am; Asn Trop Biol; Am Asn Naturalists; Soc Conserv Biol. **Research Statement & Publications:** Research on the ecology and conservation of tropical ecosystems; ecological research emphasizes the structure and function of communities of mammals; conservation focuses on monitoring of biodiversity status. **Mailing Address:** Conservation International, 1919 M St, NW Ste 600, Washington, DC 20036. **Fax:** 202-912-0772. **E-Mail:** t.lacher@conservation.org

LACHICA, R VICTOR, CONTROL & MONITORING OF FOOD-BORNE PATHOGENS, MICROBIAL SPOILAGE OF FOODS. **Personal Data:** b Cebu, Philippines, February 24, 1943; American citizen; m 1974, Lois. **Education:** Wartburg Col, BS, 1963, Iowa State Univ, PhD (bact), 1967. **Professional Experience:** RES MICROBIOLOGIST, NATICK RES, DEVELOP & ENG CTR, US ARMY, 1984-; vis microbiologist, USDA Eastern Res Ctr, Philadelphia, 1983-1984; adj prof food microbiol, Univ Ariz, Tucson, 1981-1983; chief, Microbiol Br, WHO, Guatemala, 1974-1980; asst res microbiologist, Univ Calif-Davis, 1969-1974; res assoc, Univ Wis-Madison, 1967-1969. **Memberships:** Am Soc Microbiol; Inst Food Technologists; AAAS; Sigma Xi. **Research Statement & Publications:** Accelerated detection and identification of bacterial pathogens and indicator organisms in foods including staphylococcus aureus, Yersinia enterocolitica and Listeria monocytogenes; control of growth of these pathogens in foods. **Mailing Address:** US Army Natick Res, 241 Indian Camp Lane, Lincoln, MA 01760. **Fax:** 508-651-5274.

LACHIN, JOHN MARION, III, CLINICAL TRIALS. **Personal Data:** b New Orleans, La, July 4, 1942; m 1966, Teresa; c Ellen, Mark & Andrea. **Education:** Tulane Univ, BS, 1965; Univ Pittsburgh, ScD(biostatist), 1972. **Honors & Awards:** American Association of Publishers award for "The Outstanding Professional And Scholarly Title Of 2002 In Mathematics And Statistics" for the book co-authored with W Rosenberger entitled Randomization in Clinical Trials; Theory and Practice, John Wiley and Sons, 2002 President, Society for Clinical Trials, 2002-3 Joseph Ciminera Lecture, Merck and Company, 2002 John C Forbes Graduate Student Honors Colloquium Medical College of Virginia, 1995 Co-recipient, the Charles H Best Medal for Distinguished Service in the Cause of Diabetes Awarded to the Diabetes Control and Complications Trial Study Group (J Lachin, Director, Coordinating Center) American Diabetes Association, 1994 Elected Member, International Statistical Institute, 1993 Distinguished Graduate Award, Graduate School of Public Health, University of Pittsburgh, 1992 Delta Omega National Honor Society, 1991 Elected Fellow, Royal Statistical Society, 1991 Elected Fellow, American Statistical Association, 1989. **Professional Experience:** PROF BIOSTATIST & EPIDEMIOL, GEORGE WASH UNIV, as of 2003; dir, Biostatist Ctr, 1988-2000; co-dir, Biostatist Ctr, 1985-1988; PROF STATIST, GEORGE WASH UNIV, 1984-; Dir, Grad Pgm in Biostatist and Epidemiol, 1995-2004; Dir, Coordinating Center, National Cooperative Gallstone Study, 1980-1984; Lupus Nephritis Collab Study, 1981-1986; Diabetes Control & Complications Trial, 1982-1998; Epidemiology of Diabetes Interventions and Complications, 1985-; Type 1 Diabetes TrialNet, 2001-2008; many others. Author of Biostatistical Methods (Wiley, 2000), co-author of Randomization in Clinical Trials (Wiley, 2002). Named author of over 90 major papers plus contributor to over 100 additional papers. **Memberships:** Biomet Soc; fel Am Statist Asn; Soc Epidemiol Res; Soc Clin Trials; Inst Math Stat; Int Soc Clin Biostatist; fel Royal Statist Soc; Int Stat Inst; International Chinese Stat Assoc; Soc for Epidemiologic Research; Am Diabetes Assoc; European Assoc Study Diabetes; Int Diabetes Epidemiology Group; Drug Information Asn. **Research Statement & Publications:** Design, coordination and analysis of medical clinical trials; statistical methodology for design and analysis of clinical trials; medical research in diabetes, renal disease, gallstone disease. **Mailing Address:** Biostatist Ctr, George Wash Univ 6110 Executive Blvd Ste 750, Rockville, MD 20852. **Fax:** 301-881-0179. **E-Mail:** jml@biostat.bsc.gwu.edu

LACHLAN, A H, MATHEMATICS. **Education:** Univ Cambridge, PhD, 1964. **Professional Experience:** PROF EMER, DEPT MATHS, SIMON FRASER UNIV, CAN, as of 2006. **Mailing Address:** Dept Math, Simon Fraser Univ, Burnaby, BC V5A 1S6, Can.

LACHMAN, IRWIN MORRIS, CERAMICS ENGINEERING. **Personal Data:** b New York, NY, August 2, 1930; m 1959, c 2. **Education:** Rutgers Univ, BSc, 1952; Ohio State Univ, MSc, 1953, PhD (ceramic eng), 1955. **Professional Experience:** RETIRED; res assoc ceramics, Corning Glass Works, 1960-1995; staff mem, Sandia Corp, 1958-1960; sr scientist ceramics, Thermo Mat, Inc, 1957-1958. **Memberships:** AAAS; fel Am Ceramic Soc; Brit Ceramic Soc; Soc Automotive Engrs. **Research Statement & Publications:** Mechanical and thermal properties of ceramics. **Mailing Address:** 19 E Fifth St, Corning, NY 14830.

LACHMAN, LAWRENCE B, CELLULAR BIOLOGY. **Personal Data:** b Denver, Colo, November 13, 1947. **Education:** Univ Colo, BA, 1969; Boston Univ, PhD (biochem), 1973. **Professional Experience:** Mem, AIDS & Related Res Rev Group, NIH-Dept Health & Human Serv, 1990-; PROF, DEPT CELL BIOL, M D ANDERSON CANCER CTR, UNIV TEX, HOUSTON, 1988-; NIH grants, 1984-1987, 1986-1989, 1988-1989 & 1987-1992; assoc prof, Dept Cell Biol, M D Anderson Cancer Ctr, Univ Tex, Houston, 1983-1988; ed-in-chief, Lymphokine Res, 1982-; sr staff scientist, Immunex Corp, Seattle, Wash, 1982-1983; mem, Biol Response Modifiers Prog, Decision Network Comt, 1982-1983; mem, Duke Comprehensive Cancer Ctr, 1981; med res asst prof, Dept Microbiol & Immunol, Div Immunol, Duke Univ Med Ctr, 1979-1982; med res assoc, Dept Microbiol & Immunol, Div Immunol, Duke Univ Med Ctr, 1978-1979; res assoc, Dept Microbiol & Immunol, Div Immunol, Duke Univ Med Ctr, 1976-1978; Res assoc pharmacol, Sch Med, Yale Univ, 1973-1976. **Memberships:** Am Asn Immunol. **Research Statement & Publications:** Lymphokines and cytokines; interleukin-1; author or co-author of numerous publications; recipient of one patent. **Mailing Address:** Dept Cell Biol, Univ Tex M D Anderson Cancer Ctr, 1515 Holcombe Blvd, Houston, TX 77030. **Fax:** 713-797-9764. **E-Mail:** llachman@mdanderson.org

LACHMAN, LEON, PHARMACY, QUALITY CONTROL & QUALITY ASSURANCE. **Personal Data:** b Bronx, NY, January 29, 1929; m 1951, Joan; c Larry & Julie. **Education:** Columbia Univ, BSc, 1951, MSc, 1953; Univ Wis, PhD, 1956. **Honorary Degrees:** Dr, Columbia Univ, 1976. **Honors & Awards:** Indust Pharmaceut Technol Award, Acad Pharmaceut Sci, 1970. **Professional Experience:** Vis prof, Rutgers Univ Col Pharm, 1983-; CONSULT, LACHMAN CONSER SERVS INC, 1979-; sr vpres sci & technol, United Lab Inc, 1979-1981; mem bd trustees, Col Pharm, Columbia Univ, 1974-1978; vpres develop & control, Du Pont Pharmaceut, 1969-1979; dir, Res & Develop Div, Ciba Pharmaceut Co, NJ, 1968-1969; asst dir pharm, Res & Develop Div, Ciba Pharmaceut Co, NJ, 1956-1968; vis scientist, Am Asn Cols Pharm. **Memberships:** Fel Acad Pharmaceut Sci; hon mem Parenteral Drug Asn (pres, 1981-1983); Am Chem Soc; Am Asn Pharmaceut Scientists; pres Acad Pharmaceut Sci. **Research Statement & Publications:** Process and equipment design; research and development of pharmaceutical dosage forms; analytical research; quality control practices; medical research; regulatory affairs; Food and Drug Administration regulatory submissions and compliance. **Mailing Address:** Lachman Cons Serv Inc, Ste 604 1600 Stewart Ave, Westbury, NY 11590-6611. **Fax:** 516-683-1887.

LACHS, GERARD, ELECTRONICS. **Personal Data:** b Essen, Ger, August 2, 1934; American citizen; m 1957, Sandra; c Gregory & Melanie. **Education:** NY Univ, BS, 1956; Univ Rochester, MS, 1961; Syracuse Univ, PhD (elec eng), 1964. **Professional Experience:** PROF ELEC ENG, UNIV SFLA, 1984-; from asst prof to prof elec eng, Pa State Univ, 1964-1984; instr elec eng, Syracuse Univ, 1961-1964; sr res staff mem commun, Gen Dynamics/Electronics, 1958-1961; asst engr, Sperry Gyroscope Co, 1957-1958. **Memberships:** Inst Elec & Electronics Engrs; Acoust Soc Am. **Research Statement & Publications:** Coherent fiber optic communication systems; digital communication systems; coding of orthogonal wave shapes; audition and psycho-acoustics; bioengineering. **Mailing Address:** Dept Elec Eng, Univ S Fla, Tampa, FL 33620. **E-Mail:** lachs@ssunburn.ec.usf.edu

LACK, LEON, BIOCHEMISTRY. **Personal Data:** b New York, NY, January 7, 1922. **Education:** Brooklyn Col, AB, 1943; Mich State Univ, MS, 1948; Columbia Univ, PhD (biochem), 1953. **Professional Experience:** ASSOC PROF, SCH PSYCHOL, FLINDERS UNIV, as of 2003; PROF PHARMACOL, MED CTR, DUKE UNIV, 1971-; from asst prof to assoc prof, Med Ctr, Duke Univ, 1965-1971; from instr to asst prof pharmacol, Sch Med, Johns Hopkins Univ, 1955-1964; Fel, Duke Univ, 1953-1955. **Memberships:** Am Soc Biol Chemists; Am Soc Pharmacol & Exp Therapeuts. **Research Statement & Publications:** Metabolism of aromatic substances; intestinal active transport; pharamacology of androgen related disorders. **Mailing Address:** Sch Psychol, Flinders Univ, PO Box 2100, Adelaide, Australia. **E-Mail:** leon.lack@flinders.edu.au

LACKEY, CAROLYN JEAN, COMMUNITY NUTRITION. **Personal Data:** b Shelby, NC, November 24, 1948. **Education:** Univ NC, Greensboro, BSHE, 1971; Univ Tenn, Knoxville, MS, 1973, PhD (food sci), 1974. **Professional Experience:** PROF, FOOD & NUTRIT, NC AGR EXTEN SERV, NC STATE UNIV, 1983-; proj dir, Nutrit Educ Grant, Mich Dept Educ, 1978; from asst prof to assoc prof community nutrit, Mich State Univ, 1976-1983; asst prof foods & nutrit, Purdue Univ, 1974-1976. **Memberships:** Soc Nutrit Educ; Inst Food Technologists. **Research Statement & Publications:** Investigation of determinants of food behavior and food behavior modification; development, implementation and evaluation of food and nutrition education materials. **Mailing Address:** Dept Family Consumer Sci, NCSU Campus Box 7605, Raleigh, NC 27615-7605. **Fax:** 919-515-2786. **E-Mail:** carolyn_lackey@ncsu.edu

LACKEY, HOMER BAIRD, APPLIED CHEMISTRY. **Personal Data:** b Freewater, Ore, November 23, 1920; m 1942, c 3. **Education:** Ore State Univ, BS, 1947, MS, 1948. **Professional Experience:** Consult, chem concrete, 1982-; MGR REGULATORY AFFAIRS, CHEM PROD DIV, CROWN ZELLERBACH CORP, 1980-; mgr prod res, Chem Prod Div, 1968-1980; supvr prod res, Chem Prod Div, 1955-1968; res chemist, Cent Res Dept, Crown Zellerbach Corp, 8-1955; Asst, Ore State Univ, 1947-1948. **Memberships:** Am Chem Soc; Am Soc Testing & Mat; Am Concrete Inst. **Research Statement & Publications:** Forest byproduct utilization. **Mailing Address:** 804 NW 19th Ave, Camas, WA 98607.

LACKEY, JAMES ALDEN, MAMMALOGY. **Personal Data:** b Glens Falls, NY, November 25, 1938; div, c Jesse S & Christopher J. **Education:** Cornell Univ, BS, 1961; Calif State Univ, San Diego, MA, 1967; Univ Mich, PhD (zoology), 1973. **Professional Experience:**

PROF ZOOLOGY, STATE UNIV NY, OSWEG O, 1973-. **Memberships:** Am Soc Mammalogists; Sigma Xi; AAAS. **Research Statement & Publications:** Reproduction, growth, development and population ecology of mammals; biochemical genetics. **Mailing Address:** Biol Dept, State Univ NY, Oswego, NY 13126. **E-Mail:** lackey@oswego.edu

LACKEY, LAURENCE, GEOMORPHOLOGY, ENGINEERING GEOLOGY. **Personal Data:** American citizen. **Education:** Principia Col, BS, 1969; Univ Mich, PhD (geol), 1974. **Professional Experience:** ASSOC PROF & CHMN GEOL, PRINCIPIA COL, 1981-; mem proposal rev panel, Inst Sci Equip Prof, NSF, 1981; asst prof, Principia Col, 1979-1980; consult eng geol, 1975- & Off Energy Info Validation, US Dept Energy, 1978; prin investr, US Nuclear Regulatory Comn Contract, 1977-1978; Dir, Tenn Earthquake Info Ctr, 1977-1978; asst prof geol, Memphis State Univ, 1975-1978; Asst prof geol, Mich State Univ, 1974-1975. **Memberships:** AAAS; Geol Soc Am; Am Quaternary Asn; Nat Asn Geol Teachers. **Research Statement & Publications:** Computer applications in geology and quaternary geology. **Mailing Address:** 1002 Spruce St, Boulder, CO 80302-4029.

LACKEY, ROBERT T, FISHERIES & WILDLIFE MANAGEMENT. **Personal Data:** b Kamloops, BC, May 18, 1944; American citizen; m 1967, Lana; c Christopher R & Karen M. **Education:** Humboldt State Univ, BS (Fisheries), 1967; Univ Maine, Orono, MS (Zoology), 1968; Colo State Univ, PhD (fisheries & wildlife), 1971. **Professional Experience:** Senior Fisheries Biologist, EPA Research Laboratory 2000-; Professor of Fisheries, Oregon State University 1982-, Professor of Political Science, Oregon State University 1995-; ASSOC DIR, CTR ANALYSIS ENVIRON CHANGE, 1991-1997; DEP LAB DIR, ORE STATE UNIV, 1989-; br chief, Environ Res Lab, Corvallis, 1987-1989; assoc br chief, Environ Res Lab, Corvallis, 1985-1987; PROF FISHERIES, ORE STATE UNIV, 1982-; sr ecologist, Environ Res Lab, Corvallis, 1981-1985; group leader, Nat Water Res Analysis Group, 1979-1981; vis prof, Univ Mich, 1978; vis prof, George Mason Univ, 1976-1977; fish & wildlife adminr, US Fish & Wildlife Serv, 1976-1977; US Dept Agr, 1973-1978 & US Forest Serv, 1975-1978; Brandermill Corp, 1974-1975 & US Army Corps Engrs, 1975-1976; assoc prof fisheries, Fisheries Sci, 1974-1979; consult, US Fish & Wildlife Serv, 1974-1976; Res grants, US Nat Marine Fisheries Serv, 1972-1978; Res grants, Off Econ Opportunity & Celanese Corp, Off Water Res, 1972-1977; sect leader, Fisheries Sci, 1971-1972 & 1975-1977; Asst prof, Va Polytech Inst & State Univ, 1971-1974. **Memberships:** Inst Fishery Res Biologists; Am Fisheries Soc. **Research Statement & Publications:** Long-term forecast of the future of salmon in western North America: fisheries management, including structure and management of aquatic renewable natural resources; systems analysis; environmental assessment; ecological risk assessments; ecosystem management; ecological risk assessment. **Mailing Address:** Environ Protection Agency, 200 SW 35th St, Corvallis, OR 97333. **Fax:** 541-754-4799. **E-Mail:** lackey.robert@epamail.epa.gov

LACKEY, WALTER JACKSON, CERAMIC & METALLURGICAL ENGINEERING. **Personal Data:** b Shelby, NC, February 6, 1940; m 1961, Betty; c 2. **Education:** NC State Univ, BS (metall eng) & BS (ceramic eng), 1961, MS, 1963, PhD (ceramic eng), 1970. **Honors & Awards:** Roland B Snow Award, Am Ceramic Soc, 1996. **Professional Experience:** PROF MECH ENG, GA INST TECHNOL, 1997-; prin res scientist, Ga Inst Technol, 1986-1996; group leader, Metals & Ceramics Div, Oak Ridge Nat Lab, 1969-1984; res asst electronic ceramics, NC State Univ, 1966-1969; mat engr, Douglas Aircraft Corp, 1965-1966; res scientist, Battelle-Northwest Lab, 1963-1965. **Memberships:** Fel Am Ceramic Soc; Am Soc Metals. **Research Statement & Publications:** Fabrication, characterization and testing of nuclear fuels and waste forms; mechanisms and measurement of electrical conduction in ceramic insulators; ceramic coatings and composites; ceramic superconductors. **Mailing Address:** 3129 Wendwood Dr, Marietta, GA 30062. **Fax:** 404-894-9342. **E-Mail:** jack.lackey@me.gatech.edu

LACKNER, HENRIETTE, HEMATOLOGY. **Personal Data:** b Vienna, Austria, February 27, 1922; American citizen; m 1949, c 3. **Education:** Univ Leeds, MB & ChB, 1945, MD, 1948. **Honorary Degrees:** FRCP, Univ Leeds, 1996. **Professional Experience:** PROF HEMAT, SCH MED, NY UNIV, 1975-; assoc vis physician, Bellevue Hosp, NY, beginning 1975; assoc med, Univ Hosp, beginning 1975; from asst prof clin med to asst prof med, Sch Med, NY Univ, 1967-1975; asst, Univ Hosp, 1966-1975; clin asst vis physician, Bellevue Hosp, NY, 1965-1975; instr med, Sch Med, NY Univ, 1965-1967; res scientist, Am Nat Red Cross, beginning 1963; res assoc, Sch Med, NY Univ, 1963-1965; physician-in-chg & asst physician med outpatient clin, Arthritis Clin, 1956-1962; res asst, Groote Schuur Hosp, Cape Town, SAfrica, 1955-1962; jr lectr med, Univ Cape Town, 1955-1962; asst physician, Arthritis Clin, 1955-1956. **Memberships:** Soc Study Blood; Am Soc Hemat. **Research Statement & Publications:** Blood coagulation disorders and pathological fibrinolysis. **Mailing Address:** Dept Med, NY Univ Med Ctr, New Bellevue, 462 First AV, New York, NY 10016-6451.

LACKNER, JAMES ROBERT, AEROSPACE MEDICINE. **Personal Data:** b Virginia, Minn, November 11, 1940; m 1970, Ann. **Education:** Mass Inst Technol, BSc, 1966, PhD, 1970. **Honors & Awards:** Arnold B Tuttle Award, Aerospace Med Asn. **Professional Experience:** Comn space, Biol & Med, beginning 1991; mem, Comn Vision, 1987-1992; provost & dean fac, Dept Psychol, 1986-1989; mem, Comt Hearing, Bioacoust & Biomech, Nat Res Coun, 1985-1989; space sci bd, Sensory Motor Panel, Nat Acad Sci, 1984-1986; dir, Ashton Graybiel Spatial Orientation Lab, Brandeis Univ, 1982-; fabricant comt life sci exp for a space sta, 1982; RIKLIS PROF PHYSIOL, BRANDEIS UNIV, 1977-; chmn dept psychol, Dept Psychol, 1975-1983; res assoc dept psychol & clin res ctr, Mass Inst Technol, Cambridge, 1970-1980; from asst prof to assoc prof, Dept Psychol, 1970-1979. **Memberships:** Am Soc Gravitional & Space Biol; Aerospace Med Asn; Soc Neuroscience; Psychonomics Soc; Int Brain Res Orgn; hon mem Barany Soc; hon mem Int Acad Astronaut. **Research Statement & Publications:** Human sensory-motor and spatial orientation. **Mailing Address:** Brandeis Univ, Dept Psychol, 415 S St MS 033, Waltham, MA 02154-2700. **Fax:** 781-736-2031. **E-Mail:** lackner@brandeis.edu

LACKO, ANDRAS GYORGY, BIOCHEMISTRY. **Personal Data:** b Budapest, Hungary, November 10, 1936; Canadian citizen; m 1964, c 4. **Education:** Univ BC, BSA, 1961, MSc, 1963; Univ Wash, PhD (biochem), 1968. **Professional Experience:** PROF BIOCHEM, IMMUNOL & MOLECULAR BIOL, UNIV NTEX HEALTH SCI CTR, FT WORTH, 1983-; assoc prof, Dept Biochem & Molecular Biol, Univ Ntex Health Sci Ctr, Ft Worth, 1975-1983; asst prof med, Med Sch, Temple Univ, 1972-1975; mem staff, Med Sch, Temple Univ, 1971-1972; asst mem, Albert Einstein Med Ctr, 1969-1971; NIH fel, Albert Einstein Col Med, 1968-1969; Res asst biochem, Univ Wash, 1963-1968. **Memberships:** Am Soc Biochem & Molecular Biol; Am Heart Asn. **Research Statement & Publications:** Structure and function of enzymes and lipoproteins; Drug delivery. **Mailing Address:** Dept Molecular Biol & Immunol, Univ N Tex Health Sci Ctr, RES-416K, 3500 Camp Bowie Blvd, Ft Worth, TX 76107. **Fax:** 817-735-2118. **E-Mail:** alacko@hsc.unt.edu

LACKRITZ, HILARY, CHEMICAL ENGINEERING. **Education:** Northwestern Univ, BSE, 1985, PhD (mat sci & eng), 1990. **Professional Experience:** SR STAFF ENGR, LOCKHEED MARTIN SPACE SYSTS CO, ADVAN TECHNOL CTR, PALO ALTO, CALIF, 2004-; cofounder, Lightwave BioApplications, Cupertino, Calif, 2002-2005; LECTR, CHEM ENG, SAN JOSE STATE UNIV, 2002-; assoc dir, Microtechnol & Mat, Aclara BioSciences, Mountain View, Calif 1999-2002; dir mat, Gemfire Corp, Palo Alto, Calif, 1997-1999; from asst prof to assoc prof, Purdue Univ, 1991-1996. **Mailing Address:** San Jose State Univ, One Wash Sq Eng 385F, San Jose, CA 95192-0082. **Fax:** 408-924-4057. **E-Mail:** hilary.lackritz@sjsu.edu

LACKRITZ, HILARY S, CHEMICAL ENGINEERING. **Professional Experience:** CHMN NANOBIOTECHNOLOGY FORUM, NANOSIG, as of 2003. **Mailing Address:** Nanosig, 2000 Univ Ave, East Palo Alto, CA 94303. **E-Mail:** hlackritz@nanosig.org

LACKS, SANFORD, GENETICS, MOLECULAR BIOLOGY. **Personal Data:** b New York, NY, January 28, 1934; m Elaine; c Jennifer, Daniel & Julia. **Education:** Union Univ, NY, BS, 1955; Rockefeller Univ, PhD, 1960. **Professional Experience:** SR GENETICIST EMERITUS, BROOKHAVEN NAT LAB, 2002-; from asst geneticist to sr geneticist, Brookhaven Nat Lab, 1961-2002; Instr biol, Harvard Univ, 1960-1961. **Memberships:** Am Soc Microbiol; Am Soc Biol Chem; Genetics Soc Am; DNA Methylation Soc. **Research Statement & Publications:** Bacterial transformation; DNA repair; DNA methylation; restriction enzymes; folate biosynthesis. **Mailing Address:** Biol Dept, Brookhaven Nat Lab, Upton, NY 11973-5000. **Fax:** 631-344-3407. **E-Mail:** lacks@bnl.gov

LACKSONEN, JAMES W(ALTER), CHEMICAL ENGINEERING. **Personal Data:** b Ashtabula, Ohio, October 17, 1936; m 1957, c 2. **Education:** Ohio State Univ, BS & MS, 1959, PhD (chem eng), 1964. **Professional Experience:** Prof emer chem eng, Univ Toledo, beginning 1992; asst dean, Col Eng, 1971-1992; from asst prof to prof, Univ Toledo, 1967-1992; sr develop engr chem-plastics div, Gen Tire & Rubber Co, Ohio, 1966-1967; proj engr, Pittsburgh Plate Glass Co, 1965-1966; res engr, Battelle Mem Inst, 1960-1965. **Memberships:** AAAS; Am Inst Chem Engrs; Am Chem Soc; Electrochem Soc. **Research Statement & Publications:** Kinetics and surface chemistry processes; fuel cells; transport of gases in microporous media; reactor design; reinforced plastics; foam; mass transfer. **Mailing Address:** 4758 S Crestridge Rd, Toledo, OH 43623.

LA CLAIRE, JOHN WILLARD, II, PLANT CELL BIOLOGY, PHYCOLOGY. **Personal Data:** b Utica, NY, July 1, 1951; m 1994, Julie. **Education:** Cornell Univ, BS, 1973; Univ SFla, MA, 1975; Univ Calif, Berkeley, PhD (bot), 1979. **Professional Experience:** Prin investr marine biotechnol, ONR, 1995-; vis assoc prof, Dept Cell Biol, Stanford Univ, 1989; prin investr plant growth develop, USDA, 1987-; PROF, SCH BIOL SCI, UNIV TEX, 1999-; assoc prof Dept Bot, Univ Tex, 1985-1999; prin investr, Cell Biol Sect, NSF, 1981-; asst prof, Dept Bot, Univ Tex, 1979-1985. **Memberships:** AAAS; Am Soc Cell Biol; Bot Soc Am; Brit Phycol Soc; Int Phycol Soc; Phycol Soc Am (secy, 2000-2002). **Research Statement & Publications:** Cell biology and molecular biology of algae; cell motility phenomena; cellular wound healing, mitosis, cytokinesis and cytoplasmic streaming; cytoskeleton of plant cells; plasmid like DNA. **Mailing Address:** Sch Biol Sci, Univ Tex, One Univ Sta A6700, Austin, TX 78712. **E-Mail:** laclaire@uts.cc.utexas.edu

LACOMBE, ROBERT H, MATHEMATICS. **Professional Experience:** CHAIR, MAT SCI & TECH, CONFERENCES LLC, as of 2005. **Memberships:** Glassfibre Reinforced Concrete Asn. **Mailing Address:** Conferences LLC, 3 Hammer Dr, Hopewell Junction, NY 12533. **Fax:** 212-656-1016. **E-Mail:** rhlacombe@compuserve.com

LACOSS, RICHARD THADDEE, SIGNAL PROCESSING, COMPUTERIZED SENSOR DATA INTERPRETATION. **Personal Data:** b Gardner, Mass, August 19, 1937; m 1984, Cynthia; c Zelda & Remi. **Education:** Columbia Univ, BA, 1959, BS, 1960; Univ Calif, Berkeley, MS, 1962, PhD (elec eng, info & control theory), 1965. **Professional Experience:** SR STAFF, LINCOLN LAB, as of 2006; group leader, Lincoln Lab, Mass Inst Technol beginning 1969; mem staff, 1965-1969. **Memberships:** Inst Elec & Electronics Engrs; Sigma Xi; Asn Comput Mach. **Research Statement & Publications:** Signal processing; object recognition; radar signal analysis; neural networks; image processing; model-based algorithms; intelligent systems; atmospheric acoustics; distributed algorithms; system engineering. **Mailing Address:** Lincoln Lab, Mass Inst Technol, S3-479 77 Mass Ave, Cambridge, MA 02139-4307. **E-Mail:** lacoss@LL.MIT.EDU

LACOSTE, RENE JOHN, ANALYTICAL CHEMISTRY, PESTICIDE CHEMISTRY. **Personal Data:** b New York, NY, February 19, 1927. **Education:** Rensselaer Polytech Inst, BS, 1950; Univ Chicago, MS, 1953. **Professional Experience:** RETIRED; foreign regulatory mgr agr chem, Rohm & Haas Co, 1980-1990; regional regulatory mgr, Rohm & Haas Co, 1975-1980; Agr indust rep UN, Codex Comt Pesticide Residues, 1970-1990; int registr agr & sanit chem, Rohm & Haas Co, 1969-1975; sr chemist, Rohm & Haas Co, 1968-1969; chemist, Rohm & Haas Co, 1953-1968; Chemist, Am Dent Asn, 1950-1953. **Memberships:** Fel AAAS; Am Chem Soc; Am Inst Chem; NY Acad Sci; Sigma Xi. **Research Statement & Publications:** Physical and chemical methods of analysis; electrochemical analysis; separations of organic mixtures; developed methods for analysis of chemicals in products of industrial production; national and international industry and government groups concerned with drafting and adopting regulations regarding production and use of agricultural pesticide chemicals. **Mailing Address:** 5353 Arlington Expressway Apt 11-B, Jacksonville, FL 32211-5588.

LACOUNT, ROBERT BRUCE, ORGANIC CHEMISTRY. **Personal Data:** b Martinsburg, WVa, September 16, 1935; m 1964, Virginia; c Victoria & Robert. **Education:** Shepherd Col, BS, 1957; Univ Pittsburgh, MLitt, 1962, PhD (org chem), 1965. **Professional Experience:** PROF CHEM, WAYNESBURG COL, 1991-; tech dir, ViRoLac Ind, 1989-; res chemist, Dept Energy, 1977-1989; res chemist, Energy Res & Develop Admin, 1975-1977; prof & chmn dept chem & physics, Waynesburg Col, 1971-1991; res chemist, US Bur Mines, 1970-1975; from asst prof chem to prof & chmn dept, Waynesburg Col, 1965-1971; res grant, Petrol Res Fund, 1965-1967; res assoc fundamental org chem, Mellon Inst, 1958-1965. **Memberships:** Am Chem Soc. **Research Statement & Publications:** Synthetic organic chemistry; organic sulfur chemistry; production of low-sulfur fuels from coal; instrumental methods. **Mailing Address:** Dept Chem, Waynesburg Col, 309 Stewart Sci Hall, Waynesburg, PA 15370. **E-Mail:** rlacount@waynesburg.edu

LACOURSE, WILLIAM CARL, GLASS SCIENCE & ENGINEERING. **Personal Data:** b Schenectady, NY, June 19, 1943; m 1966, Patricia; c Brian C & Elisa (Rogers). **Education:** State Univ NY, Stony Brook, BS, 1966, MS, 1967; Rensselaer Polytech Inst, PhD (mat eng), 1970. **Professional Experience:** ASSOC DIR, CTR GLASS RES, NSF, as of 2000; VPRES, SAXON GLASS TECHNOL, 1996-; dir, Ctr Glass res, Alfred Univ, 1996-1997; vis scientist, St Gobair res, Paris, 1987 & Univ Modera, Italy, 1995; PROF GLASS SCI, COL CERAMICS, ALFRED UNIV, 1970-; Nat res Coun postdoctoral fel, Naval res lab, 1970. **Memberships:** Fel Am Ceramic Soc; Soc Glass Technol. **Research Statement & Publications:** Authored over 70 publications in general area of glass science, with special emphasis on chemical and mechanical properties development of special compositions for new or improved properties. **Mailing Address:** Dept Ceramic Eng & Mat Sci, Sch Eng, Alfred Univ, 160 Binns-Merrill Hall, Alfred, NY 14802. **Fax:** 607-871-2392. **E-Mail:** lacourse@alfred.edu

LACOURSE, WILLIAM R, ANALYTICAL CHEMISTRY. **Education:** Northeastern Univ, PhD, 1987. **Professional Experience:** PROF, DEPT CHEM & BIOCHEM, UNIV MD BALTIMORE CO, as of 2006. **Research Statement & Publications:** electrochemical detection in high performance liquid chromatography. **Mailing Address:** Dept Chem & Biochem, Univ MD Baltimore Co, 1000 Hill Top Circle, Baltimore, MD 21228. **Fax:** 410-455-2608. **E-Mail:** lacourse@umbc.edu

LACOUTURE, PETER GEORGE, PHARMACOLOGY, PHYSIOLOGY. **Personal Data:** b Worcester, Mass, October 26, 1951; m 1978, Sheila; c Alyssa, Bryan & Timothy. **Education:** Col Holy Cross, AB, 1973; Mass Col Pharm & Allied Health Sci, MS, 1981, PhD (pharmacol & physiol), 1986. **Professional Experience:** PRES, MAGIDOM DISCOVERY, LLC, 2001-; sr dir, Purdue Pharma, LP, 1997-2001; dir, Purdue Frederick, 1994-1997; assoc dir, Purdue Frederick, 1992-1994; asst dir, Wyeth-Ayerst Res, 1990-1992; examr, Am Bd Appl Toxicol, 1989; sr clin scientist, Wyeth-Ayerst Res, 1988-1990; asst med, Dept Med, Children's Hosp Boston, 1988-1989; instr pediat, Harvard Med Sch, 1988; res fel path, Harvard Med Sch & develop officer, Clin Labs, Children's Hosp Boston, Mass, 1987; res affil toxicol, Div Clin Pharmacol & Toxicol, Children's Hosp, Boston, 1985-1987; consult, Drug Epidemiol Unit, Boston Univ Med Ctr, 1980-1987; sr res asst physiol, Harvard Sch Pub Health, 1980-1985; consult, Mass Poison Control Syst, 1977-1987. **Memberships:** Am Acad Clin Toxicol; Am Soc Pharmacol & Exp Therapeut; Am Soc Clin Pharmacol & Therapeut; Am Thoracic Soc; Am Col Allergy & Immunol; Am Pain Soc. **Research Statement & Publications:** Rheumatology, anti-inflammatory drugs; immunology, anti-allergy and pulmonary drugs; general toxicology; pharmacoepidemiology; regulatory affairs; author of over 100 technical publications. **Mailing Address:** Magidom Discovery, LLC, 1771 Post Rd E No 228, Newton, CT 06470-1774.

LACROIX, GUY, MARINE ECOLOGY. **Personal Data:** b Que, April 10, 1930; m 1960, c 2. **Education:** Laval Univ, BA, 1952, LPh, 1953, DSc, 1968; Univ Montreal, BSc, 1957, MSc, 1959. **Professional Experience:** RETIRED; assoc dir, Sch Grad Studies, 1985-1997; dir, Grad Studies Biol, 1983-1985; ed, Can Naturalist, 1979-1986; mem bd, Laval Univ, 1974-1977; Sci Comt Oceanic Res, Can Nat Comt, 1974-1978; exec secy, Interuniv Group Oceanog Res, Que, 1970-1977; from asst prof to prof biol oceanog, Dept Biol, Laval Univ, 1968-1997; zooplanktonologist, Grande Riviere Marine Biol Sta, Que, 1958-1968. **Memberships:** Marine Biol Asn UK; Am Soc Limnol & Oceanog; Plankton Soc Japan. **Research Statement & Publications:** Zooplankton; invertebrate zoology; primary production; marine invertebrates. **Mailing Address:** 1155 Ave Turnbull, Apt 403, Quebec, PQ G1R 5G3, Can.

LACROIX, JEAN-MICHEL, MOLECULAR BIOLOGY. **Honorary Degrees:** Dr, Univ Paris III, New Sorbonne, 1978. **Professional Experience:** DIR, CNED, CAN, as of 2006; CTR INFECTIONS & BIOMAT RES, UNIV TORONTO, beginning 1995. **Memberships:** Int Coun Can Studies. **Mailing Address:** Toronto Hosp, Bell Wing Rm G631, Toronto, ON M5G 2C4, Can. **Fax:** 416-978-7307. **E-Mail:** lacroix@medac.med.utoronto.ca

LACROIX, MONIQUE, FOOD SCIENCE. **Education:** Laval Univ, BSc, 1980, MSc, 1982, PhD (nutrit), 1986. **Professional Experience:** PROF, INST ARMAND FRAPPIER RES CTR, as of 2004; RESEARCHER, CAN IRRADIATION CTR, INST ARMAND FRAPPIER RES CTR, as of 2004. **Mailing Address:** Inst Armand-Frappier Res Ctr, 531 Boul des Prairies CP 100, Laval, PQ H7V 1B7, Can. **Fax:** 450-687-5792. **E-Mail:** monique.lacroix@inrs-iaf.uquebec.ca

LACROIX, NORBERT HECTOR JOSEPH, MATHEMATICS, BIOLOGICAL SCIENCES. **Personal Data:** b Sarsfield, Ont, October 26, 1940; m 1965, Ghislaine; c Eric, Hugo & Carl (deceased). **Education:** Univ Ottawa, BSc, 1962; Univ Notre Dame, PhD (math), 1966. **Professional Experience:** PROF MATH, LAVAL UNIV, 1977-; chmn dept, Laval Univ, 1970-1977; from asst prof to assoc prof, Laval Univ, 1966-1977; instr math, Univ Notre Dame, 1962-1966. **Memberships:** Can Math Soc; Asn Canadienne-Francaise Advan Sci; Can Appl Math Soc; Can Soc Theoret Biol; Am Math Soc. **Research Statement & Publications:** Organisational principles in developmental and structural biology; mathematical models. **Mailing Address:** Dept Math, Laval Univ, Quebec, PQ G1K 7P4, Can. **Fax:** 418-656-2817. **E-Mail:** nlacroix@mat.ulaval.ca

LACY, ANN MATTHEWS, GENE STRUCTURE & FUNCTION-FUNGI, MOLECULAR GENETICS, & HUMAN GENETICS. **Personal Data:** b Boston, Mass, May 29, 1932. **Education:** Wellesley Col, BA, 1953; Yale Univ, MS, 1956, PhD (microbiol), 1959. **Professional Experience:** EMER PROF BIOL SCI, GOUCHER COL, 1998-; Elizabeth Connolly Todd prof, Goucher Col, 1994-1998; chmn, Fac Natural Sci & Math, Goucher Col, 1988-1991; prof biol sci, Goucher Col, 1973-1998; chmn, Dept Biol Sci, Goucher Col, 1969-1972, 1986-1987, 1989-1998; sr res fel, Bot Dept, Univ Glasgow, Scotland, 1968-1969; from asst prof to assoc prof, Goucher Col, 1961-1973; prin investr, genetics tryptophan synthase in neurospora crassa, NSF res grants, Goucher Col, 1960-1970; instr genetics, Goucher Col, 1959-1961; res asst, Dept Genetics, Carnegie Inst, Washington, Cold Spring Harbor, 1953-1954. **Memberships:** AAAS; Genetics Soc Am; Am Asn Univ Profs; Sigma Xi. **Research Statement & Publications:** Gene-enzyme relationships and gene regulation in Neurospora crassa (gene organization, cross-pathway regulation), especially in the tryptophan biosynthetic pathway. **Mailing Address:** Dept Biol Sci Goucher Col, 1021 Dulaney Valley Rd, Towson, MD 21204.

LACY, GEORGE HOLCOMBE, PHYTOPATHOLOGY, BACTERIAL GENETICS. **Personal Data:** b Washington, DC, November 13, 1943; m 1964, c 2. **Education:** Calif State Univ, Long Beach, BS, 1966, MS, 1971; Univ Calif, Riverside, PhD (phytopath), 1975. **Professional Experience:** RETIRED; prof plant path, VA Polytech Inst & State Univ, beginning, 1988-; Environ Protection Agency, NSF grant, 1987-1991; NSF grant, USDA grant, 1983-1989; from asst prof to assoc prof, VA Polytech Inst & State Univ, 1980-1988; asst plant pathologist, Conn Agr Exp Sta, 1977-1980; NSF grant, Univ Wis-Madison, 1976-1977, 1987-; res assoc plant path, Univ Wis-Madison, 1975-1977; NIH grant, 1975-1976; scientist II soil microbiol, Jet Propulsion Lab, Calif Inst Technol, 1969-1971; biol instr, US Peace Corps, Corozal Town, Belize, 1966-1968; lab technician qual control, Am Chem & Plastics Co, Stauffer Chem Co, Calif, 1963-1965. **Memberships:** Am Phytopath Soc; Am Microbiol Soc. **Research Statement & Publications:** Molecular basis for plant pathogenesis and biological control of plant disease ecological impact of release of genetically engineered microorganisms into the environment. **Mailing Address:** Dept Plant Path Physiol & Weed Sci Va Polytech Inst & State Univ, Rm 202 435 Old Glade Rd, Blacksburg, VA 24061-0330. **Fax:** 540-231-5755. **E-Mail:** lacygh@vt.edu

LACY, LEWIS L, GEOMECHANICS & ROCK MECHANICS & MICROGRAVITY SCIENCES, MATERIAL ANALYSIS & APPLIED PHYSICS FOR PETROLEUM PRODUCTION. **Personal Data:** b Bluefield, WVa, March 25, 1941; m 1964, Peggy; c Gregory S Lacy & Robert L Lacy. **Education:** Va Polytech Inst & State Univ, BS, 1963, MS, 1965; Univ Tenn, Knoxville, PhD (physics), 1971. **Honors & Awards:** Marshall Space Flight Ctr Dirs Commendation Award, NASA, 1971 & NASA Manned Flight Awareness Award, 1974; NASA Group Achievement Award, Johnson Space Flight Ctr, 1976; NASA New Technol Awards, 1980, 1984, 1993. **Professional Experience:** DIR, GEOMECHANICS, CORE LAB, as of 1999; SR RES SCIENTIST, BJ SERV, 1993-1999; mem, Comt Advance Hydraul Fracturing, Soc Petrol Engrs, 1986-1989; sr res staff, Exxon Prod Res Co, 1981-1993; supervisory space scientist NASA, 1975-1981; br chief, Solid State & Solidification Br, 1977-1981; mat & appl physics scientist, Space Sci Lab, 1968-1977; exp physicist, Space Sci Lab, Marshall Space Flight Ctr, NASA, 1965-1968; Res assoc solid state physics, Los Alamos Sci Lab, 1964. **Memberships:** Am Phys Soc; Soc Petrol Engrs; Am Rock Mechanics Soc. **Research Statement & Publications:** Geomechanics and rock mechanics laboratory testing and engineering analysis; borehole stability and sand control testing and analysis; data for hydraulic fracturing designs; acoustics and ultrasonics for exploration and production; gleeble welding simulation experiments and fracture toughness of offshore platform steels; hydraulic fracture geometry and orientation, triaxial borehole seismic, tiltmeter arrays and fracture mapping; solidification and crystal growth, containerless supercooling and low-gravity solidification, low temperature and superconducting materials. **Mailing Address:** Core Lab, 6316 Windfern, Houston, TX 77040. **E-Mail:** lewis.lacy@corelab.com

LACY, MELVYN LEROY, PLANT PATHOLOGY, EPIDEMIOLOGY. **Personal Data:** b Henry, Nebr, October 24, 1931; m 1954, Shirley Chenoweth; c Matthew & Miles. **Education:** Univ Wyo, BS, 1959, MS, 1961; Ore State Univ, PhD (plant path), 1964. **Honors & Awards:** Distinguished Serv Award, Am Phytopath Soc. **Professional Experience:** RETIRED; From asst prof to prof plant path, Mich State Univ, 1965-1996. **Memberships:** Am Phytopath Soc; Can Phytopath Soc; Am Potato Asn. **Research Statement & Publications:** Soil-borne fungus diseases, epidemiology and control; pesticides for disease control; epidemiology, disease forecasting and disease management. **Mailing Address:** Dept Bot & Plant Path, Mich State Univ, East Lansing, MI 48823. **E-Mail:** lacyml@aol.com

LACY, PAUL ESTON, pathology; deceased, see previous edition for last biography

LACY, PRITI S, ANATOMY. **Education:** Allahabad Univ, India, BS; Lucknow Univ, India, MS; Univ Nebr Med Ctr, PhD. **Professional Experience:** PROF ANAT, OSTEOP MED CTR, DES MOINES UNIV, as of 2006. **Mailing Address:** Des Moines Univ, Osteop Med Ctr, Rm 330, Des Moines, IA 50312. **Fax:** 515-271-1400.

LACY, W(ILLARD) C(ARLETON), GEOLOGICAL ENGINEERING. **Personal Data:** b Waterville, Ohio, July 17, 1916; m 1940, Jo Wipior; c 6. **Education:** DePauw Univ, AB, 1938; Univ Ill, MS, 1940; Harvard Univ, PhD (geol), 1950. **Honors & Awards:** Fulbright Lectr, Univ Queensland, 1967; Henry Krumb Lectr, 1985; Ben Dickerson Award, 1991; Medal of Honor, Mining Hall of Fame, 1993. **Professional Experience:** EMER CONSULT, JAMES COOK UNIV, NQUEENSLAND, 1983-; emer prof geol, James Cook Univ, Nqueensland, 1981-1993; found chair geol, James Cook Univ, Nqueensland, 1972-1981; prof mining & geol eng & head dept, Univ Ariz, 1964-1971; prof geol, Univ Ariz, 1955-1964; Vis lectr, Harvard Univ, 1953; from asst chief to chief geologist, Cerro Del Pasco Corp, 1950-1955; petrologist, Cerro Del Pasco Corp, 1946-1950; Geologist, Titanium Alloy Mfg Co, 1942-1943; prin, Lacy & Assocs, Consults. **Memberships:** Fel Geol Soc Am; Soc Econ Geol; Am Inst Mining Metall & Petrol Engrs; Int Soc Rock Mech; hon fel Australasian Inst Mining & Metall; Asn Eng Geologists. **Research Statement & Publications:** Mining geology; localization of ore deposits; ground stabilization. **Mailing Address:** 8700 N La-Cholla Blvd, Tucson, AZ 85742.

LACY, W(ILLIAM) J(OHN), CHEMICAL ENGINEERING. **Personal Data:** b Meriden, Conn, May 26, 1928; m 1950, c William P, Gregory D & Debra (Gwen). **Education:** Univ Conn, BS, 1950, New York Univ, 1951, Orins, 1957, PhD. **Honorary Degrees:** DSc, Paul Sabatier Univ, France, 1983. **Honors & Awards:** Gold Medal, Am Water Works Asn, 1960; Paul Sabatier Univ Medal, France, 1983; Bronze Medal, Environ Protection Agency, 1983; US Distinguished Serv Medal, 1984; Govern Thailand Environ Medal, 1984; Lublin Polytech Univ Medal, 1988; Madam Curie Medal, Poland, 1989; Polish Acad Sci Medal, 1992; Washington Acad Sci Medal, 1992; High Inst Pub Health Medal, Egypt, 1993; Leonard Gloub Chem Award. **Professional Experience:** Italy, 1987 & Hong Kong, 1990; VI, Belgium, 1985; PRES, LACY & CO, ENVIRON & INDUST CONSULTS, 1983-; VI, France, 1983; co-chair III, IV, V & VI, X, Int Conf Chem, Protect Environ, Poland, 1981 & 1989; Egypt, 1979 & Italy, 1981; dir water, waste & hazardous mat res, 1979-1983; sci dir, US Deleg, India, 1978; rep, Environ Protection Agency, World Cong Berlin, 1977; deleg, Tokyo Conf, 1977; co-chmn, Third Int Conf, Sorrento, Italy, 1976; head, US Deleg UN Environ Prog, Paris, 1975 & 1978; dep dir, US deleg, USSR, 1975, 1976 & 1978; prin eng sci adv, Appl Sci & Technol Div, 1974-1979; dir, Appl Sci & Technol Div, 1971-1974; chief indust pollution control res & develop, Fed Water Pollution Control Admin, Environ Protection Agency, 1967-1971; asst dir, Post Attack Res Div, Off Civil Defense, Wash, DC, 1962-1967; chief radiochemist, Off Civil Defense & Mobilization, 1959-1962; chief test sta, Oak Ridge Nat Lab, Tenn, 1958-1959; chmn adv comt spec weapons, Atomic Energy Comn, 1956-1958; mem Nat Adv Bd Water Decontamination, 1954-1956; Partic sanit eng conf, Atomic Energy Comn, 1952, 1954 & 1956; chemist & sr proj engr, Eng Res & Develop Labs, Va, 1951-1958; Asst chemist & res assoc, NY Univ, 1950-1951; vpres, Int & Exec Comt Chem Protection Environ; lectr, numerous US univs; consult pollution prev; US Dept Energy, waste minimization, USAID & environ activ Cent Europ, Dept Com; chmn (ad hoc) Environ Protection Agency Hazardous Waste Res Lab Comt Waste Minimization. **Memberships:** Am Soc Testing & Mat; Am Chem Soc; Sigma Xi; fel Am Inst Chem Engrs; Am Acad Environ Engrs; life mem Int Ozone Asn. **Research Statement & Publications:** Industrial waste water treatment; pollution prevention waste minimization; reactor waste disposal problems; hazardous waste monitoring and disposal; author of 201 publications and granted 4 patents. **Mailing Address:** 9114 Cherry Tree Dr, Alexandria, VA 22309-2905. **Fax:** 703-780-2184.

LAD, PRAMOD MADHUSUDAN, RECEPTOR PHARMACOLOGY, MEMBRANE BIOPHYSICS & BIOCHEMISTRY. **Personal Data:** b Bombay, India, December 25, 1948; American citizen; m 1978, c 1. **Education:** London Univ, BSc, 1970; Cornell Univ, PhD (chem), 1974. **Professional Experience:** ADJ ASSOC PROF, UNIV SOUTHERN CALIF, 1986-; vis assoc res fac, Calif Inst Technol, Pasadena, 1981-; KAISER REGIONAL RES LAB, KAISER FOUND INST, LOS ANGELES, 1981-. **Memberships:** Am Soc Pharmacol & Exp Therapeut; Biophys Soc; Endocrine Soc; AAAS; Am Chem Soc; Reticuloendothelial Soc. **Research Statement & Publications:** Major pathways of receptor mediated signaling in cells of the immune response; cells involved in inflammatory reactions such as neutrophils, lymphocytes, and mast cells; platelet-leukocyte interactions and their role in thrombus formation. **Mailing Address:** Regional Res Lab, Kaiser Found Hosp, 4900 Sunset Blvd, Los Angeles, CA 90027-5337.

LAD, ROBERT AUGUSTIN, CHEMISTRY. **Personal Data:** b Chicago, Ill, May 8, 1919; m 1944, Delores; c 9. **Education:** Univ Chicago, SB, 1939, SM, 1941, PhD (inorg chem),

1946. **Professional Experience:** RETIRED; mem solid state sci panel, Nat Acad Sci, Nat Res Coun, 1963-1978; chief, Mat Sci Br, 1959-1978; aeronaut res scientist, Nat Adv Comt Aeronaut, Lewis Res Ctr, NASA, 1946-1959; asst, Nat Defense Res Comt, Univ Chicago, 1942-1946. **Memberships:** AAAS; Am Phys Soc; fel Am Inst Chem. **Research Statement & Publications:** Physics and chemistry of surfaces; radiation chemistry; materials science. **Mailing Address:** 3114 W 159th St, Cleveland, OH 44111.

LAD, ROBERT JOSEPH, PHYSICS. **Education:** Northwestern Univ, BS, 1980; Cornell Univ, MS, 1982, PhD, 1986. **Professional Experience:** DIR, LAB SURFACE SCI & TECH, 1997-; PROF PHYSICS, UNIV MAINE, 1997-; from asst prof to assoc prof, Univ Maine, 1988-1997. **Research Statement & Publications:** Surface and Interface Properties of Materials; Synthesis and Processing of Ceramic and Semiconducting Thin Films; Electronic Properties of Materials; Thin Film Sensor Materials; Metal-Ceramic and Ceramic-Ceramic Interfaces; Defect Microstructure of Surfaces; Scanning Probe Microscopy; Tribology of Hard Coatings; Reactivity and Degradation of Ceramic Surfaces; Chemical Sensors; Biosensors. **Mailing Address:** Dept Physics & Astron, Univ Maine, 5764 Sawyer Res Ctr, Orono, ME 04469-5764. **Fax:** 207-581-2255. **E-Mail:** RJLAD@MAINE.EDU

LADA, CHARLES JOSEPH, ASTRONOMY. **Personal Data:** b Webster, Mass, March 18, 1949; m 1984, c 2. **Education:** Boston Univ, BA, 1971; Harvard Univ, AM, 1972, PhD (astron), 1975. **Professional Experience:** SR ASTROPHYSICIST, SMITHSONIAN ASTROPHYS OBSERV, 1990-; vis assoc prof, Univ Calif, Berkeley, 1988-1989; fel, Alfred P Sloan Found, 1981-1984; from asst prof to assoc prof, Steward Observ, Univ Ariz, 1980-1990; fel astron, Bart Bok, Steward Observ, Univ Ariz, 1978-1980; res fel, Harvard Univ, 1977-1978; Fel, Ctr Astrophys, Harvard Col Observ & Smithsonian Astrophys Observ, 1975-1977. **Memberships:** Am Astron Soc; Int Astron Union. **Research Statement & Publications:** Formation of stars; interstellar gas dynamics; structure and evolution of interstellar molecular clouds; structure and evolution of our galaxy. **Mailing Address:** Harvard Smithsonian Ctr Astrophys Mail Stop 72, 60 Garden St, Cambridge, MA 02138. **Fax:** 617-496-7507. **E-Mail:** clada@cfa.harvard.edu

LADA, ELIZABETH A, ASTRONOMY. **Honors & Awards:** Annie Jump Cannon Award, Am Astron Soc, 1992. **Professional Experience:** PROF ASTRON, UNIV FLA, as of 2002; fmr astron, Harvard Smithsonian Ctr, Cambridge, Mass. **Memberships:** Am Astron Soc. **Research Statement & Publications:** Astronomy. **Mailing Address:** Dept Astron Univ Fla, PO Box 112055, Gainesville, FL 32611. **Fax:** 352-392-5089. **E-Mail:** lada@astro.ufl.edu

LADANYI, BRANKA MARIA, THEORETICAL CHEMISTRY, PHYSICAL CHEMISTRY. **Personal Data:** b Zagreb, Croatia, September 7, 1947; Canadian citizen; m 1974, Marshall. **Education:** McGill Univ, BSc, 1969; Yale Univ, MPhil, 1971, PhD (chem), 1973. **Professional Experience:** Assoc ed, J Chem Physics, 1994-; vis fel, Joint Inst Lab Astrophys, 1993-1994; PROF CHEM, COL STATE UNIV, 1987-; Camille & Henry Dreyfus Teacher-Scholar, 1983-1986; Alfred P Sloan fel, 1982-1985; from asst prof to assoc prof, Col State Univ, 1979-1987; res assoc chem, Yale Univ, 1974-1979; vis asst prof chem, Univ Ill, Urbana, 1974. **Memberships:** Am Chem Soc; fel Am Phys Soc; fel AAAS; Asn Women Sci; Sigma Xi. **Research Statement & Publications:** Statistical mechanics of fluids; structure and dynamics of molecular liquids; light scattering and nonlinear optical response of fluids; solvation in fluids and clusters; dielectric properties of fluids; solvent effects on chemical reactions; supercritical fluids; confined liquids and microemulsions; published over 15 articles. **Mailing Address:** Dept Chem, Colo State Univ, Ft Collins, CO 80523-1872. **Fax:** 970-491-3361. **E-Mail:** bl@lamar.colostate.edu

LADANYI, BRANKO, GEOTECHNICAL ENGINEERING. **Personal Data:** b Zagreb, Croatia, December 14, 1922; Canadian citizen; m 1946, Nevenka; c Branka, Thomas & Marc. **Education:** Univ Zagreb, BEng, 1947; Univ Louvain, PhD (civil eng), 1959. **Honors & Awards:** R F Legget Geotech Award, 1981; E E De Beer Geotech Award, 1987; Elbert F Rice Mem Award, Am Soc Civil Engrs, 1991; Roger J E Brown Mem Award, Can Geotech Soc, 1993; Horst Leipholz Medal, Can Soc Civil Eng, 1996; Northern Sci Award, Govt Can, 1996. **Professional Experience:** PROF EMER CIVIL ENG, ECOLE POLYTECH, UNIV MONTREAL, 1994-; prof geotech eng, Dept Civil Eng, 1977-1982; dir, Northern Eng Centre, beginning 1972; prof civil eng, Ecole Polytech, Univ Montreal, 1967-1994; from assoc prof to prof geotech eng, Laval Univ, Que, 1962-1967; res engr soil mech, Belg Geotech Inst, Ghent, 1958-1962; asst prof soil mech & found eng, Univ Zagreb, 1952-1958; design engr found & hydraul struct, Dept Transport, Zagreb, 1947-1952. **Memberships:** Fel Eng Inst Can; Can Inst Mining & Metall; fel Am Soc Civil Engrs; fel Can Soc Civil Engrs; fel Royal Soc Can; Tunnelling Asn Can (pres, 1982-1984); Can Rock Mech Asn (pres, 1984-1987); fel Can Acad Eng. **Research Statement & Publications:** Soil and rock mechanics; permafrost engineering; mechanics of permafrost and ice; problems of foundation engineering, tunnelling and arctic offshore construction. **Mailing Address:** Dept Civil, Geol & Mining Eng, Ecole Polytech, Univ Montreal, Box 6079 Centre-Ville Sta, Montreal, PQ H3C 3A7, Can.

LADAS, GERASIMOS, DIFFERENTIAL EQUATIONS. **Personal Data:** b Lixuri, Greece, April 25, 1937; American citizen; m 1965, c 2. **Education:** Nat Univ Athens, BS, 1961; NY Univ, 1966, MS, 1966, PhD (math), 1968. **Professional Experience:** Dir, Doctor Philosophy Prog, Appl Math Sci, Univ RI, 1992-1997; dept chairperson, Univ RI, 1982-1986; PROF MATH, UNIV RI, 1975-; chmn dept, Univ RI, 1972-1978; from asst prof to assoc prof, Univ RI, 1969-1975; asst prof math, Fairfield Univ, 1968-1969; fel, NY Univ, 1964-1968. **Memberships:** Am Math Soc. **Research Statement & Publications:** Ordinary, functional and abstract differential equations. **Mailing Address:** Math Dept, Univ RI, Kingston, RI 02881. **Fax:** 401-792-4617, 401-874-4454. **E-Mail:** gladas@math.uri.edu

LADD, CHARLES CUSHING, III, CIVIL ENGINEERING, GEOTECHNICAL ENGINEERING. **Personal Data:** b Brooklyn, NY, November 23, 1932; m 1954, Carol; c Melissa, Charles, Ruth & Matthew. **Education:** Bowdoin Col, BA, 1955; Mass Inst Technol, BS, 1955, SM, 1957, DSc (soil eng), 1961. **Honors & Awards:** Croes Medal, 1973; Norman Medal, 1976; Terzaghi Lectr, 1986; Hogentogler Award, 1990; Middlebrook Award, Am Soc Chem Engrs, 1996. **Professional Experience:** PROF EMER, DEPT CIVIL & ENVIRON ENG, MASS INST TECHNOL, as of 2005; vis sr scientist, Norweg Geotech Inst, 1983; prof civil & environ eng, Mass Inst Technol, beginning 1970; vis consult, Haley & Aldrich, Inc, 1967-1968; from instr to assoc prof, Mass Inst Technol, 1957-1970. **Memberships:** Nat Acad Eng; Am Soc Civil Engrs; Am Soc Testing & Mat; Am Soc Eng Educ; Nat Soc Prof Engrs; hon mem Am Soc Chem Engrs; Can Geotech Soc; Brit Geotech Soc. **Research Statement & Publications:** Engineering properties of soils, soft ground and offshore construction as applied to civil engineering projects. **Mailing Address:** Dept Civil & Environ Eng, Mass Inst Technol, 77 Mass Ave, Cambridge, MA 02139-4307. **Fax:** 617-253-6044. **E-Mail:** ccladd@mit.edu

LADD, CONRAD MERVYN, POWER PLANT PROJECT MANAGEMENT, NUCLEAR & ENVIRONMENTAL ENGINEERING. **Personal Data:** b Lakewood, Ohio, December 16, 1926; m 1947, Bonnie; c Craig, Sue A, Patricia & Deborah. **Education:** Univ Mich, BSME, 1949. **Honors & Awards:** Dedicated Serv Award, Am Soc Mech Engrs, 1987. **Professional Experience:** Chmn energy comt, Task Force Acid Rain, 1987-1990; CHMN & CHIEF EXEC OFFICER, SR MGT CONSULT INC, 1985-; co-chmn, Task Force Acid Rain, 1985-1986; chmn, Task Force Clean Coal Technol, 1985-1986; chmn, Power Div, Am Soc Mech Engrs, 1981-1982; mem exec comt, Power Div, Am Soc Mech Engrs, 1978-1983; mgr bus develop & proj exec, Stearns Roger, Inc, 1976-1985; asst mgr mkt, Stone & Webster Engrs, 1974-1976; mkt mgr, Atomics Int, Div Rockwell Int, 1963-1974; prod mgr, Brush Beryllium Corp, 1959-1963; sr engr, Atomic Power Develop Asn/ Commonwealth Asn, 1952-1959; intermediate engr, Westinghouse Atomic Power Div, 1951-1952; student engr, Duquesne Light Co, 1949-1951. **Memberships:** Fel Am Soc Mech Engrs. **Research Statement & Publications:** Engineering, development and testing of basic nuclear equipment and systems and nuclear fuel fabrication and processing; two infield patents. **Mailing Address:** Sr Mgt Consults Inc, 1780 S Bellaire Ste 809, Denver, CO 80222.

LADD, JOHN HERBERT, physical chemistry, physics; deceased, see previous edition for last biography

LADD, KAYE VICTORIA, INORGANIC CHEMISTRY, PHYSICAL CHEMISTRY. **Personal Data:** b Seattle, Wash, August 26, 1941. **Education:** Reed Col, BA, 1963; Brandeis Univ, MA, 1965, PhD (inorg chem), 1974. **Professional Experience:** Consult, Corff & Shapiro, 1977; emer mem fac chem, Evergreen State Col, 1975-2000; consult, New Eng Aquarium, 1970-1975; assoc prof chem, Suffolk Univ, 1968-1975; staff scientist chem biol, Tyco Labs Inc, 1965-1968. **Memberships:** Am Chem Soc; AAAS; Sci Inst Publ Info. **Research Statement & Publications:** Environmental inorganic research, especially the transport of trace metals in metabolic process within and between organisms. **Mailing Address:** 1704 24th Ave NW, Olympia, WA 98502. **E-Mail:** laddk@elwha.evergreen.edu

LADD, THYRIL LEONE, ENTOMOLOGY. **Personal Data:** b Albany, NY, October 10, 1931; m 1956, c Karen, Valerie & Diana. **Education:** State Univ NY, Albany, AB, 1956, MA, 1958; Cornell Univ, PhD (entom), 1963. **Professional Experience:** RETIRED; adj prof entom, Ohio State Univ, 1971-1992; res leader, Hort Insects Res Lab, 1969-1992; res entomologist, Agr Res Sta, USDA, 1962-1992. **Memberships:** AAAS; Entom Soc Am; Am Entom Soc; Sigma Xi; Coun Agr Sci & Technol. **Research Statement & Publications:** Effects of radiation and chemicals on insect reproduction; integrated insect control; insect responses to attractants and repellents; effects of insect feeding on plant yields; improved procedures for applications of insecticides. **Mailing Address:** 1258 S W 44th Terrace, Deerfield Beach, FL 33442-8260.

LADDA, ROGER LOUIS, PEDIATRICS, CLINICAL GENETICS. **Personal Data:** b Highland, Ill, October 28, 1936; m 1957, c 5. **Education:** Wesleyan Univ, BA, 1958; Sch Med, Univ Chicago, MD, 1963. **Professional Experience:** PROF PEDIAT, COL MED, PA STATE UNIV, 1983-; app mem, sci adv bd, Geront Res Ctr, Nat Inst Aging, 1982-1984; CHIEF, DIV GENETICS, MILTON S HERSHEY MED CTR, PA STATE UNIV, 1974-; from asst prof to assoc prof, Div Genetics, 1974-1983; res & clin fel, Children's Serv & Genetics Unit, Mass Gen Hosp, Sch Med, Harvard Univ, 1972-1974. **Memberships:** Am Pediat Soc; Soc Pediat Res; AAAS; Sigma Xi. **Research Statement & Publications:** Growth regulating factors and cell division. **Mailing Address:** Milton S Hershey Med Ctr, Pa State Univ, PO Box 850, Hershey, PA 17033-0850. **Fax:** 717-531-0276. **E-Mail:** rladda@psu.edu

LADDE, GANGARAM SHIVLINGAPPA, DIFFERENTIAL EQUATIONS, APPLIED SYSTEMS ANALYSIS. **Personal Data:** b Jalkot, India, March 9, 1940; American citizen; m 1965, c 3. **Education:** Marathwada Univ, BSc, 1963, MSc, 1965; Univ RI, PhD (math), 1972. **Professional Experience:** Res assoc, Univ Santa Clara, Calif, 1981 & 1987; PROF MATH, UNIV TEX, ARLINGTON, 1980-; vis prof math, Univ Rome, Italy, 1978 & Univ Tex, Arlington, 1979-1980; grant-in-aid, Res Found, State Univ NY, Albany, 1978-1979; fel, Univ Santa Clara, Calif, 1974; from asst prof to assoc prof, State Univ NY, Potsdam, 1973-1980; instr, Univ RI, 1971-1973; teaching asst, Univ RI, 1967-1971; ed, Stochastic Analysis & Appln. **Memberships:** Am Math Soc; Indian Math Soc; Sigma Xi; Soc Indust & Appl Math; Inst Elec & Electronics Engrs; NY Acad Sci. **Research Statement & Publications:** Biomathematics; competitive analysis; differential games; deterministic analysis; mathematical modeling in biological, medical, physical, and social sciences; nonlinear boundary value problems; oscillation theory; stability theory; stochastic andlysis; systems analysis; filtering and control theory. **Mailing Address:** Dept Math, Univ Tex, PO Box 19408, Arlington, TX 76019-0001. **Fax:** 817-272-5802. **E-Mail:** ladde@exchange.uta.edu

LADDU, ATUL R, EXPERIMENTAL BIOLOGY. **Personal Data:** b August 23, 1940; American citizen. **Education:** MB & BS, 1962, MD, 1967. **Professional Experience:** PRIN, CARDIOVASC, 1990-; dir clin res, Cardiovasc & Neuroscience, Abbott Labs, 1988-1990; dir clin res, DuPont Critical Care, 1982-1988; proj leader, Ives Labs, Inc, Div Am Home Prod Inc, 1978-1982; assoc med dir, Ives Labs, Inc, Div Am Home Prod Inc, 1976-1978; asst med dir, Ives Labs, Inc, Div Am Home Prod Inc, 1976; sr clin invest assoc, Ciba-Geigy Corp, 1975-1976; group leader, Cardiovasc Div, Lederle Labs, Div Am Cyanamid Co, 1973-1975; from 1st instr to asst prof, Dept Pharmacol, Med Col Wis, 1971-1973; postdoctoral fel, Dept Pharmacol, Med Col Wis, 1968-1971; Instr pharmacol, Maulana Azad Med Col, New Delhi, 1963-1968; Assoc ed, J Clin Pharmacol, Int J Clin Pharmacol. **Memberships:** Fel Am Col Cardiol; fel Am Soc Clin Pharmacol & Therapeut; fel Am Col Clin Pharmacol; Am Soc Hypertension; Am Fedn Clin Res; NY Acad Sci; Am Soc Pharmacol & Exp Therapeut; Soc Exp Biol & Med; Sigma Xi; Int Study Group Res Cardiac Metab. **Research Statement & Publications:** Conducting clinical trials with cardiovascular products and neuropharmacological agents; author or co-author of several publications. **Mailing Address:** 26 Chicopee Dr F, Princeton, NJ 08540.

LADE, ROBERT WALTER, SOLID STATE ELECTRONICS. **Personal Data:** b Fond du Lac, Wis, April 3, 1935; m 1956, Nancy; c Kipton, Carey, Scot & Andrew. **Education:** Marquette Univ, BEE, 1958, MS, 1961; Carnegie Inst Technol, PhD (elec eng), 1962. **Professional Experience:** FOUNDER, LADE'S INTERNET SERVICE, 1994-; res mgr, Eaton Corp, 1984-1991; mem staff, RWL Eng, 1977-1984; prof elec eng & chmn dept, Marquette Univ, 1967-1977; assoc prof, NC State Univ, 1963-1967; instr, Marquette Univ, 1959-1961 & Carnegie Inst Technol, 1961-1962; engr, AC Spark Plug, Wis, 1959-1960. **Memberships:** Inst Elec & Electronics Engrs. **Research Statement & Publications:** Electrical properties of free and passivated semiconductor surfaces under the influence of high energy radiation fields; computer-aided circuit design and power semiconductor device design. **Mailing Address:** 2941 SW TENTH Pl, Cape Coral, FL 33909. **E-Mail:** rwlade@cyberstreet.com

LADECOLA, COSTANTINO, NEUROSCIENCES. **Personal Data:** b Aquino, Italy, March 15, 1953; m 1987, c 1. **Education:** Univ Rome, MD & PhD (physiol), 1977. **Honors & Awards:** McHenry Award, Hist Neurol, 1990. **Professional Experience:** PROF NEUROL, UNIV MINN, TWIN CITIES, as of 2003; ASST PROF NEUROL, UNIV MINN, 1990-; neurol residency, 1986-1990; asst prof neurobiology, Cornell Univ Med Col, 1984-1986; instr neurol, Cornell Univ Med Col, 1982-1983; instr physiol, Univ Rome, 1978-1979. **Memberships:** Am Physiol Soc; Neuroscience Soc; Am Acad Neurol; Soc Cerebral Blood Flow. **Research Statement & Publications:** Regulation of blood circulation to the brain with respect to intrinsic neural pathways and neuro transmitters, in health and in the disease state; published over 50 articles. **Mailing Address:** Dept Neurol, Univ Minn, PO Box 295 420 Del St SE, Minneapolis, MN 55455. **Fax:** 612-625-7950. **E-Mail:** iadec001@umn.edu

LADEFOGED, PETER NIELSEN, linguistics, phonetics; deceased, see previous edition for last biography

LA DELFE, PETER CARL, PHYSICS, OPTICS. **Personal Data:** b Woburn, Mass, February 19, 1943; m 1978, Carol. **Education:** Clarkson Col Technol, BS, 1968, MS, 1971. **Professional Experience:** STAFF MEM, OPTICAL SENSORS & RADIOMETRIC INSTRUMENTS, LOS ALAMOS NAT LAB, 1990-; mgr, Aurora Optics, 1988-1990; proj leader, Phoenix Beam Transp, 1985-1988; staff mem, Coating Sect, 1982-1985; sect leader, Coating Sect, 1979-1982; staff mem optical films, Los Alamos Nat Lab, 1978-1979; consult pvt pract, 1974-1977; sr physicist optical films, Spectrum Systs Div, Barnes Eng Co, 1971-1974. **Memberships:** Am Vacuum Soc; Optical Soc Am; Int Soc Optical Eng. **Research Statement & Publications:** Design and development of optical interference filters including research in the materials science of producing optical films; instrument design and system analysis for optical sensing systems. **Mailing Address:** 600 Los Pueblos, Los Alamos, NM 87544. **Fax:** 505-667-3815. **E-Mail:** pladelfe@lanl.gov

LADEN, G M, AERONAUTICS. **Professional Experience:** VPRES & ASST GEN MGR, MISSILE SYST DIV, LOCKHEED MISSILES & SPACE CO, 1987. **Memberships:** Nat Aeronaut Asn. **Mailing Address:** Lockheed Missiles & Space Co, MSD D 80-01 181 1111 Lockheed Way, Sunnyvale, CA 94809-1212.

LADENHEIM, HARRY, REACTOR ENGINEERING, PROCESS ENGINEERING. **Personal Data:** b Vienna, Austria, October 17, 1932; American citizen; m 1955, c 2. **Education:** City Col New York, BS, 1954; Polytech Inst Brooklyn, PhD (org polymer chem), 1958. **Professional Experience:** RETIRED; PC trainer, Data Processing Trainers, Inc, 1996-1997; consult, 1987-1996; sr process engr, Air Prods & Chem Inc, Paulsboro, NJ, 1982-1994; process engr, Air Prods & Chem Inc, Marcus Hook, Pa, 1982-1987; prin res engr, Air Prods & Chem Inc, Marcus Hook, Pa, 1979-1981; sr develop engr, Houdry Process & Chem Co, 1976-1979; sr res chemist, Houdry Process & Chem Co, 1970-1976; res chemist, Houdry Process & Chem Co, 1963-1970; res chemist, Esso Res & Eng Co, 1959-1963; Fel chem, Ill Inst Technol, 1958-1959. **Memberships:** Am Chem Soc. **Research Statement & Publications:** Mechanisms in physical organic chemistry; exploratory and process study in petroleum technology; use of polymers as enzyme models; catalysis; catalytic chemistry. **Mailing Address:** 459 Levering Mill Rd, Bala Cynwyd, PA 19004-2726.

LADENSON, JACK HERMAN, CLINICAL CHEMISTRY. **Personal Data:** b Philadelphia, Pa, April 8, 1942; m 1968, Ruth; c Michele S & Jeffrey L. **Education:** Pa State Univ, BS, 1964; Univ Md, PhD (analytical chem), 1971. **Honors & Awards:** Outstanding Contrib Educ Award, Am Asn Clin Chem, 1989; Distinguished Scientist Award, Clin Ligand Assay Soc, 1994. **Professional Experience:** ACTG DIR, RESIDENCY PROG CLIN PATH, WASH UNIV, ST LOUIS, as of 2003; mem, bd trustees, Van Slyke Soc, 1993-; OREE M CARROLL & LILLIAN B LADENSON CHMN CLIN CHEM, WASH UNIV SCH MED, beginning 1993; PROF PATH & CLIN CHEM MED, WASH UNIV SCH MED, beginning 1984; mem, bd dirs, Am Asn Clin Chem, 1981-1983 & 1985-1987; HEAD, CLIN CHEM & COMPUT, SCH MED WASH UNIV, 1980-; DIR CLIN CHEM, BARNES HOSP, beginning 1980; dir, Am Bd Clin Chem, 1979-1985; co-dir, Barnes Hosp, 1976-1979; from asst prof to assoc prof, Barnes Hosp, 1972-1984; asst dir clin chem, Barnes Hosp, 1972-1976; fel clin chem, Hartford Hosp, 1970-1972; NSF fel, 1966-1970. **Memberships:** Am Asn Clin Chem (pres, 1986); Acad Clin Lab Physicians & Scientists. **Research Statement & Publications:** Development of monoclonal antibodies and assays for cardiac proteins and detection of myocardial infarction. **Mailing Address:** Div Lab Med, Sch Med, Wash Univ, PO Box 8118, 660 S Euclid Ave, St Louis, MO 63110-1093. **Fax:** 314-362-1461, 314-454-5208. **E-Mail:** ladenson@labmed.wustl.edu

LADERMAN, JULIAN DAVID, MATHEMATICS, COMPUTER SCIENCE. **Personal Data:** b New York, NY, October 15, 1948. **Education:** NY Univ, BA, 1970, MS, 1972, PhD (comput sci), 1976. **Professional Experience:** ASSOC PROF MATH & COMPUT SCI, LEHMAN COL, 1984-; consult, Systs Revisited, 1978-; from instr to asst prof math, Lehman Col, 1973-1983. **Memberships:** Am Math Soc; Math Asn Am; Asn Comput Mach. **Research Statement & Publications:** Computational complexity; mathematical programming; statistics; game theory; probability; operations research; programming languages; numerical analysis. **Mailing Address:** Dept Math & Comput Sci, Lehman Col, City Univ NY, G-204 250 Bedford Park Blvd W, Bronx, NY 10468-1589. **E-Mail:** laderman@lehman.cuny.edu

LADESIC, JAMES G, AEROSPACE ENGINEERING. **Education:** Embry-Riddle Aeronaut Univ, BS, 1967; Univ Cent Fla, MS, 1973; Univ Fla, PhD (mech eng), 1983. **Professional Experience:** PROF, AEROSPACE ENG, EMBRY-RIDDLE AERONAUT UNIV, as of 2005. **Memberships:** Am Soc Eng Educ. **Mailing Address:** Embry Riddle Aeronaut Univ, 600 S Clyde Morris Blvd, Daytona Beach, FL 32114-3900. **Fax:** 386-226-6747. **E-Mail:** ladesicj@erau.edu

LADINSKY, HERBERT, PHARMACOLOGY, BIOCHEMISTRY. **Personal Data:** b New York, NY, July 22, 1935; m 1967, Silvana Consolo. **Education:** City Col New York, BS, 1958; State Univ NY, PhD (pharmacol), 1966. **Professional Experience:** HEAD DEPT BIOCHEM & MOLECULAR PHARMACOL, BOEHRINGER INGELHEIM ITALIA, MILAN, 1985-; vis scientist, Weizman Inst, Rehovot, Israel, 1979; Consult, Multinat Pharmaceut Co, 1974-1984; lab chief, Mario Negri Inst, 1969-1984; Fel pharmacol, Royal Caroline Inst, Stockholm, 1966-1967 & Mario Negri Inst, 1967-1969; NIH fel, 1966-1968. **Memberships:** Ital Pharmacol Soc; Int Soc Neurochem; Am Soc Neurosci; Ital Soc Neurosci. **Research Statement & Publications:** Biochemistry, neurochemistry, and neuropharmacology of the central cholinergic and serotonergic systems; location and function of subtypes of muscarinic and serotoninergic receptors; nerve and receptor plasticity. **Mailing Address:** Dept Biochem & Molecular Pharmacol, Milan 20139, Italy. **Fax:** 392-535-5368.

LADINSKY, JUDITH L, ENDOCRINOLOGY, PUBLIC & INTERNATIONAL HEALTH. **Personal Data:** b Los Angeles, Calif, June 16, 1938; m 1961, Jack; c Morissa & Mark. **Education:** Univ Mich, BS, 1961; Univ Wis-Madison, MS, 1964, PhD (reproductive physiol), 1968. **Professional Experience:** ASSOC PROF, POP HEALTH SCI, as of 2006; DIR, OFF INT HEALTH, 1985-; assoc prof prev med, Sch Med, Univ Wis, Madison, beginning 1975; from instr to asst prof prev med, Dept Gynec-Obstet, 1968-1974; proj assoc, Dept Gynec-Obstet, 1961-1968; Dept Anat, 1958-1960 & Dept Surg, 1960-1961; res asst, Dept Neuropath, Univ Mich, 1956-1958; med technologist, Clin Labs, St Mary's Hosp, Mich, 1955-1956; chmn, US Comt Sci Coop with Vietnam & Laos; consult, Ministries Health, Southeast Asia. **Memberships:** Am Soc Cell Biol; NY Acad Sci; Tissue Cult Asn; Am Pub Health Asn; Asn Teachers Prev Med; Nat Coun Int Health; Nat Asn Pub Health Policy (secy, 1984-1986); Sigma Xi. **Research Statement & Publications:** Cell kinetics of normal and neoplastic tissues; automated methods of cancer detection; endocrinology of tumors; community medicine; neonatology; health care delivery; international health. **Mailing Address:** Dept Pop Health Sci, Univ Wis Med Ctr, 1760 Med Sci Ctr 1300 Univ Ave, Madison, WI 53706-1585. **Fax:** 608-262-2327. **E-Mail:** jlladins@facstaff.wisc.edu

LADISCH, MICHAEL R, BIOCHEMICAL ENGINEERING. **Personal Data:** b Upper Darby, Pa, January 15, 1950; m 1975, c 2. **Education:** Drexel Univ, BS, 1973; Purdue Univ, MS, 1974, PhD (chem eng), 1977. **Honors & Awards:** James M Van Laren Serv Award, Am Chem Soc, 1990; US Presidential Young Investr Award, 1984; Peterson Award, Am Chem Soc, 1977. **Professional Experience:** DIR, LAB RENEWABLE RESOURCES ENG, PURDUE UNUV, as of 2004; DISTINGUISHED PROF, BIOMED ENG, PURDUE UNIV, as of 2003; DISTINGUISHED PROF, AGR, BIOL ENG, PURDUE UNIV, as of 2003; PROF FOOD, AGR & CHEM ENG, PURDUE UNIV, 1985-; group leader, res & proces eng, lab renewable resources, beginning 1978; from asst prof to assoc prof, Purdue Univ, 1978-1981; res eng, biochem, 1977-1978. **Memberships:** Am Chem Soc; Am Inst Chem Engrs; Am Soc Agr Engrs; fel Am Inst Med & Biol Eng; Nat Acad Eng. **Research Statement & Publications:** Cellulose conversion; bioseparations; enzyme and chemical kinetics; liquid chromatography; Published over 15 articles. **Mailing Address:** Lab Renewable Resources Eng, Potter Ctr Purdue Univ, West Lafayette, IN 47906. **Fax:** 765-496-1115. **E-Mail:** ladisch@ecn.purdue.edu

LADISCH, STEPHAN, TUMORGENICITY, GLYCOBIOLOGY. **Personal Data:** b Garmisch-Partenkirchen, WGer, July 18, 1947; American citizen; m 1974, Brigitte; c Gwenola & Virginie. **Education:** Univ Pa, Philadelphia, BS, 1969, MD, 1973. **Professional Experience:** DIR, CTR CANCER & TRANSPLANTATION BIOL, CHILDREN'S RES INST, as of 2002; PROF PEDIAT & BIOCHEM & MOLECULAR BIOL, GEORGE WASH UNIV, SCH MED, as of 2002; PROF PEDIAT, DIV HEMAT-ONCOL, SCH MED, beginning 1986; inst pasteur, Paris, 1986-1987; Career Develop Award, 1982-1987; scholar, Leukemia Soc Am, 1982-1987; vis scientist, Lausanne Br, Ludwig Inst for Cancer Res, Epalinges, Switz, 1981-1982; NIH res grants, 1980-1984 & 1983-; Nat Found-March Dimes res grant, 1980-1984; SR MEM, HUMAN IMMUNOBIOL GROUP, UNIV CALIF, LOS ANGELES, beginning 1978; from asst prof to assoc prof, Div Hemat-oncol, Sch Med, 1978-1986; investr, Pediat Oncol Br, Nat Cancer Inst, Bethesda, Md, 1977-1978; clin assoc, Pediat Oncol Br, Nat Cancer Inst, Bethesda, Md, 1975-1977; intern & resident pediat, Children's Hosp Med Ctr, Boston, Mass, 1973-1975; NSF res grants, 1968-1969 & 1972. **Memberships:** Am Soc Hemat; AAAS; Soc Pediat Res; Am Asn Immunologists; Am Fedn Clin Res. **Research Statement & Publications:** Modulation of the immune response by gangliosides, membrane glycolipids shed by tumor cells and role of this process in tumorgenicity. **Mailing Address:** Dept Immunol, George Wash Univ, 111 Mivh Ave NW, Washington, DC 20010. **Fax:** 202-884-3929. **E-Mail:** ladisch@gwu.edu

LADISH, JOSEPH STANLEY, ATOMIC & MOLECULAR PHYSICS. **Personal Data:** b Worcester, Mass, August 9, 1943; m 1964, c 2. **Education:** Mass Inst Tech, BS, 1965; Yale Univ, MS, 1966, MPhil, 1967, PhD (physics), 1974. **Professional Experience:** RETIRED; group leader, Hydrodyn Group, Physics Div, Los Alamos Nat Lab, as of 1998; adj fac, Univ NMex, Los Alamos, 1983-; res staff, Los Alamos Nat Lab, beginning 1974. **Memberships:** Am Phys Soc. **Research Statement & Publications:** Production of polarized electrons; carbon dioxide laser fusion research; detection by Cerenkav radiation; optical transition radiation. **Mailing Address:** 260 Aragon Ave, Los Alamos, NM 87544.

LADKANY, SAMAAN GEORGE, FINITE ELEMENT ANALYSIS, EXPERIMENTAL MECHANICS. **Personal Data:** b Damascus, May 16, 1941; American citizen; m 1982, c 2. **Education:** Am Univ Beirut, BS, 1963; Univ Wis-Madison, BS, 1965, MS, 1967, MS, 1975, PhD (civil eng), 1975. **Professional Experience:** Mem, Steel Bridges Comt, Am Soc Civil Engrs, 1995-; mem, Tubular Struct Comt, Struct Stability Res Coun, 1993-; mem, Double Curved Shells Comt, 1993-; dir, High Level Nuclear Waste Prog, Univ Nev, Las Vegas/Dept Energy, 1991-1996; PROF CIVIL ENG, UNIV NEV, 1988-; DIR, NUCLEAR WASTE STORAGE PROG, 1988-; expert witness/consult, Clark Co Attorneys, 1985-; co-prin investr, Univ Nev Las Vegas/Army Res Off Robotics, 1985-1991; assoc prof & prin investr, Nuclear Waste Storage Prog, Univ Nev, 1984-1988; co-prin investr, Univ Nev, Las Vegas/Am Soc Heating, Refrig & Air Conditioning Engrs Prop Fans, 1984-1986; asst prof, Johns Hopkins Univ, 1979-1984; adj asst prof & scientist, Eng Res Sta, Univ Wis-Madison, 1975-1979. **Memberships:** Struct Stability Res Coun; Am Soc Civil Engrs; Am Concrete Inst; Am Soc Eng Educ; Sigma Xi. **Research Statement & Publications:** Applications of linear and nonlinear finite element analysis to flexible robots, plates and shell structures; experimental investigations of large pipes, dented under extreme conditions; photoelastic studies of faulted tunnel systems. **Mailing Address:** Dept Civil Eng, Univ Nev, 4505 Md Pwky PO Box 454015, Las Vegas, NV 89154-4015. **Fax:** 702-895-3936. **E-Mail:** samaan@ce.unlv.edu

LADMAN, AARON J(ULIUS), ANATOMY. **Personal Data:** b Jamaica, NY, July 3, 1925; m 1982, Patricia A Bergbauer; c Susan (Brown), Thomas J & Peter. **Education:** NY Univ, AB, 1947; Ind Univ, PhD (anat), 1952. **Professional Experience:** ADJ PROF NEUROBIOLOGY & ANAT, ALLEGHENY UNIV HEALTH SCI, MCP HAHNEMANN SCH MED, HAHNEMANNUNIV, PHILADELPHIA, 1996-; prof anat, Sch Allied Health, 1981-1996; dean, Sch Allied Health, 1981-1986; ed, Anat Record, 1968-; mem res career award comt, Nat Inst Gen Med Sci, 1967-1971; prof anat & chmn dept, Univ NMex, 1964-1981; USPHS career develop award, 1962-1964; assoc prof, Med Units, Univ Tenn, 1961-1964; assoc anat, Harvard Med Sch, 1955-1961; Res fel anat, Harvard Med Sch, 1952-1955. **Memberships:** Am Soc Cell Biol; Coun Biol Ed; Histochem Soc; Am Asn Anatomists (2nd vpres 1980-1981 & 1st vpres 1981-1982); fel AAAS. **Research Statement & Publications:** Cytochemistry; electron microscopy; endocrinology; experimental cytology; retina lung; tumor biology; scientific writing. **Mailing Address:** Dept Neurobiology & Anat Allegheny, Univ Health Sci MCP Hahnemann Sch Med, Ctr City Campus Broad & Vine, Philadelphia, PA 19102-1192. **E-Mail:** ladmana@allegheny.edu

LADNER, DAVID WILLIAM, QUANTITATIVE STRUCTURE-ACTIVITY RELATIONSHIPS. **Personal Data:** b Meadville, Pa, June 22, 1947; m 1973, Cathy Tillman; c Rebecca & Deborah. **Education:** Pa State Univ, BS, 1969; Univ Ga, PhD (org chem), 1974. **Professional Experience:** AT, AM CYANAMID CORP, as of 2000; RES MGR CHEM DISCOVERY, AGR RES DIV, AM CYANAMID, 1996-; sr group leader herbicide synthesis, Agr Res Div, Am Cyanamid, 1993-1996; group leader, Agr Res Div, Am Cyanamid, 1983-1993; sr res chemist herbicide synthesis, Agr Res Div, Am Cyanamid, 1980-1983; res chemist herbicide synthesis, Agr Res Div, Am Cyanamid, 1977-1980; sr scientist, N L Industs, 1976-1977; res fel org synthesis, Syntex, SA, Mex, DF, 1975-1976; Res assoc org systhesis, Dept Chem, Univ Wash, 1974-1975. **Memberships:** Am Chem Soc. **Research**

Statement & Publications: Design and synthesis of herbicides and plant regulants, particularly those affecting enzymes in amino acid biosynthetic pathways; quantitative structure-activity relationships, techniques to model activity, translocation and uptake of pesticides; high throughput synthesis. **Mailing Address:** Am Cyanamid Corp, Pearl River, NJ 10965.

LADNER, RICHARD E, COMPUTER SCIENCE. **Personal Data:** b Berkeley, Calif, August 22, 1943; c 2. **Education:** St Marys Col, Calif, BS, 1965; Univ Calif, Berkeley, PhD (math), 1971. **Honors & Awards:** Presidential Award Excellence Sci, Math & Eng Mentoring, 2004. **Professional Experience:** Fel, Victoria Univ, Wellington, NZ, 1993; fulbright travel grant, NZ, 1992-1993; prog comt mem, Comput Profs Social Responsibility, 1992; assoc ed, J Comput & Syst Sci, 1989-; prog comt mem, Comput Profs Social Responsibility, 1988; fel, Math Sci Res Inst, 1986; Guggenheim fel, 1985-1986; vis appts, Gallaudet Univ, 1985; BOEING PROF COMPUT SCI & ENG, UNIV WASH, 1981-; ed, J Comput, Soc Indust & Appl Math, 1980-1983; vis appts, Yale Univ, 1978; vis appts, Univ Toronto, 1977; from actg asst prof to assoc prof, Univ Wash, 1971-1981. **Memberships:** Fel Asn Comput Mach; Inst Elec & Electronics Engrs Comput Soc; Am Math Soc; Asn Symbolic Logic. **Research Statement & Publications:** Design and analysis of algorithms; parallel and distributed computation theory; computational complexity; computer networks; lossy data compression. **Mailing Address:** Dept Comput Sci & Eng, Univ Wash, Paul G Allen Ctr Comput Sci & Eng Rm 632 Box 352350, Seattle, WA 98195. **Fax:** 206-543-2969. **E-Mail:** ladner@cs.washington.edu

LADNER, SIDNEY JULES, PHYSICAL CHEMISTRY. **Personal Data:** b Houston, Tex, March 12, 1936; m 1959, c 2. **Education:** Univ Houston, BS, 1959, PhD (phys chem), 1965. **Professional Experience:** Assoc prof chem, Houston Baptist Univ, beginning 1969; asst prof, Houston Baptist Univ, 1967-1969; chemist, Shell Develop Co, Tex, 1966-1967; fel chem, Univ NMex, 1965-1966. **Memberships:** Am Chem Soc. **Research Statement & Publications:** Molecular spectroscopy; decay processes and the decay kinetics of molecules in excited electronic energy states; chemical education. **Mailing Address:** Dept Chem, Houston Baptist Univ, 7502 Fondren Rd, Houston, TX 77074-3204.

LADO, FRED, THEORY OF LIQUIDS. **Personal Data:** b La Coruna, Spain, June 5, 1938; American citizen; m, c 3. **Education:** Univ Fla, BS, 1960, PhD (physics), 1964. **Professional Experience:** Guest scientist, Inst Rocasolano, CSIC, Madrid, Spain, 1997; guest scientist, Int Ctr Theoret Physics, Trieste, Italy, 1987; PROF PHYSICS, NC STATE UNIV, 1985-; fulbright sr lectr, Spain, 1971-1972; from asst prof to assoc prof, NC State Univ, 1968-1985; staff mem, Los Alamos Sci Lab, 1965-1968; Fel physics, Univ Fla, 1964-1965. **Memberships:** Am Phys Soc. **Research Statement & Publications:** Statistical mechanics; equilibrium and non-equilibrium theory of liquids; many-body problem. **Mailing Address:** Dept Physics, NC State Univ, Raleigh, NC 27695-8202. **Fax:** 919-515-6538. **E-Mail:** fred_lado@ncsu.edu

LA DU, BERT NICHOLS, BIOCHEMICAL PHARMACOLOGY. **Personal Data:** b Lansing, Mich, November 13, 1920; m 1947, c 4. **Education:** Mich State Col, BS, 1943; Univ Mich, MD, 1945; Univ Calif, PhD (biochem), 1952. **Professional Experience:** Dir res, Dept Anesthesiol, beginning 1991; PROF EMER PHARMACOL, UNIV MICH MED SCH, ANN ARBOR, 1988-; prof, Dept Anesthesiol, 1974-1988; chmn dept, Dept Anesthesiol, 1974-1980; prof pharmacol & chmn dept, Med Sch, NY Univ, 1963-1974; instr, Bellevue Med Ctr, 1951-1954; from sr asst surgeon to med dir, NIH, 1950-1963; res assoc, Goldwater Mem Hosp Res Serv, NY Univ, 1950-1954; asst biochem, Mich State Col, 1946-1947; asst biochem, Univ Calif, 1947-1950; intern, Rochester Gen Hosp, NY, 1945-1946. **Memberships:** Am Soc Biol Chemists; Am Chem Soc; Am Soc Pharmacol & Exp Therapeut (pres, 1978-1979); Am Soc Human Genetics; NY Acad Sci (pres, 1970). **Research Statement & Publications:** Drug metabolism; metabolism of tyrosine; inborn errors of metabolism; pharmacogenetics. **Mailing Address:** Univ Mich, Med Sch, Dept Pharmacol, 1301 MSRB III, Ann Arbor, MI 48109-0632. **Fax:** 734-763-4450. **E-Mail:** bladu@umich.edu

LADUKE, JOHN CARL, SYSTEMATIC BIOLOGY, BIOLOGICAL SCIENCES. **Personal Data:** b Jackson, Mich, November 21, 1950; m 1973, c 1. **Education:** Tex Tech Univ, BS, 1973, MS, 1975; Ohio State Univ, PhD (bot), 1980. **Honors & Awards:** Ralph E Alston Award, Bot Soc Am, 1979. **Professional Experience:** PROF BIOL, UNIV NDAK, as of 2003; assoc prof biol, Univ NDak, beginning 1985; asst prof, Univ NDak, 1980-1985. **Memberships:** Int Asn Plant Taxon; Am Soc Plant Taxonomists; Bot Soc Am; Soc Syst Zool; Sigma Xi. **Research Statement & Publications:** Plant systematics; chemosystematics; Sphaeralcea Malvacae including gathering morphological, cytological, flavonoid chemical data, molecula. **Mailing Address:** Dept Biol, Univ NDak, PO Box 9019, Grand Forks, ND 58202-9019. **E-Mail:** john_laduke@und.nodak.edu

LADWIG, HAROLD ALLEN, NEUROLOGY. **Personal Data:** b Manilla, Iowa, May 11, 1922; m 1946, c Stephen & Rosemary. **Education:** Univ Iowa, MD, 1947, BA, 1952; Am Bd Psychiat & Neurol, dipl. **Professional Experience:** FAC, EEG LAB, WILSON MEM HOSP, NC, 1983-; assoc prof, Sch Med, Creighton Univ, 1966-1983; Dept Neurol, Univ Nebr Med Ctr, 1966-1983; dir, EEG Lab, Children's Mem Hosp, 1963-1970 & Archbishop Bergan Mercy Hosp, 1964-1983; consult physician, Vet Admin Hosp, 1959-1963; assoc dir, EEG Lab, Creighton Mem St Joseph's Hosp, 1958-1964; mem med staff, Nebr Children's Ther Ctr, 1956-1964; Dir, EEG Lab, Creighton Mem St Joseph's Hosp, 1954-1970; attend physician, Vet Admin Hosp, 1954-1959; asst dir rehab ctr, EEG Lab, Creighton Mem St Joseph's Hosp, 1954-1958; from instr to asst prof neurol & psychiat, Sch Med, Creighton Univ, 1954-1956; Clin instr neurol, Univ Minn, 1950-1953. **Memberships:** Am EEG Soc; AMA; Am Col Physicians; Am Cong Rehab Med; Am Acad Neurol. **Research Statement & Publications:** Diagnostic neurology and rehabilitation of neurological patients; care of the aged; electroencephalography. **Mailing Address:** PO Box 3049, Wilson, NC 27895-3049.

LADY, EDWARD R, MECHANICAL ENGINEERING. **Education:** Univ Louisville, BME, 1947; Mass Inst Technol, SM, 1949; Univ Mich, PhD, 1963. **Professional Experience:** PROF EMER, MECH ENG DEPT, UNIV MICH, as of 2006. **Mailing Address:** Dept Mech Eng & Appl Mech, Univ Mich, 2016 AL, Ann Arbor, MI 48109 -2133. **Fax:** 734-936-0426. **E-Mail:** erlady@umich.edu

LADY, RICHARD L, ENVIRONMENTAL CHEMISTRY. **Professional Experience:** CO-ORDR, DEL MAXIMIS INC, as of 2001. **Mailing Address:** De Maximis Inc, 9041 Executive Park Dr Suite 601, Knoxville, TN 37923.

LAEMLE, LOIS K, DEVELOPMENTAL NEUROBIOLOGY, VISUAL SYSTEMS. **Personal Data:** b New York, NY, May 26, 1941. **Education:** City Univ NY, BS, 1962; Columbia Univ, PhD (anat), 1968. **Professional Experience:** ASSOC PROF, OPTHAL, INST OPTHAL & VISUAL SCI, UNIV MED & DENT NJ, as of 2004; assoc ed, Am J Anat, beginning 1989; vis prof, Dept Ophthal, NY Med Sch, 1983; ASSOC PROF, NEUROANAT & HISTOL, UNIV MED & DENT NJ, 1977-; prin investr, NIH res grant, 1973-1981, 1982-1986; asst prof, Univ Med & Dent NJ, 1972-1977; res fel, Neuroscience, Rose F Kennedy Ctr Ment Retardation, 1969-1972; fel anat, Albert Einstein Col Med, 1968. **Memberships:** Am Asn Anatomists; Soc Neuroscience; Sigma Xi; NY Acad Sci; Cajal Club. **Research Statement & Publications:** Morphology and development of the central nervous system; fiber connections, neuronal maturation, and neurotransmitters in the visual system; mechanisms of arcadian timekeeping; Published over 10 articles. **Mailing Address:** Dept Opthal, Inst Opthal & Visual Sci, Univ Med & Dent NJ, 100 Berben St, Newark, NJ 07103. **E-Mail:** laemle@umdnj.edu

LAEMMLE, JOSEPH THOMAS, ORGANIC CHEMISTRY, METAL WORKING LUBRICANTS. **Personal Data:** b Louisville, Ky, February 7, 1941; m 1965, Patricia; c Scott, Adam & Lillian. **Education:** Bellarmine Col, BA, 1964; Ga Inst Technol, MS, 1968, PhD (org chem), 1971; Ga State Univ, MBA, 1976. **Honors & Awards:** Union Camp fel 1970-1971, Sigma Xi Award. **Professional Experience:** SR TECHNICAL CONSULT, ALCOA LAB, 1997-; div mgr, Surface Tech Div, Alcoa Labs, 1986-1997; sr tech supvr, Alcoa Labs, 1981-1986; tech supvr, Alcoa Labs, 1981; staff scientist, Alcoa Labs, 1980-1981; sr scientist, Alcoa Labs, 1977-1980; asst prof chem, Kennesaw Col, 1973-1977; NDEA, fel 1970; from asst res chemist to asst, Ga Inst Technol, 1967-1973; NASA, trainee, 1969. **Memberships:** Am Chem Soc; Soc Tribologist & Lubrication Engrs; Sigma Xi. **Research Statement & Publications:** Determination of the structure of organometallic compounds; lubricant testing and development; descriptions of organometallic reaction mechanisms and sterechemistry of additions with Ketones; metal working lubricants including formation, handling, reclamation and disposal. **Mailing Address:** Surface Tech Div, Alcoa Tech Ctr, 100 Technical Dr, Alcoa Ctr, PA 15069-0001. **Fax:** 412-337-2809.

LAEMMLEN, FRANKLIN, PLANT PATHOLOGY, ENTOMOLOGY, VEGETABLE CROPS. **Personal Data:** b Reedley, Calif, March 8, 1938; m Anne; c Teresa & Louise. **Education:** Univ Calif, Davis, BS, 1960, PhD (plant path), 1970; Purdue Univ, West Lafayette, MS, 1967. **Professional Experience:** RETIRED(Emeritus), DIR, SANTA BARBARA & SAN LUIS OBISPO COUNTIES, UNIV CALIF, as of 2002; FARM ADV, SANTA BARBARA & SAN LUIS OBISPO COUNTIES, UNIV CALIF, 1992-; farm adv, Imp Co Coop Exten, 1980-1992; vis colleague, Dept Plant Path, Univ Calif, Berkeley, 1978-1979; from asst prof to assoc prof plant path, Mich State Univ, 1976-1980; assoc ed, Plant Dis Reporter, 1974-1977; asst prof, Univ Hawaii, 1970-1972; Res asst plant path, Univ Calif, Davis, 1966-1970. **Memberships:** Sigma Xi; Am Phytopath Soc; NACAA. **Research Statement & Publications:** Extension plant pathology; ornamental plant diseases; plant disease diagnostic laboratory; field and vegetable crop diseases. **Mailing Address:** UCCE Santa Barbara County, Santa Maria, CA 93455. **Fax:** 805-934-6333. **E-Mail:** fflaemmlen@ucdavis.edu

LAESSIG, RONALD HAROLD, CLINICAL CHEMISTRY, PUBLIC HEALTH & PUBLIC HEALTH LABORATORY ADMINISTRATION. **Personal Data:** b Marshfield, Wis, 1940; m Joan; c 1. **Education:** Wis State Univ-Stevens Point, BS, 1962; Univ Wis-Madison, PhD (analytical chem), 1965, Post Doc Princeton Univ, 1966 Post Doc CDC Atlanta 1966. **Honors & Awards:** DIFCO Award, Am Pub Health Asn, 1974; Outstanding Contrib through Serv to Profession of Clin Chem Award, Am Asn Clin Chem, 1990, Natelson Award for Advan Clin Chem, 1990. **Professional Experience:** Mem bd, Am Asn Clin Chem, 1985-1988; pres, Nat Comt Clin Lab Stand, 1980-1982; DIR, STATE LAB HYG, 1979-; PROF PREV MED & PATH, MED CTR, UNIV WIS, MADISON, 1976-; chmn diag prod comt, Food & Drug Admin, 1972-1974; Mem, Inst Bd Anal Chem, 1971-; assoc prof, State Lab Hyg, 1971-1976; asst dir, State Lab Hyg, 1970-1979; chief chem, State Lab Hyg, 1966-1979; Fel, Princeton Univ, 1965-1966 & Ctr Dis Control, Atlanta, 1966. **Memberships:** Am Asn Clin Chem; Am Chem Soc; Am Pub Health Asn. **Research Statement & Publications:** Automation; newborn screening; computerization of laboratory operation; public health laboratory applications of test procedures. **Mailing Address:** State Laboraory Hygiene, 465 Henry Mall - Univ Wis, Madison, WI 53706. **Fax:** 608-262-3257. **E-Mail:** rhl@mail.slh.wisc.edu

LAETSCH, THEODORE WILLIS, MATHEMATICAL ANALYSIS. **Personal Data:** b St Louis, Mo, January 7, 1940; m 1961. **Education:** Wash Univ, St Louis, BS, 1961; Mass Inst Technol, SM, 1962; Calif Inst Technol, PhD (appl math), 1968. **Professional Experience:** HEAD, MATH DEPT, 1978-; ASSOC PROF MATH, UNIV ARIZ, 1971-; Nat Acad Sci-Nat Res Coun resident res associateship, Wright-Patterson AFB, Ohio, 1970-1971; asst prof math, Ill State Univ, 1968-1970; asst prof physics, Col Idaho, 1962-1965. **Memberships:** Am Math Soc; Soc Indust & Appl Math. **Research Statement & Publications:** Functional analysis in partially ordered spaces; boundary value problems for ordinary and partial differential equations. **Mailing Address:** Dept Math, Univ Ariz, 617 N Santa Rita PO Box 210089, Tucson, AZ 85721-0089. **Fax:** 520-621-8322. **E-Mail:** laetsch@math.arizona.edu

LAETSCH, WATSON MCMILLAN, BOTANY. **Personal Data:** b Bellingham, Wash, January 19, 1933; m 1958, c 2. **Education:** Wabash Col, BA, 1955; Stanford Univ, PhD (biol), 1961. **Honorary Degrees:** DSc, Wabash Col, 1985. **Professional Experience:** EMER PROF BOT, UNIV CALIF, BERKELEY, as of 2005; mem, Indo-US Subcomn Educ & Cult, 1983-; vice chancellor Under grad Affairs, Univ Calif, Berkeley, 1980-; pres, Asn Sci-Tech Ctrs, 1977-1978; dir, Lawrence Hall Sci, 1972-1980; prof Bot, Univ Calif, Berkeley, 1971-; dir, Univ Bot Garden, 1969-1973; assoc dir, Lawrence Hall Sci, 1969-1972; NSF sr fel, Univ Col, London, 1968-1969; from asst prof to assoc prof bot, Univ Calif, Berkeley, 1963-1971; asst prof biol, State Univ NY, Stony Brook, 1961-1963; Fulbright fel, Univ Delhi, India, 1956-1957. **Memberships:** AAAS; Bot Soc Am; Am Soc Plant Physiol; Soc Exp Biol & Med. **Research Statement & Publications:** Plant development; structure and function of the photosynthetic apparatus; science education. **Mailing Address:** 1554 LeRoy Ave, Berkeley, CA 94708-1942. **Fax:** 510-548-6260.

LA FEHR, THOMAS ROBERT, GEOPHYSICS. **Personal Data:** b Los Angeles, Calif, February 6, 1934; m 1957, c 5. **Education:** Univ Calif, Berkeley, AB, 1958; Colo Sch Mines, MSc, 1962; Stanford Univ, PhD (geophys), 1964. **Professional Experience:** PRES, LCT, 1989-; pres, Edcon, 1975-1989; adj prof geophys, Colo Sch Mines, 1975-1989; consult, GAI-GMS Div, EG&G, Inc, 1969-1970 & Explor Data Consult, 1970-1989; assoc prof, Colo Sch Mines, 1969-1975; dir tech develop, GAI-GMX Div, EG&G Inc, 1967-1969; vpres tech develop, GAI-GMX Inc, 1966-1967; geophysicist, Geophys Assocs, Int, 1964-1966; Lectr, Stanford Univ, 1964; Geophysicist, US Geol Surv, 1962-1964. **Memberships:** Hon mem Soc Explor Geophys; Am Asn Petrol Geol; Am Geophys Union. **Research Statement & Publications:** Gravity and magnetic exploration; potential field theory; integrated seismic, gravity, well log data; borehole gravity. **Mailing Address:** 9566 Briar Forest Dr, Houston, TX 77063.

LAFERRIERE, ARTHUR L, ORGANIC CHEMISTRY, INORGANIC CHEMISTRY. **Personal Data:** b Willimantic, Conn, December 3, 1933; m 1955, c 3. **Education:** Brown Univ, BS, 1955; Rutgers Univ, MS, 1958; Univ RI, PhD (chem), 1960. **Professional Experience:** PROF CHEM, RI COL, 1962-; Res chemist, Minerals & Chem Corp, 1956-1958 & Am Cyanamid Co, 1960-1962. **Memberships:** Am Chem Soc. **Research Statement & Publications: Inorganic solution chemistry; organic redox mechanisms. **Mailing Address:** Dept Chem, RI Col 600Mt Pleasant Ave, Providence, RI 02908. **E-Mail:** alaferriere@ric.edu

LAFEVER, HOWARD N, PLANT BREEDING, GENETICS. **Personal Data:** b Hagerstown, Ind, May 13, 1938; m 1958, c 2. **Education:** Purdue Univ, BS, 1959, MS, 1961, PhD (plant breeding & genetics), 1963. **Honors & Awards:** Crops & Soils Award, Am Soc Agron, 1977. **Professional Experience:** RETIRED; from asst prof to prof genetics & plant breeding, Ohio Agr Res & Develop Ctr, 1965-1992; res geneticist, Boll Weevil Res Lab, USDA, 1963-1965; asst prof genetics, Purdue Univ, 1963; instr bot, Wis State Univ, LaCrosse, 1963. **Memberships:** Am Soc Agron; Crop Sci Soc Am. **Research Statement & Publications:** Breeding new wheat varieties for distribution and production in midwest; genetic studies of wheat. **Mailing Address:** 500 Danberry Dr, Wooster, OH 44691.

LAFEVERS, JAMES RONALD, MANAGEMENT OF RESEARCH & DEVELOPMENT, MANAGEMENT OF MULTIDISCIPLINARY RESEARCH IN ENERGY DEVELOPMENT. **Personal Data:** b Oakland, Calif, November 16, 1944; m 1965, Judy Isbell; c Sandra, Terri & Jamie. **Education:** Univ Cent Ark, BS, 1968; Univ Southern Miss, MS, 1970; Ind State Univ, PhD (econ geog), 1974. **Professional Experience:** EXEC DIR & DEP VPRES ARGONNE NAT LAB, UNIV CHICAGO, 1992-; mem, Cong Sci & Technol Adv Comt, 1991-1994; actg assoc vpres res & lab, Univ Chicago Argonne Nat Lab, 1991-1992; dir sci & technol rev, Univ Chicago Argonne Nat Lab, 1983-1991; lectr sci & environ policy, Northwestern Univ, 1982-1984; consult energy & environ sci, Los Alamos Tech Assocs, 1981-1982; environ scientist & prog mgr, Argonne Nat Lab, 1979-1982; asst scientist & prog mgr, Argonne Nat Lab, 1974-1979; consult energy & environ res, Argonne Nat Lab, 1973-1974; res assoc, River Basin Res Ctr, 1971-1972; res assoc, Crane Ctr Econ Develop, 1970-1971; instr phys geog & resource mgt, Univ Southern Miss, 1970-1971; Instr phys sci, Columbia Acad, 1969-1970; Consult resource mgt, Southern Miss Develop Comn, 1968-1969. **Memberships:** AAAS; Asn Am Geographers; Am Nuclear Soc; Am Phys Soc; Am Mgt Asn; Inst Environ Sci. **Research Statement & Publications:** Energy resource and facility development and related economic and environmental impacts, including the effects of legislation and policy decisions on both the energy industry and the environment; application of both basic and applied research methods. **Mailing Address:** Off Vpres Argonne, Univ Chicago, 9700 S Cass Ave, Bldg 201, Argonne, IL 60439-4832. **Fax:** 630-252-5329. **E-Mail:** jlafevers@anl.gov

LAFFERTY, JAMES FRANCIS, BIOMEDICAL ENGINEERING, MECHANICAL ENGINEERING. **Personal Data:** b Pampa, Tex, December 23, 1927; m 1956, Vivian; c 3. **Education:** Univ Ky, BS, 1955; Univ Southern Calif, MS, 1957; Univ Mich, MS, 1966, PhD (nuclear eng), 1967. **Professional Experience:** Pres, lafferty eng, 1992 EMER PROF & DIR BIOMED ENG CTR, 1990-; BIOMED ENG CONSULT, UNIV KY, 1990-; prof & dir, Biomed Eng Ctr, 1985-1990; prof mech eng & lab dir, Werner-Gren Res Lab, Univ Ky, 1973-1985; actg lab dir, Werner-Gren Res Lab, Univ Ky, 1967-1973; assoc prof mech eng, Werner-Gren Res Lab, Univ Ky, 1962-1973; NSF fac fels, Univ Mich, 1961-1962 & 1965-1966; asst prof nuclear eng, Werner-Gren Res Lab, Univ Ky, 1957-1962; mem tech staff, Hughes Aircraft Co, 1955-1957; Asst, Wenner-Gren Res Lab, Univ Ky, 1954-1955. **Memberships:** Orthop Res Soc; Soc Automotive Eng. **Research Statement & Publications:** Biomechanics of the skeletal and cardiovascular systems; response of biosystems to impact, vibration, acceleration. **Mailing Address:** 693 Andover Village Pl, Lexington, KY 40509. **Fax:** 828-743-0531. **E-Mail:** aerie344@cs.com

LAFFERTY, JAMES M(ARTIN), PHYSICAL ELECTRONICS, POWER ELECTRONICS. **Personal Data:** b Battle Creek, Mich, April 27, 1916; m 1942, c 4. **Education:** Univ Mich, BSE, 1939, MS, 1940, PhD (elec eng), 1946. **Honors & Awards:** Naval Ord Develop Award, 1946; Lamme Medalist, Inst Elec & Electronics Engrs, 1979. **Professional Experience:** Group leader, People to People Citizen Embassador Prog, 1984-1988; INDEPENDENT CONSULT, 1981-; mgr, Power Electronics Lab, Res & Develop Ctr, 1978-1981; mgr, Electronic Power Conditioning & Control Lab, 1975-1978; mgr, Physics & Electronic Eng Lab, 1974-1975; mgr, Physics & Elec Eng Lab, 1972-1974; mgr, Gen Physics Lab, 1968-1972; mgr, Plasma & Vacuum Physics Br, 1956-1968; res assoc, Gen Elec Co, 1942-1956; radio proximity fuse res, Carnegie Inst Wash, 1941; Mem staff, Eastman Kodak Co, NY, 1939. **Memberships:** Nat Acad Eng; fel AAAS; fel Am Phys Soc; fel Inst Elec & Electronics Engrs; hon mem Am Vacuum Soc; Int Union Vacuum Sci Tech Applns (pres 1981-1983). **Research Statement & Publications:** Electrometer and microwave tubes; electron guns; lanthanum boride cathodes; color television picture tubes; gas discharge tubes; hot-cathode magnetron ionization gauge; triggered vacuum gap; vacuum switch; electric vehicles. **Mailing Address:** 1202 Hedgewood Lane, Schenectady, NY 12309.

LAFFERTY, KEVIN D, MATHEMATICAL MODELLING, PARASITE ECOLOGY. **Personal Data:** b Glendale, Calif, September 8, 1963; m 1992, Cristina. **Education:** Univ Calif, Santa Barbara, BA, 1985, MA, 1988, PhD (ecol), 1991. **Professional Experience:** ADJ PROF, UNIV CALIF, LOS ANGELES, 1993-; res biologist, Univ Calif, Santa Barbara, 1993; fel, Nat Marine Sanctuary, 1992-1993; lectr parasitol, Univ Calif, Santa Barbara, 1990-1992. **Memberships:** Western Soc Naturalists. **Research Statement & Publications:** Effects that parasites have on the ecology and evolution of their hosts; degradation of the marine environment. **Mailing Address:** 6352 Via Real, Carpinteria, CA 93013.

LAFFERTY, WALTER J, PHYSICAL CHEMISTRY. **Personal Data:** b Wilmington, Del, February 10, 1934; m 1958, Mary; c Anne, Maura, Clare, Ellen, Paula & Brenda. **Education:** Univ Del, BS, 1956; Mass Inst Technol, PhD (phys chem), 1961. **Honors & Awards:** Silver Medal, Dept Com Iber droke visiting prof, CSIC, Madad. **Professional Experience:** SCIENTIST EMER, 1997-; vis prof, Univ Paris (VI), 1987, 1991 & 1993; Leverhulme vis fel, Univ Reading, England, 1970-1971; chemist, Nat Inst Stand & Technol, 1962-1996; res assoc, Johns Hopkins Univ, 1961-1962. **Memberships:** Coblentz Soc. **Research Statement & Publications:** Infrared and microwave spectroscopy. **Mailing Address:** Optical Technol Div, Nat Inst Stand & Technol, Bldg 221 Rm B250, Gaithersburg, MD 20899. **E-Mail:** walter.lafferty@mst.gov

LAFFIN, ROBERT JAMES, MICROBIOLOGY. **Personal Data:** b New Haven, Conn, April 16, 1927; m 1974, Judith; c 4. **Education:** Yale Univ, BS, 1949, PhD (microbiol), 1955; Am Bd Med Lab Immunol, dipl. **Professional Experience:** PROF MICROBIOL, ALBANY MED COL, 1976-; assoc prof, Albany Med Col, 1967-1976; asst prof, Albany Med Col, 1964-1967; instr obstet & gynec, med sch, Tufts Univ, 1962-1964; immunologist, St Margaret's Hosp, 1962-1964; from instr to assoc prof, Creighton Univ, 1955-1962; instr microbiol, Womans Col, Univ NC, 1953-1955. **Memberships:** Emer mem Am Asn Immunologist. **Research Statement & Publications:** Microbiology. **Mailing Address:** Dept Microbiol, Albany Med Col, Union Univ, 47 New Scotland Ave, Albany, NY 12208-3479. **Fax:** 518-262-5748. **E-Mail:** riaffin@ccgateway.amc.edu

LAFFLER, THOMAS G, GENETICS. **Personal Data:** b Detroit, Mich, May 10, 1946; m 1968, c 3. **Education:** Mass Inst Technol, BS, 1968; Univ Wash, PhD (genetics), 1974. **Professional Experience:** CONSULT, 1989-; asst prof microbiol, Med & Dent Schs, Northwestern Univ, 1980-1989; res assoc, McArdle Lab Cancer Res, 1978-1980; fel oncol, McArdle Lab Cancer Res, 1974-1978. **Memberships:** Genetics Soc Am; Sigma Xi. **Research Statement & Publications:** Study of molecular basis of cell cycle control using Physarum polycephalum as a lower enkorycote model; cell cycle mutants and the regulation of tubulin biosynthesis and DNA replication. **Mailing Address:** 1964 Pinehurst Ct, Libertyville, IL 60048.

LAFFOON, JOHN, ELECTRON MICROSCOPY. **Personal Data:** b Albia, Iowa, June 20, 1955. **Education:** Univ Iowa, BS, 1979. **Professional Experience:** ULTRA MICROTOMY DENT RES, 1979-; Electron microscopy, Dent Col, Univ Iowa, 1979-1988. **Research Statement & Publications:** Electron microsopy in dental research for the past nine years; tem and sem and micro probe, soft and hard tissue. **Mailing Address:** Electron Probe Microanalysis Facil Dows Inst Dent Res, Univ Iowa Col Dent, N441 Dent Sci Bldg, Iowa City, IA 52242.

LAFLAMME, GASTON, EPIDEMIOLOGY, MYCOLOGY. **Personal Data:** b St Prosper, Beauce, Que, July 15, 1945; m 1980, c 1. **Education:** Laval Univ, Que, BSc App, 1968, MSc, 1971; Swiss Fed Inst Technol, Zurich, DSc App(forest path & mycol), 1975. **Professional Experience:** RES SCIENTIST, CAN FORESTRY SERV, QUE, 1980-; forest pathologist, Dept Land & Forest, Que, 1978-1980; res scientist forest path, Can Forestry Serv, Nfld, 1975-1978. **Memberships:** Can Phytopath Soc; Poplar Coun Can; Can Forestry Inst. **Research Statement & Publications:** Decay of living trees; taxonomy of fungi; scleroderris canker and other tree diseases; endophytic fungi. **Mailing Address:** Laurentian Forestry Ctr, Can Forest Serv, PO Box 3800 1055 rue du PEPS, St Foy, PQ G1V 4C7, Can. **Fax:** 418-648-5849. **E-Mail:** ung@cfl.forestry.ca

LA FLEUR, JAMES KEMBLE, MECHANICAL ENGINEERING. **Personal Data:** b Los Angeles, Calif, April 23, 1930; m 1964, c 3. **Education:** Calif Inst Technol, BSME, 1952, Pepperdine, MBA, 1980. **Professional Experience:** RETIRED; chmn, pres & chief exec officer, GTI Corp, 1975-1990; pres, Indust Cryogenics Inc, 1966-1975; chmn bd, 1957-1960 & LaFleur Corp, 1965-1966; Dynamic Res Inc, 1957-1960 & LaFleur Corp, 1960-1965; pres, Kemsco Inc, 1956-1957; Engr, AiResearch Mfg Co, 1952-1956. **Memberships:** Am Soc Mech Engrs; Cryogenic Soc Am; Int Solar Energy Soc; Int Asn Hydrogen Energy; Am Wind Energy Asn. **Research Statement & Publications:** Applying knowledge gained in the development of normal turbo-machinery to the field of low temperature to develop new low temperature processes. **Mailing Address:** PO Box 2327, North Hollywood, CA 91602.

LAFLEUR, KERMIT STILLMAN, TEXTILE CHEMISTRY, SOIL SCIENCE. **Personal Data:** b Waterville, Maine, February 14, 1915; m 1939, c 1. **Education:** Colby Col, BA, 1937; Clemson Univ, MS, 1964, PhD, 1966. **Professional Experience:** PROF EMER, AGRON & SOILS, CLEMSON UNIV, as of 2003; prof, Clemson Univ, 1975-1980; assoc prof soil chem, Clemson Univ, 1967-1975; sr scientist, Deering Milliken Res Corp, 1966-1967; consult chemist, Deering Milliken Res Corp, 1962-1966; group leader wool res, Deering Milliken Res Corp, 1959-1962; tech supt, Excelsior Mills, 1956-1958; res chemist, Excelsior Mills, 1952-1956; chief chemist, Deering Milliken Maine Mills, 1947-1952; chief chemist, Wyandotte Worsted Co, Maine, 1940-1946; asst chemist, Wyandotte Worsted Co, Maine, 1937-1940. **Memberships:** AAAS; Am Soc Agron; Soil Sci Soc Am. **Research Statement & Publications:** Wool chemistry; soil chemistry. **Mailing Address:** 150 Downs Blvd, Clemson, SC 29631.

LAFLEUR, LOUIS DWYNN, ACOUSTICS, ULTRASONICS. **Personal Data:** b Elton, La, December 28, 1940; m 1964, c 4. **Education:** Univ Southwestern La, BS, 1962; Univ Houston, PhD (physics), 1969. **Professional Experience:** PROF PHYSICS, UNIV SOUTHWESTERN LA, as of 2000; assoc prof Physics, Univ Southwestern La, beginning 1974; asst prof, Univ Southwestern LA, 1970-1974; asst prof physics, Drury Col, 1969-1970; aerospace technologist, Manned Spacecraft Ctr, NASA, 1965-1966; res scientist assoc, Defense Res Lab, Univ Tex, Austin, 1964-1965. **Memberships:** Am Phys Soc; Am Asn Physics Teachers; Acoust Soc Am. **Research Statement & Publications:** Acoustics and ultrasonics; electroacoustics; mossbauer spectroscopy. **Mailing Address:** Dept Physics, Univ Southwestern La, PO Box 44210, Lafayette, LA 70504. **Fax:** 337-482-6699. **E-Mail:** lafleur@louisiana.edu

LAFLEUR, MICHEL, BIOPHYSICAL CHEMISTRY, SPECTROSCOPY OF BIOMOLECULES. **Personal Data:** b Montreal, Que, March 14, 1960. **Education:** Univ Sherbrooke, BSc, 1982; Univ Laval, PhD (chem), 1987. **Professional Experience:** PROF PHYS CHEM, UNIV MONTREAL, 2001-; assoc prof phys chem, Univ Montreal, 1995-2001; asst prof, Univ Montreal, 1990-1995; Postdoctoral fel, Dept Biochem, Univ BC, 1987-1990. **Memberships:** Can Asn Advan Sci; Spectros Soc Can; Can Soc Chem; Fedn Am Soc Exp Biol; Biophys Soc. **Research Statement & Publications:** Establish the physico-chemical laws dictating the behavior of biomolecules by characterizing the structure and dynamics by spectroscopic methods. **Mailing Address:** Dept Chem, Univ Montreal, Montreal, PQ H3C 3J7, Can. **Fax:** 514-343-7586. **E-Mail:** michel.lafleur@umontreal.ca

LAFLEUR, ROBERT GEORGE, HYDROLOGY & WATER RESOURCES. **Personal Data:** b Albany, NY, March 31, 1929; m 1950, c 3. **Education:** Univ Rochester, AB, 1950; Rensselaer Polytech Inst, MS, 1953, PhD, 1961. **Professional Experience:** PRIN GEOLOGIST, SPECTRA ENVIRON GROUP INC, 1994-; PROF EMER, GLACIAL GEOL & WATER RESOURCES, RENSSELAER POLYTECH INST, 1993-; prof, glacial geol & water resources, Rensselaer Polytech inst, 1982-1993; from asst prof to assoc prof, Glacial Geol & Water Resources, Rensselaer Polytech inst, 1955-1982; instr geol, Glacial Geol & Water Resources, Rensselaer Polytech inst, 1952-1955; consult, NY State Educ dept & US Geol Surv. **Memberships:** Fel Geol Soc Am; Nat Asn Geol Teachers; Am Geophys Union; Arctic Inst NAm; Soc Econ Paleontologists & Mineralogists; Sigma Xi; Am Inst Prof Geologist; Am Inst Hydrol. **Research Statement & Publications:** Glacial geology; hydrogeology. **Mailing Address:** Spectra Environ Group Inc, 307 S Townsend St, Syracuse, NY 13202. **Fax:** 315-471-2111.

LAFON, GUY MICHEL, GEOCHEMISTRY, PHYSICAL CHEMISTRY. **Personal Data:** b Bordeaux, France, June 5, 1943. **Education:** Paris Sch Mines, Civil Ing Mines, 1964; Univ Alta, MSc, 1965; Northwestern Univ, Ill, PhD (geol), 1969. **Professional Experience:** SR RES GEOLOGIST, RES ASSOC, EXXON PROD RES CO, 1979-; asst prof geol, Johns Hopkins Univ, 1972-1979; asst prof geol, State Univ NY Binghamton, 1970-1972; Res Found fel, State Univ NY Binghamton, 1969-1970. **Memberships:** Sigma Xi; AAAS; Geochem Soc; Soc Econ Paleont & Mineral; Geol Soc Am; Am Chem Soc. **Research Statement & Publications:** Geochemistry of natural water systems; thermodynamic properties of brines and minerals; equilibrium models; experimental study of mineral-fluid reactions, hydrothermal simulation of geological processes. **Mailing Address:** PO Box 2189, Houston, TX 77252-2189.

LAFON, STEPHEN WOODROW, ANTIMICROBIAL THERAPY. **Personal Data:** b Owasso, Mich, August 3, 1953; m 1974, c 2. **Education:** Olivet Nazarene Col, BA, 1975; WVa Univ, MSc, 1978. **Professional Experience:** CLIN RES SCIENTIST I, DEPT INFECTIOUS DIS, BURROUGHS WELLCOME CO, as of 1993; clin res assoc III, dept infectious dis, 1987-1989; prog coordr, dept proj coord, 1986-1987; res scientist II, dept exp ther, Burroughs Wellcome Co, 1981-1986; res scientist I, dept exp ther, Burroughs Wellcome Co, 1978-1981; res asst, dept exp ther, Burroughs Wellcome Co, 1977-1978. **Memberships:** Am Soc Biol Chemists. **Research Statement & Publications:** Metabolism and pharmacokinetics of numerous potential therapeutic agents; purine metabolism and nucleic acid synthesis in mammalian cells and protozoa; DNA damage assays and repair research; early HIV diseases and opportunist infections; author of numerous publications. **Mailing Address:** Dept Infectious Dis & Immunol, Burroughs Wellcome Co, 3030 Cornwallis Rd, Research Triangle Park, NC 27709-2700.

LAFOND, ANDRE, FORESTRY. **Personal Data:** b Montreal, Que, July 1, 1920; m 1946, c 3. **Education:** Jean-de-Brebeuf Col, BA, 1942; Laval Univ, BA, 1945, BASc, 1946; Univ Wis, PhD, 1951. **Professional Experience:** RETIRED; pres, Res Found, 1975; dean fac forestry, Laval Univ, 1971-1985; prof forest ecol & physiol, Laval Univ, 1951-1985; forester, Que Forest Serv, 1946-1951; consult, Que Northshore Paper Co, World Bank & Can Int Develop Agency. **Memberships:** Can Soc Soil Sci; Can Soc Plant Physiol; Fr-CanAsn Advan Sci; Can Inst Forestry; Int Soc Soil Sci. **Research Statement & Publications:** Forest ecology, particularly soil vegetation relationships; forest physiology, particularly mineral nutrition of trees and fertilization; forest management, particularly site classification. **Mailing Address:** 2071 Marie-Victorin, St Nicolas, PQ G7A 4H4, Can.

LAFONTAINE, JEAN-GABRIEL, CELL BIOLOGY, ELECTRON MICROSCOPY. **Personal Data:** b Sherbrooke, Que, August 4, 1928; m 1952, c 3. **Education:** Laval Univ, Lic es Sci, 1950; Univ Wis, MS, 1952, PhD (zool), 1954. **Honors & Awards:** Que Asn Advan Sci Prize, 1982. **Professional Experience:** PROF BIOL, SCI FAC, LAVAL UNIV, 1968-; assoc prof biol, Med Sch, 1964-1968; asst prof path, Med Sch, 1960-1964; Rockefeller Inst, 1956-1958 & Montreal Cancer Inst, 1958-1960; Damon Runyon fel, 1954-1956; Res asst cytol, Sloan Kettering Inst, 1954-1956. **Memberships:** Am Soc Cell Biol; Can Soc Cell Biol; Royal Soc Can 1984; NY Acad Sci 1985. **Research Statement & Publications:** Cytochemistry and ultrastructure of the cell nucleus. **Mailing Address:** Dept Biol, Laval Univ, Quebec, PQ G1K 7P4, Can.

LAFONTAINE, THOMAS E, AIR & WATER POLLUTION CONTROL, THERMAL PROCESS DESIGN. **Personal Data:** b Clarksburg, Mass, January 2, 1952; m 1981, Catherine Hackett; c Christina & Colima. **Professional Experience:** VPRES & TECH DIR, INTERCON PAC INC, 1990-; Pac Aqua-Tech, Ltd, 1990-; PRES/OWNER, TELTECH CO, 1988-; Consult, Ralston Brokers Int, 1988-; vpres, ATESA USA, Inc, 1987-1988; tech dir, Cameron-Yakima Inc, 1981-1987; Pres, T&C Res, 1978-1980. **Memberships:** Int Carbon Soc; Nat Pollution Control Fedn; Nat Air Pollution Control Asn; Am Water Works Asn. **Research Statement & Publications:** Chemically treated activated carbons for special applications; manufacture of special purpose activated carbons; conversion of organic waste from landfills into activated carbon; process development for the disposal of waste tires. **Mailing Address:** PO Box 2784, Yakima, WA 98907. **Fax:** 509-965-5963.

LAFORNARA, JOSEPH PHILIP, CHEMISTRY, ENVIRONMENTAL SCIENCES. **Personal Data:** b Buffalo, NY, December 5, 1942; wid, c 2. **Education:** Canisius Col, BS, 1964; Univ Fla, PhD (inorg chem), 1970. **Professional Experience:** CHIEF ENVIRON RESPONSE TEAM, US ENVIRON PROTECTION AGENCY, 1987-; Spill Control Syst, 1978-; phys scientist, Environ Response Team, 1978-1987; mem, Task Force for Nitrosamine Control & Task Force for Kepone Control, US Environ Protection Agency, 1975-; Oil & Hazardous Mat Spills Br, Indust Environ Res Lab, 1975-1978; tech adv, Hazardous Mat Adv Comt, Nat Res Coun-Nat Acad Sci, 1971-; res chemist, Nat Environ Res Ctr, 1971-1975; res chemist, Edison Water Qual Lab, Fed Water Qual Admin, Dept Interior, 1970-1971; chmn, Hazardous Mat Div, Am Soc Testing & Mat Comt, No F-20. **Memberships:** Am Soc Testing & Mat; Am Chem Soc; Water Pollution Control Fedn. **Research Statement & Publications:** Application of chemical technology to control of spills of hazardous materials; chemical analysis of inorganic and organic water and air pollutants; ultimate disposal of chemical wastes. **Mailing Address:** Environ Response Team US Environ Protection Agency, 1200 Pa Ave N W, Washington, DC 20460. **E-Mail:** lafornara.joseph@epa.gov

LAFOUNTAIN, JAMES ROBERT, CELL BIOLOGY. **Personal Data:** b Richmond, Va, January 8, 1944; m 1970, c 2. **Education:** Princeton Univ, AB, 1966; State Univ NY, Albany, PhD (biol sci), 1970. **Professional Experience:** PROF, BIOL SCI, STATE UNIV NY, BUFFALO, 1986-; from asst prof to assoc prof, State Univ NY, Buffalo, 1972-1986; fel, Eidgenossi Tech Univ, Switz, 1971-1972. **Memberships:** Am Soc Cell Biol. **Research Statement & Publications:** Physiology of cell division and cell motility; Published over 10 articles. **Mailing Address:** Dept Biol Sci, State Univ NY, 657 Cooke Hall, Buffalo, NY 14260. **Fax:** 716-645-2975. **E-Mail:** jrl@acsu.buffalo.edu

LAFOUNTAIN, LESTER JAMES, GEOLOGY. **Personal Data:** b Marinette, Wis, September 27, 1942; m 1964, c 1. **Education:** Univ Wis, BS & MS, 1964; Univ Colo, PhD (geol), 1973. **Professional Experience:** CONSULT, BRYANA STIRRAT & ASSOC, 1992-; consult, Emot, 1990-1992; vpres, Converse Environ Consults Calif, 1988-1990; asst prog mgr, Battelle Off Nuclear Waste Isolation, 1985-1988; vpres, Technos, 1984-1985; gen mgr corp, D'Appolonia Geophys Corp, 1980-1984; chief geologist int oper, D'Appolonia Geophys Corp, 1978-1979; proj geologist, D'Appolonia Geophys Corp, 1976-1977; asst proj geologist, D'Appolonia Geophys Corp, 1975-1976; res assoc rock mech, Dept Geol, Univ NC, 1971-1974; geologist, Texaco Inc, 1966; party chief geol, US Steel Corp, 1965; field geologist, US Steel Corp, 1964. **Memberships:** Geol Soc Am; Am Geophys Union; AAAS; Sigma Xi; Am Soc Civil Engrs; Nat Water Well Asn; Soc Explor Geophysicists. **Research Statement & Publications:** The mechanisms and physical aspects of rock dilation, stick slip and earthquake precursors; the tectonics of the mid-continent and its relationship to seismicity. **Mailing Address:** 61 Hidden Valley Ave, Monrovia, CA 91016.

LAFRAMBOISE, JAMES GERALD, PLASMA PHYSICS. **Personal Data:** b Windsor, Ont, July 26, 1938; m 1962, c 2. **Education:** Univ Windsor, BSc, 1957; Univ Toronto, BASc, 1959, MA, 1960, PhD (aerospace studies), 1966. **Professional Experience:** PROF EMER PHYSICS & ASTRON, YORK UNIV, as of 2006; assoc ed, J Geophys Res, Space Physics, 1983-1985; prof physics & astron, York Univ, beginning 1977; assoc prof, York Univ, 1971-1977; asst prof physics, York Univ, 1967-1971; asst prof math, Univ Windsor, 1965-1967; mem prog team, WISP Shuttle Exp. **Memberships:** Can Asn Physicists; Am Geophys Union; Planetary Soc. **Research Statement & Publications:** High-voltage electrical charging of spacecraft; electrode devices for plasma diagnostics; high-voltage antennas in space plasmas; spacecraft-plasma interactions. **Mailing Address:** Dept Physics & Astron, York Univ, 4700 Keele St, Downsview, ON M3J 1P3, Can. **Fax:** 416-736-5516. **E-Mail:** laframboise@quasar.phys.yorku.ca

LAFRAMBOISE, MARC ALEXANDER, mathematics; deceased, see previous edition for last biography

LAFRANCHI, EDWARD ALVIN, ELECTRICAL ENGINEERING. **Personal Data:** b Petaluma, Calif, July 23, 1928; m 1954, c 3. **Education:** Univ Santa Clara, BS, 1950. **Professional Experience:** RETIRED; dep assoc dir eng, Dept Electronics Eng, 1986-1991; dept head, Dept Electronics Eng, 1973-1986; div leader, Lawrence Livermore Lab, 1966-1973; group leader, Lawrence Livermore Lab, 1958-1966; design engr, Lawrence Livermore Lab, 1956-1958; opers engr, Lawrence Livermore Lab, 1953-1956. **Memberships:** Inst Elec & Electronics Engrs. **Research Statement & Publications:** Computer science and engineering; engineering management. **Mailing Address:** 359 Polk Way, Livermore, CA 94550.

LAFRENZ, DAVID E, MICROBIOLOGY. **Personal Data:** b Waterloo, Iowa, August 13, 1947; c 2. **Education:** Ariz State Univ, BS, 1971; Univ Iowa, PhD, 1978. **Professional Experience:** RES MICROBIOLOGIST, H S TRUMAN MEM VET ADMIN HOSP, COLUMBIA, 1988-; ASST PROF & ASSOC DIR, CELL & IMMUNOBIOL CORE FACIL & DIR FLOW CYTOMETRY FACIL, DEPT MICROBIOL, SCH MED, UNIV MO, COLUMBIA, 1988-; assoc res scientist, Dept Internal Med, 1987-1988; adj asst prof, Dept Internal Med, 1987-1988; Mem, Res & Develop Comt, Vet Admin Med Ctr, Iowa City, Iowa, 1987-1988; res health sci specialist, Vet Admin Med Ctr, Iowa City, 1983-1988; dir, Animal Care Facil, 1983-1988; postdoctoral res affil, Howard Hughes Med Inst, Stanford Univ Sch Med, 1981-1983; Postdoctoral fel, Howard Hughes Med Inst, Stanford Univ Sch Med, 1978-1981. **Memberships:** Am Asn Immunologists; AAAS; Am Soc Microbiol; Soc Anal Cytol. **Research Statement & Publications:** Cellular immunology; immunologic memory; molecular immunology; molecular biology. **Mailing Address:** Dept Res, H S Truman Mem Hosp 800 Hospital Dr, Columbia, MO 65201-5275. **Fax:** 573-443-2511 Ext 6453.

LAFUZE, JOAN ESTERLINE, PEDIATRICS. **Personal Data:** b Indianapolis, Ind. **Education:** Ind Univ, AB, 1959; Ball State Univ, MS, 1975, Ind Univ, PhD (physiol), 1981. **Professional Experience:** PROF BIOL, SCH MED, IND UNIV, as of 2004; ASSOC DIR PEDIAT HEMAT-ONCOL, SCH MED, IND UNIV, as of 2004; asst prof biol, Ind Univ E, 1987; res assoc pediat hemat-oncol, Sch Med, Ind Univ, beginning 1985; asst prof, Dept Physiol & Biophys, Sch Med, Ind Univ, 1984-1987; res technologist pediat hemat-oncol, James Whitcomb Riley Hosp Children, Ind, 1981-1985; res & teaching asst, Dept Physiol & Biophys, Sch Med, Ind Univ, 1975-1981; educ coordr, Ind Voc Tech Col, 1968-1971; teaching supvr, In-Serv Lab, Educ Prog, Reid Mem Hosp, 1965-1968; med technologist, Richmond Med Lab, 1963-1965; student technologist, Sch Med Technol, St Vincent Hosp, 1960-1961; lab tech & asst supvr, Gen Lab, Methodist Hosp, 1959-1960. **Memberships:** Am Soc Clin Pathologists; Am Physiol Soc; Tissue Cult Asn; AAAS. **Research Statement & Publications:** Construction of a Molt-3 cDNA library; construction and characterization of a subtracted T-cell ALL cDNA library; construction of a subtracted T-cell ALL probe; sequencing; effect of neutrophil activation on respiration, blood pressure and absolute granulocyte count of rabbits and cats; use of antioxidants to attenuate the in vivo and in vitro effects of chemotactic agents; adherence of neutrophils to culture vascular endothelium; transendothelial migration of activated neutrophils. **Mailing Address:** Dept Pediat, Ind Univ Sch Med Riley Hosp C 702 Barnhill Dr Rm 2720, Indianapolis, IN 46202-5225. **Fax:** 317-631-0941. **E-Mail:** jlafuze@indiana.edu

LAGACE, LISETTE, MOLECULAR BIOLOGY & PROTEIN, BIOCHEMISTRY & CELL BIOLOGY. **Personal Data:** b October 13, 1951; c 2. **Education:** Univ Que, BS, 1975; Laval Univ, PhD (physiol), 1979. **Professional Experience:** SR SCIENTIST, BIOMEGA INC, 1989-; asst prof, Laval Univ, 1984-1989; Instr cell biol, Baylor Col Med, 1982-1984. **Memberships:** Am Soc Cell Biol; Antiviral Res Soc. **Research Statement & Publications:** Molecular biology; protein biochemistry; cloning expression and purifictaion of recombinant proteins; study of the role or veral protein in the virus cycle. **Mailing Address:** Dept Biochem Biomega Inc, 2100 Cunard, Laval, PQ H7S 2G5, Can.

LAGACE, PAUL ALFRED, MATERIALS & STRUCTURES ENGINEERING, COMPOSITE MATERIALS. **Personal Data:** b Lewiston, Maine, July 27, 1957; m 1983, Robin. **Education:** Mass Inst Technol, SB, 1978, SM, 1979, PhD (aeronaut & astronaut), 1982. **Honors & Awards:** Von Karman Lectr, Israeli Aerospace Sci Orgn, 1993; Coombes Lectr, Australian Aeronaut & Astronaut Soc, 1997; World fel Intn'l Com on Composite Materials, 2001; AIAA Fellow, 2000; ASC Fellow, 2005; Stinchcomb Award, ASTM, 2000; MacVicar Faculty Fellow, MIT, as of 1995. **Professional Experience:** CO-DIR, LEADERS MANUFACTURING/SYSTS DESIGN & MGT, MASS INST TECHNOL, 1998-2003; ASSOC DIR, ENG SYSTS DIV, MASS INST TECHNOL, 1998-2001; DIR, TECHNOL LAB ADVAN Mat and Structures, MASS INST TECHNOL, as of 1983; Pres, Int Comt Composite Mat, 1993-1999; PROF AERONAUT & ASTRONAUT & ENG SYSTS, MASS INST TECHNOL, 1993-; actg head, Dept Aeronaut & Astronaut, 1991-1993; exec officer, Dept Aeronaut & Astronaut, 1990-1991; from asst prof to assoc prof, Mass Inst Technol, 1982-1993. **Memberships:** fel Am Inst Aeronaut & Astronaut; Am Soc Composites; Am Soc Testing & Mat; Soc Advan Mat & Process Engrs. **Research Statement & Publications:** Composite materials and structures, their fracture, durability, damage tolerance and applications; ukn. **Mailing Address:** Dept Aeronaut & Astronaut & Eng Systs, Mass Inst Technol, 77 Mass Ave, Rm 33- 310, Cambridge, MA 02139. **E-Mail:** pal@mit.edu

LAGAKOS, STEPHEN WILLIAM, BIOSTATISTICS. **Personal Data:** b Philadelphia, Pa, June 18, 1946; m 1968, c 2. **Education:** Carnegie-Mellon Univ, BS, 1968; George Wash Univ, MPhil & PhD (math & statist), 1972; Harvard Univ, MA, 1986. **Honors & Awards:** Spiegelman Gold Medal, 1986. **Professional Experience:** HENRY PICKERING WALCOTT PROF BIOSTATISTICS, HARVARD SCH PUB HEALTH, as of 2004; prof, Harvard Sch Pub Health, beginning 1986; assoc prof, Harvard Sch Pub Health, 1980-1985; asst prof statist sci, Statist Lab, State Univ NY Buffalo, 1973-1980; protocol statistician, Eastern Coop Oncol Group, 1972-; coord statistician, Working Party Ther Lung Cancer, 1972-; statistician biostatist, Statist Lab, State Univ NY Buffalo, 1972-1980; math statistician, Naval Ord Sta, 1968-1970. **Memberships:** Biomet Soc; Royal Statist Soc; Inst Math Statist; Int Asn Study Lung Cancer; Am Statist Asn. **Research Statement & Publications:** The planning, design and analysis of clinical trials with particular emphasis on survival-type data. **Mailing Address:** Dept Biostatistics, Harvard Sch Pub Health, 677 Huntington Ave, Boston, MA 02115-6023. **Fax:** 617-739-1781, 617-432-2832. **E-Mail:** lagakos@hsph.harvard.edu

LAGALLY, MAX GUNTER, MATERIALS SCIENCE & SURFACE PHYSICS, NANOTECHNOLOGY & BIOTECHNOLOGY. **Personal Data:** b Darmstadt, Ger, May 23, 1942; American citizen; m 1969, Shelley; c Eric, Douglas & Karsten. **Education:** Pa State Univ, BS, 1963; Univ Wis, MS, 1965, PhD (physics), 1968. **Honors & Awards:** Tibbetts Award, US Small Business Association, 2002; Elected, National Academy of Engineering, 2001; Elected Member, Deutsche Akademie der Naturforscher - Leopoldina(German National Academy of Science), 1999; Outstanding Science Alumnus Award, Pennsylvania State University, 1996; Davisson-Germer Prize, American Physical Society, 1995; MRS Medal,

Materials Research Society, 1994; David Adler Lectureship Award, American Physical Society, 1994; Medard W Welch Award, American Vacuum Society, 1991. **Professional Experience:** Founder, SonoPlot LLC 2003; Founder, president, now COB, nPoint, Inc. 1997; E.W. Mueller Professor of Materials Science and Physics, 1993- Humboldt sr res fel, Juelich, Ger, 1992; Gordon Godfrey vis prof physics, Univ NSW, Sydney, Australia, 1987; John Bascom prof surface sci & technol, Univ Wis-Madison, 1986-; DIR THIN-FILM DEPOSITION & APPLS CTR, UNIV WIS-MADISON, 1985-1993; PROF MAT SCI & ENG, UNIV WIS, MADISON, 1977-; H I Romnes fel, 1976-1980; vis scientist surface physics, Sandia Nat Lab, 1974; Sloan Found fel, 1973-1977; from asst prof to assoc prof, Univ Wis-Madison, 1971-1977; instr physics & res assoc surface physics, Univ Wis-madison, 1970-1971; Vis fel physics, Fritz Haber Inst, Max Planck Soc, 1968-1969. **Memberships:** Fel Am Phys Soc; Mat Res Soc; Fel Am Vacuum Soc; fel Australian Inst Physics; Fel AAAS; SPIE; OSA; Sigma Xi. **Research Statement & Publications:** Nanoscale properties of surfaces, interfaces, thin films, and dimensionally confined structures primarily of semiconductors; atom-scale mechanisms of film growth; relationship of morphology to localized electronic, optoelectronic, and magnetic properties. Development of advanced instrumentation for surface and interface studies, in particular diffraction, scanned-probe microscopies, and metrology. Bioarray technology and instrumentation. **Mailing Address:** Dept Mat Sci & Eng, Univ Wis, 1509 Univ Ave, Madison, WI 53706. **Fax:** 608-265-4118. **E-Mail:** lagally@engr.wisc.edu

LAGANIS, EVAN DEAN, INFRARED SYNTHESIS, ORGANOSILICONE CHEMISTRY. **Personal Data:** b Detroit, Mich, June 6, 1953; m 1977, c 2. **Education:** State Univ NY, Geneseo, BA, 1975; Dartmouth Col, PhD (org chem), 1980. **Professional Experience:** AT ASAHI GLASS FLUOROPOLYMERS, USA, as of 2003; southeast REGIONAL MGR, DUPONT SAFETY & ENVIRON MGT & SERV, 1993-; ACCOUNT MGR, OPTICAL DISK MEDIA, PHOTOSYSTS & ELECTRONIC PROD DEPT, E I DU PONT Del NEMOURS & CO INC, 1992-; RES CHEMIST, OPTICAL DISK MEDIA, PHOTOSYSTS & ELECTRONIC PROD DEPT, E I DU PONT Del NEMOURS & CO INC, 1985-; res chemist organofluorine, organosilicon & polyacetylene chem, Cent Res & Develop Dept, 1981-1984; fel organometallic & cyclophane chem, Univ Ore, 1979-1981. **Memberships:** Am Chem Soc. **Research Statement & Publications:** Preparation of infrared dyes for use as the active layer in Optical Disk Media; organosilicon reagents for organic synthesis. **Mailing Address:** AGC Chems Am Inc, 229 E 22nd St, Bayonne, NJ 07002. **Fax:** 610-380-6201. **E-Mail:** evan_langanis@agfusa.com

LAGARIAS, JEFFREY CLARK, MATHEMATICS. **Personal Data:** b Pittsburgh, Pa, November 16, 1949. **Education:** Mass Inst Technol, SB & SM, 1972, PhD (math), 1974. **Honors & Awards:** Lester Ford Award, Math Asn Am, 1987. **Professional Experience:** MEM, ALGORITHMS & OPTIMIZATION RES DEPT, AT & T LABS, as of 1999; vis assoc prof comput sci, Rutgers Univ, 1984; vis asst prof, Univ Md, 1978-1979; MEM TECH STAFF, BELL TELEPHONE LABS, 1974-. **Memberships:** Am Math Soc; Math Asn Am; Soc Indust & Appl Math; Inst Elec & Electronics Engrs; Asn Comput Mach; Math Prog Soc. **Research Statement & Publications:** Computational complexity theory; cryptography; number theory; discrete mathematics, dynamical systems. **Mailing Address:** AT & T Labs Res, Rm C235 180 Park Ave, Florham Park, NJ 07932-0971. **Fax:** 973-360-8178. **E-Mail:** jcl@research.att.com

LAGARIAS, JOHN S(AMUEL), PHYSICS, ELECTRONICS. **Personal Data:** b Rochester, NY, July 4, 1921; m 1947, Virginia J Clark; c Jeffrey C, Peter C & J Clark. **Education:** Rensselaer Polytech Inst, BS, 1948. **Professional Experience:** Mem, Calif Air Resources Bd, 1985-; PRES LAGARIAS ASSOCS, INC, 1984-; Conf chmn, 1st Int Conf Electro Precipitation, 1981; dir environ qual, Kaiser Engrs Inc, 1971-1984; Conf chmn, 2nd Int Clean Air Cong, 1970; pres, Resources Res, Inc, Va, 1967-1971; exec vpres, Resources Res, Inc, Va, 1966-1967; vpres, Resources Res, Inc, Va, 1965-1966; mgr, Res & Develop, Am Instrument Co, 1963-1965; mgr, Physics & Phys Chem Lab, 1961-1963; mgr, Metal Prod Res, 1956-1961; mgr, Precipitation Br, 1953-1955; physicist, Koppers Co, Inc, Pa, 1951-1953; Engr, Res Dept, Westinghouse Elec Corp, 1948-1951. **Memberships:** Fel hon mem Air Pollution Control Asn (pres 1968-1969); Am Phys Soc; sr mem Inst Elec & Electronics Engrs; Am Acad Environ Engrs; fel Int Soc Electrostatic Precipitation. **Research Statement & Publications:** Industrial gas cleaning equipment including electrostatic precipitators, bag filters, and scrubbers; environmental controls. **Mailing Address:** Lagarias Assocs Inc, 5954 Autumnwood Dr No 5C, Walnut Creek, CA 94595.

LAGE, GARY LEE, PHARMACOLOGY, TOXICOLOGY. **Personal Data:** b Hinsdale, Ill, November 11, 1941; m 1964, c 2. **Education:** Drake Univ, BS, 1963; Univ Iowa, MS, 1965, PhD (pharmacol), 1967. **Honorary Degrees:** Dipl, Am Bd Toxicol, 1980. **Professional Experience:** TOXICOLOGIST, TOXILOGICS INC, as of 2003; prof toxicol & dir toxicol progs, Philadelphia Col Pharm & Sci, 1978-1984; USPHS res career develop award, 1975-1980; assoc prof pharm, Univ Wis-Madison, 1973-1978; from asst prof to assoc prof pharmacol, Sch Pharm, Univ Kans, 1967-1973; chmn dept pharmacol & toxicol. **Memberships:** Soc Toxicol (treas 1985-1987); Am Pharmaceut Asn; AAAS; Am Soc Pharmacol & Exp Therapeut; Am Asn Col Pharm. **Research Statement & Publications:** Study of drug distribution and metabolism in relation to drug toxicity, distribution and/or metabolism, especially cardiac glycosides; hepatotoxicity mechanisms. **Mailing Address:** 22 Bernard Dr, Ewing, NJ 08628. **Fax:** 609-883-9044. **E-Mail:** glage@comcast.net

LAGE, JANICE M, PATHOLOGY. **Personal Data:** b Exeter, Calif, July 5, 1951. **Education:** Calif State Univ, Fresno, BS, 1973; Wash Univ, Mo, MD, 1980; Am Bd Path, cert, 1985. **Professional Experience:** PROF & CHAIR, DEPT PATH & LAB MED, CHILDREN'S HOSP, as of 2004; NIH grant, 1990; pathologist, Brigham & Women's Hosp, beginning 1987; asst prof, Harvard Med Sch, beginning 1987; instr, Brigham & Women's Hosp, 1984-1987; assoc pathologist, Brigham & Women's Hosp, Boston, Mass, 1984-1987; fel, Dept Path, 1983-1984; asst path, Sch Med, Wash Univ, 1983; obstet & gynec, Wash Univ, 1982-1983; instr obstet/gynec, Sch Med, Wash Univ, 1982; resident path, Wash Univ, 1981-1982; instr path, Sch Med, Wash Univ, 1981; instr path, Sch Med, Stanford Univ, 1980. **Memberships:** US Acad Path; Can Acad Path; Am Asn Pathologists; Int Soc Gynec Pathologists; Soc Pediat Pathologists. **Research Statement & Publications:** Gestational trophoblastic diseases; perinatal and obstetric pathology, with emphasis on congenital malformations; application of flow cytometry to surgical pathology of obstetric and gynecologic tumors. **Mailing Address:** Dept Path & Lab Med, Children's Hosp, Rm 304 171 Ashley Ave, Charleston, SC 29425. **Fax:** 843-792-0555. **E-Mail:** lagejm@musc.edu

LAGERGREN, CARL ROBERT, PHYSICS. **Personal Data:** b St Paul, Minn, November 21, 1922; m 1947, c 3. **Education:** State Col, Wash, BS, 1944, MS, 1949; Univ Minn, PhD (physics), 1955. **Professional Experience:** RES ASSOC, RADIOL SCI DEPT, PAC NORTHWEST LABS, BATTELLE MEM INST, 1968-; mgr mass spectrometry, Radiol Sci Dept, Pac Northwest Labs, Battelle Mem Inst, 1965-1968; Sr physicist, Hanford Atomic Prod Oper, Gen Elec Co, 1955-1965. **Memberships:** Am Phys Soc; Sigma Xi. **Research Statement & Publications:** Mass spectrometry; electron impact phenomena; isotopic abundances; surface ionization; ion optics. **Mailing Address:** 2110 Howell Ave, Richland, WA 99352-2012.

LAGERGREN, ERIC S, STATISTICS. **Professional Experience:** QUAL & PROD SECT, KRAFT FOOS RES, NABISCO as of 2002. **Memberships:** Am Statistical Asn. **Mailing Address:** Kraft Foods, Nabisco, 200 DeForest Ave, East Hanover, NJ 07936-1944. **Fax:** 973-503-4781. **E-Mail:** LagergrenE@nabisco.com

LAGERSTEDT, HARRY BERT, PLANT PHYSIOLOGY, HORTICULTURE. **Personal Data:** b Glen Ridge, NJ, August 2, 1925; m 1952, c 5. **Education:** Ore State Univ, BS, 1954, MS, 1957; Tex A&M Univ, PhD (plant physiol), 1965. **Professional Experience:** RETIRED; res horticulturist, Agr Res Serv, beginning 1967; assoc prof, Ore State Univ, beginning 1967; from instr to asst prof hort, Ore State Univ, 1957-1967; Northwest Germplasm Repository. **Memberships:** Am Soc Plant Physiol; Am Soc Hort Sci; Sigma Xi. **Research Statement & Publications:** Plant growth regulators; nut crops. **Mailing Address:** 34151 N E Electric Rd, Corvallis, OR 97333.

LAGESON, DAVID R, GEOLOGY. **Education:** Western State Col, Colo, BA, 1973; Univ Wyo, 1977, PhD, 1980. **Professional Experience:** PROF & HEAD, DEPT GEOL, MONT STATE UNIV, as of 2003. **Mailing Address:** Dept Earth Sci, Mont State Univ, Traphagen Hall 202, Bozeman, MT 59717. **E-Mail:** lageson@montana.edu

LAGHARI, JAVAID RASOOLBUX, ELECTRICAL ENGINEERING. **Personal Data:** b Hyderabad, Pakistan, June 25, 1950; American citizen; m 1982, Shahida; c Zaid. **Education:** Sind Univ, Pakistan, BE, 1971; Middle East Tech Univ, Turkey, MS, 1975; State Univ NY, Buffalo, PhD (elec eng), 1980. **Professional Experience:** CHIEF EXEC OFFICER, ZAB SOLUTIONS, as of 2006; dir grad studies, State Univ NY, Buffalo, beginning 1993; prof elec eng, State Univ NY, Buffalo, beginning 1992; chmn, Tech Prog Comt, Int Symp Elec Insulation, 1992; mem, ADCOM, Inst Elec & Electronics Engrs, beginning 1991; mem, Tech Prog Comt, Int High Voltage Symp, 1989; mem, Tech Prog Comt, Int Symp Elec Insulation, 1988-1990; chmn, Radiation Soc Comt, Inst Elec & Electronics Engrs, 1986-; prin investr, Off Naval Res, 1986-1987; prin investr, Air Force Off Sci Res, 1983-1990; from asst prof to assoc prof, State Univ NY, Buffalo, 1980-1992; asst exec engr, Airports Develop Agency, Pakistan, 1975-1976; asst eng, Indust Grindery, Pakistan, 1971-1972; mem, Comt Man & Radiation. **Memberships:** Inst Elec & Electronics Engrs. **Research Statement & Publications:** High voltage and pulsed power; electrical insulation and dielectrics, as applicable to space power technology, including energy storage and transport devices; high speed diagnostics; Super vision and guidance under graduate and engineering studies. **Mailing Address:** 90 Clifton, Karachi, 75600, Pakistan. **Fax:** 92-21-5830446. **E-Mail:** info@zabsolutions.com

LAGNESE, JOHN EDWARD, MATHEMATICS. **Personal Data:** b Pittsburgh, Pa, March 7, 1937; m 1960, c 3. **Education:** Univ Dayton, BS, 1959; Univ Md, Col Park, MA, 1961, PhD (math), 1963. **Professional Experience:** RETIRED; prof emer math, Georgetown Univ, ending 2005; prof math & chmn dept, georgetown univ, beginning 1972; consult, AID, 1970; from asst prof to assoc prof, Georgetown Univ, 1964-1972; Nat Acad Sci-Nat Res Coun fel, Nat Bur Stand, 1963-1964. **Memberships:** Am Math Soc; Math Asn Am. **Research Statement & Publications:** Partial differential equations; operator theory. **Mailing Address:** Dept Math, Georgetown Univ, 256 Reiss Sci Bldg, Washington, DC 20057-0001. **Fax:** 202-687-6067. **E-Mail:** agnese@math.georgetown.edu

LAGO, JAMES, PROCESS RESEARCH & DEVELOPMENT, FERMENTATION & ISOLATION. **Personal Data:** b New York, NY, November 7, 1921; m 1968, Barbara. **Education:** Polytech Inst Brooklyn, BChE, 1944; Mass Inst Technol, MS, 1947. **Honors & Awards:** Merck Dir Award. **Professional Experience:** CONSULT, 1986-; vpres process res & develop, Merck & Co Inc, Rahway, 1979-1985; dir chem eng res & develop, Merck & Co Inc, Rahway, 1969-1979; mgr, Merck & Co Inc, Rahway, 1964-1969; sect mgr, Merck & Co Inc, Rahway, 1957-1964; group leader chem eng, Merck & Co Inc, Rahway, 1951-1957; jr engr, Merck & Co Inc, Rahway, 1947-1951; Asst, Manhattan Proj, 1944-1946. **Memberships:** emer mem Nat Acad Eng; Am Chem Soc; Am Inst Chem Engrs; AAAS. **Research Statement & Publications:** Development of processes for the preparation of medicinals; design and startup of manufacturing facilities for the processes developed. **Mailing Address:** Los Olivos, CA 93441. **Fax:** 509-493-3498.

LAGO, PAUL KEITH, ENTOMOLOGY. **Personal Data:** b Worthington, Minn, June 24, 1947; m 1969, Barbara; c Eric. **Education:** Bemidji State Col, BA, 1969, MA, 1971; NDak State Univ, PhD (entom), 1977. **Professional Experience:** PROF BIOL, UNIV MISS, 1976-. **Memberships:** Coleopterists Soc; Entom Soc Am; Am Entom Soc; Sigma Xi; NY Entom soc; Entomol Soc Wash; Miss Acad Sci. **Research Statement & Publications:** Insect taxonomy, principally coleoptera and aquatic insects; insect ecology. **Mailing Address:** Dept Biol, Univ Miss, Univ, MS 38677. **Fax:** 662-915-5144. **E-Mail:** plago@olemiss.edu

LAGOWSKI, JEANNE MUND, BIOCHEMICAL & MOLECULAR GENETICS. **Personal Data:** b St Louis, Mo, November 17, 1929; m 1954, Joseph. **Education:** Bradley Univ, BS, 1951, MS, 1952; Univ Mich, PhD (org chem), 1957. **Professional Experience:** ASSOC DEAN, COL NATURAL SCI & PROF NEUROBIOLOGY, UNIV TEX, AUSTIN, 1981-; asst dean, Div Gen & Comp Studies, Univ Tex, Austin, 1978-1981; ASSOC, DANFORTH FOUND, 1977-; assoc prof zool, Div Gen & Comp Studies, Univ Tex, Austin, 1974-1981; lectr zool, Col Natural Sci & Prof Zool, Univ Tex, Austin, 1973-1974; asst dean, Div Gen & Comp Studies, Univ Tex, Austin, 1972-1978; res career develop award, NIH, 1964-1969; res scientist, Col Natural Sci & Prof Zool, Univ Tex, Austin, 1963-1973; assoc res scientist biochem genetics, Col Natural Sci & Prof Zool, Univ Tex, Austin, 1959-1963; res fel phys org chem, Cambridge Univ, 1957-1959; res chemist, Mich State Univ, 1956-1957; instr analytical chem, Bradley Univ, 1951-1952. **Memberships:** Am Chem Soc; Int Soc Heterocyclic Chemists. **Research Statement & Publications:** Chemistry of nitrogen heterocycles; biochemical genetics. **Mailing Address:** Sch Biol Sci, Dept Neurobiology, Univ Tex, One Univ Sta A2900, Austin, TX 78712-1099. **E-Mail:** jmlagowski@mail.utexas.edu

LAGOWSKI, JOSEPH JOHN, INORGANIC CHEMISTRY. **Personal Data:** b Chicago, Ill, June 8, 1930; American citizen; m 1954, Jeanne M. **Education:** Univ Ill, BS, 1952; Univ Mich, MS, 1954; Mich State Univ, PhD (inorg chem), 1957; Cambridge Univ, PhD (inorg chem), 1959. **Honors & Awards:** Piper Prof Award, Nat Chem Mfg Asn, 1981; Chem Educ Award, Am Chem Soc, 1989; James Flack Norris Award, Chem Edu. **Professional Experience:** PROF CHEM, UNIV TEX, AUSTIN, 1967-; from asst prof to assoc prof, Univ Tex, Austin, 1959-1967. **Memberships:** Am Chem Soc; The Chem Soc; AAAS. **Research Statement & Publications:** Liquid ammonia solutions; organometallic compounds; borazines and derivatives; electrochemistry; development of computer-based teaching methods; non-aqueous solution chemistry, chemical education; metal atom reactions. **Mailing Address:** Dept Chem, Univ Tex, WEL 4 328, Austin, TX 78712-0165. **Fax:** 512-471-3288. **E-Mail:** jjl@mail.utexas.edu

LAGRAFF, JOHN ERWIN, AERODYNAMICS, GAS TURBINE HEAT TRANSFER. **Personal Data:** b Schenectady, NY, July 24, 1940; m 1962, Susan; c John R & Thomas. **Education:** Mass Inst Technol, BS, 1962; Oxford Univ, DPhil(eng sci), 1970. **Honors & Awards:** Ralph Teetor Award, Soc Automotive Engrs, 1972; Nat Fac Adv Award, Am Inst Aeronaut & Astronaut, 1990. **Professional Experience:** Vpres, Edu, 2003-2006; chair, dept Mech, Aerospace & mfg Eng, Syracuse Univ, 1997-2002; chair, div Aerospace, 1995-1996; dir, Ctr Htoersonics, 1993-1998; dir, Aerospace Eng Prog, Syracuse Univ, 1986-1994; dep dir edu, 1984-1994; vis prof, Oxford Univ, 1983; DIR, ENG YEAR ABROAD PROG, SYRACUSE UNIV, 1980-; PROF FLUIDS-AERODYN, DEPT MECH & AERODYN ENG, 1970-; assoc scientist, res & Advan Develop div, Avco Corp, 1962-1966; assoc sci, res & Develop Div, Wlmington Mass, 1962-1966. **Memberships:** Assoc fel Am Inst Aeronaut & Astronaut; Am Soc Mech Engrs; Am Asn Univ Prof; Am Asn Eng Educ. **Research Statement & Publications:** Unsteady aerodynamics; heat transfer associated with gas turbines; boundary layer transition-hypersonics. **Mailing Address:** Dept Mech, Aerospace & Mfg Eng, Syracuse Univ Col Eng, 151 Link Hall, Syracuse, NY 13244. **E-Mail:** jlagraff@syr.edu

LAGRANGE, WILLIAM SOMERS, FOOD MICROBIOLOGY, FOOD SAFETY. **Personal Data:** b Ames, Iowa, April 23, 1931; m 1954, c 3. **Education:** Iowa State Univ, BS, 1953, PhD (dairy bact), 1959. **Professional Experience:** PROF EMER, IOWA STATE UNIV, 2000-; exten food technologist, Iowa State Univ, 1962-2000; exten technologist dairy mfg, Univ Ky, 1959-1962. **Memberships:** Int Asn Milk Food & Environ Sanit; fel Inst Food Technologists; Am Dairy Sci Asn. **Research Statement & Publications:** Dairy manufacturing quality control; dairy and foods microbiology; foods processing and control. **Mailing Address:** Dept Food Technol, Iowa State Univ, 2312 Food Sci Bldg, Ames, IA 50011. **Fax:** 515-294-8181. **E-Mail:** foodsci@exnet.iastate.edu

LAGRASSA, SUSAN, MATHEMATICS EDUCATION, COMMUTATIVE SEMIRINGS. **Personal Data:** b Kansas City, Mo, March 29, 1965; m 1995, Kevin. **Education:** NE Mo State Univ, BSE (mathematics education), 1987, MA (mathematics), 1989; Univ Iowa, PhD (math), 1995. **Professional Experience:** ASSOC PROF MATH & MAE-MATH DIR, TRUMAN STATE UNIV, 1995-; proj dir, Goals 2000 Math Proj, 1996-2001; trainer, Mid Sch Math Mentoring Inst, 1995-1997; res coordr, Connie Belin Nat Ctr Gifted Educ, 1992-1994; instr math, NE Mo State Univ, 1989-1991. **Memberships:** Am Math Soc; Math Asn Am; Nat Coun Teachers Math; Missouri council of Teachers of Mathematics; Missouri Mathematical Asn for the Advancement of Teacher Training. **Research Statement & Publications:** Master of Arts Education program in mathematics; ideals in and polynomials over commutative semirings. **Mailing Address:** Div Math & Comput Sci, Truman State Univ, Kirksville, MO 63501. **E-Mail:** lagrassa@truman.edu

LAGU, AVINASH L, ANALYTICAL CHEMISTRY OF RDNA DERIVED PROTEINS, CAPILLARY ELECTROPHORESIS. **Personal Data:** b Belgaum, India, February 14, 1941. **Education:** Bombay Univ, India, BSc, 1961; Univ Cincinnati, MS, 1972, PhD (analytical chem), 1974. **Professional Experience:** RES SCIENTIST, LILLY RES LABS, 1988-; sranalytical chemist, Eli Lilly & Co, 1979-1987; scientist, Ortho Pharmaceut Corp, Johnson & Johnson, 1976-1979; Sr analytical chemist, Norwich Pharmacol, Proctor & Gamble, 1974-1976. **Memberships:** Am Chem Soc; Sigma Xi. **Research Statement & Publications:** Developing methods for the analysis of recombinant DNA derived proteins and peptides; biotechnology related problems; application of capillary electrophoresis and high-performance liquid chromatography to the analysis of DNA fragments and proteins. **Mailing Address:** Lilly Corp Ctr, DC 3224, Indianapolis, IN 46285. **Fax:** 317-276-5499. **E-Mail:** allagu@lilly.com

LAGUNOFF, DAVID, PATHOLOGY. **Personal Data:** b New York, NY, March 14, 1932; m 1958, Susan Powers; c Rachel, Liza & Michael. **Education:** Univ Chicago, MD, 1957. **Professional Experience:** PROF PATH, ST LOUIS UNIV, 1979-; chmn path, St Louis Univ, 1979-1996; Nat Cancer Inst spec fel path, Sir William Dunn Sch Exp Path, Oxford Univ, 1969-1970; Nat Heart Inst spec fel physiol, Carlsberg Lab, Denmark, 1962-1964; from instr to prof path, Univ Wash, 1960-1979; Nat Heart Inst fel path, USPHS trainee, 1959-1960; Nat Heart Inst fel path, Univ Wash, 1958-1959; intern, San Francisco Hosp, Calif, 1957-1958; Asst microbiol, Univ Miami, 1951-1953. **Memberships:** Am Soc Invest Path; Am Soc Cell Biol; Am Asn Immunol. **Research Statement & Publications:** Mast cell structure and function; cell secretion; inflammation; endothelial motility, angiogenesis. **Mailing Address:** Dept Path Sch Med, St Louis Univ 1402 S Grand Blvd, St Louis, MO 63104-1079. **Fax:** 314-268-5649. **E-Mail:** lagunofd@slucare1.sluh.edu

LAGUNOWICH, LAURA ANDREWS, ANATOMY. **Personal Data:** b November 29, 1960; c 1. **Education:** Dickinson Col, BSc, 1983; Thomas Jefferson Univ, PhD (path & cell biol), 1987. **Professional Experience:** ASSOC DIR TOXICOL, RUTGERS UNIV, 1992-; assoc mem, Environ & Occup Health Sci Inst, 1991-; Johnson & Johnson scholar develop neurotoxicol, Environ & Occup Health Sci Inst, 1991-1996; res asst prof, Neurotoxicol Labs, Dept Pharmacol & Toxicol, Col Pharm, 1990-1992; instr, Dept Anat, Pa Sch Podiat Med, 1988-1989; Nat Res Serv award, Nat Eye Inst, 1987-1990; Fel, Dept Anat & Develop Biol, Thomas Jefferson Univ, 1987-1990; NIH training grant develop biol & teratology, 1987. **Memberships:** Int Soc Differentiation; Soc Develop Biol; Soc Neuroscience. **Research Statement & Publications:** Genetic control of disease; clinical aspects of neoplasia; environmental and nutritional disorders; teratology; translational and pasttranslational control of proteins; hemostasis and red blood cells; cardiac function and blood pressure. **Mailing Address:** Regeneron Pharmaceut, 777 Old Saw Mill River Rd Bldg 2, Tarrytown, NY 10591.

LAGUROS, JOAKIM GEORGE, SOIL MECHANICS, HIGHWAY ENGINEERING. **Personal Data:** b Istanbul, Turkey, February 4, 1924; American citizen; m 1957, c 1. **Education:** Robert Col, Istanbul, BS, 1946; Iowa State Univ, MS, 1955, PhD (soil mech), 1962. **Professional Experience:** DAVID ROSS BOYD PROF EMER, CIVIL ENG & ENVIRON SCI, UNIV OKLA, as of 2002; prof civil eng & environ Sci, Univ Okla, beginning 1980; prof soils & hwys, Univ Okla, 1969-1980; mem, Physicochem Phenomena Soils Comt, Hwy Res Bd, Nat Acad Sci-NatRes Coun, 1964-1967; assoc prof, Univ Okla, 1963-1969; asst prof soil mech, Univ Ohio, 1962-1963; Robert Col, 1958 & McFadzen, Everly & Assocs, 1961; asst prof, Robert Col, 1956-1959; res asst soils, Exp Sta, Iowa State Univ, 1954-1956, 1959-1962; consult, Neth Harbor Works Co, Turkey, 1952; instr civil eng, Robert Col, 1951-1954; asst engr, Naval Shipyard, Turkey, 1948-1951. **Memberships:** Am Soc Civil Engrs; Am Soc Eng Educ; Clay Minerals Soc. **Research Statement & Publications:** Behavior of soils under load application; improvement of soil properties by admixtures; quality control of materials. **Mailing Address:** Dept Civil Eng & Environ, Univ Okla, 202 W Boyd St, Rm 334, Norman, OK 73019-1024. **Fax:** 405-325-4217. **E-Mail:** bgfinch@ou.edu

LAHAIE, IVAN JOSEPH, ELECTROMAGNETIC SCATTERING & IMAGING, RADAR CROSS-SECTION ANALYSIS & MEASUREMENT TECHNOLOGY. **Personal Data:** b Bay City, Mich, May 21, 1954; m 1993, Kathy R Hill; c Katelyn L (Hill) & Alexandra R. **Education:** Mich State Univ, BS, 1976; Univ Mich, MS, 1977, PhD (elec eng), 1981. **Honors & Awards:** Radar Systs Panel Award, Inst Elec & Electronics Engrs Aerospace & Electronic Systs Soc, 1991. **Professional Experience:** SR SCIENTIST, ENVIRON RES INST MICH, 1991-; Assoc ed, Inst Elec & Electronics Engrs Antennas & Propagation, 1986-; res engr, Environ Res Inst Mich, 1980-1991; Res asst, Radiation Lab, Univ Mich, 1976-1980. **Memberships:** Inst Elec & Electronics Engrs; Sigma Xi; Optical Soc Am. **Research Statement & Publications:** Application of electromagnetic scattering, inverse scattering, and signal processing techniques to the analysis of radar cross-section measurements and synthetic aperture radar. **Mailing Address:** Environ Res Inst Mich, PO Box 134001, Ann Arbor, MI 48113-4001. **Fax:** 734-994-0944. **E-Mail:** lahaie@erim.org

LAHAM, SOUHEIL, INHALATION TOXICOLOGY, CANCER. **Personal Data:** b Port-au-Prince, Haiti, April 17, 1926; m 1955, Marie Grintchenko; c Nadia & Beatrice. **Honors & Awards:** William P Yant Award in Toxicol & Indust Hyg. **Professional Experience:** SCI CONSULT, as of 2002; head, Inhalation Toxicol Unit, Environ Health Directorate, 1979-1981; Carleton Univ, beginning 1977 & Univ Calif, Berkeley, beginning 1981; Ohio State Univ, Columbus, beginning 1974; vis prof, Univ Que, beginning 1973; vis prof, Univ Ottawa, beginning 1971; sr res scientist & consult, Environ Toxicol Prog, Occup Health Div, 1962-1979; chief, Environ Toxicol Prog, Occup Health Div, 1962-1971; head, Biochem Sect, Environ Health Directorate, 1958-1962; guest scientist, Can Dept Health & Welfare, 1956-1958; Guest scientist, Nat Res Coun Can, 1956-1958; Res assoc, Univ Paris, 1954-1956; head, Occup Toxicol Res Sect. **Memberships:** Am Indust Hyg Asn; Toxicol Soc Can; Europ Soc Toxicol; Soc Toxicol; AAAS; Europ Asn Cancer Res. **Research Statement & Publications:** Inhalation toxicity and metabolism of toxic and carcinogenic substances; environmental and occupational cancer; chemical carcinogenesis; neurotoxicology; peripheral neuropathy induced by industrial chemicals; inhalation toxicity of indoor air pollutants. **Mailing Address:** 249 Latchford Rd, Ottawa, ON K1Z 5W3, Can. **Fax:** 613-728-8301.

LAHAMER, AMER S, HYPERFINE INTERACTIONS USING MOSSBAUER SPECTROSCOPY, ENDOHEDRAL METALLOFULLERENES CHARACTERIZATION BY TIME-OF-FLIGHT MASS SPECTROMETERY. **Personal Data:** b Ganzour, Libya, July 24, 1956. **Education:** Univ Iowa, BSEE, 1980, MSEE, 1981, MS, 1984; Vanderbilt Univ, PhD (solid state physics), 1990. **Professional Experience:** PROF & CHMN PHYSICS, BEREA COL, as of 2004; hon res asst, Univ Tenn, 1997-; assoc prof physics, Berea Col, beginning 1996; actg chmn dept, Berea Col, 1995-1996; asst prof, Berea Col, 1990-1996; instr, Berea Col, 1989-1990. **Memberships:** Am Phys Soc; Am Asn Univ Profs. **Research Statement & Publications:** Hyperfine interactions by Mossbauer spectroscopy; production analysis and characterization of endohedral metallofullerenes. **Mailing Address:** Dept Physics, Berea Col, CPO 1872, 2191 Campus Dr, Berea, KY 40404. **Fax:** 859-985-3917. **E-Mail:** lahamera@berea.edu

LAHERU, KEN L, STRESS ANALYSIS. **Professional Experience:** STAFF, THIOKOL CORP, as of 2006. **Memberships:** Am Inst Aeronaut & Astronaut. **Mailing Address:** Thiokol Corp, PO Box 707 MS 254, Brigham City, UT 84302-0707. **Fax:** 801-863-6023.

LAHEY, M EUGENE, PEDIATRICS. **Personal Data:** b Ft Worth, Tex, December 28, 1917; m 1942, c 6. **Education:** Univ Tex, BA, 1939; St Louis Univ, MD, 1943. **Professional Experience:** PROF EMER PEDIAT, UNIV UTAH, as of 2001; pres, AMA, beginning 1965; res dir, Children's Hosp, East Bay, 1964-1965; mem residency rev comt, AMA, 1961-1965; mem, Scope Panel, US Pharmacopeia, beginning 1960; hemat training grant comt, Nat Inst Arthritis & Metab Dis, 1959-1963; mem med adv bd, Leukemia Soc, beginning 1958; prof, Univ Utah, 1958-1983; head dept, Univ Utah, 1958-1974; from asst prof to assoc prof, Univ Cincinnati, 1952-1958; asst prof pediat, Univ Utah, 1951-1952; Nat Res Coun fel med sci, Univ Utah, 1949-1951; vis prof, Children's Hosp, Honolulu. **Memberships:** Am Soc Hemat; Am Pediat Soc; Soc Pediat Res. **Research Statement & Publications:** Pediatric hematology. **Mailing Address:** 50 N Medical Dr, Salt Lake City, UT 84132-1001.

LAHEY, RICHARD THOMAS, HEAT TRANSFER, FLUID MECHANICS. **Personal Data:** b St Petersburg, Fla, February 20, 1939; m 1961, Eleanor; c Steven, Patrick & Kathleen. **Education:** US Merchant Marine Acad, BS, 1961; Rensselaer Polytech Inst, MS, 1964; Columbia Univ, ME, 1966; Stanford Univ, PhD (mech eng), 1971. **Honors & Awards:** Glen Murphy Award, Am Soc Eng Educ, 1985; Tech Achievement Award, Am Nuclear Soc, 1985, Arthur Holly Compton Award, 1989, Glenn T Seaborg Medal, 1992; E O Lawrence Mem Award, US Dept Energy, 1988. **Professional Experience:** Dean eng, Rensselaer Polytech Inst, 1994-1998; Alexander von Humbolt sr scientist fel, 1994-1995; dir, Ctr Multiphase Res, Rensselaer Polytech Inst, 1991-1994; EDWARD E HOOD JR PROF ENG, RENSSELAER POLYTECH INST, 1989-; prof, Mechanical Aerospace& Nuclear Eng, Rensselaer Polytech Inst, 1987-; prof, Dept Chem Eng, Rensselaer Polytech Inst, 1987-; adj prof, Univ Pisa, Italy & Claude Bernard Univ, France, 1987; ed, J Nuclear Eng & Design, 1983-1994; Fulbright fel, Magdalen Col, Oxford Univ, 1983-1984; comnr, Eng Manpower Comn, 1981-; pres, R T Lahey, Inc, 1981-1983; mem, Advan Code Rev Group & LOFT Rev Group, US Nuclear Regulatory Comn, 1976-1998; mem, Sci Adv Comt, EG & G Idaho Inc, 1976-1998; chmn, Dept Nuclear Eng, Rensselaer Polytech Inst, 1975-1987; mgr core & safety develop, Nuclear Energy Div, Gen Elec, 1966-1975; res assoc, Columbia Univ, 1964-1966; engr, Knolls Atomic Power Lab, 1961-1964. **Memberships:** Nat Acad Eng; Russian Academy of Sci; fel Am Nuclear Soc; Sigma Xi; NY Acad Sci; Am Soc Eng Educ; fel Am Soc Mech Engrs; Am Inst Chem Engrs. **Research Statement & Publications:** Two-phase flow and boiling heat transfer technology; nuclear reactor thermal-hydraulics and safety. **Mailing Address:** Sch Eng, Rensselaer Polytech Inst, 110 Eighth St, Troy, NY 12181. **Fax:** 518-276-3055. **E-Mail:** laheyr@rpi.edu

LAHIRI, SUKHAMAY, PHYSIOLOGY. **Personal Data:** b Calcutta, India, April 1, 1933; m 1965. **Education:** Univ Calcutta, BSc, 1951, MSc, 1953, DPhil(physiol), 1956; Oxford Univ, DPhil(physiol), 1959. **Honors & Awards:** Premchand-Roychand Gold Medal, Univ Calcutta, 1962. **Professional Experience:** PROF PHYSIOL, UNIV PA, as of 2004; assoc prof physiol, Univ Pa, beginning 1973; assoc prof environ physiol, Univ PA, 1969-1973; sr res assoc, Cardiovasc Inst, Michael Reese Hosp & Med Ctr, Chicago, Ill, 1967-1969; vis fel & asst prof, State Univ NY Downstate Med Ctr, 1965-1967; hon lectr, Univ, 1960-1965; asst prof physiol, Presidency Col, Univ Calcutta, 1959-1965; Govt WBengal scholar, Oxford Univ, 1956-1959. **Memberships:** NY Acad Sci; Am Physiol Soc. **Research Statement & Publications:** High altitude physiology; regulation and adaptation; gas exchange; chemoreceptors. **Mailing Address:** Dept Physiol, Univ Pa Med Sch, B400 Richards Bldg, Philadelphia, PA 19104-6085. **Fax:** 215-573-5851. **E-Mail:** lahiri@mail.med.upenn.edu

LAHIRI, SYAMAL KUMAR, MATERIALS SCIENCE, ADVANCED CERAMICS. **Personal Data:** b Rangoon, Burma, January 1, 1940; m 1970, c 3. **Education:** Univ Calcutta, BE,

1961; Univ Notre Dame, MS, 1964; Northwestern Univ, PhD (mat sci), 1969. **Honors & Awards:** Outstanding Invention Award, IBM Corp, 1976. **Professional Experience:** AT CENT GLASS RES INST, CALCUTTA, INDIA, as of 2002; adj prof, IIT, Uharagpur, India, 1988-1989; T J Watson Res Ctr, IBM Corp, 1987; Nat Phys Lab & Cent Electronics Inst, New Delhi, India, 1984-1986; vis scientist, Nat Phys Lab & Indian Inst Technol, New Delhi, India, 1978-1979; res staff mem, T J Watson Res Ctr, IBM Corp, 1968-1984; sr sci asst, Defence Metall Res Lab, Govt of India, 1961-1962. **Memberships:** Am Phys Soc; Inst Elec & Electronics Engrs; fel Inst Engrs India. **Research Statement & Publications:** Thin film properties; fabrication of thin film devices; physical metallurgy; Josephson tunneling devices; microelectronic packaging; mechanical properties of materials; electronic ceramics. **Mailing Address:** Sch Appl Sci, Nanyang Tech Univ Nanyang Ave, Singapore 639798, Singapore.

LAHITA, ROBERT GEORGE, IMMUNOLOGY, RHEUMATOLOGY. **Personal Data:** b Elizabeth, NJ, December 30, 1945; m 1971, Terry; c Jason & Eric. **Education:** St Peter's Col, BS, 1967; Thomas Jefferson Univ, MD, 1973, PhD (microbiol), 1973. **Honors & Awards:** Knowles Lectr, 1997; Fedelitas Award, Lupus Found, 1996. **Professional Experience:** CHIEF, RHEUMATOLOGY, ST VINCENT HOSP, NEW YORK CIYT, as of 2005; ASSOC PROF, UNIV COLUMBIA, 1991-; physician, Rockefeller Hosp, beginning 1983; NY Serv Life Eval Found, Serv Life Eval Found Am, beginning 1983; mem, exec bd, NY Arthritis Found, 1982-; consult, Medcom, 1981-; lectr, Mt Sinai Med Ctr, 1981-; assoc prof, med & pharmacol, Cornell Med Col, 1980-1990; from asst prof to assoc prof immunol, Rockefeller Univ, 1980-1987; clin scholar, Rockefeller Univ; chmn bd, Lupus Found Am; chief, rheumatology, St Luke's Roosevelt Hosp, NY; bd gov, NY Arthritis Found; attend physician, Hosp Joint Dis, NY; attend phys, Hosp Spec Surg, NY. **Memberships:** Am Rheumatism Asn; Am Soc Microbiol; NY Acad Sci; Harvey Soc; AAAS; Clin Immunol Soc. **Research Statement & Publications:** Effect of sex steroids on immune response; disease systemic lupus erythematosus. **Mailing Address:** Columbia Univ, 432 W 58th St, New York, NY 10019. **Fax:** 201-447-6437. **E-Mail:** rlahita@mem.po.com

LAHOTI, GOVERDHAN DAS, MATERIALS SCIENCE ENGINEERING. **Personal Data:** b Jaipur, India, May 4, 1948; American citizen; m 1975, Sheila; c 4. **Education:** Univ Burdwan, BEng, 1969, Univ Calif, Berkeley, MS, 1970, PhD (mech eng), 1973. **Honors & Awards:** Gold Medal, Univ Burdwan, 1970. **Professional Experience:** DIR R&D MANUFACT TECHNOL 1996-; RES SCIENTIST, TIMKEN RES, CANTON, OHIO, 1982-; res scientist, Batelle Mem Inst, Columbus, Ohio, 1974-1981; consult mech engr, 1973-1974; res asst, Univ Calif, Berkeley, 1972-1973; teaching asst mech eng, Univ Calif, Berkeley, 1970-1972. **Memberships:** Soc Mfg Engrs; Am Soc Metals; Am Soc Mech Engrs; CIRP; pres North Am Mfg Res Inst; Soc Mech Engrs. **Research Statement & Publications:** Development and optimization of metalworking processes, such as forging, rolling, and extrusion; computer aided modeling of metal working techniques. **Mailing Address:** 4105 Glenmoor Rd NW, Canton, OH 44718.

LAHR, CHARLES DWIGHT, MATHEMATICAL ANALYSIS. **Personal Data:** b Philadelphia, Pa, February 6, 1945; m 1986, c 4. **Education:** Temple Univ, BA, 1966; Syracuse Univ, MA, 1968, PhD (math), 1971. **Professional Experience:** PROF MATH & COMPUT SCI, DARTMOUTH COL, 1984-; prof math & comput sci & dean fac, Dartmouth Col, 1984-1989; assoc dean fac sci & dean grad studies, Dartmouth Col, 1981-1984; from asst prof to assoc prof math, Dartmouth Col, 1975-1984; vis asst prof math, Savannah State Col, 1973-1974 & Amherst Col, 1974-1975; Mathematician, Bell Labs, 1971-1973. **Memberships:** Am Math Soc; Sigma Xi; Math Asn Am; AAAS. **Research Statement & Publications:** Banach algebras, particularly convolution algebras in harmonic analysis; use of computers in secondary school teaching. **Mailing Address:** Dept Math & Comput Sci, Dartmouth Col, 6188 Bradley Rm 410, Hanover, NH 03755. **Fax:** 603-646-1312. **E-Mail:** dwight.lahr@dartmouth.edu

LAHR, GILBERT M, METALLURGICAL ENGINEERING, FAILURE ANALYSIS OF ENGINE COMPONENTS. **Personal Data:** b Detroit, Mich, September 18, 1922; wid Marie; c Patricia A (Boone), David G & Janis E (Visser). **Education:** Gen Motors Inst (Now Kettering Univ), BSIndustE, 1946. **Professional Experience:** RETIRED; chief metallurgist in charge mat eng, Mat Qual Control, Failure Analysis & Metall Processing Diesel Engines, 1977-1985; asst chief metallurgist, Detroit Diesel Eng Div, Gen Motors, 1962-1977; Metallurgist, Detroit Diesel Eng Div, Gen Motors, 1947-1962; Fel-Am Soc formetals. **Memberships:** Fel Am Soc Metals. **Research Statement & Publications:** High strength cold-worked steel; development of materials and processes for manufacturing of cylinder liners; holder of two patents. **Mailing Address:** 45152 Byrne Ct, Northville, MI 48167.

LAHR, JOHN CLARK, EARTHQUAKE LOCATION, EDUCATION OUTREACH. **Personal Data:** b Indianapolis, Ind, November 11, 1944; m 1978, Janice; c Taya, Nils & Elizabeth. **Education:** Rensselaer Polytech Inst, BS, 1966; Columbia Univ, MS, 1971, PhD (seismol), 1975. **Professional Experience:** GEOPHYSICIST SEISMOL, US GEOL SURV, 1971-. **Memberships:** Seismol Soc Am; Am Geophys Union; Nat Sci Teachers Asn. **Research Statement & Publications:** Seismicity and tectonics of Alaska, especially as related to hazards assessment. **Mailing Address:** PO Box 548, Corvallis, OR 97339. **E-Mail:** lahr@usgs.gov

LAHTI, LESLIE ERWIN, CHEMICAL ENGINEERING. **Personal Data:** b Floodwood, Minn, July 27, 1932; m 1956, Alma; c David, Mark & Paul. **Education:** Tri State Col, BS, 1954; Mich State Univ, MS, 1958; Carnegie Inst Technol, PhD (chem engr), 1964. **Honors & Awards:** Tecedo Engr Yr Award, 1986. **Professional Experience:** RETIRED; emer prof chem engr, Univ Toledo, 1990-1995; dean engr, Univ Toledo, 1980-1989; stubbs, Overbeck, 1979-1981; consult, Inland Chem Co, beginning 1970; from assoc prof to prof & chmn dept, Univ Toledo, 1967-1980; consult, Am Oil, Great Lakes Chem, 1967-1969; asst prof chem engr, Purdue Univ, 1963-1967; assoc prof, Tri State Col, 1958-1960; develop engr, Ren Plastics, 1957; glass technologist, Corning Glass Works, 1955-1957. **Memberships:** Fel Am Inst Chem Engrs; Am Chem Soc; Am Soc Engr Educ; Nat Soc Prof Engrs. **Research Statement & Publications:** Fundamentals of nucleation and crystallization from solutions; polymerization processes. **Mailing Address:** 4813 Dressage Lane, Sylvania, OH 43560.

LAHUE, ROBERT S, BIOCHEMISTRY. **Education:** Univ Va, BA; Univ Calif, PhD. **Professional Experience:** DIR EPPLEY'S CANCER RES TRAINING PROG, UNIV NEBR MED CTR, as of 2005; ASSOC PROF, EPPLEY INST, as of 2005. **Mailing Address:** Univ Nebr Med Ctr, Box 986805, Omaha, NE 68198-6805. **E-Mail:** rlahue@unmc.edu

LAI, CHII-MING, METABOLISM. **Personal Data:** b Taiwan, China, May 25, 1935; c 2. **Education:** Kaohsiung Med Col, BS, 1965; Univ Ga, MS, 1971; State Univ NY, Buffalo, PhD (pharmaceut), 1977. **Professional Experience:** PRIN RES SCIENTIST, CLIN MONITORING, QUEST PHARMACEUT SERV LLC, 2002-; sr res assoc, Stine-Haskell Res Ctr, Du Pont Merck Pharmaceut Co, beginning 1991; sr res assoc, Du Pont Pharmaceut, 1989-1990; res fel, Du Pont Critical Care, Newark, Del, 1986-1989; res fel, Am Critical Care, McGaw Park, Ill, 1981-1986; sr res investr, Am Critical Care, McGaw Park, Ill, 1978-1981; res investr, Am Critical Care, McGaw Park, Ill, 1977-1978; res asst pharmaceut, Sch Pharm, State Univ NY, Buffalo, 1971-1977; teaching asst pharm, Sch Pharm, Univ Ga, 1969-1971; pharmacist, Develop Dept, Taiwan Tanabe Pharmaceut Co, 1966-1969. **Memberships:** Am Pharmaceut Asn; Am Asn Pharmaceut Scientists; Am Soc Pharmacol & Exp Therapeut; NY Acad Sci. **Research Statement & Publications:** Biopharmaceutics, pharmacokinetics, drug metabolism and detoxication; animal screening and screening techniques; linear and nonlinear model fitting and stimulation; statistical methods; bioanalytical methods development; isotope tracer techniques; control theory and biological feedback mechanisms; physical pharmacy and bio-organic chemistry. **Mailing Address:** Quest Pharmaceut Serv LLC, Del Tecnol Park, Three Innovation Way, Ste 240, Newark, DE 19711. **Fax:** 302-369-5602.

LAI, CHING-SAN, CELL BIOPHYSICS, MEMBRANE BIOPHYSICS. **Personal Data:** b Taiwan, November 27, 1946; m 1971, Shan-Lan Liu; c Jennifer Y & Shawn S. **Education:** Nat Taiwan Norm Univ, BS, 1970; Univ Hawaii, PhD (biophys), 1978. **Professional Experience:** PROF, MED COL WIS, 1991-; assoc prof, Med Col Wis, 1985-1990; NIH grantee, 1982-; asst prof biophys, Med Col Wis, 1981-1984; res assoc, Med Col Wis, 1979-1980; Fel biophys, Univ Hawaii, 1978. **Memberships:** Biophys Soc; AAAS; Int Electron Paramagnetic Resonance Soc. **Research Statement & Publications:** Molecular dynamics of cell adhesive glycoproteins; development and applications of electron spin resonance spectroscopy to biomedical systems. **Mailing Address:** Dept Radiol, Med Col Wis 8701 Watertown Plank, Milwaukee, WI 53226-3548.

LAI, CHINTU (VINCENT C), COMPUTATIONAL HYDRAULICS, HYDROMECHANICS. **Personal Data:** b Changhua, Formosa, August 5, 1930; m 1963, c 2. **Education:** Taiwan Univ, BS, 1954; Univ Iowa, MS, 1957; Univ Mich, PhD (civil eng), 1962. **Professional Experience:** RES HYDROLOGIST, WATER RESOURCES DIV, US GEOL SURV, RESTON, 1973-; Ore, 1963-1965 & Arlington, Va, 1965-1973; Res hydraul engr, Wash, DC, 1961-1963. **Memberships:** Am Soc Civil Engrs; Asn Comput Mach; Int Asn Hydraul Res; Am Geophys Union; Sigma Xi. **Research Statement & Publications:** Computational hydraulics-surface water problems; transient flows in closed and open conduits; numerical modelling and computer simulation of unsteady flows in rivers, estuaries, embayments, closed conduits and other areas in hydromechanics and hydrologic process. **Mailing Address:** 6814 Glenmont St, Falls Church, VA 22042-4105.

LAI, CHUN-YEN, ENZYMOLOGY, BACTERIAL TOXIN. **Education:** Univ Ill, PhD (biochem), 1961. **Professional Experience:** RETIRED; adj prof biochem, Med Col, Cornell Univ, beginning 1979; res investr, Roche Res Ctr, beginning 1973; res chief, Hoffman-La Roche Inc. **Mailing Address:** 4404 Sunflower Dr, Rockville, MD 20853.

LAI, DAVID CHIN, ELECTRONICS & RADAR, PATTERN RECOGNITION. **Personal Data:** b Beijing, China, November 11, 1931; American citizen; m 1963, c 2. **Education:** Nat Taiwan Univ, BSEE, 1954; Johns Hopkins Univ, DEng, 1960. **Professional Experience:** SR STAFF MEM, GA TECH RES INST, 1996-; prin res engr, Gleason Res Assocs, 1995-1996; sr staff mem, Martin Marietta Orlando Aerospace, 1985-1995; Vis prof elec eng, Stanford Univ, 1971-1975; from assoc prof to prof elec eng, Univ Vt, 1965-1985; assoc prof elec eng, Northeastern Univ, 1962-1965; Asst prof eng, Brown Univ, 1960-1962. **Memberships:** Sr mem, Inst Elec & Electronics Engrs. **Research Statement & Publications:** Signal processing; radar signals; pattern recognition; automatic target recognition; multi-sensor fusion; granted 2 US patents. **Mailing Address:** 175 Spring Chase Circle, Altamonte Springs, FL 32714.

LAI, DAVID YING-LUN, STRUCTURAL-ACTIVITY RELATIONSHIPS, RISK ASSESSMENT. **Personal Data:** b Canton, China, August 1, 1947; American citizen; m 1984, c 2. **Education:** Chinese Univ, Hong Kong, BSc, 1970; Med Col, Ga, PhD (biochem), 1977. **Professional Experience:** SR TOXICOLOGIST, EXISTING CHEM ASSESSMENT BR, RISK ASSESSMENT DIV, as of 2000; toxicologist, Us Environ Protection Agency, beginning 1987; sr toxicologist consult, Sci Applns Int Corp, 1979-1987; instr, Dept Med, Med Ctr, Tulane Univ, 1977-1979; instr biol & biochem, Dept Biol, Chinese Univ, Hong Kong, 1970-1972. **Memberships:** Soc Toxicol; Am Col Toxicol; Am Asn Cancer Res; Am Soc Pharmacol & Exp Therapeut; Soc Risk Analysis; Europ Asn Cancer Res. **Research Statement & Publications:** Development and evaluation of hazard and risk assessment of toxic substances. **Mailing Address:** Div Risk Assessment, Existing Chem Assessment Br, US Environ Protection Agency, 401 M St SW, Washington, DC 20460. **E-Mail:** lai.david@epa.gov

LAI, ELAINE Y, CELL BIOLOGY. **Personal Data:** b Brit Hong Kong, November 11, 1949; m 1981. **Education:** Iowa State Univ, BS, 1973; Brandeis Univ, PhD (biol), 1978. **Honors & Awards:** Estherlee Runoto Gilbert Merit Award, 1977. **Professional Experience:** PROF, DEPT BIOLOGY, BRANDEIS UNIV, as of 2003; organizer, EMBO Course, Max Planck Inst, WGer, 1986; Max-Planck fel, Munich, 1986; SR RES ASSOC BIOL, BRANDEIS UNIV, 1982-; vis lectr cell-free translation, Univ NC, Chapel Hill, 1979. **Memberships:** Am Soc Cell Biol. **Research Statement & Publications:** Regulation of eukaryotic gene expression during cell differentiation; emphasis on dissection of the coordinate expression of flagellar calmodulin and tubulin genes in the amebo-flagellate, Naegleria gruberi. **Mailing Address:** Dept Biol, Brandeis Univ, 415 SSt, Waltham, MA 02254-9110. **Fax:** 781-736-3107. **E-Mail:** elai@brandeis.edu

LAI, FENG CHYUAN, HEAT TRANSFER, ENERGY CONVERSION. **Personal Data:** b Taipei, Taiwan, August 6, 1956; American citizen; m 1986, Hongshing; c Cathy B & Anthony C. **Education:** Nat Tsing Hua Univ, Taiwan, BS, 1978; Univ Del, MS, 1985, PhD (mech eng), 1988. **Professional Experience:** ASSOC PROF MECH ENG, UNIV OKLA, as of 2003; Co-prin investr, Dept Energy, 1994-1996 & NASA, 1996; prin investr, Okla Ctr Advan Sci & Technol, 1995-1997; asst prof mech eng, Univ Okla, beginning 1992; res assoc, Colo State Univ, 1986-1992; asst engr, Energy Res Lab, Taiwan, 1980-1982. **Memberships:** Am Soc Mech Engrs; Am Soc Heating Refrig & Air-Conditioning Engrs; Am Soc Eng Educ; Am Inst Aeronaut & Astronaut. **Research Statement & Publications:** Heat and mass transfer in porous media, heat transfer enhancement using electrical field; manufacturing of composite materials and indoor air quality. **Mailing Address:** Sch Aerospace & Mech Eng, Col Eng, Felgar Hall, Rm 218A, Univ Okla, Norman, OK 73072. **Fax:** 405-325-1088. **E-Mail:** flai@ou.edu

LAI, FONG M, CARDIOVASCULAR PHARMACOLOGY. **Personal Data:** b Taiwan, August 17, 1942; m 1969, c 2. **Education:** Taipei Med Col, BS, 1966; Taiwan Univ, MS, 1969; Med Col Va, PhD (pharmacol), 1974. **Professional Experience:** GROUP LEADER & PRIN PHARMACOLOGIST, LEDERLE LABS, AM CYANAMID CO, 1976-; Res fel, Roche Inst Molecular Biol, 1974-1976. **Memberships:** Am Soc Pharmacol & Exp Therapeut. **Research Statement & Publications:** Mechanisms of the hypertension and the cerebral vasculative pharmacology. **Mailing Address:** Wyeth-Averst Res CN8000, Princeton, NJ 08543. **Fax:** 732-274-4004. **E-Mail:** laif@erols.com

LAI, JAI-LUE, ACOUSTICS, STRUCTURAL DYNAMICS. **Personal Data:** b Taipei, Taiwan, December 9, 1940; American citizen; m 1968, c 2. **Education:** Nat Taiwan Univ, BS, 1962; Polytech Inst Brooklyn, MSE, 1966; Princeton Univ, PhD (mech eng), 1969. **Professional Experience:** MGR, PRATT & WHITNEY, 1992-; dir, Gencorp Automotive, 1987-1991; assoc res & develop fel, B F Goodrich Co, 1968-1989; engr satellite struct, RCA Corp, 1967. **Memberships:** Am Inst Aeronaut & Astronaut; Am Soc Mech Engrs; Soc Advan Mat Process Eng; Soc Petrol Engrs; Soc Automotive Engrs. **Research Statement & Publications:** Application of new material composite structure as new products or components. **Mailing Address:** 106 Barrington Way, Glastonbury, CT 06033-4343.

LAI, JUEY HONG, CHEMICAL ENGINEERING, POLYMER CHEMISTRY. **Personal Data:** b Taipei, Taiwan, December 4, 1936; m 1968, Li-Huey; c Eric Yo-Ping Lai & Bruce Yo-Sheng Lai. **Education:** Nat Taiwan Univ, BS, 1959; Univ Wash, MS, 1963, PhD (phys chem), 1969. **Honors & Awards:** H W Sweatt Award, Honeywell Inc, 1980. **Professional Experience:** Mem, spl rev panel, Nat Inst Dent Craniofacial Rsch/NIH, 2000-2005; Small Bus Innovation res award, Dept Health & Human Serv, 1990, 1993-1994, 1995, 1996-1998, 1997, 1999-2001; PRES, LAI LABS, INC., 1989-; lectr, State Univ NY, New Paltz, 1983; from prin res scientist to staff scientist, polymer mat & tech., Honeywell Technol Ctr, 1973-1987; res specialist, polymer chem, Univ Minn, 1969-1972. **Memberships:** Fellow: Acad Dent Mat, Am Inst Chemists; member, Am Chem Soc, Int Asn Dent Res, Sigma Xi, AAAS. **Research Statement & Publications:** Rschr. on polymers for dental and electronic applications, gas removal tech., solid state chemistry; Holder of 9 patents and author of 52 publications. **Mailing Address:** LAI Laboratories, Inc, 14617 White Oak Dr, Burnsville, MN 55337-4152. **E-Mail:** jlai@aol.com

LAI, KAI SUN, ENGINEERING. **Personal Data:** b Hong Kong, China, American citizen. **Education:** Pa State Univ, BSc, 1959. **Professional Experience:** ENGR, UNITED TECHNOL, 1986-; eng specialist, Teledyne McCormick Selph, 1982-1986; sr scientist, Teledyne McCormick Selph, 1980-1982; mgr, Teledyne McCormick Selph, 1968-1980; sr analyst, Atlantic Res Corp, 1962-1968; Engr, Aerojet Gen Corp, 1959-1962. **Research Statement & Publications:** Combustion process and thermochemical analysis of solid fuels and additives, including boranes; propulsion for aerospace applications and use of explosives and pyrotechnics for safety applications. **Mailing Address:** 855 W Eighth St, Gilroy, CA 95020. **Fax:** 408-842-7355. **E-Mail:** klai@gilroy.com

LAI, KUO-YANN, PHYSICAL CHEMISTRY, SURFACE & COLLOID SCIENCE. **Personal Data:** b Miao-Li, Taiwan, September 13, 1946; m 1972, Jane; c Melody, Amy & Peter. **Education:** Cheng Kung Univ, Taiwan, BS, 1969; Univ Tex, El Paso, MS, 1974; Clarkson Col Technol, PhD (chem), 1977. **Honors & Awards:** Pres Award for Tech Excellence, Colgate-Palmolive, 1985; Asian Am Corp Achieve Award, Org Chinese Am, 1992. **Professional Experience:** ASSOC DIR, GLOBAL MAT SOURCING, COLGATE-PALMOLIVE CO, 1996-; assoc dir, household surface care prod develop, 1993-1995; mgr oral prod develop, Colgate-Palmolive Co, 1987-1993; sr sect head chem res, Colgate-Palmolive Co, 1986-1987; sect head, Colgate-Palmolive Co, 1983-1986; res assoc, Colgate-Palmolive Co, 1983; sr res chemist, Colgate-Palmolive Co, 1980-1983; res chemist, Colgate-Palmolive Co, 1977-1980; NSF fel, 1974-1977; Robert A Welch fel, 1972-1974. **Memberships:** Am Chem Soc; Am Oil Chemists Soc. **Research Statement & Publications:** Adhesional wetting; scavenging of aerosols; surfactants and detergents; oral hygiene prods. **Mailing Address:** Colgate-PalmoliveCo, 330 Park Ave, New York, NY 10022. **E-Mail:** huo_yann_lai@colpal.com

LAI, MICHAEL MING-CHIAO, VIROLOGY, VIRAL HEPATITIS. **Personal Data:** b Tainan, Taiwan, September 8, 1942; m 1971, Cathy; c Cindy & Jennifer. **Education:** Nat Taiwan Univ Col Med, MD, 1968; Univ Calif, Berkeley, PhD (molecular biol), 1973. **Honors & Awards:** Elected academician, Academia Sinica, Taiwan, 1992. **Professional Experience:** INVESTR, HOWARD HUGHES MED INST, 1990-; PROF MICROBIOL & NEUROL, SCH MED, UNIV SOUTHERN CALIF, 1983-; Nat Mult Sclerosis Soc, beginning 1982; prin investr grants, NIH, beginning 1975; prin investr grants, Nat Cancer Inst & Am Cancer Soc, 1973-1985; from asst prof to assoc prof microbiol, Howard Hughes Med Inst, 1973-1983; molecular biologist, Univ Calif, Berkeley, 1973; med officer, Chinese Marine Corps, 1968-1969. **Memberships:** Am SocMicrobiol; Am Soc Virol; Fedn Am Soc Exp Biol; AAAS; RNA Cos; Soc Chinese Bioscientists Am (pres, 1991-1992). **Research Statement & Publications:** Molecular biology of hepatitis viruses and coronaviruses; mechanism of viral pathogenesis and viral replication. **Mailing Address:** Dept Microbiol Sch Med, Univ Southern Calif 2011 Zonal Ave, Los Angeles, CA 90033. **Fax:** 323-442-9555. **E-Mail:** michlai@hsc.usc.edu

LAI, MING, DESIGN & ENGINEERING SOLID-STATE LASER SYSTEMS, LASER PHYSICS. **Personal Data:** b Guangdong, China, May 9, 1957; m 1985, Meijuan Yuan. **Education:** Univ Zhongshan, China, BSc, 1982; Univ Toronto, Can, MSc, 1986; Univ NMex, PhD (optical sci), 1990. **Professional Experience:** DIR, RES & DEVELOP DIV, 1995-; SR LASER SCIENTIST, NOVATEC LASER SYSTEMS INC, 1994-; laser scientist, Res & Develop Div, 1992-1994; res assoc, Univ NMex, 1990-1992. **Memberships:** Optical Soc Am; Am Phys Soc. **Research Statement & Publications:** Solid-state lasers and medical laser systems for eye surgery; laser physics and technology, particularly on ultra short laser pulse generation, amplification and application. **Mailing Address:** 2705 Avenida De Anita No 31, Carlsbad, CA 92008. **E-Mail:** mlai003@aol.com

LAI, MING-CHIA DANIEL, ENGINE COMBUSTION & SPRAY PROCESSES, COMBUSTION LASER DIAGNOSTICS & COMPUTATIONAL FLUID DYNAMICS. **Personal Data:** b Taipei, Taiwan, July 28, 1957; American citizen; m 1985, c 4. **Education:** Nat Taiwan Univ, BS, 1979; Pa State Univ, MS & PhD (mech eng), 1985. **Professional Experience:** PROF MECH ENG, WAYNE STATE UNIV, as of 2004; consult, Honda NAm Res & Develop & Ford Motor Co, 1997; mem, Combustion & Fuel Comt, Int Gas Turbine Inst, 1996-; charles devlieg prof mech eng, Wayne State Univ, beginning 1996; consult, Gen Motor Corp, 1994-1996; vis prof mech eng, Univ Hiroshima, Japan, 1994; consult, Inst Gas Technols, 1993; consult, CFD Res Corp, 1990; tech assoc, Internal Combustion Div, Am Soc Mech Engrs, 1987-; from asst prof to assoc prof, Wayne State Univ, 1987-1996; postdoctoral assoc, Mass Inst Technol, 1986-1987; postdoctoral res fel, Univ Mich, 1985-1986. **Memberships:** Am Soc Mech Engrs; Soc Automotive Engrs; Am Inst Aeronaut & Astronaut; Combustion Inst; Inst Liquid Atomization & Spray Syst. **Research Statement & Publications:** Applying and developing laser diagnostics and computational fluid dynamics techniques to automotive and aeronautic propulsion and manufacturing systems; spray and mixture formation process; combustion; emission and control strategies in internal combustion engine and gas turbine engines. **Mailing Address:** Dept Mech Eng, Wayne State Univ, 2129 Eng Bldg 5050 Anthony Wayne, Detroit, MI 48202. **Fax:** 313-577-8789. **E-Mail:** lai@moon1.eng.wayne.edu

LAI, PATRICK KINGLUN, IMMUNOVIROLOGY, MOLECULAR IMMUNOLOGY. **Personal Data:** b Hong Kong, October 10, 1944; Australian citizen; m Priscilla; c Lee J & Chay A. **Education:** Univ Western Australia, PhD (microbiol), 1978. **Professional Experience:** SCI REV ADMINR, CTR SCI REV, as of 2006; dir, molecular biol & biotechnology prog & chmn, Bioscience dept, beginning 1993; ASSOC, DEPT BIOSCIENCE, SALEM INT UNIV, SALEM, WVA, 1993-; mem virol, Tampa Bay Res Inst, 1990-1996; asst mem, Tampa Bay Res Inst, 1987-1990; from instr to asst prof immunol, Univ Nebr Med Ctr, 1984-1987; sr res officer immunol, Royal Postgrad Med Sch, UK, 1982-1984; vis prof, Alta Heritage Fund, Univ Alta, 1982; Europ Molecular Biol Orgn fel, Univ Zurich, 1981; res fel, Imp Cancer Res Funds, UK, 1979-1982; immunol, Univ Col London, UK, 1979-1982; res fel biol, Univ Ottawa, Can, 1978-1979; WHO fel, Rush-Presby St Luke Med Ctr, Chicago, 1976-1977; vis scholar, Int Agency Res Cancer, France, 1975. **Memberships:** Am Asn Immunologists; AAAS; NY Acad Sci; Am Soc Microbiol; Am Soc Virol. **Research Statement & Publications:** Study interaction between viruses and cellular components that give diseases; Use molecular techniques and DNA technology to develop the next generation of vaccines. **Mailing Address:** Salem Int Univ, 223 W Main St, Salem, WV 26426-0500. **Fax:** 304-782-5579. **E-Mail:** lai@salemiu.edu

LAI, POR-HSIUNG, PROTEIN. **Education:** Mass Col Pharm, PhD (med chem), 1977; Kaohsiung Med Col, bs, 1970. **Professional Experience:** PRES & CO-FOUNDER, BIO-SYSTEMS CO, LTD, 2001-; PRES & CO-FOUNDER, LIFE SCIENCES CO, LTD, 2000-; CO-FOUNDER, VITATECH VENTURE CAPITAL INVESTMENT, 1998-; CO-FOUNDER, PROTEIN INST INC, 1990-. **Mailing Address:** Protein Inst Inc, PO Box 550, Broomall, PA 19008-0550.

LAI, RALPH WEI-MEEN, SURFACE CHEMISTRY, MINERAL SCIENCE & ENGINEERING. **Personal Data:** b Tou-Lu, Taiwan, December 17, 1936; American citizen; m 1966, c 2. **Education:** Cheng Kung Univ, Taiwan, BS, 1959; SDak Sch Mines & Technol, MS, 1964; Univ Calif, Berkeley, PhD (mat sci & eng), 1970. **Professional Experience:** Pres, Toshi Co, 1986-; SCIENTIST, US DEPT ENERGY, 1985-; pres, Western Prospect Co, 1978-; sr proj engr metall eng, Kennecott Develop Ctr, Kennecott Copper Corp, 1974-1985; mineral processing scientist process develop, Anglo-Am Clays Corp, 1973-1974; res scientist mat res, Cyprus Mines Corp, 1969-1972. **Memberships:** Am Inst Mining Metall & Petrol Engrs; Japan Inst Mining & Metall; Clay Minerals Soc; Am Chem Soc. **Research Statement & Publications:** Surface chemistry of oxide minerals; coal preparation and utilization; theory on linea-nonlinear physical law and model. **Mailing Address:** Dept Energy, Nat Energy Technol Lab, PO Box 10940, Pittsburgh, PA 15236-0940. **Fax:** 412-386-4810. **E-Mail:** ralphwlai@aol.com

LAI, SAN-CHENG, CHEMICAL ENGINEERING. **Personal Data:** b Taiwan, China, December 8, 1940; m 1968. **Education:** Taiwan Univ, BS, 1963; Univ Mo-Rolla, MS, 1966, PhD (chem eng), 1968. **Professional Experience:** MEM TECH STAFF, ATOMICS INT, 1977-; sr res engr, Am Potash & Chem Corp, 1968-1977. **Memberships:** Am Inst Chem Eng; Electrochem Soc; Am Chem Soc. **Research Statement & Publications:** Electrodeposition of manganese dioxide; alkaline battery and magnesium can battery development; sodium chlorate and perchlorate process development; manganese metal process improvement; fluidized bed cell development. **Mailing Address:** 1478 Kingston Circle, Westlake Village, CA 91362.

LAI, SHU TIM, SPACECRAFT INTERACTIONS, SPACE PHYSICS. **Personal Data:** b Hong Kong, May 23, 1938; American citizen; m 1972. **Education:** Brandeis Univ, MA, 1967, PhD (physics), 1971. **Professional Experience:** Chmn, AIAA Atmospheric & Space Environ Tech Comt, 2003-2005; chmn, AIAA Atmospheric & Space Environ Stand Comt, 1996-2002; chmn, IEEE Nuclear & Plasma Chapter, IEEE New England Sect, 1993-1996; SR PHYSICIST, USAF RES LAB, 1981-; sr mem res staff, Boston Col, 1979-1980; mem res staff, Lincoln Lab, Mass Inst Technol, 1978-1979. **Memberships:** Am Geophys Union; Am Phys Soc; Am Asn Physics Teachers; Inst Elec & Electronics Engrs; Am Inst Aeronaut & Astronaut. **Research Statement & Publications:** Space plasma physics, spacecraft charging; electron, ion and neutral beams emitted from spacecrafts; atmospheric physics; spacecraft interactions with space environment; digital signal processing. **Mailing Address:** USAF Res Lab, PO Box VSBS, 29 Randolph Rd, Hanscom AFB, MA 01731-3010. **Fax:** 781-377-5571. **E-Mail:** shu.lai@hanscom.af.mil

LAI, TZE LEUNG, MATHEMATICS, STATISTICS. **Personal Data:** b Hong Kong, June 28, 1945; American citizen; m 1975, Letitia; c 2. **Education:** Univ Hong Kong, BA, 1967; Columbia Univ, MA, 1970, PhD (statist), 1971. **Honors & Awards:** Comt of Presidents Statist Soc Award, 1983. **Professional Experience:** PROF STATIST, STANFORD UNIV, 1987-; John Simon Guggenheim fel, 1983-1984; vis prof, Math Sci Res Inst, Berkeley, 1983; vis prof statist, Stanford Univ, 1978-1979; vis assoc prof math, Univ Ill, Urbana-Champaign, 1975-1976; from asst prof to prof statist, Columbia Univ, 1971-1987. **Memberships:** Fel Am Statist Asn; fel Inst Math Statist; Academia Sinica; Int Statist Inst; Biometric Soc; Drug Info Asn. **Research Statement & Publications:** Sequential methods in statistics; statistical quality control and clinical trials; time series analysis; limit theorems in probability; renewal theory and random walks; martingales and potential theory; system identification and control; cardiorespiratory physiology; medical informatics; quant finance and economics. **Mailing Address:** Dept Statist, Stanford Univ, 390 Serra Mall, Stanford, CA 94305-4065. **Fax:** 650-725-8977. **E-Mail:** lait@stat.stanford.edu

LAI, WAYNE M, IMMUNOLOGY. **Education:** Univ Tex Southwestern Med Sch, PhD. **Professional Experience:** RES FEL, UNIV TEX SOUTHWESTERN MED SCH, as of 2006. **Mailing Address:** Univ Tex Southwestern Med Sch, 5323 Harry Hines Blvd, Dallas, TX 75235-7200. **Fax:** 214-648-4033. **E-Mail:** wayne.lai@utsouthwestern.edu

LAI, W(EI) MICHAEL, MECHANICAL ENGINEERING. **Personal Data:** b Amoy, China, November 29, 1931; American citizen; m 1963, Linda C; c David & Michelle. **Education:** Nat Taiwan Univ, BS, 1953; Univ Mich, Ann Arbor, MS, 1959, PhD (eng mech), 1962. **Honors & Awards:** Melville Medalist, Am Soc Mech Engrs, 1982; Best Paper Award, Bioeng Div, ASME, 1991; Founding Fel, Am Inst Biomed, Biol Eng, 1995; Distinguished Faculty Teaching Award, Columbia Eng Schl, 2000; Lissner Medal, ASME, 2001. **Professional Experience:** Prof & chair, Dept Mech Eng, Columbia Univ, 1996-2002; PROF MECH ENG & ORTHOP BIOENG, COLUMBIA UNIV, 1987-; From asst prof to prof mech, Rensselaer Polytech Inst, 1961-1989. **Memberships:** F el Am Soc Mech Engrs; Am Soc Biomech; AAAS; Ortho Res Soc. **Research Statement & Publications:** Hydrodynamic stability; continuum mechanics; biomechanics. **Mailing Address:** 215 W 95th St Apt 9H, New York, NY 10025-6340. **Fax:** 212-854-3304.

LAI, YIH-LOONG, PHYSIOLOGY. **Education:** Taiwan Normal Univ, BS, 1963; Kans State Univ, PhD (physiol), 1972. **Professional Experience:** RES PROF PULMONARY PHYSIOL, DEPT PHARMACOL, UNIV KY, 1992-; res assoc prof, Dept Pharmacol, Univ KY, 1984-1992; assoc mem, Mayo Clin, 1981-1984; asst mem, Mayo Clin, 1976-1981; NIH fel, Mayo Clin, 1972-1974. **Memberships:** Am Physiol Soc; Am Heart Asn. **Research Statement & Publications:** Physiology. **Mailing Address:** Dept Physiol, Nat Taiwan Univ Med Col 1 Jen-Ai Rd First Sec, Taipei, Taiwan.

LAI, YING-SAN, VALVE DESIGN & DEVELOPMENT, VALVE APPLICATIONS. **Personal Data:** b Taiwan, China, September 9, 1937; American citizen; m 1966, Nancy; c Nolan, Ormond & Lynna. **Education:** Nat Taiwan Univ, BS, 1960; Univ Iowa, MS, 1963; Northwestern Univ, PhD (mech eng), 1973. **Professional Experience:** VPRES ENG, TELEDYNE FLUID SYSTS, 1993-; dir eng, Valve Div, Dresser Industs, 1984-1992; eng dir, Dresser Dewrance Ltd, UK, 1983-1984; chief engr, Valve Div, Dresser Industs, 1973-1983; stress analyst, CBI Industs, 1972-1973; design engr, CBI Industs, 1963-1969. **Memberships:** Am Soc Mech Engrs; Am Petrol Inst. **Research Statement & Publications:** Pressure relief valves and line valves for industrial applications. **Mailing Address:** 4878 Dublin Dr, North Royalton, OH 44133.

LAI, YUAN-ZONG, WOOD CHEMISTRY. **Personal Data:** b Taiwan, China, March 11, 1941; m 1968, c 2. **Education:** Nat Taiwan Univ, BS, 1963; Univ Wash, MS, 1966 & 1967, PhD (wood chem), 1968. **Professional Experience:** SR RES ASSOC, PAPER SCI ENG, STATE UNIV NY, COL ENV SCI FORESTRY, SYRACUSE, as of 2006; assoc prof forestry, Dept Forestry, Mich Technol Univ, beginning 1977; asst prof wood chem, Dept Forestry, Mich Technol Univ, 1975-1977; sr res assoc wood chem, Univ Mont, 1970-1975; from res asst to res assoc wood chem, Col Forest Resources, Univ Wash, 1964-1970. **Memberships:** Tech Asn Pulp & Paper Indust; Am Chem Soc; Sigma Xi. **Research Statement & Publications:** Lignin, cellulose and extractive chemistry; thermal properties of wood components. **Mailing Address:** Col Environ Sci & Forestry, State Univ NY, 419 Walters Hall, Syracuse, NY 13210. **Fax:** 315-470-6593. **E-Mail:** yzlai@syr.edu

LAI, YU-CHIN, POLYMER CHEMISTRY. **Personal Data:** b February 2, 1949; m 1979, Pi-Ching; c Leslie & Sophia. **Education:** Nat Tsing Hua Univ, Taiwan, BS, 1971; Carnegie-Mellon Univ, MS, 1975; Univ Fla, PhD (chem), 1980. **Professional Experience:** PRIN SCIENTIST, BAUSCH & LOMB, 1992-; sr scientist, Bausch & Lomb, 1990-1992; sr polymer chemist, Bausch & Lomb, 1986-1990; res chemist polymer chem, Corp Res & Develop, Allied corp, 1981-1986; res assoc, Univ Mass, 1980-1981; mem, Tech Prog Comt Polymeric Mat Sci & Eng, Am Chem Soc. **Memberships:** Am Chem Soc. **Research Statement & Publications:** Synthesis of organic compounds: monomers and polymers; kinetics and mechanism of polymerization; structure-properties relationships in polymers. **Mailing Address:** Contact Lens Div Res & Develop, Bausch & Lomb Inc, 1400 N Goodman St PO Box 450, Rochester, NY 14603-0450. **Fax:** 585-338-5304. **E-Mail:** yu-chin_lai@bausch.com

LAIA, JOSEPH R, STRATEGY, TECHNOLOGY LEVERAGING & IMPLEMENTATION. **Personal Data:** m 1980, Jill Jensen; c 2. **Education:** State Univ NY, Stony Brook, BS, 1980, MS, 1983, PhD (mat sci & eng), 1986. **Professional Experience:** SR DIR, STRATEGIC MARKETING, NOVELLUS, as of 1999; dir, Energy Technol Prog, Los Alamos Nat Lab, beginning 1994; co-dir, Advan Mat Lab, 1993-1994; group leader, Los Alamos Nat Lab, 1990-1994; sect leader, Los Alamos Nat Lab, 1988-1990; Staff mem, Los Alamos Nat Lab, 1987-1988. **Research Statement & Publications:** Vapor phase processing of material, reactivity of solids, strategy in technology development, research and development portfolio management and leveraging into core business lines. **Mailing Address:** Novellus Systems Inc, 4000 N First St, San Jose, CA 95134. **Fax:** 408-943-3422.

LAIBINIS, PAUL EDWARD, CHEMICAL ENGINEERING. **Personal Data:** b Wilkes-Barre, Pa, December 8, 1963. **Education:** Mass Inst Technol, SB, 1985; Harvard Univ, MA, 1987, PhD (chem), 1991. **Honors & Awards:** Victor K LaMer Award, Am Chem Soc, 1994; Presidential Early Career Awardfor Scientists & Engrs, 1996. **Professional Experience:** ASSOC PROF CHEM ENG, RICE UNIV, as of 2003; Off Naval Res young investr, beginning 1996; Doherty asst prof, Mass Inst Technol, beginning 1996; Beckman Fedn young investr, beginning 1995; Texaco-Mangelsdorf asst prof, 1994-1996; asst prof, Cambridge, 1993-1994; postdoctoral fel, Calif Inst Technol, Pasadena, 1991-1993; teaching/res asst, Harvard Univ, Cambridge, 1985-1991. **Memberships:** AAAS; Am Inst Chem Engrs; Am Chem Soc; Mat Res Soc. **Research Statement & Publications:** Contributed over 40 science publications on self-assembling strategies for surface modification controlling interfacial properties and sensor design; one patent in area of thin films and nanotechnology. **Mailing Address:** Dept Chem Eng, Rice Univ, MS-362, PO Box 1892, Houston, TX 77251-1892. **Fax:** 713-348-5478. **E-Mail:** pel@rice.edu

LAIBLE, JON MORSE, ALGEBRA. **Personal Data:** b Bloomington, Ill, July 25, 1937; m 1959, Jo; c Kathy J, Kenneth R, Jackie A & Michael H. **Education:** Univ Ill, Urbana, BS, 1959, PhD (math), 1967; Univ Minn, Minneapolis, MA, 1961. **Professional Experience:** EXEC OFFICER, EASTERN ILLNIOS UNIV FOUND, as of 2002; dean, Col Lib Arts & Sci, 1981-1993; prof math, Eastern Ill Univ, 1979-1994; from asst prof to assoc prof, Eastern Ill Univ, 1964-1979; asst prof math, Western Ill Univ, 1961-1964. **Memberships:** Math Asn Am; Sigma Xi. **Mailing Address:** Eastern Ill Univ Found, 600 Lincoln Ave, Charleston, IL 61920.

LAIBLE, ROY C, POLYMER PHYSICS, CHEMISTRY. **Personal Data:** b Boston, Mass, June 16, 1924. **Education:** Northeastern Univ, BS, 1945; Boston Univ, MA, 1948; Mass Inst Technol, PhD, 1970. **Honors & Awards:** Technol US Army Res & Study Fel Europe, 1961-1962. **Professional Experience:** CONSULT, TEL-TECH, 1988-; consult, properties plastics & elastomers, 1987-2001; chief, Polymers & Org Mat Br, 1976-1987; chief, Textile Res Sect, 1970-1976; physics scientist, US Army Natick Labs, 1963-1970; secy Army res & study fel viscoelastic properties polymers, Sweden & Scotland, 1962-1963; phys sci adminr, US Army Natick Labs, 1958-1963; org chemist, US Army Natick Labs, 1953-1958; org chemist, Cent Intel Agency, 1952-1953; res assoc polymerization, Univ RI, 1950-1952. **Research Statement & Publications:** Allyl polymerization; viscoelastic properties of fibrous and non-fibrous polymers; ballistic properties of polymers; chemical and mechanical properties of polymers especially elastomers; editor of one book; ballistic materials and penetration mechanics editor. **Mailing Address:** 101 Overbrook Dr, Wellesley, MA 02482.

LAIBOWITZ, ROBERT (BENJAMIN), APPLIED PHYSICS. **Personal Data:** b Yonkers, NY, March 24, 1937; m 1958, c 3. **Education:** Columbia Col, BA, 1959; Columbia Univ, BS, 1960, MS, 1963; Cornell Univ, PhD (appl physics), 1967. **Professional Experience:** ADJ SR RES SCIENTIST, DEPT ELEC ENG, COLUMBIA UNIV, as of 2005; adj assoc prof, Dept Elec Eng, Columbia Univ, as of 2000; RES STAFF MEM, THOMAS J WATSON RES CTR, 1966-. **Memberships:** fel Am Phys Soc; fel Am Vacuum Soc. **Research Statement & Publications:** Electrical and optical properties of materials; superconductivity. **Mailing Address:** Int Bus Mach Res Div, Thomas J Watson Res Ctr, PO Box 218, Yorktown Heights, NY 10598. **Fax:** 914-945-2141. **E-Mail:** laibow@us.ibm.com

LAIBSON, PETER R, OPHTHALMOLOGY. **Personal Data:** b New York, NY, December 11, 1933; m Ruth; c David I, Rebecca (Popell) & Rachel. **Education:** Univ Vt, BA, 1955; State Univ NY, Downstate Med Ctr, MD, 1959; Am Bd Ophthal, dipl, 1965. **Professional Experience:** CO-DIR, CORNEA SERV, as of 2004; ATTENDING SURGEON, WILLS EYE HOSP, as of 2004; PROF OPHTHAL, SCH MED, THOMAS JEFFERSON UNIV, 1973-; consult lectr, US Naval Hosp, Philadelphia, 1968-; assoc prof ophthal, Sch Med, Temple Univ, 1966-1973; fel corneal dis, Retina Found & Mass Eye & Ear Infirmary, 1964-1965; attend surgeon & dir cornea serv, Wills Eye Hosp; mem ophthal staff, Lankenau Hosp, Philadelphia. **Memberships:** Asn Res Ophthal; Am Acad Ophthal; AMA; Am Ophthal Soc. **Research Statement & Publications:** Corneal diseases and surgery of the cornea, particularly viral external diseases, herpes simplex and adenoviruses. **Mailing Address:** Wills Eye Hosp, 840 Walnut St Ste 920, Philadelphia, PA 19107-5109. **Fax:** 215-928-3854.

LAIDLAW, JOHN COLEMAN, ENDOCRINOLOGY. **Personal Data:** b Toronto, Ont, February 28, 1921; m 1957, Ann; c Kate & Meg. **Education:** Univ Toronto, BA, 1942, MD, 1944, MA, 1947; Univ London, PhD (biochem), 1950; FRCP (C), 1955; FRSC, 1975; FRCP, 1981. **Professional Experience:** AT, MCMASTER UNIV, as of 2004; PROF EMER MED, UNIV TORONTO, as of 2004; VPRES, RES & EDUC, ONT CANCER TREATMENT & RES FOUND, 1986-; prof med, Univ Toronto, beginning 1986; exec dir med affairs, Can Cancer Soc, 1986-1992; sci adv to pres, Med Res Coun, Ottawa, 1985-1986; dean, fac health sci, 1981-1985; prof med & chmn dept, McMaster Univ, 1975-1981; dir inst med sci, Univ Toronto, 1967-1975; sr physician, Toronto Gen Hosp, 1959-1975; from asst prof to prof med, Univ Toronto, 1956-1975; physician, Toronto Gen Hosp, 1954-1959; assoc, Univ Toronto, 1954-1956; jr assoc, Peter Bent Brigham Hosp, Boston, 1953-1954; instr, Harvard Med Sch, 1953-1954; res fel, Harvard Med Sch, 1951-1953; Asst, Peter Bent Brigham Hosp, Boston, 1951-1953; sr intern med, Toronto Gen Hosp, 1950-1951; lectr biochem, Univ London, 1947-1950; demonstr biochem, Univ Toronto, 1946-1947; Jr intern, Toronto Gen Hosp, 1944. **Memberships:** Endocrine Soc; Am Soc Clin Invest; Can Soc Clin Invest (pres, 1962); Can Soc Endocrinol & Metab (pres, 1975). **Mailing Address:** Dept Med, Univ Toronto, 620 Univ Ave, Toronto, ON M5G 2L7, Can. **Fax:** 416-971-6888. **E-Mail:** jlaidlaw@cancercare.on.ca

LAIDLAW, WILLIAM GEORGE, THEORETICAL CHEMISTRY. **Personal Data:** b Wingham, Ont, March 13, 1936; m 1961, Lucia; c David K & Michael K. **Education:** Univ Western Ont, BSc, 1959; Calif Inst Technol, MSc, 1961; Univ Alta, PhD (theoret chem), 1963. **Professional Experience:** PROF EMER CHEM, UNIV CALGARY, 1993-; FAC PROF CHEM, UNIV CALGARY, 1993-; from asst prof to prof chem, Univ Calgary, 1965-1993; NATO fel, Math Inst, Univ Oxford, 1964-1965; adj prof physics, Univ Hawaii. **Memberships:** Chem Inst Can; Can Asn Physics. **Research Statement & Publications:** Hydrodynamics; flow of fluids in porous media; fluid systems near instabilities. **Mailing Address:** Dept Chem, Univ Calgary, 2500 Univ Dr NW, Calgary, AB T2N 1N4, Can. **Fax:** 403-289-9488. **E-Mail:** laidlaw@ucalgary.ca

LAIDLER, KEITH JAMES, PHYSICAL CHEMISTRY, CHEMICAL KINETICS & HISTORY OF CHEMISTRY. **Personal Data:** b Liverpool, Eng, January 3, 1916; m 1943, Mary Auchincloss; c Margaret (deceased), Audrey (deceased) & James. **Education:** Oxford Univ, BA, 1937, MA, 1955, DSc, 1956; Princeton Univ, PhD (phys chem), 1940. **Honorary Degrees:** LLD, Simon Fraser Univ, 1997. **Honors & Awards:** Medal, Chem Inst Can, 1971; Queen's Jubilee Medal, 1977; Centenary Medal, Royal Soc Can, 1982, Henry Marshall Tory Medal, 1987; Dexter Award Excellence, Am Chem Soc, 1996. **Professional Experience:** PROF EMER CHEM, UNIV OTTAWA, 1981-; commonwealth vis prof, Sussex Univ, 1966-1967; vice dean fac pure & appl sci, Univ Ottawa, 1962-1966; chmn dept, Univ Ottawa, 1961-1966; prof, Univ Ottawa, 1955-1981; from asst prof to assoc prof chem, Cath Univ Am, 1946-1955; chief sci officer & supt phys & math wing, Can Armaments Res & Develop Estab, 1944-1946; sci officer, Can Armaments Res & Develop Estab, 1942-1944; Res chemist, Nat Res Coun Can, 1940-1942. **Memberships:** Royal Soc Chem; fel Royal Soc Can; fel Chem Inst Can. **Research Statement & Publications:** Chemical kinetics of gas reactions; surface, solution and enzyme reactions; photochemistry; history of physical chemistry. **Mailing Address:** Dept Chem, Univ Ottawa, Ottawa, ON K1N 6N5, Can.

LAI-FOOK, JOAN ELSA I-LING, ZOOLOGY. **Personal Data:** b Port of Spain, Trinidad, August 3, 1937. **Education:** Univ Col WI, BSc, 1961; Western Reserve Univ, PhD (biol), 1966. **Professional Experience:** RETIRED; assoc prof zool, Univ Toronto, beginning 1973; asst prof, Univ Toronto, 1966-1973. **Memberships:** Am Soc Cell Biol. **Research Statement & Publications:** Fine structure of insect development and physiology. **Mailing Address:** Dept Zool, Univ Toronto, Toronto, ON M5S 1A1, Can.

LAI-FOOK, STEPHEN J, BIOMEDICAL ENGINEERING. **Personal Data:** b Trinidad & Tobago, August 28, 1940; American citizen; m 1974, Michele; c Kristin & Thomas. **Education:** Loughborough Univ, Eng, BS, 1964; Southhampton Univ, Eng, MS, 1966; Univ Wash, Seattle, PhD (mech eng), 1972. **Professional Experience:** Assoc ed, J Appl Physiol, 1993-; PROF PHYSIOL, UNIV KY, 1991-; PROF BIOMED ENG, WENNER GREN RES LAB, UNIV KY, 1987-; assoc mem, Cardiovasc Res Inst, 1984-1987; adj assoc prof physiol, Sch Pediat, 1984-1987; lectr, Sch Pediat, 1983, 1984 & 1986; instr orgn physiol, Pulmonary Physiol Lab, 1982-1985; assoc prof physiol & biophys, Mayo Med Sch, 1981; adj asst prof physiol & med, Univ Calif, San Francisco, 1981; consult, Mayo Clin, 1980-1981; res career develop award, 1980; assoc prof physiol & med, Mayo Med Sch, 1978-1981; assoc consult thoracic dis, Mayo Clin, 1977-1980; NIH young investr award, 1976; instr biophys, Mayo Med Sch, 1975-1978; fel, Dept Aerospace Eng & Mech, Univ Minn, 1973-1974; res engr, Boeing Co, 1966-1969. **Memberships:** Am Physiol Soc; Am Soc Mech Engrs; Biomed Eng Soc; Microcirculation Soc; Am Thoracic Soc; Am Heart Asn; Am Acad Mech. **Research Statement & Publications:** Pulmonary mechanics; mechanical properties of the lung; mechanics of lung interstitium and the pleural space in relation to liquid and solute exchange; mathematical modeling of physiological systems. **Mailing Address:** Dept Physiol Col Med, Univ Ky, Lexington, KY 40506. **Fax:** 606-257-1836. **E-Mail:** lai-fook@cbme.uky.edu

LAIHING, KENNETH, NONLINEAR OPTICS, LASER SPECTROSCOPY. **Personal Data:** b Trinidad, WI, American citizen; m 1980, Esther Adolph; c Steven K. **Education:** Col Staten Island, BS, 1972; Long Island Univ, MS, 1981; Univ Ga, PhD (chem), 1988. **Honors & Awards:** Martin Reynolds Smith Mem Prize, Am Chem Soc, 1987. **Professional Experience:** PROF & CHMN, DEPT CHEM, OAKWOOD COL, 1996-; prin investr, NSF, beginning 1992; fel, NSF, 1991 & 1992; res fel, Am Chem Soc, 1991; res fel, US Army, 1989 & 1990; from asst prof to assoc prof, dept chem, Oakwood Col, 1988-1995. **Memberships:** Am Chem Soc; Optical Soc Am; Am Phys Soc; Int Union Pure & Appl Chem. **Research Statement & Publications:** Preparation and characterization of novel inorganic and organometallic compounds for nonlinear applications; new techniques for identification and sequencing of biological molecules using matrix assisted time-of-flight mass spectrometry. **Mailing Address:** Dept Chem, Oakwood Col, 7000 Adventist Blvd NW, Huntsville, AL 35896. **Fax:** 205-726-7111. **E-Mail:** laihing@oakwood.edu

LAIKEN, NORA DAWN, MEDICAL PHYSIOLOGY, MEDICAL EDUCATION. **Personal Data:** b Chicago, Ill, June 28, 1946; m 1967, Stuart; c 2. **Education:** Univ Chicago, BS, 1967; Rockefeller Univ, PhD (life sci), 1970. **Professional Experience:** Mem, Undergrad

Teaching Proj Comt, Am Gastroenterol Asn, 1985-1991; LECTR MED, UNIV CALIF, SAN DIEGO, 1983-; ASST DEAN CURRIC & STUDENT AFFAIRS, UNIV CALIF, SAN DIEGO, 1983-; asst adj prof med, 1980-1983; mem test adv, Asn Am Med Col, 1974-1978; lectr med, 1974-1980; DIR TUTORIAL PROG, UNIV CALIF, SAN DIEGO, 1973-; sci curric adv physics, biol & chem, Adaptive Learning Prog, 1972-1973; USPHS fel & res assoc phys biochem, Univ Calif, San Diego, 1971-1972; USPHS fel & res assoc phys biochem, Inst Molecular Biol, Univ Ore, 1970-1971. **Research Statement & Publications:** Development of innovative instructional materials and methods in the basic medical sciences, particularly in medical physiology and pharmacology; applications of computers to biomedical problems. **Mailing Address:** Univ Calif San Diego, 9500 Gilman Dr, La Jolla, CA 92093-0606. **Fax:** 858-822-0343. **E-Mail:** nlaiken@ucsd.edu

LAINE, RICHARD MASON, ORGANOMETALLIC CHEMISTRY. **Personal Data:** b San Fernando, Calif, October 31, 1947. **Education:** Calif State Univ, Northridge, BS, 1969; Univ Southern Calif, PhD (chem), 1973. **Professional Experience:** PROF, DEPT MATSCI & ENG, UNIV MICH, as of 2005; assoc prof, dept mat sci & eng/dept chem, Univ Mich, beginning 1990; fac, Dept Mat Sci & Eng, Univ Wash, Seattle, 1987-1990; proj leader, NIH Grant, 1978-1981; prin investr, NSF Chem Eng Grant, 1978-1979; phys inorg chemist, SRI Int, 1977-1987; dept Chem & Dept Chem & Nuclear Eng, Stanford Res Inst, 1976-1977; Dept Chem & Nuclear Eng, Univ Calif, Santa Barbara, 1974-1976; fel chem, Univ Del, 1973-1974. **Memberships:** Am Chem Soc; Catalysis Soc; Sigma Xi. **Research Statement & Publications:** Homogeneous catalysis of the water-gas shift reaction and the catalysis of related reactions wherein water serves as a source of hydrogen. **Mailing Address:** Dept Mat Sci & Eng, Univ Mich, 2114 Dow, Ann Arbor, MI 48109-2136. **Fax:** 734-763-4788. **E-Mail:** talsdad@engin.umich.edu

LAINE, ROGER ALLAN, BIOCHEMISTRY, ANALYTICAL CHEMISTRY. **Personal Data:** b Cloquet, Minn, January 28, 1941; div, c 4. **Education:** Univ Minn, Minneapolis, BA, 1964; Rice Univ, Houston, PhD (biochem), 1970. **Professional Experience:** ADJ PROF, DEPT ENTOMOL, LA STATE UNIV, 2001-; PROF, DIV BIOCHEM & MOLECULAR BIOL, DEPT BIOL SCI & DEPT CHEM, LA STATE UNIV, BATON ROUGE, 1997-; PRES & FOUNDER, ANOMERIC INC, BATON ROUGE, 1997-; chief scientist, Glycomed, Inc, 1988-1991; chmn, Dept Biochem, La State Univ, Baton Rouge, 1983-1988; from asst prof to assoc prof biochem, Col Med, Univ Ky, 1975-1988; fel Pathobiology, Univ Wash, 1972-1974; fel biochem, Mich State Univ, East Lansing, 1970-1972. **Memberships:** Am Chem Soc; Soc Complex Carbohydrates; Am Soc Mass Spectrometry; Am Soc Biol Chemists. **Research Statement & Publications:** Biochemistry of complex carbohydrates, microbial diagnostics; chemical ecology of termites, other insects. **Mailing Address:** Div Biochem & Molecular Biol, Dept Biol Sci, La State Univ, 512 Choppin Hall, Baton Rouge, LA 70803. **Fax:** 225-578-4695. **E-Mail:** rlaine@usa.net

LAING, JOHN E, ENTOMOLOGY, ECOLOGY. **Personal Data:** b Ottawa, Ont, October 17, 1939; m 1964, c 2. **Education:** Carleton Univ, BSc, 1963, MSc, 1964; Univ Calif, Berkeley, PhD (entom), 1968. **Professional Experience:** PROF EMER, DEPT ENVIRON BIOL, UNIV GUELP, as of 2004; from asst prof to assoc prof environ biol, Univ Guelph, 1973-1996; asst res entomologist & lectr, Div Biol Control, Univ Calif, Berkeley, 1968-1973. **Memberships:** Entom Soc Can (secy, 1978-1981); Entom Soc Am; Ecol Soc Am; Int Asn Ecol; Int Orgn Biol Control; Sigma Xi. **Research Statement & Publications:** Ecology of tetranychid mites; populations dynamics of arthropods; ecology and control of orchard pests; biological control of insect pests and weeds. **Mailing Address:** Dept Biol & Environ, Univ Guelph, Guelph, ON N1G 2W1, Can.

LAING, PATRICK GOWANS, ORTHOPEDIC SURGERY. **Personal Data:** b Barnes, Eng, November 8, 1923; American citizen; m 1956, c 4. **Education:** Univ Southampton, MB & BS, 1940; FRCS, 1948; FRCS(C), 1954, Am Bd Orthop Surg, dipl, 1960. **Professional Experience:** CLIN PROF ORTHOP SURG, UNIV PITTSBURGH, 1963-; ORTHOP SURGEON, AIKEN MED, 1956-; chief serv, Vet Admin Hosp, 1956-1992; assoc prof orthop surg, Aiken Med, 1956-1963; Fel cerebral palsy, Univ Pittsburgh, 1955-1956; chief resident surg, Vet Hosp, St John, NB, 1954-1955; sr registr, Bradford Hosp, Yorkshire, 1952-1954; orthop surg, Lewisham Hosp, London, 1948-1950 & Pembury Hosp, Kent, 1950-1952; gen & orthop surg, Queen Mary's Hosp, Sidcup, 1948; registr orthop surg, Royal Hampshire Co Hosp, Winchester, 1946-1947; House surgeon, Kings Col Hosp, London, Eng, 1945-1946. **Memberships:** Orthop Res Soc; Am Orthop Asn; Am Soc Testing & Mat; NY Acad Sci; Brit Orthop Asn. **Research Statement & Publications:** Blood supply and the dynamics of circulation in bones and joints; metallurgy and engineering in orthopedics; radioisotopes in clinical orthopedics. **Mailing Address:** Univ Pittsburgh, Pittsburgh, PA 15232.

LAING, RONALD ALBERT, BIOPHYSICS. **Personal Data:** b Seattle, Wash, December 9, 1933. **Education:** Reed Col, BA, 1956; Rice Univ, MA, 1958, PhD (low temperature physics), 1960. **Professional Experience:** RETIRED; res prof ophthal, Med Sch, Boston Univ, ending 2004; assoc prof ophthal, Med Sch, Boston Univ, beginning 1970; vis scientist, Univ Tokyo, 1969-1970; sr scientist, Space Sci Inc, 1968-1970; vis lectr, Univ Mass, Boston, 1967-1968; consult, Space Sci Inc, 1967-1968; NIH fel, Mass Inst Technol, 1966-1967; NSF sci fac fel, Harvard Univ, 1965-1966; asst prof physics, Tulane Univ, 1960-1968. **Memberships:** Biophys Soc; Asn Res in Vision & Ophthalmol; Optical Soc Am; AAAS; Sigma Xi. **Research Statement & Publications:** Ophthalmic biophysics; bioengineering. **Mailing Address:** Dept Ophthal, Boston Univ Sch Med, Lexington, MA 02173-3829.

LAIPIS, PHILIP JAMES, MOLECULAR BIOLOGY, GENETICS. **Personal Data:** b Charleston, SC, April 20, 1944; m 1970, c 2. **Education:** Calif Inst Technol, BS, 1966; Stanford Univ, PhD (genetics), 1972. **Professional Experience:** ASSOC CHMN, DEPT BIOCHEM & MOLECULAR BIOL, UNIV FLA, 1997-; vis affil, Whitehead Inst, Mass Inst Technol, 1987-1988; SCI DIR, BIOL COMPUT FACIL, INTERDISCIPLINARY CTR BIOTECHNOL RES, UNIV FLA, 1987-; PROF BIOCHEM & MOLECULAR BIOL, UNIV FLA, 1986-; vis scholar biochem, Harvard Univ, 1981-1982; from asst prof to assoc prof, Univ Fla, 1974-1986; Nat Cancer Inst fel, Princeton Univ, 1972-1974. **Memberships:** AAAS; Am Soc Microbiol; Sigma Xi; Am Soc Biol Chem; Am Soc Cell Biol. **Research Statement & Publications:** Gene organization and variation in mammalian mitochondrial DNA; mechanisms of maternal inheritance, mitochondrial amplification and embryonic distribution of mitochondria on mammals; gene organization and variation in mammalian carbonic anhydrase genes; site directed mutation of human carbonic anhydrase isozymes and expression in bacterial systems. **Mailing Address:** Dept Biochem & Molecular Biol, Col Med, Univ Fla, PO Box 100245, Gainesville, FL 32610. **Fax:** 352-392-6870. **E-Mail:** plaipis@ufl.edu

LAIR, ALAN VAN, PARABOLIC & ELLIPTIC PARTIAL DIFFERENTIAL EQUATIONS. **Personal Data:** b Anna, Tex, May 2, 1948; m 1978, Vickie. **Education:** Univ NTex, BA, 1970; Tex Tech Univ, MS, 1972, PhD (math), 1976. **Professional Experience:** DEPT HEAD, DEPT MATH & STAT, AIR FORCE INST TECHNOL, 1993-; PROF MATH, AIR FORCE INST TECHNOL, 1991-; from asst prof to assoc prof, Air Force Inst Technol, 1982-1991; Reviewer, Math Rev, 1980-; From asst prof to assoc prof math, Univ SDak, 1976-1982. **Memberships:** Am Math Soc; Soc Indust & Appl Math. **Research Statement & Publications:** Existence and properites of solutions to partial differential equations; A Rellich compactness theorem for sets of finite volume; Uniqueness for a nonlinear abstract Cauchy problem; Finite extinction time for solutions of nonlinear parabolic equations. **Mailing Address:** Dept Math & Stat, Air Force Inst Technol, 2950, P St, Wright-Patterson, OH 45433-7765. **Fax:** 937-656-4413. **E-Mail:** alair@afit.edu

LAIRD, CAMPBELL, PHYSICAL METALLURGY. **Personal Data:** b Ardrishaig, Scotland, June 17, 1936; m 1964, Beckwith; c Katherine F, Andrew K & Lucy M. **Education:** Cambridge Univ, BS, 1959, MA, 1963, PhD (metall), 1963. **Professional Experience:** PROF MAT SCI & ENG, UNIV PA, 1980-; Battelle vis prof, Ohio State Univ, 1968-; prof metall, Univ PA, 1968-1980; prin scientist, Sci Lab, Ford Motor Co, 1963-1968; Res fel metall, Christ's Col, Cambridge Univ, 1961-1965; vis prof physics, Univ Vienna; hon prof, Academia Sinica. **Memberships:** Am Inst Mining Metall & Petrol Engrs; Am Soc Testing & Mat; Electron Micros Soc Am; Royal Inst Gt Brit; Brit Inst Metals; fel Am Soc Metals. **Research Statement & Publications:** Fracture of materials, especially by fatigue; superconductivity; diffusional phase transformations; electron microscopy; cyclic stress-strain response of materials; environmental effects on fractive; properties of composite materials; published over 270 articles. **Mailing Address:** Dept Mat Sci & Eng, Univ Pa, 3231 Walnut St, Philadelphia, PA 19104-6272. **Fax:** 215-573-2128. **E-Mail:** laird@lrsm.upenn.edu

LAIRD, CHARLES DAVID, CELL BIOLOGY, HUMAN GENETICS. **Personal Data:** b Portland, Ore, May 12, 1939; m 1961, c 4. **Education:** Univ Ore, BA, 1961; Stanford Univ, PhD (genetics), 1966. **Honors & Awards:** Wassenberg Mem Lectr, San Diego State Univ, 1990. **Professional Experience:** Mem, Fred Hutchinson Cancer Res Ctr, 1990-; RES AFFIL, CHILD DEVELOP & MENT RETARDATION CTR, 1989-; vis scholar, Cambridge Univ, 1978-1979; Distinguished vis lectr, Univ Tex, Austin, 1977; PROF ZOOL & ADJ PROF GENETICS, UNIV WASH, 1975-; assoc prof zool & adj assoc prof genetics, Child Develop & Ment Retardation Ctr, 1971-1975; asst prof zool, Univ Tex, Austin, 1968-1971; NIH fel genetics, Univ Wash, 1967-1968. **Memberships:** AAAS; Am Soc Human Genetics; Genetic Soc Am. **Research Statement & Publications:** Encoding the three dimensional structure of chromosomes; mechanisms of transcription control; chromosome structure and function; human genetics. **Mailing Address:** Dept Zool, Univ Wash Box 351800, Seattle, WA 98195. **Fax:** 206-543-1620. **E-Mail:** cdlaird@u.washington.edu

LAIRD, CHRISTOPHER ELI, NUCLEAR PHYSICS, QUANTUM MECHANICS. **Personal Data:** b Anniston, Ala, November 29, 1942; m 1966, Mary; c 2. **Education:** Univ Ala, BS, 1963, MS, 1966, PhD (physics), 1970. **Professional Experience:** Vis res prof, Marshall Space Flight Ctr, 1982, 1983 & 1996; vis res prof, Univ Ky, 1979-1981 & 1986; fac res mem, Argonne Nat Lab, 1977-1978; FOUND PROF PHYSICS, EASTERN KY UNIV, 1975-; fac res mem, Vanderbilt Univ, 1969; from asst prof to assoc prof, Eastern KY Univ, 1967-1975. **Memberships:** Am Phys Soc; Sigma Xi; Sci Res Soc; Am Nuclear Soc. **Research Statement & Publications:** Theoretical and experimental nuclear physics with primary emphasis in beta decay; atomic effects during beta decay; proton induced nuclear reactions; experimental measurements of proton-induced reaction cross-sections; analysis of this data using various nuclear models; activation of spacecraft materials. **Mailing Address:** Dept Physics & Astron, Eastern Ky Univ, 351 Moore Hall, Richmond, KY 40475. **Fax:** 859-622-1020. **E-Mail:** chris.laird@eku.edu

LAIRD, CLEVE WATROUS, PHYSIOLOGY, GENETICS. **Personal Data:** b Montclair, NJ, March 29, 1938; m 1965, Elizabeth; c Kevin W & Brian C. **Education:** Gettysburg Col, BA, 1961; Univ Nebr, MS, 1963; Rutgers Univ, PhD (endocrinol & reproductive physiol), 1967. **Honors & Awards:** Can Heart Prize, 1976. **Professional Experience:** PRES & CONSULT, DRIAL CONSULT, 1986-; dir, Lab Serv Clin, Chem & Physiol, Remote Imaging Syst, 1981-1986; sr scientist & group leader, Union Carbide, med prod, 1977-1980; instr, Harvard Med Sch, 1974-1980; sr scientist, Block Eng, 1974-1977; adj asst prof, Boston Univ, 1972-1977; res assoc, Biores Inc, 1972-1974; adj assoc prof, Baylor Col Med, 1969-1972; biol sect head, Hycel Inc, 1969-1972; staff, NATO mammalian genetics course, 1968; postdoctoral fel, NIH, 1967-1969; Cyto chem consult, Coulter Electronics. **Memberships:** Am Physiol Asn; Am Heart Asn; Am Asn Clin Chem; Am Soc Vet Clin Pathologists; Soc Reproductive Physiol; Sigma Xi. **Research Statement & Publications:** Clinical chemistry; impact of genetics and disease on the physiology and biochemistry of animals and humans. **Mailing Address:** Drial Consults Inc, 2139 Tapo St Ste 228, Simi Valley, CA 93063-1085. **Fax:** 805-522-1526. **E-Mail:** diabetes@ix.netcom.com

LAIRD, DON M, CLINICAL CHEMISTRY. **Personal Data:** b Johnstown, NY, August 27, 1953. **Education:** Campbell Univ, BS, 1977; Wake Forest Univ, PhD (energy metab), 1983. **Professional Experience:** AT ABBOTT LABS, 1994-; tech specialist, Abbott Labs, 1992-1994; sr res scientist, Monsanto Co, 1987-1992; NIH res fel, Johns Hopkins Univ Med Sch, Baltimore, 1983-1987. **Memberships:** Am Asn Clin Chem. **Research Statement & Publications:** Clinical chemistry. **Mailing Address:** Abbott Labs, Bldg AP8 One Abbott Park Rd, North Chicago, IL 60064.

LAITIN, HOWARD, SYSTEMS ANALYSIS & DESIGN. **Personal Data:** b Brooklyn, NY, November 18, 1931; m 1961, c 3. **Education:** Brooklyn Col, BA, 1952; Harvard Univ, MA, 1953, PhD (statist, pub health & econ), 1956. **Professional Experience:** CONSULT, 1995-; chief scientist, Hughes Aircraft Co, 1982-1995; adj prof, Sch Eng, Univ Southern Calif, 1966-1990; mgr proj anal, Hughes Aircraft Co, 1962-1982; Clin assoc prof pub health, Univ Calif, Los Angeles, 1959-1973; sr economist, Rand Corp, 1959-1962; proj dir, Army Med Serv, 1957-1959; dir, Michael Saphier & Assoc, 1956; med economist, Hosp Coun Greater NY, 1954-1956; adv to var orgn & govt agencies. **Research Statement & Publications:** Technical analysis; military affairs; public health; solid and hazardous waste management; air pollution; transportation; safety; economic studies. **Mailing Address:** 4916 White Ct, Torrance, CA 90503.

LAITY, DAVID SANFORD, CHEMICAL ENGINEERING. **Personal Data:** b Mt Kisco, NY, November 20, 1926; m 1950, Mary; c David Jr & Robert. **Education:** Haverford Col, BA, 1949; Mass Inst Technol, MS, 1950; NY Univ, ScD (chem eng), 1956. **Professional Experience:** RETIRED; vpres, Process Res Dept, 1986-1992; chmn, Adv Coun, Sch Chem Eng, Cornell Univ, 1981-1991 & Worcester Polytech Inst, 1985-1987; mgr, Process Design Div, Chevron Corp, 1973-1986; staff planner, Chevron Oil Europe, 1971-1973; asst proj mgr, Belg Refinery, 1969-1971; staff econ analyst, Comptrollers Analysis Div, 1967-1969; supv res engr, Process Design Div, Chevron Res Co, 1959-1966; plant process engr & supvr, Eng Serv Div, E I DuPont de Nemours & Co, 1950-1959. **Memberships:** Am Inst Chem Eng; Sigma Xi. **Research Statement & Publications:** Process engineering and research management in chemical and petroleum industries. **Mailing Address:** 96 Silverwood Dr, Lafayette, CA 94549. **E-Mail:** dslaity@attbi.com

LAITY, JOHN LAWRENCE, INDUSTRIAL CHEMISTRY, PETROLEUM CHEMISTRY. **Personal Data:** b Helena, Mont, February 23, 1942; m 1964, c 2. **Education:** Stanford Univ, BS, 1964; Univ Wash, PhD (chem), 1968. **Professional Experience:** CHEMIST & SUPVR, SHELL OIL CO, 1968-. **Memberships:** Am Chem Soc. **Research Statement & Publications:** Photochemical smog; automotive and engine research; combustion; gasoline and oil additives; compositions of fuels and solvents; exhaust emissions; catalysts; atmospheric reactions; air and water pollution; polymer chemistry. **Mailing Address:** 14207 Withersdale, Houston, TX 77077.

LAJTAI, EMERY ZOLTAN, GEOLOGY. **Personal Data:** b Hungary, October 28, 1934; Canadian citizen; m 1959. **Education:** Univ Toronto, BASc, 1950, MASc, 1961, PhD (Pleistocene geol), 1966. **Professional Experience:** PROF EMER CIVIL ENG, UNIV MAN, as of 2005; prof, Dept Civil & Geol Eng, Univ Man, as of 1999; prof geol, Univ Nb, beginning 1977; Nat Res Coun Can res grants, 1971-1977; assoc prof eng geol & rock mech, Univ NB, 1970-1977; govt can, Geol Surv grants, 1967-1968; asst prof, Univ NB, 1967-1970; Nat Res Coun Can res grants, 1966-1968; vis lectr eng geol, Univ NB, 1965-1967; eng geologist, H G Acres & Co Ltd, Ont, 1963-1965; soils engr, Subway Construct Br, Toronto Transit Comn, 1961-1963. **Memberships:** Can Geotech Soc; Can Rock Mech Group. **Research Statement & Publications:** Brittle fracture of rocks under compressive loading with application in structural and engineering geology. **Mailing Address:** Dept Civil & Geol Eng, Univ Man, 411 Eng Bldg, Winnipeg, MB R3T 5V6, Can. **Fax:** 204-474-7514. **E-Mail:** lajtai@cc.umanitoba.ca

LAJTHA, ABEL, BIOCHEMISTRY, TOXICOLOGY. **Personal Data:** b Budapest, Hungary, September 22, 1922; m 1953, Marie; c Terry & Kate. **Education:** Eotvos Lorand Univ, Budapest, PhD (chem), 1945. **Honorary Degrees:** Dr, Univ Padua, Italy. **Honors & Awards:** Mem of the Hungarian acad of sci; Slovenian acad of sci & the armenian acad of sci. **Professional Experience:** PROF EXP PSYCHIAT, SCH MED, NY UNIV, 1971-; DIR, NY STATE RES INST NEUROCHEM, 1966-; prin res scientist, Sch Med, NY Univ, 1962-1966; assoc res scientist, NY State Psychiat Inst, 1957-1962; asst prof, Col Physicians & Surgeons, Columbia Univ, 1956-1969; sr res scientist, NY State Psychiat Inst, 1950-1957; asst prof, Inst Muscle Res, Mass, 1949-1950; res fel, Royal Inst Gt Brit, 1948-1949; fel, Zoology Sta, Italy, 1947-1948; asst prof biochem, Eotvos Lorand Univ, 1945-1947; pres, Am Soc Neurochem & Int Soc Neurochem. **Memberships:** Int Brain Res Orgn; Am Soc Biol Chemists; Am Acad Neurol; Am Col Neuropsychopharmacol; Int Soc Neurochem; Am Chem Soc. **Research Statement & Publications:** Mechnisms of reward and congnitive effects of drugs of abuse Neurochemistry; amino acid and protein metabolism of the brain and the brain barrier system. **Mailing Address:** Ctr Neurochem, NS Kline Inst, 140 Old Orangeburg Rd, Orangeburg, NY 10962. **Fax:** 845-398-5531.

LAJTHA, KATE, BIOGEOCHEMISTRY, ENVIRONMENTAL PHYSIOLOGY. **Personal Data:** b New York, NY, July 16, 1957; m 1987, Sherman. **Education:** Harvard Univ, AB, 1979; Duke Univ, PhD (bot), 1986. **Honors & Awards:** Murray Buell Award, Ecol Soc Am, 1986. **Professional Experience:** INTERIM DIR, ENIVRON SCI PROG, ORE STATE UNIV, 2002-; PROF, DEPT BOT PLANT PATH, ORE STATE UNIV, 2000-; from asst prof to assoc prof, dept biol, Boston Univ, 1987-1995. **Memberships:** Ecol Soc Am; Am Inst Biol Sci; AAAS. **Research Statement & Publications:** Environmental biogeochemistry; nitrogen saturation in coastal ecosystems; trace metal geochemistry in the Danube Delta. **Mailing Address:** Dept Bot & Plant Path, Ore State Univ, 2082 Cordley Hall, Corvallis, OR 97331-2902. **Fax:** 541-737-3574. **E-Mail:** lajthak@Sci.oregonstate.edu

LAKATOS, ANDRAS IMRE, THIN FILM DEVICES, LIQUID CRYSTAL DISPLAYS. **Personal Data:** b Budapest, Hungary, August 23, 1937; m 1972, c 1. **Education:** Alfred Univ, BS, 1962, MS, 1963; Cornell Univ, PhD (appl physics), 1967. **Professional Experience:** MGR, JOSEPH C WILSON CTR RES & TECHNOL XEROX CORP, as of 2000; MGR THIN FILM DEVICE AREA, WEBSTER RES CTR, XEROX INC, 1978-; scientist photoelec properties displays, 1966-1978. **Memberships:** Sr mem Inst Elec & Electronics Engrs; fel Soc Info Display; Am Phys Soc; Soc Photog Sci & Eng. **Research Statement & Publications:** Development of thin film transistors for the addressing of one and two dimensional marking or display arrays. **Mailing Address:** Xerox Corp, 800 Phillips Rd, Webster, NY 14580. **Fax:** 716-422-8548.

LAKATTA, EDWARD G, INTERN MED, CARDIOL, PHYSIOL. **Personal Data:** b Scranton, Pa, May 1944; m 1968, Loretta; c Edward Alexander, Christiana & Lucas. **Education:** Univ Scranton, BS, 1966; Georgetown Univ, MD, 1970. **Honorary Degrees:** Dr Honoris Causa, Univ D'Auvergne, France. **Honors & Awards:** Georgtown Hosp Spec Awd in Med; Mosby Scholarship Bk Awd; Eli Lilly Fellow in Med Sci, Am Coll of Physicians, 1975; Public Health Serv Commendation Medal, 1982, 1990; Elected Fellow, Cardiovasc Sec, Am Physiol Soc; Elected Fellow, Am Soc Clin Invest; Elected Fellow, Internation Soc Heart Res; Nat Inst Health Dir Awd, 1985, 1996; Paul Dudley White Awd in Cardiol, 1992; Allied Signal 1993 Achievement Awd in Aging; Hon Prof, Dept of Biol, Beijing Univ, 1994; Member, Asn Am Phys; Chair, Gordon Conference on Mech of Cardiac Regul, 1994; Chair, Sci Program Committee, Internation Soc Heart Res World Congress, 1998, 2004; Novartis Prize for Gerontol Res, 1999; Distinguished Serv Medal, Public Health Serv, Nat Inst Health, Nat Inst Aging, 2000; Irving Wright Awd of Distinction, Am Fed for Aging Res, 2000; Inaugural Fellow, Counc on Basic Cardiovasc Sci, Am Heart Asn, 2001; Elected Fellow, Am Heart Asn, 2001; Frank J O'Hara Alumni Awd, Univ of Scranton, 2001; Elected Fellow, Int Acad Cardiovasc Sci, 2002; Schober Awd, Universitaet Halle Wittenberg, 2003. **Professional Experience:** SR INVESTR CHIEF, CARDIAC FUNCTION SECT, GERONT RES CTR, NIH; SR INVESTR CHIEF, LAB CARDIOVASC SCI, GERONT RES CTR, NIH; prof physiol, Univ Md Sch Med, Baltimore, Md; prof med, Johns Hopkins Sch Med, Baltimore, Md. **Memberships:** Am Physiol Soc; Am Heart Asn; Am Soc Clin Invest; Biophys Soc; Internation Soc Heart Res; Physiol Soc; Asn Am Phys; Heart Fail Soc Am. **Research Statement & Publications:** The overall goals of the Laboratory of Cardiovascular Sciences that Dr. Lakatta directs are (1) to identify age-associated changes that occur within the cardiovascular system and to determine the mechanisms fo-r these changes; (2) to study myocardial structure and function and to determine how age interacts with chronic disease states to alter function; (3) to study basic mechanisms in excitation-contraction coupling and how these are modulated by surface receptor signaling pathways in cardiac muscle; (4) to determine mechanisms of normal and abnormal pacemaker function and arrhythmias; (5) to discover mechanisms of stem cell committment to the cardiovascular lineage and the steps that govern the development of cardiac cells; (6) to determine mechanisms that govern neuro-hormonal behavioral aspects of hypertension; (7) to determine mechanisms of normal and abnormal function of vascular smooth muscle and endothelial cells; and (8) to establish the potentials and limitations of new therapeutic approaches such as gene transfer techniques and stem cell therapies. Dr. Lakatta has authored over 270 original publications in top, peer reviewed cardiovascular journals, written over 180 invited reviews/book chapters and delivered over 320 invited lectures. **Mailing Address:** Lab Cardiovasc Sci, Geront Res Ctr, Nat Inst Health, Rm 3-B-04, 5600 Nathan Shock Dr, Baltimore, MD 21224-6825. **Fax:** 410-558-8150. **E-Mail:** lakattae@grc.nia.nih.gov

LAKE, BRUCE M, OCEAN REMOTE SENSING. **Personal Data:** b November 22, 1941. **Education:** Princeton Univ, BSE, 1963; Calif Inst Technol, MS, 1964, PhD (aeronaut), 1969. **Professional Experience:** MGR COMPUT PHYSICS BUS, TRW SPACE & TECHNOL GROUP, 1996-; Mem, Naval Studies Bd Boundary Layer Dynamics Panel, 1992-1995; mgr, Ocean Technol Dept, 1981-1996; Technol staff, Fluid Mechs Dept, 1969-1981. **Memberships:** Nat Acad Eng; Am Phys Soc; Sigma Xi. **Research Statement & Publications:** Surface-wave hydrodynamics and non-acoustic anti-submarine warfare; nonlinear hydrodynamics and ocean remote sensing; wave stability, dynamics and radar scattering; author or coauthor of over 35 articles. **Mailing Address:** Dept Ocean Technol/Sensors Lasers & Res Ctr, TRW Space & Technol Div One Space Park R1/1008B, Redondo Beach, CA 90278. **Fax:** 310-814-2359. **E-Mail:** blake@amelia.sp.trw.com

LAKE, CHARLES RAYMOND, PSYCHOPHARMACOLOGY. **Personal Data:** b Nashville, Tenn, July 6, 1943; m 1967, c 2. **Education:** Tulane Univ, BS, 1965, MS, 1966; Duke Univ, PhD (physiol & pharmacol), 1971, MD, 1972. **Professional Experience:** Psychiat consult, Nat Naval Med Ctr, Bethesda, Md, 1980-; PROF PHARMACOL & PROF PSYCHIAT, UNIFORMED SERV UNIV HEALTH SCI, 1979-; attend physician, sect Exp therapeut, NIMH, 1978-1980; clin assoc, Lab Clin Sci, 1975-1977; res assoc, Duke Univ Med Ctr, 1974-1975; resident psychiat, Duke Univ Med Ctr, 1972-1974. **Memberships:** Am Soc Pharmacol & Exp Therapeut; Soc Biol Psychiat; Am Soc Neurochem; Am Col Neuropsychopharmacol; Int Soc Hypertension. **Research Statement & Publications:** Biogenic amine metabolism as related to neuropsychiatric disease and blood pressure regulation; endorphins and neuropsychiatric disorders; endogenous opioid and catecholamine interrelationships. **Mailing Address:** Univ Health Sci, 4301 Jones Bridge Rd, Bethesda, MD 20814-4799.

LAKE, DAVID ALLEN, PHYSICAL THERAPY, HEALTH PROFESSIONS EDUCATION. **Personal Data:** b Ypsilanti, Mich, February 10, 1951. **Education:** Univ Calif, Irvine, BS, 1972; Ind State Univ, MS, 1975; Tex Tech Sch Med, PhD (physiol-neurosci), 1978. **Professional Experience:** PROF & DEPT HEAD PHYS THER, ARMSTRONG ATLANTIC STATE UNIV, 1994-; assoc prof & dept head, Northeastern Univ, 1988-1994; asst prof phys ther, Northeastern Univ, 1985-1988; Vis prof, St George Sch Med, 1981-1982; asst prof biol, Kean Col, NJ, 1980-1985; actg asst prof zool, NC State Univ, 1978-1980; res assoc, Univ Mich, 1972-1973. **Memberships:** Am Physiol Soc; Am Phys Ther Asn; Sigma Xi; Fedn Am Socs Exp Biol; Am Col Sports Med. **Research Statement & Publications:** Innovative teaching methodologies including cooperative learning, problem-based learning and other active learning metholdologies; volunteer programs for the elderly and teaching methods in geriatrics. **Mailing Address:** Dept Phys Ther, Armstrong Atlantic State Univ, 11935 Abercorn St, Savannah, GA 31419. **Fax:** 912-921-5838. **E-Mail:** lakedavi@mail.armstrong.edu

LAKE, GEORGE RUSSELL, DYNAMICS OF GALAXIES, COSMOLOGY. **Personal Data:** b Washington, DC, June 12, 1953; c Astrid & Caitlin. **Education:** Haverford Col, BA, 1975; Princeton Univ, MA, 1977, PhD (physics), 1980. **Honors & Awards:** Dudley Prize. **Professional Experience:** PROF, UNIV WASH, 1986-; mem tech staff, Bell Labs, 1981-1986; Fel, Univ Calif, Berkeley, 1979-1980; Fel, Churchill Col, Cambridge, 1980-1981; Proj scientist, NASA. **Research Statement & Publications:** Dynamics of galaxies, galaxy formation and cosmology; low mass stars; search for extraterrestrial intelligence. **Mailing Address:** Dept Astron, Univ Wash, FM 20, Seattle, WA 98195. **Fax:** 206-685-0403. **E-Mail:** lake@astro.washington.edu

LAKE, JAMES ALBERT, MOLECULAR & CELL BIOLOGY. **Personal Data:** b Nebr, m 1967, c 2. **Education:** Univ Colo, BA, 1963; Univ Wis, Madison, PhD (physics), 1967. **Honors & Awards:** Irma T Hirschl Found Award, 1974; Burton Award, Electron Micros Soc Am, 1975. **Professional Experience:** Fel, Churchill Col, Cambridge, UK, 1983; PROF MOLECULAR CELL & DEVELOP BIOL, UNIV CALIF, LOS ANGELES, 1976-; from asst prof to assoc prof cell biol, Med Sch, NY Univ, 1972-1976; asst prof cell biol, Rockefeller Univ, 1970-1972; res fel, Harvard Univ, 1969-1970; NIH fel molecular biol, Mass Inst Technol, 1967-1968 & Children's Cancer Res Found, Mass, 1968-1970; Fel physics, Univ Wis, 1967. **Memberships:** Fel AAAS; Fel Linnean Soc London: Fel Am Academy Microbiology. **Research Statement & Publications:** Molecular evolution and molecular structure of biological molecules; ribosome function and structure; protein synthesis. **Mailing Address:** Dept Molecular Cell & Develop Biol, Univ Calif, 242 MBI, 242 Boyer Hall, Los Angeles, CA 90095. **Fax:** 310-206-7286. **E-Mail:** lake@mbi.ucla.edu

LAKE, JAMES ALLAN, NUCLEAR POWER. **Education:** Ga Inst Tech, BS, MS, PhD. **Professional Experience:** ASSOC LAB DIR, NUCLEAR & ENERGY SYSTS ENG, IDAHO NAT ENG & ENVIRON LAB, as of 2006. **Memberships:** Am Nuclear Soc. **Mailing Address:** Idaho Nat Lab, PO Box 1625, Idaho Falls, ID 83415. **Fax:** 208-526-0884.

LAKE, LARRY WAYNE, PETROLEUM ENGINEERING. **Personal Data:** b Del Norte, Colo, January 31, 1946; m 1975, Carole; c Lelie S & Jeffrey W. **Education:** Ariz State Univ, BS, 1967; Rice Univ, PhD, 1973. **Honors & Awards:** Reservoir Engr Award, Soc Petrol Engrs. **Professional Experience:** W A TEX MONCRIEF CENTENNIAL CHAIR, UNIV TEX, AUSTIN, 1998-; PROF PETROL & GEOSYSTEMS ENG, COL ENG, UNIV TEX, AUSTIN, 1978-; sr res eng, Shell Develop Co, Houston, 1973-1978; Prog engr, Motorola Co, Phoenix, 1968-1970; consult enhanced oil recovery. **Memberships:** Nat Acad Eng; Soc Mining Engrs; Soc Petrol Engrs; Am Inst Chem Engrs. **Research Statement & Publications:** Petroleum engineering; enhanced oil recovery. **Mailing Address:** Dept Petrol & Geosystems Eng, Col Eng, Univ Tex, PO Box C0300, Austin, TX 78712. **Fax:** 512-471-9605. **E-Mail:** larry_lake@mail.utexas.edu

LAKE, ROBERT D, POLYMER CHEMISTRY, UNSATURATED POLYESTER & VINYLESTER RESINS. **Personal Data:** b Lansing, Mich, September 7, 1930; m 1964, Angeline M Fricioni; c Carolyn A & Jeffrey R. **Education:** Mich State Univ, BS, 1952; Ind Univ, PhD (org chem), 1956. **Professional Experience:** RETIRED; consult, 1990-1996; mgr, flame retardant resins, 1989-1990; develop group mgr, Reichold Chem, 1980-1989; proj tech coordr, Res Dept, 1977-1980; sr scientist, Res Dept, 1972-1977; group mgr explor res, Koppers Co, Inc, 1966-1972; scientist, Koppers Co, Inc, 1960-1966; fel chem res, Mellon Inst, 1957-1960; Am Petrol Inst fel, Northwestern Univ, 1956-1957. **Research Statement & Publications:** Synthesis and properties of vinyl and condensation polymers; preparation and properties of unsaturated polyester resins; smoke and flammability behavior of polymers; development of thermoset polyester molding compounds; flame retardant and corrosion resistant polyester and vinylester resins. **Mailing Address:** 215 Thornwood Ct, Coraopolis, PA 15108. **E-Mail:** rdaml@usaor.net

LAKEIN, RICHARD BRUCE, SUPERCOMPUTING, PARALLEL COMPUTING. **Personal Data:** b Baltimore, Md, March 5, 1941; m 1964, c 2. **Education:** Yale Univ, BA, 1962; Univ Md, MA, 1964, PhD (math), 1967. **Professional Experience:** COMPUT SYSTS ANALYST, NAT SECURITY AGENCY, 1982-; mathematician, Nat Security Agency, 1975-1982; asst prof math, State Univ NY, Buffalo, 1968-1974; lectr math, Univ Md, 1967-1968.

Memberships: Am Math Soc; Asn Comput Mach. **Research Statement & Publications:** Parallel computing; number theory. **Mailing Address:** 8711 Bunnell Dr, Potomac, MD 20854-3606.

LAKER, KENNETH R, ELECTRICAL ENGINEERING. **Professional Experience:** ALFRED FITLER MOORE PROF, ELEC ENG, UNIV PA, as of 2006. **Memberships:** Inst Elec & Electronics Engrs. **Mailing Address:** Univ Pa, 200 S 33RD St, Philadelphia, PA 19104-6390. **Fax:** 215-898-0587.

LAKES, RODERIC STEPHEN, LASERS & OPTICS, MECHANICAL ENGINEERING. **Personal Data:** b New York, NY, August 10, 1948; m 1971. **Education:** Rensselaer Polytech Inst, BS, 1969, PhD (physics, biophys), 1975. **Honors & Awards:** Burlington Northern Found Award, 1987. **Professional Experience:** DISTINGUISHED PROF ENG PHYSICS, BIOMED ENG, UNIV WIS, 1998-; prin investr, Study Viscoelastic Elastomers, 1986-1988; vis prof, dept mat, Queen Mary Col, Univ London, 1984; prin investr, proj bone biomech, NIH, 1979-1982; from asst prof to prof, biomedical & med eng, Univ Iowa, 1978-1998; vis asst prof biomed eng, Rensselaer Polytech Inst, 1978; asst prof physics, Tuskegee Inst, 1977-1978; res assoc appl sci, Yale Univ, 1975-1977; NIH fel, Yale Univ, 1975-1977. **Memberships:** Am Phys Soc; Soc Photo Optical Instrumentation Engrs; Sigma Xi; fel Am Soc Mech Engrs; fel AAAS; Soc Rheology; fel Am Inst Med & Bio Eng. **Research Statement & Publications:** Novel structured materials; bone biomechanics and bioelectricity; properties of piezoelectric solids and composite materials; applied optics; holographic interferometry; published over 150 articles and granted four US patents. **Mailing Address:** Dept Biomed Eng, Univ Wis, 541 Eng Res Bldg 1500 Eng Dr, Madison, WI 53706-1687. **Fax:** 608-263-7451. **E-Mail:** lakes@engr.wisc.edu

LAKEY, WILLIAM HALL, GENITO-URINARY SURGERY. **Personal Data:** b Medicine Hat, Alta, November 12, 1927; m 1957, c 4. **Education:** Univ Alta, BSc, 1949, MD, 1953; FRCPS(C), 1960. **Professional Experience:** RETIRED; dir, Div Urol, Univ Hosp, Edmonton, 1971-1997; prof surg, Fac Med, Univ Alta, 1960-1997. **Memberships:** Fel Am Col Surg; Am Urol Asn; Can Urol Asn; Can Acad Genito-Urinary Surg; Am Asn Genito-Urinary Surg. **Research Statement & Publications:** Renal transplantation; renal hypertension and use of diagnostic tests; kidney preservation. **Mailing Address:** Dept Surg-Urol, Univ Alta, Edmonton, AB T6G 2B7, Can.

LAKHTAKIA, AKHLESH, T-MATRIX WAVE SCATTERING & ELECTRODYNAMICS OF CHIRAL MATERIALS & BIANISOTROPIC MATERIALS, SCULPTURED THIN FILMS & PHOTONIC BANDGAP MATERIALS. **Personal Data:** b Lucknow, India, July 1, 1957; m 1982, Mercedes; c Natalya S. **Education:** Banaras Hindu Univ, India, BTech, 1979; Univ Utah, MS, 1981 & PhD (elec eng), 1983. **Honors & Awards:** Faculty Scholar Medal, Penn State, 2004; Outstanding eng teaching Award, Penn State, 2004; Outstanding eng res Award, Penn State, 1996; Certificate of Appreciation, IEEE EMC soc, 1994; Novel eng Application Award (ANNIE' 94), 1994. **Professional Experience:** DISTINGUISHED PROF, PA STATE UNIV, 2003-; visiting prof physics, Imperial College, London, 2004; prof, PA State Univ 1997-2003, Scottish Amicable lectr, Univ Glasgow, 1995; traveling lectr, Int Comn Optics, 1992; int lectr, Optical Soc Am, 1992, 2003; assoc prof, Pa State Univ, 1991-1997; visiting prof physics, Buenos Aires, 1990, 1992, ed-in-chief, Speculations in Sci & Technol, 1994-1996; asst prof, PA State Univ, 1984-1991; scholar, PA State Univ, 1983-1984; res asst, Univ Utah, 1979-1983. **Memberships:** fel Optical Soc Am; fel Int Soc Optical Eng; fel Inst Physics. **Research Statement & Publications:** Author and co-author of over 695 papers and conference publications on wave-material interaction, electromagnetics, chiral media, complex media fractals, chaos, bioelectromagnetics; materials science; sculptured thin films; nanotechnology; fractals; chaos; author/editor of 11 research books. **Mailing Address:** 212 EES Bldg, Univ Park, PA 16802. **Fax:** 814-865-9974. **E-Mail:** axl4@psu.edu

LAKIN, JAMES D, ALLERGIES, CLINICAL IMMUNOLOGY. **Personal Data:** b Harvey, Ill, October 4, 1945; m 1972, Sally; c Margaret K & Matthew A. **Education:** Northwestern Univ, BSc, 1968, PhD, 1968, MD, 1969. **Professional Experience:** MANAGING PARTNER, MINN ALLERGY & ASTHMA CONSULT LLP, as of 2004; LAB DIR, OXBORO CLIN, 1993-; CHMN DEPT ALLERGY & IMMUNOL, OXBORO CLIN, 1990-; chmn, dept allergy, 1989; diving med officer, Nat Oceanic & Atmospheric Admin, 1988-; dir, Okla Med Res Found, 1982-; dir, Okla Allergy Clin, 1980-; dir, Frontiers Sci, 1979-1981; mem, Res Comt, Presby Hosp, Oklahoma City, 1977; mem, Comt Allergy & Clin Immunol, Am Col Chest Physicians, 1977; dir, Adolescent Allergy Clin, Children's Mem Hosp, 1976-; from clin asst prof to clin prof internal med & pediat, Univ Okla Health Sci Ctr, Oklahoma City, 1976-1989; asst prof, Georgetown Univ Med Ctr, 1975-1976; pvt pract, Okla Allergy Clin, 1975-1989; lt commander, Med Corps, Naval Med Res Inst, USNR, 1974-1976; dir allergy-res training, Allergy Res Lab, Nat Naval Med Ctr, 1974-1976; dep dir, Clin Immunol Fiv, Naval Med Res Inst, Nat Naval Med Ctr, 1974-1975; staff investr & lab dir, Allergy Res Lab, Nat Naval Med Ctr, 1974; fel, Allergy Sect, 1973; resident, Dept Internal Med, Univ Mich Med Ctr, 1971-1972; intern, Dept Internal Med, Univ Mich Med Ctr, 1970; Passavant Hosp Sch Nursing, 1966-1968 & Wesley Mem Hosp Sch Nursing, 1966-1968; Instr, Dept Microbiol, NorthwesternUniv Med Sch, 1966-1968; staff mem, Baptist Med Ctr, St Anthony Hosp, Children's Mem Hosp, Univ Hosp, Presby Hosp, Mercy Mem Hosp & Deaconess Hosp, Oklahoma City, Okla; spec consult, Vet Admin Hosp, Oklahoma City, Okla. **Memberships:** Am Asn Immunologists; fel Am Col Physicians; fel Am Col Chest Physicians; AMA; Am Soc Internal Med; Fedn Am Socs Exp Biol; fel Am Acad Allergy & Immunol; Undersea Med Soc. **Research Statement & Publications:** Classification of hypersensitivity reactions; immune response and hypersensitivity reactions. **Mailing Address:** Minn Allergy & Asthma Consult, LLP, 303 E Nicollet Blvd, Ste 362, Burnsville, MN 55337-4559. **Fax:** 952-223-3041. **E-Mail:** jdlakin@minnesotaallergy.com

LAKKARAJU, H S, SURFACE SCIENCE, NONLINEAR OPTICS. **Personal Data:** b Bapatla, India, September 20, 1946; m 1969, c 2. **Education:** Andhra Univ, India, BSc, 1965, MSc, 1967; Fairleigh Dickinson Univ, MS, 1973; State Univ NY, Buffalo, PhD (physics), 1979. **Professional Experience:** PROF PHYSICS, SANJOSE STATE UNIV, 1981-; vis asst prof, Tex A&M Univ, 1979-1981; sr sci asst, Radiosci Div, Nat Phys Lab, 1970-1971. **Memberships:** Am Phys Soc; Optical Soc Am; Int Soc Optical Eng. **Research Statement & Publications:** Laser spectroscopy and nonlinear optics, and the applications of these in the surface science; condensed matter physics and biophysics. **Mailing Address:** Dept Physics, San Jose State Univ, 148 Sci Bldg, San Jose, CA 95192. **E-Mail:** slakkara@email.sjsu.edu

LAKOSKI, JOAN MARIE, NEUROPHARMACOLOGY, NEUROENDOCRINOLOGY. **Personal Data:** b Poughkeepsie, NY, March 28, 1953; c 2. **Education:** Mount Holyoke Col, BA, 1975; Univ Iowa, PhD (pharmacol), 1981. **Professional Experience:** ASST VICE CHANCELLOR, OFF ACAD CAREER DEVELOP, UNIV PITTSBURGH HEALTH SCI, as of 2004; PROF, DEPT PHARMACOL, SCH MED, UNIV PITTSBURGH, as of 2004; chmn, Com Women Aspet, 2002-2005; interim chmn, 2000-2001; mem, Ethics Adv Com, Endocrinology Soc, 1998-; mem Biochem endocrinol studies sec, NIH, 1998-2002; prof pharmacol, Pa State Univ Col Med, beginning 1993; mem, Young Scientists Bd, Inst Develop Neuroscience & Aging 1992-; asst prof human biol chem & genetics, Univ Tex Med Br, Galveston, 1992-1993; co-chmn, Symp Serotonin & Drugs Abuse, 1992; chmn, Preprof Subcomt Educ, Am Soc Pharmacol & Exp Therapeut, 1991-1993; mem, Coord Ctr Aging Adv Comt, Univ Tex Med Br, 1990-1993; chmn, Comt Res, Univ Tex Med Br, 1990-1991; assoc ed, Molecular & Cellular Neuroscience, beginning 1989; res career develop award, Nat Inst Aging, 1989-1994; mem, Teaching & Eval Mat Subcomt, Am Soc Pharmacol & Exp Therapeut, 1989-1991; adj mem, Marine Biomed Inst, 1988-1993; mem, Initial Rev Group Pharmacol Spec Rev Comt, Nat Inst Drug Abuse, 1987; asst prof pharmacol, Univ Tex Med Br, Galveston, 1984-1992; fel neuropharmacol, Yale Univ Sch Med, 1981-1984; post doc fel, Yale Univ Sch Med, 1981-1984; biologist, NIH, 1975-1977. **Memberships:** Soc Neuroscience; Endocrine Soc; Sigma Xi; Serotonin Club; AAAS; Int Soc Develop Neuroscience; Int So c Neuroendocrinol; Am Soc Pharmacol & Exp Ther. **Research Statement & Publications:** Neuropharmacology of age-related changes in central nervous system function mediating serotonin neural systems including modulation by steroid hormones estrogen and corticosterone. **Mailing Address:** Dept Pharmacol, Univ Pittsburgh, 3550 Terrace St PO Box 850 Ste 401 Scaife Hall, Hershey, PA 15261. **Fax:** 717-531-0419. **E-Mail:** jlakoski@hs.pitt.edu

LAKOWICZ, JOSEPH RAYMOND, BIOPHYSICS, BIOCHEMISTRY. **Personal Data:** b Philadelphia, Pa, March 15, 1948; c 2. **Education:** La Salle Col, BA, 1970; Univ Ill, Urbana, MS, 1971, PhD (biochem), 1973. **Professional Experience:** ADJ PROF, ELEC ENG, UNIV MD, 1993-; head, Molecular Graphics Fac, Univ Md Sch Med, 1989-1993; SR STAFF SCIENTIST, MED BIOTECHNOL CTR, UNIV MD, 1988-; DIR BIOCHEM & MOLECULAR BIOL, UNIV MD, 1988; PROF BIOCHEM, SCH MED, UNIV MD, 1984-; assoc prof, Sch Med, Univ MD, 1980-1984; estab investr, Am Heart Asn, 1977; asst prof biochem, Univ Minn, 1975-1980; NATO fel biochem, Oxford Univ, 1973-1974. **Memberships:** AAAS; Am Chem Soc; Biophys Soc; Am Soc Photobiol; Sigma Xi; Am Soc Biol Chemists; Optical Soc Am; Am Phys Soc; Protein Soc. **Research Statement & Publications:** Fluorescence spectroscopy; membrane transport of chlorinated hydrocarbons and carcinogens; rapid relaxationphenomena in biopolymers; frequency-domain fluorometry; energy transfer; molecular dynamics; time-domain fluorometry. **Mailing Address:** Dept Biol Chem, Univ Md Sch Med, 108 N Greene St, Baltimore, MD 21201-1503. **Fax:** 410-705-8408. **E-Mail:** lakowicz@umbi.emd.edu

LAKRITZ, JULIAN, ORGANIC CHEMISTRY. **Personal Data:** b Antwerp, Belg, February 13, 1930; American citizen; c 2. **Education:** NY Univ, BA, 1952; Univ Mich, MS, 1954, PhD (org chem), 1960. **Professional Experience:** VPRES SALES & MKT, ANSCOTT-SIGNAL CHEM CO, 1975-; tech dir, Anscott-signal Chem CO, 1975-1990; dir res & develop, Am Permac Inc, Garden City, NY, 1968-1975; Res chemist, Esso Res & Eng Co, 1958-1968. **Memberships:** Am Chem Soc; Am Asn Textile Chem & Colorists. **Research Statement & Publications:** Chemistry and technology for solvent processing of textiles.

LAKS, DAVID BEJNESH, DEFECT CALCULATIONS IN SOLIDS. **Personal Data:** b Brooklyn, NY, March 31, 1962; m 1984, c 1. **Education:** Columbia Univ, BS, 1983, MS, 1984, PhD (solid state physics), 1990. **Professional Experience:** STAFF MEM, T J WATSON RES CTR, 1992-; fel, Solar Energy Res Inst, 1990-1992. **Memberships:** Am Phys Soc; Mat Res Soc. **Research Statement & Publications:** Theoretical investigations of defects in zinc-selenide and doping problems in wide band-gap semiconductors; semiconductor interface structures; Auger recombination in semiconductors. **Mailing Address:** T J Watson Res Ctr, PO Box 218, Yorktown Heights, NY 10598.

LAKS, PETER EDWARD, WOOD PRESERVATION. **Personal Data:** b Brisbane, Australia, July 15, 1953; Canadian citizen; m 1973, c 3. **Education:** Simon Fraser Univ, BSc, 1976, MSc, 1979; Univ BC, PhD (wood sci), 1984. **Professional Experience:** PROF, SCH FOREST RES & ENVIRON SCI, MICH TECHNOL UNIV, as of 2002; sr res sci, Mich Technol Univ, beginning 1985; adj prof, 1985-. **Memberships:** Am Chem Soc; Am Soc Pharmacog. **Mailing Address:** Sch Forestry & Wood Prod, Mich Technol Univ, 120 Noblet Bldg, Houghton, MI 49931. **E-Mail:** plaks@mtu.edu

LAKSHMAN, M RAJ, LIPIDS, ALCOHOLISM. **Personal Data:** b Calcutta, India, August 3, 1938; American citizen; m 1966, Malathi; c Vijay & Madhu. **Education:** Poona Univ, BS, 1958, MS, 1959; Inst Sci, PhD (biochem), 1966. **Professional Experience:** RES PROF, GEORGE WASH UNIV, 1990-; assoc res prof, Dept Vet Affairs Med Ctr, Wash, DC, 1983-1990; mem, Exp Adv Group Nutrit, Food & Drug Admin, 1983; CHIEF LIPID RES, DEPT VET AFFAIRS MED CTR, Wash, DC, 1980-; res chemist, Nat Inst Alcohol Abuse & Alcoholism, 1978-1980; res prof, Am Univ, 1976; vis scientist, NIMH, 1974-1978; proj assoc, Vet Admin Med Ctr, Wis, 1971-1974; sr res adv, Rockefeller Found, Bangkok, 1967-1971; Nat Res Coun fel, Dept Nat Health & Welfare, Can, 1966-1967. **Memberships:** Am Soc Biol Chem; Res Soc Alcoholism; Am Inst Nutrit; Int Soc Biochem Res Alcoholism. **Research Statement & Publications:** Lipid and lipoprotein regulation, alcoholic hyperlipidemia, hormonal control, regulation of alcohol dehydrogenase, mechanism of absorption, action of tetrachloro-dibenzo p-dioxin, cholesterol deposition and removal, obesity. **Mailing Address:** Dept Vet Affairs Med Ctr, Lipid Res Lab, 151T50 Irving St, Washington, DC 20422.

LAKSHMANAN, NEELA, MATHEMATICS. **Education:** Univ Buffalo, MA, 1984, PhD 1987. **Professional Experience:** FAC, DEPT MATHS, UNIV SCRANTON, as of 1999. **Mailing Address:** Math Dept, Univ Scranton, Scranton, PA 18510-4501. **Fax:** 570-941-6369.

LAKSHMANAN, P R, ORGANIC POLYMER CHEMISTRY. **Personal Data:** b Jamshedpur, Bihar, India, April 28, 1939. **Education:** Univ Calcutta, BS, 1958; Univ Bombay, BS, 1961; NDak State Univ, MS, 1965, PhD (polymers & coating), 1966. **Professional Experience:** RETIRED; tech dir, Baychem Int, Inc, beginning 1983; dir new prods res & develop, 1980-1985; res chemist plastics & sr res chemist coatings & adhesives, Gulf Oil Chem Co, 1966-; sect supvr, 1966-1980. **Memberships:** Am Chem Soc; Oil & Color Chemists Asn; Soc Plastic Engrs; Am Inst Chemists. **Research Statement & Publications:** Relationship between structure and performance of adhesives and coatings; mechanism of adhesion, polymer blends and alloys. **Mailing Address:** Baychem Int Inc, Ste 400 5625 FM 1960 W, Houston, TX 77069-4211.

LAKSHMANAN, V S, COMPUTER SCIENCE. **Education:** AC Col Eng & Technol, India, BEng, 1981; Indian Inst Sci, India, MEng, 1983, PhD (comput sci), 1987. **Professional Experience:** PROF, DEPT COMPUT SCI, UNIV BC, CAN, as of 2006. **Mailing Address:** Dept Comput Sci Univ BC, 2366 Main Mall, Vancouver, BC V6T 1Z4, Can. **Fax:** 604-822-5485. **E-Mail:** laks@cs.ubc.ca

LAKSHMANAN, VAIKUNTAM IYER, METALLURGICAL CHEMISTRY, HYDROMETALLURGY. **Personal Data:** b Pazhaya Kayal, Madras, India, July 10, 1940; m 1968. **Education:** Univ Bombay, BSc, 1961, MSc, 1963, PhD (chem), 1968. **Honors & Awards:** Bosworth Smith Inst Award, Brit Inst Mining & Metall, 1974; Flavelle Award Technol Develop &

Transfer; Sherritt Hydrometall Award; Standelman Award Tech Excellence. **Professional Experience:** VCHMN & CHEIF EXEC OFFICER, PROCESS RES ORTECH INC, as of 2005; prog dir, Environ & Mat Processing, Ortech Corp, as of 2002; mgr mineral resources, Ortech Int, beginning 1981; res chemist, Eldorado Nuclear Ltd, 1977-1981; assoc scientist extractive metall sect, Noranda Res Ctr, Montreal, 1976-1977; fel metall chem sect, Canmet, Dept Energy, Mines & Resources, Ottawa, 1975-1976; lectr, Univ Birmingham, 1972-1975; res fel minerals eng, Univ Birmingham, 1969-1972; chief chemist, H&R Johnson India (PVT) Ltd, 1968-1969; adj prof, Dept Metall & Mat Sci, Univ Toronto; assoc, Dept Chem Eng. **Memberships:** Metall Soc; Royal Inst Chem; Brit Inst Mining & Metall; Soc Chem Indust; Can Inst Mining & Metall; Am Soc Mining Eng. **Research Statement & Publications:** Solution chemistry; solution treatment precipitation; solvent extraction; ion exchange; treatment of effluents; radiotracer studies; precious and rad metals recovery; technology development and transfer in the areas of hydrometallurgy, environmental and materials processing. **Mailing Address:** Process Res Ortech Inc, 2350 Sheridan Park Dr, Mississauga, ON L5K 2T4, Can. **Fax:** 905-823-9537. **E-Mail:** lsequeria@processtech.com

LAKSHMIKANTHAM, VANGIPURAM, MATHEMATICS. **Personal Data:** b Hyderabad, India, August 8, 1926; American citizen; m 1942, Sarojamma; c Sreekantham, Neerada & Niropama. **Education:** Osmania Univ, India, PhD (math), 1959. **Honors & Awards:** Ashbell Smith Res Prof; Distinguished Res Award, 1981. **Professional Experience:** Prof and Head, math sci, FLA inst technol, 1989-; PROF APPL MATH, UNIV TEX, ARLINGTON, 1989-; Ashbel Smith prof, Univ Tex, Arlington, 1986; DIR, DIV INTERDISCIPLINARY SCI, 1983-; prof math & chmn dept, Univ Tex, Arlington, 1973-1986; prof & chmn dept, Univ RI, 1966-1973; prof & chmn dept, Marathwada Univ, India, 1964-1966; assoc prof, Univ Alta, 1963-1964; vis mem, Res Inst Advan Study, 1962-1963; vis mem, Math Res Ctr, Univ Wis-Madison, 1961-1962; Res assoc math, Univ Calif, Los Angeles, 1960-1961; assoc ed, J Math Anal & Applns, Applicable Analysis, Appl Math & Comput, J Math & Phys Sci, J Differential Equations & Dynamic Systs, J Nonlinear Differential Equations; Ed, Nonlinear Analysis, Nonlineal World & Stochastic Analysis & Appl. **Memberships:** Am Math Soc; Indian Math Soc; Indian Nat Acad Sci; Soc Indust & Appl Math; Int Nat Fedn Nonlinear Analysts(pres). **Research Statement & Publications:** Differential inequalities; theory and applications, including stability theory by Liapunov's second method; nonlinear analysis. **Mailing Address:** Dept Appl Math Fla Inst Technol, 150 W University Blvd, Melbourne, FL 32901. **Fax:** 321-984-8461. **E-Mail:** lakshmik@fit.edu

LAKSHMINARAYAN, S, RESPIRATORY DISEASES. **Personal Data:** b Madras, India, July 2, 1943; American citizen. **Education:** India Inst Med Sci, New Delhi, MBBS, 1964; Royal Col Physicians, London, MRCP, 1969, FRCP, 1983. **Professional Experience:** Chmn, Intensive Care Comt, Vet Admin Med Ctr, Seattle, beginning 1988; Royal Postgrad Med Sch & Hammersmith Hosp, London, 1986; vis prof, St Johns Med Col, Bangalore, India, 1985-1986; PROF MED, SCH MED, UNIV WASH, 1982-; MED DIR RESPIRATORY THER UNIT & PULMONARY FUNCTION LAB & CHIEF PULMONARY CRITICAL CARE MED SECT, VET ADMIN MED CTR, SEATTLE, WASH, 1975-; assoc prof, Vet Admin Med Ctr, Seattle, Wash, 1975-1982; from instr to asst prof med, Pulmonary Div, Univ Colo Med Ctr, 1972-1975; Brompton Hosp, 1970-1971 & Univ Colo Med Ctr, 1971-1972; fel, Pulmonary Div, Westminster Hosp, London, 1969-1970. **Memberships:** Am Col Chest Physicians; Am Thoracic Soc; Am Fedn Clin Res; Am Heart Asn; Am Physiol Soc; NY Acad Sci. **Research Statement & Publications:** Pulmonary medicine; respiratory therapy. **Mailing Address:** Vet Affairs Puget Sound Health Care Syst, 1660 S Columbian Way, Seattle, WA 98108. **Fax:** 206-764-2659.

LAKSHMINARAYANA, J S S, PHYCOLOGY, WATER POLLUTION. **Personal Data:** b Penumantra, India, September 22, 1931; m 1960, c 2. **Education:** Andhra Univ, India, BSc, 1952; Banaras Hindu Univ, MSc, 1954, PhD (bot), 1960. **Professional Experience:** RETIRED; assoc prof to prof, Dept Biol, Univ Moncton, 1970-1997; fel, Mem Univ Nfld, 1970; lectr, Visvesvaraya Regional Col Eng, India, 1966-1969; Fr Govt fel, ASTEF, Paris, 1965-1966; scientist & head biol, Nat Environ Eng Res Inst, India, 1959-1970; Lectr bot, Banaras Hindu Univ, 1955. **Memberships:** Fel Linnean Soc UK; fel Marine Biol Asn, India. **Research Statement & Publications:** Algology, limnology and oceanography in relation to pollution; coastal zone management; primary productivity in relation to fishery development. **Mailing Address:** 271 Argyle St, Moncton, NB E1C 3V5, Can.

LAKSHMINARAYANAN, KRISHNAIYER, BIOCHEMISTRY, INDUSTRIAL MICROBIOLOGY. **Personal Data:** b Bikshandarkoil, India, July 5, 1924; m 1960, Kamakshi; c Gayathri & Venkatesh. **Education:** Univ Madras, BSc, 1945, MSc, 1950, PhD (biochem), 1955. **Professional Experience:** PRES, BIO-TECH INC, BENSENVILLE, ILL, 1975-; mgr process develop, Searle Biochem, Div G D Searle & Co, 1971-1975; res & develop, Dawe's Fermentation Prod, Inc, 1971; dir fermentation develop, Dawe's Fermentation Prod, Inc, 1969-1971; sr indust enzymologist, Dawe's Fermentation Prod, Inc, 1967-1969; hon lectr, Univ Western Ont, 1964-1967; proj leader, John Labatt Ltd, 1963-1967; sr res scientist, John Labatt Ltd, 1962-1963; res scientist indust microbiol, John Labatt Ltd, 1961-1962; plant biochemist, Cent Bot Lab, Allahabad, 1960-1961; Sci & Indust Res, Govt India, 1959-1960; Nat Res Coun Can fel, Univ Man, 1956-1958; Imp Chem Industs fel, Nat Inst Sci India, 1955-1956; asst prof microbiol, Birla Col, Pilani, 1952; biochemist, Stanley Hosp, Madras, 1950-1951; Jr chemist, King Inst Prev Med, India, 1945-1947. **Memberships:** Fel Chem Inst Can; fel Royal Inst Chemists. **Research Statement & Publications:** Microbial enzymology; plant biochemistry; toxicology; immunology; chromatography; microtechniques; industrial fermentations; enzyme production; immobilization; enzymes for clinical diagnostics and food applications.

LAKSHMIVARAHAN, SIVARAMAKRISHNAN, COMPUTER SCIENCE. **Personal Data:** b Karaikurichi, India, June 12, 1944; m 1973, Shantha; c Subha & Bharathram. **Education:** Univ Madras, India, BSc, 1964; Indian Inst Sci, Bangalore, BE, 1967, ME, 1969, PhD (algorithms), 1973. **Professional Experience:** George Lynn Cross res prof, Col Eng, 1995; Nat Tsing-Huo Univ, Indian Inst Sch, 1993; Nat Tsing-Huo Univ, Taiwan, 1992; PROF, SCH COMPUT SCI, UNIV OKLA, 1992-; Tech Inst Higher Studies, Mex, 1988, 1990 & 1993; assoc distinguished lectr, Col Eng, 1986-1987; Amoco Prod Res Ctr, Nat Inst Stand & Technol, 1985; prof, Col Eng, 1984-1992; Hallibuurton distinguished lectr, Col Eng, 1984-1986; Amoco Prod Res Ctr, Tulsa, 1983; Univ Laval, Can, 1982; Vis prof, Univ Bonn, 1980 & 1982; assoc prof, Sch Elec Eng & Comput Sci, Univ Okla, 1978-1984; asst prof, Dept Eng & Appl Sci, Yale Univ, New Haven, 1976-1978; vis asst prof, Div Appl Math, Brown Univ, Providence, 1975-1976; lectr & asst prof, Dept Comput Sci, Madras, 1973-1975; proj asst, Sch Automation, 1973; Res asst, Indian Inst Sci, Bangalore, 1969-1973; consult, Amoco Res Ctr, Nat Inst Stand & Technol. **Memberships:** Fel Inst Elec & Electronics Engrs; fell Asn Comput Mach. **Research Statement & Publications:** Author and editor of numerous books; contributed various articles to science journals. **Mailing Address:** Sch Comput Sci, Univ Okla, Norman, OK 73019. **Fax:** 405-325-4044. **E-Mail:** varahan@ou.edu

LAKSO, ALAN NEIL, POMOLOGY, PLANT PHYSIOLOGY. **Personal Data:** b Auburn, Calif, January 3, 1948. **Education:** Univ Calif, Davis, BS, 1970, PhD (plant physiol), 1973. **Honors & Awards:** Gourley Award, Am Soc Hort Sci, 1980. **Professional Experience:** CHMN, DEPT HORT SCI, NY STATE AGR EXP STA, CORNELL UNIV, as of 2002; PROF HORT SCI, NY STATE AGR EXP STA, CORNELL UNIV, 1986-; assoc prof hort, Sci Dept, 1980-1986; asst prof pomol, NY State Agr Exp Sta, Cornell Univ, 1973-1980. **Memberships:** Int Soc Hort Sci; Am Soc Hort Sci; Am Soc Enol & Viticult; Sigma Xi. **Research Statement & Publications:** Environmental physiology and the physiological bases of yield and quality of apples and grapes. **Mailing Address:** Dept Hort Sci, NY State Agr Exp Sta, Cornell Univ, Geneva, NY 14456. **E-Mail:** anl2@cornell.edu

LAL, DEVENDRA, NUCLEAR PHYSICS, GEOCHEMISTRY & GEOPHYSICS. **Personal Data:** b Banaras, India, February 14, 1929; m 1955. **Education:** Banaras Hindu Univ, BSc, 1947, MSc, 1949; Univ Bombay, PhD (physics), 1958. **Honorary Degrees:** DSc, Banaras Hindu Univ, Varanasi, 1981. **Honors & Awards:** Krishnan Medal, Indian Geophys Union, 1965; S S Bhatnagar Award, 1967; Krishnan Medal Lectr, Indian Nat Sci Acad, 1981; Jawaharlal Nehru Award for Phys Sci; Raman Birth Centenary Award, 1996. **Professional Experience:** FEL, PHYS RES LAB, AHMEDABAD, INDIA, 1989-; sr prof, Scripps Inst Oceanog, Univ Calif, San Diego, 1983-1989; mem sci adv comt to Cabinet, Govt India, 1981-1982; dir, Scripps Inst Oceanog, Univ Calif, San Diego, 1972-1987; PROF NUCLEAR PHYSICS, SCRIPPS INST OCEANOG, UNIV CALIF, SAN DIEGO, 1967-; from res fel to sr prof, Tata Inst Fundamental Res, Bombay, India, 1949-1972. **Memberships:** Foreign assoc Nat Acad Sci; fel Indian Acad Sci; fel Indian Nat Sci Acad; assoc mem Royal Astron Soc; fel Royal Soc. **Research Statement & Publications:** Cosmic rays; astrophysics; meteoritics; oceanography; meteorology; hydrology; geophysics; glaciology and geomorphology; published recently 5 books. **Mailing Address:** Scripps Inst Oceanog, UCSD, 9500 Gilman Dr, La Jolla, CA 92093-0244. **Fax:** 858-822-3310. **E-Mail:** dlal@ucsd.edu

LAL, HARBANS, PHARMACOLOGY. **Education:** Univ Kans, MS, 1958; Univ Chicago, PhD (pharmacol), 1962. **Professional Experience:** PROF EMER & CHMN EMER, DEPT PHARMACOL & BIOL SCI, TEX COL OSTEOP MED, UNIV NTEX, 2000-; prof biol sci, Tex Col Osteop Med, Univ NTex, beginning 1980; chmn, dept pharmacol, Univ NTex, beginning 1980; adj prof chem & behav, Tex Christian Univ, beginning 1980; clin psychopharmacologist, RI Inst Ment Health, 1978-1980; dir psychopharmacol, Inst Behav Med, 1977-1979; res & develop scientist, Janssen Pharmaceut, 1973-1974; prof psychol, Univ RI, 1970-1980; res assoc, RI Inst Ment Health, 1969-1978; from assoc prof to prof pharmacol & toxicol, Univ RI, 1967-1980; assoc prof pharmacol & toxicol, Univ Kans, 1965-1967; res assoc neurol & psychiat, Med Sch Northwestern Univ, 1962-1965; res pharmacologist, IIT Res Inst, 1961-1965; res fel, Univ Chicago, 1958-1961; teaching asst & lectr, Univ Chicago; grants, var corp & orgn; nat grant rev panels ad hoc appts, NSF, Nat Inst Drug AbuseStudy Sect, Harry Frank Guggenheim Found, Human Embryol & Develop Study Sect; consult, Boehinger Pharmaceut Co, Burroughs Welcome Pharmaceut Co, Hoechst-Roussel Pharmaceut Co, Upjohn Pharmaceut Co, Ciba-Geigy Pharmaceut Co, McNeill Pharmaceut Co, Ortho Pharmaceut Co & Sterling-Winthrop Pharmaceut Co; co-instr, Chicago Med Sch, Chicago Col Osteop Med, Univ Kans, Univ RI, Brown Univ Med Sch, Tex Col Osteop Med & Univ NTex. **Memberships:** Am Col Neuropsychopharmacol; Asn Med Sch Pharmacol; Am Soc Pharmacol & Exp Therapeut; Soc Neuroscience; Soc Toxicol; Behav Pharmacol Soc; fel Am Col Clin Pharmacol; Soc Biol Psychiat; Am Psychol Asn; Fedn Am Socs Exp Biol. **Research Statement & Publications:** Pharmacology; toxicology; psychopharmacology. **Mailing Address:** Dept Pharmacol, Tex Col Osteop Med, Univ NTex Health Sci Ctr, 3500 Camp Bowie, Ft Worth, TX 76017-2699. **Fax:** 817-735-2091.

LAL, MANOHAR, ENGINEERING SYSTEM MODELS, MATHEMATICAL PHYSICS. **Personal Data:** b Lakki Marwat, India, April 11, 1934; m 1963, Urmila; c Gaurav, Gunjan & Garima-Lal. **Education:** Allahabad Univ India, BSc, 1955; Indian Inst Sci, DIISc, 1958; Univ Ill, Urbana, MS, 1961, PhD (elec eng), 1963. **Professional Experience:** Sr res assoc, Amoco Tulsa Tech Ctr, beginning 1992; spec res assoc, Amoco Tulsa Tech Ctr, 1986-1992; res assoc 1982-1986; adj prof, Univ Tulsa, 1981; sr staff scientist, Amoco Tulsa Tech Ctr, 1980-1982; sr res scientist math physics, Amoco Tulsa Tech Ctr, 1978-1980; vis res prof, Coord Sci Lab, Univ Ill & Elec Eng & Comput Sci Dept, Univ Santa Clara, 1975; prof elec eng, Wichita State Univ, 1974-1978; Khosla res award, Univ Roorkee, India, 1971; from asst prof to prof, Univ Roorkee, India, 1963-1974; lectr electronics & commun, Univ Roorkee, India, 1958-1960. **Memberships:** Inst Elec & Electronics Engrs; Soc Petrol Engrs. **Research Statement & Publications:** Electricial systems and circuits; Engineering systems modeling and control, fluid mechanics, drilling and production research in petroleum, fluid flow and wave propagtion in earth models, digital signal processing, solids control, rock mechanics and wellbore stability. **Mailing Address:** Amoco Prod Co Res Ctr, PO Box 3385, Tulsa, OK 74102.

LAL, MOHAN, MATHEMATICS. **Personal Data:** b Dharmkot, Punjab, May 8, 1932; Canadian citizen; m 1964. **Education:** D M Col, Punjab, India, BA, 1952; Aligarh Muslim Univ, MSc, 1955; Univ BC, PhD (nuclear physics), 1962. **Professional Experience:** EMER PROF MATH, MEM UNIV NFLD, 1975-; comput specialist, Fed & Prov Land Inventory Studies, Dept Mines & Natural Resources, Can, 1967; from asst prof to assoc prof math, Mem Univ Nfld, 1964-1975; asst prof math & physics, Mt Allison Univ, 1963-1964; res assoc, Univ Alta, 1962-1963; res asst, Univ BC, 1957-1961; lectr physics, D A V Col, Punjab, India, 1955-1957. **Memberships:** Can Math Cong. **Research Statement & Publications:** Numerical analysis; applied mathematics and elementary number theory. **Mailing Address:** Dept Math & Statist, Mem Univ Nfld Elizabeth Ave, St John's, NL A1C 5S7, Can.

LAL, RATTAN, SOIL PHYSICS, TROPICAL SOILS. **Personal Data:** b Karyal, Punjab, September 5, 1944; m 1971, Sukhvarsha; c Priva, Pratibha, Abhishek & Vivek. **Education:** Punjab Agr Univ, Ludhiana, India, BSc, 1963; Indian Agr Res Inst, New Delhi, MSc, 1965; Ohio State Univ, PhD (soil physics), 1968. **Honors & Awards:** Int Soil Sci Award, Soil Sci Soc Am, 1988; Distinguished Scientist Award, Asn Sci Indian Origin, 1990. **Professional Experience:** DIR, CARBON MGT & SEQUESTRATION CTR, OHIO STATE UNIV, 2003-; PROF SOIL PHYSICS, OHIO STATE UNIV, COLUMBUS, OHIO, 1989-; soil sci appl res award, 1992; bd mem, Orgn Trop Studies, 1989-1993; pres, Int Soil Tillage Res Orgn, Holland, 1988-1991; pres, Ankeny, Iowa, 1988-1991; assoc prof, Ohio State Univ, Columbus, Ohio, 1987-1989; bd mem, Int Soil Tillage Res Orgn, Holland, 1984-1988; coordr, Upland Prod Systs, Int Inst Trop Agr, Ibadan, Nigeria, 1984-1987; chmn, Working Group ISSS, Soil Erosion Res Methods, 1983-1988; World Asn Soil & Water Conserv, Ankeny, Iowa, 1983-1987; vpres, Int Comt Continental Erosion, IAHS, UK, 1982-1987; soil physicist, Int Inst Trop Agr, Ibadan, Nigeria, 1970-1987; sr res fel soil physics, Univ Sydney, Australia, 1968-1969. **Memberships:** World Asn Soil & Water Conserv (pres, 1988-1991); Int Soil Tillage Res Orgn (pres, 1988-1991); fel Soil Sci Soc Am; fel Am Soc Agron; Int Soc Soil Sci; Soil & Water Conserv Soc. **Research Statement & Publications:** Management of soil and water resources with particular relevance to the tropics and sub-tropics; processes of soil degradation under intensive management including accelerated erosion, compaction, anaerobiosis, transport of sediment-related pollutants, emission of radiatively active gases from soils and deterioration of soil structure; soil conservation; soils and greenhouse effect. **Mailing Address:** Sch Natural Resources, Col Food, Agr & Environ Sci, Ohio State Univ, 422B Kottman Hall 2021 Coffey Rd, Columbus, OH 43210. **Fax:** 614-292-7432. **E-Mail:** lal.1@osu.edu

LAL, RAVINDRA BEHARI, MATERIALS SCIENCE-CRYSTAL GROWTH NONLINEAR OPTICAL MAT. **Personal Data:** b Agra, India, October 5, 1935; American citizen; m 1962, Usha; c Amit K. **Education:** Agra Univ, BSc, 1955, MSc, 1958, PhD (physics), 1963. **Honors & Awards:** New Technol Invention Award, 1981, 1983. **Professional Experience:** Prin investr space shuttle experiment, First Int Microgravity Lab, NASA, 1992; PROF PHYSICS, ALA A&M UNIV, 1979-; assoc prof, Ala A&M Univ, 1975-1979; asst prof physics, Paine Col, 1973-1975; sr res assoc, Univ Ala, Huntsville, 1971-1973; asst prof, Indian Inst Technol, Delhi, 1968-1970; Nat Acad Sci-Nat Res Coun resident res assoc, Marshall Space Flight Ctr, NASA, 1964-1967; Lectr physics, REI Col, Agra Univ, 1958-1959 & Delhi Polytech, 1963-1964. **Memberships:** Am Phys Soc; Sigma Xi; Am Asn Crystal Growth, SPIE (fel). **Research Statement & Publications:** Solid state physics; crystal growth and characterization of materials; magnetic and electrical properties of II-VI and III-V compounds; infra-red detector materials; manufacturing in space; selected by NASA as an investigator for an experiment on International Microgravity Lab (1ML-1) for 1992; growth of nonlinear optical materials for second harmonic generation; Room temperature IR detectors. **Mailing Address:** Dept Physics, Ala A&M Univ PO Box 71, Normal, AL 35762. **Fax:** 256-851-5622. **E-Mail:** rlal@aamu.edu

LAL, SAMARTHJI, NEUROPSYCHIATRY. **Personal Data:** b London, Eng, March 23, 1938; Canadian citizen; m 1974, Maureen; c Sikander. **Education:** Univ London, MB, BS, 1962; McGill Univ, dipl psychiat, 1967; FRCP (C), 1970; Am Bd Psychiat & Neurol, 1978. **Honors & Awards:** Heinz Lehmann Award, 1986; Joey & Toby Tannenbaum Distinguished Scientist Award, 1997. **Professional Experience:** CO DIR, SCHIZOPHRENIA NEURODEVLOPMENTAL DIS RES THEME, DOUGLAS HOSP RES CTR, as of 2006; DIR, MCGILL CTR RES SCHIZOPHRENIA, as of 2006; actg dir, McGill Ctr Res Schizophrenia, beginning 1992; PROF, DEPT PSYCHIAT, MCGILL UNIV, 1983-; examr, Royal Col Phys Surg, Can, 1981-1982; bd dirs, Res Ctr, beginning 1980; sr psychiatrist, Montreal Gen Hosp, beginning 1978; staff psychiatrist, Douglas Hosp, beginning 1976; consult, Psychiat Consultation Serv, beginning 1975; dir, Clin & Basic Res Psychiat, Montreal Gen Hosp, beginning 1975; assoc psychiatrist, Montreal Gen Hosp, 1974-1978; from asst prof to assoc prof, Montreal Gen Hosp, 1973-1983; staff psychiatrist, Montreal Gen Hosp, beginning 1971; consult psychiatrist, Queen Mary Vet Hosp, 1971-1978; chief consult serv, Montreal Gen Hosp, 1971-1975; med res coun can res fel psychiat, 1967-1971. **Memberships:** Can Soc Clin Invest; Can Psychiat Asn; fel Am Psychiat Asn; fel Can Col Neuropsychopharmacol; Soc Biol Psychiat; Int Soc Psychoneuroendrinol. **Research Statement & Publications:** Monoaminergic mechanisms in anterior pituitary secretionand in neurological and psychiatric disorders. **Mailing Address:** Douglas Hosp Res Ctr, Pavilion Perry 6875 LaSalle Blvd, Montreal, PQ H4H 1R3, Can. **Fax:** 514-888-4064. **E-Mail:** samarthji.lal@muhc.mcgill.ca

LALA, JAYNARAYAN H, AERONAUTICS. **Professional Experience:** ENG FEL, RAYTHEON, as of 2006. **Memberships:** Inst Elec & Electronics Engrs. **Mailing Address:** Raytheon Co, 2461 S Clark St Suite 1000, Arlington, VA 22202. **Fax:** 703-419-1348. **E-Mail:** jay_lala@Raytheon.com

LALA, JAYNARAYAN HOTCHAND, COMPUTER ENGINEERING. **Personal Data:** b Hyderabad, Pakistan, January 12, 1951; m 1977, Michele. **Education:** Indian Inst Technol, SB, 1971; Mass Inst Technol, SM, 1973, ScD, 1976. **Professional Experience:** ENG FEL, INTEGRATED DEFENSE SYST, RAYTHEON, as of 2004; VCHMN, FAULT TOLERANT COMPUT, INST ELEC & ELECTRONICS ENGRS TECH COMT, as of 2004; prin mem tech staff, Charles Stark Draper Lab Inc, 1993-1999; mem, Battle Mgt Panel, Strategic Defense Initiative, 1992; leader, Advan Comput Archit Group, 1991-1993; div leader, Fault Tolerant Systs Div, 1985-1991; Adv, USN Combat Syst Archit Adv Panel, 1985-1986; chief systs archit sect, NASA Dept, 1983-1985; Tech staff, Charles Stark Draper Lab, Inc, Cambridge, 1976-1983. **Memberships:** Fel Am Inst Aeronaut & Astronaut; Indian Inst Technol Soc New Eng (vpres 1995-); Int Fedn Info Processing; fel Inst Elec & Electronics Engrs. **Research Statement & Publications:** Fault tolerant computer designs; contributed articles to professional journals. **Mailing Address:** Charles Stark Draper Lab Inc, 555 Technol Sq, Cambridge, MA 02139-3539. **E-Mail:** jay_lala@raytheon.com

LALA, PEEYUSH KANTI, CANCER, IMMUNOLOGY. **Personal Data:** b Chittagong, Brit India, November 1, 1934; m 1992, Shipra; c Probal & Prason. **Education:** Univ Calcutta, MB, BS, 1957, PhD (med biophys), 1962. **Professional Experience:** PROF ANATCELL BIOL, UNIV WESTERN ONT, 1993-; pres, Can Asn Anat, 1991-1993; JCB grant award, Can Asn Anat, 1990; PROF ONCOL, UNIV WESTERN ONT, 1989-; vpres, Can Asn Anat, 1989-1990; counr, Int Soc Reprod Immunol, 1986; prof & chair anat, Univ Western Ont, 1983-1993; vis prof, Walter & Eliza Hall Inst Med Res, Melbourne Univ, 1977-1978; USPHS grant, 1975-; res dir, Med Res Coun Can grant, 1968- & Nat Cancer Inst Can grant, 1969-; from asst prof to prof anat, McGill Univ, 1968-1983; res assoc biol & health physics, Chalk River Nuclear Labs, Atomic Energy Can Ltd, 1967-1968; res scientist, Radiobiol Lab, Univ Calif, San Francisco, 1964-1966; res assoc biol & med res, Argonne Nat Lab, 1963-1964; Fulbright travel scholar, 1962; demonstr path & hemat, NRS Med Col, 1961-1962; Demonstr path, Calcutta Med Col, 1959-1960. **Memberships:** Am Asn Immunol; Am Asn Cancer Res; Int Soc Exp Hemat; Int Soc Reprod Immunol; Am Asn Anat; Am Soc Reprod Immunol (vpres 1985); Soc Leuko Biol. **Research Statement & Publications:** Studies of cell population kinetics during normal hematopoiesis, leukemias and cancer; host-tumor cell interactions in vivo; biology of tumor-host and fetomaternal relationship; author of more than 150 research publications and 14 book chapters on hematology, immunology, cancer and reproduction; discoverer of a new mode of cancer therapy applied to human trial; biology of the placenta, invasion and metastasis. **Mailing Address:** Dept Anat Cell Biol, Univ Western Ont, London, ON N6A 5C1, Can. **Fax:** 519-661-3936. **E-Mail:** pklala@julian.uwo.ca

LALANCETTE, JEAN-MARC, INORGANIC CHEMISTRY, ENVIRONMENTAL CHEMISTRY. **Personal Data:** b Drummondville, Que, April 21, 1934; m 1958, c 3. **Education:** Univ Montreal, BSc, 1957, MSc, 1958, PhD (chem), 1961. **Honors & Awards:** Manning Award, 1985; Award, Can-Fr Asn Advan Sci, 1985. **Professional Experience:** AT, INOTEL INC, as of 2004; PRES & CONSULT CHEMIST ENVIRON & HIGH TEMPERATURE CHEM, INOTEL INC, 1985-; vpres res & develop, Net Asbestos Soc, 1980-1985; from asst prof to prof chem, Univ Sherbrooke, 1960-1987. **Memberships:** Chem Inst Can. **Research Statement & Publications:** Organometallic chemistry; chemistry of graphite intercalates, both catalytic and synthetic properties; photochemical reactions; use of natural materials for protection of environment; peat moss. **Mailing Address:** Inotel Inc, 470 Irene-Coutre St, Sherbrooke, PQ J1L 1J4, Can. **Fax:** 819-346-8248.

LALANCETTE, ROGER A, ANALYTICAL CHEMISTRY, STRUCTURAL CHEMISTRY. **Personal Data:** b Springfield, Mass, July 30, 1939; m 1978, c Christopher & Brian. **Education:** Am Int Col, BA, 1961; Fordham Univ, PhD (analytical chem), 1967. **Professional Experience:** PROF CHEM, RUTGERS UNIV, NEWARK, 1987-; Vis scientist, Univ Calif, San Francisco, 1980-1981; assoc prof, Rutgers Univ, Newark, 1976-1987; asst prof analytical chem, Rutgers Univ, Newark, 1969-1976; res chemist photopolymerization, Photo Prod Dept, E I du Pont Del Nemours & Co, Inc, NJ, 1967-1969; Res fel, Brookhaven Nat Lab, 1966-1967. **Memberships:** Am Chem Asn; Am Mat Soc; Am Crystallog Asn. **Research Statement & Publications:** Preparation and structural studies; x-ray powder and single crystal analysis; GC/MS of pesticides in soil and water. **Mailing Address:** Dept Chem Rutgers Univ Newark Campus, 73 Warren St, Newark, NJ 07102-1814. **Fax:** 973-353-1264. **E-Mail:** rogerlal@andromeda.rutgers.edu

LALANDE, MARC, GENETICS. **Education:** Univ Toronto, PhD. **Professional Experience:** PROF & CHMN, GENETICS & DEVELOP BIOL, HEALTH CTR, UNIV CONN, as of 2005. **Mailing Address:** Univ Conn Health Ctr, Farmington, CT 06030. **Fax:** 860-679-8345. **E-Mail:** lalande@neuron.uchc.edu

LALAS, DEMETRIUS P, DYNAMIC METEOROLOGY, ENVIRONMENTAL FLUID DYNAMICS. **Personal Data:** b Athens, Greece, September 28, 1942; m 1967, c 2. **Education:** Hamilton Col, AB, 1962; Cornell Univ, MAeroE, 1965, PhD (aerospace), 1968. **Professional Experience:** DIR, NAT OBSERV ATHENS & PRES GOV BD, GREEK WIND ENERGY ASN, 1994-; adv, Ministry Energy & Indust & Ministry Environ & pres, 1993-1994; managing dir, Lomda Tech, Ltd, 1989-1994; pres, Ctr Renewable Energy Sources, Athens, Greece, 1988-1991; prof, Dept Mech Eng, 1979-1990; prof & chmn dept & dir, Meteorol Inst, 1979-1983; assoc prof, Dept Meteorol, Univ Athens, Greece, 1976-1977; consult, Coop Inst Res Environ Eng, Univ Colo, 1974-1975; assoc prof, Dept Eng Mech & Dept Mech Eng, Wayne State Univ, 1973-1979; Vis fel, Coop Inst Res Environ Eng, Univ Colo, 1973-1974; Asst prof, Dept Eng Mech & Dept Mech Eng, Wayne State Univ, 1968-1973. **Memberships:** Am Meteorol Soc; Am Geophys Union; Greek Meteorol Soc; Am Soc Mech Eng. **Research Statement & Publications:** Dynamics of micro and mesoscale wave dynamics, their excitation, stability and properties; solar and wind energy; air pollution modelling; environmental fluid mechanics; lubrication theory. **Mailing Address:** Papanastasiou 27, Neo Psychiko, Athens 15451, Greece. **Fax:** 301-342-1019.

LALCHANDANI, ATAM PRAKASH, OPERATIONS RESEARCH, PLANNING. **Personal Data:** b India, October 20, 1943; American citizen; div, c 1. **Education:** Indian Inst Technol, Bombay, BTech, 1963; Cornell Univ, MS, 1966, PhD (oper res), 1967. **Professional Experience:** CONSULT, 1992-; vpres finance & admin, Nat Adv Systs, 1983-1992; treas, Nat Adv Systs, 1981-1983; dir planning & analysis, Nat Semiconductor Corp, 1977-1981; dir indust serv, Control Analysis Corp, 1973-1977; vis lectr, Grad Sch Bus, Univ Santa Clara, 1969-1977; dir appl syst, Optimum Systs Inc, Santa Clara, Calif, 1969-1973; Univ Cincinnati, 1969; Xavier Univ, Ohio, 1969; sr oper res analyst, Procter & Gamble, 1967-1969. **Memberships:** Opers Res Soc Am; Inst Mgt Sci; Financial Exec Inst. **Research Statement & Publications:** Finance. **Mailing Address:** Los Altos, CA 94022. **E-Mail:** ataml@worldnet.att.net

LALEHZARIAN, HAMO, HUMAN FACTORS/ERGONOMICS & DESIGN OF EXPERIEMENT, STTISITICAL PROCESS CONTROL & STATISTICAL QUASLITY CONTROL. **Personal Data:** b Isfahan, Iran, December 22, 1952; American citizen; m 1991, Carine; c Serjlc & Arin. **Education:** Univ Texas, Arlington, BS 1980; MS 1981, & Ph.D. 1987. **Honors & Awards:** Midwest Decision Science Institute Certificate of Appreciation; Quality Management Track Chair, for significant contributions to the thirtieth annual meeting of the Midwest Decision Science Institute in Springfield, Illinois, April 22-21, 1999 Society of Manufacturing Engineering for individual contribution and outstanding support of Student Chapter, California State University, Fresno, 1994 Gold Coin Award for individual contribution, leadership and outstanding support of the student chapter, Institute of Industrial Engineers, California State University, Fresno, 1989. **Professional Experience:** J.G. Boswell Company: Porterville, California; Dole Food Processing: Fowler, CA; Gottschalk's Department Store: Madera, California Visiting Professor American University of Armenia, 1993; Professor of Industrial Engineering, CALIFORNIA STATE UNIVERSITY, FRESNO, 1987- 2004; Management Engineer Financial analyst, Merchantil National Bank, 1981-1984. **Memberships:** Phi Theta Kappa, Bee County College Honor Society Alpha Pi Mu, Industrial Engineering Honor Society Omega Rho Operations research Honor Society Institute of Industrial Engineers Human Factors Society Society of Manufacturing Engineering (SME) Robotics International (RI/SME). **Research Statement & Publications:** Effects of mental work load on the p300 component of evoked brain potentials and various levels of automation. **Mailing Address:** Deptartment Mechancial & Industrial Eng, Calif State Univ, 2320 E San Ramon Ave, Fresno, CA 93740-8030. **E-Mail:** hamol@csufresno.edu

LALEZARI, PARVIZ, MEDICINE, PHYSIOLOGY. **Personal Data:** b Hamadan, Iran, August 17, 1931; m 1958, Cecilia; c Jacob Paul & Renee. **Education:** Univ Teheran, MD, 1954. **Professional Experience:** PRES, CHIEF EXEC OFFICER & MED DIR, BERGEN COMMMUNITY REGIONAL BLOOD CTR, 1994-; PROF PATH, ALBERT EINSTEIN COL MED, YESHIVA UNIV, 1989-; Am Cancer Soc res grant, 1989-1994; PROF MED, ALBERT EINSTEIN COL MED, 1979-; from asst prof to assoc prof, Chief Exec Officer & Med Dir, Bergen Community Regional Blood Ctr, 1967-1979; NIH res grant, 1965-; dir immuno hemat & blood bank, Montefiore Hosp & Med Ctr, 1960-1996; City NY Res Counc res grant, 1960-1964. **Memberships:** Am Soc Hemat; Am Soc Clin Invest; Am Asn Immunol; Am Asn Blood Banks. **Research Statement & Publications:** Leukocyte immunology; red cell immunology autoimmune diseases, hematopoietic progenitor cells, blood substitutes. **Mailing Address:** Albert Einstein Col Med, Yeshiva Univ, 1300 Morris Park Ave, Bronx, NY 10461.

LALIBERTE, GARLAND E, AGRICULTURAL ENGINEERING. **Personal Data:** b Walkerburn, Man, December 28, 1936; m 1959, c 2. **Education:** Univ Sask, BS, 1956, MS, 1961; Colo State Univ, PhD (agr eng), 1966. **Honors & Awards:** Maple Leaf Award, Can Soc Agr Eng, 1981; Agr Eng Yr Award, Am Soc Agr Eng, 1990. **Professional Experience:** EMER DEAN, UNIV MAN, 1996-; prof agr eng, Univ Man, 1986-1996; Can Soc Agr Eng fel, 1984; Agr Inst Can fel, 1983; prof & head dept, Univ Man, 1969-1986; assoc prof, Univ Man, 1967-1969; res scientist, Can Dept Agr, 1961-1967; engr, Can Dept Agr, 1956-1961. **Memberships:** Am Soc Agr Engrs; Can Soc Agr Eng (pres 1978-1979); Sigma Xi; fel Agr Inst Can. **Research Statement & Publications:** Drainage engineering; irrigation engineering; soil and water conservation. **Mailing Address:** Dept Biosysts Eng, Univ Man, E2-376 Eng Bldg, Winnipeg, MB R3T 5V6, Can. **Fax:** 204-474-7512. **E-Mail:** glalib@ms.umanitoba.ca

LALIBERTE, LAURENT HECTOR, ELECTROCHEMISTRY, CORROSION. **Personal Data:** b Ottawa, Ont, October 7, 1943; m 1966, c 2. **Education:** Univ Ottawa, BSc, 1966, PhD (chem), 1969. **Honors & Awards:** Weldon Medal, Can Pulp & Paper Asn. **Profes-**

sional Experience: MGR PROCESS CONTROL TECH, INT PAPER, PINEVILLE MILL, 1990-; mgr tech serv, Int Paper, Pineville Mill, 1987-1990; group mgr, Int Paper, Pineville Mill, 1979-1987; sr res assoc, Int Paper, Pineville Mill, 1978-1979; scientist corrosion, Pulp & Paper Res Inst Can, 1971-1978; fel chem, Univ Ottawa, 1969-1971. **Memberships:** Nat Asn Corrosion Engrs; Tech Asn Pulp & Paper Indust. **Research Statement & Publications:** Corrosion of materials used in pulp and paper industry process equipment; chemical engineering; process control. **Mailing Address:** Int Paper, 1285 Tri Ridge Blvd, Loveland, OH 45140.

LALL, ABNER BISHAMBER, VISUAL ELECTROPHYSIOLOGY, NEUROETHOLOGY. **Personal Data:** b Bareilly, UP, India, January 28, 1933; m 1968, Jean; c Sarojini. **Education:** Univ Delhi, BSc, 1954; Boston Univ, STB, 1959; Syracuse Univ, MS, 1962; Univ Md, PhD (zoology), 1971. **Professional Experience:** ASSOC PROF BIOL, HOWARD UNIV, 1988-; res scientist, Dept Biophys, Johns Hopkins Univ, 1985-1988; asst prof, Univ Miami, 1982-1983; assoc res scientist, Dept Biol, McCollum Pratt Inst, 1979-1982 & 1983-1985; asst prof, Skidmore Col, 1977-1978; sr assoc, Howard Univ Col Med, 1976-1977, 1978-1979; fel neurophysiol, Johns Hopkins Univ Sch Med, 1974-1975; asst prof, City Col NY, 1972-1974; Grass Found fel neurophysiol, Marine Biol Lab, Woods Hole, Mass, 1970; investr, Eye Res Found Bethesda, 1969-1972. **Memberships:** Asn Res Vision & Opthal; Soc Integr Comp Biol; Int'l Soc Neuroethology; Soc Neuroscience; Int'l Soc Biolumin Chemilumin. **Research Statement & Publications:** Neural mechanisms of visual behavior among anthropods. Retinal function in mutant zebrafish. **Mailing Address:** Dept Biol, Howard Univ, 415 Col St NW, Washington, DC 20059. **Fax:** 202-806-4564. **E-Mail:** alall@howard.edu

LALL, B KENT, CIVIL ENGINEERING, TRANSPORTATION ENGINEERING. **Personal Data:** b Sargodha, India, February 4, 1939; American citizen; m 1970, Margaret; c Niren N. **Education:** Panjab Univ, India, BSc, 1961; Univ Roorkee, ME, 1964; Univ Birmingham, PhD (transp), 1969. **Professional Experience:** Chair, 1994-1995 & chair, Transp Cong, 1995; mem, Unsig Intersect Comt, Transp Res Bd, 1990-; secy, Exec Comt, Urban Transp Div, 1990-1992; chmn, Pub Transp Comt, Urban Transp Div, Am Soc Civil Engrs, 1988-1990; consult, Nat Rds Bd, Ministry Works, NZ, 1986; vis prof, Univ Adelaide, SAustralia, 1985; PROF DEPT CIVIL & ENVIRON ENG, PORTLAND STATE UNIV, 1984-; mem, Geometric Design Hwys Comt, 1980-; mem, Pub Transp Comt, Urban Transp Div, Am Soc Civil Engrs, 1979-; assoc prof, Portland State Univ, 1977-1984; assoc prof, Univ Man, 1975-1977; asst prof & lectr civil eng, Indian Inst Technol, Delhi, 1964-1975; Teaching fel hwy, Univ Roorkee, 1961-1964. **Memberships:** fel Am Soc Civil Engrs; Sigma Xi; Inst Transp Engrs; High Speed Ground Transp Asn Am. **Research Statement & Publications:** Urban transportation; traffic management and video imaging technologies, intelligent transportation systems, transportation planning and systems; pavement design; highway and traffic engineering; highway materials and construction; highway capacity and geometric design. **Mailing Address:** Dept Civil & Environ Eng, Portland State Univ, PO Box 751, Portland, OR 97207-0751. **E-Mail:** kent@cecs.pdx.edu

LALL, PRITHVI C, NUCLEAR PHYSICS, ACOUSTICS. **Personal Data:** b Panjab, India, September 20, 1931. **Education:** Panjab Univ, MS, 1954; Ore State Univ, PhD (physics), 1962; George Wash Univ, JD, 1969. **Professional Experience:** ASSOC COMNR, DEPT NAVY, NAVAL UNDERWATER SYST CTR, 1971-; asst prof, Howard Univ, 1962-1971. **Memberships:** Am Phys Soc; Sigma Xi. **Mailing Address:** Off Patent Coun, Naval Underwater Syst Ctr Bldg 112T, Newport, RI 02841.

LALL, SANTOSH PRAKASH, NUTRITIONAL BIOCHEMISTRY. **Personal Data:** b Motihari, India, September 8, 1944; Canadian citizen; m 1974, Barbara; c Carolyn & Julie. **Education:** Allahabad Univ, BSc, 1964; Univ Guelph, MSc, 1968, PhD (nutrit), 1973. **Honors & Awards:** Research Award of Excellence (2000) - Aquaculture Association of Canada. **Professional Experience:** HEAD, AQUACULT SECT, HALIFAX LAB, 1994-; res scientist fish nutrit, Aquacult Sect, Halifax Lab, 1974-1993; fel, Nutrit Dept, Univ Guelph, 1973; Res asst, Nutrit Dept, Univ Guelph, 1968; Res asst animal nutrit, Allahabad Agr Inst, 1964-1965. **Memberships:** Can Soc Nutrit Sci; Aquacult Asn Can; NY Acad Sci; World Aquacult Soc; Comp. Nutr. Soc. **Research Statement & Publications:** Nutrient requirements of salmonid and marine fishes in fresh water and sea water. **Mailing Address:** Inst Marine Biosci Nat Res Coun, 1411 Oxford St, Halifax, NS B3H 3Z1, Can. **Fax:** 902-426-9413. **E-Mail:** santosh.lall@nrc.ca

LALLEY, EDWARD T, PATHOLOGY, IMMUNOLOGY. **Personal Data:** b Pittsburgh, Pa, March 30, 1943. **Education:** Univ Pa, BS, 1965, PhD (path), 1978; Univ Pittsburgh, DMD, 1968. **Professional Experience:** PROF PATH, UNIV PA, 1991-; from asst prof to assoc prof, Univ PA, 1978-1991; instr, Univ PA, 1971-1978; Residency path, Univ Pa, 1971-1973. **Memberships:** Am Cancer Soc. **Research Statement & Publications:** Pathology; immunology. **Mailing Address:** Univ Pa, 4001 Spruce St, Philadelphia, PA 19104-6003.

LALLEY, PETER AUSTIN, HUMAN GENETICS, BIOCHEMICAL GENETICS. **Personal Data:** b Lackawanna, NY, February 19, 1940; m 1967, c 3. **Education:** Siena Col, BS, 1961; Cath Univ Am, MS, 1969; State Univ NY, Buffalo, PhD (human genetics), 1974. **Professional Experience:** PROF, ROCHESTER INST TECHNOL, as of 2003; DIR, CTR BACCALAURATE & GRAD STUDIES, NAT TECH INST DEAF, ROCHESTER INST TECHNOL, 1993-; fac, Ctr Molecular Biol, Wayne State Univ, 1988-1993; fac, Inst Med Res, Bennington, Vt, 1985-1988; contract genetic basis mutagenesis & carcinogenesis, Dept Energy, 1978-1985; sr investr biochem genetics, Biol Div, Oak Ridge Nat Lab, 1977; mem, Int Comt Human Gene Mapping, 1975-1992; mem staff biochem genetics, Vet Admin Oncol Br, Nat Cancer Inst, 1975-1977; fel human genetics, Roswell Park Mem Inst, 1974-1975. **Memberships:** AAAS; Am Soc Human Genetics; Genetics Soc Am. **Research Statement & Publications:** Comparative genetics; gene mapping; somatic cell hybrids; genetics of carcinogenesis; mutagenesis; genetics of inherited diseases. **Mailing Address:** Ctr Baccalaureate & Grad Studies, Nat Tech Inst Deaf, Rochester Inst Tech, 52 Lomb Memorial Dr, Rochester, NY 14623-5604. **Fax:** 585-475-6130. **E-Mail:** palbgs@rit.edu

LALLEY, PETER MICHAEL, NEUROPHYSIOLOGY, NEUROPHARMACOLOGY. **Personal Data:** b Scranton, Pa, January 21, 1940; m 1963, Ruth; c Maureen, Christopher, Angela & Jacqueline. **Education:** Philadelphia Col Pharm & Sci, BS, 1963, MS, 1965, PhD (pharmacol), 1970. **Professional Experience:** PROF EMER, DEPT PHYSIOL, SCH MED, UNIV WIS, MADISON, as of 2005; Prof Physiol, Univ Wis Sch Med, as of 1998; Univ Gottingen, Fed Repub Ger, 1988; vis prof, physiol, Univ Heidelberg, Fed Repub Ger, 1985-1987; assoc prof, Physiol, sch med, Univ Wis, Madison, beginning 1980; asst prof, Sch Med Univ Wis, Madison, 1976-1980; asst prof, pharmacol, Col Med, Univ Fla, 1974-1976; asst prof, Sch Med, Univ Pittsburgh, 1973-1974; lectr, neurosci pharmacol, Sch Med, Univ Pittsburgh, 1972-1973; Fel, neuropharmacol, Sch Med, Univ Pittsburgh, 1970-1973; Consult, US Pharmacopoeia & Dispensing Info. **Memberships:** Soc Neuroscience; Sigma Xi; Am Physiol Soc; AAAS; Am Pharmaceut Asn; Am Heart Asn. **Research Statement & Publications:** Identifying the neurotransmitters in the brainstem and spinal cord which control respiration and blood pressure, and determining the conditions under which they are operative; Published over 10 articles. **Mailing Address:** Dept Physiol, Univ Wis Med Ctr 1300 Univ Ave, Madison, WI 53706-1509. **Fax:** 608-265-5512. **E-Mail:** pmcolley@facollaff.ivcoc.edu

LALLEY, THOMAS L, BEHAVIORAL SCIENCE. **Personal Data:** b Baltimore, Md, January 22, 1928. **Education:** Loyola Col, BA, 1947; Georgetown Univ, MA, 1950. **Professional Experience:** RETIRED; chief, Serv Res Br, 1987-1996; dep chief, Antisocial & Violent Behav Br, NIMH, 1976-1987. **Mailing Address:** 3713 Yuma St NW, Washington, DC 20016-2211.

LALLI, CAROL MARIE, MARINE BIOLOGY. **Personal Data:** b Toledo, Ohio, December 5, 1938. **Education:** Bowling Green State Univ, BS & BEd, 1960, MA, 1962; Univ Wash, PhD (zoology), 1967. **Professional Experience:** RES SCI, UNIV BC, as of 2004; res assoc, Univ BC, beginning 1980; from asst prof to assoc prof marine sci, McGill Univ, 1969-1979; lectr zool, McGill Univ, 1968-1969. **Memberships:** Marine Biol Asn. **Research Statement & Publications:** Ecological studies of planktonic and benthonic gastropod molluscs. **Mailing Address:** Zool Dept, Univ BC, Vancouver, BC V6T 1Z4, Can.

LALLY, PHILIP M(ARSHALL), ELECTRICAL ENGINEERING, VACUUM ELECTRONICS. **Personal Data:** b New York, NY, September 30, 1925; m 1947, Mary; c Philip J, Stephen A & James W. **Education:** Mass Inst Technol, SB, 1948, SM, 1949. **Professional Experience:** RETIRED; mgr design eng, Vacuum Electronics Bus Unit, 1993-1995; mgr elec eng, Low Power Prod Line, Teledyne Electronics Technol, 1990-1993; adv develop mgr, Low Power Prod Line, Teledyne Electronics Technol, 1985-1990; mgr eng, Low Power Prod Line, Teledyne Electronics Technol, 1968-1985; mgr res & advan devices, Electronic Tube Div, Sperry-Rand Corp, 1964-1968; prod eng mgr, Electronic Tube Div, Sperry-Rand Corp, 1960-1964; asst prod eng supt, Electronic Tube Div, Sperry-Rand Corp, 1960; eng dept head, Electronic Tube Div, Sperry-Rand Corp, 1959-1960; lectr, Adelphi Col, 1955-1956 & Univ Fla, 1958-1959; eng supvr res & develop, Electronic Tube Div, Sperry-Rand Corp, 1957-1959; eng sect head, Electron Tube Dept, Sperry Gyroscope Co, 1955-1957; sr engr, Electron Tube Dept, Sperry Gyroscope Co, 1954-1955; engr, Electron Tube Dept, Sperry Gyroscope Co, 1949-1954; asst elec eng, Mass Inst Technol, 1948-1949. **Memberships:** Sr mem, Inst Elec & Electronics Engrs. **Research Statement & Publications:** Microwave vacuum tubes, especially traveling wave tubes and klystrons. **Mailing Address:** 738 De Soto Dr, Palo Alto, CA 94303.

LALLY, VINCENT EDWARD, meteorology, electronics; deceased, see previous edition for last biography

LALONDE, DONNA E, MATHEMATICS. **Education:** Univ Kans, MA, 1985. **Professional Experience:** DEAN & ASSOC PROF, DEPT MATH & STATIST, WASHBURN UNIV, as of 2004. **Mailing Address:** Math Dept, Washburn Univ Topeka, Topeka, KS 66621. **Fax:** 785-670-1426. **E-Mail:** donna.lalonde@washburn.edu

LALONDE, ROBERT THOMAS, TOXICOLOGY. **Personal Data:** b Bemidji, Minn, May 7, 1931; m 1957, Suzanne; c Robert J, Judith M, Mary C, Jane F, Suzanne, Jerome V & Thomas A. **Education:** St John's Univ, Minn, BA, 1953; Univ Colo, PhD, 1957. **Professional Experience:** PROF EMER CHEM, STATE UNIV NY, COL ENV SCI & FORESTRY, as of 2005; Fed Rep Ger Exchange, 1980; prof chem, State Univ Ny, Col Env Sci & Forestry, beginning 1968; NIH fel, 1965-1966; from asst prof to assoc prof, State Univ NY, 1959-1968; res assoc, Univ Ill, 1958-1959; sr res engr chem, Jet Propulsion Lab, Calif Inst Technol, 1957-1958. **Memberships:** Am Chem Soc; Am Soc Pharmacol; Environ Mutagen Soc; Sigma Xi. **Research Statement & Publications:** Chemistry of natural products; chemistry of alkaloids, terpenoids, steroids and fatty acid derivatives; origin, synthesis, structure-activity relations and modes of inactivation of halogen containing mutagens; geogenesis of organo-sulfur compounds. **Mailing Address:** State Univ NY, Col Environ Sci & Forestry, Dept Chem, 321 Jahn Lab, Syracuse, NY 13210. **Fax:** 315-470-6856. **E-Mail:** rtlalond@syr.edu

LALOR, WILLIAM FRANCIS, COTTON PRODUCTION & PROCESSING, TROPICAL FOOD CROPS. **Personal Data:** b Dublin, Ireland, September 30, 1935; American citizen; m 1961, c 4. **Education:** Univ Col, Dublin, B Agr Sc, 1958; Mich State Univ, MS, 1962; Iowa State Univ, PhD (agr eng), 1968. **Professional Experience:** VPRES, AGR RES, COTTON INC, 1991-; dir, Agr Res, 1973-1990; scientist agr eng, Int Inst Trop Agr, 1971-1973; prof agr eng, Auburn Univ, 1968-1971; lectr agr, Univ Col, Dublin, 1962-1965; prof engr, dept consumer-affairs, Calif. **Memberships:** Am Soc Agr Engrs. **Research Statement & Publications:** Development of production and processing systems for cotton and cottonseed. **Mailing Address:** Cotton Inc, 6399 Weston Pkwy, Cary, NC 27513. **Fax:** 919-678-2230.

LALWANI, NARENDRA DHANRAJ, DRUG DEVELOPMENT, INVESTIGATIVE & MECHANISTIC TOXICOLOGY. **Personal Data:** b Gujarat, India, September 25, 1952; American citizen; m 1985, Leena; c Nalin & Neeraj. **Education:** Gujarat Univ, BS, 1973; Univ Bombay, MS, 1976, PhD (biophys), 1979. **Professional Experience:** SR MGR, DEPT PATH & EXP TOXICOL, PARKE-DAVIS PHARMACEUT RES, 1993-; res assoc, Dept Path & Exp Toxicol, Parke-davis Pharmaceut Res, 1991-1993; sr scientist, Dept Path & Exp Toxicol, Parke-davis Pharmaceut Res, 1990-1991; prin investr, Va Commonwealth Univ, 1989; asst prof, Med Col Va, Va Commonwealth Univ, 1987-1990; prin investr, Am Cancer Soc, 1987-1988; prin investr, Nat Cancer Inst, 1984-1987; asst prof & res scientist, Northwestern Univ Med Sch, 1984-1987; res assoc, Northwestern Univ Med Sch, 1981-1983; fel, Northwestern Univ Med Sch, 1979-1981; jr res fel, Cancer Res Inst, Bombay, India, 1976-1979; res student, Cancer Res Inst, Bombay, India, 1974-1976. **Memberships:** Am Soc Cell Biol; Am Asn Cancer Res; Soc Toxicol; Am Soc Microbiol; AAAS. **Research Statement & Publications:** Signal transduction in cell proliferation and differentiation; cellular and molecular aspects of apoptosis; mechanisms of chemical toxicity in liver and pancreas; xenobiotic effects on peroxisomes; receptor mediated gene expression. **Mailing Address:** Dept Path & Exp Toxicol, Parke-Davis Pharmaceut Res, 2800 Plymouth Rd, Ann Arbor, MI 48106-1047. **Fax:** 313-996-5001. **E-Mail:** lalwann@aa.wl.com

LAM, CHAN F, IMAGE PROCESSING, CONFORMAL DOSE PLANNING FOR STEREOTACTIC RADIOSURGERY. **Personal Data:** b Kwantung, China, October 23, 1943; m 1967, c 2. **Education:** Calif Polytech State Univ, BS, 1965; Clemson Univ, MS, 1967, PhD (elec & comp eng), 1970. **Professional Experience:** PROF RADIOL, BIOMED IMAGE & SIGNAL PROCESSING LAB, 1991-; DIR, BIOMED IMAGE & SIGNAL PROCESSING LAB, 1987-; Spec Study Sect, Biomed Res Technol Rev Comt, 1986-1990; vis res prof, Dept Elec Eng, Cheng Kung Univ, Tainan, Taiwan, 1985; PROF BIOMED, MED UNIV SC, 1980-; dir, Biomed Comput Ctr, 1980-1985; Spec Study Sect, NIH, 1979; dir, Time Share & Hybrid Comput Systs, 1975-1980; dir, Opers& Chief Prog, Med Univ SC, 1971-1972; from asst prof to assoc prof biomed eng, Opers& Chief Prog, Med Univ SC,

1970-1980; res asst comp analysis, Clemson Univ, 1966-1970; Res asst, Grad Inst Technol, Univ Ark, 1965-1966. **Memberships:** Sigma Xi; Inst Elec & Electronics Engrs; Pattern Recognition Soc; Soc Math Biol. **Research Statement & Publications:** Modeling of enzyme kinetic reaction mechanisms; biomedical signal and image processing; optimal dose planning for stereotactic radiosurgery; pattern recognition. **Mailing Address:** Dept Biomet, Med Univ SC 171 Ashley Ave, Charleston, SC 29425. **Fax:** 803-792-0539. **E-Mail:** lam@tigger.musc.edu

LAM, CHEUNG-WEI, ELECTROMAGNETIC INTERFERENCE, SIGNAL INTEGRITY. **Personal Data:** b Hong Kong, March 5, 1965; m 1993, Hoi-Man; c Isaac S. **Education:** Chinese Univ Hong Kong, BS, 1987; Mass Inst Technol, MS, 1989, PhD (elec eng), 1993. **Honors & Awards:** Inst Elec & Electronics Engrs Prize, 1987. **Professional Experience:** SR EMC ENGR, APPLE COMPUT, as of 2003; EMC DISTINGUISHED LECT, APPLE COMPUT, as of 2003; tech staff, Quad Design Technol, beginning1993; researcher, Schlumberger-Doll Res, 1990. **Memberships:** Inst Elec & Electronics Engrs; Sigma Xi. **Research Statement & Publications:** Design of efficient electromagnetic interference simulator; development of nonlinear models for superconducting transmission lines; high-speed electronic interconnection and packaging; acoustic logging in borehole structures. **Mailing Address:** Apple Comput Inc, 1 Infinite Loop MS 26A, Cupertino, CA 95014. **Fax:** 408-862-5061. **E-Mail:** lam@apple.com

LAM, CHIU-WING, TOXICOLOGY. **Professional Experience:** AT SPACE & LIFE SCI, JOHNSON SPACE CTR, NASA, as of 2004. **Mailing Address:** Space & Life Sci, Johnson Space Ctr, NASA, Houston, TX 77058. **E-Mail:** chiu-wing.lam@jsc.nasa.gov

LAM, DANIEL J, PHYSICAL METALLURGY & CHEMISTRY. **Personal Data:** b Hong Kong, December 30, 1930; m 1959, c 3. **Education:** Rensselaer Polytech Inst, BMetE, 1956, MMetE, 1958, PhD (phys metall), 1960. **Professional Experience:** RETIRED; group leader, Argonne Nat Lab, 1978-1996; sr scientist, Argonne Nat Lab, 1974-1996; metallurgist, Argonne Nat Lab, 1972-1974; assoc metallurgist, Argonne Nat Lab, 1966-1972; asst metallurgist, Argonne Nat Lab, 1960-1966; instr, Rensselaer Polytech Inst, 1958-1960; res assoc metall, Rensselaer Polytech Inst, 1956-1958. **Memberships:** AAAS; Am Phys Soc; Am Inst Mining, Metall & Petrol Engrs. **Research Statement & Publications:** Electronic structure and related physical and chemical properties of actinide metals, alloys and compounds; electronic structure and related physical properties of multicomponent oxides. **Mailing Address:** 10318 SW 49th Lane, Gainesville, FL 32608-7161.

LAM, FUK LUEN, CHEMISTRY. **Personal Data:** b Hong Kong, November 7, 1937; American citizen; m 1968, Irene Chan; c David & Eugene. **Education:** Univ SC, PhD (org chem), 1966. **Professional Experience:** MGR QUAL ASSURANCE, PARKE-DAVIS, WARMER-LAMBERT CO, 1980-; assoc, Sloan-Kettering Inst, 1975-1979; res assoc chem oncogenesis, Sloan-Kettering Inst, 1970-1975; Brandeis Univ, 1968-1969; Fel chem, Mass Inst Technol, 1966-1967. **Memberships:** Am Chem Soc. **Research Statement & Publications:** Organic and analytical chemistry. **Mailing Address:** 92 Westminster Rd, Chatham, NJ 07928. **Fax:** 973-631-7722.

LAM, GABRIEL KIT YING, RADIATION BIOPHYSICS, CANCER RADIOTHERAPY. **Personal Data:** b Hong Kong, January 1, 1947; m 1974, c 3. **Education:** Univ Hong Kong, BSc, 1970; Univ Western Ont, MSc, 1971; Univ Toronto, PhD (biophys), 1974. **Professional Experience:** MED PHYSICIST, OTTAWA REGIONAL CANCER CTR, 1997-; biophysicist, BC Cancer Agency, 1984-1996; hon asst prof, Univ BC, 1981-; Staff biophysicist, BC Cancer Res Ctr, 1976-1984; Med Res Coun fel, Univ BC, 1974-1976. **Memberships:** Radiation Res Soc; Am Asn Physicists Med; Can Orgn Med Physicists; fel Can Col Physicists Med. **Research Statement & Publications:** Biophysical studies in the use of particle radiation for cancer radiotherapy; theoretical studies of radiation action. **Mailing Address:** Ottawa Hosp Regl Cancer Ctr, 503 Smyth Rd, Ottawa, ON K1H 1C4, Can. **Fax:** 613-247-3507. **E-Mail:** glam2001@hotmail.com

LAM, GILBERT NIM-CAR, PHARMACOKINETICS, DRUG METABOLISM. **Personal Data:** b Shanghai, China, November 10, 1951. **Education:** State Univ NY, Buffalo, BS, 1976; Univ Ill, PhD (pharm), 1981. **Professional Experience:** PRES & CEO, MICROCONSTANTS INC, as of 2002; assoc dir, Dupont Merck Pharmaceut Co, beginning 1991; res biochemist, E I DuPont Del Nemours & Co, Inc, 1981-1991. **Memberships:** Am Asn Pharmaceut Scientists; Int Soc Study Xenobiotics. **Research Statement & Publications:** Pharmacokinetics; biopharmaceutics; drug metabolism and analytical methodology of pharmaceuticals. **Mailing Address:** MicroConstants, Inc, 10110 Sorrento Valley Rd, Ste A, San Diego, CA 92121. **Fax:** 858-362-5698.

LAM, HARRY CHI-SING, THEORETICAL HIGH ENERGY PHYSICS. **Personal Data:** b Hong Kong, November 10, 1936. **Education:** McGill Univ, BSc, 1958; Mass Inst Technol, PhD (physics), 1963. **Professional Experience:** PROF EMER PHYSICS, MCGILL UNIV, 2004-; chmn dept, Mcgill Univ, 1976-1980; Rutherford prof physics, Mcgill Univ, 1975-2004; asst ed, Can J Physics, beginning 1973; from asst prof to assoc prof, Mcgill Univ, 1965-1975; res assoc physics, Univ Md, 1963-1965. **Memberships:** Am Phys Soc; Can Asn Physicists. **Research Statement & Publications:** Quantum field theory; particle theory. **Mailing Address:** Dept Physics, McGill Univ, Rutherford Physics Bldg, 3600 Univ St, Montreal, PQ H3A 2T8, Can. **E-Mail:** lam@physics.mcgill.ca

LAM, JOHN LING-YEE, CLASSICAL & QUANTUM ELECTRODYNAMICS. **Personal Data:** b Hong Kong, May 28, 1940; American citizen. **Education:** Rice Univ, BA, 1962; Calif Inst Technol, PhD (physics), 1967. **Professional Experience:** PRIN ENGR, BOEING DEFENSE & SPACE GROUP, 1988-; sr tech specialist, Northrop Corp, 1981-1988; sr res physicist, Dikewood Corp, 1974-1981; Nat Res Coun Can, 1969-1971 & Max Planck Inst Physics & Astrophys, Munich, 1971-1973; res fel, Univ Miami, 1968-1969; res fel, Calif Inst Technol, 1966-1968. **Memberships:** Am Phys Soc. **Research Statement & Publications:** Interaction between radiation and matter in both the classical and quantum regimes, and in both the microscopoic and macroscopic aspects. **Mailing Address:** 4821 Kent-Des Moines Rd Apt 303, Kent, WA 98032.

LAM, KAI SHUE, PHYSICS, CHEMICAL PHYSICS. **Personal Data:** b Hong Kong, February 22, 1949. **Education:** Univ Calif, Berkeley, AB, 1970; Mass Inst Technol, PhD (physics), 1976. **Professional Experience:** PROF, DEPT PHYSICS, CAL POLY UNIV, as of 2002; sr res assoc chem physics, Dept Chem, Univ Rochester, beginning 1980; fel & instr chem physics, 1976-1980. **Memberships:** Am Phys Soc; Sigma Xi. **Research Statement & Publications:** Atomic and molecular collision physics; atom-surface collisions; interaction of collision systems with laser radiation; spectral line broadening. **Mailing Address:** Physics Dept, Calif State Polytech Univ, Bldg 8 Rm 226, Pomona, CA 91768. **Fax:** 909-869-5090. **E-Mail:** kslam@csupomona.edu

LAM, KIN, COMPUTATIONAL FLUID MECHANICS & NUCLEAR REACTOR SAFETY, MULTI-PHYSICS MANUFACTURING SIMULATIONS & SOFTWARE VERIFICATION & VALIDATION. **Personal Data:** m. **Professional Experience:** LOS ALAMOS NAT LAB. **Mailing Address:** Los Alamos Nat Lab, PO Box 1663, Los Alamos, NM 87545. **E-Mail:** klam@lanl.gov

LAM, KUI CHUEN, MATHEMATICAL PROGRAMMING & ACCURACY ANALYSIS, ASTRONAUTICAL GUIDANCE. **Personal Data:** b Hong Kong, September 22, 1943; m 1974, c 1. **Education:** Univ Hong Kong, BS gen hons, 1967, BS spec hons, 1968; Univ Ore, MS, 1971, PhD (physics), 1974. **Professional Experience:** TECH STAFF ASTRONAUT GUID, C S DRAPER LABS INC, 1980-; res assoc radio astron, Mass Inst Technol, 1979-1980; res specialist atmospheric physics, Cloud Physics Dept, Univ Mo, Rolla, 1976-1979; lab supvr foreign lang, Western Carolina Univ, 1976; asst prof physics, Pahlaui Univ, Shiraz, Iran, 1975-1976; res assoc physics, Univ Ga, 1974-1975. **Memberships:** Am Phys Soc. **Research Statement & Publications:** Numerical analysis; mathematical physics; control and decision astronautical guidance; particle theory. **Mailing Address:** Mass Inst Technol, PO Box 172, Cambridge, MA 02139.

LAM, KWOK-WAI, BIOCHEMISTRY. **Personal Data:** b Kowloon, Hong Kong, September 21, 1935; m 1961, c 2. **Education:** E Tex Baptist Col, BS, 1957; Univ Pittsburgh, PhD (biochem), 1963. **Professional Experience:** RETIRED; vis scientist, Wilmer Ophthal Inst, Johns Hopkins, as of 2003; prof ophthal, Univ Tex, Health Sci Ctr, 1982-1996; res prof ophthal, Albany Med Col, 1981; res assoc prof biochem, 1973-1981; asst prof biochem, Boston Univ, Sch Med, 1970-1973; career develop award, NIH, 1967; assoc enzymol, Retina Found, Boston, 1966-1973; fel enzymol & geront, Nat Inst Child Health & Human Develop, 1963-1965. **Memberships:** Nat Acad Clin Biochem; Am Chem Soc; Asn Res Vision & Ophthal; Fedn Am Socs Exp Biol; Nat Registry Clin Chem. **Research Statement & Publications:** Mechanism of oxidative phosphorylation; clinical enzymology. **Mailing Address:** Johns Hopkins Hosp, 600 N Wolfe St, Baltimore, MD 21287.

LAM, LEO KONGSUI, INERTIAL GUIDANCE INSTRUMENTS. **Personal Data:** b Hong Kong, September 12, 1946; American citizen; m 1983, Florence; c Stephen & Jonathan. **Education:** Univ Hong Kong, BSc, 1969; Columbia Univ, MA, 1970, PhD (physics), 1975. **Professional Experience:** SR MEM TECH STAFF, GUIDANCE & CONTROL SYSTS DIV, LITTON INDUSTS INC, 1988-; mem tech staff, Guidance & Control Systs Div, Litton Industs Inc, 1981-1988; mem fac, Univ Southern Calif, 1979-1981; res asst prof physics, Univ Mo, Rolla, 1977-1979; res assoc physics, Joint Inst Lab Astrophys, Univ Col, 1975-1977; guest worker physics, Boulder Labs, Nat Bur Stands, 1975-1977. **Memberships:** Optical Soc Am. **Research Statement & Publications:** Fiber optics gyroscopes; erbium doped fiber amplifiers. **Mailing Address:** Litton Guid & Control, 5500 Canoga Ave Mail Sta Seven, Woodland Hills, CA 91367. **Fax:** 818-715-4351. **E-Mail:** lam@littongcs.com

LAM, LOUISA, SCIENTIFIC COMPUTATION. **Education:** Wellesley Col, BA; Univ Toronto, MSc, PhD (math). **Professional Experience:** ED BD, INT J COMPUT PROCESSING ORIENT LANG, as of 2006; ADJ ASSOC PROF, DEPT COMPUT SCI & SOFTWARE ENG, CONCORDIA UNIV, as of 2005. **Mailing Address:** Dept Comput Sci & Software Eng, Concordia Univ, 145 de Maisonneuve Blvd W, 606, Montreal, PQ H3G 1M8, Can. **Fax:** 514-848-2830. **E-Mail:** llam@cenparmi.concordia.ca

LAM, NGHI QUOC, METAL PHYSICS & RADIATION EFFECTS. **Personal Data:** b Vietnam, October 4, 1945; American citizen; m 1969, Hien; c Albert, Alice & Tina. **Education:** Laval Univ, BS, 1968; McMaster Univ, PhD (mat sci), 1971. **Honors & Awards:** Mat Sci Res Award, Dept Energy, 1984. **Professional Experience:** OBSERVER, ARGONNE NAT LAB, as of 2004; CHMN & ED, APPL PHYSICS LETT, ARGONNE NAT LAB, as of 2003; sr scientist, Argonne Nat Lab, beginning 1988; scientist, Argonne Nat Lab, 1977-1988; vis scientist, Ctr Nuclear Studies, Saclay, France, 1976-1981 & 1986-1988; adj prof, Div Med Physics & Bioengineering, Chicago Med Sch, 1976-1981 & 1986-1988; asst scientist, Argonne Nat Lab, 1974-1977; fel metal physics, Argonne Nat Lab, 1971-1974. **Memberships:** Am Phys Soc; Mat Res Soc; Bohmische Physikalische Gesellschaft. **Research Statement & Publications:** Radiation effects; atomic defects; diffusion; segregation; phase transformation; sputtering; ion implantation; electron microscopy; computer modeling and simulations. **Mailing Address:** Argonne Nat Lab, 9700 S Cass Ave, Argonne, IL 60439-4871. **Fax:** 630-252-4973. **E-Mail:** apl@jap.anl.gov

LAM, SAU-HAI, APPLIED MATHEMATICS, AEROSPACE & MECHANICAL ENGINEERING. **Personal Data:** b Macao, December 18, 1930; American citizen; m Patsy; c Nelson, Karen & Philip. **Education:** Rensselaer Polytech Inst, BE, 1954; Princeton Univ, PhD (aeronaut eng), 1958. **Professional Experience:** Assoc ed, Physics Fluids, 1983-1999; chmn, dept mech & aerospace eng, 1983-1989; co-chmn, prog appl & computational math, 1983-1986; assoc dean eng, Eng Physics Prog, 1980-1981; Edwin Wilsey chaired prof, Princeton Univ, 1973-1999; chmn, Eng Physics Prog, 1972-1981; prof aeronaut eng, Princeton Univ, 1967-1999; sr NSF fel, 1966-1967; from asst prof to assoc prof aerospace eng, Princeton Univ, 1960-1967; asst prof, Cornell Univ, 1959-1960; res assoc, Princeton Univ, 1958-1959; Res asst, Princeton Univ, 1956-1958. **Memberships:** Fel Am Inst Aeronaut & Astronaut; Am Phys Soc; Am Soc Mech Engrs. **Research Statement & Publications:** Theoretical gas dynamics; chemical kinetics; ionized gas flows; non-linear dynamics and control. **Mailing Address:** Dept Mech & Aerospace Eng, Princeton Univ, D209 Eng Quadrangle, Princeton, NJ 08544. **Fax:** 609-258-6109. **E-Mail:** lam@princeton.edu

LAM, SHEUNG TSING, APPLIED NUCLEAR PHYSICS, INFORMATION TECHNOLOGY. **Personal Data:** b Hong Kong, December 11, 1934; Canadian citizen. **Education:** Univ Hong Kong, BSc, 1959; Univ Ottawa, MSc, 1962; UnivAlta, PhD (physics), 1967. **Professional Experience:** TECHNOL TRANSFER & INFO, UNIV ALTA, 1991-; AMS proj coordr, Nuclear Res Ctr, 1987-1991; staff physicist & safety officer, Nuclear Res Ctr, 1972-1986; Frederick Gardner Cottrell Res Corp grant, 1971-1972; asst prof, Univ Va, 1970-1972; Can Nat Coun fel & res assoc nuclear physics, Univ Toronto, 1967-1970; Attached staff mem, Chalk River Nuclear Labs, Atomic Energy Can Ltd, 1967-1970; Demonstr physics, Univ Hong Kong, 1959-1960. **Memberships:** Am Phys Soc. **Research Statement & Publications:** Nuclear structure studies using electrostatic accelerators and fast neutron induced fission studies; neutron-neucleus scattering and analysis using optical potentials; study of 3-body interacton using n-D breakup reaction; trace element analysis using proton-induced X-ray emission; trace isotope analysis using accelerator mass spectrometry; use of internet for communication of data. **Mailing Address:** Centre Subatomic Res, Univ Alta, Edmonton, AB T6G 2N5, Can. **E-Mail:** lam@phys.unlberton.ca

LAM, SIMON SHIN-SING, COMPUTER SCIENCE, COMPUTER NETWORKS. **Personal Data:** b Macao, July 31, 1947; m 1971, Amy; c Eric. **Education:** Wash State Univ, BS, 1969; Univ Calif, Los Angeles, MS, 1970, PhD, 1974. **Honors & Awards:** Leonard G Abraham Prize, Inst Elec & Electronics Engrs, 1975 William R Bennett Prize, Inst Elec & Electronic Eng, 2001. **Professional Experience:** REGENTS CHAIR COMPUT SCI, UNIV TEX, AUSTIN, 2001-; chair dept, Univ Tex, Austin, 1992-1994; David S Bruton Centennial prof, Univ Tex, Austin, 1985-1988; PROF COMPUT SCI, UNIV TEX, AUSTIN, 1983-; NSF grant, 1978-; from asst prof to assoc prof, Univ Tex, Austin, 1977-1983; res staff mem,

IBM Watson Res Ctr, Yorktown Heights, NY, 1974-1977; res engr, ARPA Network Measurement Ctr, Univ Calif, Los Angeles, 1971-1974; chancellor's teaching fel, Univ Calif, Los Angeles, 1969-1973; ed-in-chief, IEEE-ACM Transactions Networking, 1995-1999. **Memberships:** fel Inst Elec & Electronics Engrs; fel Comput Mach. **Research Statement & Publications:** Computer science; contributed articles to professional journals; researched computer network, protocol design; distributed multimedia and internet security services. **Mailing Address:** Dept Comput Sci, Univ Tex, One Univ Sta C0500, Austin, TX 78712. **Fax:** 512-471-8885. **E-Mail:** lam@cs.utexas.edu

LAM, STANLEY K, SEPARATION SCIENCE, CLINICAL CHEMISTRY. **Personal Data:** b Hong Kong, American citizen. **Education:** Calif State Univ, BA, 1974; State Univ NY, Buffalo, PhD (chem), 1980. **Professional Experience:** ASSOC PROF LAB MED, ALBERT EINSTEIN COL MED, 1978-. **Memberships:** Am Chem Soc; Am Asn Clin Chem. **Research Statement & Publications:** Chromatographic methods for the monitoring of therapeutic agents and development of chromatographic techniques. **Mailing Address:** 2240 VanCortlandt Circle, Yorktown Heights, NY 10598.

LAM, TENNY N(ICOLAS), TRANSPORTATION ENGINEERING, OPERATIONS RESEARCH. **Personal Data:** b Hong Kong, November 28, 1940; m 1966, c 1. **Education:** Univ Calif, Berkeley, BS, 1963, MEng, 1964, DEng(transp sci), 1967. **Professional Experience:** RETIRED; dean eng, Univ Hong Kong, 1992-1994; prof, Univ Hong Kong, 1991-1994; reader, Univ Hong Kong, 1987-1989; from assoc prof to prof civil eng, Univ Calif, Davis, 1974-1986; assoc ed, Transp Sci, 1974-1977 & 1980-1986; sr res engr, Dept Theoret Physics, Gen Motors Res Labs, 1968-1974; asst prof civil eng, Univ Mo, Columbia, 1966-1968. **Memberships:** Opers Res Soc Am; Am Soc Civil Engrs. **Research Statement & Publications:** Traffic flow theory; transportation systems planning and analysis. **Mailing Address:** Univ Calif, 3100 Shelter Cove, Davis, CA 95616.

LAM, TSIT-YUEN, ALGEBRA. **Personal Data:** b Hong Kong, February 6, 1942; m 1970, Chee-King; c Juwen, Fumei, Juleen & Tsai-Yu. **Education:** Hong Kong Univ, BA, 1963; Columbia Univ, PhD (math), 1967. **Honors & Awards:** Steele Prize, Am Math Soc, 1983. **Professional Experience:** Guggenheim fel, 1981-1982; Miller prof, Univ Calif, 1978-1979; PROF MATH, UNIV CALIF, BERKELEY, 1976-; vchmn dept, Univ Calif, 1975 & 1980-1981; Alfred P Sloan Found fel, 1972-1974; from asst prof to assoc prof, Univ Calif, 1969-1976; lectr, Univ Calif, 1968-1969; instr, Univ Chicago, 1967-1968; fel math, Univ Ill, Urbana, 1967. **Memberships:** Am Math Soc; Math Asn Am. **Research Statement & Publications:** Finite groups and group representation theory; quadratic forms; ring theory. **Mailing Address:** Dept Math, Univ Calif, 871 Evans Hall, Berkeley, CA 94720-3840. **Fax:** 510-642-8204. **E-Mail:** lam@math.berkeley.edu

LAM, VINH-TE, PHYSICAL CHEMISTRY. **Personal Data:** b Saigon, South Vietnam, December 12, 1939; Canadian citizen; m 1980. **Education:** Univ Montreal, BS, 1962, PhD (phys chem), 1967. **Professional Experience:** PROF CHEM, COL BOIS-DEL-BOULOGNE, 1972-; lectr phys chem & Nat Res Coun Can grant, Univ Sherbrooke, 1969-1972; fel, Nat Res Coun Can, 1967-1969; Prof org chem, Col St Laurent, 1966-1967. **Memberships:** Am Chem Soc; Chem Inst Can. **Research Statement & Publications:** Thermodynamics; thermochemistry; static and dynamic microcalorimetry; critical phenomena; surface and polymer chemistry; molecular interactions; structure of liquids and solutions. **Mailing Address:** 6728 Chateaubriand, Montreal, PQ H2S 2N8, Can. **E-Mail:** vinhteel@collegebdeb.qc.ca

LAM, YIU-KUEN TONY, ORGANIC CHEMISTRY. **Personal Data:** b Hong Kong, June 5, 1947; American citizen; m 1977, c 3. **Education:** Chinese Univ, Hong Kong, BSc, 1971; Univ NB, PhD (org chem), 1974. **Professional Experience:** RES FEL, MERCK & CO, INC, 1984-; sr res chemist, Merck & CO, Inc, 1979-1983; asst prof, Univ Alta, 1977-1979; Res assoc, Univ Tex, Austin, 1975-1977. **Memberships:** AAAS; Am Chem Soc; Am Soc Pharmacog. **Research Statement & Publications:** Discovery and chemistry of novel biologically interesting principles from microbial, herbal and animal sources. **Mailing Address:** 6 Hilltown Ct, Plainsboro, NJ 08536.

LAMAN, JERRY THOMAS, INSITU SOLUTION MINING, RESTORATION OF GROUND WATER. **Personal Data:** b Muskogee, Okla, March 1, 1947. **Education:** Colo Sch Mines, che, 1969. **Professional Experience:** PRES & BD DIR, SOLUTION MINING CORP, LARAMIE, 1989-; VPRES, IN-SITU INC, LARAMIE, WYO, 1984-; proj mgr, Solution Mining Corp, Laramie, 1983-1984; chief metallurgist, Cleveland Cliffs Iron Co, 1977-1983; asst mine supt, Cliffs Copper Corp, 1972-1977; Refinery engr, ARCO, Torrance, Calif, 1969-1971. **Research Statement & Publications:** Solution mining and ground water restruction. **Mailing Address:** 11512 Tin Cup Dr Apt 202, Austin, TX 78750. **E-Mail:** jlaman@ev1.com

LAMANNA, JOSEPH CHARLES, NEUROPHYSIOLOGY, OPTICAL INSTRUMENTATION. **Personal Data:** b Bronxville, NY, July 12, 1949; m 1971, c 3. **Education:** Georgetown Univ, BS, 1971; Duke Univ, PhD (physiol), 1975. **Honors & Awards:** Young Investr Award, NIH, 1977. **Professional Experience:** PROF & CHMN, DEPT ANAT, 1993-; PROF, DEPT NEUROL, CASE WESTERN RES UNIV, 1990-; Merit Rev Bd, Vets Admin, 1987-1990; Brain, Lung & Develop Res Study Comt, Am Heart Asn, 1986-1989; assoc prof, Dept Anat, 1981-1990; Semmelweiss Med Sch, Budapest, Hungary, 1980; Res Career Develop Award, NIH, 1978-1981; from asst prof to assoc prof, Dept Neurol & Physiol-Biophys, Med Sch, Univ Miami, 1977-1981; Postdoctoral fel, NIH, 1975-1977; NIH fel & res assoc physiol, Duke Univ Med Ctr, 1975-1977; vis investr neurosurg Loma Linda Med Univ, Calif, 1975. **Memberships:** Am Physiol Soc; optical soc Am; Int Soc Oxygen Transp Tissues; Soc Neuroscience; biomed eng soc; Microcirculatory Soc; AAA; Int Soc Cerebral Blood Flow Metabolism. **Research Statement & Publications:** Determining the role of oxygen and oxidative energy metabolism in the function of the central nervous system in mammals. **Mailing Address:** Dept Anatomy, Case Western Res Univ Sch Med 10900 Euclid Ave, Cleveland, OH 44106-4930. **Fax:** 216-368-1144. **E-Mail:** joseph.lamanna@case.edu

LAMANNA, WILLIAM J, AERONAUTICS. **Professional Experience:** DIR ENG ADVANCED SUPPORT CONCEPTS, BOEING CO, as of 2003. **Memberships:** Am Inst Aeronaut & Astronaut. **Mailing Address:** Phantom Works, Boeing Co, M/S S 100-1163 PO Box 516, St Louis, MO 63166-0516. **Fax:** 314-233-6208. **E-Mail:** william.j.lamanna@boeing.com

LA MANTIA, CHARLES R, CHEMICAL ENGINEERING. **Personal Data:** b New York, NY, June 12, 1939; m 1961, c 2. **Education:** Columbia Univ, BA, 1960, BS, 1961, MS, 1963, ScD(chem eng), 1965. **Honors & Awards:** Egleston Medal, Columbia Univ, 2001. **Professional Experience:** BD DIR, NEUROMETRIX, 2004-; DIR, STATE ST CORP, BOSTON, MASS, 1993-; pres, chief exec officer, Arthur D Little, Inc, Cambridge, 1986-1999; pres, Koch Process Systs Inc, Westborough, Mass, 1981-1986; vpres, chem & metall eng, Arthur D Little Inc, Cambridge, 1967-1981; res & develop proj off, Defense Atomic Support Agency, 1965-1967; mem staff, Charles F Bonilla & Assocs, 1965. **Memberships:** Am Inst Chem Engrs. **Research Statement & Publications:** Chemical process design, analysis and development; air pollution control; energy technology; cryogenic technology. **Mailing Address:** 3 Goodwin Rd, Lexington, MA 02173.

LA MAR, GERD NEUSTADTER, STRUCTURAL CHEMISTRY. **Personal Data:** b Brasov, Romania, December 21, 1937; American citizen; m 1964, c 2. **Education:** Lehigh Univ, BS, 1960; Princeton Univ, PhD (chem), 1964. **Professional Experience:** DIR, UNIV CALIF, DAVIS, NUCLEAR MAGNETIC RESONANCE FACILITY, 1989-; fel, John Simon Guggenheim Mem Found, 1975; PROF CHEM, UNIV CALIF, DAVIS, 1974-; fel, Alfred P Sloan Found, 1972; from asst prof to assoc prof, Univ Calif, Davis, 1971-1974; res chemist, Shell Develop Co, 1967-1970; NATO fel, 1966-1967; NSF fel, 1964-1966. **Memberships:** Am Chem Soc. **Research Statement & Publications:** The use of magnetic resonance spectroscopy as a tool for elucidating structure-function relationships in metallo-enzymes and their model complexes. **Mailing Address:** Dept Chem, Univ Calif-Davis, Davis, CA 95616-5224. **Fax:** 530-752-8995. **E-Mail:** lamar@chem.ucdavis.edu

LAMAR, RICHARD T, SOIL MICROBIOLOGY. **Education:** NC State Univ, PhD, 1986. **Professional Experience:** DIR RES & APPLN, EARTHFAX DEVELOP CORP, as of 2003. **Mailing Address:** EarthFax Develop Corp, 1770 North Res Pkwy Suite 190, North Logan, UT 84341. **Fax:** 435-787-2749. **E-Mail:** earthfax@mtwest.net

LAMARCA, MICHAEL JAMES, DEVELOPMENTAL BIOLOGY. **Personal Data:** b Jamestown, NY, June 4, 1931; m 1954, c 3. **Education:** State Univ NY Albany, AB, 1953; Cornell Univ, PhD (zool), 1961. **Professional Experience:** RETIRED; vis lectr biol chem, Harvard Med Sch, 1977-1978; prof, Lawrence Univ, 1976-; NSF sci fac fel biol sci, Purdue Univ, 1971-1972; chmn dept, Lawrence Univ, 1970-1974; resident dir, Assoc Cols Midwest Argonne Semester Prog, Argonne Nat Lab, 1968-1969; from asst prof to assoc prof biol, Lawrence Univ, 1965-1976; NSF res grant, 1963-1965; asst prof, Rutgers Univ, 1963-1965; Instr zool, Rutgers Univ, 1961-1963. **Research Statement & Publications:** RNA and protein synthesis in echinoderm, amphibian, and mammalian development. **Mailing Address:** 2109 Beacon St SW, Rochester, MN 55902.

LAMARCHE, FRANCOIS, SURFACE ACTIVITY OF PROTEINS, PROTEIN STRUCTURE. **Personal Data:** b Montreal, Que, January 2, 1960; m 1986, c 2. **Education:** Univ Que, Trois-Rivieres, BS, 1982, PhD (biophys), 1988. **Professional Experience:** RES SCIENTIST PROTEIN STRUCT, FOOD RES & DEVELOP CTR, AGR & AGRI-FOOD CAN, 1988-. **Memberships:** Biophys Soc; Protein Soc. **Research Statement & Publications:** Study of the behavior of proteins at air-water and oil-water interface; importance of structural factors of protein on their surface properties. **Mailing Address:** Food Res & Develop Ctr, Agr & Agri-Food, 3600 Casavant Blvd W, St-Hyacinthe, PQ J2S 8E3, Can. **Fax:** 450-773-8461. **E-Mail:** lamarchef@agr.gc.ca

LAMARCHE, J L GILLES, PHYSICS. **Personal Data:** b Montreal, Que, May 31, 1927; m 1961, AnneMarie; c Marie & Pierre. **Education:** Univ Montreal, BSc, 1950; Univ BC, MA, 1953, PhD (physics), 1957. **Professional Experience:** ADJ PROF PHYSICS, UNIV OTTAWA, 1992-; from asst prof to prof, Univ Ottawa, 1957-1992. **Memberships:** Am Phys Soc; Can-Fr Asn Advan Sci; Can Asn Physicists. **Research Statement & Publications:** Low temperature physics; semimagnetic semiconductor magnetism; nuclear magnetism. **Mailing Address:** Dept Physics, Univ Ottawa, Ottawa, ON K1N 6N5, Can. **Fax:** 613-562-5190. **E-Mail:** lamarche@physics.uottawa.ca

LAMARCHE, PAUL H, GENETICS, PEDIATRICS. **Personal Data:** b Boston, Mass, September 5, 1929; m 2000, Rolande; c Paul Jr, Marian, Claire, Patricia, Phillip, Rachelle, Darel & David. **Education:** Boston Col, BS, 1956; Boston Univ, MD, 1960; Mass Inst Technol, ScM, 1974. **Honorary Degrees:** MA, Brown Univ 1974. **Honors & Awards:** March Of Dimes- Franklin Delairo Roosevelt Award; Children Miracle Network- Miracle Dr Award, (WYETH). **Professional Experience:** DIR, HUSSON COL RES INST, BANGOR, as of 2004; MED DIR, EASTERN MAINE MED CTR, 1985-; prof pediat, Sch Med, Tufts Univ, 1981; PROF GENETICS, UNIV MAINE, 1974-; chief pediat & genetics, Univ Maine, 1974-1985; assoc physician-in-chief pediat, Birth Defects Ctr, 1969-1975; consult, Child Study Ctr, Brown Univ, 1967-1974; med dir child develop ctr, Birth Defects Ctr, 1966-1975; consult, Providence Lying-In Hosp, 1966-1974; med dir, Birth Defects Ctr, 1965-1975; prin investr Nat Cancer Inst grant, 1964-1969; res assoc path & dir genetics lab, RI Hosp, 1963-1975; asst pediatrician, Providence Lying-In Hosp, 1963-1974. **Memberships:** AAAS; Genetics Soc Am; Tissue Cult Asn. **Research Statement & Publications:** Genetics and cytogenetics of teratogenesis and oncogenesis; electron microscopy of fine structure of somatic cellular phenotypes normal and abnormal in the human. **Mailing Address:** Res Inst, Husson Col, One Col Circle, Bangor, ME 04401-2999. **Fax:** 207-941-7139. **E-Mail:** phlammd2@pol.net

LAMARCHE, PAUL HENRY, PLASMA-MATERIALS INTERACTIONS, ULTRA-HIGH VACUUM SCIENCE. **Personal Data:** b Norwood, Mass, April 21, 1953; m 1996, Susan; c Keirnan, Reilly, Casey, Colleen & Denis. **Education:** Boston Col, BS, 1975; Yale Univ, MS, 1976, PhD (physics), 1981. **Professional Experience:** DEPT MGR, PHYSICS DEPT, PRINCETON UNIV, as of 2004; DEPT HEAD, TRITIUM SYST DIV, PRINCETON UNIV, 1993-; chmn, Plasma Sci & Technol Div, Am Vacuum Soc, 1989; Consult, 1984-; Head, Vacuum Systs Group, 1984-1993; res assoc, Univ Chicago, 1982-1984; Res physicist, Exxon Prod Res Co, 1981-1982. **Memberships:** Am Phys Soc; Am Vacuum Soc; NY Acad Sci. **Research Statement & Publications:** The interaction of energetic plasma ions with solids as embodied in fusion research devices; interfacial processes at vacuum-wall boundary; consulting work on vacuum vessel and system design; management of professional and technical staff. **Mailing Address:** Dept Physics, Princeton Univ, 213 Jadwin Hall, Trenton, NJ 08638. **E-Mail:** lamarche@princeton.edu

LAMASTRO, ROBERT ANTHONY, GLASS TECHNOLOGY. **Personal Data:** b New York, NY, September 11, 1956; m 1981, c 1. **Education:** Rutgers Univ, BA & BS, 1979, MS, 1981, PhD (ceramic eng), 1982. **Professional Experience:** ADJ PROF MATH, ROWAN UNIV, as of 2004; adj prof, Cumberland Co Col, beginning 1989; mgr glass res & develop, Wheaton Industs, 1984-1989; glass technologist, Wheaton Industs, 1982-1984. **Memberships:** Am Ceramic Soc; Soc Glass Technol; Parenteral Drug Asn; Am Chem Soc; AAAS. **Research Statement & Publications:** Development of specialty glass formulations for the pharmaceutical and cosmetic packaging industries. **Mailing Address:** Dept Math, Rowan Univ, Robinson Hall, Glassboro, NJ 08332-2003. **E-Mail:** lamastro@rowan.edu

LAMATTINA, JOHN LAWRENCE, HETEROCYCLIC CHEMISTRY, MEDICINAL CHEMISTRY. **Personal Data:** b Brooklyn, NY, January 22, 1950; m 1971, c 3. **Education:** Boston Col, BS, 1971; Univ NH, PhD (chem), 1975. **Professional Experience:** PRES, PFIZER GLOBAL RES & DEVELOP, 2003-; DIR, THERMO ELECTRON CORP, 2002-; SR VPRES, PFIZER INC, 1999-; sr vpres, Worldwide Develop, 1999; sr vpres, Worldwide Discovery Oper, 1998; vpres, US Discovery Oper, 1993; dir med chem, Pfizer Inc, beginning 1987; res scientist med chem, Pfizer Inc, beginning 1977; NIH fel, Princeton Univ, 1975-1977. **Memberships:** Am Chem Soc. **Research Statement & Publications:** Design and synthesis of compounds which possess intriguing biological properties. **Mailing Address:** Thermo Electron Corp, 81 Wyman St, Waltham, MA 02454-9046. **Fax:** 781-622-1207.

LAMAZE, GEORGE PAUL, NEUTRON DEPTH PROFILING, EXPERIMENTAL NUCLEAR PHYSICS. **Personal Data:** b Algiers, Algeria, January 15, 1945; American citizen; m 1965, Catherine; c Theresa & Melissa. **Education:** Fla State Univ, BA, 1965; Duke Univ, PhD (physics), 1972. **Honors & Awards:** Award Merit, Am Soc Testing & Mat. **Professional Experience:** PHYSICIST, NUCLEAR ANAL METHODS GROUP, NAT INST STAND & TECHNOL, as of 2004; vchair, Subcomt Nuclear Radiation Metrol & chmn, Comt Nuclear Technol Applns, beginning 1994; secy comt, Nuclear Technol & Applns, Am Soc Testing & Mat, 1990-1992; physicist, Inorg Analysis Res Div, Nat Inst Stand & Technol, beginning 1989; sci asst to rep George Brown, Calif, 1978-1979; physicist neutron stand, Nat Bur Stand, 1972-1989. **Memberships:** Am Phys Soc; fel Am Soc Testing & Mat. **Research Statement & Publications:** Measurement of neutron depth profiling; radioactivity measurements; cold neutron fluence rates. **Mailing Address:** Nuclear Anal Methods Group, Anal Chem Div, Nat Inst Stand & Technol, Rm B173 Bldg 235 100 Bur Dr, Gaithersburg, MD 20899-8395. **Fax:** 301-208-9279. **E-Mail:** george.lamaze@nist.gov

LAMB, BRIAN K, POLLUTION. **Education:** Idaho State Univ, BS, 1973; Calif Inst Technol, PhD, 1978. **Professional Experience:** REGENTS PROF, DEPT CIVIL & ENVIRON ENG, WASH STATE UNIV, as of 2006. **Mailing Address:** Dept Civil & Environ Eng, Wash State Univ, Pullman, WA 99164. **Fax:** 509-335-7632. **E-Mail:** blamb@wsu.edu

LAMB, DAVID E(RNEST), CHEMICAL ENGINEERING, COMPUTER SCIENCE. **Personal Data:** b Pampa, Tex, April 6, 1932; m 1956, c 5. **Education:** Yale Univ, BE, 1953; Princeton Univ, MS, 1954, PhD (chem eng), 1962. **Professional Experience:** Mem adv comt, Off Comput Activities, NSF, 1968-1971; mem steering comt, Simulation Coun, 1965-; PROF CHEM ENG, STATIST & COMPUT SCI & CHMN DEPT, UNIV DEL, 1965-; assoc prof& dir comput ctr, Statist & Comput Sci & Chmn Dept, Univ Del, 1963-1965; mem theory comt, Am Automatic Control Coun, 1961-; Ethyl Corp, 1960 & Prentice-Hall, Inc, 1960-; asst prof chem eng, Statist & Comput Sci & Chmn Dept, Univ Del, 1958-1963; Consult, Sun Oil Co, 1957-; res engr, Sun Oil Co, Pa, 1957; Instr chem eng, Princeton Univ, 1956. **Memberships:** Asn Comput Mach; Simulation Coun. **Research Statement & Publications:** Continuous and discrete system simulation; computer graphics. **Mailing Address:** 101 B Smith Hall Univ Del, Newark, DE 19716.

LAMB, DENNIS, CLOUD PHYSICS. **Personal Data:** b Chicago, Ill, February 3, 1941; m 1981, Pat; c Julie. **Education:** Kalamazoo Col, BA (physics), 1963; Univ Wash, PhD (atmospheric sci), 1970. **Professional Experience:** PROF, METEOROL DEPT, PA STATE UNIV, UNIV PARK, 1997-; assoc prof meterol dept, Pa State Univ, Univ Park, 1986-1997; from asst to res prof, Atmospheric Sci Ctr, Desert Res Inst, Univ Nev, Reno, 1972-1986; NATO res assoc meteorol, Univ Frankfurt, 1971-1972; gen physicist data assessment, Naval Weapons Ctr, China Lake, Calif, 1963-1965. **Memberships:** Am Meteorol Soc; Sigma Xi; Am Geophys Union. **Research Statement & Publications:** Nucleation and growth of solids from the liquid and vapor phases; formation of cloud nuclei; cloud physics/ weather modification; atmospheric chemistry. **Mailing Address:** Meteorol Dept, Pa State Univ, 519 Walker Bldg, Univ Park, PA 16802. **E-Mail:** lno@ems.psu.edu

LAMB, DONALD JOSEPH, PHARMACY. **Personal Data:** b Pittsburgh, Pa, October 29, 1931; m 1956, c 2. **Education:** Ohio State Univ, BSc, 1954, MSc, 1955, PhD (pharm), 1960. **Professional Experience:** RETIRED; dir proj mgt, Upjohn Co, 1988-; dir proj support, Upjohn Co, 1983-1988; res mgr pharmaceut res, Upjohn Co, 1970-1983; res head, Upjohn Co, 1965-1970; Res assoc pharmaceut res & develop, Upjohn Co, 1960-1965. **Memberships:** Am Pharmaceut Asn; Am Acad Pharmaceut Sci; Am Chem Soc; Sigma Xi. **Research Statement & Publications:** Design and evaluation of drug dosage forms, including design and evaluation of drugs to fit specific dosage forms. **Mailing Address:** 5128 Allardowne St, Portage, MI 49002.

LAMB, DONALD QUINCY, ASTROPHYSICS. **Personal Data:** b Manhattan, Kans, June 30, 1945; m 1978, Linda; c Michael. **Education:** Rice Univ, BA, 1967; Univ Liverpool, MSc, 1969; Univ Rochester, PhD (physics), 1974. **Professional Experience:** Dept chmn, Univ Chicago, 1988-1991; adv bd, Aspen Ctr Physics, 1987-; vis prof physics, Inst Theoret Physics, Univ Calif, Santa Barbara, 1987; PROF ASTRON & ASTROPHYS, UNIV CHICAGO, 1985-; sect, Aspen Ctr Physics, 1985-1986; trustee, Aspen Ctr Physics, 1981-1987; physicist, Smithsonian Ctr Astrophys, Harvard Univ, 1980-1985; lectr astron, Harvard Univ, 1980-1985; vis scientist, Smithsonian Ctr Astrophys, Harvard Univ, 1979-1980; Guggenheim fel, 1978-1979; vis assoc prof physics, Mass Inst Technol, 1978-1979; from asst prof to prof, Univ Ill, 1975-1980; res asst prof physics, Univ Ill, 1973-1975; Marshall scholar, 1967-1969. **Memberships:** Fel Am Phys Soc; Am Astron Soc; fel Royal Astron Soc; Brit Inst Physics; Europ Phys Soc. **Research Statement & Publications:** Evolution and structure of white dwarfs and neutron stars; physics of compact x-ray and gamma-ray sources, supernovae; properties of matter at high densities. **Mailing Address:** Dept Astron & Astrophys, Univ Chicago, 5640 S Ellis Ave, Chicago, IL 60637. **Fax:** 773-702-8212. **E-Mail:** lamb@oddjob.uchicago.edu

LAMB, DONALD R(OY), CIVIL ENGINEERING. **Personal Data:** b Yuma, Colo, May 6, 1923; m 1943, c 3. **Education:** Hastings Col, BA, 1947; Univ Wyo, BS, 1951, MS, 1953, CE, 1958; Purdue Univ, PhD, 1962. **Professional Experience:** PROF CIVIL ENG & HEAD DEPT, UNIV WYO, 1970-; from supply instr to assoc prof, Univ Wyo, 1951-1970; coach, Nebr, 1947-1949; Supt high schs, Nebr, 1946-1947. **Memberships:** Am Soc Eng Educ; Am Soc Civil Engrs; Nat Soc Prof Engrs; Sigma Xi. **Research Statement & Publications:** Use of radioisotopes in the study of portland cement, asphalt concrete and soils; portland cement concrete and associated aggregates; transportation; recreational engineering; engineering geology. **Mailing Address:** 417 Stetson Ct, Laramie, WY 82070.

LAMB, FREDERICK KEITHLEY, ASTROPHYSICS. **Personal Data:** b Manhattan, Kans, June 30, 1945; m 1971, c 2. **Education:** Calif Inst Technol, BS, 1967; Oxford Univ, DPhil(theoret physics), 1970. **Professional Experience:** DIR, CTR THEORET ASTROPHYS, 1999-; BRAND & MONICA FORTNER ENDOWED CHMN THEORET ASTROPHYS, UNIV ILL, URBANA, 1998-; vis scholar, Stanford Univ Ctr Space Sci & Astrophys, 1985-1986; sci fel, Ctr Int Security & Arms Control, Stanford Uni, 1985-1986; fel, John Simon Guggenheim Found, 1985-1986; PROF ASTRON, UNIV ILL, URBANA, 1980-; PROF PHYSICS, UNIV ILL, URBANA, 1978-; vis assoc, Caltech, 1977-1978; vis fel, Inst Astron, Cambridge, UK, 1975-1976; fel commorer, Churchill Col, Cambridge, UK, 1975-1976; res fel, Alfred P Sloan Found, 1974-1978; assoc, Ctr Advan Study, Univ Ill, Urbana, 1973-1974; from asst prof to assoc prof, Univ Ill, Urbana, 1972-1978; instr & res assoc, Univ Ill, Urbana, 1970-1972; fel physics, Magdalen Col, Oxford Univ, 1970-1972. **Memberships:** Fel Am Phys Soc; Am Astron Soc; fel Royal Astron Soc; Int Astron Union. **Research Statement & Publications:** White dwarfs, neutron stars, and black holes; plasma theory and applications to pulsars and cosmic X-ray sources; the interaction of radiation with matter; arms control and international security. **Mailing Address:** Dept Physics, Univ Ill, 237B Loomis Lab 1110 W Green St, Urbana, IL 61801-3080. **Fax:** 217-333-9819. **E-Mail:** fkl@uiuc.edu

LAMB, GEORGE ALEXANDER, PEDIATRICS, INFECTIOUS DISEASES. **Personal Data:** b Glens Falls, NY, September 25, 1934; m 1956, c 3. **Education:** Swarthmore Col, BS, 1955; State Univ NY Upstate Med Ctr, MD, 1959. **Professional Experience:** PROF PEDIAT, BOSTON UNIV SCH MED, 1979-; assoc prof prev & social med, Harvard Med Sch, 1972-1979; fel infectious dis, beginning 1964; from asst prof to assoc prof, State Univ NY Upstate Med Ctr, 1964-1972; resident, State Univ NY Upstate Med Ctr, 1960-1962; intern pediat, State Univ NY Upstate Med Ctr, 1959-1960. **Research Statement & Publications:** Infectious diseases of children, especially the epidemiology of respiratory illnesses; community child health. **Mailing Address:** Boston Univ, Dept Health & Hosps, 818 Harrison Ave, Boston, MA 02118-2999.

LAMB, GEORGE LAWRENCE, PHYSICS. **Personal Data:** b Norwood, Mass, April 28, 1931; m 1959, c 4. **Education:** Boston Col, BS, 1953, MS, 1954; Mass Inst Technol, PhD (physics), 1958. **Professional Experience:** PROF EMER MATH, UNIV ARIZ, as of 2004; prof math & optical sci, Univ Ariz, beginning 1974; physicist, United Aircraft Res Labs, Conn, 1963-1974; staff mem, Los Alamos Sci Lab, 1958-1963. **Memberships:** Am Phys Soc; Sigma Xi; Acoust Soc Am. **Research Statement & Publications:** Nonlinear waves and solitons; acoustic wave propagation. **Mailing Address:** Univ Ariz, 2942 Ave Del Conquistador RR 2, Tucson, AZ 85749-9304.

LAMB, GEORGE MARION, MICROPALEONTOLOGY, STRATIGRAPHY. **Personal Data:** b Little Rock, Ark, December 23, 1928; m 1953, c 2. **Education:** Emory Univ, BA, 1950, MS, 1954; Univ Colo, Boulder, PhD (geol), 1964. **Professional Experience:** PROF EMER GEOL, UNIV SALA, as of 2002; asst to pres, Univ Sala, beginning 1989; prof geol, 1964-1989; geologist, Stand Oil Calif, Inc, 1955-1961. **Memberships:** Am Asn Petrol Geol; Geol Soc Am; Am Inst Prof Geologists. **Research Statement & Publications:** Ecology and paleoecology of Foraminifera; biostratigraphic relationships; groundwater and environmental geology; beach erosion and development. **Mailing Address:** Rte 2 Box 48, Stevenville, TX 76401.

LAMB, H RICHARD, PSYCHIATRY. **Personal Data:** b Philadelphia, Pa, September 18, 1929; m Doris; c Jonathan, Carolyn & Thomas. **Education:** Univ Pa, BA, 1950; Yale Univ, MD, 1954. **Honors & Awards:** Presidential Commendation, Am Psychiat Asn, 1985; Arnold L van Ameringen Award in Psychiatric Rehabilitation & Treatment of the Chronically Mentally Ill, Am Psychiat Asn, 1998; National Alliance for the Mentally Ill, Don and Peggy Richardson Memorial Award For Distinguished Service to Persons Afflicted With Serious Mental Illness, 2003. **Professional Experience:** PROF PSYCHIAT, SCH MED, UNIV SOUTHERN CALIF, 1980-; Ed-in-chief, New Directions Ment Health Serv J, 1978-; mem comt rehab, Am Psychiat Asn, 1978-1984; Chair, Task Force on the Homeless Mentally Ill, 1983-1985 & 1989-1991, Am psychiat Asn, Committee on Jails and Prisons, 2002-Present, Am Psychiat Asn; assoc prof, Sch Med, Univ Southern Calif, 1976-1980; Consult, NIMH, 1975-; Chief rehab serv, San Mateo Co Ment Health Serv, 1968-1976; mem, Group Advan Psychiat 1982- National Board of Directors, National Alliance on Mental Illness (NAMI), 2005-present. **Memberships:** Fel Am Psychiat Asn; fel Am Col Psychiatrists; Group Advan Psychiat. **Research Statement & Publications:** Social and community psychiatry and community mental health with a major focus on the long-term severely disabled psychiatric patient in the community. **Mailing Address:** Dept Psychiat & Behav Sci, Sch Med, Univ Southern Calif, 2020 Zonal Ave, Los Angeles, CA 90033. **Fax:** 323-226-4268. **E-Mail:** hlamb@usc.edu

LAMB, JAMES C(HRISTIAN), III, SCIENCE EDUCATION, RESEARCH ADMINISTRATION. **Personal Data:** b Warsaw, Va, August 20, 1924. **Education:** Va Mil Inst, BS, 1947; Mass Inst Technol, SM, 1948, SE, 1952, ScD(sanit eng), 1953. **Professional Experience:** CONSULT, 1991-; judge, US Nuclear Regulatory Comn, 1974-; from assoc prof to prof, Univ NC, Chapel Hill, 1959-1987; adj prof, Newark Col Eng, 1956-1959; sanit engr, Am Cyanamid Co, 1955-1959; res assoc, Mass Inst Technol, 1953-1955; asst sanit eng, Mass Inst Technol, 1951-1953; lectr, Wash & Lee Univ, 1949-1950 & Exten Div, State Dept Educ, Mass, 1951-1952; Consult engr, 1948-1950, 1952-1955, 1959-; Instr civil eng, Va Mil Inst, 1948-1950. **Memberships:** Am Soc Civil Engrs; Am Water Works Asn; Water Pollution Control Fedn. **Research Statement & Publications:** Industrial wastes; sewage treatment; water supply; saline water conversion; corrosion; stream pollution; refuse disposal; steam pollution, regulatory controls and standards; civil engineering. **Mailing Address:** 2401 Old Ivy Rd, Charlottesville, VA 22903.

LAMB, JAMES L, MICROPALEONTOLOGY. **Personal Data:** b Los Angeles, Calif, January 17, 1925; m 1945, c 2. **Education:** Univ Southern Calif, BS, 1953. **Professional Experience:** CONSULT, 1981-; paleontologist, Exxon Prod Res Co, 1964-1981; Paleontologist, Richfield Oil Corp, 1953-1957 & Creole Petrol Corp, 1957-1964. **Memberships:** Soc Econ Paleont & Mineral; Am Asn Petrol Geologists; Venezuelan Asn Geol Mining & Petrol. **Research Statement & Publications:** Historical geology and paleontology; geologic distribution of planktonic foraminifera; tertiary microfossils; Pleistocene epoch. **Mailing Address:** 1358 Lawnridge St, Medford, OR 97504-6246.

LAMB, J(AMIE) PARKER, MECHANICAL & AEROSPACE ENGINEERING. **Personal Data:** b Boligee, Ala, September 21, 1933; m 1955, Nancy; c David & Stephen P. **Education:** Auburn Univ, BS, 1954; Univ Ill, MS, 1958, PhD (mech eng), 1961. **Honors & Awards:** Founders Award, Am Soc Mech Engrs, 1975; Centennial Award, Am Soc Mech Engrs, 1980; Joe J King Prof Eng Award, 1984. **Professional Experience:** PROF EMER MECH ENG, UNIV TEX, AUSTIN, as of 2003; dir eng prog, Univ Tex, Pan-Am, 1993-1994; gen chmn, Tenth US Nat Cong, Appl Mech, 1986; Ernest Cockrell Jr Mem prof, Uinv Tex, Austin, beginning 1981; chmn aerospace eng, Col Eng, 1981-1988; Vought Aerospace Corp, Tex, 1969-1970 & Mobil Oil Corp, Tex, 1977-1978; assoc dean, Col Eng, 1976-1981; assoc tech ed, J Fluids Eng, 1976-1979; chmn dept, Univ Tex, Austin, 1970-1976; NASA, Ala, 1969-1970; Tracor, Inc, Tex, 1965-1967; from asst prof to prof mech eng, Univ Tex, Austin, 1963-1981; consult, ARO, Inc, Tenn, 1963-1965; asst prof eng mech, NC State Univ, Raleigh, 1961-1963; proj engr, Flight Control Lab, Wright Air Develop Ctr, Ohio, 1955-1957. **Memberships:** fel Am Soc Mech Engrs; assoc fel Am Inst Aeronaut & Astronaut; Am Soc Eng Educ; Nat Soc Prof Engrs. **Research Statement & Publications:** Heat transfer and fluid mechanics in separated flow regions; compressible turbulent boundary layers; heat, mass and momentum transfers in free turbulent jets; energy conversion processes for low temperature sources. **Mailing Address:** Dept Mech Eng, Univ Tex, One Univ Sta C2200, Austin, TX 78712-0292. **Fax:** 512-471-1045. **E-Mail:** jplamb@mail.utexas.edu

LAMB, JOHN DAVID, MACROCYCLIC HOST-GUEST CHEMISTRY, SEPARATIONS CHEMISTRY. **Personal Data:** b Brockville, Ont, October 10, 1949; m 1976, Betty; c Michael, Jeremy, Joshua, Zachary, Matthew & Jacob. **Education:** Brigham Young Univ, BS, 1971, PhD (inorg phys chem), 1978. **Honors & Awards:** Carnegie Professor of the

Year, 2000. **Professional Experience:** Eliot A. Butler Professor, Brigham Young Univ, 2000-; Associate Dean, Undergraduate Education, BYU, 2000-; visiting lecturer, Univ Pavia, Italy, 1995; co-ed-in-chief, J Inclusion Phenomena & Macrocyclic Chem, 1992-; chair, Intl Org Comm, Intl Symposium on Macrocyclic Chem, 1995-; PROF CHEM, BRIGHAM YOUNG UNIV, 1991-; visiting lect, Sichuan Univ, China, 1991; exec dir res & creative work, Brigham Young Univ, 1990-1992; Univ Parma, Italy, 1990 & 1991; vis prof, Univ Catania, Italy, 1989; prin investr, Dionex Corp, beginning 1986; dir res admin, Brigham Young Univ, 1985-1990; pin investr, US Dept Energy, beginning 1984; prog mgr separations & analysis, US Dept Energy, 1982-1984. **Memberships:** Am Chem Soc. **Research Statement & Publications:** Macrocyclic ligands in making chemical separations by ion chromatography, liquid membranes, solvent extraction and capillary electrophoresis; multimedia computer materials for chemistry instruction. **Mailing Address:** Dept Chem & Biochem, Brigham Young Univ, Provo, UT 84602. **Fax:** 801-422-0263. **E-Mail:** john_lamb@byu.edu

LAMB, MARY ROSE, GENETIC & MOLECULAR BIOLOGY OF PHOTOTAXIS IN CHLAMYDOMONAS, ORGANELLE GENETICS. **Personal Data:** b Glen Falls, NY, August 8, 1952. **Education:** Reed Col, BA, 1974; State Univ NY, Albany, MLS, 1975; Ind Univ, PhD (zool), 1984. **Professional Experience:** PROF, DEPT BIOL, UNIV PUGET SOUND, 2001-; assoc prof, Dept Biol, Univ Puget Sound, 1990-2001; asst prof, Dept Biol, Univ Puget Sound, 1984-1990; asst prof biol, Bryn Mawr Col, 1983-1984. **Memberships:** Genetics Soc Am; Am Soc Microbiol; Sigma Xi; aaas. **Research Statement & Publications:** Genetics and molecular biology of phototaxis in chlamydomonas reinhardil; identified four genes that affect the assembly of the eyespot and are characterizing those genes. **Mailing Address:** Dept Biol, Univ Puget Sound, Tacoma, WA 98416-1088. **Fax:** 253-879-3500. **E-Mail:** mrlamb@ups.edu

LAMB, MINA MARIE WOLF, NUTRITION, FOOD PREPARATION. **Personal Data:** b Sagerton, Tex, August 14, 1910; m 1941, c 1. **Education:** Tex Tech Col, BA, 1932, MS, 1937; Columbia Univ, PhD (nutrit, chem), 1942. **Honors & Awards:** Piper Award, 1965; Medallion Award, Am Dietetic Assoc, 1986; Serv Award, 1987. **Professional Experience:** PROF EMER FOOD & NUTRIT, TEX TECH UNIV, 1975-; Margaret W Weeks distinguished prof, Tex Tech Univ, 1969-1975; lectr & adv foreign students, Dept Food & Nutrit, 1960-1971; head, Dept Food & Nutrit, 1955-1969; from lab asst to prof, Tex Tech Univ, 1940-1969; teacher & res worker food & nutrit, 1935-1937; Teacher, elem & high sch, 1933-1935. **Memberships:** AAAS; Am Dietetic Asn; Am Home Econ Asn; Am Men Sci. **Research Statement & Publications:** Basal metabolism of college girls and children of various ages older than two years; needs of children and adults; dietary studies of children, college girls and families; animal feeding work with albino rats determining growth and reproduction responses to various diets and foods. **Mailing Address:** Dept Food sci & Nutrit, Tex Tech Univ, Lubbock, TX 79407-3102.

LAMB, PETER JAMES, METEOROLOGY, CLIMATE DYNAMICS. **Personal Data:** b Nelson, NZ, June 21, 1947; New Zealander & American citizen; c Karen D Lockwood & Brett T Lamb. **Education:** Univ Canterbury, Christ Church, NZ, BA, 1969, MA, 1971, Hons, 1972; Univ Wis, PhD, 1976, Univ Canterbury, Christ CHurch, NZ, DSC, 2002. **Honors & Awards:** Margary Lectr, 1991. **Professional Experience:** PROF & DIR, SCH METEOROL, UNIV OKLA, NORMAN, 1991-; sect head, Ill State Water Surv, Champaign, 1984-1990; consult, Dept State, Dept Energy, Agency Int Develop, Nat Oceanic & Atmospheric Admin, NSF, World Meteorol Orgn, Kingdom Morocco, Univ Wis, Univ Adelaide, Univs Space Res Asn & Environ Protection Agency, 1983-; adj prof, Univ Ill, Urbana, 1983-1994; sr scientist, Ill State Water Surv, Champaign, 1979-1991; Vis res assoc, Univ Miami, Fla, 1978-1979; lectr, Univ Adelaide, Australia, 1976-1979; res assoc, Univ Wis-Madison, 1976; res asst, Univ Wis-Madison, 1971-1976; numerous res grants from US & Fed Agencies. **Memberships:** Am Meteorol Soc; Royal Meteorol Soc; Am Asn State Climatologists; Sigma Xi. **Research Statement & Publications:** Research on heat transport by the Atlantic Ocean; role of the ocean in causing droughts in Sahelian Africa; investigations of precipitation variability in North America and North Africa-; investigation of societal impacts of short-term climate variations. **Mailing Address:** Univ Okla, CIMMS-Sarkeys Energy Ctr, 100 E Boyd Rm 1110, Norman, OK 73019. **Fax:** 405-325-7614. **E-Mail:** plamb@ou.edu

LAMB, RICHARD C, GAMMA RAY ASTRONOMY, ELEMENTARY PARTICLE PHYSICS. **Personal Data:** b Lexington, Ky, September 8, 1933; m 1959, Jane Oldham; c Cheryl, Richard, David & Wayne. **Education:** Mass Inst Technol, BS, 1955; Univ Ky, PhD (physics), 1963. **Professional Experience:** VIS ASSOC PHYSICS, CALIF INST TECH, as of 2001; sr assoc, Jet Propulsion Lab, Nat Res Coun, 1982-1983; prin investr prog observational gamma-ray astron, 1980-; vis scientist, NASA-Goddard Space Flight Ctr, 1975-1976; prof Physics, Iowa State Univ, 1972-1996; assoc prof, Iowa State Univ, 1967-1972; Asst scientist, Argonne Nat Lab, 1963-1967. **Memberships:** Fel Am Phys Soc; Am Astron Soc; Int Astron Union. **Research Statement & Publications:** Very high energy gamma ray astronomy using the atmospheric Cerenkov technique; identification of gamma ray sources. **Mailing Address:** Dept Physics, Calif Inst Tech, 220-47 Space Radiation Lab, Pasedena, CA 91125. **Fax:** 626-449-8676. **E-Mail:** lamb@srl.caltech.edu

LAMB, ROBERT ANDREW, VIROLOGY, MOLECULAR BIOLOGY. **Personal Data:** b London, Eng, September 26, 1950; American citizen; m 1989, Reay; c Alexander, Duncan & Gabriella. **Education:** Univ Birmingham, BS, 1971; Univ Cambridge, PhD (virol), 1974. **Honorary Degrees:** ScD, Univ Cambridge, 1991. **Honors & Awards:** Phoebe Weinstein Award Negative Strand Virus Res, 1980; Merit Award, NIH, 1987 & 1997; Wallace P Rowe Award Excellence Virol Res, NIH, 1990. **Professional Experience:** Ed-in-chief, Virol, 1994-; INVESTR, HOWARD HUGHES MED INST, 1991-; PROF MICROBIOL & IMMUNOL, NORTHWESTERN UNIV, 1991-; JOHN EVANS PROF MOLECULAR & CELLULAR BIOL, NORTHWESTERN UNIV, 1990-; ed, J Virol, 1987-1993; from assoc prof to prof, Northwestern Univ, 1983-1990; estab investr, Am Heart Asn, 1982-1987; assoc ed, Virol, 1980-1993; Irma T Hirschl career scientist award, 1979-1983; from asst prof to assoc prof virol, Rockefeller Univ, 1977-1982; Fulbright-Hays travel award, 1974-1977; res assoc, Rockefeller Univ, 1974-1977. **Memberships:** Nat Acad Sci; fel Am Acad Microbiol; Am Soc Cell Biol; Am Soc Virol (pres, 2001-2002); Am Soc Microbiol; Am Soc Biochem & Molecular Biol; Soc Gen Microbiol; Am Soc Virol; fel AAAS. **Research Statement & Publications:** Virology; replication of influenza virus and paramyxoviruses; cell biology of integral membrane proteins. **Mailing Address:** Dept Biochem Molecular & Cell Biol, Northwestern Univ, 2153 N Campus Dr, Evanston, IL 60208-3500. **Fax:** 847-491-2467. **E-Mail:** ralamb@northwestern.edu

LAMB, ROBERT CARDON, DAIRY SCIENCE. **Personal Data:** b Logan, Utah, January 8, 1933; m 1953, c 5. **Education:** Utah State Univ, BS, 1956; Mich State Univ, MS, 1959, PhD (dairy cattle breeding), 1962. **Professional Experience:** HEAD ANIMAL DAIRY & VET SCI, UTAH STATE UNIV, 1990-; res leader, Agr Res Serv, USDA, 1972-1990; res dairy husbandman, Agr Res Serv, USDA, 1964-1972; asst prof, Utah State Univ, 1961-1964; Instr dairy sci, Mich State Univ, 1958-1960. **Memberships:** Am Dairy Sci Asn. **Research Statement & Publications:** Use of incomplete records in dairy cattle selection; genetics by nutrition interactions; inheritance of abnormalities in livestock; feed utilization efficiency in dairy cattle; dairy herd management; exercise for dairy cows; integrated reproduction management; stress in dairy cattle; dairy cattle housing; use of BST in dairy cattle. **Mailing Address:** Animal Sci, Utah State Univ, Logan, UT 84322-0001.

LAMB, ROBERT EDWARD, ANALYTICAL CHEMISTRY. **Personal Data:** b Sharon, Pa, July 12, 1945; m 1973, c 2. **Education:** St Louis Univ, BA, 1969, BS, 1970; Univ Ill, MS, 1974, PhD (analytical chem), 1975. **Professional Experience:** PROF CHEM, OHIO NORTHERN UNIV, 1988-; from asst prof to assoc prof, Ohio Northern Univ, 1978-1988; asst prof chem, Southern Methodist Univ, 1975-1978; lectr analytical chem, sch chem sci, Univ Ill, 1975. **Memberships:** Am Chem Soc. **Research Statement & Publications:** Pulse polarography and stripping analysis; liquid chromatography; analysis of trace metal complexes; environmental applications of analytical techniques. **Mailing Address:** Dept Chem, Ohio Northern Univ, Meyer Hall Sci 267, Ada, OH 45810. **Fax:** 419-772-2985. **E-Mail:** r-lamb@onu.edu

LAMB, SANDRA INA, ORGANIC CHEMISTRY, ENVIRONMENTALCHEMISTRY. **Personal Data:** b New York, NY, April 20, 1931; m 1950, c 4. **Education:** Univ Calif, Los Angeles, BS, 1954, PhD (phys org chem), 1959. **Professional Experience:** RETIRED; lectr chem, Univ Calif, as of 1999; lectr chem, Univ Calif, Santa Barbara, 1993-; lectr chem, Univ Calif, Los Angeles, 1976-1993; Mt St Mary's Col, Calif, 1971-1976; lectr, Med Sch, Univ Calif, 1970; from asst prof to assoc prof chem, Mt St Mary's Col, Calif, 1969-1976; chmn, Dept Phys Sci & Math, Mt St Mary's Col, Calif, 1969-1975; asst res pharmacologist, Med Sch, Univ Calif, 1966-; instr, Exten Div, Univ Calif, 1961-1969; asst prof, San Fernando Valley State Col, 1960-1961; instr chem, Santa Monica City Col, 1959. **Memberships:** AAAS; Am Chem Soc; Sigma Xi. **Research Statement & Publications:** Analytical applications of gas chromatography in chemistry and medicine with special interest in analysis of acetylcholine andvarious cholinergic agents; mechanism of action of muscarinic agents; analytical applications of gas chromatography and ion chromatography air pollution; synthesis of small ring compounds. **Mailing Address:** 430 Zimpher Dr, Sebastopol, CA 95472.

LAMB, WALTER ROBERT, PHYSICS, GRAVITATION RESEARCH. **Personal Data:** b Weiser, Idaho, September 26, 1922; m 1946, Jean M MacArthur; c Gayna D (Bang). **Education:** Univ Calif, AB, 1948. **Professional Experience:** PRES, ENERGY SYSTS & SOLAR INC, 1990-; consult, Elec Power Res Inst, 1989-1990; eng mgr, Acrian, 1985-1989; eng mgr, 1963-1964 & Union Carbide Corp, 1978-1985; physicist, Raytheon Co, 1971-1977; physicist, Fairchild Semiconductor Corp, 1968-1971; mgr advan processing, Stewart-Warner Microcircuits, 1965-1968; Fairchild Semiconductor, 1963-1964 & Union Carbide Corp, 1964-1965; solid state physicist, Res & Develop Dept, Raytheon Semiconductor Co, 1959-1963; Physicist, US Naval Radiol Defense Lab, 1948-1959. **Memberships:** AAAS; Am Phys Soc. **Research Statement & Publications:** Solid state, nuclear radiation, optical, luminescent, thermodynamic and gravitational phenomena; insolation. **Mailing Address:** 148 Jacinto Way, Sunnyvale, CA 94086. **E-Mail:** 71700.1261@compuserve.com

LAMB, WILLIS EUGENE, QUANTUM MECHANICS, ATOMIC PHYSICS. **Personal Data:** b Los Angeles, Calif, July 12, 1913; m 1939, Ursula. **Education:** Univ Calif, Berkeley, BS, 1934, PhD, 1938; Univ Pa, DS, 1953; Oxford Univ, MA, 1956. **Honorary Degrees:** MA, Yale Univ, 1961; LHD, Yeshiva Univ, 1965; DSc, Gustavus Adolphus Col, 1975, Columbia Univ, 1990. **Honors & Awards:** Nobel Prize in Physics, 1955; Nat Medal Sci, 2000; Rumford Medal, Am Acad Arts & Sci, 1953; Loeb Lectr, Harvard Univ, 1953-1954; Award, Res Corp, 1955; Fulbright Lectr, Univ Grenoble, 1964; Gordon Shrum Lectr, Simon Fraser Univ, 1972; Einstein Medal, Soc Optical & Quantum Electronics, 1992. **Professional Experience:** REGENTS PROF EMER OPTICAL SCI, UNIV ARIZ, 2003-; REGENTS PROF EMER PHYSICS, UNIV ARIZ, 2003-; REGENTS PROF EMER, ARIZ RES LAB, UNIV ARIZ, 2003; Vikrom Sarab-hai prof, Physics Res Lab, 1997; sr fel, Alexander von Humboldt Found, 1992-1994; Univ Ariz Regents Prof, Univ Ariz, 1989-2003; prof, Ariz Res Labs, 1983-2003; prof physics & optical sci, Univ Ariz, 1974-2003; Henry Ford II prof, Josiah Willard Gibbs prof, 1972-1974; Henry Ford II prof, Yale Univ, 1962-1972; vis prof, Columbia Univ, 1961; Guggenheim fel, 1960-1961; vis prof, Japan Soc Promo Sci, Res Inst Fundamental Res, Kyoto Univ & Tata Inst Fundamental Res, Bombay, 1960; fel, New Col & Wykeham prof, Oxford Univ, 1956-1962; prof, Stanford Univ, 1951-1956; from asst prof to prof physics, Columbia Univ, 1945-1952; mem staff, Radiation Lab, Columbia Univ, 1943-1952; assoc, Columbia Univ, 1943-1945; instr, Columbia Univ, 1938-1943; asst physics, Univ Calif, 1934-1935 & 1936-1937; consult, Philips Labs Inc, NASA, Bell Tel Labs & Perkin-Elmer Corp. **Memberships:** Nat Acad Sci; fel Am Phys Soc; hon mem NY Acad Sci; hon fel Brit Inst Physics; hon fel Royal Soc Edinburgh; hon fel Inst Physics; fel Optical Soc Am; hon fel Phys Soc. **Research Statement & Publications:** Theoretical physics; atomic and nuclear structure; microwave spectroscopy; fine structure of hydrogen and helium; magnetron oscillators; statistical mechanics; masers and lasers; quantum theory of measurement. **Mailing Address:** Optical Sci Ctr, Univ Ariz, Meinel Bldg 1630 E Univ Blvd, Tucson, AZ 85721. **E-Mail:** willis@primus.opt-sci.arizona.edu

LAMBA, RAM SARUP, INORGANIC CHEMISTRY, ORGANIC CHEMISTRY. **Personal Data:** b Calcutta, India, December 29, 1941; American citizen; m 1969, c 2. **Education:** Delhi Univ, India, BS, 1962, MSc, 1964; ETex State Univ, DEd(inorg chem, educ), 1973. **Professional Experience:** Dean acad affairs & prof, Univ PR, Cayey, 1998-2001; PROF CHEM, UNIV PR, CAYEY UNIV CAMPUS, 1998-; prof chem, Inter Am Univ PR, 1981-1998-; prof, math & physics, 1983-1987; dean acad affairs, math & physics, 1977-1982; assoc prof chem, math & physics, 1973-1983; chmn dept natural sci, Inter Am Univ PR, 1973-1977; asst prof & chmn dept, Inter Am Univ PR, 1970-1971; instr chem, Inter Am Univ PR, 1969-1970; chemist & supt dyeing & finishing, Beaunit Corp NC, Humacao, PR, 1968-1969; res asst, Indian Inst Petrol, Dehradun, India, 1964-1965. **Memberships:** Royal Inst Chem; Am Chem Soc; The Chem Soc; fel Inst Educ Leadership. **Research Statement & Publications:** To develop innovative methods in the teaching of college chemistry and to integrate with biological sciences; synthesis and study of chromium III, complexes; construction of low cost equipment in chemistry. **Mailing Address:** Dept Chem, Univ PR, PO Box 1943, Cayey, PR 00736. **Fax:** 787-738-8510. **E-Mail:** rlamba@cayey.upr.edu

LAMBA, SURENDAR SINGH, PHARMACY, PHARMACOGNOSY. **Personal Data:** b India, March 3, 1936; m 1967, Betty; c Sunjai. **Education:** Agra Univ, BS, 1954; Univ Rajasthan, BPharm, 1957; Panjab Univ, India, MPharm, 1960; Univ Nebr, MS, 1963; Univ Colo, PhD (pharmacog), 1966. **Honors & Awards:** Lederle Fac Award, 1975. **Professional Experience:** SECT LEADER & PROF MED CHEM/NATURAL PROD, FLA A&M UNIV, 1988-; vis prof, Univ Panama, 1977-1978 & Univ Benin, Nigeria, 1981-1982; from assoc prof to prof pharmacog, Fla A&M Univ, 1966-1988. **Memberships:** Am Pharmaceut Asn; Acad Pharmaceut Sci; NY Acad Sci; Am Soc Pharmacog; Sigma Xi; Am Asn Col Pharm. **Research Statement & Publications:** Evaluation of potential antisickling agents from natural and synthetic sources; phytochemistry. **Mailing Address:** Col Pharm & Pharmaceut Sci, Fla A&M Univ, Tallahassee, FL 32307. **E-Mail:** surendar.lamba@famu.edu

LAMBDIN, PARIS LEE, ENTOMOLOGY. **Personal Data:** b St Charles, Va, October 13, 1941; m 1964, Linda; c Miranda L & Michael L. **Education:** Hiwassee Col, AA, 1962; Lincoln Mem Univ, BA, 1964; Va Polytech Inst & State Univ, MS, 1972, PhD (entom), 1974. **Honors & Awards:** W S Overton Faculty Award of Merit, 2002; Nat Assoc Colleges & Teachers of Agriculture Teaching Award, 2002; ESA Outstanding Poster Award, 2001; Dogwood Arts Festival Book Award, 1992; ISSIS-VI Res Award, 1990; Inst Res Award, 1990; Literary Hall of Fame (LMU), 1989; Sigma Xi Res Award, 1973. **Professional Experience:** PROF ENTOM, DEPT ENTOMOL & PLANT PATH, UNIV TENN, 1974-; U.S. Marine Corps, 1967-1969, Spotsylvania High School, Teacher biol. 1969-1970, Bassett High Sch, 1964-1966. **Memberships:** Entomol Soc Am; Entomol Soc Georgia; Entomol Soc SCarolina; Entomol Soc Tenn (pres, 1995-1996); Entomol Soc Washington. **Research Statement & Publications:** Systematics of species in the superfamily Coccoidea; biological control of ornamental and forest insect pests. **Mailing Address:** Dept Entom & Plant Path, Univ Tenn, Knoxville, TN 37901-1071. **Fax:** 865-974-4744. **E-Mail:** plambdin@utk.edu

LAMBE, JOHN JOSEPH, SOLID STATE PHYSICS. **Personal Data:** b Cork, Ireland, December 1, 1926; American citizen; m 1950, c 2. **Education:** Univ Mich, BSE, 1948, MS, 1950; Univ Md, PhD (physics), 1954. **Professional Experience:** CONSULT, 1986-; consult, Jet Propulsion Lab, Pasadena, Calif, 1979-1986; staff scientist solid state physics, Ford Motor Co, 1959-1979; physicist microwave res, Univ Mich, 1956-1959; physicist solid state physics, Naval Res Lab, 1951-1956; Eng physics, Airborne Instruments Lab, 1948-1951. **Memberships:** Fel Am Phys Soc. **Research Statement & Publications:** Solid state physics; magnetic resonance; luminescence; super conductivity; electron tunneling. **Mailing Address:** 205 224th Ave SE, Sammamish, WA 98074.

LAMBE, ROBERT CARL, PLANT PATHOLOGY. **Personal Data:** b Minneapolis, Minn, November 25, 1927; m 1950, c 2. **Education:** Univ Southern Calif, AB, 1952; Univ Calif, MS, 1955; Ore State Col, PhD (plant path), 1960. **Professional Experience:** ASSOC PROF EMER PLANT PATH, VA POLYTECH INST & STATE UNIV, as of 2002; assoc prof plant path, Va Polytech Inst & State Univ, 1967-1980; exten plant pathologist, Iowa State Univ, 1963-1967; plant pathologist, Area Exten, Tex A&M Univ, 1960-1963; jr plant pathologist, Ore State Col, 1958-1960. **Research Statement & Publications:** Fungicides and extension plant pathology. **Mailing Address:** Dept Plant Path, Va Polytech Inst & State Univ, 210 Burruss Hall, Blacksburg, VA 24061.

LAMBE, THOMAS ANTHONY, OPERATIONS RESEARCH, ENGINEERING SCIENCE. **Personal Data:** b Victoria, BC, December 27, 1930; m 1964. **Education:** Univ BC, BASc, 1952; Stanford Univ, MSc, 1958, PhD (eng sci), 1968. **Professional Experience:** PROF EMER, SCH PUB ADMIN, UNIV VICTORIA, as of 1996; assoc Prof, Sch Pub Admin, Univ Victoria, beginning 1974; assoc prof indust eng, Univ Toronto, 1968-1974; proj leader opers res, BC Res Coun, 1958-1965; res engr, BC Res Coun, 1954-1957; engr, Can Westinghouse, 1952-1954. **Memberships:** Can Oper Res Soc; Opers Res Soc Am. **Research Statement & Publications:** Economic analysis of engineering systems, particularly the transportation and natural resource industries; decision theory and individual choice behavior. **Mailing Address:** Dept Pub Admin, Univ Victoria, Rm 7326, PO Box 1700, HSD Bldg, Victoria, BC V8W 2Y2, Can.

LAMBE, T(HOMAS) WILLIAM, GEOTECHNICAL ENGINEERING. **Personal Data:** b Raleigh, NC, November 28, 1920; m 1947. **Education:** NC State Univ, BS, 1942; Mass Inst Technol, SM, 1944, ScD(soil mech), 1948. **Honors & Awards:** Collingswood Prize, Am Soc Civil Engrs, 1952, Arthur M Wellington Prize, 1961 & 1984, Norman Medal, 1964, Terzaghi Lectr, 1970 & Karl Terzaghi Award, 1975; Desmond Fitzgerald Medal, Brit Soc Civil Engrs, 1954 & 1956; R P Davis Lectr, Univ WVa, 1973; Terzaghi Mem Lectr, Istanbul, Turkey, 1973; Rankine Lectr, Brit Inst Civil Engrs, 1973; Moh Lectr, Taipei, Taiwan, 1980, Indonesia & Singapore, 1981; Ardaman Lectr, Univ Fla, 1985; Shaw Lectr, NC State Univ, 1985. **Professional Experience:** EDMUND K TURNER PROF EMER CIVIL ENG, MASS INST TECHNOL, 1981-; Edmund K Turner prof, Geotech Div, 1969-1981; prof geotech eng & head, Geotech Div, 1959-1969; assoc prof & dir, Soil Stabilization Lab, 1952-1959; Consult geotech eng, 1945-; from instr to asst prof soil mech, Mass Inst Technol, 1945-1952; soil engr, Dames & Moore, San Francisco, 1944-1945; struct & found engr, Univ Calif, San Francisco, 1944; field engr airbase construct, US Navy, Brunswick, Maine, 1943; instr civil eng, Univ NH, 1942-1943; field engr, Olsen Consult Engrs, Edenton, NC, 1942; Struct detailer, Am Bridge Co, Pa, 1942. **Memberships:** Nat Acad Eng; hon mem Am Soc Civil Engrs; fel Brit Inst Civil Engrs; hon mem Venezuelan Soc Soil Mech & Found Eng; hon mem Southeast Asian Soc Geotech Eng. **Research Statement & Publications:** Soil testing, stabilization and mineralogy; soil engineering; earth and rock dams. **Mailing Address:** Mass Inst Technol, Dept Civil & Envioron Eng, Cambridge, MA 02139-4307.

LAMBECK, KURT, GEOPHYSICS. **Personal Data:** b Utrecht, Neth, September 20, 1941; m 1967, Bridget M Nicholls; c Alexis & Fiona. **Education:** Univ NSW, BS, 1963; Oxford Univ, PhD, 1968, DSci, 1976. **Honorary Degrees:** DEng, Nat Tech Univ, Greece, 1994. **Honors & Awards:** Macelwane Medal, Am Geophys Union, 1976, Charles A Whitten Medal, 1993; Sir Harold Jeffreys Lectr, Royal Astron Soc, 1989; Alfred Wegener Medal, 1997 Eur Union Geosci Jaeger Medal Aust Acad Sc 1995; George Lemaitre Prize, Univ of Louvain la Neuve, 2001; Tage Erlander prof, Swedish Res Council 2001. **Professional Experience:** Dir, Res Sch Earth Sci, Australian Nat Univ, 1984-1992; PROF GEOPHYS, RES SCH EARTH SCI, AUSTRALIAN NAT UNIV, 1977-; prof geophysics, Dept Earth Sci, Univ Paris, 1973-1977; dir sci, Group Res Geodesie Spatiale, Observ Paris, 1970-1973; Geodesist, Smithsonian Astrophys Observ, 1967-1970; Assoc, Harvard Col Observ, 1967-1970; chmn, Comt Int Union Geodesy & Geophys Study Earth's Deep Interior; chmn, Bilateral Sci & Tech Progs, Dept Indust, Tech & Com. **Memberships:** Fel Am Geophys Union; Australian Acad Sci; foreign mem Norweg Acad Sci & Lett; foreign mem Royal Neth Acad Art & Sci; fel Royal Soc, UK Foreign Mem Acad Europea. **Research Statement & Publications:** Geophysics, including satellite geodesy, geodynamics and climate. **Mailing Address:** Res Sch Earth Sci, Australian Nat Univ, Canberra ACT 0200, Australia. **Fax:** 612-624-95443.

LAMBEK, JOACHIM, MATHEMATICS. **Personal Data:** b Leipzig, Ger, December 5, 1922; Canadian citizen; m 1948, c 3. **Education:** McGill Univ, BSc, 1946, MSc, 1947, PhD, 1951. **Professional Experience:** PETER REDPATH PROF EMER MATH, MCGILL UNIV, as of 2006; prof math, Mcgill Univ, beginning 1963; mem, Inst Advan Study, 1959-1960; assoc prof, Mcgill Univ, 1954-1963. **Memberships:** Am Math Soc; Math Asn Am; Can Math Cong; Sigma Xi. **Research Statement & Publications:** Algebra. **Mailing Address:** Dept Math, McGill Univ, Burnside Hall 805 Sherbrooke St W, Montreal, PQ H3A 2K6, Can. **Fax:** 514-398-3899. **E-Mail:** lambek@math.mcgill.ca

LAMBERG, STANLEY LAWRENCE, ANATOMY & PHYSIOLGY, HISTOLOGY. **Personal Data:** b Brooklyn, NY, October 2, 1933; m 1963, Charlotte; c Steven K & Eric M. **Education:** Brooklyn Col, BS, 1955; Oberlin Col, MA, 1957; Tufts Univ, MS, 1962; NY Univ, PhD (biol), 1968. **Honors & Awards:** Founder's Day Award, NY Univ, 1969 Chancellor's Award for Excellence in Teaching, State Univ NY, 1976. **Professional Experience:** RETIRED SUFFOLK CO COM COL, AdjProfAnat& Physio, 1987-present, adjassocprof, 1986-1987, adjasstprof, 1981-1986; STATE UNIV NY FARMINGDALE, ProfMedLabTech, 1975-1995, assocprof, 1973-1975, asstprof, 1970-1973, adj profbiol, 1980-2002; LongIsland Univ Conolly Col, Asstprofbiol, 1967-1970, adjprof, 1975-1978, adjassocprof, 1973-1975, adjasstprof, 1970-1973; City Col NY, lectbiol, 1966-1967; NY Univ, Col Dent, Guggheim Inst Dent Res, Asst Res Sci, 1968-1969; Col Dent, Nat Inst Dent Res Felhistol, 1961-1966; Tufts Univ, Sch Med, Charlton Res Felphysiol, 1958-1961; Cornell Univ, Sch Med, Chief Techbiochem, 1957-1958; Oberlin Col, Grad Teaching Asstbiol, 1955-1957. **Memberships:** AAAS; NY Acad Sci; Sigma Xi; Nat Soc Histotechnol. **Research Statement & Publications:** Mitochondrial phosphorylation reactions during embryonic development; Effect of ultraviolet irradiation and various inhibitors and uncoupling reagents on mitochondrial phosphorylation reactions. **Mailing Address:** Dept Nat Sci, Grant Campus, Suffolk County Comm Col, Crooked Hill Rd, Brentwood, NY 11717. **E-Mail:** lambers@sunysuffolk.edu

LAMBERG-KARLOVSKY, CLIFFORD CHARLES, ANTHROPOLOGY, ARCHAEOLOGY. **Personal Data:** b Praque, Czech, October 2, 1937; m 1959, Martha; c Karl E Othmar & Christopher W. **Education:** Dartmouth Col, AB, 1959; Univ Pa, MA, 1964, PhD, 1965. **Honorary Degrees:** MA, Harvard Univ, 1970. **Honors & Awards:** Reckitt Lectr, Brit Acad, 1973. **Professional Experience:** Can lectr, Beersheva Univ, 1993; DIR, AM SCH PREHISTORIC RES, 1992-; STEPHEN PHILLIPS PROF ARCHAEOL, HARVARD UNIV, 1991-; excavation projs, USSR, 1990-1991, Anau, Turkmenistan; Nat Endowment Humanities grant, 1977-; Nat Endowment Arts grant, 1977-; dir, Peabody Mus Archaeol & Ethnol, 1977-1990; excavation projs, Saudia Arabia, 1977-1980; trustee, Am Inst Yemeni Studies, 1976-1977; assoc, Columbia Univ, 1969-; CUR NEAR EASTERN ARCHAEOL, PEABODY MUS ARCHAEOL & ETHNOL, 1969-; trustee, Am Sch Oriental Res, 1969-1971; trustee, Am Inst Iranian Studies, 1968-; excavation projs, Tepe Yahya, Iran, 1967-1975; NSF grant, 1966-1975; from asst prof to prof anthrop, Am Sch Prehistoric Res, 1965-1990; Dir archaeol surv, Syria, 1965; asst prof sociol & anthrop, Franklin & Marshall Col, 1964-1965. **Memberships:** Fel Soc Antiquaries Gt Brit & Ireland; Am Anthrop Asn; AAAS; NY Acad Sci; Soc Am Archaeol; Archeol Inst Am; Am Acad Arts & Sci. **Research Statement & Publications:** Ancient civilization; archaeological surveys and excavations in Iran, Saudi Arabia, Syria and Central Asia. **Mailing Address:** Harvard Univ, 57J Peabody Mus, Cambridge, MA 02138. **Fax:** 617-496-8041. **E-Mail:** karlovsk@fas.harvard.edu

LAMBERSON, LEONARD ROY, INDUSTRIAL & MANUFACTURING ENGINEERING. **Personal Data:** b Stanwood, Mich, November 18, 1937; m 1975, c 3. **Education:** Gen Motors Inst, BME, 1961; NC State Univ, MS, 1963; Tex A&M Univ, PhD (indust eng), 1967. **Honors & Awards:** Craig Award, Am Soc Qual Control, 1978. **Professional Experience:** CONSULT, as of 2002; dean eng, Western Mich Univ, Kalamazoo, 1989-1999; chmn dept, Wayne State Univ, 1982-1989; prof indust eng, Wayne State Univ, 1979-1989; reliability engr, US Army Tank Auto Command, 1977-1978; assoc prof, Wayne State Univ, 1970-1979; chmn dept, Gen Motors Inst, 1969-1970; asst prof, Tex A&M Univ, 1965-1968; from asst prof to prof indust eng, Gen Motors Inst, 1964-1970; prod foreman, Chevrolet Div, Gen Motors Corp, 1961-1964. **Memberships:** Am Inst Indust Engrs; Am Soc Qual Control; Am Soc Eng Educ. **Research Statement & Publications:** Development of techniques and procedures to improve thereliability of commercial products; published over 20 articles. **Mailing Address:** Indust & Mfg Eng, Western Mich Univ, E 207 Parkview Campus, Kalamazoo, MI 49008-5336. **Fax:** 269-387-4024. **E-Mail:** leonard.lamberson@wmich.edu

LAMBERSON, ROLAND H, ECOLOGICAL MODELLING, CONSERVATION BIOLOGY. **Personal Data:** m 1990, Michele; c Robyn (Verkamp) & Laurie (O'Keeffe). **Education:** Hastings Col, BA, 1963; Univ Wyo, MS, 1965; Univ Northern Colo, DA, 1974. **Professional Experience:** Univ Natal, SAfrica, 1993; Univ Perugia, Italy, 1982; PROF MATH & DIR, ENVIRON SYSTS GRAD PROGS, HUMBOLDT STATE UNIV, 1980-; vis prof math, Univ BC, 1979-1980, 1987; chmn, Math Dept, Des Moines Area Community Col, 1974-1980; asst prof math, Hastings Col, 1967-1974; chmn, Physics Dept, Minot State Col, 1965-1967. **Memberships:** Resource Modeling Asn (pres, 1985-1986, exec secy, 1989-); Math Asn Am; Soc Conserv Biol; Soc Math Biol. **Research Statement & Publications:** Development of mathematical models for viability analysis or managementof threatened or endangered species particularly the northern spotted owl and other forest dwelling species; published numerous articles. **Mailing Address:** Math Dept, Humboldt State Univ, Arcata, CA 95521. **Fax:** 707-826-3140. **E-Mail:** rhl1@humboldt.edu

LAMBERT, ALAN L, MATHEMATICS. **Personal Data:** b New York, NY, November 28, 1943. **Education:** Univ Miami, BS, 1966, MS, 1967; Univ Mich, PhD, 1970. **Professional Experience:** PROF MATH, UNIV NC, CHARLOTTE, 1983-. **Memberships:** Am Math Soc; Irish Math Soc. **Research Statement & Publications:** Properties of composition operators. **Mailing Address:** Math Dept, Univ NC, Fretwell 355C, Charlotte, NC 28223-0001. **Fax:** 704-687-6415. **E-Mail:** allamber@email.uncc.edu

LAMBERT, BRIAN KERRY, INDUSTRIAL ENGINEERING. **Personal Data:** b Spokane, Wash, November 21, 1941; m 1963, c 2. **Education:** Tex Tech Col, BS, 1964, MS, 1966, PhD (indust eng), 1967. **Professional Experience:** Assoc prof, Indust Eng, Tex Tech Univ, beginning 1971; asst prof, Tex Tech Univ, 1967-1971; Indust Eng Dept, NMex State Univ. **Memberships:** Soc Mfg Engrs; Inst Indust Engrs; Am Soc Eng Educ. **Research Statement & Publications:** Manufacturing research and development, specifically machining operations research and systems analysis, specifically reliability. **Mailing Address:** Dept Indust Eng, NMex State Univ, PO Box 30001, Las Cruces, NM 88003. **E-Mail:** blambert@nmsu.edu

LAMBERT, CAROLYN U, FOOD SCIENCE. **Education:** Univ Mo, BS; Univ Wis, MS; Univ Tenn, Knoxville, PhD. **Professional Experience:** ASSOC PROF, FOOD SYSTS MGT, PA STATE UNIV, as of 2006. **Mailing Address:** Sch Hospitality Mgt, Pa State Univ, 229 Mateer Bldg, University Park, PA 16802-1307. **Fax:** 814-863-4257. **E-Mail:** cul@psu.edu

LAMBERT, CHARLES CALVIN, DEVELOPMENTAL BIOLOGY, REPRODUCTIVE BIOLOGY. **Personal Data:** b Rockford, Ill, April 10, 1935; m 1965, c 2. **Education:** San Diego State Univ, BA, 1964, MS, 1966; Univ Wash, PhD (zool), 1970. **Professional Experience:** PROF EMER ZOOL, CALIF STATE UNIV, FULLERTON, as of 2004; Shimoda Marine Res Ctr, 1982 & Kewalo Marine Lab, 1985; vis prof, Friday Harbor Labs, 1981 & Shimoda Marine Res Ctr (UNESCO/ICRO course), 1982; Vis investr, Bermuda Biol Sta, 1980; Prof Zool, Calif State Univ, Fullerton, beginning 1979; Vis investr, Hopkins Marine Sta, 1978; Vis investr, Friday Harbor Labs, 1974-; from asst prof to assoc prof, Calif State

Univ, Fullerton, 1970-1979; NIH traineeship, Univ Wash, 1970. **Memberships:** Am Soc Zoologists; Soc Develop Biol; AAAS; Am Soc Cell Biol; Int Soc Develop Biol; Int Cell Res Orgn. **Research Statement & Publications:** Development and physiology of marine invertebrates. **Mailing Address:** Dept Biol, Calif State Univ-Fullerton, Fullerton, CA 92634. **E-Mail:** clambert@fullerton.edu

LAMBERT, DAVID L, ASTRONOMY. **Education:** Univ Col Oxford, BS, 1960; Balliol Col, PhD (astrophysics), 1965. **Honors & Awards:** Dannie Heineman Prize, Am Astron Soc, 1987. **Professional Experience:** DIR, MCDONALD OBSERV, as of 2004; ISABEL MC-CUTCHEON HARTE CENT CHAIR ASTRON, UNIV TEX, 1987-; Guggenheim fel & vis Erskine fel, Univ Canterbury, NZ, 1985; PROF ASTRON, UNIV TEX, 1974-; res fel, Calif Inst Technol, Pasadena & Mt Wilson Palomar Observ. **Memberships:** fel Royal Astron Soc; Am Astron Soc; Int Astron Union. **Research Statement & Publications:** Astronomy. **Mailing Address:** Dept Astron, Univ Tex, Austin, TX 78712-1083. **Fax:** 512-471-6016.

LAMBERT, DIANE, MATHEMATICAL STATISTICS. **Personal Data:** American citizen. **Education:** Univ Rochester, PhD (statist), 1979. **Professional Experience:** Bell Labs Fel, 2001; HEAD STATIST & DATA MINING RES, BELL LABS, LUCENT TECHNOLOGIES, 1997-; Distinguished mem tech staff, Bell Labs, Lucent Technologies, 1996. **Memberships:** Fel Inst Math Statist (exec secy 1990-1993); fel Am Statist Asn; Int Statist Inst. **Research Statement & Publications:** Developing, analyzing and applying innovative statistical models for nonstandard applications such as the risk of disclosure in publicly released databases and the probability of detecting low levels of environmental contaminants. **Mailing Address:** Bell Labs, Lucent Technologies, Rm 2C-256, 600 Mountain Ave, Murray Hill, NJ 07974-0636. **Fax:** 908-582-3340. **E-Mail:** dl@bell-labs.com

LAMBERT, EDWARD HOWARD, medical physiology, neuromuscular disorders; deceased, see previous edition for last biography

LAMBERT, FRANK LEWIS, ORGANIC CHEMISTRY. **Personal Data:** b Minneapolis, Minn, July 10, 1918; m 1943, Bernice Webster. **Education:** Harvard Univ, BA, 1939; Univ Chicago, PhD (org chem), 1942. **Professional Experience:** SCI CONSULT, GETTY CONSERV INST, 1982-; EMER PROF CHEM, OCCIDENTAL COL, 1981-; NSF fac fel, 1970-1971; NSF fac fel, 1957-1958; from asst prof to prof, Getty Conserv Inst, 1948-1980; instr chem, Univ Calif, Los Angeles, 1947-1948; head develop dept, Edwal Labs, Ill, 1946-1947; develop chemist, Edwal Labs, Ill, 1943-1944; Res & develop chemist, Edwal Labs, Ill, 1942-1943. **Memberships:** Am Chem Soc. **Research Statement & Publications:** Polarography of organic halogen compounds; halogenation of organic compounds. **Mailing Address:** 2834 Lewis Dr, La Verne, CA 91750-4308.

LAMBERT, GEORGE, VETERINARY MICROBIOLOGY. **Personal Data:** b Etobicoke, Ont, October 8, 1923; American citizen; m 1948, c 3. **Education:** Univ Guelph, DVM, 1947; Iowa State Univ, MS, 1966. **Professional Experience:** RETIRED; res leader immunol res, 1985-1989; asst dir, Nat Animal Dis Ctr, 1975-1980; chief virol res lab, Nat Animal Dis Ctr, 1970-1975; asst dir biol dept, Diamond Labs Inc, 1967-1970; res virol, Nat Animal Dis Lab, 1965-1967; res vet bact, Nat Animal Dis Lab, 1957-1965; asst state vet epidemiol, Va Dept Agr, 1953-1957; coop agt, Univ Wis & USDA, 1950-1953; asst prof, WVa Univ, 1948-1950; instr vet path, Ont Vet Col, Univ Guelph, 1947-1948. **Memberships:** Am Vet Med Asn; US Animal Health Asn; Conf Res Workers Animal Dis. **Research Statement & Publications:** Administration of animal disease research. **Mailing Address:** 1375 231st Rd, Boone, IA 50036.

LAMBERT, GLENN FREDERICK, biochemistry; deceased, see previous edition for last biography

LAMBERT, HELEN HAYNES, ENDOCRINOLOGY. **Personal Data:** b Baton Rouge, La, July 25, 1939; div, c 2. **Education:** Wellesley Col, BA, 1961; Univ NH, MS, 1963, PhD (zoology), 1969. **Professional Experience:** Prof emer biol, Northeastern Univ, as of 2003; assoc prof biol, Northeastern Univ, beginning 1975; asst prof, Northeastern Univ, 1970-1975; asst prof biol, Simmons Col, 1969-1970; instr zool, Univ NH, 1967-1968; mem, Sex Info & Educ Coun US. **Memberships:** AAAS; Sigma Xi; Am Inst Biol Sci; Am Soc Zool. **Research Statement & Publications:** Environmental factors affecting reproduction and sexual behavior; sex determination and development of sex differences. **Mailing Address:** Dept Biol, Northeastern Univ, 360 Huntington Ave, Boston, MA 02115-5096.

LAMBERT, HOWARD W, TOPOLOGY. **Personal Data:** b Oakland, Calif, August 2, 1937; m 1957, c 3. **Education:** Univ Calif, Berkeley, BA, 1960; Iowa State Univ, MS, 1961; Univ Utah, PhD (math), 1966. **Professional Experience:** Prof math, Western NMex Univ, beginning 1980; from asst prof to prof math, Univ Iowa, 1966-1980. **Memberships:** Am Math Soc; Math Asn Am; Am Asn Univ Professors; Soc Indust & Appl Math. **Research Statement & Publications:** Upper semi-continuous decompositions of topological spaces, 3-manifolds. **Mailing Address:** 760 Encanto Dr, Sparks, NV 89436.

LAMBERT, IAIN B, BIOLOGY. **Education:** Guelph Univm BSc, 1981; McMaster Univ, PhD, 1990. **Professional Experience:** ASSOC PROF, DEPT BIOL, CARLETON UNIV, 1996-; asst prof, Carleton Univ, 1992-1996; IBMC du CNRS Strasbourg, France, 1990-1992. **Research Statement & Publications:** Bacterial nitroreductases; genomics; mutagenesis and DNA Repair; environmental microbiology. **Mailing Address:** Dept Biol, Carleton Univ, 1125 Colonel By Dr, Ottawa, ON K1S 5B6, Can. **Fax:** 613-520-3539. **E-Mail:** iain_lambert@carleton.ca

LAMBERT, JAMES LEBEAU, ORGANIC CHEMISTRY, ANALYTICAL CHEMISTRY. **Personal Data:** b Sanford, Fla, February 11, 1934. **Education:** Spring Hill Col, BS, 1959; Johns Hopkins Univ, PhD (chem), 1963. **Professional Experience:** PROF EMER CHEM, SPRING HILL COL, as of 2002; chmn Dept, Spring Hill Col, beginning 1982; prof chem, Spring Hill Col, beginning 1979; acad dean, Spring Hill Col, 1976-1978; from asst prof to assoc prof, prof chem, Spring Hill Col, 1968-1979. **Memberships:** AAAS; Am Chem Soc; Sigma Xi. **Research Statement & Publications:** Mechanisms of organic reactions; carbanions. **Mailing Address:** Dept Chem, Spring Hill Col 4000 Dauphin St, Mobile, AL 36608-1791.

LAMBERT, JAMES MORRISON, NUCLEAR PHYSICS. **Personal Data:** b Chicago, Ill, February 18, 1928; m 1953, c 3. **Education:** Johns Hopkins Univ, BA, 1955, PhD (physics), 1961. **Professional Experience:** PROF EMER, GEORGETOWN UNIV, as of 2004; prof physics, Georgetown Univ, beginning 1974; res consult, Naval Res Lab, beginning 1966; from asst prof to assoc prof, Georgetown Univ, 1964-1974; asst prof, Univ Mich, 1961-1963; instr physics, Johns Hopkins Univ, 1960-1961. **Memberships:** Am Phys Soc; AAAS; Sigma Xi. **Research Statement & Publications:** Experimental medium energy nuclear physics; nuclear reaction studies using particle accelerators; experimental surface physics. **Mailing Address:** Dept Physics, Georgetown Univ, Washington, DC 20007. **E-Mail:** lambert@georgetown.edu

LAMBERT, JERRY ROY, AGRICULTURAL ENGINEERING, AGRICULTURAL INFORMATION SYSTEMS. **Personal Data:** b Benton, Ill, September 16, 1936; div, c 3. **Education:** Univ Fla, BAgrE, 1958, MS, 1962; NC State Col, PhD (agr eng), 1964. **Professional Experience:** PROF EMER AGR & BIOL ENG, CLEMSON UNIV, as of; comput coordr, Clemson Univ, beginning 1985; prof agr eng, Clemson Univ, beginning 1972; from asst prof to assoc prof, Clemson Univ, 1964-1972; design eng trainee, Soil Conserv Serv, USDA, 1958-1960. **Memberships:** Am Soc Eng Educ; Am Soc Agr Engrs. **Research Statement & Publications:** Water relations of plants; evapotranspiration; water movement in soils; simulation of agricultural systems; microcomputer applications to agriculture information delivery systems. **Mailing Address:** Dept Agr Eng, Clemson Univ, Clemson, SC 29633.

LAMBERT, JOHN B(OYD), METALLURGY & PHYSICAL METALLURGICAL ENGINEERING, MATERIALS SCIENCE ENGINEERING. **Personal Data:** b Billings, Mont, July 5, 1929; wid, c William, Thomas, Stephanie, Patricia, Catherine & Karen. **Education:** Princeton Univ, BS, 1951; Univ Wis, PhD (chem eng), 1956. **Honors & Awards:** Co-Recipient, Charles Hatchett Award, Inst Metals, 1986. **Professional Experience:** Pres., JBL Consulting LLC, 1992-; CONSULT, 1992-; corp tech dir & vpres, Fansteel, Inc., 1991-1992; gen mgr & vpres, Metals Div, 1988-1990; mkt mgr, Metals Div, 1987-1988; corp tech dir & vpres, Fansteel, Inc., 1980-1987; mgr mfg eng, V R Wesson Div, 1973-1980; plant mgr, Metals Div, 1971-1972; mkt mgr, Fansteel Inc, 1969-1971; sr res engr, Pigments Dept, Del, 1963-1968; Res engr, Indust & Biochem Dept, E I du Pont de Nemours & Co, 1956-1963; Instr, Am Chem Soc. **Memberships:** emer mem Am Chem Soc; emer mem Am Inst Chem Engrs; sr mem Am Soc Metals; sr mem Sigma Xi. **Research Statement & Publications:** Inorganic colloid chemistry; physical and powder metallurgy; surface chemistry, drying, machining and metal cutting; ceramic cutting tools; technical management; refractory metals, including tantalum, niobiom, and hard metals. **Mailing Address:** 617 E Greenbriar Lane, Lake Forest, IL 60045-3214. **Fax:** 847-234-7649. **E-Mail:** drjbl@aol.com

LAMBERT, JOSEPH B, ORGANIC CHEMISTRY. **Personal Data:** b Ft Sheridan, IL, July 4, 1940; m 1967, Mary; c Laura K, Alice P & Joseph C. **Education:** Yale Univ, BS, 1962; Calif Inst Technol, PhD (org chem), 1965. **Honors & Awards:** Eastman Kodak Award, 1965; Nat Fresenius Award, 1976; Norris Award for Teaching Chem, Am Chem Soc, 1987; Fryxell Award in Sci Archaeol, Soc Am Archaeol, 1989; Nat Catalysis Award, Chem Mfrs Asn, 1993; Frederic Stanley Kipping Award in Silicon Chem, Am Chem Soc, 1998; Mosher Award, Am Chem Soc, 2003; Sidney M Edelstein Award, Am Chem Soc, 2004. **Professional Experience:** Charles Deering McCormick Prof Teaching Excellence 1999-2002; distinguished lectr, Sigma Xi, 1997-1998; chmn, Div Hist Chem, Am Chem Soc, 1996-; CLARE HAMILTON HALL PROF CHEM, NORTHWESTERN UNIV, 1991-; USAF Off Sci Res fel, 1990; vis scholar, Polish Acad Sci, 1981 & Chinese Acad Sci, 1988; ed-in-chief, J Phys Org Chem, 1986-; chmn dept, 1986-1989; Nat Acad Sci exchange fel, 1985; dir, Integrated Sci Prog, 1982-1985; Guggenheim fel, 1973; vis assoc, Brit Mus Res Lab, 1973; Alfred P Sloan Found fel, 1968-1970; From asst prof to prof, Northwestern Univ, 1965-1991. **Memberships:** Fel AAAS; Sigma Xi; Am Chem Soc (chair div hist chem 1996); fel Brit Interplanetary Soc; Soc Archeol Sci (pres int off 1986-1987); fel Japan Soc Prom Sci. **Research Statement & Publications:** Organosilicon chemistry, other main group chemistry, organic reaction mechanisms, archaeological chemistry. **Mailing Address:** Dept Chem Northwestern Univ, Rm Tech M194, 2145 Sheridan Rd, Evanston, IL 60208-3113. **E-Mail:** jlambert@northwestern.edu

LAMBERT, JOSEPH MICHAEL, APPROXIMATION THEORY, NUMERICAL METHODS. **Personal Data:** b Philadelphia, Pa, November 19, 1942; m 1973, c 3. **Education:** Drexel Univ, BS, 1965; Cornell Univ, MS, 1967; Purdue Univ, PhD (math), 1970. **Professional Experience:** SR ASSOC DEAN, INFO SCI & TECHNOL, PA STATE UNIV, as of 2005; vis assoc prof comput sci, Cornell Univ, Ithaca, 1986-1987; ASSOC PROF & DEPT HEAD COMPUT SCI, PA STATE UNIV, 1982-; actg head, Col Sci, 1980-1982; asst dean, Col Sci, 1979-1982; vis assoc prof math, Univ Tenn, Knoxville, 1977-1978; from asst prof to assoc prof math, Pa State Univ, 1970-1981. **Memberships:** Am Math Soc; Asn Comput Mach; Inst Elec & Electronics Engrs. **Research Statement & Publications:** Functional analysis; approximation theory; numerical analysis; operations research; software metrics. **Mailing Address:** Dept Comput Sci & Eng, Pa State Univ, 332G Info Sci & Technol Bldg, Univ Park, PA 16802-0001. **Fax:** 814-865-5664. **E-Mail:** j9l@psu.edu

LAMBERT, JOSEPH PARKER, dentistry; deceased, see previous edition for last biography

LAMBERT, LAURIE E, IMMUNOLOGY. **Personal Data:** b Springfield, Mass. **Education:** Univ Wis, PhD (immunol), 1987. **Professional Experience:** SR ASSOC SCIENTIST, MARION MERRELL DOW, 1993-. **Research Statement & Publications:** Immunology. **Mailing Address:** Dept Immunol Marion Merrell Dow, 2110 E Galbraith Rd, Cincinnati, OH 45215-6300.

LAMBERT, MARY PULLIAM, BIOCHEMISTRY, NEUROBIOLOGY. **Personal Data:** b Birmingham, Ala, April 27, 1944. **Education:** Birmingham-Southern Col, BS, 1966; Northwestern Univ, PhD (biochem), 1971. **Professional Experience:** SR RES ASSOC, NORTHWESTERN UNIV, 1997-; res assoc, Northwestern Univ, 1983-1997; NIH res fel, Northwestern Univ, 1982-1983; fel reproductive biol, Northwestern Univ, Ill, 1981-1982; instr biochem, Northwestern Univ, Ill, 1970-1972. **Memberships:** Sigma Xi; Soc Neuroscience. **Research Statement & Publications:** Neurotransmitter receptors; receptor biochemistry; receptor development; mechanism of receptor function; Alzheimer's disease. **Mailing Address:** Dept Neurobiol & Physiol, Northwestern Univ, Evanston, IL 60208. **Fax:** 847-491-5211. **E-Mail:** mlambert@northwestern.edu

LAMBERT, MAURICE C, PHYSICAL CHEMISTRY. **Personal Data:** b Roosevelt, Utah, April 14, 1918; m 1942, c 5. **Education:** Brigham Young Univ, BS, 1939, MA, 1941. **Professional Experience:** RETIRED; sr res scientist, Westinghouse Hanford Co, 1970-1982; sr res scientist, Battelle Northwest Labs, 1965-1970; sr chemist, Gen Elec Co, 1964; chemist, Hanford Atomic Prod Oper, 1948-1964; assoc chemist, Indust Lab, Mare Island Naval Shipyard, 1941-1946. **Memberships:** Am Chem Soc; Soc Appl Spectros. **Research Statement & Publications:** Spectrometry, absorptiometry and diffraction; atomic absorption and flame emission spectrometry; separations of trace elements; gas-solid reactions; properties of inorganic oxides; fused salt studies; surface analysis by electron spectroscopy; automation of analytical techniques. **Mailing Address:** 1514 Mahan Ave, Richland, WA 99352.

LAMBERT, MURIEL WIKSWO, DNA REPAIR, CHROMATIN STRUCTURE IN DNA REPAIR. **Personal Data:** b Teaneck, NJ. **Education:** Sweet Briar Col, AB, 1966; Northwestern Univ, PhD (biol sci), 1970. **Professional Experience:** PROF MED, DIV DERMAT, 1993-; mem, NIH Study Sect, Nat Inst Arthritis & Musculoskeletal & Skin Dis Res Core Ctr Grants, 1992-; PROF PATH, UNIV MED & DENT, NJ MED SCH, 1991-; Prin investr, NIH, 1986-; from asst prof to assoc prof, Div Dermat, 1978-1991; assoc, Div Dermat, 1976-1978; res fel, Sch Med, Yale Univ, 1972-1976; NIH fel, Harvard Univ, Sch

Dent med, 1970-1972; NSF fel, Northwestern Univ, 1966-1970. **Memberships:** Am Asn Cancer Res; Environ Mutagen Soc; Soc Invest Dermat; Am Soc Photobiol; Fedn Am Soc Exp Biol; Am Acad Dermat. **Research Statement & Publications:** DNR repair of specific types of damage with emphasis on mammalian systems; the role of chromatin structure and protein DNA interaction on the repair process is being investigated; defects in these repair processes in certain genetic diseases such as xeroderma pigmentosum and Fanconi anemia. **Mailing Address:** Dept Path Med Sch, Univ Med & Dent NJ, 185 S Orange Ave, Newark, NJ 07103. **Fax:** 973-982-7293.

LAMBERT, PAUL WAYNE, GEOMORPHOLOGY, PHOTOGRAPHY. **Personal Data:** b Ft Worth, Tex, October 27, 1937; m 1959, Janice M O'Neil; c Dean P. **Education:** Tex Tech Univ, BA, 1959; Univ NMex, MS, 1961, PhD (geol), 1968. **Professional Experience:** ADJ PROF GEOG, SOUTHERN METHODIST UNIV, 1997-; adj cur geol, Panhandle-Plains Hist Mus, WTex A&M Univ, Canyon, 1994-; assoc prof geol, WTex A&M Univ, 1981-1996; geologist, US Geol Surv, 1973-1981; geologist, Dept Prehist, Nat Inst Anthrop & Hist, Mex, 1972-1973; Res grants, Geol Soc Am & Sigma Xi, 1968-1969 & NSF, 1969-1970; assoc prof, WTex State Univ, 1968-1970; asst prof geol, Cent Mo State Col, 1965-1968; Geologist, Texaco Inc, NMex, 1961-1962. **Memberships:** Geol Soc Am; Soc Am Archaeol; Asn Am Geographers; Royal Geog Soc; Explorers Club. **Research Statement & Publications:** Photographic documentation of physical and cultural geographic features in western United States and Mexico. **Mailing Address:** 151 Del Oro Cir, Colorado Spgs, CO 80919. **Fax:** 806-656-2928.

LAMBERT, REGINALD MAX, BACTERIOLOGY, IMMUNOLOGY. **Personal Data:** b Delta, Ohio, February 25, 1926; m 1952, c 3. **Education:** Butler Univ, BA, 1950; Univ Buffalo, MA, 1952, PhD (bact & immunol), 1955. **Professional Experience:** PROF MICROBIOL & IMMUNOL, STATE UNIV NY, BUFFALO, as of 2004; dir, Buffalo Regional Red Cross Bldg Prog, 1973-; assoc prof Microbiol, State Univ NY, Buffalo, beginning 1967; dir blood bank, Shands Teaching Hosp, Univ Fla, 1964-1967; asst prof path, Col Med, Univ Fla, 1964-1967; consult, 1960-1963 & 1967- & Buffalo Gen Hosp, 1963-1964; asst prof, Sch Med, State Univ NY Buffalo, 1959-1964; consult, E J Meyer Mem Hosp, Buffalo, 1958; assoc, Sch Med, State Univ NY Buffalo, 1957-1959; assoc dir, Blood Group res Unit, 1955-1964 & 1967-1976; instr, Sch Med, State Univ NY Buffalo, 1955-1957; asst bact & immunol, Sch Med, State Univ NY Buffalo, 1951-1955. **Memberships:** AAAS; Am Soc Microbiol; Int Soc Blood Transfusion; Int Soc Hemat; Sigma Xi. **Research Statement & Publications:** Blood groups; immunohematology; transfusion genetics. **Mailing Address:** Dept Microbiol & Immunol, State Univ NY, 233 Shermin Hall, S Campus, Buffalo, NY 14214. **E-Mail:** rlambert@buffalo.edu

LAMBERT, RICHARD BOWLES, PHYSICAL OCEANOGRAPHY. **Personal Data:** b Clinton, Mass, April 20, 1939; m 1964, Sherrill; c Lisa Beth L. **Education:** Lehigh Univ, AB, 1961; Brown Univ, ScM, 1964, PhD (physics), 1966. **Honors & Awards:** Ocean Sci Award, Am Geophysical Union, 1999. **Professional Experience:** Prog dir phys oceanog, NSF, 1991-1999; assoc prog dir, NSF, 1984-1991; assoc prog dir oceanog, Ocean Physics Div, 1984-1990; sr res oceanogr, Ocean Physics Div, 1982-1984; asst vpres, Ocean Physics Div, 1980-1982; mgr, Ocean Physics Div, 1979-1981; res oceanogr, Sci Appln Inc, 1977-1984; prog dir phys oceanog, NSF, 1975-1977; from asst prof to assoc prof oceanog, Univ RI, 1967-1975; Fulbright fel aerodyn, Munich Tech, 1966-1967. **Memberships:** Am Geophys Union; Oceanog Soc; Chartee Life Memam, Sci, Affil. **Research Statement & Publications:** Hydrodynamic stability; oceanic turbulence; diffusion energy transfer; air-sea interaction; program management. **Mailing Address:** 11312 Gainsborough Rd, Potomac, MD 20854. **E-Mail:** rblamert@erols.com

LAMBERT, ROBERT F, ELECTRICAL ENGINEERING, ACOUSTICS. **Personal Data:** b Warroad, Minn, March 14, 1924; m 1951, c 3. **Education:** Univ Minn, BEE, 1948, MS, 1949, PhD, 1953. **Honors & Awards:** John Johnson Mem Educ Award, Inst Noise Control Engrs, 1984. **Professional Experience:** PROF EMER ELEC ENG, UNIV MINN, MINNEAPOLIS, as of 2002; NASA Langley Res Ctr, Hampton, Va, 1979; assoc dean, Inst Technol, 1967-1968; vis scientist, Ill Phys Inst, Univ Goettingen, Ger, 1964; prof elec eng, Univ Minn, Minneapolis, beginning 1959; vis asst prof, Mass Inst Technol, 1953-1955; from instr to assoc prof, Univ Minn, Minneapolis, 1949-1959; asst elec eng, Univ Minn, Minneapolis, 1948-1949. **Memberships:** Am Soc Eng Educ; fel Acoust Soc Am; fel Inst Elec & Electronics Engrs; Sigma Xi; Inst Noise Control Engrs. **Research Statement & Publications:** Signal analysis including random processes and noise; acoustics including flow ducts, wave filters, porous materials, wave propagation, noise control; communication technology including ink jet printing, ultrasonic scanning, speech and electroacoustics; random processes; author of numerous publications. **Mailing Address:** Dept Elec Eng Inst Technol, Univ Minn 200 Union St SE, Minneapolis, MN 55455. **E-Mail:** lambert@ece.umn.edu

LAMBERT, ROBERT HENRY, ATOMIC PHYSICS. **Personal Data:** b Bayshore, NY, November 3, 1930; div, c Rober L & Suzanne M. **Education:** St Lawrence Univ, BS, 1952; Harvard Univ, MS, 1954, PhD (physics), 1963. **Professional Experience:** PROF PHYSICS, UNIV NH, 1968-; grant, NSF, 1965-1971; res grants, Univ NH, 1962-1963, 1965-1966; from asst prof to assoc prof, Univ NH, 1961-1968; asst, Harvard Univ, 1957-1960; instr physics, Univ NH, 1955-1957. **Memberships:** Am Phys Soc. **Research Statement & Publications:** Measurement of hyperfine structure using optical pumping. **Mailing Address:** Dept Physics, Univ NH, Rm 203 DeMeritt Hall, Durham, NH 03824. **Fax:** 603-862-2998. **E-Mail:** rlambert@christa.unh.edu

LAMBERT, ROGER GAYLE, PLANT PHYSIOLOGY. **Personal Data:** b Minneapolis, Minn, January 22, 1930; m 1956, c 3. **Education:** Univ Minn, BS, 1953, MS, 1957, PhD (plant physiol), 1961. **Professional Experience:** RETIRED; Fel bot & plant path, Potato Virus Lab, Colo State Univ, 1970-1971; from actg head to head, Dept Biol, 1963-1966; from asst prof to prof, Univ Louisville, 1961-1993; Instr plant physiol, Univ Minn, 1957-1961. **Memberships:** Am Soc Plant Physiol; Sigma Xi. **Research Statement & Publications:** Plant competition and trophic structure of ecosystems. **Mailing Address:** RR 3 Box 305, Georgetown, IN 47122.

LAMBERT, ROGERS FRANKLIN, ORGANIC CHEMISTRY. **Personal Data:** b Kamas, Utah, July 12, 1929; m 1951, c 4. **Education:** Brigham Young Univ, BS, 1953; Purdue Univ, PhD (org chem), 1958. **Professional Experience:** PROF EMER CHEM, RADFORD COL, as of 2004; prof chem, Radford Col, beginning 1965; res supvr, Thiokol Chem Corp, 1961-1965; res chemist, Ethyl Corp, 1958-1961; chemist, US Bur Mines, 1953. **Memberships:** Am Chem Soc. **Research Statement & Publications:** Polymers; chemical reductions; transition metal carbonyls; reactions of heterocyclics. **Mailing Address:** Dept Chem, Radford Univ, E Main St, Radford, VA 24142.

LAMBERT, ROYCE LEONE, SOILS, AGRONOMY. **Personal Data:** b Coatesville, Ind, November 3, 1933; m 1953, c 3. **Education:** Purdue Univ, Lafayette, BS, 1964, MS, 1966, PhD (soil physics), 1970. **Professional Experience:** FAC EMER SOIL SCI, CALIF POLYTECH STATE UNIV, as of 2005; soil conservationist, Nat Park Serv, 1971; assoc prof soils, Calif Polytech State Univ, San Luis Obispo, 1969-1994. **Memberships:** Am Soc Agron; Soil Sci Soc Am; Soil Conserv Soc Am. **Research Statement & Publications:** Soil management. **Mailing Address:** Dept Soil Sci, Calif Polytech State Univ, San Luis Obispo, CA 93407-0001.

LAMBERT, WALTER PAUL, CIVIL ENGINEERING. **Personal Data:** b Glendale, WVa, September 25, 1944; m 1972. **Education:** Univ Cincinnati, BS, 1967, MS, 1969; Univ Tex, Austin, PhD (civil eng), 1975. **Honors & Awards:** Medal, Int Ozone Inst, 1977. **Professional Experience:** AT MONTGOMERY WATSON, INC, as of 1994; mgr, res & develop, Roy F Weston, Inc, 1981-?; lectr, Hood Col, 1979-1981; environ eng staff officer, Hq, US Army Med Res & Develop Command, 1977-1981; res area mgr, Med Bioengineering Res & Develop Lab, US Army, Ft Detrick, 1975-1977; fel, Univ Tex, Austin, 1972-1975. **Memberships:** Am Water Works Asn; Water Pollution Control Fedn; Soc Am Military Engrs; Am Defense Preparedness Asn; Am Soc Testing & Mat. **Research Statement & Publications:** Mathematical modeling of water resource systems; wastewater reuse; research management decision theory; human factors engineering; hazardous materials; decontamination of contaminated soils and sediments. **Mailing Address:** Montgomery Watson Inc, 301 N Lake Ave, Pasadena, CA 91101.

LAMBERT, WILLIAM M, JR, MATHEMATICS. **Personal Data:** b Wausau, Wis, April 6, 1936. **Education:** Univ Wis, BA, 1958; Univ Calif, Los Angeles, MA, 1959, PhD (math), 1965. **Professional Experience:** RETIRED; prof, Dept Math, Univ Costa Rica, 1974-1985; assoc prof, Univ Detroit, 1969-1974; from asst prof to assoc prof, Loyola Univ, Calif, 1963-1969; res asst, Univ Calif, Los Angeles, 1960-1963; teaching asst, Univ Calif, Los Angeles, 1959-1960; Teaching asst math, Univ Wis, 1957-1958. **Memberships:** Math Asn Am; Asn Symbolic Logic. **Research Statement & Publications:** Effective processes of general algebraic structures; metamathematics of algebra. **Mailing Address:** Apdo 111-2070, Sabanilla 2070, Montes de Oca, Costa Rica.

LAMBERTI, GARY ANTHONY, STREAM ECOLOGY, PLANT-HERBIVORE INTERACTIONS. **Personal Data:** b Oakland, Calif, October 5, 1953; m 1990, Donna; c Matthew & Sara. **Education:** Univ Calif, Davis, BS, 1975; Univ Calif, Berkeley, PhD (aquatic biol), 1983. **Honors & Awards:** John A Kaneb award for teching excellence, univ of Notre Dame (2001); pres, north Am Benthological soc (1997-1998); prof of the term award; Mortarboard soc, Oregon state univ (1987); best student paper award; north Am Benthological soc annual meeting, Ann Arbor Mi (1982); distinguished teaching asst; univ of Calif, Berkeley (1981); outstanding graduate student award; dept of Entomological sci, UC Berkeley (1981). **Professional Experience:** PROF & ASST CHAIR, DEPT OF BIOL SCI, UNIV NOTRE DAME, 2001-; assoc ed, J NAm Benthological Soc, 1991-1994; prin investr, NSF, 1990-1993; assoc prof biol, Univ Notre Dame, 1995-2000; asst prof, Univ Notre Dame, 1989-1995; res asst prof, Ore State Univ, 1986-1989; assoc, Ore State Univ, 1984-1986; consult, Clear Lake Algae Res Unit, 1976-1977. **Memberships:** Ecol Soc Am; NAm Benthological Soc; Am Inst Biol Sci; AAAS Indiana acad of sci. **Research Statement & Publications:** Ecology of streams and rivers; benthic communities the importance of algal-herbivore interactions; the retention and processing of nutrients and organic matter; the impacts of exotic species, especially zebra mussels. **Mailing Address:** Dept Biol Sci, Univ Notre Dame, Notre Dame, IN 46556-0369. **Fax:** 574-631-7413.

LAMBERTS, AUSTIN E, MARINE ZOOLOGY, NEUROSURGERY. **Personal Data:** b East Saugatuck, Mich, November 30, 1914; div, c Catherine (LeGalley), Barbara (Law), Marcia & Conrad P. **Education:** Calvin Col, AB, 1936; Univ Mich, Ann Arbor, MD, 1941, MS, 1950; Am Bd Neurosurg, dipl, 1952; Univ Hawaii, PhD (marine zool), 1973. **Professional Experience:** Res grant, Nat Sci Asn, 1978; res grant, Nat Geog Soc, 1974 & 1978; INDEPENDENT RES, REEF ECOL, 1973-; teaching asst marine zool, Univ Hawaii, 1969-1973; consult neurosurg, St Mary's Hosp, GrandRapids, 1950-1976; pvt pract neurosurg, St Mary's Hosp, Grand Rapids, 1950-1968; Resident & instr neurosurg, Univ Mich, 1945-1950. **Memberships:** Fel Explorers Club; Am Asn Neurosurgeons; Cong Neurosurgeons; Am Med Asn. **Research Statement & Publications:** Study of natural life cycles of reef corals and unexplained coral kills; coral growth using the dye alizarin; effects of pesticides on coral growth; collecting and identification of modern Pacific reef corals; cataloging. **Mailing Address:** 1520 Leffingwell NE, Grand Rapids, MI 49505.

LAMBERTS, BURTON LEE, BIOCHEMISTRY. **Personal Data:** b Fremont, Mich, October 24, 1919. **Education:** Calvin Col, BS, 1949; Mich State Univ, PhD (chem), 1958. **Professional Experience:** RETIRED; chief biochemist, Dent Res Facil, Naval Dent Res Inst, 1960-1988; instr, Mich State Univ, 1958-1960; asst chem, Mich State Univ, 1955-1958; chemist, Northern Regional Res Lab, Ill, 1951-1954. **Memberships:** Am Chem Soc; Int Asn Dent Res. **Research Statement & Publications:** Dental caries; salivary gland secretions; relationship of oral microbial products to periodontal disease. **Mailing Address:** 1320 Minard Lane, Libertyville, IL 60048.

LAMBERTS, ROBERT L, PHOTOGRAPHIC OPTICS, PHYSICAL OPTICS. **Personal Data:** b Fremont, Mich, September 8, 1926; m 1951, Margaret Van Mouwerik; c Ruth (DuMont), Margaret (Bendroth), Nancy (Black), William J, Robert J & Peter J. **Education:** Calvin Col, AB, 1949; Univ Mich, MS, 1951; Univ Rochester, PhD (optics), 1969. **Professional Experience:** RETIRED; pres, Sine patters llc, pittsford, ny, as of 2002; Nazareth Col, Rochester, 1986-1989; teaching, Daystar Univ Col, Nairobi, Kenya, 1984-1985; teaching, Roberts-Wesleyan Col, 1983-1984; sr res assoc, Kodak Res Labs, Eastman Kodak Co, 1951-1983; Sine Patterns, Pittsford NY. **Memberships:** Fel Optical Soc Am. **Research Statement & Publications:** Image structure of optical systems and photographic materials; physical optics. **Mailing Address:** 236 Henderson Dr, Penfield, NY 14526.

LAMBERTSEN, CHRISTIAN JAMES, PHARMACOLOGY. **Personal Data:** b Westfield, NJ, May 15, 1917; wid, c Christian, David, Richard & Bailey. **Education:** Rutgers Univ, BS, 1939; Univ Pa, MD, 1943. **Honorary Degrees:** DSc, Northwestern Univ, 1977. **Honors & Awards:** Ocean Sci & Eng Award, Marine Technol Soc, 1972; Environ Sci Award, NY Acad Sci, 1974 & Aerospace Med Asn, 1979; Boerema Award, Undersea & Hyperbaric Med Soc, 1992. **Professional Experience:** Life Sci Div, Environ Biomed Sci Working Group, 1991-; mem, Radiation & Environ Health Working Group, NASA, 1989-1991; DISTINGUISHED PROF EMER ENVIRON MED, MED CTR, UNIV PA, 1985-; DIR, ENVIRON BIOMED RES DATA CTR, 1985-; med adv, SubSea Int, Inc, US & Brit, 1983-; mem, Comt Undersea Physiol & Med, Nat Res Coun, 1972- & Comt Hyperbaric Oxygenation; mem, US Oceanogr Adv Bd, 1970-; dir, Inst Environ Med, 1968-1985; consult, Man Space Comt, Space Sci Bd, Nat Acad Sci, 1962-1980; chmn, Man Space Comt, Space Sci Bd, Nat Acad Sci, 1960-1962; consult, Sci Adv Bd, USAF, 1959-1961; consult neuropharmacol, Del State Hosp, 1957-1961; consult & lectr, Off Surgeon Gen, USN, 1957-1960; consult, US Army Chem Ctr, 1955-1959; basic sci secy bd, Pharmacol Comt, Nat Bd Med Examrs, 1954-; mem, Pharmacol Comt, Nat Bd Med Examrs, 1954-1955; prof pharmacol & exp therapeut, Univ Pa, 1953-1985; mem, Comt Undersea Warfare & Comt Naval Med Res, Nat Res Coun, 1953-1972 & panel underwater swimmers, 1953-1956; vis res assoc prof, Univ Col, London, 1951-1952; mem, Panel Shipboard & Submarine Med, Off Secy Defense Res Develop Bd, 1950-1953; assoc med, Univ Hosp, Univ Pa, 1948-1977; Markle scholar, 1948-1953; from instr to assoc prof pharmacol, Univ Pa, 1946-1952; Intern, Hosp Univ Pa, 1943; mem adv panel med sci, Off Secy Defense; chmn, Comt Manned Undersea Activ, Off Secy Navy. **Memberships:** Nat Acad Eng; fel Am Soc Clin Pharmacol & Therapeut; Am Physiol Soc (pres, 1954-1955); Am Soc Clin Invest; Am Soc Pharmacol & Exp Therapeut; Am Col Clin Pharmacol & Chemother; Asn Am Med Cols; Europ Undersea Biomed Soc; Int Acad Astronaut; Int Astronaut Fedn; Sigma Xi. **Research Statement & Publications:** Respiratory physiology and pharmacology; aerospace and diving medicine; breathing apparatus for underwater swimmers; granted 10 US patents. **Mailing Address:** Inst Environ Med Med Ctr, Univ Pa, One John Morgan Bldg, 3620 Hamilton Walk, Philadelphia, PA 19104-6068. **E-Mail:** clambert@mail.med.upenn.edu

LAMBERTSEN, RICHARD H, PATHOBIOLOGY, PATHOPHYSIOLOGY. **Personal Data:** b Philadelphia, Pa, February 11, 1953. **Education:** Univ Pa, BA, 1975, VMD, 1979, PhD (comp med & exp hemat), 1980. **Professional Experience:** RES ASSOC, ECOSYSTS TECHNOL TRANSFER INC, 1988-; fel, Comt Challenges Modern Soc, NATO, 1987-1989; adv ecotoxicol, Ctr Doc & Res Marine Pollution, France, 1987-1989; mem, Working Group on Assessment Risk Associated Maritime Shipment Dangerous Prod, NATO/CCMS, 1987; consult, Div Res Resources, NIH, 1987; mem sci comn, Int Whaling Comn, 1986; dir, Inst Biomed Aquatic Studies, 1984-1988; asst prof physiol, Col Vet Med, Univ Fla, 1982-1988; guest investr, Coastal Res Ctr, Woods Hole Oceanog Inst, 1982, 1983, 1986, 1991; vis scientist, Inst Exp Path, Univ Iceland, 1981-1988; scholar, Woods Hole Oceanog Inst, 1981-1982. **Memberships:** Int Asn Aquatic Animal Sci; Am Soc Anatomists; Soc Marine Mammal; Am Soc Zoologists; AAAS; Oceanog Soc; Int Union Conserv Nature. **Research Statement & Publications:** Investigations of fundamental and societal implications of the maximization of kinetic energy through processes of organic and technologic evolution; spatiokinetic organization of hematopoietic microenvironments; baleen whale feeding mechanics and biological momentum transfer processes; large whale pathobiology and pathophysiology; marine ecotoxicology and conservation; maintenance of freedom of scientific inquiry; marine policy. **Mailing Address:** Ecosysts Technol Transfer Inc, PO Box 6788, Titusville, FL 32782. **E-Mail:** rlambert@iu.net

LAMBERTSON, GLEN ROYAL, ACCELERATOR SCIENCE, PARTICLE DYNAMICS. **Personal Data:** b Paonia, Colo, January 14, 1926; m 1950, Jean Smith; c Tali, Roy & Dean. **Education:** Univ Colo, BS, 1948; Univ Calif, Berkeley, MA, 1951. **Honors & Awards:** 1991 Prize for Achievement in Accelerator Physics and Techol, US Particle Accelerator Sch; three patents. **Professional Experience:** CONSULT, 1991-; group leader, Lawrence Berkeley Lab, 1973-1991; staff sr scientist, Lawrence Berkeley Lab, 1971-1991; res physicist, Lawrence Berkeley Lab, 1964-1971; Vis scientist, Europ Orgn Nuclear Res, Geneva, 1963-1964; Res physicist, Lawrence Radiation Lab, Berkeley, 1951-1954 & 1955-1963 & Brookhaven Nat Lab, 1954-1955. **Memberships:** Fel Am Phys Soc; AAAS. **Research Statement & Publications:** Analysis, design specification, and development of particle accelerator components; items that interact electromagnetically with the beam. **Mailing Address:** 6401 Castle Dr, Oakland, CA 94611.

LAMBERTSON, W ROGER, AERONAUTICS. **Professional Experience:** DIR, GOVT RES REQ, LOCKHEED CORP, as of 2006. **Memberships:** Nat Acad Press. **Mailing Address:** Lockheed Missiles & Space Co, 1725 Jefferson Davis Hwy, Arlington, VA 22202-4102. **Fax:** 703-413-5805.

LAMBETH, DAVID N, MAGNETISM. **Personal Data:** b Carthage, Mo, March 18, 1947; m 1969, c 1. **Education:** Univ Mo-Columbia, BS, 1969; Mass Inst Technol, PhD (physics), 1973. **Professional Experience:** DIR, INTEVAC INC, 1996-; assoc dir, Data Storage Syst, Carnegie Mellon Univ, 1989-1999; PROF, ELEC, COMPUT ENG & MAT SCI ENG, CARNEGIE MELLON UNIV, 1989-; OWNER, LAMBETH SYSTS, 1988-; sr res physicist, Eastman Kodak Co, 1973-1988. **Memberships:** Inst Elec & Electronics Engrs; Magnetics Soc; Am Phys Soc. **Research Statement & Publications:** Magnetism and magneto-optics of thin film materials. **Mailing Address:** Dept Elec & Comp Eng, Carnegie Mellon Univ, 329 Roberts Eng Hall, Pittsburgh, PA 15213. **Fax:** 412-268-4916. **E-Mail:** lambeth@ece.cmu.edu

LAMBETH, DAVID ODUS, BIOCHEMISTRY. **Personal Data:** b Carthage, Mo, June 16, 1941; m 1962, Sharon; c Gregory S & Judith C. **Education:** Univ Mo, Columbia, BS, 1962; Purdue Univ, MS, 1967; Univ Wis-Madison, PhD (biochem), 1971. **Professional Experience:** CHESTER FRITZ DISTINGUISHED PROF BIOCHEM, SCH MED, UNIV NDAK, 1984-; from asst prof to assoc prof, Sch Med, Univ Ndak, 1977-1984; asst prof chem, Univ SFla, 1973-1977; NIH fel biochem, Univ Mich, 1971-1973; Instr chem, Columbia Pub Schs, 1962-1967. **Memberships:** Sigma Xi; Am Chem Soc; Am Soc Biochem & Molecular Biol. **Research Statement & Publications:** Enzymology; role of GTP in metabolism; mitochondrial bioenergetics. **Mailing Address:** Dept Biochem, Sch Med & Health Sci, Univ NDak, 501 N Columbia Rd, Grand Forks, ND 58203. **Fax:** 701-777-2382. **E-Mail:** dlambeth@medicine.nodak.edu

LAMBETH, J DAVID, BIOCHEMISTRY. **Personal Data:** b El Paso, Tex, August 26, 1950; m Victoria Stevens; c Jonathan D, Benjamin H & Dylan R. **Education:** Southern Methodist Univ, BA, 1972; Duke Univ, PhD (biochem), 1976, MD, 1977. **Professional Experience:** CHMN, DEPT BIOCHEM, EMORY UNIV SCH MED, 1994-; PROF, DEPT BIOCHEM, EMORY UNIV SCH MED, 1991-; Prin investr, NIH, 1980-; from asst prof to assoc prof, Dept Biochem, Emory Univ Sch Med, 1980-1991; NIH fel, Dept Biochem, Duke Univ, 1977-1980. **Memberships:** Am Soc Biochem & Molecular Biol; AAAS; Endocrine Soc. **Research Statement & Publications:** Enzymology, regulation and signal transductions relating to oxidative systems; neutrophil superoxide generation and its receptor-coupled regulation, including phospholipase D; cholesterol metabolism and trafficking in the adrenal cortex. **Mailing Address:** Dept Biochem, Emory Univ, 1510 Clifton Rd, Atlanta, GA 30322. **E-Mail:** dlambe@emory.edu

LAMBETH, VICTOR NEAL, vegetable crops, tomato breeding; deceased, see previous edition for last biography

LAMBOOY, JOHN PETER, BIOCHEMISTRY. **Personal Data:** b Kalamazoo, Mich, December 6, 1914; m 1942, Irene; c John P, Peter K, Philip J & Kathleen A. **Education:** Kalamazoo Col, AB, 1937, MS, 1938; Univ Ill, MA, 1939; Univ Rochester, PhD (physiol chem), 1942. **Honors & Awards:** Sci Achievement Award, Sigma Xi Md Sect, 1974; Md Chemist Award, Am Chem Soc, 1985. **Professional Experience:** PROF EMER, SCH DENT, UNIV MD, as of 2006; prof biochem, sch dent, Univ Md, Baltimore, beginning 1985; prof & chmn dept, Sch Med, 1974-1985; dean grad studies & res, Sch Med, 1971-1974; prof biol chem, Sch Med, 1969-1974; assoc dean, Grad Sch, Baltimore Campuses, Univ Md, 1969-1971; prof biochem, Eppley Inst Cancer Res, Col Med, Univ Nebr, 1964-1969; prof chem pharmacol & sect head biochem pharmacol, Eppley Inst Cancer Res, Col Med, Univ Nebr, 1963-1968; from instr to assoc prof physiol, Univ Rochester, 1946-1963. **Memberships:** Am Chem Soc; Sigma Xi; Am Soc Biochem & Molecular Biol. **Research Statement & Publications:** Synthesis and biological acitivity of vitamin analogs, amino acid analogs, anesthetics, sympathomimetic amines, bacteriostatic agents, carcinolytic agents and carcinogenic agents. **Mailing Address:** Sch Med, Univ Md, Baltimore, MD 21286.

LAMBORN, BJORN N A, PLASMA PHYSICS. **Personal Data:** b Stockholm, Sweden, April 2, 1937. **Education:** Univ Calif, Berkeley, AB, 1958, MA, 1960; Univ Fla, PhD (physics, math), 1962. **Professional Experience:** PROF EMER PHYSICS, FLA ATLANTIC UNIV, as of 2005; assoc dean, Col Sci, Fla Atlantic Univ, beginning 1995; prof physics, Fla Atlantic Univ, beginning 1975; chmn dept, Col Sci, 1970-1973 & 1979-1991; from asst prof to assoc prof, Col Sci, 1965-1975; res physicist, Inst Plasmaphysik, GmbH, Munich, Ger, 1963-1965; instr physics, Univ Miami, 1963; bd trustees, Thiouracil. **Memberships:** Sigma Xi; Am Phys Soc. **Research Statement & Publications:** Theoretical plasma physics; wave interaction in relativistic plasmas; nonadiabatic particle motion; diffusion; nonlinear wave coupling; space plasmas. **Mailing Address:** Dept Physics, Fla Atlantic Univ, Rm 438 Sci & Eng Bldg, Boca Raton, FL 33431. **E-Mail:** lamborn@physics.fau.edu

LAMBRAKIS, KONSTANTINE CHRISTOS, AEROSPACE ENGINEERING. **Personal Data:** b Piraeus, Greece, January 30, 1936; American citizen. **Education:** Univ Bridgeport, BSEE, 1962, MSME, 1965; Rensselaer Polytech Inst, PhD (aerospace eng), 1971. **Professional Experience:** PROF MECH ENG, UNIV NEW HAVEN, as of 2005; consult, Times Fiber Commun Inc, 1986-1987; consult, Textron Inc, 1986-1987; consult, United Nuclear Corp, 1984-1985; dean eng, Univ New Haven, beginning 1976; chmn mech eng dept, Univ New Haven, 1974-1976; prof eng & gas dynamics, Univ New Haven, beginning 1972-; assoc prof gas dynamics, Univ New Haven, 1969-1972; asst prof thermodynamics, Univ New Haven, 1966-1969; sr mech eng, MB Electronics, 1964-1966; develop elec engr, Skinner Pridision Industs, 1961-1964. **Memberships:** Am Soc Mech Eng; AAAS; Am Soc Elec Eng; Am Soc Aeronaut Eng. **Research Statement & Publications:** Compressible fluid flow and thermal sciences; new computational techniques for solving non-linear partial differential equations occurring in thermal-fluid sciences and field theory. **Mailing Address:** Dept Mech Eng, Univ New Haven, 300 Orange Ave Buckman Hall B112, West Haven, CT 06516-1916. **Fax:** 203-931-6087. **E-Mail:** klambrakis@newhaven.edu

LAMBRECHT, RICHARD MERLE, RADIOPHARMACEUTICAL CHEMISTRY, NUCLEAR MEDICINE. **Personal Data:** b Salem, Ore, April 8, 1943; div, c Curtis W, Lars A & Luke B. **Education:** Ore State Univ, BS, 1965; Univ Nebr, PhD (phys chem), 1969. **Honors & Awards:** IR 100 Award Innovation, 1984, 1985 & 1986; M Chamberland Award, Am Chem Soc, 1987. **Professional Experience:** DIR, BIOMED & HEALTH PROG, AUSTRALIAN NUCLEAR SCI & TECHNOL ORGN, 1985-; chmn & prin scientist, King Faisal Specialist Hosp & Res Ctr, Saudi Arabia, 1985-1990; ed, J Radioanal Chem, 1978-; chemist, Brookhaven Nat Lab, 1974-1985; assoc, Brookhaven Nat Lab, 1970-1974; Res assoc chem, Brookhaven Nat Lab, 1969-1970; prof chem, Univ Wollongong, Australia; fel, Sch Med, Univ Sydney, Australia. **Memberships:** Soc Nuclear Med; fel Royal Soc Chem; Am Chem Soc; Royal Australian Inst Chem; Australian & NZ Soc Nuclear Med. **Research Statement & Publications:** Radiopharmaceutical chemistry and nuclear medicine with emphasis on reactor and accelerator production and use of short-lived radionuclides; radiopharmaceutical design and development. **Mailing Address:** ANSTO, Bio Med & Health Prog, Menai 2234, Australia. **Fax:** 612-717-9262.

LAMBREMONT, EDWARD NELSON, ENTOMOLOGY, NUCLEAR SCIENCE. **Personal Data:** b New Orleans, La, July 29, 1928; m 1990, c 4. **Education:** Tulane Univ, BS, 1949, MS, 1951; Ohio State Univ, PhD (entom), 1958. **Professional Experience:** PROF EMER NUCLEAR SCI & DIR EMER NUCLEAR SCI CTR, LA STATE UNIV, BATON ROUGE, as of 2004; vis scientist, Int Atomic Energy Agency, Vienna, beginning 1988; southeast regional dir, bd dir, Sigma Xi, 1983-1990; bd dirs, Oak Ridge Assoc Univs, Med & Health Sci Div, 1979-1984; vis scientist, Oak Ridge Assoc Univs, Med & Health Sci Div, beginning 1977; prof nuclear sci & dir nuclear sci ctr, la state univ, baton rouge, beginning 1974; assoc prof nuclear sci, LA State Univ, Baton Rouge, 1966-1974; entomologist, Insect Physiol, Entom Res Div, Agr Res Serv, USDA, La, 1958-1966; asst entom, Ohio State Univ, 1954-1956; asst zool, Tulane Univ, 1948-1951; consult nuclear sci & technol, pub info & radiation safety, energy issues. **Memberships:** AAAS; Entom Soc Am; Sigma Xi; Nuclear Soc. **Research Statement & Publications:** Physiology and biochemistry of insects, especially lipid metabolism, synthesis and utilization of fatty acids, phospholipids and glycerolipids and lipid enzyme systems; radiotracer and nuclear science methodology as applied to biological problems; insect radiation biology and physiology of tumorous tissues. **Mailing Address:** Nuclear Sci Ctr, La State Univ, Baton Rouge, LA 70803-5820. **Fax:** 225-578-2094.

LAMBROPOULOS, PETER POULOS, THEORETICAL PHYSICS. **Personal Data:** b Tripolis, Greece, October 5, 1935; American citizen. **Education:** Athens Tech Univ, dipl, 1958; Univ Mich, MSE, 1962, MS, 1963, PhD (nuclear sci), 1965. **Professional Experience:** CONSULT, 1994-; co-chmn dept, Univ Southern Calif, 1981-1983; prof, Univ Southern Calif, 1979-1994; assoc prof physics, Univ Southern Calif, 1975-1979; from asst to assoc prof, Tex A&M Univ, 1973-1975; vis fel, Joint Inst Lab Astrophys, 1972-1973; asst physicist, Argonne Nat Lab, Ill, 1967-1972; sr physicist, Bendix Res Lab, Mich, 1965-1967; Engr, Orgn Telecommun, Greece, 1959-1960. **Memberships:** AAAS; Am Phys Soc; Fedn Am Scientists. **Research Statement & Publications:** Atomic physics; interaction of radiation with matter; quantum optics; strong electromagnetic fields. **Mailing Address:** Max Planck Inst fui Quantenoptik Postfach 1513, Hans Kopfermann Strasse, 85748 Garching, Ger.

LAMBROS, JOHN, COMPOSITE MATERIALS, FRACTURE MECHANICS. **Personal Data:** b Athens, Greece, April 10, 1967. **Education:** Imp Col, London, BEng, 1988; Calif Inst Technol, MS, 1989, PhD (aeronaut), 1994. **Professional Experience:** Assoc prof mech eng, Univ Del, 2000; ASSOC PROF AERONAUT & ASTRONAUT ENG, UNIV ILL, 2000-; asst prof mech eng, Univ Del, 1995-2000; res fel aeronaut, Calif Inst Technol, 1994-1995. **Memberships:** Am Soc Mech Engrs; Soc Exp Mech; Am Acad Mech. **Research Statement & Publications:** Dynamic fracture mechanics; advanced materials; optical techniques; high speed photography and thermography; dynamic friction. **Mailing Address:** Dept Aeronaut & Astronaut Eng Univ Ill, 310 Talbot Lab 104 S Wright St, Urbana, IL 61801. **E-Mail:** lambros@uiuc.edu

LAMBSON, ROGER O, ANATOMY. **Personal Data:** b Provo, Utah, February 5, 1939; c 3. **Education:** Univ Mont, BA, 1961; Tulane Univ, PhD (anat), 1965. **Professional Experience:** RETIRED; vchancellor admin, Univ Kans, beginning 1989; prof anat, Univ Kans, beginning 1984; vchancellor, health policy & prog develop, 1984-1988; assoc dean basic sci, Col Med, Univ Ky, 1976-1984; assoc dean acad affairs, Col Med, Univ Ky, 1975-1976; assoc dean student affairs & dir admis, Col Med, Univ Ky, 1971-1975; from instr to prof anat, Col Med, Univ Ky, 1965-1984. **Memberships:** Asn Am Med Col; Am Asn Anatomists; Am Asn Med Clins. **Mailing Address:** Univ Kans Med Ctr, Kansas City, KS 66160-7100.

LAMDEN, MERTON PHILIP, BIOCHEMISTRY. **Personal Data:** b Boston, Mass, September 7, 1919; m 1942, Bernice; c Carol B (Sacks) & Deborah J (Lamden). **Education:** Univ Mass, BS, 1941; Mass Inst Technol, PhD (food technol), 1947. **Professional Experience:** PROF EMER BIOCHEM, COL MED, UNIV VT, 1985-; vis res biochem, Dept Food Sci & Technol, Univ Calif, Davis, 1975; commonwealth Fund fel & NSF-Orgn Europ Econ Coop sr vis fel, Univ Col, Univ London, 1961-1962; from asst prof to prof, Col Med, Univ VT, 1947-1985; mem res staff, Food Technol Labs, 1943-1944; asst, Mass Inst Technol, 1941-1942. **Memberships:** AAAS; Am Chem Soc; Am Inst Nutrit; Brit Biochem Soc. **Research Statement & Publications:** Vitamin content and retention in foods; nutritional status of humans; biochemical studies on ascorbic and oxalic acids; role of ascorbic acid in metabolism. **Mailing Address:** Univ Vt, 17 Wildwood Dr, Burlington, VT 05401. **E-Mail:** merton.lamden@uvm.edu

LAMDIN, EZRA, clinical trials, hypertension; deceased, see previous edition for last biography

LAMEIER, STEVEN H, MATHEMATICS. **Education:** Univ Cincinnati, MA, 1966, Phd, 1973. **Professional Experience:** ASSOC PROF MATH, THOMAS MORE COL, as of 2005. **Mailing Address:** Thomas More Col, Crestview Hills, KY 41017. **Fax:** 859-344-3345.

LAMEIRO, GERARD FRANCIS, KNOWLEDGE TECHNOLOGY, COMPLEX MODELS. **Personal Data:** b Paterson, NJ, October 3, 1949. **Education:** Colo State Univ, BS, 1971, MS, 1973, PhD (mech eng), 1977. **Honors & Awards:** Nat Distinguished Serv Award, Asn Energy Engrs, 1981. **Professional Experience:** MKT DEVELOPER, HEWLETT PACKARD, 1996-; SR RES FEL, LAMEIRO RES INST, 1992-; DIR, LAMEIRO RES INST, 1991-; independent mgt strategist, Comput Corp, 1988-1991; columnist, HP Chronicle, 1988-1991; prod mgr, Hewlett-Packard Co, 1984-1988; pres, Successful Automated Off Systs, Inc, 1982-1984; mem, Nat Bd Dirs, Asn Energy Engrs, 1980-1981; asst prof mgt sci & info systs, Solar Energy Res Inst, 1978-1983; sr scientist, Solar Energy Res Inst, 1977-1978; fel, NSF fel solar energy, 1977; fel, Solar Energy Appln Lab, Colo Energy Res Inst, Colo State Univ, 1974-1977. **Memberships:** Asn Energy Engrs (pres-elect, 1979 & pres, 1980). **Research Statement & Publications:** Knowledge technology and knowledge revolution and its impact on corporation; economy and society; national economic growth; complex models. **Mailing Address:** PO Box 9580, Ft Collins, CO 80525-0500.

LAMELAS, FRANCISCO JAVIER, SYNCHROTRON X-RAY SCATTERING, MOLECULAR BEAM EPITAXY GROWTH & SURFACE SCIENCE. **Personal Data:** b Havana, Cuba, February 6, 1959; American citizen. **Education:** Univ Wis-Milwaukee, BS, 1980, Madison, MS, 1982; Univ Mich, Ann Arbor, MS, 1987, PhD (physics), 1990. **Professional Experience:** ASSOC PROF, BOISE STATE UNIV, as of 2004; mem tech staff, At&T Bell Labs, Murray Hill, Nj, beginning 1990; sr assoc engr, Int Bus Mach, East Fishkill, NY, 1982-1984. **Memberships:** Am Phys Soc. **Research Statement & Publications:** Synchrotron-based x-ray scattering studies of thin film and surface structures; molecular beam epitaxy growth of metallic superlattices; semiconductor growth processes. **Mailing Address:** Boise State Univ, 1910 Univ Dr, Boise, ID 83725-1570. **Fax:** 208-426-4330. **E-Mail:** lamelas@boisestate.edu

LAMENSDORF, DAVID, ELECTRICAL ENGINEERING. **Personal Data:** b NY, November 22, 1937; m Joyce. **Education:** Cornell Univ, BS, 1960; Harvard Univ, MS, 1961, PhD (appl physics), 1967. **Professional Experience:** PRIN ENGR, MITRE CORP, 2000-; group leader, Mitre Corp, 1985-2000; sr res sect head, Sperry Defense Electronics, 1983-1985; res assoc, Univ Col London, 1972-1973; mem tech staff, Sperry Res Ctr, 1967-1983. **Memberships:** AAAS; sr mem Inst Elec & Electronics Engrs; Sigma Xi. **Research Statement & Publications:** Electromagnetic theory; transient analysis of antennas; microwave antennas, networks and electronics; adaptive arrays and radar. **Mailing Address:** Mitre Corp, MS M114 Burlington Rd, Bedford, MA 01730. **E-Mail:** davidl@mitre.org

LA MERS, THOMAS HERBERT, ELECTRO CHEMICAL SENSORS, BIOSENSORS. **Personal Data:** b New York, NY, April 23, 1945; m 1969. **Education:** Antioch Col, BSES, 1968. **Professional Experience:** DESIGN CONSULT, MECH DEVICES, YELLOW SPRINGS INSTRUMENT CO INC, 1989-; consult, Ventura Labeling Co, 1984-1985; prod res & develop, Mech Devices, Yellow Springs Instrument CO Inc, 1969-1989; aircraft designer, SRL Corp, 1969; machine designer, Vernay Labs, 1968-1969. **Memberships:** AAAS. **Research Statement & Publications:** Integrating science and technology to accomplish new objectives in engineering design; gas sensors; thermometry; ceramic sensors. **Mailing Address:** 777 Dayton St, Yellow Springs, OH 45387. **Fax:** 937-767-9187.

LAMEY, HOWARD ARTHUR, PLANT PATHOLOGY CONSULTANT, ROW CROP DISEASES. **Personal Data:** b Bloomington, Ind, December 20, 1929; m 1956, Cynthia; c Timothy, Thaddeus, Linda, Suzan & Laura. **Education:** Ohio Wesleyan Univ, BA, 1951; Univ Wis-Madison, PhD (plant path), 1954. **Professional Experience:** PLANT PATHOL CONSULT & PRES, AGART LLC, 2001-; exten plant pathologist & prof, Exten Serv, NDak State Univ, 1977-2001; consult, Cent Am & Mex, 1976; proj mgr, Food & Agr Orgn, Suweon, Korea, 1971-1975; coordr plant protection prog & chmn, Res Comt, 1970-1971; consult, Food & Agr Orgn, UN, Bangkok, Thailand, 1970; plant pathologist, Int Inst Trop Agr, Ibadan, Nigeria, 1969-1971; proj mgr, Food & Agr Orgn, UN, Bangkok, Thailand, 1967-1968; rice virologist, Food & Agr Orgn, UN, Bangkok, Thailand, 1966-1967; sr res plant pathologist, Baton Rouge, La, 1960-1969; plant pathologist, USDA, Camaguey, Cuba, 1958-1960; asst plant pathologist, US Army, Md, 1956-1957; proj assoc, Dept Plant Path, Univ Wis, 1954-1955, 1957-1958; res asst, Dept Plant Path, Univ Wis, 1951-1954. **Memberships:** fel AAAS; Am Phytopath Soc; Canadian Phytopathological Soc. **Research Statement & Publications:** Diseases of sugarbeets, sunflower, dry edible beans, soybeans, and canola; fungicides, foliar and seed treatment, epidemiology. **Mailing Address:** Dept Plant Path, NDak State Univ, Box 5012, Fargo, ND 58105. **Fax:** 701-231-7851. **E-Mail:** alamey@ndsuext.nodak.edu

LAMEY, STEVEN CHARLES, ANALYTICAL CHEMISTRY, ORGANIC CHEMISTRY. **Personal Data:** b Lock Haven, Pa, March 5, 1944; m 1970, Charlotte. **Education:** Lock Haven State Col, BA, 1968; WVa Univ, MS, 1973, PhD (analytical chem), 1975. **Professional Experience:** RES CHEMIST ENERGY RES, MORGANTOWN ENERGY TECHNOL CTR, 1975-; res chemist org synthesis, Am Aniline Corp, 1968-1970. **Memberships:** Am Chem Soc; AAAS; Coblentz Soc; Sigma Xi. **Research Statement & Publications:** Characterization of coal tars; electrochemistry; instrument development for coal characterization; environmental analysis; characterization of coal combustion products; mild gasification of coal-waste management-environmental chemistry; on-line instrumentation for trace element analysis; coal technology. **Mailing Address:** Morgantown Energy Technol Ctr, Collins Ferry Rd, Morgantown, WV 26505.

LAMIE, EDWARD LOUIS, COMPUTER SCIENCE. **Personal Data:** b Kingsley, Mich, August 27, 1941; m 1960, Frances; c David, Jennifer, William, Kate, Andrew, Marla & Melissa. **Education:** San Diego State Univ, AB, 1969; Univ Southern Calif, MS, 1971; Mich State Univ, PhD (comput sci), 1974. **Professional Experience:** PROF EMER DEPT COMPUT SCI, CALIF STATE UNIV, STANISLAUS, as of 2004; DIR INST RES, CALIF STATE UNIV, STANISLAUS, 1993-; prof & chmn dept, Cent Mich Univ, 1982-; prof dept comp sci, Calif State Univ, Stanislaus, beginning 1982; assoc prof comput sci, Cent Mich Univ, 1971-1982; mem tech staff, Rockwell Int, 1969-1971. **Memberships:** Asn Comput Mach; Inst Elec & Electronics Engrs. **Research Statement & Publications:** Database systems; discrete simulation; artificial intelligence. **Mailing Address:** Dept Comp Sci, Calif State Univ, 801 W Mont Vista Ave, Turlock, CA 95382. **E-Mail:** lamie@altair.csustan.edu

LAMIELL, JAMES MICHAEL, MATHEMATICS. **Education:** Univ Colo Sch Med, MD. **Professional Experience:** CHIEF, DEPT CLIN INVESTS, BROOKE ARMY MED CTR, TEX, as of 2006. **Mailing Address:** 64 Granburg Circle, San Antonio, TX 78218. **Fax:** 210-916-6488.

LAMKEY, KENDALL RAYE, QUANTITATIVE GENETICS, APPLIED STATISTICS. **Personal Data:** b Springfield, Ill, November 22, 1958; m 1981, Becky; c Collin, Nickolas & Jacob. **Education:** Univ Ill, BS, 1980, MS, 1982; Iowa State Univ, PhD (plant breeding), 1985. **Professional Experience:** Assoc ed, Crop Sci Soc Am, 1991; assoc prof & collabr, Iowa State Univ, 1990-1997; asst prof & collabr, Iowa State Univ, 1985-1990; RES GENETICIST PLANTS, USDA, AGR RES SERV, 1984-; prof & Collabr, Iowa State Univ, beginning 1997. **Memberships:** Am Soc Agron; Crop Sci Soc Am; Biometrics Soc; Genetics Soc Am. **Research Statement & Publications:** Application of quantitative genetics and selection theory to more effectively and efficiently improve and broaden the genetics base of corn. **Mailing Address:** Dept Agron, Iowa State Univ, Ames, IA 50011-0001. **Fax:** 515-294-9359. **E-Mail:** krlamkey@iastate.edu

LAMM, FOSTER PHILIP, POLYMER CHEMISTRY. **Personal Data:** b Whittier, Calif, April 18, 1950; m 1977, c 2. **Education:** Univ Calif, San Diego, BA, 1972; Wesleyan Univ, PhD (chem), 1979. **Professional Experience:** SR RES SCIENTIST, POLYMER SCI, UNITED TECHNOL RES CTR, as of 2000; res scientist, United Technol Res Ctr, beginning 1979. **Memberships:** Am Chem Soc; Soc Mfg Engrs. **Research Statement & Publications:** Chemistry and processing of high performance adhesives; new materials and processing techniques for electrical insulating; organic materials failure analysis. **Mailing Address:** United Technol Res Ctr, One Financial Plaza, Hartford, CT 06101. **Fax:** 860-728-7879.

LAMM, LARRY O, PHYSICS. **Education:** E Carolina Univ, BS, 1978, MS, 1983; Univ Notre Dame, PhD (physics) 1989. **Professional Experience:** RES PROF PHYSICS, UNIV NOTRE DAME, as of 2006. **Mailing Address:** Dept Physics, Univ Notre Dame, Notre Dame, IN 46556. **Fax:** 574-631-7716. **E-Mail:** llamm@nd.edu

LAMM, MICHAEL EMANUEL, IMMUNOLOGY, PATHOLOGY. **Personal Data:** b Brooklyn, NY, May 19, 1934; m 1961, Ruth Kumin; c Jocelyn & Margaret. **Education:** Univ Rochester, MD, 1959; Western Res Univ, MS, 1962; Am Bd Path, dipl, 1965. **Professional Experience:** PROF PATH, CASE WESTERN RES UNIV, 1981-; chmn, dept path, Case Western Res Univ, 1981-2001; from asst prof to prof path, Sch Med, NY Univ, 1964-1981; res assoc, NIH, 1962-1964; from intern to resident path, Univ Hosps, Cleveland, Ohio, 1959-1962. **Memberships:** US & Can Acad Path; Am Soc Invest Path; Clin Immunol Soc; Am Asn Immunol; Soc Mucosal Immunol. **Research Statement & Publications:** Mucosal immunity; immunopathology. **Mailing Address:** Dept Path, Case Western Res Univ, Cleveland, OH 44106. **Fax:** 216-368-0494. **E-Mail:** michael.lamm@case.edu

LAMM, WARREN DENNIS, BEEF CATTLE MANAGEMENT, COOPERATIVE EXTENSION ADMINISTRATION. **Personal Data:** b West Reading, Pa, January 27, 1947; m 1971, Jean; c Kevan & Dana. **Education:** Del Valley Col Sci & Agr, BS, 1969; Iowa State Univ, MS, 1972; Univ Nebr, PhD (ruminant nutrit), 1976. **Professional Experience:** DIR, MASTER AGR, COLO STATE UNIV, as of 2005; asst dir, Agr & Natural Resources, Coop Exten, Colo State Univ, 1986-2005; Kellogg fel, 1988; exten beef specialist, Dept Animal Sci, 1981-1986; asst prof beef cattle nutrit & eval, Va Polytech Inst & State Univ, 1976-1981; Exten agt, Exten Serv, Colo State Univ, 1972-1973. **Memberships:** Am Soc Animal Sci. **Research Statement & Publications:** Beef nutrition and management; energetic efficiency; protein utilization; use of underutilized feedstuffs and animal waste refeeding. **Mailing Address:** Colo State Univ, 124 Shepardson Ste A, Ft Collins, CO 80523-1101. **Fax:** 970-491-4895. **E-Mail:** dlamm@vines.colostate.edu

LAMMERS, PETER J, BIOCHEMISTRY. **Education:** Univ Idaho, BS; Portland State Univ, PhD (Chem), 1982. **Professional Experience:** ASSOC PROF, CHEM & BIOCHEM & DIR, MOLECULAR BIOL PROG, NMEX STATE UNIV, as of 2005. **Research Statement & Publications:** Bioinformatic approaches to protein structure; genomics of symbiotic fungi. **Mailing Address:** Dept Chem & Biochem, NMex State Univ, POBox 30001 Dept 3MLS, Las Cruces, NM 88003-0001. **Fax:** 505-646-6846. **E-Mail:** plammers@nmsu.edu

LAMMERS, WIM, PHYSIOLOGY. **Personal Data:** b Rome, Italy, October 12, 1947; Dutch citizen. **Education:** Univ Amsterdam, MD, 1981; Univ Limburg, Neth, PhD (physiol), 1987. **Professional Experience:** ASST DEAN, RES & GRAD STUDIES, 1990-; ASSOC PROF PHYSIOL, FAC MED & HEALTH SCI, UNITED ARAB EMIRATES UNIV, 1989-; asst prof, Res & Grad Studies, 1988-1989; Asst prof physiol, Fac Med, Univ Limburg, Neth, 1975-1988. **Memberships:** Am Physiol Soc; NY Acad Sci; Europ Soc Cardiol. **Research Statement & Publications:** Normal and abnormal electrical propagation in cardiac and smooth muscle. **Mailing Address:** Dept Physiol, Fac Med & Health Sci PO Box 17666, Al Ain, United Arab Emirates. **E-Mail:** wlammers@uaeu.ac.ae

LAMMERTSMA, KOOP, CHEMISTRY. **Personal Data:** b Makkum, Frysland, Neth, August 29, 1949. **Education:** Univ Groningen, Neth, MS, 1975; Univ Amsterdam, PhD, 1979. **Professional Experience:** PROF, UNIV ALA, 1992-; from asst prof to assoc prof, Univ Ala, 1983-1992; res fel, Univ Southern Calif, Los Angeles, 1981-1983; Univ Erlangen, Nurnberg, Ger, 1980-1981; Fel, Univ Col London, Eng, 1980. **Memberships:** Am Chem Soc. **Research Statement & Publications:** Author of numerous publications; chemistry. **Mailing Address:** Dept Chem, Vrije Univ, Amsterdam, Netherlands.

LAMMIE, JAMES L, TRANSIT. **Personal Data:** b Homestead, Pa, September 19, 1931. **Education:** US Mil Acad, BS, 1953; Purdue Univ, MS, 1957; George WashUniv, MS, 1969; US Army Command & Gen Staff Col, MMAS, 1975. **Honors & Awards:** Civil Eng of Yr Award, Am Soc Civil Engrs, 1991, Parcel/Sverdrup Civil Eng Mat Award, 1991. **Professional Experience:** DIR, PARSONS BRINCKEROFF INC, 1996-; mem, Indust Policy Adv, US Trade Rep, 1996; pres & chief exec officer, Parsons Brinckeroff Inc, 1990-1996; pres & chief operating officer, Parsons Brinckeroff Inc, 1982-1990; proj dir, Parsons Brinckeroff Inc, 1975-1982; dir syst develop, Harding Larson assoc, 1974-1975; dist engr,

1972-1974; US Army Colonel, 1953-1974; asst prof mil eng, Colo Sch Mines. **Memberships:** Nat Acad Eng; fel & hon mem Am Soc Civil Engrs; fel Soc Am Mil Engrs; Am Pub Transit Asn. **Mailing Address:** Parsons Brinckerhoff Inc, 1 Penn Plaza, New York, NY 10119. **Fax:** 212-465-5096.

LAMMIE, PATRICK J, PARASITOLOGY. **Education:** Tulane Univ, PhD, 1983. **Professional Experience:** RES SCIENTIST, DIV PARASITIC DIS, CTR DIS CONTROL, DEPT CELLULAR BIOL, UNIV GA, as of 2004; RES BIOLOGIST, CTR DIS CONTROL, 1989-. **Mailing Address:** Div Parasitic Dis Ctr Dis Control Dept Cellular Biol Univ Ga, 724 Biol Sci Bldg, Atlanta, GA 30602-2607. **Fax:** 770-488-4108. **E-Mail:** pjl1@cdc.gov

LAMMI-KEEFE, CAROL J, NUTRITION. **Personal Data:** b Acushnet, Mass, June 11, 1947. **Education:** UnivMinn, PhD (nutrit), 1980. **Professional Experience:** Asst prof nutrit sci, Univ Conn, as of 2002; PROF, DEPT NUTRIT SCI, UNIV CONN, 1995-; HEAD, DEPT NUTRIT SCI, UNIV CONN, 1995-; prof, dept nutrit sci, Univ Conn, 1995-1998. **Mailing Address:** Dept Nutrit Sci, Univ Conn, Storrs, CT 06269-4017. **Fax:** 860-486-3764. **E-Mail:** clammi@canr.uconn.edu

LAMOLA, ANGELO ANTHONY, PHOTOBIOLOGY, PHOTOCHEMISTRY. **Personal Data:** b Newark, NJ, August 12, 1940; m 1963, c 2. **Education:** Mass Inst Technol, BS, 1961; Calif Inst Technol, PhD (chem), 1965. **Honors & Awards:** Baekeland Award, Am Chem Soc, 1977. **Professional Experience:** BD DIR, NGIMAT CO, 2002-; dir emerging technol, Rohm & Haas Co, 2001-2002; chief scientist, Rohm & Haas Co, 1998-2002; vpres res & develop, shirley Co, beginning 1988; sci adv, Advan Magnetics Corp, 1986-; dir chem res, Polaroid Corp, 1985-1988; Snider Found lectr, Univ Toronto, 1981; head, Molecular Biophys Res Dept, 1980-1985; mem study sect biophys & biophys chem, NIH, 1978-1983; Welch Found lectr, 1978; adj prof, Dept Dermat, Columbia Col Physicians & Surgeons, 1975-1985; mem res staff, Bell Labs, 1966-1980; asst prof chem, Univ Notre Dame, 1964-1966; ed, Molecular Photochem; mem photobiol comt, Nat Res Coun-Nat Acad Sci. **Memberships:** AAAS; Am Chem Soc; Am Soc Photobiol (pres, 1976-1977); Int Soc Optical Eng. **Research Statement & Publications:** Photochemistry; imaging chemistry; medical applications of fluorescence. **Mailing Address:** nGimat Co, 5315 Peachtree Indust Blvd, Atlanta, GA 30341. **E-Mail:** alamola@rohmhaas.com

LAMOND, BERNARD F, MATHEMATICS. **Education:** Univ Montreal, BSc, MSc; Univ BC, PhD (mgt sci). **Professional Experience:** PROF, DEPT OPERS, UNIV LAVAL, as of 2006. **Memberships:** Can Oper Res Soc. **Mailing Address:** Dept Oper & Dec Syst Sch Bus Admin, Univ Laval, Quebec, PQ G1K 7P4, Can. **Fax:** 418-656-2624. **E-Mail:** Bernard.Lamond@fsa.ulaval.ca

LAMONDE, ANDRE M, PHARMACY. **Personal Data:** b St Lambert, Que, October 5, 1936; m 1966. **Education:** Univ Montreal, BPharm, 1961; Purdue Univ, MSc, 1963, PhD (indust pharm), 1965. **Professional Experience:** MGR PHARMACEUT TECHNOL, GLEXO-WELLCOME, 1989-; qual control dir, Schering Can, 1979-1989; qual control dir, Med Div, Syntex Ltd, 1972-1979; qual control mgr, Med Div, Syntex Ltd, 1970-1972; regulatory affairs coordr, Med Div, Syntex Ltd, 1968-1970; asst prof pharm, Univ Montreal, 1965-1968. **Research Statement & Publications:** Basic pharmaceutics and pharmaceutical analysis. **Mailing Address:** 1875 Georgeville Rd, Magog, PQ J1X 3W4, Can.

LAMONDIA, JAMES A, NEMATOLOGY, SOIL MICROBIOLOGY. **Personal Data:** b Springfield, Mass, December 3, 1957; m 1979, Bonnie; c Jeffrey & Patrick. **Education:** Fitchburg State Col, BS, 1979; Cornell Univ, MS, 1982, PhD (plant path), 1984. **Professional Experience:** RES SCIENTIST, DEPT PLANT PATH, VALLEY LAB, CONN AGR EXP STA, 1998-; assoc scientist res, Dept Plant Path, Conn Agr Exp Sta, beginning 1989; assoc ed, J Nematol, 1988-1991; pathologist, Valley Lab, Windsor, 1987-1989; asst scientist res, Dept Plant Path, Conn Agr Exp Sta, 1986-1989; res assoc plant path, Cornell Univ, 1984-1986. **Memberships:** Am Phytopath Soc; Soc Nematologists. **Research Statement & Publications:** Ecology and integrated management of soilborne plant pathogens, especially plant parasitic nematodes and fungi involved in complex diseases. **Mailing Address:** Dept Plant Path & Ecol, Conn Agr Exp Sta, Valley Lab, 153 Cook Hill Rd, Windsor, CT 06095. **Fax:** 860-683-4987. **E-Mail:** james.lamondia@po.state.ct.us

LAMONT, GARY BYRON, CONTROL OF AUTONOMOUS VEHICLES, BIO- INSPIRED COMPUTATION. **Personal Data:** b St Paul, Minn, February 14, 1939; m 1966, Delores; c Jon, Heather & Michael. **Education:** Univ Minn, BPhysics, 1961, MSEE, 1967, PhD (control sci), 1970. **Honors & Awards:** teacher of the year (Eta Kappa Nu, 2001). **Professional Experience:** PROF AIR FORCE INSTITUTE of TECHNOLOGY, Dept of Electrical and Computer Engineering, as of 1980; from asst prof to assoc prof, Air Force Inst Technol, 1970-1980; systs analyst, Honeywell Inc, 1965-1967; Develop engr, Honeywell Inc, 1961-1965. **Memberships:** Inst Elec & Electronics Engrs; Am Soc Eng Educ; Asn Comput Mach; Soc Indust & Appl Math; Tau Beta Pi. **Research Statement & Publications:** Major research: control engineering; intelligent systems; parallel distributed computing; evolutionary computation; developing bio-inspired algorithms for autonomous vehicles(reconnaissance, parallel simulation), artificial immune systems (intrusion detection), and optimization (engineering/scientific applications). **Mailing Address:** Air Force Inst Technol, Wright-Patterson AFB AFT/ENG, Dayton, OH 45433. **Fax:** 937-656-4055. **E-Mail:** gary.lamont@afit.edu

LAMONT, JOHN THOMAS, MEDICINE, GASTROENTEROLOGY. **Personal Data:** b Lockport, NY, October 2, 1938; m 1964, c 3. **Education:** Canisius Col, BS, 1960; Univ Rochester, MD, 1965. **Professional Experience:** FAC, SCH MED.HARVARD UNIV, as of 2003; Prof Gastroenterol, Univ Hosp, Boston Univ, beginning 1985; Consult gastroenterologist, Peter Bent Brigham Hosp, Boston Hosp Women & WRoxbury Vet Admin Hosp, 1975-1980 & Univ, Boston City Hosp, 1980-; assoc prof & chief, Univ Hosp, Boston Univ, 1980-1985; res grants, Am Cancer Soc & Nat Found for Ileitis Colitis, 1977-1978; asst prof med, Harvard Med Sch, 1975-1980; NIH career investr award, 1975; instr, Harvard Med Sch, 1973-1975; Fel, Mass Gen Hosp, 1971-1973. **Memberships:** Am Soc Clin Res; Am Gastroenterol Asn; Am Soc Study Liver Dis. **Research Statement & Publications:** Structure and function of colonic glycoproteins; biochemistry of intestinal tract in health and disease; colon cancer; gallstones, ulcer; bacterial toxins. **Mailing Address:** Dept Gastroenterol, Harvard Univ, Boston, MA 02115. **E-Mail:** jlamont@bidmc.harvard.edu

LAMONT, JOHN W(ILLIAM), ELECTRICAL ENGINEERING, COMPUTER SCIENCE. **Personal Data:** b Cape Girardeau, Mo, March 7, 1942; m 1968, c 2. **Education:** Univ Mo-Rolla, BSEE, 1964; Univ Mo-Columbia, MSEE, 1966, PhD, 1970. **Professional Experience:** PROF, DEPT ELEC & COMPUT ENG, IOWA STATE UNIV, 1987-; proj mgr, Elec Power Res Inst, 1977-1987; asst prof, dept elec eng, Univ Tex, Austin, 1973-1977; asst prof, Univ Southern Calif, 1970-1973; instr elec eng, Univ Mo-Columbia, 1966-1970. **Memberships:** Nat Soc Prof Engrs; Inst Elec & Electronics Engrs; Sigma Xi. **Research Statement & Publications:** Application of computers to power systems. **Mailing Address:** Dept Elec & Comput Eng, Iowa State Univ, 324 Town Hall, Ames, IA 50011. **Fax:** 515-294-6760. **E-Mail:** jwlamont@ee.iastate.edu

LAMONT, PATRICK, INTELLIGENT SYSTEMS, COMPUTER ALGEBRA NUMBER THEORY. **Personal Data:** b Dublin, Ireland, August 29, 1936. **Education:** Glasgow Univ, BSc, 1958, PhD (math), 1962. **Professional Experience:** Prof comput sci, Wetern Ill Univ, beginning 1991; assoc prof math & comput sci, St Johns Univ, 1988-1989; assoc prof, Western Ill Univ, 1983-1991; asst prof quant info sci, Western Ill Univ, 1979-1983; asst prof math, Monmouth Col, Ill, 1976-1979; chmn, Deep Springs Col, California, 1974-1976; assoc prof math, St Mary's Col, Ind, 1970-1974; asst prof, Univ Notre Dame, 1966-1968; lectr pure math, Univ Birmingham, 1964-1970; Dept Sci & Indust Res traveling fel, State Univ Utrecht & Univs Gottingen & Munich, 1962-1964; asst lectr math, Royal Col Sci & Technol, Scotland, 1961-1962. **Memberships:** Am Math Soc; London Math Soc; Asn Comput Mach. **Research Statement & Publications:** Arithmetic theory of nonassociative algebras and intelligent software systems; cryptology; general computer sciences. **Mailing Address:** 141 Chandler Blvd, Macomb, IL 61455-1414. **Fax:** 309-298-2302. **E-Mail:** mfpjl@uxa.ecn.bgu.edu

LAMONT, SUSAN JOY, IMMUNOGENETICS, DISEASE RESISTANCE. **Personal Data:** b Hammond, Ind, December 26, 1953; m 1974, Gregory; c 1. **Education:** Trinity Christian Col, BA, 1975; Univ Ill Med Ctr, PhD (anat), 1980. **Professional Experience:** CHARLES F CURTISS DISTINGUISHED PROF, IOWA STATE UNIV, 2004-; HEAD, DEPT ANIMAL SCI, IOWA STATE UNIV, 2001-; asst dir res, Iowa Agr & Home Economics Experiment Station, 1994-1997; PROF ANIMAL SCI, IOWA STATE UNIV, 1992-; vis scientist, Spelderholt, Neth, 1990; from asst prof to assoc prof, Iowa State Univ, 1983-1991; postdoctoral fel, Univ Mass, 1980-1983. **Memberships:** Conf Res Workers Animal Dis; Am Asn Immunologists; Poultry Sci Asn; World Poultry Sci Asn; Int Soc Animal Genetics. **Research Statement & Publications:** Structure and function of the chicken major histocompatibility complex; genetic resistance to disease in poultry; biomedical disease models in avian species; genetics of growth and body composition; author of various articles. **Mailing Address:** Dept Animal Sci, Iowa State Univ, 2255 Kildee Hall, Ames, IA 50011. **Fax:** 515-294-2401. **E-Mail:** sjlamont@iastate.edu

LA MONTAGNE, JOHN RING, microbiology; deceased, see previous edition for last biography

LAMOREAUX, PHILIP ELMER, GEOLOGY, HYDROLOGY. **Personal Data:** b Chardon, Ohio, May 12, 1920; m 1943, Ura Mae Munro; c Philip E Jr, James W & Karen L. **Education:** Denison Univ, BA, 1943, DSc; Univ Ala, MA, 1949. **Honors & Awards:** Ian Campbell Medal, Am Geol Inst, 1990, William B Heroy Award, 1995; Commander's Medal, US Corps Eng, 1990. **Professional Experience:** RETIRED; sr biologist, PE Lamoreauz &Assocs, Inc, beginning 1990; chmn bd, PE Lamoreaux &Assocs, Inc, 1987-1990; mem bd trustee, Denison Univ, 1987; mem, Med Tech Reference Group, Oak Ridge Nat Lab, 1984-1988; ed-in-chief, J Environ Geol, 1982-; pres, PE Lamoreaux &Assocs, Inc, 1976-1987; pres, Comt Publ, Am Geol Inst, 1971-1972; chmn, Comt Publ, Am Geol Inst, 1968-1970; dir, Environ Inst Waste Mgt Studies, 1967-1978; Mauritania, Africa, Senegal & Colombia, 1964; vice chmn, Interstate Oil Compact Comn, 1963; Consult, Surinam, 1963; from assoc prof to prof, Univ Ala, Tuscaloosa, 1961-1978; state geologist & oil & gas supvr, Geol Surv Ala, 1961-1977; Consult, Philippines, 1961; chief, Groundwater Br, 1959-1961; div hydrologist, US Geol Surv, 1958-1959; Consult, Thailand, 1954, 1961, 1976; Consult, Egypt, 1953, 1959, 1961, 1963-1964, 1965, 1970, 1980; lectr geol, Univ Ala, Tuscaloosa, 1948-1959; dist geologist, US Geol Surv, 1947-1948; asst geologist, US Geol Surv, 1945-1947; Jr geologist, US Geol Surv, 1943-1945; chmn bd trustees, Geol Soc Am. **Memberships:** Nat Acad Sci; Nat Acad Eng; Geol Soc Am; Am Asn Petrol Geologists; Int Asn Hydrogeologists (vpres, 1973-1977, pres, 1977-1980); Am Inst Prof Geologists; Soc Econ Geol; Am Inst Hydrol; Am Soc Testing & Mat; Am Geophys Union; Am Inst Mech Engrs; Int Union Geol & Geophys. **Research Statement & Publications:** Groundwater geology; fluoride in groundwater; stratigraphy of Gulf Coastal Plain; hydrogeology of Karst areas. **Mailing Address:** P E LaMoreaux & Assocs Inc, 2610 University Blvd, Tuscaloosa, AL 35401-1566. **Fax:** 205-752-4043. **E-Mail:** pel@dbtech.net

LAMOTTE, CAROLE CHOATE, IMMUNOCYTOCHEMISTRY, ELECTRON MICROSCOPY. **Personal Data:** b Washington, DC, May 15, 1947; m 1970, c 2. **Education:** Univ Okla, BS, 1967; Georgetown Univ, MS, 1969; Johns Hopkins Univ, PhD (physiol), 1972. **Honors & Awards:** Jacob Javitz Neuroscience Investr Award, 1988-1995. **Professional Experience:** Regular mem, NIH Neurol Sci & Study Sect, 1985-1988; assoc prof neurosurg, Sch Med, Yale Univ, 1983-; prin investr, NIH Grant, 1978-1995; asst prof neuroanat & neurosurg, Sch Med, Yale Univ, 1978-1983; res assoc neurosurg, Sch Med, Yale Univ, 1977-1978; asst prof anat, Sch Med, Johns Hopkins Univ, 1975-1977; instr anat, Sch Med, Johns Hopkins Univ, 1974-1975; NIH fel anat, Sch Med, Johns Hopkins Univ, 1972-1974. **Memberships:** Am Asn Anatomists; Soc Neuroscience; Am Pain Soc. **Research Statement & Publications:** Anatomy and physiology of pain and temperature sensation; sprouting and reorganization in injured spinal cord. **Mailing Address:** Res Lab, Yale Univ Sch Med 333 Cedar St, New Haven, CT 06510.

LAMOTTE, CLIFFORD ELTON, PLANT PHYSIOLOGY. **Personal Data:** b Alpine, Tex, June 24, 1930; m 1974, c 2. **Education:** Tex A&M Univ, BS, 1953; Univ Wis, PhD (bot), 1960. **Professional Experience:** VIS PROF BIOL, WASH UNIV, ST LOUIS, 2004; PROF EMER BOT, IOWA STATE UNIV, as of 2003; prof bot, Iowa State Univ, beginning 1980; fac leave Univ Col Wales, UK, 1974-1975; assoc prof bot & plant path, Iowa State Univ, 1966-1980; from instr to asst prof, Boston Univ, 1961-1966; res assoc biol, Princeton Univ, 1960-1961. **Memberships:** Bot Soc Am; AAAS; Am Soc Plant Physiol. **Research Statement & Publications:** Hormonal regulation of development and orientation in plants; plant morphogenesis using tissue culture methods; growth and development in plants. **Mailing Address:** Dept Biol, Wash Univ, Busch Lab 251, Box 1137, St Louis, MO 63130. **E-Mail:** clamotte@biodec.wustl.edu

LAMOTTE, LOUIS COSSITT, MICROBIOLOGY, EPIDEMIOLOGY. **Personal Data:** b Clinton, SC, January 21, 1928; m 1948, Lila; c Barbara, Robert, Nancy, Diane & Cynthia. **Education:** Duke Univ, AB, 1948; Univ NC, MSPH, 1951; Johns Hopkins Univ, ScD(virol, entom), 1958. **Honors & Awards:** Pub Health Serv Super Serv Award, 1981. **Professional Experience:** RETIRED; dir, Div Tech Eval & Assistance, Ctr Dis Control, 1982-1986; dir, Licensure & Proficiency Testing Div, 1972-1982; adj prof, Ga State Univ, beginning 1971; chief, Microbiol Br, 1970-1972; dept chief, Pesticides Prog, 1969-1970; chief community studies, Pesticides Prog, 1966-1969; asst chief, Dis Ecol Sect, 1965-1966; mem grad fac, Colo State Univ, 1959-1966; chief, Virus Invest Unit, Dis Ecol Sect, Tech Br, Nat Commun Dis Ctr, 1958-1965; virologist, Chem Corps, US Dept Army, 1951-1958; bacteriologist, State Bd Health, NC, 1948-1951. **Memberships:** AAAS; Sigma Xi; Am Soc Trop Med & Hyg; Am Pub Health Asn; Am Soc Microbiol. **Research Statement & Publications:** Epidemiology of arthropod-borne viruses; virology, bacteriology, parasitology and epidemiology of infectious diseases. **Mailing Address:** 4820 Leeds Ct, Atlanta, GA 30338. **Fax:** 770-394-7977. **E-Mail:** llamotte@aol.com

LAMOTTE, ROBERT HILL, NEUROSCIENCES. **Personal Data:** b Washington, DC, November 4, 1940; m 1970. **Education:** Trinity Col, BS, 1963; Kans State Univ, PhD (psychol), 1969. **Professional Experience:** PROF ANESTHESIOL & PHYSIOL, MED SCH, YALE UNIV, as of 2005; assoc prof anesthesiol & physiol, Med Sch, Yale Univ, beginning 1977; asst prof neurophysiol, Sch Med & asst prof psychol, Johns HopkinsUniv, 1973-1977; Fel neurophysiol, Johns Hopkins Univ, 1973-1977; instr, Johns Hopkins Univ, 1970-1973. **Memberships:** Soc Neuroscience; AAAS. **Research Statement & Publications:** Neurophysiology and psychophysics of somesthesis. **Mailing Address:** Dept Anesthesiol Yale Univ, Sch Med 333 Cedar St, New Haven, CT 06510-3219. **E-Mail:** robert.lamotte@yale.edu

LAMOUREUX, GERALD LEE, BIOCHEMISTRY. **Personal Data:** b Bottineau, NDak, April 13, 1939; m 1969. **Education:** Minot State Col, BS, 1961; NDak State Univ, PhD (chem), 1966. **Professional Experience:** RETIRED; adj prof, NDak State Univ, beginning 1974; res chemist, Metab & Radiation Res Lab, Agr Res Serv, USDA, beginning 1966. **Memberships:** Am Chem Soc; Sigma Xi; Weed Sci Soc; Int Union Pure & Appl Chem. **Research Statement & Publications:** Elucidation of metabolic pathways utilized by plants and animals in the metabolism of herbicides, insecticides and other exenobiotics; glutathione-S-transferase mediated reactions; herbicide mode of action. **Mailing Address:** 2449 Lilac Lane, Fargo, ND 58102-2123.

LAMOYI, EDMUNDO, IMMUNOCHEMISTRY, IMMUNOPARASITOLOGY. **Personal Data:** b Oaxaca, Mex, May 6, 1952; m 1990, Judith Dominguez; c Carla & Renata. **Education:** Nat Univ Mex, BS, 1975; Brandeis Univ, PhD (biol), 1981. **Professional Experience:** Lectr, Sci & Humanities Col, Nat Univ Mex, 1987-; SR INVESTR, BIOMED RES INST, NAT UNIV MEX, 1986-; Nat researcher, Nat Syst Res, Pub Educ Secretariat, Mex, 1986; vis assoc, Nat Inst Allergy & Infectious Dis, NIH, 1983-1986; Postdoctoral res assoc, Brandeis Univ, 1981-1983. **Memberships:** Am Asn Immunologists. **Research Statement & Publications:** Studies of the human immune response to the parasite entamoeba histolytica; analysis of parasite antigens with monoclonal antibodies. **Mailing Address:** Dept Immunol, Inst Invest Biomed UNAM APDO 70-228, Mexico City DF 04510, Mex. **Fax:** 525-550-0048.

LAMP, BENSON J, MARKETING & DEVELOPMENT, AGRICULTURAL ENGINEERING. **Personal Data:** b Cardington, Ohio, October 7, 1925; m 1948, Martha; c Elaine, Marlene, Linda & David. **Education:** Ohio State Univ, BS (agr) & BS (agr eng), 1949, MS, 1952; Mich State Univ, PhD (agr eng), 1960. **Honors & Awards:** Gold Medal, Am Soc Agr Engrs. **Professional Experience:** PRES, BMJ INC, 1991-; PROF EMER AGR ENG, OHIO STATE UNIV, COLUMBUS, 1991-; bus planning mgr, Ford Tractor Opers Div, Ford Motor Co, Troy, Mich, 1978-1987; vpres mkt & develop, Ford Aerospace Div, Dearborn, 1976-1978; mkt mgr, Ford Tractor Opers Div, Ford Motor Co, Troy, Mich, 1971-1976; prod planning mgr, Ford Tractor Opers Div, Ford Motor Co, Troy, Mich, 1966-1971; prod mgr, Massey Ferguson Ltd, Toronto, 1961-1966; prof, B J Companies, 1949-1961, 1987-1991. **Memberships:** Fel Am Soc Agr Engrs (pres 1985-1986). **Research Statement & Publications:** Agricultural engineering; harvesting and management. **Mailing Address:** Col Food, Agr & Environ Sci, 260a Ag Eng, 590 Woody Hayes Dr, Columbus, OH 43210. **E-Mail:** lamp.2@osu.edu

LAMP, HERBERT F, PLANT ECOLOGY, PRAIRIE ECOLOGY. **Personal Data:** b Davenport, Iowa, August 6, 1919; wid, c Barbara, Majorie, Herbert Jr, Laurie, Jonathan & K athryn. **Education:** Chicago Teacher Col, BEd, 1941; Univ Chicago, SM, 1947, PhD (bot), 1951. **Professional Experience:** Vol, Herbarium, Morton Arboretum, 1985-; EMER PROF BIOL SCI, NORTHEASTERN ILL UNIV, 1985-; assoc dean, Arts & Sci, 1983-1984; prof biol sci & chmn dept, Northeastern Ill Univ, 1966-1983; prof biol, Northeastern Ill Univ, 1964-1966; from assoc prof to prof, Ill Teachers Col Chicago-S, 1959-1964; chmn dept natural sci, Ill Teachers Col Chicago-S, 1956-1964; Res assoc, Univ Chicago, 1952-1956; teacher biol, Ill Teachers Col Chicago-S, 1950-1959; Instr bot, Fla State Univ, 1947-1950. **Memberships:** Bot Soc Am; Ecol Soc Am; Sigma Xi. **Research Statement & Publications:** Physiological ecology of range grasses; bromus inermis leyss; prairie ecology; commmunity ecology. **Mailing Address:** 180 Linden Ave, Elmhurst, IL 60126-3605. **E-Mail:** hlamp@compuserve.com

LAMP, WILLIAM OWEN, POPULATION ECOLOGY, BIOLOGICAL CONTROL. **Personal Data:** b Omaha, Nebr, June 19, 1951; m 1973, c 2. **Education:** Ohio State Univ, MS, 1976; Univ Nebr, BS, 1972, PhD (entom), 1980. **Professional Experience:** ASST PROF ENTOM, UNIV MD, 1985-; res assoc, Ill Natural Hist Surv, 1980-1985. **Memberships:** Entom Soc Am; Weed Sci Soc Am. **Research Statement & Publications:** Ecological interactions in agroecosystems, especially mutiple pest interactions, and their economic and environmental impact for crop protection. **Mailing Address:** Dept Entom, Univ Md, College Park, MD 20742-0001. **Fax:** 301-314-9290. **E-Mail:** wl1@umail.umd.edu

LAMPE, MARTIN, PLASMA PHYSICS, CHARGED PARTICLE BEAMS. **Personal Data:** b Brooklyn, NY, April 29, 1942; m 1964, Barbara; c William T & Rebecca I. **Education:** Harvard Univ, AB, 1962; Univ Calif, Berkeley, MA, 1963, PhD (physics), 1967. **Honors & Awards:** E O Hulburt Award, Naval Res Lab, 1985. **Professional Experience:** SR SCIENTIST, NAVAL RES LAB, 1995-; supvr res physicist, Naval Res Lab, 1975-1995; res physicist, Naval Res Lab, 1969-1975; res assoc, NY Univ, 1967-1969. **Memberships:** Fel Am Phys Soc; Inst Elec & Electronics Engrs; Sigma Xi. **Research Statement & Publications:** Theory of plasma instabilities; non-linear theory and propagation of relativistic electron beams; modeling of plasma processing and low-temperature discharges. **Mailing Address:** Naval Res Lab Code, 4555 Overlook Ave SW, Washington, DC 20375-5346. **Fax:** 202-767-1607. **E-Mail:** lampe@nrl.navy.mil

LAMPERT, CARL MATTHEW, ALTERNATIVE ENERGY ENGINEERING, OPTICAL SWITCHING TECHNOLOGY. **Personal Data:** b Portland, Ore, February 20, 1952. **Education:** Univ Calif, Berkeley, BS (electronic eng) & BS (mat sci), 1974, MS, 1977, PhD (mat sci), 1979. **Professional Experience:** CHAIR, STAR SCI, as of 2005; ed-in-chief, Star Sci, as of 2005; OWNER & SCI CONSULT, STAR SCI, 1996-; Elf Atochem, France, 1990-; Optical Coating Labs Inc, Santa Rosa, 1988-; lectr, Inst Theoret Physics, Trieste, Italy, 1985-; UN Develop Prog, NY, 1985-; consult, Lyon & Lyon, Los Angeles, 1985; proj leader, Int Energy Agency, Paris, France, 1984-1996; ed-in-chief, Solar Energy Mat J, 1982-; conf chmn, Int Optical Eng Soc, 1982-; prin investr & staff scientist, Lawrence Berkeley Lab, Calif, 1979-1996; res asst, Lawrence Berkeley Lab, Calif, 1974-1979; comput programmer, US Forestry Serv, 1972-1974; electronics technician, Contra Costa Col, San Pablo, 1970-1972. **Memberships:** Fel Int Optical Eng Soc; Inst Elec & Electronics Engrs; Am Vacuum Soc; Int Solar Energy Soc; Sigma Xi. **Research Statement & Publications:** Development of new optical materials and coatings for glass and plastic products, application to buildings, automotive and aerospace glazing; engineering and materials for energy conversion components; large scale optical switching and display products; author of over 100 papers, 1 book, 2 patents, lectured in 16 countries. **Mailing Address:** Star Sci, 8730 Water Rd, Cotati, CA 94931-4252. **Fax:** 707-794-0323. **E-Mail:** cmlstar@juno.com

LAMPERT, SEYMOUR, SOLAR ENERGY & ALTERNATE ENERGY APPLICATIONS. **Personal Data:** b Brooklyn, NY, March 5, wid Shirley; c Rachel B, David A & Martin D. **Education:** Ga Inst Technol, BS, 1943; Calif Inst Technol, MS, 1947, AE, 1948, PhD (aeronaut eng & math), 1954. **Professional Experience:** PROF EMER ENG, UNIV SOUTHERN CALIF, 1993-; vpres, Davato Corp, 1985-; ed-in-chief, J Solar Sci, 1981-1982; prof eng, Univ Southern Calif, 1975-1993; sci adv, Dept Defense, 1968-1969; vpres, Syst Assoc Inc, 1967-1971; Consult, Jet Propulsion Lab, Calif Inst Technol, 1967-1968; dir advan systs, NAm Aviation Space & Info Systs, 1962-1967; mgr appl mech, Ford Aeronotronic, 1956-1962; chief engr, Odin Assocs, 1955-1956; asst prof eng, Univ Southern Calif, 1954-1955; res engr, Jet Propulsion Lab, Calif Inst Technol, 1951-1954; res scientist, Ames Lab, Nat Adv Comt Aeronaut, 1944-1951; Instr math, Ga Sch Technol, 1943-1944. **Memberships:** Sigma Xi; Sci Res Soc Am. **Research Statement & Publications:** Structures for spacecraft; spacecraft design; methodology for developing area transportation; fluid mechanics; wing theory; solar energy. **Mailing Address:** Univ Southern Calif, PO Box 4719, Irvine, CA 92716-4719. **E-Mail:** sylamp@aol.com

LAMPERTI, ALBERT A, RADIATION BIOLOGY, NEUROANATOMY. **Personal Data:** b Bronx, NY, October 24, 1947; m 1972, c 2. **Education:** Manhattan Col, BS, 1969; Univ Cincinnati, PhD (anat), 1973. **Professional Experience:** PROF, DEPT ANAT & CELL BIOL, TEMPLE UNIV SCH MED, 1998-; ASST DEAN STUD AFFAIRS, TEMPLE UNIV SCH MED, 1997-; assoc prof, dept anat, Temple Univ Sch Med, beginning 1980; Asst prof anat, Univ Cincinnati, 1973-1980. **Memberships:** Am Asn Anatomists; Radiation Res Soc; Asn Am Med Cols. **Research Statement & Publications:** Reproductive neuroendocrinology; radiation biology. **Mailing Address:** Dept Anat & Cell Biol, Temple Univ Sch Med, 3400 N Broad St, Philadelphia, PA 19140-5196. **Fax:** 215-707-2966. **E-Mail:** lamperti@temple.edu

LAMPERTI, JOHN WILLIAMS, STOCHASTIC PROCESSES. **Personal Data:** b Montclair, NJ, December 20, 1932; m 1957, Claudia; c Matthew D, Steven J, Aaron M & A Noelle. **Education:** Haverford Col, BS, 1953; Calif Inst Technol, PhD (math), 1957. **Professional Experience:** PROF EMER, DARTMOUTH COL, 1999-; vis prof, Nat Atonomous Univ Nicaragua, 1990; consult, Am Friends Serv Comt, 1980, 1985, 1991; vis prof, Aarhus Univ, 1972-1973; sci exchange visitor, USSR, 1970; PROF MATH, DARTMOUTH COL, 1968-; assoc prof, Dartmouth Col, 1963-1968; res assoc, Rockefeller Inst, 1962-1963; vis asst prof, Dartmouth Col, 1961-1962; from instr to asst prof math, Stanford Univ, 1957-1961. **Memberships:** Fedn Am Scientists; fel Inst Math Statist; Union Concerned Scientists. **Research Statement & Publications:** Probability theory, particularly properties of stochastic processes. **Mailing Address:** Dept Math, Dartmouth Col, Hanover, NH 03755. **Fax:** 603-646-1312. **E-Mail:** john.lamperti@dartmouth.edu

LAMPI, RAUNO ANDREW, FOOD SCIENCE & TECHNOLOGY & FOOD SERVICE SYSTEMS, CHEMICAL ENGINEERING. **Personal Data:** b Gardner, Mass, August 12, 1929; m 1951, Betty; c Steven, Martin, Karin & Eric. **Education:** Univ Mass, BS, 1951, MS, 1955, PhD (food technol), 1957. **Honors & Awards:** Rohland Isker Award, Res & Develop Assocs, 1969; Indust Achievement Award, Inst Food Technol, 1978; Riegter-Davis Award, Inst Food Technol Packaging Div, 1995. **Professional Experience:** CONSULT, 1990-; chief, Adv Equip Br, Technol Acquisition Div, Natick Res Develop & Eng Ctr, 1988-1989; chief, Food Equip Div, 1976-1988; chief, Systs Develop Br, Packaging Div, 1969-1976; res phys scientist, Packaging Div, 1967-1969; packaging technologist, Container Div, Natick Labs, US Army, 1966-1967; mgr, Food Technol Sect, Cent Eng Labs, FMC Corp, 1962-1966; tech dir, New Eng Appl Prod Co, 1959-1962; asst mgr indust instrumentation, Food Div, Foxboro Co, 1957-1959; res instr food technol, Univ Mass, 1953-1957. **Memberships:** Fel Inst Food Technol. **Research Statement & Publications:** Continuous applesauce and juice processes; stability of freeze dried foods; thermal processing of foods in flexible packages and flat metal containers; development of food service systems; design concepts for NASA Space Station Feeding System. **Mailing Address:** 20 Wheeler Rd, Westborough, MA 01581. **Fax:** 508-366-8069.

LAMPKY, JAMES ROBERT, MICROBIOLOGY. **Personal Data:** b Battle Creek, Mich, June 19, 1927; m 1971, Shirley. **Education:** Eastern Mich Univ, BS, 1959; Univ Mo, MA, 1961, PhD (microbiol), 1966. **Professional Experience:** Lectr, Brookgreen Gardens 1993-1999; adv, Sc Poison Control Ctr, 1993-1999; PROF EMER BIOL, CENT MICH UNIV, 1992-; from asst prof to prof, Cent Mich Univ, 1966-1992; from instr to asst prof bact, Wis State Univ, 1963-1966. **Research Statement & Publications:** Cellulolytic fruiting myxobacteria of the genus Polyangium with emphasis on morphology and ultrastructure. **Mailing Address:** Dept Biol, Cent Mich Univ, 217 Brooks Hall, Mt Pleasant, MI 48859. **Fax:** 989-774-3462.

LAMPMAN, GARY MARSHALL, ORGANIC CHEMISTRY. **Personal Data:** b South Gate, Calif, October 8, 1937; m 1971, Marian; c Elizabeth & Karl. **Education:** Univ Calif, Los Angeles, BS, 1959; Univ Wash, PhD (chem), 1964. **Professional Experience:** Res fel, Univ Col London, 1978, 1981 & 1986; PROF ORG CHEM, DEPT CHEM, WESTERN WASH UNIV, 1973-; from asst prof to assoc prof, Western Wash Univ, 1964-1973. **Memberships:** Am Chem Soc; Sigma Xi. **Research Statement & Publications:** Synthetic organic chemistry; organometallic chemistry; chemical education; cobaloxime chemistry; published over 5 articles. **Mailing Address:** Dept Chem, Western Wash Univ, 516 High St Campus Box 340, Bellingham, WA 98225-9150. **Fax:** 360-650-2826. **E-Mail:** lampman@chem.wwu.edu

LAMPORT, DEREK THOMAS ANTHONY, BIOCHEMISTRY. **Personal Data:** b Brighton, Eng, December 1, 1933; m 1963, c 5. **Education:** Univ Cambridge, BA, 1958, PhD (biochem), 1963. **Professional Experience:** VIS SR RES FEL BIOL SCI, UNIV SUSSEX, as of 2004; PROF BIOCHEM, DOE PLANT RES LAB, MICH STATE UNIV, 1974-; from asst prof to assoc prof, Doe Plant Res Lab, Mich State Univ, 1964-1974; staff scientist, Res Inst Advan Studies, Martin Marietta Corp, Md, 1961-1964. **Memberships:** Am Chem Soc. **Research Statement & Publications:** Plant cell wall proteins; role of hydroxyproline-rich glycoproteins, notably extensin, in plant growth. **Mailing Address:** PO Box 423, Potterville, MI 48876. **E-Mail:** d.t.a.lamport@sussex.ac.uk

LAMPORT, LESLIE B, CONCURRENT & DISTRIBUTED COMPUTING. **Personal Data:** b New York, NY, February 7, 1941. **Education:** Mass Inst Technol, BS, 1960; Brandeis Univ, MA, 1963, PhD (math), 1972. **Professional Experience:** AT MICROSOFT RES, 2001-; sr consult engr, Digital Equip Corp, 1985-2001; SRI Int, 1977-1985; Mass Comput Assocs, 1970-1977; prof math, Marlboro Col, 1965-1969. **Memberships:** Nat Acad Eng; Inst Elec & Electronics Engrs. **Mailing Address:** Microsoft Corp, 1065 La Avenida, Mtain View, CA 94043.

LAMPPA, GAYLE K, GENETICS, BIOLOGY. **Education:** Reed Col, BA, 1973; Univ Wash, PhD (bot), 1980. **Professional Experience:** ASSOC PROF, DEPT MOLECULAR GENETICS & CELL BIOL, UNIV CHICAGO, as of 2004; Mem study sect, Prog Plant Growth & Develop, Competitive Res Grants Off, USDA, 1988, 1989, & 1990; chmn, Univ Biosafety Comt, Univ Chicago, 1986-1987; Zeisler fac award, 1985; Andrew Mellon fel,

1985; asst prof, Dept Molecular Genetics & Cell Biol, Univ Chicago, beginning 1985; NIH postdoctoral fel, 1982-1985; Damon Runyon-Walter Winchell Res Fund postdoctoral fel, 1982-1984; Postdoctoral fel, Lab Plant Molecular Biol, Rockefeller Univ, 1981-1984; mem, Ctr Photochem & Photobiol & Comt Genetics; ad hoc reviewer, Dept Energy & NSF. **Memberships:** Sigma Xi; Am Soc Plant Physiol; Int Soc Plant Molecular Biol; Am Soc Cell Biol. **Mailing Address:** Dept Molecular Genetics & Cell Biol, Univ Chicago, Rm 827A 920 E 58th St, Chicago, IL 60637. **E-Mail:** gklamppa@midway.uchicago.edu

LAMPSON, BUTLER WRIGHT, Computer systems, human-computer interaction. **Personal Data:** b Washington, DC, December 23, 1943; m 1967, Lois; c Michael & David. **Education:** Harvard Univ, AB, 1964; Univ Calif, Berkeley, PhD (comput sci), 1967. **Honorary Degrees:** DSc, Swiss Fed Inst Technol, Zurich, 1986, DSc, Univ of Bologna, 1996. **Honors & Awards:** Software Systs Award, Asn Comput Mach, 1985, Turing Award, 1992; IEEE Comput Pioneer Award, 1996; IEEE von Neumann Medal, 2001; National Computer Systems Security Award, NIST/NSA, 1998; Nat Acad Eng Draper Prize 2004. **Professional Experience:** Technical Fellow, Microsoft, 1995-; sr corp consult engr, Digital Equip Corp, Cambridge, Mass, 1985-1994; sr res fel, Xerox Palo Alto Res Ctr, 1980-1984; res fel, Xerox Palo Alto Res Ctr, 1971-1980; dir syst develop, Berkeley Comput Corp, 1969-1971; from asst prof to assoc prof comput sci, Univ Calif, Berkeley, 1967-1971. **Memberships:** Nat Acad Eng; fel Asn Comput Mach; Am Acad Arts & Sci; Nat Acad Sci. **Research Statement & Publications:** Computer architecture, programming languages, operating systems, computer security, user interfaces. **Mailing Address:** Microsoft, 180 Lakeview Ave, Cambridge, MA 02138. **Fax:** 617-547-9580. **E-Mail:** blampson@microsoft.com

LAMPSON, FRANCIS KEITH, METALLURGICAL ENGINEERING, MATERIALS ENGINEERING. **Personal Data:** b Minneapolis, Minn, August 7, 1924; m 1945, Margaret; c Michael K, Jan C, Andrea L & Kevin D. **Education:** Univ Ill, BS, 1949. **Professional Experience:** Pres, F K Lampson Assocs, beginning 1974; DIR MAT ENGRS, MARQUARDT CO, DIV CCI CORP, 1965-; Pacific Coast area tech rep, Allegheny-Ludlum Steel Corp, Los Angeles, 1957-1965; group leader, Mat & Processing, Marquardt Co, Van Nuys, Calif, 1954-1957; exp metallurgist, Allison Div, Gen Motors Corp, 1951-1954; jr metallurgist, NEPA Div, Fairchild Eng & Air Corp, 1949-1951. **Memberships:** Am Soc Metals; Soc Aeroscpace Mat Process Engrs; Am Soc Testing Mats; Am Inst Mining Engrs. **Research Statement & Publications:** Propulsion technology materials; ferrous and super alloy materials; refractory materials and related disilicide coatings; biomedical materials. **Mailing Address:** 10000 Aldea Ave N, Northridge, CA 91325.

LAMPSON, GEORGE PETER, biochemistry; deceased, see previous edition for last biography

LAMPSON, LOIS ALTERMAN, IMMUNE RESPONSES. **Education:** Univ Calif, Berkeley, BA, 1968, PhD (immunol), 1976. **Professional Experience:** ASSOC PROF NEUROSURG, HARVARD MED SCH, 1999-; ASSOC NEUROL, HARVARD MED SCH, 1990-; IMMUNOLOGIST, BRIGHAM & WOMENS HOSP, 1990-; adj prof neurol, Univ Pa Sch Med, 1986-1987; asst prof anat, Sch Med, Univ Pa, 1979-1986. **Research Statement & Publications:** Role of major histocompatibility complex in neural tissue; immune response to neural tumor. **Mailing Address:** Brigham & Women's hosp & Harvard Med Sch, 221 Longwood Ave, Boston, MA 02115. **Fax:** 617-547-9580. **E-Mail:** lampson@rics.bwh.harvard.edu

LAMPTON, MICHAEL LOGAN, X-RAY ASTRONOMY. **Personal Data:** b Williamsport, Pa, March 1, 1941. **Education:** Calif Inst Technol, BS, 1962; Univ Calif, Berkeley, PhD (physics), 1967. **Professional Experience:** SR SPACE FEL, SPACE SCI LAB, UNIV CALIF, BERKELEY, as of 2005; sen res physicist, Space Sci Lab, Univ Calif, Berkeley, as of 2003; NSF fel, Univ Calif, Berkeley, 1968-1969; asst res physicist, Space Sci Lab, Univ Calif, Berkeley, beginning 1967. **Memberships:** Am Geophys Union; Am Astron Soc. **Research Statement & Publications:** Ultraviolet astronomy. **Mailing Address:** 10821 Sterling Ave, Berkeley, CA 94703-7450. **Fax:** 510-643-2624. **E-Mail:** mlampton@ssl.berkeley.edu

LAMSTER, HAL B, GENERAL COMPUTER SCIENCE, OPERATIONS RESEARCH. **Personal Data:** b New York, NY, July 12, 1941; m 1967, c 1. **Education:** NY Univ, BS, 1963, MS, 1970. **Professional Experience:** FOUNDER, LAMSTER CONSULT as of 2005; chmn comt, Asn Comput Mach, beginning 1986; exec vpres, Telmar Info Serv Corp, 1971-2002; pres & founder, Time Sharing Sci Inc, 1970-1971; Consult, Gen Analysis, 1968-1969. **Memberships:** Inst Elec & Electronics Engrs; Asn Comput Mach. **Research Statement & Publications:** Microcomputing application; data communications; man-machine interactions. **Mailing Address:** Lamster Consult, 399 E 72nd St 19C, New York, NY 10021. **Fax:** 212-249-5575. **E-Mail:** hal@lamster.org

LAMSTER, IRA BARRY, DENTISTRY, BIOCHEMISTRY. **Personal Data:** b New York, NY, March 6, 1950; m 1971, c 2. **Education:** Queens Col, NY, BA, 1971; Univ Chicago, SM, 1972; State Univ NY, Stony Brook, DDS, 1977; Harvard Univ, MMSc, 1980; Am Bd Oral Med, cert, 1984. **Professional Experience:** PROF DENT & ORAL SURG, COLUMBIA UNIV, as of 2004; DEAN, SCH DENT & ORAL SURG, COLUMBIA UNIV, as of 2004; assoc prof dent & dir periodont, Columbia Univ, beginning 1988; grants, NIH, 1982-1986, 1985-; dent student res training award, NIH, Nat Inst Dent Res, 1982; prin investr, res contracts & grants, Lever Res Inc, Warner-Lambert Co, Johnson & Johnson & Block Drug Co, 1980-; from asst prof to assoc prof periodont & oral med, Fairleigh Univ, 1980-1988; res fel, Lab Surg Res, Med Sch, Harvard Univ; teaching fel periodontol, Sch Dent Med, 1977-1980. **Memberships:** Sigma Xi; Am Dent Asn; Am Acad Periodontol; AAAS; Am Acad Oral Med. **Research Statement & Publications:** Host response in human periodontal disease; diagnostic techniques for periodontal disease; application of a biochemical profile of gingival crevicular fluid. **Mailing Address:** Columbia Univ Sch Dent & Oral Surg, 630 W 168 St Dean Off Box 20, New York, NY 10032. **Fax:** 212-305-7134. **E-Mail:** ibl1@columbia.edu

LAMUNYON, CRAIG WILLIS, DEVELOPMENTAL GENETICS, SEXUAL SELECTION BY SPERM COMPETITION. **Personal Data:** b Fullerton, Calif. **Education:** Calif State Univ, Fullerton, BA, 1984; Cornell Univ, PhD (chem ecol), 1992. **Professional Experience:** Assistant Professor, California State Polytechnic Univ., 2003-present; Assistant Professor, Florida Atlantic Univ., 2000-2003; Assistant Research Professor, Univ. of Arizona, 1996-2000; Research Associate, Univ. of Arizona, 1993-1996; Res assoc, Cornell Univ, Ithaca, NY, 1992-1993. **Memberships:** Entomological Soc of Am; Genetics Soc of Am; International Soc of Behavioral Ecology. **Research Statement & Publications:** Sexual conflict and its ramifications, especially the genetics, evolution and mechanism of sperm development, maternal mitochondrial inheritance and sperm competition. **Mailing Address:** Deptartment Biological Sci, Calif State Polytechnic Univ, Pomona, CA 91768. **Fax:** 909-869-4078. **E-Mail:** cwlamunyon@csupomona.edu

LAMUTH, HENRY LEWIS, APPLIED PHYSICS, ELECTRICAL ENGINEERING. **Personal Data:** b Painesville, Ohio, April 15, 1942; m 1969, c 2. **Education:** Ohio State Univ, BS, 1966, PhD (physics), 1970. **Professional Experience:** AT, ALPHACOMM INC, COMPUT SYSTS, 1987-; Sperry Corp, 1987; mgr, Sensors, Electronics & Controls Group, Columbus Labs, Battelle Mem Inst, beginning 1974; mem tech staff electro-optics, Orlando Div, Martin Marietta Aerospace, 1972-1974; assoc res physicist optics, Willow Run Labs, Inst Sci & Technol, Univ Mich, 1970-1972. **Memberships:** AAAS; Am Phys Soc; Sigma Xi; Inst Elec & Electronics Engrs. **Research Statement & Publications:** Electro-optics, infrared, radar sensors and sensing; missile systems; atmospheric transmission; fiber and integrated optics; communication systems and techniques with optical radiation; electronic control systems; analog-digital electronic systems. **Mailing Address:** 4922 Brookwood Meadows Dr, Brighton, MI 48116.

LAN, CHUAN-TAU EDWARD, AERODYNAMICS, STABILITY & CONTROL. **Personal Data:** b Taiwan, China, April 21, 1935; American citizen; m 1961, Sumy; c Susan, Justin & Austin. **Education:** Nat Taiwan Univ, BS, 1958; Univ Minn, MS, 1963; NY Univ, PhD (aeronaut), 1968. **Honors & Awards:** Cert of Recognition, NASA Langley Res Ctr, 1978, 1980, 1982 & 1986; Aerodynamics Award; Am Inst of Aeronautics & Astronautics, 2000. **Professional Experience:** J L CONSANT DISTING PROF AEROSPACE ENG, UNIV KANS, 1998-; consult, Vigyan Res Assoc, Inc, 1986-; prof, Univ Kans, 1978-1992; consult, Aeronaut Res Lab, Taiwan, 1977-; reviewer, J Aircraft & Am Inst Aeronaut & Astronaut, 1975-; prin investr, NASA Langely Res Ctr, 1973-; from asst prof to assoc prof, Univ Kans, 1968-1978; assoc res scientist aeronaut, Aerospace Labs, NY Univ, 1968; asst civil engr hydraul, Bd Water Supply, NY, 1963-1965. **Memberships:** Am Inst Aeronaut & Astronaut, assoc fel. **Research Statement & Publications:** Steady and unsteady aerodynamics; flight dynamics. **Mailing Address:** Dept Aerospace Eng, Univ Kans, Lawrence, KS 66045. **Fax:** 785-864-3597. **E-Mail:** vortex@ku.edu

LAN, MING-JYE, POLYMER SYNTHESIS, POLYMER COMPOSITE. **Personal Data:** b Kaohsiung, Taiwan, November 3, 1953; m 1980, c 1. **Education:** Nat Tsing-Hua Univ, Taiwan, BS, 1976; Univ Mich, MS, 1981, PhD (chem & macromolecular sci & eng), 1985. **Professional Experience:** STAFF PROD DEVELO, FRESENIUS MED CARE N AM, as of 2005; res chemist, baxter inc, 1992-; sr res chemist, Allied-Signal Inc, 1987-1992; res chemist, Allied-Signal Inc, 1985-1987; teaching asst org chem, Univ Mich, 1979-1984. **Memberships:** Am Chem Soc; Soc Advan Mat & Process Eng. **Research Statement & Publications:** Bipolar membranes for water splitting; synthesis and characterization of biopolymers as anti-viral agents; synthesis of monomers and polymers; thermoset polymers for composites. **Mailing Address:** Fresenius Med Care N Am, 95 Hayden Ave, Lexington, MA 02420-9192.

LAN, SHIH-JUNG, DRUG METABOLISM. **Personal Data:** b Kwangtung, China, September 15, 1938; m 1967, c 2. **Education:** Univ Tunghai, BS, 1960; Okla State Univ, MS, 1964; Univ Minn, PhD (biochem), 1968. **Professional Experience:** AT XENOBIOTIC LAB, as of 2003; res group leader, Bristol-Myers Squibb Pharmaceut Co, beginning 1975-; sr res investr, Squibb Inst Med Res, 1973-1974; res investr drug metab, Squibb Inst Med Res, 1969-1973; Fel physiol chem, Univ Wis, 1967-1969. **Memberships:** Am Chem Soc; Am Soc Pharmacol & Exp Therapeut. **Research Statement & Publications:** Microsomal drug metabolism enzyme systems; mechanism of drug action. **Mailing Address:** Xenobiotic Lab, 107 Morgans Lane, Plainsboro, NJ 08536. **Fax:** 609-799-7497. **E-Mail:** sjlan@xbl.com

LANAM, RICHARD DELBERT, METALLURGY OF PLATINUM GROUP METALS. **Personal Data:** b Denver, Colo, May 31, 1943; m 1965, Anna; c Richard III, Amy & Catherine. **Education:** Northwestern Univ, BS, 1966; Drexel Univ, MS, 1969, PhD (mat eng), 1972. **Professional Experience:** RETIRED; tech mgr, Engelhard Corp, 1988-2005; tech oper mgr, Engelhard Corp, 1982-1988; metall section head, Engelhard Corp, 1979-1982; sr metall eng, Pfizer Inc, 1974-1979; eng Specialist, Olin Corp, 1970-1974. **Memberships:** Am Soc Metals; Am Inst Metall Eng. **Research Statement & Publications:** General refining and use of platinum group metals; sputter-coated ruthenium for electrical contact applications; author of ten publications and holder of nine US patents. **Mailing Address:** 655 Fourth Ave, Westfield, NJ 07090.

LANCASTER, BRICK, HEALTH EDUCATION ADMINSTRATION. **Personal Data:** b Detroit, MI, July 20, 1949; m 2004, Becky; c 4. **Education:** Central Michigan Univ, BS, Biology, 1971, MA, Public Health Education, 1972. **Honors & Awards:** Sarah MazelisAward, Am Pub Health Asn, 1993; Health Prom & Educ Advocacy Award, Asn State & Territorial Dirs Health Prom & Pub Health Educ, 1996; Distinguished Fellow, Society for Public Health Education, 2001. **Professional Experience:** Chief, Program Services Branch, Office on Smoking and Health, Centers for Disease Control and Prevention, 2001-present; ASSOC DIR HEALTH EDUC PRACT & POLICY, NAT CTR CHRONIC DIS, CTR DIS CTRL & PREV, CDC, 1992-2001; Chief, Office of Health Prom & Educ, Ariz Dept Health Serv, 1986-1992; Assitant Director for Managemen, Kent County Health Dept. Grand Rapids, Mich. 1983-1986; Deputy Director, Office of Health Education, Michigan Dept. of Public Health, 1979-1983; Chief, Health Education, Central Michigan District Health Department, 1971-1979. **Memberships:** Asn State & Territorial Dirs Pub Health Educ (pres, 1990-1992); Soc Pub Health Educ (vpres, 1982 & secy 1990-1992); Int Union Health Promotion Educ. **Mailing Address:** Office on Smoking & Health/CDC, Mailstop K-50, 4770 Buford Hwy NE, Atlanta, GA 30341-3724. **Fax:** 770-488-1220. **E-Mail:** blancas997@aol.com

LANCASTER, CLEO, ANIMAL PHYSIOLOGY. **Personal Data:** b Rocky Mount, NC, December 10, 1948. **Education:** Elizabeth City State Univ, NC, BS, 1971; Western Mich Univ, MS, 1979. **Professional Experience:** SR RES BIOLOGIST, UPJOHN CO, 1971-; res asst, Brookhaven Nat Lab, 1971. **Memberships:** AAAS; NY Acad Sci. **Research Statement & Publications:** Experimental gastroenterology; development of experimental models of ulcers, gastric lesions, pancreatitis and surgical methods to study gastric secretion; helped develop the cytoprotection concept, antisecretory property of prostaglandins and the antipancreatitis effect of opioid agonists. **Mailing Address:** Safety Pharmacol, Upjohn Co, Kalamazoo, MI 49001.

LANCASTER, GEORGE MAURICE, DIFFERENTIAL GEOMETRY. **Personal Data:** b Penrith, Eng, July 18, 1934; m 1964, Georgia Reid; c John & Sarah. **Education:** Univ Liverpool, BSc, 1956; Univ Sask, PhD (math), 1967. **Professional Experience:** Nat Res Coun Can grants, Univ Sask, 68-7O; RETIRED; dean sci & eng, Royal Rds Mil Col, 1987-1995; prof math, Royal Rds Mil Col, 1980-1995; head dept, Royal Rds Mil Col, 1978-1987; spec lectr, Univ Victoria, 1971; assoc prof, Royal Rds Mil Col, 1970-1980; asst prof, Univ Sask, 1967-1970; lectr math, Royal Roads Mil Col, 1960-1964; opers res analyst, Northern Elec Co Ltd, Montreal, 1958-1960; Res analyst, Weapons Res Div, A V Roe & Co Ltd, Woodford, Eng, 1956-1958. **Memberships:** Am Math Soc; Tensor Soc. **Research Statement & Publications:** Differential geometry; imbedding of Riemannian manifolds. **Mailing Address:** 1229 St Patrick St, Victoria, BC V8S 4Y3, Can.

LANCASTER, JACK R, BIOENERGETICS, ELECTRON TRANSFER. **Personal Data:** b Memphis, Tenn, August 27, 1948; m Judith; c Tonya & Madeline. **Education:** Univ Tenn,

Martin, BS, 1970, PhD (biochem), 1974. **Professional Experience:** NAT LECTR, SIGMA XI, 1994-; PROF PHYSIOL & MED, LA STATE UNIV, NEW ORLEANS, 1994-; assoc prof, Univ Pittsburgh, 1992-1995; estab investr, Am Heart Asn, 1983-1988; from asst prof to assoc prof biochem, Utah State Univ, 1980-1992; res assoc biochem, Cornell Univ, 1974-1976 & Duke Univ, 1976-1980; NSF trainee, 1970-1973; mem, Coun Basic Sci, Am Heart Asn. **Memberships:** Am Chem Soc; Am Soc Biol Chemists; Biophys Soc; Sigma Xi; Am Heart Asn. **Research Statement & Publications:** Basic biochemical mechanisms of biological actions of nitric oxide and immune cytotoxicity; bioenergetics; electron transfer. **Mailing Address:** Depts Physiol & Med, La State Univ Med Ctr, 1901 Perdido St, New Orleans, LA 70112. **Fax:** 504-568-6158. **E-Mail:** ilanca@lsumc.edu

LANCASTER, JAMES D, AGRONOMY. **Personal Data:** b Randolph, Miss, June 11, 1919. **Education:** Miss State Col, BS, 1947, MS, 1948; Univ Wis, PhD, 1954. **Professional Experience:** RETIRED; agronomist, Exp Sta & prof agron, Miss State Univ, 1957-1985; asst agronomist, Exp Sta & asst prof agron, 1951-1957. **Memberships:** Am Soc Agron; Soil Sci Soc Am; AAAS. **Research Statement & Publications:** Soil fertility and testing; fertilizer evaluation; crop fertilization. **Mailing Address:** 1250 Oktoc Rd, Starkville, MS 39759.

LANCASTER, JESSIE LEONARD, JR, ENTOMOLOGY. **Personal Data:** b Horatio, Ark, January 26, 1923; m 1946, c 4. **Education:** Univ Ark, BSA, 1947; Cornell Univ, PhD (econ entom), 1951. **Professional Experience:** PROF EMER EMTOM, UNIV ARK, FAYETTEVILLE, as of 2004; NIH spec res fel, Rocky Mountain Lab, 1963-1964; prof entom, Univ Ark, Fayetteville, beginning 1960; from asst prof to assoc prof, Univ Ark, Fayetteville, 1951-1960; Asst, Cornell Univ, 1947-1951. **Memberships:** Entom Soc Am. **Research Statement & Publications:** Medical veterinary entomology and mosquito control. **Mailing Address:** 1923 E Joyce Blvd Apt 270, Fayetteville, AR 72703.

LANCASTER, JOHN, MICROBIAL GENETICS. **Personal Data:** b Bolton, Miss, August 30, 1937; m 1964. **Education:** Miss State Univ, BS, 1959, MS, 1961; Univ Tex, PhD (microbiol), 1964. **Professional Experience:** Dir lab animal resources, Univ Okla, beginning 1988; dir scholar-leadership enrichment prog, Univ Okla, beginning 1987; assoc dean, Univ Okla, 1984-1988; prof microbiol, Univ Okla, beginning 1983; from asst prof to assoc prof, Univ Okla, 1968-1983; NIH grant, 1966; NIH trainee, Univ Tex, 1963-1964. **Memberships:** AAAS; Am Soc Microbiol; Hist Sci Soc; Am Asn Lab Animal Sci. **Research Statement & Publications:** Mechanism of conjugation in Escherichia coli; animal behavior in relations to animal rights; biological perspectives on environmental ethics. **Mailing Address:** Dept Microbiol, Univ Okla, 770 Van Fleet Oval, Norman, OK 73019-6130. **Fax:** 1644. **E-Mail:** jlancaster@ou.edu

LANCASTER, JOHN S, MATHEMATICS. **Education:** Ind Univ, Phd (operator theory), 1972. **Professional Experience:** PROF MATH, MARSHALL UNIV, as of 2005. **Mailing Address:** Math Dept SH 717, Marshall Univ, Huntington, WV 25755. **Fax:** 304-696-4646. **E-Mail:** lancaste@marshall.edu

LANCASTER, MALCOLM, CARDIOLOGY, GERIATRICS. **Personal Data:** b Amarillo, Tex, July 28, 1931; m 1959, Patricia; c Pamela (Lancaster-Elzinga), Kimberly (Russell), Lisa & Timothy. **Education:** Univ Tex Southwestern Med Sch, MD, 1956; Univ Colo, Denver, MS, 1960. **Honors & Awards:** Casimir Funk Award, Asn Mil Surgeons US, 1971; USAF Res & Develop Award, 1971; John Jeffries Award, Am Inst Aeronaut & Astronaut, 1974; Arnold D Tuttle Award, Aerospace Med Asn, 1975. **Professional Experience:** RETIRED; prof clin med, Dept Family Pract, Univ Tex Health Sci Ctr, San Antonio, beginning 1985; pres, Systemics Inc, San Antonio, Tex, beginning 1981; chief med serv & clin dir, San Antonio State Chest Hosp, 1978-1981; chief, Clin Sci Div, 1972-1978; chief, Internal Med Br, Sch Aerospace Med, Brooks AFB, Tex, 1966-1973; chief, Cardiopulmonary Serv, USAF Hosp, Wright Patterson AFB, 1965-1966; chmn, Dept Med, USAF Hosp, Wright Patterson AFB, 1965-1966; chief med serv, 48th Tactical Hosp, Royal Air Force, Lakenheath, Eng, 1960-1963. **Memberships:** Fel Aerospace Med Asn; fel Am Col Cardiol; fel Am Col Physicians; Am Geriat Soc; fel Am Col Prev Med. **Research Statement & Publications:** Medical aspects of aerospace operations; cardiovascular disease epidemiology; computers and electrocardiography; computer aided design; geriatrics aerospace medicine. **Mailing Address:** 101 Hibiscus Lane, San Antonio, TX 78213.

LANCASTER, PETER, MATHEMATICS. **Education:** Univ Liverpool, BSc, 1952, MSc, 1956, DSc, 1987. **Professional Experience:** PROF EMER, DIV APPL MATHS, UNIV CALGARY, CAN, as of 2006. **Mailing Address:** Univ Calgary Dept Math & Statist, Rm 558 Math Sci Bldg, Calgary, AB T2N 1N4, Can. **E-Mail:** lancaste@math.ucalgary.ca

LANCE, GEORGE M(ILWARD), MECHANICAL & ELECTRICAL ENGINEERING. **Personal Data:** b Youngstown, Ohio, December 4, 1928. **Education:** Case Inst Technol, BS, 1952, MS, 1954. **Professional Experience:** EMER PROF MECH ENG, UNIV IOWA, 1991-; chmn eng prog, Univ Iowa, 1974-1985; assoc dean undergrad progs & student affairs, Univ Iowa, 1974-1979; prof mech eng, Univ Iowa, 1970-1991; from asst prof to prof, Univ Iowa, 1961-1970; sr systs engr, Moog Servocontrols, Inc, 1960-1961; lectr mech eng, Univ Wash, St Louis, 1956-1960; res engr, TRW, Inc, 1954-1956; Instr eng, Case Inst Technol, 1952-1954. **Memberships:** Am Soc Mech Engrs. **Research Statement & Publications:** Theory of automatic control; hydraulic servosystems; system design. **Mailing Address:** 609 S Summit, Univ Iowa, Iowa City, IA 52240.

LANCE, R(ICHARD) H, MECHANICS. **Personal Data:** b Geneva, Ill, November 29, 1931; m 1953, c 3. **Education:** Univ Ill, Urbana, BS, 1954; Ill Inst Technol, MS, 1957; Brown Univ, PhD (solid mech), 1962. **Professional Experience:** PROF EMER THEORET & APPL MECH, COL ENG, CORNELL UNIV, 1998-; prof theoret & appl mech, col eng, Cornell Univ, beginning 1981; sr scientist, Hughes Aircraft Co, 1980-1981, 1986-1987; assoc dean eng, Cornell Univ, 1974-1986; Lectr, Int Bus Mach Corp, NY, 1966; from asst prof to assoc prof theoret & appl mech, Cornell Univ, 1962-1981; res assoc, Brown Univ, 1962; mech engr, Ingersoll Milling Mach Co, Ill, 1957-1958; test engr, Minneapolis Honeywell Regulator Co, 1954. **Memberships:** Am Soc Mech Engrs; AAAS; Am Acad Mech. **Research Statement & Publications:** Mechanical behavior of solids; engineering structural mechanics; plasticity; numerical methods in engineering. **Mailing Address:** 453 Heron Point, Chestertown, MD 21620. **E-Mail:** rhl1@cornell.edu

LANCE, VALENTINE A, REPRODUCTIVE PHYSIOLOGY, COMPARATIVE ENDOCRINOLOGY. **Personal Data:** b London, Eng, February 14, 1940; wid, c 2. **Education:** Long Island Univ, BS, 1966; Col William & Mary, MA, 1968; Univ Hong Kong, PhD (zoology), 1974. **Professional Experience:** CTR REPRODUCTION ENDANGERED SPECIES, as of 2002; HEAD, ENDOCRINOL, SAN DIEGO ZOO, as of 1999; endocrinologist, San Diego Zoo, beginning 1987; asst prof, Sch Med, Tulane Univ, 1982-1987; ASST PROF PHYSIOL, LA STATE UNIV, 1978-; res assoc endocrinol, Boston Univ, 1974-1978; Demonstr zool, Univ Hong Kong, 1968-1974; grant rev, NSF; reviewer, Gen & Comp Endocrinol, J Exp Zool, Peptides, Herpetologica J Wildlife Dis. **Memberships:** Endocrine Soc; Soc Study Reproduction; Am Soc Zoologists; Soc Study Amphibians & Reptiles; Herpetologists League; Sigma Xi; AAAS. **Research Statement & Publications:** Evolution of the endocrine system; evolution of pituitary control of gonadal steroidogenesis; role of hypothalamic hormones and related reptiles in non-mammalian vertebrates; hormonal control of seasonal reproduction; physiology and endocrinology of non-mammalian vertebrates; endocrinology of pregnancy, pancreatic hormones and peptides in non-mammalian and mammalian vertebrates. **Mailing Address:** Ctr Reproduction Endangered Species, San Diego Zoo, PO Box 120551, San Diego, CA 92112.

LANCET, MICHAEL SAVAGE, PHYSICAL CHEMISTRY, CHEMICAL ENGINEERING. **Personal Data:** b Detroit, Mich, December 11, 1944; m 1969, c 1. **Education:** Rose Hulman Inst Technol, BS, 1966; Univ Chicago, MS, 1971, PhD (nuclear chem), 1972. **Professional Experience:** RES SCIENTIST COAL CONVERSION RES, CONSOL COAL CO, 1974-; res assoc nuclear cosmo chem, Carnegie-Mellon Univ, 1972-1974; fel, Carnegie-Mellon Univ, 1972-1974. **Memberships:** AAAS; Am Chem Soc; Sigma Xi. **Research Statement & Publications:** Conversion of coal to substitute natural gas and synthetic liquids; utilization of all other forms of energy. **Mailing Address:** Chem Res Div, Consolidation Coal Co, Library, PA 15129.

LANCIANI, CARMINE ANDREW, ECOLOGY. **Personal Data:** b Leominster, Mass, May 16, 1941; m 1964, c 2. **Education:** Cornell Univ, BS, 1963, PhD, 1968. **Professional Experience:** PROF EMER ZOOL, UNIV FLA, as of 2003; prof zool, Univ Fla, beginning 1980-; assoc prof zool, Univ Fla, 1973-1980; asst prof zool & biol sci, Univ Fla, 1970-1973; interim asst prof zool, Univ Fla, 1968-1970. **Memberships:** Ecol Soc Am; Entom Soc Am; Am Soc Limnol & Oceanog; Soc Study Evolution. **Research Statement & Publications:** Population ecology of aquatic organisms, particularly life cycles, growth, reproduction and competition of parasitic water mites; effect of parasitism on host ecology. **Mailing Address:** Dept Zool Univ Fla, Box 118525, Gainesville, FL 32611. **Fax:** 352-392-3704. **E-Mail:** carmine@zoo.ufl.edu

LAND, CHARLES EVEN, STATISTICS, EPIDEMIOLOGY. **Personal Data:** b San Francisco, Calif, July 13, 1937; m Vera; c David & Graham. **Education:** Univ Ore, BA, 1959; Univ Chicago, MA, 1964, PhD (statist), 1968. **Honors & Awards:** Outstanding Serv Medal, USPHS, 1991 Meritorious Serv Medal, USPHS, 1994 Director's Award, NIH, 1986 Individual Merit Award, NIH, 2004 Group Merit Award, NIH, 2004 Honorary Member, NCRP, 2005. **Professional Experience:** SR INVESTR, DIV CANCER EPIDEMIOL & GENETICS, NIH, as of 2004; HEALTH STATISTICIAN, RADIATION EPIDEMIOL BR, NAT CANCER INST, NIH, 1984-; health statistician, Environ Epidemiol Br, 1977-1984; expert math statistician, Biometry Br, 1975-1977; res assoc statist, Atomic Bomb Casualty Comn & Radiation Effects Res Found, 1973-1975; asst prof, Ore State Univ, 1968-1973; res assoc statist, Atomic Bomb Casualty Comn, Nat Acad Sci, 1966-1968; mem comt 1 on risk assessment, Int Comn Radiol Protection, 1985-2005; Hon mem, Nat CounRadiation Protection & Measurement. **Memberships:** Radiation Res Soc; fel Am Col Epidemiol; fel Am Statist Asn; Biomet Soc; AAAS; Am Epidemiol Soc. **Research Statement & Publications:** Risk analysis; inference problems associated with transformations of data; radiation carcinogenesis in human populations; epidemiology; biometry. **Mailing Address:** Div Cancer Epidemiol & Genetics, NCI, NIH, Rm 7046, Exec Plaza S, Bethesda, MD 20892-7238. **Fax:** 301-402-0207. **E-Mail:** landc@mail.nih.gov

LAND, DAVID J(OHN), ATOMIC & MOLECULAR PHYSICS, MATERIALS ANALYSIS. **Personal Data:** b Boston, Mass, February 15, 1939. **Education:** Boston Col, BS, 1959; Brown Univ, PhD (physics), 1966. **Professional Experience:** RES PHYSICIST, NAVAL SURFACE WEAPONS CTR, 1968-; Nat Acad Scires assoc, Naval Surface Weapons Ctr, 1966-1968; res asst physics, Brown Univ, 1959-1966. **Memberships:** Am Phys Soc; Optical Soc Am. **Research Statement & Publications:** Atomic collision physics; modelling and simulation of atomic collision processes. **Mailing Address:** Carderock Div Naval Surface Warfare Ctr, Code 682 841 MacArthur Blvd, West Bethesda, MD 20817-5700. **Fax:** 301-227-4733. **E-Mail:** landd@casys.dt.navy.mil

LAND, GEOFFREY ALLISON, HISTOCOMPATIBILITY & IMMUNOGENETICS, MEDICAL MICROBIOLOGY. **Personal Data:** b Jeannette, Pa, July 9, 1942; m 1966, Maxine; c Kevin, Melissa & Kyle. **Education:** Univ Tex, Arlington, BSc, 1968; Tex Christian Univ, MSc, 1970; Tulane Univ, PhD (med mycol), 1973. **Honors & Awards:** Pres Award, Med Mycol Soc Am, 1990; Meridian Award for Outstanding MedMycologist, 1992. **Professional Experience:** CHAIR, DEPT HISTOCOMPATIBILITY & IMMUNOL, METHODIST HOSP, as of 2006; PROF HISTOCOMPATIBILITY, BAYLOR COL, as of 2004; ASSOC ADMIN DIR PATH & LABS, METHODIST HOSP, 1989-; dir, Histocompatibility & Immunogenetics Lab, Stewart Regional Blood Ctr, beginning 1987; DIR, HISTOCOMPATIBILITY & IMMUNOGENETICS, METHODIST HOSP, 1983-; consult, ClinMicrobiol Labs, Univ Tex Health Sci Ctr, Dallas, beginning 1981; adj assoc prof biol, Tex Christian Univ, beginning 1981; DIR MICROBIOL & IMMUNOL, METHODIST HOSP, 1981-; dir mycol & assoc dir-microbiol, Univ Cinn Med Ctr, 1979-1981; assoc ed, J Oncol & Hematol, 1975-1979; adj prof biol &chem, NTex State Univ, 1975-1979; vis scientist, dept virol, Cent Pub Health Lab State SerumInst, Helsinki, 1975; NTex Soc Med Technologists, beginnig 1975; instr & lectr, Tex Soc Clin Microbiologists, beginning 1974; chmn & dir med mycol, Wadley Inst Molecular Med, 1974-1979; vis asst prof, NC Cent Univ, 1973-1974; teaching asst microbiol, Tex Christian Univ, 1968-1970; inhalation therapist, Baylor Univ Med Ctr, Dallas, 1966-1968. **Memberships:** Am Soc Microbiol; Med Mycol Soc Am (secy-treas, 1978-1989, pres, 1991-1992); IntSoc Human & Animal Mycol; Am Soc Histocompatibility & Immunogenetics; Am Asn BloodBanks; NY Acad Sci. **Research Statement & Publications:** The molecular basis and early diagnosis of fungal infections in the compromised host; relationship of the human immune system and transplantation. **Mailing Address:** Methodist Med Ctr, 1441 N Beckley Ave, Dallas, TX 75203. **Fax:** 214-947-3586.

LAND, LYNTON S, GEOLOGY, GEOCHEMISTRY. **Personal Data:** b Baltimore, Md, December 30, 1940. **Education:** Johns Hopkins Univ, AB, 1962, MA, 1963; Lehigh Univ, PhD (geol), 1966. **Professional Experience:** RETIRED; prof emer geol sci, Univ Tex, Austin, as of 2003; prof geol sci, Univ Tex, Austin, beginning 1977; asst prof, Univ Tex, Austin, 1967-1977; res fel geol, Calif Inst Technol, 1966-1967. **Memberships:** Soc Econ Paleontologists & Mineralogists; Int Asn Sedimentol. **Research Statement & Publications:** Sedimentology; carbonate sedimentation; diagenesis; sedimentary geochemistry; stable isotope geochemistry. **Mailing Address:** Dept Geol Sci, Univ Tex, Austin, TX 78712-1026. **E-Mail:** lynton@mail.utexas.edu

LAND, MARGARET F, MATHEMATICS. **Mailing Address:** Tex A & M Univ-Kingsville, Math Dept Campus Box 172, Kingsville, TX 78363-8201.

LAND, MING HUEY, CAD APPLICATIONS. **Personal Data:** b Hsinchu, Taiwan, July 10, 1940; American citizen; m 1970, Whel-ing; c Judy Karen & Michael Henry. **Education:** Taiwan Normal Univ, BS, 1963; Northern Ill Univ, MS, 1968; Utah State Univ, EdD, 1970. **Honors & Awards:** Spec Recognition Award, Int Technol Educ Asn, 1990. **Professional Experience:** DEAN FINE & APPL ARTS, APPALACHIAN STATE UNIV, 1989-; vis prof, Ne Univ Technol, China, 1986; chair technol, Appalachian State Univ, 1983-1989; Fulbright lectr, Chungnam Nat Univ Korea, 1980-1981; prof indust educ, Miami Univ, 1971-1983; asst prof technol, Eastern Ill Univ, 1970-1971. **Memberships:** Am Soc Eng Educ; Am Voc Asn; Int Technol Educ Asn; Nat Asn Indust Technol. **Research Statement & Publications:** Theories of engineering graphics; descriptive geometry; applications in computer graphics. **Mailing Address:** 320 Univ Circle, Boone, NC 28607.

LAND, PETER L, SOLID STATE PHYSICS, CERAMICS. **Personal Data:** b Leasburg, Mo, November 20, 1929; m 1966, Kathleen J Wysong; c Stephanie M, Jennifer S & Debora D. **Education:** Univ Mo, BS, 1958, MS, 1960, PhD (physics), 1964. **Professional Experience:** RETIRED; RES SCIENTIST, HARDENED MAT BR, WRIGHT LABS, WRIGHT-PATTERSON AFB, OHIO, 1975-; Res scientist, Metall & Ceramics Lab, Aerospace Res Labs, 1964-1975. **Memberships:** Sigma Xi. **Research Statement & Publications:** New or improved nonlinear optical materials; optical properties of solids and liquids; laser effects on materials; optical filton theory. **Mailing Address:** 502 Land Dr, Dayton, OH 45440-3701. **E-Mail:** pland@siscom.net

LANDA, EDWARD ROBERT, ENVIRONMENTAL RADIOACTIVITY, TRACE ELEMENTS IN SOILS. **Personal Data:** b New York, NY, October 29, 1948; m 1992, Judith. **Education:** City Col NY, BS, 1970; Univ Minn, MS, 1972, MPH, 1974, PhD (soil sci), 1975. **Professional Experience:** Vis fac, St Mary's Col, Md, 1991; RES HYDROLOGIST, US GEOL SURV, 1978-; res assoc, Depts Agr Chem & Soil Sci, Ore State Univ, 1975-1978; Res asst, Dept Soil Sci, Univ Minn, 1970-1975. **Memberships:** Soil Sci Soc Am; Health Physics Soc; Am Geophy Union. **Research Statement & Publications:** Fate and transport of radionuclides and traffic-related contaminants in aquatic and terrestrial environments; uranium mill tailings. **Mailing Address:** US Geol Surv, 430 National Ctr, Reston, VA 20192. **Fax:** 703-648-5484. **E-Mail:** erlanda@usgs.gov

LANDAU, BARBARA RUTH, physiology; deceased, see previous edition for last biography

LANDAU, BERNARD ROBERT, MEDICINE, BIOCHEMISTRY. **Personal Data:** b Newark, NJ, June 24, 1926; m 1956, Lucille; c Steven, Deborah & Rodger. **Education:** Mass Inst Technol, SB, 1947; Harvard Univ, MA, 1949, PhD (chem), 1950; Harvard Med Sch, MD, 1954. **Honorary Degrees:** MD (Honor), Karolinska Inst, 1993. **Professional Experience:** PROF BIOCHEM, CASE WESTERN RES UNIV, 1979-; prof pharmacol, Case Western Res Univ, 1970-1978; PROF MED, CASE WESTERN RES UNIV, 1969-; dir dept biochem, Merck Inst Therapeut Res, 1967-1969; asst prof biochem & from asst prof to assoc prof med, Case Western Res Univ, 1959-1967; estab investr, Am Heart Asn, 1959-1964; sr res physician, Peter Bent Brigham Hosp, Boston, Mass, 1958-1959; tutor, Harvard Med Sch, 1957-1959; USPHS res fel biochem, Harvard Med Sch, 1957-1958; clin assoc, Nat Cancer Inst, 1955-1957; Med house officer, 1954-1955. **Memberships:** Endocrine Soc; Soc Biol Chem; Am Physiol Soc; Asn Am Physicians; Am Diabetes Asn. **Research Statement & Publications:** Metabolism; endocrinology; diabetes mellitus. **Mailing Address:** Dept Med, Case Western Res Iniv Hosps 10900 Euclid Ave, Cleveland, OH 44106-4951. **Fax:** 216-368-4927. **E-Mail:** brl@po.curu.edu

LANDAU, BURTON JOSEPH, OUTCOMES ASSESSMENT IN MEDICAL EDUCATION, MICROBIOLOGY & VIROLOGY. **Personal Data:** b Boston, Mass, May 6, 1933; m, c 2. **Education:** Boston Univ, AB, 1954; Univ NH, MS, 1957; Univ Mich, PhD (microbiol), 1967. **Honors & Awards:** Lindback Award. **Professional Experience:** ASSOC DEAN for Medical Education, SCH MED, Drexel University, Professor of Microbiology and Immunology. **Mailing Address:** Drexel Univ Col Med, 2900 Queen Lane, Philadelphia, PA 19129. **Fax:** 215-843-5495. **E-Mail:** blandau@drexelmed.edu

LANDAU, DAVID PAUL, MAGNETISM, STATISTICAL MECHANICS. **Personal Data:** b St Louis, Mo, June 22, 1941; m 1966, Heidi; c 2. **Education:** Princeton Univ, BA, 1963; Yale Univ, MS, 1965, PhD (physics), 1967. **Honors & Awards:** Jesse Beams Medal, 1987, Aneesur Rahman Prize Computational Physics, Am Physical Soc, 2002; Lamar Dodd Res Award, 2003. **Professional Experience:** Sr fel, US scientist Humboldt, Univ Mainz, 1988; DISTINGUISHED RES PROF PHYSICS, UNIV GA, 1984-; Alexander von Humboldt fel, Univ Saarland, 1975; Guest scientist, KFA Jlich, WGer, 1974; from asst prof to prof, Univ GA, 1969-1984; lectr eng & appl sci, Yale Univ, 1968-1969; asst res physics, Nat Ctr Sci Res, Grenoble, France, 1967-1968. **Memberships:** Fel Am Phys Soc; Sigma Xi. **Research Statement & Publications:** Critical phenomena associated with phase transitions; properties of magnetic solids, computer-simulation methods, phase transitions in binary alloys and adsorbed monolayers. **Mailing Address:** Dept Physics & Astron, Univ Ga, 307A Physics Bldg, Athens, GA 30601. **Fax:** 706-542-2492. **E-Mail:** dlandau@hal.phsast.uga.edu

LANDAU, EMANUEL, EPIDEMIOLOGY, BIOSTATISTICS. **Personal Data:** b New York, NY, November 28, 1919; m 1948, Davetta Goldberg; c Elizabeth L (Rabin). **Education:** City Col New York, BA, 1939; Am Univ, PhD (econ), 1966. **Honors & Awards:** Super Serv Award, HEW, 1963. **Professional Experience:** Chmn, Comt Statist & Environ, Am Statist Asn, 1984-1985; PROJ DIR & STAFF EPIDEMIOLOGIST, AM PUB HEALTH ASN, 1975-; consult, Bur Radiol Health, Food& Drug Admin, 1975-1983; assoc ed, J Air Pollution Control Asn, 1972 & J Clin Data & Analysis, 1974-; adv, Dept Transp, 1972-1974; chief, Epidemiol Studies Br, Bur Radiol Health, Food &Drug Admin, USPHS, 1971-1975; epidemiologist, Adminr Res & Monitoring, Environ ProtectionAgency, 1971; epidemiologist, Adminr Res & Develop, Environ Health Serv, 1969-1971; nat AirControl Admin tech liaison rep, Adv Comt Toxicol, Nat Acad Sci, 1968-1969; adv air qualcriteria, Karolinska Inst, Sweden, 1968; mem, comt study lung cancer among uranium miners, USPHS, 1967; advair qual criteria, WHO, Switz, 1967; mem, Comt Long-term Training OutsideServ, USPHS, 1966-1968; statist adv, Nat Air Pollution Control Admin, 1965-1969; mem, Career Serv Bd Math & Statist, Dept Health, Educ & Welfare, 1965-1969; head, Lab & ClinTrials Sect, Nat Cancer Inst, 1962-1964; chief, Biomet Sect, Div Air Pollution, USPHS, 1959-1962; mem staff, Calif State Dept Pub Health, 1957-1959; chief, Family Statist Sect, Bur-Census, 1948-1956; Bus economist, Econ Date Analysis Br, Off Price Admin, 1941-1942 &1946-1947. **Memberships:** Fel Am Pub Health Asn; fel Royal Soc Health; Air & Waste Mgt Asn; Am StatistAsn; Soc Occup & Environ Health. **Research Statement & Publications:** Problems of environmental health; public health statistics; chronic disease epidemiology. **Mailing Address:** Am Pub Health Asn, 1015 15th St NW, Washington, DC 20005. **Fax:** 202-789-5661.

LANDAU, HENRY J, MATHEMATICS. **Education:** Harvard Univ, PhD (Maths), 1957. **Professional Experience:** STAFF, DEPT MATHS, AT&T BELL LABS, as of 2004. **Memberships:** Am Math Soc. **Mailing Address:** AT&T Bell Labs, 600 Mountain Ave, Murray Hill, NJ 07974-0636. **Fax:** 908-582-2379. **E-Mail:** hjl@research.att.com

LANDAU, JOSEPH VICTOR, MOLECULAR BIOLOGY. **Personal Data:** b New York, NY, January 9, 1928; m 1950, c 3. **Education:** City Col NY, BS, 1947; NY Univ, MSc, 1949, PhD, 1953. **Professional Experience:** RETIRED; prof biol, Rensselaer Polytech Inst, beginning 1967; chmn dept biol, Rensselaer Polytech Inst, beginning 1972; head accelerated biomed prog, Rensselaer Polytech Inst, beginning 1967; adj assoc prof, Rennselaer Polytech Inst, 1964-1967; res assoc oncol, Albany Med Col, Union, 1957-1966; chief biol sect, Basic Sci Res Lab, Vet Admin Hosp, Albany, 1957-1966; instrphysiol, Russell Sage Col, 1956-1957; runyon cancer res fel, NY Univ, 1952-1955; USPHS resasst, Naples Zool Sta, Italy, 1952; USPHS asst, NY Univ, 1949-1951. **Memberships:** Am Soc Cell Biol; Biophys Soc; Am Inst Biol Sci; Am Soc Microbiol; Sigma Xi. **Research Statement & Publications:** Protein and nucleic acid synthesis; barobiology; contractility. **Mailing Address:** Rensselaer Polytech Inst, 110 Eigth St, Troy, NY 12180-3590.

LANDAU, JOSEPH WHITE, MEDICINE, DERMATOLOGY. **Personal Data:** b Buffalo, NY, May 23, 1930; m 1985, c 5. **Education:** Cornell Univ, BA, 1951, MD, 1955; Am Bd Pediat, dipl, 1962; Am Bd Dermat, dipl, 1965, cert dermatopath, 1975. **Professional Experience:** CLIN PROF, MED CTR, UNIV CALIF LOS ANGELES, as of 2004; prof, med ctr, Univ Calif, Los Angeles, beginning 1999; assoc clin prof med dermat, Med Ctr, Univ Calif Los Angeles, 1974-1999; attend physician, Wadsworth Vet Admin Hosp, beginning 1966; attend physician, Student Health Serv, 1965-1986; from asst prof to assoc prof med & dermat, Univ Calif Los Angeles, 1964-1974; asst res dermatologist, Univ Calif Los Angeles, 1964; fel mycol, Med Ctr, Univ Calif Los Angeles, 1962-1963; US Pub Health Serv fel hemat, Children's Hosp, Los Angeles, 1961-1962; Med Ctr, Univ Calif Los Angeles, 1960-1961; Children's Hosp, Boston, 1959-1960; resident pediat, Children's Hosp, Buffalo, 1956; intern, Gen Hosp, Buffalo, 1955-1956. **Memberships:** Am Acad Dermat; Soc Invest Dermat. **Research Statement & Publications:** Host-parasite relationships in mycology; genodermatoses. **Mailing Address:** Parkside Med Ctr, 428 Santa Monica Blvd, Ste 401, Santa Monica, CA 90404-2047.

LANDAU, MATTHEW PAUL, AQUACULTURE, CRUSTACEAN PHYSIOLOGY. **Personal Data:** b New York, NY, December 16, 1949; m 1985, Brenda; c Rose & Isaac. **Education:** St John's Univ, BS, 1972; Long Island Univ, MS, 1976; Fla Inst Technol, PhD (oceanog), 1983. **Professional Experience:** PROF MARINE SCI, RICHARD STOCKTON COL, as of 2004; assoc prof marine sci, Richard Stockton Col, beginninng 1990; asst prof, Richard Stockton Col, 1988-1990; res scientist aquacult, Oceanic Inst, 1984-1985; postdoctoral aquacult, Harbor Br Oceanog Inst, 1983-1984 &biol, Univ Conn, 1985-1988; technician biochem, USDA, Gainesville, Fla, 1975-1978 & biol, Univ WFla, 1978-1979; res fel biol, NY Ocean SciLab, 1974-1975. **Memberships:** World Aquacult Soc; Am Soc Zoologists; Crustacean Soc; Am Fisheries Soc. **Research Statement & Publications:** General aquaculture systems, especially as they relate to crustaceans; reproductive endocrinology of crustaceans, in particular concerning the mandibular organ. **Mailing Address:** Richard Stockton Col, PO Box 195, Pomona, NJ 08240. **E-Mail:** mlandau@stockton.edu

LANDAU, RALPH, chemical engineering; deceased, see previous edition for last biography

LANDAU, RICHARD LOUIS, ENDOCRINOLOGY. **Personal Data:** b St Louis, Mo, August 8, 1916; m 1943, c 3. **Education:** Wash Univ, BS & MD, 1940. **Professional Experience:** EMER PROF MED, UNIV CHICAGO, 1988-; Ed, Perspectives in Biol & Med, 1973-; From asst prof to prof, Univ Chicago, 1948-1988. **Memberships:** Am Soc Clin Invest; Endocrine Soc; AMA; Sigma Xi. **Research Statement & Publications:** Hormonal regulation of growth processes; reproductive endocrinology; metabolic influence of progesterone; effect of steroid hormones on electrolyte metabolism. **Mailing Address:** 505 N Lakeshore D Apt 5710, Chicago, IL 60611.

LANDAU, WILLIAM, microbiology; deceased, see previous edition for last biography

LANDAU, WILLIAM M, NEUROLOGY, NEUROPHYSIOLOGY. **Personal Data:** b St Louis, Mo, October 10, 1924; m 1947, c 4. **Education:** Wash Univ, MD, 1947. **Professional Experience:** PROF NEUROL, SCH MED, WASH UNIV, as of 2006; chmn, Nat Comt Res Neurol & Commun Dis, 1980-; CO-HEAD, DEPT NEUROL & NEUROSURG, beginning 1975; pres, Am Bd Psychiat & Neurol, 1975; head, Dept Neurol, Sch Med, Wash Univ, 1970-1991; vis prof, Univ Munich, 1963; From instr to assoc prof, Dept Neurol & Neurosurg, 1952-1963; sr asst surgeon & neurophysiologist, NIMH & Nat Inst Neurol Dis & Blindness, 1952-1954. **Memberships:** Am Physiol Soc; Am EEG Soc; Am Neurol Asn (pres, 1977); Asn Univ Profs Neurol (pres, 1978); Am Acad Neurol. **Research Statement & Publications:** Sensory and motor systems. **Mailing Address:** Dept Neurol, Sch Med, Wash Univ, Campus Box 8111, 660 S Euclid, St Louis, MO 63110. **Fax:** 314-747-1345. **E-Mail:** landauw@neuro.wustl.edu

LANDAUER, MICHAEL ROBERT, NEUROTOXICOLOGY. **Personal Data:** b New York, NY, September 24, 1946. **Education:** Rutgers Univ, BS, 1968; Univ Ill, Urbana, MS, 1970, PhD (biopsychol), 1975. **Professional Experience:** Grant recipient, Vet Admin & Dept Defense, 1991-1996; RES TOXICOLOGIST, ARMED FORCES RADIOBIOL RES INST, 1984-; vis res scientist, US Army Chem Res & Develop Ctr, 1982-1984; res assoc, pharmacol, Med Col Va, 1982-1984; grant, NIMH, 1979; fel, toxicol & pharmacol, Med Col, Va Commonwealth Univ, 1979-1982; vis asst prof biol, Barnard Col, Columbia Univ, 1976-1979; lectr, Philadelphia Zoo, 1976; res assoc psychol, Beaver Col, 1974-1976. **Memberships:** Radiation Res Soc; Animal Behav Soc; Am Soc Zoologists; Europ Soc Radiation Biol; Am Col Toxicologists; Asn Govt Toxicologists (pres, 1997-1998); Behav Toxicol Soc; Int Neurotoxicology Soc. **Research Statement & Publications:** Behavioral effects of ionizing radiation and chemical radiation protectors; neurotoxicology; psychopharmacology. **Mailing Address:** Dept Radiation Pathophysiol & Toxicol, Armed Forces Radiobiol Res Inst, Bldg 42 8901 Wis Ave, Bethesda, MD 20889-5603. **E-Mail:** landauer@afrri.usuhs.mil

LANDAW, STEPHEN ARTHUR, INTERNAL MEDICINE, HEMATOLOGY. **Personal Data:** b Paterson, NJ, June 20, 1936; c Jared & Nicole. **Education:** Univ Wis-Madison, BS, 1957; George Wash Univ, MD, 1959; Univ Calif, Berkeley, PhD (med physics), 1969; Am Bd Internal Med, dipl, 1972, cert hemat, 1972, cert medoncol, 1975; Am Bd Nuclear Med, dipl, 1972. **Honors & Awards:** Kosmos Achievement Award, NASA, 1975 & 1977. **Professional Experience:** PROF MED, STATE UNIV NY HEALTH SCI CTR, 1978-; mem attend staff med, Vet Admin Hosp, 1973-; mem attend staff med, Univ Hosp & Crouse-Irving Mem Hosp, 1973-1995; assoc chief staff res, Vet Admin Hosp, Syracuse, NY, 1973-1995; assoc prof med & radiol, State Univ NY Health Sci Ctr, 1973-1978; chief isotope lab, Alameda Co Hosp, Oakland, Calif, 1971-1973; Nat Heart & Lung Inst career develop award, 1970-1973; asst physician, Donner Lab, Univ Calif, Berkeley, 1970-1973; lectr med physics, Univ, 1970-1972; attend staff physician, Alameda Co Hosp, Oakland, Calif, 1969-1973; Nat Heart Inst fel med physics, DonnerLab, Univ Calif, Berkeley, 1963-1970; NIH fel med & hemat, Med Col Va, 1962-1963; asst resident internal med, Mt Sinai Hosp, NY, 1960-1961; intern, Mt Sinai Hosp, NY, 1959-1960. **Memberships:** fel Am Col Physicians; Am Soc Hemat; Am Fedn Clin Res; Soc Exp Biol & Med; Soc Pediat Res. **Research Statement & Publications:** Bilirubin kinetics; quantitative red blood cell kinetics; polycythemic disorders; carbon monoxide kinetics. **Mailing Address:** Med Serv (III) Vet Admin Med Ctr, 800 Irvine Ave, Syracuse, NY 13210. **Fax:** 315-477-4570. **E-Mail:** landaw.stephen@syracuse.va.gov

LANDAY, ALAN LEE, MICROBIOLOGY. **Personal Data:** b Pittsburgh, Pa, February 13, 1955. **Education:** Pa State Univ, BS, 1976; Univ Pittsburgh, PhD, 1981. **Professional Experience:** ASSOC CHMN, DEPT IMMUNOL & MICROBIOL, RUSH MED COL, RUSH UNIV, as of 2002; PROF, DEPT MICROBIOL & IMMUNOL, RUSH MED COL, RUSH UNIV, as of 2002; grants, AMAC Corp, 1991-1992; grants, Coulter Immunol, 1990-1991; assoc prof immunol/microbiol path & med, Rush Med Col, beginning 1988; grants, Loyd Frye Found, 1988-1991; grants, NIH, 1986-1989 &1987-1992; asst prof path, Path & Med, 1985-1988; grants, Rush Univ, 1985-1986; grants, RushMed Ctr, 1985-1986; grants, Leukemia Res Found, 1985-1986; grants, Am Cancer Soc, 1985-1986; DIR CLIN IMMUNOL LAB & FLOW CYTOMETRY LAB, OFF CONSOL SERV, RUSH-PRESBY-ST LUKE'S MED MED CTR, CHICAGO, 1983-; asst prof immunol/microbiol, Path & Med, 1983-1988; postdoctoral, Cellular Immunobiol Unit, Univ Ala Sch Med, Birmingham, 1981-1983; Adv, Freedon Proj, Col Am Pathologists Diag & NASA Space Sta; chmn, NatComt Clin Lab & Qual Control & Stand Comt, Soc Analytical Cytol; mem, Stand Subcomt FlowCytometry, Immunol Res Comt, Flow Cytometry Adv Comt, NIH. **Memberships:** AAAS; NY Acad Sci; Int Soc Analytical Cytol; Am Soc Histocompatability &Immunogenetics; Am Soc Clin Path; Am Fedn Clin Res; Am Asn Immunologists; Clin ImmunolSoc; Am Soc Hemat; Am Asn Pathologists. **Research Statement & Publications:** Effects of Vitamin C on growth characteristics of cultured cells; effects of radiation, chemotherapy & immunotherapy on a transplan; biology; pathology; numerous technical publications. **Mailing Address:** Dept Immunol Microbiol, Rush Med Col, Rush Univ, Suite 616, 1735 West Harrison St, Chicago, IL 60612-3833. **Fax:** 312-942-2808. **E-Mail:** alanday@rush.edu

LANDBORG, RICHARD JOHN, CHEMISTRY, SCIENCE EDUCATION. **Personal Data:** b Manchester, Iowa, May 13, 1933; m 1955, c 4. **Education:** Luther Col, Iowa, BA, 1955; Univ Iowa, MS, 1957, PhD (chem), 1959. **Professional Experience:** Fulbright exchange prof, Univ Santa Maria Antigua, Panama, 1967; chmn dept, Augustana Col, Sdak, 1965-1967; ASSOC PROF CHEM, AUGUSTANA COL, SDAK, 1963-; asst prof, Augustana Col, Sdak, 1959-1963; Part-time instr chem, Cornell Col, 1957-1958. **Memberships:** AAAS; Am Chem Soc; Sigma Xi. **Research Statement & Publications:** Chemistry of diazomethane particularly the addition cyclization reactions with activated olefinic systems. **Mailing Address:** 1109 W 37th St, Sioux Falls, SD 57105-0678.

LANDE, ALEXANDER, THEORETICAL NUCLEAR PHYSICS. **Personal Data:** b Hilversum, Neth, January 5, 1936; American citizen. **Education:** Cornell Univ, BA, 1957; Mass Inst Technol, PhD (theoret physics), 1964. **Professional Experience:** PROF PHYSICS, INST THEORET PHYSICS, STATE UNIV GRONINGEN, 1980-; Chmn, Inst Theoret Physics, 1976-1983; assoc prof, Inst Theoret Physics, State UnivGroningen, 1972-1980; vis assoc prof, Nordic Inst Theoret Atomic Physics, 1970-1972; asst prof, Niels Bohr Inst, 1968-1970; NSF fel, Niels Bohr Inst, 1966-1968; Instr, Palmer Phys Lab, Princeton Univ, 1963-1966. **Memberships:** Am Phys Soc; Europ Phys Soc; Neth Phys Soc. **Research Statement & Publications:** Theoretical nuclear structure. **Mailing Address:** Inst Theoret Physics Groningen Univ, Nijenborgh 4, Groningen 9747 AG, Netherlands. **Fax:** 315-036-34947. **E-Mail:** lande@th.rug.ne

LANDE, KENNETH, ASTROPHYSICS, ELEMENTARY PARTICLE PHYSICS. **Personal Data:** b Vienna, Austria, June 5, 1932; American citizen; c 3. **Education:** Columbia Univ, AB, 1953, AM, 1955, PhD (physics), 1958. **Professional Experience:** Assoc ed astrophys, Phys Rev Letters, 1987; actg chmn, Astron & Astrophys, 1984-; PROF PHYSICS, UNIV PA, 1974-; from instr to assoc prof, Univ PA, 1959-1974; asst physics, Columbia Univ, 1954-1957. **Memberships:** Am Phys Soc; Sigma Xi; Am Astron Soc. **Research Statement & Publications:** Neutrino physics; cosmic rays. **Mailing Address:** Dept Physics, Univ Pa, 209 S, 33rd St, Philadelphia, PA 19104-6396. **Fax:** 215-898-2010. **E-Mail:** klande@sas.upenn.edu

LANDE, RUSSELL SCOTT, POPULATION GENETICS, EVOLUTION. **Personal Data:** b Jackson, Miss, August 10, 1951. **Education:** Univ Calif, Irvine, BS, 1972; Harvard Univ, PhD (biol), 1976. **Honors & Awards:** MacArthur Fel, John D & Catherine T MacArthur Found, 1997. **Professional Experience:** PROF BIOL, UNIV ORE, 1989-; asst prof biophys & theoret biol, Univ Chicago, 1978-1989; fel genetics, Univ Wis-Madison 1976-1978. **Research Statement & Publications:** Population genetics and evolution, especially of quantitative characters and chromosomal rearrangements. **Mailing Address:** Dept Biol, Univ Ore, Eugene, OR 97403. **E-Mail:** russ@aylmer.uoregon.edu

LANDE, SAUL, BIOCHEMISTRY, ORGANIC CHEMISTRY. **Personal Data:** b Philadelphia, Pa, August 7, 1930; m 1954, c 4. **Education:** Ursinus Col, BS, 1948; Univ Pittsburgh, PhD (biochem), 1960. **Professional Experience:** STAFF, ST JOSEPHS HOSP, 1989-; assoc clin prof dermat, Sch Med, YaleUniv, 1977-1989; assoc prof biochem med, Sch Med, Yale Univ, 1963-1976; sr res chemist, Squibb Res Inst, 1961-1963. **Memberships:** Am Chem Soc. **Research Statement & Publications:** Chemistry of biologically active peptides. **Mailing Address:** 35 Point Beach Dr, Milford, CT 06902.

LANDE, SHELDON SIDNEY, ENVIRONMENTAL CHEMISTRY, RISK ASSESSMENT. **Personal Data:** b Chicago, Ill, July 16, 1941; m 1964, c 2. **Education:** Ill Inst Technol, BS, 1962; Mich State Univ, PhD (chem), 1966. **Professional Experience:** ENVIRON SPECIALIST, 3M CO, 1979-; res assoc, Syracuse Univ Res Corp, 1975-1979; pub health adminr, Allegheny Co Health Dept, Pa, 1972-1975; res assoc water chem, Grad Sch Pub Health, Univ Pittsburgh, 1971-1972; res chemist, Gulf Res & Develop Co, 1970-1971; mult fel petrol, Mellon Inst, 1968-1970. **Memberships:** Air & Waste Mgt Asn; Am Chem Soc; Soc Exposure Analysis; Soc Risk Analysis. **Research Statement & Publications:** Fate of organic substances in soil and water; analysis of organic chemicals in the environment; health risk analysis. **Mailing Address:** Corp Prod Responsibility Dept, 3M Ctr, Bldg 290-04-01, St Paul, MN 55144. **Fax:** 651-736-9278. **E-Mail:** sslande@mmm.com

LANDECKER, PETER BRUCE, SPACECRAFT INSTRUMENTATION. **Personal Data:** b New York, NY, October 1, 1942. **Education:** Columbia Univ, BA, 1963; Cornell Univ, PhD (exp physics), 1968. **Honors & Awards:** Hughes Aircraft Co Inventor Awards, 1983, 1988, 1989, 1990, 1991, 1992, 1993, 1994, 1995, 1996, 1997, 1998. **Professional Experience:** SR STAFF SCIENTIST, TRW SPACE & TECHNOLOGY, 2000-; consult, Sumware Corp, 1986; lab scientist, Space & Commun Group, Hughes Aircraft Co, 1982-2000; consult, Aerospace Corp, 1982-1983; Instr, El Camino Col, 1977 & 1986-1988; prin investr, Solar X-ray satellite Payload, 1974-1982; mem tech staff, Aerospace Corp, 1974-1982; consult, Columbia Univ, 1974-1975; res assoc, Columbia Univ, 1970-1974; asst res physicist, Univ Calif, Irvine, 1968-1970; instr physics, Cornell Univ, 1967-1968. **Memberships:** Int Astron Union; Am Phys Soc. **Research Statement & Publications:** Instruments on remote sensing spacecraft; x-ray astronomy; cosmic ray physics; solar physics; spacecraft and photography; star sensing attitude determination; acronyms; magnetic fields; granted four patents; author of 76 publications. **Mailing Address:** Northrop Grumman Space Technol, One Space Park, Redondo Beach, CA 90278. **Fax:** 310-812-1584. **E-Mail:** plandecker@yahoo.com

LANDEFELD, THOMAS DALE, REPRODUCTIVE ENDOCRINOLOGY, BIOCHEMISTRY. **Personal Data:** b Columbus, Ohio, March 24, 1947; div, c 2. **Education:** Marietta Col, AB, 1969; Univ Wis-Madison, BS & PhD (reproductive endocrinol), 1973. **Professional Experience:** Prof, Biology Department, ASSOC DEAN, FAC AFFAIRS & SCHOLARLY ACTIV, COL ARTS & SCI, CALIF STATE UNIV, DOMINGUEZ HILLS, 1996-2004; asst dean res & grad studies, Univ Mich, 1989-1993; assoc prof, dept pharmacol, Univ Mich, Ann Arbor, beginning 1987; asst prof, DeptPath, Univ Mich, Ann Arbor, 1982-1987; co-investr, NIH res grant, Univ Mich, 1979-1990 &1983-1990; prin investr, NIH res grant, Univ Mich, 1978-1990; asst res scientist, Dept Path, 1978-1982; from res assoc to sr res assoc, Univ Mich, Ann Arbor, 1976-1978; fel obstet & gynecdept, Sch Med, Wash Univ, 1974-1976; fel endocrinol div, Med Col, Cornell Univ, 1973-1974; Fel, Comt Inst Coop. **Memberships:** Endocrine Soc; Soc Study Reproduction; Sigma Xi; NY Acad Sci; Am SocBiochem & Molecular Biol; Soc Sci Study Sex. **Research Statement & Publications:** Pituitary gonadotropins; isolation, purification, and biochemical characterization; mechanisms and control of biosynthesis; mRNA purification and translation; gene expression and regulation; recombinant DNA and cloning. **Mailing Address:** California State Univ, 1000 E Victoria St, Dominguez HIlls, CA 90747. **Fax:** 734-763-4450. **E-Mail:** tlandefeld@cas.csudh.edu

LANDEL, ROBERT FRANKLIN, PHYSICAL CHEMISTRY, RHEOLOGY. **Personal Data:** b Pendleton, NY, October 10, 1925; m 1953, Aurora; c Carlisle P, Grace P, Hans F, Robert F Jr, Kevin L & Matthew N. **Education:** Univ Buffalo, BA, 1950, MA, 1951; Univ Wis, PhD (phys chem), 1954. **Honors & Awards:** Except Sci Achievement Award, NASA, 1976; Except Serv Award, 1988; Humboldt Prize, Ger, 1990. **Professional Experience:** RETIRED; vis prof, Swiss Fed Tech Inst, Lausanne, Switz, 1993-1994, 1997; vis prof, Univ Philippines, Manila, 1993-1994, 1997; dept mgr, Appl Mech Technol Sect, 1983-1985; consult, Sandia Corp, 1983; mgr, Mat Res & Biotechnol Sect, CalTech Jet Propulsion Lab, 1982-1983; sr res scientist, Control & Energy Conversion Div, 1981-1992; div technologist, Control & Energy Conversion Div, 1979-1980; res affil, Rancho Los Amigos Hosp, Downey, Calif, beginning 1976; mgr, Energy & Mat Res Sect, 1976-1979, 1980-1982; mgr, Propulsion & Mat Res Sect, 1975-1976; sr fel, Ctr Res Macromolecules, France, 1972; sr Fulbright fel, Italy, 1971-1972; sr res fel, CalTech Jet Propulsion Lab, Calif Inst Technol, 1965-1969; chief, Polymer Res Sect, 1961-1975; chief, Solid Propellant Chem Sect, 1959-1961; sr res engr, Jet Propulsion Lab, Calif Inst Technol, 1955-1959; res assoc, Univ Wis, 1954-1955. **Memberships:** Am Phys Soc; Am Chem Soc; Soc Rheology (pres, 1985-1987). **Research Statement & Publications:** Dependent of mechanical preparation of polymers on time, tempearture chemistry and network structure, amount and type of filler, from infiniteserival straint to rupture and in time and maulti-oxical response. **Mailing Address:** 300 Tahimik Trail, Santa Cruz, CA 95065. **E-Mail:** rflandel@cruzio.com

LANDEN, ERNEST W, HEALTH SCIENCES. **Education:** NW Mo State Teacher's Col, BA, 1931; Univ Mo-Columbia, MS, 1933, PhD (biophys), 1938. **Professional Experience:** RETIRED; proj mgr, Caterpillar Tractor Co, as of 2000. **Mailing Address:** 307 Kickapoo Terr, Peoria, IL 61604. **Fax:** 309-675-6155.

LANDER, ARTHUR DOUGLAS, COGNITIVE SCIENCE. **Personal Data:** b Brooklyn, NY, September 12, 1958. **Education:** Yale Univ, BS, 1979; Univ Calif, San Francisco, PhD (neuroscience), 1985. **Professional Experience:** CHMN, DEPT DEVELOP & CELL BIOL, UNIV CALIF, IRVINE, as of 2004; ASSOC DIR, UC IRVINE DEVELOP BIOL CTR, as of 2004; SCI DIR, UC IRVINE TRANSGENIC MOUSE FACIL, as of 2004; David & Lucile Packard fel sci & eng, 1988-1993; Edward J Poitras asst profhuman biol & exp med, Dept Brain & Cognitive Sci & Dept Biol, Mass Inst Technol, 1988-1991; asst prof, Dept Brain & Cognitive Sci & Dept Biol, Mass Inst Technol, beginning 1987; assoc, Howard Hughes Med Inst, Ctr Neurobiology & Behav, Col Physicians & Surgeons, Columbia Univ, 1985-1987. **Memberships:** Soc Neuroscience; Soc Develop Biol; NY Acad Sci; Am Soc Cell Biol; Am Soc Clin Invests. **Research Statement & Publications:** Molecular mechanisms of axon outgrowth and guidance; cellular responses to extracellular matrix; biologic functions of proteoglycans. **Mailing Address:** Dept Develop & Cell Biol, Univ Calif, 5205A Biol Sci II McGaugh Hall, Irvine, CA 92697-2300. **Fax:** 949-824-4709. **E-Mail:** adlander@uci.edu

LANDER, ERIC STEVEN, GENETICS. **Personal Data:** b Brooklyn, NY, February 3, 1957. **Education:** Princeton Univ, BA, 1978; Oxford Univ, PhD (math), 1981. **Honors & Awards:** Christian A Herter Distinguished Lectr, NY Univ, 1993; Gladstone Distinguished lectr, Gladstone Inst, 1994; Herman Beerman lectr, Soc Investigative Dermat, 1995; Rhoads Mem Award Excellence Cancer Res, Am Asn Cancer Res, 1995; Herbert Boyer Lect Genetics, Univ Calif, San Francisco, 1995; Kroc Distinguished lectr, Univ Wash, 1996. **Professional Experience:** Mem, Genetics Working Group, NIMH, 1997-; mem, Develop Diagnostics Working Group, Nat Cancer Inst, 1996-1997; US Pres Comn Nat Medal Sci, 1995-1997; Ralph R Braund distinguished vis prof, Univ Tenn, 1994; PROF, DEPT BIOL, MASS INSTTECHNOL, 1993-; GENETICIST MED, MASS GEN HOSP, 1993-; DIR, WHITEHEAD/MASS INST CTR GENOME RES, 1990-; mem, DNA Technol Forensic Sci, 1990-1993; MEM, WHITEHEAD INST BIOMED RES, 1989-; assoc prof, Mass Gen Hosp, 1989-1993; mem, Comt Math & Molecular Biol, Nat Acad Sci, 1989-1990; MacArthur prize felres human genetics & med, 1987-1992; assoc prof, Grad Sch Bus, Harvard Univ, 1987-1990; fel, Whitehead Inst Biomed Res, 1986-1989; vis scientist, Mass Gen Hosp, 1984-1989; asst prof, Grad Sch Bus, Harvard Univ, 1981-1986. **Memberships:** Nat Acad Sci; Human Genome Orgn; Genetics Soc Am; Am Soc Human Genetics; Math Asn Am; fel AAAS; Am Acad Forensic Sci; Am Asn Cancer Res. **Research Statement & Publications:** Human, mouse and rat genetics; study of traits with complex inheritance; construction of genetic, physical and sequence maps of human, mouse and rat genomes; development and application of tools for function genomics. **Mailing Address:** Whitehead Inst/Mass Inst Technol Ctr Genome Res, 320 Charles St, Cambridge, MA 02139-1561. **Fax:** 617-258-0903. **E-Mail:** lander@broad.mit.edu

LANDER, JAMES FRENCH, GEOPHYSICS, TSUNAMIS. **Personal Data:** b Bristol, Va, August 24, 1931; m 1960, Corinne Earle; c Jamie S, James Jr & Vivian G. **Education:** Pa State Univ, BS, 1958; Am Univ, MS, 1962, MA, 1968. **Honors & Awards:** Nakashizuka Award, Tsunami Soc, 1988. **Professional Experience:** Secy, Tsunami Comn, Int Union Geod & Geophys, 1996; mem, Tsunami Comn, Int Union Geod & Geophys, 1991; RES ASST, UNIV COLO, 1988-; dep dir, Nat Geophys &Solar-Terrestrial Data Ctr, Nat Oceanic & Atmospheric Admin, 1973-1988; dir, World DataCtr-A Solid Earth Geophys, 1973-1983; staff, Exec Off Pres, Off Emergency Preparedness, 1970-1971; chief, Nat Earthquake Info Ctr, 1966-1973; chief seismol invests br, Environ ResLabs, 1963-1973; chief seismol invests sect, US Coast & Geol Surv, Nat Oceanic & AtmosphericAdmin, 1962-1963; geophysicist, US Coast & Geol Surv, Nat Oceanic & Atmospheric Admin, 1958-1962. **Memberships:** AAAS; Seismol Soc Am; Am Geophys Union; Sigma Xi; Tsunami Soc; Int SocPrevent & Mitication Natural Hazards. **Research Statement & Publications:** US tsunamis; earthquake intensity; tsunami warning; diaster studies; natural hazard risks;

digitaldata bases. **Mailing Address:** Univ Colo, CIRES Campus, PO Box 449, Boulder, CO 80309-0449. **Fax:** 303-497-6513. **E-Mail:** jlander@ngdc.noaa.gov

LANDER, PHILIP HOWARD, DIAGNOSTIC RADIOLOGY, SPINAL IMAGING & DIAGNOSIS. **Personal Data:** b Montreal, Que, September 17, 1941; m 1967, Freema; c 3. **Education:** McGill Univ, Can, BSc, 1964, MD, 1966. **Professional Experience:** ASSOC PROF DIAG RADIOL, UNIV ALA BIRMINGHAM HEALTH SYST, as of 2006; assoc prof, Mcgill Univ, 1987-; sr radiologist, Sirmortimer B Davis Gen Hosp, 1972-. **Memberships:** Radiol Soc NAm; Am Roentgen Ray Soc; Int Skeletal Soc; Soc Int Spine injection; Can Asn Radiologists. **Research Statement & Publications:** Correlation of Paget's disease, bone with radiographic pathology, histopathology and clinical findings involving the weight bearing joints and the spine; diagnostic imaging of painful intervertebral segments of the cervical and lumbar spine; correlation to provocative and analgesic clinical tests; investigation of electrocoagulation of dorsal ramii of painful vertebral segments. **Mailing Address:** Univ Ala Sch Med, 1530 Third Ave S, Birmingham, AL 35294-3412. **E-Mail:** plander@uabmc.edu

LANDER, RICHARD LEON, PHYSICS. **Personal Data:** b Oakland, Calif, April 23, 1928; div c 3. **Education:** Univ Calif, Berkeley, BA, 1950, PhD (physics), 1958; Ohio State Univ, MA, 1951. **Professional Experience:** PROF PHYSICS, UNIV CALIF, DAVIS, 1970-; assoc dean res, Grad Div, 1970-1973; assoc prof physics, Univ Calif, Davis, 1966-1970; vis scientist, Europ Orgn Nuclear Res, Switz, 1966-1967; assoc res physicist, Univ Calif, San Diego, 1961-1966; res specialist nuclear physics, Boeing Co, 1960-1961; staff physicist, Lawrence Radiation Lab, Univ Calif, 1958-1960. **Memberships:** AAAS; Am Phys Soc. **Research Statement & Publications:** Experimental elementary particle physics. **Mailing Address:** Dept Physics, Univ Calif, Davis, CA 95616. **E-Mail:** lander@physics.ucdavis.edu

LANDERL, HAROLD PAUL, organic chemistry; deceased, see previous edition for last biography

LANDERS, JOHN HERBERT, JR, ANIMAL NUTRITION. **Personal Data:** b Stockton, Mo, January 24, 1921; m 1943, Mary Hanna; c Steven, Patricia & David. **Education:** Univ Mo, BS, 1942, MS, 1950; Kans State Univ, PhD (animal nutrit), 1966. **Professional Experience:** EMER PROF, ORE STATE UNIV, 1977-; from asst prof to prof & exten animal scientist, Ore State Univ, 1950-1977; instr animal sci, Univ Mo, 1949-1950; Co agent agr, Univ Mo, 1945-1949. **Memberships:** Am Romney Sheep Breeders Asn (secy, 1961-1998); Am Soc Animal Sci. **Research Statement & Publications:** Counseling and advising livestock growers in more efficient production of meat and fiber. **Mailing Address:** 29515 NE Weslinn Dr, Corvallis, OR 97333.

LANDERS, ROGER Q, JR, PLANT ECOLOGY, RANGE MANAGEMENT. **Personal Data:** b Menard, Tex, July 23, 1932; m 1954, Helen Benson; c Roger III & Amy (Ness). **Education:** Tex A&M Univ, BS, 1954, MS, 1955; Univ Calif, Berkeley, PhD (bot), 1962. **Professional Experience:** EMER EXTENRANGE SPECIALIST, TEX A&M UNIV SYST, 1994-; extenrange specialist, Tex A&M Univ Syst, 1979-; prof, Iowa State Univ, 1971-1979; From asst prof toassoc prof plant ecol, Iowa State Univ, 1962-1971. **Memberships:** Ecol Soc Am; Soc Range Mgt; Sigma Xi. **Research Statement & Publications:** Grasslands; management of grazing land by chemical, mechanical and biological methods; prescribed burning to control undesirable brush and cactus and enhance productivity of desirable forage species for livestock and wildlife. **Mailing Address:** Res & Exten Ctr, Tex A&M Univ Syst, 7887 N Hwy 87, San Angelo, TX 76901.

LANDES, HUGH S(TEVENSON), PHYSICS, ELECTRICAL ENGINEERING. **Personal Data:** b Waynesboro, Va, July 4, 1924; m 1946, c 1. **Education:** Univ Va, BS, 1953, PhD (physics), 1956. **Professional Experience:** ASSOC PROF EMER ELEC ENG, UNIV VA, as of 2000; assoc Prof Elec Eng, Univ Va, 1960-1993; asst prof elec eng, Univ VA, 1957-1960; asst prof physics, Univ SC, 1956-1957. **Memberships:** Nat Soc Prof Engrs; Am Asn Physics Teachers; Inst Elec & Electronics Engrs. **Research Statement & Publications:** Electric circuit theory; electromagnetic field theory; microwave devices; ferrite phenomena. **Mailing Address:** Dept Elec Eng, Univ Va, PO Box 400743, Charlottesville, VA 22904-4743. **Fax:** 434-924-8818.

LANDES, JOHN D, FRACTURE MECHANICS. **Personal Data:** b Sellersville, Pa, June 28, 1942; m 1964, Anne Ruth; c Jennifer, Kristina, Rebecca & David. **Education:** Lehigh Univ, BS, 1964, MS, 1965, PhD (mech), 1970. **Honors & Awards:** Irwin Medal, Am Soc Testing & Mat, 1980, Award of Merit, 1989; Fracture Mech Medal, 1995. **Professional Experience:** PROF MECH & AEROSPACE ENG & ENG SCI, UNIV TENN, 1995-; prof eng sci & mech, Univ Tenn, 1987-1995; mgr, Am Welding Inst, 1985-1987; adv engr, Westinghouse Elec Co, 1978-1985; fel engr, Westinghouse Elec Co, 1976-1978; sr engr, Westinghouse Elec Co, 1970-1976; grad asst mech, Lehigh Univ, 1966-1970; Res assoc, Pratt & Whitney Aircraft, 1965-1966. **Memberships:** Am Soc Testing & Mat; Am Welding Soc; Soc Eng Sci. **Research Statement & Publications:** Research in fracture and fatigue, fracture of ductile materials; metals and polymers including testing standards and methods of applications. **Mailing Address:** Univ of Tenn, 310 Perkins Hall, Knoxville, TN 37996-2030. **Fax:** 423-974-7663.

LANDESBERG, JOSEPH MARVIN, ORGANIC CHEMISTRY. **Personal Data:** b New York, NY, April 21, 1939; m 1964, Lucy; c 2. **Education:** Rutgers Univ, BS, 1960; Harvard Univ, MA, 1962, PhD (chem), 1965. **Professional Experience:** PROF CHEM, GRAD SCH ARTS & SCI, ADELPHI UNIV, 1975-; assoc prof, Adelphi Univ, 1970-1975; asst prof, Adelphi Univ, 1966-1970; NIH res fel, Columbia Univ, 1964-1966. **Memberships:** Am Chem Soc; Am Asn Univ Prof. **Research Statement & Publications:** Heterocyclic chemistry; synthetic applications of organometallic compounds; synthesis of strained, small-membered rings. **Mailing Address:** Dept Chem, Adelphi Univ, Sci Bldg Rm 218, Garden City, NY 11530. **Fax:** 516-877-4485. **E-Mail:** landesbj@adelphi.edu

LANDESMAN, BARBARA TEHAN, WAVE PROPAGATION & DIFFRACTION, IMAGE PROCESSING. **Personal Data:** b Louisville, Ky, February 23, 1955. **Education:** Univ Louisville, BS, 1976; Stanford Univ, MS, 1977; Univ Ariz, MS, 1984, PhD (optical scis), 1988. **Professional Experience:** OPTICAL ENGR, SPECIALIST, LOCKHEED-MARTIN ADVANCED TECHNOL CENTER, as of 2002; sr scientist, Appl Technol Assocs, 1993-2001; dir res & develop, Appl Technol Assocs, 1993-1996; res scientist, Lockheed Missiles & Space, 1989-1993; sr mem optical staff, Talandic Res Corp, 1987-1989; sr engr electro optics, Itek Corp, 1979-1980; asst prof, Elec Eng Linear Systs, San Jose Univ, 1979-1980; subsyst engr, Ford Aerospace & Communs, 1977-1979. **Memberships:** Inst Elec & Electronics Engrs; Optical Soc Am; Soc Photo Optical Instrumentation Engrs. **Research Statement & Publications:** Gaussian beam propagation diffraction and interaction with ice crystal clouds; laser resonator design and semiconductor laser; actively illuminated satellite targets imaged by ground based telescopes. **Mailing Address:** 13333 Arch Ct NE, Albuquerque, NM 87112.

LANDESMAN, EDWARD MILTON, MATHEMATICS. **Personal Data:** b Brooklyn, NY, March 19, 1938. **Education:** Univ Calif, Los Angeles, BA, 1960, MA, 1961, PhD (math), 1965. **Honors & Awards:** Math Asn Am- Deborah & Franklin Tepper Haimo Nat Award, 1966; Phi Kappa Northern Calif Excellence Award, 1987; Math Asn Am-Northern Calif Distinguished Teaching Award, 1995. **Professional Experience:** PROF EMER MATH, CROWN COL, UNIV CALIF, SANTA CRUZ, as of 2003; prof math, Crown Col, Univ Calif, Santa Cruz, beginning 1980; assoc prof, Crown Col, Univ Calif, Santa Cruz, 1971-1980; Air Force Off Sci Res grant, Univ Calif, Santa Cruz, 1970-1971; asst prof, Crown Col, Univ Calif, Santa Cruz, 1969-1971; asst prof, Univ Calif, Los Angeles, 1968-1969; asst prof, Univ Calif, Santa Cruz, 1966-1968; asst prof inresidence math, Univ Calif, Los Angeles, 1965-1966. **Memberships:** AAAS; Am Math Soc; Math Asn Am. **Research Statement & Publications:** Partial differential equations; combinatorial theory; calculus. **Mailing Address:** Acad Systs Math, 444 Castro St Ste 1200, Mtain View, CA 94041. **E-Mail:** elandesm@academic.com

LANDESMAN, HERBERT, INORGANIC CHEMISTRY. **Personal Data:** b Newark, NJ, April 22, 1927; m 1953, c 2. **Education:** Harvard Univ, BS, 1948; Purdue Univ, PhD (chem), 1951. **Professional Experience:** PROF EMER CHEM, LOS ANGELES S W COL, as of 2001; prof chem, Los Angeles S W Col, beginning 1969; vpres, EnvironResources, Inc, 1968-1969; chem consult, West Precipitation Group, Joy Mfg Co, 1966-1968; Olin Mathieson Chem Corp, 1952-1959 & Nat Eng Sci Co, 1959-1966; Res chemist, Naval Ord TestSta, 1951-1952. **Memberships:** Air Pollution Control Asn; Am Chem Soc. **Research Statement & Publications:** Organosilicon chemistry; chemistry of boron hydrides; fire extinguishants; fluorocarbons; hazards analysis; air and water pollution. **Mailing Address:** Dept Chem, Los Angeles S W Col, 1600 W Imperial Hwy, Los Angeles, CA 90047.

LANDESMAN, RICHARD, DEVELOPMENTAL BIOLOGY. **Personal Data:** b Brooklyn, NY, January 30, 1940. **Education:** NY Univ, BA, 1961, MS, 1963; Univ BC, PhD (zoology), 1966. **Professional Experience:** PROF EMER, UNIV VT, as of 2006; prof zool, Univ Vt, as of 1997; NIH & Nat Inst Dent Res, 1984-1985; assoc prof zool, Univ Vt, beginning 1969; NIH fel biol, Mass Inst Technol, 1966-1969. **Memberships:** Soc Develop Biol. **Research Statement & Publications:** Cellular and molecular basis of limb regeneration; fracture healing in the newt; differentiation and morphogenesis of the regenerating newt limb-role of hormones and secondary growth factors in regeneration; osteoinductive potential of demineralized bone matrix and bone proteins. **Mailing Address:** Dept Zool, Univ Vt, Marsh Life Scis, Burlington, VT 05405-0001. **E-Mail:** Richard.Landesman@uvm.edu

LANDGRAF, RONALD WILLIAM, FATIGUE, FRACTURE. **Personal Data:** b Freeport, Ill, March 7, 1939; m 1962, Nancy; c 2. **Education:** Carnegie Inst Technol, BS, 1961; Univ Ill, Urbana, MS, 1966, PhD (theoret & applmech), 1969. **Professional Experience:** PROF, ENG SCI & MECH, VA POLYTECHNIC INST & STATE UNIV, 1990-; vis prof, eng sci & mech, VA Polytechnic Inst & State Univ, 1988-1990; vis prof, UnivIll, Urbana-Champaign, 1985; assoc ed, fatigue eng, Mat & Struct, beginning 1979; staff scientist, eng & res staff, 1979-1988; mem eng & res staff, Sci Res Staff, Ford Motor Co, 1977-1979; res scientist, sci res staff, Ford Motor Co, 1968-1977; res assoc theoret & appl mech, Univ Ill, Urbana, 1966-1968; mat engr, micro switch div, Honeywell Inc, 1961-1965. **Memberships:** Am Soc Metals; Am Inst Mining Metall & Petrol Engrs; fel Am Soc Testing &Mat; Soc Automotive Engrs; Am Soc Eng Educ. **Research Statement & Publications:** Cyclic deformation and fracture behavior of metals and alloys; influence of metallurgical structure on fatigue crack initiation and propagation; development of fatigue design procedures. **Mailing Address:** Dept Eng Sci & Mech, VA Polytechnic Inst & State Univ, 219 Norris Hall 0219, Blacksburg, VA 24061. **Fax:** 540-231-4574. **E-Mail:** mc@landgraf.esm.vt.edu

LANDGRAF, WILLIAM CHARLES, PHARMACEUTICAL CHEMISTRY, SOFTWARE SYSTEMS. **Personal Data:** b Elizabeth, NJ, January 10, 1928; m 1953, c 3. **Education:** Seton Hall Univ, BS, 1950; Stanford Univ, PhD (chem), 1959; Univ Santa Clara, MBA, 1975. **Professional Experience:** HEAD, APEX CONSULT GROUP, LTD, as of 2003; mgr, Syntex Labs, beginning 1970; mgr & res scientist, Varian Assocs, Calif, 1963-1970; proj leader & lab supt, Ampex Corp, 1961-1963; Sr scientist chem, LockheedResLabs, Lockheed Missile Systs Div, 1958-1961. **Memberships:** Am Chem Soc; Am Pharmaceut Asn. **Research Statement & Publications:** Physical, biophysical and organic chemistry; kinetics; computer assisted experimentation; analytical chemistry; physical organic chemistry. **Mailing Address:** Apex Consult Group, Ltd, Palo Alto, CA 94303-4413.

LANDGREBE, ALBERT R, CHEMISTRY. **Personal Data:** b New Rochelle, NY, March 4, 1933; m 1958, c 2. **Education:** Fordham Univ, BS, 1957; Univ Md, PhD (chem), 1964. **Professional Experience:** RETIRED; div energy storage systs, Dept Energy, Wash, ending 1999; br chief chem storage, Energy Res & Develop Admin, beginning 1975; chemist & chmn comt sci & tech symposia, AEC, 1968-1975; radiochemist, Nat Bur Standards, Md, 1963-1968; inorg chemist, USDA, 1960-1963. **Memberships:** AAAS; Soc Nuclear Med; Sigma Xi; Am Chem Soc. **Research Statement & Publications:** Use of radioisotopes in analytical and inorganic chemistry; radio chromatographic methods; substoichiometric radioisotopic dilution analysis; removal of radioisotopes from milk; activation analysis; trace and micro analysis. **Mailing Address:** B 14 Suffex Lane, Millsboro, DE 19966.

LANDGREBE, DAVID ALLEN, ELECTRICAL ENGINEERING, SIGNAL PROCESSING & REMOTE SENSING. **Personal Data:** b Huntingburg, Ind, April 12, 1934; m (Margaret); c James D, Carole & Mary. **Education:** Purdue Univ, BS, 1956, MS, 1958, PhD (elec eng), 1962. **Honors & Awards:** Except Sci Achievement Medal, NASA, 1973; Geosci & Remote Sensing Soc Except Serv Award, Inst Elec & Electronics Engrs, Edinburgh, Scotland, 1988; William T Pecora Award, NASA & US Dept Interior, 1991; Sci Achievement Award, Inst Elec& Electronics Engrs Geosci & Remote Sensing Soc, 1992; Educ Award, Inst Elec & Electronics Engrs Geoscience & Remote Sensing Soc, 2003; Member National Academy of Engineering, 2005. **Professional Experience:** Actg head elec & comput eng, 1995-1996; assoc dean eng & dir, Eng Exp Sta, 1981-1984; PROF EMER ELEC ENG, PURDUE UNIV, 1970-; dir, Lab Applications Remote Sensing, 1969-1981; Consult, Earlham Col, 1963 & Douglas Aircraft Co, 1964-1970; From asst prof to prof, Purdue Univ, 1962-1970; res scientist, Douglas Aircraft Co, Newport Beach, Calif, 1962; electronics engr, Interstate Electronics Corp, Anaheim, Calif, 1958-1959; mem tech staff, Bell Tel Labs, Murray Hill, NJ, 1956. **Memberships:** Life Fel Inst Elec & Electronics Engrs; Am Soc Eng Educ; Fel Am Soc Photogram & Remote Sensing; Fel Am Asn Advan Sci 1999. **Research Statement & Publications:** Representation and analysis of signals; data processing. **Mailing Address:** Dept Elec & Comput Eng, Purdue Univ, West Lafayette, IN 47907-1285. **Fax:** 765-494-3358. **E-Mail:** landgreb@ecn.purdue.edu

LANDGREBE, JOHN A, REACTION MECHANISMS, REACTIVE INTERMEDIATES. **Personal Data:** b San Francisco, Calif, May 6, 1937; m 1961, Carolyn; c Carolyn J &

John F. **Education:** Univ Calif, Berkeley, BS, 1959; Univ Ill, Urbana, PhD (org chem), 1962. **Honors & Awards:** Chancellors Club Career Teaching Award, 1999; Excellence in-Teaching Award, 2000. **Professional Experience:** PROF EMER CHEM, UNIV KANS, 2002-; prof chem, Univ Kans, 1971-2002; chmn, Chem Dept, Univ Kans, 1970-1980; assoc chmn, Chem Dept, Univ Kans, 1967-1970 and 1995-2002; From asst prof to assoc prof, Univ Kans, 1962-1971. **Memberships:** Am Chem Soc. **Research Statement & Publications:** Organic reaction mechanisms; small ring compounds; carbene intermediates; reactions of carbonyl ylides. **Mailing Address:** Dept Chem, Univ Kans, 4029 Malott, Lawrence, KS 66045-7582. **Fax:** 785-864-5396. **E-Mail:** jlandgrebe@ku.edu

LANDGREN, CRAIG RANDALL, PLANT TISSUE CULTURE, PLANT DEVELOPMENT. **Personal Data:** b St Paul, Minn, December 20, 1947; m 1983, Susan; c Gari A R & Cynthia E. **Education:** Albion Col, BA, 1969; Harvard Univ, MA, 1970, PhD (biol), 1974. **Professional Experience:** PROF EMER BIOL, MIDDLEBURY COL, as of 2004; DIR, ACAD FACIL PLANNING, MIDDLEBURY COL, 1996-2004; prof, Middlebury Col, beginning 1996; dean instrnl resources, Freshman Writing Prog, 1995-1996; col Writing Prog, Freshman WritingProg, 1992-1993; dir, Freshman Writing Prog, 1990-1991; dir, SCIENS Prog, 1987-1990 &1992; chmn, Nat Sci Div, 1985-1988; dir, Northern Studies, 1984-1987; chmn dept, MiddleburyCol, 1982-1988 & 1992-1996; vis scientist, US-USSR Nat Acad Sci Exchange Prog, 1980; res assoc, Univ Ore, 1978-1981; asst prof biol, Middlebury Col, 1977-1996; vis asst prof, Univ Ore, 1976-1977; res grant, George Mason Found, 1975-1976; Asst prof, George Mason Univ, 1974-1977. **Memberships:** Sigma Xi. **Research Statement & Publications:** Studies in the culture and differentiation of isolated plant cells and plant cell protoplasts; genetic engineering through organelle transplantation and cell fusion; plant stress physiology; over wintering of plants; ethics in science. **Mailing Address:** Middlebury Col, Middlebury, VT 05753. **E-Mail:** landgren@middlebury.edu

LANDGREN, JOHN JEFFREY, MATHEMATICS, FUNCTIONAL ANALYSIS. **Personal Data:** b St Paul, Minn, November 16, 1947; m 1977, c 3. **Education:** Univ Minn, BS, 1969, MS, 1971, PhD (math), 1976. **Professional Experience:** SR RES SCIENTIST, GA INST TECHNOL, 1980-; asst prof math, UnivTenn, 1978-1980; Vis asst prof math, Ga Inst Technol, 1976-1978. **Memberships:** Sigma Xi; Soc Indust & Appl Math. **Research Statement & Publications:** Electronic warfare; simulation of radar/jamming systems; applied mathematics; radar countermeasures and radar signal processing; adaptive antenna arrays. **Mailing Address:** GTRI ELSYS Ga Inst Technol, Atlanta, GA 30332-0840. **E-Mail:** jack.landgren@gtri.gatech.edu

LANDICK, ROBERT, REGULATION OF TRANSCRIPTIONAL ELONGATION, STRUCTURE-FUNCTION OF RNA POLYMERASE. **Personal Data:** b Salem, Mass, December 9, 1951. **Education:** Univ Mich, BS, 1975, PhD (biol chem), 1983. **Honors & Awards:** Pres Young Investr Award, NSF, 1989. **Professional Experience:** PROF BACT, UNIV WIS-MADISON, as of 2004; vis scholar, Stanford Univ, 1992-1993; assocprof, Wash Univ, 1991-; presidential young investr, 1989-1993; asst prof biol, Wash Univ, 1987-1991; Searle Scholar Award, Chicago Community Trust, 1987-1990; NIH fel, StanfordUniv, 1983-1986. **Memberships:** Am Chem Soc; Am Soc Microbiol; AAAS; Am Soc Biochem & Molecular Biol. **Research Statement & Publications:** Studies of the mechanisms that control RNA synthesis by RNA polymerase after initiation; genetic and biochemical dissection of RNA polymerase structure and function during RNA chain elongation. **Mailing Address:** Dept Bact, Univ Wis, Rm 190 Biochem 420 Henry Mall 1550 Linden Dr, Madison, WI 53706-1567. **Fax:** 608-262-9865. **E-Mail:** landick@bact.wisc.edu

LANDING, ED, BIOSTRATIGRAPHY & SYSTEMATICS OF EARLY-MIDDLE CAMBRAIN SHELLED ORGANISMS, DEPOSITIONAL ENVIRONMENTS OF CONTINENTAL SLOPE & PLATFORMAL SHALE BASINS. **Personal Data:** b Milwaukee, Wis, August 10, 1949. **Education:** Univ Wis, BSc, 1972; Univ Mich, MSc, 1975, PhD (paleont), 1978. **Professional Experience:** PRIN SCIENTIST PALEONT, NY STATE MUS, as of 2004; STATE PALEONTOLOGIST, NY STATE GEOL SURV, 1986-; adj asstprof, State Univ NY, Albany, 1983-; fel, Univ Toronto, 1980; res assoc, Nat res Coun US, 1979; fel, Univ Walterloo Can, 1978. **Memberships:** Paleont Soc; Soc Econ Paleontologists & Mineralogists. **Research Statement & Publications:** Reconstructing the evolutionary relationships, habitats, paleogeography and biostratigraphic utility of the earliest skeletalized metazoans. **Mailing Address:** NY State Mus, 125 Manning Blvd, Albany, NY 12203. **Fax:** 518-473-8496. **E-Mail:** elanding@.mail.nysed.gov

LANDIS, ABRAHAM L, CHEMISTRY. **Personal Data:** b New York, NY, May 25, 1928; m 1957, Eileen; c Daniel & Lawrence. **Education:** City Col NY, BS, 1951; Univ Kans, PhD (chem), 1955. **Professional Experience:** RETIRED; sr staff scientist, Lockheed Missile Res & Develop Co, 1991-1994; sr staff scientist, Lockheed Aeronaut Syst Co, 1986-1991; sr scientist, Hughes Aircraft Co, El Segundo, Calif, 1980-1986; sr staff chemist, Hughes Aircraft Co, El Segundo, Calif, 1961-1980; sr res chemist, Atomics Int Div, NAm Rockwell, Inc, 1956-1961; aeronaut res scientist, Nat Adv Comt Aeronaut, 1955-1956; polymers consult. **Memberships:** Am Chem Soc; Sigma Xi; Am Inst Chem; Am Ceramic Soc; Soc Advan Mat & Process Eng. **Research Statement & Publications:** High temperature polymers; polymer chemistry; vacuum technology; organic synthesis; organometallic polymers; aerospace materials. **Mailing Address:** 1457 Bellevue Ave No 9, Burlingame, CA 94010. **E-Mail:** allandis@aol.com

LANDIS, ARTHUR MELVIN, HETEROPOLY COMPLEXES, SEPARATIONS SCIENCE. **Personal Data:** b Lancaster, Pa, January 21, 1944; m Linda; c Margaret & Ben. **Education:** Elizabethtown Col, BS, 1966; Ohio Univ, MS, 1970; Georgetown Univ, PhD (chem), 1977. **Professional Experience:** ASSOC PROF CHEM, EMPORIA STATE UNIV, EMPORIA, Kans, 1991-; asst prof, Emporia State Univ, Emporia, Kans, 1987-1991; consult, Springfiled Wire, 1986-1989; lectr chem, Western New Eng Col, beginning 1984; asst prof chem, Col Our Lady Elms, Chicopee, Kans, 1983-1987; vis prof chem, Georgetown Univ, 1983; mem, Gordon Res Conf, 1980-1982; sr res chemist, UOP, Inc, Signal-Allied Co, Des Plaines, Ill, 1977-1982; vis prof chem, Dickinson Col, Carlisle, Pa, 1975-1977; vis prof, Georgetown Univ, Wash, DC, 1973-1975; head teaching fel chem, Georgetown Univ, Wash, DC, 1970-1975. **Memberships:** sr mem Am Chem Soc; sr mem Sigma Xi. **Research Statement & Publications:** Heteropolies and polyoxometallates; preparation and properties of organo-heteropoly polymers; configurations and conformations of species; separation theory of solutes via interaction with inorganic solids, for example, preparative liquid chromatography. **Mailing Address:** Dept Chem, Emporia State Univ, 211E Sci Hall, Emporia, KS 66801-6314. **E-Mail:** landisar@emporia.edu

LANDIS, DENNIS MICHAEL DOYLE, NEUROLOGY, NEUROSCIENCE. **Personal Data:** b Boston, Mass, August 12, 1945; m 1970, Story; c Michael C. **Education:** Harvard Col, AB, 1967; Harvard Med Sch, MD, 1971; Am Bd Internal Med, dipl, 1975; Am Bd Psychiat & Neurol, dipl, 1979. **Honors & Awards:** teacher investr award, Javits Neurosci investr award, 1989. **Professional Experience:** GILBERT HUMPHREY PROF & CHMN, CASE WESTERN RES UNIV, 1995-; prof neurol & neuroscil, Sch Med, Case Western Res Univ, 1988-1995; assoc prof neurol & Ctr Neuroscience, develop genetics & anat, Case Western Res Univ, 1988-1990; NEUROLOGIST, UNIV HOSPS CLEVELAND, 1985-; attend physician, Neurol Serv, Vet Admin Hosp, Cleveland, 1985-; dir, Lab Neurocytol, 1985-; Neurol & Consult Serv, Univ Hosps Cleveland, 1985-; assoc prof neurol, develop genetics & anat, Case Western Res Univ, 1985-1988; asst prof neurol-Neuroscience, Harvard Med Sch, 1983-1985; asst neurologist, Neurol Serv & Neurol Consult Serv & dir, Muscular Dystrophy Asn Clin, 1979-1985; lectr, Mass Gen Hosp, Marine Biol Lab & Case Western Res Univ, 1978-; attend physician, Neurol Serv & Neurol Consult Serv & dir, Muscular Dystrophy Asn Clin, 1978-1985; assoc neuropathologist, Eunice Kennedy Shriver Ctr Ment Retardation, Waltham, Mass, 1978-1985; from instr to asst prof neurol, Harvard Med Sch, 1978-1983; asst neurol, Mass Gen Hosp, 1978-1979; teacher investr award, Nat Inst Neurol & Communicative Dis & Stroke, 1978; Instr Neurobiology, Marine Biol Labs, Woods Hole, Mass, 1977-. **Memberships:** Soc Neuroscience; Am Acad Neurol; Am Soc Cell Biol; Am Neurol Asn; Asn of University Professors of Neurology. **Research Statement & Publications:** Structure and function at synaptic junctions in the central nervous system; membrane and cytoplasmic structure in astrocytes; astrocyte function during development, in the adult, and in the response to injury; thrombolytic therapy for acute ischemic stroke. **Mailing Address:** Dept Neurol, Univ Hosp cleveland, 11100 Euclid Ave, Cleveland, OH 44106. **Fax:** 216-844-7443. **E-Mail:** dennis.landis@case.edu

LANDIS, E K, CHEMICAL ENGINEERING. **Personal Data:** b Pulaski, Va, June 17, 1930; m 1965, c 1. **Education:** Va Polytech Inst, BS, 1954; Univ Va, MChE, 1955; Carnegie Inst Technol, PhD (chem eng), 1959. **Professional Experience:** PROF & HEAD EMER, UNIV ALA, as of 2005; Ford Found prof, Carnegie Inst Technol, 1964; consult, US ArmyMissile Command, 1961- & US Bur Mines, 1962-; from asst prof to prof chem eng, Univ Ala, Tuscaloosa, 1959-1988. **Memberships:** Am Inst Chem Engrs; Am Soc Eng Educ. **Research Statement & Publications:** Combustion instability; thermodynamics of solution; mass transfer in fixed beds; mass and energy transfer across living cell walls. **Mailing Address:** 3309 Royal Scots Way, Ft Smith, AR 72908-9327.

LANDIS, FRED, mechanical engineering; deceased, see previous edition for last biography

LANDIS, JOHN W, nuclear power safety; deceased, see previous edition for last biography

LANDIS, PHILLIP SHERWOOD, ORGANIC CHEMISTRY, AGRICULTURE & FOOD CHEMISTRY. **Personal Data:** b York, Pa, July 29, 1922; m 1986, Cornelia; c Michael & Bryan. **Education:** Franklin & Marshall Col, BS, 1943; Univ Ky, MS, 1947; Northwestern Univ, PhD (chem), 1958. **Honors & Awards:** Outstanding Sci Award, Am Chem Soc, 1986. **Professional Experience:** RETIRED; consult, Int Lubricants Inc, beginning 1986; consult, Mobil Res & Develop, 1983-1985; adj prof, Glassboro State Col, 1981-1994; mgr prod res group, Mobil Res & Develop Corp, 1969-1983; sr res assoc, Mobil Oil Corp, 1966-1969; res assoc, Mobil Oil Corp, 1963-1966; res chemist, Mobil Oil Corp, 1947-1963; chemist, Cities Serv Refining Corp, 1943-1945. **Memberships:** Am Chem Soc; Sigma Xi. **Research Statement & Publications:** Mechanisms and kinetics of organic reactions; pyrolysis of organic compounds; organo-sulfur compounds; petrochemicals; radical reactions; chemistry of jojoba oil; chemistry of plant oils; lubricant additives from plant oils. **Mailing Address:** 5753 Independence Circle, Alexandria, VA 22312-2629. **E-Mail:** shiblandis@aol.com

LANDIS, STORY CLELAND, NEUROBIOLOGY. **Personal Data:** b New York, NY, May 14, 1945; m 1969. **Education:** Wellesley Col, BA, 1967; Harvard Univ, MA, 1970, PhD (biol), 1973. **Professional Experience:** DIR, NAT INST NEUROL DIS & STROKE, as of 2003; scientific dir, NAT Inst Neurol Dis & Stroke, beginning 1995; assoc prof, dept pharmacol, Case Western Res Univ, beginning 1985; res fel neurobiology, Harvard Med Sch, 1975-, instr, beginning 1980; NIH fel neuropath, 1973-1975. **Memberships:** Am Asn Anatomists; Soc Neuroscience; Am Soc Cell Biol. **Research Statement & Publications:** Developmental neurobiology; cell biology. **Mailing Address:** Off Dir, Nat Inst Neurol Dis & Stroke, Rm 8A52, Bldg 31, Bethesda, MD 20892-2540.

LANDIS, VINCENT J, INORGANIC CHEMISTRY. **Personal Data:** b Minneapolis, Minn, October 27, 1928; m 1950, c 6. **Education:** Wash State Univ, BS, 1950; Univ Minn, PhD (inorg chem), 1957. **Professional Experience:** PROF EMER CHEM, SAN DIEGO STATE UNIV, as of 2003; prof chem, San Diego State Univ, 1965-1997; Richland fac fel, Univ-Wash, 1964-1965; From instr to assoc prof, San Diego State Univ, 1954-1965. **Memberships:** Am Chem Soc. **Research Statement & Publications:** Metal coordination compounds; radiochemistry. **Mailing Address:** Dept Chem, San Diego State Univ, San Diego, CA 92182-0001.

LANDIS, WAYNE G, AQUATIC TOXICOLOGY, METABOLISM OF XENOBIOTICS. **Personal Data:** b Washington, DC, January 20, 1952. **Education:** Wake Forest Univ, BA, 1974; Ind Univ, MA, 1978, PhD (zoology), 1979. **Professional Experience:** PROF & DIR, INST ENVIRON TOXICOL, HUXLEY COL ENVIRON, WESTERN WASH UNIV, as of 2005; CHAIR, DEPT ENVIRON SCI, HUXLEY COL ENVIRON, WESTERN WASH UNIV, as of 2005; RES BIOLOGIST, TOXICOL DIV, CHEM RES & DEVELOP CTR, 1982-; environ & health scientist, environ & health studies group, Franklin Res Ctr, 1979-1982; assoc instr biol, Dept Biol, Ind Univ, 1974-1979. **Memberships:** Genetics Soc Am; Soc Protozoologists; Am Soc Testing & Mat; Soc StudyEvolution; AAAS; Sigma Xi; Soc Environ Toxicol & Chem. **Research Statement & Publications:** Toxicity, fate and impact on community structure of environmental toxicants on aquatic systems; characterization of the DF Pases in Tetrahymena thermophila; ecology and evolution of paramecium; structure activity derivations for toxicologic endpoints; holds two US patents. **Mailing Address:** Inst Environ Toxicol, Huxley Col Western Wash Univ, 516 High St ES 518, Bellingham, WA 98225-9180. **Fax:** 360-650-6556. **E-Mail:** landis@cc.wwu.edu

LANDIS, WILLIAM JOEL, STRUCTURAL BIOLOGY, BIOMINERALIZATION. **Personal Data:** b Clarksville, Tenn, March 1, 1943. **Education:** Univ Mass, BA, 1965, SM, 1967; Mass Inst Technol, MS, 1967, PhD (biophys), 1972. **Honors & Awards:** C E Hall Award, Electron Micros Soc Am, 1991. **Professional Experience:** PROF, DEPT MICROBIOLOGY, N EASTRN OHIO UNIV COL MED, 2005-; MEM GRAD FAC, KENT STATE UNIV, 1999-; prof & chmn, Dept Biochem & Molecular Path, N Eastern Ohio Univ Col Med, 1998-2004; prin investr, NASA, 1988-; sr res scholar, Fulbright Found, 1988-1989; assoc prof orthop surg, cellular biol & anat, Harvard Med Sch, 1984-1996; prin investr, William F Milton Fund, 1984-1986; asst prof Orthop Surg, Harvard Med Sch, 1981-1984; prin investr, Whitaker Health Sci Found, 1981-1983; sr res assoc, Children's Hosp, Boston, 1980-1998; prin investr, NIH, 1980-1983 & 1992-; sci consult, var co & corp, 1975-; res assoc, Children's Hosp, Boston, 1975-1980; res assoc, anat, 1974-1981; res asst Orthop Surg, Children's Hosp, Boston, 1972-1975; assoc, Orthop Surg, Harvard Med Sch, 1972-1974. **Memberships:** Orthop Res Soc; Microbeam Analysis Soc; Int Asn Dent Res; Electron MicroscopeSoc Am; Am Soc Gravitational & Space Biol; Fulbright Asn. **Research Statement & Publications:** Characterizing the effects of force (mechanical, electromagnetic and gravitational) on the structure of the skeleton and dentition and mineralized tissues. **Mailing Address:** Col Med, NorthEastern Ohio Univ, 4209 St Rt 44 PO Box 95, Rootstown, OH 44272-0095. **Fax:** 330-325-5925. **E-Mail:** wjl@neoucom.edu

LANDISS, DANIEL JAY, FORENSIC ENGINEERING, COMPUTERS IN EDUCATION. **Personal Data:** b Alton, Ill, June 11, 1943. **Education:** Wash Univ, St Louis, BS, 1964, MS, 1966. **Professional Experience:** Vis prof, Czech Tech Univ, Prague, 1988-1989; assoc, Senne, Kelsey & Assocs, 1985-; PROF TECHNOL, ST LOUIS COMMUNITY COL, 1985-; OWNER & CHIEF EXEC OFFICER, QUEST INSTRUMENTS LTD, 1979-; chief engr, Artronix, Inc, 1972-1973; dir, Eng Tech Serv, Wash Univ, 1967-1969 & Biomed Eng Lab, Lewis-Howe Co, 1969-1972; dir, Eng Technical Serv, Wash Univ, 1967-1969; Res engr, Mallinckrodt InstRadiol, 1966-1967; res engr, Mallinckrodt Inst Radiol, 1966-1967; teaching assist & res assist, Biomed Eng Lab, Wash Univ, 1964-1966. **Memberships:** Am Radio Relay League; Am Soc Eng Edu; Am Tech Edu Assoc; Am Voc Assoc; Assoc Career & Tech Edu; Assoc Comput Machinery; Inst Elect & Electronics Engs. **Research Statement & Publications:** Biomedical ultrasound diagnostics; Digital data logging and analysis; Forensic engineering; International education. **Mailing Address:** St Louis Community Col, 3400 Pershall Rd, St Louis, MO 63135. **Fax:** 314-513-4718. **E-Mail:** dan@stlcc.info

LANDMAN, ALFRED, ATOMIC PHYSICS. **Personal Data:** b Vienna, Austria, June 29, 1933; American citizen; m 1967, c 2. **Education:** Univ Pa, AB, 1954; Columbia Univ, PhD (physics), 1963. **Professional Experience:** GEN ENGR, TRANSP SYSTS CTR, US DEPT TRANSP, 1970-; physicist, NASA Electronics Res Ctr, 1967-1970; adv res engr, Gen Tel & Electronics Labs, 1966-1967; res engr physics, Gen Tel & Electronics Labs, 1965-1966; res assoc chem physics, Inst StudyMetals, Univ Chicago, 1963-1964; res assoc, Columbia Univ, 1963; Lectr physics, Brooklyn Col, 1959-1962. **Memberships:** Am Phys Soc. **Research Statement & Publications:** Spectroscopy; optical pumping; gas laser molecular stark effect; synthetic fuels. **Mailing Address:** 29 Tyler Rd, Lexington, MA 02173.

LANDMAN, DONALD ALAN, THEORETICAL & COMPUTATIONAL PLASMA, ATOMIC PHYSICS. **Personal Data:** b New York, NY, April 23, 1938; m 1970, c 2. **Education:** Columbia Univ, AB, 1959, MA, 1961, PhD (physics), 1965. **Professional Experience:** RES PHYSICIST, MISSION RES CORP, 1985-; from assoc astron to astron, Inst Astron, Univ Haw, 1972-1985; res scientist, Cornell Aeronaut Lab, Buffalo, 1970 & Advan Res Instrument Systs Inc, 1971; asst prof physics, NY Univ, Bronx, 1965-1969. **Memberships:** NY Acad Sci; Am Phys Soc; Int Astron Union. **Research Statement & Publications:** Theoretical and computational plasma and atomic physics applied to atmospheric problems; research in solar physics. **Mailing Address:** Mission Res Corp, 735 State St PO Drawer 719, Santa Barbara, CA 93102. **Fax:** 805-962-8530.

LANDMAN, MARGARET, ECONOMICS. **Personal Data:** b Providence, RI, September 4, 1953; c Cyntha Guretin, Melissa, Robert Barber & Benjamin. **Education:** Brown Univ, AB, 1981, AM, 1983, PhD, 1989. **Professional Experience:** CHAIR, DEPT ECON, BRIDGEWATER STATE COL, as of 2005; DIR, CTR ECON EDUC, BRIDGEWATER STATE COL, as of 2005; pi Mass Dept Edu grant, Mass Dept Edu, 2002; pi 2CII grant, Commonwealth Info Techol, 2001; staff mem, Jordan Fiore Justice Sch, Bridgewater State Col, 2000-2001; PROF ECONS, BRIDGEWATER STATE COL, 1987-; instr econs, Univ RI, 1983-1984. **Memberships:** Am Econ Asn; Eastern Econ Asn; Western Econ Asn; Comt Status of Women in Econ Profession. **Mailing Address:** Bridgewater State Col, Dept Econ, Hunt Hall Rm Rm 115, Bridgewater, MA 02325. **Fax:** 508-531-6136. **E-Mail:** mlandman@bridgew.edu

LANDMAN, UZI, MICROMECHANICS, CHEMICAL PHYSICS. **Personal Data:** b Tel-Aviv, Israel, May 22, 1944. **Education:** Hebrew Univ, Israel, BSc, 1966; Weizman Inst Sci, Israel, MSc, 1967; Israel InstTechnol, DSc(theoret chem), 1969. **Professional Experience:** FULLER E CALLAWAY CHAIR COMPUT MAT SCI, GA INST TECHNOL, as of 2003; DIR, CTR COMPUTATIONAL MAT SCI, 1992-; Ed, J Computational Mat Sci, 1991-; REGENTS PROF, SCH PHYSICS, GA INST TECHNOL, 1988-; assoc dean res, Col Sci & LibStudies, 1988-1989; NORDITA PROF, CHALMERS UNIV TECHNOL, INST THEORETPHYSICS, GOTEBORG, SWEDEN, 1984-; from assoc prof to prof, Chalmers Univ Technol, Inst Theoret Physics, Goteborg, Sweden, 1975-1988; sr fel, Inst Fundamental Studies, DeptPhysics & Astron, Univ Rochester, 1975-1977; scientist, Webster Xerox Res Lab, 1972-1975; resasst prof physics, Univ Ill, Urbana, 1971-1972; vis asst prof chem, Univ Calif, Santa Barbara, 1970-1971; asst prof chem, Israel Inst Technol, 1969-1970. **Memberships:** Fel Am Phys Soc; Am Vacuum Soc. **Research Statement & Publications:** Formulation and application of a multiple scattering theory of inelastic electron diffraction from metal surfaces leading to the earliest precision determination of surface plasmon dispersion relation for aluminum; statistical physics; chemical physics; computational physics. **Mailing Address:** Sch Physics, Ga Inst Technol, Howey-W411/W410, Atlanta, GA 30332. **Fax:** 404-894-7747. **E-Mail:** uzi.landman@physics.gatech.edu

LANDMESSER, LYNN THERESE, PHYSIOLOGY, NEUROBIOLOGY. **Personal Data:** b Santa Ana, Calif, November 30, 1943. **Education:** Univ Calif, Los Angeles, BA, 1965, PhD (neurophysiol), 1969. **Honors & Awards:** Yntema Mem Lectr, State Univ NY, Syracuse, 1981; Twelfth Ann TrotterLectr, Dept Anat & Neurobiology, Wash Univ, 1987. **Professional Experience:** GARVIN PROF & CHMN, DEPT NEUROSCIENCES, CASE WESTERN UNIV, as of 2003; Mem sci adv bd, Nat Inst Child Health & Develop, NIH, 1989-; Wiersma visprof neuroscience, Calif Inst Technol, 1989; dir, NIH Postdoctoral Training Grant Neuroscience, 1988-; NSF grant, 1988-1991; Arturo Rosenblueth distinguished prof, Ctr Advan Studies, Mexico City, 1987; prof, dept physiol & neurobiology, Univ Conn, Storrs, beginning 1985; Jacob Javitsinvestr award, 1985-1992; Grass Found vis scientist, Anat Dept, Emory Univ, Ga, 1984; prof, Physiol Sect, Biol Sci Group, 1983-1985; mem, NIH Study Sect Neurol B, 1982-1985; SocialIssues Comt, Soc Neuroscience, 1982-1985; assoc ed, J Neuroscience, 1981-1985; mem, Sci Adv Comt, Nat Spinal Cord Injury Found, 1979-1987; assoc ed, Develop Biol, 1977-1981; NIH grant, 1972-1985; from asst prof to prof biol, Dept Biol, Yale Univ, 1972-1983; NIH fel, Physiol Dept, Col Med, Univ Utah, 1969-1971, Dept Regulatory Biol, Univ Conn, 1971-1972. **Memberships:** Soc Neurosci; Am Physiol Soc; Soc Develop Biol (pres 1988-1989); fel AAAS. **Research Statement & Publications:** Neurophysiology. **Mailing Address:** Dept Neurosciences, Sch Med, Case Western Res Univ, Rm E653, 10900 Euclid Ave, Cleveland, OH 44106-4975. **Fax:** 216-368-4650. **E-Mail:** ltl@case.edu

LANDO, BARBARA ANN, ALGEBRA. **Personal Data:** b Elizabeth, NJ, December 7, 1940; m 1965. **Education:** Georgian Court Col, BA, 1962; Rutgers Univ, New Brunswick, MS, 1964, PhD (math), 1969. **Professional Experience:** STATE DIR, ELDERHOSTEL, 1990-; from asst prof to prof, Univ Alaska, Fairbanks, 1979-1990; instr math, Douglass Col, Rutgers Univ, NB, 1969. **Memberships:** Am Math Soc; Math Asn Am; Inst Elec & Electronics Engrs; Asn Comput Mach. **Research Statement & Publications:** Differential algebra; formal language theory. **Mailing Address:** 1881 Yankovich Rd, Fairbanks, AK 99709.

LANDO, JEROME B, POLYMER SCIENCE. **Personal Data:** b Brooklyn, NY, May 23, 1932; m 1962, Geula; c Jeffrey, Daniel & Avital. **Education:** Cornell Univ, BA, 1953; Polytech Inst Brooklyn, PhD (chem), 1963. **Honors & Awards:** Distinguished Alumnus Citation, Polytech Univ, 1990; Int Res Award, Soc Plastics Engrs, 1994; Int Education Award, Soc Plastics Engrs, 1999. **Professional Experience:** PRES, EDISON POLYMER INOVATION CORP, 2000-; dir, Polymer Microdevices Lab, 1987-; vis prof, Weismann Inst, Israel, 1987; tech dir, Edison Polymer Inovation Corp, 1985-2000; chmn dept, Case Western Res Univ, 1978-1985; vis prof, Univ Mainz, 1974; PROF MACROMOLECULAR SCI, CASE WESTERN RES UNIV, 1974-; Humboldt Found Sr Am Scientist Award, 1974; assoc prof, Case Western Res Univ, 1968-1974; asst prof polymer sci & eng, Case Western Res Univ, 1965-1968; res chemist, Camille Dreyfus Lab, Res Triangle Inst, 1963-1965; fel, Polytech Inst Brooklyn, 1963; mem adv bd, J Molecular Electronics, Mat Lett & Polymers Advan Technol. **Memberships:** Am Chem Soc; Am Crystallog Asn; Am Phys Soc; Sigma Xi; Soc Plastics Engrs. **Research Statement & Publications:** Polymer physical chemistry; solid state reactions, especially polymerization reactions and polymer crystal structure; synthesis of stereoregular polymers, pyroelectric and piezoelectric polymers; electronic and optical properties of polymers and thin film. **Mailing Address:** Dept Macromolecular Sci, Case Western Res Univ, Cleveland, OH 44106. **E-Mail:** jbl2@po.cwru.edu

LANDOLFI, NICHOLAS F, MOLECULAR IMMUNOLOGY. **Personal Data:** b Ashtabula, Ohio, September 2, 1955; m 1988. **Education:** Ohio State Univ, BS, 1977; Miami Univ, MS, 1980; Univ Tex, PhD (immunol), 1984. **Professional Experience:** STAFF SCIENTIST, PROTEIN DESIGN LABS, 1988-; Res fel, Univ TexSouthwestern Med Sch, 1985-1988 & Leukemia Soc Am, 1987-1988. **Memberships:** Am Asn Immunologists; AAAS; Sigma Xi. **Research Statement & Publications:** Structure and function analysis of molecules involved in immune response; differential control of genes in the cells of the immune system. **Mailing Address:** 34801 Campus Dr, Fremont, CA 94555.

LANDOLL, LEO MICHAEL, POLYMER CHEMISTRY. **Personal Data:** b Cleveland, Ohio, October 11, 1950; m 1971, Mary; c 2. **Education:** Kent State Univ, BA, 1970; Univ Del, MBA, 1982; Univ Akron, PhD (polymer sci), 1975. **Professional Experience:** RES ASSOC, APPL EXTR TECH Films 1999-current; Dir. Technology APPL. EXTR TECH Nets 1994-1999; Hercules, Inc, 1974-1994. **Memberships:** Am Chem Soc. **Research Statement & Publications:** Acrylic UV polymerization; Polymer synthesis and processing related to thermoplastic and thermoset systems, fibers, films, property correlations; Synthesis and structure property relations of natural and synthetic water soluble polymers. **Mailing Address:** AET Inc, 15 Read's Way, New Castle, DE 19720. **Fax:** 302-326-5503. **E-Mail:** slandoll@aetinc.com

LANDOLPH, JOSEPH RICHARD, CHEMICAL & GENETIC TOXICOLOGY, MOLECULAR BIOLOGY OF CHEMICAL CARCINOGENESIS. **Personal Data:** b Upper Darby, Pa, November 9, 1948; m 1980, Alice; c Joseph R III & Louis S. **Education:** Drexel Univ, BS, in Chemistry, 1971; Univ Calif, Berkeley, PhD (chem), 1976; Postdoctoral Fellow, Univ Southern Calif, Comprehensive Cancer Center, Los Angeles, Calif, I977-I980. **Honors & Awards:** Merck Award Dept Chem Drexel Inst Technol, Phila PA, 1971; Superior Cadet Award, US Army ROTC Drexel Inst of Technol, Phile PA, 1971; Robert Cleland Excellence in Teaching Award, Dept of Pathol, USC Sch of Med, 1985; ICI Traveling Lectureship Award, from US Soc of Toxicology, 1990. **Professional Experience:** Review panel mem, Nat Res Coun & Nat Acad Sci, 1989-1999; investgr, Environ Health, US NIEHS, 1994, 1995, 1999; grant reviewer, Alcohol or Toxicology Study section IV, NIH, 1999-2000; grant reviewer, Path Study Sect, NIH, 1997, 1999; ICI Traveling Lectureship, U. S. Soc Toxicol, 1990; Howard Hughes fellowship reviewer, Genetics Panel, Nat Res Coun, 1989, I998, I999, 2000, 2001; ASSOC PROF MOLECULAR MICROBIOL & IMMUNOL, PATH & MOLECULAR PHARMACOL & TOXICOL WITH TENURE, USC/NORRIS COMPREHENSIVE CANCER CTR, KECK SCH MED, UNIV SOUTHERN CALIF, 1987-; consult, Am Petrol Inst, 1985-1987; prin investr, Nat Cancer Inst, Nat Inst Environ Health Sci & Environ Protection Agency grants, 1983-2001; asst prof, microbiol & path, Comprehensive Cancer Ctr, Univ Southern Calif, 1982-1987; asst prof path, Comprehensive Cancer Ctr, Univ Southern Calif, 1980-1982; postdoctoral res fel chem carcinogenesis, Comprehensive Cancer Ctr, Univ Southern Calif, 1977-1980; postdoctoral fel, Am Cancer Soc, 1977-1979; res asst chem, Dept Chem, Univ Calif, Berkeley, 1971-1976; 2nd LT-CAPT, US Army reserve, 1971-1977; chem technician, Smith Kline & Fr Co, Philadelphia, Pa, 1969; Qual control chemist, Rohn Haas Co, Philadelphia, Pa, 1968; consult, Ozone Criteria Doc, Environ Protection Agency, US; Grant reviewer, U. S E. P. A., I984-I989; Grant reviewer, NIEHS, I985, I994, I995, I999, 2004, 2005. **Memberships:** Am Asn Cancer Res; Am Soc Cell Biol; U. S. Soc of Toxicology; Vice-Pres elect Metals Specialty Section, U. S. Soc of Toxicology, 2000-2001; Vice-Pres Metals Specialty Section, U. S. S. O. T, 2001-2002; Pres, Metals Specialty Section of U. S. SOT 2002-2003; Counsilor, Metals Specialty Section, U. S. SOT, 2003-2004. **Research Statement & Publications:** Mechanisms of chemical carcinogenesis studied in cultured mammalian cells; molecular biology of oncogene activation and tumor suppressor gene in-activation caused by organic chemical carcinogens and carcinogenic metal salts, including nickel, chromium, and arsenic compounds; human carcinogenesis mechanisms; molecular oncology. **Mailing Address:** Cancer Res Lab, Rm #218, 1303 N Mission Rd, USC/Norris Comprehensive Cancer Center, Keck Sch Med, Univ Southern Calif, Los Angeles, CA 90033. **Fax:** 323-224-7679. **E-Mail:** landolph@usc.edu

LANDOLT, ARLO UDELL, ASTRONOMY. **Personal Data:** b Highland, Ill, September 29, 1935; m 1966, Eunice J Casper; c Lynda, Barbara, Vicky, Debra & Jennifer. **Education:** Miami Univ, BA, 1955; Ind Univ, MA, 1960, PhD (astron), 1963. **Honors & Awards:** George van Biesbroeck Prize, 1995 Awarded the 1995 Van Biesbroeck award for service to Astron; LSU distinguished fac award, 1998. **Professional Experience:** Space Telescope Sci Inst grant, 1985-1990; mem, US Nat Comt, Int Astron Union, 1980-1989 & 1995-; pres fac senate, dept physics & astron, La State Univ, Baton Rouge, 1979-1980; Air Force Off Sci Res, grants, 1977-1987; prog dir, NSF, Washington, DC, 1975-1976; actg chmn, dept physics & astron, La State Univ, Baton Rouge, 1972 & 1973; dir observ, LA State Univ, Baton Rouge, 1970-1988; secy, sect D Astron, AAAS, 1970-1978; PROF PHYSICS & ASTRON, LA STATE UNIV, BATON ROUGE, 1968-; NASA, 1965 & 1992; Grad Res Coun res grants, La State Univ, Baton Rouge, 1964-1976; res grants, 1964, 1966, 1969, 1971, 1973, 1975 & 1992-1997; Res Corp, 1964; from asst prof to assoc prof, LA State Univ, Baton Rouge, 1962-1968; Mem first wintering-over party, Int Geophys Year Amundson-Scott S Pole Sta, Antarctica, 1957; scientist aurora & airglow, US Int Geophys Year Comt, 1956-1958; guest investr, Dyer Observ, Vanderbilt Univ, Goethe Link Observ, Ind Univ, Kitt Peak Nat Observ, Cerro Tololo Inter-Am Observ & Las Campanas Observ, La Serena, Chile. **Memberships:** Fel AAAS; Int Astron Union; Am Astron Soc (secy, 1980-1989 & 1995-); Royal Astron Soc Eng; Sigma Xi; Explorer's Club Mem Am asn advancement of sci Newcomb Cleveland prize comm of Judges 1975-1977; Mem, LSU fac senate review and long range planning comm, 1990-1992; chair 1991-1992; Mem steering comm of LSU self-study for accreditation, 1981-1983; (chair of Stannford V - comm on faculty); Mem oversight comm to review Astron centers sections of the nat sci found, 1984; Vice chairman of US nat Delegation to XVIIIth int astron union general assembly, Patras, Greece, 1982; mem, nominating comm of AIP governing Board (1985-1987) and chair of comm, 1986; mem comm on comms Am inst of physics (AIP), 1996-1999; mem and chair (1997-2002), comm on Physics prog policy physics resources comm. Am inst of Physics (AIP), 1996-2002; mem nominating comm section D (Astronomy), Am. **Research Statement & Publications:** Photometric investigations of star clusters, variable stars, and eclipsing binaries; standard astronomical photometric systems; galactic structure. **Mailing Address:** Dept Physics & Astron, La State Univ, Baton Rouge, LA 70803-4001. **Fax:** 225-578-5855. **E-Mail:** landolt@rouge.phys.lsu.edu

LANDOLT, JACK PETER, SPATIAL DISORIENTATION, BIODYNAMICS. **Personal Data:** b Zurich, Switz, March 17, 1934; Canadian citizen; m 1964, C Gwendolyn Delmas; c Lydia M, Phillip L, Monica A, Christian L & Mark D. **Education:** Univ Ottawa, BASc, 1959, MSc, 1962; Iowa State Univ Sci & Technol, PhD (elec eng), 1968. **Honors & Awards:** A Jaan Saber Mem Award, Can Aeronaut & Space Inst, 1992; Sidney P Leverett, Jr, Environ Sci Award, Aerospace Med Asn, 1994; NTW Award Excellence, Transp Asn Can, 1995; Hon memb, Civil Aviation Medical Asn, 2002. **Professional Experience:** HEAD, PLANS & POLICY, DEFENSE & CIVIL INST ENVIRON MED, (R&D CANAND-TORONTO) 1989-; sect head, aerospace physiol, 1986-1989; sect head biophys, Defense & Civil Inst Environ Med, 1980-1986; Aerospace Med Panel, Adv Group, Aerospace Res & Develop, NATO, 1978-; Mem, Can Adv Comt, Int Stand Org, 1977-1989; sect head disorientation biodynamics, Defense & Civil Inst Environ Med, 1976-1980; group head motion sickness biodynamics, Defense & Civil Inst Environ Med, 1975-1976; defense scientist vestibular physiol, Defense & Civil Inst Environ Med, 1968-1975; Defense scientist oper res, Can Army Oper Res Estab, 1961-1965. **Memberships:** Soc Neurosci; Barany Soc. **Research Statement & Publications:** Neurobiology of peripheral vestibular apparatus; space adaptation syndrome and circular vection; vestibular-visual interactions; motion cues in simulation sickness; impact protection of the human; author or coauthor of over 100 publications; high altitude and high acceleration physiology. **Mailing Address:** Defense R&D Canada-Toronto, 1133 Sheppard Ave W, Toronto, ON M3M 3B9, Can.

LANDOLT, PETER JOHN, INSECT COMMUNICATION, CHEMICAL ECOLOGY. **Personal Data:** b Cincinnati, Ohio, June 13, 1952. **Education:** Northern Mich Univ, BS, 1974; Wash State Univ, MS, 1976, PhD (entom), 1978. **Professional Experience:** RES LEADER & LOCATION COORDR, USDA AGR RES SERV, WAPATO, 2002-; RES ENTOMOLOGIST, USDA AGR RES SERV, WAPATO, 1996-2002; res entomologist, USDA Agr Res Serv, Gainesville, 1984-1996; res entomologist, Miami, 1981-1983; Res assoc, Fresno, 1979-1981; res asst entomol, Wash State Univ, 1974-1978. **Research Statement & Publications:** Study of chemically mediated behavior important to host, food, and mate-finding strategies of insects, with emphasis on cabbage looper moths and tephritid fruit flies. **Mailing Address:** USDA Agr Res serv, Yakima Agr Res Lab, 5230 Konnowac Pass Rd, Wapato, WA 98951.

LANDOLT, ROBERT GEORGE, ORGANIC CHEMISTRY. **Personal Data:** b Houston, Tex, April 4, 1939; m 1962, c 3. **Education:** Austin Col, BA, 1961; Univ Tex, PhD (org chem), 1965. **Professional Experience:** Dir, Res Div, Tex Higher Educ Coord Bd, 1991; Cong fel, Am Chem Soc, 1986-1987; consult & contractor, US Navy, 1982-1984; PROF, TEX WESLEYAN UNIV, 1981-; chmn, Chem Dept, 1981-1985; sr scientist, Radian Corp, 1980-1981; Resident consult, Columbus Labs, Battelle Mem Inst, 1974-1975; chmn dept, Muskingum Col, 1971-1974; from asst prof to assoc prof org chem, Muskingum Col, 1967-1980; Res assoc org chem, Univ Ill, 1965-1967. **Memberships:** AAAS; Am Asn Univ Prof; Am Chem Soc; Sigma Xi. **Research Statement & Publications:** Abnormal claisen rearrangement and reactions in aprotic polar solvents; nitroso aromatic compounds; oxidation of coal and coal model compounds; computer assisted information retrieval; origin of organic pollutants in water; hypochlorite reactions with organics. **Mailing Address:** Dept Chem, Tex Wesleyan Univ, Ft Worth, TX 76105. **Fax:** 817-531-4425. **E-Mail:** landoltr@txwes.edu

LANDOLT, ROBERT RAYMOND, HEALTH PHYSICS. **Personal Data:** b Sherman, Tex, May 11, 1937; m 1970, Alice; c Sarah, Doris & George. **Education:** Austin Col, BA, 1959; Univ Kans, MS, 1961; Purdue Univ, PhD (bionucleonics), 1967. **Professional Experience:** PROF EMER HEALTH SCI, PURDUE UNIV, West Lafayette, IND, as of 2004; prof health sci, Purdue Univ, West Lafayette, Ind, beginning 1981; from instr to assoc prof, Purdue Univ, West Lafayette, Ind, 1964-1981; reactor health physicist, Phillips Petrol Co, Idaho, 1961-1964. **Memberships:** Health Physics Soc. **Research Statement & Publications:** Radioactive aerosol production during reactor decommissioning; low-level radioactive waste management. **Mailing Address:** Sch Health Sci, Purdue Univ, West Lafayette, IN 47907. **Fax:** 765-496-1377. **E-Mail:** landoltr@purdue.edu

LANDON, DAVID B, ARCHEOLOGY, ANTHROPOLOGY. **Education:** Boston Univ, PhD, 1991. **Professional Experience:** ASSOC DIR ANDREW FISKE MEM CTR ARCHAEL RES & ADJ PROF ANTHROPOL, CTR SR SCIENTIST ENVIRON ARCHAEL, UNIV MASS, as of 2006. **Research Statement & Publications:** Archaeology of historic and industrial period sites; environmental archaeology; zooarchaeology; and archaeological science. **Mailing Address:** Dept Anthrop, Col Lib Arts, Univ Mass, 100 Morrissey Blvd, Boston, MA 02125-3393. **E-Mail:** david.landon@umb.edu

LANDON, ERWIN JACOB, BIOCHEMISTRY. **Personal Data:** b Cleveland, Ohio, January 22, 1925; m 1965. **Education:** Univ Chicago, BS, 1945, MD, 1948; Univ Calif, PhD (biochem), 1953. **Professional Experience:** ASSOC PROF EMER PHARMACOL, SCH MED, VANDERBILT UNIV, as of 2006; assoc prof pharmacol, sch med, vanderbilt Univ, beginning 1967; asst prof, Sch Med, Vanderbilt Univ, 1959-1967; sr res fel pharmacol, Sch Med, Yale Univ, 1957-1959; intern, Harper Hosp, Detroit, Mich, 1948-1949. **Memberships:** Am Chem Soc; Am Soc Pharmacol & Exp Therapeut; Sigma Xi. **Research Statement & Publications:** Biochemistry of renal transport; cell calcium regulation. **Mailing Address:** Dept Pharmacol, Sch Med, Vanderbilt Univ, 460 Preston Res Bldg, Nashville, TN 37232-6300. **Fax:** 615-343-4522.

LANDON, JOHN CAMPBELL, VIROLOGY, CANCER. **Personal Data:** b Hornell, NY, January 3, 1937; m 1958, c 4. **Education:** Alfred Univ, AB, 1959; George Wash Univ, MS, 1962, PhD (biol), 1967. **Professional Experience:** CHMN BD, CHIEF EXEC OFFICER, BIOQUAL INC, 1986-; pres, Semna Inc, 1985-1991; PRES, BIOQUAL INC, 1982-; pres, Mason Res Inst, 1975-1982; dir sci, Frederick Cancer Res Ctr, 1972-1975; dir spec prog develop, Litton Bionetics, Inc, 1971-1972; dir dept virol & cell biol, Litton Bionetics, Inc, 1968-1971; head virol, Litton Bionetics, Inc, 1965-1968; biologist, Nat Cancer Inst, 1960-1965. **Memberships:** AAAS; Am Soc Cell Biol; NY Acad Sci; Am Soc Microbiol. **Research Statement & Publications:** Viral oncology; tissue culture; general human and simian virology; cell biology; environmental biology. **Mailing Address:** Bioqual Inc, 9600 Med Ctr Dr, Rockville, MD 20850-3336. **Fax:** 301-251-1260. **E-Mail:** jlandon@bioqual.com

LANDON, SHAYNE J, ORGANOSILICON & ORGANOMETALLIC CHEMISTRY. **Personal Data:** b Alexandria Bay, NY, July 21, 1954; m 1979, Martha; c Thomas P. **Education:** State Univ NY, Plattsburgh, BA, 1976, MA, 1979; Univ Del, PhD, 1984. **Professional Experience:** TECH MGR, CROMPTON CORP, 2000-; group mgr, OSI Specialty Group, Witco Corp, 1997-2000; RES SCIENTIST, OSI SPECIALTIES GROUP, WITCO CORP, 1994-; proj scientist, Spec Chems Div, Union Carbide Corp, 1990-1994; sr chemist, Spec Chems Div, Union Carbide Corp, 1985-1990; res assoc, Pa State Univ, 1984-1985. **Memberships:** Am Chem Soc; Sigma Xi. **Research Statement & Publications:** Organosilicon chemistry; silicone surfactants; urethanes; spectroscopy; reaction mechanisms and kinetics; silicon modified polymer. **Mailing Address:** OSI Specialties Group, Crompton Corp, 777 Old Saw Mill River Rd, Tarrytown, NY 10591. **Fax:** 914-784-4803. **E-Mail:** landosh@cromptoncorp.com

LANDON, SUSAN MELINDA, PETROLEUM GEOLOGY. **Personal Data:** b Mattoon, Ill, July 2, 1950; m 1993, Richard. **Education:** Knox Col, BA, 1972; State Univ NY, MA, 1975. **Honors & Awards:** Martin Van Couvering Award, Am Inst Prof Geologists, 1991; Ben H Parker Memorial Medal, Am inst prof geol, 2001; Honorary mem, Am assoc of petrol geol, 2000. **Professional Experience:** Ed, Interior Rift Basins, 1993; mem bd, Earth Sci & Resources, Nat Res Coun, 1992-; mem & chmn, Colo Geol Surv Adv Comt, Denver, 1991-1993; INDEPENDENT GEOLOGIST, DENVER, 1990-; mgr, Explor Training, Amoco, Houston, 1987-1989; instr petrol geol & explor, Bur Land Mgt, US Forest Serv, Nat Park Serv Indust, 1978-; petrol geologist, Amoco Prod Co, Denver, 1974-1987. **Memberships:** Am Asn Petrol Geologists (treas); Am Inst Prof Geologists; geol soc of Am. **Research Statement & Publications:** Frontier explorations for hydrocarbons in US and in midcontinent rift system. **Mailing Address:** Thomasson Partner Assocs, 1100 Stout St Ste 1400, Denver, CO 80202. **Fax:** 303-436-1935. **E-Mail:** susanlandon@att.net

LANDOR, JOHN HENRY, SURGERY. **Personal Data:** b Canton, Ohio, September 30, 1927; m 1953, c 6. **Education:** Univ Chicago, PhB, 1948, MD, 1953. **Professional Experience:** CHIEF, DEPT SURG, RARITAN VALLEY HOSP, GREEN BROOK, 1973-; prof & chief gen surg, Col Med & Dent NJ, Rutgers Med Sch, 1972-; prof, Col Med, Univ Fla, 1969-1972; Commonwealth Found fel, Royal Postgrad Med Sch, London, 1966-1967; from instr to prof, Sch Med, Univ Mo-Columbia, 1959-1969; instr surg, Sch Med, Univ Chicago, 1958. **Memberships:** Am Col Surgeons; Soc Univ Surgeons; Am Gastroenterol Asn; Soc Surg Alimentary Tract; Int Soc Surgeons. **Research Statement & Publications:** Physiology of the stomach. **Mailing Address:** State Univ NY, Health Sci Ctr Dept Surg, 450 Clarkson Ave PO Box 40, Brooklyn, NY 11203. **E-Mail:** jhlbecket@aol.com

LANDOWNE, DAVID, PHYSIOLOGY, BIOPHYSICS. **Personal Data:** b Chicago, Ill, December 26, 1942; m 1966, Edith; c Mahayana & Youme. **Education:** Mass Inst Technol, BS, 1963; Harvard Univ, PhD (physiol), 1968. **Professional Experience:** PROF PHYSIOL & BIOPHYS, SCH MED, UNIV MIAMI, 1991-; assoc prof physiol & biophys, Sch Med, Univ Miami, 1975-1991; asst prof physiol & biophys, Sch Med, Univ Miami, 1972-1975; NSF fel, Univ London, 1970-1971; Grass Found fel, 1970; res assoc pharmacol, Sch Med, Yale Univ, 1968-1972; fel pharmacol, Yale Univ, 1968-1970. **Memberships:** Biophys Soc; Soc Gen Physiol. **Research Statement & Publications:** Excitable membranes; ion movements and optical measurements of the movement of excitable molecules; published over 5 articles. **Mailing Address:** Dept Physiol & Biophys, Miller Sch Med, Univ Miami, Rosenstiel Med Sci Bldg Rm 4059, Miami, FL 33101-6430. **E-Mail:** dl@miami.edu

LANDOWNE, MILTON, INTERNAL MEDICINE, CIRCULATORY PHYSIOLOGY. **Personal Data:** b New York, NY, November 19, 1912; m 1941, Eleanor; c David, Stephen, Joseph, Martha & Ruth. **Education:** City Col NY, BS, 1932; Harvard Univ, MD, 1936. **Professional Experience:** RETIRED; med adv, US Army Res Inst Environ Med, 1976-1985; dir med lab, US Army Res Inst Environ Med, 1965-1976; asst clin prof, Harvard Univ, 1965-1974; head divcardiol & chronic dis, Sinai Hosp, Baltimore, 1958-1965; med dir, Levindale Hebrew Home & Infirmary, Baltimore, Md, 1957-1965; asst prof, Johns Hopkins Univ, 1955-1965; assoc chief geront sect, Nat Heart Inst, 1949-1957; chief cardiovasc res unit, Vet Admin Hosp, 1948-1949; asst prof med, Univ Chicago, 1946-1948; instr, Univ Chicago, 1941-1946; Libman fel, MichaelReese Hosp, Chicago, 1939-1941; Mt Sinai Hosp, New York, 1936-1939. **Memberships:** AAAS; Am Soc Clin Invest; Am Physiol Soc; Soc Exp Biol & Med; Am Heart Asn. **Research Statement & Publications:** Disorders of the circulation; biology aging; clinical medicine; physiology of blood and circulation; metabolic and renal diseases; environmental medicine. **Mailing Address:** 67 Woodchester Dr, Weston, MA 02193.

LANDRETH, GARY E, SIGNAL TRANSDUCTORS. **Personal Data:** b Van Nuys, Calif, April 26, 1950. **Education:** Univ Kans, BA, 1972; Univ Mich, PhD (neurobiol), 1977. **Professional Experience:** PROF NEUROSCIENCE, CASE WESTERN RES UNIV, as of 2000; assoc prof neuroscience, Case Western Res Univ, beginning 1989; asst prof neuroscience, Case Western Res Univ, 1986-1989; asst prof, Med Col Univ SC, 1980-1986; fel neurobiology, Stanford Univ, 1977-1980. **Memberships:** Am Soc Biol Chemists; Soc Neurosci. **Research Statement & Publications:** Signal transductors. **Mailing Address:** Alzheimer Res Lab, Sch Med, Case Western Res Univ, E504, Cleveland, OH 44106-4928. **Fax:** 216-368-3079. **E-Mail:** gel2@po.cwru.edu

LANDRETH, KENNETH S, ANATOMY. **Personal Data:** b Galax, Va, August 22, 1947; m 1976, c 2. **Education:** Univ Wash, Seattle, PhD (biol struct), 1980. **Professional Experience:** PROF MICRO BIOL & IMMUNOL, SCH MED, WVA UNIV, 1991-; mem, Mary Babb Randolph Cancer Ctr, WVa, 1990-; assoc profmicrobiol, Sch Med, WVa Univ, 1985-1991; sr res scientist, Okla Med Res Found, 1982-1985; res fel, Sloan-Kettering Cancer Ctr. **Memberships:** Am Asn Immunologists. **Research Statement & Publications:** Regulation of B lymphocyte production in the bone marrow; lemopoiesis. **Mailing Address:** Dept Microbiol Immunol & Cell Biol, WVa Univ Sch Med, Morgantown, WV 26506-0002. **E-Mail:** klandret@wvumbrcc1.hsc.wvu.edu

LANDRETH, RONALD RAY, WASTE REUSE, SULFUR OXIDE. **Personal Data:** b Mattoon, Ill, June 15, 1949; m 1971, Laura; c L Paige, Matthew C & Brittany J. **Education:** Northwestern Univ, BA, 1971; Pa State Univ, PhD (environ chem), 1975. **Professional Experience:** VPRES, PROJ MGT, SORBENT TECHNOL CORP, as of 2003; mgr opers & technol, Advan Graphite Technol, Inland steel, Co, 1992-2003; prog mgr new ventures, Inland Steel, 1990-1992; new ventures, Inland Steel, 1988-1990; scientist res, Inland Steel, 1986-1988; sr environ consult eng, Inland Steel, 1985-1986; proj mgr sorbent injection, Inland Steel, 1984-1986; group leader environ res, InlandSteel, 1979-1985; res engr, Inland Steel, 1975-1979; res fel chem, Pa State Univ, 1972-1975. **Memberships:** Air & Waste Mgt Asn; Am Chem Soc. **Research Statement & Publications:** Environmental sciences, primarily air and solids; airwork included air monitoring, source identification and development of innovative desulfurization controls (patented); solid waste work included recycling and reuse technology development. **Mailing Address:** Sorbent Technol Corp, 1664 E Highland Rd, Twinsburg, OH 44087. **Fax:** 219-942-4574.

LANDRIGAN, PHILIP J, ENVIRONMENTAL EPIDEMIOLOGY, OCCUPATIONAL MEDICINE. **Personal Data:** b Boston, Mass, June 14, 1942; m 1976, c 3. **Education:**

Harvard Med Sch, MD, 1967; Univ London MSc, 1977. **Professional Experience:** ETHEL H WISE PROF MED, MT SINAI SCH MED, as of 2006; ED-IN-CHIEF, AM J INDUSL MED, as of 2006; DIR, CTR CHILDREN'S HEALTH & ENVIRON, MT SINAI SCH MED, as of 2006; CHMN COMMUNITY MED & DIR, DIV ENVIRON MED, 1990-; prof environ med, Mt Sinai Sch Med, beginning 1985; chmn, Comt Environ Hazard, Am Acad Pediat, 1983-1987; vice chair, Bd Environ Sci & Technol, Nat Acad Sci, 1981-1986; dir surveillance hazard& eval, Occup epidemiol, Nat Inst Occup Safety & Health, 1979-1985; chief, Environ HazardsActiv, Ctr Dis Control, 1970-1973. **Memberships:** Inst Med-Nat Acad Sci; Am Epidemiol Soc; Royal Soc Med; Am Acad Pediat; Am Pub Health Asn; Am Occup Med Asn; NY Acad Sci. **Research Statement & Publications:** Occupational and environmental epidemiology; Lema poisoning; occupational respiratory diseases; reproductive dysfunction and neurotoxicology. **Mailing Address:** Dept Commun Med, Mt Sinai Sch Med, One Gustave L Levy Pl, Box 1057, New York, NY 10029. **Fax:** 212-996-0407. **E-Mail:** phil.landrigan@mountsinai.org

LANDRUM, BILLY FRANK, ORGANIC CHEMISTRY, POLYMER CHEMISTRY. **Personal Data:** b Atlanta, Ga, June 7, 1920; m 1948, Marjorie Rakestraw; c Douglas F, Charles T & Barbara E (Bozarth). **Education:** Emory Univ, AB, 1947, MS, 1949, PhD (chem), 1950. **Professional Experience:** RETIRED; tech serv mgr, comput mat dept, 1981-1985; mgr, Mkt Develop, Plastics & Additives Div, 1974-1978; staff scientist, Com Develop Dept, Ciba-Geigy Corp, 1967-1974; staff scientist, Whittaker Corp, 1966-1967; mgr advan projs, FMC Corp, NJ, 1962-1966; head polymer sect, Minn Mining & Mfg Co, 1957-1962; res supvr pilot plant, M WKellogg Co, 1953-1957; Res chemist polymer chem, M W Kellogg Co, 1950-1953. **Memberships:** Am Chem Soc; Sigma Xi; Soc Advan Mat & Processing Eng. **Research Statement & Publications:** Organo-metallic reactions; polymers; fluorocarbons; urethanes; coal and coke; activated carbon; composite materials. **Mailing Address:** 1748 Percheron Dr, New Prt Rchy, FL 34655.

LANDRUM, LESLIE ROGER, SYSTEMATICS, PHYTOGEOGRAPHY. **Personal Data:** b St Louis, Mo, December 1, 1946; m 1973, Sonia. **Education:** NY State Col Forestry, BS, 1969; Univ Mich, MS, 1975, PhD (bot), 1980. **Honors & Awards:** B A Krukoff Res Assoc, NY Bot Garden, Bronx, 1980-1983. **Professional Experience:** Fulbright fel, Paraguay & Brazil, 1995; co-ed, J Ariz-Nev Acad Sci, 1991-1994; co-ed, Vascular Plants Ariz Proj, beginning 1987; comn mem, Orgn Flora Neotropica, beginning 1986; SR RES SCIENTIST & HERBARIUM CUR, DEPT BOT, ARIZ STATE UNIV, TEMPE, 1986-; vis lectr, Univ Calif, Berkeley, 1986; vis lectr, San Francisco State Univ, 1985; teaching asst, Div Biol Sci, Univ Mich, Ann Arbor, 1973-1980; Peace Corp vol, Sch Forestry, Univ Chile, Santiago, 1969-1973. **Memberships:** Am Soc Plant Taxonomists; Int Asn Plant Taxon; Soc Econ Bot. **Research Statement & Publications:** Systematics of American Myrtaceae; flora and phytogeography of temperate South America, especially Chile; analysis of phylogenetic patterns; phytogeography of Southern South America; flora of Arizona; numerical phylogenetic analysis; author of numerous publications. **Mailing Address:** Dept Bot, Herbarium Cur, Ariz State Univ, Tempe, AZ 85287-1601. **Fax:** 602-965-6899. **E-Mail:** les.landrum@asu.edu

LANDRUM, PETER FRANKLIN, AQUATIC TOXICOLOGY SPECIALIZING IN BIOACCUMULATION PROCESSES. **Personal Data:** b Scotia, Calif, October 15, 1947. **Education:** Calif State Col, San Bernardino, BS, 1974; Univ Calif, Davis, PhD (pharmacol & toxicol), 1979. **Honors & Awards:** Founders Award, 1999; Admin Award, 1999; ISI Highly Cited Researcher, 2002. **Professional Experience:** Adj assoc prof, Dept Zoology, Southern Ill Univ, 2002; RES CHEM, NAT OCEANIC & ATMOSPHERIC ADMIN/GREAT LAKES ENVIRON RES LAB, 2000-; chief sci br, Nat Oceanic & Atmospheric Admin/Great Lakes Environ Res Lab, 1997-1999; actg dir, US Dept Comm Great Lakes Environ Res Lab, 1996-1997; supvry chemist, US Dept Com Great Lakes Environ Res Lab, 1994-2000; adj assoc prof, Dept Entom, Ohio State Univ, 1994-2003; adj assoc prof, Sch Pub Health, Univ Mich, 1993-; fel, Coop Inst Limnol & Ecosyst Res, 1992-; assoc ed, J Great Lakes Res, 1992-; assoc ed, Critical Reviews Environ Sci & Technol, 1992-; lectr toxicol, Eastern Mich Univ, 1984-1991; res chemist, US Dept Com Great Lakes Environ Res Lab, 1981-1994; res assoc, Savannah River Ecol Lab, 1979-1981. **Memberships:** Soc Environ Toxicol & Chem; Am Chem Soc; Am Soc Testing & Mat; Int Asn Great Lakes Res. **Research Statement & Publications:** Exposure and effects of organic contaminants to aquatic organisms with a special emphasis on the processes and environmental factors affecting the bioavailabilty of sediment-associated contaminants of benthos. **Mailing Address:** Nat Oceanic & Atmospheric Admin, Great Lakes Environ Res Lab, 2205 Commonwealth Blvd, Ann Arbor, MI 48105-1593. **Fax:** 734-741-2055. **E-Mail:** peter.landrum@noaa.gov

LANDRUM, RALPH AVERY, GEOPHYSICS. **Personal Data:** b Memphis, Tenn, October 2, 1926; m 1949, c 3. **Education:** Rice Inst, BS, 1949; Univ Tulsa, MS, 1964. **Professional Experience:** RETIRED; sr res geophysicist, Western Geophys Co Am, 1974-1993; res assoc, Res Ctr, Amoco Prod Co, 1971-1974; staff res scientist, Pan Am Petrol Corp, 1967-1971; staff res engr, Pan Am Petrol Corp, 1963-1967; res engr, Pan Am Petrol Corp, 1956-1963; res seismic observer, Stanolind Oil & Gas Co, 1951-1956; asst seismic observer, Amerada PetrolCorp, 1949-1951. **Memberships:** Am Soc Explor Geophys; Inst Elec & Electronics Engrs; Europ Asn ExplorGeophys. **Research Statement & Publications:** Exploration geophysics; design of seismic instrumentation; mathematics of seismic data processing. **Mailing Address:** 1707 Valley Vista Dr, Houston, TX 77077.

LANDRY, JAMES M, CHEMISTRY. **Education:** Xavier Univ, BS & MS; Miami Univ, PhD (Inorg Chem). **Professional Experience:** GETTY RES INST, as of 2006. **Mailing Address:** Res & Educ Dept, Getty Res Inst, 1200 Getty Ctr Dr Suite 1100, Los Angeles, CA 90049-1688.

LANDRY, MICHAEL RAYMOND, MARINE ZOOPLANKTON, PROTOZOAN ECOLOGY. **Personal Data:** b Berlin, NH, April 16, 1948; m 1972, Christine; c Steve M & Scott R. **Education:** Univ Calif, Santa Barbara, BA, 1970; Univ Wash, PhD (oceanog), 1976, MBA, 1986. **Honors & Awards:** Spec Creativity Award, NSF, 1990; Regent's Medal, Excellence Res, Univ Hawaii, 2001. **Professional Experience:** Intern, Global Commun Systs working group on numerical modeling, beginning 1995; joint Global Ocean Flux Study Prog Steering Comt, beginning 1995; chmn, Dept Oceanog, Univ Hawaii, 1993-1996; PROF OCEANOG, DEPT OCEANOG, UNIV HAWAII, 1989-; assoc chmn, Dept Oceanog, Univ Hawaii, 1989-1992; assoc prof, Dept Oceanog, Univ Hawaii, 1987-1989; res assoc prof biol oceanog, Sch Oceanog, 1983-1987; Coordr, NW Regional Oceanog Prog, US Dept Energy, 1982-1985; res asst prof, Univ Wash, 1978-1983; res biologist, Scripps Inst Oceanog, Univ Calif, San Diego, 1976-1978. **Memberships:** Am Soc Limnol & Oceanog; Western Soc Naturalists; Soc Protozoologists; Intern Soc Copepodiologists; fel AAAS; Am Geophys union. **Research Statement & Publications:** Feeding behavior and population dynamics of marine zooplankton; marine microbial ecology; marine ecosystem research and modeling; carbon and nitrogen cycling. **Mailing Address:** Dept Oceanog, Univ Hawaii-Manoa, Honolulu, HI 96822. **Fax:** 808-956-9516. **E-Mail:** landry@soest.hawaii.edu

LANDRY, RICHARD GEORGES, APPLIED STATISTICS. **Personal Data:** b Manchester, NH, November 7, 1942; m 1966, c 3. **Education:** Oblate Col, BA, 1964; Boston Col, MEd, 1967, PhD (res & statist), 1970. **Professional Experience:** CHESTER FRITZ DISTINGUISHED PROF, EDUC FOUNDATIONS & RES, UNIV NDAK, as of 2004; prof measurement & statist, Ctr Teaching & Learning, Univ NDak, beginning 1980; res coordr, Nat Inst Educ Proj, Univ NDak, 1973-; eval consult, Grand Rapids Sch Dist, Minn, 1973-; eval auditor, numerous ESEA Title III Projs, 1970-; assoc prof, Ctr Teaching & Learning, Univ Ndak, 1970-1980; asst prof, Ctr Teaching & Learning, UnivNdak, 1969-1973. **Memberships:** Am Asn Univ Prof; Am Educ Res Asn; Am Statist Asn; Nat Coun Measurement-Educ. **Research Statement & Publications:** Applied educational statistics; educational measurement and evaluation in affective domain; foreign language learning and creativity. **Mailing Address:** Educ Found & Res, Univ NDak, PO Box 7189, Grand Forks, ND 58202. **E-Mail:** richard_landry@und.nodak.edu

LANDRY, STEPHEN G, MATHEMATICS. **Education:** Wesleyan Univ, PhD, 1989. **Professional Experience:** CHIEF INFO OFFICER, SETON HALL UNIV, NJ, as of 2006. **Mailing Address:** Math Dept Seton Hall Univ, 400 S Orange Ave, South Orange, NJ 07079. **Fax:** 973-761-7942. **E-Mail:** landryst@shu.edu

LANDRY, STUART OMER, ZOOLOGY. **Personal Data:** b New Orleans, La, September 30, 1924; m 1950, c 2. **Education:** Harvard Univ, BS, 1949; Univ Calif, PhD (zoology), 1954. **Professional Experience:** PROF EMER BIOL, STATE UNIV N, BINGHAMTON, as of 2004; Actg dean grad sch, State Univ NY Binghamton, 1966-1968; prof Biol State Univ NY Binghamton, beginning 1963; assoc prof biol & chmn dept, La State Univ, 1959-1963; from instr to asst prof anat, Univ Mo, 1954-1959; assoc, Univ Calif, 1953-1954; asstzool, Univ Calif, 1952-1953; Curatorial asst, Mus Vert Zool, Calif, 1950-1952. **Memberships:** AAAS; Soc Syst Zool; Am Soc Mammal; Am Asn Anat; Am Soc Zoologists. **Research Statement & Publications:** Comparative anatomy and classification of mammals; functional anatomy of mammals. **Mailing Address:** Dept Biol Sci, State Univ NY, Vestal Pkwy East, P O Box 6000, Binghamton, NY 13902-6000. **E-Mail:** slandry@binghamton.edu

LANDS, WILLIAM EDWARD MITCHELL, BIOCHEMISTRY. **Personal Data:** b Chillicothe, Mo, July 22, 1930; c 4. **Education:** Univ Mich, Ann Arbor, BS, 1951; Univ Ill, PhD (biol chem), 1954. **Honors & Awards:** Gold Medal Bond Award, Am Oil Chemists Soc, 1965; Glycerine Res Award, 1969; Verhagen Lectr, 1979-1981; Pfizer Biomed Res Award, 1985. **Professional Experience:** DIR, OMEGA PROTEIN CORP, 1998-; dir, div basic res, Nat Inst Alcohol Abuse & Alcoholism, beginning 1990; prof, Univ Ill Med Ctr, 1985-1990; head biochem, Univ Ill Med Ctr, 1980-1985; ed, Biochem & Biophys Acta, J Lipid Res, 1978-; ed, Can J Biochem, 1972-1978; Danforth Assoc, 1966-; chmn subcomt biochem nomenclature, Nat Acad Sci, 1962-1964; from instr to profbiochem, Univ Mich, Ann Arbor, 1955-1980; NSF fel, Calif Inst Technol, 1954-1955. **Memberships:** AAAS; Am Chem Soc; Am Soc Biochem & Molecular Biol; Am Oil Chemists Soc; Sigma Xi; Am Inst Nutrit. **Research Statement & Publications:** Metabolism of glycerides and long-chain aliphatic acids and aldehydes; formation of membranes and regulation of membrane function; prostaglandin biochemistry and control of its biosynthesis. **Mailing Address:** Omega Protein Corp, 1717 St James Pl, Suite 550, Houston, TX 77056. **Fax:** 713-940-6122.

LANDSBAUM, ELLIS M(ERLE), CHEMICAL ENGINEERING. **Personal Data:** b Chicago, Ill, February 28, 1925; m 1952, c 2. **Education:** Ill Inst Technol, BSc, 1949; Northwestern Univ, MSc, 1953, PhD (chem eng), 1955; Univ Calif Los Angeles, cert nuclear tech, 1967, cert bus mgt, 1972. **Professional Experience:** SR STAFF ENGR, PROPULSION DEPT, AEROSPACE CORP, 1984-; sect mgr, Propulsion Dept, Aerospace Corp, 1961-1984; res group supvr, Jet Propulsion Lab, Calif Inst Technol, 1955-1961; jr engr, Socony Oil Co, 1949-1951. **Memberships:** Assoc fel Am Inst Aeronaut & Astronaut. **Research Statement & Publications:** Solid propellant rockets; combustion; nozzles; system analysis. **Mailing Address:** Aerospace Corp, 2350 E El Segundo Blvd, El Segundo, CA 90245-4691. **Fax:** 310-336-5000. **E-Mail:** ellis.m.landsbaum@aero.org

LANDSBERG, ARNE, CHEMICAL ENGINEERING. **Personal Data:** b Des Moines, Iowa, June 10, 1933; c Karin & Eric. **Education:** Univ Colo, BS, 1955; Ore State Univ, PhD (chem eng), 1964. **Professional Experience:** RETIRED; chem res engr, US Bur Mines, Albany, 1966-1991; peace corps volfor prof, Chem Eng Prog, Costa Rica, 1964-1966; Chem engr, US Bur Mines, 1961-1964. **Memberships:** Sigma Xi; Am Chem Soc. **Research Statement & Publications:** Chemical kinetics of gas-solid reactions; vapor-solid equilibrium. **Mailing Address:** 1415 NW Greenwood Pl, Corvallis, OR 97330-1827.

LANDSBERG, DENNIS R, AERONAUTICS. **Professional Experience:** PRES, LANDSBERG ENG, NY, as of 2006. **Memberships:** NY Capital Region Chap AEE, (pres, 2004 & 2005). **Mailing Address:** Landsberg Eng, 37 Timberwick Dr PO Box 556, Clifton Park, NY 12065-6238. **Fax:** 518-383-9406. **E-Mail:** dlandsberg@landsbergeng.com

LANDSBERG, JOHANNA D (JOAN), ANALYTICAL CHEMISTRY, RESEARCH ADMINISTRATION. **Personal Data:** b Medford, Ore, July 15, 1940; c Karin & Eric. **Education:** Ore State Univ, Phd, 1992, BS, 1962, MS, 1964. **Professional Experience:** RETIRED; project leader, Pac Northwest Res Sta, Silvicult Lab, Forest Serv, USDA, Bend, Ore, 1989-; prin investr, US-Spain Res Proj, 1986-1989; res chemist, Bend Res, Inc, 1977-1978, res chemist, Bend Res, Inc, 1979-1989; res asst, dept food sci & technol, Ore State Univ, 1976-1977. **Memberships:** Am Chem Soc; Sigma Xi; AAAS; Soc Am Foresters. **Research Statement & Publications:** Effects of prescribed fire on soil, forest floor and foliar nutrients in Central Oregon ponderosa pine and mixed conifer lands. **Mailing Address:** 1741 Nw Vicksburg Ave, Bend, OR 97701.

LANDSBERG, LEWIS, METABOLISM. **Personal Data:** b New York, NY, November 23, 1938. **Education:** Williams Col, AB, 1960; Yale Univ, MD, 1964. **Professional Experience:** VICE PRES MED AFFAIRS & DEAN, FEINBERG SCH MED, as of 2004; physician-in-chief, Dept Med, Northwestern Mem Hosp, beginning 1990; irving scutter prof & chmn, Dept Med, Med Sch, Northwestern Univ, 1990-2000; dir, ctr endocrinol, metab & nutrit, beginning 1990; sr physician, Beth Israel Hosp, 1988-1990; physician, Beth Israel Hosp, 1979-1988; assoc physician, Beth Israel Hosp, 1974-1979; assoc visphysician, Boston City Hosp, 1973-1974; from asst prof to prof med, Harvard Med Sch, 1972-1990; assisting physician, Boston City Hosp, 1972-1973; attend physician, West Haven Vet Admin Hosp, 1970-1972; from instr to asst prof med, Sch Med, Yale Univ, 1969-1972; from assoc physician to attend physician, Yale-New Haven Hosp, 1969-1972. **Memberships:** Am Fedn Clin Res; Endocrine Soc; NY Acad Sci; Am Heart Asn; Am SocPharmacol & Exp Therapeut; fel Am Col Physicians; AAAS; Am Physiol Soc; Am Soc ClinInvest; Asn Am Physicians. **Research Statement & Publications:** Catecholamines and the sympathoadrenal system; nutrition and the sympathetic nervous system; obesity and hypertension; numerous publications. **Mailing Address:** Dept Med, Feinberg Sch Med, Northwestern Univ, Morton Bldg, Rm 4-656, Chicago, IL 60611-2950. **Fax:** 312-908-9032.

LANDSBERGER, FRANK ROBBERT, PHYSICAL BIOCHEMISTRY, VIROLOGY. **Personal Data:** b Amsterdam, Neth, August 10, 1943; American citizen; div, c 1. **Education:** Cornell Univ, BA, 1964; Brown Univ, PhD (physics), 1970. **Professional Experience:** DIR, MOJAVE THERAPEUTICS INC, as of 2003; dir off sci & tech develop, Mt Sinai Med Ctr, 1991-1997; adj assoc prof, Rockefeller Univ, 1987-1991; from asst prof to assoc prof, Andrew W Mellon found fel, 1980-1987; from asst prof to assoc prof, Rockefeller Univ, 1974-1987; asst prof chem, Ind Univ, Bloomington, 1971-1974; res fel biochem, Div Endocrinol, Sloan-Kettering Inst Cancer Res, 1969-1971; res asst physics, Brown Univ, 1964-1969. **Memberships:** AAAS; Biophys Soc; fel NY Acad Sci; Am Soc Microbiol; Am Chem Soc; SigmaXi. **Research Statement & Publications:** Use of physical biochemical studies of the structure and function of biological and model membranes with emphasis on enveloped viruses and parasites and their interaction with cell surfaces. **Mailing Address:** Mojave Therapeutics, Inc, 22 Saw Mill River Rd, Hawthorne, NY 10532-1533. **Fax:** 914-347-0292.

LANDSBURG, ALEXANDER CHARLES, COMMERCIAL SHIP DESIGN & OPERATIONS & SHIP MANEUVERABILITY, HUMAN FACTORS & COST & RISK ASSESSMENT. **Personal Data:** b Saginaw, Mich, December 23, 1942; m 1967, Lorin; c Lori A, Alexander G, Jessica L & Eliot N. **Education:** Univ Mich, BS, 1966, MS, 1969; Harvard Bus Sch, PMD, 1979. **Honors & Awards:** Gold Medal Award, Dept Transportation, 2000; Bronze Medal, Maritime Adminsitration, 1977; Distinguished Service Award, Soc of Naval Arch & Marine Engr, 1988; Society of Naval Architects and Marine Engineers (SNAME) Cochrane Award for Best Paper Award in 2005, 1976 and 1973; Distinguished Service Award SNAME, 1988. **Professional Experience:** Coordinator RES AND DEVEL, Assoc Admin of Financial Approvals and Cargo Preference, MARITIME ADMIN, 2000-; PROG MGT SYSTS SAFETY & HUMAN FACTORS, OFF MARITIME LAB TRAINING & SAFETY, MARITIME ADMIN, 1995-; prog mgr, ship performance & safety, Off Technol Assessment, 1988-1995; naval architect, Off Ship Construct, 1987-1988; liaison, Off Advan Ship Opers, 1985-1987; comput-aided cost analysis, Off Shipbldg Costs, 1978-1985; mgr, comput-aided ship design, 1976-1978; mgr, ship design develop, 1974-1976; chief, Environ Activ, Off Shipbldg Costs, 1974-1976; naval archit, Off Ship Construct, 1967-1974; trainee, Maritime Admin, 1966-1967. **Memberships:** Soc Naval Architects & Marine Engrs; life mem regional VP and mem of council 1992-1994; Chairman Chesapeake Section 1983-1984. **Research Statement & Publications:** Innovative ship design and operations; computer-aided ship design and operations; ship maneuverability; information and training for shipboard personnel; ship design and operations for military sealift; cost analysis; human factors research. **Mailing Address:** Maritime Admin, Dept Transp, 307 Williamsburg Dr, Silver Spring, DC 20590. **Fax:** 202-366-3128. **E-Mail:** alexlandsburg@comcast.net

LANDSCHOOT, PETER J, AGRICULTURE. **Education:** Pa State Univ, BS, 1982, MS, 1984; Univ RI, PhD (Plant Path), 1988. **Professional Experience:** PROF TURFGRASS SCI, DEPT CROP SOIL SCI, PA STATE UNIV, 2003-; from asst prof to assoc prof, turfgrass sci, Pa State Univ, 1989-2003. **Memberships:** Am Phytopathological Soc; Crop Sci Soc Am; Am Soc Hort Sci. **Mailing Address:** Penn State Univ, 413 Agr Sci & Indust Bldg, University Park, PA 16802. **Fax:** 814-863-7043. **E-Mail:** pjl1@psu.edu

LANDSEA, CHRISTOPHER W, METEOROLOGY. **Honors & Awards:** Banner I Miller Award, Am Meteorol Asn, 1994. **Professional Experience:** RES METEOROLOGIST, HURRICANE RES DIV, as of 2004; PROF, DEPT ATMOSPHERIC SCI, COLO STATE UNIV, as of 2001. **Mailing Address:** Hurrican Res Div, 4301 Rickenbacker Causeway, Miami, FL 33149. **Fax:** 305-361-4402. **E-Mail:** landsea@aoml.noaa.gov

LANDSKROENER, PETER, PROCESS ENGINEERING FOR PAPER INDUSTRY, PAPER FILM & FOIL. **Personal Data:** b Woodbury, NJ, December 3, 1928. **Education:** Univ Del, BS, 1950, MS, 1951; Cath Univ Am, PhD (phys chem), 1954. **Professional Experience:** CONSULT, 1982-; pres coating, laminating & printing, John Dusenbery Co, 1976-1982; gen mgr, Columbia Magnetics, 1969-1976; vpres res & develop com develop, AnninIndust, 1966-1969. **Memberships:** Am Chem Soc; Am Inst Chemists; Sigma Xi. **Mailing Address:** 418 Poppasquash Rd, Bristol, RI 02809.

LANDSMAN, DAVID, MOLECULAR BIOLOGY, GENETICS. **Personal Data:** b Cape Town, SAfrica, October 5, 1953; m 1982, Dawn; c Marc & Kevin. **Education:** Univ Cape Town, S Africa, BSc, 1976, PhD (biochem), 1984. **Professional Experience:** SR RES SCIENTIST, NAT CTR BIOTECHNOLOGY INFO, NIH, as of 2005; MOLECULAR BIOLOGIST & COMPUTATIONAL MOLECULAR BIOLOGIST, NIH, as of 2004; vis assoc, Nat Cancer Inst, Lab Molecular Carcinogenesis, NIH, 1987-1989; vis fel, Nat Cancer Inst, NIH, 1984-1987; vis scientist, Nat Ctr Biotechnology Info Naval Ordinance Lab & NIH. **Memberships:** Am Soc Biochem & Molecular Biol. **Research Statement & Publications:** Structure and function of interphase chromatin and nuclei; molecular and cellular interactions controlling the regulation of gene expression. **Mailing Address:** Nat Ctr Bio-Technol Info Nat Inst Health, Bldg 38A Rm 6N601 8600 Rockville Pike MSC 6075, Bethesda, MD 20894-6075. **Fax:** 301-480-9241. **E-Mail:** landsman@quagga.nlm.nih.gov

LANDSMAN, DOUGLAS ANDERSON, PHYSICAL CHEMISTRY. **Personal Data:** b Dundee, Scotland, May 31, 1929; div, c 4. **Education:** Univ St Andrews, BSc, 1949, Hons, 1950, PhD (thermodyn), 1957. **Professional Experience:** ED, JOHN WILEY & SONS LTD, as of 2003; Sr proj engr, Int Fuel Cells, 1972-1991; res supvr, Mat Eng Res Lab, Pratt & Whitney Aircraft Div, Middletown, 1965-1972; prin sci officer, Chem Div, Atomic Energy Res Estab, UK Atomic Energy Authority, Eng, 1960-1965; Harwell sr fel, Chem Div, Atomic Energy Res Estab, UK Atomic Energy Authority, Eng, 1958-1960; Nat Res Coun Can fel, 1957-1958; Sr sci officer, Chem Div, Atomic Weapon Res Estab, UK Atomic Energy Authority, Eng, 1953-1957; CONSULT, FUEL CELL CHEM. **Memberships:** Fel Royal Soc Chem; Am Chem Soc. **Research Statement & Publications:** Thermodynamics of ionization in aqueous solutions; chemistry of the hydrogen isotopes; isotope separation; gas chromatography; chemonuclear reactors; energy conversion; fuel cells. **Mailing Address:** John Wiley & Sons Ltd, West Sussex, UK.

LANDSTREET, JOHN DARLINGTON, STELLAR MAGNETISM, STELLAR ATMOSPHERES. **Personal Data:** b Philadelphia, Pa, March 13, 1940; m 1986, Barbara; c David & Sarah. **Education:** Reed Col, BA, 1962; Columbia Univ, MA, 1963, PhD (physics), 1966. **Honors & Awards:** Carlyle S Beals Award, Canadian Astronomical Society, 2002. **Professional Experience:** Adjunct research professor of physics and astronomy, University of Western Ontario, 2005-2008; past president, Canadian Astronomical Society, 1998-2000; visscientist, Observatoire Midi-Pyrenees, Toulouse, France, 1997-1998; president, Canadian Astronomical Society, 1996-1998; chmn, Telescope Corp, Can, France, Hawaii, 1996-1997; vice-president, Canadian Astronomical Society, 1994-1996; vchmn, TelescopeCorp, Can, France, Hawaii, 1994-1995; chmn dept, Univ Western Ont, 1992-1996; secy, Telescope Corp, Can, France, Hawaii, 1992-1993; mem bd dirs, Telescope Corp, Can, France, Hawaii, 1991-1997; visscientist, Observatoire Midi-Pyrenees, Toulouse, France, 1991-1992; distinguished res prof, UnivWestern Ont, 1987-1988; mem, Coun Admin, Astron Observ, Mont Megantic, 1985-1990; visscientist, Inst Theoret Astrophys, Univ Heidelberg, 1984-1985; chmn, Sci Adv Coun, Can-France-Hawaii Telescope Corp, 1982-1983; chmn, Grant Selection Comt Space & Astron, Natural Sci & Eng Res Coun Can, 1982-1983; mem, Sci Adv Comt, Can Ctr Space Sci, 1981-1983; vchmn, Sci Adv Coun, Can-France-Hawaii Telescope Corp, 1981; mem, Sci Adv-Coun, Can-France-Hawaii Telescope Corp, 1980-1983; mem, grant selection comtaSpace &Astron, Natural Sci & Eng Res Coun Can, 1980-1983; PROF, DEPT PHYSICS & ASTRON, UNIV WESTERN ONT, 1976-2005; from asst prof to assoc prof, Univ Western Ont, 1970-1976; asst prof, ColumbiaUniv, 1970; res assoc astron, Columbia Univ, 1967-1970; asst prof, Mt Holyoke Col, 1966-1967; instr physics, Mt Holyoke Col, 1965-1966; mem bddirs, Can Astron Soc. **Memberships:** Am Astron Soc; Can Astron Soc (vpres, 1994-1996, pres, 1996-1998); fel Royal AstronSoc; Int Astron Union. **Research Statement & Publications:** Observation of circular and linear polarization in stars and extragalactic objects, especially white dwarfs; observation, interpretation and modelling of stellar magnetic fields and of stellar spectra One book published: Physical Processes in the Solar System (Keenan and Darlington 2003). **Mailing Address:** 18 Rollingwood Circle, London, ON N6G 1P7, Can. **Fax:** 519-473-4174. **E-Mail:** jlandstr@astro.uwo.ca

LANDSTROM, D(ONALD) KARL, NATURAL GAS TECHNOLOGY, HVAC. **Personal Data:** b Portland, Ore, October 12, 1937. **Education:** Mass Inst Technol, BS, 1959. **Professional Experience:** DEP DIR, GAS APPLIANCE TECHNOL CTR, COLUMBUS LABS, BATTELLE MEM INST, 1991-; proj mgr energy & thermal technol, Gas Appliance Technol Ctr, Columbus Labs, Battelle Mem Inst, 1980-1990; prin res scientist solar mat analysis, Gas Appliance Technol Ctr, Columbus Labs, Battelle Mem Inst, 1965-1980; res engr mat environ, NAm Aviation, 1963-1965; supvr electron micros, Goodyear Atomic Corp, 1959-1963. **Memberships:** AAAS; Int Solar Energy Soc; Am Soc Heating Refrig & Air Conditioning Engrs. **Research Statement & Publications:** Solar energy; environmental impact analysis; thermal analysis; materials research; physical and chemical analysis; electron microscopy; electron probe analysis; nuclear waste; energy and environmental systems; agricultural controlled environment system; heat pumps and alternative energy systems; gas fired heat pumps; heating, ventilating and air conditioning systems; gas appliance technology; granted 4 patents. **Mailing Address:** 903 Neil Ave, Columbus, OH 43215. **Fax:** 614-424-3534.

LANDUCCI, LAWRENCE L, ORGANIC CHEMISTRY, NUCLEAR MAGNETIC RESONANCE. **Personal Data:** b St Paul, Minn, May 20, 1939; m 1969, c 3. **Education:** Univ Minn, BS, 1962, PhD (org chem), 1967. **Professional Experience:** Organizer, First Int Workshop Nuclear Magnetic Resonance & Wood Sci, Vancouver, BC, 1985; RES CHEMIST & NUCLEAR MAGNETIC RESONANCE SPECTROSCOPIST, US FOREST PROD LAB, 1967-. **Memberships:** Am Chem Soc. **Research Statement & Publications:** Lignin and lignin model compound chemistry; methods of lignin degradation; mechanism of anthraquinone pulping; nuclear magnetic resonance characterization of lignin and reaction products; application of state-of-the-art nuclear magnetic resonance methods to characterization of wood components. **Mailing Address:** Forest Prod Lab, USDA Forest Serv, One Gifford Pinchot Dr, Madison, WI 53726-2398. **Fax:** 608-231-9592.

LANDWEBER, LAWRENCE H, COMPUTER SCIENCE. **Personal Data:** b New York, NY, November 29, 1942; m 1966. **Education:** Brooklyn Col, BS, 1963; Purdue Univ, MS & PhD (comput sci), 1966. **Professional Experience:** PROF EMER COMPUT SCI & CHMN DEPT, UNIV WIS, MADISON, as of 2003; prof comput sci & chmn dept, Univ Wis, Madison, beginning 1977; from asst prof to assoc prof, Univ Wis-Madison, 1967-1977. **Memberships:** Am Math Soc; Asn Comput Mach; Sigma Xi. **Research Statement & Publications:** Theoretical computer science; computer networks; computer conferencing and mail. **Mailing Address:** Dept Comput Sci, Univ Wis, 1210 W Dayton St, Madison, WI 53706. **Fax:** 608-262-9777. **E-Mail:** lhl@cs.wisc.edu

LANDWEBER, PETER STEVEN, MATHEMATICS. **Personal Data:** b Washington, DC, August 17, 1940; m 1964, c 2. **Education:** Univ Iowa, BA, 1960; Harvard Univ, MA, 1961, PhD (math), 1965. **Professional Experience:** Chmn, Russian Translations Comt, Am Math Soc, 1989-1992; NSF grad felcommemorative lectr, 1989; PROF MATH, RUTGERS UNIV, NEW BRUNSWICK, 1974-; NATO fel, Univ Cambridge, 1974-1975; assoc prof, Rutgers Univ, New Brunswick, 1970-1974; asst prof, Yale Univ, 1968-1970; mem sch math, Inst Advan Study, 1967-1968 & 1986-1987; asst prof math, Univ Va, 1965-1968. **Memberships:** Am Math Soc; Math Asn Am. **Research Statement & Publications:** Cobordism theory of differential manifolds. **Mailing Address:** Dept Math, Univ Rutgers, 110 Frelinghuysen Rd Rm 526, Princeton, NJ 08854. **Fax:** 732-445-5530. **E-Mail:** landwebe@math.rutgers.edu

LANDWEHR, JAMES M, STATISTICAL APPLICATIONS & COLLABORATIONS, RESEARCH ON APPLIED STATISTICS METHODOLOGIES. **Personal Data:** b Philadelphia, Penn, January 12, 1945; m 1967, c 3. **Education:** Yale Univ, BA, 1966; Univ Chicago, PhD (statist), 1972. **Honors & Awards:** Outstanding Statist Appln Award, Am Statist Asn, 2003; Frank Wilcoxon Award, Am Soc Qual, 2002. **Professional Experience:** DIR, DATA ANALYSIS RES DEPT, AVAYA LABS, 2000-; Distinguished Mem Tech Staff, AT&T Bell Labs, 1993-2000; Panel mem, Nat Acad Sci, Nat Res Coun, 1984-1988; co-prin investr, Quant LitProj, Am Statist Asn, Nat Coun Teachers Math, 1984-1987; Statist, Math Sci Res Ctr, Research Supvr, AT & T Bell Labs, 1982-1993; tech staff & supvr, AT&TBell Labs, Murray Hill, 1973-1982; Lectr & asst prof statist, Univ Mich, Ann Arbor, 1970-1973. **Memberships:** Fel AAAS; Fel Am Statist Asn (BoD, 2000-2002); Inst Math Statist; Math Asn Am. **Research Statement & Publications:** Statistical experimentation and data analysis for technological and business systems and applications; categorical data analysis and logistic regression; graphical methods; precollege statistics education; statistical applications. **Mailing Address:** Avaya Labs Research, Rm 2D-24, 233 Mount Airy Rd, Basking Ridge, NJ 07920. **Fax:** 908-696-5402. **E-Mail:** jml@avaya.com

LANDY, ARTHUR, BIOCHEMICAL GENETICS, GENE REGULATION. **Personal Data:** b Philadelphia, Pa, March 17, 1939; m 1965, Eva; c 2. **Education:** Amherst Col, BA, 1961; Univ Ill, PhD (microbiol & biochem), 1965. **Honors & Awards:** National Academy of Sciences 1999-; American Academy of Arts and Sciences 1999-. **Professional Experience:** Mem, Microbiol Genetics Study Sect, NIH, 1987-1991; chmn nucleic acids, GordonRes Conf, 1983; mem recombinant DNA adv comt, NIH, 1981-1986; assoc ed, Cell, 1979-1985; mem advbd, Am Cancer Soc, 1978-1983; PROF MED SCI, BROWN UNIV, 1978-; fac res assoc, Am CancerSoc, 1975-1981; assoc prof, Brown Univ, 1975-1977; asst prof, Brown Univ, 1968-1974; fel, AmCancer Soc, 1968; res fel biochem genetics, Med Res Coun Lab Molecular Biol, Cambridge, Eng, 1966-1968; NATO fel, 1966-1967. **Memberships:** Am Soc Microbiol; Am Soc Biochem.and Molec. Biology. **Research Statement & Publications:** mechanisms of site-specific recombination; gene structure and regulation. **Mailing Address:** Div Biol & Med, Brown Univ Box G, Providence, RI 02912-0001. **E-Mail:** arthur_landy@brown.edu

LANDZBERG, ABRAHAM H(AROLD), SEMICONDUCTOR PROCESS ENGINEERING. **Personal Data:** b New York, NY, September 10, 1929; m 1955, Joan; c Judith E, Carol A

& Steven J. **Education:** NY Univ, BSME, 1951; Princeton Univ, MSE, 1953. **Professional Experience:** CONSULT, SEMICONDUCTOR & ELECTRONIC PACKAGING DEVELOP & MFG, 1993-; sr eng mgr, Packaging Develop Eng, 1985-1993; sr eng mgr, Semiconductor Develop Eng, 1976-1985; advan mfg mgr, Components Div, 1971-1976; dept mgr integrated circuits, Components Div, 1965-1970; dept mgr appl mech, Res Div, IBM, 1959-1965; develop engr, Gen Elec Co, 1952-1959. **Memberships:** Inst Elec & Electronics Engrs. **Research Statement & Publications:** Physics of failure of integrated circuits; mechanical properties of materials; applied mechanics, application to electronic computer components; turbines; electrical machinery; manufacturing systems and processes for integrated circuits; electronic component packaging development; microelectronics reliability. **Mailing Address:** 685 Fieldstone Ct, Yorktown Heights, NY 10598.

LANE, ALFRED GLEN, ANIMAL NUTRITION. **Personal Data:** b Stoutland, Mo, August 21, 1932; m 1957, Ann; c Kenny J & Glenda A. **Education:** Univ Mo, BS, 1959, MS, 1960, PhD (animal nutrit), 1965. **Professional Experience:** RETIRED; dairy specialist, Tex A&M Univ, 1982-1994; pvt consult, 1977-1982; mgr diary res, Allied Mills Inc, 1970-1977; asst prof, Univ Mo, Columbia, 1965-1970; asst dairy husb, Univ Mo, Columbia, 1963-1965; instr voc agr, Parkersburg Community Sch, Iowa, 1960-1963. **Memberships:** Am Dairy Sci Asn; Am Soc Animal Sci. **Research Statement & Publications:** Ruminant nutrition; physiology. **Mailing Address:** PO Box 58, Stephenville, TX 76401.

LANE, BARTON GEORGE, PHYSICS. **Education:** Mass Inst Technol, PhD (physics), 1981. **Professional Experience:** FOUNDER, PLASMA DYNAMICS LAB, 1990. **Mailing Address:** Plasma Dynamics, 60 Hurd Rd, Belmont, MA 02178. **Fax:** 978-988-0186.

LANE, BENJAMIN CLAY, PHARMACOLOGY. **Personal Data:** b Raleigh, NC, February 8, 1952. **Education:** Wash State Univ, BS, 1974, MS, 1976, PhD (bact), 1980. **Professional Experience:** SR RES SCIENTIST, IMMUNOSCI PROG, ABBOTT LABS, ILL, 1989-; srres investr, Immunosci Prog, Abbott Labs, Ill, 1988-1989; res pharmacologist, Immunosci Prog, Abbott Labs, Ill, 1985-1988; res fel, Arthritis Found, 1983-1984; NIH fel, Med Ctr, Duke Univ, 1981-1982; res assoc, Div Rheumatic Dis, Med Ctr, Duke Univ, 1981-1985; res scholar, DivClin Immunol & Rheumatic Dis, Med Ctr, Univ Southern Calif, 1979-1981; lab instr, Dept Bact & Pub Health, Wash State Univ, 1975-1978. **Mailing Address:** Abbott Labs 100 Abbott Park Rd, Info Nat Libr Med NIH Bldg 38A Rm 8N807, Abbott Park, IL 20894-0001.

LANE, BENNIE RAY, MATHEMATICS. **Personal Data:** b Deming, NMex, July 2, 1935; m 1956, c 4. **Education:** Colo State Col, BA, 1956, MA, 1957; George Peabody Col, PhD (math), 1962. **Professional Experience:** PROF EMER, DEPT MATH & STATIST, EASTERN KY UNIV, as of 2001; prof, Dept Math, Eastern Ky Univ, beginning 1966; chmn dept, Eastern KY Univ, 1966-1978; from asst prof to assoc prof, George Peabody Col, 1963-1966; asst prof math, ColoState Col, 1962-1963; instr appl math, Vanderbilt Univ, 1961-1962; Asst prof math, UnivChattanooga, 1959-1961. **Memberships:** Am Math Asn. **Research Statement & Publications:** Mathematics education; teaching mathematics by television; abstract algebra; programmed instruction. **Mailing Address:** Dept Math & Statist, Eastern Ky Univ, Acad Comput & Telecommunications, Combs 207, Wallace 313, Richmond, KY 40475. **Fax:** 859-622-3051.

LANE, BERNARD PAUL, PATHOLOGY. **Personal Data:** b Brooklyn, NY, June 27, 1938; m 1962, Dorthy; c Erika, Andrew & Matthew. **Education:** Brown Univ, AB, 1959; NY Univ, MD, 1963; State Univ NY, MA, 1992. **Professional Experience:** Vet Admin Hosp, Northport, NY, beginning 1971 & Stony Brook Univ Hosp, beginning 1979; PROF PATH, HEALTH SCI CTR, STATE UNIV NY STONY BROOK, 1976-; assoc prof, Health Sci Ctr, State Univ NY Stony Brook, 1971-1976; vis scientist, Armed Forces Inst Path, 1971; attend pathologist, Bellevue & NY Univ Hosp, 1969-1971; from asst prof to assoc prof path, Sch Med, NY Univ, 1966-1971; NIH trainee exp path, Sch Med, NY Univ, 1965-1966; chief cell injury labs, Armed Forces Inst Path. **Memberships:** Am Soc Cell Biol; Int Acad Path; Am Asn Path; Am Soc Clin Path; Am Asn Cancer Res. **Research Statement & Publications:** Experimental pathology; electron microscopy; cellular injury. **Mailing Address:** Dept Path, State Univ NY Health Sci Ctr, Stony Brook, NY 11790.

LANE, BYRON GEORGE, BIOCHEMISTRY. **Personal Data:** b Toronto, Ont, May 16, 1933; m 1961. **Education:** Univ Toronto, BA, 1956, PhD (biochem), 1959. **Honors & Awards:** Ayerst Award, Can Biochem Soc, 1971. **Professional Experience:** EMER PROF BIOCHEM, UNIV TORONTO, as of 2004; prof biochem, Univ Toronto, beginning 1968; assoc prof, Univ Alta, 1964-1968; asst prof, Univ Alta, 1961-1963; res assoc, Rockefeller Inst, 1960-1961; Jr res asstbiochem, Med Ctr, Univ Calif, San Francisco, 1959-1960. **Memberships:** Am Soc Biol Chemists. **Research Statement & Publications:** Biochemical investigations of germin, the marker protein for onset of growth in germinating wheat embryos. **Mailing Address:** Dept Biochem, Univ Toronto One Kings College Circle, Toronto, ON M5S 1A8, Can. **E-Mail:** byron.lane@utoronto.ca

LANE, CARL LEATON, FOREST SOILS. **Personal Data:** b Raleigh, NC, February 11, 1928; m 1952, c 1. **Education:** NC State Univ, BS, 1952, MS, 1961; Purdue Univ, PhD (forest soil microbiol), 1968. **Professional Experience:** RETIRED; coordr, Res & Grad Progs, Dept Forestry, 1985-1990; from asst prof to prof forestry, Clemson Univ, 1960-1990; forest mgr, State Hosp Butner, NC, 1952-1959. **Memberships:** Soc Am Foresters. **Research Statement & Publications:** Forest soils microbiology; forest soil tree disease relationships; nitrogen fixation; effluent utilization. **Mailing Address:** 150 Folgers St, Clemson, SC 29631.

LANE, CHARLES A, ORGANIC CHEMISTRY. **Personal Data:** b Wichita, Kans, November 18, 1932. **Education:** Univ Okla, BS, 1954; Yale Univ, MS, 1959; Univ Calif, PhD (chem), 1963. **Professional Experience:** ADJ PROF PHYSICS & CHEM, UNIV ALASKA, ANCHORAGE, as of 2004; ASSOC PROF ORG CHEM, UNIV TENN, KNOXVILLE, 1973-; asst prof, Univ Tenn, Knoxville, 1964-1973; asst prof, Univ Calif, 1963-1964; asst prof org chem, Univ Nigeria, 1961-1963; org chemist, Lederle Labs, Am Cyanamid Co, 1956-1958. **Research Statement & Publications:** Theoretical chemistry. **Mailing Address:** Dept Physics & Astron Univ Alaska, 3211 Providence Dr, Anchorage, AK 99508. **E-Mail:** clane@ibm.net

LANE, DENNIS DEL, AIR POLLUTION MONITORING & CONTROL, AEROSOL SCIENCE. **Personal Data:** b Peoria, Ill, February 16, 1950; m 1969, Kristine; c Thomas D, Jeffrey T, T Matthew & Theresa B. **Education:** Univ Ill, Urbana, BS, 1972, MS, 1973, PhD (environ eng), 1976. **Honors & Awards:** Award Res Excellence, US Environ Protection Agency, 1991, Bronze MedalRes Achievements, 1993. **Professional Experience:** N T VEATCH DISTINGUISHED PROF ENVIRON ENG, UNIV KANS, beginning 1993; mem, Subcomt Great Lakes Appl Health, USPHS, 1992-1993; mem bd sci counrs, AgencyToxic Substances & Dis Registry, 1988-1994; US Environ ProtectionAgency, beginning 1985; State Kans Atty Gen, beginning 1977; prin investr, US Environ Protection Agency, beginning 1981; consult, Midw Res Inst, 1977-1991; from asst prof to prof, Univ Kans, 1976-1993. **Memberships:** Air & Waste Mgt Asn; Am Soc Civil Engrs; Am Soc Aerosol Res; AAAS; AsnEnviron Eng Profs. **Research Statement & Publications:** Aerosol science (physics and chemistry of particles moving in the air); air quality monitoring; air pollution control; water-related areas in environmental engineering and science. **Mailing Address:** Dept Civil & Envoirn Eng, Univ Kans, 4112B Learned, Lawrence, KS 66045. **E-Mail:** lane@ukans.edu

LANE, DONALD WILSON, PETROLEUM GEOLOGY. **Personal Data:** b Fayetteville, Tenn, June 23, 1934; m 1960, Joanne; c 3. **Education:** Dartmouth Col, BA, 1956; Univ Ill, MS, 1958; Rice Univ, PhD (geol), 1961. **Professional Experience:** RETIRED; geologist, Ohm Remediation Serv, 1992-1997; geologist, Jones & Neuse, 1991-1992; geologist, ERM-Southwest, 1988-1991; consult geologist, 1987-1988; sr geologist, Britoil Ventures, 1985-1986; consult geologist, 1976-1984; Mgr Exp Geol & Rocky Mountain Area, Mich & Wis Pipeline Co, 1973-1976; staff geologist, Geol Surv Wyo, 1970-1973; regional geologist, Royal Resources Corp, 1970; geologist, Tenneco Oil Co, 1961-1970. **Memberships:** Am Asn Petrol Geol. **Research Statement & Publications:** Lower Paleozoic stratigraphy and hydrocarbon potential of the northeastern United States; Wyoming stratigraphy and stratigraphic resources; Lower Cretaceous stratigraphy of northwestern Colorado; eocene and cretaceous stratigraphy of Texas Gulf Coast; Pennsylvanian stratigraphy of North Texas. **Mailing Address:** 12214 Mossycup Dr, Houston, TX 77024-4224.

LANE, EDWIN DAVID, FISH CULTURE, FISH ECOLOGY. **Personal Data:** b Vancouver, BC, May 9, 1934; m 1958, c 2. **Education:** Univ BC, BSc, 1959, MSc, 1962; Univ Tex, PhD (zoology), 1966. **Professional Experience:** COORDR, FISHERIES & AGR DEPT, MALASPINA COL, NANAIMO, BC, 1979-; head coop res, Can Wildlife Serv, Can Dept Environ, 1974-1979; res grant, Calif StateUniv, Long Beach, 1968-1969 & 1971-1974; assoc prof zool, Calif State Univ, Long Beach, 1968-1974; fisheries expert, Food & Agr Orgn, 1967-; res scientist, Res Br, Ont Dept Land &Forest, 1966-1968; staff mem, Fisheries Invest Off, NZ Marine Dept, 1962-1963. **Memberships:** Can Soc Zoologists; NZ Limnol Soc; Am Fish Soc. **Research Statement & Publications:** Salmonid culture especially feeding; ecology of fishes, especially in streams, estuaries and coastal bay systems; environmental impact of development, especially in the North. **Mailing Address:** Fisheries & Agr Dept, Malaspina Col 900 5th St, Nanaimo, BC V9R 5S5, Can.

LANE, ERIC TRENT, MICROCOMPUTER ANIMATION GRAPHICS. **Personal Data:** b Baton Rouge, La, August 30, 1938; m Chantana; c Carmen & Vivian. **Education:** La State Univ, BS, 1960; Rice Univ, MA, 1963, PhD (physics), 1967. **Honors & Awards:** Proj Seriphim Grand Prize Software, 1987; Educom/Ncrptl Award, 1988. **Professional Experience:** PROF PHYSICS, UNIV TENN, CHATTANOOGA, 1977-; assoc prof, Univ Tenn, Chattanooga, 1967-1977; vis lectr physics, La State Univ, New Orleans, 1963-1965; coordr exhibs, Challenger Learning Ctr; NSF grant, Microcomput Course Develop. **Memberships:** Am Phys Soc; Am Asn Physics Teachers; Sigma Xi. **Research Statement & Publications:** Microcomputer animation graphics for science and physics education; research applied to improvement of teaching and human relationships. **Mailing Address:** Dept Physics, Univ Tenn, 823 Oaks St, Chattanooga, TN 37403-2598. **Fax:** 423-425-4683.

LANE, ERNEST PAUL, TOPOLOGY. **Personal Data:** b Greene Co, Tenn, November 14, 1933; m 1961, c 2. **Education:** Berea Col, BA, 1955; Univ Tenn, MA, 1957; Purdue Univ, PhD (math), 1965. **Professional Experience:** PROF MATH, APPALACHIAN STATE UNIV, 1975-; assoc prof, Appalachian State Univ, 1970-1975; asst prof, Va Polytech Inst, 1965-1970; instr math, Berea Col, 1958-1960; programmer, Army Ballistic Missile Agency, Ala, 1957-1958. **Memberships:** Math Asn Am; Am Math Soc. **Research Statement & Publications:** Abstract spaces; metrization; real-valued functions on abstract spaces. **Mailing Address:** Dept Math, Appalachian State Univ, Boone, NC 28608-0001. **E-Mail:** epl@math.appstate.edu

LANE, FORREST EUGENE, PLANT PHYSIOLOGY, PLANT BIOCHEMISTRY. **Personal Data:** b Enola, Ark, June 24, 1934; m 1954, Leota; c Sharon R, Laura K, Linda M, Dwight H & Ellen S. **Education:** Univ Ark, BA, 1956, MEd, 1959, MS, 1963; Univ Okla, PhD (plant physiol), 1965. **Professional Experience:** RETIRED; from asst prof to assoc prof, Dept Bot & Bact, Univ Ark, Fayetteville, 1967-1996; asst prof biol, Kans State Col Pittsburg, 1965-1967; NSF fel, 1963-1965; instr biol, Univ Ark, 1958-1963; teacher, Hall High Sch, Ark, 1957-1958. **Memberships:** Sigma Xi; Am Soc Plant Physiol; Scand Soc Plant Physiol; Bot Soc Am; Phytochem Soc NAm. **Research Statement & Publications:** Dormancy in plant structures such as seeds, fruits, tubers and buds; relationship between dormancy and plant phenolics; enzymes associated with hormone control and plant growth; anthocyanin pigments. **Mailing Address:** 5450 Huntsville Rd, Univ Ark, Fayetteville, AR 72701.

LANE, GARY (THOMAS), ANIMAL NUTRITION, BIOCHEMISTRY. **Personal Data:** b Center, Ky, November 8, 1941; m 1963, c 3. **Education:** Berea Col, BS, 1963; Purdue Univ, West Lafayette, MS, 1965, PhD (animal nutrit), 1968. **Professional Experience:** DIR, TECH SERV, BERKMANN MILLS, 1986-; assoc exten prof dairy, UnivKy, 1977-1986; from asst prof to assoc prof animal nutrit, Tex A&M Univ, 1967-1977; res asstanimal nutrit, Purdue Univ, West Lafayette, 1963-1967. **Memberships:** Am Dairy Sci Asn; Am Soc Animal Sci. **Research Statement & Publications:** Ration additives for ruminants; ration and its relation to milk composition and yield; mechanisms of milk synthesis; chemical preservation of high-moisture grain. **Mailing Address:** 1124 Secretariat Dr E, Danville, KY 40422.

LANE, GEORGE ASHEL, APPLIED CHEMISTRY, MATERIALS SCI, ACQUATIC ECOL. **Personal Data:** b Norman, Okla, May 9, 1930; m 2000, Mary-Susan Haske Lane; c Brook Haske & Michael James Haske. **Education:** Grinnell Col, AB, 1952; Northwestern Univ, PhD (phys chem), 1955. **Honors & Awards:** IR-100 Award, 1980. **Professional Experience:** Consultant, 1997- RES ASSOC, OMNITECH INT, 1992- 1997; res assoc, Dow Chem USA, 1980-1992; sr res specialist, Dow Chem USA, 1973-1980; res specialist, Dow Chem USA, 1969-1973; sr res chemist, Dow Chem USA, 1966-1969; proj leader, Dow Chem USA, 1963-1966; chemist, Dow Chem USA, 1958-1963; staff asst, Dow Chem USA, 1956-1958; spec projs chemist, Dow Chem USA, 1955-1956; asst, Northwestern Univ, 1952-1955; Asst chem, Grinnell Col, 1951-1952. **Memberships:** emer mem, Am Chem Soc; assoc mem, Sigma Xi. **Research Statement & Publications:** Solar energy; energy storage; oxygen isotope effects; trout ecology; auto crash protection; rocket propellant testing and evaluation; pyrotechnics; ceramics. **Mailing Address:** 3802 Wintergreen Dr, Midland, MI 48640.

LANE, H CLIFFORD, EXPERIMENTAL BIOLOGY. **Personal Data:** b Detroit, Mich, June 15, 1950. **Education:** Univ Mich, BS, 1972, MD, 1976; Am Bd Internal Med, cert, 1979; Am Bd Infectious Dis, cert, 1984; Am Bd Allergy & Immunol, cert, 1986. **Professional Experience:** Prof med, George Wash Univ, 1993-; CLIN DIR, IMMUNOPATHOGENESIS SEC, DIV INTRAMULAR RES, NIH 1991-; CHIEF, CLIN & MOLECULAR RETROVIROL SECT, LAB IMMUNOREGULATION, 1989-; dep clin dir, Nat Inst Allergy & Infectious Dis, NIH, beginning 1985; sr investr, Lab Immunoregulation, 1982-1989; clin assoc, Lab Immunoregulation, 1979-1982; resident, Univ Hosp, Ann Arbor, Mich, 1977-1979; intern internal med, Univ Hosp, Ann Arbor, Mich, 1976-1977. **Memberships:** Am Fedn Clin Res; Am Asn Immunologists; Am Col Physicians; fel Infectious DisSoc Am; Am Soc Clin Invest; Am Asn Physicians. **Research Statement & Publications:** Mechanisms of activation, proliferation and differentiation of human lymphoid cells in the normal immune response; clinical, pathophysiologic, immunologic, molecular biologic, virologic and therapeutic aspects of disease states including the vasculitic syndromes, Sjogren's syndrome, and AIDS. **Mailing Address:** Nat Inst Allergy & Infectious Dis, NIH, Rm 11S231 Bldg 10, Bethesda, MD 20892-6612. **E-Mail:** cl17d@nih.gov

LANE, HAROLD RICHARD, PALEONTOLOGY, STRATIGRAPHY. **Personal Data:** b Danville, Ill, March 7, 1942; m 1968, Sherry; c Christopher Richard & Erich Thomas. **Education:** Univ Ill, Urbana, BS, 1964; Univ Iowa, MS, 1966, PhD (geol), 1969. **Honors & Awards:** Fellow-Geological Society of America. **Professional Experience:** PROG DIR, DIRECTORATE GEOSCIENCE, DIV EARTH SCI, NSF, as of 2006; mgr worldwide paleont. and stratigraphy, Amoco Prod Co, Houston, beginning 1989; Sr res scientist and Research Supervisor, Res Ctr, 1968-1989. **Memberships:** Int Palaeont Asn; Soc Econ Paleont & Mineral; Paleontological Society, AAAS, Cushman Foundation, Geological Soc of Am. **Research Statement & Publications:** Evolution, biostratigraphy, and systematic paleontology of microfossils, conodonts, especially in Devonian through Middle Pennsylvanian strata of North America for the solution of problems relating to paleogeography and paleoclimatology. **Mailing Address:** Sedimentary Geology & Paleobiology Program, Surface Earth Processes Sec, Earth Sci Division, National Sci Found, 4201 Wilson Blvd, Rm 789, Arlington, VA 22230. **Fax:** 703-292-9025. **E-Mail:** hlane@nsf.gov

LANE, HELEN W, BIOMEDICINE. **Personal Data:** b Cleveland, Ohio, June 22, 1945. **Education:** Univ Calif, Berkeley, BS, 1968; Univ Wis-Madison, MS, 1971; Univ Fla, PhD (animal nutrit), 1978. **Professional Experience:** PRIN INVESTR, JOHNSON SPACE CTR, NASA, HOUSTON, as of 2000; prin coord sci cheif nutritionist, special asst to dir, 1991-1996; dir clin labs, Johnson Space Ctr, Houston, 1991-1996; adj prof, Dept Prev Med, Univ Tex Med Br, Galveston, beginning 1989; DIR NUTRIT BIOCHEM, JOHNSON SPACE CTR, HOUSTON, 1989-; Am Inst Cancer Res Study Sect, 1986-1991 & Am Dietetic Asn, 1989; Nat Cancer Inst, NIH, 1986; prof, Dept Nutrit & Foods, Auburn Univ, 1984-1989; assoc prof, Prog Nutrit & Dietetics & Grad Sch Biomed Sci, 1982-1984; grant reviewer, USDA, 1981, 1983-1985, 1987 & 1989; adj appt, Dept Chem, Houston Baptist Univ, 1978-1984; asst prof, Prog Nutrit & Dietetics, Univ Tex Health Sci Ctr, Houston, 1977-1982; grad teaching asst, Prog Clin & Commun Dietetics, 1975-1977; asst gastroenterol, Dept Internal Med, 1974-1975; instr, Dept Food Sci, Univ Fla, 1972-1974; asst gastroenterol, Dept Internal Med, Univ Wis-Madison, 1970-1972. **Memberships:** Am Asn Cancer Res; Am Dietetic Asn; Am Home Econ Asn; Am Inst Nutrit; Am Soc Clin Nutrit; Inst Food Technologists; Sigma Xi. **Research Statement & Publications:** Nutritional sciences; preventive medicine; dietetics. **Mailing Address:** Biomed Opers & Res, Johnson Space Ctr, NASA, Rm 920D, SA Bldg 1, 2101 NASA Rd One, Houston, TX 77058-3963. **Fax:** 281-483-2086. **E-Mail:** hlane@ems.jsc.nasa.gov

LANE, I WILLIAM, CANCER ONCOLOGY MEDICINE. **Education:** Rutgers Univ, Phd. **Professional Experience:** CHMN, CARTILAGE CONSULTS INC, as of 2003. **Memberships:** Am Med Assoc. **Mailing Address:** Cartilage Consults Inc, 80 Woodland Rd Ste 4, Short Hills, NJ 07078. **Fax:** 201-236-9091.

LANE, JAMES DALE, VERTEBRATE ZOOLOGY. **Personal Data:** b Las Cruces, NMex, August 28, 1937; m 1958, c Christopher. **Education:** NMex State Univ, BS, 1959, MS, 1962; Univ Ariz, PhD (zoology), 1965. **Professional Experience:** Prof zool, McNeese State Univ, beginning 1970; asst prof biol, Mcneese StateUniv, 1965-1970; asst geochronology, Univ Ariz, 1965; asst zool, Univ Ariz, 1962-1965; asst biol, NMex State Univ, 1959-1962. **Memberships:** AAAS; Soc Syst Zool; Am Soc Mammal; Soc Vert Paleont; Am Inst Biol Sci. **Research Statement & Publications:** Ecology and systematics of various mammalians taxons, especially rodents. **Mailing Address:** Dept Biol, McNeese State Univ, PO Box 92000, Lake Charles, LA 70605-4511.

LANE, JOSEPH M, ORTHOPAEDIC SURGERY. **Personal Data:** b New York, NY, October 27, 1939; m 1963, Barbara; c Debra & Jennifer. **Education:** Columbia Univ, BA, 1957; Harvard, Univ, MD, 1965. **Professional Experience:** ASSOC DIR TRAUMA SERV, MBD UNIT SPEC SURG, NEW YORK, 1996-; MED DIR, METAB BONE DIS SERV & OSTEOPOROSIS PREV, 1996-; chmn orthop, Univ Calif, Los Angeles, 1993-1996; dir, res div, 1990-1993; assoc dir, MultiPurpose Arthritis Ctr, New York, 1988-; CHIEF, MBD UNIT SPEC SURG, NEW YORK, 1976-; surg intern, chief MBD Sect, 1973-1976; chief resident, Hosp Univ Pa, Philadelphia, 1972-1973; resident, Hosp Univ Pa, Philadelphia, 1969-1972; res fel, Philadelphia Gen Hosp, 1969-1970; res assoc, NIH, Nat inst Dent res, Bethesda, Md, 1967-1969; resident gen surg, Hosp Univ Pa, Philadelphia, 1966-1967; surg intern, Hosp Univ Pa, Philadelphia, 1965-1966; consult & collabr, Collagen Corp, Warsaw, Ind, Genetics inst, Andover, Mass, EBI, Fairfield, NJ; dir, Orthop lab Appl Clin res & Tissue Eng. **Memberships:** Fel Am Acad Orthop Surgeons; AMA; Am Soc Bone & Mineral Res; Musculoskeletal Tumor Soc (pres 1982-1983); Orthop Res Soc (pres 1984-1985). **Research Statement & Publications:** Orthopaedic surgery; oncology; characterize connective tissue injury and repair; bone regeneration with growth factors (BMP). **Mailing Address:** Hosp Spec Surg, 535 E, 70th St, New York, NY 10021. **Fax:** 212-772-1061. **E-Mail:** lanej@hss.edu

LANE, JOSEPH ROBERT, PHYSICAL METALLURGY, METALLURGICAL ENGINEERING. **Personal Data:** b Chicago, Ill, March 3, 1917; m 1949, Wyvona Alexander. **Education:** Univ Ill, BS, 1943; Mass Inst Technol, ScD(metall), 1950. **Professional Experience:** RETIRED; sr staff metallurgist, Nat Mat Adv Bd, Nat Acad Sci, 1955-1989; brhead, Naval Res Lab, 1950-1955; res asst, Mass Inst Technol, 1945-1950; Metallurgist, UnivChicago, Metall Lab, 1943-1945. **Memberships:** Fel Am Soc Metals Int. **Research Statement & Publications:** Superalloys, refractory metals and various aerospace structural materials. **Mailing Address:** 7211 Rebecca Dr, Alexandria, VA 22307.

LANE, KEITH ALDRICH, ANALYTICAL CHEMISTRY. **Personal Data:** b Gridley, Kans, November 11, 1921. **Education:** Oglethorpe Univ, AB, 1942, MA, 1943. **Professional Experience:** RETIRED; environ chemist, Indust Chems Div, 1970-1983; group leader analytical res, Solvay Process Div, Allied Chem Corp, 1964-1970; chemist, Solvay Process Div, Allied Chem Corp, 1958-1964; group leader analytical res, Mutual Chem Co Am, 1951-1958; chemist, Mutual Chem Co Am, 1943-1951. **Research Statement & Publications:** All phases of chromium chemistry; organic and inorganic analytical method development; environmental studies and pollution control. **Mailing Address:** 122 Royal Rd, Liverpool, NY 13088.

LANE, KENNETH D, PHYSICS. **Education:** Ga Inst Technol, BS, MS; Johns Hopkins Univ, PhD. **Professional Experience:** PROF PHYSICS, BOSTON UNIV, as of 2005. **Mailing Address:** Dept Phys, Boston Univ, 590 Commonwealth Ave, Boston, MA 02215. **Fax:** 617-353-6062. **E-Mail:** lane@physics.bu.edu

LANE, LAWRENCE JUBIN, ELECTRICAL ENGINEERING. **Personal Data:** b Morganton, NC, February 19, 1927; m 1975, Helen; c Priscilla (Purks) & Richard. **Education:** NC State Col, BEE, SO, 1950; Univ Va, MSEE, 1971. **Professional Experience:** RETIRED; consult engr, Salem, VA, 1983-1995; sr systs design engr, Salem, VA, 1978-1983; sr develop engr, Waynesboro, 1963-1978; develop engr, Waynesboro, 1955-1963; class supvr, Philadelphia, 1954-1955; engr, Gen Elec Co, Schenectady, 1950-1954. **Memberships:** Fel Inst Elec & Electronics Engrs. **Research Statement & Publications:** Patentee in field. **Mailing Address:** 1601 Chatham Rd, Waynesboro, VA 22980-3203. **E-Mail:** juh_lane@cfw.com

LANE, LEONARD JAMES, HYDROLOGY. **Personal Data:** b Tucson, Ariz, April 25, 1945; m 1964, c 2. **Education:** Univ Ariz, BS, 1970, MS, 1972; Colo State Univ, PhD (civil eng), 1975. **Honors & Awards:** Super Serv Award, USDA, 1981; Arthur S Flemming Award, 1983. **Professional Experience:** RES LEAD, HYDROLOGIST, AGR RES SERV, USDA, 1984-; adj assoc prof renewablenatural resouces, Univ Ariz, 1982-; staff mem, Univ Calif, 1981-1984; Fac affil civil eng, ColoState Univ, 1973-1974; Hydrologist, Agr Res Serv, USDA, 1970-1981. **Memberships:** Am Geophys Union; Am Soc Civil Engrs; Am Water Resources Asn; BritGeomorphol Res Group; Am Soc Agr Engrs; Sigma Xi. **Research Statement & Publications:** Hydrology of semiarid regions; runoff and sediment simulation models incorporating geomorphic features, land use and management; improved erosion prediction technology; climatic fluctuations and change. **Mailing Address:** US Dept Agr, Agr Res Serv, SW Watershed Res Ctr, 2000 E Allen Rd, Tucson, AZ 85719. **Fax:** 520-670-5550. **E-Mail:** ljlane@tucson.ars.ag.gov

LANE, LESLIE CARL, PLANT VIROLOGY. **Personal Data:** b Stamford, Conn, April 5, 1942; m 1977, c 2. **Education:** Univ Wis, BS, 1965, PhD (biochem), 1971. **Professional Experience:** PROF PLANT PATH, UNIV NEBR LINCOLN, as of 2005; assoc prof plant path, Univ Nebr Lincoln, beginning 1981; asst prof, Univ Nebr lincoln, 1975-1981; fel virol, Univ Nebr lincoln, 1973-1975; fel virol, John Innes Inst, Norwich, Eng, 1971-1973. **Memberships:** Am Phytopath Soc; Electrophoresis Soc; Am Soc Virol. **Research Statement & Publications:** Structure and replication of plant viruses; virus directed protein and nucleic acid synthesis; virus-host interactions; gel electrophoretic separations; fluorescence detection methods. **Mailing Address:** Dept Plant Path, Univ Nebr, 406L Plant Sci Hall, Lincoln, NE 68521-1010. **E-Mail:** llane1@unl.edu

LANE, LEWIS BEHR, HAND SURGERY, CLINICAL & BASIC SCIENCE RESEARCH IN ORTHOPAEDICS. **Personal Data:** b NY, December 16, 1948; m Nancy. **Education:** Columbia Col, BA, 1970, MD, 1974; Am Bd OrthopSurg, cert, 1981 & 1989, cert surg hand, 1989. **Honors & Awards:** Philip D Wilson Prize; Lewis Clark Wagner Prize. **Professional Experience:** Clin assoc prof orthop surg, Cornell Univ Med Col, beginning 2000; CHIEF HAND SURG, DEPT ORTHOP, LONG ISLAND JEWISH MED CTR, 1997-; CLIN ASST PROF ORTHOP SURG, ALBERT EINSTEIN COL MED, 1997-; clin assoc prof orthop surg, Cornell Univ Med Col, 1992-1997, beginning 2000; assoc ed, Am J Hand Surg, 1991-; attend orthop surgeon, Hosp Spec Surg, 1990-; vis scientist, Hosp Spec Surg, 1980-1989; fel hand surg, St Lukes-Roosevelt Hosp, 1979-1980; resident orthop surg, Hosp Spec Surg, 1975-1976; fel orthop res, Hosp Spec Surg, 1975-1976; intern surg, NY Hosp, 1974-1975. **Memberships:** Am Soc Surg Hand; fel Am Acad Orthop Surgeons; fel Am Col Surgeons; Orthop Res Soc; Amer Orthopedic Association. **Research Statement & Publications:** Hand surgery, both clinical and basic science; tenosynovitis; infection; arthritis. **Mailing Address:** 800 Community Dr, Manhasset, NY 11030. **Fax:** 516-365-1634.

LANE, LOIS KAY, PROTEIN CHEMISTRY. **Education:** Dartmouth Col, PhD (biol), 1974. **Professional Experience:** ASSOC PROF EMER, DEPT PHARMACOL & CELL BIOPHYS, COL MED, UNIV CINCINNATI, as of 2003; Assoc prof, Dept Pharmacol & Cell Biophys, Col Med, Univ Cincinnati, beginning 1977. **Mailing Address:** Dept Pharmacol, Col Med, Univ Cincinnati, 231Albert Sabin Way, Cincinnati, OH 45267. **Fax:** 513-558-1169. **E-Mail:** lois.lane@uc.edu

LANE, MALCOLM DANIEL, BIOCHEMISTRY, MOLECULAR BIOLOGY. **Personal Data:** b Chicago, Ill, August 10, 1930; m 1951, Patricia; c Claudia J & Malcolm D Jr. **Education:** Iowa State Univ, BS, 1951, MS, 1953; Univ Ill, PhD, 1956. **Honors & Awards:** Mead Johnson Award, Am Inst Nutrit, 1966; William C Rose Award, 1981. **Professional Experience:** Bd Sci Coun, Nat Heart, Lung & Blood Inst, 1986-1992; DELAMAR PROF BIOL CHEM & CHMN DEPT, MED SCH, JOHNS HOPKINS UNIV, 1978-; prof physiol chem, Med Sch, Johns Hopkins Univ, 1970-1978; mem, Biochem Study Sect, NIH, 1970-1974; from assoc prof biochem to prof, Sch Med, NY Univ, 1964-1970; sr fel, Max Planck Inst Cell Chem, 1962-1963; from assoc prof biochem & nutrit to prof, Va Polytech Inst, 1956-1964; res asst, Iowa State Univ, 1951-1953. **Memberships:** Nat Acad Sci; Am Chem Soc; Am Soc Biochem & Molecular Biol (pres, 1991); Am Inst Nutrit; AAAS; Am Soc Cell Biol; Harvey Soc; fel Am Acad Arts & Sci. **Research Statement & Publications:** Transcriptional control of gene expression during differentiation; differentiation of preadipocytes into adipocytes; insulin action; glucose transport; diabetes. **Mailing Address:** Dept Biol Chem, Sch Med, Johns Hopkins Univ, 725 N Wolfe St, Baltimore, MD 21205. **Fax:** 410-955-0903. **E-Mail:** dlane@jhmi.edu

LANE, MEREDITH ANNE, SYSTEMATICS, EVOLUTION. **Personal Data:** b Mesa, Ariz, August 4, 1951; div. **Education:** Ariz State Univ, BS, 1974, MS, 1976; Univ Tex, PhD (bot), 1980. **Honors & Awards:** Cooley Award, Am Soc Plant Taxonomists, 1982. **Professional Experience:** Prof, dept Ecol & Evolutionary Biol & Cur Natural Hist Mus, Univ Kans, as of 1998; mem coun, Int Orgn Plant Biosyts, 1990-1992; cur-in-charge, R L McGregor herbarium, Univ Kans, 1990-1998; DIR, R L MCGREGOR HERBARIUM, UNIV KANS, 1989-; ASSOC PROF BOT, UNIV KANS, 1989-; consult ed, plant taxon, Encyc Sci & Eng, McGraw-Hill, 1986-1993; adj asst prof bot, dept Bot, Univ Wyo, Laramie, 1986-1989; prog dir, Am Soc Plant Taxonomists, 1985-1989; actg cur, Rocky Mountain Herbarium, Univ Wyo, 1985-1986; chmn, Systs Sect, Bot Soc Am, 1984-1986; vis asst prof, dept Bot, Univ Tex, 1982; assoc prof bot, dept EPO Biol, Univ Colo, Boulder, 1980-1989. **Memberships:** Int Asn Plant Taxon; Am Soc Plant Taxonomists (secy 1985-1987); Bot Soc Am; Int Orgn Plant Biosysts. **Research Statement & Publications:** Angiosperm systematics, specifically of southwestern North American and Mexican Compositae(Astereae), using cytotaxonomic, ecogeographic, scanning electron microscopic, biogeographic and cladistic techniques; pollination biology of Compositae, especially micromorphological pollinator cues; forensic botany. **Mailing Address:** Dept Bot Univ Kans, 2045 Constant Ave Campus W, Lawrence, KS 66047-3729. **Fax:** 913-864-7364. **E-Mail:** mlane@kuhub.cc.ukans.edu

LANE, NANCY JANE, CELL BIOLOGY, NEUROBIOLOGY. **Personal Data:** b Halifax, NS, 1936; m 1969, R N Perham; c Temple D & Quentin S. **Education:** Dalhousie Univ, BSc, 1958, MSc, 1960; Oxford Univ, DPhil (cytol), 1963; CambridgeUniv, PhD, 1968. **Honorary Degrees:** ScD, Cambridge Univ, 1981; LLD, Dalhousie Univ, 1985; DSc, Salford Univ, 1994. **Professional Experience:** Non-exec dir, Smith & Nephew & Peptide

Therapeut; chair, govt working partywomen sci & eng, 1993; WELLCOME FEL, CAMBRIDGE UNIV, 1991-; grad tutor, GirtonCol, Cambridge Univ, 1975-; off fel & lectr cell biol, Girton Col, Cambridge Univ, 1970-; sr prinsci officer & head electron micros, Agr Res Coun Res Unit Insect Neurophysiol & Pharmacol, Dept Zool, Cambridge Univ, 1968-1990; res fel, Girton Col, Cambridge Univ, 1968-1970; resstaff biologist, Yale Univ, 1965-1968; res asst prof path, Albert Einstein Col Med, 1964-1965. **Memberships:** Am Soc Cell Biol; Brit Soc Cell Biol (secy, 1982-1990); Soc Exp Biol; fel RoyalMicros Soc; fel Zool Soc; fel Royal Soc Arts. **Research Statement & Publications:** Freeze-fracture and tracer analysis of invertebrate central nervous systems; accessibility of nervous systems to tracer molecules; structure and biochemistry of tight junctions in endothelial cells; alzheimer's disease. **Mailing Address:** Dept Zool, Downing St, Cambridge CB2 3EJ, UK. **Fax:** 442-233-36676.

LANE, NEAL F, ATOMIC PHYSICS. **Personal Data:** b Oklahoma City, Okla, August 22, 1938; m 1960, Joni; c Christy (Saydjari) & John P. **Education:** Univ Okla, BSc, 1960, MS, 1962, PhD (physics), 1964. **Honorary Degrees:** DSc, Univ Ala, 1994, Mich State Univ, 1995, Ohio State Univ, 1996; DHL, Univ Okla, 1995, Marymount Univ, 1995. **Honors & Awards:** George R Brown Prize, 1973-1974, 1976-1977; Pres Award, Am Soc Mech Eng Int, 1999. **Professional Experience:** EDWARD A & HERMENA HANCOCK KELLY UNIV PROF PHY & ASTRON, RICE UNIV, 2001-; asst pres, sci & technol & dir, Off Sci & Technol, Policy 1998-2001; dir, NSF, 1993-1998; provost, Dept Physics, 1986-1993; non-resident fel, Joint Inst Lab Astrophys, Univ Colo, 1984-1993; chancellor, Univ Colo, Colo Springs, 1984-1985; Distinguished Karcher lectr, Univ Okla, 1983; distinguished vis scientist, Univ Ky, 1980; dir, Physics Div, NSF, 1979-1980; chmn, Dept Physics, 1977-1982; vis fel, Joint Inst Lab Astrophys, Univ Colo, 1975-1976; prof physics & space physics & astron, Rice Univ, Houston, Tex, 1972-1984; Alfred P Sloan res fel, 1967-1973; from asst prof to assoc prof physics, Rice Univ, Houston, Tex, 1966-1972; vis fel, Joint Inst Lab Astrophys, Univ Colo, 1965-1966; NSF res fel physics, Queen's Univ, Belfast, 1964-1965. **Memberships:** fel Am Phys Soc; fel AAAS; Am Asn Phys Teachers; Sigma Xi; fel Am Acad Arts& Sci; Am Inst Phys. **Research Statement & Publications:** Theoretical studies of collision processes involving electrons, atoms and molecules. **Mailing Address:** Dept Phys & Astron MS 108, 6100 Main St, Houston, TX 77005. **Fax:** 713-348-5143. **E-Mail:** neal@rice.edu

LANE, NORMAN GARY, PALEONTOLOGY. **Personal Data:** b French Lick, Ind, February 19, 1930; m 1958, c 3. **Education:** Oberlin Col, AB, 1952; Univ Kans, MS, 1954, PhD (geol), 1958. **Professional Experience:** PROF EMER PALEONT & GEOL SCI, IND UNIV, BLOOMINGTON, 1994-; chmn dept, Ind Univ, Bloomington, 1984-1987; prof paleont, Ind Univ, Bloomington, 1973-1994; res assocpaleont, Smithsonian Inst, 1971-; fulbright prof, Trinity Col, Dublin, 1971-1972; from asst prof to prof geol, Univ Calif, Los Angeles, 1958-1973; Fulbright scholar, Univ Tasmania, 1955-1956. **Memberships:** Paleont Soc (pres 1988); Soc Econ Paleontologists & Mineralogists; Soc VertPaleont; Paleont Asn. **Research Statement & Publications:** Functional morphology and community relations of fossil crinoids. **Mailing Address:** Dept Geol Sci, Ind Univ, GY513, 1001 E 10th St, Bloomington, IN 47405-1405. **Fax:** 812-855-7899. **E-Mail:** lane@indiana.edu

LANE, ORRIS JOHN, JR, ROAD PAVEMENT. **Personal Data:** b Sigourney, Iowa, April 21, 1932. **Education:** Iowa State Univ, BS, 1957. **Professional Experience:** Stand Comt Direct Design Buried Concrete Pipe, Am Soc Civil Engrs, 1990-; TESTING ENGR, IOWA DEPT TRANSP, 1987-; Portland cement concrete engr, Iowa DeptTransp, 1983-1987; dist mat engr, Iowa Dept Transp, 1973-1983; Mem, C-13 Tech ComnConcrete Pipe, Am Soc Testing & Mat, 1967-1973 & 1983-; Asst dist mat engr, Portland cementconcrete engr, 1963-1973; spec invest eng, Iowa Hwy Comn, 1962-1963; Asst dist mat engr, Iowa Hwy Comn, 1957-1962. **Memberships:** Nat Soc Prof Engrs. **Research Statement & Publications:** A principle in development of the Iowa System for concrete bridge floor repair and rehabilitation; a principle in development of the Iowa Fast Track system for concrete pavement which permits early return of the new pavement to service. **Mailing Address:** 1111 Garfield, Ames, IA 50014.

LANE, PETER, ORNITHOLOGY. **Honors & Awards:** Commemorative Medal, Confederation Can, 1993. **Research Statement & Publications:** Author of two books. **Mailing Address:** 210 Chemin de l'Eperon CP 1654, Lac Beauport, PQ G0A 2C0, Can.

LANE, RAYMOND OSCAR, NUCLEAR PHYSICS. **Personal Data:** b Asbury Park, NJ, September 25, 1924; m 1949, c 3. **Education:** Iowa State Univ, PhD (physics), 1953. **Professional Experience:** RETIRED; distinguished prof physics, Ohio Univ, beginning 1974; prof physics, OhioUniv, 1966-1974; assoc physicist, Argonne Nat Lab, 1953-1966; res asst, Inst Atomic Res, Iowa State Col, 1949-1953. **Memberships:** Am Phys Soc. **Research Statement & Publications:** Penetration of electrons in matter; beta ray spectroscopy; neutron scattering; neutron polarization; nuclear structure. **Mailing Address:** 10 Canterbury Dr, Athens, OH 45701.

LANE, RICHARD DURELLE, MONOCLONAL ANTIBODY TECHNOLOGY, ENZYMOLOGY. **Personal Data:** b Detroit, Mich, May 14, 1953; m 1975, c 3. **Education:** Bowling Green State Univ, BS, 1975; Med Col Va, PhD (anat), 1980. **Professional Experience:** PROF NEUROBIOLOGY, MED COL OHIO, as of 2004; assoc prof neurobiology, Med Col Ohio, beginning 1987; asst prof, Med ColOhio, 1984-1987; instr, Med Col Ohio, 1980-1983; NIH res technician, Med Col Ohio, 1975-1976. **Memberships:** Soc Neurosci; AAAS; Am Asn Immunologists. **Research Statement & Publications:** Investigating the reorganization of the somatosensory system in response to peripheral nerve injury. **Mailing Address:** Dept Anat, Med Col Ohio, Rm 103, Health Sci Bldg, 3035 Arlington Ave, Toledo, OH 43614. **Fax:** 419-383-4126. **E-Mail:** rlane@mco.edu

LANE, RICHARD L, CERAMICS, ELECTRONIC MATERIALS. **Personal Data:** b Franklinville, NY, March 11, 1935; m 1958, Helen; c 4. **Education:** State Univ NY, Alfred, BS, 1957, PhD (ceramic sci), 1962. **Honors & Awards:** Tech Innovation Awards, NASA. **Professional Experience:** PROF EMER, MICROELECTRONIC ENG, ROCHESTER INST TECHNOL, 2001-; prof microelectronic eng, Rochester inst Technol, 1987-2001; dir, Technol Ctr, Kayex Corp, 1978-1987; dir eng, Hamco div, 1974-1978; mgr res & develop, Hamco Mach & Electronics Corp, 1970-1974; proj leader, Hamco Mach & Electronics Corp, 1968-1970; res scientist, Fundamental res lab, 1965-1968; res scientist, Appl res lab, Xerox Corp, 1962-1965. **Research Statement & Publications:** chemical-mechanical planarization of integrated circuits; chemistry of glass, surface properties and reactions, high temperature reactions and crystal-glass interactions; chemical and physical properties of crystalline ceramic materials; semiconductor materials processing; plasma etching. **Mailing Address:** Rochester Inst Technol, Rochester, NY 14623. **Fax:** 585-475-5041. **E-Mail:** rllemc@ritvax.isc.rit.edu

LANE, RICHARD NEIL, MATHEMATICS, ELECTRICAL ENGINEERING. **Personal Data:** b Richmond, Va, September 1, 1944. **Education:** Calif Inst Technol, BS, 1965, PhD (math), 1968. **Professional Experience:** PRES, REV CONSULT LTD, 1975-; dir commun studies, Systs Applns, Inc, 1970-1975; sr scientist, Systs Applns, Inc, 1969-1970; mem prof staff math, Gen Elec Co, 1968-1969; PRES, LANE WESTLY INC. **Memberships:** Am Math Soc; Inst Elec & Electronics Engrs. **Research Statement & Publications:** Systems analysis and modeling of cost and performance of communications systems, especially mobile radio and common carrier systems. **Mailing Address:** Lane Westly Inc, 2813 Easton Dr, Hillsborough, CA 94010-6009. **Fax:** 650-347-0160. **E-Mail:** richardl@revconsultants.com

LANE, ROBERT HAROLD, BIOINORGANIC CHEMISTRY, INORGANIC CHEMISTRY. **Personal Data:** b Tampa, Fla, September 4, 1944. **Education:** Univ NC, BS, 1966; Univ Fla, PhD (chem), 1971. **Professional Experience:** Soc Plastic Engr, Oilfield Chem Prog Comt, 2001-; Soc Plastic Engr, Distinguished Lectr Comt, 2002-; Soc Plastic Comt distinguished lect, 1999-2000; CONSULT, NSTAR TECHNOL INT, 1995-; prin staff engr, ARCO Alaska, Inc, Anchorage, 1990-1995; res dir, ARCO Res & Tech Serv, Plano, Tex, 1985-1990; proj leader, ARCO Corp Tech, Chatsworth, CA, 1983-1985; sr res scientist, Occidental Res Corp, Irvine, CA, 1980-1983; asst prof chem, Univ Ga, 1975-1980; instr, Univ Ga, 1973-1980; sr res fel, Ore Grad Ctr, 1973; NIH fel, Ore Grad Ctr, 1973; assoc phys biochem, Ore Grad Ctr, 1971-1972. **Memberships:** Am Chem Soc. **Research Statement & Publications:** Theoretical and experimental aspects of transition metal electron transfer in multinuclear systems; highly dispersed metal species on ordered supports. **Mailing Address:** NStar Technol Int, Houston, TX 77005.

LANE, ROBERT KENNETH, ENVIRONMENTAL SCIENCE, RESOURCE MANAGEMENT. **Personal Data:** b Brandon, Man, February 7, 1937; m 1961, c 1. **Education:** Brandon Col, BSc, 1957; Ore State Univ, MS, 1962, PhD (oceanog), 1965. **Honors & Awards:** Centennial Medal, Govt Can, 1967, Merit Award, 1977. **Professional Experience:** PRIN PROJ MGR, WESTERN ENVIRON PERSPECTIVES LTD, as of 2004; PRES, WESTERN ENVIRON PERSPECTIVES LTD, 1992-; dir, Environ Protection Serv, 1982-1992; dir water proj, Can W Found, 1979-1981; sci adv, Environ Can, 1975-1979; chmn, Int Joint Comn Upper Great Lakes Water Qual Bd, 1972-1975 & Poplar River Bd, 1978-1980; res scientist, Environ Can, 1966-1975; instr oceanog, Ore State Univ, 1963-1966; oceanogr, Fisheries Res Bd Can, 1959-1961; forecaster, Meteorol Serv Can, 1957-1958; prin investr, Landsat & Skylab, NASA. **Memberships:** Am Soc Limnol & Oceanog; Am Geophys Union; Royal Meteorol Soc; Int Asn GtLakes Res (pres, 1974-1975); Am Meteorol Soc; Sigma Xi. **Research Statement & Publications:** Physical oceanography and limnology, especially heat and radiation exchange; remote sensing; meteorology. **Mailing Address:** Western Environ Perspectives Ltd, PO Box 65053, St Albert, AB T8N 5Y3, Can.

LANE, ROBERT SIDNEY, MEDICAL ENTOMOLOGY, MICROBIOLOGY. **Personal Data:** b Worcester, Mass, March 7, 1944; m 1968, c 2. **Education:** Univ Calif, Berkeley, BA, 1966, PhD (entom), 1974; San Francisco State Col, MA, 1969. **Professional Experience:** ASSOC PROF, DEPT ENTOM SCI, UNIV CALIF, BERKELEY, 1984-; assoc specialist, Dept Entom Sci, Univ Calif, Berkeley, 1980-1984; lectr, BiolDept, San Francisco State Univ, 1979-1980; assoc pub health biologist, Vector Biol & ControlSect, State Dept Health, Calif, 1977-1979; asst pub health biologist, Vector Biol & Control Sect, State Dept Health, Calif, 1974-1977; fel, Calif Acad Sci. **Memberships:** Entom Soc Am; Wildlife Dis Asn; Am Soc Trop Med & Hyg; Soc VectorEcologists; Sigma Xi. **Research Statement & Publications:** Biosystematics of Tabanidae (Diptera); ecology and epidemiology of tick-borne disease, particularly Lyme disease and other spirochetoses. **Mailing Address:** Dept Entom Sci, Univ Calif, 411 201 Wellman Hall, Berkeley, CA 94720-3112. **Fax:** 510-642-7428. **E-Mail:** blane@nature.berkeley.edu

LANE, ROGER LEE, ZOOLOGY, EMBRYOLOGY. **Personal Data:** b Mt Carmel, Ill, July 4, 1945; m 1968, Paulette; c Leigh S, Brooke C & Taylor C. **Education:** Univ Nebr, BS, 1968, MS, 1971, PhD (zoology), 1974. **Professional Experience:** PROF BIOL SCI, KENT STATE UNIV, 1980-; asst prof, Kent State Univ, 1975-1980; vis lectr zool, John F Kennedy Col, 1973-1975. **Memberships:** Crustacean Soc; Am Malacol Union; Am Micros Soc; Nat Asn Biol Teachers. **Research Statement & Publications:** Histology and histochemistry of terrestrial isopod crustaceans and terrestrial pulmonate gastropods. **Mailing Address:** Dept Biol Sci, Kent State Univ, 3325 W 13 St, Ashtabula, OH 44004. **Fax:** 216-964-4257. **E-Mail:** lane@ashtabula.kent.edu

LANE, STEPHEN MARK, PHYSICS. **Personal Data:** b Scott Air Force Base, Ill, November 22, 1948. **Education:** San Jose State Univ, BA, 1971; Univ Calif, Davis, MS, 1973, PhD (appl sci), 1979. **Professional Experience:** ASSOC DIR, SCI & TECHNOL, LAWRENCE LIVERMORE NAT LAB, as of 2003; DIR, PHYSICS & ADV TECHNOL, LAWRENCE LIVERMORE NAT LAB, as of 2003; SR SCIENTIST, LAWRENCE LIVERMORE NAT LAB, 1992-; physicist, Laser Fusion, Lawrence Livermore Nat Lab, 1978-1984. **Memberships:** Am Phys Soc. **Research Statement & Publications:** Atomic and nuclear spectroscopy as applied to laser fusion research. **Mailing Address:** Lawrence Livermore Nat Lab, 7000 E Ave, Livermore, CA 94551. **Fax:** 925-424-2778. **E-Mail:** slane@llnl.gov

LANE, WILLIAM JAMES, ANALYTICAL CHEMISTRY. **Personal Data:** b Zanesville, Ohio, December 5, 1925; m 1950, c 3. **Education:** Denison Univ, BA, 1947; Miami Univ, MS, 1953; Iowa State Univ, PhD (chem), 1957. **Professional Experience:** LAB SUPVR, ANAL RES & SCHEDULING, UOP, INC, 1981-; labsupvr, spectroscopy & anal res, 1978-1981; group leader anal chem res & develop, Universal Oil Prod Co, 1974-1978; res coordr anal chem, Universal Oil Prod Co, 1969-1974; res anal chemist, Chem Div, 1964-1969; anal group supvr, Columbia-Southern Chem Corp, Pittsburgh Plate Glass Co, 1960-1964; anal chemist, Columbia-Southern Chem Corp, Pittsburgh Plate Glass Co, 1957-1960; res asst anal chem, Ames Lab, Iowa State Univ, 1952-1957; asst chemist, AEC, Mound Lab, Monsanto Chem Co, 1948-1951. **Memberships:** Am Chem Soc. **Research Statement & Publications:** General wet chemical analysis; polarography; chromatography; spectrophotometry. **Mailing Address:** 444 W Norman Ct, Des Plaines, IL 60016-2443.

LANE, WILLIAM W, ELECTRONICS ENGINEERING. **Personal Data:** b Roanoke, Va, February 25, 1934; m 1978, Ronnie G; c Jonathan D, Drew H & Craig M. **Education:** Brooklyn Col, BA, 1956; Cornell Univ, MBA, 1958. **Professional Experience:** PRES, W LANE & ASSOC INC, NEW YORK, 1992-; chmn, Emerson Comput Corp, 1989-1991; chmn, Maj Exco Imports Inc, 1977-1985; chmn & dir, Emerson, Hong Kong, 1976; chmn, chief exec officer & dir, Emerson Radio Corp, North Bergen, NJ, 1974-1991; vchmn & dir, Int Chia Hsin, Taipai, Taiwan, 1973-1976; vpres & dir, Int Transistor Corp, Burbank, 1971-1973; chmn & dir, Major Electronics Corp, 1970; pres, Majorette Enterprises, 1961-; vpres, MajorElectronics Corp, 1959-1970; mem bus adv bd, USSenate; chmn, H H Scott, Inc Cardiac Resuscitator Corp; chmn, Emerson Investment Corp; chmn, Major Realty Corp; chmn, Emteck Technol Ltd. **Mailing Address:** 760 Park Ave, New York, NY 10021-4152.

LANFORD, OSCAR E, III, MATHEMATICAL PHYSICS, ANALYSIS & FUNCTIONAL ANALYSIS. **Personal Data:** b New York, NY, January 6, 1940; m 1961, Regina Krigman;

c Lizabeth M. **Education:** Wesleyan Univ, BA, 1960; Princeton Univ, MA, 1962, PhD (physics), 1966. **Honorary Degrees:** ScD, Wesleyan Univ, 1990. **Honors & Awards:** Award in Appl Math & Numerical Analysis, Nat Acad Sci, 1986. **Professional Experience:** PROF MATH, SWISS FED INST TECHNOL, ZURICH, 1987-; prof physics, Inst des Haute Estudes Sci, Bures-sur-Yvette, France, 1982-1987; exchange prof, Univ Aix-Marseille, 1971; mem, Inst Advan Studies, 1970; Alfred Sloan Found res fel, 1969-1971; vis profphysics, Inst des Haute Estudes Sci, Bures-sur-Yvette, France, 1967-1968; from asst prof to profmath, Univ Calif, Berkeley, 1966-1987; instr math, Princeton Univ, 1965-1966. **Memberships:** Am Math Soc. **Research Statement & Publications:** Mathematical physics, especiallystatistical mechanics and dynamical systems theory. **Mailing Address:** D-Math, ETH - Zentrum, Zurich 8092, Switzerland. **E-Mail:** lanford@math.ethz.ch

LANFORD, ROBERT ELDON, IMMUNOLOGY, VIROLOGY. **Personal Data:** b Ft Worth, Tex, April 18, 1951; m 1972, Deborah Hanna; c Shane & Jeremiah. **Education:** Univ Tex, BS, 1974; Baylor Col Med, PhD (virol), 1979. **Professional Experience:** Adj prof, Dept Microbiol, Univ Tex Health Sci Ctr, San Antonio, 1991-; SCIENTIST, DEPT VIROL & IMMUNOL, SOUTHWEST FOUND BIOMED RES, SANANTONIO, TEX, 1990-; assoc scientist, Dept Virol & Immunol, Southwest Found Biomed Res, San Antonio, 1986-1989; from adj prof to adj assoc prof, Dept Microbiol, Univ Tex Health SciCtr, San Antonio, 1984-1991; asst scientist, Dept Virol & Immunol, Southwest Found BiomedRes, San Antonio, 1984-1985; asst prof, Dept Virol & Epidemiol, Baylor Col Med, Houston, Tex, 1982-1984. **Memberships:** Am Soc Microbiol; Am Soc Virol; Am Soc Cell Biol. **Research Statement & Publications:** Hepatitis B virus; hepatitis C virus; lipoprotein (a). **Mailing Address:** Dept Virol & Immunol, SW Found Biomed Res, 7620 NW Loop 410, San Antonio, TX 78228-0147. **E-Mail:** rlanford@icarus.sfbr.org

LANFORD, WILLIAM ARMISTEAD, ION BEAM ANALYSIS OF MATERIALS, THIN FILM PHYSICS. **Personal Data:** b Albany, NY, November 15, 1944; c Catherine, William & Anne. **Education:** Univ Rochester, BS, 1966, PhD (physics), 1972. **Honors & Awards:** Semiconductor Res Corp Inventor Recognition Award, 1994, 1996 & 1998. **Professional Experience:** Vis prof, Univ Uppsala, Sweden, 1994-1996; guest researcher, Royal Swedish Acad Sci, 1994-1996; chmn, Physics Dept, State Univ NY, Albany, 1990-1992; chair physics dept, State Univ NY, Albany, 1990-1992; coun rep, NY State Sect, Am Phys Soc, 1989-1991; dir, Accelerator Lab, State Univ NY, Albany, 1988-1994; chmn, NY State Sect, Am Phys Soc, 1987-1989; consult, Nat Semiconductor, 1984 & Bell Labs, 1985-1992; vchmn, NY State Sect, Am Phys Soc, 1985-1987; PROF PHYSICS, STATE UNIV NY, ALBANY, 1983-; ed, Radiation Effects, 1983-1989; mem, Int Adv Comt, Ion Beam Analysis Conf, 1981-; consult, IBM, 1980-; consult, Exxon, 1979-1993; assoc ed, Appl Nuclear Sci, 1979-1992; fel, Alfred P Sloan Found, 1979-1983; assoc prof, State Univ NY, Albany, 1979-1983; consult, Sotheby's, 1979; from asst prof to assoc prof physics, Yale Univ, 1973-1979; asst prof, Mich State Univ, 1972-1973; res assoc, Mich State Univ, 1971-1972. **Memberships:** Am Ceramic Soc; Am Phys Soc; Mat Res Soc; Hist Metall Soc; Bohmtsche Phys Soc; Sigma Xi; AAAS. **Research Statement & Publications:** Use of neuron beams in the study of materials including nuclear reaction analysis of hydrogen in materials; reaction of glass with water; microelectronic materials; archaeological materials. **Mailing Address:** Dept Physics, State Univ NY, Albany, NY 12222. **Fax:** 518-442-4486. **E-Mail:** lanford@albany.edu

LANG, BRUCE Z, PARASITOLOGY, IMMUNOLOGY. **Personal Data:** b St Joseph, Mo, May 31, 1937; m 1959, c 2. **Education:** Chico State Col, BS, 1960; Univ NC, Chapel Hill, MSPH, 1961, PhD (parasitol), 1966. **Professional Experience:** PROF EMER, BIOL, EASTERN WASH UNIV, as of 2005; chmn dept biol, Eastern Wash Univ, 1978-1980; mem grad fac, Wash State Univ, 1977-; USDA grants, 1977-1983; affil fac mem, Univ Idaho, 1975-; prof biol, Eastern Wash Univ, 1974-; NSF grants, 1969-1972; from asst prof to assoc prof, Eastern Wash Univ, 1967-1974; vis asst prof zool, Univ Okla, 1966-1967; NIH fel zool, Univ Okla, 1966-1967. **Memberships:** AAAS; Am Soc Parasitol; Am Soc Zoologists; Am Soc Trop Med & Hyg; Am Inst Biol Sci. **Research Statement & Publications:** Host-parasite relationships; ecology of parasitism; ecology of fresh-water gastropod molluscs. **Mailing Address:** Dept Biol, Eastern Wash Univ, Cheney, WA 99004-2440. **E-Mail:** blang@mail.ewu.edu

LANG, C MAX, LABORATORY ANIMAL MEDICINE. **Personal Data:** b Paris, Ill, December 29, 1937; m 1965, Sylvia; c Karen E, John A & Susan C L (Swiegert). **Education:** Univ Ill, BS, 1959, DVM, 1961. **Honors & Awards:** Res Award, Am Asn Lab Animal Sci, 1979 & 1980; Charles River Prize, 1987. **Professional Experience:** GEORGE T HARREL PROF, DEPT COMP MED, COL MED, MILTON S HERSHEY MED CTR, PA STATE UNIV, as of 2005; CHMN, DEPT COMP MED, COL MED, MILTON S HERSHEY MED CTR, PA STATE UNIV, 1966-. **Memberships:** Am Col Lab Animal Med (secy-treas, 1981-1990, pres-elect, 1990-1991, pres, 1991-1992). **Research Statement & Publications:** Environmental factors that can influence interpretation of research data; published over 20 articles. **Mailing Address:** Milton S Hershey Med Ctr, Pa State Univ PO Box 850, Hershey, PA 17033-0850. **Fax:** 717-531-5001. **E-Mail:** cml7@psu.edu

LANG, CALVIN ALLEN, GERONTOLOGY, NUTRITION. **Personal Data:** b Portland, Ore, June 13, 1925; m 1949, c 4. **Education:** Princeton Univ, AB, 1947; Johns Hopkins Univ, ScD(biochem), 1954. **Honors & Awards:** Tanner Lectr, Inst Food Tech, 1973. **Professional Experience:** Nat Sigma Xi lectureship, 1990; DIR, LOUISVILLE LONGITUDINAL LONGEVITY PROG, 1983-; PROF BIOCHEM, SCH MED, UNIV LOUISVILLE, 1972-; dir biomed aging res prog, Louisville Longitudinal Longevity Prog, 1971-1974; NIH fel, 1957-1959 & res career develop award, 1967-1972; from asst prof to assoc prof, Louisville Longitudinal Longevity Prog, 1959-1972; res assoc, Sch Hyg & Pub Health, Johns Hopkins Univ, 1956-1959; Fel, Sch Hyg & Pub Health & McCollum-Pratt Inst, Johns Hopkins Univ, 1956-1959; asst scientist insect biochem, Conn Agr Exp Sta, 1954-1956; Res collabr, Brookhaven Nat Labs, 1949-1951. **Memberships:** Am Soc Biol Chem; Am Inst Clin Nutrit; Soc Exp Biol & Med; fel Geront Soc (vpres, 1971); Sigma Xi. **Research Statement & Publications:** Biochemistry of growth and aging; insect and nutritional biochemistry; glutathione detoxification and aging. **Mailing Address:** Dept Biochem MDR 412, Univ Louisville Sch Med, Louisville, KY 40292-0001.

LANG, CHARLES H, INSULIN RESISTANCE, TRACER METHODOLOGY. **Personal Data:** b Pittsburgh, Pa, July 7, 1954; m 1981, c 3. **Education:** Westminster Col, BS, 1976; Hahnemann Med Col, MS, 1979, PhD (physiol), 1981. **Professional Experience:** PROF & VICE CHMN, CELLULAR & MOLECULAR PHYSIOL, PA STATE COL MED, HERSHEY, 1997-; PROF SURG, PA STATE COL MED, HERSHEY, 1997-; PROF SURG, UNIV HOSP, STATE UNIV NY STONY BROOK, 1992-; from asst prof to assoc prof metab & shock, La State Univ Med Ctr, 1986-; res asst prof metab & shock, La State Univ Med Ctr, 1984-1986; fel metab, La State Univ Med Ctr, 1981-1984. **Memberships:** Shock Soc; Am Physiol Soc; Am Diabetes Asn; Internal Endotoxin Soc; Res Soc Alcoholism; Surg Infection Soc. **Research Statement & Publications:** The role of glucose counter-regulatory hormones in mediating insulin action in various pathophysiological conditions, including sepsis, diabetes, chronic alcoholism and burn; the influence of various cytokines on carbohydrate homeostasis and their putative role in endotoxemia and sepsis. **Mailing Address:** Dept Cellular & Molecular Physiol, Penn State Univ Col Med, 500 Univ Dr, Hershey, PA 17033. **Fax:** 717-531-7667. **E-Mail:** clang@psu.edu

LANG, CONRAD MARVIN, PHYSICAL CHEMISTRY, INORGANIC CHEMISTRY. **Personal Data:** b Chicago, Ill, July 1, 1939; m 1961, Louise; c Kevin Alan, Kurtis Erik & Kenneth Marvin. **Education:** Elmhurst Col, BS, 1961; Univ Wis-Madison, MS, 1964; Univ Wyo, PhD (chem), 1970. **Honors & Awards:** Helen M Free Award, Pub Outreach, Am Chem Soc, 1997; Eugene Katz Distinguished L&S prof, Univ Wis, 2001. **Professional Experience:** PROF EMER & HON UNIV ASSOC, 2006-; vis prof chem, Univ Wis, Madison, Bd dirs, Am Chem Soc, 1989-1995; W B King vis prof chem, Iowa State Univ, 1976-1977; PROF CHEM, UNIV WIS, STEVENS POINT, 1978-; NSF res grant, Univ Wis, Stevens Point, 1971-1973; CONSULT, CROWNS, MERKLIN, MIDTHUN & HILL, ATTORNEYS LAW, 1970-; from instr to assoc prof, Univ Wis, Stevens Point, 1964-1978; res asst, Univ Wis-Madison, 1963-1964; teaching asst chem, Univ Wis, Madison, 1961-1963. **Memberships:** Am Chem Soc; Hon lifetime foreign mem, Finnish Chem Soc. **Research Statement & Publications:** Application of electron spin resonance to molecular structure and macromolecular aspects of binary fluid mixtures; semiempirical quantum chemical calculations on systems of biological interest; physiochemical aspects of vision; chemical philately; chemical demonstrations; history of science. **Mailing Address:** Dept Chem, Univ Wis, Stevens Point, WI 54481. **Fax:** 715-346-2640. **E-Mail:** cmlang@uwsp.edu

LANG, DAVID (VERN), SEMICONDUCTORS, PHYSICS. **Personal Data:** b Willmar, Minn, July 11, 1943; m 1968, c 3. **Education:** Concordia Col, Moorhead, Minn, BA, 1965; Univ Wis-Madison, PhD (physics), 1969. **Honors & Awards:** Morris E Leeds Award, Inst Elec & Electronics Engrs, 1988. **Professional Experience:** ADJ MAT PHYSICS DIR, SEMICONDUCTOR ELECTRONICS RES DEPT, LUCENT TECHOL, 1996-; SEMICONDUCTOR ELECTRONICS RES DEPT, LUCENT TECHNOL, 1987-; head, Semiconductor Electronics Res Dept, Bell Labs, 1981-1987; mem tech staff, Bell Labs, 1972-1981; res asst prof, Univ Ill, Urbana, 1970-1972; res assoc physics, Univ Ill, Urbana, 1969-1970. **Memberships:** fel Am Phys Soc; sr mem Inst Elec & Electronics Engrs. **Research Statement & Publications:** Capacitance spectroscopy (Deep Level Transient Spectroscopy); defects in III-V semiconductors; recombination enhanced solid state defect reactions; radiation damage in semiconductors; gap states in amorphous semiconductors. **Mailing Address:** Lucent Technol, Rm 1C-327 700 Mountain Ave, Murray Hill, NJ 07974-0636. **Fax:** 908-582-2043. **E-Mail:** dvl@bell-labs.com

LANG, DIMITRIJ ADOLF, BIOPHYSICS, MOLECULAR BIOLOGY. **Personal Data:** b Berlin, Ger, August 30, 1926; m 1959, c 2. **Education:** Univ Frankfurt, MS, 1953, PhD (biophys), 1959. **Professional Experience:** RETIRED; NIH res career develop awards, 1967-1971 & 1972-1976; from asstprof to prof biol, Univ Tex, Dallas, 1965-1991; res asst biophys, Max Planck Inst Biophys, 1953-1958 & Hyg Inst, Univ Frankfurt, 1958-1965. **Memberships:** Electron Micros Soc Am; Biophys Soc. **Research Statement & Publications:** Electronics; physics of ionizing radiations; high-output x-ray machines; standard dosimetry of x-rays; electron microscopy of bacteria, viruses and nucleic acids; physical chemistry of nucleic acids. **Mailing Address:** 802 St Lukes Dr, Richardson, TX 75080.

LANG, ENID ASHER, PSYCHIATRY. **Personal Data:** b Los Angeles, Calif, August 28, 1944; m Norton; c Eugene & Aaron. **Education:** Radcliffe Col, AB, 1966; Univ Southern Calif, MD, 1970; Columbia Univ, MS, 1974. **Honorary Degrees:** MPN, Columbia Univ, 1974. **Professional Experience:** CLIN ASSOC PROF & FAC MEM PSYCHIAT, MT SINAI SCH MED, NY, 1981-, dir, Socialization Prog Psychiat Outpatients, 1975-; dir, Group Psychiat & Training Psychiat Residents, Bellevue Hosp, Sch Med, NY Univ, 1975-; facmem, Sch Med, NY Univ, 1975-1980; res fel, Columbia Univ Health Serv, 1974-1975; resident psychiat, Columbia Psychiat Inst, 1972-1974; med intern, Beth Israel Hosp, NY, 1971-1972; process groups psychiat residents training, Mt Sinai Med Ctr, Dept Psychiat, Psychoanal & Lit, teaching course fac. **Memberships:** Am Psychiat Asn; NY Acad Sci; Am Women's Med Asn. **Research Statement & Publications:** A longitudinal comparative study of treatment-outcome of discharged psychiatric outpatients who receive group therapy with medication versus individual therapy with medication only. **Mailing Address:** Dept Psychiat, Mt Sinai Sch Med, PO Box 1230 One Gustave L Levy Pl, New York, NY 10029. **Fax:** 212-860-3945.

LANG, ERICH KARL, RADIOLOGY, INTERVENTIONAL RADIOLOGY. **Personal Data:** b Vienna, Austria, December 7, 1929; American citizen; m 1956, Nicole; c Erich C & Cortney A. **Education:** Columbia Univ, MS, 1951; Univ Vienna, MD, 1953. **Honors & Awards:** Distinguished Serv Awd, Amer Board of Radiology. **Professional Experience:** DIR COMPUT TOPOGRAPHY, SCH MED, TULANE UNIV, as of 2004; prof radiol, Univ Med & Dent NJ, 1995-; PROF RADIOL, SCH MED, TULANE UNIV, 1976-; prof radiol & urol, sch med, la state univ, new orleans, beginning 1976; prof radiol & chmn dept, Sch Med, La State Univ, Shreveport, 1967-1976; chmn dept, Sch Med, Tulane Univ, 1967-1976; radiologist, Methodist Hosp, Indianapolis, Ind, 1961-1967; assoc radiologist, Johns Hopkins Hosp & Univ, 1959-1961; assoc radiol, Johns Hopkins Hosp & Univ, 1956-1959. **Memberships:** AMA; Radiol Soc NAm; Soc Nuclear Med; Am Col Radiol; Am Col Chest Physicians; pres Soc of Uroradiology; pres Soc of Gynecoradiolgy. **Research Statement & Publications:** Diagnostic, vascular roentgenographic examinations; diagnostic roentgenographic evaluation of tumors and tumor diagnosis. **Mailing Address:** Tulaue Health Sci Center, 1430 Tulaue Ave, New Orleans, LA 70110. **Fax:** 504-568-8955. **E-Mail:** elang1@tulane.edu

LANG, FRANK ALEXANDER, SYSTEMATIC BOTANY. **Personal Data:** b Olympia, Wash, May 14, 1937; m 1959, Suzanne; c Thomas & Amy. **Education:** Ore State Univ, BS, 1959; Univ Wash, MS, 1961; Univ BC, PhD (bot), 1965. **Professional Experience:** PROF EMER BIOL, SOUTHERN ORE UNIV, 1998-; chmn, dept, Southern Ore State Col, 1990-1998; vis scholar, Harvard Univ, Herbaria, 1981-1982; prof biol, Southern Ore State Col, beginning 1977; chmn dept, Southern Ore State Col, 1976-1981 & 1990-1996; from asst prof to assoc prof, Southern Ore State Col, 1966-1977; asst prof biol, Whitman Col, 1965-1966. **Memberships:** Am Fern Soc; Calif Bot soc. **Research Statement & Publications:** natural mist for the hoi polli flora of the Siskiyou mountains; native plant conservation. **Mailing Address:** Dept Biol, Southern Ore Univ, 1250 Siskiyou Blvd, Ashland, OR 97520. **E-Mail:** frlang@charter.net

LANG, FRANK THEODORE, PHYSICAL CHEMISTRY. **Personal Data:** b New York, NY, January 25, 1938; m 1963, c 3. **Education:** St Francis Col, NY, BS, 1959; Rensselaer Polytech Inst, PhD (phys chem), 1964. **Professional Experience:** RETIRED; prof chem, Fairleigh Dickinson Univ, Florham-Madison, beginning 1980; chmn, Dept Chem, 1970-1973 & 1989-1993; assoc prof phys chem, Fairleigh DickinsonUniv, Florham-madison, 1967-1980; res assoc-instr energy transfer, Univ NC, Chapel Hill, 1965-1967; res assoc photochem, Univ Sheffield, 1964-1965. **Memberships:** Am Chem Soc. **Research Statement & Publications:** Charge transfer complexes; flash photolysis; low temperature photochemistry; energy transfer processes; luminescene studies; oscillating reactions. **Mailing Address:** Dept Chem, Fairleigh Dickinson Univ, Madison, NJ 07940. **E-Mail:** lang@fdu.edu

LANG, GEORGE E, TOPOLOGY. **Personal Data:** b Chicago, Ill, June 29, 1942; m 1968, c 2. **Education:** Loyola Univ Chicago, BS, 1964; Univ Dayton, MS, 1966; Purdue Univ, PhD (math), 1970. **Professional Experience:** PROF MATH & COMPUT SCI, FAIRFIELD UNIV, as of 2004; assoc prof math & comput sci, Fairfield Univ, beginning 1970; teaching asst, Purdue Univ, 1967-1969 & Univ Dayton, 1964-1966. **Memberships:** Am Math Soc; Math Asn Am; Am Asn Univ Profs; Asn Comput Mach. **Research Statement & Publications:** Homotopy theory; subgroups of homotopy groups; direct limits of CW complexes with an eye to group theoretic applications. **Mailing Address:** Dept Math & Comput Sci, Fairfield Univ, 1073 N Benson Rd, Fairfield, CT 06824. **Fax:** 203-254-4163. **E-Mail:** lang@cs.fairfield.edu

LANG, GERALD EDWARD, PLANT ECOLOGY. **Personal Data:** b Chicago, Ill, March 1, 1945; m 1973, Joyce; c Stephanie R. **Education:** Western Ill Univ, BS, 1968; Univ Wyo, MS, 1969; Rutgers Univ, PhD (bot), 1973. **Professional Experience:** PROVOST & VPRES, ACAD AFFAIRS & RES, WVA UNIV, 1996; interim provost & Vpres, Acad Affairs & Res, Wva Uiv, 1995-1996; dean, Wva Univ, 1993-1996; dean, Eberly Col Art & Sci, 1987-1993; interim dean, Col Arts & Sci, Wva Univ, 1986-1987; NASA res grant, 1985-1988; PROF BIOL, WVA UNIV, 1984-; asst dean, Wva Univ, 1984-1986; Environ Protection Agency res contract, 1982-1985; Army Corps Engrs res contract, 1979-1982; from asst prof to assoc prof, WVa Univ, 1976-1984; NSF res grants, 1974-1985; res instr terrestrial ecol, Dartmouth Col, 1973-1976; teaching asst, Dept Bot, Rutgers Univ, 1969-1970; from teaching asst to res asst, Dept Bot, Univ Wyo, 1967-1969. **Memberships:** AAAS; Brit Ecol Soc; Ecol Soc Am. **Research Statement & Publications:** Vegetation patterns and biogeochemical processes in high-elevation wetland ecosystems in the Appalachian Mountains; decomposition rates for leaf and wood litter; concomitant elemental mineralization patterns in forest ecosystems. **Mailing Address:** Dept Biol, WVa Univ, 206 Stewart Hall PO Box 6203, Morgantown, WV 26506-6203. **E-Mail:** gelang@mail.wvu.edu

LANG, GERHARD HERBERT, MEDICAL MICROBIOLOGY, VETERINARY MEDICINE. **Personal Data:** b Neunkirchen, WGer, January 6, 1927; Canadian citizen; m 1959, c 2. **Education:** Univ Lyons, France, DVM, 1955; Pasteur Inst, Paris, cert bact, 1955; Univ Toronto, MVSc, 1962. **Professional Experience:** RETIRED; animal health expert virol, Food & Agr Orgn, Rome, 1971-1973; from asst prof to assoc prof vet virol, Ont Vet Col, Univ Guelph, 1961-1992; assoc vet, Beauquesne, France, 1955-1957. **Memberships:** Am Asn Avian Pathologists; World Vet Poultry Asn; Can Soc Microbiologists; AmSoc Microbiologists; Can Vet Med Asn. **Research Statement & Publications:** Animal and human virus infections, their diagnosis and control; medical and veterinary microbiology. **Mailing Address:** 87 Hearn Ave, Guelph, ON N1H 5Y6, Can.

LANG, HARRY GEORGE, PHYSICS. **Personal Data:** b Pittsburgh, Pa, June 2, 1947; m 1973, Bonnie. **Education:** Bethany Col, WVa, BS, 1969; Rochester Inst Technol, MS, 1974; Univ Rochester, EdD, 1979. **Honors & Awards:** Award from CEASD, 2001; James C Marsters Promotion Award for Outstanding Contributions Presented by TDI, 2001; Edmund Lyon Founders Award for Exceptional Prof Contributions to the Educ of Persons Who Are Deaf, Rochester Sch for the Deaf, 2001 Rochester Inst of Tech Eisenhart Outstanding Teacher for 1983. **Professional Experience:** PROF, DEPT EDUC RES & DEVELOP, ROCHESTER INST TECHNOL, NAT TECH INST DEAF, 1990-; vis lectr, Univ Leeds, Eng, 1988; coordr, Off Fac Develop, 1984-1990; vis prof, Univ Rochester, 1981-; prof physics, Rochester Inst Technol, Nat Tech Inst Deaf, 1980-1984; Consult, Proj Handicapped Sci, AAAS, 1978-; Asst prof, Rochester Inst Technol, Nat Tech Inst Deaf, 1970-1980; ed, Testing Phys Handicapped Students in Sci; consult, Res Better Sch, Inc; consult, Am Printing House for Blind. **Memberships:** Nat Sci Teachers Asn; AAAS; Asn Col Educators-Deaf & Hard Hearing; Nat Asn Res Sci Teaching; Asn Educ Teachers Sci. **Research Statement & Publications:** Test measurement theory; criterion referenced measurement; science curriculum research; digital computer analysis and synthesis of speech; historical contributions of deaf persons to science; research on effective teaching. **Mailing Address:** Nat Tech Inst for the Deaf, 96 Lomb Mem Dr, Rochester, NY 14623. **E-Mail:** harry.lang@rit.edu

LANG, IVAN MARSHALL, SWALLOWING, VOMITING. **Personal Data:** b Wilkes-Barre, Pa, October 26, 1947; m 1973, c 2. **Education:** Univ Pittsburgh, BS, 1969; Temple Univ, MS, 1975, PhD (physiol & biophys), 1980; Univ Wis, DVM, 1996. **Professional Experience:** ASSOC PROF MED, MED COL WIS, as of 2004; adj assoc prof med, Med Col Wis, beginning 1996; from asst prof to assocprof surg, Med Col Wis, 1983-1992. **Memberships:** Am Physiol Soc; Am Gastroenterol Asn; Soc Neuroscience; Am Motility Soc; Am VetMed Asn. **Research Statement & Publications:** Physiology of swallowing with special interest in bolus transport from pharynx to stomach and in the mechanisms of airway protection; physiology of vomiting and belching; peripheral and central neurol control of these phenomena. **Mailing Address:** Dept Gastroenterol & Hepatology, Med Col Wis, 8701 Watertown Plank Rd, Milwaukee, WI 53226. **E-Mail:** imlang@post.its.amcw.edu

LANG, JAMES D, AERONAUTICS. **Professional Experience:** RETIRED; dir technol, New Aircraft & Missile prod, McDonnel Douglas Aerospace, 1998-2001. **Memberships:** Hon fel Am Inst Aeronautics & Astronaut. **Mailing Address:** McDonnell Douglas Aerospace, Mailcode 0013422 PO Box 516, St Louis, MO 63166-0516. **Fax:** 314-232-9207.

LANG, JAMES FREDERICK, DRUG METABOLISM. **Personal Data:** b Dayton, Ohio, March 19, 1931; m 1958, c 2. **Education:** Univ Cincinnati, BS, 1958, MS, 1970. **Professional Experience:** RETIRED; group leader, drug metab clin res support, 1985-1990; sr res biochemist, Merrell Dow Res Inst, 1982-1985; sect head drug metab, Merrell Dow Pharmaceut, Inc, 1972-1982; from res asst biochem to biochemist, Merrell Dow Pharmaceut, Inc, 1963-1972; res asst toxicol & drug metab, Christ Hosp Inst Med Res, Subsid Elizabeth Gamble DeaconessHome Asn, 1958-1963. **Research Statement & Publications:** Isolation and identification of drug metabolites, pharmacokinetics; development and application of analytical methods for trace analysis of drug residues in biological media. **Mailing Address:** 2894 Pineridge Ave, Cincinnati, OH 45208-2818.

LANG, JEFFREY W, BIOLOGY. **Professional Experience:** PROF BIOL, UNIV NDAK, as of 2001. **Mailing Address:** Dept Biol, Univ NDak, PO Box 7144, Grand Forks, ND 58202-9019.

LANG, JOHN CALVIN, PHYSICAL CHEMISTRY. **Personal Data:** b Montclair, NJ, May 6, 1942; m 1966, Elizabeth; c Phebe D. **Education:** Wesleyan Univ, BA, 1964; Cornell Univ, MS, 1968, PhD (chem), 1972. **Professional Experience:** ASST TECH DIR, ALCON LABS, 1986-; adj assoc prof chem, Univ Tex, Arlington, 1986-; res assoc, Arco Oil & Gas Co, 1984-1986; res scientist phys chem, Procter & Gamble Co, 1975-1984; fel, Cornell Univ, 1972 & 1973-1975; fel, Univ Reading, Eng, 1972-1973; adv, Ctr Surface Sci & Eng, Univ Fla. **Memberships:** Am Phys Soc; Sigma Xi; Am Chem Soc; Controlled Release Soc. **Research Statement & Publications:** Phase equilibria; phase transitions; critical phenomena; thermodyamics of aqueous solutions; magnetic resonance; light scattering; surfactant, polymer and colloid physical chemistry; drug delivery, especially ophthalmalogic; drug assessment. **Mailing Address:** Alcon Res Ltd, 6201 S Freeway R0 11, Ft Worth, TX 76134-2099. **Fax:** 817-551-4584. **E-Mail:** john.lang@alconlabs.com

LANG, JOSEPH EDWARD, THEORETICAL PHYSICS. **Personal Data:** b Covington, Ky, August 10, 1942. **Education:** Thomas More Col, AB, 1964; Univ Ill, MS, 1965, PhD (physics), 1970; Wright State Univ, MS, 1988. **Professional Experience:** ASSOC PROF, COMPUT SCI DEPT, UNIV DAYTON, as of 2006; assoc prof physics, Univ Dayton, beginning 1981; vis scientist, Air Force Mat Lab, Wright-Patterson Air Force Base, 1978-1979; asst prof physics, Thomas More Col, 1971-1980; NSF fel, Lawrence Radiation Lab, Univ Calif, Berkeley, 1970-1971. **Memberships:** Am Phys Soc; Am Asn Physics Teachers; Sigma Xi. **Research Statement & Publications:** Elementary particle physics; magnetic anisotropy; computers in education. **Mailing Address:** Comput Sci Dept, Univ Dayton, Anderson Ctr Rm 146, Dayton, OH 45469-2160. **E-Mail:** joseph.lang@notes.udayton.edu

LANG, KENNETH LYLE, FRESHWATER ECOLOGY. **Personal Data:** b Cuba City, Wis, April 12, 1936; m 1961, c 1. **Education:** Iowa State Col, BS, 1959; Univ Iowa, MS, 1966, PhD (zoology), 1970. **Professional Experience:** ASSOC PROF EMER ZOOL, HUMBOLDT STATE UNIV, 2001-; assoc prof zool, Humboldt State Univ, 1977-2001; assoc prof biol, Humboldt State Univ, 1970-1977. **Memberships:** Am Soc Zool; Am Soc Limnol & Oceanog. **Research Statement & Publications:** Freshwater zooplankton populations; dispersion patterns and species diversity of benthic and planktonic Cladoceran assemblages. **Mailing Address:** Dept Biol, Humboldt State Univ, One Harpst St, Arcata, CA 95521-8299. **Fax:** 707-826-3201. **E-Mail:** kll1@axe.humboldt.edu

LANG, LAWRENCE GEORGE, SOLID STATE PHYSICS. **Personal Data:** b Pittsburgh, Pa, March 25, 1931; m 1953, c 2. **Education:** Carnegie Inst Technol, BS, 1952, MS, 1953, PhD (physics), 1957. **Professional Experience:** PROF EMER PHYSICS, PA STATE UNIV, 1997-; prof, Pa State Univ, 1973-1996; res physicist, Atomic Energy Res Estab, Eng, 1963-1965, 1966-1973; Nat AcadSci-Nat Res Coun fel, 1963-1964; asst prof to assoc prof physics, Carnegie Inst Technol, 1960-1966; eng specialist, Philco Corp, 1957-1958; res physicist, Carnegie Inst Technol, 1956-1957 & 1958-1960. **Memberships:** Am Phys Soc. **Research Statement & Publications:** Angular correlation of radiation from positron annihilation in solids; Mossbauer effect in compounds; paramagnetic and diamagnetic salts; biological macromolecules. **Mailing Address:** Dept Physics, Pa State Univ, 104 Davey Lab, Univ Park, PA 16802-6300. **Fax:** 814-865-3604. **E-Mail:** gx1@psu.edu

LANG, MARTIN, ENVIRONMENTAL ENGINEERING. **Professional Experience:** PVT CONSULT ENGR, 1989-. **Memberships:** Nat Acad Eng. **Mailing Address:** 11 Pine Dr N Apt A, Roslyn, NY 11576.

LANG, MARTIN T, COMPUTER IN MATHEMATICS EDUCATION. **Personal Data:** b Yokohama, Japan, May 7, 1936; m 1965, Barbara; c Rebecca, Ruth & Jonathan. **Education:** NCent Col, BA, 1959; Univ Kans, MA, 1963; Univ Tex-Austin, PhD (math educ), 1973. **Professional Experience:** PROF EMER, CALIF POLYTECH STATE UNIV, 1999-; prof math, Calif Polytech State Univ, 1978-1999; from asst prof to assoc prof, Calif Polytech State Univ, 1969-1978; from lectr to asst prof math, San Diego State Univ, 1964-1969; asst instr math, Univ Kans, 1963-1965; Nat Woodrow Wilson fel, 1959. **Memberships:** Math Asn Am; Nat Coun Teachers Math; Am Asn Univ Profs; Nat Educ Asn. **Research Statement & Publications:** Use of computers in math education at the college level; computer augmented instruction. **Mailing Address:** Dept Math, Calif Polytech State Univ, San Luis Obispo, CA 93407. **E-Mail:** mlang@calpoly.edu

LANG, MELVIN S, MATHEMATICS. **Professional Experience:** ASSOC VPRES ACAD ADMIN, WALLA WALLA COL, as of 2001; CHMN ACAD STAND ADMIS GRAD COUN, WALLA WALLA COL, as of 2001. **Mailing Address:** Walla Walla Col, 204 S Col Ave, College Place, WA 99324. **Fax:** 509-527-2253. **E-Mail:** scotbe@wwc.edu

LANG, NEIL CHARLES, CHEMICAL PHYSICS. **Personal Data:** b Montreal, Que, January 24, 1948; American citizen. **Education:** McGill Univ, BSc, 1968; Mass Inst Technol, PhD (phys chem), 1974. **Professional Experience:** CHEMIST, LASER PROG, LAWRENCE LIVERMORE LAB, 1976-; Fel, Nat Res Coun Can, 1974-1976. **Memberships:** Am Phys Soc; Sigma Xi. **Research Statement & Publications:** Chemical physics, reaction dynamics and energy transfer processes in gas phase collisions; applications in laser technology and isotope enrichment. **Mailing Address:** 670 Vernon St No 404, Oakland, CA 94610.

LANG, NORMA JEAN, PHYCOLOGY. **Personal Data:** b Memphis, Tenn, July 25, 1931. **Education:** Ohio State Univ, BS, 1952, MA, 1958; Ind Univ, PhD (bot), 1962. **Honors & Awards:** Darbaker Award in phycol, 1969. **Professional Experience:** PROF EMER BOT, UNIV CALIF, DAVIS, as of 2003; Guggenheim fel, Westfield Col, London, 1969-1970; NSF res grant, 1965-1967; from asst prof to assoc prof bot, Univ Calif, Davis, 1963-1974; NIH res fel algae, Univ Tex, 1962-1963. **Memberships:** Phycol Soc Am (treas, 1971-1973, vpres, 1974, pres, 1975); Brit Phycol Soc; Electron Micros Soc Am; Int Phycol Soc; Bot Soc Am. **Research Statement & Publications:** Electron microscopic studies of development in unicellular green algae, colonial green algae and cyanobacteria, especially diferentiation of hetercysts; desiccation survival and development of colonial form. **Mailing Address:** Dept Bot, Univ Calif, Davis, CA 95616. **E-Mail:** njlang@ucdavis.edu

LANG, NORMA M, NURSING, & PUBLIC POLICY. **Personal Data:** b Wausau, Wis, December 27, 1939; m Glenn; c Brian & Elizabeth. **Education:** Alverno Col, BS, 1961; Marquette Univ, MS, 1963, PhD, 1974. **Honorary Degrees:** MA, Univ Pa, 1992; DSc, State Univ NY, 1996; PhD, Marquette Univ, 2003. **Honors & Awards:** Jessie M Scott Award, American Nurses Association, 2002; Ernest A Codman Award, Joint Commission on Accreditation of Healthcare Organizations (JCAHO), 2001; Outstanding Leadership Award for the Advancement of Nursing Diagnosis, North American Nursing Diagnosis Association (NANDA), 1998; Fellow, The College of Physicians of Philadelphia, 1992; American Nurses Association Distinguished Membership Award, 1992. **Professional Experience:** 2005- University of Wisconsin System Distinguished Professor and Aurora Distinguished Professor of Healthcare Quality and Informatics at the University of Wisconsin-Milwaukee; Professor and Dean Emeritus, University of Pennsylvania; 2004-2005 Aurora Distinguished Professor of Healthcare Quality and Informatics at the University of Wisconsin-Milwaukee; 2000-2005 Professor and Lillian S. Brunner Chair in Medical Surgical Nursing at the School of Nursing, University of Pennsylvania; 1992-2000 Margaret Bond Simon Dean & Professor, School of Nursing, University of Pennsylvania; dean, Sch Nursing, Univ Wis, Milwaukee, 1980-1992; proj dir res develop grant, Sch Nursing, Univ Wis, Milwaukee, 1977-1979; ctr scientist, Urban Res Ctr, 1977-1979; res assoc, SchNursing, Univ Wis, Milwaukee, 1977; from asst prof to prof, Sch Nursing, Univ Wis, Milwaukee, 1968-1992; nursing coodr, Wis Regional Med Prog, 1968-1973; instr & asst prof, Sch Nursing, Univ Wis, Milwaukee, 1965-1969; instr & coodr med-surg nursing, St Mary's Sch Nursing, 1964-1965; staff nurse & asst instr, St Joseph's Hosp, 1961-1962. **Memberships:** Fellow, Institute of Medicine, National Academy of Science, 1988-; Fellow, Am Academy of Nursing, 1976-; Honorary Fellow, Royal Academy of Nursing, London, England, 1994-; Member, Am Medical Informatics Asn Association, 2000-; Am Asn of University Professors, 1968-; Am Public Health Association, 1968-; Am Nurses Association, 1961-. **Research Statement & Publications:** Nursing; nursing and public policy; education administration; quality health care; nursing taxonomy; informatics. **Mailing Address:** Univ Wis-Milwaukee, 1921 E Hartford Ave, Milwaukee, WI 53211. **Fax:** 414-229-6474. **E-Mail:** nlang@uwm.edu

LANG, NORTON DAVID, PHYSICS. **Personal Data:** b Chicago, Ill, July 5, 1940; m 1969, Enid; c Eugenie & Aaron. **Education:** Harvard Univ, AB, 1962, AM, 1965, PhD (physics), 1968. **Honors & Awards:** Davisson-Germer Prize, Am Phys Soc, 1977. **Professional Experience:** Adj prof electrical engineering, Columbia Univ, 2005-; Chmn, Davisson-Germer Prize Comt, 1990; chmn of the fel comt, Div Condensed Matter Physics, Am Phys Soc, 1985-1987; mgr, Elec Struct Theory Group, 1984-1993; assoc ed, Phys Rev Lett, 1980-1983; RES STAFF MEM, IBM CORP, 1969-; asst res physicist, Univ Calif San Diego, 1967-1969. **Memberships:** Fel NY Acad Sci; fel Am Phys Soc; senior member, IEEE; Am Chem Soc. **Research Statement & Publications:** Condensed matter physics; surface science; molecular electronics. **Mailing Address:** Int Bus Mach Res Ctr, Yorktown Heights, NY 10598. **E-Mail:** langn@us.ibm.com

LANG, PATRICIA L, INFRARED MICROSPECTROSCOPY. **Personal Data:** b Kingstown, RI, October 21, 1954; m Howard. **Education:** Ball State Univ, BS, 1983; Miami Univ, PhD (chem), 1987. **Professional Experience:** PROF CHEM, BALL STATE UNIV, 1998-; from asst to assoc prof, Dept Chem, Ball State Univ, 1987-1998. **Memberships:** Am Chem Soc; Soc Appl Spectros; Indiana Acad Sci; Sigma Xi. **Research Statement & Publications:** Infrared spectroscopy applied to the analysis of a wide range of materials which include bacteria, asbestos, parchment, paper, polymers, pigmnets and monolayers of gold surfaces. **Mailing Address:** Dept Chem, Ball State Univ, CP 409P, Muncie, IN 47306. **Fax:** 765-285-2351. **E-Mail:** plang@bsu.edu

LANG, PETER MICHAEL, CHEMICAL & NUCLEAR ENGINEERING. **Personal Data:** b Vienna, Austria, September 3, 1930; American citizen; m 1974, Marlene. **Education:** Mass Inst Technol, SB, 1951, SM, 1952, ScD(chem eng), 1955. **Professional Experience:** PROG MGR, DEPT ENERGY, 1977-; div mgr, Aerojet Nuclear Co, 1973-1977; staff consult, NUS Corp, 1966-1973; vis scientist, Swiss Fed Inst Reactor Res, 1962-1964; lectr, Univ Md, 1960; nuclear engr, ACF Industs, 1956-1959 & Allis-Chalmers Mfg Co, 1959-1966; chem engr, Shell Develop Co, 1955-1956; res asst chem eng, Mass Inst Technol, 1952-1953 & 1954-1955. **Memberships:** Am Nuclear Soc. **Research Statement & Publications:** Development of nuclear power plant improvements, design, economics, and safety of nuclear plants; nuclear fuel improvements; ultra-safe reactor designs. **Mailing Address:** US Dept Energy, Washington, DC 20585.

LANG, PHILIP CHARLES, ORGANIC CHEMISTRY. **Personal Data:** b Jamestown, NY, November 16, 1934; m 1955, c 3. **Education:** Allegheny Col, BS, 1957; Ohio Univ, MS, 1959; Rensselaer Polytech Inst, PhD (orgchem), 1966. **Professional Experience:** SR RES CHEMIST & DIR CHEM, CIBA-GEIGY CORP, 1980-; res chemist, GAF Corp, 1967-1973 & Toms River Chem Corp, 1973-1980; assoc res chemist, Sterling WinthropRes Inst, 1962-1967; Res chemist, Diamond Alkali Co, 1959-1962. **Memberships:** Am Chem Soc. **Research Statement & Publications:** Synthetic medicinal chemistry; heterocyclic and acteylene compounds; aromatics and synthetic dyes. **Mailing Address:** 216 Edgemere Dr RD 5, Toms River, NJ 08755.

LANG, RAYMOND W, MICROBIOLOGY. **Personal Data:** b Syracuse, NY, August 1, 1930; m 1953, c 5. **Education:** LeMoyne Col, NY, BS, 1952; Mich State Univ, MS, 1957, PhD (microbiol), 1959. **Professional Experience:** Consult, Ohio Dept Health, beginning 1983; PROF MED MICROBIOL, COL MED, OHIO STATE UNIV, 1972-; consult training prog, Nat Inst Dent Res, 1972-1975; assoc prof, Col Med, Ohio State Univ, 1968-1972; consult urol res sect, Millard Fillmore Hosp, 1964-1966; from instr to asst prof bact & immunol, Sch Med, State Univ NY Buffalo, 1963-1968; fel bact & immunol, Sch Med, State Univ NY Buffalo, 1962-1963; asst prof microbiol, St John's Univ, NY, 1959-1962. **Memberships:** AAAS; Am Soc Microbiol; Am Asn Immunol. **Research Statement & Publications:** Immunochemistry of tissue antigens; autoimmunity. **Mailing Address:** Dept Med Microbiol, Ohio State Univ Col Med 333 W TENTH Ave, Columbus, OH 43210-1238. **E-Mail:** lang.1@osu.edu

LANG, ROBERT PHILLIP, physical chemistry; deceased, see previous edition for last biography

LANG, ROGER H, COMMUNICATION THEORY. **Personal Data:** b New York, NY, July 8, 1940. **Education:** Polytech Inst Brooklyn, BSEE, 1962, MSEE, 1964, PhD (electrophys), 1968. **Professional Experience:** CHMN DEPT, GEORGE WASH UNIV, 1984-; PROF ENG APPL SCI, GEORGE Wash UNIV, 1970-; fel, Nat Res Coun. **Memberships:** Fel Inst Elec & Electronics Engrs. **Mailing Address:** Dept Elec Eng & Comput Sci, George Wash Univ, 801 22nd St NW Rm 627 Phillips Hall, Washington, DC 20052. **Fax:** 202994-0227. **E-Mail:** lang@seas.gwu.edu

LANG, ROY, PHYSICS. **Personal Data:** b Tokyo, Japan, April 5, 1942; m 1972, Junko; c Eugene & Mariko. **Education:** Univ Tokyo, BS, 1966; Mass Inst Technol, PhD (physics), 1971. **Honors & Awards:** Sakurai Mem Award, Optoelectronics Indust & Tech Develop Asn, 1992. **Professional Experience:** RES FEL, RES & DEVELOP GROUP, NEC CORP, JAPAN, 1997-; gen mgr, Fundamental Res Labs, 1991-1997; researcher, Ctr Res Labs, 1973-1991; Res assoc, Inst LabAstrophys, Univ Colo & Nat Bur Stand, 1971-1973. **Memberships:** Fel Inst Elec & Electronics Engrs; Japan Appl Physics Soc; Japan Phys Soc. **Research Statement & Publications:** Contribution to development of optoelectronic devices, especially of semiconductor lasers; granted 16 Japanesepatents in field. **Mailing Address:** Res & Develop Group NEC, 4-1-1 Miyazaki, Miyamae-ku Kawasaki 216, Japan. **Fax:** 814-485-62130. **E-Mail:** lang@rdq.cl.nec.co.jp

LANG, SERGE, number theory, algebraic geometry; deceased, see previous edition for last biography

LANG, STANLEY ALBERT, ORGANIC CHEMISTRY. **Personal Data:** b Cleveland, Ohio, March 30, 1944. **Education:** John Carroll Univ, BS, 1966; Brown Univ, PhD (org chem), 1970. **Professional Experience:** RES PROF CHEM, STEVENS INST TECHNOL, as of 2006; DIR, INFECTIOUS DIS CHEM RES, WYETH-AYERST RES, as of 2004; vpres chem, Chem Diversity Lab, as of 2002; HEAD, CHEM DEPT, INFECTIOUS DIS THER SECT, MED RES DIV, AMCYANAMID INC, 1980-; group leader, Info Dis Ther Sect, 1977-1980; group leader, Info DisTher Sect, 1974-1977; res chemist, Lederle Labs, Am Cyanamid Inc, 1974; res fel, Nat CancerInst fel, 1971; res fel, Ohio State Univ, 1970. **Memberships:** Am Chem Soc. **Research Statement & Publications:** Synthetic organic chemistry; medicinal drugs; antibiotics, anticancer agents; immunoregulants. **Mailing Address:** Chem Diversity Labs, Inc, 11558 Sorrento Valley Rd, San Diego, CA 92121. **Fax:** 858-794-4931. **E-Mail:** slang@chemdiv.com

LANG, THOMAS G(LENN), MECHANICAL ENGINEERING. **Personal Data:** b San Jose, Calif, July 28, 1928; m 1962, c 2. **Education:** Calif Inst Technol, BS, 1948 & 1950; Univ Southern Calif, MS, 1953; Pa State Univ, PhD (aerospace eng), 1968. **Professional Experience:** PRES, SEMI-SUBMERGED SHIP CO, 1979-; consult, 1978-1979; head, Advan Concepts Div, 1973-1978; head, Advan Concepts Group, 1970-1973; head advan design, Systs Analysis Group, Naval Undersea Ctr & Naval Ocean SystsCtr, 1968-1970; tech consult, Ocean Technol Dept, Naval Undersea Warfare Ctr, 1968; US NavalOrd Test Sta scholar, Pa State Univ, 1966-1968; head hydrodyn res group, US Naval Ord TestSta, 1961-1966; head oceanic res group, US Naval Ord Test Sta, 1958-1961; hydrodynamicist, US Naval Ord Test Sta, 1952-1958; designer, US Naval Ord Test Sta, 1951-1952; stress analyst, NAm Aviation, Inc, 1950-1951; Operator, Southern Calif Coop Wind Tunnel, 1948-1949; HYDRODYNAMICS CONSULT. **Memberships:** Am Inst Aeronaut & Astronaut; Marine Technol Soc; Soc Naval Architects &Marine Engrs. **Research Statement & Publications:** Hydrodynamics, especially stability and control, propulsion, boundary layer control, vented hydrofoils, sea animal hydrodynamics, polymer additives for drag reduction; semisubmerged ship design. **Mailing Address:** Semi Submerged Ship Corp, San Diego, CA 92075.

LANG, VALERIE ILONA, ATMOSPHERIC SCIENCES, SPECTROSCOPY & PHYSICAL CHEMISTRY. **Personal Data:** b New Market, Ont, March 24, 1959. **Education:** McGill Univ, BSc, 1979; Univ Miami, MS, 1982; Dartmouth Col, PhD (phys chem), 1986. **Professional Experience:** SR PROJ ENGR, CORP CHIEF ENGR OFF, AEROSPACE CORP, as of 2003; proj engr govt & environ progs, Aerospace Corp, beginning 1993; cong sci fel, Am Geophys Union, 1992-1993; mem tech staff, Aerospace Corp, 1988-1992; Resident res assoc, Nat Res Coun, Jet Propulsion Lab, NASA, 1986-1988. **Memberships:** Am Geophys Union; AAAS; Am Chem Soc. **Research Statement & Publications:** Chemical kinetics; atmospheric spectroscopy; space launch chemistry. **Mailing Address:** Corp Chief Engr Off, Aerospace Corp, M1/131, PO Box 92957, Los Angeles, CA 90009. **Fax:** 310-540-2348. **E-Mail:** valerie.lang@aero.org

LANG, WILLIAM WARNER, ACOUSTICAL & NOISE CONTROL ENGINEERING. **Personal Data:** b Boston, Mass, August 9, 1926; m 1954, Asta; c Robert. **Education:** Iowa State Univ, BS, 1946, PhD (physics), 1958; Mass Inst Technol, MS, 1949. **Honors & Awards:** Achievement Award, Inst Elec & Electronics Engrs Group Audio & Electroacoust, 1972, Centennial Medal, 1984; Silver Medal, Acoust Soc Am, 1984; Pro Silentio Medal, Hungarian Optical Acoust & Film Tech Soc, 1989. **Professional Experience:** PRES EMER, INT INST NOISE CONTROL ENG, 2002-; sr tech staff mem, IBM, Acoust lab, 1991-1992; adj prof physics, Vassar Col, 1979-1996; prog mgr acoust technol, Acoust lab, 1975-1990; mem eval panel, Mech div, Nat Bur Stand, 1974-1975; sr physicist & mgr, Acoust lab, 1964-1975; adv physicist, IBM Corp, 1958-1964; spec engr, E I du Pont Del Nemours & Co, Inc, 1955-1957; instr physics, US Naval Post-Grad Sch, 1951-1955; Acoust engr, Bolt, Beranek & Newman, Inc, 1949-1951. **Memberships:** Nat Acad Eng; Inst Noise Control Eng (pres, 1978); Acoust Soc Am (treas, 1995-1999); fel Inst Elec & Electronics Engrs; fel Audio Eng Soc; fel Inst Acoust Eng; AAAS. **Research Statement & Publications:** Acoustics; effects and control of noise; theory and design of acoustical materials; determinations of sound power levels of noise sources; national noise policy. **Mailing Address:** 29 Hornbeck Ridge, Poughkeepsie, NY 12603-4205.

LANGACKER, PAUL GEORGE, THEORETICAL PHYSICS, ELEMENTARY PARTICLE PHYSICS. **Personal Data:** b Evanston, Ill, July 14, 1946. **Education:** Mass Inst Technol, BS, 1968; Univ Calif, Berkeley, MA, 1969, PhD (physics), 1972. **Honorary Degrees:** MS, Univ Pa, 1981. **Honors & Awards:** Humboldt Award, 1987. **Professional Experience:** Chmn, Dept Physics & Astron, Univ Pa, 1996-2001; William Smith prof physics, Univ Pa, 1993-1998; Alexander von Humboldt award, 1987-1988; PROF, DEPT PHYSICS & ASTRON, UNIV PA, 1985-; from res assoc to prof, Dept Physics & Astron, Univ Pa, 1974-1993; res assoc, Rockefeller Univ, 1972-1974. **Memberships:** Fel Am Phys Soc; fel AAAS. **Research Statement & Publications:** Theoretical elementary particle physics especially the experimental consequences of fundamental theories. **Mailing Address:** Dept Physics & Astron, Univ Pa, 209 S 33rd St, Philadelphia, PA 19104-6396. **E-Mail:** pgl@electroweak.hep.upenn.edu

LANGAGER, BRUCE ALLEN, POLYMER CHEMISTRY. **Personal Data:** b Willmar, Minn, January 17, 1942; m 1964, c 2. **Education:** Augsburg Col, BA, 1964; Univ Minn, Minneapolis, PhD (org chem), 1968. **Professional Experience:** TECH SUPVR, 3M CO, 1978-; res specialist, 3M Co, 1974-1978; sr res chemist, 3M Co, 1968-1974. **Memberships:** Sigma Xi. **Research Statement & Publications:** Life sciences; surface chemistry. **Mailing Address:** 3M Innovative Properties CO, 3M Ctr Bldg 0201-01-S-13, St Paul, MN 55144.

LANGAN, THOMAS AUGUSTINE, BIOCHEMISTRY. **Personal Data:** b Providence, RI, July 25, 1930; m 1960, c 2. **Education:** Fordham Univ, BS, 1952; Johns Hopkins Univ, PhD (biochem), 1959. **Professional Experience:** PROF PHARMACOL, MED SCH, UNIV COLO, DENVER, 1983-; assoc prof, Med Sch, Univ Colo, Denver, 1971-1983; sr investr, C F Kettering Res Lab, 1970-1971; from asst prof to assoc prof, Antioch Col, 1967-1971; investr, C F Kettering Res Lab, 1967-1970; staff scientist, C F Kettering Res Lab, 1965-1967; res assoc biochem, Rockefeller Inst, 1962-1965; mem res staff, Wenner-Gren Inst, Stockholm, Sweden, 1961-1962; guest investr biochem, Rockefeller Inst, 1960-1961; NSF fel, 1959-1962; mem res staff, Med Nobel Inst, Stockholm, Sweden, 1959-1960. **Memberships:** Am Soc Biol Chemists; Am Soc Cell Biol; Am Soc Pharmacol & Exp Therapeut. **Research Statement & Publications:** Metabolism and function of histones and nuclear phosphoproteins; control of histone phosphorylation by cyclic adenosine monophosphate and cell growth; regulation of nucleic acid synthesis in eukaryotes; effects of histone phosphorylation on chromotin structure; role of cdc2 protein kinase substrates in control of cell cycle progression. **Mailing Address:** Dept Pharmacol, Univ Colo Med Ctr, Sci Ctr PO Box 6511, Denver, CO 80262. **Fax:** 303-724-3663. **E-Mail:** thomas.langan@uchsc.edu

LANGARI, REZA, MATHEMATICS. **Education:** Univ Calif, BS, 1980, MS, 1983, PhD (Mech Eng), 1991. **Professional Experience:** PROF, DEPT MECH ENG, TEX A&M UNIV, as of 2006. **Mailing Address:** Tex A & M Univ, Dept Mech Eng M/S 3123, College Station, TX 77843-3123. **Fax:** 979-845-3081. **E-Mail:** rlangari@tamu.edu

LANGDALE, GEORGE WILFRED, management of crop residues, conservation tillage; deceased, see previous edition for last biography

LANGDON, ALLAN BRUCE, PLASMA THEORY, COMPUTATIONAL PHYSICS. **Personal Data:** b Edmonton, Alta, December 14, 1941; m 1966, c 3. **Education:** Univ Man, BSc, 1963; Princeton Univ, PhD (astrophys), 1969. **Professional Experience:** Assoc div leader, physics dept, Lawrence Livermore Lab, 1991-; affil mem, Ctr Plasma Physics & Fusion Eng, Univ Calif, Los Angeles, 1977-1978; staff physicist, Physics Dept, Lawrence Livermore Lab, 1970-1991; lectr elec eng, Univ Calif, Berkeley, 1969-1973 & 1981-1982; actg asst prof elec eng, Univ Calif, Berkeley, 1967-1969. **Memberships:** Fel Am Phys Soc; Sigma Xi; Can Asn Physicists; Asn Comput Mach. **Research Statement & Publications:** Plasma theory; computational physics; computer simulation of plasmas; numerical analysis. **Mailing Address:** L-472 Lawrence Livermore Lab, PO Box 808, Livermore, CA 94550. **Fax:** 925-423-9208. **E-Mail:** langdon1@llnl.gov

LANGDON, EDWARD ALLEN, MEDICINE, RADIOLOGY. **Personal Data:** b Los Angeles, Calif, February 9, 1922. **Education:** Western Res Univ, BS, 1942; Univ Mich, MD, 1945. **Professional Experience:** RETIRED; prof & vice chmn, Dept Radiol Oncol & asst dean student affairs, beginning 1970; prof radiol & chief, Radiother Div & asst dean student affairs, 1970-1978; from asst prof to assoc prof, Sch Med, Univ Calif, Los Angeles, 1959-1970. **Memberships:** AMA; Am Col Radiol; Radiol Soc NAm; Soc Nuclear Med; Asn Univ Radiol. **Research Statement & Publications:** Radiation therapy. **Mailing Address:** 200 UCLA Med Plaza Ste B265, Los Angeles, CA 90024.

LANGDON, GLEN GEORGE, COMPUTER ENGINEERING & COMPUTER SCIENCE, DATA COMPRESSION IMAGE CODING. **Personal Data:** b Morristown, NJ, June 30, 1936; m 1963, Marian; c Karen. **Education:** Wash State Univ, BSEE, 1957; Univ Pittsburgh, MSEE, 1963; Syracuse Univ, PhD (elec eng), 1968. **Professional Experience:** PROF EMER COMPUT ENG, UNIV CALIF, SANTA CRUZ, as of 2003; prof comput eng, Univ Calif, Santa Cruz, beginning 1987; mem gov bd, Comput Soc, Inst Elec & Electronics Engrs, 1984-1985; lectr, Stanford Univ, 1980, 1984-1985; lectr, Univ Santa Clara, 1975-1978; res staff comput sci, IBM Corp, 1974-1987; vis prof, UnivSao Paulo, Brazil, 1971-1972; lectr, Syracuse Univ, NY, 1968-1969; engr, IBM Corp, 1963-1973; engr, Westinghouse Elec Corp, 1960-1963. **Memberships:** Fel Inst Elec & Electronics Engrs; Asn Comput Mach. **Research Statement & Publications:** Data compression and arithmetic coding; image compression and processing; computer logic design. **Mailing Address:** 220 Horizon Way, Aptos, CA 95003-2739. **E-Mail:** langdon@cse.ucsc.edu

LANGDON, HERBERT LINCOLN, GROSS ANATOMY, DEVELOPMENTAL ANATOMY. **Personal Data:** b Malone, NY, July 7, 1935; m 1972. **Education:** St Lawrence Univ, BS, 1957; Univ Mo, MA, 1963; Univ Miami, PhD (biol struct), 1972. **Professional Experience:** ASSOC PROF ANAT, SCH DENT MED, UNIV PITTSBURGH, 1978-; Resconsortium, Cleft Palate Ctr, Univ Pittsburgh, 1976; asst prof, Sch Dent Med, Univ Pittsburgh, 1972-1978; Asst prof biol, Miami-Dade Community Col, 1965-1968. **Memberships:** Am Cleft Palate Asn; Sigma Xi; Am Asn Anatomists. **Research Statement & Publications:** Normal and abnormal morphology and development of human tongue and velopharyngeal mechanism; craniofacial development and growth; neuroanatomy. **Mailing Address:** Univ Pittsburgh, Pittsburgh, PA 15261. **E-Mail:** hll17@pitt.edu

LANGDON, JOAN STERLING, MATHEMATICS. **Education:** Hampton Univ, BA, 1973; Col William & Mary, MA, 1977; Old Dom Univ, MS, 1985; Am Univ, PhD, 1989. **Professional Experience:** DEAN, SCH ARTS & SCI, BOWIE STATE UNIV, as of 2005. **Mailing Address:** Bowie State Univ, 1709 Albert Terr, Mitchellville, MD 20721. **Fax:** 301-464-7521. **E-Mail:** joan.langdon@bowiestate.edu

LANGDON, KENNETH R, PLANT TAXONOMY, ENDANGERED SPECIES. **Personal Data:** b Cache, Okla, August 20, 1928; m 1961, c 3. **Education:** Okla State Univ, BS, 1958, MS, 1960; Univ Fla, PhD (plant path, nematol, bot), 1963. **Professional Experience:** RETIRED; nematologist & botanist, Div Plant Indust, Fla Dept Agr & Consumer Serv, 1963-1991. **Memberships:** Soc Europ Nematologist; Int Asn Plant Taxon; Am Soc Plant Taxonomists. **Research Statement & Publications:** Plant systematics. **Mailing Address:** 2216 NW 49th Terr, Gainesville, FL 32605.

LANGDON, ROBERT GODWIN, BIOCHEMISTRY. **Personal Data:** b Dallas, Tex, January 18, 1923; m 1945, c 4. **Education:** Univ Chicago, MD, 1945, PhD (biochem), 1953. **Professional Experience:** RETIRED; chmn dept, Univ Va, 1977-1982; prof biochem, Univ Va, 1969-1982; prof biochem & chmn dept, Col Med, Univ Fla, 1967-1969; Lederle award, 1954-1957; from instr to prof physiol chem, Sch Med, Johns Hopkins Univ, 1953-1967; USPHSfel, Univ Chicago, 1951-1953. **Memberships:** Am Soc Biol Chemists; Am Chem Soc. **Research Statement & Publications:** Membrane biochemistry; glucose transport; mechanism of hormone action. **Mailing Address:** Buck Creek Farm, PO Box 464, Nemo, TX 76070.

LANGDON, TERENCE G, MECHANICAL PROPERTIES CREEP & SUPERPLASTICITY, ULTRA-FINE GRAINED MATERIALS. **Personal Data:** b Trowbridge, Eng, January 24, 1939; m 1968, Mady. **Education:** Univ Bristol, physics, BSc, 1961, DSc, 1980; Univ London, PhD (phys metal), 1965. **Honorary Degrees:** Dr Honoris Causa, Russ Acad Sci, 2003. **Honors & Awards:** Hon Academician, Acad Sci Bashkortostan Rep, Russia, 1993; Henry Marian Howe Medal, ASM Int'l, 2000; Fel Royal Acad Eng, 2002; Struct Mater Div Disting Sci/Engineer Award, TMS, 2005; Somiya Award, IUMRS, 2005. **Professional Experience:** WILLIAM E. LEONHARD PROF ENG, UNIV SOUTHERN CALIF, 2003-; RESEARCH PROF, ENG SCIENCES, Univ Southhampton, 2005-; vis prof, Kyushu Univ, 2001-; vis prof, Danish Tech Univ, 1998; vis scientist, Riso Nat Lab, Denmark, 1984; prof, Univ NSW, 1984; vs prof, Univ Melbourne, 1977-1978; prof, Univ Southern Calif, 1976-2003; assoc prof, Univ Southern Calif, 1971-1976; res assoc, Univ BC, 1969-1971; res fel, Cavendish Lab, Univ Cambridge, 1968-1969; vis scientist, US Steel Corp, 1967-1968; Res metallurgist, Univ Calif, Berkeley, 1965-1967. **Memberships:** Fel Inst Physics; fel Inst Materials; fel Am Ceramic Soc; fel ASM Int'l; fel TMS; hon member Japan Inst Metals. **Research Statement & Publications:** Mechanical properties at high temperatures of crystalline materials including metals, ceramics and composites; deformation mechanisms in creep and superplasticity; processing of metals using severe plastic deformation. **Mailing Address:** Dept Aerospace & Mech Eng, Univ Southern Calif, Los Angeles, CA 90089-1453. **Fax:** 213-740-8071. **E-Mail:** langdon@usc.edu

LANGDON, WILLIAM KEITH, organic chemistry; deceased, see previous edition for last biography

LANGE, BARRY CLIFFORD, PROCESS RESEARCH, FORMULATION CHEMISTRY. **Personal Data:** b Philadelphia, Pa, June 14, 1952; m 1974, Linda Leedom; c Julianna & Jillian. **Education:** Stevens Inst Technol, BS, 1974; Pa State Univ, PhD (chem), 1979, MIT 1980. **Professional Experience:** RES MGR, JOHNSON & JOHNSON CO, 2001-; MIT Post doc, 1979-1980; res mgr, Rohm & Haas Co, 1984-1987; agr chem discovery chemist, Rohm & Haas CO, 1984-1987; process chemist, Rohm & Haas Co, 1980-1984; res assoc, Mass Inst Technol, 1980. **Memberships:** Am Chem Soc. **Research Statement & Publications:** Research management, design of biologically active compounds, chemical process research, kinetics and mechanisms of organic reactions; synthesis of penicillin and cephalosporin analogs and other antibiotics; physical organic chemistry including enolate alkylation; polymer chemistry; agricultural and food chemistry; biochemistry. **Mailing Address:** 1031 Barley Way, Lansdale, PA 19446-3200.

LANGE, BRUCE AINSWORTH, CHEMISTRY OF SURFACES, CEMENT CHEMISTRY. **Personal Data:** b Springfield, Mass, August 3, 1948; m 1977, c 2. **Education:** Lowell Technol Inst, BS, 1970; Univ NH, PhD (chem), 1974. **Professional Experience:** DIR, WASTE MGT & DECOMMISSIONING OPERS, ATOMIC ENERGY, CAN, 2006-; br mgr, Chalk River Lab, 1991-1996; from group leader to br mgr anal chem, Pinawa, Man, Atomic Energy Can, 1983-1991; groupleader chem, W R Grace & Co, Cambridge, Mass, 1979-1983; res chemist, Nat Inst Occup Safety& Health, Cincinnati, Ohio, 1976-1979; fel chem, Univ Cincinnati, 1975-1976; fel chem, Northwestern Univ, 1974-1975. **Memberships:** Am Ceramic Soc. **Research Statement & Publications:** X-ray crystallography; inorganic synthesis; radiopharmaceuticals; development of analytical methods for hazardous materials; surface chemistry; cement chemistry; comminution of minerals; process design; computer modelling; analytical chemistry. **Mailing Address:** Chalk River Labs, Chalk River, ON K0J 1J0, Can.

LANGE, CARINA BEATRIZ, MARINE PHYTOPLANKTON, DIATOMS. **Personal Data:** b Buenos Aires, Arg, July 27, 1955; c Alexander Pillard. **Education:** Univ Buenos Aires, Licenciada, 1980, PhD (marine biol), 1988. **Professional Experience:** ASSOC RESEARCHER, SCRIPPS INST OCEANOG, 1996-; lectr, Univ Concepcion, Chile, 1992-1993 & Cath Univ, Puerto Rico, 1995; vis scientist, Univ Oslo, 1991 & Univ Breinen, 1991-1993 & 1996; assoc specialist, Scripps Inst Oceanog, 1991-1995; asst specialist, Scripps Inst Oceanog, 1990-1991; SRA, Scripps Inst Oceanog, 1986-1989. **Memberships:** Am Soc Limnol & Oceanog; Am Geophys Union; Int Soc Diatom Res; Oceanog Soc. **Research Statement & Publications:** Annual and interannual variations of marine phytoplankton fluxes to the sea floor; paleoproductivity; morphological studies on marine diatoms; toxic diatoms. **Mailing Address:** Geol Res Div, Scripps Inst Oceanog, Univ Calif, La Jolla, CA 92093-0215. **Fax:** 619-534-0784. **E-Mail:** clange@ucsd.edu

LANGE, CHARLES FORD, BIOCHEMISTRY, IMMUNOLOGY. **Personal Data:** b Chicago, Ill, February 16, 1929; m 1953, c 3. **Education:** Roosevelt Univ, BS, 1951, MS, 1953; Univ Ill, PhD (biochem), 1959; Am Bd Med Lab Immunol, dipl, 1981. **Professional Experience:** EMER PROF MICROBIOL, 1996-; consult immunologist, Hines Vet Admin Hosp, 1975-1995; from assoc to prof microbiol, Loyola Univ, 1970-1995; head phys chem, Hektoen Inst Med Res, Cook Co Hosp, 1963-1969; res assoc, Hektoen Inst Med Res, Cook Co Hosp, 1961-1963; res assoc biochem, Univ Ill, 1960-1961. **Memberships:** Am Chem Soc; Am Soc Biochem & Molecular Biol; Transplantation Soc; Am Soc Microbiol; Am Asn Immunol; AAAS. **Research Statement & Publications:** Urinary glycoproteins; immunochemistry of streptococcal related glomerulonephritis; streptococcal M-proteins; transplantation antigens; immunology of aging; autoimmune diseases; monoclonal antitissue antibodies. **Mailing Address:** Dept Microbiol, Stritch Sch Med, Loyola Univ, Maywood, IL 60153. **E-Mail:** clange@luc.edu

LANGE, CHRISTOPHER STEPHEN, RADIATION BIOPHYSICS, GENOME STRUCTURE. **Personal Data:** b Chicago, Ill, February 11, 1940; m 1964, Eleanor; c Tamara A & Theodore O. **Education:** Mass Inst Technol, Cambridge, BS, 1961; Oxford Univ, Eng, DPhil (Radiation bio), 1968. **Professional Experience:** NIH/Div Res Grants, SBIR Special Study Sect-2, 1993; prof physiol & biophys, Sch Grad Studies, beginning 1992; scholar adv comt, Kosciuszko Found, 1989-; mem, Tumor Biol Comt & tumor repository utilization comt, Radiation Ther Oncol Group, Nat Proj, NIH/NCI, 1988- & 1993-; guest scientist, Brookhaven Nat Lab, 1983-; PROF RADIATION ONCOL & DIR RADIATION RES, COL MED, STATE UNIV NY, HEALTH SCI CTR BROOKLYN, 1980-; presidential distinguished lectr, Univ Hirosaki, Japan, 1979; vis prof chem, Univ Calif, San Diego, 1975-1976; vis radiobiologist, Am Inst Biol Sci, 1973-1979; prin investr, Grants USDOE, NSF, NCI, NIGMS, Mathers Found, etc, 1972-; res career develop award, USDHEW/NCI, 1972-1977; asst prof radiol, radiobiol, biophys, Sch Med & Dent, Univ Rochester, 1969-1980; NHS sr res officer radiobiol, 1968-1969; NHS res officer radiobiol, Christie Hosp & Holt Radium Inst, Manchester, Eng, 1962-1968; Med Res Coun res asst radiobiol, Churchill Hosp, Headington, Oxford, 1961-1962. **Memberships:** Radiation Res Soc; Biophys Soc; NY Acad Sci; Sigma Xi (NW regional dir, 1999-2005) exec coord, 2002-2003); AAAS. **Research Statement & Publications:** Molecular and cellular bases of cellular and organisimal radiation effects and aging; DNA damage and repair; DNA structure in mammalian chromosomes; viscoelastometry and other hydrodynamic behavior of DNA; differentiation control (polarity) in tissues; assays for improved cancer therapy. **Mailing Address:** State Univ NY Downstate Ctr, 450 Clarkson Ave PO Box 1212, Brooklyn, NY 11203. **E-Mail:** lange_c@downstate.edu

LANGE, EUGENE ALBERT, STRUCTURAL INTEGRITY TECHNOLOGY, FRACTURE MECHANICS. **Personal Data:** b Stevens Pt, Wis, October 22, 1923; m 1951, Lois June Lange. **Education:** Univ Wis, BS, 1945, MS, 1951. **Honors & Awards:** Res Pub Award, Naval Res Lab, 1968. **Professional Experience:** RETIRED; consult, Eugene A Lange, 1980-1990; Lectr, Union Col, Schenectady, NY, 1970-1988; surv res metal, Naval Res Lab, 1956-1980; res engr, Gray Iron Res Inst, 1953-1956; Res metal, Univ Wis, 1951-1953. **Memberships:** Sr mem, pres Washington Chapter, Am Soc Metals. **Research Statement & Publications:** Casting technology; non-magnetic steels; fracture mechanics; dynamic fracture toughness. **Mailing Address:** 9503 Veirs Dr No 3, Rockville, MD 20850.

LANGE, GAIL LAURA, ALGEBRA. **Personal Data:** b Chicago, Ill, June 28, 1946. **Education:** Univ Md, BS, 1967; Univ NH, MS, 1969, PhD (math), 1975. **Professional Experience:** CONSULT, 1980-; PROF, DEPT MATH & COMPUT SCI, as of 2006; asst prof, Univ Maine, Farmington, 1975-1980; instr math, Univ Maine, Farmington, 1972-1975. **Memberships:** Am Math Soc; Math Asn Am. **Research Statement & Publications:** Investigation of which finite p-groups can be the Frattini subgroup of finite p-groups. **Mailing Address:** Shaw Hill Rd, Rd One PO Box 1203, Farmington, ME 04938. **Fax:** 207-778-7125. **E-Mail:** lange@maine.edu

LANGE, GORDON DAVID, NEUROPHYSIOLOGY, BIOLOGICAL OCEANOGRAPHY. **Personal Data:** b Douglas, Ariz, January 15, 1936; c 3. **Education:** Calif Inst Technol, BS, 1958; Rockefeller Univ, PhD (biophys), 1965. **Professional Experience:** NEUROPHYSIOLOGIST, NAT INST NEUROL & COMMUN DIS &STROKE, NIH, 1984-; assoc prof, Neuroscience, Univ Calif, San Diego, 1974-1984; asst prof, UnivCalif, San Diego, 1968-1974; asst res neuroscientist, Univ Calif, San Diego, 1966-1968; res assoc biophys, Rockefeller Univ, 1965-1966. **Memberships:** Soc Neuroscience; NY Acad Sci; Sigma Xi. **Research Statement & Publications:** Neurophysiology of sensory systems; studies of the dynamics of interactions among nerve cells; mathematical and computer models of interactions of organisms. **Mailing Address:** Nat Inst Neurol Dis & Stroke, Bldg 10 - Magnuson CC, Rm 5S227 10 Ctr Dr, Bethesda, MD 20892. **Fax:** 301-480-2492. **E-Mail:** gl2c@nih.gov

LANGE, GORDON LLOYD, TERPENOID SYNTHESIS, PHOTOCHEMICAL CYCLOADDITIONS. **Personal Data:** b Edmonton, Alta, March 1, 1937; m 1964, Gail; c Stephen & Margot. **Education:** Univ Alta, BS, 1959; Univ Calif, Berkeley, PhD (org chem), 1963. **Honors & Awards:** Union Carbide Award, Chem Educ, 1986. **Professional Experience:** PROF EMER CHEM & BIOCHEM, UNIV GUELPH, 2001-; fel, 3M, 1991; prof chem & biochem, Univ Guelph, beginning 1985; from asst prof to assoc prof chem, Univ Guelph, 1967-1984; lectr org chem, Univ Western Ont, 1965-1967; res chemist, Procter & Gamble Co, 1962-1965. **Memberships:** Am Chem Soc; fel Chem Inst Can. **Research Statement & Publications:** Synthesis of natural products and compounds with potential biological activity; organic photochemistry; structural elucidation of natural products; free radical fragmentation reactions. **Mailing Address:** Dept Chem & Biochem, Univ Guelph, 161 C&M, Guelph, ON N1G 2W1, Can. **Fax:** 519-766-1499. **E-Mail:** lange@chembio.uoguelph.ca

LANGE, IAN M, GEOLOGY, GEOCHEMISTRY. **Personal Data:** b New York, NY, November 11, 1940. **Education:** Dartmouth Col, BA, 1962, MA, 1964; Univ Wash, PhD (geol), 1968. **Professional Experience:** PROF EMER GEOL, UNIV MONT, as of 2004; prof geol & chmn dept, Univ Mont, beginning 1977; prof Econ Geol, Univ Mont, 1972-1977; asst prof geol, Fresno State Col, 1968-1972; vis prof, Dartmouth Col, 1971-; asst prof geol, Fresno State Col, 1968-1972. **Memberships:** Geochem Soc; Geol Soc Am; Soc Econ Geologists; Soc Exploration Geochemists; Am Geophys Union; Sigma Xi. **Research Statement & Publications:** Isotope geology, economic geology. **Mailing Address:** Dept Geol, Univ Mont, SC 329, Missoula, MT 59802-0001. **E-Mail:** gardener@selway.umt.edu

LANGE, JAMES NEIL, PHYSICS. **Personal Data:** b Bridgeport, Conn, May 4, 1938; m 1958, c 2. **Education:** Pa State Univ, PhD (physics), 1964. **Professional Experience:** Prof emer physics, Okla State Univ, as of 2004; VPRES, INTERCOMP INC, STILLWATER, 1985-; regents prof physics, Okla State Univ, beginning 1981; vis prof, Nat Univ Mex, 1978; sr vis fel, Gt Brit, 1976; vis prof, Univ Nottingham, 1976; prof physics, Okla State Univ, beginning 1971; from asst prof to assoc prof, Okla State Univ, 1965-1971. **Memberships:** Am Phys Soc; Am Geophys Union. **Research Statement & Publications:** Acoustics; geophysics. **Mailing Address:** Dept Physics, Okla State Univ, 145 Physical Sci, Stillwater, OK 74078-3072. **Fax:** 405-744-6811.

LANGE, KENNETH L, GENETICS & MEDICAL IMAGING, COMPUTATIONAL PROBABILITY & STATISTICS. **Personal Data:** b Angola, Ind, June 16, 1946; m 1970, c 2. **Education:** Mich State Univ, BS, 1967; Mass Inst Technol, MS, 1968 & PhD (math), 1971. **Honors & Awards:** Fellow of the American Institute for Medical And Biomedical Engineering, elected 2001; George W Snedecor Award, 1993. **Professional Experience:** Chair, Dept Human Genetics, Univ Calif, Los Angeles, as of 2004; Rosenfeld Professor of Computational Genetics, Univ Calif, Los Angeles, as of 2003; Prof Statistics, Dept of Statistics, Univ Calif, Los Angeles, as of 2000; Prof of Biomath & Human Genetics, Depts of Biomath & Human Genetics, Univ Calif, Los Angeles, as of 1998; Pharmacia & Upjohn Foundation Research Professor & Prof Math, Univ Mich, 1996-1998; Prof Biostat, Univ Mich 1994-1998; Vis Prof Statistics, Harvard Univ, 1990-1991; Dept Chair, Biomath, Univ Calif, Los Angeles, 1985-1994; Vis Prof Statistics, Mass Inst Tech, 1983-1984; mem, Joint Comm Mathematics in Life Sciences, Am Math Soc & Soc Indust & Appl Math, 1984-1987; Prof Biomath, Univ Calif, Los Angeles, 1983-1996; NIH Research Career Development Award, Univ Calif, Los Angeles, 1979-1984; from asst prof to assoc prof, Univ Calif, Los Angeles, 1974-1983; NIH postdoc Fellow, Biomath, Univ Calif, Los Angeles, 1972-1974; Asst Prof Math, Univ NH, 1971-1972. **Memberships:** Soc Indust & Appl Math; Am Soc Human Genetics; Am Statist Asn. **Research Statement & Publications:** Biomathematical modeling in genetics, medical imaging, demography, and physiology; applied stochastic processes and computational statistics. **Mailing Address:** Dept Biomath, 10833 Le Conte Ave, AV-515 CHS, Univ Ca, Los Angeles, CA 90095-1766. **E-Mail:** klange@ucla.edu

LANGE, KLAUS ROBERT, PHYSICAL CHEMISTRY, SURFACE CHEMISTRY, DETERGENCY. **Personal Data:** b Berlin, Ger, January 15, 1930; American citizen; m 1951, Sulvia Pollack; c Stephen M & Karen J. **Education:** Univ Pa, AB, 1952; Univ Del, MS, 1954, PhD (phys chem), 1956. **Professional Experience:** CONSULT, 1990-; sr tech adv, Quaker Chem Corp, 1986-1990; res dir, Quaker Chem Corp, 1975-1986; Mem bd dir, Chem Data Systs, 1970-1975; lab mgr, Betz Lab Inc, 1969-1974; res assoc, Philadelphia Quartz Co, 1967-1969; sr res chemist, Philadelphia Quartz Co, 1959-1967; Res chemist, Atlantic Refining Co, 1955-1959. **Memberships:** Am Chem Soc; Tech Asn Pulp & Paper Inst. **Research Statement & Publications:** Physical adsorption; heterogeneous catalysis; surface chemistry of silica and related solids; silicate solutions, fundamental properties; colloidal suspensions; detergency; pollution control; polymer applications; lignin and paper chemistry; defoamers; detergents. **Mailing Address:** 805 Lombard St, Philadelphia, PA 19147-1316.

LANGE, LEO JEROME, MATHEMATICS. **Personal Data:** b New Rockford, NDak, August 29, 1928; m 1955, c 4. **Education:** Regis Col, Colo, BS, 1952; Univ Colo, MA, 1956, PhD (math), 1960. **Professional Experience:** Dept chmn, Univ MO, Columbia, 1988-1991; PROF MATH, UNIV MO, COLUMBIA, beginning 1983; from asst prof to assoc prof, Univ MO, Columbia, 1960-1983; asst, UnivColo, 1958-1960; mathematician, Boulder Labs, Nat Bur Stand, 1956-1960; instr math, UnivColo, 1952-1956. **Memberships:** Math Asn Am; Am Math Soc. **Research Statement & Publications:** Continued fractions; complex analysis; approximations & expansions. **Mailing Address:** Dept Math, Univ Mo, 315 Math Sci Bldg, Columbia, MO 65211-0001. **E-Mail:** langel@missouri.edu

LANGE, LESTER HENRY, MATHEMATICS. **Personal Data:** b Concordia, Mo, January 2, 1924; m 1962, c 5. **Education:** Valparaiso Univ, AB, 1948; Stanford Univ, MS, 1950; Univ Notre Dame, PhD, 1960. **Honors & Awards:** L R Ford Sr Award, Math Asn Am, 1972; spec asst todean, moss landing marine lab, calif, beginning1988. **Professional Experience:** PROF EMER, MOSS LANDING MARINE LAB, CALIF, as of 2004; EMER DEAN & EMER PROF MATH, SAN JOSE STATE UNIV, 1988-; SPEC ASST TODEAN, MOSS LANDING MARINE LAB, CALIF, 1988-; dean sch sci, San Jose State Univ, 1970-1988; chmn dept, San Jose State Univ, 1962-1970; actg head dept, San Jose State Univ, 1961-1962; from asst prof to prof, San Jose State Univ, 1960-1970; instr, Univ Notre Dame, 1956-1957 & 1959-1960; asst prof, Valparaiso Univ, 1954-1956; Instr math, Valparaiso Univ, 1950-1953. **Memberships:** AAAS; Math Asn Am; London Math Soc; Nat Coun Teachers Math. **Research Statement & Publications:** Complex variable; topology. **Mailing Address:** Moss Landing Marine Lab, PO Box 450, Moss Landing, CA 95039-0450. **E-Mail:** lange@mlml.calstate.edu

LANGE, ROBERT CARL, magnetic resonance imaging, radiological physics; deceased, see previous edition for last biography

LANGE, ROBERT ECHLIN, WILDLIFE DISEASES, WILDLIFE DISEASE PREVENTION. **Personal Data:** b Janesville, Wis, m 1970. **Education:** Colo State Univ, BS, 1968, 1970, MS, 1973, DVM, 1974. **Professional Experience:** CHIEF, DIV FED AID, US FISH & WILDLIFE SERV, 1994-; dept asst regional dir Fed Aid, Fish & Wildlife, 1988-1994; field diagnostician, Nat Wildlife Health Lab, 1980-1988; adj prof, NMex State Univ, 1978-1980; adj prof, Biol Dept, NMex Highlands Univ, 1975-1977; wildlifevet wildlife dis, NMex Dept Game & Fish, 1974-1980; Wildlife dis consult, Colo Wild Animal DisCtr, 1972-1974. **Memberships:** Wild Animal Dis Asn; Am Vet Med Asn; Wildlife Soc; Am Asn Wildlife Vet (secytreas, 1981-). **Research Statement & Publications:** Investigation into the game management implications of wildlife diseases in elk, Rocky Mountain bighorn sheep and other mammals; wildlife disease management in migratory waterfowl; mammals and wildlife disease prevention. **Mailing Address:** Div Fed Aid, US Fish & Wildlife Serv, Rm 140, 4401 N Fairfax Dr, Arlington, VA 22203.

LANGE, WILLIAM JAMES, SURFACE PHYSICS. **Personal Data:** b Sandusky, Ohio, January 20, 1930; m 1951, Jeanne; c 4. **Education:** Oberlin Col, AB, 1951; Mass Inst Technol, PhD (physics), 1956. **Professional Experience:** RETIRED; mgr vacuum physics, Res Labs, Westinghouse Elec Corp, 1964-1988; physicist, Res Labs, Westinghouse Elec Corp, 1956-1964; asst phys electronics, Mass Inst Technol, 1951-1956. **Memberships:** Am Phys Soc; Am Vacuum Soc. **Research Statement & Publications:** Ultrahigh vacuum; interaction of gases with surfaces. **Mailing Address:** 3917 Hickory Hill Rd, Murrysville, PA 15668.

LANGE, WINTHROP EVERETT, PHARMACY. **Personal Data:** b Appleton, Wis, September 22, 1925; m 1948, c 2. **Education:** Univ Wis, BS, 1952, MS, 1953, PhD (pharm, chem), 1955. **Professional Experience:** Adj prof, A&M Schwartz Col Pharm & Health Sci, 1978-1982; VPRES, INTDIR TECH SERV, PURDUE FREDERICK CO, 1974-; dir labs, Int Dir Tech Serv, PurdueFrederick Co, 1968-1974; prof & chmn dept, Mass Col Pharm, 1966-1968; from asst prof toassoc prof, Mass Col Pharm, 1958-1966; asst prof, SDak State Col, 1955-1958; asst pharm, UnivWis, 1952-1954. **Memberships:** Am Chem Soc; Am Pharmaceut Asn; Soc Cosmetic Chem; Acad Pharmaceut Sci; Int Fedn Socs Cosmetic Chem (pres 1976-1977). **Research Statement & Publications:** Synthesis of metal chelates as pro-drugs; pharmaceutical analysis. **Mailing Address:** 525 Kings Way, Naples, FL 34104.

LANGE, YVONNE, MEMBRANE BIOGENESIS, CHOLESTEROL MOVEMENT IN CELLS. **Personal Data:** b Durban, SAfrica, April 5, 1941; m 1982. **Education:** London Univ, BSc, 1962; Oxford Univ, DPhil (theoret physics), 1966. **Professional Experience:** PROF BIOCHEM & PATH, RUSH MED COL, 1984-; assoc prof, Rush Med Col, 1981-1986; from asst prof to assoc prof, Sch Med, Boston Univ, 1976-1981; res fel, Sch Med, Boston Univ, 1975-1976; lectr, Harvard Med Sch, 1973-1975; instr biophys, Harvard Med Sch, 1970-1972. **Memberships:** Am Soc Biol Chemists; Am Soc Cell Biol. **Research Statement & Publications:** Intracellular movement of newly synthesized cholesterol in cultured cells with the objective of elucidating mechanisms by which eukaryotic cells regulate their membrane cholesterol content. **Mailing Address:** Dept Biochem, Rush Univ 1653 W Congress Pkwy, Chicago, IL 60612. **Fax:** 312-942-8233.

LANGEBARTEL, RAY GARTNER, MATHEMATICS, ASTRONOMY. **Personal Data:** b Quincy, Ill, April 27, 1921; m 1945, c 4. **Education:** Univ Ill, AB, 1942, AM, 1943, PhD (math), 1948. **Professional Experience:** PROF EMER MATH, UNIV ILL, URBANA, as of 2003; prof math, Univ Ill, Urbana, beginning 1970; vis res assoc, Stockholm Observ, 1950-1951; from instr to assoc prof, Univ Ill, Urbana, 1948-1970; asst math, Univ Ill, Urbana, 1946-1948. **Research Statement & Publications:** Function theory; stellar dynamics. **Mailing Address:** Dept Math, Univ Ill, Champaign, IL 61820.

LANGELAND, KAARE, DENTAL MATERIALS, EXPERIMENTAL PATHOLOGY. **Personal Data:** b Saltdal, Norway, November 3, 1916. **Education:** Vet Col Norway, grad, 1938; Norweg State Dent Sch, DDS, 1942; Univ Oslo, PhD, 1957. **Honors & Awards:** Badge of Honor in Silver & Prize, Norweg Dent Asn, 1959. **Professional Experience:** Adj prof, Dept Endodontics, Sch Grad Dent, Boston Univ, 1992-; PROF EMER, DEPT RESTORATIVE DENT & ENDODONTOLOGY, SCH DENT MED, UNIV CONN HEALTH CTR, FARMINGTON, 1987-; Off Naval Res Contract, 1971-1977; prof & chmn, Dept Endodontics, Univ Conn Health Ctr, Farmington, 1970-1987; Univ Conn Res Found grants, 1970-1973 & 1976-1977; prof, Dept Gen Dent, Sch Dent Med, Univ Conn Health Ctr, Farmington, 1969-1970; Serco grant, 1966-1967; mem, Working GroupDent Terminology, Int Orgn Stand, 1965; prof oral biol, Univ & proj dir, Minn Mining & Mfg, State Univ NY Buffalo, 1964-1969; 3M grant, 1963-1969; USPHS grants, 1963-1968, 1969-1970, 1977-1979; assoc prof oral histol & chmn dept, Univ & proj dir, Minn Mining & Mfg, State Univ NY Buffalo, 1963; USPHS grants, Res Found, State Univ NY Buffalo, 1963; Norwegstate rep, Inter-Nordic Comt Planning NordicBur Stand Dept Mat, 1961-1962; ed, Scand Dent J, 1957-1963; res assoc, Norweg Inst Dent Res, 1952-1963; teacher, Norweg State Dent Sch, 1948-1949; asst, Dent DiagDept, Gaustad Hosp, 1942-1952; mem, Coun StandDent Mat & Devices, Am Mat Stand Inst; vchmn comn dent res, Int Dent Fedn, chmn workinggroup biol testing dent mat; vis lectr, Boston Univ. **Memberships:** Norweg Dent Asn; hon mem Dent Asn SAfrica; hon mem Dent Asn SouthRhodesia; hon mem SAfrican Prosthodont Soc; corresp mem Finnish Dent Soc. **Research Statement & Publications:** Experimental pathology regarding biomaterials; evaluation of the biologic properties of methods; devices, and materials used in dentistry before they are released for general use; author of numerous books, chapters, articles and abstracts. **Mailing Address:** Dept Endodontology, Univ Conn Health Ctr, 263 Farmington Ave, Farmington, CT 06030-1715.

LANGENAU, EDWARD E, WILDLIFE BIOLOGY, PSYCHOLOGY. **Personal Data:** b Brooklyn, NY, October 28, 1946; m 1969, Diana; c Erik & David. **Education:** Rensselaer Polytech Inst, BS, 1968; Mich State Univ, MS, 1973, PhD (wildlife mgt), 1976; MPA, 1981. **Professional Experience:** RETIRED; BIG GAME SUPVR, STATE MICH, 1986-; wildlife res biologist, State Mich, 1974-1985. **Memberships:** Soc Am Foresters; Wildlife Soc. **Research Statement & Publications:** Public behavior; white-tailed deer behavior; forest recreation; attitude toward clearcutting; hunter behavior; natural resource policy analysis; public administration. **Mailing Address:** PO Box 1067, Indian River, MI 49749-1067.

LANGENBERG, DONALD NEWTON, SOLID STATE PHYSICS. **Personal Data:** b Devils Lake, NDak, March 17, 1932; m Patricia; c Karen, Julia, John & Amy. **Education:** Iowa State Univ, BS, 1953; Univ Calif, Los Angeles, MS, 1955, Berkeley, PhD (physics), 1959. **Honorary Degrees:** MA, Univ Pa, 1971, DSc, 1985; DSc, State Univ of NY, 1998. **Honors & Awards:** John Price Wetherill Medal, Franklin Inst, 1975. **Professional Experience:** PROFESSOR, UNIV MD, COL PARK, as of 1990; chancellor, Univ Syst Md, 1990-2002; PROF & CHANCELLOR EMER, UNIV MD, 2002-; chancellor, Univ Ill, Chicago, 1983-1990; dep dir, NSF, 1980-1982; mem, chmn & bd dir, Nat Asn State Univ & Land-Grant Col, 1991; mem, bd trustees, Univ Pa, 1990-2000; president, American Physical Society 1993; president, American Association for the Advancement of Research 1982; Nat Comn Res, 1978-1980; Coun Govt Relations & chmn, Adv Coun, 1977-1980; prof elec eng & sci, Univ PA, beginning 1976; trustee, Assoc Univs, Inc, 1975-1980; vprovost grad studies & res, Univ Pa, 1974-1979; mem, Adv Comt Res, NSF, 1974-1977; guest researcher,

Cent Inst Low Temperature Study, Bayer Acad Sci & Tech Univ Munich, 1974; dir lab res struct matter, Univ Pa, 1972-1974; vis prof, Calif Inst Technol, 1971; chmn, Nat Acad Sci-Nat Acad Eng-Nat Res Coun Panel Adv to Cryogenics Div, Nat Bur Stand, 1970-1975; mem, Comn I, Int Union Radio Sci, 1969-; mem, Nat Acad Sci-Nat Acad Eng-Nat Res Coun Panel Adv to Cryogenics Div, Nat Bur Stand, 1969-1970; distinguished vis scientist, Mich State Univ, 1969; Guggenheim Found fel, 1966-1967; assoc prof, Advan Normal Sch, Univ Paris, 1966-1967; Sloan Found fel, 1962-1964; from asst prof to assoc prof physics, Univ Pa, 1960-1967; NSF fel, 1959-1960; actg instr physics, Univ Calif, Berkeley, 1958-1959. **Memberships:** Fel AAAS (pres 1990); fel Am Phys Soc (pres 1993). **Research Statement & Publications:** Cyclotron resonance and Fermi surface studies in metals and semiconductors; tunneling and Josephson effects in superconductors; precision measurement and fundamental physical constants; low temperature physics; nonequilibrium phenomena in superconductors. **Mailing Address:** Dept Physics, Univ MD, 4211 Toll Physics Bldg, College Park, MD 20742. **Fax:** 301-314-9525. **E-Mail:** dnl@usmd.edu

LANGENBERG, PATRICIA WARRINGTON, BIOSTATISTICS, CLINICAL TRIALS & WOMENS HEALTH. **Personal Data:** b Des Moines, Iowa, September 10, 1931; m 1953, Donald N; c Karen K, Julia A, John N & Amy P. **Education:** Iowa State Univ, BS, 1953; Temple Univ, MA, 1975, PhD (math), 1978. **Professional Experience:** PROF BIOSTATISTICS, UNIV MD SCH MED, BALTIMORE, 1996-; VICE CHAIR, DEPT EPIDEMIOL & PREV MED, UNIV MD SCH MED, BALTIMORE, 1996-; assoc prof biostatistics, Univ Md, Baltimore, 1990-1996; assoc prof biomet, Sch Pub Health, Univ Ill, 1983-1990; asst prof statist, Temple Univ, 1980-1983; from instr to asst prof math, LaSalle Col, 1975-1980. **Memberships:** Am Statist Asn; Biomet Soc; Caucus Women Statist; Soc Clin Trials. **Research Statement & Publications:** Clinical trials; biostatistics; mathematical statistics; women's health. **Mailing Address:** Dept Epidemiol & Prev Med, Univ Md, 660 W Redwood St, Baltimore, MD 21201. **Fax:** 410-706-8013. **E-Mail:** plangenb@umaryland.edu

LANGENBERG, WILLEM G, PLANT PATHOLOGY, PLANT VIROLOGY. **Personal Data:** b Djombang, Indonesia, April 16, 1928; American citizen; m 1955, c 3. **Education:** Calif State Col Long Beach, BS, 1963; Univ Calif, Berkeley, PhD (plant path), 1967. **Professional Experience:** PROF, LIFE SCI DEPT, UNIV NEBR-LINCOLN, 1980-; RES PLANT PATHOLOGIST, AGR RES SERV, USDA, 1967-; assoc prof plant path, Univ Nebr-Lincoln, 1967-1980. **Memberships:** Am Phytopath Soc. **Research Statement & Publications:** Study of plant-virus-vector relationships with labeled antibodies or viruses; light and electron microscopy radioautography. **Mailing Address:** Dept Plant Path, Univ Nebr, Lincoln, NE 68583.

LANGENHEIM, JEAN HARMON, PLANT BIOCHEMICAL ECOLOGY & EVOLUTION. **Personal Data:** b Homer, La, September 5, 1925; div. **Education:** Univ Tulsa, BS, 1946; Univ Minn, MS, 1949, PhD (bot, geol), 1953. **Professional Experience:** RES PROF, UNVI CALIF, SANTA CRUZ, 2001-; PROF EMER BIO, UNIV CALIF, SANTA CRUZ, 1993-; mem, US Nat Comt, Int Union Biol Sci, 1989-1994; mem, ecol adv comm, Environ Protection Agency, 1977-1981; mem, NSF comn floral inventory Amazon, 1975-1987; acad vpres, Org Trop Studies, 1975-1977; chmn, Biol Dept, 1974-1976; vis prof biol, Harvard Univ, 1974; prof biol, Univ Calif, Santa Cruz, beginning 1973; mem exec comt, Org Trop Studies, 1972-1977; from asst prof to assoc prof, Univ Calif, Santa Cruz, 1966-1973; res assoc, Bot Mus, 1963-1966; scholar, Radcliffe Inst Independent Study, 1963-1964; Asn Univ Women fel, Harvard Univ, 1962-1963; teaching assoc, Univ Ill, 1959-1962; from instr to asst prof, San Francisco Col Women, 1956-1959; lectr, Mills Col, 1955-1956; mem teaching staff & bd trustees, Rocky Mountain Biol Lab, 1954-1965; res assoc, Univ Calif, Berkeley, 1954-1959; investr, Nat Geol Serv, Colombia, 1953. **Memberships:** Int Soc Chem Ecol (pres, 1986-1987); Bot Soc Am; Ecol Soc Am (vpres, 1980-1981, pres, 1986-1987); fel AAAS; Asn Trop Biol (pres, 1985); Soc Econ Biol (pres, 1993-1994). **Research Statement & Publications:** Paleoecological studies of amber; evolutionary and physioecological studies of tropical resin-producing and other terpene-producing p; concepts of ecology; plants and human affairs. **Mailing Address:** Dept Ecol & Evolutionary Biol, Sinsheimer Labs, Univ Calif, Santa Cruz, CA 95064. **Fax:** 831-459-3139. **E-Mail:** lang@biology.ucsc.edu

LANGENHEIM, RALPH LOUIS, PALEONTOLOGY, STRATIGRAPHY. **Personal Data:** b Cincinnati, Ohio, May 26, 1922; m 1994, Casey; c Victoria & Ralph L. **Education:** Univ Tulsa, BS, 1943; Univ Colo, MS, 1947; Univ Minn, PhD (geol), 1951. **Professional Experience:** PROF EMER GEOL, UNIV ILL, URBANA, 1992-; CUR EMER PALEONT, MUS NATURAL HIST, 1992-; consult curric & prog, Fac Geol & Mining, Polytech Univ Albania, 1992; cur paleont, Mus Natural Hist, 1983-1992; partner, Lanman Assocs; consult geologists, 1974-; foreign assoc, Geol Surv Iran, 1973; from asst prof to prof geol, Mus Natural Hist, 1959-1992; adv, Geol Surv Can, 1957 & Cent Geol Surv, Repub China, 1981; foreign expert, Inst Geol Nac, Colombia, 1953; asst prof paleont, Univ Calif, 1952-1959; asst prof geol, Coe Col, 1950-1952. **Memberships:** Geol Soc Am; Paleont Soc (secy, 1962-1970); Am Asn Petrol Geol; fel AAAS; fel Explorers Club; Nat Assoc Geosci Teachers. **Research Statement & Publications:** Invertebrate paleontology and stratigraphy; Paleozoic of western and central North America; Tertiary of southern Mexico; Permian and Carboniferous of Iran; petroleum and energy geology; approximately 125 publications. **Mailing Address:** Dept Geol Univ Ill, 334 NHB 1301 W Green St, Urbana, IL 61801. **E-Mail:** rlangenh@uiuc.edu

LANGER, ARTHUR M, MINERALOGY, ENVIRONMENTAL SCIENCES. **Personal Data:** b New York, NY, February 18, 1936; m 1967, c 4. **Education:** Hunter Col, BA, 1956; Columbia Univ, MA, 1962, PhD (mineral), 1965. **Professional Experience:** DEP EXEC OFFICER, EARTH & ENVIRON SCI, BROOKLYN COL, CITY UNIV NY, as of 2004; DEP DIR, CTR APPL STUDIES ENVIRON, CITY UNIV NY, as of 2004; PROF, ENVIRON SCI LAB, BROOKLYN COL, CITY UNIV NY, as of 2004; consult, Consumer Prod Safety Comn, Wash, DC, 1986; DIR, ENVIRON SCI LAB, INST APPL SCI, BROOKLYN COL, CITY UNIV NY, 1985-; assoc prof, polypeptide & membrane res, Brooklyn Col, City Univ NY, 1985; consult, Ctr Dis Control, Nat Acad Sci, 1984; consult, Ctr Dis Control, Atlanta, 1984; consult, Int Metalworkers Fedn, Geneva, 1980; consult, Ministry Mines, Johannesburg, Safrica, 1977; consult, Inst Pub Health, Norway, 1977; consult, NIH, Bethesda Md, 1974; consult, Int Agencies Res Cancer, Lyon WHO, 1974; adj assoc prof, Queens Col, NY, 1968-1970; asst prof mineral, Environ Sci Lab, Inst Appl Sci, Brooklyn Col, City Univ New York, 1966-1968; res assoc environ sci, Environ Sci Lab, Inst Appl Sci, Brooklyn Col, City Univ New York, 1965-1966; assoc dir, Environ Sci Lab, Mt Sinai Sch Med, 1965-1986; res assoc mineral, Columbia, 1962-1965; assoc prof mineral, Mt Sinai Sch Med, Environ Sci Lab, Inst Appl Sci, Brooklyn Col, City Univ NY. **Memberships:** AAAS; Geol Soc Am; Electron Probe Analysis Soc Am; Geochem Soc; MineralSoc Am. **Research Statement & Publications:** Metamorphic and igneous petrology; clay mineralogy; secondary mineralization; instrumentation; microparticulate identification, analysis and interaction in the human environment. **Mailing Address:** Environ Sci Lab, Brooklyn Col, City Univ NY, 5144 Ingersoll Hall, Brooklyn, NY 11210. **E-Mail:** alanger@brooklyn.cuny.edu

LANGER, DIETRICH WILHELM, SOLID STATE PHYSICS. **Personal Data:** b Berlin, Ger, August 13, 1930; American citizen; m 1961, c 4. **Education:** Tech Univ Berlin, MS, 1957, PhD (physics), 1960. **Honors & Awards:** Alexander von Humboldt Award, 1972. **Professional Experience:** PROF ELECTRICAL ENG, UNIV PITTSBURGH, 1987-; fel, Indust Col ArmedForces, 1975-1976; adv, Max Planck Inst Solid State Study, 1972-1973; group leader, electronicproperties, Semiconductors Group, 1965-1987; grant, Ecole Normale Superieure, Paris, 1964-1965; eve lectr, Univ Dayton, 1959-1960; from res physicist to sr res physicist, AerospaceRes Labs, Wright-Patterson Air Force Base, 1957-1965. **Memberships:** Fel Am Phys Soc; sr mem Inst Elec & Electronics Engrs. **Research Statement & Publications:** Optical, electronic and electrooptical properties of semiconductors and devices; materials research; research and development administration. **Mailing Address:** Elec Eng Dept, Univ Pittsburgh, 348 Benedum Hall 3700 O Hara St, Pittsburgh, PA 15261. **Fax:** 412-624-8003. **E-Mail:** dwl@ee.pitt.edu

LANGER, GLENN A, MEDICINE. **Personal Data:** b Nyack, NY, May 5, 1928; m 1954, c 1. **Education:** Colgate Univ, BA, 1950; Columbia Univ, MD, 1954. **Professional Experience:** CASTERA EMER PROF CARDIOL, MED CTR, UNIV CALIF, LOS ANGELES, as of 2001; DIR, CARDIOVASC RES LAB, UNIV CALIF, LOS ANGELES, as of 2001; PROF EMER MED & PHYSIOL, MED CTR, UNIV CALIF, LOS ANGELES, as of 2001; dir, Cardiovasc Res Lab, Univ Calif, Los Angeles, beginning 1987; Macy fac scholar, 1979-1980; Griffith vis prof cardiol, 1979; castera prof cardiol, Med Ctr, Univ Calif, Los Angeles, beginning 1978; chmn exec comt, BasicSci Coun & bd dirs, Am Heart Asn, 1976-1978; prof med & physiol, Med Ctr, Univ Calif, Los Angeles, beginning 1969; vice chmn, Dept Physiol, Univ Calif, Los Angeles, 1967-1987; assoc dir, Cardiovasc Res Lab, Univ Calif, Los Angeles, 1966-1987; assoc prof, Univ Calif, LosAngeles, 1966-1969; asst prof med, Columbia Univ, 1963-1966; clin instr, Los Angeles CoCardiovasc Res Lab & Med Ctr, Univ Calif, Los Angeles, 1960-1962; sr resident, Mass GenHosp, 1959-1960; asst res, Columbia-Presby Med Ctr, 1957-1958; intern, Mass Gen Hosp, 1954-1955. **Memberships:** Am Heart Asn; Am Physiol Soc; Am Soc Clin Invest; Am Asn Physicians; Soc Gen Physiologists. **Research Statement & Publications:** Myocardial physiology and metabolism. **Mailing Address:** Dept Med & Physiol, Univ Calif, 675 Circle Dr S, Los Angeles, CA 90095-1361.

LANGER, HORST G, INORGANIC CHEMISTRY. **Personal Data:** b Breslau, Ger, December 29, 1927; American citizen; m 1955, c 2. **Education:** Brunswick Tech Univ, Dipl, 1954, Dr rer nat(chem), 1956. **Professional Experience:** ASSOC SCIENTIST, DOW CHEM USA, 1968-; sr res chemist, Dow ChemUSA, 1964-1968; res chemist, Dow Chem USA, 1958-1964; res assoc inorg chem, Ind Univ, 1956-1958; Asst inorg analytical chem, Brunswick Tech Univ, 1951-1956. **Memberships:** Am Chem Soc; Am Soc Mass Spectrometry; Int Confedn Thermal Analysis; felNAm Thermal Analytical Soc; Ger Chem Soc. **Research Statement & Publications:** Analytical, dental and organometallic chemistry; mass spectrometry; thermal analysis; fire retardants; catalysts. **Mailing Address:** 28 Joyce Rd, Wayland, MA 01778-4516.

LANGER, JAMES STEPHEN, STATISTICAL MECHANICS. **Personal Data:** b Pittsburgh, Pa, September 21, 1934; m 1958, Elinor; c Ruth, Stephen & David. **Education:** Carnegie Inst Technol, BS, 1955; Univ Birmingham, PhD, 1958. **Honors & Awards:** Oliver Buckley Prize, Am Phys Soc, 1997. **Professional Experience:** VPRES, NAT ACAD SCI, as of 2004; dir, Inst Theoret Physics, 1989-1995; PROF MAT & PHYSICS, UNIV CALIF, SANTA BARBARA, 1982-; Guggenheim fel, Harvard Univ, 1974-1975; assoc dean, Mellon InstSci, 1971-1974; vis assoc prof, Cornell Univ, 1966-1967; from asst prof to prof, Carnegie-Mellon Univ, 1964-1982; instr physics, Carnegie-Mellon Univ, 1958-1964. **Memberships:** Nat Acad Sci; fel Am Phys Soc; Am Acad Arts & Sci; fel AAAS. **Research Statement & Publications:** Theoretical solid state physics; kinetics of phase transformations. **Mailing Address:** Dept Physics, Univ Calif, Santa Barbara, CA 93106. **Fax:** 805-893-2902. **E-Mail:** langer@physics.ucsb.edu

LANGER, ROBERT MARTIN, CHEMICAL ENGINEERING. **Personal Data:** b Boston, Mass, May 29, 1925. **Education:** Yale Univ, BS, 1945, DEng, 1952; Mass Inst Technol, SM, 1948. **Professional Experience:** RETIRED; vpres & treas, Badger Co Inc, Cambridge, Mass, 1983-1987; sr vpres, Badger Am Inc, Cambridge, 1981-1983; vpres proj admin, Badger Co Inc, Cambridge, Mass, 1978-1980; mgr dir, Badger BV, The Hague, Neth, 1974-1978; dep mgr dir, Badger BV, Hague, Neth, 1970-1974; sales mgr, Badger Co Inc, Cambridge, Mass, 1968-1970. **Memberships:** Am Inst Chem Engrs. **Mailing Address:** 280 Commonwealth Ave, Boston, MA 02116-2422.

LANGER, ROBERT SAMUEL, BIOENGINEERING, BIOMEDICAL SCIENCE. **Personal Data:** b August 29, 1948; American citizen; m 1988, Laura; c Michael & Susan. **Education:** Cornell Univ, BS, 1970; Mass Inst Technol, ScD, 1974. **Honorary Degrees:** Dr, Eidgenossische Tech Sch, Zurich, 1996. **Honors & Awards:** Walter F Enz Lectr, Univ Kans, 1989; Founders Award, Controlled ReleaseSoc, 1989; Creative Polymer Chem Award, Am Chem Soc, 1989; Clemson Award, Soc Biomat, 1990; Prof Prog Award, Am Inst Chem Engrs, 1990; Outstanding Pharmaceut Paper Award, 1990 & 1992; Charles M A Stine Award, 1991; OrganonTeknika Award, Europ Soc Artificial Organs, 1991; Perlman Mem Award Lectr, 1992; Phillips Award, 1992; Distinguished Pharmaceut Scientist Award, Am Asn Pharmaceut Scientists, 1993; Ebert Prize, Am Pharmaceut Asn, 1995 & 1996; William Walker Award, 1996. **Professional Experience:** Chmn, Am Inst Med & Biol Eng Col Fels, 1995-1996; Priestley Lectr, Pa State Univ, 1993; Kurt Wohl Mem Lectr, Univ Del, 1993; Kelly Distinguished Lectr, Purdue Univ, 1992; Miles Distinguished Lectr, Univ Pittsburgh, 1992; pres, Controlled Release Soc, 1991-1992; Sidney Riegelman Lectr, Univ Calif, San Francisco, 1991; Louis W Busse Lectr, Univ Wis, 1991; Sandoz-Dorsey lectr, Ohio State Univ, 1991; Ashton-CaryLectr, Ga Inst Technol, 1991; GERMESHAUSEN PROF, DEPT CHEM ENG, MASS INST TECHNOL, 1988-; prof, Dept Appl Biol Sci, Mass Inst Technol, 1985-1988; ed, Biomat, 1983-; from asst prof to assoc prof, Dept Nutrit & Food Sci, Mass Inst Technol, 1978-1985; vis asst prof nutrit & food sci, Mass Inst Technol, 1977-1978; RES ASSOC SURG, BOSTON CHILDREN'S HOSP, 1974-; consult, numerous co. **Memberships:** Nat Acad Sci; Inst Med - Nat Acad Sci; Biomed Engr Soc; Controlled Release Soc; Am Soc Artificial Internal Organs; Am Chem Soc; fel Soc Biomat; fel Am Inst Med & Biol Eng; Am Inst Chem Engrs; Am Acad Arts & Sci; Sigma Xi. **Research Statement & Publications:** Polymer drug delivery systems; tumor neovascularization; applicationof enzymes in medicine; biomaterials; tissue engineering. **Mailing Address:** Dept Chem Eng, Mass Inst Technol, E25-342, Cambridge, MA 02139. **Fax:** 617-258-8827. **E-Mail:** rlanger@mit.edu

LANGER, SIDNEY, INORGANIC CHEMISTRY. **Personal Data:** b New York, NY, December 15, 1925. **Education:** NY Univ, AB, 1949; Ill Inst Technol, PhD (chem), 1955. **Professional Experience:** 1984-1989; RETIRED; sr scientist, Sci Appl Int, 1989-1993; mgr gas cooled fast breeder reactor fuels, Nuclear Fuels Group, Res & Develop Div, Gulf Gen Atomic, 1977-1981; Group leader fuels & mat develop, gas-cooled fast reactor project, Gen Atomic Co, 1971-; mem sr res staff, Nuclear Fuels Group, Res & Develop Div, Gulf Gen Atomic, 1969-1983; group leader, Nuclear Fuels Group, Res & Develop Div,

Gulf Gen Atomic, 1969-1971; mem res staff, Gen Atomic Div, Gen Dynamics Corp, 1960-1969; Chemist, Oak Ridge Nat Lab, 1954-1960; prin prog specialist, TMI-2 Accident Eval Prog, EG&G Idaho, Inc. **Memberships:** AAAS; Sigma Xi; Am Chem Soc; fel Am Nuclear Soc, Phi Beta Kappa. **Research Statement & Publications:** Nuclear reactor chemistry; physical chemistry and thermodynamics of high temperature systems; phase equilibria; fission product behavior in fuels; fission product release; fuel processing and reprocessing; nuclear reactor safety. **Mailing Address:** PO Box 22062, San Diego, CA 92192. **Fax:** 858-587-8289. **E-Mail:** skllane@aol.com

LANGERMAN, NEAL RICHARD, CHEMICAL & ENVIRONMENTAL SAFETY. **Personal Data:** b Philadelphia, Pa, March 11, 1943. **Education:** Franklin & Marshall Col, AB, 1965; Northwestern Univ, PhD (chem), 1969. **Professional Experience:** Ed adv bd, Lab Safety & Environ Mgt, 1999-; PRES, ADV CHEM SAFETY, 1997-; pres, Chem Safety Asn, San Diego, Calif, 1982-1997; assoc prof chem, Utah State Univ, 1977-1983; asst prof, Utah State Univ, 1975-1977; asst prof biochem, Sch Med, Tufts Univ, 1970-1975; NIH fel chem, Yale Univ, 1969-1970. **Memberships:** Am Soc Biol Chemists; Biophys Soc; Calorimetry Soc; Undersea Med Soc; Am Chem Soc. **Research Statement & Publications:** Thermodynamic studies of protein reactions, especially flavin-flavoprotein interactions; microcalorimetry; fluorescence spectroscopy; analytical ultracentrifugation; chemical safety; management of hazardous waste; chemical resource recovery; around 50 publication. **Mailing Address:** Advanced Chem Safety, 7563 Convoy Ct, San Diego, CA 92111. **Fax:** 858-874-8239. **E-Mail:** chemsaf@ix.netcom.com

LANGFELDER, LEONARD JAY, GEOTECHNICAL & COASTAL ENGINEERING. **Personal Data:** b Lynbrook, NY, February 5, 1933; m 1955, c 3. **Education:** Univ Fla, BSCE, 1959, MSE, 1960; Univ Ill, PhD (civil eng), 1964. **Professional Experience:** PROF EMER, NC STATE UNIV, as of 2002; CONSULT ENGR, 1988-; vpres & mgr dir, Harbor Br, Oceanog Inst, Inc, 1986-1988; asst secy, Nat Resources, NC, 1982-1983; prof & head, Dept Marine, Earth & Sci, 1980-1985; prof marine sci & eng & head dept, NC State Univ, 1978-1980; from asst prof to profcivil eng, NC State Univ, 1969-1978; dir, Ctr Marine, Earth, Atmospheric Sci, NC State Univ, 1969-1978; mem soils, geol & found cmt, Hwy Res Bd, Nat Acad Sci-Nat Res Coun, 1965-; vislectr civil eng, Univ Ill, 1964; res assoc coastal eng, Univ Fla, 1960-1962. **Memberships:** Am Soc Civil Engrs. **Research Statement & Publications:** Soil properties, principally shear strength and compaction properties of cohesive soils; improved foundation engineering principles; coastal processes. **Mailing Address:** Dept Marine, Earth & Atmospheric Sci, NC State Univ, PO Box 8208, Raleigh, NC 27695-8208.

LANGFITT, THOMAS WILLIAM, neurosurgery; deceased, see previous edition for last biography

LANGFORD, COOPER HAROLD, III, PHYSICAL INORGANIC CHEMISTRY, ENVIRONMANTAL CHEMISTRY. **Personal Data:** b Ann Arbor, Mich, October 14, 1934; m 1967, Martha; c Robert, Cooper & Holly. **Education:** Harvard Univ, AB, 1956; Northwestern Univ, PhD (chem), 1959. **Honors & Awards:** Fellow, Royal Society of Canada, 1991; Fellowship of NOW (Univ Amsterdam)1990; Fellow, Americal Association for the Advancementof Science, 1981; Alfred P Sloan Fellow, 1968-1970. **Professional Experience:** FACULTY PROF, UNIV CALGARY 2004-; PROF CHEM, UNIV CALGARY 1992-2004; COORD SCI & TECH & SOCI PROG, UNIV CALGARY, 1999- VPRES RES, UNIV CALGARY, 1992-1998; Dir phys & math sci, Nat Sci & EngRes Coun Can, 1990-1992; Assoc vrector res, Concordia Univ, 1987-1990; mem, strategic grants comt, open sect, Nat Sci Eng Res Coun Can, 1985-; chem chmn, Coun Can Univ, 1981-1983; prof chem & chmn dept, Concordia Univ, 1980-1987; chmn, Chem Grants Comt, Nat Res Coun Can, 1977-1978; consult, Nat Health & Welfare Can, 1977; mem, Chem Grants Comt, Nat Res CounCan, 1975-1978; consult, Inland Waters Directorate, Can, 1973; Alfred P Sloan Found fel, 1968-1970; from assoc prof to prof, Carleton Univ, 1967-1980; vis asst prof, Columbia Univ, 1964; from asst prof to assoc prof, Amherst Col, 1960-1967; instr chem, Amherst Col, 1960-1961; NSF fel, Univ Col, London, 1959-1960. **Research Statement & Publications:** Inorganic and environmental photochemistry; humic substances; kinetics in analysis; solution physical chemistry; described in four books and over 250 papers. **Mailing Address:** Dept Chem, Univ Calgary, 2500 Univ Dr NW, Calgary, AB T2N 1N4, Can. **Fax:** 403-289-9488. **E-Mail:** chlangfo@ucalgary.ca

LANGFORD, DAVID, MECHANICAL ENGINEERING, NUCLEAR ENGINEERING. **Personal Data:** b New York, NY, May 6, 1934; m 1990, c Laura J, Meryl D, Jennie H & Joshua B. **Education:** NY Univ, BS, eng, 1956; MS, nuclear eng, 1957; Ill Inst Technol, MS, mathmetics, 1959; Rensselaer Polytech Inst, DEngSc, 1965. **Professional Experience:** RETIRED; engr, US Nuclear Reg Comn, 1982-1991; regional radiation & noise rep, US Environ Protection Agency, 1972-1982; from asst prof to assoc prof mech eng, Drexel Univ, 1966-1972; from sr analytical engr to asst proj engr, Pratt & Whitney Aircraft, United Aircraft Corp, 1959-1966; from asst physicist to assoc physicist, IIT Res Inst, 1957-1959. **Research Statement & Publications:** Psychology and education of engineers; nuclear engineering; magnetohydrodynamics; superconductivity; conduction heat transfer; fluid flow; environmental science/Nuclear Environmental Protection Agency. **Mailing Address:** 1201 Seminole Blvd Apt 94, Largo, FL 33770.

LANGFORD, DEAN TED, LIGHTING & PRECISION. **Personal Data:** b June 19, 1939; m Nancy; c Douglas T & John P. **Education:** Univ Ill, BS, 1962. **Honorary Degrees:** LHD, Salem State Col, 1990. **Professional Experience:** Bd dir, Osram Sylvania, as of 2003; co-chmn, Alliance Save Energy, as of 2003; chief exec officer, Osram Sylvania Inc, 1996-2001; pres, Osram Sylvania Inc, beginning 1993; pres, GTE Elec Prod, 1984-1993; vpres mkt, GTE Commun Systs, 1983-1984; group dir commun, Ryebrook, NY, 1982-1983; corpdir mgt develop, Armonk, 1981-1982; Regional sales mgr, IBM, 1980-1981. **Memberships:** Nat Elec Mfg Asn; Phys Sci Inc. **Mailing Address:** Osram Sylvania Inc, 100 Endicott St, Danvers, MA 01923-3623.

LANGFORD, ERIC SIDDON, MATHEMATICS. **Personal Data:** b New York, NY, May 23, 1938; m 1959, c 1. **Education:** Mass Inst Technol, SB, 1959; Rutgers Univ, MS, 1960, PhD (math), 1963. **Honors & Awards:** L R Ford Award, Math Asn Am, 1971. **Professional Experience:** PROF EMER MATH, CALIF STATE UNIV, CHICAGO, as of 2006; prof math, Calif State Univ, Chicago, beginning 1982; prof, Univ Maine, Orono, 1977-1982; vis distinguished prof math, Calif Polytech State Univ, San Luis Obispo, 1977-1978; vis scholar, Univ Calif, Berkeley, 1976; vis assoc prof math, Calif Inst Technol, 1972-1973; assoc ed, Am Math Monthly, 1971-1975; assoc prof math, Univ Maine, Orono, 1969-1977; collab ed, Am Math Monthly, 1969-1971; vis assoc, Daniel H Wagner, Assocs, 1966; asst prof math, Naval Postgrad Sch, 1964-1969; res specialist, Autonetics Div, NAmRockwell, 1963-1964. **Research Statement & Publications:** Geometrical aspects of Banach spaces; Riesz spaces. **Mailing Address:** Dept Math & Statist, Calif State Univ, Chicago, CA 95929-0525. **E-Mail:** elangford@csuchico.edu

LANGFORD, FRED F, ECONOMIC GEOLOGY. **Personal Data:** b Toronto, Ont, December 19, 1929; m 1953, c 3. **Education:** Univ Toronto, BA, 1953; Queen's Univ, Ont, MA, 1955; Princeton Univ, PhD (geol), 1960. **Professional Experience:** PROF GEOL SCI, UNIV SASK, 1971-; assoc prof, Univ Sask, 1962-1971; assoc prof geol, Univ Kans, 1958-1962; geologist, Ont Dept Mines, 1954-1957; geologist, ImpOil Co, 1953-1954. **Memberships:** Mineral Asn Can; Geol Asn Can. **Research Statement & Publications:** Economic geology; potash geology; uranium deposits. **Mailing Address:** Dept Geol Sci, Univ Sask, Saskatoon, SK S7N 0W0, Can.

LANGFORD, GEORGE, PHYSICAL & MECHANICAL METALLURGY. **Personal Data:** b Chicago, Ill, December 26, 1936; m 1968, c 2. **Education:** Mass Inst Technol, BS. **Honorary Degrees:** DSc (metall), Mass Inst Technol, 1966. **Professional Experience:** VPRES & PRIN CONSULT, AMENEX ASSOCS INC, WESTTOWN, 1986-; prin consult & mgr metall dept, Lehigh Testing Lab, Inc, New Castle, 1981-1986; assoc prof, Dept Mat Eng, Drexel Univ, 1975-1981; res specialist, Monsanto Triangle Park Develop Ctr, Res Triangle Park, 1972-1975; scientist, Edgar C Bain Lab Fundamental Res, US Steel Corp, Monroeville, 1966-1971; res asst metall dept, Mass Inst Technol, Cambridge, 1963-1966; instr metall dept, Mass Inst Technol, Cambridge, 1959-1962. **Memberships:** AAAS; Am Soc Metals; Am Inst Mining Metall & Petrol Engrs; Sigma Xi. **Research Statement & Publications:** Optical and electron metallography of heavily deformed metals and theory of their strain hardening; wire drawing; steel casting by diffusion solidification and liquid infiltration. **Mailing Address:** Amenex Assoc, Inc, PO Box 1041, Westtown, PA 19395-1041. **Fax:** 610-647-5828. **E-Mail:** amenex@amenex.com

LANGFORD, GEORGE MALCOLM, CELL BIOLOGY, CYTO SKELETON. **Personal Data:** b Halif, NC, August 26, 1944; m 1968, Sylvia; c Joy, Grant & George III. **Education:** Fayetteville State Univ, BS, 1966; Ill Inst Technol, MS, 1969, PhD (cell biol), 1971. **Honorary Degrees:** MA, Dartmouth Col, 1994; LHD, Beloit col. **Professional Experience:** ADJ PROF, DEPT PHYSIOL, DARTMOUTH MED SCH, as of 2004; PROF, DARTMOUTH COL, 1991-; Ernest Everett Just Prof Natural Sci, Dept Biol Sci, Fac Arts & Sci, 1991-; cell biol prog dir, NSF, 1988-1989; NSF Adv Comt Cell Molecular Biol, 1984-; trustee, Marine Biol Lab, 1984-; consult, Marine Biol Lab, 1982-; consult, NIH, 1981-; from assoc prof to prof cell biol, Sch Med, Univ NC, Chapel Hill, 1979-1991; Macy fel, Steps fel, 1978; Col Med, Howard Univ, 1977-1979; Macy fel, Marine Biol Lab, 1976 & 1977; asst prof cell biol, Univ Mass, 1973-1976; NIH fel, 1971-1973; Fel biophys cytol, Univ Pa, 1971-1973; chair, Educ & Human Resources Comt, Nat Sci Bd. **Memberships:** AAAS; Am Soc Cell Biol; Sigma Xi; NY Acad Sci. **Research Statement & Publications:** Vesicle transport on axoplasmic microtubules and actin filaments; the structure and function of microtubules and actin filaments; wave propagation in the microtubular axostyle; properties of axonal and dendritic microtubules; axonal transport; Published over 5 articles. **Mailing Address:** Dartmouth Col Dept Biol Sci, 6044 Gilman Rm 416, Hanover, NH 03755-3576. **Fax:** 603-646-1347.

LANGFORD, PAUL BROOKS, PHYSICAL ORGANIC CHEMISTRY. **Personal Data:** b Lockesburg, Ark, August 11, 1930; m 1959, c 1. **Education:** Okla State Univ, BS, 1952, MS, 1954; Ga Inst Technol, PhD (chem), 1962. **Professional Experience:** DISTINGUISHED PROF CHEM, DAVID LIPSCOMB COL, as of 2004; chmn dept, David Lipscomb Col, beginning 1980; prof chem, David Lipscomb Col, beginning 1970; from asst prof to assoc prof, David Lipscomb Col, 1962-1970; instrchem, Ga Inst Technol, 1956-1962. **Memberships:** Am Chem Soc. **Research Statement & Publications:** Rates and mechanisms of reactions of organic halogen compounds; charge transfer complex compounds. **Mailing Address:** Dept Chem, David Lipscomb Univ, 3901 Granny White Pike, Nashville, TN 37204-3951. **E-Mail:** beverly.langford@lipscomb.edu

LANGFORD, ROBERT BRUCE, ORGANIC CHEMISTRY, CHEMICAL EDUCATION. **Personal Data:** b San Francisco, Calif, March 7, 1919; m 1957, Wilma R Ostrander. **Education:** Univ Calif, Los Angeles, BS, 1948; Univ Southern Calif, MS, 1963, PhD, 1972. **Professional Experience:** ADJ PROF CHEM, L A PIERCE COL, 1992-; EMER PROF CHEM, E LOS ANGELES COL, 1986-; chmn dept, L A Pierce Col, 1968-1974; from instr to prof, L A Pierce Col, 1964-1986; teacher chem, Los Angeles City Schs, 1961-1964; lab mgr org synthesis, Cyclo Chem Corp, 1958-1961; res chemist pesticides, Stauffer Chem Co, 1954-1958; Chemist petrol analysis, Southern Pac Co, 1949-1954. **Memberships:** Am Chem Soc; Sigma Xi. **Research Statement & Publications:** Organic synthesis; sulfur compounds; photochemistry. **Mailing Address:** 644 Haverkamp Dr, Glendale, CA 91206.

LANGFORD, ROLAND EVERETT, TOXICOLOGY. **Personal Data:** b Owensboro, Ky, April 11, 1945; m 1967, Son; c John E & Lee S. **Education:** Ga Southern Univ, BS, 1967; Univ Ga, MS, 1971, PhD (phys chem), 1974; Univ NC, PhD (health physics), 1994. **Professional Experience:** Adj fac, Purdue Univ, 1995; LT COLONEL MED SERV CORP, US ARMY, 1992-; CONSULT HAZARDOUS MAT & INDUST HYG, US ARMY, 1985-; comdr environsanitation team, Fifth Prevent Med Unit, 1981-1983; adj fac, Univ MD Korea, 1981-1983; sanitengr & environ sci officer, US Army Environ Hyg Agency, 1979-1981; chief, Clin Chem Lab SciDiv, US Army Acad Health Sci, 1978-1979; asst prof chem, Ga Southern Col, 1977-1978; head, Sci Dept, 1976-1977; asst prof chem & geol, Ga Mil Col, 1975-1977; res assoc, Chem Dept, Univ Ga, 1974; instr chem & math, Bainbridge Col, 1973-1974; chemist & instr, Environ Sci Educ Agency, 1971-1972. **Memberships:** Am Chem Soc; fel Am Inst Chemists; Asn Mil Surgeons US; Nat Environ HealthAsn; Am Acad Sanitarians; Royal Asiatic Soc; Health Physics Soc. **Research Statement & Publications:** Toxiology of mlitary releant chemicals and exposures especially weapon system combustion products. **Mailing Address:** US Army Med Res Detachment, MCMR-UWW 2800Q St Bldg 824, Wright-Patterson AFB, OH 45433-7947. **E-Mail:** langfordr@falcon.al.mil

LANGFORD, RUSSELL HAL, HYDROLOGY, ENVIRONMENTALCHEMISTRY. **Personal Data:** b North Platte, Nebr, November 14, 1925; m 1946, Mary Imogene Ellenbecker; c Stephen R, David G, Amy L & Russell J. **Education:** Univ Nebr, BSc, 1949. **Professional Experience:** RETIRED; assoc chief hydrologist, Off Water Data Coord, 1980-1985; chief, Off Water Data Coord, 1968-1980; asst chief, Off Water Data Coord, 1966-1968; Hydrologist, US Geol Surv, 1949-1966; alt chmn, US Nat Comt Sci Hydrol; US mem comn hydrol, World Meteorol Org, Intergovt Coun, Int Hydrolog Prog, UNESCO; Mem, Int Souris-Red River Eng Bd, Int Joint Comn US & Can. **Memberships:** Am Chem Soc; Am Water Works Asn; Am Geophys Union; Water Pollution Control Fedn; AAAS. **Research Statement & Publications:** Water chemistry; geochemistry; hydrology of the Missouri River basin, Colorado River basin, great basin. **Mailing Address:** 8380 Greensboro Dr Apt 926, McLean, VA 22102.

LANGFORD, WILLIAM FINLAY, DIFFERENTIAL EQUATIONS, BIFURCATION THEORY. **Personal Data:** b Thunder Bay, Ont, September 11, 1943; m 1992, Anne Ellis; c Cathena, Anne, Allison & Robert. **Education:** Queens Univ, Can, BSc, 1966; Calif Inst Technol, PhD (appl math), 1971. **Honors & Awards:** Pres distinguished prof award, univ Guelph, 2001. **Professional Experience:** Res vis, Math res Ctr, Univ Warwick, Coventry, England, 2002; Chercheur assoc, Inst Non Lineaire de Nice, France, 2001-2002; res vis, Inst Math

& Appl, Minn, 1998; BC Mattews Alumni fel, 1996; dep dir, Fields Inst Res Math Sci, 1996-1999; prog organizer, Fields Inst Res Math Sci, 1992-1993; chair, Dept Math & Statist, 1990-1996; Univ Guelph Forster fel, 1989; Can-UK Bilateral Exchange fel, 1989; res visitor, Inst Math & Appl, Minn, 1989; PROF MATH, UNIV GUELPH, CAN, 1988-; vis prof, Tianjin Univ China, 1987; mem bd dirs, Can Math Soc, 1985-1989; vis prof math, Univ Houston, 1985-1987; adj prof appl math, Univ Waterloo, 1983-; assoc prof, Univ Guelph, Can, 1982-1987; res visitor, Univ Nice, France, 1979-1980; from asst prof to assoc prof math, McGill Univ, 1970-1982. **Memberships:** Am Math Soc; Soc Indust & Appl Math; Can Math Soc; Can Appl Math Soc; Can Math soc. **Research Statement & Publications:** Theory of bifurcation for nonlinear differential equations; effects of symmetry; numerical algorithms for bifurcation problems and applications in science and engineering. **Mailing Address:** Dept Math & Statist, Univ Guelph, Guelph, ON N1G 2W1, Can. **Fax:** 519-837-0221. **E-Mail:** wlangfor@uoguelph.ca

LANGHAM, ROBERT FRED, PATHOLOGY. **Personal Data:** b Grand Ledge, Mich, January 31, 1912; m 1937, c 5. **Education:** Calvin Col, AB, 1935; Mich State Univ, MS, 1937, DVM, 1942, PhD, 1950. **Professional Experience:** EMER PROF VET PATH, MICH STATE UNIV, beginning 1988; actg chmn, Dept Path, Col Vet Med, Mich State Univ, 1973-1975; from instr to prof vet path, Mich State Univ, 1938-1988. **Memberships:** Am Vet Med Asn; Am Col Vet Path; Conf Res Workers Animal Dis; Int Acad Path. **Research Statement & Publications:** Leptospirosis; neoplasms and joint disease in animals; co-author and author. **Mailing Address:** 330 Shoesmith, Haslett, MI 48840.

LANGHANS, ROBERT W, FLORICULTURE. **Personal Data:** b Flushing, NY, December 29, 1929; m 1952, c 3. **Education:** Rutgers Univ, BS, 1952; Cornell Univ, MS, 1954, PhD (floricult), 1956. **Honors & Awards:** Blauvelt Award, 1955; Kenneth Post Award, Am Soc Hort Sci, 1965. **Professional Experience:** RETIRED; prof floricult, Cornell Univ, beginning 1968; from asst prof to assocprof, Cornell Univ, 1956-1968. **Memberships:** Am Soc Hort Sci; Am Soc Plant Physiol; Int Soc Hort Sci. **Research Statement & Publications:** Effects of photoperiod and temperature on growth and flowering. **Mailing Address:** Dept Floriculture, Cornell Univ Col Agr 15-D Plant Sci Bldg, Ithaca, NY 14853. **Fax:** 607-255-4457. **E-Mail:** rwl2@cornell.edu

LANGHEINRICH, ARMIN P(AUL), CHEMISTRY, FUEL ENGINEERING. **Personal Data:** b Planitz, Ger, September 1, 1926; American citizen; m 1949, c 3. **Education:** Univ Utah, BS, 1958, MA, 1962. **Professional Experience:** MGR, TECH & ADMIN SERV, KENNECOTT MINERALS CO, 1979-; srscientist, Res Dept, Metal Mining Div, 1971-1979; Spec instr chem, Salt Lake Ctr ContinuingEduc, Brigham Young Univ, 1963-1977; from asst scientist to scientist, Res Ctr, Western MiningDiv, 1962-1971; jr scientist, Res Ctr, Western Mining Div, 1959-1962; Asst chemist, UtahCooper Div, 1959. **Memberships:** Am Chem Soc; Am Soc Testing & Mat (secy 1977-1982). **Research Statement & Publications:** Application of x-ray fluorescence techniques to laboratory and on-stream analyses; energy dispersion x-ray analysis with conventional and radioisotope excitation; optical emission spectroscopy applied to geochemical samples and to refined copper; development of high purity copper standards; environmental analysis. **Mailing Address:** 230 M St, Salt Lake City, UT 84103-3544.

LANGHOFF, CHARLES ANDERSON, chemical physics; deceased, see previous edition for last biography

LANGHOFF, PETER WOLFGANG, COMPUTATIONS, APPLIED SCIENCE. **Personal Data:** b New York, NY, January 19, 1937; m 1962, Judith; c Lisa, Kristen (Grunnan) & Alison. **Education:** Univ Hofstra, BS, 1958; State Univ NY, Buffalo, PhD (physics), 1965. **Professional Experience:** Vpres res, SRT, Inc, 1986-1988; prof chem & fac assoc, Supercomput Res Inst, Fla State Univ, 1985-1986; vis prof, Univ Paris, Orsay, 1981; vis fel, Nat Res Coun fel, 1978-1979; prof chem, Ind Univ, Bloomington, beginning 1977; vis prof, Univ Colo, Boulder, 1976; vis fel, Joint Inst Lab Astrophys, 1975-1976; from asst prof to assoc prof, Ind Univ, Bloomington, 1969-1977; fel, Harvard Univ, 1967-1969; physicist, Cornell Aeronaut Labs, Inc, Cornell Univ, 1962-1965. **Memberships:** Am Phys Soc; Am Chem Soc. **Research Statement & Publications:** Atomic and molecular physics; interaction of radiation and matter; atomic and molecular structure; molecular photoionization; supercomputer computations; advanced solar energy technology; hydrogen production; x-ray photophysics and chemistry. **Mailing Address:** Dept Chem, Ind Univ, Bloomington, IN 47405. **Fax:** 812-855-8300. **E-Mail:** langhoff@othello.ucs.indiana.edu

LANGILLE, ALAN RALPH, CROP PHYSIOLOGY. **Personal Data:** b Amherst, NS, April 2, 1938; m 1967, c 1. **Education:** McGill Univ, BS, 1960; Univ Vt, MS, 1962; Pa State Univ, PhD (agron), 1967. **Professional Experience:** COOP PROF BOT, UNIV MAINE, as of 2006; PROF AGRON, UNIV MAINE, 1979-; Vis prof, dept plant path, Kans State Univ, 1979-1980; from asst prof to assoc prof agron, Univ Maine, Orono, 1973-1979. **Memberships:** Am Soc Agron; Am Soc Hort Sci; Potato Asn Am. **Research Statement & Publications:** Hormonal control of tuber initiation and subsequent growth in the potato; growth regulator physiology; salt tolerance in conifers; protoplast regeneration; published over 5 articles. **Mailing Address:** Dept Plant Soil & Environ Sci, Univ Maine, 5722 Deering Hall, Orono, ME 04469-5722. **Fax:** 207-581-2999. **E-Mail:** alanl@maine.edu

LANGILLE, BRIAN LOWELL, CARDIOVASCULAR CELL BIOLOGY. **Personal Data:** b Victoria, BC, July 26, 1947; m 1993, Susan Lee Adamson; c Ellen Rebecca. **Education:** Univ BC, BSc, 1969, MSc, 1970, PhD (zool), 1975. **Professional Experience:** PROF PATH, OBSTET & GYNEC, UNIV TORONTO, as of 1999; assoc prof path, Obstet & Gynec, Univ Toronto, beginning 1994; counr, Biophys Soc Can, 1991-; career investr, Heart & StrokeFound, Ont, 1989-; assoc prof path, Obstet & Gynec, Univ Toronto, 1985-1994; asst prof physiol, Univ Western Ont, 1979-1985; sr res fel, Heart & Stroke Found, Ont, 1978-1979; asst prof biophys, Univ Western Ont, 1977-1979; mem, Coun Basce Sci, Am Heart Asn. **Memberships:** Am Asn Pathologists; AAAS; Biophys Soc Can; Can Atherosclerosis Soc; AmHeart Asn. **Mailing Address:** Toronto Hosp, CCRW 1-836, 200 Elizabeth St, Toronto, ON M5G 2C4, Can.

LANGLAND, OLAF ELMER, RADIOLOGY, DENTISTRY. **Personal Data:** b Madrid, Iowa, May 30, 1925; wid, c 4. **Education:** Univ Iowa, DDS, 1951, MS, 1961; Am Bd Oral & Maxillo-Facial Radiol, dipl, 1981; Am Bd Oral Med, dipl, 1984. **Honors & Awards:** Merit Award, Coun Int Rels, Am Dent Asn, 1975. **Professional Experience:** PROF EMER DENTAL DIAG SCI, UNIV TEX HEALTH SCI CTR, 1999-; mem Nat Bd Test Const Comt Oral Path & Dent Radiol, Am Dent Asn, 1979-1983; prof & head, Div Oral & Maxillofacial Dent Radiol, Dent Diagsci, Sch Dent, Health Sci Ctr, Univ Tex, San Antonio, beginning 1975; prof, Dept Radiol, Sch Med, Univ Tex, beginning 1975; chmn, oral diag-med sect, Am Asn Dent Schs, 1973, & dent radiol sect, 1984; vis prof, Univ Fed Alagoas, Maceio, Brazil, 1973; staff dentist, Charity Hosp, New Orleans, 1969-1975; prof oral diag-med-radiol & head dept, Sch Dent, La State Univ, New Orleans, 1969-1975; consult, Wilford Hall USAF Hosp, Lackland, Tex, 1968-1977; mem subcomt proposed dent x-ray mach, Am Nat Stand Inst, 1968-1974; head dept, Col Dent, UnivIowa, 1964-1969; USPHS grant, Col Dent, Univ Iowa, 1964-1966; from instr to assoc prof oraldiag & radiol, Col Dent, Univ Iowa, 1959-1969. **Memberships:** fel Am Col Dent; Am Acad Dent Radiol (pres, 1984); Orgn Teachers Oral Diag (pres, 1973); Am Asn Dent Schs; Int Asn Oral & Maxillo-Facial Radiol. **Research Statement & Publications:** Panoramic radiography; educational research in dentistry; clinical research in oral manifestations of systemic disease; application of modern intensifying screens in diagnostic radiology. **Mailing Address:** Dept Dent Diag Sci, Univ Tex Health Sci Ctr, 7703 Floyd Cur Dr, San Antonio, TX 78284-7768.

LANGLANDS, ROBERT P, MATHEMATICS. **Personal Data:** b New Westminster, BC, October 6, 1936; m 1956, Charlotte; c William, Robert, Sarah & Thomasin. **Education:** Univ BC, BA, 1957, MA, 1958; Yale Univ, PhD (math), 1960. **Honorary Degrees:** DSc, Univ BC, McMaster Univ, City Univ NY Grad Ctr, 1985, Univ Waterloo, 1988, Univ Paris VII, 1989, McGill Univ, 1992, Toronto, 1993. **Honors & Awards:** Wilbur Cross Medal, Yale Univ, 1975; Cole Prize, Am Math Soc, 1982; Common Wealth Award, Sigma Xi Res Soc, 1984; Nat Acad Sci Award in Math, 1988; Wolf Prize, 1996. **Professional Experience:** HERMANN WEYL PROF MATH, INST ADVAN STUDY, as of 2006; res prof, Ctr Math, 1994-; PROF MATH, INST ADVAN STUDY, 1972-; prof math, Yale Univ, 1967-1972; Sloan fel, 1964-1966; Miller fel, Univ Calif, Berkeley, 1964-1965; from asst prof to assoc prof, Princeton Univ, 1962-1967; mem, Inst Advan Study, 1962-1963; lectr, Princeton Univ, 1961-1962; instr math, Princeton Univ, 1960-1961. **Memberships:** Nat Acad Sci; Royal Soc London; Am Math Soc; Can Math Soc; AAAS; SigmaXi; Royal Soc Can. **Research Statement & Publications:** Group representations; automorphic forms. **Mailing Address:** Sch Math Inst Advan Study, 115 Fuld Hall, One Einstein Dr, Princeton, NJ 08540. **E-Mail:** rpl@math.ias.edu

LANGLEBEN, MANUEL PHILLIP, GLACIOLOGY, MICROMETEOROLOGY. **Personal Data:** b Poland, April 9, 1924; Canadian citizen; m 1948, c 3. **Education:** McGill Univ, BSc, 1949, MSc, 1950, PhD (physics), 1953. **Professional Experience:** PROF EMER PHYSICS, MCGILL UNIV, 1989-; asst chmn, McGill Ctr Northern Studies & Res, 1984-1989; dir, McGill Ctr Northern Studies & Res, 1977-1980; prof, McGill Ctr Northern Studies & Res, 1969-1989; from asst prof to assoc prof, McGill Univ, 1959-1969; lectr, McGill Univ, 1957-1959; res atmospheric physics, McGill Univ, 1953-1957. **Memberships:** Royal Meteorol Soc; Glaciol Soc; Am Geophys Union; Sigma Xi; fel Royal Soc Can. **Research Statement & Publications:** Physics of ice; sea ice; ice drift. **Mailing Address:** Dept Physics, McGill Univ, Rutherford Physics Bldg, 3600 Univ St, Montreal, PQ H3A 2T8, Can. **Fax:** 514-398-8434. **E-Mail:** plangl@physics.lan.mcgill.ca

LANGLEY, ALBERT E, PHARMACOLOGY, TOXICOLOGY. **Personal Data:** b July 2, 1943. **Education:** Waynesburg Col, BS, 1967; Ohio State Univ, Columbus, PhD (pharmacol), 1974. **Professional Experience:** PROF EMER PHARMACOL & TOXICOL, SCH MED, WRIGHT STATE UNIV, DAYTON, as of 2002; ASSOC DEAN ACAD AFFAIRS, SCH MED, WRIGHT STATE UNIV, DAYTON, OHIO, 1990-; consult, Eurand Am, Inc, 1984-; mem, Lab Animal Utilization Comt, 1982-1987 & chmn, RadiationSafety Comt, 1984-; invited lectr, var asns, univs & insts, 1982-; chmn dept, Dept Pharmacol & Toxicol, Wright State Univ, 1982-1985; vice chair dept, DeptPharmacol & Toxicol, Wright State Univ, 1980-1982; res grants, var insts & asns, 1979-; coursedir med pharmacol, Wright State Univ, 1978-1983; from asst prof to prof, Dept Pharmacol &Toxicol, Wright State Univ, 1977-1990; scientist, Cardiovasc Sect, Warner-Lambert Res Inst, Morris Plains, NJ & Ann Arbor, Mich, 1976-1977; postdoctoral fel, Dept Pharmacol, Med Ctr, Univ Colo, Denver, 1974-1976. **Memberships:** Am Soc Pharmacol & Exp Therapeut; Asn Med Sch Pharmacol; Soc Toxicol. **Research Statement & Publications:** Autonomic and ocular drugs; antihypertensives, antilipidemics, and antiarrythmics; diuretics; cardiotonics; histamine and antihistamines; vasoactive peptides; drugs used to treat migraine; alcohols; antianginals; respiratory drugs; thrombolytics. **Mailing Address:** Dept Pharmacol & Toxicol, Sch Med, Wright State Univ, 3640 Colonel Glen Hwy, Dayton, OH 45435. **Fax:** 937-775-7221. **E-Mail:** albert.langley@wright.edu

LANGLEY, CHARLES H, GENETICS. **Education:** Univ Tex, BA 1968, PhD (zoology), 1971. **Professional Experience:** PROF GENETICS, UNIV CALIF, as of 2005. **Mailing Address:** Univ Calif, 3342B Storer Hall Off 752-4085, Davis, CA 95616. **Fax:** 530-752-1449. **E-Mail:** chlangley@ucdavis.edu

LANGLEY, G R, INTERNAL MEDICINE, HEMATOLOGY. **Personal Data:** b Sydney, NS, October 6, 1931; m 1957, Jean M Ballentyne; c Joanne, Mark R & Richard. **Education:** Mt Allison Univ, BA, 1952; Dalhousie Univ, MD, 1957; FRCP (C), 1961, FACP, 1965. **Honorary Degrees:** FRCP (E), 1983. **Honors & Awards:** Queens Jubilee Medal, 1977; Medal, Nat Can Inst, 1985. **Professional Experience:** PHYSICIAN, QEII HEALTH SCI CTR, as of 2004; wightman vis prof, royal col physicians & surgeons, 1990; sr physician, Victoria Gen Hosp, 1982-; head dept med, victoria gen hosp, 1974-1982; head dept, DalhousieUniv, 1974-1982; head dept med, camp hill hosp, 1969-1974; PROF MED, DALHOUSIEUNIV, 1968-; from asst prof to assoc prof med, Dalhousie Univ, 1964-1968; John & Mary RMarkle scholar med, 1963-1968; lectr internal med, Dalhousie Univ, 1963-1964; med res coun can fel, sch med & dent, Univ Rochester, 1961-1962 & Dalhousie Univ, 1963; J Arthur Haatzfel hemat, Univ Melbourne, 1960-1961; asst resident internal med, Victoria Gen Hosp & TorontoGen Hosp, 1957-1960. **Memberships:** Fel Am Col Physicians; Can Soc Clin Invest; Can Soc Bioethics; Am Soc Hemat; Royal Col Physicians & Surgeons Can; Am Soc Clin Oncol. **Research Statement & Publications:** Hematological oncology; quantitative analysis of bioethical issues. **Mailing Address:** Dept Med, QEII Health Sci Ctr, Dalhousie Univ, Rm 442, Bethune Bldg, 1278 Tower Rd, Halifax, NS B3H 2Y9, Can. **Fax:** 902-428-4436. **E-Mail:** langley@ac.dal.ca

LANGLEY, KENNETH HALL, LASER LIGHT SCATTERING. **Personal Data:** b Ft Collins, Colo, September 1, 1935; m Joan E.. **Education:** Mass Inst Technol, BS, 1958; Univ Calif, Berkeley, PhD (physics), 1966. **Professional Experience:** PROF PHYSICS, UNIV MASS, AMHERST, 1981-; actg asst prof & res assoc physics, Univ Calif, Berkeley, 1966; from asst prof to assoc prof, Univ Mass, Amherst, 1963-1981; cofounder, Langley-Ford Instruments. **Memberships:** Am Phys Soc; AAAS. **Research Statement & Publications:** Experimental dynamic light scattering from polymers and biological macromolecules; dynamic nuclear orientation; light scattering from critical point fluids; biological systems. **Mailing Address:** Dept Physics & Astron, Univ Mass, Amherst, MA 01003. **E-Mail:** langley@phast.umass.edu

LANGLEY, NEAL ROGER, POLYMER CHEMISTRY. **Personal Data:** b Sumas, Wash, July 27, 1939. **Education:** Univ Wash, BS, 1961; Univ Wis, PhD (chem), 1968. **Honors & Awards:** Tech Achievement Award, Dow Corning Corp, 1996. **Professional Experience:** REHOLOGY & MECH PROPERTIES SPECIALIST, IMPACT ANAL, 2001-; vis scientist, Univ Wash, 1995; res scientist, process characterization, Dow Corning Corp, 1994-1999; HH Doan vis scientist, Va Technol, 1987-1988; ASSOC RES SCIENTIST, DOW CORNING CORP, 1980-; chemist, Dow Corning Corp, 1968-1980; sr res scientist, Pac Northwest Lab, Battelle Mem Inst, 1967-1968. **Memberships:** Am Chem Soc; Am Inst Chem Engrs; Soc Rheology. **Research Statement & Publications:** Structure and viscoelastic properties of cross-linked polymers; structure and thermo-mechanical properties of ceramic fibers; published over 50 articles. **Mailing Address:** Impact Anal, 1910 W St Andrews Rd, Midland, MI 48640. **Fax:** 989-832-5560.

LANGLEY, ROBERT ARCHIE, VACUUM TECHNOLOGY, MATERIAL SCIENCE. **Personal Data:** b Athens, Ga, October 21, 1937; div, c Laura, Anne & David. **Education:** Ga Inst Technol, BS, 1959, MS, 1960, PhD (physics), 1963. **Professional Experience:** RETIRED; staff Scientist, Sandia Nat Labs, 2000; staff scientist, Oak Ridge Nat Lab, 1981-1996; prog coordr, Oak Ridge Nat Lab, 1978-1980 & Int Atomic Energy Agency, 1980-1981; staff mem, Sandia National Labs, 1968-1978; physicist, Air Force Cambridge Res Labs, 1963-1965 & Oak Ridge Nat Lab, 1966-1968; asst physics, Ga Inst Technol, 1959-1963. **Memberships:** Am Phys Soc; Soc of Vacuum Coaters; emer mem Am Vacuum Soc. **Research Statement & Publications:** Plasma-wall interactions in controlled fusion devices; ion implantation; hydrogen and helium migration in metals; surface physics; ion backscattering; nuclear microanalysis; material science. **Mailing Address:** 374 Marney Cove Rd, Kingston, TN 37763.

LANGLEY, ROBERT CHARLES, ORGANIC CHEMISTRY. **Personal Data:** b NJ, April 11, 1925; m 1954, c 1. **Education:** St Peters Col, BS, 1949. **Professional Experience:** SECT HEAD, RES & DEVELOP DIV, ENGELHARD INDUSTS, INC, 1962-; res dir, Hanovia Div, 1954-1962; Chemist, E I du Pont Del Nemours & Co, 1950-1954. **Memberships:** Am Chem Soc; Am Ceramic Soc. **Research Statement & Publications:** Organic compounds of metals; thin films; gas purification. **Mailing Address:** 214 Old Forge Rd, Millington, NJ 07946.

LANGLEY WOOD, ROBERTSON HARRIS, ENVIRONMENTAL PHYSIOLOGY. **Personal Data:** b Lynchburg, Va, August 22, 1924; m 1951, c 5. **Education:** Col William & Mary, BS, 1949; Columbia Univ, AM, 1950; Cornell Univ, PhD (biol), 1965. **Professional Experience:** RETIRED; prof environ studies & dir prog, Sweet Briar Col, 1972-1982; prof zool & chmn dept, Univ NH, 1969-1972; sr marine scientist & head dept environ physiol, Va Inst Marine Sci, 1967-1969; asst prof, Univ Va, 1963-1969; from asst prof to assoc prof, Col William& Mary, 1961-1969; assoc marine scientist & head dept, Va Inst Marine Sci, 1961-1967; res asst biol, Lerner Lab, Am Mus Natural Hist, 1959-1960; res asst biol, Inst Fish Res, Univ NC, 1959; res asst biol, Woods Hole Oceanog Inst, 1957-1958; researcher, Bur Com Fisheries, US Fish &Wildlife Serv, 1956-1957; pvt bus, 1952-1956; instr sociol, Winthrop Col, 1950-1951. **Memberships:** AAAS; Am Soc Limnol & Oceanog; Am Soc Zoologists; Animal Behav Soc; Estuarine Res Soc. **Research Statement & Publications:** Physiological and behavioral effects upon marine organisms of changes in sensory and biochemical characteristics of environment. **Mailing Address:** 104 Monacan Pl, Madison Heights, VA 24572-3411. **Fax:** 804-384-6380.

LANGLOIS, BRUCE EDWARD, FOOD MICROBIOLOGY. **Personal Data:** b Berlin, NH, September 16, 1937; m 1960, c 2. **Education:** Univ NH, BS, 1959; Purdue Univ, PhD (dairy microbiol), 1962. **Professional Experience:** PROF EMER ANIMAL SCI, UNIV KY, as of 2006; prof animal sci, Univ KY, beginning 1974; from asst prof to assoc prof dairy sci, Univ KY, 1964-1974; Asst prof dairy, Purdue Univ, 1962-1964. **Memberships:** Am Soc Microbiol; Inst Food Technologists; Int Asn Milk Food & Environ Sanit; Sigma Xi. **Research Statement & Publications:** Staphyloccocal mastitis; transferable drug resistance in farm animals; microflora of dairy and meat products; published over 15 articles. **Mailing Address:** Dept Animal Sci, Univ Ky, 500 S Limestone St, Lexington, KY 40506-0001.

LANGLOIS, GORDON ELLERBY, PHYSICAL CHEMISTRY. **Personal Data:** b Burley, Idaho, August 30, 1918; m 1944, c 3. **Education:** Northwestern Univ, BS, 1942; Univ Calif, PhD (phys chem), 1952. **Professional Experience:** Mgr, Synthetic Fuels Div, 1973-1978; sr res chemist, Calif Res Corp, ChevronRes Co, 1969-1973; Sr res chemist, Calif Res Corp, Chevron Res Co, 1943-1969. **Memberships:** Am Chem Soc. **Research Statement & Publications:** Catalytic reactions of hydrocarbons, as polymerization, alkylation and isomerization; synthetic fuels technology. **Mailing Address:** 33 Linda Ave Apt 1901, Piedmont, CA 94611.

LANGMAN, CRAIG BRADFORD, METABOLIC BONE DISEASE, KIDNEY STONE DISEASE. **Personal Data:** b Philadelphia, Pa, February 15, 1953. **Education:** Temple Univ, BS, 1973; Hahnemann Univ, MD, 1977. **Professional Experience:** PROF PEDIAT, NORTHWESTERN UNIV, 1993-; Assoc chair pediat, Northwestern Univ, 1989-1992; assoc prof, Northwestern Univ, 1987-1993; Asst prof pediat, Univ Chicago, 1981-1985. **Memberships:** Am Soc Pediat Nephrology; Nat Kidney Found; Int Soc Kidney & Urinary Tract; Am Soc Bone & Mineral Res; Soc Pediat Res. **Research Statement & Publications:** Clinical expression and basic mechanisms of metabolic bone and stone disease in children, including the expression of forerunners of adult diseases such as osteoporosis; bone cell biology; cytokine regulation. **Mailing Address:** Feinerg Sch Med, Northwestern UNiv, Children's Mem Hosp, 2300 Children's Plaza, Chicago, IL 60614.

LANGMUIR, CHARLES H, GEOCHEMISTRY. **Personal Data:** b Ont, November 24, 1950. **Education:** Harvard Univ, BA, 1973; State Univ NY, Stony Brook, PhD (geol), 1980. **Honors & Awards:** Bowen Award, Am Geophys Union, 1996. **Professional Experience:** PROF GEOCHEM, HARVARD UNIV, as of 2005; adj sr res scientist, Lamont-Doherty Earth Observ, Columbia Univ, beginning 2003; Arthur Sloane res fel, 1984; ARTHUR STORKE PROF GEOL, DEPT EARTH & ENVIRON SCI, LAMONT-DOHERTY EARTH OBSERV, COLUMBIA UNIV. **Memberships:** Fel Am Geophys Union. **Mailing Address:** Dept Earth & Planetary Sci, 20 Oxford St Rm 110, Cambridge, MA 02138. **E-Mail:** langmuir@ldeo.columbia.edu

LANGMUIR, DONALD, GEOCHEMISTRY. **Personal Data:** b Nashua, NH, April 5, 1934; c 2. **Education:** Harvard Univ, AB, 1956, MA, 1961, PhD (geol sci), 1965. **Professional Experience:** PROF EMER GEOCHEM, COLO SCH MINES, as of 1995; pres, Colo Mountain Club, 1990; mem, President's Nuclear Waste Tech RevBd, 1989; dir, Earth Search, Inc, 1981-1985; vis prof inorg chem, Univ Sidney, Australia, 1980; pres, Hydrochem Systs Corp, beginning 1979; prof geochem, Colo sch Mines, beginning 1978; assoc ed, Geochim Cosmochim Acta, 1975-1980; adj prof geochem, DesertRes Inst, Univ Nev, Reno, 1974-1975; from asst prof to prof geochem, Pa State Univ, Univ Park, 1967-1978; lectr water resources, Rutgers Univ, 1966-1967; Geochemist, Water Resources Div, US Geol Surv, 1964-1966. **Memberships:** Fel AAAS; Am Chem Soc; Am Geophys Union; fel Mineral Soc Am; GeochemSoc; Sigma Xi; Soc Environ Geochem & Health. **Research Statement & Publications:** Geochemistry of subsurface waters; thermodynamic properties of minerals and dissolved species in water; adsorption of dissolved inorganic species on geological materials; geochemistry of exploration for ore deposits, of solution mining, and of groundwater pollution and restoration. **Mailing Address:** Dept Geochem, Colo Sch Mines, 1500 Ill St, Golden, CO 80401.

LANGMUIR, MARGARET ELIZABETH LANG, PHYSICAL CHEMISTRY, PHOTOCHEMISTRY. **Personal Data:** b Chicago, Ill, November 11, 1935; m 1962, Bruce; c Lisa D (Maypother) & Jonathan B. **Education:** Culver-Stockton Col, BA, 1956; Purdue Univ, PhD (chem), 1963. **Professional Experience:** VPRES, COVALENT ASSOCS, as of 1998; sr scientist, Covalent Assoc, Inc, beginning 1984; sr scientist, Giner, Inc, 1981-1983; sr scientist, EIC Corp, 1978-1981; res assoc, Northeastern Univ, 1976-1978; consult, 1969-1974; phys chemist, Pioneering Res Div, US Army Natrick Labs, 1963-1969; instr anal & inorg chem, Wellesley Col, 1960-1963. **Memberships:** AAAS; Am Chem Soc; Electrochem Soc; Sigma Xi. **Research Statement & Publications:** Organic photochemistry; acidity functions; flash photolysis; fast reaction mechanisms; excited state proton transfer; fluorescence, phosphorescence and charge transfer spectra; electrochemistry; implantable electrodes; isomerization; semiconductor electrochemistry; photoelectrochemical cells; solar cells; polymer modified electrodes, ion selective electrodes, ion selective fluorophores; electrochemistry. **Mailing Address:** Covalent Assoc Inc, 10 State St, Woburn, MA 01801-6820. **Fax:** 978-443-7878.

LANGNER, EUGENE E, JR, METALLURGY. **Honors & Awards:** William J Grede Award, Am Foundry Soc, 1992 **Professional Experience:** RETIRED; dir, Am Foundry Soc, 1988; from metall engr to vpres & works mgr, Am Cast Iron Pipe Co, Birmingham, Ala, 1952-1992. **Memberships:** Am Foundry Soc. **Mailing Address:** Am Cast Iron Pipe Co Mfg Div, PO Box 2727, Birmingham, AL 35202-2727.

LANGNER, GERALD CONRAD, PHYSICS. **Personal Data:** b Austin, Minn, February 13, 1944; m 1973, c 1. **Education:** St John's Univ, BA, 1966; NDak State Univ, MA, 1968. **Professional Experience:** MEM, INDUST HYG SECT, LOS ALAMOS NAT LAB, as of 1997; MEM STAFF, NONDESTRUCTIVE TESTING, LOS ALAMOS NAT LAB, 1974-; scientist II physics, Albuquerque Div, EG&G Inc, 1969-1973; physicist control syst eng, US Navy, 1968-1969. **Memberships:** Am Soc Nondestructive Testing; Am Phys Soc. **Mailing Address:** Los Alamos Nat Lab, PO Box 1663, Los Alamos, NM 87545. **Fax:** 505-667-0433. **E-Mail:** langnerg@lanl.gov

LANGNER, RONALD O, BIOCHEMICAL PHARMACOLOGY. **Personal Data:** b Chicago, Ill, May 10, 1940; m 1963, c 2. **Education:** Blackburn Col, BA, 1962; Univ RI, MS, 1966, PhD (pharmacol), 1969. **Professional Experience:** PROF PHARMACOL, UNIV CONN, as of 2003; assoc prof pharmacol, Univ Conn, beginning 1969. **Memberships:** Am Biol Chem. **Research Statement & Publications:** Metabolism of collagen and its relationship to experimental atherosclerosis. **Mailing Address:** Dept Pharmacol, Sch Pharmacol, Univ Conn, 69 N Eagleville Rd Unit 3092, Storrs, CT 06269-2092. **Fax:** 860-486-4998. **E-Mail:** ronald.langner@uconn.edu

LANGONE, JOHN JOSEPH, BIO-ORGANIC CHEMISTRY. **Personal Data:** b Cambridge, Mass, August 20, 1944; m 1967, c 2. **Education:** Boston Col, BS, 1966; Boston Univ, PhD (org chem), 1972. **Professional Experience:** CHIEF MOLECULAR BIOL, NAT CANCER INST, as of 2004; staff fel immunochem, Nat Cancer Inst, beginning 1975; sr res assoc biochem, Brandeis Univ, 1972-1975; fel org chem, Boston Univ, 1971-1972. **Memberships:** Am Chem Soc; Am Soc Biol Chemists. **Research Statement & Publications:** Immunopharmacology and immunochemistry of biologically active compounds; cancer immunochemistry. **Mailing Address:** Molecular Biol Br, Food & Drugs Admin, OST HFZ-113 12709 Twinbrook Pkwy, Rockville, MD 20852-1719.

LANGRANA, NOSHIR A, COMPUTER AIDED DESIGN, BIOMECHANICS. **Personal Data:** b Bombay, India, October 1, 1946; American citizen; m 1972, Dinaz; c 2. **Education:** Univ Bombay, India, BE, 1968; Cornell Univ, MS, 1971, PhD (mech eng), 1975. **Honors & Awards:** Ralph R Teetor Award, Soc Automotive Engrs, 1977. **Professional Experience:** PROF, DEPT MECH & AEROSPACE ENG, RUTGERS UNIV, as of 2004; PROF, DEPT BIOMED ENG, RUTGERS UNIV, as of 2004; Mary W Raisler Distinguished Teaching Chair Prof, 2001-2004; adj prof surg, NJ Med Sch, 1995-; undergrad dir, Mech & Aerospace Eng Prog, Rutgers Univ, 1989-1998; from asst prof to assoc prof, Col Eng, Rutgers Univ, 1976-1987. **Memberships:** Am Soc Mech Engrs; Orthop Res Soc; NAm Spine; Sigma Xi; fel Am Soc Mech Engrs; Biomed Eng Soc; Am Inst Med & Biol Eng. **Research Statement & Publications:** Computer-aided design technology in the investigation of musculoskeletal problems; designing and developing layered manufacturing, virtual reality and devices for medical use. **Mailing Address:** Mech Engr, Rutgers Univ Busch Campus PO Box 909, Piscataway, NJ 08855. **Fax:** 732-445-3124.

LANGRETH, DAVID CHAPMAN, THEORETICAL CONDENSED MATTER PHYSICS, THEORETICAL SURFACE PHYSICS. **Personal Data:** b Greenwich, Conn, May 22, 1937; m 1966, Ellen; c Robert & Katrina. **Education:** Yale Univ, BS, 1959; Univ Ill, MS, 1961, PhD (physics), 1964. **Honorary Degrees:** Dr Technol, Chalmers Univ Technol, 2004. **Honors & Awards:** Special Creativity Award, NSF, 1986. **Professional Experience:** Vis prof, Chalmers Univ, Goteborg, Sweden, 1988 & 1993; Nordita vis prof, Sweden, 1988; chmn, Davisson-Germer Prize Comt, 1988; vis scientist, Univ Calif, Santa Barbara, 1983; coordr surface physics prog, Inst Theoret Physics, Santa Barbara, 1983; PROF II PHYSICS, RUTGERS UNIV, NEW BRUNSWICK, 1980-; guest prof, Nordita, Copenhagen, 1975-1976; Rutgers res coun fel, Univ Calif, San Diego, 1973-1974; assoc chmn physics dept & dir grad prog physics, Rutgers Univ, New Brunswick, 1970-1973; prin investr, NSF grants, 1969-; from asst prof to prof, Rutgers Univ, New Brunswick, 1967-1980; res assoc physics, Univ Chicago, 1964-1965 & Cornell Univ, 1965-1967. **Memberships:** AAAS; fel, Am Phys Soc; Int Eval Comt. **Research Statement & Publications:** Theoretical solid state physics, specializing in the many body problem; theoretical surface physics; published over 70 articles. **Mailing Address:** Dept Physics & Astron, Rutgers Univ, 136 Frelinghuysen Rd, Piscataway, NJ 08855-8019. **Fax:** 732-445-4400. **E-Mail:** langreth@physics.rutgers.edu

LANGRIDGE, ROBERT, MOLECULAR BIOLOGY. **Personal Data:** b Essex, Eng, October 26, 1933; m 1960, c 2. **Education:** Univ London, BSc, 1954, PhD (crystallog), 1957. **Professional Experience:** Vis prof biochem biophys, Ore State Univ, 1994-; PROF EMER, PHARMACEUT CHEM & BIOCHEM & BIOPHYS, UNIV CALIF, 1994-; prof, Dept Pharmaceut Chem, 1977-1994; prof biochem & biophys, Sch Med, Univ Calif, 1977-1994; dir, Comput Graphics Lab, 1977-1994; prof biochem, Princeton Univ, 1968-1976; prof biophys & info sci, Univ Chicago, 1966-1968; lectr, HarvardUniv, 1964-1966; res assoc, Harvard Univ, 1963-1964; res assoc biophys, Mass Inst Technol, 1959-1961 & Children's Hosp, Med Ctr, Boston Univ, 1961-1966; res fel biophys, Yale Univ, 1957-1959. **Memberships:** Inst Med-Nat Acad Sci; Biophys Soc; Am Crystallog Asn; Am Chem Soc; AAAS. **Research Statement & Publications:** X-ray diffraction and physical-chemical studies of the structures of biological macromolecules, particularly nucleic acids, nucleoproteins, viruses and ribosomes; applications of high speed digital computers. **Mailing Address:** Dept Biochem & Biophys, Univ Calif, San Francisco, CA 94143-0446. **E-Mail:** rl@cgl.ucsf.edu

LANGRIDGE, WILLIAM HENRY RUSSELL, VIROLOGY, DEVELOPMENTAL BIOLOGY. **Personal Data:** b New York, NY, January 30, 1938; m 1960, c 2. **Education:** Univ Ill, Urbana, BS, 1962, MS, 1964; Univ Mass, PhD (biochem), 1973. **Professional Experience:** PROF BIOCHEM, CTR MOLECULAR BIOL & GENE THER, SCH MED, LOMA LINDA

UNIV, as of 2006; Juv Diabetes Found grant, 2000; NIH fel virol, Boyce Thompson Inst, Ithaca, NY, 1974-1987. **Memberships:** AAAS; Soc Invert Path; Am Soc Microbiol; Sigma Xi. **Research Statement & Publications:** Metabolism of baculoviruses and vertebrate and insect poxviruses; the mechanism of infection and the structure of the virus genome and virus protein; plant molecular biology; published over 5 articles. **Mailing Address:** Dept Biochem, Ctr Molecular Biol & Gene Ther, Sch Med, Loma Linda Univ, 161 Mortensen Hall, Loma Linda, CA 92350. **Fax:** 909-558-4887. **E-Mail:** blangridge@llu.edu

LANGS, DAVID A, X RAY CRYSTALLOGRAPHY. **Professional Experience:** AT MED FOUND BUFFALO, as of 1992. **Mailing Address:** Med Found Buffalo, 73 High St, Buffalo, NY 14203-1196.

LANGSAM, MICHAEL, POLYMER CHEMISTRY. **Personal Data:** b Brooklyn, NY, November 4, 1938; m 1962, c 3. **Education:** Rensselaer Polytech Inst, BS, 1959; Polytech Inst Brooklyn, PhD (polymer sci), 1964. **Professional Experience:** AIR PROD & CHEM INC, as of 1997; MGR POLYMER PROCESS DEVELOP, AIR PROD & CHEM INC, 1975-; sr res chemist, Air Prod & Chem, Inc, 1967-1975; res chemist polymer, B F Goodrich Lab, Brecksville, Ohio, 1964-1967. **Memberships:** Sigma Xi; Am Chem Soc. **Research Statement & Publications:** Polymer synthesis, rheology, polymer kinetics, and particle morphology. **Mailing Address:** Air Prod & Chem, Inc, 7201 Hamilton Blvd, Allentown, PA 18195.

LANGSAM, YEDIDYAH, CHEMISTRY. **Education:** Brooklyn Col, BS, 1973, MA, 1976; Polytech Inst NY, PhD, 1978. **Professional Experience:** CHAIR, DEPT COMPUT & INFO SCI, BROOKLYN COL, 1981-; Murray Koppelman prof, Brooklyn Col, 2004-2006. **Mailing Address:** Brooklyn Col, City Univ NY, 2900 Bedford Ave, Brooklyn, NY 11210. **Fax:** 718-951-5000. **E-Mail:** langsam@sci.brooklyn.cuny.edu

LANGSDORF, WILLIAM PHILIP, PHYSICAL ORGANIC CHEMISTRY. **Personal Data:** b Cambridge, Ohio, April 6, 1919; m 1995, Margret; c Philip David, Kathleen & Linda. **Education:** Ohio State Univ, BSc, 1941; Mass Inst Technol, PhD (chem), 1949. **Professional Experience:** RETIRED; res assoc, Indust & Biochem Dept, E I Du Pont de Nemours & Co, Inc, 1962-1979; res chemist, Indust & Biochem Dept, E I Du Pont de Nemours & Co, Inc, 1949-1962. **Memberships:** Sigma Xi. **Research Statement & Publications:** Organic reactions; mechanism of organic reactions; kinetics. **Mailing Address:** 2149 Culver Dr, Wilmington, DE 19810-1309. **E-Mail:** langsdorfhome@aol.com

LANGSETH, ROLLIN EDWARD, ELECTRICAL ENGINEERING, MATHEMATICS. **Personal Data:** b St Paul, Minn, April 13, 1940; m 1966, c 2. **Education:** Univ Minn, Minneapolis, BS, 1962, MSEE, 1965, PhD (elec eng), 1968. **Professional Experience:** SUPVR, AT&T BELL LABS, as of 2004; dist mgr, Am Tel & Tel Co, beginning 1981; Mem tech staff, Bell Tel Labs, 1968-1980. **Memberships:** Inst Elec & Electronics Engrs. **Research Statement & Publications:** Communication in multipath propagation media; diversity systems; effects of noise and interference; data networks; satellite systems. **Mailing Address:** AT&T Bell Labs, Rm 3M 526, Crawfords Corner Rd, Holmdel, NJ 07733.

LANGSJOEN, ARNE NELS, ORGANIC CHEMISTRY. **Personal Data:** b Dalton, Minn, April 6, 1919; m 1943, Carol L Gaustad; c Karen (Zins), Peter L & Thor V (deceased). **Education:** Gustavus Adolphus Col, BA, 1942; Univ Iowa, MS, 1943, PhD, 1949. **Professional Experience:** RETIRED; Univ Alaska, Fairbanks, 1982-1983; vis prof chem, Tunghai Univ, Taichung, Taiwan, 1969-1970; NSF res fel, Uppsala & Royal Inst Technol, Sweden, 1958-1959; prof chem, Gustavus Adolphus Col, 1956-1986; chmn dept, Gustavus Adolphus Col, 1956-1966; From asst prof to assoc prof, Gustavus Adolphus Col, 1948-1956. **Memberships:** Am Chem Soc; Sigma Xi. **Research Statement & Publications:** Biological chemistry. **Mailing Address:** 410 N Fourth St, St Peter, MN 56082.

LANGSLEY, DONALD GENE, psychiatry, psychoanalysis; deceased, see previous edition for last biography

LANGSTON, CHARLES ADAM, SEISMOLOGY. **Personal Data:** b 1949. **Education:** Case Western Res Univ, BS, 1972; Calif Inst Technol, MS, 1974, PhD (geophys), 1976. **Professional Experience:** PROF SEISMOL & EARTH STRUCT, UNIV MEMPHIS, as of 2001-; distinguished vis prof, Univ Memphis, 2000-2001; mem, Comt Seismol, Nat Res Coun, 1991-1997; bd dirs, Seismol Soc Am, 1988-1991; prof geophys, Pa State Univ, beginning 1986; prof, Pa State Univ, 1986-2001; dir, Seismic Observ, Pa State Univ, 1985-; assoc ed, J Geophys Res, 1980-1982; from asst prof to assoc prof, PA State Univ, 1977-1986; res fel, Calif Inst Technol, 1976-1977; res asst, Calif Inst Technol, 1975-1976; res asst geophys, Louis D Beaumont fel, 1974-1975; res asst geophys, Calif Inst Technol, 1972-1974. **Memberships:** Am Geophys Union; Seismol Soc Am (pres, 1990-1991); Geol Soc Am. **Research Statement & Publications:** Theoretical and observation seismology; wave propagation in elastic media; seismic source parameter estimation; crustal and upper mantle structure. **Mailing Address:** Dept Earth Sci, Univ Memphis, 3876 Cent Ave Ste One Campus Box 526590, Memphis, TN 38152-3050. **Fax:** 901-678-4734. **E-Mail:** clangstn@memphis.edu

LANGSTON, CLARENCE WALTER, MICROBIOLOGY. **Personal Data:** b Gainesville, Tex, July 4, 1924; m 1948, c 2. **Education:** Southern Methodist Univ, BS, 1949; NTex State Univ, MA, 1951; Univ Wis, PhD (bact), 1955. **Professional Experience:** PRES, LANGSTON LABS, INC, KANS & PR, 1971-; head bact sect, Midwest Res Inst, 1966-1971; chief virus & rickettsial div, Directorate Biol Opers, Pine BluffArsenal, US Army, Ark, 1962-1966; bacteriologist, Dairy Cattle Res Br, Agr Res Serv, USDA, 1954-1962; asst, Univ Wis, 1951-1954; Bacteriologist, Kraft Foods Co, 1950-1951. **Memberships:** Am Acad Microbiol; Am Soc Microbiol; Soc Indust Microbiol. **Research Statement & Publications:** Dairy and food bacteriology; microbiology and chemistry of fermentations; physiology of bacteria; taxonomy and nomenclature of bacteria; research development and production of viruses and rickettsiae. **Mailing Address:** 10520 Walmer St, Overland Park, KS 66212.

LANGSTON, DAVE THOMAS, ENTOMOLOGY. **Personal Data:** b Chickasha, Okla, April 19, 1945; m 1965, c 4. **Education:** Southwestern Okla State Univ, BS, 1967; Okla State Univ, MS, 1970; Univ Ariz, PhD (entom), 1974. **Professional Experience:** SPECIALIST, DEPT ENTOM, UNIV ARIZ, as of 2003; assoc prof entom, Univ Ariz, beginning 1980; exten specialist entom, Univ Ariz, beginning 1974; res assoc, Univ Ariz, 1970-1974; res asst, Okla State Univ, 1967-1970. **Memberships:** Entom Soc Am. **Research Statement & Publications:** Insect management as it influences production agriculture, specifically those insects which are economically important in the Southwestern United States. **Mailing Address:** Dept Entom, Univ Ariz, Maricopa Agr Ctr PO Box 2100, Tucson, AZ 85721-0036. **Fax:** 520-621-1150.

LANGSTON, GLEN IRVIN, RADIO ASTRONOMY. **Personal Data:** b Marion, Ohio, November 22, 1956; m 1987, c 1. **Education:** Mass Inst Technol, BS, 1981, PhD (physics), 1987. **Professional Experience:** SCIENTIST, NAT RADIO ASTRON OBSERV, GREEN BANK, 1999-; proj mgr, Nat Radio Astron Observ, 1989-1998; Scientist, Max Plancklnst, 1987-1988 & Naval Res Lab, 1988-1989. **Research Statement & Publications:** Gravitational lensing. **Mailing Address:** Nat Radio Astron Observ, PO Box 2, Green Bank, WV 24944. **Fax:** 304-456-3032.

LANGSTON, JAMES HORACE, ORGANIC CHEMISTRY. **Personal Data:** b Garrison, Tex, October 8, 1917; m 1984, Edith. **Education:** Stephen F Austin State Col, BA, 1937; Univ NC, MA, 1939, PhD (org chem), 1941. **Professional Experience:** RETIRED; chmn, Div Natural Sci & Math, 1968-1972; Fulbright lectr & resconsult, Nat Univ Honduras, 1967-1968; Fulbright lectr, Cent Univ & Nat Polytech Sch, Ecuador, 1959-1960; prof chem, Samford Univ, 1958-1984; head dept, Samford Univ, 1958-1978; from assoc prof to prof textile chem & dyeing, Clemson Col, 1946-1958; res chemist, Columbia Chem Div, Pittsburgh Plate Glass Co, 1941-1946; asst chem, Univ NC, 1937-1940. **Memberships:** Am Chem Soc; fel Am Inst Chemists. **Research Statement & Publications:** Drugs; polymers; plastics; plasticizers; catalysis; fibers; textile finishing materials; sulfone formation. **Mailing Address:** 542 Hillyer High Rd, Anniston, AL 36207-6246.

LANGSTON, JOANN H, ENGINEERING. **Education:** Col New Rochelle, BA; George Mason Univ, PhD (pub policy); Univ Md Law Sch, JD. **Professional Experience:** ASST DIR, ARMY CONTRACTING AGENCY, as of 2005; MEM, ARMY ACQUISITION CORPS, as of 2005. **Mailing Address:** 14514 Faraday Dr, Rockville, MD 20853. **Fax:** 703-697-7748. **E-Mail:** joann.langston@hqda.army.mil

LANGSTON, WANN, VERTEBRATE PALEONTOLOGY. **Personal Data:** b Oklahoma City, Okla, July 10, 1921; m 1946, c 2. **Education:** Univ Okla, BS, 1943, MS, 1947; Univ Calif, PhD (paleont), 1952. **Professional Experience:** DIR EMER, VERT PALEONT LAB, as of 2005; prof emer geol sci, Univ Tex, Austin, as of 2003; Yaeger prof, Univ Tex, Austin, beginning 1983; prof geol sci, Univ Tex, Austin, beginning 1975; res assoc, Cleveland Mus Natural Hist, 1974-; dir, Vert Paleont Lab, Tex Mem Mus, 1969-; res scientist, Tex Mem Mus, 1962-; vert paleontologist, Nat Mus Can, 1954-1962; lectr, Mus-Paleont, Univ Calif, 1951-1952; preparator, Mus Paleont, Univ Calif, 1949-1954; instr geol, TexTech Col, 1946-1948; VPRES LAB, BALCONES RES CTR, AUSTIN. **Memberships:** Geol Soc Am; Soc Vert Paleont (vpres, 1973-1974 & pres, 1974-1975); Am Soc Icthyol& Herpet; Am Asn Petrol Geologists; Sigma Xi. **Research Statement & Publications:** Fossil amphibians and reptiles; stucture and relationships of extinct crocodylia and large pterosaurs; cretaceous non-mammalian tetrapods in texas. **Mailing Address:** Univ Tex Balcones Res Ctr, Vert Paleont, Austin, TX 78712. **E-Mail:** wannl@mail.utexas.edu

LANGTON, STACY G, MATHEMATICS. **Education:** Harvard Univ, PhD (maths), 1972. **Professional Experience:** PROF, DEPT MATHS & COMPUT SCI, UNIV SAN DIEGO, CA, as of 2006. **Mailing Address:** Math & Comput Sci Dept, Univ San Diego, San Diego, CA 92110. **E-Mail:** langton@sandiego.edu

LANGVARDT, PATRICK WILLIAM, MASS SPECTROMETRY, CHROMATOGRAPHY. **Personal Data:** b Dodge City, Kans, March 20, 1950. **Education:** Kans State Teachers Col, BS, 1972; Purdue Univ, MS, 1974. **Professional Experience:** DIR, ANAL SCI & SOLUTIONS, DOW CORNING CORP, as of 2003; RES LEADER ANALYTICAL CHEM, DOW CHEM CO, 1974-. **Memberships:** Am Soc Mass Spectrometry; Sigma Xi; Am Chem Soc. **Research Statement & Publications:** Analytical chemistry in support of toxicology studies; metabolite identification; analytical toxicology; trace determinations in biological matrices; automated sample preparation and analysis. **Mailing Address:** Anal Sci & Solutions, Dow Corning Corp, C03101, Midland, MI 48686-0994.

LANGWAY, CHESTER CHARLES, JR, EARTH SCI, ICE CORESCI. **Personal Data:** b Worcester, Mass, August 15, 1929; m 1959, c Nancy Jo, Mary E, Joann k & Thomas J. **Education:** Boston Univ, AB, 1955, MA, 1956; Univ Mich, PhD (geol, glaciol), 1965. **Honorary Degrees:** PhD Univ of Bern, Switzerland, 1992, PhD, Univ Copenhagen, Denmark, 1996. **Honors & Awards:** Collegium of Distinguished Alumni, Boston Univ, 1996; Mt Langwan, Antarctica, USNSF/USNAS, 1971 Forigen Mem, Danish Royal Acad, Arts & Sci, 1994. **Professional Experience:** Vis prof, Univ Copenhagen 1996; PROF EMER GEOL, STATE UNIV NY, BUFFALO, 1994-; vis prof, Univ Bern, 1981; vis prof, Nat Inst Polar Res, Tokyo, Japan, 1990; prof geol sci & chmn dept, State Univ NY Buffalo, 1977-1994; mem panel glaciol, Comt Polar Res, Nat Acad Sci, 1969-1975; chief snow & ice br, US Army Cold Regions Res & Eng Lab, 1966-1977; res glaciologist, US Army Cold Regions Res & Eng Lab, 1961-1965; res assoc properties of snow & ice, Res Inst, Univ Mich, 1959-1961; res geologist, US Army Snow, Ice & Permafrost Res Estab, 1956-1959. **Memberships:** AAAS; fel Geol Soc Am; Fel Am Geophys Union; fel Arctic Inst NAm; Sigma Xi, fel phi kappa Phi. **Research Statement & Publications:** Basic and applied research related to the properties of snow and ice, including field and laboratory techniques of analyzing polar regions shallow and deep ice cores for stratigraph ic history and age dating purposes; isotopic and ionic constituents, terrestrial and extraterrestrial inclusions and pales environmental. **Mailing Address:** 25 Wendys Way, Harwich, MA 02645.

LANGWEILER, MARC, FLOW CYTOMETRY. **Personal Data:** b Astoria, NY, January 27, 1952. **Education:** Cornell Univ, BS, 1972, DVM, 1975, MS, 1980, PhD, 1983. **Professional Experience:** INSTR & TECH SPECIALIST DEPT PATH, DARTMOUTH-HITCHCOCK MED CTR, 1988-; res tech, Dept Radiation Biol/Oncol, Sch Med, ECarolina Univ, 1986-1988; res assoc, Dept Path, State Univ NY Med Ctr, 1984-1985; clin immunol fel, NIH, Dept Microbiol/Immunol, Duke Univ Med Ctr, 1983-1984; postdoctoral res fel, NIH, Dept Microbiol/Immunol, Duke Univ Med Ctr, 1982-1984; grad vet asst, NY State Col Vet Med, Cornell Univ, Ithaca, 1979-1982; grad res asst, NY State Col Vet Med, Cornell Univ, Ithaca, 1977-1979; Henry Bergh Mem Hosp, New York, 1976-1977; vet clinician, Flushing Vet Hosp, NY, 1975-1976. **Memberships:** Int Soc Analytical Cytol; Clinical Cytometry Soc. **Research Statement & Publications:** clinical flow cytometry. **Mailing Address:** Dept Path, Dartmouth-Hitchcock Med Ctr, One Medical Ctr Dr, Lebanon, NH 03756. **E-Mail:** marc.langweiler@dartmouth.edu

LANGWIG, JOHN EDWARD, FOREST PRODUCTS, WOOD SCIENCE. **Personal Data:** b Albany, NY, March 5, 1924; m 1946, Margaret Kirk; c Nancy A (Davis). **Education:** Univ Mich, Ann Arbor, BS, 1948; State Univ NY Col Forestry, Syracuse Univ, MS, 1968, PhD (wood sci), 1971. **Professional Experience:** PROF EMER WOOD SCI, OKLA STATE UNIV, 1986-; exten prof, deptforestry, 1981-1986; chmn, dept forestry, 1975-1981; from asst prof to prof, Okla State Univ, 1971-1986; Instr wood prod eng, State Univ NY Col Forestry, Syracuse Univ, 1969-1970. **Memberships:** Soc Wood Sci & Technol; Forest Prod Res Soc; Soc Am Foresters; Sigma Xi; Tech Asn Pulp & Paper Indust. **Research Statement & Publications:** Neutron activation analysis of trace elements in wood and effects on physical properties; physical properties of wood-polymer composites. **Mailing Address:** Dept Forestry, Okla State Univ, Stillwater, OK 74078-0491.

LANGWORTHY, HAROLD FREDERICK, MATHEMATICS, OPTICS. **Personal Data:** b White Plains, NY, August 1, 1940; m 1965, Nikki; c Katherine, Kristen & Thomas. **Educa-**

tion: Rensselaer Polytech Inst, BS, 1962; Univ Minn, PhD (math), 1970. **Professional Experience:** DIR MFG RES & ENG, EASTMAN KODAK CO, ROCHESTER, 1992-; assoc dir, MR&E, 1991-1992; gen mgr thermal printing, IISG, 1990-1991; dir res, Ill-Ind Sea Grant, 1989-1990; dir, Res Labs, CISG, 1986-1989; dir, Physics Div, Kodak Res Labs, 1983-1986; asst dir, Res Labs, Eastman Kodak Co, Rochester, 1981-1983; lab head, Res Labs, Eastman Kodak Co, Rochester, 1979-1981; res assoc, Res Labs, Eastman Kodak Co, Rochester, 1967-1979. **Memberships:** Optical Soc Am; AAAS. **Research Statement & Publications:** Mathematical optics; rheology. **Mailing Address:** 732 Hightower Way, Webster, NY 14580. **E-Mail:** hal@kodak.com

LANGWORTHY, JAMES BRIAN, NUCLEAR PHYSICS, MATHEMATICAL PHYSICS. **Personal Data:** b Billings, Mont, February 18, 1934; m 1965, Alva Lawhorne; c Alan & Shelby. **Education:** Univ Colo, BS, 1956; Univ Md, MS, 1966. **Professional Experience:** RES PHYSICIST RADIATION DAMAGE, RADIATION EFFECTS BR, CONDENSED MATTER & RADIATION SCI DIV, NAVAL RES LAB, 1976-; Pres, YouthResources Ctr, Inc, 1971-1987; res physicist particle transp, Theory Br, Nuclear Physics Div, 1969-1976; Physicist math physics, Radiation Div, 1959-1969. **Memberships:** Am Phys Soc; AAAS; Sigma Xi. **Research Statement & Publications:** Radiation damage, hardening and shielding; energetic particle transport by Monte Carlo computer codes; microdosimetry in single event upset of memory cells; chord distributions; radiation hardening of satellite electronics. **Mailing Address:** Code 6613, Naval Res Lab, Washington, DC 20375-5345. **E-Mail:** langworthy@radef.nrl.navy.mil

LANGWORTHY, THOMAS ALLAN, MICROBIAL PHYSIOLOGY. **Personal Data:** b Oak Park, Ill, August 7, 1943; m 1988, Jane; c 2. **Education:** Grinnell Col, BA, 1965; Univ Kans, PhD (microbiol), 1971. **Honors & Awards:** Alexander von Humboldt US Sr Scientist Prize, 1984; Burlington Northern Found Award, 1987. **Professional Experience:** PROF MICROBIOL, UNIV SDAK, 1995-; prof & interim chmn microbiol, Univ SDak, 1991-1995; prof microbiol, Univ SDak, 1982-1991; from asst prof to assoc prof, Univ SDak, 1972-1982; res assoc, Univ SDak, 1971-1972. **Memberships:** Am Soc Microbiol; AAAS; Am Acad Microbiol; Int Orgn Mycoplasmology. **Research Statement & Publications:** Structure and function of the membranes and cell surfaces of bacteria from extreme environments, mycoplasmas, archaebacteria and cellular evolution. **Mailing Address:** Dept Microbiol Sch Med, Univ SDak, Vermillion, SD 57069-2390. **Fax:** 605-677-5658. **E-Mail:** tlangwor@usd.edu

LANGWORTHY, WILLIAM CLAYTON, ORGANIC CHEMISTRY, ENVIRONMENTAL CHEMISTRY. **Personal Data:** b Watertown, NY, September 3, 1936; m 1958, Margaret; c Kenneth & Geneva. **Education:** Tufts Univ, BSChem, 1958; Univ Calif, Berkeley, PhD (org chem), 1962. **Professional Experience:** VPRES ACAD AFFAIRS, FT LEWIS COL, 1983-; dean sch sci & math, Calif Polytech State Univ, San Luis Obispo, 1976-1983; prof chem & head dept, Calif Polytech State Univ, San Luis Obispo, 1973-1976; assoc dean, Sch Lett, Arts & Sci, CalifState Col, Fullerton, 1970-1973; dir environ studies prog, Sch Lett, Arts & Sci, Calif State Col, Fullerton, 1970-1972; from asst prof to prof, Calif State Col, Fullerton, 1965-1973; asst prof, Alaska Methodist Univ, 1962-1965; NIH fel chem, Mass Inst Technol, 1961-1962. **Memberships:** AAAS; Am Chem Soc; Sigma Xi. **Research Statement & Publications:** Physical organic chemistry; organic reactions in liquid ammonia; environmental chemistry, especially analysis and effects of trace pollutants. **Mailing Address:** Ft Lewis Col, 1000 Rim Dr, Durango, CO 81301-3999. **Fax:** 970-247-7680.

LANHAM, RICHARD HENRY, EDUCATIONAL ADMINISTRATION. **Personal Data:** b Shelbyville, Ill, m 1959, c 2. **Education:** Ohio Col Podiatric Med, DPM, 1958; Univ Louisville, MEd, 1980. **Professional Experience:** PRES EMER, CALIF COL PODIATRIC MED, SAMUEL MERRITT COL, as of 2003; prof podiatric med, vpres & dean acad affairs, Calif Colpodiatric Med, beginning 1985; adj clinician, Ohio Col Podiatric Med, beginning 1981; clin investr, SutterBiomed, 1979-1985; clin investr, Dow Corning Corp, 1979-1982; pvt pract, Clarksville, 1959-1985. **Memberships:** Am Podiatric Med Asn (pres, 1985-1986); Am Col Foot Surgeons; Am Col FootOrthopedists (pres, 1970-1971); Am Pub Health Asn; Am Bd Podiatric Orthop; Am Bd Podiatric Surg. **Research Statement & Publications:** Clinical investigation of three designs for foot implants; author of articles on foot surgery, drug use surveys and case reports. **Mailing Address:** Samuel Merritt Col Calif Col Podiatric Med, 370 Hawthorne Ave, Oakland, CA 94609.

LANIER, LEWIS L, EXPERIMENTAL BIOLOGY. **Personal Data:** b Memphis, Tenn, July 1, 1953. **Education:** Va Polytech Inst & State Univ, BS, 1975; Univ NC, PhD (microbiol & immunol), 1978. **Professional Experience:** VICE CHMN, DEPT MICROBIOL & IMMUNOL, UNIV CALIF, SAN FRANCISCO, 2003-; PROF, DEPT MICROBIOL & IMMUNOL & CANCER RES INST, UNIV CALIF, SAN FRANCISCO, 1999-; dir, Dept Immunobiol, Dnax Res Inst, 1997-1999; assoc dir, Dept Human Immunol, Dnax Res Inst, 1993-1996; sr sci staff, Dept Immunol, Dnax Res Inst, 1991-1992; mem, Inst Health Reviewers Res, NIH, 1989-1993; transmitting ed, Int Immunol, 1988-; assoc res dir, Becton Dickinson Monoclonal Ctr, 1988-1990; res assoc, Cancer Res Inst, Sch Med, Univ Calif, San Francisco, 1987-; assoc ed, J Immunol, 1986-; sr res scientist, Becton Dickinson Monoclonal Ctr, 1981-1988; res asst prof, Dept Path, Damon Runyon-Walter Winchell Cancer Fund, Sch Med, Univ NMex, 1981; fel, Dept Path, Damon Runyon-Walter Winchell Cancer Fund, Sch Med, Univ NMex, 1979-1981. **Memberships:** Am Asn Immunologists; Soc Anal Cytol; Clin Immunol Soc; Sigma Xi. **Research Statement & Publications:** Experimental biology. **Mailing Address:** Dept Microbiol & Immunol, Univ Calif, PO Box 0414, San Francisco, CA 94143-0414. **Fax:** 415-502-8424. **E-Mail:** lanier@itsa.ucsf.edu

LANIER, ROBERT GEORGE, NUCLEAR PHYSICS. **Personal Data:** b Chicago, Ill, October 27, 1940; div, c 2. **Education:** Lewis Col, BS, 1962; Fla State Univ, PhD (nuclear chem), 1968. **Professional Experience:** STAFF MEM, NUCLEAR CHEM DIV, LAWRENCE LIVERMORE NAT LAB, UNIV CALIF, 1971-; fel, Nuclear Chem Div, Lawrence Livermore Nat Lab, Univ Calif, 1969-1971; US AEC fel, Chem Div, Oak Ridge Nat Lab, 1967-1969. **Memberships:** AAAS; Am Phys Soc. **Research Statement & Publications:** Experimental low energy nuclear structure studies; charged-particle reaction spectroscopy, cross section measurements and in-beam gamma ray spectroscopy. **Mailing Address:** Nuclear Chem Div L 232, Univ Calif Lawrence Livermore Nat Lab, PO Box 808, Livermore, CA 94550. **E-Mail:** lanier1@llnl.gov

LANING, J HALCOMBE, MANUFACTURING AUTOMATION. **Personal Data:** b Kansas City, Mo, February 14, 1920; m 1943, Betty; c Christine, James, Susan & Linda. **Education:** Mass Inst Technol, BA, 1940, PhD (appl math), 1947. **Professional Experience:** RETIRED; head, Automation Technol Dept, 1985-1989; sr fel automation, mfg & comput dept, C S Draper Lab, Inc, 1982-1985; head, mfg & comput dept, C S Draper Lab, Inc, 1973-1982; sr staff mem, Instrumentation Lab, Mass Inst Technol, 1945-1973. **Memberships:** Nat Acad Eng; Asn Comput Mach; Am Math Soc; Am Inst Aeronaut & Astronaut; Soc Indust & Appl Math; Inst Elec & Electronics Engrs. **Mailing Address:** 130 Temple St, West Newton, MA 02165.

LANING, STEPHEN HENRY, ANALYTICAL CHEMISTRY. **Personal Data:** b Albany, NY, October 18, 1918; m 1946, Marjorie; c Barbara A & Malcolm H. **Education:** Union Col, NY, BS, 1941; Rutgers Univ, PhD (phys chem), 1947. **Professional Experience:** RETIRED; supvr res & tech serv, Chem Div, Pittsburg Plate Glass Co, 1967-1986; supvr res & tech serv, Chem Div, Pittsburg Plate Glass Co, 1961-1967; res chemist, Chem Div, Pittsburg Plate Glass Co, 1947-1961; instr, Rutgers Univ, 1945-1946; asst, Rutgers Univ, 1941-1944. **Memberships:** Am Chem Soc; AAAS; Soc Appl Spectros. **Research Statement & Publications:** Development of methods for x-ray analysis of glass, silica and titania pigments, minerals, cements and other types of materials; developed x-ray methods for determining quartz in airborne dusts. **Mailing Address:** 1219 Greenvale Ave, Akron, OH 44313-6745.

LANKFORD, EDWARD B, MUSCLE MECHANICS, CARDIAC MECHANICS. **Personal Data:** b Salisbury, Md, January 31, 1958. **Education:** Va Polytech Inst & State Univ, BS, 1980; Univ Md, MD, 1984; Johns Hopkins Univ, PhD (biomed eng), 1991. **Professional Experience:** Res. Asst. Prof., Pathology, Anatomy, & Cell Biology, Thomas Jeffeson University & Medicine/Cardiology 1999-; ASST PROF, CARDIOVASC SECT, HOSP UNIV PA, 1995-1999; Instr, Cardiovasc Sect, Hosp Univ PA, 1994-1995; Fel, Cardiovasc Sect, Hosp Univ PA, 1990-1994; Resident, Hershey Med Ctr, 1988-1990. **Memberships:** Am Col Physicians Biophysics Society. **Research Statement & Publications:** Mechanics of muscle in human diseased states; cardiac mechanics in hypertrophic cardiomyopathy and dilated cardiomyopathy; Regulation of cardiac contraction. **Mailing Address:** 545 Jefferson Alumni Hall, 1020 Locust St, Philadelphia, PA 19107. **Fax:** 215-503-2046. **E-Mail:** ed@pcsb620.tju.edu

LANKFORD, JAMES, MATERIALS SCIENCES. **Professional Experience:** DIR, DEPT MAT ENG, SOUTHWEST RES INST, TEX, as of 2003. **Memberships:** Am Soc Metals. **Mailing Address:** Dept Mat Sci, Southwest Res Inst 6220 Culebra Rd, San Antonio, TX 78228-0510.

LANKFORD, J(OHN) L(LEWELLYN), PROPULSION, HYPERBALLISTICS. **Personal Data:** b Hampton, Va, September 13, 1920; m 1945, Mary C; c John F & Susan C. **Education:** Va Polytech Inst, BS, 1942 Masters-Sci/Aerohautical Eng. **Professional Experience:** RETIRED; assoc staff & consult energy prog, Univ Md, 1979-1980; lectr, Montgomery Col, 1978-1979; consult, energy & heat transfer, 1976-; consult & prog mgr, US Navy, 1970-1975; prin investr & mgr rain erosion & hypersonic reentry mat, Naval Surface Weapons Ctr, White Oak, Md, 1965-1970; Consult, Bur Weapons, US Navy, 1964-1975; actg chief, Missile Dynamics Div, Naval Ord Lab, 1964-1965; chief adv studies lunar logistics flight systs, NASA, 1962-1964; aeronaut res engr, Naval Ord Lab, 1958-1962; head, dept gas dynamics, Exp Inc, 1954-1958; res engr, Cent Res Lab, Melpar, 1953-1954; Aeronaut res scientist, Nat Adv Comt Aeronaut, 1945-1953. **Memberships:** Assoc fel Am Inst Aeronaut & Astronaut; AAAS. **Research Statement & Publications:** Supersonics; hypersonics; propulsion aerodynamics; inlets; aeroballistics. **Mailing Address:** 1717 Marymont Rd, Silver Spring, MD 20906.

LANKFORD, WILLIAM FLEET, NUCLEAR & SOLID STATE PHYSICS. **Personal Data:** b Charlottesville, Va, January 9, 1938. **Education:** Univ Va, BA, 1960; Univ SC, MS, 1964, PhD (physics), 1969. **Professional Experience:** PRES, CENT AM SOLAR ENERGY PROJ, 1991-; PROF PHYSICS, GEORGE MASON UNIV, 1978-; fel, Col William & Mary, 1969; Instr physics, Univ NC, Greensboro, 1962-1963; from asst prof to assoc prof, George Mason Univ, 1959-1978. **Memberships:** Am Inst Physics; Am Phys Soc. **Research Statement & Publications:** Experimental solid state research. **Mailing Address:** Dept Physics & Astron, George Mason Univ, Rm 309 Sci & Technol Bldg, Fairfax, VA 22030. **Fax:** 703-993-1269. **E-Mail:** wlankfor@osf1.gmu.edu

LANKFORD, WILLIAM T, METALLURGY. **Professional Experience:** FEL MEM, US STEEL CORP, as of 2005. **Memberships:** Am Soc Mech Engrs. **Mailing Address:** US Steel Corp, 600 Grant St, Pittsburgh, PA 15230. **Fax:** 412-433-5733.

LANKS, KARL WILLIAM, PATHOLOGY, MOLECULAR BIOLOGY. **Personal Data:** b Philadelphia, Pa, November 1, 1942. **Education:** Pa State Univ, BS, 1963; Temple Univ, MD, 1967; Columbia Univ, PhD (path), 1971. **Professional Experience:** DIR PATH, STATEN ISLAND UNIV HOSP, NY, as of 2004; PROF PATH, STATE UNIV NY DOWNSTATE MED CTR, 1988-; from asstprof to assoc prof, State Univ NY Downstate Med Ctr, 1974-1988; instr path, Columbia Univ, 1971-1972; NIH res fel, Dept Chem, Harvard Univ, 1971-1972; intern, Columbia-Presby Hosp, 1967-1968. **Memberships:** Am Soc Biol Chemists; Am Soc Exp Path; Am Soc Cell Biol. **Research Statement & Publications:** Structure and metabolism of messenger ribonucleic acids; mechanism of cell attachment; regulation of protein and RNA messenger synthesis in cultured cells; structure and function of heat shock proteins. **Mailing Address:** Staten Island Univ Hosp, 475 Seaview Ave, Staten Island, NY 10305.

LANMAN, JOSEPH T, JR, GENETICS. **Education:** Ind Univ, PhD. **Professional Experience:** CLIN ASST PROF PATH, STATE UNIV NY, as of 2006. **Mailing Address:** Clinical Labs Univ Hosp State Univ NY, Rm L3-500, Stony Brook, NY 11794.

LANMAN, ROBERT CHARLES, BIOCHEMICAL PHARMACOLOGY, TOXICOLOGY. **Personal Data:** b Bemidji, Minn, October 2, 1930; m 1957, Dorothy; c Michael, Dianne, Douglas & Krista. **Education:** Univ Minn, BS, 1956, PhD (pharmacol), 1967. **Professional Experience:** EXEC VPRES, KANSAS CITY ANALYTICAL SERV, 1991-; chmn, Div Pharmacol, Univ Mo, Kansas City, 1987-1992; vpres, Kansas City Analytical Serv, 1984-1991; PROF PHARMACOL & MED, UNIV MO, KANSASCITY, 1981-; assoc prof pharmacol & med, Univ Mo, Kansas City, 1966-1981; pharmacologist, Sect Biochem Drug Action, Lab Chem Pharmacol, Nat Heart Inst, 1962-1966; teaching asst, ColPharm, Univ Minn, 1958-1959; consult, Marion Merrell Dow, Inc. **Memberships:** Am Asn Cols Pharm; Am Soc Pharmacol & Exp Therapeut; Fedn Am Socs ExpBiol; Am Asn Pharmaceut Scientists; Am Pharmaceut Asn. **Research Statement & Publications:** Passage of drugs across body membranes; mechanism and kinetics of drug absorption, distribution, metabolism and excretion; analysis of drugs in biological fluids and tissues. **Mailing Address:** 12400 Shawnee Mission Pkwy, Shawnee Msn, KS 66216. **Fax:** 913-268-3240.

LANN, JOSEPH SIDNEY, ORGANIC CHEMISTRY. **Personal Data:** b Washington, DC, September 16, 1917. **Education:** Univ Md, BS, 1937, PhD (org chem), 1941. **Professional Experience:** RETIRED; mgr develop prod, Freon Prod Div, 1968-1980; asst dist mgr, Freon Prod Div, 1965-1968; asst mgr new prod & mkt develop, Freon Prod Div, 1964-1965; dir, Freon Prod Lab, 1954-1964; res chemist, Jackson Lab, E I du Pont de Nemours & Co, Inc, 1946-1954. **Memberships:** sr mem Am Chem Soc. **Research Statement & Publications:** Surface active agents and neoprene; organic compounds; fluorinated hydrocarbons. **Mailing Address:** 608 Haverhill Rd, Sharpley, Wilmington, DE 19803-2437.

LANNER, RONALD MARTIN, FOREST GENETICS, TREE PHYSIOLOGY. **Personal Data:** b Brooklyn, NY, November 12, 1930; m 1957, Harriette; c Deborah & David. **Education:** Syracuse Univ, BS, 1952, MF, 1958; Univ Minn, Minneapolis, PhD (forestry), 1968. **Professional Experience:** PROF EMER FOREST GENETICS & DENDROL, UTAH STATE UNIV, as of 2003; ed, Western J Appl Forestry, 1984-1996; vis prof, Univ Wash, 1982-1983; res fel, UnivFla, 1973-1974; consult, Forestry Proj, Food & Agr Orgn, UN, Taiwan, 1969; prof, Utah StateUniv, 1967-1995; res forester, Pac Southwest Forest & Range Exp Sta, US Forest Serv, 1958-1964. **Memberships:** Soc Am Foresters. **Research Statement & Publications:** Morphogenesis and growth of woody plants; evolution and ecology of pines with bird-dispersed seeds; author of books about trees. **Mailing Address:** Dept Forest Res, Utah State Univ, Logan, UT 84322-5230. **Fax:** 435-797-3796.

LANNERS, H NORBERT, ELECTRON MICROSCOPY. **Personal Data:** b Volkmarsen, Ger, June 23, 1943; m 1973. **Education:** Univ Tubingen, Ger, Dr rer nat, 1973. **Professional Experience:** ASST PROF, ROCKEFELLER UNIV, 1980-; res assoc, Cornell Univ MedCol, 1976-1980; adj res assoc, Rockefeller Univ, 1976-1979; Vis scientist, Agr Exp Sta, UnivPuerto Rico, 1976; Fel, Rockefeller Univ, 1973-1976. **Memberships:** Soc Protozoologists; Electron Microsc Soc Am. **Research Statement & Publications:** Cultivation of human malaria parasites. **Mailing Address:** 4552 N Palm Ave, Fresno, CA 93704.

LANNERT, KENT PHILIP, INDUSTRIAL ORGANIC CHEMISTRY. **Personal Data:** b Belleville, Ill, November 29, 1944; m 1970, c 2. **Education:** Southern Ill Univ, Carbondale, BA, 1966; Vanderbilt Univ, PhD (chem), 1969. **Professional Experience:** MGR TECHNOL, MONSANTO CO, 1986-; sr group leader, Monsanto Co, 1983-1986; group leader, Monsanto Co, 1982-1983; sr res specialist, Monsanto Co, 1976-1982; res specialist, Monsanto Co, 1972-1976; Res chemist, Monsanto Co, 1969-1972. **Memberships:** Am Chem Soc. **Research Statement & Publications:** Organic synthesis; chelation; synthesis of chelants and other detergent related chemicals; phosphates processing. **Mailing Address:** Monsanto, 800 N Lindbergh Blvd, St Louis, MO 63166.

LANNI, FREDERICK, BIOLOGY. **Education:** Harvard Univ, PhD. **Professional Experience:** ASSOC PROF, DEPT BIOL, CARNEGIE-MELLON UNIV, as of 1996; SR RES SCIENTIST, DEPT BIOL, CARNEGIE-MELLON UNIV, 1990-. **Mailing Address:** Dept Biol Sci, Carnegie-Mellon Univ, 4400 Fifth Ave PO Box 32, Pittsburgh, PA 15213-2683. **Fax:** 412-268-7129. **E-Mail:** lanni@andrew.cmu.edu

LANNING, DAVID D(AYTON), NUCLEAR ENGINEERING. **Personal Data:** b Baker, Ore, March 30, 1928; m 1950, c 3. **Education:** Univ Ore, BA, 1951; Mass Inst Technol, PhD (nuclear eng), 1963. **Professional Experience:** Consult, Stone & Webster Eng Corp, 1977-1978; prof nuclear eng, Mass Inst Technol, beginning 1969; sect mgr, Battelle-Northwest, 1966-1969; unit mgr reactor physics, Battelle-Northwest, 1965-1966; from asst prof to assoc prof nucleareng, Mass Inst Technol, 1962-1965; asst dir res reactor, Mass Inst Technol, 1962-1965; res assoc& reactor supt, Mass Inst Technol, 1957-1962; physicist, Hanford Atomic Prod Oper, Gen ElecCo, 1951-1957; Mem, Monticello Nuclear Power Reactor Safety Audit Comt, Nat Res Coun, NSF; consult, Boston Edison Co; PROF EMER NUCLEAR ENG, MASS INST TECHNOL. **Memberships:** Am Nuclear Soc. **Research Statement & Publications:** Nuclear engineering education; design, safety, control and operation of nuclear reactor systems. **Mailing Address:** Dept Nuclear Eng, Mass Inst Technol 77 Massachusetts Ave, Cambridge, MA 02139-4307.

LANNING, WILLIAM CLARENCE, PHYSICAL CHEMISTRY. **Personal Data:** b Boicourt, Kans, December 9, 1913; wid, c Patricia L, John G & Marianne. **Education:** Sterling Col, AB, 1934; Univ Kans, AM, 1936, PhD (chem), 1938. **Professional Experience:** RETIRED; res chemist, Bartlesville Energy Res Ctr, ERDA, 1974-1980; sect mgr, Phillips Petrol Co, 1957-1973; res chemist, Phillips Petrol Co, 1946-1973; res chemist & sect mgr, Naval Res Lab, 1938-1945; asst instr chem, Univ Kans, 1935-1938. **Memberships:** Am Chem Soc; Sigma Xi. **Research Statement & Publications:** Non-aqueous solutions; inorganic preparations; catalytic hydrocarbon and petroleum processes; fundamentals of crude oil production; refining of synthetic crude oils. **Mailing Address:** 1530 Pecan Pl, Bartlesville, OK 74003.

L'ANNUNZIATA, MICHAEL FRANK, ANALYSIS OF RADIONUCLIDES, INTERNATIONAL CONSULTING. **Personal Data:** b Springfield, Mass, October 14, 1943; m 1973, Maria Del Carmen Salazar; c Michael, Helen & Frank E. **Education:** St Edward's Univ, BS, 1965; Univ Ariz, MS, 1967, PhD (agr chem & soils), 1970. **Honorary Degrees:** Hon Teaching Dipl, Cent Univ Ecuador, 1978. **Professional Experience:** Ethiopian Sci & Technol Com, Addis Ababa, Ethiopia, 1996; Nat Radiation Com, Arusha, Tanzania, 1996; MANAGING DIR, WORLDTECH INT TECH SERV, OCEANSIDE, CALIF, 1995-; Packard Instrument Co, Meriden, Conn, 1995-1997; Egypt Atomic Energy Authority, Cairo, Egypt, 1995-1996; Sudan Atomic Energy Com, Khartoum, Sudan, 1995; Ministry Educ, Jakarta, Indonesia, 1995; Forest Res Inst Nigeria, Ibadan, 1994-1995; Nat Coun Sci Res, Lusaka, Zambia, 1994; Int Atomic Energy Agency, Vienna, Austria, 1993; hon prof, Zhejiang Agr Univ, Hangzhou, China, 1992; Nuclear Energy Comn, Santiago, Chile, 1992; Ministry Energy Resources, Bejing, China, 1992; managing dir, Cornado, Calif, 1991-1994; Nat Atomic Energy Agency, Baton, Jakarta, Indonesia, 1991-1994; consult, Romania, 1991; consult, Korea, 1991; consult, Israel, 1990; consult, Hungary, 1990; consult, Belg, 1990; consult, Italy, 1990; consult, Sweden, 1989, 1990; consult, Mex, 1989; consult, Ger Dem Repub, 1989; consult, Czech, 1989; mem bd gov, Uppsala Univ, Int Sci Progs, Uppsala, Sweden, 1988-1991; consult, Poland, 1988, 1990; consult, Vietnam, 1988; consult, Thailand, 1988; consult, China, 1988; consult, France, 1987, 1988; consult, Fed Rep Ger, 1987; sr officer, head fel & training sect, 1986-1991; consult, US Dept State, 1985, 1989; first officer, Int Atomic Energy Agency, Vienna, 1983-1986; vis lectr, Univ Guanajuato, Mex, 1981; consult, USSR State Comt Utilization Atomic Energy, 1980, 1985; second officer, Int Atomic Energy Agency, Vienna, 1980-1983; consult, Uruguay, 1980; consult, Spain, 1980; consult, Panama, 1980; consult, Arg, 1980; consult, Guatemala, 1979; consult, Columbia, 1979; consult, Costa Rica, 1978, 1980; consult, Govt Nicaragua, 1978; Atomic Energy Comn, Quito, Ecuador, 1978; assoc officer, Int Atomic Energy Agency, Vienna, 1977-1980; res investr, Nat Inst Nuclear Energy, Mex, 1975-1977; prof & res investr, Univ Chapingo, Mex, 1973-1975; consult & lectr, Atomic Sch Trop Agr, Cardenas, Mex, 1973; res assoc, Univ Ariz, 1972-1973; consult health veg, Caborca, Mex, 1972; res chemist herbicides, Amchem Prod Inc, 1971-1972; vis lectr, Timiryazev Agr Acad, Moscow; vis lectr, Inst Nuclear Appln Vet Sci, Turkey. **Memberships:** Sigma Xi; AAAS. **Research Statement & Publications:** Detection and measurement of radio nuclides; analysis of radioactivity; use of radioisotopes in fertilizer use efficiency studies; use of isotopes in the elucidation of biochemical pathways and mechanisms. **Mailing Address:** 4317 Cassanna Way No 1608, Oceanside, CA 92057-7621. **E-Mail:** lannunzi@sprynet.com

LANOU, ROBERT EUGENE, EXPERIMENTAL PHYSICS. **Personal Data:** b Burlington, Vt, February 13, 1928; m Cornelia; c Katharine B, Gregory P, Elizabeth M & Steven M. **Education:** Worcester Polytech Univ, BS, 1952; Yale Univ, PhD (physics), 1957. **Professional Experience:** PROF EMER & RES PROF, BROWN UNIV, 2001-; Chmn dept, Brown Univ, 1985-1992; chmn, High Energy Discussion Group, Brookhaven Nat Lab, 1981-1983; prof physics, Brown Univ, 1966-2001; mem fac, Brown Univ, 1959-; physicist, Lawrence Radiation Lab, Univ Calif, 1957-1959; mem, exec comt, Div Particles & Fields, Am Phys Soc; mem, High Energy Physics Adv Panel Comt, Future High Energy Comput, Solar Neutrino Res; consult, Brookhaven Nat Lab & US Dept Energy. **Memberships:** Fel AAAS; fel Am Phys Soc. **Research Statement & Publications:** Elementary particle physics; particle astrophysics. **Mailing Address:** Dept Physics, Brown Univ, Providence, RI 02912. **Fax:** 401-863-2024. **E-Mail:** lanou@physics.brown.edu

LANOUE, ALCIDE MOODIE, HEALTH CARE ADMINISTRATION. **Personal Data:** b Tonawanda, NY, November 2, 1934; m 1986, Beth Gortner; c Claire L, Alcide J, George E & Michelle. **Education:** Harvard Univ, BA, 1956; Yale Univ, MD, 1960; Am Bd Orthop Surg, dipl. **Professional Experience:** RETIRED; surgeon gen, Dept Army General's Off, Comdr, Army Med Command, Ft Sam Houston, beginning 1994; Maj Gen, US Army Med Corps, 1988; comdt, Acad Health Sci, Us Army, Ft Sam Houston, beginning 1986; cmndg gen, Dwight David Eisenhower Army Med Ctr, Ft Gordon, Ga, 1984-1986; mem staff, US Army MEDDAC, Ft Benning, Ga, 1982-1984; comdr, US Army MEDDAC, Ft Stewart, Ga, 1980-1982; mem staff, Hanau Clin, Ger, 1977-1980; mem staff, Walter Reed Army Med Ctr, Wash, DC, 1973-1977; mem staff, Command & Gen Staff Col, Kans, 1970-1971; mem staff, Valley ForgeGen Hosp, Pa, 1967-1973; mem staff, 24th Evacuation Hosp, Repub Vietnam, 1967; mem staff, 2nd Surg Hosp, Repub Vietnam, 1966-1967; res orthop surg, Brooke Army Med Ctr, Tex, 1963-1966; intern, Brooke Army Med Ctr, Tex, 1960-1961. **Memberships:** Fel Am Chem Soc; Am Acad Orthop Surg. **Research Statement & Publications:** Orthopedic surgery; contributed many chapters to books and articles to professional journals. **Mailing Address:** 416 Dickman Rd, San Antonio, TX 78234-1019.

LA NOUE, KATHRYN F, BIOCHEMISTRY, CELL PHYSIOLOGY. **Personal Data:** b Camden, NJ, December 21, 1934; m 1958, c Claire Louise, Alcide Joseph, George Edwin & Michele. **Education:** Bryn Mawr Col, AB, 1956; Yale Univ, PhD (biochem), 1960. **Professional Experience:** PROF PHYSIOL, MILTON S HERSHEY MED CTR, PA STATE UNIV, 1981-; assoc prof, Milton S Hershey Med Ctr, PA STATE UNIV, 1974-1981; Dr W D Stroud estab investr, Am Heart Asn, 1971-1976; asst prof, Johnson Res Found, Sch Med, Univ Pa, 1971-1974; res assoc, Johnson Res Found, Sch Med, Univ Pa, 1970; NIH fel, Johnson Res Found, Sch Med, Univ Pa, 1968-1970; res chemist, US Army Surg Res Unit, 1961-1967. **Memberships:** AAAS; Am Chem Soc; Am Soc Biol Sci; Biophys Soc; Am Physiol Soc. **Research Statement & Publications:** Control of mitochondrial metabolism; membrane transport mechanisms; mechanism of transmembrane signalling. **Mailing Address:** Dept Cell & Molecular Biol, Pa State Univ, Milton S Hershey Med Ctr, Hershey, PA 17033. **Fax:** 717-531-7667. **E-Mail:** klanoue@psu.edu

LANOUX, SIGRED BOYD, INORGANIC CHEMISTRY. **Personal Data:** b New Orleans, La, November 1, 1931; m 1954, Emily; c Yvonne & Jeannine. **Education:** Southwestern La Univ, BS, 1957; Tulane Univ, PhD (inorg chem), 1962. **Professional Experience:** PROF CHEM, UNIV SOUTHWESTERN LA, 1974-; dean sci, Dept Chem, 1986-1992; head, Dept Chem, 1972-1986; from asst prof to assoc prof chem, Univ Southwestern La, 1966-1974; res chemist, Textile Fibers Dept, E I du Pont de Nemours & Co, Inc, 1962-1966; res assoc, Univ Ill, Urbana, 1961-1962. **Research Statement & Publications:** Phosphazene chemistry. **Mailing Address:** 104 Ridgewood, Lafayette, LA 70506-3222. **Fax:** 318-482-5676. **E-Mail:** lonaux@louisiana.edu

LANPHERE, MARVIN ALDER, GEOLOGY, GEOCHEMISTRY. **Personal Data:** b Spokane, Wash, September 29, 1933; m 1961, Joyce; c Christine, Darcy & Andrew. **Education:** Mont Sch Mines, BS, 1955; Calif Inst Technol, MS, 1956, PhD (geol), 1962. **Honors & Awards:** Meritorious Serv Award, Interior Dept. **Professional Experience:** Vis fel, Australian Nat Univ, 1975-1976; vis prof, Stanford Univ, 1972; secy, Volcanol, Geochem & Petrol Sect, Am Geophys Union, 1970-1972; RES GEOLOGIST, US GEOL SURV, CALIF, 1969-; dep asst chief geologist, Wash, DC, 1967-1969; geologist, US Geol Surv, Calif, 1963-1967; postdoctoral fel, Calif Inst Technol, 1962-1963. **Memberships:** Fel Geol Soc Am; Am Geophys Union. **Research Statement & Publications:** Geochronology, application of techniques of radioactive age determination of rocks and minerals to geological problems; isotope tracer studies of geological processes. **Mailing Address:** US Geol Surv, MS 937, 345 Middlefield Rd, 1036 Oakland Ave, Menlo Park, CA 94025. **E-Mail:** alder@usgs.gov

LANPHIER, ROBERT C, III, ENGINEERING. **Personal Data:** b November 13, 1932; American citizen; m 1999, Jeanne; c Robert C IV, Edward O II, Jonathan M Sr & Margaret L (Howd). **Education:** Yale Univ, BEEE, 1956, BSIA, 1957. **Honors & Awards:** mem nat acad of eng, 1993. **Professional Experience:** PRES & CEO, AGMED INC, 1988-; pres, chief exec officer, Dickey-joh corp, 1968-1988. **Memberships:** ASAE (pres, 1990-1991); Nat Acad Eng. **Mailing Address:** AGMED Inc, 713 W Prospect, Springfield, IL 62704. **Fax:** 217-744-0630. **E-Mail:** rclanphier@aol.com

LANSBURY, PETER THOMAS, ORGANIC CHEMISTRY. **Personal Data:** b Vienna, Austria, February 24, 1933; American citizen; m 1957, c 3. **Education:** Pa State Univ, BS, 1953; Northwestern Univ, PhD (chem), 1956. **Professional Experience:** PROF EMER CHEM, STATE UNIV NY, BUFFALO, as of 2004; res award, Ciba-Geigy Corp, 1973-1974; PROF CHEM, STATE UNIV NYBUFFALO, 1965-; consult, Hooker Chem Corp, 1965-1974; fel, Alfred P Sloan Found, 1963-1967; vis prof chem, Univ Ill, Urbana, 1963-1964; Prin investr, NSF res grants, 1960-; from asst prof to assoc prof, State Univ NY Buffalo, 1959-1965; lectr org chem, Univ Del, 1958-1959; res scientist chem, E I du Pont Del Nemours & Co, Inc, 1956-1958. **Memberships:** Am Chem Soc; Sigma Xi. **Research Statement & Publications:** organosynthetic methodology and natural products total synthesis. **Mailing Address:** Dept Chem, State Univ NY, Buffalo, NY 14221.

LANSFORD, EDWIN MYERS, JR, BIOCHEMISTRY, MICROBIOLOGY. **Personal Data:** b Houston, Tex, June 26, 1923; m 1981, Ingrid Gimm; c Elayne, Daniel & Ralph. **Education:** Univ Calif, Los Angeles, BA, 1946; Rice Univ, BA, 1948; Univ Tex, MA, 1951, PhD (biochem), 1951. **Professional Experience:** RETIRED; prof biochem, Southwestern Univ, Georgetown, Tex, 1967-1993; res scientist, Clayton Found Biochem Inst, Univ Tex, 1953-1967; Fel, Univ Ill, 1951-1952. **Memberships:** Am Chem Soc; Sigma Xi. **Research Statement & Publications:** Microbial intermediary metabolism; amino acid activating enzymes; metabolic effects of alcohol; single carbon unit metabolism and its control. **Mailing Address:** 1202 Peachtree St, Georgetown, TX 78626.

LANSING, ALLAN M, CARDIOVASCULAR SURGERY, ORGAN TRANSPLANTATION. **Personal Data:** b St Catherines, Ont, September 12, 1929; m 1951, c 3. **Education:** Univ Western Ont, MD, 1953, PhD (physiol), 1957; FRCS(C), 1959. **Honorary Degrees:** LHD, Bellarmine Col, Louisville, Ky, 1985; DSc, Transylvania Univ, Lexington, Ky, 1985. **Honors & Awards:** Hon G Ferguson Trophy, Western Ont Fac Med, 1953. **Professional Experience:** RETIRED; med dir cardiovasc surg, Norton Audubon Heart Inst, 1993-2001; bd mem, Nat Kidney Found, Louisville, Western Ky, Bellarmine Col, Louisville, Ky, beginning 1985; bd mem, Nat Kidney Found, Transylvania Univ, Lexington, Ky, beginning 1985;

dir cardiovasc surg, Humana Heart Inst Int, Louisville, Ky, 1983-1993; prog surg thoracic & cardiovasc, Sect Cardiovasc Surg, Univ Louisville, 1980-1984; prof surg, Sect Cardiovasc Surg, Univ Louisville, 1969-1980; chief, Sect Cardiovasc Surg, Univ Louisville, 1969-1974; assoc prof, Sch Med, Univ Louisville, 1963-1969; Markle scholar med sci, beginning 1961; asst prof surg & physiol, Fac Med, Univ Western Ont, 1961-1963; Nat Res Coun Can scholar, Univ Western Ont, 1955-1957. **Memberships:** Fel Am Col Surg; fel Am Col Cardiol; Soc Univ Surg; Royal Col Surg Can; Warren H Cole Soc. **Research Statement & Publications:** Cardiovascular physiology and shock; pulmonary atelectasis; renal transplantation; open heart surgery; research in heart replacement, including transplantation and the mechanical heart and the major fields at present; promotion and improvement of college education. **Mailing Address:** 3200 Boxhill Lane, Louisville, KY 40222. **E-Mail:** lansing@deltau.org

LANSINGER, JOHN MARCUS, GEOPHYSICS, IONOSPHERIC PHYSICS. **Personal Data:** b July 20, 1932; American citizen; m 1953, c 2. **Education:** Lewis & Clark Col, BS, 1954; Univ Alaska, MS, 1956. **Professional Experience:** PVT CONSULT, QUITEK, 1980-; staff mem, Phys Dynamics Inc, 1976-1979; vpres, Boeing Sci Res Labs, Northwest Environ Technol Labs, Inc, 1969-1976; staff assoc, Boeing Sci Res Labs, Northwest Environ Technol Labs, Inc, 1959-1969; sr engr, Philco Corp, 1957-1959; Instr geophys, Univ Alaska, 1956-1957. **Memberships:** Am Geophys Union; Inst Elec & Electronics Engrs; Air Pollution Control Asn; AmPhys Soc. **Research Statement & Publications:** Environmental sciences; ionospheric research; atmospheric propagation at optical wavelengths. **Mailing Address:** 1717 Nw 99th St, Seattle, WA 98117.

LANSKA, DOUGLAS JOHN, ADULT & GERIATRIC NEUROLOGY, NEUROEPIDEMIOLOGY & DEMENTIA. **Personal Data:** b Milwaukee, Wis, August 6, 1959; m 1982, Mary; c Joseph & John. **Education:** Univ Wis, BS, 1980; Med Col Wis, MS, 1984, MD, 1984; Univ Ky, MSPH, 1996. **Honors & Awards:** Career Investr Develop Award, Nat Inst Neurol Dis & Stroke, 1991; McHenryAward, Am Acad Neurol, 1997. **Professional Experience:** Am Bd Psychiat & Neurol Test Comt, 1992- & Dept Vet Affairs Comt, 1993-1994; fac res award, Col Med, Univ Ky, 1993; staff neurologist, Vet Affairs Med Ctr, Lexington, 1991-; consult, Internal Med Ctr Advan Res & Educ, 1991-; adv panel mem, Am Med Asn, 1991-; consult, Commonwealth Ky Ctr Excellence Stroke, 1991; consult, Ky Med Rev Bd, 1989-; assoc, Sanders Brown Ctr Aging, 1989-; assoc med staff, Div Maternal & Child Health, CommonwealthKy, 1989-; STAFF NEUROLOGIST, VET AFFAIRS MED CTR, 1989-; ASSOC PROF NEUROL, PREV MED & ENVIRON HEALTH, UNIV KY, 1989-; asst prof neurol, Vet AffairsMed Ctr, 1989-1992; instr neurol, Univ Hosps Cleveland, 1988-1989; resident physician, UnivHosps Cleveland, 1984-1988; consult comput programmer, CSI Corp, 1982-1984. **Memberships:** Am Acad Neurol; World Fedn Neurol; Am Heart Asn Stroke Coun; Am ColPhysician Execs; Am Neurol Asn; Asn Univ Profs Neurol. **Research Statement & Publications:** Epidemiologic studies of neurologic diseases especially investigations of factors producing temporal trends and large scale patterns of morbidity and mortality; stroke, dementia, Alzheimer's disease, Parkinson's disease, amyotrophic lateral sclerosis and Huntington's disease. **Mailing Address:** Dept Neurol Univ Ky, Ky Clin L-412, Lexington, KY 40536-0284. **Fax:** 606-323-5943. **E-Mail:** djlansva@ukcc.uky.edu

LANSKA, MARY JO, PEDIATRICS, NEUROLOGY. **Personal Data:** b Burlington, Wis, December 30, 1958; m 1982, James; c Joseph Thomas, James Michael & John Robert. **Education:** Univ Wis, Milwaukee, BS, 1980; Med Col Wis, Milwaukee, MS & MD, 1984. **Honors & Awards:** Dr's Houghton Award, Wis State Med Soc, 1984; Merck Award for Scholastic Achievement, Merck Corp, 1984; Glasgow Mem Achievement Citation/Am Med Women's Assoc, 1984; Warren Wheeler Teacher Award, Univ Ky, 1989-1990. **Professional Experience:** STAFF PEDIATRICIAN & NEUROLOGIST, GUNDERSON LUTHERAN CLIN, 2000-; STAFF NEUROLOGIST, DEPT VETERANS AFFAIRS, TOMAH, WIS, 1999-; neurodevelop consult, Divot Maternal & Child Health, 1997-1998; cobs pediat neurologist, Lex-Fayaatte County Sch Sys, Lexington, Ky 1996-1998; asst prof neurol & pediat, Univ Ky, Wrighton, 1989-1994. **Research Statement & Publications:** Population bases; epidemiologic studies of neonatal seizures using national hospital discharge survies; other studies in clinical neurology, pediatrics and health service and epidemiology. **Mailing Address:** Gundersen Lutheran - Tomah Clin, 500 E Veterans St, Bldg 12, Tomah, WI 54660. **Fax:** 608-372-3253.

LANSKI, CHARLES PHILIP, NONCOMMUTATIVE RING THEORY. **Personal Data:** b Chicago, Ill, October 19, 1943. **Education:** Univ Chicago, SB, 1965, SM, 1966, PhD (math), 1969. **Professional Experience:** PROF MATH, UNIV SOUTHERN CALIF, 1982-; sr visit fel, Univ Leeds, Eng, 1976; from asst prof to assoc prof, Univ Southern Calif, 1969-1982; NSF grant, 1971-1978. **Memberships:** Am Math Soc; Math Asn Am. **Research Statement & Publications:** Noncommutative ring theory; rings with involution; derivations and identities of prime rings; cardinality conditions in rings. **Mailing Address:** Univ Southern Calif, Denney Res Bldg DRB 155, Los Angeles, CA 90089-2532. **Fax:** 213-740-2424. **E-Mail:** clanski@math.usc.edu

LANTERMAN, ELMA, analytical chemistry; deceased, see previous edition for last biography

LANTERMAN, WILLIAM STANLEY, III, PLANT PATHOLOGY. **Personal Data:** b Portsmouth, Va, September 8, 1947; m 1975, Denise; c Samuel MacDonald & Ian Kennedy. **Education:** Univ Maine, BS, 1980; Cornell Univ, MPS, 1982, PhD, 1985. **Professional Experience:** DIR, PLANT PROTECTION DIV, 1994-; chmn, Comt Cert Stand, NAm PlantProtection Orgn, Ottawa, Ont, beginning 1989; dir & exec mem coop adv bd, Univ Victoria, BC, beginning 1988; DIR CTR PLANT HEALTH, AGR CAN RES & QUARANTINE STA, SIDNEY, BC, 1987-; head, Plant Quarantine Sect, 1985-1987. **Research Statement & Publications:** Plant pathology and regulatory aspects of the international movement of plant germ plasm. **Mailing Address:** Agr Can Ctr Plant Health, 8801 E Saanich Rd, Sidney, BC V8L 1H3, Can. **Fax:** 250-363-6661. **E-Mail:** lantermanw@em.agr.ca

LANTERO, ORESTE JOHN, BIOCHEMISTRY, ORGANIC CHEMISTRY. **Personal Data:** b Chicago, Ill, August 26, 1942; m 1967, c 2. **Education:** Purdue Univ, BS, 1964; NDak State Univ, PhD (biochem), 1971. **Professional Experience:** RES SCIENTIST BIOCHEM, SOLVAY INC, 1973-; Res fel, Merrell Nat Lab, 1971-1973. **Memberships:** AAAS. **Research Statement & Publications:** Isolation and characterization of enzymes; preparation and characterization of immobilized enzymes. **Mailing Address:** 59731 Ridgewood Dr, Goshen, IN 46526.

LANTOS, P(ETER) R(ICHARD), CHEMICAL ENGINEERING. **Personal Data:** b Budapest, Hungary, July 18, 1924; American citizen; m 1947, c 4. **Education:** Cornell Univ, BChE, 1945, PhD (chem eng), 1950. **Professional Experience:** PRES, TARGET GROUP INC, 1980-; vpres, Arco Polymers, Inc, 1978-1979; dir res &develop, Arco Polymers, Inc, 1976-1977; gen mgr, Plastics Div, Rhodia Inc, 1975; vpres res &develop, Sun Chem Corp, 1970-1975; dir develop, Sun Chem Corp, 1969-1970; mgr res &develop, Celanese Plastics Co, 1964-1969; mgr appln & prod develop, Celanese Plastics Co, 1961-1963; res supvr, E I du Pont Del Nemours & Co, Inc, 1955-1960; res engr, E I du Pont deNemours & Co, Inc, 1950-1955; develop chemist, Gen Elec Co, 1946-1947; chmn, Res Mgt Group, Philadelphia; chmn, Chem Mkts & Econ, Div Am Chem Soc. **Memberships:** Asn Consult Chemists & Chem Engrs; Am Chem Soc; Am Inst Chem Engrs; Plastic Inst Am; Soc Plastics Engrs. **Research Statement & Publications:** Polymers; plastics; fibers. **Mailing Address:** The Target Group Inc, 1000 Harston Lane, Glenside, PA 19038. **Fax:** 215-836-2518. **E-Mail:** peterrl@aol.com

LANTZ, THOMAS LEE, POWER HYDRAULICS, LUBRICATION OF INDUSTRIAL MACHINERY. **Personal Data:** b Clarksburg, WVa, July 12, 1936; m 1961, c 2. **Education:** WVa Univ, BS, 1959; Univ Pittsburgh, MA, 1967. **Professional Experience:** SECY, SOC TRIBOLOGISTS & LUBRICATION ENGR, as of 2004; Instr hydraul, drafting, eng, WVa Northern Community Col, 1987-; instr techmath & physics, Belmont Tech Community Col, 1977-1987; comt mem, Asn Iron & Steel Engrs, 1975-; Dir, Am Soc Lubrication Engrs, 1974-1984; PLANT HYDRAUL & LUBRICATION ENGR, WHEELING-PITTSBURGH STEEL, 1967-; MTCE engr, Wheeling-pittsburgh Steel, 1959-1967. **Memberships:** Fel Am Soc Lubrication Engrs (vpres 1974-1984). **Research Statement & Publications:** Power hydraulics; lubrication of industrial machinery; several technical articles. **Mailing Address:** 124 E Cardinal Ave, Wheeling, WV 26003-2602. **E-Mail:** tomlantz1@yahoo.com

LANYI, JANOS K, BIOCHEMISTRY. **Personal Data:** b Budapest, Hungary, June 5, 1937; American citizen; m 1988, c Brigitte Schobert. **Education:** Stanford Univ, BS, 1959; Harvard Univ, MA, 1961, PhD (biochem), 1963. **Honors & Awards:** Except Sci Achievement Medal, NASA, 1977; H Julian Allen Award, 1978; Alexander von Humbolt Prize, 1979. **Professional Experience:** DEPT CHMN, UNIV CALIF, IRVINE, 1995-; PROF PHYSIOL & BIOPHYS, UNIV CALIF, IRVINE, 1980-; res scientist, Planetary Biol Div, Ames Res Ctr, NASA, 1966-1980; Nat Acad Sci-Nat Res Coun res assoc biochem, 1965-1966; NIH fel genetics, Sch Med, Stanford Univ, 1963-1965. **Memberships:** Biophys Soc; Am Soc Biol Chem; Hungarian Acad Sci. **Research Statement & Publications:** Structure and function of enzymes and membranes in halophilic microorganisms; bacteriorhodopsin, halorhodopsin; energetics and mechanism of proton and chloride transport. **Mailing Address:** Dept Physiol & Biophys, Univ Calif, Irvine, CA 92717. **Fax:** 949-824-8540. **E-Mail:** jklanyi@uci.edu

LANYON, HUBERT PETER DAVID, SOLID STATE PHYSICS. **Personal Data:** b Halesowen, Eng, June 25, 1936; m 1979, c 5. **Education:** Cambridge Univ, BA, 1958, MA, 1962; Leicester Univ, PhD (physics), 1961. **Professional Experience:** PROF EMER ELEC ENG, WORCESTER POLYTECH INST, as of 2003; prof elec eng, Worcester Polytech Inst, beginning 1977; assoc prof, Worcester Polytech Inst, 1967-1977; assoc prof elec eng, Carnegie Inst Technol, 1966-1967; mem tech staff, RCA Labs, 1963-1966; res assoc elec eng, Univ Ill, Urbana, 1961-1963; res demonstr physics, Leicester Univ, 1958-1961. **Memberships:** Inst Elec & Electronics Engrs; Sigma Xi. **Research Statement & Publications:** Physics of solid state devices; device modelling; integrated circuits; solar cell physics; instrumentation. **Mailing Address:** Elec Eng & Comput Dept, Worcester Polytech Inst, 100 Inst Rd, Worcester, MA 01609-2247. **Fax:** 508-831-5491. **E-Mail:** lanyon@ece.wpi.edu

LANYON, SCOTT MERRIL, ORNITHOLOGY, BIOCHEMICAL SYSTEMATICS. **Personal Data:** b Tucson, Ariz, July 17, 1956; m 1981, Vicki Umbach; c Ashley & Cassandra. **Education:** State Univ NY Col Geneseo, BA, 1977; Ind Univ, MA, 1980; La State Univ, PhD (evolutionary biol), 1985. **Professional Experience:** PROF, ECOL, EVOLUTION & BEHAV, UNIV MINN, as of 2003; DIR, BELL MUS NATURAL HIST, as of 2003; dir, James Ford Bell Mus Natural Hist, 1995; counr, Am Ornith Union, beginning 1993; adj prof, Univ Ill, Chicago, 1993-1995; pritzker cur systematic biol, Field Mus Natural Hist, 1992-1995; chmn, Dept Zool, 1990-1993; counr, Wilson Ornith Soc, 1990-1991; adj prof, Ill State Univ, 1988-2000; prin investr, NSF Grant, 1986-1989, 1987-1990, 1991-1996; lectr, Univ Chicago, 1985-; From asst cur to assoc cur, Field Mus Natural Hist, 1985-1992. **Memberships:** Fel Am Ornithologists Union; Wilson Ornithol Soc; Cooper Ornithol Soc; Soc Syst-Zoologists; Soc Study Evolution. **Research Statement & Publications:** Using DNA sequence data to construct and test hypotheses of evolutionary relationships for birds; studies of the evolution of behavior, morphology and ecology. **Mailing Address:** Bell Mus Natural Hist, Univ Minn, 10 Church St SE, Minneapolis, MN 55455. **Fax:** 612-624-6777. **E-Mail:** slanyon@biosci.cbs.umn.edu

LANYON, WESLEY EDWIN, ORNITHOLOGY. **Personal Data:** b Norwalk, Conn, June 10, 1926; m 1951, c 2. **Education:** Cornell Univ, AB, 1950; Univ Wis, MS, 1951, PhD (zoology), 1955. **Honors & Awards:** Brewster Award, Am Ornith Union, 1968. **Professional Experience:** RETIRED; adj prof, City Univ New York, beginning 1968; cur, Am Mus Natural Hist, 1967-1986; assoc cur, Am Mus Natural Hist, 1963-1967; res dir, Kalbfleisch Field Res Sta, AmMus Natural Hist, Huntington, 1958-1980; asst cur, Am Mus Natural Hist, 1957-1963; asst prof, Miami Univ, 1956-1957; instr zool, Univ Ariz, 1955-1956. **Memberships:** Am Ornith Union (pres, 1976-1978); Cooper Ornith Soc; Wilson Ornith Soc; SocSyst Zool; Soc Study Evolution. **Research Statement & Publications:** Application of compararive behavior and ecology of closely related populations of birds to avian systematics, especially vocalizations in avian taxonomy; use of morphology in the systematics of higher categories of birds. **Mailing Address:** 138 Prince St, New York, NY 10012.

LANZA, GIOVANNI, PHYSICS. **Personal Data:** b Trieste, Italy, August 5, 1926; m 1950, c 4. **Education:** Univ Trieste, PhD, 1950. **Professional Experience:** Consult, Saunders Assocs, 1963-; PROF PHYSICS, NORTHEASTERN UNIV, 1960-; consult, Lab Electronics, Inc, 1958-; assoc prof, Northeastern Univ, 1958-1960; res fel, Harvard Univ, 1955-1958; vis physicist nuclear physics, Mass Inst Technol, 1954-1955; Fulbright& Smith Mundt scholars, 1954; prof, Univ Cagliari, Univ Sardinia & Univ Padua, 1952-1954; asst-prof quantum theory, Univ Trieste, 1950-1952. **Memberships:** Ital Phys Soc; Sigma Xi. **Research Statement & Publications:** Magnetohydrodynamics; plasma physics; energy conversion techniques; nuclear physics; physics of upper atmosphere. **Mailing Address:** PO Box 1083, Campton, NH 03223.

LANZA, GUY ROBERT, AQUATIC ECOLOGY. **Personal Data:** b Englewood, NJ, January 27, 1939; m 1968, c 2. **Education:** Fairleigh Dickinson Univ, BS, 1961; Univ Ky, MS, 1969; Va Polytech Inst & StateUniv, PhD (zoology), 1972. **Professional Experience:** PROF & DIR, DEPT ENVIRON SCI, UNIV MASS, as of 2006; prof environ health, Etenn State Univ, beginning 1989; assoc profenviron sci, Univ Tex, Dallas, 1975-1990; aquatic ecologist, Univ Tex, Dallas, 1975-1989; subcomt partic, NatComn Water Qual, 1975; asst dir, Aquatic ecol prog, NY Univ Med Ctr, 1973-1975; aquatic ecologist, Smithsonian Inst, 1971-1973 & NY Univ, 1973-1975; consultecologist, Int Ctr Med Res & Training, Malaysia, 1972-1973; res biologist, Merck Inst TherapeutRes, 1963-1969. **Memberships:** AAAS; Water Pollution Control Fedn. **Research Statement & Publications:** Structure and function of aquatic ecosystems; pollution ecology and the environmental physiology and energetics of aquatic organisms. **Mailing Address:** Dept Environ Sci Prog, Univ Mass, 312 Stockbridge Hall, Amherst, MA 01003. **Fax:** 413-545-4860. **E-Mail:** glanza@nre.umass.edu

LANZA, RICHARD CHARLES, NUCLEAR SCIENCE, RADIOGRAPHY. **Personal Data:** b New York, NY, April 28, 1939; m 1963, Sylvia; c 1. **Education:** Princeton Univ, AB, 1959; Univ Pa, MS, 1961, PhD (physics), 1966. **Professional Experience:** SR RES SCIENTIST, CASTSCAN RES PROG, MASS INST TECHNOL, 1983-; res fel, Mass Gen Hosp, 1975-1976; assoc radiol, Harvard Med Sch & Peter Bent Brigham Hosp, 1974-; mem res staff, Mass Inst Technol, 1974-1983; asst prof, Mass Inst Technol, 1968-1974; res assoc physics, MassInst Technol, 1966-1968. **Memberships:** AAAS; Inst Elec & Electronics Engrs; Am Phys Soc. **Research Statement & Publications:** Experimental particle physics, nuclear and electronic instrumentation, medical instrumentation, especially in radiology and nuclear medicine; imaging for nondestructive testing and evaluation; radiation imaging; development of new radiation resources. **Mailing Address:** Dept Nuclear Sci & Eng, Mass Inst Technol, 77 Mass Ave NW13-221, Cambridge, MA 02139-4307. **Fax:** 617-253-2343. **E-Mail:** lanza@mit.edu

LANZA-JACOBY, SUSAN, NUTRITION, INFECTION. **Personal Data:** m 1978, c 1. **Education:** Hunter Col, BS, 1965; Columbia Univ, MS, 1968; Rutgers Col, PhD (nutrit biochem), 1979. **Professional Experience:** PROF, DEPT SURG, THOMAS JEFFERSON UNIV, 1979-; instr, Philadelphia Gen Hosp Sch Nursing, 1972-1977; lectr, Hunter Col, 1968-1972. **Memberships:** Am Inst Nutrit; Am Dietetic Asn; Shock Soc; Am Soc Parenteral Nutrit. **Research Statement & Publications:** Lipid metabolism in infection, tumor growth, and parenteral feeding; lipids and lipoproteins. **Mailing Address:** Dept Surg, Thomas Jefferson Univ, 1025 Walnut St, Philadelphia, PA 19107-5001. **Fax:** 215-923-1420. **E-Mail:** susan.lanza-jacoby@jefferson.edu

LANZANO, BERNADINE CLARE, COMPUTER SCIENCE, MATHEMATICS. **Personal Data:** b Stanberry, Mo, October 29, 1933; m 1957. **Education:** Benedictine Col, BS, 1955. **Professional Experience:** SR STAFF ENGR COMPUT SCI, TRW SYSTS GROUP, 1957-; Mathematician, Lockheed Corp, 1956-1957. **Memberships:** Math Asn Am; Soc Indust & Appl Math. **Research Statement & Publications:** Design and development of computer software in the areas of trajectory analysis, optimization, targeting, and in the fields of information processing of financial and scientific data; management of database management systems applications software development, installation, and operational support. **Mailing Address:** 1630 Eagle Nest Circle, Winter Springs, FL 32706.

LANZANO, PAOLO, APPLIED MATHEMATICS, SPACE PHYSICS. **Personal Data:** b Cairo, Egypt, November 29, 1923; American citizen; m 1957. **Education:** Univ Rome, BS, 1943, PhD (math), 1947. **Professional Experience:** SR RES SCIENTIST, NAVAL RES LAB, 1976-; head math res ctr, Naval ResLab, 1972-1976; assoc prof math, Nicholls State Univ, 1971-1972; prin scientist, Space & InfoSysts Div, NAm Aviation, 1961-1971; res scientist, Nortronics Div, Northrop Corp, 1960-1961; mem tech staff, Space Tech Labs, Calif, 1958-1960; design specialist, Douglas Aircraft Co, Calif, 1956-1958; Asst prof math, Univ Rome, 1946-1949 & St Louis Univ, 1950-1956; Fel, Inst AdvanStudies, Univ Rome, 1946-1948. **Memberships:** Am Math Soc; Am Geophys Union Soc; Soc Indust & Appl Math; assoc fel AmInst Aeronaut & Astronaut. **Research Statement & Publications:** Celestial mechanics; theory of relativity; Riemannian geometry; space physics; geodesy; geophysics. **Mailing Address:** 1630 Eagle Nest Circle, Winter Springs, FL 32708.

LANZARO, GREGORY, ENTOMOLOGY & GENETICS. **Personal Data:** b NY, m Christina. **Education:** kans State univ, BS, 1972; Univ Ariz, Tuscon, MS, 1978; univ Florica, Gainsville, Fla, PhD (Entomol) 1986. **Professional Experience:** DIR CTR VECTOR-BORNE DIS, UNIV CALIF-DAVIS, 2006-; DIR, MOSQUITO RES PROG, DEPT ENTOMOL, UNIV CALIF-DAVIS, 2002-; prof, Dept Pathol, Univ Tex Med Br, 2001-2002; from asst to assoc prof, Dept Pathol, Univ Tex Med Br, Galvenston, 1993-1997; guest researcher, McArthur fel, lab Malaria Res, NIH, 1991-1993; fel, Dept Entomol, Univ Calif-Davis, 1988-1990; asst entomologist, Miss State Univ, 1986-1988. **Mailing Address:** Dept Entomol, Univ Calif-Davis, One Shields Ave, davis, CA 95616-8579. **Fax:** 530-752-1537. **E-Mail:** gclanzaro@ucdavis.edu

LANZEROTTI, LOUIS JOHN, GEOPHYSICS, SPACE PHYSICS. **Personal Data:** b Carlinville, Ill, April 16, 1938; m 1965, c 2. **Education:** Univ Ill, BS, 1960; Harvard Univ, MA, 1963, PhD (physics), 1965. **Honors & Awards:** Lisle Abbott Rose Eng Award, 1960; NASA Distinguished Pub Serv Medal, 1988; 24th Harry G Armstrong Lectr, Aerospace Med Asn, 1989; Dean John R BentonLectr, Col Eng, Univ Fla, 1994; Antarctica Geog Feature named in honor, Mt Lanzeratti. **Professional Experience:** DISTINGUISHED RES PROF, DEPT PHYSICS, NJ INST TECHNOL, 2002-; Regents lectr, Univ Calif, Los Angeles, 1987; mem, Adv Coun, 1984-; mem, Space & Earth Sci Adv Comt, 1984-1988; DISTINGUISHED MEM TECH STAFF, BELL LABS LUCENT TECHNOLOGIES, 1982-; mem, Polar Res Bd, 1982-1990; mem, Space SciBd, Nat Acad Sci, 1979-1983 & 1988-; adj prof, Univ Fla, 1978-; mem, Space Sci Adv Comt, NASA, 1975-1979; assoc ed, J Geophys Res, 1971-1973; mem, Bell Labs Lucent Technologies, 1967-1982; fel, Bell Labs Lucent Technologies, 1965-1967. **Memberships:** Nat Acad Eng; fel Am Phys Soc; fel Am Geophys Union; sr mem Inst Elec &Electronics Engrs; Soc Terrestial Magnetism & Elec Japan; assoc fel Am Inst Aeronaut &Astronaut; fel AAAS; Int Acad Astronaut; Am Astron Soc; Europ Geophys Soc. **Research Statement & Publications:** Particles and fields in planetary magnetospheres; solar cosmic ray composition and propagation; ionosphere-magnetosphere coupling; planetary magnetospheres; geomagnetic depth sounding; impacts of space effects on technologies. **Mailing Address:** Ctr Solar-Terrestrial Res, NJ Inst Technol, Newark, NJ 07102. **Fax:** 908582-3972. **E-Mail:** louis.j.lanzerotti@njit.edu

LANZEROTTI, MARY YVONNE DEWOLF, PHYSICAL CHEMISTRY. **Personal Data:** b Phoenix, Ariz, November 7, 1938; m 1965, Louis; c Mary & Louis. **Education:** Univ Calif, Berkeley, BS, 1960; Harvard Univ, PhD (phys chem), 1965. **Honors & Awards:** Res & Develop Achievement Award, Dept Army Res, 1995. **Professional Experience:** RES PHYS SCIENTIST, E&W DIV, US ARMY ARDEC, 1965-; res chemist, Mithras Inc, Mass, 1964-1965; asst, Harvard Univ, 1960-1964; chemist, US Naval Ord Test Sta, 1960. **Memberships:** AAAS; Am Chem Soc; Am Phys Soc; Am Soc Mech Engrs; Am Defense Preparedness Asn; Mat Res Soc. **Research Statement & Publications:** Mechanical behavior of materials under high acceleration; power spectral analysis of fracture surface topography; crystal growth of energetic materials during high acceleration using an ultracentrifuge. **Mailing Address:** E&W Div Bldg 3022, US Army ARDEC, Picatinny Arsenal, NJ 07806-5000.

LANZKOWSKY, PHILIP, PEDIATRICS, HEMATOLOGY. **Personal Data:** b Cape Town, SAfrica, March 17, 1932; m 1955, c 5. **Education:** Univ Cape Town, MB ChB, 1954, MD, 1959; Royal Col Physicians & Surgeons, diplchild health, 1960; Am Bd Pediat, dipl, 1966, cert pediat hematol-oncol, 1975; FRCP (E), 1973. **Honorary Degrees:** DSc, St Johns Univ NY, 1995. **Honors & Awards:** Joseph Arenow Prize, 1959. **Professional Experience:** EXE DIR, SCHNEIDER C HOSP, NY, as of 2004; VPRES, C HEALTH NETWORK, NY, as of 2004; PROF PEDIAT, STATE UNIV NY STONY BROOK, 1970-; pediatrician-in-chief, chmn pediat & chief pediat hemat, Long Island Jewish-Hillside Med Ctr, 1970-; pediatrician-in-chief, Queens Hosp Ctr, 1970-; mem pediat adv comt, NY City DeptHealth, 1970-1973; assoc prof, NY Hosp-Cornell Med Ctr, 1967-1970; dir pediat hemat, NewYork Hosp-Cornell Med Ctr, 1965-1970; asst prof pediat, NY Hosp-Cornell Med Ctr, 1965-1967; lectr, Univ Cape Town, 1963-1965; consult pediatrician & pediat hematologist, Red Cross War Mem C's Hosp, 1963-1965; res fel, Col Med, Univ Utah, 1962-1963; clin & resfel pediat hemat, Duke Univ, 1961-1962; Benger Labs traveling grant, 1961; registr pediat unit, St Mary's Hosp Med Sch, Univ London, 1961; Cecil John Adams mem traveling fel & Hill-Pattison-Struthers bursary, 1960; Dr C L Herman res grants, 1958 & 1964; from registr to srregistr, Red Cross War Mem Children's Hosp, 1957-1960; gen pract, 1956-1957; from intern to srintern, Groote Schuur Hosp, Univ Cape Town, 1955-1956. **Memberships:** Am Soc Hemat; Am Acad Pediat; Am Soc Clin Oncol; Am Asn Cancer Res; AmPediat Soc. **Research Statement & Publications:** Nutritional anemias in children, especially iron, folate and protein deficiency; pediatric oncology. **Mailing Address:** Schneider C's Hosp, 269-01 76th Ave, New Hyde Park, NY 11040.

LANZKRON, ROLF W, ASTROPHYSICS, AERONAUTICAL & ASTRONAUTICAL ENGINEERING. **Personal Data:** b Hamburg, Ger, December 9, 1929; American citizen; m 1961, Virginia; c Paul, Sophie & Lisa. **Education:** Milwaukee Sch Eng, BS, 1954; Univ Wis, MS, 1955, PhD, 1956. **Honors & Awards:** Outstanding Achievement Award, NASA, 1964 Clifford Burtoioi award, FAA, 1995. **Professional Experience:** PRES, R W L ASSOCS, 1995-; dir, Air Traffic Control, 1993-1995; dep dir, Air Traffic Control, 1983-1992; graphic systs mgr, Fed Aviation Admin Display Systs, Raytheon Co, 1981-1983; opers mgr graphic oper, Fed Aviation Admin Display Systs, Raytheon Co, 1978-1981; prog mgr, prog mgr Air Force AN-TPN/19 Prog, 1973-1978; prog mgr, Fed Aviation Admin Display Systs, Raytheon Co, 1968-1973; chief flight projs, Div, Apollo, NASA, 1962-1968; design engr, Martin Co, 1957-1962; asst res & develop, Univac Div, Sperry Rand Corp, 1956-1957; asst, Univ Wis, 1955-1956. **Memberships:** Am Inst Aeronaut & Astronaut; Sigma Xi; Math Asn Am; Inst Elec & Electronics Engrs. **Research Statement & Publications:** Several papers on control system; several papers on automatic checkout of space craft; paper on display technology; research in air traffic control; vessel traffic control. **Mailing Address:** Two Mallard Way, Gloucester, MA 01930. **Fax:** 978-282-4897.

LANZONI, VINCENT, PHARMACOLOGY, CLINICAL MEDICINE. **Personal Data:** b Kingston, Mass, February 23, 1928; m 1960, Phoebe Krey; c Susan, Karen & Margaret. **Education:** Tufts Univ, PhD (pharmacol), 1953; Boston Univ, MD, 1960. **Professional Experience:** DEAN & PROF MED, GRAD SCH BIOMED SCI, UNIV MED & DENT NJ, 1987-; dean & prof med, NJ Med Sch, 1975-1987; prof pharmacol, Sch Med, Boston Univ, 1973-1975; assoc dean sch med, Sch Med, Boston Univ, 1969-1975; assoc prof pharmacol &med, Sch Med, Boston Univ, 1966-1973; asst prof pharmacol & instr med, Sch Med, BostonUniv, 1963- 1966; fel med, Boston City Hosp, 1963-1965; from intern to resident, Boston CityHosp, 1960-1963; Res fel, NIH, 1953-1954; Instr pharmacol, Sch Med, Tufts Univ, 1953-1954. **Memberships:** Sigma Xi. **Research Statement & Publications:** Cardiovascular pharmacology. **Mailing Address:** Univ Med & Dent, Med Sci Bldg-C-690, 185 S Orange Ave, Newark, NJ 07103-2714. **Fax:** 201-982-7148.

LAO, BINNEG YANBING, ELECTRONICS ENGINEERING, APPLIED PHYSICS. **Personal Data:** b Szechwan, China, February 25, 1945; American citizen; m 1970, Jennifer; c Catherine & Richard. **Education:** Univ Calif, Los Angeles, BS, 1967; Princeton Univ, MA, 1969, PhD (physics), 1971. **Professional Experience:** CHIEF SCIENTIST & CO-FOUNDER, SIERRA MONOLITHICS INC, 1988-; consult, 1986-1988; mgr, Microelectronics Magnavox Res Oper, Magnavox Adv Prod & Syst Co, 1980-1986; prin physicist appl physics, Bendix Res Labs, Bendix Corp, 1976-1980; sr res physicist instrumentation, Eastern Div Res Labs, Dow Chem Co, 1973-1976; NSF fel solid state physics, Ctr Theoret Physics, Univ Md, 1971-1973. **Memberships:** Am Phys Soc; Sigma Xi; Inst Elec & Electronics Engrs. **Research Statement & Publications:** Radio frequency and microwave system development; superconducting sensors and electronics; wireless systems; nonlinear and excitonic effects in semiconductors; sensors and solid state devices. **Mailing Address:** Sierra Monolithics, 103 W Torrance Blvd, Redondo Beach, CA 90277-3631. **Fax:** 310-318-8635. **E-Mail:** blao@monolithics.com

LAO, CHANG SHENG, MEDICAL DEVICE & CLINICAL TRIALS REVIEW, IN-VITRO DIAGNOSTIC TESTS ANALYSIS. **Personal Data:** b Shanghai City, China, December 10, 1935; American citizen; m 1966, Ching; c Allen, Lawrence & Cathy. **Education:** Nat Taiwan Univ, BA, 1960; Univ Mass, MS, 1966; Yale Univ, PhD (biostatist), 1973. **Professional Experience:** MATH STATISTICIAN, CTR RADIOL HEALTH DEVICES, FOOD &DRUG ADMIN, 1987-; supvry math statistician, Ctr Drugs Eval & Res, 1986-1987; lectr medstatist, Howard Univ Sch Med, 1983; math statistician, Ctr Drugs Eval & Res, Food & DrugAdmin, 1974-1980; math statistician, Ctr Radiol Health Devices, 1980-1986; epidemiologist, US Environ ProtectionAgency, 1980; Statist reviewer, Asn Off Analytical Chemists, 1977-1991; med res scientist, PaDept Health, 1973-1974; statistician, E I du Pont Del Nemours & Co Inc, 1966-1968. **Memberships:** Am Statist Asn; Biomet Soc; Asn Off Analytical Chemists. **Research Statement & Publications:** Statistical reviews of medical devices clinical trials; analyze the statistical and epidemiological data related to public health; design and analyze laboratory data on heart valve study; ethylene oxide study; in-vitro diagnostic tests. **Mailing Address:** 15429 Narcissus Way, Rockville, MD 20853. **Fax:** 301-443-8559. **E-Mail:** csl@fdadr.cdrh.fda.gov

LAO, LANG LI, PHYSICS. **Education:** Calif Inst Technol, BS & MS, 1976; Univ Wis-Madison, MS, 1977, PhD (nuclear eng), 1979. **Professional Experience:** SR STAFF SCIENTIST & MGR, INTEGRATED MODELING BR, THEORY & COMPUT SCI, FUSION GROUP, GEN ATOMICS, as of 2005. **Memberships:** Am Phys Soc. **Mailing Address:** Gen Atomics, PO Box 85608, San Diego, CA 92186. **Fax:** 619-455-3586. **E-Mail:** lang.lao@gat.com

LAO, LANG LI, NUCLEAR FUSION. **Personal Data:** b Hai Duong, Vietnam, January 28, 1954; m 1979, Ngan; c Bert J & Brian J. **Education:** Calif Inst Technol, BS & MS, 1976; Univ Wis-Madison, MS, 1977 PhD, 1979. **Honors & Awards:** Award for Excellence in Plasma Physics, Am Phys Soc, 1994. **Professional Experience:** SR STAFF SCIENTIST & MGR, THEORY & COMPUTATIONAL SCI DIV, GEN ATOMICS, as of 2003; PRIN SCIENTIST, GEN ATOMICS, 1982-; Tactical Recon Wing, RedondoBeach, Calif, 1981-1982; staff scientist, Oak Ridge Nat Lab, Tenn, 1979-1981. **Memberships:** fel Am Phys Soc. **Research Statement & Publications:** Equilibrum analysis of magnetic fusion; plasma physics experiments; developed a widely used computer code; published numerous articles; published 10 books. **Mailing Address:** Gen Atomics, PO Box 85608, San Diego, CA 92186. **Fax:** 858-455-3586. **E-Mail:** lang.lao@gat.com

LAO, YAN-JEONG, CHEMICAL ENGINEERING, ENVIRONMENTAL HEALTH. **Personal Data:** b Nanking, China, February 5, 1936; American citizen; m 1965, c 2. **Education:**

Nat Taiwan Univ, BS, 1958; Univ Mich, MS, 1962; PhD (chem eng), 1969. **Professional Experience:** Dept Chmn, Ecarolina Univ, 1985-1997; PROF ENVIRON HEALTH, ECAROLINA UNIV, 1981-; from asst prof to assoc prof, Ecarolina Univ, 1973-1981; sr engr, Monsanto Co, 1972-1973; Res engr chem eng, E I du Pont Del Nemours & Co, Inc, 1969-1971. **Memberships:** Nat Environ Health Asn; Am Indust Hyg Asn; Sigma Xi. **Research Statement & Publications:** Monitoring and analyzing environmental pollutants, the study of their effects and health related problems. **Mailing Address:** Dept Environ Health, ECarolina Univ, Greenville, NC 27858.

LAPALME, DONALD WILLIAM, PHOTOGRAPHIC ENGINEERING, PHYSICAL CHEMISTRY. **Personal Data:** b Woonsocket, RI, July 27, 1937; m 1961, c 4. **Education:** St John's Univ NY, BS, 1959, MS, 1961, PhD (chem), 1968. **Professional Experience:** VPRES OPERS, GAF BLDG Mat CORP, 1981-; plant mgr prod, PhotoDiv, 1978-1981; tech dir process eng, Res & Develop, 1976-1978; prod mgr reprographics, Photo Div, Gaf Bldg Mat Corp, 1974-1976; sr prod engr, Photo Div, Gaf Bldg Mat Corp, 1972-1974; Sr res chemist photo eng, Photo Div, Gaf Bldg Mat Corp, 1967-1972. **Memberships:** Soc Photog Scientists & Engrs (pres 1973-1974); Am Chem Soc. **Research Statement & Publications:** Photographic science. **Mailing Address:** 3002 Tudor Dr, Wayne, NJ 07444.

LAPENTA, GIOVANNI M, SPACE PLASMA, COMPUTER SIMULATIONS. **Personal Data:** b Torino, Italy, October 29, 1965. **Education:** Ministry Science, PhD (plasma phys), 1993. **Professional Experience:** SCIENTIST, UNIV CALIF LANL, 2000-; vis scientist, LANL, 1996-2000; prof Computational, Politecnico Di Torino, 1995-2001; fel, LANL, 1994-1995; vis scientist, LANL, 1993-1994; vis Scientist, MIT, 1992-1993. **Research Statement & Publications:** Theoretical and simulation study of processes in space and astrophysical plasmas. **Mailing Address:** Los Almos Nat Lab, Los Alamos, NM 87544. **Fax:** 505-665-3107. **E-Mail:** lapenta@lanl.gov

LAPETINA, EDUARDO G, PLATELET AGGREGATION, PHOSPHOLIPIDS. **Education:** Univ Buenos Aires, Argentina, PhD (biochem), 1967. **Professional Experience:** PROF MED, CASE WESTERN RES UNIV, 1976-; Group leader molecularbiol, Wellcome Res Labs, Burroughs Wellcome Co, 1976-. **Research Statement & Publications:** Thrombosis. **Mailing Address:** Molecular Cardiovasc Res Ctr Dept Med, Case Western Res Univ 10900 Euclid Ave, Cleveland, OH 44106-4958.

LAPEYRE, GERALD J, SOLID STATE PHYSICS, SURFACE PHYSICS. **Personal Data:** b Riverton, Wyo, January 3, 1934; m 1960, c 3. **Education:** Univ Notre Dame, BS, 1956; Univ Mo, MA, 1958, PhD (physics), 1962. **Professional Experience:** PROF EMER PHYSICS, MONT STATE UNIV, as of 1999; prof physics, Mont State Univ, beginning 1974; from asst prof to assoc profphysics, Mont State Univ, 1962-1974. **Memberships:** Fel Am Phys Soc; Am Asn Physics Teachers; Am Vacuum Soc. **Research Statement & Publications:** Solid state physics surface science with emphasis on synchrotron photoemission and electronic structure. **Mailing Address:** Dept Physics, Mont State Univ, EPS 213 PO Box 173840, Bozeman, MT 59717-3840. **Fax:** 406-994-4452. **E-Mail:** lapeyre@physics.montana.edu

LAPEYRE, JEAN-NUMA, MOLECULAR PATHOLOGY. **Personal Data:** b Los Angeles, Calif, October 17, 1945. **Education:** Univ Calif, Los Angeles, BS, 1967, MS, 1969; Univ Southern Calif, PhD (molecularbiol), 1975. **Professional Experience:** Mem, NSF Rev Bd, 1990-; ASSOC BIOCHEMIST & ASSOC PROF BIOCHEM, EXP PATH SECT, M D ANDERSON CANCER CTR, UNIV TEX, 1985-; mem, NIH Study Sect, Clin Sci IV, 1985-1989; vis exchange scientist, Nat Ctr Sci Res, Inst Molecular Biophys, Orleans, France, 1982; from instr to asst prof & asst biochemist, Exp Path Sect, M D Anderson Cancer Ctr, UnivTex, 1979-1985; res assoc, Exp Path Sect, M D Anderson Cancer Ctr, Univ Tex, 1978-1979; proj investr, Exp Path Sect, M D Anderson Cancer Ctr, Univ Tex, 1977-1978; lectr chem embryol, Molecular Biol Grad Sch, Univ Geneva, 1976; Fogarty Int fel, Swiss NSF, Univ Geneva, 1975-1977; lectr cell biol & dent biochem, Univ Southern Calif, 1973-1975; Consult, DNA Sci, Inc, Houston & Cytol Technol, Inc. **Memberships:** Am Soc Biochem & Molecular Biol; AAAS; Biophys Soc; Am Asn Cancer Res. **Research Statement & Publications:** DNA chemical synthetic methods and DNA sequencing; DNA structure and conformation; author of numerous scientific publications. **Mailing Address:** Dept Gene Therapeut Tampa Bay Res Inst, 10900 Roosevelt Blvd, St Petersburg, FL 33716.

LAPHAM, LOWELL WINSHIP, NEUROPATHOLOGY. **Personal Data:** b New Hampton, Iowa, March 20, 1922; div, c Joan, Steven, Judith & Jennifer. **Education:** Oberlin Col, BA, 1943; Harvard Med Sch, MD, 1948. **Honors & Awards:** award for mentitornis contrubationa in neuropathology miven by Am assoc of neuropathologists. **Professional Experience:** EMER PROF NEUROPATH, MED CTR, UNIV ROCHESTER, 1992-; prof, Med Ctr, Univ Rochester, 1969-1992; assoc prof path, Med Ctr, Univ Rochester, 1964-1969; from asst prof to assoc prof, path Case Western Res Univ, 1957-1964; Nat Mult Sclerosis Soc fel cytochem, Case Western Res Univ, 1956-1958; Sr instr path, Case Western Res Univ, 1955-1957. **Memberships:** sr mem Am Asn Neuropath; Sigma Xi. **Research Statement & Publications:** Studies of developmental diseases of nervous system; brain tumors; nature and function of glia; effects of environmental substances on nervous system. **Mailing Address:** 121 Kendal Dr, Oberlin, OH 44074.

LAPICKI, GREGORY, ATOMIC COLLISIONS, INNER SHELL IONIZATION. **Personal Data:** b Warsaw, Poland, February 14, 1945; American citizen. **Education:** Warsaw Univ, MS (physics), 1967; NY Univ, PhD (physics), 1975. **Professional Experience:** Fulbright award, Arg, 1991-1992; PROF PHYSICS, E CAROLINA UNIV, 1988-; panel reviewer, Off Naval Technol Postdoc Fel, 1987; prin investr, Nat Bur Stand, 1982-1984; partic, Oak Ridge Nat Lab, 1981-1987; assoc prof, E Carolina Univ, 1981-1987; asst prof physics, Northwestern State Univ La, 1980-1981; vis asst prof physics, Tex A & M Univ, 1979-1980; res scientist, NY Univ, 1977-1978; post doc physics, NY Univ, 1975-1976. **Memberships:** Am Phys Soc; Fulbright Asn; Sigma Xi. **Research Statement & Publications:** Penetration of charged particles in matter; development of theories of inner shell direct ionization and electron capture; study of asymmetric and symmetric ion atom collisions; published over 100 refereed articles. **Mailing Address:** Dept Physics, E Carolina Univ, Greenville, NC 27858. **Fax:** 252-328-6314. **E-Mail:** lapickig@ecu.edu

LAPIDUS, ARNOLD, MATHEMATICS. **Personal Data:** b Brooklyn, NY, November 6, 1933; m 1952, Nancy. **Education:** Brooklyn Col, BS, 1956; NY Univ, MS, 1960, PhD (math), 1967. **Professional Experience:** ENTREPRENEUR, ADVAN MATH, 1987-; sr engr, Singer Electronic Syst Corp, 1986-1987; prof & chmn, Dept Comput & Decision Syst, 1983-1985; assoc prof quant analysis, Fairleigh Dickinson Univ, 1977-1983; asst math prof, Fairleigh Dickinson Univ, 1971-1976; sci prog mgr, Comput Applns Inc-NASA, 1969-1971; math analyst, Comput Applns Inc-NASA, 1968-1969; assoc res scientist, AEC comput facil, 1961-1968; asst res scientist, AEC comput facil, 1961-1965; asst math, Courant Inst, NY Univ, 1958-1960. **Memberships:** Soc Indust & Appl Math; Math Asn Am; Am Math Soc; AAAS; Am Asn Univ Prof. **Research Statement & Publications:** Partial and ordinary differential equations; Monte Carlo methods; scientific programming; artificial intelligence; tedious algebraby computer; fluid dynamics by computer; shock calculations; numerical methods and analysis; linear programming; kalman filters; analysis of biological graphics. **Mailing Address:** 401 Fergus Way, Tobyhanna, PA 18466.

LAPIDUS, HERBERT, PHARMACY, PHARMACOLOGY. **Personal Data:** b New York, NY, August 10, 1931; m 1952, Iris; c Lani R & William S. **Education:** Columbia Univ, BS, 1953, MS, 1955; Rutgers Univ, PhD (pharm), 1967. **Professional Experience:** VPRES RES & DEVELOP, COMBE INC, 1977-; tech dir, Combe Inc, 1970-1977; dept head, Bristol-Myers Co, 1967-1970; group leader, Bristol-Myers Co, 1963-1967; proj leader pharm, Bristol-Myers Co, 1960-1963; Proj leader, Julius Schmid Co, 1957-1960. **Memberships:** Am Chem Soc; Sigma Xi; Soc Cosmetic Chemists; NY Acad Sci; AmSoc ClinPharmacol & Therapeut; Am Asn Pharmaceut Scientists. **Research Statement & Publications:** Development of pharmaceutical dosage forms, especially sustained release medication, biopharmaceutics and percutaneous absorption; development of new technology, such as hair dyes, skin and dental products, and veterinary products; granted 16 patents in the chemical and drug fields. **Mailing Address:** Combe Inc, 1101 Westchester Ave, White Plains, NY 10604.

LA PIDUS, JULES BENJAMIN, MEDICINAL CHEMISTRY. **Personal Data:** b Chicago, Ill, May 1, 1931; m 1970, Anne M LuPidus; c Steven, Amy, Mark & Marilyn. **Education:** Univ Ill, BS, 1954; Univ Wis, MS, 1957, PhD (pharmaceut chem), 1958. **Professional Experience:** Pres, Coun Grad Sch, US, 1984-; PRES, COUN GRAD SCHS, US, 1984-; vprovost res & dean, Grad Sch, 1974-1984; assoc dean res, Grad Sch, 1972-1974; Consult, Prog Comt, 1971-1975; PROF MED CHEM, OHIO STATE UNIV, 1967-; Consult, Pharmacol & Toxicol Training Grants Comt, Nat Inst Gen Med Sci, NIH, 1965-1967; From asst prof to prof, Ohio State Univ, 1958-1967. **Memberships:** Am Chem Soc; fel AAAS. **Research Statement & Publications:** Structure-action relationships; autonomic pharmacology. **Mailing Address:** Coun Grad Schs, One Dupont Circle NW Suite 430, Washington, DC 20036-1173.

LAPIDUS, MICHEL LAURENT, FRACTAL GEOMETRY, MATHEMATICAL PHYSICS. **Personal Data:** b Casablanca, Morocco, July 4, 1956; m 1980, Odile; c Julie A & Michael A. **Education:** Univ Pierre & Marie Curie, Paris VI, MS, 1977, DEA, 1978, Dr (Math), 1980, Doctoral d'Etat es Sci Math, 1986, Habilitation, 1987. **Honors & Awards:** Michael Award Res Sci, Univ Ga, Athens, 1989-1990; Creative Research Medal, Univ Ga, 1989-1990. **Professional Experience:** Mem, Inst Henri Poincare, Paris, 2004; vis prof, Univ. of Copenhagen, Denmark and Univ. of Rome, Italy (many times between 2001 and 2005); mem, Math Sci Res Inst, Berkeley, 1999 & 2001; vis prof, Newton Inst of Math. Sci., Univ. of Cambridge, UK, 1999, vis prof, Inst Higher Sci Studies, Paris, 1995-1996, 1997, 1998, 2000; PROF MATH, UNIVCALIF, RIVERSIDE, 1990-; vis prof, Yale Univ, 1990-1991; creative res medal, Univ Ga, Athens, 1989-1990; assoc prof math, Univ Ga, Athens, 1986-1990; vis asst prof, Univ Iowa, Iowa City, 1985-1986; mem, Math Sci Res Inst, Berkeley, 1984-1985; Award, Fac Res &Innovation Fund, Univ Southern Calif, 1984; asst prof math, Univ Southern Calif, Los Angeles, 1980-1985; Georges Lurcy fel math, Univ Calif, Berkeley, 1979-1980; Res assoc, math, Rectoratde Paris, Inst Pure Math, Univ Paris VI, 1978-1980. **Memberships:** Amer Math Soc; Fr Math Soc; AAAS; Int Asn Math Physicists; Soc Indust & ApplMath; Amer Phys Soc. **Research Statement & Publications:** Mathematical research in analysis, partial differential equations, dynamical systems, and mathematical physics; study of the Trotter-Lie formula and modification of the Feynman integral; Feynman path integrals in quantum mechanics; Feynman's operational calculus for noncommuting operators; eigenvalues and eigenfunctions of elliptic boundary value problems with indefinite weights; spectral and fractal geometry; vibrations of fractal drums; origin of fractality in nature; connections with number theory, particularly the theory of the Riemann zeta function and the Riemann Hypothesis; fractal geometry and noncommutative geometry; fractal membranes and fractal string theory. **Mailing Address:** Dept Math, Univ Calif, Off Surge 231, Riverside, CA 92521-0135. **Fax:** 951-827-7314. **E-Mail:** lapidus@math.ucr.edu

LAPIERRE, YVON DENIS, PSYCHOPHARMACOLOGY. **Personal Data:** b Bonnyville, Alta, October 19, 1936; m 1960, Nicole; c Michel, Denis & Stephan. **Education:** Ottawa Univ, BA, 1957, MD, 1961; Univ Montreal, MSc, 1970; FRCP (C), 1972. **Honors & Awards:** Medal Hon, Can Col Neuropschopharmacol, 1988; Tait-MacKenzie Medal, Ottawa Acad Med, 1980. **Professional Experience:** PSYCHIATRIST CHIEF, ROYAL OTTAWA HOSP, 1986-; CHMN, PSYCHIAT DEPT, 1986-; chmn, Expert Standing Comt Psychotrop Drugs, 1982; PROF, PSYCHIAT & PHARMACOL, UNIV OTTAWA, 1981-; dir, outpatient clin, Royal Ottawa Hosp, 1980-1985; dir res & psychiat, Royal Ottawa Hosp, 1979-1986; dir, psychopharmacol, Ottawa Gen Hosp, 1976-1979; from asst prof to assoc prof, Psychiat Dept, 1973-1981; sci dir psychiat, Pierre Janet Hosp, Que, 1970-1976; lectr, Psychiat Dept, 1970-1973. **Memberships:** Can Col Neuropsychopharmacol; fel Royal Col Physicians & Surgeons Can; Soc Biol Psychiat; Col Int Neuropsychopharmacol; fel Am Psychiat Asn; fel Am Col Psychiat. **Research Statement & Publications:** Drugs used in the treatment of psychiatric disorders plus biochemical clinical and electrophysiological research in the underlying biological factors contributing to mental illness. **Mailing Address:** Royal Ottawa Hosp, 1145 Carling Ave, Ottawa, ON K1Z 7K4, Can.

LAPIETRA, JOSEPH RICHARD, PHYSICAL CHEMISTRY, THERMODYNAMICS. **Personal Data:** b New York, NY, July 20, 1932. **Education:** Marist Col, BA, 1954; Cath Univ Am, PhD (chem), 1961. **Professional Experience:** PROF EMER CHEM, MARIST COL, as of 2003; prof chem, Marist Col, beginning 1977; acad dean, Marist Col, 1969-1975; from asst prof to assoc prof, Marist Col, 1964-1977; instr chem, Cath Univ Am, 1960-1961; teacher high sch, NY, 1954-1956. **Memberships:** Am Chem Soc. **Research Statement & Publications:** Chemistry of transition metal complexes; thermochemistry; history of science; electrochemistry. **Mailing Address:** Dept Chem, Marist Col, DN 228B, Poughkeepsie, NY 12601. **E-Mail:** richard.lapietra@marist.edu

LAPIN, A I E, ELECTRICAL ENGINEERING. **Personal Data:** b Montreal, Que, May 13, 1938; m 1964, Ruth; c Kathleen, Heather & Amy. **Education:** McGill Univ, BEng, 1960; Univ Sheffield, PhD (elec eng), 1963. **Professional Experience:** PRIN SCIENTIST ENGR, HUGHES MISSILE SYSTS CO, 1992-; eng staff specialist, Gen Dynamics Corp, 1970-1992; mem tech staff, Bell Tel Labs Inc, 1963-1970. **Memberships:** Inst Elec & Electronics Engrs. **Research Statement & Publications:** Microwave diode and transistor circuitry; microwave systems for tactical missiles. **Mailing Address:** 1302 Albright Ave, Upland, CA 91786. **Fax:** 909-868-4716.

LAPIN, ABRAHAM, CHEMICAL ENGINEERING, MATHEMATICS. **Personal Data:** b Cairo, Egypt, September 30, 1923; American citizen; wid, c Jonathan & Josh. **Education:** Univ Mich, BScE(chem eng) & BScE(math), 1949; Polytech Inst Brooklyn, MSc, 1955; Lehigh Univ, PhD (chem eng), 1963. **Professional Experience:** RETIRED; lectr, Lehigh Univ, 1964; lectr, Pa State Univ, 1961; sect mgr cryogeniceng res & develop, Air Prod & Chem, Inc, 1963-1975; group leader, Air Prod & Chem, Inc, 1959-1963; proj engr, Air Prod & Chem, Inc, 1957-1959; chem engr, Air Prod & Chem, Inc, 1955-1957; chem engr,

Mineral Beneficiation Lab, Columbia Univ, 1954; mat engr, US CorpsEng, 1953; sales mgr, Dapor Trading Co, Inc, 1951-1952; asst port engr, Am Israeli Shipping Co, Inc, 1949-1951. **Memberships:** Am Chem Soc; Am Inst Chem Engrs; fel Am Inst Chemists; Am Soc Heating, Refrig & Air-Conditioning Eng; Am Soc Testing & Mat. **Research Statement & Publications:** Cryogenic engineering; low temperature separation; distillation; heat transfer; insulation; fluid flow. **Mailing Address:** The Pavillion, 845 Palmer Ave, Mamaroneck, NY 10543.

LAPIN, DAVID MARVIN, BIOLOGY. **Personal Data:** b New York, April 12, 1939; m 1967, c 2. **Education:** NY Univ, BA, 1960, MS, 1963, PhD (biol), 1968. **Professional Experience:** PROF BIOL SCI & CHMN BIOL DEPT, TOURO COL, 1985-; chmn dept, Fairleigh Dickinson Univ, 1976-1985; Grants aid, Fairleigh Dickinson Univ, 1968-1972; Frominstr to prof biol sci, Fairleigh Dickinson Univ, 1966-1985. **Memberships:** AAAS; Am Soc Hemat. **Research Statement & Publications:** Kinetics of hematopoiesis; humoral regulation of hematopoiesis. **Mailing Address:** 1439 E 28th St, Brooklyn, NY 11210. **E-Mail:** davidlap@touro.edu

LAPIN, EVELYN P, NEUROCHEMISTRY, ENZYMOLOGY. **Personal Data:** b Montreal, Que, August 29, 1933; c 3. **Education:** McGill Univ, BSc, 1954, PhD (biochem), 1957. **Professional Experience:** Res asst prof, Mt Sinai Sch Med, 1981-1988; instr neurochem, Mt Sinai SchMed, 1974-1981; LECTR, QUEEN'S COL, NY, 1973-; NIH fel, Mt Sinai Sch Med, 1970-1973; lectr biochem, McGill Univ, 1965-1966; instr math & chem, Herzliah Acad, 1962-1965; Am Cancer Soc fel, Dept Path, Albert Einstein Col Med, 1957-1959; vis asst prof, Stern Col Women, Yeshiva Univ, NY; vis assoc prof, Columbia Univ. **Memberships:** Brit Biochem Soc; Am Soc Neurochem; Can Fedn Univ Women; Int Soc-Neurochem; NY Acad Sci. **Research Statement & Publications:** Subcellular compartmentalization of respiratory activity and energy metabolism; protein and lipid chemistry of nervous system, localization, separation and identification and function; biochemical mechanisms of hydrocarbon neurotoxins in central and distal axonopathy; brain catecholamines, dopamine, sub P, CCK in selected areas in animal Parkinsonian model. **Mailing Address:** 142-05 Roosevelt Apt 325, Flushing, NY 11354.

LAPIN, GREGORY D, ELECTROMAGNETIC BIOEFFECTS, RADIO FREQUENCY DEVICES. **Personal Data:** b Chicago, Ill, July 28, 1956; m 1980, Jill; c Ashley, Marni & Joel. **Education:** Northwestern Univ, BS, 1978, MS, 1979, PhD (elec eng), 1987. **Professional Experience:** Consult, Digital Design Lab, 1995-; ASST PROF BIOMED ENG & NEUROL, NORTHWESTERN UNIV, 1988-1995. **Memberships:** Sr mem Inst Elec & Electronics Engrs; mem Bioelectromagnetics Soc. **Mailing Address:** 1206 Somerset Ave, Deerfield, IL 60015-2819. **E-Mail:** g.lapin@ieee.org

LAPINS, MARIS, AERONAUTICS. **Education:** Univ Va, PhD (aerospace eng); Long Island Univ, MBA (finance). **Professional Experience:** DIR DEVELOP, NORTHROP GRUMMAN INTEGRATED SYST, as of 2006. **Mailing Address:** Grumman Aerospace Corp, M/S C17-05 Aircraft Syst Div, Bethpage, NY 11714. **Fax:** 516-575-2164.

LAPITAN, NORA L, PLANT GENOME ORGANIZATION & EVOLUTION, GENOME MAPPING. **Personal Data:** b Manila, Philippines, August 23, 1956; American citizen; m 1981, Ronald; c Ronald & Reginald. **Education:** Univ Philippines, BS, 1978; Kans State Univ, MS, 1983, PhD (genetics), 1986. **Professional Experience:** PROF, COLO STATE UNIV, 2002-; assoc prof, Colo State Univ, 1995-2002; prin investr, USDA, 1990-; prin investr, Agr Exp Sta, Colo State Univ, 1989-1995; asst prof genetics, Colo State Univ, 1989-1995; consult, UN Develop Prog, 1988; assoc, Cornell Univ, 1986-1989. **Memberships:** Am Soc Agron; Sigma Xi. **Research Statement & Publications:** Use of molecular techniques to genetically improve crop plants; use of DNA markers to locate and isolate genes for important traits, such as resistance to diseases and insects; molecular organization of plant genomes. **Mailing Address:** Dept Soil Sci, Colo State Univ, Ft Collins, CO 80523-0001. **Fax:** 970-491-0564. **E-Mail:** nora.lapitan@colostate.edu

LAPKIN, MILTON, POLYMER CHEMISTRY. **Personal Data:** b New York, NY, July 29, 1929; m 1964, c 3. **Education:** Polytech Inst New York, BS, 1951, PhD (org chem), 1955. **Professional Experience:** DIR RES, ICI RESINS, USA, 1986-; dir res, Beatrice Foods, Polyvinyl ChemIndust, 1973-1986; dir res, Olin Corp, 1969-1973; sect leader, Olin Corp, 1959-1960; Groupleader, Olin Corp, 1955-1959. **Memberships:** Am Chem Soc; AAAS; Am Inst Chem; Fedn Soc Coating Technol. **Research Statement & Publications:** Free radical polymerization; polyvinyl chloride; acrylic and methacyclic polymers; epoxies; propylene oxide; ethylene oxide; polyutheranes; suspension polymerization; emulsion polymerization. **Mailing Address:** 194 Greenwood Ave, Beverly Farms, MA 01915.

LAPLANCHE, LAURINE A, PHYSICAL CHEMISTRY. **Personal Data:** b New York, NY, July 4, 1938; m Glenn. **Education:** Univ Md, BS, 1959; Mich State Univ, PhD (chem), 1963. **Professional Experience:** RETIRED; prof chem, Northern Ill Univ, 1991-1994; vis prof pharmaceut chem, Univ Calif, San Francisco, 1984-1985; from asst prof to assoc prof, Northern Ill Univ, 1965-1991; asst prof physics, WVa State Col, 1964-1965. **Memberships:** Am Chem Soc; Sigma Xi. **Research Statement & Publications:** Nuclear magnetic resonance; two dimensional nuclear magnetic resonance; energy barriers to internal rotation; molecular structure of biological molecules; proton exchange; hydrogen bonding; lanthanide shift reagents and conformational analysis. **Mailing Address:** 5265 Redman Rd, Las Cruces, MN 88011-7558.

LAPLANTE, JEAN-PIERRE, CHEMISTRY. **Professional Experience:** PROF, DEPT CHEM & CHEM ENG, ROYAL MIL COL CAN, as of 2004. **Mailing Address:** Dept Chem & Chem Eng, Royal Military Col Can, Kingston, ON K7L 5P9, Can. **E-Mail:** laplante-j@rmc.ca

LAPLAZA, MIGUEL LUIS, MATHEMATICS. **Personal Data:** b Zaragoza, Spain, March 20, 1938; m 1969, c 4. **Education:** Univ Barcelona, MD, 1960; Univ Madrid, Espana, PhD (math), 1965. **Professional Experience:** PROF MATH, UNIV PR, MAYAGUEZ, 1976-; assoc prof, Univ PR, Mayaguez, 1967-1976; from asst prof to assoc prof, Univ Madrid, 1960-1966; instr math, Univ Barcelona, 1960-1961. **Memberships:** Am Math Soc; Math Asn Am. **Research Statement & Publications:** Category theory. **Mailing Address:** Dept Math, Univ PR, PO Box 9000, Mayaguez, PR 00681-9000.

LAPOINTE, JACQUES, PROTEIN BIOSYNTHESIS, MOLECULAR GENETICS. **Personal Data:** b Montreal, Que, November 22, 1942; m 1967, c 1. **Education:** Univ Montreal, BSc, 1964, MSc, 1966; Yale Univ, PhD (molecular biophys), 1972. **Professional Experience:** PROF BIOCHEM, UNIV LAVAL, 1981-; Vis assoc prof molecular biophys &biochem, Yale Univ, 1980-1981; assoc prof, Univ Laval, 1977-1981; adj prof, Univ Laval, 1973-1977. **Memberships:** Am Soc Microbiol; Am Soc Biochem & Molecular Biol; Can Biochem Soc. **Research Statement & Publications:** Regulation of the expression of genes encoding aminoacyl-t RNA synthetases in gram-negative and gram-positive bacteria; structure-function studies of bacterial aminoacyl-t RNA systhetases. **Mailing Address:** Dept Biochem, Univ Laval, Quebec City, PQ G1K 7P4, Can. **Fax:** 418-656-7176. **E-Mail:** Jacques.Lapointe@bcm.ulaval.ca

LA POINTE, JOSEPH L, ZOOLOGY. **Personal Data:** b Harvey, Ill, September 7, 1934; m 1966, c 3. **Education:** Portland State Col, BA, 1960; Univ Calif, Berkeley, PhD (zool), 1966. **Professional Experience:** PROF ENDOCRINOL, NMEX STATE UNIV, 1980-; NIH res grant, 1972-1973; assoc prof biol, Nmex State Univ, 1971-1980; asst prof, Nmex State Univ, 1968-1971; Nat Inst Child Health & Human Develop fel, 1966-1968; Assoc instr zool, Univ Calif, Berkeley, 1964-1966. **Memberships:** Am Soc Ichthyol & Herpet; Am Soc Zool; Brit Soc Endocrinol; Europ Soc Comp Endocrinol. **Research Statement & Publications:** Effect of perietal eye on circadian rhythms in lizards; thermoregulation in antusiid lizards; ultrastructure of reptilian pituitary; physiology of neurohypophysial hormones in lower vertebrates; fat mobilization in lizards. **Mailing Address:** Dept Biol, NMex State Univ, Las Cruces, NM 88003.

LAPOINTE, LEONARD LYELL, SPEECH PATHOLOGY. **Personal Data:** b Iron Mountain, Mich, June 28, 1939; m 1963, Corinne; c Chris & Adrienne. **Education:** Mich State Univ, BA, 1961; Univ Colo, MA, 1966, PhD (speech path), 1969. **Honors & Awards:** Award, Sci Exhib, XV World Cong Logopedics & Phoniatrics, 1971. **Professional Experience:** FRANCIS EPPES PROF, COMMUN DIS, FLA STATE UNIV, as of 2006; prof, Dept Speech & Hearing Sci, Ariz State Univ, Tempe, 1992-2000; chmn, Dept Speech & Hearing Sci, Ariz State Univ, Tempe, 1984-1992; mem res fac neuroling, Ctr Neurol-Behav Ling Res, 1974-; res investr speech sci, Vet Admin Med Ctr, Gainesville, 1971-1984; adj prof commun dis, Univ Fla, 1969-; coordr & instr audiol & speech path, Vet Admin Med Ctr, Gainesville, 1969-1984; asst prof phonetics, Univ Colo, Denver, 1968-1969; Felneurogenic commun dis, Vet Admin Hosp, Denver, 1968-1969; speech pathologist, Gen Rose-Mem Hosp, 1966; dir speech path commun dis, Bd Educ, Menasha, Wis, 1961-1964; consult, Vet Admin Med Ctr, Phoenix & Vet Admin Outpatient Clin, Los Angeles. **Memberships:** Acad Aphasia; fel Am Speech-Lang-Hearing Asn; Int Asn Logopedics & Phoniatrics; Int Neuropsychol Soc; Nat Aphasia Asn. **Research Statement & Publications:** Development of measurement strategies of human oral sensation-perception; oral physiology and neurolinguistics; diagnosis and treatment strategies in aphasia and related neurogenic communication impairments; developing reading tests for aphasia; memory attention disorders in left and right hemisphere damage; cognitive-linguistic interactions. **Mailing Address:** Dept Commun Dis, Fla State Univ, Tallahassee, FL 32306. **Fax:** 480-965-8516. **E-Mail:** lapointe@neuro.fsu.edu

LAPONSKY, ALFREDBAER, PHYSICAL ELECTRONICS. **Personal Data:** b Cleveland, Ohio, November 24, 1921; m 1957, Ellen; c Mark & Laura. **Education:** Lehigh Univ, BS, 1943, MS, 1947, PhD (physics), 1951. **Professional Experience:** RETIRED; fel engr, Indust & Govt Tube Div, Westinghouse Elec Corp, 1966-1983; assoc prof elec eng, Univ Minn, Minneapolis, 1963-1966; physicist electron physics, Res Lab, Gen Elec Co, 1951-1963; instr physics, Lehigh Univ, 1947-1951. **Memberships:** Sigma Xi. **Research Statement & Publications:** Electron physics; electro-optics; image sensing and display techniques. **Mailing Address:** 176 Greenridge Dr, Horseheads, NY 14845.

LAPORTE, DAVID COLEMAN, REGULATION OF GENE EXPRESSION, PROTEIN PHOSPHORYLATION CASCADES. **Personal Data:** b Bryn Mawr, Pa, July 31, 1951; m 1975, Donna; c David W & Joan M. **Education:** Univ Wis, BSc, 1976; Univ Ill, PhD (biochem), 1980. **Professional Experience:** PROF BIOCHEM, MOLECULAR BIOL & BIOPHY, UNIV MINN, as of 2005; asst prof biochem, molecular biol & biophy, Univ Minn, beginning 1983; fel, Univ Calif, Berkeley, 1980-1983. **Memberships:** Am Soc Biochem & Molecular Biol; Genetics Soc Am; Am Soc Microbiol. **Research Statement & Publications:** Regulation of cellular functions; regulation of glycogen metabolism in yeast and of the glyoxylate bybass in E coli, these systems employ protein phosphorylation and control of transcription as regulatory strategies. **Mailing Address:** Dept Biochem, Molecular Biol & Biophys, Univ Minn, 6-116 MCB, Minneapolis, MN 55455-0347. **Fax:** 612-625-2163. **E-Mail:** DLaPorte@umn.edu

LAPORTE, LEO FREDERIC, GEOLOGY. **Personal Data:** b Englewood, NJ, July 30, 1933; m 1985, Margaret Liniecki; c Leo G, Eva R & Noel A. **Education:** Columbia Univ, AB, 1956, PhD (geol), 1960. **Honors & Awards:** honor mem soc sedimentany geology, 1999. **Professional Experience:** Prof emeriters 1998-; assoc vchancellor, Undergrad Educ, 1994-1998; chair, US Nat Off, Hist Geol, Nat Res Coun, 1994-1996; provost, Crown Col, 1993-1998; secy, US Nat Off, Hist Geol, Nat Res Coun, 1991-1993; Co ed, Palaios, 1986-1989; PROF EARTH SCI, UNIV CALIF, SANTA CRUZ, 1971-1998; From instr to prof geol, Brown Univ, 1959-1971. **Memberships:** calif acad of sci; Geol Soc Am; Soc Sedimentary Geol (pres, 1995-1996); Hist Earth Sci Soc (pres, 1994); AAAS. **Research Statement & Publications:** Paleoecology and environmental stratigraphy; history and evolution of life; history of paleontology. **Mailing Address:** Univ Calif, 430 Nimity Ave, Redwood city, CA 94061.

LAPORTE, RONALD EDWARD, EPIDEMIOLOGY. **Personal Data:** b Buffalo, NY, May 29, 1949; American citizen; m 1971. **Education:** State Univ NY, Buffalo, BA, 1971; Univ Pittsburgh, MS (psychol), 1974, PhD (psychol), 1976, MS (epidemiol), 1980. **Honors & Awards:** Kelly W Memorial Award, Am Diabetes Asn, 1988. **Professional Experience:** PROF, DEPT PEDIAT & DEPT EPIDEMIOL, UNIV PITTSBURGH, 1990-; prin investr, WHO, 1990-1999; dir ctr diabetes registries & training epidemiol, WHO, 1988-; assoc prof, dept epidemiol, Univ Pittsburgh, 1983-1990; prog chmn, diabetes epidemiol coun, Am Diabetes Asn, 1983-1985; asst prof, dept epidemiol, Univ Pittsburgh, 1979-1983; epidemiologist, dept epidemiol, Univ Pittsburgh, 1978-; Fel dept epidemiol, Univ Pittsburgh, 1976-1979; teaching fel, dept Psychol, Univ Pittsburgh, 1974-1976; res asst, dept Psychol, Univ Pittsburgh, 1971-1974. **Memberships:** AAAS; Soc Epidemiol Res; Am Psychol Asn; Am Epidemiol Soc; WHO. **Research Statement & Publications:** Chronic disease epidemiology; investigating possible protective factors of coronary heart disease and diabetes epidemeology; published over 100 articles. **Mailing Address:** Dept Epidemiol, Univ Pittsburgh, Rm A529 130 DeSoto St, Pittsburgh, PA 15237. **Fax:** 412-692-8329. **E-Mail:** rlaporate@vms.cis.pitt.edu

LAPOSA, JOSEPH DAVID, PHYSICAL CHEMISTRY. **Personal Data:** b St Louis, Mo, July 21, 1938; m 1968, Karen; c Rebecca, Jessica & Judith. **Education:** St Louis Univ, BS, 1960; Univ Chicago, MS, 1962; Loyola Univ, Ill, PhD (chem), 1965. **Professional Experience:** PROF EMER CHEM, MCMASTER UNIV, as of 2006; prof chem, Mcmaster Univ, 1986-; from asst prof to assoc prof, Mcmaster Univ, 1967-1986; NIH fel chem, Cornell Univ, 1965-1967. **Research Statement & Publications:** Molecular luminescence. **Mailing Address:** Dept Chem, McMaster Univ, 1280 Main St W, Hamilton, ON L8S 4M1, Can. **Fax:** 905-522-2509. **E-Mail:** laposaj@mcmaster.ca

LAPOSATA, MICHAEL, EXPERIMENTAL BIOLOGY. **Personal Data:** b Johnstown, Pa, April 22, 1952. **Education:** Am Bd Path, dipl, 1989; Bucknell Univ, BS, 1974; Johns Hopkins Univ, MD, 1981, PhD (cellular & molecular biol), 1982. **Professional Experience:**

PROF PATH, HARVARD MED SCH, 1999-; DIR CLIN LABS, MASS GEN HOSP, 1989-; chief, Div Clin Labs, Mass Gen Hosp, beginning 1989; assoc physician lab med, Dept Med, Mass Gen Hosp, beginning 1989; assoc pathologist, Dept Path, Mass Gen Hosp, beginning 1989; assoc prof path, Harvard Med Sch, 1989-1999; Sheryl N Hirsch Award, Lupus Found, 1987-1988; co-dir, Hemostasis Lab, Hosp Univ Pa, 1986-1989; asst prof path & lab med, Med Sch Univ Pa, 1985-1989; asst dir, Hemostasis Lab, Hosp Univ Pa, 1985-1986; chief resident, Div Lab Med, Depts Path & Med, 1984-1985; resident, Div Lab Med, Depts Path & Med, 1983-1984; postdoctoral res fel, Div Hemat-Oncol, Dept Med, Sch Med Wash Univ, MO, 1981-1982. **Memberships:** Am Asn Clin Res; Am Asn Pathologists; Acad Clin Lab Physicians & Scientists; Am Heart Asn; NY Acad Sci; Am Soc Clin Pathologists. **Research Statement & Publications:** Cellular and molecular biology; pathology; hematology, coagulation and blood transfusion. **Mailing Address:** Harvard Med Sch, Mass Gen Hosp, Rm 235 Gray Bldg, Boston, MA 02114. **Fax:** 617-726-3256. **E-Mail:** mlaposata@partners.org

LAPOSTOLLE, PIERRE MARCEL, DYNAMICS OF PARTICLES IN ELECTROMAGNETIC FIELDS, SPACE CHARGE PHENOMENA. **Personal Data:** b Vanves, France, May 29, 1922; m 1947, Descolas; c Bertrand, Xavier, Emmanuel, Anne & Benedicte. **Education:** Paris Univ, PhD (traveling wave tube theory), 1947. **Professional Experience:** CONSULT, 1985-; consult, Europ Orgn Nuclear Res & Los Alamos Nat Lab, 1985-; sci adv, Ganil Caen, France, 1978-1985; sci dir, Nat Ctr Telecommun, Paris, 1972-1978; physicist, Europ Orgn Nuclear Res, Geneva, 1954-1971; engr, Nat Ctr Telecommun, Paris, 1945-1954. **Memberships:** Fel Inst Elec & Electronics Engrs; Soc France Physique. **Research Statement & Publications:** Theory of the interaction between an electromagnetic wave and a beam of particles; amplification in a traveling wave tube; acceleration of particles in a linear accelerator. **Mailing Address:** 3 Rue Victor Daix, Neuilly Sur Seine 92200, France.

LAPOTA, DAVID, BIOLOGICAL OCEANOGRAPHY, ENVIRONMENTAL TOXICOLOGY. **Personal Data:** b June 1, 1949; m 1975, Jeannette Harward. **Education:** San Diego State Univ, BS, 1973, MA, 1982; Univ Calif, Santa Barbara, PhD, 1997. **Professional Experience:** PROJ DIR, ENVIRON QUALITY BR, SPAWAR SYSTS CTR, as of 2004; SR SCIENTIST (DP-III), NAVAL COMMAND, CONTROL & OCEANSURVEILLANCE CTR, 1982-; biol lab technician, Naval Command, Control & Ocean Surveillance Ctr, 1980-1982; biologist, Naval Command, Control & Ocean Surveillance Ctr, 1979-1980; data analyst, San Diego State Univ Found, 1974-1979; comt Biol Effects, Am Soc Testing & Mat. **Memberships:** Am Geophys Union; Oceanog Soc; fel Explorer's Club; AAAS. **Research Statement & Publications:** Bioluminescence projects involved with at sea expeditions; biological tests for environmental risk assessment; author of approximately 30 publications and granted 4 patents. **Mailing Address:** Environ Quality Br, Spawar Systs Ctr, 53475 Strothe Rd, San Diego, CA 92152-6310. **Fax:** 619-553-6305. **E-Mail:** david.lapota@navy.mil

LAPP, H(ERBERT) M(ELBOURNE), AGRICULTURAL ENGINEERING. **Personal Data:** b Alameda, Sask, February 2, 1922; m 1950, c 3. **Education:** Univ Sask, BE, 1949; Univ Minn, MS, 1962. **Professional Experience:** RETIRED; emer prof agr eng, Univ Man, beginning 1989; Int Develop Res Ctr, India, 1983; Lavalin-Crippen Int, Honduras, 1983; US Agency Int Develop, Peru, 1982; US Agency Int Develop, Can Int Develop Agency, 1982; Int Bank Reconstruct & Develop, Brazil Agr ResDept, 1981; Int Bank Reconstruct & Develop, Pakistan, 1977; Int Bank Reconstruct & Develop, Philippines, 1976; consult engr, Vancouver, Honduras, 1974; consult, Can Int Develop Agency, Nigeria, 1973, 1976; local prog head develop grad studies agr eng, Latin Am region, Nat Agrarian Univ, Peru, 1967-1970; plan adv, Colombo Khon Kaen Univ, Thailand, 1965-1967; head dept, Univ Man, 1958-1967; from asst prof to prof, Univ Man, 1953-1989; exten engr, Man Dept Agr, 1951-1953; water develop, Prairie Farm Rehab Admin, Dom Govt Can, 1949-1951. **Memberships:** Fel Can Soc Agr Eng (pres, 1975-1976); Am Soc Agr Engrs; Agr Inst Can. **Research Statement & Publications:** Farm structure; soil and water. **Mailing Address:** 592 Borebank St, Winnipeg, MB R3N 1E9, Can.

LAPP, M(ARSHALL), LASER GAS DIAGNOSTICS, LIGHT SCATTERING. **Personal Data:** b Buffalo, NY, August 20, 1932; m 1980, c 2. **Education:** Cornell Univ, BEngPhys, 1955; Calif Inst Technol, PhD (eng sci), 1960. **Professional Experience:** Actg mgr, Combustion Inst, 1981-; Sci Res Coun sr visfel, Sch Physics, Univ Newcastle, 1968-1969; physicist, Corp Res & Develop, Gen Elec Co, 1960-1980; SANDIA NAT LAB. **Memberships:** AAAS; fel Am Phys Soc; fel Optical Soc Am; Am Inst Aeronaut & Astronaut; fel Brit Inst Physics. **Research Statement & Publications:** Optical diagnostics of flames; laser Raman spectroscopy; radiative properties of metal vapors and gases; optical diagnostics of gases and surfaces; atomic and molecular physics; physics of fluids. **Mailing Address:** PO Box 3500, Walnut Creek, CA 94598-0500.

LAPP, MARTIN STANLEY, CONIFER BIOTECHNOLOGY. **Personal Data:** b Toronto, Ont. **Education:** York Univ, BSc, 1969, MSc, 1972; Univ Alta, PhD (plant path), 1977. **Professional Experience:** RETIRED; res officer numerical taxon, Nat Res Coun Can, 1980-1996; Resassoc, Nat Res Coun Can, 1977-1980. **Memberships:** Can Phytopath Soc. **Research Statement & Publications:** Micropropagation of conifers; genetic engineering. **Mailing Address:** 763 Wilkinson Way, Saskatoon, SK S7N 3L8, Can.

LAPP, N LEROY, MEDICINE, PULMONARY DISEASES. **Personal Data:** b May 16, 1932; m 1956, Catherine; c Thomas & Anne. **Education:** Eastern Mennonite Col, BS, 1956; Temple Univ, MD, 1961. **Professional Experience:** EMER PROF, SCH MED, WVA UNIV, MORGANTOWN, 1996-; chmn, Dept Med, Pulmonary Dis Sect, 1978-1988; asst dean, WVa Univ, 1975-1977; from instr to prof, WVa Univ, 1966-1996. **Memberships:** Fel Am Col Physicians; fel Am Col Chest Physicians; Cent Soc Clin Res; Am Thorac Soc; Am Physiol Soc; Brit Thorac Soc. **Research Statement & Publications:** Studies on subjects occupationally exposed to a variety of inorganic mineral dusts; investigating mechanisms of lung fibrosis and the cytokines which are involved in this process. **Mailing Address:** Dept Med, Health Sci Ctr Univ WVa PO Box 9166, Morgantown, WV 26506.

LAPP, NEIL ARDEN, PLANT PATHOLOGY, NEMATOLOGY. **Personal Data:** b Bloomington, Ill, December 7, 1942; m 1967, c 2. **Education:** Goshen Col, BA, 1964; WVa Univ, MS, 1967; NC State Univ, PhD (plant path), 1970. **Professional Experience:** FIELD DEVELOP FEL, MERCK & CO, 1981-; adj assoc prof, NC State Univ, 1977-; plant pathologist, Plant Protection Div, NC Dept Agr, 1971-1981; adj asst prof plant path, NC State Univ, 1971-1977. **Memberships:** Am Phytopath Soc; Soc Nematologists. **Research Statement & Publications:** Plant disease and nematode survey and detection; chemical control. **Mailing Address:** 7208 Madiera Ct, Raleigh, NC 27615.

LAPP, P(HILIP) A(LEXANDER), GEOMATICS, SPACE TECHNOLOGY. **Personal Data:** b Toronto, Ont, May 12, 1928; m 2001, Colleen; c David, Douglas & Aimee. **Education:** Univ Toronto, BASc, 1950; Mass Inst Technol, SM, 1951, ScD(Instrumentation), 1954. **Honorary Degrees:** LLD, McMaster Univ, 1987; DSc York Univ, 1994. **Honors & Awards:** Officer of the Order of Canada, 1995 Fellow, Royal Society of Canada, 1982 Centennial Medal, 1967 Honorary Member, Engineering Institute of Canada, 1973 Fellow, Canadian Aeronautics abd Space Institute, 1965 Fellow, Canadian Academy of Engineering, 1987 Companion of the Order of Honour, (PEO), 1984 Engineering Alumni Medal, (univ of Toronto), 1984 Fellow of Ryerson University, 1987 C D Howe Award (CASI), 1987 Beach (Toronto) Roll of Honour, 1989 Meritorious Service Award, Canadian Council of Professional Engineers, 1992 Gold Medal, Association of Professional Engineers of Ontario, 1992 Queen's Golden Jubilee Medal, 2002. **Professional Experience:** Consultant, Chmn, GEOIDE board of directors, as of 2006; Fel, Ryerson Polytech Inst, 1985; mem, Bd Govs, York Univ, 1980-; mem, CanAccreditation Bd, 1971-1975; Chmn working group sensors, Can Ctr Remote Sensing, 1970-1976; PRES, PHILIP A LAPP LTD, 1969-1998; sr vpres, Spar Aerospace Prod Ltd, 1968-1969; dir tech opers, Spec Prod & Appl Res Div, 1965-1968; chief engr, Spec Prod & ApplRes Div, 1960-1965; proj engr, Guided Missile Div, 1955-1960; systs eng, Del Havilland AircraftCan Ltd, 1954-1956; res assoc, Mass Inst Technol, 1953-1954; Instr aeronaut eng, Mass InstTechnol, 1952-1953. **Memberships:** Am Inst Aeronaut & Astronaut; Inst Elec & Electronics Engrs, Senior Member; Canadian Aeronautics and Space Inst, Fellow; American Inst. of Aeronautics and Astronautics, Senior member; Canadian Remote Sensing Society. **Research Statement & Publications:** Dynamics of vehicles; guidance and control of missiles and aircraft; military and industrial instrumentation and automatic control; educational planning and research on public policy; remote sensing applied to resource management and environmental monitoring. **Mailing Address:** 128 Elgin St, Thornhill, ON L3T 1W6, Can. **Fax:** 905-731-8279. **E-Mail:** phil.lapp@rogers.com

LAPP, THOMAS WILLIAM, ENVIRONMENTAL CHEMISTRY, RISK ASSESSMENT. **Personal Data:** b Joliet, Ill, October 6, 1937; m 1961. **Education:** Coe Col, BA, 1959; Kans State Univ, MS, 1961, PhD (inorg chem), 1963. **Professional Experience:** PRIN ENVIRON SCIENTIST, MIDWEST RES INST, 1987-; sr chemist, Midwest Res Inst, 1977-1987; assoc chemist, Midwest Res Inst, 1974-1977; mem staff, Univ Mo, Kansas City, 1970-1974; assoc chemist, Midwest Res Inst, Mo, 1966-1969; asst prof nuclearchem, Univ WVa, 1964-1966; Fel radiation chem, NAm Aviation Sci Ctr, 1963-1964. **Research Statement & Publications:** Production and utilization of industrial chemicals suspected of possessing toxic properties; environmental transport and fate; risk assessment; hazardous waste incineration studies. **Mailing Address:** Midwest Res Inst, 510 Se Southwood Trl, Stuart, FL 34997.

LAPP, WAYNE STANLEY, TRANSPLANTATION BIOLOGY. **Personal Data:** b Stevensville, Ont, November 11, 1936; m 1964, c 4. **Education:** UnivToronto, BSA, 1962, MSA, 1964; McGill Univ, Montreal, PhD (transplantationphysiol), 1967. **Professional Experience:** RETIRED; prof physiol & immunol, Dept Physiol, Mcgill Univ, 1982-2005; assoc mem, Dept Med, McGill Univ, Montreal, 1980-; guest prof immunol, Ger CancerRec Ctr, Heidelberg, 1977-1978; from asst prof to assoc prof, Dept Physiol, McGill Univ, 1968-1982; fel transplantation immunol, Karolinska Inst, Stockholm, 1967-1968; counr, Can Soc Immunol. **Memberships:** Can Physiol Soc; Can Soc Immunol; Am Asn Immunol; Transplantation Soc; NYAcad Sci. **Research Statement & Publications:** Graft-versus-host induced immunosuppression of T and B lymphocyte functions; effect of the GVH reaction on T and B cell ontogency and thymus function. **Mailing Address:** Dept Physiol Ctr Clin Immunobiol & Transplant, McGill Univ McIntyre Med Sci Bldg 3655 Drummond St, Montreal, PQ H3G 1Y6, Can. **E-Mail:** wayne.lapp@mcgill.ca

LAPPAS, LEWIS CHRISTOPHER, PHARMACEUTICAL CHEMISTRY. **Personal Data:** b Lynn, Mass, May 14, 1921; m 1949, Arlene Rockwood; c John, Robert & Janet. **Education:** Mass Col Pharm, BS, 1943, MS, 1948; Purdue Univ, PhD (pharmaceut chem), 1951. **Professional Experience:** CONSULT, 1984-; Res scientist, Eli Lilly & Co, 1951-1984. **Research Statement & Publications:** Drug encapsulation processes; basic gelatin research as applied to capsular forms; study of filmogens as drug release mechanisms; stabilization of drugs and drug forms; pharmaceutical aspects of drug absorption; investigation of new antimicrobials in drug and cosmetic formulations. **Mailing Address:** 12240 Brompton Rd, Carmel, IN 46033.

LAPPE, RODNEY WILSON, CARDIOVASCULAR. **Personal Data:** b Breese, Ill, September 12, 1954; c 2. **Education:** Blackburn Col, BA, 1976; Ind Univ, PhD (pharmacol), 1980. **Professional Experience:** DIR CARDIOVASC RES, CIBA-GEIGY PHARMACEUT DIV, 1990-; res fel, Hypertension Sect, Rorer Cent Res, 1988-1990; mem, Animal Use Comt, Wyeth-Ayerst Res, 1988; mgr, Vascular Dis Sect, Wyeth-Ayerst Res, 1987-1988; chmn, Cardiovasc Subcomt, 1987 & 1988; mgr, Hypertension Sect, Wyeth Labs, Inc, 1985-1987; res scientist, Hypertension Sect, Wyeth Labs, Inc, 1982-1985; Res fel, Iowa Cardiovasc Ctr Inst, 1982; Postdoctoral pharmacol, Univ Iowa, 1980-1982. **Memberships:** Am Soc Hypertension; Am Soc Pharmacol & Exp Therapeut; Inter-Am Soc Chemother; Coun High Blood Pressure. **Research Statement & Publications:** Cardiovascular system. **Mailing Address:** Cardiovasc Res, Ciba-Geigy 556 Morris Ave, Summit, NJ 07901-1398.

LAPPIN, ALEXANDER GRAHAM, INORGANIC CHEMISTRY. **Education:** Univ Glasgow, BSc, 1972, PhD, 1975. **Professional Experience:** PROF & CHMN, DEPT CHEM & BIOCHEM, UNIV NOTRE DAME, as of 2006; lectr, Univ Glasgow, ending 1982; fel Univ Leeds, 1977-1978. **Research Statement & Publications:** Mechanistic inorganic chemistry; substitution reactions and redox processes of transition metal ion complexes and range from reactions of metalloproteins in biological systems to the corrosion chemistry associated with chemical reactors. **Mailing Address:** Dept Chem & Biochem, Univ Notre Dame, 234 Nieuwland Hall, Notre Dame, IN 46556-5670. **Fax:** 574-631-6652. **E-Mail:** Alexander.G.Lappin.1@nd.edu

LAPPIN, GERALD R, CHEMISTRY. **Personal Data:** b Caro, Mich, April 14, 1919; m 1945, c 2. **Education:** Alma Col, BS, 1941; Northwestern Univ, PhD (org chem), 1946. **Professional Experience:** RETIRED; res assoc, Tenn Eastman Co Div, Eastman Kodak Co, 1969-1983; sr res chemist, Tenn Eastman Co Div, Eastman Kodak Co, 1951-1969; asst prof, Antioch Col, 1946-1949 & Univ Ariz, 1949-1951; Consult, Vernay Labs, Ohio, 1946-1949; asst, NorthwesternUniv, 1944-1946; interim instr chem, Northwestern Univ, 1944; Asst, Northwestern Univ, 1941-1943. **Memberships:** Am Chem Soc. **Research Statement & Publications:** Additives for foods; plastics and petroleum products; chemistry of polyesters; technology forecasting as applied to research and development planning. **Mailing Address:** 4047 Skyland Dr, Kingsport, TN 37664.

LAPPORTE, SEYMOUR JEROME, ORGANIC & PETROLEUM CHEMISTRY, MATERIALS CHEMISTRY. **Personal Data:** b Chicago, Ill, March 26, 1930; m 1964, Anne; c Daniel & Michael. **Education:** Univ Chicago, MS, 1953; Univ Calif, Los Angeles, PhD (chem), 1957. **Professional Experience:** PROG DIR, NSF, 1991-; prog officer, NSF, 1987-1990; sr res scientist, Pioneering Div, 1980-1986; mgr, Pioneering Div, 1974-1986; vis scholar, Stanford Univ, 1968-1969; teacher, Exten, Univ Calif, 1960-; sr res assoc, Chevron Res Co, 1956-1974; asst, Univ Calif, Los Angeles, 1953-1956. **Memberships:** Am Chem Soc; Royal Soc Chem; Mat Res Soc. **Research Statement & Publications:**

Organic reaction mechanisms; organometallics; oxidation; transition metal chemistry; homogenous catalysis; ultraviolet stabilization; polymers; solid state chemistry; materials chemistry. **Mailing Address:** NSF, 4201 Wilson Blvd Rm 1059, Arlington, VA 22230. **Fax:** 510-376-8333. **E-Mail:** slapporte@note.nsf.gov

LAPRADE, MARY HODGE, ZOOLOGY. **Personal Data:** b Oakland, Calif, February 6, 1929; m 1958, c 2. **Education:** Wilson Col, AB, 1951; Radcliffe Col, AM, 1952, PhD (biol), 1958. **Professional Experience:** Dir, Clark Sci Ctr, 1973-1990; LECTR BIOL SCI, SMITH COL, 1965-; Instr, NSF Serv Inst High Sch Biol Teachers, 1965-1966; instr zool, Smith Col, 1958-1960 &1964-1965; Instr biol, Simmons Col, 1952-1955. **Memberships:** Sigma Xi. **Research Statement & Publications:** Growth and regeneration, particularly in crustaceans; fine structure of endocrine organs in crustaceans. **Mailing Address:** Dept Biol Sci, Smith Col, Northampton, MA 01063-0048.

LAPUCK, JACK LESTER, FOOD CHEMISTRY, BACTERIOLOGY. **Personal Data:** b Jamaica Plain, Mass, August 28, m Ruth; c Robert, Susan & Debra. **Education:** Northeastern Univ, BS, 1946; Univ Mass, MS, 1949; Calvin Coolidge Col, DSc, 1960. **Professional Experience:** Owner & mgr, Lapuck Labs, 1966-1993; instr, Univ Exten, Mass Dept Educ, 1955-1971; lab dir & vpres, Waltham Labs, Inc, 1955-1966; chemist, Waltham Labs, Inc, 1951-1955; food chemist, Food & Drug Res Labs, NY, 1951; food sanitarian, Montgomery Co Health Dept, Md, 1950-1951; past pres, Analytical Group NE Sect. **Memberships:** Am Chem Soc; Am Soc Microbiol; Inst Food Technologists; Nat Environ Health Asn Past chair-ne sec analyticals group Als past chairman ne assoc of testing Labs.ma health officers. **Research Statement & Publications:** Food technology; microbiology; analytical chemistry; environmental analyses; public health. **Mailing Address:** pobox590311, newton, MA 02459. **E-Mail:** healthman@rcn.com

LAQUATRA, IDAMARIE, NUTRITION. **Education:** Pa State Univ, BS, 1975, MS, 1979, PhD (appl nutrit), 1983. **Professional Experience:** TECH CONSULT, SHAPE UP AM, as of 2002; mgr nutrit Serv, Weight Watchers Div, Heinz Usa, Pittsburgh, Pa, beginning 1990; adv group, Plan V Dietetics Prog, Pa State Univ, 1988- & Coun Res, Am Dietetic Asn, 1989-; mem, Col Bd Adv, Col Home Econ, Ohio State Univ, 1986-1989; nutritionist, Heinz USA, 1984-1989; consult, Clin Nutrit Staff, Vet Admin Med Ctr, Bronx, NY, 1983-1984; adj fac, Home Econ Dept, Montclair State Col, NJ, 1983-1984; postdoctoral fel, Prev Cardiol Prog, Univ Med & Dent NJ, 1982-1984; pvt nutrit consult, State Col, Pa, 1980-1982; instr & consult, Pa State Univ, Univ Park, 1978-1982; lab asst, Pa State Univ, 1978 & 1979; grad asst, Pa State Univ, 1977-1981; clin dietitian, Custom Mgt Corp, 1976-1977. **Memberships:** Am Dietic Asn; Inst Food Technologists. **Mailing Address:** Shape Up Am, 15009 Native Dancer Rd, N Potomac, MD 20878. **Fax:** 240-632-1075.

LAQUER, HENRY L, CRYOGENICS, SUPERCONDUCTIVITY. **Personal Data:** b Frankfurt-am-Main, Ger, November 28, 1919; American citizen; m 1947, Justine; c Frederic C, Emily K, Lydia J & H Turner. **Education:** Temple Univ, AB, 1943; Princeton Univ, MA, 1945, PhD (phys chem), 1947. **Professional Experience:** RETIRED; prin, Cryopower Assocs, 1984-1998; consult, 1977-1983; adj prof, Los Alamos Residence Ctr, Univ NMex, 1970-1973; mem staff, Los Alamos Sci Lab, Univ Calif, 1947-1977; res chemist, Ladox Labs, Pa, 1946. **Memberships:** Am Phys Soc. **Research Statement & Publications:** High magnetic fields; applied superconductivity; dielectric studies; elastic properties of metals; cryogenics; high temperature superconductivity materials and applications. **Mailing Address:** Rte 5 Box 445, Espanola, NM 87532-8906. **E-Mail:** laquerhl@cybermesa.com

LARABELL, CAROLYN A, DEVELOPMENTAL BIOLOGY. **Personal Data:** b Detroit, Mich, December 16, 1947. **Education:** Mich State Univ, BA, 1970; Ariz State Univ, BS, 1981, PhD (zoology), 1988. **Professional Experience:** DIR, NAT CTR X-RAY TOMOGRAPHY, LAWRENCE BERKELEY NAT LAB, as of 2005; MGR, WEST COAST FACIL INTERMEDIATE VOLTAGE ELECTRON MICROS, LAWRENCE BERKELEY LAB, UNIV CALIF, BERKELEY, as of 2002; NIH reprod biol training grant, Univ Calif, Davis, 1989; scholar, Dept Biochem & Biophys & Dept Zool, Davis, 1988-1990; res assoc, Dept Zoology, Ariz State Univ, 1983-1988; teaching asst, Dept Zoology, Ariz State Univ, 1983; supvr, Dept Neurophysiol, Good Samaritan Hosp, Phoenix, 1971-1975. **Memberships:** Am Soc Cell Biol; Soc Develop Biol; AAAS; Micros Soc Am. **Research Statement & Publications:** Egg cytoskeleton and its modification during fertilization and development; signal transduction at fertilization. **Mailing Address:** Lawrence Berkeley Lab Univ Calif, 160A Donner Lab, Berkeley, CA 94143-0452. **Fax:** 510-486-6488. **E-Mail:** larabell@lbl.gov

LARA-BRAUD, CAROLYN WEATHERSBEE, BIOCHEMISTRY. **Personal Data:** b Waco, Tex, January 4, 1940; m 1970. **Education:** Univ Tex, Austin, BA, 1962, PhD (chem), 1969. **Professional Experience:** ASSOC PROF EMER, UNIV IOWA, as of 2005; assoc prof, Univ Iowa, beginning 1995; DIR PHYS EDUC SKILLS, UNIV IOWA, 1995-; asst prof to assoc prof, home econ, Univ Iowa, 1975-1992; asst res scientist biochem, Univ Iowa, 1973-1975; res assoc biochem, Clayton Found Biochem Inst & lectr home econ, Nutrit Div, Univ Tex, Austin, 1971-1973. **Memberships:** AAAS; Am Chem Soc; Sigma Xi Inst Food Technol; Am Home Econ Asn. **Research Statement & Publications:** Intermediary metabolism; regulation of inducible enzyme systems. **Mailing Address:** 810 W Benton 313-B, Iowa City, IA 52246-5924. **Fax:** 319-335-6669. **E-Mail:** carolyn-lara-braud@uiowa.edu

LARAGH, JOHN HENRY, PHYSIOLOGY, MEDICINE. **Personal Data:** b Yonkers, NY, November 18, 1924; m 1974, c 3. **Education:** Cornell Univ, MD, 1948. **Honors & Awards:** Stouffer Prize Med Res, 1969. **Professional Experience:** HILDA ALTSCHUL MASTER PROF MED, MED COL, CORNELL UNIV, as of 2002; DIR CARDIOVASC CTR, NY HOSP-CORNELL MED CTR, 1975-; mem bd sci coun, Hypertension Detection & Follow-Up Prog, Nat Heart & Lung inst, 1974-; vchmn chg medaffairs, Bd Trustees, 1974; mem adv bd, Am Soc Contemp Med & Surg, 1974; mem policy advbd, Hypertension Detection & Follow-Up Prog, Nat Heart & Lung Inst, 1971-; dir, HypertensionCtr & Nephrol div, Columbia-Presby Med Ctr, 1971-1975; attend physician, Presby Hosp, NY, 1969-1975; chmn, Coun High Blood Pressure res, Am Heart Asn, 1968-1972; from asst prof to-prof clin med, Col Physicians & Surgeons, Columbia Univ, 1967-1975; consult cardiovasc studysect, USPHS, 1964-1968 & heart prog proj A, 1967-1972; mem med adv bd, Coun High BloodPressure res, Am Heart Asn, 1961; assoc, Presby Hosp, New York, 1957-1959; instr, PresbyHosp, New York, 1955-1957; from asst attend physician to assoc attend physician, Presby Hosp, NY, 1954-1969; NY Heart Asn res fel, 1951-1952; asst, Presby Hosp, New York, 1950-1955; asst physician, Presby Hosp, NY, 1950-1954; Nat Heart inst trainee, 1950-1951; asst resident, Presby Hosp, New York, 1949-1950; intern med, Presby Hosp, New York, 1948-1949. **Memberships:** Am Soc Clin Invest; fel Am Col Physicians; Am Soc Nephrol; assoc Harvey Soc; Asn Am Physicians. **Research Statement & Publications:** Cardiovascular and renal diseases; endocrinology. **Mailing Address:** NY Hosp, Cornell Med Col, 525 E 68th St Starr H, New York, NY 10021-4873.

LARAMORE, GEORGE ERNEST, PHYSICS, MEDICINE. **Personal Data:** b Ottawa, Ill, November 5, 1943; m 1987, Shelley; c Parker & Patricia. **Education:** Purdue Univ, BS, 1965; Univ Ill, Urbana, MS, 1966, PhD (physics), 1969; Univ Miami, MD, 1976. **Honors & Awards:** Fellow, Am College Radiology 2003. **Professional Experience:** CHMN, Dept. Radiation Oncol., 1999-; VICE CHMN, DEPT RADIATION ONCOL, 1995-1999; PROF, DEPT RADIATION ONCOL, UNIV WASH, 1985-; from asst prof to prof, Dept Radiation Oncol, 1978-1985; res physicist, Sandia Labs, 1971-1975; res assoc physics, Univ Ill, Urbana, 1970-1971; NSF fel, Univ Ill, Urbana, 1969-1970. **Memberships:** Am Phys Soc; Am Vacuum Soc; AMA; Am Radium Soc; Am Soc Therapeut Radiol & Oncol; Am College Radiology. **Research Statement & Publications:** Theory of low-energy electron diffraction; fast neutron radiotherapy for human malignancies; interaction of fast electrons with solids; boron neutron capture therapy; radiation oncology. **Mailing Address:** Dept Radiation Oncol, Med Ctr, Univ Wash, 1959 NE Pac St, PO Box 356043, Seattle, WA 98195-6043. **Fax:** 206-598-3498. **E-Mail:** georgel@u.washington.edu

LARBALESTIER, DAVID C, SUPERCONDUCTIVITY. **Personal Data:** b Somerset, UK, May 22, 1943. **Education:** Imp Col, BS, 1965; Univ London, PhD (metal), 1970. **Honors & Awards:** IR-100 Award, Indust Res, 1979; Particle Accelerator Technol Award, Inst Elec & Electronics Engrs, 1991. **Professional Experience:** GRAINGER PROF SUPERCONDUCTIVITY, APPL SUPERCONDUCTIVITY CTR, UNIV WIS, MADISON, 1996-; vis prof, Univ Rennes, France, 1992; L V SHUBNIKOV PROF MAT SCI ENG, UNIV WIS, MADISON, 1991-; chair, Univ Wis, 1989-; vis scientist, Brookhaven Nat Lab, 1978; from asst prof to prof, Appl Superconductivity Ctr, Univ Wis, 1976-1981; sr sci officer, Rutherford Lab, UK, 1973-1976; scientist, Batelle Res Lab, Switz, 1970-1972. **Memberships:** Fel Am Phys Soc; Mat Res Soc. **Research Statement & Publications:** Critical current density of high field superconducting materials; developed conductors at the state of the art made from both low and high temperature superconductors. **Mailing Address:** Dept Mat Sci Eng, Univ Wis-Madison, 915 Eng Res Bldg 1500 Eng Dr, Madison, WI 53706. **Fax:** 608-263-1087. **E-Mail:** larbales@engr.wisc.edu

L'ARCHEVEQUE, REAL VIATEUR, NUCLEAR ENGINEERING & ELECTRONICS, RESEARCH & DEVELOPMENT. **Personal Data:** b Montreal, Que. **Education:** Polytech Inst, Montreal, BSc, 1960; Univ London, PhD (electronics), 1964. **Professional Experience:** SR EXEC ADV, CAN SPACE AGENCY, 1992-; sr vpres, Res & Technol, SNC Inc, 1983-1992; pres, Canatom, 1980-1983; asst to pres, Canatom, 1977-1980; Head, Electronics Br, Atomic Energy Can Ltd, 1965-1977. **Memberships:** Can Acad Eng. **Research Statement & Publications:** Hybrid microelectronics; thick film microcircuits; nuclear instruments development and design; on-line computer data acquisition systems development; geographic information systems; environmental depollution systems. **Mailing Address:** Can Space Agency, 6767 Rte De L'Aeroport, St Hubert, PQ J3Y 8Y9, Can.

LARCOM, LYNDON LYLE, PHOTOBIOLOGY, CARCINOGENESIS. **Personal Data:** b Olean, NY, April 11, 1940; m 1998, Diane; c 2. **Education:** Carnegie-Mellon Univ, BS, 1962; Univ Pittsburgh, MS, 1965, PhD (biophysics), 1968. **Professional Experience:** PROF PHYSICS & ASTRON, CLEMSON UNIV, 1981-; CONSULT, 1972-; From assst to assoc prof physics & microbiol, Clemson Univ, 1972-1981; res assoc, Univ Pittsburgh, 1970-1972; NIH fel chem, UnivPittsburgh, 1968-1970. **Memberships:** Am Soc Photobiol; Am Soc Microbiol; Sigma Xi; Am Asn Advan Sci. **Research Statement & Publications:** Mechanisms of DNA damage and repair; the biophysical properties of nucleic acids; molecular quantum mechanics; DNA-protein interactions; mechanisms of carcinogenesis; dietary cancer prevention. **Mailing Address:** Dept Physics & Astron, Clemson Univ, Clemson, SC 29634-0978. **Fax:** 864-656-0805. **E-Mail:** lllrcm@clemson.edu

LARD, EDWIN WEBSTER, ANALYTICAL CHEMISTRY. **Personal Data:** b Ala, July 17, 1921; m 1945, c 4. **Education:** Ark State Col, BS, 1949; Memphis State Univ, MA, 1961. **Professional Experience:** RETIRED; chem engr, Naval Sea Systs Command, Wash, DC, 1974-1984; res supvr, Res Div, Clarksville, Md, 1962-1974; sr chemist, Nitrogen Prod Div, W R Grace & Co, Tenn, 1954-1962; chemist, Chemstrand Corp, 1952-1954; chemist, Ethyl Corp, 1949-1952. **Memberships:** Am Chem Soc. **Research Statement & Publications:** Trace gas analysis with infrared; separation anddetermination of argo, oxygen and nitrogen by chromatography; trace analysis of acetylene, methane, carbon monoxide and carbon dioxide; synthesis of aryl dimethyl sulfonium chloride compounds; chemical warfare agents; unsaturates in auto emissions; water energy conservation on naval ships; issued 23 patents and author of 17 publications. **Mailing Address:** 12703 Beaverdale Lane, Bowie, MD 20715.

LARDNER, JAMES F, COMPUTER DESIGN, SCIENCE ADMINISTRATION. **Personal Data:** b Davenport, Iowa, May 24, 1924. **Education:** Cornell Univ, BME, 1945. **Professional Experience:** RETIRED; dir, Sears Mfg Co, beginning 1995; chmn, Mfg Studies Bd, 1990-; Comt DefenseMfg Strategy, Panel Pvt Contractors, 1990-; mem, Foundations Mfg Comt, 1989-; dir, Potash Corp, Sask, beginning 1989; mem, Comt Labor Mkt Adjustments, 1987; mem, Panel MfgEng, Bd Assessment Nat Inst Stand & Technol, 1986-1991; vpres, Component Group, 1985-1990; Mem, Cross-Disciplinary Eng Res Comt, 1985-1987; mem, Mfg Studies Bd, beginning 1984; dir, Am Stand, 1984-1990; mem, Comn Eng & Tech Systs, 1984-1986; Mem, Comt Indust/AcadCoop Mfg, 1984-1985; mem, Panel Eng Res Ctrs, Nat Acad Eng, 1984; Mem, Panel ComputDesign & Mfg, 1983; vpres, Govt Prod & Component Sales, 1982-1985; dir, Comput Aided MfgInt Inc, 1981-1984; vpres mfg develop, Corp Plant & Prod Eng Dept, 1980-1982; mem, ComtComput-Aided Mfg, Nat Res Coun, 1980-1981; corp dir mfg eng, Corp Plant & Prod Eng Dept, 1970-1980; mgr, Corp Plant & Prod Eng Dept, 1969-1970; asst gen mgr, Harvester Works, 1968-1969; asst gen mgr, Des Moines Works, 1967-1968; managing dir, John Deer Iberica SA, 1962-1967; mgr, Overseas Mfg Group, 1956-1962; eng & mfg mgr, Deere & Co, 1946-1956. **Memberships:** Nat Acad Eng; fel Soc Mgr Eng; fel Soc Mfg Engrs. **Mailing Address:** 2752 Nichols Lane, Davenport, IA 52803.

LARDNER, ROBIN WILLMOTT, APPLIED MATHEMATICS, COMPUTATIONAL MECHANICS & OCEANOGRAPHY. **Personal Data:** b Leicester, Eng, February 9, 1938; m 1979, Niki; c 4. **Education:** Cambridge Univ, BA, 1959, PhD (appl math), 1963, ScD, 1986. **Professional Experience:** PROF EMER MATH, SIMON FRASER UNIV, as of 2005; sr res scientist, KFUPM Res Inst, Dhahran, Saudi Arabia, 1995-1997 & 1991-1993; prof appl math, Univ Petrol & Minerals, Dhahran, Saudi Arabia, 1982-1987; chmn dept, Simon Fraser Univ, 1971-1973; prof, Simon Fraser Univ, 1970-1995; assoc prof, Simon Fraser Univ, 1967-1970; lectr math & physics, Univ EAnglia, 1965-1967; NATO fel appl math & theoret physics, Peterhouse Col, CambridgeUniv, 1963-1965; Res assoc physics, Columbia Univ, 1961-1963. **Research Statement & Publications:** Numerical solution of partial differential equations; numerical tidal modelling and modelling of other oceanographic flows; pollutant transport modelling; inverse problems in oceanography, data assimilation; nonlinear vibrations and waves in solids and fluids. **Mailing Address:** Dept Math & Statist, Simon Fraser Univ, TLX 10548 8888 Univ Dr, Burnaby, BC V5A 1S6, Can. **Fax:** 604-291-4947. **E-Mail:** rwl@cs.sfu.ca

LARDNER, THOMAS JOSEPH, ENGINEERING MECHANICS. **Personal Data:** b New York, NY, July 19, 1938; m 1964, Anne Jeanne; c Joseph, Theresa & Deborah. **Educa-**

tion: Polytech Inst Brooklyn, BAeroE, 1958, MS, 1959, PhD (appl mech), 1961. **Professional Experience:** PROF CIVIL ENG, UNIV MASS, 1978-; prof theoret & appl mech, Univ Ill, Urbana, 1973-1978; assoc prof mech eng, Mass Inst Technol, 1970-1973; asst prof appl math, Mass Inst Technol, 1967-1970; Fulbright lectr, Univ Nepal, 1965-1966; instr math, Mass Inst Technol, 1963-1967; res engr, Jet Propulsion Lab, Calif Inst Technol, 1962-1963; res assoc appl mech, Polytech Inst Brooklyn, 1959-1961. **Memberships:** Fel Am Soc Mech Engrs; Soc Indust & Appl Math. **Research Statement & Publications:** Applied mathematics and mechanics; applied solid mechanics. **Mailing Address:** Dept Civil & Environ Eng, Univ Mass, Amherst, MA 01003-5205. **Fax:** 413-577-4940. **E-Mail:** lardner@ecs.umass.edu

LARDY, HENRY ARNOLD, CELL BIOLOGY, ENDOCRINOLOGY. **Personal Data:** b Roslyn, SDak, August 19, 1917; m 1943, Annrita; c Nicholas, Diana, Jeffrey & Michael. **Education:** SDak State Univ, BS, 1939; Univ Wis, MS, 1941, PhD (biochem), 1943. **Honorary Degrees:** DSc, SDak State Univ, 1978. **Honors & Awards:** Lewis Award, Am Chem Soc, 1949; Neuberg Medal, 1956; Wolf Found Award Agr, 1981; Nat Award Agr Excellence, Agr Mkt Asn, 1982; Carl Hartman Award, Soc Study Reproduction, 1984; Amory Prize, Am Acad Arts & Sci, 1984; William Rose Award Biochem, Am Soc Biol Chemists, 1988. **Professional Experience:** PROF EMER BIOCHEM, UNIV WIS, MADISON, 1988-; vilas prof, UnivWis-Madison, 1966-1988; chmn, Res Dept, Enzyme Inst, 1950-1988; from asst prof to prof biolsci, Univ Wis-Madison, 1945-1950; fel, Nat Res Coun, Banting Inst, Univ Toronto, 1944-1945. **Memberships:** Nat Acad Sci; Am Philos Soc; Am Chem Soc; Am Soc Biol Chem (pres, 1964); Am Acad Arts & Sci; Soc Study Reproduction; hon mem Japanese Biochem Soc. **Research Statement & Publications:** Enzymes; intermediary metabolism; hormones; sperm storage for artificial insemination; induction of thermogenic enzymes by thyroid hormone and by specific steriods. **Mailing Address:** Dept Biochem, Univ Wis, 1710 Univ Ave, Madison, WI 53726-4087. **Fax:** 608-265-2904. **E-Mail:** halardy@facstaff.wisc.edu

LARDY, LAWRENCE JAMES, NUMERICAL ANALYSIS. **Personal Data:** b Sentinel Butte, NDak, August 23, 1934; m 1956, c 2. **Education:** NDak State Col, Dickinson, BS, 1957; Univ NDak, MS, 1959; Univ Minn, PhD (math), 1964. **Professional Experience:** Dept chmn, Syracuse Univ, 1982-1988; PROF MATH, SYRACUSE UNIV, 1975-; vis assoc prof, Univ Md, 1973-1974; res fel, Yale Univ, 1967-1968; from asst prof toassoc prof, Syracuse Univ, 1964-1974; Instr math, Univ NDak, 1959-1960 & Univ Minn, 1962-1964. **Memberships:** Soc Indust & Appl Math; Math Asn Am; Am Math Soc; Sigma Xi. **Research Statement & Publications:** Functional analysis. **Mailing Address:** Dept Math, Syracuse Univ, 213 A Carnegie, Syracuse, NY 13244-1200. **Fax:** 315-443-1475. **E-Mail:** jalindbe@syr.edu

LARDY, MATHIAS M, NUCLEAR & ANALYTICAL CHEMISTRY, HEALTH PHYSICS. **Personal Data:** b Sentinel Butte, NDak, May 24, 1932; m 1958, Deanna; c Steven, Renee, Cheryl & Robert. **Education:** Dickinson State Univ, BS, 1954; Ore State Univ, MS, 1958; Univ Mont, MS, 1962. **Professional Experience:** TECH DIR, QUANTERRA ENVIRON SERV, 1994-; tech dir, IT Corp, 1990-1994; asst vpres, US Testing Co, 1974-1990; lab dir radiobioassay & radiochem, Clin LabImprovement Act, 1968 & 1970; mgr, US Testing Co, 1967-1974; supvr radiochem anal, USTesting Co, 1966-1967; chemist radioanal, US Testing Co, 1965-1966; chemist radioanal, GenElec, 1962-1964; instr, Anaconda Sr High Sch, 1958-1960; instr, Culbertson High Sch, 1954-1957. **Memberships:** Am Chem Soc; Health Physics Soc; Am Soc Testing & Mat. **Research Statement & Publications:** Analysis of environmental and biological samples for radionuclides from tritium to curium; standards for quality assurance of radiochemical laboratories. **Mailing Address:** 1967 Pine St, Richland, WA 99352. **Fax:** 509-375-5590.

LAREW, H(IRAM) GORDON, CIVIL ENGINEERING, SOIL MECHANICS. **Personal Data:** b Independence, WVa, June 5, 1922; m 1946, Mary Jo Thompson; c Jane Jo, Hiram G III & Elizabeth T. **Education:** Univ WVa, BS, 1944; Purdue Univ, MS, 1951, PhD, 1960. **Professional Experience:** EMER PROF CIVIL ENG, UNIV VA, 1992-; from assoc prof to prof, Univ VA, 1956-1992; consult, prin, H.Gordon Larew, consult geotech eng, 1954-; instr civil eng, Purdue Univ, 1947-1956; Jr engr, NY Cent Syst, 1946. **Memberships:** Fel Am Soc Civil Engrs; Am Soc Eng Educ. **Research Statement & Publications:** Utilization of solid wastes; the effects of repeated loads upon soils; soil strength; earth dams; blast damage; building foundations. **Mailing Address:** 2500 Hillwood Pl, Charlottesville, VA 22901.

LARGE, RICHARD L, SOIL SCIENCE, AGRONOMY. **Personal Data:** b Rochester, Ind, June 9, 1940; m 1962, c 3. **Education:** Purdue Univ, BSc, 1962; Okla State Univ, MSc, 1966; Ohio State Univ, PhD (soil sci), 1969. **Professional Experience:** PRES, A&L ANAL LABS INC, as of 1999; vpres, A&L agr Labs inc, beginning 1971; STAFF MEM, A&L AGR LABS INC, 1971-; agronomist, US Testing Co, Inc, 1969-1971. **Memberships:** Soil Sci Soc; Am Soc Agron; Coun Agr Sci & Technol. **Research Statement & Publications:** Soil fertility; crop nutrition; land application of sludge. **Mailing Address:** A&L Anal Lab Inc, 2790 Whitten Rd, Memphis, TN 38133. **Fax:** 901-213-2440.

LARGENT, DAVID LEE, MYCOLOGY. **Personal Data:** b San Francisco, Calif, October 30, 1937; m 1970. **Education:** San Francisco State Col, BA, 1960, MA, 1963; Univ Wash, PhD (bot), 1968. **Professional Experience:** PROF EMER BIOL, HUMBOLDT STATE UNIV, 2001-; prof bot, Humboldt State Col, 1977-2001; assoc prof, Humboldt State Col, 1974-1977; asst prof bot, Humboldt State Col, 1968-1974; instr bot & biol, Phoenix Jr Col, 1963-1964; instr bot, Foothills Jr Col, 1963. **Memberships:** Am Soc Plant Taxon; Mycol Soc Am; Am Bryol & Lichenological Soc; Sigma Xi. **Research Statement & Publications:** Taxonomy and ecology of the Rhodophylloid fungi on the Pacific coastal states of America; cryptogamic botany. **Mailing Address:** Dept Biol, Humboldt State Univ, One Harpst St, Arcata, CA 95521-8299. **Fax:** 707-826-3201. **E-Mail:** dll2@axe.humboldt.edu

LARGENT, MAX DALE, DENTISTRY. **Personal Data:** b Winchester, Va, February 28, 1923; m 1954, c 2. **Education:** Med Col Va, DDS, 1950. **Professional Experience:** ASSOC DEAN EMER, AS OF 2006; prof & assoc dean, Baylor Col Dent, 1972-1990; chmn, Dept Pedodontics, Med Col Va, 1969-1972; dir postgrad pedodontics, Dept Pedodontics, Med Col Va, 1957-1969; from instr to prof pedodontics, Med Col Va, 1952-1972. **Memberships:** Am Dent Asn; Am Asn Dent Schs; fel Am Col Dent. **Mailing Address:** 9222 Loma Vista Dr, Dallas, TX 75243.

LARGIS, ELWOOD EUGENE, BROWN ADIPOSE TISSUE METABOLISM, HYPOGLYCEMIC DRUGS. **Education:** Univ NDak, PhD (biochem), 1970. **Professional Experience:** RES PHARMACOLOGIST, DEPT METAB DIS, LEDERLE LABS, 1973-. **Mailing Address:** Prin Sci Wyeth-Ayerst Res CN 8000 Rm 1806, Princeton, NJ 08543-8000.

LARGMAN, COREY, BIOCHEMISTRY. **Personal Data:** c 2. **Education:** Reed Col, BA, 1966; Mass Inst Technol, PhD (org chem), 1970. **Professional Experience:** DIR MOLECULAR HEMATOPOIESIS RES, UNIV CALIF, SAN FRANCISCO, as of 2004; PROF RESIDENCE, DEPT MED, UNIV CALIF, 1999-; RES SCIENTIST, NORTHERN CALIF INST RES & EDU, 1998-; CAREER SCIENTIST, VETERANS AFFAIRS RES SERV, VA MED CTR, 1992-; Merit rev bd, Vet Admin, Wash, DC, 1990-; RES PROF INTERNALMED & BIOL CHEM, SCH MED, UNIV CALIF, DAVIS, 1990-; Dept Nutrit Res Training Ctr, Univ Calif, Davis, 1990-; actg assoc chief staff res, Enzym Res Lab, Martinez Vet Med Ctr, Calif, 1989; res prog specialist basic sci, Vet Admin, Wash, DC, 1987-1990; assoc career scientist, Vet Admin, 1985-1991; assoc res prof, Vet Admin, 1984-1989; vis scientist, Dept Biochem, Univ Calif, San Francisco, 1983-1984; dir, Core Biochem Lab, 1982-1992; asst adj prof, Vet Admin, 1978-1982; asst dir, Enzym Res Lab, Martinez Vet Med Ctr, Calif, 1974-1982; fel biochem, Univ Calif, Berkeley, 1971-1974. **Memberships:** Am Soc Biol Chemists; AAAS. **Research Statement & Publications:** Expression of homeotic genes during differentiation; structure and function of proteolytic enzymes; role of homeobox genes in hematopoiesis; elastase structure and function. **Mailing Address:** Dept Med & Dermatol, Sch Med, Univ Calif, PO Box 0120, San Francisco, CA 94143-0120. **Fax:** 415-221-4262. **E-Mail:** largman@cgl.ucsf.edu

LARGMAN, THEODORE, ORGANIC CHEMISTRY. **Personal Data:** b Philadelphia, Pa, November 16, 1923; wid, c Susan, Robert, Richard & Michele. **Education:** Temple Univ, AB, 1948; Ind Univ, PhD (org chem), 1952. **Professional Experience:** RETIRED; consult, Triad Enterprises, 1990- & Teltech, 1996-; sr res assoc, Corp Chem Res Lab, 1988-1989; res assoc, Corp Chem Res Lab, 1981-1988; scientist, Cent Res Labs, 1966-1968; Sr res chemist, Nitrogen Div, Allied Signal Corp, 1962-1966; res group leader, Corp Chem Res Lab, 1951-1981. **Research Statement & Publications:** Organic synthesis; fine chemicals; agricultural pesticides; flame retardant chemicals and polymers; uranium extraction; polymer adhesion; bioresorbable polymers; fiber research; granted 35 US patents. **Mailing Address:** Seven Upper Field Rd, Morristown, NJ 07960.

LARIMER, FRANK WILLIAM, PROTEIN ENGINEERING, MOLECULAR GENETICS. **Personal Data:** b Mt Pleasant, Mich, February 26, 1948; m 1972, Constance A Zendel. **Education:** Albion Col, BA, 1971; Fla State Univ, MS, 1973, PhD (genetics), 1975. **Professional Experience:** DEPUTY DIR, CTR MOLECULAR & CELLULAR SYST, as of 2004; GROUP LEADER, GENOME ANAL & SYST MODELING, as of 2004; PROF, GRAD SCH GENOME SCI & TECHNOL, UNIV TENN, OAK RIDGE, as of 2004; ADJ PROF, DEPT BIOCHEM, CELLULAR & MOLECULAR BIOL, UNIV TENN, KNOXVILLE, as of 2004; SR RES STAFF MEM, LIFE SCI DIV, OAK RIDGE NAT LAB, 1997-; Cell, Molecular & Develop Biol Prog, Univ Tenn, Knoxville, 1989-; sr res scientist, Protein Eng Prog, Biol Div, Oak Ridge Nat Lab, 1988-1997; adj prof, biotech concentration, Bio Consortium, 1985-; Adj prof, Oak Ridge Grad Sch Biomed Sci, UnivTenn, 1977-; Res scientist, Chem Mutagenesis Prog, Biol Div, 1976-1984. **Memberships:** Am Soc Microbiol; Am Soc Biochem & Molecular Biol; Genetics Soc Am; Int SocPlant Molecular Biol; Protein Soc. **Research Statement & Publications:** Protein engineering: enzyme structure/function analysis, modeling of binding sites and catalytic complexes, subunit interactions and assembly; molecular genetics of mutagenesis and DNA repair. **Mailing Address:** Genome Anal & Syst Modeling Group, Life Sci Div, Oak Ridge Nat Lab, Oak Ridge, TN 37831-8077. **Fax:** 865-241-1965. **E-Mail:** larimerfw@ornl.gov

LARIMER, JAMES LYNN, NEUROBIOLOGY. **Personal Data:** b Washington Co, Tenn, January 7, 1932; div, c Linda & Bret. **Education:** E Tenn State Univ, BS, 1953; Univ Va, MA, 1954; Duke Univ, PhD, 1959. **Honors & Awards:** Javits Neuroscience Res Award, 1988-1995. **Professional Experience:** PROF, NEUROBIOLOGY, SCH BIOL SCI, UNIV TEX AUSTIN, 1999-; Mem marine sci panel, NSF, 1986; actg chmn dept, Univ Tex, Austin, 1973-1974; mem physiol study sect, NIH, 1972-1986; PROF BIOL SCI, UNIV TEX, AUSTIN, 1968-; Guggenheim fel, 1967-1968; from asst prof to assoc prof, Univ Tex, Austin, 1959-1968. **Memberships:** Soc Neuroscience; Am Physiol Soc; Sigma Xi; fel AAAS. **Research Statement & Publications:** Comparative physiology; behavior and neurophysiology of invertebrates. **Mailing Address:** Sch Biol Sci, Univ Tex, One Univ Sta C0930, Austin, TX 78712-1104. **E-Mail:** neuroserf@mail.utexas.edu

LARIMER, JOHN WILLIAM, GEOCHEMISTRY. **Personal Data:** b Pittsburgh, Pa, September 4, 1939; m 1965, Sarah; c Natasha A & J Jesse. **Education:** Lehigh Univ, BA, 1962, MS, 1963, PhD (geol), 1966. **Honors & Awards:** Nininger Award, 1966. **Professional Experience:** Vis prof, Calif Inst Technol, 1978-1979; PROF GEOL, ARIZ STATE UNIV, 1977-; NATO fel, Max Planck Inst, 1975-1976; from asst prof to assoc prof, Ariz State Univ, 1974-1977; prin investr, Lunar & Planetary Sci Prog, NASA, beginning 1972; NASA-AEC res assoc geochemistry, Enrico Fermi Inst, Univ Chicago, 1966-1969. **Memberships:** Fel AAAS; Geochem Soc; Am Geophys Union; fel Meteoritical Soc; Sigma Xi. **Research Statement & Publications:** Cosmochemistry; mineralogy and composition of meteorites. **Mailing Address:** Dept Geol, Box 871404, Tempe, AZ 85287-1404. **Fax:** 480-965-8102. **E-Mail:** jlarimer@asu.edu

LARIMORE, RICHARD WELDON, FISH BIOLOGY. **Personal Data:** b Rogers, Ark, February 10, 1923; m 1947, c 3. **Education:** Univ Ark, BS, 1946; Univ Ill, MS, 1947; Univ Mich, PhD (zoology), 1950. **Honors & Awards:** Fisheries Pub Award, Wildlife Soc, 1957; Am Fisheries Soc Award, 1960. **Professional Experience:** PROF EMER, UNIV ILL, URBANA, 1989-; sr lectr, Fulbright Comn, 1980, 1983, 1990; prof zool, Univ Ill, Urbana, 1970-1976; prof environ eng, Univ Ill, Urbana, 1969-1988; fishery expert, Food & Agr Orgn, 1963-1964 & 1972-1973; aquatic biologist, IllState Natural Hist Surv, 1958-1989; assoc, Univ Ill, Urbana, 1954-1958; asst aquatic biol, UnivIll, Urbana, 1946-1954. **Memberships:** Am Soc Ichthyol & Herpet; Am Fisheries Soc; Am Inst Fishery Res Biol. **Research Statement & Publications:** Ecology of stream and reservoir fishes; dynamics of cooling lakes; utilization of tropical aquatic resources. **Mailing Address:** Ctr Aquatic Ecol, Ill Natural Hist Surv, 172 Natural Resources Bldg, 607 E Peabody Dr, Champaign, IL 61820. **Fax:** 217-265-0374. **E-Mail:** rllarimo@inhs.uiuc.edu

LARIS, PHILIP CHARLES, PHYSIOLOGY. **Personal Data:** b Perth Amboy, NJ, September 5, 1931; m 1956, c 4. **Education:** Rutgers Univ, BS, 1952; Princeton Univ, MA, 1954, PhD (physiol), 1956. **Professional Experience:** PROF EMER, UNIV CALIF, as of 2006; prof biol, Univ Calif, Santa Barbara, 1975-; assoc prof, UnivCalif, Santa Barbara, 1966-1975; assoc prof, Franklin & Marshall Col, 1965-1966; from asst profto assoc prof, Univ Calif, 1958-1965; instr biol, Univ Calif, 1956-1958. **Memberships:** Am Physiol Soc; Soc Gen Physiol. **Research Statement & Publications:** Cell permeability membrane potentials; amino acid and ion transport. **Mailing Address:** 132 W Alamar Ave, Santa Barbara, CA 93105. **Fax:** 805-893-4724. **E-Mail:** laris@lifesci.ucsb.edu

LARIVEE, JACQUES, CONSERVATION. **Mailing Address:** 194 Ouellet, Rimouski, PQ G5L 4R5, Can. **E-Mail:** jlarive@cgocable.ca

LARK, CYNTHIA ANN, MICROBIOLOGY. **Personal Data:** b Shawnee, Okla, December 31, 1928; m 1951, c 4. **Education:** Mt Holyoke Col, BA, 1950; St Louis Univ, PhD, 1962. **Professional Experience:** PROF EMER BIOL, UNIV UTAH, as of 2003; assoc prof biol, Univ Utah, beginning 1972; assoc res prof biochem, UnivUtah, 1970-1972; asst prof microbiol, Kans State Univ, 1963-1970; NIH fel, Wash Univ, 1962-1963; res asst, Univ Geneva, 1955-1956 & St Louis Univ, 1959-1962; lab technician, CarnegieInst, 1950-1951

& Sloan-Kettering Inst Cancer Res, 1951-1953. **Research Statement & Publications:** Microbial genetics; molecular biol; DNA reproducing bacteria. **Mailing Address:** Univ Utah, 3605 Mill Circle, 201 S Biol Bldg, Salt Lake City, UT 84112-1196.

LARK, KARL GORDON, MOLECULAR BIOLOGY, GENETICS. **Personal Data:** b Lafayette, Ind, December 13, 1930; m 1951, c 4. **Education:** Univ Chicago, PhB, 1949; NY Univ, PhD (microbiol), 1953. **Professional Experience:** DISTINGUISHED PROF EMER BIOL, UNIV UTAH, as of 2003; mem, Nat Inst Gen Med Sci Coun, beginning 1979; ad hoc mem, Nat Inst Gen Med SciCoun, 1978-1979; prof biol, Univ Utah, beginning 1977; mem, Genetics Study Sect, NIH, 1971-1975; chmn dept, Univ Utah, 1970-1977; consult, Eli Lilly & Co, 1968-1974; mem, Genetics Panel, NSF, 1966-1969; Nat Inst Gen Med Sci career develop award, 1963-1970; prof, Kans State Univ, 1963-1970; from asst prof to assoc prof, Sch Med, St Louis Univ, 1958-1963; sr instr, Sch Med, St Louis Univ, 1957-1958; instr microbiol, Sch Med, St Louis Univ, 1956-1957; Nat Found res fel, Biophys Lab, Univ Geneva, 1955-1956; Am Cancer Soc res fel, Statenserum Inst, Denmark, 1953-1955. **Memberships:** Biophys Soc; Am Soc Cell Biol; Am Soc Biol Chem; Am Soc Microbiol. **Research Statement & Publications:** Cell growth and division; DNA replication and segregation in bacteria and eucaryotes; plant genetics and tissue culture. **Mailing Address:** Dept Biol, Univ Utah, 201 Biol Bldg, Salt Lake City, UT 84112. **E-Mail:** lark@bioscience.utah.edu

LARK, NEIL LAVERN, NUCLEAR PHYSICS. **Personal Data:** b Baker, Ore, September 10, 1934; m 1958, c 2. **Education:** Chico State Col, BA, 1955; Cornell Univ, PhD (phys chem), 1960. **Honors & Awards:** Sigma Xi. **Professional Experience:** PROF EMER PHYSICS, UNIV PAC, as of 2004; Vis astronr, Univ Hawaii, 1986, 1987; vis fel, Australian Nat Univ, 1976; prof Physics, Univ PAC, beginning 1975; vis physicist, Brookhaven Nat Lab, 1975; res collabr, BrookhavenNat Lab, 1971-1972; NSF lectr, Tex A&M Univ, 1970; consult & res collabr, Los Alamos SciLab, 1969; Ford Found fel & Fulbright grantee, Niels Bohr Inst, Copenhagen, Denmark, 1967-1968; from asst prof to prof natural sci, Raymond Col, 1962-1975; res assoc, Inst Nuclearres, Amsterdam, Neth, 1962; NATO fel, Inst Nuclear Res, Amsterdam, Neth, 1961-1962; res assoc, Brookhaven Nat Lab, 1960-1961; jr res assoc, Brookhaven Nat Lab, 1958-1959; res asst, Brookhaven Nat Lab, 1957; res asst, Los Alamos Sci Lab, 1955-1956; res asst, Univ NMex, 1954. **Memberships:** Am Phys Soc; Am Asn Physics Teachers; Am Astron Soc; Am Asn Univ Prof. **Research Statement & Publications:** Nuclear spectroscopy; teaching of physics and astronomy. **Mailing Address:** Dept Physics, Univ Pac, 3601 Pacific Ave, Stockton, CA 95211. **E-Mail:** nlark@comcast.net

LARKE, R(OBERT) P(ETER) BRYCE, VIROLOGY, INFECTIOUS DISEASES. **Personal Data:** b Blairmore, Alta, November 14, 1936; m 1960, Shirle; c Krista, Bryce Jr & Donald. **Education:** Queen's Univ, Ont, MD & CM, 1960; Univ Toronto, DCISc, 1966. **Honors & Awards:** Parkin Prize, Royal Col Physicians, Edinburgh, 1966. **Professional Experience:** PROF EMER PEDIAT, UNIV ALTA, 2001-; med dir, Prov Aids Prog, Alta Health, beginning 1990; dep med dir, CanRed Cross Blood Transfusion Serv, beginning 1988; dir, Univ Alta, 1988-1990; prof med microbial & infectious dis, Univ Alta, beginning 1986; vis scientist, Viral Oncol Unit, Pasteur Inst, Paris, France, 1986-1987; assoc med dir, Can Red Cross Blood Transfusion Serv, Edmonton, Alta, 1985-1988; hon prof med, Div Infectious Dis, 1977-1986; prof pediat, Univ Alta, 1975-2001; clin virologist, Prov Lab Pub Health, 1975-1985; assoc prof pediat, Univ Alta, 1975-1976; assoc prof pediat & path, McMaster Univ, 1972-1975; dir virol lab, St Joseph's Hosp, Hamilton, Ont, 1971-1975; asst prof path, McMaster Univ, 1971-1972; asst prof pediat, McMaster Univ, 1969-1972; sr instr, Sch Med, Case Western Res Univ, 1968; instr prev med, Sch Med, Case Western Res Univ, 1966-1968; Med Res Coun Can res fel, 1964-1966; fel microbiol, Sch Hyg, Univ Toronto, 1963-1966; res fel virol, Res Inst, 1962-1966; resident pediat, Hosp for SickChildren, Toronto, Ont, 1961-1962; Intern, St Michael's Hosp, Toronto, Ont, 1960-1961. **Memberships:** Am Soc Microbiol; Am Soc Virol; Am Pediat Soc; Infectious Dis Soc Am; CanPediat Soc; Can Soc Clin Invest. **Research Statement & Publications:** Clinical virology and infectious diseases of children and adults; mechanisms of host resistance to viral infections; interaction between viruses and blood platelets; epidemiology of viral infections; immunization against hepatitis B. **Mailing Address:** Dept Pediat, Univ Alta, 2C3 Walter C Mackenzie Ctr, Edmonton, AB T6G 2R7, Can. **Fax:** 780-407-8538.

LARKIN, DAVID, ELECTROCHEMISTRY. **Personal Data:** b London, Eng, October 6, 1941. **Education:** Loughborough Univ Technol, BTech, 1965, PhD (electrochem), 1968; Royal Inst Chem, ARIC, 1970. **Professional Experience:** PROF CHEM, TOWSON UNIV, as of 2005; assoc prof chem, Towson State Univ, beginning 1980; asst prof, TowsonState Univ, 1973-1980; asst prof chem, Fla Technol Univ, 1972-1973. **Memberships:** Am Chem Soc; Royal Soc Chem; Sigma Xi. **Research Statement & Publications:** Study of electro kinetics at solid metal electrodes. **Mailing Address:** Dept Chem, Towson Univ, Rm 563 Smith Hall, Towson, MD 21204. **E-Mail:** dlarkin@towson.edu

LARKIN, EDWARD CHARLES, HEMATOLOGY. **Personal Data:** b Waltham, Mass, August 7, 1937; m 1965, c 2. **Education:** Harvard Col, BA, 1959; Yale Univ Sch Med, MD, 1963. **Professional Experience:** PROF MED & PATH, UNIV CALIF, DAVIS, 1983-; chief hemat oncol, Marinez Va Hosp, 1975-1984; from assoc prof to prof med, Univ Calif, Davis, 1975-1983; assoc prof, Univ Tex Med Br, 1974-1975; asst prof med, Univ Tex Med Br, 1970-1974. **Memberships:** Am Soc Hemat; Int Soc Hemat; Am Col Physicians; Western Soc Clin Res. **Mailing Address:** Dept Internal Med & Path, Univ Calif Med Ctr, 4400 V St, Sacramento, CA 95817-2283. **Fax:** 916-734-0299. **E-Mail:** eclarkin@ucdavis.edu

LARKIN, JOHN MICHAEL, ORGANIC CHEMISTRY. **Personal Data:** b York, Nebr, August 11, 1937; m 1965, Sheila; c Ellen, Paul & Michael. **Education:** Univ Nebr, Lincoln, BS, 1959; Univ Colo, Boulder, MS, 1963, PhD (org chem), 1965. **Professional Experience:** CHAIR, CENT TEX LOCAL SEC, AM CHEM SOC, as of 2001; CONSULT, HUNTSMAN CORP, as of 2000; sr res supvr, Huntsman Chem Corp, beginning 1993; supvr res sect, TexacoChem Co, Austin, Tex, 1987-1993; sr proj chemist, Jefferson Chem Co, Austin, Tex, 1976-1987; sr res chemist, Texaco Inc, Beacon, 1974-1976; res chemist, Texaco Inc, Beacon, 1970-1974; from chemist to sr chemist, Texaco Inc, Beacon, 1965-1970; chemist, Qual Water Br, US GeolSurv, Nebr, 1959-1960. **Memberships:** Am Chem Soc. **Research Statement & Publications:** Organic synthesis; structure elucidation; reaction mechanisms; organic nitrogen compounds; free radical rearrangements; steroidal heterocycles; air pollution; lubricant additive synthesis; chemicals from synthesis gas; heterogeneous catalysis. **Mailing Address:** Huntsman Corp, 12414, Dorsett Rd, Austin, TX 78727-5820. **E-Mail:** jackamine@aol.com

LARKIN, JOHN MONTAGUE, MICROBIAL PHYSIOLOGY, MICROBIAL ECOLOGY. **Personal Data:** b Philadelphia, Pa, April 7, 1936; div, c Laura & Jennifer. **Education:** Ariz State Univ, BS, 1961, MS, 1963; Wash State Univ, PhD (microbiol), 1967. **Professional Experience:** ASSOC DEAN GRAD SCH, LA STATE UNIV, BATON ROUGE, 1994-; PROF MICROBIOL, LA STATE UNIV, BATON ROUGE, 1981-; from asst prof to assoc prof, LA State Univ, Baton Rouge, 1967-1981; asst microbiol, Ariz State Univ, 1961-1963 & Wash State Univ, 1963-1967. **Memberships:** Am Soc Microbiol; emer mem. **Research Statement & Publications:** Bacterial taxonomy; biology of gliding bacteria; filamentous sulfur bacteria; microbiology of cold, hydrocarbon marine seeps. **Mailing Address:** Grad Sch, La State Univ, Baton Rouge, LA 70803. **Fax:** 225-388-1370. **E-Mail:** jmlarki@aol.com

LARKIN, JOHN W, NUTRITION. **Personal Data:** b Ossining, NY, August 2, 1954. **Education:** Ohio State Univ, BS, 1978, MA, 1980; Mich State Univ, PhD (food sci), 1984. **Professional Experience:** CHIEF, FOOD PROCESS HAZARD ANALYSIS BR, CTR FOOD SAFETY & APPL NUTRIT, as of 2006. **Mailing Address:** Ctr Food Safety & Appl Nutrit, 6502 S Archer Rd, Summit-Argo, IL 60501. **Fax:** 708-728-4177. **E-Mail:** john.larkin@fda.hhs.gov

LARKIN, K(ENNETH) T(RENT), ELECTRICAL ENGINEERING. **Personal Data:** b Fowler, Colo, November 11, 1920; m 1946, c 2. **Education:** Southern Methodist Univ, BS, 1943. **Professional Experience:** Pres, Technicon Med Info Systs Corp, 1971-; dirinfo systs, Res & Develop Div, 1965-1971; dir, Res & Develop Div, 1963-1965; asst dir eng, Res& Develop Div, 1963; assoc dir eng electronics, Lockheed Missiles & Space Co, 1962-1963; assoc dir electronics res & develop, Lockheed Missiles & Space Co, 1958-1962; mgr electronicsdiv, Lockheed Missiles & Space Co, 1957-1958; mgr telecommun dept, Lockheed Missiles &Space Co, 1956-1957; dept mgr radar & radar develop, Santa Barbara Labs, 1955-1956; mgrreceiver & indicators br, Waltham Labs, Raytheon Mfg Co, 1946-1955; scientist, US Naval ResLab, DC, 1943-1945; instr radio eng, Southern Methodist Univ, 1942-1943; Jr engr, Lone StarGas Co, 1939-1942; PALO ALTO MGT GROUP. **Memberships:** Sr mem Inst Elec & Electronics Engrs. **Research Statement & Publications:** Computer systems, especially as applied to health care. **Mailing Address:** 215 Golden Hills Dr, Portola Valley, CA 94028.

LARKIN, LAWRENCE A(LBERT), FINITE ELEMENT ANALYSIS, ELASTO-PLASTIC FLOW. **Personal Data:** b Kansas City, Mo, January 5, 1937; m 1960. **Education:** Univ Kans, BA, 1959, MS, 1960, PhD (civil eng), 1964. **Professional Experience:** CONSULT ENGR, DATA SYSTS DIV, A O SMITH CORP, 1974-; res scientist, Data Systs Div, A O Smith Corp, 1970-1974; Asst prof civil eng, State Univ NY Buffalo, 1964-1969. **Memberships:** Am Soc Civil Engrs. **Research Statement & Publications:** Development of finite element computer codes; finite element computation of elasto-plastic response of vehicle structures during crash conditions. **Mailing Address:** 7728 W Coventry Dr, Franklin, WI 53132.

LARKIN, LYNN HAYDOCK, ANATOMY, REPRODUCTIVE BIOLOGY. **Personal Data:** b Highland Co, Ohio, January 29, 1934; div, c 2. **Education:** Otterbein Col, BS, 1956; Univ Colo, PhD (anat), 1967. **Professional Experience:** PROF EMER, DEPT ANAT & CELL BIOL, UNIV FLA, as of 2004; prof anat, Col Med, Univ Fla, beginning 1979; from asst prof to assoc prof, Col Med, Univ Fla, 1968-1979; res assoc molecular, cellular & develop biol, 1967-1968; instranat, Sch Med, Univ Colo, 1966-1967. **Memberships:** Sigma Xi; Am Asn Anatomists; Soc Study Reproduction; Am Asn Clin Anatomists. **Research Statement & Publications:** Role of relaxin in pregnancy and parturition. **Mailing Address:** Dept Anat & Cell Biol Univ Fla, 100235 Health Sci Ctr, Gainesville, FL 32610. **Fax:** 352-392-3305. **E-Mail:** larkin@anatomy.med.ufl.edu

LARKIN, ROBERT HAYDEN, ANALYTICAL CHEMISTRY. **Personal Data:** b New York, NY, March 26, 1946; m 1967, c 4. **Education:** Providence Col, BS, 1968; Univ Mass, PhD (phys chem), 1972. **Professional Experience:** DIR REGULATORY AFFAIRS, ROHM & HAAS CO, 1986-; sect mgrenviron sci, Rohm & Haas Co, 1984-1986; sect mgr analytical res, Rohm & Haas Co, 1979-1984; res chemist, Rohm & Haas Co, 1973-1979; Res assoc chem, Mass Inst Technol, 1972-1973. **Memberships:** Am Chem Soc; Nat Agr Chem Asn. **Research Statement & Publications:** Determination of the environmental fate and metabolism of agricultural pesticides. **Mailing Address:** Rohm & Haas Co, 100 Independence Mall W, Philadelphia, PA 19106. **Fax:** 215-592-3377.

LARKIN, RONALD PAUL, WILDLIFE ECOLOGY IN DISTURBED ENVIRONMENTS, CHARACTERIZATION OF ANIMALS MOVEMENTS. **Personal Data:** b St Louis, Mo, July 27, 1945. **Education:** Univ Mo, Columbia, AB, 1967; Rockefeller Univ, PhD, 1973. **Professional Experience:** ADY ASSOC PRO WILDLIFE ECOLOGIST, UNIV ILL, URBANA, as of 2004; Attendee & lectr, Next Generation Weather Radar Oper Support Facil, USAF, Fed Aviation Admin & Nat Weather Serv, 1993; consult & lectr, Soc Protection Nature, Israel, 1989; mem & lectr, Bird Strike Comt Europe, Copenhagen, Madrid, 1986 & 1988; consult & lectr, Bird Hazard Team, USAF, 1985-; DEPT AFFIL, DEPT ECOL, ETHOLOGY & EVOLUTION, UNIV ILL, 1981-; ASSOC PROF SCIENTIST & WILDLIFE ECOLOGIST, ILL NATURAL HIST SURV. 1980-; prin investr, USAF, US Fish & Wildlife Serv, USN, NSF, US Army & State Ill, 1978-; asst prof, Rockefeller Univ, 1975-1980; Res assoc, Rockefeller Univ, 1973-1975; adj assoc prof, Dept Nat Resources & Environ Sci. **Memberships:** Am Ornithologists' Union; Animal Behav Soc; Am Soc Naturalists; Nat Ctr Sci Educ; Am Meteorol Soc; Sigma Xi. **Research Statement & Publications:** Interdisciplinary approaches; computer applications in ecology, especially spatial statistics and automated systems for locating and recognizing animals; bird flight, migration, orientation, dispersal, radar ornithology, bird hazards to aircraft, and birds' use of atmospheric structure; bioacoustics. **Mailing Address:** Ill Natural Hist Surv, 607 E Peabody Dr, Champaign, IL 61820. **Fax:** 217-333-6294. **E-Mail:** r-larkin@uiuc.edu

LARKIN, WILLIAM ALBERT, GLASS COATINGS, POLYMER ADDITIES. **Personal Data:** b Boston, Mass, December 17, 1926; m 1953, Winifred Swierczek; c Sharon, Cynthia, William, David, Patricia, Maureen & Diane. **Education:** Boston Col, BS, 1949. **Honors & Awards:** Lifetime Innovation Award, Soc Nat Elf Aquitane, Paris, France, 1993. **Professional Experience:** Atafine chemical, 1991-; CONSULT, TECHNOL, 1992-; dir technol, Atochem NAm, 1982-1992; plant gen mgr, Atochem NAm, 1980-1981; tech dir, Atochem NAm, 1973-1980; mgr prod develop, Atochem NAm, 1968-1973; mgr tech serv, Atochem NAm, 1961-1968; dist mgr, Atochem NAm, 1957-1961; Dist mgr, McKesson & Robbins Inc, 1953-1957; Consult polymer additives & functional glass coatings. **Memberships:** Soc Plastics Engrs; Am Chem Soc. **Research Statement & Publications:** Polymer stabilizers; flame retardants; modifiers; glass coatings for strengthening and electroconductivity; organometallic, organotin chemistry and applications; holder of 35 US patents. **Mailing Address:** 38 Sylvania Ave, Avon By The Sea, NJ 07717. **Fax:** 732-774-2422. **E-Mail:** 1quest4@aol.com

LARKINS, BRIAN ALLEN, PLANT PHYSIOLOGY, PLANT BIOCHEMISTRY. **Personal Data:** b Bellville, Kans, August 12, 1946; m 1969, Pamela; c Aaron C & Philip J. **Education:** Univ Nebr, BSEd, 1969, PhD (bot), 1974. **Honors & Awards:** Fellow, American Association for the Advancement of Science, 2003; National Academy of Sciences, USA, 1996; Dennis Robert Hoagland Award, Am Soc Plant Physiologists, 1997; Regents prof, Univ of Arizona, 2001; Charles Albert Schull Award, Am Soc Plant Physiologists, 1983. **Professional Experience:** Harry W. and Elsie M. Porterfield and Regents Professor, Univ of Arizona; Professor and Head of Plant Scineces, Univ of Arizona; Hovde distinguished prof, Purdue Univ, 1986; PROF GENETICS, PURDUE UNIV, 1984-; from asst prof to assoc prof, Purdue Univ, 1976-1983; Res assoc biochem genetics, Purdue Univ, 1975-1976; Porterfield prof plant sci, Univ Ariz. **Memberships:** Nat Acad Sci; AAAS; Sigma Xi; Am Soc Biochem & Molecular Biol; Soc Develop Biol; Am Soc Plant Physiologists. **Research Statement & Publications:** Protein and nucleic acid biosynthesis; seed storage protein metabolism; regulation of gene activity during seed formation; regulation of seed Development and the synthesis of seed storage proteins. **Mailing Address:** Dept Plant Sci, Univ Ariz, Tucson, AZ 85721. **Fax:** 520-621-3692. **E-Mail:** larkins@ag.arizona.edu

LARKINS, THOMAS HASSELL, INORGANIC CHEMISTRY. **Personal Data:** b Dickson, Tenn, March 1, 1939; m 1960, c 3. **Education:** Austin Peay State Col, BS, 1960; Vanderbilt Univ, MA, 1962, PhD (chem), 1963. **Professional Experience:** RES ASSOC, EASTMAN CHEM DIV, EASTMAN KODAK CO, 1980-; sr res chemist, Tenn Eastman Co, 1963-1980. **Memberships:** Am Chem Soc. **Research Statement & Publications:** Coordination chemistry; catalysis; coal gasification; chemicals from coal. **Mailing Address:** 614 E Main Blvd, Church Hill, TN 37642.

LARKY, ARTHUR I(RVING), ELECTRICAL ENGINEERING, COMPUTER ENGINEERING. **Personal Data:** b Bound Brook, NJ, February 27, 1931; m 1981, Joan; c Susan, David, Steven, Wayne, Barbara & Melissa. **Education:** Lehigh Univ, BS, 1952; Princeton Univ, MS, 1953; Stanford Univ, PhD (elec eng), 1957. **Professional Experience:** PROF EMER ELEC & COMPUT ENG, LEHIGH UNIV, 1995-; prof comput eng, Lehigh Univ, 1964-1995; CONSULT, 1962-; from res asst prof to prof elec eng, Lehigh Univ, 1956-1995. **Memberships:** Inst Elec & Electronics Engrs. **Research Statement & Publications:** Computer design; automated testing. **Mailing Address:** Dept Elec & Comput Eng, Lehigh Univ, 215 Packard Bldg 19, Bethlehem, PA 18015. **Fax:** 609-487-3016. **E-Mail:** ail0@lehigh.edu

LARMAN, BRIAN T, AERONAUTICS. **Professional Experience:** SR STAFF, CARNEGIE MELLON UNIV, as of 2006. **Memberships:** Inst Elec & Electronic Engrs. **Mailing Address:** Software Eng Inst, Carnegie Mellon Univ, 4500 5th Ave., Pittsburgh, PA 15213-3890. **Fax:** 412-268-5758. **E-Mail:** btl@sei.cmu.edu

LARMIE, WALTER ESMOND, floriculture; deceased, see previous edition for last biography

LARMORE, LAWRENCE LOUIS, MATHEMATICS. **Personal Data:** b Washington, DC, November 23, 1941; m 1964, c 2. **Education:** Tulane Univ, BS, 1961; Northwestern Univ, PhD (math), 1965. **Professional Experience:** PROF COMPUT SCI, SCH COMPUT SCI, UNIV NEVADA LAS VEGA, as of 2004; PROF MATH, CALIF STATE COL, DOMINGUEZ HILLS, 1977-; assoc prof, Calif State Col, Dominguez Hills, 1970-1977; Asst prof math, Univ Ill, Chicago Circle, 1965-1968 & Occidental Col, 1968-1970. **Memberships:** Am Math Soc. **Research Statement & Publications:** Algebraic topology; obstruction theory; classification of liftings, embeddings and immersions; twisted extraordinary cohomology. **Mailing Address:** Dept Comput Sci, sch Comput Sci, Univ Nevada Las Vega, Las Vegas, NV 89154-4019. **E-Mail:** larmore@cs.unlv.edu

LARNER, ANDREW CHARLES, MOLECULAR BIOLOGY. **Personal Data:** b St Louis, Mo, April 1, 1953. **Education:** Haverford Col, BA, 1975; Univ Va, PhD (pharmacol), 1981, MD, 1982. **Professional Experience:** STAFF, DEPT IMMUNOL, LERNER RES INST, as of 2004; SR RES SCIENTIST, DEPT CYTOKINE BIOL, FOOD & DRUG ADMIN, 1988-; residency path, Nat Cancer Inst, 1985-1988; res fel inteferons, Rockefeller Univ, 1982-1985. **Memberships:** Am Soc Exp Pathologists; Int Soc Interferon Res. **Research Statement & Publications:** Molecular biology. **Mailing Address:** Dept Immunol, Lerner Res Inst, NB30 9500 Euclid Ave, Cleveland, OH 44195. **Fax:** 216-445-9329. **E-Mail:** larnera@ccf.org

LARNER, JOSEPH, BIOCHEMISTRY, PHARMACOLOGY. **Personal Data:** b Brest-Litovsk, Poland, January 9, 1921; American citizen; m 1947, Frances; c Andrew, James & Paul. **Education:** Univ Mich, BS, 1942; Columbia Univ, MD, 1945; Univ Ill, MS, 1949; Wash Univ, PhD (biochem), 1951. **Honorary Degrees:** Dr, Univ Barcelona, 1983; Univ Ceara Taleza Brazil, 2000. **Honors & Awards:** David Rumbaugh Award, Juv Diabetes Found, 1980; Sandoz Lectr, Can Soc Endocrinol & Metab, 1981; Banting Lectr Can Diabetes Asn, Univ Toronto, 1981; E W Sutherland Mem Lectr, Univ Miami, 1981; Paul K Smith Mem Lectr, George Washington Univ, 1982; Diaz Christobal Award, Int Diabetes Fedn, 1982; Claude P Brown Mem Lectr, Am Asn Clin Pathologists, 1983; William Creacy Estab Lectr, Temple Univ Med Sch, 1983; Doc Honor Causa, Univ Barcelona, 1983; John Lynch Lectr, Univ Notre Dame, 1984; Res Award, Japan Soc Starch Res, 1985; Res Award, Asn Am Med Col, 1987; Banting Medal, Am Diabetes Asn, 1987; Lifetime Sci Achievement Award, Commonwealth Va, 1992; Doc Honor Causa Univ Ceara, Taleza Brazil, 2000. **Professional Experience:** Prin scientist ins med, Inc Glen Allen VA, 2001-; ALUMNI PROF EMER PHARMACOL, UNIV VA, 1990-; alumni prof pharmacol, Univ Va, 1974-1990; dir, Univ Diabetes Res & Training Ctr, 1974-1991; mem rev bd, Am Cancer Soc, 1970-1974; prof pharmacol & chmn dept, Sch Med, 1969-1990; mem, Training Comt, Nat Inst Arthritis & Metab Dis, 1966; mem, Subcomt Enzymes, Nat Res Coun-Nat Acad Sci, 1964-; Hill prof metab enzym, Col Med Sci, Univ Minn, Minneapolis, 1964-1969; NIH res career award, 1963-1964, Commonwealth Fund fel, Lab Molecular Biol, Cambridge Univ, 1963-1964; mem, Metab Study Sect, NIH, 1962-1966; from assoc prof to prof pharmacol, Sch Med, Western Res Univ, 1957-1964; asst prof, Noyes Chem Lab, Univ Ill, 1953-1957; instr biochem, Wash Univ, 1951-1953. **Memberships:** Inst Med Nat Acad Sci; Am Soc Biol Chemists; fel Royal Col Med; Am Soc Pharmacol & Exp Therapeut; hon mem Japan Biochem Soc; Am Chem Soc; hon mem Can Soc Endocrinol & Metab; NY Acad Sci; Sigma Xi; Am Diabetes Asn; Am Inst Chemists; fel AAAS. **Research Statement & Publications:** Enzymatic aspects of intermediary carbohydrate metabolism, genetic and hormonal control. **Mailing Address:** Dept Pharmacol, Univ Va Health Syst, Charlottesville, VA 22903. **Fax:** 804-924-1992. **E-Mail:** jlgd@virginia.edu

LARNER, KENNETH LEE, EXPLORATION GEOPHYSICS. **Personal Data:** b Chicago, Ill, November 1, 1938; m 1976, c 2. **Education:** Colo Sch Mines, GpE, 1960; Mass Inst Technol, PhD (geophys), 1970. **Professional Experience:** DIR, CTR WAVE PHENOMENA, COLO SCH MINES, as of 2003; CHARLES HENRY GREEN PROF GEOPHYS, COLO SCH MINES, 1988-; vpres & develop, Western Geophys Co, 1980-1988; mgr res & develop explor geophys, Western Geophys Co, 1975-1980; lectr geophys, Univ Houston, 1973-1974; sr res geophysicist, Western Geophys Co, 1970-1974; res scientist image enhancement, EG&G, Inc, 1967-1969. **Memberships:** Soc Explor Geophysicists; Seismol Soc Am; Europ Asn Explor Geophysicists; Sigma Xi. **Research Statement & Publications:** Seismic signal enhancement and wave propagation; estimation of geophysical parameters from seismic measurements. **Mailing Address:** Dept Geophys, Colo Sch Mines, CO 80401-1887. **Fax:** 303-273-3478. **E-Mail:** klarner@mines.edu

LARNEY, VIOLET HACHMEISTER, MATHEMATICS. **Personal Data:** b Chicago, Ill, May 19, 1920; m 1950. **Education:** Ill State Univ, BEd, 1941; Univ Ill, AM, 1942; Univ Wis, PhD (math), 1950. **Professional Experience:** RETIRED; emer prof, State Univ NY, Albany, 1982; from assoc prof to profmath, State Univ NY, Albany, 1952-1982; asst prof, Kans State Univ, 1950-1952; instr, ExtenDiv, 1948-1950; asst math, Univ Wis, 1944-1948; Teacher high sch, Ill, 1942-1944. **Memberships:** Math Asn Am; Am Math Soc. **Research Statement & Publications:** Abstract algebra. **Mailing Address:** 573 Leisure World, Mesa, AZ 85206-3129.

LARNTZ, KINLEY, APPLIED STATISTICS, MATHEMATICAL STATISTICS. **Personal Data:** b Coshocton, Ohio, October 2, 1945; m 1965, c 3. **Education:** Dartmouth Col, AB, 1967; Univ Chicago, PhD (statist), 1971. **Professional Experience:** PROF EMER APPL STATIST, UNIV MINN, MINNEAPOLIS, 1998-; STASTICAL ADV, Orthop Rehabilitative Devices Panel FDA, as of 2005; chmn appl statist, Univ Minn, St Paul, 1971-1998. **Memberships:** Am Statist Asn; Royal Statist Soc; Biomet Soc; Inst Math Statist; Sigma Xi; AAAS. **Research Statement & Publications:** Analysis of qualitative data; comparison of small sample distributions for chi-square goodness-of-fit statistics; data analysis applied statistical methods. **Mailing Address:** Dept Appl Statist, Univ Minn, 1994 Buford Ave, St Paul, MN 55108. **Fax:** 612-624-8868. **E-Mail:** kinley@stat.umn.edu

LAROCCA, ANTHONY JOSEPH, PHYSICS, ELECTRICAL ENGINEERING. **Personal Data:** b New Orleans, La, May 15, 1923; m 1954, Anne-Marie; c 6. **Education:** Tulane Univ, BS in EE, 1949; Univ Mich, MS, 1952. **Professional Experience:** Res physicist, Environ Res Inst Mich, Univ Mich, beginning 1973; adj prof, Univ Mich, beginning 1973; from assoc res physicist to res physicist, Inst Sci & Technol, Univ Mich, Ann Arbor, 1960-1973; res assoc, Inst Sci & Technol, Univ Mich, Ann Arbor, 1958-1960; res asst, Inst Sci & Technol, Univ Mich, Ann Arbor, 1956-1958; res asst physics, Tulane Univ, 1949-1951. **Memberships:** AAAS; Optical Soc Am. **Research Statement & Publications:** Infrared and optical technology; radiation phenomena; propagation and attenuation; techniques of measurement of radiation; design and use of electrooptical devices; standards of radiation; study of techniques of remote sensing of environment. **Mailing Address:** Univ Mich, Dept Elec Eng, 1301 Beal Ave, Ann Arbor, MI 48109-2122. **Fax:** 734-763-1503.

LA ROCCA, PAUL JOSEPH, CELL PHYSIOLOGY. **Personal Data:** b Newburgh, NY, January 30, 1954; c 2. **Education:** George Washington Univ, BS, 1977; Univ Ill, Chicago, PhD (cell & develop biol), 1982. **Professional Experience:** SCIENTIST, BECTON DICKINSON LABWARE, as of 1996; MGR BIOL SCI & TECHNOL, BECTON DICKINSON LABWARE, 1986-; mgr biol res, Becton Dickinson Labware, 1984-1986; fel, NIH, 1983-1985; Res fel physiol, Div Cell Growth & Regulation, Dana-Farber Cancer Inst & Dept Physiol & Biophys, Harvard Med Sch, 1982-1984; Nat res serv award, NIH, 1982-1983. **Memberships:** Sigma Xi; Tissue Cult Asn; Am Soc Cell Biol; NY Acad Sci; Am Chem Soc. **Research Statement & Publications:** Product development and testing; manufacturing technologies; new technologies that impact cell culture. **Mailing Address:** Dept Res & Develop, Becton Dickinson Labware, One Becton Dr, Franklin Lakes, NJ 07417-1886. **Fax:** 800-743-6200.

LAROCHE, ANDRE, IDENTIFICATION OF DNA MARKERS & GENES FOR DISEASE RESISTANCE, FREEZING TOLERANCE IN HIGHER PLANTS. **Personal Data:** b Que, May 31, 1956; m 1980, Mireille; c Guillaume, Philippe, Francois J & Antoine. **Education:** Univ Sherbrooke, Que, BS, 1979, MS, 1983; Univ Western Ont, PhD (plant sci), 1987. **Professional Experience:** Adj prof, Dept Biol Sci, Univ Lethbridge, Alta, beginning 1992; RES SCIENTIST, AGRCAN RES CTR, LETHBRIDGE, ALTA, 1989-; vis fel, Agr Can Plant Res Ctr, Ottawa, Ont, 1987-1989. **Memberships:** Am Soc Plant Physiologists; Can Soc Plant Physiologists; Int Soc Plant MolecularBiol; Can-Fr Asn Advan Sci. **Research Statement & Publications:** Identification of markers linked to different disease resistance genes in cereals; identification of DNA sequences involved in the vernalization process of wheat; identification of DNA fragments unique to specific plant pathogens. **Mailing Address:** Agr & Agri-Food, Lethbridge Res Ctr, 5403, First Ave S, PO Box 3000, Lethbridge, AB T1J 4B1, Can. **Fax:** 403-382-3156. **E-Mail:** laroche@agr.gc.ca

LA ROCHE, GILLES, ENDOCRINOLOGY, WATER POLLUTION TOXICOLOGY. **Personal Data:** b Bienville, Que, July 11, 1922. **Education:** Univ Montreal, BS, 1947; McGill Univ, MS, 1951; Univ Wash, PhD (biochem), 1956. **Professional Experience:** Sci advr, Int Joint Comn Great Lakes, 1980-1985; PRES, VIT-VITAILLE-VIRON INC, 1979-; prof toxicol, McGill Univ Inst Oceanog, 1972-1981; prof toxicol & endocrinol, Sch Oceanog, RI Univ, 1966-1972; res biochemist & dir metab unit, Univ Calif, Berkeley, 1958-1966; Researcher, Univ Calif, Berkeley, 1956-1958. **Memberships:** AAAS; Am Physiol Soc; Endocrine Soc; Asn Clin Scientists. **Research Statement & Publications:** Endocrinology; water pollution toxicology. **Mailing Address:** Vit-Vitaille-Viron Inc, 1455 Sherbrooke St W PH-3, Montreal, PQ H3G 1L2, Can.

LAROCHELLE, DONALD R, CIVIL ENGINEERING. **Professional Experience:** CONSULT, CONSTRUCT INSPECTION SERV, as of 2004; fel, Am coun eng co, as of 2004. **Mailing Address:** Construct Inspection Serv, 146-3 Flintlock Village, Wells, ME 04090.

LAROCHELLE, JACQUES, ANIMAL ECOPHYSIOLOGY. **Personal Data:** b Que, September 4, 1946; m 1972, c 2. **Education:** Laval Univ, BA, 1966, BS, 1971. **Honors & Awards:** DSc, Laval Univ, 1976. **Professional Experience:** PROF PHYSIOL, LAVAL UNIV, 1992-; from asst prof to assoc prof, Laval Univ, 1977-1992; Que Ministry Educ fel & vis scholar zool, Duke Univ, 1976; Lectr physiol, Laval Univ, 1974-1975. **Memberships:** Can Soc Zoologists. **Research Statement & Publications:** Temperature regulation and locomotion in birds and mammals. **Mailing Address:** Dept Biol, Laval Univ, Quebec, PQ G1K 7P4, Can. **Fax:** 418-656-2043. **E-Mail:** jacques.larochelle@bio.ulaval.ca

LAROCK, BRUCE E, CIVIL ENGINEERING, HYDRODYNAMICS, NUMERICAL MODELING. **Personal Data:** b Berkeley, Calif, December 24, 1940; m 1968, Susan; c Lynne M & Jean E. **Education:** Stanford Univ, BS, 1962, MS, 1963, PhD (civil eng), 1966. **Honors & Awards:** Sr US scientist award, Alexander von Humboldt-Stiftung, 1986-1987. **Professional Experience:** PROF EMER CIVIL & ENVIRON ENG, UNIV CALIF, DAVIS, as of 2001; prof, civil & Environ Eng, Univ Calif, Davis, 1979; from asst prof to assoc prof, Univ Calif, Davis, 1966-1979. **Memberships:** Am Soc Civil Engrs; Sigma Xi. **Research Statement & Publications:** Hydraulics and fluid mechanics; finite element methods. **Mailing Address:** Dept Civil & Environ Eng, Univ Calif, Davis, CA 95616. **Fax:** 530-752-7872. **E-Mail:** belarock@ucdavis.edu

LAROCK, PAUL ANTHONY, ENVIRONMENTAL SCIENCES, GEOMICROBIOLOGY, MICROBIOLOGY. **Personal Data:** b New York, NY, November 18, 1937. **Education:** Rensselaer Polytech Inst, BCE, 1960, MS, 1964, PhD (environ eng), 1968. **Honors & Awards:** Nat Tech Achievement Award, NAm Lakes Mgt Soc, 1987 Lipsey award for excellence in teaching, 2004. **Professional Experience:** ADJ PROF BIOL SCI & SYST ECOL & EVOLUTION, LA STATE UNIV, as of 2004; prof, Dept Oceanog & Coastal Sci, La State Univ, beginning 1992; Assoc prof, Univ Hawaii, 1975-1976; From asst prof to prof, Fla State Univ, 1968-1992. **Memberships:** Am Soc Microbiol; Am Geophys Union; Estuarine

Research Federation. **Research Statement & Publications:** Environmental microbiology and biogeochemical cycling of minerals and toxic materials; Marine microbiology, bacterial cycling of minerals, stormwater effects on receiving bodies and microbial ecology. **Mailing Address:** Dept Oceanography & Coastal Scis, La State Univ, Baton Rouge, LA 70803. **Fax:** 504-388-6307. **E-Mail:** oclaro@lsu.edu

LAROCK, RICHARD CRAIG, ORGANIC CHEMISTRY. **Personal Data:** b Berkeley, Calif, November 16, 1944. **Education:** Univ Calif, Davis, BS, 1967; Purdue Univ, PhD (chem), 1972. **Honors & Awards:** Regents Award Fac Excellence, 1998; ACS Edward Leete Award, 2003; Paul Rylander Award, Org Reactions Catalysis Soc, 2004; ACS Arthur C Cope Sr Scholar Award, 2004. **Professional Experience:** UNIV PROF CHEM, IOWA STATE UNIV, 1999-; prof chem, Iowa State Univ, 1985-1999; A P Sloan fel, 1977-1979; Du Pont Young fac scholar, 1975-1976; from instr to assoc prof, Iowa State Univ, 1972-1985. **Memberships:** Am Chem Soc; Sigma Xi. **Research Statement & Publications:** Synthesis of biologically active compounds; new synthetic methods; organometallic and heterocyclic chemistry; polymer chemistry. **Mailing Address:** Iowa State Univ, Ames, IA 50011-3111. **Fax:** 515-294-0105. **E-Mail:** larock@iastate.edu

LAROSE, BENOIT, MATHEMATICS. **Education:** Univ Montreal, BSc, 1988, MSc, 1990, PhD (Math), 1993. **Professional Experience:** ADJ PROF, DEPT MATH & STATIST, CONCORDIA UNIV, 2000-; INSTR, DEPT MATH, CHAMPLAIN REGIONAL COL, 1998-. **Mailing Address:** LACIM-UQAM CP 8888, Succ centre-ville, Montreal, PQ H3C 3P8, Can. **Fax:** 450-672-9299. **E-Mail:** larose@mathstat.concordia.ca

LAROSSA, ROBERT ALAN, AGRICULTURE PRODUCTION. **Personal Data:** b New York, NY, January 29, 1951; c 2. **Education:** Johns Hopkins Univ, BA, 1973; Yale Univ, Mphil, 1976, PhD (molecular biophys & biochem), 1977. **Professional Experience:** SR RES DIR, CENT RES & DEVELOP, BIOCHEM SCI & ENG, DUPONT CO, as of 2001; SR RES BIOLOGIST, AGR PRODS DEPT, E I DU PONT Del NEMOURS &CO INC, 1990-; spec reviewer, Microbial Genetics & Physiol Study Sect II, NIH, 1989; adj asstprof, Sch Life & Health Sci, Univ Del, 1983-1986; lectr molecular genetics, DuPont ContinuingEduc Prog, 1981; prin investr, Cent Res & Develop Dept, E I du Pont Del Nemours & Co, Inc, 1980-1990; res assoc, Dept Biochem, Stanford Univ, 1980; invited lectr, numerous insts & univs, beginning 1979; NSF postdoctoral fel, 1979-1980; postdoctoral fel, Dept Biochem, Stanford Univ, 1977-1980; Am Chem Soc postdoctoral fel, 1977-1979; postdoctoral fel, Dept MolecularBiophys & Biochem, Yale Univ, 1977; teaching asst, Yale Univ, 1973-1974. **Memberships:** Am Soc Microbiol; Genetics Soc Am; Am Soc Biochem & Molecular Biol. **Mailing Address:** Cent Res & Develop, Biochem Sci & Eng, DuPont Co, PO Box 80173, Exp Sta, Wilmington, DE 19880-0173. **Fax:** 302-695-9183. **E-Mail:** robert.a.larossa@usa.dupont.co

LAROW, EDWARD J, AQUATIC ECOLOGY, INVERTEBRATE ZOOLOGY. **Personal Data:** b Albany, NY, December 22, 1937; m 1963, Nancy; c Mary A, Edward Jr, John & Catherine. **Education:** Siena Col, BS, 1959; Kans State Univ, MS, 1965; Rutgers Univ, PhD (zoology), 1968. **Professional Experience:** PROF BIOL, SIENA COL, NY, 1974-; vis lectr, Col Environ Sci & Forestry, 1976-1985; chmn dept, Siena Col, NY, 1971-1980; vis lectr, State Univ NY Albany, 1970-1975; Nat Res Coun Int Biol Prog grant, 1970-1974; From asst prof to assoc prof, Siena Col, NY, 1968-1974. **Memberships:** Ecol Soc Am; Am Soc Limnol & Oceanog; Int Soc Limnol. **Research Statement & Publications:** Biological rhythms and their role in the vertical migration of zooplankton; secondary production of zooplankton; effect of acid precipitation on zooplankton populations. **Mailing Address:** Dept Biol, Siena Col, 515 Loudon Rd, Loudonville, NY 12211-1462.

LARRABEE, ALLAN ROGER, BIOCHEMISTRY. **Personal Data:** b Flushing, NY, February 24, 1935; m 1960, c 3. **Education:** Bucknell Univ, BS, 1957; Mass Inst Technol, PhD, 1962; Ore Inst Sci & Technol, MS, 1986. **Professional Experience:** RETIRED; systs programmer, Boeing Comput Serv, Bellevue, beginning 1986; consult, 1981- 1986; from assoc prof to prof chem, Memphis State Univ, 1972-1983; NSF resgrant, 1970-1975; NIH res grant, 1967-1970; asst prof chem, Univ Ore, 1966-1972; staff felbiosynthesis fatty acids, NIH, 1964-1966. **Memberships:** Am Soc Biol Chemists. **Research Statement & Publications:** Role of vitamin B-12, folic acid and pantothenate as coenzymes; biosynthesis of fatty acids; multienzyme complexes; protein turnover; parallel computers. **Mailing Address:** Boeing Info & Support Syst, PO Box 3707, Seattle, WA 98124-2207.

LARRABEE, R(OBERT) D(EAN), OPTICAL METROLOGY, SEM METROLOGY. **Personal Data:** b Flushing, NY, November 29, 1931; m 1953, Ramona; c David A & Susan (Albohn). **Education:** Bucknell Univ, BS & MS, 1953; Mass Inst Technol, SM, 1955, ScD, 1957; Rider Col, MBA, 1976. **Honors & Awards:** Bronze Metal Award, US Dept Commerce, 1999. **Professional Experience:** GUEST RESEARCHER, NAT INST STAND & TECHNOL, 1994-; group leader, Nat Inst Stand & Technol, 1981-1993; mem adj fac, Univ Md, 1981-1982; physicist, Nat Inst Stand & Technol, 1976-1981; sr engr, Advan Technol Lab, 1972-1976; res engr, David Sarnoff Res Ctr, RCA Corp, 1957-1971. **Memberships:** AAAS; sr mem Inst Elec & Electronics Engrs; Am Phys Soc; Sigma Xi. **Research Statement & Publications:** Semiconductor materials and devices; solid-state plasma physics; semiconductor microwave oscillators and amplifiers; infrared physics and detectors; characterization of semiconductor materials; optical and scanning electron microscope submicrometer metrology; granted 9 patents. **Mailing Address:** 18801 Woodway Dr, Derwood, MD 20855.

LARRICK, JAMES WILLIAM, HUMAN MONOCLONAL ANTIBODIES, CANCER THERAPEUTICS. **Personal Data:** b Englewood Colo, January 4, 1950; m 1995, Zi Hua; c 14. **Education:** Colo Col, BA, 1972; Duke Univ, PhD (immunol), 1979, MD, 1980. **Professional Experience:** VPRES & CHIEF TECH OFFICER, PLANET BIOTECHNOLOGY, as of 2003; dir explor res, Genelabs Inc, 1990; FOUNDER, PANORAMA RES INST, 1988-; dir, Genelabs Inc, 1985-1988; sr scientist, Cetus Immune Res Labs, 1985; scientist & proj leader, Cetus Immune Res Labs, 1982-1984; intern, Stanford Med Ctr, Palo Alto, 1981; Thomas J Watson fel. **Memberships:** Am Asn Immunologists; Am Fedn Clin Res; AAAS. **Research Statement & Publications:** Discovery and characterization of novel biopharmaceuticals for therapy and diagnosis of diseases; human monoclonal antibodies, cytokines. **Mailing Address:** Planet Biotechnology Inc, 25571 Clawiter Rd, Hayward, CA 94545. **E-Mail:** jwlarrick@aol.com

LARROWE, BOYD T, ELECTRONIC ENGINEERING. **Personal Data:** b Merriam, Kans, May 6, 1923; m 1959, Kathryn; c Ann (Baca), John, Martha (Henry) & David. **Education:** Univ Kans, BS, 1950; Univ Ill, MS, 1951. **Professional Experience:** RETIRED; res engr, Environ Res Inst Mich, 1973-1989; res engr, Inst Sci Technol, Univ Mich, 1964-1973; chief engr, Comput Displays, Burroughs Corp Labs, Mich, 1962-1964; sr engr, Strand Eng Co, 1957-1962; res assoc, Univ Mich, 1952-1957; Mem staff digital comput design, Univ Ill, 1950-1951. **Memberships:** Inst Elec & Electronics Engrs. **Research Statement & Publications:** Digital computer design; automatic radar image interpretation; display techniques; real time electronic processor design for synthetic aperture radar. **Mailing Address:** 403 Seneca St, Tecumseh, MI 49286-1022.

LARROWE, VERNON L, ELECTRICAL ENGINEERING. **Personal Data:** b Galax, Va, February 21, 1921; m 1966, Florence Glinicki; c Victoria. **Education:** Univ Kans, BS, 1950; Univ Ill, MS, 1951; Univ Mich, PhD (elec eng), 1964. **Professional Experience:** EMER MEM TECH STAFF, ENVIRON RES INST MICH, 1989-; sr res engr, Environ Res Inst Mich, 1983-1986; res engr, Environ Res Inst Mich, 1973-1983; res engr, Infrared & Optics Lab, Willow Run Labs, 1965-1973; res engr, Inst Sci & Technol, Univ Mich, Ann Arbor, 1957-1965; head analog comput lab, Inst Sci & Technol, Univ Mich, Ann Arbor, 1953-1965; assoc res engr, Inst Sci & Technol, Univ Mich, Ann Arbor, 1953-1957; res assoc, Inst Sci & Technol, Univ Mich, Ann Arbor, 1951-1953; Asst elec eng, Univ Ill, 1950-1951. **Memberships:** Inst Elec & Electronics Engrs; Soc Comput Simulation; Soc Photo-Optical&Instrumentation Engrs; NY Acad Sci. **Research Statement & Publications:** Application of electronic analog computers; data processing; information theory; remote sensing; automatic pattern recognition; high density digital recording; servo controls. **Mailing Address:** Environ Res Inst Mich, Box 134001, Ann Arbor, MI 48113-4001. **E-Mail:** vernon2616@aol.com

LARRY, JOHN ROBERT, PHYSICAL CHEMISTRY. **Personal Data:** b Mt Clare, WVa, November 13, 1939; m 1963, c 3. **Education:** WVa Univ, BS, 1961; Ohio State Univ, PhD (chem), 1966. **Honors & Awards:** Tech Achievement Award, Int Soc Hybrid Microelectronics, 1982. **Professional Experience:** RES MGR, ELECTRONICS DEPT, RES & DEVELOP DIV, E I DU PONT DE NEMOURS & CO INC, WILMINGTON, DEL, 1984-; res supvr, E I du Pont Del Nemours& Co, Inc, 1977-1984; sr res chemist, E I du Pont Del Nemours & Co, Inc, 1974-1976; reschemist, E I du Pont Del Nemours & Co, Inc, 1966-1974. **Memberships:** Am Chem Soc; Int Soc Hybrid Microelectronics. **Research Statement & Publications:** Charge transfer and molecular complexes; ultracentrifugation; emulsion polymerization; colloid chemistry; rheology; solid state conductors; solid state resistors; multilayer capacitors. **Mailing Address:** DuPont Co, Corp Info Ctr, Wilmington, DE 19880-0334.

LARSEN, A M, JR, AERONAUTICS. **Professional Experience:** COCHAIR, NASA LYNDON B JOHNSON SPACE CTR, as of 2002. **Memberships:** Am Asn Advan Sci. **Mailing Address:** NASA, Lyndon B Johnson Space Ctr, Houston, TX 77058. **Fax:** 713-483-1207.

LARSEN, ARNOLD LEWIS, BOTANY, AGRONOMY. **Personal Data:** b Audubon, Iowa, September 7, 1927; m 1950, c 2. **Education:** Univ Iowa, BA, 1950; Iowa State Univ, MS, 1961, PhD (econ bot), 1963. **Honors & Awards:** Award of Merit, Asn Off Seed Analysts. **Professional Experience:** RETIRED; res assoc prof seed technol, Colo State Univ, beginning 1970; dir, Colo Seed Lab, Colo State Univ, beginning 1970; botanist, Field Crops & Animal Prod Seed Res Lab, Agr Res Serv, USDA, 1963-1970; from assoc to res asst bot, Seed Lab, Iowa State Univ, 1957-1963; farmer, Audubon Co, Iowa, 1953-1957. **Memberships:** Am Soc Agron; Crop Sci Soc Am; Asn Off Seed Analysts; Coun Agr Sci &Technol; Int Seed Testing Asn; hon mem Soc Com Seed Technologists. **Research Statement & Publications:** Developmental procedures for determining quality of seeds. **Mailing Address:** Colo Seed Lab, Colo State Univ, Ft Collins, CO 80523. **E-Mail:** allarsen@frii.com

LARSEN, AUBREY ARNOLD, MEDICINAL CHEMISTRY. **Personal Data:** b Rockford, Ill, September 27, 1919; m 1943, Helen; c 5. **Education:** Antioch Col, BS, 1943; Mich State Col, MS, 1944; Cornell Univ, PhD (org chem), 1946. **Professional Experience:** RETIRED; vpres res & develop, Mead Johnson & Co, 1975-1982; vpres & sci dir, Bristol-Myers Int, 1970-1975; vpres phys sci, Mead Johnson & Co, Ind, 1967-1970; dir chem res, Mead Johnson & Co, Ind, 1963-1967; asst dir org chem, Mead Johnson & Co, Ind, 1960-1963; Mem staff, Sterling-Winthrop Res Inst, 1946-1960. **Memberships:** AAAS; NY Acad Sci; Am Chem Soc; Sigma Xi. **Research Statement & Publications:** Pharmaceutical and nutritional research and development. **Mailing Address:** 2920 Cypress Ct, Evansville, IN 47711-6725.

LARSEN, AUSTIN ELLIS, VETERINARY MEDICINE, MICROBIOLOGY. **Personal Data:** b Provo, Utah, November 1, 1923; m 1945, c 4. **Education:** Wash State Univ, BS, 1948, DVM, 1949; Univ Utah, MS, 1956, PhD (microbiol), 1969. **Professional Experience:** RETIRED; assoc prof cellular, viral & molecular virol, Col Med, Univ Utah, 1980-1987; mem, Health Task Force Utah; mem, Adv Comt Fur Farmers Res Inst; non-med medasst res, Vet Admin, 1969-; consult vet, Res Lab, Fur Breeders Agr Coop Lab, 1968-; dir, Vivarium, Col Med, Univ Utah, 1968-1987; asst prof, Col Med, Univ Utah, 1968-1980; consult, Schering Corp, 1963-; clin instr microbiol, Col Med, Univ Utah, 1961-1968; vet & dir, Res Lab, Fur Breeders Agr Coop Lab, 1952-1968; vet pvt pract, Utah, 1949-1968. **Memberships:** Am Soc Microbiol; Am Soc Exp Path; Am Soc Lab Animal Pract; Sigma Xi. **Research Statement & Publications:** Slow virus research. **Mailing Address:** 1825 S 230 E, Salt Lake City, UT 84108.

LARSEN, BARBARA SELIGER, MASS SPECTROMETRY. **Personal Data:** b Englewood, NJ, October 22, 1956; m 1980, c 2. **Education:** Santa Clara Univ, BS, 1978; Univ Del, PhD (phys chem), 1983. **Professional Experience:** SR RES ASSOC, DUPONT CO, as of 2004; RES SCIENTIST, CENT RES, DUPONT CO, 1984-; NSF postdoctoral fel, Johns Hopkins Univ, 1983-1984; res assoc, Int Diagnostics Tech, 1978-1979. **Memberships:** Am Soc Mass Spectrometry; Am Chem Soc; Int Protein Soc. **Research Statement & Publications:** Mass spectrometry as applied to the area of life sciences including sequence of proteins, identification of metabolites; new ionization techniques to expand the application of mass spectrometry. **Mailing Address:** Dupont Co, PO Box 80228, Wilmington, DE 19898. **E-Mail:** barbara.s.larsen@usa.dupont.co

LARSEN, CHARLES MCLOUD, MATHEMATICS EDUCATION. **Personal Data:** b Staten Island, NY, December 6, 1924; m 1948, c 4. **Education:** Cornell Univ, AB, 1945, AM, 1950; Stanford Univ, PhD (educ), 1960. **Professional Experience:** EMER PROF MATH, SAN JOSE STATE UNIV, 1988-; Vis prof, Beijing AgrUniv, China, 1985 & 1986-1987; From instr to prof, San Jose State Univ, 1954-1988. **Memberships:** Math Asn Am; Nat Coun Teachers Math. **Research Statement & Publications:** History of mathematics; mathematics education. **Mailing Address:** 1675 Ellis Hollow Rd, Ithaca, NY 14850.

LARSEN, CHARLES ROBERT, SYSTEMS ENGINEERING, MANAGEMENT. **Personal Data:** b Independence, Mo, August 7, 1944; div, c Peter Charles, Caryn Elizabeth, Jaime Lynn & Lauren Elizabeth. **Education:** Univ Calif, Berkeley, BS, 1966. **Professional Experience:** AEROSPACE ENGR, FED AVIATION ADMIN, US DEPT TRANSP, 1994-; consult & aerospace engr, Aerospace Consult Group, Inc, 1994; tech staff specialist, Fairchild Space & Defense Corp, 1991-1994; sr advan prog mgr, Aerospace Div, Gen Elec, 1983-1991; payloads & mech systs mgr, Ford Aerospace & Commun Corp, 1972-1983; sr proj engr, Bendix Aerospace, 1970-1972; lead thermal systs engr, Aerojet-Gen Corp, 1967-1970. **Memberships:** Assoc fel Am Inst Aeronaut & Astronaut. **Research Statement & Publications:** Aerospace safety of launch vehicles, with emphasis on the X-33 and X-34 programs leading to the development of the commercial reusable vehicle. **Mailing Address:** 30 Steeple Ct, Germantown, MD 20874. **Fax:** 202-267-5463. **E-Mail:** chuck.larsen@faa.dot.gov

LARSEN, CURTIS E, QUATERNARY GEOLOGY, COASTAL GEOMORPHOLOGY. **Personal Data:** b Elmhurst, Ill, October 8, 1939. **Education:** Univ Ill, BS, 1964; Western Wash Univ, MA, 1971; Univ Chicago, PhD (anthrop), 1980. **Professional Experience:** ASSOC EASTERN REGIONAL GEOLOGIST, GEOL DIV, US GEOLSURV, 1995-; res geologist, Geol Div, US Geol Surv, 1980-1995. **Memberships:** Am Quaternary Asn. **Mailing Address:** US Geol Surv, 954 Nat Ctr 12201 Sunrise Valley Dr, Reston, VA 20192. **Fax:** 703-648-6032. **E-Mail:** clarsen@usgs.gov

LARSEN, DAVID M, THEORETICAL PHYSICS. **Personal Data:** b Hawthorne, NJ, March 8, 1936; m 1958, c 3. **Education:** Mass Inst Technol, SB, 1957, PhD (physics), 1962. **Professional Experience:** PROF, UNIV MASS, LOWELL, 1987-; staff physicist, Francis Bitter NatMagnet Lab, 1976-1987; staff physicist, Lincoln Lab, Mass Inst Technol, 1964-1976; Nat Res Coun-Nat Bur Stand fel physics, Nat Bur Stand, Wash, DC, 1962-1964. **Memberships:** Fel Am Phys Soc. **Research Statement & Publications:** Impurities in semiconductors; polaron theory. **Mailing Address:** 6 Fessenden Way, Lexington, MA 02173. **E-Mail:** davidlarsen@uml.edu

LARSEN, DAVID W, PHYSICAL CHEMISTRY. **Personal Data:** b Chicago, Ill, February 21, 1936; m 1963. **Education:** Dana Col, BA, 1958; Northwestern Univ, PhD (phys chem), 1963. **Professional Experience:** PROF EMER, UNIV MO-ST LOUIS, as of 2006; prof, Univ MO-ST Louis, beginning 1980; assoc prof chem, Univ Mo-st Louis, 1966-1980; asst prof, Univ Mo-st Louis, 1964-1966; res assoc nuclear magnetic resonancespectros, Wash Univ, 1963-1964. **Memberships:** Am Chem Soc. **Research Statement & Publications:** Nuclear magnetic resonance spectroscopy; exchange reactions of Lewis acids and bases in non-aqueous media; ionic interactions in aqueous media; environmental chemistry; special gasification techniques; more than 10 publications. **Mailing Address:** Dept Chem, Univ Mo-St Louis, St Louis, MO 63121. **Fax:** 314-516-5342. **E-Mail:** dlarsen@umsl.edu

LARSEN, EDWARD WILLIAM, APPLIED MATHEMATICS. **Personal Data:** b Flushing, NY, November 12, 1944; m 1974. **Education:** Rensselaer Polytech Inst, BS, 1966, PhD (math), 1971. **Professional Experience:** Consult, Los Alamos Nat Lab, as of 2001; Consult, Lawrence Livemore Nat Lab, as of 2001; PROF, DEPT NUCLEAR ENG, UNIV MICH, 1986-; mem staff math, Los Alamos Nat Lab, 1977-1986; ed, TransportTheory & Statist Physics, 1975-; J Appl Math, 1976-; assoc prof, Univ Del, 1976-1977; asst prof math, NY Univ, 1971-1976. **Memberships:** Soc Indust & Appl Math; Am Nuclear Soc. **Research Statement & Publications:** Asymptotic expansions; spectral theory; numerical analysis; transport theory. **Mailing Address:** Univ Mich, Dept Nuclear Eng, 2929 Cooley Bldg N Campus 2355 Bonisteel Blvd, Ann Arbor, MI 48109-2104. **Fax:** 734-764-4540. **E-Mail:** edlarsen@umich.edu

LARSEN, ELLEN WYNNE, DEVELOPMENTAL GENETICS, EVOLUTION. **Personal Data:** b Paterson, NJ, April 28, 1942; American & Canadian citizen; c 1. **Education:** Univ Mich, BSc, 1963, MSc, 1967, PhD (zoology), 1969. **Professional Experience:** PROF ZOOL, UNIV TORONTO, as of 2004; assoc Prof Zool, Univ Toronto, beginning 1979; asst prof, Dept Zool, Univ Toronto, 1974-1979; fel genetics, Simon Fraser Univ, 1970-1974; Felcytogenetics, York Univ, 1969-1970. **Memberships:** AAAS; Genetics Soc Am; Genetics Soc Can. **Research Statement & Publications:** Genes and morphogenesis in fruit fly; imaginal discs evolutionary development biology; Research_Pubs: Tissue strategies as developmental constraints: implications for animal evolution; Time- and concentration-dependent response of the Drosophila antenna imaginal disc to Antennapedia; Antenna to leg transformations: dynamics of developmental competence; Evolution of development: The shuffling of ancient modules by ubiquitous bureaucracies; Are entrenched characters developmentally constrained? Creating biramous limbs in an insect; Genes, cell behaviour and form in Origination of Form. **Mailing Address:** Dept Zool, Univ Toronto, 25 Harbord St, Toronto, ON M5S 1A1, Can. **Fax:** 416-978-8532. **E-Mail:** ellenw@zoo.utoronto.ca

LARSEN, ERIC RUSSELL, organic chemistry; deceased, see previous edition for last biography

LARSEN, FENTON E, HORTICULTURE, POMOLOGY. **Personal Data:** b Preston, Idaho, March 22, 1934; m 1954, ReNae Buxton; c Steven, Kent, JulieAnn & Michael. **Education:** Utah State Univ, BS, 1956; Mich State Univ, PhD (hort), 1959. **Professional Experience:** Ecuador, 1985 & Jordan, 1988; Consult, Indonesia, 1982; vis prof, Univ Jordan, Amman, 1979; Consult, Costa Rica, 1979, 1987, 1988; Consult, Venezuela, 1977; Consult, Columbia, 1975; PROF & HORTICULTURIST, WASH STATE UNIV, 1973-; From asst horticulturist to assoc horticulturist, Wash State Univ, 1959-1973. **Memberships:** Emer mem Am Soc Hort Sci; emer mem Am Pomol Soc; emer mem Int Plant Propagators Soc; emer mem Sigma Xi emer mem. **Research Statement & Publications:** Pomology; propagation; rootstocks, growth regulators; leaf abscission and branching of nursery stock. **Mailing Address:** Dept Hort, Wash State Univ, Pullman, WA 99164-6414. **Fax:** 509-335-9503. **E-Mail:** flarsen@wsu.edu

LARSEN, FREDERICK DUANE, GEOMORPHOLOGY. **Personal Data:** b St Johnsbury, Vt, March 20, 1930; m 1952, c 4. **Education:** Middlebury Col, BA, 1952; Boston Univ, MA, 1960; Univ Mass, PhD (geol), 1972. **Professional Experience:** PROF EMER GEOL, NORWICH UNIV, 2000-; VT & NH Geol Surv, beginning 1983; prof geol, Norwich Univ, 1980-2000; US geol surv, 1968-1982; from instr to asst prof geol, Norwich Univ, 1957-1989. **Memberships:** Geol Soc Am; Soc Sedimentary Geol; Nat Asn Geol Teachers. **Research Statement & Publications:** Glacial geology if the Connecticut Valley of Mass, Vermont and New Hampshire; glacial geology of central Vermont. **Mailing Address:** Dept Earth Sci, Norwich Univ, 65 S Main St, Northfield, VT 05663-1004.

LARSEN, GREGORY N, MATHEMATICS. **Professional Experience:** STAFF, INST DEFENSE ANAL, as of 2005. **Memberships:** Inst Elec & Electronics Engr. **Mailing Address:** 2121 Jamieson Ave 1-2003, Alexandria, VA 22314. **Fax:** 703-845-2588.

LARSEN, HARRY STITES, FORESTRY. **Personal Data:** b Pittsburgh, Pa, August 12, 1927; m 1956, c 3. **Education:** Rutgers Univ, BS, 1950; Mich State Univ, MS, 1953; Duke Univ, PhD, 1963. **Professional Experience:** ASSOC PROF EMER, DEPT FORESTRY, 1991-; assoc prof forestry, Dept Forestry, 1989-1991; assoc prof silvicult, Dept Forestry, 1971-1980; asst prof, Auburn Univ, 1959-1971; forester, Southern Timber MgtServ, 1953-1956. **Memberships:** Ecol Soc Am; Soc Am Foresters. **Research Statement & Publications:** Tree physiology; nursery seedling quality. **Mailing Address:** 316 Buena Vista Dr, Lillian, AL 36549.

LARSEN, HOWARD JAMES, DAIRY NUTRITION. **Personal Data:** b Duluth, Minn, January 21, 1925; m 1946, c 2. **Education:** Univ Wis, BS, 1950; Iowa State Col, MS, 1952, PhD (dairy husb), 1953. **Professional Experience:** PROF EMER DAIRY SCI, UNIV WIS, MADISON, 1988-; consult, US Feed Grains Coun, 1981; from asst prof to prof, Marshfield Exp Sta, Univ Wis, 1955-1988; assoc & instr dairy husb, Iowa State Col, 1954-1955. **Memberships:** Fel AAAS; Coun Agr Sci & Technol; Am Soc Animal Sci; Am Dairy Sci Asn; Sigma Xi. **Research Statement & Publications:** Forage utilization by dairy cattle; forage and concentrate preservation and utilization by dairy cattle; environmental studies with ruminants. **Mailing Address:** Dept Dairy Sci, Univ Wis, 266 Animal Sci Bldg 1675 Observ Dr, Madison, WI 53706-1284. **Fax:** 608-263-9412.

LARSEN, HOWLAND AIKENS, CHEMICAL ENGINEERING. **Personal Data:** b Seattle, Wash, June 29, 1928; m 1962, c 6. **Education:** Mass Inst Technol, SB, 1950; Univ Ill, MS, 1951, PhD (chem eng), 1957. **Professional Experience:** RES ASSOC, PLASTICS PROD DEPT, E I DU PONT DEL NEMOURS &CO INC, 1980-; sr supvr, Fluorocarbons Div, 1969-1980; res supvr, E I du Pont Del Nemours &Co, Inc, 1967-1968; sr res engr, E I du Pont Del Nemours & Co, Inc, 1964-1966; res engr, E I duPont Del Nemours & Co, Inc, 1957-1964; jr engr, Shell Develop Co, 1951-1953. **Memberships:** Am Chem Soc. **Research Statement & Publications:** Thermoplastics; irreversible chemical effects of high pressure and shear. **Mailing Address:** 1360 Market St, Parkersburg, WV 26101.

LARSEN, JAMES BOUTON, COMBUSTION TOXICOLOGY, NATURAL TOXINS. **Personal Data:** b Detroit, Mich, July 28, 1941; m 1964, Anne; c Nathan & Susan. **Education:** Kalamazoo Col, BA, 1963; Univ Miami, MS, 1966, PhD (marine biol), 1968. **Professional Experience:** PROF EMER BOIL SCI, UNIV SOUTHERN MISS, as of 2001; prof biol, Univ Southern Miss, beginning 1993; res prof, Sch Pharm, Univ Conn, 1987; investr, Marine Biol Lab, Woods Hole, 1982; from asst prof to assoc prof, UnivSouthern Miss, 1973-1993; asst prof biol, Hamline Univ, 1968-1973; fel biochem, Colo StateUniv, 1967-1968. **Memberships:** AAAS; Sigma Xi; Am Soc Zoologists; Int Soc Toxinology. **Research Statement & Publications:** Physiological effects of carbon monoxide; combustion toxicology of polymers; physiology, toxicology and pharmacology of natural toxins. **Mailing Address:** Dept Biol Sci, Univ Southern Miss, 118 Col Dr, Hattiesburg, MS 39406-0001. **Fax:** 601-266-5797. **E-Mail:** jlarsen@ocean.st.usm.edu

LARSEN, JAMES VICTOR, CHEMICAL & MATERIALS ENGINEERING. **Personal Data:** b Salt Lake City, Utah, June 16, 1942; m 1966. **Education:** Univ Utah, BS, 1967; Univ Md, College Park, MS, 1969, PhD (chem eng), 1971. **Professional Experience:** PRES, WESTECH ENG, 1984-; pres, Molded Prod Div, 1977-; pres, Eng Dept, 1977-1984; gen mgr, opers, Eimco PMD, 1976-1977; gen mgr, Eimcomet Plastics, 1973-1976; sales mgr, Eimco Div, Envirotech Corp, 1971-1973; Chem engr, US Naval Ord Lab, 1967-1971. **Memberships:** Am Inst Chem Engrs; Am Inst Mining Engrs. **Research Statement & Publications:** Nonmetallic materials; carbon fiber composites; plastics. **Mailing Address:** 2906 Kennedy Dr, Salt Lake City, UT 84108.

LARSEN, JOHN HERBERT, VERTEBRATE ZOOLOGY. **Personal Data:** b Tacoma, Wash, July 20, 1929; m 1951. **Education:** Univ Wash, BA, 1955, MS, 1958, PhD (zoology), 1963. **Professional Experience:** PROF EMER ZOOL, WASH STATE UNIV, as of 2003; DIR, ELECTRON MICROS CTR, 1983-; chmn dept, Electron Micros Ctr, 1978-1984; prof zool, Wash State Univ, beginning 1975; from asst prof to assoc prof, Electron-Micros Ctr, 1965-1975; cur & instr zool, USPHS sr fel electron micros, 1964-1965; cur & instrzool, NIH res fel, 1963-1964; cur & instr zool, Univ Wash, 1961-1962; instr biol, Univ PugetSound, 1960-1961; instr embryol, Univ Wash, 1960. **Memberships:** Am Inst Biol Sci; Am Soc Zoologists; Sigma Xi; Soc Syst Zool; Am SocIchthyologists & Herpetologists. **Research Statement & Publications:** Evolution and functional morphology of feeding systems in amphibians; implications of neoteny to urodele evolution; mechanisms of ovulation in lower vertebrates. **Mailing Address:** Dept Zool, Sch Biol Sci, Wash State Univ, PO Box 644236, Pullman, WA 99164-4236. **Fax:** 509-335-3184. **E-Mail:** larsonj@mail.wsu.edu

LARSEN, JOHN W, ORGANIC CHEMISTRY, ORGANIC GEOCHEMISTRY. **Personal Data:** b Hartford, Conn, October 30, 1940; m, c 3. **Education:** Tufts Univ, BS in Chemistry, 1962; Purdue Univ, PhD in Chemistry, 1966. **Honors & Awards:** Storch Award, Am Chem Soc. **Professional Experience:** Senior Scientist Penn State, 2003- Prof., Dept. Chem., Lehigh Univ. 1984-2003; prof, Univ Tenn, Knoxville, 1978-1984; at chem div, Oak Ridge Nat Lab, 1976-1984; from asst prof to assoc prof chem, Univ Tenn, Knoxville, 1968-1978; res fel chem, Univ Pittsburgh, 1966-1968. **Memberships:** AAAS; Am Chem Soc; Sigma Xi. **Research Statement & Publications:** CHEMISTRY OF COALS AND KEROGENS; CARBON CATALYZED REACTIONS. **Mailing Address:** The Energy Inst, 209 Academic Projects Bldg, The Pa State Univ, Univ Park, PA 16802. **E-Mail:** JWL15@psu.edu

LARSEN, KENNETH MARTIN, APPLIED MATHEMATICS. **Personal Data:** b Ogden, Utah, June 26, 1927; m 1955, Merlee Smith; c 9. **Education:** Univ Utah, BA, 1950; Brigham Young Univ, MA, 1956; Univ Calif, Los Angeles, PhD (math), 1964. **Professional Experience:** EMER PROF MATH, BRIGHAM YOUNG UNIV, 1989-; from asst prof toprof, Brigham Young Univ, 1960-1989; Teaching asst math, Brigham Young Univ, 1954-1955 & UnivCalif, Los Angeles, 1956-1960. **Memberships:** Sigma Xi; Soc Indust & Appl Math. **Research Statement & Publications:** Numerical analysis; ordinary and partial differential equations; plasma confinement and stability. **Mailing Address:** Brigham Young Univ, 2270 N 300 E, Provo, UT 84604-5860.

LARSEN, LAWRENCE HAROLD, psychiatry; deceased, see previous edition for last biography

LARSEN, LELAND MALVERN, ALGEBRA. **Personal Data:** b Blair, Nebr, August 20, 1915; m 1940, c 3. **Education:** Dana Col, BA, 1941; Univ Nebr, MA, 1948, PhD, 1967. **Professional Experience:** PROF MATH, KEARNEY STATE COL, 1967-; head dept, Kearney StateCol, 1967-1980; assoc prof, Kearney State Col, 1948-1967; instr, Univ Nebr, 1943-1944; suptschs, Nebr, 1941-1943; Pub sch teacher, Nebr, 1936-1941. **Memberships:** Math Asn Am; Nat Coun Teachers Math. **Research Statement & Publications:** Theory of fields; various algorithms. **Mailing Address:** 4311 Sunset Trail, Kearney, NE 68847.

LARSEN, LLOYD DON, FOOD MICROBIOLOGY, EARLY DETECTION OF MICROBES. **Personal Data:** b Terre Haute, Ind, September 13, 1944; m 1969, Joyce; c Michael, David, Peter, Joanna, Nathan, James, Gregory & Kathryn. **Education:** Brigham Young Univ, BS, 1969, MS, 1974; Univ Minn, PhD (food microbiol), 1979. **Professional Experience:** MICROBIOLOGIST, DUGWAY, UTAH, 1984-; Sr scientist, Carnation Res Lab, 1979-1984. **Memberships:** Am Soc Microbiol; Inst Food Technol. **Research Statement & Publications:** Plasmids in industrial microorganisms including group N streptococci; improving fermentations via biotechnology; development of substitute dairy products; microbial detection kits. **Mailing Address:** 115 E 2075 S, Orem, UT 84058-8174. **Fax:** 435-833-5716. **E-Mail:** lloydlar@earthlink.net

LARSEN, LYNN ALVIN, NUTRITION. **Personal Data:** b Grand Forks, NDak, August 2, 1943; m 1966, Bette J Tandberg; c Rachel A & Kirk D. **Education:** Univ NDak, BS, 1965; Univ Wash, PhD (inorg chem), 1971. **Professional Experience:** CHIEF, OFF PUB HEALTH & SCI, FOOD SAFETY & INSPECTION SERV, USDA, 2002-; DIR, DIV NUTRIT & SCI POLICY, OFF NUTRIT PROD, CTR FOOD SAFETY & APPL NUTRIT, as of 2002;

dir, Div Nutrit Sci & Policy, Off Nutrit Prod, Labeling & Dietary Suppl, Ctr Food Safety & Appl Nutrit, Food & Drug Admin, 2000-2002; dir, Off Spec Nutrit, Ctr Food Safety & Appl Nutrit, Food & Drug Admin, 1998-2000; exec secy, Food Adv Comn, Ctr Food Safety & Appl Nutrit, Food & Drug Admin, 1992-1998; dir, exec opers staff, Ctr Food Safety & Appl Nutrit, Food & Drug Admin, 1991-1992; sci policy analyst, Ctr Food Safety & Appl Nutrit, Food & Drug Admin, 1990-1991; assoc dir prog develop, Div Nutrit, Ctr Food Safety & Appl Nutrit, Food & Drug Admin, 1981-1990; instr, Prog Educ Gifted, Prince William Co, Va, 1979-1983; consumer safety officer, Ctr Food Safety & Appl Nutrit, Food & Drug Admin, 1978-1981; chemist, GRAS Rev Br, Div Food & Color Additives, Ctr Food Safety & Appl Nutrit, Food & Drug Admin, 1977-1978; Wash State Heart Asn fel, Div Nephrology, Dept Med, Univ Wash, 1972-1974; res assoc, Div Nephrology, Dept Med, Univ Wash, 1971-1977. **Memberships:** Am Chem Soc; AAAS; Inst Food Technologists. **Mailing Address:** Div Nutrit & Sci Policy, Ctr Food Safety & Nutrit, 200 C St Southwest, Washington, DC 20204. **Fax:** 202-260-8957.

LARSEN, MARLIN LEE, CLINICAL CHEMISTRY. **Personal Data:** b Grand Island, Nebr, November 22, 1942; m 1964, c 3. **Education:** Kearney State Col, BS, 1964; Wash State Univ, PhD (chem), 1968. **Professional Experience:** PRES, HARVARD LAB & XRAY INC, ROSEBURG, ORE, 1981-; CONSULT, Harvard Lab & Xray Inc, Roseburg, Ore, 1979-; Dir res & develop, ICN Med Labs, Inc, 1968-1979. **Memberships:** Am Asn Clin Chemists; Am Asn Bioanalysts; Am Chem Soc. **Research Statement & Publications:** Automation and methodology research of medical laboratory procedures. **Mailing Address:** 160 Rivershore Dr, Roseburg, OR 97470.

LARSEN, MAX DEAN, ALGEBRA. **Personal Data:** b Pratt, Kans, January 23, 1941; m 1962. **Education:** Kans State Teachers Col, BA, 1961; Univ Kans, MA, 1963, PhD (math), 1966. **Professional Experience:** Dean, Col Arts & Sci, Univ Nebr-Lincoln, 1974-1982; PROF MATH, UNIVNEBR-LINCOLN, 1973-; NSF res grant, 1968-1970; from asst prof to assoc prof, UnivNebr-Lincoln, 1966-1973. **Memberships:** Am Math Soc; Math Asn Am; Nat Coun Teachers Math; Sigma Xi. **Research Statement & Publications:** Extension of integral domain concepts to general commutative rings, particularly valuation theory; module theory over commutative rings. **Mailing Address:** 641 Haverford Circle, Lincoln, NE 68510-2313.

LARSEN, MIGUEL FOLKMAR, MESOSCALE & RADAR METEOROLOGY. **Personal Data:** b Caracas, Venezuela, June 2, 1953; American citizen; m 1978. **Education:** Univ Rochester, BS, 1975; Cornell Univ, MS, 1977, PhD (meteorol), 1979. **Professional Experience:** PROF PHYSICS, CLEMSON UNIV, as of 2003; GRAD COORDR, CLEMSON UNIV, as of 2003; prin investr, Air Force Off Sci Res grant, 1985-1988; NASA grant, 1986-1988; mem, sci adv comt, Arecibo Observ, 1985-1987; asst Prof Physics, Clemson Univ, beginning 1984; res assoc ionospheric physics, Cornell Univ, 1979-1984. **Memberships:** Am Geophys Union; Am Meteorol Soc. **Research Statement & Publications:** Mesoscale meteorological research using radar wind profilers; studies of neutral and ion interactions in the auroral zone thermosphere using sounding rockets and radars. **Mailing Address:** Dept Physics, Clemson Univ, 203 Kinard Lab, Clemson, SC 29634. **Fax:** 864-656-0805. **E-Mail:** mlarsen@clemson.edu

LARSEN, PAUL M, EDUCATION, PATHOPHYSIOLOGY. **Personal Data:** b Evanston, Ill, October 2, 1947; m 1984, Moira; c Jens, Rebeca, Ethan & Zachary. **Education:** Univ MD, PhD, 1987. **Honors & Awards:** NISOD Excell Awd, Univ of Texas, 1999; Phi Kappa Phi. **Professional Experience:** PROF BIOL, ANNE ARUNDEL COMMUNITY COL, 1998-; asst prof biol, Anne Arundel Community Col, 1994-1998; res assoc bot, Univ Md, 1987-1994. **Memberships:** Amer Soc for Cell Bio; Micros Soc of Aner. **Research Statement & Publications:** Coullar Physuicilgy and the melltamison in mitdsis and cell secretion. **Mailing Address:** Dept Biol, Anne Arundel Community Col, 101 Col Pkwy, Arnold, MD 21012-1895.

LARSEN, PETER FOSTER, BIOLOGICAL OCEANOGRAPHY. **Personal Data:** b Mt Kisco, NY. **Education:** Univ Conn, BA, 1967, MS, 1969; Col William & Mary, PhD (marine sci), 1974. **Professional Experience:** Adj prof life sci, Univ New Eng, 1996-2005; grad fac, U. Maine, 1997-2002; prin investr, Kennebec Area Res Endowment, beginning 1991; gov bd, Estuarine Res Fedn, 1980-1984 & secy, 1981-1983; SR RES SCIENTIST, BIGELOW LAB OCEAN SCI, 1977-; res scientist, Kennebec Area Res Endowment, 1976-1977; consult, Res Inst Gulf Maine, 1973- & Bigelow Lab Ocean Sci, 1975-1976; pres, Coastal Sci, beginning 1973; state oceanogr, Maine Dept Marine Resources, 1973-1976; asst marine scientist ecol, Va Inst Marine Sci, 1972-1973; res asst marine biol, Va Inst Marine Sci, 1970-1972; lectr chem, Norwalk Community Col, 1968-1970. **Memberships:** New Eng Estuarine Res Soc (secy-treas 1980-1982 pres 1982-1984 past pres 1984-1986); Estuarine & Coastal Sci Asn; Estuarine Res Fedn. **Research Statement & Publications:** The documentation of benthic community structure and function in the estuarine and marine environments of the Gulf of Maine region; environmental quality of the New England estuaries and their influence on the coastal ocean; Remote sensing of shallow marine environments. **Mailing Address:** Bigelow Lab Ocean Sci, 180 McKown Pt Rd PO Box 475, West Boothbay Harbor, ME 04575-0475. **Fax:** 207-633-9641. **E-Mail:** plarsen@bigelow.org

LARSEN, PHILIP O, PLANT PATHOLOGY, TURFGRASS PATHOLOGY. **Personal Data:** b Audubon Co, Iowa, December 1, 1940; m 1961, c 3. **Education:** Iowa State Univ, BS, 1963; Univ Ariz, MS, 1967, PhD (plant path), 1969. **Professional Experience:** PROF, DEPT PLANT PATH, UNIV MINN, as of 2004; DEPT HEAD, DEPT PLANT PATH, UNIV MINN, 1985-; SR ASSOC DEAN, RES COL AGR, UNIV MINN, 1985-; from asst prof to prof plantpath, Ohio State Univ, 1969-1985. **Memberships:** Am Phytopath Soc. **Research Statement & Publications:** Diseases of turf grasses. **Mailing Address:** Dept Plant Path, Univ Minn, 1991 Upper Buford Circle St, St Paul, MN 55108. **Fax:** 612-625-9728. **E-Mail:** phill@umn.edu

LARSEN, RALPH IRVING, ENVIRONMENTAL ENGINEERING, MATHEMATICAL MODELING OF AIR POLLUTANT CONCENTRATIONS & EFFECTS. **Personal Data:** b Corvallis, Ore, November 26, 1928; m 1991, Anne Harmon Larsen; c Karen, Eric, Kristine, Jan, Vikki K (Ball), Terri K (Readling) & Cindi K (King). **Education:** Ore State Univ, BS, 1950; Harvard Univ, MS, 1955, PhD (air pollution, indust hyg), 1957. **Honors & Awards:** Commendation Medal, USPHS, 1979. **Professional Experience:** ENVIRON RES ENGR, HUMAN EXPOSURE & ATMOSPHERIC SCIENCES DIV, NAT ENVIRON RES LAB, US ENVIRON PROTECTION AGENCY, 1988-; environ res engr, Environ Opers Br, Meteorol & Assessment Div, Atmospheric Sci Res Lab, 1971-1988; res engr, Off Criteria & Stand, 1967-1971; asst chief Field Studies Br, 1965-1967; chief, Biomet Sect, Field Studies Br, 1963-1965; chief tech serv, State & Community Serv Sect, Nat Air Pollution Control Admin, 1957-1961; Sanit engr, Div Water Pollution Control, USPHS, 1950-1954. **Memberships:** Air & Waste Mgt Asn; Sigma Xi; AAAS. **Research Statement & Publications:** Studies on the concentration, effects and control of air pollution; mathematical modeling; computer analyses. **Mailing Address:** 4012 Colby Dr, Raleigh, NC 27609-6045.

LARSEN, ROBERT PAUL, HORTICULTURE, UNIVERSITY ADMINISTRATION. **Personal Data:** b Vineyard, Utah, December 1, 1926; m 1948, Lorna; c Nanette (Dunford), Peggy (Rinehart), Mark & Cynthia (Bennett). **Education:** Utah State Univ, BS, 1950; Kans State Univ, MS, 1951; Mich State Univ, PhD (hort), 1955. **Professional Experience:** RETIRED; vpres univ exten, Utah State Univ, 1982-1992; prof hort & supt, Tree Fruit Res Ctr, Wash State Univ, 1968-1982; from asst prof to prof hort, Mich State Univ, 1955-1968. **Memberships:** Fel Am Soc Hort Sci (pres, 1975-1976); Int Soc Hort Sci; fel AAAS. **Research Statement & Publications:** Physiology, nutrition and management of tree fruit crops. **Mailing Address:** 1175 N Cedar Heights Dr, Logan, UT 84341.

LARSEN, RONALD JOHN, MATHEMATICAL ANALYSIS. **Personal Data:** b Chicago, Ill, January 1, 1937; m 1962, c 1. **Education:** Mich State Univ, BS, 1957, MS, 1959; Stanford Univ, PhD (math), 1964. **Professional Experience:** Adj assoc prof, Clarkson Col Technol, 1977-1978; vis assoc prof, State Univ NY, Binghamton, 1975-1976 & Albany, 1976-1977; vis asst, Univ Oslo, 1973-1974; Fulbright-Hays travel award, Norway, 1973-1974; assoc prof math, Wesleyan Univ, 1970-1975; Fulbright-Hays advan res grant, Univ Oslo, 1968-1969; asst prof, Cowell Col, Univ Calif, Santa Cruz, 1965-1970; Instr math, Yale Univ, 1963-1965. **Memberships:** Am Math Soc; Math Asn Am; Norweg Math Soc. **Mailing Address:** 174 County Rte 35, Canton, NY 13617.

LARSEN, RUSSELL D, CHEMICAL PHYSICS, STATISTICS. **Personal Data:** b Muskegon, Mich, June 6, 1936; m 1958, c 2. **Education:** Kalamazoo Col, BA, 1957; Kent State Univ, PhD (chem), 1964. **Professional Experience:** Pres, Southwestern & Rocky Mountain Div, 1987-1988; DEPT CHEM, TEX TECH UNIV, LUBBOCK, 1983-; assoc prof, dept chem, Univ Mich, 1977-1983; actg assoc prof, dept chem, Univ Nev, Reno, 1976-1977; asst prof chem, Tex A&M Univ, 1972-1976; asst prof, Ill Inst Technol, 1966-1972; Robert A Welch fel, RiceUniv, 1965-1966; res assoc, Princeton Univ, 1964-1965; asst instr, Kent State Univ, 1964; Teaching asst chem, Univ Cincinnati, 1958-1960. **Memberships:** Am Chem Soc; Am Phys Soc; Am Statist Asn; Sigma Xi; AAAS. **Research Statement & Publications:** Chemical and biomedical signal processing; spectral analysis; Walsh functions; spline representations; zero-based signal representations; chemical education, chaos. **Mailing Address:** Tex Dept Health T801, 1100 W 49th St, Austin, TX 78756.

LARSEN, SIGURD YVES, THEORETICAL PHYSICS. **Personal Data:** b Brussels, Belg, August 14, 1933; American citizen. **Education:** Columbia Univ, AB, 1954, MA, 1956, PhD (physics), 1962. **Professional Experience:** PROF EMER PHYSICS, TEMPLE UNIV, as of 1996; prof physics & chmn dept, Temple Univ, beginning 1975; vis prof, Mex Inst Petrol, 1971-1972 & Nat Univ Mex, 1972; assoc prof, Temple Univ, 1968-1975; consult, Nat Bur Stand, 1968-1971; consult, Lawrence Radiation Lab, 1967-1972; mem panel quantum fluids, Int Union Pure & Appl Chem, 1966-; consult, Los Alamos Sci Lab, 1964; physicist, Wash, DC, 1963-1968; nat acad sci-nat res coun assoc, 1962-1963; consult, Nat Bur Stand, 1962; asst physics, Columbia Univ, 1954-1957 & 1960-1962. **Memberships:** Am Phys Soc; Ital Phys Soc; Sigma Xi. **Research Statement & Publications:** Statistical physics; quantum theory; numerical analysis. **Mailing Address:** Dept Physics, Temple Univ, Philadelphia, PA 19122. **Fax:** 215-787-5652. **E-Mail:** syl@temple.edu

LARSEN, STEVEN H, AAV GENE THERAPY VECTORS & CHLAMYDIA TRACHOMATIS, HETEROLOGOUS GENE EXPRESSION. **Personal Data:** b Bringham City, Utah, August 28, 1944; m 1968, Mary; c Jill, Bert, Hans, Jacob & Kimberly. **Education:** Utah State Univ, BA, 1968, MS, 1970; Univ Wis, PhD (biochem), 1974. **Professional Experience:** ASSOC PROF MICROBIOL, IND UNIV SCH MED, 1995-; vis prof, Tokushimo Univ, 1991; Eli Lilly Young Scientist Res Awards, 1983-1985; consult, Human Amylase Cloning Group, Dept Genetics, Ind Univ, 1980-1986; asst prof, Ind Univ Sch Med, 1979-1995; instr, Johns Hopkins Univ Sch Med, 1977; fel microbiol, Johns Hopkins Univ Sch Med, 1975-1979; fel genetics, Univ Wis, 1974-1975; trainee biochem, Univ Wis, 1970-1974; teaching asst chem & physics, Utah State Univ, 1966-1970. **Memberships:** Am Soc Microbiol; AAAS. **Research Statement & Publications:** Development of eukaryotic cloning vectors; Chlamydia trachomatics genetics. **Mailing Address:** Dept Microbiol & Immunol, Ind Univ Sch Med, 635 Barnhill Dr, Indianapolis, IN 46202. **Fax:** 317-274-4090. **E-Mail:** slarsen@iupui.edu

LARSEN, TED LEROY, PHYSICS, SEMICONDUCTORS. **Personal Data:** b Jerome, Idaho, March 18, 1935; m 1957, c 2. **Education:** Univ Calif, Berkeley, BS, 1961, MS, 1962; Stanford Univ, PhD (mat sci), 1970. **Professional Experience:** DIR RES & DEVELOP, ENG OPTOELECTRONICS DIV, GENINSTRUMENT CORP, 1979-; res & develop sect mgr semiconductors, Hewlett-Packard Co, 1971-1979; res & develop group leader, Hewlett-Packard Co, 1968-1971; mem tech staff, Hewlett-Packard Co, 1962-1965. **Memberships:** Electrochem Soc; Inst Elec & Electronics Engrs. **Research Statement & Publications:** III-V compound materials and devices for optoelectronic and microwave applications, including single crystal and epitaxial growth, crystalline defects, impurity diffusion and minority carrier recombination processes; III-IV and silicon device and product development including led lamps and displays and optocouplers. **Mailing Address:** 1109 Hamilton Ave, Palo Alto, CA 94301.

LARSEN, WILLIAM L(AWRENCE), CORROSION, FAILURE ANALYSIS. **Personal Data:** b Crookston, Minn, July 16, 1926; m 1954, Gracie Richey; c Eric & Thomas. **Education:** Marquette Univ, BME, 1948; Ohio State Univ, MS, 1950, PhD (metall eng), 1956. **Professional Experience:** Prof emer and consult metallurgical eng, Iowa state univ, 1993-; prof, dept of materials sci and eng, Iowa state univ, 1976-1993; prof, dept of metallurgy, Iowa state univ, 1973-1976; from assoc prof to prof metall, Iowa state univ, 1969-1973; CONSULT PROF METALL ENGR, 1962-; from assoc metallurgist to metallurgist, Ames Lab of the AEC, 1958-1969; asst prof mech eng & chem, Iowa State Univ, 1958-1962; res metallurgist, E I du Pont de Nemours & Co, Inc, 1956-1958; Res assoc metall eng, Ohio State Univ res found, 1951-1956; lab asst, inst for the study of metals, univ of chicago, 1950-1951; res fel, Battelle memorial inst, Columbus, Oh, 1948-1950; prof engr, Iowa; Consult mat design, mat failure & educ progs for superior students. **Memberships:** Am Soc Metals Int; Nat Asn Corrosion Engrs Int; Am Soc Eng Educ (former chair, materials division); Am Soc Testing & Mat; Nat Soc Prof Engrs; Nat collegiate honors council (former nat exec cmt mem). **Research Statement & Publications:** Metallurgical engineering design and failure analysis; expert witness-product liability; consultant to industry and legal profession. **Mailing Address:** 335 N Franklin Ave, Ames, IA 50014-3424. **E-Mail:** slarsenpe@aol.com

LARSEN-BASSE, JORN, MATERIALS SCIENCE, CORROSION. **Personal Data:** b Maribo, Denmark, October 14, 1934. **Education:** Tech Univ Danish, MS, 1958, PhD (metall), 1961. **Professional Experience:** VIS SCIENTIST, NAT INST SCI & TECHNOL, 1988-; PROG DIR, SURFACE ENG & TRIBOLOGY, NSF, 1988-; prog dir, NSF, 1988-1991; prof mech eng, Ga Inst Technol, 1986-1991; chmn dept, Univ Hawaii, 1976-1980 & 1982-1985; hon vis prof, Univ NSW, 1971 & Commonwealth Sci & Indust Res Orgn, Melbourne, 1972; Ford Found resident indust, 1968-1969; from asst prof to prof mech eng,

Univ Hawaii, 1964-1986; asst prof, San Jose State Col, 1963-1964; res assoc mat sci, Stanford Univ, 1963; researcher, Soderfors Bruk, Sweden, 1961-1962; actg asst prof metall, Tech Univ Denmark, 1959-1961. **Memberships:** Am Inst Mining Metall & Petrol Engrs; Nat Asn Corrosion Engrs; Am Soc Mech Engrs; Sigma Xi; Soc Tribologists & Lubrication Engrs; fel Am Soc Metals. **Research Statement & Publications:** Abrasion resistance of metals; corrosion in marine and volcanic environments; ocean thermal energy conversion; microstructure-property relations; surface engineering. **Mailing Address:** Tribology Prog, NSF, 4201 Wilson Blvd Rm 545, Arlington, VA 22230. **Fax:** 703-292-9053. **E-Mail:** jlarsenb@nsf.gov

LARSON, ALLAN, SYSTEMATIC BIOLOGY. **Personal Data:** b Silver Spring, Md, November 7, 1953. **Education:** Univ Md, Col Park, BS, 1975, MS, 1977; Univ Calif, Berkeley, PhD (genetics), 1982. **Professional Experience:** PROF BIOL, WASH UNIV, as of 2001; assoc ed, Am Naturalist, 2002-; assoc ed, Syst Biol, 1992-1998; assoc prof, dept biol, Wash Univ, 1992-1997; Assoc ed, Evolution, 1992-1996; asst prof, Dept Biol, Wash Univ, 1986-1992; res assoc, Dept Biochem, Univ Calif, Berkeley, 1983-1986. **Memberships:** Am Soc Naturalists; Genetics Soc Am; Herpetologist's League; Soc Study Evolution; Soc Molecular Biol & Evolution; Soc Syst Biologists. **Research Statement & Publications:** Molecular population genetics and systematics, especially of amphibians and lizards; laboratory activities include amplification and sequencing of mitochondrial and nuclear DNA, and use of DNA sequence variation to study phylogenetic relationships among species and the genetic structures of populations. **Mailing Address:** PO Box 2904, St Louis, MO 63130-0304. **Fax:** 314-935-4432. **E-Mail:** larson@wustlb.wustl.edu

LARSON, ALLAN BENNETT, INDUSTRIAL PHARMACY, COSMETIC CHEMISTRY. **Personal Data:** b Chicago, Ill, February 9, 1943; m 1971, Virginia L House; c Michael A & Jacie L. **Education:** Drake Univ, BS, 1966; Univ Wis, MS, 1969; Purdue Univ, PhD (phys & industpharm), 1972. **Professional Experience:** DIR PROCESS RES & DEVELOP, WYETH-AYERST RES, AM HOMEPROD, 1987-; dir, process res & develop, Ayerst Labs, 1984-1987; mgr tech serv, Vicks PersonalCare Div, 1980-1984; group leader, Vick Divs Res & Develop, 1977-1980; sr pharmaceutscientist, Richardson-Merrell, Inc, 1976-1977; sr res pharmacist, Dorsey Labs Div, Sandoz-Wander Inc, 1972-1976. **Memberships:** Am Pharmaceut Asn; Acad Pharmaceut Sci; Soc Cosmetic Chemists; Am AsnPharmaceut Scientists; Drug Info Asn. **Research Statement & Publications:** Pharmaceutical and skin care product development and stability, preformulation, uniformity of mixing, scale-up technology, process improvements, process validation; process optimization; technology transfer. **Mailing Address:** 5 Bouchard Dr, Peru, NY 12972-9714.

LARSON, ANDREW HESSLER, EXTRACTIVE CHEMICAL METALLURGY. **Personal Data:** b Peru, Ill, September 14, 1931. **Education:** Mo Sch Mines, BS, 1953, MS, 1954; Univ Mo, PhD (metall), 1959. **Professional Experience:** METALL CONSULT, 1988-; dir metals eng, GNB Inc, 1984-1988; dir prod develop & eng, Metals Div, Gould Inc, 1978-1984; mgr res & develop, Bunker Hill Co, 1969-1978; sr res metallurgist, Bunker Hill Co, 1968-1969; Ford Found Prog prod specialist, Tex Div, Dow Chem Co, 1966-1967; from assoc prof to prof, Colo Sch Mines, 1963-1968; From asst prof to assoc prof metall eng, Mo Sch Mines, 1959-1963. **Memberships:** emer mem Am Inst Mining Metall & Petrol Engrs; emer mem Sigma Xi. **Research Statement & Publications:** High temperature thermodynamic and kinetic studies of metallurgical systems involving the extraction and refining of metals. **Mailing Address:** 4116 Strawberry Lane, Eagan, MN 55123-1421.

LARSON, ARVID GUNNAR, SIGNAL PROCESSING, COMPUTER ARCHITECTURE. **Personal Data:** b Chicago, Ill, July 26, 1937; m 1989, Nicole; c Gregory Monte Larson. **Education:** Ill Inst Tech, BS, 1959; Stanford Univ, MS, 1966, PhD (elec eng), 1973. **Honors & Awards:** Centennial Medal, Inst Elec & Electronics Engrs, 1984; Prof Achievement Award, Inst of Elec and Electronics Engrs, 1987. **Professional Experience:** CHMN, NICOLE LARSON ASSOC, 1991-; program mgr, Mitre Corp, 1999-; chief sci, Walcoff Assoc, 1993-1999; res prof, George Mason Univ, 1991-1992; sr vpres, Syntek Eng & Comput Systs, 1989-1990; prin, Booz, Allen & Hamilton Inc, 1986-1989; vpres, Analytical Disciplines Inc, 1985-1986; div mgr, Advan Res & Appln Corp, 1980-1985; proj mgr, Syst Planning Corp, 1978-1980; mgr, Appl Res Group, Planning Res Corp, 1974-1978; res engr, Stanford Res Inst, 1964-1974. **Memberships:** Sigma Xi; fel Inst Elec & Electronics Engrs, vpres 1992; Am Assoc Engr Societies, chair R&D 1994-1998; Cosmos Club, treas 1997-1999. **Research Statement & Publications:** Computer systems and network architecture, high speed signal processing; software engineering; systems science. **Mailing Address:** Nicole Larson Associates, PO Box 83130, San Diego, CA 92138-3130. **Fax:** 858-274-6226. **E-Mail:** larsons@n2.net

LARSON, BENNETT CHARLES, X-RAY DIFFRACTION, CRYSTAL DEFECTS. **Personal Data:** b Buffalo, NDak, October 9, 1941. **Education:** Concordia Col, BA, 1963; Univ NDak, MS, 1965; Univ Mo, PhD (physics), 1970. **Honors & Awards:** Bertram E Warren Diffraction Physics Award, Am Crystallog Asn, 1985; Sidhu Award, Pittsburg Diffraction Soc, 1974. **Professional Experience:** GROUP LEADER & DISTINGUISHED STAFF SCIENTIST, CONDENSED MATTER SCI DIV, OAK RIDGE NAT LAB, as of 2003; sect head, Solid State Div, Oak Ridge Nat Lab, 1990-2001; group leader, 1980-1990; guest scientist, KFA-Julich, Ger, 1974-1975; group leader, Solid State Div, Oak Ridge Nat Lab, 1973-2001; physicist, 1969-1979; res staff, Solid State Div, Oak Ridge Nat Lab, 1969-1973. **Memberships:** Am Phys Soc; Am Crystallog Asn; Mat Res Soc; Advan Photon Source Proposal Eval Panel; Chess Policy & Adv board. **Research Statement & Publications:** X-ray diffraction study of intrinsic and induced defects in crystalline solids using diffuse scattering; x-ray diffraction study of pulsed-laser annealing; x-ray diffraction using synchrotron radiation; inelastic scattering; published over 10 articles. **Mailing Address:** Oak Ridge Nat Lab, PO Box 2008 MS6030, Oak Ridge, TN 37831-6030. **Fax:** 865-574-4143. **E-Mail:** larsonbc@ornl.gov

LARSON, BRUCE LINDER, BIOCHEMISTRY, NUTRITION. **Personal Data:** b Minneapolis, Minn, June 24, 1927; m 1954, Marjorie; c Eric, David & Brian. **Education:** Univ Minn, BS, 1948, PhD (biochem), 1951. **Honors & Awards:** Gold Medal, Am Chem Soc, 1966. **Professional Experience:** EMER PROF, DEPT ANIMAL SCI & NUTRIT SCI, UNIV ILL, URBANA-CHAMPAIGN, 1990-; head, Dept Dairy Sci, 1979-1981; prin investr, Nat Dairy Coun, 1976-1979; mem nutrit sci fac, Dept Dairy Sci, 1972-1990; prin investr, NIH, 1972-1975; mem, Milk Synthesis Comn, 1969; prin investr, NSF, 1959-1974, 1979-1982; mem, Milk Proteins Comn, Am Dairy Sci Asn, 1955-1986; from instr to prof biol chem, Univ Ill, Urbana, 1951-1990; asst, Univ Minn, 1948-1951. **Memberships:** Fel AAAS; Am Chem Soc; Am Soc Biochem & Molecular Biol; Am Dairy Sci Asn. **Research Statement & Publications:** Lactation and mammary gland metabolism in the formation of mammary secretions; cellular ejection of products and biological significance of colostrum and milk; pathways of radioactive contaminants into milk and other foods. **Mailing Address:** Dept Animal Sci, Univ Ill, 312 Animal Sci Lab MC-630, Urbana, IL 61801. **E-Mail:** bllarso@uiuc.edu

LARSON, CHARLES FRED, MECHANICAL ENGINEERING, RESEARCH & TECHNOLOGY MANAGEMENT. **Personal Data:** b Gary, Ind, November 27, 1936; m 1959, Joan; c Gregory P & Laura A. **Education:** Purdue Univ, BS, 1958; Fairleigh Dickinson Univ, Rutherford, MBA, 1973. **Professional Experience:** SECY, INDUST RES INST RES CORP, 1975-; EXEC DIR, INDUST RES INST INC, 1975-; asst dir, Welding Res Coun, 1960-1975; proj engr, Combustion Eng, Inc, 1958-1960. **Memberships:** Fel AAAS; Am Soc Mech Engrs; Soc Res Adminr; Nat Soc Prof Engrs. **Research Statement & Publications:** Pressure vessels; fatigue of welded structures; fracture toughness of metals; nondestructive examination; heavy-section steels; research management; research and technical management. **Mailing Address:** Indust Res Inst Inc, 2200 Clarendon Blvd Ste 1102, Arlington, VA 22201. **Fax:** 703-647-2581.

LARSON, CURTIS L(UVERNE), AGRICULTURAL & CIVIL ENGINEERING. **Personal Data:** b Cottonwood, Minn, October 10, 1920; m 1944, c 3. **Education:** Univ Minn, BAgrE, 1943, MS, 1949; Stanford Univ, PhD (civil eng), 1965. **Professional Experience:** PROF EMER AGR ENG, INST AGR, UNIV MINN, ST PAUL, as of 2003; Chile, 1976 & Panama, 1978; Water mgt consult, Nicaragua, 1975; Water mgtconsult, Colombia, 1972-1973; prof agr eng, inst agr, Univ Minn, St Paul, beginning 1965; From instr to assoc prof, Inst Agr, Univ Minn, St Paul, 1948-1965. **Memberships:** Am Soc Agr Engrs; Am Geophys Union; Am Water Resources Asn; Soil ConservSoc Am. **Research Statement & Publications:** Surface water hydrology; watershed modeling; erosion control; water resources. **Mailing Address:** 1666 Coffman St Apt 305, St Paul, MN 55108.

LARSON, D WAYNE, PHYSICAL CHEMISTRY. **Personal Data:** b Prince Albert, Sask, December 2, 1938. **Education:** Univ Sask, BA, 1961, MA, 1962; Univ Toronto, PhD (inorg chem), 1965. **Professional Experience:** From asst to dean, Fac Grad Studies & Res, Univ Regina, 1973-1979; ASSOC PROF CHEM, UNIV REGINA, 1971-; asst prof, Univ Regina, 1968-1971; Mem res staff, Can Forces Inst Aviation Med, 1965-1968. **Memberships:** Chem Inst Can; Can Nuclear Soc. **Research Statement & Publications:** Science education, attitudes toward science; technology assessment, ethics, public policy; social issues, perceptions of risk, energy resources; uranium development in Saskatchewan. **Mailing Address:** Dept Chem, Univ Regina, Regina, SK S4S 0A2, Can.

LARSON, DANIEL JOHN, LASER SPECTROSCOPY, NEGATIVE IONS. **Personal Data:** b Minneapolis, Minn, November 8, 1944. **Education:** St Olaf Col, Minn, BA, 1966; Harvard Univ, Mass, MA, 1967, PhD (physics), 1971. **Professional Experience:** DEAN, EBERLY COL SCI, PA STATE UNIV, 1998-; prof physics, Univ VA, 1996-1998; chair dept, Physics Dept, 1991-1997; Vis scientist, Nat Bur Stand, 1985-1986 & Lab Aime Cotton, Orsay, France, 1991; assoc dean, Fac Arts & Sci, 1989-1991; vis prof, Chalmers Univ, Gothenburg, Swed, 1986; from assoc prof to prof, Univ Va, 1978-1996; From asst prof to assoc prof physics, Harvard Univ, 1970-1978. **Memberships:** Am Phys Soc; Optical Soc Am. **Research Statement & Publications:** High resolution optical and microwave spectroscopy of atoms and ions, especially negative ions, using tunable lasers and atom and ion storage and beam techniques; atomic structure and interactions in strong fields. **Mailing Address:** PA State Univ, 517 Joab L Thomas Bldg, Univ Park, PA 16802. **Fax:** 814-863-0491. **E-Mail:** djlarson@psu.edu

LARSON, DAVID MICHAEL, VASCULAR CELL BIOLOGY, INTERCELLULAR COMMUNICATION & GAP JUNCTION. **Personal Data:** b St Paul, Minn, January 12, 1951; m Susan. **Education:** Univ Minn, BS, 1972, PhD (zoology), 1980. **Professional Experience:** ASST PROF PATH LAB MED, BOSTON UNIV SCH MED, as of 2000; special sci staff, Boston Med Ctr, beginnning 1996; prin investr, Mallory Inst Path, 1984-; special sci staff, Boston City Hosp, 1984-1996; asst prof, Boston Univ Sch Med, 1984-1995; Fel, Mallory InstPath, 1983-1984; fel cytoskeletal & vascular smooth muscle cell differentiation, Brigham & Women's Hosp, 1980-1983. **Memberships:** Am Soc Cell Biol; AAAS; Microcirculatory Soc; NY Acad Sci; Am Heart Asn; NAm Vascular Biol Orgn. **Mailing Address:** Boston Univ, Sch Med, Mallory Inst Path, 784 Mass Ave, Boston, MA 02118. **Fax:** 617-534-5315. **E-Mail:** davlar@bu.edu

LARSON, DENNIS LUVERNE, RENEWABLE ENERGY ENGINEERING, SYSTEMS ENGINEERING APPLICATIONS. **Personal Data:** b Mason City, Iowa, February 3, 1940; m Cheryl; c Scott, Kristine, Steven & Kathryn. **Education:** Iowa State Univ, BS, 1963; Univ Ill, MS, 1964; Purdue Univ, PhD (agr eng), 1971. **Honors & Awards:** 1996 AZ soc ASAE engr of yr. **Professional Experience:** Fulbright scholar, Alexandria Univ, 2005-2006; Visit scholar Unicamp, Campinas, Brazil, 1994, 2002; Vis prof agr eng, Univ Melbourne, 1983-1984; ASSOC PROF AGR & BIOSYSTS ENG, UNIV ARIZ, TUCSON, 1979-; asst prof agr eng, Univ Ariz, Tucson, 1973-1979; exten agr engr, Mich State Univ, 1973; asst prof, Univ Nebr at Nat Univ, Medellin, Colombia & Nat Res Ctr, Bogota, Colombia, 1971-1973; proj design engr, John Deere Planter Works, 1966-1968; Lt, Signal Corps, US Army, Ger, 1964-1966. **Memberships:** Am Soc Agr Engrs; Am Solar Energy Soc; Am Soc Eng Educ. **Research Statement & Publications:** Renewable energy applications and energy use management; systems engineering analysis of agricultural resource management issues; evaluation of electro-migration for control of chemical movement in soils. **Mailing Address:** Univ Ariz Dept ABE, PO Box 210038, Tucson, AZ 85721. **Fax:** 520-621-3963. **E-Mail:** larson@ag.arizona.edu

LARSON, DONALD ALFRED, BOTANY. **Personal Data:** b Chicago, Ill, September 15, 1930; m 1953, c 3. **Education:** Wheaton Col, Ill, BS, 1953; Univ Ill, MS, 1955, PhD (bot), 1959. **Professional Experience:** PROF EMER BIOL SCI, STATE UNIV NY, BUFFALO, as of 2004; Prof Biol Health Sci, State Univ NY, Buffalo, beginning 1973; assoc vpres health sci, State Univ NY, Buffalo, 1973-1981; prof & dir health prof, Univ Tex, Austin, 1969-1973; assoc prof bot, Univ Tex, Austin, 1959-1969. **Memberships:** Bot Soc Am; Am Soc Cell Biologists. **Research Statement & Publications:** Electron microscopy; cytology; palynology; taxonomic uses; paleobotany. **Mailing Address:** Dept Biol Sci, State Univ NY, 621 Hoschstetter Hall, N Campus, Buffalo, NY 14260-0001.

LARSON, DONALD CLAYTON, SOLID STATE PHYSICS. **Personal Data:** b Wadena, Minn, January 29, 1934; m 1960, Susan; c Tor & Erika. **Education:** Univ Wash, BS, 1956; Harvard Univ, SM, 1957, PhD (appl physics), 1962. **Professional Experience:** PROF PHYSICS, DREXEL UNIV, 1983-; assoc prof, Drexel Univ, 1967-1983; Asst prof physics, Univ Va, 1962-1967. **Memberships:** Am Phys Soc; Int Solar Energy Soc; Am Soc Testing & Mat. **Research Statement & Publications:** Electrical properties of metallic, organic and amorphous semiconducting films; biomechanics; solar energy; insulation studies; integrated optics; biomedical optics. **Mailing Address:** Dept Physics, Drexel Univ, Philadelphia, PA 19104. **Fax:** 215-895-5934. **E-Mail:** donlarson@drexel.edu

LARSON, DONALD W, AGRICULTURAL ECONOMICS, AGRIBUSINESS. **Personal Data:** b Avoca, Minn, August 7, 1940; m 1962, c 3. **Education:** SDak State Univ, BS, 1962; Mich State Univ, MS, 1964, PhD (agr econ), 1968. **Honors & Awards:** Distinguished pol contribution award, am agr econ asn, 1989; Int award of merit, Gamma sigma delta, 1997. **Professional Experience:** Consult, Asian Develop Bank, 2000; consult, Inter-Am Develop Bank, 1999; PROF AGR ECON, OHIO STATE UNIV, 1982-; consult, mkt & price policy, World Bank, 1978, 1980, 1982, 1984, 1986, 1987, 1992, 1993; Loan consult, US AID, 1974, 1985, 1986-1993, 1999; mkt consult, 1973; from asst prof to assoc prof, Ohio

State Univ, 1970-1982; asst prof agr econ, Mich State Univ, 1968-1970. **Memberships:** Am Agr Econ Asn; Int Asn Agr Economists; Brazilian Agr Econ Asn. **Research Statement & Publications:** Grain marketing and transportation systems, marketing and market policy in developing countries; rural financial markets in developing countries. **Mailing Address:** Ohio State Univ, Dept Agr Econ, Columbus, OH 43210.

LARSON, EDWARD WILLIAM, STRUCTURAL ENGINEERING. **Personal Data:** b New Haven, Conn, April 17, 1923; m 1952, Lila; c John Edward & Susan Diane Black. **Education:** Ind Technol Col, BSCE, 1943; Northwestern Univ, MS, 1948, PhD (civil eng), 1953. **Professional Experience:** RETIRED; lectr, Calif State Univ, 1986-1992; dir, design technol, 1979-1986; assoc chief engr, Rocketdyne Div, Rockwell Int, 1975-1979; mgr tech specialties, Rocketdyne Div, Rockwell Int, 1969-1975; sect chief & mgr turbomach, Rocketdyne Div, Rockwell Int, 1963-1969; group leader dynamic sci, Rocketdyne Div, Rockwell Int, 1962-1963; supv stress analysis, Rocketdyne Div, Rockwell Int, 1957-1962; res engr, Lockheed Aircraft Corp, 1955-1957; lectr, Univ Calif, Los Angeles, 1953-1964; engr, Hughes Tool Co, Calif, 1953-1955; instr struct eng, Northwestern Univ, 1952-1953; res assoc struct, Northwestern Univ, 1949-1952; physicist, David Taylor Model Basin, 1944-1946; jr engr, Bur Ships, US Dept Navy, 1943-1944. **Memberships:** Soc Exp Stress Analysis; Am Inst Aeronaut & Astronaut; Sigma Xi; Am Soc Eng Educ. **Research Statement & Publications:** Failure investigation of engine components under actual operating conditions and structural behavior of liquid rocket engines to transient, steady state and flow-induced vibrations. **Mailing Address:** 18621 Ringling St, Tarzana, CA 91356.

LARSON, EDWIN E, GEOPHYSICS, GEOLOGY. **Personal Data:** b Los Angeles, Calif, January 5, 1931. **Education:** Univ Calif, Los Angeles, BA, 1954, MA, 1958; Univ Colo, PhD (geol), 1965. **Professional Experience:** PROF EMER GEOL SCI, UNIV COLO, BOULDER, as of 2003; prof geol sci, Univ Colo, Boulder, beginning 1975; from asst prof to assocprof, Univ Colo, Boulder, 1966-1975; NSF fel, 1965-1966; explor geologist, Humble Oil &Refining Co, 1957-1960. **Memberships:** AAAS; Geol Soc Am; Am Geophys Union; Sigma Xi. **Research Statement & Publications:** Investigation of rock magnetic properties; paleomagnetism and its application to the solution of geological problems; lunar magnetism. **Mailing Address:** Dept Geol, Univ Colo Campus, PO Box 250, Boulder, CO 80309-0250.

LARSON, ELAINE LUCILLE, NURSING. **Personal Data:** b April 27, 1943. **Education:** Univ Wash, Seattle, BS, 1965, MS, 1969, PhD (epidemiol), 1981. **Professional Experience:** PROF PHARMACEUT & THERAPEUT RES, COLUMBIA UNIV SCH NURSING, as of 2005; PROF EPIDEMIOL, SCH PUB HEALTH, COLUMBIA UNIV, as of 2005; dean, Sch Nursing, Georgetown Univ, 1992-1998; prof & dir, Sch Nursing, Georgetown Univ, 1991-1998; mem, Planning Panel Health Effects Stress & Emotions, 1991; mem, Gov Coun Prog Planning Comt, 1990-1992; prof & dir, Ctr Nursing Res, 1990-1991; mem, Gov Coun & Priorities & Planning Comt, Am Acad Nursing, 1988-1989; ed, Annals Int Med, 1988; mem, Comt Study Resources Clin Invest, Inst Med, 1988; mem, Task Force Severity Illness Adjusters, Soc Hosp Epidemiologists Am, 1987-1988; mem, Res Comt, Asn Practr Infection, 1986-1988; consult, Keck Found & Columbia Univ, NY, 1986; M Adelaide Nutting chmn clin nursing, Sch Nursing, Johns Hopkins Univ, 1985-1991; consult, Purdue Frederick Co, Norwalk, 1985; consult, Philadelphia Naval Hosp, 1984; ed, Sour Am Med Asn, 1983-; ed, Riv Mag, 1983-1987; mem, Cert Bd Infection Control, 1983-1986; clin nurse, Robert Wood Johnson Sch Nursing, Univ Pa, 1983-1985; assoc dir nursing, staff develop, 1981-1983; consult, Wash State Dept Social & Health Serv & Ctrs Dis Control, 1980; clin asst prof, Dept Physiol Nursing, 1978-1981; consult, Health Sci Learning Resource Ctr, Univ Wash, 1978; nursing res coordr, staff develop, 1977-1981; nurse coordr, staff develop, 1976-1977; nursepractr coronary care, Kaiser-Permanente Sunnyside Med Ctr, Portland, 1975-1976; consult, St Elizabeth's Hosp, 1971; asst prog dir, Sch Nursing, Univ Wash, 1969-1970; hosp epidemiologist, cardiovasc nursing, 1967-1970; clin specialist, cardiovasc nursing, 1966-1967; instr, cardiopulmonary resuscitation, Regional Med Prog & Wash State Red Cross, 1966-1967; staff nurse, Univ Wash Hosp, Seattle, 1965-1966; recipient, Biomed Res Support Grant, Robert Wood Johnson Found clin nurse fel, Ctr Dis Control grant. **Memberships:** Inst Med-Nat Acad Sci; Am Nurses Asn; Am Pub Health Asn; Asn Practr Infection Control; Soc Hosp Epidemiol Am; Soc Res Nursing Educ Forum; Am Soc Microbiol; fel Am Acad Nursing; Sigma Xi. **Research Statement & Publications:** Author of over 99 articles, journals and books. **Mailing Address:** Dept Epidemiol, Sch Pub Health, Columbia Univ, Georgian Bldg 617 W 168th St Rm 246, New York, NY 10032. **Fax:** 212-305-0722. **E-Mail:** ell23@columbia.edu

LARSON, ERIC GEORGE, PHOTOCHEMISTRY. **Personal Data:** b Chicago, Ill, April 25, 1957; m 1985, c 1. **Education:** Purdue Univ, BS, 1980; Northwestern Univ, MS, 1981, PhD (org chem), 1985. **Professional Experience:** SR RES SPECIALIST, ABRASIVES SYSTS DIV, 3M CO, 1991-; resspecialist, Corp Res Lab, 3M Co, 1988-1991; Indust Abrasives Div, Corp Res Lab, 3M Co, 1986-1988; Sr chemist, Corp Res Lab, 3M Co, 1984-1986. **Memberships:** Am Chem Soc. **Research Statement & Publications:** High performance polymers; structural adhesives; rapid cure resins; radiation curable resins; photochemistry; new polymer synthesis. **Mailing Address:** 251-1A-03 3M Ctr, St Paul, MN 55144-1000.

LARSON, ERIC HEATH, POLYELECTROLYTE CHEMISTRY, POLYMERIZATION REACTION ENGINEERING. **Personal Data:** b Medford, Mass, April 8, 1950; m 1975, Maria V Contreras; c Richard & Peter. **Education:** Tufts Univ, BS, 1972; Yale Univ, MS, 1974; Syracuse Univ, PhD (chem eng), 1977. **Professional Experience:** SR ENGR, INTERACT MULTIMEDIA, INC, MONMOUTH JUNCTION NJ, 2000-; PRIN SCIENTIST, RHONE POULENC SPECIALTY CHEMS, 1994-; Consult Scientist, Rhodia, Inc, Cranbury Res Ctr, Cranbury, NJ, 1994-1999; Group Leader, Rhodia, Inc, Cranbury Res Ctr, Cranbury, NJ, 1992-1994; group leader, Rhone Poulenc Specialty Chems, 1990-1994; res assoc, Allied Signal Corp, 1984-1990; sr res engr, Allied Signal Corp, 1981-1984; Res engr III, Allied Signal Corp, 1978-1981. **Memberships:** Tech Asn Pulp & Paper Indust; Am Chem Soc. **Research Statement & Publications:** Investigate polyelectrolyte synthesis, structure-property relationships, applications in various water treatment related industries; inverse emulsion synthesis and reactor engineering, including advanced control strategies. **Mailing Address:** 132 Derby Dr, Freehold, NJ 07228. **E-Mail:** eric@ehlarson.com

LARSON, FRANK CLARK, MEDICINE. **Personal Data:** b Columbus, Nebr, January 17, 1920. **Education:** Nebr State Teachers Col, AB, 1941; Univ Nebr, MD, 1944; Am Bd Internal Med, dipl. **Professional Experience:** PROF EMER PATH & LAB MED, UNIV WIS, MADISON, 1963-; dir, Clin Labs, Hosp, beginning 1958; from asst prof to assoc prof, Univ Wis-Madison, 1956-1963; chief invest med serv, Vet Admin Hosp, Madison, 1952-1956; asst clin prof, Univ Wis-Madison, 1951-1956; asst chief med & tuberc serv, Vet Admin Hosp, Madison, 1951-1956; instr, Univ Wis-Madison, 1950-1951. **Memberships:** Endocrine Soc; Am Col Physicians; Cent Soc Clin Res; Sigma Xi. **Research Statement & Publications:** Thyroid metabolism. **Mailing Address:** Dept Path & Lab Med, Med Sch, Univ Wis, 323 Clin Sci Ctr C5 600 Highland Ave, Madison, WI 53792. **E-Mail:** fclarson@facstaff.wisc.edu

LARSON, FREDERIC ROGER, FOREST MANAGEMENT, SYSTEMS ANALYSIS. **Personal Data:** b Los Angeles, Calif, March 26, 1942; m 1974, Angela DiSandro; c 1. **Education:** Northern Ariz Univ, BSF, 1966, MS, 1968; Colo State Univ, PhD (forestry), 1975. **Professional Experience:** RES FORESTER, PAC NORTHWEST EXP STA, US FOREST SERV, 1979-; adj prof, Northern Ariz Univ Forestry Sch, 1975-1978; Prof, Northern Ariz Univ ForestrySch, 1971-1972; res forester, Rocky Mountain Exp Sta, 1967-1978; Forester, Kaibab & NezPerce Nat Forests, 1965-1967. **Memberships:** Soc Am Foresters; Am Soc Photogram; Soc Range Mgt; Wildlife Soc; Sigma Xi. **Research Statement & Publications:** Quantifying and simulating growth and management of southwestern coniferous forests; computer simulation models ecosystems; forest multi-resource inventories. **Mailing Address:** 3301 C St Suite 200, Anchorage, AK 99503-3954. **Fax:** 907-271-2898.

LARSON, GARY EUGENE, BOTANY, BIOPHYSICS. **Personal Data:** b Jersey Shore, Pa, August 10, 1936. **Education:** State Univ NY Albany, BS, 1958, MS, 1960; Rutgers Univ, PhD (bot), 1964. **Professional Experience:** RETIRED; prof bot, Bethany Col, 1981-2003; dir, Health Sci Prog, Bethany Col, WVa, beginning 1981; AAAS rep to West African Sci Asn meeting, Lome, Togo, 1979; vis fulbright lectr, Dept Biol, Univ Ile, Nigeria, 1977-1978; exec dir, Brooke-Hancock Comprehensive Health Planning Asn, 1974-1975; dir, Nat Defense Educ Act Title I Proj, 1972-1973; peace Corps sci curric adv, Gambian Govt, 1970-1971; chmn dept, Bethany Col, WVa, 1968-1981; teacher & dir, Col Educ Prog, WVa Penitentiary, 1968-1978; WVa Heart Asn grant, 1967-1968; assoc prof, Bethany Col, WVa, 1966-1981; asst prof, Bethany Col, WVa, 1964-1966; instr biol, Douglass Col, 1962-1964; asst bot, Rutgers Univ, 1961-1962. **Memberships:** Fel AAAS; Sigma Xi; Am Inst Biol Sci; Audubon Soc. **Research Statement & Publications:** Bioelectric potentials surrounding the roots of plants; computer aided instruction; audio-tutorial education. **Mailing Address:** Dept Biol, Bethany Col, Bethany, WV 26032. **E-Mail:** glarson@bethanywv.edu

LARSON, GEORGE H(ERBERT), AGRICULTURAL ENGINEERING. **Personal Data:** b Lindsborg, Kans, January 28, 1915; m 1941, Susan Spearie; c Laurence G. **Education:** Kans State Univ, BS, 1939, MS, 1940; Mich State Univ, PhD, 1955. **Professional Experience:** PROF EMER AGR ENG, KANS STATE UNIV, 1984-; consult with Kans State Univ Proj, USAID, Central Luzon State Univ, Philippines, 1978-1980; prof agr eng & head dept agron with Kans State Univ Proj, USAID, Ahmadu Bello Univ, Nigeria, 1972-1974; prof & proj leader agr eng, Nebr Mission, USAID, Bogota, Colombia, 1970-1972; head dept, Kans State Univ, 1956-1970; prof agr eng, Kans State Univ, 1950-1984; assoc prof agr eng, Kans State Univ, 1946-1950; jr instr, US Dept Navy, 1942-1943; instr, Panhandle Agr & Moch Col, 1942; asst instr agr eng, Univ Wis, 1940-1942; asst, Kans State Univ, 1939-1940. **Memberships:** Am Soc Agr Engrs; Nat Soc Prof Engrs. **Research Statement & Publications:** Utilizing liquefied petroleum gas for weed control by flaming; power and machinery, utilizing liquefied petroleum gas in tractors; operating costs of field machinery; agricultural mechanization in developing countries. **Mailing Address:** 419 Oakdale Dr, Manhattan, KS 66502. **E-Mail:** glarson@ksu.edu

LARSON, GERALD LOUIS, ORGANIC CHEMISTRY, SYNTHETIC INORGANIC & ORGANOMETALLIC CHEMISTRY. **Personal Data:** b Tacoma, Wash, January 14, 1942; m 1966, Marilyn; c Michael E & Jeris K. **Education:** Pac Lutheran Univ, BSc, 1964; Univ Calif, Davis, PhD (chem), 1968. **Honors & Awards:** Igarravides Award, Am Chem Soc, 1987. **Professional Experience:** VPRES RES PROD, GELEST INC, as of 2005; LAB DIR CHEM TECHNOL, SILICON APPL, HULS AM, 1993-; HEAD, SILICON APPL, HULS AM, 1990-; mgr res chem, Huls Am Petrarch Systs, 1988-1990; mgr res prods, Huls Am Petrarch Systs, 1986-1988; Wurzburg Univ, 1986; La State Univ, 1984-1985; Bari Univ, Italy, 1983; vis prof, Polytech Inst Mex, 1982; chmn, PR Sect, Am Chem Soc, 1976; from asst prof to prof chem, Univ PR, Rio Piedras, 1970-1986; fel chem, Mass Inst Technol, 1969-1970; fel chem, Wash State Univ, 1968-1969. **Memberships:** Am Chem Soc; Sigma Xi. **Research Statement & Publications:** Organosilicon chemistry with an emphasis on the synthetic applications of organosilanes; new routes to organosilicon compounds, new applications of organosilicones in industry. **Mailing Address:** Gelest Inc, 11 E Steel Rd, Morrisville, PA 19067. **Fax:** 215-547-2484.

LARSON, G(USTAV) OLOF, ORGANIC CHEMISTRY. **Personal Data:** b Cedar City, Utah, December 24, 1926; m 1955, c 4. **Education:** Univ Utah, BS, 1948, MA, 1951; Wash State Univ, PhD, 1959. **Professional Experience:** PROF CHEM, FERRIS STATE UNIV, 1971-; assoc prof, Ferris State Univ, 1966-1971; NSF fac fel, Univ Colo, 1965-1966; assoc prof & head dept, Westminster Col, Utah, 1962-1965; asst prof chem, Utah State Univ, 1957-1962. **Memberships:** AAAS; Am Chem Soc. **Research Statement & Publications:** Organic reaction mechanisms; stereochemistry; teaching aids, including patents on paper steromodels and pK-pH calculator. **Mailing Address:** 285 Shoshane Ave, Rexburg, ID 83440-2228.

LARSON, HAROLD JOSEPH, MATHEMATICAL STATISTICS. **Personal Data:** b Eagle Grove, Iowa, November 16, 1934; m 1962, c 4. **Education:** Iowa State Univ, BS, 1956, MS, 1957, PhD (math, statist), 1960. **Professional Experience:** PROF EMER OPERS RES & STATIST, NAVAL POSTGRAD SCH, as of 2003; prof opers res & statist, Naval Postgrad Sch, beginning 1980; fulbright prof, Univ Sao Paulo, 1970-1971; Data Dynamics, Inc, 1965-1967 & Field Res Corp, 1965-1969; consult, Autonetics Div, NAm Aviation, Inc, 1963-1964; prof opers analysis, NavalPostgrad Sch, 1962-1980; math statistician, Stanford Res Inst, 1960-1962; instr statist, IowaState Univ, 1959-1960. **Memberships:** Am Statist Asn. **Research Statement & Publications:** Probability theory; general statistical methods. **Mailing Address:** Dept Opers Res, Naval Postgrad Sch, Glasgow Hall 292, Monterey, CA 93943-5000. **Fax:** 831-656-2595. **E-Mail:** hlarson@nps.navy.mil

LARSON, HAROLD OLAF, ORGANIC CHEMISTRY. **Personal Data:** b Port Wing, Wis, May 27, 1921. **Education:** Univ Wis, BS, 1943; Purdue Univ, MS, 1947; Harvard Univ, PhD, 1950. **Professional Experience:** RETIRED; from asst prof to prof chem, Univ Hawaii, 1958-1990; res fel, Purdue Univ, 1957-1958; asst prof, Univ WVa, 1955-1957; res fel chem, Harvard Univ, 1954-1955; chemist, Hercules Powder Co, 1950-1954; Navigator, Pan Am Airways, 1944-1945. **Memberships:** Am Chem Soc. **Mailing Address:** Dept Chem, Univ Hawaii, Honolulu, HI 96822.

LARSON, HAROLD PHILLIP, ASTRONOMY. **Personal Data:** b Hartford, Conn, July 13, 1938; m 1960, c 2. **Education:** Bates Col, BS, 1960; Purdue Univ, MS, 1963, PhD (physics), 1967. **Professional Experience:** PROF, DEPT PLANETARY SCI, UNIV ARIZ, as of 2004; res prof, lunar & planetary lab, Univ Ariz, beginning 1983; from asst prof to assoc prof astron, Lunar & Planetary Lab, Univ Ariz, 1971-1976; fel, Aime-Cotton Lab, Nat Ctr Sci Res, France, 1968-1969; res assoc physics, Purdue Univ, 1967-1968. **Memberships:** Am Astron Soc. **Research Statement & Publications:** Infrared astronomy of planetary atmospheres and surfaces. **Mailing Address:** Lunar & Planetary Lab Univ Ariz, 421 Space Sci, Tucson, AZ 85721. **E-Mail:** hplarson@email.arizona.edu

LARSON, INGEMAR W, ZOOLOGY, PARASITOLOGY. **Personal Data:** b Clarissa, Minn, December 4, 1928; m 1962. **Education:** Concordia Col, Moorhead, Minn, AB, 1951; Kans

State Univ, MS, 1957, PhD (parasitol), 1964. **Professional Experience:** CONSULT, 1983-; chmn dept biol, Augustana Col, Ill, 1977-1983; from asst prof to prof biol, Augustana Col, Ill, 1963-1983; res assoc, Ore State Univ, 1963-1966; from instrto asst zool, Kans State Univ, 1957-1963; asst parasitol, Biol Sta, Univ Mich, 1957; asst zool, Kans State Univ, 1955-1957; instr biol, Concordia Col, 1951-1952. **Memberships:** Am Soc Parasitologists; Am Micros Soc; Sigma Xi. **Research Statement & Publications:** Parasitic protozoa; floodplain insects. **Mailing Address:** 2128 31st St, Rock Island, IL 61201.

LARSON, JAMES D, BEAM TRANSPORT ANALYSIS, ACCELERATOR TECHNOLOGY. **Personal Data:** b Kansas City, Mo, February 16, 1935. **Education:** Mass Inst Technol, BS, 1957; Calif Inst Technol, MS, 1959, PhD (physics), 1965. **Professional Experience:** RETIRED; at, Columbia Univ, Upton, NY, 1971-1972; at, Brookhaven Nat Lab, Upton, NY, 1966-1971; at, Calif Inst Tech, Pasadena, 1965-1966. **Memberships:** Am Phys Soc. **Mailing Address:** 10011 E 35th St Terr, Independence, MO 64052.

LARSON, JAY MICHAEL, ENGINE VALVE TRAIN DESIGN, MATERIALS & METALLURGY. **Personal Data:** m 1966, Karen; c Kristin, Jeffrey, Gregory & Danielle. **Education:** Univ Wash, BS, 1965, MS, 1968, PhC, 1969, PhD (metall), 1970; Western MichUniv, MBA, 1990. **Professional Experience:** CONSULT, LARSON ENTERPRISES, as of 2004; mem, Oaklawn Hosp Develop Bd, beginning 1996; tech dir, Eaton Corp, beginning 1996; chmn, Iron & Steel Tech Comt, Soc Automotive Engrs, 1995-1997; mgr eng, Eaton Corp, 1991-1996; mat & serv, Eaton Corp, 1985-1991; prof, Kellogg Community Col, 1978; chief engrmats & basic proc, Eaton Corp, 1976-1985; res metallurgist, Int Nickel, 1970-1976. **Memberships:** Fel Soc Automotive Engrs; fel Am Soc Metals Int; Am Inst Mech Engrs; Sigma Xi. **Research Statement & Publications:** Patentee in field; electron microscopy; superconductors; alloy development; valve train design; standards on valve train materials; order-disorder phenomenon; ultralite engine valves; new product development process. **Mailing Address:** Larson Enterprises, LLC, PO Box 642, Marshall, MI 49068. **Fax:** 616-781-2745. **E-Mail:** larson337@voyager.net

LARSON, JAY REINHOLD, MECHANICAL & NUCLEAR ENGINEERING. **Personal Data:** b Urbana, Ill, December 6, 1932; m 1958, c 4. **Education:** Univ Ill, Urbana, BS, 1955; Univ Wash, MS, 1960; Purdue Univ, PhD (mech eng), 1964. **Professional Experience:** RETIRED; affil prof, Univ Idaho; scientist & eng supvr, EG&G Idaho Inc, 1977-1994; assoc scientist, Aerojet Nuclear Co, 1964-1977; engr, Gen Elec Co, 1960-1961. **Memberships:** Am Soc Mech Engrs; Nat Soc Prof Engrs. **Research Statement & Publications:** Heat transfer; nuclear reactor safety research. **Mailing Address:** 1033 E 25 St, Idaho Falls, ID 83404. **Fax:** 208-524-3595.

LARSON, JERRY KING, CLINICAL PHARMACOLOGY. **Personal Data:** b Willmar, Minn, May 15, 1941; m 1964, c 2. **Education:** Macalester Col, BA, 1963; Mass Inst Technol, PhD (org chem), 1967. **Professional Experience:** MGR CLIN SCI SERV, PFIZER CENT RES, PFIZER INC, 1976-; asst to dirclin res, Pfizer Cent Res, Pfizer Inc, 1970-1976; Res chemist, Chas Pfizer & Co, Inc, 1967-1970. **Memberships:** Am Chem Soc. **Research Statement & Publications:** Clinical trials with new potential drug candidates, particularly the administration and monitoring of such trials. **Mailing Address:** Pfizer Cent Res, Eastern Point Rd, Groton, CT 06340-5196.

LARSON, JOHN GRANT, CATALYSIS, SURFACE SCIENCE. **Personal Data:** b Galesburg, Ill, August 17, 1933; m 1959, c 2. **Education:** Bradley Univ, BS, 1955; Univ Ill, Urbana, PhD (phys chem), 1962. **Professional Experience:** HEAD, PHYSICS DEPT, GEN MOTORS RES LABS, 1985-; head, Phys Chem Dept, 1973-1985; dir, Chem Physics Sect, 1970-1973; supvr, Chem Physics Sect, 1966-1969; group leader, Gulf Res & Develop Co, 1964-1966; fel, Mellon Inst, 1961-1964; Projofficer, Mat Lab, Wright Field, USAF, 1955-1957. **Memberships:** Catalysis Soc; Am Chem Soc; Sigma Xi; Am Phys Soc. **Research Statement & Publications:** Catalysis, both oxide and supported metals especially for emission control; combustion chemistry; surface chemistry; magnetic materials; metal physics; layered materials. **Mailing Address:** Physics Dept, Gen Motors NAO Res & Develop Ctr 30500 Mound Rd, Warren, MI 48090.

LARSON, JOSEPH STANLEY, WETLAND ECOLOGY & POLICY. **Personal Data:** b Stoneham, Mass, June 23, 1933; m Wendy; c Marion Elizabeth & Sandra Frances. **Education:** Univ Mass, BS, 1956, MS, 1958; Va Polytech Inst, PhD (zoology), 1966. **Honors & Awards:** Conserv Award for Except Pub Serv in the Cause of Conserv, Chevron, 1990 dir Award for support of marine educ & res, NOAA, nat marine fisheries service, 2000. **Professional Experience:** PROF EMER, DEPT NATURAL RESOURCES CONSERVATION, UNIV MASS, AMHERST, 2000-; mem, Mass Fisheries & Wildlife Board, 2000-2010; chmn, US Nat Ramsar Comt, 1989-1996; deleg, Ramsar Conv Wetlands Int Importance, 1987, 1990 & 1993; dir, Environ Inst, 1983-2000; chmn dept, Mass Coop Wildlife Res Unit, Univ Mass, Amherst, 1980-1983; exec chmn, Nat Wetlands Tech Coun, 1977-; prof, Dept Nat Resources conserv, Univ Mass, Amherst, 1977-2000; assoc prof, Mass Coop Wildlife Res Unit, Univ Mass, Amherst, 1969-1977; adj asst prof wildlife ext & asst unit leader, Mass Coop Wildlife Res Unit, Univ Mass, Amherst, 1967-1969; res asst prof wildlife, Conserv Educ Div, Natural Resources Inst, Univ Md, 1965-1967; head, Conserv Educ Div, Natural Resources Inst, Univ Md, 1960-1962; state ornithologist & asst to dir, Mass Div Fisheries & Game, 1959-1960; Exec secy, Wildlife Conserv Inc, Mass, 1958-1959; adv wetlands & mem ecol comn ecosyst mgt, Int Union Conserv Nature & Natural Resources, Switz; consult wetland ecol to var pub, pvt & int agencies & foreign govts. **Memberships:** AAAS; Wildlife Soc; Ecol Soc Am; Am Soc Mammal; Soc Wetland Scientists. **Research Statement & Publications:** Wetland ecology and management specializing in techniques for assessing functions of wetlands and wetland policy; beaver behavior. **Mailing Address:** 27 Arnold Rd, Pelham, MA 01002-9757. **E-Mail:** larson@tei.umass.edu

LARSON, KENNETH ALLEN, IMMUNOLOGY, VETERINARY MEDICINE. **Personal Data:** b Havre, Mont, July 6, 1935; m 1961, c 4. **Education:** Wash State Univ, DVM, 1961, MS, 1965, PhD (immunol), 1966. **Professional Experience:** PRES, ELARS BIORES LABS INC, 1976-; assoc prof vet med & microbiol, Colo State Univ, 1969-1976; asst prof vet med, Colo State Univ, 1966-1969; Vet pvt pract, Mont, 1961-1963. **Memberships:** AAAS; Am Soc Microbiol; Am Vet Med Asn. **Research Statement & Publications:** Immunology of tumors in animals. **Mailing Address:** 1305 Teakwood Dr, Ft Collins, CO 80525.

LARSON, KENNETH BLAINE, BIOPHYSICS, BIOMATHEMATICS. **Personal Data:** b Mesa, Ariz, January 16, 1930; m 1958, c 4. **Education:** Colo Sch Mines, MetE, 1951; Mass Inst Technol, SM, 1954 & 1958, PhD (metall & physics), 1964. **Professional Experience:** Consult, NIH, 1978-; INSTR BIOMED ENG & RES ASSOC, BIOMED COMPUT LAB, SCH MED, WASH UNIV, 1970-; res staff, Cent Res Dept, Monsanto Co, 1965-1970; staff mem, Gen Atomic Div, Gen Dynamics Corp, Calif, 1964-1965; res asst metall, Mass Inst Technol, 1958-1964; White Sands Proving Ground, NMex, 1954-1955; staff mem, Engr Res & Develop Labs, US Army, Ft Belvoir, Va, 1954; Instr & res asst metall, Mass Inst Technol, 1951-1953. **Memberships:** AAAS. **Research Statement & Publications:** Ion-exchange resins; diffusion in liquid metals; measurement of thermal diffusivity and heat capacity of thin films; experimental design and statistics; structure of liquids; semiconductor crystal growth; mathematical modeling in physiology; tracer kinetics; biomedical engineering; physics of cancer radiotherapy. **Mailing Address:** 1486 S Mason Rd, St Louis, MO 63131.

LARSON, KENNETH C, COMPUTER SCIENCE. **Education:** Phd, Univ Calif, 1976. **Professional Experience:** PROF EMER COMPUT SCI, SOUTH ORE UNIV, as of 2006. **Mailing Address:** Southern Ore State Col, 1250 Siskiyou Blvd, Ashland, OR 97520. **Fax:** 541-552-6329.

LARSON, KENNETH CURTIS, PAPER CHEMISTRY, WOOD CHEMISTRY. **Personal Data:** b Madison, Wis, July 7, 1940. **Education:** Calif Inst Technol, BS, 1962; Lawrence Univ, MS, 1964, PhD (wood chem), 1967. **Honors & Awards:** E J Albert Award, Tech Asn Pulp & Paper Indust. **Professional Experience:** DIR, WORLDWIDE CONSUMER TOWEL PROD DEVELOP, SCOTT PAPER CO, PHILADELPHIA, 1981-; Mgr Res & Develop, Scott Paper Co, Philadelphia, Pa, 1980-1981; proj head, Scott Paper Co, Philadelphia, Pa, 1977-1980; sci assoc, Scott Paper Co, Philadelphia, Pa, 1974-1977; Sci specialist res & develop, Scott Paper Co, Philadelphia, Pa, 1967-1974. **Memberships:** Tech Asn Pulp & Paper Indust. **Research Statement & Publications:** Colloid and surface chemistry of wood pulp fibers; product and process development. **Mailing Address:** Kimberly Clark 2300 Winchester Rd, PO Box 2007, Neenah, WI 54957-2007.

LARSON, LARRY LEE, REPRODUCTIVE PHYSIOLOGY. **Personal Data:** b Horton, Kans, November 18, 1939; m 1963, c 2. **Education:** Kans State Univ, BS, 1962, MS, 1965, PhD (animal breeding), 1968. **Professional Experience:** ASSOC PROF REPRODUCTIVE PHYSIOL, UNIV NEBR, LINCOLN, 1977-; asst prof, Univ Nebr, Lincoln, 1972-1977; asst prof reproductive physiol, Cornell Univ, 1970-1972; NIH fel, Cornell Univ, 1968-1970. **Memberships:** Soc Study Reproduction; Brit Soc Study Fertil; Am Soc Animal Sci; Am Dairy Sci Asn. **Research Statement & Publications:** Estrus control and determination; conception failures; management factors to improve reproductive performance. **Mailing Address:** Dept Animal Sci, Univ Nebr E Campus C203 Animal Sci, Lincoln, NE 68583-0001. **Fax:** 402-472-6362. **E-Mail:** llarson2@unl.edu

LARSON, LAURENCE ARTHUR, PLANT PHYSIOLOGY, BIOLOGY EDUCATION. **Personal Data:** b Cleveland, Ohio, March 17, 1930; m 1956, c 2. **Education:** Ohio Univ, BS, 1956; Univ Tenn, MS, 1959; Purdue Univ, PhD (amino acid metab), 1963. **Professional Experience:** PROF EMER BOT, OHIO UNIV, as of 2002; prof bot, Ohio Univ, beginning 1975; from asst prof to assoc prof, Ohio Univ, 1963-1975; instr bot, Univ Tenn, 1959; phys oceanogr, US Navy Hydrographic Off, 1956-1957. **Memberships:** Am Inst Biol Sci; Asn Am Biol Teachers; Inst Relig Age Sci. **Research Statement & Publications:** Germination physiology. **Mailing Address:** Dept Biol Sci, Ohio Univ, Athens, OH 45701-2979. **E-Mail:** larsonl@bright.net

LARSON, LAWRENCE T, ECONOMIC GEOLOGY, MINERALOGY. **Personal Data:** b Waukegan, Ill, December 3, 1930; m 1957, c 3. **Education:** Univ Ill, BS, 1957; Univ Wis, MS, 1959, PhD (geol), 1962. **Professional Experience:** PROF EMER ECON GEOL, MACKAY SCH MINES, UNIV NEV, RENO, 1997-; prof econ geol, Mmackay Sch Mines, Univ Nev, Reno, beginning 1990; Fulbright lectr, UN Develop Prog, 1990; Fulbright lectr, Turkey, 1985-1986; prof geol & chmndept, Mackay Sch Mines, Univ Nev, Reno, 1975-1990; partner, Appl Explor Concepts, 1972-1979; consult, Oak Ridge Nat Lab, 1963-1969 & mining firms, 1968-; from asst prof to prof geol, Univ Tenn, Knoxville, 1961-1975; consult, UN Develop Prog, WHO & US Dept Energy. **Memberships:** Geol Soc Am; Am Inst Mining Metall & Petrol Engrs; Soc Econ Geologists. **Research Statement & Publications:** Manganese mineralogy and ore deposits; ore microscopy; uranium mineralization in Great Basin; geologic thermometry; ceramic and high alumina clay deposits; applied geochemistry and gold exploration; ore deposit geology of Turkey. **Mailing Address:** Dept Geol Sci, Univ Nev, Reno, NV 89557-0001.

LARSON, LEE EDWARD, PHYSICS. **Personal Data:** b Bristol, Conn, December 2, 1937; m 1963, c 2. **Education:** Bates Col, BS; Dartmouth Col, MA; Univ NH, PhD (ionospheric physics), 1967. **Honors & Awards:** Distinguished Serv Citation, Am Asn Physics Teachers. **Professional Experience:** PROF EMER PHYSICS, DENISON UNIV, 1998-; prof physics, Denison Univ, 1978-1998; from asst prof to assoc prof, Denison Univ, 1966-1978; instr physics, Allegheny Col, 1961-1963. **Memberships:** Am Asn Physics Teachers; Am Geophys Union. **Research Statement & Publications:** High resolution molecular spectroscopy. **Mailing Address:** Dept Physics Denison Univ, One Main St, Granville, OH 43023. **Fax:** 740-587-6240. **E-Mail:** larson@cc.denison.edu

LARSON, LESTER LEROY, veterinary medicine, diseases of reproduction; deceased, see previous edition for last biography

LARSON, M(ILTON) B(YRD), MECHANICAL ENGINEERING. **Personal Data:** b Portland, Ore, July 3, 1927; m 1950, Wilma E; c Steven Leroy, Gregory Lawrence, Arnold William & Linda Louise. **Education:** Ore State Univ, BS, 1950, MS, 1955; Yale Univ, MEng, 1951; Stanford Univ, PhD (mech eng), 1961. **Professional Experience:** PROF MECH ENG, ORE STATE UNIV, 1969-; Ford Found resident, Washington Works, E I Du Pont de Nemours & Co, Inc, 1968-1969; dean eng, Univ NDak, 1964-1968; From instr to assoc prof mech eng, Ore State Univ, 1952-1964. **Memberships:** Am Soc Mech Engrs; Am Soc Eng Educ. **Research Statement & Publications:** Heat transfer. **Mailing Address:** Dept Mech Eng, Ore State Univ 204 Rogers Hall, Corvallis, OR 97331-6001. **E-Mail:** miltlarson@aol.com

LARSON, NANCY MARIE, NEUTRON PHYSICS, DATA ANALYSIS & EVALUATION. **Personal Data:** b Dickinson, ND, September 30, 1946; m 1968, Duane; c Linnea M. **Education:** Mich State Univ, BS, 1967, MS, 1969, PhD (computational physics), 1972. **Professional Experience:** SR RES STAFF, NUCLEAR SCI & TECHNO DIV, OAK RIDGE NAT LAB, UT-BATTELLE, 1972-. **Memberships:** Am Phys Soc; Am Nuc Soc. **Research Statement & Publications:** Generalized least square (Bayes method); Reich-Moore R-matrix theory; analysis of neutron scattering data; data reduction and uncertainty propagation; covariances. **Mailing Address:** Oak Ridge Nat Lab Bldg 5700, MS 6171 PO Box 2008, Oak Ridge, TN 37831-6171. **Fax:** 865-574-8481. **E-Mail:** larsonnm@ornl.gov

LARSON, OMER R, ENTOMOLOGY. **Personal Data:** b Roseau, Minn, December 1, 1931; m 1960, Patricia A Saumur; c Kristin, Katherine, Elizabeth & Margaret. **Education:** Univ NDak, BA, 1954; Univ Minn, MS, 1960, PhD (fish parasites), 1963. **Professional Experience:** PROF EMER BIOL, UNIV NDAK, 1995-; vis prof biol, USAF Acad, 1990-1991; chmn dept, Univ NDak, 1978-1980; prof biol, Univ NDak, 1976-1995; assoc dean arts & sci, Univ NDak, 1969-1970 &1975-1976; actg chmn dept, Univ NDak, 1966-1967; from asst prof to assoc prof, Univ NDak, 1964-1976; Instr biol, Minot State Col, 1963-1964. **Memberships:** Am Soc Parasitologists; Wildlife Dis Asn; Sigma Xi; Soc Vector Ecologists; AmEntom Soc. **Research Statement & Publications:** Helminth life cycles;

parasites and diseases of fish; biogeography and cold tolerance of fleas. **Mailing Address:** Dept Biol, Univ NDak, 411 Twamley Hall, Grand Forks, ND 58202.

LARSON, PHILIP RODNEY, FOREST PHYSIOLOGY, PLANT ANATOMY. **Personal Data:** b North Branch, Minn, November 26, 1923; m 1948, c 2. **Education:** Univ Minn, BS, 1949, MS, 1952; Yale Univ, PhD (forestry), 1957. **Honors & Awards:** Barrington Moore Biol Res Award, Soc Am Foresters, 1975; New York Bot Garden Award, Bot Soc Am, 1977. **Professional Experience:** RETIRED; leader physiol wood formation, Pioneering Res Unit, NCent Forest Exp Sta, 1962; plant physiologist, Lake States Forest Exp Sta, 1956-1962; res forester, US Forest Serv, Fla, 1952-1954. **Memberships:** Am Soc Plant Physiologists; Soc Am Foresters; fel Int Acad Wood Sci; Bot SocAm; Int Asn Wood Anatomists. **Research Statement & Publications:** Wood formation; vascular anatomy; physiology of growth and development. **Mailing Address:** 16054 W Copper Crest Ln, Surprise, AZ 85374.

LARSON, REGINALD EINAR, AIR MASS TRACERS, NUCLEAR SPECTROSCOPY. **Personal Data:** b Milo, Maine, July 27, 1934; m 1966, c 1. **Education:** Univ Maine, BS, 1955; Univ Md, MS, 1966. **Professional Experience:** NUCLEAR PHYSICS CONSULT, CONSOL CONTROLS CORP, 1985-; RES PHYSICIST, NAVAL RES LAB, 1959-. **Memberships:** Am Phys Soc; Am Meteorol Soc; Am Geophys Union; Sigma Xi. **Research Statement & Publications:** Nuclear physics; atmospheric physics research; author or coauthor of over 80 publications. **Mailing Address:** 1106 Montezuma, Ft Washington, MD 20744-6923.

LARSON, RICHARD ALLEN, ENVIRONMENTAL ORGANIC CHEMISTRY. **Personal Data:** b Minot, NDak, July 9, 1941; m 1963, c 2. **Education:** Univ Minn, Minneapolis, BA, 1963; Univ Ill, Urbana, PhD (org chem), 1968. **Professional Experience:** PROF EMER ENVIRON CHEM, UNIV ILL, URBANA, as of 2005; Nat Res Coun sr res assoc, Environ Protection Agency, Athens, Ga, 1985-1986; prof, inst environ studies, Univ Ill, Urbana, beginning 1979-2003; spec lectr, UnivPa, 1973-1974; asst cur, Stroud Water Res Ctr, Acad Natural Sci Philadelphia, 1972-1979; res assoc bot, Univ Tex, Austin, 1970-1972; USPHS fels, Univ Liverpool, 1968-1969 & Cambridge Univ, 1969-1970. **Memberships:** Phytochem Soc NAm; Am Chem Soc; Am Soc Photobiol; Sigma Xi. **Research Statement & Publications:** Natural products; phytochemistry; aquatic organic chemistry; photobiology. **Mailing Address:** 372 Nat Soyabean Res Ctr, 1101 W Peabody Dr, Urbana, IL 61801. **Fax:** 217-333 8046. **E-Mail:** ralarson@uiuc.edu

LARSON, RICHARD BONDO, STAR FORMATION, GALACTIC EVOLUTION. **Personal Data:** b Toronto, Ont, January 15, 1941. **Education:** Univ Toronto, BSc, 1962, MA, 1963; Calif Inst Technol, PhD (astron), 1968. **Professional Experience:** Tinsley vis prof, Univ Tex, 1990; chmn astron dept, Yale Univ, 1981-1987; PROF ASTRON, YALE UNIV, 1975-; dir undergrad studies astron, Yale Univ, 1971-1981, 2000-; From asst prof to assoc prof, Yale Univ, 1968-1975. **Memberships:** Int Astron Union; Am Astron Soc; Royal Astron Soc Can; Royal Astron Soc; Sigma Xi. **Research Statement & Publications:** Theoretical studies of star formation and early stellar evolution; stellar dynamics, formation and evolution of galaxies. **Mailing Address:** Dept Astron Yale Univ, Box 208101, New Haven, CT 06520-8101. **Fax:** 203-432-5048. **E-Mail:** richard.larson@yale.edu

LARSON, RICHARD CHARLES, QUEUEING THEORY, LOGISTICS. **Personal Data:** b New York, NY, April 10, 1943; m 1979, Elizabeth; c Erik, Evan & Ingrid. **Education:** Mass Inst Technol, BS 1965, MS, 1967, PhD (elec eng), 1969. **Honors & Awards:** Lanchester Prize, Opers Res Soc Am, 1972; Cecil T Holmes Math Lectr, Bowdoin Col, 1991; Phillip M Morse Lectureship, Inst Operation Res & Mgt Sci, 1997-1999; Omega Rho lectr, 1999; Invited testimony before US Congress, House Comm Sci, 2000; Sir Edward Youde Memorial Fund Vis Professorship, Univ Hong Kong, 2000. **Professional Experience:** Dir, Ctr Advan Educ Serv, 1995-2003; consult, United Artists & Johnson Controls, 1993; prin investr, Mass Inst Technol Ctr Transp Studies/US Dept Transp, 1991-1993; consult, Coca-Cola Corp, 1991-1992; Wharton Sch distinguished lectr, Univ Pa, 1991; Queues-Enforth Develop, Inc, 1990-2000; Structured Decisons corp, 2000-; consult, Kuwait Found Advan Sci, 1989; PROF ELEC ENG, MASS INST TECHNOL, 1988-; consult, First Boston Corp, 1987-1988; consult, Harvard Univ, 1985-1989; consult, Union Carbide Corp, 1983-1985; vis prof opers res, Tech Univ Denmark, 1981; consult, Nat Inst Justice, 1980-1993; chmn, Enforth Corp, 1980-1990; prof elec eng & urban studies & planning, Opers Res Ctr, 1979-1988; co-dir, Opers Res Ctr, 1977-1986 & 1991-1995; prin investr, US Dept Justice, 1977-1979, 1980-1982, 1983-1985, 1984-1985, 1985-1987; vis assoc prof opers res, Dept Indust Eng & Opers Res, Univ Calif, Berkeley, 1976; founder & pres, Pub Systs Eval, Inc, 1974-1985; prin investr, NSF, 1973-1976, 1984-1987, 1987-1990, 1988-1991, 1992-1995; assoc prof urban studies & planning, elec eng & comput sci, 1972-1979; asst prof urban studies & planning & elec eng, Mass Inst Technol, 1971-1972; asst prof elec eng, Mass Inst Technol, 1969-1971; mem, Sci & Technol Task Force, President's Comn Law Enforcement & Admin Justice, Inst Defense Analysis, 1966. **Memberships:** Nat Acad Eng; Opers Res Soc Am (pres, 1993-1994); Inst Mgt Sci; Sigma Xi; AAAS; Inst Elec & Electronics Engrs; Prod & Opers Mgt Soc; Inst Operation Res & Mgt Sci. **Research Statement & Publications:** Operations research, especially decisions involving the allocation of resources; complex operational systems involving queueing type congestion, logistics distribution, scheduling of personnel, location of facilities, assisted command and control and statistical inference from transactional data; using advanced technologies for distance learning; operations research applied to private and public systems; transportation and logistics; psychology of queueing, queueing theory; criminal justice and municipal public safety. **Mailing Address:** Dept Civil & Environ Eng, Mass Inst Technol, 77 Mass Ave Rm 9-215, Cambridge, MA 02139. **Fax:** 617-252-1566. **E-Mail:** rclarson@mit.edu

LARSON, RICHARD GUSTAVUS, COMPUTER MATHEMATICS, HOPF ALGEBRAS. **Personal Data:** b Pittsburgh, Pa, May 16, 1940; m 1994, Roberta; c 3. **Education:** Univ Pa, AB, 1961; Univ Chicago, MS, 1962, PhD (math), 1965. **Honors & Awards:** Fulbright lectr, Philippines, 1978. **Professional Experience:** PROF MATH, STATIST & COMPUT SCI, UNIV ILL, CHICAGO, 1977-; from asst prof to assoc prof, Univ Ill, Chicago, 1967-1977; Instr math, Mass Inst Technol, 1965-1967. **Memberships:** Am Math Soc; Asn Comput Mach; Math Asn Am; Soc Indust & Appl Math; Asn for Women in Math. **Research Statement & Publications:** Algebraic and arithmetic structure of Hopf algebras; symbolic algorithms; computational problems of algebra; theoretical computer science; applications of hopf algebras to control theory; quantum groups. **Mailing Address:** Dept Math, Statist & Comput Sci, Univ Ill at Chicago, M/C 249, 851 S Morgan St, Chicago, IL 60607. **E-Mail:** rgl@uic.edu

LARSON, RICHARD I, CHEMICAL ENGINEERING. **Personal Data:** b Chicago, Ill, December 29, 1937; m 1961, c 3. **Education:** Northwestern Univ, BSChE, 1960; Cornell Univ, MChE, 1963; Rensselaer PolytechInst, PhD (chem eng), 1969. **Professional Experience:** PRIN ENGR, NUCLEAR FUEL DEPT, GEN ELEC CO, 1975-; proj engr, Knolls Atomic Power Lab, Schenectady, 1968-1977; Consult, Atomic Energy Comn, 1966-1968; Engr, Nuclear Fuel Dept, Gen Elec CO, 1963-1966. **Memberships:** Am Inst Chem Engrs; Am Chem Soc; Am Nuclear Soc. **Research Statement & Publications:** Nuclear fuel processing, turbulent flow-heat and mass transfer; colloidal and surface chemistry; numerical solution; ordinary and partial differential equations; system analysis; fluidization production equipment. **Mailing Address:** 2009 Spanish Wells Dr, Wilmington, NC 28405-4283.

LARSON, ROBERT ELOF, PHARMACOLOGY, TOXICOLOGY. **Personal Data:** b Spokane, Wash, October 9, 1932; m 1957, c 3. **Education:** Wash State Univ, BS, & BPharm, 1957, MS, 1962; Univ Iowa, PhD (pharmacol), 1964. **Professional Experience:** PROF EMER PHARMACOL & TOXICOL, SCH PHARM, ORE STATE UNIV, as of 2004; prof pharmacol & toxicol, Sch Pharm, Ore State Univ, beginning 1976; chmn dept, Sch Pharm, Ore State Univ, 1970-1976; from asst prof to assoc prof, SchPharm, Ore State Univ, 1965-1976; staff fel toxicol, Nat Cancer Inst, 1964-1965; pharmacist, Manito Pharm, Wash, 1957-1959. **Memberships:** Soc Toxicol; Am Soc Pharmacol & Exp Therapeut; Soc Exp Biol Med; Sigma Xi. **Research Statement & Publications:** Hepatotoxicity and nephrotoxicity of halogenated hydrocarbons; toxicity of nitrosoureas. **Mailing Address:** Col Pharm, Ore State Univ, 203 Pharmacy Bldg, Corvallis, OR 97331.

LARSON, ROGER, MARINE GEOPHYSICS, TECTONICS. **Personal Data:** b Stratford, Iowa, January 12, 1943. **Education:** Iowa State Univ, BS, 1965; Univ Calif, San Diego, PhD (oceanog), 1970. **Honors & Awards:** Newcomb-Cleveland Prize, AAAS, 1980. **Professional Experience:** PROF MARINE GEOPHYS, UNIV RI, 1980-; sr res assoc, Lamont-Doherty Geol Observ, Columbia Univ, 1976-1980; res assoc, Lamont-Doherty Geol Observ, 1971-1976; res scientist, Lamont-Doherty Geol Observ, 1970-1971. **Memberships:** Fel Geol Soc Am; fel Am Geophys Union. **Research Statement & Publications:** Marine geophysics, tectonics; published over 30 articles. **Mailing Address:** Dept Geophys, Grad Sch Oceanog, Univ RI, S Ferry Rd, Narragansett, RI 02882. **Fax:** 401-874-6811. **E-Mail:** rlar@gsosun1.gso.uri.edu

LARSON, ROLAND (RON) EDWIN, MATHEMATICS. **Personal Data:** b Ft Lewis, Wash, October 31, 1941; m 1960, Deanna; c Timothy & Jill. **Education:** Lewis & Clark Col, BS, 1966; Univ Colo, Boulder, MA, 1968, PhD (math), 1970. **Professional Experience:** FOUNDER & AUTHOR, LARSON TEXTS INC, as of 2006; PROF MATH, BEHREND COL, PA STATE UNIV, 1983-; from asst prof to assoc prof, Behrend Col, PA State Univ, 1970-1983; mem, Nat Coun Teachers Math. **Memberships:** Am Math Soc; Math Asn Am; Nat Coun Teachers Math; Am Math Asn Two Yr Col. **Research Statement & Publications:** Author of numerous publications. **Mailing Address:** Larson Texts Inc, 1762 Norcross Rd, Erie, PA 16510. **Fax:** 814-824-6377. **E-Mail:** odx@psu.edu

LARSON, RONALD G, PHYSICS. **Education:** Univ Minn, PhD (Chem Eng), 1980. **Professional Experience:** CHMN & GEORGE GRANGER BROWN PROF CHEM ENG, UNIV MICH, as of 2006. **Mailing Address:** Univ Mich, 3074F Dow, Ann Arbor, MI 48109-2136. **Fax:** 734-763-0459. **E-Mail:** rlarson@umich.edu

LARSON, RUBY ILA, CYTOGENETICS. **Personal Data:** b Hatfield, Sask, May 30, 1914. **Education:** Univ Sask, BS, 1942 & 1943, MA, 1945; Univ Mo, PhD (genetics), 1952. **Professional Experience:** RETIRED; cytogeneticist, Res Sta, 1959-1979; cytogeneticist, Sci Serv Lab, Can Dept Agr, 1948-1959; cytogeneticist, Cereal Div, Dom Exp Sta, Sask, 1945-1948. **Research Statement & Publications:** Wheat cytogenetics. **Mailing Address:** 20 Third St S Unit 410, Lethbridge, AB T1J 4P1, Can.

LARSON, RUSSELL EDWARD, AGRICULTURAL EDUCATION, ACADEMIC ADMINISTRATION. **Personal Data:** b Minneapolis, Minn, January 2, 1917. **Education:** Univ Minn, BS, 1939, MS, 1940, PhD (genetics, plant breeding), 1942. **Honorary Degrees:** DSc, Del Valley Col Sci & Agr, 1966. **Honors & Awards:** Vaughan Award, Am Soc Hort Sci, 1948. **Professional Experience:** PROVOST EMER, DEAN EMER & PROF EMER HORT, PA STATE UNIV, UNIV PARK, 1977-; CONSULT AGR, PA STATE UNIV, UNIV PARK, 1977-; adv sci affairs, Am Cocoa Res Inst, 1977-1988; provost, Col Agr, 1972-1977; chmn comn educ agr & natural resources, Nat Acad Sci-Nat Res Coun, 1966-; dean & dir, Col Agr, 1963-1974; dir agr & home econ exten, Dept Hort, 1961-1963; Sci aide, Mex Agr Prog, Rockefeller Found, 1960; head, Dept Hort, 1952-1961; prof, Col Agr, 1947-1977; assoc prof plant breeding, Pa State Univ, 1945-1947; asst prof veg gardening, Pa State Univ, 1944-1945; Asst hort, Univ Minn, 1939-1941. **Memberships:** AAAS; Am Soc Hort Sci; Genetics Soc Am; Am Genetics Asn. **Research Statement & Publications:** Administration of agricultural research development and education. **Mailing Address:** 608 Elwood, State College, PA 16801.

LARSON, RUSSELL L, BIOCHEMISTRY. **Personal Data:** b Bridgewater, SDak, December 9, 1928; wid, c 1. **Education:** SDak State Univ, BS, 1957, MS, 1959; Univ Ill, PhD (biochem), 1962. **Professional Experience:** RES CHEMIST, USDA, UNIV MO, COLUMBIA, 1965-; Fel microbiol, OreState Univ, 1962-1964. **Memberships:** Am Chem Soc; Phytochem Soc NAm; Am Soc Plant Physiol. **Research Statement & Publications:** Biochemistry of disease resistance in plants; alteration in metabolic processes in maize as a result of alteration in the genetic systems in maize. **Mailing Address:** 438 Airwood Ave, Springfield, MO 65802.

LARSON, SANFORD J, NEUROANATOMY, NEUROSURGERY. **Personal Data:** b Chicago, Ill, April 9, 1929. **Education:** Wheaton Col, Ill, BA, 1950; Northwestern Univ, MD, 1954, PhD (anat), 1962. **Professional Experience:** PROF EMER NEUROSURG, MED COL WIS, as of 2004; chief neurosurg, Vet Admin Hosp, Wis, 1991, Milwaukee Co Gen Hosp & Froedtert Mem Lutheran Hosp; prof neurosurg, Med Col Wis, beginning 1968; chmn dept, med col wis, beginning 1963; assoc prof, Med Col Wis, 1963-1968; dir neurosurg educ, Cook Co Hosp, Chicago, 1962-1963; USPHS res fel, 1961-1962; resident neurosurg, Northwestern Univ, 1955-1957 & 1959-1961; consult, columbia & milwaukee children's hosps, Wis & Shriners Hosps Crippled Children, Chicago, Ill. **Memberships:** Soc Univ Surg; Am Asn Neurol Surg; Am Col Surg; Soc Neurol Surgeons. **Research Statement & Publications:** Neurophysiology; neurological surgery. **Mailing Address:** Dept Neurosurg, Med Col, Univ Wis, 9200 W Wis Ave, Milwaukee, WI 53226.

LARSON, STEVEN MARK, NUCLEAR MEDICINE, CANCER MEDICINE. **Personal Data:** m 1964, Elaine; c Nathan P & Justine J. **Education:** Univ Wash, MD, 1968. **Honors & Awards:** Nat Inst Health. **Professional Experience:** DIR LAURENT & ALBERTA GERSCHELL PET CTR, DEPT RADIOL, MEM SLOAN KETTERING CANCER CTR, 1988-; CHIEF NUCLEAR MED SERV, DEPTRADIOL, MEM SLOAN KETTERING CANCER CTR, 1988-; PROF RADIOL, MED COL, CORNELL UNIV, 1988-; chief nuclear med, NIH, 1983-1988; Captain, USPHS, 1983-1988. **Memberships:** Inst Clin Pet (pres 1994-1995); Soc Nuclear Med. **Research Statement & Publications:** Development and application of radiolasers for diagnosis and therapy in oncology. **Mailing Address:** Mem Sloan Kettering Cancer Ctr, 1275 York Ave, New York, NY 10021. **Fax:** 212-639-3263. **E-Mail:** larsons@mskcc.org

LARSON, THOMAS D, TRANSPORTATION MANAGEMENT. **Personal Data:** b September 28, 1928. **Education:** Pa State Univ, BS, 1952, MS, 1959, PhD (civil eng), 1962. **Honors & Awards:** Secy's Gold Medal Award for Outstanding Achievement, Secy Transp, 1990. **Professional Experience:** RETIRED; pvt consult transp, beginning 1992; adminr, Fed Hwy Admin, 1989-1992; secy transp, Commonwealth Pa, 1979-1987; prof, Col Bus Admin & Col Eng, Pa State Univ, 1962-1989; chmn, Nat Gov's Task Force New Fed Transp Legis. **Memberships:** Nat Acad Eng; fel Nat Soc Civil Engrs; fel Nat Acad Pub Admin. **Mailing Address:** 132 Norle, Lemont, PA 16851.

LARSON, THOMAS E, PHYSICAL CHEMISTRY, ORGANIC CHEMISTRY. **Personal Data:** b Waupaca, Wis, April 13, 1926; m 1949, Erla Mae; c Caryn Womack, Kathy Jacobs & Greta Hanson. **Education:** Lewis & Clark Col, BA, 1950; Johns Hopkins Univ, MA, 1951, PhD (phys chem), 1956. **Honors & Awards:** Award of Excellence, Los Alamos Nat Lab, 1982; Dept Energy, Fogbank, 1984, Terrazzo, 1985; Stagecoach, 1998; High Heat Safety, 1999. **Professional Experience:** RETIRED; DOE consult, 1991-; Assoc, Los Alamos Nat Lab, 1991-; group leader explosive technol, Los Alamos Nat Lab, 1984-1991; staff mem, alt group leader WX-2, 1975-1984; staff mem, Los Alamos Nat Lab, 1956-1975; res asst, Inst Coop Res, 1953-1956; Jr instr chem, Johns Hopkins Univ, 1950-1953. **Memberships:** Am Chem Soc. **Research Statement & Publications:** Kinetics of exchange reactions in boron hydrides; sensitivity of explosives to various stimuli; radioactive materials; formulation, manfacture & performance of explosives; chemistry of tritium; radioactive waste reactions & storage. **Mailing Address:** 2711 Walnut St, Los Alamos, NM 87544.

LARSON, VAUGHN LEROY, VETERINARY MEDICINE. **Personal Data:** b Mondovi, Wis, February 21, 1931; m 1961, c 1. **Education:** Univ Minn, BS, 1958, DVM, 1960, PhD (vet med), 1968. **Professional Experience:** PROF VET MED, UNIV MINN, ST PAUL, 1974-; from asst prof to assocprof, Univ Minn, St Paul, 1968-1974; med scientist animal res, Brookhaven Nat Lab, 1968; felbovine leukemia, Univ Minn, 1961-1968; vet, 1960-1961. **Memberships:** Am Vet Med Asn; Am Asn Equine Pract; Int Leukemia Res Asn; Sigma Xi. **Research Statement & Publications:** Transmission and pathogenesis studies on bovine leukemia; clinical, pathological and therapeutic studies on chronic obstructive pulmonary disease in the equine. **Mailing Address:** 1211 Josephine Rd, St Paul, MN 55113.

LARSON, VERNON C, AGRICULTURE, ACADEMIC ADMINISTRATION. **Personal Data:** b Stambough, Mich, April 8, 1923; m 1946, Marion P; c 3. **Education:** Mich State Univ, BS, 1947, MS, 1950, EdD (educ admin), 1954. **Professional Experience:** PROF EMER, KANS STATE UNIV, 1991-; AID consult, Brazil 1989; asst provost & dir int prog, Kans State Univ, 1987-1991; AID consult, Paraguay, Botswana, 1987; AID consult, Paraguay, Nepal, Morocco, 1985; AID consult, Paraguay, 1978; AID consult, Philippines, 1977; AID consult, Sierre Leon, 1975; dir int agr progs, Kans State Univ, 1972-1987; chief party, AID & Kans State Univ Team India, 1970-1972; AID consult, Colombia, 1969; dir int agr progs, Kans State Univ, 1968-1970; AID consult, Kenya, 1968; prof agr sci & dean agr, Ahmadu Bello Univ, Nigeria & chief party, AID & Kans State Univ Team Nigeria, 1966-1968; prof dairy agr & dir int agr prog, Kans State Univ, 1962-1965; AID consult, Cyprus & Sudan, 1961; AID consult, Jordan, 1960; prof agr & asst dean, Am Univ, Beirut, 1959-1962; from asst prof to assoc prof dairy & asst to dean, Mich State Univ, 1947-1959. **Memberships:** AAAS; Nat Asn State Univs & Land-Grant Cols. **Research Statement & Publications:** Agricultural administration. **Mailing Address:** 1951 Bluestem Terr, Manhattan, KS 66502.

LARSON, VIVIAN M, VIROLOGY. **Personal Data:** b Erie, NDak, October 3, 1931. **Education:** NDak State Col, BS, 1953; Univ Mich, MPH, 1958, PhD (virol), 1963. **Professional Experience:** RETIRED; dir, NIH Virus Lab, 1980-1990; dir, NIH Virus Lab, 1971-1980; from res fel to sr res fel virol, Merck Sharp & Dohme Res Labs, 1963-1971; bacteriologist, Detroit Dept Health Labs, Mich, 1953-1959. **Memberships:** Am Soc Microbiol; Am Acad Microbiol; AAAS. **Research Statement & Publications:** Cell biology; immunology; viral; vaccines. **Mailing Address:** 362 Park Dr, Harleysville, PA 19438.

LARSON, WILBUR JOHN, ANALYTICAL CHEMISTRY. **Personal Data:** b Rockford, Ill, November 19, 1921; m 1945, Betty; c Kurt E, Gail D (Akins) & Neil F. **Education:** Augustana Col, Ill, BA, 1946; Univ Wis, MS, 1948, PhD, 1951. **Professional Experience:** RETIRED; qual control mgr, Mallinckrodt Inc, 1984-1986; res assoc, Mallinckrodt Inc, 1972-1984; asst dir qual control, Anal Develop Lab, 1964-1972; head, Anal Develop Lab, 1957-1963; chemist, Mallinckrodt Chem Works, 1951-1957. **Memberships:** Am Chem Soc; Sigma Xi. **Research Statement & Publications:** Trace analysis; quality control; electronic grade chemicals; reagent chemicals. **Mailing Address:** 1364 Stein Ave, Ferguson, MO 63135-1709.

LARSON, WILBUR S, INORGANIC CHEMISTRY, ANALYTICAL CHEMISTRY. **Personal Data:** b Downing, Wis, January 28, 1923. **Education:** Wis State Univ, River Falls, BS, 1945; Univ Wyo, MS, 1958, PhD (inorg chem), 1964. **Professional Experience:** PROF EMER, DEPT CHEM, UNIV WIS, OSHKOSH, as of 2001; prof chem, Univ Wis, Oshkosh, beginning 1976; assoc prof, Univ Wis, Oshkosh, 1963-1976; asst gen chem, Univ Wyo, 1955-1963; Teacher high schs, Wis, 1944-1955. **Memberships:** Am Chem Soc; Sigma Xi. **Research Statement & Publications:** Colorimetric sulfide, sulfite and thiosulfate analysis; stability of antimony addition compounds; equilibrium exchange mechanisms of metallic sulfides; mechanism studies of antimony pentachloride. **Mailing Address:** Dept Chem, 1538 Kentucky St, Oshkosh, WI 54901.

LARSON, WILLIAM EARL, SOIL SCIENCE. **Personal Data:** b Creston, Nebr, August 7, 1921; m 1947, c 4. **Education:** Univ Nebr, BS, 1944, MS, 1946; Iowa State Univ, PhD, 1949. **Honorary Degrees:** DSc, Univ Nebr, 1982. **Honors & Awards:** Bennett Award, Soil Conserv Soc, 1985; BlackAward, 1987; Soil Sci Award, Am Soc Agron. **Professional Experience:** PROF EMER SOIL SCI, UNIV MINN, ST PAUL, 1989-; prof, Univ Minn, StPaul, 1967-1989; Fulbright scholar, Australia, 1965-1966; vis prof, Univ Ill, 1960 & Univ Minn, 1963; from assoc prof to prof soils, Iowa State Univ, 1954-1967; Soil scientist, USDA, IowaState Univ, 1954-1967; soil scientist, USDA, Mont State Col, 1951-1954; Asst prof agron, IowaState Univ, 1949-1950. **Memberships:** Fel AAAS; fel Am Soc Agron; fel Soil Sci Soc Am; Int Soc Soil Sci; fel SoilConserv Soc Am. **Research Statement & Publications:** Soil structure and mechanics; water infiltration; nutrient interrelations in plants; crop response to soil moisture levels and soil temperature; tillage requirements of crops; utilization of sewage wastes on land. **Mailing Address:** 3334 Richmond Ave, St Paul, MN 55126.

LARTER, EDWARD NATHAN, GENETICS, PLANT BREEDING. **Personal Data:** b Can, February 13, 1923. **Education:** Univ Alta, BSc, 1951, MSc, 1952; State Col Wash, PhD (genetics, plant breeding), 1954. **Professional Experience:** PROF EMER PLANT SCI, UNIV MAN, 1989-; Rosner res chair prof plant sci & dir tritical res prog, Univ Man, 1969-1989; assoc prof genetics & plant breeding, Univ Sask, 1954-1969. **Memberships:** Genetics Soc Can; Can Soc Agron; Agr Inst Can. **Research Statement & Publications:** Plant breeding and cytogenetics of barley, triticale and related species. **Mailing Address:** Dept Plant Sci, Univ Man, 222 Agr Bldg, Winnipeg, MB R3T 2N2, Can. **Fax:** 204-474-7528.

LARTER, RAIMA, NONLINEAR DYNAMICS. **Personal Data:** b Kingsville, Tex, May 1, 1955; m 1977, Kenneth; c Nathan & Benjamin. **Education:** Mont State Univ, BS, 1976; Ind Univ, Bloomington, PhD (phys chem), 1980. **Honors & Awards:** Top Three Med Physics News Stories of 1999, "A New Model of Epilepsy, " APS News, Vol 9, No 4, April 2000, p 4. **Professional Experience:** PROG DIR, NSF, as of 2006; CHAIR, DEPT CHEM, IND UNIV-PURDUE UNIV, INDIANAPOLIS, 2000-; assoc dean gen educ, Ind Univ-Purdue Univ, Indianapolis, 1996-1998; PROF CHEM, IND UNIV-PURDUE UNIV, INDIANAPOLIS, 1992-; assoc prof, Ind Univ-Purdue Univ, Indianapolis, 1988-1991; prin investr, Petrol Res Fund, Am Chem Soc & NSF, 1987-; asst prof, Ind Univ-Purdue Univ, Indianapolis, 1983-1987; vis asst prof, Ind Univ-Purdue Univ, Indianapolis, 1981-1983; res assoc chem, Princeton Univ, 1980-1981. **Memberships:** Am Chem Soc; Am Phys Soc; Asn Women Sci (secy, 1986-1988). **Research Statement & Publications:** Chemical oscillations, chaos, self-organization phenomena and biochemical and biophysical applications; dynamical diseases, esp epilepsy. **Mailing Address:** Chem Dept, IUPUI, 402 N Blackford St, Indianapolis, IN 46202. **Fax:** 317-274-4701. **E-Mail:** larter@chem.iupui.edu

LARTIGUE, DONALD JOSEPH, BIOCHEMISTRY, ENZYMOLOGY. **Personal Data:** b Baton Rouge, La, September 7, 1934; wid Barbara G (deceased); c Carol L Rabb & David A. **Education:** La State Univ, BS, 1957, MS, 1959, PhD (biochem), 1965. **Honors & Awards:** dipl am board clin chem. **Professional Experience:** RETIRED; clin chemist, Vet Admin Med Ctr, New Orleans, 1990-1995; asst prof path, La State Univ Med Ctr, 1990-1995; assoc prof med technol, La State Univ Med Ctr, 1987-1989; clin chemist, Southern Baptist Hosp, 1976-1987; clin chemist, Ochsner Clin, 1974-1976; sr res biochemist, Corning Glass Works, 1971-1974; sr clin biochemist, J T Baker Chem Co, 1970-1971; Vis prof, Wake Forest Univ, 1968; R J Reynolds Tobacco Co, NC, 1965-1970; assoc, La State Univ, 1963-1965; asst biochem, La State Univ, 1962-1963; biochemist, USPHS Hosp, Carville, La, 1960-1962; marine biologist, Marine Lab, Univ Miami, 1960; Analyst, US Food & Drug Admin, 1959-1960. **Memberships:** Am Asn Clin Chemists. **Research Statement & Publications:** Clinical chemistry; industrial enzymology; immobilized enzymes. **Mailing Address:** 135 Belle Grove Circle, Vidalia, LA 71373.

LARUE, JAMES ARTHUR, mathematics; deceased, see previous edition for last biography

LA RUE, JERROLD A, METEOROLOGY. **Personal Data:** b San Bernardino, Calif, June 22, 1923; m 1946, Geoigene; c 2. **Education:** Univ Calif, Los Angeles, BA, 1948. **Professional Experience:** RETIRED; meteorologist in-chg, Weather Serv Off, Wash, DC, 1969-1980; br chief, US Weather Bur, Nat Weather Serv, 1968-1969; sect supvr meteorol, US Weather Bur, Nat Weather Serv, 1964-1968; quant precipation meteorologist, US Weather Bur, Nat Weather Serv, 1960-1964; meteorologist proj analyst, US Weather Bur, Nat Weather Serv, 1957-1960; forecast meteorologist, US Weather Bur, Nat Weather Serv, 1955-1957; gen meteorologist, US Weather Bur, Nat Weather Serv, 1951-1955. **Memberships:** Am Meteorol Soc; Nat Weather Asn. **Research Statement & Publications:** Objective methods adapted to operational meteorology; verification of met products, NIOP. **Mailing Address:** 5550 Rio Vida Lane, Sebastopol, CA 95472. **E-Mail:** jcrrlarue@aol.com

LARUE, JOHN CHAUNCEY, PHYSICS. **Education:** Univ Calif, PhD. **Professional Experience:** ASSOC DEAN & PROF, DEPT MECH & AEROSPACE ENG, UNIV CALIF, as of 2005. **Mailing Address:** Dept Mech & Aerospace Eng, Univ Calif, S3226 Eng Gateway, Irvine, CA 92697-2750. **Fax:** 949-824-7966. **E-Mail:** JCLaRue@uci.edu

LA RUSSA, JOSEPH ANTHONY, ELECTRO-OPTICS, ENGINEERING PHYSICS. **Personal Data:** b New York, NY, May 10, 1925; m 1946, c 3. **Education:** City Col NY, BME, 1949; Columbia Univ, MS, 1955. **Honors & Awards:** De Florez Award, Am Inst Aeronaut & Astronaut, 1968. **Professional Experience:** PRES & FOUNDER, ELECTRO VISUAL ENG INC, as of 2003; lectr flight simulation, Univ Dayton, 1980; bd mem, Microsurg res Found, 1975-; PRES, SURG MICROSYST INC, 1972-; sr vpres & tech dir, Farrand Optical Co Inc, 1952-1988. **Memberships:** NY Acad Sci; Am Inst Aeronaut & Astronaut. **Research Statement & Publications:** Development of many optical systems for spaceflight simulators including Mercury, Gemini, Apollo, LEM, T-27 and for major air force simulators; developed many surgical instruments for ophthalmological surgeons; research on implantable artificial kidney; implantable artificial heart; implantable heart valves; 31 patents in engineering technologies. **Mailing Address:** Electro Visual Eng, Inc, 171 Brady Ave, Hawthorne, NY 10532.

LA RUSSO, NICHOLAS F, MEDICINE BIOLOGY. **Professional Experience:** PROF & CHMN, DIV GASTROENTEROL & DIR, CTR BASIC RES DIGESTIVE DIS, MAYO MED SCH CLIN & FOUND, 1977-. **Mailing Address:** Dept Internal Med, Div Gastroenterol, Mayo Clin, 200 First St SW, Rochester, MN 55905-0001. **Fax:** 507-284-0762.

LASAGA, ANTONIO C, GEOCHEMISTRY, PHYSICAL CHEMISTRY. **Personal Data:** b Havana, Cuba, December 17, 1949. **Education:** Princeton Univ, BA, 1971; Harvard Univ, MS, 1973, PhD (chem physics), 1976. **Honors & Awards:** F W Clarke Medal, Geochem Soc, 1979; Award, Mineral Soc Am, 1985. **Professional Experience:** PROF GEOCHEM, YALE UNIV, 1984-; Guggenheim fel, as of 2000; vis assoc prof, Yale Univ, 1981; NSF prin investr, 1978-1985; from asst prof to prof geochem, Pa State Univ, 1977-1984; lectr chem & geol, Harvard Univ, 1976-1977; res asst chem, Harvard Univ, 1973-1976. **Memberships:** Geochem Soc; Am Geophys Union; fel Mineral Soc Am. **Research Statement & Publications:** Kinetics and thermodynamics of geochemical processes, particularly modeling diagenetic reactions in the oceans; geochemical cycles; diffusion in silicates; non-equilibrium aspects of geothermometry; quantum mechanics of bonding in silicates; structure of silicate melts. **Mailing Address:** Dept Geol & Geophys, Yale Univ, PO Box 208109, 210 Whitney Ave, New Haven, CT 06520-8109. **E-Mail:** lasaga@quantm.geology.yale.edu

LASALA, EDWARD FRANCIS, PHARMACEUTICAL CHEMISTRY, ORGANIC CHEMISTRY. **Personal Data:** b Lynn, Mass, June 15, 1928. **Education:** Mass Col Pharm, BS, 1953, MS, 1955, PhD (pharmaceut chem), 1958. **Professional Experience:** RETIRED; chmn dept, Mass Col Pharm, 1977-1991; from instr to prof chem, Mass Col Pharm, 1958-1991. **Memberships:** Am Chem Soc; Am Pharmaceut Asn. **Research Statement & Publications:** Synthesis and biological studies of medicinal agents, chiefly analgesics and antiradiation agents. **Mailing Address:** 37 Highland Ave, Saugus, MA 01906.

LASATER, ERIC MARTIN, RETINAL NEUROPHYSIOLOGY. **Personal Data:** b Stuttgart, Ger, January 6, 1953. **Education:** Colo State Univ, BS, 1975; Univ Calif, Davis, MS, 1977; Univ Tex, PhD (physiol & biohys), 1980. **Honors & Awards:** William & Mary Greve Int Res Scholar, Res Prev Blindness, Inc, 1991. **Professional Experience:** PROF OPH-

THAL, DEPT OPHTHAL, UNIV UTAH, 1992-; vchmn & dir res, dept ophthal, Univ Utah, beginning 1991; mem visual sci A2 study sect, Div Res Grants, NIH, beginning 1990; assoc prof, Dept Ophthal, 1988-1992; dir res, Dept Ophthal, 1987-1990; res asst prof, Univ Utah, 1985-1988; lectr biol, Harvard Univ, 1984-1985; fel, Harvard Univ, 1980-1984. **Memberships:** Soc Neurosci; Asn Res Vision & Ophthal; Int Soc Eye Res; Sigma Xi; Int Brain Res Orgn. **Research Statement & Publications:** How retinal neurons process visual information; study anatomy and connectivity, physiology, and neuropharmacology of individual retinal neurons to understand how these cells function in both health and disease states; technical management. **Mailing Address:** John A Moran Eye Ctr, Univ Utah, 175 N Med Dr E, Rm 5415, Salt Lake City, UT 84132. **Fax:** 801-581-3357. **E-Mail:** eric.lasater@hsc.utah.edu

LASATER, HERBERT ALAN, MATHEMATICAL STATISTICS, APPLIED STATISTICS. **Personal Data:** b Paris, Tenn, September 11, 1931. **Education:** Univ Tenn, BS, 1957, MS, 1962; Rutgers Univ, PhD (statist), 1969. **Professional Experience:** EXEC VPRES, TENN ASSOCS INT, INC, 1984-; assoc prof statist, Univ Tenn, Knoxville, 1971-; ed, J Qual Technol, 1971-1974; asst prof, Univ Tenn, Knoxville, 1962-1965 & 1968-1971; Lectr statist, Univ Tenn, 1959-1962; assoc statistician, Nuclear Div, Union Carbide Corp, 1958-1962; Instr statist, Univ Tenn, Knoxville, 1957-1958. **Memberships:** Am Statist Asn; fel Am Soc Qual Control; Sigma Xi. **Research Statement & Publications:** Statistical quality control techniques. **Mailing Address:** 452 Wyndahm Hall Way, Knoxville, TN 37922.

LASCA, NORMAN P, QUATERNARY GEOLOGY, GEOARCHAEOLOGY. **Personal Data:** b Detroit, Mich, October 20, 1934. **Education:** Brown Univ, AB, 1957; Univ Mich, MS, 1961, PhD (geol), 1965. **Professional Experience:** Actg vchancellor, Univ Wis-Milwaukee, 1981-1982; chmn dept, Univ Wis-Milwaukee, 1980-1981 & 1984-1988; assoc dean grad sch, Univ Wis-Milwaukee, 1977-1980; sr scientist, Ctr Great Lakes Studies, Univ Wis-Milwaukee, 1976-; PROF GEOL SCI, UNIV WIS-MILWAUKEE, 1976-; asst to chancelor, Univ Wis-Milwaukee, 1975-1977; fel acad admin, Am Coun Educ, 1974-1975; assoc scientist, 1971-1976; assoc prof geol, Univ Wis-Milwaukee, 1971-1976; asst prof, Univ Wis-Milwaukee, 1966-1971; NATO res fel, Inst Geol, Univ Oslo, 1965-1966; teaching fel, Univ Mich, 1961-1965; res asst geol, Univ Mich, 1960-1961. **Memberships:** Fel Geol Soc Am; Am Asn Quaternary Res; Int Asn Quaternary Res; Glaciol Soc; Swedish Soc Anthrop & Geog; Sigma Xi. **Research Statement & Publications:** Glacial geology and geomorphology of polar regions; river and lake ice formation and processes; Glacial-Pleistocene geology in Wisconsin, Geoarcheology in upper midwest. **Mailing Address:** Dept Geosci, Univ Wis, Lapham 374, Milwaukee, WI 53201. **E-Mail:** nplasca@uwm.edu

LASCANO, ROBERT J, SOIL PHYSICS. **Education:** Tex A&M Univ, BS, 1974, MS, 1977, PhD (oil physics), 1982. **Professional Experience:** PROF, DEPT SOIL & CROP SCI, TEX A&M UNIV, as of 2003. **Mailing Address:** Tex A&M Univ, USDA-ARS, 3810 Fourth St, Lubbock, TX 79415. **Fax:** 806-723-5271. **E-Mail:** r-lascano@tamu.edu

LASCELLES, JUNE, microbiology, biochemistry; deceased, see previous edition for last biography

LASCHEVER, NORMAN LEWIS, electrical engineering; deceased, see previous edition for last biography

LASEK, RAYMOND J, NEUROBIOLOGY. **Personal Data:** b Chicago, Ill, November 25, 1940. **Education:** Utica Col, BA, 1961; State Univ NY, PhD (anat), 1967. **Professional Experience:** PROF ANAT, CASE WESTERN RES UNIV, 1979-; assoc prof, Case Western Res Univ, 1974-1978; asst prof, Case Western Res Univ, 1969-1973; neurobiology, Univ Calif, San Diego, 1968-1969; NIH res fel neuropath, McLean Hosp, Harvard Med Sch, 1966-1968. **Research Statement & Publications:** Axonal transport; regulation of growth and differentiation in neurons; evolutionary neurobiology. **Mailing Address:** 2119 Abington Rd, Cleveland, OH 44106.

LASENBY, DAVID C, BIOLOGY. **Education:** Trent Univ, BSc; Toronto Univ, PhD. **Professional Experience:** PROF BIOL, WORSFOLD WATER QUAL CTR, TRENT UNIV, CANADA, as of 2006. **Research Statement & Publications:** Contaminants in lake sediments; focuses on the vertical migration of invertebrates that feed on lake sediments as a pathway for the transport and reintroduction of contaminants and nutrients back into the water column; measurement of the rates of uptake, accumulation and transport of trace metals from the sediments to the water column by organisms such as Mysis; Diporeia; Gammarus and Chaoborus. **Mailing Address:** Dept Biology, Trent Univ, 1600 West Bank Dr, Peterborough, ON K9J 7B8, Can. **E-Mail:** dlasenby@trentu.ca

LA SEUR, NOEL EDWIN, METEOROLOGY. **Personal Data:** b Stanhope, Iowa, June 25, 1922; m 1944, c 3. **Education:** Univ Chicago, SB, 1947, SM, 1949, PhD (meteorol), 1953. **Professional Experience:** RETIRED; prof meteorol, Fla State Univ, 1958-2002; dir, Nat Hurricane Exp Meteorol, 1975-1977; from asst prof to assoc prof, Fla State Univ, 1953-1958; from asst to instr, Univ Chicago, 1948-1952. **Memberships:** AAAS; Am Meteorol Soc; Am Geophys Union; Royal Meteorol Soc. **Research Statement & Publications:** Synoptic meteorology of temperature and tropical latitudes. **Mailing Address:** Dept Meteorol, Fla State Univ, Tallahassee, FL 32306-1096.

LASFARGUES, ETIENNE (STEVE) YVES, ONCOLOGY, VIROLOGY. **Personal Data:** b Milhars, France, May 5, 1916; American citizen; wid, c John E & Michele R (Di Leo). **Education:** Univ Paris, BS, 1935, DVM, 1941. **Honors & Awards:** Jensen Prize, Fr Acad Med, 1946. **Professional Experience:** RETIRED; mem, Breast Cancer Task Force Comt, Nat Cancer Inst, 1979-1982; head, Dept Tumor Cell Biol, 1977-1982; assoc mem, Dept Cytol Biophys, Inst Med Res, 1966-1977; asst prof, Col Physicians & Surgeons, Columbia Univ, 1959-1966; assoc microbiol, Col Physicians & Surgeons, Columbia Univ, 1955-1959; head lab virol, Pasteur Inst, France, 1950-1955; res fel cytol, Am Cancer Soc, Inst Cancer Res, Pa, 1947-1950; asst virol, Pasteur Inst, France, 1944-1947; res fel microbiol, Pasteur Inst, France, 1942-1944. **Memberships:** Am Asn Cancer Res; Soc for Invitro Biol; Harvey Soc. **Research Statement & Publications:** Viral oncology; cell transformation; cytogenetics. **Mailing Address:** 309 Bridgeboro Rd Apt 2460, Moorestown, NJ 08057-1428.

LASH, TIMOTHY DAVID, HETEROCYCLIC CHEMISTRY, CHEMISTRY EDUCATION. **Personal Data:** b Salisbury, Eng, October 13, 1953; m 1981, Susan. **Education:** Univ Exeter, BS, 1975; Univ Wales, MSc, 1977, PhD (org chem), 1979. **Professional Experience:** DISTING PROF ORGANIC CHEM, ILL STATE UNIV, 2000-; Camille & Henry Dreyfus shlar, beginning 1996; prof org chem, Ill State Univ, 1993-2000; res grant, NIH, 1992-1999; res grant, NSF, 1990, beginning 1992; res grant, Petrol Res Fund, beginning 1985; from asst prof to assoc prof, Ill State Univ, 1984-1993; asst prof org chem, Northern State Univ, 1982-1984; vis asst prof chem, Univ Wis-River Falls, 1981-1982; assoc, Univ Tex, Arlington, 1979-1981. **Memberships:** Royal Soc Chem; Am Inst Chemists; Am Chem Soc; Int Soc Heterocyclic Chem; Sigma Xi; AAAS; Porphyrins & Pathalocyanines Soc. **Research Statement & Publications:** Synthetic and spectroscopic studies of heterocyclic compounds, particularly pyrroles, porphyrins and oxophlorins; synthesis and geochemical origins of petroporphyrins; studies of normal and abnormal heme biosynthesis; published over 100 articles. **Mailing Address:** Dept Chem, Ill State Univ, Normal, IL 61790-4160. **Fax:** 309-438-5538. **E-Mail:** tdlash@ilstu.edu

LASHEEN, ALY M, PLANT PHYSIOLOGY, HORTICULTURE. **Personal Data:** b Cairo, Egypt, December 27, 1919. **Education:** Cairo Univ, BS, 1942; Univ Calif, Los Angeles, 1949; Agr & Mech Col Tex, PhD (plant physiol, hort), 1954. **Professional Experience:** RETIRED; prof hort, Aid Contract, Univ Minn, 1977-1979; hort adv & chief party, Univ Minn proj, Morocco, 1970-1979; prof hort, AID Contract, Univ Ky, Indonesia, 1967-1977; prof, AID Contract, Univ Ky, Indonesia, 1965-1967; assoc prof plant physiol, AID Contract, Univ Ky, Indonesia, 1961-1965; asst prof hort, Wash State Univ, 1957-1961; jr plant pathologist, Wash State Univ, 1955-1957; res assoc plant physiol, Agr & Mech Col Tex, 1954-1955; asst hort, Agr & Mech Col Tex, 1950-1953. **Memberships:** Am Soc Hort Sci; Am Soc Plant Physiol. **Research Statement & Publications:** Chemical analysis of macro and micro elements in plants; biochemical analysis of sugars and amino, organic and nucleic acids in plants; dormancy in seeds; effects of additives on plants; cold hardiness in plants; nature of dwarfing in apples. **Mailing Address:** 3607 Salisbury Dr, Lexington, KY 40510.

LASHEN, EDWARD S, MICROBIOLOGY. **Personal Data:** b New York, NY, August 11, 1934; m 1957, Marilyn; c Lori (Spector), David & Jennifer (Caplin). **Education:** Brooklyn Col, BS, 1956; Rutgers Univ, MS, 1962, PhD (microbiol), 1965. **Professional Experience:** RETIRED; res sect mgr biocides, Res Labs, Rohm & Haas Co, 1981-1992; head proj leader biocides, Res Labs, Rohm & Haas Co, 1975-1981; sr microbiologist, Res Labs, Rohm & Haas Co, 1964-1975; res asst hemat & pharmacol, Wallace Labs Div, Carter Prod Inc, 1957-1961; Res asst blood res, Jewish Chronic Dis Hosp, Brooklyn, NY, 1956-1957. **Memberships:** Am Soc Testing & Mat; Am Soc Microbiol; Soc Indust Microbiol. **Research Statement & Publications:** Microbial transformation of thiourea and substituted thioureas; biodegradation of surfactants by sewage sludge and river water microflora; broad spectrum anti-microbial agents for application as industrial biocides. **Mailing Address:** 95 Valley Dr, Furlong, PA 18925.

LASHER, GORDON (JEWETT), ASTROPHYSICS. **Personal Data:** b Denver, Colo, February 1, 1926. **Education:** Rensselaer Polytech Inst, BS, 1949; Cornell Univ, PhD (theoret physics), 1954. **Professional Experience:** Vis scholar, Stanford Univ, 1980; vis prof, Cornell Univ, 1969-1970; RES STAFF MEM, IBM-THOMAS J WATSON RES CTR, 1958-; proj physicist, Res Lab, IBM Corp, 1956-1958; assoc physicist, Res Lab, IBM Corp, 1955-1956; staff physicist, Lawrence Radiation Lab, Univ Calif, 1953-1955. **Memberships:** Fel Am Phys Soc; Int Astron Union. **Research Statement & Publications:** Applied mathematics with computer applications; solid state physics; superconductivity; theory of liquid crystals; general relativity; cosmology; theory of supernovae; lattice gauge theory; silicon dioxide and its silicon interface. **Mailing Address:** IBM-Thomas J Watson Res Ctr, Yorktown Heights, NY 10598.

LASHKARI, REZA S, INDUSTRIAL ENGINEERING. **Education:** PhD, Kans state Univ, 1977. **Professional Experience:** PROF, DEPT INDUST & SYSTEMS ENG, UNIV WINDSOR, as of 2006. **Mailing Address:** Univ Windsor, 401 Sunset Ave, Windsor, ON N9B 3P4, Can. **Fax:** 519-973-7062. **E-Mail:** lash@uwindsor.ca

LASHLEY, GERALD ERNEST, NUMERICAL ANALYSES. **Personal Data:** b Johnstown, Pa, September 26, 1935. **Education:** Eastern Nazarene Col, BS, 1957; Boston Univ, AM, 1961; Boston Univ, EdD (math educ), 1969. **Professional Experience:** PROF EMER MATH & COMPUT SCI, POINT LOMA NAZARENE UNIV, as of 2002; prof comput sci & math, Acad Comput Ctr, beginning 1980; dir, Acad Comput Ctr, 1977-1980; chmn, Div Natural Sci, Mt Vernon Nazarene Col, 1972-1976; chmn dept, Eastern Nazarene Col, 1970-1972; assoc prof math, Eastern Nazarene Col, 1964-1972; dir & instr, NSF In-Serv Inst Secondary Teachers, 1964-1972; High sch teacher, Mass, 1958-1963. **Memberships:** Asn Comput Mach; Math Asn Am. **Mailing Address:** Dept Math & Comput Sci, Point Loma Nazarene Univ, 3900 Lomaland Dr, San Diego, CA 92106-2810. **Fax:** 619-849-2579.

LASHMET, PETER K(ERNS), CHEMICAL ENGINEERING. **Personal Data:** b Ann Arbor, Mich, August 28, 1929. **Education:** Univ Mich, BSE(chem eng) & BSE(math), 1951, MSE, 1952; Univ Del, PhD (chem eng), 1962. **Professional Experience:** DEPT EXEC OFFICER, RENSSELAER POLYTECH INST, 1977-; ASSOC PROF CHEM ENG, RENSSELAER POLYTECH INST, 1965-; sr cryogenic specialist, Air Prod & Chem, Inc, 1962-1965; mgr cryostat eng, Air Prod & Chem, Inc, 1960-1962; from chem engr to sr chem engr, Air Prod & Chem, Inc, 1958-1960; process design engr, M W Kellogg Co, 1952-1953. **Memberships:** Am Chem Soc; Am Inst Chem Engrs. **Research Statement & Publications:** Catalytic properties of ion exchange resins; cryogenic refrigeration processes; miniature and compact heat exchangers; heat exchanger dynamics; computer simulation of chemical processes; chemical separation processes. **Mailing Address:** Dept Chem Eng, Rensselaer Polytech Inst, 110 Eigth St, Troy, NY 12180.

LASHMORE, DAVID S, MATERIALS SCIENCE, PHYSICAL METALLURGY. **Personal Data:** b Hempstead, NY, July 9, 1946. **Education:** Univ Fla, BS, 1969; Mich Technol Univ, MS, 1970; Univ Va, PhD (mat sci), 1977. **Honors & Awards:** Bronze Medal, Dept Com; ELectrodeposition Res Award, ELectrochem Soc; Blum Award. **Professional Experience:** GROUP LEADER ELECTRODEPOSITED COATINGS, NAT BUR STAND, 1979-; Consult, B-08 Comt Aluminum Coatings, Am Soc Testing & Mat, 1978-; Res assoc metallurgist coatings, Nat Bur Stand, 1977-1979; Int Sci Orgn, TC107. **Memberships:** Sigma Xi; Am Soc Metals; Am Electroplaters; Am Soc Testing & Mat; Am Soc Mech Engrs; Electrochem Soc; Int Sci Orgn. **Research Statement & Publications:** Surface and interface properties; transmission electron microscopy; diffraction; electrocrystallization; anodizing; powder metallurgy superlattices; magnetic thin films. **Mailing Address:** Sect 855, Dept Com Nat Inst Sci Technol, Washington, DC 20234. **Fax:** 301-926-7679. **E-Mail:** cashmore@enh.nist.gov

LASHNER, BRET AUERBACH, GASTROENTEROLOGY, INTERNAL MEDICINE. **Personal Data:** b Philadelphia, Pa, July 27, 1954. **Education:** Haverford Col, AB, 1976; NY Univ, MD, 1980; Univ Ill, Chicago, MPH, 1988. **Professional Experience:** ASSOC ED, AM J GASTROENTEROL & INFLAMMATORY BOWEL DIS, as of 2005; DIR, CTR INFLAMMATORY BOWEL DIS, CLEVELAND CLIN FOUND, 1993-; asst prof med & gastroenterol, Univ Chicago, 1986-1993; fel gastroenterol, Univ Chicago. **Memberships:** Am Gastroenterol Asn; Am Col Gastroenterol. **Research Statement & Publications:** Clinical epidemiology of gastrointestinal diseases, principally inflammatory bowel diseases. **Mailing Address:** Cleveland Clin Found, Desk S-40 9500 Euclid Ave, Cleveland, OH 44195. **Fax:** 216-444-6305. **E-Mail:** lashneb@ccf.org

LASHOF, JOYCE COHEN, MEDICINE, PUBLIC HEALTH. **Personal Data:** b Philadelphia, Pa, March 27, 1926; m 1950, Richard; c Judith, Carol & Daniel. **Education:** Duke Univ,

AB, 1946; Women's Medical Col Pennsylvania, MD, 1950. **Honorary Degrees:** DSc, Med Col Pa, 1983. **Honors & Awards:** The Sedgwich Medal, Am Public Health Asn, 1995. **Professional Experience:** PROF EMER PUB HEALTH, SCH PUB HEALTH, UNIV CALIF, BERKELEY, 1994-; prof, Sch Pub Health, 1991-1994; dean, Sch Pub Health, 1982-1991; asst dir, Off Technol Assessment, US Cong, 1978-1981; dep asst secy health progs, Dept HEW, 1977-1978; dir, Dept Pub Health, State Ill, 1973-1977; chmn dept prev med, Sect Community Med, 1972-1973; prof, Rush Med Col, 1971-1977; dir, Sect Community Med, 1966-1972; assoc prof prev med, Sch Med, Univ Ill, 1964-1971; assoc attend physician, Presby-St Luke's Hosp, 1961-; dir, Sect Prev Med & Clin Labs, Rush-Presby-St Luke's Med Ctr, 1961-1966; clin asst prof med, Sch Med, Univ Ill, 1961-1964; asst attend physician, Presby-St Luke's Hosp, 1960-1961; staff physician, Union Health Serv Inc, 1960-1961; from instr to asst prof, Sch Med, 1956-1960; asst med & physician, Stud Health Serv, Univ Chicago, 1954-1956; nat Found Infantile Paralysis fel, Yale Univ, 1953-1954; asst resident med, Montefiore Hosp, 1952-1953; asst resident med, Bronx Hosp, New York, 1951-1952; intern, Bronx Hosp, New York, 1950-1951. **Memberships:** Inst Med-Nat Acad Sci; fel Am Col Physicians; fel Am Pub Health Asn (pres, 1991); Soc Med Adminr; fel Asn Teachers Prev Med; fel Am Col Prev Med. **Research Statement & Publications:** Internal medicine; medical care; author of numerous articles and publications. **Mailing Address:** Sch Pub Health, Univ Calif, 140 Warren Hall, Berkeley, CA 94720-7360. **Fax:** 510-642-2857. **E-Mail:** jlashof@uclink.berkeley.edu

LASHOF, RICHARD KENNETH, MATHEMATICS. **Personal Data:** b Philadelphia, Pa, November 9, 1922. **Education:** Univ Pa, BS, 1943; Columbia Univ, PhD (math), 1954. **Professional Experience:** Vis prof, Math Sci Res Inst, 1990; PROF EMER MATH, UNIV CHICAGO, 1988-; vis prof, Univ Calif, Berkeley, 1985-1989; sr res fel, UK, 1981; chmn dept, Univ Chicago, 1967-1970; vis scholar, Oxford Univ, 1964-1965; NSF fel, 1960-1961; vis scholar, Univ Va Advan Inst, 1978-1979 & Inst Advan Study, Princeton, NJ, 1960, 1970; from instr to prof math, Univ Chicago, 1954-1988. **Memberships:** Am Math Soc; fel AAAS. **Research Statement & Publications:** Algebraic topology; differential geometry. **Mailing Address:** Dept Math, Univ Chicago, 5734 S Univ Ave, Chicago, IL 60637. **Fax:** 773-702-9787.

LASHOMB, JAMES HAROLD, ENTOMOLOGY. **Personal Data:** b Potsdam, NY, October 25, 1942; m 1969, c 2. **Education:** Cornell Univ, BS, 1970; Univ Md, Col Park, MS, 1973, PhD (entom), 1975. **Professional Experience:** DIR GRAD PROG ENTOM & CHMN, DEPT ENTOM, RUTGERS UNIV, as of 2006; assoc prof entom, Rutgers Univ, beginning 1984; asst prof, Rutgers Univ, 1978-1984; res assoc entom, Miss State Univ, 1975-1978. **Memberships:** AAAS; Entom Soc Am; Ecol Soc Am; Int Orgn Biol Control Noxious Animals & Plants. **Research Statement & Publications:** Sampling of insect populations and natural enemies; parasitic insect distribution within plants and parasitic insect biology. **Mailing Address:** Dept Entom, Rutgers Univ, 93 Lipman Dr, New Brunswick, NJ 08901-8520. **Fax:** 732-932-7229. **E-Mail:** lashomb@rci.rutgers.edu

LASIA, ANDRZEJ, ELECTROCHEMISTRY. **Personal Data:** b Warsaw, Poland, December 23, 1944; m 1964, c 1. **Education:** Univ Warsaw, Poland, MS, 1967, PhD (electrochemistry), 1975. **Professional Experience:** PROF, UNIV SHERBROOKE, 1993-; assoc prof, Univ Sherbrooke, 1987-1993; asst prof, Univ Sherbrooke, 1983-1987; res assoc, Univ Guelph, Ont, 1982-1983; asst prof, Univ Warsaw, Poland, 1977-1982; vis prof, Univ Sao Paulo, Sao Carlos, 2005, 1999, 1987; Univ. Louis Pasteur, Strasbourg 1998; Johannes Kepler UniversitSt, 1988, University of Warsaw, several times; Fel, Univ Guelph, Ont, 1975-1976. **Memberships:** Canadian Soc for Chemistry; Electrochem Soc; ACFAS. **Research Statement & Publications:** hydrogen adsorption, absorption into metals; hydrogen evolution; electrochemical impedance spectroscopy; new materials for electrocatalysis; porous electrrodes; SOFC. **Mailing Address:** Dept Chem, Univ Sherbrooke, Sherbrooke, PQ J1K 2R1, Can. **Fax:** 819-821-8017. **E-Mail:** a.lasia@usherbrooke.ca

LASIECKA, IRENA, APPLIED MATHEMATICS, PARTIAL DIFFERENTIAL EQUATIONS & CONTROL THEORY. **Personal Data:** b Warsaw, Poland, February 4, 1948. **Education:** Univ Warsaw, MS, 1972, PhD (appl math), 1975. **Honors & Awards:** Silver Core Award, Int Fedn Info Processes, 1992. **Professional Experience:** PROF, DEPT MATH, UNIV VA, 1998-; prof, dept appl math, Univ Va, 1987-1998; assoc ed, Int J Math & Math Sci, 1985-, Soc Indust & Appl Math J Control, Inst Elec & Electronics Engrs, Computational Optimization; assoc ed, J Appl Math & Optimization, 1984-; from assoc prof to prof differential equation, Math Dept, Univ Fla, Gainesville, 1980-1987; vis scholar control theory, Univ Calif, Los Angeles, 1978-1980; asst prof appl math, Polish Acad Sci, Warsaw, 1975-1978. **Memberships:** Int Fedn Info Processes; Am Math Soc; Soc Indust & Appl Math. **Research Statement & Publications:** Applied mathematics; control theory and optimization; partial differential equations; numerical analysis; author of approximately 100 research papers published in major journals. **Mailing Address:** Dept Math, Univ Va, Charlottesville, VA 22903. **Fax:** 434-982-3084. **E-Mail:** il2v@virginia.edu

LASINSKI, BARBARA FORMAN, PLASMA PHYSICS. **Personal Data:** b New York, NY, November 28, 1941. **Education:** Barnard Col, BA, 1962; Univ Rochester, PhD (physics), 1968. **Professional Experience:** PHYSICIST, PLASMA PHYSICS, LAWRENCE LIVERMORE LAB, 1972-; Res assoc high energy physics, Enrico Fermi Inst, Univ Chicago, 1968-1971. **Memberships:** Am Phys Soc. **Research Statement & Publications:** Computational simulation of plasmas; laser-plasma interactions; computational physics. **Mailing Address:** Lawrence Livermore Lab, PO Box 808, L-38, Livermore, CA 94551. **Fax:** 925-423-9208. **E-Mail:** blasinski@llnl.gov

LASINSKI, THOMAS A, PHYSICS. **Education:** Univ Chicago, PhD (Physics), 1971. **Professional Experience:** DEP DIR OPER, CTR APPL SCI COMPUT, LAWRENCE LIVERMORE NAT LAB, as of 2006. **Mailing Address:** 2204 Jeffrey St, Box 808, Livermore, CA 94550. **Fax:** 925-423-2993. **E-Mail:** tal@llnl.gov

LASKA, EUGENE, MATHEMATICS, STATISTICS. **Personal Data:** b New York, NY, March 17, 1938; m 1959, Estelle; c 3. **Education:** City Col New York, BS, 1959; NY Univ, MS, 1961, PhD (math), 1963. **Professional Experience:** WHO COLLABORATING CTR RES & TRAINING, MENT HEALTH PROG MGT, NATHAN S KLINE INST PSYCHIAT RES, ORANGEBURG, NY, 1985-; DIR, STATIST SCI & EPI DIV, 1984-; assoc comnr, NY State Dept Ment Hyg, 1980; RES PROF PSYCHIAT, NY UNIV MED CTR, 1979-; mem, Comput & Biomath Sci Study Sect, NIH, 1972-1976; consult comput psychiat, USSR, Israel, Italy, Iran, Peru & Indonesia, China, Chile, Ecuador, Cuba, 1968; NIMH grants, 1967-1978; dir info sci div, Nathan S Kline Inst Psychiat Res, Orangeburg, NY, 1963-1984; systs engr, IBM, NJ, 1962-1963; res assoc math, Courant Inst Math Sci, 1961-1962; Asst res scientist, Comput Lab, Res Div, NY Univ, 1959-1961. **Memberships:** Fel AAAS; Inst Math Statist; fel Am Statist Asn; Am Soc Clin Pharmacol & Therapeut; Biomet Soc. **Research Statement & Publications:** Mathematical statistics, including estimation theory; applied statistics, including biostatistics and clinical trial methodology; computers applications in medicine. **Mailing Address:** 34 Dante St, Larchmont, NY 10538.

LASKAR, RENU CHAKRAVARTI, MATHEMATICS. **Personal Data:** b Bhagalpur, India, August 8, 1930; American citizen; m 1962, Amulya; c Joy & Sonjoy Raja. **Education:** Univ Bihar, BS, 195 0; Univ Bhagalpur, MS, 195 7; Univ Ill, Urbana, PhD (group theory), 1962. **Professional Experience:** PROF MATH, CLEMSON UNIV, 1976-; Guest mathematician, Univ Paris, 1975-1976; assoc prof, Clemson Univ, 1968-1976; fel, Univ NC, Chapel Hill, 1965-1968; lectr, Indian Inst Technol, Kharagpur, 1962-1965; Lectr math, Ranchi Women's Col, India, 195 5-1958. **Memberships:** SIAM; founding fel ICA. **Research Statement & Publications:** Graph theory, in partcular, coloring problems, domination Group theory; combinatorial mathematics, especially graph theory; published more than one hundred journal articles, wrote three book chapters, edited two volumes. **Mailing Address:** Dept Math Sci Box 341907, Clemson Univ, Clemson, SC 29634-1907. **E-Mail:** rclsk@clemson.edu

LASKARIS, EVANGELOS TRIFON, MECHANICAL & ELECTRICAL ENGINEERING. **Personal Data:** b Cairo, Egypt, January 14, 1944. **Education:** Nat Tech Univ Athens, BS, 1966; Rensselaer Polytech Inst, MS, 1971, PhD (mech eng), 1974. **Honors & Awards:** IR-100 Award, Indust Res Mag, 1977; Gold & Silver Patent Awards, Corp Res & Develop, Gen Elec Co. **Professional Experience:** CHIEF TECHNOLOGIST, IMAGING TECHNOLOGIES, GE GLOBAL RES, as of 2003; mgr appl superconductivity prog, engr systs lab, Gen Elec Co, beginning 1977; cryog br, Power Generation & Propulsion lab, 1973-1977; Mech engradvan eng, Large Steam-Turbine Generator dept, 1967-1973. **Memberships:** Greek Chamber Engrs. **Research Statement & Publications:** Superconductivity; cryogenics; computational fluid dynamics; rotating machinery; intense magnetic fields. **Mailing Address:** Res & Develop Bldg, Gen Elec Global Res Co, K-1 Rm EP117, 1, Res Circle, Niskayuna, NY 12309.

LASKER, GEORGE ERIC, INFORMATION SCIENCES, PSYCHOLOGY. **Personal Data:** b Prague, Czech. **Education:** Prague Tech Univ, EC, 1957; Charles Univ, Prague, DP, 1961. **Professional Experience:** DIR, INT INST ADVAN STUDY SYS RES & CYBERNET, UNIV WINDSOR, as of 2004; dir, Int Inst Advan Studies Systs Res Cybernet, 1983; chmn, Soc Gen Systs Res Conf, 1982-1983; pres, Int Cong Appl Systs Res & Cybernet, 1980-; distinguished vis, Inst Elec & Electronics Engrs Comput Soc Prog, 1979-1982; vis scholar, Dept Comput & Commun Sci, Univ Mich, Ann Arbor, 1974-; ed bd, Int J Gen Systs, 1974-; PROF COMPUT SCI, UNIV WINDSOR, 1968-; assoc prof comput sci, Univ Man, 1966-1968; Nat Res Coun Can grant, Univ Man, 1966-1968; Asst prof math, Univ Sask, 1965-1966. **Memberships:** Can Comput Sci Asn; World Orgn Gen Systs & Cybernet; NY Acad Sci. **Research Statement & Publications:** Diagnostic methodology; artificial intelligence; biomimetic engineering; expert systems; cerebrometic design of computers; simulation models; behavioral prediction; computer controlled conditioning; mathematical psychology; forecasting methodology; computer applications; psychotronics; psychocybernetics; quality of life; expert educational systems; systems models of brain; synergetics. **Mailing Address:** Dept Comput Sci, Univ Windsor, 401 Sunset Ave, Windsor, ON N9B 3P4, Can. **E-Mail:** lasker@uwindsor.ca

LASKER, HOWARD ROBERT, MARINE BENTHIC ECOLOGY, ECOLOGY OF GORGONIAN CORALS. **Personal Data:** b New York, NY, February 8, 1952; c 2. **Education:** Univ Rochester, BS, 1972, MS, 1973; Univ Chicago, PhD (geophys sci), 1978. **Professional Experience:** Biol ed, Coral Reefs, 2001-; res assoc, Smithsonian Trop Res Inst, 1999-; PROF BIOL SCI, STATE UNIV NY, BUFFALO, 1994-; vis res, Smithsonian Trop Res Inst, 1979-1998; from asst prof to assoc prof, State Univ NY, Buffalo, 1979-1994; fel, Rosenstiel Sch Marine & Atmospheric Sci, Univ Miami, 1978-1979. **Memberships:** Ecol Soc Am; Soc Integrative & Comp Biol; Am Soc Naturalists; Int Soc Reef Studies. **Research Statement & Publications:** Ecology of corals and coral reefs; reproductive biology of benthic invertebrates ecology of algal-coelenterate symbioses; population biology of benthic invertebrates. **Mailing Address:** Dept Biol Sci, State Univ NY, Buffalo, NY 14260. **Fax:** 716-645-2975. **E-Mail:** hlasker@buffalo.edu

LASKER, SIGMUND E, PHYSICAL CHEMISTRY, BIOPHYSICS. **Personal Data:** b New York, NY, September 5, 1923. **Education:** Brooklyn Col, BS, 1949; NY Univ, MS, 1951; Stevens Inst Technol, PhD (phys chem), 1965. **Professional Experience:** PROF MED RES, NY MED COL, 1982-; assoc prof, NY Med Col, 1975-1982; asst prof pharmacol, NY Med Col, 1972-1975; Adj assoc prof, Rockefeller Univ, 1968-1980; asst prof biophys, NY Med Col, 1966-1972; res assoc phys chem, Stevens Inst Technol, 1960-1966; asst instr biochem, NY Med Col, 1958-1960; Res assoc surg, NY Med Col, 1957-1960. **Memberships:** Soc Magnetic Resonance Med; Biophys Soc; Am Chem Soc; NY Acad Sci; Am Heart Asn; Sigma Xi; NY Acad Med. **Research Statement & Publications:** Magnetic resonance imaging; polyelectrolytes; experimental thermal injuries; anticoagulants. **Mailing Address:** Dept Med, NY Med Col, Valhalla, NY 10595. **Fax:** 914-993-4694.

LASKI, BERNARD, PEDIATRICS, HEMATOLOGY. **Personal Data:** b Ont, November 11, 1915. **Education:** Univ Toronto, MD, 1939, FRCP (C), 1949; Am Acad Pediat, FAAP, 1949. **Professional Experience:** PROF PEDIAT, UNIV TORONTO, 1977-; Chief Pediat, Mt Sinai Hosp, 1954-; sr physician, Hosp for Sick Children, 1949. **Memberships:** Am Pediat Soc; Am Soc Pediat Res; Can Pediat Soc; Am Soc Hemat; Am Acad Pediat. **Mailing Address:** 99 Avenue Rd, Toronto, ON M5S 2G5, Can.

LASKIN, ALLEN I, MICROBIAL TRANSFORMATIONS & BIODEGRADATION. **Personal Data:** b Brooklyn, NY, December 7, 1928. **Education:** City Col New York, BS, 1950; Univ Tex, MA, 1952, PhD, 1956. **Honors & Awards:** Selman A Waksman Hon Lectr, Theobald Smith Soc, 1974; I M Lewis Award, 1977; Charles A Thom Award, Soc Indust Microbiol, 1992. **Professional Experience:** PRES, LASKIN & LAWRENCE ASSOC, as of 2002; Vis scholar, Rutgers Univ, 1992-1993; RES FEL, CHARLES A DANA RES INST, DREW UNIV, 1989-; pres, Matrix Res Labs, 1988-1989; vpres res & develop, Ethigen Corp, 1986-1989; vpres res & develop, Matrix Res Labs, 1986-1988; assoc dir, NJ Ctr Adv Biotechnol & Med, 1985-1986; sr res assoc, 1974-1984; head, Bioscience Res, Exxon Res & Eng Co, 1971-1985; res assoc, 1969-1974; asst dir microbiol, Squibb Inst Med Res, 1967-1969; res supvr microbiol, Squibb Inst Med Res, 1964-1967; sr res microbiologist, Squibb Inst Med Res, 1955-1964; Res scientist, Univ Tex, 1953-1955. **Memberships:** Soc Indust Microbiol (pres 1978-1979); Am Soc Microbiol; Am Chem Soc; fel Am Acad Microbiol; fel NY Acad Sci. **Research Statement & Publications:** Cell-free protein synthesis; mode of action of antibiotics; mechanisms of bacterial resistance to antibiotics; microbial transformations of steroids; petroleum microbiology; microbial enzymes; transformations and biodegradation of hydrocarbons and related compounds; BIOREMEDIATION. **Mailing Address:** Laskin & Lawrence Assoc, 383 S Middlebush Rd, Somerset, NJ 08873. **Fax:** 732-873-8618. **E-Mail:** ailaskin@aol.com

LASKIN, DANIEL M, ORAL SURGERY, MAXILLOFACIAL SURGERY. **Personal Data:** b New York, NY, September 3, m Eve; c Jeffrey, Gary & Marla. **Education:** Ind Univ, BS & DDS, 1947; Univ Ill, MS, 1951; Am Bd Oral & Maxillofacial Surg, dipl; FRCS (eng); FRCPS(G). **Honorary Degrees:** DSc, Ind Univ, 2001. **Honors & Awards:** Francis N Reichman Lectr, 1971; Distinguished Serv Award, Am Soc Oral Surgeons, 1972; Simon P

Hullihen Mem Award, WVA Univ, 1976; Arnold K Maislen Mem Award Oral Surg, 1977; Arnold K Maislen Mem Award, 1977; Res Recognition Award, Am Asn Oral & Maxillofacial Surgeons, 1978; William J Gies Oral Surg Award, 1979; Cordwainer Lectr, Univ London, 1980; Hinman Medallion, 1981; W Harry Archer Award, 1981; Heidbrink Award, Am Dent Soc Anesthesiol, 1983; Rene LeFort Medal, Brazilian Col Oral & Maxillofacial Surg & Traumatology, 1985; Edward C Hinds Lectr, 1990; Norton M Ross Award Excellence Clin Res, 1994. **Professional Experience:** Head, Dept Dent, Med Col Va Hosps, 1986-2001; attend oral & maxillofacial surgeon, Richmond Eye & Ear Hosp & Med Col Va Hosps, 1984-; PROF & CHMN, DEPT ORAL & MAXILLOFACIAL SURG, MED COL VA, 1984-1992; PROF EMER, 1992- PROF EMER ORAL & MAXILLOFACIAL SURG, UNIV ILL, 1973-1983; consult oral surgeon, Ill Masonic Hosp, 1965-1983 & Bethany Methodist Hosp, 1978-1983; bd dirs, Am Pain Soc, 1978-1980; dep chmn, Cook County Hosp, 1977-1983; attend oral surgeon, Skokie Valley Community Hosp, 1977-1983; head, Dept Dent, 1976-1983; dep chmn, Div Oral Surg, Cook County Hosp, 1976-1983; head dept, Col Dent, Univ Ill, 1973-1983; ed-in-chief, J Oral & Maxillofacial Surg, 1972-2002; ed-in-chief, J Oral & Maxillofacial Surg, 1972-2001; Swed Covenant Hosp, 1979-1983 & Edgewater Hosp, head dept, 1970-1983; chmn dept oral surg, Cook County Hosp, 1967-1977; chmn & atten oral surgeon, Div Oral Surg, Cook County Hosp, 1967-1976; assoc head dept, Col Dent, Univ Ill, 1962-1973; dir, Temporamandibular Joint & Facial Pain Res Ctr, 1961-1983; clin prof surg, Univ Ill Hosp, 1961-1983; prof oral & maxillofacial surg, Col Dent, Univ Ill, 1960-1983; from instr to assoc prof, Col Dent, Univ Ill, 1951-1960; res asst, Col Dent, Univ Ill, 1950-1951; Resident, Cook County Hosp, 1950-1951; clin asst, Col Dent, Univ Ill, 1949-1950; Intern oral surg, Jersey City Med Ctr, 1947-1948; ed, Am Asn Oral Maxillofacial Surgons AAOMS Today, 1996- & J Oral & Maxillofacial Surgery, 1972-2002. **Memberships:** Sigma Xi; Int Asn Dent Res; Soc Exp Biol & Med; Am Soc Exp Path; Am Dent Asn; Am Asn Dent Res; fel AAAS; Am Asn Oral & Maxillofacial Surgeons (pres 1976-1977); Int Asn Oral & Maxillofacial Surgeons (pres 1983-1986, secy-gen 1989-1995; Am Dent Soc Anesth (pres 1976-1978); Nat Acad Prac (Pres 2002-2004). **Research Statement & Publications:** Temporomandibular joint; metabolism of bone and cartilage; sutural growth; calcification and resorption of bone; over 700 publications in fields of oral and maxillofacial surgery and dental research and author or co-author of 15 books. **Mailing Address:** Dept Oral & Maxillofacial Surg, Va Commonwealth Univ, PO Box 980566, Richmond, VA 23298-0566. **E-Mail:** dmlaskin@vcu.edu

LASKIN, ROBERT A, AERONAUTICS. **Education:** Yale Col, BS, 1974; Stanford Univ, MS, 1979; Columbia Univ, PhD, 1982. **Professional Experience:** PROJECT TECHNOLOGIST, SPACE INTELFEROMETRY MISSION, JET PROPULSION LAB, 1997-. **Mailing Address:** Jet Propulsion Lab, Calif Inst Technol, 4800 Oak Grove Dr PO Box 301-486, Pasadena, CA 91109-8099. **Fax:** 301-209-0843. **E-Mail:** Robert.A.Laskin@jpl.nasa.gov

LASKO, PAUL, BIOLOGY. **Education:** Mass Inst Technol, PhD (biol). **Professional Experience:** PROF & CHAIR, DEPT BIOL, MCGILL UNIV, 1999-. **Mailing Address:** Dept Biol McGill Univ, 1205 Ave Docteur Penfield Rm W4/6, Montreal, PQ H3A 1B1, Can. **Fax:** 514-398-5069. **E-Mail:** paul_lasko@maclan.mcgill.ca

LASKOWSKI, EDWARD L, COMPUTER INTEGRATED MANUFACTURING, SENSORS. **Personal Data:** b Cleveland, Ohio, March 13, 1943. **Education:** Univ Detroit, BEE, 1966; Ohio State Univ, MSEE, 1968; Cleveland State Univ, DEng, 1978. **Professional Experience:** OWNER, EL ASSOCS, as of 2003; vpres technol, Acme Cleveland Corp, beginning 1986; dir res, Bendix Corp, 1985-1986; mgr advan systs, Bendix Corp, 1979-1985; Res engr, Gen Elec Co, 1968-1979. **Memberships:** Inst Elec & Electronics Engrs; Soc Mfg Engrs; Nat Elec Mfrs Asn. **Research Statement & Publications:** Intelligent sensors and systems; manufacturing computer systems; systems modeling; analysis of physical processes to be used as component of control system model; marketing new products. **Mailing Address:** 6154 Winchester Dr, Independence, OH 44131.

LASKOWSKI, LEONARD FRANCIS, JR, MEDICAL MICROBIOLOGY, CLINICAL MICROBIOLOGY. **Personal Data:** b Milwaukee, Wis, November 16, 1919; m 1946, Frances Bielinski; c Leonard F III, James & Thomas. **Education:** Marquette Univ, BS, 1941, MS, 1948; St Louis Univ, PhD (med bact), 1951; Am Bd Med Microbiol, dipl. **Professional Experience:** EMER PROF PATH & INTERNAL MED, SCH MED, ST LOUIS UNIV, 1990-; St Elizabeth's Hosp, Granite City, Ill, 1978- & St Louis Co & City Med Examr, 1978-; assoc prof internal med, St Louis Univ, 1977-1990; Mogul Diag Div, St Francis Hosp, 1974-1977; consult, Jefferson Barracks, Vet Hosp, 1972-; Mogul Diag Div, Mogul Corp, 1972-1979; St Elizabeth's Hosp, Belleville, Ill, 1968- & St Louis Co Hosp, 1969-; referee mycol, USPHS Commun Dis Ctr Prog Testing Clin Diag Labs, 1968-; consult clin microbiol, John Cochran Vet Hosp, 1966-; dir, Clin Microbiol Sect, St Louis Univ Hosps, 1965; attend, Vet Admin Hosp, health & tech training coordr, Latin Am Peace Corps Projs, 1962-1966; consult, St Mary's Group Hosp, 1957-; from asst prof to prof path, St Louis Univ, 1957-1990; fel trop med, La State Univ, 1957; China Med Bd fel, Latin Am, 1957; asst prof microbiol, St Louis Univ, 1954-1957; sr instr, St Louis Univ, 1953-1954; Instr bact, St Louis Univ, 1946-1948 & 1951-1953. **Memberships:** NY Acad Sci; Am Soc Microbiol; AAAS; fel Am Acad Microbiol; Med Mycol Soc Americas; Sigma Xi. **Research Statement & Publications:** Mechanism of intracellular parasitism; mechanism of action of therapeutic compounds. **Mailing Address:** 6229 Robertsville Rd, Villa Ridge, MO 63089.

LASKOWSKI, MICHAEL JR, BIOCHEMISTRY. **Personal Data:** b Warsaw, Poland, March 13, 1930; American citizen; m 1957, Joan Heyer; c Michael & Marta. **Education:** Lawrence Col, BS, 1950; Cornell Univ, PhD (phys chem), 1954. **Honors & Awards:** McCoy Award, Purdue Univ, 1975; Alfred Jurzykowski Found Award, 1977. **Professional Experience:** Prof chem, Purdue univ, 1965-; Head, biotech div, Purdue univ, 1967-1977; Visiting prof, UCSF, 1986, 1995, 2002; vis prof, Osaka univ, 1984; vis prof, Alberta, 1981-1983; vis prof, Yale, 1971; counr, Am Chem Soc, 1984-1987; Chmn, Proteolytic Enzymes & Inhibitors, 1982; mem, Biophys & Biophys Chem Study Sect, NIH, 1967-1971; Chmn, Gordon Res Conf Physics & Phys Chem Biopolymers, 1966; PROF CHEM, PURDUE UNIV, 1965-; from asst prof to assoc prof, Purdue Univ, 1957-1965; NIH fel, Cornell and Yale univs, 1955-1956; res assoc, Cornell univ, 1954-1955; NIH fel, Cornell univ, 1952-1954; instr, Cornell Univ, 1956-1957; Asst chem, USPHS fel, 1952-1956; Asst chem, Cornell Univ, 1950-1952; res asst, Marquette univ, 1949-1950. **Memberships:** AAAS; Am Chem Soc; Am Soc Biol Chemists; Polish Inst Arts & Sci Am; Biophys Soc; Protein Soc. **Research Statement & Publications:** Protein chemistry; role of individual amino acid residues in proteinase inhibitor-proteinase interaction; evolution; enzymes and their inhibitors. **Mailing Address:** Dept Chem, Purdue Univ, West Lafayette, IN 47907-1393. **Fax:** 765-494-0239. **E-Mail:** michael.laskowski.1@purdue.edu

LASKOWSKI, MICHAEL BERNARD, EXPERIMENTAL BIOLOGY. **Personal Data:** b Chicago, Ill, April 20, 1943. **Education:** Loyola Univ, BS, 1966; Univ Okla, PhD (physiol), 1970. **Professional Experience:** PROF PHYSIOL, DEPT BIOL SCI, UNIV IDAHO, 1988-; DIR, WAMI PROG, 1988-; dir, Regional Med Educ Prog, Univ Idaho/Wash State Univ, 1988; actg chmn dept, St Louis Univ Sch Med, 1987-1988; asst dean students, St Louis Univ Sch Med, 1985-1988; vis scientist, Dept Physiol & Biophys, Wash Univ, 1984-1985; from asst prof to prof physiol, St Louis Univ Sch Med, 1976-1988; Andrew Mellon career develop award, 1974-1976; asst prof, Vanderbilt Univ, 1974-1976; instr, Vanderbilt Univ, 1972-1974; Dept Pharmacol, Vanderbilt Univ, 1971-1972; Muscular Dystrophy Asn postdoctoral fel, Dept Biol Sci, Nwestern Univ, 1970-1971. **Memberships:** Sigma Xi; Am Physiol Soc; Am Acad Neurol; Soc Neuroscience. **Mailing Address:** Stud Health Ctr, Univ Idaho, Rm 302, Moscow, ID 83844-3051. **E-Mail:** mlaskow@uidaho.edu

LASKY, JACK SAMUEL, ORGANIC CHEMISTRY, POLYMER CHEMISTRY. **Personal Data:** b New York, NY, March 14, 1930; m 1952, Martha; c MIchael & Susan. **Education:** City Col New York, BS, 1951; Univ Md, PhD (chem), 1955. **Professional Experience:** CONSULT, 1995-, vpres res & eng, Onkonite Co, 1976-1995; vpres res, Onkonite Co, 1970-1976; dir polymer res, Onkonite Co, 1969-1970; Res chemist, US Rubber Co, 1955-1969. **Memberships:** Am Chem Soc; Inst Elec & Electronics Engrs; Power Eng Soc. **Research Statement & Publications:** Synthetic polymers; rubber; plastics; stereospecific polymerization; heterogeneous catalysis; kinetics of reactions; electrical insulating and covering materials. **Mailing Address:** 29 Newman Ave, Verona, NJ 07044.

LASKY, LAWRENCE ALAN, MOLECULAR BIOLOGY, CELL ADHESIONS & INFLAMMATION. **Personal Data:** b Los Angeles, Calif, April 15, 1951. **Education:** Univ Calif, Los Angeles, BS, 1973, PhD (molecular biol), 1978. **Professional Experience:** STAFF SCIENTIST, GENENTECH, 1991-; sr scientist, Genentech, 1985-1991; res scientist, Genentech, 1982-1985; sr scientist, Genetics Inst, 1981-1982; fel develop biol, Calif Inst Technol, 1978-1981. **Memberships:** Am Soc Cell Biol; Am Soc Invest Path. **Research Statement & Publications:** Molecular biology; cell adhesions and inflammation. **Mailing Address:** Dept Molecular-Oncol, Genetech Inc, 460 Pt San Bruno Blvd, South San Francisco, CA 94080. **Fax:** 415-399-9879. **E-Mail:** larry@lvpcapital.com

LASKY, RICHARD DAVID, ANALYTICAL BIOCHEMISTRY, GLYCOBIOLOGY. **Personal Data:** b Galesburg, Ill, August 23, 1950. **Education:** Occidental Col, BA, 1972; San Francisco State Univ, MA, 1981; Univ Calif, Davis, PhD (biochem), 1983. **Professional Experience:** SCIENTIST IV, CHARACTERIZATION, HYLAND DIV, BAXTER HEALTHCARE CORP, 1992-; res scientist, Imreg, Inc, 1988-1991; staff scientist, Barnett Inst Chem Analysis, Northeastern Univ, 1987-1988; Dept Biochem, Univ Calif-Berkeley, 1985-1987; Fel, Lab Carbohydrates Res, Harvard Med Sch, 1983-1985. **Memberships:** Soc Glycobiol; Am Soc Biochem & Molecular Biol; Protein Soc. **Research Statement & Publications:** Characterization of recombinant monoclonal antibodies and recombinant Factor VIII (rAHF); SDS-PAGE analysis, SEC-HPLC, IEF, capillary electrophoresis, peptide mapping, protein sequence analysis and oligosaccharide analysis. **Mailing Address:** Hyland Div Baxter Biotech, 1720 Flower Ave, Duarte, CA 91010. **Fax:** 626-357-8348. **E-Mail:** rickster1@aol.com

LASLEY, BILL LEE, REPRODUCTIVE PHYSIOLOGY. **Personal Data:** b Ottumwa, Iowa, June 4, 1941. **Education:** Calif State Univ, Chico, BA, 1963; Univ Calif, Davis, PhD (physiol), 1972. **Professional Experience:** PROF POP HEALTH & REPRODUCTION, UNIV CALIF, DAVIS, as of 1999; res endocrinologist, San Diego Zool Garden, beginning 1975; fel reproductive biol, Rockefeller Found, 1972-1975; Teacher math & sci, Roseville Union High Sch, 1964-1967. **Memberships:** Endocrin Soc; Soc Gyn Invest; Soc Study Reproduction. **Research Statement & Publications:** Reproductive endocrinology with emphasis on comparative studies. **Mailing Address:** Dept Pop Health & Reproduction, Univ Calif, 1136 Tupper Hall, Davis, CA 95616. **Fax:** 530-752-4278. **E-Mail:** bllasley@ucdavis.edu

LASLEY, STEPHEN MICHAEL, NEUROTOXICOLOGY, NEUROCHEMISTRY. **Personal Data:** b Louisville, Ky, February 12, 1950; m 1974, Carolyn; c Michael & David. **Education:** Univ Louisville, MEng, 1973, PhD (neuropsychopharmacology), 1979. **Professional Experience:** ADJ ASSOC PROF, DEPT BIOL SCI, ILL STATE UNIV, as of 2002; PROF, DEPT BIOMED & THER SCI, COL MED, UNIV ILL, PEORIA, 2003-; ed bd Toxicol Appl Pharmacol, 2001-; dir placement comt, Soc Toxicol, 1996-1997; ed bd, Toxicol Sci, 1993-2001; assoc prof, Dept Biomed & Ther Sci, Col Med, Univ Ill, Peoria, 1994-2003; mem placement comt, Soc Toxicol, 1992-1996; asst prof, Dept Basic Sci, Col Med, Univ Ill, Peoria, 1986-1994; res asst prof pharmacol, Tex Col Osteop Med, Ft Worth, 1985-1986; sci assoc pharmacol, Tex Col Osteop Med, Ft Worth, 1983-1985; res assoc, Col Med, Univ Cincinnati, 1982-1983; fel neurotoxicol, Col Med, Univ Cincinnati, 1979-1982. **Memberships:** AAAS; Soc Neuroscience; Soc Toxicol; Am Soc Pharmacol & Exp Therapeut; Soc Toxicol. **Research Statement & Publications:** neurotoxicity from chronic exposure to depleted uranium exposure; mechanistic bases of neurotoxicity from chronic lead exposure. **Mailing Address:** Dept Biomed & Therapeut Sci, Col Med, Univ Ill, PO Box 1649, Peoria, IL 61656. **Fax:** 309-671-8403. **E-Mail:** sml@uic.edu

LASS, JONATHAN H, CORNEA & EXTERNAL DISEASES, OPHTHALMOLOGY. **Personal Data:** b Orange, NJ, July 14, 1949. **Education:** Boston Univ, BA, 1972, MD, 1973. **Honors & Awards:** Honor Award, Am Acad Ophthal, 1987. **Professional Experience:** Dir ophthal, Univ Hosp, 1994; CHMN & CHARLES I THOMAS PROF, DEPT OPHTHAL, CASE WESTERN RES UNIV, 1994-; ophthalmologist & actg dir ophthal, Univ Hosps, Cleveland, beginning 1993; assoc prof, Dept Ophthal, Case Western Res Univ, beginning 1993; actg chmn ophthal, Dept Ophthal, 1993-1994; assoc ophthalmologist, Univ Hosps, Cleveland, 1985-1993; corneal consult, courtesy staff, Mt Sinai Med Ctr, 1981-; asst ophthalmologist, MetroHealth Med Ctr, 1979-; from asst prof to assoc prof, Dept Ophthal, 1979-1993; actg staff ophthal, Winchester Hosp, Mass, 1977-1980; clin fel ophthal, Mass-Eye & Ear Infirmary, 1977-1979. **Memberships:** Int Soc Refractive Keratoplasty; Asn Res Vision & Ophthal; Am Acad Ophthal; Eye Bank Asn Am; Contact Lens Asn Ophthalmologists. **Research Statement & Publications:** Role of cytokines in the pathogenesis of onchocercal keratitis; develop improved methods for corneal preservation. **Mailing Address:** 11100 Euclid Ave, Cleveland, OH 44106-5068. **Fax:** 216-983-0544. **E-Mail:** jhl7@po.cwru.edu

LASS, NORMAN J(AY), EXPERIMENTAL PHONETICS, SPEECH & HEARING SCIENCES. **Personal Data:** b Brooklyn, NY, September 20, 1943; m 1967, Martha; c Laura S & Jonathan E. **Education:** Brooklyn Col, City Univ NY, BA, 1965; Purdue Univ, MS, 1966, PhD (speech path, speech & hearing sci), 1968. **Professional Experience:** PROF SPEECH PATH & AUDIOL, WVA UNIV, 1977-; consult, Audiol & Speech Path Serv, Vet Admin Med Ctr, Martinsburg, WVa, 1975-1983; chmn dept, Wva Univ, 1974-1983; from asst prof to assoc prof, Wva Univ, 1969-1977; res fel, Bur Child Res, Univ Kans Med Ctr, Kansas City, 1968-1969. **Memberships:** Fel Am Speech-Lang Hearing Asn; Am Asn Phonetic Sci; WVa Speech-Lang-Hearing Asn. **Research Statement & Publications:** Listener attitudes toward accented English speakers; listener attitudes toward regional dialects; ethnic speaker identification. **Mailing Address:** Dept Speech Path & Audiol, WVa Univ, PO Box 6122, Morgantown, WV 26506-6122. **Fax:** 304-293-7565. **E-Mail:** nlass@wvu.edu

LASSEN, LAURENCE E, FORESTRY. **Personal Data:** b Milwaukee, Wis, December 16, 1932. **Education:** Iowa State Univ, BS, 1954, MS, 1958; Univ Mich, PhD (forestry), 1967.

Professional Experience: RETIRED; dir, Intermountain Res Sta, Ogden, Ut, 1983-1992; dir, Southern Forest Exp Sta, New Orleans, 1976-1983; dep dir, Wash, DC, 1974-1976; chief forest prod technol res, Wash, DC, 1972-1974; staff asst res admin, US Forest Serv, 1971-1972; proj leader, Forest Prod Lab, Wis, 1967-1971; res forest prod technologist, Forest Prod Lab, Wis, 1958-1967. **Memberships:** Soc Am Foresters; Sigma Xi; Soc Range Mgt. **Research Statement & Publications:** Forestry research. **Mailing Address:** 4882 Knollwood Dr, Ogden, UT 84403-4424.

LASSER, ELLIOTT CHARLES, MEDICINE, RADIOLOGY. **Personal Data:** b Buffalo, NY, November 30, 1922. **Education:** Harvard Univ, BS, 1943; Univ Buffalo, MD, 1946; Univ Minn, MS, 1953. **Professional Experience:** PROF EMER RADIOL, SCH MED, UNIV CALIF, SAN DIEGO, as of 2003; prof radiol, Sch Med, Univ Calif, San Diego, beginning 1968; chmn dept, Sch Med, Univ Calif, San Diego, 1968-1977; consult, Vet Admin Hosp, Pittsburgh, Pa, 1957-1968; prof & chmn dept, Sch Med, Univ Pittsburgh, 1956-1968; asst prof, Sch Med, Univ Buffalo, 1954-1956; assoc, Sch Med, Univ Buffalo, 1953-1954; instr radiol, Grad Sch Med, Univ Minn, 1952-1953. **Memberships:** AAAS; Radiol Soc N Am; Am Med Asn; Am Col Radiol. **Research Statement & Publications:** Radiology of the vascular system. **Mailing Address:** Dept Radiol, Univ Calif San Diego, San Diego, CA 92092-0001.

LASSER, HOWARD GILBERT, CHEMICAL ENGINEERING, ELECTROCHEMISTRY. **Personal Data:** b New York, NY, November 24, 1926; m 1950, Barbara; c Cathy, Ellen (LeVee) & Alan. **Education:** Lehigh Univ, BS, 1950; Columbia Univ, ChemE, 1951. **Honorary Degrees:** Dr (Ing), Darmstadt Polytech Inst, Ger, 1956. **Honors & Awards:** Sci Res Award, Sigma Xi, 1968, Dept of the Army Commendations 1968, 1969, 1970, 1972, 1972 Dept of the Navy, 1981. **Professional Experience:** OWNER, MAT RES CONSULTS, SPRINGFIELD & ALEXANDRIA, VA, 1983-; Chmn, Coatings Comt, Dept Defense, 1974-1982; mat eng consult coatings & electrochem, Naval Facil Eng Command, Dept Navy, 1973-1983; metallic & org coatings, Eng Res & Develop Ctr, Army Corps Engrs, 1956-1968 & electrochem, Electronics Command, 1968-1973; metal prod, Gen Serv Admin, 1955-1956; cryog, Bur Ships, Dept Navy, 1953-1955; Chem engr indust gases, Eng Res & Develop Labs, Army Corps Engrs, 1951-1953; consult org & electrodeposited coatings & corrosion processes. **Memberships:** Fel Oil & Colour Chemists Asn; Am Electroplaters Soc; Am Inst Chem Engrs; fel Am Inst Chemists; fel AAAS; Nat Asn Corrosion Engrs. **Research Statement & Publications:** Corrosion prevention through the use of metallic and organic coatings; development of anodic films on aluminum; transport theory as related to corrosion processes; application of lasers to etching semiconductors and other. **Mailing Address:** 5912 Camberly Ave, Springfield, VA 22150. **Fax:** 703-683-4635. **E-Mail:** mareco@erols.com

LASSER, SUE, ENGINEERING. **Professional Experience:** DIR, PROG EDUC ENRICHMENT & RETENTION, CLEMSON UNIV, as of 2004. **Mailing Address:** Prog Educ Enrichment & Retention, Clemson Univ, 104 Riggs Hall, Clemson, SC 29634. **E-Mail:** slasser@ces.clemson.edu

LASSETER, KENNETH CARLYLE, CLINICAL PHARMACOLOGY, INTERNAL MEDICINE. **Personal Data:** b Jacksonville, Fla, August 12, 1942; m 1977, Kathy Lasseter; c Kenneth c III, Susan Sherman & frank Graves. **Education:** Stetson Univ, BS, 1963; Univ Fla, MD, 1967; Am Bd Clin Pharmacol, dipl, 1992. **Honors & Awards:** Res Award, Interstate Postgrad Med Asn, 1974. **Professional Experience:** Adj assoc prof pharmacol, Barry Univ Sch Podiat Med, 1987-; VPRES & MED DIR, CLIN PHARMACOL ASSOC. INC, 1981-; CLIN ASSOC PROF PHARMACOL, UNIV MIAMI, 1981-; assoc prof pharmacol & med, Sch Med, Univ Miami, 1974-1981; Attend physician, Jackson Mem Hosp, 1971-; asst prof, Sch Med, Univ Miami, 1971-1974; fel clin pharmacol, Sch Med, Univ Miami, 1970-1971; From intern to resident med, USPHS fel cardiol, 1969-1970; From intern to resident med, Univ Ky Hosp, 1967-1969. **Memberships:** Am Soc Pharmacol & Exp Therapeut; Am Soc Clin Pharmacol & Therapeut; Am Col Physicians; Am Col Clin Pharmacol; Sigma Xi. **Research Statement & Publications:** Clinical Pharmacokinetics all Pharmacodynamics of drugs in the human species especially as modified by diseases. **Mailing Address:** Clin Pharmacol Assoc Inc, 2060 NW 22 Ave, Miami, FL 33142. **Fax:** 305-633-4904. **E-Mail:** lasseter@clinpharmmiami.com

LASSETER, ROBERT H, ELECTRICAL ENGINEERING. **Education:** Univ Pa, PhD, 1972. **Professional Experience:** PROF EMER, UNIV WIS, as of 2005. **Mailing Address:** Univ Wis, 2559A Engineering Hall, 1415 Engineering Drive, Madison, WI 53706. **Fax:** 608-262-1267. **E-Mail:** lasseter@engr.wisc.edu

LASSETER, ROBERT H, ENGINEERING. **Personal Data:** b Miami, Fla, April 4, 1938; m 1979, Lucy; c Courtney M, Malahn P, Robert M & Lauren L. **Education:** NC State Univ, BS, 1963, MS, 1967; Univ Pa, PhD (physics), 1971. **Professional Experience:** Vis Ershine fel, Univ Caterbury, NZ, 1998; Elec Power Res Inst, Palo Alto, Calif, 1990-; Formas Centrais, Brazil, 1986-1988; PROF, UNIV WIS-MADISON, 1985-; Sr consult engr, Siemens AG, Ger, 1985-1986; assoc chmn, Univ Wis-madison, 1984-1985; Formas Centrais, Gen Elec NY & Pa, 1982-; consult, LA Power & Water, 1982-1988; from asst prof to assoc prof, Univ Wis-madison, 1980-1985; consult engr, Gen Elec Co, Phila, 1973-1980; Postdoctoral, Univ Pa, 1971-1973; dir, Power Syst Eng Res Ctr, Wis. **Memberships:** Fel Inst Elec & Electronics Engrs. **Research Statement & Publications:** Application of power electronics to power systems; technical issues of utility restructuring; harmonic interactions; simulation methods; power electronic circuits and controls; distributed generation; microgrids; published numerous articles. **Mailing Address:** Dept Elec & Comput Eng Univ Wis, 1415 Eng Dr, Madison, WI 53506. **E-Mail:** lasseter@engr.wisc.edu

LASSILA, KENNETH EINO, HIGH ENERGY PHYSICS, THEORETICAL NUCLEAR PHYSICS. **Personal Data:** b Hancock, Mich, April 27, 1934. **Education:** Univ Wyo, BS, 1956; Yale Univ, MS, 1959, PhD (theoret physics), 1961. **Honors & Awards:** Fulbright lectr, Univ Oulu, Finland & Univ Oslo, Norway, 1973, Fermi Nat Accelerator Lab, 1980-1981 & 1988. **Professional Experience:** PROF EMER PHYSICS & ASTRON, as of 2004; organizer, Fifth Int Workshop Weak Interations, 1978; docent, Univ Helsinki, beginning 1973; prof, Nordic Inst Theoret Atomic Physics, 1972; prof physics, Iowa State Univ, beginning 1969; from asst prof to assoc prof physics, Iowa State Univ, 1966-1969; res assoc, Stanford Univ, 1966; Fulbright res fel, Res Inst Theoret Physics, Univ Helsinki, 1965; sr res assoc, Res Inst Theoret Physics, Univ Helsinki, 1964-1966; asst prof physics, Iowa State Univ, 1963-1964; res assoc theoret physics, Case Inst Technol, 1961-1963. **Memberships:** AAAS; fel Am Phys Soc; Finnish Phys Soc. **Research Statement & Publications:** Nucleon-nucleon interaction; radiation-field theory; elementary particle interactions and quark-gluon interactions in nuclei. **Mailing Address:** Dept Physics, Iowa State Univ, A525 Physics Bldg, Ames, IA 50011. **Fax:** 515-294-3747. **E-Mail:** klassila@iastate.edu

LASSITER, RAY ROBERTS, ECOLOGY, ENVIRONMENTAL SCIENCE. **Personal Data:** b Hertford Co, NC, April 8, 1937. **Education:** NC State Col, BS, 1959, MS, 1962; NC State Univ, PhD (animal ecol), 1971. **Professional Experience:** BIOGEOCHEMIST EARTH SYSTS MODELLING, ATHENS ENVIRON RES LAB, ENVIRON PROTECTION AGENCY, 1991-; RES ECOLOGIST, ATHENS ENVIRON RES LAB, ENVIRON PROTECTION AGENCY, 1983-; resident res scientist, Inst Ecol, Univ Ga, 1981-1983; res grant, Environ Protection Agency, 1981; Mem, Inst Ecol, Univ Ga, 1977-; chief environ systs, Br Environ Sci, Athens Environ Res Lab, Environ Protection Agency, 1975-1981; biol statistician environ sci, Freshwater Ecosysts Br, 1970-1975; systs analyst environ statist, Pollution Surveillance Br, Southeast Water Lab, Environ Protection Agency, 1967-1970; asst statistician quant ecol, NC State Univ, 1963-1967; Instr biol, Campbell Col, NC, 1962-1963. **Research Statement & Publications:** Quantitative ecology; population and community dynamics; experimental ecology using laboratory ecosystems; mathematical modeling of ecosystem processes; fate of toxic chemicals in aquatic ecosystems; predicting effects of toxic chemicals on aquatic ecosystem populations and functions. **Mailing Address:** Environ Protection Agency, 960 College Station Rd, Athens, GA 30605-2720.

LASSITER, WILLIAM EDMUND, PHYSIOLOGY, NEPHROLOGY. **Personal Data:** b Wilmington, NC, July 21, 1927. **Education:** Harvard Univ, AB, 1950, MD, 1954. **Professional Experience:** EMER PROF MED, SCH MED, UNIV NC, CHAPEL HILL, 1993-; mem cardiovasc & pulmonary res A study sect, NIH, 1969-1973 & gen med B study sect, 1978-1982; co-dir NIH surv res needs nephrol & urol, 1974-1978; sect ed, Renal & Electrolyte Physiol, Am J Physiol & J Appl Physiol, 1974-1976; mem coun kidney cardiovasc dis, Am Heart Asn, 1971-; Nat Inst Arthritis & Metab Dis career develop award, 1967-1972; Markle scholar, 1963-1968; vis investr, Physiol Inst, Berlin, 1963-1964; Estab investr, Am Heart Asn, 1962-1967; from instr to prof, Sch Med, Univ NC, Chapel Hill, 1960-1993; Life Ins Med Res Fund fel, Univ NC, Chapel Hill, 1958-1960; Donner res fel, Mass Gen Hosp, Boston, 1957-1958; sr asst resident, NC Mem Hosp, 1956-1957; Intern & asst resident med, Mass Gen Hosp, Boston, 1954-1956. **Memberships:** emer AAAS; emer Am Soc Clin Invest; emer Am Physiol Soc; emer Am Col Physicians; emer Am Soc Nephrology. **Research Statement & Publications:** Micropuncture studies of mammalian kidney function; tubular transport processes in mammalian kidney; calcium and phosphorus metabolism. **Mailing Address:** 303 N Elliott Rd, Chapel Hill, NC 27514.

LASSITER, WILLIAM STONE, ENGINEERING MANAGEMENT, NOISE & POLLUTION CONTROL. **Personal Data:** b Spring Hope, NC, July 7, 1939; m 1971, c 2. **Education:** NC State Univ, BS, 1961, PhD (mech eng), 1971; Col William & Mary, MS, 1968, MBA, 1973. **Professional Experience:** HEAD, STRUCT & THERMAL ANAL BR, LANGLEY RES CTR, NASA, as of 2004; ENGR, ANALYSIS & TEST ENG BR, AEROSPACE MECH SYSTS DIV, LANGLEY RES CTR, NASA, 1976-; pollution sensing res, Langley Res Ctr, NASA, 1970-1975; mat engr, Langley Res Ctr, NASA, 1965-1970; facil engr, Langley Res Ctr, NASA, 1963-1965; adj instr, George Wash Univ, Christopher Newport Col, & Golden Gate Univ. **Memberships:** Am Soc Mech Engrs. **Research Statement & Publications:** Noise control; pollution sensing; thermal, structural and fluid analysis. **Mailing Address:** Langley Res Ctr, NASA, Mail Stop 431, Hampton, VA 23681-0001. **Fax:** 757-864-7202. **E-Mail:** w.s.lassiter@larc.nasa.gov

LASSLO, ANDREW, medicinal chemistry; deceased, see previous edition for last biography

LAST, JEROLD ALAN, INHALATION TOXICOLOGY, LUNG DISEASE. **Personal Data:** b New York, NY, June 5, 1940; m 1975, Elaine; c Matthew, Michael & Andrew. **Education:** Univ Wis, BS, 1959, MS, 1961; Ohio State Univ, PhD (biochem), 1965. **Honors & Awards:** Frank R Blood Award, Soc Toxicol, 1980; ICI Traveling Lectureship, Soc Toxicol, 1992. **Professional Experience:** Prof dept internal med, Pulmonary/Critical Care Div, Univ Calif, Davis, 1983-, from asst prof to assoc prof, 1976-1983; Vice-Chair, Internal Medicine 1985-1997, Acting Chair, Biochemistry and Molecular Medicine, 2004. Res assoc, Dept Biochem & Molecular Biol, Harvard Univ, 1973-1976; managing ed, Proc Nat Acad Sci, USA, 1971-1973; consult, NIH, 1971-1973; asst managing ed, Proc Nat Acad Sci, USA, 1970-1971; sr res scientist, Squibb Inst Med Res, NJ, 1967-1969 & Rockefeller Univ, 1969-1970; Am Cancer Soc fel biochem, Med Sch, NY Univ, 1966-1967; Biochemist, Corn Prod Co, Ill, 1961-1962; visiting prof Bishop col, Dallas Tex, 1982; Catholic univ, Ponce, PR, 1985; Tuskegee univ, Tuskegee Ala, 1990 (all three sponsored by NIH MARC program); assoc ed, Toxicol & appl pharmacol, 1994-2008; journ ed boards, Toxicol & Appl Pharmacol, 1984-1994, Toxicol, 1980-1984, Experimental Lung Res, 1980-1983. **Memberships:** Am Soc Biochem & Molecular Biol; Am Fedn Clin Res; Soc Toxicol. **Research Statement & Publications:** Antibiotics biosynthesis and mechanism of action; lung disease; protein biosynthesis; nucleic acids; collagen biosynthesis; mucus glycoproteins; lung biochemistry; pulmonary fibrosis; health effects of air pollutants; health effects of tobacco smoke; lung disease; asthma. **Mailing Address:** Dept Med Div Pulmonary Med, Univ Calif, Davis, CA 95616. **Fax:** 530-752-8632. **E-Mail:** jalast@ucdavis.edu

LAST, JOHN MURRAY, EPIDEMIOLOGY, INTERNATIONAL HEALTH. **Personal Data:** b Tailem Bend, Australia, September 22, 1926; m 1957, Janet Wendelken; c Rebecca, David & Jonathan. **Education:** Univ Adelaide, MB & BS, 1949, MD, 1968; Univ Sydney, DPH, 1960. **Honorary Degrees:** MD, Uppsala Univ, Sweden, 1993. **Honors & Awards:** Wade Hampton Frost Award, Am Pub Health Asn, 1989; Spec Recognition Award, Am Col Prev Med, 1991; Abraham Lilienfeld award, Am col of Epidemiology 1997 (for lifetime contributions of epidemiology); Honorary life mem, int Epidemiological assoc, 1996. **Professional Experience:** EMER PROF, UNIV OTTAWA, 1992-; assoc ed, Am J Prev Med, 1986-1991; 1976 & environ health, WHO, 1984, 1990-1991, 1995-1997; sci ed, Can J Pub Health, 1981-1991; Mem, Nat Health Grant Rev Comt, NIH, 1970-1976 & Epidemiol Study Sect, 1972-1976; consult med educ, WHO, 1972-1973, 1974; prof epidemiol & community med & chmn dept, Univ Ottawa, 1970-1992; sr lectr social med, Univ Edinburgh, 1965-1969; asst prof epidemiol, Univ Vt, 1963-1964; lectr pub health, Univ Sydney, 1962-1963; Australian Postgrad Med Found fel, Social Med Res Unit, Med Res Coun UK, 1961-1962; fel, Fac Community Med, UK. **Memberships:** Int Asn Epidemiol; fel Am Pub Health Asn; fel Royal Australasian Col Physicians; fel Am Col Prev Med (pres, 1987-1989); fel Am Col Epidemiol. **Research Statement & Publications:** Environmental epidemiology; international health; biomedical ethics (history/philosophy of medicine); author of textbooks on public health and epidemiology. **Mailing Address:** Facil Med, Univ Ottawa, Ottawa, ON K1H 8M5, Can. **Fax:** 613-562-5665. **E-Mail:** last@zeus.med.uottawa.ca

LASTER, DANNY BRUCE, ANIMAL SCIENCES. **Personal Data:** b Scotts Hill, Tenn, November 29, 1942. **Education:** Univ Tenn, Knoxville, BS, 1963; Univ Ky, Lexington, MS, 1964; Okla State Univ, PhD (animal breeding), 1970. **Professional Experience:** DIR EMER, ROMAN L HRUSKA MEAT ANIMAL RES CTR, CLAY CTR, USDA, 1988-; nat prog leader & assoc dep adminr, Beef & Sheep, 1981-1988; res leader, Reproduction Res Unit, Clay Ctr, Agr Res Serv, USDA, Nebr, 1971-1978; asst prof endocrin, Iowa State Univ, 1970-1971; res specialist, Univ Ky, Lexington, 1965-1968. **Memberships:** Am Soc Animal Sci. **Research Statement & Publications:** Twinning, dystocia and embryonic mortality in beef cattle. **Mailing Address:** US Meat Animal Res Ctr Agr Res Serv, USDA PO Box 166, Clay Center, NE 68933-0166. **Fax:** 402-762-4111. **E-Mail:** laster@email.marc.usda.gov

LASTER, LEONARD, MEDICINE, SCIENCE POLICY. **Personal Data:** b New York, NY, August 25, 1928. **Education:** Harvard Univ, AB, 1949, MD, 1950; Am Bd Internal Med, dipl, 1961; Am Bd Gastroenterol, dipl, 1966. **Professional Experience:** EMER CHANCELLOR, MED CTR, UNIV MASS, as of 2004; DISTINGUISHED PROF MED, SCH MED, UNIV MASS, as of 2003; prof med, Sch Med & Pres, Ore Health Sci Univ, beginning 1978; vpres acad & clin affairs & dean, Col Med, State Univ NY Downstate Med Ctr, 1974-1978; asst dir human resources, Off Sci & Technol, Exec Off President, 1971-1974; staff mem, Off Sci & Technol, Exec Off Pres, 1969-1971; prof lectr, Sch Med, George Wash Univ, beginning 1966; chief sect gastroenterol, Metab Dis Br, Nat Inst Arthritis & Metab Dis, 1959-1969; Res fel gastroenterol, Mass Mem Hosps, 1958-1959; clin instr, Sch Med, George Wash Univ, 1955-1958; sr clin investr, Nat Inst Arthritis & Metab Dis, 1954-1958; vis investr purine metab, Pub Health Res Inst, New York, Inc, 1953-1954; from intern to resident med, Mass Gen Hosp, 1950-1953. **Memberships:** Am Soc Biol Chemists; Am Fedn Clin Res; Am Gastroenterol Asn; Am Col Physicians; Am Soc Clin Invest. **Research Statement & Publications:** Biochemical aspects of human disease; inborn errors of metabolism; disturbances of the gastrointestinal tract. **Mailing Address:** Univ Mass, Med Ctr, Ste 800 120 Front St, Worcester, MA 01608-1404. **E-Mail:** leonard.laster@umassmed.edu

LASTER, MARION LYNN, TEST & EVALUATION OF AEROSPACE SYSTEMS. **Personal Data:** b Obion County, Tenn, m 2002, Patricia; c Carol, Cheryl, Michelle & Casey. **Education:** Air War Col, 1979; Auburn Univ, BS, 1956; Ga Inst Technol, MS, 1958; Univ Tenn, PhD (aeronaut & mech eng), 1971. **Honors & Awards:** outstanding alumni, Auburn Univ. **Professional Experience:** CONSULT ENGR, 1997-; tech dir, Arnold Eng Develop Ctr, Arnold AFB, Tenn, 1991-1997; mem, Ground Test Tech Comt, Am Inst Aeronaut & Astronaut, 1990-1992; tech adv corp planning, Arnold Eng Develop Ctr, Arnold AFB, Tenn, 1987-1991; dir technol, Arnold Eng Develop Ctr, Arnold AFB, Tenn, 1980-1987; US deleg, NATO/Adv Group Aeronaut Res & Develop, 1980-1987; dir testing eng, Arnold Eng Develop Ctr, Arnold AFB, Tenn, 1978-1980; tech adv res, Arnold Eng Develop Ctr, Arnold AFB, Tenn, 1971-1978; res engr, Arnold Eng Develop Ctr, Arnold AFB, Tenn, 1961-1971; aeronaut eng, Arnold Eng Develop Ctr, Arnold AFB, Tenn, 1958-1961; USAF, Arnold Eng Develop Ctr, USAF, 1956-; aeronaut engr, Arnold Eng Develop Ctr, Arnold AFB, Tenn, 1956-1957. **Memberships:** Am Inst Aeronaut & Astronaut assoc fel; fel, ARNOLD ENG DEVELOP CTR, ARNOLD AFB, TENN; Rotary Int. **Research Statement & Publications:** Test engineering; aeronautical systems testing; test facility research and development. **Mailing Address:** 709 Holt Lane, Tullahoma, TN 37388. **E-Mail:** mlaster@edge.net

LASTER, RICHARD, CHEMICAL ENGINEERING & AGRICULTURAL BIOTECHNOLOGY, FOOD SCIENCE. **Personal Data:** b Vienna, Austria, November 10, 1923; American citizen; m 1948, Liselotte; c Susan & Thomas. **Education:** Polytech Inst Brooklyn, BChE, 1943. **Honors & Awards:** Food & Bioeng Award, Am Inst Chem Engrs, 1972. **Professional Experience:** CHMN, WENGER INC 1998-; mgt consult, 1994-1998; dir, DNA Plant Technol Corp, 1992-1994; chmn, DNA Plant Technol Corp, 1988-1994; pres & chief exec officer, DNA Plant Technol Corp, 1982-1992; exec vpres & dir, Maxwell House Coffee div, 1974-1982; group vpres coffee & food serv, Maxwell House Coffee div, 1972-1974; vpres corp & pres, Maxwell House Coffee div, 1971-1972; asst gen mgr corp, Maxwell House Coffee div, 1969-1971; opers mgr, Maxwell House Coffee div, 1967-1969; dir corp qual assurance, Jello div, 1967; opers mgr res & new prod develop, Jello div, 1964-1967; oper mgr, Atlantic Gelatin div, 1962-1964; oper mgr, Franklin Baker div, 1960-1962; mgr mfg & eng, Franklin Baker div, 1958-1960; res mgr, Walter Baker div, 1954-1958; asst lab dir eng res & develop, Cent labs, Gen Foods Corp, 1944-1954; trustee, Polytech Univ; chmn, Purchase Col Found. **Memberships:** AAAS; Am Chem Soc; Am Inst Chem Engrs; NY Acad Sci; Inst Food Tech. **Research Statement & Publications:** Chemical engineering research as applied to food processing; spray drying; atomization and leaching; chemistry of fats and oils; chocolate processing; agricultural biotechnology; genetic engineering of plants; relation of food to human genome. **Mailing Address:** 23 Round Hill Rd, Chappaqua, NY 10514.

LASTER, WILLIAM RUSSELL, VETERINARY MEDICINE, EXPERIMENTAL ONCOLOGY. **Personal Data:** b Ala, October 20, 1926. **Education:** Auburn Univ, DVM, 1951. **Professional Experience:** RETIRED; head, Cancer Screening Div, 1966-1992; head, Cancer Screening Sect, 1956-1966; virologist, Southern Res Inst, 1951-1956. **Memberships:** Am Asn Cancer Res. **Research Statement & Publications:** Cancer chemotherapy; experimental oncology. **Mailing Address:** 5529 Timber Hill Rd, Birmingham, AL 35242.

LASURE, LINDA LEE, MICROBIAL GENETICS, FUNGAL BIOPROCESS RESEARCH, RESEARCH MANAGEMENT. **Personal Data:** b Bartlesville, Okla, November 23, 1946. **Education:** St Cloud State Col, BS, 1968; Syracuse Univ & State Univ NY, PhD (genetics), 1973. **Honors & Awards:** Porter Award SIM AAAS Fellow. **Professional Experience:** STAFF SCIENTIST, BATTELLE PAC NW NAT LAB, 2000-; pres, Lasure & Assoc, 1997-2000; pres, Lasure & Crawford Consult Co, 1993-1997; pres, Worldwide Res & Develop, 1993-1995; vpres, US Labs, Panlabs, Inc, 1990-1993; sr dir, US Labs, Panlabs, Inc, 1989-1990; dir bioprod res, Miles Lab Inc, 1984-1989; supvr mutation & screening, Miles Lab Inc, 1980-1984; sr res scientist, Miles Lab Inc, 1979-1980; res scientist microbiol, Miles Lab Inc, 1974-1979; res fel, NY Bot Garden, 1972-1974. **Memberships:** AAAS; Am Soc Microbiol; Soc Industrial Microbiol Soc Indust Microbiol (pres 1997-1998). **Research Statement & Publications:** Studies of mutagenesis, inheritance, and physiological control of sexual reproduction, selection of strains of fungi with improved yields of enzymes and organic acids; molecular biology and morphology of filamentous fungi; fungal bioprocessing of renewable biomass. **Mailing Address:** Pac NW Nati Lab, PO Box 999, Richland, WA 99352. **E-Mail:** linda.lasure@pnl.gov

LASWELL, TROY JAMES, GEOLOGY. **Personal Data:** b Ottawa, Ky, November 12, 1920. **Education:** Berea Col, AB, 1942; Oberlin Col, AM, 1948; Univ Mo, PhD (geol), 1953. **Professional Experience:** PROF EMER GEOL, MISS STATE UNIV, 1985-; prof, Miss State Univ, 1962-1985; head dept, Miss State Univ, 1962-1985; from assoc prof to prof, La Polytech Inst, 1957-1962; consult geologist, South River Mining Co, 1957; consult geologist, Humble Oil & Refining Co, 1955-1958; consult geologist, Va Mins, Inc, 1955-1956; from asst prof to assoc prof, Wash & Lee Univ, 1953-1957; Geologist, Mo Geol Surv, 1952-1953. **Memberships:** Geol Soc Am; Am Asn Petrol Geologists; Am Asn Geol Teachers; Sigma Xi. **Research Statement & Publications:** Stratigraphy; sedimentation. **Mailing Address:** Dept Geosciences, Miss State Univ, 109 Hilbun Hall, PO Box 5448, Mississippi State, MS 39762-5448. **Fax:** 662-325-9423.

LASZEWSKI, RONALD M, EXPERIMENTAL NUCLEAR PHYSICS, ACOUSTICS. **Personal Data:** b Chicago, Ill, June 22, 1947. **Education:** Univ Ill, Urbana, BS, 1969, MS, 1972, PhD (physics), 1975. **Professional Experience:** RETIRED, as of 2005; prin res physicist, Univ Ill, Urbana, 1990-; from res asst prof physics to sr res physicist, Univ Ill, Urbana, 1978-1990; res assoc physics, Argonne Nat Lab, 1975-1978. **Memberships:** Am Phys Soc. **Research Statement & Publications:** Photonuclear physics and medium energy physics. **Mailing Address:** 206 W Vt Ave, Urbana, IL 61801.

LASZLO, CHARLES ANDREW, BIOMEDICAL ENGINEERING. **Personal Data:** b July 8, 1935. **Education:** McGill Univ, BE, 1961, ME, 1966, PhD (biomed eng), 1968. **Honors & Awards:** Award of Merit, Can Hard of Hearing Asn, 1990. **Professional Experience:** PROF EMER, DEPT ELEC & COMPUT SCI, UNIV BC, as of 2006; CHMN, ASSISTIVE LISTENING DEVICE SYSTS INC, as of 2004; assoc Comt Res & Develop Rehab Disabled Persons, Nat Res Coun, 1990-; res grant eval comt, Health Develop Fund Sci Coun, BC, 1989-; comt Telecommun Devices, Can Stand Asn, 1988; chmn, Bd Hearing Aid Dealers & Consult, Ministry Health, BC, 1987-; Royal Jubilee Hosp, G F Strong Rehab Ctr, 1986-; mem, Comt Hearing Aid Stand, 1986-; Royal Jubilee Hosp, Children's Hosp & St Paul Hosp, 1984-; consult, Royal Columbian Hosp, 1983-; assoc men, Dept Health Care & Epidemiol & Sch Audiol & Speech Sci, Univ BC, 1980-; prof, Dept Elec Eng, Univ Bc, beginning 1980; DIR, CLIN ENG PROG, 1980-; mem, Adv Comt Med Devices, Bur Med Devices, Health Protection Br, Health & Welfare Can, 1979-; assoc dir, Div Health Systs, 1974-1985; dir, Biomed Eng Unit, 1970-1974; assoc prof, Biomed Eng Unit & Dept Otolarygol, McGill, 1968-1974; biomed engr, OTL Res Labs, Royal Victoria Hosp, Montreal, Que, 1962-1968; design engr, Northern Elec Co & RCA Victor Co, Ltd, Montreal, Que, 1961-1962. **Memberships:** Sr mem Inst Elec & Electronics Engrs; sr mem Instrument Soc Am; fel Am Asn Med Systs & Info. **Research Statement & Publications:** Over 120 publications; electrical engineering; biomedical engineering. **Mailing Address:** Elec Eng Dept, Univ BC, 2356 Main Mall, Vancouver, BC V6T 1Z4, Can. **E-Mail:** laszlo@ece.ubc.ca

LATANISION, RONALD MICHAEL, CORROSION ENGINEERING, MATERIALS PROCESSING. **Personal Data:** b Richmondale, Pa, July 2, 1942; m 1964, Carolyn; c Ivan & Sara. **Education:** Pa State Univ, BS, 1964; Ohio State Univ, PhD (metall eng), 1968. **Honors & Awards:** Campbell Award, Nat Asn Corrosion Engrs 1973; Krumb Lectr, 1984; McFarland Award, Pa State Univ, 1986; W R Whitney Award, Nat Asn Corrosion Engrs Int, 1994; Mentor Nat Acad of Eng, Am Acad of Arts & Sci; Fel ASM Int; Distin Alumni Ohio Stae Univ Col of Eng; Honorary Alumni MIT; Fel, NACE Int. **Professional Experience:** PROF EMER MAT SCI, MASS INST TECHNOL, as of 2004; Founder, Altran Mat Eng, 1992; mem adv comt, Mass Off, Sci & Technol, 1990-1991; vis prof, Univ Naples, Italy, 1989-; dir, Mat Processing Ctr, 1984-1991; prof mat sci, H H Uhlig Corrosion Lab, Mass Inst Technol, beginning 1983; Sci adv, US House Rep Comt Sci & Technol, 1982-1983; DIR, H H UHLIG CORROSION LAB, MASS INST TECHNOL, 1975-; prof mat sci & eng, H H Uhlig Corrosion Lab, Mass Inst Technol, 1975-1983; Actg head, Mat Sci Group, Martin Marietta Labs, Baltimore, Md, 1970-1974. **Memberships:** Nat Acad Eng; Nat Asn Corrosion Engrs; Am Inst Mining Metall & Petrol Engrs; Electrochem Soc; Am Soc Metals. **Research Statement & Publications:** Corrosion of new materials (composites, magnetic alloys, etc); materials for construction of engineering systems; materials processing. **Mailing Address:** Dept Mat Sci, Mass Inst Technol, Rm 8-309, 77 Mass Ave, Cambridge, MA 02139. **E-Mail:** lats@mit.edu

LATCH, DANA MAY, ALGEBRA, TOPOLOGY. **Personal Data:** b New York, NY, August 29, 1943. **Education:** Harpur Col, BA, 1965; Queens Col, NY, MA, 1967; City Univ NY, PhD (math), 1971. **Professional Experience:** RETIRED; Alexander von Humboldt res fel, Munich, Fed Repub Ger, 1983; vis scholar comput sci, Univ NC, Chapel Hill, 1982; assoc prof math, NC State Univ, 1979-2000; vis prof math, Universitat Konstanz, Ger, 1979; NSF res grant, Rutgers Univ, 1972-1973 & NC State Univ, 1978-1980 & 1981-1983; study grant, Ger Acad Exchange Serv, Univ Konstanz, Ger, 1978; asst prof, NC State Univ, 1976-1979; Carnegie Found fac develop award, Lawrence Univ, 1975; asst prof, Douglass Col, Rutgers Univ, 1971-1974 & Lawrence Univ, 1974-1976; lectr, Queens Col, NY, 1966-1967; teaching asst math, Queens Col, NY, 1965-1966. **Memberships:** Am Math Soc; Asn Women Math. **Research Statement & Publications:** Algebraic topology of small categories; applications of category theory to the theory of program behaviors; applications of categorical methods to homotopy theory and the theory of localizations. **Mailing Address:** Dept Math, NC State Univ, Raleigh, NC 27695.

LATEEF, ABDUL BARI, FORENSIC SCIENCE, CHEMISTRY. **Personal Data:** b Faisalabad, Pakistan, April 4, 1939. **Education:** Punjab Univ, Pakistan, BS, 1959, MS, 1961; Univ Newcastle, PhD (chem), 1966. **Professional Experience:** DIR, TRI-STATE LABS INC, 1981-; prof forensic sci, Youngstown State Univ, 1981; from asst prof to assoc prof, Tri-state Labs Inc, 1971-1981; from instr to asst prof chem, Tri-state Labs Inc, 1969-1971; Nat Res Coun Can fel, Univ Calgary, 1966-1969. **Memberships:** Am Acad Forensic Sci; Forensic Soc London; Acad Criminal Justice; Sigma Xi. **Research Statement & Publications:** Spectroscopic and chromatographic analytical techniques in forensic science; role of forensic science in criminal justice system. **Mailing Address:** Tri-State Labs, 2870 Salt Springs Rd, Youngstown, OH 44509-1036.

LATERRA, JOHN J, NEURO-ONCOLOGY, NEUROLOGY. **Personal Data:** b Providence, RI, May 18, 1955. **Education:** Wash Univ, St Louis, BA, 1977; Case Western Res Univ, PhD (microbiol), 1982, MD, 1984. **Professional Experience:** PROF, NEUROL, ONCOL & NEUROSCIENCE, JOHNS HOPKINS UNIV SCH MED, beginning 2002; DIR, DEPT NEUROL, JOHNS HOPKINS UNIV SCH MED, 1994-; assoc prof, neurol, oncol & neuroscience, Johns Hopkins Univ Sch Med, 1994-2002; asst prof, dept neuroscience & oncol, Johns Hopkins Univ Sch Med, 1992-1994; asst prof, dept neurol, Johns Hopkins Univ Sch Med, 1990-1994; instr, Johns Hopkins Univ Sch Med, 1988-1990; residency neurol, Univ Mich, 1984-1988. **Memberships:** AAAS; Am Soc Neurochem; Am Soc Cell Biol. **Research Statement & Publications:** Neuro-oncology; neurology. **Mailing Address:** Dept Neurol, Kennedy Kreiger Inst, 707 N Broadway, Baltimore, MD 21205-0001. **Fax:** 410-614-9569. **E-Mail:** laterra@kennedykrieger.org

LATHAM, ARCHIE J, plant pathology, mycology; deceased, see previous edition for last biography

LATHAM, DAVID WINSLOW, ASTRONOMY. **Personal Data:** b Boston, Mass, March 19, 1940. **Education:** Mass Inst Technol, BS, 1961; Harvard Univ, MA, 1965, PhD (astron), 1970. **Professional Experience:** SR LECTR ASTRON, HARVARD UNIV, as of 2000; lectr astron, Harvard Univ, 1971-; ASTRONR, SMITHSONIAN ASTROPHYS OBSERV, 1965-. **Memberships:** Am Astron Soc; Royal Astron Soc; Int Astron Union. **Research Statement & Publications:** Frequency and characteristics of stellar binaries; extrasolar planets. **Mailing Address:** Harvard-Smithsonian Ctr Astrophys, 60 Garden St, Cambridge, MA 01451-1415. **Fax:** 617-495-7467. **E-Mail:** dlatham@cfa.harvard.edu

LATHAM, DEWITT ROBERT, PETROLEUM CHEMISTRY. **Personal Data:** b Chugwater, Wyo, October 26, 1928. **Education:** Univ Wyo, BS, 1950. **Professional Experience:** RETIRED; proj leader, Laramie Energy Tech Ctr, Dept Energy, 1964-1984; res chemist, Laramie Energy Res Ctr, US Bur Mines, 1960-1964; chemist, Laramie Energy Res Ctr, US Bur Mines, 1954-1960; Analytical chemist, Rocky Mountain Arsenal, US Army Chem Corps, Colo, 1952-1954. **Memberships:** Am Chem Soc; Sigma Xi. **Research Statement & Publications:** Nitrogen and oxygen compounds in petroleum; development of methods of analysis for petroleum shale, oil and coal liquids; separation and characterization of fossil fuel energy sources. **Mailing Address:** 1467 N 17th St, Laramie, WY 82070-2308.

LATHAM, DON JAY, ATMOSPHERIC SCIENCES. **Personal Data:** b Lewiston, Idaho, December 21, 1938. **Education:** Pomona Col, BA, 1960; NMex Inst Mining & Technol, MS, 1964, PhD, 1968. **Professional Experience:** SR RES SCIENTIST, INTERMOUNTAIN FIRE SCI LAB, USDA FOREST SERV, as of 2001; proj leader fire behav, Northern Forest Fire Lab, beginning 1997; mem, Atmospheric Elec Comt, Am Meteorol Soc, 1981-1983; fac affil, Univ Mont, beginning 1975; res meteorologist & physicist, Northern Forest Fire Lab, 1975-1997; assoc prof, Rosenstiel Sch Marine & Atmospheric Sci, Univ Miami, 1972-1975; NSF grants, Univ Miami, 1969-1975; asst prof atmospheric sci, Rosenstiel Sch Marine & Atmospheric Sci, Univ Miami, 1968-1972; sr res scientist, Rosenstiel Sch Marine & Atmospheric Sci, Univ Miami, 1967-1968; res asst, NMex Inst Mining & Technol, 1961-1967. **Memberships:** Am Meteorol Soc; Am Geophys Union. **Research Statement & Publications:** Atmospheric electricity; radar meteorology; combustion physics; artificial intelligence. **Mailing Address:** Intermountain Fire Sci Lab, USDA Forest Serv, PO Box 8089, Missoula, MT 59807. **Fax:** 406-329-4825. **E-Mail:** dlatham@fs.fed.us

LATHAM, MICHAEL CHARLES, NUTRITION, TROPICAL PUBLIC HEALTH. **Personal Data:** b Kilosa, Tanzania, May 6, 1928. **Education:** Univ Dublin, BA, 1949, MB, BCh & BAO, 1952; Univ London, DTM&H, 1958; Harvard Univ, MPH, 1965. **Honorary Degrees:** FFCM, Royal Col Physicians, London, 1973. **Honors & Awards:** Food Cycle Trophy Award, Ministry Health, Tanzania, 1978. **Professional Experience:** RETIRED; Exec Comt, Soc Int Nutrit Res, 1990- & World Alliance Breastfeeding Action, 1991-; UNESCO, Paris, 1988 & UNICEF, 1991-1993; team leader, UNICEF-WHO Rev JNSP, Ethiopia, 1987-1988 & Swed Int Develop Authority, Tanzania Eval, 1991-1992; external examr, Univ Nairobi, Kenya 1989-1990; vis scientist & chief res officer, Kenya Med Res Inst, Nairobi, Kenya, 1989-1990; panel collaborators, J Acta Tropica, Switz, 1987-; ed bd, Nutrit-Int J Appl & Basic Nutrit Sci, 1987; mem bd dir, Soc Nutrit Ed, 1986-; adj prof, Inst Agronomique et Veterinaire Hassan II, Morocco, 1986-; bd dirs, Soc Nutrit Educ, 1986-1989; consult, Swed Int Develop Agency, Tanzania, 1986; Meals for Millions Found, Calif, 1986; Bd Int Health, Nat Acad Sci & Inst Med, 1983-1988; Tanzania, 1979 & Philippines, 1981; US AID consult, Guyana, 1977 & 1978; World Bank consult, Indonesia, 1975; mem expert adv panel nutrit, WHO, 1974-; vis prof, Univ Nairobi, Kenya, 1974-1975; mem exec comt pest control, Nat Acad Sci, 1973-1978; UNICEF consult, Thailand & Malaysia, 1973; mem, Nat Acad Sci-Nat Res Coun Int Nutrit Comt, 1970-1976; consult, WHO, Manila, 1970 & UN Food & Agr Orgn, 1964 & Zambia, 1970; chmn panel, White House Conf Food, Nutrit & Health & vchmn panel, Follow-Up Conf, 1969-1971; prof int nutrit & dir, prog int nutrit, div nutrit sci, Cornell univ, beginning 1968; contrib ed, Nutrit Rev, 1968-1974; res assoc & asst prof nutrit, Harvard Univ, 1964-1968; dir nutrit unit, Tanzania Ministry Health, 1962-1964; med officer, Tanzania Ministry Health, 1955-1964; sr house officer, NMiddlesex Hosp, London, 1954-1955; rotating physician, Methodist Hosp, Los Angeles, 1953-1954; Vis exchange fel, Methodist Hosp, Los Angeles, 1953-1954; House surgeon, High Wycombe Hosp, Buckinghamshire, Eng, 1952-1953; assoc scientist, Kenya Med Res Inst, Nairobi. **Memberships:** Am Inst Nutrit; Brit Nutrit Soc; Am Soc Clin Nutrit; fel Royal Soc Trop Med & Hyg; fel Am Pub Health Asn; Nat Acad Sci. **Research Statement & Publications:** International nutrition problems; nutrition and health of low income populations; xerophthalmia; infant feeding practices; nutrition and intellectual development; protein-energy malnutrition of children; evaluation of applied nutrition programs; lactose intolerance; nutritional surveillance; nutrition and parasitic infections; author or co-author of over 300 publications including 6 books. **Mailing Address:** Dept Nutrit Sci, Cornell Univ, Ithaca, NY 14853. **Fax:** 607-255-1033. **E-Mail:** mcl6@cornell.edu

LATHAM, PATRICIA SUZANNE, HEPATOLOGY. **Personal Data:** b Annapolis, Md, August 22, 1946. **Education:** Simmons Col, BS, 1968; Univ Southern Calif, MD, 1972. **Professional Experience:** Asst prof Med & Path, Univ Md Hosp & Baltimore Vet Admin Hosp, beginning 1981; ASSOC PROF PATH, GEORGE WASH UNIV, INST BIOMED SCI, 1981-. **Memberships:** Am Asn Study Liver Dis; Am Gastroenterol Asn. **Research Statement & Publications:** Investigation of liver diseases with emphasis on structure and function; hepatocytes; Kupffer cells; endotoxin; viral pathogenesis. **Mailing Address:** Biochem & Molecular Genetics Prog, George Wash Univ, 2300 I St NW Ross Hall Ste 605, Washington, DC 20037. **Fax:** 202-994-0967. **E-Mail:** platham@mfa.gwu.edu

LATHAM, ROGER EARL, PLANT COMMUNITY ECOLOGY, CONSERVATION BIOLOGY. **Personal Data:** b Bellefonte, Pa, May 6, 1950. **Education:** Swarthmore Col, BA, 1983; Univ Pa, PhD (biol), 1990. **Professional Experience:** CONSULT & CONTRACTOR, 2000-; asst prof, Dept Biol, Swarthmore Col, 1996-2000; resful, Dept Geol, Univ Pa, 1992-1996; stewardship ecologist, Nature Conservancy, 1990-1992; dir sci & stewardship, Nature Conservancy, 1988-1990; field investr, Morris Arboretum, 1982-1983; environ planner, Fahringer McCarty Grey Inc, 1973-1980. **Memberships:** Am Inst Biol Sci; Ecol Soc Am; Natural Areas Asn; Sigma Xi; Soc Conserv Biol. **Research Statement & Publications:** Community ecology, biogeochemistry and conservation biology; restore and safeguard biological resources in two large bioreserves; fire ecology and the biogeography of global biodiversity patterns. **Mailing Address:** Continental Conserv, PO Box 57, Rose Valley, PA 19086-0057. **Fax:** 610-565-3504. **E-Mail:** rel@continentalconservation.us

LATHEM, WILLOUGHBY, MEDICINE. **Personal Data:** b Atlanta, Ga, October 9, 1923. **Education:** Emory Univ, BS, 1944, MD, 1946; Am Bd Internal Med, dipl, 1954. **Professional Experience:** VPRES SCI AFFAIRS, STERLING INT, STERLING DRUG INC, 1985-; vpres & med dir, Sterling Int, Sterling Drug, Inc, 1980-1985; vis prof, Mt Sinai Sch Med, 1980; field staff, Salvador, Bahia & Brazil, 1978-1980; regional officer, Asia, Bangkok & Thailand, 1975-1977; assoc dir health sci, Rockefeller Found, 1972-1978; dep dir biomed sci, Rockefeller Found, 1966-1972; sci rep, Off Int Res, NIH, Eng, 1962-1966; Hon res assoc, Univ Col, Univ London, 1962-1965; from asst prof to assoc prof, Sch Med, Univ Pittsburgh, 1956-1964; asst clin prof, Yale Univ, 1953-1956; asst med, Col Physicians & Surgeons, Columbia Univ, 1952-1953. **Memberships:** Am Soc Clin Invest; Harvey Soc; Am Fedn Clin Res. **Research Statement & Publications:** International health. **Mailing Address:** 122 Old Logging Rd, Stamford, CT 06903-4805.

LATHERS, CLAIRE M, CARDIO-RENAL DRUG PRODUCTS, PHARMACOLOGY. **Personal Data:** b Brooklyn, NY. **Education:** Union Univ, BS, 1969; State Univ NY, Buffalo, PhD (pharmacol), 1973. **Professional Experience:** DIR, OFF NEW ANIMAL DRUG EVAL, CTR VET MED, as of 2001; vis scientist, Johnson Space Ctr, NASA, 1989-; PHARMACOLOGIST, CARDIO-RENAL DRUG PROD, FOOD & DRUG ADMIN, 1989-; vis scientist sabbatical, Johnson Space Ctr, NASA, 1988; Dept Pharmacol, Schs Med & Dent, State Univ NY, Buffalo, 1987-1988; vis prof, Dept Pharmacol & Toxicol, Philadelphia Col Pharm & Sci, 1987; mem, Subcomt Women Phamacol, Pharmacol Soc, 1984-1992; Hoechst-Roussel Med Col Pa, 1982-1983; Gwynedd Mercy Col, 1978-1989; lectr pharmacol, Pa Col Optom, 1976-1977; from instr to assoc prof, Dept Pharmacol, 1975-1988; lectr pharmacol, Smith Kline & Fr, 1975-1983; NIH postdoctoral fel, Med Col Pa, 1973-1975. **Memberships:** Aerospace Med Asn; Am Soc Pharmacol & Ex Therapeut; Soc Exp Biol & Med; Sigma Xi; NY Acad Sci; Am Fedn Clin Res; Int Study Group Res Cardiac Metab; Am Col Clin Pharmacol (treas, 1990-). **Mailing Address:** Ctr Vet Med, Food & Drug Admin, 5600 Fishers Lane, Rockville, MD 20857-0001.

LATHI, BHAGAWANDAS PANNALAL, COMMUNICATION SYSTEMS, SIGNAL PROCESSING. **Personal Data:** b Bhokar, Maharashtr, India, December 3, 1933. **Education:** Poona Univ, BEEE, 1955; Univ Ill, MSEE, 1957; Stanford Univ, PhD (elec eng), 1961. **Professional Experience:** PROF ELEC ENG, CALIF STATE UNIV, 1980-; vis prof, Univ Iowa, 1978-1979; prof, Campinas State Univ, Brazil, 1972-1978; assoc prof elec eng, US Naval Acad, 1969-1972; assoc prof elec eng, Bradley Univ, 1962-1969; consult semiconductor indust, India, 1961-1962; res engr, Gen Electric Co, Syracuse, 1960-1961; res asst, Stanford Univ, 1957-1960; res asst, Univ Ill, 1956-1957. **Memberships:** Fel Inst Elec & Electronics Engrs. **Research Statement & Publications:** Systems and communication; random signals and communication theory; published numerous articles and books. **Mailing Address:** Dept Elec, 6000 J St, Sacramento, CA 95819-6019.

LATHROP, ARTHUR LAVERNE, PHYSICS. **Personal Data:** b Kittitas, Wash, November 21, 1918. **Education:** Wash State Univ, BS, 1943; Univ Ill, MS, 1946; Rice Univ, PhD (physics), 1952. **Professional Experience:** RETIRED; from asst prof to prof physics, Western Ill Univ, 1965-1988; res assoc, Inst Paper Chem, Lawrence, 1958-1965; res asst physics, Inst Paper Chem, Lawrence, 1953-1958; res engr, Boeing Airplane Co, Wash, 1952-1953; instr physics, Univ Tulsa, 1947-1949; physicist, Ames Aeronaut Lab, Moffett Field, Calif, 1944-1945; instr physics, Wash State Univ, 1943-1944. **Mailing Address:** 1400 Dalles Military Rd Apt G2, Walla Walla, WA 99362.

LATHROP, JAY WALLACE, SOLID STATE PHYSICS, ELECTRICAL ENGINEERING. **Personal Data:** b Bangor, Maine, September 6, 1927; wid deceased; c Margaret & Victoria. **Education:** Mass Inst Technol, BS, 1948, MS, 1949, PhD (physics), 1952. **Honors & Awards:** Dept of Army Meritorius Civilian Service Award, Us Army, 1959; Cert of Recognition, NASA, 1983; McQueen Quattle Baum Faculty Achievement Award, Clemson Univ, 1985; Outstanding South Carolina Educator, Inst Elec & Electronics Engrs, 1991. **Professional Experience:** PROF EMER ELEC ENG, CLEMSON UNIV, 1989-; dir, Ctr Semiconductor Device Reliability Res, 1984-1989; prof, Clemson Univ, 1968-1989; mgr advan technol, Semiconductor Components Div, Tex Instruments Inc, 1958-1968; Electronic scientist, Nat Bur Stand, 1952-1958. **Memberships:** Fel Inst Elec & Electronics Engrs. **Research Statement & Publications:** Microelectronics; integrated circuits; solar cells; semiconductor devices reliability. **Mailing Address:** 680 Winston Way, West Union, SC 29631. **E-Mail:** jlathrop@hubcap.clemson.edu

LATHROP, KATHERINE AUSTIN, nuclear medicine; deceased, see previous edition for last biography

LATHROP, KAYE DON, COMPUTER SCIENCE. **Personal Data:** b Bryan, Ohio, October 8, 1932. **Education:** US Mil Acad, BS, 1955; Calif Inst Technol, MS, 1959, PhD (mech eng, physics), 1962. **Honors & Awards:** E O Lawrence Mem Award, 1976. **Professional Experience:** PROF EMER APPL RES, STANFORD LINEAR ACCELERATOR CTR, 1994-; chmn, Environ, Safety & Health Coordr Coun, 1994; Nat Lab Adv Comt, Dept Energy Strategy, 1989-1990; external adv comt, Nuclear Technol & Eng Div, Los Alamos Nat Lab, 1988-1993; Study Mat Control & Acct Dept Energy Nuclear Fuel Complex, Energy Res Adv Bd Panel Access Cand Reactor Technologies New Prod Reactor, 1988; Study Mat Control & Acct Dept Energy Nuclear Fuel Complex, Nat Acad Sci, 1987-1988; head, Tech Div, 1984-1994; assoc lab dir & prof, Stanford Linear Accelerator Ctr, 1984-1994; Eng Nat Adv Comt, Univ Mich, 1983-1992; Steering Comt, Energy Eng Res Prog, Joint Mass Inst Technol-Idaho Nat Eng Lab, 1980-1990; Eng Adv Comt, Univ NMex, 1980-1984; mem, Am Nuclear Soc Deleg People's Repub China, 1980; assoc dir eng sci, Comput Sci & Serv Div, 1979-1984; mgt adv comt, Y-12 Div, Union Carbide Corp, 1979-1982; vis comt, Reactor Physics Div, Argonne Nat Lab, 1978-1983; div leader, Comput Sci & Serv Div, 1978-1979; alt div leader, Energy Div, 1977-1978; tech prog chmn, Nat Trop Meeting, Am Nuclear Soc, 1977; assoc div leader nuclear safeguards, Reactor Safety & Technol Div, 1975-1977; mem, Adv Comt Reactor Physics, US Energy Res & Develop Admin, 1973-1977; T-1 alt group leader, T-div asst div leader, 1973-1975; T-1 alt group leader, 1972-1975; guest lectr, Int Atomic Energy Agency, Poland, 1969; consult, Gulf Gen Atomic, 1968-1973; Sci Applns Inc, 1971-1974; T-1 alt group leader, Los Alamos Nat Lab, 1968-1972; staff mem & group leader reactor physics methods develop, Nuclear Analysis & Reactor Physics Dept, Gen Atomic Div, Gen Dynamics Corp, 1967-1968; adj prof, Univ NMex, 1966-1967; vis prof, Univ NMex, 1964-1965; staff mem reactor math, Los Alamos Sci Lab, 1962-1967. **Memberships:** Nat Acad Eng; Am Phys Soc; fel Am Nuclear Soc (treas 1977-1979). **Research Statement & Publications:** Analytic and numerical solutions of equations of neutron and photon transport; reactor safety; computer systems and communications. **Mailing Address:** Stanford Linear Accelerator Ctr Mail Stop 07, PO Box 4349, Stanford, CA 94309. **E-Mail:** kdon@slac.stanford.edu

LATHROP, RICHARD C(HARLES), ELECTRICAL & AERONAUTICAL ENGINEERING. **Personal Data:** b Wauwatosa, Wis, September 6, 1924. **Education:** Univ Wis, BS, 1948, MS, 1950, PhD (elec eng), 1951. **Professional Experience:** CONSULT ENGR, 1974-; tech dir, Air Force Flight Test Ctr, 1971-1974; exec officer, Cent Inertial Guide Test Facil, Air Force Missile Develop Ctr, Holloman AFB, NMex, 1968-1970; pilot, Fourth Air Commando Squadron, 1967-1968; prof & head dept, Pakistan Air Force Col Aeronaut Eng, 1965-1967; assoc prof elec eng, USAF Acad, 1961-1965; commandant, Wright Air Develop Ctr, USAF, 1959-1961; proj engr, staff mem Test Pilot Sch, 1955-1959; proj engr, Wright Air Develop Ctr, USAF, 1951-1955; Res asst, Univ Wis, 1951. **Memberships:** Sr mem Inst Elec & Electronics Engrs; assoc fel Am Inst Aeronaut & Astronaut; sr mem Simulation Coun. **Research Statement & Publications:** Analog and digital computers; automatic controls; aircraft flight testing; aircraft dynamics; microcomputers. **Mailing Address:** 920 St Ann Dr, Paso Robles, CA 93446.

LATIES, ALAN M, OPHTHALMOLOGY. **Personal Data:** b Beverly, Mass, February 8, 1931. **Education:** Harvard Univ, AB, 1954; Baylor Col, MD, 1959; Am Bd Ophthal, dipl, 1965. **Honors & Awards:** Res to Prevent Blindness Professorship Award, 1964; Friedenwald Award for Res in Ophthal, 1972. **Professional Experience:** HAROLD G SCHEIE RES PROF OPHTHAL, MED SCH, UNIV PA, 1983-; Given prof, Hosp Univ Pa, 1970-1983; asst prof, Hosp Univ Pa, 1966-1970; assoc, Hosp Univ Pa, 1964-1966; attend ophthal, Vet Admin Hosp, 1963-; asst attend physician, Philadelphia Gen Hosp, 1963-; assoc ophthal, Children's Hosp Philadelphia, 1963-; spec fel, 1963-1964; instr, Hosp Univ Pa, 1963-1964; NIH trainee, 1961-1963; resident, Hosp Univ Pa, 1960-1963; Intern, Mt Sinai Hosp, New York, 1959-1960; mem vision res & training comt, Nat Eye Inst. **Memberships:** AMA; Asn Res Vision & Ophthal; Histochem Soc; Am Asn Anat; Am Acad Ophthal & Otolaryngol. **Research Statement & Publications:** Histochemistry; visual pathways; experimental myopia. **Mailing Address:** Dept Ophthal, Univ Pa, 3700 Hamilton Walk, D-603 Richards Bldg, Philadelphia, PA 19104. **Fax:** 215-898-0528. **E-Mail:** laties@mail.med.upenn.edu

LATIES, VICTOR GREGORY, PSYCHOPHARMACOLOGY, BEHAVIOR ANALYSIS. **Personal Data:** b Racine, Wis, February 2, 1926. **Education:** Tufts Univ, AB, 1949; Univ Rochester, PhD (psychol), 1954. **Professional Experience:** PROF EMER ENVIRON MED, ENVIRON HEALTH SCI CTR, UNIV ROCHESTER, 1993-; DIR, ENVIRON STUDIES & INDUST HYG PROG, UNIV ROCHESTER, 1982-; mem bd toxicol & environ health hazards, 1977-1980; mem toxicol info prog comt, 1982-1985; dir, toxicol training prog, 1978-1991 & 1995-1996; pres, Div Exp Anal Behav, 1978-1982; mem, Nat Res Coun Panel Carbon Monoxide, Nat Acad Sci, 1973-1977; ed, J Exp Analytical Behav, 1973-1977; prof toxicol, pharmacol & psychol, 1971-1993; pres, Div Psychopharmacol, Environ Protection Agency, 1968-1969; mem, Sci Rev Panel Health Res, Environ Protection Agency, 1968-1969; mem preclin psychopharmacol res rev comt, NIMH, 1967-1971; exec ed, J Exp Analytical Behav, 1966-; assoc prof radiation biol, biophys, pharmacol & psychol, Univ Rochester, 1965-1971; from instr to asst prof, Sch Med, Johns Hopkins Univ, 1955-1965; teaching intern, Brown Univ, 1954-1955; res assoc, Univ Rochester, 1953-1954. **Memberships:** Am Psychol Asn; Am Soc Pharmacol & Exp Therapeut; Behav Pharmacol Soc (pres 1966-1968); Soc Toxicol; Asn Behav Anal; Soc Exp Anal Behav (secy-treas 1966-). **Research Statement & Publications:** Behavioral pharmacology; experimental analysis of behavior; behavioral toxicology. **Mailing Address:** Environ Health Sci Ctr, Sch Med & Dent, Univ Rochester, Rochester, NY 14642. **Fax:** 585-256-2791. **E-Mail:** victor_laties@urmc.rochester.edu

LATIMER, BRUCE MILLIKIN, BIOMECHANICS OF LOCOMOTION, HOMINID PALEONTOLOGY. **Personal Data:** b Hamilton, Ohio, August 23, 1953. **Education:** Univ Ariz, BA, 1975; Case Western Res Univ, MA, 1978; Kent State Univ, PhD (biomed sci), 1988. **Professional Experience:** EXEC DIR, THE CLEVELAND MUS NATURAL HIST, as of 2002; ASSOC PROF, DEPT ANAT, CASE WESTERN RES UNIV, SCH MED, as of 2002; supvr, Collections & Res Div, Cleveland Mus Natural Hist, beginning 1993; supvr, Collections & Res Div, beginning 1993; cur & head phys anthrop, Cleveland Mus Natural Hist, beginning 1988; asst prof anat, Case Western Res Univ, beginning 1988; from asst cur to assoc cur, Case Western Res Univ, 1985-1988. **Memberships:** Am Asn Phys Anthropologists; Am Asn Anatomists; Sigma Xi. **Research Statement & Publications:** Pleistocene hominis evolution; comparative primate anatomy. **Mailing Address:** Cleveland Mus Natural Hist, One Wade Oval Dr, Cleveland, OH 44106.

LATIMER, CLINTON NARATH, NEUROPHYSIOLOGY. **Personal Data:** b New York, NY, August 30, 1924. **Education:** Columbia Univ, AB, 1948; Syracuse Univ, PhD (physiol), 1956. **Professional Experience:** DIR DRUG SAFETY EVAL, DIR, RES DEVELOP PHARMACEUT DIV, PENNWALT CORP, 1980-; study dir toxicol, Lederle labs div, 1976-1980; Group leader neuropharmacol, Am Cyanamid Co, 1958-1976; Nat inst Neurol Dis & Blindness res fel neurophysiol, Univ Wash, 1956-1958. **Memberships:** AAAS; Am Soc Pharmacol & Exp Therapeut; Soc Neuroscience; Am Physiol Soc; AmCol Toxicol; Sigma Xi. **Research Statement & Publications:** Neuropharmacology; function of the central nervous system as delineated by extra and intracellular recordings of neuronal activity under influence of drugs and in control states; psychopharmacology; safety evaluation of all classes of compounds; physiologic toxicology; long-term alteration of function by drugs; computer applications; research administration, toxicology, pathology, drug safety evaluation. **Mailing Address:** 2785 Rush-Mendon Rd, Honeoye Falls, NY 14472-9312.

LATIMER, GEORGE WEBSTER, ANALYTICAL CHEMISTRY. **Education:** George Wash Univ, BS, 1955; Princeton Univ, PhD (analytical chem), 1961. **Professional Experience:** Consult, USAF, 1992; STATE CHEMIST, OFF TEX STATE CHEMIST, TEX A&M UNIV, 1990-; mem, Houston, 1990; consult, FGIS/USDA CONASUPO Negotiations, 1990; mem, Tex State Legis Comt Naturally Occurring Radioactive Mat, San Antonio, 1989; actg state chemist, Agr Analytical Systs, 1988-1990; chief, Agr Analytical Systs, 1986-1992; mgr corp qual control, Norwood Industs, Malvern, Pa, 1984-1986; lectr, Air Univ, Maxwell AFB, Ala, 1981-1986; mgr corp qual control, Bulk Chem Div, SFB, 1981-1984; admins liaison counr, Hq Air Force Acad, 1978-1986; asst mgr qual assurance, Whitehall Labs, Elkhart, Ind, 1978-1981; asst prof sci, Univ Evansville, 1974-1976; chief nutrit qual control & sr group leader pharm & nutrit qual control, Mead Johnson, Evansville, Ill, 1973-1978; consult, Kennecott Copper, 1966-1967; consult, Desert Industs, 1966-1967; Asst prof analytical chem & dir lab, Univ Utah, Salt Lake City, 1965-1967; group leader analytical serv & sr res chemist, PPG Industs, Corpus Christi, Tex, 1962-1964 & 1967-1973. **Memberships:** Am Asn Feed Control; Sigma Xi. **Research Statement & Publications:** Research in method for determining deimethysulfoxide in triampterene. **Mailing Address:** Off Tex State Chemist, Tex A&M Univ, PO Box 3160, College Station, TX 77841-3160. **Fax:** 979-845-1389. **E-Mail:** g-latimer@tamu.edu

LATIMER, HOWARD LEROY, PLANT GENETICS, PLANT ECOLOGY. **Personal Data:** b Seattle, Wash, July 18, 1929. **Education:** Wash State Univ, BS, 1951, MS, 1955; Claremont Cols, PhD (bot), 1959. **Professional Experience:** PROF EMER BIOL, CALIF STATE UNIV, FRESNO, 1992-; prof Biol, Calif State Univ, Fresno, beginning 1968; from asst prof to assoc prof, Calif State Univ, Fresno, 1958-1968. **Memberships:** Soc Study Evolution; Ecol Soc Am. **Research Statement & Publications:** Reproductive ecology of plants. **Mailing Address:** Dept Bio, Calif State Univ, Fresno, CA 93650. **Fax:** 559-278-3963.

LATIMER, PAUL HENRY, BIOPHYSICS. **Personal Data:** b New Orleans, La, November 25, 1925. **Education:** Univ Ill, MS, 1950, PhD (biophys), 1956. **Professional Experience:** PROF EMER PHYSICS, AUBURN UNIV, 1992-; contractor, US Army, 1977; consult, Southern Res Inst, Birmingham, 1976; prof physics, Auburn Univ, beginning 1971; assoc prof, Auburn Univ, 1962-1971; asst prof physics, Vanderbilt Univ, 1957-1962; investr, Howard Hughes Med Inst, 1957-1962; res fel plant biol, Carnegie Inst Technol, 1956-1957; asst bot, Univ Ill, 1953-1956; instr physics, Col William & Mary, 1950-1951. **Memberships:** Biophys Soc; Am Phys Soc; Optical Soc Am. **Research Statement & Publications:** Light scattering; biological optics; fluorescence; photosynthesis. **Mailing Address:** Dept Physics, Auburn Univ, Auburn, AL 36830.

LATIN, RICHARD, PHYTOPATHOLOGY, BIOLOGY. **Personal Data:** b Teaneck, NJ, October 4, 1951; m 1975, Barbara; c Eric W & David R. **Education:** Waynesburg Col, BS, 1973; Pa State Univ, MS, 1977, PhD (plant path), 1980. **Professional Experience:** PROF, DEPT BOT & PLANT PATH, PURDUE UNIV, 1993-, from asst prof to assoc prof, 1981-1993. **Memberships:** Am Phytopath Soc. **Research Statement & Publications:** Epidemiology and management of diseases of turfgrass and vegs. **Mailing Address:** Purdue Univ, West Lafayette, IN 47907-1968. **Fax:** 765-494-0363. **E-Mail:** rlatin@purdue.edu

LATINA, MICHAEL RONALD, MATHEMATICS. **Education:** Worcester Polytech Inst, BS, 1968; Brown Univ, MS, 1970, PhD, 1979. **Professional Experience:** PROF, DEPT MATHS, COMMUNITY COL RI, beginning 1970. **Memberships:** Math Asn Am. **Mailing Address:** Dept Math, Community Col RI, 84 Richland Rd, Cranston, RI 02910-4229. **Fax:** 401-825-2418.

LATORELLA, A HENRY, GENETICS, ALGOLOGY. **Personal Data:** b Winthrop, Mass, March 12, 1940. **Education:** Boston Col, BS, 1961, MS, 1964; Univ Maine, Orono, PhD (zoology & genetics), 1971. **Professional Experience:** PROF BIOL, STATE UNIV NY, GENESEO, as of 2000; assoc prof biol, State Univ NY, Col Geneseo, beginning 1970; Asst prof biol, Salem State Col, 1966-1968. **Memberships:** Am Genetic Asn; Phycol Soc Am; AAAS; Genetics Soc Am; Sigma Xi. **Research Statement & Publications:** Algal genetics and physiology; regulation of DNA replication and genetics and biochemistry of salinity adaptation by phytoflagellates. **Mailing Address:** Dept Biol, State Univ NY Geneseo, Geneseo, NY 14454. **Fax:** 585-245-5007. **E-Mail:** latorell@geneseo.edu

LATORRE, DONALD RUTLEDGE, MATHEMATICS. **Personal Data:** b Charleston, SC, May 4, 1938. **Education:** Wofford Col, BS, 1960; Univ Tenn, MA, 1962, PhD (math), 1964. **Professional Experience:** PROF EMER MATH, CLEMSON UNIV, as of 2004; prof math, Clemson Univ, beginning 1976; from asst prof to assoc prof, Clemson Univ, 1967-1976; asst prof math, Univ Tenn, 1967. **Memberships:** Am Math Soc; Math Asn Am. **Research Statement & Publications:** Abstract algebra, especially semigroups. **Mailing Address:** Dept Math Sci, Clemson Univ, Clemson, SC 29631-1907.

LATORRE, ROBERT GEORGE, SHIP HYDRODYNAMICS, NAVAL ARCHITECTURE. **Personal Data:** b Toledo, Ohio, January 9, 1949. **Education:** Univ Mich, BS, 1971, MS, 1972; MSE, 1975; Univ Tokyo, PhD, 1979. **Professional Experience:** PROF, SCH NAVAL ARCHIT & MARINE ENG, UNIV NEW ORLEANS, 1989-; chmn naval archit & marine eng, Univ New Orleans, beginning 1989; assoc prof, Dept Mech Eng, Univ Tokyo, Japan, 1986-1987; assoc prof, Univ New Orleans, 1984-1987; res scientist, Bassin d Essais des Carenes, Paris, 1983-1984; res scientist, David W Taylor Navel Ship Res & Develop Ctr, 1980-1981; asst prof naval archit & marine eng, Univ Mich, 1979-1983. **Memberships:** Am Soc Mech Engrs; Soc Naval Archit & Marine Engrs; Japan Soc Naval Archit; Royal Inst Naval Archit. **Research Statement & Publications:** Development of the design of shallow water river pushboats and estimating methods for ship resistance; towed ship safety and towed vessel course stability; design and use of 125 ft by 7 ft deep-ship - offshore model testbasin in deep and shallow water; numerical hydrodynamics; ship design using computer aided engineering; cavitation noise and underwater acoustics. **Mailing Address:** Sch Naval Archit & Marine Eng, Univ New Orleans, Sch NAME En 911, New Orleans, LA 70148. **Fax:** 504-280-5542. **E-Mail:** rglna@uno.edu

LATORRE, V(ICTOR) R(OBERT), ELECTRICAL ENGINEERING. **Personal Data:** b Brooklyn, NY, November 17, 1931. **Education:** Univ Ariz, BSEE, 1956, MS, 1957, PhD (elec eng), 1960. **Professional Experience:** RES ENGR, LAWRENCE LIVERMORE LAB, UNIV CALIF, LIVERMORE, 1976-; assoc div head, Electronic Eng Dept, 1972-1976; electronics engr, Univ Calif, Davis, 1967-1972; asst prof elec eng, Univ Calif, Davis, 1964-1967; lectr, Seattle Univ, 1962; res specialist commun systs, Boeing Co, Wash, 1961-1964; sr res engr, Frederick Res Corp, Ariz, 1960-1961; from instr to asst prof elec eng, Univ Ariz, 1957-1961; consult, electromagnetic radiation effects on equipment & humans, microwave non-destructive anal mat. **Memberships:** Sr mem Inst Elec & Electronics Engrs; Am Soc Eng Educ; Sigma Xi; NY Acad Sci. **Research Statement & Publications:** Biotelemetry systems; meteoric and tropospheric scatter propagation; design and statistical analysis of secure and jam-resistant communication systems; transportation systems research; microwave non-destructive analyses; electromagnetic interference. **Mailing Address:** Lawrence Livermore Lab L-156, Univ Calif, Box 808, Livermore, CA 94550.

LATOUR, PIERRE RICHARD, CHEMICAL ENGINEERING, PROCESS CONTROL. **Personal Data:** b Buffalo, NY, April 15, 1940. **Education:** Va Polytech Inst, BSChE, 1962; Purdue Univ, MS, 1964, PhD (chem eng), 1966. **Professional Experience:** CONSULT, FIT INC, as of 2004; PRES, SETPOINT RIGHT INC, TEX, 1997-; vpres, Aspen Technol Inc, Tex, 1996-1997; VPRES, DYNAMIC MATRIX CONTROL CORP, TEX, 1995-; Lehigh Univ, Univ Houston & Purdue Univ, 1985; dir & chmn bd, Setpoint Japan Inc, 1984-1990; Lehigh Univ, Univ Tex, 1984; Lehigh Univ, 1969 & Univ Calif, Santa Barbara, 1980, 1981; consult engr & vpres, Setpoint Inc, Tex, 1977-1995; mgr process control eng, Davis Comput Systs, Inc, NY & Tex, 1970 & Biles & Assocs, Inc, Tex, 1971-1977; sr engr, head off, Mfg Technol Dept, Shell Oil Co, 1969; Houston Res Lab, Univ Houston, 1968; tech asst to chief, Simulation Br, 1967-1968; mathematician, Theory & Analysis Off, Manned Spacecraft Ctr, NASA, Houston, 1967; Res engr, Comput Control Group, 1966-1967; Res engr, Math Group, Houston Res Lab, Shell Oil Co, Tex, 1966, 1967; Lectr, Purdue Univ, 1966; Houston Res Lab, Shell Oil Co, 1966. **Memberships:** Am Chem Soc; Am Inst Chem Engrs; Instrument Soc Am; Sigma Xi. **Research Statement & Publications:** Automatic process control; applied mathematics; digital computation; crude oil distillation; computer control of petroleum refining; cracking; simulation; process dynamics; plant economics; optimization; process engineering; computer control justification; sales; business development; marketing. **Mailing Address:** Fit Inc, 1800 Palace Court, Denton, TX 76210. **Fax:** 940-497-2166.

LATOURETTE, HAROLD KENNETH, ORGANIC CHEMISTRY. **Personal Data:** b Seattle, Wash, April 10, 1924; m 1944, Beverly; c Helen M, Lorene, Marcia S & Stephen. **Education:** Whitman Col, AB, 1947; Univ Wash, PhD (org chem), 1951. **Professional Experience:** RETIRED; environ mgr Toxic Substances, FMC Corp, Pa, 1977-1983; mgr eval, Chem Group, 1972-1976; mgr planning & eval, Cent Res Dept, NJ, 1965-1972; europ tech dir, Chem Div & vpres, FMC Chem, SA, Switz, 1962-1965; mgr org chem res, Inorg Chem Div, NJ, 1958-1962; mgr org res & develop, Becco Chem Div, NY, 1957-1958; supvr org res, Cent Res Labs, NJ, 1956-1957; dir pioneering res, Westvaco Chlor-Alkali Div, 1954-1956; res chemist, Westvaco Chem Div, FMC Corp, WVa, 1951-1954; res assoc, Univ Wash, 1948-1951. **Memberships:** Sigma Xi; Am Chem Soc. **Research Statement & Publications:** Organic reaction mechanisms; aromatic substitution; peroxides; epoxides; isocyanates; phosphorus and sulfur organics; halogenation; industrial processes. **Mailing Address:** 1526 Deception Rd, Anacortes, WA 98221.

LATOURRETTE, JAMES THOMAS, COMPUTER LANGUAGES. **Personal Data:** b Miami, Ariz, December 26, 1931; m 1955, Muriel Ashe; c Mary B, John E, J Thomas & Joanne C. **Education:** Calif Inst Technol, BS, 1953; Harvard Univ, MA, 1954, PhD (physics), 1958. **Professional Experience:** PROF EMERITUS, POLYTECH UNIV, 1993-; assoc dir, Weber Res Inst, 1987-1991; prof elec eng & comput sci, Polytech Univ, 1967-1993; sect head gas laser, TRG, Inc Div, Control Data Corp, 1966-1967; sr supvry scientist, TRG, Inc Div, Control Data Corp, 1962-1966; physicist, Gen Elec Res Lab, 1960-1962; NSF fel, Univ Bonn, 1959-1960; lectr, Harvard Univ, 1958-1959; res fel physics, Harvard Univ, 1957-1958. **Memberships:** Inst Elec & Electronics Engrs. **Research Statement & Publications:** Computer languages, systems and applications; gas laser research and applications; saturated resonance spectroscopy and laser frequency stabilization. **Mailing Address:** 2 Candlewood Ct, Huntington, NY 11743.

LATSCHAR, CARL ERNEST, PHYSICAL CHEMISTRY. **Personal Data:** b Newton, Kans, May 24, 1919; m 1941, c 5. **Education:** Kans State Univ, BS, 1941, MS, 1947; Univ Wis, PhD (phys chem), 1950. **Professional Experience:** RETIRED; sr res chemist, E I Du

Pont De Nemours & Co, Inc, beginning 1962; res chemist, E I Du Pont De Nemours & Co, Inc, 1950-1962. **Memberships:** Am Chem Soc. **Research Statement & Publications:** Textile fiber process and product development. **Mailing Address:** PO Box 1273, Salina, KS 67402-1273.

LATSHAW, DAVID RODNEY, ANALYTICAL CHEMISTRY. **Personal Data:** b Allentown, Pa, November 4, 1939. **Education:** Muhlenberg Col, BS, 1961; Lehigh Univ, MS, 1963, PhD (chem), 1966. **Professional Experience:** RES ASSOC SPECTROS, ALLENTOWN LABS, AIR PROD & CHEM INC, 1987-; mgr analytical serv, Air Prod & Chem Inc, 1980-1987; group leader, Air Prod & Chem Inc, 1969-1980; res chemist, Air Prod & Chem Inc, 1966-1969; res asst, Lehigh Univ, 1963-1966. **Memberships:** Am Chem Soc; Sigma Xi. **Research Statement & Publications:** Infrared spectroscopy. **Mailing Address:** 944 Belford Rd, Allentown, PA 18103.

LATSHAW, J DAVID, ANIMAL SCIENCE & NUTRITION. **Personal Data:** b Reading, Pa. **Education:** Pa State Univ, BS, 1964; Wash State Univ, PhD (nutrit), 1970. **Professional Experience:** PROF POULTRY SCI, OHIO STATE UNIV, 1984-; from asst prof to assoc prof, Ohio State Univ, 1970-1984. **Memberships:** Poultry Sci Asn; Am Inst Nutrit. **Research Statement & Publications:** Nutritional needs of egg-type and meat-type chickens; nutrients such as selenium, amino acids, and energy; effects of feedstuff processing. **Mailing Address:** 230D Plumb, 2027 Coffey Rd, Columbus, OH 43210-1056. **E-Mail:** latshaw.1@osu.edu

LATTA, BRYAN MICHAEL, SOLID STATE THIN FILM ELECTROCHROMICS, PARTICLE SOLID INTERACTION THEORY & MODELING. **Personal Data:** b Oshawa, Ont, October 25, 1946; m 1995, Suzhen; c Hope. **Education:** Queen's Univ, BSc, 1970, MSc, 1975, PhD (physics), 1978. **Professional Experience:** HEAD PHYSICS, ACADIA UNIV, 2001-; PROF PHYSICS, ACADIA UNIV, 1992-; prin investr, Thin Film Lab, Acadia Univ, 1988-; asst prof physics, Mem Univ Nfld, 1985-1992; Nat Sci & Eng Res Coun Can Univ res fel, Mem Univ Nfld, 1981-1984; asst prof physics, Acadia Univ, 1978-1981. **Memberships:** Can Asn Physicists; Am Phys Soc. **Research Statement & Publications:** Use detailed solid state charge distributions to evaluate the electronic and nuclear stopping power; Monte-Carlo and numerical modeling of particle-solid collision phenomena; multiple layer thin film coating and optical performance evaluation; particle solid interaction theory and modeling; electric discharge in gases; electronic instrumentation. **Mailing Address:** Physics Dept, Acadia Univ, Wolfville, NS B0P 1X0, Can. **Fax:** 902-585-1816. **E-Mail:** bryan.latta@acadiau.ca

LATTA, HARRISON, PATHOLOGY. **Personal Data:** b Los Angeles, Calif, April 5, 1918; m 1985, Lya; c William, John Gilbert & Ann. **Education:** Univ Calif, Los Angeles, BA, 1940; Johns Hopkins Univ, MD, 1943. **Professional Experience:** PROF EMER PATH, SCH MED, UNIV CALIF, LOS ANGELES, as of 2005; prof path, sch med, Univ Calif, Los Angeles, beginning 1960; assoc prof, Sch Med, Univ Calif, Los Angeles, 1954-1960; asst prof path, Sch Med, Case Western Res Univ, 1951-1954; res assoc biol, Mass Inst Technol, 1949-1951; Res fel, Children's Hosp, Boston & Harvard Med Sch, 1948-1949; instr, Johns Hopkins Univ, 1945-1946; from asst resident to resident path, Johns Hopkins Hosp, 1944-1946; intern, Church Home & Hosp, Md, 1944. **Memberships:** AAAS; Am Soc Cell Biol; us & Canadian Acda Pathal. **Research Statement & Publications:** Ultrastructure and diseases of the kidney. **Mailing Address:** UCLA Medical Center, Los Angeles, CA 90095-1732.

LATTA, JOHN NEAL, COMPUTER SCIENCE, ELECTRICAL ENGINEERING. **Personal Data:** b Ottumwa, Iowa, April 11, 1944. **Education:** Brigham Young Univ, BES, 1966; Univ Kans, MS, 1969, PhD (elec eng), 1971. **Professional Experience:** PRES & FOUNDER, FOURTH WAVE INC, 1989-; pres, Adroit Systs Inc, 1983-1989; sr staff scientist, Sci Applns, Inc, 1977-1983; sr res engr, Environ Res Inst Mich, 1973-1977; res engr, Radar & Optics Lab, Univ Mich, Ann Arbor, 1969-1973; mem tech staff holography, Bell Tel Labs, NJ, 1969; res asst optics, Ctr Res Eng Sci, Univ Kans, 1967-1968; Mem tech staff holography, RCA Labs, NJ, 1967. **Memberships:** Inst Elec & Electronics Engrs; Asn Comput Mach; Sigma Xi. **Research Statement & Publications:** Multimedia computing; digital image processing; visual displays; system engineering; digital system architecture; software engineering; holography; optical design. **Mailing Address:** 4th Wave Inc, Ste 200 1900 Elkin St, Alexandria, VA 22308. **Fax:** 703-360-2311. **E-Mail:** jnl@fourthwave.com

LATTA, WILLIAM CARL, FISH BIOLOGY, ICHTHYOLOGY. **Personal Data:** b Niagara Falls, NY, May 18, 1925; m 1950, Harriet; c 5. **Education:** Cornell Univ, BS, 1950; Univ Okla, MS, 1952; Univ Mich, PhD (fishery biol), 1957. **Professional Experience:** EMER CHIEF RES SECT, INST FISHERIES RES, STATE DEPT NATURAL RESOURCES, MICH, 1992-; chief res sect, Fisheries Div, 1976-1992; Adj prof fisheries & wildlife, Sch Natural Resources and Environment, Univ Mich, Ann Arbor, 1973-; in-charge, Inst Fisheries Res, 1966-1976; FISHERY BIOLOGIST, INST FISHERIES RES, STATE DEPT NATURAL RESOURCES, MICH, 1955-; Aquatic biologist, State Conserv Dept, NY, 1950. **Memberships:** Am Fisheries Soc; Am Soc Ichthyol & Herpet; emer mem Wildlife Soc; emer mem Ecol Soc Am; emer mem Am Inst Fishery Res Biologists; Soc Conserv Biol. **Research Statement & Publications:** Fish population dynamics; management of freshwater fisheries; biology of endangered and threatened fishes. **Mailing Address:** Inst Fisheries Res, Univ Mus Annex, Ann Arbor, MI 48109.

LATTERELL, RICHARD L, GENETICS. **Personal Data:** b Paynesville, Minn, March 14, 1928. **Education:** Univ Minn, Duluth, BA, 1950; Pa State Univ, MS, 1955; Cornell Univ, PhD (genetics), 1958. **Professional Experience:** PROF EMER SCI & MATHS, SHEPHERD COL, 1992-; vis assoc prof agron, Colo State Univ, 1979-1980; from assoc prof to prof biol, Shepard Col, 1968-1992; geneticist, Union Carbide Res Inst, 1963-1968; geneticist, Div Radiation & Organisms, Smithsonian Inst, 1960-1963; Nat Cancer Inst fel genetics, Brookhaven Nat Lab, 1958-1960. **Memberships:** Genetics Soc Am; Bot Soc Am; Sigma Xi; Am Inst Biol Sci. **Research Statement & Publications:** Radiation genetics of maize; space biology; stress tolerance of higher plants; plant cytogenetics. **Mailing Address:** Dept Biol, Shepherd Col, PO Box 3210, Shepherdstown, WV 25443-3210. **Fax:** 304-876-3101. **E-Mail:** rlattere@shepherd.edu

LATTIME, EDMUND CHARLES, IMMUNOLOGY. **Personal Data:** b Newburyport, Mass, January 18, 1951. **Education:** Gettysburg Col, BA, 1973; Rutgers Univ, MS & PhD (zoology), 1977. **Professional Experience:** ASSOC DIR, DEPT SURG, CANCER INST NJ, as of 2005; mem, Oncol Rev Bd, US Vet Admin, 1988-; lab asst mem immunol, Sloan-Kettering Inst Cancer Res, 1985-; scholar, Leukemia Soc Am, 1984; instr immunol, Grad Sch, Cornell Univ, Sloan-Kettering Inst, beginning 1981; res assoc, Grad Sch, Cornell Univ, Sloan-Kettering Inst, 1979-1984; fel immunol, Grad Sch, Cornell Univ, Sloan-Kettering Inst, 1977-1979. **Memberships:** Am Asn Immunologists; Am Asn Cancer Res; Am Chem Soc. **Research Statement & Publications:** Natural immunity with emphasis on mechanisms of lytic factor release and actions. **Mailing Address:** Dept Surg, Cancer Inst NJ 195 Little Albany St, New Brunswick, NJ 08901. **Fax:** 732-235-8098. **E-Mail:** lattimec@umdnj.edu

LATTIMER, JAMES MICHAEL, NUCLEAR ASTROPHYSICS, NEUTRINO ASTROPHYSICS. **Personal Data:** b Marion, Ind, April 12, 1950; c 4. **Education:** Univ Notre Dame, BS Physics, 1972; Univ Tex, Austin, PhD Aastronomy, 1976. **Honors & Awards:** American Physical Society Fellow, 2001; John Simon Guggenheim Fellow, 1999-2000; Ernst F Fullam fel, 1985-1986; Alfred P Sloan Res Fel, 1982-1984. **Professional Experience:** PROF ASTRON, STATE UNIV NY, STONY BROOK, 1988-; Visiting Prof, Nordita, Copenhagen, Denmark, 1985-1986; from Asst Prof to Assoc Prof, State Univ NY, Stony Brook, 1979-1988; Res. Assoc., Univ Ill, Urbana-Champaign, 1976-1979; Res. Assoc., Univ Chicago, 1976. **Memberships:** Am Astron Soc; Int Astron Union; Am Phys Soc; Am Geophys Union; Astron Soc Pac, Am. Chem. Soc. **Research Statement & Publications:** Supernovae; neutron stars; equation of state at high densities and temperatures; meteoritics; grain formation in novae and supernovae; nuclear physics; neutrino astrophysics. **Mailing Address:** Physics & Astron Dept, State Univ NY, Stony Brook, NY 11794-3800. **Fax:** 631-632-1745. **E-Mail:** lattimer@astro.sunysb.edu

LATTIMER, ROBERT PHILLIPS, ANALYTICAL CHEMISTRY, POLYMER CHEMISTRY. **Personal Data:** b Kansas City, Mo, February 2, 1945. **Education:** Univ Mo-Columbia, BS, 1967; Univ Kans, PhD (chem), 1971. **Honors & Awards:** Sparks-Thomas Award. **Professional Experience:** SR RES CHEMIST, NOVEON INC, as of 2003; sr res & develop assoc anal chem, B F Goodrich Co, beginning 1974; Fel chem, Univ Mich, Ann Arbor, 1972-1974. **Memberships:** Am Chem Soc; Am Soc Mass Spectrometry; Sigma Xi. **Research Statement & Publications:** Analysis of polymers; mass spectrometry of polymers; degradation of polymers. **Mailing Address:** Noveon Inc, 9911 Brecksville Rd, Brecksville, OH 44141. **Fax:** 216-447-5575. **E-Mail:** bob.lattimer@noveoninc.com

LATTIN, DANNY L(EE), MEDICINALCHEMISTRY. **Personal Data:** b Smith Ctr, Kans, January 9, 1942. **Education:** Univ Kans, BS, 1965; Univ Minn, Minneapolis, PhD (med chem), 1970. **Professional Experience:** DEAN & PROF, COL PHARM, SDAK STATE UNIV, BROOKINGS, 1995-; Vpres, EPSCOR Ark Sci & Technol Authority, 1994-1995; prof, Col Pharm, Univ Ark Med Sch, Little Rock, 1980-1995; from asst prof to assoc prof med chem, Col Pharm, Univ Ark Med Sch, Little Rock, 1970-1975. **Memberships:** Am Chem Soc; Am Asn Cols Pharm. **Research Statement & Publications:** Synthesis of novel opiate antagonists; synthesis and evaluation of novel opiate receptor affinity labels; study of sterochemical properties of drug receptors. **Mailing Address:** Col Pharm, SDak State Univ, Box 2202C, Brookings, SD 57007-0099. **Fax:** 605-688-6232. **E-Mail:** DANNY-LATTIN@sdstate.edu

LATTIN, JOHN D, ENTOMOLOGY. **Personal Data:** b Chicago, Ill, July 27, 1927. **Education:** Iowa State Univ, BS, 1950; Univ Kans, MA, 1951; Univ Calif, Berkeley, PhD (entom), 1964. **Honors & Awards:** Loyd Carter Award, Ore State Univ, 1961. **Professional Experience:** PROF EMER ENTOM, ORE STATE UNIV, 1968-; consult, USDA, 1981-1982; asst dean sci, Agr Exp Sta, Ore State Univ, 1967-1973; NSF fac fel, Univ Wageningen, 1965-1966; CUR, SYST ENTOM LAB, ORE STATE, 1961-1966 & 1974-; from instr to assoc prof, Agr Exp Sta, Ore State Univ, 1955-1968; asst entomologist, Agr Exp Sta, Ore State Univ, 1955-1961; jr vector control specialist, Bur Vector Control, Calif Dept Pub Health, 1954-1955; aquatic entomologist, Dept Limnol, Acad Natural Hist, Philadelphia, 1951. **Memberships:** Entom Soc Am; Soc Syst Zool. **Research Statement & Publications:** Systematics of the Pentatomoidea, Leptopododoidea and Miridae; origin, distribution and phylogeny of the Heteroptera; evolution and zoogeography of the insecta; aquatic entomology; scientific education; education of talented students; introduced insects; applied systematic entomology. **Mailing Address:** Dept Bot & Plant Path, Col Sci, Ore State Univ, 128 Kidder Hall, Corvallis, OR 97331-4608. **Fax:** 541-737-3643. **E-Mail:** lattinj@bcc.orst.edu

LATTMAN, EATON EDWARD, MOLECULAR BIOPHYSICS, STRUCTURAL BIOLOGY. **Personal Data:** b Chicago, Ill, May 15, 1940; m 1966, Susan; c Laura Joy. **Education:** Harvard Col, BA, 1962; Johns Hopkins Univ PhD (biophysics), 1969. **Honors & Awards:** Res Career Develop Award, NIH. **Professional Experience:** Dean of Research and Grauduate Education, SCH ARTS & SCI, JOHNS HOPKINS UNIV 2004-present. PROF & CHMN, DEPT BIOPHYS, SCH ARTS & SCI, JOHNS HOPKINS UNIV, 1996-2005; from asst prof to prof, Dept Biophys, Johns Hopkins Univ, 1976-1996; NIH fel biophys, Brandeis Univ, 1974-1976; fel, Max Planck Inst Biochem, 1974; res scientist, Johns Hopkins Univ, 1970-1973; NIH fel biophys, Johns Hopkins Univ, 1969-1970; ed-in-chief, Proteins: Structure, Function & Genetics; dir, Intercampus Prog Molecular Biophys. **Memberships:** Am Crystallog Asn Protein Soc Biophys Soc. **Research Statement & Publications:** Protein crystallography; mutants of staphylococcal nuclease; physical studies of protein folding; rational drug design; crystallographic methods development; electrostatics. **Mailing Address:** Johns Hopkins Univ Meergenthaler 237, 3400 N Charles St, Baltimore, MD 21218-2685. **Fax:** 410-516-4100. **E-Mail:** lattman@jhu.edu

LATTMAN, LAURENCE HAROLD, GEOLOGY -REMOTE SENSING. **Personal Data:** b New York, NY, November 30, 1923; m 1946, Hanna; c Martin & Barbara. **Education:** City Col NY, BChE, 1948; Univ Cincinnati, MS, 1951, PhD (geol), 1953. **Honors & Awards:** Fulbright Lectr, Moscow State Univ, 1975; Mineral Indust Educ Award; Am Inst Mining Metall & Engr, 1986. **Professional Experience:** EMER PRES, NMEX INST MINING TECHNOL, as of 2005; pres, Nmex Inst Mining Technol, 1983-1993; dean, Col Mines & Mineral Indust & Col Eng, Univ Utah, 1975-1983; prof geol & head dept, Univ Cincinnati, 1970-1975; mem, Nat Res Coun, 1959-1962; from asst prof to prof geomorphol, Pa State Univ, 1957-1970; asst head, Photogeol Sect, 1956-1957; photogeologist, Gulf Oil Corp, 1953-1956; instr geol, Univ Mich, 1952-1953; instr geol, Univ Cincinnati, 1951. **Memberships:** Fel Geol Soc Am; Am Soc Photogram; Am Asn Petrol Geologists; Sigma Xi. **Research Statement & Publications:** Remote sensing of environment; geomorphology; fracture analysis on aerial photographs. **Mailing Address:** 11509 Penfield Lane NE, Albuquerque, NM 87111-6526. **Fax:** 505-237-2382.

LATTMAN, MICHAEL, MAIN-GROUP CHEMISTRY, HYPERVALENT MOLECULES. **Personal Data:** b New York, NY, June 2, 1950; m 1974, Michele; c Allison & Lauren. **Education:** City Col NY, BS, 1972; City Univ NY, PhD (inorg chem), 1977. **Honors & Awards:** Camille & Henry Dreyfus Scholar, Camille & Henry Dreyfus found, 1997-1999. **Professional Experience:** PROF CHEM, SOUTHERN METHODIST UNIV, 1993-; Vis res scientist, E I Du Pont de Nemours &Co, 1986-1987; from asst prof to assoc prof, Southern Methodist Univ, 1979-1993; Fel, Univ Tex, Austin, 1976-1979. **Memberships:** Am Chem Soc; Sigma Xi; Coun Undergrad Res. **Research Statement & Publications:** Synthesis, structure and reactivity of macrocyclic-stabilized hypervalent main-group elements; reactions at coordinated ligands; new ligands which alter reactions at transition-metal centers; Calixerenes. **Mailing Address:** Chem Dept, Southern Methodist Univ, Dallas, TX 75275-0314. **Fax:** 214-768-4089. **E-Mail:** mlattman@mail.smu.edu

LAU, BRAD W C, BIOCHEMISTRY. **Personal Data:** b Macaw, China, March 23, 1950. **Education:** Univ NDak, BS, 1972, MS, 1975, PhD (biochem), 1979. **Professional Experience:** SR CHEMIST RES & DEVELOP, SIGMA DIAGNOSTICS, 1988-; res & serv, Med Ctr, Wash Univ, 1986-1988; Young investr award, Am Clin Lab Physicians & Scientists, 1986; postdoctoral fel res, Biol Res Lab, Syracuse, Wis, 1982-1985; Res assoc, Human Nutrit Res Ctr, USDA, 1979-1982. **Memberships:** Am Asn Clin Chem; Am Soc Molecular Biol & Biochem; Sigma Xi; Clin Ligand Assay Soc. **Research Statement & Publications:** Developing test reagent kits for analyses of metabolites and other chemicals in human specimens including semen, plasma, urine, and cerebral spinal fluid to be used in the clinical chemistry laboratory in hospitals and reference laboratories. **Mailing Address:** 9 Rainfield Ct, St Louis, MO 63021-7414.

LAU, CATHERINE Y, MOLECULAR BIOLOGY, IMMUNOLOGY. **Personal Data:** b Hong Kong, February 11, 1951. **Education:** Ind Univ, BS, 1972; Yale Univ, MPhil, 1974, PhD (biochem), 1976. **Honors & Awards:** Pharmaceut Res Inst Discovery Award. **Professional Experience:** EMPLOYEE, ORTHO BIOTECH DIV, JANSSEN-ORTHO INC, TORONTO, CAN, as of 2006; dir biol res, R W Johnson Pharmaceut res Inst, beginning 1989; mgr biotechnol res, Ortho Pharmaceut Ltd, Can, 1987-1988; proj mgr immunopharmacol, Ortho Pharmaceut Ltd, Can, 1985-1987; asst prof, Dept Immunol, Univ Toronto, 1984-; supvr immunopharmacol, Ortho Pharmaceut Ltd, Can, 1977-1984; res fel immunol, Ont Cancer Inst & Princess Margaret Hosp, Toronto, 1976-1977. **Memberships:** Sigma Xi; Am Asn Immunologists; Int Soc Immunopharmacol. **Research Statement & Publications:** Discover immunologically active molecules and develop them into human therapeutics. **Mailing Address:** Ortho Biotech Div, Janssen-Ortho Inc, Toronto, ON M3C 1L9, Can.

LAU, CHEUK KUN, LEUKOTRIENES, SYNTHETIC METHODS. **Personal Data:** b Hong Kong, September 3, 1951. **Education:** McMaster Univ, BSc, 1974; Univ BC, PhD (chem), 1978. **Honors & Awards:** Boris Monsaroff Mem Medal, Chem Inst Can, 1974. **Professional Experience:** SR INVESTR, MED CHEM, MERCK FROSST CTR THERAPEUT RES, as of 2003; SR RES CHEMIST MED CHEM, MERCK FROSST CAN INC, 1980-; res fel chem, Wayne State Univ, 1978-1980. **Memberships:** Am Chem Soc; Chem Inst Can. **Research Statement & Publications:** Synthesis of leukotrienes and its related products of the lipoxygenase enzymes and the design of inhibitors of this enzyme. **Mailing Address:** Ctr Therapeutic Res, Merck Frosst Can Ltd, 16711 Trans Canada Hwy, Kirkland, PQ H9H 3L1, Can. **Fax:** 514-428-4900. **E-Mail:** lau@merck.com

LAU, CLIFFORD JAMES, POLYURETHANES, POLYMER BLENDS. **Personal Data:** b Red Bank, NJ, April 9, 1955. **Education:** Northeastern Univ, MS, 1982; Ohio State Univ, BS, 1977, PhD (org chem), 1987. **Professional Experience:** GROUP LEADER, ADHESIVE & SEALANT LAB, BAYER INC, as of 1998; ASSOC SCIENTIST, BAYER INC, 1996-; assoc res scientist, Bayer Inc, 1992-1996; sr develop chemist, Miles Inc, 1987-1992; assoc scientist, Polaroid Corp, 1977-1982. **Memberships:** Am Chem Soc; Soc Plastics Engrs. **Research Statement & Publications:** Polymer blends, polyurethemers and organic chemistry; modification of thermoplastic polyurethanes, polycarbonates and mylores; development of polyurethane and polyurea materials for application in exterior automotive body panels. **Mailing Address:** 218 Thornwood Ct, Coraopolis, PA 15108. **Fax:** 519-339-7719. **E-Mail:** clifford.lau.b@bayer.com

LAU, FRANCIS YOU KING, MEDICINE. **Personal Data:** b Honolulu, Hawaii, January 5, 1924; m 1948, bernita M Anderson; c Gerald E, Ronald D, Carol A & Kathleen M. **Education:** Loma Linda Univ, MD, 1947. **Professional Experience:** CLIN PROF MED & RADIOL, SCH MED, UNIV SOUTHERN CALIF, 1979-; prof med, Loma Linda Univ, 1972-; prof, Univ Southern Calif, 1970-1979; chief cardiol, Adult Cardiovasc Catheterization Lab, Los Angeles Co-Univ Southern Calif Med Ctr, 1970-1979; mem attend staff & chief, Adult Cardiovasc Catheterization Lab, Los Angeles Co-Univ Southern Calif Med Ctr, 1965-1979; prof med, Univ Southern Calif, 1964-; asst prof, Sch Med, Univ Calif, San Francisco, 1959-1960; From clin instr to clin prof med, Loma Linda Univ, 1954-2002; fel coun clin cardiol, Am Heart Asn; consult, Vet Admin & Glendale Hosps. **Memberships:** Fel Am Col Cardiol; fel Am Col Physicians fel AMA; fel SCA and I. **Research Statement & Publications:** Cardiology; cardiac catheterization, arrhythmias and pacemakers; artificial heart-lung preparations; balloon valvuloplasty. **Mailing Address:** 1313 S Fann, Anaheim, CA 92804.

LAU, JARK CHONG, LASER APPLICATIONS. **Personal Data:** b Singapore, October 18, 1935; wid. **Education:** Calif Inst Technol, MS, 1963, AE, 1964; Univ Southampton, Eng, PhD (fluid mech), 1971. **Professional Experience:** AT, KIMBERLY-CLARK CORP, as of 2001; PRIN RES FEL, KIMBERLY-CLARK CORP, 1990-; sr res fel, Kimberly-clark Corp, 1980-1990; tech consult fluid & acoust, Lockheed-Ga Co, 1975-1980; assoc prof fluid & thermodyn, Univ Singapore, 1971-1975. **Memberships:** assoc fel Am Inst Aeronaut & Astronaut(chmn, 1999-2000). **Research Statement & Publications:** Characterize the structure of free shear turbulence; development of better techniques of forming fibrous webs; consultant service to many mills; development of a laser technology base. **Mailing Address:** Kimberly-Clark Corp, 1400 Holcomb Bridge Rd, Roswell, GA 30076. **Fax:** 770-587-8136. **E-Mail:** jlau@kcc.com

LAU, JOHN H, MECHANICAL ENGINEERING, ENGINEERING PHYSICS. **Personal Data:** b China, June 17, 1946; American citizen; m 1972, Teresa; c Judy M. **Education:** Nat Taiwan Univ, BE, 1970; Univ BC, MASc, 1973; Univ Wis-Madison, MS, 1974; Fairleigh Dickinson Univ, MS, 1981; Univ Ill-Urbana, PhD (theoret & appl mech), 1977. **Professional Experience:** SCIENTIST, AGILENT TECHNOLOGIES INC, as of 2005; sr engr electronics & mech eng, Hewlett Packard Labs, beginning 1984; mem tech staff stress analysis, Sandia Nat Labs, 1983-1984; sr engr nuclear eng, Bechtel Power Corp, 1981-1983; sr engr mech eng, Ebasco Serv Inc, 1979-1981; res assoc paper physics, Int Paper Co Res Ctr, 1978-1979; engr struct, Exxon Prod & Res Co, 1977-1978; teaching asst mech, Univ Ill-Urbana, 1974-1977; session chmn, tech comt mem & workshop speaker, Inst Elec & Electronics Engrs & Am Soc Mech Eng Tech Conf; assoc tech ed, Inst Elec & Electronics Engrs, Trans Components, Hybrids & Mfg Technol, Am Soc Mech Engrs, Trans J Electronic Packaging. **Memberships:** NY Acad Sci; AAAS; fel Inst Elec & Electronics Engrs; fel Am Soc Mech Engrs; Sigma Xi. **Research Statement & Publications:** Structural engineering; applied mechanics; nuclear engineering; operations research; materials science engineering; mechanical vibrations; electronics packaging and interconnection; published over 200 articles. **Mailing Address:** Agilent Technologies Inc, 395 Page Mill Rd, Palo Alto, CA 94303. **Fax:** 650-752-5633.

LAU, JOSEPH T Y, GLYCOBIOLOGY. **Personal Data:** b Hong Kong, March 21, 1953. **Education:** Univ Wash, Seattle, BS, 1975; Purdue Univ, PhD (biochem), 1981. **Professional Experience:** RES MEM, DEPT MOLECULAR BIOL & CELLULAR BIOL, ROSWELL PARK CANCER INST, BUFFALO, as of 2004; cancer res scientist IV, Roswell Park Cancer Inst, 1990-; asst res prof molecular biol, State Univ Ny, beginning 1986; cancer res scientist III, 1986-1990; res assoc, Johns Hopkins Sch Med, 1984-1985; fel molecular biol, Johns Hopkins Sch Med, 1981-1984. **Memberships:** Soc Complex Carbohydrates; Am Soc Biol Chemists; AAAS. **Research Statement & Publications:** Function and regulation of glycoconjugates; molecular biology of glycosyltransferases; expression of cellular differentiation epitopes. **Mailing Address:** Dept Cell & Molecular Biol, Roswell Park Cancer Inst, Elm & Carlton Sts, Buffalo, NY 14263. **Fax:** 716-845-5908. **E-Mail:** joseph.lau@roswellpark.org

LAU, KEI MAY, ELECTRICAL ENGINEERING. **Education:** Univ Minn, BS & MS; Rice Univ, PhD (Elec Eng), 1981. **Honors & Awards:** NSF Fac Award Women Scientists & Engrs. **Professional Experience:** CHAIR, DEPT ELEC & ELECTRONIC ENG, HONG KONG UNIV SCI & TECHNOL, 2005-; PROF, DEPT ELEC & ELECTRONIC ENG, HONG KONG UNIV SCI & TECHNOL, 2000-; vis prof, Dept Elec & Electronic Eng, Hong Kong Univ Sci & Technol, 1998; prof, Dept Elec & Electronic Eng, Univ Mass, beginning 1993; sr engr, M/A-COM Gallium Arsenide Prod Inc, 1980-1982. **Research Statement & Publications:** High frequency; high speed and photonic devices: light emitting diodes (LEDs); heterostructure field-effect and bipolar transistors (HFETs and HBTs); metalorganic chemical vapor deposition (MOCVD) of compound semiconductors including III-nitrides; III-As/P/Sb and dilute nitride alloys; nano-structures; selective-area heteroepitaxy; material and device characterization. **Mailing Address:** Dept Elec & Comput Eng, Hong Kong Univ Sci & Technol, Clear Water Bay, 01033, Hong Kong. **E-Mail:** eekmlau@ust.hk

LAU, KENNETH W, CHEMISTRY, FLUOROPOLYMERS. **Personal Data:** b Lamoure, NDak, November 27, 1941. **Education:** Univ NDak, BS, 1963, PhD (chem), 1969; Univ Sask, Regina, MSc, 1968. **Professional Experience:** MKT MGR, SPECIALITY POLYMERS DIV, E I DU PONT DEL NEMOURS & CO, INC, 1985-; mkt mgr, Fluoropolymers Div, 1979-1985; area supt-tech, Plastic Prod & Resins Dept, 1976-1979; develop supvr, Film Dept, Richmond, Va, 1973-1976; res chemist, E I Du Pont Del Nemours & Co, Inc, 1969-1973; Chemist, Rock Island Arsenal Lab, US Army, 1963-1964. **Memberships:** Am Chem Soc; Sigma Xi. **Research Statement & Publications:** Ylid chemistry. **Mailing Address:** 3 Briarwood Ct, Landenberg, PA 19350.

LAU, KIN-HING WILLIAM, BONE & MINERAL RESEARCH. **Personal Data:** b Hong Kong, China, July 4, 1953. **Education:** State Univ NY, Plattsburg, BA, 1976; Iowa State Univ, PhD (biochem), 1982. **Professional Experience:** ASSOC PROF ENZYMOL & KINETICS, LOMA LINDA UNIV, 1990-; asst prof enzymol & kinetics, Loma Linda Univ, 1984-1990; RES SCIENTIST, JERRY L PETTIS MEM VET ADMIN HOSP, 1982-; res fel, Loma Linda Univ, 1982-1984. **Memberships:** Am Soc Biochem & Molecular Biol; Am Soc Bone & Mineral Res; Am Soc Cell Biol; Endocrine Soc; Am Fedn Clin Res. **Research Statement & Publications:** Bone and mineral research. **Mailing Address:** Jerry L Pettis Mem Vet Admin Hosp, 11201 Benton St, Loma Linda, CA 92357-0001.

LAU, L(EUNG KU) STEPHEN, HYDROLOGY, HYDRAULIC & SANITARY ENGINEERING. **Personal Data:** b Shanghai, China, September 9, 1929; American citizen; m 1959, Virginia; c Ronald D, Kristina G (Tong) & Melina C (Doong). **Education:** Univ Calif, Berkeley, BS, 1953, MS, 1955, PhD (hydraul & sanit engr), 1959. **Honors & Awards:** George Warren Fuller Award, Am Waterworks Asn, 1989. **Professional Experience:** EMER PROF CIVIL ENGR, UNIV HAWAII, 1992-; UN, 1981; World Bank, 1978; adj res assoc, East-West Ctr, 1980-1981; consult, AMAX, 1978; consult, WHO, 1974; Fulbright vis prof, Univ Malaya, 1973-1974; consult, Univ Guam, 1972 & 1975; dir, Water Resources Res Ctr, 1971-1990; actg dir, Water Resources Res Ctr, 1970; vis assoc prof, Univ Calif, Berkeley, 1965-1966; assoc dir, Water Resources Res Ctr, 1964-1970; dir, USPHS training grant, Univ Hawaii, 1964-1965; Ground water consult, Honolulu Bd Water Supply, 1960-1964; from asst prof to prof, Univ Hawaii, 1959-1992; Res engr sea water intrusion, Univ Calif, Berkeley, 1953-1954; ground water pollution, 1955-1956. **Memberships:** Am Waterworks Asn; Am Geophys Union; Am Soc Civil Engrs; Water Environ Fedn; Nat Ground Water asn. **Research Statement & Publications:** Water reuse; groundwater; water pollution assessment; hydrologic evaluation of water resources; flood computations; water resources research administration; water resources policies; Hydrology and water resources of the Hawaiian Islands; hydrology instruction. **Mailing Address:** Water Resources Res Ctr, Univ Hawaii, Honolulu, HI 96822. **Fax:** 808-956-5044.

LAU, NGAR-CHEUNG, ATMOSPHERIC GENERAL CIRCULATION, ATMOSPHERIC VARIABILITY. **Personal Data:** b Hong Kong, July 21, 1953; American citizen; m 1979, Chih-Ping; c Michelle. **Education:** Chinese Univ, Hong Kong, BSc, 1974; Univ Wash, PhD (atmospheric sci), 1978. **Honors & Awards:** Clarence Leroy Meisinger Award, Am Meteorol Soc, 1990; Unusually Outstanding Performance Award, US Dept Com/Nat Oceanic & Atmospheric Admin, 1991; Hong Kong Observatory 120th Anniversary Distinguished Meteorologist, 2003. **Professional Experience:** Mem, International Science Program Committee, International Sympposium on the Winter Monsoon Experiment, 2006; mem, Advisory Panel, US Climate Variability Research Program, 2005-; mem, Scientific Advisory Board, NOAA Climate Test Bed, 2005-; vice chairman, International Committee, WMO Third International Workshop on Monsoon, 2004; mem, advisory academic committee, Institute of Atmospheric Physics, Chinese Academy of Sciences, 2001-; acting Dir., Geophysical Fluid Dynamics Lab, 2000-2001, 1990; ed, Advances in Atmospheric Sciences, 1999-; ed, World Scientific Series on Meterorology of East Asia, 1999-; Sci adv, Hong Kong Observ, 1996-; ed, J Atmospheric Sci, 1996- 2000; LEAD SCIENTIST, OBSERVATIONAL STUDIES PROJ, NAT OCEANIC & ATMOSPHERIC ADMIN, US DEPT COM, 1996-; C N Yang vis fel, Chinese Univ Hong Kong, 1993; SR RES METEOROLOGIST, GEOPHYS FLUID DYNAMICS LAB, PRINCETON UNIV, 1992-; vis lectr, Nat Res Coun, Taiwan, 1992; Int Reviewer, Nat Res Coun Taiwan, 1991-1994; mem, Comt Climate Variations, Am Meterol Soc, 1990-1993; vis scientist, Bur Meteorol Res Ctr, Melbourne, Australia, 1989; ed, Comt, Dynamics Atmospheres & Oceans, 1988-; US deleg, US/Japan Elnino-Southern Oscillation Workshop, 1987; US deleg, US/China Monsoon Workshop, 1987; Grad.Work Committee, Atmospheric and Oceanic Program, Princeton Univ, 1986-1989, 1995-1998, 2003-; mem, Coun Equatorial Pac Ocean Climate Studies, US Dept Com, 1985-1994; res meteorologist, Geophys Fluid Dynamics Prog, 1984-1992; lectr with rank assoc prof, prof, atmospheric & oceanic sci, Princeton Univ, 1982-; mem res staff, Geophys Fluid Dynamics Prog, 1981-1984; vis scientist, Geophys Fluid Dynamics Prog, 1978-1981; Asst atmospheric sci, Nat Ctr Atmospheric Res, 1976-1977; Res asst atmospheric sci, Univ Wash, 1974-1978. **Memberships:** Fel Am Meteorol Soc; World Meteorol Orgn; Am Geophys Union; Hong Kong Meteorol Soc. **Research Statement & Publications:** Diagnosis of large-scale circulation system in observed and model-simulated atmospheres; processing of meteorological data sets for studying nature and causes of atmospheric variability on different time scales; studying the influences of air-sea interaction on weather and climate. **Mailing Address:** Geophys Fluid Dynamics Lab, Nat Oceanic & Atmospheric Admin Princeton Univ PO Box 308, Princeton, NJ 08542. **Fax:** 609-987-5063. **E-Mail:** gabriel.lau@noaa.gov

LAU, PHILIP T S, ORGANIC CHEMISTRY, PHOTOGRAPHIC SCIENCE. **Personal Data:** b Kuala Lumpur, Malaysia, February 13, 1935; American citizen; m 1959, Harriet Y; c

Linda, Steven & David. **Education:** Alfred Univ, BS, 1958; Syracuse Univ, PhD (org chem), 1962. **Professional Experience:** Chmn, Eastman Kodak Res Coun, 1989-1991; RES FEL, COLOR PHOTOG DIV, RES LABS, EASTMAN KODAK CO, 1979-; res assoc, Color Photog Div, Res Labs, Eastman Kodak CO, 1968-1979; sr res chemist, Color Photog Div, Res Labs, Eastman Kodak CO, 1963-1968; Fel & res assoc chem, Univ Calif, Berkeley, 1962-1963; mem, Eastman Kodak distinguished inventors gallery; Lectr Photog Chem. **Memberships:** Am Chem Soc. **Research Statement & Publications:** New synthetic methodologies to novel heterocyclic and aromatic compounds; regioselective and regiospecific reactions, photographic developers, couplers, stabilizers, dyes, polymer synthesis and applications. **Mailing Address:** 345 St Andrews Dr, Rochester, NY 14626. **Fax:** 585-722-2327. **E-Mail:** plau@kodak.com

LAU, ROLAND, ORGANIC CHEMISTRY. **Personal Data:** b China, May 5, 1943. **Education:** Wayne State Univ, BA, 1965; Purdue Univ, PhD (chem), 1972. **Professional Experience:** MGR PHARMACEUT CHEM, HARDWICKE CHEM CO, SUBSID ETHYL CORP, 1980-; sr res investr, E R Squibb, Inc, 1977-1980; res investr org chem, E R Squibb, Inc, 1973-1977; fel, Syntex Res Div, Syntex Corp, 1972-1973; res chemist, Ash-Stevens, Inc, 1965-1966; Clin chemist, Henry Ford Hosp, 1965. **Memberships:** Am Chem Soc. **Research Statement & Publications:** Commercial developments of medicinal agents. **Mailing Address:** Interchem Corp, 120 Rte 17 N, Paramus, NJ 07652.

LAU, S S, ELECTRONICS ENGINEERING. **Personal Data:** b Chungking, China, July 31, 1941. **Education:** Univ Calif, Berkeley, BS, 1964, MS, 1966, PhD, 1969. **Professional Experience:** PROF MICROELECTRONICS, UNIV CALIF, SAN DIEGO, 1980-; mem staff, Calif Inst Technol, 1972-1980; mem staff, Bell Labs, 1969-1972. **Memberships:** Bohemian Phys Soc; Inst Elec & Electronics Engrs. **Research Statement & Publications:** Metal semiconductor interactions; ion-beam processes; Rutherford backscattering spectrometry; electronic materials. **Mailing Address:** Dept Elec Eng & Comput Sci, Univ Calif, 9500 Gilman Dr Mail Code 0407, La Jolla, CA 92093-0401. **Fax:** 858-534-0556. **E-Mail:** lau@ece.ucsd.edu

LAU, YIU-WA AUGUST, MATHEMATICS. **Personal Data:** b August 22, 1948. **Education:** Univ Houston, BS & MS, 1968, PhD (math), 1971. **Professional Experience:** SR RES SPECIALIST, EXXON PROD RES, 1985-; mem staff, Johnson Space Ctr, NASA, 1980-1981; From asst prof to assoc prof math, NTex State Univ, 1971-1980. **Memberships:** Am Math Soc. **Research Statement & Publications:** Topological semigroups; topology. **Mailing Address:** Exxon Explor Co, PO Box 4778, Houston, TX 77210-4778.

LAU, YUEN-SUM, PHARMACOLOGY, NEUROSCIENCE. **Personal Data:** b Shanghai, China, December 24, 1950. **Education:** Univ Hawaii, Honolulu, BS, 1973, MS, 1977, PhD (pharmacol), 1978. **Honors & Awards:** John Kane Res Award, Creighton Univ, 1985, Young Investr Award, 1986. **Professional Experience:** PROF & CHMN, DIV PHARMACOL, UNIV MO, KANSAS, as of 2003; prof & chmn, div pharmacol, Univ Wis, beginning 1994; prof, Creighton Univ Sch Med, 1990-1994; from asst prof to assoc prof neuropharmacol, Creighton Univ Sch Med, 1980-1990; fel pharmacol, Univ Mich, Ann Arbor, 1978-1980. **Memberships:** Chinese Bioscientists Am. **Research Statement & Publications:** Pharmacology; neuroscience. **Mailing Address:** Div Pharmacol, Univ Mo, Sch Pharm 2411 Holmes St, Kansas City, MO 64108. **E-Mail:** lauy@umkc.edu

LAU, YUE-YING, PHYSICS. **Education:** Mass Inst Technol, PhD (elec eng). **Honors & Awards:** Sigma-Xi. **Professional Experience:** PROF, DEPT NUCLEAR ENG & RADIOL SCI, UNIV MICH COL ENG, as of 2006. **Mailing Address:** Dept Nuclear Eng, Univ Mich, 2923 Cooley Bldg, Ann Arbor, MI 48109. **Fax:** 734-764-4540. **E-Mail:** yylau@umich.edu

LAUB, ALAN JOHN, SCIENTIFIC COMPUTATION, NUMERICAL ANALYSIS. **Personal Data:** b Edmonton, Alta, August 6, 1948. **Education:** Univ BC, BS, 1969; Univ Minn, MS, 1972, PhD (control sci), 1974. **Honors & Awards:** Control Systs Technol Award, Inst Elec & Electronics Engrs Control Systs Soc, 1993. **Professional Experience:** DIR, INST DIGITAL RES & EDUC, UNIV CALIF LOS ANGELES, as of 2006; dean, Col Eng, Univ Calif, Davis, 1996-2000; PROF, DEPT COMPUT SCI, UNIV CALIF, DAVIS, 1996-; pres, Control Systs Soc, 1991; dir, Am Automatic Control Coun, Inst Elec & Electronics Engrs, 1990-1991; chmn dept, Univ Calif, Santa Barbara, 1989-1992; Math Control, Signals & Systs, 1986- & Linear & Multilinear Algebra, 1987-1992; J Control & Optimization, Soc Idust & Appl Math, 1985-1989; prof, Univ Calif, Santa Barbara, 1983-1986; assoc ed, Int J Control, 1980-1987; assoc prof elec eng, Univ Southern Calif, 1979-1983; assoc ed, Inst Elec & Electronics Engrs Trans Automatic Control, 1979-1981; res scientist control eng, Lab Info & Decision Systs, Mass Inst Technol, 1977-1979; asst prof elec eng, Univ Toronto, 1975-1977; ast prof systs eng, Case Western Res Univ, 1974-1975. **Memberships:** Fel Inst Elec & Electronics Engrs; Soc Indust & Appl Math; Asn Comput Mach. **Research Statement & Publications:** Numerical analysis; mathematical software; scientific computation; computer-aided control system design; linear and large-scale control and filtering theory. **Mailing Address:** Dept Comput Sci, Univ Calif, One Shields Ave, Davis, CA 95616-8562. **Fax:** 530-752-4767. **E-Mail:** laub@ucdavis.edu

LAUB, BERNARD, AERONAUTICS. **Professional Experience:** STAFF AEROCAPTURE THERMAL PROTECTION, NASA AMES RES CTR, as of 2002. **Memberships:** Am Inst Aeronauts & Astronauts. **Mailing Address:** NASA Ames Res Ctr, Moffett Field, CA 94035. **Fax:** 650-604-1592. **E-Mail:** blaub@mail.arc.nasa.gov

LAUB, RICHARD STEVEN, PALEONTOLOGY, SEDIMENTOLOGY. **Personal Data:** b Brooklyn, NY, November 15, 1945. **Education:** Queen's Col, NY, BA, 1966; Cornell Univ, MS, 1968; Univ Cincinnati, PhD (paleont), 1976. **Professional Experience:** Mem, Distinguished Lectureship Comt, Buffalo Soc Natural Sci, 1978-; adj fac geol, State Univ NY Buffalo, beginning 1977; corresp, Fossil Cnidaria Newsletter, beginning 1976; adj fac, Empire State Col, 1976-1978; Supvr, Morse Creek Fossil Salvage Proj, 1976; CUR GEOL, BUFFALO MUS SCI, 1973-. **Memberships:** Paleont Soc; Paleont Asn; Am Asn Petrol Geologists; Sigma Xi; Paleont Res Inst. **Research Statement & Publications:** Early Paleozoic corals, their systematics, morphology, ecology and distribution; axial torsion in rugose corals; systematics and biology of auloporid tabulate corals. **Mailing Address:** Dept Geol, Buffalo Mus Sci, 1020 Humbolt Pkwy, Buffalo, NY 14211. **Fax:** 716-897-6723. **E-Mail:** rlaub@sciencebuff.org

LAUBACH, GERALD D, PHARMACEUTICAL CHEMISTRY. **Personal Data:** b Bethlehem, Pa, January 21, 1926. **Education:** Univ Pa, AB, 1947; Mass Inst Technol, PhD (chem), 1950. **Honorary Degrees:** Mt Sinai Sch Med, City Univ New York, DHLett, 1988; DL, Conn Col, 1986; Hofstra Univ, DSc, 1979. **Honors & Awards:** Int Palladium Medal, Am Sect, Soc Indust Chem, France, 1985. **Professional Experience:** RETIRED; pres, Pfizer, Inc, 1972-1991; exec vpres, Pfizer Pharmaceut, 1971; pres, Pfizer Pharmaceut, 1969-1971; vpres, Med Prods Res, 1964; group dir med res, Dept Med Chem, 1963; dir, Dept Med Chem, 1961; mgr, Med Prods Res, 1958-1961; Lab scientist, Pfizer Inc, 1950-1958; Ensign, USNR, 1944-1946. **Memberships:** Nat Acad Eng; Inst Med-Nat Acad Sci; NY Acad Sci; hon fel Am Inst Chemists; AAAS; Soc Chem Indust; Am Chem Soc; Am Mgt Asn. **Research Statement & Publications:** Industrial chemistry; corporate competition; pharmaceutical manufacturing. **Mailing Address:** 50 E 89th St, New York, NY 10128.

LAUBER, JOHN K, HUMAN RELATIONS. **Personal Data:** b Archbold, Ohio, December 13, 1942. **Education:** Ohio State Univ, BS, 1965, MS, 1967, PhD (neuropsychol), 1969. **Honors & Awards:** R F Longacre Award, Aerospace Med Asn, 1990; Joseph T Nall Mem Award, Nat Air Traffic Controllers Asn, 1992; Paul T Hansen Lectr, 1993; Forrest & Dominique Bird Award, Civil Aviation Med Asn, 1994. **Professional Experience:** VPRES SAFETY & TECH AFFAIRS, AIRBUS INDUST, N AM, as of 2004; mem, Res Eng & Develop Adv Comt, Fed Aviation Admin, 1995-; vpres corp safety & compliance, Delta Air Lines, Atlanta, beginning 1995; mem aeronaut adv comt, NASA, 1987; mem, Nat Transp Safety Bd, Wash, 1985-1995; chief aeronaut human factors off, NASA Ames Res Ctr, Moffett Field, 1973-1985; res psychologist, US Naval Training Equip Ctr, 1969-1973. **Memberships:** Fel Aerospace Med Asn; Human Factors Soc. **Research Statement & Publications:** Published numerous articles; safety and compliance. **Mailing Address:** Dept 025 Delta Air Lines, Hartsfield Int Airport, Atlanta, GA 30320.

LAUBER, THORNTON STUART, ELECTRIC POWER ENGINEERING. **Personal Data:** b Cornwall, Ont, January 5, 1924. **Education:** Cornell Univ, BSEE, 1944; Ill Inst Technol, MSEE, 1951; Univ Pa, PhD (elec eng), 1964. **Professional Experience:** Mem, Int Conf Large High Voltage Elec Systs, 1972; S B CRARY PROF ENG, RENSSELAER POLYTECH INST, 1970-; PROF ELEC POWER ENG, RENSSELAER POLYTECH INST, 1969-; sr analytical engr, Power Circuit Breaker Dept, 1958-1969; develop engr, Large Power Transformer Dept, Gen Elec Co, 1951-1958; Engr, Commonwealth Serv, Inc, Mich, 1946-1950; comt mem, Am Nat Stand Inst; Consult, Gen Elec Co & Hydro-Quebec. **Memberships:** Sr mem Inst Elec & Electronics Engrs; Am Soc Mech Engrs; Sigma Xi. **Research Statement & Publications:** Electric power engineering; power system transients; electromagnetic field theory. **Mailing Address:** 1005 Seminole Rd, Scotia, NY 12302.

LAU-CAM, CESAR A, Pharmacology, Toxicology & Analytical Chemistry. **Personal Data:** b Lima, Peru, November 24, 1940; American citizen; m 1967, Aurora; c Cesar Jr & David. **Education:** San Marcos Univ, Lima, BS, 1963; Univ RI, MS, 1967, PhD (pharmacog), 1969. **Professional Experience:** Instr-consult, Harlem Med Ctr, NY, 1989-1996; Prof pharmaceut sci, Dept Pharmaceut Sci, Col Pharm & Allied Health Professions, St John's Univ, NY, 1980-present; Sci adv, US Food & Drug Admin, 1979-1988; from asst prof to assoc phytochem, Dept Pharmaceut Sci, Col Pharm & Allied Health Professions, St John's Univ, NY, 1969-1980; Lab instr pharmacog, Univ RI, 1967; Instr pharm bot, San Marcos Univ, Lima, 1962-1963. **Memberships:** AAAS; Am Soc Pharmacog; Am Pharmaceut Asn; NY Acad Sci; Amer Assoc Pharmaceut Sci; Am Assoc Clin Chem. **Research Statement & Publications:** Analytical methods applied to natural products; clinical chemistry; pharmacology and toxicology of natural products; pharmacology and toxicology of alcohol; pharmaceutical drug analysis; biochemical and pharmacological aspects of taurine and taurine-related compounds; delivery of drugs and natural products using lipid-based formulations; nasal, transdermal and rectal drug delivery. **Mailing Address:** Dept Pharmaceut Sci, Col Pharm, St John's Univ, 8000 Utopia Pkwy, Jamaica, NY 11439. **Fax:** 718-990-5763. **E-Mail:** claucam@usa.net

LAUCHLE, GERALD CLYDE, ACOUSTICS, NOISE CONTROL ENGINEERING. **Personal Data:** b Williamsport, Pa, September 20, 1945; American citizen; m 1996, Esther; c Keith A & Paul M. **Education:** Pa State Univ, BS, 1968, MS, 1970, PhD (engr acoust), 1974. **Honors & Awards:** Martin Hirschorn IAC Award for Noise Control, Inst Noise Control Engr of USA, 2002; President of Inst Noise Control Engr of USA, 2005. **Professional Experience:** PROF ACOUST, PA STATE UNIV, 1990-; sr scientist, Appl Res Lab, PA State Univ, 1985-1990; from res asst to sr res assoc, Appl Res Lab, PA State Univ, 1968-1985. **Memberships:** Fel (1993) Acoust Soc Am; Board Certified(1984) Inst Noise Control Engr. **Research Statement & Publications:** Noise generated by fluid flow; general acoustics; acoustic noise control; acoustic sensors. **Mailing Address:** Penn State U Grad Prog in Acoust, 218 B Applied Sci Bldg, Univ Park, PA 16802. **Fax:** 814-865-7595. **E-Mail:** gcl1@psu.edu

LAUCK, DAVID R, ENTOMOLOGY. **Personal Data:** b Alton, Ill, June 6, 1930. **Education:** Univ Ill, BS, 1955, MS, 1958, PhD (entom), 1961. **Professional Experience:** PROF EMER ZOOL, HUMBOLDT STATE UNIV, 1986-; chmn, Div Biol Sci, 1966-1972; from asst prof to prof zool, Humboldt State Univ, 1961-1986; cur invert entom, Chicago Acad Sci, 1959-1961. **Memberships:** Entom Soc Am; Entom Soc Can. **Research Statement & Publications:** Aquatic and forest entomology. **Mailing Address:** Dept Biol Sci, Humboldt State Univ, 1 Harpst St, Arcata, CA 95521. **Fax:** 707-826-3201.

LAUD, PURUSHOTTAM WAMAN, MATHEMATICAL STATISTICS, APPLIED PROBABILITY. **Personal Data:** b Bombay, India, November 25, 1948. **Education:** Bombay Univ, BSc, 1969; Lamar Univ, MS, 1971; Univ Mo-Columbia, MA, 1973, PhD (statist), 1977. **Professional Experience:** PROF, DIV BIOSTATISTICS, MED COL, WIS, 1994-; asst prof math, Northern Ill Univ, beginning 1980; asst prof statist, Northern Ill Univ, 1977-1980. **Memberships:** Inst Math Statist. **Research Statement & Publications:** Bayesian nonparametric inference; reliability theory; stochastic processes. **Mailing Address:** Dept Biostatistics, Med Col Wis, 8701 Watertown Plank Rd, Milwaukee, WI 53226. **E-Mail:** laud@mcw.edu

LAUDANO, ANDREW P, BIOCHEMISTRY. **Education:** Univ Calif, San Diego, PhD, 1981. **Professional Experience:** ASSOC PROF, DEPT BIOCHEM & MOLECULAR BIOL, UNIV NH, as of 2006. **Mailing Address:** Dept Biochem & Molecular Biol Univ NH, Rudman Hall 46 Col Rd, Durham, NH 03824. **E-Mail:** alaudano@cisunix.unh.edu

LAUDE, HORTON MEYER, agronomy, botany; deceased, see previous edition for last biography

LAUDENSLAGER, JAMES BISHOP, CHEMICAL PHYSICS. **Personal Data:** b Harrisburg, Pa, June 8, 1945. **Education:** Temple Univ, AB, 1967; Univ Calif, Santa Barbara, PhD (phys chem), 1971. **Professional Experience:** VPRES, LASER SYSTS & ADVAN INT SYSTS, IRVINE, CALIF, 1986-; sr res sci chem physics, Jet Propulsion Lab, 1973-1986; Res assoc space sci, Jet Propulsion Lab, 1971-1973. **Memberships:** Am Phys Soc; Optical Soc Am; Soc Photoelectronics & Optics. **Research Statement & Publications:** Fundamental properties of charge transfer and metastable rare gas reactions in the gas phase for use in laser development and mass spectrometry. **Mailing Address:** 230 Granada Ave, Long Beach, CA 90803.

LAUDENSLAGER, MARK LEROY, PSYCHONEUROIMMUNOLOGY, PHYSIOLOGICAL PSYCHOLOGY. **Personal Data:** b Charlotte, NC, May 13, 1947. **Education:** Univ NC, AB, 1969; Univ Calif, Santa Barbara, PhD (psychol), 1975. **Professional Experience:** ASSOC PROF PSYCHIAT, HEALTH SCI CTR, UNIV COLO, 1991-; Counr, Psychoneurolimmunol Res Soc, 1993-; dir, Behav Immunol Lab, beginning 1986; asst prof, Denver Univ, 1986-1990; asst clin prof, Denver Univ, 1984-1986; ASST RESEARCHER,

DENVER UNIV, 1983-; lectr, Denver Univ, 1981-1983; asst res psychologist, Univ Calif, Santa Barbara, 1977-1980; NIMH fel, Scripps Inst Oceanog, 1975-1977; lectr, Univ Calif, Santa Barbara, 1974; teaching asst physiol psychol, Univ Calif, Santa Barbara, 1973; res asst neuropsychol, Univ Calif, Santa Barbara, 1971-1972; teaching asst introductory psychol, Univ Calif, Santa Barbara, 1970-1971; numerous NIMH & other res grants. **Memberships:** Int Soc Develop Psychobiol; AAAS; Am Physiol Soc; Soc Neuroscience; Psychoneuroimmunol Res Soc (Sec 2001-2003). **Research Statement & Publications:** effects of stress and affective disorders on immunocompetence and health, role of emotions, social support and temperament on health. **Mailing Address:** Dept Psychiat, Univ Colo Health Sci Ctr, 4455 E 12th Ave, Box A011-09, Denver, CO 80220-3706. **Fax:** 303-315-9570. **E-Mail:** mark.laudenslager@uchsc.edu

LAUDER, JEAN MILES, CELL BIOLOGY, ANATOMY. **Personal Data:** b Haverhill, Mass, June 29, 1945. **Education:** Univ Maine, Orono, BA, 1967; Purdue Univ, PhD (biol sci), 1972. **Professional Experience:** Chair, 1987-1989 & vchair, Gordon Conf Neural Develop, 1989; chmn, 1987-1989 & vchair, Gordon Conf Neural Develop, 1987; PROF, DEPT CELL BIOL & ANAT, SCH MED, UNIV NC, CHAPEL HILL, 1985-; vchmn, Gordon Res Conf Cent Nervous Syst-Neural Develop, 1985-1987; dir, Prog Develop Neuroscience, Div Behav & Neural Sci, NSF, 1984-1985; Mem bd dirs & asst treas, Inst Develop Neuroscience & Aging, 1983-; assoc prof, Dept Anat, 1978-1985; asst prof-in-residence, Dept Behav Sci, 1976-1978; res assoc, Lab Neuromorphol, Dept Behav Sci, Univ Conn, Storrs 1974-1975; NIMH staff fel, Lab Neuropharmacol, St Elizabeth's Hosp, Wash, DC, 1972-1974. **Memberships:** Soc Neurosci; Women Neurosci; Int Soc Develop Neurosci (pres-elect 1986-1988 pres 1988-1990); AAAS; Am Asn Anatomists; Am Soc Cell Biol; Int Soc Psychoneuroendocrinol; Sigma Xi; Int Brain Res Orgn; NY Acad Sci. **Mailing Address:** Dept Cell Biol & Anat, Sch Med, Univ NC, CB# 7090, 344 Taylor Hall, Chapel Hill, NC 27599-7090. **E-Mail:** unclau@med.unc.edu

LAUDERDALE, JAMES W, REPRODUCTIVE PHYSIOLOGY, ENDOCRINOLOGY. **Personal Data:** b Washington, DC, December 21, 1937. **Education:** Auburn Univ, BS, 1962; Univ Wis, MS, 1964, PhD (reproductive physiol, endocrinol), 1968. **Honors & Awards:** Animal Physiol & Endocrinol Award, Am Soc Animal Sci, 1986. **Professional Experience:** CONSULT, PHARMACIA & UPJOHN CO, as of 2000; res scientist & res dir, Upjohn Co, as of 2000; scientist, Upjohn Co, beginning 1967. **Memberships:** Am Soc Animal Sci; Soc Study Reproduction. **Research Statement & Publications:** Reproductive, growth and endocrinological function of large animals. **Mailing Address:** 16700 E D Ave, Augusta, MI 49012.

LAUDON, THOMAS S, SEDIMENTARY PETROLOGY, GRAVITY. **Personal Data:** b Sac City, Iowa, June 14, 1932. **Education:** Univ Wis, BSc, 1955, MSc, 1957, PhD (geol), 1963. **Professional Experience:** PROF EMER GEOL, UNIV WIS-OSHKOSH, as of 2005; NSF res grants, 1984-1985; consult geol & geophys, 1979-; Nat Acad Sci res grants, 1971-1972; NSF res grants, 1970-1971; Chmn dept geol, Univ Wis-oshkosh, 1969-1972; prof geol, Univ Wis-oshkosh, 1963-1997; NSF res grants, 1962-1967. **Memberships:** Sigma Xi; Geol Soc Am; Am Asn Petrol Geologists; Am Geophys Union; Nat Asn Geol Teachers. **Research Statement & Publications:** Geologic exploration of Antarctica; gravity, tectonics and sedimentation in modern and ancient mobile belts. **Mailing Address:** Dept Geol, Univ Wis, 800 Algoma Blvd, Oshkosh, WI 54901. **E-Mail:** laudon@uwosh.edu

LAUENROTH, WILLIAM KARL, PLANT ECOLOGY. **Personal Data:** b Carthage, Mo, July 31, 1945. **Education:** Humboldt State Col, BS, 1968; NDak State Univ, MS, 1970; Colo State Univ, PhD (plant ecol), 1973. **Honors & Awards:** Outstanding Achievement Award, Soc Range Mgt, 1989. **Professional Experience:** PROF, DEPT RANGE SCI, COLO STATE UNIV, 1987-; assoc prof, Dept Range sci, Colo State Univ, 1981-1987; res ecologist, Natural Resource Ecology Laboratory, Colo State Univ, 1973-1981. **Memberships:** Ecol Soc Am; Soc Range Mgt; Bot Soc Am; AAAS; Int Soc Ecol Modelling. **Research Statement & Publications:** Primary production and water relations of native plant communities, particularly temperate grasslands; ecosystem analysis of natural and agricultural ecosystems including simulation modelling. **Mailing Address:** Dept Range Sci, Colo State Univ, Ft Collins, CO 80523-0001. **Fax:** 970-491-2156. **E-Mail:** billl@cnr.colostate.edu

LAUER, B(YRON) E(LMER), SCIENCE EDUCATION, CHEMICAL ENGINEERING. **Personal Data:** b Glencoe, Okla, April 14, 1907. **Education:** Ore State Univ, BS, 1927; Univ Minn, MS, 1929, PhD (chem eng), 1931. **Professional Experience:** RETIRED; Jet Propulsion Lab, 1983-1984; Western Interstate Comn Higher Educ, 1982-1988; PROF EMER CHEM ENG, UNIV COLO, BOULDER, 1975-; ed, Televised Higher Educ, Assoc Western Univs, Inc, 1975-1982; consult, Interam Transp, 1968-1971; consult, PEC Corp, 1964-1965; consult, Nat Bur Stand, 1961-1964; head dept, Univ Colo, Boulder, 1947-1961; prof, Univ Colo, Boulder, 1946-1975; from asst prof to prof chem eng, NC State Univ, 1935-1942; res chem engr, Northern Paper Mills, 1931-1934; Crown-Zellerbach Corp, 1934-1935; asst instr, Univ Minn, 1927-1931. **Memberships:** Am Chem Soc; Am Soc Eng Educ; Tech Asn Pulp & Paper Indust; Am Inst Chem Engrs. **Research Statement & Publications:** Pulp and paper; testing methods; heat transfer; oil shale retorting; information storage and retrieval. **Mailing Address:** Dept Chem & Biol Eng, Univ Colo, PO Box 424, Boulder, CO 80309-0424.

LAUER, DAVID ALLAN, SOIL SCIENCE, AGRONOMY. **Personal Data:** b Creston, Iowa, September 25, 1944. **Education:** Iowa State Univ, BS, 1966; Colo State Univ, MS, 1969, PhD (soil sci), 1971. **Professional Experience:** RES SOIL SCIENTIST, AGR RES, USDA, 1976-; asst prof, Univ Ga, 1975-1976; Res assoc agron, Cornell Univ, 1971-1975. **Memberships:** Am Soc Agron; Crop Sci Soc; Soil Sci Soc; AAAS; Sigma Xi. **Research Statement & Publications:** Application of soil chemical and plant physiological principles to management of crop production systems with emphasis on plant nutrition. **Mailing Address:** 605 Lincoln Ct, Prosser, WA 99350.

LAUER, EUGENE JOHN, PLASMA PHYSICS. **Personal Data:** b Red Bluff, Calif, April 11, 1920. **Education:** Univ Calif, BS, 1942, PhD (physics), 1951. **Professional Experience:** PHYSICIST, LAWRENCE LIVERMORE LAB, UNIV CALIF, 1951-; asst physics, Univ Calf, 1946-1951. **Memberships:** Am Phys Soc. **Research Statement & Publications:** Discharge through gases; particle accelerator design; nuclear and plasma physics; controlled thermonuclear energy; relativistic beams. **Mailing Address:** Lawrence Livermore Nat Lab, 7000 E Ave, 431/2079 L-535, Livermore, CA 94550-9234. **Fax:** 925-424-5449. **E-Mail:** lauer1@llnl.gov

LAUER, FLORIAN ISIDORE, HORTICULTURE. **Personal Data:** b Richmond, Minn, September 13, 1928. **Education:** Univ Minn, BS, 1951, PhD, 1957. **Honors & Awards:** Potato Research of Yr, 1991. **Professional Experience:** RETIRED; prof potato breeding, Univ Minn, St Paul, beginning 1966; from asst prof to assoc prof, Univ Minn, St Paul, 1959-1966. **Memberships:** Am Soc Hort Sci; hon mem, Potato Asn Am. **Research Statement & Publications:** Potato breeding and genetics. **Mailing Address:** 1736 Tatum St, St Paul, MN 55113. **Fax:** 612-624-4914.

LAUER, GEORGE, PHYSICAL CHEMISTRY. **Personal Data:** b Vienna, Austria, February 18, 1936; wid. **Education:** Univ Calif, Los Angeles, BS, 1961; Calif Inst Technol, PhD (chem), 1967. **Professional Experience:** SR CONSULT, ATLANTIC RICHFIELD INC, 1988-; pres, EMSI Inc, 1981-1988; dir, Environ Monitoring & Serv Ctr, Rockwell Int Sci Ctr, 1978-1984; mgr environ res & technol, Measurement Sci, 1976-1978; dir air qual monitoring res, Measurement Sci, 1972-1975; group leader, Measurement Sci, 1971-1972; mem tech staff, Sci Ctr, NAm Rockwell Corp, 1966-1971; staff assoc, Sci Ctr, NAm Rockwell Corp, 1962-1966. **Memberships:** AAAS; Am Chem Soc; Air & Waste Mgt Asn; Am Meteorol Soc. **Research Statement & Publications:** Development of chronocoulometric techniques in electrochemistry; study of electroactive adsorbed species at electrodes; development of computer controlled instrumentation; instrumental methods in air pollution monitoring; air quality simulation modeling; environmental assessment. **Mailing Address:** 4449 Park Arroyo, Calabasas, CA 91302. **Fax:** 213-486-2021. **E-Mail:** glauer@is.arco.com

LAUER, GERALD J, AQUATIC ECOLOGY, LIMNOLOGY. **Personal Data:** b Montgomery City, Mo, October 18, 1934. **Education:** Quincy Col, BS, 1956; Univ Wash, MS, 1959, PhD (zool), 1963. **Professional Experience:** SR SCIENTIST & VPRES, EA SCI & TECHNOL, 1975-; Adj assoc prof biol, NY Univ, 1970-; asst dir, Lab Environ Studies, Med Ctr, NY Univ, 1969-1975; assoc cur, Limnol Dept, Acad Natural Sci, Philadelphia, 1967-1969; leader, Fisheries Coop Unit & assoc prof fisheries & limnol res, Ohio State Univ, 1966-1967; chief, Training Br, 1966; prin biologist, Southeast Water Lab, 1963-1966; staff biologist, USPHS, 1960-1962; teacher high sch, Mo, 1959-1960; asst, Univ Wash, 1956-1959; Lab aide limnol, Quincy Col, 1954-1956. **Memberships:** AAAS; Am Soc Limnol & Oceanog; Am Fisheries Soc; Am Littoral Soc; Ecol Soc Am. **Research Statement & Publications:** Population dynamics and community diversity of aquatic organisms; effects of pollutants and other environmental stresses on aquatic life. **Mailing Address:** Monroe, NY 10950.

LAUER, JAMES LOTHAR, MATERIALS SCIENCE, SPECTROSCOPY. **Personal Data:** b Vienna, Austria, August 2, 1920. **Education:** Temple Univ, AB, 1942, MA, 1944; Univ Pa, PhD (physics), 1948. **Honors & Awards:** Innovative Res Award, Soc Mech Engrs. **Professional Experience:** Vis scholar, Ctr Magnetic Rec Res, 1995-; EMER PROF MECH ENG, RENSSELAER POLYTECH INST, 1993-; sr res scientist, Ctr Magnetic Rec Res, 1993-1995; researcher, Surface Sci & Tribology Br, NASA-Lewis Res Ctr, Cleveland, Ohio, 1993-1995; NSF res grant, 1987- & US Army Res Off, 1986-; dir, Inst Wear Control & Tribology, 1985-1993; lectr friction & lubrication, Gordon Res Conf, 1982; prof, Rensselaer Polytech Inst, 1978-1993; prin investr, Off Naval Res, 1978-1985; lectr, Coblentz, 1978; prin investr, Air Force Off Sci Res & NASA-Lewis Res Ctr, 1973-1985; fel aerospace eng, Univ Calif, San Diego, 1964-1965; res scientist, Sun Oil Co, 1962-1977; res assoc, Sun Oil Co, 1958-1962; sr physicist, Sun Oil Co, 1954-1958; Lectr, Univ Del, 1952-1956; asst prof, Univ Pa, 1952-1954; res physicist, Sun Oil Co, 1947-1954; phys chemist, Sun Oil Co, 1944-1945; Asst instr org chem, Temple Univ, 1942-1944. **Memberships:** Am Chem Soc; Am Phys Soc; Soc Appl Spectros; Optical Soc Am; Mat Res Soc. **Research Statement & Publications:** Fourier spectroscopy; Raman and infrared spectroscopy; refraction and dispersion; theory of molecular structure; mathematical physics; x-ray spectra of polymers; combustion; shock waves in gases; adsorption and desorption; applications of molecular, mainly infrared emission, spectroscopy to problems of lubrication and tribology; optical methods of non-contacting surface analysis; electrostatics; boundary lubrication, studied by modern methods of surface analysis and applied to machinery at high operating temperatures. **Mailing Address:** 7622 Palmilla Dr No 78, San Diego, CA 92122. **Fax:** 619-458-1786.

LAUERMAN, LLOYD HERMAN, VETERINARY MICROBIOLOGY, VETERINARY IMMUNOLOGY. **Personal Data:** b Everett, Wash, February 5, 1933. **Education:** Wash State Univ, BA, 1956, DVM, 1958; Univ Wis, MS, 1959, PhD, 1968; Am Col Vet Microbiol, dipl, 1974. **Professional Experience:** ADJ PROF, VET DIAG LAB, AUBURN UNIV, as of 2004; affil prof pathobiology, Auburn Univ, 1981-; VET, DIAG LAB, MICRO SECT, STATE ALA, 1981-; vis assoc prof microbiol, Sch Dent, Univ Colo, Denver, 1974-1975; head bact sect, Diag Lab, Dept Path, 1973-1981; assoc prof, Colo State Univ, 1972-1981; Colo State Univ-AID prof microbiol, Univ Nairobi, 1968-1972; res dir vet biol, Biol Specialties Corp, 1963-1968; proj asst, Univ Wis, 1960-1963; res asst vet med, Univ Wis, 1958-1960. **Memberships:** Am Soc Microbiologists; Am Asn Vet Lab Diagnosticians; Am Vet Med Asn; US Am Health Asn; Am Asn Avian Pathologists. **Research Statement & Publications:** Diagnosis and prevention of infectious diseases of animals; research and development of laboratory diagnostic techniques and animal vaccines; biotechnology. **Mailing Address:** Vet Diag Lab, Auburn Univ, PO Box 2209, Auburn, AL 36831-2209. **Fax:** 334-826-3592. **E-Mail:** lanerll@vetmed.auburn.edu

LAUF, PETER KURT, PHYSIOLOGY, IMMUNOLOGY. **Personal Data:** b Wuerzburg, Ger, September 25, 1933; American citizen; m Norma; c Cornelia, Bettina & Adrian. **Education:** Univ Freiburg, MD, 1960. **Professional Experience:** PROF PHYSIOL & BIOPHYS & CHMN, SCH MED, WRIGHT STATE UNIV, DAYTON, OHIO, 1985-; NIH res career develop award, 1971-1975; asst prof immunol, Duke Univ Med Ctr, 1970-1980; from asst prof to prof physiol, Duke Univ Med Ctr, 1968-1985; asst prof biochem, Wayne State Univ, 1966-1967; res assoc biochem, Child Res Ctr Mich, Detroit, 1965-1967; res assoc path, Inst Path, Univ Marburg, Ger, 1964; res fel biochem, Max Planck Inst Immunobiol, Freiburg, 1962-1964; Res assoc path, Inst Path, Univ Freiburg, 1960-1962. **Memberships:** Soc Gen Physiol; Am Soc Hemat; Biophys Soc; Am Soc Physiol; Am Physiological Soc. **Research Statement & Publications:** Membrane physiology; modulation of membrane transport processes of active and passive cation by immunological reactions in red blood cells; isolation and identification of membrane transport proteins and functionally associated surface antigens; regulation and molecular mechanism of electroneutral potassium-chloride contransport in erythrocytes and epithelial cells. **Mailing Address:** Dept Pathology, Wright State Univ Sch Med, Dayton, OH 45435. **Fax:** 937-775-2759. **E-Mail:** peter.lauf@wright.edu

LAUFER, ALLAN HENRY, PHOTOCHEMISTRY, CHEMICAL KINETICS. **Personal Data:** b New York, NY, March 27, 1936; m 1959, Sondra; c Terri M & Andrea J. **Education:** NY Univ, BA, 1956; Lehigh Univ, MS, 1958, PhD (phys chem), 1962. **Professional Experience:** RETIRED; br chief, Fundamental Interactions Br, US Dept Energy, beginning 1986; chemist & prog mgr, Chem Sci Div, Off Basic Energy Sci, 1983-1986; res chemist, Nat Bur Stand, 1964-1983; res chemist, Gulf Res & Develop Co, 1962-1964. **Memberships:** AAAS; Am Chem Soc; Am Phys Soc; Sigma Xi; Inter-Am Photochem Soc. **Research Statement & Publications:** Vacuum ultraviolet photochemistry; gas phase radical reactions and kinetics; chemistry of excited states. **Mailing Address:** 5106 Russett Rd, Rockville, MD 20853.

LAUFER, DANIEL A, ORGANIC CHEMISTRY. **Personal Data:** b Affula, Israel, May 30, 1938. **Education:** Mass Inst Technol, BS, 1959; Brandeis Univ, PhD (org chem), 1964. **Professional Experience:** RETIRED; prof chem, Univ Mass, Boston, 1980-2002; res grant, 1967-1970, 1972-1974 & 1979-1984; from asst prof to assoc prof, Univ Mass, Boston, 1966-1980; NIH trainee, 1965-1966; res fel biol chem, Harvard Med Sch, 1964-1966; res assoc org chem, Columbia Univ, 1963-1964. **Memberships:** Am Chem Soc; AAAS. **Research Statement & Publications:** Peptide synthesis; new reagents for organic synthesis macrocyclic complexations analytic applications of NMR. **Mailing Address:** Dept Chem, Univ Mass, 100 Morrissey Blvd, Boston, MA 02125-3393. **E-Mail:** daniel.laufer@umb.edu

LAUFER, HANS, BIOTECHOLOGY & ENDOCRINOLOGY, MOLECULAR BIOLOGY & CELL BIOLOGY. **Personal Data:** b Ger, October 18, 1929; m 1953, Evelyn; c Jessica, Marc & Leonard. **Education:** City Col NY, BS, 1952; Brooklyn Col, MA, 1954; Cornell Univ, PhD (zoology), 1958. **Honors & Awards:** Sr Res Serv Award Harvard Univ, 1989. **Professional Experience:** Dozer fel & vis prof, Ben Gurion Univ, 1997; vis prof, Harvard Univ, 1988-1989; chmn, Div Develop Biol, Am Soc Zoologists, 1981-1982; vis prof, Karolinska Inst, Stockholm, 1972 & Yale Univ, 1980; mem exec comt, Corp Marine Biol Lab, 1979-1980; trustee, Corp Marine Biol Lab, 1978-1982; partic, Nat Acad Sci-Czech Acad Sci Exchange Prog, 1974 & 1977; NATO fel rev panel, NSF, 1974 & 1976; PROF BIOL, UNIV CONN, 1972-; mem nat bd on grad educ, Conf Bd Assoc Res Couns, 1971-1975; assoc ed, J Exp Zool, 1969-1973, 1989-; staff embryol course, Marine Biol Lab, Woods Hole, Mass, 1967-1972; assoc prof biol, Univ Conn, 1965-1972; mem, Corp Marine Biol Lab, 1962-; Lalor fel, Marine Biol Lab, Woods Hole, Mass, 1962-1963; Vis scholar, Case Western Res Univ, 1962; asst prof biol, Johns Hopkins Univ, 1959-1965; asst, Cornell Univ, 1955-1957. **Memberships:** Soc for int step comparative biol (council mem, 1979-1982); Soc Develop Biol; Am Soc Cell Biol; Tissue Cult Asn; fel AAAS; (chair sectn biol) internat soc develop biologists; European soc corp; fel of the royal entom; soc of London connecticut acad of sci & eng. **Research Statement & Publications:** Developmental physiology and biochemistry; molecular interactions in development; proteins and enzymes in ontogeny, regeneration and metamorphosis; chromosomal puffing in Diptera; gene action as related to development; hormone action during invertebrate development and reproduction. **Mailing Address:** Dept Molecular & Cell Biol, Univ Conn, U- 3 125 75 N Eagleville Rd, Storrs, CT 06269-3125. **Fax:** 860-486-4331. **E-Mail:** laufer@uconn.edu

LAUFER, IGOR, GASTROINTESTINAL RADIOLOGY. **Personal Data:** b Czech, August 6, 1944; m Bernice; c Miriam & Jacob. **Education:** Univ Toronto, BSc, 1966, MD, 1967. **Honors & Awards:** Cannon Medal, Soc Gastrointestinal Radiologists, 1989. **Professional Experience:** PROF RADIOL, SCH MED, 1980-; CHIEF GASTROINTESTINAL RADIOL, HOSP UNIV PA, 1976-1990; assoc prof, Sch Med, 1976-1980; staff radiol, McMaster Univ Med Ctr, 1972-1976; chief resident, Beth Israel Hosp, Boston, 1971-1972; Clin fel radiol, Harvard Med Sch, 1969-1972; asst resident, Diag Radiol, 1969-1971; med resident, Toronto Western Hosp, 1968-1969; Intern, New Mt Sinai Hosp, Toronto, 1967-1968. **Memberships:** Soc Gastrointestinal Radiologists (pres 1987); Am Roentgen Ray Soc; Am Col Radiol; Radiol Soc NAm; Am Gastroenterol Asn. **Research Statement & Publications:** Early diagnosis of inflammatory and neoplastic disorders of the gastrointestinal tract; double contrast radiology. **Mailing Address:** Dept Radiol, Hosp Univ Pa, 3400 Spruce St, Philadelphia, PA 19104-4219. **Fax:** 2156627263. **E-Mail:** igor.laufer@uphs.upenn.edu

LAUFER, ROBERT J, ORGANIC CHEMISTRY. **Personal Data:** b Pittsburgh, Pa, May 10, 1932. **Education:** Carnegie Inst Technol, BS, 1953, MS, 1956, PhD (org chem), 1958. **Professional Experience:** RETIRED; vpres corp planning, Orbis Prod Div, 1981-1982; vpres & gen mgr, Orbis Prod Div, 1980-1981; vpres aromatics, Norda Inc, 1979-1980; corp dir res & develop, Norda Inc, 1977-1978; dir aromatic technol, Norda Inc, 1975-1977; dir, Int Flavors & Fragrances Inc, 1972-1975; assoc dir fragrance res, Int Flavors & Fragrances Inc, 1969-1972; proj leader, Int Flavors & Fragrances Inc, 1968-1969; proj supvr res div, Consol Coal Co, 1958-1968. **Memberships:** AAAS; Am Chem Soc. **Research Statement & Publications:** Research management; aroma chemicals; terpenoids; fragrance applications research. **Mailing Address:** Six Greenhill Rd, Colts Neck, NJ 07722-1595.

LAUFERSWEILER, JOSEPH DANIEL, ECOLOGY, BOTANY. **Personal Data:** b Columbus, Ohio, August 13, 1930. **Education:** Univ Notre Dame, BS, 1952; Ohio State Univ, MSc, 1954, PhD (ecol), 1960. **Professional Experience:** PROF EMER BIOL, UNIV DAYTON, 1995-; Bd trustees, Dayton Mus Natural Hist, 1982-1992; from asst prof to assoc prof, Univ Dayton, 1963-1995; asst prof biol, Drake Univ, 1961-1963; Instr bot & ecol, Ohio State Univ, 1959-1961; adv bd & exec comt, Ohio Biol Surv. **Memberships:** Bot Soc Am; Ecol Soc Am; Am Inst Biol Sci. **Research Statement & Publications:** Reproduction of plant communities; distribution of original vegetation and its influence on man; early history of the US Atomic Engergy Commission environmental sciences program. **Mailing Address:** Dept Biol, Univ Dayton, Dayton, OH 45469-2320. **Fax:** 937-229-2021. **E-Mail:** laufersw@neelix.udayton.edu

LAUFF, GEORGE HOWARD, LIMNOLOGY, ZOOLOGY. **Personal Data:** b Milan, Mich, March 23, 1927. **Education:** Mich State Univ, BS, 1949, MS, 1951; Cornell Univ, PhD (limnol, zool), 1953. **Professional Experience:** PROF EMER ZOOL, FISHERIES & WILDLIFE, MICH STATE UNIV, 1992-; prof, W W Kellogg Biol Sta, 1964-1992; dir, W W Kellogg Biol Sta, 1964-1990; res coordr, Sapelo Island Res Found, Ga, 1962-1964; assoc prof & dir marine inst, Univ Ga, 1960-1962; res assoc, Oak Ridge Inst Nuclear Studies & Oak Ridge Nat Lab, 1960; from asst prof to assoc prof, Univ Mich, 1957-1962; res assoc, Great Lakes Res Inst, 1954-1959; instr, Univ Mich, 1953-1957; zool, Cornell Univ, 1952-1953; biol asst, Cornell Univ, 1951-1952; asst phycol, Point Barrow, Alaska, 1951; fisheries res technician, Mich State Dept Conserv, 1950. **Memberships:** AAAS; Am Inst Biol Sci; Am Soc Limnol & Oceanog (treas 1958-1961 secy 1958-1964 1967-1970 vpres 1971-1972 pres 1972-1973); Ecol Soc Am; Int Asn Theoret & Appl Limnol. **Mailing Address:** 3818 Heights Dr, Hickory Corners, MI 49060.

LAUFFENBURGER, DOUGLAS ALAN, MOLECULAR & CELLULAR BIOENGINEERING. **Personal Data:** b Des Plaines, Ill, May 6, 1953; m 1979, Linda; c Julie & Wendy. **Education:** Univ Ill, BS, 1975; Univ Minn, PhD (chem eng), 1979. **Honors & Awards:** Alan P Colburn Award, Am Inst Chem Engrs, 1988, Bioengineering Div Award, 1993; Curtis W McGraw Award, Am Soc Eng Educ, 1992; Amgen Award Biochem Engr, 1999. **Professional Experience:** DIR BIOTECHNOL PROCESS ENG CTR, MASS INST TECHNOL, as of 2005; PROF, DEPT CHEM ENG, MASS INST TECHNOL, 1999-; CO-DIR & BIOENGINEERING & ENVIRON HEALTH DIV, MASS INST TECHNOL, 1998-; J R Mares Prof, Dept Chem Eng, Mass Inst Technol, 1995-1999; prof chem eng, cell & struct biol, bioengineering & biophys, Univ Ill, 1990-1994; vis prof, Dept Chem Eng, Univ Wis, 1989-1990; J S Guggenheim fel, 1989; from asst prof to prof chem eng, bioengineering & cell biol, Univ Pa, 1979-1990. **Memberships:** Am Inst Chem Engrs; Biomed Eng Soc; Am Soc Cell Biol. **Research Statement & Publications:** Quantitative investigation of receptor-mediated cell phenomena, including growth, adhesion, migration, chemotaxis and trafficking. **Mailing Address:** Dept Chem Engg, Mass Inst Technol, Rm 56-341 / 16-429, Cambridge, MA 02139. **Fax:** 617-252-0204. **E-Mail:** lauffen@mit.edu

LAUFFENBURGER, JAMES C, SOLID STATE PHYSICS. **Personal Data:** b Buffalo, NY, August 23, 1938. **Education:** Canisius Col, BS, 1960; Univ Notre Dame, PhD (solid state physics), 1965. **Professional Experience:** PROF & CHMN, DEPT PHYSICS, CANISIUS COL, as of 2003. **Memberships:** Sigma Xi; Am Asn Physics Teachers. **Research Statement & Publications:** X-rays. **Mailing Address:** Dept Physics, Canisius Col, 020 Horan O'Donnell Sci Bldg, Buffalo, NY 14208. **Fax:** 716-888-3112. **E-Mail:** lauffen@canisius.edu

LAUFFER, DONALD EUGENE, PHYSICS. **Personal Data:** b Lebanon, Pa, July 29, 1940. **Education:** Ohio State Univ, BS, 1964, PhD (physics), 1968. **Professional Experience:** RETIRED; sr res assoc, Phillips Petrol Co, 1988-2001; explor & prod planning mgr, Phillips Petrol Co, 1986-1988; br mgr geophys, Phillips Petrol Co, 1984-1986; supvr geophys, Phillips Petrol Co, 1976-1984; sr res physicist, Phillips Petrol Co, 1968-1976. **Memberships:** Am Phys Soc; Am Chem Soc. **Research Statement & Publications:** Geophysics; wave propagation and signal processing; computational chemistry. **Mailing Address:** Phillips Petroleum Co, 205 CPL PRC, Bartlesville, OK 74004. **Fax:** 918-662-1097. **E-Mail:** del@ppco.com

LAUFFER, MAX AUGUSTUS, JR, BIOPHYSICS. **Personal Data:** b Middletown, Pa, September 2, 1914; m 1964, Erika Erskine; c Edward W, Susan K, Max E & John E. **Education:** Pa State Univ, BS, 1933, MS, 1934; Univ Minn, PhD (biochem), 1937. **Honors & Awards:** Award, Eli Lilly & Co, 1945; Priestley Lectr, Pa State Univ, 1946; Gehrmann Lectr, Univ Ill, 1951; Pittsburgh Award, Am Chem Soc, 1958. **Professional Experience:** Adj prof, Lebanon Valley Col, 1988-1990; EMER PROF, UNIV PITTSBURGH, 1984-; consult to provost, Univ Pittsburgh, 1984-1986; chmn dept biophys & microbiol, Div Natural Sci, 1971-1976; ed, Biophys J, 1969-1973; Max Planck Inst Virus Res, Tubingen, 1965-1966 & Univ Philippines, 1967; mem sci adv bd, Delta Regional Primate Res Ctr, Tulane Univ, 1964-1967; Andrew Mellon prof biophys, Div Natural Sci, 1963-1984; mem adv coun, Nat Inst Gen Med Sci, 1963-1967; chmn dept, Univ Pittsburgh, 1963-1967; chmn, Nat Inst Gen Med Sci, 1962-1963; mem prog proj comt, Nat Inst Gen Med Sci, 1961-1963; dean, Div Natural Sci, 1956-1963; co-ed, Adv Virus Res, 1953-1985; mem sci adv comt, Boyce Thompson Inst Plant Res Inc, 1953-1982; mem, Panel Virol & Immunol, Sect Biol, Comt Growth, 1953-1956; assoc dean res natural sci, Univ Pittsburgh, 1953-1954; vis prof, Theodor Kocher Inst, Bern Univ, 1952; prof biophys, Univ Pittsburgh, 1949-1963; head dept, Univ Pittsburgh, 1949-1956; mem, Nat Res Coun Comn Macromolecules, 1947-1953; res prof physics & physiol chem, Univ Pittsburgh, 1947-1949; chmn dept physics, Univ Pittsburgh, 1947-1948; assoc res prof, Univ Pittsburgh, 1944-1947; prin investr, Comt Med Res, 1944-1946; assoc, Rockefeller Inst, 1941-1944; Spec lectr, Stanford Univ, 1941; asst, Rockefeller Inst, 1938-1941; fel plant path, Rockefeller Inst, 1937-1938; instr biochem, Univ Minn, 1936-1937; Asst, Univ Minn, 1935-1936. **Memberships:** Am Chem Soc; Am Soc Biol Chemists; Biophys Soc (pres elect 1960 pres 1961); Fedn Am Sci; NY Acad Sci. **Research Statement & Publications:** Electrokinetics; ultracentrifugation; viscometry; biophysics of viruses; kinetics of virus disintegration; size and shape of macromolecules; polymerization of virus protein; hydration of proteins; entropy-driven processes in biology. **Mailing Address:** 190 Lauffer Rd, Middletown, PA 17057.

LAUFMAN, HAROLD, VASCULAR SURGERY. **Personal Data:** b Milwaukee, Wis, January 6, 1912; wid June Friend Moses (deceased); c Dionne Weigert & Laurein Kogut. **Education:** Univ Chicago, BS, 1932, Rush Med Col, MD, 1937; Northwestern Univ, MS, 1946, PhD (surg), 1948; Am Bd Surg, dipl. **Professional Experience:** Emer dir, Inst Surg Studies, Montefiore Hosp, 1981-; prof lectr surg, Mt Sinai Sch Med, 1979-; PROF LECTR SURG, MT SINAI SCH MED, 1979-; PRES, HLA SYSTS, INC, 1979-; emer prof surg, Albert Einstein Col Med, 1977; dir, Inst Surg Studies, Montefiore Hosp, 1965-1981; prof, Albert Einstein Col Med, 1965-1977; James IV traveling prof, Israel, 1962; attend, Passavant Mem & Vet Admin Res Hosps, 1954-1965; adj attend, Michael Reese Hosp, Chicago, 1948-1954; attend, Hines Vet Admin Hosp, 1948-1950; Assoc attend surgeon, Cook County Hosp, 1946-1948; From clin asst to prof surg, Med Sch, Northwestern Univ, 1940-1965. **Memberships:** Am Surg Asn; Soc Vascular Surg; fel Am Col Surg; Am Med Writers Asn (pres, 1969); Asn Advan Med Instrumentation (pres, 1974-1975); Sigma Xi Chicago Surgical soc, 1948. **Research Statement & Publications:** Surgical physiology, especially mesenteric and peripheral vascular diseases; surgical design and facilities engineering. **Mailing Address:** 31 E 72nd St, New York, NY 10021. **Fax:** 212-737-4628. **E-Mail:** hlauf@aol.com

LAUGHLIN, ALEXANDER WILLIAM, GEOCHEMISTRY, ECONOMIC GEOLOGY. **Personal Data:** b Hot Springs, Ark, November 9, 1936. **Education:** Mich Technol Univ, BSc, 1958; Univ Ariz, MSc, 1960, PhD (geol), 1969. **Honors & Awards:** Res & Develop 100 Award, 1996. **Professional Experience:** SR SCIENTIST, ICF KAISER ENGRS, 1994-; dep group leader, Los Alamos Nat Lab, Univ Calif, 1987-1994; group leader, Los Alamos Nat Lab, Univ Calif, 1978-1980; adj prof, Univ NMex, 1975; mem staff, Los Alamos Nat Lab, Univ Calif, 1974-1978 & 1980-1987; from asst prof to assoc prof, Kent State Univ, 1970-1974; res assoc geol, Univ NMex, 1969-1970; res assoc isotope geochem, Univ Ariz, 1966-1969. **Memberships:** Am Geophys Union; Int Asn Geochem & Cosmochem; fel Geol Soc Am. **Research Statement & Publications:** Geochronology; trace element geochemistry; origin of ultramafic inclusions and basalts; economic geology; geothermal energy extraction from dry hot rock, geothermal exploration techniques, petrology of precambrian rocks; potassic mafic rocks. **Mailing Address:** Environ & Energy Group, ICF Kaiser Engrs 1086 17th St, Los Alamos, NM 87544.

LAUGHLIN, ALICE, BIOCHEMISTRY, ANALYTICAL CHEMISTRY. **Personal Data:** b Malone, NY, February 19, 1918. **Education:** St Joseph Col, Conn, BS, 1949; Univ Vt, MS, 1954; Columbia Univ, EdD(col sci teaching), 1965. **Professional Experience:** PROF CHEM, JERSEY CITY STATE COL, 1974-; chmn dept, Jersey City State Col, 1969-1970; consult, NSF meeting on chem curric jr cols, Rutgers Univ, 1969; Resource mem long range planning bd, Sch Nursing, St Francis Hosp, 1963-; from asst prof sci to assoc prof chem, Jersey City State Col, 1962-1974; sci instr, Sch Nursing, St Michael Hosp, 1961-1962; res asst hemat & chemother, Columbia-Presby Med Ctr, Columbia Univ, 1957-1961; res chemist, Nat Biscuit Co, 1956-1957; asst biochemist, Vt State Agr Exp Sta, 1952-1956; teaching asst biochem, Univ Vt, 1950-1952; Lab technician, Clin Lab, Staten Island Hosp, 1949-1950. **Memberships:** Am Chem Soc; Am Asn Higher Educ; fel Am Inst Chemists; NY Acad Sci; Am Microchem Soc; Am Asn Univ Women (pres 1987-1989). **Research Statement & Publications:** Human nutrition; science education. **Mailing Address:** 1225 76th St 8C, North Bergen, NJ 07047-4602.

LAUGHLIN, CATHERINE, ANTIVIRAL RESEARCH. **Professional Experience:** CHIEF, VIROLOGY BR, NAT INST ALLERGY & INFECTIOUS DIS, as of 2004. **Mailing Address:** Nat Inst Allergy & Infectious Dis, Antiviral Res Br, NIH, 6700-B Rockledge Dr, Bethesda, MD 20817.

LAUGHLIN, CHARLES WILLIAM, NEMATOLOGY. **Personal Data:** b Iowa City, Iowa, December 9, 1939. **Education:** Iowa State Univ, BS, 1963; Univ Md, MS, 1966; Va Polytech Inst & State Univ, PhD (plant path & physiol), 1969. **Professional Experience:** RETIRED; coop state Res, Educ & Exten Serv, USDA, 1999-2000; coordr, Exp Sta Comm Orgn & Policy, Leadership Develop Prog, Acad Comm Orgn & Policy, beginning 1992; dir & prof, Colo Agr Exp Sta, Colo State Univ, 1992-1996; assoc dir, Ga Agr Exp Sta, Univ Ga, 1983-1992; dept head plant path & weed sci, Miss State Univ, 1980-1983; dir, Mich State Univ, 1978-1980; asst dir acad & student affairs, Mich State Univ, 1973-1978; from asst prof to prof nematol, Mich State Univ, 1969-1980; Asst exten nematologist, Univ Fla, 1968-1969. **Memberships:** Soc Nematologists; Brazilian Soc Nematol; Am Phytopath Soc; AAAS. **Research Statement & Publications:** Management of agro-ecosystems with the goal of developing management strategies for the protection of the crop plants from plant parasitic nematodes and associated microorganisms. **Mailing Address:** IANR News Serv, Univ Nebr-Lincoln, 203 Ag Communs Bldg, Lincoln, NE 68583-0918.

LAUGHLIN, DAVID EUGENE, PHYSICAL METALLURGY, ELECTRON MICROSCOPY. **Personal Data:** b Philadelphia, Pa, July 15, 1947. **Education:** Drexel Univ, BSc, 1969; Mass Inst Technol, PhD (metall), 1973. **Professional Experience:** Ed, Metall & Mat Trans, as of 2003; PROF MAT SCI & ENG, CARNEGIE-MELLON UNIV, as of 2003; PROF METALL, CARNEGIE-MELLON UNIV, 1982-; assoc ed, Metall Trans, 1982, 1987-; consult, 1980-; pres, Trinity Christian Sch Bd Dirs, 1978-1983; from asst prof to assoc prof, Carnegie-Mellon Univ, 1974-1982; res assoc, Nat Bur Stand, 1973-1974; NEDO grant. **Memberships:** Fel Am Soc Metals; Am Inst Mining Metall & Petrol Engrs; Am Soc Eng Educ; Am Sci Affil; Inst Elec & Electronics Engrs. **Research Statement & Publications:** X-ray diffraction; innovative teaching; phase transformations; differential scanning calorimetry; electron microscopy; magnetic materials. **Mailing Address:** Dept Mat Sci & Eng, Carnegie-Mellon Univ, 5000 Forbes Ave, Pittsburgh, PA 15213-3816. **Fax:** 412-268-3113. **E-Mail:** dl0p@andrew.cmu.edu

LAUGHLIN, ETHELREDA R, biochemistry, science education; deceased, see previous edition for last biography

LAUGHLIN, JAMES STANLEY, STATISTICS, OPERATIONS RESEARCH. **Personal Data:** b Guilford, Mo, September 23, 1936; m 1960, c 2. **Education:** Northwest Mo State Univ, BS, 1958; Univ Northern Colo, MA, 1961; Univ Denver, PhD (higher educ, math), 1968. **Professional Experience:** PROF MATH, WOODRIVER HIGH SCH, 1991-; asst prof math, Idaho State Univ, 1984-1991; dir instnl res, Idaho State Univ, 1975-1983; dir instnl studies, Kans State Teachers Col, 1970-1975; Kans State Dept Educ grant, 1969-1970; assoc prof math, Kans State Teachers Col, 1968-1975; res asst, Denver Pub Schs, Colo, 1967-1968; teacher math, Denver Pub Schs, Colo, 1959-1967; teacher chem & math, Grand Community Schs, Boxholm, Iowa, 1958-1959. **Memberships:** Math Asn Am; Am Educ Res Asn; Nat Coun Teachers Math. **Research Statement & Publications:** Teaching of mathematics. **Mailing Address:** Dept Math, Wood River High Sch PO Box 948, Hailey, ID 83333.

LAUGHLIN, JOHN SETH, medical physics; deceased, see previous edition for last biography

LAUGHLIN, ROBERT B, PHYSICS. **Personal Data:** b Visalia, Calif, November 1, 1950; m Anita. **Education:** Univ Calif, Berkeley, AB, 1972; Mass Inst Technol, PhD (physics), 1979. **Honors & Awards:** Nobel Prize in Physics, 1998; E O Lawrence Award for Physics, 1985; Oliver E Buckley Prize, 1986; Eastman Kodak Lectr, Univ Rochester, 1989; Van Vleck Lectr, 1994. **Professional Experience:** ANNE BASS & ROBERT M BASS PROF, PROF APPL PHYSICS, 1993-; PROF PHYSICS, SCH HUMANITIES & SCI, STANFORD UNIV, 1989-; assoc prof physics, prof Appl Physics, 1985-1989; RES PHYSICIST, LAWRENCE LIVERMORE NAT LAB, 1982-; Bell Tel Labs, 1979-1981; Int Bus Mach, fel, 1976-1978. **Memberships:** Nat Acad Sci; fel AAAS; fel Am Phys Soc; fel Am Acad Arts & Sci. **Mailing Address:** Dept Physics, Stanford Univ, LAM Rm 342 McCullough Bldg 476 Lomita Mall, Stanford, CA 94305-4045. **Fax:** 650-723-9389. **E-Mail:** rbl@large.stanford.edu

LAUGHLIN, R(OBERT) G(ARDINER) W(ILLIS), CHEMICAL ENGINEERING, WASTE MANAGEMENT. **Personal Data:** b London, Eng, October 11, 1942. **Education:** Univ Col, Univ London, BSc, 1964, PhD (chem eng), 1967. **Professional Experience:** DIR, WASTE MGT TECHNOL, ENVIRON TECHNOL DIV, ORTECH, 1967-; chair, Ont Minister Environ Hazardous Waste Adv Comt. **Memberships:** Can Soc Chem Eng; Asn Prof Engrs Ont. **Research Statement & Publications:** Environmental engineering; industrial waste exchange; spontaneous combustion phenomena; industrial and municipal solid waste utilization; industrial waste treatment; biomass to energy conversion systems; waste treatment systems; waste reduction and minimization; environmental technologic assessment and development. **Mailing Address:** Recycling Technol, Ortech Sheridan Park, 2395 Speakman Dr, Mississauga, ON L5K 1B3, Can. **Fax:** 905-822-7630. **E-Mail:** blaughlin@ortech.on.ca

LAUGHLIN, ROBERT GENE, PHASE SCI, SURFACTANT SCI, CAROTEN OID SCI. **Personal Data:** b Sullivan, Ind, August 9, 1930; div, c Steven K & Kenneth B. **Education:** Purdue Univ, BS, 1951; Cornell Univ, PhD (Org Chem), 1955, Hickrill Found, PD, 1956. **Honors & Awards:** Samuel Rosen Mem Award, Am Oil Chemists Soc, 1992 Otto van Warburg Found Award, Bayreuth, Ger, 2001. **Professional Experience:** RETIRED; adj prof, Chem, Clarkson Univ Potsdam, NY, 2002-; res fel, Miami Valley Labs, Procter & Gamble Co, 1992-1999; sect head, Miami Valley Labs, Procter & Gamble Co, 1968-1992; res chemist, Miami Valley Labs, Procter & Gamble CO, 1956-1968; fel org chem, Hickrill Res Labs, NY, 1955-1956. **Memberships:** Emer mem Royal Soc Chem; Am Chem Soc. **Research Statement & Publications:** Synthesis, phase science, colliod science and technology of surfactant molecules; correlation of molecular structure with aqueous phase equilibria; development of new phase study methods and principles; physical science of carotenoids; all aspects of surfactant sci (synthesis, phys chem, tech, biochem); phase sci, and development of new methods for phase studies physical & anal sci of carotenoids. **Mailing Address:** 11641 Bank Rd, Cincinnati, OH 45251. **Fax:** 513-742-4790. **E-Mail:** rglaugh@zoomtown.com

LAUGHLIN, WINSTON MEANS, SOIL SCIENCE. **Personal Data:** b Fountain, Minn, May 2, 1917; m 1947, Dorothy Fuelihan; c Ellen, Laurence, Keith & Brian. **Education:** Univ Minn, BS, 1941; Mich State Univ, MS, 1947, PhD (soil sci), 1949. **Professional Experience:** SOIL SCIENTIST, ALASKA AGR EXP STA, 1949-; asst, Mich State Univ, 1941-1942; Soil surveyor, Univ Minn, 1940-1941. **Memberships:** AAAS; Am Soc Agron; Soil Sci Soc Am; Am Sci Affil; Int Soc Soil Sci. **Research Statement & Publications:** Soil fertility, chemistry and classification with emphasis on Arctic conditions. **Mailing Address:** Agr & Forestry Exp Sta, 533 E Fireweed, Palmer, AK 99645.

LAUGHON, ALLEN S, GENETICS. **Education:** Univ Utah, Ph.D, 1983. **Professional Experience:** PROF GENETICS & MED GENETICS, UNIV WIS, as of 2006. **Mailing Address:** Lab Genetics Univ Wis, 4262 Genetics/Biotech, Madison, WI 53706-1501. **E-Mail:** alaughon@wisc.edu

LAUGHON, ROBERT BUSH, RADIOACTIVE & HAZARDOUS WASTE DISPOSAL, ENVIRONMENTAL MANAGEMENT. **Personal Data:** b Greensboro, NC, April 20, 1934; m 1957, Barbara A Jinnette; c Francia & Colin. **Education:** Colo Col, BA, 1960; Univ Colo, Boulder, MS, 1963; Univ Ariz, PhD (geol), 1970. **Professional Experience:** CONSULT GEOLOGIST, 1994-; res leader, Mich LLRW Proj, 1991-1994; geotechnol mgr, Mich LLRW Proj, 1990-1991; chief geoscientist, Proj Mgt Div, 1981-1990; mgr, Geol Explor Dept, Batelle Mem Inst, 1978-1981; proj mgr, Nuclear Div, Union Carbide Corp, 1976-1978; lectr, Moody Col, Tex A&M Univ, 1974; geologist, Manned Spacecraft Ctr, NASA, 1967-1976; instr, Univ Ariz, 1966-1967; geologist, Anaconda Co, 1964-1965; geologist, US Geol Surv, 1962-1963. **Research Statement & Publications:** Waste management; mineralogy-crystallography. **Mailing Address:** 657 Indian Mound Rd, Columbus, OH 43213.

LAUGHTER, ARLINE H, IMMUNOLOGY. **Professional Experience:** SR RES ASSOC, DEPT IMMUNOL, VET ADMIN MED CTR, 1968-. **Mailing Address:** Dept Immunol Res Vet Admin Med Ctr, Bldg 109 Rm 226 2002 Holcombe Blvd, Houston, TX 77030-4298.

LAUGHTON, PAUL MACDONELL, ORGANIC CHEMISTRY. **Personal Data:** b Toronto, Ont, September 8, 1923. **Education:** Univ Toronto, BA, 1945; Dalhousie Univ, MSc, 1947; Univ Wis, PhD (chem), 1950. **Professional Experience:** Vis prof, Stanford Univ, 1962 & Kings Col, London, 1972-1973; PROF CHEM, CARLETON UNIV, 1965-; Am Chem Soc-Petrol Res Fund fel, Univ Calif, Berkeley, 1962-1963; from asst prof to assoc prof chem, Carleton Univ, 1951-1965; Nat Res Coun Can fel, Dalhousie Univ, 1950-1951; Res assoc, Univ Wis, 1950. **Memberships:** Am Chem Soc; fel Chem Inst Can; Royal Soc Chem; Sigma Xi. **Research Statement & Publications:** Mechanism studies; isotope effects. **Mailing Address:** 928 Muskoka Ave, Ottawa, ON K2A 3H9, Can.

LAUKHUF, WALDEN LOUIS SHELBURNE, CHEMICAL ENGINEERING, DISTILATION, MASS TRANSFER. **Personal Data:** b Maysville, Ky, July 25, 1943; m 1967, Lana; c Heather & Matthew. **Education:** Univ Louisville, BS, 1966, MS, 1967, PhD (chem eng), 1969. **Professional Experience:** ASSOC CHMN, UNIV LOUISVILLE, 2000-; PROF CHEM ENG, UNIV LOUISVILLE, 1986-; assoc chmn, Univ Louisville, 1985-1989; consult, Univ Louisville, 1980-; interim chmn, Univ Louisville, 1979-1980; from asst prof to assoc prof, Univ Louisville, 1974-1986; develop eng specialist, Air Force Mat Lab, 1971-1973; USAF, 1969-1973; proj engr, Air Force Rocket Propulsion Lab, 1969-1971; engr, Humble Oil & Refining Co, 1969. **Memberships:** Am Inst Chem Engrs. **Research Statement & Publications:** Distillation; process controls; mass transfer and thermodynamics; digital control. **Mailing Address:** Dept Chem Eng, Univ Louisville, 14104 Tree Crest Ct, Louisville, KY 40245. **Fax:** 502-852-6355. **E-Mail:** scrap@lovisville.edu

LAUKONIS, JOSEPH VAINYS, PHYSICS. **Personal Data:** b Mich, April 1, 1925. **Education:** Univ Detroit, BS, 1951; Univ Cincinnati, PhD, 1957. **Professional Experience:** RETIRED; Sr res physicist, Gen Motors Corp, 1957-1990. **Memberships:** Am Phys Soc. **Research Statement & Publications:** Iron whiskers; metal surfaces; high temperature oxidation; formability of sheet metals; electron microscopy; ultrahigh vacuums; oxidation-reduction catalysts. **Mailing Address:** 32405 Northampton, Warren, MI 48093.

LAUL, JAGDISH CHANDER, GEOCHEMISTRY, COSMOCHEMISTRY. **Personal Data:** b India, September 1, 1939; m 1970, c 3. **Education:** Punjab Univ, India, BS, 1959; Purdue Univ, MS, & PhD (radio geochem), 1969. **Honors & Awards:** Group Achievement Award, NASA, 1973. **Professional Experience:** SR RES SCIENTIST CHEM, PHYS SCI DEPT, PAC NORTHWEST DIV, BATTELLE MEM INST, 1972-; res assoc, Enrico Fermi Inst, Univ Chicago, 1969-1971; res assoc, Radiation Ctr, Ore State Univ, 1971-1975. **Memberships:** Am Chem Soc; Geochem Soc; Meteoritical Soc. **Research Statement & Publications:** Studies of trace elements and their implications in lunar, meteorite, terrestrial, environmental, nuclear waste and fossile fuel samples; development of radioanalytical methods and instrumentation in neutron activation area. **Mailing Address:** 607 Cherrywood Lane, Richland, WA 99352.

LAULAINEN, NELS STEPHEN, ATMOSPHERIC SCIENCE. **Personal Data:** b Longview, Wash, October 22, 1941; div, c David, Frans, Alan, Soren, Kirsten, Trevor, Kevin & Travis. **Education:** Univ Wash, BS, 1963, MS, 1965, PhD (physics), 1968. **Professional Experience:** SR RES SCIENTIST ATMOSPHERIC SCI, BATTELLE-PAC NW LABS, as of 1999; vis scientist, Fraunhofer Inst Atmospheric Environ Res, Garmisch-Partenkirchen, Ger, 1989-1990; prog mgr earth sci, Atmospheric & Precipitation Chem Sect, Earth Sci, 1987-1994; mgr, Atmospheric & Precipitation Chem Sect, Earth Sci, 1982-1987; tech adv, US Environ Protection Agency, Wash, DC, 1981-1982; sr res scientist atmospheric sci, Battelle-Pac NW Labs, 1974-1982; lectr physics, Univ Wash, 1972-1974; res assoc geophys & astron, Geophys Prog, 1971-1974; res assoc med physics, Med Radiation Physics & Radiol, Univ Wash, 1970-1971; Res scientist, Fulbright Travel Stipend, 1968-1970; res scientist physics, First Phys Inst, Heidelberg Univ, 1968-1970. **Memberships:** Am Phys Soc; Sigma Xi; Am Geophys Union; Am Asn Aerosol Res assoc. **Research Statement & Publications:** Atmospheric aerosol physics; solar radiation and its interaction with atmospheric constituents; atmospheric pollutant transformation and removal processes; climate effects ofenergy production; acid deposition field studies and modeling. **Mailing Address:** Battelle-NW Labs MSIN K9-30, Atmospheric Sci PO Box 999, Richland, WA 99352. **E-Mail:** nels.laulainen@prl.gov

LAUNDON, CAROLINE H, GENETICS. **Education:** NC State Univ, BS; Emory Univ, PhD. **Professional Experience:** DIR, GENECARE MED GENETICS CTR, as of 2005; ADJ PROF GYNEC, GEORGE WASH UNIV, as of 2005. **Mailing Address:** Genecare Med Genetics Ctr, 120 Conner Dr Suite 201, Chapel Hill, NC 27514.

LAUNDRE, JOHN WILLIAM, WILDLIFE BEHAVIOR, ECOLOGY. **Personal Data:** b Green Bay, Wis, January 30, 1949. **Education:** Univ Wis, Green Bay, BSc, 1971; Northern Mich Univ, MA, 1974; Idaho State Univ, PhD (ecol), 1979. **Professional Experience:** AFFIL FAC BIOL SCI, IDAHO STATE UNIV, as of 2004; ASST PROF ECOL, SOUTHWEST STATE UNIV, 1979-; Instr anat, Northeast Wis Tech & Voc Inst, 1974-1976. **Memberships:** Wildlife Soc; Animal Behav Soc; Am Soc Mammalogist; Sigma Xi. **Research Statement & Publications:** Ecology and behavior of mammals, including coyotes, deer, cats and small mammals. **Mailing Address:** Dept Biol Sci, Idaho State Univ, 921 S 8th Ave, Pocatello, ID 83209. **E-Mail:** launjohn@isu.edu

LAUNER, PHILIP JULES, INFRARED SPECTROSCOPY, SILICONE TECHNOLOGY. **Personal Data:** b Philadelphia, Pa, November 20, 1922. **Education:** Drew Univ, AB, 1943; Columbia Univ, MA, 1947. **Professional Experience:** DIR RES, LAB FOR MAT INC, 1987-; pres, lab For Mat Inc, 1973-1987; specialist spectros, Silicone Prod dept,

Gen Elec Co, 1955-1972; proj chemist petrol chem, res dept, Stand Oil Co, Ind, 1948-1955; teaching asst quant analysis, Columbia Univ, 1947-1948. **Memberships:** Am Chem Soc; Soc Appl Spectros; fel Am Inst Chemists; Coblentz Soc. **Research Statement & Publications:** Infrared spectroscopy; silicone technology; identification of industrial materials. **Mailing Address:** Lab Mat Inc, 156 Lawrence St Apt 303, Saratoga Spgs, NY 12866.

LAUPUS, WILLIAM E, medicine; deceased, see previous edition for last biography

LAURANCE, NEAL L, COMPUTER SCIENCE. **Personal Data:** b Winsted, Minn, August 19, 1932. **Education:** Marquette Univ, BS, 1954, MS, 1955; Univ Ill, PhD (physics), 1960. **Professional Experience:** ED, ISO 9506, as of 2006; SR STAFF SCIENTIST, FORD MOTOR CO, 1985-; mgr analytical sci, eng & res staff, 1979-1985; mgr, Control Systs Dept, 1973-1979; res scientist, Sci Lab, Ford Motor Co, 1960-1973. **Memberships:** Am Phys Soc; fel Inst Elec & Electronics Engrs. **Research Statement & Publications:** Simulation systems; manufacturing automation, OSI computer networks; real-time systems. **Mailing Address:** Ford Motor Co, 15303 Commerce Park S, Ste 100, Dearborn, MI 48104. **Fax:** 313-390-8817. **E-Mail:** nlauranc@ford.com

LAURENCE, ALFRED EDWARD, INDUSTRIAL CHEMISTRY. **Personal Data:** b Breslau, Ger, December 12, 1910. **Education:** LLD, Breslau, Ger, 1933; dipl, Poitiers, 1934, Caen, 1936. **Professional Experience:** Vis prof, Univ Utah, 1969, 1970; CONSULT, 1968-; researcher, Economist Intel Univ, London, 1967-1968; econ planning adv, Lewis Berger, Gt Brit Ltd, 1965-1966; Consult, UN & UNESCO, 1964; dir res, Int Develop & Invest Co, Ltd, Bahamas, 1962-1963; mgr indust & chem prods, Europ Res Off, Minn Mining & Mfg Co, Ltd, 1954-1961; export mgr org chem, Propane Co, Eng, 1952-1954; chemist & technologist, Shell Chem Corp, Shell Oil Co, Calif & NY, 1946-1952; chemist, Res & Develop Dept, Atlantic Ref Co, Pa, 1941-1946; chemist & metallurgist, Indian Smelting & Ref Co, 1940-1941; chem sales technologist, Shell Oil Co, 1938-1940; Chemist, Serv Lab, Am Corn Prod Co, India, 1937-1938. **Research Statement & Publications:** Organic chemistry; petrochemistry; analytical methods; corporation finance and economics; international and patent law; sociology of industry. **Mailing Address:** La Mer 7 Sisters Rd, St Lawrence PO38 1UZ, Isle of Wight, UK.

LAURENCE, GEOFFREY CAMERON, FISH BIOLOGY, ECOLOGICAL MODELLING. **Personal Data:** b Quincy, Mass, March 24, 1943. **Education:** Univ Maine, BA, 1965; Fla State Univ, MS, 1967; Cornell Univ, PhD (fishery sci), 1971. **Honors & Awards:** Gold Medal, US Dept Com, 1981. **Professional Experience:** SUPVRY FISHERY BIOLOGIST, NAT MARINE FISHERIES SERV, NAT OCEANIC ATMOSPHERIC ADMIN, 1972-; fishery biologist, Bur Sport Fisheries & Wildlife, 1970-1972; res asst fishery sci, Cornell Univ, 1967-1970; Asst biol, Fla State Univ, 1965-1967. **Memberships:** Am Fisheries Soc; Am Inst Fishery Res Biologists; Am Soc Limnol & Oceanog; Sigma Xi. **Research Statement & Publications:** Larval fish ecology and physiology as they pertain to growth and survival; ecological and mathematical modelling of larval survival in relation to stock-recruitment problems in fishery management; biological oceanography. **Mailing Address:** 1164 Slocum Rd, Saunderstown, RI 02874-1601.

LAURENCE, JOHN A, ENVIRONMENTAL STRESS, COMPUTER MODELING & ASSESSMENTS. **Personal Data:** b Berea, Ohio, December 16, 1949. **Education:** Pa State Univ, BS, 1971; Univ Minn, MS, 1973, PhD (plant path), 1976. **Professional Experience:** PLANT PATHOLOGIST, BOYCE THOMPSON INST, as of 2005; MEM, GRAD FIELDS PLANT PATH, NAT RESOURCES, & ENVIRON TOXICOL, CORNELL UNIV, as of 2005; PROG DIR, BOYCE THOMPSON INST PLANT RES, 1991-; SCIENTIST, BOYCE THOMPSON INST PLANT RES, 1988-; adj prof, Dept Plant Path, Cornell Univ, 1983-; assoc scientist, Boyce Thompson Inst Plant Res, 1982-1988; asst scientist, Boyce Thompson Inst Plant Res, 1977-1982. **Memberships:** Am Phytopath Soc; Sigma Xi. **Research Statement & Publications:** Assessment of effects of air pollutants and other environmental stresses on plant growth and yield; modeling tree and forest response to the environment. **Mailing Address:** Boyce Thompson Inst, 200 SW 35th St, Corvallis, OR 97333. **Fax:** 541-754-4605. **E-Mail:** laurence@mail.cor.epa.gov

LAURENCE, KENNETH ALLEN, MICROBIOLOGY, PHYSIOL OF REPRODUCTION. **Personal Data:** b Cleveland, Ohio, November 4, 1928; m 1949, Elaine; c Kirk A & Denise L (Clough). **Education:** Marietta Col, AB, 1951; Univ Iowa, MS, 1953, PhD Zoology, 1956. **Professional Experience:** EMER PROF ZOOL, UNIV IDAHO, 1993-; dir, Int Progs Off, Univ Idaho, 1990-1993; res develop coordr, Univ Idaho, 1985-1994; Supreme Coun Univ Foreign Relations Unit, Cairo, Egypt, 1984; dep exec dir, Consortium Int Develop, Tucson, Ariz, 1983-1985; prin contact officer & alt trustee, Consortium Int Develop, Tucson, Ariz, 1980-1983; dir grants & contracts, Univ Idaho, 1980-1983; consult, Egyptian Univ, Rockefeller Found, 1980; prof & head, Dept Biol Sci, Univ Idaho, 1976-1980; proj specialist, Ford Found, Cairo, Egypt, 1973-1974; assoc dir, Biomed Div, 1968-1976; Ford Found consult physiol reprod, Egyptian Univs Prog, 1966-1967; asst med dir, Pop Coun Inc, 1960-1968; asst prof, Med Col, Cornell Univ, 1959-1960; instr microbiol & immunol, Med Col, Cornell Univ, 1957-1959; NIH fel immunol, Univ Iowa, 1956-1957. **Research Statement & Publications:** Physiology of reproduction; immunology; parasitology; medical bacteriology; immunologic studies of the reproductive processes. **Mailing Address:** 1000 Timber Lane, Moscow, ID 83843-8787. **E-Mail:** klavren@uidaho.edu

LAURENCE, ROBERT L(IONEL), CHEMICAL ENGINEERING, POLYMER SCIENCE. **Personal Data:** b West Warwick, RI, July 13, 1936; m 1959, Carol; c Jonathan, Lisa & Andrew. **Education:** Mass Inst Technol, BS, 1957; Univ RI, MS, 1960; Northwestern Univ, PhD (chem eng), 1966; Inst Nat Polytech, DSc, 1989. **Honorary Degrees:** DSc, Inst Nat Polytech Toulouse, Univ Toulouse, France, 1989. **Professional Experience:** PROF EMER, DEPT CHEM ENG, UNIV MASS, AMHERST, 2001-; vis prof, Ecole Nat Superieure du Ingenieurs, Genie Chemique (Toulouse), 1990; vis prof, Universidad Nac del Sur, 1989-1990; consult, Gen Elec Corp Res & Develop, 1989-1990; head dept, Polymer Sci & Eng, Univ Mass, Amherst, 1982-1989; vis prof, Col de France, 1982; vis prof Universidad Nac del Sur, Bahia Blanca, Arg, 1978; vis prof, Imp Col Sci & Technol, 1974-1975; prof chem eng, Polymer Sci & Eng, Univ Mass, Amherst, 1973-2001; assoc prof, Polymer Sci & Eng, Univ Mass, Amherst, 1968-1973; asst prof chem eng, Johns Hopkins Univ, 1965-1968; engr, Elastomers Dept, Tex, 1961-1963; engr, Eng Res Lab, E I du Pont de Nemours & Co, Del, 1960-1961; res engr, Elec Boat Div, Gen Dynamics Corp, Conn, 1957-1958. **Memberships:** Fel Am Inst Chem Engrs; Am Chem Soc; fel Am Inst Chemists. **Research Statement & Publications:** Fluid mechanics-hydrodynamic stability; polymerization reaction engineering; diffusion in polymers; polymer processing; diffusion in zeolites. **Mailing Address:** Dept Chem Eng, Univ Mass, Amherst, MA 01003-3110. **Fax:** 413-545-1647. **E-Mail:** rlaurence@ecs.umass.edu

LAURENCOT, HENRY JULES, DRUG METABOLISM, ANIMAL SCIENCE. **Personal Data:** b Brooklyn, NY, December 14, 1929. **Education:** St Peter's Col, NJ, BS, 1951; Fordham Univ, MS, 1955, PhD (biol), 1965. **Professional Experience:** RES INVESTR, HOFFMAN-LA ROCHE, INC, 1966-; Asst plant physiol. **Memberships:** Am Soc Pharmacol & Exp Therapeut; NY Acad Sci; Sigma Xi; AAAS. **Research Statement & Publications:** In vivo and in vitro metabolic studies of radioactive experimental drugs. **Mailing Address:** Bldg 735 Rm 117, Hoffmann-La Roche Inc 22-10 Rte 208 S, Fair Lawn, NJ 07410.

LAURENDEAU, NORMAND MAURICE, MECHANICAL ENGINEERING, PHYSICAL CHEMISTRY. **Personal Data:** b Lewiston, Maine, August 16, 1944. **Education:** UnivNotre Dame, BS, 1966; Princeton Univ, MS, 1968; Univ Calif, Berkeley, PhD (mech eng), 1972. **Professional Experience:** REILLY PROF COMBUST ENG, PURDUE UNIV, 1995-; fel, Japan Soc Prom Sci, 1992; vis prof, Dept Chem, Northwestern Univ, 1988; PROF MECH ENG, PURDUE UNIV, 1982-; dir, Coal Res Ctr, Purdue Univ, 1981-1984; res engr, Arthur D Little, Inc, 1980-1981; from asst prof to assoc prof, Purdue Univ, 1972-1982. **Memberships:** Am Soc Mech Engrs; Am Chem Soc; Combustion Inst; Optical Soc Am. **Research Statement & Publications:** Combustion; chemical kinetics; combustion diagnostics; air pollution; laser-induced fluorescence; engineering ethics. **Mailing Address:** Sch Mech Eng, Purdue Univ, 585 Purdue Mall, West Lafayette, IN 47907-2088. **Fax:** 765-494-0539. **E-Mail:** laurende@purdue.edu

LAURENSON, ROBERT MARK, MECHANICAL ENGINEERING. **Personal Data:** b Pittsburgh, Pa, October 25, 1938; m 1961, c 2. **Education:** Mo Sch Mines, BS, 1961; Univ Mich, Ann Arbor, MSE, 1962; Ga Inst Technol, PhD (mech eng), 1969. **Honors & Awards:** Award, McDonnell Douglas Astronaut Co, McDonnell Douglas Corp, 1971. **Professional Experience:** Tech specialist, McDonnell Douglas Corp, 1975-1992; staff engr, McDonnell Douglas Corp, 1974-1975; group dynamics engr, McDonnell Douglas Corp, 1971-1974; Lectr, Dept Eng Mech, St Louis Univ, 1969-1971; sr dynamics engr, McDonnell Douglas Corp, 1968-1971; Dynamics engr, McDonnell Aircraft Co, 1962-1964. **Memberships:** Am Inst Aeronaut & Astronaut; Am Soc Mech Engrs. **Research Statement & Publications:** Vibrations of structures and machine elements; response of elastic and flexible structures to transient loadings. **Mailing Address:** 1104Jasper Ct, Crofton, MD 21114.

LAURENT, GILLES J, NEUROBIOLOGY. **Education:** Univ Toulouse, BA, 1978, PhD, 1985, DVM, 1985. **Professional Experience:** PROF BIOL & COMPUT & NEURAL SYSTS, CALIF INST TECHNOL, as of 2003. **Mailing Address:** Div Biol, Calif Inst Technol, 139-74, Pasadena, CA 91125. **E-Mail:** laurentg@its.caltech.edu

LAURENT, PIERRE, ELECTRON MICROSCOPY. **Personal Data:** b Thionville, France, July 25, 1925. **Education:** Acad Lille, BSc, 1944; Univ Nancy, MSc, 1948; Univ Paris, Sorbonne, DSc, 1958. **Professional Experience:** Res consult, 1980-; CVP Div Hosp, Univ Pa, Philadelphia, 1976-1980; RES DIR, CNRS, STRASBOURG, 1974-; res dir, Col France, 1969-1973; Vis prof, Michael Rease Hosp, Chicago, 1968; sr researcher, CNRS, Paris, 1957-1968; res fel, CNRS, Paris, 1950-1956; asst prof, Univ Lille, 1949-1950; Teacher natural sci, Col d'Armentieres, 1948-1949. **Memberships:** Am Physiol Soc; Soc Exp Biol; Am Soc Zoologists; Soc Physiol. **Research Statement & Publications:** Structural and physiological approach of adaptative processes in vertebrates, more particularly fishes; osmoregulation, circulation and respiration; gill morphology and physiology, acid-base regulation and ion transport; immunocytochimie of carbonic anhydrase, cortisol, prolactine; cell kinetics. **Mailing Address:** 18 Rue de la Scierie, Ittenheim F 67117, France. **Fax:** 338-869-0813.

LAURENT, ROGER, GEOLOGY. **Personal Data:** b Geneva, Switz, June 23, 1938. **Education:** Univ Geneva, Lic es sci, 1962, Ing Geol, 1964, Dr es Sci(geol & mineral sci), 1967. **Professional Experience:** RETIRED; vis prof, Univ Geneve, Switz, 1989; vis prof, Univ Nancy, France, 1980; prof petrol, Laval Univ, beginning 1979; assoc prof, Laval Univ, 1973-1979; adj prof, Laval Univ, 1971-1973; asst prof mineral & petrog, Middlebury Col, 1967-1971; res asst geochronol, Sci Res Nat Corp Switz, 1965-1967; asst mineral, Univ Geneva, 1963-1965. **Memberships:** Fel Geol Asn Can; Swiss Soc Mineral & Petrol; Swiss Geol Soc; fel Geol Soc Am. **Research Statement & Publications:** Study of ophiolites, asbestos and chromite in the field and in the labs by petrography; petrology; geochronometric determinations and geochemical studies; study of platinum in ultramafic rocks. **Mailing Address:** Dept Geol, Laval Univ, Quebec, PQ G1K 7P4, Can. **E-Mail:** laurent@ggl.ulaval.ca

LAURENT, SEBASTIAN MARC, catalysis, zeolite science; deceased, see previous edition for last biography

LAURENT, TORVARD CLAUDE, BIOCHEMISTRY. **Personal Data:** b Stockholm, Sweden, December 5, 1930. **Education:** Karolinska Inst, BM, 1950, MD, 1958. **Honorary Degrees:** MD, Turku Univ, Finland, 1993; PharmD, Bologna Univ, Italy, 1994. **Professional Experience:** SCI SECY, WENNER-GREU FOUND, 1993-; Mem, Nobel Comt Chem, 1992-; vis prof biochem, Monash Univ, Australia, 1979-1980; chair, Dept Med & Physiol Chem, 1973-1977 & 1987-1991; Mem, Swed Med Res Coun, 1970-1977; Mem, Swed Natural Sci Res Coun, 1968-1970; prof med & physiol chem, Univ Uppsala, Sweden, 1966-1996; assoc prof, Univ Uppsala, Sweden, 1961-1966; res fel & assoc, Retina Found, 1953-1954 & 1959-1961; Instr histol & chem, Karolinska Inst, 1949-1952 & 1955-1958. **Memberships:** Royal Swed Acad Sci (pres, 1991-1994); Swed Biochem Soc (secy, 1967-1970). **Research Statement & Publications:** Chemistry of connective tissue, physical properties, physiological functions; turnover and medical applications of the polysaccharide hyaluronan; opthalmic biochemistry, physical chemistry of polysaccharide networks; transport processes in polysaccharide solutions, biochemical separation techniques; methods for cell separation. **Mailing Address:** Inst Med/Physiol Chem Univ Uppsala, BMC Box 575, Uppsala S-751 23, Sweden.

LAURENZI, BERNARD JOHN, CHEMICAL PHYSICS. **Personal Data:** b Philadelphia, Pa, December 23, 1938. **Education:** St Joseph's Col, Pa, BS, 1960; Univ Pa, PhD (chem), 1965. **Professional Experience:** PROF CHEM, STATE UNIV NY, ALBANY, 1984-; from asst prof to assoc prof, State Univ NY, Albany, 1969-1983; asst prof chem, Univ Tenn, Knoxville, 1966-1968 & Bryn Mawr Col, 1968-1969; NSF fel, Pa State Univ, 1965-1966; res chemist, Rohm & Haas Chem Co, 1960-1961. **Memberships:** Am Chem Soc; Am Phys Soc. **Research Statement & Publications:** Quantum chemistry; use of Green's functions in atomic and molecular calculations; properties of isoelectronic molecules. **Mailing Address:** Dept Chem, Univ Albany, 1400 Wash Ave, Albany, NY 12222. **Fax:** 518-442-3462. **E-Mail:** bjl01@albany.edu

LAURENZI, GUSTAVE, MEDICINE. **Personal Data:** b Orange, NJ, July 19, 1926. **Education:** NY Univ, BA, 1949; Georgetown Univ, MD, 1953; Am Bd Internal Med, dipl; Am Bd Pulmonary Dis, dipl. **Professional Experience:** CLINICAL PROF MED, SCH MED, TUFTS UNIV, 1975-; assoc prof, Sch Med, Tufts Univ, 1970-1975; chief med, St Vincent Hosp, Worcester, Mass, 1968-; assoc prof med, NJ Col Med & Dent, 1963-1968; Am Thoracic Soc Edward L Trudeau fel, 1962-1964; asst prof med & dir div respiratory dis, NJ Col Med & Dent, 1960-1963; consult, Harvard Med Serv, Boston City Hosp, 1959-1960; channing res fel bact & immunol, Mallory Inst Path, Harvard Univ & res fel, Am

Thoracic Soc, 1959-1960; chief resident physician chest serv, Bellevue Med Ctr, 1958-1959; Nat Found training fel, Am Trudeau Soc, 1958-1959; USPHS res fel, 1957-1958; Res fel, Cardiopulmonary Lab, Columbia-Presby Med Ctr, 1956-1957; asst resident, Columbia Med Serv, Bellevue Hosp, NY, 1955-1956; intern med, Yale Med Serv, Grace-New Haven Hosp, Conn, 1954-1955; Intern path, Mallory Inst Path, Boston City Hosp, 1953-1954; dir respiratory care serv, Newton-Wellesley Hosp. **Memberships:** Fel Am Col Physicians; Am Thoracic Soc; Am Fedn Clin Res. **Research Statement & Publications:** Chest disease; chronic bronchitis and pulmonary emphysema. **Mailing Address:** Tufts Univ, Sch Med, Dept Med, 136 Harrison Ave, Boston, MA 02111.

LAURIE, GORDON WILLIAM, CELL BIOLOGY, EXTRACELLULAR MATRIX. **Personal Data:** b Hamilton, Ont, December 28, 1953; m 1981, c 2. **Education:** McMaster Univ, BSc, 1976; McGill Univ, MSc, 1979, PhD (anat), 1982. **Honors & Awards:** Ralph D Lillie Award, Am Histochem, Soc, 1982. **Professional Experience:** ASSOC PROF, DEPT CELL BIOL, UNIV VA, 1994-; asst prof, Dept Cell Biol, Univ VA, 1988-1994; from vis fel to vis assoc, NIH, 1983-1988. **Memberships:** Am Asn Anatomists; Am Soc Cell Biol; Soc Develop Biol. **Research Statement & Publications:** Molecular assembly and sythesis of basement membrane and its relation to cell receptors. **Mailing Address:** Dept Anat & Cell Biol, Univ Va, PO Box 439 Jordan 3-94 Health Syst, Charlottesville, VA 22908. **Fax:** 434-982-3912. **E-Mail:** gwl6s@virginia.edu

LAURIE, JOHN SEWALL, EXPERIMENTAL BIOLOGY. **Personal Data:** b Gloucester, Mass, May 30, 1925. **Education:** Ore State Univ, BS, 1950; Johns Hopkins Univ, ScD, 1956. **Professional Experience:** RETIRED; from assoc prof to prof biol, ECarolina Univ, 1963-1990; mem staff water pollution study, USPHS, 1962-1963; asst prof exp biol, Univ Utah, 1959-1962; instr zool, Tulane Univ, 1957-1959; Res fel parasite physiol, Inst Parasitol, McGill Univ, 1956-1957. **Memberships:** Am Soc Parasitol; Wildlife Dis Asn; Am Soc Zoologists; Sigma Xi. **Research Statement & Publications:** Physiology of parasites; physiology, ultrastructure and ecology of helminth parasites. **Mailing Address:** 1900 S Charles Blvd, Greenville, NC 27858.

LAURIE, VICTOR WILLIAM, PHYSICAL CHEMISTRY. **Personal Data:** b Columbia, SC, June 1, 1935. **Education:** Univ SC, BS, 1954; Harvard Univ, AM, 1956, PhD (chem), 1958. **Professional Experience:** PROF EMER CHEM, PRINCETON UNIV, as of 2005; prof, Princeton Univ, 1971-1980; John S Guggenheim fel, 1970; assoc prof chem, Princeton Univ, 1966-1971; Alfred P Sloan fel, 1963-1967; asst prof chem, Stanford Univ, 1960-1966; NSF fel, Univ Calif, 1959-1960; fel, Nat Res Coun, Nat Bur Stand, 1957-1959. **Memberships:** Sigma Xi; AAAS; Am Chem Soc; Am Phys Soc. **Research Statement & Publications:** Molecular spectroscopy and structure. **Mailing Address:** Dept Chem, Princeton Univ, Princeton, NJ 08544.

LAURIENTE, MIKE, METALLURGY, SPACE ATMOSPHERES. **Personal Data:** b Trail, BC, June 26, 1922. **Education:** Mich Technol Univ, BS, 1943, MS, 1947. **Honorary Degrees:** DrEng, Johns Hopkins Univ, 1955. **Professional Experience:** RETIRED; tech mgr, Goddard Space Flight Ctr, Nasa, Greenbelt, Md, 1983-1997; asst secy transp, Off Systs Eng, US Dept Transp, Wash, DC, 1971-1983; adv engr, Aerospace Div, Westinghouse Elec Corp, Md, 1962-1971; fel engr, Aerospace Div, Westinghouse Elec Corp, Md, 1956-1962; consult, Ballistics Res Lab, Ord Dept, US Army, Aberdeen Proving Ground, 1951-1955; res staff asst metal physics, Johns Hopkins Univ, 1949-1955; metallurgist, Int Harvester Co, Ill, 1947-1949. **Memberships:** Am Phys Soc; fel Am Soc Metals; Sigma Xi. **Research Statement & Publications:** Magnetic thin films; active and passive electronic devices; radiation damage; electrical insulation; magnetic anisotropic metals; technological advances having application to transportation safety and security; fracture mechanics; nondestructive testing; space environment. **Mailing Address:** 6608 White Gate Rd Clarksville Ridge, Clarksville, MD 21029. **Fax:** 301-286-1742. **E-Mail:** laurient@envnet.gsfc.nasa.gov

LAURIN, PUSHPAMALA, ELECTROMAGNETISM, TELECOMMUNICATIONS. **Personal Data:** b Bangalore City, India, American citizen; m 1964, c Nicole & Erik. **Education:** Gujarat Univ, India, BSc, 1956; Karnatak Univ, India, MSc, 1958; Univ Mich, Ann Arbor, MSE, 1962, PhD (physics), 1967. **Professional Experience:** SR PROJ MGR, SATELLITE COMMUN, MOTOROLLA INC, 1989-; VP Business develop Telesoft Inc, 2001-; sr resource mgr, Cellular Intrastruct Group, Motorola Inc, 1989-2001; at AT&T Bell Labs, Maperville, Ill, 1986-1989; vpres, Greame Publ Co, Wilborheim, Mass, 1984-1986 & AT&T Bell Labs, 1986-1989; dir info resources, Gould Inc, Rolling Meadows, Ill, 1976-1986; instr electronics & physics, Harper Col, 1971-1976; lectr elec eng & physics, Southern Ill Univ, 1970-1971; res scientist physics, McDonnell-Douglas Corp, Mo, 1968-1969; asst prof math, Eastern Mich Univ, 1967-1968; asst res physicist, Radiation Lab, 1962-1967; res asst meteorol, Univ Mich, Ann Arbor, 1961-1962; sales engr, Toshniwal Bros, Bombay, 1959-1960; jr sci asst, Nat Sugar Inst, Kanpur, India, 1958-1959. **Memberships:** Inst Elec & Electronics Engrs. **Research Statement & Publications:** Electromagnetic interactions. **Mailing Address:** 2703 W Ironwood Dr, Chandler, AZ 85224. **E-Mail:** mlaurin@indts.com

LAURITZEN, PETER O, POWER ELECTRONICS & SEMICONDUCTOR DEVICE MODELING. **Personal Data:** b Valparaiso, Ind, February 14, 1935; m 1963, Helen Janzen; c Beth & Margo. **Education:** Calif Inst Technol, BS, 1956; Stanford Univ, MS, 1958, PhD (elec eng), 1961. **Honors & Awards:** Emeritus pvt elec enor, Univ Wash, 1999-; fulbright sr lecturer, Indian Inst Technol, Madras, India, 1997, danfoss prof, Aalborg Univ, Denmark, 1999. **Professional Experience:** Eng mgr, Avtech Corp, 1979-1980; Adj prof social mgt technol, Univ Wash, 1977-1982; PROF ELEC ENG, UNIV WASH, 1973-; from asst prof to assoc prof, Univ Wash, 1965-1973; mem tech staff, Fairchild Semiconductor Div, 1961-1965. **Memberships:** Inst Elec & Electronics Engrs; AAAS. **Research Statement & Publications:** Semiconductor device modeling; power electronics. **Mailing Address:** Dept Elec Eng Box 352500, Univ Wash, Seattle, WA 98195. **E-Mail:** plauritz@ee.washington.edu

LAURS, MICHAEL, OCEANOGRAPHY. **Education:** Ore State Univ, BS, 1961. **Professional Experience:** RETIRED; mem adv bd, Large Pelagics Res Ctr, Univ NH, as of 2005. **Mailing Address:** Large Pelagics Res Ctr Univ NH, Spaulding Hall 46 Col Rd, Durham, NH 03824. **Fax:** 603-862-3442.

LAURS, R(OBERT) MICHAEL, OCEANOGRAPHY, FISHERIES. **Personal Data:** b Oregon City, Ore, January 27, 1939; m 1982, Betty; c Brendan M & Meghan M. **Education:** Ore State Univ, BS, 1961, MS, 1963, PhD (oceanog), 1967. **Honors & Awards:** Silver Medal, Dept Com, 1980. **Professional Experience:** LAB DIR, PAC FISH ENVIRON LAB, NAT MARINE FISHERIES SERV, 2004-2005; LAB DIR, HONOLULU LAB, NAT MARINE FISHERIES SERV, 1994-2004 sci subgroup, Intergov Oceanog Comn, Intergrated Global Ocean Sta Syst, 1981-; Sci adv, AmFisherman's Res Found, 1971-; Oceanogr, Southwest Fisheries Ctr, La Jolla Lab, Calif, 1967-1994. **Memberships:** AAAS; Marine Biol Asn UK; Am Soc Limnol & Oceanog; Am Inst Fishery Res Biologists; Eastern Pac Oceanic Conf; Am Fisheries Soc. **Research Statement & Publications:** Fishery forecasting; environmental conditions affecting the distribution and abundance of tunas; albacore tuna ecology; vertical distribution and migration of micronektonic organisms; satellite oceanography. **Mailing Address:** R Michael Laurs, 555 Grove St, Jacksonville, OR 97530. **E-Mail:** mike.laurs@noaa.gov

LAURSEN, E(MMETT) M(ORTON), HYDRAULIC ENGINEERING. **Personal Data:** b Fairmount, NDak, January 24, 1919. **Education:** Univ Minn, BCE, 1941; Univ Iowa, PhD (mech, hydraul), 1958. **Honors & Awards:** Hilgard Prize, Am Soc Civil Engrs, 1959, Res Prize, 1961. **Professional Experience:** RETIRED; Consult, 1985-; PROF CIVIL ENG, UNIV ARIZ, beginning 1962; head dept, Univ Ariz, 1962-1968; assoc prof civil eng, Mich State Univ, 1958-1962; res engr, Inst Hydraul Res, Univ Iowa, 1948-1958; res assoc, Inst Hydraul Res, Univ Iowa, 1947-1948; asst, Inst Hydraul Res, Univ Iowa, 1945-1947; asst scientist, St Anthony Falls Hydraul Lab, Minn, 1945; jr engr, Al Johnson Construct Co, 1942-1943; Asst, St Anthony Falls Hydraul Lab, Minn, 1941-1942. **Memberships:** Am Soc Civil Engrs; Am Geophys Union; Int Asn Hydraul Res. **Research Statement & Publications:** Sediment transportation; fluid mechanics and its applications. **Mailing Address:** 926 W Comobabi Dr, Tucson, AZ 85704.

LAURSEN, GARY A, MYCOLOGY, ARCTIC ECOLOGY. **Personal Data:** b Seattle, Wash, August 13, 1942; m Elizabeth; c Shawna Lea & Heather Frances (Johnson). **Education:** Western Wash Univ, BA, 1965; Univ Mont, MST, 1970; Va Polytech Inst & State Univ, PhD (bot/mycol), 1975. **Honors & Awards:** Sigma Xi Res Award, Va Polytech Inst & State Univ, 1977 Presidential Award for Sci Teaching Excellance, NSF, 1987; Outstanding Biology Teachers Educators, Alaska, 1992; Technology Scholar, Tandy Corp, 1994. **Professional Experience:** Adj prof biol, dept biol, Univ Alaska, Fairbanks, 2000-; SR RES PROF, INST ARCTIC BIOL, UNIV ALASKA, FAIRBANKS, 1997-; proj officer cold prog, Off Naval Res, Arlington, 1980-1982; prof officer cold prog, Off Naval Res, Arlington, 1980-1982; actg tech dir admin & sci, Naval Arctic Res Lab, Univ Alaska, 1976-1977 & Remote Sensing Prog, 1977-1978; prin investr, Animal Res Facil, Univ Alaska, 1976-; asst dir sci, Naval Arctic Res Lab, 1976-1980; res assoc, Va Polytech Inst & State Univ, 1975-1976; res asst mycol, Va Polytech Inst & State Univ, 1971-1975; biol instr, Toppenish, Wash, Sch Dist, 1965-1971. **Memberships:** Mycol Soc Am; Sigma Xi; National Sci Teachers Assoc; North Am Soc; Phi Delta Keppa; Beta Sigma Phi. **Research Statement & Publications:** Systematic and ecological treatments of Arctic, Alpine and Meratime tundra fleshy fungi, their role and significance within these environmentally harsh ecosystems. **Mailing Address:** Dept Biol Sci Inst Arctic Biol Univ Alaska, PO Box 757000, Fairbanks, AK 99775. **Fax:** 907-474-6185. **E-Mail:** ffgal@uaf.edu

LAURSEN, PAUL HERBERT, GENERAL CHEMISTRY. **Personal Data:** b Ord, Nebr, March 28, 1929. **Education:** Dana Col, BA, 1954; Ore State Univ, PhD (org chem), 1961. **Professional Experience:** PROF EMER CHEM, NEBR WESLEYAN UNIV, as of 2004; provost, Nebr Wesleyan Univ, beginning 1978; acad dean, Nebr Wesleyan Univ, 1976-1978; NSF sci fac fel, Univ Calif, Los Angeles, 1967-1968; prof chem, Nebr Wesleyan Univ, beginning 1964; from asst prof to assoc prof chem, Nebr Wesleyan Univ, 1959-1964. **Memberships:** AAAS; Am Chem Soc. **Research Statement & Publications:** Synthesis of nitrogen heterocycles; identification of natural products. **Mailing Address:** Dept Chem, Nebr Wesleyan Univ, 5000 St Paul Ave, Lincoln, NE 68504-2794.

LAURSEN, RICHARD ALLAN, BIO-ORGANIC CHEMISTRY, PROTEIN CHEMISTRY. **Personal Data:** b Normal, Ill, May 1, 1938; m 1971, Irene; c Michael & Sarah. **Education:** Univ Calif, Berkeley, BS, 1961; Univ Ill, PhD (chem), 1964. **Honors & Awards:** Pehr Edman Award, 1988. **Professional Experience:** Vis scientist metrop mus art, Ny, NY, 1999; specialist protein chem, int panel, Chinese Prov Univ Develop, Worlk Banak, Hunan Normal Univ, Chsngsha, People's Repub China, 1990; mem sci adv comt on clin invest, NSF Biol Instrumentation Prog, 1984-1988; PROF CHEM, BOSTON UNIV, 1976-; mem sci adv comt on clin invest, Am Cancer Soc, 1975-1979; Alfred P Sloan fel, 1972-1974; guest scientist, Max Planck Inst Molecular Genetics, 1971; NIH res career develop award, Boston Univ 1969-1974; from asst prof to assoc prof, Boston Univ, 1966-1976; NIH fel, Harvard Univ, 1964-1966. **Memberships:** Fel AAAS; fel AAAS; Am Chem Soc; Am Soc Biochem & Molecular Biol; Protein Soc; Peptide Soc. **Research Statement & Publications:** Development of methods and materials for the synthesis of peptide microarrays; development of analytical methods for and anlysis of artists materials. **Mailing Address:** Dept Chem, Boston Univ, 590 Commonwealth Ave, Boston, MA 02215. **Fax:** 617-353-6466. **E-Mail:** laursen@bu.edu

LAURSEN, TOD ALAN, COMPUTATIONAL & CONTACT MECHANICS. **Personal Data:** b Corvallis, Ore, March 3, 1964. **Education:** Ore State Univ, BS, 1986; Stanford Univ, MS, 1989, PhD (mech eng), 1992. **Honors & Awards:** Career Award, NSF, 1997. **Professional Experience:** PROF CIVIL & ENVIRON ENG, DUKE UNIV, as of 2003; SR ASSOC DEAN EDUC, DUKE UNIV, as of 2003; Young investr award, Off Naval res, 1997; consult, Lawrence Livermore Nat Lab, 1992-; asst prof civil eng, Duke Univ, beginning 1992; engr, Lawrence Livermore Nat Lab, 1986-1992. **Memberships:** Am Soc Mech Engrs; Am Soc Civil Engrs; Am Acad Mech; Sigma Xi; US Asn Comput Mech. **Research Statement & Publications:** Continuum and computational mechanics; formulations and numerical descriptions for systems featuring contact and impact phenomena. **Mailing Address:** Dept Civil & Environ Eng, Duke Univ, Box 90287 127 Hudson Hall, Durham, NC 27708-0287. **Fax:** 919-660-5219. **E-Mail:** laursen@duke.edu

LAUSCH, ROBERT NAGLE, IMMUNOBIOLOGY. **Personal Data:** b Chambersburg, Pa, February 22, 1938. **Education:** Muhlenberg Col, BS, 1960; Pa State Univ, MS, 1962; Univ Fla, PhD (microbiol), 1966. **Professional Experience:** PROF MICROBIOL & IMMUNOL, COL MED, UNIV SOUTH ALA, 1985-; assoc prof, Col Med, Univ South Ala, 1977-1985; assoc prof microbiol, Col Med, Pa State Univ, 1975-1977; asst prof, Col Med, Pa State Univ, 1969-1975; Fel virol, Baylor Col Med, 1966-1969. **Memberships:** Am Soc Microbiol; Am Asn Cancer Res; Am Asn Immunologists; Fedn Am Socs Exp Biol; Asn Res Vision Ophthal. **Research Statement & Publications:** Virus immunology; Study of mechanisms operative in ocular inflammation. **Mailing Address:** Dept Microbiol & Immunol, Col Med, Univ S Ala, MSB 2096, Mobile, AL 36688. **Fax:** 251-460-7931. **E-Mail:** rlausch@jaguar1.usouthal.edu

LAUSH, GEORGE, MATHEMATICS. **Personal Data:** b Barrackville, WVa, September 17, 1921; wid Dolores M (deceased). **Education:** Univ Pittsburgh, BS, 1943; Cornell Univ, PhD, 1949. **Professional Experience:** Prof emer, univ of Pittsburgh, 1983-; PROF MATH, UNIV PITTSBURGH, 1962-; from asst prof to assoc prof, Univ Pittsburgh, 1949-1962; asst math, Cornell Univ, 1946-1949; res assoc, Manhattan Dist, Univ Rochester, 1944-1946; Asst chem, Univ Pittsburgh, 1943-1944. **Memberships:** Am Math Soc; Math Asn Am. **Research Statement & Publications:** Infinite series; real functions; functional analysis. **Mailing Address:** 181 Pearce Mill Rd, Wexford, PA 15090-8508.

LAUSHMAN, ROGER H, POPULATION GENETICS, CONSERVATION BIOLOGY. **Personal Data:** b Ida Grove, Iowa, May 3, 1950. **Education:** Univ Ga, PhD (bot), 1988; Univ Kans, BS, 1979; Iowa State Univ, MS, 1983. **Professional Experience:** ASSOC PROF BIOL, OBERLIN COL, as of 2006; vis asst prof evolution & ecol, Oberlin Col, beginning

1989; postdoctoral fel, Friday Harbor Labs, Univ Wash, 1988-1989. **Memberships:** Bot Soc Am; Ecol Soc Am; Soc Conserv Biol; Soc Study Evol; Am Soc Naturalists. **Research Statement & Publications:** Population genetics of aquatic vascular plants, particularly those with water-pollination; conservation biology, particularly of threatened plant species and aquatic habitats. **Mailing Address:** Dept Biol, Sci Ctr, Oberlin Col, K123, 119 Woodland St, Oberlin, OH 44074-1097. **Fax:** 440-775-8960. **E-Mail:** roger.laushman@oberlin.edu

LAUTENBERGER, WILLIAM J, APPLIED STATISTICS, PHYSICAL & POLYIMIDE CHEMISTRY. **Personal Data:** b Flushing, NY, March 11, 1943; m 1979, Anita Spiegel; c Gemma, Will, Joanna. **Education:** Muhlenberg Col, BS, 1964; Univ Pa, PhD (phys chem), 1967. **Professional Experience:** 1996-2001, quality manager, HD Microsystems (JV between Dupont & Hitachi Chemical); RES SUPVR, ELECTRONICS DEPT, E I DU PONT DEL NEMOURS & CO, WILMINGTON, 1981-; 1981-1996, research supervisor, Electronic Dept.; develop specialist, indust hyg, Du Pont Fabrics & Finishes Dept, Appl Technol Div, 1978-1981; statist prog consult, Org Chem Dept, Exp Sta, Wilmington, 1974-1978; res chemist, Org Chem Dept, Exp Sta, Wilmington, 1971-1974; Res chemist, Dye Div, Org Chem & Res & Develop Dept, Jackson Labs, NJ, 1967-1971. **Memberships:** Am Chem Soc; Sigma Xi. **Research Statement & Publications:** Reaction mechanisms; photochemistry; heterogenous catalysis; mechanisms of dyeing; emulsion science; solid-solid adsorption; consulting in design and analysis of experiments; air sampling; gas diffusion mechanisms; gas adsorption, desorption phenomena, electronic materials, semiconductors and packaging materials PWB laminates, photo polymers; polyimide polymers. **Mailing Address:** 506 Ott Rd, Bala Cynwyd, PA 19004-2510. **Fax:** 610-668-1536.

LAUTENS, MARK, ASYMMETRIC SYNTHESIS, CATALYSIS. **Personal Data:** b Hamilton, Ont, July 9, 1959; c 2. **Education:** Univ Guelph, BSc, 1981; Univ Wis-Madison, PhD (chem), 1985. **Honors & Awards:** FRSC, Royal soc of Can, 2001; Merck Frosst Awardee, Can Soc Chem, 1994; Rutherford Prize, Royal Soc Can, 1994, AC Cope Scholar, Am Chem Soc, 2006; R Lemieux Award, Can Soc Chem, 2004; A Bader Award, Can Soc Chem, 2004. **Professional Experience:** ASTRAZENECA PROF OF ORGANIC SYNTHESIS, UNIV Toronto, 1998- MERCKFROSST/NSERC INDUSTRIAL RESEARCH CHAIR, UNIV Toronto, 2003-; PROF CHEM, UNIV TORONTO, 1995-; Steacie res fel, Natural Sci & Eng Res Coun, 1994-1996; Eli Lilly Awardee, 1992-; Alfred P Sloan Found fel, 1991; Biomega young investr, 1989-1993; from asst prof to assoc prof chem, Univ Toronto, 1987-1995; Res assoc, Harvard Univ, 1985-1987. **Memberships:** Am Chem Soc; Can Soc Chem. **Research Statement & Publications:** Synthesis of biologically active or structurally novel compounds; metal catalyzed reactions for control of stereochemistry; asymmetric synthesis; multicomponent reactions. **Mailing Address:** Dept Chem, Univ Toronto, Toronto, ON M5S 1A1, Can. **Fax:** 416-946-8185. **E-Mail:** mlautens@chem.utoronto.ca

LAUTENSCHLAEGER, FRIEDRICH KARL, ORGANIC CHEMISTRY. **Personal Data:** b Gefell, Ger, June 27, 1934. **Education:** Univ Heidelberg, BA, 1956; Univ Toronto, MA, 1960. **Professional Experience:** SR SCIENTIST, TREMCO RES CTR, DUNLOP CO, LTD, TORONTO, 1985-; group leader, Dunlop Res Ctr, 1972-1985; res chemist, NAm Res Ctr, 1961-1972; Res asst org chem, Univ Toronto, 1957-1959. **Memberships:** Am Chem Soc. **Research Statement & Publications:** Stereochemistry of organic compounds; synthesis of small ring compounds; organic sulfur chemistry; reactive intermediates; vulcanization chemistry and physics; radiation vulcanization/cure for pressure-sensitive products. **Mailing Address:** 2562 Cushing Rd, Mississauga, ON L5K 1X1, Can.

LAUTENSCHLAGER, EUGENE PAUL, BIOMATERIALS. **Personal Data:** b Chicago, Ill, April 5, 1937; m Patricia. **Education:** Ill Inst Technol, BS, 1958; Northwestern Univ, MS, 1960, PhD (mat sci), 1966. **Honors & Awards:** F4 Award of Merit, Am Soc Testing & Mat. **Professional Experience:** DIR, SKINNER LAB BIOMAT RES, as of 2004; CLIFFORD C RAISBECK, PROF ORTHOP SURG, NORTHWESTERN UNIV, as of 2003; div dir, North-Western Univ, 1988-2001; vis prof, Free Univ Berlin, 1984; prof biol mat, NorthWestern Univ, 1974-2001; consult, Bioengineering Comt, Am Acad Orthop Surgeons, 1973-1985; NIH career develop award, 1971-1975; from asst prof to assoc prof, Northwestern Univ, 1966-1974; res metallurgist, Allis-Chalmers Mfg Co, 1960-1962. **Memberships:** Am Soc Testing & Mat; Am Inst Mining Metall & Petrol Eng; Int Asn Dent Res; Am Soc Metals; Acad Dent Mat. **Research Statement & Publications:** Biological and dental materials; medical implant materials; kinetics of cementing media for implant stabilization; computer assisted instruction. **Mailing Address:** Skinner Lab Biomat Res, Northwestern Univ, 311 E Chicago Ave, Chicago, IL 60611. **Fax:** 312-503-2440. **E-Mail:** epl560@nwu.edu

LAUTERBACH, GEORGE ERVIN, PHYSICAL CHEMISTRY. **Personal Data:** b Bushnell, Ill, June 13, 1927. **Education:** Monmouth Col, BS, 1949; Bradley Univ, MS, 1953; Purdue Univ, PhD (biochem), 1958. **Professional Experience:** MGR NEW PRODS RES & DEVELOP, MARINE COLLOIDS INC, 1978-; assoc prof chem & res assoc, Div Natural Mat & Systs, Inst Paper Chem, 1965-1978; res org chemist, Paper Lab, Kimberly Clark Corp, 1957-1965 & Pioneering & Advan Develop Lab, 1965; Chemist, Starch & Dextrose Div, Northern Regional Res Lab, 1949-1953. **Memberships:** Am Chem Soc; Tech Asn Pulp & Paper Indust; Am Asn Cereal Chemists. **Research Statement & Publications:** Polysaccharide chemistry; enzymic and chemical modification of starch; high temperature starch cooking; hemicelluloses; starch in paper coatings; top sizes and internal sizing of paper products. **Mailing Address:** PO Box 213, Thomaston, ME 04861-0213.

LAUTERBACH, HANS, PHARMACEUTICAL SCIENCE. **Personal Data:** b 1934. **Professional Experience:** PRES, DIAG DIV, MILES INC, 1992-; Staff, Bayer AG, Leverkusen, Ger, 1951-1991. **Mailing Address:** Bayer Corp, 100 Bayer Rd, Pittsburgh, PA 15205-9741.

LAUTERBACH, JOHN HARVEY, CARBOHYDRATE CHEMISTRY, TOBACCO CHEMISTRY. **Personal Data:** b Jersey City, NJ, April 2, 1944; div. **Education:** Worcester Polytech Inst, BS, 1966; Ohio State Univ, MSc, 1968, PhD (chem), 1970. **Professional Experience:** DIR RES SERV, BROWN & WILLIAMSONTOBACCO CORP, 1992-; Mgr Res Serv, Brown & Williamson Tobacco Corp, 1989-1993; mgr mat res, Brown & Williamson Tobacco Corp, 1987-1989; analytical res div head, Brown & Williamson Tobacco Corp, 1980-1987; dir chem, Prof Serv Indust, Inc, 1979-1980; mgr chem, Pillsbury Co, 1978-1979; Chmn, Environ Comn, Borough Raritan, NJ, 1976-1978; mgr, Cent Tech Eval, Nat Starch & Chem Corp, 1974-1978; proj supvr, Cent Tech Eval, Nat Starch & Chem Corp, 1971-1973; res assoc, 1967-1968 & org chem, 1970-; chemist analytical chem, Union Carbide Chem & Plastics Co, 1970-1971; chief asst, 1967-1968 & org chem, 1968-1969; Asst analytical chem, Ohio State Univ, 1966-1967; chmn & bd dirs, Tobacco Inst Testing Lab, Bethesda, Md. **Memberships:** Am Chem Soc; fel Am Inst Chemists; fel Royal Soc Chem; Sigma Xi; Am Soc Testing & Mat; Am Mgt Asn; Inst Food Technol. **Research Statement & Publications:** Polysaccharide chemistry, particularly structure determinations and modifications; high performance liquid chromatography and nuclear magnetic resonance spectroscopy; new techniques for managing service departments in research and development organizations; tobacco chemistry; gas chromatography, liquid chromatography and mass spectrometry. **Mailing Address:** Brown & Williamson Tobacco, 2600 Weaver Rd, Macon, GA 31298. **Fax:** 502-568-8210.

LAUTERBACH, RICHARD THOMAS, POLYMER CHEMISTRY, ORGANIC CHEMISTRY. **Personal Data:** b Rochester, Pa, December 29, 1946. **Education:** Johns Hopkins Univ, BS, 1968; Northwestern Univ, PhD (chem), 1975. **Professional Experience:** GROUP LEADER, OIL FIELD SERV, RICHARDSON CO, 1981-; group leader protective coatings, Daubert Chem Co, 1980-1981; Group leader water soluble polymers, Daubert Chem Co, 1975-1980. **Memberships:** Am Chem Soc; Soc Cosmetic Chem. **Research Statement & Publications:** Water soluble polymers for wastewater treatment and paper production additives; corrosion preventive coatings. **Mailing Address:** 632 S Tenth Ave, La Grange, IL 60525-3036.

LAUTERBUR, PAUL CHRISTIAN, PHYSICALCHEMISTRY, MEDICAL IMAGING. **Personal Data:** b Sidney, Ohio, May 6, 1929; American citizen. **Education:** Case Inst Technol, BS, 1951; Univ Pittsburgh, PhD (chem), 1962. **Honorary Degrees:** Dr, Univ Liege, Belg, 1984, Nicolaus Copernicus Med Acad, Poland, 1988; DSc, Carnegie Mellon Univ, 1987, Wesleyan Univ, 1989, State Univ NY, 1990. **Honors & Awards:** Nobel Prize Physiol Med 2003; Gold Medal, Soc Magnetic Resonance Med, 1982; Smith Kline & Fr Lectr, Univ Col London, 1983; Biol Physics Prize, Am Phys Soc, 1983; Jesse Beams Lectr, Univ Va, 1983; H H Iddles Lectr Chem, Univ NH, 1984; Howard N Potts Medal, Franklin Inst, 1984; Albert Lasker Clin Res Award, 1984; Gairdner Found Int Award, 1985; Kosar Mem Award, Soc Photog Scientists & Engrs, 1985; Charles F Kettering Prize, Gen Motors Cancer Res Found, 1985; Distinguished Res Biomed Sci Award, Asn Am Med Col, 1986; Medal Honor, Inst Elec & Electronics Engrs, 1987; Nat Medal Sci, 1987; Roentgen Medal, 1987; Nat Medal Technol, 1988; Gold Medal Award, Soc Comput Body Tomog, 1989; Laufman-Greatbatch Award, Asn Advan Med Instrumentation, 1989; Int Soc Magnetic Resonance Award, 1992; Kyoto Prize, Inamori Found (Japan), 1994. **Professional Experience:** PROF CHEM, UNIV ILL, URBANA, as of 2001; DISTINGUISHED UNIV PROF, COL MED, UNIV ILL, CHICAGO, 1990-; prof Bioeng, Dept Elect & Comput Eng & prof biophys, Dept Physiol & Biophys, 1988-; prof, Ctr Advan Study, Univ Ill, Urbana-Champaign, 1987-; adj prof, State Univ NY, Stony Brook, 1985-; HEAD, DEPT MED INFO SCI & DEPT CHEM, URBANA- CHAMPAIGN, 1985-; DIR, BIOMED MAGNETIC RESONANCE LAB, 1985-; prof, Biomed Magnetic Resonance Lab, 1985-1990; univ prof, State Univ NY, Stony Brook, 1984-1985; leading prof chem, State Univ NY, Stony Brook, 1983-1984; ed-in-chief, Magnetic Resonance Med, 1982-1983; res prof radiol, State Univ NY, Stony Brook, 1978-1985; vis scholar, Dept Chem, Stanford Univ, 1969-1970; Alfred P Sloan fel, 1965-1967; from assoc prof to prof chem, State Univ NY, Stony Brook, 1963-1983; chmn, subcomt E-13.7 Nuclear Magnetic Resonance, Soc Testing & Mat, 1960-1962; fel, Mellon Inst, 1955-1963; jr fel, Mellon Inst, 1953; res assoc, Mellon Inst, 1952-1953; res asst, Mellon Inst, 1951-1952. **Memberships:** Nat Acad Sci; fel Am Phys Soc; Am Chem Soc; fel AAAS; Soc Magnetic Resonance Med (pres 1981-1983); Sigma Xi; Radiol Soc NAm; Inst Elec & Electronics Engrs; Biophys Soc; Soc Neuroscience. **Research Statement & Publications:** Nuclear magnetic resonance studies of structure and properties of molecules, crystals and biological systems; imaging by magnetic resonance zeugmatography, including biological and medical applications; published numerous articles in various scientific journals. **Mailing Address:** Dept Chem Univ Ill, 600 S Mathews 51-6 MC-712, Urbana, IL 61801. **Fax:** 217-244-0445. **E-Mail:** pcl@uiuc.edu

LAUTERIO, THOMAS J, NUTRITION BIOCHEMISTRY. **Professional Experience:** ASSOC PROF, DIABETES INST, EASTERN VA MED SCH, as of 2000. **Mailing Address:** Diabetes Inst, Eastern Va Med Sch, Norfolk, VA 23502.

LAUTT, WILFRED WAYNE, LIVER FUNCTIONS, HEPATIC CIRCULATION, TYPE 2 DIABETES. **Personal Data:** b Lethbridge, Alta, June 29, 1946. **Education:** Univ Alta, BSc (Honors physiology), 1968; Univ Man, MSc, 1970; PhD (pharmacol), 1972; Univ Montreal, MRC Toxicology Fellowship 1972-1974. **Honors & Awards:** Michael Smith Prize in Health Research Finalist Award for recognition and support of outstanding research presented by the Canadian Institutes of Health Research, 2004-2006; Dr RE Beamish Award for excellence in cardiovascular research presented by the Heart & Stroke Foundation of Manitoba, 2002, 1999, 1996; Univ of Manitoba Graduate Students Teaching Award, 1999; Ernesto Roma Award for contribution to diabetes research presented by the Portuguese Diabetes Association, 1999; Sigma Xi Senior Scientist Award, 1999; First J A F Stevenson Award Contrib Physiol, Can Physiol Soc, 1980; Ciba Geigy Award Contrib Pharmacol, Pharmacol Soc Can, 1995. **Professional Experience:** Founder, President and CSO of DiaMedica Inc. 2000-present; Advisory Board Member, Journal of Pharmacological Sciences, 2003-2007; Associate Editor, Can J Physiol Pharmacol, 1990-2006; Editoral Board Member, Am J Physiol Gastrointest Liver Physiol, 1988-1998; Pres, Western Pharmacol Soc, 1994; coun mem, Western Pharmacol Soc, 1992-1994; PROF PHARMACOL & THERAPEUT, UNIV MAN, 1989-; dept head, Hepatorenal Res Unit, 1989-1994; prof pharmacol & therapeut & sect head, Univ Man, 1984-1989; sci officer, Grants Comt, Can Heart Found, 1982-1988; mem, Med Adv Bd, Can Liver Found, 1982-1987; mem coun, Can Physiol Soc, 1982-1985; J A F Stevenson vis prof, Can Physiol Soc, 1980; from assoc prof to prof physiol, Can Liver Found, Univ Sask, 1978-1982; asst prof & res scholar, Can Liver Found, Univ Sask, 1974-1978; Med Res Coun Can fel toxicol, Univ Montreal, 1972-1974. **Memberships:** Can Physiol Soc; Am Physiol Soc; Can Pharmacol Soc; Am Asn Study Liver Dis; Can Asn Study Liver Dis (vpres 1985 pres 1987-1988); Am Soc Pharmacol & Exp Therapeut; Can Soc Clin Investr. **Research Statement & Publications:** Peripheral vascular physiology and hepatic physiology, pharmacology and toxicology; vascular and metabolic consequences of autonomic nerve activity in the liver; local control of intestinal and hepatic blood flow; hepatic parasympathetic nerve control of skeletal muscle insulin sensitivity - novel diagnostics and therapeutics for type 2 diabetes. **Mailing Address:** Dept Pharmacol & Therapeut, Univ Man Fac Med, 753 McDermot Ave, A210 Chown Bldg, Winnipeg, MB R3E 0T6, Can. **Fax:** 204-975-7784. **E-Mail:** wlautt@cc.umanitoba.ca

LAUTZENHEISER, CLARENCE ERIC, METALLURGY. **Personal Data:** b Lincoln, Nebr, May 21, 1921. **Education:** Mass Inst Technol, BS, 1952. **Professional Experience:** PRES, INT ENGRS, 1986-; VPRES EMER, NDE SCI & TECHNOL DIV, SOUTHWEST RES INST, 1985-; vpres, Qual Assurance Systs & Eng Div, 1974-1985; from asst dir to dir spec eng serv, Southwest Res Inst, 1969-1974; mgr metall eng, Southwest Res Inst, 1967-1969; Consult, Reliability & Qual Assurance Div, NASA, 1965-1967; sr res engr, Southwest Res Inst, 1962-1967; maintenance specialist, Dow Chem Co, 1960-1962; maintenance engr, Dow Chem Co, 1952-1960; Res engr, Dow Chem Co, 1952-1953. **Memberships:** Am Soc Metals; fel Am Soc Nondestructive Testing (pres 1975-1976); Am Welding Soc; fel Am Soc Mech Engrs; Nat Asn Corrosion Engrs; Sigma Xi. **Research Statement & Publications:** New methods of magnesium production; corrosion; failure analysis; welding; nondestructive inspection in petrochemical industry fabrication quality control and in-service inspection of nuclear reactor power systems. **Mailing Address:** Int Engrs, PO Box 800, Medina, TX 78055.

LAUVER, DEAN C, AERONAUTICAL & ASTRONAUTICAL ENGINEERING. **Personal Data:** b Warren, Pa, June 8, 1920. **Education:** Pa State Univ, BS, 1942. **Professional Experience:** SR PROJ ENGR, AEROSTRUCTURES, INC, 1984-; Navy liaison officer, Adv Group Aerospace Res & Develop, NATO, 1976-1980; dep asst chief technol, Air Progs, Off Naval Res, 1967-1980; Off Naval Res mem Dept Defense res & eng panel supporting res & technol, Aeronaut & Astronaut Coord Bd, 1966-; tech dir, Air Progs, Off Naval Res, 1962-1967; Mem Fed Aviation Agency-Air Force-NASA working groups supersonic transport res progs & Fed Aviation Agency rep on NASA screening comt on mat, 1962; chief, Struct & Mat Br, Fed Aviation Agency, 1961-1962; air craft & missile specialist, Chief Naval Opers, 1959-1961; tech asst & asst head, Contract Struct Design Sect, 1957-1959; head, Struct Design & Analytical Unit, 1949-1957; stress analyst, Air Frame Design Div, Bur Aeronaut, Dept Navy, 1946-1949; Jr engr, Mesta Mach Co, Pa, 1942. **Memberships:** Am Inst Aeronaut & Astronaut. **Research Statement & Publications:** Naval vehicle and weapon research and technology, including sensors, electronics, acoustics and operational analysis. **Mailing Address:** 6538 Cedarwood Ct, Falls Church, VA 22041.

LAUVER, MILTON RENICK, plasma physics; deceased, see previous edition for last biography

LAUVER, RICHARD WILLIAM, PHYSICAL CHEMISTRY, PROJECT MANAGEMENT. **Personal Data:** b Monmouth, Ill, March 15, 1943; m 1972, Lorna; c Ned William Lauver. **Education:** Knox Col, AB, 1965; Univ Ill, Urbana, PhD (chem), 1970. **Professional Experience:** PROJ MGR, GLENN RES CTR, NASA, as of 2002; RES CHEMIST, LEWIS RES CTR, NASA, 1974-; Nat Res Coun res assoc, 1972-1974. **Memberships:** Am Chem Soc; Soc Adv Mat & Process Eng; Soc Plastic Eng; Coblentz Soc. **Research Statement & Publications:** Physical and chemical characterization of polymer materials; Design/Development of space flight instrumentation; Program/Project management. **Mailing Address:** Glenn Res Ctr, NASA, 21000 Brookpark Rd, Cleveland, OH 44135-3191. **E-Mail:** richard.w.lauver@grc.nasa.gov

LAUX, DAVID CHARLES, IMMUNOLOGY, BACTERIOLOGY. **Personal Data:** b Sarver, Pa, January 1, 1945. **Education:** Wash & Jefferson Col, BA, 1966; Miami Univ, Ohio, MS, 1968; Univ Ariz, PhD (microbiol), 1971. **Professional Experience:** Chmn, dept microbiol, Univ RI, beginning 1988; vis scientist, Oxford Univ, 1988 & 1995; PROF IMMUNOL, DEPT CELL MOLECULAR, UNIV RI, 1983-; res grant, Nat Inst Allergy & Infectious Dis, 1980, 1983 & 1986; res grant, Nat Cancer Inst, 1974, 1978; from asst prof to assoc prof, Dept Microbiol, 1973-1978; fel immunol, dept microbiol, Sch Med, Pa State Univ, 1971-1973. **Memberships:** Am Soc Microbiol; Am Asn Immunol; Am Asn Advan Sci. **Research Statement & Publications:** Molecular basis of large intestine colonization; bacterial/mucosal surface interactions. **Mailing Address:** Dept Cell & Molecular Biol Univ RI, Morrill Sci Bldg, Kingston, RI 02881. **E-Mail:** laux@uri.edu

LAUZON, RODRIGUE VINCENT, COLLOID SCIENCE, PAPER CHEMISTRY. **Personal Data:** b Ottawa, Ont, October 24, 1937. **Education:** Univ Toronto, BA, 1960; Univ Conn, MS, 1962; Clarkson Col Technol, PhD (colloid chem), 1971. **Honors & Awards:** Petrol Engr Int, Offshore Technol Conf, 1982; Meritorious Award for Eng Innovation. **Professional Experience:** RES SCIENTIST, HERCULES INC, 1983-; group leader, Hercules Inc, 1983-1990; colloid consult, 1982-1983; vis scientist, Indust Res Inst, 1982; Chmn colloid & surface chem group, Southeastern Sect, Am Chem Soc, 1979-1983; sr res scientist colloid, NL Baroid, NL Industs, Inc, 1978-1982; dir latex res & develop, Dart Industs, 1975-1978; res assoc colloid chem, Celanese Res Co, 1974-1975; Res specialist latex, Dow Chem Co, 1970-1974; mem, Colloid Div. **Memberships:** Am Chem Soc; Trade Asn Pulp & Paper Indust; Asn Consult Chemists & Chem Engrs; Nat Homeopathic Soc. **Research Statement & Publications:** Inorganic colloids; clays, oxides, halides; polymer colloids: latexes, water-soluble polymers, natural polymers; rheology of disperse systems; drilling muds; foams and emulsions; coagulation; adsorption from solution; electrokinetics; paper and paper chemicals. **Mailing Address:** 63 Quail Hollow Dr, Hockessin, DE 19707. **Fax:** 302-995-3694.

LAVAIL, JENNIFER HART, NEUROANATOMY, NEUROVAROLOGY. **Personal Data:** b Evansville, Ind, April 2, 1943; c Matthew H & Katherine H. **Education:** Trinity Col, DC, BA, 1965; Univ Wis, PhD (anat), 1970. **Honors & Awards:** Charles Judson Herrick Award, Am Asn Anatomists, 1975. **Professional Experience:** Affiliated prof Univ Autonoma de Nuevo Leon, Monterrey, Mexico 2002-; prof Oththalmology, Univ Calif, San Francisco, 1993-; bd sci counr, Nat Inst Neurol & Commun Dis & Stroke, 1986-; PROF ANAT, UNIV CALIF, SAN FRANCISCO, 1983-; mem neurol study sect, NIH, 1982-1986; assoc prof, Univ Calif, San Francisco, 1976-1986; Alfred P Sloan fel, 1976-1979; spec fel, Harvard Med Sch, 1973-1976; from instr to asst prof neuropath, Harvard Med Sch, 1973-1976; Nat Inst Neurol Dis & Stroke res fel neuropath, Harvard Med Sch, 1970-1973; res fel, Sch Med, Wash Univ, 1969-1970; vis fel anat, Sch Med, Wash Univ, 1968-1969; Woodrow Wilson fel, 1965. **Memberships:** Am Asn Anatomists; Soc Neuroscience; Asn Res Vision Ophthl; Soc Cell Biol; Am soc Microbiol. **Research Statement & Publications:** Development of the central nervous system; anterograde and retrograde axonal transport; Neurotropic Virus Invasion of the Nervous sys. **Mailing Address:** Dept Anat, Univ Calif, Campus Box 0452, San Francisco, CA 94143-0452. **Fax:** 415-476-4845. **E-Mail:** LavailJ@vision.ucsf.edu

LAVAIL, MATTHEW MAURICE, NEUROSCIENCES, CELL BIOLOGY. **Personal Data:** b Abilene, Tex, January 7, 1943. **Education:** NTex State Univ, BA, 1965; Univ Tex Med Br, PhD (anat), 1969. **Honors & Awards:** Res Award, Sigma Xi, 1970; Fight Sight Citation, 1975; Sundial Award, Retina Found, 1976; Friedenwald Award, Asn Res Vision & Ophthal, 1981. **Professional Experience:** PROF ANAT, MED SCH, UNIV CALIF, SAN FRANCISCO, as of 2004; actg chmn, Med Sch, Univ Calif, San Francisco, 1981-1982; assoc Prof Anat, Med Sch, Univ Calif, San Francisco, beginning 1976; Nat Eye Inst res career develop award, 1974-1979; res assoc Neuroscience, Children's Hosp Med Ctr, 1973-1976; asst prof neuropath, Harvard Med Sch, 1973-1976; Nat Eye Inst fel neuropath, Harvard Med Sch, 1970-1973; res fel, Harvard Med Sch, 1969-1973. **Memberships:** Asn Res Vision & Ophthal; Soc Cell Biol; AAAS; Am Asn Anat; Soc Neuroscience. **Research Statement & Publications:** Photoreceptor-pigment epithelial cell interactions; retinal development; inherited retinal degeneration; neuroembryology; retrograde axonal transport. **Mailing Address:** Dept Anat, Univ Calif, Sch Med, 10 Kirkham St PO Box 0730, San Francisco, CA 94143-0730. **Fax:** 415-476-0709. **E-Mail:** mmlv@itsa.ucsf.edu

LAVAL, WILLIAM NORRIS, GEOLOGY. **Personal Data:** b Seattle, Wash, January 27, 1922. **Education:** Univ Wash, BS, 1943, MS, 1948, PhD (geol), 1956. **Professional Experience:** RETIRED; prof geol & earth sci, Lewis-Clark State Col, 1963-1995; chmn div natural sci, Lewis-clark State Col, 1963-1975; assoc prof geol & geol eng, SDak Sch Mines & Technol, 1960-1962; asst prof geol, Colo State Univ, 1956-1960; consult, 1954-1956 & 1962-1963; resident geologist, Yale Dam, Ebasco Serv, Inc, Wash, 1951-1953; geologist, Corps Eng, US Army, 1949-1951; geologist, US Geol Surv, 1943-1945 & 1948-1949; Field asst, US Geol Surv, 1942. **Memberships:** Fel Geol Soc Am; Sigma Xi. **Research Statement & Publications:** Stratigraphy, structure and petrology of Columbia Plateau; environmental geology. **Mailing Address:** Dept Geol, Lewis-Clark State Col, 500 8th Ave, Lewiston, ID 83501.

LAVALLE, H CLAUDE, CHEMICAL ENGINEERING. **Personal Data:** b Cap-Sante, Que, July 28, 1938. **Education:** Univ Laval, Que, BScA, 1964, MScA, 1965, DSc, 1970. **Professional Experience:** Adminr, John Meunier Inc, Montreal, 1991-; PRES, H C LAVALLEE INC, DONNACONA, QUE, 1989-; Consult, Roche Ltee, Quebec City, 1988-; DIR, PULP & PAPER RES CTR, UNIV QUE-TROIS-RIVIERES, 1987-; head, Pulp & Paper Indust, Minister Environ, Govt Que, 1986-1987; sr engr, Pulp & Paper Indust, Minister Environ, Govt Que, 1974-1987; prof chem eng, Univ Que Trois-Rivieres, 1970-1974; Researcher, Defense Res Estab Valcartier, Govt Can, Que, 1965-1967. **Memberships:** Tech Asn Pulp & Paper Indust. **Research Statement & Publications:** Chemical engineering; research in pulp and paper. **Mailing Address:** Ctr Res Pulp & Paper, 3351 Blvd des Forges, Trois-Rivieres, PQ G9A 5H7, Can.

LAVALLE, PLACIDO DOMINICK, GEOMORPHOLOGY. **Personal Data:** b New York, NY, May 13, 1937; m Rita; c Dawn, Lori & Dominick. **Education:** Columbia Univ, BA, 1959; Univ Southern Ill, MA, 1961; Univ Iowa, PhD (geog), 1965. **Professional Experience:** ADJ PROF GEOG, UNIV WINDSOR, as of 2004; vis prof, Keele Univ, Eng, 1976; assoc prof geog, Univ Windsor, beginning 1969; asst prof, Univ Calif, Los Angeles, 1964-1967 & Univ Ill, Urbana, 1967-1969; res asst geog, Univ Iowa, 1962-1963; consult, Parks, Can. **Memberships:** AAAS; Asn Am Geogrs; Can Asn Geogr; Nat Speleol Soc. **Research Statement & Publications:** Soil geography; quantative analysis of karst geomorphology in Kentucky and Puerto Rico; spatial patterns of soil toxin distribution in Lebec, California; dynamics of shoreline change at Point Pelee, Ontario, Canada. **Mailing Address:** Dept Earth Sci, Univ Windsor, 401 Sunset Ave, Windsor, ON N9B 3P4, Can. **Fax:** 519-973-7081. **E-Mail:** plavall@uwindsor.ca

LAVALLEE, ANDRE, WHITE PINE BLISTER RUST. **Personal Data:** b Joliette, Que, August 31, 1936. **Education:** Montreal Univ, BA, 1956; Laval Univ, BSc, 1960, DSc, 1969; McGill Univ, MSc, 1963. **Professional Experience:** RETIRED; scientist forest path, Forest Inst Dis Surv, 1985-1991; prog mgr forest protection, Forest Inst Dis Surv, 1979-1984; sect head, Forest Inst Dis Surv, 1975-1978; res scientist, Can Forestry Serv, Que, 1970-1975; biologist forest path, Can Forestry Serv, Que, 1960-1969. **Memberships:** Can Phytopath Soc; Can Inst Forestry. **Research Statement & Publications:** Characterization of white pine plantation sites with respect to white pine blister rust and weevil susceptibility; elaborate and evaluate integrated forest pest control prescriptions within intensive forest management practices. **Mailing Address:** 2250 Robitaille, Quebec, PQ G1P 2M3, Can.

LAVALLEE, DAVID KENNETH, INORGANIC CHEMISTRY, BIOCHEMISTRY. **Personal Data:** b Malone, NY, October 1, 1945; m 1997, Eileen; c Jeffrey, Gregory & Jocelyn. **Education:** St Bonaventure Univ, BS, 1967; Univ Chicago, SM, 1968, PhD (inorg chem), 1971. **Honors & Awards:** Catalyst Award, Chem Mfrs Asn, 1986 Fulbright Senior Research Fellowship, 1985-1986. **Professional Experience:** PROVOST & VPRES, ACAD AFFAIRS, STATE UNIV NY, NEW PALTZ, as of 1999; fulbright fel, 1985-1986; PROF CHEM, HUNTER COL, 1984-; res collabr, Brookhaven Nat Lab, 1979-; mem grad fac biochem & chem, City Univ New York, 1978-; assoc prof, Hunter Col, 1978-1983; asst prof chem, Colo State Univ, 1972-1978; vis scientist, Argonne Nat Lab, 1971-1972; USPHS fel, Dept Anat, Univ Chicago, 1971-1972. **Memberships:** Am Chem Soc; AAAS; Sigma Xi; NY Acad Sci; Soc Nuclear Med. **Research Statement & Publications:** Synthesis, spectroscopy, reaction mechanisms and structural chemistry of metalloporphyrins; applications of porphyrins to medicine. **Mailing Address:** State Univ NY, 75 S Manheim Blvd, New Paltz, NY 12561. **Fax:** 845-257-3284. **E-Mail:** lavallee@newpaltz.edu

LAVALLEE, LORRAINE DORIS, MATHEMATICS. **Personal Data:** b Holyoke, Mass, May 31, 1931. **Education:** Mt Holyoke Col, AB, 1953; Univ Mass, Amherst, MA, 1955; Univ Mich, PhD (math), 1962. **Professional Experience:** EMER PROF MATH, UNIV MASS, AMHERST, 1993-; assoc head, Dept Math & Statist, univ MASS, Anherst, 1971-1972 & 1977; From instr to prof, 1959-1993. **Memberships:** Am Math Soc; Asn Women in Math; Math Asn Am. **Research Statement & Publications:** General topology. **Mailing Address:** 123 Granby Rd, South Hadley, MA 01075-2909.

LAVANCHY, ANDRE C(HRISTIAN), MECHANICAL ENGINEERING. **Personal Data:** b Switz, November 17, 1922. **Education:** Swiss Fed Inst Technol, ME, 1946. **Professional Experience:** MGR CENTRIFUGE DEVELOP, PENNWALT CORP, 1965-; chief analytical engr, Sharples Res Labs, 1956-1965; Design engr, Am Viscose Corp, 1955; res engr, Sharples Res Labs, 1950-1955; Design & test engr, Brown & Boveri, Switz, 1946-1949. **Memberships:** Am Soc Mech Engrs; Am Chem Soc. **Research Statement & Publications:** Stress and vibration analysis; applied dynamics; powder technology; liquid-liquid and solid-liquid separation; fluid flow; aerodynamics; thermodynamics. **Mailing Address:** 11 Coniston Dr, West Chester, PA 19382.

LAVANISH, JEROME MICHAEL, ORGANIC CHEMISTRY. **Personal Data:** b Cleveland, Ohio, March 10, 1940. **Education:** Case Inst Technol, BS, 1962; Yale Univ, MS, 1963, PhD (chem), 1966. **Professional Experience:** ASST VPRES GLOBAL FORMULATIONS RES, AGR RES DIV, AM CYANAMID CO, 1996-; dir, Am Cyanamid Co, 1995-1996; Mgr Chem Discovery, Am Cyanamid Co, 1991-1995; group leader, Am Cyanamid Co, 1988-1991; mgr biochem synthesis, PPG Industs, 1981-1988; Res chemist, PPG Industs, 1966-1981. **Memberships:** Am Chem Soc; Sigma Xi. **Research Statement & Publications:** Synthetic organic chemistry; synthesis and action of herbicides and plant growth regulators; design and action of agrochemicals; formulation and process development, agrochemicals. **Mailing Address:** Agr Res Div, Am Cyanamid Co PO Box 400, Princeton, NJ 08543-0400.

LAVE, ROY E(LLIS), INDUSTRIAL ENGINEERING, OPERATIONS RESEARCH. **Personal Data:** b Homewood, Ill, September 23, 1935. **Education:** Univ Mich, BS & MBA, 1958, MS, 1960; Stanford Univ, PhD (indust eng), 1965. **Honors & Awards:** Outstanding Young Fac, Am Soc Eng Educ, 1971. **Professional Experience:** CHIEF EXEC OFFICER, SYSTAN INC, as of 2003; DIR, BANK LOS ALTOS, 1995-; chair, Paratransit Comt, Transp Res Bd, 1993-; mem, Paratransit Comt, Transp Res Bd, 1982-1985; comnr, Metrop Transp Comn, San Francisco Bay Area, 1980-1987; mayor, City Los Altos, 1976-1978; coun mem, City Los Altos, 1974-1982; dir, Phoenix housing develop corp, 1969-1977 & Consumer Alliance, 1971-1973; assoc prof & assoc chmn dept, Stanford Univ, 1968-1972; consult, Inter-Am Develop Bank, 1968-1972 & Unido, 1968-1970; assoc prof eng-econ systs & dir fed internships & interdisciplinary projs, Stanford Univ, 1967-1968; DIR & CHMN BD, SYSTAN INC, 1966-; agency Int develop, 1965-1967 & Ford Found, 1966; consult, Coun Int Prog Mgt, 1963; asst prof indust eng, Stanford Univ, 1962-1968; consult, Rand Corp, 1961-1965; asst opers res, Univ Mich, 1957-1960. **Memberships:** Opers Res Soc Am; Inst Mgt Sci; Inst Indust Engrs; Transp Res Bd. **Research Statement**

& Publications: Systems analysis in international development planning; managements control systems; national and urban transportation planning and policy analysis; decision budgeting; information systems design; project management. **Mailing Address:** Systan Inc, 343 Second St, PO Box U, Los Altos, CA 94022-4021. **Fax:** 650-949-3395.

LAVELLE, ARTHUR, NEUROCYTOLOGY. **Personal Data:** b Fargo, NDak, November 29, 1921; m 1947, Faith W; c Audrey. **Education:** Univ Wash, BS, 1946; Johns Hopkins Univ, MA, 1948; Univ Pa, PhD (anat), 1951. **Professional Experience:** EMER PROF ANAT, UNIV ILL COL MED, 1988-; vis prof dept anat & brain res inst & Guggenheim fel, Univ Calif, Los Angeles, 1968-1969; USPHS-NIH res grant, Univ Ill, 1953-1970; from instr to prof, Univ Ill Col Med, 1952-1988; USPHS fel, Univ Pa, 1951-1952; asst instr anat, Sch Med, Univ Pa, 1948-1951; jr instr biol, Johns Hopkins Univ, 1946-1948; Asst zool, Univ Wash, 1944-1946. **Memberships:** emer mem AAAS; emer mem Am Asn Anat; emer mem Biol Stain Comn (pres, 1981-1986); emer mem; emer mem Am Soc Cell Biol; emer mem Soc Neurosci; Sigma XI. **Research Statement & Publications:** Neurocytology; cytological development of nerve cells; experimental alteration of development of nerve cells. **Mailing Address:** 462 Highland Ave, Elmhurst, IL 60126-2208. **E-Mail:** arthurlavelle@cs.com

LAVELLE, FAITH WILSON, HISTOLOGY, NEUROEMBRYOLOGY. **Personal Data:** b St Johnsbury, Vt, March 14, 1921; m 1947, Arthur; c Audrey. **Education:** Mt Holyoke Col, BA, 1943, MA, 1945; Johns Hopkins Univ, PhD (biol), 1949. **Professional Experience:** RETIRED; emer prof anat, Stritch Sch Med, Loyola Univ, Chicago, 1987-; actg chmn dept, Stritch Sch Med, Loyola Univ, Chicago, 1984-1985; from asst prof to prof anat, Stritch Sch Med, Loyola Univ, Chicago, 1970-1986; res assoc anat, Univ Ill Col Med, 1955-1970; USPHS res grant, Univ Ill Col Med, 1953-1970; instr, Univ Ill Col Med, 1953-1955; lectr, Univ Ill Col Med, 1952-1953; instr anat, Med Sch, 1951-1952; admin asst zool, Univ Pa, 1948-1951; Lab instr zool, Mt Holyoke Col, 1943-1945. **Memberships:** emer mem; Am Asn Anat; emer mem Soc Neurosci; emer mem Sigma Xi; emer mem AAAS. **Research Statement & Publications:** Experimental alteration of development of nerve cells; proteins in neural development. **Mailing Address:** 462 Highland Ave, Elmhurst, IL 60126. **E-Mail:** arthurlavelle@cs.com

LAVELLE, JOHN WILLIAM, GEOLOGICAL OCEANOGRAPHY, PHYSICAL OCEANOGRAPHY. **Personal Data:** b Sacramento, Calif, April 26, 1943. **Education:** Univ Calif, Berkeley, BA, 1965; Univ Calif, San Diego, MS, 1968, PhD (physics), 1971. **Professional Experience:** OCEANOGR, PAC MARINE ENVIRON LAB, NAT OCEANOG & ATMOSPHERIC ADMIN, 1977-; geol oceanogr, Environ Res Labs, Miami, 1973-1977; Marine geophysicist, 1972-1973. **Memberships:** Am Geophys Union. **Research Statement & Publications:** Theoretical studies of centered on particle transport and deposition in marine environments. **Mailing Address:** Pac Marine Environ Lab, NOAA, 7600 Sand Point Way NE, Bldg 3, Seattle, WA 98115-0070. **Fax:** 206-526-6054. **E-Mail:** j.william.lavelle@noaa.gov

LAVENDEL, HENRY W, CHEMICAL ENGINEERING, METALLURGY. **Personal Data:** b Warsaw, Poland, April 23, 1919. **Education:** Univ Milan, PhD (indust chem), 1951. **Professional Experience:** RETIRED; sr staff scientist, Palo Alto Res Labs, Lockheed Missiles & Space Co, Lockheed Aircraft Co, 1961-1987; assoc chem engr, Argonne Nat Lab, 1957-1960; res assoc, Sintercast Corp, 1955-1957; res scientist powder metall, Am Electro Metal Co, NY, 1952-1955. **Memberships:** Sigma Xi; Am Inst Mining Metall & Petrol Engrs; Am Soc Metals; Am Chem Soc. **Research Statement & Publications:** High temperature materials. **Mailing Address:** 1511 Hamilton Ave, Palo Alto, CA 94303-2825.

LAVENDER, DENIS PETER, PLANT PHYSIOLOGY. **Personal Data:** b Seattle, Wash, October 13, 1926. **Education:** Univ Wash, BS, 1949; Ore State Univ, MSc, 1958, PhD, 1962. **Professional Experience:** PROF EMER, FOREST PHYSIOL, ORE STATE UNIV, as of 2002; MEM STAFF, UNIV BC, VANCOUVER, CAN, as of 2002; prof, Sch Forestry, begining 1970; assoc prof, Ore Forest Res Lab, 1963-1970; in charge forest physiol, Forest Res Ctr, 1957-1963; Res asst, Ore State Bd Forestry, 1950-1957. **Memberships:** Sigma Xi. **Research Statement & Publications:** Development of hardy coniferous seedlings; nutrition of second growth Douglas fir stands; reduction of the juvenile period of conifers; dormancy in Douglas fir seedlings and conifers; mineral nutrition and precocious flowering in conifers. **Mailing Address:** Dept Forest Sci, Col Forestry, Ore State Univ, Corvallis, OR 97333.

LAVENDER, DEWITT EARL, MATHEMATICS, STATISTICS. **Personal Data:** b Jackson Co, Ga, November 9, 1938. **Education:** Univ Ga, BS, 1962, MA, 1963, PhD (math, statist), 1966. **Professional Experience:** CHMN EMER & ASSOC PROF EMER MATH, GA SOUTHERN COL, as of 2003; head dept, Ga Southern Col, beginning 1970; from asst to assoc prof math, Ga Southern Col, 1966-1998. **Memberships:** Am Math Soc; Math Asn Am; Inst Math Statist. **Research Statement & Publications:** Mathematical statistics. **Mailing Address:** Dept Math, Ga Southern Univ, Statesboro, GA 30458. **E-Mail:** ekl@frontiernet.net

LAVENDER, JOHN FRANCIS, VIROLOGY, MICROBIOLOGY. **Personal Data:** b November 16, 1929. **Education:** Drake Univ, BA, 1951; Univ Ill, Champaign, MS, 1953; Univ Calif, Los Angeles, PhD (infectious dis), 1962. **Professional Experience:** RES SCIENTIST MOLECULAR BIOL, ELI LILY & CO, 1985-; res virologist, Eli Lily & CO, 1972-1985; sr virologist, Eli Lily & CO, 1964-1972; NIMH fel virol, Univ Calf, Los Angeles, 1962-1963. **Memberships:** Am Soc Microbiol; Sigma Xi; NY Acad Sci. **Research Statement & Publications:** Psychological stress and viral disease resistance; drugs and the entry of viruses across the blood brain barrier; development of parainfluenza, rabies, canine distemper and measles vaccines; Herpes Simplex vaccines types 1 and 2; chemotherapy of virus diseases; molecular biology; cell culture for mass production of proteins. **Mailing Address:** 543 West Dr, Indianapolis, IN 46202.

LAVER, MURRAYLANE, ORGANIC CHEMISTRY, WOOD CHEMISTRY. **Personal Data:** b Warkworth, Ont, March 7, 1932; m 1963, c Ann Margaret & Elizabeth Clara. **Education:** Ont Agr Col, BScA, 1955; Ohio State Univ, PhD (org chem), 1959. **Professional Experience:** RETIRED; Vis lectr biol chem, Harvard Univ, 1977-1978; ASSOC PROF FOREST PRODS CHEM, ORE STATE UNIV, 1969-; res instr chem, Univ Wash, 1968-1969; prof specialist res div, Weyerhaeuser Co, 1966-1968; res scientist, Weyerhaeuser Co, 1964-1966; res chemist wood sci, Rayonier Can, Inc, 1963; Res chemist food sci, Westreco Co, 1959-1963. **Memberships:** Am Chem Soc; Am Asn Univ Prof. **Research Statement & Publications:** Pulp and paper, carbohydrate, food and wood chemistry. **Mailing Address:** Dept Forest Prods, Ore State Univ, Corvallis, OR 97331-5703.

LAVERDIERE, MARC RICHARD, SOIL CONSERVATION, SOIL CHEMISTRY. **Personal Data:** b Coaticook, Que, May 28, 1946. **Education:** Laval Univ, BSc, 1969, MSc, 1971; Cornell Univ, PhD (agron), 1976. **Professional Experience:** PROF SOIL & WATER CONSERV, LAVAL UNIV, 1989-; head, Dept Soil Sci & prof soil conserv & land use, 1985-1989; guest lectr, Fac Agr, Alimentation Dept Soils, Laval Univ, 1977; res scientist, Clay Miner, Can Dept Agr, 1976-1985; res Off Pedogenesis, 1971-1973. **Memberships:** Soil Conserv Soc; Am Soc Agron; Soil Sci Soc Am; Can Soil Sci Soc; Int Soc Soil Sci. **Research Statement & Publications:** Soil conservation; control of soil degradation; surface composting. **Mailing Address:** Univ Laval, Paul-Comtois House Rm 2207, PQ G1K 7P4, Can. **E-Mail:** marc.laverdiere@sga.ulaval.ca

LAVERGNE, JULIO A, CELLULAR IMMUNOLOGY, MOLECULAR IMMUNOLOGY. **Personal Data:** b Panama City, Panama, December 17, 1942. **Education:** Univ Costa Rica, licenciature, 1970; Univ Tex, PhD (immunol & microbiol), 1979. **Professional Experience:** Vis scientist, Ctr Dis Control, Ga, 1996; PROF IMMUNOL, SCH MED, UNIV PR, 1989-; from assoc chair to chair, Dept Microbiol, 1987-1996; DIR, LAB LASER FLOW CYTOMETRY & MED SCI, UNIV PR, 1986-; dir, Hybridoma Lab, 1985-1989; guest researcher, Nat Inst Allergy & Infectious Dis, Bethesda, Md, 1983; Sci adv, PR Health Dept, 1982-1984; from asst prof to assoc prof, Sch Med, Univ PR, 1980-1989; instr immunol, Sch Med, Univ PR, 1979-1980; Instr biol, Univ Panama, 1970-1972; mem, Res Comt, HispanoAm Biomed Asn. **Memberships:** Am Soc Microbiol; AAAS; Int Soc Analytical Cytol; NY Acad Sci; Am Asn Vet Immunologists; HispanoAm Biomed Asn. **Research Statement & Publications:** Apoptosis regulation in HIV-infected cells; role of cytokines, nitric oxide, reactive oxygen species, dehydrogenases, cytochrome oxidases, mitochondrial membrane electron transport and membrane potential; BCL-2, MnSOD and cyclin expression in apoptosis. **Mailing Address:** Dept Microbiol & Zool, Sch Med, Univ Puerto Rica, PO Box 365067, San Juan, PR 00936-5067. **Fax:** 787-758-4808. **E-Mail:** jlavergne@rcm.upr.edu

LAVERNE, JAY A, PHYSICAL CHEMISTRY. **Education:** Lamar Univ, BS, 1972; Univ Nebr, PhD, 1981. **Professional Experience:** PROF SPECIALIST & CONCURRENT PROF, DEPT PHYSICS, UNIV NOTRE DAME, as of 2006. **Research Statement & Publications:** Radiation Chemical Effects with Heavy Ions. **Mailing Address:** Radiation Lab, Univ Notre Dame, 225 Nieuwland Sci Hall, Notre Dame, IN 46556. **Fax:** 574-631-8068. **E-Mail:** laverne.1@nd.edu

LAVERNIA, ENRIQUE JOSE, SOLIDIFICATION PROCESSING, METAL MATRIX COMPOSITES. **Personal Data:** b Havana, Cuba, July 30, 1960. **Education:** Brown Univ, BS, 1982; Mass Inst Technol, MS, 1984, PhD (mat eng), 1986. **Professional Experience:** DEAN COL ENG, UNIV CALIF, DAVIS, 2002-; CHAIR, UNIV CALIF, IRVINE, 1998-; vis prof, Max Planck Inst, Ger, 1997; PROF, UNIV CALIF, IRVINE, 1995-; Alexander Von Humboldt fel, Ger, 1995; from asst prof to assoc prof, Univ Calif, Irvine, 1987-1995; res assoc; MIT, 1986-1987; res assoc, MIT, 1982-1986. **Memberships:** Sigma Xi; Am Soc Metals; Mat Res Soc; Metall Soc; Am Powder Industs Fedn. **Research Statement & Publications:** Structure and mechanical behavior of metals and alloys processed under rapid solidification conditions; spray atomization and deposition of metals and alloys; solidification processing of metal matrix composites; mathematical modeling of solidification. **Mailing Address:** Col Eng Univ Calif, One Shields Ave, Davis, CA 95616-5294. **Fax:** 530-752-8058. **E-Mail:** lavernia@ucdavis.edu

LAVERTY, JOHN JOSEPH, PLASTIC ENGINEERING. **Personal Data:** b Chicago, Ill, May 27, 1938. **Education:** Eastern Ill Univ, BS, 1964; Univ Ariz, MS, 1966. **Professional Experience:** STAFF RES SCIENTIST, POLYMER DEPT, GEN MOTORS RES LABS, 1981-; sr res chemist, Gen Motors Res Labs, 1978-1981; assoc sr res chemist, Gen Motors Res Labs, 1971-1978; Res chemist, Gen Motors Res Labs, 1966-1971. **Memberships:** Am Chem Soc; Soc Plastic Engrs. **Research Statement & Publications:** Plastic engineering and polymer physics; structure-property relationship of block copolymers and polymer blends; durability of engineering plastics and the recyclability of engineering thermoplastics. **Mailing Address:** 34066 Chatsworth, Sterling Heights, MI 48312-4604. **Fax:** 313-986-1207.

LAVERY, JOHN EDWARD, COMPUTATIONAL GEOMETRY, NUMERICAL SOLUTION OF DIFFERENTIAL & INTEGRAL EQUATIONS. **Personal Data:** b Columbus, Ohio, November 23, 1945; m 1995, Monica; c Kristen, Eileen, Kevin & Eric. **Education:** Mich State Univ, BA, 1965; Univ Akron, MS, 1968; Univ Md, PhD (math), 1973. **Professional Experience:** Sr Prog Mgr, Math Div, Army Res Off, 1997-; assoc dir, Math & Comput Sci Div, Army Res Off, 1995-1997; Sole Proprietor, L1 Assocs, 1994-; dir, Bd Math Sci, Nat Res Coun, 1991-1994; prog mgr, Off Naval Res, 1989-1991; adj assoc prof math, Case Western Res Univ, 1987-1989; consult, Gen Elec, 1984-1986; assoc prof math, Case Western Res Univ, 1982-1986; vis assoc prof math, Humboldt Found & Tech Univ Munich, 1980-1982; math researcher, US Nat Acad Sci & Comput Ctr, Siberian Br, Acad Sci, USSR, 1979-1980; from assoc prof to prof math, Soochow Univ, Taiwan, 1975-1979; exchange scholar, US Nat Acad Sci & Czech Acad Sci, 1974; assoc prof math, Tunghai Univ, Taiwan, 1973-1974; aerospace technologist, NASA, 1968-1973 & 1986-1989. **Research Statement & Publications:** Curve and surface fitting for computer aided geometric design, image analysis, topography and medical imaging; numerical solutions of differential and integral quations of electromagnetics, acoustics, fluid flow and elasticity. **Mailing Address:** Mathematics Division, Army Res Office, PO Box 12211, Research Triangle Park, NC 27709-2211. **Fax:** 919-549-4354. **E-Mail:** john.lavery2@us.army.mil

LAVI, ABRAHIM, ELECTRICAL ENGINEERING, COMPUTER SCIENCE. **Personal Data:** b Iran, January 12, 1934. **Education:** Purdue Univ, BS, 1957; Carnegie Inst Technol, MS, 1958, PhD (elec eng), 1959. **Professional Experience:** Mem staff, Dept Energy, Wash, DC, 1976-1978; PROF ELEC ENG, CARNEGIE-MELLON UNIV, 1968-; from asst prof to assoc prof elec eng, Carnegie-mellon Univ, 1959-1968; res asst, Carnegie-mellon Univ, 1957; consult, Graphic Arts Technol Found, Pa. **Memberships:** sr mem Inst Elec & Electronics Engrs; Marine Technol Soc; Int Solar Energy Soc. **Research Statement & Publications:** System modelling and optimization; low temperature difference energy conversion; control and instrumentation. **Mailing Address:** Dept Elec & Comput Eng, Carnegie-Mellon Univ, 5000 Forbes Ave, Pittsburgh, PA 15213. **Fax:** 412-268-2860.

LAVIA, LYNN ALAN, OBSTETRICS & GYNECOLOGY, CANCER. **Personal Data:** b Des Moines, Iowa, October 30, 1948. **Education:** Briar Cliff Col, BS, 1970; Drake Univ, MA, 1976; Univ Nebr, PhD (med sci), 1981; Wichita State Univ, BS, 1992. **Professional Experience:** Clin dir, Texnoma Family Clin, 1993-1994; clin dir, Wellington Hosp, 1992-1993; peer reviewer, Am Asn Physicians Assts, 1991-1992; consult, Derby Coastal Oil Refinery, 1990-; mem fac morphometry course, USAF Inst Path, 1989-; SR SCIENTIST RES, IMAGE ANALYTICAL RES, 1989-; asst prof anat & embryol, Biol Dept, Wichita State Univ, 1988-1990; dir res, Obstet & Gynec Dept, Univ Kans Med Sch, Wichita, 1981-1989; grad fel internal med, Univ Nebr Med Ctr, 1978-1980; Instr anat & physiol, Iowa Western Community Col, 1976-1978; emergency med tech, Mercy Hosp Emergency Rm, 1972-1974; Medic, US Army, 1970-1972. **Memberships:** Int Soc Stereology; Am Asn Physician Assts. **Research Statement & Publications:** Currently involved in how estrogen-stimulated stroma-epithelial cell interaction in uterine endometrium induces hyperplasia and neoplasia. **Mailing Address:** 211 Circle Dr, Guymon, OK 73942. **Fax:** 580-423-7551.

LA VIA, MARIANO FRANCIS, IMMUNOPATHOLOGY, FLOW CYTOMETRY. **Personal Data:** b Rome, Italy, January 29, 1926; American citizen; m 1991, June Faulkner; c William, Maria, Charles, Jacqueline, Susan, Christopher & Thomas. **Education:** Univ Messina, MD, 1949. **Professional Experience:** PROF EMER, MED UNIV SC, 1995-; prof path & lab med, Div Diag Immunol, 1987-1995; dir, Div Diag Immunol, 1979-1988; prof lab med, Med Univ SC, 1979-1987; prof, Bowman Gray Sch Med, 1968-1971 & Sch Med, Emory Univ, 1971-1979; from asst prof to assoc prof, Sch Med, Univ Colo, Denver, 1960-1968; instr, Univ Chicago, 1957-1960; asst path, Univ Chicago, 1952-1957; asst gen path, Univ Palermo, 1950-1952. **Memberships:** Clin Immunol Soc; Am Asn Immunol; Am Soc Invest Path; Soc Leukocyte Biol; Int Soc Analytical Cytol; Clin Cytom Soc. **Research Statement & Publications:** Subtype response to stress and its significance in immunomodulation and morbidity. **Mailing Address:** 718 Deepwood Dr, Charleston, SC 29412. **Fax:** 803-792-3814. **E-Mail:** mlavia@prodigy.net

LAVIGNE, DAVID M, BIOLOGY MANAGEMENT OF MARINE MAMMALS. **Personal Data:** b Watford, Eng, March 18, 1946. **Education:** Univ Western Ont, BSc, 1968; Univ Guelph, MSc, 1971, PhD (zool), 1973. **Professional Experience:** PROF ZOOL, UNIV GUELPH, 1987-; chmn, Sect CSZ, Wildlife Biologists, 1985-1986; vis scientist, Brit Antarctic Surv, Cambridge, UK, 1980-1981; Mem, Seal Specialists Group, Int Union Conserv Nature & Natural Resources, 1977-; from asst prof to assoc prof, Univ Guelph, 1973-1987. **Research Statement & Publications:** Population ecology of marine mammals; ecological energetics and life history traits of mammalian populations; management of marine mammal population. **Mailing Address:** PO Box 60, Rockwood, ON N0B 2K0, Can.

LAVIGNE, ROBERT JAMES, ENTOMOLOGY. **Personal Data:** b Herkimer, NY, May 30, 1930. **Education:** Am Int Col, BA, 1952; Univ Mass, MS, 1958, PhD (entom), 1961. **Professional Experience:** PROF EMER ENTOM, UNIV WYO, as of 2002; chief party, Wyo Team, Somalia, 1985-1988; prof, Univ Wyo, beginning 1971; from asst prof to assoc prof, Univ Wyo, 1959-1971; res instr entom, Univ Mass, 1956-1959. **Memberships:** Entom Soc Am; Pan-Pac Entom Soc; Orthopterist's Soc; NAm Benthological Soc; Australian Entom Soc. **Research Statement & Publications:** Insect taxonomy, especially Diptera; insect behavior, especially robber flies, Asilidae; environmental entomology; biocontrol of weeds; forest entomology; rangeland entomology. **Mailing Address:** Univ Wyo, 2013 Agr Bldg, Laramie, WY 82071. **Fax:** 307-766-6403.

LAVIK, PAUL SOPHUS, BIOCHEMISTRY. **Personal Data:** b Camrose, Alta, February 11, 1915. **Education:** St Olaf Col, AB, 1937; Univ Wis, MS, 1941, PhD (biol chem), 1943; Western Res Univ, MD, 1959. **Professional Experience:** Pres, Radiation Ther Consults, 1982-; emergency clin, Cleveland Clin, 1981-; Staff physician radiotherapy, Cleveland Clin, 1974-1981; ASSOC CLIN PROF RADIOL, SCH MED, CASE WESTERN RES UNIV, 1970-; assocprof, Sch Med, Case Western Res Univ, 1952-1970; asst prof biochem, Sch Med, Case Western Res Univ, 1947-1952; from instr to asst prof, Baylor Col Med, 1943-1947; Instr biochem, Sch Med, La State Univ, 1943. **Memberships:** Am Soc Biol Chemists; Radiation Res Soc; Am Asn Cancer Res; Am Soc Therapeut Radiologists; Am Col Radiol. **Research Statement & Publications:** Nucleic acid metabolism; radiation biochemistry; radiation therapy. **Mailing Address:** 2202 Acacia Park Dr 2702, Lyndhurst, OH 44124-3858.

LAVILLA, ROBERT E, PHYSICAL CHEMISTRY. **Personal Data:** b New York, NY, May 8, 1926. **Education:** Bethany Col, BS, 1953; Cornell Univ, PhD (phys chem), 1960. **Professional Experience:** RETIRED; x-ray spectroscoper, Nat Inst Stand & Technol, beginning 1988; x-ray spectroscoper, Nat Inst Stand & Technol, 1960-1988; fel, Nat Res Coun-Nat Bur Stand, 1960-1961. **Memberships:** Am Phys Soc. **Research Statement & Publications:** Electron diffraction of solids and gases; optical properties of materials; x-ray absorption and emission; symchrotron radiation. **Mailing Address:** Montgomery Village, MD 20886.

LAVIN, J GERARD, MATERIALS SCIENCE ENGINEERING, ENGINEERING PHYSICS. **Personal Data:** b Manchester, Eng, October 7, 1932; American citizen; m 1962, Lora Harrer; c Elinor (Hays) & Jennifer. **Education:** Univ Mich, MScE, 1959, ScD(chem eng), 1963. **Professional Experience:** RETIRED; Du Pont fel, Cent Res & Develop, E I du Pont de Nemours & Co, 1991-2000; sr res fel, Pioneering Res Lab, E I du Pont de Nemours & Co, 1985-1991; res mgr, Eng Non-Woven Struct Div, E I du Pont de Nemours & Co, 1983-1985; mfg mgr, Old Hickory Plant, Tenn, E I du Pont de Nemours & Co, 1982-1983; tech supt, Old Hickory Plant, Tenn, E I du Pont de Nemours & Co, 1978-1981; process supt, Cape Fear Plant, NC, E I du Pont de Nemours & Co, 1976-1978; sr supvr, Camden Plant, SC, E I du Pont de Nemours & Co, 1973-1976; supvr res & develop, Kingston Plant, NC, E I du Pont de Nemours & Co, 1971-1973; supvr res & develop, Pioneering & Carothers Res Labs, E I du Pont de Nemours & Co, 1968-1971; res engr, Pioneering Res Lab, Du Pont Fibers Inc, E I du Pont de Nemours & Co, 1963-1968. **Memberships:** Sigma Xi; Am Carbon Soc; Mat Res Soc. **Research Statement & Publications:** Man-made fibers; non-woven fabric forms; research and development cultures and their results; carbon nanoparticles. **Mailing Address:** 15 Wellesley Rd, Swarthmore, PA 19081. **E-Mail:** lavinjg@a1.esvax.umc.dupont.com

LAVIN, PETER MASLAND, GEOPHYSICS. **Personal Data:** b Philadelphia, Pa, April 16, 1935. **Education:** Princeton Univ, BSE, 1957; Pa State Univ, PhD (geophys), 1962. **Professional Experience:** PROF EMER GEOPHYS, PA STATE UNIV, 1992-; from instr to prof, Pa State Univ, 1960-1991. **Memberships:** Soc Explor Geophys; Am Geophys Union. **Research Statement & Publications:** Exploration geophysics with emphasis on gravity and magnetic interpretation; time-series analysis; crustal structure and tectonic history; environmental and groundwater geophysics. **Mailing Address:** Dept Geophys, Pa State Univ, 503 Deike Bldg, Univ Park, PA 16802. **Fax:** 814-863-7823.

LAVIN, PHILIP TODD, BIOSTATISTICS. **Personal Data:** b Rochester, NY, November 21, 1946; m 1970, Mary; c 2. **Education:** Univ Rochester, BA, 1968; Brown Univ, PhD (appl math), 1972. **Professional Experience:** Dermat, Food & Drug Admin, 1992-1995; co-investr, Nat Cancer Inst, 1988-; ASSOC PROF SURG, MED SCH, HARVARD UNIV, 1987-; prin investr, DITOH Study, 1985-1989; pres, Consult Statist, Inc, 1984-1987; PRES & CHIEF EXEC OFFICER, AVERIN INC, 1983-; panel mem ophthalmic, dent & radiologic devices, Food & Drug Admin, 1983-1986; from asst prof to assoc prof biostatistics, Sch Pub Health, 1977-1986; biostatistician, Dana-Farber Cancer Inst, 1977-1984; coord statistician, Eastern Coop Oncol Group, 1976-1978; prin investr, Gastrointestinal Tumor Study Group, 1975-1979; biostatistician, US deleg Japan, Sci Exchange Comt Gastric Oncol, Nat Cancer Inst, 1975; res asst prof biostatist, State Univ NY, Buffalo, 1974-1977; res asst prof appl math, Brown Univ, 1972-1974. **Memberships:** Am Statist Asn; Biomet Soc; Drug Info Asn; Regulatory Affairs Prof Soc. **Research Statement & Publications:** Biostatistics; clinical trials; pattern analysis; experimental design; statistical computing; health care evaluation; biomarkers in design and analysis of clinical trials for drugs, biologics, and medical devices; research interests in screening studies, longitudinal data bases, and natural history of disease. **Mailing Address:** Averion Inc, Four Calif Ave, Framingham, MA 01701. **Fax:** 508-416-2796. **E-Mail:** plavin@averioninc.com

LAVINE, ADRIENNE GAIL, Heat transfer. **Personal Data:** b Norristown, Pa, August 14, 1958; m 1982, Gregory; c Elias B & Jacob S. **Education:** Brown Univ, ScB, 1979; Univ Calif, Berkeley, MS, 1983, PhD (mech eng), 1984. **Honors & Awards:** NSF presidential young investr award, 1988; Taylor Medal, Int Inst Prod Engrs, 1990; ASME fel, 1999. **Professional Experience:** Prof Mech Eng, Univ Calif Los Angeles, 1997-; Assoc Prof Mech Eng, Univ Calif Los Angeles, 1991-1997; Asst prof, Univ Calif, Los Angeles, 1984-1991; Assoc engr, Owens-Corning Fiberglas Tech Ctr, Granville, OH, 1979-1981. **Memberships:** Fellow, Am Soc Mech Engrs. **Research Statement & Publications:** Thermal issues in nanoscale manufacturing; Coupled thermal and mechanical phenomena, especially in shape memory alloy devices; Thermal aspects of manufacturing processes; natural and mixed convection heat transfer. **Mailing Address:** Mech & Aerospace Eng Dept, Univ Calif, Los Angeles, CA 90095-1597. **Fax:** 310-206-2302. **E-Mail:** lavine@seas.ucla.edu

LAVINE, JAMES PHILIP, THEORETICAL & COMPUTATIONAL PHYSICS. **Personal Data:** b Syracuse, NY, December 3, 1944; m 1971, Carolyn; c Gregory D. **Education:** Mass Inst Technol, BS, 1966; Univ Md, PhD (physics), 1971. **Professional Experience:** Mem, Tech Adv Bd Semiconductor Res Corp, 1991-2002; Res fel, 1998-, PHYSICIST, 1976, EASTMAN KODAK CO, res assoc physics, Univ Rochester, 1974-1976; res asst prof, Laval Univ, 1973-1974; res assoc physics, Univ Liege, 1971-1973. **Memberships:** Am Phys Soc; Mat Res Soc; Micros Soc Am; Am Asn Adv Sci; Electrochem Soc. **Research Statement & Publications:** Semiconductor device modeling and simulation of semiconductor device fabrication; optical properties of solids; transport in solids; defects in solids. **Mailing Address:** Eastman Kodak Co, Res Labs Bldg 81, Rochester, NY 14650-2008.

LAVINE, LEROY S, orthopedic surgery; deceased, see previous edition for last biography

LAVINE, RICHARD BENGT, MATHEMATICAL ANALYSIS. **Personal Data:** b Philadelphia, Pa, June 27, 1938. **Education:** Princeton Univ, AB, 1961; Mass Inst Technol, PhD (math), 1965. **Professional Experience:** PROF MATH, UNIV ROCHESTER, 1976-; assoc prof, Univ Rochester, 1972-1976; mem staff, Inst Advan Study, 1971-1972; vis prof, Inst Theoret Physics, Univ Geneva, 1971; asst prof, Cornell Univ, 1966-1971; instr math, Aarhus Univ, 1965-1966. **Memberships:** Am Math Soc. **Research Statement & Publications:** Mathematics of quantum mechanics; functional analysis. **Mailing Address:** Univ Rochester, Hylan 909, Rochester, NY 14627. **Fax:** 585-244-6631. **E-Mail:** lavine@math.rochester.edu

LAVINE, ROBERT ALAN, NEUROPHYSIOLOGY, PSYCHOLOGY. **Personal Data:** b Chicago, Ill, February 18, 1941. **Education:** Univ Chicago, BS, 1962, PhD (physiol), 1969. **Professional Experience:** Int res fel rev, Fogarty & NIH, 1983-; ASSOC PROF PHYSIOL & NEUROL, SCH MED, GEORGE WASH UNIV, 1980-; guest scientist, NIMH, 1973-; from instr to asst prof, Sch Med, George Wash Univ, 1969-1975; NIH fel, George Wash Univ, 1969-1970. **Memberships:** Soc Neuroscience; Soc Psychophysiol Res. **Research Statement & Publications:** Human psychophysiology and experimental neuropsychology; clinical applications of averaged evoked potentials; clinical neurophysiology, computer applications in psychology. **Mailing Address:** Dept Physiol, George Wash Univ Med Sch, 2300 I St NW, Washington, DC 20037-2337. **E-Mail:** laviner@gwu.edu

LA VIOLETTE, PAUL ESTRONZA, SATELLITE OCEANOGRAPHY. **Personal Data:** b New York, NY, April 11, 1930; m 1975, Stella M Prucnal; c 2. **Education:** Univ Ill, BS, 1952. **Professional Experience:** OCEANOGR REMOTE SENSING, MISS STATE UNIV RES CTR, 1990-; Doude, Western Mediter Circulation Exp, 1986-1987; Doude, Va, 1984; Little Window II Sahara Upwelling Explor, US & Spain Ocean Exp, 1973 & Grand Banks Explor, US & Can Ocean Exp, 1979-1980; oceanogr remote sensing, Naval Ocean Res & Develop Activ, 1976-1990; Prin investr, US & Mex Ocean Exp, 1971; Oceanogr descriptive oceanog, Naval Oceanogr Off, 1960-1976. **Memberships:** Am Geophys Union; AAAS; Marine Technol Soc; Res Soc Am. **Research Statement & Publications:** Basic and applied research in satellite oceanography. **Mailing Address:** Heron Labs, PO Box 87, Waveland, MS 39576. **Fax:** 228-466-4372.

LAVIZZO-MOUREY, RISA J, HEALTH POLICY. **Education:** Harvard Univ, MD, 1979; Univ Pa, MBA, 1986. **Professional Experience:** PRES & CHIEF EXEC OFFICER, ROBERT WOOD JOHNSON FOUND, 2003-; mem, Adv Comn Consumer Protection & Qual Health Care Indust, beginning 1997; Sylvan Eisman prof med & health care systs, Inst Aging, Univ Pa, beginning 1997; dir, Inst Aging, Univ Pa, beginning 1994; assoc exec vpres health policy, Inst Aging, Univ Pa, beginning 1994; assoc ed, J Gen Internal Med, 1994; dep adminr, Agency Health Policy & Res, 1992-1994; chair, Minority Health Subcomt, Nat Comt Vital & Health Statist, 1989-; co-chair, Task Force Minority Health, Am Geriat Soc, 1989-1992; fac, Inst Aging, Univ PA, 1984-1995; Med dir, Elmira Jefferies Mem Home, 1984; chief, Div Geriatric Med, Med Sch; mem, White House Task Force Health Care Reform, Task Force Aging Res, Off Technol Assessment Panel Prev Serv Medicare Beneficiaries; mem, Panel Dis & Disability Prev Among Older Adults, Inst Med-Nat Acad Sci; Fac, Temple Univ & Harvard Med Sch. **Memberships:** Inst Med-Nat Acad Sci. **Research Statement & Publications:** Health policy; health promotion for the elderly; quality of care; minority populations. **Mailing Address:** Robert Wood Johnson Found, PO Box 2316, Col Rd E & Rte One, Princeton, NJ 08543.

LAVKULICH, LESLIE MICHAEL, SOIL SCIENCE. **Personal Data:** b Coaldale, Alta, April 28, 1939. **Education:** Univ Alta, BSc, 1961, MSc, 1963; Cornell Univ, PhD (soil sci), 1967. **Professional Experience:** DIR, INST RESOURCES & ENVIRON & SUSTAINABILITY, UNIV BC, as of 2003; CHMN, RESOURCE MGT & ENVIRON STUDIES, UNIV BC, 1990-; head dept, Univ Bc, 1980-1990; PROF SOIL SCI, UNIV BC, 1975-; from asst prof to assoc prof, Univ Bc, 1966-1975. **Memberships:** Am Soc Agron; Can Agr Res Coun; Am Soc Soil Sci; Can Soc Soil Sci (pres, 1980-1981); Int Soc Soil Sci. **Research Statement & Publications:** Soil genesis and classification; weathering of minerals; soil claymineralogy; soil-plant relationships; mine waste characterization; resource allocation; natural resource management. **Mailing Address:** Dept Soil Sci, Univ BC, 2206 E Mall, Vancouver, BC V6T 1Z3, Can. **Fax:** 604-822-9250. **E-Mail:** lml@ires.ubc.ca

LAVOIE, ALVIN CHARLES, EMULSION POLYMERIZATION, ACRYLATES. **Personal Data:** b Fall River, Mass, January 26, 1956. **Education:** Southeastern Mass Univ, BS, 1977; Univ Wis-Madison, PhD (org chem), 1981. **Professional Experience:** DIR, TECH RECRUITING, ROHM & HAAS CO, as of 2001; res sect mgr, Rohm & Haas Co, beginning 1992; sr scientist, 1981-1992. **Memberships:** Am Chem Soc. **Research Statement & Publications:** Utilization of vinyl sulfides as enolonium equivilants in organic synthesis; applications of organosulfer intermediates in organic synthesis; emulsion polymerization of acrylates. **Mailing Address:** Rohm & Haas Co, 727 Norristown Rd, Spring House, PA 19477-0904. **E-Mail:** rssacl@rohmhaas.com

LAVOIE, DANIEL, BIOLOGY. **Education:** St Michael's Col, BA, 1971; Univ Vt, PhD (Biochem), 1977. **Professional Experience:** ASSOC PROF BIOL, ST ANSELM COL, as of 2004; 1978 - Fel, Albert Einstein Col Med, 1978. **Research Statement & Publications:** The enzymology and physiology of pyruvate kinase from the photosynthetic bacterium Chromatiun vinosum; the biochemistry and role in cancer of the iron storing protein ferritin in Homo sapiens; the biochemistry of iron and iron binding siderophores in nutritional immunity against the bacterial pathogen Pasteurella multocida infecting Oryctolagus cuniculus (rabbits). **Mailing Address:** Dept Biology, St Anselm Col, 100 Saint Anselm Dr, Manchester, NH 03102. **Fax:** 603-222-4012. **E-Mail:** dlavoie@anselm.edu

LAVOIE, EDMOND J, SYNTHETIC ORGANIC & NATURAL PRODUCTS CHEMISTRY. **Personal Data:** b New York, NY, January 11, 1950. **Education:** Fordham Univ, BS, 1971; State Univ NY, Buffalo, PhD (med chem), 1975. **Professional Experience:** PROF MED CHEM, COL PHARM, RUTGERS UNIV, as of 2004; CHMN PHARMACEUT CHEM, COL PHARM, RUTGERS UNIV, as of 2004; ASSOC MEM, ENVIRON CARCINOGENESIS DIV, AM HEALTH FOUND, 1980-; HEAD SECT METAB BIOCHEM, ENVIRON CARCINOGENESIS DIV, AM HEALTH FOUND, 1977-; assoc, Environ Carcinogenesis Div, Am Health Found, 1976-1979; Res assoc, Environ Carcinogenesis Div, Am Health Found, 1975-1976; Asst res prof, Dept Urol, NY Med Col. **Memberships:** Am Chem Soc; Am Asn Cancer Res; Environ Mutagen Soc. **Research Statement & Publications:** Experimental and environmental carcinogenesis; environmental analysis; tobacco sciences. **Mailing Address:** Dept Med Chem, Col Pharm, Rutgers Univ, 160 Frelinghuysen Rd, Piscataway, NJ 08854-8020. **Fax:** 732-445-6312. **E-Mail:** elavoie@rci.rutgers.edu

LAVOIE, JEAN-MARC, PHYSIOLOGY. **Education:** Univ Wis, BSc, 1971; Univ Montreal, MSc, 1973, PhD (exercise physiol), 1979. **Professional Experience:** DIR, METABOLIC RES LAB LIVER & EXERCISE, UNIV MONTREAL, as of 2003; PROF METAB, DEPT PHYS EDUC, UNIV MONTREAL, 1989-; from asst prof to assoc prof, Univ Montreal, 1979-1989. **Memberships:** Am Physiol Soc; Can Asn Sports Sci; Am Col Sports Med. **Research Statement & Publications:** Physiology. **Mailing Address:** Metabolic res lab liver & exercise, Univ Montreal, CP 6128 Succ Centre Ville, Montreal, PQ H3C 3J7, Can. **E-Mail:** jean-marc.lavoie@umontreal.ca

LAVOIE, MARCEL ELPHEGE, ZOOLOGY. **Personal Data:** b Manchester, NH, July 16, 1917. **Education:** St Anselm's Col, BA, 1940; Univ NH, MS, 1952; Syracuse Univ, PhD (zoology), 1956. **Professional Experience:** RETIRED; from asst prof to assoc prof zoology, Univ NH, 1955-1984; lectr zoology, Syracuse Univ, 1952-1955; instr biol, Univ NH, 1950-1952; instr chem, St Anselm's Col, 1946-1947. **Research Statement & Publications:** Mammalian anatomy and physiology. **Mailing Address:** 43 Madbury Rd, Durham, NH 03824.

LAVOIE, RONALD LEONARD, METEOROLOGY. **Personal Data:** b Manchester, NH, April 21, 1933. **Education:** Univ NH, BA, 1954; Fla State Univ, MS, 1956; Pa State Univ, PhD, 1968. **Professional Experience:** DIR, OFF METEOROL, NAT WEATHER SERV, NAT OCEANIC & ATMOSPHERIC ADMIN, 1990-; chief, Prog Requirements & Develop, Nat Weather Serv, 1982-1990; dir, Atmospheric Progs, Off Res Develop, 1979-1982; dir, Environ Modification Off, Nat Oceanic & Atmospheric Admin, 1973-1979; assoc dir meteorol prog, NSF, 1972-1973; assoc prof, Pa State Univ, 1968-1972; NSF sci fac fel, 1963-1964; asst prof meteorol, Univ Hawaii, 1959-1968; Chief observer, Mt Wash Observ, 1957-1959. **Memberships:** AAAS; Am Meteorol Soc; Am Geophys Union; Nat Weather Asn. **Research Statement & Publications:** Cloud physics and weather modification; numerical modeling on the mesoscale; tropical meteorology. **Mailing Address:** 16905 Briardale Rd, Derwood, MD 20855.

LAVOND, DAVID G, PSYCHOLOGY. **Education:** Ohio State Univ, MA, 1976, PhD (Psychol), 1979; Santa Clara Univ, BS, 1975. **Honors & Awards:** Troland Res Award, Nat Acad Sci, 1994; John W Streff Vision Achievement Award, NORA Int, 2003. **Professional Experience:** PROF PSYCHOL, UNIV CALIF, LOS ANGELES, as of 2003. **Mailing Address:** Dept Psychol Biol Sci, Univ Southern Calif, Los Angeles, CA 90024. **Fax:** 213-740-5687. **E-Mail:** lavond@neuro.usc.edu

LAVY, TERRY LEE, WEED SCIENCE, SOIL CHEMISTRY. **Personal Data:** b Greenville, Ohio, February 9, 1936. **Education:** Ohio State Univ, BS, 1958, MS, 1959; Purdue Univ, PhD (plant nutrit), 1962. **Professional Experience:** DIR, PESTICIDE RESIDUE LAB, UNIV ARK, 1978-; from asst prof to prof agron, Univ Nebr-Lincoln, 1962-1978; Lab supvr soil chem classification, Ohio State Univ, 1958-1959. **Memberships:** Weed Sci Soc Am; Am Soc Agron; Am Chem Soc. **Research Statement & Publications:** Factors affecting the mobility and degradation of pesticides in the soil profile; evaluating exposure of pesticide applicators; monitoring irrigation and domestic wells for pesticide contamination. **Mailing Address:** Dept Agron, Altheimer Lab, 276 Altheimer Dr, Fayetteville, AR 72704. **Fax:** 501-575-3975.

LAW, ALAN GREENWELL, APPROXIMATION & COMPUTING, MEDICAL IMAGING. **Personal Data:** b Seaham, Eng, August 21, 1936. **Education:** Univ BC, BA, 1958, MA, 1961; Ga Inst Technol, PhD (math), 1968. **Honors & Awards:** M A Ferst Res Award, Sigma Xi, 1968. **Professional Experience:** DEAN SCI, MEM UNIV NFLD, 1994-; head comput sci, Univ Regina, 1990-1994; Univ Minn, Duluth, 1985; vis prof, Univ Col Swansea, Wales, 1984; vis staff mem, Los Alamos Meson Physics Facil, 1976-1977; from asst prof to prof, Univ Regina, 1968-1994; Instr math, Ga Inst Technol, 1961-1968. **Memberships:** Math Asn Am; Sigma Xi; Soc Indust & Appl Math; Can Info Processing Soc. **Research Statement & Publications:** Numerical analysis and computing; modelling in sciences; digital image processing; large-scale computational problems; interdisciplinary analysis in natural and computational sciences. **Mailing Address:** Fac Sci, Mem Univ Nfld, St John's, NL A1B 3X7, Can. **Fax:** 709-737-3316. **E-Mail:** alaw@morgan.ucs.mun.ca

LAW, ALBERT G(ILES), CIVIL ENGINEERING, HYDROLOGY. **Personal Data:** b Ottawa, Ill, July 1, 1931. **Education:** Univ Ill, Urbana, BS, 1954; Univ Wis, MS, 1960, PhD (civil eng), 1965. **Professional Experience:** RETIRED; fel eng hydrol sci, Rockwell Hanford Opers, 1994; mgr hydrol sci, Rockwell Hanford Opers, 1977-1994; dir water resources engr, Clemson Univ & consult, US Geol Surv, 1975-1977; Vis assoc prof, Colo State Univ, 1971-1972; from asst prof to assoc prof civil eng, Clemson Univ, 1962-1977; instr civil eng, Univ Wis, 1958-1962; Design engr, Warzyn Eng Co, Wis, 1956-1958. **Memberships:** Nat Water Well Asn; Soc Mining Engrs; Am Soc Civil Engrs; Am Geophys Union; Am Water Resources Asn. **Research Statement & Publications:** Ground water hydrology, ground water flow, radioactive waste disposal. **Mailing Address:** 417 Snyder Rd, Richland, WA 99352.

LAW, AMY STAUBER, CLINICAL BIOCHEMISTRY. **Personal Data:** b Philadelphia, Pa, June 26, 1938; div. **Education:** Mt Holyoke Col, AB, 1959; Univ Del, MS, 1963, PhD (chem), 1969. **Professional Experience:** RES ASSOC I PLANT & SOIL SCI, UNIV DELAWARE, as of 2000; CLIN BIOCHEMIST, MED CTR DEL, 1969-; chief lab sect, Meat Inspection Div, Del State Bd Agr, 1968-1969; res chemist, AviSun Corp, 1961-1965. **Memberships:** AAAS; Am Chem Soc; Am Asn Clin Chemists; Asn Women Sci. **Research Statement & Publications:** Development of clinical methods; clinical applications of protein biochemistry; hemoglobinopathies; clinical toxicology. **Mailing Address:** Spec Chem-Christiana Hosp, Med Ctr Del, PO Box 6001, Newark, DE 19718-6001.

LAW, BRUCE MALCOLM, CONDENSED MATTER SURFACE PHYSICS, LIGHT SCATTERING. **Personal Data:** b Lower Hutt, NZ, June 23, 1956. **Education:** Victoria Univ, BS, 1978, BS, 1979, PhD (physics), 1986. **Professional Experience:** PROF PHYSICS, KANS STATE UNIV, as of 2005; asst prof, Kans State Univ, beginning 1989; res assoc, Univ Md, 1985-1989. **Memberships:** Am Phys Soc. **Research Statement & Publications:** Condensed matter surface physics/chemistry; application of light scattering techniques to both bulk and surface phases; non-equilibrium steady states. **Mailing Address:** Dept Physics, Kans State Univ, 327 Cardwell Hall, Manhattan, KS 66506. **Fax:** 785-532-6806. **E-Mail:** bmlaw@phys.ksu.edu

LAW, CECIL E, OPERATIONS RESEARCH, MICRO COMPUTER APPLICATIONS. **Personal Data:** b Vancouver, BC, November 27, 1922. **Education:** Univ BC, BA, 1950. **Honors & Awards:** Coronation Medal, 1953; Award Merit, Can Opers Res Soc, 1991. **Professional Experience:** RETIRED; emer prof opers, Res Sch Bus, 1990-1993; dir, Inst Community & Occup Health, 1985-1988; dir, Comput Lab, 1984-1988; dir, Visway TPT Inc, 1983-1988; exec dir, Can Inst Guided Transport, 1971-1983; prof comput sci, Queen's Univ, Ont, 1969-1983; prof oper res, Queen's Univ, Ont, 1966-1990; coordr opers analysis, Can Nat Rwy, 1964-1966; Lectr, Exten Dept, McGill Univ, 1964-1966; sr opers res analyst, Can Nat Rwy, 1962-1964; opers res mgr, Can Industs Ltd, 1961-1962; supvr opers res, Can Industs Ltd, 1960-1961; head oper gaming & tactics sect, Can Army Oper Res Estab, 1958-1960; head weapons effects & field trials sect, Can Army Oper Res Estab, 1955-1958; head arctic oper res sect, Defence Res Northern Lab, 1951-1954; Head animal field exp sect, Suffield Exp Sta, Defence Res Bd, 1951. **Memberships:** Opers Res Soc Am; Opers Res Soc UK; Can Int Proc Soc; Can Opers Res Soc (vpres, 1966, pres, 1967). **Research Statement & Publications:** Wildlife ecology and population dynamics, particularly Arctic; operations research, especially military and civil operational gaming and simulation; theoretical and applied critical path analysis and program evaluation and review technique; transportation research; micro-computer applications. **Mailing Address:** Sch Bus, Queen's Univ, Kingston, ON K7L 3N6, Can. **E-Mail:** lawc@qucdn.queensu.ca

LAW, CHUNG K, MECHANICAL ENGINEERING, AEROSPACE ENGINEERING. **Education:** Univ Alta, BSc, 1968; Univ Toronto, MSc, 1970; Univ Calif, PhD (eng physics), 1973. **Honors & Awards:** Energy Systs Award, 1999. **Professional Experience:** ROBERT H GODDARD PROF, MECH & AEROSPACE ENG DEPT, PRINCETON UNIV, 1998-. **Memberships:** Am Soc Mech Engrs; Nat Acad Eng. **Mailing Address:** Dept Mech & Aerospace Eng, Princeton Univ, D325 Eng Quad, Princeton, NJ 08540-5263. **Fax:** 609-258-6233. **E-Mail:** cklaw@pucc.princeton.edu

LAW, CHUNG KING, MECHANICAL ENGINEERING. **Education:** Univ Alta, BS, 1968; Univ Toronto, MA, 1970; Univ Calif, PhD (Eng Physics), 1973. **Professional Experience:** ROBERT H GODDARD PROF, DEPT MECH & AEROSPACE ENG, PRINCETON UNIV, 1988-; prof, Dept Mech Eng, Univ Calif, 1984-1988. **Mailing Address:** Dept Mech & Aerospace Eng, Princeton Univ, Princeton, NJ 08540-5263. **Fax:** 609-258-6233. **E-Mail:** cklaw@princeton.edu

LAW, CHUNG KING, COMBUSTION, PROPULSION. **Personal Data:** b Shanghai, China, September 21, 1947; m 1973, Helen; c Jonathan, Jennifer & Jeffrey. **Education:** Univ Alta, BS, 1968; Univ Toronto, MS, 1970; Univ Calif, San Diego, PhD, 1973. **Honors & Awards:** Curtis W McGraw Award, Am Soc Eng Educ, 1984; Silver Medal, Combustion Inst, 1990; Propellants & Combustion Award, Am Inst Aeronaut & Astronaut, 1994; Heat Transfer Memorial Award, Am Soc Mech Eng, 1997; Energy Systems Award, Am Inst Aeronaut & Astronaut, 1999; Pendray aerospace Literature Award, Am Inst Aeronaut & Astronaut, 2004. **Professional Experience:** ROBERT H GODDARD PROF MECH & AEROSPACE ENG, PRINCETON UNIV, 1995-; prof mech & aerospace eng, Princeton Univ, 1988-1995; prof, Univ Calif, Davis, 1984-1988; from assoc prof to prof, Northwestern Univ, 1976-1984; res staff, Princeton Univ, 1975-1976; assoc sr res engr, Gm Res Lab, 1973-1975. **Memberships:** Fel Am Inst Aeronaut & Astronaut; fel Am Soc Mech Engrs; Combustion Inst; US National Academy Eng. **Mailing Address:** Dept Mech & Aerospace Eng, Princeton Univ, D325 Eng Quadrangle, Princeton, NJ 08540-5263. **Fax:** 609-258-6233. **E-Mail:** cklaw@princeton.edu

LAW, DAVID H, INTERNAL MEDICINE, GASTROENTEROLOGY. **Personal Data:** b Milwaukee, Wis, July 24, 1927; m 1949, Patricia; c 5. **Education:** Cornell Univ, AB, 1950, MD, 1954. **Honors & Awards:** except serv award of the secty for veterans affairs, 1996, 2002; Mark Walton Award for excellence in clin care leadership from Veterons Health Admin, 2000; Hon fel, Am Acad Med Admin, 1993. **Professional Experience:** ASSOC CHIEF STAFF EDUC, VET ADMIN MED CTR, BAY PINES, 1996-; actg chief, Patient Care off, 1995-1996; asst chief med dir, Hosp Based Serv, Vet Admin Hq, 1986-1995; prof med, George Wash Med Sch, 1985-1996; dir med serv, Vet Admin Cent Off, Wash, DC, 1985-1986; prof med, Sch Med, Univ NMex, beginning 1969; chief med serv, Albuquerque Vet Admin Hosp, 1969-1985; attend physician, Thayer Vet Admin Hosp, 1962-1969; spec consult interdept comt nutrit for nat defense, NIH, 1962-1963; med dir out-patient dept & chief div gastroenterol, Vanderbilt Univ Hosp, 1960-1969; physician out patients & dir personnel health serv, NY Hosp, 1958-1960; asst physician outpatients, NY Hosp, 1957-1958; NIH fel, Nat Cancer Inst, 1957-1958; asst resident, NY Hosp, 1955-1957; intern med, NY Hosp, 1954-1955. **Memberships:** Fel Am Col Physicians; Am Soc Clin Nutrit; Am Gastroenterol Asn; Am Inst Nutrit; Western Soc Clin Invest; Western Asn Physicians. **Research Statement & Publications:** Inflammatory bowel disease; malabsorption; gastric secretion; medical care; nutrition; out-patient clinics; delivery of health care. **Mailing Address:** Vet Admin Med Cent 11B, PO Box 5005, Bay Pines, FL 33744. **Fax:** 727-398-9556. **E-Mail:** law.d@bay-pines.va.gov, david.law@med.va.gov

LAW, ERIC W, DIAGENESIS-METAMORPHISM, NEURAL NETWORK. **Personal Data:** b Taipei, Taiwan, July 14, 1949. **Education:** Case Western Res Univ, PhD (geol), 1983. **Professional Experience:** ASSOC PROF GEOL, MUSKINGUM COL, as of 2004; asst prof geol, Muskingum Col, beginning 1984. **Research Statement & Publications:** Petrology; geochronology; Taiwan; subduction; slate; K-Ar; computer; neural network; diagenesis; clay minerals; granite; metamorphism; sandstone. **Mailing Address:** Dept Geol, Muskingum Col, 163 Stormont St, New Concord, OH 43762.

LAW, FRANCIS C P, DRUG METABOLISM, TOXICOKINETIC MODELLING. **Personal Data:** b Hong Kong, October 12, 1941; m 1981, Rosemary; c Genevieve, Angela, Gerald & Vanessa. **Education:** Univ Alta, BS, 1966, MS, 1969; Univ Mich, PhD (drug metab), 1972. **Professional Experience:** PROF, SIMON FRASER UNIV, 1987-; assoc prof environ toxicol prog, Dept Biol Sci, 1983-1987; assoc prof, Col Pharm, Dalhousie Univ, 1981-1982; asst prof drug metab & toxicol, Col Pharm, Dalhousie Univ, 1975-1981; vis fel, Nat

Inst Environ Health Sci, 1972-1975. **Memberships:** Pharmacol Soc Can; Soc Toxicol Can; Am Soc Pharmacol & Exp Therapeut; Soc Environ Toxicol & Chem. **Research Statement & Publications:** Disposition, metabolism and toxicity of drugs; environmental pollutants and other chemicals in living organisms including humans; development of physiologically based toxicokinetic models; human health risk assessment; ecological risk assessment. **Mailing Address:** Dept Biol Sci, Environ Toxicol Prog, Simon Fraser Univ, Burnaby, BC V5A 1S6, Can. **Fax:** 604-291-3496. **E-Mail:** flaw@sfu.ca

LAW, GEORGE ROBERT JOHN, POULTRY GENETICS. **Personal Data:** b Vermilion, Alta, June 4, 1928. **Education:** Univ BC, BSA, 1950; Wash State Univ, MS, 1957; Univ Calif, Davis, PhD (genetics), 1961. **Professional Experience:** AGR PROJ MGR, SAN DIEGO STATE UNIV FOUND, 1989-; int counr, Col Agr Sci, 1988-1989; counr, Div Continuing Educ, 1981-1988; asst to dean, Col Agr Sci, 1978-1981; assoc prof animal sci, Colo State Univ, 1973-1978; Immuno-geneticist, Hy-Line Int, Pioneer Hawaii-Bred Int Inc, 1961-1972. **Research Statement & Publications:** Immuno-genetic studies of turkeys and chickens including blood type variation, serum protein, egg white protein and isozyme polymorphism; teaching, research and application of studies to breeding of poultry. **Mailing Address:** ENARP San Diego State Univ Found, 6330 Alvarado Ct, San Diego, CA 92120.

LAW, HSIANG-YI DAVID, OPTOELECTRONICS, SEMICONDUCTOR MATERIAL. **Personal Data:** b Hong Kong, February 12, 1949; American citizen; m 1973, Ruby H Yee; c Jeremy & George. **Education:** Univ Wash, BSEE, 1972; Cornell Univ, MSEE, 1975, PhD (elec eng), 1977. **Professional Experience:** PRES, ARTERNET CORP, 1993-; vpres technol, PCO, Inc, 1984-1991; mgr, Semiconductor Device Lab, Technol Res Ctr, TRW Inc, 1980-1984; Mem tech staff, Sci Ctr, Rockwell Int Corp, 1977-1980. **Memberships:** Sr mem Inst Elec & Electronics Engrs; Am Phys Soc. **Research Statement & Publications:** III-V alloys material study; avalanche photodiodes; double heterostructure lasers; integrated optoelectronic devices; ionization coefficients of III-V materials; ion implantation, anodic oxidation and other surface passivation methods. **Mailing Address:** 29776 Woodbrook Dr, Agoura Hills, CA 91301. **Fax:** 818-222-0736. **E-Mail:** hdlaw@pacbellnet.com

LAW, JIMMY, THEORETICAL PHYSICS, COMPUTATIONAL PHYSICS & ASTROPARTICLE PHYSICS. **Personal Data:** b Seremban, Malaysia, September 23, 1942. **Education:** Univ London, BSc, 1963, PhD (physics), 1968. **Professional Experience:** RETIRED; PROF PHYSICS, UNIV GUELPH, 1984-2005; Emeritus Univ Guelph 2005. **Memberships:** Brit Inst Physics; Can Asn Physicists. **Research Statement & Publications:** Theoretical calculations in nuclear and hypernuclear physics; inner shell vacancy creation mechanisms in atomic physics; Anyon physics and chaos; Solar Neutrino Physics (SNO). **Mailing Address:** Dept Phys, Univ Guelph, Guelph, ON N1G 2W1, Can. **Fax:** 519-836-9967. **E-Mail:** jlaw@uoguelph.ca

LAW, JOHN, POWER SYSTEMS, ELECTRIC MACHINERY. **Personal Data:** b Cleveland, Ohio, December 8, 1930. **Education:** Case Inst Technol, BS, 1957; Univ Wis-Madison, MS, 1960, PhD (elec eng), 1962. **Professional Experience:** Planning engr, Idaho Power Co, 1981; vis prof elec eng, Wash State Univ, 1980; PROF EMER ELEC ENGR, UNIV IDAHO, 1979-; vis engr, Eng Soc Comn Energy, 1979; mem, Fac Improvement Comt, NSF, 1978; NSF fel, Elec Power Res Inst, 1978; engr, Idaho Nat Eng lab, 1977; consult, Idaho Power Co, 1976; assoc prof, Univ Idaho, 1975-1979; vis assoc prof elec eng, Bogazici Univ, Turkey, 1974-1975; sr staff engr, Carrier Corp, 1974; chief engr, Carrier Corp, 1965-1974; sr elec engr, Carrier Corp, 1963-1965; assoc prof elec eng, Mont State Univ, 1962-1963; instr, Univ Wis, 1957-1961. **Memberships:** Inst Elec & Electronics Engrs; Nat Soc Prof Engrs. **Research Statement & Publications:** Computer methods in power systems analysis; response of AC servomotors with nonsinusoinal and discontinuous impedance source voltage. **Mailing Address:** Dept Elec Eng, Univ Idaho, Buchanan Eng Lab, Moscow, ID 83844. **Fax:** 208-885-7579. **E-Mail:** johnlaw@ece.uidaho.edu

LAW, JOHN HAROLD, ENTOMOLOGY. **Personal Data:** b Cleveland, Ohio, February 27, 1931; m 2000, Jeannette. **Education:** Case Inst Technol, BS, 1953; Univ Ill, PhD (chem), 1957. **Honorary Degrees:** HC, Sofia Univ, Bulgaria, 1995; HC, Univ South Bohemia, Czech Republic, 2004. **Honors & Awards:** Gregor Mendel Medal, J E Purkinje Medal, Czech Acad Sci. **Professional Experience:** ADJUNCT PROF, UNIV. GEORGIA, 2004-; REGENTS PROF EMERITUS, UNIV ARIZ, 2002-; Wellcome vis prof, Univ Mass, 1993; regents prof, biochem dept, univ ariz, 1992-2002; dir biotechnol, Ctr Insect Sci, 1986-1992; dept head, Ctr Insect Sci, 1981-1986, 1993-1998; prof chem, Univ Chicago, 1967-1981; prof biochem, Univ Chicago, 1965-1981; from instr to asst prof, Harvard Univ, 1959-1965; instr chem, Northwestern Univ, 1958-1959; Res fel, Harvard Univ, 1957-1958. **Memberships:** Nat Acad Sci; Am Soc Biol Chemists; fel AAAS; Am Chem Soc; fel Entom Soc Am. **Research Statement & Publications:** Insect biochemistry; lipid metabolism; protein chemistry; iron metabolism. **Mailing Address:** Entomol Dept 413 Biol Sci, Univ GA, Athens, GA 30602-2816. **E-Mail:** jhlaw@bugs.ent.uga.edu

LAW, MARGARET ELIZABETH, EXPERIMENTAL HIGH ENERGY PHYSICS. **Personal Data:** b Birmingham, Eng, May 6, 1934; m 1957. **Education:** Univ Birmingham, Eng, BSc, 1955, PhD (high energy physics), 1958; Boston Univ, MBA, 1984. **Professional Experience:** DIR, PHYSICS LAB, HARVARD UNIV, 1989-; SR LECTR, HARVARD UNIV, 1986-; registr, Fac Arts & Sci, 1978-1989; lectr, Harvard Univ, 1972-1978, 1983-1985; sr res assoc high energy physics, Harvard Univ, 1971-1978; res assoc, Harvard Univ, 1967-1971; res fel, Harvard Univ, 1961-1967; Nat Res Coun fel nuclear physics, McMaster Univ, 1958-1960. **Research Statement & Publications:** Experimental research in strong interactions. **Mailing Address:** Lyman Lab, Harvard Univ, Rm 233, Arlington, MA 02474. **E-Mail:** law@physics.harvard.edu

LAW, MARK EDWARD, COMPUTER ENGINEERING. **Education:** Stanford Univ, PhD, 1988. **Professional Experience:** PROF & CHMN ELEC & COMPUT ENG, UNIV FLA, as of 2004. **Mailing Address:** Dept Elec & Comput Eng Univ Fla, 535 NEB PO Box 116130 216 Larsen Hall, Gainesville, FL 32611-6130. **Fax:** 352-392-8381. **E-Mail:** law@tec.ufl.edu

LAW, PAUL ARTHUR, CLINICAL CHEMISTRY. **Personal Data:** b Lowell, Mass, September 19, 1934; m 1981, c 4. **Education:** Lowell Technol Inst, BS, 1956; Mich State Univ, PhD (org chem), 1962. **Professional Experience:** GEN MGR MOTION PICTURE & TELEVISION PROD, EASTMAN KODAK CO, 1986-; asst supt med prod, Eastman Kodak Co, 1980-1986; gen supvr, Eastman Kodak Co, 1978-1980; tech assoc, Eastman Kodak Co, 1969-1978; sr res chemist, Eastman Kodak Co, 1963-1969; fel polypeptide synthesis, Fla State Univ, 1962-1963; Res chemist, Dow Corning Corp, 1956-1958. **Memberships:** Am Asn Clin Chemists. **Research Statement & Publications:** Color photographic chemistry. **Mailing Address:** Eastman Kodak Co, 343 State St, Rochester, NY 14650.

LAW, PETER KOI, NEUROMUSCULAR ELECTROPHYSIOLOGY. **Personal Data:** b Chengsha, China, February 25, 1946; Chinese & Canadian citizen. **Education:** McGill Univ, BSc, 1968; Univ Toronto, MSc, 1969, PhD (neurophysiol), 1972. **Professional Experience:** CHIEF EXEC OFFICER, CELL THER RES FOUND, as of 2004; CHMN, CELL THER RES FOUND, 1991-; prof, Univ Tenn, 1988-1991; NIH grants, 1983-1993; assoc prof neurol physiol & biophys, Univ Tenn, 1979-1988; NSF res grant, 1979-1982; NIH res grant, 1978-1979; muscular dystrophy asn res grant, 1975-1988; Vanderbilt Univ res coun res grant, 1975-1979; electromyography consult, Vanderbilt Univ Hosp, Nashville, 1975-1979; asst prof neurol, Sch Med, Vanderbilt Univ, 1975-1979; sr investr, Jerry Lewis Neuromuscular Dis Res Ctr, Nashville, Tenn, 1975-1979; baptist hosp, 1975-1979; St thomas hosp, 1975-1979; muscular dystrophy asn can fel, 1972-1975; fel, med ctr, McMaster Univ, 1972-1975. **Memberships:** Asn Am Med Cols; AAAS; NY Acad Sci; Soc Neuroscience; Can Soc Neuroscience. **Research Statement & Publications:** Developmental membrane biophysics; motor-unit electrophysiology; muscular dystrophy; myogenesis and muscle regeneration; genetic complementation and therapy; acupuncture analgesia; myogenic cell transplant treatment for muscle disease. **Mailing Address:** Cell Ther Res Found, 1770 Moriah Woods Ste 18, Memphis, TN 38117.

LAW, S EDWARD, BIOLOGICAL ENGINEERING, AGRICULTURAL ENGINEERING. **Personal Data:** b September 10, 1939. **Education:** NC State Col, BS, 1961; NC State Univ, Raleigh, MS, 1964, PhD (biol & agr eng), 1968. **Honors & Awards:** Tyler Prize Environ Achievement, Electrostatics Soc Am, 1994. **Professional Experience:** D W BROOKS DISTINGUISHED PROF, BIOL & AGR ENG DEPT, UNIV GA, 1988-; prof, Agr Eng Dept, 1982-1988; from asst to assoc prof, Agr Eng Dept, 1970-1982; res engr, Gourdine Environ Systs Inc, 1969-1970; Nat Acad Sci postdoctoral res assoc, Just Res Lab, USDA-Agr Res Serv. **Memberships:** Nat Acad Eng; fel Inst Elec & Electronics Engrs; fel Am Soc Agr Engrs; Electrostatics Soc Am; Int Ozone Asn; Entom Soc Am; Sigma Xi. **Research Statement & Publications:** Light-scattering properties of optically dense biological particulate systems; charged-particulate technology and electrogas dynamics; research and development of electrostatics for agriculture and biological applications; granted 14 domestic and foreign patents; published 8 articles in last 5 years. **Mailing Address:** Dept Biol & Agr Eng Univ Ga, Rm 111 Driftmier Eng Ctr, Athens, GA 30602-4435. **Fax:** 706-542-8806. **E-Mail:** edlaw@engr.uga.edu

LAW, WILLIAM BROUGH, PLASMA PHYSICS. **Personal Data:** b Elko, Nev, October 11, 1932. **Education:** Univ Nev, BSc, 1954; Ohio State Univ, PhD (nuclear physics), 1960. **Professional Experience:** PROF EMER PHYSICS, COLO SCH MINES, as of 2005; assoc prof physics, Colo Sch Mines, beginning 1968; asst prof, Colo Sch Mines, 1965-1968; staff mem, Sandia Lab, 1960-1965; physicist, Armour Res Found, 1960. **Memberships:** Am Phys Soc. **Research Statement & Publications:** Gamma ray spectroscopy; accelerator physics. **Mailing Address:** Dept Physics, Colo Sch Mines, Rm 433 Meyer Hall, Golden, CO 80401. **E-Mail:** wlaw@mines.edu

LAWFORD, GEORGE ROSS, BIOCHEMISTRY, CELL BIOLOGY. **Personal Data:** b Toronto, Ont, February 27, 1941. **Education:** Univ Toronto, BSc, 1963, PhD (biochem), 1966. **Professional Experience:** PROF HEALTH SCI, MCMASTER UNIV, as of 2003; PRES & CONSULT, ROSS LAWFORD & ASSOC, 1993-; pres, Ortech Int, 1989-1993; tech dir & gen mgr, Weston Res Ctr, 1977-1989; mem staff, Weston Res Ctr, 1973-1977; asst prof biochem, McMaster Univ, 1968-1973; Can Med Res Coun fel, 1966-1968; mem, Nat Biotechnol Adv Comt Can. **Memberships:** Can Res Mgt Asn; Can Inst Food Sci & Technol; Am Asn Cereal Chemists. **Research Statement & Publications:** Functional significance of interactions between subcellular components; regulation of protein biosynthesis and the adenyl cyclase system; food chemistry; fermentation; research management. **Mailing Address:** Ross Lawford & Assoc, 23 Runsey Rd, Toronto, ON M4G 1N7, Can. **E-Mail:** rlawford@allstream.net

LAWING, WILLIAM DENNIS, STATISTICS. **Personal Data:** b Charlotte, NC, March 29, 1935. **Education:** NC State Col, BS, 1957, MS, 1959; Iowa State Univ, PhD (statist), 1965. **Professional Experience:** PROF EMER INDUST ENG & EXP STATIST, UNIV RI, as of 2004; assoc prof indust & exp statist, Univ Ri, beginning 1969; adj assoc prof, NC State Univ, 1968-1969; vis lectr, Iowa State Univ, 1967-1968; adj prof, Duke Univ, 1966-1967; statistician, Res Triangle Inst, 1965-1969. **Memberships:** Am Statist Asn. **Research Statement & Publications:** Industrial applications of statistics; quality control; operations research; sequential analysis; decision theory; survey sampling. **Mailing Address:** Dept Indust & Exp Statist, Univ Ri, Kingston, RI 02881.

LAWLER, ADRIAN RUSSELL, AQUACULTURE, TOXICOLOGY. **Personal Data:** b Etowah, Tenn, November 25, 1940; div. **Education:** Univ Rochester, AB, 1962; Col William & Mary, Va, MS, 1964, PhD (marine biol), 1971. **Professional Experience:** RETIRED; aquarium supvr, Marine Educ Ctr, Biloxi, 1984-1998; co-chmn toxicol prog & head exp organism cult, Gulf Coast Res Lab, 1976-1984; marine biologist, Gulf Coast Res Lab, beginning 1975; Consult, Nat Aquaculture Info Syst, 1975-; assoc marine biologist, Gulf Coast Res Lab, 1973-1975; teaching fel, Gulf Coast Res Lab, 1971-1973; grad asst, Va Inst Marine Sci, 1962-1971; NSF summer student, Va Inst Marine Sci, 1962. **Research Statement & Publications:** Culture of marine and freshwater organisms, birds and mammals for experimentation; toxicity testing; external parasites of marine and freshwater fishes; larval fish development; display of organisms in Mississippi's marine science aquarium; disease diagnosis and control in captive organisms on public display; aquarium design and maintenance. **Mailing Address:** Aquarium Supvr, JL Scott Marine Educ Ctr & Aquarium, 115 E Beach Blvd, Biloxi, MS 39530. **E-Mail:** alawler@hotmail.com

LAWLER, GREGORY FRANCIS, PROBABILITY. **Personal Data:** b Alexandria, Va, July 14, 1955; m 1990, Marcia. **Education:** Univ Va, BA, 1976; Princeton Univ, MA, 1977, PhD (math), 1979. **Honors & Awards:** Fellow, American Academy of Arts and Sciences, 2005 Fellow, Institute of Mathematical Statistics, 1992. **Professional Experience:** PROF MATH, CORNELL UNIV, as of 2001; From Asst Prof to A. Hollis Edens Professor, Duke Univ, 1979-2003. **Memberships:** Am Math Soc; Int Asn Math Physics; fel Int Math Statist. **Research Statement & Publications:** Random walks; processes from statstical physics such as self-avoiding walks. **Mailing Address:** Dept Math, Cornell Univ, 567 Malott Hall, Ithaca, NY 14853-4201. **Fax:** 607-255-7149. **E-Mail:** lawler@math.cornell.edu

LAWLER, JACK (JOHN) W, PHYSICS. **Personal Data:** b Newton, Mass, May 2, 1949. **Education:** Villanova Univ, BS, 1971; Boston Col, PhD (physics), 1976. **Professional Experience:** Res comput comt, Brigham & Womens Hosp, 1992-; Prin investr, NIH, 1989-1994; ASSOC PROF PATH, HARVARD MED SCH, 1988-; ASSOC PROF PATH, BRIGHAM & WOMENS HOSP, HARVARD MED SCH, 1988-; Prin investr, NIH, 1988-1990; inst biosafety comt, St Elizabeths Hosp, 1988; health site vis comt, NIH, 1985-1992; vis scientist, Mass Inst Technol, 1985-1989, res affil, & 1992-; investr, Dept Biomed Res, St Elizabeths Hosp, 1985-1988; comt intellectual property, Tufts Univ, Sch Med, 1985-1986; chmn, Tufts Univ, Sch Med, 1985-1986; sci affairs comt, Tufts Univ, Sch Med, 1984-1988; assoc investr, Dept Biomed Res, St Elizabeths Hosp, 1983-1985; prin investr, NIH, 1982-1995; from asst prof to assoc prof, Tufts Univ, Sch Med, 1982-1988; asst investr, Dept Biomed Res, St Elizabeths Hosp, 1982-1983; res assoc, Dept Biomed Res, St Elizabeths Hosp, 1980-1982; res fel, Dana-Farber Cancer Inst, 1976-1980. **Member-**

ships: Int Soc Thrombosis & Hemostasis; NY Acad Sci; Am Soc Hemat; AAAS; Am Soc Cell biol. **Research Statement & Publications:** Structural and functional organization of thrombospondin; the role of thrombospondin and its receptor in the normal and abnormal vascular cell function; the function of thrombospondin in tissue genesis and repair; author of over 50 publications. **Mailing Address:** Dept Path, Beth Israel Deaconess Med Ctr Harvard Med Sch, RN 270c, 330 Broookline Ave, Boston, MA 02115. **Fax:** 617-667-3591. **E-Mail:** jlawler@bidmc.harvard.edu

LAWLER, JAMES E, PSYCHOLOGY. **Personal Data:** b January 15, 1946. **Education:** Cornell Col, BA, 1967; Wake Forest Univ, MA, 1970; Univ NC, Chapel Hill, PhD (physiol psychol), 1973. **Professional Experience:** PROF, DEPT ANAT & NEUROBIOLOGY, CTR HEALTH SCI, 1987-; chancellor's fac res scholar award, 1987; res incentive award, Sci Alliance, Univ Tenn, beginning 1985; PROF & HEAD, DEPT PSYCHOL, UNIV TENN, KNOXVILLE, 1985-; vis scientist, Minority Access Res Career, Fedn Am Socs Exp Biol, beginning 1983; vis assoc prof, Dept Med, Cardiovasc Res & Training Ctr, Sch Med, Univ Ala, 1983-1984; consult progs & planning, Am Psychol Asn, 1980; Sudden Cardiac Death Rev Comt, Nat Heart, Lung & Blood Inst, NIH, 1978; mem, High Blood Pressure Res Coun, Am Heart Asn, beginning 1977; from asst prof to assoc prof, Dept Anat & Neurobiology, Ctr Health Sci, 1975-1985; res assoc, Cardiovasc Labs, Sch Pub Health, Harvard Univ, 1973-1975; res asst psychiat, Sch Med, Univ NC, 1972-1973; NIH fel neurobiology, Sch Med, Univ NC, 1970-1972; grad asst, Wake Forest Univ, 1967-1968. **Memberships:** AAAS; Am Physiol Soc; Soc Behav Med; Soc Neuroscience; Soc Psychophysiol Res. **Research Statement & Publications:** Author of numerous publications. **Mailing Address:** 306 Austin Peay Bldg, Knoxville, TN 37996-0900. **Fax:** 865-974-3330. **E-Mail:** jlawler@utk.edu

LAWLER, JAMES EDWARD, SPECTROSCOPY, PLASMA SCIENCE. **Personal Data:** b St Louis, Mo, June 29, 1951; m 1973, Katherine; c Emily C & Catherine M. **Education:** Univ Mo, BS, 1973; Univ Wis-Madison, MS, 1974, PhD (physics), 1978. **Honors & Awards:** W P Allis Prize, Am Phys Soc; Penning Award, Int Conf Phenomena Ionized Gases. **Professional Experience:** ARTHUR & AURELIA SCHAWLOW PROF PHYSICS, UNIV WIS, 1989-; H I Romnes fac fel, Univ Wis 1987-1992; from asst prof to assoc prof, Univ Wis, 1980-1989; res assoc, Physics Dept, Stanford Univ, 1978-1980. **Memberships:** Fel Am Phys Soc; Fel Optical Soc Am; Sigma Xi. **Research Statement & Publications:** Physics of gas discharge plasmas; laser spectroscopy; laboratory astrophysics; atomic physics. **Mailing Address:** Dept Physics, Univ Wis, 1150 Univ Ave, Madison, WI 53706. **Fax:** 608-265-2334. **E-Mail:** jelawler@wisc.edu

LAWLER, JAMES HENRY LAWRENCE, CHEMICAL ENGINEERING, NUCLEAR ENGINEERING. **Personal Data:** b Detroit, Mich, January 31, 1936; m 1989, Lidia Zelmiva Palomico; c M Jennette, Mary, Duncan, James, Thomas, Bruce, Heather & Meaghan. **Education:** Univ Louisville, BChE, 1959, MEngr, 1972; Brigham Young Univ, MS, 1966; Univ Utah, ME & PhD (chem eng), 1969. **Honorary Degrees:** doc and permanent visiting prof, univ of San Marcos, Lima, Peru. **Professional Experience:** Consult, Alliance Aircraft, 1999-2002; consult, Brole Inc, 1994-1997; consult Pamasia, 1994; teacher, Toronto Col, 1997-1999 CONSULT, 1994-; physics res engr, Super Conducting Super Collider, 1991-1994; engr, Gen Dynamics Nat Aerospace Plane, 1986-1991; staff engr, Rockwell Hanford Oper, 1980-1986; chmn chem technol, Univ Dayton, 1977-1980; head nuclear eng technol, Trident Technol Col, SC, 1973-1977; AEC fel, Kans State Univ, 1972; asst prof chem, Dixie Col, 1969-1973; eng, Boeing Co, 1962-1965; engr, Wright Patterson AFB, 1959-1962; engr, Radio Sta WKYW, 1958-1959; engr, Radio Sta WKLO, 1957-1958; radio engr, Louisville Free Pub Libr, 1952-1954. **Memberships:** Am Inst Chem Eng; Am Chem Soc. **Research Statement & Publications:** Materials; cyclic history; socio-mathematics; quantization of space-time; unified theory of gravity, strong and weak nuclear forces, electromagnetic forces, proton theory. **Mailing Address:** 3765 Wedgworth Rd S, Ft Worth, TX 76133.

LAWLER, JOHN PATRICK, SANITARY ENGINEERING, MATHEMATICS. **Personal Data:** b Brooklyn, NY, January 30, 1934. **Education:** Manhattan Col, BCE, 1955; NY Univ, MCE, 1958; Univ Wis, PhD (sanit eng), 1960. **Professional Experience:** PARTNER, LAWLER, MATUSKY & SKELLY ENGRS, 1977-; partner, Quirk, Lawler & Matusky Engrs, 1965-1977; lectr summer inst water resources, Clemson Univ, 1965 & 1966; lectr summer inst stream analysis, Manhattan Col, 1964-1966; assoc, Cosulich & Quirk, Water Resources Engrs, 1964-1965; vis assoc prof, Manhattan Col, 1963-; Consult, Humble Oil & Refining Co, NJ, 1961-1962; asst prof, Rutgers Univ, 1960-1965; instr civil eng, Manhattan Col, 1956-1958; Civil engr, F G Davidson, Inc, NY, 1955-1956. **Memberships:** Am Soc Civil Engrs; Water Pollution Control Fedn; Sigma Xi. **Research Statement & Publications:** Mathematical analysis of the transport processes and reaction kinetics associated with stream and estuarine pollution; water resources systems; water and waste treatment operations. **Mailing Address:** Lawler Matusky & Skelly Engrs, One Blue Hill Plaza, Pearl River, NY 10965.

LAWLER, MARTIN TIMOTHY, FLUID MECHANICS, HEAT TRANSFER. **Personal Data:** b Rochester, Minn, April 6, 1937. **Education:** Milwaukee Sch Eng, BS, 1961; Case Inst Technol, MS, 1965, PhD (eng), 1967. **Professional Experience:** MANAGING PARTNER, LAWLER & ASSOCS, 1972-; vpres, Swenberg Eng Inc, 1970-1972; prin res scientist, Corp Res Ctr, Honeywell Inc, Minn, 1967-1970; res asst, Fluid, Thermal & Aerospace Sci, Case Inst Technol, 1964-1967; Nat Defense fel, Comt Acad Sci & Eng, Inst Technol, 1961-1964; Instr mech eng & physics, Milwaukee Sch Eng, 1959-1961. **Memberships:** Am Soc Mech Engrs; Nat Soc Prof Engrs; Am Soc Heating Refrig & Air Conditioning Engrs; Sigma Xi; Am Asn Energy Engrs. **Research Statement & Publications:** Fluid-particle and two-phase flows; heat transfer; solar systems, energy consumption and conservation. **Mailing Address:** Lawler Eng/Div JSA, Pkwy W & Rte 60, Pittsburgh, PA 15244-0508.

LAWLER, RONALD GEORGE, PHYSICAL ORGANIC CHEMISTRY. **Personal Data:** b Centralia, Wash, May 19, 1938. **Education:** Calif Inst Technol, BS, 1960; Univ Calif, Berkeley, PhD (chem), 1964. **Professional Experience:** PROF EMER CHEM, BROWN UNIV, as of 2005; prof chem, Brown Univ, beginning 1973; Alfred P Sloan res fel, 1970-1971; from asst prof to assoc prof, Brown Univ, 1965-1973; res assoc chem, Columbia Univ, 1963-1965; NSF fel, 1963-1964. **Memberships:** Am Chem Soc. **Research Statement & Publications:** Theoretical organic chemistry; electron and nuclear magnetic resonance; chemistry of free radicals and radical ions; radiation chemistry; in vivo nmr. **Mailing Address:** Dept Chem, Brown Univ, Providence, RI 02912. **E-Mail:** ronald_lawler@brown.edu

LAWLESS, EDWARD WILLIAM, TECHNICAL MANAGEMENT, ENVIRONMENTAL CHEMICALS ASSESSMENT. **Personal Data:** b Jacksonville, Ill, April 9, 1931. **Education:** Ill Col, AB, 1953; Univ Mo, PhD (phys chem), 1960. **Honorary Degrees:** DSc, Ill Col, 1979. **Professional Experience:** Chem prof, Metrop Community Col, Kansas City, Mo, beginning 1992; SR ADV ENVIRON SCI, MIDWEST RES INST, 1991-; head, Environ Assessment Sect, 1987-1991; sr adv, Technol & Health Assessment, 1982-1987; head, Technol Assessment Sect, 1973-1982; prin chemist, Midwest Res Inst, 1966-1973; sr chemist, Midwest Res Inst, 1964-1966; assoc chemist, Midwest Res Inst, 1959-1964. **Memberships:** Am Chem Soc; Soc Risk Anal; Int Asn Impact Assessment (pres, 1983-1984). **Research Statement & Publications:** Hazardous waste incineration and management; technology forecast, risk assessment and societal effects analysis; environmental chemistry and pollution control; evaluation of health and environmental hazards of industrial, consumer product and agricultural chemicals; chemistry of pesticides, fluorine, metal hydrides; correlations of chemical structures with properties; analysis of agricultural innovation; chemical kinetics. **Mailing Address:** Appl Eng Dept, Midwest Res Inst 425 Volker Blvd, Kansas City, MO 64110. **Fax:** 816-753-8420.

LAWLESS, HARRY THOMAS, PSYCHOLOGY, FOOD SCIENCE. **Personal Data:** b Hackensack, NJ, March 20, 1952. **Education:** Yale Univ, BA, 1974; Brown Univ, ScM, 1976, PhD (psychol), 1978. **Professional Experience:** PROF & DIR GRAD STUDIES, DEPT FOOD SCI, CORNELL UNIV, as of 2005; William Evans vis fel, Univ Otago, 1995; Fulbright res fel, Finland, 1995; assoc prof, Dept Food Sci, NY State Col Agr & Life Sci, Cornell Univ, beginning 1993; asst prof, Dept Food Sci, NY State Col Agr & Life Sci, Cornell Univ, 1989-1992; prof, Dept Foods & Nutrit, Univ Ill, 1987-1988; instr, Dept Psychol, Univ Wis, Parkside, 1987-1988; sr scientist, Prod Eval Dept, SC Johnson & Son, 1984-1988; asst prof, Dept Food Sci, Univ Del, 1982-1984; asst prof res, Dept Otolaryngol, Thomas Jefferson Med Col, 1982-1984; asst mem, Monell Chem, Senses Ctr, 1981-1984; vis scientist, Gen Foods Tech Ctr, 1980; Instr, Northeastern Univ, 1979-1980; postdoctoral assoc, Food Sci Lab, US Army Natick Res & Develop Command, 1978-1980; mem, Nat Adv Bd, Nat Inst Deafness & Commun Dis; mem, Grad Field Food Sci & Grad Field Psychol, Cornell Univ. **Memberships:** Sigma Xi; Inst Food Technologists; Psychonomic Soc; Am Soc Testing & Mat; Asn Chemoreception Sci; Soc Consumer Psychol; Soc Study Ingestive Behav; Am Soc Enol & Viticult; Am Psychol Asn. **Research Statement & Publications:** Sensory evaluation of foods; advanced concepts in sensory evaluation; sensory evaluation of dairy products; flavors analysis and applications. **Mailing Address:** Dept Food Sci, Cornell Univ, 106 Stocking Hall, Ithaca, NY 14853-7201. **Fax:** 607-254-4868. **E-Mail:** htl1@cornell.edu

LAWLESS, JAMES GEORGE, ANALYTICAL CHEMISTRY. **Personal Data:** b Brooklyn, NY, August 18, 1942. **Education:** Lafayette Col, BS, 1964; Purdue Univ, MS, 1966; Kans State Univ, PhD (chem), 1969. **Professional Experience:** DIV CHIEF, EARTH SYST SCI DIV, AMES RES CTR, NASA, as of 1994; co-investr returned lunar samples, NASA, 1970-; res scientist mass spectrometry, NASA, 1969-. **Memberships:** Am Soc Mass Spectrometry; Geochem Soc; Meteoritic Soc. **Research Statement & Publications:** Mass spectrometry of organic compounds; analysis of lunar samples and meteorites for carbon compounds. **Mailing Address:** MS 239-20, Ames Res Ctr, Moffett Field, CA 94035.

LAWLESS, KENNETH ROBERT, MATERIALS SCIENCE. **Personal Data:** b Key West, Fla, August 21, 1922. **Education:** Lynchburg Col, BS, 1946; Univ Va, PhD (chem), 1951. **Professional Experience:** PROF EMER MAT SCI, UNIV VA, 1986-; chmn dept, Univ Va, 1976-1986; prof mat sci, Univ Va, 1968-1980; from asst prof to assoc prof, Univ Va, 1960-1968; res assoc chem, Univ Va, 1952-1960; Fulbright fel, Univ Norway, 1951-1952. **Memberships:** Electron Micros Soc Am; Am Crystallog Asn; Inst Mining, Metall & Petrol Engrs; Microbeam Anal Soc. **Research Statement & Publications:** Chemistry and physics of solids and surfaces; x-ray diffraction; electron diffraction and electron microscopy. **Mailing Address:** Dept Mat Sci & Eng, Univ Va, Thornton Hall, Charlottesville, VA 22903. **Fax:** 804-982-5660. **E-Mail:** krl@virginia.edu

LAWLESS, PHILIP AUSTIN, ENGINEERING PHYSICS. **Personal Data:** b Tulsa, Okla, June 7, 1943. **Education:** Rice Univ, BA, 1965; Duke Univ, PhD (physics), 1974. **Professional Experience:** SR RES PHYSICIST, RES TRIANGLE PARK, 1985-; physicist, Res Triangle Inst, 1974-1985. **Research Statement & Publications:** Theoretical and experimental investigations of electrostatic precipitators for particulate control. **Mailing Address:** ResTriangle Inst, 3040 Cornwallis Rd, Research Triangle Park, NC 27709. **Fax:** 919-541-8737.

LAWLESS, WILLIAM N, SOLID STATE PHYSICS. **Personal Data:** b Denver, Colo, September 15, 1936. **Education:** Colo Sch Mines, EMet, 1959; Rensselaer Polytech Inst, PhD (physics), 1964. **Professional Experience:** STAFF, LAKE SHORE CRYOTRONICS INC, 1980-; guest worker, Cryogenics Div, Nat Bur Stand, Boulder, 1973-1975; res assoc physics, Res & Develop Labs, Corning Glass Works, 1969-1980; sr res physicist, Res & Develop Labs, Corning Glass Works, 1966-1968; fel solid state physics, Swiss Fed Inst Technol, 1964-1966. **Memberships:** AAAS; Am Inst Physics; Cryogenic Soc Am; Am Phys Soc. **Research Statement & Publications:** Ferroelectricity; doped alkali halides; glass-ceramic technology. **Mailing Address:** Ceramphysics, Inc, 921 Eastwind Dr, Ste 110, Westerville, OH 43081. **Fax:** 614-882-1437.

LAWLEY, ALAN, METALLURGY, MATERIALS SCIENCE. **Personal Data:** b Birmingham, Eng, August 29, 1933; American citizen; m 1960, Nancy; c Carolyn A, Elizabeth A & Jennifer A. **Education:** Univ Birmingham, BS (phys metall), 1955, PhD (phys metall), 1958. **Honors & Awards:** Krumb Lectr, Am Inst Mining Metall & Petrol Eng, 1985; Distinguished Serv Powder Metall Award, Metal Powder Indust Fedn, 1991; ASM Gold Medal 1996; Jenkins Award Inst of Materials, 1996; National Acad of Engineering 1998; Fellow APMI International, 1998; Educator Award, TMS, 2002. **Professional Experience:** PROF EMER MAT SCI & ENG, DREXEL UNIV, as of 2004; consult, Cabot Corp, 1981; prof metall eng, Drexel Univ, beginning 1979; consult, Open Univ, UK, 1975; chmn, Mat Eng Dept, 1969-1979; assoc prof metall eng, Drexel Univ, 1966-1969; lab mgr phys metall, Res Labs, Franklin Inst, Pa, 1961-1966; res assoc metall, Univ Pa, 1958-1961. **Memberships:** fel Am Soc Metals Int; Am Soc Eng Educ; fel Am Powder Metall Inst; Inst Mat; TMS (pres, 1982); AIME (pres, 1987). **Research Statement & Publications:** Powder metallurgy; physical and mechanical metallurgy; engineering education; materials engineering design. **Mailing Address:** Dept Mat Sci & Eng, Drexel Univ, Wynnewood, PA 19096-1925. **Fax:** 215-895-6760. **E-Mail:** alan.lawley@drexel.edu

LAWLEY, THOMAS J, DERMATOLOGY. **Professional Experience:** DEAN SCH MED, EMORY UNIV, 1996-; PROF & CHMN, DEPT DERMAT, EMORY UNIV, 1989-. **Memberships:** Amn Soc Clin Invest; Asn Amn Prof. **Research Statement & Publications:** written more than 200 book chapters, research articles. **Mailing Address:** Dept Dermat, Emory Univ Sch Med, 1440 Clifton Rd NE, Rm 321, Atlanta, GA 30322. **Fax:** 404-727-0473. **E-Mail:** cfost01@emory.edu

LAWMAN, MICHAEL JOHN PATRICK, EXPERIMENTAL BIOLOGY. **Personal Data:** b September 30, 1949. **Education:** Guildford Co Tech Col, HNC, 1972; Ewell Co Tech Col, LIBiol, 1973, MIBiol, 1975; Univ Surrey, PhD, 1979. **Professional Experience:** ADJ ASSOC PROF & DIR RES, DEPT PEDIAT, DIV HEMAT-ONCOL, 1989-; ASSOC PROF IMMUNOL, DEPT IMMUNOL & MED MICROBIOL, COL MED, UNIV FLA, 1988-; Nat Acad

Sci, 1985 & USAID, 1988-1990; co-investr & consult porcine immunity to African swine fever virus, USAID, 1987-1990; Prin investr, Natural Sci & Eng Res Coun Can, 1986-1989 & 1987-1990; res scientist & prog coordr immunol, Vet Infectious Dis Orgn, Univ Sask, 1985-1988; NSF travel scholar, Nat Acad Sci travel scholar, 1985; Prin investr, USDA, 1984-1987; consult, Upjohn, 1984; NSF travel scholar, Ruminant Immunol Conf, Kenya, 1984; asst prof immunol, Dept Comp & Exp Path, 1983-1985; asst prof, Dept Immunol & Med Microbiol, Col Med, 1982-1985; Prin investr, USDA, 1982-1986; Prin investr, USDA, 1981-1984; asst prof immunol, Dept Prev Med, Col Vet Med, Univ Fla, 1981-1983; asst prof virol-immunol, Dept Microbiol, Sch Vet Med, Auburn Univ, 1980-1981; NIH res fel, Dept Microbiol & Immunol, Univ Tenn, 1979-1980; higher sci officer, Dept Exp Path, Animal Virus Res Inst, 1976-1979; sci officer, Dept Exp Path, Animal Virus Res Inst, 1972-1976; Asst sci officer, Dept Exp Path, Animal Virus Res Inst, 1969-1972. **Memberships:** Inst Biol; Conf Res Workers Animal Dis; Asn Am Immunologists; Am Soc Microbiol; Am Vet Immunologist Asn; NY Acad Sci. **Research Statement & Publications:** Foot-and-mouth disease virus in British deer; epizootic haemorrhagic disease of deer virus in domestic farm animals and in British deer; in vitro characteristics of epizootic haemorrhagic disease of deer virus; pathogenesis of bluetongue virus in sheep; peste des petits ruminants; vertical transmission of bluetongue virus in sheep; electrophoretic studies on the double stranded RNA genome of orbviruses; stimulation and growth of macrophage of various animals species in in vitro culture. **Mailing Address:** 1117 Heron Rd, Key Largo, FL 33037.

LAWRASON, F DOUGLAS, INTERNAL MEDICINE. **Personal Data:** b St Paul, Minn, July 30, 1919. **Education:** Univ Minn, BA, 1941, MA & MD, 1944. **Professional Experience:** CONSULT, 1984-; mem bd dirs, Morristown Mem Hosp, 1980- & NJ State Sci Adv Comt, 1980-; sr vpres sci, Sci Affairs & pres, Res Div, Schering-Plough Corp, 1980-1984; sr vpres, Sci Affairs & pres, Res Div, Schering-Plough Corp, 1973-1980; dean, Univ Tex Health Sci Ctr Dallas, 1972-1973; prof internal med, Univ Tex Health Sci Ctr Dallas, 1969-1973; assoc dean acad affairs, Univ Tex Health Sci Ctr Dallas, 1969-1972; vpres med res, Merck Sharp & Dohme Res Labs, Pa, 1966-1969; exec dir med res, Merck Sharp & Dohme Res Labs, Pa, 1961-1966; training grant comt, Nat Res Coun, 1959-1964; prof internal med, provost med affairs & dean med ctr, Univ Ark, 1955-1961; inst grant comt, Am Cancer Soc, 1955-1960; comt blood & related probs, Nat Acad Sci, 1953-1957; asst prof & asst dean, Sch Med, Univ NC, 1953-1955; mem hemat study sect, NIH, 1951-1953; Assoc Prof, Nat Res Coun, 1950-1953; from instr to asst prof med, Sch Med, Yale Univ, 1949-1950; James Hudson Brown res fel, Yale Univ, 1948-1949; from intern to resident, Sch Med, Yale Univ, 1944-1949; Instr anat, Med Sch, Univ Minn, 1941-1943. **Memberships:** AAAS; Am Fedn Clin Res; Am Col Cardiologists; NY Acad Sci; Am Soc Internal Med. **Research Statement & Publications:** Cancer and leukemia in inbred strains of mice; hematology; medical education and administration; research management. **Mailing Address:** 2 Carriage Hill Dr, Morristown, NJ 07960.

LAWRENCE, ADDISON LEE, SHRIMP FARMING. **Personal Data:** b Cape Girardeau, Mo, December 19, 1935. **Education:** SE MO State Univ, BSc, 1956; Univ Mo, MA, 1958, PhD (physiol), 1962. **Professional Experience:** PROF, WILDLIFE & FISHERIES SCI & AGRI RES EXTEN CTR, TEX A&M UNIV, as of 2004; maricult coordr, Tex A&M Sea Grant Prog, 1979-1986; dir, Marine Sci Prog, 1977-1978; assoc dir res, Univ Houston, 1975-1977; prof, Univ Houston, 1964-1979; vis instr, Hopkins Marine Sta, Stanford Univ, 1963; fel physiol, Stanford Univ, 1962-1964; asst prof biol, Westminster Col, Fulton, Mo, 1961-1962; NIH fel. **Memberships:** Am Soc Zoologists; Soc Exp Biol Med; World Aquacult Soc; Nat Shellfish Soc; Western Soc Naturalists; Crustacean Soc. **Research Statement & Publications:** Nutrition; physiology; biochemistry; shrimp mariculture; shrimp reproduction; shrimp raceway and pond production; shrimp larviculture; author of over 160 technical publications. **Mailing Address:** Dept Wildlife & Fisheries Sci, Tex A&M Univ, Shrimp Mariculture Res, 1300 Port St, Port Aransas, TX 78373-1450. **Fax:** 512-749-5756.

LAWRENCE, ALONZO WILLIAM, ENVIRONMENTAL ENGINEERING. **Personal Data:** b Rahway, NJ, April 11, 1937; m 1960, c 3. **Education:** Rutgers Univ, BS, 1959; Mass Inst Technol, MS, 1960; Stanford Univ, PhD (civil eng), 1967. **Honors & Awards:** Eng Sci Award, Am Asn Environ Eng Prof, 1977. **Professional Experience:** VPRES ENVIRON RESOURCES, KOPPERS CO, 1984-; GEN MGR, CHEM SYSTS SECTOR, KOPPERS CO, PITTSBURGH, 1984-; vpres sci & technol, Chem Systs Sector, Koppers CO, Pittsburgh, 1981-1984; vpres environ resources & occup health, Chem Systs Sector, Koppers CO, Pittsburgh, 1976-1981; from asst prof to assoc prof environ eng, Cornell Univ, 1967-1976; asst prof civil eng, Drexel Inst Technol, 1965-1967. **Memberships:** Am Soc Civil Engrs; Water Pollution Control Fedn. **Research Statement & Publications:** Wastewater treatment technology; wastewater reclamation and reuse; biokinetics; solid wastes disposal; occupational safety and health; technological innovation; strategic management of technology. **Mailing Address:** Koppers Inc, 436 Seventh Ave, Pittsburgh, PA 15219-1800.

LAWRENCE, BONITA A, MATHEMATICS. **Education:** Univ Tex, PhD (dynamical syst). **Professional Experience:** ASSOC PROF MATH, COL SCI, MARSHALL UNIV, as of 2006. **Mailing Address:** Dept Math, Marshall Univ, SH 745, Rocky Mtain, NC 27804. **Fax:** 304-696-4646. **E-Mail:** lawrence@marshall.edu

LAWRENCE, CHRISTINE, HEMATOLOGY, RHEUMATOLOGY. **Personal Data:** b New York, NY, October 18, 1930. **Education:** Univ Mich, BS, 1952; Columbia Univ, MD, 1956. **Professional Experience:** PROF EMER MED, ALBERT EINSTEIN COL MED, as of 2004; prof med, Albert Einstein Col Med, beginning 1986; DIR CLIN HEMAT, JACOBI MED CTR, 1972-; assoc prof, Albert Einstein Col Med, 1971-1986; asst prof med, Albert Einstein Col Med, 1966-1971. **Memberships:** AmCol Physicians; Am Fedn Med Res; Am Soc Hemat. **Research Statement & Publications:** Clinical hematology, particularly in genetic disorders of erythrocytes and hemoglobin. **Mailing Address:** Albert Einstein Col Med, 1300 Morris Park Ave, Bronx, NY 10461. **Fax:** 718-918-7460.

LAWRENCE, CHRISTOPHER WILLIAM, GENETICS, RADIOBIOLOGY. **Personal Data:** b London, Eng, October 2, 1934. **Education:** Univ Wales, BSc, 1956; Univ Birmingham, PhD (genetics), 1959. **Professional Experience:** PROF EMER BIOCHEM & BIOPHYS, UNIV ROCHESTER, as of 2005; prof biochem & biophys, Univ Rochester, as of 2004; prof radiation biol, Univ Rochester, beginning 1982; assoc prof, Univ Rochester, 1970-1982; Vis asst prof radiation biol, Univ Rochester, 1969; sr sci officer, Wantage Labs, UK Atomic Energy Authority, 1961-1970; sci officer radiation biol, Wantage Labs, UK Atomic Energy Authority, 1959-1961. **Memberships:** AAAS; Genetics Soc Am; Biophys Soc. **Research Statement & Publications:** Radiation molecular genetics of Saccharomyces cerevisiae. **Mailing Address:** Dept Biophys, Univ Rochester Med Sch, 601 Elmwood Ave Box 712, Rochester, NY 14642. **Fax:** 585-275-6007. **E-Mail:** christopher_lawrence@urmc.rochester.edu

LAWRENCE, DALE NOLAN, INTERNAL MEDICINE & INFECTIOUS DISEASES, GENETICS OF HUMAN IMMUNE RESPONSES. **Personal Data:** b Covington, Ky, February 24, 1944. **Education:** Duke Univ, MD, 1969; Emory Univ, MPH, 1989; Am Bd Internal Med, cert, 1973; Am Bd Infectious Dis, cert, 1975. **Honors & Awards:** Spec Award, Nat Hemophilia Found, 1990. **Professional Experience:** SR SCI ADV COORDR FOR AIDS VACCINE, INT STUDIES, VACCINE RES & DEVELOP BR, BASIC RES & DEVELOP PROG, DIV AIDS, NAT INST ALLERGY & INFECTIOUS DIS, NIH, 1991-; prog officer AIDS panel, US-Japan Coop Med Sci Prog, 1991-; consult, Global Prog on AIDS, WHO, 1991-; sect chief clin develop, 1989-1991; field investr team loader, Ctrs Dis Control-Mayo Clin Collab Reinvest: Swine Influenza Vaccine-Guillain Barre Syndrome, 1985-1987; vis fel, Harvard Inst Health Res, 1984-1985; task force mem & epidemiologist, AIDS Task Force & Div Host Factors, 1982-1989; ed consult, J AMA, J Nat Cancer Inst, J Infectious Dis, J AIDS, Sci & Am J Epidemiol, 1979-; chief immunogenetics, Clin Med Br, Divs Immunol & Host Factors, Ctr Infectious Dis, 1979-1982; physician mem med adv bd, Ctrs Dis Control, 1979-1981; vis scientist human leukocyte antigen genetics, Genetics Lab, Dept Biochem, Univ Oxford, UK, 1978-1979; med officer, Genetics Res Prog, NSF, Amazonas, Brazil, 1976; med officer immunol & parasitol, Clin Immunol Lab, Immunochem Br, Parasitol Div, Bur Labs, 1975-1977; resident gen prev med & epidemiol, Ctrs Dis Control, 1974-1976; epidemiol intel serv officer, Field Serv Div, Ctr Dis Control, USPHS, Miami, Fla, 1973-1975; intern, resident & fel internal med & infectious dis, Univ Tex Health Sci Ctr, San Antonio, 1969-1973. **Memberships:** Fel Infectious Dis Soc Am; fel Am Col Epidemiol; Asn Immunologists; fel Am Col Physicians; fel Am Col Prev Med; Am Soc Histocompatibility & Immunogenetics. **Research Statement & Publications:** Early infectious disease epidemiologic investigations; studies of human leukocyte antigen genetics; vaccine immunology and development of AIDS vaccine. **Mailing Address:** AIDS Div, Nat Inst Allergy & Infectious Dis, NIH, 6610 Rockledge Dr MSC 6612, Bethesda, MD 20892-6612. **E-Mail:** dlawrence@niaid.nih.gov

LAWRENCE, DAVID A, IMMUNOLOGY. **Personal Data:** b Paterson, NJ, January 9, 1945. **Education:** Rutgers Univ, BA, 1966; Boston Col, MS, 1968, PhD (biol), 1971. **Professional Experience:** RES SCIENTIST, WADSWORTH CTR, as of 2004; PROF IMMUNOL & INFECTIOUS DIS, WADSWORTH CTR, as of 2004; CHIEF, LAB ENVIRON & CLIN IMMUNOTOXICOL, WADSWORTH CTR, 1993-; path, Albany Med Col, 1989-1993; pharm & toxicol, Albany Med Col, 1988-1993; assoc prof med, Albany Med Col, 1984-1988; from asst prof to prof microbiol & immunol, Albany Med Col, 1974-1991; USPHS fel, Scripps Clin & Res Found, 1971-1974; NIH Toxicol Study Sect; Environ Protection Agency Health Res Rev Panel. **Memberships:** NY Acad Sci; Am Soc Microbiol; Am Asn Immunologists; Soc Toxicol. **Research Statement & Publications:** Cellular and subcellular events resulting from antigen activation and regulation of immune response; tumor immunology; immunotoxicology. **Mailing Address:** Wadsworth Ctr, NY State Dept Health, PO Box 509, Albany, NY 12201. **Fax:** 518-474-1412. **E-Mail:** david.lawrence@wadsworth.org

LAWRENCE, DAVID JOSEPH, ELECTRONIC MATERIALS, PHOTONIC DEVICES. **Personal Data:** b Johnson City, NY, June 15, 1951. **Education:** Syracuse Univ, BS, 1973; Cornell Univ, MS, 1975, PhD (electrical engineering), 1977. **Professional Experience:** PROF, DEPT INTEGRATED SCI & TECHNOL, JAMES MADISON UNIV, as of 2005; MICROELECTRONIC PROG MGR, VA MFG INNOVATION CTR, as of 1999; assoc prof, James Madison Univ, beginning 1993; res physicist semiconductor mat, Eastman Kodak Res Lab, 1978-1993; develop engr, western elec co, 1977-1978. **Memberships:** Am Asn Crystal Growth; Inst Elec & Electronics Engrs; Mat Res Soc; Am Soc Eng Educ. **Research Statement & Publications:** III-V compounds; epitaxial growth; solid state light emitters and detectors; transparent conductors; oxide films; chemical vapor deposition. **Mailing Address:** Dept Integrated Sci & Technol James Madison Univ, ISAT 320 MSC 4102, Harrisonburg, VA 22807. **Fax:** 540-568-2768. **E-Mail:** lawrendj@jmu.edu

LAWRENCE, DAVID M, PREVENTIVE MEDICINE. **Education:** Amherst Col, BA; Univ Ky, MD; Univ Wash, MPH; Am Bd Prev Med, cert. **Honors & Awards:** Trust Award, Health Res Educ Trust, 2003. **Professional Experience:** DIR PACIFIC GAS & ELECTRIC CO & RAFFLES MED GROUP INC, as of 2004; SR FEL HEALTH POLICY, MALCOLM WIENER CTR SOCIAL POLICY, as of 2003; CHMN EMER, KASIER FOUND HEALTH PLAN INC, 2002-; DIR, AGILENT TECHNOL INC, 1999-; chmn, Kasier Found Health Plan, 1992-2002; cheif exec officer, Kasier Found Health Plan, 1991-2002; mem fac, Sch Pub Health & Community Med & Sch Med, Univ Wash; Peace Corps physician, Dominican Repub & Wash, DC; health officer & dir, Human Serv, Multnomah Co, Ore. **Memberships:** Inst Med-Nat Acad Sci. **Mailing Address:** Agilent Technol Inc, 395 Page Mill Rd, Palo Alto, CA 94306.

LAWRENCE, DAVID REED, GEOLOGY, INVERTEBRATE PALEONTOLOGY. **Personal Data:** b Woodbury, NJ, October 11, 1939. **Education:** Johns Hopkins Univ, AB, 1961; Princeton Univ, PhD (geol), 1966. **Professional Experience:** PROF EMER GEOL & MARINE SCI, UNIV SC, 1997-; NSF sci fac fel, Univ Tubingen, Ger, 1971-1972; assoc prof geol & marine sci, Univ SC, beginning 1969; asst prof, Univ SC, 1966-1969; assoc prof, Princeton Univ, 1966; asst geol, Princeton Univ, 1963-1964. **Memberships:** Int Paleont Union; Geol Soc Am; Paleont Soc. **Research Statement & Publications:** Evolutionary, ecologic and biogeographic aspects of fossil invertebrates; taphonomy; historiography of the earth sciences. **Mailing Address:** Geol Dept, Univ SC, Columbia, SC 29208-0001.

LAWRENCE, DEBORAH A, MODELS OF DISEASE TRANSMISSION. **Personal Data:** b Troy, NY, December 9, 1965; m, c 2. **Education:** Russell Sage Col, BA, 1988; State Univ NY, Albany, MA, 1990, PhD (dynamical systs), 1992. **Professional Experience:** ASSOC PROF MATH, RUSSELL SAGE COL, 2000-; chmn, Dept Math & Comput Sci, Russell Sage Col, 1998-2002; asst prof math, Russell Sage Col, 1994-2000; asst prof math, Clarion Univ, Pa, 1992-1994. **Memberships:** Am Math Soc; Asn Women Math; Math Asn Am; Soc Math Biol. **Research Statement & Publications:** Dynamics of disease transmission; human papilloma virus as it is related to cervical cancer. **Mailing Address:** Dept Math & Comput Sci, Russell Sage Col, Educ 4 A Troy Campus 45 ferry st, Troy, NY 12180-4013. **E-Mail:** lawred@sage.edu

LAWRENCE, DONALD GILBERT, NEUROLOGY, NEUROANATOMY. **Personal Data:** b Kingston, Ont, January 18, 1932. **Education:** Bishop's Univ, BSc, 1953; McGill Univ, MDCM, 1957; Royal Col Physicians & Surgeons, FRCP (C), 1974. **Honors & Awards:** Osler Medal, Am Asn Hist Med, 1958. **Professional Experience:** ASSOC DEAN, FAC MED, 1984-; PROF NEUROL & NEUROSURG, MCGILL UNIV, 1980-; assoc physician, Montreal Gen Hosp, beginning 1977; assoc prof anat, Mcgill Univ, beginning 1972; head, lab neuroanat, Montreal Neuro Inst, 1972-1984; assoc prof neurol & neurosurg, Fac Med, 1972-1980; asst physician, Montreal Gen Hosp, 1972-1977; from asst prof to assoc prof neuroanat, Erasmus Univ, 1968-1972; Nat Mult Sclerosis Soc fel neurophysiol, Univ Lab Physiol, Oxford Univ, 1966-1968; res fel neuroanat, Western Res Univ, 1965-1966. **Memberships:** Cajal Club; Am Asn Hist Med; Am Asn Anat; Soc Neuroscience; Am Acad Neurol; Can Asn Neuroscience. **Research Statement & Publications:** Anatomical, behavioral and clinical investigations of motor pathways in the central nervous system;

regeneration in the central nervous system. **Mailing Address:** Neurosci Unit, Montreal Gen Hosp 1650 Cedar Ave, Montreal, PQ H3G 1A4, Can.

LAWRENCE, FRANCIS JOSEPH, PLANT BREEDING. **Personal Data:** b Glen Arm, Md, May 12, 1925. **Education:** Univ Md, BS, 1951, MS, 1958, PhD (hort, bot), 1965. **Professional Experience:** RETIRED; res horticulturist, Corvallis Res Sta, USDA, 1965-1990; from instr to asst prof, Univ Md, 1962-1965; Asst hort, Univ Md, 1953-1962. **Memberships:** Am Soc Hort Sci; Am Pomol Soc. **Research Statement & Publications:** Breeding of Fragaria and Rubus. **Mailing Address:** 1430 NW 27th St, Corvallis, OR 97330-2447.

LAWRENCE, FREDERICK VAN BUREN, METALLURGY, CIVIL ENGINEERING. **Personal Data:** b Hyannis, Mass, May 16, 1938. **Education:** Swarthmore Col, BS, 1960; Mass Inst Technol, SM, 1962, CE, 1965, ScD(mat sci), 1968. **Professional Experience:** PROF EMER CIVIL ENG, UNIV ILL, URBANA, as of 2005; prof civil eng, Univ Ill, Urbana, as of 2004, head civil eng, Univ Ill, Urbana, as of 2004; head civil eng, Univ Ill, Urbana, beginning 1996; assoc prof metall & civil eng, Univ Ill, Urbana, beginning 1968; ed, J Mat Civil Eng, Am Soc Civil Engrs. **Memberships:** Am Welding Soc; Am Soc Metals; Am Inst Mining Metall & Petrol Engrs; Sigma Xi; Am Soc Civil Engrs. **Research Statement & Publications:** Fatigue strength of welded joints; microstructure of cementitious materials. **Mailing Address:** 205 N Matthews Ave, Newark Rm 1110, Urbana, IL 61801-2350. **Fax:** 217-333-9464. **E-Mail:** flawrenc@uiuc.edu

LAWRENCE, GEORGE MELVIN, PHYSICS. **Personal Data:** b Salt Lake City, Utah, March 26, 1937. **Education:** Univ Utah, BS, 1959; Calif Inst Technol, PhD (physics), 1963. **Professional Experience:** RETIRED; sr res assoc, Lab Atmospheric & Space Physics, Univ Colo, Boulder, as of 2003; sr res assoc, lab atmospheric & space physics, Univ Colo, Boulder, beginning 1975; res assoc, Joint Inst Lab Astrophys Lab Atmospheric & Space Physics, 1971-1974; vis fel, Joint Inst Lab Astrophys, Lab Atmospheric & Space Physics, 1970-1971; vis assoc, Calif Inst Technol, 1968-1970; res scientist, McDonnell Douglas Advan Res Lab, Calif, 1967-1970; staff physicist, Princeton Univ, 1965-1967; res assoc astrophys sci, Princeton Univ, 1963-1965. **Memberships:** Fel Am Phys Soc; Am Geophys Union; Am Inst Aeronaut & Astronaut. **Research Statement & Publications:** Transition probabilities; cross sections; physical chemistry; detectors; space science; science education. **Mailing Address:** Lab Atmospheric & Space Physics, Univ Colo, Campus Box 392, Boulder, CO 80309-0575. **Fax:** 303-492-6444. **E-Mail:** george.lawrence@lasp.colorado.edu

LAWRENCE, IRVIN E, JR, EMBRYOLOGY, HISTOLOGY. **Personal Data:** b Raleigh, NC, April 18, 1926. **Education:** Univ NC, AB, 1950; Univ Wyo, MS, 1955; Univ Kans, PhD (anat), 1963. **Professional Experience:** PROF ANAT, ECAROLINA UNIV, 1978-; NIH res grant, 1975-; assoc prof, Ecarolina Univ, 1970-1978; assoc prof biol, Ecarolina Univ, 1964-1970; USPHS res grant, 1964-1965; Univ Res fel, Univ Wyo, 1963-1964; asst prof zool, Univ Wyo, 1960-1964; instr biol, Louisburg Col, 1955-1957; Teacher high sch, NC, 1951-1954. **Memberships:** Am Soc Zool; Soc Develop Biol; Sigma Xi; Pan-Am Asn Anat; Soc Study Reproduction. **Research Statement & Publications:** Biogenic amines in development; epithelial-mesenchymal interactions in organogenesis of pancreatic islets and of ovary; ovarian nerves and reproductive function. **Mailing Address:** Dept Anat, ECarolina Univ, Fifth St, Greenville, NC 27858-4353.

LAWRENCE, JAMES FRANKLIN, MATHEMATICS. **Personal Data:** b Okemah, Okla, August 20, 1950. **Education:** Okla State Univ, BS, 1972; Univ Wash, PhD (math), 1975. **Professional Experience:** PROF MATH, GEORGE MASON UNIV, as of 2002; assoc prof math, George Mason Univ, beginning 1986; asst prof, George Mason Univ, 1983-1986; vis asst prof, Univ Mass, Boston, 1981-1982; asst prof, Univ Ky, 1979-1983; res assoc, Nat Bur Stand, 1977-1979; instr math, Univ Tex, Austin, 1975-1977. **Memberships:** Math Asn Am; Am Math Soc; Sigma Xi. **Research Statement & Publications:** Field of combinatorics; study of oriented matroids. **Mailing Address:** Dept Math, George Mason Univ, Rm 253 Sci & Technol Bldg I, Fairfax, VA 22030. **Fax:** 703-993-1491. **E-Mail:** lawrence@gmu.edu

LAWRENCE, JAMES HAROLD, JR, MECHANICAL ENGINEERING. **Personal Data:** b Beatrice, Nebr, February 9, 1932; m 1955, JANE; c 2. **Education:** Tex Tech Col, BS, 1956, MS, 1960; Tex A&M Univ, PhD (mech eng), 1965. **Professional Experience:** RETIRED; assoc dean, Tex Tech Univ, 1992-1995; chmn dept, Tex Tech Univ, 1972-1983; prof mech eng, Tex Tech univ, 1971-; assoc prof, Tex Tech Univ, 1964-1971; from instr to asst prof, Tex Tech Univ, 1956-1962. **Memberships:** Am Soc Mech Engrs. **Research Statement & Publications:** Conduction; convection; radiation heat transfer; systems engineering. **Mailing Address:** Dept Mech Eng, Tex Tech Univ, Lubbock, TX 79409-0001.

LAWRENCE, JAMES NEVILLE PEED, HEALTH PHYSICS, PHYSICS. **Personal Data:** b Norfolk, Va, May 29, 1929. **Education:** Johns Hopkins Univ, BA, 1950; Vanderbilt Univ, MA, 1958, PhD (physics), 1968. **Professional Experience:** RETIRED; sr scientist, Los Alamos Nat Lab, Univ Calif, 1988-1992; asst group leader, Los Alamos Nat Lab, Univ Calif, 1980-1988; assoc group leader, Los Alamos Nat Lab, Univ Calif, 1968-1980; mem staff, Los Alamos Nat Lab, Univ Calif, 1954-1968; res asst health physics, Los Alamos Nat Lab, Univ Calif, 1951-1954. **Memberships:** Health Physics Soc. **Research Statement & Publications:** Theoretical treatment of nuclear fission, especially liquid drop applications; health physics, especially dosimetry, internal exposure calculations and radionuclide identification. **Mailing Address:** 206 El Conejo St, Los Alamos, NM 87544.

LAWRENCE, JEANNE BENTLEY, GENE MAPPING, IN SITU HYBRIDIZATION. **Personal Data:** b Sweetwater, Tex, December 10, 1951. **Education:** Stephens Col, BA, 1973; Rutgers Univ, MS, 1975; Brown Univ, PhD (molecular & cell biol), 1982. **Honors & Awards:** Jr Outstanding Cell Biologist Career Develop Award, Women Cell Biol, 1989. **Professional Experience:** PROF, DEPT CELL BIOL, UNIV MASS MED SCH, as of 2004; res career & develop award, Nat Ctr Human Genome Res, NIH, 1990; assoc prof, Dept Cell Biol, Univ Mass Med Ctr, beginning 1988; instr cell biol, Dept Anat, 1985-1988; fel, Dept Cell Biol, Univ Mass, Med Ctr, 1982-1985; res assoc, Yale Univ, 1975-1977. **Memberships:** AAAS; Am Soc Cell Biologists; Am Asn Human Genetics. **Research Statement & Publications:** Analysis of genome and nuclear organization using fluorescence in situ hybridization; human gene mapping and the functional relationship of DNA/RNA to nuclear structure. **Mailing Address:** Dept Cell Biol, Univ Mass Med Sch, 55 Lake Ave N, Worcester, MA 01655-0106. **Fax:** 508-856-5650. **E-Mail:** jeanne.lawrence@umassmed.edu

LAWRENCE, JOHN, AQUATIC ECOSYSTEM & WATER RESOURCE MANAGEMENT RESEARCH, ANALYTICAL QUALITY CONTROL. **Personal Data:** b UK, March 23, 1943; m Margaret; c 2. **Education:** Bristol Univ, BSc, 1964, PhD (chem), 1967. **Professional Experience:** DIR, AQUATIC ECOSYS MANAGEMENT RESEARCH DIVISION, NAT WATER RES INST, CAN, 2000-; dir, Aquatic Ecosys Protection Br, 1993-1996; adj prof, Carlton Univ, Ottawa, 1991-1994; dir, Res & Appln Br, 1987-1993; res mgr environ analytical methodology, Nat Water Res Inst, Can, 1980-1987; res scientist environ toxic contaminants, Nat Water Res Inst, Can, 1973-1980; res chemist semiconductors, Bell-Northern Res, 1971-1973; Res assoc electrochem, Univ Ottawa, 1967-1969 & Colo State Univ, 1969-1971. **Memberships:** Int Asn Great Lakes Res; Can Asn Environ Analysis Labs. **Research Statement & Publications:** Aquatic ecosystem and water resource management, water chemistry; water and wastewater treatment; fate and effects of toxic contaminants; analytical methods; quality assurance; environmental research. **Mailing Address:** Nat Water Res Inst, PO Box 5050, Burlington, ON L7R 4A6, Can. **Fax:** 905-336-6430. **E-Mail:** j.lawrence@ec.gc.ca

LAWRENCE, JOHN KEELER, GENERAL RELATIVITY, ASTROPHYSICS. **Personal Data:** b New York, NY, October 11, 1940. **Education:** Harvard Univ, AB, 1962; Northeastern Univ, MS, 1964, PhD (physics), 1968. **Professional Experience:** PROF EMER PHYSICS & ASTRON, CALIF STATE UNIV, 1991-; prof physics & astron, Calif State Univ, 1980-1991; assoc prof physics & astron, Calif State Univ, 1976-1980; chmn, Dept Physics & Astron, Calif State Univ, beginning 1976; asst prof, Calif State Univ, 1973-1976; fel, Univ Windsor, 1972-1973; vis res assoc, Northeastern Univ, 1971-1972; Univ asst physics, Univ Vienna, 1968-1971; vis asst prof physics & astron, Univ Ga, 1967-1968. **Memberships:** Am Phys Soc; AAAS; Austrian Phys Soc; Sigma Xi. **Research Statement & Publications:** Deflection of null radiation by gravitational fields; cosmological models; cosmological coincidences; galactic structure; active galaxies and quasars. **Mailing Address:** Calif State Univ, 18111 Nordhoff Str, Northridge, CA 91330-8268. **Fax:** 818-677-3234. **E-Mail:** john.lawrence@csun.edu

LAWRENCE, JOHN M, PHYSIOLOGY. **Personal Data:** b Cape Girardeau, Mo, October 11, 1937. **Education:** Southeast Mo State Col, BS, 1958; Univ Mo, AM, 1960; Stanford Univ, PhD (biol), 1966. **Honorary Degrees:** Dr, Univ Mediterranee, France, 2000. **Professional Experience:** PROF DEPT BIOL, UNIV SFLA, 1975-; fel, Marine Biol Lab, Hebrew Univ Israel, 1969-1970; from asst prof to assoc prof, Univ Sfla, 1965-1975; instr physiol, Stanford Univ, 1964-1965. **Memberships:** Am Soc Zool; Marine Biol Asn UK; Sigma Xi. **Research Statement & Publications:** Nutritional and reproductive physiology of marine invertebrates. **Mailing Address:** Dept Biol, Univ SFla, 4202 Fowler Ave, Off SCA 132, Tampa, FL 33620-9951. **E-Mail:** lawr@cas.usf.edu

LAWRENCE, JOHN MCCUNE, BIOCHEMISTRY. **Personal Data:** b Carmichaels, Pa, February 17, 1916. **Education:** Carnegie Inst Technol, BS, 1937, MS, 1939; Univ Pittsburgh, PhD (biochem), 1943. **Professional Experience:** RETIRED; agr chemist, Wash State Univ, 1958-1981; assoc chemist, Wash State Univ, 1948-1958; from instr to asst prof biochem, Dept Dairy Indust, Cornell Univ, 1945-1948; Nutrit Found fel, Dept Dairy Indust, Cornell Univ, 1943-1945; res asst, Mellon Inst, 1939-1941. **Memberships:** AAAS; Am Soc Plant Physiol; Sigma Xi. **Research Statement & Publications:** Enzymes; proteins; amino acids; biochemistry of seed germination and nutritional quality of seeds. **Mailing Address:** 535 N W Mountain Laurel Circle, Corvallis, OR 97330.

LAWRENCE, JOSEPH D, SYSTEMS DESIGN & SYSTEMS SCIENCE, SEMICONDUCTOR BURN-IN & TEST EQUIPMENT. **Personal Data:** b Anderson, SC, November 6, 1924. **Education:** Va Polytech Inst, BS, 1951. **Professional Experience:** RETIRED; vpres, Reliability Inc, 1987-1993; pres, Reliability Japan Inc, 1987-1990; vpres & dir technol, Reliability Inc, 1982-1987; mgr res & develop, Reliability Inc Tex, 1978-1982; pres, Datac Co, 1977-1978; vpres, Datac Co, 1973-1977; mgr digital systs eng, Camco, 1970-1973; engr/mgr, Tex Instruments, 1966-1970; engr mgr, Sperry Rand, 1960-1966; prog engr, Burroughs, 1957-1960; sr engr, Sperry Rand, 1953-1957; test engr, Gen Elec, 1951-1953. **Research Statement & Publications:** Pioneered development of burn-in and test equipment for semiconductor memories; designed computers; designed computerized traffic light control systems; granted 13 US Patents. **Mailing Address:** 115 Gershwin, Houston, TX 77079.

LAWRENCE, KELECHI, BIOCHEMISTRY, INTEGRIN SIGNALLING. **Personal Data:** b Owerri, January 17, 1959. **Education:** Southern Conn State Univ, BS, 1984; Med Univ SC, PhD (pharmacol), 1991. **Professional Experience:** SR RES SCIENTIST, DUPONT MERCK PHARM CO, 1995-; res assoc, Columbia Univ, 1993-1994; fel, Columbia Univ, 1992-1993. **Memberships:** Am Heart Asn; Fedn Am Socs Exp Biol; NY Acad Sci; AAAS; Asn Res Vision & Ophthal; Asn Black Cardiologists. **Research Statement & Publications:** Understnding the role of the integrin in angiogenesis; elaboration of angiogenic factors by retinal pigment epithelial cells; degenerative retinal diseases. **Mailing Address:** Cardio Dis Res, DuPont Merck Pharm Co, PO Box 80400 Exp Sta, Wilmington, DE 19880. **Fax:** 302-695-8210. **E-Mail:** lawrenk@aol.com

LAWRENCE, KENT L(EE), MECHANICAL ENGINEERING, ENGINEERING MECHANICS. **Personal Data:** b Beatrice, Nebr, January 23, 1937. **Education:** Tex Tech Col, BS, 1959, MS, 1960; Ariz State Univ, PhD (eng mech), 1965. **Professional Experience:** PROF MECH ENG, UNIV TEX, ARLINGTON, 1977-; ENG CONSULT, UNIV TEX, ARLINGTON, 1965-; assoc prof, Univ Tex, Arlington, 1961-1962 & 1964-1977; instr mech, Univ Ill, 1960-1961. **Memberships:** Am Soc Mech Engrs; Am Helicopter Soc. **Research Statement & Publications:** Vibrations; dynamics; structural mechanics; finite element methods. **Mailing Address:** Dept Mech Eng, Univ Tex, Arlington, Box 19023 300D Woolf Hall, Arlington, TX 76019-0001. **E-Mail:** lawrence@uta.edu

LAWRENCE, KURT C, DIELECTRICS HYPERSPECTRAL IMAGING. **Personal Data:** b Decatur, Ga, July 9, 1962; m 1985, Laurie; c Kimberly Sara & Casey. **Education:** Univ Ga, BS, 1985, MS, 1987 phd 1997. **Professional Experience:** AGR ENGR, AGR RES SERV, USDA, 1985-. **Memberships:** Assoc mem Am Soc Agr Engrs. **Research Statement & Publications:** Measurement of dielectric properties of agricultural products; determination of moisture content by dielectric properties measurements; hyperspecitral imaging of surface contaminats for popltry food society. **Mailing Address:** 1241 Fernwood Dr, Watkinsville, GA 30677.

LAWRENCE, MERLE, PHYSIOLOGY OF HEARING. **Personal Data:** b Remsen, NY, December 1915; m 1942, Roberta H. lAWRENCE; c Linda A Lawrence, Roberta H.L Henderson, James B Lawrence. **Education:** Princeton Univ, AB, 1938, MA, 1940, PhD (psychol), 1941. **Honors & Awards:** Distinguished Lifetime Achievement Award, Am Acad Audiol; Gold Medal, Am Otol Soc; Award ofMerit, Am Acad Opthalmol & Otolaryngol; Award of Merit, Asn Res Otolaryngol. **Professional Experience:** PROF EMER, MED SCH, UNIV MICH, ANN ARBOR, 1985-; communicative Dis Rev Comt, Nat Adv Neurol & Commun Dis & Stroke Coun, 1976-1980; communicative Dis Rev Comt, Nat Inst Neurol & Communicative Dis & Stroke, 1972-1976; mem, Commun Dis Res Training Comt, Nat Inst Neurol Dis & Stroke, 1961-1965 & Commun Sci Study Sect, NIH, 1965-1970; dir, Kresge Hearing Res Inst, 1961-1982; prof physiol, Med Sch, Univ Mich, Ann Arbor, 1959-1965; prof otolaryngol & psychol, Med Sch, Univ Mich, Ann Arbor, 1957-1985; consult, Surgeon Gen Off, 1953- & Secy Defense, 1955-1958; res assoc, Inst Indust Health, 1952-1985; assoc prof physiol acoust, Med Sch, Univ Mich, Ann Arbor, 1952-1957; from asst prof to assoc prof psychol, Princeton Univ, 1946-1952; nat res coun fel, Johns Hopkins Univ,

1941. **Memberships:** Fel Acoust Soc Am; Am Laryngol Rhinol & Otol Soc; Am Otol Soc; Col Oto-Rhino-Laryngol Amicitiae Sacrum; Asn Res Otolaryngol; Soc Univ Otolaryngologist; Am Acad Otolaryngol; Walter P Work Soc. **Research Statement & Publications:** Main research achievements in acoustic properties of the middle ear and blood and fluid circulation. **Mailing Address:** Apt I-213, 7720 Indian Oaks Dr, Vero Beach, FL 32966. **E-Mail:** merlawrn@aol.com

LAWRENCE, PAUL J, BIOCHEMISTRY. **Personal Data:** b Hazleton, Pa, December 18, 1940. **Education:** King's Col, Pa, BS, 1962; Univ Wis-Madison, MS, 1964, PhD (biochem), 1967. **Professional Experience:** VPRES, LITMUS CONCEPTS INC, 1985-; dir, diag res & develop, 1979-1985; dir immunol res & develop, Smith Kline Instruments, 1977-1981; From asst prof to assoc prof biochem, Col Med, Univ Utah, 1968-1977; NIH fel, 1967-1969; Fel biochem, Univ Wis, 1967-1968; pres, Lawrence Assay, Inc. **Memberships:** AAAS; Am Chem Soc; Fedn Am Socs Exp Biol; Am Soc Microbiol; NY Acad Sci. **Research Statement & Publications:** Mechanisms of drug action; development of diagnostic tests. **Mailing Address:** Litmus Concepts Inc, 2981 Copper Rd, Santa Clara, CA 96051-0701.

LAWRENCE, PAULINE OLIVE, INSECT ENDOCRINOLOGY & BIOCHEMISTRY, HOST-PARASITE INTERACTIONS. **Personal Data:** b November 10, 1945. **Education:** Univ WI, Jamaica, BS Hons, 1968; Univ Fla, Gainesville, MS, 1972, PhD (entom), 1975. **Honors & Awards:** Career Advan Award Women, NSF, 1988. **Professional Experience:** PROF, DEPT ENTOM & NEMATOL, UNIV FLA, 1994-; prof res & teaching, Dept Zool, 1989-1993; competitive res grants, entom & nematol, USDA, 1987-1990 & 1990-1993; mem & chmn, Nat Res Coun & NSF Minority Grad Fel Eval Panel Biol Sci, Biochem, Biophys & Biomed Sci, 1987-1989; McKnight found fel, 1986-1987; vis assoc prof, Dept Entom, Cornell Univ, 1984-1985; prin investr, regulatory biol, NSF, 1981-1984, 1985-1988, & 1990-; from asst prof to assoc prof, Dept Entom, Univ Fla, Gainesville, 1976-1989; res asst, Dept Entom, Univ Fla, Gainesville, 1972-1975; grad res fel, Dept Entom, Univ Fla, Gainesville, 1969-1972; asst entomologist res, Ministry Agr, Jamaica, Wis, 1968-1969; assoc, Danforth Found & USDA Competitive Grants rev panel. **Memberships:** AAAS; Am Soc Zoologists; Entom Soc Am; Sigma Xi; Tissue Cult Asn; Soc Invert Path; Int Soc Endocrinol. **Research Statement & Publications:** Parasite biology and the influence of host hormones on parasite development; role of symbiotic virus in parasite-host interactions; biochemistry and molecular biology of symbiotic viruses in parasitic wasps. **Mailing Address:** 3930 nw 30th pl, Gainesville, FL 32606-6146. **Fax:** 904-392-0190. **E-Mail:** peggylaw@ufl.edu

LAWRENCE, PHILIP LINWOOD, GEOPHYSICS, OIL SEARCH. **Personal Data:** b New Bedford, Mass, March 27, 1923. **Education:** Colo Sch Mines, Geol, 1949, Southern Methodist Univ, MS, 1960. **Professional Experience:** CONSULT, OIL EXPLORATION, MOBIL OIL CORP, 1981-; corp geophysicist, Geophys Serv Ctr, Tex, 1969-1981; unit supvr, Geophys Serv Ctr, Tex, 1966-1968; staff adv, NY, 1963-1965; Lectr elec eng, Southern Methodist Univ, 1960-1962; Res physicist, Magnolia Petrol Co, Tex, 1949-1962. **Memberships:** Sigma Xi. **Research Statement & Publications:** Seismic, magnetic, gravity data gathering, processing and interpretation techniques and development for mineral exploration. **Mailing Address:** 467 Harvest Glen, Richardson, TX 75081-5550.

LAWRENCE, R(AYMOND) JEFFERY, SHOCK WAVE PHYSICS. **Personal Data:** b Cornwall, NY, February 25, 1939; m 1963, Jane; c Janet B (Sanchez) & David J. **Education:** Lawrence Col, BA, 1961; Univ NMex, MS, 1970. **Professional Experience:** Prin mem of the technol staff, Sandia labs 1995-; prog mgr, Defense Nuclear Agency, 1993-1994; MEM TECH STAFF SHOCK WAVE PHYSICS, SANDIA LABS, 1967-; res physicist shock wave physics, Air Force Weapons Lab, Kirtland AFB, NMex, 1963-1967. **Memberships:** Am Phys Soc. **Research Statement & Publications:** Shock wave physics; numerical wave propagation computer code development and application; constitutive model development; application of these fields to various dynamic phenomena; program management for interactions with former Soviet Union. **Mailing Address:** 1308 Kirby St NE, Albuquerque, NM 87112. **E-Mail:** rjlawre@sandia.gov

LAWRENCE, RICHARD AUBREY, BIOCHEMISTRY, NUTRITION. **Personal Data:** b Logan, Utah, February 17, 1947. **Education:** Brigham Young Univ, BS, 1971; Univ Wis-Madison, PhD (biochem), 1975. **Professional Experience:** RES ASST PROF, DEPT MED, UNIV TEX HEALTH SCI CTR, as of 1994; asst prof med & biochem, Sch Med, LA State Univ, Shreveport, 1979-?; instr, Sch Med, La State Univ, Shreveport, 1978-1979; instr med, Univ Tex Health Sci Ctr, Dallas, 1977-1978; fel med, Univ Tex Health Sci Ctr, Dallas, 1975-1977. **Memberships:** Am Inst Nutrit; Sigma Xi. **Research Statement & Publications:** Selenium nutrition and metabolism; role of lipid peroxidation in tissue injury and disease and physiological mechanisms for protection against it; mechanism of lipid peroxidation; mechanisms of oxygen toxicity. **Mailing Address:** Dept Med, Univ Tex Health Sci Ctr, Audie L Murphy Va Hosp 7400 Merton Minter Blvd, San Antonio, TX 78284-0001. **Fax:** 210-567-4654.

LAWRENCE, RICHARD D, MATHEMATICS. **Education:** Stanford Univ, BS; Univ Ill, PhD (nuclear eng). **Professional Experience:** RES STAFF MEM & MGR, EMARKETPLACE & SUPPLY CHAIN ANAL, INT BUS MACHINES RES CTR, as of 2006. **Mailing Address:** Int Bus Machines Res Div, T J Watson Res Ctr, MS 28 204 PO Box 218, Yorktown Heights, NY 10598-0218. **Fax:** 914-945-3434. **E-Mail:** ricklawr@us.ibm.com

LAWRENCE, ROBERT D, GEOLOGY, STRUCTURE & TECTONICS OF HIMALAYA. **Personal Data:** b Ithaca, NY, May 24, 1943; m 1966, Nina. **Education:** Earlham Col, BA, 1965; Stanford Univ, PhD (geol), 1968. **Professional Experience:** Exec Dir, US Education found Pakistan, 2000-1901; Fulbright prof, Peshawar Univ, Pakistan, 1981-1982 & 1986-1987 1997-1998; ASSOC PROF GEOL, ORE STATE UNIV, 1977-; asst prof, Ore State Univ, 1970-1977; Asst prof geol, Earlham Col, 1968-1970. **Memberships:** Geol soc Am, fel. **Research Statement & Publications:** Major faults of western North America; tectonics of Pakistan; tectonic history of Pacific Northwest. **Mailing Address:** retired, Corvallis, OR.

LAWRENCE, ROBERT G, ZOOLOGY. **Personal Data:** b Wilmington, NY, February 14, 1921. **Education:** Eastern Nazarene Col, AB, 1944; Boston Univ, MA, 1946; Okla State Univ, PhD, 1964. **Honorary Degrees:** LHD, Mt Vernon Col, 1987. **Professional Experience:** RETIRED; vpres acad affairs, Mt Vernon Nazarene Col, Ohio, 1976-1987; prof biol, Mt Vernon Nazarene Col, Ohio, 1975-1987; acad dean, Mt Vernon Nazarene Col, Ohio, 1975-1987; acad dean, Mid-Am Nazarene Col, 1974-1975; dir instnl res, Mid-Am Nazarene Col, 1971-1974; prof biol sci, Mid-Am Nazarene Col, 1968-1975; assoc dean, Mid-Am Nazarene Col, 1968-1971; chmn div natural sci, Bethany Nazarene Col, 1949-1968; prof biol & head dept, Bethany Nazarene Col, 1947-1968; teacher, Henry Ford's Boys Sch, Mass, 1945-1946; mem, Am Conf Acad Deans. **Memberships:** Am Ornith Union; Nat Audubon Soc; Wilson Soc; Am Asn Higher Educ. **Research Statement & Publications:** Ornithology; relation of weather factors to migration of water fowl. **Mailing Address:** 1251 N 21st St Apt F38, Laramie, WY 82072.

LAWRENCE, ROBERT MARSHALL, anesthesiology; deceased, see previous edition for last biography

LAWRENCE, ROBERT SWAN, PREVENTIVE MEDICINE, Health Policy. **Personal Data:** b Philadelphia, Pa, February 6, 1938; m Cynthia; c Job S, Matthew S, Hannah S, Jin S & Sang B. **Education:** Harvard Univ, AB, 1960; Harvard Med Sch, MD, 1964. **Honors & Awards:** Spec Recognition Award, Am Col Prev Med, 1988; John Atkinson Ferrell Prize, 1997; Albert Schweitzer Humanitarian Prize, 2002. **Professional Experience:** Edyth Schoenrich Prof Preventive Medicine, 2005-; PROF MED, SCH MED, 1996-; PROF HEALTH POLICY & ASSOC DEAN, HOPKINS SCH PUB HEALTH, 1995-; adj prof, Sch Med, NY Univ, 1992-; dir, Health Sci Div, Rockefeller Found, 1991-1995; ed, Am J Prev Med, 1990-1992; chmn, US Prev Serv Task, Dept Health & Human Serv, 1984-1989; chmn bd, Prev Med Div, Inst Med-Nat Acad Sci, 1984; Chief, Dept Med, Cambridge Hosp, 1980-1991; from asst prof to assoc prof med, Harvard Med Sch, 1974-1991; dir, Div Primary Care, 1974-1991; from asst prof med to assoc prof, Sch Med, Univ NC, 1970-1974; sr resident, Mass Gen Hosp, 1969-1970; asst surgeon epidemiol, Epidemic Intel Serv, Ctr Dis Control, USPHS, Atlanta, 1966-1969; Intern & jr resident, Mass Gen Hosp, 1964-1966. **Memberships:** Inst Med-Nat Acad Sci; master Am Col Physicians; Soc Teachers Prev Med; Am Col Prev Med; Am Pub Health Asn; Physicians for Human Rights (pres, 1998-2002). **Research Statement & Publications:** P ublic health; author of various publications; clinical preventive services; community preventive services; sustainability policy. **Mailing Address:** Johns Hopkins Sch Pub Health, 615 N Wolfe St, Baltimore, MD 21205. **Fax:** 410-502-7579. **E-Mail:** rlawrenc@jhsph.edu

LAWRENCE, SIGMUND J(OSEPH), CHEMICAL ENGINEERING. **Personal Data:** b Chicago, Ill, May 20, 1918; div, c Clifford, Keith, Clandia, Karen, Joan & Mary. **Education:** Ill Inst Technol, BS, 1939; Univ Iowa, MS, 1942, PhD (chem eng), 1943. **Professional Experience:** CONSULT ENGR, 1991-; supv eng design chem plants, Catalytic Inc & United Engrs & Constructors, Philadelphia, 1974-1991; consult engr indust process systs, Reentry & Environ Systs Div, 1969-1973; mgr sensor progs, Instrument Dept, 1967-1969; appln engr spec sensors, Instrument Dept, 1967; appln engr, Process Comput Control, Syst Sales & Eng, 1960-1967; chem engr, Gen Eng Lab, 1957-1959; process engr, Chem Div, Silicone Prods Dept, 1952-1957; res assoc, Res Lab, 1951-1952; res assoc, Knolls Atomic Power Lab, 1948-1951; chem engr, Gen Elec Co, Wash, 1946-1948; chem engr, Shell Develop Co, Calif, 1943-1946; res chem engr, Armour Res Found, Ill Inst Technol, 1940-1941; apprentice engr, Caterpillar Tractor Co, Ill, 1939-1940. **Memberships:** Am Chem Soc; Am Inst Chem Eng. **Research Statement & Publications:** Process instrumentation, automation and control, computer monitoring and control; air, water and waste monitoring; pollution control; instrument development and design; process analysis and design; process design of chemical equipment. **Mailing Address:** 100 Linda Lane, Media, PA 19063.

LAWRENCE, VINNEDGE MOORE, ENTOMOLOGY, ECOLOGY. **Personal Data:** b Bangor, Maine, February 19, 1940; m 1966, Betty J Heinly; c Malinda (Robbin). **Education:** Miami Univ Ohio, BS, 1962, MA, 1964; Purdue Univ, PhD (entom), 1968. **Professional Experience:** Prof biol, Washington & Jefferson Col, 1986-2002; mem citizen's adv coun, Pa Dept Environ Resources, 1971-1981; vis prof zool, Rice Creek Biol Field Sta, State Univ Col, Oswego, NY, 1970; vis prof entom, Rice Creek Biol Field Sta, State Univ Col, Oswego, NY, 1969; from asst prof to assoc prof, Washington & Jefferson Col, 1968-1986; instr biol, Xavier Univ Ohio, 1964-1965. **Memberships:** AAAS; Sigma Xi; Asn Biol Lab Educ. **Research Statement & Publications:** Population dynamics of Odonata naiads in farm-pond ecosystems; distribution of Odonata in Pennsylvania; microdistribution of capniid Plecoptera; breeding behavior of Henslow's sparrow. **Mailing Address:** 210 North Ave, Washington, PA 15301-3513. **E-Mail:** vlawrence@washjeff.edu

LAWRENCE, WALTER JR, SURGERY SUR ONCOLOGY. **Personal Data:** b Chicago, Ill, May 31, 1925; m 1947, Susan Shryock; c W Thomas, Elizabeth, W Amos & Edward G. **Education:** Univ Chicago, PhB, 1945, SB, 1946, MD, 1948. **Honors & Awards:** Sloan Award Cancer Res, 1964; Horsley Award, 1973; Distinguished Serv Award, Univ Chicago, 1976; VA cultural Laureate award, 1992; Beckstrand found cancer fighter year, 1999; Presidential medallion, Va Commonwealth Univ, 2000; heritage honoree, Soc Surg Oncol, 2002; life achievement award, Sci Mus Va, 2002. **Professional Experience:** PROF EMER SURG, MED COL VA, 1994-; DIR EMER, MED COL VA, 1988-; dir, Massey Cancer Ctr, 1974-1976; Am Cancer Soc prof clin oncol, Med Col Va, 1972-1977; prof surg, med col va, 1966-1990; chmn div surg oncol, Med Col Va, 1966-1990; clin assoc prof, Med Col, Cornell Univ, 1963-1966; assoc vis surgeon, Mem Hosp, 1962-; assoc vis surgeon, James Ewing Hosp, 1962-1966; assoc mem & assoc chief div exp surg, Sloan-Kettering Inst Cancer Res, 1960-1966; asst attend surgeon, Mem Hosp, 1959-1962; asst prof, Med Col, Cornell Univ, 1958-1963; mem surg staff, NY Hosp, 1957-1966; asst vis surgeon, James Ewing Hosp, 1957-1962; Asst mem, Sloan-Kettering Inst Cancer Res, 1957-1960; clin asst attend surgeon, Mem Hosp, 1957-1959; instr surg, Med Col, Cornell Univ, 1957-1958; res fel exp surg, Mem Ctr Cancer & Allied Sci, 1956; resident, Mem Ctr Cancer & Allied Dis, 1951-1952 & 1954-1956; Halsted fel, Johns Hopkins Hosp, 1950; asst resident & asst, Sch Med, Johns Hopkins Univ, 1949-1950; intern surg, Johns Hopkins Hosp, 1948-1949. **Memberships:** Halsted Soc (pres, 1975); fel Am Col Surg; Am Surg Asn; Soc Surg Oncol (pres, 1980); Soc Univ Surgeons; Soc Head & Neck Surgeons; hon life mem Am Cancer Soc (pres, 1992) Southern Surg asn (1st v p, 2000); fel, Soc Black Acad Surgs Am, 2002. **Research Statement & Publications:** Surgery, particularly cancer and clinical cancer research. **Mailing Address:** Box 980011 Dept Surg, Med Col Va, Richmond, VA 23298. **Fax:** 804-828-4808.

LAWRENCE, WALTER EDWARD, THEORETICAL SOLID STATE PHYSICS. **Personal Data:** b Albany, NY, May 22, 1942. **Education:** Carnegie Inst Technol, BS, 1964; Cornell Univ, PhD (physics), 1970. **Honors & Awards:** Baush-Lomb Sci Award. **Professional Experience:** Vis Prof, Ohio State Univ, 1991-1992; PROF PHYSICS, DARTMOUTH COL, 1986-; assoc prof physics, Dartmouth Col, 1977-1986; asst prof, Dartmouth Col, 1971-1977; res assoc physics, Stanford Univ, 1969-1971. **Memberships:** Am Phys Soc; Sigma Xi. **Research Statement & Publications:** Solid state theory, principally superconductivity; transport theory of metals; published over 10 articles. **Mailing Address:** Dept Physics, Dartmouth Col, 249 Wilder, Hanover, NH 03755. **Fax:** 603-646-1446. **E-Mail:** jay.lawrence@dartmouth.edu

LAWRENCE, WILLARD EARL, STATISTICS. **Personal Data:** b Chassell, Mich, April 8, 1917. **Education:** Marquette Univ, BS, 1951, MS, 1953; Univ Wis, MS, 1962, PhD (statist), 1964. **Professional Experience:** PROF EMER MATH & STATIST, MARQUETTE UNIV, 1987-; statistician, Oak Ridge Nat Lab, 1979-1980; chmn dept math & statist, Marquette Univ, 1973-1979; prof, Marquette Univ, 1969-1987; Consult, NSF, 1966-1969; asst chmn dept, Marquette Univ, 1958-1963; From instr to assoc prof, Marquette Univ, 1953-1969. **Memberships:** Math Asn Am. **Research Statement & Publications:** Experimental design; response surface designs which minimize variance and bias errors; designs for mixtures; probability. **Mailing Address:** Dept Math Statist & Comput Sci, Marquette Univ, PO Box 1881, Milwaukee, WI 53201-1881. **Fax:** 414-288-5472.

LAWRENCE, WILLIAM CHASE, VIROLOGY, MOLECULAR BIOLOGY. **Personal Data:** b Cambridge, Mass, July 10, 1934. **Education:** Univ Mass, BS, 1955; Univ Pa, VMD, 1959, PhD (microbiol), 1966. **Professional Experience:** USDA Res Grant, 1975-; USPHS res grant, 1967-1974; from asst prof to assoc prof, Univ PA, 1965-1982; PROF MICROBIOL, UNIV PA. **Memberships:** AAAS; Am Vet Med Asn; Am Soc Microbiol; NY Acad Sci; Sigma Xi; Am Soc Virol. **Research Statement & Publications:** Molecular virology; vaccine development. **Mailing Address:** Dept Pathobiology, Sch Vet Med, Univ Pa, 3800 Spruce St, Philadelphia, PA 19104. **E-Mail:** wclaw@vet.upenn.edu

LAWRENCE, WILLIAM HOMER, TOXICOLOGY, PHARMACOLOGY. **Personal Data:** b Magnet Cove, Ark, March 20, 1928; div. **Education:** Col Ozarks, BS, 1950; Univ Md, MS, 1952, PhD (pharmacol), 1955. **Professional Experience:** RETIRED; vchmn, Dept Drug & Mat Toxicol, 1990-1997; fel, Acad Toxicol Sci, 1989; dipl, Acad Toxicol Sci, 1984-; prof med chem, Dept Drug & Mat Toxicol, 1983-1997; mem ed bd, J Pharmacol Sci, 1982-1988; actg chmn, Dept Drug & Mat Toxicol, 1981-1983; mem ed bd, J Toxicol Environ Heath, 1978-; assoc dir, Mat Sci Toxicol Labs, 1975-1985; adv, Neurostimulation Subcomt, Am Asn Med Implants, 1974-1978; head, Animal Toxicol Sect, 1967-1985; asst dir, Mat Sci Toxicol Labs, 1967-1975; consult, Vet Admin Hosp, Houston, 1964-1966 & Memphis, 1967-1972; from assoc prof to prof toxicol, Univ Tenn Health Sci Ctr, 1966-1983; vis scientist, Dept Pharmacol & Toxicol, Univ Tex Med Br, Galveston, 1965; vis scientist, Dept Pharmacol & Toxicol, Med Br at Galveston, 1965; lectr, Dept Pharmacol & Toxicol, Med Br at Galveston, 1964-1967; consult, Drug-Plastic Res & Toxicol Labs, 1963-1968; Vis scientist, Univ Tex, 1963; from asst prof to assoc prof pharmacol & physiol, Col Pharm, Univ Houston, 1956-1966; asst pharmacol, Sch Pharm, 1951-1954; Instr materia medica, Sch Nursing, Univ Md, 1951; mem, Gen Toxicity & Screening Task Force, Int Dent Fedn. **Memberships:** Soc Toxicol; Am Pharmaceut Asn; Sigma Xi. **Research Statement & Publications:** Toxicity of biomaterials and medical devices, especially dental materials, blood bags, intravenous administration tubings, extracorporeal devices, implantable devices and carcinogenic studies of plastics; in vivo activity and toxicity of some novel inhibitors of platelet aggregation. **Mailing Address:** 3341 Joslyn, Memphis, TN 38128.

LAWRENCE, WILLIAM MASON, FISHERIES, NATURAL RESOURCES. **Personal Data:** b Brooktondale, NY, October 2, 1918. **Education:** Cornell Univ, BS, 1938, PhD (fishery biol), 1941. **Honors & Awards:** Seth Gordon Award, Int Asn Fish & Wildlife, 1976. **Professional Experience:** RETIRED; consult, 1974-1985; chmn, Atlantic States Marine Fisheries Comn, 1971-1973; US comnr, Great Lakes Fishery Comn, 1965-1988; dep comnr, NY State Dept Environ Conserv, 1964-1974; asst comnr, NY State Conserv Dept, 1958-1964; dir fish & game, NY State Conserv Dept, 1955-1958; chief bur fish, NY State Conserv Dept, 1952-1955; sr aquatic biologist, NY State Conserv Dept, 1946-1952; Biometrician bur game, NY State Conserv Dept, 1941-1942. **Memberships:** Am Fisheries Soc (pres, 1959); Int Asn Fish & Wildlife Agencies (pres, 1969). **Research Statement & Publications:** Fish and wildlife conservation; water resources. **Mailing Address:** 991 White Church Rd, Brooktondale, NY 14817.

LAWRENZ, FRANCES PATRICIA, EVALUATION, IN-SERVICE TEACHER TRAINING. **Personal Data:** b Milwaukee, Wis, November 6, 1947. **Education:** Univ Minn, Minneapolis, BS, 1968, MA, 1971, PhD (educ, chem & math), 1974. **Professional Experience:** ASSOC DEAN RES, UNIV MINN, as of 2004; Med Sch, Northern Ariz Univ, 1985-; eval consult, Native Am Sci Educ Asn, 1984-; Med Sch, Univ Ariz, 1984-; ed, Ariz Health Educ Newsletter & assoc ed, Sch Sci & Math, 1983-; eval consult, YMCA, 1982-; Surv researcher, Ariz Dept Energy, 1982-1983; asst prof Sci Educ, Ariz State Univ beginning 1981; evaluator health, Area Health Educ Ctr, 1979-1980; consult adult educ, Govt Yukon, 1978-1979; proj mgr, NSF, 1977-1978; asst prof sci & phys sci educ, State Univ NY, Buffalo, 1975-1977; sci consult, Nat Assessment Ed Prog, 1974-1975; asst prof chem, St Mary's Jr Col, 1971-1974; vol, Peace Corps, Ankara, Turkey, 1969-1970. **Memberships:** Am Educ Res Asn; Nat Asn Res Sci Teaching; Asn Educ Teachers Sci; Sch Sci & Math Asn; Eval Network; Am Sch Health Asn. **Research Statement & Publications:** Evaluation of in-service teacher training programs in physical science and health, improvement of the quality of training and determination of what variables affect outcomes; author of various articles. **Mailing Address:** Educa Psychol, col Educa & Human Develop, Univ Minn, 331 Burton Hall, Minneapolis, MN 55455. **E-Mail:** lawrenz@umn.edu

LAWREY, JAMES DONALD, LICHENOLOGY. **Personal Data:** b Arlington, Va, December 15, 1949. **Education:** Wake Forest Univ, BS, 1971; Univ SDak, MA, 1973; Ohio State Univ, PhD (bot), 1977. **Professional Experience:** PROF ENVIRON SCI & POLICY, GEORGE MASON UNIV, as of 2003; assoc prof environ sci & policy, George Mason Univ, beginning 1977. **Memberships:** Am Bryol & Lichenological Soc; Ecol Soc Am; Brit Lichen Soc; Mycol Soc Am; Bot Soc Am. **Research Statement & Publications:** Population and community ecology of lichens; ecological significance of lichen secondary compounds; use of lichens as biological indicators of atomospheric pollution. **Mailing Address:** Dept Environ Sci & Policy, George Mason Univ, 10900 Univ Blvd, Manassas, VA 20110-2203. **Fax:** 703-993-8430. **E-Mail:** jlawrey@gmu.edu

LAWRIE, DUNCAN H, COMPUTER SCIENCE, COMPUTER ENGINEERING. **Personal Data:** b Chicago, Ill, April 26, 1943. **Education:** DePauw Univ, BA, 1966; Purdue Univ, BSEE, 1966; Univ Ill, MS, 1969, PhD (comput sci), 1973. **Professional Experience:** PROF EMER COMPUT SCI, UNIV ILL, URBANA-CHAMPAIGN, 1998-; head, dept comput sci, Univ Ill, Urbana, 1990-1996; prof comput sci, Univ Ill, Urbana, 1984-1998; from asst prof to assoc prof, Univ Ill, Urbana-Champaign, 1974-1984; vis res asst prof, Univ Ill, Urbana-Champaign, 1973-1974; sr res programmer, Univ Ill, Urbana-Champaign, 1970-1973. **Memberships:** Fel Inst Elec & Electronics Engrs; Asn Comput Mach; Inst Elec & Electronics Engrs Comput Soc (pres, 1991). **Research Statement & Publications:** Computer system organization; especially very large systems; memory hierarchies. **Mailing Address:** Dept Comput Sci, Univ Ill, 1304 W Springfield Ave, Urbana, IL 61801. **Fax:** 217-265-6738. **E-Mail:** lawrie@uiuc.edu

LAWROSKI, HARRY, CHEMICAL & NUCLEAR ENGINEERING. **Personal Data:** b Dalton, Pa, October 10, 1928. **Education:** Pa State Univ, BS, 1950, MS, 1956, PhD (chem eng), 1959. **Professional Experience:** PRES, H LAWROSKI & ASSOC, as of 2002; Consult, 1979-; asst gen mgr, Idaho Chem Progs, Allied Chem Corp, 1976-1979; gen mgr environ, Nuclear Serv Corp, 1973-1976; supt, EBR II Opers, 1968-1973; chmn, Nuclear Div, Am Inst Chem Engrs, 1967-1968; tech mgr, Zero Power Plutonium Reactor, 1963-1968; Instr, Nat Reactor Testing Sta, Univ Idaho, 1959-; assoc chem engr, Idaho Div, Argonne Nat Lab, 1958-1963; instr petrol refining, Pa State Univ, 1956-1958; Asst, Pa State Univ, 1950-1956. **Memberships:** Fel Am Nuclear Soc (treas 1971-1977 vpres 1979-1980 pres 1980-1981); fel Am Inst Chem Engrs. **Research Statement & Publications:** Reactor engineering; petroleum refining. **Mailing Address:** 5135 W Shoshone Dr, Wilson, WY 83014.

LAWS, EDWARD ALLEN, OCEANOGRAPHY & WATER POLLUTION. **Personal Data:** b Columbus, Ohio, February 4, 1945; m 1981, Stephanie Laws; c Ryan & Jennifer. **Education:** Harvard Univ, BA, 1967, PhD (chem physics), 1972. **Professional Experience:** DEAN, SCH COAST & ENVIRONMENT, LA UNIV, as of 2005; prof, Dept Oceanog, Univ Hawaii, Manoa, 1983-2004; assoc prof oceanog, Univ Hawaii, Manoa, 1980-1984; asst prof, Univ Hawaii, 1974-1980; instr oceanog, Fla State Univ, 1971-1974. **Memberships:** Am Soc Limnol & Oceanog; Am Geophys Union; Soc Environ Toxicol & Chem. **Research Statement & Publications:** Metabolism of carbon and nitrogen by marine phytoplankton; water pollution; marine food webs. **Mailing Address:** Dept Oceanog, Univ Hawaii, Manoa, 1000 Pope Rd Marine Sci Bldg, Honolulu, HI 96822. **Fax:** 808-956-9225. **E-Mail:** elaws@hawaii.edu

LAWS, EDWARD RAYMOND, NEUROSURGERY. **Personal Data:** b New York, NY, April 29, 1938; m 1962, Margaret; c Elizabeth, Margaret, Victoria & Eleanor. **Education:** Princeton Univ, AB, 1959; Johns Hopkins Univ, MD, 1963. **Professional Experience:** W GAYLE CRUTCHFIELD PROF NEUROL SUR, UNIV VA, CHARLOTTESVILLE, 1999-; prof Neurosurg & Med, Univ Va, Charlottesville, beginning 1992; prof & chmn, Med Ctr, George Wash Univ, 1987-1992; neurol surgeon, Mayo Med Sch, Mayo Clin, 1972-1987; from assoc prof to prof neurol surg, Mayo Med Sch, Mayo Clin, 1972-1987; asst prof neurol surg & neurol surgeon, Johns Hopkins Hosp, 1966-1972; asst chief toxicol, Commun Dis Ctr, USPHS, Ga, 1964-1966; fel surg, Johns Hopkins Univ, 1963-1964; intern, Johns Hopkins Hosp, 1963-1964; Henry Strong Denison fel, 1962-1963; USPHS res grants, 1960-1962. **Memberships:** Sigma Xi; Am Acad Neurol Surg; Am Col Surgeons; Child Neurol Soc. **Research Statement & Publications:** Neurooncology; pituitary surgery; epilepsy surgery. **Mailing Address:** Dept Neurol Surg, Health Sci Ctr, Univ Va, Third FlClinical Wing PO Box 800212, Charlottesville, VA 22908-0212. **Fax:** 434-924-5894. **E-Mail:** el5g@virginia.edu

LAWS, KENNETH LEE, METEOROLOGY, ELECTRONICS, BIOMECHANICS. **Personal Data:** b Pasadena, Calif, May 30, 1935; m 1965, Priscilla; c Kevin A & Virginia. **Education:** Calif Inst Technol, BS, 1956; Univ Pa, MS, 1959; Bryn Mawr Col, PhD (physics), 1962. **Professional Experience:** PROF EMER PHYSICS, DICKINSON COL, 2000-; prof physics, Dickinson Col, 1978-2000; from asst dean to assoc dean, Dickinson Col, 1971-1977; from asst prof to assoc prof, Dickinson Col, 1962-1978; instr physics, Hobart & William Smith Cols, 1958-1959. **Memberships:** Am Asn Physics Teachers; Am Meteorol Soc; Sigma Xi. **Research Statement & Publications:** Biomechanics; physics of dance. **Mailing Address:** Dickinson Col, Carlisle, PA 17013-2896. **E-Mail:** laws@dickinson.edu

LAWS, LEONARD STEWART, MATHEMATICS. **Personal Data:** b Pocasset, Okla, December 29, 1917; m 1943, Janet O; c Gregory, Kenneth, David & Rebecca. **Education:** Willamette Univ, AB, 1939; Stanford Univ, MA, 1941; Mich State Univ, EdD, 1953. **Honorary Degrees:** Doctors of Art and Literature, Southwestern col, KS, 2001. **Professional Experience:** Nsf fel, stanford univ 1962-1963; mgt consult, 1964-; NSF fel, Stanford Univ, 1961-1962; PROF MATH, SOUTHWESTERN COL, KANS, 1955-; chmn, Natural Sci Div, 1955-1974; dean & registr, Southwestern Col, Kans, 1953-1955; Asst, Mich State Univ, 1947 & 1953; from instr to asst prof, Univ Minn, 1942-1952; asst math & mech, Univ Minn, 1941-1942; Asst math, Stanford Univ, 1939-1941. **Memberships:** Am Soc Qual Control; Am Statist Asn. **Research Statement & Publications:** Industrial reliability; design of experiments. **Mailing Address:** 311 Houston St, Winfield, KS 67156.

LAWS, PRISCILLA WATSON, NUCLEAR STRUCTURE, HEALTH PHYSICS. **Personal Data:** b New York, NY, January 18, 1940; m 1965, Kenneth; c kevin & virginia. **Education:** Reed Col, BA, 1961; Bryn Mawr Col, MA, 1963, PhD (physics), 1966. **Honors & Awards:** Dana Award, Pioneering Achievement Educ, 1993; Milliken Award, Am Asn Physics Teachers, 1996; Robert A Millikan Medal. **Professional Experience:** RES PROF PHYSICS & ASTRON, DICKSON COL, as of 2006; pres, Creative Technol Inc, 1982-1991; chmn, Dept Physics& Astron, 1982-1983; prof physics, Dickson Col, 1979-2002; mem med radiation adv comt, Bur Radiation Health, Food & Drug Admin, HEW, 1974-1978; from asst prof to assoc prof, Dickson Col, 1965-1979; sr tech aide, Bell Labs, 1962; asst physics, Bryn Mawr Col, 1961-1963; consult, Off Technol Assessment, US Cong. **Memberships:** Am Asn Physics Teachers; NSF. **Research Statement & Publications:** Nuclear beta decay; environmental radiation; effects of medical x-rays, energy and environment; development of activity-based curriculum materials entered by computer-based research tools for high school and college students. **Mailing Address:** Dept Physics Astron, Dickinson Col, Carlisle, PA 17013. **Fax:** 717-245-1642. **E-Mail:** lawsp@dickinson.edu

LAWSON, ANDREW COWPER, II, PHYSICS. **Personal Data:** b Chicago, Ill, October 21, 1946. **Education:** Pomona Col, BA, 1967; Univ Calif, San Diego, MS, 1969, PhD (physics), 1972. **Professional Experience:** At, LOS ALAMOS NAT LAB, as of 1998; STAFF MEM, PHYS METALLURGY GROUP, LOS ALAMOS NAT LAB, 1983-; assoc prof, Mech Engr, Calif State Univ, Long Beach, 1982-1983; asst prof physics, Pomona Col, 1977-1982; asst res physicist, Inst Pure & Appl Physics, Univ Calif, San Diego, 1972-1977. **Memberships:** AAAS; Am Phys Soc; Am Asn Physics Teachers; Am Crystallog Asn. **Research Statement & Publications:** Superconductivity in relation to crystal structure; behavior of the electrical resistance of metals; occurance of crystallographic transformations at low temperatures; applications of neutron scattering to materials science. **Mailing Address:** Los Alamos Nat Lab, PO Box 1663, Los Alamos, NM 87545. **Fax:** 505-665-2676. **E-Mail:** lawson@lanl.gov

LAWSON, ANTON ERIC, SCIENCE EDUCATION. **Personal Data:** b Lansing, Mich, October 24, 1945. **Education:** Univ Ariz, BS, 1967; Univ Ore, MS, 1969; Univ Okla, PhD (sci educ), 1973. **Honors & Awards:** Res in Sci Teaching Award, Nat Asn for Res in Sci Teaching, 1976. **Professional Experience:** PROF SCI EDUC, ARIZ STATE UNIV, as of 2005; assoc prof sci educ, Ariz State Univ, beginning 1980; asst prof, Ariz State Univ, 1977-1980; res educr, Univ Calif, Berkeley, 1974-1977; res assoc biol educ, Purdue Univ, 1973-1974; instr sci educ, Univ Okla, 1972-1973; teacher math & sci, Ralston Intermediate Sch, Belmont, Calif, 1969-1971. **Memberships:** Nat Asn Res Sci Teaching; Asn Educ Teachers Sci; Sch Sci & Math Asn; Nat Asn Biol Teaching; AAAS. **Research Statement & Publications:** Development of formal reasoning; psychology of teaching science and mathematics. **Mailing Address:** Dept Zool, Ariz State Univ, Tempe, AZ 85287-1501. **Fax:** 408-965-2519. **E-Mail:** anton.lawson@asu.edu

LAWSON, BENJAMIN F, ORAL MEDICINE, PERIODONTOLOGY. **Personal Data:** b Montgomery, Ala, May 29, 1931. **Education:** Auburn Univ, BS, 1953; Emory Univ, DDS, 1961; Ind Univ, MSD, 1963; Univ Ala, cert periodont, 1968. **Professional Experience:** RETIRED; int consult health educ, Thailand, 1983; int consult health educ, Pakistan, 1981; dean, Col Appl Health Sci, 1972-1990; chmn dept, Col Dent Med, 1970-1972; Warner-Lambert drug study grants, 1970; from assoc prof to prof oral med & periodont, Sch Dent, Univ SC, 1968-1972; chmn dept, Sch Dent, Univ SC, 1968-1970; asst prof, Sch Dent, Univ Ala, 1966-1968; consult, Vet Admin, Birmingham & Charleston, Ft Benning, Ft Jackson & Charleston Co & Med Univ hosps, 1964 & 1967-1969; gen practr, 1963-1966; asst prof oral diag & chmn dept, Sch Dent, Emory Univ, 1963-1966; drug study grants, Eli Lilly & Co, 1962, 1965, 1967 & 1970; NIH training grant, 1961-1963. **Memberships:** Am Dont Asn; Am Soc Allied Health Professions. **Research Statement & Publications:** Histology-histopathologyof dental pulp, ceramic and titanium implants; vital pulpal therapy. **Mailing Address:** 531 Savannah Hwy, Charleston, SC 29407.

LAWSON, CHARLES ALDEN, ROCK MAGNETISM, EXPERIMENTAL PETROLOGY. **Personal Data:** b Philadelphia, Pa, May 2, 1951. **Education:** Univ Calif, Santa Cruz, BS, 1973; Princeton Univ, MA, 1976, PhD (geol), 1981. **Professional Experience:** SR ADV SCI & TECHNOL, US DEPT STATE, 1996-; spec asst sci & technol, US Dept State, 1992-1996; sci attache, US Embassy, Tel Aviv, 1989-1992; prog officer, US Dept State, 1987-1989; Tellers comt, Mineral Soc Am, 1985-1986; geologist, US Geol Surv, 1984-1987; Rock magnetism working group comt, Int Asn Geomagnetism & Aeronomy, 1983-1987; NASA-Johnson Space Ctr, 1982-1984 & Princeton Univ, 1981-1982; res fel, Geophys Lab, Carnegie Inst Wash, 1977-1979; geologist, Bechtel Corp, 1973-1974. **Memberships:** Am Geophys Union; Sigma Xi. **Research Statement & Publications:** Chemical and physical properties of iron-titanium oxides; correlation of microstructures and magnetic properties of ilmenite-hematite minerals; scanning and transmission electron microscopy of geologic materials; international multilateral negotiations; middle east water resources and environmental issues. **Mailing Address:** US Dept State, 2201 C St NW, Washington, DC 20520. **Fax:** 202-647-7837. **E-Mail:** lawnsonca@state.gov

LAWSON, CHARLES L, MATHEMATICS. **Personal Data:** b Idaho, 1931. **Education:** Univ Calif Berkeley, BS, 1952; UCLA, PhD (math), 1961. **Professional Experience:** CONSULT, 1996-; supvr appl math group, Jet Propulsion Lab, Calif Tech Inst, beginning 1960. **Memberships:** Asn Comput Mach; Soc Indust & Appl Math; Math Asn Am. **Research Statement & Publications:** Algorithms in numerical linear algebra; development of mathematical software. **Mailing Address:** 301 Calle Pueblo, San Clemente, CA 92672.

LAWSON, DAVID EDWARD, SEDIMENTOLOGY. **Personal Data:** b Moncton, NB, September 17, 1939. **Education:** Univ NB, BSc, 1960, MSc, 1962; Univ Reading, PhD (geol), 1971. **Professional Experience:** ASSOC PROF SEDIMENTARY GEOL, UNIV WATERLOO, 1976-; asst prof, Univ Waterloo, 1968-1976; lectr, Univ Waterloo, 1966-1968; res geologist, Sedimentology Res Lab, Univ Reading, 1962-1966. **Memberships:** Int Asn Sedimentology; Soc Econ Paleontologists & Mineralogists; fel Geol Asn Can. **Research Statement & Publications:** Environmental fluvial sedimentology; nearshore sedimentation; primary sedimentary structures; volcanic sediments; continental shelf sedimentation; torridonian sediments of northwest Scotland. **Mailing Address:** Dept Earth Sci, Univ Waterloo, Waterloo, ON N2L 3G1, Can. **Fax:** 519-746-7484. **E-Mail:** delawson@sciborg.uwaterloo.ca

LAWSON, DAVID FRANCIS, POLYMER ORGANIC CHEMISTRY, GENERATION OF POLYMERS. **Personal Data:** b Chicago, Ill, June 24, 1945; m 1985, Nel; c Amy, David & Erin. **Education:** Lewis Univ, BA, 1967; Iowa State Univ, PhD (org chem), 1971. **Professional Experience:** SECT MGR, POLYMER SYNTHESIS, BRIDGESTONE/FIRESTONE RES, INC, 1994-; Vis scholar, Ohio Acad Sci, 1990-1993; assoc scientist, Firestone Cent Res Labs, 1982-1994; sr res scientist, Firestone Cent Res Labs, 1975-1981; res scientist, Firestone Cent Res Labs 1970-1975; Instr chem, Iowa State Univ, 1968-1969. **Memberships:** Am Chem Soc; Adhesion Soc; Sigma Xi. **Research Statement & Publications:** Organic polymer chemistry; anionic polymerization; combustion, smoke, and flammability of polymers; synthetic and physical organic chemistry; elastomer synthesis; engineering thermoplastics; adhesives; polymer surface chemistry and adhesion; organolithium chemistry. **Mailing Address:** 11621 Garden Lane NW, Uniontown, OH 44685.

LAWSON, DAVID MICHAEL, REPRODUCTIVE ENDOCRINOLOGY, LACTATION. **Personal Data:** b Denver, Colo, November 13, 1943. **Education:** Va Polytech Inst, BS, 1965, MS, 1967; Cornell Univ, PhD (physiol), 1970. **Professional Experience:** PROF PHYSIOL, SCH MED, WAYNE STATE UNIV, 1993-; from asst prof to assoc prof, Dept Physiol, Sch Med, Wayne State Univ, 1973-1993; res assoc, Sch Med, Wayne State Univ, 1971-1973; NIH trainee physiol, Cornell Univ, 1971; grad res asst, Cornell Univ, 1967-1970; grad res asst, Va Polytechnic Inst, 1965-1967. **Memberships:** Endocrine Soc; Soc Exp Biol & Med. **Research Statement & Publications:** Control of prolactin secretion; molecular nature of prolactin form synthesis through release; endocrine control of mammary gland function; Published over 10 articles. **Mailing Address:** Dept Physiol, Sch Med, Wayne State Univ, 5203 Scott Hall 540 E Canfield, Detroit, MI 48201. **Fax:** 313-577-5494. **E-Mail:** davelawson@wayne.edu

LAWSON, DEWEY TULL, ACOUSTICS. **Personal Data:** b Kinston, NC, February 6, 1944; m 1966, Elizabeth; c Jonathan D & Neal B. **Education:** Harvard Univ, AB, 1966; Duke Univ, PhD (physics), 1972. **Honors & Awards:** Presidential Citation, Am Otolog Soc, 1997. **Professional Experience:** DIR, CTR AUDITORY PROTHESIS RES, RTS INT, 2002-; ast dir, Ctr Auditory Prothesis Res, Res Triangle Inst, ending 2002; prof otolaryngol, Duke Univ, 1992-; consult archit & environ acoust & adj prof physics, Duke Univ, 1980-; SR SCIENTIST, RES TRIANGLE INST, 1979-; asst prof physics, Duke Univ, 1974-1979; res assoc physics, Lab Atomic & Solid State Physics, Cornell Univ, 1972-1974. **Memberships:** Am Phys Soc; Am Asn Physics Teachers; Sigma Xi. **Research Statement & Publications:** Signal processing and electrical stimulation for implanted auditory prostheses, musical acoustics, hearing. **Mailing Address:** Res Triangle Inst, 3040 Cornwallis Rd PO Box 12194, Research Triangle Park, NC 27709. **E-Mail:** dtl@rti.org

LAWSON, EDWARD EARLE, PEDIATRICS, NEONATOLOGY. **Personal Data:** b Winston-Salem, NC, August 6, 1946. **Education:** Harvard Univ, BA, 1968; Sch Med, Northwestern Univ, MD, 1972. **Professional Experience:** CONSULT, DEPT PEDIAT, JOHNS HOPKINS MED, as of 2006; vice chmn pediat, Univ NC, Chapel Hill, beginning 1995; interim chmn, Dept Pediat, 1993-1995; dir, Div Neonatal/Perinatal Med, 1988-1995; Alexander von Humboldt res fel, WGer, 1985-1986; res career develop award, NIH, 1982-1987; prin investr, NIH res grants, 1979-; attend pediatrician, NC Mem Hosp, 1978-; from asst prof to assoc prof, Univ NC, Chapel Hill, 1978-1986; E L Trudeau fel, Am Lung Asn, 1978-1981; instr pediat, Harvard Med Sch, 1977-1978; fel neonatology, Harvard Med Sch, 1975-1978; Residency pediat, Children's Hosp, Boston, 1972-1975. **Memberships:** Am Thoracic Soc; Soc Pediat Res; Am Physiol Soc; Am Acad Pediat; Am Pediat Soc; Perinatal Res Soc. **Research Statement & Publications:** Neural mechanisms of central respiratory control, particularly in newborns. **Mailing Address:** Dept Pediat, Johns Hopkins Med, 601 N Caroline St, Baltimore, MD 21287. **E-Mail:** ned.pedslan@mhs.unc.edu

LAWSON, HERBERT BLAINE, MATHEMATICS. **Personal Data:** b Norristown, Pa, January 4, 1942. **Education:** Brown Univ, ScB & AB, 1964; Stanford Univ, PhD (math), 1968. **Honors & Awards:** Steele Prize, Am Math Soc, 1975. **Professional Experience:** DISTINGUISHED PROF MATH, STATE UNIV NY, STONY BROOK, 1993-; Tata Inst Fundamental Res, Bombay, India, 1987; mem, Coun Am Math Soc, 1986-; Sloan fel & JSPS fel, Kyoto Univ, Japan, 1986; vis prof, Ecole Polytech, France, 1983-1984; Guggenheim fel, 1983; prof, State Univ NY, Stony Brook, 1980-1993; IHES, Bures-sur-Yvette, France, 1977-1978; mem, Inst Advan Study, Princeton, 1972-1973; from assoc prof to prof, Univ Calif, Berkeley, 1971-1980; Sloan Found fel, Univ Calif, Berkeley, 1970-1972; vis prof, Inst Pure & Appl Math, Rio Del Janeiro, Brazil, 1970-1971; Lectr math, Univ Calif, Berkeley, 1968-1970; mem, Nat Comt Math. **Memberships:** Nat Acad Sci; Am Math Soc (vpres, 1997). **Research Statement & Publications:** Minimal surfaces; Riemannian geometry; foliations; several complex variables; mathematical physics; algebraic geometry. **Mailing Address:** Dept Math, State Univ NY, Stony Brook, NY 11794-3651. **Fax:** 631-632-7631. **E-Mail:** blaine@math.sunysb.edu

LAWSON, JAMES EVERETT, ZOOLOGY. **Personal Data:** b Derby, Va, January 8, 1933. **Education:** ETenn State Univ, BS, 1958, MA, 1959; Va Polytech Inst, PhD (zool), 1967. **Professional Experience:** RETIRED; from assoc prof to prof, ETenn State Univ, 1964-1994; instr, Va Polytech Inst, 1961-1962; Instr biol, ETenn State Univ, 1959-1961; Dir, Off Preprofessional Advert. **Research Statement & Publications:** Ecology and systematics of pseudoscorpions. **Mailing Address:** 114 Chadwick Cir, Johnson City, TN 37601.

LAWSON, JAMES W, ANTI-RHYTHMIC DRUGS. **Education:** Univ Okla, PhD (pharmacol), 1955. **Professional Experience:** PROF, DEPT MED CHEM, UNIV TENN, MEMPHIS, 1964-. **Mailing Address:** Univ Tenn, 800 Madison Ave, Memphis, TN 38163-0001.

LAWSON, JIMMIE DON, TOPOLOGICAL ALGEBRA. **Personal Data:** b Waukegan, Ill, December 6, 1942; m 1964, Laura; c Michal & John K. **Education:** Harding Col, BS, 1964; Univ Tenn, PhD (math), 1967. **Professional Experience:** BOYD PROF MATH, LA STATE UNIV, BATON ROUGE, as of 2004; ed, Am Math Monthly, 1996-; vis prof, Tech Univ, Darmstadt, Ger, 1992-1993; vis prof, Oxford Univ, 1984; chair, LA State Univ, Baton Rouge, 1990-1992; ed, Semigroup Forum, 1988-; alexander von Humboldt fel & hon Fulbright fel, Tech Univ, Darmstadt, W Ger, 1980-1981; PROF MATH, LA STATE UNIV, BATON ROUGE, 1976-; vis assoc prof, Univ Houston, 1976; NSF grants, prin investr, 1969-1994; from asst prof to assoc prof, LA State Univ, Baton Rouge, 1968-1975; asst prof math, Univ Tenn, 1967-1968. **Memberships:** Am Math Soc; Math Asn Am. **Research Statement & Publications:** Topological algebra; algebraic topology and semigroups; topology; continuous lattices; lie semigroups; control theory; topological dynamics; author of various articles; co-author of two research monographs; co-editor of one research monograph. **Mailing Address:** Dept Math, La State Univ, Lockett 216, Baton Rouge, LA 70803. **Fax:** 504-388-4276. **E-Mail:** lawson@math.lsu.edu

LAWSON, JOEL S(MITH), PHYSICS, ELECTRONICS. **Personal Data:** b New York, NY, July 3, 1924; m 1946, c 4. **Education:** Williams Col, BA, 1947; Univ Ill, MS, 1949, PhD (physics), 1953. **Honors & Awards:** Distinguished Civilian Serv Awd, US Navy, 1967. **Professional Experience:** RETIRED; consult, 1985-1993; chief scientist, Naval Electronics Systs, 1981-1984; tech dir, Naval Electronics Systs, 1974-1981; dir, Naval Labs, Wash, DC, 1968-1974; res & eng consult, Comdr-in-Chief Pac, 1967-1968; spec asst electronics, Off Asst Secy Navy, 1965-1967; sr staff mem, Sci Eng Inst, 1958-1965; from res asst prof to res assoc prof, Control Systs Lab, Univ Ill, 1955-1957; res assoc, Control Systs Lab, Univ Ill, 1953-1955. **Memberships:** Fel AAAS. **Research Statement & Publications:** Applications of digital data processing techniques to information handling; communications systems; radar techniques; development of advanced electronic devices for military applications; theory of military command control. **Mailing Address:** 3089 La Pietra Circle, Honolulu, HI 96815.

LAWSON, JOHN DOUGLAS, COMPUTER SCIENCE, NUMERICAL ANALYSIS. **Personal Data:** b Meaford, Ont, September 2, 1937; m Sue; c 3. **Education:** Univ Toronto, BASc, 1959; Univ Waterloo, MSc, 1960, PhD (appl math), 1965. **Professional Experience:** VPRES INFO TECHNOL, TULANE UNIV, as of 2002; pres, Algoma Univ Col, beginning 1987; chmn dept comput sci, 1974-1978, 1983-1984; prof comput sci, Univ Waterloo, 1973-1987; vis lectr, Univ Dundee, 1971-1972; assoc dean math, Univ Waterloo, 1968-1971; from asst prof to assoc prof, Univ Waterloo, 1964-1973; asst scientist, Med Div, Oak Ridge Inst Nuclear Studies, 1964-1965; lectr, 1960-1964; teaching fel math, 1959-1960. **Research Statement & Publications:** Numerical solution of ordinary differential equations; programming languages for scientific applications; approximation theory. **Mailing Address:** Tulane Univ, 201A Richardson, New Orleans, LA 70118. **E-Mail:** jlawson@tulane.edu

LAWSON, JOHN EDWARD, medicinal chemistry; deceased, see previous edition for last biography

LAWSON, JOHN EDWIN, ANIMAL BREEDING. **Personal Data:** b Shoal Lake, Man, November 28, 1933. **Education:** Univ Man, BSAgr, 1956, MSA, 1963. **Professional Experience:** RETIRED; res scientist beef cattle breeding, Res Br, Agr Can Res Sta, 1957-1988; head, Animal Sci Sect, Agr Can Res Sta. **Research Statement & Publications:** Evaluation of cattle breeds and crosses for reproductive performance and efficiency of production in specific environments; investigation of genotype-environment interactions; direct and correlated response to single trait selection. **Mailing Address:** 2843 Lakeview Dr, Lethbridge, AB T1K 3G2, Can.

LAWSON, JUAN (OTTO), PHYSICS. **Personal Data:** b Bluefield, WVa, April 18, 1939. **Education:** Va State Col, BS, 1960; Howard Univ, MS, 1962, PhD (physics), 1966. **Professional Experience:** RETIRED; dean, Col Sci, 1975-1980; prof physics, Grad Sch, 1974-1992; asst dean, Grad Sch, 1970-1971; From asst prof to assoc prof, Univ Tex El Paso, 1967-1974. **Memberships:** Am Phys Soc; Sigma Xi. **Research Statement & Publications:** Mathematical physics; solid state theory. **Mailing Address:** 8712 Cielo Vista Dr, El Paso, TX 79925.

LAWSON, KENNETH DARE, ELECTRON MICROSCOPY. **Personal Data:** b Clinchport, Va, May 12, 1934. **Education:** E Tenn State Univ, BA, 1959; Univ Fla, MS, 1961, PhD (chem), 1963. **Professional Experience:** SECT HEAD, MIAMI VALLEY LABS, PROCTER & GAMBLE CO, 1963-. **Memberships:** AAAS; Am Chem Soc. **Research Statement & Publications:** Nuclear magnetic resonance spectroscopy; structure of mesomorphic phases; biophysics. **Mailing Address:** 460 Whitestone Ct, Cincinnati, OH 45231-2716.

LAWSON, KENT DELANCE, PHYSICS EDUCIVE (SCI) PHYSICS. **Personal Data:** b Binghamton, NY, February 17, 1921; m 1942, Jane Hulbirt; c Lee, Nancy & Ardie. **Education:** Cornell Univ, BA, 1943; Rensselaer Polytech Inst, MS, 1951, PhD (physics), 1956. **Professional Experience:** EMER DISTINGUISHED TEACHING PROF, STATE UNIV NY COL, ONEONTA, 1991-; distinguished teaching prof, State Univ NY Col, Oneonta, 1975-1991; dir, EDUX Prog, 1970-1991; prof physics, State Univ NY Col, Oneonta, 1965-1975; Res & educ prof consult, 1956-1970; mem fac, Bennington Col, 1953-1966; Instr physics, Rensselaer Polytech Inst, 1946-1952. **Memberships:** Am Phys Soc; Am Asn Physics Teachers sr mem in both. **Research Statement & Publications:** Education theory unified theory of physical reality, man and awareness; learning how to think physics (vs memoriaing physics). **Mailing Address:** 53 Center St, Oneonta, NY 13820. **E-Mail:** klawson@dmcom.net

LAWSON, LARRY DALE, LIPID BIOCHEMISTRY, GARLIC ANALYSIS & PLANT ANALYSIS. **Personal Data:** b Elkhart, Ind, December 23, 1946; m 1973, Carol; c April, Lisa, Adam, Charity, Sarah & Julie. **Education:** Purdue Univ, BS, 1968; Brigham Young Univ, MS, 1973; Univ Ill, PhD (nutrit sci), 1979. **Professional Experience:** RES DIR, PLANT BIOACTIVES RES INST, as of 2000; res & develop mgr, Murdock Madaus Schwabe Co, beginning 1986; res assoc, Univ NC, 1983-1985; Fel, Hormel Inst, Univ Minn, 1978-1983. **Memberships:** Am Soc Nutrition; Soc Med Plant Res. **Research Statement & Publications:** Sulfur biochemistry of garlic, aanlaysis of plants, lipid nutrition. **Mailing Address:** Plant Bioactives Res Inst, 95 S Mountain Way Dr, Orem, UT 84058. **Fax:** 801-226-3083. **E-Mail:** lawson@plant-bioactives.com

LAWSON, MARLENE T, MATHEMATICS, STATISTICIAN. **Personal Data:** b Washington, DC. **Education:** Univ Dist Columbia, bs, 1962; Ssouthern CT State Univ, MA, 1970; Geo Wash Univ, MS, 1971; Geo Wash Univ, EdD, 1983. **Honors & Awards:** Advisor, Black Student Alliance, Trinity College; recog of completion of 7 int'l Study Missions, Geo Wash Univ. **Professional Experience:** MATH TEACHER, MAGGIE WALKER GOV SCHOOL GOVT & INT STUDIES, RICHMOND, VA, 2001-; math teacher, Brooke Point H School, Stafford County, VA, 1994-2001; from asst to assoc prof, Trinity College& Mt Vernon College, 1986-1994; from asst to assoc profl lectr, Geo Wash Univ, 1972-1975. **Memberships:** Nat Counl Teachers Math; Va Edu Assoc. **Research Statement & Publications:** Adapting oper research to the high school and middle school classroom. **Mailing Address:** Gov Sch Govt & Int Studies, 1000 N Lombardy St, Richmond, VA 23220. **Fax:** 804-354-6939. **E-Mail:** mlawson@gsgis.k12.va.us

LAWSON, MERLIN PAUL, CLIMATOLOGY. **Personal Data:** b Jamestown, NY, January 12, 1941; m 1964, Nina; c Keith, Kenneth & Kristin. **Education:** State Univ NY Buffalo, BA, 1963; Clark Univ, MA, 1966, PhD (geog-climat), 1973. **Professional Experience:** Professor of Geosciences, 2002- Dean Emeritus 2002- Dean of Int Affairs, Univ Nebr, 1997-2001; Treas, Midwestern Asn Grad Schs 1995-2002; DEAN GRAD STUDIES, UNIV NEBR, LINCOLN, 1992-2002; asst vchancellor res & assoc dean grad studies, Univ Nebr, Lincoln, 1987-1992; PROF CLIMAT, UNIV NEBR, LINCOLN, 1982-2002; chmn dept geog, Univ Nebr, Lincoln, 1980-1987; from asst prof to assoc prof climat, Univ Nebr, Lincoln, 1968-1982; Instr climat, Northeastern Univ, 1967-1968. **Memberships:** Sigma Xi; Am Meteorol Soc; Asn Am Geogrs; Am Assoc for the Advancement of Sci; Fulbright asn. **Research Statement & Publications:** Climate Change; Historical climate of the Great American Desert; severe droughts since 1700 in the western United States; descriptive climatic change; coral reef-global warming. **Mailing Address:** 7700 Portsche Lane, Lincoln, NE 68516. **E-Mail:** mlawson@unl.edu

LAWSON, MILDRED WIKER, MATHEMATICS, COMPUTER SCIENCES. **Personal Data:** b New London, Conn, November 10, 1922. **Education:** Univ Md, BS, 1947, MA, 1949. **Professional Experience:** RETIRED; from assoc mathematician to sr mathematician, Appl Physics Lab, Johns Hopkins Univ, Laurel, 1958-1985; asst chief prog, Corps Engrs, Army Map Serv, 1957-1958; proj leader math & comput prog, Corps Engrs, Army Map Serv, 1955-1957; mathematician, Corps Engrs, Army Map Serv, 1951-1955; cartog compilation aide, Corps Engrs, Army Map Serv, 1950-1951; instr, Univ Md, 1949-1950; asst math, Univ Md, 1947-1949. **Research Statement & Publications:** Analysis and programming of computer solutions of problems arising in scientific projects; computer language training. **Mailing Address:** 5113 Durham Rd E, Columbia, MD 21044.

LAWSON, NEAL D(EVERE), CHEMICAL ENGINEERING. **Personal Data:** b 1916. **Education:** Pa State Col, BS, 1938, MS, 1942, PhD (chem eng), 1946. **Professional Experience:** RETIRED; spec asst tech info res & develop, Ill, 1977-1980; supvr new prod develop, Ill, 1966-1977; develop specialist, Ill, 1965-1966; tech mgr, Ill, 1958-1956; additives mgr, Cent Region, 1956-1958; head chem div, E I Du Pont de Nemours & Co Inc, 1950-1956; group leader petrol chem lab, E I Du Pont de Nemours & Co Inc, 1947-1950; instr, Pa State Col, 1942-1947; asst petrol ref lab, Pa State Col, 1938-1942. **Memberships:** Am Chem Soc; Soc Automotive Engrs; Am Soc Lubrication Engrs; Am Soc Testing & Mat. **Research Statement & Publications:** Stability of petroleum products; additives for lubricating oils and gasoline; fuel oil stabilizers; additives and thickeners for greases. **Mailing Address:** 903 Chickadee Lane, West Chester, PA 19382.

LAWSON, NORMAN C, PLANT BREEDING. **Personal Data:** b Glasgow, Scotland, November 3, 1929. **Education:** Glasgow Univ, BSc, 1953; Univ Reading, dipl agr, 1954; McGill Univ, MSc, 1958, PhD, 1961. **Professional Experience:** RETIRED; dir dipl prog, McGill Univ, 1973-1989; assoc prof agron, McGill Univ, 1967-1989; res scientist, Res Sta, Sask, 1965-1967; res off, Exp Farm, Can Dept Agr, BC, 1961-1965. **Memberships:** Am Soc Agron; Crop Sci Soc Am; Genetics Soc Can; Agr Inst Can; Can Soc Agron. **Research Statement & Publications:** Genetics and breeding of forage and oil crop species. **Mailing Address:** 20826 Lake Shore Rd, Baie-D'urfe, PQ H9X 1R9, Can.

LAWSON, ROBERT BERNARD, NEGOTIATIONS, PSYCHOLOGY. **Personal Data:** b New York, NY, June 20, 1940; div, c Christine, Megan, Steven Robert & Jennifer Erin. **Education:** Monmouth Univ NJ, BA, 1961; Univ Del, MA, 1963, PhD (psychol), 1965. **Professional Experience:** CHMN, DEPT PSYCHOL, UNIV VT, 2002-; dir, Master Pub Admin Prog, Col Arts & Sci, Univ Vt, 1999-2002; actg dir, Master Pub Admin Prog, Col Arts & Sci, Univ Vt, 1998-1999; prof pub admin, Sch Bus Admin, Univ Vt, 1990-1995; interim chair, Dept Pub Admin, Sch Bus Admin, Univ Vt, 1990-1995; dir, Gen-Exp Psychol Prog, Univ Vt, 1988-1990; pres, Alliance, Mgt consult firm, 1987-; chmn, Univ Press New Eng, 1979-1980; mem bd govs, Univ Press New Eng, 1978-; assoc vpres res & grad dean, Univ Vt, 1978-1986; PROF PSYCHOL, UNIV VT, 1974-; dir, Visual Perception Lab, Univ Vt, 1974-1978; consult, IBM, 1974-1977; interim chair, Dept Psychol, Univ Vt, 1970-1971; consult supvr, Behavior Therapy Team, Dannemora State Hosp, NY, 1968-1972; from asst prof to assoc prof, Univ VT, 1966-1974; asst prof psychol, Villanova Univ, Pa, 1965-1966; NASA fel, 1962-1964; numerous res grants, NIH, NSF, NASA & USAID. **Memberships:** AAAS; NY Acad Sci; Sigma Xi; Am Psychol Asn; Am Soc Pub Admin; Eastern Psychol Asn; Nat Asn Schools Pub Affairs Admin; NY Acad Sci. **Research Statement & Publications:** Orginaonal culture leadership; published over 100 articles. **Mailing Address:** Dept Psychol, Univ Vt, John Dewey Hall, Burlington, VT 05405-0134. **Fax:** 802-656-8783. **E-Mail:** robert.lawson@uvm.edu

LAWSON, ROBERT DAVIS, THEORETICAL PHYSICS. **Personal Data:** b Sydney, Australia, July 14, 1926. **Education:** Univ BC, BASc, 1948, MASc, 1949; Stanford Univ, PhD, 1953. **Professional Experience:** RETIRED; resident assoc, Argonne Nat Lab, beginning 1996; nordita fel, Niels Bohr Inst, Copenhagen, 1976-1977; vis prof, State Univ NY, Stony Brook, 1972-1973; weizmann sr fel, Weizmann Inst Sci, Israel, 1967-1968; sr physicist, Argonne Nat Lab, 1966-1996; vis physicist, UK Atomic Energy Authority, Harwell, Eng, 1962-1963; assoc physicist, Argonne Nat Lab, 1959-1966; res physicist, Enrico Fermi Inst Nuclear Studies, Ill, 1957-1959; jr res physicist, Univ Calif, 1953-1957; asst, Stanford Univ, 1949-1953; asst, Univ BC, 1947-1948. **Memberships:** Am Phys Soc. **Research Statement & Publications:** Nuclear physics. **Mailing Address:** Appl Physics, Argonne Nat Lab, MS 316, Argonne, IL 60439. **Fax:** 630-252-3903.

LAWSON, ROGER H, HORTICULTURE. **Personal Data:** b Portland, Ore, January 21, 1937. **Education:** Ore State Univ, BS, 1960, PhD (plant pathol), 1963. **Professional Experience:** Emeritus fellow of HRI, as of 2006; NAT PROG LEADER HORT & SUGAR CROPS, USDA, 1995-. **Mailing Address:** Nat Prog Lab, Agr Res Serv, USDA, BARC W Bldg 005, Beltsville, MD 20705.

LAWSON, WILLIAM, FACIAL PLASTIC SURGERY, MAXILLOFACIAL SURGERY. **Personal Data:** b New York, NY, November 23, 1934. **Education:** NY Univ, BA, 1956, DDS, 1961, MD, 1965. **Professional Experience:** Attend surgeon otolaryngol, Elmhurst Gen Hosp, 1982-; PROF OTOLARYNGOL, MT SINAI SCH MED, 1982-; ATTEND SURGEON, MT SINAI HOSP, NY, 1982-; chief head & neck surg, Bronx Vet Hosp, 1975-. **Memberships:** Am Acad Facial Plastic Reconstruct Surg (vpres, 1987-1989); Am Soc Head & Neck Surgeons; Am Soc Maxillofacial Surgeons; Am Laryngol Soc; Am Rhinologic Laryngol Otol Soc; Am Col Surgeons. **Research Statement & Publications:** Melanocytic system of head and neck, discovery of melanocytes in larynx, nasal cavity, orbit and dental lamina; experimental proof of the neurocrine nature of glomus cells of the head and neck; paraganglyonic chemoreceptor system; discovery of paraganglia in laryna; author of sourcebook with 3000 references. **Mailing Address:** Dept Otolaryngol, Mt Sinai Sch Med, New York, NY 10029-6501. **E-Mail:** w.lawson@mssm.edu

LAWTON, ALEXANDER R, III, MEDICINE. **Personal Data:** b November 8, 1938. **Education:** Yale Univ, BA, 1960; Vanderbilt Univ, MD, 1964. **Professional Experience:** EDWARD C STAHLMAN PROF PEDIAT PHYSIOL & CELL METAB, VANDERBILT UNIV, as of 2003; PROF MICROBIOL & IMMUNOL, VANDERBILT UNIV, as of 2003; HEAD PEDIAT ALLERGY, IMMUNOL & RHEUMATOLOGY, VANDERBILT UNIV, as of 2003; fac, sch med, vanderbilt Univ, nashville, 2002; prof pediat & microbiol, Sch Med, Univ Ala, Birmingham, 1976-1986; from asst prof to assoc prof, Univ Ala, 1971-1976; NIH spec fel immunol, Sch Med, Univ Ala, Birmingham, 1969-1971; clin investr, Lab Clin Invest, Nat Inst Allergy & Infectious Dis, 1968-1969; clin assoc, Lab Clin Invest, Nat Inst Allergy & Infectious Dis, 1966-1968; asst resident, Vanderbilt Univ Hosp, 1965-1966; intern, Vanderbilt Univ Hosp, 1964-1965. **Memberships:** Sigma Xi. **Research Statement & Publications:** Pediatrics; microbiology; immunology; author of numerous publications. **Mailing Address:** Dept Pediat, Sch Med, Vanderbilt Univ, 311 Oxford House 4144, Nashville, TN 37232-2580.

LAWTON, ALFRED HENRY, GERIATRICS. **Personal Data:** b Carson, Iowa, July 26, 1916; m 1974, Ruth; c George W, Dianna M (Fisel) & Lola M (Finch). **Education:** Simpson Col, AB, 1937; Northwestern Univ, MS, 1939, BM, 1940, MD, 1941, PhD (physiol), 1943. **Honorary Degrees:** ScD, Simpson Col, 1958. **Professional Experience:** RETIRED; dir gerontol educ, Advent Christian village, beginning 1982; clin prof community health & family prac, Univ Fla Sch Med & dir gerontol, 1978-1982; dir geriat res, Educ & Clin Ctr & assoc chief staff res & develop, Vet Admin Ctr, 1975-1978; exec dir tech adv comn aging res, US Dept Health, Educ & Welfare, 1973-1974; actg vpres acad affairs, Univ SFla, 1970-1973; actg dean, Col Med, Univ SFla, 1968-1970; from asst to assoc dean acad affairs, Univ SFla, 1966-1970; dir study ctr, Nat Inst Child Health & Human Develop, 1962-1966; asst dir prof serv res & educ & chief intermediate serv, US Vet Admin Ctr, Bay Pines, 1955-1962; med res adv, US Dept Air Force, 1951-1955; liaison mem coun arthritis & metab dis, USPHS, 1950-1955; asst clin prof, Sch Med, George Wash Univ, 1948-1955; chief res div, US Vet Admin, Wash, DC, 1948-1951; dean & prof physiol & pharm, Univ NDak, 1947-1948; asst prof med, physiol & pharm, Sch Med, Univ Ark, 1946-1947; resident, Henry Ford Hosp, Detroit, 1941-1942; intern, Passavant Mem Hosp, Chicago, 1940-1941; mem exec coun, Nat Res Coun, US Armed Forces Vision Comt & Nat Coun Aging. **Memberships:** Am Physiol Soc; Am Soc Pharmacol & Exp Therapeut; Am Geriat Soc; Geront Soc; Am Pub Health Asn. **Research Statement & Publications:** Aging; chronic diseases. **Mailing Address:** Advent Christian Village, Dowling Park, FL 32060.

LAWTON, EMIL ABRAHAM, SYNTHETIC CHEMISTRY, WATER CHEMISTRY. **Personal Data:** b Detroit, Mich, October 12, 1922; m 1976, Cynthia Block; c Gil, Ron & Leoa. **Education:** Wayne State Univ, AB, 1946; Purdue Univ, PhD (inorg chem), 1952. **Honors & Awards:** Civilian Patriotic Award, US Army, 1984. **Professional Experience:** Consult chemist, 1989-; CONSULT, 1989-; mem tech staff, Jet Propulsion Lab, Calif Inst Technol, 1983-1989; mgr advan prog, Shock Hydrodynamics Div, Whittaker Corp, 1977-1982; vpres res & develop, Tech & Mgt Consults, 1976-1977; proj mgr, Neus, Inc, 1975-1976; sect head, Wasatch Div, Thiokol Corp, 1972-1975; prog mgr, Rocketdyne Div, Rockwell Int, 1957-1972; proj leader, Battelle Mem Inst, 1953-1957; Res chemist, Nat Bur Stand, 1952-1953. **Memberships:** Am Chem Soc; AAAS; Sigma Xi. **Research Statement & Publications:** Combustion; explosives and propellants; lubricants; gun-propellants; fluorine. **Mailing Address:** 13025 Hesby St, Sherman Oaks, CA 91423.

LAWTON, JOHN G, ELECTRICAL ENGINEERING. **Personal Data:** b Vienna, Austria, June 3, 1923. **Education:** City Col New York, BEE, 1949; Mass Inst Technol, SM, 1951; Cornell Univ, PhD, 1960. **Professional Experience:** PRES, LAWTRONICS, INC, 1983-; pres, J & J Technologies, Inc, 1978-1983; staff scientist, Cornell Aeronaut Lab, Inc, 1970-1978; from asst engr to prin staff engr, Cornell Aeronaut Lab, Inc, 1954-1970; Jr engr electronics, Stanford Res Inst, 1951. **Memberships:** Inst Elec & Electronics Engrs. **Research Statement & Publications:** Communications; modulation; information and communications theory; fire control; guidance equipment; computers; statistics. **Mailing Address:** Northstar Aeronaut, 8353 Westfield Rd, Seville, OH 44273.

LAWTON, MICHAEL P, TOXICOLOGY. **Personal Data:** b Tacoma, Wash, June 26, 1963. **Education:** Univ Calif, Davis, BS, 1986; NC State Univ, PhD (toxicol), 1991. **Professional Experience:** SR RES INVESTR, PFIZER INC, GROTON, as of 2002; INTRAMURAL RES TRAINING AWARD FEL, NAT INST ENVIRON HEALTH SCI, NIH, 1991-; lab tech, Lawrence Livermore Nat Lab, 1986-1987. **Memberships:** Am Soc Biochem & Molecular Biol. **Research Statement & Publications:** Toxicology. **Mailing Address:** Pfizer Inc, Eastern Point Rd, Groton, CT 06340. **Fax:** 860-715-7455. **E-Mail:** michael_lawton@groton.pfizer.com

LAWTON, RICHARD G, SYNTHETIC ORGANIC CHEMISTRY, BIO-ORGANIC CHEMISTRY. **Personal Data:** b Berkeley, Calif, August 29, 1934. **Education:** Univ Calif, Berkeley, BS, 1956; Univ Wis, PhD (chem), 1962. **Professional Experience:** PROF EMER ORG CHEM, UNIV MICH, ANN ARBOR, as of 2004; John S Guggenheim Found fel, 1978-1979; consult, German Wool res inst, Aachen, WGer, 1979-1980; prof org chem, Univ Mich, Ann Arbor, beginning 1970; consult, Colgate-Palmolive res Labs, 1970-; vis prof, Univ Wis, 1970-1971; from instr to assoc prof, Univ Mich, Ann Arbor, 1962-1970; asst org chem, Univ Wis, 1959-1962; asst isolation & identification, Merck Sharp & Dohme res labs, 1956-1957. **Memberships:** AAAS; Am Chem Soc. **Research Statement & Publications:** Synthetic organic chemistry including peptide chemistry, alkaloids, terpenes and polycyclic aromatic hydrocarbons. **Mailing Address:** Dept Chem Univ Mich, 930 N Univ, Ann Arbor, MI 48105-1055. **Fax:** 734-647-4865. **E-Mail:** richy@umich.edu

LAWTON, ROBERT ARTHUR, ELECTRONICS, ELECTROOPTICS. **Personal Data:** b Sanford, Colo, July 2, 1932. **Education:** Brigham Young Univ, BS, 1960; Univ Colo, MS, 1968, PhD (elec eng), 1972. **Honors & Awards:** Super Accomplishment, Nat Bur Standards, 1966 & 1975, Outstanding Performance, 1977 & Spec Achievement, 1978. **Professional Experience:** CONSULT, 1992-; group leader electromagnetic waveform meteorol, Nat Bur Standards, 1980-1992; Sci & Technol Fel energy & power, US House Rep, Dept Com, 1978-1979; physicist pulsed electro-optics, Nat Bur Standards, 1974-1992; pulse measurement, Nat Bur Standards, 1970-1974; Physicist radio freq standards, Nat Bur Standards, 1960-1970. **Memberships:** Inst Elec & Electronics Engrs; Optical Soc Am; Sigma Xi. **Research Statement & Publications:** Electrical and optical pulse generation and measurement including time domain autocorrelation and power spectral analysis; laser pulse demodulation; signaldetection in noise; electromagnetic field effects in materials. **Mailing Address:** 546 W 40 N, Orem, UT 84057.

LAWVERE, FRANCIS WILLIAM, ALGEBRA. **Personal Data:** b Muncie, Ind, February 9, 1937; m 1966, Fatima; c Marco, John, Philip, Danilo & Silvana. **Education:** Ind Univ, BA, 1960; Columbia Univ, MA & PhD (math), 1963. **Professional Experience:** PROF EMER MATH, STATE UNIV NY BUFFALO, as of 2005; prof math, State Univ NY Buffalo, beginning 1974-; vis prof, Aarhus Univ, 1971-1972 & Nat Res Inst Italy, 1972-1974; res prof, Dalhousie Univ, 1969-1971; Sloan fel, Swiss Fed Inst Technol, 1968-1969; assoc prof, Grad Ctr, City Univ New York, 1967-1968; asst prof, Univ Chicago, 1966-1967; res assoc, Swiss Fed Inst Technol, 1965-1966; NATO fel, Swiss Fed Inst Technol, 1964-1965; asst prof math, Reed Col, 1963-1964; syst analyst, Litton Industs, Inc, 1962-1963. **Memberships:** Am Math Soc. **Research Statement & Publications:** Foundations of category theory; categorical foundations of mathematics; algebraic theories and equational doctrines; axiomatic theory of topoi; closed categories and metric spaces; synthetic differential geometry; functorial thermodynamics and continuum mechanics. **Mailing Address:** Dept Math, State Univ NY Buffalo, 244 Mathematics Bldg, Buffalo, NY 14260. **Fax:** 716-829-2299. **E-Mail:** wlawvere@ubunix.buffalo.edu

LAWWILL, STANLEY JOSEPH, MATHEMATICS. **Personal Data:** b London, Ohio, May 23, 1916; m 1940, Martha Fulford; c Judith, Patricia, Lois, Lawrence & Kenneth. **Education:** Univ Cincinnati, AB, 1937, MA, 1939, PhD (math), 1941. **Professional Experience:** RETIRED; pres, Analytical Servs, Inc, 1958-1981; tech dir, Sci Analytical Off, Melpar, Inc Div, Westinghouse Air Brake Co, 1958; dep chief scientist, Atomic Capabilities Div, 1954-1958; chief, Atomic Capabilities Div, 1950-1954; dep chief, Opers Analysis Off, 1948-1950; opers analyst, HQ Strategic Air Command, 1946-1948; gunnery analyst, 2nd & 20th Air Forces, USAF, 1944-1946; mathematician appl math group, Columbia Univ, 1944; Instr math, Northwestern Univ, 1941-1944. **Memberships:** Opers Res Soc Am; Sigma Xi. **Research Statement & Publications:** Orthogonal functions; overconvergence of approximations in terms of rational harmonic functions; operations analysis; weapon systems evaluation. **Mailing Address:** 6532 Copa Ct, Falls Church, VA 22044.

LAWYER, ARTHUR L, EXPERIMENTAL BIOLOGY. **Education:** Univ Calif, Davis, BS; Yale Univ, MPhil, 1977, PhD (molecular biochem & biophys), 1979. **Professional Experience:** VPRES & MANAGING DIR, STATE AFFAIRS DIV, TECHNOL SCI GROUP INC, as of 2002; Chmn, Calif-Environ Agency Task Force, Western Agr Chem Asn, 1991-; DIR, STATE AFFAIRS DIV, TECHNOL SCI GROUP INC, 1991-; sr proj mgr, State Govt Affairs, Valent USA Corp, 1990; mgr, State Govt Affairs, Valent USA Corp, 1989-1990; chmn, Environ Initiative Task Force, 1989-1990; chmn, Govt Affairs Comt & Calif Rep Comt, 1988-1990; chmn, Proposition 65 Task Forces, Western Agr Chem Asn, 1987-1990; Mem, State Affairs Comt, Nat Agr Chem Asn, 1987-1990; sr state regulatory specialist, Valent USA & Chevron Chem Co, 1987-1989; regulatory specialist-state liaison, Biotechnol Group, Chevron Chem Co, 1986-1987; res biochemist, Biotechnol Group, Chevron Chem Co, 1981-1986; Rockefeller Found fel, Calvin Lab, Lawrence Berkeley Labs, Univ Calif, 1979-1981. **Research Statement & Publications:** Thirteen publications covering enzymatic mechanisms, photosynthetic metabolism, plant biotechnology and prediction of groundwater contamination. **Mailing Address:** Technol Sci Group, 1101 17th St, NW, Suite 500, Washington, DC 20036.

LAX, BENJAMIN, SOLID STATE PHYSICS, PLASMA PHYSICS. **Personal Data:** b Miskolz, Hungary, December 29, 1915. **Education:** Cooper Union, BS, 1941; Mass Inst Technol, PhD (physics), 1949. **Honorary Degrees:** DSc, Yeshiva Univ, 1975. **Honors & Awards:** Buckley Prize, Am Phys Soc, 1960; Gano Dunn Medal, Cooper Union Alumni Asn, 1969. **Professional Experience:** Adv bd, EPSCOR, Ky & adv comt, Weber Res Inst, 1986-; Lincoln Lab, Mass Inst Technol, 1986-; PROF EMER PHYSICS, MASS INST TECHNOL, 1986-; Gen Motors Res Lab, 1983- & Amoco Res Ctr, Stand Oil Co, 1985-; assoc prog adv comt & chmn, Physics Panel, 1983-1984; adv comt, Am Friends Jerusalem Col Technol, 1982-1983; DIR EMER & PHYSICIST, FRANCIS BITTER NAT MAGNETIC LAB, 1981-; Guggenheim fel, 1981-1982; mem bd dirs, Infrared Indust, 1973-1976 & Barnes Eng Co, 1978-; Assoc ed, J Appl Physics, 1957-1959 & Barnes Eng Co, 1978-; consult, Raytheon Co, 1976-; chmn, 10th Int Conf Physics Semiconductors, & Int Union Pure & Appl Physics Comn Quantum Electronics, 1976-; Solid State Sci Panel, Nat Res Coun, 1970-1981; Joint Coun Quantum Electronics, 1964-1981 & chmn, 1966-1968; prof, Lincoln Lab, 1965-1986; assoc dir, Lincoln Lab, 1964-1965; mem, Coun Am Phys Soc, 1963-1967; dir, Solid State Div, 1960-1981; head, Solid State Div, 1958-1964; assoc head, Commun Div, 1957-1958; head, Ferrites Group, 1953-1955 & Solid State Group, 1955-1957; mem staff, Lincoln Lab, Mass Inst Technol, 1951-1953; mem staff, Air Force Cambridge Res Ctr, 1946-1951; radar officer, Radiation Lab, Mass Inst Technol, 1944-1946; mech engr, US Eng Off, 1941-1942. **Memberships:** Nat Acad Sci; NY Acad Sci; Sigma Xi; fel Am Phys Soc; fel Am Acad Arts & Sci; fel Optical Soc Am; fel AAAS. **Research Statement & Publications:** Nonlinear effects in solids and plasmas; interaction of submillimeter radiation with plasmas and solids; laser produced plasmas; semiconductors and ferrites; radar and millimeter waves. **Mailing Address:** Dept Physics, Mass Inst Technol, Cambridge, MA 02139. **Fax:** 617-253-5405.

LAX, EDWARD, CRYOGENICS. **Personal Data:** b Toronto, Ont, August 29, 1931. **Education:** Univ Calif, Los Angeles, AB, 1952, MA, 1959, PhD (physics), 1960. **Professional Experience:** RETIRED; mem tech staff, Autonetics Div, Rockwell Int Corp, 1967-1996; mem tech staff, Aerospace Corp, 1961-1967; Sr physicist, Ultrasonic Systs, Inc, 1960-1961. **Memberships:** Am Phys Soc; Inst Elec & Electronics Engrs. **Research Statement & Publications:** Electron-phonon effects in metals at low temperatures; acoustical-optical effects; cryogenic heat transfer and thermodynamics; hypersonics and delay lines; infrared systems. **Mailing Address:** 5637 Wilhelmina Ave, Woodland Hills, CA 91367.

LAX, MELVIN DAVID, RANDOM DIFFERENTIAL EQUATIONS. **Personal Data:** b Boston, Mass, March 20, 1947. **Education:** Rensselaer Polytech Inst, BS, 1969, MS, 1971, PhD (math), 1974. **Professional Experience:** PROF MATH, CALIF STATE UNIV, LONG BEACH, 1986-; from asst prof to assoc prof, Calif State Univ, Long Beach, 1977-1986; vis asst prof, Okla State Univ, 1976-1977; Lectr math, Southern Ill Univ, Carbondale, 1974-1976. **Memberships:** Am Math Soc; Soc Indust & Appl Math. **Research Statement & Publications:** Approximate solution of random differential equations and random integral equations. **Mailing Address:** Dept Math & Statist, Calif State Univ, 1250 Bellflower Blvd, Long Beach, CA 90840. **Fax:** 562-985-8227. **E-Mail:** mlax@csulb.edu

LAX, PETER DAVID, PARTIAL DIFFERENTIAL EQUATIONS. **Personal Data:** b Budapest, Hungary, May 1, 1926; American citizen; m 1948, c 2. **Education:** NY Univ, AB, 1947, PhD, 1949. **Honors & Awards:** Nat Medal of Sci; Lester R Ford Award, 1966 & 1973; von Neumann Lectr, Soc Indust & Appl Math, 1969; Hermann Weyl Lectr, 1972; Hedrick Lectr, 1973; Chauvenet Prize, Math Asn Am, 1974; Norberg Prize, Am Math Soc, 1975; Wolf Prize, 1987; Steele Prize, 1992. **Professional Experience:** Mem, Nat Sci Bd, 1980-1986; dir, Courant Math & Comput Lab, 1980; head, Dept Math & Comput Sci & dir, Courant Inst Math Sci, 1972-1980; dir, AEC Comput & Appl Math Ctr, 1963-1972; asst to dir, Math Ctr, 1959-1963; PROF MATH, NY UNIV, 1958-; from asst prof to assoc prof math, NY Univ, 1951-1957; staff mem, Manhattan Proj, Los Alamos Sci Lab, 1950; consult, Los Alamos Sci Lab, 1950; mem, Manhattan Proj, Los Alamos Sci Lab, 1945-1946. **Memberships:** Nat Acad Sci; Am Acad Sci; NY Acad Sci; Math Asn Am; Am Math Soc (pres, 1979-1980); Russ Acad Sci; Fr Acad Sci; Chinese Acad Sci; Hungary Acad Sci; Am Soc Arts & Sci; Soviet Acad Sci; Beijing Acad Sci; Moscow Math Soc. **Research Statement & Publications:** Theory of partial differential equations; numerical analysis; scattering theory; functional analysis; fluid dynamics. **Mailing Address:** NY Univ Courant Inst Math Sci, 251 Mercer St, New York, NY 10012. **Fax:** 212-995-4121. **E-Mail:** lax@cims.nyu.edu

LAXER, CARY, COMPUTER GRAPHICS. **Personal Data:** b Brooklyn, NY, July 16, 1955; m 1990, Norma; c Phillip. **Education:** NY Univ, BA, 1976; Duke Univ, PhD (biomed eng), 1980. **Professional Experience:** PROF & HEAD, COMPUT SCI & SOFTWARE ENG, ROSE-HULMAN INST TECHNOL, as of 2004; from asst prof to assoc prof, Rose-hulman Inst Technol, 1981-1993; res asst prof, comput sci, Duke Univ, 1980-1981. **Memberships:** Inst Elec & Electronics Engrs; Asn Comput Mach; Am Soc Eng Educ. **Research Statement & Publications:** Computer analysis of cardiac electrical signals with relation to myocardial infarct geometry; biomedical computing. **Mailing Address:** Rose-Hulman Inst Technol, 5500 Wabash Ave Campus Box 100, Terre Haute, IN 47803-3999. **Fax:** 812-872-6060. **E-Mail:** laxer@rose-hulman.edu

LAXPATI, SHARAD R, ANTENNAS, ELECTROMAGNETIC THEORY. **Personal Data:** b Bombay, India, July 16, 1938; American citizen; m 1983, Maureen; c Nealen G & Leela J. **Education:** Gujarat Univ, India, BE, 1957; Univ Ill, MS, 1961, PhD (elec eng), 1965. **Professional Experience:** Associate Dean for Undergraduate Administration, College of Engineering, Univ Ill, Chicago, 2005 - present, assoc head instr, Elec Eng & Comput Sci, Univ Ill, Chicago, 1993-2000; consult, Symmetron Inc, 1987-2005; owner, LMS Eng, Chicago, Ill, 1985-; consult, Locus, Inc, Alexandria, VA, beginning 1984-1987; consult, Naval Res Lab, Wash, DC, 1979-1990; dir, Matrix Publ Priv LTD, India, 1978-1985; vis sr assoc, Syst Res Ltd, Richmond, UK, 1976-1977; ASSOC PROF ELEC ENG & COMPUT SCI, UNIV ILL, CHICAGO, 1973-; asst prof info eng, Elec Eng & Comput Sci, Univ Ill, Chicago, 1969-1973; asst prof elec eng, Pa State Univ, 1965-1969; jr sci officer, Reactor Control Div, Atomic Energy Estab, India, 1958-1960. **Memberships:** Inst Elec & Electronics Engrs; (Sr. mem) Int Union Radio Sci, Commission B (mem); SECY (2000-2002). **Research Statement & Publications:** Radiation and propagation of electromagnetic waves; applied mathematics; computational electromagnetics; optical communication; educational technology for personalized instruction. **Mailing Address:** Dept Elec Eng & Comput Eng Univ Ill, 851 S Morgan St, Chicago, IL 60607-7042. **Fax:** 312-996-6465. **E-Mail:** laxpati@uic.edu

LAY, DAVID CLARK, OPERATOR THEORY, LINEAR ALGEBRA. **Personal Data:** b Los Angeles, Calif, March 1, 1941; m 1970, Lillian; c Christina, Deborah & Melissa. **Education:** Aurora Col, BA, 1962; Univ Calif, Los Angeles, MA, 1965, PhD (math), 1966. **Professional Experience:** Air Force USR grants, 1987-1990; vis prof, Univ Amsterdam, 1980; PROF MATH, UNIV MD, COL PARK, 1977-; res grant, Neth Orgn Advan Pure Res, 1973; NSF res grants, Univ Md, Col Park, 1968-1973, 1976-1977, 1990-1992; from asst prof to assoc prof, Univ MD, Col Park, 1966-1977; teaching asst math, Univ Calif, Los Angeles, 1963-1964. **Memberships:** Am Math Soc; Math Asn Am; Sigma Xi; Soc Indust & Appl Math. **Research Statement & Publications:** Functional analysis; spectral theory of linear operators; operator-valued analytic functions, linear algebra; research papers; books called introduction to functional analysis, second edition; calculus and its applications; linear algebra and its applications, second edition. **Mailing Address:** Dept Math, Univ Md, College Park, MD 20742. **Fax:** 301-314-0827. **E-Mail:** lay@math.umd.edu

LAY, DOUGLAS M, ANATOMY, ZOOLOGY. **Personal Data:** b Jackson, Miss, July 3, 1936. **Education:** Millsaps Col, BS, 1958; La State Univ, MS, 1961; Univ Chicago, PhD (anat), 1968. **Professional Experience:** ASSOC PROF ANAT, UNIV NC, CHAPEL HILL, 1973-; asst prof zool & cur mammals, Univ Mich, 1969-1973; Instr anat, Univ Chicago, 1968-1969. **Memberships:** Am Soc Mammal; Am Soc Zool; Soc Study Evol; Soc Syst Zool; Soc Vert Palaeont. **Research Statement & Publications:** The adaptive significance of specializations of mammals for life in deserts, particularly the structure and function of the ear in desert rodents; origin, evolution, functional anatomy, biology and systematics of rodents. **Mailing Address:** 100 1/2 Moon Pt, Chapel Hill, NC 27514.

LAY, JOHN CHARLES, VETERINARY DIAGNOSTIC PATHOLOGY, PULMONARY PATHOLOGY. **Personal Data:** b Ponca City, Okla, March 6, 1948; wid. **Education:** Univ Mo, Columbia, BS, 1971, DVM, 1975; Cornell Univ, PhD, 1986. **Professional Experience:** ASST PROF, DEPT VET PATH, TEX A&M UNIV, 1983-; fel trainee exp path, NY State Col Vet Med, Cornell Univ, 1978-1983; gen vet practr, Lakin, Kans, 1977-1978; Assoc scientist vet med, Inhalation Toxicol Res Inst, Lovelace Found for Med Educ & Res, 1975-1977. **Memberships:** Am Vet Med Asn. **Research Statement & Publications:** Bovine Respiratory Disease; pulmonary inflammatory response and mechanisms of deep lung clearance and lung defense. **Mailing Address:** 311 Brandywine Rd, Chapel Hill, NC 27516.

LAY, KENNETH W(ILBUR), CERAMICS, MATERIALS SCIENCE. **Personal Data:** b Ringgold Co, Iowa, February 4, 1939. **Education:** Iowa State Univ, BS, 1961; Northwestern Univ, PhD (mat sci), 1966. **Professional Experience:** MAT SCIENTIST, GEN ELEC RES & DEVELOP CTR, 1987-; mgr ceramics processing, Gen Elec Res & Develop Ctr, 1975-1987; commun & admin mgr mat sci & engr, Gen Elec Res & Develop Ctr, 1973-1975; res scientist, Gen Elec Res & Develop Ctr, 1965-1973. **Memberships:** Fel Am Ceramic Soc; Mat Res Soc. **Research Statement & Publications:** Ceramics processing and properties; diffusion; nuclear fuels; non-stoichiometric compounds; oxide superconductors. **Mailing Address:** Gen Elec Res & Develop Ctr, PO Box 8, Schenectady, NY 12301.

LAY, STEVEN R, MATHEMATICS. **Personal Data:** b Los Angeles, Calif, November 28, 1944. **Education:** Aurora Col, BA, 1966; Univ Calif, Los Angeles, MA, 1968, PhD (math), 1971. **Professional Experience:** CONSULT, 1990-; prof math, Aurora Univ, 1980-1990; Assoc prof, Aurora Univ, 1971-1980. **Memberships:** Am Math Soc; Math Asn Am; Nat Coun Teachers Math. **Research Statement & Publications:** Combinatorial geometry and convexity; the separation of convex sets; mathematics education. **Mailing Address:** 80-1517 Tenjin Cho, Ono Shi 675-13, Japan.

LAY, THORNE, SEISMOLOGY. **Personal Data:** b Casper, Wyo, April 20, 1956; m 1993, Susan; c Griffin Reedlay. **Education:** Univ Rochester, BS, 1978; Calif Inst Technol, MS, 1980, PhD (geophys), 1983. **Honors & Awards:** Macelwane Medal, Am Geophys Union, 1991; Plaque of Appreciation, Air Force Technical App Ctr, 1997; Citation for Excellence in Referring, Am Geophys Union. **Professional Experience:** DIR INST GEOPHYSICS AND PLANETARY PHYSICS, 2000-; chmn, earth sci dept, 1994-2000; mem, comt seismol, nat res coun, 1992-1999; chmn, Panel CTBT Res, 1995-1997; chmn, Panel Seismic Data Requirements, 1994-1995; mem, Comt Seismol, Nat Res Coun, 1992-1999; dir, Inst Tectronics, 1990-1994; Defense Advan Res Projs Agency Proposal Rev Panel, 1991 & NSF Geophys Panel, 1990-1993; chmn, SEDI Comt, US Am Geophys Union, 1990-1992; PROF SEISMOL, UNIV CALIF, SANTA CRUZ, 1989-; ed, EOS, Am Geophys Union, 1989-1991; panelist, Air Force Geophys Lab Panel, 1988-1992; panelist, US Geol Surv Rev Panel, 1988-1990; panelist, Air Force Tech Appln Ctr Panel, 1987-; dir, Seismog Sta, 1987-1989; presidential young investr, NSF, 1985-1990; Shell fac fel, Shell Found, 1985-1988; Sloan Found fel, 1985-1987; from asst prof to assoc prof seismol, Univ Mich, 1984-1989; researcher, Calif Inst Technol, 1983; NSF Graduate fel, 1978-1981. **Memberships:** Seismol Soc Am; fel Am Geophys Union; fel Royal Astron Soc; AAAS; Soc Explor Geophysicists; Am Asn Prof Geologists. **Research Statement & Publications:** Earthquake seismology; structure of the earths interior; author of over 170 papers in professional journals and books. **Mailing Address:** Earth Sci Dept, Univ Calif Santa Cruz, Santa Cruz, CA 95064. **Fax:** 831-459-3074. **E-Mail:** tlay@es.ucsc.edu

LAYCHOCK, SUZANNE GALE, PHOSPHOLIPIDS, CYCLIC NUCLEOTIDES & INSULIN. **Personal Data:** b Brooklyn, NY, April 28, 1949. **Education:** Brooklyn Col, BS, 1971; City Univ NY, MA, 1973; Med Col Va, PhD (pharmacol), 1976. **Professional Experience:** PROF PHARMACOL, STATE UNIV NY, BUFFALO, 1989-; from asst prof to assoc prof, Med Col Va, 1978-1989; res assoc pharmacol, Vanderbilt Univ, 1977-1978. **Memberships:** Endocrine Soc; Am Soc Pharmacol & Exp Therapeut; Am Diabetes Asn. **Research Statement & Publications:** Investigation of the signal transduction mechanisms which regulate insulin secretion from islets of Langerhans; role of phospholipid turnover, cyclic nucleotides, eicosanoids and calcium in regulation of metabolism and insulin release in the beta cell. **Mailing Address:** Dept Pharmacol, Sch Med, State Univ NY, 102 Farber Hall, Buffalo, NY 14214-3000. **Fax:** 716-829-2801. **E-Mail:** laychock@acsu.buffalo.edu

LAYCOCK, MAURICE VIVIAN, NATURAL PRODUCTS, MARINE ALGAE. **Personal Data:** b Liverpool, Eng, September 3, 1938. **Education:** Liverpool Univ, BSc, 1962, PhD (plant physiol), 1965. **Professional Experience:** RETIRED; res officer biochem, Nat Res Coun Can, 1968-1996. **Research Statement & Publications:** Protein chemistry; biochemistry of nitrogen compounds in algae; chemistry of marine toxins. **Mailing Address:** Nat Res Coun, 1411 Oxford St, Halifax, NS B3H 3Z1, Can. **Fax:** 902-426-9413. **E-Mail:** maurice@imb.lan.nrc.ca

LAYCOCK, WILLIAM ANTHONY, PLANT ECOLOGY. **Personal Data:** b Ft Collins, Colo, March 17, 1930. **Education:** Univ Wyo, BS, 1952, MS, 1953; Rutgers Univ, PhD (bot), 1958. **Honors & Awards:** Outstanding Achievement Award, Soc Range Mgt, 1985, Renner Award, 1993. **Professional Experience:** Consult, continuing comt, Int Rangeland Cong, 1996-; PROF EMER, RANGELAND ECOL & WATERSHED MGT, UNIV WYO, 1996-; mem, continuing comt, Int Rangeland Cong, 1991-1999; head, Dept Range Mgt, 1985-1996; range scientist, Agr Res Serv, USDA, 1976-1985; affil fac, Colo State Univ, 1974-; asst dir, Rocky Mountain Forest Range Exp Sta, US Forest Serv, 1974-1976; coordr site dir western coniferous biomed, US Int Biol Prog, 1971-1972; NZ Nat Res Adv Coun-NZ Forest Serv sr res fel, 1969-1970; Collabr range sci, Utah State Univ, 1964-1974; range scientist, Intermountain Forest & Range Exp Sta, 1958-1974; Asst, Rutgers Univ, 1955-1958. **Memberships:** Ecol Soc Am; fel Soc Range Mgt (pres 1988). **Research Statement & Publications:** Ecology and management of rangelands; autecology of range species; snow management on rangelands. **Mailing Address:** Dept Range Mgt, PO Box 3354, Laramie, WY 82071. **E-Mail:** blaycock@uwyo.edu

LAYDEN, GEORGE KAVANAUGH, MATERIALS SCIENCE. **Personal Data:** b Greenport, NY, April 13, 1929. **Education:** Lafayette Col, BS, 1953; Pa State Univ, MS, 1959, PhD (ceramic technol), 1961. **Professional Experience:** RETIRED; mat scientist, Unitet Technol Res Ctr, 1961-. **Memberships:** Am Ceramic Soc; AAAS; Sigma Xi. **Research Statement & Publications:** Fabrication and characterization ofaerospace materials, including fibrilar carbon and graphite, structrual ceramics, nickel based superalloys and fiber and whisker reinforced glass/ceramic matrix composites. **Mailing Address:** 1071 Farmington Ave, West Hartford, CT 06107.

LAYE, RONALD CURTIS, CLINICAL HEALTH PSYCHOLOGY, APPLIED PSYCHOPHYSIOLOGY. **Personal Data:** b New York, NY, November 27, 1945; m 1967, Estarisa; c Aviva, Basya, Shira, Devora & Aaron. **Education:** Clarkson Col Technol, BS, 1967; Univ Alta, MSc, 1973, PhD (psychol), 1976. **Honors & Awards:** Outstanding Paper Award, Asn appl psycolophysiol & Biofeedback, 1996; Registered Psycologist; British Columbia 508 Ceritified in biofeedback. **Professional Experience:** PROF, PSYCHOL DEPT, UNIV COL FRASER VALLEY, 1977-; dept head, Psychol Dept, Univ Col Fraser Valley, 1988-1990; pvt pract, Clin Pyschol, 1982-2002; consult Clin Psychologist, Chilliwack Mental Health Ctr, 1979-1993; vis asst prof, State Univ NY Oswego, 1976-1977; psychol Instr, Univ Alta, 1973-1976; Clin psychologist, Univ Alta Hosp, 1973-1976. **Memberships:** Asn Appl Psychophysiol & Biofeedback; Can Psychol Asn Bristish Columbia Psychological Assoc. **Research Statement & Publications:** Psychophysiol and health impact of television; psychophysiol and personality variables in stress reactions; psychophysiol assessment. **Mailing Address:** Dept Psychol, Univ Col Fraser Valley, 33844 King Rd, Abbotsford, BC V2S 7M9, Can. **Fax:** 604-855-7558. **E-Mail:** laye@ucfv.bc.ca

LAYER, ROBERT WESLEY, ORGANIC CHEMISTRY. **Personal Data:** b Brooklyn, NY, August 11, 1928; wid Barabara A Nelson; c Steven R, David N & Caren S. **Education:** NY Univ, AB, 1950; Univ Cincinnati, PhD, 1955. **Honors & Awards:** Melvin Mooney Award, Rubber Div, Am Chem Soc, 1992. **Professional Experience:** Consult, BF Goodwrench, 1994-; RES FEL, B F GOODRICH CO, 1990-; sr res assoc, B F Goodrich Co, 1979-1990; res assoc, B F Goodrich Co, 1971-1979; sr res chemist, B F Goodrich Co, 1957-1971; sr tech mgr, B F Goodrich Co, 1955-1957; Control chemist, Naugatuck Chem Co, 1950-1952. **Memberships:** Am Chem Soc; Rubber & Polymer Divs, Akron Rubber Group. **Research Statement & Publications:** Rubber chemicals; reactions of ozone; chemistry of p-phenylenediamines and of anils; antioxidants; accelerators. **Mailing Address:** 4621 A Cox Dr, Stow, OH 44224.

LAYLOFF, THOMAS, ANALYTICAL CHEMISTRY. **Personal Data:** b Granite City, Ill, January 29, 1937. **Education:** Wash Univ, BA, 1958, MS, 1961; Univ Kans, PhD (analytical chem), 1964. **Professional Experience:** QUAL ASSURANCE MGR, SUPPLY CHAIN MGT SYST, PRESIDENT'S EMERGENCY PLAN AIDS RELIEF, as of 2005; PRIN PROG ASSOC, CTR PHARMACEUT MGT, MGT SCI HEALTH, as of 2005; dir, div drug analysis, Food & Drug Admin, beginning 1976; adj prof chef, St Louis Univ, 1976-; sci adv, Nat Ctr Drug Analysis, Food & Drug Admin, 1967-1976; From asst prof to prof, Div Drug Analysis, Food & Drug Admin, 1964-1976; vpres & dir, Pharmaceutl Stand Div, US Pharmacopeia. **Memberships:** AAAS; Sigma Xi; Am Chem Soc; Asn Off Anal Chem; fel Am Asn Pharmaceut Scientists. **Research Statement & Publications:** Data acquisition and processing; chemometrics. **Mailing Address:** Ctr Pharmaceut Mgt, Mgt Sci Health, 165 Allandale Rd, Boston, MA 02130. **Fax:** 617-524-2825. **E-Mail:** tom@layloff.net

LAYMAN, DALE PIERRE, MEDICAL & BIOLOGICAL SCIENCES TERMINOLOGY, COMPUTER-LIKE MODES OF HUMAN THINKING. **Personal Data:** b Niles, Mich, July 3, 1948; m 1970, Kathleen; c Andrew, Alexis, Allison & Amanda. **Education:** Univ Mich, BS, 1971, MS, 1974; Ball State Univ, EDs, 1979, Univ Ill, PhD (health & safety studies), 1986. **Professional Experience:** PROF HUMAN ANAT & PHYSIOL & MED TERMINOLOGY, JOLIET JR COL, 1975-; prof anat & physiol, Lake Super State Univ, 1974-1975; pres & founder, Robowatch. **Memberships:** Human Anat Physiol Soc; corp mem Text & Acad Authors Asn; corp mem Soc Leading Intellectuals World; London Diplomatic Acad; Sci Fac Int Ctr. **Research Statement & Publications:** Author of books in biology, human anatomy, physiology, and medical terminology; research in epidemiology of running injuries; research and authoring in biological order, disorder; founder of Robowatch. **Mailing Address:** 509 Westridge Lane, Joliet, IL 60431. **E-Mail:** drdlayman@aol.com, drdale@robowatch.org

LAYMAN, DON LEE, ANATOMY. **Personal Data:** b Johnston, Pa, May 20, 1938. **Education:** Juniata Col, BS, 1961; Syracuse Univ, MS, 1965; George Wash Univ, PhD (cell biol), 1970. **Professional Experience:** ASSOC PROF, DEPT ANAT, MED CTR, LA STATE UNIV, as of 2003; asst prof, Dept Med, Ore Health Sci Univ, Dept Anat, 1977-1984; asst prof, Dept Med, Ore Health Sci Univ, 1975-1977; res asst prof, Dept Path, Baylor Col Med, 1973-1975; Spec fel, NIH, 1971-1973; NIH spec fel, Dept Path, Univ Wash, Seattle, 1971-1973; res chemist, Lab Biochem, Nat Inst Dent Res, 1970-1971; biologist, Nat Eye Inst & Nat Inst Dent Res, 1968-1970. **Memberships:** Sigma Xi; Am Soc Cell Biol; NY Acad Sci; AAAS; Tissue Cult Asn; Am Asn Dent Res. **Research Statement & Publications:** Periodontitis. **Mailing Address:** Dept Anat & Cell Biol, La State Univ Med Ctr 1100 Fla Ave, New Orleans, LA 70119-2714. **Fax:** 504-619-8741. **E-Mail:** dlayma@lsusd.lsuhsc.edu

LAYMAN, DONALD KEITH, HUMAN NUTRITION, SPORTS NUTRITION. **Personal Data:** b Kewanee, Ill, February 15, 1950; m Jerelyn; c 2. **Education:** Ill State Univ, BS, 1972, MS, 1974; Univ Minn, PhD (nutrition), 1978. **Honors & Awards:** Young Investr Award, NIH, 1982, Shannon Award, 1992; Bio Serv Award, Am Inst Nutrit, 1986. **Professional Experience:** PROF NUTRIT, UNIV ILL, 1989-; bd, Human Sci, 1998-2001; assoc dean, Col Agr, Consumer & Environ Sci, Univ Ill, 1995-1999; dir, Sch Human Res & Family Studies, Univ Ill, 1991-1995; chair, Div Food & Nutrit, Univ Ill, 1990-1991; adj prof, Inst Agron & Vet, Rabat, Morroco, 1986-1990; consult, Shriner's Hosp Barred Children, 1986; consult, Nat Aeronaut & Space Admin, 1983; consult, nutrition, Regional Office Educ, Ill, 1979-1980; from asst prof to assoc prof, Univ Ill, 1978-1989. **Memberships:** Am Soc Nutrit Sci. **Research Statement & Publications:** Regulation of protein turnover and energy metabolism in skeletal muscle; amino acid metabolism in skeletal muscle and its role in adult health, obesity, diabetes and athletic performance. **Mailing Address:** Dept Food Sci & Human Nutrit, Univ Ill, 437 Bevier Hall, Urbana, IL 61801. **E-Mail:** dlayman@uiuc.edu

LAYMAN, WILBUR A, ANALYTICAL CHEMISTRY, PHYSICAL CHEMISTRY. **Personal Data:** b Blair, Nebr, January 9, 1929; m 1953, Alice Schultz; c Mike, Karen, Judi, Gregg & Rodney. **Education:** Dana Col, BS, 1953; Univ Nebr, MS, 1958; Mont State Univ, PhD (analytical chem), 1963. **Professional Experience:** RETIRED; prof chem & chmn, Phys Sci Dept, Easternmont Col, 1967-1982; assoc prof, Adams State Col, 1966-1967; asst prof, SDak State Univ, 1963-1966; instr chem, Hastings Col, 1958-1960 & Dana Col, 1962-1963; Chemist, Harris Labs, 1954-1958. **Memberships:** Am Chem Soc. **Research Statement & Publications:** Stability constants of metal complexes; polarized infrared spectroscopy of thin crystal films. **Mailing Address:** 619 Ave C, Billings, MT 59102.

LAYNE, CLYDE BROWNING, APPLIED PHYSICS. **Personal Data:** b El Paso, Tex, February 19, 1947. **Education:** Princeton Univ, AB, 1969; Univ Calif, Davis, MS, 1973, PhD (appl sci), 1975. **Professional Experience:** INITIATIVE MGR, INT SECURITY, SANDIA NAT LAB, as of 2002; TECH STAFF, COMBUSTION PHYSICS DIV, SANDIA NAT LAB, LIVERMORE, CALIF, 1980-; physicist, Div Laser Physics, Lawrence Livermore Lab, Univ Calif, 1969-1980. **Memberships:** Am Phys Soc; Optical Soc Am. **Research Statement & Publications:** Relaxation and energy transfer in ions in solids; atomic vapor-laser isotope separation of uranium; lasersapplied to combustion diagnostics. **Mailing Address:** Sandia Nat Labs, PO Box 5800 MS-1230, Albuquerque, NM 87185.

LAYNE, DONALD SAINTEVAL, BIOCHEMISTRY. **Personal Data:** b Lime Ridge, Que, April 5, 1931. **Education:** McGill Univ, BSc, 1953, MSc, 1955, PhD, 1957. **Professional Experience:** CHMN, SCIENTIFIC ADV BD, PHEROMONE SCI CORP, as of 2006; vpres, Toronto Gen Hosp, beginning 1982; vpres, Connaught Lab, Ltd, 1979-1982; prof biochem, Univ Ottawa, 1968-1979; head Physiol & Endocrinol Sect, Food & Drug Directorate, Can, 1966-1968; from scientist to sr scientist, Worcester Found Exp Biol, 1959-1966; res assoc psychiat, Queen's Univ Ont, 1958-1959; Fel biochem, Univ Edinburgh, 1957-1958. **Memberships:** AAAS; Endocrine Soc; Am Soc Biol Chemists; Royal Soc Can. **Research Statement & Publications:** Biochemistry of estrogenic hormones. **Mailing Address:** Pheromone Sci Corp, 443 King St E, Toronto, ON M5A 1L5, Can.

LAYNE, JAMES NATHANIEL, MAMMALOGY, VERTEBRATE BIOLOGY. **Personal Data:** b Chicago, Ill, May 16, 1926; m 1950, Lois; c Linda C, Kimberly, Jamie, Susan & Rachel. **Education:** Cornell Univ, BA, 1950, PhD (zoology), 1954. **Honors & Awards:** C Hart Merriam Award, Am Soc Mammalogists, 1976; Medalist Fla Acad of Sci, 1995. **Professional Experience:** EMER SR RES BIOLOGIST, ARCHBOLD BIOL STA, 1994-; sr res biologist, Archbold Biol Sta & Archbold Cur Dept Mammal & mem bd dir, Archbold Expeds, Am MusNatural Hist, 1985-1993; res assoc, Am Mus Natural Hist, 1982-1990; exec dir & mem bd dirs, Archbold Biol Sta & Archbold Cur Dept Mammal & mem bd dir, Archbold Expeds, Am MusNatural Hist, 1976-1985; consult, WHO, 1969; adj prof, Univ SFla, 1968-1989; res dir, Archbold Biol Sta & Archbold Cur Dept Mammal & mem bd dir, Archbold Expeds, Am MusNatural Hist, 1967-1976; asst prof zool, Cornell Univ, 1963-1967; assoc prog zool, Cornell Univ, 1963-1967; res assoc, Fla State Mus, 1963-1965; Vis scientist, Pvt Ecol Sect, Lab Perinatat Physiol, NINDB, 1961-1962; from asst prof to assoc prof biol, Univ Fla, 1955-1963; from asst cur to assoc cur biol sci, Fla State Mus, 1955-1963; asst prof zool, Southern Ill Univ, 1954-1955; Asst vert zool, Cornell Univ,

1950-1954; res assoc, Fla State Collection Arthropods. **Memberships:** Fel AAAS; Am Soc Zoologists; hon mem Am Soc Mammalogists (vpres, 1965-1970, pres, 1970-1972); Wildlife Soc; Ecol Soc Am; Orgn Biol Field Stas (vpres, 1984-1985, pres, 1986-1987). **Research Statement & Publications:** Mammalian ecology, systematics, behavior and morphology; general vertebrate biology and ecology of Florida. **Mailing Address:** Archbold Biol Sta, PO Box 2057, Lake Placid, FL 33856. **Fax:** 863-699-1927. **E-Mail:** jlayne@strato.net

LAYNE, PORTER PRESTON, BIOCHEMISTRY. **Personal Data:** b Martin, Ky, September 20, 1945. **Education:** Univ Ky, BS, 1966, PhD (biochem), 1971; Boston Univ, MBA, 1978. **Professional Experience:** DIR REGULATORY AFFAIRS, SMITH KLINE CORP, 1986-; dir, Preregis Affairs, 1985-1986; assoc dir clin info, Preregis Affairs, 1985; asst dir, Preregis Affairs, 1983-1984; SR INVESTR DEVELOP, SMITH KLINE CORP, 1982-; asst dir clin data sci, Smith Kline Corp, 1982-1983; assoc investr develop, Smith Kline Corp, 1980-1981; Actg chmn, Div Chem, Sch Med, Tufts Univ, 1975-1976; asst prof, Sch Med, Tufts Univ, 1974-1980; Fel protein chem, Sch Med, Tufts Univ, 1971-1973. **Memberships:** Sigma Xi; Drug Info Asn; Regulatory Affairs Prof Soc. **Research Statement & Publications:** Extra chromosomal inheritance; bacterial physiology; enzyme mechanism (phosphoglucomutase); adenylate cyclase and tuftsin research. **Mailing Address:** RR 4, Pottstown, PA 19465-9804.

LAYNE, RICHARD C, PLANT BREEDING. **Personal Data:** b St Vincent and the Grenadines, West Indies, December 14, 1936; m 1963, c 2. **Education:** McGill Univ, B.Sc. (Agriculture) 1959; Univ Wisconsin, M.S.(Agronomy, Plant Pathology)1960; Univ Wisconsin, Ph.D. (Agronomy, Plant Pathology) 1963. **Honors & Awards:** Shepard Award, Am Pomol Soc, 1967 & 1983, Wilder Medal, Am Pomol Soc 1996; Carrol R Miller Award, Am Soc Hort Sci, 1977, 1978, 1982, 1985; Outstanding Researcher Award, Am Soc Hort Sci, 1993; HonLife Member, Can Soc Hort Sci, 1996. **Professional Experience:** "RETIRED"; int consult hort, 1996-; Res scientist, Res Sta, Agriculture Canada 1963-1996; Head, Hort Sci Sect, Harrow Res Sta. 1990-1996. **Memberships:** Canadian Soc Hort Sci (Honorary Life Member 1996-). **Research Statement & Publications:** Breeding cultivars and rootstocks of peach, nectarine, apricot and pear for cold hardiness and disease resistance; environmental and genetic factors affecting cold hardiness; rootstock-scion physiology; orchard management. **Mailing Address:** PO Box 132, Harrow, ON N0R 1G0, Can. **E-Mail:** layne@mnsi.net

LAYSON, WILLIAM M(CINTYRE), PHYSICS, MECHANICAL ENGINEERING. **Personal Data:** b Lexington, Ky, September 24, 1934; m 1967, c 2. **Education:** Mass Inst Technol, BS, 1956, PhD (physics), 1963. **Professional Experience:** DIR, WOLF TRAP FOUND, as of 2004; vpres, Continuum Mech Div, Sci Appln Inc, beginning 1976; vpres & mgr, Wash Div, 1970-1976; mgr dept, Gen Res Corp, 1969-1970; mem tech staff, Gen Res Corp, 1967-1969; sr systs engr tech staff, Pan Am World Airways, 1964-1967; lectr physics, Univ Calif, 1963-1964; Res physicist, Univ Calif, 1962-1963. **Memberships:** Am Phys Soc; Am Inst Aeronaut & Astronaut; Inst Elec & Electronics Engrs. **Research Statement & Publications:** Nuclear weapons effects; dust and debris clouds; radiation transport; ground coupling; fireball effects; radar systems; fluid mechanics; electromagnetic propagation; atmospheric physics; systems analysis. **Mailing Address:** Wolf Trap Found, 1645 Trap Rd, Vienna, VA 22182.

LAYTON, DAVID WARREN, RISK ANALYSIS, WATER RESOURCES. **Personal Data:** b Woburn, Mass, September 19, 1948; m 1977, c 3. **Education:** Bridgewater State Col, BA, 1970; Univ Ariz, PhD (water resources admin), 1975. **Professional Experience:** SR ENVIRON SCIENTIST RISK ANAL WATER RESOURCES & ENERGY, LAWRENCE LIVERMORE NAT LAB, as of 2002. **Memberships:** Am Water Resources Asn; Soc Risk Analysis. **Research Statement & Publications:** Risk analysis; environmental studies; pollution control technologies; geothermal energy. **Mailing Address:** Lawrence Livermore Nat Lab, Livermore, CA 94550. **E-Mail:** layton1@llnl.gov

LAYTON, EDWIN THOMAS, JR, HISTORY OF TECHNOLOGY. **Personal Data:** b September 13, 1928. **Education:** Univ Calif, Los Angeles, BA, 1950, MA, 1953, PhD (hist), 1956. **Honors & Awards:** Dexter Prize, Soc Hist Technol, 1970, Leonardo da Vinci Medal, 1990. **Professional Experience:** PROF EMER HIST SCI & TECHNOL, UNIV MINN, as of 2003; Adv ed, Bus & Prof Ethics J, 1981-; mem, Nuclear Manpower Studies Comn, Nat Acad Sci-Nat Res Coun, 1981; Adv ed, Isis, 1979-1981; prof hist sci & technol, Univ Minn, beginning 1975; assoc prof hist sci & technol, Case Western Res Univ, 1965-1975; asst prof, Purdue Univ, 1960-1965; Instr hist, Ohio State Univ, 1957-1960; Instr hist, Univ Wis, 1956-1957. **Memberships:** Soc Hist Technol (pres 1985-1986); Hist Sci Soc; fel AAAS; Soc Social Studies Sci. **Research Statement & Publications:** Interaction of science and technology in nineteenth century America; nature and role engineering sciences; history of engineering. **Mailing Address:** 2816 Webster Ave SE, Minneapolis, MN 55416.

LAYTON, HAROLD, MATHEMATICS & BIOLOGY. **Education:** Asbury Col, AB, 1979; Univ KY, MS, 1980; Duke Univ, phD (math), 1986. **Professional Experience:** PROF, DEPT MATH, DUKE UNIV, 2001-; dir, Undergrad Studies, Dept Math, Duke Univ, 1995-1998; from asst prof to assoc prof, Dept Math, Duke Univ, 1988-2001; fel, Courant Inst math Sci, NY Univm 1986-1988. **Memberships:** Am Physiol Soc; Am Soc Nephrology; Soc Indust & Appl Math; Soc Math Biol. **Research Statement & Publications:** Mathematical physiology. **Mailing Address:** Dept Math, Duke Univ, POBox 90320, Durham, NC 27708. **E-Mail:** layton@math.duke.edu

LAYTON, JACK MALCOLM, PATHOLOGY. **Personal Data:** b Ossian, Iowa, September 27, 1917. **Education:** Luther Col, AB, 1939, DSc, 1974; Univ Iowa, MD, 1943; Am Bd Path, dipl, 1950. **Professional Experience:** RETIRED; trustee, Am Bd Path, 1974-; Actg dean, Col Med & actg dir, Med Ctr, Univ Ariz, 1971-1973; prof path & head dept, Col Med, Univ Ariz, 1967-1988; dir clin path, Ariz Health Serv, 1967-1988; from asst prof to prof, Univ Iowa Hosp, 1950-1967; assoc, Univ Iowa Hosp, 1949-1950; instr, Univ Iowa Hosp, 1947-1949; asst path, Univ Iowa Hosp, 1946-1947; Intern, Univ Iowa Hosp, 1943. **Memberships:** Am Soc Clin Path (pres, 1973); Col Am Path; Am Asn Path & Bact; Am Soc Exp Path; Int Acad Path (pres, 1975-1976); Sigma Xi. **Research Statement & Publications:** Virology; host-parasite relationships in viral and rickettsial diseases; comparative pathology of inflammation; ultramicroscopic pathologic anatomy of infectious diseases; biological activities of teratomas; influenza and psittacosis-lymphogranuloma groups of viruses. **Mailing Address:** 5815 N Placita Del Baron, Tucson, AZ 85718.

LAYTON, RICHARD GARY, PHYSICS, CLOUD PHYSICS. **Personal Data:** b Salt Lake City, Utah, December 24, 1935; m 1963, Susan; c Catherine, Paul & Spencer. **Education:** Univ Utah, BA, 1960, MA, 1962; Utah State Univ, PhD (physics), 1965. **Professional Experience:** PROF EMER PHYSICS, NORTHERN ARIZ UNIV, 1999-; chair, Physics Dept, Northern Ariz Univ, 1986-1992; chair, Dept Physics & Astron, 1985-1992; interim chair, Physics Dept, Northern Ariz Univ, 1985-1986; prof phys, Northern Arizona univ, 1983-; sci collabr, Grand Canyon Nat Park, 1972-1975; res assoc, Lowell Observ, 1972 & 1971; assoc prof, Northern Ariz Univ, 1969-1983; from asst prof to assoc prof physics, State Univ NY Col, Fredonia, 1965-1969; asst res physicist electro-dynamics Labs, Utah State Univ, 1963-1964; asst physics, Univ Utah, 1960-1962. **Memberships:** Am Asn Physics Teachers; Am Phys Soc; Sigma Xi. **Research Statement & Publications:** Ice nucleation surfaces, ellipsometry; atmospheric optics; frost damage prevention for plants; science education. **Mailing Address:** Dept Physics, Northern Ariz Univ, Box 6010, Flagstaff, AZ 86011-6010. **Fax:** 520-523-1371. **E-Mail:** gary.layton@nau.edu

LAYTON, TERRY NORTH, MEDICAL PRODUCT DESIGN & MEDICAL TECHNOLOGY ASSESSMENT, GMP & REGULATORY REQUIREMENTS FOR MEDICAL PRODUCTS. **Personal Data:** m 1969, c 2. **Education:** Univ Wyo, BS, 1966; Univ Ill, MS, 1972; Univ Va, PhD (biomed eng), 1975. **Professional Experience:** Technical Officer, Laytech, Inc-.BUS DEVELOP & REGULATORY TECHNOLOGIST, BIOMED ACOUSTICS RES CO, 2001-; Adj Prof, Dept BIOENGINEERING, Univ Ill, 2000-; ASSOC BIOMED ENG, PACKER ENG, 2000-; CHIEF TECH OFFICER, LAYTECH, INC, 1999-; dir biomed eng, Packer Eng, 1991-1994; chief tech officer, Laytech, 1990-1991; mgr, Baxter, 1988-1990; mgr, Kendall Co, 1980-1988; sect head, Kendall Co, 1978-1980; sr res engr, Kendall Co, 1976-1978; Res engr, Kendall Co, 1975-1976. **Memberships:** Inst Elec & Electronics Engrs; Plastics Eng; Urodynamics Soc. **Research Statement & Publications:** Design and commercialization of medical products, with expertise in new technologies, design, engineering and manufacturing in the areas of anesthesia, cathetic, intravenous products and urology. **Mailing Address:** Laytech, Inc, 1771 RFD Andrew Court, Long Grove, IL 60047. **Fax:** 847-438-3678. **E-Mail:** tlayton71@aol.com

LAYTON, THOMAS WILLIAM, PHYSICS. **Personal Data:** b Kaysville, Utah, February 24, 1927. **Education:** Calif Inst Technol, BS, 1951, PhD (physics, math), 1957. **Professional Experience:** RETIRED; consult, Defense & Space Systs Group, 1991-1997; sr staff engr, Defense & Space Systs Group, 1964-1991; mgr, Inertial Guid Dept, Thompson-Ramo-Wooldridge Inc, 1959-1964; mem tech staff, Inertial Guid Dept, Thompson-Ramo-Wooldridge Inc, 1955-1959; res engr, Jet Propulsion Lab, Calif Inst Technol, 1953-1955. **Memberships:** Am Phys Soc; Am Inst Aeronaut & Astronaut. **Research Statement & Publications:** Cosmic rays; navigation and guidance systems for ballisticmissiles and space flight vehicles. **Mailing Address:** 4836 W Elmdale Dr, Rolling Hills, CA 90274. **Fax:** 310-378-1692.

LAYZER, ARTHUR JAMES, THEORETICAL PHYSICS. **Personal Data:** b Cleveland, Ohio, August 21, 1927. **Education:** Case Western Res Univ, BS, 1950; Columbia Univ, PhD (physics), 1960. **Professional Experience:** ASSOC PROF EMER PHYSICS & ENG PHTSICS, STEVENS INST TECHNOL, as of 2003; US Dept Educ grant deafness res & reading, 1978-1980; assoc prof eng physics, Stevens Inst Technol, beginning 1977; assoc prof physics, Stevens Inst Technol, beginning 1968; resident visitor comput music, Acoust Div, Bell Labs, 1967-1983; vis res scientist, Brookhaven Nat Lab, 1966; asst prof, Stevens Inst Technol, 1964-1967; res scientist, Courant Inst, NY Univ, 1960-1963. **Memberships:** AAAS; Am Educ Res Asn. **Research Statement & Publications:** Quantum mechanical theory of critical phenomena, especially superconductivity; sound-analogic text representations in deafness and language; score-mediated generation of music and text; test measures and analysis in reading and writing; language and art media applications of computer science. **Mailing Address:** 161 W 75th St Apt 5E, New York, NY 10023.

LAYZER, DAVID, ASTRONOMY. **Personal Data:** b Ohio, December 31, 1925; m 1959, c 6. **Education:** Harvard Univ, AB, 1947, PhD (theoret astrophys), 1950. **Honors & Awards:** Bok Prize, 1960. **Professional Experience:** DONALD H MENZEL PROF EMER ASTROPHYS, HARVARD UNIV, as of 2003; donald h menzel prof astrophys, Harvard Univ, beginning 1980; prof astron, Harvard Univ, 1960-1980; consult, Geophys Corp Am, 1959-1965; res fel & lectr, Harvard Univ, 1955-1960; res assoc, Harvard Univ, 1953-1955; res assoc physics, Princeton Univ, 1952-1953; lectr astron, Univ Calif, Berkeley, 1951-1952; Nat Res Coun res fel, 1950-1951. **Memberships:** Am Acad Arts & Sci; Am Astron Soc; Int Astron Union; Royal Astron Soc. **Research Statement & Publications:** Cosmology and cosmogony; theoretical astrophysics and atomic physics; ionospheric physics. **Mailing Address:** Dept Astron, Harvard Univ, Observ 60 Gordon St MS 16, Cambridge, MA 02138-3800. **E-Mail:** layzer@fas.harvard.edu

LAZAR, ANNA, METHOD DEVELOPMENT FOR DETECTING DIETHYLSTILBESTROL RESIDUES IN TISSUES, LIQUID CHROMATOGRAPHIC METHOD DEVELOPMENT FOR THE ANALYSIS OF INSULIN. **Personal Data:** b Budapest, Hungary, January 10, 1931. **Education:** Eotros Lorand Sci Univ, Budapest, Dipl, 1955. **Professional Experience:** RETIRED; chemist, Food & Drug Admin, beginning 1970; Hercules Inc, 1964-1969 & Cancer Res Inst, 1969-1970; Chemist, Stanford Univ, 1962-1963; chemist, Wilkens Instr & Res, 1961-1962; chemist, Arthur D Little, 1959-1961; chemist, Harvard Univ, 1957-1959. **Research Statement & Publications:** Analytical method development for the determination and identification of protein hormones, monoclonal antibody purity assessment, and measurements of a variety of pharmaceutical residues in a number of different matrices; analytical method evaluation of new drug applications. **Mailing Address:** 428 Montgomery Ave, Haverford, PA 19041.

LAZAR, NORMAN HENRY, PLASMA & NUCLEAR PHYSICS. **Personal Data:** b Brooklyn, NY, June 21, 1929. **Education:** City Col NY, BS, 1949; Ind Univ, MS, 1951, PhD (physics), 1953. **Professional Experience:** RETIRED; TRW Defense & Space Syst, 1978-1993; physicist, Oak Ridge Nat Lab, Union Carbide Nuclear Co, 1953-1978. **Memberships:** Fel Am Phys Soc; fel AAAS. **Research Statement & Publications:** Controlled thermonuclear reactions; beta and gamma ray spectroscopy; plasma physics. **Mailing Address:** 38194 S Golf Course Dr, Tucson, AZ 85739. **E-Mail:** nlazar@juno.com

LAZARCHICK, JOHN, HEMATOLOGY & HEMOSTASIS. **Personal Data:** b Pottsville, Pa, November 1, 1942; m 1960, c John J. **Education:** Lafayette Col, AB, 1964; Thomas Jefferson Med Univ, MD, 1968. **Professional Experience:** PROF PATHOL, MED UNIV SC, as of 2004; DIR HEMAT & HEMATPATHOL FEL PGM, MED UNIV SC, as of 2004; assoc prof hemat, Med Univ Sc, beginning 1982; asst prof, Med Univ SC, 1979-1982; asst prof hemat, Health Ctr, Univ Conn, 1977-1979. **Memberships:** Am Fedn Clin Res; AAAS; Asn Clin Scientists; World Hemophilia Fedn. **Research Statement & Publications:** Role of protein kinase C in platelet function; release reaction and the pathophysiologic basis of fibronectin elavation in preeclampsia. **Mailing Address:** Dept Pathol & Lab Med, Med Univ SC Med Ctr, PO Box 250908 165 Ashley Ave, Charleston, SC 29425-0001. **Fax:** 843-792-1248. **E-Mail:** lazarj@musc.edu

LAZARETH, OTTO WILLIAM, SPACE NUCLEAR POWER, MAGNETICALLY LEVITATED VEHICLES. **Personal Data:** b Brooklyn, NY, September 16, 1938. **Education:** Wagner Col, BS, 1961; Queens Col, MA, 1968; City Univ NY, PhD (physics), 1973. **Professional Experience:** CHMN, BROOKHAVEN NAT LAB, as of 1996; PHYSICIST, BROOKHAVEN NAT LAB, 1974-; physics assoc, Brookhaven Nat Lab, 1967-1973; res asst physics, Queens Col, 1965-1967. **Memberships:** Am Phys Soc; Am Nuclear Soc. **Research**

Statement & Publications: Nucleonics; radiation damage and effects in solids; modeling physical systems with computers. **Mailing Address:** Brookhaven Nat Lab, Bldg 475B, Upton, NY 11973.

LAZARIDES, ELIAS, PHARMACOLOGY, CELL BIOLOGY. **Personal Data:** b Athens, Greece, May 3, 1950. **Education:** Wesleyen Univ, BS, 1971; Harvard Univ, PhD (biochem), 1975. **Professional Experience:** PRES, CHIEF EXEC OFFICER & DIR, TARGETED MOLECULES CO, as of 2004; exec dir res pharmacol, Merck Res Labs, beginning 1991; from asst prof to prof cell biol, Calif Inst Technol, 1977-1991; Fel cell biol, Univ Colo, Boulder, 1975-1977. **Memberships:** Am Soc Cell Biol; Am Soc Hemat. **Research Statement & Publications:** Pharmacology; cellbiology. **Mailing Address:** Targeted Molecules Co, Suite 318, 3030 Bunker Hill St, San Diego, CA 92109. **Fax:** 858-777-2810.

LAZARIDIS, ANASTAS, ENERGY ENGINEERING, HEAT TRANSFER. **Personal Data:** b Istanbul, Turkey, December 8, 1940. **Education:** Robert Col, Turkey, BS, 1963; Columbia Univ, MS, 1964, DSc (Eng), 1969. **Professional Experience:** RETIRED; prof, Dept Mech Eng, Widener Univ, beginning 1997; fulbright scholar, Democritas Univ, Thrace, Greece, 1997-1998; chmn, dept mech eng, Widener Univ, beginning 1994; US Army, 1985 & USAF, 1988-1990; from asst prof to assoc prof, Dept Mech Eng, Widener Univ, 1983-1997; fac res grants, Am Soc Eng Educ & Dept Energy, 1983; pres, Helios Inc, Wilmington, Del, 1976-1983; regional mkt mgr process control, Control Automation Technol Co, 1975-1976; heat transfer specialist-process eng, Day & Zimmermann Inc, Philadelphia, 1972-1975; adj prof mech eng, Drexel Univ, 1972-1975; textile fibers dept, E I Du Pont Del Nemours & Co Inc, 1969-1972; lectr mech eng, Manhattan Col, 1965-1967 & Richmond Col, City Univ New York, 1967-1968; heat & mass transfer lab, Columbia Univ, 1965-1968; res engr, Exxon Res & Eng Co, 1965; fulbright scholar award, Boese scholar award, 1964-1965; fulbright scholar award, Columbia Univ, 1963-1964; tech paper reviewer, Heat Transfer J & Solar Energy Eng J, Am Soc Mech Engrs, Int J Heat & Mass Transfer, Int J Numerical Heat Transfer. **Memberships:** Am Soc Eng Educ; Am Soc Mech Eng. **Research Statement & Publications:** Energy; heat transfer; thermodynamics of energetic materials; textile engineering; combustion and detonation; mathematical modeling; contributed over 30 articles to professional publications. **Mailing Address:** Dept Mech Eng, Widener Univ, One Univ Pl, Chester, PA 19013. **Fax:** 610-499-4059. **E-Mail:** anastas.lazaridis@widener.edu

LAZARIDIS, CHRISTINA NICHOLSON, MATERIALS SCIENCE, ELECTRONIC MATERIALS. **Personal Data:** b New York, NY, January 12, 1942. **Education:** Mt Holyoke Col, AB, 1962; Columbia Univ, MA, 1963, PhD (chem), 1966. **Professional Experience:** RES ASSOC, E I DU PONT DEL NEMOURS & CO INC, 1968-; res chemist, Colgate-Palmolive Co, 1966-1968. **Memberships:** Am Chem Soc. **Research Statement & Publications:** Photosensitive systems, including conventional silver halide as well as novel photopolymeric materials; thick film materials for electronics, polymeric and cermet systems, membrane touch switch inks, ultraviolet curable products, conductors, dielectrics and resistors for screen-printing applications and photoresists; polyimides and photodefinable polyimides. **Mailing Address:** Electronics Mat, du Pont Co Exp Sta PO Box 80336, Wilmington, DE 19880-0336. **Fax:** 302-695-8196. **E-Mail:** lazaridi@esvax.dnet.dupont.com

LAZARIDIS, NASSOS A(THANASIUS), MECHANICAL METALLURGY, PHYSICAL METALLURGY MATERIALS ENGINEERING, PRODUCT APPLICATION. **Personal Data:** b Athens, Greece, October 6, 1943; American citizen; m 1973, Linda; c Christine & Laura. **Education:** Nat Tech Univ, Athens, BS & MS, 1967; Univ Wis-Madison, MS, 1970, PhD (metall eng), 1971. **Professional Experience:** STAFF CONULT, AUTOMOT PROD APPLIED, 2000-; consult, Automotive Prod Appln, 1994-2000; metall technol mgr, I/N Kote, Joint Venture Inland Steel Co & Nippon Steel Corp, 1989-1994; sect mgr flat prod, Qual Dept, 1987-1988; sect mgr, Mat Eng, Prod Appl Res, 1985-1988; supvr res engr, Res Lab, 1980-1985; spec consult, Sec Steel Refining & Continuous Casting, 1979-1980; adj prof, Purdue Univ, Calumet Campus, 1978-1986; sr res engr, Inland Steel Co, 1975-1979; lectr & proj assoc, Univ Wis-Madison, 1974-1975; proj assoc, Am Motors Corp, 1974-1975; prod engr metal working, Nat Can Corp, Greece, 1973-1974. **Memberships:** Am Soc Metals Int; Greek Tech Chamber Prof Engrs; Sigma Xi; Soc Automotive Engrs. **Research Statement & Publications:** Fracture toughness; fatigue; product development; formability, effect of metallurgy on machinability; hot deformation of steel and other alloys; materialsEngineering; hot dip and electrogalvanizing of sheet steel, product testing, corrosion resistance; applications of sheet steels to automotive design; material selection; automotive materials. **Mailing Address:** 15593 Spring Meadow Lane, Granger, IN 46530-9063. **Fax:** 219-399-6562. **E-Mail:** nassos.laxaridis@ispal.com

LAZARO, ERIC JOSEPH, SURGERY. **Personal Data:** b Muttra, India, December 28, 1921. **Education:** Univ Madras, MBBS, 1946; Georgetown Univ, MS, 1955; Am Bd Surg, dipl, 1955; FRCS(C), 1956. **Professional Experience:** PROF SURG, COL MED & DENT NJ, 1962-; assoc prof, Col Med & Dent NJ, 1962; prof surg, All India Inst Med Sci, 1961-1962; Colombo Plan fel, 1961; prof thoracic surg, All India Inst Med Sci, 1960-1961; assoc prof, All India Inst Med Sci, 1958-1960; Rockefeller Found fels, 1957 & 1962; Instr surg, Georgetown Univ, 1954-1957. **Memberships:** AAAS; fel Am Col Surg; Soc Surg Alimentary Tract; AMA. **Research Statement & Publications:** Pathogenesis of pancreatitis; biologic effects of splenic extracts. **Mailing Address:** Dept Surg, Univ Med Dent, Med Sch, 185 S Orange Ave, Newark, NJ 07103-2757.

LAZAROFF, NORMAN, GEOCHEMICAL ACTIVITIES OF MICROORGANISMS, USING CYANOBACTERIA TO SCREEN FOR NEW ANTIBIOTICS. **Personal Data:** b Brooklyn, NY, November 24, 1927; m Sandra; c Alan & Deborah. **Education:** Syracuse Univ, AB (chem), 1950, MS (microbiol), 1952; Yale Univ, PhD (microbiol), 1960. **Professional Experience:** Fndr & dir, Fdn Microbiol Anal, 1997-; owner, Micronostix, 1993-1997; EMER ASSOC PROF BIOL & RES PROF, STATE UNIV NY BINGHAMTON, 1990-; assoc prof, (Biol. Sciences) 1966-1990; sr res scientist, Res Corp, Syracuse, 1964-1966; asst prof biol sci, Univ Southern Calif, 1962-1964; microbiologist, BC Res Coun, 1961-1962; fel microbiol, Brandeis Univ, 1960-1961; consult, Evans Res & Develop Corp, 1957-1959; proj leader, Evans Res & Develop Corp, 1956-1957; bacteriologist, Schwarz Labs, Inc, 1955-1956; Asst enzymol, Res Found, State Univ NY, 1955. **Memberships:** Am Soc Microbiol; Am Chem Soc; Phycol Soc Am. **Research Statement & Publications:** photophysiology of cyanobacterial differentiation and morphogenesis; antibiotic screening; antiadhesin antibiotics; bio and geochemical role of sulfate in chemolithotrophic iron oxidation and mineral deposition; bacterio-electric leaching. **Mailing Address:** Found for Microbiological Analysis (Micro-Nostix), 312 Front St, Vestal, NY 13850. **Fax:** 607-786-3683. **E-Mail:** micronostix@stny.rr.com

LAZAROW, PAUL B, CELL BIOLOGY, INTRACELLULAR TRANSPORT & ASSEMBLY. **Personal Data:** b May 6, 1945. **Education:** Univ Chicago, AB, 1967; Rockefeller Univ, PhD (biochem cytol), 1972. **Professional Experience:** PROF EMER, DEPT CELL BIOL & ANAT, MT SINAI SCH MED, NY, 2000-; chmn, dept cell biol & anat, Mt Sinai Sch Med, Ny, 1989-2000; adj prof, Rockefeller Univ, NY, NY, beginning 1989; prof, dept cell biol & anat, Mt Sinai Sch Med, Ny, 1989-2000; from asst prof to assoc prof, Rockefeller Univ, New York, NY, 1975-1989; Damon Runyon fel, dept Biol Sci, Stanford Univ, Palo Alto, Calif, 1973-1975; NIH int fel, lab Molecular Embryol, Naples, Italy, 1972-1973. **Memberships:** Harvey Soc Am (secy); Soc Cell Biol; Am Soc Biochem & Molecular Biol; Am Soc Human Genetics Marine Biol Lab Corp. **Research Statement & Publications:** Peroxisome biogenesis in yeast (mutants, genes and the cellular roles of gene products in assembling peroxisomes); inherited human diseases caused by defects in peroxisome function or biogenesis. **Mailing Address:** Dept Cell Biol & Anat, Mt Sinai Sch Med, Fifth Ave & 100th St Box 1007, New York, NY 10029. **Fax:** 212-860-1174. **E-Mail:** paul.lazarow@mssm.edu

LAZARSFELD, ROBERT K, Algebraic geometry. **Education:** Brown Univ, PhD 1980. **Honors & Awards:** Sloan Fellow, 1884, Presidential Young Investigator, 1985 Guggenheim Fellow, 1998 AMS Colloquium Lecturer, 2005. **Professional Experience:** Professor of Mathematics, Univ. of Mich, 1996-pres Professor of Mathematics, UCLA, 1987-1997 Assoc. Prof. of Math., UCLA, 1984-1987. **Mailing Address:** Dept Mathematics, Univ Mivh, Ann Arbor, MI 48109. **Fax:** 734-763-0937. **E-Mail:** rlaz@umich.edu

LAZARTE, JAIME ESTEBAN, HORTICULTURE & DEVELOPMENT PHYSIOLOGY, PROTEIN PRODUCTION & BIOTECHNOLOGY. **Personal Data:** b Lima, Peru, July 26, 1943; American citizen. **Education:** Agrarian Univ, BS & Ing Agr, 1966; Rutgers Univ, MS, 1970, PhD (hort), 1976. **Honors & Awards:** Fullbright Fel, 1990, 1991 & 2001. **Professional Experience:** LECTR, HARVARD MED SCH, 1991-; DIR, PROTEIN PROD & CTR BLOOD RES, 1991-; Diagenics Int, Inc., IRCAD, Strawbourg, France, 2001-2002; fel, Gas Poxycell and Fulbright 1990, 1991 & 2001; vis prof, Davis Pasteur Univ, Strasbourg France, 2000; Dir, Inst Biotechnol, Univ Nat Agraria, La Molina, Peru, 1998; Dir of Res & Development, BRAD, 1997; res, Tex A&M Univ, 1989-1991; pres, PRI, 1983-1988; asst prof, Hort, Tex A&M Univ, 1978-1982; res assoc, Veg Crops, Univ Fla, 1976-1978; lab supvr, Tissue Cult, Rutgers Univ, 1973-1976. **Research Statement & Publications:** Flower initiation and sex expression; sex modification; morphology and embryology horticultural crops; asparagus officinalis; plant tissue culture; biotechnology; protein production; insect cell-baculovirus; bioreactors; cyclic guanosine monophosphate facility design; cyclic guanosine, monophosphate protein production. **Mailing Address:** 127 Booth St, Needham, MA 02194. **E-Mail:** lazarte@cbr.med.harvard.edu

LAZARUS, ALLAN KENNETH, CHEMISTRY. **Personal Data:** b Bangor, Maine, May 20, 1931. **Education:** NY Univ, BA, 1952, MS, 1955, PhD (org chem), 1957. **Professional Experience:** RETIRED; asst prof chem, Trenton State Col, 1972-1997; group leader synthetic lubricants, Intermediates Div, Tenneco Chem Inc, 1966-1971; Esso Res & Eng Co, 1965-1966; Inorg Chem Div, FMC Corp, 1959-1965; chemist, Cities Serv Res & Develop Co, 1957-1959. **Memberships:** Sigma Xi; Sci Res Soc Am. **Research Statement & Publications:** Stereochemistry; organic synthesis; product and process development; fuels; automatic transmission fluids; synthetic lubricants. **Mailing Address:** One Gardenways Ct, Lakewood, NJ 08701.

LAZARUS, DAVID, SOLID STATE PHYSICS. **Personal Data:** b Buffalo, NY, September 8, 1921; m 1943, Betty; c Barbara, William, Mary Ann & Richard. **Education:** Univ Chicago, PhD (physics), 1949. **Professional Experience:** PROF EMER PHYSICS, UNIV ILL, URBANA CAMPAIGN, 1987-; mem gov bd, Am Inst Physics, 1981-; chmn, Coun Mat Sci, US Dept Energy, 1981-1986; ed-in-chief, Am Phys Soc, 1980-1991; vis prof, Harvard Univ & Mass Inst Technol, 1978-1979; Guggenheim fel, 1968-1969; vis prof, Univ Paris, 1968-1969; from instr to prof, Univ Ill, Urbana, 1949-1987; instr, Univ Chicago, 1949; asst physics, Univ Chicago, 1946-1949; res assoc, Radio Res Lab, Harvard Univ, 1943-1945; instr electronics, Univ Chicago, 1942-1943. **Memberships:** Fel Am Phys Soc; fel Am Asn Physics Teachers; fel AAAS. **Research Statement & Publications:** Defect and electronic properties of solids; high pressure physics. **Mailing Address:** 502 W Vt Ave, Urbana, IL 61801.

LAZARUS, GERALD SYLVAN, DERMATOLOGY. **Personal Data:** b New York, NY, February 16, 1939. **Education:** Colby Col, BS, 1959; George Wash Univ, MD, 1963. **Honorary Degrees:** MA, Univ Pa, 1982. **Honors & Awards:** Sultzberger Award, Am Acad Dermat; Montagna Award, Soc Invest Dermat. **Professional Experience:** DEAN EMER, SCH MED, UNIV CALIF, DAVIS, as of 2001; adj prof, Dermat, Univ Calif, San Francisco, as of 2001; dean, Sch Med, Univ Calif, Davis, beginning 1982; Milton B Hartzell prof & chair, Dept Dermat, Univ Pa, 1982-1993; prof med, Div Dermat, Duke Univ Med Ctr, 1975-; chmn, J Lamar Calloway chair prof dermat, 1975-1982; chmn, Div Dermat, Duke Univ Med Ctr, 1975-1978; sr investr, Arthritis Found, 1972-1977; head, Sect Dermat, Dept Med, Montefiore Hosp, 1972-1975; assoc prof med & co-dir dermat training prog, Albert Einstein Col Med, 1972-1975; Carl Herzog fel, 1970-1972; vis scientist, Strangeways Labs, Univ Cambridge, Eng, 1970-1972; res fel, Arthritis Found, 1970-1972; consult dermat, Addenbrookes Hosp, Cambridge, Eng, 1970-1972; chief resident dermat, Dept Dermat, Harvard Med Sch, 1969-1970; clin & res assoc, Dept Dermat, Harvard Med Sch, 1968-1970; prin investr, Lab Histol & Path, Nat Inst Dent Res, 1967-1968; clin assoc, Med Neurol Br, Nat Inst Neurol Dis & Blindness, 1965-1967; med resident, Univ Mich Med Ctr, 1964-1965; med intern, Univ Mich Med Ctr, 1963-1964; vis fel, Clare Hall, Cambridge. **Memberships:** Am Rheumatism Asn; Soc Invest Dermat (pres-elect, 1997-1998); Am Fedn Clin Res; fel Am Col Physicians; Royal Soc Med; Am Soc Clin Invest; Asn Am Physicians; Am Dermat Asn. **Research Statement & Publications:** Study of the role of proteinases in catabolic processes in skin and evaluation of the mechanisms by which these proteinases can instigate an inflammatory response; role of proteinases in inflammation generally and skin diseases particularly. **Mailing Address:** Off Dean Sch Med, Univ Calif, Davis, CA 95616. **E-Mail:** gslazarus@ucdavis.edu

LAZARUS, LAWRENCE H, OPIOID PEPTIDES, RECEPTORS. **Education:** Univ Calif, Los Angeles, PhD (cellular physiol), 1966. **Professional Experience:** DIR, DIV INTRAMURAL RES ENVIRON TOXICOL PROG, LAB COMPUT BIOL & RISK ANAL, NIH, as of 2004; HEAD, PEPTIDE NEUROCHEM SECT, NIH, 1983-; RES CHEMIST, NAT INST ENVIRON HEALTH SCI, NIH, 1977-. **Memberships:** AAAS; Am Soc Biochem & Molecular Biol; Int Neuropeptide Soc; Am Chem Soc; Am Peptide Soc. **Research Statement & Publications:** Peptide biochemistry; peptide mode of action; neuropeptides. **Mailing Address:** Div Intramural Res, Nat Inst Environ Health Sci, NIH, MD C3-04, PO Box 12233, Research Triangle Park, NC 27709. **Fax:** 919-541-0626. **E-Mail:** lazarus@niehs.nih.gov

LAZARUS, MARC SAMUEL, PHYSICAL INORGANIC CHEMISTRY. **Personal Data:** b Brooklyn, NY, September 9, 1946. **Education:** City Univ NY, BS, 1968; Princeton Univ, MA, 1971, PhD (chem), 1974. **Professional Experience:** PROF CHEM, HERBERT H LEHMAN COL, CITY UNIV NEW YORK, 1984-; from asst prof to assoc prof, Herbert H Lehman Col, City Univ New York, 1974-1984; res collabr, Brookhaven Nat Lab, 1974-1984; res assoc chem, Lawrence Berkeley Lab, Univ Calif, 1973-1974. **Memberships:**

Am Chem Soc; Am Phys Soc. **Research Statement & Publications:** Applications of x-ray photoelectron spectroscopy to the study of transition metal compounds and alloys. **Mailing Address:** Dept Chem, City Univ NY Herbert H Lehman Col, Bedford Park Blvd W, Bronx, NY 10468. **Fax:** 718-960-8750. **E-Mail:** mlazarus@lehman.cuny.edu

LAZARUS, ROGER BEN, THEORETICAL PHYSICS. **Personal Data:** b New York, NY, June 3, 1925. **Education:** Harvard Univ, AB, 1947, MA, 1948, PhD (physics), 1951. **Professional Experience:** MEM STAFF, LOS ALAMOS NAT LAB, 1973-; div leader, Los Alamos Sci Lab, 1968-1973; group leader, Los Alamos Sci Lab, 1958-1968; mem staff, Los Alamos Sci Lab, 1951-1958. **Memberships:** NY Acad Sci; Am Phys Soc; Asn Comput Mach. **Research Statement & Publications:** Simultaneous partial differential equations; computing machines. **Mailing Address:** Los Alamos Nat Lab, PO Box 1663, Los Alamos, NM 87545.

LAZARUS, STEVEN S, MARKETING. **Personal Data:** b Rochester, NY, June 16, 1943. **Education:** Cornell Univ, BS, 1966; Polytech Univ NY, MS, 1967; Univ Rochester, PhD, 1974. **Professional Experience:** CONSULT, 1994-; MKT CONSULT, CLIN REF SYSTS, DENVER, 1986-; IMX, Louisville, Ky, 1986-1987; sr vpres, Pal Assocs Inc, Denver, 1984-1985; assoc prof, Metro State Col, Denver, 1983-1984; dir, Sci Appln Intern Corp, Englewood, Colo, 1979-1984; pres, Mgt Systs Analysis Corp, Denver, 1977-1994; consult, State Colo, Denver, 1976-1981; speaker, Med Group Mgt Asn, 1975-; assoc & exec dir, Ctr Res, Ambulatory Health Care Admin. **Memberships:** Sr mem Inst Indust Eng; Med Group Mgt Asn; Opers Res Soc Am. **Research Statement & Publications:** Strategic planning; marketing; industrial engineering. **Mailing Address:** 7023 E Eastman Ave, Denver, CO 80224.

LAZAR-WESLEY, ELIANE M, PHYSIOLOGY. **Personal Data:** b Strasbourg, France, January 24, 1953. **Education:** Univ Louis Pasteur, France, BSc, 1975, PhD, 1982. **Professional Experience:** HEALTH SCIENTIST ADMINR, NAT INST DRUG ABUSE, NIH, as of 2003; patent examr, Patent & trademark Off, as of 2002; sr staff fel, lab physiol & pharmacol studies, Nat Inst Alcohol Abuse & Alcoholism, Rockville, Md, beginning 1989; sr staff fel, lab molecular Oncol, Inst Sci Cancer res, 1987-1989; vis fel, lab chemoprev, Nat cancer Inst, NIH, Bethesda, 1984-1987; sr researcher, Nat Ctr Sci res, France, 1982-1984; researcher, nat ctr sci res, France, 1979-1982. **Mailing Address:** Nat Inst Drug Abuse, NIH, Rm 220 6101 Exec Blvd MSC 8401, Bethesda, MD 20892-8401. **Fax:** 301-443-0538. **E-Mail:** el6r@nih.gov

LAZAY, PAUL DUANE, SOLID STATE PHYSICS. **Personal Data:** b Philadelphia, Pa, June 2, 1939. **Education:** Trinity Col, Conn, BS, 1961; Mass Inst Technol, PhD (physics), 1968. **Professional Experience:** SR TECH ADV, QUEST TURNAROUND ADV, as of 2004; vpres & gen manager, Cisco Sys Inc, 1995-1997; Bd dirs, SpecTran Corp, Sturbridge, Mass, beginning 1987; vpres mkt, pres & gen mgr, 1987-1988; pres & chief exec off, Telco Systems Corp, 1986-1993; vpres eng, Telco Systems Corp, 1986-1987; vpres eng, ITT-EOPD, Roanoke, Va, 1983-1986; Supvr, Optical Measurement & Process Automation, Bell labs, 1969-1983. **Memberships:** Am Phys Soc; Optical Soc Am; Sigma Xi; Inst Elec & Electronics Engrs. **Research Statement & Publications:** Optical fiber research and optical communications. **Mailing Address:** Quest Turnaround Adv Inc, 37 Purchase St, Rye, NY 10580. **Fax:** 914-921-2136.

LAZDA, VELTA ABULS, IMMUNOLOGY, MOLECULAR BIOLOGY. **Education:** Purdue Univ, BS, 1962; Northwestern Univ, PhD (microbiol), 1967. **Professional Experience:** GRAD FAC, DEPT SURG, COL MED, UNIV ILL, as of 2006; adj assoc prof, Univ Ill Med Ctr, beginning 1991; DIR, HISTOCOMPATIBILITY LAB, GIFT HOPE ORGAN & TISSUE DONOR NETWORK, 1987-; asst prof, Dept Surg, 1977-1991; DIR, TISSUE TYPING LAB, UNIV ILL MED CTR, 1977-; USPHS Career Develop Award, 1972-1977; res assoc, Immunol Div, Res Inst, Am Dent Asn Health Found, 1969-1977; Am Cancer Soc Postdoc fel, Northwestern Univ, 1967-1969. **Memberships:** AAAS; Am Asn Immunologists; Am Soc Microbiol; Am Soc Histocompatibility & Immunogenetics; Transplantation Society. **Research Statement & Publications:** Transplantation immunology. **Mailing Address:** 660 N Indust Dr, Elmhurst, IL 60126. **Fax:** 630-758-2602. **E-Mail:** vlazda@giftofhope.org

LAZELL, JAMES DRAPER, POPULATION BIOLOGY, BIOGEOGRAPHY. **Personal Data:** b New York, NY, September 5, 1939. **Education:** Univ South, Sewanee, BA, 1961; Univ Ill, MS, 1963; Harvard Univ, MA, 1966; Univ RI, PhD (biol), 1970. **Professional Experience:** Assoc, Miss Mus Natural Sci, 1990-; assoc, Bishop Mus, 1987-; curatorial affil, Yale Peabody Mus, 1982-; PRES, CONSERV AGENCY, 1979-; assoc, Mus Comp Zool, 1977-; sanctuary dir, Mass Audubon Soc, 1975-1979; prin investr, Earthwatch, 1973-; collabr, Nat Park Serv, 1969-; sci staff, Mass Audubon Soc, 1967-1976; Head, Dept Sci, Palfrey Street Sch, 1966-1974. **Memberships:** Am Soc Ichthyologists & Herpetologists; Am Soc Mammalogists; Am Soc Zoologists; Soc Study Amphibians & Reptiles; fel Explorers Club. **Research Statement & Publications:** Vertebrate systematics; endangered species conservation; ecology; demographics; distribution of rare and little-known animals; exploration as of 1990; author of 120 scientific papers and three books. **Mailing Address:** Conserv Agency, 8 Swinburne St, Jamestown, RI 02835. **Fax:** 580-364-0543. **E-Mail:** hq@theconservationagency.org

LAZERSON, EARL EDWIN, ALGEBRA, NUMBER THEORY. **Personal Data:** b Detroit, Mich, December 10, 1930. **Education:** Wayne State Univ, BS, 1953; Univ Mich, MA, 1954, PhD, 1982. **Professional Experience:** PRES EMER, SOUTHERN ILL UNIV, 1994-; pres, Southern Ill Univ, 1979-1993; actg pres, Sch Sci & Technol, 1979-1980; vpres & provost, Sch Sci & Technol, 1977-1979; actg vpres & provost, Sch Sci & Technol, 1976-1977; prof math, Southern Ill Univ, beginning 1973; dean, Sch Sci & Technol, beginning 1973; chmn, Dept Math, Southern Ill Univ, 1972-1973; actg chmn, Dept Math, Southern Ill Univ, 1971-1972; NSF res grant, 1962-1967. **Memberships:** Am Math Soc; Math Asn Am; London Math Soc; Soc Math France. **Mailing Address:** Southern Ill Univ, Edwardsville, IL 62026.

LAZO, JOHN STEPHEN, ONCOLOGY, BIOCHEMICAL PHARMACOLOGY. **Personal Data:** b Philadelphia, Pa, December 15, 1948; m 1974, Jacqui; c Jacquelyn. **Education:** Univ Johns Hopkins, BA, 1971; Univ Mich, Ann Arbor, PhD (pharmacol), 1976. **Professional Experience:** Vis scientist, Nat Cancer Res Inst, Tokyo, Japan, 1990; PROF PHARMACOL & CHMN DEPT, UNIV PITTSBURGH, SCH MED, 1987-; Vis scientist, Sloan-Kettering Inst Cancer Res, 1985-1986; from asst prof to assoc prof pharmacol, Univ Yale, 1978-1987; fel, Univ Yale, 1976-1978; USPHS-NIH trainee, Dept Pharmacol, Univ Mich, Ann Arbor, 1971-1976; lab asst, Dept Chem, Univ Johns Hopkins, 1971; Lab asst, Dept Pharmacol, Thomas Jefferson Med Col, 1968-1969. **Memberships:** Am Soc Pharmacol & Exp Therapeut; Tissue Culture Asn; Am Asn Cancer Res; NY Acad Sci; AAAS; Am Soc Biochem & Molecular Biol; Am Cancer Soc. **Research Statement & Publications:** Pharmacology and toxicology of antitumor agents; use of cultured cells to study drug actions; action of drugs on lung tissue; Published over 6 articles. **Mailing Address:** 5128 Pembroke Pl, Pittsburgh, PA 15232. **Fax:** 412-648-9009. **E-Mail:** lazo@pop.pitt.edu

LAZOWSKA, EDWARD DELANO, Computer Systems. **Personal Data:** b Washington, DC, August 3, 1950. **Education:** Brown Univ, AB, 1972; Univ Toronto, MS, 1974, PhD, 1977. **Honors & Awards:** Member, National Academy of Engineering; Fellow, Am Acad Arts & Sci; Fellow, ACM; Fellow, Inst Elec & Electronics Engrs; Fellow, AAAS; Computing Research Assn Distinguished Service Award, 2005. **Professional Experience:** Co-Chmn, President's Info Technol Adv Comt, 2003-2005; Mem, Technl Adv Bd, Microsoft Res, 1991-; Bill & Melinda Gates Chair, Comput Sci & Eng, Univ Wash, 2000-; Prof, Comput Sci & Eng, Univ Wash, 1977-; Chair, DARPA Information Science & Technology Study Group, 2004-2006; Chair, Computing Research Assn, 1997-2001; Chair, NSF CISE Advisory Committee, 1998-1999; Member, NRC Computer Science & Telecommunications Board, 1996-2002. **Research Statement & Publications:** Computer systems: modelling and analysis; design and implementation; distributed and parallel systems. **Mailing Address:** Comput Sci & Eng, Box 352350, Univ Wash, Seattle, WA 98195-2350. **E-Mail:** lazowska@cs.washington.edu

LAZZARA, RALPH, MEDICINE. **Personal Data:** b Tampa, Fla, August 14, 1934. **Education:** Univ Chicago, BA, 1955; Tulane Univ, MD, 1959. **Honors & Awards:** Regents Award for Superior Res, Univ OK 1984; Geo L Cross Res Prof, Univ OK 1988; Natalie O Warren Prof Med, Univ OK 1989; Pres, Heart Rhythm Soc (NASPE)1995-6; Distinguished Scientist Award, NASPE 1999; Regent's Professor, Univ OK 2003. **Professional Experience:** GEORGE LYNN CROSS RES PROF MED, UNIV OKLA; NATALIE O WARREN PROF MED, SCH MED, UNIV OKLA; Dir CARI, Univ OK, 1998; Regents Prof, Univ OK 2003; chief sect cardiol, Univ Okla Health Sci Ctr & Vet Admin Hosp, Oklahoma City, 1978-1998; prof med, Sch Med, Univ Okla, beginning 1978; chief sect cardiol, Vet Admin Hosp, 1974-1978, Univ Miami, prof med, Sch Med, Univ Miami; assoc prof, Sch Med, Univ Miami, 1972-1977; dir coronary care unit, Vet Admin Hosp, Miami, 1972-1975; asst prof med, Sch Med, Univ Miami, 1971-1972; staff cardiologist & chief sect electrophysiol, Mt Sinai Hosp, Miami Beach, 1970-1972; staff mem & dir cardiovasc res lab, Ochsner Clin & Ochsner Found Hosp, New Orleans, 1965-1967; research fel, Col Physicians & Surgeons, Columbia Univ, 1964-1965; resident, Med Sch, Tulane Univ & Charity Hosp, 1963-1964; instr med, Tulane Univ, 1960-1967; asst, Charity Hosp, New Orleans, 1960-1964. **Memberships:** Soc Clin Invest, Assoc Am Phys; Heart Rhythm Soc; Am Coll Cardiol; Am Heart Assoc; European Soc Cardiol. **Research Statement & Publications:** Cardiac electrophysiology. **Mailing Address:** Cardiac Arrhythmia Research Inst, 1200 Everett Dr, Rm 6E103, Oklahoma City, OK 73104. **Fax:** 405-271-7455. **E-Mail:** ralph-lazzara@ouhsc.edu

LAZZARINI, ALBERT JOHN, SYSTEMS ENGINEERING, OPTICAL SYSTEMS DESIGN. **Personal Data:** b Lucca, Italy, October 11, 1952. **Education:** Mass Inst Technol, SB, 1974, PhD (nuclear physics), 1978. **Professional Experience:** DATA & COMPUT GROUP LEADER, LASER INTERFEROMETER GRAVITATIONAL WAVE OBSERV, CALIF INST TECHNOL, as of 2006; prin investr, Kaman Inst/kaman Sci Corp, beginning 1988; sr scientist, Kaman Inst/kaman Sci Corp, 1984-1988; res asst prof physics, Univ Wash, 1980-1984; res assoc Except Nuclear Physics, Univ Wash, 1978-1980. **Memberships:** Am Soc Phys; Int Soc Optical Eng. **Research Statement & Publications:** Overall responsibility for end-to-end system design and performance analysis of complex electro-optical systems operating in the visible and infrared; design of adaptive optics systems; adaptive control, AI methods for information processing. **Mailing Address:** Laser Interferometer Gravitational Wave Observ, Calif Inst Technol, Mail Stop 18-34 609 Millikan, Pasadena, CA 91125. **Fax:** 626-304-9834. **E-Mail:** azzarini_a@ligo.caltech.edu

LAZZARINI, ROBERT A, MOLECULAR GENETICS. **Personal Data:** b New York, NY, October 14, 1931. **Education:** Univ Calif, Los Angeles, BS, 1955, PhD (biol chem), 1960. **Honors & Awards:** Quastel Lectr Molecular Sci, McGill Univ, Can, 1985; Pfizer Lectr, Univ Montreal, Can, 1985; Meritorious Exec Rank Award Sr Sci Serv, 1986. **Professional Experience:** PROF MOLECULAR CELL & DEVELP BIOL, MT SINAI SCH MED, as of 2004; adv Coun Microbiol & Virol, Am Cancer Soc, 1982-1984 & Alzheimer Dis Adv Bd, Am Health Assistance Found, 1989-; DIR, BROOKDALE CTR MOLECULAR BIOL, MT SINAI SCH MED, NY, 1988-; mem, Virol Study Sect, div res Grants, NIH, 1980 & Neurol C Study Sect, 1988-1989; chief, lab Molecular Genetics, 1981-1988; mem, Adv Coun Basic Sci, Mult Sclerosis Soc, 1981-1987; chmn, RNA Virus div, Am Soc Microbiol, 1981-1983; chmn, Conf Mech Viral Resistance, Mult Sclerosis Soc, Colo, 1980; head, Sect Molecular Virol, 1974-1981; Session chmn, Gordon res Conf, 1974 & 1975; head, Sect Regulation Nucleic Acid Synthesis, 1970-1974; res scientist, Nat inst Neurol & Commun Dis & Stroke, 1965-1970; Lab Molecular Biol, Nat inst Neurol & Commun Dis & Stroke, 1964-1965; staff fel, lab Biochem, Nat inst Dent res, NIH, 1963-1964; Postdoctoral fel, Johns Hopkins Univ, 1960-1963. **Memberships:** Am Soc Biol Chemists; Am Soc Microbiol; Am Soc Neurochem; Am Soc Virol. **Research Statement & Publications:** Published more than 25 articles. **Mailing Address:** Dept Develop & Molecular Biol, Mt Sinai Sch Med, One Gustave L Levy Pl, PO Box 1126, New York, NY 10029. **E-Mail:** robert.lazzarini@mssm.edu

LE, CHAP THAN, STATISTICS, BIOMETRICS. **Personal Data:** b Vietnam, August 1, 1948. **Education:** Calif State Univ, BA, BS & MA, 1971; Univ NMex, PhD (statist), 1978. **Professional Experience:** PROF BIOSTATISTICS, SCH PUB HEALTH, UNIV MINN, MINNEAPOLIS, as of 2003; DIR BIOSTATISTICS, CANCER CTR, UNIV MINN, MINNEAPOLIS, s 2003; asst prof biomet, Univ Minn, beginning 1978. **Memberships:** Biomet Soc. **Research Statement & Publications:** Reliability and life testing; nonparametric statistics; survey sampling; theory of survivorship; epidemiology. **Mailing Address:** Pub Health Box 197 Mays, Univ Minn Med Sch 420 Del St SE, Minneapolis, MN 55455-0374. **E-Mail:** lexxx001@umn.edu

LE, GUAN, SPACE PHYSICS. **Personal Data:** b Chengdu, China, September 14, 1962. **Education:** Univ Sci & Technol China, BS, 1984; Univ Calif, Los Angeles, MS, 1989, PhD (geophys & space physics), 1991. **Professional Experience:** ASTROPHYSICIST, GODDARD SPACE FLIGHT CTR, NASA, 2000-; res geophysicist, Inst Geophys & Planetary Physics, Univ Calif, Los Angeles, 1991-2000. **Memberships:** Am Geophys Union. **Research Statement & Publications:** Ultraflow frequency waves upstream of collisionless shocks, the earth's magneto pause and boundary layers, and solar wind- magnetosphere interaction; analysis and interpretation of spacecrafts data and ground-based data as they related to these research areas. **Mailing Address:** Lab Extraterrestrial Physics, NASA, Code 696, Greenbelt, MD 20771. **Fax:** 301-286-1648. **E-Mail:** Guan.Le.1@nasa.gov

LE, SHU-YUN, BIOINFORMATICS, STRUCTURAL BIOLOGY. **Personal Data:** b Shanghai, China, June 9, 1947; Canadian citizen; m Jing-Jing; c Seann Yi. **Education:** Shanghai Jiaotong Univ, China, cert, 1970; Shanghai Inst Biochem, Chinese Acad Sci, China, MS, 1981, PhD, 1982. **Professional Experience:** STAFF SCIENTIST, NAT CANCER INST, NIH, 1997-; vis scientist, Div Biol Sci, 1992-1996; res assoc, Nat Res Coun, Can, 1989-1992; vis assoc, Lab Math Biol, Div Cancer Biol & Diag, Nat Cancer Inst, NIH, 1988-1989; NIH Fogarty vis fel, NIH, 1985-1989; vis fel, Lab Math Biol, Div Cancer Biol & Diag, Nat Cancer Inst, NIH, 1985-1988; asst prof, Shanghai Inst Biochem,

Chinese Acad Sci, 1983-1985; res assoc, Shanghai Inst Biochem, Chinese Acad Sci, 1982-1983; col teacher math, Shanghai Zhong-Hua Chuang Chang, 1975-1978; asst engr, Shanghai Zhong-Hua Chuang Chang, 1972-1975; Technician, Shanghai Zhong-Hua Chuang Chang, 1970-1972. **Research Statement & Publications:** Computational biology; genomic search for ncRNA and functional structured RNA; computation of higher order structures of RNA; research on viruses and cells by computational analysis; published more the 90 papers. **Mailing Address:** Ctr for Cancer Research Nanobiology Program, CCR, NCI, NIH, Bldg 469 Rm 151, Frederick, MD 21702. **Fax:** 301-846-5598. **E-Mail:** shuyun@ncifcrf.gov

LEA, ARDEN OTTERBEIN, ENTOMOLOGY. **Personal Data:** b Cleveland, Ohio, October 19, 1926. **Education:** Univ Rochester, BA, 1948; Ohio State Univ, MSc, 1950, PhD (entom), 1957. **Professional Experience:** PROF EMER ENTOM, UNIV GA, AS 2005; prof, Univ Ga, 1974-1992; mem, Trop Med & Parasitol Study Sect, NIH, 1974-1978; assoc prof entom, Univ Ga, 1969-1974; USPHS spec res fel, Denmark, 1960-1961; chief, Physiol Sect, Entom Res Ctr, State Bd Health, Fla, 1958-1969; insect nutrit, Ohio State Univ, 1956-1958; USPHS med entomologist, Onchocerciasis Proj, Pan Am Sanit Bur, Guatemala, 1951-1953; res assoc insecticide testing, Ohio State Univ, 1950-1951; mem, Sci Adv Panel Onchocerciasis, WHO. **Memberships:** AAAS; Am Soc Trop Med & Hyg; Am Mosquito Control Asn. **Research Statement & Publications:** Endocrine physiology of Diptera; physiology and behavior of mosquitoes; peptide hormones. **Mailing Address:** 360 Millstone Circle, Athens, GA 30605.

LEA, GEORGE KOO, HIGH PERFORMANCE COMPUTING, FLUID MECHANICS. **Personal Data:** b Shanghai, China, October 20, 1938. **Education:** George Wash Univ, BSME, 1960; Va Polytech Inst, PhD (eng mech), 1966. **Professional Experience:** RETIRED; prog dir, Commun & Comput Systs, NSF, 1987-1999; vis res scientist, David Taylor Res & Develop Ctr, 1985-1986; prog dir fluid mech, Commun & Comput Systs, NSF, 1972-1985; assoc prog dir, Commun & Comput Systs, NSF, 1970-1972; asst prof mech eng, George Wash Univ, 1965-1971. **Memberships:** Am Phys Soc. **Research Statement & Publications:** Perturbation and asymptotic methods in mechanics, gasdynamics, radiative heat transfer, nonlinear water waves. **Mailing Address:** Elec & Commun Systs, NSF, 4201 Wilson Blvd, Arlington, VA 22230. **Fax:** 703-306-0305. **E-Mail:** glea@nsf.gov

LEA, JAMES DIGHTON, SYSTEMS SCIENCE. **Personal Data:** b Monticello, Ill, April 9, 1933. **Education:** Tex Western Col, BA, 1957; Univ Tex, MA, 1960, PhD (physics), 1963. **Professional Experience:** RES ASSOC SYSTS, EXXON PROD RES CO, EXXON CORP, 1975-; explor systs adv, Exxon Co USA, 1973-1975; sr prof systs analyst, Humble Oil & Refining Co, 1969-1973; Sr res scientist physics, Esso Prod Res Co, Stand Oil NJ, 1963-1969. **Memberships:** Am Math Soc; Am Phys Soc; Soc Explor Geophysicists; Am Asn Petrol Geologists. **Research Statement & Publications:** Application of computer science to geological problems. **Mailing Address:** 6230 Bayou Bridge, Houston, TX 77096-3706.

LEA, JAMES WESLEY, TOPOLOGY, ALGEBRA. **Personal Data:** b Lebanon, Tenn, March 17, 1941. **Education:** Tenn Polytech Inst, BS, 1963, MS, 1965; La State Univ, PhD (math), 1971. **Professional Experience:** PROF MATH, MIDDLE TENN STATE UNIV, 1981-; vis assoc prof math, Univ Tenn, Knoxville, 1976-1977; from asst prof to assoc prof, Middle Tenn State Univ, 1971-1981; instr, Tenn Technol Univ, 1966-1967; instr math, Univ Tenn, Martin, 1965-1966. **Memberships:** Am Math Soc; Math Asn Am; Sigma Xi. **Research Statement & Publications:** Lattice theory. **Mailing Address:** Dept Math Sci, Middle Tenn State Univ, PO Box 222, Murfreesboro, TN 37132-0001. **E-Mail:** jwlea@mtsu.edu

LEA, MICHAEL ANTHONY, BIOCHEMISTRY. **Personal Data:** b Leeds, Eng, December 26, 1939; American citizen; wid, c Gareth D & Catrin J. **Education:** Univ Birmingham, BSc, 1961, PhD (biochem), 1964. **Professional Experience:** PROF BIOCHEM, UNIV MED & DENT NJ, 1978-; from asst prof to assoc prof, Univ Med & Dent NJ, 1967-1978; instr, Sch Med, Ind Univ, 1966-1967; Res assoc pharmacol, Sch Med, Ind Univ, 1964-1966. **Memberships:** AAAS; Am Chem Soc; Am Soc Cell Biol; Am Asn Cancer Res; Am Soc Biochem Molecular Biol. **Research Statement & Publications:** Control of nucleic acid synthesis and growth in normal and neoplastic cells. **Mailing Address:** Dept Biochem, 185 S Orange Ave, Univ Med & Dent NJ, Newark, NJ 07103-2714. **Fax:** 973-972-5594. **E-Mail:** lea@umdnj.edu

LEA, ROBERT MARTIN, PHYSICS. **Personal Data:** b New York, NY, November 4, 1931. **Education:** Union Col, NY, BS, 1953; Yale Univ, PhD (physics), 1957. **Professional Experience:** PROF EMER PHYSICS, CITY COL NY, as of 2002; dir, NRCSE, 1981-1988; chmn dept, City Col New York, 1970-1974 & 1987-1989; dir, NSF Dept Develop Grant, 1970-1974; prin investr, NSF res grants, City Col New York, 1959-1970; vis physicist, Brookhaven Nat Lab, 1959-1970; prof physics, City Col New York, beginning 1957. **Memberships:** Am Phys Soc; Am Asn Physics Teachers. **Research Statement & Publications:** High energy experimental physics. **Mailing Address:** Dept Physics, City Col NY, J-419 Marshak Sci Bldg 138th St Convent Ave, New York, NY 10031. **Fax:** 212-650-6940.

LEA, SUSAN MAUREEN, ASTROPHYSICS, PHYSICS EDUCATION. **Personal Data:** b Cardiff, Wales, UK, July 10, 1948; m 1974, Michael; c Jennifer. **Education:** Cambridge Univ, BA, 1969, MA, 1973; Univ Calif, Berkeley, PhD (astron), 1974. **Professional Experience:** PROF, DEPT PHYSICS & ASTRON, SAN FRANCISCO STATE UNIV, 1984-; assoc prof, Dept Physics & Astron, San Francisco State Univ, 1980-1984; asst res astron, Univ Calif, Berkeley, 1977-1980; res fel, Univ Md, College Park, 1976-1977; res assoc astrophys, Ames Res Ctr, NASA, 1974-1976. **Memberships:** Am Astron Soc; Royal Astron Soc; Int Astron Union; Am Phys Soc. **Research Statement & Publications:** High energy astrophysics, especially x-ray and radio astronomy; numerical hydrodynamics; compact galactic x-ray sources, clusters of galaxies, intergalactic matter and cosmology. **Mailing Address:** Dept Physics & Astron, San Francisco State Univ 1600 Holloway Ave, San Francisco, CA 94132-1722.

LEA, WAYNE ADAIR, COMPUTER RECOGNITION OF SPEECH. **Personal Data:** b Helena, Mont, January 16, 1940; m Gayle; c 7. **Education:** Mont State Col, BS, 1962, MS, 1964; Mass Inst Technol, SM & EE, 1966, Purdue Univ, PhD, 1972. **Professional Experience:** Actg mgr, Speech Group, A I Lab, Nynex S&T, 1987; pres, Speech J C Inst, 1985; DIR, PRES, SPEECH SCI INST, 1985-; sr vpres & dir, Ctr Speech Res & Educ, VCS Corp, 1983-1984; adj assoc prof, Dept Elec & Comput Eng, Univ Calif, Santa Barbara, 1981-1983; dir, Speech Sci Publ, beginning 1980; consult speech recognition var co, beginning 1979; chmn, Acad Forensic Appl Commun Sci, 1978-1982; adj assoc prof, Dept Ling, Univ Southern Calif, 1978-1983; res scientist, Speech Commun Res Lab, 1977-1981; prin investr, Defense Systs Div, Sperry Univac, 1972-1977; instr elec eng, Res Found, Purdue Univ, 1970-1972; proj leader, Electronics Res Ctr, NASA, 1966-1970; NSF fel, Electronics Res Lab, Mass Inst Technol, 1964-1966; res assoc, Electronics Res Lab, Mont State Col, 1962-1964. **Memberships:** Sr mem Inst Elec & Electronics Engrs; Acoust Soc Am; Am Acad Forensic Sci; Am Asn Phonetic Sci; Sigma Xi; Soc Automotive Engrs. **Research Statement & Publications:** Computer recognition of speech; intonation, linguistic stress and rhythm; acoustic phonetics, forensic phonetics; usability engineering for voice interfaces. **Mailing Address:** Speech Sci Inst, 201 W Burnsville Parkway, Ste 134, Burnsville, MN 55337. **E-Mail:** speechSciinst@msn.com

LEABO, DICK ALBERT, APPLIED STATISTICS, ECONOMIC STATISTICS. **Personal Data:** b Walcott, Iowa, October 30, 1921; m 1955, c 1. **Education:** Univ Iowa, BS, 1949, MA, 1950, PhD (statist, econ), 1953. **Honors & Awards:** Order of Artus, Hon Econs Soc. **Professional Experience:** FRED M TAYLOR DISTINGUISHED PROF EMER STATIST, UNIV MICH, ANN ARBOR, 1984-; Fred M Taylor Distinguished prof, Grad Sch Bus, 1978-1984; Consult, Brookings Inst, 1957-1959 & NCent Accrediting Asn, 1974-1984; dir PhD Prog, Grad Sch Bus, 1965-1981; exchange prof, Rotterdam Sch Econ, 1965; prof, Grad Sch Bus, 1963-1979; assoc dean, Grad Sch Bus, 1962-1965; from asst prof to assoc prof statist, Univ Mich, Ann Arbor, 1957-1963; asst prof econ & asst dir, Bur Econ & Bus Res, Mich State Univ, 1956-1957; asst prof econ & asst dir, Bur Bus & Econ Res, Univ Iowa, 1953-1956; res assoc, Bur Bus & Econ Res, Univ Iowa, 1949-1953; Res asst econ, Bur Bus & Econ Res, Univ Iowa, 1948-1949. **Memberships:** Am Statist Asn; Am Econ Asn; Asn Bus Economists. **Research Statement & Publications:** Regional economic research and the application of regression and correlation techniques. **Mailing Address:** 2115 Nature Cove Ct No 105, Ann Arbor, MI 48104-4977.

LEACH, BARRIE WILLIAM, APPLIED MATHEMATICS, ELECTRICAL ENGINEERING. **Personal Data:** b Winnipeg, Man, November 25, 1945. **Education:** Univ Man, BSc, 1967, MSc, 1968, PhD (elec eng), 1972. **Professional Experience:** Assoc res officer, Flight Res, Nat Res Coun Can, beginning 1980; asst res officer, Nat Res Coun Can, 1972-1980. **Memberships:** Inst Elec & Electronics Engrs. **Research Statement & Publications:** Optimal parameter and state estimation; aeromagnetics; geophysical and anti-submarine warfare applications; digital filtering techniques multi-sensor navigation techniques. **Mailing Address:** Inst Aerospace Res, Nat Res Council Can, Montreal Rd Bldg U-61, Ottawa, ON K1A 0R6, Can.

LEACH, BERTON JOE, ZOOLOGY, SCIENCE ADMINISTRATION. **Personal Data:** b Tuscola, Ill, March 30, 1932; m 1955, Barbara; c Laura A (Weiss) & Berton F. **Education:** Wash Univ, AB, 1957; Univ Mo, MA, 1960, PhD (zoology), 1963. **Professional Experience:** RETIRED; dir, Human Neurobiol Educr, 1994; guest researcher, Brain & Behav Lab, NIH, 1991-1992; adj prof neuroscience, Georgetown Univ Med Sch, 1989-2002; gen reader, Marine Biol Lab, 1985-1987; sr scientist, Capital Syst Group, 1978-1981; comput data bases, US Govt Contracts Pvt Indust, 1976-1981; chief consult, Berton J Leach Assoc, Rockville, Md, 1976-1978; exec secy, Cardiovasc & Pulmonary Study Sect, Div Res Grants, NIH, 1974-1976; med technol educ adv, Jewish Hosp, St Louis, 1972; prof biol, F H Dearing prof, 1970-1974; vis scholar, Harvard Univ, 1969; chmn dept biol & geol, Cent Methodist Col, 1968-1974; prof biol, Cent Methodist Col, 1968-1970; asst prog dir, Col Sci Improv Prog, 1967-1968; res evaluator, USPHS, 1966-1967; asst prog dir, Undergrad Stud Prog, NSF, 1966-1967; assoc prof, George Wash Univ, 1966; asst prof, George Wash Univ, 1963-1966; grant, NSF Equip, 1973-1974; asst zool, USPHS, 1962-1963; instr, Univ Mo, 1960-1962; asst zool, Univ Mo, 1958-1960. **Memberships:** Sigma Xi; Am Soc Mammalogists; AAAS; Marine Biol Lab Asn. **Research Statement & Publications:** Cancer construction data base; vertebrate biology computer courseware; mammalian neuroanatomy; mammalian behavior; vocalizations of Talpidae. **Mailing Address:** 12707 Weiss St, Rockville, MD 20853. **Fax:** 301-929-8467. **E-Mail:** bertjleach@aol.com

LEACH, CHARLES MORLEY, PLANT PATHOLOGY, MYCOLOGY. **Personal Data:** b Sacramento, Calif, October 28, 1924. **Education:** Queen's Univ, Ireland, BS, 1949, BAgr, 1950; Ore State Univ, PhD (plant path), 1956. **Professional Experience:** PROF EMER, DEPT BOT & PLANT PATH, ORE STATE UNIV, 1989-; NZ sr sci fel, 1973-1974 & Cambridge Univ, 1984-1985; prof plant path, Ore State Univ, 1966-1989; NSF fel, Univ Bristol, 1962-1963; from asst plant pathologist to assoc plant pathologist, Ore State Univ, 1957-1966; Instr bot, Ore State Univ, 1951-1957. **Memberships:** Am Phytopath Soc; Mycol Soc Am; Brit Mycol Soc; Int Soc Plant Path; Can Plant Path Soc; Int Asn Aerobiology. **Research Statement & Publications:** Biology of plant pathogenic fungi, especially reproduction and spore discharge, seed-borne diseases of agricultural crops, electrical nature of plant surfaces and active spore discharge. **Mailing Address:** Dept Bot & Plant Path, Ore State Univ, 2082 Cordley Hall, Corvallis, OR 97330-2902. **E-Mail:** jorcl@proaxis.com

LEACH, ERNEST BRONSON, MATHEMATICS. **Personal Data:** b Huchow, China, December 21, 1924; div. **Education:** Case Inst Technol, BS, 1949; Mass Inst Technol, PhD (math), 1953. **Professional Experience:** PROF EMER, DEPT MATH, CASE WESTERN RES UNIV, 1988-; prof, Case Western Res Univ, 1982-1988; partic, Inelec Proj, Inst Nat Elec & Electronics, Boumerdes, Algeria, 1976-1978; mem staff, Northwestern Univ Proj, Univ Khartoum, 1966-1967; Partic, Indo-Am Prog, Indian Inst Technol, Kanpur, 1963-1964; assoc prof math, Case Western Res Univ, 1959-1982; From instr to asst prof, Case Western Res Univ, 1953-1959. **Research Statement & Publications:** Algebraic topology; functional analysis. **Mailing Address:** Dept Math, Case Western Res Univ, 10900 Euclid Ave, Cleveland, OH 44106-7058.

LEACH, FRANKLIN ROLLIN, BIOCHEMISTRY. **Personal Data:** b Gorman, Tex, April 2, 1933; m 1970, Anna; c Alan, Barry, Carol (Huddle), Carolyn (Proctor), Ja net (Weiss) & Barbara (Perkins) Net (Weiss), Barbara (Perkins). **Education:** Hardin-Simmons Univ, BA, 1953; Univ Tex, PhD (chem), 1957. **Professional Experience:** PROF EMERITUS, OKLA STATE UNIV, 1998-; assoc dept head, Okla State Univ, 1990-1998; chmn grad fac genetics, Okla State Univ, 1976-1978; prof biochem, Okla State Univ, 1968-1998; res fel, Calif Inst Technol, 1965-1966; NIH res career develop award, 1962-1972; from asst prof to assoc prof biochem, Okla State Univ, 1960-1968; Soc Am Bacteriologists pres fel, Univ Ill, 1960; res assoc, Okla State Univ, 1959-1960; Nat Acad Sci fel med sci, Univ Calif, 1957-1959; res scientist I, Biochem Inst, 1953-1956. **Memberships:** AAAS; Am Chem Soc; Am Soc Microbiol; Am Soc Biochem & Molecular Biol; Am Soc Photobiol; Coun Biol Ed; Protein Soc; Int Soc Biolumin Chemilumin. **Research Statement & Publications:** Bioluminescence; analytical biochemistry; enzymology; environmental biochemistry. **Mailing Address:** Dept Biochem & Molecular Biol, Okla State Univ, Stillwater, OK 74078-3035. **Fax:** 405-744-7799. **E-Mail:** firefly@biochem.okstate.edu

LEACH, JAMES L(INDSAY), MECHANICAL ENGINEERING. **Personal Data:** b Lawrenceville, Ill, April 9, 1918. **Education:** Univ NMex, BS, 1942; Univ Ill, MS, 1950; Ill State Univ, PhD, 1976. **Professional Experience:** PROF EMER MECH ENG, UNIV ILL, URBANA, as of 2003; consult, Acad Educ Develop, Tehran, Iran, 1973-1975; adv to dean eng, Utter Pradesh Agr Univ, 1969; Inst Coimbatore, Indian, Pradesh Agr Univ, 1967; guest prof, Sch Bengal Eng Col, Calcutta, 1964; installation engr, Universal Bleacher Co, Kuwait, 1962; guest prof, Indian Inst Tech, Kharagpur, Indian, 1960-1961; prof mech eng,

Univ Ill, Urbana, beginning 1959; Caterpillar Tractor Co, 1955-1956 & Universal Bleacher Co, 1956-; Consult, Aluminum Co Am, 1952-1953; Consult, USAF, 1950-1951; from asst prof to assoc prof, Univ Ill, Urbana, 1948-1959; Pac Bridge Co, USN Cont Dock & Yards Comb & Control Eng, Southwest Pac, 1943; US Ord Res & Gage Dept, Wash, DC, 1942; Engr, Tex Co, Ill, 1940-1941. **Memberships:** Am Foundrymen's Soc; Sigma Xi; Am Soc Mech Engrs; Am Soc Mil Engrs; Am Soc Petrol Engrs; Nat Soc Prof Engr; Fedn Am Scientists. **Research Statement & Publications:** Carbon dioxide process for hardening molds and cores for casting metal; shell molding. **Mailing Address:** RR 2 No 171B, Flat Rock, IL 62427.

LEACH, JOHN KLINE, CARDIOLOGY, PHYSIOLOGY. **Personal Data:** b Buffalo, NY, July 11, 1922; m 1945, Priscilla; c Barbara, Catherine, David, Elizabeth & William. **Education:** Baldwin-Wallace Col, BS, 1943; Albany Med Col, MD, 1947; Am Bd Internal Med, dipl, 1968; Am Bd Cardiovasc Dis, dipl, 1969. **Professional Experience:** PROF EMER MED & NEUROSCIENCES, MED SCH, UNIV, NMEX, 1986-; from asst prof to prof med & physiol, Med Sch, Univ, Nmex, 1972-1985; vis assoc prof, Med Ctr, Univ Calif, Los Angeles, 1971-1972; consult med, Bataan Hosp, Albuquerque, 1969-1983; consult med & cardiol, St Joseph Hosp, Albuquerque, 1969-1983; consult cardiol, Presby Hosp, Albuquerque, 1969-1983; assoc chief staff res, Vet Admin Hosp, Albuquerque, 1969-1973; res grant cardiol, Univ NMex, 1969-1972; attend med, Univ Hosp, Albuquerque, NMex, beginning 1966; chief cardiol sect, Vet Admin Hosp, Albuquerque, 1966-1972, 1977-1983; from asst prof to assoc prof med, Med Sch, Univ Nmex, 1966-1976; lectr, Med Ctr, Univ Kans, 1963-1964; assoc chief staff res, Vet Admin Ctr, Wadsworth, Kans, 1963-1964; asst prof physiol, Albany Med Col, 1962-1963; NIH res fel physiol, Albany Med Col, 1961-1963; instr med, Albany Med Col, 1955-1962; clin asst & asst attend, Albany Hosp, 1955-1962. **Memberships:** Fel Am Col Cardiol; Am Fedn Med Res; Am Heart Asn; fel Am Col Physicians; Am Physiol Soc; Heart Failure Soc of America. **Research Statement & Publications:** Cardiovascular research; cardiac muscle mechanics and hemodynamics; shortening deactivation of cardiac muscle-mechanisms and significance; cardiac muscle physiology. **Mailing Address:** Dept NeuroSci, Sch Med, Univ NMex, Albuquerque, NM 87131. **Fax:** 505-272-8082.

LEACH, JOSEPH HENRY, LIMNOLOGY, FISHERIES BIOLOGY. **Personal Data:** b Sturgeon Falls, Ont, February 20, 1931. **Education:** Univ Toronto, BSA, 1954; Univ Guelph, MSc, 1966; Univ Aberdeen, PhD (marine ecol), 1969. **Honors & Awards:** Anderson-Everett Award, Int Asn Great Lakes Res, 1992. **Professional Experience:** RETIRED; adj prof, Univ Windsor, beginning 1993; sr scientist, Ont Ministry Natural Resources, 1986-1996; res scientist, Ont Ministry Natural Resources, 1969-1985. **Memberships:** Am Fisheries Soc; Int Asn Great Lakes Res (pres, 1978-1979); Int Asn Theoret Appl Limnol. **Research Statement & Publications:** Limnology and fisheries of the Great Lakes; impacts of cultural perturbations, particularly eutrophication and introduced species. **Mailing Address:** 111 Division St S, Kingsville, ON N9Y 1P5, Can. **Fax:** 519-825-3163.

LEACH, KAREN LYNN, CELL BIOLOGY. **Education:** Ohio Wesleyan Univ, BA, 1977; Univ Mich, Ann Arbor, PhD (pharmacol), 1981. **Professional Experience:** SR RES SCIENTIST, DEPT CELL BIOL, UPJOHN CO, KALAMAZOO, 1990-; assoc ed, J Immunol, 1990-1992; Organizer, Sixth Int Symp Cell Endocrinol, Lake Placid, NY, 1990; res scientist, Dept Cell Biol, Upjohn CO, Kalamazoo, 1984-1989; Postdoctoral fel, Lab Cellular Carcinogenesis & Tumor Prom, Nat Cancer Inst, 1984; reviewer, Cancer Res, J Biol Chem, J Immunol & J Cell Biol; invited lectr, numerous univs. **Memberships:** Soc Neurosci; Am Soc Cell Biol; Am Soc Biochem & Molecular Biol. **Mailing Address:** Dept Cell Biol, Uphohn Co 301 Henrietta St, Kalamazoo, MI 49001.

LEACH, LEONARD JOSEPH, TOXICOLOGY, ENVIRONMENTAL HEALTH. **Personal Data:** b Rochester, NY, August 3, 1924. **Education:** Brigham Young Univ, BS, 1949. **Professional Experience:** RETIRED; asst prof radiation biol & biophys, Sch Med & Dent, 1965-1986; speaker, Gordon Res Conf Toxicol & Safety Eval, NH, 1960; instr indust hyg, Atomic Energy Proj, Univ Rochester, 1957-1965; assoc indust hygienist, Atomic Energy Proj, Univ Rochester, 1955-1957; phys chemist, Army Chem Ctr, Md, 1951-1952. **Memberships:** Am Soc Toxicol; Am Acad Indust Hyg; Pan-Am Med Asn; Am Indust Hyg Asn; NY Acad Sci. **Research Statement & Publications:** Inhalation toxicity of airborne agents related to air pollution and all aspects of environmental health. **Mailing Address:** 47 Pickdale Dr, Rochester, NY 14626.

LEACH, ROBERT ELLIS, SPORTS MEDICINE, ORTHOPEDIC SURGERY. **Personal Data:** b Sanford, Maine, November 25, 1931. **Education:** Princeton Univ, BA, 1953; Columbia Univ, MD, 1957; Am Bd Orthop Surg, dipl. **Honors & Awards:** Sports Med Man Yr Award, Sports Med Soc, 1988. **Professional Experience:** ED EMER, AM J SPORTS MED, 2002-; ed-in-chief, Am j Sports Med, 1989-2002; chmn, Sports Med Coun, US Comt, 1985-1993; head physician, Olympic Team, USA, 1980-1984; Am, Brit & Can traveling fel, 1971; lectr, Tufts Univ, 1970-; PROF ORTHOP SURG, MED SCH, BOSTON UNIV, 1970-; Dir orthop serv, Boston City Hosp, 1970-1976; chmn orthop, Lahey Clin Found, 1967-1970. **Memberships:** Am Orthop Asn (pres, 1994); Am Orthop Soc Sports Med (pres, 1983); Am Acad Orthop Surgeons. **Research Statement & Publications:** Synthetic ligament reconstruction. **Mailing Address:** Dept Orthop Surg, Boston Univ, One Sherborn St, Boston, MA 02215. **Fax:** 781-736-0607.

LEACH, ROBIN J, BIOLOGY. **Education:** Univ Utah, PhD, 1984. **Professional Experience:** PROF, DEPT CELLULAR & STRUCT BIOL, UNIV TEX HEALTH SCI CTR, as of 2005; DIR GRAD COLLOQUIUM & INSTR GENETICS COURSE, UNIV TEX HEALTH SCI CTR, as of 2005. **Mailing Address:** Dept Cell & Structural Biol Univ Tex Health Sci Ctr, 7703 Floyd Curl Dr Rm 2 0541/2V, San Antonio, TX 78284-7762. **E-Mail:** leach@uthscsa.edu

LEACH, ROLAND MELVILLE, INFLUENCE OF NUTRITION & ENDOCRINE SYSTEM ON SKELETAL DEVELOPMENT. **Personal Data:** b Framingham, Mass, August 27, 1932. **Education:** Univ Maine, BS, 1954; Purdue Univ, MS, 1956; Cornell Univ, PhD (nutrit), 1960. **Honors & Awards:** Am Feed Mfrs Asn Award, Poultry Sci Assoc, 1980. **Professional Experience:** WALTHER H OTT PROF AVIAN BIOL, PA STATE UNIV, as of 2005; DISTINGUISHED PROF POULTRY SCI & NUTRIT, PA STATE UNIV, UNIV PARK, as of 2004; prof poultry sci, pa state Univ, university park, beginning 1973; assoc prof poultry sci, Pa State Univ, Univ Park, 1968-1973; asst prof animal nutrit, Cornell Univ, 1960-1968; chemist, Plant Soil & Nutrit Lab, USDA, 1959-1968. **Memberships:** Poultry Sci Asn; Am Inst Nutrit; AAAS; Am Soc Bone & Mineral Res. **Research Statement & Publications:** Mineral nutrition of animals; role of trace elements in bone formation; role of autocrine growth factors in skeletal development. **Mailing Address:** Dept Poultry Sci & Nutrit, Pa State Univ, 205 Henning Bldg, Univ Park, PA 16802. **Fax:** 814-865-5691. **E-Mail:** lnr@psu.edu

LEACH, RONALD J, SOFTWARE SYSTEMS. **Personal Data:** b Baltimore, Md, February 5, 1944; m 1965, Mary; c John, Anne & David. **Education:** Univ Md, BS, 1964, MA, 1966; Johns Hopkins Univ, PhD (comput sci), 1971, MS, 1983. **Professional Experience:** CHAIR, HOWARD UNIV, 1997-; NASA fel, 1984-1985; Am Soc Eng Educ fel, 1984-1985; PROF, DEPT SYSTS & COMPUT SCI, HOWARD UNIV, 1969-. **Memberships:** Asn Comput Mach; Comput Soc; Am Math Asn; Inst Elec & Electronics Engrs. **Research Statement & Publications:** Authored five books and nearly seventy technical papers. **Mailing Address:** Dept Systs & Comput Sci Sch Eng Howard Univ, 2300 Sixth St NW, Washington, DC 20059. **Fax:** 202-806-4531.

LEACH, WILLIAM MATTHEW, CELL BIOLOGY, RADIOBIOLOGY. **Personal Data:** b Pine Mountain, Ky, June 26, 1933; m 1960, Marion; c Jennifer Megan, William Marcus & Steven Drew. **Education:** Berea Col, BA, 1956; Univ Tenn, MS, 1962, PhD (zoology), 1965. **Professional Experience:** ASSOC DIR SCI, OFF SCI & TECHNOL, CTR DEVICES & RADIOL HEALTH, FOOD & DRUG ADMIN, 1986-; dir Div Life Sci, Bur Radiol Health, 1985-1986; adj prof genetics, George Wash Univ, 1972-; chief exp studies br, Bur Radiol Health, 1971-1984; trustee, Environ Educ Ctr, Pine Mountain Settlement Sch, Ky, 1967-; chief radiation cytol lab, Div Biol Effects, Bur Radiol Health, 1967-1971; res biologist, Radiation Bio-Effects Prog, Nat Ctr Radiol Health, 1966-1967; USAEC res assoc zoology & entom, Inst Radiation Biol, Univ Tenn, 1964-1966. **Memberships:** AAAS; Am Soc Cell Biol; Am Genetic Asn; Sigma Xi. **Research Statement & Publications:** Cell responses to radiation in relation to the cell cycle; cell synthetic activities during the cell cycle; behavior of particulates and molecules in cells; developmental biology; microwave radiation research. **Mailing Address:** Food & Drug Admin, 5600 Fishers Lane, Rockville, MD 20857-0001. **E-Mail:** william.leach@nih.hhs.gov

LEACH-HUNTOON, CAROLYN S, ENDOCRINOLOGY, PHYSIOLOGY. **Personal Data:** b Leesville, La, August 25, 1940. **Education:** Northwestern State Col, La, BS, 1962; Baylor Univ, MS, 1966, PhD (physiol), 1968. **Honors & Awards:** Louis H Bauer Founder's Award, Aerospace Med Asn. **Professional Experience:** RETIRED; consult, 1989-2004; dir space & life sci, Biomed Labs Br, 1987-1989; assoc dir, Biomed Labs Br, 1984-1987; chief, Biomed Labs Br, 1976-1984; chief, Space Metab & Bioichem Br, 1974-1976; adj asst prof, Baylor Col Med, 1970-; Proj Tektite II, NASA-Dept Interior, 1970; assoc investr, Inst Environ Med, Sch Med, Univ Pa, 1970; proj Tektite I, US Navy-NASA-Gen Elec-Dept Interior, 1969; head, Endocrine & Biochem Labs, Johnson Space Ctr, NASA, 1968-1974; adj instr physiol, Baylor Col Med, 1968-1970; res assoc, Nat Res Coun-Nat Acad Sci, Manned Spacecraft Ctr, NASA, 1968-1970; consult, Proj Sea Lab, US Navy, 1968-1969; spec med technologist, M D Anderson Hosp & Tumor Inst, Univ Tex, Houston, 1964-1968; med technologist, M D Anderson Hosp & Tumor Inst, Univ Tex, Houston, 1962-1964; mem res staff, Marine Biomed Inst, Univ Tex. **Memberships:** Fel Aerospace Med Asn; Int Astronaut Fedn; Endocrine Soc; Am Physiol Soc; Am Soc Med Technol; Am Soc Clin Path; Am Inst Aeronaut & Astronaut. **Research Statement & Publications:** The study of the physiological adaptation of man to changing environments, particularly the endocrine mechanisms involved in adaptation; aerospace medicine. **Mailing Address:** 4154 Sue Ellen St, Houston, TX 77087.

LEACOCK, ROBERT JAY, ASTRONOMY. **Personal Data:** b New York, NY, March 1, 1939. **Education:** Univ Fla, BS, 1960, MS, 1962, PhD (astron), 1971. **Professional Experience:** ASSOC CHMN, UNIV FLA, 1980-; ASSOC PROF PHYS SCI & ASTRON, UNIV FLA, 1976-; asst prof, Univ Fla, 1971-1976; res asst astron, Univ Fla, 1963-1971; instr physics, Pensacola Jr Col, 1962-1963. **Memberships:** AAAS; Am Astron Soc. **Research Statement & Publications:** Nonthermal radio observations of the major planets; optical variations of extragalactic radio sources. **Mailing Address:** Dept Astron, Univ Fla, Gainesville, FL 32605. **E-Mail:** leacock@astro.ufl.edu

LEADABRAND, RAY LAURENCE, ELECTRONICS ENGINEERING. **Personal Data:** b Pasadena, Calif, October 12, 1927. **Education:** San Jose State Col, BS, 1950; Stanford Univ, MS, 1953. **Professional Experience:** SR VPRES, SCI APPLNS INT CORP, 1985-; sr vpres, Eng Res Group, 1980-1985; exec dir, Electronics & Radio Sci Div, 1968-; mgr, Radio Physics Lab, 1960-1968; head propagation group, SRI Int, 1959-1960; res engr, SRI Int, 1955-1958; asst, Stanford Univ, 1952-1955; Field engr, Philco Corp, 1950-1952. **Memberships:** AAAS; fel Inst Elec & Electronics Engrs; Am Geophys Union; Int Union Radio Sci; Sigma Xi. **Research Statement & Publications:** Ionospheric radio propagation; auroral radar; moon and satellite reflection and transmission; propagation studies related to nuclear explosions and missile flight; radio and radar astronomy research of solar systems. **Mailing Address:** 3161 E Rivernest Dr, Boise, ID 83706.

LEADBETTER, EDWARD RENTON, MICROBIOLOGY. **Personal Data:** b Barnesboro, Pa, January 26, 1934; m 1956, Gloria; c Aletha, Garth, Briana & Jared. **Education:** Franklin & Marshall Col, BS, 1955; Univ Tex, PhD (bact), 1959. **Honorary Degrees:** MA, Amherst Col, 1970. **Professional Experience:** Course dir, Marine Biol Lab, Woods Hole, 1995-1999; prog dir, Cellular Biochem, NSF, 1990-1991; found microbiol lectr, Am Soc Microbiol, 1989-1990; PROF, DEPT MOLECULAR & CELL BIOL, UNIV CONN, 1985-; Nat Acad Sci-Hungarian Acad Sci Exchange, Szeged, 1985, 1988; head, Dept Microbiol, Univ Conn, 1984-1985; prof, Biol Sci Group, Univ Conn, 1978-1985; head dept, Biol Sci Group, Univ Conn, 1978-1983; NATO sr fel, Univ Seville, 1972; mem corp, Marine Biol Lab, Woods Hole, 1971-; instr, Marine Biol Lab, Woods Hole, 1971-1978; vis prof, Hampshire Col, 1971; prof biol, Amherst Col, 1970-1978; chmn dept, Amherst Col, 1967-1971; NIH spec fel, Univ Mass, 1966-1967; NSF fel, Hopkins Marine Sta, Pac Grove, Calif, 1962-1963; from asst prof to assoc prof, Amherst Col, 1961-1970; instr, Amherst Col, 1959-1961. **Memberships:** Am Soc Microbiol; Soc Gen Microbiol. **Research Statement & Publications:** Microbial ecology, physiology, and biochemistry; amine metabolism; photosynthesis; myxobacteria; oral microbiology; hydrocarbon oxidation; ultrastructure; gliding motility, sulfonate formation and degradation. **Mailing Address:** Dept Molecular & Cell Biol, Univ Conn, 354 Mansfield Rd Unit 2131, Storrs Manfield, CT 06269-2131. **Fax:** 860-486-1936. **E-Mail:** erl@uconnvm.uconn.edu

LEADER, GORDON ROBERT, PHYSICAL CHEMISTRY. **Personal Data:** b Milwaukee, Wis, January 27, 1916; m 1946, Helen Kendrick; c Richard, Julie, Malcolm & James. **Education:** Univ Wis, BS, 1937; Univ Minn, PhD (phys chem), 1940. **Professional Experience:** RETIRED; consult, Elf Atochem, 1986-1996; sr res chemist, Pennwalt Corp, 1964-1986; sr res chemist, Thiokol Chem Corp, 1958-1964; res chemist, Olin Mathieson Chem Corp, 1953-1958; res chemist, Mallinckrodt Chem Works, Mo, 1951-1953; asst prof chem, Univ Ky, 1947-1951; Nat Defense Res Comt, Manhattan Dist Proj, Univ Chicago, 1943-1947; Nat Defense Res Comt, Northwestern Univ, 1942-1943; res chemist, Monsanto Chem Co, Mo, 1940-1942. **Memberships:** Am Chem Soc. **Research Statement & Publications:** Chemical process development; Raman and nuclear magnetic resonance spectroscopy; radiochemistry; conductance and dielectric constants of organic solutions. **Mailing Address:** 726 Loveville Rd Apt 211, Hockessin, DE 19707-1505. **E-Mail:** cokesbury1@aol.com

LEADER, JOHN CARL, STATISTICAL OPTICS, LASER INTERACTIONS. **Personal Data:** b St Louis, Mo, October 25, 1938; m 1961, Kay; c Tracy & Susan. **Education:**

Rensselaer Polytech Inst, BS, 1960, PhD (nuclear physics), 1969. **Professional Experience:** Consult, Mcdonnell Douglas Corp, beginning 1996; proj mgr, McDonnell Douglas Res Labs, 1991-1996; dir res, McDonnell Douglas Res Labs, 1987-1991; ed, Proc Soc Photo-Optical Instrumentation Engrs, 1983; chief scientist radiation sci, McDonnell Aircraft Reconnaissance Lab, McDonnell Douglas Corp, 1981-1987; sr scientist, McDonnell Aircraft Reconnaissance Lab, McDonnell Douglas Corp, 1974-1981; sr engr, McDonnell Aircraft Reconnaissance Lab, McDonnell Douglas Corp, 1969-1974. **Memberships:** Optical Soc Am; Soc Photo-Optical Instrumentation Engrs; Union Radio Sci Int. **Research Statement & Publications:** Theoretical research on radiation scattering from rough surfaces; optical propagation through atmospheric turbulence; partial coherence theory; laser radar; charged particle beam propagation; laser interactions with materials. **Mailing Address:** 1016 Julianna Dr, Manchester, MO 63011. **E-Mail:** jcleader@concentric.net

LEADER, SOLOMON, MATHEMATICS. **Personal Data:** b Spring Lake, NJ, November 14, 1925. **Education:** Rutgers Univ, BS, 1949; Princeton Univ, MA, 1951, PhD (math), 1952. **Professional Experience:** PROF EMER MATH, RUTGERS UNIV, NEW BRUNSWICK, as of 2004; prof math, Rutgers univ, New Brunswick, beginning 1961; From instr to assoc prof, Rutgers Univ, New Brunswick, 1952-1961. **Memberships:** Am Math Soc; Math Asn Am; Sigma Xi. **Research Statement & Publications:** Functional analysis; general topology. **Mailing Address:** Dept Math, Rutgers Univ, New Brunswick, NJ 08903-2101.

LEADERS, FLOYD EDWIN, JR, pharmacology, research administration; deceased, see previous edition for last biography

LEADON, BERNARD M(ATTHEW), FLUID MECHANICS. **Personal Data:** b Farmington, Minn, November 29, 1917. **Education:** Col St Thomas, BS, 1938; Univ Minn, MS, 1942, PhD (fluid mech), 1955. **Professional Experience:** Chmn, Third US Nat Conf Wind Eng, 1978; PROF EMER ENG SCI, UNIV FLA, 1975-; Martinez & Costa & Assocs, 1971 & 1978 & Pratt & Whitney Aircraft Corp, 1974 & 1976-1982; NATO fel, 1972; consult, AMF Beaird, 1969; consult, USAF, 1966; prof, Univ Fla, 1964-1975; consult, Gen Dynamics/Convair, 1964-1965; vis prof, San Diego State Col, 1962-1964; sr staff scientist, Gen Off, Gen Dynamics/Convair, 1957-1964; consult, Minneapolis-Honeywell Regulator Corp, 1956-1957; scientist, Rosemount Aeronaut Lab, 1948-1957; lectr, Univ Minn, 1946-1957; chief aerodynamicist, Rosemount Aeronaut Lab, 1946-1948; head propulsion exp sect, Cornell Aeronaut Lab, 1945-1946; sr aerodynamicist, Curtiss-Wright Corp, NY, 1944-1945; instr, Univ Buffalo, 1944-1945; aerodynamicist, Curtiss-Wright Corp, NY, 1943-1944; instr, Univ Minn, 1942-1943; asst aerodyn, Univ Minn, 1942; engr, Pac Gas & Elec Co, Calif, 1941. **Memberships:** Am Inst Aeronaut & Astronaut; Sigma Xi. **Research Statement & Publications:** Heat transfer; aerodynamics; airplane design. **Mailing Address:** Dept Eng Univ Fla, 328-B MAE-A, Gainesville, FL 32601-4323. **E-Mail:** bml@mae.ufl.edu

LEADS, DAN, CERAMIC ENGINEERING. **Honors & Awards:** Samuel Geitsbeek Award, Am Ceramic Soc, 1994. **Professional Experience:** ARTECH INC, CLARKSVILLE, as of 2002. **Mailing Address:** PO Box 848, Ft Smith, AR 72902.

LEAF, ALEXANDER, INTERNAL MEDICINE. **Personal Data:** b Yokohama, Japan, April 10, 1920. **Education:** Univ Wash, BS, 1940; Univ Mich, MD, 1943. **Honorary Degrees:** AM, Harvard Univ, 1961. **Honors & Awards:** Homer Smith Award Renal Physiol, 1981; Kuber Medal, Asn Am Physicians, 1995; A N Richards Award, Int Soc Nephrology. **Professional Experience:** MASS GEN HOSP, as of 2006; Distinguished physician, Vet Affairs, 1992-1996; JACKSON EMER PROF CLIN MED, SCH MED, HARVARD UNIV, 1990-; Ridley Watts prof prev med & chmn, Dept Prev Med & Clin Epidemiol, 1980-1990; John Simon Guggenheim Mem Found fel, Balliol Col, Oxford Univ, 1971-1972; chief med serv, Mass Gen Hosp, 1966-1981; Jackson prof clin med, Harvard Univ, 1966-1981; physician, Mass Gen Hosp, 1962-; from asst prof to assoc prof, Harvard Univ, 1956-1965; from asst physician to assoc physician, Mass Gen Hosp, 1953-1962; assoc, Harvard Univ, 1953-1956; Instr med, Univ Mich, 1947-1949. **Memberships:** Nat Acad Sci; Inst Med-Nat Acad Sci; Am Physiol Soc; Asn Am Physicians; Am Acad Arts & Sci; Am Soc Clin Invest; foreign mem Royal Danish Acad Sci & Lett. **Research Statement & Publications:** Ion transport and membrane physiology; kidney physiology; nutrition; certain polyunsaturated fatty acids in fish oils; prevention of fatal ischemia-induced ventricular arrhythmias; free fatty acids; protective fatty acids that stabilize electrically every cardiac myocyte in the heart; modulating the sodium and calcium ion channel currents in the cell membranes. **Mailing Address:** Mass Gen Hosp, 149 13th St, Boston, MA 02129. **Fax:** 617-726-6144.

LEAF, BORIS, STATISTICAL MECHANICS, ELECTRODYNAMICS. **Personal Data:** b Yokohama, Japan, March 4, 1919; American citizen; m 1947, Genevieve; c Evelyn M, David A & Michael L. **Education:** Univ Wash, BS, 1939; Univ Ill, PhD (phys chem), 1942. **Professional Experience:** PROF EMER PHYSYCS, STATE UNIV NY COL CORTLAND, as of 2000; partic, State Univ NY-Moscow State Univ, USSR, 1981; assoc ed, Am J Physics, 1976-1979; scholar exchange prof, Res Found, State Univ NY, beginning 1974; vis prof, Cornell Univ, 1973-1974; fac fel & grants-in-aid, Res Found, State Univ NY, 1970-1972; prof, State Univ NY, Binghamton, 1967-1971; prof physics, State Univ NY Col Cortland, 1965-1989; chmn dept, State Univ NY Col Cortland, 1965-1982; res fel, Brussels, 1958-1960; prof, Kans State Univ, 1954-1965; assoc prof physics, Kans State Univ, 1946-1954; fel, Yale Univ, 1945-1946; spec asst, Nat Defense Res Comt, Univ Ill, 1945; assoc chemist, Metall Lab, Univ Chicago, 1944-1945; instr phys chem, Univ Ill, 1943-1944; spec asst chem, Univ Ill, 1942-1943. **Memberships:** Fel AAAS; fel Am Phys Soc; Am Asn Physics Teachers; NY Acad Sci. **Research Statement & Publications:** Thermodynamic theory; transport processes; quantum theory. **Mailing Address:** 11039 39th Ave NE, Seattle, WA 98125.

LEAHEY, DOUGLAS MCADAM, ATMOSPHERIC CHEMISTRY & PHYSICS. **Personal Data:** b Truro, NS, August 23, 1942. **Education:** Dalhousie Univ, BS, 1963; McGill Univ, MS, 1966; NY Univ, PhD (air pollution), 1971. **Professional Experience:** STAFF SCIENTIST, BOVAR ENVIRON SERV, 1988-; mgr air qual serv, Bovar Environ Serv, 1971-1988; res assoc, NY Univ, 1968-1971; Meteorologist, Can Govt, 1963-1968. **Memberships:** Am Meteorol Soc; Can Meteorol & Oceanog Soc; Air & Waste Mgt Asn. **Research Statement & Publications:** Atmospheric turbulence, plume dispersion, urban air pollution and wind flow regimes. **Mailing Address:** 3036 Second St SW, Calgary, AB T2S 1T3, Can.

LEAHY, DENIS ALAN, X-RAY ASTRONOMY, SUPERNOVA REMNANTS. **Personal Data:** b Taber, Alta, June 13, 1952. **Education:** Univ Waterloo, BSc, 1975; Univ BC, MSc, 1976, PhD (physics), 1980. **Professional Experience:** PROF, DEPT PHYSICS & ASTRON, UNIV CALGARY, 1993-; from asst prof to assoc prof, Univ Calgary, 1988-1993; res fel physics, Univ Calgary, 1983-1988; sessional instr, Univ Calgary, 1982-1983; res assoc, Marshall Space Flight Ctr, 1980-1982. **Memberships:** Am Astron Soc; Can Astron Soc; Sigma Xi; Can Asn Physicists; Int Astronaut Union. **Research Statement & Publications:** X-ray astronomy, data analysis and interpretation; supernova remnants; x-ray binaries; symbiotic stars; pulsar magnetospheres. **Mailing Address:** Dept Physics & Astron, Univ Calgary, 2500 Univ Dr NW, Calgary, AB T2N 1N4, Can. **Fax:** 403-289-3331. **E-Mail:** leahy@iras.ucalgary.ca

LEAHY, JOHN V, MATHEMATICS. **Professional Experience:** PROF & VICE PROVOST, DEPT MATH, UNIV ORE, as of 2004. **Mailing Address:** Dept Math, Univ Ore, 459 Willamette, Eugene, OR 97403-1222. **E-Mail:** leahy@math.uoregon.edu

LEAHY, MARY GERALD, INSECT PHYSIOLOGY, ACAROLOGY. **Personal Data:** b San Francisco, Calif, October 11, 1917. **Education:** Univ Southern Calif, BA, 1945; Cath Univ Am, MA, 1947; Univ Notre Dame, PhD (biol), 1962. **Professional Experience:** FAC, ST ANTHONYS CONVENT, 1985-; prin investr, NIH grant, 1974-1977; vis scientist, Ga Southern Col, 1974-1975; sr res scientist, Nairobi, Kenya, 1973-1974; collab scientist, EAfrican Vet Res Orgn, Kenya, 1973-1974; WHO grant, Israel Inst Biol Res, Ness Ziona & Hebrew Univ Jerusalem, 1968-1969; fel trop pub health, Harvard Univ, 1966; chmn dept, Mt St Mary's Col, 1962-1965; NSF res grants, 1962-1964, 1965-1967, 1970-1971; from asst prof to prof biol, Mt St Mary's Col, 1947-1985; exchange scientist tick pheromones & hormones, Poland, Czech & Russia, Nat Acad Sci. **Memberships:** AAAS; Entom Soc Am; Am Inst Biol Sci. **Research Statement & Publications:** Mosquitoes and ticks; pheromones and reproductive physiology. **Mailing Address:** Carondelet Ctr, 11999 Chalon Rd, Los Angeles, CA 90048.

LEAHY, RICHARD GORDON, GEOCHEMISTRY. **Personal Data:** b Buffalo, NY, March 6, 1929; m 1953, c 3. **Education:** Yale Univ, BS, 1952; Harvard Univ, AM, 1954, PhD (geol), 1957. **Professional Experience:** RETIRED; exec dir, New Eng Consortium Undergrad Sci Educ, 1988-; chmn, Consortium Sci Comput, 1986-1988; asst to pres civic & govt rels, Div Eng & Appl Physics, 1970-1971; ASSOC DEAN FAC ARTS & SCI, HARVARD UNIV, 1968-; dir labs, Div Eng & Appl Physics, 1960-1968; Mem US tech panel geochem, Int Geophys Year, 1957-1958; asst to dir & res assoc geol, Woods Hole Oceanog Inst, 1956-1960; Asst geochem, Yale Univ, 1952-1953. **Memberships:** AAAS; Am Geophys Union; NY Acad Sci. **Research Statement & Publications:** Geochemistry of heavy isotopes in sea water and marine sediments; chemical processes of submarine weathering; variation of carbon dioxide in the atmosphere and its relation to air mass properties. **Mailing Address:** Sci Ctr, Harvard Univ, Cambridge, MA 02138.

LEAIST, DEREK GORDON, ELECTROCHEMISTRY, DIFFUSION. **Personal Data:** b Akron, Ohio, January 5, 1955. **Education:** Queen's Univ, Kingston, Ont, BSc, 1977; Yale Univ, MSc, 1978, PhD (phys chem), 1980. **Honors & Awards:** Lash Miller Award, Electrochem Soc, 1989. **Professional Experience:** PROF, CHEM DEPT, UNIV WESTERN ONT, LONDON, CAN, 1990-; from asst prof to assoc prof, Chem Dept, Univ Western Ont, London, Can, 1982-1990; res assoc chem, Nat Res Coun, Ottawa, Can, 1981-1982. **Research Statement & Publications:** Theoretical and experimental studies of diffusion in liquids, with emphasis on coupled transport inmulticomponent electrolyte mixtures; micelle solutions; thermal diffusion in liquids; author of various articles. **Mailing Address:** Dept Chem, Univ Western Ont, Off Rm 067 Chem Bldg, London, ON N6A 5B7, Can. **E-Mail:** dleaist@uwo.ca

LEAK, JOHN CLAY, DRUG REGULATION, RADIO PHARMACEUTICALS. **Personal Data:** b Washington, DC, August 31, 1928. **Education:** Univ Vt, BS, 1949; Univ Ill, PhD (chem), 1954. **Professional Experience:** RES CHEMIST, FOOD & DRUG ADMIN, 1979-; res chemist, Food & Drug Admin, 1976-1979; mgr prod opers, Life Group, 1975-1976; sr staff chemist, ICN Pharmaceut, Inc, 1969-1975; sr staff chemist, Tracerlab, 1967-1969; mgr chem dept, Tracerlab, 1965-1967; vpres, ChemTrac Corp, 1962-1965; oper mgr, Baird-Atomic, Inc, Mass, 1962-1965; tech dir, ChemTrac Corp, 1961-1962; res dir, Cyclo Chem Corp, 1960-1961; dir carbon-14 dept, Isotopes Specialties Co, 1959-1960; chemist, Isotopes Specialties Co, 1956-1959; res assoc animal nutrit, Univ Ill, 1955-1956; Fulbright scholar, Ger, 1954-1955; asst, Univ Ill, 1951-1954. **Memberships:** Sigma Xi. **Research Statement & Publications:** Mechanism of organic reactions; metabolic fate of labeled hydroxy-proline in rats; synthesis of labeled compounds; applications for stable and radioactive isotopes; manufacture and control of radiopharmaceuticals; drug analysis. **Mailing Address:** Food & Drug Admin, Annapolis, MD 21403-4661.

LEAK, LEE VIRN, CELL & MOLECULAR BIOLOGY, PROTEOMICS. **Personal Data:** b Chesterfield, SC, July 22, 1932; m 1964, Eleanor Carrol Merrick; c Alice Elizabeth (Dillon)& Lee V, Jr. **Education:** SC State Col, BS, 1954; Mich State Univ, MS, 1959, PhD (cell biol), 1962. **Honors & Awards:** Adelle Melbourne Holmes Mem Award, Am Heart Asn. **Professional Experience:** Speaker, Gordon Res Conf, Lymphatic Vascular Syst, 2004; ad hoc mem, Nat Heart Lung & Blood Inst, Exp Cardiovasc Syst Sect, 2002; NIH res grant, 1994-1998; mem bd trustees, St Andrew Episcopal Sch, 1992-1994; NSF res grant, 1990-1993; RES PROF, COL MED, HOWARD UNIV, 1983-; mem adv coun, Pulmonary Dis Br, Nat Heart, Lung & Blood Inst, 1982-1986; mem panel basic biomed sci, Nat Res Coun, 1980; mem, Div Cancer Biol, Diag Bd, Nat Cancer Inst, 1979; PROF, GRAD SCH ART & SCI, 1976-; NIH res grant, 1974-1984; mem, Marine Biol Lab Corp, 1973-1976; mem, Nat Bd Med Examr, 1973-1976; founder/dir, EE Just Lab Cellular Biol, 1972-; mem, Div Biol & Agr, Nat Res Coun, 1972-1975; mem, Anat Sci Training Comt, 1972-1973; PROF ANAT, COL MED, HOWARD UNIV, 1971-; Nat Heart, Lung & Blood Inst res grant, 1971-1986; chmn dept, Grad Sch Art & Sci, 1971-1981; from instr to asst prof anat, Harvard Med Sch, 1967-1971; consult, Shriners Burns Res Inst, 1967-1971; Am Heart Asn res grant, 1967-1970; USPHS res grant, 1966-1998; mem, Nat Inst Allergy Infectious Dis, 1966-1985; asst biol, Harvard Med Sch, 1965-1968; asst surg, Mass Gen Hosp, 1964-1965; res fel electron micros, Mass Gen Hosp & Harvard Med Sch, 1962-1964; asst prof biol sci, Mich State Univ, beginning 1962; mem, Res Comt, Am Heart Asn; guest scientist, Clin Proteomics Prog Therapeutic Protect, Food & Drug Admin. **Memberships:** Am Asn Anat; Am Soc Cell Biol; Am Soc Zool; Genetics Soc Am; Sigma Xi; Am Physiol Soc; Int Soc Lymphol; Tissue Cult Asn; NAm Vascular Org; Soc In Vitro Biol. **Research Statement & Publications:** Biology of the lymphatic vascular system and its role during the inflammatory response; pulmonary lymphatic drainage; ontogeny of the lymphatic system; pericarditis; chemotaxis; cell adhesion & migration; cell culture of lymphatic endothelium; lymphangiogenesis in vitro. **Mailing Address:** Dept Anat, Col Med, Howard Univ, 520 W St SW, Washington, DC 20059. **Fax:** 202-265-7055. **E-Mail:** lleak@fac.howard.edu

LEAKE, DON H, MATHEMATICS. **Education:** Univ Mo-Columbia, BS, MS; Wash Univ, PhD. **Professional Experience:** PROF MATH, UNIV WIS-RIVER FALLS, as of 2006. **Mailing Address:** Dept Math, Univ Wis, River Falls, 214 E N Hall, River Falls, WI 54022. **Fax:** 715-425-3590. **E-Mail:** Don.Leake@uwrf.edu

LEAKE, LOWELL JR, MATHEMATICS EDUCATION. **Personal Data:** b Denver, Colo, May 25, 1928; m 1959, Jane Acomb; c Katherine J & L Gregory. **Education:** Tufts Col, AB, 1950; Univ Wis, MS, 1956, PhD (math, educ), 1962. **Professional Experience:** PROF MATH, UNIV CINCINNATI, 1974-; from instr to assoc prof math, Univ Cincinnati, 1960-1974; high sch teacher, Ill, 1956-1958; Traffic chief, Northwestern Bell Tel Co, 1950-

1954; US Army, 1951-1953. **Memberships:** Emer Mem Math Asn Am; emer mem Nat Coun Teachers Math; emer mem Am Asn Univ Professors. **Research Statement & Publications:** Training of secondary and elementary mathematics teachers at undergraduate and graduate levels; learning of mathematics; PIAGET and probability; computers in education; helping teaching assistants learn to teach. **Mailing Address:** Dept Math Sci/0025 Old Chem 819C, Univ Cincinnati, Cincinnati, OH 45221. **Fax:** 513-556-3417. **E-Mail:** leakel@msn.com

LEAKE, MARTHA A, PLANETARY SCIENCE. **Education:** Univ Ariz, PhD. **Professional Experience:** PROF PHYSICS & ASTRON, VALDOSTA STATE UNIV, as of 2005. **Mailing Address:** Dept Physics Astronomy & Geology, Valdosta State Univ, Valdosta, GA 31698-0055.

LEAKE, PRESTON HILDEBRAND, ORGANIC CHEMISTRY, AMINO ACIDS, PAPER CHEMISTRY TOBACCO TECHNOLOGY. **Personal Data:** b Proffit, Va, August 8, 1929; m 1954, Elizabeth; c Luther H & Lawrence A. **Education:** Univ Va, BS, 1950; Duke Univ, MA, 1953, PhD (chem), 1954. **Honors & Awards:** Distinguished Serv Award, Va Sect, Am Chem Soc, 1976. **Professional Experience:** RETIRED; vpres res, Res & Develop Dept, Am Tobacco Co, 1989-1992; dir res & develop dept, Res & Develop Dept, Am Tobacco Co, 1987-1989; asst dir, Res & Develop Dept, Am Tobacco Co, 1970-1987; asst managing dir, Res & Develop Dept, Am Tobacco Co, 1968-1970; asst to managing dir, Res & Develop Dept, Am Tobacco Co, 1965-1968; adj prof, Richmond Prof Inst, 1963-1964; asst res dir, Albemarle Paper Mfg Co, 1960-1965; res supvr org chem, Nitrogen Div, Allied Chem Corp, 1954-1960. **Memberships:** Am Chem Soc; Am Inst Chemists; Tech Asn Pulp & Paper Indust; Sigma Xi; Tobacco chem. **Research Statement & Publications:** Polycyclic aromatic chemistry: Psychorr synthesis; amino acids and cyanuric acid derivatives; polyethylene; sizing; silica fume; specialty and filter papers; tobacco; plant physiology. **Mailing Address:** 401 Delton Ave, Hopewell, VA 23860-1815. **Fax:** 804-452-5484.

LEAKEY, JULIAN EDWIN ARUNDELL, BIOCHEMICAL PHARMACOLOGY, PROTEIN CHEMISTRY. **Personal Data:** b Settle, Yorkshire, UK, June 12, 1951. **Education:** Univ Dundee, UK, PhD, 1976. **Professional Experience:** RES BIOLOGIST, DEPT HEALTH & HUMAN SERV, NAT CTR TOXICOL RES, FOOD & DRUG ADMIN, as of 2005; PROF TOXICOL, UNIV ARK MED SCI, as of 2005; res biologist, Div Biometry & Risk Assessment, 1991; ADJ PROF, UNIV ARK, MED SCI, 1987-; SR STAFF TOXICOL, DIV REP DEV TOXICOL, NAT CTR TOXICOL RES, 1985-; vis scientist, Develop Toxicol, 1983; res fel, Dept Biochem, Univ Dundee, 1978-1985; fel toxicol, Inst Environ Health & Sci, Res Triangle Park, 1977-1978. **Memberships:** Teratology Soc; Int Soc Xenobiotics; Soc Exp Bld Med. **Research Statement & Publications:** Hormonal development, nutrition and environmental regulation of drug metabolizing enzymes in relation to toxicology, pharmacokinetics and carcinogenesis. **Mailing Address:** Dept Health & Human Serv, Nat Ctr Toxicol Res, Food & Drug Admin, Rm 103 200 Independence Ave, Washington, DC 20201. **Fax:** 870-543-7576. **E-Mail:** julian.leakey@fda.hhs.gov

LEAKEY, RICHARD ERSKINE, ANTHROPOLOGY. **Personal Data:** b Nairobi, Kenya, December 19, 1944. **Honorary Degrees:** DSc, Wooster Col, 1978, Rockford Col, 1983, Univ Aberdeen, 1994; LittD, Univ Kent, 1987; LhD, Ohio Univ, 1990. **Honors & Awards:** Franklin Burr Prize, 1965 & 1973; Centennial Award, Nat Geog Soc, 1988, Hubbard Medal, 1994; James Smithson Medal, Smithsonian Inst, 1990; Gold Medal, Royal Geog Soc London, 1990; Medal, Port Archaeol Soc, 1990. **Professional Experience:** DIR, KENYA WILDLIFE SERV, 1989-; head, Wildlife Conserv Dept, 1989-1990; chmn, EAfrica Wildlife Soc, 1985-1989; mem, WTurkana Res Prof, 1982, 1984-1986; mem, Buluk-Early Miocene Proj, 1982; mem, Nakali/Suguta Valley Exped, 1978; dir & chief exec, Nat Mus Kenya, 1974-1989; vchmn, Environ Prep Group, Kenya, 1972-1974; leader & coordr, Koobi Fora Res Proj, Lake Turkana, 1969-; admin dir, Nat Mus Kenya, 1968-1974; Leader, ERudolph Exped, 1968; Leader, Int Omo River Exped SEthiopia, 1967; Asst dir, Ctr Prehist & Paleont, 1966-1967; Leader, Exped West Baringo Kenya, 1966. **Memberships:** Fel Royal Anthrop Inst; fel AAAS; fel Kenya Acad Sci; fel Inst Cultural Res UK; Pan African Asn Prehist Studies; Sigma Xi; EAfrica Wildlife Soc. **Research Statement & Publications:** Numerous publications and scholarly lectures in the United States and abroad; author of five books; contributed various chapters to books and articles to professional journals. **Mailing Address:** PO Box 24926, Nairobi, Kenya.

LEAL, GEORGE D, CIVIL ENGINEERING. **Personal Data:** b San Francisco, Calif, February 28, 1934. **Education:** Calif Inst Technol, MS, 1958; Univ Chicago, MBA, 1965. **Professional Experience:** CHMN, DAMES & MOORE, 1981-. **Memberships:** Nat Acad Eng; Am Soc Civil Eng. **Mailing Address:** Dames & Moore Inc, 911 Wilshire Blvd Suite 700, Los Angeles, CA 90017. **Fax:** 213-683-0401.

LEAL, JOSEPH ROGERS, ORGANIC CHEMISTRY. **Personal Data:** b New Bedford, Mass, September 14, 1918. **Education:** Univ Mass, BS, 1949; Ind Univ, PhD (chem), 1953. **Professional Experience:** PRES, CRESCENT CONSULTS, 1983-; sr staff assoc, Celanese Res Co, 1967-1983; mgr contract rels, Wash, DC, 1963-1967; tech rep govt res liaison, Wash, DC, 1957-1963; res chemist, Am Cyanamid Co, 1952-1957; asst chemist, Revere Copper & Brass Co, 1942-1943 & 1945-1946; Res asst, Corn Prod Refining Co, 1940-1942. **Memberships:** AAAS; Am Chem Soc; NY Acad Sci; Am Inst Chemists; Soc Advan Mat Process Eng. **Research Statement & Publications:** High temperature resistant aromatic and heterocyclic polymers; nonflammable fibers; high strength, high modulus reinforcement materials. **Mailing Address:** 10 S Crescent, Maplewood, NJ 07040-2711.

LEAL, L GARY, FLUID MECHANICS, POLYMER PHYSICS. **Personal Data:** b Bellingham, Wash, March 18, 1943; m 1965, Mary; c Heather Noel, Kamaron Brie & Farrah Aimee. **Education:** Univ Wash, BS, 1965; Stanford Univ, MS, 1968, PhD (chem engr), 1969. **Honors & Awards:** Allan Colburn Award, Am Inst Chem Engrs, 1978, William H Walker Award, 1993; Allan Colburn Mem Lectr, Univ Del, 1978; Stanley Corrsin Lectr, Johns Hopkins Univ, 1990; Stanley Katz Mem Lectr, City Col City Univ, NY, 1991; Reilly Mem Lectr, Univ Notre Dame, 1992; Robert Pigford Lectr, Univ Del, 1994; Julian Smith Lectr, Cornell Univ, 1995; Rothschild Visiting Prof, Isaac Newton Inst Math, Univ Cambridge, UK; Julian C Smith Lect, Sch Chem Engr, Cornell Univ, 1996; Rutgers Collaboratus X Lect, Dept Chem & Biochem Engr, Rutgers Univ, 2000; George K Batchelor Lect Fluid Mech, Dept App Math Theoretical Physics, Univ Cambridge, 2000; Distinguished Alumni Award, Dept Chem Engr, Univ Wash, 2000; Bingham Medal, Soc Rheology, Am Inst Physics, 2000; NCE Cullimore Memorial Lect, NJIT, 2001; Fluid Dynamics Prize, Am Phys Soc, 2002. **Professional Experience:** Congress comm IUTAM, 2000-; CHEM ENGR ADV BD, VA TECH, 2000-; IUTAM Fluids Symposia Panel, 2000-; ed bd, App Rheology, 1999-; ed bd, Advans chem engr, 1998-; adv bd, Cambridge Univ Press, Series Chem, 1998-; ed, Physics of Fluids, Am inst Physics, 1998-; Rothschild vis prof, Cambridge Univ, 1995; mem, Policy Comt, Nat Acad Engr, beginning 1994; chmn, US Nat Comt Theoret & Appl Math, 1994-1996; mem, Nat Res Coun Space Studies Bd Comt, Microgravity Res, 1993-; US deleg chair, IUTAM Can Assembly, 1992-; rep, Gen Assembly Union Theoretical & App Mech, 1992-1998; mem, US Nat Comt Theoret & Appl Math, 1991-; Dowell-Schlumberger, 1985-1988 & Univ Okla, 1991-; PROF & CHAIR CHEM & NUCLEAR ENGR, UNIV CALIF, SANTA BARBARA, 1989-; from asst prof to prof chem engr, Chevron prof, 1986-1989; NSF engr, Fluid mech Workshop, Savanannah, Ga; 1986-1987; assoc ed, Int J Multiphase Flow, beginning 1985; consult ed, J Am Inst Chem Engrs, 1985-1987; consult, Dynamics Technol Inc, 1982-1991; consult, Firestone Res, 1981-1989; sr vis appl math, Cambridge Univ, 1976-1977; Guggenheim fel, Cambridge Univ, 1976-1977; prin investr, NSF, 1971- & Off Naval Res, 1975-; consult, Richards of Rockford, 1975-1979; Petrol Res Fund grant, Calif Inst Technol, beginning 1970; from asst prof to prof chem engr, Calif Inst Technol, 1970-1986; NSF fel, Cambridge Univ, 1969-1970. **Memberships:** Nat Acad Engr; Soc Rheol; Brit Soc Rheol; fel Am Phys Soc; Am Inst Chem Engrs; Am Soc Engr Educ. **Research Statement & Publications:** Fluid mechanics; suspension mechanics; rheology; mechanical and optical properties of polymeric liquids; multiphase flows; colloid physics; published numerous articles. **Mailing Address:** 1560 Hillcrest Rd, Santa Barbara, CA 93103. **E-Mail:** lglzo@Eng.ucsb.edu

LEAMNSON, ROBERT N, MICROBIOLOGY. **Education:** Univ Ill, PhD (biol), 1973. **Professional Experience:** PROF BIOL, UNIV MASS, DARTMOUTH, as of 2005. **Mailing Address:** Dept Biol, Univ Mass, North Dartmouth, MA 02747. **Fax:** 508-999-8196. **E-Mail:** rleamnson@umassd.edu

LEAMON, TOM B, ERGONOMICS, HUMAN FACTORS & SAFETY. **Personal Data:** b Ossett, Yorkshire, Eng, April 16, 1940; American citizen; m 1967, Geraldine; c Amanda C, Jonathan M & Genevieve E. **Education:** Univ Manchester, UK, BS, 1961; Cranfield Inst Technol, UK, MS, 1968, PhD (indust eng), 1982; Univ Aston, UK, MS, 1970. **Honors & Awards:** Sir Ben Williams Silver Medal, Inst Prod Engrs, 1969; Ergonomics Div Award Outstanding Contrib Enhancement Ergonomics, Inst Indust Eng, 1993; Otto Edholm Medal Res, Ergonomics Society; 2000, Soc 2000 Lec, Ergonomics Soc, 1998; Pres Award, Int Ergonomics Assoc. **Professional Experience:** Lectr, Harvard Univ, Sch Pub Health, 1993; VPRES & DIR, RES CTR, LIBERTY MUTUAL INS CO, 1991-; trustee, Am Soc Safety Engrs, Fed Europ Engrs; consult var groups; assoc reader ergonomics, Univ Loughborough, UK; chair, Ergo Div, Inst Indust Engrs, 1990-1991; prof & chair indust eng, Tex Tech Univ, 1987-1991; chair, Tech Interest Group Indust Ergonomics, Human Factors Soc, 1983-1985; prof & chair indust eng, Northern Ill Univ, 1982-1987; dir, Grad Safety Prog, Univ Ill, Chicago, 1981-1982; br head ergonomics, Nat Coal Bd, UK, 1975-1981; gen secy, Ergonomics Soc, 1973-1979; conf secy, Ergonomics Soc, 1971-1973; dir ergonomics, Ergo Lab, Cranfield Inst, 1970-1975; indust secy, Ergonomics Soc, 1969-1972; chartered eng, Eng Coun Great Brit, 1966; mgr ergonomics, Pilkington Glass, UK, 1964-1970. **Memberships:** fel Human Factors & Ergonomics Soc; fel Ergonomics Soc; fel Inst Prod Engrs; Inst Indust Eng; Am Soc Safety Eng. **Research Statement & Publications:** Ergonomics and human factors considerations in industry and daily living, including slips and falls, computer application, workplace design, equipment design and the human and work performance of the disabled. **Mailing Address:** Liberty Mutual Res Ctr Safety & Health, 71 Frankland Rd, Hopkinton, MA 01748. **Fax:** 508-435-8136. **E-Mail:** com.leamon@libertymutual.com

LEAMY, LARRY JACKSON, QUANTITATIVE GENETICS. **Personal Data:** b Alton, Ill, November 15, 1940. **Education:** Eastern Ill Univ, BS, 1962; Univ Ill, Urbana, MS, 1965, PhD (zoology), 1967. **Professional Experience:** Vis prof, Wash Univ Sch Med, 1995-; PROF BIOL, UNIV NC, CHARLOTTE, 1988-; chmn dept, Univ NC, Charlotte, 1988-1994; vis prof entom & genetics, Univ Wis-Madison, fac grant-in-aid, 1982-1986; NSF grant, 1981-1982; chmn dept, Calif State Univ, Long Beach, 1978-1988; fac grant-in-aid, Calif State Univ, Long Beach, 1969-1970, 1973, 1978-1981; from asst prof to prof biol, Calif State Univ, Long Beach, 1967-1988; Calif State Univ Found new fac grant, Calif State Univ, Long Beach, 1967-1968. **Memberships:** Genetics Soc Am; Am Genetic Asn; Soc Study Evolution. **Research Statement & Publications:** Quantitative genetics of mice. **Mailing Address:** Dept Biol, Univ NC, UNCC 9201 Univ City, Charlotte, NC 28223-0002. **Fax:** 704-687-3128. **E-Mail:** ljleamy@email.uncc.edu

LEAN, DAVID ROBERT SAMUEL, BIOLOGY, CHEMISTRY. **Personal Data:** b Peterborough, Ont, October 18, 1937; div, c 3. **Education:** Univ Toronto, BASc, 1962, PhD (zoology), 1973. **Professional Experience:** NSERC INDUST CHAIR ECTOXICOLOGY, DEPT BIOL, UNIV OTTAWA, as of 2004; PROF IOL, UNIV OTTAWA, as of 2001; res scientist biol & limnol, Can Dept Environ, beginning 1972; lectr ecol, Univ Toronto, 1971-1973; engr chem, Union Carbide Corp, 1963-1967. **Memberships:** Am Soc Limnol & Oceanog; Int Asn Theoret & Appl Limnol; Soc Prof Engrs. **Research Statement & Publications:** Interrelationships of carbon, nitrogen, phosphorous and iron on algae growth and decomposition in lakes. **Mailing Address:** Dept Biol, Univ Ottawa, MacDonald Hall 150 Louis-Pasteur, Ottawa, ON K1N 6N5, Can. **E-Mail:** dlean@Sci.uottawa.ca

LEAN, ERIC GUNG-HWA, ACOUSTICS, OPTICS. **Personal Data:** b Fukien, China, January 1, 1938. **Education:** Cheng Kung Univ, Taiwan, BS, 1959; Univ Wash, MS, 1963; Stanford Univ, PhD (elec eng), 1967. **Professional Experience:** FEL & VPRES, INDUST TECHNOL RES INST, HSINCHU, TAIWAN, as of 2000; GEN DIR, OPTO-ELECTRONICS & SYST LAB, INDUST TECHNOL RES INST, as of 2000; CHMN, BD CHINESE ASN MAGNETIC TECHNOL, as of 2000; mgr, optical & magnetic storage technol, T J Watson Res Ctr, IBM Corp, beginning 1981; mgr, Printer Technol, 1979-1981; mgr, Optical Solid State Technol, 1971-1979; mgr acoust & optical physics, T J Watson Res Ctr, 1969-1971; mem res staff nonlinear optics, T J Watson Res Ctr, 1967-1969; res assoc microwave acoust & laser, Hanson Lab Physics, Stanford Univ, 1967; res asst microwave acoust, Hanson Lab Physics, Stanford Univ, 1963-1967; Res asst elec eng, Univ Wash, 1961-1963. **Memberships:** Fel Inst Elec & Electronics Engrs; Sigma Xi; Optical Soc Am. **Research Statement & Publications:** Microwave acoustic waves in solids; nonlinear optics; optical signal processing devices; surface wave devices; laser applications; integrated optics; fiber optics; printers. **Mailing Address:** Indust Technol Res Inst, 195 Chung Hsing Rd, Chu Tung, Taiwan. **Fax:** 886-3-582-0045.

LEAN, JUDITH L. **Education:** Australian Nat Univ, BS, 1974; Univ Adelaide, Australia, PhD (atmospheric physics), 1980. **Professional Experience:** RES PHYSICIST, SPACE SCI DIV, NAVAL RES LAB, WASH, DC, 1986-. **Memberships:** Nat Acad Sci; Am Astron Soc; fel Am Geophys Union; Am Meteorol Soc; Int Asn Geomagnetism & Aeronomy. **Mailing Address:** Space Sci Div, Naval Res Lab, 4555 Overlook Ave SW, Washington, DC 20375. **E-Mail:** lean@demeter.nrl.navy.mil

LEANDER, JOHN DAVID, PSYCHOPHARMACOLOGY. **Personal Data:** b Mt Vernon, Wash, April 8, 1944; m 1965, c 3. **Education:** Pac Lutheran Univ, BA, 1966; Western Wash State Col, MA, 1967; Univ Fla, PhD (psychol), 1971; Ind Univ, MBA, 1985. **Professional Experience:** RES ADV, LILLY RES LAB, ELI LILLY & CO, 1990-; sr res scientist, Lilly Res Lab, Eli Lilly & Co, 1985-1989; res scientist, Lilly Res Lab, Eli Lilly & CO, 1981-1984; from asst prof to assoc prof pharmacol, Univ NC, Chapel Hill, 1974-1981; instr,

Univ NC, Chapel Hill, 1973-1974; Fel neurobiology prog, Univ NC, Chapel Hill, 1971-1973. **Memberships:** AAAS; Behav Pharmacol Soc; Am Soc Pharmacol & Exp Therapeut. **Research Statement & Publications:** Behavioral pharmacology; effects of drugs on behavior and the interaction of drugs with ongoing behavior. **Mailing Address:** Neuroscience Res, Lilly Res Labs, Eli Lilly & Co, Indianapolis, IN 46285-0001. **Fax:** 317-276-9276.

LEANING, WILLIAM HENRY DICKENS, TECHNICAL MANAGEMENT, PARASITOLOGY. **Personal Data:** b Whakatane, NZ, February 24, 1934; m 1956, c 4. **Education:** Univ Sydney, BVSc, 1956. **Professional Experience:** EXEC DIR TECH SERV, MERCK SHARP & DOHME CO, INC, AGVET, 1981-; exec dir animal sci res develop res & admin, Merck Sharp & Dohme Co, Inc, 1975-1981; sr dir clin res animal sci res, Merck Sharp & Dohme Co, Inc, 1972-1974; dir mkt develop large animal prod, Merck Sharp & Dohme Co, Inc, 1969-1972; vet tech dir appl res parasitol, Merck Sharp & Dohme NZ Ltd, 1962-1969; Vet gen pract, Nth Canterbury Vet Club, NZ & Putaruru Vet Club, NZ, 1957-1962. **Memberships:** NZ Vet Asn; Am Asn Vet Parasitologist; World Asn Adv Vet Parasitol; Am Vet Med Asn; Am Asn Indust Vet. **Research Statement & Publications:** Concepts of applied preventive medicine on whole herd/flock basis throughout productive life of animal/bird; primary areas helminthology, entomology; innovation in formulation and treatment application; applied parasitology and agri-economic benefits of year-round parasite control programs. **Mailing Address:** 163 Sherwood Lane, Stirling, NJ 07980.

LEAP, DARRELL IVAN, WATER RESOURCES, AQUIFER ANALYSIS. **Personal Data:** b Huntington, WVa, October 19, 1937. **Education:** Marshall Univ, BS, 1960; Ind Univ, MA, 1966; Pa State Univ, PhD (geol), 1974. **Professional Experience:** PROF HYDROGEOL, PURDUE UNIV, as of 2004; assoc Prof Hydrogeol, Purdue Univ, beginning 1980; prin investr, Hydrol Nev Test Site, Nev Nuclear Waste-Storage Invest, US Dept Energy, 1978-1980; hydrologist, US Geol Surv, 1974-1980; geologist, SDak State Geol Surv, 1966-1971; instr geol, Univ SDak, 1966-1969; ground Water Contamination Studies, Purdue Univ. **Memberships:** Am Geophys Union; AAAS; Sigma Xi; Geol Soc Am; Nat Asn Ground Water Scientists & Engrs. **Research Statement & Publications:** Regional aquifer systems for recharge-discharge relationships and water resources; ground-water modeling; ground-water tracers; radioactive-waste disposal; flow in fractured rocks; flow in glaciated terranes; glacial geology; ground water contamination. **Mailing Address:** Dept Earth & Atmospheric Sci Purdue Univ, 550 Stadium Mall Dr, West Lafayette, IN 47907-2051. **Fax:** 765496-1210. **E-Mail:** dileap@purdue.edu

LEAPMAN, RICHARD DAVID, ELECTRON MICROSCOPY, ELECTRON SPECTROSCOPY. **Personal Data:** b Bath, Eng, December 6, 1950; American citizen; m 1979, Gisele; c Neil, Michael & Juliana. **Education:** Cambridge Univ, Eng, BA, 1973, MA, 1976, PhD (physics), 1977. **Honors & Awards:** Burton Medal, Micros Soc Am, 1985; Birks Award, Microbeam Anal Soc, 1985, Heinrich Award, 1989. **Professional Experience:** CHIEF, SUPRAMOLECULAR STRUCT & FUNCTION RESOURCE, DBEPS, ORS, NIH, as of 2006; ACTG DIR, DIV BIOENGINEERING & PHYSICAL SCI, NIH, as of 2006; lectr & consult, Philips Electron Optics, 1991-1993; head, Biomed Eng & Instrumentation Prog, Nat Ctr Res Resources, NIH, beginning 1988; vis scientist, Electron Beam Imaging & Microspectros Group Biomed Eng & Instrumentation Prog, Nat Ctr Res Resources, NIH, 1980-1988; res assoc, Sch Appl & Eng Physics, Cornell Univ, 1977-1979; res fel, Dept Metall & Mat Sci, Oxford Univ, 1976-1977. **Memberships:** Am Phys Soc; Micros Soc Am; Microbeam Analysis Soc; NY Acad Sci; Mat Res Soc. **Research Statement & Publications:** Development of analytical electron microscopy for application to biological systems; electron-energy-loss spectroscopy; cryo-scanning transmission electron microscopy of cellular organelles and macromolecular assemblies; elemental mapping at nanometer resolution. **Mailing Address:** Div Bio Eng & Physical Sci, Off Res Serv, NIH, Rm 3N17 Bldg 13, Bethesda, MD 20892. **Fax:** 301-496-6608. **E-Mail:** leapman@helix.nih.gov

LEAR, BERT, plant pathology; deceased, see previous edition for last biography

LEARN, ARTHUR JAY, SOLID STATE PHYSICS. **Personal Data:** b Lewistown, Mont, March 25, 1933; m 1959, c 2. **Education:** Reed Col, BA, 1954; Mass Inst Technol, PhD (physics), 1958. **Professional Experience:** VPRES, CVD TECHNOL, SILICON VALLEY GROUP INC, 1983-; eng mgr, Supertex, Inc, 1981-1983; prog mgr, Intel Corp, 1976-1981; sr mem res staff, Fairchild Camera & Instrument Corp, 1970-1976; mem staff, Electronics Res Ctr, NASA, 1967-1970; Mem tech staff, TRW Systs, Calif, 1958-1967; exec mem tech staff, Anicon, Inc. **Memberships:** Am Phys Soc; Electrochem Soc; Am Vacuum Soc. **Research Statement & Publications:** X-ray diffraction; electron microscopy; properties of thin films; thin film superconductor and semiconductor devices; metallization; chemical vapor deposition; thermal oxidation. **Mailing Address:** 10822 Wilkinson Ave, Cupertino, CA 95014-4732.

LEARN, GERALD H, BOTANY. **Education:** Univ Louisville, BS, MS; Wash Univ, PhD (pop biol). **Professional Experience:** RES SCIENTIST, JIM MULLINS' LAB, UNIV WASH SCH MED, as of 2005. **Mailing Address:** Dept Microbiol Univ Wash, Box 358070 960 Repulican St, Seattle, WA 98109-4325. **E-Mail:** learn@u.washington.edu

LEARNED, JOHN GREGORY, NEUTRINO OSCILLATIONS & NEUTRINO ASTRONOMY & NEUTRINO PHENOMENOLOGY, GEO-NEUTRINOS & VARIOUS MEANS OF ULTRA-HIGH ENERGY DETECTION INCLUDING RADIO & ACOUSTIC MEASUREMENTS. **Personal Data:** b Plattsburgh, NY, April 12, 1940; m 2001, Coleen; c Alison Jennifer Learned-Wolf & Bryan David Learned. **Education:** Columbia Col, NY, BS, 1961; Univ Pa, Philadelphia, MS, 1963; Univ Wash, Seattle, PhD (physics), 1968. **Honors & Awards:** Rossi Prize, Asahi Prize, Regents Medal. **Professional Experience:** PROF PHYSICS & ASTRON., UNIV. HAWAII, 1980-; neutrino studies, neutrino oscillations, geo-neutrinos, ultrahigh energy neutrinos, neutrino astronomy, neutrino phenomenology. **Research Statement & Publications:** Leader in efforts for first high energy neutrino astronomy; published papers in particle astrophysics; played key role in discovery of muon neutrino oscillations (and hence mass); initiated many new projects in particle astrophysics. **Mailing Address:** Dept Physics & Astron, Univ Hawaii, 2505 Correa Rd, Honolulu, HI 96822. **Fax:** 808-956-2930. **E-Mail:** jgl@phys.hawaii.edu

LEARNED, ROBERT EUGENE, ECONOMIC GEOLOGY, GEOCHEMISTRY. **Personal Data:** b Glendale, Calif, July 3, 1928; m 1956, c 2. **Education:** Occidental Col, AB, 1955; Univ Calif, Los Angeles, MA, 1962; Univ Calif, Riverside, PhD (geol), 1966. **Professional Experience:** RETIRED; geologist, US Geol Surv, 1967-1992; asst prof geol, Chapman Col, 1965-1967; geologist, Aerogeophys Co, Calif, 1955-1956. **Memberships:** Geol Soc Am; Geochem Soc; Asn Explor Geochemists; Soc Econ Geologists; Asn Geoscientists Int Develop; Sigma Xi. **Research Statement & Publications:** Geology and geochemistry of ore deposits; geochemical exploration methods. **Mailing Address:** 825 Windbell Circle, Tucson, AZ 85745-9671.

LEARY, FRANCIS CHRISTIAN, MODULES OVER COMMUTATIVE RINGS, ALGEBRAIC CODING THEORY. **Personal Data:** b West Hartford, Conn, April 23, 1949; m 1976, c 3. **Education:** Univ Conn, BA, 1971; State Univ NY, Albany, MA, 1974, PhD (math), 1979. **Professional Experience:** ASSOC PROF MATH, ST BONAVENTURE UNIV, 1989-; asst prof, St Bonaventure Univ, 1985-1989; asst prof math, Transylvania Univ, 1980-1985; instr & asst prof, Skidmore Col, 1979-1980; adj asst prof, Union Col, Schenectady, 1975-1976; lectr math, Waterbury State Tech Col & Post Jr Col, 1973. **Memberships:** Am Math Soc; Sigma Xi; Math Asn Am. **Research Statement & Publications:** Rings and modules; algebraic coding theory. **Mailing Address:** Dept Math, St Bonaventure Univ, St Bonaventure, NY 14778-9999.

LEARY, HARVEY LEE, NUTRITION. **Education:** NC State Univ, BS, 1971, MS, 1975, PhD (animal sci-immunol), 1978. **Professional Experience:** SR RES SCIENTIST, MEAD JOHNSON NUTRIT GROUP, BRISTOL-MYERS SQUIBB CO, 1988-; sr scientist, Mead Johnson Nutrit Group, Bristol-myers Squibb CO, 1985-1988; sr res scientist, Immuno Biotech, Inc, Overland Park, Kans, 1983-1985; postdoctoral res assoc, Dept Biochem, Col Health Sci, Univ Kans, 1982-1984; postdoctoral res assoc, Dept Dairy Sci, Univ Ill, Urbana-Champaign, 1978-1982; res asst, Dept Animal Sci, NC State Univ, 1972-1978. **Memberships:** Am Asn Immunologists; Am Soc Microbiol. **Research Statement & Publications:** Radiometric and enzyme immunoassay development; Western blotting; gel precipitation analysis; preparation and characterization of radiotracers and antibody-enzyme conjugates; immunization of animals and purification of antibody; enzymatic digestion of immunoglobulias and purification of biologically active fragments; antigen localization methods with both light and electron microscopy; protein and virus purification and characterization. **Mailing Address:** Mead Johnson Res Ctr, 2400 W Lloyd Expressway R-10, Evansville, IN 47721-0001.

LEARY, JAMES FRANCIS, BIONANOTECHNOLOGY, FLOW CYTOMETRY/CELL SORTING. **Personal Data:** b Portsmouth, NH, April 12, 1948; American citizen; m 1978, Rosemary; c Charles, Elaine, Selena & Michael. **Education:** Mass Inst Technol, BS (aeronaut & astronaut) & BS (phil & hist), 1970; Univ NH, MS, 1974; Pa State Univ, PhD (biophys), 1977. **Honors & Awards:** NY Acad Sci, 1985; Sigma Xi Hon, 1985; Whos Who Tech Today, 1994; Whos Who Am, 2000. **Professional Experience:** ASST DIR, BIOMED ENF CTR, 2002-; SR SCIENTIST, SEALY CTR VACCINE DEVELOP, 2001-; PROF INTERNAL MED, UNIV TEX MED BR, GALVESTON, 1994-; assoc prof pediat, Med Sch, Univ Rochester, 1985-1994; assoc prof path & lab med, Med Sch, Uinv Rochester, 1985-1994; asst prof path, Med Sch, Univ Rochester, 1981-1985; postdoc biophys & instrumentation, Los Alamos Sci Lab, 1977-1978; dir, Cell Analysis & Sorting Facil. **Memberships:** Int Soc Anal Cytol; AAAS; Optical Soc Am. **Research Statement & Publications:** Development of new automated laser flow cytometric instrumentation and clinically useful diagnostic tests; breast cancer diagnostics; bionanotechnology; molecular biosensors; nanomedicine; optical biochips. **Mailing Address:** Univ Tex Med Br, Mary Moody Northern Pavilion 4 216, Galveston, TX 77555-0435. **Fax:** 409-772-6527. **E-Mail:** jleary@utmb.edu

LEARY, JOHN DENNIS, PHYTOCHEMISTRY, NATURAL PRODUCTS. **Personal Data:** b New Bedford, Mass, December 6, 1934; m 1957, c 4. **Education:** Mass Col Pharm, BS, 1956, MS, 1958; Univ Conn, PhD (pharmacog), 1964. **Professional Experience:** Chmn, Dept Chem & Physics, 1984-1987; PROF BIOCHEM, MASS COL PHARM & ALLIED HEALTH SCI, 1983-; assoc prof biochem, Mass Col Pharm & Allied Health Sci, 1974-1983; assoc prof pharmacog & bot, Mass Col Pharm & Allied Health Sci, 1968-1974; from asst prof to assoc prof phytochem, St John's Univ, NY, 1963-1968; asst prof, Ore State Univ, 1959-1961; Asst pharmacog, Univ Conn, 1958-1959. **Memberships:** Am Asn Col Pharm; Am Soc Pharmacog. **Research Statement & Publications:** Phytochemical studies, primarily Solanaceae and Meliaceae; chemotaxonomy and biogenesis; microbial transformation of organic compounds. **Mailing Address:** Dept Chem & Physics, Mass Col Pharm, 179 Longwood Ave, Boston, MA 02115-5896.

LEARY, RALPH JOHN, ORGANIC CHEMISTRY. **Personal Data:** b Elizabeth, NJ, November 3, 1929; m 1952, c 6. **Education:** Seton Hall Univ, BS, 1951; Univ Ill, PhD (chem), 1957. **Professional Experience:** RETIRED; sr res assoc, Exxon Res & Eng Co, 1980-1987; sect head, Exxon Res & Eng Co, 1978-1987; res assoc, Exxon Chem Co USA, 1978-1980; lab head, Exxon Chem Co USA, 1975-1977; group leader & res assoc, Esso Res & Eng Co, 1967-1975; group leader, Esso Res & Eng Co, 1957-1967; jr chemist, Merck & Co, Inc, 1951-1954. **Memberships:** Am Chem Soc; Sigma Xi. **Research Statement & Publications:** Gas chromatography and automation of laboratory instruments; Am Soc Testing and Mat. **Mailing Address:** 211 Oak Lane, Cranford, NJ 07016.

LEARY, RICHARD LEE, PALEOBOTANY, PALEOECOLOGY. **Personal Data:** b Portsmouth, Va, September 19, 1936; m 1961, Eleanor; c Seth & Sara. **Education:** Va Polytech Inst, BS, 1959; Univ Mich, MS, 1961, PhD (geol), 1980. **Professional Experience:** CUR EMER GEOL, ILL STATE MUS, as of 2006; Fulbright res award, Arg & Brazil, 1991; NSF grantee, 1981-1984, 1985, 1986, 1994; adj asst prof environ geol, Sangamon State Univ, 1973-1978; cur geol, Ill State Mus, beginning 1961. **Memberships:** Geol Soc Am; Bot Soc Am; Paleobot Sec; Int Orgn Paleobot; Latin-Am Asn Paleobot & Paleonol. **Research Statement & Publications:** Late Paleozoic fossil plants, paleoecology, paleoenvironments and plant evolution; comparisons of Southern Hemisphere glossopterids and Northern Hemisphere lesleya. **Mailing Address:** ISM Res & Collections Ctr, 1011 E Ash St, Springfield, IL 62703. **Fax:** 217-785-2857. **E-Mail:** leary@museum.state.il.us

LEARY, ROLFE ALBERT, FOREST MENSURATION. **Personal Data:** b Waterloo, Iowa, March 5, 1938; m 1967, c 2. **Education:** Iowa State Col, BS, 1959; Purdue Univ, MS, 1961, PhD (forest mgt), 1968. **Professional Experience:** ASSOC PROF, US FOREST SERV, as of 2003; PRIN MENSURATIONIST FORESTRY, US FOREST SERV, N CENT FOREST EXP STA, 1972-; mensurationist, US Forest Serv, N Cent Forest Exp Sta, 1968-1972; instr forest mensuration, Southern Ill Univ, 1964-1965; vol forester, US Peace Corps, St Lucia, Wis, 1961-1963. **Memberships:** AAAS; Ecol Soc Am; Sigma Xi; Coun Unified Res & Educ. **Research Statement & Publications:** Boundary value problem method of calibrating forest growth models; generalized forest growth projection system; philosophy and methods of forest research; multiple-use decision-making. **Mailing Address:** USDA Forest Serv, 1400 Independence Ave SW, Washington, DC 20250-0003. **E-Mail:** rleary@forestry.umn.edu

LEASK, R(AYMOND) A(LEXANDER), PULP & PAPER. **Personal Data:** b Edmonton, Alta, January 15, 1919; m 1942, Barbara; c Barbara E, Susanne J, Sally D & Martha J. **Education:** Univ Alta, BSc, 1941, MSc, 1947. **Professional Experience:** RETIRED; consult, 1983-1993; asst res dir, Ont Paper Co, 1973-1983; process engr, Sandwell & Co, 1971-1973; dir res, Bauer Bros Co, 1964-1971; supvr pulping sect, Cent Res Div, Abitibi Power & Paper Co, 1950-1964; chem engr, Powell River Co, 1948-1950; res asst, Res Coun Alta, 1945-1947; res chemist, Can Int Paper Co, 1942-1944; chemist, Brit-Am Oil Co, 1941. **Memberships:** Fel Tech Asn Pulp & Paper Indust; Can Pulp & Paper Asn; Asn Prof Engrs; Rotary Int. **Research Statement & Publications:** Pulping methods on a pilotplant scale and on a commercial scale; improving paper machine performance and improving newsprint quality. **Mailing Address:** 3 Mayholme Ct, St Catharines, ON L2N 4C1, Can.

LEATH, KENNETH T, PLANT PATHOLOGY, SELECTION FOR DISEASE RESISTANCE. **Personal Data:** b Providence, RI, April 29, 1931; m 1955, Marie; c Kenneth, Steven, Kevin & Maria B. **Education:** Univ RI, BS, 1959; Univ Minn, MS & PhD (phytopath), 1966. **Honors & Awards:** Merit Cert, Am Forage & Grassland Coun, 1983; Res Award, Nat Alfalfa Seed Coun, 1993. **Professional Experience:** CONSULT, 1994-; plant pathologist, Regional Pasture Res Lab, USDA, 1966-1994; adj prof, Dept Plant Path, Pa State Univ, 1966-1994; res technician cereal rusts, Cereal Rust Lab, Minn, 1959-1966. **Memberships:** Am Phytopath Soc; Am Soc Agron; Am Forage & Grassland Coun; Int Soc Root Res; Sigma Xi. **Research Statement & Publications:** Clover and alfalfa diseases; host-parasite interaction; biocontrol; disease resistance methodology; develops protocol for selecting plants resistant to diseases; germplasm evaluation; advising on forage, field and turf crops. **Mailing Address:** 1438 Willowbrook Dr, Boalsburg, PA 16827.

LEATH, PAUL LARRY, SOLID STATE PHYSICS. **Personal Data:** b Moberly, Mo, January 9, 1941; m Rosemary; c 1. **Education:** Univ Mo, Columbia, BS, 1961, MS, 1963, PhD (physics), 1966. **Professional Experience:** CHAIR, PHYSICS & ASTRON DEPT, 1995-2004; provost, Rutgers Univ, New Brunswick, 1987-1992; PROF PHYSICS, RUTGERS UNIV, NEW BRUNSWICK, 1978-; assoc provost, Rutgers Univ, New Brunswick, 1978-1987; assoc dept, Rutgers Univ, New Brunswick, 1973-1975; from asst prof to prof, Rutgers Univ, New Brunswick, 1967-1978; Res assoc theoret physics, Oxford Univ, 1966-1967. **Memberships:** AAAS; Am Phys Soc; Sigma Xi; Brit Inst Physics; NY Acad Sci. **Research Statement & Publications:** Theoretical solid state physics; inelastic neutron scattering; vibrational and electronic properties of alloys; anharmonic crystals; disordered and dilute magnets; percolation processes; breakdown phenomena. **Mailing Address:** Dept Physics & Astron, Rutgers Univ, Piscataway, NJ 08854-8019. **Fax:** 732-445-4343. **E-Mail:** leath@physics.rutgers.edu

LEATHEM, WILLIAM DOLARS, MEDICAL NUTRITION, MEDICAL PARASITOLOGY. **Personal Data:** b Chicago, Ill, January 6, 1931; m 1952, c 3. **Education:** Univ Wis, BS, 1961, MS, 1963, PhD (zool), 1965. **Professional Experience:** MGR NUTRIT RES, ABBOTT LABS, 1978-; med monitor nutrit, Abbott Labs, 1976-1978; asst dir clin nutrit, Eaton Labs, 1974-1976; res assoc, Norwich Pharmacal Co, 1969-1974; asst prof, NSF grants, 1967-1969; asst prof, Univ Wis, Waukesha Ctr, 1966-1969; asst prof biol, Wis State Univ, Whitewater, 1965-1966; Asst zool, Univ Wis, 1962. **Memberships:** AAAS; Am Soc Parasitol; Soc Protozool; Am Soc Trop Med & Hyg; Am Soc Parenteral & Enteral Nutrit; Sigma Xi. **Research Statement & Publications:** General parasitology and protozoology. **Mailing Address:** 1488 Camden Dr, Gurnee, IL 60031.

LEATHER, GERALD ROGER, PLANT PHYSIOLOGY. **Personal Data:** b Smithsburg, Md, October 16, 1937; m 1963, c 3. **Education:** Shepherd Col, BS, 1968; Hood Col, MA, 1973; Va Polytech Inst & State Univ, PhD (plant physiol), 1976. **Professional Experience:** Adj prof, Va Polytech Inst & State Univ, 1980-; PLANT PHYSIOLOGIST, US DEPT AGR, 1976-; LECTR, HOOD COL, 1976-; biologist, US Dept Agr, 1974-1976; Biologist, US Army, 1970-1974. **Memberships:** Weed Sci Soc Am; Am Soc Plant Physiologists; Sigma Xi. **Research Statement & Publications:** Secondary plant chemicals in the allelopathic interaction of weeds and crops; dormancy and germination mechanisms in weed seeds; maternal influence on the physiology and biochemistry of seed dormancy. **Mailing Address:** 759 Stayman Dr, Falling Waters, WV 25419. **E-Mail:** leatherhomes@prodigy.net

LEATHERLAND, JOHN F, ENDOCRINOLOGY, PHYSIOLOGY. **Personal Data:** b Nottingham, Eng, July 5, 1943; Canadian citizen; m 1965, Ann Murphy; c Steven & Rachel. **Education:** Sheffield, Eng, BSc, 1964; Leeds, Eng, PhD (endocrinol), 1967. **Honorary Degrees:** DSc, Sheffield Univ, Eng, 1993. **Honors & Awards:** Excellence in Res, Sigma Xi, 1989. **Professional Experience:** PROF & CHAIR, ONT VET COL, UNIV GUELPH, as of 2004; Ed-in-chief, Fish Physiol & Biochem, 1983-; vis prof, Murdoch Univ, Australia, 1980 & 1987; Vis fel, Univ Bath, UK, 1979; from asst prof to assoc prof, Dept Zool, Univ Guelph, Can, 1971-1983; Univ Hull, UK, 1969-1971; Fel endocrinol, Univ BC, 1967-1969. **Memberships:** Soc Endocrinol; Can Soc Zool; Sigma Xi. **Research Statement & Publications:** Endocrine control of metabolism, growth and reproduction of fish, particularly the role of the pituitary, thyroid and adrenal glands. **Mailing Address:** Dept Biomedical Sci, Ont Vet Sci, Univ Guelph, Guelph, ON N1G 2W1, Can. **Fax:** 519-767-1656. **E-Mail:** jleatherland@ovc.uoguelph.ca

LEATHERMAN, NELSON E(ARLE), BIOENGINEERING. **Personal Data:** b Grand Rapids, Mich, March 22, 1939; m 1968. **Education:** Univ Mich, BSE, 1962, MSE, 1963, PhD (bioeng), 1967. **Professional Experience:** RES ASSOC, DEPT MED, DUKE UNIV, as of 2003; res assoc, Vt Lung Ctr, Univ Vt, 1977-; asst prof, Ind Univ, Bloomington, 1968-1977; res asst physiol, Univ Mich, 1967-1968. **Memberships:** Biomed Eng Soc. **Research Statement & Publications:** Modeling of biological control systems; particularly identification of nonlinear systems. **Mailing Address:** Med Ctr Duke Univ, 321 Bell Bldg Box 3861, Durham, NC 27710.

LEATHERMAN, STEPHEN PARKER, OCEANOGRAPHY, STRATIGRAPHY-SEDIMENTATION. **Personal Data:** b Charlotte, NC, November 6, 1947; m 1987. **Education:** NC State Univ, BS, 1970; Univ Va, PhD (environ sci), 1976. **Professional Experience:** PROF, FLA INT UNIV, AS OF 2005; DIR, INT HURRICANE RES CTR, FLA INT UNIV, 1997-; DIR, LAB COSTAL RES, FLA INT UNIV, 1997; dir bd, Climate Inst, Wash DC, 1987-; dir, Lab Coastal Res, Univ Md, beginning 1987; expert testimony, US Senate, 1986, 1987, 1988; consult, Heritage Coast Proj, Wales, UK, 1985-; mem, Nat Acad Sci Comt Sea Level Impacts, 1984-1987; from asst prof to assoc prof geog, Lab Coastal Res, Univ MD, 1981-1987; tech consult, US Dept Interior Task Force Barrier Islands, 1980-1981; mem, Expert Panel Selection Global Coastal Biospheres, UNESCO, 1980; dir res unit, Univ Mass, 1977-1981; sci adv & team leader, Earthwatch Sci Expeds, Belmont, Mass, 1976-1981; asst prof geol, Boston Univ, 1975-1977; petrol geologist, Texaco Inc, Houston, Tex, 1970-1972. **Memberships:** Soc Econ Paleontogists & Mineralogists; fel Geol Soc Am; Int Geol Correlation Prog; AAAS. **Research Statement & Publications:** Beaches and barrier islands; has authored/edited 8 books and over 50 refeered journal articles, including Science and Nature. **Mailing Address:** Lab Coastal Res, Fla Int Univ, Miami, FL 33199. **Fax:** 305-348-1761. **E-Mail:** leatherm@fiu.edu

LEATHERS, CHESTER RAY, MYCOLOGY. **Personal Data:** b Claremont, Ill, May 15, 1929; m 1953, c 4. **Education:** Eastern Ill Univ, BS, 1950; Univ Mich, MS, 1951, PhD (bot), 1955. **Professional Experience:** RETIRED; EMER PROF MICROBIOL, ARIZ STATE UNIV, 1990-; ASSOC PROF BOT, ARIZ STATE UNIV, 1961-; asst prof, Ariz State Univ, 1957-1961; Res mycologist, Biol Warfare Labs, US Army, Md, 1955-1957. **Memberships:** Fel AAAS; Mycol Soc Am; Am Phytopath Soc; Am Inst Biol Sci. **Research Statement & Publications:** Mycology and plant pathology, particularly fleshy fungi, cereal and vegetable diseases; allergenic fungi; medical mycology. **Mailing Address:** Dept Bot & Microbiol, Ariz State Univ, Tempe, AZ 85287-1601.

LEATHERWOOD, JAMES M, animal nutrition; deceased, see previous edition for last biography

LEATHRUM, JAMES FREDERICK, COMPUTER SCIENCE, COMPUTER ENGINEERING. **Personal Data:** b Dover, Del, December 24, 1937; m 1960, c 3. **Education:** Univ Del, BChE, 1959; Princeton Univ, MA, 1961, PhD (chem eng), 1963. **Professional Experience:** PROF ELEC & COMPUT ENG, CLEMSON UNIV, 1980-; consult, US Army, 1968-1983 & Burroughs Corp, 1969-1973; from asst prof to assoc prof comput sci, Univ Del, 1967-1980; proj scientist, Union Carbide Corp, 1965-1967. **Memberships:** Asn Comput Mach; Am Inst Chem Engrs; Sigma Xi; Inst Elec & Electronics Engrs. **Research Statement & Publications:** Programming systems for real time and interactive computers; software engineering. **Mailing Address:** Elec & Comput Eng Dept, Clemson Univ, 313C Riggs Hall, Clemson, SC 29634-0915. **Fax:** 864-656-5910. **E-Mail:** james.leathrum@ces.clemson.edu

LEAV, IRWIN, PATHOLOGY. **Personal Data:** b Brooklyn, NY, July 4, 1937; m 1961, c 2. **Education:** Ohio State Univ, BA, 1959, DVM, 1965; Am Col Vet Pathologists, dipl, 1970. **Honors & Awards:** Pfizer Res Award, 1995. **Professional Experience:** PROF PATH, SCH MED, VET MED, TUFTS UNIV, 1987-; assoc dean res, Sch Vet Med, 1983-1993; Nat Cancer Inst, grant, 1981-; assoc dean basic sci, Sch Med, Vet Med, Tufts Univ, 1978-1983; grant, Nat Cancer Inst, 1978-1981; consult, US Armed Forces Inst Environ Med, 1974- & Angell Mem Hosp, 1976-; assoc dir path, Angell Mem Hosp, 1974-1976; assoc prof, Sch Med, Vet Med, Tufts Univ, 1970-1987; res assoc, Steroid Biochem Lab, 1969-; ASST PATH, HARVARD MED SCH, 1968-; res fel path, NIH spec fel, 1968-1970; res fel path, Harvard Med Sch, 1965-1968. **Memberships:** Int Acad Path; Am Col Vet Pathologists; Am Vet Med Asn. **Research Statement & Publications:** Mechanisms of action of sex hormones on normal, hyperplastic and neoplastic male accessory sex organs. **Mailing Address:** Dept Path & Anat, Sch Vet Med, Tufts Univ, 200 Westboro Rd, North Grafton, MA 01536. **E-Mail:** ileav@juno.com

LEAVELL, WALTER F, MEDICINE. **Professional Experience:** HEALTH ADV & CONSULT, HOWARD UNIV, WASH, as of 2004; dean, Meharry Med Col, 1982-1987; interim vpres health affairs, Howard Univ. **Mailing Address:** Howard Univ, Howard Univ Hosp Tower, Suite 6000, 2041 Ga Ave, NW, Washington, DC 20060.

LEAVENS, PETER BACKUS, MINERALOGY. **Personal Data:** b Summit, NJ, June 20, 1939; m 1980, Sharon Fitzgerald; c Karla. **Education:** Yale Univ, BA, 1961; Harvard Univ, MA, 1964, PhD, 1966. **Professional Experience:** Assoc ed, Can Min, 1996-; PROF GEOL, UNIV DEL, 1988-; regist prof geologist, State Del, 1987-; cur minerals, Univ Del, 1978-; res assoc, Smithsonian Inst, 1967-1990; from asst prof to assoc prof, Univ Del, 1967-1988; res assoc, dept mineral sci, Smithsonian Inst, 1965-1967. **Memberships:** Fel Mineral Soc Am. **Research Statement & Publications:** Crystal structure analysis; description of new mineral species; conditions of mineral occurrence and stability; mineralogy and geochemistry of pegmatites; carbonate metamorphism; asbestos mineralogy. **Mailing Address:** Dept Geol, Univ Del, Newark, DE 19716. **Fax:** 302-831-4158. **E-Mail:** pbl@udel.edu

LEAVENWORTH, HOWARD W, JR, METALLURGY, RESEARCH ADMINISTRATION. **Personal Data:** b Waterbury, Conn, June 3, 1928; m 1955, c 3. **Education:** Stevens Inst Technol, ME, 1951; Yale Univ, MS, 1953. **Honors & Awards:** NASA Award, 1967; President's Award, Am Soc Microbiol, 1970 & 1971; Meritorious Serv, 1983. **Professional Experience:** RETIRED; res supvr, Bur Mines, Albany Res Ctr, 1976-1988; metallurgist, Bur Mines, Albany Res Ctr, 1967-1988; asst mgr, Am Mach & Foundry Co, 1962-1967; prog mgr solid state physics, Air Force Off Sci Res, 1961-1962; sr scientist, Pratt & Whitney Aircraft Co, 1955-1961 & Oak Ridge Nat Lab, 1955-1957; Metallurgist, Franklin Inst, 1953-1955. **Memberships:** Fel AAAS; Sigma Xi; Am Inst Mining, Metall & Petrol Engrs. **Research Statement & Publications:** Alloy development; corrosion; surface science; wear; extractive metallurgy; concrete; wire rope; powder metallurgy. **Mailing Address:** 20 Bayview Lane, Port Townsend, WA 98368.

LEAVENWORTH, RICHARD S, INDUSTRIAL ENGINEERING & OPERATIONS RESEARCH, QUALITY CONTROL & CAPITAL BUDGETING. **Personal Data:** b Oak Park, Ill, September 30, 1930; m 1955, JoAnne. **Education:** Stanford Univ, BSIE, 1961, MSIE, 1962, PhD (indust eng), 1964. **Professional Experience:** PROF EMER INDUST & SYSTS ENG, UNIV FLA, 1988-; consult, Total Qual Mgt, Naval Aviation Depot, Jacksonville, Fla, 1988; consult, Off Chief Economist, TVA, 1984-1988; expert consult, Temple, Barker & Sloane, 1984; actg chmn dept, Indust & Systs Eng, Univ Fla, 1979; adv, Eng Soc Comn Energy, 1978-1979; ed, Eng Economist, 1976-1980; mfg educ serv, Gen Elec Co, NY, 1965-1967 & Manhattan Industs, 1970-1973; prof, Indust & Systs Eng, Univ Fla, 1966-1988; consult, Off Transp Res, US Dept Com, 1965-1966; asst prof indust eng, Va Polytech Inst, 1964-1966; eng asst, Light Div, Dept Pub Utilities, Tacoma, Wash, 1956-1959. **Memberships:** Fel Inst Indust Engrs (vpres, 1977-1979 & 1982-1984); Am Soc Qual Control; Am Soc Eng Educ. **Research Statement & Publications:** Engineering economics; statistical quality control; development of process control systems for Naval Aviation depots; author in quality assurance, quality management and engineering economics. **Mailing Address:** Dept Indust & Systs Eng, 477 Weil Hall, Gainesville, FL 32611. **Fax:** 352-392-3537. **E-Mail:** leavenwo@ise.ufl.edu

LEAVIS, PAUL CLIFTON, MUSCLE RESEARCH, PROTEIN SCIENCE. **Personal Data:** b May 17, 1944; American citizen; m 1970, Judith; c Jeremy & Allison. **Education:** Univ Notre Dame, BS, 1966; Tufts Univ, PhD (physiol), 1971. **Professional Experience:** Pres, Analytical Biotechnol Servs, 1991-; ASSOC PROF PHYSIOL, SCHS DENT, MED & VET MED, TUFTS UNIV, 1989-; SR SCIENTIST, BOSTON BIOMED RES INST, 1988-; mem, Molecular Aspects Excitable Tissues Res Study Comt, 1986-1989; prin scientist, Schs Dent, Med & Vet Med, Tufts Univ, 1986-1988; asst prof physiol, Sch Dent Med & Sch Vet Med, Tufts Univ, 1978-1989; staff scientist, Dept Muscle Res, Boston Biomed Res Inst, 1978-1986; estab investr, Am Heart Asn, 1978-1983; res assoc, Dept Neurol, Harvard Med Sch, 1978; res assoc, Dept Muscle Res, Boston Biomed Res Inst, 1975-1978; lectr, Tufts Univ, 1974-; res fel, Dept Neurol, Harvard Med Sch, 1974-1978; res fel, Dept Muscle Res, Boston Biomed Res Inst, 1972-1975; lab instr, Med Sch, Tufts Univ, 1969-1971. **Memberships:** AAAS; Biophys Soc; NY Acad Sci; Am Soc Biochem & Molecular Biol. **Research Statement & Publications:** Protien Chem, Biochemistry of embryonic cell growth factors, peptide chem; Biochemistry of contractile and regulatory proteins in mammalian skeletal and cardiac muscle and non-muscle motile cells; structure and function of calcium binding proteins; effects of protein-protein interactions on the metal binding proteins of troponin C; use of rare earth ions as probes of metal binding sites; supramolecular structure of muscle protein complexes; molecular cytoskeleton structure and function; protein structure and characterization. **Mailing Address:** Boston Biomed Res Inst, 64 Grove St, Watertown, MA 02472. **E-Mail:** leavis@bbri.org

LEAVITT, CHRISTOPHER PRATT, PHYSICS. **Personal Data:** b Boston, Mass, November 20, 1927; m 1959, c 5. **Education:** Mass Inst Technol, BS, 1948, PhD (physics), 1952. **Professional Experience:** PROF EMER PHYSICS, UNIV NMEX, 1996-; mem, Nuclear Physics Steering Comt, 1970-1971; mem, Tech Adv Panel, Los Alamos Meson Physics Facil, 1969-1971; mem, Particles & Fields Subcomt, NASA, 1965-1967; actg chmn, Dept Physics & Astron, 1958-1960; from asst prof to prof, Univ Nmex, 1956-1995; directorate res & develop, Air Force Missile Develop Ctr, Holloman AFB, 1956-1960; Consult, Res Directorate, Physics Div, Kirtland AFB, 1956-1960; assoc physicist, Brookhaven Nat Lab, NY, 1954-1956; Res assoc physics, Brookhaven Nat Lab, NY, 1952-1954. **Memberships:** Am Phys Soc. **Research Statement & Publications:** Nuclear and high energy physics; cosmic rays; space physics. **Mailing Address:** Dept Physics & Astron, Univ NMex, Albuquerque, NM 87131. **E-Mail:** leavitt@unm.edu

LEAVITT, FRED W, APPLIED MATHEMATICS. **Personal Data:** b Elizabeth, NJ, October 16, 1928. **Education:** Newark Col Eng, BS, 1950; Rensselaer Polytech Inst, MS, 1955, PhD (chem eng), 1957. **Professional Experience:** SR ENGR, LINDE DIV, UNION CARBIDE CORP, 1963-; group leader, Linde Div, Union Carbide Corp, 1961-1963; chem engr, Linde Div, Union Carbide Corp, 1957-1961; Chem engr, Biol Labs, US Army, Camp Detrick, 1952-1954. **Memberships:** AAAS; Am Chem Soc. **Research Statement & Publications:** Development of adsorptive separation processes; automatic data logging; development of computer systems for reducing, analyzing and correlating data and making design calculations; chemical kinetics and equilibria. **Mailing Address:** 150 Arielle Ct Apt G, Williamsville, NY 14221-1976.

LEAVITT, JOHN ADAMS, ION BEAM ANALYSIS, ATOMIC PHYSICS. **Personal Data:** b Lewis, Colo, December 8, 1932; m 1955, Shirley; c Genevieve, Anne, John, Andrew & Matthew. **Education:** Univ Colo, BA, 1954, Harvard Univ, MA, 1956, PhD (physics), 1960. **Professional Experience:** EMER PROF PHYSICS, UNIV ARIZ, 1995-; from asst prof to prof, Univ Ariz, 1960-1995. **Memberships:** Am Phys Soc. **Research Statement & Publications:** Developing and using new techniques for analyzing thin films using ion beams from a 6 MV Van de Graaff accelerator. **Mailing Address:** Dept Physics, Univ Ariz, 1118 E Fourth St PO Box 210081, Tucson, AZ 85721. **Fax:** 520-323-9606. **E-Mail:** jleav5@aol.com

LEAVITT, JULIAN JACOB, licensing, technology acquisition; deceased, see previous edition for last biography

LEAVITT, LAURENCE D, AERONAUTICS. **Professional Experience:** DIR RES, LANGLEY RES CTR, NASA, as of 2006. **Memberships:** Am Inst Aeronaut & Astronaut; Soc Automotive Engrs. **Mailing Address:** Langley Res Ctr, NASA, 11 W Taylor St MS 280, Hampton, VA 23681. **Fax:** 804-864-7722. **E-Mail:** Laurence.D.Leavitt@nasa.gov

LEAVITT, MARC LAURENCE, NEUROSCIENCE, ANIMAL PHYSIOLOGY. **Personal Data:** b St Louis, Mo, April 30, 1947; m 1971, Linda Brunell; c Michelle. **Education:** Southern Ill Univ, BA, 1969, MA, 1971; Univ Iowa, PhD (physiol & biophys), 1975. **Professional Experience:** ASST PROF PSYCHIAT, MED COL PA, ALLEGHENY CAMPUS, 1988-; SR SCIENTIST, NEUROSCIENCE RES LAB, ALLEGHENY-SINGER RES INST, PITTSBURGH, 1986-; sr res fel hypertension res, Allegheny-Singer Res Inst, 1985-1986; assoc prof, Biomed Sci Dept, 1982-1986; vis investr, Dept Anesthesia Res, Michael Reese Hosp & Med Ctr, Chicago, 1980; asst prof, Biol Dept, Southwest Mo State Univ, Springfield, 1978-1982; Fel, Dept Pharmacol & Med, Col Med, Univ Ky, Lexington, 1975-1978; Kroc Found fel, 1975-1977. **Memberships:** Am Physiol Soc; Am Soc Hypertension; Soc Neurosci; NY Acad Sci; AAAS; Soc Cryobiol; Int Behav Neurosci Soc. **Research Statement & Publications:** Psychopharmacology of behavior-aggression and delerium; techniques for profound hypothermic cardiac arrest in conjunction with blood substitution; pharmacological modulation of intracranial pressure; brain cancer models; neurotrophic factors and Parkinson's disease. **Mailing Address:** Neuroscience Res Ctr, Allegheny-Singer Res Inst, Pittsburgh, PA 15212.

LEAVITT, WENDELL WILLIAM, ENDOCRINOLOGY, REPRODUCTIVE BIOLOGY. **Personal Data:** b Conway, NH, January 15, 1938; m 1959, c 4. **Education:** Dartmouth Col, AB, 1959; Univ NH, MS, 1961, PhD (zool), 1963. **Professional Experience:** Prof biochem, health sci ctr & prof obstet & gynec, Sch Med, Tex Tech Univ, 1983-1989; mem Pop Res Comn, Nat Inst Child Health & Human Develop, NIH, 1983-1987; prof obstet & gynec, Med Sch, Univ Mass, 1978-1983; adj prof, Boston Univ, 1978-1983; sr scientist endocrinol, Worcester Found Exp Biol, 1977-1983; mem, regulatory biol panel, NSF, 1977-1979; Vis scientist, Univ Wis-Madison, 1967-1968 & Med Ctr, Vanderbilt Univ, 1972-1973; from asst prof to prof physiol, Col Med, 1967-1977; asst prof biol, Univ Cincinnati, 1964-1967; res assoc endocrinol & instr zool, Agr Exp Sta, Univ NH, 1963-1964; Res analyst zool, Agr Exp Sta, Univ NH, 1960-1963. **Memberships:** Sigma Xi; Am Soc Zoologists; Endocrine Soc; Soc Study Reproduction; Am Physiol Soc; Am Soc Cell Biol; Am Soc Biol Chemists. **Research Statement & Publications:** Mechanism of pituitary function in relation to gonadotrophin secretion; control of female reproductive processes; estrogens and pituitary function; neuroendocrinology and aging of the reproductive system; steroid hormone receptor systems; mechanism of steroid hormone action. **Mailing Address:** Dept Biol Sci, Wichita State Univ, 441 Hubbard Hall, Wichita, KS 67208. **Fax:** 316-978-3772. **E-Mail:** wendell.leavitt@wichita.edu

LEAVITT, WILLIAM GRENFELL, ALGEBRA. **Personal Data:** b Omaha, Nebr, March 19, 1916; wid, c Carol (Eveland), Robert & Elizabeth (Deceased). **Education:** Univ Nebr, AB, 1937, MA, 1938; Univ Wis, PhD (math), 1947. **Professional Experience:** PROF EMER MATH, UNIV NEBR, LINCOLN, as of 2006; Univ Nebr Res Coun vis fel, Leeds, Eng, 1973; NSF fel, 1959-1960; prof math, Univ Nebr, Lincoln, 1956-1986; chmn dept, Univ Nebr, Lincoln, 1954-1964; from instr to assoc prof, Univ Nebr, Lincoln, 1947-1956; actg instr math, Univ Wis, 1946. **Memberships:** Am Math Soc; Math Asn Am. **Research Statement & Publications:** Ring theory; theory of modules; theory of radicals. **Mailing Address:** Dept Math, Univ Nebr, 810 oldfather Hall, Lincoln, NE 68588-0323. **Fax:** 402-472-8466. **E-Mail:** wleavitt@unl.edu

LEAVY, PAUL MATTHEW, REMOTE SENSING, SELF-REGULATING AUTONOMOUS VEHICLE OPERATION. **Personal Data:** b Jackson, Mich, April 15, 1923; m 1944, Jeanne; c William & Paula. **Education:** US Naval Acad, BS, 1944. **Professional Experience:** PRES, PAUL LEAVY ASSOCS, 1990-; dir, Develop Progs, Teledyne CME, 1984-1990; mgr mkt, Western Div, GTE EOO, 1978-1984; vpres, ITT EOPD, 1972-1978; mem, Counter Terrorism, Nat Acad Eng, 1972; mgr, Radiation Div, Sanders Assocs, 1962-1972; pres, Trident Corp, 1959-1962; Consult, Nat Acad Sci, ASW, 1959-1960; mgr adv progs, Lab Electronics, 1957-1959; Mgr navy projs, Arma Div, Am Bosch Arma, 1954-1957. **Memberships:** Soc Photo-Optical Instrumentation Engrs; Am Inst Aeronaut & Astronaut; AAAS; Unmanned Vehicle Asn. **Research Statement & Publications:** Original invention and development of various active OCM and IRCM systems; development of C W sensing lasar radar; development of chemical/bio mass spectrometer for rapid sensing of subtoxic levels of CW or biowarfare threat substances. **Mailing Address:** 110 Wood Rd Apt H101, Los Gatos, CA 95030-6724.

LEBACQZ, J V, FLIGHT DYNAMICS. **Professional Experience:** PROG MGR, NASA AMES RES CTR, as of 2006. **Memberships:** Am Inst Aeronauts & Astronauts. **Mailing Address:** NASA Ames Res Ctr, M/S 211-2, Moffett Field, CA 94035. **Fax:** 415-694-5792.

LEBARON, FRANCIS NEWTON, NEUROCHEMISTRY, LIPID CHEMISTRY. **Personal Data:** b Framingham, Mass, July 26, 1922; m 1953, c 1. **Education:** Mass Inst Technol, BS, 1944; Boston Univ, MA, 1948; Harvard Univ, PhD (biochem), 1951. **Professional Experience:** RETIRED; vis scholar, Mass Inst Technol, 1974-1975; chmn dept, Sch Med, Univ NMex, 1971-1978; from assoc prof to prof biochem, Sch Med, Univ NMex, 1964-1983; assoc, Harvard Med Sch, Harvard Univ, 1959-1964; tutor, Harvard Med Sch, Harvard Univ, 1957-1964; assoc biochemist, McLean Hosp, Mass, 1957-1964; res assoc, Harvard Med Sch, Harvard Univ, 1956-1959; fel, Maudsley Hosp, 1953-1954; asst biochemist, McLean Hosp, Mass, 1952-1953, 1954-1957; asst biochemist, McLean Hosp, Waverley, Mass, 1951-1952. **Memberships:** AAAS; Am Soc Neurochemistry; Am Soc Biol Chem; Am Inst Nutrit. **Research Statement & Publications:** Biochemistry of the nervous system, especially the chemistry of proteins and lipids and their nervous complexes as they occur in mammalian nervous tissues; role of polyunsaturated fatty acids in nervous tissues. **Mailing Address:** 1111 Heatherwood, Yarmouthport, MA 02675.

LE BEAU, MICHELLE M, GENETICS. **Education:** Univ Ill, PhD, 1981. **Professional Experience:** PROF, DEPT MED, UNIV CHICAGO, as of 2005; DIR, THE CANCER RES CTR, as of 2005. **Mailing Address:** Dept Med Sect Hematol-Oncol Cytogen Lab Univ Chicago, 5841 S Md Ave MC2115, Chicago, IL 60637-1463. **E-Mail:** mlebeau@medicine.bsd.uchicago.edu

LEBEL, JACK LUCIEN, RADIOLOGY, RADIATION BIOLOGY. **Personal Data:** b Montreal, Que, September 16, 1933; American citizen; m 1960, c 2. **Education:** Univ Montreal, DVM, 1958; Colo State Univ, MS, 1966, PhD (radiation biol), 1967; Am Col Vet Radiol, dipl, 1968. **Professional Experience:** Consult, Wildlife Pharmaceut, 1990-; PROF RADIOL & RADIATION BIOL, COL VET MED & BIOMED SCI, COLO STATE UNIV, 1973-; consult, Rockewell Int, 1973-; asst dean, Curric Col, Colo State Univ, 1970-1972; consult, Orthop Found Animals, 1969-; assoc prof radiol & radiation biol, Col Vet Med & Biomed Sci, Colo State Univ, 1968-1973; assoc prof radiol, Univ Montreal, 1967-1968; asst prof vet med, Univ Montreal, 1961-1964. **Memberships:** Am Vet Med Asn; Am Vet Radiol Soc. **Research Statement & Publications:** Bone pathology; biological effects of plutonium contamination; densitometry; pulmonary physiology. **Mailing Address:** Dept Radiol, Colo Sate Univ, Ft Collins, CO 80523. **E-Mail:** jlebel@vth.colostate.edu

LEBEL, JEAN EUGENE, MATHEMATICS. **Personal Data:** b Can, March 21, 1922. **Education:** McGill Univ, BS, 1944; Univ Toronto, MA, 1950, PhD (appl math), 1958. **Professional Experience:** DIR, MCGILL UNIV, as of 2004; assoc prof math, Univ Toronto, beginning 1965; from asst prof to assoc prof math, Georgetown Univ, 1958-1965; lectr, McGill Univ, 1955-1957; theoret physicist, Newmont Explor, Ltd, Ariz, 1952-1954. **Memberships:** Am Math Soc; Can Math Cong. **Research Statement & Publications:** Analysis; applied mathematics. **Fax:** 418-657-2132. **E-Mail:** jean.lebel@inrs.ucs.uquebec.ca

LEBEL, NORMAN ALBERT, organic chemistry, reaction mechanisms, synthesis; deceased, see previous edition for last biography

LEBEL, ROLAND GUY, PHYSICAL CHEMISTRY, CHEMICAL ENGINEERING. **Personal Data:** b Edmundston, NB, February 10, 1932; m 1964, c 1. **Education:** NS Tech Col, BEng, 1955; Mass Inst Technol, SM, 1956; McGill Univ, PhD (phys chem), 1962. **Professional Experience:** ASSOC PROF, UNIV MONCTON, as of 2002; Dean, Sch Forest Sci, Univ Moncton, 1985-1997; dir res & develop, Papeterie Reed Ltd, 1980-1985; tech dir, Papeterie Reed Ltd, 1969-1980; res & develop proj coordr pulp & paper, Reed Inc, 1965-1969; sr develop engr, Anglo Paper Prod Ltd, 1963-1965; demonstr, McGill Univ, 1959-1962; Res engr, Fraser Pulp & Paper Co Ltd, 1958-1959. **Memberships:** Sr mem Can Pulp & Paper Asn. **Research Statement & Publications:** Planning, organization and coordination of research and development of projects related to the manufacture of newsprint and other paper products. **Mailing Address:** Sch Forest Sci, Univ Moncton, 165 Blvd Hebert, Edmundston, NB E3V 2S8, Can.

LEBEL, SUSAN, MOLECULAR BIOLOGY, MOLECULAR IMMUNOLOGY. **Personal Data:** b July 5, 1959; Canadian citizen; m 1989, Steve N Slilaty; c Catherine E. **Education:** Montreal Univ, Que, BSc, 1982, PhD (molecular biol), 1987. **Professional Experience:** PRES, GENOMICS ONE CORP, 1995-; vpres, Quantum Biotechnol Inc, 1991-1995; sr scientist, Biotechnol Res Inst, Biomira Inc, 1989-1992; Vis res fel, Natural Sci & Eng Res Coun Can, 1987-1988; Fel, Biotechnol Res Inst, Biomira Inc, 1987-1988. **Research Statement & Publications:** Anecoti based expression system and human cell expression system; design and devlopment of molecular biology products, kits for research. **Mailing Address:** 270 Blvd Samson Suite 105, Laval, PQ H7X 2Y9, Can. **E-Mail:** slebel@genomicsone.com

LEBEN, CURT (CHARLES), PLANT PATHOLOGY. **Personal Data:** b Chicago, Ill, July 7, 1917; m 1944, Margaret J; c Clay & Monte. **Education:** Ohio Univ, BS, 1940; Univ Wis, PhD (plant path), 1946. **Honorary Degrees:** Phi Beta Kapa, 1944; Fellow American Phtopathological Soc, 1954. **Professional Experience:** RETIRED; prof plant path, Agr Res & Develop Ctr, 1967-1988; actg chmn, Ohio State Univ, 1967-1968; prof bot & plant path & assoc chmn dept, Ohio State Univ, 1959-1967; head agr res labs, Eli Lilly & Co, Ind, 1957-1959; plant pathologist, Eli Lilly & Co, Ind, 1955-1957; asst prof, Univ Wis, 1949-1955; res assoc, Univ Wis, 1946-1949; asst plant path, Univ Wis, 1942-1946; asst, Univ Wis, 1942; Asst bot, Ohio Univ, 1939-1940. **Memberships:** AAAS; fel Am Phytopath Soc; Sigma Xi. **Research Statement & Publications:** Antibiotics and antibiosis in relation to plant diseases; microbiology; epiphytic microorganisms; bacterial and decay diseases; forest tree diseases; biological control. **Mailing Address:** 923 Thorne Ave, Wooster, OH 44691.

LEBENBAUM, MATTHEW T(OBRINER), ELECTRONICS ENGINEERING. **Personal Data:** b Portland, Ore, November 29, 1917; m 1942, c 2. **Education:** Stanford Univ, BA, 1938; Mass Inst Technol, MS, 1945. **Professional Experience:** RETIRED; dir, Appl Electronics Div, Airborne Instruments Lab, Cutler-Hammer, Inc, 1945-; res assoc, Radio Res Lab, Harvard Univ, 1942-1945; asst syst planning engr, Am Gas & Elec Corp, 1941-1942; Asst elec eng, Stanford Univ, 1938-1939 & Mass Inst Technol, 1939-1941. **Memberships:** Fel Inst Elec & Electronics Engrs; Int Union Radio Sci. **Research Statement & Publications:** Radio receivers, especially microwave; methods and techniques of noise measurement; intermediate frequency amplifiers; application of electronic methods to power systems; radio astronomy instrumentation; low noise devices. **Mailing Address:** 286 Route 30, Middlebury, VT 05753.

LEBENTHAL, EMANUEL, GASTROENTEROLOGY, PEDIATRICS. **Personal Data:** b Jerusalem, Israel, April 12, 1936; American citizen; c 5. **Education:** Hebrew Univ, Israel, MD, 1964. **Honors & Awards:** Int Prize Mod Nutrit, Int Dairy Fedn, Switz, 1984. **Professional Experience:** DIR, INT INST INFANT NUTRIT & GASTROINTESTINAL DIS, 1984-; prof pediat gastroenterol, State Univ NY, Buffalo, 1980-; PROF PEDIAT GASTROENTEROL, STATE UNIV NY, BUFFALO, 1980-; CHIEF PEDIAT GASTROENTEROL, CHILDREN'S HOSP BUFFALO, 1980-; Consult to clin staff, Roswell Park Mem Inst, 1977-; assoc prof pediat, State Univ NY, Buffalo, 1976-1980; assoc prof pediat, Int Inst Infant Nutrit & Gastrointestinal Dis, 1976-1980; assoc, Children's Hosp, Boston, 1974-1976; Asst med, Children's Hosp, Boston, 1972-1974. **Memberships:** Soc Pediat Res; NAm Soc Pediat Gastroenterol; Am Pancreatic Asn; Am Asn Study Liver Dis; Am Soc Clin Nutrit; Am Inst Nutrit. **Research Statement & Publications:** Impact of the ontogeny of the gut on feeding the compromised and premature infant, specifically the ontogeny of the pancreas; determinants that affect acture diarrhea to develop into chronic diarrhea in children. **Mailing Address:** Dept Peds, Hadassah Medical Organization, Mt Scopus, Jerusalem, Israel. **Fax:** 197-228-23515.

LEBER, PHYLLIS ANN, REACTION MECHANISMS, PLANT GROWTH REGULATORS. **Personal Data:** b Scranton, Pa, 1949; c 1. **Education:** Albright Col, Pa, BS, 1976; Univ NMex, PhD (chem), 1981. **Professional Experience:** DR E PAUL & FRANCES H REIFF PROF CHEM, FRANKLIN & MARSHALL COL, PA, as of 2004; PROF CHEM, FRANKLIN & MARSHALL COL, PA, 1996-; chmn, Dept Chem, Franklin & Marshall Col, 1989-1994; assoc prof, Franklin & Marshall Col, Pa, 1988-1996; vis asst prof org chem, Univ NMex, 1983; asst prof, Franklin & Marshall Col, Pa, 1982-1988; asst prof org chem, Pomona Col, Claremont, Calif, 1981-1982; jr chemist, Am Color & Chem Co, Reading, Pa, 1971-1976. **Memberships:** Am Chem Soc; Sigma Xi. **Research Statement & Publications:** Physical organic chemistry as it relates to the elucidation of reaction mechanisms of thermal unimolecular isomerizations, both uncatalyzed and catalyzed; synthens and biology of autin cholire ester anpyates. **Mailing Address:** Dept Chem, Franklin & Marshall Col, Lancaster, PA 17604-3003. **Fax:** 717-291-4343. **E-Mail:** phyllis.leber@fandm.edu

LEBER, SAM, METALLURGY. **Personal Data:** b Rockford, Ill, November 15, 1925; m 1952, c 2. **Education:** Univ Ill, BS, 1948, MS, 1949. **Professional Experience:** RETIRED; mgr metals eval subsect, Refractory Metals Dept, 1971-1986; supvr struct eval unit, Lamp Metals & Components Dept, Gen Elec Co, 1966-1971; metallurgist, Lamp Metals & Components Dept, Gen Elec Co, 1955-1966; X-ray crystallographer, Horizons Inc, 1950-1955. **Memberships:** Am Soc Metals; Am Inst Mining, Metall & Petrol Engrs. **Research Statement & Publications:** Physical metallurgy; x-ray, optical and electron metallurgy. **Mailing Address:** 2495 Deborah Dr, Beachwood, OH 44122.

LEBERMANN, KENNETH WAYNE, FOOD SCIENCES. **Personal Data:** b Davenport, Iowa, December 5, 1937; m 1962, c 2. **Education:** Univ Ill, Urbana, BS, 1959, PhD (food sci), 1964; Univ Calif, Davis, MS, 1961. **Professional Experience:** RETIRED; vpres res, Quaker Oats Co, 1979-; dir, Quaker Oats Co, 1978-1979; asst dir, Quaker Oats Co, 1978; mgr pet food res, Quaker Oats Co, 1975-1978; sect mgr pet foods, Quaker Oats Co, 1970-1975; sect mgr bakery prod, Quaker Oats Co, 1969-1970; sr group leader bakery prod, Quaker Oats Co, 1967-1969; group leader cereals, Quaker Oats Co, 1966-1967; scientist, CPC Int, 1964-1966. **Memberships:** Inst Food Technologists; Sigma Xi. **Research Statement & Publications:** Industrial research related to new product development, pet food research. **Mailing Address:** 250 Monument Ave, Barrington, IL 60010.

LEBHERZ, HERBERT G, BIOCHEMISTRY. **Personal Data:** b San Francisco, Calif, July 27, 1941; div. **Education:** San Francisco State Univ, BA, 1964, MA, 1966; Univ Wash, PhD (biochem), 1970. **Professional Experience:** PROF EMER BIOCHEM, SAN DIEGO STATE UNIV, 1996-; prof biochem, San Diego State Univ, 1980-1996; assoc prof, San Diego State Univ, 1976-1980; cancer res sci biochem, Roswell Park Mem Inst, 1975-1976; from res assoc to sr res assoc cell biol, Swiss Fed Inst Technol, 1971-1975. **Memberships:** Am Heart Asn; Am Soc Biol Chemists; AAAS. **Research Statement & Publications:** Elucidation of the mechanisms involved in the regulation of protein synthesis and protein degradation in developing adult and diseased organisms. **Mailing Address:** Dept Chem, San Diego State Univ, San Diego, CA 92182-0328.

LEBIEDZIK, JOZEF, QUANTITATIVE MICROSCOPY, MATERIALS SCIENCE. **Personal Data:** b February 13, 1940; American citizen; m 1969, c 1. **Education:** Pa State Univ, BS, 1970, MS, 1972, PhD (solid state sci), 1975. **Professional Experience:** PRES, ADVAN RES INSTRUMENTS CORP, as of 2004; pres, Modern Instrumentation Technol, Inc, beginning 1980; vpres res & develop quant micros, Lemont Sci Inc, 1976-1986; res assoc, Mat Res Lab, Pa State Univ, 1975-1976; res asst quant micros, Mat Res Lab, Pa State Univ, 1970-1975. **Memberships:** Microbeam Analysis Soc; Am Vacuum Soc. **Research Statement & Publications:** Microbeam analysis on automated scanning electron microscopes or electron probe systems; laboratory automation; surface analysis systems - instrumentation. **Mailing Address:** Advan Res Inst Co, 5151 Ward Rd, Wheat Ridge, CO 80033. **Fax:** 303-463-5505. **E-Mail:** aricorp@aricorp.com

LEBIEN, TUCKER W, LABORATORY MEDICINE, PATHOLOGY. **Personal Data:** b Minneapolis, Minn, December 8, 1948. **Education:** NDak State Univ, BS, 1970, MS, 1973; Univ Nebr, PhD (med microbiol-immunol), 1977. **Honors & Awards:** McFadden Lectr, Nebr Med Ctr, 1987; Stohlman Mem Award, Leukemia Soc Am, 1989. **Professional Experience:** DIR, UNIV MINN, COMBINED MD & PHD PROG & NIH MED SCIENTIST TRAINING PROG, MINNEAPOLIS, 2003-; DEP DIR, UNIV MINN CANCER CTR, 1997-; ASSOC DIR BASIC RES, UNIV MINN CANCER CTR, 1994-; assoc ed, Blood, 1991-1993; dir, NIH Immunol Training Prog, 1989-2002; PROF, DEPT LAB MED & PATH, 1989-; dir grad studies, Pathobiology Grad Prog, Univ Minn, 1988-1993; vis assoc prof path, Lab Molecular Immunol, Harvard Med Sch, 1986; assoc dir, Pathobiology Grad Prog, 1985-1987; assoc ed, J Immunol, 1984-1988; organizing fac, Fermentation Biotechnol Ctr, Univ Minn, 1983-; New investr award, Nat Cancer Inst, 1980-1982; from instr to assoc prof, Dept Lab Med & Path, Univ Minn, 1979-1989; res fel, Dept Lab Med & Path, Univ Minn, 1977-1979; res asst, Dept Med Microbiol, Nebr Med Ctr, 1974-1977. **Memberships:** Am Asn Immunologists; Am Asn Cancer Res; Am Soc Hemat; Am Soc Microbiol; Sigma Xi; Fedn Am Scientists; AAAS. **Research Statement & Publications:** Neutral endopeptidase; differentiative programs of lymphoid progenitor cells; published more than 50 articles. **Mailing Address:** Dept Lab Med & Path, Univ Minn, PO Box 609, Minneapolis, MN 55455-0315. **E-Mail:** lebie001@tc.umn.edu

LEBLANC, ADRIAN DAVID, RADIOLOGICAL PHYSICS, NUCLEAR MEDICINE. **Personal Data:** b Salem, Mass, May 21, 1940; m 1966, c 2. **Education:** Univ Mass, BA, 1962; Iowa State Univ, MS, 1966; Univ Kans, PhD (radiation biophys), 1972; Am Bd Health Physics, cert; Am Bd Radiol, cert in nuclear med physics. **Professional Experience:** DIR DIV SPACE LIFE SCI, UNIV SPACE RES ASSOC, as of 2005; PROF MED NUCLEAR MED, BAYLOR COL MED, 1972-; radiation physicist, Vet Admin Hosp, beginning 1967; health physicist, hosp & radiol physicist, dept nuclear med, Methodist Hosp, beginning 1966. **Memberships:** Health Physics Soc; Soc Nuclear Med; Am Asn Physicists in Med; Sigma Xi. **Research Statement & Publications:** Coronary blood flow; neutron activation analysis; x-ray fluorescence; health physics. **Mailing Address:** Div Space Life Scis, Univ Space Res Assoc, 3600 Bay Area Blvd, Houston, TX 77058. **Fax:** 281-244-2006. **E-Mail:** leblanc@dsls.usra.edu

LEBLANC, ARTHUR EDGAR, GEOLOGY, PALYNOLOGY. **Personal Data:** b Moncton, NB, September 29, 1923; American citizen; m 1952, c 2. **Education:** Univ Mass, Amherst, BS, 1952, MS, 1954. **Professional Experience:** SR PROJ GEOLOGIST, GULF OIL RES & DEVELOP CO, 1977-; proj palynologist, Gulf Oil Res & Develop CO, 1969-1977; sr res scientist, Res Ctr, Pan Am Petrol Corp, Okla, 1965-1969; Paleontologist, Shell Oil Co, Tex, 1954-1962 & Calif, 1962-1965. **Memberships:** AAAS; Am Asn Petrol Geologists; Soc Econ Paleontologists & Mineralogists; Am Asn Stratig Palynologists. **Research Statement & Publications:** Stratigraphic Paleozoic palynology; Mesozoic and Cenozoic stratigraphic palynology. **Mailing Address:** 11622 Spriggs Way, Houston, TX 77024.

LEBLANC, DONALD JOSEPH, PLASMID BIOLOGY, MICROBIAL PHYSIOLOGY. **Personal Data:** b Shirley, Mass, July 3, 1942; m 1966, c 4. **Education:** St Michael's Col, BA, 1964; Fordham Univ, MS, 1966; Univ Mass, Amherst, PhD (microbiol), 1970. **Honors & Awards:** Dr John C Hartnett Lectr, St Michaels Col, 1980. **Professional Experience:** Mem BM2 study sect, NIH, 1992-; PROF MICROBIOL, MED SCH, UNIV TEX, SAN ANTONIO, 1988-; vis scientist, Am Soc Microbiol Minority Student Sci Careers Support Prog, 1987-1992; mem, Am Soc Microbiol Culture Collection Subcomt, Pub Affairs Con, 1987-1992; sect head, plasmid biol, 1981-1988; consult, Food & Drug Admin, 1978-1992; res microbiologist, plasmid biol, 1977-1981; sr staff fel, Georgetown Univ Sch Med & Dent, 1975-1977; staff fel, NIH, 1972-1975; fel, Georgetown Univ Sch Med & Dent, 1970-1972. **Memberships:** NY Acad Sci; Am Soc Microbiol; AAAS. **Research Statement & Publications:** Molecular, genetic, and biochemical techniques to identification and characterization of chromosomal and extrachromosomal genetic traits. **Mailing Address:** Dept Microbiol Med Sch Univ Tex, 7703 Floyd Curl Dr, San Antonio, TX 78284-6200.

LEBLANC, FRANCIS ERNEST, NEUROPHYSIOLOGY, NEUROSURGERY. **Personal Data:** b North Sydney, NS, June 10, 1935; m 1961, c 3. **Education:** St Francis Xavier Univ, BSc, 1955; Univ Ottawa, MD, 1959; Univ Montreal, MSc, 1962, PhD (neurophysiol), 1964; FRCS(C), 1968. **Professional Experience:** CONSULT, NEUROSURG, as of 2003; CHMN, KING FAISAL SPECIALIST HOSP & RES CENTRE, as of 2003; assoc dean clin serv, Univ Calgary, 1983-; prof surg, Univ Calgary, 1980-; CHIEF, DIV NEUROSURG, FOOTHILLS HOSP, CALGARY, 1974-; from asst prof to assoc prof, Univ Calgary, 1971-1979; consult neurosurgeon, Foothills Hosp, 1971-1974; asst prof, McGill Univ, 1968-1970; vis neurosurgeon, Royal Victoria Hosp, Montreal, 1968; asst neurosurgeon, Montreal Neurol Inst, 1968; res scholar, Montreal Neurol Inst, 1967-1970; lectr neurosurg, McGill Univ, 1967-1968; consult, Queen Mary Vet Hosp, Montreal, 1967; clin fel & chief resident, Montreal Neurol Inst, 1966-1967; demonstr neurol, McGill Univ, 1964-1967; res fel, Univ Montreal, 1962-1964; lectr physiol, Univ, 1961-1964; Med Res Coun fel, Univ Montreal, 1961-1964; res asst, Neurol Sci Lab, Univ Montreal, 1961-1962; jr asst resident surg, Queen Mary Vet Hosp, Montreal, 1960-1961; Intern, Montreal Gen Hosp, Que, 1959-1960. **Memberships:** Can Neurosurg Soc; Cong Neurol Surg; Asn Acad Surg; fel Am Col Surg. **Research Statement & Publications:** Cerebrovascular physiology; epilepsy; movement disorders. **Mailing Address:** King Faisal Specialist Hosp & Res Ctr, PO Box 3354, Riyadh, Saudi Arabia. **E-Mail:** neuron@kfshrc.edu.sa

LEBLANC, GABRIEL A, GEOPHYSICS, SEISMOLOGY. **Personal Data:** b Montreal, Que, June 24, 1927; American citizen; m 1968, Katherine; c Genevieve. **Education:** Univ Montreal, BA, 1952; L'Immaculee-Conception, Montreal, LPh, 1953; Boston Col, MSc, 1958, SThL, 1960; Pa State Univ, PhD (geophys), 1966. **Professional Experience:** SR PRIVATE CONSULT, SEISMOL, 1993-; consult, Weston Geophys Corp, 1986-1992; sr staff consult & sr seismologist, Weston Geophys Corp, 1977-1986; sr res scientist, Seismol Div, Dept Energy, Mines & Resources, Can, 1971-1976; assoc prof geophys, Laval Univ, 1966-1971; res asst seismol, Pa State Univ, 1963-1966. **Memberships:** Am Geophys Union; Can Geophys Union; Seismol Soc Am. **Research Statement & Publications:** Regional tectonics and local seismicity; seismic hazard analysis; strong motion; induced seismicity; local arrays. **Mailing Address:** 17 Byard Lane, Westborough, MA 01581. **Fax:** 508-393-7674. **E-Mail:** kandgleblanc@mindspring.com

LEBLANC, JACQUES ARTHUR, PHYSIOLOGY. **Personal Data:** b Quebec City, Que, August 23, 1921; American citizen; m 1951, c 3. **Education:** Laval Univ, BA, 1943, BSc, 1947, PhD (physiol), 1951. **Professional Experience:** PROF EMER HUMAN PHYSIOL, FAC MED, LAVAL UNIV, asw 2004; prof human physiol, Fac Med, Laval Univ, beginning 1958; Physiologist human physiol, Defence Res Bd, Can Dept Nat Defence, 1949-1956. **Memberships:** AAAS; Am Physiol Soc; Fedn Am Socs Exp Biol; Soc Exp Biol & Med; FrCan Asn Advan Sci. **Research Statement & Publications:** Amines in stress conditions; tranquilizers; mast cells; basic and applied work in environmental physiology. **Mailing Address:** Dept Physiol, Sch Med Laval Univ, Pavillon Vandry House 2205B, Quebec, PQ G1K 7P4, Can. **Fax:** 418-656-7898. **E-Mail:** jacques.leblanc@phs.ulaval.ca

LEBLANC, JERALD THOMAS, PHOTOGRAPHIC SCIENCE, ORGANIC CHEMISTRY. **Personal Data:** b Baton Rouge, La, March 10, 1943; m 1968. **Education:** Birmingham-Southern Col, BS, 1965; Fla State Univ, PhD (org chem), 1970. **Professional Experience:** PROF MP TECH STAFF, EASTMAN KODAK CO, as of 2002; sr chemist res labs, Eastman Kodak Co, beginning 1970. **Memberships:** Imaging sci & tech Royal Photog Soc; Am Chem Soc. **Research Statement & Publications:** Silver halide chemistry and physics; organic dye synthesis. **Mailing Address:** PO Box 92988, Rochester, NY 14692.

LEBLANC, LARRY JOSEPH, TELECOMMUNICATION NETWORKS, OPERATIONS RESEARCH. **Personal Data:** b New Orleans, La, July 21, 1947; m 1969, Marguerite; c Aimee & Sara. **Education:** Loyola Univ, New Orleans, La, BS, 1969; Northwestern Univ, Evanston, IL, MS, 1971, PhD (opers res), 1973. **Honors & Awards:** Scientific Advisor to France Telecom, 1996 and 1997 Japanese Gov Res Award Foreign Specialists, 1994. **Professional Experience:** Vis prof, Univ Chile, 2005, 2002, 1988 & 1978; Vis prof, Tel Aviv Univ, Israel, 1997; vis prof, Univ Ulster, Northern Ireland, 1993; vis prof, Univ Thessaloniki, Greece, 1992; vis prof, NISTEP, Japan, 1992; vis prof, Neth Orgn Appl Sci Res, 1991; PROF OPER MGT & INFO TECHNOL, VANDERBILT UNIV, 1988-; coun mem, telecommun spec interest group, Opers Res Soc Am, 1988-1990; vis prof, Ecole Centrale Paris, 1987; chmn transp sci sect, Opers Res Soc Am, 1984-1986; vis prof, Technion, Israel, 1984; vis prof, Univ Ulm, Ger, 1981, 1982, 1984, 1985; assoc prof, Vanderbilt Univ, 1980-1988; NSF grants, 1980-1981 & 1982-1983; vis prof, Linkoping Inst Tech, Sweden, 1980; consult, Ingram Barge, Nu-kote Intl, Miss Chem Corp, Dr Pepper Co, Trailways,

McDermott, WFAA Radio, Pan Technol, Urban Systs, US Army Inventory Res Off, Port Everglades Steel Co, Eaton Corp, Carbon/Graphite Group & John Hamburg & Assoc, Inc, 1977-; from asst prof to assoc prof opers res, Southern Methodist Univ, 1973-1980; Fel, 1969-1972; grant, US Dept Transp, 1979-1980. **Memberships:** Inst Opers Res & Mgt Sci Beta Gamma Sigma. **Research Statement & Publications:** Applying real-world optimization models of supply chains in spreadsheets, telecommunication network design and analysis, and computer implementation of algorithms for large-scale optimization models. **Mailing Address:** Owen Grad Sch Mgmt, Vanderbilt Univ, 401 21st Ave South, Nashville, TN 37203. **Fax:** 615-343-7177. **E-Mail:** larry.leblanc@owen.vanderbilt.edu

LEBLANC, LEONARD JOSEPH, SOLID STATE PHYSICS. **Personal Data:** b Moncton, NB, November 6, 1937; m 1959, c 3. **Education:** St Joseph's Univ, NB, BSc, 1959; Univ Notre Dame, PhD (physics), 1964. **Professional Experience:** RETIRED; vpres acad, Univ Moneton, 1980-1996; dean fac sci & eng, Univ Moneton, 1975-1980; vdean fac sci, Univ Moneton, 1969-1974; from asst prof to prof physics, Univ Moneton, 1964-1996. **Memberships:** Am Asn Physics Teachers; Can Asn Physicists. **Research Statement & Publications:** Optical and photoelectric properties of metals in the vacuum ultraviolet. **Mailing Address:** Dept Physics, Univ Moncton, Moncton, NB E1A 3E9, Can.

LEBLANC, LESTER L, MARINE SCIENCE. **Education:** Univ RI, PhD. **Professional Experience:** PROF EMER, OCEAN ENG, FLA ATLANTIC UNIV, as of 2006. **Mailing Address:** Ocean Eng Dept, Fla Atlantic Univ, Boca Raton, FL 33431.

LE BLANC, MARCEL A R, PHYSICS, SUPERCONDUCTIVITY. **Personal Data:** b Gravelbourg, Sask, March 25, 1929. **Education:** Univ Sask, BSc, 1952, MA, 1954; Univ BC, PhD (physics), 1958. **Professional Experience:** PROF EMER PHYSICS, UNIV OTTAWA, 1994-; chmn, Dept Physics, 1980-1986; prof, Univ Ottawa, 1968-1994; mem tech staff & consult, Aerospace Corp, 1963-1968; asst prof elec eng, Univ Southern Calif, 1963-1968; consult, Spectromagnetic Industs, 1962-1963; consult, Varian Assocs, 1961-1962; asst prof, San Jose State Col, 1961-1962; res assoc physics, Stanford Univ, 1959-1963. **Memberships:** Fel Am Phys Soc; Can Asn Physicists. **Research Statement & Publications:** Photonuclear cross-sections; nuclear polarization; low temperature physics; superconductivity. **Mailing Address:** Dept Physics, Univ Ottawa, Macdonald Hall, 150 Louis Pasteur, Ottawa, ON K1N 6N5, Can. **Fax:** 613-562-5190.

LEBLANC, MICHAEL H, PEDIATRICS, NEONATOLOGY. **Personal Data:** b Birmingham, Ala, October 19, 1950; American citizen; m 1975, Janice; c Arthur, Vivian & Eric. **Education:** Auburn Univ, BS, 1972; Univ Ala, MD, 1975. **Honors & Awards:** Young Investr Award, Am Acad Pediat, 1982; Earnest G P Spivey Res Award, Am Heart Asn, 1987, John P Mallone Res Award, 1991. **Professional Experience:** PROF PEDIAT, UNIV MISS SCH MED, as of 2002; chmn res comt, Am Heart Asn, 1992-1994; counr, Southern Soc Pediat Res, 1989-1991; from asst prof to assoc prof, Univ Miss Sch Med, 1981-1992; fel neonatol, Univ Cincinnati, 1981; resident pediat, Univ Cincinnati, 1978; partic infant incubator task force, Am Acad Pediat, Asn Advan Med Instrumentation, Food & Drug Admin. **Memberships:** AMA; Soc Pediat Res; Am Physiol Soc; Southern Soc Pediat Res (secy-treas 1991-1995 pres 1996-1997); Asn Advan Med Instrumentation; Am Acad Pediat. **Research Statement & Publications:** Heat transfer and thermo regulation in infants; effect of polycythemia on the newborn; agents that amelrorate the effect of hypoxic ischemia on the brain in the newborn; use of surfactants in hyaline membrane disease in human infants. **Mailing Address:** Dept Med Ctr, Univ Miss, 2500 N State St, Jackson, MS 39216-4505. **Fax:** 601-984-5266. **E-Mail:** mleblanc@ped.umsmed.edu

LEBLANC, OLIVER HARRIS, JR, PHYSICAL CHEMISTRY. **Personal Data:** b Beaumont, Tex, November 14, 1931; m 1956, Ann Jones; c Catherine. **Education:** Rice Univ, BA, 1953; Univ Calif, PhD, 1957. **Professional Experience:** RETIRED; Phys chemist, Res & Develop Ctr, Gen Elec Co, 1957-1994. **Research Statement & Publications:** Electrochemistry; inorganic chemistry; membrane biophysics. **Mailing Address:** 2958 Grinnel Dr, Davis, CA 95616.

LEBLANC, RICHARD J, JR, COMPUTER SCIENCE. **Education:** La State Univ, BS, 1972; Univ Wis-Madison, MS, 1974 & PhD (comput sci), 1977. **Professional Experience:** PROF & ASSOC DEAN, COL COMPUT, GA INST TECHNOL, beginning 1978. **Mailing Address:** Ga Inst Tech, Atlanta, GA 30332. **Fax:** 404-894-9846. **E-Mail:** rich@cc.gatech.edu

LEBLANC, ROBERT BRUCE, FLAMMABILITY & FLAME RESISTANCE. **Personal Data:** b Alexandria, La, January 28, 1925; m 1996, Donna; c 7. **Education:** Loyola Univ, BS, 1947; Tulane Univ, MS, 1949, PhD (chem), 1950. **Professional Experience:** PRES & FOUNDER, LEBLANC RES CORP, 1970-; res mgr, Nat Cotton Coun, 1968-1970; textile chem develop mgr, ADM Chem Div, Ashland Oil Co, 1967-1968; sr textile specialist, Org Res Dept, Dow Chem Co, 1963-1967; res specialist, Org Res Dept, Dow Chem Co, 1952-1963; asst prof chem, Tex A&M Univ, 1950-1952; mem, Info Coun Fabric Flammability. **Memberships:** Am Chem Soc; Am Asn Textile Chemists & Colorists; Am Soc Testing & Mat; Nat Fire Protection Asn. **Research Statement & Publications:** Textile chemistry and phosphorus chemistry; flammability and fire retardance of textiles and plastics. **Mailing Address:** LeBlanc Res Corp, PO Box 391, Tallulah, LA 71284-0391.

LEBLANC, ROGER M, SURFACE CHEMISTRY, BIOLOGICAL MEMBRANES. **Personal Data:** b Trois-Rivieres, Que, January 5, 1942; m 1928, Micheline; c Daniel, Hugues, Marie-Jose & Nancy. **Education:** Laval Univ, Can, BSc, 1964. **Honorary Degrees:** DSc (phys chem), Laval Univ, Can, 1968. **Honors & Awards:** Vincent Award, Fr Can Asn Advan Sci, 1978; Noranda Award, Chem Inst Can, 1982; Barringer Award, Spectros Soc Can, 1983; John Labatt Ltd Award, Can Soc Chem, 1992; Medal Gov Can, 1993. **Professional Experience:** CHMN, DEPT CHEM, UNIV MIAMI, CORAL GABLES, FLA, 1993-; PROF, DEPT CHEM, UNIV MIAMI, CORAL GABLES, FLA, 1993-; chmn, Cell Biol & Genetics Selection Comt, Natural Sci & Eng Res Coun Can, 1990-1991; mem, Analytical & Phys Chem Selection Comt, 1988-1990; chmn, Cell Biol & Genetics Selection Comt, Natural Sci & Eng Res Coun Can, 1982-1983; chmn, Ctr Photobiophys, 1981-1991; mem, Cell Biol & Genetics Selection Comt, Natural Sci & Eng Res Coun Can, 1980-1982; dir, Group Biophys Res, 1978-1981; chmn, Dept Chem-Biol, Univ Que, 1971-1975; prof phys chem, Dept Chem-Biol, 1970-1993; fel phys chem, Davy Faraday Res Lab, Royal Inst, London, Eng, 1968-1970; chmn & prof phys chem, Dept Chem, Univ Miami, Coral Gables, Fla. **Memberships:** Chem Inst Can; Am Chem Soc; Biophys Soc; Europ Photochem Asn; Brit Biophys Soc; Am Soc Photobiol. **Research Statement & Publications:** The interaction of chlorophyll with itself and with various chloroplast components; the specific interaction in a two dimensional array is being studied with monolayer and photophysics techniques. **Mailing Address:** Chem Dept, Univ Miami, 315 Cox Sci Bldg, Coral Gables, FL 33124. **Fax:** 305-284-6367. **E-Mail:** rml@miami.edu

LEBLANC, RUFUS JOSEPH, GEOLOGY. **Personal Data:** b Erath, La, October 12, 1917; m 1940, c 4. **Education:** La State Univ, BS, 1939, MS, 1941. **Honors & Awards:** Sidney Powers Medal, Am Asn Petrol Geologists, 1988. **Professional Experience:** OWNER, LEBLANC SCH CLASTIC SEDIMENTS, HOUSTON, Tex, 1986-; mem, Staff Explor Training Dept, clastic sediments, 1965-1986; sr staff geologist, Explor Dept, Offshore Div, 1961-1965; sr geologist, Tech Serv, 1957-1960; mgr, Dept Geol Res, 1953-1956; Mem, Comt Fundamental Res Occurrence & Recovery Petrol, Am Petrol Inst, 1952-1957; sr res geologist, Shell Oil Co, 1948-1952; chief geol sect, Miss River Comn, US War Dept, 1947-1948; geologist, Miss River Comn, US War Dept, 1944-1946; Asst geologist, La State Univ, 1941-1943; assoc ed, J Am Asn Petrol Geologists. **Memberships:** Fel Geol Soc Am; hon mem Soc Econ Paleont & Mineral; hon mem Am Asn Petrol Geologists. **Research Statement & Publications:** Fundamental research in stratigraphy and sedimentology; exploration for oil and gas; quaternary geology; exploration training; environmental geology gulf coast. **Mailing Address:** 3751 Underwood St, Houston, TX 77025-1805.

LEBLOND, CHARLES PHILIPPE, HISTOLOGY, ENDOCRINOLOGY. **Personal Data:** b Lille, France, February 5, 1910; m 1936, Gertrude; c Philippe, Paul, Pierre, Marie & Pascale. **Education:** Univ Nancy, Lic es S, 1932; Univ Paris, MD, 1934; Univ Montreal, PhD (iodine metab), 1942; Univ Sorbonne, DSc, 1945. **Honorary Degrees:** DSc, Acadia Univ, 1972, Mc Gill Univ, 1982, Univ Montreal, 1985, York Univ, 1986. **Honors & Awards:** Wilson Medal, Am Soc Cell Biol, 1982. **Professional Experience:** Chmn dept, McGill Univ, 1957-1975; PROF ANAT, MCGILL UNIV, 1948-; from asst prof to assoc prof, McGill Univ, 1943-1948; lectr histol & embryol, McGill Univ, 1941-1943; asst, Lab Del Synthese Atomique, Paris, 1938-1940; Rockefeller fel, Sch Med, Yale Univ, 1936-1937; asst histol, Med Sch Paris, 1934-1935. **Memberships:** Am Asn Anat; Histochem Soc; fel Royal Soc; fel Royal Soc Can. **Research Statement & Publications:** Histological localization of vitamin C; uptake of iodine by thyroid; tracing of radio elements and labelled precursors of nucleic acids, proteins and glycoproteins by means of radioautography; cell dynamics in gastro-intestinal tract; chromosome condensation. **Mailing Address:** Dept Anat & Cell Biol, McGill Univ, 3640 Univ St, Montreal, PQ H3A 2B2, Can. **Fax:** 514-398-5047. **E-Mail:** cleblond@medcor.mcgill.ca

LEBLOND, PAUL HENRI, PHYSICAL OCEANOGRAPHY, FISHERIES. **Personal Data:** b Que, December 30, 1938; div, c 3. **Education:** Laval Univ, BA, 1957; McGill Univ, BSc, 1961; Univ BC, PhD (physics), 1964. **Honorary Degrees:** DSc, Mem Univ, Nfld, 1992. **Honors & Awards:** Wooster Award, North Pacific Marine Sci Org 2004; Foreign Fellow, Academy of Natural Sciences of the Russian Federation, 1992; Tully Medal, CanMeteorol Oceanog Soc, 1991; Fellow, Royal Society of Canada, 1982; President's Prize, Can Meteorol Oceanog Soc, 1981. **Professional Experience:** Trustee, Canadian Foundation for Climate and Atmospheric Sciences, 2001-; Pacific Fisheries Resource Conservation Council, 1998-; chair, 2005-; Fisheries Resource Conserv Coun, 1993-1997; PROF EMER, DEPT EARTH & OCEAN SCI, UNIV BC, 1992-; prog leader, Ocean Prof Enhancement Network, 1991-1993; assoc dean, Fac Sci, Univ BC, 1983-1985; vis prof, Laval Univ, 1979-1980; head oceanog, Univ BC, 1987-1992; prof physics & oceanog, Univ BC, 1975-1996; vis prof. Univ Marseille 1985-1986; vis scientist, Inst Oceanol, USSR Acad Sci, Moscow, 1973-1974; Vis assoc prof, Simon Fraser Univ, 1970; Nat Res Coun Can fel, Inst Meereskunde, Kiel, Ger, 1964-1965. **Memberships:** Can Meteorol Oceanog Soc; Am Geophys Union. **Research Statement & Publications:** Ocean waves and currents, fisheries resource conservation, marine cryptozoology. **Mailing Address:** S42, C7, RR#2, Galiano Island, BC V0N 1P0, Can. **E-Mail:** leblond@gulfislands.com

LEBO, GEORGE ROBERT, PHYSICS, RADIO ASTRONOMY. **Personal Data:** b Chadron, Nebr, September 27, 1937; m 1958, c 2. **Education:** Wheaton Col, BS, 1959; Univ Ill, MS, 1960; Univ Fla, PhD (physics), 1964. **Professional Experience:** ASSOC PROF EMER PHYSICS & ASTRON, UNIV FLA, as of 2004; assoc prof physics & astron, Univ Fla, beginning 1977; asst prof, Univ Fla, 1965-1977; res assoc radio astron, Univ Fla, 1964-1965. **Memberships:** Am Astron Soc; Am Geophys Union; Am Phys Soc. **Research Statement & Publications:** Study of decametric radiation from the planets, particularly Jupiter. **Mailing Address:** Dept Astron, Univ Fla, PO Box 112055, Gainesville, FL 32611-2055. **E-Mail:** lebo@astro.ufl.edu

LEBO, ROGER VAN, GENETIC NEUROPATHY, PRENATAL DIAGNOSIS. **Personal Data:** b Pottsville, Pa, March 1, 1948; m 1972, Susan; c Franklin & Paul. **Education:** Pa State Univ, BS, 1970; Duke Univ, PhD (genetics), 1974. **Professional Experience:** DIR, CYTOGENETICS LAB, 1993-; consult, Genetype Corp, 1991-1992; res liaison, Charcot-Marie-Tooth Asn, 1990-; prin investr, NIH, 1988-1992; assoc prof dept obstet & gynec, Sch Med, Univ Calif, San Fransico, beginning 1987; dir, Molecular Genetics Lab, 1987-1993; prin investr, Muscular Dystrophy Asn, 1984-1994; assoc res biochemist, Dept Med, 1983-1986; dir, cell sorting facil & assoc, 1980-1986; consult, Nat Cert Agency, Med Lab Personnel, Cytogenetic Subcomt, 1980-1985; res assoc, Howard Hughes Med Inst, 1978-1980; asst res biochemist, Dept Med, Univ Calif, San Francisco, 1976-1983; res biochemist, Dept Med, Univ Calif, San Francisco, 1974-1976. **Memberships:** Am Soc Human Genetics; NY Acad Sci; Human Genome Orgn; Peripheral Neuropathy Asn; Am Fedn Clin Res. **Research Statement & Publications:** Human genetic disease studies included positionally cloning the Charcot-Marie-Tooth 1B gene, developing in-situ prenatal diagnostic tests for gene and chromosome aneuploidy and developing gene mapping by chromosome sorting. **Mailing Address:** Akron Hosp, Cytogenetics Lab, Akron, OH 94122-2722. **Fax:** 330-543-3226. **E-Mail:** rlebo@chmca.org

LEBOEUF, JEAN-NOEL G, PHYSICS. **Education:** Inst Nat de la Recherche Scientifique, PhD, 1976. **Professional Experience:** GROUP LEADER, OAK RIDGE NAT LAB, as of 1998. **Mailing Address:** Bldg 9201-2 Oak Ridge Nat Lab, PO Box 2009, Oak Ridge, TN 37831. **Fax:** 865-574-3940. **E-Mail:** leboeuf@fed.ornl.gov

LEBOFSKY, LARRY ALLEN, PLANETARY SCIENCES. **Personal Data:** b Brooklyn, NY, August 31, 1947; m 1980, Nancy; c Miranda. **Education:** Calif Inst Technol, BS, 1969; Mass Inst Technol, PhD (earth & planetary sci), 1974. **Professional Experience:** SR RES SCIENTIST, UNIV ARIZ, 1989-; from res assoc to assoc planetary sci, Univ Ariz, 1977-1989; res assoc planetary sci, Jet Propulsion Lab, 1975-1977. **Memberships:** Am Astron Soc; Int Astron Union; Am Geophys Union; Meteoritical Soc; Nat Sci Teachers Asn; Astron soc pacific. **Research Statement & Publications:** Remote sensing of the visual, near infrared and thermal infrared spectra of asteroids and satellites for the study of composition; related studies of laboratory reflection spectra. **Mailing Address:** Lunar & Planetary Lab, Univ Ariz 2333 E Seventh St, Tucson, AZ 85719-5610. **Fax:** 520-621-1532. **E-Mail:** lebofsky@lpl.arizona.edu

LEBOLD, WILLIAM K, ENGINEERING, GENERAL. **Education:** Univ Minn, BEE, 1945; Northwestern Univ, MS, 1953; Purdue Univ, PhD (psychol), 1957. **Professional Experience:** PROF EMER ENG & EDUC PSYCHOL, DEPT FRESHMAN ENG, PURDUE UNIV, as of 2004; prof eng & educ psychol, Dept Freshman Eng, Purdue Univ, ending 2001. **Mailing Address:** Dept Freshman Eng, Purdue Univ, 1286 Eng Admin, West Lafayette, IN 47907-1286. **Fax:** 765-494-5819. **E-Mail:** lebold@ecn.purdue.edu

LEBOLD, WILLIAM KERNS, EDUCATIONAL RESEARCH & INFORMATION SYSTEMS IN ENGINEERING, EQUITY RESEARCH & CAREER DEVELOPMENT. **Personal Data:** b Chicago, Ill, August 23, 1923; m 1945, Donna Seterdahl; c William Jr, Sandra J & Thomas L. **Education:** Univ Minn, BS, 1945; Northwestern Univ, MS, 1953; Purdue Univ, PhD (psychol), 1957. **Honors & Awards:** Distinguished Serv Award, Am Soc Eng Educ, 1991, Centennial Medallion, 1993; Distinguished Serv Award, Inst Elec & Electronics Engrs, 1992; Benjamin Dasher Award, Am Soc Eng Educ & Inst Elec & Electronics Engrs, 1993; Harold Amrine Visionary Award, Nat Soc Black Engrs, 1996; Sugamove of the Wabush, State of Indiana. **Professional Experience:** PROF EMER, PURDUE UNIV, 2002-; comdn, Eng Workforce Comn, as of 1990; vis prof, Univ Minn, 1988-1989 & 1995-1996; res dir, Eng Workforce Comn, 1984-1987; chair, Info Systs, 1982-1983; consult, Alfred Sloan Found, 1978; res assoc, Nat Res Coun, 1972-1973; interim dir, Measurement & Res Ctr, 1971; proj coordr, Am Soc Eng Educ, 1963-1970; prof eng, Purdue Univ, 1962-2001; vis prof, Univ Calif, Los Angeles, 1961-1965; asst to dean eng, Purdue Univ, 1958-1971; assoc prof, Purdue Univ, 1958-1961; examr, N Cent Asn Cols & Univs, 1957-1980; chair, Educ Res & Methods Div, Am Soc Eng Educ, 1957-1965; consult, Gen Elec Co, 1955-1956; res asst, Purdue Univ, 1954-1957; asst prof elec eng, Univ Ill, Chicago, 1953-1954; engr, Commonwealth Edison, 1950-1951; instr & staff counr, Univ Ill, Chicago, 1947-1953; elec engr, Automatic Elec, 1945-1947. **Memberships:** Fel Am Soc Eng Educ; fel Am Psychol Asn; Chair 1999-2000, V.Chair-Secy. 1997-1998, Asee Academy of Fellowship. **Research Statement & Publications:** Engineering education research and information systems; survey research, career development, equity research, equal opportunities, engineering retention, self concepts, longitudinal studies of engineers, optimal placement, applied statistics; computer literacy. **Mailing Address:** 3430 List Pl Apt 1105, Minneapolis, MN 55416-4549. **Fax:** 765-494-5819. **E-Mail:** lebold@ecn.purdue.edu

LEBOUTON, ALBERT V, MICROSCOPIC ANATOMY, CELL BIOLOGY. **Personal Data:** b La Salle, Ill, July 10, 1937; m 1959, c 3. **Education:** San Diego State Col, BS, 1960; Univ Calif, Los Angeles, PhD (anat), 1966. **Professional Experience:** ASSOC PROF EMER ANAT, UNIV ARIZ, 1999; actg head dept, Univ Calif, Los Angeles, 1972-1974; asst prof anat, Univ Calif, Los Angeles, 1966-1972. **Memberships:** AAAS; Am Inst Biol Sci; Fedn Am Sci; Am Soc Cell Biol; Am Asn Anat. **Research Statement & Publications:** Radioautography, radiobiochemistry, and immunocytochemistry of protein metabolism and growth in the liver. **Mailing Address:** Col Med, Univ Ariz, Rm Isn 444 PO Box 245044, Tucson, AZ 85724.

LEBOVITZ, NORMAN RONALD, APPLIED MATHEMATICS, ASTROPHYSICS. **Personal Data:** b New York, NY, September 27, 1935; m 1971, Ruth; c David & Michael. **Education:** Univ Calif, Los Angeles, AB, 1956; Univ Chicago, MS, 1957, PhD (physics), 1961. **Professional Experience:** Guggenheim Found fel, 1977; PROF MATH, UNIV CHICAGO, 1969-; Sloan Found fel, 1967; from asst prof to assoc prof, Univ Chicago, 1963-1969; Moore instr math, Mass Inst Technol, 1961-1963; managing ed, Soc Indust & Appl Math. **Memberships:** Soc Indust & Appl Math; Amer Phys Soc. **Research Statement & Publications:** Stability theory; bifurcation theory; rotating fluid masses; singular perturbation theory. **Mailing Address:** Dept Math, Univ Chicago, 5734 S Univ Ave, Chicago, IL 60637-1514. **Fax:** 773-702-9787. **E-Mail:** lebovitz@cs.uchicago.edu

LEBOVITZ, ROBERT MARK, NEUROPHYSIOLOGY, BIOMATHEMATICS & BIOENGINEERING. **Personal Data:** b Scranton, Pa, May 6, 1937; c 3. **Education:** Calif Inst Technol, BS, 1959, MS, 1960; Univ Calif, Los Angeles, PhD (neurophysiol), 1967. **Professional Experience:** PROF NEUROPHYSIOL, UNIV TEX HEALTH SCI CTR, DALLAS, 1980-; Nat Inst Environ Health Sci grant, 1977- & Off Naval Res Contracts, 1978-; Food & Drug Admin grant, 1974-; prof bd, Home Health Serv, Dallas, 1974-; Sloan Consortium scholar, 1974-1975; NIH grants, 1971-; Energy Conversion Devices, 1971 & Equitable Environ Health, 1971-; adj prof, Inst Technol, Southern Methodist Univ, 1971-1974; Neurosyst Inc, 1971; Neurosyst, Dallas Epilepsy Asn, 1971; assoc prof, Univ Tex Health Sci Ctr, Dallas, 1970-1980; NSF fel, Univ Tex Regents, 1970-1972; staff chief technical officer, Centra-Guard Inc & Neighborhood Coop Patrol, 1969-1971; staff scientist auditory & visual info processing, Recognition Equip Inc, 1969-1970; res assoc neural models, Ctr Theoret Biol, State Univ NY Buffalo, 1969; Recognition Equip Inc, 1969; consult, Dept Path & Eng Sci, Rand Corp, 1969; NSF fel, Sch Med, NY Univ, 1967-1969; resident consult, Dept Math, Rand Corp, 1967; mem tech staff, Hughes Aircraft Co, 1959-1962. **Memberships:** Am Physiol Soc; NY Acad Sci; Biophys Soc; Inst Elec & Electronics Engrs; Soc Neuroscience. **Research Statement & Publications:** Neural networks and neural modelling; neurophysiology of epilepsy and behavior; modification and control of behavior via drugs and implanted or extraneous brain stimulating arrays; microwave interactions with the nervous system and behavior; electronic medicine. **Mailing Address:** Dept Physiol, Univ Tex SW Med Ctr, 5323 Harry Hines Blvd, Dallas, TX 75235-8570.

LEBOW, IRWIN L(EON), TELECOMMUNICATIONS, Satellite communications. **Personal Data:** b Boston, Mass, April 27, 1926; m Grace; c Judith, William & David. **Education:** Mass Inst Technol, SB, 1948, PhD (physics), 1951. **Professional Experience:** Adjunct Professor U MD, University College, 1998-; CONSULT, 1987-; vpres, Syst Res & Appln Corp, 1984-1987; vpres eng, Am Satellite Co, 1981-1984; chief scientist & assoc dir technol, Defense Commun Agency, 1975-1981; assoc div head, Lincoln Lab, Mass Inst Technol, 1970-1975; group leader, Lincoln Lab, Mass Inst Technol, 1965-1970; assoc group leader, Lincoln Lab, Mass Inst Technol, 1960-1965; Mem staff, Lincoln Lab, Mass Inst Technol, 1951-1960; Mem, Comt Commun & Info Processing, Inst Elec & Electronics Engrs; AUTHOR: Theory and Design of Digital Machines, McGraw Hill, 1962 (with others); The Digital Connection, W.H.Freeman, 1991; Information Highways and Byways, IEEE Press, 1995; Understanding Digital Transmission and Recording, IEEE Press, 1998; Coping with Your Difficult Older Parent, Avon, 1999 (with others). **Memberships:** Fel Am Phys Soc; fel Inst Elec & Electronics Engrs; AAAS; Sigma Xi. **Research Statement & Publications:** Communication systems, including satellite communications, command and control systems and information processing systems; author on information technology. **Mailing Address:** 5600 Wis Ave, #909, Chevy Chase, MD 20815. **E-Mail:** irwinle@cs.net

LEBOW, MICHAEL DAVID, BEHAVIORAL MEDICINE, HEALTH PSYCHOLOGY. **Personal Data:** b Detroit, Mich, June 24, 1941; m 1969, c 2. **Education:** Univ Calif, Los Angeles, BS, 1964; Univ Utah, MA, 1967, PhD (psychol), 1969. **Professional Experience:** Chmn, Psychol Intervention Subcomt, Task Force Treatment Obesity, Can Health & Welfare, 1986-; PROF PSYCHOL, UNIV MAN, 1979-; assoc prof, Univ Man, 1974-1979; adj asst prof, psychol, Dartmouth Col, 1973-1974; asst prof med psychol, Med Sch Dartmouth, Univ, 1972-1974; asst prof psychol, Univ Man, 1972-1973. **Memberships:** Sigma Xi; Am Psychol Asn; Soc Behav Med; Can Psychol Asn; Asn Advan Behav Therap. **Research Statement & Publications:** Treatment programs for the obese; attitudes, perceptions and practices of children, adolescents and adults towards the obese. **Mailing Address:** Dept Psychol, Univ Man, Winnipeg, MB R3T 2N2, Can. **Fax:** 204-474-7599. **E-Mail:** mlebow@cc.umanitoba.ca

LEBOWITZ, BARRY D, GERIATRICS. **Personal Data:** b Boston, Mass, February 11, 1942. **Education:** McGill Univ, BA, 1964; Ind Univ, MA (comp sociol), 1967; Cornell Univ, MA (sociol), 1967, PhD (sociol), 1970. **Honors & Awards:** Meritorious Achievement, Ment Health Serv, 1982; Super Serv Award, USPHS, 1991. **Professional Experience:** CHIEF, ADULT & GERIATRIC TREATMENT & PREV INTERVENTIONS RES BR, NAT INST MENTAL HEALTH, as of 2001; CHIEF, MENT DIS AGING RES BR, NAT INST ALCOHOL ABUSE & ALCOHOLISM, NIH, 1983-. **Memberships:** Am Psychiat Asn; Am Asn Geriat Psychiat. **Mailing Address:** Adult & Geriatric Treatment & Prev Interventions Res Br, NIMH, NIH, Rm 7160, 6001 Exec Blvd, MSC 9663, Bethesda, MD 20892-9663. **Fax:** 301-443-4279.

LEBOWITZ, JACOB, MOLECULAR BIOLOGY, BIOCHEMISTRY. **Personal Data:** b Brooklyn, NY, October 20, 1935; m 1978, Candace. **Education:** Brooklyn Col, BS, 1957; Purdue Univ, PhD (phys chem), 1962. **Honors & Awards:** scholar award, Am Cancer Soc, 1982-1983. **Professional Experience:** RETIRED; prof microbiol, Med Ctr, Univ Ala, Birmingham, beginning 1977; assoc prof, Med Ctr, Univ Ala, Birmingham, 1974-1977; career develop award, NIH, 1972-1977; from asst prof to assoc prof biochem, Syracuse Univ, 1966-1974; res fel biophys chem, Calif Inst Technol, 1962-1966. **Memberships:** AAAS; Am Chem Soc; Am Soc Microbiol; Am Soc Biol Chem & Molecular Biol; Biophys Soc; Protein Soc. **Research Statement & Publications:** Analysis of RNA polymerase-promoter interactions; structural transitions in supercoiled DNA in relation to biological activity; characterization protein-DNA and proteial-protein interactions using analytical ultra centrifugation. **Mailing Address:** Dept Microbiol, Univ Ala, Med Ctr 520 CHSB, Birmingham, AL 35294-2041. **E-Mail:** jack_lebowitz@micro.microbio.uab.edu

LEBOWITZ, JACOB MORDECAI, NUCLEAR PHYSICS. **Personal Data:** b New York, NY, March 21, 1936; m 1965, c 2. **Education:** Yeshiva Univ, BA, 1957; Columbia Univ, MA, 1960, PhD (physics), 1965. **Professional Experience:** ASSOC PROF PHYSICS, BROOKLYN COL, 1970-; from instr to asst prof, Brooklyn Col, 1959-1970. **Memberships:** Am Phys Soc; Sigma Xi. **Research Statement & Publications:** Nuclear forces; fission. **E-Mail:** jmloc@cunyvm.cuny.edu

LEBOWITZ, JOEL LOUIS, STATISTICAL MECHANICS, MATHEMATICAL PHYSICS. **Personal Data:** b Taceva, Czech, May 10, 1930; American citizen; m 1953. **Education:** Brooklyn Col, BS, 1952; Syracuse Univ, MS, 1955, PhD (physics), 1956. **Honorary Degrees:** Dr Hon Causa, Ecole Polytech Fed Lausanne, 1977. **Honors & Awards:** A Cressy Morrison Award in Natural Sci, NY Acad Sci, 1986, Heinz R Pagels Human Rights of Scientists Award, 1996; Delmar S Fahrney Medal, The Franklin Inst, 1995. **Professional Experience:** Ed/co-ed, Annals NY Acad Sci, Collective Phenomena, beginning 1980; mem, Sci Comt Sci Matters, Inst desHautes Etudes Scientifiques, Bures-sur-Yvette, France, 1979-1982; GEORGE WILLIAM HILL PROF MATH & PHYSICS & DIR, CTR MATH SCI RES, RUTGERS UNIV, 1977-; guggenheim fel, 1976-1977; ed-in-chief, J Statist Physics, 1975; from asst prof to prof, Grad Sch Sci, Yeshiva Univ, 1957-1977; asst prof physics, Stevens Inst Technol, 1957-1959; NSF res fel, Yale Univ, 1956-1957; vis prof, Sch Med, Cornell Univ; mem, Inst Theoret Physics. **Memberships:** Fel Nat Acad Sci; NY Acad Sci (pres-elect 1977-1979 pres 1979); fel Am Phys Soc; Am Math Soc; fel AAAS; Int Union Pure & Appl Physics (secy 1982-1984 pres 1985-1987). **Research Statement & Publications:** Statistical mechanics of equilibrium and nonequilibrium processes; theory of liquids. **Mailing Address:** Dept Math, Hill Ctr, Rutgers Univ, 110 Frelinghuysen Rd, piscataway, NJ 08854. **Fax:** 732-445-3923. **E-Mail:** lebowitz@math.rutgers.edu

LEBOWITZ, MICHAEL DAVID, EPIDEMIOLOGY, PULMONARY DISEASES. **Personal Data:** b New York, NY, December 21, 1939; m 1960, Joyce; c Jon, Kira & Debra. **Education:** Univ Calif, Berkeley, AB, 1957, MA, 1965; Univ Wash, PhC, 1969, PhD (epidemiol & int health), 1971. **Honors & Awards:** Am Epidemiol Soc, 1980; Int Acad Indoor Air Sci, 1992; fel, Am Col Epidemiol, 1994; J Weselowski Award, Int Soc Expos Anal, 2003. **Professional Experience:** DIR, ARIZ PREV CTR, ARIZ COL PUB HEALTH, UNIV ARIZ, 2004-; past chair, Steering Comt, Nat Prev Res Ctr, 2002-2003; counr, Exec Comt, Int Soc Exposure Anal, 2001; PROF PUB HEALTH & MED, MEL & ENID ZUCKERMAN COL PUB HEALTH, UNIV ARIZ, 2000-; DIR & CHAIR EPIDEMIOL & BIOSTATISTICS, MEL & ENID ZUCKERMAN COL PUB HEALTH, UNIV ARIZ 2000-; chair-elect & chair, Epidemiol Coun, Assoc Schs Pub Health, 2000-; ed bd, Indoor Air, 2000-; prin investr grants, Nat Inst Environ Health Sci, 2000-2002; from vice chair to chair, Nat Prev Res Centers Steering Comt, 2000-2002; pres-elect, pres, & past pres, Int Soc Exposure Anal, 1999-2001; dir, Ariz Prev Res Ctr, Univ Ariz, 1998-; prin investr grants, Ctrs Dis Control, 1998-; mem, Nat Res Coun/Nat Acad Sci Panel Strategies Protect Health US Deployed Forces, 1998-2000; collabor, Special Invest Unit Gulf War Illness, US Senate Veteran's Affairs Comm, 1997-1998; assoc dept head & dir epidemiol unit, Ariz Prev Ctr Dept, Col Med, Univ Ariz, 1996-2000; consult, Nat Res Coun/Nat Acad Sci/Inst Med Comn Environ Justice, 1996; mem, Ariz-Sonora Binat'l Work Groups, 1995-; chair, Epidemiol Grad Prog, Univ Ariz, 1994-2003; assoc ed, J Toxicol Indust Health, 1994-; vis prof, Univ Groningen, 1993; vis prof, Univ Pisa, 1993; sr fel, Ital Nat Res Coun, 1993; mem, WHO &EURO Exposure Assessment Working Group, 1993, 1995; consult, EC/EU COST, Environ Epidemiol Directorate, 1993; ed bd, J Respiratory Critical Care Med, 1993-1998; consult, Europ Community Concerted Action Airway Obstructive Dis, 1993-1995; assoc ed, J Exposure Anal Environ Epidemiol, 1992-1999; mem, Comm Indoor Allergens, Nat Res Coun Inst Med, 1991-1993; mem, Nat Res Coun/Nat Acad Sci Working Group Mult Chem Sensitivities, 1991; reviewer, Nat Res Coun/Nat Acad Sci Environ Epidemiol Comts, 1991; consult, WHO Environ Health Centers Europe 1991-; mem, WHO/EC Comn Air Pollution Exposure & Health Hazards & Abatement Strategies, 1990-1993; vis prof & NZMRC consult, Univ Otago, 1989; chair, Peak Flow Work Group, Europ Respiratory Soc, 1989-1997; counr, Exec Comt, Int Soc Exposure Anal, 1989-1993; mem steering comt, Int Soc Environ Epidemiol, 1988-1993; consult & peer rev panel, Nat Ctr Environ Health, Ctr Dis Control, 1987-; Ariz Gov Spec Environ investr, 1987-1994; consult & reviewer, US Cong Off Technol Assessment, 1987-1988; consult, Nat Res Coun/Nat Acad Sci Comn Assessing Human Exposure, 1987-1990; vis prof, Polish Acad Sci, 1986; facil chair, Environ Inventory Questionnaire Stand Work Group, Environ Protection Agency, 1986-1989; partic, WHO/EURO Air Qual Guidelines, 1985-1987; consult, Sci Adv Bd, Environ Protection Agency, 1984-; mem, Working Group Approaches Invest Cancer Risk Passive Smoking, Int Agency Res Cancer, 1984; ed bd, J Air Pollution Control Asn, 1984-1988; vis prof, Univ Pisa, 1982; sr fel, Ital Nat Res Coun, 1982; mem, WHO/EURO Environ Work Group, 1982-1995; vis prof, Polish Acad Sci, 1981; consult, Polish & Hungarian NIHs, 1981-2003; vis prof, Univ Pisa, 1979, 1980; sr fel, Ital Nat Res Coun, 1979, 1980; WHO adv, 1979-; ad hoc mem, Epidemiol Study Sect, NIH, 1979-1984; co-chmn, Comt Indoor Pollutants, Nat Res Coun, Nat Acad Sci, 1979-1981; fel, Univ London Postgrad Cardiothoracic Inst, 1978-1979; mem, WHO Comn, 1978-1995; preceptor, NIH fel, Am Thoracic Soc, Fogarty Ctr fel & CNR Fel, 1978-1990; mem, Behav Study Sect, NIH, 1977; assoc prog dir, NIH Inst Training Prog, 1977-1986; prin investr grants, Environ Protection Agency, 1977-; ed bd, J Behav Med, 1977-1993; prin investr grants, Food & Drug Admin, 1976-1981; mem, Epidemiol Study Sect, NIH, 1975-1978; consult, NIH, 1975-; consult, Pan Am Health Orgn, 1975-; mem & chmn, Pima Co Air Qual Adv Coun, 1975-; asst to assoc dir, Respiratory Sci Ctr, Univ Ariz, 1974-1996; consult, Nat Heart, Lung & Blood Inst, 1972-1999; prof, dept Med, Col Med, Univ Ariz, 1971-; prin & co-prin investr grants, NIH, 1971-1999; asst dir, Specialized Ctr Res, Univ Ariz, 1971-1997; partic, NSF-Japan Soc Prom Sci Coop Sci Group Air Pollution, 1969-1970; res assoc, environ health, Med & Pub Health Sch, Univ Wash, 1967-1971; biostatistician, Calif Dept Pub Health, 1967; pub health statistician, Almeda Co Health Dept, 1962-1963. **Memberships:** Int Epidemiol Asn; Soc Epidemiol Res; Am Thoracic Soc; Int Soc Environ Epidemiol; Int Soc Exposure Analysis; Assoc Teachers Prev Med; fel Am Col Chest Physicians; fel Collegium Ramazzini; hon mem Hungarian Soc Hyg. **Research Statement & Publications:** Pulmonary, cardiovascular, diabetes and other chronic disease epidemiology; etiology and natural history of pulmonary diseases and other chronic diseases; environ health effects research; environmental exposure assessment; infectious disease epidemiol; community-based prevention/intervention research. **Mailing Address:** Ariz Prev Ctr, Mel & Enid Zuckerman Col Pub Health, Univ Ariz, 1145 N Campbell Ave PO Box 210228, Tucson, AZ 85721-0228. **Fax:** 520-326-0435. **E-Mail:** mlebowit@u.arizona.edu

LEBOY, PHOEBE STARFIELD, GENE EXPRESSION, BONE BIOLOGY. **Personal Data:** b Brooklyn, NY, July 29, 1936; m 1984, Neal. **Education:** Swarthmore Col, AB, 1957; Bryn Mawr Col, PhD (biochem), 1962. **Honorary Degrees:** MA, Univ Pa, 1971. **Honors & Awards:** Lindback award for distinguished teaching, 2004. **Professional Experience:** Secretary, Association for Women in Science; chmn, dept biochem, 1992-1996; Fogarty fel, Univ Oxford, 1989-1990; chairperson, Grad Group Molecular Biol, Univ Pa, 1984-1987; vis prof, Univ Calif, San Francisco, 1979-1980; PROF BIOCHEM, SCH DENT MED, UNIV PA, 1976-2005; NIH res grant, & NIH res career develop award, 1971-1976; NIH res grant, Univ Pa, 1968-; NATO fel, Weizmann Inst Sci, 1966-1967; from instr to assoc prof, Sch Med, Univ Pa, 1965-1976; res assoc, Sch Med, Univ Pa, 1963-1966; res assoc biochem, Bryn Mawr Col, 1961-1963. **Memberships:** Am Soc Biol Chem; Am Soc Bone Mineral Res; Am Soc Cell Biol; Orthop. Res. Soc; Assn Women in Science. **Research Statement & Publications:** Role of gene expression in tissue mineralization; molecular biology of bone formation; bone morphogenetic proteins, mesenchymal stem cells. **Mailing Address:** 1600 Hagys Ford Rd, Apt 9W, Narberth, PA 19072. **Fax:** 610-667-8578. **E-Mail:** phoebe@biochem.dental.upenn.edu

LE BRETON, GUY C, PHARMACOLOGY. **Personal Data:** b Miami, Fla, October 1, 1946. **Education:** Univ Chicago, BS, 1968, PhD (pharmacol), 1973. **Professional Experience:** Mem, Comt Pub Info, Am Soc Pharmacol & Exp Therapeut, 1986-1988; PROF, DEPT PHARMACOL, UNIV ILL, 1985-; field ed, J Pharmacol & Exp Therapeut, 1982-; estab investr, Am Heart Asn, 1982-1987; mem bd trustees, Am Asn Accreditation Lab Animal Care, 1982-1986; from instr to assoc prof, Dept Pharmacol, 1975-1985; fel trainee, Dept Pharmacol, 1973-1975; mem, Coun Thrombosis, Am Heart Asn. **Memberships:** Sigma Xi; Am Soc Pharmacol & Exp Therapeut; AAAS. **Research Statement & Publications:** Drug development; thrombosis and anti-thrombotic drugs; blood platelet: aggregating agents, aggregation, prostaglandins, prostaglandin endoperoxides, thromboxanes, thromboxane antagonists, thromboxane receptor, calcium, ion fluxes, cAMP; fluorescent cation probes; cellular secretion; cellular contraction; fatty acid metabolism. **Mailing Address:** Dept Pharmacol, Col Med, Univ Ill, 768 Col Med E 808 S Wood St, Chicago, IL 60612-3796. **Fax:** 312-996-1296. **E-Mail:** gcl@uic.edu

LEBRETON, PIERRE ROBERT, BIOPHYSICAL CHEMISTRY. **Personal Data:** b Chicago, Ill, September 17, 1942; m 1969, Laura; c David. **Education:** Univ Chicago, BS, 1964; Harvard Univ, MA, 1966, PhD (chem physics), 1970. **Professional Experience:** PROF EMER, UNIV ILL, CHICAGO, 2003-; RES ASSOC, BEN MAY INST, UNIV CHICAGO, 2002-; Blowitz-Ridgeway Found grant, 1993-1994; am Can Soc res grant, 1991-; prof chem, Univ Ill, Chicago, 1987-; Petrol Res Fund Am Chem Soc, grant, 1987-1994; NIH grants, 1987-1990; Am Can Soc res grant, 1984; NIH grants, 1980-1983; res assoc, Nat Ctr Sci Res, Univ Louis Pasteur, Strasbourg, France, 1980; Am Cancer Soc grants, 1976-1980; from asst prof to assoc prof, Univ Ill, Chicago, 1973-1987; fel chem, Jet Propulsion Lab, Calif Inst Technol, 1971-1973; fel physics, Phys Inst, Univ Freiburg, Ger, 1970-1971; bd trustees, Blowitz Ridgeway Found. **Memberships:** Am Chem Soc mem; Int Soc Quantum Biol exec comm; Biophys Soc mem; Am Asn Cancer Res mem; Blowite-Ridgeway Found (trustee). **Research Statement & Publications:** Photoelectron, theoretical quantum mechanical, and time-resolved fluorescence investigations of nucl. **Mailing Address:** Dept Chem, Univ Ill, 845 W Taylor St Rm 4500 M/C 111, Chicago, IL 60607-7061. **Fax:** 312-996-0431. **E-Mail:** lebreton@uic.edu

LEBRUN, PRISCILLA C, PHYSICAL CHEMISTRY. **Professional Experience:** MEM, AM CHEM SOC, as of 2004. **Mailing Address:** Am Chem Soc, 1155 Sixteenth St, NW, Washington, DC 20036. **Fax:** 202-776-8258.

LEBRUN, ROGER ARTHUR, MEDICAL ENTOMOLOGY, INVERTEBRATE PATHOLOGY. **Personal Data:** b Providence, RI, May 26, 1946; wid Kathleen. **Education:** Providence Col, AB, 1968; Cornell Univ, MSc, 1973, PhD (invert path), 1977. **Honors & Awards:** CARNEGIE PROF OF THE YEAR 2001 (RI); UNIV OF RI PROF OF THE YEAR 2000; DISTINGUISHED ACHIEVEMENT AWARD IN TEACHING, ENT, SOC, AMER, EASTERN BRANCH, 2000; CITATION FOR TEACHING EXCELLENCE, RI SENATE (2000); CITATION FOR TEACHING EXCELLENCE, GOV OF RI (2000). **Professional Experience:** DIR GRADUATE STUDIES, COL ENVIRON &LIFE SCI, Univ RI, 2000-2005; 1984-1985; PROF INVERT PATH, UNIV RI, 1977-; Fel, Inst Pasteur; Eli Lilly Fel. **Memberships:** Soc Invert Path; Entom Soc Am; Sigma Xi. **Research Statement & Publications:** Protozoan and fungal pathogens of medically important insects; fungal pathogens of ticks (lyme disease); host-parasite relationships; microbial ecology of pathogens. **Mailing Address:** Lab FOR INVERTEBRATE PATHOLOGY Univ RI, Univ RI 229 Woodward Hall, Kingston, RI 02881. **Fax:** 401-874-2494. **E-Mail:** lebrun@uri.edu

LEBSOCK, KENNETH L, AGRONOMY. **Personal Data:** b Brush, Colo, October 19, 1921; m 1943, c 2. **Education:** Mont State Col, BS, 1949; NDak State Univ, MS, 1951; Iowa State Col, PhD (plant breeding), 1953. **Professional Experience:** RETIRED; agr adminr, Agr Res Serv, USDA, 1972-1987; Wheat breeding & genetics, Agr Res Serv, USDA, 1953-1972. **Memberships:** Fel Am Soc Agron. **Mailing Address:** 3045 Shorewood Lane, St Paul, MN 55113.

LEBURTON, JEAN-PIERRE, THEORY & SIMULATION OF SEMICONDUCTOR S & NANO SCALE QUANTUM DEVICES. **Personal Data:** b Liege, Belg, March 4, 1949; American citizen; m 1983, Lisette. **Education:** Univ Liege, Belg, License, 1971, PhD (physics), 1978. **Honors & Awards:** Chevalier Dans l'Ordre oes Palnes Academiques, Fr Govt, 1993. **Professional Experience:** FULL TIME FAC, MOLECULAR & ELECTRONIC NANOSTRUCTURES, BECKMAN INST, as os 2004; GREGORY E STILLMAN PROF ELEC & COMPUT ENG, UNIV ILL, as of 2004; vis prof, inst micro & ono electronics, swiss federal inst technol, lausane, Switz, 2000; vis prof phys electronics, Univ Tokyo, 1992; vis prof phys electronics, Hitachi Ltd Quantum Mat Chair, 1992; prof phys Electronics & res prof, Univ Ill, beginning 1991; from asst prof & res asst prof to assoc prof & res assoc prof, Univ Ill, 1983-1991; vis asst prof, Univ Ill, 1981-1983; res scientist, Siemens AG, Munich, Ger, 1979-1981. **Memberships:** fel Inst Elec & Electronics Engrs; NY Acad Sci; fel Am Phys Soc; Electrochem Soc; fel AAAS; fel optical soc of Am. **Research Statement & Publications:** Research on electronic, transport and optical properties of nanoscale devices and low dimensional structures such as quantum wells, quantum wires and quantum dots; Nano technol-Quantum consult. **Mailing Address:** Beckman Inst, 405 N Mathews Ave, Urbana, IL 61801. **Fax:** 217-244-4333. **E-Mail:** leburton@ceg.uiuc.edu

LEBWOHL, MARK GABRIEL, INHERITED DISORDERS OF ELASTIC TISSUE, PSORIASIS. **Personal Data:** b New York, NY, April 27, 1952; m 1978, Madeleine; c 2. **Education:** Columbia Col, BA, 1974; Harvard Med Sch, MD, 1978. **Professional Experience:** CHMN, DEPT DERMAT, MT SINAI MED CTR as of 2002; PROF DERMAT, MT SINAI SCH MED, 1993-; dir, div Clin Dermat, Mt Sinai Hosp, 1983-1997. **Memberships:** Am Acad Dermat; Soc Investigative Dermat; Dermat Found; Am Dermat Asn. **Research Statement & Publications:** Genetic disorders of the skin including psoriasis, neurofibromatosis and pseudoxanthoma elasticum. **Mailing Address:** 1 Gustave Levy Pl, New York, NY 10029. **E-Mail:** mark.lebwohl@mssm.edu

LECAR, HAROLD, BIOPHYSICS. **Personal Data:** b Brooklyn, NY, October 18, 1935; m 1958, Helene; c Joshua & Matthew. **Education:** Columbia Univ, AB, 1957, PhD (physics), 1963. **Professional Experience:** PROF MOLECULAR & CELL BIOL, UNIV CALIF, BERKELEY, as of 2004; regents lectr, Univ Calif, San Diego, 1982; fel commoner, Churchill Col, Cambridge Univ, 1975-1976; Biophysicist, Lab Biophys, Nat Inst Neurol & Commun Dis & Stroke, 1963-1985. **Memberships:** AAAS; Am Phys Soc; Biophys Soc; Sigma Xi. **Research Statement & Publications:** Biophysics of nerve excitation; ion channels; membrane transport mechanisms. **Mailing Address:** Dept Molecular Cell Biol, Univ Calif, 189 LSA, Berkeley, CA 94720-3200. **Fax:** 510-643-6791. **E-Mail:** hlecar@uclink4.berkeley.edu

LECAR, MYRON, ASTROPHYSICS. **Personal Data:** b Brooklyn, NY, April 10, 1930. **Education:** Mass Inst Technol, BS, 1951; Case Inst Technol, MS, 1953; Yale Univ, PhD (astron), 1963. **Professional Experience:** LECTR ASTROPHYS, COL OBSERV, HARVARD UNIV, 1965-; ASTRONR, SMITHSONIAN ASTROPHYS OBSERV, 1965-; lectr astrophys, Yale Univ Observ, 1962-1965; astronr, Inst Space Studies, NASA, 1962-1965. **Memberships:** Am Astron Soc; Fedn Am Scientists; Royal Astron Soc; Sigma Xi. **Research Statement & Publications:** Dynamics of the solar system; stellar dynamics and galactic structure; cosmology. **Mailing Address:** Harvard-Smithsonian Ctr Astrophys, 60 Garden St, Cambridge, MA 02138. **Fax:** 617-495-7093. **E-Mail:** mlecar@cfa.harvard.edu

LECCE, JAMES GIACOMO, MICROBIOLOGY. **Personal Data:** b Williamsport, Pa, January 11, 1926; m 1950. **Education:** Dartmouth Col, BA, 1949; Pa State Univ, MS, 1951; Univ Pa, PhD (microbiol), 1953. **Professional Experience:** EMER PROF ANIMAL SCI, NC STATE UNIV, 1976-; PROF MICROBIOL, NC STATE UNIV, 1963-; from asst prof to assoc prof microbiol, NC State Univ, 1955-1963; instr prev med, Sch Vet Med, Univ Pa, 1953-1955. **Memberships:** Am Soc Microbiol. **Research Statement & Publications:** Rotavirus; passive immunity; enteric diseases. **Mailing Address:** 2729 Cambridge Rd, Raleigh, NC 27608-1141.

LECHAGO, JUAN, GASTROINTESTINAL PATHOLOGY, SURGICAL PATHOLOGY. **Personal Data:** b Barcelona, Spain, August 2, 1942; American citizen; m 1966, Lia Epstein; c John P, James B & Sarah A. **Education:** Nat Col, Monserrat, Arg, BS, 1959; Nat Univ Cordoba, Arg, MD, 1966; Queen's Univ, Can, MSc, 1967, PhD (path), 1971. **Professional Experience:** CHMN & PROF, UNIV TEX, SOUTHWESTERN MED SCH, as of 2003; CHIEF LAB SER, VETERANS AFFAIRS MED CTR, DALLAS, as of 2003; Prin investr, Nat Cancer Inst, 1995-; med dir, Sch Histotechnol, Methodist Hosp, Houston, 1991-1993; affil mem, Ctr Ulcer Res & Educ, Los Angeles, 1990-; PROF, DEPT PATH, BAYLOR COL MED, 1990-; DIR, SURG PATH SERV, METHODIST HOSP, TEX, 1990-; prof & vchair, A G Gill endowed prof, 1989-1990; Ctr Diabetes Res, Dallas, 1988-1990; prof & vchair, Dept Path, Southwestern Med Sch, Univ Tex, Dallas, 1987-1990; chief lab serv, Vet Admin Med Ctr, Dallas, Tex, 1987-1990; dir morphal core, Ctr Study Inflammatory Bowel Dis, 1985-1987; lectr & consult, Naval Reg Med Ctr, Long Beach, Calif, 1982-1987; head autopsy path serv, Harbor Med Ctr, Univ Calif, Los Angeles, 1981-1987; key investr, Ctr Ulcer Res & Educ, Los Angeles, 1974-1990; prin investr, NIH, 1974-1984, 1982-1986; Head gastrointestinal path & staff pathologist, Harbor Med Ctr, Univ Calif, Los Angeles, 1973-1987; From asst prof to prof path, Sch Med, Univ Calif, Los Angeles, 1973-1987. **Memberships:** US Can Acad Path; Am Gastroenterol Asn; Gastrointestinal Path Soc (pres 1987-1988); Latin Am Path Found (pres 1994-1996); Endocrine Path Soc; hon mem Cent Am Asn Path; hon mem Argentian Soc Path. **Research Statement & Publications:** Biology and pathology of the neuroendocrine cells of the digestive system in man and experimental species; pathobiology and molecular pathology of gastrointestinal neoplasia and precursor conditions. **Mailing Address:** Dept Path Baylor Col Methodist Hospital Rm 236, One Baylor Plaza, Houston, TX 77030. **Fax:** 713-793-1473. **E-Mail:** jlechago@bcm.tmc.edu

LECHEVALIER, HUBERT ARTHUR, MICROBIOLOGY. **Personal Data:** b Tours, France, May 12, 1926; American citizen; m 1950, Mary; c Marc & Paul. **Education:** Laval Univ, MS, 1948; Rutgers Univ, PhD (microbiol), 1951. **Honorary Degrees:** DSc, Laval Univ, 1983. **Honors & Awards:** Lindback Award, 1976; Charles Thom Award, 1982; Bergey Award, 1989; New Gerey Inventor Hall Fame, 1990. **Professional Experience:** EMER PROF MICROBIOL, WAKSMAN INST MICROBIOL, RUTGERS UNIV, NEW BRUNSWICK, NJ, 1991-; USPHS spec fel, Pasteur Inst, Paris, 1961-1962; exchange scientist, Acad Sci, USSR, 1958-1959; from asst prof to prof, Waksman Inst Microbiol, Rutgers Univ, New Brunswick, NJ, 1951-1991. **Memberships:** emer mem, Soc Indust Microbiol; Fr Soc Microbiol; Soc Actinomyeates, Japan. **Research Statement & Publications:** Morphology, classification and products of actinomycetes, including antibiotics; history of microbiology. **Mailing Address:** Goddard-Nisbet Rd, Morrisville, VT 8041. **E-Mail:** mheques@together.net

LECHEVALIER, MARY P, ACTINOMYCETES, CHEMOTAXONOMY. **Personal Data:** b Cleveland, Ohio, January 27, 1928. **Education:** Mt Holyoke Col, BA, 1949; Rutgers Univ, MS, 1951. **Honors & Awards:** Charles Thom Award, Soc Indust Microbiol, 1982; Waksman Award, Theobald Smith Soc, 1991; J Roger Porter Award, US Fed Cult Collections, 1992. **Professional Experience:** PROF EMER MICROBIOL, RUTGERS UNIV, PISCATAWAY, 1991-; res prof, Rutgers Univ, 1985-1991; from asst res prof to assoc res prof, Rutgers Univ, 1975-1985; res assoc, Rutgers Univ, 1962-1975; Res microbiologist, E R Squibb & Sons, 1960-1961. **Memberships:** AAAS sr mem NAm Mycological Asn sr mem; Sigma Xi Pres Rutgers Univ chapter 1977-1978 Soc for actnimycetes Japan Foreian Mem. **Research Statement & Publications:** Classification, ecology, physiology and natural products of actinomycetes; microbial transformations; nitrogen fixation. **Mailing Address:** RR 2 Box 2235, Morrisville, VT 05661.

LECHLEIDER, J W, MATHEMATICS, COMPUTER SOFTWARE. **Personal Data:** b Brooklyn, NY, February 22, 1933; m 1955, c 2. **Education:** Cooper Union, BME, 1954; Polytech Inst Brooklyn, MEE, 1957, PhD (elec eng), 1965. **Professional Experience:** HEAD, MDF SOFTWARE DESIGN DEPT, BELL LABS, 1976-; head loop transmission maintenance eng dept, Outside Plant & Underwater Systs Div, 1970-1976; head outside plant eng dept, Outside Plant & Underwater Systs Div, 1967-1970; supvr transmission studies, Outside Plant & Underwater Systs Div, 1965-1967; mem tech staff, Bell Tel Labs, 1955-1965; engr, Gen Elec Co, 1954-1955. **Memberships:** Sr mem Inst Elec & Electronics Engrs; Am Math Soc; Sigma Xi. **Research Statement & Publications:** Electromagnetic theory; communication theory; transmission theory. **Mailing Address:** AT & T Bell Labs, 4 Harding Terr, Morristown, NJ 07960-4204.

LECHNER, BERNARD J, RESEARCH MANAGEMENT, TELEVISION SYSTEMS. **Personal Data:** b New York, NY, January 25, 1932; m Joan. **Education:** Columbia Univ, BSEE, 1957. **Honors & Awards:** David Sarnoff Award, RCA Corp, 1962; Frances Rice Darne Award, Soc Info Display, 1971 & Beatrice Winner Award, 1983; David Saznoff Gold Medal Award, Soc Motion Picture & TV Engrs, 1996; Outstanding contributor award, Advanced television systs comm, 2000; Progress medal, soc Motion picture & TV engrs, 2001; Television eng achievement award, nat asn of Broadcasters, 2002. **Professional Experience:** CONSULT, 1987-; staff vpres, RCA Labs, 1983-1987; lab dir, RCA Labs, 1977-1983; group head, RCA Labs, 1962-1977; Mem tech staff, RCA Labs, 1957-1962. **Memberships:** Fel Inst Elec & Electronics Engrs; fel Soc Info Display (vpres, 1976-1978, pres, 1978-1980); fel Soc Motion Picture & TV Engr. **Research Statement & Publications:** Video-tape recording; high speed digital computer circuits; tunnel diodes; display devices and systems; ferroelectrics; electroluminescence; magnetic thin films; instrumentation; liquid crystals; digital television systems; TV receivers; TV tuning systems; TV broadcast equipment; cable TV systems; high definition TV; TV Standards. **Mailing Address:** 59 Carson Rd, Princeton, NJ 08540. **Fax:** 609-924-7547. **E-Mail:** tvbernie@ieee.org

LECHNER, JAMES ALBERT, APPLIED STATISTICS, RELIABILITY. **Personal Data:** b Danville, Pa, August 6, 1933; m 1956, Pegge B; c 3. **Education:** Carnegie Inst Technol, BS, 1954; Princeton Univ, PhD (math statist), 1959. **Professional Experience:** CONSULT, 1995-; math statistician, Statist Eng Div, Nat Inst Stand & Technol, 1971-1995; mem tech staff, Res Anal Corp, Va, 1967-1971; adv mathematician, Aerospace Div, Md, 1963-1967; sr mathematician, Res Labs, Westinghouse Elec Corp, Pa, 1960-1963; instr math, Princeton Univ, 1957-1958; instr, Carnegie Tech, Univ Md & George Washington Univ. **Memberships:** Am Statist Asn. **Research Statement & Publications:** Probability; theory of reliability; systems analysis; stochastic processes. **Mailing Address:** 3801 Chatham Rd, Ellicott City, MD 21042. **E-Mail:** james.lechner@att.net

LECHNER, JOHN FRED, CELL & MOLECULAR BIOLOGY, TOXICOLOGY. **Personal Data:** b Holyoke, Colo, October 27, 1942. **Education:** Cornell Univ, BS, 1964; Hahnemann Med Col, PhD (microbiol), 1970. **Professional Experience:** ASST DIR CELL & MOLECULAR BIOL, INHALATION TOXICOL RES INST, ALBUQUERQUE, NMEX, 1991-; dep lab chief, Vitro Carcinogenesis Sect, Lab Human Carcinogenesis, 1990-1991; consult, Clonetics Inc, Calif, 1989-1991; consult, Organogenesis, Inc, Mass, 1988-1990; chmn, Comt Carcinogenesis Initiative, Prostate Cancer Working Group, 1986-1987 & Tumor Tissue Request Rev Comt, Nat Dis Interchange, 1987-1990; Prostate Cancer Task Force, Nat Cancer Inst, 1986-1989; chief, Vitro Carcinogenesis Sect, Lab Human Carcinogenesis, 1985-1991; chief, Cell Cult & Media Br, Ctr Infectious Dis, Centers Dis Control, Atlanta, 1984-1985; sr staff fel, Nat Cancer Inst, NIH, 1983-1984; mem, Handicapped Employee Adv Comt, NIH, 1982 & Cellular Physiol Grant Rev Study Sect, 1982-1984; expert scientist, Nat Cancer Inst, NIH, 1979-1983; asst dir, Prostate Cancer Lab, Pasadena, 1978-1979; res investr, Pasadena Found Med Res, 1976-1978; res fel, W Alton Jones Cell Sci Ctr, Lake Placid, NY, 1975-1976; Nat res serv award, Pub Health Serv, 1975; res assoc, Mass Inst Technol, Cambridge, 1973-1975; asst prof, Div Genetics & mem, Grad Sch Fac, 1971-1973; from instr to sr instr, Div Genetics, Hahnemann Med Col, Philadelphia, 1969-1971; res asst, Div Genetics, Hahnemann Med Col, Philadelphia, 1966-1969; microbiol training fel, Ind Univ, Bloomington, Iowa, 1965-1966; grad teaching asst, Ind Univ, Bloomington, Iowa, 1964-1965. **Memberships:** Am Asn Cancer Res; Am Soc Cell Biol; Tissue Cult Asn; AAAS; Am Asn Pathologists; Fedn Am Socs Exp Biol. **Research Statement & Publications:** Cell biology-growthfactor, nutritional and hormonal control of growth and differentiation; in vitro carcinogenesis of human epithelial cells. **Mailing Address:** 623 OBS Cancer Inst, Wayne State Univ Sch Med 540 E Canfield, Detroit, MI 48201.

LECHNER, JOSEPH H, DNA SEQUENCE, MAMMALIAN STRUCTURAL PROTEINS. **Personal Data:** b Boston, Mass, November 13, 1951; c Paul, Dawn & Sarah. **Education:** Roberts Wesleyan Col, BS (chem), 1972; Univ Iowa, PhD (biochem), 1977. **Professional Experience:** PROF CHEM, MOUNT VERNON NAZARENE UNIV, 1987-; from asst prof to assoc prof, 1979-1987; teaching fel, Dent Sch, Northwestern Univ, 1978-1979. **Memberships:** Am Chem Soc; fel Am Sci Affil. **Research Statement & Publications:** Structural proteins in mammalian connective tissues; health benefits of religious practices; science fairs in secondary schools. **Mailing Address:** 800 Martinsburg Rd, Mt Vernon, OH 43050-9500. **E-Mail:** jlechner@mvnu.edu

LECHNER, ROBERT JOSEPH, SOFTWARE ENGINEERING, INFORMATION SCIENCE. **Personal Data:** b Danville, Pa, October 19, 1931; m 1955, Patricia; c Marie, Nancy, Amy, David, Stephen, John & Tony. **Education:** Carnegie Inst Technol, BS, 1952, MS, 1953; Harvard Univ, PhD (appl math), 1963. **Professional Experience:** PROF EMER COMPUT SCI, UNIV MASS, LOWELL, as of 2002; assoc prof elec eng, Northeastern Univ, 1976-1982; sr engr, Honeywell Info Systs, 1970-1975; C S Draper Lab, 1975-1976; sr eng specialist, Sylvania Electronics Corp, 1963-1970; eng specialist, Sylvania Electronics Corp, 1961-1963; adv res engr, Sylvania Electronics Corp, 1959-1961; res engr, Sylvania Electronics Corp, 1957-1959; sr engr, Sylvania Electronics Corp, 1955-1957. **Memberships:** Life mem, Inst Elec & Electronics Engrs Comput Soc; sr mem, Asn Comput Mach. **Research Statement & Publications:** Software engineering; information modeling object-oriented methods. **Mailing Address:** Univ Mass, Dept Comput Sci, One Univ Ave, Lowell, MA 01854. **E-Mail:** lechner@cs.uml.edu

LECHOWICH, RICHARD V, FOOD SCIENCE, FOOD MICROBIOLOGY. **Personal Data:** b Chicago, Ill, June 23, 1933; m 1983, Isabel; c 8. **Education:** Univ Chicago, AB, 1952, MS, 1955; Univ Ill, PhD (food sci), 1958. **Professional Experience:** RETIRED; dir, Nat Ctr Food Safety & Technol, 1989-1998; exec vpres, ABC Res Lab, Fla, 1987-1989; mgr microbiol, Gen Foods Corp, 1981-1987; prof food sci & technol & head dept, Va Polytech Inst & State Univ, 1971-1981; from asst prof to prof food sci, Mich State Univ, 1963-1971; res microbiologist, Continental Can Co, Inc, Ill, 1958-1963; res asst food sci, Univ Ill, Urbana, 1955-1958; microbiologist, Am Meat Inst Found, Ill, 1952-1955. **Memberships:** AAAS; Int Asn Milk, Food & Environ Sanitarians; fel Inst Food Technologists; Am Soc Microbiologists; Brit Soc Appl Bact; Am Soc Agr Engrs. **Research Statement & Publica-**

tions: Food safety mechanisms of bacterial spore formation and germination; chemical composition and thermal resistance phenomena of bacterial spores; food poisoning microorganisms, especially Clostridium botulinum; food safety. **Mailing Address:** 124 Carriage Way B-114, Burr Ridge, IL 60521.

LECHOWICZ, MARTIN JOHN, PLANT ECOLOGY, FOREST ECOLOGY. **Personal Data:** b Chicago, Ill, February 23, 1947; m 1977, Marcia. **Education:** Mich State Univ, BA, 1969; Univ Wis-Madison, MSc, 1973, PhD (plant ecol), 1976. **Honors & Awards:** Alan Blizzard Award, Soc Teaching & Learning in Higher Education 2002. **Professional Experience:** DIR, GAULT NATURE RESERVE, MCGILL UNIV, 1995-2010; PROF BIOL, MCGILL UNIV, 1988-; assoc prof, McGill Univ 1981-1987; asst prof, Mcgill Univ, 1976-1980; lectr ecol, Dept Bot, Univ Wis-Madison, 1975; Visiting prof: Kyoto Univ 2004, U Washington 1997, Cornell Univ 1983. **Memberships:** Ecol Soc Am; Soc Study Evolution; Am Soc Naturalists; Bot Soc Am; Bot Soc Japan. **Research Statement & Publications:** Physiological ecology and evolutionary ecology of plants, and particularly resource uptake and allocation; plant herbivore interactions; forest ecology; tree growth; community ecology. **Mailing Address:** Dept Biol, McGill Univ, Stewart Biol Bldg, 1205 Docteur Penfield, Rm W6/8A, Montreal, PQ H3A 1B1, Can. **Fax:** 514-398-5069. **E-Mail:** martin.lechowicz@mcgill.ca

LECHTENBERG, VICTOR L, AGRONOMY. **Personal Data:** b Butte, Nebr, April 14, 1945; m 1967, c 4. **Education:** Univ Nebr, BS, 1967; Purdue Univ, PhD (agron), 1971. **Honors & Awards:** Ciba-Geigy Award, Am Soc Agron. **Professional Experience:** VICE PROVOST ENGAGEMENT, PURDUE UNIV, as of 2004; CHMN, USDA AGR RES, as of 1997; dean agr, Purdue Univ, W lafayette, beginning 1994; exec assoc dean agr, Purdue Univ, W Lafayette, 1989-1993; assoc dir, Agr Exp Sta, 1982-1989; from instr to prof agron, Purdue Univ, W Lafayette, 1969-1982. **Memberships:** Fel Am Soc Agron; fel Crop Sci Soc Am (pres); Am Forage & Grassland Coun; AAAS; Coun Agr Sci & Technol. **Research Statement & Publications:** Factors that affect forage crop quality and utilization; environmental physiology of forage crops; genetic improvement of crop quality. **Mailing Address:** Purdue Univ, 610 Purdue Mall Rm 130, West Lafayette, IN 47907. **Fax:** 765-494-7420. **E-Mail:** vll@agad.purdue.edu

LECHTMAN, MAX D, MICROBIOLOGY, MEDICAL DEVICE TESTING. **Personal Data:** b Providence, RI, April 24, 1935; m 1962, Dale; c Alex N, Jay & Risa. **Education:** Univ RI, AB, 1957; Univ Mass, MS, 1959; Univ Southern Calif, PhD (bact), 1968. **Professional Experience:** INDUST CONSULT, 1971-; instr, Calif Community Col Syst, 1971-1995; mem tech staff aerospace microbiol, Autonetics Div, NAm, Rockwell Corp, Anaheim, 1967-1971; microbiologist, AiRes Mfg Co Div, 1965-1967; microbiol consult, Garrett Corp, 1964-1965; instr microbiol, Univ Southern Calif, 1964; Microbiologist, Douglas Aircraft Co, Calif, 1961-1962 & Res & Develop Div, Magna Chem Co, 1962-1964. **Memberships:** Am Soc Microbiol; Soc Indust Microbiol; AAAS. **Research Statement & Publications:** Microbial cytology, cytochemistry and physiology; bioluminescent bacteria for detection of toxic chemicals; laboratory and medical instrumentation; medical device testing. **Mailing Address:** 8641 Delray Circle, Westminster, CA 92683. **Fax:** 714-897-7759. **E-Mail:** bythemax@socal.rr.com

LECK, CHARLES FREDERICK, ORNITHOLOGY, ECOLOGY. **Personal Data:** b Princeton, NJ, June 20, 1944. **Education:** Muhlenberg Col, BS, 1966; Cornell Univ, PhD (vert zool), 1970. **Professional Experience:** ASSOC PROF ECOL, RUTGERS UNIV, NEW BRUNSWICK, as of 2004; dir ecol prog, Rutgers Univ, New Brunswick, 1974-1978; assoc prof ecol, Rutgers Univ, New Brunswick, beginning 1970; vis fac mem, West Indies Lab, Smithsonian Trop Res Inst, 1970-1973; vis res assoc, Smithsonian Trop Res Inst, 1968-1969. **Memberships:** Wilson Ornith Soc; Cooper Ornith Soc; Am Ornith Union; Sigma Xi; Asn Trop Biologists. **Research Statement & Publications:** Avian ecology and landscape ecology and conservation; tropical biology; published over 15 articles. **Mailing Address:** Dept Ecol, Univ Rutgers, 134 ENRS Bldg 14 Col Farm Rd, New Brunswick, NJ 08901. **E-Mail:** leck@aesop.rutgers.edu

LECKIE, FREDERICK ALEXANDER, ENGINEERING MECHANICS, MATERIALS ENGINEERING. **Personal Data:** b Dundee, Scotland, March 26, 1929; m 1957, c 3. **Education:** Univ St Andrew, BSc, 1949; Stanford Univ, MS, 1955, PhD (eng mech), 1958. **Professional Experience:** PROF EMER, DEPT MECH & ENVIRON ENG, UNIV CALIF, SANTA BARBARA, 1988-; prof theoret & appl mech & mech eng, Univ Ill, Urbana-Champaign, 1978-1988; prof eng, Univ Leicester, 1968-1978; lectr, Univ Cambridge, 1958-1968; res asst mech, Tech Hochsch, Hannover, Ger, 1957-1958; civil engr, Mott, Hay & Anderson, Westminister, London, 1949-1951. **Memberships:** Am Soc Mech Engrs; Am Acad Mech. **Research Statement & Publications:** Properties of load bearing mechanical components operating at elevated temperatures; creep rupture and fractures of materials at elevated temperatures. **Mailing Address:** Dept Mech & Environ Eng, Univ Calif, Rm 2325 Eng II Bldg, Santa Barbara, CA 93106-5070. **Fax:** 805-893-8651. **E-Mail:** leckie@Eng.ucsb.edu

LECKLITNER, MYRON LYNN, NUCLEAR MEDICINE, MEDICAL ULTRASOUND. **Personal Data:** b Canton, Ohio, June 16, 1942; c 1. **Education:** Pa State Univ, BS, 1964; Univ Ala, Tuscaloosa, BS, 1970, Birmingham, MD, 1974; Am Bd Nuclear Med, cert, nuclear med, 1982. **Professional Experience:** HEAD, DIV NUCLEAR MED, UNIV S ALA MED CTR, as of 2003; PROF RADIOL & ANESTHESIOL, UNIV S ALA, 1986-; Am Col Nuclear Physicians, 1986-1988 & mem bd regents & treas, chmn finance comt, 1986-1988; vis prof, Univ Oxford, UK, 1985, 1988; vis prof, Royal Postgrad Med Sch, Univ London, UK, 1985; sr scientist, Cancer Ctr, beginning 1984; assoc prof radiol & dir diag imaging, Cancer Ctr, 1983-1986; vis prof, Univ Nuevo Leon, Monterrey, Mex, 1983; mem, Acad Coun, Soc Nuclear Med, 1981-; asst prof radiol, Univ Tex, San Antonio, 1979-1983; nuclear med, Lloyd Noland Hosp, Birmingham, 1977-1979; resident med, Lloyd Noland Hosp, Birmingham, 1974-1977. **Memberships:** Soc Nuclear Med; Am Col Nuclear Med; Am Inst Ultrasound Med; Am Col Radiol; AMA; Radiol Soc Am; Am Col Nuclear Physicians; fel Am Col Nuclear Med. **Research Statement & Publications:** Basic science and clinical investigations involving human biokinetics and quality control of radiotracers; relation of physiology and pathophysiology to nuclear medicine. **Mailing Address:** Dept Radiol, Univ S Ala, 2451 Fillingim St, Mobile, AL 36617. **Fax:** 251-471-7882.

LECKONBY, ROY ALAN, PHYSICAL ORGANIC CHEMISTRY, SYNTHETIC ORGANIC CHEMISTRY. **Personal Data:** b Bethlehem, Pa, August 1, 1949; m 1971, Janice Tollerton; c Remington, Brian, Christopher & Peter. **Education:** Hamilton Col, AB, 1971; Univ Rochester, MS, 1974, PhD (chem), 1976. **Professional Experience:** MGR RES & DEVELOP, CLEANING SYSTEMS INC, as of 2004; sr develop engr, Shell Chem Co, beginning 1992; qual assurance mgr, Apple Grove, WVa, 1986-1992; plant chemist, La Porte, Tex, 1982-1986; sr res chemist, Goodyear Tire & Rubber Co, Akron, Ohio, 1977-1982; Fel res, Robert A Welch Found, Rice Univ, 1976-1977. **Memberships:** Soc Plastics Engrs. **Research Statement & Publications:** Organic synthesis; age resistors for rubbers and plastics; monomers; oxidation of organic chemicals. **Mailing Address:** Cleaning Systs Inc, PO Box 5606, 1997 Am Blvd, De Pere, WI 54115-5606. **Fax:** 920-337-9410. **E-Mail:** raleckonby@shellus.com

LECKRONE, DAVID STANLEY, ASTROPHYSICS. **Personal Data:** b Salem, Ill, November 30, 1942; m 1964, c 2. **Education:** Purdue Univ, BS, 1964; Univ Calif, Los Angeles, MA, 1966, PhD (astron), 1969. **Professional Experience:** SR PROJ SCIENTIST, PROJ HUBBLE SPACE TELESCOPE, GODDARD SPACE FLIGHT CTR, NASA, 1992-; ASTROPHYSICIST, NASA, 1969-. **Memberships:** Am Astron Soc; Int Astron Union. **Research Statement & Publications:** Ultraviolet stellar spectroscopy and photometry from space vehicles; magnetic and chemically peculiar stars; stellar atomspheres; abundances of the elements in astronomical objects; instrumentation for space astronomy. **Mailing Address:** NASA-Goddard Space Flight Ctr, Code 600, Greenbelt, MD 20771. **Fax:** 301-286-1670. **E-Mail:** david.s.leckrone.l@gsfc.nasa.gov

LECLAIRE, CLAIRE DEAN, organic chemistry; deceased, see previous edition for last biography

LECOURS, MICHEL, communications systems, signal processing; deceased, see previous edition for last biography

LECTKA, THOMAS. **Education:** Oberlin Col, BA, 1985; Cornell Univ, PhD, 1990. **Professional Experience:** John Simon Guggenheim Mem Found fel, 2003-2004; Camille Dreyfus teacher scholar, 1999; ASSOC PROF CHEM, JOHNS HOPKINS UNIV, as of 1998; Alexander von Humboldt postdoctoral fel, Univ Heidelberg; NIH postdoctoral fel, Harvard Univ. **Mailing Address:** Dept Chem, Johns Hopkins Univ, 3400 N Charles St, Baltimore, MD 21218-2685. **Fax:** 410-516-8420. **E-Mail:** lectka@jhu.edu

L'ECUYER, JACQUES, APPLIED & NUCLEAR PHYSICS. **Personal Data:** b St-Jean, Que, March 6, 1937; m 1959, c 3. **Education:** Col St Jean, BA, 1956; Univ Montreal, BSc, 1959, MSc, 1961, PhD (physics), 1966. **Professional Experience:** Head, Comn eval Col Educ, Univ Que, 1993-2005; mem, Hong Kong Coun Acad Accreditation, 1988-; mem, Que Univs Coun, 1977-1981; vpres teaching & res, Comn Eval Col Educ, Univ Que, 1988-1993; pres, Que Univ Coun, 1981-1988; mem bd gov, Univ Montreal, 1976-1979; prof, Univ Montreal, 1973-1986; from asst prof to assoc prof physics, Univ Montreal, 1969-1973; Nat Res Coun Can fel, Oxford Univ, 1967-1969; asst prof physics, Laval Univ, 1964-1967; lectr, Univ Sherbrooke, 1963-1964; lectr, Univ Montreal, 1961-1963. **Memberships:** Can Asn Physicists; Fr-Can Asn Advan Sci. **Research Statement & Publications:** Experimental nuclear physics. **Mailing Address:** 10890 Berri, Montreal, PQ H3L 2H5, Can.

L'ECUYER, MEL R, MECHANICAL ENGINEERING, HEAT TRANSFER. **Personal Data:** b Concordia, Kans, June 4, 1936; m 1962. **Education:** Purdue Univ, BS, 1959, MS, 1960, PhD (mech eng), 1964. **Professional Experience:** PROF EMER MECH ENG, PURDUE UNIV, as of 2004; prof mech eng, Purdue Univ, beginning 1976; sr eng specialist, LTV Aerospace Div, Ling-Temco-Vought, Inc, Tex, 1968-; from asst prof to assoc prof, Jet Propulsion Ctr, 1964-1976; res engr, Jet Propulsion Ctr, 1960-1964. **Memberships:** Am Inst Aeronaut & Astronaut; Am Soc Mech Engrs; Am Soc Eng Educ. **Research Statement & Publications:** Mass transfer cooling; two-phase flow; propulsion gas dynamics. **Mailing Address:** Dept Mech Eng, Purdue Univ, West Lafayette, IN 47906. **E-Mail:** lecuyer@purdue.edu

LECZYNSKI, BARBARA ANN, HUMAN & ENVIRONMENTAL MONITORING, QUALITY ASSURANCE. **Personal Data:** b Lowell, Mass, August 27, 1954. **Education:** Univ Lowell Mass, BS, 1976; Univ Conn, MS, 1979. **Professional Experience:** Chairperson, Workgroup Leaded Paint Encapsulants, Am Soc Testing Mat, 1994-1997; STAFF, OFF POLLUTION PREV & TOXICS, US ENVIRON PROTECTION AGENCY, 1993-; sr consult, David C Cox & Assocs, 1990-1993; proj mgr, Wash Consult Group, 1989-1990; proj mgr, Battelle Mem Inst, 1984-1989; appl math, Eastman Kodak Co, 1980-1984; math statistician, US Dept Labor, Bur Labor Statist, 1978-1980. **Memberships:** Am Statist Asn; Am Soc Qual Control; ASTM. **Research Statement & Publications:** Participated on several multidisciplinary projects with applications to environmental monitoring in particular human monitoring exposure, lead paint and asbestos abatement studies; consumer preference and marketing strategies and economic indicators; developed sampling designs for field studies; provided experimental designs for industrial manufactures research projects. **Mailing Address:** Off Pollution Prev & Toxics US Environ Protection Agency, 1200 Pa Ave NW, Washington, DC 20460. **Fax:** 202-564-4775. **E-Mail:** leczynski.barbara@epa.gov

LEDBETTER, DAVID H, GENETICS. **Personal Data:** b Lakehurst, NJ, 1953. **Education:** Univ Tex, PhD. **Professional Experience:** DIR CTR MED GENETICS, UNIV CHICAGO, as of 2005. **Mailing Address:** Univ Chicago Ctr Med Genetics, 5841 S Md Ave Rm L038 M/C 2050, Chicago, IL 60637-1470. **E-Mail:** dhl@genetics.bsd.uchicago.edu

LEDBETTER, HARVEY DON, MATERIALS SCIENCIE ENGINEERING. **Personal Data:** b Pierson, Ill, June 26, 1926; m 1947, c 3. **Education:** Univ Ariz, BS, 1949, MS, 1950; Univ Tenn, PhD (chem), 1954. **Professional Experience:** RES SCIENTIST, CENT RES, 1990-; sr proj mgr, Cent Res, 1983-1989; dir technol res & develop, Cent Res, 1981-1983; lab dir, Cent Res Plastics Lab, 1976-1981; tech mgr, Designed Prod Dept, 1971-1976; res supvr, Dow Chem USA, 1967-1971; res group leader, Dow Chem USA, 1953-1967; Asst gen chem, Univ Tenn, 1950-1952. **Memberships:** AAAS; Am Chem Soc; Soc Plastics Engrs; Sigma Xi; Soc Advan Math & Process Eng; Fiber Soc. **Research Statement & Publications:** Polymer nucleation and stabilization; vacuum processes; preparation and physics of composite structures; fiber processing. **Mailing Address:** Lake Pinehurst Villas No 14, Pinehurst, NC 28374.

LEDBETTER, JEFFREY A, IMMUNOTHERAPY. **Professional Experience:** CO-FOUNDER, CHIEF SCI OFFICER & DIR, TRUBION PHARMACEUT INC, as of 2004; RES FEL, DEPT IMMUNOTHERAPY, ONCOGEN, 1981-. **Mailing Address:** Trubion Pharmaceut, Inc, 2401 Fourth Ave, Ste 1050, Seattle, WA 98121. **Fax:** 206-838-0503.

LEDBETTER, JOE O(VERTON), ENVIRONMENTAL HEALTH ENG, CIVIL ENGINEERING. **Personal Data:** b New Hope, Ala, February 1, 1927; m 1992, Ann D Hagood; c Jane C Hagood & Richard Lance Hagood. **Education:** Univ Ala, BSCE, 1950; Univ Tex, MS, 1958, PhD (civil eng), 1963. **Professional Experience:** PROF EMER, UNIV TEX, AUSTIN; Prof Civil Eng, Univ Tex, Austin, 1971-1993; from instr to assoc prof, Tex Hwy Dept, 1956-1971; resident engr, Tex Hwy Dept, 1951-1956; PRES, USPHS, 1950-; Proj engr, Ala Hwy Dept, 1950-1951. **Memberships:** Am Indust Hyg Asn; Health Physics Soc. **Research Statement & Publications:** Air pollution control; sampling, evaluation, and abatement; disposal of solid radioactive and hazardous wastes; radiological and industrial health engineering; air pollution from wastewater treatment. **Mailing Address:** 1814 Rockmoor Dr, Austin, TX 78703. **E-Mail:** ledbetter@mail.utexas.edu

LEDBETTER, MARY LEE STEWART, CELL BIOLOGY, IMMUNOLOGY. **Personal Data:** b Monterrey, Mex, August 30, 1944; American citizen; m 1966, Steven; c William & Joanna. **Education:** Pomona Col, BA, 1966; Rockefeller Univ, PhD (genetics), 1972. **Honors & Awards:** Dirs Award Distinguished Teaching Scholar, NSF, 2003. **Professional Experience:** Mem rev panel, Howard Hughes Med Inst, 1994, 1998, 2006; guest scientist, Scripps Res Inst, 1994-; NSF vis professorship Women, 1994-1995; PROF BIOL, COL HOLY CROSS, 1993-; vis assoc prof, Tufts Univ, 1992; mem rev panel, NSF Young Investr Award, 1991-1993; mem rev panel, NASA Specialized Ctr Res & Training Gravitational Biol, 1990, 1994; mem cell biol adv panel, NSF, 1986-1990; from asst prof to assoc prof, Col Holy Cross, 1980-1993; res asst prof biochem, Dartmouth Med Sch, 1979-1980; res assoc psychiat, Dartmouth Med Sch, 1977-1979; instr, Dartmouth Med Sch, 1975-1978; Nat Cancer Inst fel, USPHS, Dartmouth Med Sch, 1975-1977; Leukemia Soc Am fel, Dartmouth Med Sch, 1973-1975, 1977-1978; res assoc microbiol, Dartmouth Med Sch, 1972-1975; Damon Runyon-Walter Winchell fel, Dartmouth Med Sch, 1972-1973; USPHS res trainee, Sch Med, NY Univ, 1972. **Memberships:** Am Soc Cell Biol; AAAS; Sigma Xi; Asn Women Sci. **Research Statement & Publications:** Study of metabolic regulation in cultured mammalian cells, particularly cell communication through gap junctions and ion transport and the interactions between them; published over 8 articles. **Mailing Address:** Dept Biol, Col Holy Cross, O'Neil 342 One Col St, Worcester, MA 01610. **Fax:** 508-793-2696. **E-Mail:** mledbett@holycross.edu

LEDBETTER, MYRON C, CELL BIOLOGY, BOTANY. **Personal Data:** b Ardmore, Okla, June 25, 1923. **Education:** Okla State Univ, BS, 1948; Univ Calif, MA, 1951; Columbia Univ, PhD, 1958. **Honors & Awards:** Distinguished Scientist Award, Biol Micros Soc Am, 1996. **Professional Experience:** RETIRED; adj prof, City Univ NY, beginning 1982; bd mgr, NY Bot Garden, 1982-1984; consult, Celanese Res Corp, 1981-1982; sr cell biologist, Brookhaven Nat Lab, 1974-1989; cell biologist, Brookhaven Nat Lab, 1965-1974; res assoc, Harvard Univ, 1961-1965; res assoc, Rockefeller Inst, 1961; fel training grant prog, USPHS, 1960-1961; guest investr & fel, Rockefeller Inst, 1960; guest assoc, Brookhaven Nat Lab, 1958-1960; asst plant anatomist, Boyce Thompson Inst, 1957-1960; fel plant physiol, Boyce Thompson Inst, 1953-1957; guest sr biologist, Brookhaven Nat Lab. **Memberships:** AAAS; Am Soc Cell Biol; Bot Soc Am; Electron Micros Soc Am (pres, 1978); Am Inst Biol Sci; Torrey Bot Club (pres, 1984-1985). **Research Statement & Publications:** Morphology of physiologically dwarfed tree seedlings; feeding damage to plant tissues by lygus bugs; histopathology of ozone on plants; distribution of fluorine in plants; plant fine structure, microtubules in plants; plant cell walls; electron microscopy; structure of macromolecular complexes by cluster ion bombardment. **Mailing Address:** Valley Rd, Port Jefferson, NY 11777.

LEDBETTER, STEVEN R, EXPERIMENTAL BIOLOGY. **Professional Experience:** SR RES SCIENTIST, CANCER & INFECTIOUS DIS, UPJOHN CO, 1984-. **Mailing Address:** Dept Cancer/Develop Biol, Upjohn Co 301 Henrietta St, Kalamazoo, MI 49001. **Fax:** 269-385-7373.

LEDBETTER, W(ILLIAM) B(URL), CIVIL ENGINEERING. **Personal Data:** b El Paso, Tex, September 15, 1934; c 4. **Education:** Tex A&M Univ, BS, 1956; Univ Tex, Austin, PhD (civil eng), 1964. **Honors & Awards:** K B Woods Award, Transp Res Bd, Nat Acad Sci, 1976. **Professional Experience:** PROF CIVIL ENG & RES ENGR, TEX A&M UNIV, 1971-; chmn, Transp Res Bd Comt, Nat Res Coun-Nat Acad Sci, 1970-1979; from asst res engr to assoc res engr, Tex A&M Univ, 1964-1971; from asst prof to assoc prof, Tex A&M Univ, 1964-1971; consult. **Memberships:** Nat Soc Prof Engrs; Am Soc Civil Engrs; Am Soc Eng Educ; Am Soc Testing & Mat; Am Concrete Inst; Am Soc Qual Control. **Research Statement & Publications:** Quality management; project management; construction materials; concrete materials engineering. **Mailing Address:** 1006 Challedon Way, Pendleton, SC 29670-9760.

LEDDY, JAMES JEROME, INDUSTRIAL CHEMISTRY. **Personal Data:** b Detroit, Mich, July 28, 1929; m 1951, Dorothy; c Christine, James, Kathleen, Karen, Thomas, Ann, Mary, David & Jeanne. **Education:** Univ Detroit, BS, 1951; Univ Wis, PhD (chem), 1955. **Honors & Awards:** Herbert H Dow Medal, 1987. **Professional Experience:** RETIRED; Dow res fel, Core Res & Develop, 1992-1995; dir, Bioprod Lab, 1988-1992; sr res scientist, Cent Res, 1985-1988; tech mgr, Chlor-Alkali Technol Ctr, 1980-1985; res scientist, Mich Div Inorg Res, 1973-1980; res scientist, Electrochem & Inorg Res Lab, 1971-1973; assoc res scientist, Electrochem & Inorg Res Lab, 1967-1971; sr res chemist, Electrochem & Inorg Res Lab, 1963-1967; proj leader, Electrochem & Inorg Res Lab, 1960-1963; proj leader, Dow Chem USA, 1959-1960; asst prof, Assumption Univ, 1959-1960; chemist inorg res, Dow Chem USA, 1955-1959. **Memberships:** Fel AAAS; Am Chem Soc; Sigma Xi. **Research Statement & Publications:** Chemistry of less familiar elements, especially titanium, zirconium and hafnium; coordination compounds; unfamiliar oxidation states; amalgam chemistry; electrochemistry; inorganic polymers; industrial inorganic and electrochemistry; chlor-alkali; engineering ceramics and material science; biotechnology. **Mailing Address:** 311 Cherryview Dr, Midland, MI 48640-5559.

LEDDY, JOHN PLUNKETT, IMMUNOLOGY. **Personal Data:** b New York, NY, September 10, 1931; m 1956, c 3. **Education:** FordhamUniv, BA, 1952; Columbia Univ, MD, 1956. **Professional Experience:** PROF EMER MED M & D-IMMUNO/RHEUM UNIT, UNIV ROCHESTER, as of 1999; emer prog dir, NIH Specialized Res Ctr grant immunol, 1978-; prof med & microbiol, Med Ctr, Univ Rochester, beginning 1973; dir, USPHS Training Grant, 1970-; DIR CLIN IMMUNOL UNIT, MED CTR, UNIV ROCHESTER, 1970-; NIH res grant, 1965-; sr investr, Arthritis Found, 1965-1970; from asst prof to assoc prof med, Med Ctr, Univ Rochester, 1964-1973; Nat Found fel, 1962-1964; sr instr, Med Ctr, Univ Rochester, 1962-1964; res med officer immunochem, Walter Reed Army Inst Res, 1960-1962; USPHS trainee hemat, Med Ctr, Univ Rochester, 1959-1960; from intern to resident internal med, Boston City Hosp, Harvard Med Serv, 1956-1959. **Memberships:** Am Soc Clin Invest; Am Asn Immunologists. **Research Statement & Publications:** Biology of complement system in man; erythrocyte autoantibodies in human diseases. **Mailing Address:** Dept Med, Univ Rochester Med Ctr, Box 695, Rochester, NY 14642-8695. **Fax:** 585-473-1482.

LEDDY, SUSAN, NURSING. **Personal Data:** b Jersey City, NJ, February 23, 1939; m 1972, c 2. **Education:** Skidmore Col, BS, 1960; Boston Univ, MS, 1965; NY Univ, PhD (nursing), 1973. **Professional Experience:** PROF EMER NURSING SCI, UNIV WIDENER, as of 2006; prof nursing sci, Univ Widener, as of 2004; dean, Col Health Sci, Univ Wyo, beginning 1984; dean & prof nursing, Col Health Sci, Univ Wyo, 1981-1984; chmn & prof nursing, Mercy Col, 1976-1981; independent consult, 1975-; consult nursing educ, Nat League Nursing, 1975; asst prof, Pace Univ, 1973-1975; asst prof, Columbia Univ, 1966-1970; instr nursing, New Rochelle Hosp, 1965-1966; instr nursing, Mt Auburn Hosp, 1962-1965. **Memberships:** Nat League Nursing (vpres, 1985-1987). **Research Statement & Publications:** Biological rhythms; nursing education and curriculum; health care delivery. **Mailing Address:** Sch Nursing, Widener Univ, One Univ Pl, Chester, PA 19013. **E-Mail:** susan.leddy@widener.edu

LEDEEN, ROBERT W, BIOCHEMISTRY, NEUROBIOLOGY, NEURO CHEMISTRY OF BRAIN CELLS. **Personal Data:** b Denver, Colo, August 19, 1928; m 1982, Lydia Hailparn. **Education:** Univ Calif, Berkeley, BS, 1949; Ore State Univ, PhD (org chem), 1953. **Honors & Awards:** Jacob Javits Award, 1987; Alexander von Humboldt Prize, 1988. **Professional Experience:** PROF NEUROSCI, UNIV MED & DENT NJ, 1991-; mem, Nat Mult Sclerosis Soc Study Sect, 1989-1995; dep chief ed, J Neurochem, 1982-1988; mem, Neurol Sci Study Sect, NIH, 1976-1980; prof biochem in neurol, Albert Einstein Col Med, 1975-1991; from asst prof to assoc prof biochem in neurol, Albert Einstein Col Med, 1962-1975; res chemist, Albert Einstein Col Med, 1959-1961; res chemist, Mt Sinai Hosp, New York, 1956-1959; fel, Univ Chicago, 1953-1954. **Memberships:** AAAS; Am Chem Soc; Am Soc Biol Chem; Am Soc Neurochem; Int Soc Neurochem; NY Acad Sci. **Research Statement & Publications:** Biochemistry of the nervous system; gangliosides and other lipids of the nervous system; myelin lipids; myelin enzymology and pharmacology; neuronal differentiation. **Mailing Address:** 8 Donald Ct, Wayne, NJ 07470-4608. **Fax:** 973-972-5059. **E-Mail:** ledeenro@umdnj.edu

LEDER, FREDERIC, CHEMICAL ENGINEERING. **Personal Data:** b New York, NY, November 1, 1939; m 1971, c 2. **Education:** Queens Col, BS, 1961; Columbia Univ, BS, 1961; Yale Univ, MS, 1963, PhD (chem eng), 1965. **Professional Experience:** MANAGING DIR, TECH MGT ASSOCS, WESTPORT, CONN, 1995-; ASSOC DIR, OFF COOP RES, YALE UNIV, 1995-; managing partner, Specialty Capital Group, 1985-1995; dir res, Cities Appl Res & Technol Ctr, 1976-1985; dir explor res, Occidental Res Corp, Irvine, 1974-1976; gas separations res assoc, Esso Res & Eng Co, Exxon Corp, Linden, 1973; sr res engr, Esso Res & Eng Co, Exxon Corp, Linden, 1968-1973; res engr, Esso Res & Eng Co, Exxon Corp, Linden, 1965-1968; pres, Technol Mgt Assocs. **Memberships:** Am Inst Chem Eng; Sigma Xi. **Research Statement & Publications:** Phase equilibria at high pressure; gas separations; rate processes; energy technology. **Mailing Address:** 2742 Sturges Hwy, Westport, CT 06880-1732. **Fax:** 918-481-3585.

LEDER, HARRY, LINGUISTICS. **Professional Experience:** AT DEPT ENG, UNIV AUCKLAND, as of 1994. **Mailing Address:** Dept Eng, Univ Auckland, Private Bag 92019, Auckland, New Zealand. **E-Mail:** h.leder@auckland.ac.nz

LEDER, IRWIN GORDON, BIOCHEMISTRY. **Personal Data:** b New York, NY, June 16, 1920; m 1945, c 3. **Education:** Brooklyn Col, AB, 1942; NY Univ, MS, 1947; Duke Univ, PhD (biochem), 1951. **Professional Experience:** BIOCHEMIST, NAT INST ARTHRITIS, METAB & DIGESTIVE DIS, BETHESDA, 1954-; asst, pub health res Inst Inc, NY, 1953-1954; USPHS fel, Yale Univ, 1952-1953; USPHS fel, NY Univ, 1951-1952; res assoc, Duke Univ, 1951. **Memberships:** Fedn Am Socs Exp Biol. **Research Statement & Publications:** Niacin metabolism; pyridine nucleotide synthesis; intermediary carbohydrate metabolism; enzymology. **Mailing Address:** 4004 Wexford Dr, Kensington, MD 20895.

LEDER, PHILIP, MOLECULAR GENETICS. **Personal Data:** b Washington, DC, November 19, 1934; m 1959, c 3. **Education:** Harvard Col, BA, 1956, Harvard Med Sch, MD, 1960. **Honorary Degrees:** DSc, Yale Univ, 1984, Mt Sinai Col Med, 1985. **Honors & Awards:** Nat Medal Sci, 1989; Richard Lounsberry Award, Nat Acad Sci. **Professional Experience:** DIR HEALTHCARE, SCHERING-PLOUGH CORP, 2003-; SR INVESTR, HOWARD HUGHES MED INST, 1986-; JOHN EMORY ANDRUS PROF & CHMN, DEPT GENETICS, HARVARD MED SCH, 1980-; lab chief molecular genetics, Nat Inst Child Health & Human Develop, NIH, 1972-1980. **Memberships:** Nat Acad Sci; Inst Med-Nat Acad Sci; Genetics Soc Am; Am Acad Arts & Sci; Am Soc Biol Chemists. **Research Statement & Publications:** Molecular biology and genetics. **Mailing Address:** Dept Genetics, Harvard Med Sch, Rm 356E Genetics NRB 77 Ave Louis Pasteur, Boston, MA 02115. **Fax:** 617-432-7944. **E-Mail:** leder@rascal.med.harvard.edu

LEDERBERG, ESTHER MIRIAM, GENETICS, MICROBIOLOGY. **Personal Data:** b New York, NY, December 18, 1922; m 1993. **Education:** Hunter Col, AB, 1942; Stanford Univ, MA, 1946; Univ Wis, PhD (genetics), 1950. **Honors & Awards:** Co-recipient, Pasteur Award, Soc Ill Bact, 1956. **Professional Experience:** EMER PROF MICROBIOL, STANFORD UNIV, 1985-; consult, Molecular Biol Comput Res Resource, 1986-; dir, Plasmid Ref Ctr, 1976-1986; res prof, Med Sch, Stanford Univ, 1974-1985; sr scientist, Med Sch, Stanford Univ, 1971-1974; res assoc, Med Sch, Stanford Univ, 1968-1971; Am Cancer Soc Sr Dernham fel, 1968-1970; res geneticist, Med Sch, Stanford Univ, 1959-1968; Fulbright fel, Australia, 1957; proj assoc genetics, Univ Wis, 1950-1959. **Memberships:** Fel AAAS; Genetics Soc Am; Brit Soc Gen Microbiol; Sigma Xi. **Research Statement & Publications:** Genetics of microorganisms; lysogenicity; bacterial recombination and transformation; DNA repair; phase variation of Flagellar antigens in Salmonella; R plasmids. **Mailing Address:** Dept Med Microbiol, No 5402 Stanford Med Sch, Stanford, CA 94405.

LEDERBERG, JOSHUA, GENETICS. **Personal Data:** b Montclair, NJ, May 23, 1925; m 1968, Marguerite; c David K & Anne. **Education:** Columbia Univ, BA, 1944; Yale Univ, PhD (microbiol), 1947. **Honors & Awards:** Nobel Prize, 1958; Nat Medal Sci, 1989; Allen Newell Award, 1996; Maxwell Finland Award, 1997; Benjamin Franklin Award, AM Phil Soc, 2002. **Professional Experience:** PROF EMER, MOLECULAR GENETICS & INFORMATICS, ROCKEFELLER UNIV, NY, 1995-; univ prof Sackler Found Scholar, Rockefeller Univ, 1990-1995; pres, Rockefeller Uni, 1978-1990; prof genetics & chmn dept, Med Sch, Stanford Univ, 1959-1978; prof med & genetics & chmn dept, Univ Wis, 1958-1959; from asst prof to prof genetics, Univ Wis, 1947-1958. **Memberships:** Nat Acad Sci; Inst Med-Nat Acad Sci; foreign mem The Royal Soc; NY Acad Sci (pres, 1993); Am Acad Arts & Sci; Am Philos Soc; fel AAAS. **Research Statement & Publications:** Molecular genetics and evolution; science policy; computer science; emulation of scientific reasoning. **Mailing Address:** Dept Molecular Genetics & Informatics, Rockefeller Univ, 1230 York Ave, New York, NY 10021-6399. **Fax:** 212-327-7974. **E-Mail:** jsl@rockefeller.edu

LEDERBERG, SEYMOUR, MICROBIOLOGY, GENETICS. **Personal Data:** b New York, NY, October 30, 1928; m Victoria; c Tobias Marc Lederberg & Sarah Lederberg Stone. **Education:** Cornell Univ, BA (chem), 1951; Univ Ill, PhD (bact), 1955. **Professional Experience:** Prof emer med sci, 2001-; assoc dean grad studies biol med, grad progs biol med, 1985-1995; coordr, grad progs biol med, 1978-1985; adj prof pub health law, Law Sch Ctr Law & Health Sci & sch of public health, Boston Univ, 1977-; Comt Genetic Screening Cystic Fibrosis, Nat Acad Sci-Nat Res Coun, 1974-1975 & Nat Inst Arthritis, Metab & Digestive Dis, 1975-1978; lectr, Law Sch Ctr Law & Health Sci, Boston Univ, 1973-1977; Gen Med & Sci Adv Coun, Cystic Fibrosis Found, 1972-1976; chmn microbiol sect, Brown Univ, 1970-1978; consult, Nat Inst Gen Med Sci, 1970-1974; PROF BIOL, BROWN UNIV, 1966-; USPHS fel, Inst Biol Phys Chem, Paris, 1965-1966; from asst prof to assoc prof, Brown Univ, 1958-1966; vis asst prof bact, Univ Calif, 1957-1958; Am Cancer Soc fel, Univ Calif, 1955-1957; vis scholar, Harvard Law Sch, 1972. **Memberships:** Am Soc Microbiol; Genetics Soc Am; Am Soc Human Genetics; Am Assoc Adv Sci- all emer mem 2001-. **Research Statement & Publications:** Human, microbial and viral genetics; DNA restriction and modification; genetics of cystic fibrosis; chromosomal, microtubule and cell surface functions in yeast cell cycles; genetics of microbial drug-resistance and virulence; oxidative inactivation of pathogens in water and air. **Mailing Address:** Biol & Med Box G, Brown Univ, Providence, RI 02912. **E-Mail:** seymour_lederberg@brown.edu

LEDERER, C MICHAEL, NUCLEAR CHEMISTRY, NUCLEAR STRUCTURE. **Personal Data:** b Chicago, Ill, June 6, 1938; m 2001, Christina. **Education:** Harvard Univ, AB, 1960; Univ Calif, Berkeley, PhD (nuclear chem), 1964. **Professional Experience:** RES CHEM & RES ASSOC, UNIV CALIF ENERGY INST, BERKELEY, 2001-; LEC, DEP NUCLEAR ENG, UNIV CALIF, BERKELEY, 1983-; Dep dir, Univ Calif Energy Inst, 1980-2001; head, Info & Data Analysis Dept, Lawrence Berkeley Lab, Univ Calif, Berkeley, 1978-1980; sen mem & dir Isotopes Proj, Lawrence Berkeley Lab, Univ Calif, Berkeley, 1971-1978; mem, US Nuclear Data Comt, 1970-1978; mem, Isotopes Proj, Lawrence Berkeley Lab, Univ Calif, Berkeley, 1964-1971; res asst, Nuc Chem Div, Lawrence Berkeley Lab, Univ Calif, Berkeley, 1961-1963. **Memberships:** AAAS; Am Phys Soc; Am Nuclear Soc; Sigma Xi. **Research Statement & Publications:** Energy production, use and environmental effects; experimental nuclear structure physics. **Mailing Address:** Energy Inst Univ Calif, 2547 Channing Way, Berkeley, CA 94720-5180. **Fax:** 510-643-5180. **E-Mail:** lederer@berkeley.edu

LEDERER, WILLIAM JONATHAN, CARDIAC MUSCLE, CELLULAR & MOLECULAR PHYSIOLOGY. **Personal Data:** b 1946; American citizen; m 1975, Jennie; c Miriam & Rebecca. **Education:** Harvard Univ, BA, 1970; Yale Univ, MD, 1976, PhD (physiol), 1975. **Professional Experience:** DIR & PROF PHYSIOL, UNIV MD, 1988-; Counr, Biophys Soc, 1993-; Vis researcher, Univ Col London, 1981-1990; estab investr, Am Heart Asn, 1981-1986; from asst prof to assoc prof physiol, Univ MD, 1979-1988; fel physiol, Oxford Univ, 1977-1979; Intern internal med, Univ Wash, 1976-1977. **Memberships:** Soc Gen Physiologists; Biophys Soc; NY Acad Sci; AAAS; Am Physiol Soc; Physiol Soc London; mem, Am Heart Asn. **Research Statement & Publications:** Mammalian heart muscle to determine how it functions at the cellular and molecular level; links between the electrical activity and the ion transport function of cardiac cells and how these properties relate to the force generated by the heart; cellular control of calcium, sodium and pH. **Mailing Address:** Dept Physiol, Sch Med, Univ Md, 108 N Greene St, Baltimore, MD 21201. **Fax:** 410-706-4271. **E-Mail:** jlederer@umaryland.edu

LEDERIS, KAROLIS (KARL), PHARMACOLOGY, ENDOCRINOLOGY. **Personal Data:** b Lithuania, August 1, 1920; m 1952, c 2. **Education:** Bristol Univ, BSc, 1958, PhD (pharmacol), 1961, DSc(endocrinol), 1968. **Honors & Awards:** UpJohn Award in Pharmacol, 1990. **Professional Experience:** EMER PROF PHARMACOL & THERAPEUT, MED SCH, UNIV CALGARY, 1989-; mem, Int Peer Rev Comt, Networks Ctr Excellence, 1989-1990; exec, Med Res Coun Can, 1983-1990; mem, grants comt prog grants, Med Res Coun Can, 1983-1984; Kyoto Univ, Japan, 1980 & Univ Santiago & Valdivia, Chile, 1982; chmn, grants comt prog grants, Med Res Coun Can, 1981-; Univ Bristol, Eng, 1979; vis prof, Vilnius Univ, Lithuania, USSR, 1976; prof, Med Sch, Univ Calgary, 1969-1989; reader, Bristol Univ, 1968-1969; NSF fel, Univ Calif, Berkeley, 1967-1968; sr lectr, Bristol Univ, 1966-1968; lectr, Bristol Univ, 1963-1966; Jr fel pharmacol, Bristol Univ, 1961-1963; Wellcome Trust & Ger Res Asn fel, Univ Kiel, 1961-1962; ed, Pharmacol, Int J Exp & Clin Pharmacol. **Memberships:** Int Brain Res Orgn; Endocrine Soc; Brit Soc Endocrinol; Brit Pharmacol Soc; UK Physiol Soc; Can Physiol Soc; Can Pharmacol Soc; Can Biochem Soc; NY Acad Sci; Am Soc Pharmacol & Exp Therapeut; Fedn Am Socs Exp Biol; fel Royal Soc Can. **Research Statement & Publications:** Hypothalamo-neurohypophyseal system, mechanisms of hormone storage and secretion; central nervous system of teleosts and amphibians; chemistry, pharmacology and gene expression of urotensin peptides, corticotropin releasing hormones and neurohypophyseal hormones. **Mailing Address:** 147 Carthew St, Comox, BC V9M 1T4, Can.

LEDERMAN, DAVID MORDECHAI, BIOMEDICAL ENGINEERING, MEDICAL PHYSICS. **Personal Data:** b Bogota, Colombia, May 26, 1944; American citizen; m 1967, Natalie; c Jonathan & Jeanine. **Education:** Univ Los Andes, BE, 1966; Cornell Univ, BS, 1966, ME, 1967, PhD (aerospace eng), 1973. **Honorary Degrees:** Doctor Eng, Worchester Poly Inst, 2002. **Honors & Awards:** Doctor Engr, WPI, 2002; Cor Vitae Award, Amer Heart Asn, 2002; Med Device Indust Pioneer Award, Mass Med, 2002. **Professional Experience:** VICE CHMN & DIR, NEW ENG HEALTHCARE INST, 2002-; mem, Coun Adv, Jacobs Sch Eng, Univ Calif, San Diego, 2001-; adv, Bioengineering Coun, Cornell Univ, 1998-; pres & chief exec officer & chmn bd, Abiomed Inc, beginning 1981; consult, Med Res Comt, 1981-1982; chmn, Med Res Comt, 1979-1981; prin res scientist, Avco-Everett Res Lab Inc, Avco Corp, 1976-1979; sr staff mem, Avco-Everett Res Lab Inc, Avco Corp, 1973-1976; from prof appl math fac arts & sci to dir div biomed eng fac eng, Univ Los Andes, 1972-1973. **Memberships:** AAAS; NY Acad Sci; Sigma Xi; Int Soc Artificial Organs; Am Heart Asn; Founding Fel Am Inst Biol Eng Sci; Nat Acad Eng. **Research Statement & Publications:** Development of clinical cardiovascular devices; prosthetic heart valves; blood-compatible biomaterials; hemodynamics and thrombosis; inplantable artificial hearts, advanced ventrrcula assist devices. **Mailing Address:** PO Box 426, Marblehead, MA 01945-0426. **E-Mail:** d.lederman@excite.com

LEDERMAN, FRANK L, PHYSICS, MATHEMATICS. **Personal Data:** b Buffalo, NY, August 19, 1949; m 1993, Daphna Kaplansky. **Education:** Carnegie-Mellon Univ, BS & MS, 1971; Univ Ill, Urbana, PhD (physics), 1975. **Professional Experience:** SR VPRES TECHNOL, NORANDA INC, 1992-; vpres, res & develop, 1988-1992; mgr power electronics systsbr, solid state physics & ultrasonics, Gen Elec Corp Res & Develop Ctr, 1984-1987; mgr energy systems mgt branch, solid state physics & ultrasonics, Gen Elec Corp Res & Develop Ctr, 1981-1982; mgr ultrasound imager prog, solid state physics & ultrasonics, Gen Elec Corp Res & Develop Ctr, 1978-1980; Physicist, solid state physics & ultrasonics, Gen Elec Corp Res & Develop Ctr, 1975-1978. **Memberships:** Am Phys Soc; Sigma Xi; Indust Res Inst; Can Res Mgt Asn. **Research Statement & Publications:** Solid state physics; signal processing; medical imaging; power circuits, integrated power electronics, lighting systems, motor and drives; metallurgy; metals processing; forestry; computing; Research and development. **Mailing Address:** Alcoa Tech Dr ADM-C Aluminum Co of Am, 100 Technical Dr, New Kensington, PA 15068-0001. **Fax:** 724-337-5436.

LEDERMAN, HOWARD MARK, PEDIATRICS, IMMUNOLOGY & IMMUNODEFICIENCY. **Personal Data:** b Chicago, Ill, April 3, 1952; m 1984, c 3. **Education:** Univ Mich, BS, 1972, MD, 1977, PhD (microbiol), 1978. **Professional Experience:** PROF PEDIAT, JOHNS HOPKINS UNIV SCH MED, 2003-; DIR, PEDIAT IMMUNODEFICIENCY CLIN, JOHNS HOPKINS HOSP, 1993-; assoc prof pediat, Johns Hopkins Univ Sch Med, 1991-2000; asst prof, Pediat Immunodeficiency Clin, Johns Hopkins Hosp, 1984-1990; pediat immunol fel, Hosp Sick Children, Toronto, 1981-1983; pediat residency training, Johns Hopkins Hosp, 1978-1981. **Memberships:** Am Asn Immunologists; Clin Immunol Soc; Soc Pediat Res. **Research Statement & Publications:** Defining and treating primary immunodeficiency diseases; investigating the role of fever as a host defense mechanism. **Mailing Address:** Johns Hopkins Hosp, 600 N Wolfe St, Baltimore, MD 21287-3922. **Fax:** 410-955-0229. **E-Mail:** hlederm1@jhem.jhmi.edu

LEDERMAN, LEON MAX, NUCLEAR PHYSICS, INSTRUMENTS. **Personal Data:** b New York, NY, July 15, 1922; m 1981, Ellen; c Renas, Rachel H & Jess A. **Education:** City Col NY, BS, 1943; Columbia Univ, AM, 1948, PhD (physics), 1951. **Honorary Degrees:** DSc, City Col NY, 1981, 1985, Northern Ill Univ & Univ Chicago, 1983, Ill Inst Technol, 1987, Lake Forest Col, Carnegie-Mellon Univ, 1988, Aurora Univ, Univ Ill, 1989, Univ Pittsburgh & Bradley Univ, DHL, Columbia & Rush Univ. **Honors & Awards:** Nobel Prize in Physics, 1988; Nat Medal Sci, US pres Lyndon Johnson, 1965; Wolf Prize, State of Israel, 1982, Enrico Feimi Award, Pres Bill Clinton, 1993. **Professional Experience:** PRITZKER PROF PHYSICS, ILL INST TECHNOL, as of 2005; PROF PHYSICS & FRANK E SULZBERGER PROF, UNIV CHICAGO, as of 2005; chmn, AAAS, 1991-1992; mem, Secy Energy Adv Bd, Wash, DC, 1990-; chmn, Aspen Ctr Physics, Colo, 1989-; Mus Sci Indust, Chicago, 1989-; EMER DIR, FERMILAB, BATAVIA, 1989-; physics & astron, Nat Acad Sci, 1988-; mem bd dirs, Weizmann Inst Sci, Israel, 1988-; dir, Fermilab, Batavia, 1979-1989; Higgins chair physics, Columbia Univ, 1972; mem, High Energy Physics Adv Panel, Atomic Energy Comn, 1967-1970; Ernest Kempton Adams fel, 1961 & NSF fel, 1967; dir, Nevis Labs, 1962-1979; Guggenheim & Ford Found fel, 1958-1959; assoc dir, Nevis Labs, 1953; from asst prof to prof physics, Columbia Univ, 1952-1989; res assoc, Columbia Univ, 1951-1952; collabr, Res Nevis Lab Prog, Brookhaven Nat Lab, Europ Ctr Nuclear Res, Fermilab & State Univ NY, Stony Brook; US rep, Int Comt Future Accelerators. **Memberships:** Nat Acad Sci; fel Am Phys Soc; fel Am Acad Arts & Sci; fel AAAS (pres-elect, 1990, pres, 1991-1992). **Research Statement & Publications:** Properties and interactions of elementary particles; author of over 200 publications. **Mailing Address:** Fermi Nat Accelerator Lab, PO Box 500, Batavia, IL 60510-0500.

LEDERMAN, MARCOS, MAGNETIC RECORDING, MICROSCOPY & METROLOGY. **Personal Data:** b Bogota, Columbia, December 15, 1963. **Education:** Sch Advan Physics & Chem, Paris, BA, 1987; Univ Calif, Los Angeles, MS, 1987, PhD (physics), 1991. **Professional Experience:** Sr res & develop engr, Read-Rite Corp, beginning 1995; Postdoctoral researcher, Univ Calif-San Diego, 1991-1995. **Memberships:** Am Phys Soc. **Research Statement & Publications:** Dynamics of single domain ferromagnetic particles; development of devices based on the spin valve and multilayer effects for magnetic recording including materials development and sensor design; failure analysis of magnetoresistive and spin-valve heads. **Mailing Address:** Read-Rite Corp, 44100 Osgood Rd, Fremont, CA 94539-6401. **Fax:** 510-683-7065.

LEDERMAN, PETER B, CHEMICAL & ENVIRONMENTAL ENGINEERING. **Personal Data:** b Weimar, Ger, November 16, 1931; American citizen; m 1957, Susan; c 2. **Education:** Univ Mich, BSE, 1953, MS, 1957, PhD (chem eng), 1961. **Honors & Awards:** Silver Medal, US Environ Protection Agency, 1976; Larry K Cecil Award Environ Eng, Am Inst Chem Engrs, 1987; Stanley E Kappe Award, Am Acad Environ Engrs. **Professional Experience:** RETIRED; dir, Ctr Environ Eng & Sci, NJ Inst Technol, ending 2002; exec dir, Hazardous Substances Mgt Res Ctr, beginning 2002; res prof chem eng & environ piolicy, NJ Inst Technol, ending 2002; vpres & sr tech adv, Spill Prev & Emergency Response Div, 1988-1993; vpres & gen mgr, Spill Prev & Emergency Response Div, 1983-1988; vpres hazardous/toxic Mat mgt, Roy F Weston, 1980-1983; vpres & gen mgr, Cottrell Environ Sci, 1978-1980; mgr tech develop & res, Cottrell Environ Sci, 1976-1978; dir indust waste treatment, Res & Develop, US Environ Protection Agency, 1972-1976; assoc prof chem eng, Polytech Inst Brooklyn, 1966-1972; sr chem engr, Esso Res & Eng Co, 1966; lectr, Columbia Univ, 1965-1967; engr chem develop, Esso Res & Eng Co, 1963-1965; engr, Esso Res Labs, 1961-1963; instr, Univ Mich, 1959-1961; technologist, Cent Res Div, Gen Foods Corp, 1956; teaching fel, Univ Mich, 1955-1959; jr technologist chem eng, Shell Oil Co, 1953; panel arbitrators, Am Arbit Asn. **Memberships:** Fel Am Inst Chem Engrs; Am Chem Soc; Am Soc Eng Educ; Nat Soc Prof Engrs; Air & Waste Mgt Asn; dipl Am Acad Environ Engrs; Am Soc Mech Engrs. **Research Statement & Publications:** Environmental studies; solid and hazardous material management; computer application; process optimization; polymers; mass transfer; pollution prevention; waste minimization; emergency response. **Mailing Address:** NJ Inst Technol, Univ Heights, Newark, NJ 07102-1982. **Fax:** 908-464-0654. **E-Mail:** peter.b.lederman@njit.edu

LEDERMAN, SALLY ANN, PHYSIOLOGY OF PREGNANCY & LACTATION, BODY COMPOSITION. **Personal Data:** b NY, July 8, 1937; div, c Evin & Leandra. **Education:** Brooklyn Col, BS, 1957; Columbia Univ, MS, 1976, PhD (nutrit), 1980. **Professional Experience:** SPEC LECT, COLUMBIA UNIV, MAILMAN SCH PUB HEALTH, 1998-; RES ASSOC ST LUKES HOSP DEPT MED, OBESITY RES CTR, 1996-; Ella McCollum Vahlteich prof, Human Nutrit, Teachers Col, Columbia Univ, 1994-1997; prin investr, Bur Maternal & Child Health, Dept Health & Human Serv, 1990-1995; assoc prof pub health & nutrit, Sch Pub Health, 1990-1994; mem, Subcomt Weight Gain During Pregnancy, Nat Acad Sci, 1988-1990; Travel award, Am Inst Nutr, intl nutrit conf, Brighton, Eng, 1985; asst prof, Public Health Physicians & Surgeons, 1983-1990; fellow obstet & biochem, Col Physicians & Surgeons, 1983; fellow nutrit, Columbia Univ, 1980-1982; lectr chem, Brooklyn Col, 1962-1966 & 1973-1974; Analy chemist, Food & Drug Admin, 1957-1962. **Memberships:** Asn Women Sci; NY Acad Sci; Am Inst Nutrit (Am Soc Nutr Sci); Am Pub Health Asn; AAAS. **Research Statement & Publications:** Physiological and psychosocial factors affecting the course/outcome of pregnancy and lactation with special emphasis on issues related to nutrition and to public health. **Mailing Address:** 41 Lake Dr E, Wayne, NJ 07470. **E-Mail:** sal1@columbia.edu

LEDFORD, BARRY EDWARD, BIOCHEMISTRY, MOLECULAR BIOLOGY. **Personal Data:** b Denver, Colo, February 27, 1942; m 1965, Margaret; c Brian & Molly. **Education:** Univ Colo, Boulder, BA, 1963, MS, 1965; Fla State Univ, Tallahassee, PhD (chem), 1971. **Professional Experience:** PROF EMER BIOCHEM & MOLECULAR BIOL, MED UNIT SC, CHARLESTON, as of 2004; ASSOC DEAN, COL GRAD STUDIES & DIR, PROG MOLECULAR & CELL BIOL & Pathobiology, 1989-; prof biochem & molecular biol, Med Univ SC, Charleston, beginning 1984; from asst prof to assoc prof biochem, Col Grad Studies & Dir, Prog Molecular & Cell Biol & Pathobiology, 1973-1984; USPHS postdoctoral fel, Biol Div, Oak Ridge Nat Lab, 1971-1973; USPHS biochem trainee, Dept Chem, 1967-1971; teaching asst, Fla State Univ, Tallahassee, 1966-1967; jr scientist, Lawrence Livermore Nat Lab, 1965-1966; res asst, Univ Colo, Boulder, 1964-1965; teaching asst, Univ Colo, Boulder, 1963-1964. **Memberships:** Am Soc Biochem & Molecular Biol; AAAS; Am Soc Cell Biol; Soc Develop Biol. **Mailing Address:** Dept Biochem & Molecular Biol Med, Univ SC, 171 Ashley Ave, Charleston, SC 29425. **Fax:** 843-792-8565. **E-Mail:** ledfordb@musc.edu

LEDFORD, RICHARD ALLISON, FOOD MICROBIOLOGY. **Personal Data:** b Charlotte, NC, June 30, 1931; m 1957, Martha; c Richard Jr, Roeby, Ann, Jeanne & Robert. **Education:** NC State Univ, BS, 1954, MS, 1956; Cornell Univ, PhD (food sci), 1962. **Honors & Awards:** Nordica Award, 1987. **Professional Experience:** PROF EMER, DEPT FOOD SCI, CORNELL UNIV, 2002; dir, Inst Food Sci, beginning 1988; chmn dept, Cornell Univ, beginning 1985; prof food sci, Cornell Univ, beginning 1980; assoc dir, Inst Food Sci, 1975-1977; chmn dept, Inst Food Sci, 1972-1977; from asst prof to assoc prof, Inst Food Sci, 1964-1980; dir, NY State Food Lab, NY State Dept Agr & Mkts, 1961-1964. **Memberships:** Am Soc Microbiol; Inst Food Technologists; Am Dairy Sci Asn. **Research Statement & Publications:** Microbiological aspects of food science, especially food fermentations and analytical methods. **Mailing Address:** Dept Food Sci Cornell Univ, 114 Stocking, Ithaca, NY 14853-7201. **Fax:** 607-254-4868.

LEDFORD, THOMAS HOWARD, ORGANIC CHEMISTRY. **Personal Data:** b Macon, Ga, August 24, 1942; m 1965, Joan; c Jeff & Scott. **Education:** Univ Ga, BS, 1964; Univ Fla, PhD (chem), 1973. **Professional Experience:** QUAL ASSURANCE OFFICER, LA DEPT OF ENVIRON QUAL, 2001-; chief environ chemist, Rubicon Corp, 1987-2001; sr tech develop chemist, Rubicon Corp, 1987-1993; adj assoc prof chem, La State Univ, 1981-; sr res chemist, Exxon Res & Develop, 1980-1986; res chemist fuels processing, Exxon Res & Develop, 1973-1980; res chemist polymer intermediates, Tenn Eastman Res Labs, Kingsport, Tenn, 1964-1968. **Memberships:** Am Chem Soc. **Research Statement & Publications:** Polymers; reactions in strong acids; fuel processing chemistry; sulfur chemistry; isocyanate chemistry; environmental chemistry. **Mailing Address:** 2322 W Highmeadow Ct, Baton Rouge, LA 70816-2530.

LEDIAEV, JOHN P, MATHEMATICS. **Personal Data:** b Goorgan, Iran, September 8, 1940; American citizen; div, c Ann. **Education:** Occidental Col, BA, 1963; Univ Calif, Riverside, MA, 1965, PhD (noether lattices), 1967. **Professional Experience:** ASSOC PROF MATH, UNIV, 1971-, asst prof, 1967-1971. **Memberships:** Am Math Soc; math Assoc Am. **Research Statement & Publications:** Structure; representation and embedding of Noether lattices; primary decomposition in multiplicative lattices; semi-prime operations in Noether lattices. **Mailing Address:** Dept Math, Univ Iowa, 25E MLH, Iowa City, IA 52240. **Fax:** 319-335-0627. **E-Mail:** lediaev@math.uiowa.edu

LEDIG, F THOMAS, EVOLUTION, CONSERVATION GENETICS. **Personal Data:** b Dover, NJ, August 13, 1938; div, c Colleen B, Sean C & Brendan O. **Education:** Rutgers Univ, BS, 1962; NC State Univ, MS, 1965, PhD (genetics), 1967. **Honorary Degrees:** Ms, Yale Univ, 1979. **Honors & Awards:** Fel, Am Asn Advancement of Sci, 2002; Barrington Moore Mem Award, 1992; Glaser Distinguished vis prof, Fla Int Univ, 1991-1992; Leslie L Schaffer Lectr, Univ BC, 1988-1989; Distinguished serv award, Int Union of forest res org 2000; outstinding scientist award USDA forest serv, 1988. **Professional Experience:** SR SCIENTIST, INST FOREST GENETICS, USDA FOREST SERV, 1988-; dir, Inst Forest Genetics, USDA Forest Serv, 1979-1988; res geneticist, Inst Trop Forestry, Rio Piedras, PR, 1978; from asst prof to prof forest genetics, Yale Univ, 1966-1980. **Memberships:** Forest genetic resources working group NA forest comm/FAO/UN; AAAS; Soc Am Foresters; Soc Conserv Biol; Int Soc Trop Foresters; Botanical soc of Am; Amn soc of plant taxonomists; calif bot soc. **Research Statement & Publications:** Population genetics and evolution; conservation of genetic resources; genecology, eucalypt biomass fuel breeding. **Mailing Address:** Inst Forest Genetics, 2480 Carson Rd, Placerville, CA 95667. **Fax:** 530-754-9366. **E-Mail:** tledig@ucdavis.edu

LEDIN, GEORGE, COMPUTER SCIENCE, STATISTICS. **Personal Data:** b Seekirchen, Austria, January 28, 1946; American citizen; m 1968, Suzanne; c Kathryn & Alexander. **Education:** Univ Calif, Berkeley, BS, 1967; Univ San Francisco, JD, 1982. **Professional Experience:** CHAIR, DEPT COMPUT SCI, 1994-; PROF COMPUT SCI, SONOMA STATE UNIV, 1984-; chair, Comp Sci Dept, 1976-1982; prof comput sci, Univ San Francisco, 1975-1984; US rep, Int Fedn Info Processing, 1972-1974; sr res assoc, Inst Chem Biol, 1970-1975; lectr math & comput sci, Univ San Francisco, 1968-1974; consult comput sci & statist, 1966-; statistician & mathematician, Univ San Francisco, 1965-1970. **Memberships:** AAAS; Am Math Soc; Assocn Comput Mach; Math Assocn Am; NY Acad Sci; Am Assocn Artificial Intel; Soc Indust & Appl Math. **Research Statement & Publications:** Comp security/data mining and knowledge discovery; comp graphics/debrification; programming methodology; heuristic programming; pattern recognition; mathematical models for biosciences; number theory; combinatorics; graph theory; game theory; information theory. **Mailing Address:** Dept Comput Sci, Sonoma State Univ, 1801 E Cotati Ave Darwin 121, Rohnert Park, CA 94928-3613. **Fax:** 707-664-2807. **E-Mail:** george.ledin@sonoma.edu

LEDINKO, NADA, VIROLOGY. **Personal Data:** b Girard, Ohio, December 16, 1925. **Education:** Ohio State Univ, BS, 1946; Pa State Col, MS, 1949; Yale Univ, PhD (microbiol), 1952. **Professional Experience:** PROF EMER BIOL, UNIV AKRON, 1990-; assoc dir, Toolan Inst Med Res, 1990-1992; prof, Univ Akron, 1971-1989; Res career develop award, NIH, 1966-1971; assoc investr & NIH res career develop awardee, Putnam Mem Hosp Inst Med Res, Bennington, Vt, 1965-1971; USPHS fel, Carnegie Inst Genetics Res Unit & Salk Inst Biol Studies, 1963-1965; virologist, Pub Health Res Inst, 1956-1962; Nat Found Infantile Paralysis fel, Walter & Eliza Hall Inst, Australia, 1953-1955; res asst virol, Yale Univ, 1952-1953. **Memberships:** AAAS; Am Asn Path & Bact; Tissue Cult Asn; Am Soc Microbiol; Am Asn Cancer Res. **Research Statement & Publications:** Genetical and biochemical aspects of viral growth; cancer research. **Mailing Address:** Dept Biol, Univ Akron, 302 Buchtel Hall, Akron, OH 44325.

LEDLEY, FRED DAVID, PEDIATRICS, GENE THERAPY. **Personal Data:** b Washington, DC, November 27, 1954; m 1976, Tamara; c 2. **Education:** Univ Md, Col Park, BS, 1974; Georgetown Univ, MD, 1978. **Honors & Awards:** Upjohn Achievement Award, Georgetown Univ, 1978. **Professional Experience:** FOUNDER & CHMN, MYGENOME INC, as of 2005; pres & chief exec officer, Variagenics Inc, as of 2003; vpres, clin & regulatory, Genemed Inc, beginning 1993; assoc prof cell biol & pediat, Baylor Col Med, 1989-1993; asst investr, Howard Hughes Med Inst, 1985-1992; asst prof to assoc prof cell biol, Baylor Col Med, 1983-1989; fel genetics, Mass Inst Technol, 1981-1983; fel genetics, Harvard Med Sch, Children's Hosp, 1981-1983; fel, Am Can Soc, 1981-1983; Janeway scholar, Harvard Med Sch, Children's Hosp, 1981; resident pediat, Harvard Med Sch, Children's Hosp, 1978-1981. **Memberships:** Am Soc Human Genetics; Soc Pediat Res; Soc Inherited Metab Dis; Am Fedn Clin Res; Am Soc Study Liver Dis. **Research Statement & Publications:** The development of methods for gene therapy; study of technical, clinical, commercial, and ethical issues of gene therapy. **Mailing Address:** Mygenome Inc, Needham, MA 02139.

LEDLEY, ROBERT STEVEN, BIOPHYSICS, COMPUTER SCIENCE. **Personal Data:** b New York, NY, June 28, 1926; m 1949, c 2. **Education:** NY Univ, DDS, 1948; Columbia Univ, MA, 1949. **Honors & Awards:** Nat Inventors Hall of Fame, 1990; Nat Medal of Technol, 1997. **Professional Experience:** Prof physiol, biophys & radiol, med ctr, Georgetown Univ, beginning 1970; pres, Digital Info Sci Corp, 1970-1975; prof elec eng, Sch Eng & Appl Sci, George Wash Univ, 1968-1970; PRES & RES DIR, NAT BIOMED RES FOUND, 1960-; instr pediat, Sch Med, Johns Hopkins Univ, 1960-1963; mem staff, Nat Acad Sci-Nat Res Coun, 1957-1961; assoc prof elec eng, Sch Eng, George Wash Univ,

1957-1960; consult mathematician, Data Processing Systs Div, Nat Bur Stand, 1957-1960; opers res analyst, Opers Res Off, Strategic Div, Johns Hopkins Univ, 1954-1956; physicist, External Control Group, Electronic Comput Lab, 1953-1954; vis scientist, Nat Bur Stand, 1951-1952; instr physics, Radiation Lab, Columbia Univ, 1949-1950; res physicist, Radiation Lab, Columbia Univ, 1948-1950; affil rep, Pattern Recognition Soc. **Memberships:** Soc Math Biophys; Inst Elec & Electronics Engrs; Biophys Soc; NY Acad Sci; Pattern Recognition Soc. **Research Statement & Publications:** Applications of computers to medical instrumentation; computer softwaresystems and applications in medicine and biology; computer aids to medical diagnosis; computer information science; medical imaging; pattern recognition; medical informatics. **Mailing Address:** Nat Biomed Res Found, Georgetown Univ Med Ctr, 3900 Reservoir Rd NW, Washington, DC 20007-2187. **Fax:** 202-687-1662. **E-Mail:** ledley@nbrf.georgetown.edu

LEDLEY, TAMARA SHAPIRO, EARTH SYSTEM SCIENCE, CLIMATOLOGY. **Personal Data:** b Washington, DC, May 18, 1954; m 1976, Fred; c Miriam E & Johanna S. **Education:** Univ Md, BS, 1976; Mass Inst Technol, PhD (meteorol), 1983. **Professional Experience:** SR SCIENTIST, CTR SCI TEACHING & LEARNING, TERC, as of 2005; PRIN INVESTR, CTR SCI TEACHING & LEARNING, TERC, as of 2004; mem comt, Global & Environ Chg, Am Geophys Union, 1993-; assoc ed, J Geophys Res-Atmospheres, 1993-; vis lectr geol & geophys, Rice Univ, 1993; asst dir, Solar Inst, 1993; sr fac fel, Climate/Earth Syst Sci, Rice Univ, beginning 1990; dir, Weather & Climate Proj, Teacher Training Prog Observational Sci, George Observ, 1990-1992; lectr space physics & astron, Rice Univ, 1990 & 1991; mem, Alaska SAR Facil Archive Working Team, 1988 & McMurdo SAR Facil Sci Working Team, 1990; consult, Broader Perspectives Inc, 1990; assoc res scientist, Rice Univ, 1990; consult, Sci Connection Elem Sci Curric Proj, Houston Mus Natural Sci, 1989-1990; coordr, Nat Week Educ, Union Concerned Scientists, 1989; Prin investr, NSF grants, 1985-; Tex Advan Technol Prog grants, 1987-1992; asst res scientist, Rice Univ, 1985-1990; res assoc climat, Rice Univ, 1983-1985. **Memberships:** AAAS; Am Meteorol Soc; Am Geophys Union; Oceanog Soc; Sigma Xi. **Research Statement & Publications:** Understanding the role of the polar regions in shaping climate on a wide range of time scales by examining how atmosphere-sea ice-ocean interactions influence climate change. **Mailing Address:** TERC, Ctr Sci Teaching & Learning, 2067 Mass Ave, Cambridge, MA 02492. **Fax:** 617-349-3535. **E-Mail:** tamara_ledley@terc.edu

LEDNEY, GEORGE DAVID, RADIATION BIOLOGY, HEMATOLOGY. **Personal Data:** b Sharon, Pa, June 25, 1937. **Education:** Youngstown Univ, BS, 1960; Univ Notre Dame, PhD (biol), 1965. **Professional Experience:** Team leader, radiation injury treatment, Armed Forces Radiobiol Res Inst, beginning 1995; CHMN, RADIATION MED DEPT, RADIATION INJURY TREATMENT, ARMED FORCES RADIOBIOL RES INST, 1995-; proj mgr microbiol-immunol, div immunol, 1988-1995; head, div immunol, 1973-1988; assoc prof, med units, Univ Tenn, Memphis, 1970-1973; am cancer soc grants, 1968 & 1970; Nat Cancer Inst fel, 1965-1967; asst prof radiation biol, med units, Univ Tenn, Memphis, 1965-1967. **Memberships:** Am Asn Lab Animal Sci; Asn Gnotobiotics. **Research Statement & Publications:** Radiation biology; radiation and immune functioning; bone marrow transplantation; wound trauma; radiation and susceptibility to infection. **Mailing Address:** Dept Radiation Med, Armed Forces Radiobiol Res Inst, Bldg 42 8901 Wis Ave, Bethesda, MD 20889-5603. **Fax:** 301-295-6503. **E-Mail:** ledney@afrri.usuhs.mil

LEDNICER, DANIEL, ORGANIC CHEMISTRY. **Personal Data:** b Antwerp, Belg, October 15, 1929. **Education:** Antioch Col, BS, 1952; Ohio State Univ, PhD (chem), 1955. **Professional Experience:** CONSULT, 1994-; chemist, Nat Cancer Inst, 1988-1994; pharm mgr, ABC Labs, 1984-1988; dir Med Chem & Pharm, Adria Labs, 1980-1984; dir chem res, Mead Johnson & Co, 1976-1980; sr scientist, Upjohn Co, 1973-1976; chemist, Upjohn Co, 1959-1973; Esso Res & Develop Co fel, Univ Ill, 1958-1959; res assoc, Duke Univ, 1956-1958; sr chemist, G D Searle & Co, 1955-1956. **Memberships:** Am Chem Soc. **Research Statement & Publications:** Stereochemistry; medicinal chemistry; hypotensives; analgesics; pharmaceutical analysis. **Mailing Address:** 10401 Grosvenor Pl, Rockville, MD 20852. **Fax:** 301-581-0344. **E-Mail:** dlednicer@att.net

LEDOUX, ROBERT LOUIS, MINERALOGY. **Personal Data:** b Marieville, Que, April 19, 1933; m 1961, c 2. **Education:** Univ Montreal, BSc, 1956; Laval Univ, MScA, 1960; Purdue Univ, PhD (mineral), 1964. **Professional Experience:** RETIRED; prof petrol & mineral, Laval Univ, 1994; from assoc prof to prof mineral, Laval Univ, 1964-1994. **Memberships:** Mineral Asn Am; Can Asn Mineral; Geol Asn Can. **Research Statement & Publications:** Infrared studies of layered silicates. **Mailing Address:** 711 rue Moreau, Ste Foy, PQ G1V 3A5, Can.

LEDSOME, JOHN R, PHYSIOLOGY, MEDICINE. **Personal Data:** b Bebington, Eng, June 18, 1932; m 1957, Susan; c Henry, Mark & Sarah. **Education:** Univ Edinburgh, MB, ChB, 1955, MD, 1962. **Honorary Degrees:** DSc, Univ Edinburgh, 1989. **Professional Experience:** PROF EMER PHYSIOL, UNIV BC, as of 2005; head, Univ BC, 1980-1991; BC Heart Found res grant, 1972-1994; prof physiol, Univ Bc, beginning 1968; Med Red Coun Can res grant, 1968-1995; res grant, USPHS, 1966-1968; Med Res Coun Eng res grant, 1965-1968; USPHS int fel, 1964-1965; lectr physiol, Univ Leeds, 1959-1968. **Memberships:** Can Physiol Soc; Brit Physiol Soc; Am Physiol Soc. **Research Statement & Publications:** Neuro-humoral control of the cardiovascular system; function of left atrial receptors and arterial baroreceptors. Atrial naturetic peptide and ADH; Regulation of body fluid volumes.; Spinal cord function in microgravity. Cardio- vascular adaptation to weightlessness in humans. **Mailing Address:** 5651 Westhaven Rd, West Vancouver, BC V7W 1T5, Can. **Fax:** 604-9219691. **E-Mail:** jledsome@interchange.ubc.ca

LEDUC, ELIZABETH HORTENSE, CELL BIOLOGY. **Personal Data:** b Rockland, Maine, November 19, 1921. **Education:** Univ Vt, BS, 1943; Wellesley Col, MA, 1945; Brown Univ, PhD (biol), 1948. **Professional Experience:** PROF EMER BIOMED, BROWN UNIV, as of 2005; EMER DEAN DIV BIOL & MED, BROWN UNIV, 1973-; mem adv coun, Nat Inst Gen Med Sci, 1972-1976; prof biol, Brown Univ, beginning 1964; from asst prof to assoc prof, Brown Univ, 1953-1964; instr & assoc anat, Harvard Med Sch, 1949-1953; res assoc biol, Brown Univ, 1948-1949. **Memberships:** AAAS; Am Soc Cell Biol; Soc Francaise de Microscopie Electronique; Histochem Soc; Am Soc Exp Path. **Research Statement & Publications:** Histophysiology and pathology of the liver; cellular mechanism in antibody production; ultrastructural and cytochemical effects of cancer chemotherapeutic compounds on normal and neoplastic cells. **Mailing Address:** Div Biol & Med Sci Box G-B593, Brown Univ, Providence, RI 02912-0001. **E-Mail:** elizabeth_leduc@brown.edu

LEDUC, GERARD, FISHERIES, BIOCHEMISTRY. **Personal Data:** b Verdun, Que, September 7, 1934; m 1959, c 3. **Education:** Univ Montreal, BSc, 1958, MSc, 1960; Ore State Univ, PhD (fisheries), 1966. **Professional Experience:** INDEPENDENT RESEARCHER, 1990-; chmn dept, Sir George Williams Univ, 1969-1972; from asst prof to prof biol sci, Sir George Williams Univ, 1966-1990; Biologist, Que Wildlife Serv, 1963-1966. **Research Statement & Publications:** Fisheries problems in water pollution, mainly the long-term effects of sublethal concentrations of toxicant; artificial streams. **Mailing Address:** 6 Chemin de l'Equinox RR 3, Mansonville, PQ J0E 1X0, Can.

LEDUC, JOHN W, MATHEMATICS. **Professional Experience:** PROF EMER, DEPT MATHS, UNIV S ALA, as of 2005. **Memberships:** Am Math Asn. **Mailing Address:** Dept Math, Univ S Ala, 307 Univ Blvd N, Mobile, AL 36688-0002. **Fax:** 251-461-1537.

LEDUC, RICHARD, STRUCTURE-FUNCTION ANALYSIS, PROTEIN DESIGN. **Personal Data:** b Montreal, Que, August 5, 1957; m Johanne; c Alexandre & Catherine. **Education:** Univ Sherbrooke, BS, 1980, MS, 1982; Univ Montreal, PhD (biomed sci), 1988. **Professional Experience:** PROF, UNIV SHERBROOKE, 1992-; postdoctoral fel, Oregon Health Sciences Univ, 1989-1991. **Memberships:** Int Proteolysis Soc; Am Assoc Advan Sci. **Research Statement & Publications:** Structure-function and inhibition of mammalian convertases, calcium-dependent serine proteases involved in processing inactive precursor proteins into biologically active peptides; structure-function of G-protein coupled receptors. **Mailing Address:** Dept Pharmacol, Med Sch, Univ Sherbrooke, 3001 12th Ave N, Sherbrooke, PQ J1H 5N4, Can. **Fax:** 819-564-5400. **E-Mail:** richard.leduc@usherbrooke.ca

LEDUC, SHARON KAY, STATISTICS, CLIMATOLOGY. **Personal Data:** b Hattiesburg, Miss, April 28, 1943; m 1964, Richard; c Brian, Philip & Russell. **Education:** Eastern Ill Univ, BS, 1965; Univ Mo, Columbia, MA, 1967, PhD (statist), 1971. **Honors & Awards:** Distinguished Alumnus, Eastern Ill Univ, 1999; Gold Medal, USDOC. **Professional Experience:** DEP DIR, NAT CLIMATIC DATA CTR, 2001-; adj prof, Mea NC State Univ, 1995-2002; adj prof geog, Univ NC, 1990-2000; Environ Protection Agency, NC, 1988-2001; prof atmospheric sci, Univ Mo, 1967-1989; Nat Environ Satellite, Data & Info Serv, statistician, Ctr Environ Assessment Serv, Nat Ocean & Atmo. **Memberships:** Am Statist Asn; Am Meteorol Soc; Sigma Xi. **Research Statement & Publications:** Statistical analysis of atmospheric data for climate change; evaluation of air quality models; technological transfer methods. **Mailing Address:** 151 Patton Ave, Asheville, NC 28801. **Fax:** 828-271-4246. **E-Mail:** sharon.leduc@noaa.gov

LEDUY, ANH, BIOCHEMICAL ENGINEERING, APPLIED MICROBIOLOGY. **Personal Data:** b Vietnam, February 6, 1946; Canadian citizen; m 1977, Suzanne; c Isabelle & Dominic. **Education:** Univ Sherbrooke, BScA, 1969, MScA, 1972; Univ Western Ont, PhD (biochem eng), 1975. **Professional Experience:** PROF CHEM ENG, LAVAL UNIV, 1985-; consult, 1981-; from asst to assoc prof, Laval Univ, 1977-1985; res assoc chem eng, Univ Sherbrooke, 1975-1977. **Memberships:** NY Acad Sci. **Research Statement & Publications:** Utilization of microorganisms; enzymes systems in the production of biomass and precious metabolites from abundant raw materials, waste materials and industrial agricultural by-products. **Mailing Address:** Dept Chem Eng, Laval Univ, St Foy, PQ G1K 7P4, Can. **Fax:** 418-656-5993. **E-Mail:** anh.leduy@gch.ulaval.ca

LEDWELL, THOMAS AUSTIN, MECHANICAL ENGINEERING, ENERGY CONVERSION & ENVIRONMENTAL IMPACTS OF ENERGY. **Personal Data:** b PEI, June 13, 1938; m 1964, Mary Elaine; c 4. **Education:** NS Tech Col, BE, 1960, ME, 1965; Univ Waterloo, PhD (mech eng), 1968. **Professional Experience:** Sr adv, Sci Technol, 1994-1997; lectr physics environ, Carleton Univ, 1987-1996; dir, Renewable Energy Policy, 1986-1994; CONSULT, 1985-; chief, Demonstration Prog, 1982-1985; sr tech adv, Conserv & Renewable Energy, Energy, Mines & Resources, 1980-1982; head res coord, Renewable Energy Policy, 1978-1980; tech adv, Renewable Energy Policy, 1977-1978; Res coordr, Nat Res Coun, 1975-1977. **Memberships:** Combustion Inst. **Research Statement & Publications:** Thermodynamics; engine design and development; applied mathematics; energy research and development; environmental impacts and health impacts of energy climate change ozone layer. **Mailing Address:** Natural Resources Can, 580 Booth St 18th Flr, Rm C1, Ottawa, ON K1A 0E4, Can. **Fax:** 613-947-4120. **E-Mail:** tledwell@nrcan.gc.ca

LEDWITZ-RIGBY, FLORENCE INA, REPRODUCTIVE ENDOCRINOLOGY. **Personal Data:** b New York, NY, February 14, 1946; m 1968, c 2. **Education:** City Col NY, BS, 1966; Case Western Res Univ, MS, 1968; Univ Wis-Madison, PhD (endocrinol & reprod physiol), 1972. **Professional Experience:** ADJ PROF BIOL, UNIV WIS, as of 2006; dir affirmative action, Univ Wis, 1994-; adv, Women & Gender Relations & hon prof obstet & gynec, Univ BC, 1990-1994; prof, Dept Biol Sci, Northern Ill Univ, 1987-1990; vis res prof, Dept Genetics, Univ Ill, Chicago, 1987-1988; from asst prof to assoc prof physiol, Dept Biol Sci, Northern Ill Univ, 1975-1987; vis asst prof physiol, Dept Biol, 1974-1975; res fel reprod physiol, Sch Med, Dept Physiol, Univ Pittsburgh, 1972-1974. **Memberships:** Am Physiol Soc; Soc Study Reprod; Endocrine Soc. **Research Statement & Publications:** Endocrine and physiological control mechanisms of ovarian cell function and differentiation. **Mailing Address:** Biol Dept, Univ Wis, 340 Phillips Sci Bldg, Eau Claire, WI 54701-4800.

LEE, ALFRED M, TELECOMMUNICATIONS POLICY, TECHNOLOGY ASSESSMENT. **Personal Data:** b Bloomington, Ind, August 23, 1951. **Education:** Univ Ill, BSEE, 1973; Cornell Univ, MS, 1975, PhD (civil engr & pub policy), 1981. **Professional Experience:** AM NUMBERIG COUNCIL FED, 2001-; Inst Elec & Electronics Engrs, 1995-; Fed Networking Council, nat sci Found 1995-1997; Actix assoc Admin off Policy anal & develop NTIA US dept of comm 1990; INTERNET POLICY DEVELOP SR POLICY ADV, OFF POLICY ANALYSIS & DEVELOP, NAT TELECOMMUN & INFO ADMIN, US DEPT COM, 1990-; telecommun policy analyst, Off Policy Analysis & Develop, Nat Telecommun & Info Admin, US Dept Com, 1984-1990; assoc ed, Inst Elec & Electronics Engrs Technol & Soc Mag, 1981-1984; Mem, Transp Res Bd, Subcomt Telecommun & Transp, Trade-offs, 1980-1984; fel, Prog Sci, Technol & Sci, 1980-1982; res asst electronic message transfer, Cornell Univ, 1978-1980; res specialist mobile commun, Cornell Univ, 1975-1978. **Memberships:** Inst Elec & Electronics Engrs; Sigma Xi. **Research Statement & Publications:** Telecommunications policy; transportation-communications trade-offs and the social impact of developments in telecommunications; mobile communications; electronic message transfer. **Mailing Address:** Nat Telecommun & Info Admin H4725, US Dept Comm, Washington, DC 20230.

LEE, ALFRED TZE-HAU, ANALYTICAL CHEMISTRY, ORGANIC CHEMISTRY. **Personal Data:** b Hong Kong, July 22, 1939; American citizen; m 1970, Kitty; c Winnie & Hanson. **Education:** Univ Calif, Berkeley, BS, 1963; Univ Calif, Los Angeles, PhD (chem), 1968. **Professional Experience:** Chmn, City Col San Francisco, 1985-1990; PROF CHEM, CITY COL SAN FRANCISCO, 1968-; res scientist, Jet Propulsion Lab, Pasadena, 1968; instr chem, East Los Angeles Col, 1967-1968. **Memberships:** Am Chem Soc. **Research Statement & Publications:** Oxidation-state diagrams; pulse polarography; analytical methods in general, vacuum-ultraviolet spectra of olefins. **Mailing Address:** Dept Chem, City Col San Francisco, 76 Jordan Ave, San Francisco, CA 94118-2503. **E-Mail:** atlee@ccsf.edu

LEE, AMY SHIU, MOLECULAR BIOLOGY, BIOCHEMISTRY. **Personal Data:** b Canton, China, August 5, 1947; American citizen; m 1972, c 2. **Education:** Univ Calif, Berkeley,

BA, 1970; Calif Inst Technol, MS, 1972, PhD (biophys, molecular biol), 1975. **Honors & Awards:** Merit Award, NIH, 1988. **Professional Experience:** PROF BIOCHEM, SCH MED, UNIV SOUTHERN CALIF, 1988-; fac res award, Am Cancer Soc, 1983-1988; NIH study sect, 1980-1988; from asst to assoc prof, Sch Med, Univ Southern Calif, 1979-1987; sr res fel, Calif Inst Technol, 1978-1979; sr res fel, Calif Inst Technol, 1978-1969; Am Cancer Soc fel, NIH Pub Health Serv fel, 1977-1978; Am Cancer Soc fel, Calif Inst Technol, 1975-1976; res fel, Calif Inst Technol, 1975-1978; teaching asst biol, Calif Inst Technol, 1971-1974; res asst bact, Univ Calif, Los Angeles, 1970-1971. **Memberships:** AAAS. **Research Statement & Publications:** DNA sequence organization and gene expression in cell cycle regeneration eukaryotes; recombinant DNA technology; published over 20 articles. **Mailing Address:** Dept Biochem, Univ Southern Calif, Keck Sch Med, Bldg NOR 5307 1441 Eastlake Ave, Los Angeles, CA 90089-9176. **Fax:** 323-865-0094. **E-Mail:** amylee@usc.edu

LEE, ANTHONY, PLASMA PHYSICS. **Personal Data:** b Canton, China, December 8, 1941; American citizen; m 1969, c 2. **Education:** Drexel Univ, BS, 1966; Stevens Inst Technol, MS, 1969, PhD (physics), 1971. **Professional Experience:** Sr engr, Res & Develop Ctr, Westinghouse Elec Corp, beginning 1976; vis asst prof physics, Univ SFla, 1975-1976; adj asst prof, Univ SFla, 1973-1975; fel plasma physics, Univ Sask, 1971-1973; DIR, ADV ENG, DIV GEN MOTORS, PACKARD ELEC. **Memberships:** Am Phys Soc; Inst Elec & Electronics Engrs. **Research Statement & Publications:** Nonlinear plasma wave theory; linear and nonlinear low frequency waves in plasmas with density, potential and temperature gradients; catalytic turbulent heating of plasmas as supplementary tokamac heating. **Mailing Address:** Packard Elec, PO Box 431 Sta 93L, Warren, OH 44846.

LEE, ANTHONY L, CATALYSIS, GAS PROCESSING. **Personal Data:** b Qingdao, China, November 16, 1934; American citizen; m 1962, c 2. **Education:** Univ Calif, Berkeley, BS, 1958; Mo Sch Mines, MS, 1961, Illi Inst Technol, Phd. **Professional Experience:** PRES, CEMENT-LOCK GROUP, GAS TECHNOL INST, as of 2004; assoc dir, gas processing & catalysis, Inst Gas Technol, beginning 1988; asst dir, Catalyst Develop, 1985-1988; sr chem engr, Inst Gas Technol, 1978-1985; supvr catalytic processing, Inst Gas Technol, 1969-1978; supvr fundamental properties res, Inst Gas Technol, 1966-1969; chem engr, Inst Gas Technol, 1961-1966; chemist, Stepan Chem Co, 1960; res asst, Calif Inst Technol, 1958-1959. **Memberships:** Am Inst Chem Engrs. **Research Statement & Publications:** Transport and thermodynamic peoperties of hydrocarbons; coal gasification research; methanation, water-gas shift, hydrotreating, hydrocracking, and steam reforming catalysis; C1 chemistry; hydroforming; gas processing. **Mailing Address:** Inst Gas Technol, 1700 S Mt Prospect Rd, Des Plaines, IL 60018. **E-Mail:** tonyl@igt.org

LEE, ARTHUR CLAIR, OPHTHALMOLOGY, RADIATION RESEARCH. **Personal Data:** b Abilene, Kans, August 3, 1923; m 1951, Margaret Helzer; c Marsha, Lorraine, Douglas, Suzanne & Angela. **Education:** Colo State Univ, DVM, 1952, MS, 1963, PhD (radiation biol), 1970. **Professional Experience:** RETIRED; vet sect leader, Collab Radiol Health Lab, USPHS, 1964-1990; vet radiologist, AEC Proj, Colo State Univ, Foothills Campus, 1963-1966; Morris Found fel, 1960-1962; Practr vet med, 1952-1960. **Memberships:** AAAS; Am Vet Med Asn; Radiation Res Soc Am; Am Soc Vet Ophthal. **Research Statement & Publications:** Radiation effects on canine growth and development; ocular lesions as a result of age at exposure; cataractogenesis from heavy charged particles. **Mailing Address:** 1908 Mohawk St, Ft Collins, CO 80525-1526.

LEE, BENEDICT HUK KUN, MECHANICAL ENGINEERING, AERONAUTICS. **Personal Data:** b Hong Kong, October 17, 1940; Canadian citizen; m 1966, Alice Lau; c Karen & Alexander. **Education:** McGill Univ, BEng, 1963, MEng, 1964, PhD (mech eng), 1966. **Professional Experience:** GROUP LEADER, DEPT EXP AERODYN & AEROELASTICITY, NAT RES COUN, as of 2004; Adj prof, Dept Mech Eng, Univ Ottawa, Ont, beginning 1991; sr res scientist, Nat Res Coun, beginning 1967; Res assoc, McGill Univ, 1966-1967. **Memberships:** Am Inst Aeronaut & Astronaut; Acoust Soc Am; Can Aeronaut & Space Inst. **Research Statement & Publications:** Fluid mechanics; gas dynamics; acoustics and aerodynamics; aeroelasticity; structural dynamics. **Mailing Address:** Nat Res Coun, Rm 241, Bldg U-66, Ottawa, ON K1A 0R6, Can. **Fax:** 613998-1281.

LEE, BERNARD S, CHEMICAL ENGINEERING, PHYSICAL CHEMISTRY. **Personal Data:** b China, December 14, 1934; American citizen; m 1963, c 3. **Education:** Polytech Inst Brooklyn, BChE, 1956, PhD (chem eng), 1960. **Professional Experience:** DIR, NUI CORP, as of 2004; DIR, PEERLESS MFG CO, as of 2004; DIR, NAT FUEL GAS CO, 1994-; lectr, Am inst Chem Engrs, beginning 1981; pres, inst Gas Technol, 1978-1999; exec vpres, inst Gas Technol, 1977-1978; vpres, inst Gas Technol, 1976-1977; asst vpres process res, mgr & dir coal gasification, 1975-1976; supvr, mgr & dir coal gasification, 1965-1975; mem staff, Arthur D Little, Inc, 1960-1965. **Memberships:** Fel Am Inst Chem Engrs; Am Chem Soc; Am Inst Mining Metall & Petrol Engrs; Sigma Xi; Am Gas Asn. **Research Statement & Publications:** Energy conversion processes for its production of synthetic fuels from coal, lignite, peat, oil shale, biomass, urban and industrial wastes and efficient energy utilization systems involving solar energy and fuel cells. **Mailing Address:** Nat Fuel Gas Co, 6363 Main St, Williamsville, NY 14221. **Fax:** 716-857-7229.

LEE, BRENDAN, MICROBIOLOGY. **Education:** City Univ NY, BS, 1986; State Univ NY Health Sci Ctr, PhD, 1990, MD, 1993. **Professional Experience:** INVESTR, HOWARD HUGHES MED INST, 2005-; ASSOC PROF, DEPT MOLECULAR & HUMAN GENETICS, BAYLOR COL MED, 2001-. **Mailing Address:** Baylor Col Med, One Baylor Plaza Rm 635E, Houston, TX 77030. **Fax:** 713-798-5168. **E-Mail:** blee@bcm.tmc.edu

LEE, BURNELL, COATINGS FORMULATIONS, GENERAL FORMULATION. **Personal Data:** b Hearne, Tex, December 8, 1955; m 1978, Katherin H Corlett; c Aaron D & Kristin M. **Education:** Southwest Mo State Univ, BS, 1980; Univ Ill, Champaign-Urbana, PhD (org chem), 1987. **Professional Experience:** SR RES CHEMIST, ETHYL CORP, 1993-; res specialist, Ethyl Corp, 1990-1993; sr res chemist, Ethyl Corp, 1987-1990. **Memberships:** Am Chem Soc; Soc Cosmetic Chemists; Am Vacuum Soc; Soc Tribologists & Lubrication Engrs. **Research Statement & Publications:** Synthesis and application polyimide polymers for coatings, molding, and composite manufacture; applications of proprietary additives in a variety areas including ceramic coatings, cosmetics, agricultural products, and foams. **Mailing Address:** 15133 Seven Pines, Baton Rouge, LA 70817. **Fax:** 504-768-5607.

LEE, BURTRAND INSUNG, MATERIALS CHARACTERIZATION, MATERIALS SYNTHESIS. **Personal Data:** b Seoul, Korea, January 20, 1952; American citizen; m 1979, Connie; c Curtis J. **Education:** Southern Col, Coldale, BA, 1976; Western Mich Univ, MS, 1979; Univ Fla, Gainesville, PhD (mat engr), 1986. **Honors & Awards:** Res Excellence Award, Clemson univ, 2001 Fulbright Scholar Award, 1993 Borad of Trustee Fac Excell Award, 2000, 2003. **Professional Experience:** Affil staff Scientist, Pac NW Nat Lab, 1995-; vis sr researcher, Hitachi Res Lab, Japan, 1993; PROF MATER. SCI, CLEMSON UNIV, 1986-; distinguished vis prof, Pusan Nat Univ, Korea, 1990; Fulbright vis prof, Norweg Inst Technol, 1989; prin investr, Petrol Res Fund, Am Chem Soc, 1987-1988 & NSF, 1988-; panel comt mem, Nat Sci & Technol Ctr, 1987-1988; asst prof mat sci, Clemson Univ, 1986-1991; Lectr, State Univ NY, 1980; Chemist, Biospherics Inc, 1976-1978; ed jour ceramic processing res; ed, KCI concrete jour. **Memberships:** Am Chem Soc; Am Ceramic Soc; Mat Res Soc; Sigma Xi. **Research Statement & Publications:** Surface interactions of ceramic and polymeric materials; new methods or new materials for engineering and opto-electronic applications; chemical processing or ultrastructure processing of ceramic materials; sol-gel processing; Nanoparticles and surface/colloidal science. **Mailing Address:** Sch Mater Sci & Engr, Olin Hall, Clemson Univ, Clemson, SC 29634-0971. **Fax:** 864-656-1453. **E-Mail:** Lburtra@yahoo.com

LEE, BYUNGKOOK, PROTEIN STRUCTURE MODELING, BIOINFORMATICS. **Personal Data:** b Korea, February 7, 1941; m 1964, c 1. **Education:** Seoul Nat Univ, BS, 1961; Cornell Univ, PhD (phys chem), 1967. **Professional Experience:** HEAD MOLECULAR MODELING SECT & SR PRIN INVESTR, NAT CANCER INST, BETHESDA, MD, as of 2005; CHIEF, MOLECULAR MODELING SECT, NIH, BETHESDA, MD, 1991-; res chemist, Molecular Modeling Sect, NIH, Bethesda, MD, 1987-1991; expert, Molecular Modeling Sect, NIH, Bethesda, MD, 1980-1987; from asst prof to assoc prof chem, Univ Kans, 1970-1983; USPHS res fel, Yale Univ, 1969-1970. **Memberships:** Protein Soc; Biophys Soc. **Research Statement & Publications:** Biothermodynamics; computer modeling of biological macromolecules. **Mailing Address:** NIH Nat Cancer Inst, Lab Molecular Biol, Bldg 37 Rm 5120 37 Convent Dr MSC 4262, Bethesda, MD 20892-4292. **Fax:** 301-402-1344. **E-Mail:** bk@nih.gov

LEE, CATHERINE COYLE, BIOINORGANIC CHEMISTRY, CATALYSIS. **Personal Data:** b New York, NY, May 16, 1952; c 1. **Education:** Hunter Col, City Univ NY, BS, 1974; Calif Inst Technol, PhD (chem), 1978. **Professional Experience:** SR STAFF CHEMIST, EXXON RES & ENG, 1991-; PROJ LEADER, EXXON RES & ENG, 1990-; Alexander von Humboldt fel, 1984-1985; adj asst prof, Hunter Col, City Univ NY, 1981-1982; sr chemist, Exxon Res & Eng, 1980-1983 & 1983-1991; res chemist, Exxon Res & Eng, 1979-1980; Fel chem, Stanford Univ, 1977-1979; Res award, Sigma Xi, 1977. **Memberships:** Am Chem Soc. **Research Statement & Publications:** Bioinorganic chemistry with specific emphasis on the kinetics of metalloprotein reactions; preparation and characterization of transition metal-sulfur complexes as catalysts and lubricant additives. **Mailing Address:** Exxon Res & Eng, Rte 22 E, Annandale, NJ 08801.

LEE, CHARLES NORTHAM, ENGINEERING, FORESTRY. **Personal Data:** b Syracuse, NY, January 13, 1925; m 1952, c 4. **Education:** Syracuse Univ, BS, 1949, BCE, 1957, MCE, 1959. **Professional Experience:** PROF EMER, COL ENVIRON SCI & FORESTRY, STATE UNIV NY, as of 2004; prof forest eng, State Univ NY Col Environ Sci & Forestry, 1968-1995; DIR COMPUT CTR, COL ENVIRON SCI & FORESTRY, STATE UNIV NY, 1964-; assoc prof forest eng, State Univ NY Col Environ Sci & Forestry, 1964-1968; NSF fel Sci Fac MIT, 1963-1965; asst prof forest mgt, State Univ NY Col Environ Sci & Forestry, 1959-1963; consult geotech engr, 1957-; instr civil eng, Syracuse Univ, 1957-1959. **Memberships:** Am Soc Civil Engrs; Asn Comput Mach. **Research Statement & Publications:** Land locomotion under off-highway conditions; modulation techniques applied to roadway design; information coding content and transformations for analysis and design of engineering systems. **Mailing Address:** State Univ NY, Col Environ Sci & Forestry, 312 Bray Hall One Forestry Dr, Syracuse, NY 13210-2778. **Fax:** 315-470-6958. **E-Mail:** cnlee@suvm.edu

LEE, CHARLES RICHARD, SOIL CHEMISTRY, PLANT NUTRITION. **Personal Data:** b Tarrytown, NY, December 3, 1942; m 1965, Nancy Giles; c Laura A, Juliet M & Katherine A. **Education:** Univ Tampa, BS, 1964; Clemson Univ, MS, 1965, PhD (agron), 1968. **Honors & Awards:** US Army res & develop Achievement Award, US Army, 1983. **Professional Experience:** RES SOIL SCIENTIST, US ARMY CORPS ENGRS, ENVIRON LAB, WATERWAYS EXP STA, 1973-; Res scientist, Can Dept Agr, 1968-1973; Adj prof, Delta State Univ, Miss State Univ, Univ Miss & Univ Miss. **Memberships:** Am Soc Agron; Int Soc Soil Sci; Am Soc Agron; charter mem, fel Int Soc Soil Sci. **Research Statement & Publications:** Land treatment of wastewater; heavy metal uptake by marsh plants; soil fertility; minor elements; plant growth in high zinc, aluminum or manganese media; restoration of problem soil; environmental clean-up. **Mailing Address:** Environ Lab US Army Engr, Waterways Exp Sta 3909 Halls Ferry Rd, Vicksburg, MS 39180-0631. **Fax:** 601-634-3120. **E-Mail:** leec@wes.army.mil

LEE, CHARLOTTE, BIOCHEMISTRY, ORGANIC CHEMISTRY. **Personal Data:** b Boligee, Ala, July 13, 1930. **Education:** Knoxville Col, BS, 1953; Tuskegee Univ, MS, 1955; Univ Kans, PhD (biochem), 1959. **Professional Experience:** CHAIRPERSON SCI DEPT, TRITON COL, 1991-; INSTR CHEM, TRITON COL, 1979-; assoc prof, Southern Ill Univ, Edwardsville, 1971-1978; Asst prof chem, Nassau Community Col, 1970-1971. **Memberships:** Am Chem Soc; Nat Asn Advan Colored People. **Mailing Address:** 10214 S 84th Ter, Palos Hills, IL 60465-1374.

LEE, CHE-HUNG R, METABOLISM. **Professional Experience:** CTR BIOLOGICS EVAL & RES, FOOD & DRUG ADMIN, as of 2003; prin investr, metab res div, Naval Med Res Inst, beginning 1984. **Mailing Address:** Ctr Biologics Eval & Res, Food & Drug Admin, Bethesda, MD 20889.

LEE, CHEN HUI, FORESTRY. **Personal Data:** b Taipei, Taiwan, December 2, 1929; m 1962, c 2. **Education:** Nat Taiwan Univ, BS, 1953; Mich State Univ, MS, 1960, PhD (forestry), 1966. **Honors & Awards:** Sigma Xi Spec Sci Res Award, Univ Wis, Stevene Point Club, 1993. **Professional Experience:** PROF FORESTRY, UNIV WIS-STEVENS POINT, 1977-; US Forest Serv res grants, 1977 & 1979; from asst prof to assoc prof, Univ Wis-stevens Point, 1966-1977; res asst, Mich State Univ, 1962-1966; instr, Nat Taiwan Univ, 1959-1962; asst, Nat Taiwan Univ, 1954-1959. **Memberships:** Soc Am Foresters; Chinese Soc Forestry; Japanese Forestry Soc; Sigma Xi. **Research Statement & Publications:** Forest genetics and tree improvement, especially tree physiology, pine leaf anatomy and wood quality. **Mailing Address:** Col Natural Res, Univ Wis, Rm 0362A, Stevens Point, WI 54481. **E-Mail:** clee@uwsp.edu

LEE, CHENG-SHENG, AQUACULTURE & MARICULTURE, REPRODUCTIVE PHYSIOLOGY. **Personal Data:** American citizen. **Education:** Nat Taiwan Univ, BS, 1970, MS, 1972; Univ Tokyo, PhD (aquacult), 1979. **Professional Experience:** DIR, CTR TROP & SUBTROP AQUACULTURE, OCEANIC INST, 1997-; SCI DIR, FINFISH & ASIA PROG, OCEANIC INST, 1997-; asst vpres, Oceanic Inst, 1992-1996; FINFISH PROG MGR, OCEANIC INST, 1984-; shrimp prog mgr, Oceanic Inst, 1981-1984; Res assoc, Oceanic Inst, 1979-1981; Aquatic biologist, Tungkang Marine Lab, 1973-1976. **Memberships:** World Aquacult Soc; Asian Fisheries Soc; Am Fisheries Soc. **Research Statement & Publications:** Induction of maturation and spawning of marine finfish; evaluating optimal environment conditions for food organisms and early life stages of finfish. **Mailing Address:** Oceanic Inst, 41-202 Kalanianole Hwy, Waimanalo, HI 96795. **Fax:** 808-259-5971. **E-Mail:** cslee@oceanicinstitute.org

LEE, CHEUK MAN, ORGANIC CHEMISTRY, PHARMACEUTICAL CHEMISTRY. **Personal Data:** b China, February 22, 1929; c 2. **Education:** Univ Hong Kong, BSc, 1954, MSc, 1957; Univ Mich, PhD (pharmaceut chem), 1960. **Professional Experience:** ASSOC RES FEL, ABBOTT LABS, 1960-. **Memberships:** Am Chem Soc. **Research Statement & Publications:** Synthesis of organic compounds of biological activities; heterocyclic chemistry; anti-biotics. **Mailing Address:** 504 W Golf Rd, Libertyville, IL 60048-3516.

LEE, C(HIA) H(UAN), ELECTRICAL ENGINEERING. **Personal Data:** b China, October 1, 1919; m 1953, c 4. **Education:** Chiao Tung Univ, China, BS, 1942; Cornell Univ, MS, 1949, PhD (elec eng), 1951. **Honors & Awards:** Cert Recognition, NASA, 1973. **Professional Experience:** ENG CONSULT, AIRESEARCH MFG CO, 1983-; sr engr specialist, Airesearch Mfg CO, 1964-1982; fel engr, Westinghouse Elec Corp, 1958-1964; asst prof elec eng, Polytech Inst Brooklyn, 1955-1958; develop engr, Reliance Elec & Eng Co, Ohio, 1951-1955; distrib engr, Canton Power Co, 1947-1948; Design engr, Cent Elec Mfg Works, China, 1942-1947. **Memberships:** Inst Elec & Electronics Engrs; Am Soc Naval Engrs; China Elec Eng Soc. **Research Statement & Publications:** Electric machinery; electric power systems; electromagnetic devices; electronic components; circuit theory; land, sea and air transportation; electronic power converter; control systems. **Mailing Address:** 30584 Ganado Dr, Rancho Palos Verdes, CA 90275-6222.

LEE, CHI-HANG, NATURAL PRODUCTS CHEMISTRY, FOOD SCIENCE. **Personal Data:** b Vinh Long, South Vietnam, January 1, 1939; American citizen; m 1964, c 2. **Education:** Southern Ill Univ, Carbondale, BA, 1960; Rutgers Univ, New Brunswick, PhD (natural prod chem), 1966. **Honors & Awards:** Chairman's Award, Gen Foods Corp, 1977; Agr Comn Appreciation Award, Taiwan, Rep China, 1989. **Professional Experience:** RETIRED; dir analytical serv, Del Monte Corp, 1988-1996; chem dir, Del Monte Corp, 1985-1987; biochem mgr, Del Monte Corp, 1980-1985; sr res scientist, RJR Foods, 1978-1980; mem, Adv Comt, Econ Affairs, Repub China, 1977-1989; Vis prof, King's Col, 1973-1977; from res specialist to sr res specialist, Gen Foods Corp, 1972-1978; sr chemist, Gen Foods Corp, 1967-1971; res assoc, Rutgers Univ, 1966; Res asst, Rutgers Univ, 1961-1965. **Memberships:** Am Chem Soc; Am Sci Affil (pres, 1982). **Research Statement & Publications:** Carbohydrates; flavors; sweeteners; food chemistry, biochemistry and chemical analysis. **Mailing Address:** Del Monte Corp Res Ctr, 205 N Wiget Lane, Walnut Creek, CA 94598.

LEE, CHI-HO, PHARMACOLOGY. **Personal Data:** b Taitung, Taiwan, July 2, 1941; American citizen; m 1972, Chin-Chin Kao; c Roger. **Education:** Kaohsiung Med Col, Taiwan, BS, 1967; Univ Tokyo, MS, 1972; Sch Med Sci, Cornell Univ, PhD (pharmacol), 1976. **Professional Experience:** RES SCIENTIST, SYNTEX RES, as of 2004; STAFF RESEARCHER II, CARDIOVASC PHARMACOL, SYNTEX RES, 1981-; staff researcher I, Cardiovasc Pharmacol, Syntex Res, 1979-1981; fel, Cardiovasc Pharmacol, Syntex Res, 1978-1979; Fel pharmacol, Roche Inst Molecular Biol, 1975-1976 & Med Col, Cornell Univ, 1976-1978; mem, Am Heart Asn, High Blood Pressure Coun. **Memberships:** AAAS; Western Pharmacol Soc; Am Soc Hypertension; Int Soc Heart Res. **Research Statement & Publications:** Cardiovascular pharmacology; antihypertensive drugs; evaluation of drug mechanisms; cerebral and peripheral blood vessels; heart; hemodynamics. **Mailing Address:** Inst Pharmacol, Syntex Discovery Res, Palo Alto, CA 94304. **Fax:** 650-354-7400.

LEE, CHI-JEN, BIOCHEMICAL BASIS ON IMMUNOGENICITY OF BACTERIAL POLYSACCHARIDES, BACTERIAL POLYSACCHARIDE VACCINES. **Personal Data:** b Yi-Lan, Taiwan, February 8, 1936; American citizen; m 1960, Sue-Yuan; c Johns, Lucia & Benjamin. **Education:** Nat Taiwan Univ, BS, 1957; Johns Hopkins Univ, ScD, 1966. **Professional Experience:** Referee, CRC Press, Inc, Boca Raton, Fla, 1988; vis prof, Dept Biochem, Col Med, Nat Cheng Kung Univ, 1984; thesis dir, Dept Microbiol, Med Ctr, George Wash Univ, 1983-1984 & 1987-; mem bd adv, Dept Biochem, Col Med, Nat Cheng Kung Univ, 1983-1984; mem bd dirs, Chinese Med & Health Asn, Wash, DC, 1980; chmn, 3rd Pneumococcal Workshop, Food & Drug Admin, Bethesda, Md, 1979; mem, Nat Reconstruct Comt Med & Health, 1978; SUPVRY RES CHEMIST, CTR BIOLOGICS, FOOD & DRUG ADMIN, 1974-; sr staff fel, Nat Inst Child Health & Human Develop, NIH, Bethesda, Md, 1973-1974; asst prof, Rockefeller Univ, New York City, 1968-1973; res assoc, Rockefeller Univ, New York City, 1967-1968; res assoc, Dept Biochem, Johns Hopkins Univ, 1966-1967; pharmacist, China Chem & Pharmaceut Co, Taiwan, 1959-1962; chmn, Polysaccharide Vaccine Comt, Food & Drug Admin, Bethesda, Md. **Memberships:** Am Asn Immunologists; Am Soc Biol Chemists. **Research Statement & Publications:** Characterization of group 19 pneumolysins and cloning of their ply genes have been studied to examine the relationship of ply to virulence; inactivated pneumolysin is conjugated to pneumococcal polysaccharide to form a polysaccharide-protein conjugate to develop a more effective pneumococcal vaccine. **Mailing Address:** US Food & Drug Admin, 5600 Fishers Lane, Rockville, MD 20857-0001.

LEE, CHIN C, ELECTRICAL ENGINEERING. **Personal Data:** b Taiwan, American citizen. **Education:** Nat Chiao-Tung Univ, BS, 1970, MS, 1973; Carnegie Mellon Univ, PhD, 1979. **Professional Experience:** PROF, DEPT ELEC ENG & COMPUT SCI, UNIV CALIF, IRVINE, 1994-; from asst to assoc prof, Dept Elec Eng, Univ Calif, Irvine, 1984-1993; res specialist, Dept Elec Eng, Univ Calif, Irvine, 1980-1983; res assoc, Carnegie-Mellon Univ, 1979-1980. **Memberships:** Inst Elec & Electronics Engrs. **Mailing Address:** Dept Elec & Computer Eng, Henry Samueli Sch Eng, Univ Calif, EG 2226, Irvine, CA 92717. **Fax:** 949-824-3732. **E-Mail:** cclee@uci.edu

LEE, CHIN OK, CARDIAC ELECTROPHYSIOLOGY. **Personal Data:** b Choong-buk, Korea, June 8, 1939; American citizen; m 1969, c 2. **Education:** Seoul Nat Univ, BS, 1965, MS, 1967; Ind Univ, PhD (physiol), 1973. **Honors & Awards:** Louis N Katz Basic Sci Res Prize, 1974; Pfizer Award Outstanding Res, 1986. **Professional Experience:** PROF & CHMN, DEPT LIFE SCI, POHANG UNIV SCI & TECHNOL, as of 2003; Adj prof med, Gatsby Lab, Rockfeller Univ, 1998-; Adj prof med, Cornell Univ, 1993-; Overseas vis fel, Brit Heart Found, 1990; mem, res peer rev comt, NY Heart Asn, 1988-; vis prof, Nat Defense Med Ctr, Taipei, Repub China, 1988; prof cardiac electrophysiol, Cornell Univ Med Campus, beginning 1986; adv consult, Site Visit, NIH, 1980; from asst prof to assoc prof, Cornell Univ Med Campus, 1976-1986; fel cardiac electrophysiol, Univ Chicago, 1972-1976; Res fel biochem, Atomic Energy Res Inst, 1967-1968; Estab investr, Am Heart Asn. **Memberships:** Am Physiol Soc; Biophys Soc; NY Acad Sci; AAAS. **Research Statement & Publications:** Cardiac cellular electophysiology; regulation of intracellular Na and Ca ions in heart muscle; intracellular application of ion-selective microelectrodes, intracellular application of ion sensitive dyes. **Mailing Address:** Dept Life Sci, Pohang Univ Sci & Technol, San 31 Hyojadong, Pohang Kyungbuk, Korea. **E-Mail:** colee@vision.postech.ac.kr

LEE, CHIN-CHIU, MICROBIOLOGY, ELECTRON MICROSCOPY. **Personal Data:** b Hunan, China, August 10, 1934; m 1964, c 1. **Education:** Taiwan Norm Univ, BSc, 1955; Loyola Univ, MS, 1964; La State Univ, PhD (parasitol), 1968. **Professional Experience:** RETIRED; chmn dept, King's Col, Pa, 1977-1991; assoc prof biol, King's Col, Pa, 1968-1991; res assoc parasitol, La State Univ, 1964; res technologist biochem, La State Univ, 1963; asst instr biol, Nanyang Univ, 1959-1961; asst instr biol, Taiwan Norm Univ, 1958-1959; biol teacher, High Sch, Taiwan, 1956-1958; biol teacher, Taiwan Prov Agr Sch, 1955-1956. **Memberships:** Am Soc Parasitol; Electron Micros Soc Am; AAAS. **Research Statement & Publications:** Medical parasitology; studies on the physiological and ultrastructural aspects of parasites, particularly of parasitic nematodes. **Mailing Address:** 29 Maple Dr, Swoyersville, PA 18704.

LEE, CHING TSUNG, QUANTUM OPTICS, MATHEMATICAL PHYSICS. **Personal Data:** b Taiwan, July 1, 1937; m 1967, c 2. **Education:** Nat Taiwan Univ, BS, 1962; Rice Univ, MA, 1965, PhD (physics), 1967. **Professional Experience:** PROF EMER PHYSICS, ALA A&M UNIV, 1973-; assoc prof, Ala A&M Univ, 1969-1973; NASA fel, Rice Univ, 1968-1969; welch found fel, Tex A&M Univ, 1967-1968. **Memberships:** Am Phys Soc; Optical Soc Am. **Research Statement & Publications:** Superradiance; free-electron laser; squeezed states. **Mailing Address:** Dept Physics, Ala A&M Univ, 121 V M Chambers Bldg, PO Box 285, Normal, AL 35762-0285. **E-Mail:** lee@lee.physics.aamu.edu

LEE, CHING-TSE, ANIMAL BEHAVIOR, BEHAVIOR MEDICINE. **Personal Data:** b Sinchu, Taiwan, China, May 21, 1940; m 1969, c 2. **Education:** Nat Taiwan Univ, BS, 1963; Bowling Green State Univ, MA, 1967, PhD (psychol), 1969. **Honors & Awards:** Nat Sci Coun Award, 1979 & 1980. **Professional Experience:** PROF PSYCHOL, BROOKLYN COL, CITY UNIV NEW YORK, 1982-; fel, Dept Health Educ & Welfare, 1974; from asst prof to assoc prof, Brooklyn Col, City Univ New York, 1971-1982; fac res award, City Univ New York, 1971, 1973, 1974; fac assoc psychol, Univ Tex-Austin, 1969-1971. **Memberships:** Animal Behav Soc; Am Psychol Asn; AAAS; Behav Genetics Asn. **Research Statement & Publications:** Investigation of animal communication processes through olfaction and hormonal determinants of the production of olfactory signals; effects of neonatal hormones on behavioral differentation; mathematical models applied to animal behavior; biofeedback and behavior medicine; Chinese medicine theories; states of consciousness. **Mailing Address:** Dept Psychol, Brooklyn Col City Univ New York, 4405 James Hall 2901 Bedford Ave, Brooklyn, NY 11210-2813. **E-Mail:** clee@brooklyn.cuny.edu

LEE, CHING-WEN, ENGINEERING MECHANICS, SOLID MECHANICS. **Personal Data:** b Yunnan, China, November 19, 1921; American citizen; m 1951, c 1. **Education:** Nat Inst Technol, Chungking, China, BS, 1944; Ill Inst Technol, MS, 1956, PhD (mech), 1958. **Professional Experience:** EMER PROF ENG SCI & MECH, UNIV TENN, KNOXVILLE, 1966-; assoc prof, Univ Tenn, Knoxville, 1962-1966; asst prof eng mech, Case Inst Technol, 1960-1962; Staff mem, Res & Develop Lab, Int Bus Mach Corp, Endicott, NY, 1959-1960. **Memberships:** Am Soc Mech Engrs; Am Soc Eng Educ; Am Acad Mech. **Research Statement & Publications:** Mechanics of deformable solids; elasticity; plates and shells; thermal stresses. **Mailing Address:** 8300 Bennington Dr, Knoxville, TN 37909-2305. **E-Mail:** cwlee@utk.edu

LEE, CHI-YU GREGORY, EXPERIMENTAL BIOLOGY, OBSTETRICS & GYNECOLOGY. **Personal Data:** b Taiwan, China, April 19, 1945; American citizen; c 2. **Education:** Nat Taiwan Univ, China, BSc, 1967; Calif Inst Technol, MSc, 1971, PhD (chem), 1972. **Professional Experience:** PROF OBSTET & GYNEC, ACUTE CARE UNIT, UNIV BC, 1989-; mem, Task Force Vaccines Fertil Regulation, WHO, 1985-; DIR ANDROLOGY, ACUTE CARE UNIT, UNIV BC, 1981-; res asst prof, Dept Biochem, Univ NC, Chapel Hill, 1977-1981; sr staff fel, Lab Animal Genetics, Nat Inst Environ Health Sci, NIH, Res Triangle Park, NC, 1976-1981; vis prof, Chem Ctr, Univ Lund, Sweden, 1975; res chemist, Dept Chem, Univ Calif, San Diego, 1972-1975; consult, Beckman Instruments Inc. **Memberships:** Sigma Xi; AAAS; NY Acad Sci; Am Soc Biol Chemists; Soc Study Reproduction; Am Fertil Soc; Am Asn Clin Chem. **Research Statement & Publications:** Applications of biotechnology; sperm antigen-based immunocontraceptive vaccines; new tumor markers for early diagnosisand monitoring of cancer patients; monoclonal antibodies against human proteins-hormones and clinical applications. **Mailing Address:** Andrology Lab, Vancouver Hosp, Univ BC, 2211 Westbrook Mall, Vancouver, BC V6T 2B5, Can. **Fax:** 604-822-7675. **E-Mail:** andr@interchange.ubc.ca

LEE, CHONG SUNG, MOLECULAR BIOLOGY. **Personal Data:** b Seoul, Korea, September 4, 1939; American citizen; m 1972, Jacqueline; c Christopher & Jennifer. **Education:** Seoul Nat Univ, BS, 1964; Calif Inst Technol, PhD (chem), 1970. **Professional Experience:** Vis assoc prof, Harvard Med Sch, 1982-1983; ASSOC PROF MOLECULAR GENETICS, UNIV TEX, AUSTIN, 1978-; asst prof, Univ Tex, Austin, 1972-1978; Jane Coffin Childs Mem Fund for Med Res fel, 1970-1972; fel biochem, Harvard Med Sch, 1969-1972; grad res asst biophys, Calif Inst Technol, 1965-1969. **Memberships:** Genetics Soc Am; Am Soc Cell Biol; Am Soc Biochem & Molecular Biol; Korean Chem Soc. **Research Statement & Publications:** Molecular genetics of the rosy locus in Drosophila melanogaster. **Mailing Address:** Dept Zool, Univ Tex, Austin, TX 78712.

LEE, CHOONG WOONG, TELECOMMUNICATION SYSTEMS, EDTV & HDTV SIGNAL PROCESSING. **Personal Data:** b Pyunganpuk-Do, Korea, May 3, 1935; m 1964, c 4. **Education:** Seoul Nat Univ, BS, 1958, MS, 1960; Univ Tokyo, Dr Eng, 1972. **Honors & Awards:** Dongbaik Order of Merit. **Professional Experience:** Trustee, Korea Telecommun, 1991; pres, Korean Soc Med & Biol Eng, 1988 & Korean Inst Telematics & Electronics Engrs, 1989; chmn, Bd Utilization Radio Waves, Ministry Commun, Korea, 1986-1989; PROF, DEPT ELECTRONICS ENG, SEOUL NAT UNIV, 1981-; from asst prof to assoc prof, Dept Electronics Eng, 1971-1981; vis res fel, Dept Elec Eng, Univ Sydney, 1963 & Univ Tokyo, 1969-1971; Lectr, Dept Electronics Eng, 1964-1971; Res assoc, Commun Systs Lab, Nat Res Inst Defense, Korea, 1958-1964. **Memberships:** Fel Inst Elec & Electronics Engrs; Inst Electronics, Info & Commun Engrs Japan; Korean Inst Telematics & Electronics. **Research Statement & Publications:** Communication systems especially wide band am, fm demodulators; edtv and hdtv signal processing; medical electronics. **Mailing Address:** Seoul Nat Univ Sch of Elec Eng Office 301, 902, San 56-1 Shinlim d ong Kwanak-ku, Seoul 151742, South Korea. **Fax:** 822-875-5346. **E-Mail:** cwl@white.snu.ac.kr

LEE, CHOUNG MOOK, FLUID MECHANICS, OCEAN ENGINEERING. **Personal Data:** b Pyungtek, Korea, October 3, 1935; m 1965, c 2. **Education:** Seoul Nat Univ, BS, 1958; Univ NDak, BS, 1961; Univ Calif, Berkeley, MEng, 1963, PhD (naval archit), 1966. **Honors & Awards:** Linnard Prize, Soc Naval Architechts & Marine Engrs, 1975. **Professional Experience:** VPRES, POHANG INST SCI & TECHNOL, 1986-; sci officer fluid mech, Off Naval Res, 1982-1986; vpres, Korea Res Inst Ships, 1978-1979; Adj prof, George Washington Univ, 1972-1973; Res scientist hydrodyn, David Taylor Res Ctr, 1966-1982. **Memberships:** Soc Naval Architects & Marine Engrs; Am Soc Mech Engrs; Soc Naval Architects Japan; Sigma Xi. **Research Statement & Publications:** Theoretical, mumerical and experimental investigation of ship hydrodynamics; water waves; stability and dynamics of floating and submerged bodies; body-wave interactions; resistance of ships. **Mailing Address:** San 31 Hyojadong, Dept Mech Eng, Pohang 790-784, South Korea. **Fax:** 056-227-93199. **E-Mail:** cmlee@vision.postech.ac.kr

LEE, CHUAN-PU, BIOCHEMISTRY, PHYSICAL CHEMISTRY. **Personal Data:** b Tsing-Tao, China, September 24, 1931. **Education:** Nat Taiwan Univ, BS, 1954; Ore State Univ, PhD (biochem), 1961. **Honorary Degrees:** DPhil, Univ Stockholm, 1978. **Honors & Awards:** Silver Medal, Chinese Chem Soc, 1955; Merck Index Award, 1960. **Professional Experience:** DISTINGUISHED PROF BIOCHEM, SCH MED, WAYNE STATE UNIV, as of 2001; ed, Current Topics Bioenergetics, 1981-; prof biochem, sch med, Wayne State Univ, beginning 1975; ed, Biochimica et Biophysica Acta & Biochimica et Biophysica Acta Review on Bioenergetics, 1973-; from assoc prof to prof biochem, Johnson Found, Univ Pa, 1970-1975; USPHS career develop award, 1968-1973; mem staff, Johnson Found, Univ Pa, 1966-1975; docent, Wenner-Gren Inst, Stockholm, 1965-1966; Jane Coffin Childs Mem Fund Med Res fel physiol chem, Wenner-Gren Inst, Stockholm, 1963-1965; Johnson Found res fel, Univ Pa, 1961-1963; res assoc biochem, Ore State Univ, 1960-1961; instr chem, Nat Taiwan Univ, 1954-1956. **Memberships:** AAAS; Chinese Chem Soc; Am Soc Biol Chem; Biophys Soc; NY Acad Sci. **Research Statement & Publications:** Reaction mechanisms of electron and energy transfer in oxidative phosphorylation; neuromuscular diseases and mitochondrial metabolism. **Mailing Address:** Dept Biochem, Wayne State Univ Sch Med, Detroit, MI 48207-2803. **E-Mail:** cplee@wayne.edu

LEE, CHUNG, REPRODUCTIVE ENDOCRINOLOGY, NUTRITION. **Personal Data:** b Shanghai, China, September 18, 1936; American citizen; m 1965, c 2. **Education:** Nat Taiwan Univ, BS, 1959; WVa Univ, MS, 1966, PhD (nutrit & endocrinol), 1969. **Professional Experience:** JOHN T. GRAYHACK PROF UROL RES, NORTHWESTERN UNIV FEINBERG SCH MED, 1992-; Res consult, NuClin Diag, 1990; vis scholar, Vets Gen Hosp, Taipei, Taiwan, 1989; res consult, Lilly Res Labs, 1988-; pres, Chicago Chap, Soc Chinese Bioscientists Am, 1988-; mem, Cancer Prevention Comt, Ill Div, Am Cancer Soc, 1988-; treas & chair, Finance Comt, Soc Basic Urol Res, 1988-1990; PROF CELL & MOLECULAR & STRUCT BIOL, 1987-; Prin investr, Nat Inst Diabetes & Digestive & Kidney Dis grant, 1987-1992; PROF UROL, MED SCH, NORTHWESTERN UNIV, CHICAGO, 1985-; res consult, Upjohn Co, 1985; res consult, Travenol-Baxter, 1983-1986; Prin investr, Elsa Univ Pardee Found grant, 1982-1984; res consult, Abbott Labs, 1978-; Prin investr, Abbott Labs grant, 1978-1984; res consult, Matpath, 1978; Prin investr, Nat Inst Child Health & Human Develop, 1977-1991; lectr, Cook Col Grad Med Sch, 1977-1980; DIR, UROL RES LAB, 1974-; from asst prof to assoc prof, Urol Res Lab, 1974-1985; Prin investr, Am Cancer Soc grant, 1973-1974; assoc obstet & gynec, Urol Res Lab, 1971-1974; USPHS fel, Albany Med Col, 1969-1971. **Memberships:** Endocrine Soc; Soc Study Reproduction; Am Asn Cancer Res; Am Physiol Soc; Am Soc Cell Biol; Am Urol Asn; Nat Kidney Found. **Research Statement & Publications:** Hormonal regulation of breast and prostate cancer; mechanism of sex steroid action; cancer and hormones; protein analysis and indexing. **Mailing Address:** Feinberg Sch Med, Northwestern Univ, 303 E Chicago Ave, Tarry 16-703, Chicago, IL 60611-3008. **Fax:** 312-908-7275. **E-Mail:** c-lee7@northwestern.edu

LEE, CHUNG JA, NUTRITION. **Personal Data:** b Seoul, Korea, January 3, 1938. **Education:** Seoul Nat Univ, BS, 1961; Univ Mass, MS, 1968; Purdue Univ, PhD (human nutrit), 1970. **Professional Experience:** COMMUNITY RES SERV, KY STATE UNIV, as of 2002; PROG AREA COORDR HUMAN NUTRIT, DEPT HOME ECON, KY STATE UNIV, 1982-; PROF NUTRIT, DEPT HOME ECON, KY STATE UNIV, 1978-; from asst prof to assoc prof, Ky State Univ, 1970-1978. **Memberships:** Am Inst Nutrit; Am Dietetic Asn; Am Home Econ Asn. **Research Statement & Publications:** Nutrition. **Mailing Address:** Community Res Serv, Ky State Univ, FrankFt, KY 40601.

LEE, CHUNG N, MATHEMATICS. **Personal Data:** b Sinuiju, Korea, November 7, 1931. **Education:** Seoul Nat Univ, BA, 1954; Univ Va, MA, 1957, PhD, 1959. **Professional Experience:** EMER ASSOC PROF MATH, UNIV MICH, ANN ARBOR, 1968-; from instr to asst prof, Univ Mich, Ann Arbor, 1960-1968. **Memberships:** Am Math Soc. **Research Statement & Publications:** Algebraic topology; transformation groups; topology of manifolds. **Mailing Address:** Sci & Technol, Pohang Univ Kyung-Buk, Pohang 790-784, South Korea.

LEE, CINDY, ORGANIC GEOCHEMISTRY, MARINE CHEMISTRY. **Personal Data:** b Columbus, Ohio, February 10, 1950. **Education:** Ariz State Univ, BSE & BS, 1970; Univ Calif, PhD (oceanog), 1975. **Professional Experience:** Trustee, Bermuda Biol Sta Res, beginning 1995; guest prof, Max Planck Inst Marine Microbiol, Bremen, 1993-1994; Nat Res Coun scope, 1991-1993; chmn, Gordon Conf Chem Oceanog, 1991; PROF, STATE UNIV NY, STONY BROOK, 1990-; co-vchmn, Gordon Conf Chem Oceanog, beginning 1989; assoc prof, State Univ NY, Stony Brook, 1986-1990; assoc scientist, Woods Hole Oceanog Inst, 1981-1986; asst scientist, Woods Hole Oceanog Inst, 1977-1981; fel investr, Woods Hole Oceanog Inst, 1975-1977. **Memberships:** Geochem Soc; Am Soc Limnol & Oceanog; Am Geophys Union; Europ Asn Org Geochemists; AAAS; Oceanog Soc. **Research Statement & Publications:** Distribution and behavior of biogenic compounds in sediments and waters of open ocean and coastal areas, salt marshes, and lakes; rates and mechanisms of transformation reactions which occur as organic compounds are affected by biological, geological, and physical processes. **Mailing Address:** Marine Sci Res Ctr, State Univ NY, 109 Challenger Hall, Stony Brook, NY 11794-5000. **Fax:** 631-632-8820. **E-Mail:** cindy.lee@stonybrook.edu

LEE, DAEYONG, MECHANICAL & COMPUTER-AIDED ENGINEERING. **Personal Data:** b Ham Nam, Korea, June 16, 1933; American citizen; m 1962, Youngja; c 3. **Education:** Ripon Col, BA, 1958; Mass Inst Technol, BS, 1958, MS, 1962, ScD(metall), 1965. **Professional Experience:** PROF MECH ENG, RENSSELAER POLYTECH INST, TROY, NY, 1983-; adj prof, Rensselaer Polytech inst, Troy, 1981-1983; res staff, Gen Elec res & Develop Ctr, Schenectady, 1966-1983; staff mem, Mass inst Technol, 1965-1966; res asst metall, Mass inst Technol, 1961-1965; Mech Metall, Ladish Co, 1958-1960. **Memberships:** Am Inst Mining Metall & Petrol Engrs; Am Soc Metals; Am Soc Mech Eng; Am Deep Drawing Res; Soc Plastics Engrs. **Research Statement & Publications:** Mechanical metallurgy; plasticity theory, mechanics, constitutive equations, nuclear materials, fracture, friction and lubrication, materials processing; computer-aided engineering. **Mailing Address:** rensselaer polytech inst, 33 Cobble Hill Rd, Albany, NY 12211. **Fax:** 518-276-6025. **E-Mail:** leed@rpi.edu

LEE, DAH-YINN, CIVIL ENGINEERING, HIGHWAY MATERIALS. **Personal Data:** b Tsing-tao, China, June 4, 1934; m 1962, c 2. **Education:** Cheng Kung Univ, Taiwan, BSc, 1958; Iowa State Univ, PhD (civil eng), 1964. **Professional Experience:** PROF EMER CIVIL ENG, IOWA STATE UNIV, 1998-; prof civil eng, Iowa State Univ, 1978-1998; from asst prof to assoc prof, Iowa State Univ, 1965-1978; Res assoc, Eng Res Inst, 1964-1965; Comt mem, Hwy Res Bd, Nat Acad Sci-Nat Res Coun. **Memberships:** Am Soc Testing & Mat; Am Soc Civil Engrs; Am Concrete Inst. **Research Statement & Publications:** Asphalt durability; aggregates used for asphalt mixtures; waste materials in construction; pavement recycling; foamed asphalt; sulfur in construction. **Mailing Address:** Dept Civil Eng, Iowa State Univ, Ames, IA 50011-2010.

LEE, DAISY SI, PEDIATRICS, ALLERGY. **Personal Data:** b Peiping, China, July 21, 1934; American citizen; m 1966, Herbert; c Sharon & Melissa. **Education:** Okla Baptist Univ, BA, 1956; Bowman Gray Sch Med, MD, 1961; Am Bd Pediat, dipl; Am Bd Allergy & Immunol, dipl, 1975. **Professional Experience:** ASST CLIN PROF PEDIAT, MED CTR, UNIV ALA, BIRMINGHAM, 1976-; dir pediat allergy prog, Ctr Develop & Learning Dis, 1972-1976; asst prof, Ctr Develop & Learning Dis, 1969-1976; pediatrician, Ctr Develop & Learning Dis, 1969-1972; fel pediat, Sch Med, Stanford Univ, 1966-1969; fel, Inst Nutrit Sci, Columbia Univ & Dept Med, St Lukes Hosp Ctr, 1965-1966; resident pediat, NY Heart Asn fel med, 1964-1965; resident pediat, St Luke's Hosp Ctr, New York, 1962-1964; Intern med, Georgetown Div, Wash Gen Hosp, 1961-1962. **Memberships:** NY Acad Sci; Sigma Xi; Am Acad Allergy; Am Col Allergists. **Mailing Address:** 1025 S 18th St Ste 303, Birmingham, AL 35205. **Fax:** 205-933-8339.

LEE, DANIEL DIXON, ANIMAL NUTRITION. **Personal Data:** b Dillon, SC, September 27, 1935; m 1958, c 4. **Education:** Clemson Univ, BS, 1957, MS, 1964; NC State Univ, Raleigh, PhD (biochem & nutrit), 1970. **Professional Experience:** PROF EMER DAIRY SCI, CLEMSON UNIV, beginning 1991; head, Clemson Univ, 1987-1991; asst dean res, Sch Agr, 1976-1986; from asst prof to assoc prof mineral metab, Dept Animal Indust, Southern Ill Univ, 1970-1986; res supvr biochem, NC State Univ, 1967-1970. **Memberships:** Am Soc Animal Sci. **Research Statement & Publications:** Trace mineral metabolism; nonprotein nitrogen utilization; wintering of cattle on crop residues and feeding of recycled animal wastes to ruminants. **Mailing Address:** Dept Animal & Vet Sci, Clemson Univ 115 Poole Agr Ctr PO Box 340361, Clemson, SC 29634-0363.

LEE, DAVID ALLAN, APPLIED MATHEMATICS. **Personal Data:** b Ft Smith, Ark, November 7, 1937; m 1960, Shilah; c Jill & James. **Education:** Univ Mo, Columbia, BSEE, 1959; Brown Univ, ScM, 1961; Ill Inst Technol, PhD (mech), 1963. **Honors & Awards:** SES Meritorious Executive, 1991; Barchi Prize, 1995 DOD Medal for Distinguished Civilian Service, 1993. **Professional Experience:** SR RES FEL, LOGISTICS MGT INST, 1993-; dir, res & develop procuremen, Cost Analysis Div, Off Secy Defence, 1985-1993; sr exec fel, Sr Exec Fel Prog, J F Kennedy Sch, Harvard Univ, 1983; head, Dept Math & Comput Sci, USAF Inst Technol, 1975-1985; dir, Appl Math Res Lab, 1971-1975; vis prof, von Karman Inst Fluid Dynamics, Rhode-St-Genese, Belg, 1969-1970; res mathematician, Air Force Aerospace Res Labs, 1963-1971. **Memberships:** Ethnicity; Caucasian. **Research Statement & Publications:** Econometrics of forecasting development and procurement costs of major defense acquisitions; air traffic capacity modeling. **Mailing Address:** Logistics Mgmt Inst, 2000 Corporate Ridge, MClean, VA 22102-7805. **E-Mail:** dalee@lmi.org

LEE, DAVID ANSON, GLAUCOMA, OCULAR PHARMACOLOGY. **Personal Data:** b Pine Ridge, SDak, January 28, 1956; m 1990, Karen Q Cheng; c Scott K & Steven M. **Education:** Boston Univ, BA, 1980, MD, 1980; Univ Minn, Minneapolis, MS, 1984; Univ Calif, Los Angeles, MBA, 1993. **Honors & Awards:** Honor Award, Am Acad Ophthal, 1993. **Professional Experience:** PROF OPHTHAL, SCH MED, 1996-; Harvard Med Sch, 1992 & Univ Mich, 1993; CHIEF, GLAUCOMA DIV, JULES STEIN INST, UNIV CALIF, LOS ANGELES, 1990-; Univ Calif, Irvine, 1990; vis prof ophthal, Cleveland Clin & Baylor Col Med, 1989; vis prof ophthal, Univ Minn, 1988 & 1989; vis prof ophthal, Univ Calif, San Diego & Univ Pittsburg, 1987; from asst prof to assoc prof, Sch Med, 1986-1996; Judson Daland fel, Am Philos Soc, 1985-1987; asst ophthal, Mass Eye & Ear Infirmary, Harvard Univ, 1985-1986; fel, Heed Ophthalmic Found, 1984-1986; Glaucoma fel, Mass Eye & Ear Infirmary, Harvard Univ, Boston, 1984-1986; Internship & residency ophthal, Mayo Clin, Rochester, Minn, 1980-1984. **Memberships:** Fel Am Acad Ophthal; fel Am Col Surgeons; Soc Heed Fels; Am Col Physician Execs; Asn Res Vision & Ophthal; AAAS. **Research Statement & Publications:** Biochemistry, cell biology, and pharmacology of the ciliary body epithelium, trabecular meshwork, and aqueous humor of the eye; development and testing of new ocular drug delivery systems; modulating ocular wound healing. **Mailing Address:** Dept Ophthal, Col Med Hershey, Hershey, PA 17033.

LEE, DAVID CHARLES, MICROBIOLOGY, IMMUNOLOGY. **Personal Data:** b Manchester, Eng, June 10, 1950. **Education:** Stanford Univ, BS, 1973; Univ Wash, PhD (biochem), 1979. **Professional Experience:** PROF & CHMN BIOCHEM & BIOPHYS, UNIV NC, CHARLESTON, 1998-; Mem, Protein Eng & Molecular Genetics Prog, 1991-; assoc prof, Dept Microbiol & Immunol, 1991-1995; DIR, NUCLEIC ACID CORE FAC, LINEBERGER COMPREHENSIVE CANCER CTR, UNIV NC, CHAPEL HILL, 1989-; core mem, Cancer Cell Biol Prog, Lineberger Comprehensive Cancer Ctr, Univ NC, 1985-; asst prof, Dept Microbiol & Immunol, 1985-1991; sr scientist, Oncogen, Seattle, Wash, 1983-1985; res assoc, Dept Biol Chem, Wash Univ, 1983; Postdoctoral fel, Dept Pharmacol, 1981-1983; Helen Hay Whitney Found fel, 1980-1983; Postdoctoral fel, Dept Biol Chem, Wash Univ, 1979-1981. **Research Statement & Publications:** Regulation of transforming growth factors; immunoregulatory effects of the interferons; transgenic expression of TGFa and related growth factors. **Mailing Address:** Univ NC, 519 Mary Ellen Jones Bldg 231 CB# 7260, Chapel Hill, NC 27599-7295. **Fax:** 919-966-2852. **E-Mail:** dclee@med.unc.edu

LEE, DAVID K H, BIOCHEMISTRY. **Education:** McGill Univ, BS, 1969; Queen's Univ, PhD (biochem), 1973. **Professional Experience:** CHIEF SCIENTIFIC OFFICER, NOAB BIODISCOVERIES, 2001-; dir pharmacol, Allelix Biopharmaceut Inc, beginning 1996; mgr, Allelix Biopharmaceut Inc, 1993-1996; res mgr, Dept Biochem & Pharmacol, R W Johnson Pharmaceut Res Inst, 1989-1993; sect head, Wyeth-Ayerst Res, 1988-1989; group leader, Wyeth-Ayerst Res, 1986-1988; res assoc, Wyeth-Ayerst Res, 1980-1986; sr scientist, Wyeth-Ayerst Res, 1977-1980; assoc scientist, Royal Victoria Hosp, 1977; prof asst, McGill Univ, 1976-1977; Postdoctoral fel, McGill Univ, 1973-1976. **Memberships:** Am Soc Pharmacol & Exp Therapeut; NY Acad Sci; AAAS; Soc Neuroscience; Soc Exp Biol & Med. **Research Statement & Publications:** Focus on drug discovery activities including high throughput screens and functional assays; therapeutic areas include central nervous system, obesity and virology. **Mailing Address:** NoAb BioDiscoveries Inc, 2820 Argentia Rd, Unit 8, Mississauga, ON L5N 8G4, Can. **Fax:** 905-814-5241. **E-Mail:** dkhlee@noabbiodiscoveries.com

LEE, DAVID LOUIS, CHEMISTRY. **Personal Data:** b Oakland, Calif, October 19, 1948; m 1975, c 2. **Education:** Univ Calif, Berkeley, BS, 1970, PhD (chem), 1976; Univ Ill, Urbana, MS, 1972. **Professional Experience:** GROUP SUPVR, ICI AMERICAS, 1987-; group supvr, Stauffer Chem Co, 1985-1987; sr res chemist, Stauffer Chem Co, 1983-1984; res chemist, Stauffer Chem Co, 1980-1982; sr chemist, Cordova Chem Co, 1977-1980; Res assoc chem, Univ Calif, San Francisco, 1976-1977. **Memberships:** Am Chem

Soc. **Research Statement & Publications:** Defining the structure-activity space of new classes of herbicides. **Mailing Address:** Zeneca, 1200 S 47th St, Richmond, CA 94804-4610.

LEE, DAVID MALLIN, EXPERIMENTAL NUCLEAR PHYSICS, NUCLEAR SAFEGUARDS. **Personal Data:** b Brooklyn, NY, January 18, 1944; m 1966, c 5. **Education:** Manhattan Col, BS, 1966; Univ Va, PhD (physics), 1971. **Professional Experience:** US expert, Int Atomic Energy Agency, 1980-1981; MEM STAFF, LOS ALAMOS NAT LAB, 1974-; res assoc physics, Univ Va, 1971-1974. **Memberships:** Am Phys Soc; Sigma Xi. **Research Statement & Publications:** Medium energy nuclear physics; position sensitive detectors; beam line instrumentation. **Mailing Address:** Los Alamos Nat Lab, PO Box 1663, Los Alamos, NM 87545. **Fax:** 505-665-7920. **E-Mail:** dlee@lanl.gov

LEE, DAVID MORRIS, PHYSICS. **Personal Data:** b Rye, NY, January 20, 1931; m 1960, Dana; c Eric B & James M. **Education:** Harvard Univ, AB, 1952; Univ Conn, MS, 1955; Yale Univ, PhD (physics), 1959. **Honors & Awards:** Nobel Prize in Physics, 1996; Sir Francis Simon Mem Prize, Brit Inst Physics, 1976; Oliver Buckley Prize, Am Phys Soc, 1981. **Professional Experience:** JAMES G WHITE DISTINGUISHED PROF PHYS SCI, CORNELL UNIV, 1999-; Joseph Fourier Univ, France, 1994-; chmn, Nat Res Coun Comt Fundamental Constants & Stand, 1990-1993; Sect B Electorate Nominating Comt, AAAS, 1990-1993; Univ Calif, San Diego, 1988; lectr, Peking Univ, 1981; Japan Soc Prom Sci fel, 1977; vis prof, Univ Fla, 1974-1975 & 1994; prof physics, Cornell Univ, 1969-1999; Guggenheim fel, 1966-1967 & 1974-1975; guest assoc physicist, Brookhaven Nat Lab, 1966-1967; from instr to assoc prof, Cornell Univ, 1959-1968. **Memberships:** Nat Acad Sci; fel Am Acad Arts & Sci; fel AAAS; fel Am Phys Soc. **Research Statement & Publications:** Low temperature physics with emphasis on quantum fluids and solids, and superconductivity; solid helium three and solid helium four; normal and superfluid phases of liquid helium three; spin polarized hydrogen gas; liquid helium three helium four mixtures; magnetic resonance; ultrasonics; magnetism. **Mailing Address:** Lab Atomic & Solid Physics, Cornell Univ, 610 Clark Hall, Ithaca, NY 14853-2501. **Fax:** 607-255-6428. **E-Mail:** dml20@cornell.edu

LEE, DAVID OI, HEAT TRANSFER, ELECTRO MAGNETIC-SEISMIC GEOPHYSICS. **Personal Data:** b Hong Kong, China, February 5, 1940; American citizen; div, c Andrea. **Education:** Tex A&M Univ, BS, 1962, MS, 1964. **Professional Experience:** SR MEM TECH STAFF, SANDIA NAT LABS, 1990-; Mem tech staff, Sandia Nat Labs, 1967-1990; Mem, Subcomt Nuclear Qual Assurance, Am Soch Mech Engrs; vchmn, Subcomt Environ Res & Develop & Energy & Environ Qual Div, Am Soc Qual Control. **Memberships:** Soc Petrol Engrs; Sigma Xi; Am Soc Mech Engrs; Am Soc Qual Control. **Research Statement & Publications:** Heat transfer and fluid mechanics experimental and analytical research; system analysis including economic analysis of solar systems; instrumentation development for enhanced oil recovery; development of seismic tehniques for small event detection; development of electromagnetic techniques for sensing of tunnels and contamination plumes; quality assurance. **Mailing Address:** 12709 Northern Sky NE, Albuquerque, NM 87111.

LEE, DAVID ROBERT, HYDROLOGY, RADIOECOLOGY. **Personal Data:** b Grand Forks, NDak, May 9, 1945; m 1975, c 5. **Education:** Univ NDak, BS, 1968, MS, 1972; Va Polytech Inst & State Univ, PhD (zoology), 1976. **Professional Experience:** RES OFFICER HYDROL & RADIOECOL, ATOMIC ENERGY CAN, CHALK RIVER, ONT, 1979-as of today; adj prof, Dept Earth Sci, Univ Waterloo, Ont, 1979-; res asst prof earth sci & biol, Univ Waterloo, 1976-1979. **Memberships:** Am Geophys Union; Am Soc Limnol & Oceanog. **Research Statement & Publications:** Groundwater contaminant flux to surface waters; soil and groundwater remediation. **Mailing Address:** Environ Res Br, Atomic Energy Ca Ltd, Chalk River Labs, Chalk River, ON K0J 1J0, Can. **Fax:** 613-584-1350. **E-Mail:** leed@aecl.ca

LEE, DAVID WEBSTER, PLANT EVOLUTION, PLANT STRUCTURE & FUNCTION. **Personal Data:** b Wenatchee, Wash, December 10, 1942; m 1972, Carol Rotsinger; c Sylvia & Katherine. **Education:** Pac Lutheran Univ, BS, 1966; Rutgers Univ, MS, 1968, PhD (bot), 1970. **Professional Experience:** PROF, DEPT BIOL SCI & ENVIRON STUDIES, FLA INT UNIV, as of 2003; Indo-Am fel, 1984-1985; assoc prof, Dept Biol Sci, Fla Int Univ, beginning 1982; asst prof, Fla Int Univ, 1980-1982; maite Del conf assoc, Univ Montpellier II, 1977-1978; lectr, Univ Malaya, Kuala Lumpur, 1973-1976; Res assoc bot & microbiol, Ohio State Univ, 1970-1972; field res, Cent Am & Southeast Asia. **Memberships:** Am Bot Soc; Soc Trop Biol; Ecol Soc Am; Sigma Xi. **Research Statement & Publications:** Evolution and adaptation of plants in humid tropical forests. **Mailing Address:** Dept Biol Sci, Fla Int Univ, Miami, FL 33199. **Fax:** 305-348-1986. **E-Mail:** leed@fiu.edu

LEE, DAVID YUE-WEI, ORGANIC CHEMISTRY, MEDICINAL CHEMISTRY. **Personal Data:** b San-Tung, China, March 9, 1946; m 1972, c 3. **Education:** Calif State Univ, Sacramento, MS, 1973; Columbia Univ, MS, 1975, PhD (chem), 1978. **Professional Experience:** DIR BIOORGANIC & NATURAL PROD LAB, MC LEAN HOSP, as of 2005; ASSOC PROF, HARVARD MED SCH, as of 2003; sr res chemist synthesis, Res Triangle Inst, beginning 1978; res grad asst, Columbia Univ, 1974-1978. **Memberships:** Am Chem Soc. **Research Statement & Publications:** Synthesis of steroidal hormone for contraceptive purpose; isolation and structure determination of medicinal component from natural resources; countercurrent chromatography and its applications in natural products and recombinant protein research; isolation of bio-active components from Chinese herbal medicine. **Mailing Address:** Mc Lean Hosp, 15 Mill St, Belmont, MA 02478. **E-Mail:** dlee@mclean.harvard.edu

LEE, DER-TSAI, COMPUTER SCIENCE, COMPUTATIONAL GEOMETRY. **Personal Data:** b Taipei, Taiwan, April 5, 1949; American citizen; m 1974, c 2. **Education:** Univ Ill, Urbana-Champaign, (comput science), PhD, 1978; Univ Ill, Urbana-Champaign, MS, 1976; Nat Taiwan Univ, BS, 1971. **Honors & Awards:** Honorary Medal, Inst Information & Computing Machinery, 2002; Outstanding Res Award, Pan Wen-Yuan Found, 2001. **Professional Experience:** PROF COMPUT SCIENCE, NAT TAIWAN UNIV, 2000-; DISTING RES FEL, ACADEMIA SINICA, 1998-; prog dir, Nat Science Found, 1989-1990; consult, IBM T.J. Watson Res Ctr, 1985; prof comput science, Northwestern Univ, 1978-1998. **Memberships:** Inst Elec & Electronics Engrs, fel; Asn Computing Machinery, fel. **Research Statement & Publications:** Algorithms; computational geometry; VLSI systems; web-based computing, digital libraries, intelligent transportation systems; bioinformatics. **E-Mail:** dtlee@ieee.org

LEE, DIANA MANG, LIPOPROTEINS. **Personal Data:** b Mukden, China, American citizen; m 1960, Fu Chu; c Amy J. **Education:** Nat Taiwan Univ, BS, 1955; Utah State Univ, MS, 1960; Univ Okla, PhD (biochem), 1967. **Professional Experience:** Consultant, lab of lipids&liporoteins, Oklahoma Med Res found, 1994-; RES ASSOC PROF, RES DIV WOMEN'S HEALTH DEPT OBSTET/GYNEC, HEALTH SCI CTR, UNIV OKLA, 1994-; assoc mem, Free Radical Biol & Aging Res Prog, 1992-1994; mem, arteriosclerosis hypertension & lipid metab adv comt, Nat Heart Lung & Blood Inst, NIH, 1992-1993; consult, NIH, 1979-1981; reviewer, Biochem & Biophys Act, 1977-1983, 1987-; assoc prof biochem, Sch Med, Univ Okla, 1976-1993; assoc ed, Artery, 1975-; assoc mem lipoproteins, Okla Med Res Found, 1975-1992; mem, Coun Arteriosclerosis, Credential Comt, Am Heart Asn, 1973-1975; asst prof, Dept Biochem, Sch Med, Univ Okla, 1972-1976; NIH grant awardee, 1971-; asst mem, Okla Med Res Found, 1971-1975; Res assoc, Dept Biochem, Sch Med, Univ Okla, 1968-1971; sr investr, Okla Med Res Found, 1967-1971; trainee lipoproteins, Presby-St Luke's Hosp, 1964-1967; supvr chem, Presby-St Luke's Hosp, 1961-1964; univ asst chem eng, Nat Taiwan Univ, 1957; Chemist analytical chem, Yung-Kang Cement Corp, 1955-1957; editor of biochem et biophys acta, 1984-1987; Guest editor of progress in lipia res, 1990-1991; numerous grants awarded. **Memberships:** Am Chem Soc; Sigma Xi; AAAS; Am Oil Chemists Soc; NY Acad Sci; Am Soc Biol Chemists; Am Heart Asn. **Research Statement & Publications:** Structural aspects of human plasma lipoproteins and apolipoproteins, particularly in low density lipoproteins and apolipoprotein B; lipid peroxidation; antioxidants; estrogen and a n tiathe r osclerosis; lipolysis in renal insufficiency; cholesterol ester transfer protein and anheroselerosis. **Mailing Address:** OUHSC & Okla Medical Res Found, 825 NE 13th St, Oklahoma City, OK 73104.

LEE, DO IK, LATEX TECHNOLOGY, COATINGS TECHNOLOGY. **Personal Data:** b Chinnampo, Korea, March 6, 1937; American citizen; m 1970, Ilhae; c Albert Kimin Lee. **Education:** Seoul Nat Univ, BS, 1959; Columbia Univ, MS, 1964, EngScD(chem eng), 1967. **Honors & Awards:** Coating & Graphic Arts Div Award, Tech Asn Pulp & Paper Indust & Charles W Engelhard Medallion, 1986; Midland Sect Award, Am Chem Soc, 1989; Fel Tech Asn Pulp & Paper Indust, 1991; Fire of Genius, The Saginaw Valley Patent Law Association, 1992; Distinguished Service Award, Korea Tech Asn Pulp & Paper Indust, 2003. **Professional Experience:** ADJ PROF, DEPT PAPER ENG, CHEM ENG & IMAGING, COL ENG & APPL SCI, WESTERN MICH UNIV, as of 1997; chmn, Gordon Res Conf, Polymer Colloids, 2001; sr scientist, Dow Chem Co, 1997-2002; res scientist, Dow Chem USA, 1988-1996; sr assoc scientist, Dow Chem USA, 1982-1988; assoc scientist, Dow Chem USA, 1979-1982; sr res specialist, Dow Chem USA, 1975-1979; res specialist, Dow Chem USA, 1972-1975; res chem engr, Dow Chem USA, 1967-1972; res asst, Chem Eng Dept, Columbia Univ, 1962-1967; Meteorol officer, Korean Air Force, 1958-1961. **Memberships:** Fel Tech Asn Pulp & Paper Indust; Korea Tech Asn Pulp & Paper Indust; Korean-Am Scientist & Engrs Asn; Polymer Soc Korea. **Research Statement & Publications:** Rheology of disperse systems; coating rheology; colloid science; paper coating technology; emulsion polymerization, inverse emulsion polymerization; latex technology; structured latexes; nanostructured latexes; latex particle morphology; particle packing; thermal properties of latexes; solid and hollow plastic pigments; wet-end chemistry; papermaking. **Mailing Address:** Dept Paper Eng, Chem Eng & Imaging, Western Mich Univ, A-217 Parkview Campus, Kalamazoo, MI 49008-5462. **Fax:** 269-2763501. **E-Mail:** doiklee@aol.com

LEE, DO-JAE, PHYSICAL ORGANIC CHEMISTRY. **Personal Data:** b Namwon, Korea, January 24, 1928; American citizen; m 1957, c 2. **Education:** Long Beach State Col, BS, 1960; San Diego State Col, MS, 1964; Univ Calif, San Diego, PhD (chem), 1967. **Professional Experience:** RETIRED; res chemist, Toms River Chem Corp, 1968-1990. **Memberships:** Am Chem Soc. **Research Statement & Publications:** Development of new dyestuff and economic process for plant production. **Mailing Address:** 24 Chutney St, Toms River, NJ 08757.

LEE, DONALD GARRY, PHYSICAL CHEMISTRY, ORGANIC CHEMISTRY. **Personal Data:** b Midale, Sask, June 21, 1935; m 1959, Marilyn; c Wendy, Eric & Rebecca. **Education:** Univ Sask, BA, 1958, MA, 1960; Univ BC, PhD (chem), 1963. **Professional Experience:** Vis prof, Stanford Univ, 1980-1981; vis scholar, Univ Oslo, 1972-1973; PROF CHEM, UNIV REGINA, 1971-; assoc prof, Univ Regina, 1967-1971; res assoc, Harvard Univ, 1965-1966; RETIRED; pres, Lutheran Col, Univ Regina; PRES LUTHER COL. **Memberships:** Chem Inst Can; Am Chem Soc. **Research Statement & Publications:** Oxidation mechanisms; protonation studies; heavy oil and coal research; environmental assessment. **Mailing Address:** Dept Chem, Univ Regina 3737 Wascana Pkwy, Regina, SK S4S 0A2, Can. **Fax:** 306-585-4894.

LEE, DONALD JACK, NUTRITIONAL BIOCHEMISTRY. **Personal Data:** b Goldendale, Wash, January 28, 1932; m 1958, c 3. **Education:** WashState Univ, BS, 1958, MS, 1960; Univ Ill, PhD (nutrit, biochem), 1965. **Professional Experience:** CHMN, DEPT FOOD SCI & HUMAN NUTRIT, WASH STATE UNIV, 1986-; team leader, Lesotho Farming Systs Proj, 1984-1986; asst dir, Agr Res Ctr, 1975-1984; USPHS res grant, 1966-1975; assoc prof food sci & technol, Food Protection Sect, Ore State Univ, 1965-1975. **Memberships:** Inst Food Technologists; Am Inst Nutrit; Sigma Xi; Am Dietetic Asn. **Research Statement & Publications:** Nutritional biochemistry, especially lipid metabolism; toxicity and carcinogenicity of natural compounds. **Mailing Address:** Dept Food Sci & Human Nutrit, Wash State Univ, Pullman, WA 99164-6376. **Fax:** 509-335-4815.

LEE, DONALD WILLIAM, FLUID MECHANICS, APPLIED MECHANICS. **Personal Data:** b Buffalo, NY, November 4, 1947; m 1978, Sandra; c Eric Franklin & Andrew Robert. **Education:** Clarkson Col, BS, 1969, MS, 1973; Univ Mich, PhD (appl mech), 1977. **Honors & Awards:** Secretary, conferences & exhibition cmt, environ water resources inst, 2001-; Conf chair, CSCE/ASCE int conf on environ eng, 2002-. **Professional Experience:** Conf chair, CSCE/ASCE Int Conf on Environ Eng, 2002; secy, Conferences & Exhibition Cmte, Environ Water Resources Inst, ASCE, 2001; SR RES STAFF, ENVIRON SCI DIV, OAK RIDGE NAT LAB, 1999-; prog ldr, Radioact Waste Mgmnt & Safety Anal Prog, Oak Ridge Nat Lab, 1997-1999; chair, prof activities comt, environ eng div ASCE, 1996-1998; vice chair, prof activities comt, environ eng div ASCE, 1994-1996; chair, air& radiation mgt comm, environ eng div ASCE, 1992-1994; vchmn, Air & Radiation Mgt Comt Environ Eng Div, Am Soc Civil Eng, 1990-1992; secy, Air & Radiation Mgt Comt Environ Eng Div, Air Radration Mgt Comm Environ Eng Div, ASCE, 1992-1994; grp ldr appl phys sci, Oak Ridge Nat Lab, 1989-1997; mem, Low-Level Radioactive Waste Tech Resource Group 40CFR 193 & Low-Level Radioactive Waste Peer Rev Panel Dept Energy Order 5820-2A, 1988-1996; adj assoc prof, NC State Univ, 1987-; res staff mem, Oak Ridge Nat Lab, 1981-1989; res assoc fluid mech, Oak Ridge Nat Lab, 1977-1981; Instr gen sci, Wayne State Univ, 1975-1976; res asst appl mech, Univ Mich, 1971-1976; teaching fel mech eng, Clarkson Col Technol, 1970-1971; Engr, Ford Motor Co, 1969-1970; professional engr, Tenn& Mich; diplomat, Am Acad of environ engrs. **Memberships:** Mem Am Soc Civil Engrs; Mem Am Soc Mech Engrs; Mem Sigma Xi. **Research Statement & Publications:** Environmental fluid dynamics of surface water and groundwater; environmental impact assessment of energy technologies; low-level radioactive waste management. **Mailing Address:** 6400 Brandywine Dr, Lenoir City, TN 37772-6847. **Fax:** 865-576-8646. **E-Mail:** lees@icx.net

LEE, DONG HOON, LIE GROUPS & LIE ALGEBRAS, TOPOLOGICAL GROUPS. **Personal Data:** b Seoul, Korea, November 17, 1938; m 1968, c 2. **Education:** Seoul Nat

Univ, BS, 1961; Tulane Univ, PhD (math), 1967. **Professional Experience:** PROF MATH, CASE WESTERN RES UNIV, 1981-; vis prof math, Seoul Nat Univ, 1976-1977; from asst prof to assoc prof, Case Western Res Univ, 1967-1980. **Memberships:** Am Math Soc. **Research Statement & Publications:** Representation theory of lie groups and lie algebras. **Mailing Address:** Dept Math, Case Western Res Univ, 10900 Euclid Ave, Cleveland, OH 44106-7058. **Fax:** 216-368-5163. **E-Mail:** dhl@po.cwru.edu

LEE, DOUGLAS HARRY KEDGWIN, ENVIRONMENTAL SCIENCES. **Personal Data:** b Bristol, Eng, February 22, 1905; American & Australian citizen; m 1952, Dorothy Yingling; c Roderick K. **Education:** Univ Queensland, MSc, 1927; Univ Sydney, MB & BS, 1929, dipl trop med, 1933, MD, 1940; FRACP, 1940; Am Bd Indust Hyg, dipl. **Honorary Degrees:** MD, Univ Queensland, 1986. **Honors & Awards:** Cutter Lectr, Sch Pub Health, Harvard Univ, 1950; Order of Australia, 1995; Bancroft Medal Queenslane, Inst Med Res, 1996. **Professional Experience:** RETIRED; emer prof, Univ Queensland, 1990; fel, Queensland Inst Med Res, 1983; Consult, Mt Sinai Med Sch, 1974-1976; adj prof, NC State Univ, 1968-1974; assoc dir, Nat Inst Environ Health Sci, 1966-1973; chief occup health res & training facility, USPHS, 1960-1966; assoc sci dir res, Qm Res & Eng Command, 1958-1960; chief, Res Br, Off Qm Gen, 1955-1958; prof physiol climat & lectr environ med, Johns Hopkins Univ, 1948-1955; Consult, US Qm Corps, 1947-1955 & Food & Agr Orgn, UN, 1947-1960; dean fac med, Univ Queensland, 1938-1942; prof physiol, Univ Queensland, 1936-1948; prof physiol, King Edward VII Col Med, Singapore, 1935-1936; Med officer, Commonwealth Dept Health, Australia, 1930-1933. **Memberships:** Am Physiol Soc; fel NY Acad Sci. **Research Statement & Publications:** Climatic physiology, effects of climate on man and animals and application to clothing, housing and tropical development; occupational and environmental health. **Mailing Address:** 211/180 Swan Rd, Taringa Qld 4068, Australia.

LEE, EDWARD HSIEN-CHI, PLANT PHYSIOLOGY, ENVIRONMENTAL SCIENCE. **Personal Data:** b Taiwan, August 31, 1935; m 1967, Amy; c Tony & Michael. **Education:** Nat Taiwan Univ, BS, 1959; Univ Kans, MA, 1966; Univ Okla, PhD (bot), 1969. **Professional Experience:** RETIRED; adj prof, Dept Natural Resource Sci & Landscape Archit, Univ Md, Col Park, beginning 1985; plant physiologist, Agr Res Serv, USDA, beginning 1978; assoc prof cellular physiol, genetics & microbiol, Cent Methodist Col, Mo, 1969-1978; teaching asst gen bot & physiol, Univ Okla, 1966-1969; lab instr gen bot & taxon, Nat Taiwan Univ, 1961-1964. **Memberships:** AAAS; Am Soc Plant Physiol; Plant Growth Regulator Soc Am; Sigma Xi; Scand Soc Plant Physiol; NAm Taiwanese Prof Asn. **Research Statement & Publications:** Environmental stress; air pollution, photosynthesis and oxidative stress. **Mailing Address:** 312 Opera Ct, Silver Spring, MD 20878-3462.

LEE, EDWARD PRENTISS, PHYSICS. **Personal Data:** b Tulsa, Okla, October 3, 1942. **Education:** Calif. Inst. Technol., BS, 1964; Univ Chicago, MS, 1966, PhD (physics), 1968. **Professional Experience:** Chief Scientist for Heavy Ion Fusion Virtual National Lab. 2001-2005, Senior Scientist 1995-, Staff Scientist accelerator physics, Lawrence Berkeley National Lab. 1982-1995; staff physicist (plasma physics), Lawrence Livermore National Lab. 1970-1982; Member (plasma physics)of Inst. Advan. Study, Princeton, NJ, 1968-1970. **Memberships:** Fel Am Physical Soc. **Research Statement & Publications:** High current charged particle beams; controlled thermonuclear fusion; astrophysics; particle accelerators. **Mailing Address:** Lawrence Berkeley Nat Lab, 1 Cyclotron Rd MS/47-112, Berkeley, CA 94720. **Fax:** 510-486-5392. **E-Mail:** eplee@lbl.gov

LEE, ELHANG HOWARD, PHOTONICS, SEMI CONDUCTOR SCIENCE. **Personal Data:** b Seoul, Korea, December 19, 1947; m 1974, Namsoo Chang; c David & Jennifer. **Education:** Seoul Nat Univ, BS, 1970; Yale Univ, MS, 1973, MPhil, 1975, PhD (appl physics), 1977. **Honors & Awards:** Nat Medal Hon, Pres Korea; Outstanding Acad Contrib Award, Korean Phy Soc. **Professional Experience:** Chmn, Laser & Electro-Optic Soc, Inst Elec & Electronics Engrs (Korea), 1994-; exec dir, Int Soc Optic Engrs (Korea), 1992-; adj prof, Chungham Nat Univ, Korea, 1992-; Vis prof, Korea Advan Inst Sci & Technol, 1992; EXEC DIR & VPRES RES, KOREA ELEC & TELECOMMUN RES INST, 1990-; sr mem res staff, AT&T Bell Labs, 1984-1990; res scientist, Monsanto Co, 1980-1984; res assoc scientist, Princeton Univ, 1979-1980; Res staff scientist, Yale Univ, 1978-1979. **Memberships:** Fel Korean Phys Soc; Sigma Xi; fel Optic Soc Korea; Am Phys Soc; Optic Soc Am; NY Acad Sci; AAAS. **Research Statement & Publications:** Optoelectronics and photonics for light waves, optical communication and information processing; semiconductor physics, materials and devices for electronics, telecommunications and information technology; author of over 250 papers and 2 book publications. **Mailing Address:** ETRI Daeduck Sci Town, Yusong PO Box 106, Daejeon City 305600, South Korea. **Fax:** 824-286-06836. **E-Mail:** ehlee@ard.etri.re.kr

LEE, ELLEN SZETO, MODELING & SIMULATION, DESIGN. **Personal Data:** b Hong Kong, British citizen; c 1. **Education:** Mt Holyoke Col, BA, 1977; Univ Calif, Berkeley, MS, 1979, PhD (elec eng & computer sci), 1982. **Professional Experience:** Vis lectr, Rutgers Univ, 1987; mem tech staff, Bell Commun Res, Inc, 1984-1986; MEM TECH STAFF, AT&T BELL LABS, 1982-1984, 1986-; vis lectr, Univ Calif, Berkeley, 1981-1982. **Memberships:** Inst Elec & Electronics Engrs; NY Acad Sci. **Research Statement & Publications:** Computer-aided design for all aspects of electrical designs: digital and analog circuits, very large scale integration circuits, switch-mode power supplies; circuit theory; object-oriented computer programming. **Mailing Address:** 4501 Torino Pl, Plano, TX 75093-7020.

LEE, EMERSON HOWARD, PHYSICAL CHEMISTRY, SURFACE CHEMISTRY. **Personal Data:** b Okmulgee, Okla, February 23, 1921; m 1948, Margaret; c Stephen, Richard, Don & Thomas. **Education:** Univ Tex, BS, 1952, PhD (chem). 1955. **Professional Experience:** RETIRED; consult, 1982-1985; sciencefello, Monsanto Co, 1965-1982; res specialist, Monsanto Co, 1959-1960; res chemist, Monsanto Co, 1956-1959; res engr, Develop & Res Dept, Continental Oil Co, 1954-1956; chemist, Darco Div, Atlas Powder Co, 1946-1950. **Memberships:** Am Chem Soc; Sigma Xi. **Research Statement & Publications:** Surface chemistry and catalysis. **Mailing Address:** 48 Beaver Dr, St Louis, MO 63141.

LEE, ENG-HONG, COCCIDIOSIS VACCINES FOR COMMERCIAL CHICKENS & TURKEYS, IMPROVEMENT OF COCCIDIOSIS VACCINE THROUGH BIOTECHNOLOGY. **Personal Data:** b Butterworth, Malaysia, January 13, 1944; Canadian citizen; m Marilyn; c May M & Alan W. **Education:** Nanyang Univ, Singapore, BS, 1967; Univ Guelph, MS, 1970; Univ Mass, Amherst, PhD (zoology), 1974. **Professional Experience:** PRES, VETECH LABS INC, 1983-; res assoc, Univ Guelph, 1976-1981; fel, Nat Res Coun, Ottawa, 1974-1975. **Memberships:** Am Soc Parisitol; NY Acad Sci. **Research Statement & Publications:** Developed, patented and commercialized a live coccidiosis vaccine for chickens and turkeys which appeared to be effective and is in use worldwide; developed a gel-delivery system for vaccines and microingredients. **Mailing Address:** Vetech Labs Inc, 131 Malcolm Rd, Rockwood, ON N1K 1A8, Can. **Fax:** 519-822-9471. **E-Mail:** immucox@vetechinc.com

LEE, ERASTUS HENRY, PLASTICITY, CONTINUUM MECHANICS. **Personal Data:** b Southport, Eng, February 2, 1916; c 4. **Education:** Cambridge Univ, UK, BA, 1937, MA, 1943; Stanford Univ, PhD (mech eng), 1940. **Honors & Awards:** Timoshenko Medal, Am Soc Mech Engrs, 1976. **Professional Experience:** PROF EMER, DEPT AERONAUT & ASTRONAUT, STANFORD UNIV, as of 2006; prof eng, Rensselaer Polytech Inst, beginning 1981; prof appl mech & aero eng, Stanford Univ, 1962-1981; chmn, Div Appl Math, 1953-1958; from assoc prof to prof appl math, Brown Univ, 1948-1962; asst dir tech eng, Dept Atomic Energy, UK, 1946-1948; exp sci officer, Armaments Res Dept, Ministry Supply, UK, 1943-1946; exp sci officer, Ordnance Bd, War Off, UK, 1941-1943. **Memberships:** Nat Acad Eng; fel Am Soc Mech Engrs; fel Inst Mech Eng UK; fel Am Acad Mech; fel Soc Eng Sci. **Research Statement & Publications:** Plasticity analysis and constitutive equations. **Mailing Address:** Dept Aeronaut & Astronaut, Stanford Univ, Stanford, CA 94305.

LEE, ERIC KIN-LAM, CHEMICAL ENGINEERING, POLYMER CHEMISTRY. **Personal Data:** b Hong Kong, June 25, 1948; m 1972, c 1. **Education:** NC State Univ, BS, 1970, MS, 1972, PhD (chem eng), 1976. **Professional Experience:** VPRES RES & DEVELOP, INTEGRATED BIOSYSTEMS INC, as of 2004; vpres, Technol & Eng, Hemasure Inc, beginning 1994; dir membrane res & technol develop, Sepracor Inc, 1986-1993; sr res eng, DuPont Co, 1984-1986; proj mgr, Bend Res, Inc, 1977-1984; Res fel, Max Planck Inst Biophys, 1976-1977. **Memberships:** Am Inst Chem Engrs; Am Chem Soc; NAm Membrane Soc. **Research Statement & Publications:** Research and development of synthetic membranes and other separation media; design and engineering of devices, systems and processes for medical, biotechnical and industrial applications. **Mailing Address:** Integrated Biosystems Inc, 445 Devlin Rd, Napa, CA 94558. **Fax:** 707-226-9303.

LEE, E(RNEST) BRUCE, control engineering; deceased, see previous edition for last biography

LEE, ERNEST Y C, BIOCHEMISTRY, MOLECULAR BIOLOGY. **Professional Experience:** CHMN & PROF BIOCHEM & MOLECULAR BIOL, NY MED COL, as of 2004; prof biochem, dept biochem & molecular biol, sch med, Univ Miami, beginning 1967. **Mailing Address:** Dept Biochem & Molecular Biol, NY Med Col, Basic Sci Bldg, Valhalla, NY 10595. **Fax:** 914-594-4058. **E-Mail:** ernest_lee@nymc.edu

LEE, E(UGENE) STANLEY, OPERATIONS RESEARCH & COMPUTER SCIENCE, NEURAL NETWORK & SUPPORT VECTOR MACHINES. **Personal Data:** b Hopei, China, September 7, 1930; American citizen; m 1983, Yuan; c Linda J, Margaret H, Lynn, Jin & Ming. **Education:** Chieng-Cheng Inst Tech Taiwan, BChE, 1953; Univ NC, MS, 1957, Princeton Univ, PhD (chem eng), 1962. **Professional Experience:** Ed, Energy Sci & Technol, 1977-; vis prof, Univ Southern Calif, Los Angeles, 1972-1976; NSF grant, 1971-; PROF INDUST ENG, KANS STATE UNIV, 1971-; from asst prof to assoc prof chem eng, Kans State Univ, 1966-1971; res engr, Phillips Petrol Co, Okla, 1960-1966; Off Air Res Grantee, USDA; assoc ed, J Math Analysis & Appln & Math with Appln; assoc ed, Comput & Math with Appln. **Memberships:** Soc Indust & Appl Math; Am Inst Chem Engrs; Opers Res Soc Am; Inst Indust Engrs. **Research Statement & Publications:** Optimization theory; applied mathematics; quasilinearization and invariant imbedding; systems engineering; set theory; expert systems. **Mailing Address:** Dept Industrial & manufacturing systems Eng, Kans State Univ 237 Durland Hall, Manhattan, KS 66506-5101. **E-Mail:** eslee@ksu.edu

LEE, EUN SUL, SURVEY SAMPLING, DEMOGRAPHIC METHODS. **Personal Data:** b Gongju, Korea, September 19, 1934; American citizen; m 1964, c 2. **Education:** Seoul Nat Univ, BA, 1957; Univ Ky, MA, 1964; NC State Univ, PhD (exp statist & sociol), 1970. **Professional Experience:** PROF BIOMET & DEMOG, SCH PUB HEALTH, UNIV TEX HEALTH SCI CTR, HOUSTON, 1987-; fel hist med, Univ Cincinnati, Nat Endowment Humanities, 1980; UN Fund Pop Activ, Pop & Develop Inst, Seoul Nat Univ, 1976; vis prof, Dept Sociol, Utah State Univ, 1975; from asst prof to assoc prof, Sch Pub Health, Univ Tex Health Sci Ctr, Houston, 1972-1987; res biometrician, Sch Pub Health, Univ Tex Health Sci Ctr, Houston, 1969-1972; res assoc statist analysis, NC Bd Higher Educ, 1966-1969. **Memberships:** Biomet Soc; Am Statist Asn; Pop Asn Am; Am Pub Health Asn; Int Union Sci Study Pop. **Research Statement & Publications:** Ethnic differentials in mortality, fertility and health behavior; public health policy analysis; changing cardiovascular mortality and morbidity trends; sample survey design. **Mailing Address:** Univ Tex Health Sci Ctr, 1200 Herman Pressler Dr, Houston, TX 77030. **Fax:** 713-500-9149. **E-Mail:** eun.s.lee@uth.tmc.edu

LEE, FANG-JEN SCOTT, BIOCHEMISTRY, MICROBIOLOGY. **Personal Data:** b Taipei, Taiwan, April 20, 1957; American citizen; m 1984, Leewen Lin; c Alice & Albert. **Education:** Nat Taiwan Univ, BS, 1980; NC State Univ, MS, 1984, PhD (biotechnol & microbiol), 1986. **Professional Experience:** SR STAFF, LAB CELLULAR METAB, NAT HEART, LUNG & BLOODINST, NIH, 1990-; Res fel, Dept Genetics, Harvard Med Sch & Dept Molecular Biol, Mass Gen Hosp, 1987-1990; Consult, Yung-Shin Pharmaceut Industs Co Ltd, 1986-1990. **Memberships:** Am Soc Biochem & Molecular Biol; Am Soc Microbiol; AAAS; Protein Soc; Sigma Xi. **Research Statement & Publications:** Investigation of protein processing and signal transduction. **Mailing Address:** Inst Molecular Med Sch, Nat Taiwan Univ No 7 Chung Shan South Rd, Taipei, Taiwan, China. **E-Mail:** fangjen@ha.mc.ntu.edu.tw

LEE, FLOYD DENMAN, NUCLEAR PHYSICS. **Personal Data:** b Hays, Kans, April 27, 1938. **Education:** Univ Kans, BS, 1960, PhD (physics), 1966. **Professional Experience:** ASSOC PROF PHYSICS, MONT STATE UNIV, 1968-; Nat Acad Sci-Nat Res Coun assoc, 1966-1968; Instr physics, Univ Kans, 1965-1966. **Memberships:** Am Asn Physics Teachers; Am Phys Soc. **Research Statement & Publications:** Low-energy nuclear research with Van-de-Graaf accelerators; nuclear structure. **Mailing Address:** Dept Physics, Mont State Univ, AJM Johnson Hall, Bozeman, MT 59717-0001.

LEE, FRANKLIN Y, MEDICINE. **Education:** Med Univ SC, MD, 1983. **Professional Experience:** CONSULT, as of 2006. **Mailing Address:** 155 S Spring Mill Rd, Villanova, PA 19085.

LEE, FRANKLIN YIEN-HWEI, PHARMACOLOGY. **Personal Data:** b Taiwan, October 20, 1937; m 1968, Shan-guang; c Yishane, Yiying & Yiking. **Education:** Nat Taiwan Univ, MD, 1963; Univ Calif, Los Angeles, PhD (pharmacol), 1968. **Professional Experience:** MED DIR, LIBERTY REHAB & MED CTR, PHILADELPHIA, PA, 1993-; attend physician, Jefferson Park Hosp, Philadelphia, Pa, 1985-1992 & Thomas Jefferson Univ Hosp, 1992-; med dir, Lee Clin, Villanova, Pa, 1985-1993; consult physician, Spruce Med Ctr, Philadelphia, Pa, 1985-1991; attend hematologist oncologist, Leland Hosp, Riverdale, Md, 1984-1985; pres, L&L Clin, Inc, Rockville, Md, 1983-1985; attend hematologist oncologist, Greater Beltsville Laurel Med Ctr, Md, 1983-1985; attend hematologist oncologist, Shady Grove Adventist Hosp, Rockville, Md, 1982-1985; attend hematologist, Georgetown Univ, Wash, DC, 1982-1983; consult specialist, Bethesda Res Lab, Gaithersburg, 1981-1982; Am

Cancer Soc fel clin onocol, Sect Hemat & Oncol, Cook Co Hosp, Chicago, 1980-1981; fel sect hemat, Rush-Presby & St Luke's Hosp, Chicago, 1978-1980; staff physician, St Joseph Hosp, Chicago, 1977-1978; staff, Chicago Med Sch Hosp, 1976-1977; sect head, Abbott Labs, 1972-1976; sr investr pharmacol, Searle Res Lab, G D Searle & Co, 1968-1972; res pharmacologist, Univ Calif, Los Angeles, 1966-1968; res assoc, Neuropsychiat Inst, 1966-1968; res asst pharmacol, Univ Calif, Los Angeles, 1964-1966. **Memberships:** AAAS; Am Soc Pharmacol & Exp Therapeut; Sigma Xi; Am Chem Soc; Am Ctr Chinese Med Sci. **Research Statement & Publications:** Gastrointestinal pharmacology and physiology; biochemical pharmacology; cancer chemotherapy; experimental leukemia; hematology; oncology. **Mailing Address:** 155 S Spring Mill Rd, Villanova, PA 19085-1408. **Fax:** 215-923-7320. **E-Mail:** yhlee@bellatlantic.net

LEE, FRED C, POWER CONVERSION. **Personal Data:** American citizen; c 2. **Education:** Nat Cheng Kung Univ, Taiwan, BS, 1968; Duke Univ, Durham, MS, 1972, PhD (elec eng), 1974. **Honors & Awards:** Ralph R Teeter Award, Soc Automotive Eng, 1985; William E Newell Power Electronics Award, Inst Elec & Electronics Engrs, Power Electronics Soc, 1989. **Professional Experience:** LEWIS A HESTER CHAIR PROF, DEPT ELEC & COMPUT ENG, VA POLYTECH INST & STATE UNIV, as of 2004; adv bd, Power Integrations Inc, beginning 1988; DIR, TECHNOL DEVELOP CTR POWER ELECTRONICS, 1987-; bd dirs, Zytec Corp, beginning 1986; dir, James S Tucker Prof, beginning 1986; dir, Va Polytech Eng Ctr, Va Polytech Inst & State Univ, beginning 1985; assoc ed, Inst Elec & Electronics Engrs Trans Power Electronics, beginning 1985; mem, Power Electronics Coun, Inst Elec & Electronics Engrs, 1985-1987; from asst prof to prof, Va Polytech Inst & State Univ, 1977-1986; res asst, Spacecraft Systs Res Lab, 1972-1977; teaching asst, Duke Univ, 1970-1972. **Memberships:** Fel Inst Elec & Electronics Engrs; Inst Elec & Electronics Engrs Indust Applications Soc; Inst Elec & Electronics Engrs Power Electronics Soc (vpres, 1988-1989); Brit Inst Elec Engrs. **Research Statement & Publications:** Power conversion; power devices; high frequency resonant converters; distributed power systems; power hybrids; space power systems; nonlinear control; design optimization; system modeling; analysis and simulation. **Mailing Address:** Dept Elec & Comput Eng, Va Polytech Inst & State Univ, 648 Whittemore, Blacksburg, VA 24061-8125. **Fax:** 540-231-3362. **E-Mail:** fclee@vt.edu

LEE, G FRED, ENVIRONMENTAL SCIENCES. **Education:** San Jose State Univ, BA, 1955; Univ NC, MS, 1957; Harvard Univ, PhD, 1960. **Professional Experience:** PRES, G FRED & ASSOCS, 1989-. **Mailing Address:** G. Fred Lee & Assocs, 27298 E El Macero Dr., El Macero, CA 95618-1005. **Fax:** 530-753-9956. **E-Mail:** gfredlee@aol.com

LEE, GARRETT, CARDIOVASCULAR RESEARCH, LASER MEDICINE. **Personal Data:** b San Francisco, Calif, June 23, 1946. **Education:** Univ Calif, Berkeley, BA, 1968; Univ Calif, Davis, MD, 1972. **Professional Experience:** DIR RES, WESTERN HEART INST, SAN FRANCISCO, 1984-; dir, Laser Res Lab, Cedars Med Ctr, Fla, 1983-1984; bd dir, Am Heart Assoc, 1981-1983; chmn, cardiovasc Curric, Univ Calif, Davis, 1979-1983; dir, Cardiac Cath Lab, 1978-1983; counr, Am Fedn Clin Res, 1977-1981; asst prof med, Univ Calif, Davis, 1976-1983; med consult, Calif Comn Peace Officer Stand, 1975-1980; med dir, Aspirin Myocardial Infarction Study, Univ Calif, Davis, 1975-1978; fel cardiol, Univ Calif, Davis, 1974-1976; residency med, Univ Calif, Davis, 1973-1975; internship med, Duke Univ Med Ctr, 1972-1973. **Memberships:** Am Col Cardiol; Am Soc Laser Med & Surg; Am Col Clin Pharmacol; Am Col Angiol; Am Fedn Clin Res; Am Heart Asn. **Research Statement & Publications:** Cardiovascular pharmacology and interventional cardiology including lasers and heart disease, angioscopy, balloon angioplasty and thrombolytic therapy in accute myocardial infarction; pain management with low power lasers. **Mailing Address:** Western Heart Inst, 450 Stanyan St, San Francisco, CA 94117.

LEE, GEORGE C, STRUCTURAL ENGINEERING & EARTHQUAKE ENGINEERING, BIOMECHANICS. **Personal Data:** b Beijing, China, July 17, 1932; m, c 2. **Education:** Nat Taiwan Univ, BSE, 1955; Lehigh Univ, MS, 1958, PhD (civil eng), 1960. **Honors & Awards:** Adams Mem Award, Am Welding Soc, 1974; Super Accomplishment Award, NSF, 1977. **Professional Experience:** Special Task Director, MULTIDISCIPLINARY CTR EARTHQUAKE ENG RES, 2003 - Director, Multidisciplinary Center for Earthquake Eng. Res., 1993-2003; SAMUEL P. CAPEN PROF ENG & APPL SCI, STATE UNIV NY, BUFFALO, 1995-; Dir, Health Instrument & Device Inst, 1984-1985; assoc dir, Calspan -State Univ NY, Buffalo, 1984-1990; dean eng & appl sci, State Univ NY, Buffalo, 1978-1995; head eng mech sect, NSF, 1977-1978; chmn, Dept Civil Eng, 1972-1977; dir socio-eng prog, Dept Civil Eng, 1971-1978; dir grad studies, Dept Civil Eng, 1971-1978; actg chmn, Dept Civil Eng, 1970-1971; NIH grant & sr res fel, Dept Physiol, Harvard Univ, Sch Pub Health, 1969-1970; PROF ENG & APPL SCI, STATE UNIV NY, BUFFALO, 1967-; Spec eng consult, Struct Dynamics Dept, Bell Aerosysts Co, 1965-; assoc prof, State Univ NY, Buffalo, 1963-1967; asst prof civil eng, State Univ NY, Buffalo, 1961-1963; from res asst to res assoc, Frit Eng Lab, 1957-1961; Res fel civil eng, Lehigh Univ, 1956-1957. **Memberships:** Am Soc Civil Engrs; Am Soc Eng Educ; Am Welding Soc; Sigma Xi; AAAS. **Research Statement & Publications:** Steel structures; ultimate strength design; biomechanics; earthquake engineering; multi-hazard engineering. **Mailing Address:** State Univ NY, 429 Bell Hall, Buffalo, NY 14260. **Fax:** 716-645-3940. **E-Mail:** gclee@buffalo.edu

LEE, GEORGE H, II, ENVIRONMENTAL ANALYSIS. **Personal Data:** b Ithaca, NY, February 26, 1939; m 1964, June Esther Brown; c David & Daniel. **Education:** Rensselaer Polytech Inst, BChE, 1961, PhD (phys chem), 1965. **Professional Experience:** Tech Dir chem Div; Air Force Inst for burns & Safety & Occup Risk Anal, Anal chem consult, Air force ctr for Environ Excellence, Brooks AFB, TX 1992-1994; chief, Volatile Org Function, Occup & Environ Health Directorate, 1988-1992; assoc chief, Forensic & Doc Div, Air Force Drug Testing Lab, 1986-1988; sr res scientist, US Army Fuels & Lubricants Res Lab, 1981-1986; sr res scientist fire technol, Southwest Res Inst, 1977-1981; assoc found scientist, Southwest Found Res & Educ, 1973-1977; sr res chemist, Dept Phys & Biol Sci, Southwest Res Inst, 1971-1973; res chemist, Res Ctr, Hercules Inc, Del, 1967-1971; Res assoc, Cornell Univ, 1965-1967; Adj prof, Earth & Phys Sci, Univ Texas, San Antonio. **Memberships:** Sigma Xi; AAAS; Astron Soc Pac. **Research Statement & Publications:** Analysis of potable and non-potable waters, soils and tissues for toxic contaminants. **Mailing Address:** 11107 Whispering Wind, San Antonio, TX 78230. **Fax:** 210-536-6205. **E-Mail:** george.lee@brooks.af.mil

LEE, GLENN RICHARD, INTERNAL MEDICINE, HEMATOLOGY. **Personal Data:** b Ogden, Utah, May 18, 1932; m 1969, Pamela; c Jennifer & Cynthia. **Education:** Univ Utah, BS, 1953, MD, 1956. **Professional Experience:** RETIRED; dean, Col Med, 1978-1984; prof med, Univ Utah, 1973-1994; assoc dean acad affairs, Univ Utah, 1973-1976; from instr to assoc prof, Univ Utah, 1963-1973; res fel, Univ Utah, 1961-1963; clin fel hemat, Univ Utah, 1960-1961; asst resident, Boston City Hosp, 1957-1958; intern med, Boston City Hosp, 1956-1957. **Memberships:** Am Fedn Clin Res; Am Soc Hemat; Am Col Physicians; Am Soc Clin Invest. **Research Statement & Publications:** Clinical and experimentally induced abnormalities in heme biosynthesis; physiologic consequences of copper deficiency; iron metabolism. **Mailing Address:** 3781 S Ruth Dr, Holladay, UT 84124.

LEE, GLORIA, NEURONAL CYTOSKELETON. **Personal Data:** m 1985, Craig T Morita; c Stephen & Catherine. **Education:** Univ Calif, AB, 1974; Harvard Univ, PhD, 1981. **Professional Experience:** ASST PROF Neuroscience, DEPT NEUROL, BRIGHAM & WOMEN'S HOSP, 1986-. **Memberships:** Soc Neurosci; Am Soc Cell Biol. **Research Statement & Publications:** Regulation of cytoskeletal changes taking place during neuronal differentiation. **Mailing Address:** Brigham Group Dept Neurol, Brigham & Women's Hosp 221 Longwood Ave, Boston, MA 02115. **Fax:** 617-732-7787. **E-Mail:** glee@cnd.bwh.harvard.edu

LEE, GORDON M(ELVIN), ELECTRICAL ENGINEERING. **Personal Data:** b Minneapolis, Minn, January 3, 1917; m 2001, Betty; c Theodore, James, David & Mary. **Education:** Univ Minn, BEE, 1938; Univ Mo, MS, 1939; Mass Inst Technol, DSc(elec eng), 1944. **Honors & Awards:** Thompson Mem Prize, Inst Elec & Electronics Engrs, 1946. **Professional Experience:** CONSULT, 1981-; pres, Cent Res Labs, Inc, Sargent Industs, 1973-1981; lectr, Univ Minn, 1948; tech dir elec eng & secy-treas, Cent Res Labs, Inc, Sargent Industs, 1945-1973; mem staff, Div Indust Coop, 1944-1945; Mem, Nat Defense Res Comt, 1944; asst elec engr, Mass Inst Technol, 1939-1944; Asst elec eng, Univ Mo, 1938-1939. **Memberships:** AAAS; Am Nuclear Soc; Inst Elec & Electronics Engrs. **Research Statement & Publications:** Remote handling equipment; properties of dielectrics; high-speed oscillography; development of high-speed micro-oscillograph and remotehandling equipment. **Mailing Address:** PO Box 744, Brainerd, MN 56401. **Fax:** 218-828-0306.

LEE, GRETA MARLENE, CELL BIOLOGY, VIDEO MICROSCOPY. **Personal Data:** b El Paso, Tex. **Education:** ETenn State Univ, MS, 1983; Duke Univ, PhD (zool), 1989; Univ Mo, Columbia, BS, 1971. **Professional Experience:** RES ASSOC PROF, UNIV NC, CHAPEL HILL, as of 2003; res asst prof, Univ Nc, Chapel Hill, beginning 1992; Lawton Chiles biotechnol fel, Dept Cell Biol & Anat, 1989-1992. **Memberships:** Am Soc Cell Biol. **Research Statement & Publications:** Chondrocyte biology, dynamic structure of pericellular and extracellular matrices; movements of individual molecules on living cells using specific colloidal gold probes and video enhanced light microscopy. **Mailing Address:** Dept Orthop, Arthritis Res Ctr Univ NC 5109 Thruston -Bowles Bldg CB 7280, Chapel Hill, NC 27599-7280. **Fax:** 919-966-1856. **E-Mail:** gmlee@med.unc.edu

LEE, GRIFF C, OFFSHORE DESIGN, OFFSHORE CONSTRUCTION. **Personal Data:** b Jackson, Miss, August 17, 1926; m 1950, c 3. **Education:** Tulane Univ, BE, 1948; Rice Univ, MS, 1951. **Professional Experience:** CONSULT, GRIFF C LEE INC, as of 2004; PRES, GRIFF C LEE INC, 1983-; Mem, Marine Bd Nat Res Coun, Offshore Comt Am Petrol Inst, Adv Comt-Offshore Technol Detnorske Veritas, Welding Res Coun, Tech Panel Offshore Installations for Lloyd's Register Shipping, Comt Offshore Platforms & Bd Adv, Tulane Univ, 1980-; vpres res & develop, McDermott Inc, 1978-1983; group vpres, McDermott Inc, 1975-1978; chief engr, McDermott Inc, 1966-1975; prin engr & design engr, McDermott Inc, 1954-1966; Civil engr, Humble Oil & Refining Co, 1948-1954. **Memberships:** Nat Acad Eng; hon mem Am Soc Civil Engrs; Am Concrete Inst; Am Welding Soc; Soc Petrol Eng. **Research Statement & Publications:** Advanced engineering technology; offshore construction for the petroleum industry. **Mailing Address:** Griff Lee Inc, PO Box 70787, New Orleans, LA 70172. **Fax:** 504-539-7203.

LEE, HAROLD HON-KWONG, DEVELOPMENTAL BIOLOGY, BIOTECHNOLOGY. **Personal Data:** b China, January 31, 1934; m 1966, c 2. **Education:** Okla Baptist, AB, 1956; Univ Tenn, MS, 1958, PhD (embryol), 1965. **Professional Experience:** PROF EMER BIOL, UNIV TOLEDO, as of 2003; dir, Master Lib Studies, beginning 1988; prof biol, Univ Toledo, beginning 1975; USPHS fel, Carnegie Inst, 1965-1967. **Memberships:** Soc Develop Biologists; AAAS; Am Cancer Soc; NIH grants; United Nations grants; Lolor Found. **Research Statement & Publications:** Cell interactions and fertilization development of reproduction; biotechnology; tissue culture. **Mailing Address:** Dept Biol, Univ Toledo, 2801 W Bancroft St, Toledo, OH 43606-3328. **Fax:** 419-537-7737. **E-Mail:** hlee@uoft02.utoledo.edu

LEE, HARVEY SHUI-HONG, DYNAMICS & AERODYNAMICS OF VEHICLES ON GUIDEWAY. **Personal Data:** b China, February 7, 1949; American citizen. **Education:** Newark Col Eng, BSc, 1972; Ohio State Univ, MSc, 1974. **Professional Experience:** MECH ENGR, US DEPT TRANSP, 1975-. **Memberships:** Am Soc Mech Engrs. **Research Statement & Publications:** Assessing the safety of the dynamics of train/track interaction and the aerodynamic effects of trains on its surrounding. **Mailing Address:** US Dept Transp, John A Volpe Nat Transp Systs Ctr, 55 Broadway, Cambridge, MA 02142. **Fax:** 617-494-3616. **E-Mail:** leeh@volpe.dot.gov

LEE, HAYNES A, LASERS, GLASS TECHNOLOGY. **Personal Data:** b Johnson City, Tenn, October 14, 1932; m 1959, c 3. **Education:** Emory & Henry Col, BS, 1954; Alfred Univ, MS, 1961. **Professional Experience:** RETIRED; gen mgr, Laser Inst Am, beginning 1981; bd dir, Laser Inst Am, 1975-1980; gen mgr optical prod, Laser Inst Am, 1973-1980; chief laser scientist, Owens Ill Inc, 1968-1972; glass scientist, Owens Ill Inc, 1966-1968; glass technologist, Owens Ill Inc, 1963-1966; glass technologist, Thatcher Glass Mfg Co, NY, 1961-1963. **Memberships:** Am Ceramic Soc; Sigma Xi; Laser Inst Am; Optical Soc Am. **Research Statement & Publications:** Electronic pheonmena in glasses, particularly laser phenomena. **Mailing Address:** 5845 Viramar Rd, Toledo, OH 43611.

LEE, HENRY, ELECTRICAL ENGINEERING. **Education:** Univ Calif, Berkeley, BS, 1983, PhD, 1989. **Professional Experience:** PROF, ELEC ENG & COMPUT SCI, UNIV CALIF, as of 2006; PROF, INTEGRATED NANOSYSTEMS RES FACIL, UNIV CALIF, as of 2006. **Mailing Address:** Dept Elec & Comput Eng, Henry Samueli Sch Eng, Univ Calif, EG 2231, Irvine, CA 92697-2625. **Fax:** 949-824-3732. **E-Mail:** hplee@uci.edu

LEE, HENRY C, FORENSIC SCIENCE & CRIMINAL INVESTIGATION, BIOCHEMISTRY. **Personal Data:** b China, November 22, 1938; m 1963, Margaret; c Sherry & Stanley. **Education:** John Jay Col NY, BS, 1972; NY Univ, MS, 1974, PhD (biochem), 1975. **Honorary Degrees:** DSc, Univ New Haven, 1990; LHD, St Jospeh Univ, 1996, Bridgeport Univ, 1997; LLD, Williams Law sch, 1998. **Honors & Awards:** Distinguished Criminalist Award, Am Acad Forensic Sci, 1988, Distinguished Fel Award, 1994; John Dondero Award, Int Asn Identification, 1989, Distinguished Sci Serv Medals, 1986, 1990 & 1996 800 other Awards & medals. **Professional Experience:** Northeastern Univ, 1977-1979 & Law Sch, Univ Conn, 1993; Am J Forensic Path, 1990-; Forensic Rev, 1989-; ed, Forensic Sci, 1981-; CHIEF, CONN STATE FORENSIC SCI LAB, 1979-; PROF FORENSIC SCI, FORENSIC SCI LAB, 1978-; res grant, Univ New Haven, 1978 & 1979; vis fac, Yale Univ, 1978; DIR, FORENSIC SCI LAB, 1977-; DIR, CTR APPL RES, UNIV NEW HAVEN, 1976-; assoc prof & dirforensic sci, Conn State Forensic Sci Lab, 1976-1978; vis prof, Seton Hall Univ, 1976; dir Chair prof, Unh, Ccsu, Law sch, Conn State Forensic Sci Lab, 1975-1998-2001; comn, Conn Dept of Public Safety 2001- chief emer, State Police; res scientist, Med Ctr, NY Univ. **Memberships:** NY Acad Sci; fel Am Acad Forensic Sci; AAAS; Am Soc Testing & Mat; Am Soc Crime Lab Dirs; Int Found Sci; distinguished mem Int Asn Identification; fel Eng Fingerprint Soc. **Research Statement & Publications:** Protein biosynthesis; blood individualization, forensic science and crime scene investigation; forensic chemistry; DNA typing; fingerpirnt and trace analysis. **Mailing Address:** Forensic Sci Lab, 278 Colony St, Meriden, CT 06451-2098. **Fax:** 203-639-6485.

LEE, HENRY JOUNG, ANTI-INFLAMMATORY STEROIDS. **Personal Data:** b Seoul, South Korea, November 17, 1941; American citizen; m 1969, Hyoja; c Lois, Jae & Jenny. **Education:** Seoul Nat Univ, BS, 1964, MS, 1966; Okla State Univ, PhD (biochem), 1971. **Professional Experience:** Consult, Sandoz Pharmaceut Co, 1986-; grant reviewer, NIH, 1985; consult, Taisho Pharmaceut Co, 1985; PROF BASIC SCI, COL PHARM, FLA A & M UNIV, 1982-; prin investr, NIH, 1979-; vis scientist, Rockefeller Univ, 1979; from asst prof to assoc prof, Col Pharm, Fla A & M Univ, 1973-1982; res assoc, Mt Sinai Sch Med, 1971-1973; res asst biochem, Okla State Univ, 1967-1971; instr food technol, Seoul Women's Col, 1966-1967. **Memberships:** Sigma Xi; Am Chem Soc; Am Soc Biol Chemists. **Research Statement & Publications:** Chemical synthesis and evaluation of new anti inflammatory steroids without adverse effects. **Mailing Address:** Dept Med Chem, Fla A & M Sch Pharm, Pharm Bldg Rm 227, Tallahassee, FL 32307. **E-Mail:** henry.lee@famu.edu

LEE, H(O) C(HONG), MECHANICAL ENGINEERING. **Personal Data:** b Seoul, Korea, August 2, 1933; m 1965, c 2. **Education:** Univ Bridgeport, BS, 1957; Rensselaer Polytech Inst, MME, 1959, PhD (mech eng), 1962. **Professional Experience:** RETIRED; sr tech staff mem, Ibm Corp, beginning 1989; sr engr, IBM Corp, 1977-1989; adv engr, IBM Corp, 1970-1977; staff engr, IBM Corp, 1968-1970; adj assoc prof, Rensselaer Polytech Inst, 1968-1970; consult, Mech Tech Inc, 1962-1965 & Gen Elec Co, 1965-1968; asst prof mech eng, Rensselaer Polytech Inst, 1962-1968. **Memberships:** Am Soc Mech Engrs. **Research Statement & Publications:** Dynamics of structural elements; rotor dynamics. **Mailing Address:** 8 Tudor Dr, Endicott, NY 13760.

LEE, HOONG-CHIEN, PHYSICS. **Personal Data:** b Hong Kong, August 12, 1941; m 1965, c 3. **Education:** Nat Taiwan Univ, BSc, 1963; McGill Univ, MSc, 1967, PhD (physics), 1969. **Professional Experience:** PROF, DEPT LIFE SCI, NAT CENTRAL UNIV, 2000-; PERMANENT VIS PROF, INST THEORET PHYSICS, ACAD SCI, 2000-; DIR CTR COMPLEX SYSTS, NAT CENTRAL UNIV, 1997-; PROF, DEPT PHYSICS, NAT CENTRAL UNIV, 1995-; sr res officer theoret physics, Chalk River Nuclear Labs, Atomic Energy Can Ltd, 1985-1993; assoc res officer, Chalk River Nuclear Labs, Atomic Energy Can, Ltd, 1968-1985; Tech collabr physics, Brookhaven Nat Lab, 1967-1968. **Memberships:** Am Phys Soc; Can Asn Physicists. **Research Statement & Publications:** Theoretical nuclear physics; structure of nuclei; electromagnetic and weak interaction; structure and decay of elementary particles and nuclei. **Mailing Address:** Nat Central Univ, Dept Physics & Life Sci, No 300, Jungda Rd, Jhongli, China. **Fax:** 886-3425-1175. **E-Mail:** hclee@phy.ncu.edu.tw

LEE, HSI-NAN, ATMOSPHERIC SCIENCE, MATHEMATIC NUMERICAL TECHNIQUES. **Personal Data:** b Taiwan, July 15, 1946; m 1974, c 2. **Education:** Col Chinese Cult, BS, 1970; Univ Utah, MS, 1973, PhD (meteorol), 1977. **Professional Experience:** Res asst prof, Dept Meteorol, Univ Utah, 1980-1982; assoc meteorologist, Brookhaven Nat Lab, 1979-1980; asst meteorologist atmospheric sci, Brookhaven Nat Lab, 1977-1979; Res asst meteorol, Univ Utah, 1971-1977. **Memberships:** Sigma Xi; Am Meteorol Soc. **Research Statement & Publications:** Advanced numerical modeling study in environmental air pollution; large scale atmospheric wave structure and nonlinear interaction in wave number frequency space; mathematic numerical techniques; numerical techniques for solving partial and ordinary differential equation. **Mailing Address:** 17252 Chestnut St, Yorba Linda, CA 92886.

LEE, HSIN-YI, DEVELOPMENTAL BIOLOGY. **Personal Data:** b Hsin-Chu, Taiwan, c 1. **Education:** Nat Taiwan Univ, BS, 1959; Oberlin Col, MA, 1964; Univ Minn, Minneapolis, PhD (zool), 1967. **Professional Experience:** Chmn dept, Rutgers Univ, Camden, beginning 1984; PROF ZOOL, RUTGERS UNIV, CAMDEN, 1978-; from asst prof to assoc prof biol, Rutgers Univ, Camden, 1968-1978; res assoc tissue cult, Cardiovasc Inst, Michael Reese Hosp & Med Ctr, 1968. **Memberships:** AAAS; Am Soc Zoologists. **Research Statement & Publications:** Neural tube formation. **Mailing Address:** Dept Biol, Rutgers Univ, 315 Penn St, Camden, NJ 08102. **Fax:** 856-225-6312. **E-Mail:** hsin-yi@crab.rutgers.edu

LEE, HUA, ACOUSTIC MICROSCOPY, IMAGING ALGORITHM DESIGN. **Personal Data:** b Taipei, Taiwan, September 30, 1952; m 1976, c 2. **Education:** Nat Taiwan Univ, BS, 1974; Univ Calif, Santa Barbara, MS, 1978, PhD (elec eng), 1980. **Professional Experience:** PROF ELEC ENG, UNIV CALIF, SANTA BARBARA, 1990-; from asst prof to assoc prof elec eng, Univ Ill, 1983-1990; asst prof elec eng, Univ Calif, Santa Barbara, 1980-1983. **Memberships:** Inst Elec & Electronics Engrs; Acoust Soc Am. **Research Statement & Publications:** All aspects of the imaging technology; high-resolution high-speed imaging techniques; imaging system optimization; radar and sonar imaging; signal analysis and processing; biomedical imaging, high resolution gerome sequencing; computer vision and non-destructive evaluation. **Mailing Address:** Dept Elec & Comput Eng, Univ Calif, Rm 4115 Eng I, Santa Barbara, CA 93106-9560. **Fax:** 805-893-3262. **E-Mail:** hualee@ece.ucsb.edu

LEE, HUA-TSUN, MATHEMATICS, LINEAR & INTEGER PROGRAMMING. **Personal Data:** b Nanking, China, May 11, 1937; m 1963, Su; c Amy, Albert, Margaret & Lita. **Education:** Tunghai Univ, Taiwan, BS, 1959; Univ Pittsburgh, PhD (math), 1971. **Professional Experience:** PROF MATH, POINT PARK COL, 1982-; assoc prof, Fudan Univ, 1980-1982; from asst prof to assoc prof, Point Park Col, 1969-1982; instr biostatist, Grad Sch Pub Health, 1967-1968; asst math, Univ Pittsburgh, 1965-1967 & 1968-1969; asst physics, Univ Pittsburgh, 1961-1964; Asst physics, Tunghai Univ, Taiwan, 1961. **Memberships:** Math Asn Am. **Research Statement & Publications:** Summability methods of infinite series; linear programming; integer programming. **Mailing Address:** Dept Math, Natural Sci & Eng Technol, Point Park Univ, 605A Acad Hall 201 Wood St, Pittsburgh, PA 15222. **Fax:** 412-392-3962. **E-Mail:** hlee@ppc.edu

LEE, HULBERT AUSTIN, GEOLOGY. **Personal Data:** b Chelsea, Que, June 17, 1923; m 1947, Katherine A Yuill; c Edith, Eleanor, Thomas, Douglas & Barbara. **Education:** Queen's Univ, Ont, BSc, 1949; Univ Chicago, PhD (geol), 1953. **Professional Experience:** CONSULT GEOLOGIST, LEE GEO-INDICATORS LTD, 1969-; pres, Lee Geo-indicators Ltd, 1969-1996; Vis lectr, Univ NB, 1964-1965; Geologist, Geol Surv Can, 1950-1969. **Memberships:** Fel Geol Soc Am; Can Inst Mining & Metall; Prospectors & Developers Asn. **Research Statement & Publications:** Correlation of quaternary events around Hudson Bay, the Tyrrell Sea and Keewatin ice divide; quaternary studies in New Brunswick; esker and till methods of mineral exploration now firmly established and extensively used in the exploration industry; kimberlite petrology, engineering terrain analysis of Ontario; morphology and significance of gold particles. **Mailing Address:** 10 Alexander St Box 68, Stittsville, ON K2S 1A2, Can.

LEE, HUNG, ENVIRONMENTAL MICROBIOLOGY, BIOMASS CONVERSION & BIO-PRODUCTS. **Personal Data:** b Kaoshiung, Taiwan, November 1954; Canadian citizen; m 1990, Colleen; c Jeremy & Jasmine. **Education:** Univ BC, BSc (honors in biochem), 1977; McGill Univ, PhD (biochem), 1982. **Honors & Awards:** Citation for Res Excellence Award, Imp Oil Ltd, 1990; University of Guelph Presidential Distinguished Professor Award (2002-2004). **Professional Experience:** PROF ENVIRON BIOL, UNIV GUELPH, 1999-; vis prof, Fac Forestry, Univ BC, 2005-2006; adj prof, Sch Eng, Univ Guelph, 1992-; vis prof, Biotechnol Lab, Univ BC, 1992-1993; assoc prof environ biol, Univ Guelph, 1991-1999; asst prof, Univ Guelph, 1986-1991; fel, Med Res Coun Can, 1984; res assoc, Nat Res Coun Can, 1983-1986. **Memberships:** Am Soc Microbiol; Soc Indust Microbiol. **Research Statement & Publications:** Biotransformation and biodegradation of environmental pollutants; molecular cloning and characterization of catabolic genes; structure-function and protein engineering studies of catabolic enzymes; detection and monitoring of microorganisms in the environment; metabolism and bioconversion of hemicellulosic sugars; environmental toxicology. **Mailing Address:** Dept Environ Biol, Univ Guelph, Guelph, ON N1G 2W1, Can. **Fax:** 519-837-0442. **E-Mail:** hlee@uoguelph.ca

LEE, HYUNG MO, MEDICINE, VASCULAR & TRANSPLANT SURGERY. **Personal Data:** b Tanchon, Korea, September 27, 1926; American citizen; m 1959, c 2. **Education:** Keijo Imp Univ, BS, 1945; Seoul Nat Univ, MD, 1949. **Professional Experience:** PROF EMER SURG, VA COMMON WEALTH UNIV, 1996-; chmn, Div Vascular Surg, 1994-1996; chmn, Div Vascular & Transplant Surg, 1973-1994; dir, Clin Transplant Prog, Med Col Va, 1973-1994; from instr to emer prof, Med Col Va, 1963-1996; res fel surg, Med Col Va, 1959-1961. **Memberships:** Am Col Surgeons; Am Soc Nephrology; Transplantation Soc; Am Soc Transplant Surgeons (secy, 1981-1983, pres, 1984-1985); Int Cardiovasc Surg Soc; Int Soc Heart Transplantation; Int Soc Nephrology. **Research Statement & Publications:** Renal homotransplantation. **Mailing Address:** Dept Surg, Sch Med, Va Comman Wealth Univ, 1200 E Broad St PO Box 980645, Richmond, VA 23298-0057. **Fax:** 804-827-1016. **E-Mail:** hmlee@vcu.edu

LEE, I P, MOLECULAR BIOLOGY, ENDOCRINOLOGY. **Personal Data:** b Rupl, Korea, December 25, 1935; American citizen; m 1962, c 4. **Education:** Pac Lutheran Univ, BA, 1959; Univ Wash, MS, 1969, PhD (pharmacol), 1971. **Professional Experience:** Med Sch, Beijing polytech Univ, 1987; RES PHARMACOLOGIST MOLECULAR TOXICOL, DEPT HEALTH & HUMAN SERV, FOOD & DRUG ADMIN, 1985-; Med Sch, Yonsei Univ, 1984; Med Sch, Cath Univ, 1983; vis prof, Fed Tech Univ & Univ Zurich, Inst toxicol, 1975-1976; res pharmacologist, Nat Inst environ health serv, 1972-1985; res pharmacologist, Nat Cancer Inst, NIH, 1969-1972. **Memberships:** Am Soc Pharmacol & Exp Therapeut; Soc Toxicol; Sigma Xi. **Research Statement & Publications:** Metabolism and toxicology of chemical carcinogens in male reproductive tissues. **Mailing Address:** Dept Health & Human Serv & Molecular Toxicol, Food & Drug Admin, HFF-162 8301 Muirkirk Rd, Laurel, MD 20708.

LEE, ILZOO, SPACE SYSTEMS ENGINEERING, PROPULSION. **Personal Data:** b Seoul, Korea, January 12, 1958; American citizen. **Education:** Han Yang Uni, Seoul, Korea, BS, 1982; Alfred Univ, MS, 1984; Univ Utah, PhD (mat sci & eng), 1989. **Professional Experience:** SR PROJECT MANAGER, AEROSPACE CORP, 1997-; mat scientist, Res Dept, Naval Air Warfare Ctr, 1991-1997; post-doctoral fel, Mat Sci & Eng, Univ Utah, 1990-1991. **Memberships:** Am Ceramic Soc; Am Chem Soc; Am Inst Aeronaut & Astronaut. **Mailing Address:** PO Box 92957-M5/123, Los Angeles, CA 90009-2957. **Fax:** 310-563-3159. **E-Mail:** ilzoo.lee@aero.org

LEE, INSUP, COMPUTER & INFORMATION SCIENCES. **Personal Data:** b Seoul, Korea, March 15, 1955; c 2. **Education:** Univ NC, Chapel Hill, BS, 1977; Univ Wis, Madison, MS, 1978, PhD (comput sci), 1983. **Professional Experience:** Cecilia Fitler Moore Prof, Dept Comput & Info Sci, Univ Pa, as of 2005; assoc prof comput sci, Univ Pa, beginning 1983. **Memberships:** Fel Inst Elec & Electronics Engrs; Am Comput Mach. **Research Statement & Publications:** Distributed real-time computing. **Mailing Address:** Dept Comput & Info Sci Univ Pa Moore Sch Elec Eng, Levine Hall Rm 602 3330 Walnut St, Philadelphia, PA 19104-6389. **Fax:** 215-573-7362. **E-Mail:** lee@cis.upenn.edu

LEE, I-YANG, NUCLEAR PHYSICS. **Personal Data:** b Nanking, China, December 21, 1946; American citizen; m 1972, Eva; c Helen & Haidy. **Education:** Nat Taiwan Univ, BSc, 1968; Univ Pittsburgh, PhD (physics), 1974. **Professional Experience:** SCI DIR, LAWRENCE BERKELEY LAB, as of 2001; staff physicist nuclear physics, Lawrence Berkeley Lab, beginning 1992; Physicist, Oak Ridge Nat Lab, 1977-1992; physicist, Lawrence Berkeley Lab, 1975-1977. **Memberships:** Fel Am Phys Soc. **Research Statement & Publications:** Nuclear physics. **Mailing Address:** Nuclear Sci Div Bldg 88, Lawrence Berkeley Nat Lab, Berkeley, CA 94720. **E-Mail:** iylee@lbl.gov

LEE, J TODD, MATHEMATICS. **Education:** Guilford Col, BS; Tex Tech Univ, MS, PhD (math). **Professional Experience:** ASSOC PROF MATH, ELON UNIV, as of 2006. **Mailing Address:** Dept Math, Elon Univ, 2308 Campus Box Duke Bldg 209A, Elon, NC 27244. **Fax:** 336-278-6245. **E-Mail:** tlee@elon.edu

LEE, JA H, PLASMA PHYSICS, LASER SCIENCE & OPTICAL DIAGNOSTICS. **Personal Data:** b Hamyang, South Korea, April 25, 1925; American citizen; m 1952, Chang; c Ye-unggil, Yeung-Sook, Insook & Yeung W. **Education:** Kyungpook Nat Univ, Korea, BS, 1948; George Peabody Col, Nashville, MS, 1961; Vanderbilt Univ, Nashville, MS, 1962, PhD (physics), 1964. **Professional Experience:** SR RES SCIENTIST, NASA LANGLEY RES CTR, 1983-; adj res prof physics, Hampton Univ, 1980-; res prof physics, Vanderbilt Univ, Nashville, 1978-1983; res assoc prof, Vanderbilt Univ, Nashville, 1973-1978; prin investrgrants, Langley Res Ctr, NASA, 1969-; sr res assoc, Vanderbilt Univ, Nashville, 1969-1973; res assoc physics, NASA/Nat Acad Sci, 1967-1969; prof physics, Kyungpook Nat Univ, Daegu, Korea, 1965-1967. **Memberships:** Am Phys Soc; Inst Elec & Electronics Engrs; AIAA. **Research Statement & Publications:** Pulsed high beta plasma; high-pulsed power sources, solar pumped laser and laser pumping source development; atomic and molecular spectroscopy. **Mailing Address:** 37 E Governor Dr, Newport News, VA 23602-7405. **Fax:** 757-728-6910. **E-Mail:** j.h.lee@larc.nasa.gov

LEE, JAMES C, HUMAN BIOLOGY CHEMICAL & GENETICS. **Personal Data:** b Shanghai, China, December 16, 1941; American citizen; m 1969, Lucy; c Ching-Wen & Ching-Men. **Education:** Hope Col, BA, 1966; Case Western Res Univ, PhD (biochem), 1971. **Professional Experience:** PROF & ROBERT A WELCH CHAIR CHEM, DEPT HUMAN BIOL CHEM & GENETICS, UNIV TEX MED BR, GALVESTON, 1990-; mem, Molecular & Cellular Biophys Study Sect, NIH, 1981-1985 & spec study sect, 1989, 1990 & 1991; vis prof, State Univ NY, Stony Brook, 1986; from asst prof to prof biochem, St Louis Univ, Mo, 1976-1990; fel, Grad Dept Biochem, Brandeis Univ, Boston, Mass, 1971-1976. **Memberships:** Am Chem Soc-Div Biol Chem; fel AAAS; Biophys Soc; Am Soc Biol Chemists; Am Soc Cell Biol. **Research Statement & Publications:** Elucidate the regulatory mechanisms of biological functions at the molecular level; gene expressions; supra-macromolecular assembly; enzyme activity. **Mailing Address:** Human Biol Chem & Genetics Dept, Univ Tex Med Br, Blocker Med Res Bldg, Galveston, TX 77555-1055. **Fax:** 409-772-4298. **E-Mail:** jclee@utmb.edu

LEE, JAMES M, BIOCHEMICAL ENGINEERING, PLANT CELL CULTURE. **Personal Data:** American citizen; m. **Education:** Yon-Sei Univ, Korea, BS, 1970, MS, 1972; Univ Ky, PhD (chem eng), 1978. **Professional Experience:** PROF CHEM ENG, WASH STATE UNIV, 1988-; Program Director, Biochem Eng & Biotech Prog, National Science Foundation 2002-; Assoc Prof, Washington State Univ, 1983-1988; Assoc Prof, Cleveland State Univ, 1982-1983, Asst Prof, Cleveland State Univ, 1978-1982. **Memberships:** Am Chem Soc; Am Inst Chem Engrs. **Research Statement & Publications:** Production foreign protein products from large-scale plant suspension cell culture; mass transfer; mixing; fermentation; bioreactor design. **Mailing Address:** Chem Eng Dept, Wash State Univ, Pullman, WA 99164-2710. **Fax:** 509-335-4806. **E-Mail:** jmlee@wsu.edu

LEE, JAMES NORMAN, MAGNETIC RESONANCE IMAGING, FUNCTIONAL MAGNETIC RESONANCE IMAGING. **Personal Data:** b Santa Monica, Calif, December 20, 1956; m 1979, Kim; c Bethany, Jessica & Christina. **Education:** Univ Utah, BA, 1980, MS, 1982; Duke Univ, PhD, 1986; Brigham Young Univ, MS, 2004. **Professional Experience:** RES ASSOC, UNIV UTAH, 1999-; asst prof radiol, Univ Utah, 1988-1993; Res assoc, Duke Univ, 1986-1988. **Research Statement & Publications:** Applications of functional magnetic resonance imaging (fMRI). **Mailing Address:** Ctr Advan Med Tech, 729 Arapeen Dr, Salt Lake City, UT 84108. **Fax:** 801-585-3592. **E-Mail:** jim@ucair.med.utah.edu

LEE, JANG Y, CARDIOVASCULAR. **Professional Experience:** RES INVESTR, DEPT CARDIOVASC PHARMACOL, ABBOTT LABS, 1984-. **Mailing Address:** Dept Cardiovasc Pharmacol, Abbott Labs Dept 47-B/AP-9, Abbott Park, IL 60064-3500.

LEE, JEAN CHOR-YIN WONG, BIOCHEMISTRY. **Personal Data:** b Canton, China, August 26, 1941; m 1967, Kit Wi; c Garland & Clifford. **Education:** Chung Chi Col, Hong Kong, dipl, 1962; Univ Nebr, Lincoln, PhD (chem), 1967. **Honors & Awards:** Lewis E Harris Award for Excellence, 1989. **Professional Experience:** DIR SCI SERV, HARRIS LABS, INC, 1993-; ADJ ASST PROF, UNIV NEBR, LINCOLN, 1987-; group leader, Univ Nebr, Lincoln, 1986-1993; fel chem & res assoc, Univ Nebr, Lincoln, 1970-1986; Res instr biochem, Col Med, Univ Nebr, Omaha, 1967-1970. **Memberships:** Am Chem Soc; Am Asn Pharmaceut Sci; Clin Ligand Assay Soc. **Research Statement & Publications:** Biomembranes, structure and transport; analysis of pharmaceuticals. **Mailing Address:** PO Box 80837, Harris Lab Inc, Lincoln, NE 68501-0837.

LEE, JEN-SHIH, ENGINEERING MECHANICS. **Personal Data:** b Kwangtung, China, August 22, 1940; American citizen; m 1966, c Lionel, Grace & Albert. **Education:** Nat Taiwan Univ, BS, 1961; Calif Inst Technol, MS, 1963, PhD (aeronaut, math), 1966. **Professional Experience:** PROF & EMER BIOMED ENG, UNIV VA, as of 2004; chmn Dept, Univ Va, beginning 1988; prof biomed eng, Univ VA, beginning 1984; Nat Heart & Lung Inst res career develop award, 1975-1980; USPHS res grant, Univ Va, 1971; from asst prof to assoc prof, Univ VA, 1969-1983; San Diego Co Heart Asn advan res fel, 1966-1969; asst res engr, Univ Calif, San Diego, 1966-1969. **Memberships:** Am Physiol Soc; Biomed Eng Soc; fel Am Soc Mech Engrs; Inst Elec & Electronics Engrs; Microcirc Soc; fel Am Inst Med & Biol Eng; Biomed Eng Soc (pres-elect, 1993-1994). **Research Statement & Publications:** Hemodynamics; pulmonary mechanics and edema; indicator dilution technique as applied to microcirculation and transcapillary exchange in microvessels. **Mailing Address:** Dept Biomed Eng, Univ Va, PO Box 800759, Charlottesville, VA 22908-0759. **Fax:** 434-982-3870. **E-Mail:** jl@virginia.edu

LEE, JEONGIN, PHYSICS. **Education:** Sch Computational Sci, PhD, 1998. **Professional Experience:** STAFF, NAT RES COUN ASSOC, NASA, as of 2006. **Mailing Address:** 4201 Cathedral Ave Nw Apt 617w, Washington, DC 20016. **Fax:** 301-614-5644. **E-Mail:** jlee-at-milkyway.gsfc.nasa.gov

LEE, JOE, TRANSPORTATION ENGINEERING, TRAFFIC ENGINEERING. **Personal Data:** b Shanghai, China, March 2, 1939; American citizen; m 1970, c 2. **Education:** Nat Taiwan Univ, BSc, 1961; Asian Inst Technol, MEng, 1966; Ohio State Univ, PhD (transp & traffic eng), 1971. **Professional Experience:** Consult, UN, 1988-; PROF CIVIL ENG, UNIV KANS, 1981-; DIR, TRANSP CTR, UNIV KANS, 1977-; prin investr, Ctr Res Inc, Univ Kans, 1974-; from asst prof to assoc prof civil eng, Transp Ctr, 1971-1981; res asst, Ohio State Univ, 1966-1971; res asst, Asian Inst Technol, 1964-1966; field engr construct, BES Eng Corp, 1962-1964; installation officer maintenance, Chinese Air Force, 1961-1962; adv prof, Xian Hwy Univ, Tung Chi Univ, Hefei Indust Univ & Shandong Transp Univ. **Memberships:** Inst Transp Engrs; Am Soc Civil Engrs; Am Soc Eng Educ; Am Road & Transp Builders Asn; Am Pub Works Asn; N Am Chinese Transp Profs Asn. **Research Statement & Publications:** Traffic flow dynamics; highway design; traffic safety; traffic signal operation and general systems theory. **Mailing Address:** Dept Civil Environ & Archit Eng, Univ Kans, 2150 Learned Hall 1530 W 15th St, Lawrence, KS 66045-7609. **Fax:** 785-864-3199. **E-Mail:** jlee@ku.edu

LEE, JOHN ALEXANDER HUGH, EPIDEMIOLOGY. **Personal Data:** b Isle of Wight, Eng, October 10, 1925; m 1949, c 3. **Education:** Univ Edinburgh, BSc, 1947, MB, ChB, 1949, MD, 1955; Univ London, DPH, 1952. **Professional Experience:** EMER PROF EPIDEMIOL, UNIV WASH, 1966-; mem sci staff, Social Med Res Unit, Med Res Coun, London Hosp, 1955-1966; fel epidemiol, London Sch Hyg & Trop Med, 1952-1955. **Memberships:** Am Epidemiol Soc; Brit Soc Social Med; Brit Med Asn; Int Epidemiol Asn. **Research Statement & Publications:** Epidemiology of neoplastic diesease. **Mailing Address:** Dept Epidemiol & Int Health Box 358080, Univ Wash SC 36 1100 Fairview Ave N, Seattle, WA 98109-1024. **Fax:** 206-667-4762. **E-Mail:** jahlee@u.washington.edu

LEE, JOHN A N, PROGRAMMING LANGUAGES, SOFTWARE ENGINEERING. **Personal Data:** b Coventry, Eng, December 23, 1934; American citizen; m 1988, Delores; c Andrew, Derek, Jo-Anne, Stuart & Jamie. **Education:** Univ Nottingham, BSc, 1955, PhD (appl sci), 1958. **Honors & Awards:** Outstanding Contrib Award, Asn Comput Mach, 1981, Distinguished Serv Award, 1993; Cert Distinguished Serv, US Dept Defense, 1983. **Professional Experience:** ED-IN-CHIEF, INST ELEC & ELECTRONICS ENGRS COMPUT SOC, 1991-; dir, Ctr Innovative Technol, Inst Info Technol, Herndon, Va, 1987-1991; coun mem, Stand Comt, Asn Comput Mach, 1982-1984; ed & ed-in-chief, Am Fedn Info Processing Socs, 1980-1991; fac assoc, Santa Teresa Lab, IBM Corp, San Jose, 1980-1981; head, Dept Comput Sci, Va Tech, 1979-1980; PROF COMPUT SCI, VA TECH, 1974-; vis prof, Univ Denver, 1970-1971; prof comput sci, Univ Mass, Amherst, 1964-1974; assoc dir, Comput Ctr, 1964-1974; chair, Stand Comt, Asn Comput Mach, 1964-1973; head, Dept Comput Sci, Univ Mass, Amherst, 1964-1969; Dir, Comput Ctr, Queens Univ, Kingston, Ont, 1960-1964; asst prof civil eng, Queens Univ, Kingston, Ont, 1959-1964; asst engr, Freeman, Fox & Partners, 1957-1959. **Memberships:** Fel Asn Comput Mach (vpres, 1984-1986); Inst Elec & Electronics Engrs Comput Soc (vpres, 1995-1996); Am Fedn Info Processing Socs. **Research Statement & Publications:** Programming languages: history, compilers and design; software engineering: formal specifications, testing, integration, history of computing. **Mailing Address:** Dept Comput Sci, Va Tech, 512 McBryde Hall, Blacksburg, VA 24061-0106. **Fax:** 540-231-6075. **E-Mail:** janlee@cs.vt.edu

LEE, JOHN CHAESEUNG, REACTOR PHYSICS, ENGINEERING. **Personal Data:** b Seoul, Korea, July 29, 1941; American citizen; m 1971, Theresa; c Nina. **Education:** Seoul Nat Univ, BS, 1963; Univ Calif, Berkeley, PhD (nuclear eng), 1969. **Professional Experience:** Mem, Tech Working Group, US DepT Energy Generation IV Roadmap Proj, 2001-2003; CHAIR, DEPT NUCLEAR ENG & RADIOL SCI, 1999-2004; mem, Panel Separations Technol & Transmutation Systs, Transmutation Subgroup, Nat Acad Sci, 1991-1996; actg chmn, Dept Nuclear Eng, 1986; PROF NUCLEAR ENG, UNIV MICH, ANN ARBOR, 1981-; vis scientist, Ger, 1981-1982; Consult, Adv Comt Reactor Safeguards, US Nuclear Regulatory Comn, 1975-1994 & Los Alamos Nat Lab, 1977-1988; from asst prof to assoc prof, Univ Mich, Ann Arbor, 1974-1981; sr engr, Gen Elec Co, 1973-1974; Sr engr nuclear eng, Westinghouse Elec Corp, 1969-1973. **Memberships:** Fel Am Nuclear Soc; AAAS. **Research Statement & Publications:** Nuclear reactor physics; reactor kinetics; fuel cycle analysis; reactor safety analysis; power plant simulation and control. **Mailing Address:** Dept Nuclear Eng, Radiol Sci, Univ Mich, Ann Arbor, MI 48109-2104. **Fax:** 734-763-4540. **E-Mail:** jcl@umich.edu

LEE, JOHN CHEUNG HAN, INDUSTRIAL MICROBIOLOGY, INFECTIOUS DISEASES-ANTIBOTICS. **Personal Data:** b China, December 1, 1945; m 1977, c 1. **Education:** Rutgers Univ, BA, 1967; Long Island Univ, MS, 1972; St John's Univ, PhD (microbiol), 1979. **Professional Experience:** Supvr, Miles Pharmaceut, 1979-; sect head, Julius Schmid, Inc, 1967-1973; ASSOC DIR CELL BIOCHEM, SMITH KLINE BEECHAM. **Memberships:** Am Soc Microbiol; NY Acad Sci; Soc Indust Microbiol; Sigma Xi. **Research Statement & Publications:** In vitro activity of new antibiotics; effect of antibiotics on functions of macrophages. **Mailing Address:** Smith Kline Beecham, King of Prussia, PA 19406.

LEE, JOHN CHUNG, BIOCHEMISTRY. **Personal Data:** b Shanghai, China, March 2, 1936; American citizen; m 1963, June; c Andrew & Nathan. **Education:** Taylor Univ, AB, 1961; Purdue Univ, West Lafayette, MSc, 1964, PhD (molecular biol), 1967. **Professional Experience:** PROF BIOCHEM, UNIV TEX HEALTH SCI CTR, SAN ANTONIO, 1985-; USPHS res grant, Univ Tex Health Sci Ctr, San Antonio, 1971-; from asst prof to assoc prof, Med Sch, 1969-1985; Res assoc biochem, Mass Inst Technol, 1967-1969. **Memberships:** Am Chem Soc; Am Soc Biochem & Molecular Biol; Am Soc Bone Miner Res; Orthopedic Res Soc. **Research Statement & Publications:** Structure and function of nucleic acids and of ribosomes; RNA-protein interactions; molecular action of bone morphogenetic proteins. **Mailing Address:** Dept Biochem (MC7760), Univ Tex Health Sci Ctr, San Antonio, TX 78229-3900. **Fax:** 210-567-6595. **E-Mail:** leej@uthscsa.edu

LEE, JOHN D(AVID), AERODYNAMICS. **Personal Data:** b Barrie, Ont, August 24, 1924; American citizen; m 1949, c 3. **Education:** Univ Toronto, BSc, 1949; Inst Aerophys, Toronto, MSc, 1950, PhD (aerophys), 1952. **Professional Experience:** RETIRED; dir, Aeronaut & Astronaut Res Lab, Ohio State Univ, beginning 1968; prof aeronaut & astronaut eng, Ohio State Univ, beginning 1959; dir, Aerodyn Lab, Ohio State Univ, 1955-1968; assoc prof aeronaut eng, Ohio State Univ, 1955-1959; asst prof & res assoc, Ohio State Univ, 1953-1955; consult, Naval Ord Lab, Wright Air Develop Ctr, Fluidyne Eng Corp, Sandia Corp & US Army. **Memberships:** Am Inst Aeronaut & Astronaut; Sigma Xi. **Research Statement & Publications:** Hypersonic fluid mechanics; boundary layer phenomena; low density flows; transonic high Reynolds number flows. **Mailing Address:** Dept Aeronaut & Astronaut Eng, Ohio State Univ, 2300 W Case Rd, Columbus, OH 43235-2533. **Fax:** 614-292-5552.

LEE, JOHN DENIS, METEOROLOGY. **Personal Data:** b Trinidad, WI, April 22, 1929; m 1958, c 3. **Education:** Fla State Univ, BS, 1970, MS, 1971, PhD (meteorol), 1973. **Professional Experience:** COORDR MINORITY AFFAIRS, PA STATE UNIV, as of 2004; RES ASSOC, PA STATE UNIV, 1986-; UN expert meteorol educ & training, Saudi Arabia, 1982-1986; lectr meteorol, UN Develop Prog for Advan Training Meteorol Eng-speaking Caribbean Territories, 1978-1981; asst prof meteorol, Pa State Univ, 1974-1978; fel, Nat Ctr Atmospheric Res, 1973-1974. **Memberships:** Am Meteorol Soc; Sigma Xi; NY Acad Sci. **Research Statement & Publications:** Numerical modeling of cooling tower plumes and urban pollution; time series analysis; numerical modeling of flow over obstacles. **Mailing Address:** Col Earth & Mineral Sci, Pa State Univ, 101 Deike Bldg, Univ Park, PA 16802.

LEE, JOHN E, JR, AGRICULTURE. **Education:** Auburn University, BS, 1957, MS, 1958; Harvard Univ, PhD (econ), 1969. **Professional Experience:** HEAD EMER, DEPT AGR ECON, MISS STAE UNIV, as of 2005. **Mailing Address:** Econ Res Serv Rm 1226 USDA, 1301 NY Ave NW, Washington, DC 20005-4788.

LEE, JOHN HAK SHAN, COMBUSTION, SHOCK WAVES & EXPLOSIONS. **Personal Data:** b Hong Kong, September 7, 1938; Canadian citizen; m 1962, c 2. **Education:** McGill Univ, BSc, 1960, PhD (eng), 1965; Mass Inst Technol, MSc, 1962. **Honors & Awards:** Silver Medal, Combustion Inst, 1980 & Dionizy Smolenski Medal, 1988; Numa Manson Gold Medal, 1991. **Professional Experience:** PROF MECH ENG, MCGILL UNIV, 1973-; from asst prof to assoc prof, McGill Univ, 1964-1966; lectr, McGill Univ, 1962-1964. **Memberships:** Order Engrs Quebec; Am Phys Soc; Combustion Inst; Am Inst Aeronaut & Astronaut. **Research Statement & Publications:** Combustion and detonation phenomenon, combustion synthesis of materials; cause, effects, prevention and mitigation of accidental explosions in the production, transport, storage of flammable gases, liquids, organic, metallic and coal dusts; hydrogen combustion and vapor explosion problems pertaining to nuclear reactor accident. **Mailing Address:** Dept Mech Eng, McGill Univ, Rm 459 Macdonald Eng Bldg 817 Sherbrooke St W, Montreal, PQ H2A 2K6, Can. **Fax:** 514-398-7365. **E-Mail:** jhslee@mecheng.mcgill.ca

LEE, JOHN JOSEPH, MARINE MICROBIOLOGY, PROTOZOOLOGY. **Personal Data:** b Philadelphia, Pa, February 23, 1933; m Judith; c Monica J Tischler & James M Lee. **Education:** Queens Col, NY, BS, 1955; Univ Mass, MA, 1957; NY Univ, PhD (biol), 1960. **Honors & Awards:** JOSEPH A CUSHMAN AWARD. **Professional Experience:** RES ASSOC, PHILADELPHIA ACAD NATURAL SCI, 1985-; PROF BIOL, NEW YORK CITY COL, 1972-; RES ASSOC, LAMONT-DOHERTY GEOL OBSERV, 1970-; RES ASSOC IOLR, NATIONAL CENTER FOR MARICULTURE, EILAT ISRAEL 1983-res assoc, Living Foraminifera Lab, Am Mus Natural Hist, 1970-; dir, Marine Microbiol Ecol Lab, Inst Oceanog, City Univ New York, 1968-; from asst prof to assoc prof, New York City Col, 1966-1972; asst prof, NY Univ, 1961-1966; Res fel & dir, Living Foraminifera Lab, Am Mus Natural Hist, 1960-1968. **Memberships:** Fel AAAS; Soc Protozool (pres, 1991); Phycol Soc Am; Am Soc Microbiol; Am Micros Soc; Int Soc Symbiosis (pres, 1999-2001); fel NYAS. **Research Statement & Publications:** Cytology, fine structure, life history, ecology, cultivation and nutrition of foraminifera; algal endosymbiosis in foraminifera, meiofauna, benthic marine food webs and diatom assemblages; Mariculture. **Mailing Address:** Dept Biol, NY City Col, MR704, Marshak Sci Bldg, 138th Convent Ave, New York, NY 10031. **Fax:** 212-650-8585. **E-Mail:** jjlee@sci.ccny.cuny.edu

LEE, JOHN K, CELL & DEVELOPMENTAL BIOLOGY. **Professional Experience:** RES INSTR, VANDERBILT UNIV, TENN, 1996-; Postdoctoral fel, Univ Calif San Diego, 1994-1996; Postdoctoral fel, Cell & Develop Biol Dept, Harvard Univ, 1989-1994. **Mailing Address:** Dept Pharm, Vanderbilt Univ, 454 MRB1, Nashville, TN 37232-6600.

LEE, JOHN NORMAN, PHYSICS. **Personal Data:** b Schenectady, NY, December 2, 1944; m 1968, Lina Chan; c Jennifer & John. **Education:** Union Col, Schenectady, BS, 1966; Johns Hopkins Univ, MA, 1968, PhD (physics), 1971. **Honors & Awards:** Kingslake Medal & Prize, Soc Photo-Optical Instrumentation Engrs. **Professional Experience:** SUPVR RES PHYSICIST, NAVAL RES LAB, 1980-; physicist, Electronics Res & Develop Command, Harry Diamond Labs, 1971-1980; Res asst physics, Johns Hopkins Univ, 1969-1971. **Memberships:** Am Phys Soc; sr mem Inst Elec & Electronics Engrs; Optical Soc Am. **Research Statement & Publications:** Signal processing using acousto-optics and surface acoustic wave devices; radiation damage in optical materials and components; signal processing for optical sensors; optical devices for signal processing; optical computing. **Mailing Address:** Naval Res Lab, Code 5620, Washington, DC 20375. **Fax:** 202-767-6370. **E-Mail:** lee8@ccf.nrl.navy.mil

LEE, JOHN W, MATHEMATICS. **Education:** Stanford Univ, PhD, 1969. **Professional Experience:** PROF & ASSOC CHAIR, DEPT MATH, ORE STATE UNIV, as of 2004. **Mailing Address:** Dept Math, Ore State Univ, Rm 294C Kidder Hall, Corvallis, OR 97331-4601. **Fax:** 541-737-0517. **E-Mail:** jwlee@math.oregonstate.edu

LEE, JOHN WILLIAM, CHEMICAL PHYSICS, BIOPHYSICS. **Personal Data:** b Sydney, Australia, April 7, 1935; m 1960, c 2. **Education:** Univ NSW, BS, 1956, PhD (phys chem), 1960. **Professional Experience:** PROF BIOCHEM, UNIV GA, 1975-; assoc prof, Univ Ga, 1969-1975; staff scientist, New Eng Inst Med Res, 1963-1969; res assoc biochem, McCollum-Pratt Inst, Johns Hopkins Univ, 1961-1963. **Memberships:** Am Chem Soc; Am Phys Soc. **Research Statement & Publications:** Positron annihilation in matter; radiation chemistry; energy exchange processes in chemical and biological systems; bioluminescence; chemiluminescence; radiation physics. **Mailing Address:** Dept Biochem Univ Ga, A120A Life Sci Bldg, Athens, GA 30602-7229. **E-Mail:** jlee@uga.edu

LEE, JOHN YUCHU, ORGANIC CHEMISTRY, ORGANOMETALLICS. **Personal Data:** b Tai-Ho, China, January 25, 1948; American citizen; m 1976, c 2. **Education:** Nat Cheng-Kung Univ, Taiwan, BS, 1970; S Dak State Univ, MS, 1974; Vanderbilt Univ, PhD, 1978. **Professional Experience:** RES SPECIALIST, NEW PROJ DEVELOP, ALBERMARLE CORP, 1989-; pres, Chinese Asn, Baton Rouge, 1989-1990; sr res chem, res & develop, 1988-1989; prin & prog dir, Baton Rouge Chinese Sch, 1985-1986; res chemist indust & specialty chem, res & develop, 1980-1988; res assoc bioorg chem, Robert Welch Fel Organometallics, 1979-1980; res assoc bioorg chem, chem dept, Tex A & M Univ, 1978-1979; asst, Vanderbilt Univ, 1974-1978; asst, S Dak State Univ, 1973-1974; chem reagent officer, Chinese Air Force Acad, 1970-1971. **Memberships:** Sigma Xi; fel Am Inst Chemists; Am Chem Soc; Royal Soc Chem; Japanese Chem Soc; Chinese Am Chem Asn; AAAS; Soc Francaise Chimie. **Research Statement & Publications:** Synthesis, isolation and characterization of pharmaceutical, agricultural, surfactant and detergent intermediates, as well as process improvement; bromine chemicals; chemicals from biomass; alkylation products; flame retardants; catalysis; polymer chemistry; advanced materials. **Mailing Address:** 1524 Stoneleigh Dr, Baton Rouge, LA 70808-5776.

LEE, JON H(YUNKOO), APPLIED MATHEMATICS, NONLINEAR DYNAMICS, COMPUTER SIMULATIONS. **Personal Data:** b Seoul, Korea, March 5, 1934; American citizen; m 1970, Janet; c 4. **Education:** Seoul Nat Univ, BS, 1956; Ohio State Univ, MS, 1958, PhD (chem eng), 1962. **Honors & Awards:** Gen Foulois Res Award, 1987. **Professional Experience:** RES SCIENTIST, FLIGHT DYNAMICS LAB, WRIGHT-PATTERSON AFB, OHIO, 1975-; instr, Air Force Inst Technol, 1973; appl mathematician, Aerospace Res Labs, 1964-1975; chem engr, USAF Mat Lab, 1962-1964; adj prof, Dept Chem Eng, Univ Dayton, 1962. **Memberships:** Am Phys Soc; Sigma Xi; Am Acad Mech; Soc Indust & Appl Math. **Research Statement & Publications:** Fluid dynamics; structural vibration; stochastics and chaos; computational mechanics; dynamical systems. **Mailing Address:** 10661 Putnam Rd, Englewood, OH 45322-9764. **Fax:** 937-255-6684. **E-Mail:** jon.lee@wpafb.af.mil

LEE, JONATHAN K P, NUCLEAR PHYSICS. **Personal Data:** b Kiangsu, China, July 13, 1937; m 1967, c 3. **Education:** McGill Univ, BEng, 1960, MSc, 1962, PhD (nuclear physics), 1965. **Professional Experience:** PROF PHYSICS, MCGILL UNIV, 1981-; dir, Foster Radiation Lab, beginning 1979; from asst prof to assoc prof, Foster Radiation Lab, 1968-1981; res asst, Univ Toronto, 1966-1968; Nat Res Coun Can overseas fel, 1965-1966. **Memberships:** Can Asn Physicists; Am Phys Soc; Oper Sci Apliquees. **Research Statement & Publications:** Nuclear structure studies; laser spectroscopy. **Mailing Address:** Dept Physics, McGill Univ, Rutherford Physics Bldg 3610 Univ St, Montreal, PQ H3A 2B2, Can. **E-Mail:** jlee@physics.mcgill.ca

LEE, JONG K, METALLURGY. **Education:** Seoul Nat Univ, BS, 1964; Univ Wash, MS, 1969; Stanford Univ, PhD (Mat Sci), 1973. **Professional Experience:** PROF, DEPT MAT SCI & ENG, MICH STATE UNIV, MICH, as of 2005. **Memberships:** Am Soc metals. **Mailing Address:** Dept Metall & Mat Eng, Mich Technol Univ 1400 Townsend Dr 403 M&ME Bldg, Houghton, MI 49931. **Fax:** 906-487-2934. **E-Mail:** JKL103@mtu.edu

LEE, JONG SUN, MICROBIOLOGY. **Personal Data:** b Suwon, Korea, July 10, 1932; m 1958, c 3. **Education:** Univ Calif, Berkeley, BA, 1958; Ore State Univ, MS, 1962, PhD (microbiol), 1963. **Professional Experience:** RETIRED; Technol Ctr, Fishery Indust, Kodiak, Alaska, 1982-1993; prof food sci & tech, Ore State Univ, 1980-1982; from asst prof to prof food microbiol, Ore State Univ, 1963-1982. **Memberships:** AAAS; Am Soc Microbiol; Inst Food Technol; Brit Soc Appl Bact; Sigma Xi. **Research Statement & Publications:** Microbiology of sea foods. **Mailing Address:** 2695 SW Pickford St, Corvallis, OR 97333.

LEE, JOSEPH CHUEN KWUN, PATHOLOGY, CELL BIOLOGY. **Personal Data:** b Chungking, China, October 6, 1938; American citizen. **Education:** Univ Hong Kong, MB, BS, 1964; Univ Rochester, PhD (path), 1970; FRCP (C), 1971, Am Bd Path, 1972, FRCP (A), 1985, MRC(path), 1986. **Professional Experience:** DEAN FAC MED, CHINESE UNIV, HONG KONG, 1996-; dean fac med, Chinese Univ, Hong Kong, 1986-1989; PROF PATH, CHINESE UNIV, HONG KONG, 1982-; res fel, Armed Forces Inst Path, 1981; vis prof, NIH, 1980; asst prof to assoc prof path & oncol, Univ Rochester Med Ctr, 1972-1980; Toronto Gen Hosp, Univ Toronto, 1970-1971 & Princess Margaret Hosp, Ont Cancer Inst Can, 1971-1972; resident path, New York Hosp-Cornell Med Ctr, 1966-1967; rotating intern, St Francis Hosp, NY, 1966; Intern, Hong Kong, 1964. **Memberships:** AAAS; Am Soc Cell Biol; Soc Anal Cytol; Am Asn Path; Electron Micros Soc Am. **Research Statement & Publications:** Nasopharyngeal carcinoma. **Mailing Address:** Fac Med, Chinese Univ Hong Kong, Shatin New Territories Hong Kong, China. **Fax:** 852-263-76274. **E-Mail:** joelee@cuhk.edu.hk

LEE, JOSHUA ALEXANDER, GENETICS. **Personal Data:** b Rocky Ford, Ga, October 30, 1924; m 1956, c 2. **Education:** San Diego State Col, AB, 1950; Univ Calif, PhD (genetics), 1958. **Professional Experience:** EMER PROF CROP SCI, AGR EXP STA, NC STATE UNIV, 1993-; prof crop sci, Agr Exp Sta, NC State Univ, 1971-1993; GENETICIST, AGR EXP STA, NC STATE UNIV, 1958-; asst, Univ Calif, 1954-1956; Technician, Univ Calif, 1951-1953. **Memberships:** Crop Sci Soc Am; Soc Study Evolution. **Research Statement & Publications:** Genetical problems pertaining to the improvement of domesticated cotton species. **Mailing Address:** 118 West Lake Dr, Sylvania, GA 30467.

LEE, JUNE KEY, ENGINEERING MECHANICS. **Personal Data:** b Seoul, Korea, August 9, 1943; American citizen; m 1970, Yoon; c Jane, Judy & Julie. **Education:** Han-Yang Univ, BS, 1965; Tenn Technol Univ, MS, 1970; Univ Tex, Austin, PhD (eng mech), 1976. **Professional Experience:** PROF MECH, OHIO STATE UNIV, 1986-; consult, 1980-; co-prin investr var grants, Dept Energy, 1980-1982; prin investr, NSF & Ohio State Univ, 1978-; from asst prof to assoc prof, Ohio State Univ, 1977-1986; asst prof eng, Drexel Univ, 1976-1977; asst instr, Univ Tex, 1975-1976; res asst comput mech, Res Inst, Univ Ala, Huntsville, 1970-1973. **Memberships:** Am Acad Mech; Am Soc Mech Eng; Am soc Aut eng, Am soc eng Edu. **Research Statement & Publications:** Theory and application of the finite element method in applied mechanics; numerical methods; sheet metal forming; hygro-thermo-mechanical response of porous media; published over 15 articles. **Mailing Address:** Dept Mech Eng, Ohio State Univ, 274 Bldg One 650 Ackerman Rd, Columbus, OH 43210-1117. **Fax:** 614-292-3163. **E-Mail:** lee.71@osu.edu

LEE, KAH-HOCK, INORGANIC CHEMISTRY. **Personal Data:** b January 28, 1941; American citizen; m 1967, c 3. **Education:** Nanyang Univ, BS, 1964; Georgetown Univ, PhD (inorg chem), 1970. **Professional Experience:** PRES, ADVAN INVESTMENT MGT CO, 1977-; Res fel, Dept Chem, Grad Sch, Georgetown Univ, 1971-1973; Environ chemist, DC Dept Environ Serv, 1969-1980. **Memberships:** Am Chem Soc. **Research Statement & Publications:** Environmental toxic trace metals; effect of x-ray film developer on radiation protection; heteropoly inorganic anions exchange mechanisms. **Mailing Address:** 947 Cedar Ridge Ct, Orange Park, FL 32065-5757.

LEE, KAI NIEN, ENVIRONMENTAL MANAGEMENT, SCIENCE POLICY. **Personal Data:** b New York, NY, October 19, 1945; m 1971, c 2. **Education:** Columbia Univ, BA, 1966; Princeton Univ, PhD (physics), 1971. **Honors & Awards:** White House Fel, 1976; Kellogg Fel, 1980. **Professional Experience:** DIR & ROSENBURG PROF ENVIRON STUDIES, WILLIAMS COL, as of 2004; prof & dir environ studies, Williams Col, beginning 1991; vis prof, Kyoto Univ, Japan, 1990-1991; bd, Radioactive Waste Mgt, Nat Acad Sci, 1983-; mem, Northwest Power Planning Coun, 1983-1987; Kellogg Nat fel, 1980-1983; mem, Environ Studies Bd, 1980-1982; mem Naval Res adv comt, 1978-; mem adv panel radioactive waste disposal, Off Tech Assessment, 1978-1981; White House fel, US Dept Defense, 1976-1977; from asst prof to assoc prof, Inst Environ Studies & Dept Polit Sci, 1975-1991; mem int adv bd, Policy Sci, 1974-; res asst prof, Prog Social Mgt Technol & Dept Polit Sci, Univ Wash, 1973-1975; asst res social scientist, Inst Govt Studies, Univ Calif, Berkeley, 1972-1973; Soc Sci Res Coun res training fel, 1971-1972. **Memberships:** fel Soc Religion Higher Educ; AAAS; Am Polit Sci Asn. **Research Statement & Publications:** Energy and environmental policy and politics: energy, fish and wildlife, global climate change, environmental conflict and dispute settlement; influence of technological change on American life. **Mailing Address:** Ctr Environ Studies, Williams Col, PO Box 632, Williamstown, MA 01267. **Fax:** 413-597-3489. **E-Mail:** kai.n.lee@williams.edu

LEE, KAI-FONG, ANTENNA THEORY & DESIGN, APPLIED ELECTROMAGNETICS. **Personal Data:** b China, July 17, 1939; American citizen; m 1971, Alice; c Walter, Steven & Amy. **Education:** Queen's Univ, Can, BS, 1961, MS, 1963; Cornell Univ, PhD (elec eng), 1966. **Professional Experience:** PROF ELEC ENG & DEAN, SCH ENG, UNIV MISS, as of 2003; LaPierre prof & chmn, elec eng, Univ Toledo, 1996-2000; prof & chmn elect eng, Univ Toledo, Toledo, Ohio, 1998-1995; ASEE-NASA summer fac res fel, NASA Lewis Res Ctr, 1998-1995; prof elec eng, Univ Akron, 1985-1988; reader, Chinese Univ Hong Kong, 1984-; head dept electronic eng, City Polytech Hong Kong, 1984-1985; sr lectr, Chinese Univ Hong Kong, 1977-1983; vis reseacher, Univ Calif, Los Angeles, 1975; lectr electronics, Chinese Univ Hong Kong, 1973-1977; sr resident res assoc, Nat Res Coun-Nat Oceanic & Atmospheric Admin, 1972-1973; vis scientist, Nat Ctr Atmospheric Res, 1968-1969; from asst prof to assoc prof appl phys, Catholic Univ Am, 1967-1972; fel, Univ Calif, San Diego, 1966-1967; res asst, Nat Radio Astron Observ, 1966. **Memberships:** Sr mem Inst Elec & Electronics Engrs; fel Inst Elec & Electronics Engrs; Chartered Eng UK; Am Phys Soc; Sigma Xi. **Research Statement & Publications:** Theory and design of microstrip, helical and reflector antennas; theory of plasma waves and instabilities; author of 157 Journal articles and 124 conference papers. **Mailing Address:** Dept Elec Eng, Sch Eng, Univ Miss, 101 Carrier Hall, Oxford, MS 38677. **Fax:** 662-915-1287. **E-Mail:** leek@olemiss.edu

LEE, KAI-LIN, BIOCHEMISTRY, ENDOCRINOLOGY. **Personal Data:** b Nanking, China, September 16, 1935; m 1964. **Education:** Nat Taiwan Univ, BS, 1960; Tulane Univ, PhD (biochem), 1966. **Professional Experience:** BIOCHEMIST, BIOL DIV, OAK RIDGE NAT LAB, 1970-; res assoc, Biochem, Biol Div, 1969-1970; Hoffmann-La Roche fel, Biochem, Biol Div, 1968-1969; instr, Tulane Univ, 1967-1968; fel biochem endocrinol, Tulane Univ, 1966-1967; res asst biochem, Tulane Univ, 1962-1966; Teaching asst bot, Nat Taiwan Univ, 1961-1962. **Memberships:** AAAS; Endocrine Soc; Am Chem Soc; Am Soc Biol Chemists. **Research Statement & Publications:** Hormonal regulation of metabolic processes. **Mailing Address:** Environ Sci Div, Oak Ridge Nat Lab, Oak Ridge, TN 37831-2009.

LEE, KANG, SMART SENSOR INTERFACE, SENSOR SYSTEM INTEGRATION. **Personal Data:** b December 7, 1947. **Education:** Univ Md, MA, 1981. **Professional Experience:** Chmn, Sensor technol comt, Inst elec & electronics engrs, 1995-; GROUP LEADER SENSOR INTEGRATION, NAT INST STAND & TECHNOL, 1987-. **Memberships:** Inst Elec & Electronics Engrs. **Mailing Address:** Div Mfg Metrol, Nat Inst Stand & Technol, 822 100 Bur Dr Bldg 233 Rm B102, Gaithersburg, MD 20899-8220. **E-Mail:** kang.lee@nist.gov

LEE, KANG IN, SYNTHETIC POLYMER CHEMISTRY, POLYMERIC MATERIALS SCIENCE. **Personal Data:** b Korea, November 2, 1946; American citizen; m 1975, Miryoung; c Grace & Albert. **Education:** Murray State Univ, BA, 1970; State Univ NY Buffalo, MA, 1972; Polytech Inst NY, PhD (polymer sci), 1976. **Honors & Awards:** Seymour L Shapiro Award. **Professional Experience:** Affil prof mat sci, Wash Univ, 1985-1986; SR RES

SPECIALIST POLYMER SCI, MONSANTO CO, CHEM GROUP, 1984-; sr mem tech staff polymer sci, Fundamental Res Lab, Gen Tel & Electronics Labs, 1980-1984; res scientist polymer chem, Cent Res Labs, Firestone Tire & Rubber Co, 1977-1980; res assoc, Inst Polymer Sci, Univ Akron, 1976-1977. **Memberships:** Am Chem Soc; Sigma Xi; Korean Scientist & Engrs Am; Tech Asn Pulp & Paper Indust. **Research Statement & Publications:** Synthesis and characterization of new polymers for microelectronics application; cationic and ziegler natta polymerizations; new photoresist developments; conducting polymers, electron beam sensitive polymers, polymers for optical fiber sensor applications, and polymers for paper surface sizing applications. **Mailing Address:** Monsanto Co, 730 Worcester St, Indian Orchard, MA 01151. **Fax:** 413-730-2506. **E-Mail:** kilee@ccmail.monsanto.com

LEE, KATHRYN ADELE BUNDING, MOLECULE-SURFACE INTERACTIONS, VIBRATIONAL SPECTROSCOPY. **Personal Data:** b Chicago, Ill, m 1986, Shu; c Emily. **Education:** Univ Chicago, BA, 1971; City Univ NY, PhD (phys org chem), 1980. **Professional Experience:** RES ASSOC, NAT STARCH & CHEM CO, 1994-; sr scientist, SC Johnson Wax, 1987-1994; res chemist, Naval Res Lab, 1985-1987; res asst, Georgetown Univ, 1984-1985; vis scientist, IBM, 1982-1984; Nat Res Coun fel, Nat Bur Stand, 1980-1982. **Memberships:** Am Chem Soc; Sigma Xi; Soc Appl Spectros. **Research Statement & Publications:** Molecule-surface interactions and reactions; use of in situ spectroscopic and electrochemical techniques; Raman and Fourier transform infrared spectroscopies; optical second harmonic generation; near infared spectroscopy; reaction monitoring. **Mailing Address:** Nat Starch Co, 10 Finderne Ave, Bridgewater, NJ 08807-0500. **Fax:** 908-685-5005. **E-Mail:** kathryn.lee@nstarch.com

LEE, KEENAN, GEOLOGY. **Personal Data:** b Huntington, NY, November 20, 1936; m 1966, c 2. **Education:** La State Univ, Baton Rouge, BS, 1960, MS, 1963; Stanford Univ, PhD (geol), 1969. **Professional Experience:** PROF EMER GEOL, COLO SCH MINES, as of 2003; assoc prof geol, Colo Sch Mines, beginning 1974; asst prof, Colo Sch Mines, 1969-1974; geologist, Mobil Oil Libya, Ltd, 1963-1966; Geophys trainee, Cuban Stanalind Oil Co, Pan Am Petrol Corp, 1957-1958. **Memberships:** AAAS; Geol Soc Am; Am Soc Photogram. **Research Statement & Publications:** Hydrogeology; remote sensing; published over 20 articles. **Mailing Address:** Dept Geol & Geol Eng, Colo Sch Mines, BE 305A 1500 Ill St, Golden, CO 80401. **Fax:** 303-273-3859. **E-Mail:** klee@mines.edu

LEE, KEN, FOOD SCIENCE & TECHNOLOGY. **Personal Data:** b West Orange, NJ, September 5, 1953; c 1. **Education:** Rutgers Univ, BS, 1975; Univ Mass, Amherst, PhD (food sci & nutrit), 1980. **Professional Experience:** PROF & CHAIR, DEPT FOOD SCI & TECHNOL, COL AGR, OHIO STATE UNIV, 1990-; counr, Inst Food Technologists, beginning 1984; conf chmn, Midwest Food Processing Conf, 1984; From asst prof to assoc prof food sci, Dept Food Sci & Technol, Col Agr, Ohio State Univ, 1980-1990; chmn, Tech Adv Comt, Ctr Dairy Res. **Memberships:** Sigma Xi; Inst Food Technologists; Am Asn Cereal Chemists; Am Inst Nutrit; Am Dairy Sci Asn. **Research Statement & Publications:** Over 40 publications in peer-review research journals and over 30 published abstracts; mineral bioavailability from cured meats; analysis of nutrient inhibitors; mineral binding by dietary fiber; oxidized cholesterol compounds in foods; nitrate metabolism and analysis in foods; anti-nutrients in tea; hydrocolloids in dairy foods. **Mailing Address:** Dept Food Sci & Technol, Ohio State Univ, 2015 Fyffe Rd, Columbus, OH 43210-1007. **Fax:** 614-292-0218. **E-Mail:** lee.133@osu.edu

LEE, KENNETH, PHYSICS OF BEAMS. **Personal Data:** b China, October 9, 1943. **Education:** Ohio State Univ, BS, 1966; Univ Calif, Los Angeles, PhD (physics), 1972. **Professional Experience:** RES SCIENTIST, LOS ALAMOS NAT LAB, 1972-. **Memberships:** Am Phys Soc. **Mailing Address:** Appl Theoret & Computational Physics Div, Los Alamos Nat Lab, XCM, MS F645, PO Box 1663, Los Alamos, NM 87545. **Fax:** 505-665-3389. **E-Mail:** ken_lee@lanl.gov

LEE, KEUN MYUNG, ACOUSTIC EMISSION, SOFTWARE ENGINEERING. **Personal Data:** b Korea, October 17, 1945; m 1974, c 1. **Education:** Seoul Nat Univ, BS, 1967; State Univ NY Stony Brook, PhD (astrophys), 1979. **Professional Experience:** SR SCIENTIST ACOUST EMISSION, PHYS ACOUST CORP, 1981-; Systs analyst x-ray spectromet, Princeton Gamma Tech, Inc, 1979-1981. **Memberships:** Inst Elec & Electronics Engrs. **Research Statement & Publications:** Industrial applications and theory of x-ray spectrometry; signal processing; acoustic emission; computer applications of acoustic signal processing. **Mailing Address:** AT&T Bell Labs, Crawfords Corner, Holmdel, NJ 07733.

LEE, KI D, AERONAUTICS. **Education:** Seoul Nat Univ, BS, 1967; Univ Ill, MS, 1973, PhD (aeronaut & astronaut eng) 1976. **Professional Experience:** PROF DEPT AEROSPACE ENG, COL ENG, UNIV ILL, 1995-. **Mailing Address:** Dept Aerospace eng, Col Eng, Univ Ill, 104 S Wright St, Urbana, IL 61801. **Fax:** 217-244-0720. **E-Mail:** kdlee@uiuc.edu

LEE, KIL S, MATHEMATICS. **Education:** Univ Ga, EdD (maths), 1977. **Professional Experience:** PROF, DEPT MATHS, MANKATO STATE UNIV, MANKATO, as of 2006. **Memberships:** Am Math Asn. **Mailing Address:** Dept Math Astron & Statist, Mankato State Univ, Mankato, MN 56002-8400. **Fax:** 507-389-6376.

LEE, KING C, PHARMACOLOGY. **Personal Data:** c 3. **Education:** Eastern Ky Univ, BS, 1978; Univ Ky, Lexington, PhD (pharmacol), 1983. **Professional Experience:** VPRES, REGULATORY AFFAIRS, ACORDA THERAPEUTICS INC, 2003-; CLIN AFFAIRS MGR, IBEX TECHNOLS, 1993-; mem, Antioxidant Proj Team, Diag Image Discovering Team & Magnetic Resonance Develop Team, Sterling Res Group, 1987-; res investr, Dept Cardiovasc Pharmacol, Sterling Res Group, 1987-1993; supvr & sr pharmacologist cardiovasc pharmacol, Wyeth-Ayrst Res, 1986-1987; Co-chmn, Cardiovasc Res Subcomt, Wyeth-Ayrst Res, 1986-1987; fel, Dept Physiol & Biophys, 1983-1985; res asst, Dept Pharmacol, Col Med, Univ Ky, 1980-1983. **Memberships:** AAAS; Am Physiol Soc; Am Soc Pharmacol & Exp Therapeut; NY Acad Sci. **Research Statement & Publications:** Therapeutic agents for ischemic-reperfusion, congestive heart failure and hypertension, glaucoma and ocular ischemia; diagnostic agents for magnetic resonance and x-ray imagings. **Mailing Address:** Acorda Therapeutics Inc, 5485 Pare, Montreal, PQ H4P 1P7, Can.

LEE, KIUCK, NUCLEAR PHYSICS. **Personal Data:** b Hamhung, Korea, January 15, 1922; c 5. **Education:** Seoul Nat Univ, BS, 1947, MS, 1949; Fla State Univ, PhD (physics), 1955. **Professional Experience:** RES PROF PHYSICS, MARQUETTE UNIV, 1968-; Res assoc, Argonne Nat Lab, 1960; from asst prof to assoc prof, Marquette Univ, 1957-1968; Res assoc physics, Fla State Univ, 1955-1956 & Argonne Nat Lab, 1956-1957. **Memberships:** Am Phys Soc. **Research Statement & Publications:** Nuclear structure studies on deformed nucleus, fission and the superheavy nucleus. **Mailing Address:** Dept Physics, Marquette Univ, PO Box 1881, Milwaukee, WI 53201-1881. **Fax:** 414-288-3989.

LEE, KOK-MENG, DYNAMIC SYSTEMS & CONTROL, DESIGN & MANUFACTURING AUTOMATION. **Personal Data:** b Singapore, August 20, 1952; m 1982, c 1. **Education:** State Univ NY, Buffalo, BS, 1980; Mass Inst Technol, SM, 1982, PhD (mech eng), 1985. **Honors & Awards:** Int Hall of Fame New Technol Award, 1992. **Professional Experience:** PROF MECH ENG, GA INST TECHNOL, as of 2002; assoc prof mech eng, Ga Inst Technol, beginning 1990; Ga Tech, Gen Motors & Ford, 1989-; NSF Presidential young investr, 1989; Sigma Xi Jr, Fac Award, Ga Tech, 1989; prin investr, NSF, 1988-; consult, Milliken Textile Co, 1987 & 1988; asst prof, Ga Inst Technol, 1985-1990; res asst, Fluid Power Control Lab, Mass Inst Technol, 1980-1985. **Memberships:** Am Soc Mech Engrs; Inst Elec & Electronics Engrs; Instrument Soc Am; Am Soc Eng Educ. **Research Statement & Publications:** Dynamic system modeling, control and automation; mechatronics and their application to intelligent control systems and manufacturing automation; awarded one patent. **Mailing Address:** Dept Elect Eng Ga Inst Technol Sch Mech Eng, MARC Rm 474, Atlanta, GA 30332-0405. **Fax:** 404-894-9342. **E-Mail:** kokmeng.lee@me.gatech.edu

LEE, KOTIK KAI, MATHEMATICAL PHYSICS, NONLINEAR DYNAMICAL SYSTEMS. **Personal Data:** b Chungking, China, May 30, 1941; American citizen; c 2. **Education:** Chung-Yuan Col, BSc, 1964; Univ Ottawa, MSc, 1967; Syracuse Univ, PhD (physics), 1972. **Professional Experience:** CHIEF SCIENTIST, QET INC, 1993-; educ Comt Am Phys Soc, 1992-1994; assoc prof, Univ Colo, 1989-1993; Mem, Educ Coun, Optical Soc Am, 1989-1991; sr staff scientist, Perkin-Elmer Co, 1986-1989; sr staff scientist, Gen Elec Co, 1984-1986; scientist, TRW, 1982-1984; scientist, lab laser energetics, Univ Rochester, 1979-1982; physicist, Santa Barbara Res Ctr, 1978-1979; scientist, Lab Laser Energetics, Univ Rochester, 1977-1978; vis prof math, Univ Ottawa, 1974-1976; asst prof, Rio Grande Col, 1973-1974; instr, Syracuse Univ, 1972-1973; res asst physics, Syracuse Univ, 1968-1972; asst physics, Univ Ottawa, 1965-1967. **Memberships:** Am Math Soc; Am Phys Soc; Can Asn Physicists; Optical Soc Am; Int Soc Gen Relativity & Gravitation; Inst Elec & Electronics Engrs; NY Acad Sci. **Research Statement & Publications:** Global structures of spacetimes, singularities in general relativity, mathematical foundations of quantum field theory and statistical mechanics, differential equations, laser physics, astrophysics, nonlinear optics and nonlinear dynamical systems. **Mailing Address:** 5755 Pale Rock Terr No L, Colorado Springs, CO 80919.

LEE, KUEN HUNG, COMPUTER SCIENCE, ENGINEERING. **Personal Data:** b March 17, 1944; m 1973, Wai Kuen Yu; c Elisa Y, Melisa M, Cindy S & Edmund S. **Education:** Calif State Univ, BS, 1971; Univ Southern Calif, MS, 1973; Nova Univ, Dr(math educ), 1983. **Honors & Awards:** Outstanding teaching award for math prof to math asn of Am 1995; distinguished alumi award by California State Univ, Los Angeles, 1996. **Professional Experience:** Adj prof math, Calif State Univ, 1975-; PROF MATH, LOS ANGELES TRADE TECHNIC COL, 1974-; Adj prof math, Univ Southern Calif, 1973-1990; Comput syst analyst, Jet Propulsion Lab. **Memberships:** Math Asn Am; AAAS; Am Statist Asn. **Research Statement & Publications:** publ 8 mathematics textbooks in a unique step-by-step format with side explanations Ranging from Arithmetics, algebra to calculus and differential equations. **Mailing Address:** 5240 Haskell St, La Canada Flintridge, CA 91011. **Fax:** 818-952-3638.

LEE, KUO-HSIUNG, MEDICINAL CHEMISTRY, NATURAL PRODUCTS CHEMISTRY. **Personal Data:** b Taiwan, January 4, 1940; m 1968, c 2. **Education:** Kaohsiung Med Col, Taiwan, BS, 1961; Kyoto Univ, MS, 1965; Univ Minn, Minneapolis, PhD (med chem), 1968. **Honors & Awards:** Taite O Soine Mem Award, 1990; TM Tu's Sci Award, 1995; Merit Award, NIH, 1996. **Professional Experience:** Mem, Sci Rev & Sci Coun Comt, Nat Health Res Inst, Taiwan, Repub China, 1996; mem, NIH Reviewers Res, 1994-1998; KENAN PROF & ENDOWED CHMN, UNIV NC, CHAPEL HILL, 1992-; mem, Bioorg Natural Prod Study Sect, NIH, 1990-1994; consult, Sphinx Biotechnol Corp, 1990-1994; consult, Nat Res Inst Chinese Med, Taiwan, 1989-; consult, Genelabs, Inc, 1988-; Hollingsworth fac scholar award, 1988; mem, Phys Biochem Study Sect, NIH, 1988; mem, Bioorg & Natural Prod Study Sect, NIH, 1986, 1990; reviewer, natural prod related grant appl, NSF, 1985; mem, Chem Study Sect, NIH, 1985, 1986, 1988, 1989; mem, Develop Therapeut Contracts Rev Comt, Nat Cancer Inst, 1984-1988; DIR, NATURAL PROD LAB, SCH PHARM, UNIV NC, CHAPEL HILL, 1983-; US Army Med Res Acquisition Agency contract, 1983-1987; mem, Study Sect Psychopharmacol, NIMH, 1983-1984; ad hoc mem, Br Study Sect, Conf & Sem Prog, NIH-Fogarty Int Ctr, 1983; Am Cancer Soc grant, 1975-1981, 1986-; USPHS res grants, Univ NC, 1971-; from asst prof to prof med chem, Natural Prod Lab, Sch Pharm, Univ NC, Chapel Hill, 1970-1991; postdoctoral scholar chem, Univ Calif, Los Angeles, 1968-1970. **Memberships:** Am Chem Soc; Am Soc Pharmacog; fel Am Asn Pharm Scientists; fel Acad Pharmaceut Sci; fel AAAS; Chem Soc; Soc Synthetic Org Chem Japan; Phytochem Soc N Am. **Research Statement & Publications:** Medicinal chemistry of the bioactive natural products and their synthetic analogs including antitumor, antiviral, anti-AIDS, antibiotics anti-inflammatory, anti-fungal agents, and antimalarial agents; insect antifeedants; Chinese medicines; over 350 research articles in various journals. **Mailing Address:** Sch Pharm, Univ NC, Beard Hall Rm 315 CB 7360, Chapel Hill, NC 27599-7360. **Fax:** 919-966-3893. **E-Mail:** khlee@unc.edu

LEE, KWANG, POULTRY NUTRITION & MANAGEMENT. **Personal Data:** b Seoul, Korea, January 18, 1942; m 1970, Soon-Ja; c Albert & Susan. **Education:** Seoul Nat Univ, BS, 1964; Southern Ill Univ, MS, 1969; Mich State Univ, PhD (poultry sci & nutrit), 1973. **Professional Experience:** PROF EMER POULTRY SCI & NUTRIT, UNIV ARK, PINE BLUFF, 2002-; consult, Am Soybean Asn, 1993; prin investr, Poultry Res Projs, 1974-; prof poultry sci & nutrit, Univ Ark, Pine Bluff, 1973-2002. **Memberships:** Poultry Sci Asn; Korean Soc Animal Sci; World Poultry Sci Asn; Am Registry Prof Animal Scientists. **Research Statement & Publications:** Improve production efficiency and well-being of poultry through management and nutrition. **Mailing Address:** Dept Agr, Univ Ark, PO Box 4913, Pine Bluff, AR 71601. **Fax:** 870-543-8543. **E-Mail:** lee_k@vx4500.uapb.edu

LEE, KWANG SOO, PHARMACOLOGY. **Personal Data:** b Seoul, Korea, February 1, 1918; m 1940, c 3. **Education:** Keijo Imp Univ, Korea, MD, 1942, PhD, 1945; Johns Hopkins Univ, 1956. **Honors & Awards:** Pres Award, Repub Korea. **Professional Experience:** PROF PHARMACOL, CHUNG-ANG UNIV, SEOUL, REPUB SKOREA, 1980-; prof pharmacol, State Univ NY Downstate Med Ctr & Col Physicians & Surgeons, Columbia Univ, 1962-1980; from asst prof to assoc prof, Jefferson Med Col, 1951-1956; assoc, Jefferson Med Col, 1950-1951; instr, Jefferson Med Col, 1949-1950; Asst prof pharmacol, Seoul Nat Univ, 1948-1949. **Memberships:** Am Soc Pharmacol & Exp Therapeut. **Research Statement & Publications:** Cardiac metabolism; mechanisms of drug actions. **Mailing Address:** Dept Pharmacol, Chung-Ang Univ 221 Heuksuk Dong Dongjak KU, Seoul, South Korea.

LEE, KYUNG NO, BIOCHEMISTRY. **Personal Data:** b Korea, May 12, 1945; American citizen; m 1973, Chung S Kim; c Steve C & James C. **Education:** Korea Univ, BS; Am Univ, PhD. **Professional Experience:** ASSOC PROF, UNIV OKLA, COL MED ASST MEM, OKLA MED RES FOUND, 1993-; From asst scientist to assoc scientist, Biomed

Div, Samuel Roberts Noble Found, 1985-1993. **Memberships:** Am Chem Soc; Am Soc Biochem & Molecular Biol; Am Soc Cell Biol. **Research Statement & Publications:** Structure and function of transghitaminases and their substrates; role of factor XIII in thrombosis and hemostasis. **Mailing Address:** Dept Med Univ Okla Health Sci Ctr, PO Box 26901 BSEB 306, Oklahoma City, OK 73190. **Fax:** 405-271-3191. **E-Mail:** kyung-lee@ouhsc.edu

LEE, L(AWRENCE) H(WA) N(I), ENGINEERING MECHANICS, STRUCTURAL ENGINEERING. **Personal Data:** b Shanghai, China, January 5, 1923; American citizen; m 1948, Lydia; c Lynn Lawrence. **Education:** La Univ Utopia, China, BS, 1945; Univ Minn, MS, 1947, PhD (struct eng & mech), 1950. **Honors & Awards:** Struct Mech Res Award, Off Naval Res & Am Inst Aeronaut & Astronaut, 1971. **Professional Experience:** PROF EMER AEROSPACE & MECH ENG, UNIV NOTRE DAME, 1993-; Rock Island Arsenal, US Army, 1976 & Dodge Div, Reliance Elec Corp, 1980; prof, Univ Notre Dame, 1969-1993; consult, Gen Motors Corp, 1960-1963 & 1973; prof eng sci, Univ Notre Dame, 1960-1969; consult, Bendix Corp, 1953-1975; from asst prof to assoc prof eng mech, Univ Notre Dame, 1950-1960; instr math & mech, Univ Minn, 1949; engr, Lin-Hu Reconstruct Asn, 1945-1946. **Memberships:** Am Soc Mech Engrs; Am Soc Civil Engrs; Soc Eng Sci; Am Soc Eng Educ. **Research Statement & Publications:** Inelastic stability; dynamic plasticity; elasticity; experimental stress analysis and dynamic stability. **Mailing Address:** Dept Aerospace & Mech Eng, Grad Sch, Univ Notre Dame, 365 Fitzpatrick Hall, Notre Dame, IN 46556-5637. **Fax:** 574-631-8341. **E-Mail:** lawrence.h.lee.64@nd.edu

LEE, LELA A, DERMATOLOGY. **Personal Data:** b Gorman, Tex, September 7, 1950; m 1984, Norman; c 1. **Education:** Rice Univ, BA, 1972; Univ Tex, MD, 1976; Am Bd Internal Med, cert, 1979; Am Bd Dermat, cert, 1983. **Honors & Awards:** Stelwagon Award, Am Acad Dermat, 1983-1984. **Professional Experience:** DIR, AM BD DERMAT, as of 2005; PROF DERMAT & MED, UNIV COLO, 1997-; CHIEF DERMAT, DENVER HEALTH MED CTR, 1997-; Carl J Herzog prof, Univ Okla, 1991-1997. **Memberships:** Am Dermat Asn; Med Dermat Soc (pres, 1998-1999); Am Acad Dermat. **Research Statement & Publications:** Clinical and basic science studies concerning the definition and pathogenesis of neonatal lupus and of cutaneous lupus in adults. **Mailing Address:** Denver Health Med Ctr, 660 Bannock St Mail Code 4000, Denver, CO 80204. **Fax:** 303-436-7249. **E-Mail:** lela.lee@uchsc.edu

LEE, LIENG-HUANG, ORGANIC & POLYMER SURFACE CHEMISTRY, ADHESION SCIENCE. **Personal Data:** b Fukien, China, November 6, 1924; m 1949, Chiu-Bin Wu; c Muriel (Payne), Daniel, Robert & Grace. **Education:** Amoy (Xiamen) Univ, BSc, 1947; Case Inst Technol, MSc, 1954, PhD (chem), 1955. **Honors & Awards:** Mabery Prize, 1954. **Professional Experience:** Div Polym Matl Sci Eng, ACS, 2001; CONSULT, 1994-; hon prof, Lanzhou Inst Chem Phys, Chinese Acad Sci, 1988-; Res Ctr Solid Lubrication, Chinese Acad Sci, 1987-; vis prof chem, Xiamen Univ, China, 1986-; mem comt, Reliability of Adhesive Bonds in Severe Environs, Nat Res Coun, 1984; course organizer, Fundamentals Adhesion, 1981-1996; invited lectr, Chinese Acad Sci, 1979, 1983, 1986, 1987, 1991, 1994; adv ed, J Adhesion, 1971-; sr scientist, Xerox Corp, 1968-1994; sr res chemist, Dow Chem Co, 1963-1968; res org chemist, Dow Chem Co, 1958-1963; vis prof, Taiwan Prov Norm Univ, 1957-1958; Consult, Union Res Inst, Taiwan, China, 1957-1958; lectr, Tunghai Univ, 1956-1957; res assoc, Case Inst Technol, 1955-1956; asst res chemist, Chia-Yee Solvent Works, 1948-1951 & Rain Stimulation Res Inst, 1951-1952; Jr chemist, Nantou Sugar Factory, China, 1947-1948; R L Patrick fel, Adhesion Soc. **Memberships:** Am Chem Soc; Sigma Xi; Am Phys Soc; Adhesion Soc; NY Acad Sci (1996). **Research Statement & Publications:** Polymer friction and wear; adhesion and surface chemistry; electrophotography; tribology; published 110 papers, edited 12 technical books and granted 31 US patents; invented mobile cloud-seedings with silver iodide from locomotive. **Mailing Address:** 796 John Glenn Blvd, Webster, NY 14580. **Fax:** 585-872-2915.

LEE, LIH-SYNG, BIOCHEMISTRY, BIOPHYSICS. **Personal Data:** b China, October 28, 1945; m 1974, c 1. **Education:** Nat Taiwan Univ, BS, 1968; Yale Univ, MPh, 1971, MS, 1972, PhD (chem), 1974. **Professional Experience:** STAFF ASSOC CARCINOGENESIS, COLUMBIA UNIV, 1976-; Res scientist biochem & fel, Roswell Park Mem Inst, 1974-1976. **Memberships:** NY Acad Sci; AAAS; Am Chem Soc. **Research Statement & Publications:** Chemical carcinogenesis; tumor promotion; growth factors; hormone receptors; cell culture; transport; enzymology; DNA metabolism; cell cycle; gene transfer; membrane biophysics; drug design. **Mailing Address:** 22 Van Wyck Dr, Princeton Junction, NJ 08550-1640.

LEE, LILIAN M, CLINICAL & PROTEIN CHEMISTRY. **Personal Data:** b Hong Kong, 1938. **Education:** McGill Univ, BS, 1963; Univ BC, MS, 1965; Univ Western Ont, PhD (path chem), 1971. **Professional Experience:** HEAD PROTEIN CHEMIST, SPECTRAL DIAG INC, 1992-; res assoc, Hosp Sick Children, 1975-1992; Res fel, Clin Chem Training Prog, Univ Wash, Seattle, 1973-1975. **Research Statement & Publications:** Clinical and protein chemistry. **Mailing Address:** Spectral Diag Inc, 18 Hollywood Ave No 1407, North York, ON M2N 6P5, Can.

LEE, LINDA SHAHRABANI, ENVIRONMENTAL FATE OF ORGANICS, CONTAMINANT HYDROLOGY. **Personal Data:** b Dover, Del, July 22, 1959; div, c James R & Joshua R. **Education:** Univ Fla, BS, 1983, MS, 1989, PhD (soil chem & contaminant hydrol), 1993. **Professional Experience:** PROF ENVIRON CHEM, PURDUE UNIV, as of 2002; from asst prof to assoc prof environ Org Chem, Purdue Univ, 1993-2001; sr chemist, Univ Fla, 1989-1993; chemist I soil water sci dept, chemist III, 1988-1989; chemist I soil water sci dept, Univ Fla, 1984-1988. **Memberships:** Am Asn Agron; Am Chem Soc; Nat Ground Water Asn; AAAS; Sigma Xi. **Research Statement & Publications:** The sorption, solubility, degradation and transport of various classes of organic contaminants in aqueous, mixed-solvent and multi-phasic systems. **Mailing Address:** Dept Agron, Pudue Univ, 915 W State St, Lilly Hall Life Sci, West Lafayette, IN 47907-2054. **Fax:** 765-496-2926. **E-Mail:** lslee@purdue.edu

LEE, LIN-SHAN, ELECTRICAL ENGINEERING. **Personal Data:** b Kaohsiung, Taiwan, September 23, 1952; m 1983, Chia-Ling Mei; c Meng-Heng. **Education:** Nat Taiwan Univ, BSEE, 1974; Stanford Univ, MSEE, 1975, PhD, 1977. **Honors & Awards:** Medal Distinguished Accomplishment, Chinese Inst Elec Engrs, 1991. **Professional Experience:** Ed, J Selected Areas in Commun, Inst Elec & Electronics Engrs, 1994-1995; dir inst info sci, Academia Sinica, Taipei, 1991-; Res fel, Academia Sinica, Taipei, 1985-; PROF, NAT TAIWAN UNIV, 1982-; head, Dept Comput Sci & Info Eng, 1982-1987; assoc prof, Nat Taiwan Univ, 1979-1982; Tech consult, Edutel Commun & Devels Inc, 1977-1979. **Memberships:** Inst Elec & Electronics Engrs; Inst Elec & Electronics Engrs Commun Soc; Union Radio Sci Int; Chinese Inst Elec Engrs; Computational Linguistic Soc Repub China. **Research Statement & Publications:** Contributed various articles to professional journals; contributions in Mandarin dictation technology for input of Chinese text-to-speech systems for synthesizing Mandarin speech from unlimited Chinese texts. **Mailing Address:** 73rd Floor 58th Lane Wen-Chou St, Taipei 107, Taiwan. **Fax:** 886-278-24814. **E-Mail:** lsl@iis.sinica.edu.tw

LEE, LINWOOD LAWRENCE, NUCLEAR PHYSICS. **Personal Data:** b Trenton, NJ, August 5, 1928; m 1957, Dorothy; c Linwood III. **Education:** Princeton Univ, AB, 1950; Yale Univ, MS, 1951, PhD (physics), 1955. **Professional Experience:** PROF EMER PHYSICS, STATE UNIV NY, STONY BROOK, as of 2004; prof Physics, State Univ NY, Stony Brook, beginning 1965; dir, Nuclear Struct Lab, 1965-1984; assoc physicist, Argonne Nat lab, 1960-1965; vis asst prof physics, Univ Minn, 1959-1960; asst physicist, Argonne Nat lab, 1954-1959. **Memberships:** Fel Am Phys Soc; fel AAAS. **Research Statement & Publications:** Experimental studies of nuclear structure and spectroscopy; nucleon transfer reactions; near barrier heavy ion reactions. **Mailing Address:** Dept Physics& Astro, State Univ NY, Stony Brook, NY 11794-3800. **E-Mail:** linwood.lee@stonybrook.edu

LEE, LLOYD LIEH-SHEN, STATISTICAL MECHANICS, POLYMER TECHNOLOGY. **Personal Data:** b China, January 25, 1942; American citizen. **Education:** Nat Taiwan Univ, BS, 1963; Northwestern Univ, PhD (chem eng), 1971; Univ Nebr, MS, 1965. **Professional Experience:** C M SLIEPCEVICH PROF CHEM ENG & MAT SCI, UNIV OKLA, as of 2004; assoc prof chem eng & mat sci, Univ Okla, beginning 1980; asst prof, Univ Okla, 1976-1980; mgr textiles, Tashing Chem Co, 1973-1975; researcher liquids, Univ Paris, 1972; res engr polymer, Du Pont Chem Co, 1971-1972. **Memberships:** Am Chem Soc. **Research Statement & Publications:** Natural gas properties; electrolyte solutions; perturbation theory for liquid structure and liquid thermodynamics; Monte Carlo and molecular dynamics simulations; turbulence; high-speed spinning of polymeric filaments. **Mailing Address:** Dept Chem Eng & Mat Sci, Univ Okla, 100 E Boyd St, Norman, OK 73019-6623. **E-Mail:** lle@ou.edu

LEE, LONG CHI, EXPERIMENTAL PHYSICS. **Personal Data:** b Kaohsiung, Taiwan, October 19, 1940; m 1967, c Gloria Y & Thomas D. **Education:** Taiwan Normal Univ, BS, 1964; Univ Southern Calif, MA, 1967, PhD (physics), 1971. **Honors & Awards:** SDSU Meritorious Performance & Prof Award, 1986, 1988, 1990. **Professional Experience:** ADJ PROF CHEM, SAN DIEGO STATE UNIV, 1986-; PROF ELEC & COMPUT ENG, SAN DIEGO STATE UNIV, 1982-; sr physicist, Stanford Res Inst Int, 1979-1981; physicist, Stanford Res Inst Int, 1977-1978; adj asst prof physics, Univ Southern Calif, 1977; vis scientist, Univ Kaiserslautern, Ger, 1975; res staff physicist, Univ Southern Calif, 1972-1977; from res asst to res assoc, Univ Southern Calif, 1967-1972. **Memberships:** Am Phys Soc; Inter-Am Photochemical Soc; Inst Elec & Electronics Engrs; Am Geophys Union; Int Soc Optical Eng. **Research Statement & Publications:** Photoionization and photodissociation processes of small molecules and radicals using vacuum ultraviolet radiation; photodestruction processes of atmospheric positive and negative ions; molecular processes in electrical discharges; optical characteristics of small aerosol particles; molecular processes in chemical etching; reaction kinetics. **Mailing Address:** Dept Elec & Comput Eng, San Diego State Univ, 309 Office E-408, San Diego, CA 92182-0190. **Fax:** 619-594-3701. **E-Mail:** llee@mail.sdsu.edu

LEE, LOU-CHUANG, PLASMA PHYSICS, SPACE PHYSICS. **Personal Data:** b Taiwan, China, April 20, 1947; c 2. **Education:** Nat Taiwan Univ, BS, 1969; Calif Inst Technol, MS, 1972, PhD (physics), 1975. **Honors & Awards:** Moore Prize, 1987. **Professional Experience:** Distinguished Fulbright Scholar, 1988; PROF, GEOPHYS INST, UNIV ALASKA, 1986-; Toray vis scholar, 1986; assoc prof, Geophys Inst, Univ Alaska, 1978-1986; vis asst prof, Inst Phys Sci & Technol, Univ Md, 1977-1978; Res assoc physics, Goddard Space Flight Ctr, NASA, 1975-1977. **Memberships:** Am Phys Soc; Am Geophys Union; AAAS. **Research Statement & Publications:** Magnetospheric physics. **Mailing Address:** Dept Physics 1 Ta-Hsueh Rd, National Cheng Kung University, Tainan, Taiwan, 70101, China. **E-Mail:** loulee@plasma.phys.ncku.edu.tw

LEE, LU-YUAN, AIRWAY DISEASE, AIR POLLUTANTS & HEALTH. **Personal Data:** b June 26, 1946; m 1978, Hsiao-Hwa; c Stephanie J & Calvin Y. **Education:** Nat Taiwan Univ, BS, 1969; Univ Miss, MS, 1972, PhD (physiol), 1975. **Professional Experience:** FRED W ZECHMAN PROF PHYSIOL, UNIV KY, 2002-; PROF, CTR BIOMED ENG, UNIV KY, 2002-; co dir grad studies, Univ Ky, 1997-2000; vis scientist, Novartis inst med sci, 1997; res dir, Univ Ky, 1994-1997; PROF PHYSIOL, MED CTR, UNIV KY, 1992-; vis prof, Dept Pharmacol, Karolinoka Inst, Sweden, 1992; sr int award, Young investr award, 1992; vis scientist, Dept Physiol, Univ Tex Med Br, 1985; NIH, Young investr award, 1980; from asst prof to assoc prof, Med Ctr, Univ KY, 1978-1992; Nat res serv award, 1977; res fel, Cardiovasc Res Inst, Univ Calif, San Francisco, 1975-1978. **Memberships:** Am Physiol Soc; Am Thoracic Soc; sr mem Biomed Eng Soc. **Research Statement & Publications:** Elucidate the neurohumoral mechanisms underlying the airway responses to inhaled irritants in health and in airway diseases; pulmonary reflexes. **Mailing Address:** Dept Physiol & Biophys, Univ Ky Med Ctr, Lexington, KY 40536-0084. **Fax:** 859-323-1070. **E-Mail:** lylee@pop.uky.edu

LEE, MARIETTA Y W T, DNA REPLICATION, DNA REPAIR. **Personal Data:** b Canton, China, March 3, 1943; m 1969, Ernest Y; c Patrick. **Education:** Nazareth Col, BSc, 1965; New York Univ, MS, 1967; Univ Miami, PhD (biol), 1973. **Professional Experience:** PROF & RESEARCHER, DEPT BIOCHEM & MOLECULAR BIOL, NEW YOR MED COL, as of 2004; prof biochem & molecular biol, Univ Miami, beginning 1994; prof med, Univ Miami, beginning 1993; mem, NIH Biochem Study Sect, 1990-1994; mem, ASBMB Comt Equal Opportunity Women, 1988-1991; Estab investr, Am Heart Asn, 1984-1989; from asst prof to assoc prof, Univ Miami, 1981-1992. **Memberships:** Am Soc Univ Prof; Am Soc Biol Chemists. **Research Statement & Publications:** Inhibition of human DNA polymerases by antiviral drugs; mechanisms of DNA replication and DNA repair; over expression of DNA polymerases, PCNA and replication proteins; production of honodonal antibodies to DNA polymerases and replication protein. **Mailing Address:** Dept Biochem, Basic Scis Bldg, New York Medical Col, Valhalla, NY 10595. **E-Mail:** marietta_lee@nymc.edu

LEE, MARK, SOLID STATE PHYSICS. **Personal Data:** b Taipai, Taiwan, April 10, 1964. **Education:** Harvard Univ, BA, 1986, MA, 1986; Stanford Univ, PhD (physics), 1991. **Professional Experience:** BELL LAB, 1999-; from asst prof to assoc prof physics, Univ Va, 1993-1999. **Memberships:** Am Phys Soc; Mat Res Soc. **Mailing Address:** Dept Physics, Univ Va, McCormick Rd, Charlottesville, VA 22903. **Fax:** 804-924-4576. **E-Mail:** marklee@virginia.edu

LEE, MARTIN ALAN, ASTROPHYSICS. **Personal Data:** b Bromley, Eng, October 9, 1945; American citizen. **Education:** Stanford Univ, BSc, 1966; Univ Chicago, PhD (physics), 1971. **Professional Experience:** GRAD DIR, DEPT PHYSICS, as of 2004; PROF, SPACE SCI CTR, as of 2004; PROF PHYSICS, UNIV NH, 1990-; vis prof extraterrestrial physics, Max Planck Inst, WGer, 1985; res assoc prof, Univ NH, 1984-1990; Ed, Advances Space Res, 1984; res scientist astrophys, Univ NH, 1979-1984; asst prof physics, Wash Univ, 1974-1979; res assoc, Lab Astrophys & Space Res, Univ Chicago, 1973-1974; res assoc, Max Planck Inst Extraterrestrial Physics, WGer, 1972-1973; NATO fel astrophys, Max Planck Inst Extraterrestrial Physics, WGer, 1971-1972; prin investr, NSF grant. **Memberships:** Am Astron Soc; Am Geophys Union. **Research Statement & Publications:** Energetic particle transport and plasma processes in the solar-terrestrial environment including ion shock acceleration, solar modulation of galactic cosmic rays, plasma instabilities and wave propagation. **Mailing Address:** Dept Physics, Univ NH, 39 Col Rd, Durham, NH 03824. **E-Mail:** marty.lee@unh.edu

LEE, MARTIN JEROME, BIOCHEMISTRY. **Personal Data:** b Bayonne, NJ, May 24, 1943; m 1967, c 1. **Education:** Rutgers Univ, New Brunswick, BA, 1965, MS, 1968, PhD (biochem), 1969. **Professional Experience:** MGR, HEALTHCARE TECHNOL, as of 2003; Dir appl res, Coulter Diag, 1980-; staff scientist, Technicon Instruments Corp, 1973-1980; sr res assoc, Pharmacia Fine Chem, Inc, 1971-1973; res assoc biochem, Enzyme Inst, 1970-1971; Nat Inst Gen Med Sci fel, Univ Wis-Madison, 1969-1970; staff, Rockland Medi-Labs. **Memberships:** Biophys Soc; Am Chem Soc; Sigma Xi; NY Acad Sci. **Research Statement & Publications:** Bioenergetics; chromatography; separational techniques and instrumentation; automated cytochemistry, immunology, clinical chemistry and enzymology. **Mailing Address:** 3 Habosem St, Ashdod, Israel.

LEE, MARTIN J G, CONDENSED MATTER PHYSICS. **Personal Data:** b Kings Lynn, Eng, March 16, 1942. **Education:** Cambridge Univ, BA, 1963, MA & PhD (physics), 1967. **Professional Experience:** PROF PHYSICS, UNIV TORONTO, as of 2006; prof physics, Univ Toronto, beginning 1979; assoc prof, Univ Toronto, 1974-1979; asst prof physics, James Franck Inst & Dept Physics, Univ Chicago, 1969-1974; instr, Univ Chicago, 1967-1969. **Memberships:** Can Asn Physicists. **Research Statement & Publications:** Experimental and theoretical study of Fermi surfaces and electronic structure of metals; photo field emission phenomena; high temperature superconductivity. **Mailing Address:** Dept Physics, Univ Toronto, SW651 60 St George St, Toronto, ON M5S 1A7, Can. **Fax:** 416-978-5848. **E-Mail:** lee@utsc.utoronto.ca

LEE, MARTIN JOE, ACCELERATOR PHYSICS, MICROWAVES. **Personal Data:** American citizen. **Education:** Univ Calif, BS, 1960; NY Univ, MS, 1962; Stanford Univ, PhD (elec eng), 1967. **Professional Experience:** CONSULT, 1987-; Spec consult, Electron Storage Ring Corp, 1978-; dep chief, Pep Theory Group, Accelerator Physics, Stanford Linear Accelerator Ctr, 1978-1987; accelerator theorist, Stanford Linear Accelerator Ctr, 1969-1978; ENG PHYSICIST, SLAC, 1967-; accelerator physicist, Brookhaven Nat Lab, 1967-1969; microwave engr accelerator eng, Stanford Linear Accelerator Ctr, 1962-1967; Microwave engr commun, Bell Tel Lab, 1960-1962. **Memberships:** Inst Elec & Electronics Engrs. **Mailing Address:** Stanford Univ ARDA, Stanford Linear Accelerator Ctr, PO Box 4349 Mail Stop 26, Stanford, CA 94309. **Fax:** 650-926-2851. **E-Mail:** lmartin@slac.stanford.edu

LEE, MARY ANN, MATHEMATICS. **Education:** Purdue Univ, PhD, 1989. **Professional Experience:** PROF, DEPT MATH, MANKATO STATE UNIV, as of 2004. **Memberships:** Am Math Soc. **Mailing Address:** 123 Catalina Dr, Mankato, MN 56001. **Fax:** 507-389-1899. **E-Mail:** mary.lee@mnsu.edu

LEE, MATHEW HUNG MUN, PHYSICAL MEDICINE & REHABILITATION. **Personal Data:** b Hawaii, July 28, 1931; m 1958, c 3. **Education:** Johns HopkinsUniv, AB, 1953; Univ Md, MD, 1956; Univ Calif, MPH, 1962; Am Bd Phys Med & Rehab, dipl, 1966. **Professional Experience:** CHMN DEPT REHAB MED, GOLDWATER MEM HOSP, as of 2004; PROF REHAB MED, SCH MED, NY UNIV, 1973-; pres, Goldwater Mem Hosp, 1971-; attend physician, Bellevue Hosp Ctr, 1971-; clin assoc prof, Col Dent, NY Univ, 1970-; vpres med bd, Goldwater mem Hosp, 1969-1970; clin asst prof, Col Dent, NY Univ, 1969-1970; World Rehab Fund consult, Gordon Seagrave & Maryknoll Hosps, Korea, 1969; vis physician, Goldwater mem Hosp, 1968-; asst attend physician, Hosp, NY Univ, 1968-; DIR DEPT REHAB MED, GOLDWATER MEM HOSP, 1968-; assoc dir, dept Rehab Med, 1968; chief electrodiag unit, Goldwater mem Hosp, 1966-; Bur Adult Hyg, 1965- & Human Resources Ctr, 1966-; asst clin prof, Col Dent, NY Univ, 1966-1969; dir educ & training, dept Rehab Med, 1966-1968; from asst prof to assoc prof rehab med, Rehab Serv, 1965-1973; consult, Daughters Israel Hosp, New York, 1965-1972; assoc vis physician, Goldwater mem Hosp, 1965-1968; NY State Health Dept assignee, Rehab Serv, 1964-1965; Resident, inst Phys Med & Rehab, Med Ctr, NY Univ, 1962-1964; consult, US dept Interior. **Memberships:** AAAS; fel Am Acad Phys Med & Rehab; fel Am Col Physicians; Pan-Am Med Asn; fel Am Pub Health Asn. **Mailing Address:** Rusk Inst Rehab Med, 400 E 34th St, Ste 600, New York, NY 10016. **Fax:** 212-263-8815. **E-Mail:** leem01@popmail.med.nyu.edu

LEE, MAY D-MING (LU), NATURAL PRODUCTS ISOLATION, STRUCTURE ELUCIDATION. **Personal Data:** b China, May 12, 1949; American citizen; m 1974, c 2. **Education:** Univ BC, BS, 1972; Univ Ill, Urbana, MS, 1974, PhD (chem), 1976. **Professional Experience:** ASSOC DIR, MOLECULAR DIVERSITY, LEDERLE LABS, as of 2005; res chemist, Lederle Labs, beginning 1977; Med Res Div, Am Cyanamid Co, 1977-1994; res fel chem, Harvard Univ, 1976-1977. **Memberships:** Am Chem Soc; AAAS. **Research Statement & Publications:** Isolation, screening and structure elucidation of novel antitumor and antibacterial agents from fermentation; screening methodology. **Mailing Address:** Lederle Lab, One Cyanamid Plaza, Wayne, NJ 07470.

LEE, MELVIN, NUTRITION, BIOCHEMISTRY. **Personal Data:** b New York, NY, January 5, 1926; m 1949, c 4. **Education:** Univ Calif, Los Angeles, BA, 1947; Univ Calif, Berkeley, MA, 1952, PhD (nutrit), 1958. **Professional Experience:** Vis scientist, Gunma Univ, Japan, 1986; sci exchange fel, Japan Soc Prom, 1981; PROF NUTRIT, SCH FAMILY & NUTRIT SCI, UNIV BC, as of 1974; prof nutrit & dir, Sch Home Econ, 1967-1974; USPHS res fel, 1966; asst prof biochem, Sch Med, Univ Calif, San Francisco, 1963-1967; lectr dent, Sch Med, Univ Calif, San Francisco, 1961-1967; from instr to asst prof prev med, Sch Med, Univ Calif, San Francisco, 1958-1967. **Memberships:** AAAS; Am Inst Nutrit; Soc Environ Geochem & Health; Soc Nutrit Latin Am; Can Soc Nutrit Sci. **Research Statement & Publications:** Relation of diet to metabolic patterns; factors influencing growth; maternal alcohol and fetal development. **Mailing Address:** Sch Family Nutrit Sci, Univ BC, Vancouver, BC V6T 1W5, Can.

LEE, MEN HUI, CANCER RESEARCH. **Personal Data:** b Taiwan, April 2, 1933; American citizen. **Education:** Nat Taiwan Univ, BS, 1956; Utah State Univ, MS, 1963; Columbia Univ, PhD (biochem), 1968. **Professional Experience:** Vis prof, Div Oncol-Hemat, Ohio State Univ, 1988-1989; PROF BIOCHEM, DEPT AGR CHEM, NAT TAIWAN UNIV, 1980-; Spec fel, Leukemia Soc Am, Inc, 1974-1976; res assoc pharmacol, Dept Pharmacol, Yale Univ, 1971-1980; NIH postdoctoral, Dept Biol Chem, Harvard Univ, 1969-1971; Postdoctoral biochem, Chem Dept, Columbia Univ, 1968-1969. **Memberships:** Am Soc Pharmacol & Exp Therapeut; Am Asn Cancer Res. **Research Statement & Publications:** Cancer: fields of chemotherapy, tumor immunology involving lymphokine-activated killer cells and enzymology related to cancer. **Mailing Address:** Agr Chem Dept Biochem Lab, Nat Taiwan Univ, Taipei, Taiwan.

LEE, MICHAEL, BIOLOGY. **Education:** Ball State Univ, BS, EdD; Governors State Univ, MA. **Professional Experience:** PROF MICROBIOL & CHMN, DEPT NATURAL SCI & PHYSICAL EDUC, as of 2006. **Mailing Address:** Dept Nat Sci & Physical Educ Joliet Junior Col, E 1044 1215 Houbolt Rd, Joliet, IL 60431-8938. **E-Mail:** mlee@jjc.edu

LEE, MICHAEL CHING-HSUEH, MATERIAL COMPOSITION PROCESSING & STRUCTURE, FINITE ELEMENT ANALYSIS IN RHEOLOGY. **Personal Data:** m 1972, Amy; c Benjamin, Josephine, David & John. **Education:** Nat Cheng-Kung Univ, BS, 1970; Univ Calif, MS, 1974, PhD (mech eng), 1977. **Professional Experience:** PRIN RES ENGR, POLYMERS DEPT, GEN MOTORS RES & DEVELOP CTR, 1989-; sr tech staff, Exec Dept, 1987-1993; prog mgr, Exec Dept, 1986-1987; sr staff res engr, Polymers Dept, Gen Motors Res Labs, 1984-1989; Group leader, Polymers Dept, Gen Motors Res Labs, 1983-1987; staff res engr, Polymers Dept, Gen Motors Res Labs, 1981-1984; sr res engr, Polymers Dept, Gen Motors Res Labs, 1978-1981; Fel, Dept Chem, Univ Calif, Berkeley, 1977-1978. **Memberships:** Am Chem Soc; Soc Rheology. **Research Statement & Publications:** Unified constitutive equations for materials; rheology; composition, processing, structure and property relationships for materials; mixing rule for elastonic and plastic composites; co-injection molding process; finite element analysis for elastoner and visco elastic materials; polymer tribology and research planning. **Mailing Address:** 480-106-316 Bldg No 1-6, 30500 Mound Rd, Warren, MI 48090-9055. **Fax:** 248-641-7766. **E-Mail:** michael_c._lee@gmrnotes3.gmr.com

LEE, MING T, HYDRAULICS, WATER RESOURCES. **Personal Data:** b Taipei, Taiwan, August 15, 1940; American citizen; m 1970, c 2. **Education:** Nat Taiwan Univ, BS, 1963, MS, 1966; Univ Cincinnati, MS, 1968; Purdue Univ, PhD (civil eng), 1972. **Professional Experience:** SR WATER RESOURCES ENGR, GREINER ENG, 1993-; prof scientist hydraul, Ill State Water Surv, 1991-1993; assoc prof scientist, Ill State Water Surv, 1975-1991; res engr hydraul, Agr Econ Dept, Univ Ill, 1972-1975; hydraul engr, Vogt, Iver & Assoc, Ohio, 1968; res engr, Hydraul Lab, Water Resources Planning Comn, 1966-1967. **Memberships:** Am Geophys Union; Soil Conserv Soc Am; Am Soc Civil Engrs; Sigma Xi. **Research Statement & Publications:** Soil erosion; sediment transport; lake hydrology; watershed erosion control; hydrologic computer modeling. **Mailing Address:** 1608 Lago Vista Blvd, Palm Harbor, FL 34685-3352.

LEE, MING-LIANG, MEDICAL GENETICS, BIOCHEMISTRY. **Personal Data:** b Tainan, Taiwan, June 26, 1936; m 1965, c 3. **Education:** Nat Taiwan Univ, MD, 1962; Univ Miami, PhD (biochem), 1969. **Professional Experience:** ASSOC PROF MED GENETICS & CHIEF DIV, RUTGERS MED SCH, 1977-; chief fel med genetics, Sch Med, Johns Hopkins Univ, 1976-1977; Asst prof, Sch Med, Univ Miami, 1972-1976. **Memberships:** Am Soc Biol Scientist; Am Soc Med Genetics. **Mailing Address:** Acad Health Sci Ctr CN-19 Dept Pediat, UMDNJ-R W Johnson Med Sch, New Brunswick, NJ 08903.

LEE, MINYOUNG, MATERIALS SCIENCE, RELIABILITY ANALYSIS. **Personal Data:** b Seoul, Korea, August 11, 1938; American citizen; m 1966, Shinyoung Lee; c Michael, Albert. **Education:** Seoul Nat Univ, BS, 1961; Providence Col, MS, 1967; Brown Univ, PhD (mat sci), 1971. **Honors & Awards:** GE Coolidge Fel, 1999. **Professional Experience:** Vis scientist, Inst Solid State Physics, Tokyo Univ, 2000; vis scientist, Cavendish Lab, Cambridge Univ, 1976; metallurist, GE Global Res Ctr, 1971-2001. **Research Statement & Publications:** Development of very hard materials primarily for cutting tools and wear parts; advanced materials processing technology; tribology; sensors for factory automation. **Mailing Address:** 1133 Glen Meadow Ct, Niskayuna, NY 12309. **Fax:** 518-387-7563. **E-Mail:** leem@nycap.rr.com

LEE, M(ONHE) HOWARD, THEORETICAL PHYSICS. **Personal Data:** b Pusan, Korea, May 21, 1937; American citizen; m 1967, Margaret; c Jennifer K. **Education:** Univ Pa, BS, 1959, PhD (physics), 1967. **Professional Experience:** Adj prof, Inst adv study, Korea, 2000-; REGENTS PROF PHYSICS, UNIV GA, 1999-; sr fel, Asia-Pacific Ctr for Theoret Phys, 1997-2000; vis scientist, Gzech Acad Sci, 1990; grants, Army Res Off, 1988-1995; grants, NSF, 1987-1996; grants, Off Naval Res, 1985-1989; vis prof, Dept Physics, Seoul Nat Univ, Korea, 1980; co-chmn, 17th Eastern Theoret Physics Conf, Athens, Ga, 1979; Fulbright-Hays Sr Res Scholar Award, Univ Louvain, Belg, 1978-1979; grants, Dept Energy, 1977-1987; grants, Air Force Off Sci Res, 1977-1978; grants, NATO, 1976-1978 & 1993-1994; guest lectr, Inst Theoret Physics, Univ Leuven, Belg, 1976; from asst prof to prof, Univ GA, 1973-1999; NIH res grant & investr biomat, Health Sci & Technol, Mass Inst Technol & Harvard Univ, 1971-1973; res assoc, Dept Physics & Mat Sci Ctr, Mass Inst Technol, 1969-1971; fel physics, Theoret Physics Inst, Univ Alta, 1967-1969. **Memberships:** fel Am Phys Soc. **Research Statement & Publications:** Many-body theory; statistical mechanics; mathematical physics. **Mailing Address:** Dept Physics Univ Ga, 305D&E Physics Bldg, Athens, GA 30602. **E-Mail:** mhlee@uga.edu

LEE, NANCY L, BIOLOGICAL SCIENCE. **Professional Experience:** PROF EMER MICROBIOL, UNIV CALIF, 1965-. **Mailing Address:** Dept Biol Sci, Univ Calif, Santa Barbara, CA 93106-0001. **Fax:** 805-893-4724.

LEE, NANCY ZEE-NEE MA, PHARMACOLOGY. **Personal Data:** b Shanghai, China, October 28, 1940; American citizen; m 1965, c 2. **Education:** Southwestern Univ, Georgetown, Tex, BS, 1963; Univ Tex, Austin, PhD (biochem), 1967. **Professional Experience:** PROF, DEPT PHARMACOL, UNIV MINN MED SCH, MINNEAPOLIS, 1989-; prof, Dept Pharmacol & Langley Porter Psychiat Inst, 1987-1989; adj assoc prof, Dept Pharmacol & Langley Porter Psychiat Inst, 1984-1987; assoc res pharmacologist, Dept Pharmacol & Langley Porter Psychiat Inst, 1978-1984; asst res biochemist, Dept Pharmacol, Univ Calif, San Francisco, 1972-1978; res biochemist III-VI, Dept Pharmacol, Univ Calif, San Francisco, 1968-1972; postdoctoral fel, Dept Biochem, Northwestern Univ, Evanston, Ill, 1967; Res asst, Univ Tex, Austin, 1963-1967. **Memberships:** Sigma Xi; Soc Neurosci; Am Soc Pharmacol & Exp Therapeut; AAAS; Int Asn Women Bioscientist; Soc Chinese Bioscientists Am. **Research Statement & Publications:** Pharmacology; Biochemical mechanism for narcotic addiction. **Mailing Address:** Dept Pharmacol, Univ Minn 3-249 Millard Hall 435 Delaware St SE, Minneapolis, MN 55455-0347.

LEE, NEWTON, COMPUTER SCIENCE. **Professional Experience:** FOUNDING ED & ED CHIEF, ASSOC COMPUT MACH, as of 2004; adj Fac Mem, Woodbury Univ, as of 2004; SR STAFF ENGR, DISNEY ONLINE, as of 2004. **Mailing Address:** Asn Comput Mach, 1515 Broadway, New York, NY 10036.

LEE, NORMAN K, APPLIED MATHEMATICS. **Personal Data:** b Frankfort, Ind, February 3, 1934; m 1956, c 2. **Education:** Hanover Col, BA, 1956; Vanderbilt Univ, MA, 1958; Purdue Univ, PhD (bionucleonics), 1969. **Professional Experience:** RETIRED; admin asst dept, Ball State Univ, 1979-1982; assoc prof math, Ball State Univ, beginning 1969;

sr instr, Somerset Community Col, 1968-1969; NSF fel, 1963-1964; partic, Acad Year Inst, 1962-1963; asst prof, Ball State Univ, 1958-1966. **Research Statement & Publications:** Mathematical models. **Mailing Address:** 401 W Main St, Ridgeville, IN 47380-1119. **E-Mail:** nklee@connectiva.net

LEE, PATRICE ANNE, PHYSIOLOGY, SEPTIC SHOCK & TRAUMATIC SHOCK. **Personal Data:** b Baltimore, Md, February 24, 1960. **Education:** Univ Miami, BS, 1982; Duke Univ, PhD (physiol), 1987. **Professional Experience:** DIR PEDIAT CRITICAL CARE RES, MED CITY DALLAS HOSP, 1990-; asst res scientist, Okla Med Res Found, 1987-1990. **Memberships:** Am Thoracic Soc; Soc Critical Care Med; Shock Soc; Am Physiol Soc; Wilderness Med Soc. **Mailing Address:** Dept Pharmacol, Amgen Boulder Inc, 3200 Walnut St MS AB 30, Boulder, CO 80301.

LEE, PATRICK A, CONDENSED MATTER THEORY. **Personal Data:** b Hong Kong, September 8, 1946; American citizen; m 1969, Jeanne; c 2. **Education:** Mass Inst Technol, BS, 1966, PhD (physics), 1970. **Honors & Awards:** Oliver Buckley Condensed Matter Physics Prize, 1991. **Professional Experience:** WILLIAM & EMMA ROGERS PROF PHYSICS & DIV, ATOMIC, BIOL, CONDENSED MATTER & PLASMA PHYSICS, MASS INST TECHNOL, as of 2005; prof physics, Mass Inst Technol, beginning 1982; mem tech staff, Bell Labs, 1974-1982; asst prof physics, Univ Wash, Seattle, 1973-1974; mem tech staff, Bell Labs, 1972-1973; J W Gibbs instr physics, Yale Univ, 1970-1972. **Memberships:** Nat Acad Sci; fel Am Phys Soc; Am Acad Arts & Sci. **Research Statement & Publications:** Disordered electronic systems; quantum transport in small structures; theory of high temperature superconductivity. **Mailing Address:** Dept Physics, Mass Inst Technol, 77 Mass Ave Rm 12-117, Cambridge, MA 02139. **Fax:** 617-253-2562. **E-Mail:** palee@mit.edu

LEE, PAUL D, ASTRONOMY, ASTROPHYSICS. **Personal Data:** b Ina, Ill, February 15, 1940; m 1961, c 2. **Education:** Univ Ill, BS, 1963, MS, 1965, PhD, 1968. **Professional Experience:** PROF PHYSICS & ASTRON, MIDDLE TENN STATE UNIV, as of 2004; assoc prof physics & astron, Middle Tenn State Univ, beginning 1994; from asst prof to assoc prof physics & astron, La State Univ, Baton Rouge, 1968-1994. **Memberships:** Royal Astron Soc; Am Astron Soc. **Research Statement & Publications:** Spectrophotometry of stellar and nonstellar objects; stellar atmospheres and chemical abundances in stars. **Mailing Address:** Dept Physics & Astron, Middle Tenn State Univ, 217 Wiser Patten Sci MTSU Box X-106, Murfreesboro, TN 37132. **Fax:** 615-898-5303. **E-Mail:** plee@physics.mtsu.edu

LEE, PAUL L, MEDICAL IMAGING. **Personal Data:** b China, June 12, 1944; American citizen; m 1972, Amy; c Mayylee & Andrew S Lee. **Education:** Calif Inst Technol, BS, 1967, PhD (physics), 1972. **Professional Experience:** Vis fac, MTS, 1985-; PROF PHYSICS, CALIF STATE UNIV, NORTHRIDGE, 1983-; vis fac, Jet Propulsion Lab, Caltech, 1983-1984; vis assoc, Calif Inst Technol, 1976-1983; from asst prof to assoc prof, Calif State Univ, Long Beach, 1975-1983; lectr physics, Calif State Univ, Long Beach, 1973-1975; res fel physics, Calif Inst Technol, 1971-1973. **Memberships:** Am Phys Soc. **Research Statement & Publications:** Image processing and medical physics; nuclear magnetic resonance imaging protocols and special hardware; algorithms for analyzing X-ray angiograms; data analysis; numerical methods. **Mailing Address:** Dept Physics & Astron, Calif State Univ, Northridge, CA 91330. **Fax:** 818-677-5234. **E-Mail:** paul.lee@csun.edu

LEE, PETER CHUNG-YI, ENGINEERING MECHANICS. **Personal Data:** b Hankow, Hupei, China, September 29, 1934; m 1961, c 1. **Education:** Cheng Kung Univ, Taiwan, BS, 1957; Rutgers Univ, MS, 1961; Columbia Univ, MS, 1965, DEngSc(eng mech), 1965. **Honors & Awards:** C B Sawyer Mem Award, 1980. **Professional Experience:** PROF CIVIL ENG, PRINCETON UNIV, 1976-; from asst prof to assoc prof, Princeton Univ, 1966-1976; Sloan vis fel, 1965-1966. **Memberships:** Am Soc Mech Engrs; Am Soc Civil Engrs; Acoust Soc Am; Inst Elec & Electronics Engrs. **Research Statement & Publications:** Theory of elasticity; vibrations and wave propagation in elastic solids and pieoelectric crystals; effects of initial stresses and accelerations; temperature changes on the vibrations of elastic and crystal plates. **Mailing Address:** Dept Civil Eng & Opers Res, Princeton Univ, E-317, E-quad, Princeton, NJ 08544. **Fax:** 609-258-1270. **E-Mail:** lee@soil.princeton.edu

LEE, PETER E, PLANT VIROLOGY. **Personal Data:** b Trinidad, WI, October 18, 1930; m 1960, c 2. **Education:** Univ Man, BSc, 1958; Univ Wis, MSc, 1959, PhD (entom), 1961. **Professional Experience:** RETIRED; from asst prof to prof biol, Carleton Univ, 1965-1989; res officer virus vector studies, Can Dept Agr, 1961-1965; jr res entomologist, Univ Calif, Berkeley, 1961. **Memberships:** Electron Micros Soc Am. **Research Statement & Publications:** Characterization of leafhopper-transmitted viruses and insect viruses; virus purification and electron microscopy. **Mailing Address:** 38 Inuvik Crescent, Kanata, ON K2L 1A2, Can.

LEE, PETER H Y, FLUID MECHANICS, PLASMA. **Personal Data:** b Chungking, China, April 20, 1939. **Education:** Nat Taiwan Univ, BS, 1961; Tech Univ Aachen, Ger, dipl, 1967; Calif Inst Technol, PhD (aeronaut), 1973. **Professional Experience:** PROMAXIS CO, as of 2005; SR SCIENTIST, OCEAN TECHNOL DEPT, TRW SPACE & DEFENSE, 1991-; staff mem, Los Alamos Nat Lab, 1984-1991; physicist, Lawrence Livermore Lab, 1976-1984; mem tech staff, TRW, 1973-1976. **Memberships:** Am Phys Soc. **Mailing Address:** Promaxis Co, 7247 Crest Rd, Rancho Palos Verdes, CA 90275. **Fax:** 310-544-8763. **E-Mail:** promaxis@usa.com

LEE, PETER VAN ARSDALE, PHARMACOLOGY, MEDICINE. **Personal Data:** b San Francisco, Calif, March 31, 1923; m 1951, c 4. **Education:** Stanford Univ, AB, 1944, MD, 1947. **Professional Experience:** SR FAC CONSULT, PACIFIC AIDS EDUC TRAINING CTR, as of 2003; PROF EMER FAMILY & PREV MED, SCH MED, UNIV SOUTHERN CALIF, 1980-; vis fel, Brit Asn Study Med Educ, 1971-1972; Prof Med, Sch Med, Univ Southern CalifF, beginning 1967; prof pharmacol, Univ Southern Calif, 1967-1980; assoc prof med, Univ Southern Calif, 1960-1967; admis officer, Univ Southern Calif, 1960-1965; assoc prof pharmacol, Univ Southern Calif, 1958-1967; assoc dean, Univ Southern Calif, 1958-1960; consult, Commonwealth Fund, 1958-1959; asst prof & asst dean, Univ Southern Calif, 1955-1958; asst prof, Sch Med, Stanford Univ, 1954-1955; instr pharmacol, Sch Med, Stanford Univ, 1952-1954; clin asst, Col Med, State Univ NY, 1951-1952; Resident, King's Co Hosp, NY, 1951-1952; resident med, Stanford Univ Hosps, 1950-1951; asst resident path, Stanford Univ Hosps, 1949-1950; Intern, San Francisco Hosp, 1946-1947. **Memberships:** AAAS; Am Fedn Clin Res; Asn Am Med Cols; Brit Asn Study Med Educ; fel Royal Soc Med. **Research Statement & Publications:** Medical education; clinical pharmacology. **Mailing Address:** Dept Family Med, Keck Sch Med, Univ Southern Calif, 1420 San Pablo St, Los Angeles, CA 90033. **E-Mail:** pvlee@hsc.usc.edu

LEE, PHILIP RANDOLPH, INTERNAL MEDICINE. **Personal Data:** b San Francisco, Calif, April 17, 1924; m 1953, c 4. **Education:** Stanford Univ, AB, 1945, MD, 1948; Univ Minn, MS, 1955; Am Bd Internal Med, cert, 1956. **Honorary Degrees:** ScD, MacMurray Col, 1967. **Honors & Awards:** Hugo Schaefer Medal, Am Pharmaceut Asn, 1976. **Professional Experience:** SR ADV, SCH MED & EMER PROF, UNIV CALIF, SAN FRANCISCO, 1997-; asst secy health, Dept Health & Human Servs, Wash, 1993-1997; chair, Physician Payment Rev Comn, 1986-1993; pres, Health Comn, City San Francisco, 1985-1989; pres bd dirs, World Inst Disability, 1984-; mem, Comt Pop, Nat Res Coun-Nat Acad Sci, 1983-1986; mem adv bd, Scripps Clin & Res Found, 1980-; co-dir, Inst Health & Aging, Sch Nursing, Univ Calif, San Francisco, 1980-; Nat Coun Health Planning & Develop, Dept HEW, 1978-1980; Nat Coun Health Planning & Develop, USPHS Adv Comt, 1978; mem, Nat Coun Smoking & Pub Policy, 1977-1978; dir, Inst Health Policy Studies, 1972-1993; prof social med, Med Ctr, 1969-1993; chancellor, Univ Calif, San Francisco, 1969-1972; asst secy, Dept HEW, 1965-1969; asst secy health & sci affairs, Univ Calif, San Francisco, 1965-1969; dep asst secy health & sci affairs, Dept HEW, 1965; dir health serv, Off Tech Coop & Res, AID, 1963-1965; asst clin prof, Sch Med, Stanford Univ, 1959-1967; consult, Bur Pub Health Serv, USPHS, 1958-1963; mem, Dept Internal Med, Palo Alto Med Clin, Calif, 1956-1965; clin instr med, Sch Med, Stanford Univ, 1956-1959; asst prof clin phys med & rehab, Sch Med, NY Univ, 1955-1956. **Memberships:** Inst Med-Nat Acad Sci; AAAS; AMA; Am Pub Health Asn; Am Fedn Clin Res; Am Col Physicians; Am Geriat Soc; Asn Am Med Col. **Research Statement & Publications:** Arthritis and rheumatism, especially Rubella arthritis; cardiovascular rehabilitation; academic medical administration; health policy; author of over 10 books and many technical journal articles. **Mailing Address:** Sch Med, Univ Calif, 3333 Calif St Ste 265 Box 0936, San Francisco, CA 94118. **Fax:** 415-476-0705. **E-Mail:** smoser@itsa.ucsf.edu

LEE, PING, CELLULAR PHYSIOLOGY. **Personal Data:** b Summantra, Indonesia, April 17, 1936. **Education:** Nat Univ Taipei, BS, 1959; Duke Univ, MS, 1961, PhD (physiol), 1964. **Professional Experience:** INTERIM CHAIR, DEPT PHYSIOL, WVA UNIV, 1990-; PROF PHYSIOL, DEPT PHYSIOL, SCH MED, WVA UNIV, 1977-; from asst prof to assoc prof, Dept Physiol, Wva Univ, 1968-1977; instr med physiol, Duke Univ, 1966-1968; fel membrane transport, Duke Univ, 1964-1966. **Memberships:** Am Physiol Soc; Biophys Soc. **Mailing Address:** Dept Physiol, Sch Med, WVa Univ, Rm 3051 HSN, PO Box 9229, Morgantown, WV 26506. **E-Mail:** plee@hsc.wvu.edu

LEE, PING-CHEUNG, PEDIATRICS, CELL BIOLOGY. **Personal Data:** b Hong Kong, September 10, 1939. **Education:** Univ Hong Kong, BSc, 1963; Fla State Univ, MS, 1965, PhD, 1968. **Professional Experience:** PROF PHARMACOL & TOXICOL; RES PROF & DIR, GASTROINTESTINAL LABS, DEPT PEDIAT, MED COL WIS, MILWAUKEE, 1989-; asst ed, J Pediat Gastroenterol & Nutrit, 1982-1990; dir, Gastrointestinal & Nutrit Lab, Children's Hosp, Buffalo, NY, 1979-1989; assoc prof, Dept Pediat, State Univ NY, Buffalo, 1979-1989; vis investr, Digestive Dis Br, Inst Arthritis, Metab & Digestive Dis, NIH, 1978; asst prof, Dept Surg & Biochem, Med Col Ohio, Toledo, 1975-1979; instr, Dept Biochem, 1974-1975; Res investr, Steroid Hormone Lab, Wesley Mem Hosp, Chicago, Ill, 1972-1975; res assoc, Dept Biochem, Med Sch, Northwestern Univ, 1972-1974; Res assoc, Dept Chem, Fla State Univ, Tallahassee, 1968-1972. **Memberships:** Am Soc Biochem & Molecular Biol; Am Gastroenterol Asn; Soc Exp Biol & Med; Am Pancreatic Asn; Int Soc Study Fatty Acids & Lipids; Int Soc Study Xenobiotics; Soc Toxicol. **Research Statement & Publications:** Alternative enzyme suppplements for the treatment of pancreatic insufficiency; endocrine and reproductive toxicology of environmental contaminants. **Mailing Address:** Dept Pediat Med Col Wis, MACC Fund Res Ctr 8701 Watertown Plank Rd, Milwaukee, WI 53226. **Fax:** 414-266-6328. **E-Mail:** pclee@mail.mcw.edu

LEE, PUI KUM, OPTICS. **Personal Data:** b Peking, China, June 22, 1916; American citizen; m 1941, c 4. **Education:** Lingnam Univ, BS, 1940; Columbia Univ, MS, 1949. **Honors & Awards:** IR-100 Award, Indust Res Mag, 1978. **Professional Experience:** RETIRED; sr res specialist, Cent Res Labs, 3M Co, 1967-1982; res specialist imaging, Cent Res Labs, 3M Co, 1963-1967; sr chemist reprography, Cent Res Labs, 3M Co, 1956-1963; res assoc chem, Columbia Univ, 1949-1956; mgr, China Chem Corp, 1942-1946; res chemist, Inst Indust Res, 1941-1942; Asst chem, Nat Kwangsi Univ, China, 1940-1941. **Memberships:** Am Chem Soc; Soc Photog Sci & Eng; Optical Soc Am. **Research Statement & Publications:** Imaging optics. **Mailing Address:** 2240 Midland Grove Rd No 305, St Paul, MN 55113.

LEE, RALPH EDWARD, COMPUTER SCIENCE. **Personal Data:** b Gilliam, Mo, July 1, 1921; m 1942, c 5. **Education:** Mo Valley Col, BS, 1942; Univ Mo, MS, 1949; Ind Univ, MA, 1953. **Professional Experience:** RETIRED; dir, Comput Ctr, 1960-1988; prof, Sch Mines, Univ Mo, Rolla, 1959-1988; NSF fel, Nat Bur Stand, 1959; from instr to assoc prof math, Sch Mines, Univ Mo, Rolla, 1946-1959. **Memberships:** Data Processing Mgt Asn; Asn Comput Mach; Soc Indust & Appl Math; Asn Educ Data Systs. **Research Statement & Publications:** Numerical analysis; matrix computations. **Mailing Address:** 12651 US Hwy 63 S, Rolla, MO 65401.

LEE, RAY H(UI-CHOUNG), ELECTRICAL ENGINEERING, MATHEMATICS. **Personal Data:** b Canton, China, March 28, 1918; American citizen; c 4. **Education:** Nat Cent Univ, China, BS, 1941; Stanford Univ, MA, 1945, EE, 1946, MS, 1947. **Professional Experience:** RETIRED; consult prod develop & strategic planning, beginning 1973; chief engr, Liquid Crystal Display, Backman Instruments, 1969-1973; staff mem & mgr, Tex Instruments, 1966-1969; staff mem, David Sarnoff Res Ctr, Radio Corp Am, NJ, 1964-1966; res specialist & chief mathematician, Chromatic TV Labs & Auktometric Corp, 1955-1963; engr specialist, Boeing Airplane Co, 1951-1955; founder & prin, Honolulu Trade Sch, 1947-1951; design engr, Cent Radio Works China, 1941-1944. **Memberships:** Inst Elec & Electronics Engrs; Soc Info Display. **Research Statement & Publications:** Processings; energy; communication. **Mailing Address:** 23203 Park Esperanza, Calabasas, CA 91302.

LEE, RICHARD FAYAO, ENVIRONMENTAL CHEMISTRY, BIOLOGICAL OCEANOGRAPHY. **Personal Data:** b Shanghai, China, July 13, 1941; American citizen; m 1970, Josephine tagle; c Elizabeth & Lori. **Education:** San Diego State Col, BA, 1964, MA, 1966; Univ Calif, San Diego, PhD (marine biol), 1970. **Professional Experience:** Consult, Exxon Corp, 1975; mem adv comt, Marine Resources Res Group Biol Accumulators, UN Food & Agr Orgn, 1974-; RES PROF OCEANOG, SKIDAWAY INST OCEANOG, 1974-; Res assoc biochem, Pa State Univ, 1971-1972 & Scripps Inst Oceanog, 1972-1973; Lectr oceanog, San Diego State Univ, 1971-1973. **Memberships:** Am Chem Soc; Am Soc Limnol & Oceanog; Sigma Xi. **Research Statement & Publications:** Fate of petroleum hydrocarbons in the marine food web; role of lipids in the ecology of marine zooplankton; aquatic toxicology; vitellogenesis in marine crustaceans; environmental toxicology; mariculture. **Mailing Address:** Skidaway Inst Oceanog, Ocean Sci Circle, Savannah, GA 31411. **Fax:** 912-598-2310.

LEE, RICHARD J, SOLID STATE PHYSICS. **Personal Data:** b Minot, NDak, July 23, 1944; m 1960. **Education:** Univ NDak, BSEd, 1966; Colo State Univ, PhD (physics), 1970. **Professional Experience:** PRES, RJ LEE GROUP, INC, as of 2003; mem staff,

US Steel Corp, beginning 1974; asst prof, Purdue Univ, Ft Wayne, 1970-1974; res asst, Colo State Univ, 1968-1970; Instr physics, Lake Regional Jr Col, beginning 1966. **Memberships:** Am Phys Soc; Am Asn Physics Teachers; Am Chem Soc. **Research Statement & Publications:** Theory of quantum solids; phase transition; light scattering. **Mailing Address:** RJ Lee Group, Inc, 350 Hochbery Rd, Monroeville, PA 15146. **Fax:** 724-733-1799.

LEE, RICHARD NORMAN, ATMOSPHERIC CHEMISTRY. **Personal Data:** b Waukegan, Ill, November 3, 1939; m 1964, c 2. **Education:** Park Col, BA, 1961; Univ Kans, PhD (chem), 1968. **Professional Experience:** RES SCIENTIST, ATMOSPHERIC SCI DEPT, BATTELLE PAC NORTHWEST LABS, 1972-; asst prof chem, St Norbert Col, 1966-1972. **Memberships:** Am Chem Soc. **Research Statement & Publications:** Reaction kinetics; environmental chemistry; chemical analysis; atmospheric pollutants and tracers. **Mailing Address:** 1864 Marshall Ave, Richland, WA 99352-2460. **E-Mail:** dick.lee@pnl.gov

LEE, ROBERT BUMJUNG, TRANSPORTATION & CIVIL ENGINEERING. **Personal Data:** b Seoul, Korea, January 24, 1937; American citizen; m 1965, c 2. **Education:** Seoul Nat Univ, BSCE, 1961; Polytech Inst Brooklyn, MSTP, 1969, PhD (transp eng), 1973. **Professional Experience:** PRES, URBITRAN ASSOCS INC, 1981-; vpres consult engr, Urbitran Assoc Inc, 1980-1981; sr traffic engr, Louis Berger Int Inc, 1975-1980; asst prof, Polytech Inst Brooklyn, 1973-1975; res assoc traffic & transp, Polytech Inst Brooklyn, 1969-1973; traffic engr, Port NY Authority, 1967-1969; Hwy engr civil, Madigan-Hyland Eng Co, 1964-1967; treas, Urbitran Assoc Inc. **Memberships:** Am Soc Civil Engrs; Sigma Xi. **Research Statement & Publications:** Transportation; transit; environmental impacts. **Mailing Address:** Urbitran Assocs Inc, 71 W 23rd St, New York, NY 10010.

LEE, ROBERT E, ELECTRICAL & BIOMEDICAL ENGINEERING. **Personal Data:** b Rochester, NY, May 22, 1932; m 1957, c 4. **Education:** Univ Rochester, BS, 1954, MS, 1962, PhD (elec eng), 1966. **Professional Experience:** Consult, Eastman Kodak, 1981; ASSOC PROF ELEC ENG, ROCHESTER INST TECHNOL, 1968-; asst prof elec eng, Univ WVa, 1966-1968; tech specialist, Bausch & Lomb, Inc, 1965-1966; asst prof thermodyn, fluids, calculus & eng, Rochester Inst Technol, 1958-1962; proj engr, Gen Rwy Signal Co, 1957-1958; instr thermodyn, Univ Buffalo, 1956-1957. **Memberships:** Am Soc Eng Educ; Inst Elec & Electronics Engrs; Optical Soc Am; Sigma Xi. **Research Statement & Publications:** Visual systems, specifically latency to response of human pupil for contraction and dilation; effects of intensity, adaptation and size of change on latency. **Mailing Address:** One Lomb Mem Dr, Rochester Institute of Tech, Rochester, NY 14623.

LEE, ROBERT E, PHYSICAL CHEMISTRY, AIR POLLUTION. **Personal Data:** b Albany, NY, September 21, 1936; m 1960, c 2. **Education:** Siena Col, BS, 1958; George Wash Univ, MEA, 1964; Univ Cincinnati, MS, 1967, PhD (phys chem), 1969. **Professional Experience:** RES CHEMIST, US ENVIRON PROTECTION AGENCY, 1964-, BR CHIEF, EAB; scientist, Melpar, Inc, Va, 1962-1964; Chemist, US Army Biol Labs, Md, 1958-1962. **Memberships:** AAAS; Air Pollution Control Asn; Am Chem Soc. **Research Statement & Publications:** Air pollution chemistry. **Mailing Address:** US EPA, Mail Code 7406401 M St SW, Washington, DC 20460.

LEE, ROBERT EDWARD, PHYCOLOGY, CRYOBIOLOGY. **Personal Data:** b Worcester, Mass, September 15, 1942; m 1968, Patricia; c Nicole, Alana & Christian. **Education:** Cornell Univ, BSc, 1964; Univ Mass, PhD (biol), 1971. **Professional Experience:** FAC, COLO STATE UNIV, as of 2005; Vet Med, COLO STATE UNIV, 1981-; fel, Boston Biomed Res Inst & Harvard Med Sch, 1979-1981; assoc prof, Shiraz Univ, 1977-1979; Lectr, Univ Witwatersrand, 1971-1977. **Research Statement & Publications:** Systematics of algae; electron microscopy and freeze-fracture of biological systems; neuronal growth and development; preservation of tissues using rapid freezing. **Mailing Address:** Dept Biomed Sci, Colo State Univ, 1617 Campus Delivery, Ft Collins, CO 80523-1617. **Fax:** 970-491-7907. **E-Mail:** robert.e.lee@colostate.edu

LEE, ROBERT GUM HONG, MINING. **Personal Data:** b Montreal, Que, May 22, 1924; m Maude; c Peter, Patricia & Catherine. **Education:** McGill Univ, Montreal, BS, 1947. **Honors & Awards:** Airey Award, Can Inst Mining & Metall, 1974, Falconbridge Innovation Award, 1992. **Professional Experience:** CONSULT; dir & adv, Hydrogenics Corp, as of 2003; mem bd dirs, Montreal Chinese Hosp, 1975-1982; res engr, Can Liquid Air Ltd, Montreal, beginning 1947. **Memberships:** Soc Cryobiol; Am Inst Mining & Metall; Am Chem Soc; Can Inst Mining & Metall. **Mailing Address:** Hydrogenics Corp, 5985 McLaughlin Rd, Mississauga, ON L5R 1B8, Can. **Fax:** 905-361-3626.

LEE, ROBERT MAUNG KYAW WIN, HYPERTENSION, VASCULAR SMOOTH MUSCLE. **Personal Data:** b Burma, November 7, 1943; Canadian citizen; m 1975, Nancy; c Frederick J & Andrew J. **Education:** Univ Mandalay, Burma, BSc(Hons), 1966; Univ Rangoon, Burma, MSc, 1969; Univ Alta, PhD (entom), 1975. **Honors & Awards:** Lo Yuk Tong Found Lectr, Univ Hong Kong, 1993; Distinguished Service Award, Canadian Hypertension Society, 1999. **Professional Experience:** Pres, Can Hypertension Soc, Canada, 1995-1996; PROF ANAESTHESIA, MCMASTER UNIV, 1989-; COORDR, SMOOTH MUSCLE RES PROG, MCMASTER UNIV, 1988-; mem, Circulation Coun, Am Heart Asn, 1987-; Distinguished speaker, Kunming Med Col, China, 1985 & 1988; Ont Ministry Health Career Scientists, McMaster Univ, 1982-1992; from asst prof to assoc prof anaesthesia, McMaster Univ, 1980-1989; Rose-Levy Rosenstadt fel, McMaster Univ, 1980-1982; MRC Centennial fel hypertension, McMaster Univ, 1979-1980; res assoc, McMaster Univ, 1978-1979; fel entom, McMaster Univ, 1976-1978; fel entom, Univ Regina, 1975-1976; Lectr histol, Univ Regina, 1975. **Memberships:** Am Physiol Soc; Am Heart Asn; Can Hypertension Soc; Inter-Am Soc Hypertension; Pharmacol Soc Can; Int Soc Hypertension; Pharmacol Soc Can; Can Soc Athero Thrombo Vasc Biol. **Research Statement & Publications:** Role of structural changes of blood vessels in the development of high blood pressure (hypertension) in humans; biology of vascular smooth muscle cells; structure and function of airway cilia in health and in disease. **Mailing Address:** Dept Anesthesia, Health Sci, McMaster Univ, 1200 Main St W, Hamilton, ON L8N 3Z5, Can. **Fax:** 905-523-1224. **E-Mail:** rmkwlee@mcmaster.ca

LEE, ROBERT W, EXPERIMENTAL PHYSICS. **Personal Data:** b Cedar Rapids, Iowa, February 28, 1931; m 1951, c 3. **Education:** Mich State Univ, BS, 1953, MS, 1955. **Honors & Awards:** AIP Award, Indust Applns Physics, 1985. **Professional Experience:** RETIRED; sr res physicist, Res Labs, Gen Motors Corp, 1955-1988. **Memberships:** Sigma Xi. **Research Statement & Publications:** Permanent magnets; electro-optics; gas diffusion in solids. **Mailing Address:** 3090 Myddleton Dr, Troy, MI 43084.

LEE, ROBERT WILLIAM, PHYSICAL PHARMACEUTICAL CHEMISTRY, PHYSICAL BIOORGANIC CHEMISTRY. **Personal Data:** b Honolulu, Hawaii, July 16, 1960; American citizen; m Susan; c Brian, Ellen & Kevin. **Education:** Univ Wash, BS (chem) & BS (biol), 1982; Univ Calif, Santa Barbara, PhD (phys bioorg chem), 1990. **Honors & Awards:** Vision & Accomplishment Award, Sterling Winthrop Pharmaceut Res div, 1992. **Professional Experience:** VPRES PHARMACEUT DEVELOP, NOVAVAX INC, 2005-; sr mgr, Elan Drug Delivery Inc, beginning 2001; mgr, Elan Pharmaceut Technol, 1999-2001; mgr, Nanosystems, 1997-1999; principal res invest, Nanosystems, 1996-1997; sr res invest, Nanosystems, 1994-1996; sr res investr, Sterling Winthrop Pharmaceut Res Div, 1992-1994; adj assoc prof, Univ Kans, 1992-; res investr, Sterling Winthrop Pharmaceut Res Div, 1990-1992. **Memberships:** Am Chem Soc; Am Asn Parmaceut Scientists; PDA; asn for the advancement of med instrumentation. **Research Statement & Publications:** Development and implementation of novel technologies and computer modeling paradigms to expedite the discovery and development of pharmaceutics. **Mailing Address:** Novavax, Inc, 508 Lapp Rd, Malvern, PA 19355. **E-Mail:** robert.lee@elan.com

LEE, ROLAND ROBERT, NEURORADIOLOGY, MAGNETIC RESONANCE IMAGING & SPECTROSCOPY. **Personal Data:** b Cleveland, Ohio, July 18, 1954. **Education:** Calif Inst Technol, BS, 1975; Univ Calif, Berkeley, MA, 1977; Univ Calif, Los Angeles, MD, 1985. **Professional Experience:** ASSOC PROF RADIOL & DIR MAGNETIC SOURCE IMAGING UNIV NMEX, ALBUQUERQUE, 1997-; asst prof radiol, Johns Hopkins Hosp, 1992-1997; clin instr & res Fel neuroradiol, Dept Radiol, Univ Calif, San Francisco, 1991-1992; clin& res fel magnetic resonance imaging spectros, Long Beach Mem Magnetic Resonance Ctr, Huntington Mem Med Res Inst, 1990-1991; resident diag radiol, Harvard Med Sch, Brigham & Women's Hosp, 1986-1990; intern, Harbor Ucla Med, 1985-1986; res asst superconductivity, Univ Calif, Berkeley, 1977-1981; Physicist laser fusion & teaching asst physics, Lawrence Livermore Nat Lab, Univ Calif, Berkeley, 1975-1977. **Memberships:** Am Col Radiol; sr mem Am Soc Neuroradiol; Radiol Soc NAm; AMA; Ama; Amer Soc Spine Radiology. **Research Statement & Publications:** Clinical diagnostic radiology; neuroradiology and magnetic resonance imaging; magnetic resonance spectroscopy; medical image processing; magnetoencephalography and magnetic source neuroimaging; spinal imaging. **Mailing Address:** Va medical Ctr, univ of New Mexico, Radiology Dept, 1501 San Pedro Drive Se (114m), Albuquerque, NM 87108. **Fax:** 505-256-5708. **E-Mail:** rrlee@unm.edu

LEE, RONALD NORMAN, SURFACE PHYSICS, MATERIALS SCIENCE. **Personal Data:** b Springfield, Mo, October 21, 1935; m 1959, c 1. **Education:** Univ Ill, BS, 1958, MS, 1960; Brown Univ, PhD (physics), 1965. **Professional Experience:** TECH LEADER, SURFACE SCI GROUP, 1979-; PHYSICIST, MAT DIV, NAVAL SURFACE WARFARE CTR, 1974-; physicist, US Naval Ord Lab, 1968-1974; fel phys chem, Battelle mem Inst, Ohio, 1965-1968; res assoc physics, Brown Univ, 1964-1965; res assoc physics, Coord Sci Lab, Univ Ill, 1960. **Memberships:** Am Phys Soc; Am Vacuum Soc; AAAS; Sigma Xi. **Research Statement & Publications:** Surface science; composite materials interface properties carbon fiber surface properties corrosion bio-corrosion; physics of electron spectroscopies; physics of scanning tunneling; microscopy battery electrode chemistry; energetic materials. **Mailing Address:** Naval Surface Warfare Ctr, 10901 NH Ave, Silver Spring, MD 20903. **Fax:** 301-394-4472.

LEE, RONALD S, SHOCK COMPRESSION OF SOLIDS, DETONATION PHYSICS. **Personal Data:** b Ames, Iowa, December 29, 1938; m 1966, Jean; c Elizabeth & Karin. **Education:** Luther Col, Iowa, BA, 1961; Iowa State Univ, PhD (physics), 1967. **Professional Experience:** GROUP LEADER, LAWRENCE LIVERMORE LAB, 1992-; physicist, Lawrence Livermore Lab, 1987-1992; from asst prof to prof physics, Kans State Univ, 1964-1987. **Memberships:** Am Phys Soc; Am Defense Preparedness Asn. **Research Statement & Publications:** Shock waves in chemically reacting media; radiation effects in solids. **Mailing Address:** 1822 Vancouver Way, Livermore, CA 94550. **Fax:** 925-422-2382. **E-Mail:** lee35@llnl.gov

LEE, RONNIE, TOPOLOGY. **Personal Data:** b China, November 6, 1942. **Education:** Chinese Univ Hong Kong, BS, 1965; Univ Mich, PhD (math), 1968. **Professional Experience:** PROF MATH, YALE UNIV, as of 2004; DIR UNDERGRAD STUDIES, YALE UNIV, beginning 1977; assoc prof math, Yale Univ, beginning 1973; Sloan Found fel, 1973; asst prof, Yale Univ, 1970-1973; mem, Inst Advan Studies, 1968-1970. **Research Statement & Publications:** Differential topology. **Mailing Address:** Dept Math, Yale Univ, 402 DL, New Haven, CT 06520-8283. **Fax:** 203-432-7316. **E-Mail:** rlee@math.yale.edu

LEE, ROY Y, COMPUTER SCIENCE. **Education:** Univ Wis-Madison, PhD, 1967. **Professional Experience:** STAFF, SANDIA NAT LAB, as of 2005. **Mailing Address:** Sandia Nat Lab, PO Box 969, Livermore, CA 94551. **Fax:** 925-294-3410.

LEE, S Y, ACCELERATOR PHYSICS. **Professional Experience:** PROF, DEPT PHYSICS, IND UNIV, as of 2005. **Memberships:** Am Physics Soc. **Mailing Address:** Dept Physics, Indiana Univ, Swain W 205, Bloomington, IN 47405. **Fax:** 812-855-5533. **E-Mail:** shylee@indiana.edu

LEE, SAMUEL C, ELECTRICAL ENGINEERING, COMPUTER SCIENCE. **Personal Data:** b Hong-Chow, China, May 4, 1937; American citizen. **Education:** Nat Taiwan Univ, BS, 1960; Univ Calif, Berkeley, MS, 1963; Univ Ill, Urbana, PhD (elec eng), 1965. **Professional Experience:** PROF ELEC ENG & COMPUT SCI, UNIV OKLA, 1975-; vis assoc prof, Baylor Col Med & asst neurophysiologist, Methodist Hosp, Houston, 1972-1975; assoc prof, NY Univ, 1967-1970 & Univ Houston, 1970-1975; consult, Bell Labs, 1967-1970 & NAm Aircraft Co, Conn, 1968-1969; mem tech staff elec eng, Bell Labs, Murray Hill, 1965-1967. **Memberships:** Inst Elec & Electronics Engrs; Asn Comput Mach; Am Soc Eng Educ. **Research Statement & Publications:** Digital systems; logical design; pattern recognition; artificial intelligence. **Mailing Address:** Sch Elec Eng & Comput Eng, Univ Okla, 202 W Boyd Rm 219, Norman, OK 73019-1023. **Fax:** 405-325-7066. **E-Mail:** samlee@ou.edu

LEE, SANG M, QUALITY CONTROL. **Education:** Univ Ga, PhD (mgt), 1969. **Professional Experience:** CHAIR, MGT DEPT, UNIV NEBR, LINCOLN & EXE DIR NEBR PRODUCTIVITY & ENTREPRENEURSHIP CTR & DIR, CTR ALBANIAN STUDIES, as of 2006. **Memberships:** Pan-Pac Bus Asn. **Mailing Address:** Univ Nebr, Lincoln, PO Box 880491, Lincoln, NE 68588-0491. **Fax:** 402-472-5855. **E-Mail:** slee1@unl.edu

LEE, SHAW-GUANG LIN, BIOCHEMISTRY. **Personal Data:** b Miao-Li, Taiwan, October 9, 1944; American citizen; m 1968, c 3. **Education:** Nat Taiwan Univ, BS, 1967; Northwestern Univ, PhD (biochem), 1972. **Professional Experience:** ASSOC DIR, BIOTECHNOL & MICROBIOL, WYETH-AYERST RES, 1988-; prin scientist, Meloy Lab, 1982-1984; res biochemist molecular virol, Abbott Labs, 1975-1981; Fel biochem, Northwestern Univ, 1973-1975. **Memberships:** Am Chem Soc. **Research Statement & Publications:** AIDS vaccine developmental research; lyme disease vaccine; strombolytic agents; fibrinolysis. **Mailing Address:** Wyeth-Ayerst Res, PO Box 8299, Philadelphia, PA 19101-8299.

LEE, SHIH-SHUN, MOLECULAR GENETICS, CANCER CHEMOTHERAPY. **Personal Data:** b Taiwan, May 25, 1936; American citizen; m 1969, c 2. **Education:** Nat Taiwan Univ, BS, 1959, MS, 1964; Mont State Univ, PhD (genetics), 1969. **Professional Experience:** RETIRED; chmn tissue cult dept, Burzynski Res Inst, 1981-1993; assoc dir cancer res, Stehlin Found, 1975-1981; res assoc cancer res, Stehlin Found, 1973-1974; Fels, Indiana Univ, 1969-1970; M D Anderson Hosp & Tumor Inst, 1970-1973; res asst genetics, Mont State Univ, 1966-1969; instr agron, Prov Taiwan Agr Col, 1964-1966. **Memberships:** Sigma Xi. **Research Statement & Publications:** Tumor tissue culture; tumor chemotherapy; induction of cancer cell differentiation. **Mailing Address:** 2707 Cane Field Dr, Sugar Land, TX 77479.

LEE, SHIH-YING, MECHANICAL ENGINEERING, ENGINEERING EDUCATION. **Personal Data:** b Peking, China, April 30, 1918. **Education:** Mass Inst Technol, DSc, 1945. **Professional Experience:** CHMN & CHIEF EXEC OFFICER, SETRA SYSTS INC, 1996-; PROF EMER, MASS INST TECHNOL, 1974-; prof mech eng, Mass Inst Technol, 1966-1974; fac mem, Mass Inst Technol, 1952-1974; res engr, Mass Inst Technol, 1947-1952. **Memberships:** Nat Acad Eng. **Mailing Address:** Dept Mech Eng, Mass Inst Techonol, 77 Mass Ave, Cambridge, MA 02139. **Fax:** 617-258-6156. **E-Mail:** leesy@setra.com

LEE, SHO RONG, MATHEMATICS. **Professional Experience:** PROF, DEPT MATHS, PACE UNIV, as of 2006. **Memberships:** Math Asn Am. **Mailing Address:** Dept Math, Pace Univ, 861 Bedford Rd, Pleasantville, NY 10570. **Fax:** 212-346-1659.

LEE, SHUH-YUAN, PHYSICS. **Education:** State Univ NY, PhD, 1972. **Professional Experience:** PROF, IND UNIV, as of 2005. **Memberships:** Fel Am Phys Soc. **Mailing Address:** Dept Physics, Indiana Univ Swain Hall W 117, Bloomington, IN 47405. **Fax:** 812-855-5533. **E-Mail:** shylee@indiana.edu

LEE, SHUI LUNG, ORGANIC CHEMISTRY. **Personal Data:** b Canton, China, September 15, 1938; m 1969, c 2. **Education:** Univ Western Australia, BS, 1965, PhD (org chem), 1969. **Professional Experience:** SR CHEMIST, GANES CHEMICALS, 1980-; chemist, Ganes Chemicals, 1978-1980; sr res chemist, pigments div, Chemetron Corp, 1975-1978; sr chemist, Aldrich Chem Co, 1974-1975; Queens Univ, Can, 1971-1974; Fel org chem, McMaster Univ, 1969-1971. **Memberships:** Am Chem Soc. **Research Statement & Publications:** Medicinal and fine organic chemicals. **Mailing Address:** One Toby Terr, Towaco, NJ 07082-1413.

LEE, SHUISHIH SAGE, EXPERIMENTAL PATHOLOGY, ANATOMIC PATHOLOGY. **Personal Data:** b Soo-chow, China, January 5, 1948; m 1973, Chung; c Yvonne & Michael. **Education:** Nat Taiwan Univ, MD, 1972; Univ Rochester, PhD (path), 1976. **Professional Experience:** CLIN ASST PROF, DEPT PATH, MED SCH, IND UNIV, 1989-; PATHOLOGIST, PARKVIEW MEM HOSP, 1979-; resident path, Northwestern Mem Hosp, 1978-1979; resident, Med Ctr, Univ Rochester, 1977-1978; Intern path, Med Ctr, Univ Rochester, 1976-1977. **Memberships:** Int Acad Pathol; Am Asn Pathologists; Am Soc Clin Pathologists; Col Am Pathologists; Int Acad Cytol; Electron Micros Soc Am. **Research Statement & Publications:** Synthesis of ferritin in rat liver and hepatoma cells; cytopathology. **Mailing Address:** Dept Path, 5728 Prophet's Pass, Ft Wayne, IN 46845-9659.

LEE, SHUNG-YAN LUKE, ORGANIC CHEMISTRY. **Personal Data:** b China, September 10, 1938; American citizen; m 1962, c 2. **Education:** Univ Wis, BS, 1959; Ohio State Univ, MS, 1962, PhD (phys org chem), 1966. **Professional Experience:** RES CHEMIST PHOTOG SYST, E I DU PONT Del NEMOURS & CO, INC, 1966-, SCIENTIST. **Memberships:** Am Chem Soc. **Research Statement & Publications:** Investigations of photopolymerization systems. **Mailing Address:** 714 Foxdale Rd, Wilmington, DE 19803-1604.

LEE, SHWU-LUAN, MOLECULAR BIOLOGY, GENE REGULATION. **Personal Data:** b Taipei, Taiwan, December 20, 1954. **Education:** Nat Univ Taiwan, BS, 1977, MS, 1980; Univ Ill, PhD (pharmacol), 1987. **Professional Experience:** RES INSTR, BRIGHAM & WOMEN'S HOSP, HARVARD UNIV, 1993-; fel molecular biol, Brigham & Women's Hosp, Harvard Univ, 1991-1993; fel molecular biol, Dana Farber Cancer Inst, 1990-1991; fel regulation coronary circulation, Univ Ill, 1987-1989. **Memberships:** Am Soc Cell Biol. **Mailing Address:** Renal Div, Brigham & Women's Hosp, 75 Francis St, Boston, MA 02115.

LEE, SHYH-YUAN, ACCELERATOR PHYSICS, NUCLEAR PHYSICS. **Personal Data:** b Yuinin, Taiwan, November 17, 1943. **Education:** Univ Taiwan, BS, 1963; State Univ NY, Stony Brook, MS, 1969 & PhD (physics), 1972. **Professional Experience:** PROF PHYSICS, IND UNIV, 1990-; physicist, Brookhaven Nat Labs, 1985-1990; assoc physicist, Brookhaven Nat Labs, 1984-1985; asst prof physics, State Univ NY, Stony Brook, 1978-1984; res assoc, Univ Paris Orsay, 1976-1977 & Univ Wash Seattle, 1977-1978. **Memberships:** Am Phys Soc; Nat Geog Soc. **Research Statement & Publications:** Nonlinear physics; accelerator and spin physics. **Mailing Address:** Dept Physics, Ind Univ, Swain W 205, Bloomington, IN 47405. **Fax:** 812-855-5533. **E-Mail:** shylee@indiana.edu

LEE, SI DUK, ENVIRONMENTAL SCIENCES, BIOLOGICAL CHEMISTRY, TOXICOLOGY. **Personal Data:** b Ham Hung, Korea, January 2, 1932; American citizen; m 1957, c 3. **Education:** Seoul Nat Univ, BS, 1955; Univ Md, MS, 1959, PhD (biochem), 1962. **Honors & Awards:** Bronze Medal, US Environ Protection Agency, 1980 & 1984. **Professional Experience:** Vis scholar, Harvard Univ, 1987-; adj assoc prof, Duke Univ Med Sch, 1982-1987; SR SCI HEALTH ADV, US ENVIRON PROTECTION AGENCY, 1973-; dep chief, biol effects br, Nat Environ Res Ctr, Environ Protection Agency, 1971-1973; chief biochem sect, Nat Air Pollution Control Admin, 1969-1971; adj asst prof, Dept Biol, Col Med, Univ Cincinnati, 1967-1980 & Dept Environ Health, 1975-1980; chief biochem unit, USPHS, 1967-1969; supvry res chemist, USPHS, 1965-1967; res chemist, USPHS, 1964-1965; Res assoc biochem, Am Heart Asn adv res fel, 1963-1964; Res assoc biochem, NIH fel, 1962-1963; Res assoc biochem, Med Ctr, Duke Univ, 1961-1962. **Memberships:** AAAS; Am Chem Soc; Am Col Toxicol; Air Pollution Control Asn; Sigma Xi; Soc Toxicol. **Research Statement & Publications:** Effects of air pollutants on metabolism; lipid metabolism; effects of pollutants on aging; effects of sulfur dioxide on subcellular metabolism; environmental management. **Mailing Address:** US Environ Protection Agency, NCEA MD-52, Research Triangle Park, NC 27711-0001.

LEE, SIDNEY, CHEMICAL ENGINEERING, PHYSICAL CHEMISTRY. **Personal Data:** b Philadelphia, Pa, April 20, 1919; div, c Phillip & Candy. **Education:** Univ Pa, BS, 1939; Cornell Univ, MChE, 1940. **Professional Experience:** RETIRED; pres, Dallas Labs & Assoc Labs Inc, 1970-1985; dir, Dallas Labs & Assoc Labs Inc, 1945-1970; sr chem engr, Tex, 1942-1945; chem engr, Atlantic Refining Co, Pa, 1938-1942; dir, Am Shipbldg Co; pres, W I Investment Co & St Croix Real Estate Develop Corp; mem exec comt, W I Bank & Trust Co; chmn, Sidney Lee Assocs. **Memberships:** Am Chem Soc; Am Pub Health Asn; fel Am Inst Chemists; Am Inst Chem Engrs; Am Inst Mining, Metall & Petrol Engrs; Sigma Xi. **Research Statement & Publications:** Design and cost economics; process and product evaluation. **Mailing Address:** PO Box 130, Christiansted, St Croix, VI 00821.

LEE, SIN HANG, SURGICAL PATHOLOGY, HISTOCHEMISTRY. **Personal Data:** b Hong Kong, November 17, 1932; American citizen; m 1958, Kee; c Emil & Karen. **Education:** Wuhan Med Col, China, MD, 1956. **Professional Experience:** Guest prof, Tongji Med Univ Hankow, Wuhan, China, 1984-; PATHOLOGIST, HOSP ST RAPHAEL, NEW HAVEN, CONN, 1973-; ASSOC CLIN PROF PATH, YALE UNIV, NEW HAVEN, CONN, 1973-; assoc prof, Hosp St Raphael, New Haven, Conn, 1971-1973; asst prof, McGill Univ, Montreal, Can, 1968-1971; fel, Mem Hosp Cancer & Allied Dis, 1967-1968; resident path, NY Hosp, Cornell Med Ctr, 1964-1967; intern clin, South Baltimore Gen Hosp, 1963-1964; demonstr path, Univ Hong Kong, 1961-1963; asst lectr, Sichuan Med Col, Chengou, China, 1957-1961; postgrad bact, Sichuan Med Col, Chengou, China, 1956-1957. **Memberships:** Col Am Pathologists; Int Acad Path; Am Asn Pathologists; NY Acad Sci; AAAS; Royal Col Physicians & Surgeons Can. **Research Statement & Publications:** Histochemical localization of enzyme activities; cytochemical assays of steroid receptors in breast cancer and other target cells; mycoplasma pneumoniae antigen for the detection of specific membrane antibodies in patients for early diagnosis of infection; awarded two patents. **Mailing Address:** Dept Path, Hosp St Raphael, 1450 Chapel St, New Haven, CT 06511.

LEE, SIU-LAM, INSECT ECOLOGY, EVOLUTION. **Personal Data:** b Macao, China, October 3, 1941; m 1982, Felicia; c Terence, Timothy & Serena. **Education:** Chung Chi Col, Chinese Univ, Hong Kong, BSc, 1962; Oberlin Col, AM, 1963; Cornell Univ, PhD (entom), 1967. **Professional Experience:** RETIRED; assoc prof biol, Univ Mass, Lowell, North Campus, 1975-2004; NSF res grant, 1969-1972. **Memberships:** Am Entom Soc; Animal Behav Soc; Bee Res Asn; Sigma Xi; Archoeological Soc Amer. **Research Statement & Publications:** Learning ability of fruit fly; behavioral ecology of the leaf-cutter bee; effects of ginseng, Panax ginseng, on mamalian blood cells and malaria infecton; the flora of temperate deciduous forests. **Mailing Address:** Dept Biol, Univ Mass, N Campus, Lowell, MA 01854. **Fax:** 978-934-3044. **E-Mail:** siulam_lee@ml.edu

LEE, SOOHEE, HUMAN CELL BLOOD GROUPS. **Personal Data:** b Seoul, Korea, April 15, 1944. **Education:** Univ Ewha, Korea, BS, 1967; Univ Tex, MS, 1971; Univ Utah, PhD (pharmaceut), 1985. **Professional Experience:** ASSOC MEM, NY BLOOD CTR, as of 2004; asst mem, NY Blood Ctr, beginning 1987; fel molecular biol, Univ Med & Dent NJ, 1985-1987. **Memberships:** Am Soc Cell Biol. **Research Statement & Publications:** Calcium binding proteins. **Mailing Address:** Lab Membrane Biochem, NY Blood Ctr, 310 E 67th St, New York, NY 10021. **E-Mail:** solee@nybloodcenter.org

LEE, STANLEY L, INTERNAL MEDICINE, HEMATOLOGY. **Personal Data:** b Newburgh, NY, August 27, 1919; m 1947, Ann; c Nancy, Edward J & Kenneth R. **Education:** Columbia Univ, AB, 1939; Harvard Univ, MD, 1943. **Professional Experience:** DIR EMER HEMAT & ONCOL, BROOKDALE HOSP MED CTR, 1996-; PROF EMER MED, DOWNSTATE MED CTR, STATE UNIV NY, 1990-; dir hemat & oncol, Brookdale Hosp Med Ctr, 1982-1996; dean, Col Med & vpres acad affairs, 1981-1982; actg pres, Downstate Med Ctr, State Univ NY, 1979-1981; dean fac, Downstate Med Ctr, State Univ NY, 1978-1979; dir med, Jewish Hosp & Med Ctr, Brooklyn, 1971-1977; treas, Int Cong Hemat, NY, 1965-1968; from assoc prof to prof, Downstate Med Ctr, State Univ NY, 1959-1990; dir hemat, Maimonides Med Ctr, Brooklyn, 1959-1971; asst attend hematologist, Mt Sinai Hosp, NY, 1953-1959; asst, Mt Sinai Hosp, NY, 1949-1953; Intern, Georg Escherich fel path, 1948-1949; resident med, Mt Sinai Hosp, NY, 1946-1948; intern, Mt Sinai Hosp, NY, 1943-1944. **Memberships:** AmSoc Hemat; Am Rheumatism Asn; Soc Human Genetics; Am Fedn Clin Res; fel Am Col Physicians; Am Soc Clin Oncol. **Research Statement & Publications:** Systematic lupus erythematosus; leukemia. **Mailing Address:** Dept Med, Downstate Med Ctr, State Univ NY, PO Box 50, Rm 2-208, Bldg UH, Brooklyn, NY 11203. **Fax:** 718-240-6034.

LEE, STEPHEN, SOLID STATE CHEMISTRY. **Personal Data:** b New York, NY, October 25, 1955; m 1985, Kim. **Education:** Yale Univ, BA, 1978; Univ Chicago, PhD (chem), 1985. **Professional Experience:** PROF CHEM, CORNELL UNIV, as of 2005; PROF CHEM, UNIV MICH, 1997-; assoc prof, Univ Mich, 1993-1997; Alfred P Sloan fel, Alfred Sloan Found, 1993-1995; asst prof, Univ Mich, 1988-1993; Humboldt res fel, Univ Munster, 1987 & 1995; NATO fel, Univ Nantes, 1985-1986. **Research Statement & Publications:** Solid state chemistry synthesis; structural characterization and electronic structure of solids; materials chemistry; author of numerous publications. **Mailing Address:** Dept Chem, Cornell Univ, 160B Baker Lab, Ithaca, NY 14853-1301. **Fax:** 607-255-4137. **E-Mail:** sl137@cornell.edu

LEE, STEVE S, HERBAL PROCESS, TRADITIONAL FOLK MEDICINE. **Personal Data:** b Taiwan, November 2, 1948; American citizen; m 1979, Rosa; c Peter & Katherine. **Education:** Kaohsiung Med Col, Taiwan, BS, 1972; Duquesne Univ, MS, 1984. **Professional Experience:** Mgr, Prod Develop, Nature's Sunshine, 1993-; PLANT MGR, SUNRIDER INT, 1987-; lab mgr, Grad Sch Pub Health, Univ Pittsburgh, 1985-1987. **Memberships:** Inst Food Technologies; Asn Cosmetic Chemists; Asn Traditional Med. **Research Statement & Publications:** Extraction of Chinese folk medicinal herbs; evaluation of the extract particularly in antitumor and antibacteria. **Mailing Address:** 1742 Misty Meadows Cir, Sandy, UT 84093-3700.

LEE, STEVEN B, BIOLOGY. **Education:** John Taylor's lab, PhD, 1990. **Professional Experience:** ASSOC PROF, SAN JOSE STATE UNIV, as of 2005; DIR, FORENSIC SCI PROG, SAN JOSE STATE UNIV, as of 2005. **Mailing Address:** San Jose State Univ, One Wash Sq, San Jose, CA 95192-0050. **Fax:** 408-924-2953. **E-Mail:** steven.lee@sjsu.edu

LEE, STEVEN HUNTER, ANALYTICAL CHEMISTRY. **Personal Data:** b Battle Creek, Mich, June 17, 1953; m 1976, Heather Luchak; c Derek. **Education:** Andrews Univ, BS, 1976; Univ Wis-Madison, PhD (analytical chem), 1981. **Professional Experience:** CHMN, DEPT CHEM, WALLA WALLA COL, as of 2001; PROF CHEM, WALLA WALLA COL, 1983-; Assoc, Ind Univ, 1981-1983. **Memberships:** Am Chem Soc. **Research Statement & Publications:** Laser excited fluorescence and non-linear spectroscopy. **Mailing Address:** Dept Chem, Walla Walla Col, 204 S Col Ave, College Place, WA 99324. **Fax:** 509-527-2253.

LEE, STUART M(ILTON), MATERIALS SCIENCE. **Personal Data:** b New York, NY, April 14, 1920; m 1948, c Gary, Scott & Randy (deceased). **Education:** Long Island Univ, BS, 1941; Univ Nev, MS, 1947; Fla State Univ, PhD (org chem), 1953. **Honors & Awards:** Nat Meritorious Bronze Award, Soc Advan Mat & Process Eng, 1982; Space Award, 1995; Ed Emer Soc Advan Mat & Process Eng J. **Professional Experience:** RETIRED; int tech dir, Soc Advan Mat & Process Eng, 1989-1990; ed, Encycl Composites, 1985-1992; res polymer batteries, SRI Int, 1985-1986; ed in chief, Technomic Publ Co, 1983-1990; ed, Soc Advan Mat & Process Eng J, 1979-1995; sr staff scientist, Ford Aerospace & Commun Corp, 1971-1985; sr tech specialist, Autonetics Div, N Am Rockwell Int Corp, Calif, 1964-1971; mgr chem res & develop, Electro Optical Systs Inc, Xerox Corp, 1961-1964; res chemist, Aerojet Gen Corp, 1959-1961; sr res chemist & proj leader org res, Allied Signal Corp, 1952-1959; chief chemist org synthesis, Trinity Res Found, 1949-1950; chemist analytical develop, Gen Dyestuffs Corp, 1942-1943; chemist anal & testing, NY Testing Labs, 1941-1942; consult, SRI Int, GTE, Siemens, Teledyne & others; emer ed, Mat & Design. **Memberships:** Am Chem Soc; fel Soc Advan Mat & Process Eng.

Research Statement & Publications: Electronic materials, bioengineering materials and satellites; composites, coatings, encapsulants and sealants; instrumental failure analysis; materials and processes used for thick and thin films, dielectrics, high voltage and corona, bonding, joining, laser and electronic organics, polymer batteries and plastic packaging; systems for withstanding space environments; electronic and laser organics; high temperature and organic polymers; Sterilization and decontamination effects; approximately 80 technical publications including 13 patents; contributing author or editor of 23 books One Cd encycl; granted 13 US and foreign patents. **Mailing Address:** 20935 Heron Dr, Bodega Bay, CA 94923. **E-Mail:** smlee20@aol.com

LEE, SUE YING, VERTEBRATE MORPHOLOGY. **Personal Data:** b Schenectady, NY, January 11, 1940; m 1973, Archie; c Mathew. **Education:** State Univ NY Albany, BS, 1961, MS, 1963; Univ Ill, Urbana, PhD (zoology), 1968. **Professional Experience:** PROF EMER, BIOL SCI, HUMBOIDT UNIV, as of 2006; consult, Int Union Conserv Nature & Natural Resources, World Wildlife Fund, 1974-1975; from asst prof to prof vert morphol & humananat, Humboldt State Univ, 1969-1996; instr vert morphol & human anat, Univ Ill, Chicago, 1967-1969. **Memberships:** AAAS; Am Soc Zoology; Am Inst Biol Sci; Western Soc Naturalists; Soc Vert Paleont; Am Asn Anatomists; Am Soc Mammal. **Research Statement & Publications:** Natural landscape production. **Mailing Address:** Dept Biol Sci, Humboldt State Univ, Arcata, CA 95521. **Fax:** 707-826-3201.

LEE, SUK YOUNG, SOIL SCIENCE, ENVIRONMENTAL CHEMISTRY. **Personal Data:** b Seoul, Korea, June 18, 1940; American citizen; m 1966, c 2. **Education:** Univ Sask, MS, 1968; Univ Wis, PhD (soil sci), 1973. **Professional Experience:** RES SCIENTIST ENVIRON SCI, OAK RIDGE NAT LAB, 1977-; Univ SFla, 1975-1976 & Tex A&M Univ, 1976-1977; fel, Univ Wis, 1974-1975. **Memberships:** Am Soc Agron; Soil Sci Soc Am; Clay Minerals Soc. **Research Statement & Publications:** Transport of trace elements and radio nuclides, such as plutonium and uranium, in environment. **Mailing Address:** 12 Monaco Lane, Oak Ridge, TN 37830.

LEE, SUN, SURGERY. **Personal Data:** b Seoul, Korea, June 2, 1920; American citizen; m 1945, c William, Gloria, Thomas, Marlene, Janet & Donna. **Education:** Seoul Nat Univ, MD, 1945 Cook county graduate sch of med, Chicago, 1950. **Honorary Degrees:** PhD, Yamaguchi univ sch of med Yamaguchi, Japan, 1975; hon prres, internat microsurg soc, 1983. **Honors & Awards:** Gold Medal, Pioneer Exp Microsurg, Ger; Gold Medal, Lombardo Surg, Italy. **Professional Experience:** PROF EXP SURG, UNIV CALIF, SAN DIEGO, 1974-; assoc prof surg, Scripps Clin & Res Found, 1968-1974; ASSOC, SCRIPPS CLIN & RES FOUND, 1964-; From instr to asst prof, Univ Pittsburgh, 1957-1964; Surg fel, Univ Pittsburgh, 1955-1957. **Memberships:** Int Microsurg Soc; Int Proctol Soc Founder & mem, Internat soc f Experi Microsurg soc. **Research Statement & Publications:** Development of organ transplant in the rat to study transplantation immunology and associated physiology; techniques of heart-lung, liver, spleen, pancreas, testicle, kidney and stomach transplantation and allied microsurgical techniques in rats; develop of consecutive organ transplant tech in the inbred rats has made to solve many aspect indluding solving organ donor shortage, and many more. **Mailing Address:** 6462 Cardeno Dr, La Jolla, CA 92037. **Fax:** 619-542-1280. **E-Mail:** msurgery@joymail.com

LEE, SUNG MOOK, THEORETICAL MECHANICS, SNOW & COLD ENVIRONMENTAL RESEARCH. **Personal Data:** b Seoul, Korea, March 2, 1933; wid, c Peter, Patricia & Janet. **Education:** Yonsei Univ, BSc, 1955; Ohio State Univ, MSc, 1959, PhD (crystal dynamics), 1965. **Professional Experience:** RETIRED; vprovost res & dean, Grad Sch, 1991-2000; dean res & grad sch, Grad Sch, 1988-1991; vis sr res fel, Inst Sound & Vibration Res, Univ Southampton, Eng, 1980 & 1981; dir, Keweenaw Res Ctr, 1976-1991; NATO sr fel sci, 1974; prof physics, Mich Technol Univ, beginning 1972; from asst prof to assoc prof, Grad Sch, 1965-1972; asst prof physics, Denison Univ, 1961-1965; Teacher, Hansung Boy's High Sch, Korea, 1954-1955. **Memberships:** Am Phys Soc. **Research Statement & Publications:** Vibrational analysis of periodic systems, crystal lattices, and molecules; wave propagation in solids; mechanical properties of solids; mechanics; acoustics; optics; snow and ice. **Mailing Address:** Grad Sch, Mich Technol Univ, Houghton, MI 49931. **Fax:** 906-487-2245. **E-Mail:** smlee@mtu.edu

LEE, SUNG W, AEROSPACE ENGINEERING. **Education:** Mass Inst Technol, PhD (aeronaut & astronaut). **Professional Experience:** PROF AEROSPACE ENG, UNIV MD, as of 2006. **Memberships:** Am Soc Composites; Am Soc Aeronaut & Astronaut. **Mailing Address:** Aerospace Eng, Univ Md, College Park, MD 20742. **Fax:** 301-314-9477. **E-Mail:** lee@eng.umd.edu

LEE, SUNGGYU, Alternative Fuel Technologies, Polymer Engineering. **Personal Data:** b Kangjin-Kun, Korea, March 11, 1952; m 1980, Kyung; c Yoonjin, Yoonjo & Jonghoo. **Education:** Seoul Nat Univ, BS, 1974, MS, 1976; Case Western Res Univ, PhD (chem eng), 80. **Honors & Awards:** Louis A Hill Award, 1987; Outstanding Teacher Award, Univ Akron, 1987; Outstanding Researcher Award, Univ Akron, 1993; Distinguished Alumni Award, Seoul National Univ, 1994; National Academy of Engineering of Korea, 1998-. **Professional Experience:** C W LAPIERRE PROF, DEPT CHEM ENG, UNIV MO-COLUMBIA, 1997-; Chairman, Dept Chem Eng, 1997-2005; Dir, Process Res Ctr, 1990-1997; Robert Iredell prof chem eng & dept head, Univ Akron, 1988-1997; prof consult, 1980-; From asst prof to assoc prof, Univ Akron, 1980-1988. **Memberships:** Am Inst Chem Engrs; Am Chem Soc; Kor Inst Chem Engrs; Natl Aca Engr Korea; Am Soc Patent Holders; Sigma Xi; Tau Beta Pi; Golden Key Nat Hon Soc. **Research Statement & Publications:** Supercritical fluid technologies; clean alternative fuels; hydrogen generation; specialty and reactive polymers and polymerization; polymer nano- and micro-composites; oxygenates; high pressure reactor engineering; editor of ency chemistry processing; author of 6 books, 129 journal articles and 114 proceedings articles; granted 21 U.S. patents. **Mailing Address:** Dept Chem Eng, Univ Mo, W2033A, Eng Bldg E, Columbia, MO 65211. **Fax:** 573-884-4940. **E-Mail:** leesu@missouri.edu

LEE, SUNGSOO C, FOOD SCIENCE. **Education:** Ewha Univ, BS, 1972, MS, 1974; Univ Wis, MS, 1978, PhD (food sci), 1983. **Professional Experience:** Vchmn sub comt dietary fiber/complex carbohydrates & food nutrit & safety comt, Int Life Sci Inst, 1993-; SR SCIENTIST, KELLOGG CO, 1993-; mem, Food Nutrit Methods Comt, Asn Official Analytical Chemists, 1992-; sr res chemist, Kellogg Co, 1989-1990 & 1990-1993; res chemist, Kellogg Co, 1986-1988; assoc res chemist, Kellogg Co, 1984-1986; assoc res scientist, Kellogg Co, 1983-1984. **Memberships:** Int Life Sci Inst; Am Asn Cereal Chemists; Asn Off Anal Chemists (pres elect, 1991-1992, pres, 1992-1993); Inst Food Technologists; Am Inst Nutrit. **Research Statement & Publications:** Food scientist with special expertise in dietary fiber and carbohydrates; proficient in development of worldwide nutrition labelling, product improvements, laboratory quality control and new business opportunity programs; author of 10 publications. **Mailing Address:** Kellogg Co, 235 Porter St, Battle Creek, MI 49016-3423.

LEE, TED C K, PROTEIN PURIFICATION, PROTEIN DRUG DEVELOPMENT. **Personal Data:** b Seoul, Korea, December 3, 1940; American citizen; m 1966, Sue J Moon; c Shirley, Charles & Michelle. **Education:** Korea Univ, BS, 1965; Okla State Univ, PhD (biochem), 1971. **Professional Experience:** RES GROUP LEADER, DADE INT INC, 1992-; sr res scientist, Rhone-Poulene Rorer Inc, prin scientist, sect mgr, 1981-1992; vis prof, Cornell Univ, 1978-1981; asst prof, Howard Univ Med Col, 1973-1978; Res assoc, Rockefeller Univ, 1971-1973. **Memberships:** Am Soc Biochem & Molecular Biol; Am Chem Soc. **Research Statement & Publications:** Protein drug development; purification, refolding and formulation of proteins; assay development. **Mailing Address:** PO Box 520672, Dade Int Inc MS W-708, Miami, FL 33152-0672.

LEE, TEH HSUN, BIOCHEMISTRY. **Personal Data:** b Shaoshin, China, March 25, 1917; m 1952, Mang; c Robert. **Education:** Chekiang Univ, BS, 1938; Univ Mich, PhD, 1954. **Professional Experience:** RETIRED; vis assoc prof biochem, Albert Einstein Col Med, 1967-1984; chief, Protein Hormone Res Lab, 1966-1984; asst dir, Vet Admin Human Protein Hormone Bank, Vet Admin Hosp, 1964-1966; assoc prof, Sch Med, Univ Colo, Denver, 1964-1966; sr biochemist, Merck Sharp & Dohme, 1962-1964; asst prof exp med, Sch Med, Yale Univ, 1960-1962; res assoc, Sch Med, Yale Univ, 1955-1960; res assoc, Sch Med, Univ Ore, 1954-1955. **Memberships:** Am Chem Soc; Am Soc Biol Chem; Endocrine Soc. **Research Statement & Publications:** Pituitary hormones. **Mailing Address:** 2800 N Hwy A1A Apt 706, Ft Pierce, FL 34949.

LEE, TEH-HSUANG, SOLID STATE PHYSICS. **Personal Data:** b Shanghai, China, August 15, 1936; m 1961, c 2. **Education:** Nat Taiwan Univ, BS, 1958; Purdue Univ, West Lafayette, PhD (physics), 1967. **Professional Experience:** SR PHYSICIST, RES LABS, EASTMAN KODAK CO, 1967-. **Memberships:** Am Phys Soc. **Research Statement & Publications:** Optical properties of solids; semiconductors; magnetic semiconductors. **Mailing Address:** Eastman Kodak Co, 343 State St, Rochester, NY 14650.

LEE, TEN CHING, MEMBRANES, PHOSPHOLIPIDS. **Education:** Tulane Univ, New Orleans, PhD (biochem), 1967. **Professional Experience:** BIOCHEM RES MGR, OAK RIDGE INST, 1997-; BIOCHEMIST, UNIV TENN. **Mailing Address:** Med/Health Sci Div, Oak Ridge Assoc Univ PO Box 117, Oak Ridge, TN 37831-0117.

LEE, THERESA, RECOMBINANT DNA, BIOTECHNOLOGY. **Personal Data:** b Beijing, China, American citizen; m 1970, c 1. **Education:** Nat Taiwan Univ, BS, 1962; Univ Pittsburgh, MS, 1964; Wash Univ, PhD (biochem), 1968. **Professional Experience:** PROG OFF, DIV PRECLIN RES, NAT INST DRUG ABUSE, 1988-; chemist, Chem Div, Food & Drug Admin, 1984-1988; res chemist molecular biol, Nat Cancer Inst, NIH, 1977-1984; prof staff microbiol, Med Sch, 1971-1977; fel, Johns Hopkins Univ, 1970-1971; fel biochem, Harvard Univ, 1968-1970; fel biochem, Med Sch, Univ Wis, 1968. **Memberships:** Am Soc Biol Chemists; AAAS; Am Soc Microbiologists; NY Acad Sci; Am Chem Soc. **Research Statement & Publications:** Recombinant DNA techniques; molecular biology; proteins; biochemistry; virology. **Mailing Address:** Div Basic Res, Nat Inst Drug Abuse, NIH, 5600 Fishers Lane Rm 10A-19, Rockville, MD 20857. **Fax:** 301-594-6043. **E-Mail:** tl37h@nih.gov

LEE, THOMAS J, ENGINEERING. **Personal Data:** b Wedowee, Ala, 1935; m Jean; c Kevin & Patrick. **Education:** Univ Ala, BS, 1958, PhD, 1993. **Honors & Awards:** Exec Excellence Distinguished Serv Award, Sr Execs Asn Prof Develop League, 1992. **Professional Experience:** PRES, ALA MASTER GARDENERS INC, as of 2005; VICE PRES, ALA MASTER GARDENERS INC, 2001-2003; PVT CONSULT, 1994-; dir, Sortie Lab Task Team, 1989-1994; dep dir, Sortie Lab Task Team, 1980-1989; mgr, Sortie Lab Task Team, 1974-1980; mgr, Sortie Lab Task Team, 1973-1974; from tech asst to tech dep dir, Marshall Space Flight Ctr, NASA, 1969-1973; syst engr, Marshall Space Flight Ctr, NASA, 1960-1969; Aerospace res engr, Ballistic Missile Agency, US Army, Redstone Arsenal, Ala, 1958-1960. **Memberships:** Fel Am Inst Aeronaut & Astronaut. **Mailing Address:** Ala Master Gardeners, inc, 230 Walden Lane, New Market, AL 35761. **Fax:** 256-851-8125. **E-Mail:** bjeanlee@aol.com

LEE, THOMAS KELLEN, ORTHOPEDIC SURGERY. **Education:** MD; Cert, Am Bd Orthop Surgl; Cert, Nat Bd Med Exmr. **Professional Experience:** PHYSICIAN ORTHOP SURG, TESSON HEIGHTS ORTHOP, as of 2005. **Mailing Address:** Tesson Heights Orthop, 12152 Tesson Ferry Rd, St Louis, MO 63128. **Fax:** 314-849-2042.

LEE, T(HOMAS) S(HAO-CHUNG), ELECTRICAL ENGINEERING. **Personal Data:** b Soochow, China, November 18, 1931; m 1960, c 2. **Education:** Nat Taiwan Univ, BS, 1954; Univ Minn, Minneapolis, MS, 1956, PhD (elec eng), 1961. **Professional Experience:** RETIRED; assoc prof emer elec eng, Univ Minin, Minneapolis, as of 2005; assoc prof elec eng, Univ Minn, Minneapolis, beginning 1966; aero div, 1963-1964 & US Naval Res Lab, beginning 1965; consult, mil prod group, Honeywell Regulator Co, 1961-1962; from instr to asst prof, Univ Minn, Minneapolis, 1957-1966. **Memberships:** Am Phys Soc; Am Geophys Union. **Research Statement & Publications:** Acoustics; explosive phenomena; gas-dynamics; systems; electromagnetism; interplanetary phenomena. **Mailing Address:** Dept Elec Eng 139 Elec Eng Bldg, Univ Minn Rm 4-178 200 Union St, Minneapolis, MN 55455.

LEE, TIEN PEI, ELECTRICAL ENGINEERING. **Personal Data:** b Nanking, China, September 8, 1933; m 1963, c 2. **Education:** Taiwan Norm Univ, BS, 1957; Ohio State Univ, MS, 1959; Stanford Univ, PhD (elec eng), 1963. **Professional Experience:** RETIRED; consult, Sarnoff Corp, Princeton Univ, 2000-2002; mem tech staff, Bell Tel Labs, 1963-1984. **Memberships:** Inst Elec & Electronics Engrs; Sigma Xi. **Research Statement & Publications:** Microwave electronics; microwave solid state devices; varactor diodes; parametric amplifiers; semiconductor lasers and related optical communication. **Mailing Address:** Five Marion Dr, Holmdel, NJ 07733-1716.

LEE, TIEN-CHANG, GEOPHYSICS, HYDROGEOLOGY. **Personal Data:** b Nantou, Taiwan, July 1, 1943; m 1969, Zora; c Cin-T & Cin-Y. **Education:** Nat Taiwan Univ, BS, 1965; Univ Southern Calif, PhD (geophys), 1973. **Professional Experience:** PROF GEOPHYS, UNIV CALIF, RIVERSIDE, 1987-; assoc prof, Univ Calif, Riverside, 1979-1987; asst prof, Univ Calif, Riverside, 1974-1979; fel marine geophys, Woods Hole Oceanog Inst, 1973-1974. **Memberships:** Soc Explor Geophysicists. **Research Statement & Publications:** Computational geophysics and hydrogeology. **Mailing Address:** Dept Earth Sci, Univ Calif, Geol Bldg, Riverside, CA 92521. **Fax:** 909-787-4324. **E-Mail:** tien.lee@ucr.edu

LEE, TING Y, BIOPHYSICS. **Education:** Univ London, PhD (radiation physics), 1980. **Professional Experience:** DIR STROKE IMAGING RES, RADIOL DEPT, UNIV WESTERN ONT, 2001-. **Memberships:** Can Orgn Med Physics; Soc Magnetic Resonance Med. **Mailing Address:** Radiol Dept & Imaging Div, Lawson Res Inst, St Joseph's Health Ctr 268 Grosvenor St, London, ON N6A 4V2, Can. **Fax:** 519-646-6204. **E-Mail:** tlee@imaging.robarts.ca

LEE, TONG-NYONG, PLASMA PHYSICS, ATOMIC PHYSICS. **Personal Data:** b July 22, 1927; American citizen; m 1959, c 3. **Education:** Seoul Nat Univ, BS, 1950; Univ London,

PhD (physics), 1959. **Professional Experience:** EMER PROF PHYSICS, POHANG INST SCI & TECHNOL, 1988-; res physicist plasma physics & optical sci, Naval Res Lab, 1970-1988; assoc prof appl physics, Cath Univ Am, 1964-1970; Asst prof physics, Seoul Nat Univ, 1960-1963. **Memberships:** Am Phys Soc. **Research Statement & Publications:** Short wavelength laser generation; plasma physics and spectroscopy of high temperature; high density plasma and solar flare study. **Mailing Address:** Pohang Inst Sci & Technol, PO Box 125 HyoJa-Dong San 31, Pohang City Kyungbuk 790-784, South Korea. **Fax:** 825-622-793099. **E-Mail:** tnlee@postech.ac.kr

LEE, TONY JER-FU, PHARMACOLOGY. **Personal Data:** b Hualien, Taiwan, November 10, 1942; American citizen; m 1978, c 2. **Education:** Taipei Med Col, Taiwan, BS, 1967; WVa Univ, PhD (pharmacol), 1973. **Professional Experience:** RES PROF, SCH MED, SOUTHERN ILL UNIV, SPRINGFIELD, 2004-; PROF PHARMACOL, SCH MED, SOUTHERN ILL UNIV, SPRINGFIELD, 1987-2004; from asst prof to assoc prof, Sch Med, Southern Ill Univ, Springfield, 1975-1987; fel, Univ Calif, Los Angeles, 1973-1975; mem, High Blood Pressure Coun, Am Heart Asn; mem, Stroke Coun, Soc Neurol Sci; Am Heart Asn grant, NIH. **Memberships:** Am Soc Pharmacol & Exp Therapeut; Soc Neuroscience. **Research Statement & Publications:** Cerebral vessel innervation in health and disease. **Mailing Address:** Sch Med Pharm, Southern Ill Univ, Springfield, IL 62794-9629. **E-Mail:** tlee@siumed.edu

LEE, TSUNG DAO, THEORETICAL PHYSICS. **Personal Data:** b China, November 25, 1926; m 1950, Hui; c 2. **Education:** Univ Chicago, PhD (physics), 1950. **Honorary Degrees:** DSc, Princeton Univ, 1958; LLD, Chinese Univ Hong Kong, 1969; DSc, City Col NY, 1978, Bard Col, 1984, Peking Univ, 1985, Drexel Univ, 1986, Univ Bologna, 1988, Columbia Univ, 1990, Adelphi Univ, 1991. **Honors & Awards:** Nobel Prize in Physics, 1957; Order of Merit, Grande Ufficiale, Repub Italy, 1986; Ettore Majorana-Erice Sci Peace Prize, 1990. **Professional Experience:** Zhejiang Univ, 1988 & Shanghai Jiao Univ & Suzhou Univ, 1987; Hon prof, Nankai Univ, 1986; Hon prof, Peking Univ & Nanjing Univ, 1985; UNIV PROF, COLUMBIA UNIV, 1984-; Hon prof, Quinghua Univ, 1984; Hon prof, Jinan Univ & Fudan Univ, 1982; Hon prof, Univ Sci & Technol, China, 1981; Loeb lectr, Harvard Univ, 1964; ENRICO FERMI PROF PHYSICS, COLUMBIA UNIV, 1963-; prof, Inst Advan Study, 1960-1963; from asst prof to prof, Columbia Univ, 1953-1960; mem, Inst Advan Study, 1951-1953; res assoc physics, Univ Calif, 1950-1951; res assoc astrophys, Univ Chicago, 1950. **Memberships:** Nat Acad Sci; Acad Sci China; Am Acad Arts & Sci; Am Philos Soc. **Research Statement & Publications:** Field theory; statistical mechanics; gravity; particle physics. **Mailing Address:** Dept Off Univ Profs 829 Pupin Box 8, Columbia Univ Morningside Heights W 120th St, New York, NY 10027. **E-Mail:** tl4@columbia.edu

LEE, TSUNG TING, PLANT HORMONE, GROWTH REGULATION. **Personal Data:** b Anhwei, China, March 21, 1923; m 1950, c 3. **Education:** Nat Cent Univ, China, BS, 1947; Univ Wis, MS, 1959, PhD (plant physiol), 1962. **Professional Experience:** RETIRED; Hon lectr, Univ Western Ont, 1976-; Plant physiologist, London Res Ctr, Can Dept Agr, 1968-1988. **Memberships:** Am Soc Plant Physiol; Plant Growth Regulator Soc Am; Sigma Xi; Int Asn Plant Tissue Cult; Can Soc Plant Physiol. **Research Statement & Publications:** Plant growth regulators; auxin metabolism, concerning regulation of conjugation and oxidation of IAA. **Mailing Address:** 30 Runnymede, London, ON N6G 1Z8, Can.

LEE, TSUNG-SHUNG HARRY, NUCLEAR PHYSICS. **Personal Data:** b Taipei, Taiwan, June 7, 1943; American citizen; m 1968, Chinmei; c Thomas S. **Education:** Taiwan Norm Univ, BS, 1965; Nat Tsung-Hua Univ, MS, 1968; Univ Pittsburgh, PhD (physics), 1973. **Professional Experience:** Adj prof, Dept Physics, Univ Pittsburgh, 1994-2000; SR PHYSICIST, ARGONNE NAT LAB, 1993-; head nuclear theory group, Agronne Nat Lab, 1989-1994; physicist, Argonne Nat Lab, 1981-1992; asst physicist, Argonne Nat Lab, 1977-1980; res assoc physics, Argonne Nat Lab, 1975-1977; res assoc physics, Bartol Res Found, 1973-1975. **Memberships:** fel Am Phys Soc. **Research Statement & Publications:** Intermediate-energy and high-energy nuclear physics. **Mailing Address:** Physics Div, Argonne Nat Lab, 9700 S Cass Ave, Argonne, IL 60439-4843. **Fax:** 630-252-6008. **E-Mail:** lee@theory.phy.anl.gov

LEE, TUNG-CHING, FOOD SCIENCE & TECHNOLOGY, FOOD SAFETY. **Personal Data:** b Szechwan, China, October 28, 1941; American citizen; m 1970, c 2. **Education:** Tung-Hai Univ, Taiwan, BS, 1963; Univ Calif, Davis, MS, 1966, PhD (agr chem), 1970. **Professional Experience:** DISTINGUISHED PROF FOOD SCI & NUTRIT, CTR ADVAN FOOD TECHNOL, RUTGERS UNIV, NJ, as of 2004; DISTINGUISHED PROF, INST MARINE & COASTAL SCI, COOK COL, RUTGERS UNIV, as of 2004; prof food sci, Univ RI, beginning 1979; vis prof, Grad Inst Food Sci, Nat Taiwan Univ, 1978-1979; consult, many US & int food co, 1976-; adv, Food Indust Res & Develop Adv Comt, Repub China, beginning 1976; vis prof, Inst Biochem, Cluj, Romania, 1975; from asst prof to assoc prof, Univ RI, 1972-1979; sr food technologist, Hunt-Wesson Foods, Inc, 1970-1972; Res asst, Univ Calif, 1965-1970. **Memberships:** Fel Inst Food Technologists; Am Chem Soc; Am Inst Nutrit; Am Soc Microbiol. **Research Statement & Publications:** Nutritional and safety aspects of food processing; Maillard browning reaction; carotenoids and vitamins; food extrusion; marine food technology; biotechnological applications in food technology; fish nutrition; fishfeed technology. **Mailing Address:** Dept Food Sci & Nutrit, Cook Col, Rutgers Univ, 63 Dudley Rd, New Brunswick, NJ 08901-8520. **Fax:** 732-932-6776. **E-Mail:** lee@aesop.rutgers.edu

LEE, TZOONG-CHYH, ORGANIC CHEMISTRY, BIO-ORGANIC CHEMISTRY. **Personal Data:** b Taiwan, January 2, 1936; m 1962, c 3. **Education:** Yamagata Univ, Japan, BS, 1963; Tohoku Univ, Japan, MS, 1965; Australian Nat Univ, PhD (med chem), 1968. **Professional Experience:** RES MGR, LEA RONAL INC, 1980-; assoc, Sloan-Kettering Inst Cancer Res, 1975-1980; res assoc org chem, Sloan-Kettering Inst Cancer Res, 1971-1975; USPHS fel, Damon Runyon Res fel, 1969-1970; USPHS fel, Sloan-Kettering Inst Cancer Res, 1968-1971. **Memberships:** Am Chem Soc. **Research Statement & Publications:** Nitrogen heterocyclic chemistry; organic synthesis; structure-activity relationship; imaging chemicals. **Mailing Address:** Six Villa Lane, Larchmont, NY 10538.

LEE, VING JICK, CHEMISTRY, NATURAL PRODUCTS CHEMISTRY. **Personal Data:** b Columbus, Ohio, July 28, 1951; m 1974, c Adrianne & Derric. **Education:** Ohio State Univ, BA, 1971; Univ Ill, Urbana, MS, 1973, PhD (chem), 1975. **Professional Experience:** CHIEF EXECUTIVE OFFICER & CHIEF SCIENTIFIC OFFICER, CB R & D INC, as of 2004; Chief Scientific officer, Canamax pharamaceut, inc, 2002-; tech advisor, Inconix pharmaceut, 2001-; vp, chem& Pre-clinical Eval, microcide pharmaceut, 1993-1998; vp, res operations & tech Assessment, sr res advisor, Microcide, 1998-2001; head, Dept Chem, Infectious Dis & Molecular Biol Res, 1990-; sr res group leader, Lederle Labs, Am Cyanamid Co, 1987-1989; res chemist, Lederle Labs, Am Cyanamid Co, 1977-; NIH res assoc, Harvard Univ, 1975-1977; res assoc chem, Univ Ill, Urbana, 1971-1975; teaching assoc, Univ Ill, Urbana, 1971-1973; VPRES CHEM, MICROCIDE PHARMACEUT; Mem, Med Chem Study Sect, NIH. **Memberships:** Am Chem Soc; Int Soc Heterocyclic Chem, Am soc microbiol. **Research Statement & Publications:** Antibiotics, antivirals and natural products; drug develop. **Mailing Address:** Microcide Pharmaceut, 850 Maude Ave, Mtain View, CA 94043. **Fax:** 650-567-5555. **E-Mail:** vleed@iconixpharm.com, vlee@anamaxinc.com

LEE, VIN-JANG, HETEROGENEOUS CATALYSIS, QUANTUM THEORY. **Personal Data:** b Honan, China, February 14, 1937; div, c 1. **Education:** Ord Eng Col, Taiwan, Dipl Eng, 1953; Notre Dame Univ, MS, 1958; Univ Mich, PhD (chem eng), 1963. **Professional Experience:** PRES, CYBERDYNE INC, 1981-; pres, Lee Securities & Investment Co, 1975-1980 & Econo Trading Corp, 1980-1981; consult catalysis, Libby Corp, 1974-1977; vis prof, Dept Chem, Univ Calif, Los Angeles, 1972-1973; assoc prof chem eng, Univ Mo, Columbia, 1968-1974; res specialist, Univ Mo, Columbia, 1965-1968; res specialist, Monsanto Chem Co, 1964-1965; chem engr, 26th Arsenal, Repub China, 1952-1957. **Memberships:** Am Phys Soc; Am Chem Soc; Am Inst Chem Eng. **Research Statement & Publications:** Surface physics; catalysis and kinetics; tunneling in catalysis; physical foundations of quantum theory. **Mailing Address:** Cyberdyne Inc, 1045 Ocean Ave Ste 2, Santa Monica, CA 90403.

LEE, VIRGINIA ANN, BIOCHEMISTRY. **Personal Data:** b Grand Rapids, Mich, October 30, 1922. **Education:** Univ Ill, BS, 1944; Univ Colo, MS, 1946, PhD (biochem), 1952. **Professional Experience:** ASSOC PROF FOOD SCI & NUTRIT, COLO STATE UNIV, 1978-; asst prof, Colo State Univ, 1967-1978; asst prof, Sch Med, Univ Colo, Denver, 1959-1967; Instr biochem, Sch Med, Univ Colo, Denver, 1955-1959. **Memberships:** Am Dietetics Asn; Soc Nutrit Educ; Sigma Xi. **Research Statement & Publications:** Nutrition. **Mailing Address:** 1405 Luke St, Ft Collins, CO 80524-4227.

LEE, VIRGINIA MAN-YEE, NEUROSCIENCES. **Education:** Univ London, BSc, 1967, MSc, 1968; Univ Calif, San Francisco, PhD (biochem), 1973; Rudolf Magnus Inst Pharmacol, Utrecht, MBA, 1974; Dept Neuropath, Children's Hosp Med Ctr Harvard Med Sch, Boston, MBA, 1979; Wharton Sch, Univ Pa, MBA, 1987. **Honors & Awards:** Sen Jacob Javits Award, Nat Inst Neurol & Communicative Dis & Stroke, 1988-1995; Zenith Award Alzheimer's Dis Res, Alzheimer's Asn Inc, 1991-1994; Metrop Life Found Award Alzheimer's Dis Res, 1991; Allied Signal Award Aging Res, 1992; 1996; Rita Hayworth Award Med Res Alzheimer's Dis, 1997; Potamkin Prize Med Res in Alzheimer's Dis, 1998; Stanley Cohen Biomed Res Award, 2000; Metrop Life Found Award Med Res Alzheimer's Dis. **Professional Experience:** CO-DIR, CTR NEURODEGENERATIVE DIS RES, SCH MED, UNIV PA, as of 2004; assoc ed, J Alzheimer's Dis, 2000-; prog comt chair, Soc Neuroscience 2000; mem, exec comt, Univ Pa Med Service Training Program, 2000; JOHN H WARE 3RD PROF ALZHEIMER'S RES, INST NEUROL SCI, UNIV PA, 1999-; mem, ed bd, Neurorehabilitation & Neural Repair, 1998-; mem, Univ PA Cell & Molecular Biol Grad Grp, 1997-; mem, Comt Rev Procedures Regarding Misconduct Res, 1997; mem, Prog Comt, Soc Neuroscience, 1997-; med ctr mem, Comt Appointments & Promotions, Univ PA, 1995-; PROF PATHOL & LAB MED, SCH MED, UNIV PA, 1993-; res prof, Dept Path & Lab Med, Univ Pa Sch Med, 1990-1993; res assoc prof, Dept Pathol & Lab Med, Univ Pa Sch Med, 1986-1990; res asst prof, Dept Pathol & Lab Med, Univ Pa Sch Med, 1981-1986. **Research Statement & Publications:** Study of the neuronal cytoskeleton and the study of Alzheimer's Disease. **Mailing Address:** Dept Path & Lab Med, Ctr Neurodegenerative Dis Res, Sch Med, Univ PA, 3rd FlMaloney Bldg/4283, 3600 Spruce St, Philadelphia, PA 19104-6074. **Fax:** 215-349-5909. **E-Mail:** vmylee@mail.med.upenn.edu

LEE, W W, PHYSICS. **Education:** Northwestern Univ, PhD, 1970. **Professional Experience:** LAB FEL, PRINCETON PLASMA PHYSICS LAB, PRINCETON UNIV, as of 2006. **Mailing Address:** Princeton Plasma Physics Lab, Princeton Univ, PO Box 451, Princeton, NJ 08543. **Fax:** 609-243-0000. **E-Mail:** wwlee@pppl.gov

LEE, WAI-HON, OPTICAL PHYSICS, COMMUNICATIONS SCIENCE. **Personal Data:** b Haiphong, Vietnam, April 29, 1942; American citizen; m 1968, c 2. **Education:** Mass Inst Technol, BSc, 1965, MSc, 1967, DSc, 1969. **Professional Experience:** PRES, HOETRON INC, SUNNYVALE, CALIF, 1989-; mgr laser imaging systs, Xidex Corp, beginning 1981; staff mem res optical sci, Palo Alto Res Ctr, Xerox Corp, 1973-1981; assoc prin eng coherent optics, Electronic Syst Div, Harris Corp, 1969-1973. **Memberships:** Inst Elec & Electronics Engrs; Optical Soc Am; Soc Photo-Optical Instrumentation Engrs; Soc Photog Scientists & Engrs. **Research Statement & Publications:** Applications of grating structures for testing optical surfaces and scanning laser beam; optical methods for storing digital information at high density. **Mailing Address:** Hoetron Inc, 776 Palomar Ave, Sunnyvale, CA 94086.

LEE, WARREN FORD, AGRICULTURAL ECONOMICS. **Personal Data:** b Harriston, Ont, August 25, 1941; m 1966, c 3. **Education:** Univ Toronto, BS, 1963; Univ Ill, MS, 1967; Mich State Univ, PhD (agr econ), 1970. **Professional Experience:** PROF EMER, DEPT AGR ECON & DEVELOP ECON, OHIO STATE UNIV, as of 2006; prof agr econ, Ohio State Univ, 1980-2003; prof agr econ & rural sociol, Ohio State Univ, beginning 1980; economist, Econ Br, Agr Can, 1975-1976; assoc prof agr finance, Ohio State Univ, 1970-1980; credit adv, Farm Credit Corp, 1963-1965. **Memberships:** Am Agr Econ Asn. **Research Statement & Publications:** Agricultural credit and finance; farm firm growth; rural capital markets; bank structure and performance; financial institutions. **Mailing Address:** Dept Agr Econ, Ohio State Univ, 230 Agr Admin Bldg 2120 Fyffe Rd, Columbus, OH 43210. **Fax:** 614-292-7710. **E-Mail:** lee.69@osu.edu

LEE, WEI-KUO, PETROCHEMICAL SEPARATIONS, SOLID FLUIDIZATION TECHNOLOGY. **Personal Data:** b Hopei, China, April 29, 1943; American citizen. **Education:** Nat Taiwan Univ, BS, 1965; Univ Houston, PhD (chem eng), 1971. **Professional Experience:** TECH STAFF MEM, UNION CARBIDE CHEM & PLASTICS CO, 1988-; sr res engr, Shell Develop Co, 1986-1988; staff engr, Exxon Res & Eng Co, 1977-1986; Adj prof, Chem Eng Dept, NJ Inst Technol, 1975-1981; res engr, Celanese Res Co, 1973-1977; Unidel fel, Univ Del, 1972-1973. **Memberships:** Am Inst Chem Engrs; Soc Plastics Engrs; Soc Rheology; Am Inst Physics; Sigma Xi. **Research Statement & Publications:** Applications of fluid mechanics and rheology in various plastics technology and petrochemical engineering problems, including fibers, films, wire and cable insulations, oil field fluids, solid suspensions, composites, multiphase dispersions, fluidized solids and powders. **Mailing Address:** 328 Eileen Way, Bridgewater, NJ 08807-1961. **Fax:** 732-271-7886.

LEE, WEI-LI S, IMMUNOLOGY, BASIC SCIENCE & CLINICAL. **Personal Data:** b Kiangsi, China, February 14, 1945; m 1970, c 2. **Education:** Tunghai Univ, BS, 1966; State Univ NY, Buffalo, MA, 1969, PhD (biol), 1972. **Honors & Awards:** Res Grant from Activor, Inc; Centocor, Inc for the following tops; Synthetic peptides in angiogenesis & wound healing; Effect of Infleximab on Collagen prod in skin. **Professional Experience:** DIR, RES, STATE UNIV NY DOWNSTATE MED CTR, 1993-; ASST PROF DERMAT, STATE UNIV NY DOWNSTATE MED CTR, 1983-; Benjamin Zohn Res, Cult Fundgrant, 1983; Dermat Found grant, Soc Investigative Dermat, 1979; instr dermat med, Lab Exp Dermat, 1975-1982; res assoc immunochem, Col Physicians & Surgeons, Columbia Univ, 1972-

1975; asst biol sci, State Univ NY, Buffalo, 1966-1972; Johnson 's & Johnson's grant, Estee Lauder grant. **Memberships:** Sigma Xi; NY Acad Sci; Soc Investigative Dermat; Am Fedn Clin Res; Skin Pharmacol Soc Am acad dermato. **Research Statement & Publications:** Development of an in vitro model system to elucidate the mechanism of skin inflammation and testing of potential irritants and anti-irritants; clinical phase II and III studies; supevision of collaborative basic science and clinical research projects; research interests focused on novel methods of skin inflammative using an in vitro model system comprising human microvascular endothelial cells, leucocytes and keratinocytes; development of in vitro model systems to be used in the understanding of underlying mechanism for immunity, immune research and inflammation. **Mailing Address:** State Univ NY Downstate Med Ctr, Dept Dermat, 450 Clarkson Ave, Brooklyn, NY 11203. **Fax:** 718-207-2794. **E-Mail:** wei-li.lee@downstate.edu

LEE, WEI-MING, PHYSICAL CHEMISTRY, POLYMER CHEMISTRY. **Personal Data:** b Kiangsu, China, June 11, 1936; m 1962. **Education:** Nat Taiwan Univ, BS, 1957; Southern Ill Univ, MA, 1961; Univ Ill, PhD (phys chem), 1964. **Professional Experience:** RETIRED; sr assoc scientist, Advan Composites Lab, Central Res, Dow Chem Co, beginning 1984; assoc scientist, Dow Chem USA, 1981-1983; vis prof chem eng, Mich Tech Univ, 1980-1981; staff mem plastics res & develop, Dow Chem USA, 1978-1980; staff mem olefin plastics res & develop, Dow Chem USA, 1974-1976; sr res engr styrene molding polymers res & develop, Dow Chem USA, 1965-1974; res assoc theoret chem kinetics, Univ Calif, Santa Barbara, 1964-1965; teacher chem & math, Univ High Sch, Taiwan Norm Univ, 1959. **Memberships:** Am Chem Soc; Soc Advan Mat & Process Eng. **Research Statement & Publications:** Mechanical properties of polymeric materials and plastic foams; computer simulation of chemical and physical processes; fundamental studies of polyurethanes; composite materials science. **Mailing Address:** Central Res, Dow Chem Co, Bldg 1714, Midland, MI 48640.

LEE, WEN-HWA, GENETICS. **Personal Data:** b June 1, 1950; m Eva. **Education:** Nat Taiwan Normal Univ, BS, 1972; Nat Taiwan Univ, MA, 1977; Univ Calif, Berkeley, PhD, 1981. **Honors & Awards:** F E Shideman-Sterling Award, Univ Minn, 1999; Presidential Award, Soc Chinese Bioscientists Am, 2001. **Professional Experience:** Mem, bd Int Sci Adv, Sharf Found, 2001-; mem, Sci Coun, Found Cancer Gene Therapy, 2001-; mem, Bioenterprise Steering Adv Comt, Ministry Econ Affairs, Develop Ctr Biotechnology, Rep China, 2001-; chmn, Selecting Comt Life Sci, Presidential Sci Awd, Rep China, 2001-; F E Shideman Sterling Lectureship, Univ Minn, Dept Pharmacol, 1999; Li Shih-Chen Distinguished Lectureship, Univ Pittsburgh, 1999; chmn, Cancer Rev Panel, NIH, 1999-; mem, Search Comt Dir, Inst Drug Develop, 1999-2001; mem, Adv Comt, Univ Tex Health Sci Ctr, San Antonio, Children's Cancer Res Ctr, 1999-2000; PROF & CHMN MOLECULAR MED, UNIV TEX HEALTH SCI CTR, SAN ANTONIO, 1996-; chair, Grad Prog Molecular Sci, Univ Tex Health Sci Ctr, San Antonio, 1993-1997; ALICE P MCDERMOTT DISTINGUISHED CHAIR, DIR, UNIV TEX HEALTH SCI CTR, SAN ANTONIO, 1991-; prof path, Univ Tex Health Sci Ctr, San Antonio, beginning 1991; adj prof, Chinese Univ Sci & Technol, Hefei, 1991-1994; prof, Univ Calif, San Diego, 1990-1991; assoc prof, Univ Calif, San Diego, 1987-1990. **Mailing Address:** Dept Molecular Med, Univ Tex Health Sci Ctr, 15355 Lambda Dr, San Antonio, TX 78245-3207. **Fax:** 210-567-7377. **E-Mail:** leew@uthscsa.edu

LEE, WILLIAM CHIEN-YEH, ELECTRICAL ENGINEERING. **Personal Data:** b London, Eng, July 20, 1932; m 1964, c 2. **Education:** Chinese Naval Acad, Taiwan, BSc, 1954; Ohio State Univ, MS, 1960, PhD (elec eng), 1963. **Professional Experience:** VPRES & CHIEF SCIENTIST, AIRTOUCH COMMUN, as of 2004; vpres, Pactel Cellular, beginning 1985; mem, Nat Commun Forum Overseas Coun, beginning 1985; affil mem, Univ Calif, Irvine, beginning 1985; affil mem, Univ Calif, Davis, beginning 1985; publ chmn, Inst Elec & Electronics Engrs Transactions on VehicularTechnol, beginning 1979; sr scientist & mgr, Defense Commun Div, ITT, 1979-1984; mem tech staff commun, Bell Labs, 1964-1979. **Memberships:** Brit Inst Elec Engrs; fel Inst Elec & Electronics Engrs; Sigma Xi. **Research Statement & Publications:** Wave propagation in anisotropic medium; antennas; signal fading; communication systems, particularly those relating to the ultrahigh frequency and x-band regions; author of three books on mobile communications and more than one hundred technical articles. **Mailing Address:** Airtouch Commun Corp Tech Group, 1340 Treat Blvd Suite 500, Walnut Creek, CA 94596.

LEE, WILLIAM HUNG KAN, GEOPHYSICS. **Personal Data:** b Kwangsi, China, October 6, 1940; m 1966, c 2. **Education:** Univ Alta, BSc, 1962; Univ Calif, Los Angeles, PhD (planetary & space physics), 1967. **Professional Experience:** SCIENTIST EMER, US GEOL SURV, as of 2002; ed, Chinese Geophys J, 1978; translation bd mem, Am Geophys Union, 1975-1978; guest lectr, Stanford Univ, 1969; res geophysicist, Us Geol Surv, beginning 1967; asst res geophysicist, Univ Calif, Los Angeles, 1967; ed, Geophys Monogr 8, Am Geophys Union, 1965; secy, Heat-Flow Comt, Int Union Geod & Geophys, 1963-1965. **Memberships:** AAAS; Am Geophys Union; Seismol Soc Am; Soc Explor Geophys; Sigma Xi. **Research Statement & Publications:** Terrestrial heat-flow; thermal evolution of the planets; computer modeling of geologic processes; earthquake seismology. **Mailing Address:** US Geol Surv, 345 Middlefield Rd, MS 977, Rm 3-221A, Menlo Park, CA 94025-3591. **Fax:** 650-329-5163. **E-Mail:** lee@usgs.gov

LEE, WILLIAM JOHN, PRESSURE TRANSIENT TESTING, RESERVOIR PERFORMANCE ANALYSIS. **Personal Data:** b Lubbock, Tex, January 16, 1936; m 1961, Phyllis; c Anne P (Widdison) & Mary D Odom. **Education:** Ga Inst Technol, B Che, 1959, MS, 1961, PhD (chem eng), 1963. **Honors & Awards:** Halliburton Edu Found Award, 1982-1983; Reservoir Eng Award, 1986; Distinguished Serv Award, 1992; John Franklin Carll Award, 1995; Distinguished Lectr, Soc petrol engrs, 1978; Distinguished fac achievement award, Soc petrol engrs, 1981; hon mem 2000-edu Award, Ga tech acad dist engr acad, 2002; Tex Soc prof engrs dream way, 2002; SPE DeGolyer Distinguished Serv Medal, 2004. **Professional Experience:** L F PETERSON CHAIR, TEX A&M UNIV, 1992-; PROF PETROL ENG, TEX A&M UNIV, 1977-; Samuel Roberts Noble chair, Exec vpres technol, S A Holditch & Asscoc, 1980-1999; distinguished lectr, Soc Petrol Engrs, 1978-1992; tech adv, Exxon Co, USA, 1971-1977; assoc prof petrol eng, Miss State Univ, 1968-1971; sr res specialist, Exxon Prod Res Co, 1962-1968. **Memberships:** Nat Acad Eng; Soc Petrol Engrs; Sigma Xi; Am inst mining metal; Briaerean Soc; Phi Eta Sigma; Phi Kappa Phi; Pi Epsilon Tau; Tau Beta Pi; Theta Tau. **Research Statement & Publications:** Low permeability gas well analysis; petroleum reservoir engineering; tight gas applications; reservoir rock and fluid properties; published over 100 articles, 150 presentations, and 7 books; pressure transient testing and gas reservoir engineering. **Mailing Address:** 407C Richardson Bldg, 3116 TAMU, College Station, TX 77843-3116. **Fax:** 979-845-1307. **E-Mail:** john.lee@pe.tamu.edu

LEE, WILLIAM ORVID, FIELD CROPS. **Personal Data:** b Brigham City, Utah, July 2, 1927; m 1951, c 4. **Education:** Utah State Univ, BS, 1950, MS, 1954; Ore State Univ, PhD (farm crops), 1965. **Professional Experience:** RETIRED; res agronomist, Sci & Educ Admin, Agr Res, USDA, Utah, 1956-1983; agronomist, Wyo, 1954-1956; agronomist, Sci & Educ Admin, Agr Res, USDA, Utah, 1951-1954; soil scientist, Bur Reclamation, US Dept Interior, 1950-1951. **Memberships:** Weed Sci Soc Am. **Research Statement & Publications:** Crop science; control of weeds in forage and turf seed crops; legumes and grasses. **Mailing Address:** 1538 NW 12th St, Corvallis, OR 97701.

LEE, WILLIAM ROSCOE, GENETICS. **Personal Data:** b Little Rock, Ark, February 14, 1930; m 1953, Catherine; c 3. **Education:** Univ Ark, BSA, 1953; Univ Wis, MS, 1953, PhD (genetics, entom), 1956. **Honors & Awards:** EMS Award in Recog of Substained Res on Genetic Effects of Environ Mutagens in Drosophila, 1996; Environ Mutagen Soc. **Professional Experience:** PROF EMER BIOL SCI, LA STATE UNIV, BATON ROUGE, as of 2004; prof bio sci, LA State Univ, Baton Rouge, beginning 1973; assoc prof, LA State Univ, Baton Rouge, 1967-1973; asst prof zool, Univ Tex, Austin, 1963-1967; Res exec for H J Muller, Ind Univ, 1962-1963; from asst prof to assoc prof entom, Univ NH, 1956-1963; asst, Univ Wis, 1952-1956; dir, Inst Mutagenesis, La State Univ, Baton Rouge. **Memberships:** Genetics Soc Am; Radiation Res Soc; Environ Mutagen Soc. **Research Statement & Publications:** Radiation genetics; mechanisms of mutagenesis; recombinant DNA; southern blot experiments with both cloned and synthetic probes; relation between DNA adducts in the germ cells of Drosophila melanogaster and changes in DNA of induced mutants. **Mailing Address:** Dept Biol Sci, La State Univ Baton Rouge, Baton Rouge, LA 70803-0001. **E-Mail:** leemuta@lsu.edu

LEE, WILLIAM THOMAS, IMMUNOLOGY. **Personal Data:** b Hartford, Conn, July 18, 1958. **Education:** George Wash Univ, BA, 1980, MForensic Sci, 1982; Johns Hopkins Univ, PhD (immunol), 1986. **Professional Experience:** RES SCIENTIST, NY STATE DEPT HEALTH, DAVID AXELROD INST, NY, 1993-; asst instr, Dept Microbiol, Univ Tex Health Sci Ctr, Dallas, 1987-1992. **Memberships:** Am Asn Immunologists. **Mailing Address:** Lab Immunol David Axelrod Inst Pub Health Wadsworth Ctr, Labs & Res NY State Dept Health PO Box 2202, Albany, NY 12201-2002. **Fax:** 518-474-8366. **E-Mail:** william.lee@wadsworth.org

LEE, WILLIAM WAI-LIM, RESOURCE MANAGEMENT, ENVIRONMENTAL ENGINEERING. **Personal Data:** b Shanghai, China, August 6, 1948; American citizen. **Education:** Tulane Univ, BSE, 1969; Univ Mich, MSE, 1970; Mass Inst Technol, SMCE, 1976. **Honorary Degrees:** ScD (resources systs mgt), Mass Inst Technol, 1977. **Professional Experience:** AT DEPT NUCLEAR ENG, UNIV CALIF, BERKELEY, 1986-; proj dir, R F Weston Inc, 1982-1985; asst prof, civil & urban eng, Univ Pa, 1979-1982; proj engr decision anal, Woodward-Clyde Consults, 1977-1979; proj engr water reuse, Los Angeles County Sanit Dists, 1970-1972. **Memberships:** Am Soc Civil Engrs; AAAS; Am Geophys Union; Am Nuclear Soc; Sigma Xi. **Research Statement & Publications:** Applicability of quantitative analytical techniques in resources and environmental problems; analysis of nuclear waste management. **Mailing Address:** Environ Eval Group, 7007 Wyo Blvd NE Ste F-2, Albuquerque, NM 87109. **E-Mail:** willlee@uclink4.berkeley.edu

LEE, WILLIAM WEI, MEDICINAL CHEMISTRY. **Personal Data:** b San Francisco, Calif, May 17, 1923; m 1947, Pauline; c Peter H, Kerwin J & Roderick M. **Education:** Univ Calif, BS, 1947; Univ Minn, PhD (org chem), 1952. **Professional Experience:** RETIRED; analyst, Defense Intelligence Agency, 1981-1992; prog dir, Synthetic Cancer Drugs, 1978-1987; sr org chemist, Stanford Res Inst Int, 1956-1977; assoc chemist org chem, Stanford Res Inst Int, 1954-1956; org res chemist, Cent Res Dept, Monsanto Chem Co, 1952-1954; asst org chem, Univ Minn, 1948-1951; jr chemist org anal chem, Shell Develop Co, 1947-1948. **Memberships:** Am Chem Soc; Sigma Xi; Radiation Res Soc. **Research Statement & Publications:** Allylic and acetylenic compounds; nucleosides, amino acids and alkylating agents; enzyme chemistry; active halogen compounds; folic acid antagonists; heterocyclic chemistry; chemotherapy, particularly cancer chemotherapy; radioensitizing agents. **Mailing Address:** 991 N Calif Ave, Palo Alto, CA 94303-3407.

LEE, WONYONG, HIGH ENERGY PHYSICS. **Personal Data:** b Korea, December 29, 1930; American citizen; m 1961, Soo; c Adrian T Lee. **Education:** Calif Inst Technol, BS; Univ Calif, Berkeley, PhD (Physics), 1961. **Honors & Awards:** Asn Korean Physicists Am Medal Physics, 1992; Ho-Am Prize Basic Sci, 1996. **Professional Experience:** PROF EMER PHYSICS, COLUMBIA UNIV, as of 2005; Guggenheim Found fel, 1979; prof physics, Columbia Univ, beginning 1972; Alfred P Sloan fel, 1965; from asst prof to assoc prof physics, Columbia Univ, 1964-1972; res assoc, nevis lab, Columbia Univ, 1962-1964; res assoc physics, Lawrence Radiation Lab, Univ Calif 1961-1962. **Memberships:** Fel Am Phys Soc. **Research Statement & Publications:** High energy experimental physics. **Mailing Address:** Dept Physics, Columbia Univ, 720 Pupin, New York, NY 10027. **E-Mail:** wlee@phys.columbia.edu

LEE, WOONG MAN, PATHOLOGY. **Personal Data:** b Seoul, Korea, December 3, 1938. **Education:** Seoul Nat Univ, BS, 1960, MD, 1964; Am Bd Path, cert, 1976. **Professional Experience:** PATHOLOGIST, GLEN FALLS HOSP, NY, 1979-; attend pathologist, Vet Admin Hosp, Albany, NY, 1974-1979; asst attend pathologist, Albany Med Ctr Hosp, 1974-1979; from instr to asst prof path, Albany Med Col, NY, 1970-1979; residency, Albany Med Ctr Hosp, 1970-1972; asst residency, Albany Med Ctr Hosp, 1967-1970. **Memberships:** Col Am Path; Am Soc Clin Path; US-CAN Acad Path. **Research Statement & Publications:** Anatomical aspects and drug treatment of atherosclerosis. **Mailing Address:** Dept Path, Glens Falls Hosp, Glens Falls, NY 12801.

LEE, WOOYOUNG, POLYMER MANUFACTURING. **Personal Data:** b Pusan, Korea, January 2, 1938; m 1966, June; c Marjorie & Christina. **Education:** Seoul Nat Univ, BS, 1961; Univ Wis-Madison, MS, 1964, PhD (chem eng), 1966. **Professional Experience:** MGR, EDISON RES LAB, MOBIL CHEM CO, 1986-; mgr polyolefins process, Chem Prods Dept, 1985-1986; mgr, Chem Prods Dept, 1984-1985; synthetic fuels develop, reforming & spec process develop, 1980-1984; mgr, reforming & spec process develop, 1977-1980; res assoc, Mobil Res & Develop Corp, 1974-1977; sr res engr, Mobil Res & Develop Corp, 1969-1974; res engr, Mobil Res & Develop Corp, 1966-1969; fel chem eng, Univ Wis, 1966. **Memberships:** Am Inst Chem Engrs; Am Chem Soc; Soc Polymer Engrs. **Research Statement & Publications:** Conversion of oxygenates to hydrocarbons; aromatics and olefin upgrading process development; fluid bed catalytic cracking; kinetics and reaction engineering; lube additives and synthetic hydrocarbon fluids; polyethylene process product. **Mailing Address:** Mobil Chem Res & Develop Corp, PO Box 3029, Edison, NJ 08818-3029. **Fax:** 732-321-6343.

LEE, Y C, DATABASES, COMPUTATIONAL GEOMETRY. **Personal Data:** b Hong Kong, March 30, 1948; Canadian citizen; m 1981, c 2. **Education:** Simon Fraser Univ, BSc, 1977; Univ NB, MSc, 1980, PhD (surv eng), 1986. **Honors & Awards:** Bauch & Lomb Photogram Award, Can Inst Surv & Mapping, 1982, ACDS Graphics Award, 1991. **Professional Experience:** PROF, DEPT SURV ENG, UNIV NB, as of 2003; assoc prof gis, dept surv eng, Univ NB, beginning 1991; consult, NB Geog Info Corp, beginning 1990; mem, working group GIS, Int Soc Photogram & Remote Sensing, beginning 1989; tech comt geomatics, Can Gen Stand Bd, beginning 1989; comn Urban Cartog, Int Cartog Asn, beginning 1989; consult, Can Int Develop Agency, beginning 1988; consult, Universal

Systs Ltd, Fredericton, NB, beginning 1987; asst prof, dept surv eng, Univ Nb, 1977-1991. **Memberships:** Can Inst Surv & Mapping; Can Cartog Asn; Inst Elec & Electronics Engrs Comput Soc. **Research Statement & Publications:** Geographic information systems and automated cartography, particularly in areas of data models, data structures, geometric processing, visualization, user interfaces and spatial search algorithms. **Mailing Address:** Dept Surv Eng, Univ NB, PO Box 4400, Head Hall E-58, Fredericton, NB E3B 5A3, Can. **Fax:** 506-453-4943. **E-Mail:** yclee@unb.ca

LEE, YIM TIN, ATOMIC PROCESS IN PLASMA, LAB X-RAY LASER RESEARCH. **Personal Data:** b Canton, China, June 14, 1950. **Education:** Univ Calif, Berkeley, BA, 1972; Univ Calif, San Diego, PhD (physics), 1977. **Professional Experience:** RES PHYSICIST, LAWRENCE LIVERMORE NAT LAB, 1979-; fel physics, Univ Calif, San Diego, 1977-1979; consult, Phys Dynamics Inc, 1976-1977. **Memberships:** Am Phys Soc; AAAS; Fusion Energy Asn. **Research Statement & Publications:** Atomic processes in laser produced plasma and soft x-ray lasing. **Mailing Address:** Lawrence Livermore Nat Lab, PO Box 808 L-298, Livermore, CA 94550.

LEE, YING KAO, POLYMER CHEMISTRY. **Personal Data:** b Shanghai, China, December 14, 1932; American citizen; m 1961, Theresa Tai; c Arthur, Annette & Angela. **Education:** Tai Tung Univ, BSc, 1952; Univ Cincinnati, PhD (chem), 1961. **Honors & Awards:** Achievement Award, Chinese Inst Engrs, US, 1994. **Professional Experience:** RETIRED; Distinguished scientist & Dupont fel, E I Du Pont Del Nemours & Co, Inc, 1996; Dupont fel & chief scientist, Dupont Automotive, 1996; Hon prof, Inst Chem, Beijing, 1994; dupont fel, Marshall Res & Develop Lab, E I Du Pont Del Nemours & Co, Inc, beginning 1990; dept fel, E I du Pont Del Nemours & Co, Inc, 1989-1990; sr res fel, E I du Pont Del Nemours & Co, Inc, 1986-1989; res fel, E I du Pont Del Nemours & Co, Inc, 1976-1987; res assoc, E I du Pont Del Nemours & Co, Inc, 1970-1976; staff chemist, E I du Pont Del Nemours & Co, Inc, 1968-1970; res chemist, E I du Pont Del Nemours & Co, Inc, 1965-1968; proj leader, Tex-US Chem Co, 1965; Res chemist, Tex-US Chem Co, 1960-1963. **Memberships:** Am Chem Soc; Sigma Xi. **Research Statement & Publications:** Polymers or polymeric systems used in coating field; high temperature polymer for electronics applications; crosslinking chemistries. **Mailing Address:** Marshall Res & Develop Lab, E I du Pont de Nemours & Co Inc, Philadelphia, PA 19146. **Fax:** 215-339-6114.

LEE, YONG YUNG, ACCELERATOR PHYSICS, HIGH ENERGY PHYSICS. **Personal Data:** b Kyungpook, Korea, February 12, 1936; American citizen; m 1963, Younghee; c Susan & Paul. **Education:** Kyung-Pook Nat Univ, BS, 1958, MS, 1960; Univ Mich, PhD (physics), 1964. **Professional Experience:** PHYSICIST, BROOKHAVEN NAT LAB, 1971-; asst prof physics, State Univ NY, Stony Brook, 1967-1971; res assoc physics, Univ Wis, 1964-1967. **Memberships:** Fel Am Phys Soc. **Research Statement & Publications:** Accelerator physics. **Mailing Address:** Brookhaven Nat Lab, Bldg 817, Upton, NY 11973. **Fax:** 516-282-8374. **E-Mail:** yylee@bnl.gov

LEE, YOUNG HIE, CHEMICAL ENGINEERING, BIOCHEMICAL ENGINEERING. **Personal Data:** b Seoul, Korea, January 12, 1946; m 1972, c 2. **Education:** Seoul Nat Univ, BS, 1971; Purdue Univ, MS, 1974, PhD (chem eng), 1977. **Professional Experience:** PROF CHEM ENG, DREXEL UNIV, 1978-; prin investr, NSF proj, 1978-1990. **Memberships:** Am Inst Chem Engrs; Am Chem Soc. **Research Statement & Publications:** Transport phenomena; gas liquid reaction; waste water treatment; biomass utilization. **Mailing Address:** Dept Chem Eng, Drexel Univ, 3141 Chestnut St, Philadelphia, PA 19104-2816. **Fax:** 215-895-5837. **E-Mail:** ylee@cbis.ece.drexel.edu

LEE, YOUNG JACK, STATISTICS. **Personal Data:** b Seoul, Korea, February 25, 1942; m 1967, c 3. **Education:** Seoul Nat Univ, BSE, 1964; Ohio State Univ, MS, 1972, PhD (statist), 1974. **Professional Experience:** MATH STATISTICIAN, NIH, 1979-; asst prof statist, Univ Md, Col Park, 1974-1979; instr electronics eng, Korean Air Force Acad, 1967-1969. **Memberships:** Am Statist Asn; Biomet Soc. **Research Statement & Publications:** Nonparametric/robust design of experiment and statistical analysis in hypothesis testing, ranking and selection and estimation; applications of statistics to social science and life science; method in clinical trial, statistical design and analysis for carcinogenesis and mutagenesis bioassays. **Mailing Address:** NIH, 6100 Exec Blvd Rm 7B13, Bethesda, MD 20892.

LEE, YOUNG-HOON, SEMICONDUCTOR DEVICES. **Personal Data:** b Korea, September 18, 1935; m 1965, Kim; c Benjamin S. **Education:** Dong-Guk Univ, BS, 1961, MS, 1963; State Univ NY Albany, PhD (physics), 1972. **Professional Experience:** MEM RES STAFF, IBM THOMAS J WATSON RES CTR, 1978-; fel physics, State Univ NY, Albany, 1973-1978; sr asst physics, Dong-Guk Univ, 1963-1966. **Memberships:** Am Phys Soc; Am Vacuum Soc. **Research Statement & Publications:** Defects in solids and electron spin resonance; electronics engineering; microelectronics fabrication techniques; plasma processings. **Mailing Address:** Int Bus Mach, T J Watson Res Ctr, PO Box 218, Yorktown Heights, NY 10598. **E-Mail:** ylee@watson.ibm.com

LEE, YOUNG-ZOON, TOXICOLOGY, FISHERIES TECHNOLOGY. **Personal Data:** b Korea, October 1, 1943; Canadian citizen; m 1975, Sung-ae; c Yohan, Eric & Ruthann. **Education:** Dongguk Univ, Seoul, Korea, BS, 1966, MS, 1969; Kyushu Univ, Fukuoka, Japan, PhD (enzym), 1974. **Professional Experience:** DIR, BIOFOODS, STOLLE MILK BIOLOGICS, INC, as of 2003; DIR, EGG BIOLOGICS RES, STOLLE RES & DEVELOP CORP, 1990-; res assoc, Food Sci Dept, 1986-1989; res assoc, Poultry Sci Dept, Univ BC, 1984-1985; asst prof res, Biochem Dept, mem Univ Nfld, 1980-1984; univ res fel, Biochem Dept, mem Univ Nfld, 1978-1980; Nat Res Coun res fel, Fisheries Marine Serv, Nfld Biol Sta, Can, 1975-1977; Lectr microbiol, Dept Agrobiol, Dongguk Univ, Seoul, Korea, 1975. **Memberships:** Inst Food Technologists; Poultry Sci Asn; Am Asn Avian Pathologists; Korean Scientist & Engrs Asn Am; Soc Toxicol Can; Japan Soc Biosci Biotechnol & Agrochem. **Research Statement & Publications:** Identification and isolation of biological factors in avian eggs, animal bloods, marine products and microorganisms using supercritical fluid chromatography and extraction, affinity, high-performance liquid chromatography, gas chromatography-mass spectrometry, ultrafiltration and immunological techniques for developing pharmaceutical and functional food compounds to control human, animal and fish diseases. **Mailing Address:** Stolle Milk Biologics, Inc, 6954 Cornell Rd, Suite 400, Cincinnati, OH 45242. **Fax:** 513-489-7267. **E-Mail:** yzl@smbimilk.com

LEE, YUAN CHUAN, BIOCHEMISTRY. **Personal Data:** b Taiwan, China, March 30, 1932; m 1958, c 1. **Education:** Nat Taiwan Univ, BS, 1955, MS, 1957; Univ Iowa, PhD (biochem), 1962. **Honors & Awards:** Merit Award, NIH. **Professional Experience:** PROF BIOL, JOHNS HOPKINS UNIV, 1974-; from asst prof to assoc prof, Johns Hopkins Univ, 1965-1974; res assoc biochem, Univ Iowa, 1962 & Univ Calif, Berkeley, 1962-1965; vis prof, Kyoto Univ, Academia Sinica, Taipei & Beijing Med Univ. **Memberships:** Am Chem Soc; Am Soc Biol Chem; Japanese Biochem Soc; Chinese Biochem Soc; Am Soc Cell Biol. **Research Statement & Publications:** Complex carbohydrates; carbohydrate receptors. **Mailing Address:** Dept Biol, Johns Hopkins Univ, Levi Bldg 3400 N Charles St, Baltimore, MD 21218-2699. **Fax:** 410-516-5213. **E-Mail:** yclee@.jhu.edu

LEE, YUAN TSEH, CHEMISTRY. **Personal Data:** b Hsinchu, Taiwan, November 19, 1936; m 1963, Bernice; c Ted, Sidney & Charlotte. **Education:** Nat Taiwan Univ, BSc, 1959; Nat Tsing Hua Univ, Taiwan, MS, 1961; Univ Calif, Berkeley, PhD (phys chem), 1965. **Honorary Degrees:** Dr, Univ Waterloo, Can, 1986, Chinese Acad Sci, 1987, Chinese Univ Hong Kong, 1989, Ariz State Univ, 1990, Univ Rome, 1992, Univ Southern Calif, 1993, Chenkuna Univ, Taiwan, 1994, Hong Kong Baptist Univ, 1994, Providence Univ, 1995, Univ Md, 1996. **Honors & Awards:** Nobel Prize in Chem, 1986; Nat Medal Sci, 1986; Ernest O Lawrence Award, US Dept Energy, 1981; Harrison Howe Award, Rochester Sect, 1983; Peter Debye Award, Am Chem Soc, 1986; Michelson Award, 1987; Faraday Medal, Royal Soc Chem, 1992. **Professional Experience:** PROF EMER, DEPT CHEM, UNIV CALIF, BERKELEY as of 2005; FAC SR SCIENTIST, CHEM SCI DIV, LAWRENCE BERKELEY NAT LAB, as of 2005; RES, ACAD SINICA, 1994-; grad prof, Dept Chem, Univ calif, Berkely, beginning 1994; Nat Lab Chem Kinetics & Reaction Dynamics, Nat Taiwan Univ, 1994; Nat Lab Chem Kinetics & Reaction Dynamics, Bilkent Univ, 1993; Univ prof, Chem Sci Div, Lawrence Berkeley Lab, 1991-1994; vis prof, Univ Perugia, 1989; Nat Lab Chem Kinetics & Reaction Dynamics, Xiamen Univ, 1988; Nat Lab Chem Kinetics & Reaction Dynamics, Fuzou Inst, 1988; Nat Lab Chem Kinetics & Reaction Dynamics, Beijing Univ, 1988; Chinese Univ, Nankai Univ, 1987; Chinese Univ, Nanjing Univ, 1987; Chinese Univ, Sci & Technol, 1986; Fairchild distinguished scholar, 1983; hon prof, Inst Chem Chinese Acad Sci, 1980; hon prof, Fudan Univ, 1980; John Simon Guggenheim fel, 1976-1977; prin investr, Chem Sci Div, Lawrence Berkeley Lab, beginning 1974; prof, Chem Sci Div, Lawrence Berkeley Lab, 1974-1991; numerous named lectrs, US & foreign univs, 1973-; Alfred P Sloan fel, 1969-1971; from asst prof to prof chem, Univ Chicago, 1968-1974. **Memberships:** Nat Acad Sci; fel Am Phys Soc; fel Am Acad Arts & Sci; Am Chem Soc; fel AAAS; hon mem Int Acad Sci; corresp mem Gottingen Acad Sci. **Research Statement & Publications:** Chemical kinetics, reaction dynamics, laser chemistry and molecular interaction. **Mailing Address:** Dept Chem, Univ Calif, Rm 419 Latimer Hall, Berkeley, CA 94720-1460. **E-Mail:** ytlee@gate.sinica.edu.tw

LEE, YUEN SAN, FOODS, BIOCHEMISTRY. **Personal Data:** b Taipei, Taiwan, October 13, 1939; m 1967, Helen; c James & May. **Education:** Nat Taiwan Univ, BS, 1962; Utah State Univ, MS, 1965; Univ Md, Col Park, PhD (food sci, biochem), 1968. **Professional Experience:** PROJ RES, DEPT BIOL & ENVIRON SCI, UNIV DC, as of 2002; chmn, dept food sci, 1989-1992; prof, dept biol & environ sci, Univ Dc, beginning 1977; chemist, comn pub health, DC Govt, 1968-1977. **Memberships:** Inst Food Technol; Am Chem Soc; Am Dietetic Asn. **Research Statement & Publications:** Method development in the determination of pesticides in meat, milk and water; quality control of detecting adulteration in meat and meat products for consumer protection; heavy metals in foods. **Mailing Address:** Dept Biol & Environ Sci, Univ DC, Rm 200-04 Bldg 44 Ste 416 4200 Conn Ave NW, Washington, DC 20008. **E-Mail:** ylee@udc.edu

LEE, YUNG, MECHANICAL ENGINEERING. **Personal Data:** b Inchon, Korea, May 11, 1932; Canadian citizen; m 1960, c 1. **Education:** Seoul Nat Univ, BEng, 1959, MEng, 1961; Univ Liverpool, PhD (mech eng), 1964. **Professional Experience:** PROF EMER MECH ENG, UNIV OTTAWA, as of 2004; dir, Ottawa-Carleton Inst Mech & Aeronaut Eng, beginning 1984; prof mech eng, Univ Ottawa, beginning 1973; from asst prof to assoc prof, Ottawa-carleton Inst Mech & Aeronaut Eng, 1967-1973; res officer, Chalk River Nuclear Lab, Atomic Energy Can, Ltd, 1965-1967; Lectr mech eng, Liverpool Polytech Inst, 1964-1965. **Memberships:** Can Soc Mech Engrs; Eng Inst Can; Asn Prof Engrs Ont. **Research Statement & Publications:** Fluid flow; heat transfer. **Mailing Address:** Dept Mech Eng, Univ Ottawa, Ottawa, ON K1N 6N5, Can. **E-Mail:** ylee@genie.uottawa.ca

LEE, YUNG-CHANG, PHYSICS. **Personal Data:** b Canton, China, November 7, 1935; American citizen. **Education:** Nat Taiwan Univ, BSc, 1955; Univ Md, PhD (physics), 1963. **Professional Experience:** PROF PHYSICS, STATE UNIV NY, BUFFALO, as of 2004; physicist, Lawrence Livermore Lab, 1978-1979; vis prof, Nat Tsing Hua Univ & Nat Taiwan Univ, 1973-1974; assoc prof physics, State Univ NY, Buffalo, beginning 1967; mem tech staff, Bell Tel Lab, 1961-1967. **Memberships:** Am Phys Soc. **Research Statement & Publications:** Solid state physics and quantum optics, including superradiance in thin crystal films; excitons in thin films; Anderson localization and Thouless' maximum resistance; interaction of electromagnetic radiation with plasmas; parametric coupling in plasmas; two dimensional crystalline order; high temperature superconductivity; meissner attractive forces on dirty superconductors; density functional theory; clustered hubbard model. **Mailing Address:** Dept Physics, State Univ NY, 305 Fronczak Hall, Buffalo, NY 14260. **E-Mail:** phyyclee@buffalo.edu

LEE, YUNG-CHENG, ELECTRONIC PACKAGING, HEAT TRANSFER. **Personal Data:** b Taiwan, China, February 5, 1956; American citizen; m 1983, c 1. **Education:** Nat Taiwan Univ, BS, 1978; Univ Minn, MS, 1982, PhD (mech eng), 1984. **Professional Experience:** PROF, DEPT MECH ENG, UNIV COLO, BOULDER, as of 2000; ASSOC DIR, NSF CTR, as of 2000; assoc prof, dept mech eng, Univ Colo, Boulder, beginning 1993; NSF presidential young investr award, 1990; asst prof, dept mech eng, Univ Colo, Boulder, 1989-1993; mem tech staff, AT&T Bell Labs, Murray Hill, 1984-1989; res asst, Univ Minn, 1980-1984. **Memberships:** Am Soc Mech Engrs; Soc Mfg Engrs. **Research Statement & Publications:** Low-cost prototyping and manufacturing of electronic multichip modules; three dimensional packaging for portable supercomputers; optoelectronic packaging; mechatronics; plasma-aided manufacturing. **Mailing Address:** Dept Mech Eng Univ Colo, Cb 427, Boulder, CO 80309-0427. **Fax:** 303-492-3498. **E-Mail:** leeyc@colorado.edu

LEE, YUNG-KEUN, NUCLEAR PHYSICS. **Personal Data:** b Seoul, Korea, September 26, 1929; American citizen; m 1958, Ock-Kyung; c Ann, Arnold, Sara, Sylvia & Clara. **Education:** Johns Hopkins Univ, BA, 1956; Univ Chicago, MS, 1957; Columbia Univ, PhD (physics), 1961. **Professional Experience:** PROF EMER NUCLEAR PHYSICS, JOHNS HOPKINS UNIV, as of 2005; prof physics, Johns Hopkins Univ, beginning 1971; from asst prof to assoc prof, Johns Hopkins Univ, 1964-1971; res scientist, Columbia Univ, 1961-1964. **Memberships:** Am Phys Soc. **Research Statement & Publications:** Nuclear beta decay; nuclear reactions; Mossbauer effects; intermediate energy physics; relativistic heavy ion physics. **Mailing Address:** Dept Physics & Astron, Johns Hopkins Univ, 3400 N Charles St Bloomberg Ctr Rm 366, Baltimore, MD 21218. **Fax:** 410-516-7239. **E-Mail:** yklee@jjhu.edu

LEECH, GEOFFREY BOSDIN, RESEARCH ADMINISTRATION. **Personal Data:** b Montreal, Que, August 28, 1918; m 1946, Jean Winters; c Joan (Edwards). **Education:** Univ BC, BASc, 1942; Queen's Univ, Ont, MSc, 1943; Princeton Univ, PhD (petrol, econ geol), 1949. **Professional Experience:** RETIRED; dir, Econ Geol Div, 1979-1982; Assoc secy gen, Int Asn on Genesis of Ore Deposits, 1978-1984; head, Econ Geol Subdiv, 1973-1978; geologist, Geol Surv Can, Dept Energy, Mines & Resources, 1949-1972; chief party, BC Dept Mines, 1947-1948; geologist, Int Nickel Co Can, Ltd, Ont, 1943-1946;

Field asst, Geol Surv Can, 1940-1941 & 1942. **Memberships:** Fel Geol Soc Am; fel Soc Econ Geol; fel Royal Soc Can; Can Inst Mining & Metall; fel Geol Asn Can. **Research Statement & Publications:** Regional metallogeny; mineral resource evaluation; problems of resource adequacy. **Mailing Address:** 1113 Greenlawn Crescent, Ottawa, ON K2C 1Z4, Can.

LEECH, H(ARRY) WILLIAM, PHYSICS, COMPUTER SCIENCE. **Personal Data:** b Triadelphia, WVa, April 28, 1940; m 1988, Carolyn; c Albert B, Amy J, Alan J, William J & Julia L. **Education:** WVa Univ, BS, 1962, MS, 1964; Univ Md, PhD (physics), 1975. **Professional Experience:** RETIRED; chmn, W Liberty State Col, beginning 1992; prof physics, W Liberty State Col, beginning 1980; dean technol & commun, Jefferson Tech Col, 1986-1990; chmn, Jefferson Tech Col, 1984-1986; from assoc prof to prof eng technol, Jefferson Tech Col, 1980-1990; asst prof physics, Bethany Col, 1978-1980; asst prof physics, Southern Conn State Col, 1977-1978; mem tech staff comput sci, Comput Sci Corp, 1973-1977; from instr to asst prof physics & math, W Liberty State Col, 1964-1968. **Memberships:** Am Asn Physics Teachers. **Research Statement & Publications:** Cosmic ray astrophysics; celestial mechanics; orbit determination; scientific applications of computer science. **Mailing Address:** Dept Physics, W Liberty State Col, W Liberty, WV 26074.

LEECH, STEPHEN H, INTERNAL MEDICINE, CLINICAL IMMUNOLOGY. **Personal Data:** b March 27, 1942; c 4. **Education:** Univ Edinburgh, MB, 1965; Univ London, PhD (immunol), 1976; FRCP (C), 1971. **Professional Experience:** PROF PATH & LAB MED, MED SCH, 1993-; DIR IMMUNOL, GENETICS LAB, TEMPLE UNIV, 1993-; dir, Sentara Serol Lab, 1988-; prof clin immunol, Dept Immunol & Microbiol, Eastern Va Med Sch, 1988-1993; dir, Immunol Lab, Sentara Norfolk Gen Hosp, Va, 1987-; assoc prof, Dept Biomet & Genetics, 1985-1987; dir, B Cell Clin, 1981-1987; dir, Immunocytogenetics Lab, Med Ctr, La State Univ, 1979-1987; from asst prof to prof med statist, Dept Med, 1976-1987; dir, Allergy Clin, Charity Hosp, La State Univ, New Orleans, 1976-1987; chief, Sect Allergy & Clin Immunol, Med Ctr, La State Univ, New Orleans, 1976-1987; clin res fel, Tumor Immunol Unit, Univ Col Hosp, London, 1972-1976; fel allergy & immunol, Royal Victoria Hosp, Montreal, 1970-1972; resident internal med, Minneapolis, 1969-1970; resident internal med, Univ Minn, Mayo Clin, 1967-1969; house physician, St Mary's Hosp, Knoxville, 1967; internship, Mem Res Ctr & Hosp, Univ Tenn, Knoxville, 1966-1967; house surgeon, Edinburgh Royal Infirm, Scotland, 1965-1966; mem, Nat Histocompatability Comt, United Network Organ Sharing. **Memberships:** Am Acad Allergy & Immunol; Am Soc Histocompatability & Immunogenetics; Am Fedn Clin Res; Am Asn Immunologists; Am Soc Transplant Physicans; Clin Immunol Soc. **Mailing Address:** Temple Univ Sch Med, 3401 N Broad St, Philadelphia, PA 19140. **Fax:** 215-707-2053. **E-Mail:** flyboy42@vm.temple.edu

LEEDER, JOSEPH GORDEN, dairy products manufacture, consultant in ice cream manufacture; deceased, see previous edition for last biography

LEEDHAM, CLIVE D(OUGLAS), AUTOMOTIVE ELECTRONICS, COMPUTERS. **Personal Data:** b London, Eng, November 1, 1928; American citizen; m 1955, June; c Alexander Clive & Barry Scott. **Education:** Univ London, BSc, 1949; Mass Inst Technol, SM, 1955; Purdue Univ, PhD (elec eng), 1963. **Professional Experience:** RETIRED 1993; bus dev mgr delco electronics corp, 1990-1993; regional mgr int sales, Delco Electronics Corp, 1983-1990; bus develop mgr digital systs, Delco Electronics Corp, 1976-1983, 1990-1993; staff engr, Delco Electronics Corp, 1965-1976; consult, Delco Electronics Corp, 1963-1965; asst prof, Univ Calif, 1962-1965; consult, USAF, 1961-1962; instr, Purdue Univ, 1958-1962; teaching asst, Mass Inst Technol, 1953-1955; jr engr, Metrop Vickers Elec Co Ltd, 1951-1952; apprentice, Metrop Vickers Elec Co Ltd, 1949-1951; asst lectr elec eng, Univ London, 1948-1949. **Research Statement & Publications:** Automatic control; signal processing; acoustics; digital computers. **Mailing Address:** 1811 El Faro, Santa Barbara, CA 93109-1903. **Fax:** 805-966-2605. **E-Mail:** cliveleedham@compuserve.com

LEEDOM, JOHN MILTON, INTERNAL MEDICINE, INFECTIOUS DISEASES. **Personal Data:** b Peoria, Ill, October 18, 1933; m Anita; c Liane J & John M IV. **Education:** Univ Ill, BA, 1955, BS, 1956, MD, 1958; Am Bd Internal Med, dipl, 1967 & 1974. **Professional Experience:** PROF MED, SCH MED, UNIV SOUTHERN CALIF, 1976-; CHIEF, DIV INFECTIOUS DIS, DEPT MED, 1975-2002; from asst prof to assoc prof, Div Infectious Dis, Dept Med, 1962-1976; officer res proj, Epidemic Intel Serv, USPHS, Infectious Dis Lab, Univ Southern Calif, 1962-1964; Res fel, Univ Ill Res & Educ Hosps, 1960-1961; Resident med, Univ Ill Res & Educ Hosps, 1959-1960 & 1961-1962; consult health facil construct div, Health Serv & Ment Health Admin; Professor Medicine, Emeritus, Keck School Medicine University Southern California. **Memberships:** Am Fedn Clin Res; Am Soc Microbiol; Infectious Dis Soc Am; Western Soc Clin Invest; Western Asn Physicians; International AIDS Society. **Research Statement & Publications:** Infectious disease, particularly viral and bacterial diseases of the central nervous system; AIDS and AIDS treatment. **Mailing Address:** Dept Med, Keck Sch Med the Univ Southern Calif, Rm 635 IRD Bldg 2025 Zonal Ave, Los Angeles, CA 90033. **E-Mail:** jmleedom@usc.edu

LEEDS, J VENN, ELECTRICAL ENGINEERING, ENVIRONMENTAL ENGINEERING. **Personal Data:** b Wharton, Tex, October 26, 1932; m 1956, Jan; c David V & Elizabeth (Nuchia). **Education:** Rice Univ, BA, 1955, BSEE, 1956; Univ Pittsburgh, MSEE, 1960, PhD (elec eng), 1963; JD, Univ Houston, 1972. **Professional Experience:** EMER PROF ELEC & ENVIRON ENG, RICE UNIV, 1990-; consult, var ins co& law firms, beginning 1972; mem safety & licensing panel, US Nuclear Regulation Comn, 1971-1978; master, Sid W Richardson Col, 1970-1976; consult, Esso Prod Res Co Div, Exxon, 1963-1968 & Geospace Corp, 1968-1972; from asst prof to prof elec & environ eng, Rice Univ, 1965-1990; asst prof elec eng, Rice Univ, 1963-1965; sr engr, Bettis Atomic Lab, Westinghouse Elec Corp, 1956-1963. **Memberships:** Inst Elec & Electronics Engrs; Sigma Xi. **Research Statement & Publications:** Design and analysis of large, complex systems; applied mathematics; interactions of law and engineering; applied mathematics; electrical events; fire and explosions; artificial intelligence. **Mailing Address:** 10807 Atwell Dr, Houston, TX 77096-4939. **Fax:** 713-723-3902.

LEEDS, MORTON W, ORGANIC CHEMISTRY, PHARMACOLOGY. **Personal Data:** b Brooklyn, NY, December 18, 1916; m 1945, Norma Sterne; c Valerie. **Education:** Polytech Univ NY, BS, 1938, MS, 1939, PhD (org chem), 1944. **Professional Experience:** EXEC DIR, MED-CHEM ASSOC, 1982-; asst dir med prods mgt, Med Res Div, 1977-1982; Permanent adj prof, Kean Col, 1971-1980; mgr clin develop, Ciba-Geigy Pharmaceut Co, 1971-1977; from asst dirto assoc dir chem res, Res Labs, Air Reduction Co, 1960-1971; supvr org chem develop & res, Res Labs, Air Reduction Co, 1956-1960; head appln & develop, Res Labs, Air Reduction Co, 1952-1956; asst chief chemist, Schwarz Labs, NY, 1950-1952; sr chemist, E I du Pont Del Nemours & Co, Inc, 1948-1950; head develop dept amino acids, Biochem Div, NJ, 1945-1948; sr chemist, Res Lab, Interchem Corp, 1939-1945; Chemist, Bio-Med Res Lab, NY, 1935-1939. **Memberships:** Am Chem Soc; fel Am Inst Chem; NY Acad Sci; Sigma Xi. **Research Statement & Publications:** Organic synthesis and development; acetylene and pharmaceutical chemistry; petrochemicals; clinical pharmacology research. **Mailing Address:** 6 Sunningdale Ct, Maplewood, NJ 07040.

LEEDS, NORMA S, ISOLATION & CHEMICAL CHARACTERIZATION OF NATURAL PRODUCTS, ORGANIC & GENERAL CHEMISTRY. **Personal Data:** b 1920; m 1950, Morton W Leeds; c Valerie A. **Education:** Hunter Col, BA, 1940; Rutgers Univ, PhD (org chem), 1950. **Professional Experience:** EMER PROF ORG CHEM, KEAN COL, 1991-; dept chmn, Kean Col, 1970-1972; from assoc prof to prof, Kean Col, 1964-1991; asst prof, Caldwell Col, 1960-1964; instr chem, Fairleigh Dickinson Univ, 1958-1960; res assoc, Sloan Kettering Inst, 1955; Sr chemist, Gen Aniline & Film, 1953-1958. **Memberships:** Sigma Xi; Am Chem Soc. **Research Statement & Publications:** Partial synthesis in steroid hormone field of compounds with possible carcinogenic properties; synthesis of surfactants; isolation and characterization of natural products; history of chemistry; publications. **Mailing Address:** 6 Sunningdale Ct, Maplewood, NJ 07040-2420.

LEEDY, CLARK D, SOILS SCIENCE. **Personal Data:** b Chicago, Ill, June 3, 1933; m 1956, c 5. **Education:** Purdue Univ, BS, 1955; NMex State Univ, MS, 1964, MA, 1966; Tex A&M Univ, PhD (educ), 1974. **Professional Experience:** RETIRED; assoc soil scientist, Univ Nev, Reno, 1976; div leader, WVa Univ, 1973-1976; exten soils specialist, NMex State Univ, 1957-1971. **Memberships:** Sigma Xi. **Research Statement & Publications:** Forms, rates, methods and timingof phosphorous fertilizer application on alfalfa yield and quality. **Mailing Address:** 10405 Red Rock Rd, Reno, NV 89506.

LEEDY, DANIEL LONEY, URBAN WILDLIFE, OUTDOOR RECREATION & ECOLOGY. **Personal Data:** b North Liberty, Ohio, February 17, 1912; m 1989, Virginia L Bittenbender; c Robert & Kathleen. **Education:** Miami Univ, AB, 1934, BSc, 1935; Ohio State Univ, MSc, 1938, PhD (wildlife mgt), 1940. **Honors & Awards:** Conserv Award, Am Motors Corp, 1958; Aldo Leopold Award, Wildlife Soc, 1983. **Professional Experience:** RETIRED; Mem, res coun comts & panels, Nat Acad Sci, 1957-1974 & surface mining panel, 1978-1979; sr scientist, Nat Inst Urban Wildlife, 1975-1994; water resources res scientist, Off Water Resources Res, US Dept Interior, 1965-1974; chief div res & educ, Bur Outdoor Recreation, 1963-1965; chief br wildlife res, Coop Wildlife Res Unit Prog, 1957-1963; coordr, Coop Wildlife Res Unit Prog, 1949-1957; leader, Ohio Unit, US Fish & Wildlife Serv, 1945-1948; asst leader, Ohio Wildlife Res Unit, Ohio State Univ, 1940-1942; Lab asst geol & zool, Miami Univ, 1934-1935. **Memberships:** Wildlife Soc (pres, 1953, exec secy, 1954-1957); Am Fisheries Soc; Am Ornithologists Union; Wilson Ornith Soc; Sigma Xi. **Research Statement & Publications:** Wildlife ecology; socioeconomics of fish and wildlife and recreation; natural resources training and employment; wildlife-land use relationships; water resources; urban wildlife and ecology; ecologic impacts of water development, surface mining, highways, and electric utilities in relation to wildlife. **Mailing Address:** 12401 Ellen Ct, Silver Spring, MD 20904-2905.

LEEF, AUDREY V, MATHEMATICS. **Personal Data:** b Hoboken, NJ, July 15, 1922; m 1947, c 4. **Education:** Montclair State Col, BA, 1943; Stevens Inst Technol, MS, 1947; Rutgers Univ, EdD, 1976; Drew Univ, MDiv, 1985. **Professional Experience:** Chaplain, Montclair State Col, Upper Montclair, NJ, beginning 1990; assoc prof math, Montclair State Col, Upper Montclair, NJ, 1966-1990; Teacher & chair, Dept Math, Millburn High Sch, NJ, 1943-1948. **Memberships:** Nat Coun Teachers Math; Asn Women Math; Asn Women Educ; Am Asn Univ Women. **Research Statement & Publications:** Mathematics education; mathanxiety. **Mailing Address:** Dept Math, Montclair State Univ, Montclair, NJ 07043.

LEEF, JAMES LEWIS, CRYOBIOLOGY, IMMUNOLOGY. **Personal Data:** b San Francisco, Calif, March 6, 1937; m 1964, c 4. **Education:** Univ Calif, San Francisco, BA, 1967; Univ Tenn, PhD (biol), 1974. **Professional Experience:** DIR, BIOMED RES INST, as of 2006; PRES, BIOMED RES INST, as of 2004; exec dir, Biomed Res Inst, beginning 1982; dir, Biomed Res Inst, beginning 1982; guest scientist, Navy Med Res Inst, 1976-; sr investr cryobiol & head Malaria Res Dept, Biomed Res Inst, 1976-1982; fel, Univ Ill, 1973-1976; consult, Sci & Indust Res & Develop Co, 1967-1969. **Memberships:** Soc Cryobiol; Tissue Cult Asn; Am Asn Tissue Banks; NY Acad Sci; AAAS. **Research Statement & Publications:** Malariology; mechanisms of freezing injury; study of various developmental stages of malaria and schistosomiasis parasites as antigens in developing a malaria and schistosomiasis vaccine and preservation of these forms at low temperatures. **Mailing Address:** Biomed Res Inst, 12111 Parklawn Dr, Rockville, MD 20852. **Fax:** 301-881-7640. **E-Mail:** jleef@afbr-bri.com

LEE-FRANZINI, JULIET, EXPERIMENTAL PHYSICS. **Personal Data:** b Paris, France, May 18, 1933; American citizen; m 1964, c 1. **Education:** Hunter Col, BA, 1953; Columbia Univ, MA, 1957, PhD (physics), 1960. **Professional Experience:** ADJ PROF, LAB NAZIONALI DE FRASCATI, 1993-; vis prof, Cornell Univ, 1980-1981; NSF grant, 1972; AEC grant, 1966-1972; from asst prof to prof physics, State Univ NY, Stony Brook, 1963-1993; State Univ NY Res Found grant, 1963-1966; res fel astrophys, Nat Acad Sci-Nat Res Coun, 1962-1963; Res assoc physics, Columbia Univ, 1960-1962; vis assoc physicist, Brookhaven Nat Lab. **Memberships:** Fel Am Phys Soc. **Research Statement & Publications:** Elementary particle physics; weak interactions. **Mailing Address:** Lab Nazionali de Frascati del INFN, Via Fermi 40 CP 13, I-00044 Frascati, Italy. **Fax:** 497-216-088369. **E-Mail:** juliet@particle.uni-karlsruhe.de

LEE-HAM, DOO YOUNG, PHARMACOLOGY, TOXICOLOGY. **Personal Data:** b Seoul, Korea, March 31, 1932; American citizen; m 1966, Euiyoung; c Thomas & Deanna. **Education:** Mercer Univ, BA, 1957; Cath Univ Am, MS, 1961, PhD (physiol), 1966. **Professional Experience:** PHYSIOLOGIST, DIV ONCOL & RADIOPHARM DRUG PROD, FOOD & DRUG ADMIN, 1969-; sr scientist, Melpar, Inc, 1967-1969; spec lectr physiol & biochem, Sungshin Womans Univ & Ewha Womans Univ, 1966-1967; res scientist, Microbiol Assoc, Inc, 1962-1966. **Memberships:** NY Acad Sci. **Research Statement & Publications:** Basic and applied cell physiology; in vitro and in vivo testing of drugs and chemicals for their carcinogenic potential, mutagenicityand cell transformation. **Mailing Address:** Food & Drug Admin, Parklawn Bldg 5600 Fishers Lane, Rockville, MD 20857. **Fax:** 301-594-0499.

LEE-HUANG, SYLVIA, BIOCHEMISTRY & MOLECULAR BIOLOGY. **Personal Data:** b Shanghai, China, July 14, 1930; American citizen; m 1957, c 3. **Education:** Nat Taiwan Univ, BS, 1952; Univ Idaho, MS, 1957; Univ Pittsburgh, PhD (biophys), 1961. **Professional Experience:** PROF BIOCHEM, SCH MED, NY UNIV, as of 2004; Prin investr, beginning 1972; assoc prof biochem, Sch Med, NY Univ, beginning 1971; res assoc prof, Sch Med, NY Univ, 1970-1971; from instr to asst prof, Sch Med, NY Univ, 1967-1970; res scientist, Sch Med, NY Univ, 1966-1967; instr biochem, Med Col, Cornell Univ, 1964-1966; res assoc chem physics, Sloan-Kettering Inst, 1962-1964; NIH fel microbiol, Sch Med, Univ Pittsburgh, 1961-1962. **Memberships:** AAAS; Am Soc Biol Chemists; Biophys Soc; Harvey Soc; NY Acad Sci. **Research Statement & Publications:** Molecular mechanism of transmission and expression of genetic information; control and mechanism of differentiation and development; erythropoietin and the regulation of red cell production; mechanism of anti-HIV action of plant proteins and polycyclic compounds. **Mailing Address:** Dept Biochem, NY Univ Sch Med, 550 First Ave, New York, NY 10016. **E-Mail:** leehus01@popmail.med.nyu.edu

LEELAMMA, SRINIVASA (G), MATHEMATICS. **Personal Data:** b Mysore, India. **Education:** Osmania Univ, India, BSc, 1955, MSc, 1957; Marathwada Univ, India, PhD (math), 1965. **Professional Experience:** DISTINGUISHED PROF MATH, STATE UNIV NY COL GENESEO, as of 2004; prof math, State Univ NY Col Geneseo, beginning 1973; assoc prof, State Univ NY Col Geneseo, 1968-1973; asst prof, Univ RI, 1966-1968; instr, Calgary Univ, 1965-1966; lectr math, Women's Col, Kurnool, India, 1959-1965. **Memberships:** Am Math Soc; Math Asn Am. **Research Statement & Publications:** Qualitative analysis in differential equations; stability theory. **Mailing Address:** State Univ NY Col Geneseo, Dept Math, 330 C S Hall, Geneseo, NY 14454. **E-Mail:** leela@geneseo.edu

LEEMAN, SUSAN EPSTEIN, PHYSIOLOGY, ENDOCRINOLOGY. **Personal Data:** b Chicago, Ill, May 9, 1930; m 1957, c 3. **Education:** Goucher Col, BA, 1951; Radcliffe Col, MA, 1954, PhD, 1958. **Honorary Degrees:** DSc, State Univ NY, Utica/Rome, 1992; Dr, Goucher Col, Towson, Md, 1993. **Honors & Awards:** Astwood Award, 1981; Van Dyke Award, 1982; Louis & Bert Freedman Found Award, 1982. **Professional Experience:** Fogarty scholar, 1994; PROF PHARMACOL, BOSTON UNIV, 1992-; dir, Interdepartmental Neuroscience Prog, 1984-1992; Albert Heritage med res vis prof, 1981; mem, Endocrinol Study Sect, Div Res Grants, NIH, 1981; prof physiol, Med Sch, Univ Mass, 1980-1992; from asst prof to assoc prof physiol, Lab Human Reprod & Reprod Biol, Harvard Med Sch, 1972-1980; asst res prof, Brandeis Univ, 1968-1971; adj asst prof, Brandeis Univ, 1966-1968; USPHS career develop award, 1962-; sr res assoc biochem, Brandeis Univ, 1962-1966; fel neurochem, Brandeis Univ, 1959-1962; instr physiol, Harvard Med Sch, 1958-1959; dir, Intramural Res Sci Comt, NIMH & ad hoc comt, Recent Prog Hormone Res. **Memberships:** Nat Acad Sci; Endocrine Soc; Soc Neuroscience; AAAS; Am Physiol Soc. **Research Statement & Publications:** Neuroendocrinology. **Mailing Address:** Boston Univ, Dept Pharmacol, L-611, Boston, MA 02118. **Fax:** 617-638-4329. **E-Mail:** sleeman@bu.edu

LEEMAN, WILLIAM P, GEOCHEMISTRY. **Personal Data:** b Texas, December 17, 1945; m, c 1. **Education:** Rice Univ, BA, 1867 & MA, 1969, Univ Ore, PhD, 1974. **Professional Experience:** PROF, DEPT EARTH SCI, RICE UNIV, as of. **Research Statement & Publications:** Convergent margin volcanism and relation to subduction processes; intraplate volcanism in the western U.S. and Hawaii; geochemistry of metamorphic rocks and its bearing on crustal evolution and subduction processes; geochemistry of 'fluid-mobile' elements such as boron, arsenic, antimony, etc. and implications for evolution and distribution of geologic fluids. **Mailing Address:** Dept Geol & Geophysics, Rice Univ, 6100 Main, Houston, TX 77005-1827. **E-Mail:** leeman@rice.edu

LEEMANN, CHRISTOPH WILLY, EXPERIMENTAL & ACCELERATOR PHYSICS. **Personal Data:** b Basel, Switz, January 12, 1939; m 1969, c 2. **Education:** Univ Basel, Switz, BS, 1962, PhD (nuclear physics), 1969. **Professional Experience:** DIR, THOMAS JEFFERSON NAT ACCELERATOR FACIL, 2001-; interim dir, Thomas Jefferson Nat Accelerator Facil, 2000-2001; dep dir, Thomas Jefferson Nat Accelerator Facil, 2000; assoc dir, Thomas Jefferson Nat Accelerator Facil, 1985-2000; dep leader, Adv Accelerator Studies Group, Lawrence Berkeley Lab, 1984-1985; Sabbatical leave, Europ Orgn Nuclear Res, Geneva, Switz, 1980-1981; staff scientist accelerator physics, Lawrence Berkeley Lab, Univ Calif, 1973-1984; fel accelerator physics, Lawrence Berkeley Lab, Univ Calif, 1972-1973; fel, Lawrence Berkeley Lab, Univ Calif, 1970-1972; res assoc, Univ Basel, 1969-1970; res asst nuclear physics, Univ Basel, 1963-1969. **Memberships:** AAAS; Am Phys Soc. **Research Statement & Publications:** Design and development of particle accelerators and related devices; beam cooling techniques; colliding beam devices; relativistic heavy ion accelerators; published over 50 articles. **Mailing Address:** Thomas Jefferson Nat Accelerator Facil, 12000 Jefferson Ave, Newport News, VA 23606. **E-Mail:** leemann@jtlab.org

LEEMANS, WIM PIETER, PHYSICS. **Personal Data:** b Gent, Belg, June 7, 1963. **Education:** Free Univ, Brussels, BS, 1985; Univ Calif, Los Angeles, MS, 1987, PhD (elec eng), 1991. **Honors & Awards:** Simon Ramo Award, Am Phys Soc, 1992. **Professional Experience:** GROUP LEADER, l'OASIS, LAWRENCE BERKELEY LAB, CALIF, as of 2002; STAFF SCIENTIST, LAWRENCE BERKELEY LAB, CALIF, 1991-; Grad scholar, Inst Elec & Electronics Engrs Nuclear & Plasma Soc, 1987; mem, Francqui Found. **Memberships:** Int Soc Optical Eng; Am Phys Soc; Inst Elec & Electronics Engrs; Royal Flemish Engrs Soc. **Research Statement & Publications:** High-intensity laser-plasma interaction in preformed and laser-produced plasmas; plasma beat-wave acceleration of electrons, driven density fluctuations using collective thomson scattering of visible laser probe beam; analysis of forward and backward scattered spectra of the pump beam and hole-coupled resonator mode analysis. **Mailing Address:** Div Accelerator Fusion Res, Lawrence Berkeley Lab, One Cyclotron Rd MS 71-259, Berkeley, CA 94720. **Fax:** 510-486-7981. **E-Mail:** wpleemans@lbl.gov

LEEMING, DAVID JOHN, MATHEMATICS. **Personal Data:** b Victoria, BC, June 8, 1939; m 1966, Yvonne; c Heather, Graeme & Robert. **Education:** Univ BC, BSc, 1961; Univ Ore, MA, 1963; Univ Alta, PhD (math), 1969. **Professional Experience:** PROF EMER MATH, UNIV VICTORIA, BC, as of 2006; site dir, Univ Victoria, 2003-2004; educ coordr, Univ Victoria, 2001-2006; prof math, Univ Victoria, BC, beginning 1986; course writer, Open Learning Inst, 1979; from instr to assoc prof, Univ Victoria, BC, 1963-1986, 1975-1986; mem, Acad Coun, Open Learning Agency, Burnaby, BC; managing ed, Pi Sky Mag. **Memberships:** Math Asn Am; Can Math Soc. **Research Statement & Publications:** Approximation theory; error bounds for interpolation schemes; rational approximation. **Mailing Address:** Dept Math, Univ Victoria, PO Box 3045 D264 Clearihue Bldg, Victoria, BC V8W 3P4, Can. **Fax:** 250-721-8962. **E-Mail:** leeming@math.uvic.ca

LEENEN, FRANS H H, CARDIOLOGY, HYPERTENSION. **Personal Data:** b Linne, Neth, September 16, 1943; Canadian citizen; m 1986, Mindy; c Arjan, Bob-Willem, Sarah C, David A & Peter M. **Education:** Univ Utrecht, PhD (Pharmacology), 1971, MD, 1973; FRCP (C), 1986. **Honors & Awards:** Young Investr Award, Can Hypertension Soc, 1982; Career Investr Award, Heart & Stroke Found Ont, 1989; Pfizer Chair in Hypertension Research, 2003 -. **Professional Experience:** PROF MED & PHARMACOL, UNIV OTTAWA, 1989-; DIR, HYPERTENSION UNIT, HEART INST, 1989-; principal investr, Heart & Stroke Found Ont, 1982- & Can Inst Health Research, 1985-; coordr, Clin Pharmacol Training Prog, Univ Toronto, 1985-1988; Assistant - aAssoc prof, Dept of Medic, Univ Toronto, 1979-1989; dir, Hypertension Unit, Toronto Western Hosp, 1979-1988; resident inter med & cardiol, Univ Utrecht, Neth, 1974-1978; res fel clin pharmacol, Univ Pittsburgh Sch Med, 1972-1973; fel, Coun High Blood Pressure Res, Am Heart Asn. **Memberships:** Fel Am Physiol Soc, 1994 -; fel Am Heart Asn 1991 -; fel Int Ac Cardiovasc Sciences, 2003 - Member, Int Soc Hypertension, Am Soc Clin Pharm, Am Soc Hypertension. **Research Statement & Publications:** Pharmacology; cardiology; brain mechanisms and sympathetic hyperactivity in salt sensitive hypertension and heart failure; effects of antihypertensive drugs on the heart in both animal models and humans. **Mailing Address:** Hypertension Unit, Univ Ottawa Heart Inst, 40 Ruskin St, Ottawa, ON K1Y 4W7, Can. **Fax:** 613-761-5105. **E-Mail:** fleenen@ottawaheart.ca

LEEP, HERMAN ROSS, MANUFACTURING, ENGINEERING ECONOMY. **Personal Data:** b Louisville, Ky, October 21, 1940. **Education:** Univ Louisville, BSME, 1963; Univ Del, MMAE, 1967; Purdue Univ, PhD (indust eng), 1979. **Professional Experience:** PROF INDUST ENG, UNIV LOUISVILLE, as of 2004; lectr, GE, 1986-1988; assoc prof indust eng, Univ Louisville, beginning 1983; asst prof graphics, 1973-1979; asst prof indust eng, 1979-1983; MECH ENGR, E I DU PONT Del NEMOURS, 1963-. **Memberships:** Am Soc Metals Int. **Research Statement & Publications:** Machining of composite materials; machining of titanium alloys; measurement of tool wear; measurement of cutting forces; measurement of surface finish; metal cutting research; published extensively on metal cutting, adaptive control, intelligent feature-based process planning, design and evaluation of cellular manufacturing systems, and manufacturing cost estimating. **Mailing Address:** Dept Indust Eng, Univ Louiseville, J B Speed Bldg, Louisville, KY 40272. **Fax:** 502-852-5633. **E-Mail:** hrleep01@gwise.louisville.edu

LEEPER, DENNIS BURTON, RADIATION BIOLOGY, HYPERTHERMIC ONCOLOGY CANCER. **Personal Data:** b Glendale, Calif, May 3, 1941; m Mardys; c 5. **Education:** Univ Iowa, BS, 1964, PhD (radiation biol), 1969. **Honors & Awards:** Sci Award, Am Cancer Soc, 1986 Eugene Robinson Award, NAHS, 2002. **Professional Experience:** DIV DIR, LAB EXP RADIATION ONCOL & DIV RADIATION BIOL, DEPT RADIATION ONCOL, THOMAS JEFFERSON UNIV, as of 2006; assoc ed, Int J Hyperthermia, 1985-; Diag Radiol & Nuclear Med Study Sect, NIH, 1983-1987; counr biol, Radiation Res Soc, 1983-1986; assoc ed, Int J Radiation Biol, 1983-1986; mem, Training Grant Study Sect, NCI, 1982-1983; chmn, NAm Hyperthermia Group, 1981-1985; PROF RADIATION ONCOL, THOMAS JEFFERSON UNIV HOSP, 1980-; consult radiation biol, Franklin Inst, Pa, 1976-1982; prin investr, NIH Res Grants, 1972-; adj assoc prof biomed eng, Univ Pa, 1972-1980; from asst prof to assoc prof, Thomas Jefferson Univ Hosp, 1970-1980; affil grad fac, Colo State Univ, 1970-1972; AEC fel, Colo State Univ, 1969-1970. **Memberships:** Radiation Res Soc; Am Asn Cancer Res; Cell Kinetics Soc; AAAS; Am Soc Thermalapeut Radiol Oncol; NAm Hyperthermia Group; Sigma Xi; NY Acad Sci. **Research Statement & Publications:** Interaction of radiation, hyperthermia, and anti-cancer drugs in mammalian cells in culture and in normal and tumor tissues in vivo; cell cycle kinetics; experimental radiation oncology. **Mailing Address:** Dept Radiation Oncol, Thomas Jefferson Univ, 111 S 11th St, Philadelphia, PA 19107-5097. **Fax:** 215-955-5825. **E-Mail:** dennis.leeper@mail.tju.edu

LEEPER, HAROLD MURRAY, POLYMER CHEMISTRY. **Personal Data:** b Akron, Ohio, July 14, 1920; m 1942, Mildred; c Sheryl L (Glotzer), David G & Mark R. **Education:** Univ Akron, BS, 1942, MS, 1947. **Professional Experience:** CONSULT, 1991-; prin scientist polymers, Alza Corp, 1980-1991; res scientist, Alza Corp, 1970-1980; group leader, Monsanto Co, 1954-1970; res chemist polymers, Wm Wrigley Jr Co, 1947-1954; polymer chemist rubber, Govt Rubber Labs, 1944-1947; rubber technologist, US Eng Bd, 1942-1944. **Memberships:** Am Chem Soc; Soc Plastics Engrs; AAAS. **Research Statement & Publications:** Chemistry, physics, and technology of rubbers and plastics; drug delivery systems. **Mailing Address:** Alza Corp, 1040 Gest Dr, Mtain View, CA 94040. **E-Mail:** hal1920@aol.com

LEEPER, JOHN ROBERT, ENTOMOLOGY. **Personal Data:** b Hackensack, NJ, July 12, 1947; m 1973, Catherine; c Schuyler R & Michael Thomas. **Education:** Carthage Col, BA, 1969; Univ Hawaii, MS, 1971, PhD (entom), 1975. **Professional Experience:** TECHNOL LEADER, ASIA PAC, DU PONT INC, 1994-; res asst, Appln Technol, 1992-1994; mgr, Agr Sci Lab, Tsukuba, Japan, 1989-1992; mgr US prod develop, rice herbicides, Agr Prod Dept, 1988-1989; licensing prod mgr, New Bus Ventures, 1985-1988; sr res biologist, Du Pont Exp Sta, Du Pont Inc, 1980-1985; asst prof entom, NY State Agr Exp Sta, Cornell Univ, 1977-1980; res assoc entom, Tree Fruit Res Ctr, Wash State Univ, 1975-1977. **Memberships:** Entom Soc Am. **Research Statement & Publications:** Managing collaborative research projects throughout asia pacific. **Mailing Address:** Stine Haskell Lab 215/304A, 1094 Elkion Rd, Newark, DE 19713. **Fax:** 302-366-5236.

LEEPER, RAMON JOE, PLASMA PHYSICS, HIGH ENERGY NUCLEAR PHYSICS. **Personal Data:** b Princeton, Mo, April 1, 1948; m 1976, c 1. **Education:** Mass Inst Technol, SB, 1970; Iowa State Univ, PhD (high energy nuclear physics), 1975. **Professional Experience:** SUPVR DIAGNOSTICS DIV, SANDIA NAT LABS, 1986-; mem tech staff Plasma Physics, Sandia Nat Labs, 1976-1986; res assoc high energy nuclear physics, Ames Lab, US Dept Energy, 1975-1976; guest scientist, Argonne Nat Lab, 1971-1976. **Memberships:** Am Phys Soc; Sigma Xi. **Research Statement & Publications:** Particle beam induced controlled thermonuclear fusion; neutron physics; fusion plasma diagnostic techniques; neutron production of inertially confined high temperature fusion plasmas; high intensity pulsed neutron sources; high current ion beams; meson spectroscopy. **Mailing Address:** Diagnostics Target Experiment Div, Sandia Nat Labs, Div 1277 PO Box 5800, Albuquerque, NM 87185-1196. **Fax:** 505-845-7820. **E-Mail:** rjleepe@sandia.gov

LEERBURGER, BENEDICT ALAN, SCIENCE WRITING, JOURNALISM. **Personal Data:** b New York, NY, January 2, 1932; m 1958, Julie; c Ellen & Marian. **Education:** Colby Col, BA, 1954. **Professional Experience:** Freelance writer, 1980-; CONSULT COMPUT SCI, PHYS SCI & GEN SCI COMMUN, 1979-; ed-in-chief, McGraw-Hill Book Co, 1976-1979; publ, Kraus-Thomson Org, Ltd, 1974-1976; dir publ, NY Times, 1972-1974; vpres & ed dir, Nat Micro-Publ Corp, 1970-1972; proj dir, CCM Info Sci, Inc, 1968-1970; Storrington Printing & Pub Co, Inc, 1967-1970 & NSF Deep Freeze Prog, Antarctica, 1967; Cross, Hinshaw & Lindberg, Inc, 1965-1967; ed, Cowles Ed Corp, 1961-1968; sci ed, Grolier, Inc, 1959-1961; consult, Sci Digest, 1959-1961; asst ed, Prod Eng Mag, 1954-1959. **Memberships:** Nat Asn Sci Writers; Am Hist Asn; Nat Sci Teachers Asn; Am Soc Journalists & Authors. **Research Statement & Publications:** Physical science; Antarctica; American scientific history. **Mailing Address:** 338 Heathcote Rd, Scarsdale, NY 10583.

LEE-RUFF, EDWARD, CHEMISTRY & PHOTOCHEMISTRY, STRAINED COMPOUNDS. **Personal Data:** b Shanghai, China, January 4, 1944; Canadian citizen; div, c Daniel, Caroline & Stephane. **Education:** McGill Univ, BSc, 1964, PhD (org chem), 1967. **Honors & Awards:** Fellow of the Chemical Institute of Canada (FCIC). **Professional Experience:** PROF CHEM, YORK UNIV, 1985-; from asst prof to assoc prof, York Univ, 1974-1984; Nat Res Coun fel, Columbia Univ, 1967-1969. **Memberships:** Chem Inst Can. **Research Statement & Publications:** Organic photochemistry; reactions of strained molecules; organic chemistry; Soluble polymer Support Synthesis; Chemistry of Fluorenyl Cations. **Mailing Address:** Dept Chem, York Univ, 4700 Keele St, Toronto, ON M3J 1P3, Can. **Fax:** 416-736-5936. **E-Mail:** leeruff@yorku.ca

LEES, ALISTAIR JOHN, PHOTOCHEMISTRY, SPECTROSCOPY. **Personal Data:** b Preston, Eng, July 12, 1955; m 1979, c 2. **Education:** Univ Newcastle, BSc, 1976, PhD (chem), 1979. **Professional Experience:** PROF & CHAIR CHEM, BINGHAMTON UNIV, as of 2003; vis prof, Univ Cent Lancashire, 1992-1994; vis prof, Cambridge Univ, 1988-1989; assoc prof inorg chem, State Univ NY, Binghamton, beginning 1986; consult, Int Paper Corp, 1985-; consult, IBM Corp, 1985-1986; asst prof, State Univ NY, Binghamton, 1981-1986; fel phys chem, Univ Southern Calif, 1979-1981. **Memberships:** Am Chem Soc; Royal Soc Chem. **Research Statement & Publications:** Photochemistry and spectroscopy of transition metal compounds; organometallic chemistry; homogeneous catalysis; kinetics and mechanism; low-temperature spectroscopy and photochemistry. **Mailing Address:** Dept Chem, Binghamton Univ, Binghamton, NY 13902-6016. **Fax:** 607-777-4478. **E-Mail:** alees@binghamton.edu

LEES, ANDREW, BIOCONJUGATE CHEMISTRY, VACCINE DEVELOPMENT. **Personal Data:** b Boston, Mass, February 9, 1953; m 1987, Julie; c Adam E & Elizabeth M. **Education:** Harvey Mudd Col, BS, 1976; Johns Hopkins Univ, PhD (biophys), 1984. **Professional Experience:** 1999- Director of Macromolecular Sciences, Biosynexus. 1998- Res. Assoc prof, Dept Med, Uniformed Servs, Univ Health Sci, beginning 1993-1999 Dir Vaccine Development, Virion Systems, Inc. 1985-1988 Fel, Johns Hopkins Univ. **Memberships:** AAAS; Am Chem Soc. **Research Statement & Publications:** Developing new chemistries for convalently coupling proteins to carbohydrates with the goal of enhanced vaccine capabilities to stimulate better responses to both the carbohydrate and protein components; developing combination vaccines to minimize the total number of necessary immunizations. **Mailing Address:** Biosynexus Inc, 9119 Gaither Red, Gaithersburg, MD 20877. **Fax:** 301-990-4990. **E-Mail:** pippinrabbit@earthlink.net

LEES, DAVID ERIC BERMAN, OPTICAL MEASUREMENT TECHNOLOGY. **Personal Data:** b Boston, Mass, July 22, 1950; m 1977, c 3. **Education:** Oakland Univ, BS, 1972; Univ Rochester, MS, 1974, PhD (optics), 1979. **Professional Experience:** CONSULT, DEBL ASSOCS, 1993-; Prin investr, ONR Phase I, 1989; prin investr, Sparta, Inc, 1986-1993; prin investr, NSF Phase I Small Bus Innovation Res Award, 1984; systs engr, Automatrix, Inc, 1982-1986; prin develop engr, Honeywell, 1979-1982. **Memberships:** Optical Soc Am (secy, 1990-1991); Soc Photo-Optical Instrumentation Engrs. **Research Statement & Publications:** Machine vision for industrial applications; vision guided robots; optical gauging; speckle imaging; imaging laser radan development. **Mailing Address:** 57 Gleason Rd, Lexington, MA 02420. **Fax:** 801-640-7135. **E-Mail:** debl@world.std.com

LEES, GEORGE EDWARD, VETERINARY INTERNAL MEDICINE, VETERINARY NEPHROLOGY & UROLOGY. **Personal Data:** b Pittsburgh, Pa, February 7, 1948; m 1980, Kathleen K Schultze. **Education:** Colo State Univ, BS, 1970, DVM, 1972; Univ Minn, MS, 1979. **Professional Experience:** Chmn bd, Am Col Vet Internal Med, 1991-1992; PROF SMALL ANIMAL MED, COL VET MED, TEX A&M UNIV, 1986-; assoc prof, Col Vet Med, Tex A&M Univ, 1980-1986; clin asst prof small animal med, Col Vet Med, Univ Minn, St Paul, 1979-1980; resident small animal med, Col Vet Med, Univ Minn, St Paul, 1976-1979; Intern small animal med & surg, Sch Vet Med, Univ Calif, Davis, 1975-1976. **Memberships:** Am Col Vet Internal Med (vpres 1988-1990 pres-elect 1989-1990 pres 1990-1991). **Research Statement & Publications:** Diagnosis, treatment and prevention of spontaneous diseases of the urinary system in dogs and cats. **Mailing Address:** Dept Small Animal Med Surg, Col Vet Med, Tex A&M Univ, 4474-TAMU, College Station, TX 77843-4474. **Fax:** 979-845-6978.

LEES, GRAHAM, BIOPHYSICS. **Personal Data:** b Pemburg, Eng, February 17, 1953. **Education:** Univ Cambridge, BA, 1974, MA, 1976, PhD (neurophysiol), 1978. **Professional Experience:** Ed dir life & medsci, Academic Press, beginning 1993; ed chief, Raven Press, 1988-1993; ed mgr, Elsevier Sci Publ, 1986-1988; ed, Elsevier Sci Publ, 1980-1986; res fel biophys, Gif-Sur-Yvelle, France, 1978-1980. **Memberships:** Soc Neuroscience; Am Acad Sci. **Research Statement & Publications:** Biophysics. **Mailing Address:** Academic Press, 525 B St Ste 1900, San Diego, CA 92101.

LEES, MARJORIE BERMAN, NEUROCHEMISTRY, NEUROIMMUNOLOGY. **Personal Data:** b New York, NY, March 17, 1923; m 1946, Sidney; c David, Andrew & Eliot. **Education:** Hunter Col, BA, 1943; Univ Chicago, MS, 1945; Harvard Univ, PhD (med sci), 1951. **Professional Experience:** Mem, Panel Biomed & Biol Behav Res, NASA & NIH, 1993-; EMER PROF BIOCHEM, NEUROL DEPT, MED SCH, HARVARD UNIV, 1993-; ASSOC DIR, MENT RETARDATION RES CTR, 1993-; DIR, BIOCHEM DIV, 1990-; chief ed, J Neurochem, 1986-1990; prof, Ment Retardation Res Ctr, 1985-1993; Javits invest award, NIH, 1984-1991, 1991-1997; mem, Nat Adv Coun, Nat Inst Neurol & Communicative Disorders & Stroke, 1979-1982; BIOCHEMIST, EUNICE KENNEDY SHRIVER CTR, 1976-; sr res assoc, Harvard Med Sch, 1975-1985; prin res assoc, Harvard Med Sch, 1971-1975; assoc biochemist, McLean Hosp, 1966-1976; prin investr, NIH grants, 1962-; sr res assoc pharmacol, Dartmouth Med Sch, 1962-1966; res assoc, Harvard Med Sch, 1959-1962 & 1966-1971; assoc biochemist, McLean Hosp, 1958-1962; biochem, Neurol Div, Mass Gen Hosp, 1958; instr neuropath, Harvard Med Sch, 1955-1959; asst biochemist, McLean Hosp, 1955-1958; res asst, McLean Hosp, 1953-1955; Am Cancer Soc res fel, 1951-1953; asst, Col Physicians & Surgeons, Columbia Univ, 1945-1946; asst, Univ Chicago, 1943-1945. **Memberships:** Am Soc Biol Chem; Am Soc Neurochemistry (treas, 1975-1981, pres, 1983-1985); Soc Neuroscience; Am Asn Neuropath; Int Soc Neurochemistry; Int Soc Neuroimmunology. **Research Statement & Publications:** Chemistry of the nervous system; myelin and demyelinating diseases; neuroimmunology; brain proteins. **Mailing Address:** E K Shriver Ctr, 200 Trapelo Rd, Waltham, MA 02452. **Fax:** 781-893-4824. **E-Mail:** marjorie.lees@umassmed.edu

LEES, MARTIN H, PEDIATRICS, CARDIOLOGY. **Personal Data:** b London, Eng, May 11, 1929; m 1959, Elizabeth; c Deborah, Jacqueline & Christina. **Education:** Univ London, MB, BS, 1955, MD, 1962. **Honorary Degrees:** FRCP, 1980. **Professional Experience:** PROF PEDIAT, MED SCH, UNIV ORE, 1971-; Assoc prof, Med Sch, Univ Ore, 1962-1971; chief, pediat cardiol, Emanuel Hosp, Portland, Ore. **Memberships:** Am Pediat Soc; Am Heart Asn; Royal Col Physicians London. **Research Statement & Publications:** Pediatric cardiology; newborn and infant cardiopulmonary physiology and pathophysiology. **Mailing Address:** Dept Pediat, Univ Ore Med Sch, Portland, OR 97201. **Fax:** 503-280-4134.

LEES, NORMAN DOUGLAS, MICROBIOLOGY, MOLECULAR BIOLOGY. **Personal Data:** b Providence, RI, September 16, 1945; m 1981, c 3. **Education:** Providence Col, AB, 1967; Northwestern Univ, PhD (microbiol), 1973. **Professional Experience:** ASSOC PROF BIOL, IND UNIV-PURDUE UNIV, INDIANAPOLIS, 1980-; grants, Ind Univ-Purdue Univ, Indianapolis, 1974 & Biomed Sci Res, 1975 & 1977; asst prof, Ind Univ-purdue Univ, Indianapolis, 1973-1980; teaching asst biol sci, Northwestern Univ, 1967-1973. **Memberships:** Am Soc Microbiol; Sigma Xi. **Research Statement & Publications:** Role of sterols in biological membranes. **Mailing Address:** Dept Biol, Ind Univ-Purdue Univ, 723 W Mivh St SL-2306 B, Indianapolis, IN 46202-5132. **E-Mail:** nlees@iupui.edu

LEES, ROBERT S, MEDICINE, BIOCHEMISTRY. **Personal Data:** b New York, NY, July 16, 1934; m 1960, c 4. **Education:** Harvard Univ, AB, 1955, MD, 1959; Am Bd Internal Med, dipl. **Professional Experience:** PRES & FOUNDING DIR, BOSTON HEART FOUND, as of 2002; pres, Boston Heart Found, beginning 1991; PROF HEALTH SCI TECHNOL, HARVARD UNIV & MASS INST TECHNOL, 1971-; dir, Clin Res Ctr, 1969-1974; assoc prof, Clin Res Ctr, 1969-1971; asst prof med & attend physician, Rockefeller Univ, 1966-1969; fel coun arteriosclerosis, Am Heart Asn, 1965-; staff assoc & attend physician med, Nat Heart Inst, 1963-1966; hon asst registr cardiol, Nat Heart Hosp, Eng, 1962-1963; USPHS fel, 1962-1963; asst resident med, Mass Gen Hosp, Boston, 1961-1962; USPHS res fel med, 1960-1961; Dalton scholar, Harvard Med Sch, 1960; Intern surg, Mass Gen Hosp, Boston, 1959-1960; asst med, Mass Gen Hosp; assoc med, Peter Bent Brigham Hosp. **Memberships:** Am Heart Asn; Am Fedn Clin Res; Am Soc Clin Invest; Am Soc Pharmacol & Exp Therapeut. **Research Statement & Publications:** Cardiology, especially ischemic heart disease; lipid and lipoprotein metabolism. **Mailing Address:** Boston Heart Found, 139 Main St, Cambridge, MA 02142. **E-Mail:** rsl@mit.edu

LEES, RONALD EDWARD, OCCUPATIONAL MEDICINE, EPIDEMIOLOGY. **Personal Data:** b Carlisle, UK, February 14, 1935; Canadian citizen; m 1962, Millis; c Karen, Hilary. **Education:** Glasgow Univ, MBChB, 1958, DPH, 1962, MD, 1967. **Honorary Degrees:** fel Col Family Physicians Can, 1996. **Professional Experience:** Prof family med, Queens Univ, 1975-1999; from asst prof to prof epidemiol, Queens Univ, beginning 1969; field med officer, Rockefeller Found, NY, 1965-1968; Med officer health, Govt St Lucia, Wis, 1962-1965; PROF EMER, FAC HEALTH SCI, QUEENS UNIV. **Research Statement & Publications:** Tropical health-infant malnutrition, schistosomiasis, parasitic and infectious disease control; environmental and occupational health-epidemiologic studies in effect of toxins, noise induced heari; occupational health problems in underdeveloped countries. **Mailing Address:** Dept Community Health & Epidemiol, Queens Univ, Second Floor, Abramsky Hall, Arch St, Kingston, ON K7L 3N6, Can. **Fax:** 6113-533-6686. **E-Mail:** leesr@post.queensu.ca

LEES, RONALD MILNE, MOLECULAR SPECTROSCOPY. **Personal Data:** b Sutton, Eng, October 28, 1939; Canadian citizen; m 1962, c 2. **Education:** Univ BC, BS, 1961, MS, 1965; Bristol Univ, PhD (physics), 1967. **Professional Experience:** PROF EMER, DEPT PHYSICS, UNIV NB, FREDERICTON, as of 2006; dept chmn, Univ Nb, Fredericton, 1981-1988; prof physics, Univ NB, Fredericton, beginning 1977; vis assoc prof, Physics Dept, Univ BC, Vancouver, 1974-1975; Nat Res Coun Can grant, Univ NB, Fredericton, 1968-; assoc prof, Univ Nb, Fredericton, 1968-1977; Nat Res Coun Can fel, Nat Res Coun, Ottawa, 1966-1968; prin investr, Centres Excellence Molecular & Interfacial Dynamics, Fed Networks Centres Excellence Prog. **Memberships:** Can Asn Physicists; Am Asn Physics Teachers; Optical Soc Am; Soc Photo-Optical Instrumentation Engrs. **Research Statement & Publications:** Atomic and molecular physics; molecular spectroscopy. **Mailing Address:** Dept Physics, Univ NB, P223, Fredericton, NB E3B 5A3, Can. **E-Mail:** lees@unb.ca

LEES, SIDNEY, ENGINEERING, STRUCTURE OF HARD TISSUES. **Personal Data:** b Philadelphia, Pa, April 17, 1917; m 1946, Marjorie Berman; c David E, Andrew P & Eliot J. **Education:** City Col New York, BS, 1938; Mass Inst Technol, SM, 1948, ScD, 1950. **Professional Experience:** CHM Int Symp, Acoustical Imaging, emer 1997; joint chmn, NE Doppler Conf, 1981; chmn, Conf Ultrasonics, 1978; vis scientist, Univ Amsterdam Dent Sch, 1975; Chmn, Joint Automatic Control Conf, 1965 & Res Conf Instrumentation Sci, 1971; SR STAFF MEM & HEAD BIOENG DEPT, FORSYTH DENT CTR, BOSTON, 1966-; prof eng, Dartmouth Col, 1962-1966; pres, Lees Instrument Res Inc, 1959-1963; vpres, United Res Inc, 1959; consult instrumentation, 1957-1959; asst prof, Mass Inst Technol, 1950-1957; res assoc aeronaut, Mass Inst Technol, 1947-1950; engr, US Signal Corps, 1940-1943; Observer, US Weather Bur, 1938-1940; adj prof, Northeastern Univ. **Memberships:** Emer mem Am Phys Soc; emer mem Sigma Xi; emer mem Inst Elec & Electronics Engrs; emer mem Am Acoust Soc. **Research Statement & Publications:** Ultrasonics; bioinstrumentation; measurement systems and components; control systems; geophysical instrumentation. **Mailing Address:** 50 Eliot Mem Rd, Newton, MA 02158. **Fax:** 617-262-4021.

LEES, THOMAS MASSON, ANALYTICAL CHROMATOGRAPHY, FERMENTATION PRODUCTION. **Personal Data:** b New York, NY, June 16, 1917; wid Nola (Deceased); c David & Christine. **Education:** Long Island Univ, BS, 1939; Iowa State Univ, MS, 1942, PhD (biophys chem), 1944. **Professional Experience:** RETIRED; from prodn supvr to sr res chemist, Pfizer, Inc, 1946-1980; res chemist, Am Distilling Co, 1944-1946. **Memberships:** Am Chem Soc emer mem. **Research Statement & Publications:** Fermentative production of glycerol; antibiotics development, production and identification; analysis of medicinal compounds. **Mailing Address:** 35 Woodridge Circle, Gales Ferry, CT 06335.

LEES, WAYNE LOWRY, EXPERIMENTAL PHYSICS, ENGINEERING PHYSICS. **Personal Data:** b Washington, DC, July 18, 1914; m 1939, c 2. **Education:** Swarthmore Col, BA, 1937; Harvard Univ, MA, 1940, PhD (physics), 1949. **Professional Experience:** RETIRED; mem staff, Duracell Int Inc, 1980-1982; staff mem, lab phys sci, P R Mallory & Co Inc, Burlington, Mass, 1974-1980; proj engr, Design Automation Inc, Lexington, Mass, 1972-1973; assoc prof math, Wash Tech Inst, 1971-1972; Electronics Res Ctr, NASA, Cambridge, 1965-1970; Instrumentation Lab, Mass Inst Technol, 1958-1965; Nuclear Metals Inc, 1954-1958; Metall Proj, Mass Inst Technol, 1950-1954; Tracerlab Inc, 1949-1950; physicist, Nat Bur Standards, 1944-1946; physicist, Geophys Lab, Wash, DC, 1942-1944; asst, Bartol Res Found, Pa, 1939-1940. **Memberships:** AAAS; Am Phys Soc; Fedn Am Sci; Inst Elec & Electronics Engrs. **Research Statement & Publications:** Quasistatic electrical systems and dielectric properties; physics of high pressures and metals; electrode phenomena; electron and ion transport; engineering physics. **Mailing Address:** 29 Tower Rd, Lexington, MA 02421.

LEESE, JOHN ALBERT, REMOTE SENSING, NUMERICAL MODELING. **Personal Data:** b Manchester, Md, December 6, 1932; m 1959, c 4. **Education:** Pa State Univ, BS, 1957; Fla State Univ, MS, 1959; Univ Mich, PhD (meteorol), 1964. **Professional Experience:** VIS SCIENTIST, GLOBAL ENERGY WATER CYCLE EXP, WORLD CLIMATE RES PROG, UNIV CORP ATMOSPHERIC RES, 1993-; Dept Meteorol, Univ Md, 1992-1993; dir res, Inst Naval Oceanog, 1988-1992; sr scientist admin, World Meteorol Orgn, Geneva, Switz, 1982-1988; dep dir admin, Nat Environ Satellite Serv, 1978-1982; assoc dir data processing, Nat Environ Satellite Serv, 1975-1978; div chief res & develop, Nat Environ Satellite Serv, 1969-1975; dept mgr res & develop, Atmospheric Sci Dept, IBM Corp, 1964-1969; lectr, Univ Mich, 1961-1964; meteorologist res & develop, Air Force Cambridge Labs, 1959-1961; meteorologist, USNR, 1958-1978. **Memberships:** Am Meteorol Soc; Oceanog Soc. **Research Statement & Publications:** Digital data processing and quantitative information extraction techniques of environmental satellite data for input to numerical models of the atmosphere and the oceans. **Mailing Address:** Univ Corp Atmospheric Res, Ste 1201 100 Wayne Ave, Silver Spring, MD 20910-5603. **Fax:** 301-427-2222. **E-Mail:** leese@ogp.nasa.gov

LEESER, DAVID O(SCAR), FORENSIC MATERIALS ENGINEERING. **Personal Data:** b El Paso, Tex, August 3, 1917; m 1945, c 2. **Education:** Univ Tex, BS, 1943; Ohio State Univ, MS, 1950. **Honors & Awards:** Award, Nat Adv Comt Aeronaut, 1944; Apollo Achievement Award, NASA, 1969; Award, Off Sci Res & Develop. **Professional Experience:** CONSULT ENGR, 1987-; mgr, Eng Mat Lab, Burroughs Corp, 1975-1986; chief metallurgist, Amplex Div, 1968-1975; chief scientist, Missile Div, Chrysler Corp, 1961-1968; Int Conf Peaceful Uses Atomic Energy, Geneva, 1958 & Int Atomic Energy Agency Conf, Vienna, 1961; high temperature nuclear fuel comt, US AEC, 1957-1961; US del, World Metall Cong, 1957; mem welding forum, US AEC, 1954-1964; staff metallurgist & chief mat sect, Atomic Power Develop Assocs, Inc, 1954-1961; reactor mat engr, Nuclear Power Dept, Detroit Edison Co, 1954-1961; assoc metallurgist, Argonne Nat Lab, 1950-1954; res engr, Battelle Mem Inst, 1944-1950; metallurgist, Bradley Mining Co, Idaho, 1943-1944; mem, Atomic Indust Forum. **Memberships:** Am Soc Testing & Mat; Sigma Xi; Am Soc Mech Engrs; Am Mgt Asn; Am Soc Metals; Am Soc Metals Int. **Research Statement & Publications:** Evaluation of aerospace designs with regard to conventional and nonconventional materials applications and advanced aerospace requirements; ground and launch support equipment; materials for high-speed computer and electromechanical business machine systems under development; failure analysis in each category. **Mailing Address:** 11515 N91st St Suite 151, Scottsdale, AZ 85260.

LEESON, CHARLES ROLAND, ANATOMY. **Personal Data:** b Halifax, Eng, January 26, 1926; m 1954, c 5. **Education:** Cambridge Univ, BA, 1947, MB, BChir, 1950, MA, 1950, MD, 1959, PhD (anat), 1971. **Professional Experience:** PROF EMER ANAT, SCH MED, UNIV ILL, 1988-; vis prof anat, London Hosp Med Col, Eng, 1973-1974; prof anat & chmn dept, Univ Mo, Columbia, 1966-1978; prof anat, Univ Iowa, 1963-1966; assoc prof anat & histol, Queen's Univ, Ont, 1961-1963; assoc prof, Dalhousie Univ, 1958-1961; lectr anat, Univ Col SWales, 1955-1958. **Memberships:** Anat Soc Gt Brit & Ireland; Am Asn Anat. **Research Statement & Publications:** Post natal development, particularly inmarsupials and rodents and with reference to certain organ systems. **Mailing Address:** 19810 SW 95th St, Dunnellon, FL 34432.

LEESON, DAVID BRENT, SATELLITE & MICROWAVE COMMUNICATIONS, IONOSPHERIC PROPAGATION. **Personal Data:** b Cleveland, Ohio, April 12, 1937; m 1980, Barbara Splane; c Hugh L & Melinda A. **Education:** Calif Inst Technol, BS, 1958; Mass Inst Technol, MS, 1959; Stanford Univ, PhD (elec eng), 1962. **Honors & Awards:** WJ Cady Award, Inst Elec & Electronics Engrs, 2001; Entrepreneur Year, Stanford Grad Sch Bus; Dist Alum Award, MIT. **Professional Experience:** CONSULT & PROF, DEPT ELEC ENG, STANFORD UNIV, 1994-; chmn, chief exec officer & founder, Calif Microwave Inc, 1968-1993; Dir microwave lab, Applied Tech Inc, Palo Alto, 1964-1968; fmr Dir, Stanford Telecommunications Inc.; fmr Dir, Morphics Technology Inc. **Memberships:** Fel Inst Elec & Electronics Engrs; Am Electronics Asn (bd govs 1982-1983); Electronics Indust Asn (bd dirs 1980-1982); Tau Beta Pi; Eta Kappa Nu; Sigma Xi. **Research Statement & Publications:** Entrepreneurship, strategy, organizational life cycles; author of IEEE papers on nonlinear frequency multipliers, radar, oscillator stability; book on Yagi antennas. **Mailing Address:** Stanford Univ, 350 Serra Mall, David Packard Rm 352, Stanford, CA 94305. **Fax:** 650-723-9251. **E-Mail:** leeson@nova.stanford.edu

LEESON, LEWIS JOSEPH, BIOPHARMACEUTICS, PHARMACO-KINETICS. **Personal Data:** b Paterson, NJ, April 26, 1927; m 1953, Barbara; c Suzanne, Erica & Alexander. **Education:** Rutgers Univ, BS, 1950, MS, 1954; Univ Mich, PhD (pharmaceut chem), 1957. **Honors & Awards:** Univ Michigan, sch of pharmacy, distinguished alummus awards; Lou Busse lectr, Univ Wis. **Professional Experience:** PRES, LJL ASSOCS INC, 1993-; distinguished res fel, biopharm, Ciba-Geigy Pharmaceut Co, 1984-1993; sr res fel biopharm, Geigy Chem Corp, 1980-1984; sr dir pharm res & develop, Geigy Chem Corp, 1978-1980; dir, Geigy Chem Corp, 1973-1978; asst dir, Geigy Chem Corp, 1971-1973; asst dir pharmaceut develop, Geigy Chem Corp, 1969-1971; proj leader pharmaceut, Union Carbide Res Inst, 1967-1969; res chemist, Lederle Labs, Am Cyanamid Co, 1957-1967; asst, Rutgers Univ, 1952-1954 & Univ Mich, 1955-1956; Relief pharmacist, Frieds Pharm, 1952-1954; pharmacist, Silver Rod Drugs, 1951-1952; Intern pharm, Mack Drug Co, 1950-1951. **Memberships:** Controlled Release Soc; Am Pharmaceut Asn; fel Acad Pharmaceut Sci; Sigma Xi; fel Am Asn Pharmaceut Sci; Int Pharmaceut Fedn. **Research Statement & Publications:** Pharmaceutical product development; application of physical chemical techniques for developing various pharmaceutical dosage forms; biopharmaceutics; pharmacokinetics. **Mailing Address:** 134 Ridge Dr, Montville, NJ 07045. **Fax:** 973-335-1909. **E-Mail:** lewisleeson@erols.com

LEESON, THOMAS SYDNEY, ANATOMY. **Personal Data:** b Halifax, UK, January 26, 1926; m 1952, c 3. **Education:** Cambridge Univ, BA, 1946, MA, 1949, MD & BCh, 1950, MD, 1959, PhD, 1971. **Professional Experience:** PROF EMER CELL BIOL & ANAT, UNIV ALTA, 1991-; prof anat, Univ Alta, 1982-1991; head dept, Univ Alta, 1963-1982; from asst prof to assoc prof, Univ Toronto, 1957-1963; asst lectr anat, Univ Wales, 1955-1957. **Memberships:** Am Asn Anat; Brit Asn Clin Anatomists; Anat Soc Gt Brit & Ireland; Electron Microscopy Soc Am. **Research Statement & Publications:** Electron microscopy, histology and embryology; pancreatic centroacinar cells as they relate to acinar and ductular cells and to insular cells the latter associated with paracrine secreatin and hormonal control of exocrine secretion. **Mailing Address:** Dept Biol Sci, Univ Alta, CW 405, Biol Sci Ctr, Edmonton, AB T6G 2E9, Can. **Fax:** 780-492-9234.

LEESTMA, DAVID C, AERONAUTICS. **Personal Data:** b May 6, 1949. **Education:** U.S. Naval Post Grad Sch, MS, 1972. **Professional Experience:** ASST PROG MGR ORBITAL SPACE PLANE, JOHNSON SPACE CENTER, NASA, as of 2005. **Memberships:** Am Inst Astronaut & Aeronaut. **Mailing Address:** NASA Johnson Space Ctr, Code CA, Houston, TX 77058. **Fax:** 713-483-2724.

LEESTMA, JAN E, PATHOLOGY, NEUROPATHOLOGY. **Personal Data:** b Flint, Mich, November 30, 1938; m 1961, c 2. **Education:** Hope Col, BA, 1960; Univ Mich, MD, 1964; Northwestern Univ, MBA, 1985. **Professional Experience:** CHIEF MED OFFICER & CO-FOUNDER, NEUROPATHOLOGIST, as of 2004; ASSOC MED DIR, CHICAGO NEUROSURG CTR & CHICAGO INST NEUROSURG & NEURORESEARCH, 1987-; prof path & neurol, Univ Chicago, 1986-1987; dean student, Div Biol Sci, Pritzker Sch Med, Univ Chicago, 1986-1987; attend physician, Children's Mem Hosp, 1982-; asst med examr, Cook Co Off Med Examr, Chicago, beginning 1977; 80 W Suburban Hosp, Oak Park, Ill, 1976-1985; Great Lakes Naval Hosp, Ill, beginning 1974; Baxter-Travenol Labs, Morton Grove, Ill, 1973-1976; attend physician, Nwestern Mem Hosp, Chicago, 1971-; Vet Admin Lakeside Hosp & Vet Admin North Chicago Hosp, Ill, beginning 1971; from asst prof to assoc prof path, Sch Med, Northwestern Univ, 1971-1986; consult, DC Gen Hosp, Wash, DC, 1969-1971; Nat Naval Med Ctr, Bethesda, Md, 1969-1970; fel neuropath, Einstein Med Col & instr path, Univ Colo Med Sch, Denver, 1967-1968; resident & intern path, Univ Colo Med Sch, Denver, 1964-1967. **Memberships:** Am Asn Neuropathologists; Sigma Xi; AAAS; NY Acad Sci. **Research Statement & Publications:** Experimental neurology; neurological degenerative disease; central nervous system tissue; brain tumors; computerized data analysis; electron microscopy forensic medicine; electron microscopy, forensic neuropathology. **Mailing Address:** Chicago Neurosurgical Ctr, 5841 S Md Ave Box 69, Chicago, IL 60690-0069.

LEET, RICHARD HALE, HEALTH PHYSICS. **Personal Data:** b Maryville, Mo, October 11, 1926; m 1949, Phyllis; c Richard H II, Alan C & Dana E. **Education:** NW Mo State Col, BS, 1948; Ohio State Univ, PhD (phys chem), 1952. **Professional Experience:** RETIRED; vchmn, Amoco Corp, 1991-1992; dir, Amoco Corp, 1983-1991; pres, Amoco Chems Corp, 1978-1983; exec vpres, Amoco Chems Corp, 1977-1978; vpres mktg, Amoco Chems Corp, 1975-1977; vpres planning & admin, Amoco Chems Corp, 1974-1975; vpres supply, Atlanta, 1971-1974; regional vpres, Atlanta, 1970-1971; mgr, Mfg Dept, 1969-1970; dir, Mktg Dept, Am Oil Co, 1964-1968; res chemist, Stand Oil Co, 1953-1964. **Memberships:** Am Chem Soc; Soc Chem Indust; Am Indust Health Coun. **Mailing Address:** 3631 Lantern Dr, Gainesville, GA 30504-5420.

LEEVY, CARROLL M, MEDICINE, NUTRITION. **Personal Data:** b Columbia, SC, October 13, 1920; m 1956, Ruth S Barboza; c Carroll B & Maria S. **Education:** Fisk Univ, AB, 1941; Univ Mich, MD, 1944. **Honorary Degrees:** DSc, NJ Inst Technol, 1973; DHH, Dr Hum, Fisk Univ, 1981; BSc, Univ Nebr, 1989. **Honors & Awards:** Mod Med Award, 1972; Achievement Award, Nat Med Asn, 1987; Distinguished Serv Award, Am Asn Study Liver Dis, 1991. **Professional Experience:** DISTINGUISHED PROF MED, COL MED NJ, as of 2004; DIR, LIVER CTR, 1990-; chmn bd trustees, Asn Acad Minority Physicians, 1988-; SCI DIR, SAMMY DAVIS JR NAT LIVER INST, 1984-; consult, Food & Drug Admin, 1970-1978 & Nat Med Libr, 1980-1984; chmn & physician chief, Dept Med, 1975-1991; mem clin cancer training comt, NIH, 1969-1973; chief med, East Orange Vet Admin Hosp, 1966-1971; physician-in-chief, Martland Hosp, 1966-1968; mem dean's comt, East Orange Vet Admin Hosp, 1966-1968; actg chmn, Dept Med, 1966-1968; consult & mem med adv comt, Vet Admin Hosp, East Orange, NJ, 1964; prof med, Col Med Nj, beginning 1962; dir, Div Hepatic Metab & Nutrit, 1959-1991; assoc prof, NJ Med Sch, 1959-1962; USPHS spec res fel, 1958-1959; res assoc, Harvard Univ, 1958-1959; Intern med, dir Clin Invest & Outpatient Dept, 1948-1958; consult, US Naval Hosp, St Albans, 1948; resident, Jersey City Med Ctr, 1945-1948; Intern med, Jersey City Med Ctr, 1944-1945. **Memberships:** Soc Exp Biol & Med; Nat Med Asn; Master Am Col Physicians; Asn Am Physicians; Am Asn Study Liver Dis (pres 1970); Int Assoc Study Liver (pres 1972-1976); Asn Acad Minority Physicians (pres 1986-1988). **Research Statement & Publications:** Pathogenesis and treatment of end stage liver disease; factors which control hepatic nucleic acid and collagen synthesis; mechanism and treatment of portal hypertension, nutrition and liver disease; immunology and genetic of liver disease. **Mailing Address:** NJ Med Sch, 90 Bergen St, Suite 2100, Newark, NJ 07109. **Fax:** 973-972-6761.

LEE-WHITING, GRAHAM EDWARD, CHARGED-PARTICLE OPTICAL SYSTEMS, PHYSICAL BOUNDARY-VALUE PROBLEMS. **Personal Data:** b Iroquois Falls, Ont, March 2, 1926; m 1952. **Education:** Univ Toronto, BASc, 1948, MA, 1949; Bristol Univ, PhD (theoret physics), 1952. **Professional Experience:** RETIRED; emer researcher, Theoret Physics Br, beginning 1991; head, theoret physics br, 1969-1991; theoret physicist, Atomic Energy Can Res Co, 1952-1969. **Memberships:** Can Asn Physicists; Am Phys Soc. **Research Statement & Publications:** The theory of focusing and dispersive systems for charged particles; beta spectrometers using magnetic and or electric fields. **Mailing Address:** Chalk River Labs, AECL Res, Chalk River, ON K0J 1J0, Can.

LEEZER, ROGER W, MATHEMATICS. **Education:** Calif State Univ, Sacramento, PhD. **Professional Experience:** FAC, CALIF STATE UNIV, SACRAMENTO, as of 2006. **Mailing Address:** Dept Math, Calif State Univ, 6000 J St, Sacramento, CA 95819-6051. **Fax:** 916-278-5586. **E-Mail:** leezerr@saclink.csus.edu

LEFAR, MORTON SAUL, ORGANIC CHEMISTRY. **Personal Data:** b New York, NY, April 11, 1937; m 1961, c 2. **Education:** Brooklyn Col, BS, 1958, MA, 1962; Rutgers Univ, PhD (chem), 1965. **Professional Experience:** VPRES, EPOLIN INC, 1989-; consult, Merrill-Lynch, 1980-1989; consult pharmacuet, 1979-1981; lectr chem, Rutgers Univ, 1979-1981; dir qual control, Hoechst-Roussel Pharmaceut Inc, 1975-1978; mgr anal chem, Rhodia Inc, 1969-1974; sr scientist, Warner-Lambert Res Inst, 1968-1969; sect head org chem div nutrit, Food & Drug Admin, Wash, DC, 1966-1968; res chemist, Inst Environ Med, Med Sch, NY Univ, 1958-1960. **Memberships:** Am Pharmaceut Asn; Am Chem Soc; Sigma Xi. **Research Statement & Publications:** Natural products chemistry; analytical chemistry; photochemistry; environmental health; analytical methods development on new pharmaceuticals; new business ventures. **Mailing Address:** Epolin Inc, 358-364 Adams St, Newark, NJ 07105. **Fax:** 973-465-5353.

LEFCOE, NEVILLE, PHYSIOLOGY. **Personal Data:** b Montreal, Que, July 19, 1925; m 1954, c 4. **Education:** McGill Univ, BSc, 1946; Vanderbilt Univ, MD, 1950; FRCP (C), 1956. **Professional Experience:** PVT PRACT, 1994-; prof, Univ Western Ont, 1972-1994; from instr to assoc prof med, Univ Western Ont, 1957-1972. **Memberships:** Am Fedn Clin Res; Can Soc Clin Invest. **Research Statement & Publications:** Pulmonary physiology, chiefly exercise physiology, cellular mechanisms in bronchial smooth muscle and the domestic microenvironment. **Mailing Address:** 219 Oxford St W Ste 201, London, ON N6H 1S5, Can.

LE FEBVRE, EDWARD ELLSWORTH, ENVIRONMENTAL CHEMISTRY, ANALYTICAL CHEMISTRY. **Personal Data:** b Great Falls, Mont, March 9, 1933. **Education:** Univ Wash, BA, 1954; Univ Tex, San Antonio, MS, 1975. **Professional Experience:** CHEMIST, VA DIV CONSOL LABS, as of 2002; Comnr, Nat Cert Comn Chem & Chem Eng, 1977-1981; chief, Anal Serv Div, Occup & Environ Health Lab, USAF, beginning 1976; dep chief, Analytical Div, USAF, 1974-1976; chief, Environ Studies Br, Environ Health Lab, Kelly AFB, Tex, 1968-1974; res chemist, Sch Aerospace Med, Brooks AFB, Tex, 1966-1968; USAF, beginning 1962; chief, Analytical Div, Environ Health Lab, McClellan AFB, Calif, 1962-1966; chemist, State Health Dept, Helena, Mont, 1958-1962. **Memberships:** Am Chem Soc; Am Indust Hyg Asn; Am Inst Chemists; Am Conf Govt Indust Hygenists. **Mailing Address:** 12915 Red Chestnut Dr, Midlothian, VA 23112.

LE FEBVRE, EUGENE ALLEN, CONSERVATION ECOLOGY. **Personal Data:** b St Paul, Minn, October 18, 1929. **Education:** Univ Minn, BS, 1952, AP, 1953, MS, 1958, PhD (zoology), 1962. **Professional Experience:** ASSOC PROF EMER ZOOL, SOUTHERN ILL UNIV, 1993-; Southern Ill Univ, Carbondale, 1986-1987; grantee, Nat Register Archives, 1986; grantee, Int Documentation & Commun Ctr, 1981-1982; grantee, NSF, Midway Island, 1969-1973 & 1980-1983; from asst prof to assoc prof, Southern Ill Univ, 1966-1991; co-prin investr, NIH grant, 1963-1965; res assoc, Mus Natural Hist, 1961-1966; Res assoc, NIH grant, 1960-1965; res fel ornith, Mus Natural Hist, 1960-1961;

teaching asst ornith & zool, Univ Minn, Minneapolis, 1953-1959; co-prin investr, Nat Register Archives. **Memberships:** AAAS; Am Ornith Union; Cooper Ornith Soc; Ecol Soc Am; Am Inst Biol Sci; Brit Ornith Union; Sigma Xi. **Research Statement & Publications:** Conservation biology; habitat requirements of birds; environmental toxicology; biological diversity. **Mailing Address:** Dept Zool, Southern Ill Univ, Carbondale, IL 62901. **E-Mail:** glefebur@siu.edu

LEFEBVRE, MARIO, STOCHASTIC PROCESSES, STOCHASTIC CONTROL THEORY, HYDROLOGY. **Personal Data:** b Montreal, Que. **Education:** Univ Montreal, BS, 1979, MS, 1980; Univ Cambridge, Eng, PhD (math), 1984. **Professional Experience:** FULL PROF MATH, ECOLE POLYTECH MONTREAL, 1998-; assco prof math, Ecole Polytech Montreal, 1990-1998; asst prof, Ecole Polytech Montreal, 1985-1990; lectr math, Royal Mil Col St-Jean, 1984-1985. **Memberships:** Inst Math Statist. **Research Statement & Publications:** Applied probability and stochastic control theory; electrical and civil engineering applications. **Mailing Address:** Dept Math Ind Eng, Ecole Polytech, Montreal, PQ H3C 3A7, Can. **Fax:** 514-340-4463. **E-Mail:** mlefebvre@polymtl.ca

LEFEBVRE, PAUL ALVIN, DEVELOPMENTAL BIOLOGY. **Personal Data:** b Washington, DC, March 12, 1950; m 1981. **Education:** Univ Va, BA, 1972; Yale Univ, MPhil, 1978, PhD (biol), 1980. **Professional Experience:** PROF PLANT BIOL, UNIV MINN, TWIN CITIES, as of 2002; assoc prof genetics & cell biol, Univ Minn, beginning 1988; asst prof, Univ Minn, 1982-1988; Fel, Mass Inst Technol, 1980-1981. **Memberships:** Genetics Soc Am; Am Soc Microbiol. **Research Statement & Publications:** Regulation of expression of genes for flagellar proteins in Chlamydomonas; genetics and molecular biology of nitrate reductase. **Mailing Address:** Dept Plant Biol, Univ Minn, 250 Biol Sci Ctr, 1445 Gortner Ave, St Paul, MN 55108. **Fax:** 612-625-5754. **E-Mail:** pete@biosci.cbs.umn.edu

LEFEBVRE, RENE, MEDICINE. **Personal Data:** b Verdun, Que, April 5, 1923; m 1951, c 2. **Education:** Col Montreal, BA, 1944; Univ Montreal, MD, 1950; Univ Pa, DSc(med), 1954. **Professional Experience:** RETIRED; from asst prof to assoc prof, Univ Montreal, 1960-1970; pathologist, Hotel Dieu Hosp, 1954-1989; prof path, fac med, Univ Montreal. **Memberships:** Can Asn Path (pres-elect, 1965-1966, pres, 1966-). **Research Statement & Publications:** Pathology of kidney. **Mailing Address:** 850 38th Ave, Lachine, PQ H8T 2C3, Can.

LEFEBVRE, RICHARD HAROLD, SCIENCE EDUCATION. **Personal Data:** b Detroit, Mich, December 11, 1933; m 1959, Sandra; c Lauryl, Jeffrey & W Curtis. **Education:** Univ Mich, BS, 1957; Univ Kans, MS, 1961; Northwestern Univ, PhD (geol), 1966. **Professional Experience:** EMER PROF, GRAND VALLEY STATE UNIV, AS OF 1999; prof geol, Grand Valley State Univ, beginning 1975; geologist, US Geol Surv, 1975-1985; chmn dept, Grand Valley State Univ, 1970-1975 & 1985-1988; from asst prof to assoc prof, Grand Valley State Univ, 1967-1973; asst prof geol, Univ Ga, 1965-1967. **Memberships:** Nat Asn Geol Teachers. **Research Statement & Publications:** Flood basalts of the northwestern United States; remote sensing of Holocene basaltic lava flows, especially Craters of the Moon National Monument, Idaho. **Mailing Address:** 4555 Jacob Sw, Grandville, MI 49401. **E-Mail:** lefebvrd@gvsu.edu

LEFEBVRE, XAVIER P, BIOCHEMICAL ENGINEERING. **Personal Data:** b Montee Notre Dame, France, January 16, 1966. **Education:** Nat Upper Sch Chem Eng, France, BS, 1988; Ga Inst Technol, PhD (biochem eng), 1992. **Professional Experience:** DIR, CLINCIAL SERVS, PHASE FORWARD INC, as of 2004; SR SCIENTIST, ABIOMED, 1992-; Teaching asst, Ga Inst Technol, 1987-1992. **Memberships:** Biomed Eng Soc. **Mailing Address:** 40 Homsy Lane, Needham, MA 02194.

LEFER, ALLAN MARK, CARDIOVASCULAR PHYSIOLOGY, PHARMACOLCOGY. **Personal Data:** b New York, NY, February 1, 1936; m 1959, Mary; c Debra L, David J, Barry L & Leslie A. **Education:** Adelphi Col, BA, 1957; Western Reserve Univ, MA, 1959; Univ Ill, PhD (physiol), 1962. **Honors & Awards:** Carl Wiggers Memorial Award, 2004. **Professional Experience:** PROF EMER PHYSIOL, JEFFERSON MED COL, THOMAS JEFFERSON UNIV, 2001-; vis prof, Wellcome Found, 1985-1986; prof physiol & chmn dept, Jefferson Med Col, Thomas Jefferson Univ, 1974-2001; vis prof & USPHS sr fel, Hadassah Med Sch, Hebrew Univ, Israel, 1971-1972; estab investr, Am Heart Asn, 1968-1973; from asst prof to prof, Sch Med, Univ Va, 1964-1972; USPHS fel, 1962-1964; instr physiol, Case Western Res Univ, 1962-1964; mem, Study Sect Pharmacol, NIH; mem, Int Study Group Res Cardiac Metab & Pancreatic Study Group; mem coun basic sci, Circulation Coun, Am Heart Asn; mem comt pub affairs, Fedn Am Socs Exp Biol; ed, Circulatory Shock; consult, Task Group Shock, NIH. **Memberships:** Am Physiol Soc; Am Heart Asn; Soc Exp Biol & Med; Am Soc Pharmacol & Exp Therapeut; Soc Leukocyte Biol; Shock Soc (pres, 1983-1984); Int Soc Heart Res. **Research Statement & Publications:** Cardiovascular effects of adrenal hormones; humoral regulation of myocardial contractility; nitric oxide biology; experimental myocardial infarction; atherosclerosis pathophysiology; pathogenesis of circulatory shock; prostaglandins and thromboxanes; pharmacology of coronary circulation; PAF and other lipid mediators; endothelial function; adhesion molecules. **Mailing Address:** Jefferson Med Col, Thomas Jefferson Univ, 102 Locust St, Philadelphia, PA 19107-6799. **E-Mail:** allefer@aol.com

LEFEVER, ROBERT ALLEN, SOLID STATE CHEMISTRY, MATERIALS SCIENCE. **Personal Data:** b York, Pa, May 29, 1927; m 1946, Juanita Mae; c Janice Marie, Norma Jean & Allen Brian. **Education:** Juniata Col, BS, 1950; Mass Inst Technol, PhD (inorg chem), 1953. **Professional Experience:** RETIRED; ENG CONSULT, 1984-1990, plant mgr, Ferrite Memory Core Plant, 1980-1982; Consult, Spectrotherm Corp, 1974-1977 & Luxtron Corp, 1977-1980; mgr, Process Eng Dept, Ampex Corp, 1977-1980; dir mat preparation, Sch Eng, Univ Southern Calif, 1974-1977; supvr, Mat Res Div, Sandia Labs, 1963-1974; staff mem, Gen Tel & Electronics Labs, Inc, 1961-1963; head chem physics group, Hughes Res Labs, 1959-1961; mem tech staff, Hughes Res Labs, 1958-1959; sr scientist, Va Inst Sci Res, 1956-1958; Res chemist, Linde Co, 1953-1956. **Memberships:** Am Phys Soc; Am Chem Soc; Am Ceramic Soc; fel Am Inst Chemists; Sigma Xi; Am Asn Crystal Growth. **Research Statement & Publications:** Single crystal growth; growth mechanisms and characterization; sintering processes and mechanisms; ferrites; garnets; metal and rare earth oxides; semiconductors; phosphors; thermoelectrics. **Mailing Address:** 1940 S Broadway, Grand Junction, CO 81503. **E-Mail:** nita27@msn.com

LEFEVRE, GEORGE JR, GENETICS, CYTOGENETICS. **Personal Data:** b Columbia, Mo, September 13, 1917; m 1972, c 3. **Education:** Univ Mo, AB, 1937, AM, 1939, PhD (genetics), 1949. **Professional Experience:** RETIRED; emer prof biol, Calif State Univ, Northridge, 1984-1990; ed, Genetics, 1976-1981; prof, Calif State Univ, Northridge, 1965-1984; chmn, Calif State Univ, Northridge, 1965-1979; consult, NIH, 1962-1966, 1979-1983; dir biol labs, Harvard Univ, 1959-1965; consult, NSF, 1959-1962; prog dir genetic biol, NSF, 1956-1959; from asst prof to assoc prof biol, Univ Utah, 1949-1956; instr zool, Univ Mo, 1947-1948; res biologist, Oak Ridge Nat Lab, 1946-1947; Asst zool, Columbia Univ, 1941-1942. **Memberships:** Genetics Soc Am (treas, 1972-1975); Sigma Xi. **Research Statement & Publications:** Radiation genetics of Drosophila melanogaster; comparative mutagenesis; cytogenetics. **Mailing Address:** 14967 Marquette St, Moorpark, CA 93021.

LEFEVRE, HARLAN W, NUCLEAR PHYSICS. **Personal Data:** b Great Falls, Mont, May 19, 1929; div, c 8. **Education:** Reed Col, BA, 1951; Univ Idaho, MS, 1957; Univ Wis, PhD (physics), 1961. **Professional Experience:** PROF EMER PHYSICS, UNIV ORE, as of 2003; Lawrence Livermore Nat Lab, 1976-1977 & Univ Melbourne, 1988-1989; prof physics, Univ Ore, beginning 1971; vis physicist, Australian Nat Univ, 1968-1969; Consult, Lawrence Livermore Lab, Univ Calif, 1962-; assoc prof, Univ Ore, 1961-1971; Physicist, Hanford Atomic Prod Oper, Gen Elec Co, Wash, 1951-1958. **Memberships:** Am Phys Soc. **Research Statement & Publications:** Experimental nuclear physics; nuclear reactions; fast neutron spectrometry; scanning microscopy and analysis. **Mailing Address:** Dept Physics, Univ Ore, 145 Willamette Hall, Eugene, OR 97403. **Fax:** 541-346-5861. **E-Mail:** hwl@conch.uoregon.edu

LEFEVRE, MARIAN E WILLIS, PHYSIOLOGY. **Personal Data:** b Washington, DC, January 21, 1923; m 1948, Paul G; c Louise V, Vanessa F & Ralph S. **Education:** Iowa State Univ, BS, 1944; Univ Pa, MS, 1947; Univ Louisville, PhD (physiol), 1969. **Professional Experience:** RETIRED; scientist, Brookhaven Nat Lab, 1978-1985; assoc scientist, Brookhaven Nat Lab, 1975-1978; asst prof physiol, Mt Sinai Sch Med, 1973-1978; Res collabr, Brookhaven Nat Lab, 1968-1975; Assoc, Mt Sinai Sch Med, 1968-1973. **Memberships:** Am Physiol Soc; Am Gastroenterol Asn; Am Soc Cell Biol; Soc Exp Biol & Med. **Research Statement & Publications:** Structure and function of multicellular membranes; ion transport and metabolism; intestinal barrier function. **Mailing Address:** 15 Agassiz Rd, Woods Hole, MA 02543.

LEFF, ALAN R, MEDICINE, PULMONARY DISEASE SUBPECIALTY. **Personal Data:** b Pittsburgh, Pa, May 23, 1945; m 1975, Donna; c Marni, Karen & Alison. **Education:** Oberlin Col, BA, 1967; Univ Rochester, MD, 1971; Am Bd Internal Med, cert, 1976; Am Bd Int Med, Pulm Dis subspec, cert, 1978. **Honors & Awards:** Assoc Am Phyicians, 1995-; Am Soc Clin Invest 1984-, ATS Citation of Merit, 1999; Best Doctors in Am, 2003. **Professional Experience:** Dir, Glaxo SK, Center Excellence Asthma 2000-; ed, Am J Respir Crit Care Med, 1994-1999; PROF MED, ANAESTHESIA & CRIT CARE & COMT PHARMACOL, UNIV CHICAGO, 1989-; HEAD PULMONARY & CRIT CARE MED, ANAESTHESIA & CRIT CARE & COMT PHARMACOL, UNIV CHICAGO, 1989-; assoc prof anesthesia & crit care, Pulmonary Med Serv, Dept Med, Sect Pulmonary & Crit Care Med, 1988-1989; head, Pulm & Crit Care Med, Univ Chicago & Michael Reese Hosps, 1987-1989; mem prog comt, Am Thoracic Soc, 1986-; dir, Pulmonary Med Serv, Dept Med, Sect Pulmonary & Crit Care Med, 1984-1987; standing counr, Am Fedn Clin Res, 1983-1987; dir, Pulmonary Exercise Lab, 1983-1987; asst prof, Comt Clin Pharmacol, Div Biol Sci, 1983-1985; dir, Respiratory Serv, Hyde Park Community Hosp, 1982-1989; consult, adv respiratory dis, Dept Pub Health, Chicago, 1980-1984; dir, Pulmonary Function Labs, Univ Chicago Hosps & Clins, 1979-1987; asst prof med, Pulmonary Sect, Pritzer Sch Med, Univ Chicago, 1979-1985; postdoctoral res fel, Cardiovasc Res Inst, Univ Calif, San Francisco, 1977-1979; consult, Tuberc Prog, Dept Pub Health, San Francisco, 1977-1979; clin fel pulmonary dis, Cardiovasc Res Inst, Univ Calif, San Francisco, 1976-1977; intern internal med, Univ Mich Hosp, 1971-1972; intern internal med, House Off II, III internal med, 1974-1976; assoc attend physician, Cook Co Hosp, 1973-1974; med officer, Tuberc Br, Ctr Dis Control, USPHS, 1972-1974; asst tuberc control officer, Bd Health, Chicago, 1972-1974; PROF PEDIAT, NEUROBIOLOGY PHARM PHYSIOL. **Memberships:** Am Soc Clin Invest Assoc. Am. Physicians; Cent Soc Clin Invest; Am Thoracic Soc; Am Col Physicians; Sigma Xi; Am Soc Internal Med; Int Union Tuberc; Am Fedn Clin Res; Am Physiol Soc; Am Soc Pharmacol & Exp Therapeut. **Research Statement & Publications:** Investigate mechanisms of immunological regulation of inflammation in asthma and COPD. **Mailing Address:** Dept Med, Univ Chicago, AMB W656 (MC 6076) M/C 6076 5841 S Md Ave, Chicago, IL 60637-1463. **E-Mail:** aleff@medicine.bsd.uchicago.edu

LEFF, HARVEY SHERWIN, THERMAL PHYSICS. **Personal Data:** b Chicago, Ill, July 24, 1937; American citizen; m 1958, Ellen; c Lisa, Robyn, Jordan & Jeremy. **Education:** Ill Inst Technol, BS, 1959; Northwestern Univ, MS, 1960; Univ Iowa, PhD (physics), 1963. **Professional Experience:** PROF EMER, PHYSICS, CALIF STATE POLYTECH UNIV, POMONA, 1995-; assoc ed, Am J Physics, 1992-; workshop leader, Pre-Col Teachers Energy Ideas & Physics Toys, 1986-; prof & chair, physics dept, Calif State Poly Univ, Pomona, 1983-1995; scientist, Oak Ridge assoc Univ, 1979-1983; vis prof physics, Col Sci & Eng, Harvey Mudd Col, 1977-1978; prof physics, Dept Phys Sci, Chicago State Univ, 1975-1979; assoc prof & chmn, Dept Phys Sci, Chicago State Univ, 1971-1975; from asst prof to assoc prof, Case Inst Technol, 1964-1971; res assoc physics, Case Inst Technol, 1963-1964; physic coordr, Inst Teaching & Learning, Calif State Univ. **Memberships:** Am Asn Physics Teachers; Am Phys Soc; Sigma Xi. **Research Statement & Publications:** Foundations of thermodynamics; thermal efficiency of heat engines; Maxwell's Demon; physics of light bulbs; physics of toys; analysis of energy-related topics relevant to energy policymaking. **Mailing Address:** Dept Physics, Calif State Poly Univ, 3801 W Temple Ave Bldg 8 Rm 227, Pomona, CA 91768. **Fax:** 909-869-5090. **E-Mail:** hsleff@csupomona.edu

LEFF, JUDITH, MICROBIOLOGY, BIOTECHNOLOGY. **Personal Data:** b Vienna, Austria, July 6, 1935; American citizen; m 1961, Nathaniel; c Auraham, Anne & David. **Education:** Sorbonne, Lic natural sci, 1958, PhD (photobiol), 1961. **Professional Experience:** SR CONSULT FOOD TECHNOL, JLN ASSOCS, 1983-; appln chemist, Farrand Optical, 1979-1982; Nat Res Serv award, Albert Einstein Col Med, 1976-1977; NIH spec res fel, Albert Einstein Col Med, 1974-1979; NY Univ, 1971-1972 & Hebrew Univ, Jerusalem, 1972-1973; res assoc plant morphogenesis, Manhattan Col, 1967-1971; res assoc, Sch Med, Tufts Univ, 1966-1967; fel pharmacol, Sch Med, Tufts Univ, 1965; fel biol, Brandeis Univ, 1962-1963; res assoc photobiol, Nat Ctr Sci Res, Paris, 1961; Jr researcher photobiol seed germination, Nat Ctr Sci Res, Paris, 1960-1961. **Memberships:** Sigma Xi; Am Soc Microbiol; Inst Food Technol. **Research Statement & Publications:** Photobiology; chloroplast development; molecular biology; microbiology; nucleic acids as tools for solving physiological or developmental questions; microbiology of crown gall; replication of mitochondrial DNA in yeast; fluorescence spectroscopy; food and ingredient technology for the Kosher market. **Mailing Address:** 302 Howard Ave, Passaic, NJ 07055. **Fax:** 973-471-8389.

LEFF, TODD, MOLECULAR BIOLOGY. **Personal Data:** b Iowa City, Iowa, June 10, 1954. **Education:** Univ Iowa, BA, 1976; Ind Univ, PhD (molecular biol), 1982. **Honors & Awards:** Young Investr Award, Int Atherosclerosis Soc, 1989; Estab Investr Award, Am Heart Asn, 1990. **Professional Experience:** ASSOC PROF PATHOL, CTR INTEGRATIVE METAB & ENDOCRINE RES, WAYNE STATE UNIV, beginning 2002; res fel cell biol, Parke-Davis Pharmaceut Res, 1999-2001; assoc res fel cell biol, Parke-Davis Pharmaceut Res, 1994-1997; sr res assoc, Parke-Davis Pharmaceut, 1991-1994; asst prof biochem genetics & metab, Rockefeller Univ, 1985-1991; fel molecular biol, Univ Louie Pasteur, France, 1982-1985. **Memberships:** AAAS; NY Acad Sci; Am Soc Biochem & Molecular Biol. **Research Statement & Publications:** Molecular biology. **Mailing Address:** Dept Pathol, Sch Med, Wayne State Univ, 540 E Canfield Ave, Detroit, MI 48201.

LEFFAK, IRA MICHAEL, BIOCHEMISTRY. **Personal Data:** b New York, NY, October 13, 1947; m 1969, c 1. **Education:** City Col NY, BS, 1969; City Univ NY, PhD (biochem), 1976. **Professional Experience:** PROF BIOCHEM & MOLECULAR BIOL, WRIGHT STATE UNIV, as of 2003; NIH fel, 1976-1978; res fel biochem, Princeton Univ, 1976-1978; asst prof biochem, Wright State Univ, beginning 1970. **Memberships:** AAAS. **Research Statement & Publications:** Molecular biology of development; cell differentiation. **Mailing Address:** Dept Molecular Biol & Biol Chem, Wright State Univ, 136 Biol Sci Blg 3640 Colonel Gleen Hwy, Dayton, OH 45435-0001. **Fax:** 937-775-3730. **E-Mail:** michael.leffak@wright.edu

LEFFALL, LASALLE DOHENY, JR, SURGICAL ONCOLOGY. **Personal Data:** b Tallahassee, Fla, May 22, 1930; m 1956, c 1. **Education:** Fla A&M Univ, BS, 1948; Howard Univ, MD, 1952; Am Bd Surg, dipl, 1958. **Honorary Degrees:** DSc, Georgetown Univ, 1984, Fla A&M Univ, 1987, Clark Univ, 1989; LHD, Meharry Med Col, 1988. **Honors & Awards:** William H Sinkler Mem Award, Nat Med Asn, 1972; St George Medal, Am Cancer Soc, 1977; Florence Nightingale Award, 1982; Thomas Wyatt Turner Award, 1982; W Montague Cobb Mem Lectr, Nat Med Asn, 1984; James H Jackson Award, 1984; Roger L Brooke Distinguished Lectr, Brooke Army Med Ctr, 1986; Robert Wilson Kitchen, Jr Award, Am Cancer Soc, 1986; James Ewing Lectr & Medal, Soc Surg Oncol, 1987. **Professional Experience:** CHARLES R DREW PROF SURG, COL MED, HOWARD UNIV, 1996-; US Comt & Nat Orgn Comt, 13th Int Cancer Cong, 1979 & Nat Cancer Adv Bd, 1980; Nat Cancer Inst, 1972- & Am Cancer Soc, 1976-1977; Tissue & Organ Biol Sect, President's Panel Biomed Res, 1975; consult ed, J Nat Med Asn, 1973-; Diag Res Activ Group, Nat Cancer Inst, 1972-1975; Comt Study Surg Serv US, Am Col Surgeons & Am Surg Asn, 1972-1974; vis prof & lectr, numerous US & foreign univs, 1971-; consult, Walter Reed Army Med Ctr, 1971-; Surg Training Comt, Nat Inst Gen Med Sci, 1971-1972; prof lectr surg, Georgetown Univ, 1970-; prof surg & chmn dept, Howard Univ, 1970-1996; mem, Med & Sci Comt, Am Cancer Soc, 1970; actg dean, Howard Univ, 1970; consult, St Elizabeth's Hosp, 1966-1976; asst dean, Howard Univ, 1964-1970; actg co-ed, J Nat Med Asn, 1964-1965; pvt pract med, Wash, DC, 1962-; from asst prof to assoc prof surg, Howard Univ, 1962-1970; resident, Mem Sloan Kettering Cancer Ctr, NY, 1957-1959; Asst ed, J Nat Med Asn, 1955-1957; resident, Freedmen's Gen Hosp, Wash, DC, 1953-1957; Intern, Homer G Phillips Hosp, St Louis, 1952-1953; mem staff, Howard Univ Hosp. **Memberships:** Inst Med-Nat Acad Sci; Soc Surg Oncol (secy 1974-1976 pres 1978-1979); Am Cancer Soc (pres 1978-1979); Am Surg Asn; Am Chem Soc; AMA; fel Am Col Surgeons (secy 1983-). **Research Statement & Publications:** Cancer diseases; polyps and cancer of the coloectum; breast cancer; head and neck cancer; soft tissue sarcomas; author of more than 100 technical publications. **Mailing Address:** Dept Surg, Howard Univ, Tower Bldg Suite 4000, Washington, DC 20060. **E-Mail:** lleffall@fac.howard.edu

LEFFEK, KENNETH THOMAS, PHYSICAL ORGANIC CHEMISTRY, HISTORY OF CHEMISTRY. **Personal Data:** b Nottingham, Eng, October 15, 1934; Canadian citizen; m 1958, Janet M Wallace; c Katharine H & Geoffrey K. **Education:** Univ London, BSc, 1956, PhD (chem), 1959. **Professional Experience:** RETIRED; pres, Atlantic Can Chap, Royal Soc Arts, 1988-1991; prof chem, Dalhousie Univ, 1972-; dean grad studies, Dalhousie Univ, 1972-1990; Leverhulme vis fel, Univ Kent, Canterbury, 1967-1968; from asst prof to assoc prof, Dalhousie Univ, 1961-1972; Nat Res Coun Can fel, 1959-1961. **Memberships:** Fel Chem Inst Can (vpres, 1985-1986, pres, 1986-1987); Royal Soc Chem; Royal Soc Arts. **Research Statement & Publications:** Kinetics and mechanisms of organic reactions; primary and secondary kinetic deuterium isotope effects. **Mailing Address:** 980 Kentwood Terr, Victoria, BC V8Y 1A6, Can. **Fax:** 902-494-1310.

LEFFEL, ROBERT CECIL, PLANT BREEDING, GENETICS. **Personal Data:** b Woodbine, Md, April 26, 1925; m 1959, c 2. **Education:** Univ Md, BS, 1948; Iowa State Univ, MS, 1950, PhD, 1952. **Professional Experience:** RETIRED; FAO consult soybeans, India, 1987; FAO consult soybeans, Yugoslavia, 1983; res agronomist, agr Res Serv, 1983-1994; exec secy, Soybean Res Adv Inst, 1982-1984; staff scientist oilseed crop prod, Nat Prog Staff, USDA, 1976-1983; chief, Cell Cult & Nitrogen Fixtion Lab, 1975-1976; chief, Plant Nutrit Lab, 1972-1975; investigations leader, Agr Res Serv, 1962-1972; assoc prof agron, Univ Md, 1957-1962; res agronomist, Agr Res Serv, 1952-1957. **Memberships:** Crop Sci Soc Am; Am Soybean Asn. **Research Statement & Publications:** Soybean, forage crop and clover genetics; breeding and production; enhancing nitrogen metabolism of soybean; high protein soybeans. **Mailing Address:** 13275 Laurel Rd, Brogue, PA 17309.

LEFFELL, MARY S, IMMUNOGENETICS, IMMUNOLOGY. **Personal Data:** b Knoxville, Tenn, October 12, 1946. **Education:** Univ Tenn, BS, 1968; Univ NC, PhD (immunol), 1973; Am Bd Med Lab Immunol, dipl, 1979; Am Bd Histocompatibility & Immunogenetics, dipl, 1996. **Professional Experience:** PROF, SCH MED, MOLECULAR, MICROBIOL & IMMUNOL, JOHNS HOPKINS UNIV, as of 2006; DIR, IMMUNOGENETIC LAB, JOHNS HOPKINS UNIV, SCH MED, beginning 1989; assoc prof, dept med, Johns Hopkins Univ, 1989-2002; assoc prof surg & dir, Med Col Ga, Univ Ga, 1985-1989; from asst prof to assoc prof med, molecular, microbiol & immunol, Eastern Va Med Sch, 1979-1985; consult, EVIMEC, 1979-1985; dir, Immunol Lab, Eastern Va Med Sch, & Med Ctr Hosp, 1979-1985; fel, immunol, NC Mem Hosp, 1977-1979; res assoc, immunol, dept microbiol, Univ Tenn, 1973-1977. **Memberships:** Am Soc Histocompatability & Immunogenetics (pres 1995); Am Asn Immunologists; Am Soc Transplant Physicians; United Network Organ Sharing (vpres 1992-1993). **Research Statement & Publications:** Immunogenetics and transplanation immunology. **Mailing Address:** Dept Med, Johns Hopkins Univ, 2041 E Monument St, Baltimore, MD 21205. **Fax:** 410-955-0431. **E-Mail:** msleffel@jhmi.edu

LEFFERT, CHARLES BENJAMIN, ENERGY CONVERSION, CHEMICAL PHYSICS. **Personal Data:** b Logansport, Ind, May 22, 1922; m 1945. **Education:** Purdue Univ, BS, 1943; Univ Pittsburgh, MS, 1957; Wayne State Univ, PhD (chem eng), 1974. **Professional Experience:** PROF EMER CHEM ENG, WAYNE STATE UNIV, as of 2004; EMER DIR COL ENG ENERGY CTR, WAYNE STATE UNIV, beginning 1974; assoc prof chem eng, Wayne State Univ, beginning 1974; res asst, Res Inst Eng Sci, 1970-1974; sr res physicist, Res Labs, Gen Motors Corp, 1957-1970; asst physics, Univ Pittsburgh, 1952-1956; chem engr, Pittsburgh Consol Coal Co, 1949-1952; chem engr, res dept, Union Oil Co Calif, 1943-1949. **Memberships:** Am Phys Soc; Am Inst Chem Engrs; Sigma Xi. **Research Statement & Publications:** Chemical engineering. **Mailing Address:** Dept Chem Eng, Wayne State Univ, 1116 Eng Bldg, Troy, MI 48084-2688. **E-Mail:** c_leffert@wayne.edu

LEFFERT, HYAM LERNER, CELL BIOLOGY, ANIMAL CELL GROWTH CONTROL. **Personal Data:** b New York, NY, May 11, 1944; m 1987, Katherine; c 3. **Education:** Univ Rochester, BA, 1965; Brandeis Univ, MA, 1967; Albert Einstein Col Med, MD, 1971. **Professional Experience:** Res grant, NIH 1996-; PROF PHARMACOL & CTR MOLECULAR GENETICS, SCH MED, UNIV CALIF, SAN DIEGO, 1990-; John Simon Guggenheim fel, 1987-1988; Morton Grossman scholar, Am Gastroenterol Asn, 1987-1988; assoc prof pharmacol, Sch Med, Univ Calif, San Diego, 1982-1990; Nat Inst Arthritis, Nat Inst Alcohol Abuse & Alcoholism, 1980-; assoc prof med, Sch Med, Univ Calif, San Diego, 1980-1982; Nat Inst Arthritis, Metab & Digestive Dis, 1980; res grant, Nat Cancer Inst, 1976-1980; consult cell biol, Dept Nutrit Path, Mass Inst Technol, 1976; Nat Heart & Lung Inst, 1973- & Dept Med, Vet Admin Hosp, Dallas, 1974-; res grant, Nat Cancer Inst, NSF & Diabetes Asn Southern Calif, 1974; asst res prof cell biol, Salk Inst Biol Studies, 1973-1980; res assoc, Salk Inst Biol Studies, 1972-1973; fel, Salk Inst Biol Studies, 1971-1972. **Memberships:** Int Study Group Carcinoembryonic Proteins. **Research Statement & Publications:** Mechanism of liver regeneration, differentiation, gene expression and gene therapy. **Mailing Address:** Dept Pharmacol & Ctr Molecular Genetics, Univ Calif San Diego Med Sch, 9500 Gilman Dr Mail Code 0636, La Jolla, CA 92093-0636. **Fax:** 858-822-4184. **E-Mail:** hleffert@ucsd.edu

LEFFEW, KENNETH W, CHEMICAL ENGINEERING, POLYMER ENGINEERING. **Personal Data:** b Louisville, Ky, November 5, 1950; m 1969, c 3. **Education:** Univ Louisville, BS, 1973, MEng, 1973, PhD (chem eng), 1981. **Professional Experience:** Adj prof, Univ Louisville, 1978-1980; RES ASSOC, E I DU PONT DEL NEMOURS & CO, 1973-. **Memberships:** Am Inst Chem Engrs. **Research Statement & Publications:** Application of advanced process control to new process developments in large industrial projects. **Mailing Address:** Du Pont, Exp State Bldg 304 PO Box 80304, Wilmington, DE 19880-0304. **Fax:** 302-695-2504. **E-Mail:** kenneth.w.leffew@usa.dupont.co

LEFFINGWELL, JOHN C, ORGANIC CHEMISTRY. **Personal Data:** b Evanston, Ill, February 16, 1938; m 1960, c 3. **Education:** Rollins Col, BS, 1960; Emory Univ, MS, 1962, PhD (org chem), 1963. **Honors & Awards:** Philip Morris Award, Distinguished Achieve Tobacco Sci, Philip Morris Inc & Tobacco Sci, 1974; Rollins Col Distinguished Alumin Award, Sci, 1981. **Professional Experience:** EXEC VPRES, FOXFIRE FARMS INC as of 2006; PRES, LEFFINGWELL & ASSOCS, 1990-; dir, Foxfire Farms, Inc, 1985-; VPRES, FRANCHISE BEVERAGE PROD, DEL MONTE CORP, 1985-; vpres res & develop, Sunkist Soft Drinks, sr vpres, 1978-1985; vpres, Aromatics Int, 1975-1977; head flavor develop, R J Reynolds Tobacco Co, 1973-1975; head flavor res, R J Reynolds Industs Inc, 1970-1973; res chemist, Org Chem Div, Glidden Co, Fla, 1964-1965 & R J Reynolds Tobacco Co, 1965-1970; NIH fel, 1963-1964; res assoc org chem, Columbia Univ, 1963-1964. **Memberships:** Am Chem Soc; Royal Soc Chem; Inst Food Technologists. **Research Statement & Publications:** Natural products; flavor chemistry; olfaction; consumer products. **Mailing Address:** 4699 Arbor Hill Rd, Canton, GA 30115-8162. **E-Mail:** leffingwell@mindspring.com

LEFFLER, AMOS J, INORGANIC CHEMISTRY, PHYSICAL CHEMISTRY. **Personal Data:** b New York, NY, September 9, 1924; m 1949, c 3. **Education:** Brooklyn Col, BS, 1949; Univ Chicago, PhD (inorg chem), 1953. **Professional Experience:** RETIRED; prof chem, Villanova Univ, beginning 1975; sr res assoc, Nat Acad Sci-Nat Res Coun, 1973; assoc prof, Villanova Univ, 1965-1975; res assoc chem, Arthur D Little Inc, 1960-1965; res chemist, Stauffer Chem Co, 1955-1960; chemist, Callery Chem Co, 1952-1955; Am Inst Chemists Award, Brooklyn Col, 1949. **Memberships:** Am Chem Soc; Royal Soc Chem. **Research Statement & Publications:** Inorganic and physical chemistry, especially boron and metallorganic chemistry, catalysis and metal oxides and fluorine chemistry. **Mailing Address:** 408 N Sproul Rd, Broomall, PA 19008.

LEFFLER, CHARLES WILLIAM, CARDIOVASCULAR PHYSIOLOGY, PERINATAL PHYSIOLOGY. **Personal Data:** b Cleveland, Ohio, May 21, 1947; m 1968, Robin; c Noelle. **Education:** Univ Miami, BS, 1969; Univ Fla, MS, 1971, PhD (zoology), 1974. **Professional Experience:** DIR, LAB RES NEONATAL PHYSIOL, HEALTH SCI CTR, UNIV TENN, MEMPHIS, 1990-; prof pediat, Health Sci Ctr, Univ Tenn, Memphis, 1989; PROF PHYSIOL & BIOPHYS, HEALTH SCI CTR, UNIV TENN, MEMPHIS, 1986-; estab investr, Am Heart Asn, 1982-1987; from asst prof to assoc prof, Lab Res Neonatal Physiol, 1977-1986; asst prof physiol & biophys, Univ Louisville, 1976-1977; fel, Univ Fla, 1974-1976; coun fel, Univ Fla, 1973-1974; teaching asst zool, Univ Fla, 1969-1973. **Memberships:** Am Physiol Soc; Soc Exp Biol & Med; AAAS; Sigma Xi; Am Heart Asn; Soc Pediat Res. **Research Statement & Publications:** Vascular biology; paracrine/autocrine mediators in control of perinatal circulation; cerebral hemodynamics in the newborn; lipid mediators. **Mailing Address:** Dept Physiol & Biophys, 894 Union Ave NA427 3rd Fl Nash Res Bldg, Memphis, TN 38163. **E-Mail:** cleffler@utmem.edu

LEFFLER, ESTHER BARBARA, PHYSICAL CHEMISTRY. **Personal Data:** b Clearfield, Pa, February 1, 1925. **Education:** Pa State Univ, BS, 1945; Univ Va, PhD (chem), 1950. **Professional Experience:** CONSULT, 1988-; assoc dean, Sch Sci, 1978-1984; resident dir, Calif State Univ Int Prog UK, 1974-1975; res assoc, Oxford Univ, 1974-1975; actg chmn dept, Calif State Polytech Univ, 1973-1974; from asst prof to prof chem, Calif State Polytech Univ, 1967-1988; res assoc & vis lectr, Stanford Univ, 1966-1967; chmn dept, Sweet Briar Col, 1956-1959 & 1960-1966; from asst prof to prof chem, Sweet Briar Col, 1953-1966; instr chem, Randolph-Macon Woman's Col, 1949-1953; asst chemother, Stanford Res Labs, Am Cyanamid Co, 1945-1946. **Memberships:** Sigma Xi. **Research Statement & Publications:** Software development for science education. **Mailing Address:** 19950 Esquiline Ave, Walnut, CA 91789.

LEFFLER, HARRY REX, PLANT PHYSIOLOGY, PLANT GENETICS. **Personal Data:** b Rensselaer, Ind, September 20, 1942; m 1971, c 3. **Education:** Iowa State Univ, BS, 1964; Purdue Univ, MS, 1967, PhD (plant physiol), 1970. **Professional Experience:** AGRON CONSULT, 1992-; plant physiologist, DeKalb Pfizer Genetics Co, 1985-1992; assoc ed, Dekalb-Pfizer, 1985-1988; assoc ed, Agron J, 1982-1985; plant physiologist, Cotton Physiol & Genetics Unit, Agr Res Serv, USDA, 1972-1985; res assoc hort, Purdue Univ, 1971-1972; res assoc agron, Univ Ill, 1970-1971. **Memberships:** Am Soc Agron; Am Soc Plant Physiologists; Crop Sci Soc Am. **Research Statement & Publications:** Physiological genetics of seed development. **Mailing Address:** Mccabe Realtors Gmac Real Estate, 120 W Hillcrest Dr, Dekalb, IL 60115. **Fax:** 815-756-7258. **E-Mail:** Harry.Leffler@comcast.net

LEFFORD, MAURICE J, IMMUNOLOGY, MICROBIOLOGY. **Personal Data:** b London, Eng, November 27, 1930; American citizen. **Education:** Univ London, Eng, BS, 1955. **Professional Experience:** EMER PROF, DEPT IMMUNOL & MICROBIOL, WAYNE STATE UNIV, AS OF 2004; prof, Dept Immunol & Microbiol, Sch Med, Wayne State Univ, beginning 1985; Sci Working Group Immunol Leprosy, WHO, 1976-1980 & US Tuberculosis Panel, US-Japan Coop Med Sci Prog, 1984-1988; chmn, Mycobact Div, Am Soc Microbiol, 1984; assoc prof, Dept Immunol & Microbiol, Sch Med, Wayne State Univ, 1979-1985; mem, Sci Group Leprosy, Nat Inst Allergy & Infectious Dis, 1976; assoc mem, Trudeau Inst, NY, 1975-1979; asst mem, Trudeau Inst, NY, 1971-1975; mem, Unit Lab

Studies Tuberc, Brit Med Res Coun, Royal Postgrad Med Sch, 1963-1971; resident path, St Bartholomew's Hosp, London, 1959-1963; resident internal med, Royal Victoria Hosp, Bournemouth, 1957-1959. **Memberships:** Am Asn Immunologists; Am Soc Microbiol; Int Leprosy Asn. **Mailing Address:** Dept Benefits Admin, Wayne State Univ, 0113 Lande Campus, Detroit, MI 48201-1908. **E-Mail:** aa1904@wayne.edu

LEFKOFF, MERLE, SCIENCE ADMINISTRATION. **Education:** Emory Univ, MA, PhD. **Professional Experience:** CONSULT, MERLE LEFKOFF & ASSOC, 1977-. **Mailing Address:** Merle Lefkoff & Assoc, 624 Agua Fria St, Santa Fe, NM 87501.

LEFKOWITZ, BONNIE, PUBLIC HEALTH. **Education:** Univ Md, BA, 1960; Harvard Univ, MPA, 1975. **Professional Experience:** Co-chair, White House Task Force Health Care Reform, 1993; prog dir, Interagency Comt Infant Mortality, Health Resources & Servs Admin, Dept Health & Human Servs, USPHS, 1990-1992; ASSOC BUR DIR EVAL, ANALYSIS & RES, BUR PRIMARY HEALTH CARE, DEPT HEALTH & HUMAN SERVS, USPHS, 1983-; Fed exec fel, Brookings Inst, 1981; dir, Div Health Resources & Servs Anal, 1977-1982; prin analyst, Cong Budget Off, 1975-1977; Dir substance abuse & health servs anal, NY City Health Servs Admin, 1970-1974. **Research Statement & Publications:** strategic planning health systems; change and its impact on safety net providers; development of need criteria; state-based planning. **Mailing Address:** Bur Primary Health Care Eval Analysis & Res, HRSA, Rockville, MD 20857.

LEFKOWITZ, DORIS LYNNE, CELLULAR IMMUNOLOGY, MACROPHAGE ACTIVATION. **Personal Data:** b Ellenville, NY, June 27, 1943; m 1979, Stanley S; c Michael S. **Education:** Univ Miami, BS, 1966; Tex Tech Univ, MS, 1978, PhD (med microbiol), 1986. **Professional Experience:** ASSOC PROF BIOL SCI, TEX TECH UNIV, 1992-; asst prof, Tex Tech Univ, 1986-1992. **Memberships:** Am Soc Microbiol; Soc Exp Biol Med; Asn Med Lab Immunologists. **Research Statement & Publications:** Myeloperoxides as an endogenous immunoregulatory substance; cocaine effects on leukocyte functions. **Fax:** 806-742-2712.

LEFKOWITZ, IRVING, SYSTEMS & CONTROL ENGINEERING. **Personal Data:** b New York, NY, July 8, 1921; m 1955, MadelynMoinester; c Deborah & Daniel. **Education:** Cooper Union Sch Eng, BChE, 1943; Case Inst Technol, MS, 1955, PhD (control eng), 1958. **Honors & Awards:** Control Heritage Award, Am Automatic Control Coun. **Professional Experience:** PROF EMER SYSTS ENG, CASE WESTERN RES UNIV, as of 2004; CHIEF CONSULT, CONTROL SOFT INC, 1987-; chmn, Comt Indust Systs Control, Control Systs Soc, 1984-1985; chmn, Systs Eng Comt, Int Fedn Automatic Control, 1978-1981; res fel, Int Inst Appl Systs Anal, 1974-1975; chmn, Dept Systs Eng, 1970-1974 & 1980-1983; prof systs eng & chmn eng, Control Indust Systs Prog, 1965-1987; NATO fel, 1962-1963; dir, Control Indust Systs Prog, 1958-1985; from asst prof to assoc prof eng, Case Western Res Univ, 1958-1965; res assoc instrumentation eng, Case Western Res Univ, 1953-1958; head instrumentation res, J E Seagram & Sons, Inc, 1951-1953; instrument engr, J E Seagram & Sons, Inc, 1947-1951; instrument engr, Calvert Distilling Co, 1944-1947. **Memberships:** Fel AAAS; fel Inst Elec & Electronics Engrs; Int Fedn Automatic Control. **Research Statement & Publications:** Hierarchical computer control; control of industrial processes; energy conservation through integrated systems control. **Mailing Address:** Dept Systs Eng, Case Western Res Univ, 706 Olin Bldg, Univ Circle, Cleveland, OH 44106. **E-Mail:** ixl@po.cwru.edu

LEFKOWITZ, LEWIS BENJAMIN, MEDICINE. **Personal Data:** b Dallas, Tex, December 18, 1930; m Judith; c David H, Gerald L & Paul L. **Education:** Denison Univ, BA, 1951; Univ Tex Southwest Med Sch Dallas, MD, 1956. **Professional Experience:** PROF EMER, SCH MED, VANDERBILT UNIV, 2001-; prof prev med, Sch Med, Vanderbilt Univ, 1978-2001; assoc clin prof internal med, Meharry Med Col, 1978-1985; clin prof family & community med, Meharry Med Col, 1978-1981; consult, US Army Hosp, Ft Campbell, Ky, 1969-1985; asst clin prof internal med, Meharry Med Col, 1966-1978; from asst prof to assoc prof, Sch Med, Vanderbilt Univ, 1965-1978; USPHS trainee infectious dis, Univ Ill, 1962-1965; USPHS res fel, Univ Ill, 1961-1962; instr, Univ Tex Southwest Med Sch Dallas, 1960-1961; USPHS res fel med, Univ Tex Southwest Med Sch Dallas, 1959-1960. **Memberships:** Am Pub Health Asn; Community-Campus Partnerships Health. **Research Statement & Publications:** Epidemiology and pathogenesis of infectious diseases; health care delivery. **Mailing Address:** Vanderbilt Univ Sch Med, Nashville, TN 37232-4245. **Fax:** 615-936-3027. **E-Mail:** lewis.lefkowitz@vanderbilt.edu

LEFKOWITZ, ROBERT JOSEPH, MOLECULAR PHARMACOLOGY, MEDICAL SCIENCE. **Personal Data:** b New York, NY, April 15, 1943; m 1991, Lynn; c David, Larry, Cheryl, Mara & Joshua. **Education:** Columbia Univ, BA, 1962, MD, 1966; Am Bd Internal Med, dipl. **Honors & Awards:** Janeway Prize, 1966; John J Abel Award, Am Soc Pharmacol & Exp Therapeut, 1978; Gordon Wilson Medal, Am Clin & Climatol Asn, 1982; Ernst Oppenheimer Mem Award, Endocrine Soc, 1982; Lita Annenberg Hazen Award, 1983; Outstanding Res award, Int Soc Heart Res, 1985; Goodman & Gilman Award, Am Soc Pharmacol & Expert Therapeut, 1986; Gairdner Found Int Award, 1988; Res Award, Asn Am Med Col, 1990; Basic Res Prize, Am Heart Asn, 1990; Novo Nordisk Biotechnol Award, 1990; Giovanni Lorenzini Prize, 1992; Grand Prix Int Lefoulon-Delalande 2003; 2003Founding Distinguished Scientist Award American Heart Association; 2001 1st American Society of Biological Chemistry and Molecular Biology Herbert Tabor Lecture Award; 2004 Distinguished Faculty Award Duke University Medical Center; 2004 Doctor of Science, honoris causa Medical University of South Carolina 2004 Doctor of Science, honoris causa Mt Sinai School of Medicine of New York University. **Professional Experience:** PROF BIOCHEM, DUKE UNIV MED CTR, 1985-; JAMES B DUKE PROF MED, DUKE UNIV MED CTR, 1982-; prof med, Med Ctr, 1977-1982; investr, Howard Hughes Med Inst, 1976-; assoc prof med & asst prof biochem, Duke Univ Med Ctr, 1973-1977; Estab investr, Am Heart Asn, 1973-1976; fel cardiol, Mass Gen Hosp, Harvard Univ, 1971-1973; sr asst resident, Mass Gen Hosp, Harvard Univ, 1970-1971; clin & res assoc, Nat Inst Arthritis & Metab Dis, 1968-1970; From intern to jr asst resident, Columbia Presby Med Ctr, NY, 1966-1968. **Memberships:** Nat Acad Sci; Inst Med-Nat Acad Sci; Asn Am Physicians; Am Heart Asn; Am Soc Pharmacol & Exp Therapeut; Am Soc Clin Invest; Am Acad Arts & Sci; Endocrine Soc; Am Soc Biol Chem. **Research Statement & Publications:** Molecular pharmacology of drug and hormone receptors; author of numerous articles. **Mailing Address:** Duke Univ Med Ctr, PO Box 3821 467 Clin & Res Labs, Durham, NC 27710. **Fax:** 919-684-8875. **E-Mail:** lefko001@receptor-biol.duke.edu

LEFKOWITZ, RUTH SAMSON, MATHEMATICS. **Personal Data:** b Cincinnati, Ohio, October 7, 1910; m 1940, Charles; c Judith & Jeremy. **Education:** Hunter Col, BA, 1930; Columbia Univ, MA, 1960, EdD(math educ), 1966. **Professional Experience:** PROF EMER MATH, JOHN JAY COL CRIMINAL JUSTICE, CITY UNIV NEW YORK, 1976-; chmn dept, John Jay Col Criminal Justice, City Univ New York, 1973-1975; from assoc prof to prof, John Jay Col Criminal Justice, City Univ New York, 1967-1976; from asst prof to assoc prof, Bronx Community Col, 1960-1967; sec sch teacher math, New York City Bd Educ, 1938-1959. **Memberships:** AAAS; Math Asn Am; NY Acad Sci. **Research Statement & Publications:** Impact of the computer on the study of mathematics. **Mailing Address:** Dept Math, John Jay Col Criminal Justice, 900 W 190th St, New York, NY 10040.

LEFKOWITZ, STANLEY A, PHYSICALINORGANIC CHEMISTRY. **Personal Data:** b Philadelphia, Pa, August 5, 1943; m 1994, Debra. **Education:** Temple Univ, BA, 1965; Princeton Univ, PhD (chem), 1970. **Professional Experience:** EXEC VPRES, FALCONWOOD CORP, as of 2004; dir, Iron Mountain Depository Corp, 1979-1987; vpres, Falconwood Corp & Mocatta Metals Corp, beginning, 1975-; consult, Prof Exam Serv, 1974-1975 & Guana Island Hotel Corp, 1976-; asst dir instruct develop, Queens Col, 1973-1975; environ consult, NY State Temp Comn Powers Local Govt, 1972-1973; asst to vchancellor Urban Affairs, City Univ NY, 1970-1973. **Research Statement & Publications:** Alternative techniques for the extraction, refining and analysis of precious metals; the development and design of a solar-wind energy installation on Guana Island in the British Virgin Islands. **Mailing Address:** 565 5th Ave, New York, NY 10017. **Fax:** 212-984-1442. **E-Mail:** sl@falconfone.com

LEFKOWITZ, STANLEY S, MICROBIOLOGY, VIROLOGY. **Personal Data:** b New York, NY, November 26, 1933; m 1978, c 3. **Education:** Univ Miami, BS, 1955, MS, 1957; Univ Md, PhD (plant path), 1961; Am Bd Med Microbiol, dipl, 1974. **Professional Experience:** CLIN PROF MICROBIOL, COL MED, UNIV SFLA, as of 2003; virol consult, stedman's med dict, as of 2003; prof virol, Sch Med, Tex Tech Univ, beginning 1978; mem, Clin Cancer Educ Comt, NIH, 1978-1981; actg chairperson, Microbiol Dept & res coordr, 1978-1981; assoc scientist, Sloan Kettering Inst Cancer Res, 1977-1981; assoc dean, Sch Med, Tex Tech Univ, 1975-1981; assoc prof, Sch Med, Tex Tech Univ, 1972-1978; from asst prof to assoc prof virol, Med Col Ga, 1965-1969; res assoc, Variety Childrens Res Found, 1964-1965; fel viral oncol, Variety Childrens Res Found, 1961-1964. **Memberships:** AAAS; fel Am Acad Microbiol; Am Soc Microbiol; Tissue Cult Asn; Soc Exp Biol & Med; Reticuloendothelial Soc (treas); NY Acad Sci; Am Asn Immunol. **Research Statement & Publications:** Effects of highly abused drugs on immunity; cocaine alteration of macrophage functions; myeloperoxidase as an immunoregulatory agent; effects of highly abused drugs on immunity. **Mailing Address:** Dept Microbiol, Univ SFla, Tampa, FL 33620. **E-Mail:** dlefkowi@hsc.usf.edu

LEFORT, HENRY G(ERARD), CERAMICS ENGINEERING. **Personal Data:** b Mineola, NY, April 4, 1928; m 1955, c 3. **Education:** Clemson Col, BCerE, 1952; Univ Ill, MS, 1957, PhD (ceramic eng), 1960. **Professional Experience:** ASSOC PROF CERAMIC ENG, CLEMSON UNIV, 1962-; chemist, Lawrence Radiation Lab, Univ Calif, 1960-1962; res assoc ceramic eng, Univ Ill, 1955-1960; Ceramic engr, Nat Bur Standards, 1952-1955. **Memberships:** Am Ceramic Soc; Nat Inst Ceramic Engrs. **Research Statement & Publications:** Ceramic structural adhesives for high temperature use; ceramic coatings; procelain enamels; nuclear ceramics. **Mailing Address:** PO Box 65, Clemson, SC 29631.

LEFRAK, EDWARD ARTHUR, CARDIAC, VASCULAR & THORACIC SURGERY. **Personal Data:** b Newark, NJ, April 21, 1943; m 1973, c 5. **Education:** State Univ NY, Buffalo, BA, 1965; Ind Univ Sch Med, MD, 1969; Am Bd Surg, cert, 1976; Am Bd Thoracic Surg, cert, 1978. **Professional Experience:** CHIEF CARDIAC SURG, INOVA FAIRFAX HOSP, as of 2005; MED DIR CARDIAC TRANSPLANTATION PROG, FAIRFAX HOSP, VA, 1986-; mem Coun Cardiovasc Surg, Am Heart Asn, 1982; asst clin prof surg, Georgetown Univ Sch Med, beginning 1978; DIR CARDIAC SURG, FAIRFAX HOSP, VA, 1977-; resident cardiopulmonary surg, Univ Ore Med Sch, Portland, 1975-1977; resident gen surg, Baylor Col Med Affil Hosp, Houston, Tex, 1970-1975; intern surg, Baylor Col Med Affil Hosp, Houston, Tex, 1969-1970. **Memberships:** Fel Am Col Cardiol; fel Am Col Surgeons; AMA; fel Am Col Chest Physicians; fel Int Col Surgeons; Int Soc Heart Transplantation; Am Asn Thoracic Surg. **Research Statement & Publications:** Cardiac and vascular surgery; heart transplantation. **Mailing Address:** Inova Fairfax Hosp, 3300 Gallows Rd, Falls Church, VA 22042-3300.

LEFRANCOIS, LEO, EXPERIMENTAL BIOLOGY. **Personal Data:** b Bristol, Conn, January 6, 1956. **Education:** Colo State Univ, BS, 1978; Wake Forest Univ, PhD (immunol), 1982. **Professional Experience:** PROF MED, UNIV CONN HEALTH CTR, as of 2003; CHMN, DIV IMMUNOL, UNIV CONN HEALTH CTR, as of 2003; sr res scientist iii, dept cell biol, upjohn co, beginning 1990; res scientist, Dept Cell Biol, Upjohn CO, 1986-1990; res assoc, Dept Immunol, Scripps Clin & Res Found, La Jolla, Calif, 1982-1986; teaching asst, Dept Microbiol & Immunol, Bowman Gray Sch Med, Winston-Salem, NC, 1981-1982; Med technologist, Bristol Hosp, Conn, 1978-1979; adv coun mem, Midwest Autumn Immunol Conf; assoc ed, J Immunol. **Mailing Address:** Dept Med, Univ Conn Health Ctr, 263 Farmington Ave, Farmington, CT 06030. **E-Mail:** lefrancois@nso1.uchc.edu

LEFTIN, HARRY PAUL, PHYSICAL ORGANIC CHEMISTRY, INDUSTRIAL CHEMISTRY. **Personal Data:** b Beverly, Mass, October 23, 1926; m 1954, Selma Gordon; c Lori (Starr), Debra (Carnes) & Alyson (Leftin). **Education:** Boston Univ, AB, 1950, PhD (chem), 1955. **Professional Experience:** Consult, 1986-; assoc dir res, M W Kellogg Co, 1985-1986; MGR RES, PULLMAN KELLOGG, 1973-; ed, Catalysis Rev, 1967-1985; sr res assoc, Res & Develop Lab, 1967-1973; Instr, Fairleigh Dickinson Univ, 1960-1975; supvr chem res, Pullman Kellogg, 1960-1967; res chemist, Pullman Kellogg, 1959-1960; Res fel, Mellon Inst, 1954-1959; consult, Pullman Kellogg. **Memberships:** Am Chem Soc; Catalysis Soc NAm; Sigma Xi. **Research Statement & Publications:** Heterogeneous catalysis; chemisorption; electronic infrared and nuclear magnetic resonance spectra of molecules in the adsorbed state; petroleum and petrochemical process development; gas phase kinetics. **Mailing Address:** M W Kellogg Technol Co, Technol Develop Ctr 16200 Bark Row, Houston, TX 77084-5195.

LEFTON, LEW EDWARD, NONLINEAR DIFFERENTIAL EQUATIONS, SCIENTIFIC COMPUTING. **Personal Data:** b Albuquerque, NMex, September 24, 1960; m 1988, c 3. **Education:** NMex Inst Mining & Technol, BS, 1982; Univ Ill, Urbana, MS, 1986, PhD (math), 1987. **Professional Experience:** DIR IT, GEORGIA INST TECHNOL, as of 1999; assoc prof math, Univ New Orleans, beginning 1989; vis asst prof math, Univ Calif, Riverside, 1987-1989. **Memberships:** Am Math Soc; Math Asn Am. **Research Statement & Publications:** Existence, multiplicity, and qualitative behavior of solutions to nonlinear ordinary and partial differential equations; applying both numerical techniques and analytic methods; scientific computing and parallel processing. **Mailing Address:** Dept Math, Sch Math, Ga Inst Technol, 686 Cherry St, Skiles Bldg, Atlanta, GA 30332-0160. **Fax:** 404-894-4409. **E-Mail:** llefton@math.gatech.edu

LEFTON, PHYLLIS, MATHEMATICS, NUMBER THEORY. **Personal Data:** b Neptune, NJ, February 10, 1949; m 1979, c 1. **Education:** Barnard Col, BA, 1971; Columbia Univ, MA, 1972, MPhil & PhD (math), 1975; Jewish Theol Sem, BHL, 1975. **Professional Experience:** PROF MATH & COMPUT SCI, MANHATTANVILLE COL, 1987-; assoc prof math, Manhattanville Col, 1982-1987; asst prof, Manhattanville Col, 1977-1982; instr math, Belfer Grad Sch & Stern Col, Yeshiva Univ, 1975-1977; teaching asst calculus, Columbia Univ, 1970-1973. **Memberships:** Am Math Soc; Math Asn Am; Asn Women in Math; Nat Coun Teachers Math. **Research Statement & Publications:** Algebraic number theory; analytic number theory; group representation theory; theory of polynomials and field theory. **Mailing Address:** Dept Math & Comput Sci, Manhattanville Col, Rm BW8 Wing Sect Brownson Hall, Purchase, NY 10577. **Fax:** 914-694-2386. **E-Mail:** leftonp@mville.edu

LEGAN, SANDRA JEAN, REPRODUCTIVE PHYSIOLOGY, NEUROENDOCRINOLOGY. **Personal Data:** b Cleveland, Ohio, September 10, 1946. **Education:** Univ Mich, BS, 1967, MS, 1970, PhD (physiol), 1974. **Honors & Awards:** NSF Summer Res Fel 1966; NIH Predoctoral Traineeship 1968 to 1971; Phi Sigma Award, 1970; Nat Res Ser Award 1989-1990. **Professional Experience:** PROF PHYSIOL, UNIV KY, LEXINGTON, 1992-; from asst prof to assoc prof, Univ KY, Lexington, 1979-1992; res assoc, Reproductive Endocrinol Prog, Univ Mich, Ann Arbor, 1977-1979; NIH fel, Reproductive Endocrinol Prog, Univ Mich, Ann Arbor, 1975-1977; NIH fel physiol, Emory Univ, 1974-1975; NIH Postdoctoral fel, 1974-1976; teaching fel, Univ Mich, 1972-1973; instr physiol, Univ Mich, 1971-1972; Lab asst, Geigy Co, Basel, Switz, 1967-1968. **Memberships:** Am Physiol Soc; Endocrine Soc; Soc Study Reproduction; Soc Neuroscience; Soc Study Fertil; Am Neuroendocrine Soc. **Research Statement & Publications:** Neuroendocrine control of gonadotrophin secretion, specifically how modulations in steroid concentra; published over 35 manuscripts. **Mailing Address:** Dept Physiol, Univ Ky, 425 Health Sci Res Bldg, Lexington, KY 40536-0305. **Fax:** 859-323-1070. **E-Mail:** sjlegan@uky.edu

LEGARE, RICHARD J, POLYMER CHEMISTRY, CHEMICAL KINETICS. **Personal Data:** b Central Falls, RI, December 27, 1934; m 1957, c 2. **Education:** Providence Col, BS, 1956; Univ Minn, MS, 1960, PhD (phys chem), 1962. **Professional Experience:** RETIRED; staff scientist, Fibers Technol Ctr, Hercules Inc, beginning 1978; staff scientist, Bacchus Works, 1971-1976; staff scientist, Fibers Technol Ctr, Res Triangle Park, NC, 1976-1978; sr res chemist, Allegany Ballistics Lab, Md, 1962-1971. **Memberships:** Am Chem Soc. **Research Statement & Publications:** High speed kinetics; biophysical and polymer chemistry; rocket propellants; high temperature resins; composite materials. **Mailing Address:** 2619 Country Club Dr, Conyers, GA 30208.

LEGASPI, ADRIAN, ONCOLOGY. **Personal Data:** b Mexico City, Mex, July 13, 1952; m 1980, c 1. **Education:** Army Med Sch, Mex, MD, 1976. **Professional Experience:** SURG ONCOLOGIST, MT SINAI COMPREHENSIVE CANCER CTR, as of 2005; asst prof surg, Univ Miami Sch Med, beginning 1987; clin fel, surgery oncol, mem Sloan Kettering Cancer Ctr Med Col, 1985-1987; res fel, surgery, Cornell Univ NY Hosp, 1983-1985. **Memberships:** Europ Soc Parenteral & Enteral Nutrit; Asn Acad Sug. **Research Statement & Publications:** Treatment of cancer by means of surgery; nutritional aspects of patient support before and after surgery; injury and hospitalization on protein metabolism. **Mailing Address:** Mt Sinai Comprehensive Cancer Ctr, 4306 Alton Rd, Miami Beach, FL 33140. **Fax:** 305-535-2165.

LEGAULT, ALBERT, SYSTEMATIC BOTANY, PHYTOGEOGRAPHY. **Personal Data:** b Hull, Que, June 7, 1919; m 1957. **Education:** Univ Montreal, BA, 1948, BPed, 1953, BSc, 1955, MSc, 1958; Yale Univ, MSc, 1959. **Professional Experience:** PROF EMER, UNIV SHERBROOKE, as of 2005; prof bot, Univ Sherbrooke, beginning 1976; from asst prof to assoc prof, Univ Sherbrooke, 1962-1976; researcher palynol, Serv Biogeog, Prov Que, 1961-1962; teacher biol, St Louis Col, Montreal, 1950-1957. **Memberships:** Can Bot Asn; Int Asn Plant Taxon; Fr-Can Asn Advan Sci. **Research Statement & Publications:** Floristics of southeastern, arctic and subarctic Quebec. **Mailing Address:** Dept Bot, Univ Sherbrooke, Sherbrooke, PQ J1K 2R1, Can.

LEGECKIS, RICHARD VYTAUTAS, PHYSICAL OCEANOGRAPHY, REMOTE SENSING. **Personal Data:** b Panevezys, Lithuania, January 28, 1941; American citizen; m 1967, c 2. **Education:** City Univ NY, BS, 1965; Fla Inst Technol, MS, 1968; Fla State Univ, PhD (phys oceanog), 1974. **Professional Experience:** CHIEF, OCEAN SCI BR, NAT ENVIRON SATELLITE DATA & INFO SERV, NAT OCEANIC & ATMOSPHERIC ADM, as of 2002; scientist oceanog, Nat Environ Satellite Data & Info Serv, Nat Oceanic & Atmospheric Admin, beginning 1975; assoc oceanog, Nat Res Coun, 1974-1975; Nat Res Coun grant, 1974; res assoc fel, Fla State Univ, 1974; space engr, Grumman Corp, 1965-1970. **Memberships:** Am Geophys Union. **Research Statement & Publications:** Ocean currents and temperature fronts; application of satellite remote sensing to ocean studies. **Mailing Address:** Ocean Sci Br, NAT ENVIRON SATELLITE DATA & INFO SERV, NAT OCEANIC & ATMOSPHERIC ADM, SSMC3 Rm 3620 1315 E-W Hwy, Silver Spring, MD 20910-3282. **Fax:** 301-713-4598. **E-Mail:** richard.legeckis@noaa.gov

LEGENDRE, LOUIS, BIOLOGICAL OCEANOGRAPHY, NUMERICAL ECOLOGY. **Personal Data:** b Montreal, Que, February 16, 1945. **Education:** Univ Montreal, BSc, 1967; Dalhousie Univ, PhD (oceanog), 1971. **Honors & Awards:** Leo-Pariseau Award, Fr-Can Asn Advan Sci, 1985, Michel-Jurdant Award, 1986. **Professional Experience:** Killam Res fel, Can Coun, 1997-; vpres, Modelenviron, Univ Liege, Belg, 1993-; mem, task team photosynthesis measurements, Joint Global Ocean Flux Study, 1993-; mem, Sci Cultural Coun, Fr Univ Pac, 1990-; mem, bd Environ Policy, Royal Soc, 1990-1992; chair, Comt Actions struct, FCAR Fund Que, 1990; vpres, Que, Laval & McGill Univs, 1989-; chair, Sci Coord Group Int Arctic Polymya Programme, 1989-; group chair Life Sci, Strategic Panel Oceans, Natural Sci & Eng Res Coun Can, 1989-1992; mem, Sci Comt Oceanic Res, 1988-; mem, Int Exec Comt, Group on Aquatic Productivity, 1988-1992; mem, Comt Res Centres, FCAR Fund Que, 1988-1989, 1995-1996; chmn, Strategic Panel Oceans, Natural Sci & Eng Res Coun Can, 1988-1989; mem, working group, Sci Comt Oceanic Res, 1986; mem, Strategic Panel Oceans, Natural Sci & Eng Res Coun Can, 1985-1987; mem, Sci Comt Oceanic Res, 1983-1987; mem Comt Perfect, Inst Ocean Paris Monaco, 1981-; PROF OCEANOG, LAVAL UNIV, 1981-; res coordr, Que, Laval & McGill Univs, 1980-1986; mem Pop Biol Comt, Nat Sci Eng Res Coun Can, 1980-1983; mem Can nat comt for sci, comt oceanog res, Nat Res Coun Can, 1978-1979; assoc prof, Laval Univ, 1977-1981; secy gen interuniv group res oceanog, Que, Laval & McGill Univs, 1977-1979; asst prof, Laval Univ, 1974-1977; res assoc, Laval Univ, 1973-1974; mem, working group, Sci Comt Oceanic Res, 1973; NATO fel oceanog, Marine Sta Villefranche-sur-Mer, Univ Paris, 1971-1973. **Memberships:** Am Soc Limnol & Oceanog; fel Royal Soc Can. **Research Statement & Publications:** Marine primary production; physiological ecology of photosynthesis in marine phytoplankton; numerical analysis of ecological data sets. **Mailing Address:** Dept Biol, Laval Univ, Quebec, PQ G1K 7P4, Can. **Fax:** 418-656-2339. **E-Mail:** legendre@obs-vlfr.fr

LEGENDRE, PIERRE, NUMERICAL ECOLOGY, COMMUNITY ECOLOGY. **Personal Data:** b Montreal, Que, October 5, 1946; m 1969, c 2. **Education:** Univ Montreal, BA, 1965; McGill Univ, MS, 1969; Univ Colo, PhD (biol), 1971. **Honors & Awards:** Michel-Jurdant Prize Environ Sci, French Can Asn Advan Sci, 1986; Distinguished Statist Ecologist Award, Int Cong Ecol, 1994; Romanowski Medal, Royal Soc Can, 1995; 20th Century Distinguished Serv Award, Bowling Green State Univ, 1999; Marie-Victorin Prize, Govt Que, 2005. **Professional Experience:** Invited researcher, Secretariat Pac Community, Nouvelle-Caldonie, 2003; mem ed adv bd, Plant Ecol, 2002-; invited prof, Conservatoire National des Arts et Metiers, Paris, France, 2002; invited prof statist, Univ Waikato, NZ, 2001; invited researcher, Montpellier, France, 2001; pres, Numerical Taxon Conf, 1995-1996; assoc ed, Environ & Ecol Statist, 1993-; mem ed bd, Ann Royal Belg Zool Soc, 1989-1993; Killiam res fel, Can Coun, 1989-1991; invited prof, Cath Univ Louvain, Belg, 1989, 1988, 1987; mem ed adv bd, Can J Zool, 1987-; PROF BIOL, UNIV MONTREAL, 1984-; mem bd dirs, Rawson Acad Aquatic Sci, 1984-1988; assoc prof, Univ Montreal, 1980-1984; prof physics, Univ Que, Montreal, 1980; res assoc, Nat Sci & Eng Res Coun Can, 1977-1980; res dir environ sci, Univ Que, Montreal, 1973-1980; res assoc environ sci, Univ Que, Montreal, 1972-1973; postdoctoral fel genetics, Genetiska Inst, Lunds Univ, Sweden, 1971-1972; invited prof, Montpellier, France, 1985. **Memberships:** Royal Soc Can; Ecol Soc Am; Int Asn Ecol; Int Fedn Classification Soc (secy-treas 1988-1992). **Research Statement & Publications:** Mathematically analyzing the organization of ecological communities through space and integrating multi-scale spatial structures into population and community models in order to increase their predictive power; application to several types of ecosystems (aquatic and terrestrial); author of several textbooks on numerical ecology that have established the foundations of this new sub-discipline. **Mailing Address:** Dept Biol Sci, Univ Montreal, CP 6128 Succursale Centre-ville, Montreal, PQ H3C 3J7, Can. **Fax:** 514-343-2293. **E-Mail:** pierre.legendre@umontreal.ca

LEGER, LUBERT J, STRUCTURAL MECHANICS. **Honors & Awards:** JSC Invention Award, 1981. **Professional Experience:** COORDR, STRUCT MECH DIV, NASA JOHNSON SPACE CTR, as of 2002. **Mailing Address:** NASA Johnson Space Ctr, Struct Mech Div, Mail Code ES511 Bldg 13 Rm 110A, Houston, TX 77058. **Fax:** 713-483-2162. **E-Mail:** lleger@ems.jsc.nasa.gov

LEGER, ROBERT M(ARSH), ELECTRICAL ENGINEERING. **Personal Data:** b Foochow, China, June 3, 1921; American citizen; m 1978, Alicia; c Carol A, Betsy J & James R. **Education:** Antioch Col, BS, 1944; Ill Inst Technol, MS, 1950, PhD (elec eng), 1955. **Professional Experience:** RETIRED; eng specialist, Gen Dynamics Electronics, 1971-1986; from electronics engr to mgr info systs, Convair Astronaut Div, Gen Dynamics/ Convair, 1953-1970; asst prof, Ill Inst Technol, 1952-1953; instr, Ill Inst Technol, 1948-1952; asst elec eng, Ill Inst Technol, 1947-1948; qual control engr, Collins Radio Co, 1944-1946; final test foreman, Collins Radio Co, 1943-1944. **Memberships:** Sr mem Inst Elec & Electronics Engrs; Sigma Xi. **Research Statement & Publications:** Information handling systems; guidance and tracking systems. **Mailing Address:** 6517 Altair Ct, San Diego, CA 92120.

LEGG, DAVID ALAN, MATHEMATICAL ANALYSIS. **Personal Data:** b Elwood, Ind, September 7, 1947; m 1979, c 1. **Education:** Purdue Univ, BS, 1969, MS, 1970, PhD (math), 1973. **Professional Experience:** PROF & CHAIR MATH, IND UNIV-PURDUE UNIV, FT WAYNE, 1984-; from asst prof to assoc prof, Ind Univ-Purdue Univ, Ft Wayne, 1974-1980. **Memberships:** Am Math Soc; Math Asn Am; Sigma Xi. **Research Statement & Publications:** Approximation theory. **Mailing Address:** Dept Math, Ind Univ-Purdue Univ, 200A Kettler Hall, Ft Wayne, IN 46835-9737. **Fax:** 260-481-6880. **E-Mail:** legg@ipfw.edu

LEGG, IVAN, BIOINORGANIC CHEMISTRY. **Personal Data:** b New York, NY, October 15, 1937; m 1962, c 2. **Education:** Oberlin Col, BA, 1960; Univ Mich, MS, 1963, PhD (inorg chem), 1965. **Honors & Awards:** Malcolon E Pritt Award, Council Chem Res, 1994. **Professional Experience:** PROF, EXEC VPRES & PROVOST, NORTHERN ILL UNIV, as of 2003; exec vpres & provost N Ill Univ, 1992-2001; dean, Col Sci & Math, Auburn Univ, 1987-1992; chmn, Dept Chem, 1978-1987; assoc biochem, Wash State Univ, 1975-1978; NIH spec fel, Harvard Med Sch, 1972-1973; from asst prof to prof chem, Wash State Univ, 1966-1978; res assoc inorg chem, Univ Pittsburgh, 1965-1966. **Memberships:** Am Chem Soc, AAAS. **Research Statement & Publications:** Use of metal ions to probe structure-function relationships in metalloenzymes; development of models for metal ions binding sites in proteins. **Mailing Address:** Exec vpres & Provost N Ill Univ, 360 Admin Bldg Campus Box 526653, Dekolb, IL 60115-2886. **E-Mail:** ilegg@niu.edu

LEGG, JAMES C, ATOMIC PHYSICS, NUCLEAR PHYSICS. **Personal Data:** b Kokomo, Ind, September 17, 1936; m 1973, Marilyn; c Robert, Ted & Thomas. **Education:** Ind Univ, BS, 1958; Princeton Univ, MA, 1960, PhD (physics), 1962. **Professional Experience:** PROF EMER PHYSICS, KANS STATE UNIV, as of 2003; HEAD DEPT EMER, KANS STATE UNIV, 1987-; prof physics, Kans State Univ, beginning 1973; dir, Nuclear Sci Lab, 1972-1983; assoc prof, Kans State Univ, 1967-1973; asst prof, Rice Univ, 1963-1967; res assoc, Rice Univ, 1962-1963; instr physics, Princeton Univ, 1961-1962. **Memberships:** Am Phys Soc; AAAS; Am Asn Physics Teachers. **Research Statement & Publications:** Atomic and molecular collisions. **Mailing Address:** Dept Physics, Kans State Univ, 16 Cardwell Hall, Manhattan, KS 66506. **Fax:** 785-532-6806. **E-Mail:** legg@phys.ksu.edu

LEGG, JOHN WALLIS, PHYSICAL CHEMISTRY. **Personal Data:** b Minter City, Miss, September 20, 1936; m 1956, Betty; c David, Diane & Linda. **Education:** Miss Col, BS, 1958; Univ Fla, MS, 1960, PhD, 1964. **Professional Experience:** PROF EMER, DEPT CHEM, MISS COL, 2001-; head dept, Miss Col, beginning 1982; prof, Dept Chem, Miss Col, beginning 1971; vis prof, George Peabody Col, 1966; assoc prof, Miss Col, 1964-1971; instr, Univ Fla, 1963; asst, Univ Fla, 1962-1964; asst prof, Miss Col, 1960-1962; asst, Univ Fla, 1958-1960; chemist, Shell Oil Co, Tex, 1958. **Memberships:** Am Chem Soc; Am Sci Affil. **Research Statement & Publications:** Adsorption at solid surfaces and heterogeneous catalysis, specifically reactions over thorium oxide catalysts, primarily of the alcohols; dielectric properties of freon hydrates; coal powders and slurries. **Mailing Address:** Dept Chem, Miss Col, PO Box 4036, Clinton, MS 39058. **Fax:** 601-925-3933. **E-Mail:** johnwlegg@aol.com

LEGG, JOSEPH OGDEN, SOIL SCIENCE. **Personal Data:** b Tex, October 16, 1920; m 1944. **Education:** Univ Ark, BS, 1950, MS, 1951; Univ Md, PhD (soil fertil), 1957. **Professional Experience:** RETIRED; adj prof, Agron Dept, Univ Ark, beginning 1980; exchange scientist, USSR, 1963-1964; soil scientist, USDA, 1951-1979. **Memberships:** Fel AAAS; Soil Sci Soc Am; Am Soc Agron; Int Soc Soil Sci; Coun Agr Sci & Technol. **Research Statement & Publications:** Nitrogen transformations in soils; biological nitrogen fixation; soil organic matter. **Mailing Address:** 2400 W New Hope Rd, Rogers, AR 72758-1324.

LEGG, KENNETH DEARDORFF, ANALYTICAL CHEMISTRY. **Personal Data:** b Ogdensburg, NY, February 19, 1943; m 1967. **Education:** Union Col, BS, 1964; Mass Inst Technol, PhD (chem), 1969. **Professional Experience:** VPRES, SELFCARE, INC, as of 2004; dir res, Allied Health & Sci Prods, 1983-2002; dir res, Anal Res, 1982-1983; mgr, Anal Res, 1981-1982; prin scientist, Instrumentation Lab Inc, 1978-1981; assoc prof, Calif State Univ, Long Beach, 1975-1978; Vis prof chem, Univ Southern Calif, 1974-1975; asst prof chem, Calif State Univ, Long Beach, 1969-1974. **Memberships:** Am Asn Clin Chem; Am Chem Soc; Electrochem Soc. **Research Statement & Publications:** Study of fast photophysical processes using laser excitation; biomedical instrumentation; electrogenerated chemiluminescence; ion selective electrodes, amperometric sensors and biomedical instrumentation. **Mailing Address:** Selfcare Inc, 200 Prospect St, Waltham, MA 02453.

LEGG, MERLE ALAN, pathology; deceased, see previous edition for last biography

LEGG, MICHAEL H, WILDERNESS MANAGEMENT. **Education:** Mich State Univ, PhD (Recreation & Interpretation). **Professional Experience:** GRAD PROG ADV & PROF, COL FORESTRY, STEPHEN F. AUSTIN STATE UNIV, as of 2004. **Mailing Address:** Col Forestry, Stephen F Austin State Univ, PO Box 6109, Nacogdoches, TX 75962. **Fax:** 936-468-2489. **E-Mail:** kulhavy@titan.sfasu.edu

LEGG, THOMAS HARRY, PHYSICS, RADIO ASTRONOMY. **Personal Data:** b Kamloops, BC, May 4, 1929; m 1957, c 2. **Education:** Univ BC, BASc, 1953; McGill Univ, MSc, 1956, PhD (physics), 1960. **Professional Experience:** SR RES OFFICER, HERZBERG INST ASTROPHYS, NAT RES COUN CAN, 1960-; sci officer radio physics, Defense Res Bd Can, 1956-1957; Radar engr, Can Aviation Electronics Ltd, 1953-1954. **Memberships:** AAAS; Am Astron Soc; Can Asn Physicists; Royal Astron Soc Can; Inst Elec & Electronics Engrs; Sigma Xi. **Research Statement & Publications:** Microwave diffraction; electronic circuitry; radio interferometry. **Mailing Address:** Herzberg Inst Astrophys Nat Res Coun Can Rm 1038K Sussex Bldg, 100 Sussex Dr, Ottawa, ON K1A 0R6, Can. **Fax:** 613-952-6602. **E-Mail:** legg@hiaras.hia.nrc.ca

LEGGE, JOHN W, MATHEMATICS. **Education:** Ill Col, BA; Miami Univ, MS; Univ Okla, PhD, 1975. **Professional Experience:** PROF, DEPT MATHS, WESTERN KY UNIV, as of 2006. **Mailing Address:** WESTERN KY UNIV, TCCW 370, Pikeville, KY 41501. **E-Mail:** john.legge@wku.edu

LEGGE, NORMAN REGINALD, THERMOPLASTIC ELASTOMERS, SYNTHETIC ELASTOMERS. **Personal Data:** b Edmonton, Alta, April 20, 1919; American citizen; m 1942, c 5. **Education:** Univ Alta, BSc, 1942, MSc, 1943; McGill Univ, PhD (phys chem), 1945. **Honors & Awards:** Charles Goodyear Medalist, Rubber Div, Am Chem Soc, 1987. **Professional Experience:** Tech ed, 1985-; CONSULT POLYMER RES & DEVELOP, 1979-; mgr, Shell Chem Co, 1972-1978; mgr res & develop, Polumer Div, 1969-1971; mgr res & develop, Elastomers Res Lab, Rubber Div, Shell Chem Co, 1965-1969; dir, Elastomers Res Lab, Rubber Div, Shell Chem Co, 1961-1964; mgr, Elastomers Res, Shell Develop, 1955-1961; dir res & develop, Ky Synthetic Rubber Corp, 1951-1955; Proj leader, Polysar, Sarnia, Can, 1945-1951. **Memberships:** Fel AAAS; Am Chem Soc; Soc Plastic Engrs. **Research Statement & Publications:** Elastomers, thermoplastic elastomers, polymerization systems for polydienes and polystyrenes, elastomer latices; initiating and high energy explosives, technological forecasting. **Mailing Address:** 19 Barkentine Rd, Palos Verdes Peninsula, CA 90275-5822.

LEGGE, RAYMOND LOUIS, Applied Enzymology, Wastewater Treatment. **Personal Data:** b Calgary, Alta, June 9, 1954. **Education:** Univ Calgary, BSc, 1976; Univ Waterloo, PhD (biol), 1983. **Honors & Awards:** Invitation Fellowship, Japan Society for the Promotion of Science (2005-06); Sandford Fleming Foundation Distinguished Teaching Award (1999); Award of Merit, CIC (1997; 1998); Excellence in Research Award with C Barclay, MOE Ontario (1991); Lionel Cinq Mars Award, Can Bot Asn, 1982. **Professional Experience:** Executive Director, Biotechnology Res Ctr, 1999-2000; PROF OF CHEM ENG, UNIV WATERLOO, 2000-; Assoc Prof & Assoc Chair Chem Eng & Grad Studies, Univ Waterloo, 1996-1999; Assist. Prof Chem Eng, 1985-1996; Res Fel, NSERC, 1985-1995; NATO Fel, Univ Tex, Austin, 1983-1985; Jr Res Officer, Whiteshell Nuclear Res Est, 1978-1979; Res Assoc, Univ Calgary, 1977-1978; Lab Technician, Univ Calgary, 1976-1977. **Memberships:** Chem Inst Can; Can Soc Chem Eng; Am Chem Soc. **Research Statement & Publications:** Protein and biomimetic engineering; purification of enzymes; use of enzymes in novel reaction media; enzyme immobilization; enzyme stability; reaction kinetics; design and analysis of multienzyme reaction systems; soil bioremediation with Phanerochaete chrysosporum; plant cell culture; environmental engineering; constructed wetlands. **Mailing Address:** Dept Chem Eng, Univ Waterloo, Waterloo, ON N2L 3G1, Can. **Fax:** 519-746-4979. **E-Mail:** rllegge@engmail.uwaterloo.ca

LEGGE, THOMAS NELSON, ZOOLOGY, LIMNOLOGY. **Personal Data:** b Erie, Pa, September 23, 1936; m 1960, c 2. **Education:** Edinboro State Col, BS, 1959; Miami Univ, MAT, 1962; Univ Vt, PhD (zoology), 1969. **Professional Experience:** Dept chmn, Edinboro Univ PA, 1985-1987; PROF BIOL, EDINBORO UNIV PA, 1970-; from asst prof to assoc prof, Edinboro Univ PA, 1967-1970; instr biol, Northwestern Mich Col, 1962-1964. **Memberships:** Am Soc Limnol & Oceanog; Int Asn Gt Lakes Res. **Research Statement & Publications:** Physical and biological limnology, especially the distribution and ecology of calanoid copepods; ecology of small reservoirs. **Mailing Address:** Dept Biol & Health Sci, Edinboro Univ Pa, 219 Meadville St, Edinboro, PA 16444-0001.

LEGGETT, ANTHONY J, THEORETICAL PHYSICS. **Personal Data:** b UK. **Education:** Oxford Univ, BA, 1959, BS, 1961, PhD (physics), 1964. **Professional Experience:** CHMN, PHYSICS, UNIV ILL, URBANA, as of 2002; PROF, DEPT PHYSICS, UNIV ILL, 1983-; prof, Dept Physics, Univ Sussex, UK, 1978-1983. **Memberships:** Foreign assoc Nat Acad Sci; Am Phys Soc. **Mailing Address:** Dept Physics Univ Ill, 1110 W Green St, Urbana, IL 61801-3080. **Fax:** 217-333-9819. **E-Mail:** aleggett@uiuc.edu

LEGGETT, ROBERT DEAN, METALLURGICAL ENGINEERING, NUCLEAR FUELS & MATERIALS. **Personal Data:** b Midvale, Ohio, August 2, 1929; m 1951, Lillian; c Dean, Mark, John, Beth (Bailey), Ben & Matt. **Education:** Ohio State Univ, BMetE & MSc, 1952; Carnegie Inst Technol, PhD (metall eng), 1959. **Professional Experience:** RETIRED; pvt consult, beginning 1989; mgr, LMR Progs, 1988-1989; mgr, LMR fuel develop, 1976-1988; res assoc, Westinghouse-Hanford Co, 1972-1976; res assoc irradiation effects metals, Pac Northwest Labs, Battelle Mem Inst, 1965-1970; WADCO Corp, 1970-1971; tech specialist, Hanford Labs, Gen Elec Co, 1964-1965; sr engr, Hanford Labs, Gen Elec Co, 1959-1964; res asst, Metals Res Lab, Carnegie Inst Technol, 1958-1959; engr, Bettis Lab, Westinghouse Elec Corp, 1952-1955. **Memberships:** Am Soc Metals; fel Am Nuclear Soc. **Research Statement & Publications:** Basic mechanisms of irradiation behavior of materials, especially fissionable metals; corrosion of single crystals and bi crystals of stainless steel; hot water corrosion of uranium base alloys and stainless steel; irradiation behavior of nuclear fuels, materials and core components. **Mailing Address:** 2113 Harris Ave, Richland, WA 99352.

LEGGETT, WILLIAM C, FISH & MARINE ECOLOGY, POPULATION DYNAMICS. **Personal Data:** b Orangeville, Ont, June 25, 1939; m 1964, Claire; c David S & John W. **Education:** Waterloo Univ Col, BA, 1962; Univ Waterloo, MSc, 1965; McGill Univ, PhD (zoology), 1969. **Honorary Degrees:** DSc, Univ Waterloo, 1992, Laval Univ, 1996; LLD, Wilfrid Laurier Univ, 1994. **Honors & Awards:** D Webster Prof Award Merit, Am Fisheries Soc, 1986; Award Excellence Fisheries Educ, 1990; Oscar E Sette Award, 1996; Stevenson Lectr, 1987; Fry Medal, Can Soc Zoologists, 1990; Outstanding Biologist Award, Can Coun Biol Chmn, 1993. **Professional Experience:** PRIN EMER, QUEEN'S UNIV, 2004-; adj prof biol, McGill Univ, 1994-; prof biol, Queen's Univ, ending 2004; prin & vchancellor, Queen's Univ, 1994-2004; vprin acad, McGill Univ, 1991-1994; pres, Group Interuniv Oceanog Res Que, 1986-1991; dean fac sci, McGill Univ, 1986-1991; chmn bd, Huntsman Marine Lab, 1986-1991; chmn, Grant Selection Comt Oceans, 1985-1986; mem, Grant Selection Comt Oceans, 1984-1986; chmn dept, McGill Univ, 1981-1985; chmn, Grant Selection Comt Pop Biol, Natural Sci & Eng Res Coun Can, 1981-1982; assoc ed, J Am Fisheries Soc, 1976-1978 & Am J Fisheries Aquatic Sci, 1980-1985; pres & chmn bd, Huntsman Marine Lab, 1980-1983; mem, Grant Selection Comt Pop Biol, Natural Sci & Eng Res Coun Can, 1978-1981; mem, Grants Adv Comt, Can Nat Sportsmans Fund, 1977-1981; mem bd dirs, Memphremagog Conserv Inc, 1976-1980; mem, Comt Prof Cert, Am Fisheries Soc, 1976-1978; from asst prof to prof biol, McGill Univ, 1970-1994; res assoc, Essex Marine Lab, 1970-1978; res scientist fisheries, Essex Marine Lab, 1965-1970. **Memberships:** Can Soc Zoologists; Am Fisheries Soc; Am Soc Limnol & Oceanog; Am Soc Naturalists. **Research Statement & Publications:** Life history strategies in fishes; reproductive ecology of fish; environmental regulation of migration in fish; larval fish ecology; regulation of mortality in fish; lake ecosystem ecology; fish migrations and distributions; fish population dynamics; marine ecology. **Mailing Address:** Dept Biol, Queens Univ, Kingston, ON K7L 3N6, Can. **Fax:** 613-533-6617. **E-Mail:** wcl@post.queensu.ca

LEGLER, DAVID M, REMOTE SENSING, CLIMATE VARIABILITY. **Personal Data:** b Louisville, Ky, April 14, 1960; m 1982. **Education:** Fla State Univ, BS, 1982, MS, 1984, PhD (meteorol), 1992. **Professional Experience:** Mem, Atlantic Ocean Climate Studies Panel, World Meteorol Orgn, beginning 1994; consult, Nat Oceanic & Atmospheric Admin, 1993; DEP DIR & RES ASSOC, FLA STATE UNIV, 1992-; co-prin investr, Fla State Univ/Nat Oceanic & Atmospheric Admin, 1985-1994. **Memberships:** Am Geophys Union; Am Meteorol Soc; Oceanog Soc. **Research Statement & Publications:** Remote sensing of ocean surface conditions; variability of the ocean-atmosphere system and global climate variability. **Mailing Address:** COAPS, Fla State Univ, 2035 E Dirac Ste 200 Johnson Bldg, Tallahassee, FL 32306-2840. **Fax:** 850-644-4841. **E-Mail:** legler@coaps.fsu.edu

LEGLER, DONALD WAYNE, IMMUNOLOGY, PHYSIOLOGY. **Personal Data:** b Minneapolis, Minn, October 2, 1931; m 1957, c 4. **Education:** Univ Minn, BS, 1954, DDS, 1956; Univ Ala, PhD (physiol), 1966. **Professional Experience:** PROF EMER, COL DENT, UNIV FLA, 1994-; prof & dean, Col Dent, Univ Fla, 1983-1994; assoc dean, advan educ & res, Sch Dent, Univ Minn, 1980-1983; asst dean admin affairs, Sch Dent, Univ Ala, Birmingham, 1974-1980; prof oral biol & chmn dept, Sch Dent, Univ Ala, Birmingham, 1971-1980; asst dean, Sch Dent, Univ Ala, Birmingham, 1971-1974; Swed Med Res Coun fel, 1967-1968; from instr pedodont to assoc prof oral biol, Sch Dent, Univ Ala, Birmingham, 1963-1971; NIH trainee, 1962-1966. **Memberships:** Am Dent Asn; fel Am Col Dent; Am Soc Microbiol. **Research Statement & Publications:** Comparative immunology; germ free research; preventive dentistry. **Mailing Address:** 6426 SW 37th Way, Gainesville, FL 32608. **Fax:** 352-371-9411. **E-Mail:** donlegler@aol.com

LEGLER, JOHN MARSHALL, ZOOLOGY. **Personal Data:** b Minneapolis, Minn, September 9, 1930; m 1952, c 3. **Education:** Gustavus Adolphus Col, BA, 1953; Univ Kans, PhD (zool), 1959. **Professional Experience:** PROF EMER ZOOL, UNIV UTAH, as of 2002; res assoc, Los Angeles County Mus Natural Hist, 1975-; vis prof zool, Univ New Eng, Armidale, NSW, Australia, 1980, 1976-1977 & 1972-1974; prof zool, Univ Utah, beginning 1969; CUR REPTILES & AMPHIBIANS, UTAH MUS NATURAL HIST, 1969-; res assoc, Gorgas Mem Lab, Panama, 1964-; var individual res grants, 1959-; prof biol, Utah Mus Natural Hist, 1959-; cur herpet, Utah Mus Natural Hist, 1959-; from asst prof to assoc prof, Utah Mus Natural Hist, 1959-1969; asst instr herpet, Univ Kans, 1959; res asst physiol execise lab, Univ Kans, 1958-1959; asst instr zool, Mus Natural Hist, 1958; asst cur herpet, Mus Natural Hist, 1955-1959; asst zool, Univ Kans, 1953-1957; asst human anat, Gustavus Adolphus Col, 1952-1953. **Memberships:** Soc Study Evolution; Am Soc Ichthyologists & Herpetologists; fel Herpetologists League (pres, 1968-1970); Sigma Xi; Brit Herpet Soc. **Research Statement & Publications:** Herpetology; the biology of chelonians, the turtles of Middle America and Australia; biosystematics; evolution; ecology and morphology. **Mailing Address:** Dept Biol, Univ Utah, 201 S Biol Bldg, Salt Lake City, UT 84112-1196. **E-Mail:** legler@bioscience.utah.edu

LEGLER, WARREN KARL, COMPUTER SCIENCE, ELECTRICAL ENGINEERING. **Personal Data:** b Hiawatha, Kans, April 28, 1930; m 1952, c 3. **Education:** Univ Kans, BS, 1952, PhD (elec eng), 1969; Mass Inst Technol, MS, 1960. **Professional Experience:** SYSTS ANALYST, DIT-MCO INT, 1980-; asst prof physiol, Med Ctr, Univ Kans, 1970-1980; instr comput sci, Med Ctr, Univ Kans, 1968-1970; instr elec eng, Med Ctr, Univ Kans, 1963-1968; Physicist, US Naval Ord Test Sta, 1952-1963. **Memberships:** Inst Elec & Electronics Engrs; Asn Comput Mach; Sigma Xi. **Research Statement & Publications:** Application of computers to medical research, practice and teaching. **Mailing Address:** 1630 Illinois St, Lawrence, KS 66044-4040.

LEGNER, E FRED, ENTOMOLOGY, ECOLOGY, BIOLOG CONTROL. **Personal Data:** b Chicago, Ill, October 17, 1932; m 1960, Suzanne; c 2. **Education:** Univ Ill, Urbana, BS, 1954; Utah State Univ, MS, 1958; Univ Wis, PhD (entom), 1961. **Professional Experience:** ENTOMOLOGIST, Univ Calif, Riverside, 1975-; PROF BIOL CONTROL, UNIV CALIF, RIVERSIDE, 1973-; USPHS grants, 1964-1970 & NSF, 1972-1974; ASSOC PROF ENTOM, Univ Calif, Riverside, 1970-; from asst entomologist to assoc entomologist, Univ Calif, Riverside, 1962-1975; Consult, Africa, Australasia, SAm, Mid-E, Micronesia, WI & Europe, 1962, 1963 & 1965-1975; Asst entom, Univ Wis, 1961-1962. **Memberships:** Entom Soc Can; Am Mosquito Control Asn; Sigma Xi; Tri-county conservation leacle. **Research Statement & Publications:** Population dynamics of arthropods and their biological control; behavior of parasitic H ymenoptera. **Mailing Address:** 6158 Oswego Dr, Riverside, CA 92506. **E-Mail:** legneref@hotmail.com

LEGNER, HARTMUT H, AERONAUTICS. **Education:** Stanford Univ, PhD. **Professional Experience:** PRIN SCIENTIST, PHYS SCI INC, as of 2003. **Mailing Address:** Phys Sci Inc, 20 New England Bus Ctr, North Andover, MA 01845. **Fax:** 978-689-3232. **E-Mail:** legner@psicorp.com

LEGOFF, EUGENE, ORGANIC CHEMISTRY. **Personal Data:** b Passaic, NJ, August 18, 1934; m 1960, c 2. **Education:** Rutgers Univ, BS, 1956; Cornell Univ, PhD (org chem), 1959. **Professional Experience:** PROF EMER ORG CHEM, MICH STATE UNIV, 1978-; assoc prof, Mich State Univ, 1965-1978; fel org chem, Mellon Inst, 1960-1965; fel, Harvard Univ, 1959-1960. **Memberships:** Am Chem Soc. **Research Statement & Publications:** Synthesis of pseudoaromatics, non-benzenoid aromatics, heteroannulenes organic conductors, porphyrins new synthetic methods. **Mailing Address:** Dept Chem, Mich State Univ, 320 Chem Bldg, East Lansing, MI 48824-1322. **Fax:** 517-353-1793. **E-Mail:** legoff@msu.edu

LEGRAND, DONALD GEORGE, PHYSICAL CHEMISTRY. **Personal Data:** b Springfield, Mass, April 3, 1930; m 1951, c 4. **Education:** Boston Univ, BA, 1952; Univ Mass, PhD (chem), 1959. **Professional Experience:** CONSULT, 2000-; RETIRED, res chemist, Gen Elec Co Res Labs, 1959-1999; asst prof chem, Univ Mass, 1958-1959; res chemist, Mallinckrodt Chem Works, 1952. **Memberships:** Am Chem Soc; Am Phys Soc; Soc Rheol. **Research Statement & Publications:** Polymer physics; surface physics; rheo-optics. **Mailing Address:** CRD, Gen Elec Res Lab, One Res Circle, Niskayuna, NY 12307. **E-Mail:** legrand@sprynet.com

LEGRAND, FRANK EDWARD, GENETICS, ECOLOGY. **Personal Data:** b Mayfield, Okla, December 18, 1926; m 1949, c 5. **Education:** Okla State Univ, BS, 1959; NDak State Univ, PhD (plant breeding), 1963. **Professional Experience:** PROF EMER AGRON, OKLA STATE UNIV, as of 2002; Mem, Okla Crop Improv Asn, 1995-; dir, Okla Pedigreed Seed Serv, 1979-1995; prof agron, Okla State Univ, beginning 1974; Exten agronomist, Okla State Univ, 1963-1979. **Memberships:** Am Soc Agron. **Research Statement & Publications:** Genetic studies of wheat in relation to the inheritance of several quantitative and qualitative characters. **Mailing Address:** Dept Plant & Soil Sci, Okla State Univ, Stillwater, OK 74074. **Fax:** 405-744-5269.

LEGRAND, HARRY E, HYDROGEOLOGY. **Personal Data:** b Concord, NC, May 19, 1917; m 1945, c 2. **Education:** Univ NC, BS, 1938. **Professional Experience:** CONSULT HYDROLOGIST, 1974-; res geologist, Ground Water Br, 1962-1974; chief radiohydrol sect, Ground Water Br, 1960-1962; res geologist, Ground Water Br, 1959-1960; consult geologist, Ground Water Br, 1956-1959; dist geologist, Ground Water Br, 1949-1956; geologist, Ground Water Br, 1946-1949; Geol aide, US Geol Surv, 1938-1940. **Memberships:** AAAS; Geol Soc Am; Am Inst Prof Geologists; Am Geophys Union; Am Water Works Asn; Nat Water Well Asn. **Research Statement & Publications:** Contamination and geochemistry of ground water; ground water geology; ground water in igneous and metamorphic rocks; pollution and ground waste disposal. **Mailing Address:** 331 Yadkin Dr, Raleigh, NC 27609.

LEGROW, GARY EDWARD, ORGANIC CHEMISTRY, ORGANOSILICON CHEMISTRY. **Personal Data:** b Toronto, Ont, March 9, 1938; American citizen; m 1963, Lynda; c Lisa & Michael. **Education:** Univ Toronto, BA, 1960, MA, 1962, PhD (organosilicon chem), 1964. **Professional Experience:** ASST FLA STATE COORDR, AARP, as of 2002; PRIN SCIENTIST, CLARIANT LSM FLORIDA INC, 1995-; develop scientist, Dow Corning Corp, 1988-1995; res scientist advan ceramics, Dow Corning Corp, 1985-1988; assoc res scientist, Dow Corning Corp, 1983-1985; assoc res scientist basic mat res, Dow Corning Corp, 1980-1983; assoc res scientist resins res, Dow Corning Corp, 1977-1980; group leader resins res, Dow Corning Corp, 1973-1977; group leader organo-functional silicon chem, Dow Corning Corp, 1968-1970; lectr, Mich State Univ, 1966-1968; res chemist, Dow Corning Corp, 1965-1968; res assoc metall organosiloxanes, Dept Chem, Univ Sussex, 1964-1965. **Memberships:** Am Chem Soc; Sigma Xi; Soc Cosmetic Chemists. **Research Statement & Publications:** Creation and development of novel silicone-organic hybrid materials for use in a wide spectrum of market segments including personal care, automotive, electronic and coatings. **Mailing Address:** Clariant Lsm Fla Inc, 4404 NE 54th Ave, Gainesville, FL 32609. **Fax:** 352-373-7503. **E-Mail:** gary.legrow@clariant.com

LEGUIRE, LAWRENCE E, OPTHALMOLOGY. **Education:** PhD, MBA. **Professional Experience:** DIR EYE RES, PEDIATRIC OPTHALMOLOGY, CHILDREN'S HOSP INC, OHIO, as of 2005; PROF, DEPT OPTHALMOLOGY, OHIO STATE UNIV, as of 2005. **Mailing Address:** Children's Hosp Inc Dept Opthalmology, 700 Children's Dr, Columbus, OH 43205.

LEHEL, JENO, MATHEMATICS. **Education:** Hungarian Acad Sci, PhD, 1984. **Professional Experience:** PROF, DEPT MATH, UNIV MEMPHIS, as of 2006. **Mailing Address:** Dept Math, Univ Memphis, Rm 373 Dunn Hall, Memphis, TN 38152-3240. **Fax:** 901-678-2480. **E-Mail:** jlehel@msci.memphis.edu

LEHENY, ROBERT FRANCIS, APPLIED PHYSICS. **Personal Data:** b New York, NY, December 8, 1938; m 1962, Ann; c Ann R & Robert. **Education:** Univ Conn, BS, 1960; Columbia Univ, MS, 1963, Dr Engr Sci, 1966. **Honors & Awards:** Lasers & Electro-Optics Soc Traveling Lectr Inst Elec & Electronics Engrs, 1987-1988. **Professional Experience:** DEP DIR, DEFENSE ADVAN RES PROJS AGENCY, 2003-; prog mgr, Defense Advan Res Projs Agency, 1993-2003; div mgr, Bell Commun Res, Inc, Electronic Sci & Technol Res, 1987-1993; dist res mgr, High Speed Device Res Group, 1984-1987; mem tech staff semiconductor res & optical properties semiconductors, Bell Labs, Inc, 1967-1984; asst prof, Columbia Univ, 1966-1967; res asst, Columbia Univ, 1962-1966; engr electronic systs, Sperry Gyroscope Co, 1960-1961; mem bd dirs, Laser Electrooptic Soc, Inst Elec & Electronics Engrs. **Memberships:** AAAS; Am Phys Soc; fel Inst Elec & Electronics Engrs 1991; Sigma Xi; NY Acad Sci; Optical Soc Am. **Research Statement & Publications:** Optical properties of semiconductors; plasma physics; electromagnetic radiation; carrier transport in semiconductor; optoelectronic device research. **Mailing Address:** 3701 N Fairfax Dr, Arlington, VA 22203-1714. **Fax:** 703-696-2206. **E-Mail:** rleheny@darpa.mil

LEHISTE, ILSE, SPEECH PERCEPTION, GENERAL PHONETICS. **Personal Data:** b Tallinn, Estonia, January 31, 1922; American citizen. **Education:** Univ Hamburg, Ger, PhD, 1948; Univ Mich, Ann Arbor, PhD (ling), 1959; Univ Lund, Sweden, PhD (philos), 1982. **Honorary Degrees:** Dr, Univ Essex, Eng, 1977; PhD, Univ Lund, Sweden, 1982, Univ Tartu, Estonia, 1989, Doctor of Humane Letters, The Ohio State univ, 1999. **Honors & Awards:** Foreign mem, The Finnish acad of sci, 1998. **Professional Experience:** EMER PROF LING, OHIO STATE UNIV, 1987-; chmn ling, Dept Ling, 1985-1987; Univ Vienna, Austria, 1974 & Tokyo Univ, 1980; Guggenheim fel, 1969-1970 & 1975-1976; Univ Calif, Los Angeles, 1966; prof ling, Dept Ling, 1965-1987; chmn, Dept Ling, 1965-1971; Vis prof ling, Univ Cologne, 1965; assoc prof Slavic ling, Ohio State Univ, 1963-1965; res assoc phonetics, Commun Sci Lab, Univ Mich, 1957-1963; assoc prof, Kans Wesleyan Univ, Salina, 1950-1951 & Detroit Inst Technol, 1951-1956; Lectr ling, Univ Hamburg, Ger, 1948-1949. **Memberships:** Ling Soc Am (pres, 1980); fel Acoust Soc Am; Int Soc Phonetic Sci; Asn Advan Baltic Studies (pres, 1974-1976); Mod Lang Asn; fel Am Acad Arts & Sci. **Research Statement & Publications:** Acoustic analysis of spoken language; acoustic manifestation of syntactic structure; suprasegmental structure of various languages. **Mailing Address:** Dept Ling Ohio State Univ, 1712 Neil Ave, Columbus, OH 43210. **E-Mail:** ilsele@ling.ohio_state.edu

LEHMAN, ALFRED BAKER, MATHEMATICS. **Personal Data:** b Cleveland, Ohio, March 21, 1931. **Education:** Ohio Univ, BS, 1950; Univ Fla, PhD (math), 1954. **Honors & Awards:** Delbert Ray Fulkerson Award, Am Math Soc, 1991. **Professional Experience:** PROF MATH & COMPUT SCI, UNIV TORONTO, CAN, 1967-; vis prof, Univ Toronto, Can, 1965-1967; res mathematician, Walter Reed Army Inst Res, 1964-1967; res assoc, Rensselaer Polytech Inst, 1963; vis mem, Res Ctr, Univ Wis, 1961-1963; asst prof, Case Inst Technol, 1957-1961; mem staff, Acoust Lab & Res Lab Electronics, Mass Inst Technol, 1955-1957; Instr math, Tulane Univ, 1954. **Memberships:** Math Asn Am; Soc Indust & Appl Math. **Research Statement & Publications:** Combinatorial network theory. **Mailing Address:** Dept Comput Sci, Univ Toronto, Rm SF2304B, Sandford Fleming Bldg, 10 Kings Col Rd, Toronto, ON M5S 3G4, Can. **Fax:** 416-978-1931. **E-Mail:** lehman@cs.toronto.edu

LEHMAN, DENNIS DALE, SCIENCE EDUCATION. **Personal Data:** b Youngstown, Ohio, July 14, 1945; div, c Chris & Hillary. **Education:** Ohio State Univ, BSc, 1967; Northwestern Univ, MS, 1968, PhD (chem), 1973. **Professional Experience:** PROF CHEM & DEPT CHAIR, HAROLD WASH COL, as of 2006; DIR, RET PROG NORTHWESTERN, 2002-; CHMN, DEPT PHYS SCI, HAROLD WASH COL, 2000-; PROF PHYS SCI, HAROLD WASH COL, 1985-; PROF CHEM, LOOP COL, 1981-; vis prof, 1981- & lectr, Med Sch, 1981-1989; vis assoc prof, Dept Chem, Northwestern Univ, 1977-1981; vis scholar, Dept Chem, Northwestern Univ, 1973-; from asst prof to assoc prof, Loop Col, 1968-1981. **Memberships:** Am Chem Soc; Sigma Xi; AAAS. **Research Statement & Publications:** Center for Excellence in Teacher Preparation with the University of Illinois at Chicago for preparation of math and science teachers in K-12; Northwestern Universitys RET (Research Experience for Teachers) program for high school teachers; Internet teaching for the Programs for the Military and Center for Distance Learning; Working with the Chicago Public Schools to develop standards based instructional courses. **Mailing Address:** Dept Phys Sci, Harold Wash Col, Rm 905C 30 E Lake St, Chicago, IL 60601. **Fax:** 312-553-5787. **E-Mail:** dlehman@ccc.edu

LEHMAN, DONALD RICHARD, THEORETICAL NUCLEAR PHYSICS, CHIEF ACADEMIC OFFICER. **Personal Data:** b York, Pa, December 13, 1940; m Elyse. **Education:** Rutgers Univ, BA, 1962; Air Force Inst Technol, MS, 1964; George Wash Univ, PhD (physics), 1970. **Professional Experience:** EXEC VPRES ACAD AFFAIRS, GEORGE WASHINGTON UNIV, 2003-; vpres acad affairs, 1996-2003; assoc vpres res & grad studies, 1993-1996; vis sr scientist, Duke Univ & Triangle Univ Nuclear Lab, 1993; dir, Ctr Nuclear Studies, 1990-1993; dept chmn, George Washington Univ, 1987-1993; prin investr, Energy Dept Contract/Grant, George Washington Univ, 1986-1996; GEORGE GAMOW PROFESSOR OF THEORETICAL PHYSICS, GEORGE WASHINGTON UNIVERSITY, 2002- from asst prof, 1972, assoc prof, 1976, to prof physics, 1982-2002; co-prin investr, Energy Dept Contract/Grant, George Washington Univ, 1979-1986 & 1996-1998; vis staff mem & collabr, Los Alamos Nat Lab, 1974-2001; Guest worker, Nat Bur Stand, 1972-1989; Nat Acad Sci-Nat Res Coun res assoc nuclear physics, Nat Bur Standards, 1970-1972; instr physics, George Washington Univ, 1969-1970; Proj scientist nuclear physics, Air Force Off Sci Res, 1964-1968. **Memberships:** Am asn for the advancement of sci; Fel Am Phys Soc. **Research Statement & Publications:** Nuclear few-body problem; photonuclear physics; intermediate energy physics; hypernuclei; scattering theory. **Mailing Address:** Acad Affairs, George Wash Univ, Washington, DC 20052. **Fax:** 202-994-0907. **E-Mail:** lehman@gwu.edu

LEHMAN, DUANE STANLEY, INORGANIC CHEMISTRY. **Personal Data:** b Berne, Ind, January 18, 1932; m 1955, c 3. **Education:** Wheaton Col, Ill, BS, 1954; Ind Univ, PhD (chem), 1959. **Professional Experience:** DIR, RES & DEVELOP RECRUITING & RES DEVELOP, 1978-; res mgr high impact polystyrene, Res & Develop Recruiting & Res Develop, 1976-1978; group leader, Chem Eng Lab, lab dir, chem eng lab, Dow Chem Co, 1971-1976; proj leader, Chem Dept Res Lab, 1965-1967; Res chemist, 1958-1965. **Memberships:** Am Chem Soc; Sigma Xi. **Research Statement & Publications:** Coordination chemistry; brine chemistry; inorganic process research; basic refractories; new product development. **Mailing Address:** 704 Linwood Dr, Midland, MI 48640-3474.

LEHMAN, EUGENE H, MATHEMATICAL STATISTICS. **Personal Data:** b New York, NY, January 26, 1913; m 1961, c 4. **Education:** Yale Univ, BA, 1933; Columbia Univ, MA, 1937; NC State Univ, PhD (math statist), 1961. **Professional Experience:** Teaching Dumai, Indonesia, 1983-1984; PROF MATH, CEGEP DU QUEBEC, 1981-; prof statist, Concordia Univ, Montreal, 1978-1979; prof math, Univ Nat du Rwanda, 1976-1978; prof statist, Univ Que, Trois-Rivieres, 1970-1976; prof math, Mo Southern Col, 1969-1970; assoc prof math, Northern Mich Univ, 1966-1969; consult biostatistician, Cedars Lebanon Hosp, 1964-1966; consult statistician, Los Angeles, 1961-1964; Corresp abstractor, Math Rev, 1960-; asst prof, Univ Fla, 1955-1957 & Univ San Diego, 1957-1958; Res assoc math, Univ Alaska, 1949-1951; referee, La Rev Can Del Statist. **Memberships:** Am Math Soc; Am Statist Asn; Asn Can-French Advan Sci; Soc Statist Can; World Coun Gifted & Talented Children. **Research Statement & Publications:** Children in mathematics. **Mailing Address:** Four Viburnum Ave, Pointe Claire, PQ H9R 5A7, Can.

LEHMAN, GRACE CHURCH, ZOOLOGY, ENDOCRINOLOGY. **Personal Data:** b Mt Holly, NJ, June 10, 1941. **Education:** Drew Univ, AB, 1963; Ind Univ, Bloomington, PhD (zoology), 1967. **Professional Experience:** RETIRED; res investr zoology, Univ Mich, Ann Arbor, beginning 1974; res assoc, Univ Mich, Ann Arbor, 1971-1974; univ fel, Univ Mich, Ann Arbor, 1970-1971; US Pub Health Serv fel, Univ Mich, Ann Arbor, 1967, 1968-1970. **Memberships:** Am Soc Zoology. **Research Statement & Publications:** Endocrine interactions; influence of thyroid activity on reproduction; comparative and developmental endocrinology; reproductive biology of the amphibia. **Mailing Address:** 400 Maynard St, Ann Arbor, MI 48104.

LEHMAN, GUY WALTER, THEORETICAL PHYSICS. **Personal Data:** b Walkerton, Ind, September 21, 1923. **Education:** Purdue Univ, BS, 1948, MS, 1950, PhD (physics), 1954. **Professional Experience:** PROF EMER PHYSICS, UNIV KY, as of 2002; prof physics, Univ KY, beginning 1970; mem tech staff, Sci Ctr, 1967-1970; group leader theoret physics, Sci Ctr, 1963-1967; res specialist, Res Dept, Atomics Int Div, NAm Aviation, Inc, 1954-1962; asst physics, Purdue Univ, 1951-1954; asst physicist, Cornell Aeronaut Lab, 1951; Jr engr electronics, Eastman Kodak Co, 1948. **Memberships:** Fel Am Phys Soc. **Research Statement & Publications:** Solid state; mathematical physics; electronic structure; statistical mechanics; electromagnetic theory; lattice dynamics. **Mailing Address:** Dept Physics, Univ KY, Lexington, KY 40506.

LEHMAN, HARVEY EUGENE, DEVELOPMENTAL BIOLOGY, EMBRYOLOGY. **Personal Data:** b Yuhsien, China, American citizen; m 1958. **Education:** Maryville Col, Tenn, BA, 1941; Univ NC, MA, 1944; Stanford Univ, PhD (embryol), 1948. **Professional Experience:** PROF EMER ZOOL, UNIV NC, as of 2002; chmn dept, Univ Nc, beginning 1976; vis prof zool, Univ Vienna, 1976; chmn dept, Univ NC, 1962-1967; chg exp embryol course, Bermuda Biol Sta, 1960-1975; prof zool, Univ Nc, beginning 1959; fel, Univ Berne, 1952-1953; from asst prof to assoc prof, Univ NC, 1948-1959. **Memberships:** AAAS; Soc Develop Biol; Am Soc Zoologists; Am Micros Soc; Am Soc Cell Biol. **Research Statement & Publications:** Rhabdocoele parasitology; amphibian pigmentation; nuclear transplantation in Triton; hybridization in Echinoderms; tissue culture; cell migration and differentiation of the neural crest; invertebrate larvae and metamorphosis; cytochemistry of embryonic differentiation. **Mailing Address:** Dept Biol, Univ NC, Wilson Hall Box 3280, Chapel Hill, NC 27599.

LEHMAN, HUGH ROBERTS, CHEMICAL ENGINEERING, PHYSICS. **Personal Data:** b Ft Leavenworth, Kans, January 25, 1921; m 1945, c 3. **Education:** The Citadel, BS,

1941; Ohio State Univ, MSc, 1947; Univ Calif, Berkeley, PhD (chem eng), 1951. **Professional Experience:** RETIRED; staff mem nuclear weapons, Los Alamos Nat Lab, 1964-1991; mem, Consult Panel, Ballistics Missile Re-entry Systs, 1966-1968; staff asst nuclear disarmament, US AEC, 1962-1964; br chief, Air Force Intel Ctr, 1958-1962; dep chief, Analytical Div, Air Force Spec Weapons Ctr, 1955-1958; staff mem nuclear weapons, Los Alamos Sci Lab, 1952-1955; Armed Forces Spec Weapons Proj, 1951-1952; Air Proving Ground, Fla, 1947-1948; proj officer, Power Plant Lab, Wright Field, USAF, 1945-1946; Defense Technol Steering Group, AEC. **Memberships:** Am Nuclear Soc; Am Inst Aeronaut & Astronaut. **Research Statement & Publications:** Employment and effects of nuclear weapons; vulnerability of targets, nuclear and conventional. **Mailing Address:** 331 Potrillo Dr, Los Alamos, NM 87544.

LEHMAN, I ROBERT, BIOCHEMISTRY. **Personal Data:** b Tauroggen, Lithuania, October 5, 1924; American citizen; m 1959, Sandra; c Ellen R, Deborah & Samuel M. **Education:** Johns Hopkins Univ, AB, 1950, PhD (biochem), 1954; Univ Gothenberg, MD, 1987. **Honorary Degrees:** DSc, Univ Paris, 1992. **Honors & Awards:** Merck Award, Am Soc Biochem & Molecular Biol. **Professional Experience:** WILLIAM HUME PROF EMER, SCH MED, STANFORD UNIV, as of 2006; William Hume prof, Sch Med, Stanford Univ, as of 2005; chmn dept, Sch Med, Stanford Univ, 1974-1979 & 1984-1986; assoc ed, J Biol Chem, 1971-1974, 1981-1983, 1989-; prof biochem, Sch Med, Stanford Univ, beginning 1966; from asst prof to assoc prof, Sch Med, Stanford Univ, 1959-1966; instr microbiol, Wash Univ, 1957-1959; Am Cancer Soc fel, 1955-1957. **Memberships:** Nat Acad Sci; fel Am Acad Arts & Sci; Am Soc Biol Chem. **Research Statement & Publications:** Nucleic acid metabolism; biochemistry of virus infection. **Mailing Address:** Dept Biochem Sch Med Stanford Univ, Beckman Ctr 411a, Stanford, CA 94305. **Fax:** 650-723-6783. **E-Mail:** blehman@cmgm.stanford.edu

LEHMAN, JOE JUNIOR, ORGANIC CHEMISTRY. **Personal Data:** b Versailles, Mo, July 1, 1921; m 1943, c 4. **Education:** Bethel Col, Kans, AB, 1943; Wash State Univ, MS, 1947, PhD, 1949. **Professional Experience:** RETIRED; prof chem, Colo State Univ, 1963-1992; vis prof, US Naval Acad, 1961-1962; Res fel, Midwest Res Inst, 1958-1959; from instr to assoc prof, Colo State Univ, 1949-1964. **Memberships:** AAAS; Am Chem Soc; Am Soc Microbiol. **Research Statement & Publications:** Organic synthesis; modification of compounds by microorganisms; steric acceleration of hydrolytic reactions. **Mailing Address:** 906 E Elizabeth St, Ft Collins, CO 80524.

LEHMAN, JOHN MICHAEL, EXPERIMENTAL PATHOLOGY, VIROLOGY. **Personal Data:** b Abington, Pa, June 19, 1942; m Elizabeth; c Deborah & Eric. **Education:** Philadelphia Col Pharm & Sci, BS, 1964; Univ Pa, PhD (path), 1970. **Professional Experience:** PROF, DEPT PATH & LAB MED & ASSOC DEAN RES GRAD STUDIES, BRODY SCH MED, E CAROLINA UNIV, as of 2006; ASSOC VICE CHANCELLOR HEALTH SCI, BRODY SCH MED, E CAROLINA UNIV, as of 2006; prof & chmn, Dept Microbiol & Immunol, Albany Med Col, ending 1999; vis staff mem, Los Alamos Nat Lab, 1972-1992; from instr to assoc prof, 1971-1980; prof path, Med Sch, Univ Colo Med Ctr, Denver; NIH fel, Wistar Inst Anat & Biol, 1970; mem study sect, NIH & NSF. **Memberships:** Am Soc Microbiol; Tissue Cult Asn; Am Asn Cancer Res; Am Asn Exp Path; Am Soc Cell Biol. **Research Statement & Publications:** Tumor biology and virus transformation with oncogenic DNA viruses. **Mailing Address:** Dept Path & Lab Med, E Carolina Univ, Brody Med Sci Bldg 7S10, Greenville, NC 27834. **Fax:** 252-744-0010. **E-Mail:** lehmanj@mail.ecu.edu

LEHMAN, JOHN THEODORE, LIMNOLOGY, ECOLOGY. **Personal Data:** b Taylor, Pa, October 13, 1952; m 1974, Donna; c Jeffrey & Elizabeth. **Education:** Yale Univ, BS & MS, 1974; Univ Wash, PhD (zoology), 1978. **Professional Experience:** PROF ECOL & EVOLUTIONARY BIOL, UNIV MICH, ANN ARBOR, 1988-; asst prof biol, 1980-1988; mem, Great Lakes Res Div, beginning 1980; asst prof limnol, 1978-1980. **Memberships:** Am Soc Limnol & Oceanog (pres); Int Asn Theoret & Appl Limnol; Phycol Soc Am; Sigma Xi. **Research Statement & Publications:** Aquatic ecology; population dynamics of phytoplankton and zooplankton; mathematical models and numerical simulations of biological and chemical processes. **Mailing Address:** Dept Ecol & Evolutinary Biol, Univ Mich, 1053 Kraus Natural Sci Bldg 830 N Univ Ave, Ann Arbor, MI 48109. **Fax:** 734-647-0544. **E-Mail:** jtlehman@umich.edu

LEHMAN, MEIR M, SOFTWARE ENGINEERING, SOFTWARE DEVELOPMENT PROCESS. **Personal Data:** b Karlsruhe, Ger, January 24, 1925; British citizen; m 1953, Chava Robinson; c Machla L, Benjamin M, Yonathan D, Rafi D & Esti D. **Education:** Imp Col, BSc Hons, 1953, PhD (math), 1957; London Univ, DSc(comput sci), 1987. **Professional Experience:** Head dept, prin invest project FEAST/1, 1996-; dir proj, ICT&N, 1991-1994; SR RES FEL, IMP COL, 1989-; EMER PROF, IMP COL, 1984-; chmn, dir & consult, Imp Software Technol Ltd, 1982-1987; head dept, Imp Col, 1979-1984; Head dept, ICT&N, 1979-1984; prof comput sci, Imp Col, 1972-1984; res staff mem & mgr, Res Div, IBM, 1966-1972; head, digital comput, Sci Dept, Israel Ministry Defense, 1957-1966; Logic designer, Ferantti Ltd, 1956-1957. **Memberships:** Fel Inst Elec & Electronics Engrs; fel Brit Comput Soc; fel Asn Comput Mach; fel Royal Acad Eng; fel Inst Elec Engrs UK. **Research Statement & Publications:** Software engineering; software development process and its support; evolution in software technology; scientific framework for software technology. **Mailing Address:** Dept Comput, Imp Col 180 Queens Gate, London SW7 2BZ, UK. **Fax:** 441-715-948215. **E-Mail:** mml@doc.ac.ic.uk

LEHMAN, R SHERMAN, MATHEMATICS. **Personal Data:** b Ames, Iowa, January 25, 1930; div, c Clifford, Anne, John, Helen, Andrew & Irene. **Education:** Stanford Univ, BS, 1951, MS, 1952, PhD, 1954. **Professional Experience:** PROF EMER MATH, UNIV CALIF, BERKELEY, 1994-; from asst prof to prof, Univ Calif, Berkeley, 1958-1994; Fulbright res grant, Univ Gottingen, 1956-1957; prob analyst, Comput Lab, Ballistic Res Labs, Aberdeen Proving Ground, 1955-1956; consult, Rand Corp, 1954-1965. **Memberships:** Am Math Soc; Math Asn Am; Asn Symbolic Logic. **Research Statement & Publications:** Numerical analysis and computing; number theory. **Mailing Address:** Dept Math, Univ Calif, Berkeley, CA 94720. **E-Mail:** lehman@math.berkeley.edu

LEHMAN, RICHARD LAWRENCE, BIOPHYSICS, ENVIRONMENTAL HEALTH. **Personal Data:** b Portland, Ore, November 7, 1929; m 1963, Eva; c Gordon, Dale, Debra & Sandra. **Education:** Univ Ore, BS, 1951, MA, 1953; Univ Calif, Berkeley, PhD (biophys), 1963. **Honors & Awards:** Wellcome Trust Award, 1966. **Professional Experience:** CLIMATE ANAL CTR, NAT WEATHER SERV, NAT OCEANIC & ATMOSPHERIC ADMIN, WASH, as of 1994; PHYS SCIENTIST, CLIMATE PREDICTION CTR, NAT WEATHER SERV, NAT OCEANIC & ATMOSPHERIC ADMIN, 1981-; dept dir Off Ecol, Climate Prediction Ctr, Nat Weather Serv, Nat Oceanic & Atmospheric Admin, 1971-1981; res physicist, lab nuclear sci, Mass Inst Technol, 1968-1971; vis scientist, Swiss Fed Inst Technol, 1963 & Cambridge Univ, 1966; asst prof biophys & nuclear med, med ctr, Univ Calif, Los Angeles, 1964-1968; vis scientist, Am Inst Biol Sci, 1961-1981; physicist, Lawrence Radiation Lab, Univ Calif, 1957-1964; high sch instr math & sci, Calif, 1953-1956. **Memberships:** AAAS; Am Meteorol Soc; Am Geophys Union; Health Physics Soc. **Research Statement & Publications:** Climate data applications; definition of forecast; contigent probability distributions; climate impact assessment; software systems. **Mailing Address:** Climate Prediction Ctr, Nat Oceanic & Atmospheric Admin, Washington, DC 20233.

LEHMAN, ROBERT HAROLD, PHYSIOLOGY, ECOLOGY. **Personal Data:** b Duncannon, Pa, November 15, 1929; m 1952, c 1. **Education:** Bloomsburg State Col, BS, 1960; Univ Okla, MNS, 1965, PhD (physiol, ecol), 1970. **Professional Experience:** DEAN, GRAD SCH, 1986-; dean continuing studies, 1979-1986; ASSOC PROF BIOL, LONGWOOD COL, 1974-; asst dean, Longwood Col, 1974-1979; assoc prof bot, Longwood Col, 1970-1974; asst prof biol, Longwood Col, 1966-1970; consult, environ waste mgt & planning. **Memberships:** Sigma Xi. **Research Statement & Publications:** Allelopathic effects of caffeoylquinic acids and scopolin on vegetational patterning; land reclamination; use of sledge as fertilizers; biochemistry. **Mailing Address:** 230 Reed Rd, New Market, AL 35761-8135.

LEHMAN, ROGER H, MEDICINE, OTOLARYNGOLOGY. **Personal Data:** b Neosho, Wis, April 24, 1921; m 1957, c 3. **Education:** Univ Wis, BA, 1942, MD, 1944. **Professional Experience:** PROF EMER OTOLARYNGOL, MED COL WIS, 1989-; chmn, dept otolaryngol, Med Col Wis, ending 1986; Froedtept Mem Lutheran Hosp, 1980-1988; Milwaukee Children's Hosp, 1971-1988; prof otolaryngol, Med Col Wis, 1966-1986; chief otolaryngol, Vet Admin Med Ctr, Milwaukee Co Hosp, Wis, 1960-1988; consult, Vet Admin Ctr, Wood, 1954-1978; resident ophthal, Milwaukee Co Gen Hosp, 1951-1952; Resident otolaryngol, Vet Admin Ctr, Wood, Wis, 1948-1951. **Memberships:** AMA; Am Col Surg; Am Laryngol Rhinol & Otolaryngol Soc; Soc Univ Otolaryngol; Am Acad Otolaryngol; Sigma Xi. **Mailing Address:** Dept Otolaryngol, Med Col, 8701 Watertown Plank Rd, Milwaukee, WI 53226.

LEHMAN, THOMAS ALAN, CHEMICAL EDUCATION. **Personal Data:** b Berne, Ind, January 12, 1939; m 1961, c 2. **Education:** Bluffton Col, BS, 1961; Purdue Univ, PhD (chem), 1967. **Professional Experience:** PROF CHEM, BETHEL COL, 1981-; vis scientist, Nat Inst Environ Health Sci, 1979-1980; assoc prof, Bethel Col, 1973-1981; assoc prof chem & physics, Nat Univ Zaire, 1971-1973; Res assoc, Univ NC Chapel Hill, 1969-1970; Asst prof chem, Bluffton Col, 1966-1969. **Memberships:** Am Chem Soc; Am Soc Mass Spectrometry. **Research Statement & Publications:** Gaseous ion/molecule reactions; ion cyclotron resonance spectrometry; author and co-author scientific publications and book. **Mailing Address:** 1824 S Lakeshore Dr, Chapel Hill, NC 27514.

LEHMAN, WILLIAM JEFFREY, MUSCLE BIOCHEMISTRY & BIOPHYSICS, ELECTRON MICROSCOPY. **Personal Data:** b June 20, 1945; m 1982, Diana; c Frank Martin & John Marshall Lisle. **Education:** State Univ NY, Stony Brook, BS, 1966; Princeton Univ, PhD (biol), 1969. **Professional Experience:** PROF PHYSIOL & BIOPHYSICS, DEPT PHYSIOL, BOSTON UNIV SCH MED, 1990-; Whitaker award, 1983-1984; Estab investr, Am Heart Asn, 1982; from asst prof to assoc prof, Dept Physiol, Boston Univ Sch Med, 1973-1990; higher sci officer, Zool Dept, Oxford Univ, 1973; postdoctoral res fel, Biol Dept, Brandeis Univ, 1969-1972. **Memberships:** Am Heart Asn; Soc Gen Physiologists; Biophys Soc; Biochem Soc. **Research Statement & Publications:** Mechanism of regulation of muscle contraction. **Mailing Address:** Boston Univ, Sch Med, Dept Physiol, 80 E Concord St, Boston, MA 02118-2394. **E-Mail:** lehman@med-rana.bu.edu

LEHMANN, A(LDO) SPENCER, CHEMISTRY, CHEMICAL ENGINEERING. **Personal Data:** b Los Angeles, Calif, September 23, 1916; m 1953, Rosalie Lowther; c Larry & Bruce. **Education:** Stanford Univ, AB, 1938; Brown Univ, PhD (chem), 1941. **Honors & Awards:** Cert of Appreciation, Am Petrol Inst. **Professional Experience:** RETIRED; bd pres, San Diego Blood Bank, 1987; Dir, ACWA/Joint Powers Ins Authority, 1986-; Dir, Fallbrook Pub Utilites Dist, 1983-; gen mgr, Res Orgn & Facil, 1973-1976; gen mg, Tech Depts, 1968-1973; refinery mgr, Wilmington Refinery, Calif, 1966-1968; refinery supt, Houston Refinery, 1964-1966; chief technologist, NY Tech Dept, 1963-1964; process supt, NY Tech Dept, 1962-1963; asst mgr, NY Tech Dept, 1958-1962; mgr, Tech Dept, Wood River Refinery, Shell Oil Co, 1954-1958; asst to pres, Shell Develop Co, 1953-1954; tech rep, Shell Develop Co, 1952-1953; supvr develop, Shell Develop Co, 1950-1952; chemist, Shell Develop Co, 1946-1950; sr engr, Tenn Eastman Corp, Oak Ridge, Tenn, 1945-1946; Res chemist, 1943-1945 & Naval Res Lab, 1942-1943; Res chemist, Brown Univ, 1940-1942. **Memberships:** Am Petrol Inst; Am Chem Soc; Sigma Xi; Am Inst Chem Engrs. **Research Statement & Publications:** Infrared spectroscopy; development of reaction for producing metallic potassium; chemistry of uranium; design of special equipment for uranium recovery and processing; development of processes for production of petrochemicals; petroleum process design; research laboratory design and construction. **Mailing Address:** 1050 Ridge Heights Dr, Fallbrook, CA 92028-3671. **E-Mail:** slehmann@alumni.stanford.org

LEHMANN, CHRISTINE H, MATHEMATICS. **Education:** Valparaiso Univ, BS, 1968; NC State Univ, MA, 1970, PhD, 1985. **Professional Experience:** ASSOC PROF, DEPT UNIV, PURDUE UNIV, as of 2006. **Mailing Address:** Math & Physics Sect, Purdue Univ N Cent, Westville, IN 46391. **Fax:** 219-785-5501. **E-Mail:** clehmann@pnc.edu

LEHMANN, ELROY PAUL, RESOURCE MANAGEMENT, PETROLEUM GEOLOGY. **Personal Data:** b Tigerton, Wis, June 22, 1928; m 1951, c 2. **Education:** Univ Wis, BS, 1950, MS, 1951, PhD (geol), 1955. **Professional Experience:** PRES, MOBIL EXPLOR EGYPT LTD, as of 2005; gen mgr, Mobil Alaska Explor, 1983-1986; pres & gen mgr, Mobil Explor Egypt, Inc, 1979-1983; explor mgr new areas, Mobil Explor & Producing Serv, Inc, 1978-1979; explor mgr, Mobil Oil Libya Ltd, 1974-1978; sr staff explorationist, Int Div, Mobil Oil Corp, 1972-1974; chief geoscientist, Int Div, Mobil Oil Corp, 1969-1972; sr res geologist, Mobil Res & Develop Corp, 1967-1969; sr staff geologist, Mobil Latin Am Inc, 1965-1967; staff geologist, Mobil Oil Libya Ltd, 1963-1965; geol lab supvr, Mobil Oil Can, Libya, 1961-1963; sr paleontologist, Mobil Oil Can, Libya, 1960-1961; paleontologist, Mobil Oil Can, Libya, 1959-1960; Fulbright lectr, Karachi, 1958-1959; actg chmn, Wesleyan Univ, 1955-1957; mem educ comt, Am Geol Inst, 1955-1957; asst prof geol, Wesleyan Univ, 1952-1959. **Memberships:** AAAS; fel Geol Soc Am; Am Asn Petrol Geologists; Soc Econ Paleontologists & Mineralogists; Libya Petrol Explor Soc (treas, 1964, pres, 1965); Sigma Xi. **Research Statement & Publications:** Geoscience aspects of energy resource identification and evaluation. **Mailing Address:** Dallas, TX 75221. **Fax:** 972-732-8942.

LEHMANN, ERICH LEO, MATHEMATICAL STATISTICS. **Personal Data:** b Strasbourg, France, November 20, 1917; American citizen; m 1977, Juliet; c Stephen, Barbara & Fia. **Education:** Univ Calif, MA, 1942, PhD (math statist), 1946. **Honorary Degrees:** DSc, Univ Leiden, 1985 & Univ Chicago, 1991. **Honors & Awards:** R A Fisher Award, 1988; SS Wilks Award, 1996. **Professional Experience:** PROF EMER STATIST, UNIV CALIF, BERKELEY, 1989-; chmn dept, Univ Calif, Berkeley, 1973-1976; Guggenheim fel, 1955, 1966, & 1979; prof, Univ Calif, Berkeley, 1954-1989; ed, Ann Math Statist, 1953-1955; vis lectr, Princeton Univ, 1951; vis assoc prof, Columbia Univ, 1950 & Stanford Univ, 1951; from asst prof to assoc prof math, Univ Calif, Berkeley, 1942-1954. **Memberships:** Nat Acad Sci; Am Statist Asn; Inst Math Statist; Int Statist Inst; Am Acad Arts & Sci; hon fel

Royal Statist Soc. **Research Statement & Publications:** Theories of testing hypotheses and of estimation; history of statistics. **Mailing Address:** Dept Statist, Univ Calif, 367 Evans Hall, Berkeley, CA 94720-3860. **Fax:** 510-642-7892. **E-Mail:** lehmann@stat.berkeley.edu

LEHMANN, GILBERT MARK, GAS DYNAMICS, HEAT TRANSFER. **Personal Data:** b Libertyville, Ill, August 4, 1933; m 1958, Marilyn; c Susan H & Christopher M. **Education:** Valparaiso Univ, BS, 1955; Ill Inst Technol, MS, 1957; Purdue Univ, PhD (jet propulsion), 1966. **Professional Experience:** PROF EMER MECH ENG, VALPARAISO UNIV, as of 2002; dean, Col Eng, 1972-1979; prof mech eng, Valparaiso Univ, beginning 1956. **Memberships:** Am Soc Mech Engrs; Am Soc Eng Educ. **Research Statement & Publications:** Internal ballistics of solid propellant rockets. **Mailing Address:** Dept Mech, Valparaiso Univ, Gellersen Ctr, Valparaiso, IN 46383. **Fax:** 219-464-5065.

LEHMANN, HERMANN PETER, CLINICAL BIOCHEMISTRY. **Personal Data:** b London, Eng, June 24, 1937. **Education:** Univ Durham, BSc, 1959, PhD (phys chem), 1964. **Honors & Awards:** Distinguished Serv Award, Am Soc Clin Path, 1987-; Outstanding Contrib Educ Award, Am Asn Clin Chem, 1990. **Professional Experience:** PROF PATH, LA STATE UNIV MED CTR, NEW ORLEANS, 1982-; dir, Radionuclide Lab, Med Ctr La, New Orleans, 1977-; clin chemist, LA State Univ, Clin Lab, New Orleans, 1975-; consult, Vet Admin Hosp, New Orleans, 1973-; vis scientist, Charity Hosp La, New Orleans, 1971-; from asst prof to assoc prof, LA State Univ Med Ctr, New Orleans, 1971-1982; NIH sr fel biochem, Univ Wash, 1969-1971; res assoc, Radiation Lab, Univ Notre Dame, 1967-1969; volkswagen Found fel, Max Planck Inst, Mulheim Ruhr, W Ger, 1966-1967; weizmann fel, Weizmann Inst Sci, 1965-1966. **Memberships:** Am Chem Soc; Chem Soc; Am Asn Clin Chem; Brit Asn Clin Biochem; Am Soc Clin Path. **Research Statement & Publications:** Clinical chemistry; molecular pathology. **Mailing Address:** Dept Path, La State Univ Med Ctr, 1901 Perdido St, New Orleans, LA 70112-1328. **Fax:** 504-568-6037. **E-Mail:** hlehma@lsumc.edu

LEHMANN, JOEL P, MATHEMATICS. **Education:** DePaul Univ, MS, 1984; NC State Univ, PhD, 1978. **Professional Experience:** ASSOC PROF, DEPT MATHS, VALPARAISO UNIV, as of 2006. **Mailing Address:** Dept Math & Comput Sci, Valparaiso Univ, Gellersen Hall 216, Valparaiso, IN 46383-9978. **Fax:** 219-464-5381. **E-Mail:** joel.lehmann@valpo.edu

LEHMANN, JOHN R(ICHARD), COMPUTER SYSTEMS DESIGN, RESEARCH ADMINISTRATION. **Personal Data:** b Oak Park, Ill, March 24, 1934; m 1956, Barbara; c Nancy Jane & Richard Allen (deceased). **Education:** Univ Ill, BS, 1956, MS, 1958, PhD (elec eng), 1964. **Professional Experience:** DEP DIV DIR, MICROELECTRONIC INFO PROCESSING SYSTS DIV, NSF, 1987-; prog dir, Microelectronic Systs Archit Prog, 1986-1987; prog dir, Computer Res Equip Prog, Div Computer Res, 1982-1986; prog dir, Computer Systs Design Prog, Div Computer Res, 1970-1986; prog dir, Develop Computer Uses Prog, Off Comput Activ, 1967-1970; mem, Simulation Coun, 1965-1975; asst assoc prog dir, Eng Systs Prog, Div Eng, NSF, 1963-1967. **Memberships:** Inst Elec & Electronics Engrs; Am Soc Eng Educ; Inst Elec & Electronics Engrs Comput Soc; Sigma Xi. **Research Statement & Publications:** Computer systems design; microcomputer applications; electronics. **Mailing Address:** Microelectronic Info Processing Div NSF, 4201 Wilson Blvd, Arlington, VA 22230. **Fax:** 703-706-0610. **E-Mail:** jlehmann@nsf.gov

LEHMANN, JUSTUS FRANZ, PHYSICAL MEDICINE. **Personal Data:** b Koenigsberg, Ger, February 27, 1921; American citizen; m 1943, c 3. **Education:** Univ Frankfurt, MD, 1945. **Professional Experience:** PROF EMER REHAB MED, UNIV WASH, as of 2005; prof phys med & chmn dept phys med & rehab, Univ Wash, beginning 1957; asst prof & assoc dir dept, Ohio State Univ, 1955-1957; asst prof med, Mayo Clinic, 1951-1955; fel phys med, Mayo Clin, 1951-1955; asst physician internal med, Univ Frankfurt, 1948-1951; res asst, Max Planck Inst Biophys, 1946-1948; asst physician internal med, Univ Frankfurt, 1945-1946. **Memberships:** Biophys Soc; AMA; Am Asn Electromyog & Electrodiag; Am Acad Phys Med & Rehab; Am Cong Rehab Med. **Research Statement & Publications:** Biophysics of physical agents used in medicine; rehabilitation. **Mailing Address:** Health Sci Bldg, Univ Wash, PO Box 356490, Seattle, WA 98195. **Fax:** 206-685-3244.

LEHMANN, MILLIANNE, MATHEMATICS. **Education:** San Francisco State Univ, MA, 1963. **Professional Experience:** RETIRED; chair, Math Dept, Univ San Francisco, 1991-1996; proj dir, Univ San Francisco Middle School Math Inst, 1984-1986; prof math, Univ San Francisco, 1965-2004. **Mailing Address:** Univ San Francisco, Dept Math, 2130 Fulton Street, San Francisco, CA 94117-1080. **E-Mail:** lehmann@usfca.edu

LEHMANN, PAUL F, MEDICAL MYCOLOGY, MYCOLOGY. **Personal Data:** b Kampala, Uganda, June 1949; m 1980, Carol; c Hannah, Esther & Sophie. **Education:** Univ Cambridge, UK, BA (Hons), 1970, PhD (bot), 1974; Univ Birmingham, UK, MSc, 1976. **Professional Experience:** ACAD DIR, MED COL OHIO, as of 2006; PROF MICROBIOL, MED COL OHIO, 1993-; from asst prof to assoc prof, Med Col Ohio, 1979-1993; fel, Univ Cambridge, 1978; vis scientist, Ctr Dis Control, Atlanta, Ga, 1976-1978. **Memberships:** Am Soc Microbiol; Med Mycol Soc Am; Mycol Soc Am. **Research Statement & Publications:** Fungi causing human disease including yeasts, molds and poisonous mushrooms. **Mailing Address:** Dept Microbiol & Immuniol, Med Col Ohio, 3000 Arlington Ave, Toledo, OH 43614. **E-Mail:** pflehmann@mco.edu

LEHMANN, RUTH, GENETICS. **Education:** Univ Tubingen, Ger, PhD. **Professional Experience:** JULIUS RAYNES PROF DEVELOP GENETICS, NY UNIV CTR, as of 2005; INVESTR, HOWARD HUGHES MED INST, as of 2005. **Mailing Address:** Howard Hughes Med Inst & Develop Genetics Skirball Inst Biomolecular Med, Fourth Floor NY Univ Sch Med 540 First Ave, New York, NY 10016. **E-Mail:** lehmann@saturn.med.nyu.edu

LEHMANN, WILMA HELEN, VERTEBRATE MORPHOLOGY. **Personal Data:** b Chicago, Ill, November 14, 1929. **Education:** Mundelein Col, BA, 1951; Northwestern Univ, MS, 1954; Univ Ill, PhD (zool), 1961. **Professional Experience:** RETIRED; chairperson, Dept Biol, 1983-1991; vis res assoc, Argonne Nat Lab, 1969-1970; from asst prof to prof biol, Northeastern Ill Univ, 1967-1991; asst prof natural sci, Mich State Univ, 1964-1967; NSF instnl res grant, 1963-1964; asst prof zool, Pa State Univ, 1961-1964; Indexer, Evolution, 1960-1966; Res asst allergy, Med Sch, Northwestern Univ, 1954-1956. **Memberships:** Fel AAAS; Soc Study Evolution; Am Soc Zool; Sigma Xi. **Research Statement & Publications:** Comparative vertebrate anatomy; adaptive radiation of primates and rodents; functional mammalian anatomy; functional morphology, gross and microscopic, of bone; glaucoma. **Mailing Address:** 5859 N Kenneth Ave, Chicago, IL 60645.

LEHMBERG, ROBERT HENRY, NON-LINEAR OPTICS, LASER-PLASMA PHYSICS. **Personal Data:** b Philadelphia, Pa, December 4, 1937; m 1966, Norma Geder; c Karl Robert. **Education:** Pa State Univ, BSc, 1959; Univ Ariz, MSc, 1961; Brandeis Univ, PhD (physics), 1968. **Honors & Awards:** Excellence in Plasma Physics Res Award, Am Phys Soc, 1993. **Professional Experience:** Chmn prog comt, Conf Lasers & Electro-Optics, 1991; RES PHYSICIST, NAVAL RES LAB, WASHINGTON, DC, 1972-; Res physicist, Naval Air Develop Ctr, Warminster, Pa, 1966-1972. **Memberships:** Fel Am Phys Soc; AAAS; Sigma Xi; affil Inst Elec & Electronics Engrs. **Research Statement & Publications:** Development of optical beam smoothing techniques for laser fusion; optical design of the Naval Research Laboratory's Nike laser facility; nonlinear optics and laser-plasma interaction physics; contributed articles to professional journals; patentee in field. **Mailing Address:** 4502 Hadrian Ct, Alexandria, VA 22310-1420. **Fax:** 202-767-0046. **E-Mail:** lehmberg@this.nrl.navy.mil

LEHMKUHL, DENNIS MERLE, ENTOMOLOGY, ECOLOGY. **Personal Data:** b Pierre, SDak, August 22, 1942; m 1965, c 3. **Education:** Univ Mont, BA, 1964, MS, 1966; Ore State Univ, PhD (entom), 1969. **Professional Experience:** PROF BIOL, UNIV SASK, 1980-; from asst prof to assoc prof, Univ Sask, 1974-1980; Ecol & taxon consult. **Memberships:** NAm Benthological Soc; Entom Soc Can. **Research Statement & Publications:** Taxonomy and biology of Ephemeroptera; ecology of rivers; arctic and northern aquatic insects, especially ecological adaptations and limiting factors and the resulting zoogeographical implications. **Mailing Address:** Dept Biol, Univ Sask, 112 Sci Pl, Saskatoon, SK S7N 5E2, Can. **Fax:** 306-966-4461. **E-Mail:** lehmkuhl@duke.usask.ca

LEHN, JEAN-MARIE PIERRE, CHEMISTRY. **Personal Data:** b Rosheim, France, September 30, 1939; m 1965, Sylvie Lederer; c 2. **Education:** Univ Strasbourg, PhD, 1963. **Honorary Degrees:** PhD, Univ Jerusalem, 1984, Univ Autonoma, 1985, Univ Gottingen, 1987, Univ Bruxells, 1987, Univ Herakliou, 1989, Univ Bologna, 1989, Charles Univ, 1990, Univ Twente, 1991, Univ Sheffield, 1991, Univ Athens, 1992, Univ Polytech Athens, 1992, Polytech Univ. **Honors & Awards:** Nobel Prize Chem, 1987; Bronze, Silver & Gold Medals, Ctr Nat Sci Res; Gold Medal, Pontifical Acad Sci, 1981; Paracelsus Prize, Swiss Chem Soc, 1982; von Humboldt Prize, 1983; Karl-Ziegler Prize, 1989; Bonner Chemiepreis, 1993; Ettore Majorana-Erice-Sci Peace Prize, 1994; Gold Medal, Soc Acad Arts, Sci Letters, 1995. **Professional Experience:** Heinrich-Hertz Gast prof, Karlsruhe Univ, 1989; Barcelona Univ, 1985 & Frankfurt Univ, 1985-1986; vis prof chem, Cambridge Univ, 1984; PROF, COL FRANCE, 1979-; vis prof chem, Switz, 1977; vis prof chem, Harvard Univ, 1972 & 1974; prof chem, Univ Louis Pasteur Strasbourg, 1970-1979; assoc prof, Univ Louis Pasteur Strasbourg, 1970; asst prof, Univ Strasbourg, 1966-1969; Postdoctoral res assoc, Harvard Univ, 1963-1964; Staff, Nat Ctr Sci Res, 1960-1966. **Memberships:** Nat Acad Sci; hon mem AAAS; Royal Neth Acad; Am Philos Soc; Acad Europaea; Yougoslav Acad Arts & Sci; Indian Acad Sci; Polish Acad Sci; Royal Acad Sci Lett & Fine Arts; Korean Acad Sci & Technol; Acad Sci Ukraine; Acad Roumaine; Royal Soc. **Research Statement & Publications:** Contributed over 470 articles to scientific publications. **Mailing Address:** 6 rue des Pontonniers, Strasbourg 67000, France.

LEHN, WILLIAM LEE, MATERIALS ENGINEERING, CHEMISTRY. **Personal Data:** b Spring Valley, Ill, March 17, 1932; m 1954, Joan Schur; c Karen S, Michael J, Andrea J & Linda M. **Education:** Univ Ill, BS, 1954; Univ Rochester, PhD (chem), 1958. **Honors & Awards:** Sky Lab Achievement Award, NASA, 1974; R T Schwartz Eng Award, 1987. **Professional Experience:** CONSULT, 1991-; mat engr coatings, Air Force Mat Lab, 1981-1990; tech area mgr, Air Force Mat Lab, 1967-1981; group leader, Air Force Mat Lab, 1961-1967; res chemist, Air Force Mat Lab, 1960-1961; chemist polymers, E I du Pont Del Nemours, 1958-1960. **Memberships:** Am Chem Soc; Res Soc Am; Am Inst Aeronaut & Astronaut; Sigma Xi. **Research Statement & Publications:** Materials; coatings; protective and functional coatings and materials for aircraft and spacecraft; spacecraft survivability. **Mailing Address:** 450 Deauville Dr, Dayton, OH 45429. **E-Mail:** billbilt@siscom.net

LEHNE, RICHARD KARL, ORGANIC CHEMISTRY. **Personal Data:** b Newark, NJ, November 18, 1920; m 1945, c 4. **Education:** Muhlenberg Col, BS, 1941; Yale Univ, PhD (org chem), 1949. **Professional Experience:** RETIRED; dir regulatory affairs, Church & Dwight Co, Inc, 1971-1982; dir consumer prod res & develop, Cyanamid Int, 1966-1971; dir res & develop, Mennen Co, 1963-1966; mgr hair prod, Colgate-Palmolive Co, 1959-1963; from assoc dir to dir res & develop, Wildroot Co, 1952-1959; Process develop chemist, Gen Aniline & Film Co, 1949-1952. **Memberships:** AAAS; Am Chem Soc; Soc Cosmetic Chemists (secy, 1960-1963). **Research Statement & Publications:** Emulsion technology and viscosity versus stability; effects of phenolic additives. **Mailing Address:** 2 Wakesfield Lane, Piscataway, NJ 08854.

LEHNER, GUYDO R, TOPOLOGY. **Personal Data:** b Chicago, Ill, April 14, 1928; m 1973, Ellen. **Education:** Loyola Univ, Ill, BS, 1951; Univ Wis, MS, 1953, PhD, 1958. **Professional Experience:** PROF EMER MATH, UNIV MD, COL PARK, as of 2005; prof math, Univ Md, Col Park, beginning 1968; from instr to assoc prof, Univ MD, Col Park, 1958-1968; instr math, Univ Wis-Milwaukee, 1957-1958. **Memberships:** Am Math Soc; Math Asn Am. **Research Statement & Publications:** Abstract spaces; continua; point set topology. **Mailing Address:** Univ Md, Dept Math, 3306 Math, College Park, MD 20742-0001. **E-Mail:** grl@wam.umd.edu

LEHNER, NOEL D M, MEDICAL RESEARCH. **Education:** Wake Forest Univ, MS, 1970. **Professional Experience:** PROF EMER PATHOL, EMORY UNIV SCH MED, as of 2006. **Mailing Address:** Dept Path & Lab Med Emory Univ Sch Med, 218 Woodruff Mem Bldg Drawer TT Whitehead Bldg G 02, Atlanta, GA 30322-4510. **Fax:** 404-727-3212. **E-Mail:** nlehner@dar.emory.edu

LEHNER, PAUL E, TECHNOLOGY. **Education:** Bethany Col, BS, 1976; Univ Mich, MA, 1979, PhD 1981. **Professional Experience:** ASSOC PROF SYSTS ENG, GEORGE MASON UNIV, as of 2000. **Mailing Address:** George Mason Univ, 4400 Univ Dr, Fairfax, VA 22030. **Fax:** 301-286-1771. **E-Mail:** plehner@mason1.gmu.edu

LEHNER, PHILIP NELSON, ANIMAL BEHAVIOR, ECOLOGY. **Personal Data:** b NH, July 5, 1940; m 1967, c 2. **Education:** Syracuse Univ, BS, 1962; Cornell Univ, MS, 1964; Utah State Univ, PhD (animal behav), 1969. **Professional Experience:** PROF EMER ANIMAL BEHAV, COLO STATE UNIV, as of 2006; pres, Animal Behav Assocs Inc, 1983-; prof animal behav, Colo State Univ, beginning 1983; consult, Stearns-Roger Corp, 1970-1980; NIH grant, Colo State Univ, 1969-; from asst prof to assoc prof, Colo State Univ, 1969-1983; biologist, USPHS, 1965; res asst, Cornell Univ, 1962-1964 & Smithsonian Inst, 1964-1965; biologist, Bur Sport Fisheries & Wildlife, 1962. **Memberships:** AAAS; Animal Behav Soc; Soc Exp Anal Behav; Wildlife Soc; Am Vet Soc Animal Behav. **Research Statement & Publications:** Animal behavior, its description, analysis and the effects of environmental variables; wild and domestic species; fish and wildlife; zoology. **Mailing Address:** Dept Biol, Colo State Univ, Ft Collins, CO 80523-0001.

LEHNERT, SHIRLEY MARGARET, RADIOBIOLOGY. **Personal Data:** b London, Eng, June 2, 1934; m 1961, c 2. **Education:** Univ Nottingham, BSc, 1955; Univ London, MSc, 1958, PhD (biophys), 1961. **Professional Experience:** DIR, RADIATION BIOL, MONTREAL GEN HOSP RES INST, as of 2005; PROF MED PHYS UNIT, MCGILL UNIV, as of 2005; PROF RADIATION ONCOL, MCGILL UNIV, 1997-; vis scientist, Inst Gustav Roussy,

Paris, France, 1985; assoc prof radiation oncol, Mcgill Univ, 1982-1997; asst prof therapeut radiol, Mcgill Univ, 1974-1982; asst prof radiol, Radiol Res Lab, Col Physicians & Surgeons, Columbia Univ, 1971-1974; res assoc phys biol, Sloan-Kettering Inst Cancer Res, 1968-1971; sci serv officer, Defence Bd Can, 1965-1967; res biophysicist, Montreal Gen Hosp, 1963-1965; fel, Univ Rochester, 1961-1963. **Memberships:** AAAS; Radiation Res Soc; Am Asn Cancer Res. **Research Statement & Publications:** Biological and biochemical effects of ionizing radiation; delivery systems for radio and chemo-sensitizing drugs. **Mailing Address:** Dept Oncol, McGill Univ, 546 Pine Ave W, Montreal, PQ H2W 1S6, Can. **Fax:** 514-934-8220. **E-Mail:** mdle@musica.mcgill.ca

LEHNHOFF, TERRY FRANKLIN, MECHANICAL ENGINEERING, ENGINEERING MECHANICS. **Personal Data:** b St Louis, Mo, July 7, 1939; m 1960, Donna; c Mark, Lori, Stephen & Hope. **Education:** Univ Mo, Rolla, BS, 1961, MS, 1962; Univ Ill, Urbana, PhD (theoret & appl mech), 1968. **Professional Experience:** PROF EMER MECH & AEROSPACE ENG, UNIV MO, ROLLA, as of 2004; CMI, 1989-1993 & Paul Mueller Co, 1990-1994; pres, Enmeco, 1983-; Eaton Corp, 1980-1982 & Rockwell Int, 1981-1982; prof mech & aerospace eng, Univ Mo, Rolla, beginning 1977; consult, Detroit Tool, 1976-1985; res assoc, Rock Mech Res Ctr, 1970-1980; from asst prof to assoc prof mech eng, Univ Mo, Rolla, 1968-1977; res engr, Caterpillar Tractor Co, 1962-1965; legal consult, mech design & failure anal. **Memberships:** Sigma Xi; Am Soc Mech Engrs. **Research Statement & Publications:** Stress analysis by conventional and finite element methods; stress analysis of bolted and welded joints; solid mechanics; pressure vessel design; failure analysis of mechanical components. **Mailing Address:** Dept Mech Aerospace Eng & Eng Mech, Univ Mo, 125 Mech Eng Annex 1870 Miner Circle, Rolla, MO 65409-0050. **Fax:** 573-341-4115. **E-Mail:** lenhoff@umr.edu

LEHOCZKY, JOHN PAUL, STATISTICS, REAL-TIME COMPUTER SYSTEMS & COMPUTATIONAL FINANCE. **Personal Data:** b Columbus, Ohio, June 29, 1943; m 1966, Mary; c Jennifer L (Elliott) & Jessica A. **Education:** Oberlin Col, BA, 1965; Stanford Univ, MS, 1967, PhD (statist), 1969. **Professional Experience:** Dean, Col Humanities & Soc Sci, beginning 2000; THOMAS LORD PROF STATIST, CARNEGIE MELLON UNIV, 1997-; dept head, Carnegie Mellon Univ, 1984-1995; from asst prof to prof statist, Carnegie Mellon Univ, 1969-1997; assoc ed, J Real-Time Systs, Inst Elec & Electronics Engrs Trans Comput. **Memberships:** Fel Inst Math Statist; Fel Am Statist Asn; INFORMS; AAAS; Inst Elec & Electronics Engrs; Int Statist Inst; Asn Comput Mach. **Research Statement & Publications:** Applied probability theory; stochastic processes and their application to computer and communication systems; real-time computer systems; mathematical finance and space biostatistics. **Mailing Address:** Dept Statist, Carnegie Mellon Univ, BH 232G, Pittsburgh, PA 15213. **Fax:** 412-268-7828. **E-Mail:** jpl@stat.cmu.edu

LEHOULLIER, CRAIG S, ORGANIC CHEMISTRY. **Education:** PhD, 1982. **Professional Experience:** GLAXO SMITH KLINE, NC, as of 2005. **Research Statement & Publications:** Novel Syntheses of Polycyclic Aromatic Hydrocarbons. **Mailing Address:** GlaxoSmithKline, 5 Moore Dr PO Box 13398, Research Triangle Park, NC 27709.

LEHOUX, JEAN-GUY, BIOCHEMISTRY, ENDOCRINOLOGY. **Personal Data:** b St Severin, Que, January 9, 1939; m 1963, c Nathalie, Caroline & Martine. **Education:** Univ Montreal, BSc, 1963, MSc, 1967, PhD (biochem), 1969. **Professional Experience:** PROF, DEPT BIOCHEM, OBSTET & GYNEC, SHERBROOKE UNIV, 1981-; head, dept biochem, 1980-1992; head clin endocrinol, Sherbrooke Univ, 1974-1986; med res coun can scholar, 1974; from asst prof to assoc prof obstet & gynec, Sherbrooke Univ, 1971-1981; med res coun que & med res coun can grant, Univ Sherbrooke, 1971-1974; med res coun can fel, fac med, Univ Montreal, 1969-1970 & Dept Zool, Univ Sheffield, 1970-1971; lectr med, Univ Montreal, 1969-1971; biochemist, Hosp Maisonneuve, 1969-1970; res asst biochem, Univ Montreal, 1965-1969; chief chemist, Cyanamid Can Ltd, 1963-1965. **Memberships:** Brit Soc Endocrinol; Soc Endocrinol; NY Acad Sci. **Research Statement & Publications:** Studies on steroid hydroxylation with a special interest to aldosterone regulation; published over 20 articles. **Mailing Address:** Dept Biochem, Univ Sherbrooke, 2500 Blvd, Sherbrooke, PQ J1H 5N4, Can. **Fax:** 819-564-5340. **E-Mail:** jean-guy.lehoux@usherbrooke.ca

LEHOVEC, KURT, SEMI-CONDUCTING DEVICES, OPTO-ELECTRONICS. **Personal Data:** b Ledvice, Czech, June 12, 1918; American citizen; m 1952, c 4. **Education:** Prague Charles Univ, BS, 1938, MS, 1940, PhD (physics), 1941. **Professional Experience:** PROF EMER MAT SCI, UNIV SOUTHERN CALIF, 1988-; Univ Calif, Irvine, 1980; prof electronics, Univ Southern Calif, 1971-1988; consult, var co, 1967-; PRES, INVENTORS & INVESTORS, 1967-; adj prof, Williams, Col, 1967; dir semiconductor res & develop, Sprague Elec Co, 1952-1966; res fel, US Signal Corps, Ft Monmouth, NJ, 1947-1952; res fel, Physics Inst, Prague Univ, 1945-1946; head res lab, Physics Inst, Prague Univ, 1942-1945. **Memberships:** Fel Am Phys Soc; fel Inst Elec & Electronics Engrs. **Research Statement & Publications:** Crystal structure; phase diagrams; defects; energy levels; transistors; solar cells. **Mailing Address:** Dept Mat Sci, Univ Southern Calif, Univ Park MC 0483, Seaver Sci Ctr 522, Los Angeles, CA 90089. **Fax:** 213-740-4449.

LEHR, CARLTON G(ORNEY), electrical engineering; deceased, see previous edition for last biography

LEHR, DAVID, CARDIOVASCULAR PHARMACOLOGY, MEDICINE. **Personal Data:** b Sadagura, Austria, March 22, 1910; American citizen; div, c Karin Elisabeth & Jonothan Mathias. **Education:** Univ Vienna, Austria, BA, 1929, MD, 1935. **Professional Experience:** Consult ed, J Am Col Nutrit, 1982; co-chmn, Coun Drugs, Am Col Nutrit, 1980-; PROF EMER PHARMACOL, NY MED COL, 1980-; chmn ad hoc comt, Use New Therapeut Agents & Procedures Human Beings, assoc Med Schs, NY, 1967-; prof & chmn, dept Pharmacol, 1964-1979; vchmn, Panel Neurol & Psychiat Dis, 1961-1965; mem rev comt, Health res Coun New York, 1961-1965; Claud Bernard prof, inst Exp Med & Surg, Univ Montreal, 1961; prof & chmn, dept Physiol & Pharmacol, 1956-1964; vis physician, Metrop Hosp, Welfare Island, NY, 1954-1975; vis physician, Bird S Coler Hosp, 1954-1975; assoc attend physician, Flower & Fifth Ave Hosps, 1949-1975; assoc prof med, Ny Med Col, beginning 1949; asst attend physician, Flower & Fifth Ave Hosps, 1944-1949; asst vis physician, Metrop Hosp, Welfare Island, NY, 1942-1954; from instr to assoc prof pharmacol, NY Med Col, 1941-1954; pharmacologist & res assoc, Path dept, Newark Beth Israel Hosp, NJ, 1939-1942; instr, Univ Lund, 1938-1939; asst pharmacol, Univ Vienna, 1934-1948. **Memberships:** Fel AAAS; fel Am Col Physicians; fel Am Col Cardiol; Soc Exp Biol & Med; Am Soc Pharmacol & Exp Therapeut; Am Soc Arteriosclerosis; Am Soc Exp Path; Sigma Xi; NY Acad Sci; Harvey Soc; Int Soc Heart Res; NY Acad Medicine; Am Heart Asn. **Research Statement & Publications:** Cardiology; hypertension; arteriosclerosis; toxicity of sulfonamides; sulfonamide mixtures; chemotherapy; experimental cardiovascular necrosis; parathyroid hormone interrelations; tissue electrolytes. **Mailing Address:** Dept Pharmacol, NY Med Col, 125 W 96th St, New York, NY 10025-6419. **Fax:** 212-666-1726.

LEHR, GARY FULTON, NEW TECHNOLOGY EXPLORATION & EVALUATION. **Personal Data:** b Rockville Centre, NY, July 16, 1952; m 1981, c 3. **Education:** Manhattanville Col, AB, 1975; Brown Univ, PhD (chem), 1981. **Professional Experience:** TECH LEADER, PROTOTYPING GROUP, DU PONT FIBERS, E I DU PONT DEL NEMOURS & CO, INC, 1989-; staff specialist, Comput Consult, 1984-1989; staff scientist res, Cent Res & Develop Dept, 1981-1984; Res assoc, Dept Chem, Columbia Univ, 1979-1981. **Memberships:** Am Chem Soc; AAAS. **Research Statement & Publications:** Study of reaction mechanisms involving free radical and carbene intermediates, including radical-radical, radical-molecule photochemical, organometallic and autoxidation reactions. **Mailing Address:** 122 Chatham Pl, Wilmington, DE 19810.

LEHR, JAY H, HYDROLOGY, GROUNDWATER GEOLOGY. **Personal Data:** b Teaneck, NJ, September 11, 1936; m 1978, c 2. **Education:** Princeton Univ, BSE, 1957; Univ Ariz, PhD (hydrol), 1962. **Professional Experience:** SCI DIR, HEARTLAND INST, as of 2006; PRES, ENVIRON EDUC ENTERPRISES, as of 2003; ed-in-chief, Water Well J, 1972-; exec dir, Nat Water Well Asn, beginning 1967; ed, Ground Water, 1966-; asst prof, Ohio State Univ, 1964-1967; from instr to asst prof, Univ Ariz, 1962-1964; res assoc hydrol, Univ Ariz, 1959-1962; Hydrol field asst, Groundwater Br, US Geol Surv, NY, 1955-1956; adj prof, Ohio State Univ. **Research Statement & Publications:** Groundwater model studies utilizing consolidated porous medias; groundwater pollution; groundwater and surfacewater law; water well construction techniques. **Mailing Address:** 6011 Houseman Rd, Ostrander, OH 43061. **Fax:** 740-362-4339. **E-Mail:** e3power.com

LEHR, MARVIN HAROLD, POLYMER PHYSICS, POLYMER CHEMISTRY. **Personal Data:** b Brooklyn, NY, March 17, 1933; m 1956, Susan Quenk; c Mike, Ted, Steve & Bob. **Education:** Reed Col, BA, 1954; Yale Univ, MS, 1955, PhD (chem), 1959. **Professional Experience:** RES FEL CORP RES, B F GOODRICH RES & DEVELOP CTR, 1978-; sr res assoc, B F Goodrich Res Ctr, 1973-1978; res assoc, B F Goodrich Res Ctr, 1966-1973; sr res chemist, B F Goodrich Res Ctr, 1961-1966; Res chemist, B F Goodrich Res Ctr, 1959-1961. **Research Statement & Publications:** Viscoelastic-fracture behavior; polymer morphology; relation of polymer structure to properties; structure-property studies on polymer blends and composites; relationships of physical, mechanical and rheological properties to composition, microstructure and morphology of miscible and immiscible mixtures. **Mailing Address:** 1252 Briarhill Spur, Akron, OH 44333. **Fax:** 216-447-5249.

LEHRER, GERARD MICHAEL, NEUROLOGY, MULTIPLE SCLEROSIS. **Personal Data:** b Vienna, Austria, May 29, 1927; American citizen; m 1994, Suzanne Macahilig; c Alicia & Richard. **Education:** City Col New York, BS, 1950; NY Univ, MD, 1954. **Professional Experience:** NEUROLOGIST, COMMUNITY HOSP MONTEREY PENINSULA, 1997-; neurologist, Chief Grade, Palo Alto Vet Admin Health Care Syst, 1994-1997; attend neurologist, St Vincent Hosp, Nev, 1976-; sr staff neurologist, Bronx Vet Affairs Med Ctr, 1976-1994; attend neurologist, Mt Sinai Hosp, 1968-1994; prof neurol, Mt Sinai Sch Med, 1967-1994; consult neurologist, Vet Admin Hosp, Bronx, NY, 1967-1975; res collabr, Brookhaven Nat Lab, NY, 1967-1969; dir, Div Neurochem, Mt Sinai Hosp, NY, 1966-1974; assoc prof, Mt Sinai Hosp, NY, 1966-1967; consult, Preclin Psychopharmacol Res Rev Comt, NIMH, 1965-1969; from asst attend neurologist to assoc attend neurologist, Mt Sinai Hosp, NY, 1960-1968; NIH spec trainee neurochem & res fel pharmacol, Sch Med, Wash Univ, 1958-1961; asst neurol, Sch Med, Wash Univ, 1958-1960; resident, Mt Sinai Hosp, NY, 1958; NIH trainee, Mt Sinai Hosp, NY, 1956-1958; asst resident neurologist, Mt Sinai Hosp, NY, 1955-1957; intern, Mt Sinai Hosp, NY, 1954-1955; res asst neurol, Col Physicians & Surgeons, Columbia Univ, 1953-1954. **Memberships:** Fel Am Acad Neurol; fel NY Acad Med; Int Soc Neurochem; Am Neurol Asn; Am Soc Neurochem; Asn Res Nervous & Ment Disease. **Research Statement & Publications:** Brain maturation and metabolism; molecular mechanisms of central nervous system differentiation and disease, especially demyelination; neuroimmunology. **Mailing Address:** Neurol, Mt Sinai Hosp, 600 Univ Ave, Toronto, ON M5G 1X5, Can.

LEHRER, HAROLD Z, RADIOLOGY. **Personal Data:** b New York, NY, August 22, 1927. **Education:** Columbia Univ, AB, 1947; NY Univ, MD, 1953; Am Bd Radiol, dipl, 1960. **Professional Experience:** RETIRED; radiologist, as of 2004; dir dept radiol, Bird S Coler Hosp, Ny, beginning 1973; assoc prof neuroradiol, Ny Med Col, beginning 1968; from asst to assoc prof, Sch Med, Tulane Univ, 1965-1967; instr neuroradiol, NY Univ-Bellevue Med Ctr, 1963-1965; NIH spec fel neuroradiol, NY Univ-Bellevue Med Ctr, 1963-1965; asst adj radiologist, Beth Israel Hosp & Med Ctr, NY, 1959-1963; Am Cancer Soc fel, 1958. **Memberships:** AAAS; Radiol Soc NAm; Am Roentgen Ray Soc; Am Soc Neuroradiol. **Research Statement & Publications:** Neuroradiology, especially analysis of clinical data mathematically. **Mailing Address:** 89 River St, Box M705, Hoboken, NJ 07030-0705.

LEHRER, HARRIS IRVING, BIOCHEMISTRY, IMMUNOCHEMISTRY. **Personal Data:** b Boston, Mass, May 28, 1939. **Education:** Brandeis Univ, BA, 1960, PhD (biochem), 1965. **Professional Experience:** VPRES, BULK CHEM, SPECTRUM QUAL PRODS, as of 1997; SR IMMUNOCHEMIST, ICL SCI, 1978-; supvr, Sherman-Abrams Lab, 1977-1978; group leader, Ortho Diag, 1976-1977; sr scientist immunochem, Ortho Diag, 1969-1976; sr biochemist, Monsanto Corp, 1968-1969; Univ Palermo, 1965-1967 & Brandeis Univ, 1967-1968; NIH fel, Marine Biol Lab, Woods Hole, 1965. **Memberships:** AAAS; Am Asn Clin Chem; NY Acad Sci; Am Chem Soc. **Research Statement & Publications:** Development of new immunochemical techniques and their application to diagnostic testing. **Mailing Address:** Spectrum Lab Prods Inc, 14422 S San Pedro, Gardena, CA 90248.

LEHRER, PAUL LINDNER, PHYSICAL GEOGRAPHY. **Personal Data:** b Chicago, Ill, February 9, 1928; m 1953, c 4. **Education:** Univ Cincinnati, BS, 1949; Ohio State Univ, MA, 1951; Univ Nebr, PhD (geog), 1962. **Professional Experience:** PROF EMER GEOG, UNIV NORTHERN COLO, 1993-; prof geog, Univ Northern Colo, beginning 1969; assoc prof, Univ Northern Colo, 1966-1969; NSF sci fac fel, Univ Witwatersrand, 1964-1965; from instr to asst prof, Univ Wis-Milwaukee, 1960-1966; Instr geog, Ohio Univ, 1956-1959. **Memberships:** Asn Am Geogr; Sigma Xi. **Research Statement & Publications:** Soils and regional geography of Subsaharan Africa. **Mailing Address:** Dept Geog, Univ Northern Colo, Rm 2200, Candelaria Hall, Greeley, CO 80639. **Fax:** 970-351-2890.

LEHRER, PAUL MICHAEL, RELAXATION THERAPY, PSYCHOPHYSIOLOGY. **Personal Data:** b New York, NY, August 30, 1941; m 1965, Phyllis; c 2. **Education:** Columbia Col, AB, 1963; Harvard Univ, PhD (clin psychol), 1969. **Professional Experience:** PROF PSYCHIAT, ROBERT WOOD JOHNSON MED SCH, 1989-; act dir, Biofeedback Clinic, Robert Wood Johnson Rehabilitation Inst, John F Kennedy Hosp, 1982; vis prof, Univ London, 1980-1981; from asst prof to assoc prof, Robert Wood Johnson Med Sch, 1972-1989; Carter Wallace, Inc, 1975-1977; consult, Work Incentive prog, Middlesex Coun, NJ, 1970-1977; consult, Veterans Admi Hosp, E Orange, NJ, 1970-1975; asst prof psychol, Rutgers Univ, 1970-1972; clin instr psychol, Tufts Univ Sch Med, 1968-1970. **Memberships:** Am Psychol Asn; Biofeedback Soc Am; Soc Psychophys Res; Soc Behav Med; Asn Adv Behav Ther. **Research Statement & Publications:** Psychophysiological research on the effects of relaxation therapy on psychosomatic disease; psychophysiology of asthma, headache, back pain and anxiety; nature and treatment of stage fright; author of various articles. **Mailing Address:** Dept Psychiat, UMDNJ-Robert Wood Johnson Med Sch, Piscataway, NJ 08854. **Fax:** 732-235-4430. **E-Mail:** lehrer@umdnj.edu

LEHRER, ROBERT N(ATHANIEL), INDUSTRIAL & SYSTEMS ENGINEERING. **Personal Data:** b Sandusky, Ohio, January 17, 1922; m 1945, Patricia Lee Martin; c Joan E. **Education:** Purdue Univ, BS, 1945, MS, 1947, PhD (indust eng), 1949. **Honors & Awards:** Outstanding Indust Eng Award, Am Inst Indust Engrs, 1957; Frank & Lillian Gilbreath Indust Eng Award, Inst Elec & Electronics Engrs, 1987. **Professional Experience:** PROF EMER & DIR EMER, GA INST TECHNOL, 1981-; assoc & vis sr adv, Am Productivity Ctr, 1978-1979; Nat Acad Sci workshop panel indust & technol res, Indonesia, 1971; dir, Sch Indust & Systs Eng, Ga Inst Technol, 1966-1978; prof indust eng, Sch Indust & Systs Eng, Ga Inst Technol, 1963-1981; assoc dir, Sch Indust & Systs Eng, Ga Inst Technol, 1963-1966; adv indust eng, Eindhoven & Dutch Ministry Educ, 1962-; UNESCO expert, Guadalajara & Guanajuato, 1962-1963; adv indust & systs eng sem, Japan, 1959 & 1962; prof & chmn dept, Technol Inst, Northwestern Univ, Ill, 1958-1963; prof, Ga Inst Technol, 1954-1958; ed-in-chief, J Indust Eng, 1953-1962; Consult opers res, 1950-; res assoc, Ga Inst Technol, 1950-1958; assoc prof, Ga Inst Technol, 1950-1954; asst prof, Ore State Col, 1949-1950; Asst & instr indust eng, Purdue Univ, 1946-1949; consult ed indust eng & mgt sci ser, Reinhold Publ Corp; mem adv bd mil personnel supplies, Nat Acad Sci-Nat Res Coun. **Memberships:** Nat Acad Sci; Am Soc Eng Educ; fel Am Inst Indust Engrs (vpres 1960); Inst Mgt Sci; Sigma Xi; Opers Res Soc Am. **Research Statement & Publications:** Work simplification; operations research and management science; management of improvement; author of numerous publications. **Mailing Address:** Ga Inst Technol, PO Box 180, 765 First Dr, Atlanta, GA 30318. **Fax:** 404-894-2301. **E-Mail:** robert.lehrer@isye.gatech.edu

LEHRER, SAMUEL BRUCE, ALLERGY, IMMUNOLOGY. **Personal Data:** b New Britain, Conn, April 1, 1943; m 1971, c 4. **Education:** Upsala Col, BS, 1966; Temple Univ, PhD, 1971. **Professional Experience:** RES PROF MED & ADJ ASSOC PROF MICROBIOL & IMMUNOL, TULANE UNIV SCH MED, as of 2005; ADJ PROF ENVIRON MED, TULANE UNIV SCH MED, 1996-; co-chmn, Allergen Stand Comt, beginning 1993; exec Comt, Int Union Immunol Sci, 1991; chmn, Stand Comt, Am Acad Allergy, Asthma & Immunol, 1990-1995; scholar grant, Nat Fisheries Inst, 1984-1995; consult, Nat Heart Lung & Blood Inst, 1983; prof med, Sch Med, Tulane Univ, beginning 1983; res award, Cander Asn New Orleans, 1981-1982; adj assoc prof microbiol & immunol, Tulane Univ, beginning 1980; Nat Inst Allergy & Infectious Dis young investr award, 1978-1981; Am Lung Asn grant, 1978-1980; consult, Food & Drug Admin, 1978-1980; from asst prof to assoc prof, Sch Med, Tulane Univ, 1975-1983; NIH fel, 1974; fel, Scripps Clin & Res Found, La Jolla, 1971-1975; researcher, Univ Lausanne, Switz, 1969; Lab technician, Microbiol Dept, State Lab Hartford, 1965. **Memberships:** Am Soc Microbiol; Am Acad Allergy; Am Asn Immunologists; Am Thoracic Soc; Col Int Allergologicum; Am Acad Allergy Asthma & Immunol; Int Union Immunol Sci. **Research Statement & Publications:** Pathogenesis of allergic diseases including: seafood allergy, immunopathogenesis of food allergy, allergenicity of transgenic crops, mold allergy, occupational allergies and effects of indoor allergens and pollutants. **Mailing Address:** Tulane Univ Sch Med, 1700 Perdido St, New Orleans, LA 70112. **Fax:** 504-584-3686. **E-Mail:** sblehrer@tulane.edu

LEHRER, SHERWIN SAMUEL, MUSCLE PROTEIN INTERACTIONS. **Personal Data:** b New York, NY, April 2, 1934; m 1960, Liane Reif; c Damon & Erica. **Education:** Univ Pittsburgh, BS, 1956; Univ Calif, Berkeley, PhD (chem), 1961. **Professional Experience:** SR STAFF SCIENTIST BIOCHEM, BOSTON BIOMED RES INST, 1970-; Prin assoc, Harvard Med Sch, 1968-; res assoc, Retina Found, Mass, 1966-1970; fel biochem, Brandeis Univ, 1963-1966; Staff scientist thin magnetic films, Lincoln Lab, Mass Inst Technol, 1961-1962. **Memberships:** AAAS; NY Acad Sci; Am Soc Biol Chem; Am Chem Soc; Biophys Soc; Protein Soc. **Research Statement & Publications:** Application of fluorescence techniques to muscle protein conformation and interactions; muscle protein interactions. **Mailing Address:** Muscle and Motility Group, Boston Biomed Res Inst 64 Grove St Staniford, Watertown, MA 02472.

LEHRMAN, GEORGE PHILIP, PHARMACY ADMINISTRATION. **Personal Data:** b New York, NY, November 28, 1926; m 1948, Natalie Mortensen; c Philip, Paul & Peter. **Education:** Univ Conn, BS, 1950, PhD, 1955; Purdue Univ, MS, 1952. **Professional Experience:** EMER PROF, UNIV NMEX, 1989-; asst dean, Col Pharm, 1975-1989; assoc prof pharm, Univ Okla, 1967-1975; vpres, Owen Labs, 1964-1967; dir labs, Conal Pharmaceut, 1962-1964; pharmaceut develop mgr, Baxter Labs, 1961-1962; head develop, Cent Pharmacal Co, Ind, 1959-1961; res chemist, Am Cyanamid Co, 1957-1959; mkt analyst, Mead Johnson & Co, 1955-1957; Res fel, Univ Conn, 1953-1955; instr chem, Purdue Univ, 1952-1953; Asst pharm, Purdue Univ, 1950-1952. **Memberships:** Am Chem Soc; Am Pharmaceut Asn; Soc Cosmetic Chemists. **Research Statement & Publications:** Natural products; pharmaceutics. **Mailing Address:** 8431 Palo Duro NE, Albuquerque, NM 87111.

LEHRSCH, GARY ALLEN, SOIL PHYSICS, SOIL MANAGEMENT. **Personal Data:** b Altoona, Pa, June 16, 1954; m 1981, Cynthia; c Benjamin, Zachary & William. **Education:** PA State Univ, BS, 1976, MEPC, 1979, MS, 1981; Miss State Univ, PhD (soil physics), 1985. **Professional Experience:** SOIL SCIENTIST, NORTHWEST IRRIGATION & SOILS RES LAB, AGR RES SERV, USDA, KIMBERLY, IDAHO, 1987-; res asst prof, Utah State Univ, 1988-; affil prof soil sci, Univ Idaho, 1988-; soil scientist, Nat Sedimentation Lab, Oxford, Miss, 1986-1987; res assoc, Miss State Univ, 1980-1986; grad res asst, Pa State Univ, 1980. **Memberships:** Am Soc Agron; Soil Sci Soc Am; Soil & Water Conserv Soc. **Research Statement & Publications:** Evaluating the effects of climate, management, and amendments on soil hydraulic properties; Quantifying the effects of tillage, compaction, freezing, thawing, water content, climate and time on soil aggregate stability and size distribution; improving crop and irrigation management systems. **Mailing Address:** USDA-Agr Res Serv, 3793 N 3600 E, Kimberly, ID 83341-5076. **E-Mail:** lehrsch@nwisrl.ars.usda.gov

LEHTO, MARK R, HUMAN FACTORS ENGINEERING, SAFETY ENGINEERING. **Personal Data:** b Longview, Wash, September 29, 1956. **Education:** Ore State Univ, BS, 1978; Purdue Univ, MS, 1980; Univ Mich, PhD (eng), 1985. **Professional Experience:** Vis assoc prof psychol, Univ Western Australia, 1993; NEC fac fel, 1991; vis asst prof indust eng, Univ Mich, 1989-1990; NSF presidential young investr award, 1989; lectr, Nordic Inst Advan Training Occup Health, Turkey & Finland, 1989; ASSOC PROF INDUST ENG, PURDUE UNIV, 1986-; sr res engr, J M Miller Inc, 1983-1986. **Memberships:** Sr mem Human Factors Soc; Indust Eng Soc. **Research Statement & Publications:** Safety engineering; human factors; computer aided design methods that address product safety problems early in the design process; author of several books. **Mailing Address:** Sch Indust Eng Purdue Univ, 259 Grissom Hall, West Lafayette, IN 47906. **Fax:** 765-494-1299. **E-Mail:** lehto@ecn.purdue.edu

LEI, DAVID KAI YUI, NUTRITION. **Personal Data:** b Macau, July 30, 1944; m 1966, Po-lin; c Hestia. **Education:** Univ London, BS, 1968; Univ Guelph, MS, 1970; Mich State Univ, PhD (human nutrit), 1973. **Professional Experience:** CHAIR, DEPT NUTRIT & FOOD SCI, UNIV ARIZ, as of 2004; fel, Pew Nat Fac Sch Nutrit, 1991; PROF NUTRIT, UNIV ARIZ, 1988-; grant, USDA NRI, 1984, 1986, 1989, 1992, 1996; grant, Am Heart Asn, 1981, 1992; assoc prof, Univ Ariz, 1980-1988; grant, NIH, 1977; from asst prof to assoc prof nutrit, Miss State Univ, 1975-1980; res assoc hemat, Wayne State Univ, 1974-1975; res asst nutrit, Mich State Univ, 1970-1973. **Memberships:** Am Inst Nutrit; Am Dietetic Asn; Sigma Xi; Am Heart Asn; AAAS. **Research Statement & Publications:** Trace mineral metabolism; lipoprotein metabolism; nutrients on gene expression. **Mailing Address:** Dept Nutrit Sci, Univ Ariz, Tucson, AZ 85721. **Fax:** 520-621-9446.

LEI, KUAN-SHAUR, COMPUTER ENGINEERING MANUFACTURING AND MATERIALS ENGINEERING. **Personal Data:** b Taipei, Taiwan, November 25, 1955; American citizen; m Yuying Liu; c Tiffany & Timothy. **Education:** Nat Tsung-Hua Univ, Taiwan, BS, 1977; Va Tech Inst, MS, 1981; Ohio State Univ, PhD (metal eng), 1985. **Honors & Awards:** Judge for "R&D 100", 1994-1996. **Professional Experience:** SUPPLY CHAIN PROGRAM MANAGER, INDUSTRY STANDARD SERVERS, COMPAQ/HP, 1999-; SR MEM TECH STAFF, ADVAN TECHNOL DEPT, COMPAQ COMPUT CORP, 1990-; staff engr, Cortest Labs Inc, 1988-1990; Sr scientist, Geo-Centers Inc, 1986-1988. **Memberships:** Inst Elec & Electronics Engrs; Am Soc Metals Inc; Surface Mount Technol Asn. **Research Statement & Publications:** Advanced materials and manufacturing technologies involving computer/electronics including printed circuit boards, integrated circuits, packaging, soldering flux processes. **Mailing Address:** 20555 State Highway 249, M/S 060308, Houston, TX 77070.

LEI, SHAU-PING LAURA, AGRICULTURAL & FOOD CHEMISTRY. **Personal Data:** b Taipei, Taiwan, October 7, 1953; American citizen; m 1980, Hun-Chi Lin; c Victoria & Benita. **Education:** Nat Taiwan Univ, BS, 1976, MS, 1980; Univ Calif, Los Angeles, PhD (molecular biol), 1985. **Professional Experience:** DIR PROTEIN PURIFICATION, XOMA CORP, 1990-; proj dir, Int Genetic Eng Inc, 1986-1989 & Trigen Inc, 1989-1990; Teaching assoc anal chem, Nat Taiwan Univ, 1976-1978. **Research Statement & Publications:** Host-vector development for recombinant DNA; gene cloning and expression in bacteria system and chimeric antibody, fab fragment; fabs and Igg purification from mammalian; yeast and bacteria systems in pilot scale. **Mailing Address:** 11452 Clarkson Rd, Los Angeles, CA 90064.

LEIBACH, FREDRICK HARTMUT, BIOCHEMISTRY, PHYSIOLOGY. **Personal Data:** b Kitzingen, Ger, September 21, 1930; American citizen; wid, c John, Maria & James. **Education:** Southwest Mo State Col, BS, 1959; Emory Univ, PhD (biochem), 1964. **Honors & Awards:** The Rank Prize for Nutrition, awarded by the Rank Prize Fund, London, UK 2004 Distinguished Research Award, American Physiological Soc, Gastroand Liver, 2004. **Professional Experience:** Prof and Chair emeritus Biochem and Mol Biol, Med Coll of Georgia as of 2004. Prof and Chair, Biochem and Mol Biol, Med Coll of Georgia 1990 to 2004. Prof Biochem and Mol Biol, Med Coll of Georgia 1979 to 1990. Assoc. Prof, Biochem and Mol Biol, Med Coll of Georgia 1973 to 1979. Asst Prof, Biochem and Mol Biol, Med Coll of Georgia 1967 to 1973. Natl Acad Sci Natl Res Counc. Res Assoc, NASA Ames Res Ctr 1964 to 1967. **Memberships:** Am Soc Biol Chemists; Am Physiol Soc; Sigma Xi; Am Soc Nephrology, Am Gastroenterology Soc. **Research Statement & Publications:** Enzymes in protein and amino acid metabolism; peptidases; protein turnover; membrane transport of organic solutes; regulation of membrane transport systems by hormones and second messengers; cloning of membrane transporters from intestine, kidney and placenta. **Mailing Address:** Dept Biochem &Molecular Biol, Med Col Georgia, Augusta, GA 30912-2100. **Fax:** 706-721-6608. **E-Mail:** fleibach@mcg.edu

LEIBACHER, JOHN W, ASTROPHYSICS, RESEARCH ADMINISTRATION. **Personal Data:** b Chicago, Ill, May 28, 1941; m 1976, Lise. **Education:** Harvard Col, AB, 1963; Harvard Univ, PhD (astron), 1971. **Professional Experience:** Vis scientist, Observ Cote d'Azur, 1994; dir, Nat Solar Observ, 1988-1993; chair, Nat Acad Sci, 1987-1990; ASTRONR, NAT SOLAR OBSERV, 1985-; assoc astronr, Nat Solar Observ, 1983-1984; res scientist astrophys, Lockheed Res Labs, 1976-1982; res scientist astrophys, Lab Physique Stellaire Planetaire, 1973-1975; postdoctoral, Univ Colo, 1971-1972. **Memberships:** Am Astron Soc; Int Astron Union. **Research Statement & Publications:** Solar physics; helioseismology. **Mailing Address:** Nat Solar Observ, 950 N Cherry Ave, Tucson, AZ 85726-6732. **Fax:** 520-318-8278. **E-Mail:** leib@noao.edu

LEIBBRANDT, VERNON DEAN, ANIMAL NUTRITION. **Personal Data:** b McCook, Nebr, October 31, 1944; m 1967, c 2. **Education:** Univ Nebr, BS, 1966; Iowa State Univ, PhD (animal nutrit), 1972. **Professional Experience:** PROF EMER ANIMAL NUTRIT, UNIV WIS, MADISON, as of 2002; assoc prof animal nutrit, Univ Wis, Madison, 1980; asst prof, Univ Wis-madison, 1978-1980; asst prof animal nutrit, Univ Fla, 1975-1978; fel, Res Div, Cleveland Clin Found, 1972-1975. **Memberships:** Am Soc Animal Sci. **Research Statement & Publications:** Husbandry and nutritional aspects of swine production. **Mailing Address:** Dept Animal Sci, Univ Wis, Madison, 7317 Branford Lane, Madison, WI 53717.

LEIBEL, WAYNE STEPHAN, EVOLUTIONARY GENETICS, MOLECULAR SYSTEMATICS. **Personal Data:** b August 5, 1951; American citizen. **Education:** Dartmouth Col, AB, 1973; Yale Univ, MPhil, 1975, PhD (biol), 1979. **Professional Experience:** PROF BIOL, LAFAYETTE COL, as of 2000; HEAD, DEPT BIOL, LAFAYETTE COL, as of 2000; assoc prof biol, Lafayette Col, beginning 1983. **Memberships:** Soc Study Evolution; Am Soc Ichthyologists & Herpetologists; Am Soc Zoologists; Sigma Xi. **Research Statement & Publications:** Evolution at the molecular level; speciation and diversification of neotropical freshwater fishes. **Mailing Address:** Dept Biol Lafayette Col, Easton, PA 18042-1778. **Fax:** 610-330-5705. **E-Mail:** leibelw@lafayette.edu

LEIBFRIED, THEODORE F, JR, MATHEMATICS. **Education:** Univ Va, ME, 1969; Rice Univ, PhD (MATHS), 1971. **Professional Experience:** PROF, DEPT MATHS, UNIV HOUSTON-CLEARLAKE, as of 2006. **Mailing Address:** Univ Houston-Clearlake, 2700, Bay Area Blvd, Box 216, Houston, TX 77058. **Fax:** 713-283-3870. **E-Mail:** leibfried@cl.uh.edu

LEIBHARDT, EDWARD, SPECTROSCOPY. **Personal Data:** b New Rome, Wis, October 13, 1919. **Education:** Northwestern Univ, BA, 1954, PhD (astron), 1959. **Professional Experience:** PRES, DIFFRACTION PROD INC, as of 2005. **Memberships:** Optical Soc Am. **Research Statement & Publications:** Developed ruling engine for producing interferometrically ruled diffraction gratings; holographic gratings. **Mailing Address:** Diffraction Prod Inc, PO Box 1030, 9416 W Bull Vally Rd, Woodstock, IL 60098. **Fax:** 815-338-7167. **E-Mail:** dpine@aol.com

LEIBHOLZ, STEPHEN W, INFORMATION & COMMUNICATION SCIENCES. **Personal Data:** b Berlin, Ger, January 28, 1932; American citizen; m 1958, c 3. **Education:** NY Univ, AB, 1952. **Professional Experience:** FOUNDER & CHIEF EXEC OFFICER,

CHESAPEAKE TECH LABS, 1991-; chmn, Chesapeake Tech labs, beginning 1991; mem var adv panels, Dept Defense, 1970-; pres & chief exec officer, Analytics, 1967-1991; mgr syst design & anal, Auerbach Corp, 1966-1967; prog mgr opers res & anal, Auerbach Corp, 1964-1966; sr mem tech staff, Auerbach Corp, 1960-1964; prin engr, Repub Aviation Corp, 1957-1960; res assoc electronics, Adv Group Electron Devices, US Dept Defense, 1954-1956; tutor, Queens Col, 1953-1954; res asst & teaching fel physics, NY Univ, 1952-1953; mem, Simulation Coun; ed, Mil Oper Res Monogra. **Memberships:** Inst Elec & Electronics Engrs; Soc Indust & Appl Math; Opers Res Soc Am; Mil Oper Res Soc. **Research Statement & Publications:** Applied mathematics and operations research in areas of information systems and military systems, especially statistical problems; systems architecture and engineering in areas of information, communications, automation control and surveillance systems for industry and government. **Mailing Address:** Chesapeake Tech Labs Inc, 2333 Huntington Pike, Huntington Valley, PA 19006. **Fax:** 215-938-1551.

LEIBMAN, LAWRENCE FRED, ORGANIC CHEMISTRY. **Personal Data:** b Bronx, NY, September 10, 1947. **Education:** City Univ NY, PhD (chem), 1976. **Professional Experience:** MEM STAFF, BASF WYANDOTTE CORP, 1980-; chemist, Am Cyanamid Co, 1976-1980; fel org biochem, Columbia Univ, 1975-1976. **Memberships:** Am Chem Soc; Sigma Xi. **Research Statement & Publications:** Organic reaction mechanisms. **Mailing Address:** BASF Corp, 36 Riverside Ave, Rensselaer, NY 12144-2928.

LEIBO, STANLEY PAUL, CRYOBIOLOGY, EMBRYOLOGY. **Personal Data:** b Pawtucket, RI, April 8, 1937; m 1961, c 2. **Education:** Brown Univ, BA, 1959; Univ Vt, MS, 1961; Princeton Univ, MA, 1962, PhD (biol), 1963. **Professional Experience:** PROF BIOL SCI, UNIV NEW ORLEANS, as of 2005; adj res prof, Ctr Cryobiol Res, State Univ NY, Binghamton, 1988-1990; mem fac, Univ Wis, 1988; consult, UN Food & Agr Orgn, Rome, 1987-; adj prof biomed eng, Univ Tex, Austin, 1987-; mem, Comt Basic Sci Found Med Assisted Conception, Inst Med-Nat Acad Sci, 1987-1988; bd dirs & exec comt, Hubbs-Sea World Res Inst, Calif, 1986-1988; adj assoc sci, Southwest Found Biomed Res, Tex, 1986-1988; adv mem, Colombian Ctr Fertil & Steril, 1985-; adj prof, Health Sci Ctr, Univ Tex, 1983-; vpres, Res & Develop Div, Rio Vista Int, 1981-1988; vis scientist, Inst Immunol, Basel, Switz, 1980, 1982, 1984; mem sci staff, Inst Immunol, Basel, Switz, 1977-1978; mem fac, UNESCO-ICLA-ICRO Training Course & Roving Seminars on Deep Freeze Preserv Mouse Strains, Neth, 1975, Denmark, Hungary & Poland, 1976 & Czech, Italy & Yugoslavia, 1977; vis scientist health sci & technol, Mass Inst Technol, 1974; mem adv bd, Am Type Cult Collection, 1971-1974; lectr, Oak Ridge Grad Sch Biomed Sci, Univ Tenn, 1969-1980; staff biologist, Biol Div, 1965-1980; res assoc, USPHS res fel, 1964-1965; res assoc, Oak Ridge Nat Lab, 1963-1964; res prof, dept biomed sci, Univ Guelph; res assoc prof obstet/gynec, Baylor Col Med. **Memberships:** Soc Study Reproduction; Soc Cryobiol (vpres, 1978-1980 & 1983-1985; pres, 1985-1987); Int Embryo Transfer Soc (pres, 1990-1991); Am Fertility Soc. **Research Statement & Publications:** Cryobiology and physiology of mammalian spermatozoa and oocytes and embryos, erythrocytes, lymphocytes and tissue-culture cells; bovine reproduction and embryology; micromanipulation of embryos; immunology and cytogenetics of bovine embryos; biology of bacteriophage; cryobiology of bacteriophage, proteins and algae. **Mailing Address:** Dept Biol Sci, Univ New Orleans, CC 200C Acres, New Orleans, LA 70148. **E-Mail:** tlonerga@uno.edu

LEIBOLD, MATHEW ALBERT, COMMUNITY ECOLOGY, EVOLUTIONARY ECOLOGY. **Personal Data:** b Seville, Spain, September 7, 1956; American citizen. **Education:** Univ Ariz, BS, 1980, MS, 1981; Mich State Univ, PhD (zoology), 1988. **Professional Experience:** ASSOC PROF ECOL & EVOLUTION, UNIV CHICAGO, 1991-; Zool Dept, Duke Univ, 1989-1990; res assoc, Kellogg Biol Sta, Mich State Univ, 1988-1989. **Memberships:** Ecol Soc Am. **Research Statement & Publications:** Theoretical and experimental approaches to understanding how species interactions act to regulate the evolution, abundances distributions and species diversity of organisms in natural communities, especially in ponds and lakes. **Mailing Address:** Div Biol Sci, Univ Chicago, Zool 404, Chicago, IL 60637. **Fax:** 773-702-9740. **E-Mail:** mleibold@midway.uchicago.edu

LEIBOVIC, K NICHOLAS, NEUROSCIENCES, BIOPHYSICS. **Personal Data:** b Plunge, Lithuania, June 14, 1921; m 1943, Marianne Karpf; c 3. **Education:** Cambridge Univ, 1943; London Univ, 1952. **Professional Experience:** RETIRED; vis scholar, Harvard Univ, 1979-1980; prog dir, Neurosci Res Prog, Mass Inst Technol, 1978-1979; Hadassah Med Sch, Hebrew Univ, 1971 & Inst Ophthal, London, 1978; vis prof, Univ Calif, Berkeley, 1969; asst dir, Ctr Theoret Biol, 1967-1968; from assoc prof to prof biophys, State Univ NY, Buffalo, 1964-1974; prin mathematician, Cornell Aeronaut Lab, 1963-1964; sr mathematician, Westinghouse Res Labs, 1960-1963; mem math adv coun, Battersea Col Technol, 1959-1960; proj leader indust math, Brit Oxygen Res & Develop Co, 1956-1960; Mathematician, Dulwich Col, Eng, 1946-1953 & Courtaulds, 1953-1956; Lectr, Norwood Col, Eng, 1952-1953. **Memberships:** Soc Neurosci; Asn Res Vision & Ophthal. **Research Statement & Publications:** Information processing in the nervous system; electrophysiology and psychopyhsics of vision; nervous system theory; mathematical models in biology. **Mailing Address:** State Univ NY, 105 High Park Blvd, Buffalo, NY 14226. **Fax:** 716-446-0637. **E-Mail:** bphknl@acsu.bufflo.edu

LEIBOVICH, SIDNEY, FLUID DYNAMICS, APPLIED MATHEMATICS. **Personal Data:** b Memphis, Tenn, April 2, 1939; m 1962, c 2. **Education:** Calif Inst Technol, BS, 1961; Cornell Univ, PhD (theoret mech), 1965. **Professional Experience:** S C Thomas sr dir, Sibley Sch Mech & Aerospace Eng, Cornell Univ, 2001-; dir, Sibley Sch Mech & Aerospace Eng, Cornell Univ, 1998-; chmn, US Nat Comt Theoret & Appl Mech, 1991-1993; SAMUEL B ECKERT PROF MECH & AEROSPACE ENG, CORNELL UNIV, 1988-; chmn, Div Fluid Dynamics, Am Phys Soc, 1988-1989; chmn, Appl Mech Div, Am Soc Mech Engrs, 1987-1988; adv, Mech Eng & Appl Mech, NSF, 1984-1985; assoc ed, J Fluid Mech, 1982-; prof, Cornell Univ, 1978-1988; sr vis fel, Math Inst, Univ St Andrews, 1977; assoc ed, J Appl Mech, 1976-1983; assoc ed, Soc Indust & Appl Math J Appl Math, 1972-1975; from asst prof to assoc prof thermal eng, Cornell Univ, 1966-1978; NATO fel, London, 1965-1966. **Memberships:** Nat Acad Eng; Soc Indust & Appl Math; fel Am Soc Mech Engrs; Am Geophys Union; fel Am Phys Soc; fel Am Acad Arts & Sci. **Research Statement & Publications:** Fluid mechanics, particularly dynamics of vortex flows, geophysical fluid dynamics, hydrodynamic stability, and wave propagation phenomena in fluids. **Mailing Address:** Sibley Sch Mech & Aerospace Eng, Cornell Univ, 246 Upson Hall, Ithaca, NY 14853. **Fax:** 607-255-1222. **E-Mail:** SL23@cornell.edu

LEIBOWITZ, GERALD MARTIN, MATHEMATICAL ANALYSIS. **Personal Data:** b New York, NY, February 17, 1936; m 1963, c 4. **Education:** City Col NY, BS, 1957; Mass Inst Technol, SM, 1959, PhD (math), 1963. **Professional Experience:** PROF MATH, UNIV CONN, as of 2006; assoc prof math, Univ Conn, beginning 1969; assoc dir, Comt Undergrad Prog Math, Math Asn Am, Calif, 1968-1969; from instr to asst prof, Northwestern Univ, 1963-1968; instr math, Mass Inst Technol, 1963; asst engr, Ford Instrument Co, 1957. **Memberships:** Am Math Soc; Math Asn Am. **Research Statement & Publications:** Functional analysis; Banach algebras. **Mailing Address:** Dept Math, Univ Conn, MSB 220, Storrs, CT 06269-3009. **Fax:** 860-486-4238. **E-Mail:** leibow@math.uconn.edu

LEIBOWITZ, JACK RICHARD, CONDENSED MATTER PHYSICS, SUPERCONDUCTIVITY. **Personal Data:** b Bridgeport, Conn, July 21, 1929; m 1989, Ariel; c Jane & Jon. **Education:** NY Univ, BA, 1951, MS, 1955; Brown Univ, PhD (physics), 1962. **Honors & Awards:** Elected fel in Am Phys Soc, 1980. **Professional Experience:** EMER PROF PHYSICS, CATH UNIV AM, 1995-; assoc dean grad studies, Dept Art, 1988-1993; chmn, Dept Art, 1982-1986; Consult, Nat Broadcasting Co, 1979-1993; prof, Dept Art, 1974-1995; assoc prof physics, Cath Univ Am, 1969-1973; asst prof physics, Univ Md, College Park, 1964-1969; Res physicist, Lincoln Labs, Mass Inst Technol, 1956-1961 & Westinghouse Res Lab, 1961-1964. **Memberships:** Fel Am Phys Soc; fel Wash Acad Sci; Sigma Xi. **Research Statement & Publications:** Superconductivity; ultrasonic interactions in solids; intermediate and mixed states; Fermi surfaces; electron-phonon interaction; excitation spectra of inhomogeneous superconductors; physical acoustics of solids; Publication in range of edited physics journals. **Mailing Address:** Po Box 31761, Santa Fe, NM 87594. **Fax:** 202-319-4448. **E-Mail:** leibowitz@cua.edu

LEIBOWITZ, JULIAN LAZAR, VIROLOGY, PATHOLOGY. **Personal Data:** b New York, NY, December 14, 1947. **Education:** Alfred Univ, BA, 1968; Albert Einstein Col Med, PhD (cell biol), 1974, MD, 1975. **Professional Experience:** PROF, DEPT PATH & LAB MED, HEALTH SCI CTR, TEX A&M UNIV, HOUSTON, as of 2004; assoc prof path, Univ Tex, Health Sci Ctr, Houston, beginning 1985; asst prof, Univ Tex, Health Sci Ctr, Houston, 1983-1985; asst prof, Univ Calif, San Diego, 1979-1983; path resident, USPHS fel neuropath & virol, 1977-1979; path resident, Univ Calif, San Diego, 1975-1977; med scientist trainee med, Albert Einstein Col Med, 1974-1975; med scientist trainee virol, Albert Einstein Col Med, 1970-1974. **Memberships:** AAAS; Am Soc Microbiol; Am Soc Virol. **Research Statement & Publications:** Animal virology; virus induced demyelinating disease. **Mailing Address:** Dept Path & Lab Med, Health Sci Ctr, Tex A&M Univ, Col Sta, TX 77843-1114. **Fax:** 979-862-1299. **E-Mail:** leibowit@medicine.tamu.edu

LEIBOWITZ, LEONARD, THERMOPHYSICAL PROPERTIES. **Personal Data:** b New York, NY, February 5, 1931; m 1976, Stephanie; c Michael G, Naomi C & Zoe R. **Education:** NY Univ, BA, 1951, MS, 1954, PhD (chem), 1956. **Professional Experience:** SR CHEMIST, CHEM ENGINEERING DIV, ARGONNE NAT LAB, 1988-; chemist, Argonne Nat Lab, 1972-1988; assoc chemist, Argonne Nat Lab, 1961-1972; asst chemist, Argonne Nat Lab, 1958-1961; Chemist, Pigments Dept, E I du Pont de Nemours & Co, 1956-1958. **Memberships:** Am Chem Soc; Sigma Xi. **Research Statement & Publications:** Thermophysical properties; alloy phase diagrams; application of synchrotron radiation to materials science. **Mailing Address:** Chem Technol Div, Argonne Nat Lab, Argonne, IL 60439. **Fax:** 630-252-4466. **E-Mail:** leibowitz@cmt.anl.gov

LEIBOWITZ, LEWIS PHILLIP, ADVANCED SPACE SYSTEMS, LARGE OPTICAL SYSTEMS. **Personal Data:** b Chicago, Ill, June 22, 1942; m 1967, c 3. **Education:** Northwestern Univ, BS, 1964; Univ Calif, San Diego, MS, PhD (eng sci), 1969. **Honors & Awards:** New Technol Award, NASA, 1976. **Professional Experience:** ADVAN SYSTS LEADER, LOCKHEED MISSILES & SPACE CO, 1985-; mgr, Technol Appl, Int Power Technol, Inc, 1983-1985; prob mgr, NASA, Dept Defense Exploratory Technol, 1980-1983; mgr advan solar technol, Calif Inst Technol, Jet Propulsion Lab, 1977-1980; team leader, oil explor assessment, Jet Propulsion Lab, Calif Inst Technol, 1977; team leader geothermal energy, Calif Inst Technol, Jet Propulsion Lab, 1975-1977; mem tech staff atmospheric entry technol, Calif Inst Technol, Jet Propulsion Lab, 1969-1975. **Memberships:** Am Phys Soc; Sigma Xi. **Research Statement & Publications:** Dynamic performance of distributed communication and data processing networks, system definition and performance analysis of advanced space systems for communications, space surveillance, astrophysics investigation and robotic applications; developed experiments for the testing of large antennas and deployable optical systems in space; energy systems; solar and thermal technology; developed comprehensive system/cost effectiveness model that permits trade-off of advanced technology, reliability and maintenance. **Mailing Address:** Dept M120 Bldg 158, PO Box 3504, Sunnyvale, CA 94088-3504.

LEIBOWITZ, MARTIN ALBERT, APPLIED MATHEMATICS, OPERATIONS RESEARCH. **Personal Data:** b New York, NY, October 15, 1935. **Education:** Columbia Univ, BA, 1956; Harvard Univ, MA, 1957, PhD (appl math), 1961. **Professional Experience:** RETIRED; assoc prof appl math & statist, State Univ NY Stony Brook, 1973-1982; assoc prof eng, State Univ NY Stony Brook, 1966-1973; mem tech staff, Bellcomm, Inc, Wash, DC, 1963-1966; staff scientist, Int Bus Mach Res Ctr, 1960-1963. **Memberships:** Opers Res Soc Am; Asn Comput Mach. **Research Statement & Publications:** Random processes with application to control theory; guidance and communications; scientific programming. **Mailing Address:** 15 Charles St, New York, NY 10014.

LEIBOWITZ, MICHAEL JONATHAN, VIROLOGY, DRUG DELIVERY. **Personal Data:** b Brooklyn, NY, May 14, 1945; m 1966, c 2. **Education:** Columbia Univ, AB, 1966; Albert Einstein Col Med, PhD (molecular biol), 1971, MD, 1973. **Professional Experience:** Sci adv comt, Am Found AIDS Res, 1993-; ASSOC DEAN, GRAD SCH BIOMED SCI, 1992-; PROF MOLECULAR GENETICS MICROBIOL, IMMUNOL ROBERT WOOD JOHNSON MED SCH, UNIV MED & DENT NJ, 1986-; from asst prof to assoc prof, Rob Wood Johnson Med Sch 1977-1986; Alexandrine & Alexander L Sinsheimer Scholar, 1980-1983; sr staff fel, Lab Biochem Pharmacol, 1976-1977; guest worker, Lab Biochem Pharmacol, Nat Inst Arthritis, Metab & Digestive Dis, NIH, 1974-1976; Intern, Barnes Hosp, Wash Univ, St Louis, 1974. **Memberships:** Am Soc Cell Biol; Am Chem Soc; Genetics Soc Am; Am Soc Microbiol; Am Soc Virol; AAAS. **Research Statement & Publications:** Molecular basis of the interaction of viruses with eukaryotic host cells, ribozymes; drug delivery. **Mailing Address:** Dept Molecular Genetics & Microbiol, UMDNJ Robert Wood Johnson Med Sch 675 Hoes Lane, Piscataway, NJ 08854-5635. **Fax:** 732-235-5223. **E-Mail:** leibowitz@mbcl.rutgers.edu

LEIBOWITZ, RONALD, GEOGRAPHY. **Personal Data:** m Jessica; c David Heschel, Shoshana. **Education:** Columbia Univ, PhD (Geog), 1985. **Professional Experience:** PROF GEOG, PROVOST & EXEC VPRES, MIDDLEBURY COL, as of 2004. **Research Statement & Publications:** Russian geography; political geography; nationalities. **Mailing Address:** Georg Dept, Middlebury Col, Old Chapel Third Floor, Middlebury, VT 05753. **Fax:** 802-443-2071. **E-Mail:** liebowit@middlebury.edu

LEIBOWITZ, SARAH FRYER, PSYCHOPHARMACOLOGY, NUTRITION. **Personal Data:** b White Plains, NY, May 23, 1941; m 1966, c 3. **Education:** NY Univ, BA, 1964, PhD (physiol psychol), 1968. **Honors & Awards:** First Prize, Div Psychopharmacol, Am Psychol Asn, 1969. **Professional Experience:** ADJUN ASSOC PROF NEUROPHARMACOL, ROCKEFELLER UNIV, 1978-; Alfred P Sloan found award, 1977-1979; asst prof, Rockefeller Univ, 1970-1978; USPHS fel & guest investr, Rockefeller Univ, 1968-1970. **Memberships:** AAAS; fel Am Psychol Asn; NY Acad Sci; Am Soc Pharmacol & Exp Therapeut; Soc Neuroscience; Asn Res Neurol & Ment Dis; Sigma Xi; fem Am Psychol

Soc; fel Acad Behav Med Res. **Research Statement & Publications:** Study of neurochemical mechanisms in the brain which regulate behavioral and physiological responses. **Mailing Address:** Dept NeuroSci, Rockefeller Univ, 1230 York Ave, New York, NY 10021-6399. **Fax:** 212-327-7974.

LEIBSON, IRVING, CHEMICAL ENGINEERING. **Personal Data:** b Wilkes Barre, Pa, September 28, 1926; m 1950. **Education:** Univ Fla, BChE, 1945, MS, 1947; Carnegie Inst Technol, 1949, DSc (chem eng), 1952. **Professional Experience:** PRES, BOLD TECHNOL, STUART, as of 2004; assoc, Coal Indust Adv Bd, Int Energy Agency, 1980- & World Coal Study, 1979-1980; vpres & mgr res & eng, Bechtel Group Inc, beginning 1978; mgr process & environ sci develop, Bechtel Group Inc, 1975-1978; mgr com ventures & investment dept, Dart Indust Chem Group, 1974-1975; vpres, Dart Indust Chem Group, 1969-1974; mgr process engr, gen mgr Acrylonitrile-Butadiene-Styrene Plastic Div, 1967-1969; dir com develop, Rexall Chem Co, 1967; dir res & develop, Rexall Chem Co, 1965-1967; develop mgr, Rexall Chem Co, 1963-1965; mgr process engr, Rexall Chem Co, 1961-1963; supv engr, Humble Oil & Refining Co, 1959-1961; prof, Rice Univ, beginning 1958; staff engr, Humble Oil & Refining Co, 1957-1959; chem engr, Humble Oil & Refining, beginning 1952; mem, Eng Manpower Comn; lectr, Univ Md. **Memberships:** Am Chem Soc; Am Inst Chem Eng; fel Am Inst Chem. **Research Statement & Publications:** Unit operations. **Mailing Address:** Bold Technol, Stuart, FL 34996-0917.

LEIBSON, PAUL JOSEPH, IMMUNOLOGY. **Personal Data:** b Chicago, Ill, June 15, 1952; c 1. **Education:** Univ Ill, Urbana, BS, 1974; Univ Chicago, PhD (immunol), 1979, MD, 1981; Am Bd Pediat, cert, 1986. **Honors & Awards:** Henry Kaplan Award, 1988. **Professional Experience:** PROF, DEPT IMMUNOL, MAYO CLIN, as of 2003; asst prof, Dept Immunol, Mayo Clin, beginning 1986; fel, Nat Jewish Hosp & Res Ctr, Denver, 1984-1986; Intern & resident, Health Sci Ctr, Univ Colo, Denver, 1981-1984; Course chmn immunol, Mayo Med Sch. **Memberships:** Am Asn Immunologists; Soc Leukocyte Biol. **Research Statement & Publications:** Author of numerous publications. **Mailing Address:** Dept Immunol, Mayo Clin, 200 First St SW, Rochester, MN 55905-0001. **E-Mail:** leibson.paul@mayo.edu

LEIBU, HENRY J, CHEMISTRY. **Personal Data:** b Schlesiengrube, Ger, April 22, 1917; c 2. **Education:** Swiss Fed Inst Technol, ChemE, 1942, ScD (chem), 1945. **Professional Experience:** RETIRED; tech sales & develop, Europe, S Am & Australia, 1973-1985; sales develop, sr res chemist, Res & Develop Elastomers, 1966-1973; sales develop, Europe, S Am & Australia, 1959-1966; chemist res plant develop, Polychem Dept, E I du Pont de Nemours & Co Inc, 1949-1959; instr & res assoc indust chem, Swiss Fed Inst Technol, 1945-1949; consult, elastomers, med prod, high performance liquid chromatography. **Memberships:** Am Chem Soc. **Research Statement & Publications:** Elastomers; urethanes. **Mailing Address:** 4905 Threadneedle Rd, Wilmington, DE 19807-2527.

LEIBY, ROBERT WILLIAM, ORGANIC CHEMISTRY. **Personal Data:** b Allentown, Pa, April 2, 1949; m 1974. **Education:** Albright Col, BS, 1971; Lehigh Univ, MS, 1973, PhD (org chem), 1975. **Professional Experience:** ASST PROF CHEM, SOUTHERN ILL UNIV, 1987-; mem fac, Dept Chem, Univ RI, 1985-1987; mem fac, Dept Chem, Univ Wis-Whitewater, 1980-1985; vis asst prof chem, Duke Univ, 1978-1980; vis asst prof chem, Hampden-Sydney Col, 1977-1978; med chemist, Purdue Frederick Co, 1976-1977; Res assoc org chem, Dartmouth Col, 1975-1976. **Memberships:** Am Chem Soc; Sigma Xi. **Research Statement & Publications:** Organic mass spectroscopy; heterocyclic synthesis; synthesis of pharmaceutical agents particularly central nervous system agents and antineoplastic agents: organic rearrangements and mechanisms; development of new synthetic techniques and reagents. **Mailing Address:** 97 First St, Danville, PA 17821-1169.

LEICH, DOUGLAS ALBERT, NUCLEAR COSMOCHEMISTRY, MASS SPECTROMETRY. **Personal Data:** b Paterson, NJ, January 26, 1947; m 1972, c 1. **Education:** Colgate Univ, BA, 1968; Calif Inst Technol, PhD (physics), 1974. **Professional Experience:** Dep div leader, Lawrence Livermore Lab, Univ Calif, 1986-1989; mem, Lunar & Planetary Sample Team, Lunar & Planetary Inst, 1981-1983; CHEMIST NUCLEAR CHEM, LAWRENCE LIVERMORE LAB, UNIV CALIF, 1976-; asst res physicist, Univ Calif, Berkeley, 1973-1976. **Memberships:** Meteoritical Soc; Am Phys Soc; Am Chem Soc. **Research Statement & Publications:** Isotopic abundance variations in materials and their uses in interpreting natural and anthropagenic processes. **Mailing Address:** L-195 LLNL UCL, PO Box 808, Livermore, CA 94551.

LEICHNER, GENE H(OWARD), ELECTRICAL ENGINEERING. **Personal Data:** b Richmond, Ind, November 14, 1929; m 1959, c 1. **Education:** Univ Ill, BS, 1951, MS, 1955, PhD (elec eng), 1958. **Professional Experience:** VPRES, EPIC ENG INC, 1985-; prog mgr, Comput Systs Develop, 1972-1985; mgr eng, RCA Instnl Systs, Systs Control, Inc, Palo Alto, 1969-1972; leader systs eval, RCA Instnl Systs, Systs Control, Inc, Palo Alto, 1967-1969; dir eng, Intersci Res Inst, 1965-1967; assoc prof elec eng, Digital Comput Lab, 1958-1967; asst, Digital Comput Lab, 1956-1958; elec engr, Control Systs Lab, Univ Ill, 1955-1956; Elec engr electronics, Ballistic Res Lab, Aberdeen Proving Ground, Md, 1951-1952. **Memberships:** Inst Elec & Electronics Engrs; Asn Comput Mach. **Research Statement & Publications:** Applications of computers to business and scientific problems; computer system performance analysis and prediction; on line computer applications. **Mailing Address:** Epic Eng Inc, 5150 El Camino Real Suite A30, Los Altos, CA 94022.

LEICHNER, PETER K, DOSIMETRY, TOMOGRAPHY. **Personal Data:** b West Berlin, Ger, January 24, 1939; m 1986, c 1. **Education:** Univ Calif, Riverside, BA, 1964; Univ Kans, PhD (physics), 1969. **Honors & Awards:** R S Landauer Mem Award & Lectr, 1985. **Professional Experience:** DEPT RADIATION ONCOL, MED CTR, UNIV NEBR, as of 2000; assoc ed, Antibody Immunoconjugates & Radiopharmaceuts, 1987-; Nat Cancer Inst, Univ London, 1987; Am Soc Therapeut Radiol & Oncol, Univ London, 1987; invited lectr, Am Col Nuclear Physicians, 1986-; Univ London, Royal Postgrad Sch, 1986; Invited lectr, Soc Nuclear Med, 1985-; ASSOC PROF ONCOL, MED SCH, JOHNS HOPKINS UNIV, 1983-; invited lectr, Radiol Soc NAm, 1980-1988; from instr to asst prof, Johns Hopkins Univ Med Sch, 1977-1982; asst prof, Univ Ky, Lexington, 1971-1977; asst prof physics, McMurry Col, Abilene, Tex, 1969-1971. **Memberships:** Am Phys Soc; Am Asn Physicists Med; Soc Nuclear Med; Am Soc Therapeut Radiol & Oncol. **Research Statement & Publications:** Quantitative medical imaging and image analysis; tomographic reconstruction algorithms; radiation dosimetry for radiolabeled cancer therapy agents. **Mailing Address:** Dept Radiation Oncol, Med Ctr, Univ Nebr, 42nd & Dewey, Omaha, NE 68198-1045.

LEICHNETZ, GEORGE ROBERT, NEUROANATOMY. **Personal Data:** b Buffalo, NY, October 15, 1942; m 1967, Athalie; c Keri, Geoffrey & Joel. **Education:** Wheaton Col, Ill, BS, 1964; Ohio State Univ, MS, 1966, PhD (anat), 1970. **Honors & Awards:** SCH OF MED DISTINGUISHED MENTOR AWARD 2004. **Professional Experience:** PROF Anatomy & Neurobiology, VIRGINIA COMMONWEALTH UNIV SCH OF MED, 1970-; Graduate Program Director; NSF grant, 1978-1986 & 1990-1993; Instr anat, Ohio State Univ, 1969-1970. **Memberships:** Am Asn Anatomists; Soc Neuroscience; Cajal Club. **Research Statement & Publications:** Comparative neuroanatomy of primates; connections from cerebral cortex and cerebellum to brainstem pre-oculomotor nuclei and their role in the control of eye movement. **Mailing Address:** Dept Anat, Med Col Va, Va Commonwealth Univ, PO Box 709, Richmond, VA 23298-0709. **Fax:** 804-786-9477. **E-Mail:** gleichne@hsc.vcu.edu

LEICHTER, JOSEPH, NUTRITION, FOOD SCIENCE. **Personal Data:** b February 4, 1932; American citizen. **Education:** Cracow Col, Poland, BS, 1956; Univ Calif, Berkeley, MS, 1966, PhD (nutrit), 1969. **Professional Experience:** PROF NUTRIT, UNIV BC, as of 2003; from asst prof to assoc prof, Univ Bc, 1969-1982; Ministry Com & Indust, Haifa, Israel, Anresco Lab, Calif, 1960-1965; Ministry Com & Indust, Haifa, Israel, Anresco Lab, Calif, 1957-1960; chemist, Pharmaceut Plant, Cracow, Poland, 1956-1957. **Memberships:** Am Inst Nutrit; Can Soc Nutrit Sci. **Research Statement & Publications:** Folic acid metabolism; effect of protein-calorie malnutrition on carbohydrate digestion and absorption; effect of dietary lactose on intestinal lactase activity; effect of maternal alcohol consumption and cigarette smoking on growth and development of offspring. **Mailing Address:** Food, Nutrition & Health, Faculty Agr Sci, Univ BC, Vancouver, BC V6T 1Z4, Can. **Fax:** 604-822-5143.

LEID, R WESLEY, INFLAMMATION, BIOCHEMICAL MECHANISMS OF VIRAL SUPPRESSION OF ALVEOCAR MACROPHAGE FUNCTION. **Personal Data:** b Walla Walla, Wash, May 25, 1945; m 1966, c 2. **Education:** Cent Wash Univ, BA, 1968, MS, 1970; Mich State Univ, PhD (microbiol), 1973. **Professional Experience:** PROF VET MICROBIOL & PATH, WASH STATE UNIV, 1985-; vis prof, Walter & Eliza Hall Inst, Melbourne, 1985; assoc prof, Wash State Univ, 1980-1985; reviewer, Am J Vet Res, 1980-1983; consult, WHO, 1978; asst prof path, Mich State Univ, 1977-1980; instr med, Harvard Med Sch, 1976-1977; fel immunol, Harvard Med Sch, 1973-1976. **Memberships:** Am Asn Immunol; Am Asn Pathologists; AAAS; Reticulendothelial Soc; Am Soc Biochem & Molecular Biol. **Research Statement & Publications:** Pulmonary inflammation; immediate hypersensitivity; eosinophil, neutrophil, alveolar macrophage and mast cell and basophilic function; platelet biochemistry, molecular interactions of the complement cascade. **Mailing Address:** Dept Vet Microbiol & Path, Lab Molecular & Cellular Inflammation, Wash State Univ, Pullman, WA 99164-6320. **Fax:** 509-335-1082. **E-Mail:** wesleid@wsu.edu

LEIDER, HERMAN R, SOLID STATE CHEMISTRY, PHYSICAL CHEMISTRY. **Personal Data:** b Detroit, Mich, January 14, 1929; m 1960, Marjorie R Johnson Von Egidy; c Karen (Fichman) & Amy (Smith). **Education:** Wayne State Univ, BS, 1951, PhD (chem), 1954. **Professional Experience:** Scientist, M H Chew & Assoc, Inc, 1993-1995; task leader, Yucca Mountain Proj, 1988-1993; sect leader Phys Chem, Hydrides Group, 1970-1976 & Chem Compatibility Group, 1981-1988; group leader, Hydrides Group, 1970-1976 & Chem Compatibility Group, 1976-1981; chemist, Lawrence Livermore Lab, Univ Calif, 1956-1970; aeronaut res scientist, Solid State Physics Br, Chem Mat Sec, Nat Adv Comt Aeronaut, 1954-1956; res assoc, Wayne State Univ, 1952-1954; asst, Wayne State Univ, 1951-1952; consult, Clean Sci Inc. **Memberships:** AAAS Asn. **Research Statement & Publications:** Alkali halides; compatibility of materials; color center; luminescence; radiation effects; hydrides; dissolution of uranium oxides. **Mailing Address:** 1091 Batavia Ave, Livermore, CA 94550.

LEIDERMAN, LISA J, MEDICAL RESEARCH. **Education:** Univ Md, BS; Howard Univ, PhD (Pharmacol). **Professional Experience:** Prin, L.J. Leiderman & Assoc, 1996-2004. **Mailing Address:** Dept Cell Cult Proc Develop No 374, Amgen Inc Amgen Ctr Bldg 5, Thousand Oaks, CA 91320-1789.

LEIDERMAN, P HERBERT, PSYCHIATRY. **Personal Data:** b Chicago, Ill, January 30, 1924; m 1947, c 4. **Education:** Calif Inst Technol, MS, 1949; Univ Chicago, MA, 1949; Harvard Med Sch, MD, 1953. **Professional Experience:** PROF EMER PSYCHIAT, MED SCH, STANFORD UNIV, as of 2004; Prof Psychiat, Med Sch, Stanford Univ, 1968; assoc prof, Med Sch, Stanford Univ, 1963-1968; assoc, Harvard Med Sch, 1958-1963; res fel, Mass Ment Health Ctr, 1957-1958; resident psychiat, Mass Gen Hosp, 1956-1957; resident neurol, Boston City Hosp, 1954-1956; intern med, Beth Israel Hosp, 1953-1954; Asst psychol, Univ Chicago, 1948-1949; Consult, USPHS & Nat Res Coun. **Memberships:** AAAS; Am Psychosom Soc; Soc Res Child Develop; Am Acad Child Psychiat; Sigma Xi. **Research Statement & Publications:** Child development; psychology; transcultural psychiatry; psychophysiology. **Mailing Address:** 828 Lathrop Dr, Stanford, CA 94305.

LEIDERSDORF, CRAIG B, COASTAL ENGINEERING, ARCTIC ENGINEERING. **Personal Data:** b Mineola, NY, March 12, 1950; m 1984. **Education:** Stanford Univ, BS, 1972; Univ Calif, Berkeley, MS, 1975. **Professional Experience:** TREASURER, COASTAL FRONTIERS CORP, as of 2006; PRIN & COFOUNDER, COASTAL FRONTIERS CORP, as of 1998; guest lectr, Univ Tokyo, 1983; guest lectr, Univ Calif, Berkeley, 1982, 1984 & 1985; exec vpres coastal eng, Tekmarine, Inc, 1980-1986; coastal engr, Swan Wooster Eng Co Ltd, 1976-1977 & Tetra Tech, Inc, 1977-1980; res assoc hydraul res, Univ Calif, Berkeley, 1975-1976. **Memberships:** Am Soc Civil Engrs; Asn Environ Prof; Am Shore & Beach Preserv Asn; Permanent Int Asn Navig Cong. **Research Statement & Publications:** Coastal engineering and coastal oceanography, including field data acquisition, assessment of coastal stability and design of slope protection; arctic engineering relating to offshore structures and sea ice. **Mailing Address:** Coastal Frontiers Corp, Ste 101 9420 Topanga Canyon Blvd, Chatsworth, CA 91311-5759. **Fax:** 818-341-4498. **E-Mail:** coastalf@aol.com

LEIDHEISER, HENRY, PHYSICAL CHEMISTRY. **Personal Data:** b Union City, NJ, April 18, 1920; m 1944, Virginia; c Margaret F (LeBaron) & Henry III. **Education:** Univ Va, BS, 1941, MS, 1943, PhD (phys chem), 1946. **Honors & Awards:** J Shelton Horsley Res Prize, Va Acad Sci, 1949; Silver Medal, Am ELectroplaters' Soc, 1978; Arch T Colwell Award, Soc Automotive Engrs, 1978; Whitney Award, Nat Asn Corrosion Engrs, 1983; Humboldt Award, 1985; Silver Medal, S African Corrosion Inst, 1986; ELectrodeposition Div Res Award, ELectrochem Soc, 1987; Mattiello Award, Fedn Socs Coatings Technol, 1990; Uhlig Award, ELectrochem Soc, 1991. **Professional Experience:** RETIRED; dept chmn, Alcoa, 1988-1989; Von Humboldt Award, 1985-1986; chair prof, Alcoa, 1983-1990; consult, Marshall Space Flight Ctr, NASA, beginning 1971; NATO sr scientist fel, Cambridge Univ, 1969; prof chem & dir, Zettlemoyer Ctr Surface Studies, Lehigh Univ, 1968-1983; chmn, Gordon Conf Corrosion, 1964; dir res, Inst, 1960-1968; dir res, Lab, 1958-1960; mgr lab, Va Inst Sci Res, 1952-1958; proj dir, Va Inst Sci Res, 1949-1952; res assoc, Cobb Chem Lab, 1946-1949; res worker, Nat Adv Comt Aeronaut Proj, Univ Va, 1943-1945; mem adv comt, Oak Ridge Nat Lab. **Memberships:** Am Chem Soc; Electrochem Soc; Nat Asn Corrosion Engrs; fel AAAS. **Research Statement & Publications:**

Corrosion; surface science; electrodeposition; Mossbauer spectroscopy; polymer coatings; long-term food storage; paint adherence. **Mailing Address:** 822 Carnoustie Dr, Venice, FL 34293.

LEIDY, BLAINE I(RVIN), mechanical engineering; deceased, see previous edition for last biography

LEIDY, ROSS BENNETT, AGRICULTURAL & FOOD CHEMISTRY. **Personal Data:** b Newark, Ohio, June 1, 1939; m 1971, Nancy Antoine; c Marsha & Karl. **Education:** Tex A&M Univ, BS, 1963, MS, 1966; Auburn Univ, PhD (biochem), 1972. **Professional Experience:** Assoc mem, Dept Entom, 1996-; PROF, PESTICIDE RESIDUE RES LAB, NC STATE UNIV, 1995-; DIR, PESTICIDE RESIDUE RES LAB, NC STATE UNIV, 1992-; assoc prof, Dept Toxicol, 1990-1995; sr res scientist, Pesticide Residue Res Lab, NC State Univ, 1974-1992; supvr pesticide chem, Lab Div, NC Dept Human Resources, 1973-1974; NIH res assoc, Dept Animal Sci, NC State Univ, 1972-1973; Sch, Ft McClellan, Ala, 1966-1968; insr & lab supvr, Biol Br, Microbiol Lab, US Army Chem Ctr & Sch, Ft McClellan, Ala, 1966-1968; Res asst radiation biol, Radiation Biol Lab, Tex A&M Univ, 1965-1966; consult, pesticide residues air, soils & surfaces home & working environ. **Memberships:** Sigma Xi; NY Acad Sci; Am Chem Soc. **Research Statement & Publications:** Methodology and analyses of pesticide residues on plant products, soil, water, and indoor air related to the laboratory's research projects. **Mailing Address:** Pesticide Residue Res Lab, 3709 Hillsborough St NC State Univ, Raleigh, NC 27607. **Fax:** 919-515-7169. **E-Mail:** ross_leidy@ncsu.edu

LEIER, CARL V, MEDICAL DEVICES DIAGNOSTICS, MEDICAL PHYSICS. **Personal Data:** b Bismarck, NDak, October 20, 1944; m 1970, c 3. **Education:** Creighton Univ, BS, 1965; Creighton Univ Col Med, MD, 1969; Am Bd Internal Med, cert & dipl, 1973; Am Bd Internal Med, cert, 1978. **Professional Experience:** DIR, DIV CARDIOL, OHIO STATE UNIV COL MED, 1986-; PROF MED & PHARMACOL, OHIO STATE UNIV COL MED, 1984-; dir res, James W Overstreet prof med, 1983-; fac mem, grad sch, Ohio State Univ Col Med, 1980-; dir res, Div Cardiol, 1980-1983; mem, bd trustees, 1979-; res comt, Cent Ohio Heart Chapter, Am Heart Asn, 1977-1984; from asst prof to assoc prof, Div Cardiol, 1976-1984; pharmacol & therapeut comt, Ohio State Univ Hosps, 1976-1980; clin instr, Div Cardiol, 1974-1976; comt, Ohio State Univ Hosps, 1973-1974; chief instr, Div Cardiol, 1973-1974; mem, Internship Selection Comt, Dept Med, Ohio State Univ Col Med, 1973-1974, hosp procedures; instr med, Div Cardiol, 1971-1973; intern, Div Cardiol, 1969-1970. **Memberships:** Am Col Physicians; fel Am Col Clin Pharmacol; Am Fed Clin Res; Am Col Cardiol; AAAS; Am Soc Clin Invest; Int Soc Heart Res. **Research Statement & Publications:** Pharmacology. **Mailing Address:** Div Cardiol, Col Med Ohio State Univ Hosps, 669 Means Hall 1654 Upham Dr, Columbus, OH 43210. **E-Mail:** Carl.Leier@osumc.edu

LEIES, GERARD M, NUCLEAR WEAPON PHENOMENOLOGY. **Personal Data:** b Chicago, Ill, August 19, 1918. **Education:** Loyola Univ, Ill, BS, 1940; Univ Calif, MA, 1953; Georgetown Univ, PhD (physics), 1962. **Professional Experience:** RETIRED; command tech dir, Air Force Tech Appln Ctr, 1973-1988; asst tech dir, Air Force Tech Appln Ctr, 1962-1973; consult. **Memberships:** Am Phys Soc; Am Geophys Union. **Research Statement & Publications:** Nuclear weapon test detection. **Mailing Address:** 46541 River Meadows Ter, Sterling, VA 20165.

LEIF, ROBERT CARY, IMMUNOHEMATOLOGY, BIOMEDICAL ENGINEERING. **Personal Data:** b New York, NY, February 27, 1938; m 1963, c 2. **Education:** Univ Chicago, BS, 1959; Calif Inst Technol, PhD (chem), 1964. **Professional Experience:** VPRES & RES DIR, NEWPORT INSTRUMENTS, 1993-; corp fel, mgr adv concepts, Coulter Electronics, 1981-1993; Coulter Electronics, beginning 1975 & Photometrics, beginning 1975; adj asst prof microbiol, 1973-1976 & adj asst prof biomed eng, 1974-1976; assoc prof oncol, 1973-1976 & adj asst prof biomed eng, beginning 1980; assoc prof microbiol & biomed eng, 1973-1976 & adj asst prof biomed eng, beginning 1976; sr scientist, Papanicolaou Cancer Res Inst, 1972-1981; res scientist, Dept Microbiol, Univ Miami, 1971-1972; assoc scientist, Papanicolaou Cancer Res Inst, 1971-1972; consult, Damon Eng, 1969-1973; Solid State Radiation, Calif, 1967-1973; asst prof chem & biochem, Fla State Univ, 1967-1971; res assoc microbiol, Sch Med, Univ Southern Calif, 1966-1967; consult, Xerox Corp, 1966-1967; consult, Int Equip Corp, 1965-1973; fel, Univ Calif, Los Angeles, 1964-1966. **Memberships:** AAAS; Sigma Xi; Biomed Eng Soc; Am Chem Soc; Am Soc Cytol; sr mem Inst Elec & Electronics Engrs. **Research Statement & Publications:** Cellular differentiation; cytology automation; clinical chemistry instrumentation; cytology specimen preparation; computer based instrumentation; cytophysical and histochemical techniques to separate, purify and analyze heterogeneous cell populations; identification of biological activities with cell morphology. **Mailing Address:** Newport Instruments, 5648 Toyon Rd, San Diego, CA 92115-1022. **Fax:** 858-272-6907. **E-Mail:** rlief@rlief.com

LEIFER, CALVIN, EXPERIMENTAL PATHOLOGY, ELECTRON MICROSCOPY. **Personal Data:** b New York, NY, March 4, 1929; m 1963, c 2. **Education:** NY Univ, BA, 1950, DDS, 1954; State Univ NY Buffalo, PhD (exp path), 1971. **Professional Experience:** Pres, Philadelphia Sect, Am Asn Dent Res, 1985-1990; PROF PATH, SCH DENT, TEMPLE UNIV, 1978-; assoc prof, Sch Dent, Temple Univ, 1970-1978; USPHS fels, State Univ NY Buffalo, 1965-1970; Pvt pract, 1958-1965. **Memberships:** Am Dent Asn; hon mem Sigma Xi; AAAS; Int Asn Dent Res; Am Acad Oral Path; NY Acad Sci. **Research Statement & Publications:** Ultrastructural and biochemical alterations of the rat parotid gland following single and multiple doses of x-irradiation; ultrastructural and histochemical features of tumors of the salivary glands in humans; ultrastructure of human dental pulp. **Mailing Address:** 103 Waverly Rd, Wyncote, PA 19095.

LEIFER, HERBERT NORMAN, SOLID STATE PHYSICS. **Personal Data:** b New York, NY, January 30, 1925; m 1948, c 3. **Education:** Univ Calif, Los Angeles, BA, 1948, PhD (physics), 1952. **Professional Experience:** RETIRED; sr staff scientist, Rocketdyne Div, Rockwell Int, 1979-1990; sr staff scientist, Rand Corp, 1972-1979; High Energy Laser Lab, TRW Systs Group, 1968-1972; staff scientist, Electro optical Lab, Autonetics Div, N Am Aviation Inc, Calif, 1965-1967; mgr basic physics, Fairchild Semiconductor Corp, 1962-1965; mgr solid state electronics dept, Lockheed Missiles & Space Co, 1961-1962; Mem staff, Physics Lab, Ecole Normale Superieure, Paris, 1960; staff scientist, Lockheed Missiles & Space Co, 1955-1959; res assoc, Res Lab, Gen Elec Corp, 1952-1955; res engr, Univ Calif, Los Angeles, 1951-1952; asst physics, Univ Calif, Los Angeles, 1948-1951. **Memberships:** Am Phys Soc. **Research Statement & Publications:** Semiconductors; thermoelectric effects; electron-acoustic interactions; electrooptic effects; lasers. **Mailing Address:** 16557 Park Lane Circle, Los Angeles, CA 90049.

LEIFER, LARRY J, BIOMEDICAL ENGINEERING. **Education:** Stanford Univ, BS, 1962, MS, 1963, PhD (biomed eng), 1969. **Professional Experience:** DIR, STANNFORD DESIGN AFFIL PROG, STANFORD UNIV, as of 2004; co-founder, Ohlone Int Corp, beginning 1989; PROF MECH ENG & DIR, CTR DESIGN RES, STANFORD UNIV, 1982-; assoc prof, Ctr Design Res, Stanford Univ, 1976-1982; asst prof biomed systs anal, Swiss Fed Inst Technol, Zurich, 1973-1976; NASA res exchange fel, Man-Vehicle Lab, Mass Inst Technol, 1973; Staff mem, Ames Res Ctr, NASA, 1969-1972. **Research Statement & Publications:** Developed laboratory and curriculum for programmable electromechanical systems design; develop basic design theory and methodology through application of knowledge-based engineering technology to a wide range of industrial machine design problems. **Mailing Address:** Dept Mech Eng, Design Div, Stanford Univ, Stanford, CA 94305-4021. **Fax:** 650-493-6481. **E-Mail:** leifer@cdr.stanford.edu

LEIFER, LESLIE, PHYSICAL CHEMISTRY. **Personal Data:** b New York, NY, April 13, 1929; m 1957, c 1. **Education:** City Col NY, BS, 1950; Univ Kans, PhD (phys chem), 1959. **Honors & Awards:** Travel Awards, US AEC, Stockholm, 1962; Travel Awards, Australia, 1963; Res Award, Mich Technol Univ, 1970; Travel Awards, Stockholm, 1971. **Professional Experience:** PROF EMER CHEM, MICH TECHNOL UNIV, as of 2004; prof chem, Mich Technol Univ, beginning 1966; assoc prof, Boston Col, 1963-1966; res assoc & staff mem, Lab Nuclear Sci, Mass Inst Technol, 1961-1963; asst prof chem, Clark Univ, 1959-1960; Res assoc nuclear & inorg chem, Mass Inst Technol, 1956-1959. **Memberships:** AAAS; Am Chem Soc; Sigma Xi. **Research Statement & Publications:** Solution physical chemistry; Mossbauer spectroscopy; quantum chemistry; energy storage materials. **Mailing Address:** Dept Chem, Mich Technol Univ, 1400 Townsend Dr, Houghton, MI 49931-1295.

LEIFER, ZEV, GENETIC TOXICOLOGY, POLYAMINE BIOSYNTHESIS. **Personal Data:** b Brooklyn, NY, May 24, 1941; m 1972, c 5. **Education:** Yeshiva Univ, BA, 1963; Harvard Univ, MA, 1965; NY Univ, PhD (microbiol), 1972. **Professional Experience:** PROF MICROBIOL, NY COL PODIATRIC MED, as of 2004; res assoc prof microbiol, Ny Med COl, beginning 1981; DNA Repair Deficient Bacterial Assay Work Group, Genetic Toxicol Prog, Environ Protection Agency, 1978-1981; res asst prof, NY Med Col, 1976-1981; Queens Col, City Univ NY, 1974-1976; fel microbiol, NY Univ, 1972-1974. **Memberships:** Am Soc Microbiol; Am Chem Soc; AAAS; Environ Mutagen Soc; Sigma Xi. **Research Statement & Publications:** Development and utilization of microbiological assay systems for the detection of environment mutagens and carcinogens; biosynthesis and biological role of polyamines. **Mailing Address:** Dept Basic Sci, NY Col Podiatric Med, 1800 Park Ave, New York, NY 10035. **E-Mail:** leifer1@ix.netcom.com

LEIFIELD, ROBERT FRANCIS, INORGANIC CHEMISTRY. **Personal Data:** b St Louis, Mo, January 29, 1928; m 1952, c 7. **Education:** St Louis Univ, BS, 1952, MS, 1959. **Professional Experience:** RETIRED; pres, Leifield Inc, beginning 1986; consult, 1986-1991; dir new prod develop, Catalysts & Performance Chem Div, Mallinckrodt Inc, 1985-1986; dir res & develop, chem div, 1977-1985; tech mgr, Calsicat Div, 1970-1977; res & develop mgr, Calsicat Div, 1969-1970; assoc mgr res, Mallinckrodt Chem Works, 1966-1969; res chemist, Mallinckrodt Chem Works, 1962-1966; group leader process develop, Mallinckrodt Chem Works, 1961-1962; supvr metall & ceramics, Mallinckrodt Chem Works, 1958-1961; chemist, Mallinckrodt Chem Works, 1956-1958; chemist, Great Lakes Carbon Co, 1952-1956. **Memberships:** Catalysis Soc; Am Chem Soc; Licensing Execs Soc. **Research Statement & Publications:** Column and thin layer chromatography; analytical reagents; product and process research and development; uranium metallurgical chemistry; heterogeneous catalysis; licensing consultation. **Mailing Address:** Mallinckrodt Inc, 675 McDonnell Blvd, Hazelwood, MO 63042. **Fax:** 314-654-5381.

LEIGA, ALGIRD GEORGE, IMAGING MATERIALS. **Personal Data:** b New York, NY, March 25, 1933; m 1955, Ann; c 4. **Education:** NY Univ, BA, 1955, MS, 1960, PhD (phys chem), 1963. **Professional Experience:** CONSULT IMAGING MAT TECHNOL & MFG, 1995-; mayor, City Claremont, Calif, 1994-1997; councilman, City Claremont, Calif, 1990-2003; mgr mat technol & mfg, Supplies Bus Ctr, 1989-1995; mgr, Supplies Bus Ctr, 1988-1989; mgr mat technol opers, Xerox Med Systs, Monrovia, Calif, 1981-1987; corp res & develop staff, Xerox Corp, Palo Alto, 1977-1981; mgr mat develop, Xeroradiography, Pasadena, 1973-1977; sr scientist, Mat Sci Lab, NY, 1964-1973; res scientist, Dept Chem, NY Univ, 1962-1964. **Memberships:** Am Chem Soc; Soc Photog Scientists & Engrs; Optical Soc Am. **Research Statement & Publications:** Vacuum ultraviolet photochemistry and spectroscopy; decomposition reactions of solids; materials development for electrophotography. **Mailing Address:** 3790 Elmira Ave, Claremont, CA 91711. **E-Mail:** aleiga@eartlink.net

LEIGH, DONALD C, continuum mechanics; deceased, see previous edition for last biography

LEIGH, EGBERT GILES, TROPICAL ECOLOGY, EVOLUTIONARY POPULATION GENETICS. **Personal Data:** b Richmond, Va, July 27, 1940; m 1968, Elizabeth; c John M & Mary B. **Education:** Princeton Univ, AB, 1962; Yale Univ, PhD (biol), 1966. **Professional Experience:** STAFF SCIENTIST, SMITHSONIAN TROP RES INST, as of 2006; biologist, Smithsonian Trop Res Inst, beginning 1969; asst prof, Princeton Univ, 1966-1972; actg instr biol, Stanford Univ, 1966. **Memberships:** Ecol Soc Am; Am Soc Naturalists; Paleont Res Inst; Brit Ecol Soc. **Research Statement & Publications:** Role of mutualism in evolution; what circumstances lend effectiveness to the common interest of members in the good of their group or community; ecology of tropical forest. **Mailing Address:** Smithsonian Trop Res Inst, Unit 948, Apartado, AA 34002-0948. **Fax:** 507-212-8148. **E-Mail:** leighl@si.edu

LEIGH, RICHARD WOODWARD, ENERGY TECHNOLOGY, ELECTRIC UTILITY ANALYSIS. **Personal Data:** b New York, NY, April 26, 1942. **Education:** Oberlin Col, BA, 1965; Columbia Univ, PhD (physics), 1973 prof engr, NY state, 1996. **Professional Experience:** SR ENGR, COMMUNITY ENVIRON CTR, NY, 2001-; consult engr, efficiency elec utility, 1996-2001; sr res assoc, Brookhaven Nat Lab, 1994-1996; assoc prof physics, Pratt Inst, 1987-1993; assoc scientist energy syst, Brookhaven Nat Lab, 1980-1987; asst scientist, Brookhaven Nat Lab, 1977-1980; res fel, Lab Spectros Hertzienne, Ecole Normale Superieure, Paris, 1975-1977; adj asst prof, City Col New York, 1973-1975; res assoc physics, City Col New York, 1972-1973; consult energy conserv & utility anal, US& developing countries. **Memberships:** AAAS; Am Phys Soc. **Research Statement & Publications:** Energy technologies, especially heat exchanger materials and design; energy efficiency, storage and solar; technical, economic and infrastructural requirements and benefits; electric utility planning methods and systems; coherent optics. **Mailing Address:** 415 Central Park W 12C, New York, NY 10025. **Fax:** 212-866-4560. **E-Mail:** rwleigh@earthlink.net

LEIGH, STEFAN, STATISTICS. **Education:** Princeton Univ, BA; Univ Md, MS (Math Statist). **Professional Experience:** MATH STATISTCIAN, STATISTICAL ENG DEPT, NAT INST STAND & TECHNOL, as of 2001. **Memberships:** IMS. **Research Statement & Publications:** Exploratory data analysis; saddlepoint and small-sample asymptotics; fundamental constants; bremsstrahlung modeling; forensic DNA QA/QC; asbestos abatement metrology issues; electrochemical noise; extreme value theory - extreme winds - interval censoring; changepoint analysis; multivariate modeling of cement/concrete. **Mail-**

ing Address: Statistical Eng Div, Nat Inst Stand & Technol, NIST N Rm 353, Gaithersburg, MD 20899. **Fax:** 301-990-4127. **E-Mail:** stefan.leigh@nist.gov

LEIGHLY, HOLLIS PHILIP, physical metallurgy; deceased, see previous edition for last biography

LEIGHLY, KAREN MARIE, X-RAY ASTRONOMY, ACTIVE GALACTIC NUCLEI. **Personal Data:** b Denver, Colo, April 30, 1959. **Education:** NMex Inst Mining & Technol, BS (physics) & BS (math), 1983; Mont State Univ, MS, 1987, PhD (physics), 1991. **Professional Experience:** ASST PROF, DEPT PHYSICS & ASTRON, UNIV OKLA, 2000-; assoc res scientist, Columbia Astrophys Lab, 1997-2000; Sci & Technol Agency fel, Inst Phys & Chem Res, 1994-1996; prin investr, NASA/HST, ELIVE, IVE, ROSAT, GINGA, ASCA, XTE, SAX, beginning 1992; Nat Res Coun fel, Goddard Space Flight Ctr, NASA, 1992-1994. **Memberships:** Am Astron Soc; Int Astron Union. **Research Statement & Publications:** X-ray emission from active galactic nuclei; x-ray spectrum and the variability of these objects; analysis of data from various orbiting observatories; the x-ray emission from active galactic nuclei is important because very rapid variability observed implies the emission comes from close to the black hole believed to power these objects. **Mailing Address:** Dept Physics & Astron, Univ Okla, OK 73019-0390. **E-Mail:** leighly@mail.nhn.ou.edu

LEIGHT, WALTER GILBERT, OPERATIONS RESEARCH, STANDARDS ENGINEERING. **Personal Data:** b New York, NY, November 19, m Frances; c Claudia R & K Adam. **Education:** City Col NY, BS, 1942. **Honors & Awards:** Bronze Medal, Dept Com, 1979, Silver Medal, 1995; Meritorious Service Award, Am Nat Stand Inst, 1996. **Professional Experience:** Guest Researcher, NAT INST STANDS & TECHNOL, 2004-; DEP DIR, OFF STANDS SERV, NAT INST STANDS & TECHNOL, 1989-2003; asst assoc dir indust & stands, 1987-1988; prog mgr, Stands Code & Info, 1982-1986; chief, Off Stands Info Anal & Develop, 1981- 1982; chief, Prod Safety Technol Div, 1978-1981; chief, Off Consumer Prod Safety, Nat Inst Stands & Technol, 1974-1978; prog mgr decision systs, Tech Anal Div, Nat Bur Stands, 1971-1974; from sci analyst to dir opers anal div, Opers Eval Group & sr sci analyst, Systs Eval Group, Ctr Naval Anal, 1953-1970; res meteorologist, US Weather Bur, 1946-1953; High sch instr, NY, 1942; Govt mem coun, Am Nat Stand Inst, Z-21 comt. **Memberships:** Fel AAAS; Opers Res Soc Am; Am Meteorol Soc. **Research Statement & Publications:** Decision systems; criminal justice; search and rescue; nuclear safeguards; military systems; extended forecasting; consumer product safety; standards and trade; laboratory accreditation; conformity assessment. **Mailing Address:** 9416 Bulls Run Pkwy, Bethesda, MD 20817. **Fax:** 301-963-2871. **E-Mail:** walter.leight@nist.gov

LEIGHTON, ALEXANDER HAMILTON, PSYCHIATRIC EPIDEMIOLOGY, CULTURAL ANTHROPOLOGY. **Personal Data:** b Philadelphia, Pa, July 17, 1908; m 1966, Jane; c Doreen (Walker) & Fredrick A. **Education:** Princeton Univ, BA, 1932; Cambridge Univ, MA, 1934; Johns Hopkins Univ, MD, 1936. **Honorary Degrees:** AM, Harvard Univ, 1966; SD, Acadia Univ, 1974; SD, Univ Laval, 1991. **Honors & Awards:** Human Rels Award, Am Soc Advan Mgt, 1946; La Pouse Award, Am Pub Health Asn, 1975; Ment Health Asn Res Achievement Award, 1975; Malinowski Award, Soc Appl Anthrop, 1984; Jubin Award, Am Psychopath Asn, 1994. **Professional Experience:** PROF PSYCHIAT & COMMUNITY HEALTH EPIDEMIOL, DALHOUSIE UNIV, as of 1999; Mem, Consult Comt Ment Health Res, Dept Nat Health & Welfare, Can, 1982-; PROF EMER SOCIAL PSYCHIAT, HARVARD SCH PUB HEALTH, 1975-; Nat Health Scientist Award, Can, 1975-1984; prof psychiat & community health epidemiol, Dalhousie Univ, 1975-; mem comt effects herbicides Vietnam, Nat Acad Sci, 1971-1973; vis lectr, Cath Univ Louvain, 1971; prof social psychiat & head, Dept Behav Sci, 1966-1975; reflective fel, Carnegie Corp NY, 1962-1963; Surgeon Gen Adv Comt Indian Affairs, 1956-1959 & Peace Corps, 1961-1963; mem sub-panel behav sci, President's Sci Adv Comt, 1961-1962; Thomas W Salmon Mem lectr, NY Acad Med, 1958; mem expert adv panel ment health, WHO, 1957-1975; fel, Ctr Advan Study Behav Sci, 1957-1958; prof social psychiat, Med Col, 1956-1966; tech adv, Milbank Mem Fund, 1956-1963; dir, Prog Social Psychiat, 1955-1966; chmn comt psychiat & social sci, Social Sci Res Coun, 1950-1958; dir, Stirling Co Proj, 1948-1975; mem bd dirs, Social Sci Res Coun, 1948-1958; dir, Southwest Proj, 1948-1953; consult, Bur Indian Affairs, US Dept Interior, 1948-1950; prof sociol & anthrop, Col Arts & Sci, Cornell Univ, 1947-1966; Prof, Sch Indust & Labor Rels, 1947-1952; Guggenheim fel, 1946-1947; Social Sci Res Coun fel field work among Navajos & Eskimos, Columbia Univ, 1939-1940. **Memberships:** Fel AAAS; fel Am Psychiat Asn; Am Philos Soc; fel Am Anthrop Asn; Am Psychopath Asn; hon fel Royal Col Psychiatrists UK. **Research Statement & Publications:** Social and cultural change; social psychiatry; psychiatric epidemiology. **Mailing Address:** Harvard Sch Pub Health, Harvard Univ, 677 Huntington Ave, Boston, MA 02115.

LEIGHTON, ALVAH THEODORE, GENETICS, PHYSIOLOGY. **Personal Data:** b Portland, Maine, April 17, 1929; m 1953, c 4. **Education:** Univ Maine, BS, 1951; Univ Mass, MS, 1953; Univ Minn, PhD (poultry genetics & physiol), 1960. **Professional Experience:** VMAYOR, BLACKSBURG TOWN COUN, 1974-; prof poultry sci, Va Polytech Inst & State Univ, beginning 1971; assoc prof, Va Polytech Inst & State Univ, 1959-1971; asst poultry genetics, Univ Mass, 1951-1952 & Univ Minn, 1955-1959. **Memberships:** Sigma Xi; World Poultry Sci Asn; Am Genetic Asn; Poultry Sci Asn. **Research Statement & Publications:** Reproductive physiology and management of turkey populations. **Mailing Address:** Blacksburg Town Coun, 711 Broce Dr, Blacksburg, VA 24060. **E-Mail:** aleighton@blacksburg.gov

LEIGHTON, FRANK THOMSON, COMPUTER SCIENCE. **Education:** Princeton Univ, BS; Mass Inst Technol, PhD (math). **Professional Experience:** PROF APPL MATH, MASS INST TECHNOL, as of 2005; CHIEF SCIENTIST, AKAMAI TECHNOLOGIES, as of 2005. **Memberships:** Am Acad Arts & Sci. **Mailing Address:** Dept Math Mass Inst Technol, 2-374 32-G594 77 Mass Ave, Cambridge, MA 02139. **Fax:** 617-258-5429. **E-Mail:** ftl@math.mit.edu

LEIGHTON, FREDERICK ARCHIBALD, VETERINARY MEDICINE. **Personal Data:** b November 4, 1948. **Education:** Cornell Univ, AB, 1970; Univ Sask, DVM, 1979; NY State Col Vet Med, PhD (exp path), 1984. **Professional Experience:** EXEC DIR, CAN COOPERATIVE WIDELIFE HEALTH CTR, as of 2001; PROF & HEAD, DEPT VET PATH, WESTERN COL VET MED, UNIV SASK, as of 2001; Co-dir Can Coop Wildlife Health Ctr, 1992-; chmn, Wildlife Health Fund, 1987-; Comput Coord Comt, 1988-1989 & Electron Micros User's Comt, 1986-1990; SUPVR, ELECTRON MICROS LAB, 1985-; Comput Coord Comt, Western Col Vet Med, 1985-1987; hon vis assoc prof, Dept Biochem, Mem Univ Nfld, St John's, 1985; mem, Toxicol Group, Univ Sask, 1984-; mem mgt comt, Wildlife Health Fund, 1984-; assoc prof, Dept Vet Path, Western Col Vet Med, Univ Sask, 1984-1988; hon vis res fel, Dept Biochem, Mem Univ Nfld, St John's, 1983; instr, Dept Vet Path, Western Col Vet Med, Univ Sask, 1979-1980; student asst wildlife dis studies, Dept Vet Path, Western Col Vet Med, Univ Sask, 1975-1978; res asst wildlife ecol, Bald Eagle Proj, Besnard Lake, Sask, 1974; teacher, Crescent Collegiate, Robert's Arm, Nfld, 1972-1973. **Memberships:** Wildlife Dis Asn; Am Col Vet Pathologists; AAAS; Am Asn Pathologists; Can Vet Med Asn; Can Asn Vet Pathologists (vpres, 1987-1988, pres, 1988-1989). **Research Statement & Publications:** Wild animal diseases-pathology and surveillance; toxicopathology of petroleum oils and pesticides in wild birds. **Mailing Address:** Dept Vet Path, Western Col Vet Med, Univ Sask, 259 Toxicol Ctr Bldg, 52 Campus Dr, Saskatoon, SK S7N 5B4, Can. **E-Mail:** ted.leighton@usask.ca

LEIGHTON, FREEMAN BEACH, GEOLOGY. **Personal Data:** b Champaign, Ill, December 19, 1924; c 4. **Education:** Univ Va, BS, 1946; Calif Inst Technol, MS, 1949, PhD (geol), 1951. **Honors & Awards:** Claire P Holdredge Award, Nat Asn Eng Geologists, 1967. **Professional Experience:** RETIRED; adj res prof, Whittier Col, 1978-; state-of-the-art reviewer, US Geol Surv/HUD/Asn Bay Area Govts, 1972-1974; mem eng geol qual bd, City Los Angeles, 1962-1970; pres, Leighton & Assocs, Inc, 1960-; Dir undergrad res prog, NSF, 1959-1965; from asst prof to prof geol, Whittier Col, 1950-1978. **Memberships:** AAAS; Geol Soc Am; Am Asn Petrol Geologists; Am Asn Prof Geologists; Nat Asn Geol Teachers. **Research Statement & Publications:** Active faulting; environmental planning; landslides; hillside development; geomorphology; engineering geology. **Mailing Address:** 55970 Pebble Beach, La Quinta, CA 92253.

LEIGHTON, HENRY GEORGE, METEOROLOGY. **Personal Data:** b London, Eng, May 2, 1940; Canadian citizen; m 1962, c 3. **Education:** McGill Univ, BS, 1961, MS, 1964; Univ Alta, PhD (nuclear physics), 1968. **Professional Experience:** PROF METEOROL, MCGILL UNIV, 1980-; assoc prof meteorol, Mcgill Univ, beginning 1980; asst prof, Mcgill Univ, 1972-1980; res assoc, Mcgill Univ, 1971-1972; vis asst prof, Univ Ky, 1970-1971; res assoc nuclear physics, R J van Del Graaff Lab, Holland, 1968-1970. **Memberships:** Can Meteorol Soc; Am Meteorol Soc. **Research Statement & Publications:** Atmospheric radiation; cloud physics and cloud chemistry; published over 15 articles. **Mailing Address:** Dept Atmospheric & Oceanog Sci, McGill Univ, 805 Sherbrooke St W, Montreal, PQ H3A 2K6, Can. **E-Mail:** henry.leighton@mcgill.ca

LEIGHTON, MORRIS WELLMAN, EXPLORATION GEOLOGY, BASIN STUDIES. **Personal Data:** b Champaign, Ill, June 17, 1926; m 1947, Jean; c Randi, Kathryn & Kari. **Education:** Univ Ill, BS, 1947; Univ Chicago, MS, 1948, PhD (geol), 1951. **Professional Experience:** Trustee, Geol soc Am Found, 1996-2001; chair, Geol soc Am Found Board, 1998-2001; emer adj prof, Univ Ill, beginning 1994; EMER CHIEF, ILL STATE GEOL SURV, 1994-; distinguished lectr, Am Asn Petrol Geologists, 1990; chief, Ill State Geol Surv, 1983-1994; chief geologist, Esso InterAmerica, 1974-1983; div mgr, Esso Prod Res Co, 1972-1974; explor mgr, Esso Australia Ltd, 1970-1972; asst explor mgr, Esso Stand Oil Ltd, Australia, 1969-1970; geol adv, Esso Explor Inc, 1964-1968; sr res geologist, Jersey Prod Res Co, 1963-1964; geologist-in-chg Europ study group, Esso Mediter, 1961-1963; geol sect head, Jersey Prod Res Co, 1958-1961; res geologist, Jersey Prod Res Co, 1951-1958. **Memberships:** Fel Geol Soc Am; hon mem Asn Am State Geologists; Am Asn Petrol Geologists. **Research Statement & Publications:** Petroleum geology; basin studies; basin and play assessment; earth sciences, general; carbonate rocks. **Mailing Address:** 302 E Sherwin Dr, Urbana, IL 61802. **E-Mail:** leighton@isgs.uiuc.edu

LEIGHTON, TERRANCE J, BIOCHEMISTRY. **Personal Data:** b Twin Falls, Idaho, October 14, 1944. **Education:** Ore State Univ, BSc, 1966; Univ BC, PhD, 1970. **Professional Experience:** PROF BIOCHEM & MOLECULAR BIOL, DEPT MOLECULAR & CELL BIOL, UNIV CALIF, BERKELEY, 1989-; sr fel, Max Planck Soc, 1984-; Alexander von Humboldt-Stiftung fel, 1980-1983; Guest Ger Govt, Max Planck Inst Molecular Genetics, Berlin, WGer, 1976; from asst prof to prof microbiol, Dept Molecular & Cell Biol, Univ Calif, Berkeley, 1974-1988; asst prof, Dept Microbiol, Med Sch, Univ Mass, Worcester, 1972-1974; Postdoctoral fel, Dept Biochem & Biophys, Univ Calif, Davis, 1970-1972. **Memberships:** AAAS; Sigma Xi; Biophys Soc; Am Soc Biochem & Molecular Biol; Am Chem Soc; Am Soc Microbiol; fel Am Inst Chem; Soc Indust Microbiol. **Research Statement & Publications:** Genetic engineering of high performance bioprocess systems; molecular genetic regulation of Bacillus subtilis development; molecular genetic regulation of Bacillus subtilis translational initiation and termination; environmental mutagenesis, carcinogenesis and the role of flavonols and flavonol glycosides as dietary anticarcinogens. **Mailing Address:** Biochem Dept, 206 Barker Hal, Lafayette, CA 94720-3202. **E-Mail:** leighton@bacillus.berkeley.edu

LEIKIN, JERROLD BLAIR, TOXICOLOGY, EMERGENCY MEDICINE. **Personal Data:** b Chicago Ill, August 28, 1954. **Education:** Univ Iowa, BS 1976; Univ Chicago, MD, 1980. **Honors & Awards:** Alumnae Award, Chi Med Sch, 1999. **Professional Experience:** ASSOC DIR, COOK CO HOSP, as of 2005; DIR, Ruth A Lawrence Poison & Drug Info Ctr, Univ Rochester Med Ctr as of 2005; fel med toxicol, Univ Calif, 2000; med dir, Rush Poison Control Ctr, assoc dir, Rush Emergency Servs, 1988-2001; PROF MED, RUSH MED COL, 1988-; chmn, Res & Educ, Am Col Emergency Physicians, 1987-; ATTEND MED TOXICOL, COOK CO HOSP, 1985-; asst prof med, Univ Ill, 1984-1988; dir Med Toxicol, ENH-OMEGA, Glenview, Ill. **Memberships:** AMA; Am Acad Clin Toxicol; Am Col Physicians; Am Col Emergency Physicians; Am Col Med Toxicol. **Research Statement & Publications:** Toxicology and emergency medicine; drugs of abuse and inhalation toxins. **Mailing Address:** Dept Med, Rush Univ, 600 S Paulina St Ste 440, Chicago, IL 60612.

LEIMGRUBER, RICHARD M, PHYSICAL SCIENCE. **Professional Experience:** Chief ed, Appl Theoritical Electrophoresis, as of 1999; SR RES SPECIALIST, ANAL SCI CTR, MONSANTO CO, 1983-. **Mailing Address:** Anal Sci Ctr, Monsanto Co, BB2K, 700 Chesterfield Village Pkwy N, St Louis, MO 63198. **Fax:** 314-537-6806. **E-Mail:** rmleim@ccmax.monsanto.com

LEIMKUHLER, FERDINAND F, INDUSTRIAL ENGINEERING, OPERATIONS RESEARCH. **Personal Data:** b Baltimore, Md, December 31, 1928; m 1956, c 6. **Education:** Johns Hopkins Univ, PhD (Eng), 1962; Loyola Univ, BS, 1950; Johns Hopkins Univ, BS, 1952. **Professional Experience:** RETIRED; fulbright prof, Univ Ljubjana, Yugoslavia, 1974-1975; head, Sch Indust Eng, 1969-1974 & 1981-1993; vis prof, Univ Calif, Berkeley, 1968-1969 & 1990-1991; prof indust eng, Purdue Univ, beginning 1966; assoc prof, Purdue Univ, 1961-1966; res assoc & instr indust eng, Johns Hopkins Univ, 1957-1961; engr, E I du Pont Del Nemours & Co, 1952-1957. **Memberships:** Opers Res Soc Am; Inst Mgt Sci; fel Am Inst Indust Engrs; Am Soc Eng Educ; sci adv bd. **Research Statement & Publications:** Library operations research; engineering economic analysis; transportation of highly radioactive materials; stochastic system theory; manufacturing systems. **Mailing Address:** Sch Indust Eng, Purdue Univ, 315 N Grant St, West Lafayette, IN 47907-2023. **Fax:** 765-494-1299.

LEIN, M ROSS, ORNITHOLOGY. **Education:** Univ Sask, BA, 1966, MA, 1968; Harvard Univ, PhD, 1973. **Professional Experience:** ASSOC PROF, DEPT BIOL SCI, UNIV CALGARY, as of 2005. **Mailing Address:** Dept Biol Univ Calgary, 2500 Univ Dr NW, Calgary, AB T2N 1N4, Can. **Fax:** 403-289-9311. **E-Mail:** mrlein@ucalgary.ca

LEIN, PAMELA J, NEUROSCIENCES. **Personal Data:** b Buffalo, NY, April 16, 1959; m 1981, Richard. **Education:** Cornell Univ, BS, 1981; ETenn State Univ, MSEH, 1983; State Univ NY, PhD (pharmacol), 1990. **Professional Experience:** ASST PROF, ENVIRON HEALTH SCI, BLOOMBERG SCH PUBLIC HEALTH, JOHNS HOPKINS UNIV, as of 2005; FAC MEM, CTR ALTERNATIVE ANIMAL TESTING, as of 2005; ASST PROF BIOL, CANISIUS COL, 1993-; environ health analyst, Dames & Moore, 1992-1993; fel molecular immunol, Roswell Park Cancer Inst, 1991-1992; adj assist prof, dept pharmacol, State Univ NY, Buffalo. **Memberships:** Soc Neuroscience; Am Soc Cell Biol; Am Pub Health Asn. **Research Statement & Publications:** Epigenetic specification of neuronal form. **Mailing Address:** Dept Biol, Bloomberg Sch Pub Health, John Hopkins Univ, 615 N Wolfe St, Baltimore, MD 21205. **Fax:** 410-955-0116. **E-Mail:** plein@jhsph.edu

LEINBACH, F HAROLD, PHYSICS. **Personal Data:** b Ft Collins, Colo, January 7, 1929; wid, c 2. **Education:** SDak State Univ, BS, 1949; Calif Inst Technol, MS, 1950; Univ Alaska, PhD (geophys), 1962. **Professional Experience:** RETIRED; Actg dir, Space Environ Lab, 1982-1986; instr, Space Environ Lab, Nat Oceanog, Atmospheric Admin, Univ Colo, 1978-1979; physicist, Space Environ Lab, Nat Oceanog, Atmospheric Admin, Univ Colo, 1966-1993; asst prof physics, Univ Iowa, 1962-1966; Geophysicist, Geophys Inst, Alaska, 1950-1953 & 1956-1962. **Memberships:** Am Astron Soc; Am Geophys Union; Am Asn Physics Teachers; Sigma Xi. **Research Statement & Publications:** High latitude ionospheric absorption of cosmic radio noise; solar cosmic rays and their interaction with the ionosphere; solar physics; space physics; laboratory plasma physics. **Mailing Address:** 2015 Kohler Dr, Boulder, CO 80303.

LEINBACH, RALPH C, ALLOYS. **Personal Data:** b Esterly, Pa, November 24, 1928; m 1951, c 4. **Education:** Lehigh Univ, BS, 1954. **Honors & Awards:** Regional Tech Award, Am Iron & Steel Inst, 1963, Spec Achievement Cert, 1967; Bradley Stoughton Award, Am Soc Metals, 1971. **Professional Experience:** RETIRED; mem, Interim Core Group Mkt Develop Comt, Am Iron & Steel Inst, 1985; sr vpres technol, eng & purchasing, 1982-1987; mem bd dirs, Metal Prop Coun Inc, 1980; group vpres, Carpenter Steel Div, 1979-1982; div vpres tech, Carpenter Technol Corp, 1976-1979; vpres tech, Carpenter Technol Corp, 1975-1976; vpres metall, Carpenter Technol Corp, 1971-1975; asst vpres metall, Carpenter Technol Corp, 1970-1971; chief metallurgist, Mill Metallurgy, 1968-1970; mgr, Mill Metallurgy, 1965-1968; plant metallurgist, Bridgeport, Conn plant, 1961-1965; melting metallurgist, Bridgeport, Conn plant, 1957-1961; melting metallurgist, Electronics & Magnetics, Carpenter Technol Corp, Reading, Pa, 1956; metallurgist, Res & Develop Lab, Electronics & Magnetics, Carpenter Technol Corp, Reading, Pa, 1955; metallurgist, Atomic Power Div Res Ctr, Babcock & Wilcox Co, Alliance, Ohio, 1954. **Memberships:** Fel Am Soc Metals; Am Inst Metall Engrs; Am Iron & Steel Inst; Soc Automotive Engrs; Soc Metall Engrs; Am Welding Soc; Metals Soc; Am Vacuum Soc. **Research Statement & Publications:** Stainless steel making utilizing vacuum treatment; vacuum induction melting of specialty steels and alloys; specialty steel melting; US and Canadian patents; technical publications. **Mailing Address:** 2404 Bell Dr, Reading, PA 19609.

LEINEN, MARGARET SANDRA, PALEOCEANOGRAPHY, PALEOCLIMATE. **Personal Data:** b Chicago, Ill, September 20, 1946; c Daniel W. **Education:** Univ Ill, BS, 1969; Ore State Univ, MS, 1975; Univ RI, PhD (oceanog), 1980. **Professional Experience:** ASST DIR GEOSC, NAT SCI FOUND, 2000-; vprovost marine progs & dean, Univ RI, beginning 1992; prof & assoc dean, Univ RI, 1988-1992; from asst res prof to assoc res prof, Univ RI, 1982-1988; marine scientist, Univ RI, 1980-1982. **Memberships:** Geochem Soc; fel Geol Soc Am; Am Geophys Union; Oceanog Soc (pres, 1994-). **Research Statement & Publications:** Deep sea sedimentary processes; history of atmospheric circulation. **Mailing Address:** Dept GeoScis, Nat Sci Found, 4201 Wilson Blvd, Arlington, VA 02882-1197. **Fax:** 703-292-9042. **E-Mail:** mleinen@gsosun1.gso.uri.edu

LEINHARDT, GAEA, MATHEMATICS. **Education:** Univ Chicago, BA, 1966, MST, 1968; Univ Pittsburgh, PhD (Educ Res), 1972. **Professional Experience:** SR SCIENTIST, LEARNING RES & DEVELOP CTR, UNIV PITTSBURGH, as of 2003; PROF EDUC, UNIV PITTSBURGH, as of 2003. **Mailing Address:** Dept Math, Univ Pittsburgh, 3939 O'Hara St, Pittsburgh, PA 15213. **Fax:** 412-624-9149. **E-Mail:** gaea@pitt.edu

LEINROTH, JEAN PAUL, SEPARATION PROCESSES. **Personal Data:** b Utica, NY, July 4, 1920. **Education:** Cornell Univ, BMechEng, 1941; Mass Inst Technol, SM, 1948, ScD(chem eng), 1963. **Professional Experience:** PRES, LEINROTH ASSOC, 1988-; Mass Inst Technol, 1988-1989; vis prof, Univ Conn, 1986-1988; Gen Elec, Sterling Org, Nycomed John Brown E&C, Vanderbilt Chem Corp, Syntex, Velsicol Westex, Rohm & Haas, Clean Harbors, Mass Inst Technol Energy Lab, CPI Plants, Great Lakes Citem, Cabot Corp, 1987-; mgr spec projs, John Brown E&C, 1980-1985; process dir, John Brown E&C, 1972-1980; vis prof, Mass Inst Technol, 1971-1972; Consult, Develop Sci, 1971-1972; assoc prof chem eng, Cornell Univ, 1964-1971; Consult, Union Carbide Chem Co, 1964-1968; vis assoc prof, Mass Inst Technol, 1963-1964; instr thermodyn, Mass Inst Technol, 1960-1961; proj leader, Union Carbide Chem Co, 1956-1959; proj engr, Union Carbide Chem Co, 1948-1956; asst job engr, M W Kellogg Co, NY, 1942-1943; trainee, Stand Oil Co, Ohio, 1941-1942. **Memberships:** Am Inst Chem Engrs. **Research Statement & Publications:** Chemical kinetics; thermodynamics; staged operations; computer applications. **Mailing Address:** 33 Millstone Rd, Wilton, CT 06897. **E-Mail:** jean@leinroth.com

LEINWAND, LESLIE, IMMUNOLOGY. **Personal Data:** b New York, NY, November 18, 1950. **Education:** Cornell Univ, BS, 1972; Yale Univ, PhD (biol), 1978. **Professional Experience:** PROF, MOLECULAR BIOL, UNIV COLO, 1985-; from asst prof to assoc prof immunol, Albert Einstein Col Med, 1981-1985; fel immunol, Rockefeller Univ, 1978-1981. **Mailing Address:** Dept Cellular & Develop Biol, Univ Colo, A418, Boulder, CO 80309-0347. **Fax:** 303-492-8907. **E-Mail:** leinwand@stripe.colorado.edu

LEINWEBER, FRANZ JOSEF, DRUG METABOLISM. **Personal Data:** b Berlin, Ger, January 18, 1931; American citizen; m 1960, c 2. **Education:** Univ Tuebingen, Dr rer nat(biol), 1956. **Professional Experience:** SR SCIENTIST, HOFFMANN-LA ROCHE INC, 1977-; sr scientist, Warner-Lambert Res Inst, 1969-1977; sr scientist, McNeil Labs, Inc, 1965-1969; res assoc, Univ Tenn, 1963-1965; Fel biochem, Tex A&M Univ, 1957-1960 & Johns Hopkins Univ, 1960-1963. **Memberships:** Am Soc Pharmacol & Exp Therapeut. **Research Statement & Publications:** Photoperiodism and biological clocks; enzymology, intermediary metabolism and metabolic regulation of sulfur amino acid biosynthesis in bacteria and molds; drug metabolism and separation methods; enzymatic mechanisms of drug biotransformation. **Mailing Address:** 3 Georgian Rd, Randolph, NJ 07869-1205.

LEIPNIK, ROY BERGH, NON-LINEAR PARTIAL DIFFER ENTIAL EQUATIONS, STOCHASTIC PROCESSES & CLASSICAL ANALYSIS. **Personal Data:** b Los Angeles, Calif, May 6, 1924. **Education:** Univ Chicago, SB, 1945, SM, 1948; Univ Calif, Berkeley, PhD (math), 1950. **Honors & Awards:** Scientist of the Yr, Louisiana Tech Univ, 1998. **Professional Experience:** PROF APPL MATH & MEM ALGEBRA INST, UNIV CALIF, SANTA BARBARA, 1975-; prof, Univ Fla, 1961-1962, 1964-1965 & 1970; lectr, Univ Calif, Los Angeles, 1959-; sr res scientist, Naval Weapons Ctr, Calif, 1957-1975; Fulbright res prof, Univ Adelaide, 1955, 1963 & 1968; asst prof, Univ Wash, 1950-1957; fel, Sch Math, Inst Advan Study, Princeton, 1948-1950; from asst to assoc math, Univ Calif, 1946-1948; asst math statist & econ, Univ Chicago, 1945-1946; pres, Idactic Co. **Memberships:** Am Math Soc; Math Asn Am; Inst Math Statist; Inst Elec & Electronics Engrs; Soc Indust & Appl Math. **Research Statement & Publications:** Operator analysis; mathematical physics; control systems; stochastic processes; information theory; plasma physics; transportation theory; recursive algorithms; differential equations; engineering mechanics; hydrologic and climatic equations; fluid mechanics; micro-economics; statistical distributions. **Mailing Address:** Math Dept, Univ Calif, S Hall 6507, Santa Barbara, CA 93106. **Fax:** 805-893-2385. **E-Mail:** leipnik@math.ucsb.edu

LEIPOLD, MARTIN H(ENRY), CERAMICS. **Personal Data:** b Englewood, NJ, July 4, 1932; m 1958, c 3. **Education:** Rutgers Univ, BS, 1954; Ohio State Univ, MS, 1955, PhD (ceramics), 1958. **Honors & Awards:** Except Serv Award, NASA, 1989. **Professional Experience:** Mgr, Historically Black Cols & Univ Initiative, 1987-1990; adj prof, Univ Calif, Los Angeles, 1976-1984; MEM TECH STAFF, JET PROPULSION LAB, 1974-; assoc prof mat sci, Col Eng, Univ Ky, 1967-1974; res specialist, Jet Propulsion Lab, Calif Inst Technol, 1962-1967; sr scientist, Jet Propulsion Lab, Calif Inst Technol, 1958-1962; res assoc ceramics, Ohio State Univ Res Found, 1955-1958. **Memberships:** Fel Am Ceramic Soc; Am Inst Ceramic Engrs; Am Soc Metals. **Research Statement & Publications:** Properties, fabrication and structure of ceramics and semi-conductor materials; photovoltaic power systems; IR sensors; focal plane arraxs. **Mailing Address:** 1118 Sheraton Dr, La Canada Flintridge, CA 91011.

LEIPOLD, RICHARD A, MATHEMATICS. **Education:** Carnegie Mellon Univ, PhD. **Professional Experience:** CHAIR, DEPT MATH, WAYNESBURG COL, PA, as of 2006. **Memberships:** Am Math Soc. **Mailing Address:** 440 Beechwood Ave, Carnegie, PA 15106. **Fax:** 412-627-6416. **E-Mail:** rleipold@waynesburg.edu

LEIPUNER, LAWRENCE BERNARD, HIGH ENERGY & ELEMENTARY PARTICLE PHYSICS. **Personal Data:** b Long Beach, NY, May 27, 1928; m 1948, Rohna; c Walter, Betsy & Maresa. **Education:** Univ Pittsburgh, BS, 1950; Carnegie Inst Technol, MS, 1954, PhD (physics), 1962. **Professional Experience:** Vis prof, Yale Univ, 1967-1968; SR RES PHYSICIST, BROOKHAVEN NAT LAB, 1955-. **Memberships:** Fel Am Phys Soc. **Research Statement & Publications:** Lepton and quark experiments. **Mailing Address:** Dept Physics, Brookhaven Nat Lab, Bldg 510A, Upton, NY 11973. **Fax:** 631-334-5568.

LEIS, BRIAN NORMAN, III, FRACTURE MECHANICS, DAMAGE MECHANICS. **Personal Data:** b Kitchener, Ont, October 25, 1947; m 1969, Linda; c Shawn, Craig & Shannon. **Education:** Univ Waterloo, BASc, 1971, MASc, 1972, PhD (civil eng), 1979. **Honors & Awards:** National Research council, canada. **Professional Experience:** Sr. Res Leader, APPL MECH, BATTELLE COLUMBUS LAB, 2001-; subcomt chmn, Am Soc Testing & Mat, 1981-1985; Res Leader, Sr scientist, Battelle Columbus Lab, 1981-2001; Adj prof mech eng, Ohio State Univ, 1980-1983; staff scientist, Battelle Columbus Lab, 1979-1981; Scientist appl mech, Battelle Columbus Lab, 1974-1979. **Memberships:** Am Soc Testing & Mat; Am Soc Mech Engrs; Am Inst Metall Engrs. **Research Statement & Publications:** Damage mechanics in materials and structures, including model simulation, with emphasis on fatigue, fracture and environmental degradation; granted one patent. **Mailing Address:** Battelle Columbus Lab, Columbus, OH 43201. **Fax:** 614-424-3457. **E-Mail:** bleis@columbus.rr.com

LEIS, JONATHAN PETER, NUCLEIC ACID ENZYMOLOGY, VIROLOGY. **Personal Data:** b Brooklyn, NY, August 17, 1944; m 1970, c 2. **Education:** Hofstra Univ, BA, 1965; Cornell Univ, PhD (biochem), 1970. **Professional Experience:** PROF BIOCHEM, MED SCH, CASE WESTERN RES UNIV, 1986-; assoc prof, Med Sch, Case Western Res Univ, 1979-1986; res career develop awards, NIH, 1974-1979; asst prof surg, microbiol & immunol, Med Ctr, Duke Univ, 1974-1979; Damon Runyon res fel, 1971; fel, develop biol & cancer, Albert Einstein Col Med, 1970-1973. **Memberships:** Am Soc Biol Chemists; Am Soc Microbiol; Am Soc Virol. **Research Statement & Publications:** Control of expression of eukaryotic genes; biochemical mechanisms of replication of Retro viruses; Published over 80 articles. **Mailing Address:** Dept Biochem Med Sch, Case Western Res Univ 2119 Abington Rd, Cleveland, OH 44106. **Fax:** 216-368-4544. **E-Mail:** jxl8@po.cwru.edu

LEISE, ESTHER M, INVERTEBRATE NEUROANATOMY, LARVAL NEUROBIOLOGY. **Personal Data:** b Washington, DC, May 13, 1953. **Education:** Univ Md, BS, 1975; Univ Wash, PhD (zoology), 1983. **Professional Experience:** ASSOC PROF NEUROBIOLOGY, DEPT BIOL, UNIV NC, GREENSBORO, 1998-; asst prof neurobiology, Dept Biol, Univ NC, Greensboro, 1991-1998; asst researcher, Pac Biomed Res Ctr, Univ Hawaii, Honolulu, 1990-1991; postdoctoral res assoc, Dept Biol, Ga State Univ, 1988-1990; postdoctoral res assoc, Dept Zool, Univ Calif, Davis, 1983-1988; teaching asst, Dept Zool, Univ Wash, 1975-1983. **Memberships:** Soc Neuroscience; AAAS; Am Soc Zoologists; Int Soc Neuroethol. **Research Statement & Publications:** Neuroendocrine control of settlement and metamorphosis in marine invertebrate larvae, particularly molluscan veligers. **Mailing Address:** Dept Biol Univ NC, 312 Eberhart Bldg PO Box 26170, Greensboro, NC 27402. **Fax:** 336-334-5839. **E-Mail:** esther_leise@uncg.edu

LEISENRING, ALBERT, MATHEMATICS. **Education:** Yale Univ, BA, 1960; Univ London, PhD (Math), 1967. **Professional Experience:** RETIRED; fac, Evergreen State Col, ending 2005. **Mailing Address:** 3202 French Rd NW, Olympia, WA 98602. **Fax:** 206-866-6794.

LEISERSON, LEE, organic chemistry, physical chemistry; deceased, see previous edition for last biography

LEISMAN, GERRY, NEUROPSYCHOLOGY, CONTROL THEORY. **Personal Data:** b London, Eng, October 18, 1947; Israeli citizen; m 1996, Yael; c Yael M, Amit, Akiba J, Michelle Z & Daniel E. **Education:** Queens Col, BA, 1968; Univ Manchester, MSc, 1970, MB ChB, 1972; Union Univ, PhD (biomed eng & neuropsychology), 1979; Int Univ Complementary Med, MD, 1990. **Honors & Awards:** Outstanding Contrib Vision Sci, Am Optometric Asn, 1982. **Professional Experience:** PROF PSYCHOL, COL STATEN ISLAND, CITY UNIV NY, 2001-; assoc dean & dir, Inst Biomed Eng & Rehab Servs, 1992-2001; distinguished lectr biomed eng, Inst Elec & Electronics Engrs, 1992; prof biomed eng, Biobehav & Neuroscience, Touro Col, 1990-2001; mem, Comt Emerging Biomed Technol, Eng Med Biol Soc, 1990-; pres & chief sci officer, Nat Inst Complementary Med, 1990-1992; vis scholar, Palmer Col Chiropract, 1990; prof life sci & elec eng, NY Inst Technol, 1986-1991; vpres res & develop, Am Electromedics Corp, 1982-1986; assoc prof psychiat, neurol & ophthal, Univ Med & Dent NJ-NJ Med Sch, 1972-198179; assoc prof health sci & comput sci, City Univ NY, 1972-1981. **Memberships:** Fel Am Psychol Soc; NY Acad Sci; Am Col Forensic Examrs; sr mem Inst Elec & Electronics Engrs Eng Med & Biol Soc; Int Neuropsychol Soc; AAAS. **Research Statement & Publications:** Neurosciences, neuroimaging, and electrophysiology applied to brain organization, vision, neuropsychology, systems science, neurophysics, and related areas; brain cognition; forensic examination. **Mailing Address:** Dept Psychol, City Univ NY, Merrick, NY 11566. **E-Mail:** drgersh@yahoo.com

LEISS, ERNST L, HIGH-PERFORMANCE COMPUTING, DATA SECURITY. **Personal Data:** b Ger, July 7, 1952. **Education:** Univ Waterloo, Can, MMath, 1974; Tech Univ Vienna, Austria, Dipl Ing, 1975, Dr Techn, 1976. **Professional Experience:** PROF COMPUT SCI, UNIV HOUSTON, 1992-; Nat lectr, Asn Comput Mach, 1991-2002; dir, Res Comput Lab, 1985-1993; from asst prof to assoc prof, Univ Houston, 1979-1992; mem fac, Univ Chile, 1978 & Univ Ky, 1979; fel, Univ Waterloo 1976-1977; Vis prof, var univs, Europe & Latin Am. **Memberships:** Sr mem Inst Elec & Electronics Engrs; Asn Comput Mach; Soc Explor Geophysicists. **Research Statement & Publications:** Vector and parallel computing; seismic data processing; data security; databases; automata theory. **Mailing Address:** Dept Comput Sci, Univ Houston, Houston, TX 77204-3475. **Fax:** 713-743-3335. **E-Mail:** coscel@cs.uh.edu

LEISS, JAMES ELROY, PHYSICS. **Personal Data:** b Youngstown, Ohio, June 2, 1924; m 1945, Wilma; c 4. **Education:** Case Inst Technol, BS, 1949; Univ Ill, MS, 1951, PhD (physics), 1954. **Professional Experience:** RETIRED; dir, Off High Energy & Nuclear Physics, Dept Energy, 1978-1985; dir, Ctr Radiation Res, Nat Bur Stand, 1954-1978; asst physics, Univ Ill, 1949-1954; lab asst, Gen Elec Co, 1948-1949. **Memberships:** Am Phys Soc; AAAS; Sigma Xi. **Research Statement & Publications:** Nuclear physics, especially photonuclear reactions and photomeson reactions; design of particle accelerators; scientific research management. **Mailing Address:** Rte Two Box 142C, Broadway, VA 22815.

LEISSA, A(RTHUR) W(ILLIAM), VIBRATIONS, BUCKLING. **Personal Data:** b Wilmington, Del, November 16, 1931; m 1953, c 2. **Education:** Ohio State Univ, BME & MSc, 1954, PhD (eng mech), 1958. **Professional Experience:** PROF EMER ENG MECH, OHIA STATE UNIV, as of 2003; Ed-in-chief, Appl Mech Reviews, 1993-; res fel, Japan Soc Prom Sci, 1990; assoc ed, J Vibration Acoust, 1989-1993; chmn, Orgn Comt, Pan Am Congress Appl Mech, 1986-1989; assoc ed, Appl Mech Reviews, 1985-1993; vis prof, USAF Acad, 1985-1986; & Medtronic, Inc, 1984-1985; vis prof, Swiss Fed Inst Technol, 1972-1973; consult, Kaman Nuclear, 1968-1970; consult, Battelle Mem Inst, 1964-; Prof Eng Mech, Ohio State Univ, beginning 1964; Res Found Supvr, Ohio State Univ, beginning 1962; consult, NAm Aviation, Inc, 1958-1964; fac assoc, Boeing Airplane Co, 1957; from instr to assoc prof, Res Found, 1956-1964; res assoc, Res Found, 1955-1956; Mech engr, Ralph & Curl Engrs, 1954-1958; Assoc engr, Sperry Gyroscope Co, 1954-1955. **Memberships:** Assoc fel Am Inst Aeronaut & Astronaut; Am Soc Eng Educ; Int Asn Shell Struct; fel Am Soc Mech Engrs; fel Am Acad Mech (pres 1987-1988). **Research Statement & Publications:** Elasticity; plates and shells; vibration of continuous systems; buckling; numerical methods for solving boundary value and eigenvalue problems; composite structures. **Mailing Address:** Dept Eng Mech Ohio State Univ, 206 W 18th Ave, Columbus, OH 43210-1117. **E-Mail:** leissa.1@osu.edu

LEISTER, HARRY M, PHYSICAL CHEMISTRY. **Personal Data:** b Quakertown, Pa, March 3, 1941; m 1962, Marie; c 4. **Education:** Pa State Univ, BS, 1963; Drexel Univ, MS, 1965; Temple Univ, PhD (phys chem), 1970. **Professional Experience:** DIR, QUAKER CHEM CORP, 1988-; group lab mgr, Quaker Chem Corp, 1983-1988; sr chem, Quaker Chem Corp, 1982-1983; scientist, Amchem Prod, Inc, 1981-1982; group leader, Amchem Prod, Inc, 1973-1981; chemist, Amchem Div, Union Carbide Corp, 1971-1973; res chemist, E I Du Pont Del Nemours & Co, 1969-1970. **Memberships:** Am Chem Soc; Immunochemiluminometric Assay. **Research Statement & Publications:** Organic coatings; inorganic coatings; formulation of specialty products for metal process industry; emulsification. **Mailing Address:** Quaker Chem Corp, One Quaker Park 901 Hector St, Conshohocken, PA 19428-0809.

LEISURE, ROBERT GLENN, SOLID STATE PHYSICS. **Personal Data:** b Cromwell, Ky, January 29, 1938; m Jeanine. **Education:** Western Ky Univ, BS, 1960; Wash Univ, PhD (physics), 1967. **Honors & Awards:** US-France Exchange Scientist Award; Sci & Eng Res Coun Award, UK 1983 & 1987; Fel, Inst of Physics (UK). **Professional Experience:** Mem operating bd, Colo Advan Mat Inst 1991-1998; vis prof, Tokushima Univ, 1991; collabr, Los Alamos Nat Lab, 1990-1994, 2004-; chmn, Dept Physics, 1984-1990; sr vis fel, St Andrews Univ, Scotland, 1983 & 1987; PROF PHYSICS, COLO STATE UNIV, 1978-; Vis scientist, Univ Paris VI, 1978-1979; from asst prof to assoc prof, Colo State Univ, 1970-1978; Res scientist, Boeing Sci Res Lab, 1967-1970. **Memberships:** Am Phys Soc; Sigma Xi; Acoust Soc Am. **Research Statement & Publications:** Ultrasonics; elastic and anelastic properties of solids; resonant ultrasound spectros. **Mailing Address:** Dept Physics, Colo State Univ, Ft Collins, CO 80523-1875. **Fax:** 970-491-7947. **E-Mail:** leisure@lamar.colostate.edu

LEITCH, CRAIG H B, EARTH SCIENCE, ECONOMIC GEOLOGY. **Honors & Awards:** Barlow Medal, Can Inst Mining & Metall, 1991. **Professional Experience:** AT DEPT GEOL, UNIV BC, as of 2001. **Mailing Address:** Dept Geol, Univ BC, 2329 W Mall Vancouver, BC V6T 1Z4, Can.

LEITCH, GORDON JAMES, GASTROINTESTINAL PHYSIOLOGY, INTESTINAL PROTOZOAN PARASITES. **Personal Data:** b Karachi, Pakistan, September 1, 1937; m 1963, Linda; c Ian J, Colin T, Megan E, Simon D, Allison L & Jocelyn J. **Education:** Univ Chicago, PhD (physiol), 1964; Ohio State Univ, MS, 1960; Univ Alberta, BS, 1958. **Professional Experience:** VISITING PROF, WHITNEY LAB MARINE BIOSCIENCE, 2005-CHMN, DEPT PHYSIOL, MOREHOUSE SCH MED, 1978-2005; PROF, DEPT PHYSIOL, MOREHOUSE SCH MED, 1977-2005 ASSOC PROF, EVANSVILLE CTR, INDIANA UNIV SCH MED, 1972-1977 VISITING PROF, MAHIDOL UNIV, ROCKEFELLER FDN, 1967-1972. **Memberships:** Am Physiological Society American Soc for Microbiology Society of Protozoologists American Gastroenterological Association. **Research Statement & Publications:** Diarrhea pathophysiology; Host-parasite interactions. **Mailing Address:** The Whitney Lab for Marine BioSci, 9505 Ocean Shore Blvd, St Augustine, FL 32080-8610. **Fax:** 904-461-4052. **E-Mail:** leitch@whitney.ufl.edu

LEITCH, JAY A, ENVIRONMENTAL & RESOURCE ECONOMICS, PUBLIC FINANCE. **Personal Data:** b Fergus Falls, Minn, September 20, 1948; m 1990, Rebecca; c Philip, Forrest & Rachel. **Education:** Moorhead State Univ, Minn, BA, 1974; NDak State Univ, MS 1976; Univ Minn, PhD (agr & appl econ), 1981. **Professional Experience:** DEAN, COL OF BUS ADMIN, NDAK STATE UNIV, 1997-; assoc dir, NDak Water Resources Res Inst, 1987-1990; dir, Tri-Col Univ Ctr Environ Studies, 1986-1992; spec asst, Off Asst, 1986-1988; sr economist off policy anal, Off Secy, Dept Interior, 1986; sci adv, Secy Army, 1985-1986; DISTINGUISHED PROF AGR ECON, NDAK STATE UNIV, 1981-; Naval intel officer, USNR, 1980-1992. **Memberships:** Soc Wetland Scientists (pres, 1989-1990); Am Water Resources Asn; Can Water Resources Asn; Am Agr Econs Asn; Asn Environ Prof; Int Impact Assessment Asn. **Research Statement & Publications:** Wetland economics and policy at all levels from local to global. **Mailing Address:** Col bus admin, NDak State Univ, Fargo, ND 58105-5137. **Fax:** 701-237-7508. **E-Mail:** jleitch@ndsuext.nodak.edu

LEITE, RICHARD JOSEPH, PRELIMINARY DESIGN OF SPACECRAFT & SPACEFLIGHT PAYLOADS, DEVELOPMENT OF MINIATURIZED SENSORS & INSTRUMENTS. **Personal Data:** b Fremont, Ohio, March 8, 1923; m 1955, Barbara; c Mark R, Jeffrey H & Mary L (Berlew). **Education:** Univ Notre Dame, BNS, 1945, BSE, 1947; Univ Mich, MSE, 1948, PhD (aero eng), 1956. **Professional Experience:** RETIRED; staff mgr, Eng & Test Div, TRW Inc, Redondo Beach, Calif, 1977-1992; sr scientist, KMS Fusion Inc, 1972-1977; sr staff engr, Bendix Aerospace Corp, 1971-1972; res consult, Univ Mich, Ann Arbor, 1968-1971; prin investr, Univ Mich, Ann Arbor, 1963-1971; res engr, Univ Mich, Ann Arbor, 1958-1971; lectr, Univ Mich, Ann Arbor, 1958-1960; sr engr, Booz-Allen Appl Res, Inc, 1956-1958; res assoc, Univ Mich, Ann Arbor, 1948-1956. **Memberships:** Sigma Xi. **Research Statement & Publications:** Electrical systems design and development of spacecraft; qualification testing and electrical integration of systems components and systems; laser fusion fuel pellet development and insertion technology; spaceflight mass spectrometer development; upper atmosphere composition measurement pioneer; experimental demonstration of stability criteria for tube flow; one United States patent. **Mailing Address:** 6742 Abbottswood Dr, Rancho Palos Verdes, CA 90275-3018.

LEITER, ANDREW B, MEDICAL RESEARCH. **Education:** Univ Pa, AB, 1971; Case Western Reserve Univ, MD, PhD (biochem), 1978. **Professional Experience:** ASSOC DIR, GASTROINTESTINAL RES ABSORPTIVE & SECRETORY PROCESSES, TUFTS-NEW ENG MED CTR, as of 2004; PROF MED, TUFTS UNIV, 2000-. **Memberships:** Am Gastroenterol Asn; Am Soc Microbiol. **Mailing Address:** Tufts-New Eng Med Ctr, 750 Wash St Box 218, Boston, MA 02111-1526. **E-Mail:** aleiter@tufts-nemc.org

LEITER, EDWARD HENRY, CELL BIOLOGY GENETICS OF DIABETES MOUSE MODELS. **Personal Data:** b Columbus, Ga, April 17, 1942; m 1964, Susan. **Education:** Princeton Univ, BS, 1964; Emory Univ, MS, 1966, PhD (biol), 1968. **Honors & Awards:** Kayla & Gerold Grodsky Basic Res Scientist Award, Juv Diabetes Res Found Int, 1994. **Professional Experience:** SR STAFF SCIENTIST, JACKSON LAB, 1990-; juvenile Diabetes Found grant, 1976-; Nat inst Arthritis & Metab Dis res grant, 1974-; from assoc staff scientist to staff scientist, Jackson Lab, 1974-1989; asst prof biol, Brooklyn Col, 1971-1974; NIH trainee, Univ Tex, Austin, 1968-1971. **Memberships:** Endocrine Soc; Am Diabetes Asn; Am Asn Immunologists. **Research Statement & Publications:** Function of normal and diabetic pancreatic endocrine cells in vitro; genetic viral and environmental parameters producing pancreatic pathologies in the mouse; immunology of type one diabetes. **Mailing Address:** Jackson Lab, 600 Main St, Bar Harbor, ME 04609. **Fax:** 207-288-6077. **E-Mail:** ehl@aretha.jax.org

LEITER, JOSEPH, biochemistry; deceased, see previous edition for last biography

LEITH, ARDEAN, BIOLOGICAL COMPUTING. **Personal Data:** b Warsaw, NY, March 21, 1947; m 1982, Meeli Chew; c Eric Weiming. **Education:** Rensselaer Polytech Inst, BS, 1968, MS, 1986; Univ Rochester, PhD (biol), 1972. **Professional Experience:** COMPUT SCIENTIST, HEALTH RES INC, ALBANY, NY, 1985-; asst prof cell biol, Univ Guam, USA, 1982-1985; fac mem cell biol, Univ Pertanian Malaysia, 1978-1982; sr res assoc cell biol, Worcester Polytech Inst, Mass, 1976-1978; fac mem biophys, Nat Univ Malaysia, 1972-1976. **Memberships:** Asn Comput Mach; Inst Elec & Electronics Engrs; Am Chem Soc; AAAS. **Research Statement & Publications:** Visualization of cellular structure; display techniques for tomographic and confocal microscopy data; mathematical modeling of biological processes; computer graphics applications in biology. **Mailing Address:** Wadsworth Labs, Empire State Plaza PO Box 509, Albany, NY 12201. **E-Mail:** leith@wadsworth.org

LEITH, CARLTON JAMES, GEOLOGY. **Personal Data:** b Madison, Wis, September 24, 1919; m 1941, Marian; c Carol J (Kurumada) & Ronnie S. **Education:** Univ Wis, BA, 1940, MA, 1941; Univ Calif, PhD (geol), 1947. **Professional Experience:** PROF EMER GEOSCI, NC STATE UNIV, 1980-; head dept, NC State Univ, 1967-1980; prof geol eng, NC State Univ, 1965-1980; assoc prof, NC State Univ, 1961-1965; geologist, Holmes & Narver Inc, 1960-1961; geologist, Stand Oil Co, Calif, 1951-1960; chief petrog unit, US Engrs Testing Lab, 1949-1951; from instr to asst prof geol, Univ Ind, 1947-1949; asst geol, Univ Calif, 1946-1947; geologist, Stand Oil Co, Tex, 1946; from jr mineral economist to asst mineral economist, Mineral Prod & Econ Div, US Bur Mines, 1942-1943; asst geol, Univ Calif, 1941-1942. **Memberships:** Am Asn Petrol Geol. **Research Statement & Publications:** Engineering geology; sedimentary petrology; areal geology; gravity and magnetics. **Mailing Address:** 17960 Tanleaf Lane, Salinas, CA 93907.

LEITH, CECIL ELDON, JR, TURBULENCE, ATMOSPHERIC SCIENCES. **Personal Data:** b Boston, Mass, January 31, 1923; m 1942, Mary Henry; c Ann, John & Paul. **Education:** Univ Calif, Berkeley, AB, 1943, PhD (math), 1957. **Honors & Awards:** Meisinger Award, Am Meteorol Soc, 1967, Carl-Gustaf Rossby Res Medal, 1981. **Professional Experience:** PHYSICIST EMER, DEPT ENERGY, LAWRENCE LIVERMORE NAT LAB, 1990-; physicist, Lawrence Livermore Nat Lab, Dept Energy, 1983-1990; sr scientist, Atmospheric Anal & Prediction Div, 1981-1983; officer, Joint Sci Comt, World Climate Res Prog, 1981-1983; dir, Atmospheric Anal & Prediction Div, 1978-1981; chmn, Comt Atmospheric Sci, Nat Res Coun, 1978-1980; mem, Int Comn Dynamic Meteorol, Int Asn Meteorol & Atmospheric Physics, 1972-1980 & Int Comn Climate, 1978-1980; mem joint organizing comt, Global Atmospheric Res Prog, World Meteorol Orgn & Int Counc Sci Unions, 1976-1980; sr scientist, Nat Ctr Atmospheric Res, 1968-1978; Physicist, Lawrence Radiation Lab, Univ Calif, 1946-1968. **Memberships:** Fel AAAS; fel Am Phys Soc; fel Am Meteorol Soc; Am Math Soc. **Research Statement & Publications:** Computational fluid dynamics; statistical hydrodynamics; turbulence. **Mailing Address:** 627 Carla St, Livermore, CA 94550-2316. **E-Mail:** leith1@llnl.gov

LEITH, DAVID W G S, C P VIOLATION, RARE B DECAYS, LIGHT QUARK SPECTROSCOPY INSTRUMENTATION. **Personal Data:** b Glasgow, Scotland, September 5, 1937; m 1962, Doreen; c Evan, Roderick & Gordon. **Education:** Univ Glasgow, BSc, 1959, PhD (natural philos), 1962. **Professional Experience:** Dir res, Linear Accelerator Ctr, Stanford Univ, 1991-2000; PROF PHYSICS, LINEAR ACCELERATOR CTR, STANFORD UNIV, 1970-; Stanford Univ Senate, 1988-1990; chair, Stanford Linear Accelerator Ctr, Stanford Univ, 1980-1990; assoc prof, Linear Accelerator Ctr, Stanford Univ, 1966-1970; staff physicist, Glasgow Univ, Europ Orgn Nuclear Res, Geneva, Switz, 1963-1966; res fel pysics, Glasgow Univ, Europ Orgn Nuclear Res, Geneva, Switz, 1962-1963. **Memberships:** Fel Am Phys Soc; Brit Inst Physics & Phys Soc; dir of res, Stanford Univ (1991-2001). **Research Statement & Publications:** Strong interaction physics with emphasis on scattering experiments and investigations of resonance properties, their classification and the associated phenomenological analysis; study of electroweak interaction via the production and decay of z boson. **Mailing Address:** Stanford Univ, 754 Mayfield Ave, Stanford, CA 94305. **Fax:** 650-925-3587. **E-Mail:** leith@slac.stanford.edu

LEITH, EMMETT NORMAN, electro-optics; deceased, see previous edition for last biography

LEITH, JOHN DOUGLAS, PATHOLOGY. **Personal Data:** b Grand Forks, NDak, April 20, 1931; m 1957, c 2. **Education:** Lehigh Univ, BA, 1952; Univ Pa, MD, 1956; Univ Wis, PhD (cytol), 1964; Am Bd Path, cert anat & clin path, 1974, cert radioisotopic path, 1975. **Professional Experience:** RETIRED; actg chief pathologist, Brockton Hosp, 1991-1993; assoc pathologist, Brockton Hosp, 1975-1991; resident path, Peter Bent Brigham Hosp, Boston, 1971-1974; Univ Wis res grants 1968-1970; NSF grant, 1968-1970; from asst prof to assoc prof biol, Univ Wis-Oshkosh, 1967-1971; Health Res Serv Found res grant, 1966-1967; Am Cancer Soc Inst res grant, 1965-1966; asst prof anat & cell biol, Med Sch, Univ Pittsburgh, 1964-1967; Nat Cancer Inst spec fel, 1963-1964; asst zoology, NSF fel, 1960-1963; asst zoology, Univ Wis, 1959-1960; intern, Med Ctr, Univ Calif, San Francisco, 1956-1957. **Memberships:** Col Am Path; Am Soc Clin Path; Sigma Xi. **Mailing Address:** 162 Islington Rd, Auburndale, MA 02166.

LEITH, WILLIAM CUMMING, MECHANICAL ENGINEERING, POLLUTION CONTROL. **Personal Data:** b Kimberley, BC, April 15, 1925; m 1950, Marian; c James, Brenda & Hope. **Education:** Univ BC, BAppSc, 1948, MAppSc, 1949; McGill Univ, PhD (mech eng), 1960. **Honors & Awards:** Duggan Prize & Medal, Eng Inst Can, 1959. **Professional Experience:** CONSULT, 1990-; mech engr, Cominco Ltd, 1973-1990; res assoc prof nuclear eng, Univ Wash, 1967-1973; design engr, Cominco-Trail, BC, 1962-1964 & H G Acres Co, Ont, 1964-1967; sr res scientist, Hydronautic Inc, Md, 1961-1962; mech res engr, Dom Eng Works, Que, 1953-1961; jr engr, Dom Eng Works, Que, 1949-1950 & Cominco-Trail, BC, 1951-1952. **Memberships:** Am Soc Mech Engrs. **Research Statement & Publications:** Design of devices for access to blood circulatory systems such as cannulas, fistulas and catheters; pollution control; scrubbing of gases; uranium enrichment by gas centrifuge; cavitation correlated to vibration white finger in loggers' hands and minimum energy model of wood chip refining pulp/paper making. **Mailing Address:** PO Box 157, Trail, BC V1R 4L4, Can.

LEITMAN, MARSHALL J, APPLIED MATHEMATICS, CONTINUUM PHYSICS. **Personal Data:** b Yonkers, NY, January 16, 1941. **Education:** Rensselaer Polytech Inst, BS, 1962; Brown Univ, PhD (appl math), 1965. **Professional Experience:** PROF MATH, CASE WESTERN RES UNIV, 1981-; assoc prof, Case Western Res Univ, 1971-1981; vis asst prof, Cath Univ Louvain, 1970-1971; asst prof, Case Western Res Univ, 1966-1971; res assoc appl math, Brown Univ, 1965-1966. **Memberships:** Soc Natural Philos; Soc Indust & Appl Math. **Research Statement & Publications:** Mechanics; viscoelasticity. **Mailing Address:** Dept Math & Statist, Case Western Res Univ, Univ Circle, Cleveland, OH 44106-1749. **Fax:** 216-368-5163. **E-Mail:** mxl5@po.cwru.edu

LEITMANN, G(EORGE), MECHANICS, SYSTEMS & CONTROL. **Personal Data:** b Vienna, Austria, May 24, 1925; m 1955, Nancy Lloyd; c Josef L & Elaine M (Parker). **Education:** Columbia Univ, BS, 1949, MA, 1950; Univ Calif, PhD (eng sci), 1956. **Honorary Degrees:** DSc, Technische Univ, Vienna, 1988, Univ Paris, 1989; DIng, Technische Univ, Darmstadt, 1989. **Honors & Awards:** Pendray Aerospace Lit Award, Am Inst Aeronaut & Astronaut, 1977; Mech & Control ofFlight Award, Am Inst Aeronaut & Astronaut, 1980; Alexander von Humboldt Sr Scientist Award, 1981; Levy Medal, Franklin Inst, 1981; Alexander von Humboldt Medal, 1991; Bellman Award, 1995; Oldenburger Medal, Am Soc Mech Engrs, 1995; Order of Merit, Germany, 1996; Order of Merit, Italy, 1997; Berkeley Fellow, Univ Calif Berkeley, 2001; Disting Eng Alumni Award, Univ Calif Berkeley, 2002. **Professional Experience:** Assoc dean, Int Rel, Univ Calif, Berkeley, 2003-; assoc ed, J Optimal Theory Appln, 2001-; PROF GRAD SCH, FAC ENG, 1995-; pres, Alexander von Humboldt Asn Am, 1994-; CHAIR, FAC ENG, 1994-; EMER PROF ENG SCI, UNIV CALIF, BERKELEY, 1991-; Hughes Chair Mech Eng, Col Eng, 1990-1991; from ed to hon ed, J Math Anal Appl, 1985-; assoc dean, Col Eng, 1981-1994; chmn, Div Appl Mech, Univ Calif, Berkeley, 1968-1972; univ ombudsman, Univ Calif, Berkeley, 1968-1970; Consult, Martin Co, 1957-1958 & Lockheed Missiles & Space Co, 1958-1966; from asst prof to prof eng sci, Univ Calif, Berkeley, 1957-1991; head aeroballistics anal sect, Naval Ord Test Sta, 1955-1957; Physicist, Naval Ord Test Sta, 1950-1955. **Memberships:** Nat Acad Eng; Int Acad Astronaut; Acad Sci Bologna; fel Am Inst Aeronaut & Astronaut; Arg Acad Eng; Russ Acad Natural Sci; Bavarian Acad Sci; Georgian Acad Sci Georgian Acad Engin. **Research Statement & Publications:** Exterior ballistics of rockets and astrodynamics; variational problems in mechanics and astronautics; optimal control of dynamic systems; game theory; control of uncertain systems; applications to economics, engineering; resource. **Mailing Address:** Engr Dean's Ofc, 320 McLaughlin, Mech Engr, 5130 Etcheverry, Berkeley, CA 94720-1700. **Fax:** 510-642-6216. **E-Mail:** gleit@coe.berkeley.edu

LEITNER, ALFRED, MATHEMATICAL THEORY OF WAVE PROPAGATION, DEMONSTRATION EXPERIMENTS. **Personal Data:** b Vienna, Austria, November 3, 1921; American citizen; m 1948, Marzia O'Neil; c Kathleen, Deborah (Jones) & David. **Education:** Univ Buffalo, BA, 1944; Yale Univ, MS, 1945, PhD (physics), 1948. **Professional Experience:** EMER PROF PHYSICS, RENSSELAER POLYTECH INST, 1987-; vis prof physics, Rensselaer Polytech Inst, 1964 & US Mil Acad, West Point, 1983-1985; Ger exchange fel, Deutsches Mus, Munich, 1977-1978; prof, Rensselaer Polytech Inst, 1967-1987; consult, Proj Physics, Harvard Univ, 1966-1967; res assoc, Proj Physics, Harvard Univ, 1965-1966; Vis prof physics & Guggenheim fel, Aachen Technische Hochschule, Ger, 1958-1959; from asst prof to prof physics, Mich State Univ, 1951-1967; Res scientist, Courant Inst, NY Univ, 1947-1951. **Memberships:** Fel Am Phys Soc. **Research Statement & Publications:** Mathematical theory of wave propagation, boundary value problems and special functions; production of educational films demonstrating physical phenomena for students of physics; history of physics. **Mailing Address:** 1201 Eighth Terr N, Naples, FL 34102-5411. **E-Mail:** ltnr@aol.com

LEITNER, PHILIP, VERTEBRATE ZOOLOGY. **Personal Data:** b Peking, China, June 16, 1936; American citizen; m 1960, c 2. **Education:** St Mary's Col, Calif, BS, 1958; Univ Calif, Los Angeles, MA, 1960, PhD (zoology), 1961. **Professional Experience:** PROF BIOL, ST MARY'S COL, CALIF, 1976-; chmn dept, St Mary's Col, Calif, 1970-1976; NSF res grants, 1965-1970; NIH res grant, 1963-1965; from instr to assoc prof, St Mary's Col, Calif, 1962-1976; jr res zoologist, Univ Calif, Los Angeles, 1961-1962. **Memberships:** AAAS; Am Soc Zoologists; Soc Study Evolution; Am Soc Mammalogists. **Research Statement & Publications:** Environmental physiology of mammals, especially physiological responses to temperature and photoperiod. **Mailing Address:** Dept Biol, Sch Med, St Marys Col, PO Box 4507 1928 St Marys Rd, Moraga, CA 94575-4507. **Fax:** 925-376-4027. **E-Mail:** pleitner@stmarys-ca.edu

LEITZ, FRED JOHN, JR, PHYSICAL CHEMISTRY, NUCLEAR CHEMISTRY. **Personal Data:** b Portland, Ore, February 2, 1921; m 1945, Kathryn Kauper; c Fred, Robert & Steven. **Education:** Reed Col, BA, 1940; Univ Calif, PhD (phys chem), 1943. **Professional Experience:** CONSULT, 1984-; staff mgr technol, Westinghouse Hanford Co, 1979-1984; mgr planning & anal, Westinghouse Hanford Co, 1976-1979; sr staff scientist, Westinghouse Hanford Co, 1970-1976; consult to dir, Battelle Northwest Lab, 1969-197O; mgr steam reactor technol, Advan Prod Oper, 1966-1968; mgr fast reactor core eng & test, Advan Prod Oper, 1964-1966; develop proj engr, Atomic Power Equip Dept, Gen Elec Co, 1958-1964; nuclear engr, Atomic Power Develop Assocs, Mich, 1956-1958; chemist, Radiochem & Reactor Metall Res, Hanford Works, Gen Elec Co, Wash, 1948-1956; sr chemist, Oak Ridge Nat Lab, Tenn, 1946-1948; sr res chemist, Monsanto Chem Co, Ohio, 1944-1946; instr chem, Univ Calif, 1943-1944. **Memberships:** Am Chem Soc; Am Nuclear Soc. **Research Statement & Publications:** Heavy element and fission product chemistry; nuclear fuel cycle development; fast and steam cooled reactor design and technology. **Mailing Address:** 14019 104th Street Ct E, Puyallup, WA 98374.

LEITZ, FREDERICK HENRY, PHARMACOLOGY. **Personal Data:** b Hastings, Mich, November 20, 1928; m 1970. **Education:** Kalamazoo Col, BA, 1952; Univ Calif, Los Angeles, PhD (chem), 1962. **Professional Experience:** SR PRIN SCIENTIST, SCHERING CORP, 1970-; staff fel, Lab Chem Pharmacol, Nat Heart Inst, 1965-1970; res scientist, Lamont Geol Observ, 1963-1965; Res grant, Inst Org Chem, Royal Inst Technol, Sweden, 1962-1963. **Memberships:** Am Chem Soc; Am Soc Pharmacol & Exp Therapeut; NY Acad Sci. **Research Statement & Publications:** Drug metabolism, bioavailability, bioequivalency and pharmacokinetics. **Mailing Address:** Schering Corp, 86 Orange St, Bloomfield, NJ 07003-4744.

LEITZ, VICTORIA MARY, BIOCHEMISTRY, LABORATORY MEDICINE. **Personal Data:** b Yorkshire, Eng. **Education:** Oxford Univ, BA, 1964, DPhil(clin chem), 1968. **Professional Experience:** PRIN, INT BIOMED CONSULT, 1994-; dir clin chem, Pharmacia diag, 1990-1994; vpres int sales & mkt, Electro-Nucleonics, Inc, 1984-1989; dir mkt, Electro-Nucleonics, Inc, 1981-1984; dir tech serv, Electro-Nucleonics, Inc, 1979-1981; mgr diag chem & clin chem, Electro-Nucleonics, Inc, 1974-1979; mgr develop chem & clin chem, Becton-Dickinson, NJ, 1971-1972; chemist neurochem, Sect Child Neurol, Nat Inst Neurol Dis & Stroke, NIH, 1968-1970; Res scientist human genetics, Med Res Coun, Oxford, Eng, 1967-1968. **Memberships:** Am Asn Clin Chem; Nat Comt Clin Lab Stand; Biomed Mkt Asn. **Mailing Address:** 55 Peninsula Dr, Hilton Head Island, SC 29926.

LEITZE, ANNETTE E, MATHEMATICS. **Professional Experience:** PROF & CHAIR, DEPT MATHS, BALL STATE UNIV, as of 2005. **Memberships:** Am Math Asn. **Mailing Address:** Ball State Univ, 2000 W Univ Ave, Muncie, IN 47306. **Fax:** 765-285-2173. **E-Mail:** aleitze@bsu.edu

LEITZEL, JOAN PHILLIPS, MATHEMATICS. **Personal Data:** b Valparaiso, Ind, July 2, 1936; m 1965, c 2. **Education:** Hanover Col, BA, 1958; Brown Univ, MA, 1961; Univ Ind, PhD (algebra), 1965. **Professional Experience:** Pres, Univ NH, beginning 1996; sr vice chancelor affairs, Univ Nebr, 1992-1996; div dir, NSF, 1990-1992; assoc provost, Ohio State Univ, 1985-1990, prof math, Ohio State Univ, 1983-1992; vchmn, Math Dept, Ohio State Univ, 1973-1977; from asst prof to assoc prof, Ohio State Univ, 1965-1983; instr math, Oberlin Col, 1961-196. **Memberships:** Am Math Soc; Math Asn Am. **Research Statement & Publications:** Field theoretical proofs for cohomological results in class field theory. **Mailing Address:** Off Pres, Univ N H, Thompson 105 Main St, Durham, NH 03824.

LEITZMANN, CLAUS, BIOCHEMISTRY, NUTRITION. **Personal Data:** b Dahlenburg, Ger, February 6, 1933; m 1957, c 4. **Education:** Capital Univ, BS, 1962; Univ Minn, MS, 1964, PhD (biochem), 1967. **Honors & Awards:** Zabel prize, 1987. **Professional Experience:** DIR INST NUTRIT, UNIV GIESSEN, 1990-; PROF INST NUTRIT, UNIV GIESSEN, 1978-; Mem, Trop Inst, Univ Giessen, 1974-; assoc, Univ Giessen, 1974-1978; chief labs, Anemia & Malnutrit Res Ctr, Thailand, 1971-1974; vis prof biochem, Mahidol Univ, Thailand, 1969-1971; Nat Inst Gen Med Sci res asst molecular biol inst, Univ Calif, Los Angeles, 1967-1969. **Memberships:** AAAS; Inst Soc Nutrit; Am Soc Clin Nutrit; Am Inst Nutrit. **Research Statement & Publications:** Nutrition in developing countries; interaction of nutrition and infection; adaptations to changes in food intake; hunger and satiety; obesity; dietary fibers; vegetarianism. **Mailing Address:** Inst Nutrit, Justus-Liebig-U Wilhelmstr 20, 35392 Giessen, Ger.

LEIVA, MIRIAM A, MATHEMATICS. **Professional Experience:** PROF EMER, UNIV NC, CHARLOTTE, as of 2006. **Memberships:** TODOS Math. **Mailing Address:** Dept Math, Univ NC, Charlotte, NC 28223. **Fax:** 704-687-6415. **E-Mail:** maleiva@email.uncc.edu

LEJA, J(AN), SURFACE CHEMISTRY, METALLURGY. **Personal Data:** b Grodzisko, Poland, May 27, 1918; m 1947, c 6. **Education:** Univ London, BSc, 1945; Univ Krakow, dipl Ing, 1947; Cambridge Univ, PhD (surface chem), 1954. **Honorary Degrees:** Dr, Marie Curie-Sklodowska Univ, Poland, 1976. **Professional Experience:** PROF EMER MINING & MINERAL PROCESS ENG, UNIV BC, 1983-; prof, Univ Bc, 1965-1983; from asst prof to prof metall, Univ Alta, 1957-1965; res fel colloid sci, Cambridge Univ, 1954-1957; reduction officer, SAfrica, 1949-1952; Res metallurgist, Southwest Africa Co, Eng, 1947-1949. **Memberships:** Brit Inst Mining & Metall; fel Can Inst Chem; Can Inst Mining & Metall. **Research Statement & Publications:** Surface chemistry; infrared spectroscopy of adsorption; effluent control; dissolution of metals; corrosion. **Mailing Address:** Dept Mining & Mineral Process Eng, Univ BC, 2329 W Mall, Vancouver, BC V6T 1Z4, Can.

LEKEUX, PIERRE MARIE, VETERINARY PHYSIOLOGY, BOVINE & EQUINE DISEASES. **Personal Data:** b Liege, Belg, April 7, 1954; m 1978, Delogne Odette; c Max & David. **Education:** Univ Liege, Belg, DVM, 1978; Univ Utrecht, Neth, PRD 1984. **Honors & Awards:** Peter Bridge Award, 1991. **Professional Experience:** Bd mem, Int Comt Eprine Exercise Physiol, 1994-; chmn meeting comt, World Eprine Vet Asn, 1991-; Assoc ed-in-chief, Annals of Med Vet, 1986 & Pratipue Vet Equine, 1991; secy gen bovine, World Asn Buiatrics, 1990-; pres equine, Equine Res Funds, 1988-; DIR, LAB FUNCTIONAL INVEST, 1988-; Pres, Comp Respiratory Soc, 1988-1989; PROF PHYSIOL, UNIV LIEGE, 1986-. **Memberships:** Comp Respiratory Soc; Am Physiol Soc; World Asn Buiatrics; World Equine Vet Asn. **Research Statement & Publications:** Physiological, pathophysiological and pharmacological studies of the cardio-pulmonary function in large animals; exercise physiology. **Mailing Address:** Univ Liege Bat B42, Sart Tilman, Liege B-4000, Belgium. **Fax:** 324-156-2935.

LEKLEM, JAMES ERLING, NUTRITION. **Personal Data:** b Rhinelander, Wis, August 1, 1941; m 1967, c 2. **Education:** Univ Wis, BS, 1964, MS, 1966, PhD (nutrit), 1973. **Honors & Awards:** Borden Award, Am Home Econ Found, 1985. **Professional Experience:** PROF EMER NUTRIT, ORE STATE UNIV as of 2002; admin intern, Agr Exp Sta, 1992-1993; prof, Dept Nutrit & Food Mgt, Oregon State Univ, beginning 1985; adj prof, Dept Human Nutrit & Food Econ, Inst Agr & Vet Med, Rabat, Morocco, 1987-1990; prof nutrit, Ore State Univ, 1985-; assoc prof, Ore State Univ, 1980-1985; res assoc, Univ Wis, 1973-1975; proj assoc clin oncol, Univ Wis, 1966-1971. **Memberships:** Sigma Xi; Am Inst Nutrit. **Research Statement & Publications:** Vitamin B6; metabolism of tryptophan;

nutrient relationship to cancer etiology; obesity; diabetes. **Mailing Address:** Dept Nutrit & Food Mgt, Ore State Univ, 108 Milam Hall, Corvallis, OR 97331-5103. **Fax:** 541-737-6914. **E-Mail:** leklemj@orst.edu

LEKOUDIS, SPIRO G, AERONAUTICS. **Professional Experience:** HEAD, ENG, MAT & PHYS SCI, OFFICE NAVAL RES, as of 2001. **Memberships:** Am Inst Aeronaut & Astronaut. **Mailing Address:** Office Naval Res, 800 N Quincy St Code 1132-F, Arlington, VA 22217. **Fax:** 703-696-2558. **E-Mail:** lekouds@onr.navy.mil

LELACHEUR, ROBERT MURRAY, PHYSICS. **Personal Data:** b Ottawa, Ont, October 12, 1920; American citizen; m 1946, c 4. **Education:** Mt Allison Univ, BSc, 1942; Dalhousie Univ, MSc, 1947; Univ Va, PhD (physics), 1949. **Professional Experience:** RETIRED; mgr develop & mfg eng, Reading, 1966-1991; dir mat & chem processes res & develop, NY, 1962-1966; asst supt eng, Western Elec Co Inc, 1958-1962; mem tech staff, Bell Labs, NJ, 1953-1958; physicist, Nat Res Coun Can, 1949-1953. **Memberships:** Am Phys Soc; Inst Elec & Electronics Engrs; Sigma Xi. **Research Statement & Publications:** Materials properties and processing; semiconductor device engineering. **Mailing Address:** 1005 Wyomissing Blvd, Wyomissing, PA 19610-2509.

LELAND, FRANCES E(LBRIDGE), PHYSICAL CHEMISTRY. **Personal Data:** b Chicago, Ill, April 22, 1932. **Education:** Swarthmore Col, BA, 1954; Northwestern Univ, PhD (phys chem), 1959. **Professional Experience:** RETIRED; prof, MacMurray Col, 1973-1994; from asst prof to assoc prof chem, MacMurray Col, 1962-1973; Instr chem, Brooklyn Col, 1959-1961. **Memberships:** Am Chem Soc. **Research Statement & Publications:** Molecular quantum mechanics. **Mailing Address:** 950 Goltra Ave, Jacksonville, IL 62650.

LELAND, ROBERT, MATHEMATICS. **Education:** Oxford Univ, Phd. **Professional Experience:** MGR, COMPUT & SOFTWARE SYSTS, 2001-. **Mailing Address:** Sandia Nat Labs, Dept 1424, Albuquerque, NM 87185-1109. **Fax:** 505-844-4543. **E-Mail:** leland@sandia.gov

LELAND, STANLEY EDWARD, JR, PARASITOLOGY. **Personal Data:** b Chicago, Ill, August 1, 1926; m 1950, Jeanne L Melby; c Stanley B, Steven B & Clayton B. **Education:** Univ Ill, BS, 1949, MS, 1950; Mich State Univ, PhD (parasitol), 1953. **Honors & Awards:** Col Vet Med Res Award, Kans State Univ, 1971; Distinguished Graduate Fac Award, Kans State Univ, 1975. **Professional Experience:** PROF EMER PARASITOL, KANS STATE UNIV, as of 2003; USDA Comt Nine, 1985-1988; ASSOC DIR EMER AGR EXP STA, KANS STATE UNIV, 1975-; vis prof parasitol, Ahmadu Bello, Univ, Zaria, Nigeria, 1972-1973; actg head dept infectious dis, Kans State Univ, 1970-1972; prof parasitol, Kans State Univ, beginning 1967; assoc parasitologist, Univ Fla, 1963-1967; consult, Eli Lilly Co, 1962-1966; prof animal path, Univ Ky, 1960-1963; from assoc parasitologist to parasitologist, Univ Ky, 1953-1960; coop agent animal dis & parasite res div, USDA, 1953-1959; asst parasitol, Mich State Univ, 1950-1953. **Research Statement & Publications:** Electrophoresis; drug testing; pathology; physiology; biochemistry; in vitro cultivation; immunology as related to parasitology published in over 120 scientific papers and 12 book chapters. **Mailing Address:** 420 Shelle Rd, Manhattan, KS 66502-3833.

LELAND, WALLACE THOMPSON, LASERS. **Personal Data:** b Minn, January 21, 1922; m 1943, c 4. **Education:** Univ Minn, BEE, 1943, PhD (physics), 1950. **Professional Experience:** MEM STAFF NUCLEAR RES, LOS ALAMOS NAT LAB, 1950-; head, Instrument Develop Dept, Carbide & Carbon Chem Corp, 1946-1947. **Memberships:** Am Phys Soc; Sigma Xi. **Research Statement & Publications:** Mass spectroscopy and nuclear reactions; high energy lasers. **Mailing Address:** Los Alamos Nat Lab, PO Box 1663, Los Alamos, NM 87545.

LELE, SHREEDHAR G, ELECTRICAL ENGINEERING, PHYSICS. **Personal Data:** b Varanasi, India, April 19, 1931; m 1966, c 2. **Education:** Banaras Hindu Univ, India, MS, 1952; Univ Mich, MS, 1962, PhD (elec eng), 1966. **Professional Experience:** DIR, ENG PROG, UNIV MASS, BOSTON, 1985-; consult, 1980-; res asst elec eng, Univ Mich, 1961-1966; lectr physics, Banaras Hindu Univ, India, 1952-1960. **Memberships:** Inst Elec & Electronics Engrs. **Research Statement & Publications:** Ionospheric physics; microwave tubes; design of electron guns and solid-state devices. **Mailing Address:** Boston Harbor Campus, Univ Mass Sci Bldg Rm S-3-110, Boston, MA 02125.

LELEIKO, NEAL SIMON, PEDIATRIC GASTROENTEROLOGY, HEPATOLOGY-NUTRITION. **Personal Data:** b Brooklyn, NY, October 26, 1946; m 1967, c 2. **Education:** Brooklyn Col, BS, 1967; NY Med Col, MD, 1971; Mass Inst Technol, PhD (biochem & metab), 1979. **Professional Experience:** CHIEF & VICE CHMN, DEPT PEDIAT, MT SINAI SCH MED, as of 2005; ADJ PROF, COMMUNITY & PREV MED, MT SINAI SCH MED, as of 2005; PROF PEDIAT, MT SINAI SCH MED, as of 2001; assoc prof pediat, Mt Sinai Sch Med, beginning 1987; dir, Gen Clin Res Ctr, 1987-1990. **Memberships:** AAAS; Am Acad Pediat; NAm Soc Pediat Gastroenterol; Soc Pediat Res; Am Fedn Clin Res. **Research Statement & Publications:** Molecular biology of gene nutrient interactions; cost of illness in children and adults; treatment and cause of inflammatory bowel disease. **Mailing Address:** Dept Pediat, Mt Sinai Sch Med, One Gustave L Levy Pl PO Box 1198, New York, NY 10029. **E-Mail:** neal.leleiko@mssm.edu

LE LEVIER, ROBERT ERNEST, THEORETICAL PHYSICS. **Personal Data:** b Los Angeles, Calif, November 7, 1923. **Education:** Univ Calif, Los Angeles, PhD (physics), 1951. **Professional Experience:** RETIRED; chief scientist & bd mem, Ros Technologies, 1983-1993; chief scientist, R & D Assocs, 1980-1983; mem staff, R & D Assocs, 1971-1980; mem staff, Rand Corp, 1957-1971; mem staff, Lawrence Radiation Lab, Univ Calif, 1951-1957. **Memberships:** Am Phys Soc. **Research Statement & Publications:** Ionospheric physics; nuclear physics; geophysics. **Mailing Address:** 961 Jacon Way, Pacific Palisades, CA 90272.

LELEWER, DEBRA ANN, DATA COMPRESSION, SOFTWARE ENGINEERING. **Personal Data:** m 1972, Steven A. **Education:** Mich State Univ, BS, 1973; Calif State Polytech Univ, Pomona, MS, 1976, MS, 1985; Univ Calif, Irvine, PhD (info & comput sci), 1991. **Professional Experience:** ASSOC VPRES FAC AFFAIRS, CALIF STATE POLYTECH UNIV, POMONA, 1995-; chair comput sci, Calif State Polytech Univ, Pomona, 1992-1995; lectr, Nat Technol Univ, 1992-1993; from asst to assoc prof comput sci, Calif State Polytech Univ, Pomona, 1985-1992; PROF, DEPT COMPUT SCI, CALIF STATE POLYTECH UNIV, POMONA, 1985-; lectr math & comput sci, Calif State Polytech Univ, Pomona, 1982-1985; Teacher & dept chair math, Glendora High Sch, 1973-1982. **Memberships:** Asn Comput Mach; Inst Elec & Electronics Engrs Comput Soc; Am Asn Univ Women; Asn Women Sci. **Research Statement & Publications:** Design and analysis of algorithms, with algorithms for data compression being a particular interest; software engineering: software metrics and software testing, mutation testing in particular; artificial intelligence, specifically natural language processing and genetic algorithms. **Mailing Address:** Dept Comput Sci, Calif State Polytech Univ, Pomona, CA 91768. **Fax:** 909-869-4396. **E-Mail:** dabrum@csupomona.edu

LELKES, PETER ISTVAN, ENDOTHELIAL CELL BIOLOGY & STIMULUS-SECRETION-SYNTHESIS COUPLING & TISSUE ENGINEERING, BIOMATERIALS & SCAFFOLDS & BIOREACTORS. **Personal Data:** b Budapest, Hungary, February 28, 1949; American citizen; m 1978, Iris; c Tamar, Efrat, Nadar & Yphtach. **Education:** Univ Aachen, Germany, MS (Physics/Biophysics, 1974, PhD (Cell Biology / Biophysics), 1977. **Honors & Awards:** Forchheim vis prof, Hebrew Univ, Jerusalem Israel. **Professional Experience:** CALHOUN CHAIR & PROF CELL TISSUE ENG, DREXEL UNIV, 2000-; PROF & DIR, LAB CELL BIOL, UNIV WIS MED SCH, 1993-2000; assoc prof, Univ Wis Med Sch, 1988-1993; vis scientist, NIH, 1983-1988; scientist, Weizmann Inst Sci, 1977-1983; Hon Guest Prof, Chinese Acad Sci, Changchun, PR China, 2005; Hon Prof, Univ Appl Sci, Aachen, Germany, 2005. **Memberships:** Int Soc Appl Vascular Biol, Tissue Eng & Regenerative Med Int Soc. **Research Statement & Publications:** Endothelial cell biology; heterogeneity and adaptation to mechanical stimuli, signal transduction mechanisms; endothelialization of artificial blood pumps; neuroendocrine development and differentiation; 3-D Cell Culture, Tissue Engineering of Vital Organs, Biomaterials and Bioreactors. **Mailing Address:** Sch Biomed Eng, Drexel Univ, 3141 Chestnut St, Philadelphia, PA 19104. **Fax:** 215-895-4893. **E-Mail:** pilelkes@drexel.edu

LELLINGER, DAVID BRUCE, TAXONOMIC BOTANY. **Personal Data:** b Chicago, Ill, January 24, 1937; m 1999, Jeannette L Salom; c 2. **Education:** Univ Ill, AB, 1958; Univ Mich, MS, 1960, PhD (bot), 1965. **Professional Experience:** Ed, Pteridologia, 1985-; Nat Geog Soc & Smithsonian Res Found explor & res grantee, 1971 & 1974; ed-in-chief, Am Fern Soc, 1966-1984; cur ferns, US Nat Herbarium, Smithsonian Inst, 1963-2002; hon assoc cur pteridophytes, Mus Nat Costa Rica. **Memberships:** Int Asn Plant Taxon; Brit Pterid Soc; Am Fern Soc. **Research Statement & Publications:** Taxonomy of ferns and fern allies, especially those of the New World tropics. **Mailing Address:** 326 West St NW, Vienna, VA 22180-4151.

LELLOUCHE, GERALD S, THERMAL PHYSICS, NUCLEAR ENGINEERING. **Personal Data:** b New York, NY, June 21, 1930; m 1981, Mary V Crain. **Education:** Purdue Univ, BS, 1952; NC State Col, PhD (nuclear eng), 1960. **Professional Experience:** PRES, TECH DATA SERV, 1990-; mgt consult, S Levy Inc, 1986-1990; sr prog mgr code develop & validation, Probabilistics & Statist, Elec Power Res Inst, 1980-1986; prog mgr, Probabilistics & Statist, Elec Power Res Inst, 1974- 1980; physicist, Brookhaven Nat Lab, 1968-1974; assoc physicist, Brookhaven Nat Lab, 1964-1968; asst nuclear eng, Brookhaven Nat Lab, 1960-1964; Jr engr, Brookhaven Nat Lab, 1952-1955. **Memberships:** Am Chem Soc; Am Inst Chem Eng; Am Nuclear Soc. **Research Statement & Publications:** Reactor kinetics, nonlinear dynamics; thermal hydraulics, two-phase flow; probabilistics, risk analysis. **Mailing Address:** 6252 N Lakewood, Chicago, IL 60660.

LELONG, MICHEL GEORGES, PLANT TAXONOMY. **Personal Data:** b Casablanca, Morocco, March 20, 1932; American citizen; m 1959, c 3. **Education:** Univ Algiers, baccalaureat, 1950; Northwestern State Col, La, BS, 1959, MS, 1960; Iowa State Univ, PhD (syst bot), 1965. **Professional Experience:** RETIRED; prof biol, Univ S Ala, beginning 1977; Assoc prof, 1965-1977. **Memberships:** Am Soc Plant Taxon; Int Asn Plant Taxon. **Research Statement & Publications:** Systematics of Panicum subgenus Dichanthelium of North America; flora of the Mobile Bay region. **Mailing Address:** 159 Bit & Spur Terrace, Mobile, AL 36608.

LEM, KWOK WAI, POLYMER SYNTHESIS, MOLECULAR COMPOSITE. **Personal Data:** b Canton, China, July 14, 1952; American citizen; m 1986, Margaret; c Paul C & Richard C. **Education:** Univ Toronto, Ont, BS, 1976; Polytech Inst NY, MS, 1980; PhD (polymer sci eng), 1983. **Honors & Awards:** Melvin M Gerson Award, 1980 & 1981. **Professional Experience:** AT HONEYWELL INT INC, as of 2004; res scientist, Allied-Signal, Inc, beginning 1993; adj prof, Polytech Univ, NY, beginning 1991; sr res engr, Armors & Composites Corp Res & Technol, 1989-1993; sr res engr, polymer alloys & composites, Corp Technol, 1987-1989; res engr, polymer blends, 1986-1987; res engr, gas separation membrane, Corp Technol, Allied-Signal Inc, 1985-1986; res engr, Corp Technol, Allied Corp, 1983-1985; polymer chemist, Schenectady Chem Can, Ont, 1977-1978; chem specialist, Can Hanson Ltd, Toronto, Ont, 1976-1977. **Memberships:** Soc Plastics Engrs; Soc Physics; Soc Rheology; Sigma Xi. **Research Statement & Publications:** Polymer processing and rheology; reactive extrusion and injection molding; advanced polymer blends and synthesis; electrochemical and membrane technologies; processing-structure-property relations in polymer materials; advanced armor materials; dynamic behavior of advanced materials; impact dynamics; degradation and stability of materials; flammability materials. **Mailing Address:** Honeywell Int Inc, 101 Columbia Rd, Morristown, NJ 07962. **Fax:** 973-455-5157. **E-Mail:** kwok-wai.lem@honeywell.com

LEMAIRE, IRMA, PHARMACOLOGY. **Professional Experience:** PROF, DEPT PHARMACOL, UNIV OTTAWA, 1990-. **Mailing Address:** Dept Pharmacol, Health Sci Ctr, Sch Med, Univ Ottawa, 451 Smyth Rd, Ottawa, ON K1H 8M5, Can.

LEMAIRE, PAUL J, OPTICAL FIBER RESEARCH & DEVELOPMENT. **Personal Data:** b Colchester, Vt, August 11, 1953; m 1986, c 2. **Education:** Mass Inst Technol, BS, 1975, PhD (ceramics), 1980. **Honors & Awards:** Purdy Award, Am Ceramic Soc, 1984. **Professional Experience:** RES SCIENTIST, AT&T BELL LABS, 1980-. **Memberships:** Am Ceramic Soc; Mat Res Soc. **Research Statement & Publications:** Optical fiber research and development; optical loss; defects in glasses; waveguide design; optical fiber processing and manufacturing; hermetic coatings; fiber reliability and hydrogen-glass reactions. **Mailing Address:** 18 Ferndale Rd, Madison, NJ 07940.

LEMAISTRE, CHARLES AUBREY, INTERNAL MEDICINE, EPIDEMIOLOGY. **Personal Data:** b Lockhart, Ala, February 10, 1924; m 1952, Joyce Trapp; c Charles Frederick, William Sidney, Joyce Anne & Helen Jean. **Education:** Univ Ala, BA, 1943; Cornell Univ, MD, 1947. **Honorary Degrees:** LLD, Austin Col, 1970 & Univ Ala, 1971; DSc, Univ Dallas, 1978 & Southwestern Univ, 1981; Dr, Univ Guadalajara, 1989. **Professional Experience:** EMER COUN PHYSICIAN, UNIV TEX, M D ANDERSON CANCER CTR, 1996-; pres, Univ Tex, M D Anderson Cancer Ctr, 1978-1996; consult, Nat Coun Educ Res, 1975; mem, United Negro Col Fund Develop Coun, 1974-1978; mem, Nat Adv Coun, Inst Serv Educ, 1974-1977; trustee, Biol Humanics Found, Dallas, 1973-; mem bd comnr, Nat Comn Accrediting, 1973-1976; mem, Nat Coun Educ Res, 1973-1975; chmn, Subcomt Diversity & Pluralism, Nat Coun Educ Res, 1973-1975; mem joint task force continuing competence pharm, Am Pharmaceut Asn-Am Asn Col Pharm, 1973-1974; chancellor, Univ Tex Syst, 1971-1978; mem, Comn Non-Traditional Study, 1971-1973; mem, President's Comn White House fel, 1971; from exec vchancellor to chancellor-elect, Univ Tex Syst, 1968-1970; consult, Div Physician Manpower, 1967-1970; mem, Surgeon Gen Emergency Health Preparedness Adv Comt, Dept Health, Educ & Welfare, 1967; vchancellor health affairs, Univ Tex, Austin, 1966-1968; mem, Nat Citizens Comn Int Coop, 1965-; assoc dean, Univ Tex Southwestern Med Sch, Dallas, 1965-1966; mem, Comt Res Tobacco & Health, AMA Educ & Res Found, 1964-1966; mem, Surgeon Gen Adv Comt Smoking & Health, 1963-1964; mem, Gov Comt Eradication Tuberc, 1963-1964; Mem,

Human Ecol Study Sect, NIH, 1962-1965; prof, Univ Tex Southwestern Med Sch, Dallas, 1959-1966; prof prev med & chmn dept, Sch Med, Emory Univ, 1957-1959; assoc prof, Sch Med, Emory Univ, 1954-1959; From instr to asst prof internal med, Med Col, Cornell Univ, 1951-1954. **Memberships:** Am Cancer Soc (pres, 1986-1987). **Research Statement & Publications:** Chest diseases; Infectious dis. **Mailing Address:** 13104 Travis View Loop, Austin, TX 78732-1741.

LE MAISTRE, CHRISTOPHER WILLIAM, AUTOMATION & ROBOTICS. **Personal Data:** b Moradabad, India, August 20, 1938; Australian citizen; m 1963, c 2. **Education:** Univ Adelaide, BS, 1963 & 1964; Rensselaer Polytech Inst, PhD (mat eng), 1972. **Professional Experience:** MANAGING DIR, SCH TECHNOL CTR SUPERCONDUCTIVITY, UNIV ILL, URBANA-CHAMPAIGN, 1993-; dir, Ctr Indust Innovation, 1984-1992; asst dean eng, Ctr Indust Innovation, 1984-1992; assoc dir, Mfg Ctr, Rensselaer Polytech Inst, 1979-1984; head lab progs, Australian Defense Sci, Canberra, 1978-1979; head int progs, Australian Defense Sci, Canberra, 1977-1978; Res & develop rep, Australian High Comn, London, 1974-1977; sr res scientist, Australian Defence Sci, 1972-1979; exp officer, Australian Defence Sci, 1964-1972. **Memberships:** Am Ceramic Soc; Am Soc Metals; Am Soc Eng Educ. **Research Statement & Publications:** Near net shape (sintering); structural studies of carbon fibers; composite design and fabrication; automation and robotics; intellectual property. **Mailing Address:** 1022 Mat Res Lab, 104 S Goodwin Ave, Urbana, IL 61801. **Fax:** 217-244-8544. **E-Mail:** clem@uluc.edu

LEMAL, DAVID M, ORGANIC CHEMISTRY. **Personal Data:** b Plainfield, NJ, February 20, 1934; m 1994, Lee; c Anne-Marie, Marielle, Richard J & Corinne. **Education:** Amherst Col, AB, 1955; Harvard Univ, PhD, 1959. **Honors & Awards:** Catalyst Award, Chem Mfrs Asn, 1987. **Professional Experience:** Comt sci, Am chem soc, 1996-; Harvard Univ, 1994; chmn, Fluorine Div, 1990; ALBERT W SMITH PROF CHEM, DARTMOUTH COL, 1981-; sabbaticals, Univ Utah 1981; alt coun, Org Div, 1981-1993; mem exec comt, Fluorine Div, Am Chem Soc, 1980-1983; trustee, Gordon Res Conf, 1973-1979; chmn bd, 1977-1978; dept chair, Dartmouth Col, 1976-1979; res fel, A P Sloan Found, 1968-1970; vis lectr, Harvard Univ, 1967; from assoc prof to prof, Dartmouth Col, 1965-1981; from instr to asst prof chem, Univ Wis, 1958-1965. **Memberships:** Am Chem Soc; Sigma Xi. **Research Statement & Publications:** Organofluorine chemistry; unusual species, stable and short-lived, in organic chemistry; organic reaction mechanisms; organic photochemistry. **Mailing Address:** Dept Chem, Dartmouth Col, Hanover, NH 03755-1477. **Fax:** 603-646-3946. **E-Mail:** david.m.lemal@dartmouth.edu

LEMAN, ROBERT B, ARRHYTHMIA MANAGEMENT. **Personal Data:** b Upper Darby, Penn, December 23, 1947; m 1973, Patti; c Brian & Heather. **Education:** Ursinus Col, BS, 1969; Univ Ark, Little Rock, MD, 1976; Am Bd Internal Med, 1979, 1981, 1992. **Professional Experience:** PROF MED, MED UNIV SC, 1997-; assoc prof med, Med Univ SC, 1989-1997; dir, Adult Electrophysiol, Med Univ SC, beginning 1988; dir, Charleston Vet Admin Cardiac Catherization Lab, Vet Admin Hosp, 1986-1992; asst prof med, Med Univ SC, 1983-1989; dir, Pacemaker Surveillance, Med Univ SC, beginning 1982; instr, Internal Med & Cardiol, Med Univ SC, 1981-1982; fel cardiol, Med Univ SC, 1979-1981; resident, Med Univ SC, 1977-1979; intern internal med, Med Univ SC, 1976-1977; instr phys sci, Gloucester County Col, 1969-1970. **Memberships:** Fel Am Heart Asn; Am Col Physicians; Am Col Cardiol; NAm Soc Pacing & Electrophysiol. **Research Statement & Publications:** Arrhythmia management, devices, medicine, ablation. **Mailing Address:** MUSC Med Ctr, 135 Rutledge Ave PO Box 250592, Charleston, SC 29425. **Fax:** 803-792-7771. **E-Mail:** lemanrb@musc.edu

LEMANN, JACOB, EXPERIMENTAL BIOLOGY, MEDICINE. **Personal Data:** b New Orleans, La, August 31, 1929. **Education:** Univ Calif, Berkeley, AB, 1950; Univ Buffalo, MD, 1954; Am Bd Internal Med, cert, 1963 & 1974. **Professional Experience:** CLIN PROF, TULANE UNIV, NEW ORLEANS, LA, 1995-; prof med, Med Col Wis, Milwaukee, 1971-1994; mem, Coun Med Adv Comt, Kidney Found Wis, 1970-1994 chief Nephrology Div, Med Col Wis, Milwaukee, 1970-1994; mem, Gen Med B Study Sect, NIH, 1970-1974 & 1982-1984; assoc prof, Med Col Wis, Milwaukee, 1970-1971; assoc prof, Boston Univ Sch Med, 1968-1970; chief, Renal Sect, Boston Univ Sch Med, 1968-1970; from asst prof to assoc prof med, Marquette Sch Med & assoc dir, Clin Res Ctr, 1963-1968; instr med, Boston Univ Sch Med, 1961-1963; asst resident, New Eng Med Ctr, Boston, 1959-1960; res fel med, renal & metabol dis, 1957-1959 & clin fel, 1960-1961; Intern, Mass Mem Hosp, Boston, 1954-1955. **Memberships:** AAAS; fel Am Col Physicians; Am Fedn Clin Res; AMA; Am Physiol Soc; Am Soc Clin Invest; Am Soc Bone & Mineral Res; Am Soc Nephrology; Asn Am Physicians; Int Soc Nephrology. **Research Statement & Publications:** Medicine; Acid-Base Physiology; calicium metabolism and the regulation of urinary calcium ederediow in humans; neihrolithasis; slinical nephrology. **Mailing Address:** Nephrology Sect, Tulane Univ Sch Med, 2601 St Charles Ave, New Orleans, LA 70130-5927.

LEMANSKI, LARRY FREDERICK, DEVELOPMENT BIOLOGY, IMMUNOELECTRON MICROSCOPY. **Personal Data:** b Madison, Wis, June 5, 1943; m 1966, Sharon L Wulf; c Scott F & Jennifer L. **Education:** Univ Wis, BS, 1966; Ariz State Univ, MS, 1968, PhD (zool), 1971. **Honors & Awards:** Presidential Award, Electron Micros Soc Am; Louis N Katz Basic Sci Res Prize, Am Heart Asn. **Professional Experience:** VPRES RES & GRAD STUD, FLA ATLATIC UNIV, 2001-; prof Med Physiol & Biol, Tex A & M Univ, 1997-2001; Dir, Cell & Molecular Training Prog, 1987-1990; distinguished sci examr, Bhopal Univ, India, 1984-; prof & chmn Anat & Cell Biol, State Univ NY, 1983-1987; estab investr award, Louis Katz res prize, 1978; from assoc prof to prof anat, Univ Wis, 1977-1983; prin investr, NIH, 1976-; estab investr award, Am Heart Asn, 1976-1981; asst prof anat, Univ Calif, San Francisco, 1975-1977; Fel biol & biochem, Univ Pa, 1971-1975. **Memberships:** Am Soc Cell Biol; AAAS; Asn Anat Chairmen; NY Acad Sci; Soc Develop Biol; Sigma Xi; Am Heart Asn. **Research Statement & Publications:** Embryonic heart development using cellular and molecular biology approaches to study; the initiation and maintenance of normal heart function in vertebrates. **Mailing Address:** Div Res & Grad Stud, FL Atlatic Univ, 777 Glades Rd, Boca Raton, FL 33431-0991. **Fax:** 561-297-0777. **E-Mail:** lemanski@fau.edu

LEMANSKI, MICHAEL FRANCIS, HETEROGENEOUS CATALYSIS. **Personal Data:** b Cleveland, Ohio, November 16, 1946. **Education:** Univ Dayton, BS, 1969; Ohio State Univ, MS, 1972, PhD (inorg chem), 1975. **Professional Experience:** Vis researcher, Ctr Catalytic Sci & Technol, Univ Del, 1980; RES SCIENTIST, BP AM CORP, 1978-; sr res chemist, Diamond Shamrock Corp, 1975-1978. **Memberships:** Am Chem Soc. **Research Statement & Publications:** Heterogeneous catalysis, including selective oxidation and selective reduction of small molecules. **Mailing Address:** Shell Chem C1341, 3333 Hwy 6 S, Houston, TX 77082.

LEMASTER, EDWIN WILLIAM, SOLID STATE PHYSICS. **Personal Data:** b Perryton, Tex, April 27, 1940; m 1964, Jane; c Annie & Matthew. **Education:** W Tex State Univ, BS, 1962; Tech Tech Univ, MS, 1966; Univ Tex, PhD (physics), 1970. **Professional Experience:** ASSOC DEAN, COL SCI & ENG, UNIV TEX, PAN AM, as of 2006; DIR SCH ENG & COMPUT SCI, UNIV TEX, PAN AM, as of 2006; PROF PHYS SCI & CHMN, ENG DEPT, UNIV TEX, PAN AM, 1988-; dean sci & technol, NMex Highlands Univ, 1986-1988; chmn, Phys Sci Dept, beginning 1973; asst prof, Pan Am Univ, beginning 1970; asst prof physics, Gen Motors Inst, 1964-1966. **Memberships:** Am Phys Soc; Am Asn Physics Teachers. **Research Statement & Publications:** Metalammonia solution properties; amorphous semiconductors; remote sensing of vegetative canopies; mathematical modeling. **Mailing Address:** Dept Eng, Univ Tex Pan Am, 1201 W Univ Dr, Edinburg, TX 78539. **Fax:** 956-381-3527. **E-Mail:** elemaster@panam.edu

LEMASTERS, JOHN J, CELL BIOLOGY. **Personal Data:** b Newark, Ohio, May 29, 1947; div, c 3. **Education:** Yale Univ, BA, 1969; Johns Hopkins Univ, MD, 1975, PhD (cell biol & anat), 1975. **Professional Experience:** Prin investr, NSF, 1990-1992; dir, Cell & Molecular Imaging, 1989-; prin investr, USPHS, 1989-1994 & 1990-1994; prin investr, Off Naval Res, 1988-1991; vis prof, Div Gastroenterol & Sect Transplantation Surg, Mayo Grad Sch Med, 1987; PROF CELL BIOL & ANAT, LAB CELL BIOL, SCH MED, UNIV NC, CHAPEL HILL, 1985-; dir, Electron Microscope Lab, 1983-1990; estab investr, Am Heart Asn, 1982-1987; from asst prof to assoc prof, Lab Cell Biol, Sch Med, Univ NC, Chapel Hill, 1977-1985; dir, Grad Studies Anat, Univ NC, 1977-1984; asst prof, Dept Cell Biol, Southwestern Med Sch, Univ Tex Health Sci Ctr, 1975-1977; teaching asst neuroanat, Dept Cell Biol, Southwestern Med Sch, Univ Tex Health Sci Ctr, 1973; Teaching asst, Dept Anat, Sch Med, Johns Hopkins Univ, 1971-1972; mem, Coun Circulation, Am HeartAsn. **Memberships:** AAAS; Am Asn Study Liver Dis; Am Asn Anatomists; Am Heart Asn; Am Soc Biochem & Molecular Biol; Biophys Soc; Electron Micros Soc Am. **Research Statement & Publications:** Rescue of injured myocytes; liver preservation for transplantation; laser scanning confocal microscope; mechanisms of cell death in hepatocytes; confocal and multiphoton microscopy. **Mailing Address:** Dept Cell & Developmental Biology, Univ NC, CB 7090, 236 Taylor Hall, Chapel Hill, NC 27599-7090. **E-Mail:** lemaster@med.unc.edu

LEMASURIER, WESLEY ERNEST, GEOLOGY. **Personal Data:** b Washington, DC, May 3, 1934; m Heather; c Michelle, Susanne & John. **Education:** Union Col, BS, 1956; Univ Colo, MS, 1962; Stanford Univ, PhD (geol), 1965. **Honors & Awards:** Named by US Advisory Committee on Anarctic Names, 1969; Mount LeMasurier, 75 27's, 139 39 W In Marie Byrd Land Antaratica. **Professional Experience:** PROF GEOL, DIV NAT & PHYS SCI, UNIV COLO, DENVER, as of 2003; assoc prof, Div Nat & Phys Sci, Univ Colo, Denver, 1968-1976; asst prof geol, Cornell Univ, 1964-1968; geologist, US Geol Surv, 1961-1964. **Memberships:** AAAS; Geol Soc Am; Am Geophys Union; Int Asn Volcanol & Chem Earth's Interior; Sigma Xi. **Research Statement & Publications:** Subglacial volcanism; petrology and tectonic relationships of volcanism in Antarctica. **Mailing Address:** Geol Dept, Univ Colo, B172 UCD, Denver, CO 80217-3364. **E-Mail:** wesley.lemasurier@colorado.edu

LEMAY, CHARLOTTE ZIHLMAN, physics, solid state physics; deceased, see previous edition for last biography

LEMAY, HAROLD E, CHEMICAL EDUCATION. **Personal Data:** b Tacoma, Wash, May 28, 1940; m 1964, Carla; c John C & David E. **Education:** Pac Lutheran, BS, 1962; Univ Ill, MS, 1964, PhD (inorg chem), 1966. **Honors & Awards:** Regents Teaching Award, bil Regents, univ & Community col syst Nevada, 1997; prof of the Year, Carnegie found Advancement Teaching, Nev, 2000. **Professional Experience:** PROF CHEM, UNIV NEV, RENO, 1978-; vis prof, Univ Calif Los Angeles, 1989-1990; vis prof, Univ Col Wales, 1978; vis prof, Univ NC, Chapel Hill, 1977-1978; assoc chmn, Univ Nev, Reno, 1985-1990; chmn dept, Univ Nev, Reno, 1984-1985; vice chmn dept, Univ Nev, Reno, 1974-1976; from asst prof to assoc prof, Univ Nev, Reno, 1966-1978. **Memberships:** Am Chem Soc; Sigma Xi; Textbook Authors Assn. **Research Statement & Publications:** Preparation and characterization of coordination compounds; reactions of coordination compounds in the solid phase; writer of chemistry textbooks. **Mailing Address:** Dept Chem, Univ Nev, Reno, NV 89557-0020. **E-Mail:** lemay@equinox.unr.edu

LEMAY, JEAN-PAUL, ANIMAL PHYSIOLOGY, ANIMAL BREEDING. **Personal Data:** b St Hyacinthe, Que, July 4, 1923; m 1952, c 2. **Education:** Classical Col St Hyacinth, BA, 1945; Univ Montreal, BSA, 1949; Univ Mass, MSc, 1951; Laval Univ, PhD, 1967. **Professional Experience:** REPROCESSED PROF ANIMAL SCI, LAVAL UNIV, as of 2004; prof animal sci, Laval Univ, beginning 1962; from instr to prof animal sci, Res Sta La Pocatiere, Que, 1951-1962; Mem artificial insemination unit, Classical Col St Hyacinthe, 1948-1949. **Memberships:** Am Soc Animal Sci; Can Soc Animal Prod. **Research Statement & Publications:** Early weaning of sheep; histophysiology of sperm atogenesis and ovogenesis in sheep; sterility in dairy cattle; physiology of reproduction in dairy cattle, sheep and goat. **Mailing Address:** Dept Animal Sci, Laval Univ, Fac Agr, Ste Foy, PQ C1K 7P4, Can.

LEMBACH, KENNETH JAMES, MONOCLONAL ANTIBODIES, CELL REGULATION. **Personal Data:** b Rochester, NY, June 16, 1939; m 1965, Regis; c Lara & Aimee. **Education:** Mass Inst Technol, BS, 1961; Univ Pa, PhD (biochem), 1966. **Professional Experience:** DIR PRECLIN RES, PHARMACEUT DIV, BIOTECHNOL GROUP, BAYER CORP, 1995-; dir preclin biol, Pharmaceut Div, 1993-1995; dir cell & mollecular biol, Miles Inc, 1991-1993; mgr cell physiol res, Miles Inc, 1986-1988; prin staff scientist, Miles Inc, 1982-1986; mgr cell & molecular biol res cutter biol, Miles Inc, 1981-1991; plasma prod res sect head, Miles Inc, 1979-1982; US Nat Cancer Inst res grants, 1971-1974, 1975-1979; from asst prof to assoc prof, Sch Med, Vanderbilt Univ, 1969-1979; res assoc biochem, Mass Inst Technol, 1968-1969; USPHS fel, Mass Inst Technol, 1966-1968. **Memberships:** AAAS; Am Soc Biochem & Molecular Biol. **Research Statement & Publications:** Cytokines; immune regulation and therapies. **Mailing Address:** Preclin Res, Div Biotechnol, Bayer Corp Pharmaceut, Berkeley, CA 94710. **Fax:** 510-705-5558.

LEMBECK, WILLIAM JACOBS, microbiology, academic administration; deceased, see previous edition for last biography

LEMBERG, HOWARD LEE, BROADBAND NETWORKS, FIBER OPTIC NETWORKS. **Personal Data:** b Queens, NY, July 29, 1949; m 1970, Christine; c Kathryn & Diana. **Education:** Columbia Univ, BA (chem physics), 1969; Univ Chicago, PhD (chem physics), 1973. **Professional Experience:** EXEC DIR, TELCORDIA TECHNOLOGIES, 1999-; exec dir, Bellcore, 1996-1999; dir, Bellcore, 1992-1996; dist mgr, Bell Labs, 1984-1991; supvr, Bell Labs, 1981-1984; mem tech staff, Bell Labs, 1978-1981; asst prof chem, Univ NC, 1975-1978; res chem physics, Bell Labs, 1973-1975. **Memberships:** Inst Elec & Electronics Engrs; Armed Forces Commun & Electronics Asn. **Research Statement & Publications:** Communications networks; optical networks; optical fiber-subscriber loop networks and broadband access video networks wireles systems and networks. **Mailing Address:** Telcordia TechnologiesRm IC-265B, 445 S St, Morristown, NJ 07962. **Fax:** 973-829-4834.

LEMBERG, LOUIS, ELECTROCARDIOGRAPHY, CARDIOLOGY. **Personal Data:** b Chicago, Ill, December 27, 1916; m 1971, Miriam Weintraub; c Jerry & Laura. **Education:** Univ Ill, BS, 1938, MD, 1940; Am Bd Internal Med, dipl, 1950, recert, 1974 & 1988; Am Bd Cardiovasc Dis, dipl, 1955. **Honors & Awards:** Luis Guerrero Mem Award, Philippines. **Professional Experience:** Ed-in-chief, Current Concepts Cardiovasc Dis, 1985-1987; ed-in-chief, Accel for Nurses, 1983-1985; PROF CLIN CARDIOL, SCH MED, UNIV MIAMI, 1969-; dir coronary care unit, Jackson Mem Hosp, 1968-1974; chief div electrophysiol, Jackson Mem Hosp, 1956-1974; chief staff, Nat Children's Cardiac Hosp, Miami, 1955-1966; attend specialist, Vet Admin Hosp, 1955-1964; Dir cardiol, Dade County Hosp, 1955-1957; res, Mt Sinai Hosp, Chicago, Ill, 1945-1948; Intern, Mt Sinai Hosp, Chicago, Ill, 1940-1941; chief div cardiol, Mercy Hosp, 1976-, mem coun clin cardiol, Am Heart Asn; attend cardiologist, Mercy & Cedars of Lebanon Hosp; Louis Lemberg endowed chair cardiol, Sch Med, Univ Miami. **Memberships:** Hon mem Philippine Med Asn; fel Am Col Physicians; Am Col Chest Physicians; Am Col Cardiol; NY Acad Sci. **Research Statement & Publications:** Cardiology; pioneer in the development of the demand pacemaker. **Mailing Address:** Div Cardiol (D39), Univ Miami PO Box 016960, Miami, FL 33101. **Fax:** 305-547-3516.

LEMBERGER, AUGUST PAUL, PHARMACEUTICS. **Personal Data:** b Milwaukee, Wis, January 25, 1926; m 1947, c 7. **Education:** Univ Wis, BS, 1948, PhD (pharm), 1952. **Honors & Awards:** Kiekhofer Award, Univ Wis, 1957. **Professional Experience:** PROF EMER PHARM & EMER DEAN, SCH PHARM, UNIV WIS, MADISON as of 2003; Bd trustees, Am Pharmaceut Soc, 1985-1988; Prof Pharm & Dean, Sch Pharm, Univ Wis, Madison beginning 1980; mem, Am Coun Pharmaceut Educ, 1978-1984; mem, Tech Adv Coun Ill Dept Pub Health Drug Substitution law, 1978-1980; consult, Dept Health, Educ & Welfare, 1972-1974; prof pharm & dean, Col, Univ Ill Med Ctr, 1969-1980; coordr exten serv, Univ Wis-Madison, 1965-1969; Mem & secy, Wis Pharm Internship Comn, 1965-1969; from instr to prof pharm, Univ Wis-Madison, 1953-1969; Sr chemist pharmaceut res, Merck & Co, Inc, 1952-1953. **Memberships:** Am Pharmaceut Asn; fel Acad Pharm Res & Sci; fel AAAS; fel Am Asn Pharmaceut Scientists; Am Asn Cols Pharmacy; Am Soc Hosp Pharmacists. **Mailing Address:** 7439 Cedar Creek Trail, Madison, WI 53717.

LEMBERGER, LOUIS, CLINICAL PHARMACOLOGY. **Personal Data:** b Monticello, NY, May 8, 1937; m 1959, Myra; c Harriet Lemberger-Schor & Margo Lemberger. **Education:** Long Island Univ, BS, 1960; Albert Einstein Col Med, PhD (pharmacol), 1964, MD, 1968. **Honorary Degrees:** DSc, Long Island Univ, 1994. **Honors & Awards:** Award, Am Soc Pharmacol & Exp Therapeut, 1985; Rawls Palmer Prog Med Award, 1986; Henry Elliott Award, 1992; Harry Gold Award, 1993; Oscar B Hunter Award, 2003; Distinguished Alumnus, Long Isl Univ; Distinguished Alumnus, Albert Einstein Col Med. **Professional Experience:** PROF EMER PHARM MED & PSYCHIAT, IND UNIV as of 2003; prof pharm med & psychiatry, Sch Med, Ind Univ, beginning 1993; clin res fel, Eli Liiy & Co, 1989-1993; dir clin pharmacol, Lilly Lab Clin Res, Lilly Res Labs 1978-1989; prof, Grad Fac, 1977-; prof pharmacol, med & psychiat, 1977-; adj prof clin pharmacol, Ohio State Univ, 1975-1986; chief clinical pharm, Eli Lilly & Co, 1975-1978; assoc prof, Grad Fac, 1975-1977; assoc prof, Clin Pharmacol Training Prog, Sch Med, Ind Univ, 1973-1977; dir, Clin Pharmacol Training Prog, Sch Med, Ind Univ, 1972-1975; asst prof pharmacol & med, Clin Pharmacol Training Prog, Sch Med, Ind Univ, 1972-1973; clin pharmacologist, Eli Lilly & Co, 1971-1975; pharmacol & toxicol res assoc clin pharmacol, Lab Clin Sci, NIMH, 1969-1971; med intern, Metropolitan Hosp Ctr-NY Med Col, 1968-1969; fel pharmacol, Albert Einstein Col Med, 1964-1968; chmn, Second World Conf Clin Pharmacol, Int Union Clin Pharmacol. **Memberships:** Am Soc Pharmacol & Exp Therapeut (pres, 1987-1988); Am Soc Clin Pharmacol & Therapeut (pres, 1983-1984); fel Am Col Neuro Psychopharm; fel Am Col Physicians; Sigma Xi; Am Soc Clincial Invest. **Research Statement & Publications:** Drug metabolism and drug-drug interactions; synthesis and metabolism of biogenic amines; biochemical mechanisms of drug action; clinical psychopharmacology; pharmacology of marihuana and cannabinoids. **Mailing Address:** 3315 Walnut Creek Dr N, Carmel, IN 46032.

LEMBI, CAROLE A, AQUATIC WEED SCIENCE. **Education:** Univ Calif, BA; Univ Tenn, PhD. **Professional Experience:** PROF BOT, PURDUE UNIV, IND, as of 2005. **Memberships:** AAAS. **Mailing Address:** Dept Bot & Plant Path Purdue Univ Lilly Hall, 915 W State St, West Lafayette, IN 47907-2054. **Fax:** 765-494-0363. **E-Mail:** lembi@purdue.edu

LEMBKE, ROGER ROY, PHYSICAL CHEMISTRY, RADIATION CHEMISTRY. **Personal Data:** b Clayton Co, Iowa, April 24, 1940; m 1969, c 2. **Education:** Luther Col, BA, 1962; Univ Nebr, Lincoln, MS, 1966; Wayne State Univ, PhD (phys chem), 1973; Univ Evansville, Ind, MCSE, 1984. **Professional Experience:** PROF EMER, CENT METHODIST UNIV, as of 2006; prof chem, Cent Methodist Col, beginning 1978; chmn dept chem, Cent Methodist Col, beginning 1978; assoc prof, Cent Methodist Col, 1976-1978; asst prof, Cornell Col, 1975-1976; res assoc, Univ Fla, 1975; guest scientist, Hahn-Meitner Inst, Berlin, 1973-1974; instr chem, Hastings Col, 1965-1969. **Memberships:** Am Chem Soc; Asn Comput Mach. **Research Statement & Publications:** Radiolysis and photolysis; rate constants and mechanisms. **Mailing Address:** Dept Chem, Cent Methodist Univ, Stedman Hall Sci, Fayette, MO 65248-1198. **Fax:** 660-248-1634. **E-Mail:** rlembke@cmc.edu

LEMCOE, M M(ARSHALL), CIVIL ENGINEERING. **Personal Data:** b St Louis, Mo, m 1951, c 2. **Education:** Wash Univ, BS, 1943, MS, 1949; Univ Ill, PhD (civil eng), 1957. **Honorary Degrees:** Washington Univ, EXI, 1949. **Honors & Awards:** Award, Curtiss-Wright Corp, 1945; IR-100 Award, 1976. **Professional Experience:** CONSULT, 1983-; tech adv, Columbus Div, Battelle Mem Inst, 1971-1983; supvr exp mech & sr tech specialist, Atomics Int Div, NAm Rockwell Corp, Calif, 1961-1971; mgr, Strength Anal Sect, Dept Struct Res, 1952-1961; supvr aeroelasticity & spec consult, Southwest Res Inst, 1951-1952; mem staff, Res Found & Dept Civil Eng, Wash Univ, 1947-1951; Struct engr, Curtiss-Wright Corp, 1943-1946. **Memberships:** Soc Exp Stress Anal; Sigma Xi. **Research Statement & Publications:** Experimental stress analysis; structures; pressure vessels; high temperature materials technology and strain gage technology; high temperature behavior of structures. **Mailing Address:** 12990 Camino Ramillette, San Diego, CA 92128.

LE MEE, JEAN M, ENGINEERING, DESIGN EDUCATION. **Personal Data:** b France, June 4, 1931; American citizen; m 1964, Katharine H Wilbur; c Hannah-Therese. **Education:** Carnegie-Mellon Univ, MS, 1959, PhD (mech eng), 1963. **Honors & Awards:** Facul fel, Inst for the Humanities, NY Univ 1989-1990; Fel Am Inst of Indian studies 1983-1984; Sr Fel, South Asia Regional studies Univ of Penn, 1978-1979. **Professional Experience:** CHMN MECH ENG, COOPER UNION SCH ENG & SCI, 1986-; PROF MECH ENG, COOPER UNION SCH ENG & SCI, 1980-; assoc prof, Cooper Union Sch Eng & Sci, 1964-1980; res engr, Lawrence Radiation Lab, Univ Calif, Berkeley, 1960 & Westinghouse Res Labs, 1962-1964; teaching asst eng, Carnegie-Mellon Univ, 1959-1961; Design engr, James Gordon & Co Ltd, Eng, 1955-1958. **Memberships:** Inst Elec & Electronics Engrs; Sigma Xi; Am Soc Mech Engrs NY Acad of Sci; chmn Med, Eng, Dept Heads Com, Region II ASME (1989-91). **Research Statement & Publications:** Control systems; semiconductor devices; design process; engineering education. **Mailing Address:** 16 Mevan Ave, Tributary Woods, Englewood, NJ 07631-3863.

LEMESHOW, STANLEY ALAN, SAMPLING, EXPERIMENTAL DESIGN. **Personal Data:** b Brooklyn, NY, January 29, 1948; m 1972, c 2. **Education:** City Col New York, BBA, 1969; Univ NC, Chapel Hill, MSPH, 1970; Univ Calif, Los Angeles, PhD (biostatist), 1976. **Professional Experience:** ASSOC ED, J BIOPHARMACEUTICAL SCI, 2000-; adj prof, dept biostatistics/ epidemiol, Sch Pub Health, Univ Mass, 1999-; DIR, BIOSTATISTICS CORE, COMPREHENSIVE CANCER CTR, OHIO STATE UNIV, 1999-; PROF & DIR, CTR BIOSTATISTICS, SCH PUB HEALTH, OHIO STATE UNIV, 1999-; assoc prof biostatists, Univ Mass, Amherst, beginning 1980; prog dir, Biopharmceut Res Unit, Div Pub Health, Univ Mass, Amherst, 1978-; Dir, Coord Ctr Multicenter Clin Trial Hyperbaric Oxygen Treatment Burn Injuries, Univ Mass, 1977-1978; asst prof, Univ Mass, Amherst, 1976-1980; sr statisticin, Sch Pub Health, Univ Calif, Los Angeles, 1974-1975; anal statistician, Comn Off, Nat Ctr Health Statist, USPHS, 1970-1972; statist supvr, Health Res Training Prog, New York City Dept Health, 1969; Res asst, Dept Prev Med, NY Med Col, 1968-1969. **Memberships:** Am Statist Asn; Soc Epidemiol Res; Am Pub Health Asn. **Research Statement & Publications:** Sampling; variance estimation in complex sampling designs; sample size determination and logistic regression analysis; medical and other applied health sciences. **Mailing Address:** Sch Pub Health, Univ Mass, Amherst, MA 01003-0002.

LEMESSURIER, WILLIAM JAMES, STRUCTURAL ENGINEERING. **Personal Data:** b Pontiac, Mich, June 12, 1926; m 1953, c 3. **Education:** Harvard Univ, BA, 1947; Mass Inst Technol, MS, 1953. **Honors & Awards:** Spec Award, Am Inst Steel Construct, 1972; George Winter Award, Am Soc Civil Engrs; Pres Medal, 1996. **Professional Experience:** EMER CHMN, LEMESSURIER CONSULT INC, 1985-; adj prof, Harvard Grad Sch Design, 1982-; sr lectr, Mass Inst Technol, 1976-1977; lectr, Harvard Grad Sch Design, 1973-; chmn & chief exec officer, Sippican Consult Int, Inc, 1973-1985; Masonry Res Adv Coun, Sci Adv Comt, Nat Ctr Earthquake Eng Res 500 Allied Prof Medal, Am Inst Architects, 1968; assoc prof, Mass Inst Technol, 1964-1967; founder & partner, LeMessurier Assoc, Inc, 1961-1973; assoc prof, Harvard Grad Sch Design, 1956-1961; founder, Goldberg-LeMessurier, 1952-1961; asst prof, Mass Inst Technol, 1952-1956. **Memberships:** Nat Acad Eng; fel Am Soc Civil Engrs; fel Am Concrete Inst; hon mem Am Inst Architects. **Research Statement & Publications:** Structural engineering design; precast concrete high rise housing system; staggered truss system for high rise steel structures; tuned mass damper system used to reduce tall building motion; structural stability. **Mailing Address:** LeMessurier Consult Inc, 675 Mass Ave, Cambridge, MA 02139.

LEMIEUX, CLAUDEL, WEED SCIENCE, WEED BIOLOGY & ECOLOGY. **Personal Data:** b Montmagny, Que, August 31, 1955; m 1977, Christiane. **Education:** Laval Univ, BSc, 1979, MSc, 1983; McGill Univ, PhD (agron), 1986. **Professional Experience:** ASSOC PROF WEED SCI, LAVAL UNIV, 1991-; chmn, Expert Comt Weeds, 1991; chmn, Provintial Weed Comt, 1990-; assoc ed, Phytoprotection, 1989-; dir, Que Soc Protection Plants, 1987-1989; RES SCIENTIST, AGR & AGR-FOOD CAN, 1986-; Biologist, Laval Univ, 1983-1986. **Memberships:** Weed Sci Soc Am; Can Soc Agron; Int Weed Sci Soc. **Research Statement & Publications:** Develop integrated weed management programs to meet economic and environmental sustainability; reduce herbicide dependency. **Mailing Address:** Agr & Agri-Food Can, 2560 Hochelaga Blvd, Ste-Foy, PQ G1V 2J3, Can. **Fax:** 418-648-2402. **E-Mail:** lemieuxc@agr.gc.ca

LEMIEUX, RAYMOND URGEL, VIROLOGY, PHYSIOLOGY. **Personal Data:** b Lac la Biche, Alta, June 16, 1920; m 1948, c 6. **Education:** Univ Alta, BSc, 1943; McGill Univ, PhD (org chem), 1946. **Honorary Degrees:** DSc, Univ NB, 1967, Laval Univ, 1970, Univ Ottawa, 1975, Waterloo Univ, 1980, Mem Univ, 1981, Univ de Que, 1982, Queens Univ, 1983, McGill Univ, 1984, Univ de Sherbrooke, 1986, McMaster Univ, 1986, Univ Alta, Edmonton, 1991; Doctorate, Univ de Provence, F. **Honors & Awards:** Merck lectr, 1956; Folkers lectr, 1958; Medal, Chem Inst Can, 1964; C S Hudson Award, Am Chem Soc, 1966; Karl Pfister lectr, 1968; Medal of Serv, Order of Can, 1968; Purves lectr, 1970; Haworth Medal, Chem Soc, Eng, 1978; Killam Prize, Can Coun, 1981; Medal Hon, Can Med Asn, 1985; Gairdner Found Int Award, 1985; Rhone-Poulenc Award, Royal Soc Chem, 1989; LeSueur Award, Soc Chem Indust, 1989; King Faisal Int Prize Sci, 1990; Can Gold medal for Sci & Eng, 1991; Medal Honor, PMAC Res Found, 1992; E C Manning Nat Award Sci, 1992; Albert Einstein World Award of Sci, 1992; Spec Alta Sci & Technol Found Award, Alta Pioneer, 1993. **Professional Experience:** Chmn, Sci Adv Comt, 1990-; hon bd mem, Chembiomed Ltd, 1986-; PROF EMER ORG CHEM, UNIV ALTA, 1985-; mem bd, Chembiomed Ltd, 1977-1978 & 1983-1984; pres, Chembiomed Ltd, 1977-1978; Pres & dir res, Raylo Chem Ltd, Alta, 1966-1976; prof, Univ Alta, 1961-1985; prof chem, chmn dept & vdean fac pure & appl sci, Ottawa Univ, Can, 1954-1961; res officer chem natural prod, Prairie Regional Lab, Nat Res Coun, 1949-1954; asst prof org chem, Univ Sask, 1947-1949; Res assoc carbohydrate chem, Ohio State Univ, 1946-1947. **Memberships:** Royal Soc Chem; fel Chem Inst Can; fel Royal Soc Can. **Research Statement & Publications:** Stereochemistry; conformational analysis; carbohydrate chemistry; synthesis and conformation; especially antibiotics and blood group determinants. **Mailing Address:** Dept Chem, Univ Alberta, Edmonton, AB T6G 2G2, Can.

LEMING, CHARLES WILLIAM, PHYSICS. **Personal Data:** b Cutler, Ill, November 5, 1943; m 1965, c 1. **Education:** Eastern Ill Univ, BS, 1965; Mich State Univ, MS, 1967, PhD (physics), 1970. **Professional Experience:** CHMN, DEPT PHYSICS, HENDERSON STATE UNIV, as of 2004; res assoc, Carbondale Mining Technol Ctr, 1981; proj dir, Fac Develop Prog, NSF, 1977; proj dir, Student Sci Training Prog, 1979; res assoc, Fac Develop Prog, NSF, 1977; res assoc, Student Sci Training Prog, 1978; PROF PHYSICS, HENDERSON STATE UNIV, 1970-; mem proj staff, NSF Consortium upper level physics software. **Memberships:** AAAS; Am Asn Physics Teachers. **Research Statement & Publications:** Optical devices; radon detection; science museum programs for teacher enhancement; textbooks which integrate computer methods into undergraduate physics courses. **Mailing Address:** Dept Physics, Henderson State Univ, 1100 Henderson St Box 7802, Arkadelphia, AR 71999-0001. **Fax:** 870-230-5144. **E-Mail:** lemingc@hsu.edu

LEMIRE, ROBERT JAMES, ACTINIDE CHEMISTRY, SOLUTION CHEMISTRY. **Personal Data:** b Toronto, Ont, March 12, 1945. **Education:** Univ Toronto, BS, 1968, MS, 1971, PhD (chem), 1975. **Professional Experience:** RES CHEM, CHALK RIVER LAB, ATOMIC ENERGY CAN LTD, 1992-; res, Whiteshell Nuclear Res Estab, 1977-1992; res fel chem, Univ Ky, 1975-1977. **Memberships:** Chem Inst Can; Am Chem Soc. **Research Statement & Publications:** Properties of aqueous solutions; complexation; octinide chemistry; compilation of chemical thermodynamic databases. **Mailing Address:** Atomic Energy Can Ltd, Chalk River Labs, Chalk River, ON K0J 1J0, Can. **E-Mail:** lemirer@aecl.ca

LEMIRE, RONALD JOHN, TERATOLOGY, PEDIATRICS. **Personal Data:** b Portland, Ore, April 20, 1933; m 1993, Kathy; c Gregory, Suzanne, Jennifer, Anne, Alisa, Brian & Leisa. **Education:** Univ Wash, MD, 1962. **Professional Experience:** DIR INPATIENT

SERV, CHILDREN'S HOSP & MED CTR, SEATTLE, as of 1978; PROF PEDIAT, UNIV WASH, beginning 1977; from asst prof to assoc prof, Univ Wash, 1968-1977; chief resident, Children's Orthop Hosp & Med Ctr, 1967-1968; asst resident pediat, Univ Wash, 1965-1967; NIH fel teratology & embryol, Univ Wash, 1963-1965; Intern, King Co Hosp, Seattle, Wash, 1962-1963. **Memberships:** Soc Pediat Res; Teratology Soc. **Research Statement & Publications:** Neuroembryology; neuroteratology. **Mailing Address:** Dir Inpatient Serv Childrens Hosp & Med Ctr Mail Stop T-0111, 4800 Sand Pt Way NE PO Box 5371, Seattle, WA 98105. **Fax:** 206-987-3836. **E-Mail:** ron.lemire@seattlechildrens.org

LEMKE, CALVIN A(UBREY), CIVIL ENGINEERING. **Personal Data:** b Waco, Tex, August 25, 1921; m 1948, Wanda Wilkes; c Steve W. **Education:** Agr & Mech Col, Tex, BS, 1943, MS, 1961, PhD, 1988. **Professional Experience:** RETIRED; assoc prof civil eng, La Tech Univ, 1965-1991; asst prof, LA Tech Univ, 1956-1965; instr math, Baylor Univ, 1952-1956. **Research Statement & Publications:** Structures and highways; highway culverts; soils. **Mailing Address:** 516 Glendale Dr, Ruston, LA 71270.

LEMKE, CARLTON EDWARD, mathematics; deceased, see previous edition for last biography

LEMKE, DONALD G(EORGE), MECHANICAL ENGINEERING. **Personal Data:** b Chicago, Ill, March 25, 1932; m 1955, c 4. **Education:** Ill Inst Technol, BS, 1955; Univ Pa, MS, 1960, PhD (mech eng), 1970. **Professional Experience:** ASSOC PROF MECH ENG, UNIV ILL, CHICAGO, 1977-; asst prof mech eng, Mich Technol Univ, 1968-1977; asst prof eng mech, Mich Technol Univ, 1965-1968; res mgr aero ballistics & mech, Missile Div, Chrysler Corp, 1964-1965; assoc scientist, Missile Div, Chrysler Corp, 1963-1964; res engr, Advan Space Proj Dept, Gen Elec Co, 1962-1963; appl mech specialist, Dyna/Struct, Inc, 1960-1961; engr, Teletype Corp, 1955-1958 & Westinghouse Elec Corp, 1958-1959. **Memberships:** Am Soc Mech Engrs; Am Inst Aeronaut & Astronaut. **Research Statement & Publications:** Machine mechanics; dynamics; structural mechanics. **Mailing Address:** Dept Mech Eng Univ Ill, 2073 ERF, Chicago, IL 60612. **Fax:** 312-996-2426. **E-Mail:** donlemke@uic.edu

LEMKE, JAMES UNDERWOOD, MAGNETIC RECORDING, MAGNETIC MATERIALS. **Personal Data:** b Grand Rapids, Mich, December 26, 1929; m 1953, c 3. **Education:** Ill Inst Technol, BS, 1959; Northwestern Univ, MS, 1960; Univ Calif, Santa Barbara, PhD, 1966. **Honors & Awards:** Reynold Johnson Medal, Inst Elec & Electronic Engrs Magnetic Soc, 1995. **Professional Experience:** PRES, AEROLIFT INC, as of 2003; CHIEF TECH OFFICER & CHMN, REC ORDING PHYSICS INC, 1986-; adj prof elec & comput eng, Univ Calif, San Diego, 1986-; res fel, Eastman Kodak Res Labs, 1982-1986; pres & founder, Spin Physics Inc, 1968-1982; dir magnetic res, Bell & Howell Res Labs, 1960-1968; assoc to tech vpres, Armour Res Found, 1957-1960; vpres eng, AV Mfg Co, 1953-1956; Electronics engr prod develop, Temco, 1951-1953. **Memberships:** Nat Acad Eng; Inst Elec & Electronics Engrs; Am Phys Soc; AAAS; Am Asn Physics Teachers. **Research Statement & Publications:** Physics of magnetic recording process; development of related components, materials, processes, devices and circuits. **Mailing Address:** Aerolift, Inc, San Diego, CA 92103.

LEMKE, PAUL ARENZ, genetics, microbiology; deceased, see previous edition for last biography

LEMKE, RONALD DENNIS, THERMAL MODELS USED TO QUANTIFY COOKING METHODS, PSYCHOMETRIC MODELS. **Personal Data:** b St Paul, Minn, April 27, 1941; m 1967, c 2. **Education:** Mankato State Univ, BS, 1966; Col St Thomas, MBA, 1980. **Professional Experience:** STAFF MEM, CHECKER ENG, MINN, 1990-; dir eng, Stein Inc, 1987-1990; vpres eng & opers, Appl Vision Systs, 1985-1987; res & develop mgr, Despatch Inc, 1980-1985; eng mgr, Thermoking Div, Westing house, 1969-1980; engr, Honeywell, 1966-1969. **Memberships:** Am Soc Heating Refrig & Air Conditioning Engrs. **Research Statement & Publications:** Development of products that utilize different heat transfer methods for the preparation of food products; forced convection, latent heat and liquid immersion heat transfer. **Mailing Address:** 2701 Nev Ave, Minneapolis, MN 55427.

LEMKE, THOMAS FRANKLIN, ORGANIC CHEMISTRY, CORROSION. **Personal Data:** b Tremont, Pa, July 28, 1942; m 1965. **Education:** Wake Forest Univ, BS, 1964; Marshall Univ, MS, 1966; Lehigh Univ, PhD (chem), 1968. **Professional Experience:** RETIRED; int dir mkt, Special Metals Corp, as of 2001; mem staff mkt develop, Inco Alloys int Inc, beginning 1980; tech serv specialist, Inco Alloys Int Inc, 1972-1980; asst prof chem, Marshall Univ, 1970-1972; biochemist, Med Res Labs, Edgewood Arsenal, 1968-1970. **Memberships:** Am Chem Soc; Nat Asn Corrosion Engrs; Sigma Xi; Am Soc Metals. **Research Statement & Publications:** Synthesis of heterocyclic compounds of medicinal interest; corrosion of nickel base alloys. **Mailing Address:** Special Metals Corp, Huntington, WV 25705-3439. **Fax:** 304-526-5643.

LEMKE, THOMAS LEE, MEDICINAL CHEMISTRY. **Personal Data:** b Waukesha, Wis, June 1, 1940; m 1990, Pat; c 3. **Education:** Univ Wis, BS, 1962; Univ Kans, PhD (med chem), 1966. **Professional Experience:** Prof Emeritus, 2005-; Director of Assessment, College of Pharmacy, Univ Houston, 2004-2006; Assoc dean for prof programs, UNIV HOUSTON, 1991-2004; PROF PHARM, UNIV HOUSTON, 1984-2005; from asst prof to assoc prof, Univ Houston, 1970-1984; Res assoc org chem & patent liaison, Upjohn Co, Mich, 1966-1970. **Memberships:** Am Chem Soc; Am Pharmacy Asn; Am Asn Col Pharm; Am Asn Higher Educ; Int Pharmaceut Fedn. **Research Statement & Publications:** educational assessment; development of tools for the assessment of courses and program outcomes. **Mailing Address:** Col Pharm, Univ Houston 4800 Calhoun Rd, Houston, TX 77204-5000. **Fax:** 713-743-1259. **E-Mail:** lemke@uh.edu

LEMKEY, FRANKIN DAVID, MATERIALS SCIENCE ENGINEERING, METALLURGY & PHYSICAL METALLURGICAL ENGINEERING. **Personal Data:** b Oak Park, Ill, January 6, 1937. **Education:** Univ Mich Ann Arbor, BSE, 1960; Univ Oxford, Eng, DPhil, 1973. **Honors & Awards:** Grossman Author's Award, Am Soc Metals Int, 1970. **Professional Experience:** VIS PROF METALL ENG MAT, UNIV CONN, 1988-; dir, Microgravity Sci & Appln Div, NASA Hq, 1988-1989; pres exec exchange fel, White House, 1988; vis, Accreditation Bd Eng & Technol, 1985-; adj prof eng, Dartmouth Col, 1982-1988; expert, DWG mem, Univs Space Res Asn, 1980-1988; chmn, Exec Bd Rev, Metall Trans, Am Inst Mech Engrs, 1980-1981; counr, Mat Res Soc, 1978-1982; Sr consult scientist, United Technologies Res Ctr, 1960-. **Memberships:** Fel Am Soc Metals Int; Mat Res Soc; Am Inst Mech Engrs. **Research Statement & Publications:** Melt grown metallic and ceramic composites for high temperature applications; discovered Raney type nickel catalysts from RSR atomization of powders; shock compaction of ferrous alloy powders; high temperature austenitic stainless steel alloys for stirling engine components; high temperature oxidation and corrosion of alloys together with thermochemical properties evaluations. **Mailing Address:** 1001 Seafarer Cir Apt 105, Jupiter, FL 33477.

LEMLEY, ROBERT, COMPUTER SCIENCE. **Education:** Dallas Baptist Col, BS; Baylor Univ, MS, PhD (physics). **Professional Experience:** MGR CAMPUS SYSTS, DIEBOLD INC, as of 2003. **Mailing Address:** Diebold Inc, 4201 Lake Shore Dr Suite A, Waco, TX 76702. **E-Mail:** lemley@acm.org

LEMLICH, ROBERT, CHEMICAL ENGINEERING, BUBBLES & FOAM. **Personal Data:** b Brooklyn, NY, August 22, 1926; m 1976, Elizabeth A Murphy. **Education:** NY Univ, BChE, 1948; Polytech Inst Brooklyn, MChE, 1951; Univ Cincinnati, PhD (chem eng), 1954. **Honors & Awards:** Sigma Xi award, 1969. **Professional Experience:** PROF EMER CHEM ENG, UNIV CINCINNATI, 1985-; chmn fels, Grad Sch, Univ Cincinnati, 1976-1978; fel, Grad Sch, Univ Cincinnati, beginning 1971; Univ Arg, 1966 & Moscow Aviation Inst, 1991; Fulbright lectr, Israel Inst Technol, 1958-1959; res grants, Res Corp, Procter & Gamble, USPHS, HEW & NSF, 1954-1981 & 1985-1988; from asst prof to prof, Univ Cincinnati, 1952-1985; chem res engr, Gen Chem Div, Allied Chem & Dye Corp, 1948-1949. **Memberships:** fel AAAS; Am Chem Soc; Am Soc Eng Educ; fel Am Inst Chem Engrs; Sigma Xi. **Research Statement & Publications:** Foam fractionation and properties; convective heat transfer. **Mailing Address:** Dept Chem eng, Univ Cincinnati, Cincinnati, OH 45221-0171. **Fax:** 513-556-3473.

LEMM, ARTHUR WARREN, NEW MATERIALS DEVELOPMENT. **Personal Data:** b Biloxi, Miss, March 9, 1952; m 1972, c 5. **Education:** Marquette Univ, BS, 1974; Univ Wis-Milwaukee, MS, 1990. **Professional Experience:** SUPVR, ANALYTICAL LAB, COOPER POWER SYSTS, 1986-; res & develop mat engr, RTE Corp, 1981-1986; lab technician, RTE Corp, 1977-1981; Supv chemist, Cerac Inc, 1974-1977. **Memberships:** Am Chem Soc; Inst Elec & Electronics Engrs; Am Soc Testing & Mat; Soc Plastics Engrs; Am Soc Metals; Mat Res Soc. **Research Statement & Publications:** Investigation of new materials development and how their utilization can be used to improve and optimize the performance and reduce costs for products of the electrical and electronic industries. **Mailing Address:** W281 S 3696, Waukesha, WI 53188-9760.

LEMMERMAN, KARL EDWARD, PHYSICAL CHEMISTRY. **Personal Data:** b Willoughby, Ohio, May 30, 1923; m 1946, c 3. **Education:** Oberlin Col, AB, 1947; Cornell Univ, PhD (chem), 1951. **Professional Experience:** RETIRED; res chemist, Procter & Gamble Co, 1951-1988; Asst gen chem, Cornell Univ, 1947-1950. **Memberships:** Am Chem Soc. **Research Statement & Publications:** Kinetics of gas-phase photochemical reactions; complex inorganic electrolytes; surfactant solutions; colloids. **Mailing Address:** 1952 Compton Rd, Mt Healthy, OH 45231-4206.

LEMMERT, KURTIS H, MATHEMATICS. **Education:** Frostburg State Col, BS; W Va Univ, MS, EdD. **Professional Experience:** PROF, DEPT MATHS, FROSTBURG STATE UNIV, as of 2006. **Mailing Address:** Math Dept, Frostburg State Univ, 101 Braddock Rd, Frostburg, MD 21532-2303. **Fax:** 301-687-4795. **E-Mail:** klemmert@frostburg.edu

LEMMING, JOHN FREDERICK, NUCLEAR PHYSICS. **Personal Data:** b Dayton, Ohio, October 31, 1943. **Education:** Univ Dayton, BS, 1966; Ohio Univ, MS, 1968, PhD (physics), 1972. **Professional Experience:** SR PHYSICIST NUCLEAR SPECTROS, MONSANTO RES CORP, MOUND LAB, 1974-; nuclear infor res assoc, Nat Acad Sci, Nat Res Coun Comt Nuclear Sci, 1972-1974; fel physics, Ohio Univ, 1972-1974. **Memberships:** Am Inst Physics; Am Phys Soc. **Research Statement & Publications:** Nuclear safeguards. **Mailing Address:** 4408 Van Winkle Dr, Amarillo, TX 79121.

LEMMON, DONALD H, SPECTROSCOPY. **Personal Data:** b Sugar Grove, Pa, October 19, 1935; m 1956, c 1. **Education:** Univ Pittsburgh, PhD (chem), 1966. **Professional Experience:** SR SCIENTIST, DHL LAB, 1991-; sr engr, Westinghouse Res Ctr, 1967-1991; Fel, State Univ NY, Stony Brook, 1966-1967. **Memberships:** Am Chem Soc; Coblentz Soc. **Research Statement & Publications:** Infrared, Raman and nuclear magnetic resonance spectroscopy; mass spectrometry. **Mailing Address:** 1415 Homestead Rd, Verona, PA 15147-2439. **Fax:** 412-798-9636. **E-Mail:** wavenumber@msn.com

LEMMON, SANDRA K, GENETICS. **Education:** Univ Rochester, BA, 1973; Washi Univ, PhD (molecular biol), 1982. **Professional Experience:** PROF, DEPT MOLECULAR & CELLULAR PHARMACOL, UNIV MIAMI SCH MED, 2005-. **Mailing Address:** Dept Molecular and Cellular Pharmacol Univ Miami Scho Med, 6165 Rosenstiel Med Sci Bldg, Miami, FL 33124. **Fax:** 305-243-4555. **E-Mail:** slemmon@miami.edu

LEMNIOS, A(NDREW) Z, AERONAUTICAL ENGINEERING, APPLIED MECHANICS. **Personal Data:** b Newburyport, Mass, November 23, 1931; m 1954, Aspasia; c Karen & Keith. **Education:** Mass Inst Technol, BS, 1953; MS, 1954; Univ Conn, PhD (appl mech), 1967, Harvard Univ, Cert, 1983. **Honors & Awards:** Honorary Fel, Am Helicopter Soc, 1997, Assoc Fel, Am INST Aeronautics & Astronautics. **Professional Experience:** Vpres & Dean, Rensselaer Hartford Grad Ctr, 1999-2002, dir, Rotocraft Technol Ctr & clin prof, Rensselaer Polytech Inst, 1993-1999; asst vpres res & technol, Kaman Aerospace Corp, Bloomfield, Conn, 1990-1993; mem adv comt, Rotary Wing Technol, Rennselaer Polytech Inst, Univ Md & Ga Inst Tech, 1983-1992; mem aeronaut adv comt, NASA, 1978-1984; adj fac, Univ Mass, 1977-; dir res & technol, Kaman Corp, 1976-1989; chief res engr, Kaman Corp, 1969-1976; chief fluid mech res, Kaman Corp, 1965-1969; res proj mgr, Kaman Corp, 1963-1965; sr anal engr, Kaman Corp, 1961-1963; instr, Western New Eng Col, 1957-; res engr, Res Labs, United Aircraft Corp, 1954-1961; asst, Aeroelastic Struct & Res Labs, Mass Inst Technol, 1953-1954. **Memberships:** Am Inst Aeronaut & Astronaut; Am Helicopter Soc. **Research Statement & Publications:** Aeroelastic behavior of rotating structures; structural dynamics and vibrations; structures and structural mechanics; computer modeling; applied mathematics; research administration. **Mailing Address:** Hartford Grad Ctr, CT 06101. **Fax:** 860-548-2427.

LEMNIOS, WILLIAM ZACHARY, PHYSICS, ELECTRICAL ENGINEERING. **Personal Data:** b Athens, Greece, September 13, 1925; American citizen; m 1954, c 4. **Education:** Mass Inst Technol, BS, 1949; Univ Ill, MS, 1951. **Professional Experience:** RETIRED; div head radar measurements div, Lincoln Lab, Mass Inst Technol, beginning 1983; assoc div head, 1969-1983; group leader, 1965-1969; asst group leader, 1964-1965; staff mem systs anal, 1952-1965. **Memberships:** AAAS; Am Phys Soc; sr mem Inst Elec & Electronics Engrs; Sigma Xi; Am Inst Aeronaut & Astronaut. **Research Statement & Publications:** Computer systems and simulation; radar systems. **Mailing Address:** Lincoln Lab, Mass Inst Technol, 77 Mass Ave, Cambridge, MA 02139-4307. **Fax:** 617-258-9344.

LEMON, EDGAR ROTHWELL, SOIL SCIENCE. **Personal Data:** b Buffalo, NY, August 22, 1921; m 1944, Donna; c Wilfred T, R Bruce & Robert J. **Education:** Cornell Univ, BS, 1943, MS, 1949; Mich State Univ, PhD (soil physics), 1954. **Honors & Awards:** Soil Sci Award, Am Soc Agron, 1972; Biometeor Award, Am Meterol Soc, 1990. **Professional Experience:** RETIRED; consult, Univ Guelph, 1983-1985; Dept Sci & Indust Res fel, NZ, 1970-1971; USSR-US exchange scientist, 1969; Guggenheim & Fulbright fel, Australia, 1962-1963; prof agron, Cornell Univ, 1956-1980; soil scientist, Agr Res Serv, USDA,

1951-1980; prof agron, Tex A&M Univ, 1951-1956. **Memberships:** Fel AAAS; fel Am Soc Agron; Soil Sci Soc Am. **Research Statement & Publications:** Applied physics, particularly physical processes in the environment of agricultural crops. **Mailing Address:** 67 Ricardo, Niagara-on-the-Lake, ON L0S 1J0, Can.

LEMON, LESLIE ROY, METEOROLOGICAL RADAR SYSTEMS DESIGN, SEVERE CONVECTIVE STORM METEOROLOGY. **Personal Data:** b Greenville, SC, January 19, 1947; m 1968, Betty; c Kristen, Allison & Jonathan. **Education:** Univ Okla, BS, 1970. **Professional Experience:** RADAR SEVERE STORMS RES METEROLOGIST, BASIC COM & INDUSTS, 2000-; mgr, Weather Res & Oper, Adv Weather Systs, Unisys Corp, beginning 1994; mgr, Weather Systs Bus Develop, Paramax, 1991-1993; mgr, Nexrad Opers Compatibility Assurance Soc, Nexrad Radar Develop, Unisys Surveillance & Fire Control Systs, 1981-1991; res meteorologist, Tech Develop Unit, 1976-1981; meteorologist, Nat Severe Storms Forecast Ctr, 1976; res meteorologist, Severe Storms Res, Nat Severe Storms Lab, Nat Oceanic & Atmospheric Admin Comn Corps, 1973-1976; mem staff oceanog data collection, Severe Storms Res, Nat Severe Storms Lab, Nat Oceanic & Atmospheric Admin Comn Corps, 1970-1973; meteorologist, Severe Storms Res, Nat Severe Storms Lab, Nat Oceanic & Atmospheric Admin Comn Corps, 1969-1970; training instr, Severe Storm Structure; consult & lectr severe storms; consult, Radar, severe storms, & res Meteorologist. **Memberships:** fel Am Meteorol Soc; Nat Weather Asn (nat vice pres, 2000, pres, 2001, past pres, 2002). **Research Statement & Publications:** Understanding and documenting severe storm structure and evolution and tornado genesis, as well as operational application of conventional and meteorological Doppler radar to the warning services; radar and visual severe storm identification; understanding and documenting severe storm structure and evolution and tornado genesis, as well as operational application of conventional and meteorological Doppler radar to the warning services; radar and visual severe storm identification. **Mailing Address:** 16416 Cogan Dr, Independence, MO 64055. **Fax:** 816-373-2869. **E-Mail:** lrlemon@compuserve.com

LEMON, PETER WILLIAN REGINALD, EXERCISE PHYSIOLOGY, NUTRITION. **Personal Data:** b London, Ont, March 15, 1951; m 1979, Mary E Nageotte; c Kristina & Kimberly A. **Education:** McMaster Univ, BA & BPE, 1973; Univ Windsor, MS, 1975; Univ Wis- Madison, PhD (exercise physiol), 1979. **Honors & Awards:** Biomed Sci Award, Int Olympic Comt Pres, 1991. **Professional Experience:** PROF & WEIDER CHAIR, DEPT HEALTH SCI, CAN CTR ACTIV & AGING, as of 2004; vis scientist, McMaster Univ, 1989; prof exercise physiol, Kent State Univ, beginning 1987; from asst prof to assoc prof, Kent State Univ, 1979-1987. **Memberships:** Fel Am Col Sports Med; Am Physiol Soc; Can Soc Exercise Physiol. **Research Statement & Publications:** Protein/amino acid metabolism during both heavy resistance and endurance exercise; quantify the protein/amino acid requirements of active individuals and to identify the mechanisms responsible for any increased needs. **Mailing Address:** Can Ctr Activ & Aging, Univ Ont, 1490 Richmond St, London, ON N6G 2M3, Can. **E-Mail:** plemon@uwo.ca

LEMONDE, ANDRE, BIOCHEMISTRY, PHYSIOLOGY. **Personal Data:** b Saint-Liboire, Que, May 30, 1921; m 1953, c 2. **Education:** Univ Montreal, BA, 1942; Laval Univ, BS, 1947, ScD(biol), 1951. **Professional Experience:** Head dept, 1976-1981; prof, 1966-; from asst prof to assoc prof, 1952-1966; hon fel biochem & entom, Cornell Univ, 1951-1952; Demonstr physiol, Laval Univ, 1947-1951; EMER PROF BIOCHEM, SCH MED, LAVAL UNIV. **Memberships:** AAAS; Am Physiol Soc; Can Biochem Soc; Nutrit Soc Can. **Research Statement & Publications:** Comparative biochemistry and physiology. **Mailing Address:** Dept Biochem, Laval Univ Sch Med, Quebec, PQ J1K 7P4, Can.

LEMONE, DAVID V, NVERTEBRATE PALEONTOLOGY, BIOSTRATIGEOPHY. **Personal Data:** b Columbia, Mo, April 16, 1932; m 1955, c 2. **Education:** NMex Inst Mining & Technol, BS, 1955; Univ Ariz, MS, 1959; Mich State Univ, PhD (geol), 1964. **Professional Experience:** PROF GEOL, UNIV TEX, EL PASO, 1977-; assoc prof, Univ Tex, El Paso, 1967-1977; asst prof, Univ Tex, El Paso, 1964-1967; assoc prof geol, SMiss Univ, 1961-1964; geologist, Stanolind Oil & Gas Co, 1955-1956 & Tex Co, 1958-1959; dir, SW Biostratig Inst. **Memberships:** Fel AAAS; Am Paleont Soc; Soc Econ Paleontologists & Mineralogists; Geol Soc Am; Am Nuclear Soc; Mat Res Soc. **Research Statement & Publications:** Paleophycology; stratigraphic paleontology; systematic invertebrate paleontology and paleobotany; nuclear waste management; paleoecology. **Mailing Address:** Univ Tex, PO Box 3, El Paso, TX 79968. **E-Mail:** lemone@geo.utep.edu

LEMONE, MARGARET ANNE, CONVECTIVE STORMS, ATMOSPHERE BOUNDARY LAYER. **Personal Data:** b Columbia, Mo, February 21, 1946; m 1976, Peter; c Patrick & Sarah. **Education:** Univ Mo, AB, 1967; Univ Wash, PhD (atmospheric sci), 1972. **Professional Experience:** SR SCIENTIST, NAT CTR ATMOSPHERIC RES, 1992-; scientist, Advan Study Prog, 1973-1992; fel, Advan Study Prog, 1972-1973. **Memberships:** Nat Acad Eng; fel AAAS; Am Geophys Union; fel Am Meteorol Soc. **Research Statement & Publications:** Structure and dynamics of atmospheric boundary layer; structure and dynamics of cumulus and cumulonimbus clouds and mesoscale convective systems and their interaction with the environment, the boundary layer and larger-scale flow. **Mailing Address:** Nat Ctr Atmospheric Res, PO Box 3000, Boulder, CO 80307. **Fax:** 303-497-8181. **E-Mail:** lemone@ucar.edu

LEMONS, JACK EUGENE, BIOMATERIALS, MATERIALS ENGINEERING. **Personal Data:** b St Petersburg, Fla, January 20, 1937; m 1962, c 2. **Education:** Univ Fla, BS, 1963, MS, 1964, PhD (metall, chem, physics), 1968. **Honors & Awards:** I Lew Mem Award, Am Acad Implant Dent, 1985. **Professional Experience:** PROF, BIOMAT & SURG, DIV RES, UNIVALA, BIRMINGHAM, 1990-; prof eng & chmn dept, biomat & surg, div res, Univala, Birmingham, 1977-1990; from instr to assoc prof, biomat & surg, div res, Univala, Birmingham, 1971-1973; NIH spec fel, med sch, Univ Ala, 1971-1973; asst prof interdisciplinary studies, Clemson Univ, 1970-1971; res metall & head, phys metall, eng div, Southern Res Inst, Ala, 1968-1970; asst, Univ Fla, 1964-1968; res assoc metall & mat, Univ Fla, 1963-1964; owner & operator, J E Lemons Gen Repair & Mach Shop, 1955-1960. **Memberships:** Am Soc Metals; Am Inst Mining Metall & Petrol Engrs; Soc Biomat; Int Asn Dent Res; Orthod Res Soc. **Research Statement & Publications:** Properties of materials for applications in physiological environments; interfacial interactions between synthetic biomaterials and tissues. **Mailing Address:** 229 Richmar Dr, Birmingham, AL 35213-4415.

LEMONS, RICHARD S, GENETICS. **Education:** Univ Conn, BA; Pa State Univ, PhD (phys chem). **Professional Experience:** MED DIR & DIV CHIEF, PEDIAT HEMATONCOL, PRIMARY CHILDREN'S MED CTR, UNIV UTAH MED CTR, as of 2005. **Mailing Address:** Primary Children's Med Ctr Univ Utah Med Ctr, 100 N Med Dr HMBG Bldg 533 Rm 4440, Salt Lake City, UT 84113. **Fax:** 801-588-2662. **E-Mail:** richard.lemons@ihc.com

LEMONS, THOMAS M, REFLECTOR DESIGN, LIGHTING PRODUCT DESIGN. **Personal Data:** b Indianapolis, Ind, September 15, 1934; m 1959, Priscilla; c Kathrine F & Elizabeth B. **Education:** Purdue Univ, BS, 1956. **Honors & Awards:** Distinguished Serv Award, Illum Eng Soc, 1983. **Professional Experience:** Consult, Qualite Sports Lighting, Inc, 1985- & Wilmette Park Dist, Ill, 1986-1995; expert witness, Tech Adv Serv for Attorneys, 1984-; lectr, TLA Lighting Consults, Inc, 1980- & Mass Inst Technol, 1984-1994; group mgr, design & applications, Illum Eng Soc, 1982-1984; Co-founder & vpres, ARC Sales, Inc, 1979-2001; PRES, TLA-LIGHTING CONSULTS INC, 1970-; mgr appln eng, GTE-Sylvania Lighting Prods, 1956-1970. **Memberships:** fel Illum Eng Soc; Itl Dark Sky Assoc; Int Comn Illum; fel US Inst Theatre Technol. **Research Statement & Publications:** Energy efficient products and lighting systems; combine the latest light sources with improved optical systems to achieve unique results; author of over seventy technical papers; awarded 16 patents. **Mailing Address:** TLA-Lighting Consult Inc, Seven Pond St, Salem, MA 01970-4819. **Fax:** 508-741-4420. **E-Mail:** tmlattla@aol.com

LEMONTT, JEFFREY FIELDING, MOLECULAR GENETICS, TUMOR CELL DRUG RESISTANCE. **Personal Data:** b New York, NY, July 1, 1944; m 1970, c 2. **Education:** Rensselaer Polytech Inst, BS, 1965; Univ Calif, Berkeley, MS, 1967, PhD (biophys), 1970. **Professional Experience:** SR SCIENTIST, GENZYME CORP, 1989-; sr scientist, Integrated Genetics, Inc, 1982-1989; res staff mem yeast genetics, Oak Ridge Nat Lab, 1974-1981; lectr, Oak Ridge Grad Sch Biomed Sci, Univ Tenn, 1974-1981; res fel genetics, Nat Res Coun Can, 1970-1972 & Nat Inst Med Res, 1973-1974. **Memberships:** Genetics Soc Am. **Research Statement & Publications:** Yeast genetics and molecular biology; mechanisms of mutagenesis and DNA repair in yeast; expression of foreign genes in yeasts; yeast transformation; recombinant DNA technology; detection of pathogenic fungi; mechanisms of multidrug resistance in human tumor cell lines; bacterial and mammalian protein expression systems. **Mailing Address:** BioMain Pharm Inc, 105 Digital Dr, Novato, CA 94949.

LEMOS, ANTHONY M, THEORETICAL PHYSICS, SOLID STATE PHYSICS. **Personal Data:** b Arlington, Mass, August 31, 1930; m 1953, c 3. **Education:** Boston Col, AB, 1952; Univ Chicago, MS, 1956; Ill Inst Technol, PhD (physics), 1964. **Professional Experience:** PROF PHYSICS, ADELPHI UNIV, 1971- & CHMN DEPT, 1977-; Res collabr, Brookhaven Nat Lab, 1965-; assoc prof, Adelphi Univ, 1971- & Chmn Dept, 1964-1971; Instr physics, Lake Forest Col, 1958-1963. **Memberships:** Am Phys Soc. **Research Statement & Publications:** Theoretical understanding of the phenomena surrounding the F-center; color centers in the alkali halides. **Mailing Address:** Dept Physics, Adelphi Univ Grad Sch Arts & Sci, Garden City, NY 11530.

LEMP, JOHN FREDERICK, VIROLOGY, CELL BIOLOGY. **Personal Data:** b Alton, Ill, May 25, 1928. **Education:** Univ Ill, BS, 1951; Nat Registry Microbiologists, Regist. **Professional Experience:** RETIRED; bd dir, Advan Biotechnol Inc, Columbia, Md, beginning 1990; sr scientist, advan biotechnol Inc, Columbia, MD, beginning 1989; proj mgr retrovirus, dir cell sci lab, Electro-Nucleonics, Inc, 1971-1988; sr microbiologist & asst br chief, Biol Ctr, 1963-1971; prin investr, Process Develop Div, 1961-1963; microbiologist, Pilot Plants Div, US Army Biol Labs, Ft Detrick, Md, 1957-1961; fermentation supt & microbiologist, Ill, 1953-1957; bacteriologist, Com Solvents Corp, Ind, 1951. **Memberships:** Am Soc Microbiol; Sigma Xi; Natl Reg of Microbiol; Chesapeake Br Am Biol Safety Asn. **Research Statement & Publications:** Fermentation, purification microbial products, B-12, riboflavin and penicillin; bacitracin, alcohols, fungal amylase, continuous sterilization and culture, pH control, polarographic dissolved oxygen; mammalian tissue culture; virus propagation and purification; electrophoresis; human interferons; human lymphokines; acquired immundeficiency syndrome virus diagnostic tests; HIV-1, HIV-2 and HHV-6, -7, -8 research and development. **Mailing Address:** 14 W Broad Way, Lovettsville, VA 22080. **Fax:** 301-497-9773. **E-Mail:** jlemp@abionline.com

LEMPERT, JOSEPH, MAGNETOHYDRODYNAMICS. **Personal Data:** b North Adams, Mass, July 3, 1913; m 1941, Jean; c Eugene, Judith (Springer) & Larry. **Education:** Mass Inst Technol, BS, 1935; Stevens Inst Technol, MS, 1942. **Professional Experience:** RETIRED; consult, Eng Sect, Electronic Tube Div, 1978-1983; adv engr, Eng Sect, Electronic Tube Div, 1966-1978; res engr, Eng Sect, Electronic Tube Div, 1958-1966; sect mgr camera tubes, Eng Sect, Electronic Tube Div, 1958; adv develop, Eng Sect, Electronic Tube Div, 1956-1958; mgr, Eng Sect, Electronic Tube Div, 1953-1956; sect engr, Lamp Div, Westinghouse Res & Develop Ctr, 1944-1953; engr, Lamp Div, Westinghouse Res & Develop Ctr, 1936-1944. **Memberships:** Am Phys Soc; fel Inst Elec & Electronics Engrs. **Research Statement & Publications:** Photoemission; photoconductivity; secondary emission; thin films; vacuum tube electronics; electronic imaging; x-ray image intensification; x-rays; storage techniques; electron beams; electron beam welding; thermionic emission; magnetohydrodynamics. **Mailing Address:** 140 Spring Grove Rd, Pittsburgh, PA 15235.

LEMPERT, NEIL, BIOLOGY, CHEMISTRY. **Personal Data:** b New York, NY, November 25, 1933; m 1962, c 5. **Education:** Hamilton Col, BS, 1954. **Professional Experience:** PROF SURG, ALBANY MED COL, 1978-; dir, Histocompatibility Lab, Albany Med Col, 1972-; from asst prof to assoc prof, Albany Med Col, 1968-1978; consult surg, Vet Admin Med Ctr, 1967-; res fel surg, Mary Imogene Bassett Hosp & Clin, Cooperstown, NY, 1963-1964; from asst instr to instr, Albany Med Col, 1960-1968; resident exp surg, Albany Med Ctr, 1960-1961. **Memberships:** Am Surg Asn; Asn Acad Surg; Transplantation Soc; Am Soc Transplant Surgeons; Cent Surg Asn. **Research Statement & Publications:** Transplantation and preservation of tissues and organs; basic immunology of organ transplantation. **Mailing Address:** Dept Surg, Albany Med Col, 43 New Scotland Ave, Albany, NY 12208-3478.

LEMPERT, WALTER R, OPTICS. **Education:** Univ Utah, PhD (Physical Chem), 1981. **Professional Experience:** PROF, DEPT CHEM, OHIO STATE UNIV, as of 2005. **Memberships:** Am Inst Aeron & Astroanu Aerodyn Measurement Tech Comt. **Research Statement & Publications:** Development and application of optical techniques for probing energy transfer and nonequilibrium plasma phenomena; application of atomic and molecular spectroscopy to problems of engineering interest. **Mailing Address:** Dept Chem, Ohio State Univ, 100 W 18th Ave, Columbus, OH 43210. **E-Mail:** lempert@chemistry.ohio-state.edu

LEMPICKI, ALEXANDER, PHYSICS. **Personal Data:** b Warsaw, Poland, January 26, 1922; American citizen; m 1952, c 2. **Education:** Imp Col, Univ London, MSc, 1952, PhD, 1960. **Professional Experience:** Mgr electrooptics lab, Govt Technol Ctr, Gen Tel & Electronics Labs, Inc, 1973-; mem adv subcomt electrophys, NASA, 1969-1971; head quantum physics group, 1965-1972; Res physicist, Electronic Tube Co, Ltd, Eng, 1949-1954; RES PROF CHEM & PHYSICS, BOSTON UNIV. **Memberships:** Fel Am Phys Soc; fel Optical Soc Am. **Research Statement & Publications:** Electroluminescence; optical properties of solids; spectroscopy and molecular structure of organo metallic complexes; optical maser materials, particularly liquid luminescence; luminescence and structure of glasses; luminescent solar collectors; semiconductors; spectroscopy of transition metal ions; scintillator materials. **Mailing Address:** 590 Commonwealth Ave, Boston, MA 02115.

LEMPKE, ROBERT EVERETT, SURGERY. **Personal Data:** b Dover, NH, November 27, 1924; m 1949, Mary Baker; c Robert E Jr, Paul D, Martha B & Kari. **Education:** Yale

Univ, MD, 1948. **Professional Experience:** RETIRED; prof, surg, Sch Med, Ind Univ, Indianapolis, 1965-1993; Vis prof surg, Jinnah Postgrad Med Ctr, Karachi, Pakistan, 1964-1965; chief surg, Vet Admin Hosp, Indianapolis, 1959-1993; assoc chief of staff med res, Vet Admin Hosp, Indianapolis, 1956-1971; from instr to assoc prof, surg, Sch Med, Ind Univ, Indianapolis, 1956-1965; resident, Med Ctr, Ind Univ, Indianapolis, 1953-1955; med officer, Army Med Res Lab, Ft Knox, Ky, 1951-1953; resident, Med Ctr, Ind Univ, Indianapolis, 1949-1951; Intern surg, Johns Hopkins Hosp, Baltimore, 1948-1949. **Memberships:** Soc Surg Alimentary Tract; Cent Surg Asn; Am Col Surg; Asn Vet Admin Surgeons. **Research Statement & Publications:** Diseases of the alimentary tract. **Mailing Address:** 4029 Roland Rd, Indianapolis, IN 46208.

LEMYRE, C(LEMENT), ELECTRICAL ENGINEERING. **Personal Data:** b Shawinigan, Que, April 2, 1934; m 1962, c 4. **Education:** Laval Univ, BScEng, 1957; Univ London, PhD (transistors), 1962. **Professional Experience:** Asst dean acad affairs, Coop Educ Progs, 1986-1988; dir, Coop Educ Progs, 1980-1983; chmn dept, Univ Ottawa, 1971-1978; secy fac sci & eng, Univ Ottawa, 1970-1973; ASSOC PROF ELEC ENG, UNIV OTTAWA, 1969-; Asn Orgn Stages France fel, 1965-1966; from asst prof to assoc prof, Laval Univ, 1962-1969. **Memberships:** Sr mem Inst Elec & Electronics Engrs; fel Eng Inst Can; Can Soc Elec & Computer Eng; Am Soc Eng Educ. **Research Statement & Publications:** Characterization of transistors. **Mailing Address:** Dept Elec Eng, Univ Ottawa, Ottawa, ON K1N 6N5, Can.

LENARD, ANDREW, MATHEMATICAL PHYSICS. **Personal Data:** b Balmazujvaros, Hungary, July 18, 1927; American citizen; m 1953, E Veronica; c George L & Dorothy L. **Education:** State Univ Iowa, BA, 1949, PhD (physics), 1953. **Professional Experience:** Mem, Inst Haute Etudes Sci, 1979-1980; PROF MATH PHYSICS, IND UNIV, BLOOMINGTON, 1966-; res staff mem, Plasma Physics Lab, Princeton Univ, 1957-1965; Res assoc physics, Columbia Univ, 1955-1957. **Memberships:** Am Phys Soc; Am Math Soc. **Research Statement & Publications:** Kinetic theory; statistical mechanics; fundamental problems of quantum physics; mathematical problems related to physics. **Mailing Address:** Dept Math, Ind Univ, Bloomington, IN 47405. **E-Mail:** lenard@indiana.edu

LENARD, JOHN, VIROLOGY, PHYSIOLOGY. **Personal Data:** b Vienna, Austria, May 17, 1937; American citizen; m 1959, c 4. **Education:** Cornell Univ, BA, 1958, PhD (biochem), 1964. **Professional Experience:** PROF PHYSIOL & BIOPHYS, RUTGERS MED SCH, UNIV MED & DENT NJ, 1976-; assoc prof, Rutgers Med Sch, Univ Med & Dent NJ, 1973-1976; adj asst prof biol, Hunter Col, 1970-1973; Am Heart Asn estab investr, 1970-1972; assoc, Sloan-Kettering Inst Cancer Res, 1968-1972; asst prof biochem, Albert Einstein Col Med, 1967-1968; fel biol, Am Heart Asn advan res fel, 1965-1967; fel biol, Univ Calif, San Diego, 1964-1965; res assoc biochem, Cornell Univ, 1963-1964. **Memberships:** Am Soc Biol Chemists; Am Soc Cell Biol; Am Soc Microbiol; Biophys Soc; Am Soc Virol. **Research Statement & Publications:** Structures of biological membranes and enveloped viruses; entry and assembly of enveloped viruses; function of viral glycoproteins; endocrinology of lower eukaryotes; insulin action. **Mailing Address:** Dept Physiol & Biophys, Robert Wood Johnson Med Sch, Univ Med & Dent NJ, 675 Hoes Lane, Piscataway, NJ 08854-5635. **Fax:** 732-235-5038. **E-Mail:** lenard@umdnj.edu

LENARZ, WILLIAM HENRY, FISH BIOLOGY, BIOSTATISTICS. **Personal Data:** b Sacramento, Calif, September 18, 1940. **Education:** Humboldt State Univ, BS, 1963; Univ Wash, MS, 1966, PhD (fisheries), 1969. **Professional Experience:** FISHERY BIOLOGIST, SW FISHERIES CTR, MARINE FISHERIES SERV, TIBURON, 1976-; sci adv, US Deleg Int Comn Conserv Atlantic Tunas, 1970-1974 & Pac Fisheries Mgt Coun, 1977-1988; biologist, Fishery, La Jolla, 1968-1976. **Memberships:** Am Statist Asn; Biometric Soc; Sigma Xi; AAAS; Ecol Soc Am; Am Inst Fishery Res Biologists. **Research Statement & Publications:** Dynamics of exploited populations of fish. **Mailing Address:** Nat Marine Fisheries Serv, SW Fisheries Sci Ctr, 110 Shaffer Rd, Santa Cruz, CA 95060.

LENCH, NICHOLAS J, GENETICS. **Education:** St Mary's Hosp Med Sch, London, PhD. **Professional Experience:** DIR, WALES GENE PARK, THE MEDICENTRE, as of 2005. **Mailing Address:** Wales Gene Park, Medicentre Heath Park, Cardiff, CF14 4UJ, UK. **E-Mail:** lenchnj@cf.ac.uk

LENCHNER, NATHANIEL HERBERT, PROSTHODONTICS. **Personal Data:** b New York, NY, August 28, 1923; wid Florence (Deceased); c Jonathan, Michael & Debra (Kane). **Education:** NY Univ, BA, 1943, DDS, 1950. **Professional Experience:** Adj assoc prof biomed eng, Sch Eng & Archit, Univ Miami, 1980-1990; DENT CONSULT, COLTENE/WHALEDENT, 1977-; assoc ed, J Prosthetic Dent, 1977-1988; asst clin prof prev dent, Sch Dent & Oral Surg, Columbia Univ, 1974-1978; asst attend dentist, Long Island Col Hosp, 1964-1965; instr dent, Col Dent, NY Univ, 1950-1955. **Memberships:** Study Group Advan Dent Diag (pres, 1968-1969); Am Prosthodontic Soc; Am & Int Asn Dent Res; life mem Am Dent Asn; fel Acad Gen Dent; fel Northeastern Gnathological Soc (pres, 1966-1970) founder& life fel Northeastern Gnathological Soc. **Research Statement & Publications:** Biomedical engineering relative to dental devices; electrosurgery; the true effect of wave forms on cutting and coagulation. **Mailing Address:** Coltene/Whaledent, 104-20 Queens Blvd, Forest Hills, NY 11375. **Fax:** 718-459-2201.

LENDARIS, GEORGE G(REGORY), SYSTEMS SCIENCE, SYSTEMS DESIGN FACILITATOR. **Personal Data:** b Helper, Utah, April 2, 1935; m 1958, c 2. **Education:** Univ Calif, Berkeley, BS, 1957, MS, 1958, PhD (elec eng), 1961. **Professional Experience:** PROF SYSTS SCI & ELEC ENG, PORTLAND ST UNIV, as of 2000; vis scholar, Eng & Econ Systs Dept, Stanford Univ, 1978; Nat Acad Sci res fel, 1973-1974; vis scientist, Johnson Space Ctr, NASA, 1973-1974; mem, Ore State Senate Task Force Econ Develop, 1972-1973; consult to pres, Ore State Senate, 1971; mem, Gov Tech Adv Comt, Ore, 1970-1972; assoc prof systs sci & chmn fac, Ore Grad Ctr Study & Res, 1969-1971; sr res engr, Gen Motors Defense Res Labs, 1963-1969; sr staff scientist adaptive flight control systs, Gen Motors Defense Res Labs, 1961-1963; NSF fel, 1960-1961. **Memberships:** Fel Inst Elec & Electronics Engrs; Soc Gen Systs Res; Pattern Recognition Soc; Asn Transpersonal Psychol; Sigma Xi; Int Neural Network Soc. **Research Statement & Publications:** Developing methodologies for assisting teams of people to carry out systems design, engineering; analysis of social and human systems; models for complex systems; structural modeling; artificial intelligence; neural networks with application to conceptual graph knowledge systems. **Mailing Address:** Dept Sys Sci & Elec Eng, Portland St Univ, 206 Harder House, PO Box 751, Portland, OR 97207-0751. **Fax:** 503-725-8489. **E-Mail:** lendaris@sysc.pdx.edu

LENDER, ADAM, DIGITAL COMMUNICATIONS, SPEECH COMPRESSION. **Personal Data:** American citizen; c 2. **Education:** Columbia Univ, BS, 1954, MS, 1956; Stanford Univ, PhD (elec eng), 1972. **Honors & Awards:** Centennial Medal, Inst Elec & Electronics Engrs, 1984. **Professional Experience:** RETIRED; sr tech ed, Commun Mag, 1987-; sr consult scientist, Lockheed Palo Alto Res Labs, 1984-1993; ed-in-chief, J Selected Areas Commun, 1983-1984; ed-in-chief, Trans Commun, Inst Elec & Electronics Engrs, 1978-1984; mem bd gov, Data Commun Systs Comt, Inst Elec & Electronics Engrs, Commun Soc, 1977-1979 & 1982-1984; adj prof elec eng, Santa Clara Univ, 1976-; Chmn, Data Commun Systs Comt, Inst Elec & Electronics Engrs, Commun Soc, 1972-1976; head, Advan Develop, Gen Tel Lenkurt Labs, San Carlos, 1961-1984; proj engr, Int Tel & Tel Labs, 1960-1961; Mem tech staff, Bell Tel Labs, Murray Hill, NJ, 1954-1960. **Memberships:** Fel Inst Elec & Electronics Engrs; assoc fel Am Inst Aeronaut & Astronaut. **Research Statement & Publications:** Digital communications; invented correlative, duobinary or partial response used worldwide for efficient, fast digital communications applied to high density magnetic disk recording for computers; 30 US patents. **Mailing Address:** Lockheed Palo Alto Res Labs Org 91-50 Bldg 251, 3251 Hanover St, Palo Alto, CA 94304.

LENEL, FRITZ (VICTOR), METALLURGY. **Personal Data:** b Kiel, Ger, July 7, 1907; American citizen; m 1943, c 5. **Education:** Univ Heidelberg, PhD, 1931. **Honors & Awards:** Powder Metall Pioneer Award, Am Powder Metall Inst, 1984. **Professional Experience:** RETIRED; prof emer metall eng, Rensselaer Polytech Inst, 1973-1975; chmn dept, Rensselaer Polytech Inst, 1965-1969; from asst prof to prof, Rensselaer Polytech Inst, 1947-1973; Delco-Moraine Div, Gen Motors Corp, Ohio, 1937-1947; metallurgist, Charles Hardy Inc, NY, 1933-1937; fel, Univ Goettingen, 1931-1933. **Memberships:** Fel Am Soc Metals; Am Inst Mining, Metall & Petrol Engrs; Brit Inst Metals; fel Am Soc Testing & Mat. **Research Statement & Publications:** Powder metallurgy. **Mailing Address:** 2218 Burdett Ave, Troy, NY 12180.

LENER, WALTER, ENTOMOLOGY. **Personal Data:** b New York, NY, March 20, 1925. **Education:** NY Univ, BA, 1948, MA, 1950, PhD (biol), 1957; Rutgers Univ, MS, 1960. **Professional Experience:** NSF res grant, 1966-1968; PROF BIOL, NASSAU COMMUNITY COL, 1964-; fel trop med, Sch Med, La State Univ, 1964; Res grant, Res Found, State Univ NY, 1963-1964, 1965-1967; coordr biol sci, Geneseo, 1962-1964; from instr to prof biol, Geneseo, 1952-1964; sci consult, New Paltz, 1951-1952; Instr biol, State Univ NY Col Oneonta, 1950-1951; consult. **Memberships:** AAAS; Ecol Soc Am; Animal Behav Soc; NY Acad Sci; Sigma Xi; Entom Soc Am. **Research Statement & Publications:** Investigating the physiology, genetics and ethology of large milkweed bug, Oncopeltus fasciatus. **Mailing Address:** 682F Front St, Hempstead, NY 11550-4528.

LENES, M.D., BRUCE ALLAN, HEMATOLOGY, TRANSFUSION MEDICINE. **Personal Data:** b White Plains, NY, April 4, 1949; m 1974, Barbara; c Laura, Emilie & Juliann. **Education:** Union Col, Union Univ, BS, 1971; Albany Med Col, Union Univ, MD, 1975. **Honors & Awards:** Transfusion Medicine Academci Award - 1983 - awarded by National Heart, Lung, and Blood Institute (NHLBI). **Professional Experience:** MED DIR, COMMUNITY BLOOD CTRS S FLA, 1998 to date/ MED DIR, AM RED CROSS BLOOD SERV, SOUTH FLORIDA, 1981-1998/ ASST PROF MED & PATH, UNIV MIAMI SCHOOL OF MED, 1981- date/ PROF LAB SCIENCES, FL INT UNIV, 1981-date: CLIN ASST PROF OF MED, Georgetown Univ, 1980-1981/ FELLOW BLOOD BANING, NIH, Bethesda Md, 1980-1981/ FELLOW HEMATOLOGY, GEORGETOWN UNIV HOSP, 1978-1980/ INTERN AND MED RESIDENT, SHANDS TEACHIHNG HOSP, U OF FL, 1975-1978. **Memberships:** Sigma Xi; Am Med Asn; Am Asn Blood Banks. **Research Statement & Publications:** Clinical research in blood banking; special emphasis on diseases tranmitted by transfusion and physician education. **Mailing Address:** Community Blood Ctrs S Fl, 1700 N State Rd 7, Lauderhill, FL 33313. **E-Mail:** blenes@cbcsf.org

LENEY, LAWRENCE, wood science, microscopy; deceased, see previous edition for last biography

LENFANT, CLAUDE J M, PHYSIOLOGY. **Personal Data:** b Paris, France, October 12, 1928; American citizen; m 1949, c 5. **Education:** Univ Rennes, BS, 1948; Univ Paris, MD, 1956; FRCP, 1992. **Honorary Degrees:** DSc, State Univ NY, Buffalo, 1988. **Honors & Awards:** Distinguished Serv Award, Am Heart Asn, 1983; Forrest M Bird Contributory Award, Am Respiratory Ther Found, 1985; Breath of Life Award, Cystic Fibrosis Found, 1988; Brotherhood Award, Asn Black Cardiologists, 1990; Presidental Distinguished Exec Award, 1991; Surgeon Gen Exemplary Award, 1993; Laura Graves Award, Nat Morrow Donor Prog, 1995. **Professional Experience:** Bd gov, US Israel Binat Sci found, 1990-1993; DIR, NAT HEART, LUNG & BLOOD INST, NIH, 1982-; dir, Fogarty Int Ctr & assoc dir, Int Res, 1981-1982; peruvian Univ, Lima, Peru, 1981; hon prof, Nat Yang-Ming Med Col, Taipei, Taiwan, 1980; dir, Div Lung Dis, Nat Heart, Lung & Blood Inst, 1972-1980; actg chief, Pulmonary Res Br, 1972-1974; assoc dir lung progs & actg assoc dir collab res & develop prog, Nat Heart & Lung Inst, NIH, 1970-1972; mem, Physiol Study Sect, NIH, 1969-1970; from instr to prof med, physiol & biophys, Univ Wash, 1961-1972; assoc dir, Inst Respiratory Physiol & staff physician, Firland Sanitorium, Seattle, 1961-1968; asst prof physiol, Univ Lille, 1959-1960; res fel, Columbia Univ, 1958-1959; res fel, Univ Buffalo, 1957-1958; fulbright fel, 1956-1958; from res asst to dir res, Ctr Marie Lannelongue, France, 1954-1957. **Memberships:** Inst Med-Nat Acad Sci; Am Physiol Soc; Am Fedn Clin Res; Fr Physiol Soc; Asn Am Physicians; hon fel Am Col Chest Physicians; hon fel Am Heart Asn; hon mem Royal Soc Med; USSR Acad Med Sci; hon mem Cardiol Soc; Am Soc Clin Invest; Int Fedn Med Electronics; Am Soc Zoologists; Soc Exp Med & Biol; Undersea Med Soc; NY Acad Sci; fel Royal Col Physicians; hon fel Poland Soc Hypertension. **Research Statement & Publications:** Respiratory physiology, especially in gas exchange; comparative physiology related to the development and environmental adaptation of the respiratory system; author or co-author of 228 scientific publications. **Mailing Address:** Nat Heart, Lung & Blood Inst, Nat Inst Health, Rm 244 Bldg One One Ctr Dr, Bethesda, MD 20892-2486. **Fax:** 301-402-0818.

LENG, DOUGLAS E, CHEMICAL ENGINEERING. **Personal Data:** b Kitchener, Ont, May 28, 1928; m 1955, Marguerite; c Ronald, Janet & Douglas. **Education:** Queen's Univ, Ont, BSc, 1951, MSc, 1953; Purdue Univ, PhD (chem eng), 1956. **Honors & Awards:** H H Dow Gold Medal; N Am Mixing Forum Award. **Professional Experience:** RETIRED; sr res scientist, Dow Interdisciplinary Groups Eng, 1989-1996; mem panel M, bd assessment, Nat Bur Stand, Nat Res Coun, 1985-1988, 1992-1998; dir, Dow Interdisciplinary Groups Eng, 1982-1989; res scientist, Dow Interdisciplinary Groups Eng, 1975-1982; assoc scientist, Dow Interdisciplinary Groups Eng, 1970-1974; sr res engr, Process Fundamentals Lab, 1963-1970; res engr, Process Fundamentals Lab, 1962-1963; chem engr, Benzene Prod Lab, Cent Res Eng Lab, 1956-1961. **Memberships:** Am Chem Soc; fel Am Inst Chem Engrs. **Research Statement & Publications:** Multiphase behavior; coalescence and dispersion; mixing, micromixing. **Mailing Address:** 1714 Sylvan Lane, Midland, MI 48640-2538. **Fax:** 989-832-2624. **E-Mail:** deleng@chartermi.net

LENG, EARL REECE, GENETICS, RESEARCH ADMINISTRATION. **Personal Data:** b Williamsfield, Ill, June 12, 1921; m Jacqueline. **Education:** Univ Ill, BS, 1941, MS, 1946, PhD (agron), 1948. **Professional Experience:** EMER PROF AGRON, UNIV ILL, URBANA, 1977-; prof dir, Intsormil, Univ Nebr, Lincoln, 1979-1984; USAID & Pac Consults, Sudan, Jamaica & Mauretania, 1977-1978; crop specialist, USAID, 1975-1977; consult, World Bank, Malaysia, 1974; consult, UNDP\FAO, Yugoslavia, 1973, 1975; consult, Int Coffee Orgn, 1972; consult, Food & Agr Orgn, Thailand, 1971; adv, USAID & Midwest Univs Consortium for Int Activities, Indonesia, 1971; from asst dir to assoc dir int prog,

1969-1973; res adv, USAID & Uttar Pradesh Agr Univ, India, 1964-1966; Fulbrightsr res fel, Max Planck Inst, Ger, 1961; consult, Fed Govt Yugoslavia & USAID, 1960-1961; prof, Univ Ill, Urbana, 1958-1977; from asst prof to assoc prof, 1948-1958; asst plant genetics, 1946-1948; Spec asst agron, 1941-1942. **Memberships:** emer mem, Crop Sci Soc Am; emer mem, Am Soc Agron. **Research Statement & Publications:** Comparative international agriculture; genetics and breeding of maize; breeding systems; evolution of maize and relatives; international soybean improvement; international agricultural development, emphasis on major cereal crops. **Mailing Address:** SE 181 Arcadia Shores Rd, Shelton, WA 98584. **E-Mail:** harleng@hctc.com

LENG, MARGUERITE LAMBERT, AGRICULTURAL BIOCHEMISTRY, ANALYTICAL BIOCHEMISTRY. **Personal Data:** b Edmonton, Alta, September 25, 1926; m 1955, Douglas E; c Ronald B, Janet (Dumas) & Douglas L. **Education:** Univ Alta, BSc, 1947; Univ Sask, MSc, 1950; Purdue Univ, PhD (biochem), 1956. **Professional Experience:** PRES, LENG ASSOCS (CONSULTS), MIDLAND, MICH, 1991-; mgr int regulatory affairs, Agr Chem, 1986-1990; res assoc int regulatory affairs, Health & Environ Sci, 1980-1986; Chmn, Div Pesticide Chem, Am Chem Soc, 1980; sr regist specialist, Agr-Org Dept, 1973-1980; registr specialist, Agr-Org Dept, 1966-1973; anal chemist, Dow Chem Co, Midland, Mich, Agr Dept, 1956-1959; sr chemist, Allergy Res Lab, Univ Mich Hosp, Ann Arbor, 1950-1953; anal chemist, Nat Res Coun Can, 1948-1949; Ed asst chem & physics, Nat Res Coun Can, 1947-1948. **Memberships:** Fel Am Chem Soc; Sigma Xi; fel Am Inst Chemists; Int Soc Study Xenobiotics; NY Acad Sci. **Research Statement & Publications:** Pesticides, their toxicology, metabolism, residues, analytical methods and realistic evaluation of hazard to the environment; meaningful communication of scientific information; international regulation of hazardous chemicals. **Mailing Address:** Leng Assoc, 1714 Sylvan Lane, Midland, MI 48640-2538.

LENG, WAI-CHOI, MOLECULAR BIOLOGY & MEDICINE. **Personal Data:** b Hong Kong, May 21, 1948. **Education:** Chinese Univ Hong Kong, BS, 1970; Baylor Col Med, PhD (virol), 1974. **Professional Experience:** DIR, DIV MOLECULAR PATH, 1990-; PROF PATH, TULANE UNIV SCH MED, 1989-; from asst prof to assoc prof, microbiol, 1977-1989; fel virol, McMaster Univ, Can, 1975-1977. **Memberships:** Am Soc Biochem & Molecular Biol; Am Soc Virol. **Research Statement & Publications:** molecular biology; medicine. **Mailing Address:** 6300 Med Sch, Dept Path Tulane Univ, New Orleans, LA 70112. **Fax:** 504-587-7389. **E-Mail:** wleung@tulane.edu

LENGEL, ROBERT CHARLES, VIBROACOUSTIC MEASUREMENT & ANALYSIS, MEASUREMENT SYSTEM ENGINEERING & DEVELOPMENT. **Personal Data:** b Key West, Fla, October 1, 1957; m 1989, Barbara. **Education:** Va Polytech Inst & State Univ, BS, 1980; Univ Tex, Austin, MS, 1993. **Professional Experience:** STAFF ENGR & SCIENTIST, TRACOR APPL SCI, 1987-; sr systs engr, David Taylor Res Ctr, Dept Navy, 1982-1987; acoust engr, David Taylor Res Ctr, Dept Navy, 1981-1982; mech design engr, Geophys Serv, Inc, Tex Instruments, Inc, 1980-1981. **Memberships:** Acoust Soc Am; Inst Noise Control Engrs. **Research Statement & Publications:** Application of advanced signal processing to problems in acoustics and vibration; vibroacoustic measurement systems engineering; noise control engineering. **Mailing Address:** Tracor Appl Sci, 6500 Tracor Lane, Austin, TX 78725-2050. **Fax:** 512-929-2241. **E-Mail:** lengel@galileo.tracor.com

LENGEMANN, FREDERICK WILLIAM, PHYSICAL BIOLOGY, TRACE ELEMENT METABOLISM. **Personal Data:** b New York, NY, April 8, 1925; m 1950, Joan Doremus Lengemann; c Frederick W Jr & David Munson. **Education:** Cornell Univ, BS, 1950, MNS, 1951; Univ Wis, PhD (dairy husb), 1954. **Honors & Awards:** fel Aaas, 1966. **Professional Experience:** EMER PROF PHYSIOL, NY STATE VET COL, CORNELL UNIV, 1988-; prof phys biol, NY State Vet Col, Cornell Univ, 1967-1988; consult, FAD-IAEA, Vienna, 1966 & 1976; Biochemist, Div Biol & Med, US AEC, 1962; assoc prof, NY State Vet Col, Cornell Univ, 1959-1967; asst prof chem, Univ Tenn, 1955-1959; Res assoc radiation biol, Univ Tenn, 1954-1955. **Memberships:** Fel AAAS; Am Dairy Sci Asn; Am Inst Nutrit; Coun Agr Sci & Technol. **Research Statement & Publications:** Environmental contamination; fission product and mineral metabolism; milk secretion; mineral absorption; bone calcification. **Mailing Address:** PO Box 217, Rome, PA 18837.

LENGYEL, G(ABRIEL), ELECTRICAL ENGINEERING, OPTICAL COMMUNICATIONS. **Personal Data:** b Budapest, Hungary, April 30, 1927; American citizen. **Education:** Budapest Tech Univ, BASc, 1949; Univ Toronto, PhD (elec eng), 1963. **Professional Experience:** PROF EMER ELEC ENG, UNIV RI, as of 2005; prof elec eng, Univ RI, beginning 1976; guest scientist, res Labs, Siemens Corp, Munich, beginning 1972; assoc prof, Univ RI, 1966-1976; mem assoc comt elec insulation, Nat Res Coun Can, 1960-1964; res asst, Univ Toronto, 1960-1963; sr res fel appl, Ont res Found, 1959-1966; develop engr, Sangamo Co, Ont, 1958-1959; proj engr, E B Eddy Co, Que, 1956-1958; res engr, Elec Power Res Inst, Budapest, 1950-1956; Demonstr math, Budapest Tech Univ, 1949-1950. **Memberships:** Inst Elec & Electronics Engrs; Am Phys Soc; Optical Soc Am. **Research Statement & Publications:** Semiconductor lasers and optical modulations. **Mailing Address:** Dept Elec & Comput eng, Univ RI, Kelley Hall Rm A209 four E Alumni Ave, Kingston, RI 02881-0805. **Fax:** 401-782-6422. **E-Mail:** engyel@ele.uri.edu

LENGYEL, ISTVAN, ORGANIC CHEMISTRY & HISTORY OF SCIENCE SYNTHETIC ORGANIC NATURAL PRODUCTS CHEMISTRY, HISTORY & PHILOSOPHY OF SCIENCE. **Personal Data:** b Kaposvar, Hungary, July 12, 1931. **Education:** Eotvos Lorand, Univ Budapest, dipl, 1955; Mass Inst Technol, PhD (org chem), 1964. **Honors & Awards:** Alexander Von Humboldt Found, Ger, 1973-1974. **Professional Experience:** PROF EMER CHEM, ST JOHN'S UNIV, 1998-; chmn dept, St John's Univ, NY, 1985-1991; prof chem, St John's Univ, Ny, beginning 1973; vis prof, Tech Univ Munich, 1973-1974; NAS vis scholar, Univ Budapest, 1973; from asst prof to assoc prof, St John's Univ, NY, 1967-1973; res assoc mass spectrometry, Mass Inst Technol, 1965-1967; fel, Munich Tech Univ, 1964-1965; res assoc org synthesis, Mass Inst Technol, 1959-1964; res asst biochem, Sch Med, Johns Hopkins Univ, 1958-1959; lab chemist, Kundl Tirol Austria Pharmaceut Co, 1957-1958; sci co-worker geochem, Geophys Res Inst Hungary, 1955-1956; res chemist, G Richter Pharmaceut Co, 1954-1955. **Research Statement & Publications:** Chemistry of x-lactams. **Mailing Address:** Dept Chem, St John's Univ, 81-50 Utopia Pkwy, Jamaica, NY 11439. **Fax:** 718-297-6703, 718-990-1876.

LENGYEL, JUDITH ANN, developmental biology, molecular biology; deceased, see previous edition for last biography

LENGYEL, PETER, BIOCHEMISTRY, MOLECULAR BIOLOGY. **Personal Data:** b Budapest, Hungary, May 24, 1929; American citizen; m 1956, c 2. **Education:** Budapest Tech Univ, Dipl, 1951; NY Univ, PhD (biochem), 1962. **Honors & Awards:** Merit Award, Natl Asn of Allergy & Infectious Diseases. **Professional Experience:** PROF EMER, MOLECULAR BIOPHYS AND BIOCHEM AND SR RES SCIENTIST, YALE UNIV, 2001; prof molecular biophys & biochem, Yale Univ, 1969-2001; assoc prof molecular biophys, Yale Univ, 1965-1969; asst prof, Sch Med, NY Univ, 1964-1965; NIH spec fel, Pasteur Inst, Paris, 1963-1964; instr biochem, Sch Med, NY Univ, 1962-1963. **Memberships:** Am Soc Biochem & Molecular Biol. **Research Statement & Publications:** Protein biosynthesis; nucleic acid and protein metabolism of animal cells and viruses; interferon defense mechanism; oncogenes. **Mailing Address:** Dept Molecular Biophys & Biochem, Yale Univ, C-139 SHM 33 Cedar St, New Haven, CT 06520-8025. **Fax:** 203-732-6404. **E-Mail:** peter.lengyel@yale.edu

LENHARD, JAMES M, CELL BIOLOGY, PHYSIOLOGY. **Professional Experience:** RES ASST, MED SCH, WASH UNIV, 1989-. **Mailing Address:** Dept Immun/Physiol, Glaxo Wellcome Res & Develop, 5 Moore Dr, Research Triangle Park, NC 27709.

LENHARD, JOSEPH ANDREW, HEALTH PHYSICS, NUCLEAR PHYSICS. **Personal Data:** b Detroit, Mich, June 18, 1929; m 1983, Crissy Thompson; c Andrea & Michelle. **Education:** Vanderbilt Univ, BA, 1953, MS, 1957; Am Bd Health Physics, dipl, 1960. **Professional Experience:** MGT & TECH CONSULT, 1989-; Charter mem, Sr Exec Serv US Govt, 1979; dir res, Dept Energy, 1977-1989; dir res, energy res & develop admin, 1972-1977; dir safety & environ control div, US Atomic Energy Coun, 1967-1972; sr health physicist broad nuclear safety, US Atomic Energy Coun, 1961-1967; Health physicist radiation protection, Oak Ridge Opers Off, 1957-1961. **Memberships:** Health Physics Soc. **Research Statement & Publications:** Research administration; physical, life and engineering sciences. **Mailing Address:** 125 Newell Lane, Oak Ridge, TN 37830.

LENHARDT, MARTIN LOUIS, AUDIOLOGY, SPEECH & HEARING SCIENCES. **Personal Data:** b Elizabeth, NJ, December 14, 1944; m 1966, c 11. **Education:** Seton Hall Univ, BS, 1966, MS, 1968; Fla State Univ, PhD (audiol, speech sci), 1970. **Professional Experience:** PROF & VICE CHMN BIOMED ENG, VA COMMONWEALTH UNIV, as of 2005; DIR, BIOACOUSTICS LAB, VA COMMONWEALTH UNIV, as of 2005; mem staff adj fac, Va Inst Marine Sci, Col William & Mary, 1980-; assoc prof pediat dent, Med Col Va, Va Commonwealth Univ, 1976; assoc prof otorhinolaryngol, Med Col Va, Va Commonwealth Univ, 1971; asst prof, Med Col VA, Va Commonwealth Univ, 1971-1975; Nat Inst Neurol Dis & Stroke fel, Johns Hopkins Univ, 1970-1971. **Memberships:** Acoust Soc Am; Am Audiol Soc; Animal Behav Soc; Asn Res Otolaryngol. **Research Statement & Publications:** Psychological and physiological acoustics; speech communication; bioacoustics and linguistics. **Mailing Address:** McGuire Hall Annex, Rm 220, 1112 E Clay St, Richmond, VA 23298-0168. **Fax:** 804-828-4454. **E-Mail:** lenhardt@gems.vcu.edu

LENHART, JACK G, FLUID CONTROLS, THERMODYNAMIC SYSTEMS. **Personal Data:** b Bremen, Ohio, May 6, 1929; m 1951, c 3. **Education:** Case Inst Technol, BSME, 1951. **Professional Experience:** DIR ENG, TELEDYNE REPUB MFG, 1978-; chief engr, Scott & Fetzer-Meriam Instrument, 1975-1978; sr proj engr, chief engr, mgr ground support dept, mgr contracts admin, Accessories Div, Parker-Hannifin, 1967-1975; proj eng, TRW Equip Lab, 1956-1967; Mat res engr, NAm Aviation, 1951-1954. **Memberships:** Nat Fluid Power Asn; Am Met Soc; Am Soc Mech Eng. **Mailing Address:** 2000 Winchester Rd, Cleveland, OH 44124.

LENHART, SUZANNE MARIE, MATHEMATICS. **Professional Experience:** PROF MATH, UNIV TENN, as of 2005. **Memberships:** Soc Math Biol; Asn Women Math. **Mailing Address:** Dept Math, Univ Tenn, 121 Ayres Hall, Knoxville, TN 37996-1300. **Fax:** 865-974-6576. **E-Mail:** lenhart@math.utk.edu

LENHART, WILLIAM J, MATHEMATICS. **Education:** St. Joseph's Col, BS, 1977; Dartmouth Col, AM, 1979, PhD, 1983. **Professional Experience:** PROF, DEPT MATHS, WILLIAMS COL, as of 2006. **Mailing Address:** Bronfman Sci Ctr, Williams Col, Williamstown, MA 01267-2695. **Fax:** 413-597-4045. **E-Mail:** lenhart@cs.williams.edu

LENHERT, ANNE GERHARDT, ORGANIC CHEMISTRY. **Personal Data:** b Lynchburg, Va, April 1, 1936; m 1967, c 2. **Education:** Hollins Col, BA, 1958; Univ NMex, MS, 1963, PhD (chem), 1965. **Professional Experience:** ASST PROF CHEM, KANS STATE UNIV, 1967-; asst prof chem, Cent Mo State Col, 1965-1967; res fel, Univ NMex, 1964-1965. **Memberships:** Am Chem Soc; Sigma Xi; Int Heterocyclic Chem. **Research Statement & Publications:** Synthesis of heterocyclic ring systems as potential purine and pteridine antagonists; anti-cancer agents and anti-radiation drugs. **Mailing Address:** Dept Chem, Kans State Univ, King 204B 111 Willard Hall, Manhattan, KS 66506-3701. **Fax:** 785-832-6666. **E-Mail:** alenher@ksu.edu

LENHERT, DONALD H, EMBEDDED SYSTEMS. **Personal Data:** b Winfield, Kans, November 25, 1934; m 1967, Anne; c Earl H & David B. **Education:** Kans State Univ, BS, 1956; Syracuse Univ, MS, 1958; Univ NMex, PhD (elec eng), 1966. **Professional Experience:** Vis prof motorola, 1984, summers 1991-2000 & vis prof Delco Electronics, 1984; vis prof, Intel Corp, 1983; vis prof, Teletronix, 1983; PROF ELEC & COMPUT ENG, KANSAS STATE UNIV, 1981-; consult air force spec weapons ctr, NMex, 1960-1962 & Am Inst Prof Educ, 1977-1983; from asst prof to assoc prof elec eng, Kansas State Univ, 1966-1981; res & teaching assoc elec eng, Univ NMex, 1962-1966; res engr, Dikewood Corp, NMex, 1960-1962; syst engr, Gen Elec Co, NY, 1956-1958. **Memberships:** Inst Elec & Electronics Engrs; Nat Soc Prof Engrs. **Research Statement & Publications:** Microprocessor systems; microprocessor applications; testing of digital systems. **Mailing Address:** Dept Elec & Comput Eng, Kans State Univ, 2077 Rathbone Hall, Manhattan, KS 66506-5204. **Fax:** 785-532-1188. **E-Mail:** lenhert@ksu.edu

LENHERT, P GALEN, CRYSTALLOGRAPHY, COMPUTER SCIENCE. **Personal Data:** b Dayton, Ohio, July 31, 1933; m 1956, c 2. **Education:** Wittenburg Univ, AB, 1955; Johns Hopkins Univ, PhD (biophys), 1960. **Professional Experience:** PROF EMER PHYSICS, VANDERBILT UNIV, as of 2003; prof phys, vanderbilt univ, beginning 1982; vis scientist, WPAFB Mat Lab, 1982-1990; NSF grants, 1972-1976, 1978-1981; from asst prof to assoc prof, Vanderbilt Univ, 1964-1982; USPHS grants, 1962-1963, 1964-1975; asst prof physics, Wittenburg Univ, 1961-1964; USPHS res fel chem crystallog, Oxford Univ, 1960-1961. **Memberships:** AAAS; Am Crystallog Asn. **Research Statement & Publications:** Determination of molecular structures by x-ray crystallographic methods; phase changes and modulated structures; polymer fiber diffraction. **Mailing Address:** Dept Physics, Vanderbilt Univ, 6301 Stevenson Ctr, Nashville, TN 37235. **Fax:** 615-343-7263. **E-Mail:** galen.lenhert@vanderbilt.edu

LENHOFF, HOWARD MAER, INVERTEBRATE ZOOLOGY & HISTORY, PHILOSOPHY OF SCIENCE & MUSIC PERCEPTION. **Personal Data:** b North Adams, Mass, January 27, 1929; m Sylvia; c Gloria & Bernard. **Education:** Coe Col, BA, 1950; Johns Hopkins Univ, PhD (biol), 1955. **Honorary Degrees:** DSc, Coe Col, 1976. **Honors & Awards:** Hon mem, Soc Phys & Nat Hist, Geneva Swiss Acad Sci, 1990; Distinguished Fellow, Iowa Academy of Scciences, 1986. **Professional Experience:** PROF EMER, DEPT DEVELOP & CELL BIOL, UNIV CALIF, IRVINE, 1993-; Adjunct Prof, Univ Miss, Oxford, 2003-; vis sr res fel, Jesus Col, Oxford Univ, 1988; distinguished fel, Iowa Acad Sci, 1986; social ecol, Ben Gurion Univ, Beersheba, Israel, 1981; vis prof chem eng, Israel Inst Technol, 1973-1974; dean grad div, Univ Calif, Irvine, 1971-1973; vis prof, Hebrew Univ Jerusalem,

1970, 1971, 1977-1978; prof develop & cell biol, Univ Calif, Irvine, 1969-1992; assoc dean sch biol sci, Univ Calif, Irvine, 1969-1971; vis scientist, Polymer Lab, Weizmann Inst Sci, Israel, 1968-1969; prof, Univ Miami, Fla, 1966-1969; USPHS career develop award, 1965-1969; dir lab quant biol, Univ Miami, Fla, 1963-1969; assoc prof biol, Univ Miami, Fla, 1959-1965; investr, Biochem Labs, Howard Hughes Med Inst, 1958-1963; fel, Dept Terrestrial Magnetism, Carnegie Inst Technol, 1958; assoc consult res, George Wash Univ, 1957-1958; Vis lectr, Howard Univ, 1957-1958; actg chief, Biochem Sect, Armed Forces Insts Path, 1956-1957; USPHS fel, Loomis Lab, Nat Cancer Inst, 1954-1956. **Memberships:** Am Soc Biol Chem; Am Soc Cell Biol; Am Chem Soc; Biophys Soc; Soc Develop Biol; Hist Sci Soc; AAAS (fellow); Sigma Xi. **Research Statement & Publications:** Invertebrate biology; chemoreception; symbiosis; cellular differentiation; immobilized enzymes; enzyme immunoassays; history of experimental biology; folklore and medicine; absolute pitch in Williams syndrome. **Mailing Address:** Dept Develop & Cell biol, Univ Calif, 5205A McGaugh Hall, Irvine, CA 92697-2300. **Fax:** 949-824-4709. **E-Mail:** hlenhoff@uci.edu

LENIART, DANIEL STANLEY, PHYSICAL CHEMISTRY. **Personal Data:** b Norwich, Conn, January 5, 1943; m 1971, Elizabeth; c Keith Daniel & Kristiana Elizabeth. **Education:** The Citadel, BS, 1964; Cornell Univ, PhD (phys chem), 1969. **Professional Experience:** IMMUNOL DIAG INSTRUMENTATION, TECHNICON INSTRUMENT CORP, 1986-; Gas Chromatography-Mass Spectros, Hewlett Packard, 1981-1985; Fel, mgr EPR res & develop, 1975-1980; appln engr, Varian Assocs, 1970-1975; Fel, Varian Assocs, 1969-1970. **Memberships:** Am Phys Soc. **Research Statement & Publications:** Study of relaxation phenomena using the techniques of electron spin resonance, electron nuclear double resonance and electron-electron double resonance. **Mailing Address:** Six Guernsey Rd, Brookfield, CT 06804.

LENKE, ROGER RAND, MATERNAL FETAL MEDICINE, MEDICAL GENETICS. **Personal Data:** b Brooklyn, NY, April 6, 1946. **Education:** Columbia Univ, MD, 1971. **Professional Experience:** RETIRED; dir mat fetal med, St Vincent's Hosp & Health Serv, 1994-1996; prof obstet & gynec, Univ Colo, 1989-1994; dir maternal & fetal med, Med Col Ohio, Toledo, 1985-1994; prof obstet & gynec, 1985-1989; dir prenatal diag, Univ Wash, Seattle, 1982-1985; fel maternal & fetal med, Univ Southern Calif, Los Angeles, 1979-1981; fel neurol, Mass Gen Hosp, 1979; resident obstet & gynec, Columbia Presby, NY, 1972-1976; intern med, Roosevelt Hosp, 1971-1972. **Memberships:** Am Col Obstetricians & Gynecologists; Am Inst Ultrasound Med; Am Soc Human Genetics; Soc Perinatal Obstets; AMA; Int Soc Fetal Med & Surg. **Research Statement & Publications:** High risk obstetrics and prenatal diagnosis. **Mailing Address:** 8801 N Meridian St Ste 209, Indianapolis, IN 46260.

LENKER, SUSAN STAMM, MATHEMATICAL LOGIC, STATISTICS. **Personal Data:** b Bridgeport, Conn, November 13, 1945; m 1968, Terry; c Scott & Carl. **Education:** Western Conn State Col, BS, 1969; Univ Colo, MA, 1970; Univ Mont, PhD (math), 1975. **Professional Experience:** ASSOC PROF MATH, DEPT MATH, CENT MICH UNIV, 1991-; assoc prof software systs, Dept Info Systs & Anal 1989-1991; asst prof oper res, Dept Math, Cent Mich Univ, 1976-1988; asst prof math, Univ Louisville, 1975-1976. **Memberships:** Am Statist Asn; Opers Res Soc Am; Am Inst Decision Sci; Am Math Soc; Sigma Xi. **Research Statement & Publications:** Data base theory; decision theory including fuzzy sets; statistics; category theory. **Mailing Address:** Dept Math, Cent Mich Univ, 206F Pearce Hall 100 W Preston Rd, Mt Pleasant, MI 48859-0001. **E-Mail:** susan.s.lenker@cmich.edu

LENKOSKI, L DOUGLAS, MEDICINE, PSYCHIATRY. **Personal Data:** b Northampton, Mass, May 13, 1925; m 1952, Jeannette; c Jan Ellen, Mark, Lisa & Joanne. **Education:** Harvard Univ, AB, 1948; Western Res Univ, MD, 1953. **Professional Experience:** PROF EMER PSYCHIAT, SCH MED, CASE WESTERN RES UNIV, AS OF 2004; dir, Substance Abuse Ctr, Case Western Reserve Univ, beginning 1990; assoc dean, Sch Med, Case Western Res Univ, beginning 1982; chief staff, Univ Hosps Cleveland, 1982-1990; chmn dept, Sch Med, Case Western Res Univ, 1970-1986; prof psychiat, Sch Med, Case Western Res Univ, 1969-2004; dir dept, Univ Hosps Cleveland, 1969-1986; dir dept, Cleveland Metrop Gen Hosp, 1969-1976; assoc dir dept, Univ Hosps Cleveland, 1966-1969; consult, Cleveland Vet Admin Hosp, 1965-; actg dir dept psychiat, Univ Hosps Cleveland, 1962-1966; from instr to assoc prof, 1960-1969; consult, DePaul Maternity & Infant Home, 1958-1967; consult, & Cleveland Ctr, 1958-1961; teaching fel, 1957-1960; Fel psychiat, Yale Univ, 1955-1956. **Memberships:** Am Col Psychiat, emer mem; Am Psychiat Asn, fel; Am Psychoanal Asn, sr mem. **Research Statement & Publications:** Psychiatric education; community mental health planning. **Mailing Address:** One Bratenahl Pl, Cleveland, OH 44108.

LENLING, WILLIAM JAMES, THERMAL SPRAY COATINGS. **Personal Data:** b Madison, Wis, January 16, 1961; m 1987. **Education:** Univ Wis-Madison, BS, 1985, MS, 1987. **Professional Experience:** AT THERMAL SPRAY TECH, as of 2004; Chmn, Publicity Comt, 1993-; RES MGR, THERMAL SPRAY TECHNOLOGIES, 1991-; Mem, Mat Sci Comt, Thermal Spray Div, Am Soc Metall, 1990-; Mat engr plasma coating res & develop, Sandia Nat Labs, 1988-1990; mat engr plasma coating res & develop, Fisher-Barton, Inc, 1987-1990. **Memberships:** Am Soc Metall; Tech Asn Pulp & Paper Indust. **Research Statement & Publications:** Material science coating development of thermal spray coatings; develop coatings for a wide variety of industrial applications; author of four publications and two patents. **Mailing Address:** Thermal Spray Tech, 515 Progress Way, Sun Prairie, WI 53590. **Fax:** 608-825-2737.

LENN, NICHOLAS JOSEPH, NEUROLOGY, ANATOMY. **Personal Data:** b Chicago, Ill, November 26, 1938; m 1964, c 3. **Education:** Univ Chicago, SB, 1959, MS & MD, 1964, PhD (anat), 1967. **Professional Experience:** CHIEF PEDIAT NEUROL, STATE UNIV NY, as of 2003; PROF NEUROL, SCH MED, STATE UNIV NY, beginning 1990; from asst prof to assoc prof pediat, Univ Calif, Davis, 1974-1980; from asst prof to assoc prof neurol, Univ Calif, Davis, 1974-1980; asst prof pediat & med, Univ Chicago, 1970-1974; Res assoc neuroanat, NIH, 1964-1966; NIH fel. **Memberships:** AAAS; Am Asn Anat; Am Acad Neurol; Child Neurol Soc; Am Neurol Asn. **Research Statement & Publications:** Developmental plasticity of mammalian brain. **Mailing Address:** Dept Neurol, State Univ NY, HSC T12-20, Stony Brook, NY 11794-8121. **Fax:** 631-444-1474.

LENNARD, CHRISTOPHER J, MATHEMATICS. **Education:** Kent State Univ, PhD. **Professional Experience:** ASSOC PROF, DEPT MATHS, UNIV PITTSBURGH, as of 2006. **Mailing Address:** Dept Math & Statist, Univ Pittsburgh, Pittsburgh, PA 15260-0001. **Fax:** 412-624-8397. **E-Mail:** lennard+@pitt.edu

LENNARTZ, MICHELLE R, MEDICINE. **Education:** Univ Mich, PhD, 1984. **Professional Experience:** ASSOC DIR, ALBANY MED CTR, as of 2004; DIR MED, WASH UNIV, 1991-. **Mailing Address:** Physiol & Cell Biol, Albany Med Col, 47 New Scotland Ave, Albany, NY 12208-3412. **E-Mail:** lennarm@mail.amc.edu

LENNARZ, WILLIAM J, BIOCHEMISTRY, CELL BIOLOGY. **Personal Data:** b New York, NY, September 28, 1934; c 3. **Education:** Pa State Univ, BS, 1956; Univ Ill, PhD (chem), 1959. **Professional Experience:** Mem, Grad Prog Cell & Develop Biol, Genetics Prog, 1989-; mem, Acad Standards Coun, 1990-; DIR, INST CELLULAR & DEVELOP BIOL, STATE UNIV NY, STONY BROOK, 1990-; DISTINGUISHED PROF & CHMN, DEPT BIOCHEM & CELL BIOL, STATE UNIV NY, STONY BROOK, 1989-; Burroughs Wellcome vis prof, Univ PR, 1988; prof, Dept Biochem & Molecular Biol, M D Anderson Cancer Ctr, Univ Tex, 1984-1989; Robert A Welch prof chem & chmn, Dept Biochem & Molecular Biol, M D Anderson Cancer Ctr, Univ Tex, 1983-1989; Burroughs Wellcome vis prof, State Univ, NY, 1983; mem, Pathobiology Chem Study Sect, 1982-1986; vis prof biochem, Sch Med, WVa Univ, 1982; ad hoc mem, Molecular Biol Study Sect, 1980-1981; mem, Physiol Chem Study Sect, NIH, 1974-1978; NSF fel, 1969-1960; from asst prof to prof, Dept Biol Chem, Sch Med, Johns Hopkins Univ, 1962-1983; NIH fel, 1960-1962; postdoctoral fel, Harvard Univ, 1959-1962. **Memberships:** Am Chem Soc; Am Soc Biochem & Molecular Biol (pres-elect 1988-1989); Am Soc Microbiol; Sigma Xi; Am Soc Cell Biol; Soc Complex Carbohydrates; Am Soc Zoologists. **Research Statement & Publications:** Cancer research; author of numerous scientific publications. **Mailing Address:** State Univ NY, Dept Biochem & Cell Biol, 450 Life Sci Bldg, Stony Brook, NY 11794-5215. **E-Mail:** wlennarz@ccmail.sunysb.edu

LENNETTE, EVELYNE T, VIROLOGY. **Professional Experience:** AT VIROLAB, INC, as of 1996. **Mailing Address:** Virolab Inc, 1204 Tenth St, Berkeley, CA 94710.

LENNON, GERARD PATRICK, CIVIL ENGINEERING. **Personal Data:** b New York, NY, November 15, 1951; m 1976, Linda; c Elizabeth, Brian & Marianne. **Education:** Drexel Univ, BS, 1975; Cornell Univ, MS, 1977, PhD, 1980. **Professional Experience:** PROF & ASSOC CHAIR, DEPT CIVIL & ENVIRON ENG, LEHIGH UNIV, as of 2003; actg dir, Environ Studies Ctr, 1989-1991; assoc prof, Lehigh Univ, Bethlehem, Pa, beginning 1986; consult, Woodward-Clyde Consults & Plymouth Meeting, Pa, beginning 1985; asst prof, 1980-1986. **Memberships:** Am Soc Chem Engrs. **Research Statement & Publications:** Design of fluidization systems for coastal applications; boundary element method for solving groundwater flow problems. **Mailing Address:** Dept Civil & Environ Eng, Fritz Eng Lab, Lehigh Univ, 13 E Packer Ave, Bethlehem, PA 18015. **E-Mail:** gpl0@lehigh.edu

LENNON, PATRICK JAMES, HOMOGENEOUS CATALYSIS, MACROCYCLIC CHEMISTRY. **Personal Data:** b Amsterdam, NY, July 24, 1950. **Education:** State Univ NY, Binghamton, BA, 1972; Brandeis Univ, PhD (org chem), 1977. **Professional Experience:** SYNTHETIC CHEM CONSULT, MONSANTO CO, 1992-; sr res specialist, Monsanto Co, 1987-1992; res specialist, Monsanto Co, 1984-1987; sr res chemist, Monsanto Co, 1980-1984; Res fel, Oxford Univ, 1977-1979. **Memberships:** Am Chem Soc; Royal Soc Chem. **Research Statement & Publications:** Homogeneous catalysis of organic reactions by transition metal complexes; organosilicon chemistry; design and synthesis of enzyme inhibitors; syntheses of macrocycles; inorganic and organic phosphorus chemistry. **Mailing Address:** 50 Wilshire Ter, St Louis, MO 63119. **E-Mail:** pjlenn@ccmail.monsanto.com

LENNON, VANDA ALICE, NEUROIMMUNOLOGY. **Personal Data:** b Sydney, Australia, August 1, 1943; m 1975. **Education:** Univ Sydney, MB, BS, 1966; Univ Melbourne, PhD (immunol), 1973. **Professional Experience:** PROF NEUROL, MAYO CLIN COL MED, as of 2006; PROF NEUROL & IMMUNOL, MAYO GRAD SCH MED, 1983-; CONSULT NEUROL & IMMUNOL, MAYO CLINIC, 1978-; assoc prof neurol & immunol, Mayo Grad Sch Med, 1978-1983; assoc adj prof, Dept Neuroscience, Univ Calif, San Diego, 1977-1978; asst res prof, Salk Inst Biol Studies, 1973-1977; res assoc, Salk Inst Biol Studies, 1972-1973; fel immunol, Walter & Eliza Hall Inst Med Res, 1968-1972; from jr intern to asst med resident, Montreal Gen Hosp, 1966-1968; res asst nuclear med, Univ Sydney, 1966. **Memberships:** Am Acad Neurol; Sigma Xi; Am Asn Immunol; Soc Neuroscience; Am Soc Clin Invest; Am Asn Neuropath. **Research Statement & Publications:** Autoimmunity to antigens of central and peripheral nervous systems and muscle; identification of neural antigens on small cell lung cancer; immunologic studies of patients with neurological and paraneoplastic diseases of presumed autoimmune basis. **Mailing Address:** Neuroimmunol Lab, Depts Neurol & Immunol, Mayo Clin, Guggenheim 828 200 First St SW, Rochester, MN 55905-0001. **E-Mail:** lennon.vanda@mayo.edu

LENNON-THOMPSON, DORIS, EXERCISE PHYSIOLOGY. **Education:** City Univ NY, BA, 1973, MS, 1975; Univ Wis-Madison, PhD (exercise physiol). **Professional Experience:** SR SCIENTIST PROD DEVELOP, DESSERTS DIV, KRAFT GEN FOODS DEPT, GEN FOODS USA, TARRYTOWN, NY, 1993-; adj asst prof community & prev med, NY Med Col, 1991-; assoc dir, Nutrit & Health Sci & Sci Rels, 1991-1993; chmn, Indust Liaison Comt, Am Inst Nutrit, 1990-; MGR, CONSUMER NUTRIT AFFAIRS, KRAFT GEN FOODS, as of 1990; mgr consumer nutrit affairs, Nutrit & Health Serv, 1989-1991; tech supvr, Gen Foods Tech Ctr, 1988-1989; scientist nutrit & health sci, Gen Foods Tech Ctr, 1985-1987; adj asst prof, Biodynamics Lab, 1984-1986; sr staff scientist, Med Dept, Chem & Biol Med Sci Div, Hazelton Labs Am, Inc, 1984-1985; lectr & lab specialist, Biodynamics Lab, 1982-1984; dir exercise physiol & res, Cardiopulmonary Rehab Corp, 1982; res assoc, Clin Nutrit Ctr, 1981-1982; Marie L Carns res fel, Dept Phys Educ & Dance, Univ Wis-Madison, 1980-1981; Task Force on Dis. **Memberships:** Am Inst Nutrit; Inst Food Technol; Sigma Xi; fel Am Col Sports Med; Am Alliance Health Phys Educ Recreation & Dance. **Research Statement & Publications:** Nutrition; exercise physiology; co-author of numerous scientific publications. **Mailing Address:** Kraft Gen Foods, 555 S Broadway T33-1, Tarrytown, NY 10519.

LENNOX, ARLENE JUDITH, MEDICAL PHYSICS, ELEMENTARY PARTICLE PHYSICS. **Personal Data:** b Cleveland, Ohio, December 3, 1942. **Education:** Notre Dame Col, Ohio, BS, 1963; Univ Notre Dame, MS, 1973, PhD (physics), 1974. **Professional Experience:** DEPT HEAD, FERMILAB NEUTRON THERAPY FACIL, 1986-; staff physicist, Fermilab Neutron Therapy Facil, 1980-1986; vis physicist, Fermilab, 1978-1980; prof physics, NCent Col, 1977-1980; res assoc physics, Fermilab, 1974-1977; Regina High Sch, 1964-1965 & Shrine High Sch, 1965-1969; teacher, Marymount High Sch, 1963-1964; mem-at-large, Forum Educ, Am Phys Soc; assoc prof, Dept Radiation Oncol, Rush Med Ctr. **Memberships:** Am Phys Soc; AAAS; Am Asn Physics Teachers; Am Asn Physicists Med; Am Soc Therapeut Radiol & Oncol. **Research Statement & Publications:** Experiments to study backward peak in pi-p elastic scattering; experiments to measure pion form factor; p-p colliding beams; neutron therapy physics; medical uses for proton linacs. **Mailing Address:** Fermilab Neutron Ther Facility, Fermi Nat Accelerator Lab, PO Box 500 Mail Stop 301, Batavia, IL 60510. **Fax:** 630-840-8766. **E-Mail:** alennox@fnal.gov

LENNOX, DONALD HAUGHTON, HYDROLOGY. **Personal Data:** b Toronto, Ont, June 7, 1924; m 1947, c David M & Patricia A. **Education:** Univ Toronto, BA, 1949; Univ Alta, MSc, 1960. **Professional Experience:** RETIRED; spec adv, Inland Waters Directorate, 1985-1988; dir, Nat Hydrol Res Inst, 1979-1985; chief, Hydrol Res Div, Environ Can, 1972-1979; head, Groundwater Subdiv, 1970-1972; maritime res sect, 1968-1970; head, Groundwater Div, 1961-1968; asst res officer, Res Coun Alta, 1957-1961; Tech Off, Occup

Health Lab, Dept Nat Health & Welfare Can, 1950-1957. **Memberships:** Geol Soc Am; Geol Asn Can; Nat Water Well Asn. **Research Statement & Publications:** Application of geophysical techniques to shallow groundwater exploration; investigation of analytical methods for the determination of aquifer and well characteristics. **Mailing Address:** 18 Glendenning Dr, Nepean, ON K2H 7Y9, Can.

LENNOX, ROBERT BRUCE, BIOELECTROCHEMISTRY, INTERFACIAL CHEMISTRY, NANOCHEMISTRY. **Personal Data:** b New Orleans, La, June 5, 1957; Canadian citizen; m 1985, c 5. **Education:** Univ Toronto, BSc, 1979, MSc, 1981, PhD (chem), 1985. **Professional Experience:** CHMN, DEPT CHEM, MCGILL UNIV, as of 2003; Tomlinson Prof.2005; Full Prof. 1997, Assoc Prof 1993; Asst Prof, Mcgill Univ, 1987-1993; Res Assoc Chem, Imp Coll, Univ London, 1985-1987. **Memberships:** Electrochem Soc; Chem Inst Can; Amer Chem Soc., Materials Res. Soc. **Research Statement & Publications:** Interfacial reactivity, organized assembly chemistry, bioelectrochemistry, organic thin films, bioelectrocatalysis; Monolayers; Bioorganic mechanisms; Biosensors; Organic chemistry. **Mailing Address:** Dept Chem, Otto Maass Chem Bldg, McGill Univ 801 Sherbrooke St W, Montreal, PQ H3A 2K6, Can. **Fax:** 514-398-3797. **E-Mail:** bruce.lennox@mcgill.ca

LENNOX, WILLIAM C(RAIG), MECHANICS. **Personal Data:** b Mount Forest, Ont, May 22, 1937; m 1961. **Education:** Univ Waterloo, BASc, 1962, MSc, 1963; Lehigh Univ, PhD (mech), 1966. **Professional Experience:** Dean eng, Univ Waterloo, beginning 1982; vis prof, Col Petrol & Minerals, Saudi Arabia, 1970-1971 & Harvey Mudd Col, 1977-1979; chmn dept, Univ Waterloo, 1976-1977 & 1979-1982; prof civil eng, Univ Waterloo, 1971-2005; from asst prof to assoc prof, Univ Waterloo, 1966-1971. **Memberships:** Am Inst Aeronaut & Astronaut; Am Soc Eng Educ; Am Acad Mech. **Research Statement & Publications:** Stochastic processes; nonlinear mechanisms; stochastic processes; nonlinear mechanics; ice research. **Mailing Address:** Dept Civil Eng, Univ Waterloo, 200 Univ Ave W, Waterloo, ON N2L 3G1, Can. **E-Mail:** wclennox@uwaterloo.ca

LE NOBLE, WILLIAM JACOBUS, ORGANIC CHEMISTRY. **Personal Data:** b Rotterdam, Neth, July 19, 1928. **Education:** Advan Tech Sch, Neth, BS, 1949; Univ Chicago, PhD, 1957. **Honors & Awards:** Humboldt Sr Scientist Award. **Professional Experience:** PROF EMER CHEM, STATE UNIV NY STONY BROOK, as of 2004; prof org chem, State Univ Ny Stony Brook, beginning 1969; from asst prof to assoc prof, State Univ NY Stony Brook, 1959-1969; NSF fel & res asst, Purdue Univ, 1958-1959; instr chem, Rosary Col, 1958; Res chemist, Indust Lab, Rohm & Haas Co, 1957; sr ed, J Org Chem. **Memberships:** Am Chem Soc. **Research Statement & Publications:** Chemical kinetics, mechanisms and equilibria in liquid systems under high pressure; face selectivity. **Mailing Address:** Dept Chem, State Univ NY, Albany, NY 12201. **E-Mail:** wlenoble@notes.cc.sunysb.edu

LENOIR, WILLIAM BENJAMIN, GEOPHYSICS, ELECTRICAL ENGINEERING. **Personal Data:** b Miami, Fla, March 14, 1939; m 1964, c 1. **Education:** Mass Inst Technol, BS, 1961, MS, 1962, PhD (elec eng), 1965. **Honors & Awards:** Except Serv Medal, NASA, 1974; Space Flight Medal, NASA, 1982. **Professional Experience:** VPRES, APPL SYST DIV, BOOZ-ALLEN & HAMILTON INC, MD, 1992-; assoc adminr, Space Flight, NASA, 1989-1992; scientist, Booz-Allen & Hamilton, beginning 1984; scientist-astronaut, Johnson Space Ctr, NASA, 1967-1984; asst prof, Mass Inst Technol, 1965-1967; asst elec eng, Ford fel eng, 1965-1966; instr, Mass Inst Technol, 1964-1965; asst elec eng, Mass Inst Technol, 1962-1964. **Memberships:** AAAS; Am Geophys Union. **Research Statement & Publications:** Microwave studies of planetary atmospheres; propagation of partially polarized waves. **Mailing Address:** Booz-Allen & Hamilton Inc, 8283 Greensboro Dr, McLean, VA 22102.

LENOIR, WILLIAM CANNON, JR, BOTANY. **Personal Data:** b Loudon, Tenn, September 22, 1929; m 1956, c 3. **Education:** Maryville Col, BS, 1951; Univ Ga, MS, 1962, PhD (bot), 1965. **Professional Experience:** DEAN BOT, COLUMBUS COL, as of 2003; PROF BOT, COLUMBUS COL, 1973-; chmn div sci & math, Columbus Col, beginning 1973; from asst prof to assoc prof bot, Columbus Col, 1962-1973; asst prof biol, Columbus Col, 1960-1962; instr high sch, Tenn, 1957-1959. **Memberships:** Am Inst Biol Sci; Bot Soc Am. **Research Statement & Publications:** Role of light in morphogenesis; organogenesis in pine; morphogenesis of the leaf of Lygodium japonicum. **Mailing Address:** Dept Biol, Columbus Col, Columbus, GA 31907.

LENON, HERBERT LEE, FISH BIOLOGY. **Personal Data:** b Battle Creek, Mich, June 8, 1939; m 1962, c 3. **Education:** Albion Col, AB, 1961; Wayne State Univ, MS, 1964; Mich State Univ, PhD (fisheries), 1968. **Professional Experience:** PROF EMER FISHERIES BIOL & ICHTHYOL, CENT MICH UNIV, as of 2003; assoc prof fisheries biol & ichthyol, Cent Mich Univ, beginning 1974; asst prof, 1967-1974. **Memberships:** Am Fisheries Soc; Nat Audubon Soc; Nat Wildlife Fedn. **Research Statement & Publications:** Freshwater fish population dynamics; management evaluation. **Mailing Address:** Dept Biol, Cent Mich Univ, 150 W Prestone Dr, Mt Pleasant, MI 48859-0021. **E-Mail:** lenon1hl@cmich.edu

LENOX, RONALD SHEAFFER, POLYMER CHEMISTRY, FIRE RETARDANT CHEMISTRY. **Personal Data:** b Lancaster, Pa, January 25, 1948; m 1971, Barbara; c Jason Frederic. **Education:** Juniata Col, BS, 1969; Univ Ill, PhD (org chem), 1973. **Professional Experience:** CONSULT, 2003-; sr prin scientist, Armstrong World Industs, 1990-2003; res unit mgr, Armstrong World Industs, 1979-1990; asst prof chem, Wabash Col, Crawfordsville, Ind, 1973-1979. **Memberships:** Am Chem Soc. **Research Statement & Publications:** Sulfonyl azide chemistry; polymer blends and alloys; fire retardant chemistry; corosion chem, elastomeric foams. **Mailing Address:** 384 Grace Ridge Dr, Lancaster, PA 17601.

LENSCHOW, DONALD HENRY, METEOROLOGY. **Personal Data:** b LaCrosse, Wis, July 17, 1938; m 1964, Janette; c Christine & Audrey. **Education:** Univ Wis, BS, 1960, MS, 1962, PhD (meteorol), 1966. **Professional Experience:** SR SCIENTIST & HEAD, NAT CTR ATMOSPHERIC RES, 1988-; affil prof, Colo State Univ, 1974-1985 & Univ Colo, 1989-1994; sr scientist, Mesoscale Res Sect, Nat Ctr Atmospheric Res, 1979-1987; staff scientist, Nat Ctr Atmospheric Res, 1975-1978; actg mgr, Res Aviation Facility, Nat Ctr Atmospheric, 1974; from scientist to chief scientist, Nat Ctr Atmospheric Res, 1965-1978. **Memberships:** Fel Am Meteorol Soc. **Research Statement & Publications:** Atmospheric boundary layer; airborne turbulence measurements and airplane research instrumentation f; air/surface exchange measurements and biogeochemical cycles. **Mailing Address:** Nat Ctr Atmospheric Res, PO Box 3000, Boulder, CO 80307. **E-Mail:** lenschow@ncar.ucar.edu

LENSKI, RICHARD E, POPULATION BIOLOGY MICROORGANISMS. **Personal Data:** b Ann Arbor, Mich, August 13, 1956. **Education:** Oberlin Col, BA, 1977; Univ NC, PhD (zool), 1982. **Honors & Awards:** Pres Award, Am Soc Naturalists, 1986 & 1992; MacArthur Fel, John D & Catherine T MacArthur Found, 1996. **Professional Experience:** JOHN A HANNAH DISTINGUISHED PROF MICROBIAL ECOL, MICH STATE UNIV, as of 2004; Vis fel, All Souls Col, Oxford, 1992-1993; fel, J S Guggenheim Mem Found, 1992-1993; hannah prof microbial ecol, Mich State Univ, beginning 1991; mem, Comt Life Sci, Nat Res Coun, 1990-; mem, Bd Biol, 1990-; pres young investr, NSF, 1988-1993; from asst prof to assoc prof ecol & evol biol, Univ Calif, Irvine, 1985-1991; Vis asst prof biol sci, Dartmouth Col, 1984; Res assoc, Univ Mass, 1982-1985. **Memberships:** Am Soc Microbiol; Am Soc Naturalists; Ecol Soc Am; Genetics Soc Am; Soc Study Evol. **Research Statement & Publications:** Experimental study of ecological and evolutionary dynamics using microorganisms; coevolution of parasites and hosts; causes and consequences of mutation. **Mailing Address:** Dept Zool, Mich State Univ 356 Plant & Soil Sci Bldg, East Lansing, MI 48824. **E-Mail:** lenski@msu.edu

LENSTRA, HENDRIK W, NUMBER THEORY. **Personal Data:** b Zaaadax, Neth, April 16, 1949. **Education:** Univ Amsterdam, PhD (math), 1977. **Honors & Awards:** Fulkerson Prize, AMS & Parisenne Soc, 1985; Royal Dutch Acad Serv Prize; Spinoza Prize, Dutch Orgn Scientific Res, 1998. **Professional Experience:** PROF MATH, UNIV LEIDEN, as of 2005; PROF EMER MATH, UNIV CALIF, as of 2005; prof math, Univ Amsterdam, beginning 1978. **Memberships:** Am Math Soc; Dutch Math Soc. **Research Statement & Publications:** Algorithmic number theories which interface with computersciences and algebraic number theories. **Mailing Address:** Math Inst, Univ Leiden, Postbus 9512 Niels Bohrweg One, Leiden, 2300 RA, Netherlands. **Fax:** 71-527-7101. **E-Mail:** hwl@math.leidenuniv.nl

LENTINI, EUGENE ALFRED ANTHONY, PATHOLOGY. **Personal Data:** b Boston, Mass, July 6, 1929; m 1951, c Eugene Jr, J Blaise, Mark & Dirk. **Education:** Boston Univ, AB, 1951, MA, 1955, PhD (myocardial metab), 1958. **Professional Experience:** CONSULT BIOHAZARD MED, 1985-; res assoc prof surg, Pa Med Col, 1982-1984; adj prof physiol, Sch Vet Med, Univ Pa, 1981-1984; scientist, Vet Admin Hosp, Philadelphia, 1981-1982; assoc prof, Dept Physiol & Pharmacol, Philadelphia Col Osteopath Med, 1977-1981; vis prof, Mass State Col & Univ Lowell, 1975-1977; assoc prof physiol, Albany Col Pharm, 1968-1975; asst prof, Med Col Va, 1964-1968; Heart & Lung res awards, 1960-1965 & 1969-1972; instr physiol, Med Sch, Univ Ore, 1958-1964; Nat Heart & Lung Inst fel, 1956-1958; grant awards, Nat Heart, Lung & Blood Inst, Am Heart Asn, Ore Heart, Va Heart, Am Osteop Asn, AMA & NIH. **Memberships:** Sigma Xi; NY Acad Sci; AAAS; Am Physiol Soc; Am Heart Asn; Am Asn Univ Prof. **Research Statement & Publications:** Bioelectronics, electronic micrometer, chart viewer; biophysics determination of oxygen diffusion coefficient through heart muscle; biochemical interrelation between ventricular dynamics and oxidative metabolism; effects of metabolic inhibitors on endogenous substrate; analysis of endogenous lipids and glycogen; physiological myocardial contract as related to substrate utilization; myocardial infarct model; vascular effects of catheterization; oncology and smooth muscle dynamics; 40 publications. **Mailing Address:** 221 Canterbury Dr, Broomall, PA 19008.

LENTON, PHILIP ALFRED, chemical engineering; deceased, see previous edition for last biography

LENTZ, BARRY R, BLOOD COAGULATION, CELLULAR FUSION. **Personal Data:** b Philadelphia, Pa, September 2, 1944; m 1966, c 3. **Education:** Univ Pa, BA, 1966; Cornell Univ, PhD, 1973. **Professional Experience:** Fac Dir, Univ NC Macromolecular Interactions Facil, 1996-1999; DIR, UNIV NC PROG MOLECULAR & CELLULAR BIOPHYS, 1995-; PROF, DEPT BIOCHEM, UNIV NC, CHAPEL HILL, 1988-; estab investr, Am Heart Asn, 1979-1984; from asst prof to assoc prof, Dept Biochem, Univ NC, Chapel Hill, 1975-1988; NIH fel biophys, Dept Biochem, Univ Va Sch Med, 1973-1975; vis scientist biophysics, Weitmann Inst Sci, 1972. **Memberships:** Am Chem Soc; Am Heart Asn; Am Soc Biochem & Molecular Biol; AAAS; N Am Thermal Anal Soc; Biophys Soc. **Research Statement & Publications:** Physical chemistry used for the solution of biologically relevant problems; platelet-derived membranes in blood coagulation; poly ethylene glycol induced cellular fusion. **Mailing Address:** Dept Biochem & Biophys, Univ NC, 418A Fac Lab Off Bldg 231H, Chapel Hill, NC 27514. **Fax:** 919-966-2852. **E-Mail:** uncbrl@med.unc.edu

LENTZ, CHARLES WESLEY, CHEMISTRY, SILICON CHEMISTRY. **Personal Data:** b Mt Pleasant, Mich, May 6, 1924. **Education:** Mich State Univ, BS, 1946. **Honors & Awards:** Sigma Xi Award, 1965. **Professional Experience:** RETIRED; chmn, Midland County Historical Soc, beginning 1999; bd dir, Chippewa Nature Ctr, 1989-1995; chmn, Sci Affairs Comt, Chem Specialities Mfg Asn, 1979-1981; dir health & environ sci, Dow Corning Corp, 1977-1986; mgr life sci res & develop, Dow Corning Corp, 1975-1977; mgr res, Dow Corning Corp, 1970-1975; mgr develop, Dow Corning Corp, 1968-1970; mem comt MC-B5, Hwy Res Bd, Nat Acad Sci-Nat Res Coun, 1967-1980; supvr develop, Dow Corning Corp, 1961-1968; chemist, Dow Corning Corp, 1955-1961; Columbia-Southern Div, Pittsburgh Plate Glass Co, 1952-1955; Chemist, Mich Chem Corp, 1946-1952. **Research Statement & Publications:** Study of silica as a reinforcing agent for silicone rubber, silicate minerals and the silicate structure changes that occur in portland cement during hydration. **Mailing Address:** 5105 Foxcroft, Midland, MI 48642.

LENTZ, DAVID LEWIS, MESOAMERICAN ARCHAEOLOGICAL BOTANY, ETHNOBOTANY. **Personal Data:** b Lima, Ohio, September 25, 1951. **Education:** Washington & Jefferson Col, BA, 1973; Eastern NMex Univ, MA, 1979; Univ Ala, PhD (biol & bot), 1984. **Professional Experience:** Vis prof biol, NY Univ, 1996-; asst prof adj, Sch Forestry, Yale Univ, 1996-; Adj asst prof anthrop, Columbia Univ, 1996-; DIR, GRAD STUDIES PROG, NY BOT GARDEN, 1973-. **Research Statement & Publications:** Subsistance and medicinal plant use practices of Central American people, both past and present. **Mailing Address:** NY Bot Garden, Bronx, NY 10458.

LENTZ, GARY LYNN, ECONOMIC ENTOMOLOGY. **Personal Data:** b Hollywood, Calif, July 15, 1943; m 1965, Aneita; c Carol, Jeffrey, Ann, Jonathan, Janeita & Shellaine. **Education:** Univ Mo-Columbia, AB, 1965; Iowa State Univ, PhD (entom), 1973. **Professional Experience:** ASSOC PROF ENTOM, AGR EXP STA, UNIV TENN, 1980-; asst prof, Agr Exp Sta, Univ Tenn, 1974-1980; asst prof, Univ Ariz, 1972-1974; res assoc entom, Iowa State Univ, 1968-1972. **Memberships:** Entom Soc Am. **Research Statement & Publications:** Pest management of cotton and soybean insects. **Mailing Address:** Dept Entom, Univ Tenn, 605 Airways Blvd, Jackson, TN 38301. **Fax:** 731-425-4760. **E-Mail:** glentz@utk.edu

LENTZ, MARK STEVEN, ENERGY CONSERVATION, SPECIALTY ENVIRONMENT DESIGN. **Personal Data:** b Madison, Wis, July 3, 1949; m 1980, Duyuan. **Education:** Univ Wis-Madison, BSME, 1978. **Honors & Awards:** Energy Award, Am Soc Heating, Refrigerating & Air Conditioning Engrs, 1988. **Professional Experience:** PRES, LENTZ ENG ASSOC INC, 1995-; sr proj engr, PSJ Eng, Inc, 1991-1995; corresp mem, TC 9.8-Large Bldg Air Conditioning Appln, Am Soc Heating, Refrigerating & Air Conditioning Engrs, Inc, 1988-; mem, TC 9.2-Indust Air Conditioning, Am Soc Heating, Refrigerating & Air Conditioning Engrs, Inc, 1985-1989; chmn, TC 9.8-Large Bldg Air Conditioning Appln, Am Soc Heating, Refrigerating & Air Conditioning Engrs, Inc, 1984-1988; sr mech engr, Donohue & Assocs, Inc, 1983-1991; proj engr, Affil Engrs, Inc, 1976-1981 & Stanley Consults, 1981-1983. **Memberships:** Am Soc Heating Refrigerating & Air Conditioning Engrs; Nat Fire Protection Asn. **Research Statement & Publications:** Advanced systems design for high-tech laboratory and specialty environment employing variable-volume ventilation and evaporative cooling; author of three publications. **Mailing Address:** Lentz Eng Assoc Inc, Sheboygan Falls, WI 53044. **Fax:** 920-467-1255. **E-Mail:** mlentz@lentzEng.com

LENTZ, MICHAEL R, MEDICAL RESEARCH. **Education:** Muhlenberg Col, BS, 1981; Univ Ala, PhD, 1986. **Professional Experience:** ASSOC PROF & PREMEDICAL ADV, UNIV N FLA, as of 2005. **Mailing Address:** Dept Biol Univ N Fla, 4567 St Johns Bluff Rd S, Jacksonville, FL 32224-2661. **E-Mail:** mlentz@unf.edu

LENTZ, PAUL JACKSON, BIOCHEMISTRY, X-RAY CRYSTALLOGRAPHY. **Personal Data:** b Niagara Falls, NY, October 10, 1944; m 1968, c 2. **Education:** Univ Alaska, BS, 1966; Purdue Univ, PhD (molecular biol), 1971; Univ Miami, MD, 1984. **Professional Experience:** MED PRACT, 1987-; med resident, Univ Mich Hosps, 1984-1987; asst prof biol, Kings's Col, 1978-1982; lectr chem, Univ Mich, 1976-1978; scholar chem, Univ Mich, 1975-1978; fel biol, Wallenberg Lab, Uppsala Univ, Sweden, 1971-1975; NIH grant, 1971-1973. **Memberships:** AMA; Am Acad Family Phys. **Research Statement & Publications:** X-ray crystallographic structure determination of proteins, nucleic acids and viruses. **Mailing Address:** 304 State St, Adrian, MI 49221-2933.

LENTZ, PAUL LEWIS, MYCOLOGY. **Personal Data:** b Indianapolis, Ind, May 26, 1918; m 1943, c 2. **Education:** Butler Univ, AB, 1940; Univ Iowa, MS, 1942, PhD (mycol), 1953. **Professional Experience:** RETIRED; chief, Mycol Lab, Sci & Educ Admin-Age Res, 1972-1983; instr advan educ sci, Grad Sch-Found, 1958-1971; mycologist, Plant Sci Res Div, 1956-1972; assoc mycologist, Plant Indust Sta, USDA, 1947-1956; asst mycol, Univ Iowa, 1940-1942, 1946-1947; bact lab, Butler Univ, 1940; asst bot lab, Butler Univ, 1938-1940. **Memberships:** Bot Soc Am; Mycol Soc Am; Int Soc Plant Taxon; Sigma Xi. **Research Statement & Publications:** Basidiomycete taxonomy, anatomy, morphology and biology; Aphyllophorales; National Fungus Collections. **Mailing Address:** Five Orange Ct, Greenbelt, MD 20770-1609.

LENTZ, RODRICK D, SOIL PHYSICS. **Education:** Portland State Univ, BS, 1974; Ore State Univ, BS, 1979, MS, 1985; Univ Minn, PhD (soil sci), 1991. **Honors & Awards:** Advan Surface Irrig Award, Am Soc Agri Engrs, 2003. **Professional Experience:** SOIL SCIENTIST, USDA AGR RES SERV NW IRRIG SOILS RES LAB, 1995-; postdoctoral fel, USDA Agr Res Serv NW Irrig Soils Res Lab, 1991 - 1995. **Mailing Address:** USDA Agr Res Serv NW Irrig Soils Res Lab, 3793 N 3600 E, Kimberly, ID 83341. **E-Mail:** Lentz@nwisrl.ars.usda.gov

LENTZ, THOMAS LAWRENCE, ACETYLCHOLINE RECEPTOR, RABIES VIRUS. **Personal Data:** b Toledo, Ohio, March 25, 1939; m 1961, Judith; c Stephen, Christopher & Sarah. **Education:** Yale Univ, MD, 1964. **Professional Experience:** PROF CELL BIOL, SCH MED, YALE UNIV, as of 2005; VCHMN CELL BIOL, SCH MED, YALE UNIV, as of 2005; ASSOC DEAN ADMIS, SCH MED, YALE UNIV, beginning 1976; assoc prof cell biol, Sch Med, Yale Univ, 1974-1985; assoc prof cytol, Sch Med, Yale Univ, 1969-1974; From instr to asst prof anat, Sch Med, Yale Univ, 1964-1969. **Memberships:** AAAS; Am Soc Cell Biol; Soc Neuroscience. **Research Statement & Publications:** Characterization of functional domains on the acetylcholine receptor; identification of cellular receptors for rabies virus. **Mailing Address:** Dept Cell Biol, Yale Univ Sch Med 333 Cedar St, New Haven, CT 06510. **Fax:** 203-785-7226. **E-Mail:** thomas.lentz@yale.edu

LENTZNER, HAROLD, PUBLIC HEALTH & EPIDEMIOLOGY. **Personal Data:** b Chicago, Ill, May 1, 1943. **Education:** Occidental Col, BA, 1965; Univ Wis, MA, 1967; Univ Pa, PhD (demog), 1987. **Professional Experience:** CONSULT as of 2003; spec asst, chronic dis & aging studies, Off analysis, epidemiol & health prom, beginning 1993; epidemiologist, ctr dis control & prev, 1989-1993. **Memberships:** Pop Asn Am; Am Pub Health Asn. **Mailing Address:** 4211 Van Buren St, Hyattsville, MD 20782. **Fax:** 301-436-8459. **E-Mail:** pamlenz@orcasonline.com

LENZ, ALFRED C, GEOLOGY. **Personal Data:** b Olds, Alta, January 6, 1929; m 1954, c 2. **Education:** Univ Alta, BSc, 1954, MSc, 1956; Princeton Univ, PhD (paleont), 1959. **Professional Experience:** PROF GEOL, UNIV WESTERN ONT, 1980-; prof paleont & stratig, Univ Western Ont, 1975-1980; from asst prof to assoc prof, Univ Western Ont, 1964-1975; Lectr, Univ Alta, 1960-1961; Paleontologist, Calif Standard Co, 1959-1964. **Memberships:** Int Palaeont Asn; Paleont Soc; Can Palaeont Asn. **Research Statement & Publications:** Lower Paleozoic biostratigraphy; Devonian stratigraphy and paleontology; graptolite biostratigraphy; Upper Silurian and Lower Devonian brachiopods. **Mailing Address:** Dept Geol, Univ Western Ont Middlesex Coll, London, ON N6A 5B7, Can.

LENZ, GEORGE H, NUCLEAR PHYSICS. **Personal Data:** b Irvington, NJ, October 9, 1939; m 1961, c 2. **Education:** Rutgers Univ, BA, 1961, MS, 1963, PhD (physics), 1967. **Professional Experience:** RETIRED; dean dept, Sweet Briar Col, 1989-2001; Whitney-Guion prof physics, sweet Briar Col, 1976-2004; chmn dept, Sweet Briar Col, beginning 1971; assoc prof, Sweet Briar Col, 1971-1976; asst prof physics, Univ Va, 1967-1971. **Memberships:** Am Phys Soc; Am Asn Physics Teachers. **Research Statement & Publications:** Analogue states; compound nucleus and direct reactions; Coulomb energy systematics. **Mailing Address:** Dept Physics, Sweet Briar Col, Sweet Briar, VA 24595.

LENZ, GEORGE RICHARD, RESEARCH ADMINISTRATION, BIOENGINEERING & BIOMEDICAL. **Personal Data:** b Chicago, Ill, November 22, 1941; m 1970, c 3. **Education:** Ill Inst Technol, BS, 1963; Univ Chicago, MS, 1965, PhD (chem), 1967; Northwestern Univ, MBA, 1983. **Professional Experience:** DIR HEALTH CARE RES & DEVELOP, BOC GROUP TECH CTR, MURRAY HILL, NJ, 1985-; sect head, G D Searle & Co, 1971-1985; res investr, 1969-1971; Nat Cancer Inst fel, Yale Univ, 1967-1969. **Memberships:** AAAS; Am Chem Soc; Royal Soc Chem. **Research Statement & Publications:** Photochemistry; medicinal chemistry. **Mailing Address:** Grlen Res & Develop Assoc, Six Apple Blossom Rd, Andover, MA 01810.

LENZ, PAUL HEINS, PHYSIOLOGY, ENDOCRINOLOGY, CELL & MOLECULAR BIOLOGY. **Personal Data:** b Newark, NJ, March 29, 1938; m 1960, c 5. **Education:** Franklin & Marshall Col, BS, 1960; Rutgers Univ, MS, 1964, PhD (endocrinol), 1966. **Honors & Awards:** Merit Award, Am Asn Clin Chem. **Professional Experience:** RETIRED; health sci admin, Nat Inst Aging, Nat Inst Health, 1993-2000; prof biol sci, Fairleigh Dickinson Univ, 1980-1993; assoc prof physiol, Fairleigh Dickinson Univ, 1970-1980; Ciba grants, 1970-1971; Eli Lilly grant, 1970; univ res grants, 1968-1971; asst prof, Fairleigh Dickinson Univ, 1966-1970. **Memberships:** Endocrine Soc; Am Oil Chemists' Soc; Am Asn Clin Chemists; Am Heart Asn. **Research Statement & Publications:** Development of microchemical techniques; hormonal and biochemical control of lipid metabolism; platelet aggregation and its control. **Mailing Address:** PO Box 5877, Bethesda, MD 20824. **E-Mail:** paullenz@worldnet.att.net

LENZ, ROBERT WILLIAM, ORGANIC CHEMISTRY. **Personal Data:** b New York, NY, April 28, 1926; m 1953, Madeleine Leblanc; c Kathleen, Douglas, Cynthia & Suzanne. **Education:** Lehigh Univ, BS, 1949; Inst Textile Technol, MS, 1951; State Univ NY, PhD (polymer chem), 1956. **Honors & Awards:** Sr Humboldt Prize, 1979; Am Chem Soc Award in Polymer Chem, 1992. **Professional Experience:** RETIRED; adj prof chem, Univ Mass, Amherst, as of 2003; Ed-in-chief, Macromolecules, beginning 1995; prof emer polymer sci & eng, Univ Mass, Amherst, 1995-; prof emer polymer sci & eng, Univ Montpelier, France, 1994; prof emer polymer sci & eng, Univ Paris, 1995; Univ Pisa, Italy, 1987; Univ Freiburg, Ger, 1979-1980; Univ Freiburg, Japan Soc Prom Sci, 1979; Royal Inst Technol, Stockholm, Sweden, 1975; vis prof, Univ Mainz, Ger, 1972-1973; from assoc prof to prof, Univ Mass, Amherst, 1966-1995; asst dir, Fabric Res Labs Inc, 1963-1966; res chemist, Eastern Res Lab, 1961-1963; res chemist, Polymer Res Lab, Dow Chem Co, 1955-1961; res chemist, Chicopee Mfg Corp, 1951-1953. **Memberships:** Am Chem Soc; Bio/Environ Degradable Polymer Soc; Am Inst Chem Eng. **Research Statement & Publications:** Monomer and polymer synthesis; kinetics and mechanism of polymerization; structure-property relations of polymers; reactions of polymers; bacterial polyesters; biodegradation of polymers. **Mailing Address:** 43 Aubinwood Rd, Amherst, MA 01002. **Fax:** 413-545-0082. **E-Mail:** rwlenz@polysci.umass.edu

LEO, ALBERT JOSEPH, MEDICAL CHEMISTRY. **Personal Data:** b Winfield, Ill, September 29, 1947; m 1947, c 3. **Education:** Pomona Col, BA, 1948; Univ Chicago, MS, 1949, PhD (chem), 1952. **Professional Experience:** Adj prof, Med Chem Proj, Pomona Col, as of 2001; PRES BIOBYTE CORP, as of 2001; adj asst prof, med chem proj, Pomona Col, beginning 1981; DIR, MED CHEM PROJ, POMONA COL, 1971-; res assoc med chem, 1968-1971. **Memberships:** Sigma Xi; Am Chem Soc. **Research Statement & Publications:** Database of parameters useful in drug design, toxicological and environmental fate studies. **Mailing Address:** Biobyte Corp, 201 W Fourth St 204, Claremont, CA 909624-5992. **Fax:** 909-624-1398. **E-Mail:** aleo@clogp.pomona.edu

LEO, GERHARD WILLIAM, GEOCHEMISTRY, MINERALOGY-PETROLOGY. **Personal Data:** b Frankfurt, WGer, January 31, 1930; American citizen; m 1968, c 2. **Education:** Stanford Univ, BS, 1951, PhD (geol), 1961. **Professional Experience:** RETIRED; res geologist, US Geol Surv, Wash, DC, 1961-1992; vis lectr, Univ Bahia, Salvador, 1959-1961; geologist, US geol surv, Menlo Park Calif, 1957-1959; Stanford Univ, 1956. **Memberships:** Fel Geol Soc Am; Am Geophys Union; Am Soc Testing & Mat. **Research Statement & Publications:** Investigations of early paleozoic; metamorphosed plutonic and volcanic rocks in the northern Appalachians. **Mailing Address:** 1417 Crowell Rd, Vienna, VA 22182.

LEOF, EDWARD B, CELL BIOLOGY. **Personal Data:** b Pittsburgh, Pa, May 9, 1954. **Education:** Purdue Univ, BS, 1976; Univ NC, PhD (cell biol), 1982. **Professional Experience:** ASSOC PROF MED, MAYO CLIN COL MED, as of 2003; PROF BIOCHEM & MOLECULAR BIOL, MAYO CLIN COL MED, as of 2003; from asst prof to assoc prof molecular biol, Vanderbilt Univ, 1985-1992; fel, Mayo Clin, 1983-1985. **Memberships:** Am Soc Cell Biol; Am Asn Cancer Res; AAAS; Sigma Xi. **Research Statement & Publications:** Cell biology. **Mailing Address:** Mayo Clin Col Med, Rochester, MN 55905. **E-Mail:** leof.edward@mayo.edu

LEON, ARTHUR SOL, MEDICAL RESEARCH, NUTRITION. **Personal Data:** b Brooklyn, NY, April 26, 1931; m 1956, Gloria; c Denise, Harmon & Michelle. **Education:** Univ Fla, BS, 1952; Univ Wis-Madison, MS, 1954, MD, 1957. **Honors & Awards:** William G Anderson Award, Am Alliance & Health Phys Educ, 1981; Citation Award, Am Col Sports Med, 1995. **Professional Experience:** PROF, DIVISION KINESIOLOGY, UNIV MINN, MINNEAPOLIS, as of 2004; HENRY L TAYLOR PROF & DIR, LAB PHYSIOL HYG & EXERCISE SCI, DIV KINESIOLOGY, COL EDUC, UNIV MINN, MINNEAPOLIS as of 2004; pres, Hennepin Div, Am Heart Asn, 1983-1984; prof, lab physiol hyg, div epidemiol, Sch Pub Health, Univ Minn, Minneapolis, beginning 1980; sr investr mult coronary risk factor intervention & lipid res clin trials, Univ Minn, Minneapolis, 1973-; dir appl physiol, Nutrit Sect, 1973-1991; chief med cardiol & prof serv, 551st Army Hosp, Ft Snelling, Minn, 1973-1986; assoc prof, Univ Minn, Minneaplolis, 1973-1980; from instr to assoc prof, Col Med & Dent NJ, 1967-1973; dir clin pharmacol, Roche Spec Treatment Unit, Newark Beth Israel Med Ctr, 1967-1973; chief med serv, 322nd Gen Hosp, USAR, Newark, 1967-1973; res assoc, Dept Clin Pharmacol, Hoffmann-La Roche Inc, 1967-1973; mem med eval team, Gemini & Apollo Projs, 1966-1967; res cardiologist, Dept Cardiorespiratory Dis, Walter Reed Army Inst Res, 1964-1967; chief gen med & cardiol, 34th Gen Hosp, US Army, France, 1961-1964; cardiol consult, US Armed Forces, France, 1961-1964; fel cardiol, Sch Med, Univ Miami & Jackson Mem Hosp, 1960-1961; fel internal med, Lahey Clin, Boston, 1958-1960; intern, Henry Ford Hosp, Detroit, 1957-1958. **Memberships:** Am Col Cardiol; Am Col Chest Physicians; Am Physiol Asn; Am Soc Pharmacol & Exp Therapeut; Am Col Sports Med (vpres, 1977-1979); Am Asn Cardiac & Pulmonary Rehab; Am Heart Asn. **Research Statement & Publications:** Prevention of coronary heart disease by risk factor modification; metabolic and cardiovascular effects of exercise; exercise testing; effects of exercise conditioning; evaluation of new cardiovascular and lipid-lowering drugs. **Mailing Address:** Div Kinesiology, Univ Minn, 1900 Univ Ave SE 202 Cooke Hall, Minneapolis, MN 55455. **Fax:** 612-626-7700. **E-Mail:** leonx002@umn.edu

LEON, B(ENJAMIN) J(OSEPH), ELECTRICAL ENGINEERING, TELECOMMUNICATIONS. **Personal Data:** b Austin, Tex, March 20, 1932; m 1954, Maxine; c Nathaniel J, Victoria (Morris), Jennifer A & There. **Education:** Univ Tex, BS, 1954; Mass Inst Technol, SM, 1957, ScD, 1959. **Professional Experience:** RETIRED; prof elec & comput eng, Univ Southwestern La, beginning 1990; sr staff officer, Nat Res Coun, 1988-1990; vis prof, Southern Methodist Univ, 1986-1987; prof elec eng, Univ Ky, Lexington, 1980-1988; chmn dept, Univ Ky, Lexington, 1980-1984; consult, Westinghouse Telecommun, 1980; elec engr, Defense Commun Agency, 1975-1976; Rome Air Develop Ctr fel & vis prof, Cornell Univ, 1968-1969; consult ed, Holt, Rinehart & Winston Series Elec Eng, Electronics & Systs, 1967-1973; ed, Trans Circuit Theory, Inst Elec & Electronics Engrs, 1967-1969; from assoc prof to prof elec eng, Purdue Univ, W Lafayette, 1962-1980; tech staff, Hughes Aircraft Co, 1959-1962; mem staff, Lincoln Lab, Mass Inst Technol, 1954-1959. **Memberships:** Nat Soc Prof Engrs; fel AAAS; fel Inst Elec & Electronics Engrs (vpres, 1979-1980). **Research Statement & Publications:** Communications systems, circuit and system theory; telecommunications management and policy. **Mailing Address:** 200 Cherry St, Lafayette, LA 70506-3626. **E-Mail:** b.leon@ieee.org

LEON, HENRY A, ENVIRONMENTAL PHYSIOLOGY, AEROSPACE BIOLOGY. **Personal Data:** b San Francisco, Calif, September 25, 1928; m 1958, c 3. **Education:** Univ Calif, Berkeley, BS, 1952, PhD (physiol), 1960. **Professional Experience:** PAYLOAD PROJ SCIENTIST, AMES RES CTR, NASA, 1981-; res scientist aerospace biol, Ames Res Ctr, NASA, 1962-1981; Milton res fel path, Harvard Med Sch, 1961-1962; mem staff, Mass Gen Hosp, Boston, 1961-1962; Nat Cancer Inst fel, Wenner-Gren Inst, Stockholm, Sweden, 1960-1961. **Memberships:** Am Physiol Soc; Aerospace Med Asn. **Research Statement & Publications:** Effect of space cabin environments on blood elements;

stress and the control of liver protein synthesis; nutrition and stress. **Mailing Address:** 2371 Richland Ave, San Jose, CA 95125-3644.

LEON, KENNETH ALLEN, FISH BIOLOGY. **Personal Data:** b New York, NY, November 19, 1937; m 1963, c Susan & David. **Education:** Ohio State Univ, BS, 1960; Col William & Mary, MS, 1963; Univ Wash, PhD (fisheries mgt), 1970. **Professional Experience:** RETIRED; regional biologist, Fisheries Rehab Enhancement Div, Douglas, 1988-1992; prin biologist, Fish Rehab, Enhancement & Develop Div, Alaska Dept Fish & Game, Juneau, 1975-1988; res biologist, Tunison Lab Fish Nutrit, US Bur Sport Fisheries & Wildlife, 1971-1974; biol consult, Ichthyol Assocs, 1970-1971. **Memberships:** Am Fisheries Soc. **Research Statement & Publications:** Enhancement and rehabilitation of salmonid species, specialty salmon incubation and hatchery design. **Mailing Address:** 5251 Myakka Valley Trail, Sarasota, FL 34241. **E-Mail:** ihunter@prodigy.com

LEON, MELVIN, EXOTIC ATOMS, MUON SPIN ROTATION. **Personal Data:** b Brooklyn, NY, September 2, 1936; m 1963, Allison; c Jennifer & David. **Education:** Univ Md, BS, 1957; Cornell Univ, PhD (physics), 1961. **Professional Experience:** LOS ALAMOS NAT LAB; mem staff, Los Alamos Nat Lab, 1972-1993; asst prof physics, Rensselaer Polytech Inst, 1966-1972; res physicist, Carnegie Inst Technol, 1963-1966; Imp Chem Industs res fel & NSF fel theoret physics, Univ Birmingham, 1961-1963. **Memberships:** Fel Am Phys Soc. **Research Statement & Publications:** Exotic atoms; muon spin rotation; muon-catalyzed fusion. **Mailing Address:** 283 El Conejo St, Los Alamos, NM 87544-2428. **E-Mail:** melleon@msn.com

LEON, MICHAEL ALLAN, EARLY LEARNING, NEUROBIOLOGY. **Personal Data:** b New York, NY, November 23, 1947; m 1970, c 2. **Education:** Brooklyn Col, BS, 1968; Univ Chicago, PhD (biopsychol), 1972. **Professional Experience:** Assoc ed, Develop Psychobiol, 1985-; PROF PSYCHOBIOL, UNIV CALIF, IRVINE, 1984-; assoc prof, Univ Calif, Irvine, 1980-1984; from asst prof to assoc prof psychol, McMaster Univ, 1972-1980. **Memberships:** Soc Neuroscience; Int Soc Develop Psychobiol; Asn Chemoreception Sci. **Research Statement & Publications:** Neurobiology of early learning; published over 20 articles. **Mailing Address:** Dept Psychobiol Univ Calif Irvine, 2205McGaugh Hall, Irvine, CA 92697-4550. **Fax:** 949-824-2447. **E-Mail:** mleon@uci.edu

LEON, MYRON A, IMMUNOLOGY. **Personal Data:** b Troy, NY, July 13, 1926. **Education:** Columbia Univ, BS, 1950, PhD (biochem), 1954. **Professional Experience:** PROF IMMUNOL, SCH MED, WAYNE STATE UNIV, as of 2004; assoc head path res, St Luke's Hosp, 1964-1974; fel, Univ Lund, Sweden, 1958; assoc surg res, St Luke's Hosp, 1953-1964. **Memberships:** Am Asn Immunol; AAAS; Am Soc Microbiol. **Research Statement & Publications:** Immunochemistry; mechanisms of natural resistance to infection; complement; myeloma proteins; lymphocyte stimulation. **Mailing Address:** Dept Immunol, Wayne State Univ Sch Med, 7374 Scott Hall 540 E Canfield, Detroit, MI 48201-1998. **E-Mail:** mleon@cms.cc.wayne.edu

LEON, RAMON V, RELIABILITY THEORY, STOCHASTIC INEQUALITIES. **Personal Data:** b Holguin, Oriente, Cuba, September 29, 1948; m 1995, Susana. **Education:** Fla State Univ, BS, 1972, MS, 1976, PhD (statist), 1979; Tulane Univ, MS, 1975. **Honors & Awards:** Ralph A Bradley Award, Fla State Univ, 1979. **Professional Experience:** ASSOC PROF, UNIV TENN, 1981-as of today; asst prof statist, Rutgers Univ, 1979-1981; vis instr statist, Fla State Univ, 1978-1979. **Memberships:** Inst Math Statist; Am Statist Asn; Am Soc Quality Control. **Research Statement & Publications:** Reliability; robust design; statistical process control. **Mailing Address:** Dept Statist, Univ Tn, 331 Stokely Mgt Ctr, Knoxville, TN 37996-0532. **Fax:** 865-974-2490. **E-Mail:** rleon@utk.edu

LEON, ROBERT LEONARD, MEDICINE, PSYCHIATRY. **Personal Data:** b Denver, Colo, January 18, 1925; m 1947, Willena; c Alexis Kay (Sigurani), Mark Robert, Jeffrey Clayton & Stacy Lee. **Education:** Univ Colo, MD, 1948. **Professional Experience:** PROF EMER, UNIV TEX HEALTH SCI CTR SAN ANTONIO, 2003-; ashbel smith prof, Univ Tex Health Sci Ctr, San Antonio, 1990-2003; consult, Audie Murphy Mem Vet Hosp, 1973-; mem psychiat training rev comt, NIMH, 1967-1995; prof psychiat & chmn dept, Univ Tex Health Sci Ctr San Antonio, 1967-1996; consult, Bur Indian Affairs, 1962-1967; consult regional off VI, NIMH, 1957-1973; from asst prof to prof psychiat, Southwest Med Sch, Univ Tex, 1957-1967; chief ment health serv, USPHS, Mo, 1954-1957; asst dir & act dir child psychiat, Greater Kansas City Ment Health Found, 1953-1954; resident child psychiat, State Dept Health, Conn, 1952-1953; resident psychiat, Med Ctr, Univ Colo, 1949-1952; intern, Univ Hosp, Ann Arbor, Mich, 1948-1949. **Memberships:** Life Fel Am Psychiat Asn; Fel Am Col Psychiatrists (pres, 1987-1988); Life Fel Am Orthopsychiat Asn; Life Fel Am Acad Child Psychiat; AMA; Fel Am Asn Soc Psychiatrists (pres, 1990-1992). **Research Statement & Publications:** Social psychiatry; Transcultural psychiatry. **Mailing Address:** Dept Psychiat, Univ Tex Health Sci Ctr, 7703 Floyd Curl Dr, San Antonio, TX 78229-3900. **Fax:** 210-567-6941. **E-Mail:** leon@uthscsa.edu

LEON, SHALOM A, BIOCHEMISTRY, RADIOBIOLOGY. **Personal Data:** b Sofia, Bulgaria, April 7, 1935; m 1962, c 3. **Education:** Hebrew Univ, Jerusalem, MSc, 1960, PhD (pharmacol), 1964. **Professional Experience:** DIR, RADIATION RES LAB, ALBERT EINSTEIN MED CTR, 1979-; ASSOC PROF RADIOBIOLOGY, SCH MED, TEMPLE UNIV, 1979-; mem bioscience staff, Sch Med, Temple Univ, 1968-; res assoc biochem, Ind Univ, 1965-1967; jr res asst pharmacol, Med Sch, Hebrew Univ, Jerusalem, 1960-1964. **Memberships:** Am Asn Cancer Res; AAAS; Radiation Res Soc; Am Chem Soc; NY Acad Sci; Am Asn Immunol. **Research Statement & Publications:** Mechanism of antibiotic action; biosynthesis of nucleic acids and proteins; use of radioactive isotopes in clinical research and diagnosis; relationship between structure and biological activity of toxins from microorganisms; effect of radioprotective agents against ionizing radiation. **Mailing Address:** Radiation Res Lab, Albert Einstein Med Ctr, York & Tabor Rd, Philadelphia, PA 19141-3098.

LEONARD, ANTHONY, ENGINEERING. **Personal Data:** b June 2, 1938; American citizen; m 1960, c 2. **Education:** Calif Inst Technol, BS, 1959; Stanford Univ, MS, 1960, PhD (nuclear eng), 1963. **Honors & Awards:** Edward Teller Award, 1963. **Professional Experience:** EMER PROF, THEODORE VON KARMAN PROF AERONAUT ENG, CALIF INST TECHNOL, 2005-; prof aeronaut eng, Theodore Von Karman, Calif Inst Technol, 2000-2005; prof aeronaut eng, Calif Inst Technol, 1985-2000; res scientist, NASA Ames Res Ctr, 1975-1985; NASA Ames Res Ctr sr fel, 1973-1975; from asst prof to assoc prof mech eng, Stanford Univ, 1966-1973; lectr, Calif Inst Technol, 1965-1966; mem tech staff, Rand Corp, 1963-1966; consult, Gen Elec Co. **Memberships:** Am Phys Soc; Soc Indust & Appl Math. **Research Statement & Publications:** Nuclear reactor theory; particle transport theory; turbulence theory; numerical fluid mechanics. **Mailing Address:** Aeronaut Labs, Calif Inst Technol, 1200 E Calif Blvd, Pasadena, CA 91125. **Fax:** 626-449-2677. **E-Mail:** tony@galcit.caltech.edu

LEONARD, ARNOLD S, SURGERY. **Personal Data:** b Minneapolis, Minn, October 26, 1930; m 1950, c 4. **Education:** Univ Minn, Minneapolis, BA, 1952, BS, 1953, MD, 1955, PhD (surg path), 1963. **Professional Experience:** PROF SURG, UNIV MINN, MINNEAPOLIS, 1973-; from asst prof to assoc prof, 1963-1973; univ fel, 1956-1963. **Memberships:** Am Soc Artificial Internal Organs; Am Soc Exp Path; Int Soc Hist Med; Soc Univ Surg; Am Pediat Surg Asn; Sigma Xi. **Research Statement & Publications:** Gastrointestinal physiology; hypothalamic stimulation and study of gastric secretion; transplantation; extracorporeal organ perfusion; pediatric surgery; computer technology. **Mailing Address:** Dept Surg, Univ Minn, Riverside Prof Bldg 606 24th Ave S, Minneapolis, MN 55454-1419. **Fax:** 612-341-2659.

LEONARD, B(ENJAMIN) F(RANKLIN), III, MINERALOGY & PETROLOGY. **Personal Data:** b Dobbs Ferry, NY, May 12, 1921; m 1950, Eleanor; c 2. **Education:** Hamilton Col, BS, 1942; Princeton Univ, MA, 1947, PhD (geol), 1951. **Honors & Awards:** Meritorious Serv Award, US Dept Interior, 1988. **Professional Experience:** RETIRED; geologist, ORE Micros Lab, US Geol Survay beginning 1993; adj prof, Colo Sch Mines, 1990-; regional counr NAm, Int Asn Genesis Ore Deposits, 1984-1989; vchmn, Int Comn Ore Micros, 1982-1986; mem, Int Comn Ore Micros, 1968-1970; geologist-in-charge, Ore Micros Lab, US Geol Surv, 1962-1993; from jr geologist to geologist, Ore Micros Lab, US Geol Surv, 1943-1993; geol field asst, Geol Surv Nfld, 1942. **Memberships:** Fel Mineral Soc Am; fel Geol Soc Am; fel Soc Econ Geol; Soc Geol Appl Mineral Deposits; Mineral Asn Can; Asn Explor Geochemists. **Research Statement & Publications:** Ore deposits, especially gold, iron and tungsten; geology of central Idaho and northwest Adirondacks; ore minerals; rock-forming minerals; geochemical and biogeochemical exploration. **Mailing Address:** US Geol Surv, Reston, VA 80401-2587.

LEONARD, BILLIE CHARLES, instructional behavior, instructional technology; deceased, see previous edition for last biography

LEONARD, BOWEN RAYDO, PHYSICS. **Personal Data:** b Houston, Tex, March 7, 1926; div, c 2. **Education:** Tex Western Col, BS, 1947; Univ Wis, MS, 1949, PhD (physics), 1952. **Professional Experience:** RETIRED; ad-hoc mem, nuclear cross sect adv group, Atomic Energy Comn, beginning 1969; sr staff scientist, Pac Northwest Lab, Battelle Mem Inst, 1967-1982; mem cross sect eval working group, nuclear cross sect adv group, Atomic Energy Comn, beginning 1966; mgr exp physics res, Pac Northwest Lab, Battelle Mem Inst, 1965-1967; mgr exp physics res, Hanford Labs, Gen Elec Co, 1957-1964; mem, nuclear cross sect adv group, Atomic Energy Comn, 1957-1963; sr scientist, Hanford Labs, Gen Elec Co, 1953-1957; physicist, Hanford Labs, Gen Elec Co, 1952-1953; asst, Univ Wis, 1947-1951. **Memberships:** Fel Am Phys Soc; Am Nuclear Soc; Sigma Xi. **Research Statement & Publications:** Neutron cross section measurements; nuclear physics; x-ray scattering; slow neutron in-elastic scattering studies of solids and liquids. **Mailing Address:** 212 S Morain St, Kennewick, WA 99336.

LEONARD, BRIAN PHILLIP, PLASMA PHYSICS, FLUID MECHANICS. **Personal Data:** b Melbourne, Australia, June 4, 1936; m 1964, c 2. **Education:** Univ Melbourne, BS, 1958; Cornell Univ, MS, 1961, PhD (aerospace eng), 1965. **Professional Experience:** PROF EMER MECH ENG, UNIV AKRON, as of 2004; prof mech eng, Univ Akron, beginning 1982; assoc prof, City Univ New York, 1976-1982; asst prof eng sci, Richmond Col NY, 1970-1976; Air Force Off Sci Res assoc plasma physics, Columbia Univ, 1969-1970; lectr appl math, Monash Univ, Australia, 1967-1968; sr lectr aeronaut eng, Royal Melbourne Inst Technol, 1966-1967; vis asst prof, Cornell Univ, 1965-1966; asst elec eng, Cornell Univ, 1964-1965; asst aerospace eng, Cornell Univ, 1961-1964. **Memberships:** Am Phys Soc; Am Inst Aeronaut & Astronaut; Am Nuclear Soc. **Research Statement & Publications:** High temperature gas dynamics; shock wave structure; magnetically driven shock waves; applied mathematics; control systems; hydrodynamics and ship stability and control; thermonuclear fusion. **Mailing Address:** Dept Mech Eng, Univ Akron, ASEC 419B 302 E Buchtel Mall, Akron, OH 44325. **Fax:** 330-972-6027. **E-Mail:** bleonard@uakron.edu

LEONARD, BYRON PETER, PHYSICS. **Personal Data:** b Morgan City, La, February 26, 1925; m 1946. **Education:** Southwestern La Univ, BS, 1943; Univ Tex, MA, 1952, PhD, 1953. **Professional Experience:** VPRES & GEN MGR EL SEGUNDO TECH OPERS & GROUP VPRES, PROGS GROUP, AEROSPACE CORP, 1968-; vpres & gen mgr, Man Orbiting Lab, Systs Eng Off, 1965-1968; dir satellite-missile observation syst prog, Progs Group, Aerospace Corp, 1960-1965; sr staff engr, Space Technol Labs, 1959-1960; chief nuclear res & develop, Gen Dynamics Corp, 1953-1959; instr physics, Southwestern La Univ, 1948-1950 & Univ Tex, 1950-1953; Proj engr, US Naval Ord Test Sta, 1946-1947. **Memberships:** Am Nuclear Soc; Am Inst Aeronaut & Astronaut; Am Chem Soc. **Research Statement & Publications:** Nuclear shielding; radiation effects to materials and operating components; radiation hazards of fission products released to the atmosphere; design of research reactors; design and use of satellite systems, particularly for surveillance applications. **Mailing Address:** 2600 W Farwell Ave, Chicago, IL 60645-4523.

LEONARD, CHARLES BROWN, BIOCHEMISTRY. **Personal Data:** b Woodbury, NJ, May 28, 1934; m 1955, c 2. **Education:** Rutgers Univ, AB, 1955; Univ Md, MS, 1957, PhD (biochem), 1963. **Professional Experience:** PROF EMER, DENT SCH, UNIV MD, BALTIMORE, as of 2006; prof Gallaudet Univ Wash, dent sch, Univ Md, Baltimore, beginnig 1993; chmn dept, Univ Md, Baltimore, 1985-1993; asst dean recruitment & admis, Univ Md, Baltimore, 1977-1985; prof biochem, dent sch, univ md, baltimore, beginning 1976; dir off admis, Univ Md, Baltimore, 1975-1977; consult, Dr H L Wollenweber, clin pathologist, 1959-1961; from instr to assoc prof, Univ Md, Baltimore, 1958-1976; asst, Univ Md, Baltimore, 1955-1958. **Memberships:** AAAS; Am Chem Soc; NY Acad Sci; Am Inst Chem; Am Asn Dent Sch; Sigma Xi. **Research Statement & Publications:** Amino acid incorporation into rat liver ribosomes; effect of divalent ions on structure of rat liver RNA; effect of o, p'-DDD on cellular metabolism; metabolic products of o, p'-DDD. **Mailing Address:** Dent Sch, Univ Md, Ellicott City, MD 21042.

LEONARD, CHRISTIANA MORISON, NEUROANATOMY, PSYCHOLOGY. **Personal Data:** b Boston, Mass, January 22, 1938; m 1982, John; c Andrew W, Amy E, Gretchen A Kuldau & J Gustav Kuldau. **Education:** Radcliffe Col, BA, 1959; Mass Inst Technol, PhD (psychol), 1967. **Professional Experience:** PROF EMER NEUROSCIENCE, COL MED, UNIV FLA, as of 2006; prof neuroscience, Col Med, Univ Fla, beginning 1986; assoc prof, Col Med, Univ Fla, 1976-1986; asst prof anat, Mt Sinai Sch Med, 1974-1976; asst prof neuropsychol, Rockefeller Univ, 1971-1974; res assoc, Rockefeller Univ, 1970-1971; USPHS trainee, Rockefeller Univ, 1967-1970. **Memberships:** AAAS; Soc Neuroscience; Sigma Xi; Am Anat Asn; Animal Behav Soc. **Research Statement & Publications:** Neurological basis of language and thought; development of language; learning disabilities and schizophrenia; functional imaging. **Mailing Address:** Dept NeuroSci, Univ Fla, Rm L3-160 100 Newell Dr, Gainesville, FL 32611. **Fax:** 352-392-8347. **E-Mail:** leonard@ufbi.ufl.edu

LEONARD, CLAIRE MARIE, DIABETES RESEARCH, DIABETIC COMPLICATIONS. **Personal Data:** b New York, NY, February 18, 1955. **Education:** Iona Col, BS, 1977; NY Med Col, MS, 1986, PhD (cell biol), 1987. **Professional Experience:** ASSOC PROF

BIOL, WILLIAM PATERSON UNIV, as of 2002; sr scientist, Alteon Inc, beginning 1990; res assoc prof, NY Med Col, 1989-1990; Fel gene regulation during development, Dept Genetics, Albert Einstein Col Med, NY, 1987-1989. **Memberships:** AAAS; Am Soc Cell Biol. **Research Statement & Publications:** Diabetes, diabetic complications. **Mailing Address:** Dept Biol, William Paterson Univ, S503A, 300 Pompton Rd, Wayne, NJ 07470. **E-Mail:** leonardc@wpunj.edu

LEONARD, DAVID E, ENTOMOLOGY. **Personal Data:** b Greenwich, Conn, December 28, 1934; m 1957, c Linda & Robyn. **Education:** Univ Conn, BS, 1956, MS, 1960, PhD (entom), 1964. **Professional Experience:** Assoc dir, Maine Agr Exp Sta, 1979-1982; Mass Agr Exp Sta, 1982-1985; Co-ed, Annals Entom Soc Am, 1978-1983; from assoc prof to prof entom, Univ Maine, Orono, 1970-1980; From asst to assoc entomologist, Conn Agr Exp Sta, 1964-1970; PROF, DEPT ENTOM, UNIV MASS, AMHERST & ACTG DEAN, COL FOOD NAT RES. **Memberships:** Entom Soc Am; Entom Soc Can; Ecol Soc Am; AAAS. **Research Statement & Publications:** Biosystematics, biology and ecology of insects; host-parasite relationships; biology of lymantriidae. **Mailing Address:** Univ Mass, Dept Entom, Fernald Hall, Amherst, MA 01003-0002.

LEONARD, EDWARD CHARLES, JR, POLYMER CHEMISTRY. **Personal Data:** b Burlington, NC, August 21, 1927; m 1952, c 1. **Education:** Univ NC, BS, 1947, PhD (chem), 1951; Univ Chicago, MBA, 1974. **Professional Experience:** FOUNDER, HUME CO INC, as of 2004; PRES & CHIEF EXEC OFFICER, HUME CO INC, 1993-; gen mgr, vpres & officer, 1983-1993; vpres res & develop, Humko Chem Div, Witco Chem Corp, beginning 1980; vpres res & develop, Humko Sheffield Chem Co Div, 1977-1980; vpres & mem Bd Dirs, Enenco, Inc, beginning 1974; tech dir, Humko Sheffield Chem Co Div, 1973-1977; mgr indust chem prod lab, Res & Develop Div, Kraft, Inc, 1967-1973; res mgr, Borden Chem Co, 1964-1967; group leader, Union Carbide Plastic Co, 1956-1964; sr res chemist, Res Dept, Bakelite Co, 1951-1956; Asst, Univ NC, 1947-1950. **Memberships:** Am Chem Soc. **Research Statement & Publications:** Synthetic surface active agents; ionic polymerizations; graft polymers; fatty acids; homogeneous catalysis; chemical economics. **Mailing Address:** Hume Co Inc, 5100 Poplar Ave, Memphis, TN 38137.

LEONARD, EDWARD (FRANCIS), CHEMICAL ENGINEERING & BIOMED ENGINEERING. **Personal Data:** b Paterson, NJ, July 6, 1932; m Gerarda; c Mary, Edward Jr, Gerald, Louise & Joseph. **Education:** Mass Inst Technol, BS, 1953; Univ Pa, MS, 1955, PhD (chem eng), 1960. **Honors & Awards:** Allan P Colburn Award, Am Inst Chem Engrs, 1969. **Professional Experience:** DIR ARTIFICIAL ORGANS RES LABS, COLUMBIA UNIV, 1968-; PROF CHEM ENG, Columbia Univ, 1967-; CHMN BIOENG COMN, Columbia Univ, 1965-1968, 1991-1994; VICE-CHAIR BiomedEngrg, 1997-2000; from asst prof to assoc prof, Columbia Univ, 1958-1967; instr chem eng, Univ Pa, 1955 & 1957-1958; Res engr, Barrett Div, Allied Chem Corp, 1953-1955; consult, Mt Sinai & St Luke's Hosp, NY, & Baxter Healthcare Corp, Am Red Cross, Medigene Corp, Cytotherapeutics Inc. **Memberships:** Fel Am Inst Chem Engrs; Am Soc Artificial Internal Organs (pres, 1972); Biomed Eng Soc; fel Am Inst Med & Biol Engrs; fel NY Acad Medicine. **Research Statement & Publications:** Heat, mass, momentum transport in fluid systems; distributed parameter chemical systems; transient behavior of chemical process systems; design of transport devices in medicine, particularly for renal and immunotherapy and cell separation; genomic engineering. **Mailing Address:** 801 Mudd Bldg Columbia Univ, New York, NY 10027. **Fax:** 212-854-3054. **E-Mail:** leonard@columbia.edu

LEONARD, EDWARD H, ANALYTICAL CHEMISTRY. **Personal Data:** b Berwick, Maine, February 21, 1919; m 1951, c 1. **Education:** Dartmouth Col, BA, 1942; Tufts Univ, MA, 1954; Univ NH, MS, 1961. **Professional Experience:** PROF EMER PHYSICS & NATURAL SCI, WORCESTER STATE COL, 1984-; assoc prof physics & natural sci, Worcester State Col, beginning 1964; sci coord, NJ, 1960-1964; head sci dept high sch, NJ, 1951-1960; res & develop engr, Eng Dept, 1946-1951; res & develop engr, Elec Res Lab, Simplex Wire & Cable Co, 1942-1946. **Memberships:** AAAS; Am Chem Soc; Am Asn Physics Teachers; Nat Sci Teachers Asn. **Research Statement & Publications:** Design and development of apparatus and aids for the teaching of physical science. **Mailing Address:** Dept Physics & Earth Sci, Worcester State Col, 486 Chandler St, Worcester, MA 01602-2597.

LEONARD, EDWARD JOSEPH, MEDICINE. **Personal Data:** b Boston, Mass, March 20, 1926; m 1956, c 3. **Education:** Harvard Med Sch, MD, 1949. **Professional Experience:** SECT CHEIF & MED OFF, LAB IMMUNOBIOL, NAT CANCER INST, as of 2004; head immunopath sect, Lab Immunobiol, Nat Cancer Inst, beginning 1976; head tumor antigen sect, Biol Br, 1973-1976; investr, Lab Immunobiol, Nat Cancer Inst, 1969-1973; from instr to assoc clin prof, George Wash Univ, 1957-1974; investr, Nat Heart Inst, 1953-1969. **Memberships:** Am Asn Immunol; Am Fedn Clin Res; Soc Gen Physiologists. **Research Statement & Publications:** Tumor immunology. **Mailing Address:** Immunopath Sect, Nat Cancer Inst, FCRDC Bldg 560 Rm 12-71, Frederick, MD 21702. **E-Mail:** leonard@ncifcrf.gov

LEONARD, ELLEN MARIE, PLASMA PHYSICS, NUCLEAR ENGINEERING. **Personal Data:** b New York, NY, November 28, 1944; m 1975, John; c Susan & Michael. **Education:** Univ Mich, BS, 1966, MS, 1968, PhD (plasma physics), 1973. **Professional Experience:** Group leader, Los Alamos Nat Lab, beginning 1993; tech staff mem 1973-1993. **Memberships:** Am Phys Soc; Am Nuclear Soc; AAAS; Inst Elec & Electronics Engrs. **Research Statement & Publications:** Nuclear nonproliferation; technology security. **Mailing Address:** Los Alamos Nat Lab, TA 3 43 C106, Los Alamos, NM 87544. **Fax:** 505-665-3456. **E-Mail:** eleonard@lanl.gov

LEONARD, HENRY SIGGINS, MATHEMATICS. **Personal Data:** b Needham, Mass, October 12, 1930; m 1954, Eva; c Alan. **Education:** Mich State Univ, BS, 1952; Harvard Univ, AM, 1953, PhD (math), 1958. **Professional Experience:** RETIRED; dir grad studies, Northern Ill Univ, 1993-1997; vis, Univ Manchester, Eng, 1987-1988; vis scholar, Univ Chicago, 1980-1981; asst chmn, Dept Math Sci, 1975-1978; vis fel, Yale Univ, 1973-1974; prof math, Northern Ill Univ, beginning 1968; vis assoc prof, Univ Ill, Urbana, 1967-1968; prin investr, NSF grants, 1959-1970; from asst prof to assoc prof math, Carnegie Inst Technol, 1958-1968. **Memberships:** Am Math Soc; Math Asn Am. **Research Statement & Publications:** Theory of groups of finite order. **Mailing Address:** Dept Math, Northern Ill Univ, DeKalb, IL 60115-2888.

LEONARD, JACK E, CHEMISTRY. **Personal Data:** b Chickasha, Okla, February 6, 1943; m 1965, c 3. **Education:** Harvard Univ, AB, 1965; Southern Methodist Univ, BD, 1967; Calif Inst Technol, PhD (chem & biol), 1971. **Professional Experience:** PRES, ENVIRON MGT INST, as of 1990; sr environ scientist, Indianapolis Ctr Advan Res, Inc, 1985-1990; fac mem, Blinn Col, 1983-1985; assoc res scientist, State Univ NY, 1961-1975 & Tex A&M Univ, 1982-1983; vis assoc prof chem, Univ Tex, El Paso, 1981-1982; sr res chemist, Allied Corp, 1980; asst prof chem, State Univ NY, 1961-1975 & Tex A&M Univ, 1975-1981. **Memberships:** Am Chem Soc; AAAS. **Research Statement & Publications:** Physical organic chemistry from mechanisms of photochemical and electrochemical reactions to laser synthesis of catalysts to mathematical group and graph theory; environmental chemical policy. **Mailing Address:** Environ Mgt Inst, 5610 Crawfordsville Rd Ste 15, Indianapolis, IN 46224. **Fax:** 317-248-4846. **E-Mail:** enutlmgt@inpui.edu

LEONARD, JACQUES WALTER, POLYMER CHEMISTRY, PHYSICAL CHEMISTRY. **Personal Data:** b Montreal, Que, August 7, 1936; m 1963, Marthe-Andree; c Anne & Simon. **Education:** Univ Montreal, BSc, 1960, MSc, 1961, PhD (chem), 1964. **Professional Experience:** Dir dept, Fac Sci & Eng, 1991-1994; Univ Del Bordeaux, France, 1991; vis fel, Inst Charles Sadron, Nat Ctr Sci Res, Strasbourg, France, 1990; vdean res, Fac Sci & Eng, 1987-1989; dir dept, Univ Laval, 1978-1981; vis prof, Univ Sussex, Eng, 1977-1978; PROF CHEM, UNIV LAVAL, 1975-; from asst prof to assoc prof chem, Univ Laval, 1966-1975; Can Nat Res Coun fel, Univ Leeds, 1964-1966. **Memberships:** Fel Chem Inst Can; Am Chem Soc. **Research Statement & Publications:** Kinetics and thermodynamics of polymerizations in solution; effect of the medium on the equilibrium of reversible cyclizations, homo- and copolymerizations; thermodynamics of polymer solutions and binary liquid mixtures. **Mailing Address:** Dept Chem, Univ Laval, Quebec, PQ G1K 7P4, Can. **Fax:** 418-656-7916. **E-Mail:** jacques.leonard@chm.ulaval.ca

LEONARD, JAMES JOSEPH, INTERNAL MEDICINE, CARDIOLOGY. **Personal Data:** b Schenectady, NY, June 17, 1924; m 1954, Helen; c James J, W Jeffrey, Paul M & Kathleen M. **Education:** Georgetown Univ, MD, 1950. **Professional Experience:** PROF MED & CHMN DEPT, UNIV HEALTH SCI, 1977-; chmn dept, sch med, Univ Pittsburgh, 1971-1977; actg chmn dept med, Sch Med, Univ Pittsburgh, 1970-1971; prof med, Sch Med, Univ Pittsburgh, 1967-1977; assoc prof med & dir div cardiol, Sch Med, Univ Pittsburgh, 1963-1967; assoc prof med & dir cardiac diag lab, Ohio State Univ, 1962-1963; dir cardiopulmonary lab, 1961-1962; from asst prof to assoc prof med, Univ Tex Med Br, 1959-1962; chief cent heart sta, DC Gen Hosp, 1957-1959; attend cardiol, Mt Alto's Vet Hosp, DC, 1957-1959; asst prof & dir, Div Cardiol, Georgetown Univ Serv, DC Gen Hosp, 1957-1959; instr, Med Sch, Duke Univ, 1956-1957; NIH cardiac trainee, Duke Univ Hosp, 1956-1957; med officer, DC Gen Hosp, 1955-1956; instr, Sch Med, Georgetown Univ, 1955-1956; resident, pulmonary Dis Div, DC gen hosp, 1954-1955; Am Trudeau Soc fel, pulmonary Dis Div, DC Gen hosp, 1954-1955; Wash Heart Asn fel cardiol, Georgetown Univ Hosp, 1953-1954; asst resident med serv, Boston City Hosp, Mass, 1952-1953; from intern to jr asst resident med, Georgetown Univ Hosp, 1950-1952. **Memberships:** Asn Am Physicians; Asn Prof Med; Asn Univ Cardiologists; Sigma Xi; Am Col Physicians; Am Clin & Climat Asn; master Am Col Physicians. **Research Statement & Publications:** Cardiopulmonary physiology. **Mailing Address:** Dept Med, Uniformed Serv Univ, 4301 Jones Bridge Rd, Bethesda, MD 20814. **Fax:** 301-295-3557.

LEONARD, JANET LOUISE, NEUROETHOLOGY, INVERTEBRATE ZOOLOGY. **Personal Data:** b Ames, Iowa, February 24, 1953. **Education:** Univ Wis-Madison, BS, 1973, PhD (zoology), 1980. **Professional Experience:** AT MARK O HATFIELD MARINE SCI CTR, ORE STATE UNIV, 1992-; vis asst prof, Hatfield Marine Sci Ctr, Ore State Univ, Newport, 1989-1992; asst prof zool, Univ Okla, 1986-1992; fel Neuroscience, Univ Calif, San Diego, 1985; fel med physiol, Univ Calgary, Can, 1981-1985; asst prof, Univ Maine, Orono, 1980-1981. **Memberships:** Animal Behav Soc; AAAS; Int Soc Neuroethologists; Soc Neuroscience; Am Soc Naturalists. **Research Statement & Publications:** Ethology and neuroethology of invertebrates; behavioral organization; mating systems; neuroethology of opisthcbranchs; coelenterate behavior. **Mailing Address:** Mark O Hatfield Marine Sci Ctr, Ore State Univ, Newport, OR 97365. **Fax:** 541-867-0105. **E-Mail:** leonarja@ccmail.orst.edu

LEONARD, JOHN ALEX, INDUSTRIAL CHEMISTRY. **Personal Data:** b Swindon, Eng, December 13, 1937; m 1961, c 2. **Education:** Univ London, BS, 1959, PhD (chem), 1962. **Professional Experience:** CHEM BUS MGR, ICI CAN, 1988-; ventures mgr, C-I-L, Inc, 1984-1988; technol & agreement mgr, C-I-L, Inc, 1977-1984; res adv, C-I-L, Inc, 1974-1977; from sr scientist catalysis to bus planning, Imperial Chem Indust, UK & USA, 1966-1974; res chemist polymers, Shell Develop Co, Calif, 1963-1966; fel, Harvard Univ, 1962-1963. **Memberships:** Am Chem Soc; Chem Soc Can; Royal Soc Chem. **Research Statement & Publications:** Catalytic, electrochemical and biological processes and research management. **Mailing Address:** ICI Can, 90 Sheppard Ave E PO Box 200, North York, ON M2N 6H2, Can.

LEONARD, JOHN EDWARD, organic chemistry, physical chemistry; deceased, see previous edition for last biography

LEONARD, JOHN JOSEPH, PHYSICAL ORGANIC CHEMISTRY. **Personal Data:** b Philadelphia, Pa, February 12, 1949; m 1972, c 2. **Education:** Drexel Univ, BS, 1972, PhD (phys org chem), 1972. **Professional Experience:** MGR CORP PLANNING, ARCO CHEM CO, DIV ATLANTIC RICHFIELD CO, 1989-; mgr res & develop, Arco Chem Co, 1985-1989; mgr catalyst res, Arco Chem Co, 1979-1985; supvr catalyst res, Arco Chem Co, 1978-1979; Adj prof math, Drexel Univ Evening Div, 1973-1980; sr res chemist, Arco Chem Co, 1973-1978; Res assoc chem, Univ Pa, 1972-1973. **Memberships:** Am Chem Soc; Int Catalysis Soc; AAAS. **Research Statement & Publications:** Kinetics and mechanisms of organic reactions especially catalysis of organic oxidation reactions(heterogeneous and homogeneous catalysis); spectroscopy of organic molecules. **Mailing Address:** 1314 Farren Lane, West Chester, PA 19380.

LEONARD, JOHN LANDER, MATHEMATICS. **Personal Data:** b Jamaica, NY, October 20, 1935; m 1965, Cecilia Luschak; c Allegra. **Education:** Carnegie Inst Technol, BS, 1957; Univ Calif, Santa Barbara, MA, 1963, PhD (math), 1966. **Professional Experience:** LECTR MATH, UNIV ARIZ, 1976-; asst prof math, Univ Ariz, 1966-1976; Fulbright lectr, Peru, 1973, Intercountry Fulbright lectr, Columbia, 1973; asst math, Univ Calif, Santa Barbara, 1961-1963, 1964-1966; mem tech staff, Tech Mil Planning Oper, 1960-1961; opers analyst, Comput Dept, Gen Elec Co, 1959-1960. **Memberships:** Math Asn Am; Sigma Xi. **Research Statement & Publications:** Graph theory, extremal problems, connectivity; real function theory; mathematical analysis. **Mailing Address:** Dept Math, Univ Ariz, Bldg 89, Tucson, AZ 85721-0089. **Fax:** 520-621-8322. **E-Mail:** jleonard@math.arizona.edu

LEONARD, JOHN W, SCIENCE ADMINISTRATION. **Personal Data:** b Washington, DC, January 19, 1925. **Education:** Mass Inst Technol, BS. **Honors & Awards:** Beavers Award, 1985. **Professional Experience:** RETIRED; sr exec, Morrison Knudsen Co Inc, 1987-1991; sr vpres eng, Morrison Knudsen Co Inc, 1985-1987; indust mem, US Nat Comt Tunneling Technol, 1982-1985; arbitor, Am Arbitration Asn, 1980-1993; mem, US Comt Large Dams, 1975-1988; vpres eng, Morrison Knudsen Co Inc, 1975-1984; chief engr, Morrison Knudsen Co Inc, 1968-1975; proj engr, Morrison Knudsen Co Inc, 1958-1961; owner, H&W Construct Co Pac NW, 1950-1953; Engr, Morrison Knudsen Co Inc, 1947-1950; Visual aide, Sch Eng, Gonzaga Univ. **Memberships:** Nat Acad Eng; fel Am Soc Civil Engrs; Sigma Xi; Soc Am Mil Engrs. **Mailing Address:** 1012 Wyndemere Dr, Boise, ID 83702-1367.

LEONARD, JOSEPH THOMAS, FUEL SCIENCE. **Personal Data:** b Scranton, Pa, August 8, 1932; m 1958, c 4. **Education:** Univ Scranton, BS, 1954; Pa State Univ, University Park, PhD (fuel technol), 1959. **Professional Experience:** RETIRED; res chemist fuels, Naval Res Lab, Wash, DC, beginning 1959; Res asst chem, Pa State Univ, University Park, 1954-1959. **Memberships:** Am Chem Soc. **Research Statement & Publications:** Electrostatic charging of hydrocarbon liquids and fuels; suppression of evaporation of hydrocarbons and smoke abatement techniques. **Mailing Address:** 6725 Buglecall Pl, Gainesville, VA 20155.

LEONARD, JOSEPH WILLIAM, MINERAL PROCESSING ENGINEERING. **Personal Data:** b Pottsville, Pa, December 24, 1930; m 1952, Josephine; c 4. **Education:** Pa State Univ, BS, 1952, MS, 1958. **Honors & Awards:** Howard N Eavenson Award, Am Inst Mining Engrs, 1969, Ersiline Ramsay Medal, 1989. **Professional Experience:** PROF EMER, UNIV KY, as of 2004; distinguished mining eng found prof, Univ KY, beginning 1992; prof, Univ KY, 1982-1992; chmn, Univ KY, 1982-1986; dir bur, William N Poundstone res prof, 1981-1982; Cortix, Bochum, WGer, 1978-1982; dean, WVa Univ, 1978-1981; prof mining, WVa Univ, 1974-1981; Pa Elec Co, Johnstown, 1971-; consult, numerous countries, 1962-; dir bur, WVa Univ, 1961-1981; res engr coal mining, US Steel Corp, Monroeville, Pa, 1958-1961; res asst coal prep, Pa State Univ, 1956-1958; asst pre engr, United Elec Coal Co, Chicago, Ill, 1954-1956; asst to div supt coal mining, Philadelphia & Reading Coal & Iron, Pottsville, Pa, 1952-1954. **Memberships:** Fel Am Inst Chemists; distinguished mem Am Inst Mining Engrs; Am Mining Cong; Sigma Xi; distinguished mem Soc Mining Engrs. **Research Statement & Publications:** Mining; coal reserve analysis; coal preparation including design; coal utilization. **Mailing Address:** Dept Mining Eng, Univ Ky, Lexington, KY 40506-0107.

LEONARD, KATHLEEN MARY, GROUND WATER STUDIES, FATE OF CONTAMINANTS. **Personal Data:** b Grand Rapids, Mich, August 14, 1954. **Education:** Univ Wis-Milwaukee, BS, 1983, MS, 1985; Univ Ala, Huntsville, PhD (environ eng), 1990. **Honors & Awards:** Engr of the Yr, Soc Am Mil Engrs, 1996. **Professional Experience:** ASSOC PROF CIVIL ENG, UNIV ALA, HUNTSVILLE, 1997-; asst prof civil eng, Univ Ala, Huntsville, 1991-1997; vpres, Optechnol, Inc, 1989-. **Memberships:** Am Soc Civil Engrs; Soc Women Engrs; Water Environ Fedn; Soc Am Mil Engrs; Int Asn Water Qual. **Research Statement & Publications:** Using optical fibers for remote chemical sensing of environmental systems, specializing in ground water and hazardous waste applications. **Mailing Address:** Dept Civil & Environ Eng Univ Ala, TH-S243, Huntsville, AL 35899. **Fax:** 256-824-6724. **E-Mail:** leonard@cee.uah.edu

LEONARD, KURT JOHN, PLANT DISEASE EPIDEMIOLOGY, PLANT HOST-PARASITE GENETICS. **Personal Data:** b Holstein, Iowa, December 6, 1939; m 1961, Maren; c Maria C, Mary A & Benjamin A. **Education:** Iowa State Univ, BS, 1962; Cornell Univ, PhD (plant path), 1968. **Honors & Awards:** Fel, Am Phytopathology Soc, 1983. **Professional Experience:** ADJ PROF, DEPT PLANT PATHOL, NCAROLINA STATE UNIV, 2001-; adj prof, Dept Plant Pathol, Univ Minn 1988-; ed, APS Pr, 1994-1997; dir, Cereal Rust Lab, Agr Res Serv-USDA, Univ Minn, 1988-2001; counr, Int Soc Plant Path, 1983-1991; ed, Phytopath, 1982-1985; mem coun, Am Pythopathol Soc, 1982-1985; res plant scientist, Agr Res Serv-USDA, NC State Univ, 1968-1988. **Memberships:** Emer mem Am Phytopath Soc. **Research Statement & Publications:** Epidemiology and genetics of cereal rust diseases; population genetics of host-parasite interactions in plant diseases. **Mailing Address:** 693 Birch Lane N, St Paul, MN 55126-1207.

LEONARD, LAURENCE, PHYSICAL METALLURGY, MATERIALS SCIENCE. **Personal Data:** b New York, NY, January 9, 1932; m 1958, c 4. **Education:** Mass Inst Technol, SB, 1954, SM, 1956, ScD(metall), 1962. **Professional Experience:** Adj assoc prof, Great Valley Grad Ctr, Pa State Univ, 1990-; Adj assoc prof, Drexel Univ, 1978-; PRIN SCIENTIST, FRANKLIN RES CTR, 1971-; group supvr, SKF Industs, Inc, 1969-1971; Asst prof metall, Case Western Res Univ, 1962-1969. **Memberships:** Am Soc Metals. **Research Statement & Publications:** Materials failure analysis; physical metallurgy of rolling contact bearings; scanning electron microscopy; metal embrittlement; x-ray diffraction; residual stresses; phase transformations; heat treatment; nondestructive testing; wear monitoring by oil analysis. **Mailing Address:** 505 Princeton Dr, King of Prussia, PA 19406.

LEONARD, MARTHA FRANCES, PEDIATRICS, CHILD DEVELOPMENT. **Personal Data:** b New Brunswick, NJ, May 10, 1916. **Education:** NJ Col Women, BSc, 1936; Johns Hopkins Univ, MD, 1940. **Honorary Degrees:** MS, Yale Univ, 1979. **Honors & Awards:** Winslow Award, 1988. **Professional Experience:** SR RES SCIENTIST & EMER PROF PEDIAT, YALE UNIV, beginning 1986; from instr to prof, Child Study Ctr, 1979-1986; fel, Child Study Ctr, 1960-1962; pvt pract, 1946-1960; asst resident pediat, NY Hosp, 1943-1946; asst resident med, Vanderbilt Univ Hosp, 1942-1943; Intern, Baltimore City Hosp, 1940-1941; consult, Area Coop Educ Serv, Village St Sch, North Haven. **Memberships:** Am Acad Pediat; Ambulatory Pediat Asn; Am Pub Health Asn. **Research Statement & Publications:** Normal and deviant child development; effects of deprivation; failure to thrive; child abuse; developmental impact of conditions such as genetic, metabolic and endocrine disorders. **Mailing Address:** Child Study Ctr, Yale Univ, New Haven, CT 06510. **Fax:** 203-488-9429. **E-Mail:** ewmfl@aol.com

LEONARD, MICHAEL STEVEN, SERVICE SYSTEMS DESIGN, QUALITY ENGINEERING. **Personal Data:** b Salsbury, NC, m 1947, Mary; c Dorothy E, Amanda B & Gabrielle F. **Education:** Univ Fla, BE, 1970, ME, 1972, PhD (syst eng), 1973. **Professional Experience:** Chair, Indust Eng, Clemson Univ, beginning 2000; mem, Board of dir, Accreditation Bd eng technol, beginning 1999; mem, Eng Accreditation Comn, Accreditation Bd Eng & Technol, 1994-1999; PROF INDUST ENG, CLEMSON UNIV, 1990-; head, Clemson Univ, 1990-1995; eval visitor, Accreditation Bd Eng & Technol, 1988-1994; chmn, Univ Mo, 1985-1990; prof, Univ Mo, 1982-1990; from asst prof to assoc prof indust eng, Univ Mo, 1975-1982; asst prof, Health Syst Res Ctr, Ga Inst Technol, 1973-1975. **Memberships:** fel Inst Indust Engrs; Soc Health Syst; Mem Inst Opers Res & Mgmt Sci, mem Am soc for Eng education; mem natl soc for prof engs. **Research Statement & Publications:** Service and information systems design; inventory control; production scheduling; facility location; quality engineering. **Mailing Address:** Dept Indust Eng, Clemson Univ, 112 Freeman Hall, Clemson, SC 29634-0920. **Fax:** 864-656-0795. **E-Mail:** mike.leonard@ces.clemson.edu

LEONARD, NELSON JORDAN, ORGANIC BIOCHEMISTRY. **Personal Data:** b Newark, NJ, September 1, 1916; m 1992, Peggy Phelps; c Kenneth Jan, Marcia Louise, James Nelson & David Anthony. **Education:** Lehigh Univ, BS, 1937; Univ Oxford, BSc, 1940, DSc, 1983; Columbia Univ, PhD (org chem), 1942. **Honorary Degrees:** ScD, Lehigh Univ, 1963; Dr, Adam Mickiewicz Univ, 1980; DSc, Univ Ill, 1988. **Honors & Awards:** Synthesis Award, Am Chem Soc, 1963, Edgar Fahs Smith Award, 1975, Roger Adams Award, 1981-1991; Medal Creative Res Synthetic Org Chem, Synthetic Org Chem Mfrs Asn, 1970; George W Wheland Award, Univ Chicago, 1991; Paul G Gassman Distinguished Service Award, Am Chem Soc, 1994 creativity award, Univ of Oregon, 1994; Arthur C Cope scholar award, Am chem soc, 1996. **Professional Experience:** FAC ASSOC, CALIF INST TECHNOL, 1992-; Sherman Fairchild distinguished scholar, Div Chem & Chem Eng, Calif Inst Technol, Pasadena, 1991; Fogarty Pasadean scholar-in-residence, NIH, Bethesda, Md, 1989-1990; REYNOLD C FUSON EMER PROF, UNIV ILL, 1986-; Reynold C Fuson prof chem & mem, Ctr Advan Study, 1981-1986; Calbiochem-Beohring lectr, Univ Calif, San Diego, 1981; pres, Bd Dirs, 1980-1988; Arapahoe lectr, Univ Colo, 1979; Edgar Fahs Smith Mem lectr, Univ Pa, 1975; prof chem & biochem, Div Org Chem, 1973-1986; mem educ adv bd & bd of selection, John Simon Guggenheim Mem Found, 1969-1988; Stieglitz lectr, 1962; mem prog comt basic phys sci, Alfred P Sloan Found, 1961-1966; Guggenheim Mem Found fel, 1959, 1967; ed-in-chief, Org Syntheses, 1956; head, Div Org Chem, 1954-1963; Am-Swiss Found lectr, 1953, 1970; ed, Org Syntheses, 1951-1958; from asst prof to prof chem, Univ Ill, Urbana, 1947-1986; Sci consult & spec investr, Field Intel Agency Tech, US Army & US Com, Europ Theatre, 1945-1946; assoc, Univ Ill, Urbana, 1944-1947; Mem, Comt Med Res, 1944-1946; instr, Univ Ill, Urbana, 1943-1944; fel & res asst chem, Univ Ill, Urbana, 1942-1943. **Memberships:** Nat Acad Sci; fel Am Acad Arts & Sci (vpres, 1990-1993); Am phili soc; Am Chem Soc; Royal Soc Chem; Swiss Chem Soc; AAAS; hon mem Pharmaceut Soc Japan. **Research Statement & Publications:** Structure, synthesis and biological activity of cytokinins; modification of nucleic acid bases; fluorescent probes of coenzyme, enzyme binding and nucleic acid structures; intramolecular interactions. **Mailing Address:** 389 California Terr, Pasadena, CA 91105.

LEONARD, PHILIP A, MATHEMATICS. **Education:** Pa State Univ, PhD, 1968. **Professional Experience:** PROF, DEPT MATHS, ARIZ STATE UNIV, as of 2003. **Mailing Address:** Math Dept, Ariz State Univ, 425 E Univ Dr, Tempe, AZ 85281. **Fax:** 480-965-8529. **E-Mail:** pal@math.la.asu.edu

LEONARD, RALPH AVERY, SOIL CHEMISTRY. **Personal Data:** b Louisburg, NC, March 2, 1937; m 1958, c 3. **Education:** NC State Univ, BS, 1959, PhD (soil chem), 1966; Purdue Univ, MS, 1962. **Professional Experience:** SOIL SCIENTIST, AGR RES SERV, USDA, 1966-; instr soil sci, NC State Univ, 1962-1966. **Memberships:** Am Chem Soc; Soil Sci Soc Am; Am Soc Agron; Sigma Xi. **Research Statement & Publications:** Physical chemistry of soils; fate of pesticides in soil and water; soil chemical aspects of waste disposal and utilization on the land. **Mailing Address:** 224 Franklin Ave, River Forest, IL 60305-2116.

LEONARD, REID HAYWARD, CHEMISTRY. **Personal Data:** b Littleton, NH, August 28, 1918; m 1946, c 3. **Education:** Univ Vt, BS, 1940; Univ W Va, MS, 1942; Univ Wis, PhD (biochem), 1947. **Professional Experience:** RETIRED; consult biochemist, beginning 1956; res chemist, Newport Industs, 1947-1956; res chemist, Salvo Chem Corp, Wis, 1946-1947; asst, Univ Wis & Forest Prod Lab, US Forest Serv, 1943-1945; asst, Exp Sta, Univ W Va, 1940-1942. **Memberships:** Am Chem Soc. **Research Statement & Publications:** Chemistry of wood; sugars from wood; lignin; levulinic acid; kidney stones; blood lipids; gas chromatography. **Mailing Address:** 537 Brent Lane, Pensacola, FL 32503.

LEONARD, ROBERT F, PHOTOLITHOGRAPHY, MICROLITHOGRAPHY. **Personal Data:** b Oceanside, NY, August 21, 1934; m 1964, c 3. **Education:** Hofstra Univ, BA, 1966; Worchester Polytech Inst, MS, 1981. **Professional Experience:** DIR RES, PROD DEVELOP, OCG MICROELECTRONICS MAT, INC, 1990-; dir res, prod develop, Philip A Hunt Chem Corp, 1984-; res mgr printing prod, 1976-1979 & photopolymer applns, 1979-1984; mgr printing prod, Rogers Corp, 1969-1976; Dir res, Litho Chem & Supply Co, 1968-1969. **Memberships:** Am Chem Soc; Am Inst Chemists; Am Soc Testing Mat; Electrochem Soc; Soc Photographer Scientists & Engrs; Soc Photo-Optical Instrumentation Engrs. **Research Statement & Publications:** Photolithographic chemicals and processes; microelectronics. **Mailing Address:** 24 Lens Ave, Dayville, CT 06241-2219.

LEONARD, ROBERT GRESHAM, MECHANICAL ENGINEERING, CONTROL ENGINEERING. **Personal Data:** b Roanoke, Va, January 27, 1937; m 1960, c 2. **Education:** Va Polytech Inst, BS, 1960, MS, 1965; Pa State Univ, PhD (mech eng), 1970. **Honors & Awards:** Homer Addams Award, Am Soc Heating Refrig & Air-Conditioning Engrs, 1975. **Professional Experience:** PROF MECH ENG & ASST DEPT HEAD, VA POLYTECH INST & STATE UNIV, 1978-; asst dir, Ray W Herrick Labs, 1976-1978; from asst prof to assoc prof mech eng, Purdue Univ, 1970-1978; lectr, Purdue Univ, 1967; instr mech eng, Va Polytech Inst, 1960-1965 & Pa State Univ, 1965-1970; eng trainee, Gen Elec Co, Va, 1956-1959. **Memberships:** Am Soc Mech Engrs. **Research Statement & Publications:** Automatic controls; dynamic systems modeling; simulation; fluid power systems; parameter identification. **Mailing Address:** Mech Eng Dept, Va Polytech Inst, 114 Randolph Hall, Blacksburg, VA 24061.

LEONARD, ROBERT STUART, GEOPHYSICS, AERONOMY. **Personal Data:** b Berkeley, Calif, January 20, 1930; m 1956, Kathryn Freeman; c Karen & Carl. **Education:** Univ Nev, BS, 1952, MS, 1953; Univ Alaska, PhD (geophys), 1961. **Professional Experience:** RETIRED; Consult, 1987-1995; exec dir, Geosci & Eng Ctr, 1986-1987; dep div dir, Radio Physics Lab, 1980-1986; dir, Radio Physics Lab, 1977-1980; asst dir, SRI Int, 1972-1977; prog mgr, SRI Int, 1969-1972; sr ionospheric physicist, SRI Int, 1962-1969; radio physicist, SRI Int, 1961-1962; instr, Geophys Inst, Univ Alaska, 1958-1960; Res asst auroral studies, Geophys Inst, Univ Alaska, 1953-1958. **Memberships:** Int Union Radio Sci; Am Geophys Union; Am Phys Soc; Inst Elec & Electronics Engrs. **Research Statement & Publications:** Chemical seeding in the ionosphere; transionospheric propagation; ionospheric disturbances; radio wave propagation. **Mailing Address:** 12837 Old Oregon Trail, Redding, CA 96003.

LEONARD, ROBERT THOMAS, PLANT PHYSIOLOGY. **Personal Data:** b Providence, RI, December 18, 1943; div, c 1. **Education:** Univ RI, BS, 1965, MS, 1967; Univ Ill, Urbana, PhD (biol), 1971. **Professional Experience:** DEPT HEAD PLANT SCI, UNIV ARIZ, 1994-; dept chmn, 1988-1994; assoc dean, Grad Div & Res Develop, 1985-1988; vchmn dept, Univ Calif, Riverside, 1978-1982; from asst prof to prof plant physiol, Univ Calif, Riverside, 1973-1982; fel plant physiol, Univ Ill & Purdue Univ, 1971-1973. **Memberships:** Am Soc Plant Biologists. **Research Statement & Publications:** Physiology and biochemistry of ion transport in plants. **Mailing Address:** Dept Plant Sci, Univ Ariz, Forbes Bldg Rm 303 PO Box 210036, Tucson, AZ 85721-0036. **Fax:** 520-621-7186. **E-Mail:** plshead@ag.arizona.edu

LEONARD, STANLEY LEE, plasma physics; deceased, see previous edition for last biography

LEONARD, THOMAS JOSEPH, DEVELOPMENTAL GENETICS. **Personal Data:** b Watertown, Mass, July 27, 1937; div, c 1. **Education:** Clark Univ, AB, 1962; Ind Univ, PhD (microbiol), 1967. **Professional Experience:** MARY DESPINA LEKAS PROF, 2003-; PROF, CLARK UNIV, 1994-; chmn biol, Clark Univ, 1994-2004; prof bot & genetics, Univ Wis-Madison, 1974-1994; assoc prof mycol, Univ Ky, 1968-1974; NIH fel, Harvard Univ, 1967-1968. **Memberships:** AAAS; Genetics Soc Am; Mycol Soc Am; Brit Mycol Soc.

Research Statement & Publications: Physiology and genetics of fungi as applied to development; genetics and physiological aspects of cell differentiation. **Mailing Address:** Dept Biol, Clark Univ, 950 Main St, Worcester, MA 01610. **E-Mail:** tleonard@clarku.edu

LEONARD, WALTER RAYMOND, ZOOLOGY, PHYSIOLOGY. **Personal Data:** b Scott Co, Va, July 5, 1923; m 1951, c 2. **Education:** Tusculum Col, BA, 1946; Vanderbilt Univ, MS, 1947, PhD (zool), 1949. **Professional Experience:** REEVES PROF BIOL & CHMN DEPT, WOFFORD COL, 1954-; assoc prof & acting chmn dept, 1950-1953; Asst prof biol, 1949-1950. **Research Statement & Publications:** Respiratory metabolism of Allomyces arbuscula; effects of activity on growth in hydra. **Mailing Address:** 350 Round Ridge Rd, Spartanburg, SC 29302.

LEONARD, WARREN J, CELL BIOLOGY. **Personal Data:** b Washington, DC, February 28, 1952; c 2. **Education:** Princeton Univ, AB, 1973; Stanford Univ, MD, 1977; Am Bd Internal Med, dipl, 1980; Am Bd Allergy & Immunol, dipl, 1983. **Professional Experience:** CHIEF, LYMPHOCYTE ACTIVATION SEC, NAT HEART, LUNG & BLOOD INST, NIH, as of 2004; CHIEF, INTRAMURAL RES PROG, NAT HEART, LUNG & BLOOD INST, NIH, as of 2004; LAB CHIEF, NAT HEART, LUNG & BLOOD INST, NIH, 1991-; med officer res, Cell Biol & Metab Br, 1987-1991; sr staff fel, Cell Biol & Metab Br, Nat Inst Child Health & Human Develop, 1985-1987; sr staff fel, Metab Br, Nat Cancer Inst, NIH, 1981-1985; res assoc, Sch Med, Wash Univ, 1980-1981; resident internal med, Barnes Hosp, St Louis, 1978-1980. **Memberships:** Sigma Xi; Am Asn Immunologists; Am Soc Clin Invest. **Research Statement & Publications:** Cell biology; two patents; numerous publications. **Mailing Address:** Nat Heart, Lung & Blood Inst, NIH, Rm 7N244 Bldg 10, Bethesda, MD 20892. **E-Mail:** wl2w@nih.gov

LEONARD, WILLIAM WILSON, MATHEMATICS. **Personal Data:** b Portland, Maine, May 1, 1934; m 1961, c 2. **Education:** Univ Tampa, BS, 1960; Univ SC, MS, 1963, PhD (math), 1965. **Professional Experience:** MEM, URBAN LIFE FAC, 1977-; PROF MATH, GA STATE UNIV, 1974-; from asst prof to assoc prof, Urban Life Fac, 1965-1974; Asst prof math, Susquehanna Univ, 1964-1965. **Memberships:** Am Math Soc; Math Asn Am; Math Soc France. **Research Statement & Publications:** Module theory; homological algebra. **Mailing Address:** 156 Cleve Tripp Rd, Poland Spring, ME 04274.

LEONARDS, KENNETH STANLEY, BIOCHEMISTRY, BIOPHYSICS. **Personal Data:** b Detroit, Mich, July 19, 1950. **Education:** Kalamazoo Col, BS, 1972; Mich State Univ, MS, 1975, PhD (biophys), 1980. **Professional Experience:** STAFF SCIENTIST, CIBA-GEIGY, 1994-; res scientist III, Ciba-geigy, 1990-1994; asst prof res, Cardiovasc Res Lab, Dept Physiol, Univ Calif, Los Angeles Sch Med, 1984-1990; fel membrane transport, Univ Va, 1982-1984; fel membrane biol, State Univ NY, Buffalo, 1980-1982. **Memberships:** Biophys Soc; Am Chem Soc; Oxygen Soc; Am Physiol Soc. **Mailing Address:** Ciba-Geigy Corp, Mail Stop 2115 LSB 556 Morris Ave, Summit, NJ 07901.

LEONBERGER, FREDERICK JOHN, INTEGRATED OPTICS, FIBER OPTICS. **Personal Data:** b Washington, DC, September 25, 1947; m 1970, Janet; c Gregory & Katharine. **Education:** Univ Mich, BSE, 1969; Mass Inst Technol, MS, 1971, PhD (elec eng), 1975. **Honors & Awards:** Quantum Electronics Award, Inst Elec & Electronics Engrs, 1993; Photonics Award, Inst Elec & Electronics Engrs, 2005. **Professional Experience:** PRIN, EOVATION TECHNOLOGIES LLC, as of 2005; DIR, AGILITY COMMUN INC, as of 2005; DIR, RF MICRO DEVICES INC, 2002-; sr vpres, Uniphase Telecommun Prod, 1999-2003; vpres & chief technol officer, Uniphase Telecommun Prod, 1995-1999; vpres & chief technol officer, Uniphase Corp, 1995-1999; co-founder & gen mgr, United Technologies Photonics Corp, 1992-1995; group leader, Lincoln Lab, Mass Inst Technol, 1981-1984; staff mem, Lincoln Lab, Mass Inst Technol, 1975-1981. **Memberships:** Fel Optical Soc Am; fel Inst Elec & Electronics Engrs; Inst Elec & Electronics Engrs Laser & Electrooptics Soc (pres, 1988). **Research Statement & Publications:** Photonic device research, with emphasis on integrated optics, fiber optics and optoelectronic devices and their applications to communication, sensing and signal processing; published over 40 articles. **Mailing Address:** RF Micro Devices, Inc, 7628 Thorndike Rd, Greensboro, NC 27409-9421. **Fax:** 336-931-7454.

LEONE, FRED CHARLES, STATISTICS. **Personal Data:** b New York, NY, August 3, 1922; m 1945, Elizabeth S Leone; c Charles, Beti, Peter, Frank, Joe, Lary & Lucy. **Education:** Manhattan Col, BA, 1941; Georgetown Univ, MS, 1943; Purdue Univ, PhD (math statist, educ), 1949. **Professional Experience:** EXEC DIR & SECY, AM STATIST ASN; exec dir & secy-treas, Am Statist Asn, 1973-198 8; NAm ed, Statist Theory & Methods Abstracts, 1969-1973; Fulbright prof, Univ Sao Paulo, Brazil, 1968-1969; prof statist & indust eng, Univ Iowa, 1966-1973; ed, Technometrics, 1963-1968; actg chmn dept, Case Western Res Univ, 1963-1965; dir statist lab, Case Western Res Univ, 1951-1965; from instr to prof math, Case Western Res Univ, 1949-1966; instr, Purdue Univ, 1943-1944 & 1946-1949; Instr, Georgetown Univ, 1942-1943. **Memberships:** Fel AAAS; fel Am Soc Qual Control; fel Am Statist Asn; Sigma Xi; Math Asn Am acey/thece Am statist asn. **Research Statement & Publications:** Experimental design and statistics applied to engineering; order statistics, especially in analysis of variance. **Mailing Address:** 201 E Wayne Ave, Silver Spring, MD 20901.

LEONE, IDA ALBA, POLLUTION BIOLOGY. **Personal Data:** b Elizabeth, NJ, April 28, 1922. **Education:** Rutgers Univ, BS, 1944, MS, 1946. **Professional Experience:** EMER PROF DEPT PLANT PATH, COOK COL, RUTGERS UNIV, 1988-; prof II, Col Agr, Rutgers Univ, 1987-1988; lectr, China, 1985; lectr, univ & inst, India, 1977; prof plant biol, Col Agr, Rutgers Univ, 1976-1987; Consult, NY State Environ Protection Bur, 1975-1976; assoc res prof, Col Agr, Rutgers Univ, 1970-1976; asst res specialist, Col Agr, Rutgers Univ, 1958-1970; res assoc, Col Agr, Rutgers Univ, 1950-1958; Asst plant path, Col Agr, Rutgers Univ, 1946-1950; dir, NJ Jr Acad Sci; US Dept Interior, NY State Dept Transp, Pa Power & Light Co, Niagara Mohawk Power Co, Rohm & Haas, Cambridge Mass Landfill Revegetation Comn, Cabot Corp. **Memberships:** Sigma Xi; Am Phytopath Soc; Am Soc Plant Physiologists; Air Pollution Control Asn; NY Acad Sci; Indian Soc Air Pollution Control. **Research Statement & Publications:** Effect of air pollution; nutritional, physiological and environmental factors on plant growth; plants as sources of air pollution; undergraduate and graduate courses in air pollution effects; effect of cooling-tower or deicing salt spray on crops; phytotoxicity of anaerobic landfill gases; role of mycorrhizae in adapting woody species to landfill conditions. **Mailing Address:** 876 Rayhon Terr, Rahway, NJ 07065-2107.

LEONE, JAMES A, PHYSICAL CHEMISTRY, INSTRUMENTATION. **Personal Data:** b Braddock, Pa, December 11, 1937; m 1961, c 1. **Education:** Univ Cincinnati, BS, 1961; Johns Hopkins Univ, MA, 1963, PhD (phys chem), 1965. **Professional Experience:** ASSOC PROF, INFO TECHNOL, ROCHESTOR INST TECHNOL, 1999-; vis asst prof info technol, Rochestor Inst Technol, 1998; prin syst analyst, Analysis & Simulation Inc, Buffalo, NY, 1995-1997; dep dir, Frontier Sci & Technol Res Found, NY, 1992-1995; prof comput sci, Canisius Col, 1990-1992; chmn, Dept Compu Sci, Canisius Col, 1983-1989; prof comput sci, Canisius Col, 1982; assoc prof chem & comput sci, Canisius Col, 1976-1981; assoc prof chem & comput sci, Canisius Col, 1976-1981; vis assoc prof, Va Polytech Inst & State Univ, 1975-1976; dir med technol, Canisius Col, 1972-1974; from asst prof to assoc prof phys chem, Canisius Col, 1967-1975; res assoc, Univ Notre Dame, 1965-1967. **Memberships:** Am Chem Soc; Sigma Xi; Soc Appl Spectros. **Research Statement & Publications:** Radiation chemistry; electron spin resonance; on-line minicomputers; minicomputer and microprocessor interfacing; minicomputers and microprocessors in instrumentation automation. **Mailing Address:** Dept Info Technol, Rochester Inst Technol, 102 Lomb Mem Dr, Rochester, NY 14623. **E-Mail:** leone@it.rit.edu

LEONE, RONALD EDMUND, SYNTHESIS OF COMPOUNDS FOR PHOTOGRAPHIC APPLICATIONS. **Personal Data:** b New York, NY, August 11, 1942. **Education:** Northwestern Univ, BA, 1964; Princeton Univ, MA, 1967, PhD (org chem), 1970. **Professional Experience:** RES ASSOC, EASTMAN KODAK CO, 1991-; sr res chemist, Eastman Kodak Co, 1971-1991; fel org chem, Yale Univ, 1969-1971. **Memberships:** Am Chem Soc; Sigma Xi. **Research Statement & Publications:** Aspects of physical organic chemistry including organic reaction mechanisms and nuclear magnetic resonance spectroscopy; synthesis of compounds for photographic applications including sensitizing dyes, silver halide fogging agents; image couplers, development inhibitor releasing couplers, bleach accelerator releasing couplers, interlayer scavengers, and latent image stabilizers. **Mailing Address:** Eastman Kodak Co, Rochester, NY 14610. **Fax:** 585-588-7611. **E-Mail:** rleone@rochester.rr.com

LEONE, STEPHEN ROBERT, CHEMICAL PHYSICS. **Personal Data:** b New York, NY, May 19, 1948. **Education:** Northwestern Univ, BA, 1970; Univ Calif, Berkeley, PhD (phys chem), 1974. **Honors & Awards:** Silver Medal Award, Dept Com, 1980, Gold Medal, 1984; Pure Chem Award, Am Chem Soc, 1982, Nobel Laureate Signature Award, 1983; Coblentz Award, 1984; Arthur S Flemming Award, 1986; Herbert P Broida Prize, Am Phys Soc, 1989; Samuel Wesley Stratton Award, Nat Inst Stand & Technol, 1992; Bourke Medal, Faraday Div, Royal Soc Chem, 1995. **Professional Experience:** PROF CHEM, UNIV CALIF, 2002-; vis prof, Chem Res Prom Ctr, Taiwan, 1992; chmn, Joint Inst Lab Astrophys, 1991-1992; vis Miller res prof, Univ Calif, 1990; John Simon Guggenheim fel, 1988; FEL, NAT INST STAND & TECHNOL, 1986-; adj prof chem, Univ Colo, 1982-2002; adj assoc prof, Nat Inst Stand & Technol, 1981-1982; fel, Joint Inst Lab Astrophys, 1978-; Alfred P Sloan Found fel, 1977; lectr, Dept Physics, Univ Colo, beginning 1976; physicist, Nat Bur Stand, 1976-1986; adj asst prof chem, Nat Inst Stand & Technol, 1976-1981; asst prof chem, Univ Southern Calif, 1974-1976. **Memberships:** Nat Acad Sci; fel Am Phys Soc; Am Chem Soc; Am Inst Physics; Sigma Xi; fel Optical Soc Am; fel AAAS; fel Japan Soc Prom Sci. **Research Statement & Publications:** Laser-excited chemical reactions; kinetics and spectroscopic investigations of excited states using specific laser excitation; energy transfer and dynamical processes of small gas phase molecules; photodissociation; new laser development; ion molecule reaction dynamics; surface dynamics; granted 3 US patents; author of 4 publications. **Mailing Address:** Dept Chem & Physics, Univ Calif, Berkeley, CA 80309-0440. **Fax:** 510-643-1376. **E-Mail:** srl@berkeley.edu

LEONG, JO-ANN CHING, VIROLOGY. **Personal Data:** b Honolulu, Hawaii, March 15, 1942; c 2. **Education:** Univ Calif, Berkeley, BA, 1964; Univ Calif, PhD (microbiol), 1971. **Honors & Awards:** Res Award, Sigma Xi, 1990. **Professional Experience:** EMER DISTINGUISHED PROF & CHAIR MICROBIOL, ORE STATE UNIV, as of 2004; Dept chair, Ore State Univ, 1996; distinguished prof, Ore State Univ, 1993; prof microbiol, Ore State Univ, beginning 1985; from asst prof to assoc prof, Ore State Univ, 1975-1985; res fel biochem, Univ Calif, San Francisco, 1973-1975; Dernham fel, Am Cancer Soc, Calif Div, 1973-1975; Giannini Found fel, 1973; from teaching assoc microbiol to res biochemist, Univ Calif, San Francisco, 1971-1973; sr res asst virol, Dept Surg, Stanford Univ Sch Med, 1965-1967; pres, Fish Health Sect, Am Fisheries Soc. **Memberships:** Am Soc Microbiologists; AAAS; Soc Gen Microbiol; NY Acad Sci; Am Asn Cancer Res; Am Soc Virol. **Research Statement & Publications:** Virus-cell interactions; tumor virology; development of recombinant DNA based vaccines for fish and shellfish. **Mailing Address:** Dept Microbiol, Ore State Univ, 220 Nash Hall, Corvallis, OR 97331-3804. **Fax:** 541-737-0496. **E-Mail:** leongj@orst.edu

LEONG, KAM CHOY, BIOCHEMISTRY, POULTRY NUTRITION. **Personal Data:** b Honolulu, Hawaii, December 17, 1920; m 1950, c 3. **Education:** Wash State Univ, BS, 1949, MS, 1950; Univ Wis, PhD (biochem, poultry), 1958. **Professional Experience:** RETIRED; asst dir nutrit, Milling Co Div, Carnation Co, 1981-1986; nutritionist, Milling Co Div, Carnation Co, 1965-1981; res chemist, Bur Com Fisheries, 1961-1965; jr poultry scientist, 1958-1961; fel, Wash State Univ, 1957-1958; asst, Univ Wis, 1954-1957; jr animal husbandman, Univ Hawaii, 1951-1954; asst, Wash State Univ, 1948-1950. **Memberships:** Am Poultry Sci Asn; Am Inst Nutrit. **Research Statement & Publications:** Amino acids; enzymes; vitamins; protein; metabolizable energy. **Mailing Address:** 410 S Las Flores Dr, Nipomo, CA 93444.

LEONG, KAM W, MATERIALS SCIENCE & ENGINEERING. **Personal Data:** b November 13, 1955; American citizen. **Education:** Univ Calif, Santa Barbara, BS, 1977; Univ Pa, Philadelphia, PhD (chem eng), 82. **Professional Experience:** PROF BIOMED ENG, JOHN HOPKINS UNIV, as of 2005; assoc prof, dept biomed eng & dept met sci & eng, Johns Hopkins Univ sch med, beginning 1991; DIR, MASTER PROG BIOMED ENG, 1990-; asst prof, Master Prog Biomed Eng, 1986-1991; Johnson & Johnson fel biomed res, Mass Inst Technol, 1983-1985; res assoc, Whitaker Col Health Sci & Technol & Dept Appl Biol Sci, Mass Inst Technol, 1982-1985. **Memberships:** Am Chem Soc; Am Inst Chem Engrs; Sigma XI; Controlled Release Soc; Soc Biomat. **Research Statement & Publications:** Biomaterials design; controlled drug delivery; tissue engineering. **Mailing Address:** Dept Biomed Eng, Johns Hopkins Univ Sch Med 3400 N Charles St, Baltimore, MD 21218-2608. **E-Mail:** kleong@eureka.wbme.jhu.edu

LEONG, SALLY A, PLANT PATHOLOGY. **Education:** Univ Calif, BA, 1976, PhD (comparative biochem), 1980. **Professional Experience:** PROF, DEPT PLANT PATH, UNIV WIS, as of 2003. **Mailing Address:** Dept Plant Path Univ Wis, 1630 Linden Dr Rm 793A Russell Labs, Madison, WI 53706. **Fax:** 608-263-2626. **E-Mail:** sal@plantpath.wisc.edu

LEONG, WILLIAM, PROCESS DEVELOPMENT. **Personal Data:** b December 26, 1961; m Fina Liotta. **Education:** Univ San Francisco, BS, 1983; Univ Calif, Davis, PhD (chem), 1988. **Professional Experience:** Councilor, Am Chem Soc, 2000-; sr principal scientist, am chem soc, 1995-; PRIN SCIENTIST, SCHERING-PLOUGH RES INST, 1994-; assoc prin scientist, Schering-plough Res Inst, 1992-1994; sr scientist, Schering-plough Res Inst, 1990-1992; Fel, Iowa State Univ, 1988-1990. **Memberships:** Am Chem Soc; Sigma Xi. **Research Statement & Publications:** Development of chemical processes for the synthesis of molecular entities of biological and medicinal interest; asymmetric synthesis and catalysis. **Mailing Address:** Schering-Plough Res Inst, 1011 Morris Ave, Union, NJ 07083. **E-Mail:** william.leong@spcorp.com

LEONHARD, WILLIAM E, CIVIL & ELECTRICAL ENGINEERING. **Personal Data:** b Middletown, Pa, December 9, 1914. **Education:** Pa State Univ, BS, 1936; Mass Inst Technol, MS, 1940. **Honorary Degrees:** LLD, Pepperdine Univ, 1987. **Honors & Awards:** George Wash Award, Inst Advan Eng, 1984. **Professional Experience:** RETIRED; chmn, pres & chief exec officer, 1978-1990; pres & chief exec officer, Parsons Corp, 1975-1978; pres, Parsons Corp, 1974-1975; sr vpres & gen mgr, Parsons Corp, 1966-1974; dir, Tittan III prog, United Technol Corp, 1964-1966; chief staff-brigadier gen, Hq Systs Command, 1961-1964; dep commdr, Missile & Space Div, 1956-1961; dir construct, USAF, 1952-1956; from lt to lt colonel, US ACE, 1936-1951. **Memberships:** Nat Acad Eng. **Mailing Address:** 455 Windmere Dr Apt 5B, State College, PA 16801. **Fax:** 814-231-2965.

LEONHARDT, EARL A, MATHEMATICS. **Personal Data:** b Council Bluffs, Iowa, April 18, 1919; m 1941, c 3. **Education:** Union Col, Nebr, BA, 1950; Univ Nebr, ME, 1952, PhD (sec educ, math), 1962. **Professional Experience:** RETIRED; from instr to prof math, Union Col, Nebr, 1952-1990; High sch instr, Nebr, 1951-1952; Mem, Nat Coun Teachers Math. **Memberships:** Math Asn Am. **Mailing Address:** 5300 CooperAve, Lincoln, NE 68506.

LEONORA, JOHN, ENDOCRINOLOGY. **Personal Data:** b Milwaukee, Wis, January 30, 1928; m 1952, c 2. **Education:** Univ Wis, BS, 1949, MS, 1954, PhD (zoology), 1957. **Honors & Awards:** Res Award Sigma Xi. **Professional Experience:** PROF MED, SCH MED, LOMA LINDA UNIV, as of 2006; CO-CHAIR PHYSIOL & PHARMACOL, SCH MED, LOMA LINDA UNIV, 1974-; PROF MED, SCH MED, LOMA LINDA UNIV, 1969-; from instr to assoc prof, sch med, Loma Linda Univ, 1959-1969; NIH fel, Univ Wis, 1957-1959; asst endocrinol, Univ Wis, 1952-1957. **Memberships:** AAAS; NY Acad Sci; Endocrine Soc; Sigma Xi. **Research Statement & Publications:** Hypothalamic-parotid endocrine axis; relationship of dentinal fluid movement to dental caries. **Mailing Address:** Dept Physiol, Sch Med, Loma Linda Univ, 25027 Mound St, Loma Linda, CA 92350-0001. **E-Mail:** jleonora@llu.edu

LEONOV, VIKTOR, STRUCTURE OPTIMIZATION OF REAL-TIME MICROPROCESSOR SYSTEMS, STRUCTURE SYNTHESIS. **Personal Data:** b Russia, February 22, 1956; m 1979, Veronika Khatala; c Yelena. **Education:** Moscow Inst Telecommun, BSEE, 1983, PhDEE(telecommun), 1992. **Professional Experience:** DESIGN ENGR, 3COM CORP, 1995-; Assoc prof, Moscow Univ Telecommuns & Informatics, 1992-1994; Chief engr res lab, Telecommun Networks & Informatics Sci Res Ctr, Moscow Univ, Telecommun & Informatics, 1983-1994. **Memberships:** Inst Elec & Electronics Engrs. **Research Statement & Publications:** Development methodology of the analysis and synthesis structure of the real time microprocessor control systems in the field of telecommunications. **Mailing Address:** 1425 Cornell Ct, Wheeling, IL 60090. **Fax:** 847-676-7312. **E-Mail:** vleonov@usr.com

LEON-PORTILLA, MIGUEL, PHILOSOPHY. **Personal Data:** b Mexico City, Mex, February 22, 1926; m 1965, Ascension Hernandez Trevino; c Marisa. **Education:** Loyola Univ, BA, 1948, MA, 1951; Nat Univ Mex, PhD, 1956. **Honorary Degrees:** DHL, Southern Meth Univ, 1980; PhD, Southern Meth Univ, 1980, Univ Yel Aviv, 1987, Southern Calif Univ, 1989, Toulouse Univ, 1990, Colima Univ & Univ La Paz, 1994. **Honors & Awards:** Nat Prize in Soc Sci, Govt Mex, 1981; Gamio Award, 1983; Ralphael Heliodoro Valle Prize in Hist, 1984. **Professional Experience:** Fulbright fel, 1975; distinguished lectr, Am Anthrop Asn, 1974; Guggenheim fel, 1969; dir, Inst Hist Res, 1966-1976; dir, Interam Indian Inst, Mex City, 1960-1966; asst dir, Interam Indian Inst, Mex City, 1958-1960; PROF FAC PHILOS, NAT UNIV MEX, 1957-; Secy, Interam Indian Inst, Mex City, 1955-1958. **Memberships:** Foreign mem Nat Acad Sci; Mex Acad Hist (pres, 1996); hon mem Am Hist Asn; Inst Different Civilizations; Soc Mex Anthrop; Am Anthrop Asn. **Mailing Address:** Coyoacan, 103 Alberto Zamora, Mexico City 04000, Mex.

LEONTE, OANA MARIANA, ELECTROCHEMISTRY, CATALYSIS. **Personal Data:** m 1964, Dinu Ioan; c Laura L. **Education:** Polytech Inst Bucharest, Romania, MS, 1967, PhD, 1986. **Honors & Awards:** Nicolae Teclu, Romanian Acad, 1978; Outstanding Contrib to Design & Technol, Inst Indust Technol Chem Indust, 1988. **Professional Experience:** AT LOW K DIELEC MAT, as of 2004; SR RES CHEMIST, EKC TECHNOL, CALIF, 1996-; sr res & develop scientist, Pinnacle Res Inst, Ga, 1995; sr res & develop chem engr/scientist, Space Systs, 1992-1994; sr res & develop scientist, Berkeley Polymer Technol, 1991-1992; sr chemist, Balazy Anal Lab, 1991; postdoctoral res, Lawrence Berkeley Lab, 1990-1991; Vis scholar, Univ Calif, Berkeley, 1990-1991; sr res & develop scientist & chem engr, Inst Phys Chem, 1976-1990; res & develop scientist & chem engr, Ctr Chem Timivoarz, Romanian Acad, 1971-1976; Chem engr, Drugs Co Bucharest, 1967-1971. **Memberships:** Am Chem Soc; Electrochem Soc; Catalysis Soc; AAAS; Am Inst Chem Engrs. **Research Statement & Publications:** Chemicals and materials with emphasis on chemical process, engineering, synthesis, formulation, characterization, technology as applied to materials science, semiconductors, storage energymaterials technology, catalysis, polymers and organic synthesis. **E-Mail:** odleonte@ix.netcom.com

LEOPOLD, ALDO CARL, PLANT PHYSIOLOGY, AGRONOMY. **Personal Data:** b Albuquerque, NMex, December 18, 1919; c 3. **Education:** Univ Wis, BA, 1941; Harvard Univ, MA, 1947, PhD (biol), 1948. **Honors & Awards:** Charles Reid Barnes Award, Am Soc Plant Physiologists, 1994; Golden Medal, Royal Galician Acad Sci, 2000. **Professional Experience:** FOUND PRES, FINGER LAKE LAND TRUST, as of 2006; CHMN, TROP FORESTRY INITIATIVE, as of 2003; SR POLICY ANALYST, NSF, as of 2003; WILLIAM C CROCKER SCIENTIST EMER, BOYCE THOMPSON INST, ITHACA, NY, 1990-; adj prof, Univ Fla, beginning 1988; bd govs, Am Inst Biol Sci & Am Soc Gravitational Space Biol, 1984; adj prof, Cornell Univ, beginning 1978; William C Crocker scientist, Boyce Thompson Inst, Ithaca, NY, 1978-1990; distinguished scientist, Boyce Thompson Inst, Ithaca, NY, 1977-1978; mem bd agr & renewable resources, Nat Res Coun, 1975-1978; grad dean & asst vpres res, Univ Nebr, 1975-1977; sr policy analyst, NSF, 1974-1975; mem panel regulatory biol, NSF, 1965; Carnegie vis prof, Univ Hawaii, 1962; from asst prof to prof hort, Purdue Univ, 1949-1975; plant physiologist, Hawaiian Pineapple Co, Hawaii, 1948-1949. **Memberships:** Fel AAAS; Am Soc Plant Physiol (vpres, 1959; pres, 1965); Am Soc Gravitational Space Biol (vpres, 1988, pres, 1989). **Research Statement & Publications:** Plant growth and development; seed viability; desiccation tolerance. **Mailing Address:** Boyce Thompson Inst, Cornell Univ, Tower Rd, Ithaca, NY 14853. **Fax:** 607-254-1242. **E-Mail:** acl9@cornell.edu

LEOPOLD, CARL, ENGINEERING EDUCATION. **Education:** Univ Wis, BA, 1941; Harvard Univ, MA & PhD, 1947. **Honors & Awards:** Charles Reid Barnes Life Mem Award, Am Soc Plant Physiol, 1994. **Professional Experience:** DISTINGUISHED SCIENTIST, BOYCE THOMPSON INST, CORNELL UNIV, as of 2003; dean Grad Col & asst vice res Univ Nebr, beginning 1975. **Memberships:** Am Soc Plant Physiol. **Mailing Address:** Boyce Thompson Inst, Cornell Univ, Tower Rd, Ithaca, NY 14853. **Fax:** 607-254-1242. **E-Mail:** acl9@cornell.edu

LEOPOLD, DANIEL J, ELECTRONIC & OPTICAL MATERIALS. **Personal Data:** b NY. **Education:** Rochester Inst Technol, BS, 1977; Wash Univ, MA, 1979, PhD (physics), 1983. **Professional Experience:** RES ASSOC PROF, WASH UNIV, beginning 1994; adj assoc prof, Physics Dept, Wash Univ, 1990-1994; scientist physics, McDonnell Douglas Res Labs, 1984-1994; postdoctoral fel physics, Harvard Univ, 1983-1984. **Memberships:** Am Phys Soc; Mat Res Soc. **Research Statement & Publications:** Optical and electronic properties of semiconductor quantum wells; molecular beam epitaxy; thin film amorphous semiconductors and conductive polymers; photonic devices. **Mailing Address:** Dept Physics, Wash Univ, Rm 242, Compton Hall, One Brookings Dr, Campus Box 1105, St Louis, MO 63130. **Fax:** 314-935-6219.

LEOPOLD, DONALD JOSEPH, FOREST ECOLOGY, DENDROLOGY. **Personal Data:** b Ft Thomas, Ky, July 13, 1956; m 1980, c 2. **Education:** Univ Ky, BS, 1978, MSF, 1981; Purdue Univ, PhD (forest ecology), 1984. **Professional Experience:** DISTINGUISHED TEACHING PROF, COL ENVIRON SCI & FORESTRY, STATE UNIV NY, as of 2001; assoc prof dendrol, Col Environ Sci & Forestry, State Univ NY, Syracuse, beginning 1985; res assoc, Univ Ga, Athens, 1985. **Memberships:** Ecol Soc Am; Soc Am Foresters; Torrey Bot Club; Soc Conserv Biologists; Int Asn Veg Sci. **Research Statement & Publications:** Vegetation responses to disturbance (natural or man-induced); restoration techniques for disturbed plant communities; rare plant management. **Mailing Address:** Col Environ Sci, State Univ NY, 333 Illick Hall, one Forestry Dr, Syracuse, NY 13210-2723. **Fax:** 315-470-6934. **E-Mail:** dendro@syr.edu

LEOPOLD, DOREEN GELLER, SPECTROSCOPY OF GAS PHASE IONS & RADICALS. **Personal Data:** b Brooklyn, NY, October 25, 1951; m 1980, Kenneth; c Karen S & Allison D. **Education:** Cornell Univ, BA 1972; Mass Inst Technol, BS, 1978; Harvard Univ, AM, 1980, PhD (chem), 1983. **Honors & Awards:** Presidential Young Investr Award, NSF, 1988. **Professional Experience:** PROF CHEM, UNIV MINN, as of 2006; assoc prof chem, Univ Minn, beginning 1993; asst prof, Univ Minn, 1986-1993; res assoc, Joint Inst Lab Astrophysics, 1983-1986. **Memberships:** Am Chem Soc; Am Phys Soc. **Research Statement & Publications:** Spectroscopy and Reactivity of metal clusters and organometallic complexes; union photoelectron spectroscopy; gas phase ion-molecule chem. **Mailing Address:** Dept Chem, Univ Minn, 207 Pleasant St SE B-1 139 Smith Hall, Minneapolis, MN 55455-0431. **Fax:** 612-626-7541. **E-Mail:** dleopold@chem.umn.edu

LEOPOLD, ESTELLA (BERGERE), BOTANY. **Personal Data:** b Madison, Wis, January 8, 1927. **Education:** Univ Wis, PhB, 1948; Univ Calif, Berkeley, MS, 1950; Yale Univ, PhD (bot), 1955. **Honors & Awards:** co-recipient, Conservationist Yr Award, Colo Wildlife Fedn, 1969; Keep Colo Beautiful Ann Award, 1979. **Professional Experience:** EMER ADJ PROF BOT, UNIV WASH, as of 2004; Zucker environ fel, Univ Cornell, 1993; prof bot, Univ Wash, Seattle, beginning, 1989; prof environ studies, Dept Bot & Col Forest Resources, 1989-1994; mem bd, Friends Earth Found, 1987-1989; mem, Mt St Helens Sci Adv Bd, US Forest Serv, 1986-1989; mem, Comt on Climate, AAAS, 1983-1984; mem, Climate Res Bd, 1983; prof, Dept Bot & Col Forest Resources, 1982-1989; chmn, US Nat Comt, Int Union Quaternary Res, 1982-1987; assoc ed, Quaternary Res, 1980-1983; vchmn, US Nat Comt, Int Union Quaternary Res, 1978-1982; mem, Environ Studies Bd, Nat Acad Sci, 1977-1980; prof bot & forest resources & dir, Quaternary Res Ctr, Univ Wash, Seattle, 1976-1982; mem, US Nat Comt, Int Union Quaternary Res, 1976-1978; mem, McIntyre Stennis Coop Forestry Res Adv Comt, 1974-1982; vis prof, Dept Bot & Inst Environ Studies, Univ Wis-Madison, 1971-1972; NSF grants, 1968-1969, 1979-1981, 1982-1983 & 1991; adj prof, Dept Biol, Univ Colo, 1967-1976; NSF travel grant to Spain, 1957, Poland, 1961, Eng, 1976, USSR, 1982, Can, 1987; res botanist, Paleont & Stratig Br, US Geol Survey, Denver, Colo, 1955-1976; Jr Sterling scholar, Sheffield Sci Sch scholar, 1954-1955; teaching asst, Dept Zool, 1954; Jr Sterling scholar, Yale Univ, 1953-1954; teaching asst, Dept Plant Sci, Yale Univ, 1952-1953; mycologist, Forest Prod Labs, Madison, Wis, 1952; res asst, Genetics Exp Sta, Smith Col, 1952; asst res hydrologist, Tree Ring Res Lab, Univ Ariz, 1951. **Memberships:** Nat Acad Sci; fel AAAS (pres-elect, 1994-); Am Quaternary Asn (pres-elect, 1980-1982, pres, 1982-1984); Bot Soc Am; Ecol Soc Am; fel Geol Soc Am; Sigma Xi. **Research Statement & Publications:** Late Cenozoic paleobotany, palynology, paleoecology and paleoclimate; pollen and spore floras of late Cenozoic age in Wyoming, Idaho, Washington, Colorado and Alaska; palynology research in late quaternary deposits of Connecticut, Washington and California; Upper Cretaceous pollen and spore floras of Alabama and Wyoming; history of western grasslands; forest history of Washington; history of Pacific Northwest forest associations; climate and vegetation patterns since glaciation. **Mailing Address:** Bot Dept, Univ Wash, PO Box 355325, Seattle, WA 98195-5325. **Fax:** 206-685-1728. **E-Mail:** eleopold@u.washington.edu

LEOPOLD, LUNA BERGERE, geomorphology; deceased, see previous edition for last biography

LEOPOLD, ROGER ALLEN, CRYBIOLOGY, EMBRYOLOGY. **Personal Data:** b Redwood Falls, Minn, March 23, 1937; m 1988, Dana; c 2. **Education:** Concordia Col, Minn, BA, 1962; Mont State Univ, PhD (entom), 1967. **Professional Experience:** Sir Frederick McMaster fel, Canberra, Australia, 1996; lead scientist, Bioscience Res Lab, Agr Res Serv, USDA, 1986-1988; res leader, Bioscience Res Lab, Agr Res Serv, USDA, 1976-1978; Adj prof zool, NDak State Univ, 1971-; RES ENTOMOLOGIST, BIOSCIENCE RES LAB, AGR RES SERV, USDA, 1967-; res asst stress physiol, Mont State Univ, 1962-1967. **Memberships:** AAAS; Entom Soc Am; Am Soc Zoologists; Soc Cryobiol. **Research Statement & Publications:** Insect reproductive physiology and development; cryobiology. **Mailing Address:** Bio Sci Res Lab, USDA Agr Res Serv, 1605 Albrecht Blvd PO Box 5674, Fargo, ND 58105-5674. **Fax:** 701-239-1348. **E-Mail:** leopoldr@fargo.ars.usda.gov

LEOPOLD, WILBUR RICHARD, III, EXPERIMENTAL CHEMOTHERAPY, TUMOR BIOLOGY. **Personal Data:** b Paterson, NJ, July 26, 1949; m 1989, Judith; c Matt, Aaron, Justin, Megan & John. **Education:** Univ Ill, BS, 1971, MS, 1973; Univ Wis, PhD (oncol), 1981. **Professional Experience:** PRES, MOLECULAR IMAGING RES INC, as of 2004; sr dir, cancer res inst, Parke-Davis Pharmaceut, beginning 1994; dir cancer res, Cancer Res Inst, Parke-Davis Pharmaceut, 1990-1994; sect dir tumor biol, Cancer Res Inst, Parke-Davis Pharmaceut, 1988-1990; sr res assoc 1986-1988; res assoc 1985-1986; sr scientist, Cancer Res Inst, Parke-Davis Pharmaceut, 1983-1985; scientist, Cancer Res Inst, Parke-Davis Pharmaceut, 1982-1983; res oncologist, Southern Res Inst, 1981-1982; chem engr, Exxon Co, 1971-1972 & 1973-1975. **Memberships:** Am Chem Soc; AAAS; Am Assoc Cancer Res. **Research Statement & Publications:** Model development for cancer therapy; evaluation of anticancer drugs; chemical carcinogenesis and toxicological evaluations. **Mailing Address:** Molecular Imaging Res Inc, 924 N Main St, Ann Arbor, MI 48104. **Fax:** 734-821-1066. **E-Mail:** leopolw@aa.wl.com

LEOSCHKE, WILLIAM LEROY, NUTRITION OF FUR ANIMALS. **Personal Data:** b Lockport, NY, May 2, 1927. **Education:** Valparaiso Univ, BA, 1950; Univ Wis, MS, 1952, PhD (biochem), 1954. **Professional Experience:** RETIRED; from asst prof to prof chem,

Valparaiso Univ, 1957-1995; consult, Mink Specialties Co, Ill, beginning 1955; proj assoc biochem, Univ Wis, 1954-1959; mem, Nat Res Coun, Sub Comt Fur Animal Nutrit. **Research Statement & Publications:** Biochemistry and nutrition of mink; fundamental nutritional requirements of mink; mink diseases of nutritional origin; composition of blood and urine of mink. **Mailing Address:** 278 W 100th S, Valparaiso, IN 46383-9615. **Fax:** 219-462-2804.

LEOVY, CONWAY B, METEOROLOGY. **Personal Data:** b Hermosa Beach, Calif, July 16, 1933; m 1958, c 4. **Education:** Univ Southern Calif, BA, 1954; Mass Inst Technol, PhD (meteorol), 1963. **Honors & Awards:** NASA Outstanding Sci Achievement Award, 1972. **Professional Experience:** PROF EMER ATMOSPHERIC SCI & GEOPHYS, UNIV WASH, as of 2003; dir, Univ Wash, 1986-1989; Solar Syst Explor Comt, NASA, 1984-1987; prof atmospheric sci & geophys & adj prof astron, Univ Wash, beginning 1974; mem, Comt Lunar & Planetary Exploration, 1974-1976 & Comt Atmospheric Sci, Nat Acad Sci, 1972-1975; assoc prof atmospheric sci, Univ Wash, 1969-1974; meteorologist, Rand Corp, Calif, 1963-1969; ed, J Atmos Sci. **Memberships:** Am Meteorol Soc; Am Geophys Union; AAAS. **Research Statement & Publications:** Dynamics, radiation and photochemistry of earth and planetary atmospheres. **Mailing Address:** Dept Atmospheric Sci, Univ Wash, ATG Bldg Rm 304 Box 351640, Seattle, WA 98195-1640. **Fax:** 206-543-0308. **E-Mail:** conway@atmos.washington.edu

LEPAGE, G PETER, PHYSICS. **Education:** McGill Univ, BSc, 1972; Stanford Univ, PhD, 1978. **Professional Experience:** PROF PHYSICS, CORNELL UNIV, 1989-. **Memberships:** Fel Am Phy Soc. **Mailing Address:** Newman Lab Nuclear Studies, Cornell Univ, Ithaca, NY 14853. **Fax:** 607-255-8463. **E-Mail:** gpl@mail.lepp.cornell.edu

LEPAGE, RAOUL, RANDOM PROCESSES, SEQUENTIAL ANALYSIS. **Personal Data:** b Detroit, Mich, March 5, 1938; m 1961, c 2. **Education:** Mich State Univ, BS, 1961, MS, 1962; Univ Minn, PhD (math statist), 1967. **Professional Experience:** PROF STATIST & PROBABILITY, MICH STATE UNIV, 1977-; assoc prof, Mich State Univ, 1972-1976; vis assoc prof statist & probability, Univ Colo, 1971; asst prof statist & probability, Columbia Univ, NY, 1967-1970; instr statist & probability, Columbia Univ, 1965-1966; consult statist. **Memberships:** Inst Math Statist. **Research Statement & Publications:** Isolating and proving significant properties of random processes; nonstandard statistical questions of an applied character and the interface between probability, statistics and computing. **Mailing Address:** Dept Statist & Probability, Mich State Univ, East Lansing, MI 48824. **E-Mail:** lepage@stt.msu.edu

LEPESKA, BOHUMIR, THERMOSET RESINS, RESIN STRUCTURE ANALYSIS. **Personal Data:** b Humpolec, Czech, November 7, 1939. **Education:** Inst Chem Technol, Czech, BS, 1962; Czech Acad Sci, PhD (organometallic chem), 1967. **Professional Experience:** Vis prof advan org chem, Univ Wis, 1974-1975; SR RES CHEMIST, PLASTICS ENG CO, 1972-; assoc org chem, Univ Notre Dame, 1969-1972; Res assoc, Inst Chem Technol, 1968-1969. **Memberships:** Sr mem Am Chem Soc; Sr mem Soc Plastics Eng; Sr mem Sigma Xi. **Research Statement & Publications:** Synthesis of new and improved thermosetting resins (polymers); structure-properties relationship of these resins; physical properties testing of molded test specimens. **Mailing Address:** 3234-B W Meadows Ct, Sheboygan, WI 53081. **Fax:** 920-458-1923. **E-Mail:** blepeska@plenco.com

LE PICHON, XAVIER, GEOPHYSICS, OCEANOGRAPHY. **Personal Data:** b Quinhon, Viet-Nam, June 18, 1937. **Honors & Awards:** Silver Medal, Nat Ctr Sci Res, 1973; Maurice Ewing Medal, Am Geophys Union, 1984; A G Huntsman Prize Oceanog Inst, Can, 1987; Wollaston Medal Geol Soc, London, 1991. **Professional Experience:** Vis prof, Oxford Univ, 1994 & Ocean Res Inst, Tokyo Univ, 1995; distinguished vis lectr, Nigerian Mining & Geosci Soc, 1994; PROF & CHAIR GEODYNAMICS, COL FRANCE, 1986-; DIR, DEPT GEOL, STAND SUPERIOR SCH, FRANCE, 1984-; prof, Univ P&M Curie, Paris, 1978-1984; sci adv to pres, Ctr Nat Exploitation Oceans, 1973-1978; chief, Dept Marine Geol, Ctr Oceanic Brit, Brest, 1969-1973; sci counr, Ctr Nat Exploitation Oceans, 1968-1969; Res asst, Univ Columbia, NY, 1963-1968. **Memberships:** Nat Acad Sci. **Research Statement & Publications:** Plate tectonics. **Mailing Address:** Ecole Normale Superieure Lab de Geol, 24 rue Lhomond, Paris 75231 Cedex 05, France. **Fax:** 330-144-322000. **E-Mail:** lepichon@sphene.ens.fr

LEPICOVSKY, JAN, AERONAUTICS. **Professional Experience:** SR RES ENGR, NASA GLEN RES CTR, as of 2006. **Memberships:** GTTC. **Mailing Address:** NASA Glenn Res Ctr, Cleveland, OH 44135. **Fax:** 216-977-1269. **E-Mail:** Jan.Lepicovsky@grc.nasa.gov

LEPIE, ALBERT HELMUT, PHYSICAL CHEMISTRY. **Personal Data:** b Malapane, Ger, August 6, 1923; American citizen; m 1956, c 1. **Education:** Aachen Tech Univ, MS, 1958; Munich Tech Univ, PhD (chem), 1961. **Honors & Awards:** Jannaf Cert of Recognition, 1985; William B McLean Award, 1988. **Professional Experience:** RES CHEMIST EMER, NAVAL WEAPONS CTR, as of 1996; Fel, Naval Weapons Ctr, 1990; res chemist, Naval Weapons Ctr, beginning 1964; Res chemist, Ger Inst Res Aeronaut, 1961-1963 & US Naval Propellant Plant, Md, 1963-1964; mem, Interagency Chem Rocket Propulsion Group. **Memberships:** AAAS; Sigma Xi; Am Chem Soc. **Research Statement & Publications:** Performance calculations of propellants; hypergolic ignitions; mechanical behavior of polymers; advanced testing methods. **Mailing Address:** 121 Desert Candles St, Ridgecrest, CA 93555-4218.

LEPINE, FRANCOIS, MASS SPECTROMETRY, ANALYSIS OF MICROBIAL METABOLITES. **Personal Data:** b Montreal, Que, March 1955. **Education:** Univ Que, Montreal, BSc, 1979, MSc, 1981; McGill Univ, PhD (chem), 1985. **Professional Experience:** PROF ANAL CHEM, INST ARMAND-FRAPPIER, 1987-; assoc, McGill Univ, 1986-1987. **Memberships:** Am Soc Mass Spectrometry. **Research Statement & Publications:** Mass spectrometry as a tool to study the decomposition of various organic compounds under physical treatment such as ultraviolet or gamma ray irradiation or microbial degradation. **Mailing Address:** Inst Armand-Frappier, 531 Des Prairies Blvd, Laval, PQ H7N 4Z3, Can. **Fax:** 514-686-5501. **E-Mail:** francois_lepine@iaf.uquebec.ca

LEPLEY, ARTHUR RAY, PHYSICAL ORGANIC CHEMISTRY. **Personal Data:** b Peoria, Ill, November 1, 1933; m 1985, c 4. **Education:** Bradley Univ, AB, 1954; Univ Chicago, SM, 1956, PhD (chem), 1958. **Professional Experience:** QUAL ASSURANCE OFFICER, LABS ADMIN, MD DEPT HEALTH & MENT HYG, DIV QUAL ASSURANCE, SAFETY & TRAINING, 1988-; resources Conserv, Bellevue, Wash, 1986; consult, Interox res & develop labs, Widnes, Eng, 1985; guest worker, lab chem physics, Nat Inst Arthritis, metabolism & digestive dis, Md, 1975-1976; vis prof, Univ Utah, 1969-1971; from assoc prof to prof chem, Marshall Univ, 1968-1988; asst prof chem, State Univ NY Stony Brook, 1960-1965; USPHS gen med fel, 1960; res assoc org chem, Univ Chicago, 1959-1960; res assoc org chem, Univ Munich, 1958-1959; NSF fel, 1958-1959. **Memberships:** AAAS; Am Chem Soc; Am Inst Chem; Sigma Xi. **Research Statement & Publications:** Flow nuclear magnetic resonance; microprocessor application in chemistry; total quality management; molecular rearrangements; free radical intermediates; continuing quality improvement; laboratory information systems; instrument interfaces; quality assurance; laboratory database. **Mailing Address:** Labs Admin, PO Box 2355, Baltimore, MD 21203. **Fax:** 410-333-5403. **E-Mail:** lepleyar@juno.com

LEPOCK, JAMES RONALD, BIOPHYSICS, PROTEINS & MEMBRANES. **Personal Data:** b Fairmont, WVa, October 20, 1948; m 2002, Natalia Kurnakova; c 3. **Education:** WVa Univ, BS, 1970, MS, 1972; Pa State Univ, PhD (biophys), 1976. **Professional Experience:** Chair, Univ Toronto, 2002-; CHAIR, UNIV WATERLOO, 1993-; PROF PHYSICS, UNIV WATERLOO, 1987-; NIH grant, 1985-; Med Res Coun Can grants, 1982-1985; Nat Sci & Eng Res Coun Can grant, 1978-; from asst prof to assoc prof, Univ Waterloo, 1977-1987; Fel radiobiol, New Eng Med Ctr, Tufts Univ, 1976-1977. **Memberships:** AAAS; Biophys Soc; Radiation Res Soc; NAm Hyperthermia Soc; Biophys Soc Can; Can Asn Physicists. **Research Statement & Publications:** Protein stability; differential scanning calorimetry; mammalian cell tissue culture; hypothermia and hyperthermia, radiation biology; fluorescence spectroscopy. **Mailing Address:** Dept of Med, Univ of Toronto, 610, Toronto, ON M5G2M9, Can. **Fax:** 416-946-2050. **E-Mail:** lepock@uhnres.utoronto.ca

LEPOFF, JACK H, PHYSICS. **Personal Data:** b Portland, Maine, July 22, 1923; m 1947, Sallie; c Bonnie & Laurie Ann. **Education:** Univ NH, BS, 1943; Columbia Univ, MA, 1948. **Professional Experience:** RETIRED; applns engr, HPA Div, Hewlett Packard Co, 1973-1992; diode appln mgr, HPA Div, Hewlett Packard Co, 1965-1973; eng specialist, Sylvania Electronic Defense Lab, Gen Tel & Electronics Corp, 1959-1965; sr staff mem, Motorola Inc, 1954-1959; Nat Bur Stands, 1951-1953; Naval Ord Lab, 1953-1954; electronic scientist, Naval Res Lab, 1950-1951; electronic scientist, Nat Bur Stands, 1949-1950. **Memberships:** Sigma Xi; Inst Elec & Electronics Engrs. **Research Statement & Publications:** Microwaves; semiconductors. **Mailing Address:** 850 Del Mar Downs Rd Apt 420, Solana Beach, CA 92075.

LEPORE, JOHN A(NTHONY), CIVIL ENGINEERING, APPLIED MECHANICS. **Personal Data:** b Philadelphia, Pa, February 19, 1935; m 1959, Patricia; c William, Thomas, Jacqueline & John Sr. **Education:** Drexel Inst, BSCE, 1957; Univ Pa, MS, 1961, PhD (appl mech), 1967. **Professional Experience:** PROF & UNDERGRAD CHAIR, DEPT SYST, UNIV PA, 1987-; prof & dept chair, dept Civil Eng, Univ Pa, 1978-1986; from assoc prof to prof, dept Civil & Urban Eng, Univ Pa, 1978-1986; Winterstein asst prof, dept Civil & Urban Eng, Univ Pa, 1971-1978; asst prof civil eng, dept Civil & Urban Eng, Univ Pa, 1968-1971; supv engr missile & space div, Gen Elec Co, 1961-1968; nuclear engr, NY Ship Bldg Corp, 1957-1961; Danforth assoc. **Memberships:** Am Soc Civil Engrs; Am Soc Eng Educ; Am Acad Mech; Earthquake Eng Res Inst. **Research Statement & Publications:** Stability of dynamic systems; applied mathematics; random processes; earthquake, wind and ocean engineering; disaster mitigation; solar energy applications. **Mailing Address:** 229 Towne Bldg, Univ Pa, Philadelphia, PA 19104. **Fax:** 215-898-5020. **E-Mail:** lepore@seas.upenn.edu

LEPOUTRE, PIERRE, POLYMER CHEMISTRY, PAPER SCIENCE. **Personal Data:** b Roubaix, France, July 28, 1933; Canadian citizen; m 1962, c 3. **Education:** Sch Advan Indust Studies, Lille, BSc, 1957; NC State Univ, MSc, 1960, PhD (chem eng), 1968. **Honors & Awards:** Coating & Graphic Arts Div Award, Tech Asn Pulp & Paper Indust. **Professional Experience:** PROF EMER CHEM ENG, UNIV MAINE, as of 2004; OBER CHAIR, UNIV MAINE, 1991-; prof chem eng, Univ Maine, beginning 1991; dir, appl Surface Sci Div, 1982-1991; head, Polymer Sect, 1978-1982; res engr, Pulp & Paper res Inst, 1971-1978; res engr, Consol Bathurst, 1968-1971; res engr, Int Cellulose res, 1963-1966; chem engr, Rohm & Haas France, 1960-1963; chem engr, Olegum, France, 1957-1958. **Memberships:** Fel Tech Asn Pulp & Paper Indust; Can Tech Asn Pulp & Paper Indust. **Research Statement & Publications:** Chemical modification of cellulose; adhesion; polymer latexes; paper coating. **Mailing Address:** Dept Chem Eng, Univ Maine, 117 Jenness Hall, Orono, ME 04469-6737. **Fax:** 207-581-2323. **E-Mail:** lepoutre@maine.edu

LEPOW, MARTHA LIPSON, PEDIATRICS, INFECTIOUS DISEASES. **Personal Data:** b Cleveland, Ohio, March 28, 1927; wid, c Lauren, David & Daniel. **Education:** Oberlin Col, BA, 1948; Case Western Res Univ, MD, 1952. **Professional Experience:** Chmn dept, Albany Med Col, 1995-1997; mem comt infectious dis, Am Acad Pediat, 1985-1991; vchmn dept, Albany Med Col, 1982-1995; PROF PEDIAT, ALBANY MED COL, 1978-; dir, Clin Studies Ctr, Albany Med Col, 1978-1987; mem study sects, NIH, 1972-1976; from assoc prof to prof pediat, Sch Med, Univ Conn, 1967-1978; sr instr & asst prof, Case Western Res Univ, 1958-1967; fel infectious dis, Cleveland Metro Gen Hosp, 1956-1958; intern & resident pediat, Case Western Res Univ, 1952-1956. **Memberships:** Am Pediat Soc; Am Asn Immunol; Infectious Dis Soc Am; emer mem Soc Pediat Res; Am Acad Pediat; Am Soc Microbiol. **Research Statement & Publications:** Clinical vaccine evaluation. **Mailing Address:** Dept Pediat, Albany Med Col, 47 New Scotland Ave Me 24, Albany, NY 12208-3478.

LEPOW, RONALD, SCIENTIFIC ADMINISTRATION. **Education:** Univ Houston, BS, 1967; Ill Col Podiatric Med, DPM, 1971. **Professional Experience:** SURG STAFF, ST. LUKES EPISCOPAL HOSP, as of 2006; SURG STAFF, ST. JOSEPH HOSP, as of 2006; FOUNDER, LEPOW FOOT & ANKLE SPECIALISTS, as of 2006. **Mailing Address:** Lepow Foot & Ankle Specialists, 6624 Fannin St Ste 1690, Houston, TX 77030.

LEPOWSKY, JAMES IVAN, MATHEMATICAL CONFORMAL FIELD THEORY. **Personal Data:** b New York, NY, July 5, 1944; m Lael. **Education:** Harvard Univ, AB, 1965; Mass Inst Technol, PhD (math), 1970. **Professional Experience:** Guggenheim fel, 1987-1988; mem, Math Sci Res Inst, 1983-1984; PROF MATH, RUTGERS UNIV, 1980-; assoc ed, Am Math Soc, 1980-1985; vis assoc prof math, Univ Paris, 1978; assoc prof, Rutgers Univ, 1977-1980; Alfred P Sloan fel, 1976-1978; mem, Sch Math, Inst Advan Study, 1975-1976, 1980, 1985, 1987-1988, 1992; asst prof math, Yale Univ, 1972-1977; lectr & res assoc math, Brandeis Univ, 1970-1972. **Memberships:** Am Math Soc; Math Asn Am; Am Phys Soc. **Research Statement & Publications:** Conformal field theory; vertex operator algebra theory; interactions with other branches of mathematics and physics; finite group theory; string theory; infinite-dimensional lie theory; combinatorics. **Mailing Address:** Hill Ctr Busch Campus, Rutgers Univ, Rm 303, New Brunswick, NJ 08854-8019.

LEPP, CYRUS ANDREW, CLINICAL BIOCHEMISTRY, DRUG ANALYSIS. **Personal Data:** b Brooklyn, NY, August 11, 1946; m 1972, Faye; c Darius H & Marcus D. **Education:** Syracuse Univ, BS, 1968, PhD (biochem), 1974. **Professional Experience:** DIR TECHNOL, OLYMPUS AM INC, 1991-; mgr, Reagent Systs Res & Develop, Ciba-Corning Diag, 1985-1991; mgr develop, Corning Med & Sci, 1980-1985; sr biochemist clin chem & biochem, Corning Glass Works, 1974-1980; lab technician clin chem, Nassau Hosp, 1968-1969. **Memberships:** Am Asn Clin Chem; Am Chem Soc. **Research Statement & Publications:** Electrophoretic separations of isoenzymes and hemoglobins; development of specific isoenzyme assay procedures; development of immunologic assays, clinical chemistry reagents, clinical chemistry controls, bloodgas reagents and controls. **Mailing Address:** Olympus Am Inc, Two Corporate Dr, Melville, NY 11747. **Fax:** 516-544-6405.

LEPPARD, GARY GRANT, CELL BIOLOGY, AQUATIC MICROBIAL ECOLOGY, CORRELATIVE MICROSCOPY. **Personal Data:** b Medicine Hat, Alta, August 6, 1940; Canadian citizen; m 1970, Kristine; c Enrico & Desiree. **Education:** Univ Sask, BA, 1962, BA hons, 1963, MA, 1964; Yale Univ, MS, 1966, MPhil, 1967, PhD (biol), 1968. **Honors & Awards:** NATO Sci Award, 1981; Comn Europ Communities Award, 1982; Japan Inst Res Innovative Technol Earth Award, 1993. **Professional Experience:** ADJ PROF, DEPT BIOL, MCMASTER UNIV, as of 2006; partner AFMNet, Can Network Centres Excellence, beginning 2003; mem/adj prof, Brockhouse Inst Materials Res, Hamilton, Ont, beginning 2002; consult fel, World Innovation Found, beginning 2002; ed, Flocculation Natural Engineered Environl Systs, 2001-2005; IUPAC fel, beginning 1998; mem, Comm Environ Anal Chem, Int Union Pure & Appl Chem, 1989-1995 & Comm Fundamental Environ Chem, 1996-1998; RITE (Japan) award, 1993; edl bd, Encycl Anall Sci, 1991-1995; prof biol, McMaster Univ, Hamilton, Ont, beginning 1988; adj prof environ biol, Univ Guelph, Ont, 1988-1992; Comn Europ Communities award, 1982; ed, Trace Element Speciation Surface Waters, 1981-1982; NATO sci award, 1981; adj prof, Dept Biol, Univ Ottawa, 1974-1975; RES SCIENTIST BIOL, CAN DEPT ENVIRON, 1971-; pres, Ottawa Biol & Biochem Soc, 1973-1974; sci res exec mem, Prof Inst Pub Serv Can, 1971-1973; biochem lab, Nat Res Coun Can, 1970-1971; Nat Res Coun Sci fel, Fac Sci, Univ Laval, 1969-1970; NATO sci fel, Inst Pharmacol, Univ Milan, 1969; NATO sci fel, Fac Med, Univ Paris, 1968. **Memberships:** Sigma Xi. **Research Statement & Publications:** Physicochemical and ecotoxicological relationships between living cells, nutrients and contaminants in aquatic ecosystems; technology transfer from biomedical sciences into aquatic sciences for analyzing the behaviour of aquatic colloid systems, biofilms and flocs. **Mailing Address:** Aquatic Ecosystem Mgt Res Div, Nat Water Res Inst, CCIW, 867 Lakeshore Rd PO Box 5050, Burlington, ON L7R 4A6, Can. **Fax:** 905-336-4420. **E-Mail:** gary.leppard@ec.gc.ca

LEPPELMEIER, GILBERT WILLISTON, PHYSICS. **Personal Data:** b Cleveland, Ohio, August 19, 1936; m 1984, Merja Lahteenaho; c Timothy G, Erika S & Kai T. **Education:** Yale Univ, BS, 1957; Univ Calif, Berkeley, PhD (physics), 1965. **Professional Experience:** RES PROF, FINNISH METEOROL INST, 1992-; res prof, Tech Res Cent, Finland, 1990-1992; sr scientist, Tech Res Cent, Finland, 1986-1992; scientist, Inst Tech Physics, Nuclear Res Ctr, Karlsruhe, Ger, 1985-1986; physicist magnetic-fusion, Lawrence Livermore Lab, 1977-1985; sr scientist laser-fusion, Lab for Laser Energetics, Univ Rochester, 1975-1977; physicist laser physics, Lawrence Livermore Lab, 1967-1975; lectr physics, Univ Sussex, 1966-1967; NATO fel physics, Free Univ Brussels, 1965-1966; Jr physicist neutron physics, Lawrence Livermore Lab, 1957-1959; Europ Space Agency & Gomos Sci adv group. **Memberships:** Am Phys Soc; Inst Elec & Electronics Engrs; Europ Phys Soc; Finnish Phys Soc. **Research Statement & Publications:** Application of small computers to instrument development and control; space instruments; atmospheric and planetary research. **Mailing Address:** Finnish Meteorol Inst/GEO, PO Box 503, Helsinki 00101, Finland. **Fax:** 358-019-29539. **E-Mail:** gilbert.leppelmeier@fmi.fi

LEPPI, THEODORE JOHN, ANATOMY, MEDICAL SCHOOL ADMINISTRATION. **Personal Data:** b Mountain Iron, Minn, May 30, 1933; wid Gloria (Deceased); c Sandra, Peter & Dorothea. **Education:** Albion Col, BA, 1959; Yale Univ, PhD (anat), 1963. **Professional Experience:** PROF EMER, SCH MED, UNIV SC, as of 2002; clinical adj prof path& anat, Unt Health Sci Ctr, Ft Worth, beginning 1999; assoc dean admis & prof anat & cell biol, Health Sci Ctr, Univ NTex, Ft Worth, 1990-1999; vis prof, Sch Med Univ Hawaii, 1988; vis scientist, Pac Biomed Res Ctr, Univ Hawaii, 1978-1979; dir admis, Sch Med, Univ Minn, Duluth, 1971-1977 & 1983-1989; assoc dean, prof Biomed Anat & Chmn Dept, Sch Med, Univ Minn, Duluth, 1971-1988; assoc dean, Sch Med, Univ Minn, Duluth, 1971-1977; Lederle Med Fac Award, 1968-1971; from asst prof to assoc prof anat, Sch Med, Univ NMex, 1966-1971; asst prof lectr, Sch Med, George Wash Univ, 1965-1966; staff fel, Lab Exp Path, Nat Inst Arthritis & Metab Dis, 1963-1966; guest lectr, Sch Med, Georgetown Univ, 1963-1964. **Memberships:** Am Asn Clin Anat. **Research Statement & Publications:** Anatomical basis for the sectional imaging modalities. **Mailing Address:** Dept Cell Biol & Anat, Sch Med, Univ SC, Columbia, SC 29208. **Fax:** 803-733-1533. **E-Mail:** jleppi@ix.netcom.com

LEPPLA, STEPHEN HOWARD, BACTERIAL TOXINS, PROTEIN PURIFICATION. **Personal Data:** b Oak Park, Ill, February 1, 1941; m 1980. **Education:** Calif Inst Technol, BS, 1963; Univ Wis-Madison, PhD (biochem), 1969. **Professional Experience:** SR INVESTR, BACTERIAL TOXINS & THERAPEUT SECT, NIH, as of 2005; res chemist, Nat Inst Dent Res, beginning 1989; res chemist, US Army Med Res Inst Infectious Dis, 1974-1989; res assoc, Div Biol & Med Sci, Brown Univ, 1971-1973; NIH fel, Dept Molecular Biol, Univ Calif, Berkeley, 1969-1971. **Memberships:** Am Soc Microbiol; Am Chem Soc; Am Soc Cell Biol. **Research Statement & Publications:** Study of bacterial protein toxins to discover mechanisms of action, structure-function relationships; vaccine design; employment of methods of protein purification; immunochemical characterizations using monoclonal antibodies; gene cloning and eukaryotic cell culture. **Mailing Address:** Bacterial Toxins & Therapeut sect, Div Intramural Res, Nat Inst Allergy & Infectious Dis, NIH, Bldg 30 Rm 303, Bethesda, MD 20892-0030. **Fax:** 301-480-0326. **E-Mail:** leppla@mail.nih.gov

LEPPLE, FREDERICK KARL, CHEMICAL OCEANOGRAPHY, GEOCHEMISTRY. **Personal Data:** b Newark, NJ, July 1, 1944; m 1975, c 2. **Education:** Univ Miami, BS, 1967, MS, 1971; Univ Del, PhD (marine studies), 1975. **Professional Experience:** PROG MGR, SHIP SAFETY & SURVIVABILITY, CHIEF NAVAL OPERS, 1989-; res chemist marine aerosols, Nat Acad Sci-Nat Res Coun, Naval Res Lab, 1976-1989; res assoc, Nat Acad Sci-Nat Res Coun, Naval Res Lab, 1974-1976; res chemist org polymers, Air Reduction Corp, 1967-1968. **Memberships:** AAAS; Am Chem Soc; Am Geophys Union. **Research Statement & Publications:** Chemistry, transport and effects of aerosols in the marine environment; marine geochemistry and oceanography; fire protection applied to navy ships. **Mailing Address:** Chief Naval Oper N86D, Pentagon Rm No 4D537, Washington, DC 20350-2000.

LEPS, THOMAS MACMASTER, CIVIL ENGINEERING, GEOTECHNICAL ENGINEERING. **Personal Data:** b Keyser, WVa, December 3, 1914; m 1940, c 1. **Education:** Stanford Univ, AB, 1936; Mass Inst Technol, MS, 1939. **Honors & Awards:** Cert of Appreciation, Am Soc Civil Engrs, 1961. **Professional Experience:** Vchmn, Exec Comt, US Comt Large Dams, 1978-1980; mem, Exec Comt, US Comt Large Dams, 1976-; mem, Peer Group Mem Comt, Nat Acad Eng, 1975-1977; CONSULT CIVIL ENGR DAMS & POWER PLANTS, THOMAS M LEPS INC, 1963-; chief engr dams & found, Shannon & Wilson, 1961-1963; mem & chmn exec comt, Soil Mech & Found Div, Am Soc Civil Engrs, 1955-1961; chief civil engr dams & power plants, Southern Calif Edison Co, 1946-1961; asst engr dams, US Bur Reclamation, 1941-1942; jr engr dams, US Corps Engrs, 1939-1941. **Memberships:** Nat Acad Eng; Am Soc Civil Engrs. **Research Statement & Publications:** Soil mechanics and seismologic engineering. **Mailing Address:** PO Box 217, Dinuba, CA 93618.

LEPSE, PAUL ARNOLD, ORGANIC CHEMISTRY. **Personal Data:** b Seattle, Wash, March 18, 1937; m 1961, c 2. **Education:** Seattle Pac Col, BS, 1958; Univ Wash, PhD (org chem), 1962. **Professional Experience:** PROF EMER CHEM, SEATTLE PAC UNIV, 2002-; prof chem, Seattle Pac Univ, 1972-2002; from asst prof to assoc prof, Seattle Pac Univ, 1963-1972; NSF fel, Univ Munich, 1961-1962. **Memberships:** AAAS; Am Chem Soc; Sigma Xi. **Research Statement & Publications:** Organic reaction mechanisms; carbene chemistry. **Mailing Address:** Dept Chem, Seattle Pac Univ, 3307 Third Ave W, Seattle, WA 98119-1899.

LEPSELTER, MARTIN P, ENGINEERING. **Personal Data:** b New York, NY, November 24, 1929; m Joan; c 3. **Education:** City Univ NY, BME, 1951. **Honors & Awards:** Jack A Morton Award, Inst Elec & Electronics Engrs, 1979; Daniel C Hughes Jr Mem Award, Int Soc Hybrid Microelectronics. **Professional Experience:** FOUNDER LEPTON INC, as of 1999; pres, Bell Telephone Labs Fel Inc, beginning 1993; chmn, pres & chief exec officer, Lepton Inc, 1986-1993; dir, Advan Very Large Scale Integration Develop Lab, AT&T Bell Labs, Murray Hill, NJ, 1957-1986. **Memberships:** Nat Acad Eng; fel Inst Elec & Electronics Engrs; Am Soc Mech Engrs. **Research Statement & Publications:** Engineering; granted 47 US patents. **Mailing Address:** Lepton Inc, 3020 Bridgeway, Sausalito, CA 94965. **Fax:** 415-703-0240.

LE QUESNE, PHILIP WILLIAM, ORGANIC CHEMISTRY. **Personal Data:** b Auckland, NZ, January 6, 1939. **Education:** Univ Auckland, MSc, 1961, PhD (chem), 1964. **Honorary Degrees:** DSc, Univ Auckland, 1979. **Professional Experience:** ASSOC DIR, BARNETT INST, 1993-; interim vice provost res & grad educ, Northeastern Univ, 1992-1993; chmn dept, Northeastern Univ, 1979-1987; PROF CHEM & MED CHEM, NORTHEASTERN UNIV, 1978-; assoc prof org chem, Northeastern Univ, 1973-1978; asst prof, Univ Mich, Ann Arbor, 1967-1973; teaching fel, Univ BC, 1966-1967; res assoc, Univ BC, 1965-1966; res assoc org chem, Oxford Univ, 1964-1965. **Memberships:** Am Chem Soc; Phytochem Soc NAm; Royal Soc Chem; NZ Inst Chem; Am Soc Pharmacog. **Research Statement & Publications:** Natural product chemistry, especiallysteroids, alkaloids, terpenoids, fungal metabolites; comparative phytochemistry; physiologically active compounds. **Mailing Address:** Dept Chem, Barnett Inst, Boston, MA 02115-5096. **Fax:** 617-373-8795. **E-Mail:** p.lequesne@neu.edu

LERBEKMO, JOHN FRANKLIN, GEOLOGY. **Personal Data:** b Alta, December 8, 1924; m 1949, c Craig, Janice, Todd & Mona. **Education:** Univ BC, BASc, 1949; Univ Calif, Berkeley, PhD (geol), 1956. **Professional Experience:** Prof, Univ Alta, ending 1991; PROF EMER SEDIMENTARY GEOL, UNIV ALTA, 1991-; assoc prof, Univ Alta, beginning 1959; asst prof geol, Univ Alta, 1956-1959. **Memberships:** Geol Soc Am; Geol Asn Can; Can Soc Petrol Geologists. **Research Statement & Publications:** Sedimentary petrology; detrital sediments; magnetostratigraphy. **Mailing Address:** Dept Earth & Atmospheric Sci, Univ Alta, 4-21 Earth Sci Bldg, Edmonton, AB T6G 2E3, Can. **Fax:** 780-492-2030. **E-Mail:** johnlerbekmo@ualberta.ca

LERCH, IRVING A, MEDICAL PHYSICS. **Personal Data:** b Chicago, Ill, June 29, 1938; m 1963. **Education:** US Mil Acad, BS, 1960; Univ Chicago, SM, 1966, PhD (med physics), 1969. **Professional Experience:** DIR, AM PHYSICS SOCI, COL PARK, as of 2004; Various corps, Int Atomic Energy Agency & WHO, 1976-; prof & sr Physicist, NY Univ Med Ctr, 1976-1993; consult med radiation physics, Int Atomic Energy Agency & WHO, 1976-1986; first officer, Int Atomic Energy Agency, Vienna, 1973-1975; res assoc med physics, Univ Chicago, 1969-1972. **Memberships:** Am Phys Soc; Am Asn Physicists in Med; Radiation Res Soc. **Research Statement & Publications:** Diagnostic radiological physics as applied to problems in image quality; cell kinetic and modelling studies as applied to problems in radiation therapy; dosimetry in radiation oncology physics; radiofrequency-induced tissue hyperthermia; computers in medicine and computer-mediated telecommunications. **Mailing Address:** The Am Physical Soc, One Physics Ellipse, Col Park, MD 20740-3844. **E-Mail:** lerch@aps.org

LERCHE, RICHARD ALLAN, LASER FUSION DIAGNOSTICS. **Personal Data:** b Chicago, Ill, February 6, 1943. **Education:** Univ Ill, BS, 1966, MS, 1967, PhD (nuclear eng), 1972. **Honors & Awards:** R&D 100 Award - 1988. **Professional Experience:** RES SCIENTIST, LASER ENG DIV, LAWRENCE LIVERMORE NAT LAB, 1972-. **Memberships:** Am Phys Soc; Inst Elec & Electronics Engrs. **Research Statement & Publications:** Laser fusion diagnostics; neutron diagnostics; streak cameras. **Mailing Address:** Lawrence Livermore Nat Lab, 7000 E Ave, Livermore, CA 94551. **E-Mail:** lerche1@llnl.gov

LERCHER, BRUCE L, MATHEMATICAL LOGIC. **Personal Data:** b Milwaukee, Wis, June 7, 1930; m 1960, c 2. **Education:** Univ Wis, BS, 1951, MS, 1952; Pa State Univ, PhD (math), 1963. **Professional Experience:** ASSOC PROF EMER MATH, STATE UNIV NY, BINGHAMTON, as of 2001; assoc prof math, State Univ Ny, Binghamton, beginning 1967; asst prof, State Univ NY, Binghamton, 1962-1967; Instr math, Univ Rochester, 1959-1962. **Memberships:** Math Asn Am; Asn Symbolic Logic. **Research Statement & Publications:** Combinatory logic. **Mailing Address:** Dept Math, State Univ NY, Binghamton, NY 13902.

LE RICHE, WILLIAM HARDING, medicine; deceased, see previous edition for last biography

LERKE, SUSAN A, CHEMISTRY. **Education:** Univ DE, PhD, 1992. **Professional Experience:** ASST DIR, JOHNSON & JOHNSON PHARMACEUT, as of 2003. **Mailing Address:** Johnson & Johnson, 802 Old Westtown Rd, Spring House, PA 19382-5277. **Fax:** 215-628-3297. **E-Mail:** slerke@prdus.jnj.com

LERMA, TONY, MATHEMATICS. **Education:** Southwest Tex State Univ, BS, 1972; Univ Tex, Austin, PhD (math), 1990. **Professional Experience:** PROF, DEPT MATH, TEX SOUTHMOST COL, UNIV TEX, BROWNSVILLE, as of 2006. **Memberships:** Math Asn Am. **Mailing Address:** Tex Southmost Col, 80 Ft Brown, Brownsville, TX 78520. **Fax:** 956-574-6637. **E-Mail:** alerma@utb1.utb.edu

LERMAN, ABRAHAM, TECHNICAL MANAGEMENT. **Personal Data:** b Harbin, China, November 14, 1935; American citizen; c 1. **Education:** Hebrew Univ, Israel, MSc, 1960; Harvard Univ, PhD (geol), 1964. **Professional Experience:** Underground injection controls, US Environ Protection Agency, beginning 1989; mem, Mat Rev Bd, 1985-1988; mem, peer rev panels nuclear repository projs, Argonne Nat Lab, beginning 1983; consult, Basalt Waste Isolation Proj, US Dept Energy, 1981-1987; vis prof, Inst Aquatic Sci, Univ Karlsruhe, 1979, 1981 & 1987; vis prof, Inst Aquatic Sci, Swiss Fed Inst Technol, Duebendorf, 1976-1977; PROF GEOL SCI, NORTHWESTERN UNIV, 1975-; assoc prof, Northwestern Univ, 1971-1975; res scientist chem limnol, Can Ctr Inland Waters, Can Dept Environ, 1969-1971; sr scientist, Weizmann Inst, Israel, 1966-1969; asst prof, Univ Ill, Chicago, 1965-1968; asst prof, Johns Hopkins Univ, 1964-1965; lectr geol, Johns Hopkins Univ, 1964; Guggenheim fel. **Memberships:** AAAS; Geochem Soc; Am Chem Soc; fel Geol Soc Am; Am Geophys Union; Sigma Xi. **Research Statement & Publications:**

Global biogeochemical cycles; water and sediment geochemistry; transport processes; nuclear wastes; surface and ground water quality. **Mailing Address:** Dept Geol Sci, Northwestern Univ, 1850 Campus Dr, Evanston, IL 60208. **Fax:** 847-491-8060. **E-Mail:** abe@earth.northwestern.edu

LERMAN, CHARLES L, COMPUTATIONAL CHEMISTRY, BIO-ORGANIC CHEMISTRY. **Personal Data:** b Elizabeth, NJ, April 23, 1948; div, c 1. **Education:** Yale Univ, BS, 1969; Harvard Univ, AM, 1970, PhD (org chem), 1974. **Professional Experience:** PRINCIPAL CHEMIST, ASTRAZENECA PHARMACEUT, 1981-; asst prof, Haverford Col, 1976-1981; asst prof chem, Juniata Col, 1974-1976. **Memberships:** Am Chem Soc; AAAS; Sigma Xi. **Research Statement & Publications:** Enzyme mechanisms and model systems; NMR studies of biochemical systems; protein modeling; comptational chemistry and information. **Mailing Address:** AstraZeneca Pharmaceuticals, 1800 Concord Pike, Wilmington, DE 19850. **E-Mail:** charles.lerman@astrazeneca.com

LERMAN, LEONARD SOLOMON, MOLECULAR BIOLOGY. **Personal Data:** b Pittsburgh, Pa, June 27, 1925; div, c Averil, Lisa & Alexander. **Education:** Carnegie Inst Technol, BS, 1945; Calif Inst Technol, PhD (chem), 1950. **Professional Experience:** RETIRED; ed, Genomics, 1990-1994; subcomt Human Genome, Dept Energy-NIH, 1989-1993; bd, Radiation Effects Res, Nat Res Coun, 1988-1996; sr lectr, Dept Biol, Mass Inst Technol, beginning 1987; mem, Health & Environ Adv Bd, Dept Energy, 1987-1992; dir diagnostics, Genetics Inst, 1984-1987; prof & chmn dept biol sci, State Univ NY, Albany, 1977-1984; Guggenheim fel, 1971-1972; NIH study sect, 1969-19732; prof molecular biol, Vanderbilt Univ, 1965-1977; mem, NSF Adv Panel, 1965-1968; USPHS res career award, 1963-1965; from asst to prof biophys, Univ Colo, 1953-1965; asst prof, Univ Colo, 1952-1953; instr pediat, Univ Colo, 1951-1952; Schenley fel, Univ Chicago, 1949-1951; asst chem, Calif Inst Technol, 1945-1949; asst org chem & explosives, Explosives Res Lab, Carnegie Inst Technol, 1945. **Memberships:** Nat Acad Sci; AAAS; Soc Human Genetics. **Research Statement & Publications:** Aspects of the physical nature of DNA as related to human genetics; mutagenesis; structure of the nucleus; recognition of genetic variations. **Mailing Address:** Mass Inst Technol, Dept Biol, Rm 68-630, Cambridge, MA 02139. **E-Mail:** islerman@mit.edu

LERMAN, MANUEL, COMPUTABILITY THEORY. **Personal Data:** b New York, NY, February 5, 1943; m 1975, c 2. **Education:** City Col NY, BS, 1964; Cornell Univ, PhD (math logic), 1968. **Professional Experience:** Mem, Math Sci Res Inst, Berkeley, 1990; Vis prof, Univ Ill, Chicago Circle, 1975-1976 & Univ Chicago, 1980; PROF MATH, UNIV CONN, 1976-; assoc prof, Univ Conn, 1973-1976; asst prof, Yale Univ, 1970-1973; Instr math, Mass Inst Technol, 1968-1970. **Memberships:** Am Math Soc; Asn Symbolic Logic. **Research Statement & Publications:** Recursive function theory; recursive model theory. **Mailing Address:** Dept Math, Univ Conn, Storrs, CT 06269. **Fax:** 860-486-4238. **E-Mail:** mlerman@math.uconn.edu

LERMAN, MICHAEL ISAAC, MOLECULAR CLONING OF HUMAN TUMOR SUPPRESSOR GENES & GENES CAUSING ALZHEIMERS DISEASE & GENES UNDERLYING GENERAL COGNITIVE ABILITIES/IQ. **Personal Data:** b Korosten, USSR, September 21, 1932; American citizen; m 1975, Eugenia; c Eugene M & Leah V. **Education:** First Moscow Med Sch, MD, 1957; Acad Med Sci, Moscow, PhD (biochem), 1961, DSc(molecular biol), 1968. **Honors & Awards:** Director's Award, NIH, 1992. **Professional Experience:** CHIEF, CANCER CAUSING GENES SECTION, LAB IMMUNOL, NAT CANCER INST, Frederick, NIH, 1990-; Consult, Diag Div, Abbott Labs, 1989-1993; expert, Lab Immunol, Nat Cancer Inst, Frederick, NIH, 1987-1990; vis scientist, Lab Immunol, Nat Cancer Inst, Frederick, NIH, 1980-1987; dir, Lab Molecular Pathobiol, 1968-1979; sr scientist, Inst Biol Med Chem, Acad Med Sci, Moscow, 1966-1978; sr scientist, Inst Molecular Biol, Acad Sci, Moscow, 1962-1964 & Bach Inst Biochem, 1964-1966; Asst prof biochem, Dept Biochem, First Moscow Med Sch, 1960-1962. **Memberships:** Am Soc Biol Chemists; AAAS; Am Soc Human Genetics; Genetic Soc Am; Int Mammalian Genome Soc; Am Asn Cancer Res. **Research Statement & Publications:** Molecular biology of protein biosynthesis; molecular biology of aging; molecular genetics of human cancers; molecular cloning of disease genes; cloning and identification of genes involved in general cognitive abilities/IQ. **Mailing Address:** Nat Cancer Inst-Frederick, Bldg 560 Rm 12-68, Frederick, MD 21702. **Fax:** 301-846-6145. **E-Mail:** lerman@ncifcrf.gov

LERMAN, STEVEN I, OCCUPATIONAL SAFETY & HEALTH, ASBESTOS. **Personal Data:** b Bronx, NY, November 14, 1944; m 1965, Ruth; c Craig, Tracy & Erica. **Education:** Queen's Col, City Univ NY, BS, 1965; Adelphi Univ, MS, 1972. **Honors & Awards:** Outstanding Serv Award, Am Soc Testing & Mat, 1988. **Professional Experience:** Tall Oaks Publ, 1989- & FED Training Ctr, 1991-; consult, Nat Inst Stand & Technol, US Dept Com, 1988-; CONSULT CHEM, SIL CONSULT, 1988-; instr, Inst Asbestos Awareness, 1988-1990; sr chemist, NY Power Authority, 1986-1988; subcomt chmn, Am Soc Testing & Mat, 1983-; cong sci counr, Am Chem Soc, 1981-1983; chemist, Con Edison NY, 1965-1986. **Memberships:** fel Am Inst Chemists; Environ Info Asn; Am Chem Soc; Am Soc Testing & Mat. **Research Statement & Publications:** Environmental laboratories; quality assurance programs for compliance; industrial health and safety; computer systems. **Mailing Address:** SIL Consult, Three Allan Gate, Plainview, NY 11803. **Fax:** 516-433-3412.

LERMAN, ZAFRA MARGOLIN, SCIENCE FOR NON-SCIENCE MAJORS, TEACHER PREPARATION & TRAINING. **Personal Data:** b Haife, Israel, January 24, 1937; American citizen. **Education:** Technion-Israel Inst Technol, BS, 1960, MS, 1964; Weizmann Inst Sci, PhD (chem), 1969. **Honors & Awards:** Natural Catalyst Award, Chem Manufacturers Asn, 1990. **Professional Experience:** DISTINGUISHED PROF SCI & PUB POLICY, DEPT SCI & MATH, as of 2003; PRES, MIMSAD, as of 2003; FOUNDER, FEET SCI, as of 2003; Prin investr, USN, 1991-; HEAD, INST SCI EDUC & SCI COMMUN, COLUMBIA, COL, 1991-; vis scholar, Grad Prog Sci, Technol & Pub Policy, George Wash, Univ, 1984-1985; chair & founder, Dept Sci & Math, 1981-1991; prin investr, NSF, 1979-1981 & 1987-; dir sci prog, Inst Sci Educ & Sci Commun, 1977-1981; vis scholar, Tech Chem Lab, ETH, Zurich, Switz, 1976-1977; res assoc, Dept Chem, Northwestern Univ, 1972-1976; fel, Dept Chem, Cornell Univ, 1969-1972; founder & chairperson, Dept Sci & Math, Columbia Col. **Memberships:** AAAS; Am Chem Soc; Int Coun Asn Sci Educ; Int Union Pure & Appl Chem; Nat Sci Teachers Asn; NY Acad Sci; Fel Am Inst Chemists; Royal Soc Chem. **Research Statement & Publications:** College science course for non-science majors future communicators; courses for pre-service teachers; teacher enhancement workshops; community-based workshops for teachers and parents together. **Mailing Address:** Inst Sci Educ & Sci Commun, Columbia Col Chicago, 600 S Mivh Ave, Chicago, IL 60605-1996. **Fax:** 312-344-8051.

LERNER, AARON BUNSEN, DERMATOLOGY, BIOCHEMISTRY. **Personal Data:** b Minneapolis, Minn, September 21, 1920; m 1989, Millie; c Peter, Michael, Ethan & Seth. **Education:** Univ Minn, BA, 1941, MS, 1942, MB & PhD (physiol chem), 1945, MD, 1945; Am Bd Dermat, dipl, 1953. **Honors & Awards:** Myron-Gordon Award, 1969; Stephen Rothman Award, 1971; Dome Lectr, 1980; Lita Annenberg Hazen Award, 1981. **Professional Experience:** EMER PROF, DEPT DERMAT, SCH MED, YALE UNIV, as of 2006; prof, Sch Med, Yale Univ, 1958-1995; chmn dept, Sch Med, Yale Univ, 1958-1985; assoc prof, Sch Med, Yale Univ, 1955-1957; assoc prof, Univ Ore, 1952-1955; asst prof dermat, Med Sch, Univ Mich, 1949-1952; Am Cancer Soc fel, Sch Med, Western Res Univ, 1948-1949; asst physiol chem, Univ Minn, 1941-1945. **Memberships:** Inst Med-Nat Acad Sci; Soc Invest Dermat; Am Acad Dermat; Am Soc Biol Chemists; Sigma Xi. **Research Statement & Publications:** Plasma proteins associated with disease; metabolism of phenylalanine and tyrosine; biochemistry of melanin pigmentation; mechanism of endocrine control of pigmentation; malignant melanomas; cryoglobulins; biochemistry of skin; author or co-author of numerous publications. **Mailing Address:** Dept Dermat, Yale Univ Sch Med, PO Box 208059, New Haven, CT 06520-8059. **Fax:** 203-397-3944. **E-Mail:** aaron.lerner@yale.edu

LERNER, ALBERT MARTIN, INTERNAL MEDICINE. **Personal Data:** b St Louis, Mo, September 3, 1929; div, c 4. **Education:** Wash Univ, BA, 1950, MD, 1954; Am Bd Internal Med, dipl, 1961. **Professional Experience:** CLIN PROF MED, COL MED, WAYNE STATE UNIV, 1982-; chief, Hutzel Hosp Med Unit, 1970-1982; clin consult bact lab, Detroit Gen Hosp, 1969-; prof med, Col Med, Wayne State Univ, 1967-1982; assoc med & path & dir bact lab, Detroit Gen Hosp, 1964-1969; consult, Vet Admin Hosp, Allen Park, Mich, 1963-1982; assoc prof med & assoc microbiol & path, Col Med, Wayne State Univ, 1963-1967; res assoc biol, Mass Inst Technol, 1962-1963; fel, Med Found Greater Boston, Inc, 1960-1963; Res fel med, Thorndike Mem Lab, Boston City Hosp & Harvard Med Sch, 1959-1962; sr asst resident, Barnes Hosp, Mo, 1958-1959; asst resident, Harvard Med Serv, Boston City Hosp, Mass, 1957-1958; lab investr, Nat Inst Allergy & Infectious Dis, 1955-1957; Intern, Barnes Hosp, St Louis, Mo, 1954-1955. **Memberships:** Fel Am Col Physicians; Am Soc Clin Invest; Inf Dis Soc Am; dipl mem Pan-Am Med Asn; Asn Am Physicians; Am Fedn Clin Res. **Research Statement & Publications:** Infectious diseases. **Mailing Address:** 31000 Lahser, Birmingham, MI 48025. **E-Mail:** ad54072@wayne.edu

LERNER, B(ERNARD) J, CHEMICAL ENGINEERING. **Personal Data:** b Brooklyn, NY, April 28, 1921; m 1951, c 3. **Education:** Cooper Union, BChE, 1943; Univ Iowa, MS, 1947; Syracuse Univ, PhD (chem eng), 1949. **Professional Experience:** PRES, BECO ENG CO, 1970-; vpres res & dir chem eng res, MK Res & Develop Co, Pa, 1968-1970; pres, Patent Develop Assocs, Inc, Pa, 1963-1968; consult, Monsanto Chem Co, 1952-1953 & Maurice A Knight Co, 1963-1966; pvt consult chem engr, 1959-1980; consult, Dominion Gulf Co, 1959-1963; group leader, Gulf Res & Develop Co, 1954-1959; asst prof, Univ Tex, 1949-1954; res engr, Inst Indust Res, Syracuse Univ, 1947-1948; Instr chem eng, Univ Iowa, 1946-1947. **Memberships:** Am Chem Soc; Am Inst Chem Engrs; Air Pollution Control Asn. **Research Statement & Publications:** Mass transfer; two-phase fluid flow; air pollution control. **Mailing Address:** Beco Eng Co, PO Box 443, Oakmont, PA 15139-0443. **Fax:** 412-828-6144.

LERNER, DAVID EVAN, MATHEMATICAL PHYSICS, SCIENTIFIC COMPUTING. **Personal Data:** b Kansas City, Mo, March 21, 1944. **Education:** Haverford Col, BA, 1964; Univ Pittsburgh, PhD (math), 1972. **Professional Experience:** PROF MATH, UNIV KANS, as of 2004; assoc prof math, Univ Kans, beginning 1980; Math Inst, Univ Oxford, 1976-1977; asst prof, Univ Kans, 1975-1979; res assoc physics, Syracuse Univ, Relativity Group, 1973-1975; instr math, Univ Pittsburgh, 1972-1973. **Memberships:** Am Phys Soc; Am Math Soc. **Research Statement & Publications:** Geometric visualization; applications and theory of nonlinear dynamics. **Mailing Address:** Dept Math, Univ Kans, 647 Snow Hall, Lawrence, KS 66045. **Fax:** 785-864-5255. **E-Mail:** lerner@math.ukans.edu

LERNER, EDWARD CLARENCE, THEORETICAL PHYSICS. **Personal Data:** b Brooklyn, NY, September 10, 1924. **Education:** Mass Inst Technol, BS, 1945, PhD (physics), 1952. **Professional Experience:** RETIRED; from assoc prof to prof physics, Univ SC, 1957-; Mem staff, Lincoln Lab, Mass Inst Technol, 1952-1958. **Memberships:** AAAS; Am Phys Soc. **Research Statement & Publications:** Electrodynamics; field theory; classical and quantum dynamics. **Mailing Address:** 12 Shadow Creek Ct, Columbia, SC 29209.

LERNER, JOSEPH, ORGANIC CHEMISTRY. **Personal Data:** b Wilkes-Barre, Pa, January 16, 1942; m 1963, Linda; c Michael & Michele. **Education:** Rutgers Univ, BS, 1963, PhD (biochem), 1967. **Professional Experience:** Pres, Tenn Coun Arts & Sci Deans, 1988; PROF CHEM, COL ARTS & SCI, TENN TECH UNIV, COOKEVILLE, 1984-; dean, Col Arts & Sci, Tenn Tech Univ, Cookeville, 1984-1994; fac fel acad higher admin, Univ NH, 1982-1983; chmn dept, Univ Maine, Orono, 1978-1983; prof, Univ Maine, Orono, 1977-1983; NIH res grant, 1974-1983; res assoc, Dept Avian Sci, Univ Calif, Davis, 1974; Hatch Fund grant, 1969-1983; from asst prof to assoc prof biochem, Univ Maine, Orono, 1968-1977; Coe Res Fund grant, 1968-1969; sr res investr biochem, Eastern Utilization Res & Develop Div, USDA, 1967-1968. **Memberships:** Am Chem Soc; Am Soc Nutrit; NY Acad Sci; Sigma Xi; AAAS. **Research Statement & Publications:** Intestinal absorption of amino acids in chicken; metabolism of small intestine; genetic aspects of transport processes; separation of nucleotide derivatives by column chromatography. **Mailing Address:** Dept Chem, Tenn Technol Univ, Box 5055, Cookeville, TN 38505-0001. **Fax:** 931-372-3434. **E-Mail:** jlerner@tntech.edu

LERNER, JULES, GENETICS, CYTOLOGY. **Personal Data:** b Englewood, NJ, October 24, 1941; m 1969, Joyce. **Education:** Bowdoin Col, BA, 1963; Johns Hopkins Univ, PhD (biol), 1967. **Professional Experience:** Prof biol, Northeastern Ill Univ, 1977-; from asst prof to assoc prof, 1967-1977. **Memberships:** AAAS. **Research Statement & Publications:** Developmental biology and genetics. **Mailing Address:** Dept Biol, Northeastern Ill Univ, 5500 N St Louis Ave, Chicago, IL 60625.

LERNER, LAWRENCE ROBERT, ORGANIC CHEMISTRY. **Personal Data:** b New York, NY, March 17, 1943; m 1964, c 2. **Education:** City Col NY, BS, 1964; Mich State Univ, PhD (org chem), 1968. **Professional Experience:** TECH MGR, MOBAY CHEM CORP, 1985-; mgr process control & develop, Harmon Colors Corp, 1981-1985; supvr org pigments, Harmon Colors Corp, 1973-1981; adj asst prof, County Col Morris, NJ, 1973-1974; group leader, Harmon Colors Corp, 1972-1973; res chemist org pigments, E I du Pont Del Nemours & Co, 1968-1972. **Memberships:** Sigma Xi; Am Chem Soc; AAAS; Inter-Soc Color Coun. **Research Statement & Publications:** Synthesis of colored organic pigments; study of the effects of structure on the photostability, color and physical properties of organic pigments. **Mailing Address:** 176 Grove Terr, Livingston, NJ 07039-4113.

LERNER, LAWRENCE S, CONDENSED MATTER PHYSICS, SCIENCE EDUCATION. **Personal Data:** b New York, NY, March 10, 1934; m 1959. **Education:** Univ Chicago, AB(Honors), 1953, MS, 1955, PhD (physics), 1962. **Honors & Awards:** Distinguished fac Teaching Award, Calif State Univ, Long Beach, 1988, Legacy lectr, Calif State Univ, Long Beach, 1996, The Ben & Elaine Whiteley Distinguished lectr, Pacific univ, 2002. **Professional Experience:** PROF EMER, NATURAL SCI & MATH, CALIF STATE UNIV, LONG BEACH, 1999-; mem, Calif Curric Framework & Criteria Comt Sci, 1988-1989; mem, Nat Fac Humanities Arts & Sci, 1978-; dir, Gen Honors Prog, 1976-1980; consult, Danforth

Assoc, 1975-; prof, Calif State Univ, Long Beach, 1973-1999; assoc prof, Calif State Univ, Long Beach, 1969-1973; res scientist, Lockheed Palo Alto Res Lab, 1967-1969; physicist, Hughes Res Labs, 1962-1965 & Hewlett-Packard Labs, Calif, 1965-1967; staff mem, Labs Appl Sci, Univ Chicago, 1958-1960. **Memberships:** AAAS; Am Phys Soc; Am Asn Physics Teachers; Hist Sci Soc; Sigma Xi Phi Beta Kappa. **Research Statement & Publications:** Fermi surfaces of metals and preparation and properties of ternary compound semiconductors; semiconductor influence of non-scientific philosophical movements on early scientific revolution; university physics texts; evaluation of state k-12 scientific standards; published over 100 aritcles. **Mailing Address:** Dept Physics & Astron, Calif State Univ, Long Beach, CA 90840. **Fax:** 562-985-7924. **E-Mail:** lslerner@csulb.edu

LERNER, LEON MAURICE, BIOCHEMISTRY, ORGANIC CHEMISTRY. **Personal Data:** b Chicago, Ill, February 2, 1938; m 1996, Fern; c Linda, Marcia & Gary. **Education:** Ill Inst Technol, BS, 1959, MS, 1961; Univ Ill, PhD (biochem), 1964. **Professional Experience:** PROF BIOCHEM, STATE UNIV NY HEALTH SCI CTR, BROOKLYN, 1980-; from instr to assoc prof, State Univ NY Health Sci Ctr, Brooklyn, 1965-1980; res assoc biochem, Col Med, Univ Ill, 1964-1965. **Memberships:** AAAS; Am Chem Soc; Sigma Xi. **Research Statement & Publications:** Potential nucleic acid antimetabolites; nucleoside analogs; chemistry and biochemistry of carbohydrates. **Mailing Address:** Dept Biochem, State Univ NY Health Sci Ctr, Brooklyn, NY 11203. **Fax:** 718-270-3316.

LERNER, LEONARD JOSEPH, CANCER, REPRODUCTION & FERTILITY. **Personal Data:** b Roselle, NJ, September 26, 1922. **Education:** Rutgers Univ, BSc, 1943, AB, 1951, MS, 1953, PhD (zoology), 1954. **Honors & Awards:** Cain Mem Award, Am Asn Cancer Res, 1989. **Professional Experience:** Adj prof, Sch Nursing, Univ Pa, 1990-; HON PROF, DEPT PHARMACOL, THOMAS JEFFERSON MED COL, 1989-; res prof, Depts Obstet & Gynec & Pharmacol, 1971-1989; dir endocrinol, Gruppo Lepetit Spa, 1971-1977; head endocrine res, Squibb Inst Med Res, 1958-1971; endocrinologist, William S Merrell Co, 1954-1958; assoc, Bur Biol Res, Rutgers Univ, 1953-1954; Pharmacist, 1946-1951; vis prof obstet & gynec, Hahnemann Med Sch; chmn & vchmn sect Biol & Med, NY Acad Sci; mem, Steering Comt Int Study Group, Steroid Hormones; mem, Breast Cancer Task Force Comt & Concept Rev Comt, Nat Cancer Inst; mem, Animal Res & Experimentation Comt, NY Acad Sci; mem bd dirs, Am Diabetes Soc; consult, pharmaceut co; Comt Animals Res, Soc Study Reprod, co-ed res steroids; assoc mem, Bur Biol Res, Rutgers Univ. **Memberships:** Endocrine Soc; Am Physiol Soc; fel NY Acad Sci; Am Soc Reproductive Med; Soc Study Reproduction; Am Asn Cancer Res; Soc Exp Biol Med; fel AAAS. **Research Statement & Publications:** Hormone antagonists; fertility control; pregnancy, ova transport and reproduction; placenta; prostaglandins; ovulation; steroids; endocrine-tumor relationships and anti-cancer research; hormone treatment pre- and post- natally effects on hormonal and behavior responses; endocrine biochemistry; central nervous system-endocrine system relationship; adrenal physiology; growth and development; diabetes, atherosclerosis and endocrine in relation to stress, hormone, blood lipids; anti-inflammation; diabetes and reproduction, diabetes and cardiovascular system; awarded 35 patents; author of numerous publications. **Mailing Address:** Dept Pharmacol, Med Col, Thomas Jefferson Univ, 1020 Locust St, Philadelphia, PA 19107. **Fax:** 215-923-7145.

LERNER, LOUIS L(EONARD), COSMETIC CHEMISTRY, MEDICAL & HEALTH SCIENCES. **Personal Data:** b Chicago, Ill, February 25, 1915; m 1949, Jean; c David L. **Education:** Cent YMCA Col, BS, 1942. **Honors & Awards:** Edward J Sparling Award, Roosevelt Univ, 2001; Hall Fame, 2001. **Professional Experience:** RETIRED; ed, Chem Bull, Am Chem Soc, 1991; consult ed, Chem Bull, Am Chem Soc, 1978-1980; phys scientist, Fed Trad Comn, US Govt, 1975-1995; consult, Seaquist Valve Co, beginning 1974; consumer protection specialist, Fed Trad Comn, US Govt, 1974; ed, Chem Bull, Am Chem Soc, 1971-1977; dir, AD Prods Corp, 1964-1966; sr scientist, Personal Care Div, Gillette Co, 1952-1974; vpres & dir res & new prod develop, Bymart Inc, 1950-1952; vpres & dir res, Kalech Res Labs, 1949-1950; exec vpres & dir res & prod, Allied Home Prods Corp, 1946-1949; instr, Cent YMCA Col, 1942-1944; dir res & prod, Consol Royal Chem Corp, 1940-1946; pres & dir res, LaLerne Labs, 1937-1940; dir, Brokers Inc, 1937-1940; chief chemist, Russian Duchess Labs, 1937; assoc chemist, Universal Merchandise Co, 1935-1937; chem asst, Universal Merchandise Co, 1934. **Memberships:** Fel AAAS; Am Chem Soc; Soc Cosmetic Chem; NY Acad Sci; Nat Asn Sci Writers. **Research Statement & Publications:** Product development, exploratory research; pharmaceuticals, proprietaries, cosmetics, detergents, emulsions, waving compositions, dyes and pigments; chemistry of polymers, proteins and enzymes; mechanical devices; surface chemistry; consumer products; environmental sciences; biology. **Mailing Address:** 900 N Lake Shore Dr, Chicago, IL 60611.

LERNER, MICHAEL PAUL, VIROLOGY, CELL BIOLOGY. **Personal Data:** b Los Angeles, Calif, May 2, 1941; m 1965, c 2. **Education:** Univ Calif, Los Angeles, BA, 1963; Kans State Univ, MS, 1967; Northwestern Univ, PhD (microbiol), 1970. **Professional Experience:** SR SCI DEAN, MCGEE EYE INST, 1984-; assoc prof microbiol, Health Sci Ctr, Univ Okla, 1973-1984; asst res biologist neurochem, Ctr Health Sci, 1972-1973; fel, NATO Advan Study Inst, Italy, 1972; Nat Inst Neurol Dis & Stroke fel, Univ Calif, Los Angeles, 1970-1971. **Memberships:** Am Soc Microbiol. **Research Statement & Publications:** Mammalian cell biochemistry and development. **Mailing Address:** 3136 Willow Brook Rd, Oklahoma City, OK 73120.

LERNER, MOISEY, software legacy systems, electrical engineering & chaos engineering; deceased, see previous edition for last biography

LERNER, NARCINDA REYNOLDS, CHEMICAL KINETICS. **Personal Data:** b Brooklyn, NY, October 10, 1933; m 1959, Lawrence S. **Education:** Hofstra Univ, BA, 1956; Univ Chicago, MS, 1959, PhD (chem), 1962. **Professional Experience:** RES SCIENTIST, AMES RES CTR, NASA, 1970-; res scientist, Lockheed Palo Alto Res Lab, 1966-1970; Mem tech staff, Hughes Res Labs Labs, Calif, 1962-1963. **Memberships:** AAAS; Am Phys Soc. **Research Statement & Publications:** Paramagnetic resonance; electron nuclear double resonance; crystalline field theory; crystal preparation; electrical properties of polymers; polymer degradation; abiotic synthesis of organic compounds. **Mailing Address:** Ames Res Ctr, NASA, MS 239-4, Moffett Field, CA 94035.

LERNER, NORMAN CONRAD, ENGINEERING ECONOMICS, INVESTMENT FEASIBILITY ANALYSIS. **Personal Data:** b New York, NY, February 13, 1936; wid, c Sheila & Julie. **Education:** Mass Inst Technol, BS, 1957; Columbia Univ, MBA, 1961; Am Univ, PhD (math econ), 1968. **Professional Experience:** Spec asst to dir, Exec Off Pres, US Off Telecommun Policy, 1971-1972; PRES, TRANSCOMM INC, 1969-; dir, Command Systs Div, Comput Sci Div, 1968-1971; proj mgr, ITT/RCA Corp, 1957-1965 & Mitre Corp, 1965-1968; rep, US-Peoples Repub China Telecommun Protocol; partic, World Admin Radio Conf, Presidential Task Force Commun Policy, Cong Off Technol Assessment-Int Telecommun, NASA Joint Study Group-Satellite Commun Underdevelop Countries & FCC Cable TV Adv Panel; mem, US State Dept Comt Ctr Telecommun Develop, Int Telecommun Union; assoc prof mgt sci, George Wash Univ. **Memberships:** Nat Soc Prof Engrs; Am Econ Asn; Inst Elec & Electronics Engrs; Nat Asn Bus Economists. **Research Statement & Publications:** Economic, financial and market development aspects of high technology industries in the US and overseas, particularly telecommunications and energy; Extensive writing addresses the privatization of telecommunications in developing countries. **Mailing Address:** 4527 Pickett Rd, Fairfax, VA 22042.

LERNER, PAULINE, NEUROCHEMISTRY. **Personal Data:** b Baltimore, Md, July 4, 1948; div. **Education:** Goucher Col, BA, 1969; Univ Md, PhD (chem), 1973. **Professional Experience:** CHEMIST, FOOD & DRUG ADMIN, 1980-; chemist, NIH, 1974-1980. **Memberships:** AAAS; Asn Women Sci; Am Chem Soc; Am Soc Neurochem; Soc Neuroscience. **Research Statement & Publications:** Regulatory work in the area of nutrition and health. **Mailing Address:** US Food & Drug Admin, 5600 Fishers Lane, Rockville, MD 20857-0001.

LERNER, RICHARD ALAN, IMMUNOLOGY. **Personal Data:** b Chicago, Ill, August 26, 1938; m 1966, c 3. **Education:** Stanford Univ, MD, 1964. **Professional Experience:** PRES, SCRIPPS RES INST, as of 2004; PROF IMMUNOCHEMISTRY, SCRIPPS RES INST, as of 2004; PRES, RES INST, SCRIPPS CLIN, LA JOLLA, 1991-; prof, Dept Chem & Dir, Res Inst, Scripps Clin, La Jolla, Calif, beginning 1974; consult, Nat Cancer Inst, beginning 1972; assoc mem, 1971-1973; assoc immunol, 1970-1971; assoc cell biol, Wistar Inst, 1968-1970; USPHS grant, Scripps Clin & Found, 1965-1968; intern med, Stanford Univ, 1964-1965. **Memberships:** Nat Acad Sci; Am Soc Path; Biophys Soc; Am Soc Microbiol; Am Soc Immunol. **Research Statement & Publications:** Molecular medicine; differentiation. **Mailing Address:** Dept Chem, The Scripps Res Inst, Rm BCC506, 0550 N Torrey Pines Rd, La Jolla, CA 92037. **Fax:** 858-784-9899. **E-Mail:** rlerner@scripps.edu

LERNER, ROBERT GIBBS, HEMATOLOGY, HEMOSTASIS & THROMBOSIS. **Personal Data:** b Brooklyn, NY, March 3, 1936; m Robert; c Lerner. **Education:** NY Univ, BA, 1956, MD, 1960. **Professional Experience:** Assoc med dir, Westchester Med Ctr, 1996-2002; ACTG CHMN, DEPT MED, beginning 1996; PROF PATH, NY MED COL, 1993-; bd dirs, Island Peer Rev Orgn, 1990-; PROF MED & CHIEF HEMAT, NY MED COL, 1980-; consult, Food & Drug Admin, 1975-1978; Prin investr var grants & projs, NY Med Col, 1970-; from asst prof to assoc prof, Dept Med, 1967-1980; instr, Sch Med, Univ Southern Calif, 1965-1967; Teaching asst, Sch Med, NY Univ, 1961-1962; mem, Coun Thrombosis, Am Heart Asn. **Memberships:** Fel Am Col Physicians; Am Soc Hemat; Nat Hemophilia Found. **Research Statement & Publications:** Hematology, specifically hemostasis and thrombosis; clinical aspects of the diagnosis and treatment of hemorrhagic and thrombotic. **Mailing Address:** NY Med Col, Dept Med, Munger Pavilion, Valhalla, NY 10595. **Fax:** 914-594-4432. **E-Mail:** lerner@nymc.edu

LERNER, TERRY JANE, GENETICS. **Education:** Rockefeller Univ, PhD, 1981. **Professional Experience:** ASST GENETICS, MOLECULAR NEUROGENETICS UNIT, MASS GEN HOSP, as of 2005. **Mailing Address:** Molecular Neurogenetics Lab Mass Gen Hosp, 13th St Bldg 149, Charlestown, MA 02129. **Fax:** 617-726-5736. **E-Mail:** lerner@helix.mgh.harvard.edu

LEROI, GEORGE, CHEMICAL PHYSICS. **Personal Data:** b London, Eng, June 23, 1936; American citizen; m Ellen. **Education:** Univ Wis, BA, 1956; Harvard Univ, AM, 1958, PhD (chem), 1960. **Honors & Awards:** Coblentz Prize, 1972. **Professional Experience:** DEAN, COL NAT SCI, MICH STATE UNIV, as of 2004; guest res, Brookhaven Nat Lab, 1985; Syncrotron Ultraviolet Radiation Facil fel, US Nat Bur Stand, 1981-1982; Japan Soc Prom Sci vis prof, 1977; guest prof, Lab Phys Chem, Swiss Fed Inst Technol, 1974-1975; PROF CHEM, MICH STATE UNIV, 1972-; assoc prof, Mich State Univ, 1967-1972; asst prof, Princeton Univ, 1964-1967; lectr, Princeton Univ, 1962-1964; res assoc chem, Univ Calif, Berkeley, 1960-1962; Ford Found fel, 1952-1956; mem, Phys Chem Div, Am Chem Soc. **Memberships:** Am Phys Soc; Am Chem Soc. **Research Statement & Publications:** Molecular spectroscopy and structure; vacuum ultraviolet, visible, infrared, far infrared, Raman; ion/molecule chemistry; laser spectroscopy and photochemistry. **Mailing Address:** Dept Chem, Mich State Univ, 103 Natural Sci Bldg, East Lansing, MI 48824-1115. **E-Mail:** geleroi@msu.edu

LEROITH, DEREK, MEDICINE, DIABETES. **Personal Data:** b Cape Town, SAfrica, January 3, 1945; m 1979, c 3. **Education:** Univ Cape Town, MB, ChB, 1967, PhD (med), 1972. **Professional Experience:** CHIEF, DIABETES BR, NAT INST DIABETES & DIGESTIVE & KIDNEY DIS, NIH, as of 2004; sr investr diabetes, NIH, beginning 1984; assoc prof med, Univ Cincinnati, 1983-1984; vis scientist diabetes, NIH, 1979-1983; sr lectr med, Univ Ben Gurion, Israel, 1976-1979; sr registr med, Middlesex Med Sch, London, England, 1975; registr med, Univ Cape Town, SAfrica, 1972-1975. **Memberships:** Fel Am Col Physicians; Am Endocrine Soc. **Research Statement & Publications:** Evolutionary origins of the vertebrate endocrine systems; hormonal substances in invertebrates; brain insulin receptors. **Mailing Address:** Diabetes Br, Nat Inst Diabetes & Digestive & Kidney Dis, NIH, Rm 8D12 Bldg 10, Bethesda, MD 20892-1758. **Fax:** 301-480-4386. **E-Mail:** derek@helix.nih.gov

LEROUX, EDGAR JOSEPH, INSECT ECOLOGY, ENTOMOLOGY. **Personal Data:** b Ottawa, Ont, January 23, 1922; m 1944, Ardis M Andrew; c Estelle, Pierre & Elizabeth. **Education:** Carleton Univ, Can, BA, 1950; McGill Univ, MSc, 1952, PhD (entom), 1954. **Honorary Degrees:** DSc, McGill Univ, 1973; DU, Univ Ottawa, 1986. **Honors & Awards:** Grace Griswold lectr, Cornell Univ, 1971; Jubilee Medal, Governor Gen Can, 1977; Armand Frappier Medal, 1984; Gold Medal, Entom Soc Can, 1986; Golden Award, Can Feed Indust Asn, 1986; Merit Award, Pub Serv Can, 1987; Officer Order Can, Gov Gen Can, 1988, Commemorative Medal ConfederationCan, 1992. **Professional Experience:** RETIRED; mem, Nat Biotechnol Adv Comt, 1983-1987; assoc comt biotechnol, Nat Res Coun, 1983-1987; Co-chmn, Can/USSR Agr Working Group & Can/Romania Comt Cooperation Agr, 1981-1987; mem, Nat Res Coun Can, 1980-1986; indept panel, Energy Mines & Resources Can, 1978-1987; chmn, Fed Interdept Comt Pesticides, 1978-1987; asst dep minister res, Res Br, Can Dept Agr, 1978-1987; interdept comt, Can Ministry State Sci & Technol, 1978-1984; chmn, comt agr, Orgn Environ Coop & Develop, 1978-1980; vchmn, Can Agr Res Coun, 1977-1987; vchmn, Agr Stabilization Bd & Agr Prod Bd, 1977-1980; mem, coord comt, Can Agr Servs, 1975-1987; dir gen, Res Br, Can Dept Agr, 1975-1978; negotiated grants comt & adv comt biol, Nat Res Coun, 1973-1978; pres Biol Coun Can, 1970-1971; pres, Biol Coun Can, 1970-1971; hon prof, MacDonald Col, McGill Univ, 1970-1971; asst dir gen, Res Br, Can Dept Agr, 1968-1975; mem, World Hort Coun, 1968-1970; dir, Can Soc Zool, 1968-1970; off cor entom, Commonwealth Inst Biol Control, 1967-1973; Can rep, Int Soc Hort Sci, 1967-1973; panel experts integrated pest control, Food & Agr Orgn, 1966-1971; dir, Biol Coun Can, 1966-1970; sci ed, Can J Plant Sci, 1965-1968; res coordr, Res Br, Can Dept Agr, 1965-1968; Entom Soc Can, 1969-1970 & Entom Soc Que, 1965-1966; adv comt entom probs, Defense Res Bd, Dept Nat Defense,

1964-1967; assoc prof, MacDonald Col, McGill Univ, 1962-1965; mem orchard protection comt, Info & Res Serv, Que Dept Agr, 1959-1963; lectr, MacDonald Col, McGill Univ, 1958-1962; asst, MacDonald Col, McGill Univ, 1953-1954; res scientist, Res Br, Can Dept Agr, 1950-1962; Demonstr, MacDonald Col, McGill Univ, 1950-1951; Asst entomologist, Fruit Insect Invests, Sci Serv, 1949-1950. **Memberships:** Emer mem Entom Soc Can (pres, 1969-1970); Can Seed Grower's Asn; fel Agr Inst Can; Asn Advan Sci Can (hon treas, 1970-1972). **Research Statement & Publications:** Insect ecology; integrated pest control; morphology; toxicology; author of over 100 publications and three memoirs books; quantitative population (dynamics) ecology studies of some key orchard, field and forest insect pests resulting in improved crop protection programs via integrated pest control approaches with heavy emphasis on use of beneficial species that feed on these crop pests. **Mailing Address:** 27 Keppler Cres, Nepean, ON K2H 5Y1, Can.

LEROUX, EDMUND FRANK, HYDROLOGY. **Personal Data:** b Muskegon Heights, Mich, March 8, 1925; m 1949, c 3. **Education:** Mich State Univ, BS, 1948. **Professional Experience:** RETIRED; asst dist chief hydrol, Manpower Sect, 1964-; chief, Manpower Sect, 1961-1964; Geologist, US Geol Surv, 1949-1960. **Memberships:** Am Geophys Union; Int Asn Hydrogeologists; AAAS. **Research Statement & Publications:** Ground water temperature; hydrology of glacial terrain in a semiarid climate. **Mailing Address:** 1675 Illinois Ave SW, Huron, SD 57350-2469.

LEROUX, PIERRE, MATHEMATICS. **Personal Data:** b Quebec City, Que, August 18, 1942; m 1964, c 2. **Education:** Univ Montreal, BSc, 1964, MSc, 1966, PhD (math), 1970. **Professional Experience:** DIR, COMBINATORICS & MATH INFO LAB, 1990-; PROF MATH, UNIV QUE, MONTREAL, 1971-. **Memberships:** Can Math Soc; Am Math Soc; Soc Indust & Appl Math. **Research Statement & Publications:** Enumerative combinatorics and special functions. **Mailing Address:** Math Dept, Univ Que CP8888 Suce Centre-ville, Montreal, PQ H3C 3P8, Can. **Fax:** 514-987-8274. **E-Mail:** leroux.pierre@uqam.ca

LEROY, ANDRE FRANCOIS, ANALYTICAL CHEMISTRY, PHYSICAL CHEMISTRY. **Personal Data:** b Philadelphia, Pa, September 30, 1933. **Education:** Yale Univ, BE, 1956; Calif Inst Technol, MS, 1957; Harvard Univ, AM, 1965, PhD (eng), 1967. **Honors & Awards:** Commendation Medal, Pub Health Serv, 1987; Clemens Herschel Prize. **Professional Experience:** Coordr, NIH-CGR Collab Res Prog Magnetic Resonance Imaging, beginning 1986; mem, Bd Sci Counrs, Life Sci Div, French AEC, 1985-1986; div res serv rep, Fogarty Int Ctr, beginning 1984; coordr, Instrumentation & Biomed Eng Sci Res, NIH-NIH & Med Res, France, 1983-; Spain, Italy, Greece, 1981 & France & Belg, 1983; CHIEF, ANALYTICAL METHODS, BIOMED ENG & INSTRUMENTATION BR, DIV RES SERV, NIH, 1980-; dir, Tech Equip Seminars, US Dept Com, France, 1980; mem staff, Sci Off, Am Embassy, Paris, France, 1978-1980; engr, NIH, Md, 1969-1978; res chemist, Northeastern Radiol Health Lab, Mass, 1963-1968; engr, Radiol Health Res Activ, US-PHS, 1958-1960. **Memberships:** Am Chem Soc; Am Inst Chem Engrs; Sigma Xi. **Research Statement & Publications:** Physical chemistry of transition metal complexes; analytical chemical and ultra-trace level isolation, characterization and quantitation of metal complex species and kinetics of protein binding and their transformations in biological systems and natural waters; high spatial resolution analysis of elements by instrumental micro analysis (electron- probe); WDX and EDX, chromatography, neutron activation analysis. **Mailing Address:** 11705 Col View Dr, Wheaton, MD 20902-2432.

LEROY, CLAUDE, NUCLEAR PHYSICS, PARTICLE PHYSICS. **Personal Data:** b Charleroi, Hainaut, Belg, September 30, 1947. **Education:** Faculte St Louis, Brussels, Mathematique Speciale, 1967; Univ Louvain, Belg, Lic en Sci, 1971, DSc, 1976. **Honors & Awards:** Rutherford Prize, Royal Soc Can, 1988. **Professional Experience:** PROF PHYSICS, UNIV MONTREAL, as of 2003; dept Energetics, Univ Florence, 1995-; hon prof, Nat Univ Peru, 1994-; Killam res fel, Can Coun, 1993-1995; attache res, dir, Nuclear Physics Lab, 1991-1994, 1978-1980; res scientist, Inst Particle Physics, Montreal, 1983-1990; assoc prof, McGill Univ, 1983-1990; researcher, Dept Develop Sci, Univ Louvain, 1981-1983; sci assoc, Ctr Europ Res Nuclear Physics, Geneva, Switz, beginning 1980; Northwestern Univ, Evanston, Ill, 1980-1981; res assoc, McGill Univ, Montreal, 1977-1980; vis res fel, Univ Southampton, Eng, 1976-1977. **Memberships:** Fel Royal Soc Can; Inst Particle Physics Can; Can Inst Physicists; Acad Sci Ill; Royal Soc. **Research Statement & Publications:** Nuclear physics; particle physics; instrumentation, high energy physics; author and co-author of over 300 scientific journals and reviews. **Mailing Address:** Dept Physics, Univ Montreal, CP 6128 Succursale Ave, Montreal, PQ H3C 3J7, Can. **Fax:** 514-343-6215. **E-Mail:** leroy@lps.umontreal.ca

LEROY, EDWARD CARWILE, RHEUMATOLOGY. **Personal Data:** b Elizabeth City, NC, January 19, 1933. **Education:** Wake Forest Univ, Winston-Salem, BS, 1955; Univ NC, Chapel Hill, MS, 1958, MD, 1960; Am Bd Internal Med, dipl, 1967. **Professional Experience:** DISTINGUISHED PROF & CHMN EMER, DEPT MICROBIOL & IMMUNOL, MED UNIV SC, CHARLESTON, 2000-; prof & chmn, dept microbiol & immunol, Med Univ Cc, charleston, 1995-2000; chmn, Dept Phys Med & Rehab, 1982-1991; sabbatical, Corpus Christi Col, Cambridge Univ, Eng, 1982-1983; fogarty sr int fel endothelial cell biol, US Dept Health & Human Serv, 1982-1983; prof med & dir, Div Rheumatology & Immunol, Dept Med, 1975-1995; am Col Rheumatology, 1989- & Am Col Physicians, 1975-1980; dir, Div Rheumatic Dic, 1971-1975; assoc attend physician & dir, Edward Daniels Faulkner Arthritis Clin, 1970-1975; vis prof & lectr, numerous US & foreign univs, 1969-1991; mem & chmn, var comts, Am Rheumatism Asn, 1967-; from asst prof to assoc prof, Dept Med, 1967-1975; asst attend physician, Presby Hosp, NY, 1967-1970; assoc, Columbia Univ Col Physicians & Surgeons, 1966-1967; NIH spec fel, 1965-1967; fel arthritis, Columbia Univ Col Physicians & Surgeons, 1965-1966; clin assoc, Nat Heart Inst, Bethesda, Md, 1962-1965; med internship & asst residency, Presby Hosp, Columbia-Presby Med Ctr, NY, 1960-1962. **Memberships:** Sigma Xi; fel Am Rheumatism Asn; Am Col Rheumatology; fel Am Col Physicians; AAAS; Am Asn Immunologists. **Research Statement & Publications:** Mechanisms involved in human connective tissue diseases; immunology; molecular and cellular mechanisms of fibrosis in the context of autoimmune disease, especially sclerodirma; author of numerous medical publications. **Mailing Address:** Dept Microbiol & Immunol, Med Univ SC, 171 Ashley Ave, Charleston, SC 29425. **Fax:** 843-792-2464. **E-Mail:** leroyc@.musc.edu

LEROY, ROBERT FREDERICK, NEUROLOGY, ELECTROENCEPHALOGRAPHY. **Personal Data:** b Passaic, NJ, July 24, 1950; m 1974, c 2. **Education:** Brown Univ, AB, 1972; Pa State Univ, MD, 1977. **Professional Experience:** DIR, EPILEPSY CTR, MED CITY HOSP, DALLAS, as of 2006; asst prof & dir clin neurophysiol, Dept Neurol, Southwestern Med Sch, Univ Tex, beginning 1982; consult, Dallas Tex Vet Admin, Med Ctr, 1982; fel, Merritt Pulnam Epilepsy Found Am, 1981-1982; resident neurol, Dept Neurol, Sch Med, Yale Univ, 1978-1981; intern, Dept Med, Baltimore City Hosp, 1977-1978. **Memberships:** Am Acad Neurol. **Research Statement & Publications:** Electroencephalography and general clinical neurophysiology as it pertains to epilepsy and its treatments. **Mailing Address:** Epilepsy Ctr, Med City Hosp, Bldg Ste 116, 7777 Forest Lane, Dallas, TX 75320.

LEROY, ROBERT JAMES, INTERMOLECULAR FORCES, MOLECULAR CLUSTERS. **Personal Data:** b Ottawa, Ont, September 30, 1943; m 1967, Virginia; c Alexander R, Sylvia M, Clara M & Monika A. **Education:** Univ Toronto, BSc, 1965, MSc, 1967; Univ Wis-Madison, PhD (chem), 1971. **Honors & Awards:** Rutherford Mem Medal, Royal Soc Can, 1984 J Heyrovsky Honorary Medal in the chem sci, acad of sci of the Czech Republic 1995. **Professional Experience:** PROF CHEM, UNIV WATERLOO, 1982-; dir, Guelph-Waterloo Ctr Grad Work Chem, 1982-1985; invited prof, Univ Paris-S Orsay, France, 1982; prof Invite, Univ Paris-Sud d'Orsay, April 1982; sr vis fel, J S Guggenheim Mem Found fel, 1979; sr vis fel, Sci Res Coun UK, 1976; A P Sloan Found fel, 1974-1976; from asst prof to assoc prof, Univ Waterloo, 1972-1982. **Memberships:** Can Asn Physicists; fel Chem Inst Can; Am Phys Soc. **Research Statement & Publications:** Empirical methods for determining intermolecular forces in simple systems; understanding and predicting the properties of simple molecules and molecular clusters. **Mailing Address:** Dept Chem, Univ Waterloo, 200 Univ Ave W, Waterloo, ON N2L 3G1, Can. **Fax:** 519-746-0435. **E-Mail:** leroy@uwaterloo.ca

LEROY, RODNEY LASH, PHYSICAL CHEMISTRY, ELECTROCHEMISTRY. **Personal Data:** b Ottawa, Ont, November 15, 1941; m 1983, c 6. **Education:** Univ Toronto, BSc, 1964, MA, 1965, PhD (phys chem), 1968; McGill Univ, dipl 1978, MBA, 1983. **Professional Experience:** MGR ENERGY & PROD APPLICATIONS LAB, NORANDA TECHNOL CTR, 1988-; exec vpres, Electrolyser Inc, 1985-1988; tech dir, Electrolyser Inc, 1980-1985; prog mgr res, Noranda Res Ctr, 1978-1979; prin scientist electrochem, Noranda Res Ctr, 1978-1979; group leader electrochem, Noranda Res Ctr, 1972-1978; assoc scientist chem, Noranda Res Ctr, 1970-1972; fel phys chem, Univ Colo & Yale Univ, 1968-1970. **Memberships:** fel Chem Inst Can; Electrochem Soc; Nat Asn Corrosion Engrs; Int Asn Hydrogen Energy; Soc Petrol Engrs; Soc Explor Geophysicists; Petrol Soc. **Research Statement & Publications:** Corrosion research; electrometallurgy of nonferrous metals, especially copper and zinc; hydrogen production by electrolysis of water; petroleum engineering. **Mailing Address:** Noranda Advan Mat, 4950 Levy St, Ste-Laurent, PQ H4R 2P1, Can.

LERSTEN, NELS R, BOTANY. **Personal Data:** b Chicago, Ill, August 6, 1932; m 1958, c 3. **Education:** Univ Chicago, BS, 1958, MS, 1960; Univ Calif, Berkeley, PhD (bot), 1963. **Professional Experience:** PROF EMER BOT, IOWA STATE UNIV, as of 2004; prof bot, Iowa State Univ, beginning 1970; From asst prof to assoc prof, 1963-1970. **Memberships:** Bot Soc Am; Sigma Xi. **Research Statement & Publications:** Systematic and developmental anatomy of angiosperms; embryology of flowering plants. **Mailing Address:** Dept Bot, Iowa State Univ, Ames, IA 50011-1020. **E-Mail:** nlersten@iastate.edu

LERTORA, JUAN J L, PHARMACOLOGY, INTERNAL MEDICINE. **Professional Experience:** HEAD, SECT CLIN PHARMACOL, 1974-; PROF PHARMACOL & MED, TULANE UNIV, SCH MED, 1970-. **Research Statement & Publications:** Pharmacology; internal medicine. **Mailing Address:** Dept Pharmacol, Tulane Univ Sch Med, 1430 Tulane Ave, New Orleans, LA 70112-2699. **Fax:** 504-588-5283. **E-Mail:** lerclpha@tulane.edu

LES, DONALD H, AQUATIC ANGIOSPERM SYSTEMATICS, ANGIOSPERM EVOLUTION. **Personal Data:** b Detroit, Mich, March 26, 1954. **Education:** Eastern Mich Univ, BS, 1976, MS, 1980; Ohio State Univ, PhD (bot), 1986. **Honors & Awards:** Hall of Fame Award (IWGS), 2002. **Professional Experience:** PROF PLANT SYSTS, UNIV CONN, 1992-; assoc prof, Univ Wis, Milwaukee, 1992; Asst prof biol, Univ Wis, Milwaukee, 1986-1992. **Memberships:** Am Soc Plant Taxonomists; Bot Soc Am; Soc Study Evolution; Aq Plant Manag Soc. **Research Statement & Publications:** Systematics, evolution, conservation and ecology of aquatic angiosperms using morphological, biochemical and molecular data. **Mailing Address:** Dept Ecol & Evolutionary Biol, Univ Conn, U-3043, Storrs, CT 06269-3043. **Fax:** 860-486-6364. **E-Mail:** les@uconn.edu

LES, EDWIN PAUL, LABORATORY ANIMAL SCIENCE. **Personal Data:** b Adams, Mass, December 28, 1923; m 1967, c 2. **Education:** Northeastern Univ, BS, 1952; Ohio State Univ, MS, 1953; PhD (genetics), 1959. **Professional Experience:** RETIRED; sr staff scientist, Jackson Lab, 1975-1990; staff scientist, Jackson Lab, 1962-1975; biologist, Biol Div, Oak Ridge Nat Lab, 1960-1962; Assoc staff scientist, Jackson Lab, 1959-1960. **Memberships:** Am Asn Lab Animal Sci. **Research Statement & Publications:** Effect of environment on reproduction, growth and survival of laboratory mice; mouse husbandry techniques and practices; laboratory animal ecology. **Mailing Address:** Indian Point Rd, Bar Harbor, ME 04609.

LESAGE, LEO G, NUCLEAR ENGINEERING, REACTOR PHYSICS. **Personal Data:** b Concordia, Kans, April 15, 1935; m 1958, Carolyn Bailey; c Annette G & Marietta L. **Education:** Univ Kans, BS, 1957; Stanford Univ, MS, 1962, PhD (nuclear eng), 1966; Univ Chicago, MBA, 1981. **Professional Experience:** RETIRED; dir, Eng Physics Div, Argonne Nat Lab, beginning 1988; US mem, Comt on Reactor Physics, Nuclear Energy Agency, 1981-; dir, Appl Physics Div, 1981-1988; Nuclear engr, Fast Breeder Reactor Develop, 1966-1981. **Memberships:** Fel Am Nuclear Soc. **Research Statement & Publications:** Fast reactor physics; fast reactor critical experiments; research management. **Mailing Address:** 303 N Third St, Watseka, IL 60970. **Fax:** 630-252-5318.

LESAGE, SUZANNE, REMEDIATION TECHNOLOGIES FOR GROUNDWATER CONTAMINATED WITH SOLVENTS OR PETROLEUM, ANALYTICAL METHODS FOR HAZARDOUS WASTES. **Personal Data:** b Quebec City, Que, March 23, 1952; div, c Francois Patrinieri & Bruno Paltrinieri. **Education:** Univ Ottawa, BSc, 1973; McGill Univ, PhD (chem), 1977. **Professional Experience:** CHIEF, AQUATIC ECOSYST MGT RES BR, NAT WATER RES INST, as of 2004; conf chair, In-situ Bioremediation, 1990-1992; res scientist Groundwater, Nat Water Res Inst, Environ Can, beginning 1989; res chemist, Nat Water Res Inst, Environ Can, 1986-1989; head, Org Chem Lab, Wastewater Technol Ctr, 1980-1986; res scientist, Agr Can, 1978-1980; fel, Agr Can, 1977-1978. **Memberships:** Am Chem Soc; Soc Environ Toxicol & Chem; Am Soc Testing & Mat. **Research Statement & Publications:** Remediation of groundwater contaminated with solvents, petroleum or landfill leachate, using biological or biochemical methods; methods and apparatus for the analysis of organic contaminants in groundwater and soil. **Mailing Address:** Nat Water Res Inst, 867 Lakeshore Rd, Burlington, ON L7R 4A6, Can. **Fax:** 905-336-6430. **E-Mail:** suzanne.lesage@ec.gc.ca

LESCARBOURA, JAIME AQUILES, PETROLEUM ENGINEERING. **Personal Data:** b Barcelona, Spain, August 29, 1937; American citizen; m 1957, c 2. **Education:** Univ Kans, BS, 1959, PhD (chem eng), 1967; Univ Wis-Madison, MS, 1961. **Professional Experience:** SR STAFF ENGR, CONOCO, INC, 1991-; res assoc, Conoco, Inc, 1984-1990; staff eng, Continental Oil Co, 1982-1984; sr res scientist, Continental Oil Co, 1976-1982; res scientist, Continental Oil Co, 1967-1976; Am Oil Found fel, 1966-1967; Engr, Cardon Refinery, Shell Oil Co Venezeula, 1961-1963. **Memberships:** Soc Petrol Engrs; Soc Rheology. **Research Statement & Publications:** Flow of Newtonian and non-Newtonian fluids; falling cylinder viscometer for non-Newtonian fluids; turbulent flow drag reduction by addition of polymers; well testing; formation evaluation; rheology of crosslinked gels, drilling muds, waxy crudes and viscous crudes; well stimulation by blasting. **Mailing Address:** Hc 89 Box 21, Hermosa, SD 57744.

LESER, ERNST GEORGE, ORGANIC CHEMISTRY. **Personal Data:** b Mineola, NY, May 3, 1943; m 1969, c Andrew, Karen & Michael. **Education:** Bucknell Univ, BS, 1965; Fordham Univ, PhD (org chem), 1970. **Professional Experience:** RES ASSOC, JACKSON LAB, E I DU PONT DE NEMOURS & CO INC, 1990-; sr res chemist, Jackson Lab, 1984-1990; prod supvr, Chamber Works, 1974-1984; res chemist, Jackson Lab, 1969-1974. **Memberships:** Am Chem Soc. **Research Statement & Publications:** Supervision of dyes and intermediates production; fluorochemical research; tetraethyl lead process assistance; carpet and textile fluoroprotectant process manufacturing assistance. **Mailing Address:** Two Orioles Nest, Elkton, MD 21921-2039.

LESH, THOMAS ALLAN, PHYSIOLOGY. **Personal Data:** b Chicago, Ill, August 6, 1929; m 1979. **Education:** Mich State Univ, BS, 1951; Ind Univ, PhD (physiol), 1968. **Professional Experience:** Assoc prof physiol & health sci, Ball State Univ & Muncie Ctr Med Educ, beginning 1977; asst prof, Ball State Univ & Muncie Ctr Med Educ, 1972-1977; asst prof physiol, Med Ctr, Univ Ark, Little Rock, 1970-1972; USPHS cardiovasc trainee, Bowman Gray Sch Med, 1968-1970; assoc ed, Howard W Sams & Co, Inc, Ind, 1955-1963. **Memberships:** Asn Am Physiol Soc; Sigma Xi. **Research Statement & Publications:** Control of blood flow. **Mailing Address:** 15803 Massey Rd, Hagerstown, IN 47346-9736.

LESHER, GARY ALLEN, DRUG METABOLISM, OCULAR PHARMACOLOGY. **Personal Data:** b Chicago, Ill, June 29, 1950; m 1973, c 2. **Education:** Carroll Col, Wis, BS, 1972; Purdue Univ, West Lafayette, MS, 1975, PhD (pharmacol), 1977. **Professional Experience:** PROF PHARMACOG, ILL COL OPTOMETRY, 1993; chmn, Basic & Health sci, Ill Col Optometry, 1999; dir res, Ill Col Optometry, 1999-. **Memberships:** Fellow, Amer Acad Of Optometry ASPET, ARVO. **Research Statement & Publications:** Ocular drug delivery by soft contact lenses, ocular pharmacokinetics, ocular metab of drugs. **Mailing Address:** Dept Basic & Health Sci, Ill Col Optom 3241 S Mivh Ave, Chicago, IL 60616-3816.

LESH-LAURIE, GEORGIA ELIZABETH, DEVELOPMENTAL BIOLOGY. **Personal Data:** b Cleveland, Ohio, July 28, 1938; m 1969. **Education:** Marietta Col, BS, 1960; Univ Wis, MS, 1961; Case Western Res Univ, PhD (biol), 1966. **Professional Experience:** RETIRED; chancellor acad affairs, Univ Colo, 1995-2003; vchancellor acad affairs, Univ Colo, 1995-1991; interim provost, Col Arts & Sci, 1989-1990; dean, Col Arts & Sci, beginning 1986; wright fel, Bermuda Biol Sta, 1984; Am Heart Asn Grant, 1982-1983; dean, Col Grad Studies, 1981-1986; prof biol, Cleveland State Univ, beginning 1977; chmn, Dept Biol, Cleveland State Univ, 1977-1981; asst dean, Western Res Col, Case Western Res Univ, 1973-1976; Am Cancer Soc instnl grant, 1973; Res Corp grant, 1971; USPHS instnl grant, 1970-1971; from asst prof to assoc prof biol, Western Res Col, Case Western Res Univ, 1969-1977; Am Cancer Soc grants, 1968-1971 & 1977-1980; asst prof biol sci, State Univ NY Albany, 1966-1969; NY State Res Found res fel, 1966-1967; Instr biol, Case Western Res Univ, 1965-1966; VCHANCELLOR ACAD AFFAIRS, UNIV COLO. **Memberships:** AAAS; Am Soc Zool; Soc Develop Biol; NY Acad Sci; Am Soc Cell Biol. **Research Statement & Publications:** Study of the neural control of developmental events in cnidarian systems and the role of nematocyst products on the mammalian cardiovascular system. **Mailing Address:** Chancellor Acad Affairs, Univ Colo, Campus Box 168, Denver, CO 80217-3364. **E-Mail:** gleshlaurie@castle.cudenver.edu

LESHNER, ALAN IRVIN, PSYCHOPHYSIOLOGY. **Personal Data:** b Lewisburg, Pa, February 11, 1944; m 1969, c 2. **Education:** Franklin & Marshall Col, AB, 1965; Rutgers Univ, MS, 1967, PhD (psychol), 1969. **Professional Experience:** DIR, NAT INST DRUG ABUSE, NIH, 1994-; actg dir, Nat Inst Drug Abuse, Nimh, 1990-1994; dep dir, Nat Inst Drug Abuse, Nimh, 1988-1990; dir, Off S & T Ctrs Develop, 1988; exec dir, Behav & Social Sci, 1985-1987; dep dir, Div Behav & Neurol Sci, 1983-1985; dep exec dir, NSB comn on precol educ, 1982-1983; proj mgr, NSF, 1980-1982; Fulbright lectr, Weizmann Inst, Israel, 1977-1978; vis scientist, Wis Regional Primate Res Ctr, 1976-1977; NIMH res grant, 1970-1971 & 1978-1980; NSF res grant, 1970-1972 & 1975-1977; from asst prof to prof psychol, Bucknell Univ, 1969-1981. **Memberships:** AAAS; fel Am Psychol Asn; Soc Neuroscience; fel NY Acad Sci. **Research Statement & Publications:** Biological basis of behavior; current and emerging science and technology policy issues; precollege and college level mathematics and science education. **Mailing Address:** Nat Inst Drug Abuse, 6001 Exec Blvd Ste 524, Bethesda, MD 20892.

LESHT, BARRY MARK, SATELLITE REMOTE SENSING, EARTH SCIENCE DATA ANALYSIS. **Personal Data:** b Chicago, Ill, November 29, 1948; m 1980, Kay; c Alison & Deanna. **Education:** Wash Univ, St Louis, BS, 1971; Univ Chicago, MA, 1973, PhD (geophys sci), 1977, MBA, 1999. **Honors & Awards:** Anderson-Everett Award, Int Asn Great Lakes Res, 1994; Editors Award, Int Asn Great Lakes Res, 1996. **Professional Experience:** ENVIRON PHYSICIST, ARGONNE NAT LAB, 2005-; Div Dir, Argonn Nat Lab, 2003-2005; Senior Fellow, Cntr Env. Sci, Univ. of Chicago, 2002-; Assoc Div Dir, Argonne Nat Lab, 1993-2003; Consult, S Fla Water Mgt Dist, NY Great Lakes Res Consortium & Int Joint Comn, 1992; physicist & group leader, Argonne Nat Lab, 1985-1992; asst physicist, Argonne Nat Lab, 1979-1984; Nat Res Coun resident fel, Atlantic Oceanog & Meteorol Labs, 1978; res assoc, Grad Sch Oceanog, Univ RI, 1977. **Memberships:** Int Asn Great Lakes Res (treas 1989-1992 secy 1993-); Am Geophys Union; Am Meteorol Soc; Int Asn Math Geol; Remote Sensing Soc. **Research Statement & Publications:** Applications statistical analysis to environmental data; analysis of satellite remote sensing data for studies of the Great Lakes; in situ profiling of atmospheric properties; benthic boundary layer processes. **Mailing Address:** 9700 S Cass Ave, Argonne, IL 60439. **Fax:** 630-252-2959. **E-Mail:** bmlesht@anl.gov

LESIEUTRE, BERNARD CHARLES, POWER SYSTEM ENGINEERING. **Personal Data:** b Detroit, Mich, January 19, 1964. **Education:** Univ Ill, BS, 1986, MS, 1988, PhD (elec eng), 1993. **Professional Experience:** ASSOC PROF ELEC ENG & COMPUT SCI, MASS INT TECHNOL, 1998-; asst prof elec eng, Mass Int Technol, 1993-1998. **Memberships:** Inst Elec & Electronics Engrs. **Research Statement & Publications:** Modeling, monitoring and analysis of large scale power systems. **Mailing Address:** Mass Inst Technol, Dept Elec Eng & Comput Sci, Rm 10-091 77 Mass Ave, Cambridge, MA 02139-4307. **Fax:** 617-258-6774. **E-Mail:** bcl@mit.edu

LESIKAR, ARNOLD VINCENT, CHEMICAL PHYSICS, PHYSICS. **Personal Data:** b Galveston, Tex, November 3, 1937; m 1976. **Education:** Rice Univ, BS, 1958; Calif Inst Technol, PhD (physics), 1965. **Professional Experience:** PROF EMER PHYSICS, ST CLOUD STATE UNIV, as of 2004; vis prof chem physics, Cath Univ Am, 1978-; prof physics, St Cloud State Univ, beginning 1966; asst physics, Tech Univ, Munich, Ger, 1965-1966; res asst physics, Calif Inst Technol, 1960-1965. **Memberships:** Sigma Xi; Am ChemSoc; Am Asn Physics Teachers; Am Phys Soc. **Mailing Address:** Dept Physics, St Cloud State Univ, Rm 314 Math & Sci Bldg 720 Fourth Ave S, St Cloud, MN 56301-4498. **Fax:** 320-308-4728. **E-Mail:** lesikar@stcloudstate.edu

LESIKAR, JAMES D, II, PHYSICS. **Education:** Rice Univ, Tex, BS, 1976, MME, 1978, MA, 1981, PhD (Physics), 1982. **Professional Experience:** PRIN ENGNR, NAT SECURITY AGENCY, SPARTA INC, 2005-. **Memberships:** Sigma Xi; Fel Nat Soc Prof Engrs. **Mailing Address:** Sparta Inc, 7075 Samuel Morse Dr 2nd Floor, Columbia, MD 21046. **Fax:** 410-872-8079. **E-Mail:** jlesikar@sparta.com

LESK, MICHAEL E, COMPUTER & INFORMATION SCIENCE. **Personal Data:** b Brooklyn, NY, May 21, 1945; m 1968. **Education:** Harvard Univ, BA, 1964, MA, 1966, PhD (chem phys), 1969. **Honors & Awards:** Flame Award, Usenix, 1994. **Professional Experience:** PROF, RUTGERS UNIV, as of 2003; head, Div Info & Intelligent Systs, NSF, 1998-2002; CHIEF RES SCIENTIST, INFO SCI RES LAB, BELLCORE, 1995-; sr res fel, Univ Col London, 1987; exec dir, Comput Sci Res Dept, 1983-1995; adj lectr comput sci, Columbia Univ, 1983-1985; mem staff, Comput Sci Res Lab, Bell Labs, 1969-1983. **Memberships:** fel Asn Comput Mach; Am Soc Info Sci. **Research Statement & Publications:** Word processing; programming languages; computer systems; information retrieval. **Mailing Address:** Libr& Info Sci, SCILS, Rutgers Univ, 4 Huntington St, Rm 306, New Brunswick, NJ 08901. **E-Mail:** lesk@scils.rutgers.edu

LESKO, KEVIN THOMAS, FISSION PROPERTIES. **Personal Data:** b April 30, 1956. **Education:** Leland Stanford, Jr Univ, BS, 1978; Univ Wash, PhD (physics), 1983. **Professional Experience:** STAFF SCIENTIST II & PHYSICIST, NUCLEAR SCI DIV, LAWRENCE BERKELEY LAB, 1987-; fel, Nuclear Sci Div, Lawrence Berkeley Lab, 1985-1987; fel, Argonne Nat Lab, 1983-1985; res asst, Accelerator Operator Instr, 1981-1983; res asst, Nuclear Physics Lab, Univ Wash, 1978-1983; teaching asst, Stanford Physics Dept, Stanford Univ, 1977-1978; tandem accelerator operator, Stanford Nuclear Physics Lab, 1976-1978. **Memberships:** Am Phys Soc. **Research Statement & Publications:** Author of several scientific journals. **Mailing Address:** Univ Calif Lawrence Berkeley Lab, One Cyclotron Rd 50B-5214 Bldg 50R5008, Berkeley, CA 94720-8158. **Fax:** 510-486-6738. **E-Mail:** ktlesko@lbl.gov

LESKO, PATRICIA MARIE, POLYMER CHEMISTRY. **Personal Data:** b Oakland, Calif, January 19, 1947; m 1993, Ronald W Novak. **Education:** Rice Univ, BA, 1968, MS, 1972, PhD (org chem), 1973. **Professional Experience:** AT JOHN WILEY & SONS, as of 1995; RES FEL, ROHM & HAAS CO, 1991-; chemist polymer chem, Res Labs, 1975-1991; Fel org chem, Syntex Corp, 1973-1975. **Memberships:** AAAS; Am Chem Soc. **Research Statement & Publications:** Emulsion polymers; coatings; leather chemistry; latex film formation. **Mailing Address:** John Wiley & Sons, NY.

LESKO, STEPHEN ALBERT, BIOCHEMISTRY. **Personal Data:** b Cassandra, Pa, December 30, 1931; m 1981. **Education:** Ind Univ, Pa, BS, 1959; Univ Md, PhD (biochem), 1965. **Professional Experience:** DIR IMAGING, CELL WORKS INC, as of 2001; ASSOC PROF BIOCHEM, JOHNS HOPKINS UNIV, 1990-; ASSOC PROF ENVIRON HEALTH SCI, JOHNS HOPKINS UNIV, 1982-; assoc prof biophys, Johns Hopkins Univ, 1982-1990; asst prof, Johns Hopkins Univ, 1973-1982; res assoc, Johns Hopkins Univ, 1968-1973; instr, Johns Hopkins Univ, 1965-1968. **Memberships:** AAAS; Am Chem Soc; Am Asn Cancer Res. **Research Statement & Publications:** Chemical carcinogenesis; nucleic acid chemistry and biology; oxygen toxicity; chromosome topography in interphase nuclei; relationship between DNA damage and cellular responses in the carcinogenic process; quantification of gene expression at the single cell level; gene mapping. **Mailing Address:** Cell Works, Inc, 6200 Seaforth St, Holabird Bus Park, Baltimore, MD 21224-6506. **Fax:** 410-633-7652. **E-Mail:** steve@cell-works.com

LESLEY, FRANK DAVID, ANALYSIS. **Personal Data:** b El Paso, Tex, December 20, 1944; m 1967, c 2. **Education:** Stanford Univ, BS, 1966; Univ Calif, San Diego, MA, 1968, PhD (math), 1970. **Professional Experience:** ASSOC CHAIR, DEPT MATH, SAN DIEGO STATE UNIV, 1994-; PROF MATH, SAN DIEGO STATE UNIV, 1976-; from asst prof to assoc prof, San Diego State Univ, 1970-1976. **Memberships:** Am Math Soc. **Research Statement & Publications:** Boundary behavior of conformal mappings, including minimal surfaces and approximation theory; published over 20 articles. **Mailing Address:** Dept Math, San Diego State Univ, San Diego, CA 92182-0001. **Fax:** 619-594-6746. **E-Mail:** lesley@math.sdsu.edu

LESLIE, CHARLES MILLER, MEDICAL ANTHROPOLOGY. **Personal Data:** b Lake Village, Ark, November 8, 1923; m 1946, Zelda; c Mario, Mira & Sam. **Education:** Univ Chicago, PhB, 1949, MA, 1950, PhD (anthrop), 1959. **Professional Experience:** Vis prof anthrop, Univ Calif, Berkeley, 1995; vis prof anthrop, McGill Univ, 1993; vis prof, Harvard Med Sch, 1992; PROF EMER, CTR SCI & CULT, UNIV DEL, 1991-; vis prof, Univ Calif, Berkeley, 1987; med anthrop ed, Social Sci & Med, 1977-1989; prof, Ctr Sci & Cult, Univ Del, 1976-1991; NSF res grant, 1974 & 1976; res assoc, Dept Anthrop, Univ Chicago, 1974-1975; prof, Anthrop Dept, Univ Col, NY Univ, 1967-1976; chmn, Anthrop Dept, Univ Col, NY Univ, 1967-1971; assoc prof, Case Western Res Univ, 1966-1967; vis prof, Univ Wash, 1965; NSF fel, Sch Oriental & African Studies, Univ London, 1962-1963; from instr to assoc prof, Pomona Col, 1956-1965; instr, Univ Minn, 1954-1956; instr anthrop, Southern Methodist Univ, 1950-1951. **Memberships:** Fel AAAS; fel Am Anthrop Asn; fel Royal Anthrop Inst Gt Brit & Ireland; Am Ethnological Soc; Soc Med Anthrop; Soc Latin Am Anthrop. **Research Statement & Publications:** World view and social change in India and Latin America; comparative study of medical systems. **Mailing Address:** Ctr Sci & Cult, Univ Del, Pub Rels, Newark, DE 19716.

LESLIE, GERRIE ALLEN, IMMUNOLOGY, IMMUNOCHEMISTRY. **Personal Data:** b Red Deer, Alta, November 19, 1941; m 1965, Anna; c Kirsten & John G. **Education:** Univ Alta, BS, 1962, MS, 1965; Univ Hawaii, PhD (microbiol), 1968. **Professional Experience:** Prof, Ore Health Sci Univ, 1981-1986; PRES, IMMUNOL CONSULTS LAB INC, 1977-; assoc prof microbiol & immunol, Ore Health Sci Univ, 1974-1981; NL Tartat res fel, 1977 & 1982; adj assoc prof microbiol, Sch Med, Tulane Univ, 1974-1980; from asst prof to assoc prof microbiol, Sch Med, Tulane Univ, 1970-1974; USPHS fel, Col Med, Univ Fla, 1968-1970; res affil, Delta Regional Primate Res Ctr, Covington, La. **Memberships:** Am Asn Immunol; Am Soc Microbiol; Am Hereford Asn. **Research Statement & Publications:** Phylogeny of immunoglobulin structure and function; regulation of the immune response; secretory immunologic system; immunoglobulin D. **Mailing Address:** Immunol Consults Lab Inc, 23558 Denali Ln, Sherwood, OR 97034. **Fax:** 503-625-1660. **E-Mail:** icleleslie@aol.com

LESLIE, JAMES, PHARMACEUTICAL CHEMISTRY. **Personal Data:** b Belfast, Ireland, April 25, 1934; m 1964, Louisa; c Ethel, Thyra & David. **Education:** Queen's Univ, Belfast, BSc, 1956, PhD (chem), 1959. **Professional Experience:** ASSOC PROF PHARM, SCH PHARM, UNIV MD, BALTIMORE, 1979-; vis, Dept Clin Physics & Bioengineering, Western Regional Hosp Bd, Glasgow, Scotland, 1971-1972; assoc prof med chem, Sch Pharm, Univ MD, Baltimore, 1966-1979; NIH res grant, 1964; asst prof, Sch Pharm, Univ MD, Baltimore, 1963-1966; asst prof chem, Wash Col, 1962-1963; asst prof & res assoc, Okla State Univ, 1961-1962; Fel, Okla State Univ, 1959-1961. **Memberships:** Am Chem Soc; Am Asn Cols Pharm. **Research Statement & Publications:** Kinetics of processes of biological interest; drug analysis. **Mailing Address:** Univ Md Sch Pharm, 100 Penn St No 540A, Baltimore, MD 21201-1082. **Fax:** 410-706-6580.

LESLIE, JAMES C, MANUFACTURING TECHNOLOGY, ADVANCED COMPOSITE MATERIALS. **Personal Data:** b Berlin, Pa, July 14, 1933; m Carmen; c James C II, Lori E, Leanne M & John C. **Education:** Pa State Univ, BSc, 1956; Ohio State Univ, MSc, 1958, PhD (chem eng), 1964. **Honors & Awards:** Judd Hall Award Outstanding Contrib to Composites Mfg, Can Mfrs Asn/Soc Mfg Engrs, 1997 fel, SME 1998; board of dir, SME, 2001. **Professional Experience:** DIR ENG, PRES & CHIEF EXEC OFFICER, ADVAN COMPOSITES & TECHNOL INC, as of 2002; mem nat bd adv, Composites Mfg Asn-SME, 1991-; mgr mkt & eng, Advan Composite Pipe & Tube, 1977-1981; contractor, Jim Leslie Consults, 1976-1980; mgr, Advan Composite Prods, Reliable Mfg, 1975-1976; group supvr, Composite Struct Group, 1966-1968; supvr, Rocket Nozzle, Case Bond & Insulation Groups, 1965-1966; group leader, Thermal Anal & High Temp Res & Develop, 1964-1965; Instr, Frostburg State Col, 1962-1963 & WVa Univ Exten Serv, Allegany Ballistics Lab, 1964-1965; sr res engr, Adv Develop Dept, Hercules Inc, 1962-1964; res asst chem eng, Res Found, 1959-1962; fel, Ohio State Univ, 1958-1959; eng exp sta, Dept Chem Eng, 1957-1958; eng exp sta, Ohio State Univ, 1956-1957; asst chem anal, Pa State Univ, 1955-1956. **Memberships:** Fel Soc Mfg Engrs; Soc Advan Mat & Process Eng (first vpres, 1973, pres, 1974). **Research Statement & Publications:** Research and development; consultant; prototype and process development in many areas of advanced composite materials fabrication; tracer techniques; development of graphite fibers; advanced composite materials and manufacturing techniques. **Mailing Address:** Advan Composite Prods & Technol Inc, 15602 Chem Lane, Huntington Beach, CA 92649-1507. **Fax:** 714-895-7766.

LESLIE, JAMES D, SOLID STATE PHYSICS. **Personal Data:** b Toronto, Ont, July 6, 1935; m 1964, c 3. **Education:** Univ Toronto, BASc, 1957; Univ Ill, MS, 1960, PhD (physics), 1963. **Professional Experience:** PROF PHYSICS, UNIV WATERLOO, 1968-; asst prof, 1963-1968. **Memberships:** Am Phys Soc; Can Asn Physicists. **Research Statement & Publications:** Low temperature physics; far infrared spectroscopy; superconductivity; electron tunneling. **Mailing Address:** Dept Physics, Univ Waterloo, 200 Univ Ave W, Waterloo, ON N2L 3G1, Can.

LESLIE, JEROME RUSSELL, WORD PROCESSING & ELECTRONIC DELIVERY OF NEWS RELEASES, PHOTOGRAPHY. **Personal Data:** b Luverne, Minn, October 11, 1939; m 1964, c 3. **Education:** SDak State Univ, BS, 1962, MS, 1990. **Professional Experience:** AGR NEWS ED, SDAK STATE UNIV, 1978-; state ed, Brookings Daily Reporter, SDak, 1973-1978; reporter-photogr & deskman, Sioux City J, Iowa, 1963-1973; reporter-photogr, Watertown Pub Opinion, SDak, 1962-1963. **Memberships:** Int Agr Commun Educ. **Research Statement & Publications:** Evaluating electronic transfer and other news delivery methods; articles on plant science, animal science, veterinary science, dairy science and economics. **Mailing Address:** SDak State Univ, PO Box 2231, Brookings, SD 57007-1897. **Fax:** 605-688-4018. **E-Mail:** leslie.jerome@ces.sdstate.edu

LESLIE, JOHN FRANKLIN, FUNGAL GENETICS. **Personal Data:** b Dallas, Tex, July 2, 1953; m 1976, Ingelin; c Timothy F & Inger J. **Education:** Univ Dallas, BA (biology), 1975; Univ Wis-Madison, MS (genetics), 1977, PhD (genetics), 1979. **Professional Experience:** PROF PLANT PATH, KANS STATE UNIV, MANHATTAN, 1996-; vis prof, fac of agric, univ Sydney, Australia, 2002; res scholar, Royal Botanic Gardens-Sydney, Australia, 2002 vis prof, Dept Microbiol, Nat Univ Rio Cuarto, Arg, 1996; editor, appl and environ microbiol, 1997-2006; assoc ed, Mycologia, 1994-1997; sr res assoc, Dept Biol Sci, Stanford Univ, Stanford, Calif, 1992-1993; from asst prof to assoc prof, Kans State Univ, Manhattan, 1984-1996; Tech adv, Inst Christian Resources, San Jose, Calif, 1981-2005; res microbiologist genetics, Int Mineral & Chem Corp, 1981-1984; fel res affil, Dept Biol Sci, Stanford Univ, Calif, 1979-1981; Fel trainee, NIH, Lab Genetics, Univ Wis-Madison, 1976-1979. **Memberships:** Genetics Soc Am; Mycol Soc Am; Am Soc Microbiol; Brit Mycol Soc; Soc Gen Microbiol; Am Phytopath Soc. **Research Statement & Publications:** Molecular, classical and population of filamentous fungi, especially Fusarium; genetics of mycotoxin production, and vegetative compatibility. **Mailing Address:** Dept Plant Path, 4002 Throckmorton Plant Sci Ctr Kans State Univ, Manhattan, KS 66506-5502. **Fax:** 785-532-5692. **E-Mail:** jfl@ksu.edu

LESLIE, PAUL WILLARD, POPULATION GENETICS, DEMOGRAPHY. **Personal Data:** b Peekskill, NY, April 23, 1948. **Education:** Bucknell Univ, BA, 1970; Pa State Univ, MA, 1972, PhD (anthrop), 1977. **Professional Experience:** PROF, DEPT ANTHROP, UNIV NC, CHAPEL HILL, as of 2003; asst prof anthrop, State Univ NY, Binghamton, beginning 1978; asst prof anthrop, Univ Tex, Austin, 1976-1978. **Memberships:** AAAS; Am Asn Phys Anthropologists; Human Biol Coun; Pop Asn Am; Soc Study Social Biol. **Research Statement & Publications:** Population genetics, demography of small populations, mathematical modeling and computer simulation; interactions among the social, demographic, and genetic structures of human populations. **Mailing Address:** Dept Anthrop, Univ NC, 306B Alumni Bldg, CB 3115, Chapel Hill, NC 27599-3115. **Fax:** 919-962-1613. **E-Mail:** pwleslie@unc.edu

LESLIE, STEVEN WAYNE, PHARMACOLOGY. **Personal Data:** b Franklin, Ind, January 23, 1946; m 1970, c 1. **Education:** Purdue Univ, BS, 1969, MS, 1972, PhD (pharmacol), 1974. **Professional Experience:** BAUERLE CENTENNIAL PROF & DOLUISIO CHMN, DEPT PHARMACOL & TOXICOL, UNIV TEX, AUSTIN, as of 2004; DEAN, COL PHARM, UNIV TEX, AUSTIN, 1998-; assoc prof pharmacol & toxicol, Univ Tex, Austin, beginning 1981; asst prof, 1974-1981. **Memberships:** Sigma Xi; AAAS. **Research Statement & Publications:** Investigations concerning the role of cellular organelles in calcium-mediated termination mechanisms in secretory tissues and the effects of various drugs on these termination mechanisms. **Mailing Address:** Col Pharm, Univ Tex, Austin, TX 78712. **Fax:** 512-471-5002. **E-Mail:** sleslie@mail.utexas.edu

LESLIE, THOMAS M, PHOTOCHEMISTRY, SYNTHETIC ORGANIC CHEMISTRY. **Personal Data:** b Philadelphia, Pa, November 11, 1954; m 1982. **Education:** Rider Col, BS, 1976; Univ Notre Dame, PhD (chem), 1980. **Professional Experience:** Res dir, Chromophore Inc, as of 1997; assoc prof, Dept Chem, Univ Ala, Huntsville, as of 1997; STAFF SCIENTIST, CELANESE RES CO, 1985-; Mem tech staff, Bell Tel Labs, 1980-1985. **Memberships:** Am Chem Soc; NY Acad Sci. **Research Statement & Publications:** Mechanism of photochemical reactions via reaction intermediates produced in laser flash photolysis; study of the effect of subtle changes in chemical constitution on materials exhibiting liquid crystal phases; liquid crystal side chain polymers; nonlinear optical materials; Published over 6 articles. **Mailing Address:** Dept Chem Univ Ala, Huntsville, AL 35899.

LESLIE, WALLACE DEAN, ANALYTICAL CHEMISTRY. **Personal Data:** b Dacoma, Okla, November 9, 1922; m 1948, c 3. **Education:** Northwestern State Col, Okla, BS, 1947; Okla State Univ, MS, 1950. **Professional Experience:** RETIRED; dir, anal res sect, 1977-1985; res group leader, res & develop dept, 1962-1977; from assoc res chemist to sr res chemist, Mfg Dept, Continental Oil Co, 1952-1962; anal chemist, Mfg Dept, Continental Oil Co, 1951-1952; instr, Northwestern State Col, Okla, 1949-1951; asst chem, Okla State Univ, 1947-1949. **Memberships:** Am Chem Soc. **Research Statement & Publications:** Analytical research and development; petroleum and petroleum products; petrochemicals. **Mailing Address:** 11 Forest Rd, Ponca City, OK 74604.

LESNAW, JUDITH ALICE, VIROLOGY, MOLECULAR BIOLOGY. **Personal Data:** b Chicago, Ill, July 30, 1940. **Education:** Univ Ill, BS, 1962, MS, 1964, PhD (cell biol), 1969. **Professional Experience:** PROF BIOL SCI, UNIV KY, 1988-; from asst prof to assoc prof, Univ KY, 1974-1988; res assoc virol, Univ Ill, 1969-1974; mem, Med Biochem Study Sect, NIH. **Memberships:** Am Soc Microbiol; Am Soc Virol; Am Soc Biochem & Molecular Biol. **Research Statement & Publications:** Structure and function of viral proteins and RNA; replication of RNA viruses; defective interfering particles; expression of recombinant proteins. **Mailing Address:** Dept Biol, Univ Ky, 225 TH Morgan Bldg, Lexington, KY 40506-0225. **Fax:** 606-257-7648. **E-Mail:** biojal@pop.uky.edu

LESNER, SHARON A, REHABILITATIVE AUDIOLOGY. **Personal Data:** b Lorain, Ohio, April 1, 1951. **Education:** Hiram Col, BA, 1973; Kent State Univ, MA, 1975; Wayne State Univ, MA (audiol), 1976; Ohio State Univ, PhD (audiol), 1979. **Professional Experience:** PROF AUDIOL, UNIV AKRON, 1979-. **Memberships:** Am Speech Lang & Hearing Asn; Acad Rehab Audiol; Acoust Soc Am; Alexander Graham Bell Asn Deaf; Am Auditory Soc; Am Acad Audiol. **Research Statement & Publications:** Visual, auditory and audio-visual reception of speech; evoked potentials including auditory and visual; hearing aid use; central auditory processing; Avdiologic rehabilitation Adults, Assistive Listening Devices and Systems, Music and Hearing, Cipreceding; Published over 6 articles. **Mailing Address:** Common Dis, The Univ Akron, Akron, OH 44325-3001. **Fax:** 330-972-7884. **E-Mail:** lesner@uakron.edu

LESNIAK, LINDA, GRAPH THEORY. **Personal Data:** b Gary, Ind, August 14, 1948; m 1983, Mark. **Education:** Western Mich Univ, BA, 1970, MA, 1971, PhD (math), 1974. **Professional Experience:** PROF MATH, DREW UNIV, 1991-; assoc prof, Drew Univ, 1985-1991; asst prof to assoc prof math, Western Mich Univ, 1978-1985; asst prof, La State Univ, Baton Rouge, 1974-1978. **Memberships:** Am Math Soc; Sigma Xi; Math Asn Am; NY Acad Sci; Asn Women in Math; Soc Indust Appl Math. **Research Statement & Publications:** Extremal problems in graph theory; generalized degree conditions. **Mailing Address:** Dept Math & Comput Sci, Drew Univ, HS 312, Madison, NJ 07940. **E-Mail:** llesniak@drew.edu

LESPERANCE, PIERRE J, INVERTEBRATE PALEONTOLOGY. **Personal Data:** b Montreal, Que, August 16, 1934; m 1960, c 3. **Education:** Univ Montreal, BSc, 1956; Univ Mich, MS, 1957; McGill Univ, PhD (geol), 1961. **Professional Experience:** Chmn dept, Univ Montreal, 1975-1979; PROF GEOL, UNIV MONTREAL, 1971-; from asst prof to assoc prof, Univ Montreal, 1961-1971; geologist, Dept Natural Resources, Que, 1960-1961. **Memberships:** Geol Soc Can; Am Asn Petrol Geol; Soc Econ Paleont & Mineral; Paleont Soc; Brit Palaeont Asn. **Research Statement & Publications:** Low and middle Paleozoic field mapping in Quebec; paleontology and biostratigraphy of Upper Ordovician to Lower Devonian trilobites and brachiopods. **Mailing Address:** Dept Geol Univ Montreal, Sta Succre Centre Ville PO Box 6128, Montreal, PQ H3C 3J7, Can.

LESSARD, CHARLES S, BIOENGINEERING. **Education:** Marquette Univ, PhD (biomed eng). **Professional Experience:** ASSOC PROF, INDUST ENG DEPT, TEX A&M UNIV, as of 2002. **Mailing Address:** Indust Eng Dept, Tex A&M Univ, College Station, TX 77843. **Fax:** 979-845-4450. **E-Mail:** clessard@iemail.tamu.edu

LESSARD, JAMES LOUIS, BIOCHEMISTRY. **Personal Data:** b Eau Claire, Wis, March 9, 1943; m 1965, c 2. **Education:** Marquette Univ, BS, 1965, PhD (biochem), 1970. **Honors & Awards:** Basil O'Connor Award, March Dimes, 1972-1976. **Professional Experience:** ASSOC DIR, CINCINNATI CHILDREN'S HOSP MED CTR, as of 2004; PROF PEDIAT, MICROBIOL & BIOCHEM, MED SCH, UNIV CINCINNATI, 1986-; assoc prof res pediat, Microbiol & Biochem, Med Sch, Univ Cincinnati, 1979-1986; PROF MOLECULAR GENETICS, MICROBIOL & BIOCHEM, MED SCH, UNIV CINCINNATI, 1974-; ASST PROF BIOL CHEM, UNIV CINCINNATI, 1974-; assoc prof, Microbiol & Biochem, Med Sch, Univ Cincinnati, 1972-1979; fel pharmacol-morphol, Pharmaceut Mfrs Asn Found, Cincinnati, Ohio, 1972-1974; res scholar biochem, Children's Hosp Res Found, 1971-1972; fel, Roche Inst Molecular Biol, Nutley, NJ, 1969-1971. **Memberships:** Am Chem Soc; AAAS; Sigma Xi. **Research Statement & Publications:** Regulatory processes in development; cell motility; immunochemistry. **Mailing Address:** Dept Pediat & Develop Biol, Univ Cincinnati, Cincinnati, OH 45236. **Fax:** 513-636-4317. **E-Mail:** james.lessard@chmcc.org

LESSARD, JEAN, ORGANIC ELECTROCHEMISTRY. **Personal Data:** b East Broughton, Que, April 29, 1936; m 1993, Francine; c Francois & Ivan. **Education:** Laval Univ, BA, 1956, BSc, 1960, PhD (org chem), 1965. **Professional Experience:** PROF CHEM, UNIV SHERBROOKE, 1976-; from asst prof to assoc prof, Univ Sherbrooke, 1969-1976; asst res officer org chem, Nat Res Coun Can, 1967-1969; Nat Res Coun Can fel, Imp Col, Univ London, 1965-1967. **Memberships:** Chem Inst Can; Royal Soc Chem; Am Chem Soc; Electrochem Soc; AAAS; Can Soc Chem; Fr Soc Chem; Int Union Pure & Appl Chem. **Research Statement & Publications:** Electrochemistry and photochemistry used to study new methods of effecting organic reactions or new organic reactions, investigation of the mechanism, scope and synthetic utility of these reactions. **Mailing Address:** Dept Chem, Univ Sherbrooke, Sherbrooke, PQ J1K 2R1, Can. **Fax:** 819-821-8017. **E-Mail:** jlessard@courrier.usherb.ca

LESSARD, RICHARD R, OIL SPILL RESPONSE TECHNOLOGY, DISPERSANT FORMULATION. **Personal Data:** b Lowell, Mass, March 15, 1943; m 1995, Nancy; c Andy & Nicolle. **Education:** Lowell Technol Inst, BS, Chem Eng, 1966; Univ Maine, MS, 1968, PhD, 1970 Chem Eng. **Professional Experience:** Retired Dist. ENG ADV, EXXONMOBIL RES & ENG CO, VA, as of 2006; OIL SPILL TECHNOL CONSULT, EXXONMOBIL RES & ENG CO, 1989-; mgr, Exxon Res & Eng Co, 1984-1989; res coordr, Exxon Res & Eng Co, 1982-1984; lab dir res & develop, Exxon Res & Eng Co, 1980-1982; mem, Fossil Energy Res Working Group III, Dept Energy, 1980; sect head, Exxon Res & Eng Co, 1976-1979; Proj staff engr, Exxon Res & Eng Co, 1970-1976. **Memberships:** Am Inst Chem Engrs; ASTM. **Research Statement & Publications:** Development of enhanced oil spill dispersants as a tool for minimizing the adverse effexts of oil spills. **Mailing Address:** 681 Penn Estates, East Stroudsburg, PA 18301. **E-Mail:** richard.r.lessard@exxonmobil.com

LESSARD, ROGER ALAIN, OPTICS. **Personal Data:** b E Broughton, Que, September 11, 1944; m 1967, c 2. **Education:** Univ Laval, BS, 1969, DSc (optics), 1973. **Professional Experience:** DIR, DEPT PHYSICS & PHYS GENIUS & OPTICS, UNIV LAVAL, as of 2004; dir, Dept Physics, Univ Laval, 2000-2001; pres, Del Laser InSpeck, Inc, 1994-1996; invited prof, Tianjin Univ, People's Repub China, 1982 & 1984; PROF OPTICS,

UNIV LAVAL, 1978-; from lectr to assoc prof 1972-1982; res officer lasers, Gentec Co, 1971-1972. **Memberships:** Can Asn Advan Sci; Can Asn Physicists; Optical Soc Am; Am Phys Soc; Soc Photo Optical Eng. **Research Statement & Publications:** Holography and optical information processing; optical memories recording media. **Mailing Address:** Dept Physics, Univ Laval, VCH-1660, Quebec, PQ G1K 7P4, Can. **Fax:** 418-656-2040. **E-Mail:** ralessard@phy.ulaval.ca

LESSELL, SIMMONS, NEUROLOGY, OPHTHALMOLOGY. **Personal Data:** b Brooklyn, NY, May 25, 1933; m 1955, c 4. **Education:** Amherst Col, BA, 1954; Cornell Univ, MD, 1958. **Professional Experience:** DIR, NEURO-OPHTHAL SERV, MASS EYE & EAR INFIRMARY, MED SCH, HARVARD UNIV, as of 2003; PROF ANAT, NEUROL & OPHTHAL, SCH MED, BOSTON UNIV, 1970-; assoc prof neurol, Neurol & Ophthal, Sch Med, Boston Univ, 1967-1970; lectr, Sch Med, Tufts Univ, beginning 1966; resident ophthal, Mass Eye & Ear Hosp, 1963-1966; resident neurol, Univ Vt, 1959-1960; physician, NIH, 1959-1960; Intern med, Cornell Univ, 1958-1959; vis surgeon, Univ Hosp; vis surgeon & dir dept ophthal, Boston City Hosp; consult ophthal, Vet Admin Hosp & Tufts-New Engl Med Ctr. **Memberships:** Asn Res Vision & Ophthal. **Research Statement & Publications:** Optic neuropathies, clinical and experimental; histochemistry and experimental pathology of the optic nerve. **Mailing Address:** Mass Eye & Ear Infirmary, 243 Charles St, Boston, MA 02114. **Fax:** 617-573-3851.

LESSEPS, ROLAND JOSEPH, DEVELOPMENTAL BIOLOGY. **Personal Data:** b New Orleans, La, August 13, 1933. **Education:** Spring Hill Col, BS, 1958; Johns Hopkins Univ, PhD (biol), 1962. **Professional Experience:** REVEREND, KASSISI MISSIONS, ZAMBIA, 1993-; mem bd trustees, Am Killfish Asn, 1986-; prof, Loyola Univ, 1981-1993; chmn dept, Loyola Univ, 1978-1983; From asst prof to assoc prof biol, Loyola Univ, 1967-1981; Vis prof, Roman Cath Univ, Nijmegen. **Memberships:** AAAS; Am Soc Zool; Electron Micros Soc Am; Soc Develop Biol; Nat Asn Biol Teachers; Am Killfish Asn. **Research Statement & Publications:** Morphogenetic movements of embryonic cells; electron microscopy of the cell surface; time-lapse filming of cell movements in living embryos. **Mailing Address:** Kassisi Missions, PO Box 30652, Lusaka, Zambia.

LESSER, GEORGE VICTOR, DENTISTRY. **Education:** DDS, 1939. **Professional Experience:** RETIRED; dent, Univ Buffalo, ending 1993. **Mailing Address:** 298 Ruskin Rd, Buffalo, NY 14226.

LESSER, MICHAEL PATRICK, EFFECTS OF ULTRA-VIOLET RADIATION ON ALGAE-INVERTEBRATE SYMBIOSES, EFFECTS OF WATER FLOW TEMPERATURE & FOOD OF THE BIOGENETICS OF MARINE INVERTEBRATES. **Personal Data:** b Bangor, Maine, October 15, 1954. **Education:** Univ NH, BA, 1983, MA, 1985; Univ Ma, PhD (zoology), 1989. **Professional Experience:** RES PROF ZOOL, UNIV NH, as of 2002; res asst zool, Univ NH, beginning 1993; consult, Pittsburgh Zoo, 1993; res scientist, Bigelow Lab for Ocean Sci, 1991-1993; chief scientist, Sea Educ Asn, 1991-1993; E-W Prog, Northeastern Univ, 1991; E-W Prog, Hawaii Inst Marine Biol, 1991, 1993; instr, Shoals Marine Lab, 1989-1993; assoc, Bigelow Lab Ocean Sci, 1989-1991. **Memberships:** Am Soc Limnol & Oceanog; Am Soc Zool; Oceanog Soc; Int Soc Study Coral Reefs; Western Soc Naturalists; Nat Shellfisheries Asn. **Research Statement & Publications:** Effects of ultraviolet radiation on corals; ultraviolet radiation effects on phytoplankton and the biogenetics of sessile suspension-feeding marine invertebrates. **Mailing Address:** Dept Zool Univ NH, Rm 202 Rudman, Durham, NH 03824-3544. **Fax:** 603-862-3784. **E-Mail:** mpl@christa.unh.edu

LESSIE, THOMAS GUY, MICROBIAL PHYSIOLOGY. **Personal Data:** b New York, NY, December 14, 1936; m 1962, c 3. **Education:** Queens Col, NY, BS, 1958; Harvard Univ, AM, 1961, PhD (biol sci), 1963. **Professional Experience:** Consult, appl environ microbiol, 1998-2001; Prof microbiol, Univ Mass, Amherst, 1981-2002; sr res scientist, US EPA Res Lab, Gulf Breeze, FL, 1993-1995; vis prof, dept biol, Yale Univ, 1988; vis prof dept microbiol, Med Col Va, 1981; ed, Boards J Bacteriol, 1976-1886, 1990-1993; vis prof, Dept Biol Sci, Purdue Univ, 1974; assoc prof, Univ Mass, Amherst, 1974-1981; asst prof, Univ Mass, Amherst, 1968-1974; res assoc microbiol, Univ Wash, 1967-1968; NIH fels biochem, Oxford Univ, 1963-1965 & biol sci, Purdue Univ, 1965-1967; Rrs asst microbiol, Haskins Labs, NY, 1958-1959. **Memberships:** Am Soc Microbiol. **Research Statement & Publications:** Biochemical genetics and genomic organisation of Burkholderia cepacia with emphasis on regulatory mechanisms governing gene expression and enzyme activity; roles of transposable gene-activating elements in evolution of new metabolic functions. **Mailing Address:** Dept Microbiol, Univ Mass, Amherst, MA 01003. **Fax:** 413-545-1578. **E-Mail:** tlessie@microbio.umass.edu

LESSIN, LAWRENCE STEPHEN, HEMATOLOGY, ONCOLOGY. **Personal Data:** b Washington, DC, October 14, 1937; m 1962, c 3. **Education:** Univ Chicago, MD, 1962. **Professional Experience:** MED DIR, WASH CANCER INST, as of 2002; consult, Walter Reed Army Med Ctr, 1975-; consult, Nat Heart, Lung & Blood Inst & US Naval Med Ctr, 1974-; prof med path & dir hemat & oncol, Sch Med, Univ George Wash, beginning 1974; assoc prof, Sch Med, Univ George Wash, 1970-1974; asst prof med, Sch Med, Univ Duke, 1968-1970; spec fel, Nat Heart Inst Hematol Med, Inst Cell Path, Paris, France, 1967-1968; instr med, Univ Pa, 1965-1967. **Memberships:** Am Col Physicians; Am Soc Hemat; Am Fedn Clin Res; Int Soc Hemat; Am Soc Clin Oncol; Sigma Xi. **Research Statement & Publications:** Red cell membrane structure in hemolytic anemias; red cell rhelogy; hematologic neoplasia; preleukemia (myelodysplasia). **Mailing Address:** Cancer Inst Wash Hosp Ctr, 110 Irving St NW, Washington, DC 20010.

LESSING, PETER, ENVIRONMENTAL GEOLOGY. **Personal Data:** b Englewood, NJ, June 15, 1938; m 1965, Katherine; c 2. **Education:** St Lawrence Univ, BS, 1961; Dartmouth Col, MA, 1963; Syracuse Univ, PhD (geol), 1967. **Professional Experience:** SR RES GEOLOGIST, WVA GEOL & ECON SURV, 1989-; chief, Geol Div, 1980-1985; adj prof, WVa Univ, 1973-; head, Environ Geol Sect, 1973-1989; environ geologist, WVa Geol Surv, 1971-1973; asst prof geol, St Lawrence Univ, 1966-1971. **Memberships:** Geol Soc Am; Asn Earth Sci Ed; Hist Earth Sci Soc. **Research Statement & Publications:** Geologic field mapping; environmental geology investigations; history of geology; landslide evaluation; geologic hazard studies; hydrology and water use. **Mailing Address:** WVa Geol & Econ Surv, PO Box 879 One Mont Chateau Rd, Morgantown, WV 26507-0879. **E-Mail:** lessing@geosrv.wvnet.edu

LESSIOS, HARILAOS ANGELOU, EVOLUTION. **Personal Data:** b Thessaloniki, Greece, March 4, 1951; m 1983, Kristin; c Nicolas & Anna. **Education:** Harvard Univ, BA, 1973; Yale Univ, MPhil, 1976, PhD (biol), 1979. **Honors & Awards:** John Spangler Nicholas Prize, Yale Univ. **Professional Experience:** STAFF SCIENTIST, SMITHSONIAN TROP RES INST, 1979-. **Memberships:** Soc Study Evolution; Soc Syst Biol. **Research Statement & Publications:** Evolution and ecology of marine organisms; ecology of coral reefs; molecular evolution recently published 5 books. **Mailing Address:** Smithsonian Trop Res Inst, Unit 948, APO, AA 34002-0948. **Fax:** 507-212-8790. **E-Mail:** Lessiosh@si.edu

LESSLER, JUDITH THOMASSON, SURVEY RESEARCH METHODS. **Personal Data:** b Charlotte, NC, October 10, 1943; m 1970, c 2. **Education:** Univ NC, Chapel Hill, AB, 1966, PhD (biostatist), 1974; Emory Univ, Ga, MAT, 1967. **Professional Experience:** SR RES LEADER & CTR DIR, BATTELLE MEM INST, 1992-; bd mem, Am Statist Asn, 1985-1987; serv fel, Nat Ctr Health Statist, 1984-1985; adj asst prof, Biostatist Dept, Univ NC, 1981-; dept mgr, Res Triangle Inst, 1980-1984; prin investr, NSF grant, 1979-1981; sr statistician, res Triangle Inst, 1978-1992; statistician, Res Triangle Inst, 1974-1978. **Memberships:** Am Statist Asn; Am Pub Health Asn; AAAS. **Research Statement & Publications:** Survey research methods; statistical treatment of nonsampling errors and multiframe-multiplicity estimators; application of cognitive psychology to survey design. **Mailing Address:** PO Box 12194, Research Triangle Park, NC 27709.

LESSMAN, CHARLES ALLEN, OOCYTE MEIOTIC MATURATION, CYTOSKELETON IN DEVELOPMENT. **Personal Data:** b St Paul, Minn, June 18, 1948; m 1971, Mary; c Shaun T & Damian C. **Education:** Univ Minn, Minneapolis, BA, 1970, MS, 1975; Univ Minn, St Paul, PhD (cell biol), 1980. **Professional Experience:** PROF, DEPT BIOL, MEMPHIS STATE UNIV, 1988-; vis prof, Univ Iowa, 1987-1988; assoc prof, St Francis Xavier Univ, 1985-1988; adj prof, Delhousie Univ, 1984-1987; asst prof, St Francis Xavier Univ, 1981-1985; fel, Johns Hopkins Univ, 1978-1981. **Memberships:** Am Soc Cell Biol; AAAS; Soc Study Reproduction; Am Soc Zoologists; Soc Develop Biol; Sigma Xi. **Research Statement & Publications:** Ovarian physiology, especially oocyte meiotic maturation in lower vertebrates; steroid (progesterone) mode of action in oocyte maturation and the cytoskeletal changes. **Mailing Address:** Dept Microbiol & Molecular Cell Sci, Univ Memphis, Memphis, TN 38152. **Fax:** 901-678-4457. **E-Mail:** clessman@memphis.edu

LESSMAN, GARY M, SOIL FERTILITY. **Personal Data:** b Hillsboro, Ill, July 15, 1938. **Education:** Southern Ill Univ, BS, 1960, MS, 1962; Mich State Univ, PhD (soil sci), 1967. **Professional Experience:** ASSOC PROF EMER AGRON, UNIV TENN, KNOXVILLE, as of 2004; assoc prof agron, Univ Tenn, Knoxville, beginning 1977; asst prof, Univ Tenn, Knoxville, 1969-1977; exten agronomist, Purdue Univ, 1967-1968. **Memberships:** Sigma Xi; Am Soc Agron. **Research Statement & Publications:** Micronutrient nutrition. **Mailing Address:** Dept Plant & Soil Sci, Univ Tenn, 375 Ellington Plant Sci Bldg 2431 Joe Johnson Dr, Knoxville, TN 37996-0001. **Fax:** 865-974-7997. **E-Mail:** lessmang@tennessee.edu

LESSMANN, RICHARD CARL, MECHANICAL ENGINEERING, FLUID MECHANICS. **Personal Data:** b New York, NY, October 14, 1942; m 1965, c 3. **Education:** Syracuse Univ, BS, 1964; Brown Univ, MS, 1966, PhD (eng), 1969. **Honors & Awards:** Am Inst Aeronaut & Astronaut. **Professional Experience:** PROF MECH ENG & APPL MECH, UNIV RI, 1983-; assoc prof mech eng & appl mech, Univ RI, 1975-1983; coordr, Fram/Allied Ctr Filtration Res Lab, 1984-; asst prof, 1969-1975; res & teaching asst, Brown Univ, 1964-1969. **Memberships:** Nat Award, Am Inst Aeronaut & Astronaut, 1964 Regional Award, Am Inst Aeronaut & Astronaut, 1966; Am Phys Soc; Sigma Xi. **Research Statement & Publications:** Turbulent flows; boundary layer theory; heat transfer. **Mailing Address:** Dept Mech Eng & Appl Mech, Univ RI, 131C Kirk Appl Eng Lab, Kingston, RI 02881. **Fax:** 401-874-2355. **E-Mail:** lessmann@egr.uri.edu

LESSNER, HOWARD E, INTERNAL MEDICINE, ONCOLOGY. **Personal Data:** b Philadelphia, Pa, February 28, 1927; m 1957, c 3. **Education:** Univ Pa, MD, 1953. **Professional Experience:** Clin dir, Comprehensive Cancer Ctr, 1974-; PROF ONCOL, UNIV MIAMI, 1974-; Dir, Comprehensive Cancer Ctr, 1972-1974; from instr to prof med, Univ Miami, 1959-1975; clin fel, Nat Cancer Inst, 1958-1959; res fel, Nat Heart Inst, Barnes Hosp, 1957-1958; clin fel, Jackson Mem Hosp, 1956-1957; sr asst resident, Jackson Mem Hosp, 1955-1956; Jr asst resident, Jackson Mem Hosp, 1954-1955. **Memberships:** Am Col Physicians; AMA; Am Soc Clin Oncol; Am Asn Cancer Res; AAAS. **Mailing Address:** 8950 N Kendall Dr No 410, Miami, FL 33176. **Fax:** 305-271-4868.

LESSO, WILLIAM GEORGE, OPERATIONS RESEARCH. **Personal Data:** b Cleveland, Ohio, March 23, 1931; m 1952, c 5. **Education:** Univ Notre Dame, BS, 1953; Xavier Univ, Ohio, MBA, 1963; Case Inst Technol, MS, 1966, PhD (opers res), 1967. **Professional Experience:** PROF EMER MECH ENG, UNIV TEX, AUSTIN, as of 2004; prof mech eng, Univ Tex, Austin, beginning 1972; assoc prof mech eng, Univ Tex, Austin, 1967-1972; proj engr, Flight Propulsion Div, Gen Elec Co, 1958-1964; design engr, Clevite Corp, 1953-1958. **Memberships:** Opers Res Soc Am; Inst Mgt Sci. **Research Statement & Publications:** Application of operations research to industrial and economic problems. **Mailing Address:** Dept Mech Eng, Univ Tex, One Univ Sta C2200, Austin, TX 78712. **Fax:** 512-471-8727.

LESSOR, DELBERT LEROY, PHYSICS, APPLIED MATHEMATICS. **Personal Data:** b 1941; American citizen; m 1962, c 2. **Education:** Ft Hays State Univ, BS, 1962; Kans State Univ, PhD (physics), 1967. **Professional Experience:** STAFF SCIENTIST, APPL PHYSICS CTR, PAC NW LABS, BATTELLE MEM INST, 1989-; sr res scientist eng physics, Appl Physics Ctr, Pac NW Labs, Battelle Mem Inst, 1980-1989; sr res scientist phys sci, Appl Physics Ctr, Pac NW Labs, Battelle Mem Inst, 1967-1980; temp asst prof physics, Kans State Univ, 1966-1967. **Memberships:** Am Phys Soc; Sci Res Soc NAm; Sigma Xi; Bioelectromagnetics Soc; Am Vacuum Soc. **Research Statement & Publications:** Electromagnetic field computation in industrial and instrument configurations; air filtration theory; nuclear particle transport; nuclear reaction theory; nuclear reactor instrumentation; geothermal chemistry; fluid flow calculation; optics theory; bioelectromagnetics effects; low energy electron diffraction analysis. **Mailing Address:** Pac NW Lab, K7-15 ISB one, Richland, WA 99352. **Fax:** 509-375-3641. **E-Mail:** del.lessor@pnl.gov

LESTER, DAVID SIMON, FLUORESCENCE MICROSCOPY, VIBRATIONAL SPECTROSCOPY IMAGING MICROSCOPY. **Personal Data:** b Sydney, Australia, February 23, 1955; m 1980, Janice; c Adam & Daniel. **Education:** Univ NSW, Australia, BSc Hons, 1977; Hebrew Univ Jerusalem, Israel, MSc, 1979; Northwestern Univ, PhD (biol). **Honors & Awards:** Outstanding Researcher, Israel Cancer Soc, 1987. **Professional Experience:** SITE HEAD, WW CLIN TECHNOL, PGRD, as of 2004; pharmacologist, DAPR, Food & Drug Admin, as of 1999; staff scientist, Food & Drug Admin, beginning 1993; vis assoc, NIH, 1990-1993; staff scientist, Harvard Univ Med Sch, 1986-1990; fel, Weizmann inst Sci, 1985-1986; fel, Muscular Dystrophy Asn, 1984-1985; fel, Harvard Univ Med Sch, 1983-1985; res assoc, Univ NC, 1981-1983; teaching asst, Northwestern Univ, 1979-1981; res asst, Hebrew Univ Jerusalem, 1978-1979. **Memberships:** Int Soc Neurochemistry; Am Soc Neuroscience; Int Brain Res Orgn; Am Asn Anatomists. **Research Statement & Publications:** Development of alternative procedures to monitor biochemical activities in simple and complex neuronal systems; new approaches to noninvasive analyses of brain function. **Mailing Address:** WW Clin Technol, PGRD, New Products Development, PGP, New York, NY 10017. **Fax:** 301-594-3037.

LESTER, DONALD THOMAS, FORESTRY. **Personal Data:** b New London, Conn, August 26, 1934; m 1962, c 2. **Education:** Univ Maine, BS, 1955; Yale Univ, MF, 1957, PhD (forest genetics), 1962. **Professional Experience:** CONSULT, FOREST GENETIC

RESOURCE MANAGEMENT CONSULT, as of 1995; SUPVR, FOREST BIOL, FORESTRY RES DIV, CROWN ZELLERBACH CORP, 1977-; From asst prof to prof forestry, Univ Wis-Madison, 1962-1977. **Memberships:** Sigma Xi. **Research Statement & Publications:** Tree breeding; genecology. **Mailing Address:** Forest Genetic Resource Management Consult, 1424 N Beach Rd, Saltspring Island, BC V8K 1B2, Can.

LESTER, FRANK K, JR, MATHEMATICS. **Education:** Ohio State Univ, Phd, 1972. **Professional Experience:** PROF, MATH EDUC COGNITIVE SCI, IND UNIV, as of 2005. **Mailing Address:** Ind Univ, Educ Bldg Rm 309, Bloomington, IN 47505-4301. **Fax:** 812-856-8116. **E-Mail:** lester@indiana.edu

LESTER, GEORGE RONALD, ENVIRONMENTAL CATALYSTS, AUTO CATALYTIC CONVERTOR. **Personal Data:** b War Eagle, WVa, September 6, 1934; m 1993, Patricia; c Julia, Kay, Brooke & David. **Education:** Berea Col, BA, 1954; Univ Ky, MS, 1956, PhD (chem), 1958. **Honors & Awards:** E V Murphree Award in Ind & Eng Chem, ACS, 2002; Welch Lecturer, 2004; Distinguished Alumni Award, Berea College, 2005. **Professional Experience:** Adj prof, Catalysis & Surface Sci Ctr, Northwestern Univ, 1995-; PRES, GEORGE LESTER INC, 1996-; sr res fel, Allied-Signal Res & Technol, 1992-1996; chair, Gordon Res Conf Catalysis, beginning 1991; res fel, Allied-Signal Res & Technol, 1990-1992; sr res scientist, Allied-Signal Engineered Mat Res Ctr, 1983-1990; dir mat sci res, UOP, Inc, 1976-1983; mgr appl catalysis, UOP, Inc, 1974-1976; assoc res coordr, UOP, Inc, 1963-1974; chemist, Universal Oil Prod Co, 1958-1963. **Memberships:** Am Chem Soc; Catalysis Soc; fel Soc Automotive Engrs. **Research Statement & Publications:** Conductivity of nonaqueous solutions; adsorption of gases on solids; heterogeneous catalysis; petrochemical processes; material science; automotive exhaust catalysis; solar systems; energy conservation; catalytic combustion; automotive gas turbine engines; electric power plant catalytic combustion; electrocatalysts for fuel cells for power plants; catalytic destruction of chemical warfare agents; catalytic incineration of hazardous pollutants; relative fossil fuel efficiencis of hybrid and fuel cell automobiles. **Mailing Address:** George Lester, Inc, Salem, VA 24153-1714. **Fax:** 540-387-2787. **E-Mail:** skygeorge@aol.com

LESTER, HENRY ALLEN, NEUROBIOLOGY, BIOPHYSICS. **Personal Data:** b New York, NY, July 4, 1945; c 2. **Education:** Harvard Col, AB, 1966; Rockefeller Univ, PhD (biophys), 1971. **Professional Experience:** CO-CHAIR, CALIF INST TECHNOL, as of 2005; BREN PROF BIOL, CALIF INST TECHNOL, 2000-; Sen Jacob Javits investr, NIH, 1985-; mem, Physiol Study Sect, 1985-1989; prof biol, Calif Inst Technol, 1983-2000; vis prof, Dept Biol Chem, Hebrew Univ, Israel, 1980-1981; res grants, NIH Res Career Develop Award, 1977-1982; assoc prof biol, Calif Inst Technol, 1976-1983; res grants, Alfred P Sloan Res fel, 1974-1976; asst prof biol, Calif Inst Technol, 1973-1976; res fel molecular Neurobiology, Inst Pasteur, 1971-1973. **Memberships:** Soc Neuroscience; Biophys Soc; Soc Gen Physiologists; fel AAAS. **Research Statement & Publications:** Excitable membranes; molecular neuroscience. **Mailing Address:** Dept Biol, Calif Inst Technol, 328A Kerckhoff, Pasadena, CA 91125. **E-Mail:** lester@caltech.edu

LESTER, JOHN BERNARD, ASTRONOMY, ASTROPHYSICS. **Personal Data:** b San Diego, Calif, March 11, 1945; m 1972, c 2. **Education:** Northwestern Univ, BA, 1967; Univ Chicago, MS, 1969, PhD (astron), 1972. **Professional Experience:** PROF, DEPT ASTRON & ASTROPHY, UNIV TORONTO, as of 2003; assoc prof astron, Univ Toronto, beginning 1981; asst prof, Univ Toronto, 1976-1981; physicist, Smithsonian Astrophys Observ, 1973-1976; presidential intern astron, Smithsonian Astrophys Observ, 1972-1973; lectr physics, Univ Wis-Milwaukee, 1969-1971. **Memberships:** Am Astron Soc; Astron Soc Pac; Int Astron Union. **Research Statement & Publications:** High dispersion stellar spectroscopy; stellar abundances; ultraviolet astronomy; infrared spectroscopy. **Mailing Address:** Dept Astron & Astrophys, Univ Toronto, Mississauga, ON L5L 1C6, Can. **Fax:** 905-828-5425. **E-Mail:** lester@astro.utoronto.ca

LESTER, JOSEPH EUGENE, PHYSICAL CHEMISTRY. **Personal Data:** b Bay City, Tex, July 2, 1942; m 1959, c 2. **Education:** Rice Univ, BA, 1964; Univ Calif, Berkeley, PhD (chem), 1968. **Professional Experience:** MGR, TECH ASSISTANCE LAB, OSRAM-SYLVANIA INC, as of 2002; ADVAN ENG SPECIALIST, OSRAM-SYLVANIA INC, 1989-; mgr mat characterization, Gulf Sci & Technol, 1985-1989; res assoc, Gulf Sci & Technol, 1981-1985; sr res chemist, GTE Labs, 1978-1981; mem staff, GTE Labs, 1973-1977; asst prof chem, Northwestern Univ, Evanston, 1967-1974. **Memberships:** Am Chem Soc; Am Phys Soc; Mat Res Soc. **Research Statement & Publications:** Kinetics and mechanisms of surface reactions; kinetics of high temperature transport reactions; thermodynamics. **Mailing Address:** Tech Assistance Lab, Osram Sylvania Inc, 71 Cherry Hill Dr, Beverly, MA 01915. **E-Mail:** joe.lester@sylvania.com

LESTER, LARRY JAMES, POPULATION GENETICS. **Personal Data:** b Bay City, Tex, July 15, 1947; m 1983, c 1. **Education:** Univ Tex, Austin, BA, 1969, PhD (pop genetics), 1975. **Professional Experience:** DIR BIOL, UNIV HOUSTON-CLEAR LAKE, as of 2000; PROF BIOL, UNIV HOUSTON, CLEAR LAKE, 1991-; from asst prof to assoc prof, Univ Houston, Clear lake, 1975-1991. **Memberships:** Sigma Xi; World Aquacult Soc; Crustacean Soc. **Research Statement & Publications:** Genetics of aquaculture species. **Mailing Address:** Dept Biol, Univ Houston Clear lake, 2700 Bay Area Blvd, Houston, TX 77058-1002. **Fax:** 281-283-3044. **E-Mail:** lester@cl.uh.edu

LESTER, MARSHA I, PHYSICS. **Education:** Douglass Col, Rutgers Univ, BA, 1976; Columbia Univ, PhD, 1981. **Professional Experience:** CHAIR & EDMUND J & LOUISE W. KAHN PROF NAT SCI, UNIV PA, as of 2005. **Memberships:** Am Phys Soc. **Mailing Address:** Dept Chem, Univ Pa, 262 T, Philadelphia, PA 19104. **Fax:** 215-573-2112. **E-Mail:** milester@sas.upenn.edu

LESTER, RICHARD GARRISON, RADIOLOGY. **Personal Data:** b New York, NY, October 24, 1925; m 1953, M Louise Kurtz; c 2. **Education:** Princeton Univ, AB, 1946; Columbia Univ, MD, 1948. **Honorary Degrees:** LHD, Meharry Med Col, 1993. **Honors & Awards:** Gold Medal, Raidol Soc NAm, 1988. **Professional Experience:** EMER PROF RADIOL, EASTERN VA MED SCH, 1993-; prof, Eastern VA Med Sch, 1984-1993; dean, Eastern VA Med Sch, 1984-1989; interim pres, Meharry Med Col, 1981-1982; prof radiol, Univ Tex Med Sch, 1976-1984; mem bd trustees, Am Bd Radiol, Meharry Med Col, 1975-1992; mem steering comt, Soc Chmn Acad Radiol Dept, 1967; mem comt acad radiol, Nat Acad Sci, 1966; prof radiol & chmn dept, Duke Univ, 1965-1976; prof & chmn dept, Med Col Va, 1961-1965; from instr to assoc prof radiol, Univ Minn, 1954-1961. **Memberships:** AMA; Am Roentgen Ray Soc; Am Col Radiol; Soc Pediat Radiol (secy-treas, 1958-1962); Am Col Chest Physicians; Radiol Soc NAm (pres, 1982-1983). **Research Statement & Publications:** Cardiovascular radiology; mammography & diagnosis of breast diseases. **Mailing Address:** PO Box 1980, Norfolk, VA 23501. **E-Mail:** rglester@aol.com

LESTER, ROBERT LEONARD, BIOCHEMISTRY. **Personal Data:** b New Haven, Conn, August 21, 1929; m 1954, Elizabeth; c Henry A & Ellen M (Stonecipher). **Education:** Yale Univ, BS, 1951; Calif Inst Technol, PhD (biochem), 1956. **Professional Experience:** PROF EMER BIOCHEM, MED SCH, UNIV KY, 1995-; consult, Merck & Co, 1987-1992; Nat Bd, Med Examiners, 1982-1985; chmn dept, Med Sch, Univ KY, 1974-1983; vis res biologist, Univ Calif, San Diego, 1969-1970; NIH res grants, 1960-; from asst prof to prof, Med Sch, Univ KY, 1960-1995; asst prof biochem, Univ Wis, 1958-1960; res fel, Inst Enzyme Res, Univ Wis, 1955-1958. **Memberships:** AAAS; Am Soc Biol Chemists; Am Chem Soc; Am Soc Microbiol; Fedn Am Sci. **Research Statement & Publications:** Lipid metabolism in yeast. **Mailing Address:** Dept Biochem, Univ Ky, Lexington, KY 40506.

LESTER, ROGER, MEDICINE. **Personal Data:** b Brooklyn, NY, December 26, 1929; m 1954, c 2. **Education:** Princeton Univ, BA, 1950; Yale Univ, MD, 1955. **Professional Experience:** ADJ PROF MED, SCH MED, EMORY UNIV, 2000-; prof gastroenterol & chief div, Sch Med, Univ Pittsburgh, beginning 1973; res grant, beginning 1965; from asst prof to prof med, Sch Med, Boston Univ, 1965-1973; NIH career develop award, 1963-1973; asst prof, Sch Med, Univ Chicago, 1962-1965; fel Thorndike Mem Lab, Harvard Univ, 1960-1962; resident, Col Med, Univ Utah, 1959-1960; NIH fel, 1956-1959; From intern to resident med, Col Med, Univ Utah, 1955-1957. **Memberships:** Am Fedn Clin Res; Am Asn Study Liver Dis; Am Soc Clin Invest; Am Gastroenterol Asn; Int Asn Study Liver. **Research Statement & Publications:** Fetal hepatic and intestinal function; effect of alcohol and liver disease on sexual function. **Mailing Address:** Dept Med, Sch Med, Emory Univ, 525 Mt Paran Rd NW, Atlanta, GA 30327. **Fax:** 404-727-0473. **E-Mail:** lescog@aol.com

LESTER, WILLIAM ALEXANDER, JR, QUANTUM MONTE CARLO. **Personal Data:** b Chicago, Ill, April 24, 1937; m 1959, Rochelle Reed; c William A III & Allison K. **Education:** Univ Chicago, BS, 1958, MS, 1959; Cath Univ, PhD (chem), 1964. **Honors & Awards:** Outstanding Serv Awd, Nat Sci Found, 1996; Percy L Julian Award, Nat Orgn Black Chemists & Chem Engrs, 1979, Outstanding Teacher Award, 1986. **Professional Experience:** PROF, DEPT CHEM, UNIV CALIF, as of 2006; FAC SR SCIENTIST, CHEM SCI DIV, LAWRENCE BERKELEY NAT LAB, as of 2006; mem, Dept Energy Adv Comn, Advan Sci Comput, 2000-2004; mem, Pres Comn Nat Medal Sci, 2000-2002. **Memberships:** Am Chem Soc; fel Am Phys Soc; Sigma Xi; Nat Orgn Black Chemists & Chem Engrs; fel AAAS; fel Calf Acad of Sci. **Research Statement & Publications:** Molecular quantum mechanics. **Mailing Address:** Dept Chem, Univ Calif, Berkeley, CA 94720-1460. **Fax:** 510-642-1088. **E-Mail:** walester@lbl.gov

LESTER, WILLIAM LEWIS, MICROBIOLOGY. **Personal Data:** b Webster City, Iowa, July 21, 1932; m 1964, c 5. **Education:** San Jose State Col, BA, 1958; Univ Calif, Davis, PhD (microbiol), 1968. **Professional Experience:** PROF EMER MICROBIOL HUMBOLDT STATE UNIV, 1998-; Health manpower coordr, mem Acad Senate, 1989-; prof microbiol, Humboldt State Univ, 1979-1998; health manpower coordr, Humboldt State Univ, 1976-1983; univ rep, Conf Assist Undergrad Sci Educ, beginning 1975; bd dirs, Redwood Health Consortium, 1973-1975; from asst prof to assoc prof, Humboldt State Univ, 1970-1979; Nat Oceanic & Atmospheric Admin sea grant, Samoa & Calif, 1970-1973; supvr res & develop, Cutter Labs, 1968-1970; Lab technician pharmacol, Univ Calif, Davis, 1962-1966. **Memberships:** AAAS; Am Soc Microbiol; Wildlife Soc; Am Soc Allied Health Prof. **Research Statement & Publications:** Biodegradation of kraft pulp mill effluent; microbial ecology; marine bioassays utilizing echino embryo. **Mailing Address:** Dept Biol, Humboldt State Univ, 1 Harpst St, Arcata, CA 95521-8299. **Fax:** 707-826-3201. **E-Mail:** wll2@humboldt.edu

LESTINGI, JOSEPH FRANCIS, ENGINEERING MECHANICS, STRUCTURAL ENGINEERING. **Personal Data:** b Long Island, NY, April 24, 1935; m 1957, Jean; c Michael, Gene, Daniel & John. **Education:** Manhattan Col, BCE, 1957; Va Polytech Inst, MS, 1959; Yale Univ, DEng(solid mech), 1966. **Honors & Awards:** Western Elec Fund Award, Am Soc Eng Educ, 1975. **Professional Experience:** Prof mech eng, Univ Dayton, Dayton, OH, 1997-2000; dean eng & prof mech eng, Univ Dayton, Dayton, OH, 1992-1997; dean eng & prof mech eng, Manhattan Col, Riverdale, NY, 1983-1992; consult eng staff, Gen Motors Corp, Warren, Mich, 1979-; prof mech eng & head dept, Dept Math & Eng Mech, Gen Motors Inst, 1979-1983; prof eng mech & chmn, Gen Motors Inst, 1978-1979; prof eng mech & chmn, Dept Math & Eng Mech, 1978-1979; from asst prof to prof civil eng, Univ Akron, 1967-1978; sr mech engr, Battelle Mem Inst, Ohio, 1965-1967; struct res engr, Elec Boat Div, Gen Dynamics Corp, Conn, 1960-1965; Instr eng mech, Va Polytech Inst, 1957-1959 & Pa State Univ, 1959-1960; Res fel, Am Soc Civil Engrs; Danforth assoc. **Memberships:** Fel Am Soc Civil Engrs; fel Am Soc Mech Engrs; Am Soc Eng Educ; Am Acad Mech; Sigma Xi; Soc Automotive Engrs. **Research Statement & Publications:** Computer assisted design; computer assisted manufacturing; finite element methods; shock and vibration analysis; computer methods. **Mailing Address:** 37637 S Terrace Park Dr, Tucson, AZ 85739. **E-Mail:** josephlestingi@hotmail.com

LESTMANN, PHILLIP E, MATHEMATICS. **Education:** Biola Univ, BS; Univ Southern Calif, PhD. **Professional Experience:** PROF, DEPT MATHS, BRYAN COL, TENN, as of 2005. **Mailing Address:** 172 Oak St, Dayton, TN 37321. **Fax:** 423-775-7330. **E-Mail:** lestmaph@bryan.edu

LESTON, GERD, ORGANIC CHEMISTRY. **Personal Data:** b Ger, September 19, 1924; American citizen; m 1950, Gloria; c Laura & Jeffrey. **Education:** City Col NY, BS, 1948; Purdue Univ, MS, 1949, PhD (chem), 1952; Univ Pittsburgh, BS, 1981. **Honors & Awards:** Pittsburgh Award, Pittsburgh Sect, Am Chem Soc, 1996. **Professional Experience:** CONSULT, 1985-; sr proj scientist, Koppers Co Inc, 1972-1985; sr group mgr, Koppers Co Inc, 1967-1972; group mgr, Koppers Co Inc, 1958-1966; sr chemist, Koppers Co Inc, 1954-1958; chemist, Koppers Co Inc, 1952-1954. **Memberships:** Am Chem Soc; Sigma Xi. **Research Statement & Publications:** Synthetic organic chemistry, particularly phenol chemistry, aromatic substitution; aromatic alkylation and dealkylation; hydrogenation; aromatic acylation; ultraviolet stabilizers; antioxidant synthesis and testing; homogenous and heterogenous catalysis; pesticides; drugs; separation techniques; organics-salt complexes. **Mailing Address:** 1219 Raven Dr, Pittsburgh, PA 15243.

LESTOURGEON, WALLACE MEADE, MOLECULAR BIOLOGY. **Personal Data:** b Alexandria, La, January 16, 1943; m 1986, c 2. **Education:** Univ Tex, Austin, BS, 1966, PhD (cell biol), 1970. **Professional Experience:** DIR UNDERGRAD STUDIES, VANDERBILT UNIV, as of 2004; prin investr, NIH grants, 1993-; PROF BIOL SCI, VANDERBILT UNIV, 1986-; dir, Cell Biol Prog, NSF, 1983-1984; from asst prof to assoc prof, Vanderbilt Univ, 1978-1986; Prin investr, NSF grants, 1975, 1978, 1981, 1985 & 1988; asst scientist, McArdle Lab Cancer Res, 1974-1978; NIH fel oncol, McArdle Lab Cancer Res, 1970-1974. **Memberships:** AAAS; Am Soc Cell Biol; Sigma Xi. **Research Statement & Publications:** Molecular biological, biochemical and physical chemical studies on the structure of 40's nuclear ribonucleoprotein particles and their role in RNA splicing and in the modulation of information flow in eucaryotes; gene regulation; published over 25 articles. **Mailing Address:** Dept Biol Sci, Vanderbilt Univ, 2425A Stevenson Ctr, Nashville, TN 37235-0001. **E-Mail:** w.m.lestourgeon@vanderbilt.edu

LESTRADE, JOHN PATRICK, HIGH-ENERGY ASTROPHYSICS, MATH PHYSICS. **Personal Data:** b New Orleans, La, March 25, 1949; m 1974, c 2. **Education:** La State Univ, New Orleans, BS, 1971; Purdue Univ, MS, 1972; Rice Univ, MS, 1976, PhD (space physics), 1978. **Honorary Degrees:** French Lang Master, Univ Aix-Marseille, France, 1968. **Professional Experience:** PROF PHYSICS, MISS STATE UNIV, 1993-; from asst prof to assoc prof, Miss State Univ, 1984-1993; asst prof physics, Tex A&M Univ, 1980-1984; res assoc planetary atmospheres, Rice Univ, 1978-1980; design scientist nuclear reactors, Westinghouse-Bettis Labs, 1973-1974. **Memberships:** Am Astron Soc. **Research Statement & Publications:** High-energy astrophysics; gamma-ray burster modelling; fractal analysis of astrophysical phenomena. **Mailing Address:** Dept Phy & Astron, Miss State Univ, PO Drawer 5167, Mississippi State, MS 39762. **Fax:** 662-325-8898. **E-Mail:** lestrade@ra.msstate.edu

LESTZ, SIDNEY J, FUEL ENGINEERING, ENGINE LUBRICATION. **Personal Data:** American citizen; m 1963, Darlene. **Education:** Pa State Univ, BS, 1957, MS, 1959. **Professional Experience:** RETIRED; dir, US Fuels & Lubricants Res Lab, SW Res Inst, 1978-1996; dir, Army Fuels & Lubricants Prog, 1976-1996; mgr fuels & lubricants eng, US Fuels & Lubricants Res Lab, Southwest Res Inst, 1971-1978; sr res engr, US Fuels & Lubricants Res Lab, Southwest Res Inst, 1970-1971; sr res engr, Exxon Res & Eng Co, 1964-1970; asst proj engr, Wright Aeronaut Div, Curtiss Wright Corp, 1961-1964; asst, Dept Petrol & Natural Gas Eng, Pa State Univ, 1958-1959. **Memberships:** Combustion Inst; Soc Automotive Engrs; Coord Res Coun; Sigma Xi. **Research Statement & Publications:** Wider boiling range fuels; synthetic fuels; alternate fuels; synthetic lubricants; universal hydraulic power transmission fluid development; safety fuels and fluids technology. **Mailing Address:** 622 Briar Oak, San Antonio, TX 78216.

LESURE, FRANK GARDNER, GEOLOGY. **Personal Data:** b Camden, SC, January 28, 1927; m 1963, c 2. **Education:** Va Polytech Inst, BS, 1951; Yale Univ, MS, 1952, PhD (geol), 1955. **Professional Experience:** RETIRED; geologist, US Geol Surv, 1955-1992. **Memberships:** Soc Econ Geol; Geol Soc Am. **Research Statement & Publications:** Genealogy. **Mailing Address:** 304 Upper Col Terrace, Frederick, MD 21701-4869.

LE SURF, JOSEPH ERIC, PHYSICAL CHEMISTRY. **Personal Data:** b London, Eng, July 21, 1929. **Education:** Univ London, BSc, 1950 & 1951. **Professional Experience:** CONSULT, 1995-; prin scientist, Vectra Tech Inc, 1988-1995; pres & chief exec officer, London Nuclear Ltd & Johnson Nuclear Serv Inc, 1984-1988; tech dir, London Nuclear Ltd, 1978-1984; head, Syst Mat Br, Atomic Energy Can Ltd, 1964-1978; sr sci officer, UK Atomic Energy Authority, 1957-1964; Sci officer corrosion, Royal Naval Sci Serv, 1951-1957. **Memberships:** Nat Asn Corrosion Engrs; Am Nuclear Soc; Can Nuclear Asn; Can Nuclear Soc. **Research Statement & Publications:** Marine corrosion; corrosion, material selection, for nuclear decontamination processing plants and nuclear power plants. **Mailing Address:** 3529 Yale Cres, Niagara Falls, ON L2J 3C4, Can.

LESYNA, LARRY, PHYSICS. **Personal Data:** b Schenectady, NY, March 20, 1958. **Education:** Calif Inst Technol, BS, 1978; Stanford Univ, PhD (appl physics), 1987. **Professional Experience:** AT, LXL TECHNOLOGY, as of 2002; Scientist, LXL Technology, 2002-; Scientist, Lockheed Martin, 1998-2002; Adj assoc prof physics & astron, Hofstra Univ, 1992-; SCIENTIST, GRUMMAN AEROSPACE, 1986-1998. **Memberships:** Am Phys Soc; Am Astron Soc. **Research Statement & Publications:** Remote sensing; low temperature physics; infrared and submillimeter astronomy. **Mailing Address:** LXL Technol, 5197 Ridge Heights St, Las Vegas, NV 89148. **Fax:** 508-374-5535. **E-Mail:** lesyna@alumni.caltech.edu

LETARTE, ALAN L, MATHEMATICS. **Education:** Univ Wisc-Madison, PhD (Maths). **Professional Experience:** STAFF, DRURY COL, as of 2003. **Mailing Address:** Drury Col, 900 N Benton Ave, Springfield, MO 65802. **Fax:** 417-873-7432. **E-Mail:** aletarte@drury.edu

LETARTE, JACQUES, PEDIATRICS, ENDOCRINOLOGY. **Personal Data:** b Montreal, Que, August 19, 1934; m 1960, c 2. **Education:** Univ Montreal, BA, 1957, MD, 1962. **Professional Experience:** DIR EXTERNAL AFFAIRS, SCHERING CAN INC, 1996-; dir govt affairs, Schering Can Inc, 1990-1996; assoc med dir, Schering Can Inc, beginning 1989; med dir, Pediat Res Ctr, Hosp Ste-Justine, 1987-1989; dir, Pediat Res Ctr, Hosp Ste-Justine, 1982-1986; prof, Univ Montreal, 1980-1990; assoc prof pediat, Univ Montreal, 1969-1980; scholar, 1969-1974; Med Res Coun Can fel, 1968-1969; res fel metab, Royal Postgrad Med Sch, London, 1968-1969; resident, Royal Postgrad Med Sch, London, 1968; res fel, Clin Biochem Inst, Geneva, 1965-1967; Queen Elizabeth II res fel, Can, 1964-1968; res fel biochem, Children's Hosp, Zurich, 1964-1965; resident pediat, St Justine Hosp, 1963-1964; Mead-Johnson fel pediat, Univ Montreal, 1963-1964; resident med, Notre Dame Hosp, Montreal, 1962. **Memberships:** AAAS; Can Soc Clin Invest; Soc Pediat Res; Endocrine Soc. **Research Statement & Publications:** Hormonal regulation of carbohydrate metabolism; hyperammonemia in children; lipid and carbohydrate metabolism in children. **Mailing Address:** Schering Can Inc, 3535 Trans-Can, Pointe Claire, PQ H9R 1B4, Can. **Fax:** 514-695-1776.

LETARTE, MICHELLE, MOLECULAR IMMUNOLOGY, LEUKEMIA. **Personal Data:** b Que, October 12, 1947. **Education:** Laval Univ, BSc, 1968; Univ Ottawa, PhD (biochem), 1972. **Professional Experience:** PROF, DEPT IMMUNOL, MED BIOPHYS & PEDIAT, UNIV TORONTO, 1987-; TERRY FOX RES SCIENTIST, NAT CANCER INST, 1985-; associateship, Med Res Coun Can, 1981-1985; SR SCIENTIST & SR INVESTR, RES INST, HOSP SICK C, 1980-; fom asst prof to assoc prof, Nat Cancer Inst, 1975-1986; Nat Cancer Inst scholar, Med Res Coun Can, 1975-1981. **Memberships:** Am Asn Histocompatibility Testing; Am Asn Immunologists; Can Soc Immunol (pres, 1997-); Can Soc Biochem; NY Acad Sci. **Research Statement & Publications:** Structure/function of endoglin its role in vascular biology and its role in the pathology of hereditary haemorrhagic telangiectasia for which it is a target gene. **Mailing Address:** Hosp Sick C, 555 Univ Ave, Toronto, ON M5G 1X8, Can. **Fax:** 416-813-6255. **E-Mail:** mablab@sickkids.on.ca

LETAW, HARRY, TECHNOLOGY. **Personal Data:** b Miami, Fla, August 7, 1926; m 1947, Joyce; c Anne Winston, Kaye Lynn, John Robert, Mary Jane, Amelia Elizabeth & James Brown. **Education:** Univ Fla, BS, 1949, MS, 1951, PhD, 1952. **Professional Experience:** CHMN, PRES, CHIEF EXEC OFFICER & BD DIRS, ESSEX CORP, 1988-; PRES, INTELLINET CORP, 1983-; chmn & pres, Radiation Systs, Inc, 1974-1978; pres, Greater Severna Park Coun, 1972-1973; chmn adv comt, Md State Dept Educ, 1969-1973; bd dirs, Econ Opportunity Comt, Anne Arundel Co, 1969-1971; pres, Logos Ltd, 1968-1972; consult, Compagnie Int Pour L'Informatique, St German-en-Laye, France, 1966-1968; PRES, SEVERN COMMUN CORP, 1965-; vpres & gen mgr, Eastern Tech Ctr, Inc, Bunker-Ramo Corp, 1964-1965; adj assoc prof bus admin, Drexel Inst, 1963-1964; dir advan progs, Elec Div, Martin Marietta, 1961-1964; Partic, DOD Joint Civilian Orientation Conf, Dept Defense, 1958 & 1995; mkt mgr, Raytheon, 1955-1961; res asst prof, Dept Elec Eng, Univ Ill, 1952-1955. **Memberships:** Sr mem Inst Elec & Electronics Engrs; Am Phys Soc; Security Affairs Support Asn; Sigma Xi. **Research Statement & Publications:** Contributed articles to professional journals; patentee in field. **Mailing Address:** Essex Corp, 9150 Guilford Rd, Columbia, MD 21046-1891. **E-Mail:** hletaw@essexcorp.com

LETCHER, DAVID WAYNE, DATABASE MANAGEMENT, BUSINESS INFORMATION SYSTEMS. **Personal Data:** b Dover, NJ, May 5, 1941; m 1963, c 4. **Education:** Rutgers Univ, BS, 1963; Univ Nebr, MS, 1965; Cornell Univ, PhD (meteorol), 1971. **Professional Experience:** PROF INFO SYSTS, SCH BUS, COL NJ, 1987-; assoc prof meteorol, Physics Dept, 1985-1986; coordr acad comput, Trenton State Col, 1981-1985; vis prof, Pub Serv Elec & Gas Co, Newark, NJ, 1977-1978; from asst prof to assoc prof meteorol, Trenton State Col, 1968-1981; co-adj prof atmospheric sci, Rutgers Univ & Mercer Co Community Col; adj prof info systs, Mercer City Community Col. **Memberships:** Asn Info Systs; Int Bus Sch Comput Asn. **Research Statement & Publications:** Development of ways to incorporate computer technology into the college business curriculum. **Mailing Address:** Sch Bus, Trenton State Col, 316 Bus Bldg Cn4700 Hillwood Lakes, Trenton, NJ 08650. **Fax:** 609-771-2845. **E-Mail:** letcher@tcnj.edu

LETCHER, JOHN HENRY, III, PHYSICS, COMPUTER SCIENCE. **Personal Data:** b Wilkes-Barre, Pa, July 18, 1936; m 1960, c 2. **Education:** Univ Tulsa, BS, 1957 & 1958; Univ Mo, MS, 1959, PhD (physics), 1963. **Honorary Degrees:** DEng Tech, Toulane Col, 1962. **Professional Experience:** Prof comput sci, Univ Tulsa, 1986-1999; vis prof comput sci, Univ Tulsa, 1985-1986; adj prof comput sci, Southern Methodist Univ Dallas, 1978-1981; mem staff, Dept Comput Sci, Southern Methodist Univ, Dallas, 1975-1979; PRES, SYNERGISTIC CONSULTS INC, 1970-; vpres systs & res, Data Res Corp, 1968-1970; mem staff, Cent Res Dept, Monsanto Co, 1964-1968; mem staff, Advan Electronics Techniques Div, McDonnell Corp, 1963-1964. **Memberships:** Sigma Xi. **Research Statement & Publications:** Computer software; hardware systems development; quantum physics and chemistry; medical physics-magnetic resonance imaging. **Mailing Address:** 7421 S Marion Ave, Tulsa, OK 74136.

LETCHER, JOHN S, JR, AERONAUTICS. **Professional Experience:** FOUND & CHMN, AEROHYDRO INC, as of 2006. **Memberships:** Am Soc Mech Engrs. **Mailing Address:** Aerohydro Inc, PO Box 684 Main St, South West Harbor, ME 04679. **Fax:** 207-244-4171.

LETCHER, STEPHEN VAUGHAN, PHYSICS, ACOUSTICS OPTICS. **Personal Data:** b Chicago, Ill, December 13, 1935; m 1959, Bettina; c Benjamin & Abby. **Education:** Trinity Col, BS, 1957; Brown Univ, PhD (physics), 1964. **Professional Experience:** PROF PHYSICS, UNIV RI, 1975-; from asst prof to assoc prof, Univ RI, 1963-1975. **Memberships:** Am Phys Soc; Fel Acoust Soc Am; Int Soc Optical Eng. **Research Statement & Publications:** Physical acoustics; physics of fluids; fiber-optic sensors. **Mailing Address:** Dept Physics, Univ RI, 2 Lippitt Rd, Kingston, RI 02881. **Fax:** 401-874-2380. **E-Mail:** sletcher@uri.edu

LETELLIER, JULIE A, MATHEMATICS. **Education:** Univ Colombo, BSc, 1983; Purdue Univ, MS, 1989, PhD, 1996. **Professional Experience:** ASSOC PROF, DEPT MATHS & COMPUT SCI, UNIV WIS-WHITEWATER, as of 2005. **Mailing Address:** Dept Math, Univ Wis-Whitewater, Baker 307, Whitewater, WI 53190. **Fax:** 262-472-5172. **E-Mail:** letellij@uww.edu

LETEY, JOHN JR, RESEARCH, ADMINISTRATION. **Personal Data:** b Carbondale, Colo, June 13, 1933; m 1955, c Laura (Petersen), Donald & Lisa (Smith). **Education:** Colo State Univ, BS, 1955; Univ Ill, PhD (soil sci), 1959. **Honors & Awards:** Soil Sci Res Award, Soil Sci Soc Am, 1973. **Professional Experience:** DIR, UNIV CALIF CTR WATER RESOURCES, as of 2004; assoc dir, ctr water & wildland resources, 1993-; Consult, India, 1987; deleg, People to People Soil Sci Deleg, China, 1983; dir, Kearney Found Soil Sci, 1980-1985; chmn, Dept Soil & Environ Sci, 1975-1980; Consult, UN Food & Agr Orgn, Bulgaria, 1973; PROF SOIL PHYSICS, UNIV CALIF, RIVERSIDE, 1968-; from asst prof to assoc prof, Riverside, 1961-1968; asst prof soil physics, Univ Calif, Los Angeles, 1959-1961; Asst agron, Univ Ill, 1955-1959. **Memberships:** Fel Am Soc Agron; fel Soil Sci Soc Am; fel AAAS. **Research Statement & Publications:** Various transport phenomena, including water movement, gas movement, ionic diffusion, pesticide and other organic chemical interaction and movement through soil. **Mailing Address:** 435 Campus View, Riverside, CA 92507. **Fax:** 909-787-3993. **E-Mail:** john.letey@ucr.edu

LETHER, FRANK G, MATHEMATICS. **Education:** Univ Utah, PhD (MATHS), 1969. **Professional Experience:** EMER PROF, DEPT MATH, UNIV GA, as of 2006. **Mailing Address:** Dept Math, Boyd Grad Res Ctr, Univ Ga, Athens, GA 30602-7403. **Fax:** 706-542-2573. **E-Mail:** fglether@math.uga.edu

LETKEMAN, PETER, CHEMISTRY. **Personal Data:** b Winkler, Man, February 12, 1938; m 1964, c 3. **Education:** Univ Man, BS, 1960, MS, 1961, PhD (chem), 1969. **Professional Experience:** PROF EMER CHEM, BRANDON UNIV, 2003-; dean sci, Brandon Univ, 1982-1993; mem staff, Tex A&M Univ, 1977-1978 & Univ Ariz, 1993-1994; prof chem, Brandon Univ, 1976-2003; pres, Western Man Sci Fair, 1976; judge-in-chief, Can Wide Sci Fair, 1975; mem bd gov & senate, Brandon Univ, 1973-1977; head dept, Brandon Univ, 1972-1980; consult, Christie Sch Supplies, Man, 1970-; grant, Univ Calif, Riverside, 1970; mem sci curric coun, Dept Educ, Man, 1968-; from asst prof to assoc prof, Brandon Univ, 1966-1976; lectr, Brandon Univ, 1963-1966; Teacher high sch, Man, Can, 1961-1963. **Memberships:** Fel Chem Inst Can; AAAS. **Research Statement & Publications:** The polarography and nuclear magnetic resonance of metal complexes in aqueous media; environmental research with regard to water and soil analysis; determination of stability constants of metal complexes; metal speciation in blood via computer modelling. **Mailing Address:** Dept Chem, Brandon Univ, 270-18th St, Brandon, MB R7A 6A9, Can. **Fax:** 204-726-4573.

LETO, SALVATORE, ANDROLOGY, CLINICAL CHEMISTRY. **Personal Data:** b Borgetto, Sicily, November 28, 1937; American citizen; m 1964, c 2. **Education:** City Col NY, BS, 1961; Georgetown Univ, PhD (biol), 1967. **Professional Experience:** DIR, CLIN LAB WASH FERTIL STUDY CTR, 1973-; dir clin lab, Baltimore, 1972-1973; supvr clin lab, Idant Corp, NY, 1971-1972; staff res fel, Nat Inst Child Health & Human Develop, NIH, 1967-1971. **Memberships:** Am Fertil Soc; Am Physiol Soc; Am Soc Andrology; Sigma Xi; Am Asn Tissue Banks; AAAS. **Research Statement & Publications:** Human male fertility; sperm cryo-preservation; immuno-infertility; endocrinology of reproduction. **Mailing Address:** Wash Fertil Study Ctr, 2600 Va Ave NW Ste 500, Washington, DC 20037-1905.

LETO, THOMAS L, MOLECULAR BIOLOGY & IMMUNOLOGY, CELL BIOLOGY. **Personal Data:** b Bridgeport, Conn, October 5, 1953. **Education:** Western Conn State, BA, 1975; Univ Va, PhD (biochem), 1980. **Professional Experience:** HEAD MOLECULAR DEFENSES SECT, LAB HOST DEFENSES, NIAID, NIH, as of 2005; SR INVESTR, LAB HOST DEFENSES, NIAID, NIH, as of 2002; STAFF SCIENTIST, NIH, 1988-; res assoc, Dept Pathol & Hemat, Yale Univ, 1983-1988; NIH fel protein struct & function, Dept Pathol & Hemat, Yale Univ, 1980-1988. **Memberships:** Am Soc Cell Biol; Am Fedn Clin Res.

Mailing Address: Lab Host Defenses, NIAID, NIH, Bldg 10 Rm 11N106, Bethesda, MD 20892-1886. **Fax:** 301-402-4369. **E-Mail:** tl2u@nih.gov

LETOURNEAU, DUANE JOHN, PLANT BIOCHEMISTRY. **Personal Data:** b Stillwater, Minn, July 12, 1926; m 1947, c Bruce Duane, Diane Elaine & Keith George. **Education:** Univ Minn, BS, 1948, MS, 1951, PhD (agr bot), 1954. **Professional Experience:** EMER PROF BIOCHEM & EMER SECY FAC, UNIV IDAHO, 1991-; secy fac, Dept Agr Biochem & Soils, 1990-1991; asst dept head, Dept Agr Biochem & Soils, 1989-1990; vis scientist, Nat Res Coun, Saskatoon, Can, 1981; prof biochem & biochemist, Dept Agr Biochem & Soils, 1973-1991; vis prof, Bot Dept, Univ Sheffield, Eng, 1973; resident res assoc, USDA, 1964-1965; prof agr biochem & agr biochemist, Dept Agr Biochem & Soils, 1963-1973; actg head, Dept Agr Biochem & Soils, 1961-1962; assoc prof & assoc agr chemist, Univ Idaho, 1958-1963; asst prof agr chem & asst agr chemist, Univ Idaho, 1953-1958; asst, Univ Minn, 1948-1953. **Memberships:** Fel AAAS; Am Soc Plant Physiol; Am Chem Soc; Am Phytopathology Soc; Mycol Soc Am. **Research Statement & Publications:** Plant biochemistry; plant cell culture techniques. **Mailing Address:** 479 Ridge Rd, Moscow, ID 83843. **Fax:** 208-885-6518.

LETOURNEUX, JEAN, THEORETICAL NUCLEAR PHYSICS. **Personal Data:** b Que, March 23, 1935; m 1970. **Education:** Laval Univ, BSc, 1959; Oxford Univ, DPhil(physics), 1962. **Professional Experience:** PROF EMER PHYSICS, UNIV MONTREAL, as of 2003; prof physics, Univ Montreal, beginning 1974; from asst prof to assoc prof, Univ Montreal, 1966-1974; asst prof, Univ Va, 1965-1966; res assoc physics, Univ Va, 1964-1965; Ciba fel, Inst Theoret Physics, Copenhagen, 1962-1964. **Memberships:** Am Phys Soc; Can Asn Physicists. **Research Statement & Publications:** Nuclear theory. **Mailing Address:** Dept Physics, Univ Montreal, C P 6128, Succursale Centre-Ville, Montreal, PQ H3C 3J7, Can. **E-Mail:** letourne@crm.umontreal.ca

LETSINGER, ROBERT LEWIS, ORGANIC CHEMISTRY. **Personal Data:** b Bloomfield, Ind, July 31, 1921; m 1943, c Reed, Sue & Louise. **Education:** Mass Inst Technol, BS, 1943, PhD (org chem), 1945. **Honorary Degrees:** DSc, Acadia Univ, Can, 1993. **Honors & Awards:** Guggenheim Fel 1956; Rosenstiel Award, 1985; Humboldt Sr Scientist Award, 1988; Arthur C Cope Scholar Award, Am Chem Soc, 1993. **Professional Experience:** PROF EMER CHEM, NORTHWESTERN UNIV, 1991-; C H Hall prof, Northwestern Univ, 1988-1991; chmn dept, Northwestern Univ, 1972-1975; med chem study sect, NIH, 1971-1975; mem, NIH Fel Rev Panel, 1965-1969; Guggenheim fel, 1956; from instr to prof, Northwestern Univ, 1946-1988; res chemist, Tenn Eastman Corp, 1946; res assoc, Mass Inst Technol, 1945-1946; asst, Mass Inst Technol, 1943-1945. **Memberships:** Nat Acad Sci; AAAS; fel Japan Soc Prom Sci; Am Chem Soc; Am Acad Arts & Sci. **Research Statement & Publications:** Bioorganic chemistry; synthesis of polynucleotides and nucleotide analogs; photochemistry; organoboron and organoalkali metal compounds; solid support synthesis. **Mailing Address:** dept chem, Northwestern Univ, 2145 Sheridan Rd, Evanston, IN 60208-3113. **E-Mail:** rletsinger@ameritech.net

LETT, GREGORY SCOTT, SCIENTIFIC COMPUTING, OPTIMIZATION. **Personal Data:** b Denver, Colo, April 20, 1958; m 1983, Elizabeth; c Michael, Patrick & Bryan. **Education:** Univ Colo, BA, 1982, PhD (comput math), 1991. **Professional Experience:** SCIENTIFIC COMPUTATIONALIST, PHYSIOME SCI INC, as of 2002; RES SYST INCORP, as of 1997; SR CONSULT ASSOC, SCI SOFTWARE-INTERCOMP INC, 1991-; sr consult, Sci Software-Intercomp Inc, 1989-1991; consult, Software Develop Lab, 1985-1986; sr engr, Martin Marietta Astronaut Group, 1983-1985 & 1986-1989. **Memberships:** Soc Indust & Appl Math. **Research Statement & Publications:** Numerical linear algebra; simulation; numerical analysis of petroleum reservoir flow; numerical analysis of groundwater flow; modelling of fluid flow in porous media; applied and computational math; numerical partial differential equations. **Mailing Address:** Sci Software - Intercomp Inc, 1801 Calif St Ste 295, Denver, CO 80202-2600. **E-Mail:** slett@ssii.com

LETT, JOHN TERENCE, BIOPHYSICS, RADIATION BIOLOGY. **Personal Data:** b London, Eng, December 23, 1933; m 1956, c 1. **Education:** Univ London, BSc, 1956, PhD (phys org chem), 1960. **Professional Experience:** PROF RADIOL & RADIATION BIOL, GRAD SCH, COLO STATE UNIV, 1968-; vis scientist, Oak Ridge Nat Lab, 1964; res assoc, Univ Calif, 1961; Sr lectr, Inst Cancer Res, Univ London, 1956-1967. **Memberships:** Radiation Res Soc; Brit Biophys Soc; Biophys Soc; Brit Asn Radiation Res. **Research Statement & Publications:** DNA structure of the chromosome; repair of radiation damage to cellular DNA; radiation and aging. **Mailing Address:** Dept Radiol, Colo State Univ, Ft Collins, CO 80523.

LETT, PHILIP W(OOD), JR, MECHANICAL SYSTEMS DESIGN. **Personal Data:** b Newton, Ala, May 4, 1922; m 1948, Katy Howell; c Kathy, Warren & Lisa. **Education:** Auburn Univ, BE, 1944; Univ Ala, MS, 1947; Univ Mich, PhD (mech eng), 1951; Mass Inst Technol, MS, 1961. **Honors & Awards:** 6 Distinguished Eng Award, Auburn Univ; Cheonsu Medal, Repub Korea; Silver Medal, Am Defense Preparedness Asn; Ben Gilmer Award. **Professional Experience:** PRES, PWL INC, 1987-; vpres res & eng, Gen Dynamics Land Systs, Warren, Mich, 1982-1987; vpres eng, Chrysler Defense Div, 1979-1982; gen mgr, Sterling Defense Div, 1976-1979; prog mgr, Mich Tank Prog, 1973-1976; operating mgr, Chrysler Defense Eng, 1961-1973; chief engr, Eng Div, Chrysler Corp, 1958-1961; asst chief engr, Eng Div, Chrysler Corp, 1954-1958; proj engr, Eng Div, Chrysler Corp, 1950-1954; instr, Univ Mich, 1948-1950; contrib author, Int Defense Rev, US Army, ending 1946; mem bd trustees Univ Ala Col Eng; distinguished eng fel, Univ Ala; consult, Gen Dynamics & US Army; chmn, Vehicle Technol Sect, Tank-Automotive Div, Am Defense Preparedness Asn; mem, Eng Coun, Auburn Univ. **Memberships:** Nat Acad Eng; Soc Automotive Engrs; Asn US Army; Am Defense Preparedness Asn. **Research Statement & Publications:** Analytical and experimental studies of dynamic stability of surface vehicles employing models in wind tunnels and full scale instrumented vehicles on roads; computer simulation of business systems using industrial dynamics techniques; combat and tactical vehicle systems research design and development and production; research on armored combat vehicle system. **Mailing Address:** PWL, Inc, 1330 Oxford, Bloomfield Hills, MI 48304.

LETTENMAIER, DENNIS P, ENVIRONMENTAL & CIVIL ENGINEERING. **Personal Data:** b December 7, 1948. **Education:** Univ Wash, BS, 1970, PhD (civil eng), 1975; George Wash Univ, MS, 1972. **Honors & Awards:** Except Achievement Award, US Geol Surv, 1986; Sci & Technol Achievement Award, US Environ Protection Agency, 1989; Huber Res Prize, Am Soc Civil Engrs, 1990. **Professional Experience:** Dir, Surface Water Hydrol Res Group, Univ Wash, as of 2003; PROF WATER RESOURCE ENG & HYDROL, UNIV WASH, 1978-; chief ed, Am Meteorol Soc J. **Memberships:** fel Am Geophys Union; Am Meteorol Soc; Europ Geophys Soc; Am Soc Civil Engrs; Am Water Resource Asn. **Mailing Address:** Dept Civil & Environ Eng, Univ Wash, 202D Wilson Ceramic Lab PO Box 352700, Seattle, WA 98195-2700. **Fax:** 206-616-6274. **E-Mail:** dennisl@u.washington.edu

LETTERMAN, HERBERT, PHARMACEUTICAL STABILITY, QUALITY CONTROL. **Personal Data:** b Brooklyn, NY, October 8, 1936; m 1957, Barbara; c Sherel, Mitchell, Allison & David. **Education:** City Col NY, BS, 1958; Brooklyn Col, MA, 1962; Seton Hall Univ, MS, 1967, PhD (anal chem) 1973. **Professional Experience:** PHARMACEUT CONSULT, 1998-; dir, Analytical Technol, Warner Lambert Pharmaceut Co, 1995-1998; consult, 1994-1995; mgr prod stability develop, Bristol Myers Prod Div, 1986-1994; mgr qual serv, Bristol Myers Prod Div, 1978-1986; head qual control, Bristol Myers Prod Div, 1966-1978; group leader phys chem res & develop, Bristol Myers Prod Div, 1963-1966; Ciba Pharmaceut Co, NJ, 1959-1963; anal chemist, Brooklyn Jewish Hosp, NY, 1958-1959. **Memberships:** Sigma Xi; Am Chem Soc; Acad Pharmaceut Sci; fel Am Soc Qual Control. **Research Statement & Publications:** Quality control; analytical method development. **Mailing Address:** 44 Del Ave, New Providence, NJ 07974-1033. **Fax:** 908-508-9015. **E-Mail:** hletter@aol.com

LETTIERI, THOMAS ROBERT, OPTICS, MICROMETROLOGY. **Personal Data:** b Scranton, Pa, September 19, 1952; m 1994, May. **Education:** Univ Miami, BS, 1973; Univ Rochester, MS, 1976, PhD (optics), 1978; Univ Md, MGA, 1987. **Honors & Awards:** IR-100 Award, 1986. **Professional Experience:** PROG MGR & TECH SPECIALIST, ADVAN TECHNOL PROG, NAT INST STANDS & TECHNOL, 1993-; physicist optics, Advan Technol Prog, Nat Inst Stands & Technol, 1979-1993; physicist high pressure, Nat Bur Stand, 1978-1979; tech monitor, Agency Int Develop Projs, Egypt & India; consult, Develop Proj, Chinese Univ. **Memberships:** AAAS; Am Soc Testing & Mat; Optical Soc Am. **Research Statement & Publications:** Optical science and technology; surface finish; microparticle measurements; light scattering; dimensional metrology. **Mailing Address:** Advan Technol Prog, Nat Inst Stand Technol, 100 Bur Dr Mail Stop 4720, Gaithersburg, MD 20899-4720. **Fax:** 301-926-9524. **E-Mail:** thomas.lettieri@nist.gov

LETTON, JAMES CAREY, PHARMACEUTICAL CHEMISTRY, ORGANIC SYNTHESIS. **Personal Data:** b Paris, Ky, June 9, 1933; m 1956, c 3. **Education:** Ky State Col, BS, 1955; Univ Ill, Chicago Med Ctr, PhD (chem), 1971. **Honorary Degrees:** LHD, Ky State Univ. **Honors & Awards:** Percy L Julian Award, Nat Orgn Prof Advan Black Chemists & Chem Engrs, 1989. **Professional Experience:** Victor Mills Soc res fel, Procter & Gamble Co, 1992-; bd dirs, Ky State Univ Found, 1985-; Nat pres, Ky State Univ Alumni Asn, 1978-1984; ORG CHEMIST, PROCTER & GAMBLE CO, 1976-; prof org chem, Dept Chem, 1973-1975; chmn, Dept Chem, 1971-1975; assoc prof org chem, Ky State Univ, 1970-1973; instr org chem, Triton Col, 1968-1970; res & develop chemist, Julian Res Inst, 1964-1969; supt prod, Smith Kline & French Labs, 1962-1964; Prod foreman, Julian Labs, 1957-1962. **Memberships:** Fel Am Inst Chemists; Am Chem Soc; hon Soc Pharmaceut Sci. **Research Statement & Publications:** Medicinal chemistry, especially beta amino ketones and analgesic properties; morphine-like compounds; steroid synthesis-carbohydrate chemistry; surface active and nonionics-synthesis; sugar derived surfactants; fat substitutes/sucrose esters. **Mailing Address:** 1247 Jeremy Ct, Cincinnati, OH 45240-2914.

LETTS, LINDSAY GORDON, RESEARCH ADMINISTRATION. **Personal Data:** b Warragul, Australia, January 9, 1948; m 1969, Barbara; c Michelle, Kathryn & David. **Education:** Monash Univ, BS, 1971; Sydney Univ, PhD (pharmacol), 1980. **Professional Experience:** SR VPRES RES & DEVELOP & CHIEF SCIENTIFIC OFFICER, NITROMED INC, as of 2003; vpres res, Nitromed, Inc, beginning 1994; mem bd, Inflammation Res Asn, 1992-; adj assoc prof, Yale Univ Sch Med, 1991-1994; mem bd, Nat Inst Community Health Educ, Quinnipiac Col, Conn, 1990-1994; mem bd, Conn United Res Excellence, 1990-1994; dir, Boehringer Ingelheim Pharmaceut, 1987-1994; sect ed, Prostaglandins, 1986-; sr res fel pharmacol, Merck Frosst Can Inc, 1982-1987; res scientist, Royal Col Surgeons Eng, 1980-1982; tutor pharmacol, Sydney Univ, 1976-1980. **Memberships:** Am Thoracic Soc; Soc Leukocyte Biol; NY Acad Sci; Am Heart Asn; Inflammation Res Asn. **Research Statement & Publications:** Inflammation research, including arachidonic acid motabolites, especially prostaglandins and leukotrienes; pulmonary inflammation including cellular influx, mediator release, airway responsiveness, asthma; elucidation of role of integrins during inflammatory responses; author of numerous publications. **Mailing Address:** Nitromed Inc, 12 Oak Park Dr, Bedford, MA 01730. **Fax:** 781-275-2282. **E-Mail:** gletts@nitromed.com

LETTVIN, JEROME Y, NEUROPHYSIOLOGY. **Personal Data:** b Chicago, Ill, February 23, 1920; m 1947, c 3. **Education:** Univ Ill, BS, 1942, MD, 1943. **Professional Experience:** PROF EMER COMMUN PHYSIOL, DEPTS BIOL, ELEC ENG & COMPUT SCI, MASS INST TECHNOL, as of 2000; lectr neurol, Harvard Med Sch, 1975-; prof commun physiol, depts biol, elec eng & comput sci, Mass Inst Technol, beginning 1966; NEUROPHYSIOLOGIST, LAB ELECTRONICS, MASS INST TECHNOL, 1951-; neuropsychiatrist & physiologist, Manteno StateHosp, 1948-1951; physiologist, Dept Psychol, Univ Rochester, 1947-1948; Intern neurol, Boston City Hosp, 1943-1944. **Memberships:** Am Physiol Soc. **Research Statement & Publications:** Experimental epistemology. **Mailing Address:** Dept Elec Eng & Comput Sci, Mass Inst Technol, 77 Mass Ave, Cambridge, MA 02139.

LEU, MING C, ROBOTICS, MANUFACTURING AUTOMATION. **Personal Data:** b Taoyuan, Taiwan, April 27, 1951; American citizen; m 1978, c 3. **Education:** Nat Univ Taiwan, BS, 1972; Pa State Univ, MS, 1977; Univ Calif, Berkeley, PhD (mech eng), 1981. **Honors & Awards:** Wood Award, Forest Prod Res Soc, 1981. **Professional Experience:** KEITH & PAT BAILEY DISTINGUISHED PROF, UNIV MO-ROLLA, as of 2005; prog chmn, Japan-US Symp on Flexible Automation, beginning 1990; chmn, Prod Eng Div, Am Soc Mech Engrs, 1989-1990; consult, AT&T, beginning 1988; prof & chmn robotics & automation, NJ Inst Technol, 1987-1999; exec comt mem, Prod Eng Div, Am Soc Mech Engrs, 1986-1989; presidential young investr award, NSF, 1985; asst prof robotics & automation, Cornell Univ, 1981-1987; consult, Moog Inc, 1981-1987; res asst vibration & control, Univ Calif, Berkeley, 1977-1981; res asst surface friction, Pa State Univ, 1975-1977. **Memberships:** Am Soc Mech Engrs; Inst Elec & Electronics Engrs; Soc Automotive Engrs; Soc Mfg Engrs; Int Soc Prod Engrs. **Research Statement & Publications:** Motion planning and control; sensors and actuators; geometric modeling; robotics; automated assembly; author of over 100 technical publications. **Mailing Address:** Dept Mech Eng, Univ MO-Rolla, 207A Mech Eng Bldg, Rolla, MO 65409-1060. **Fax:** 573-341-4607, 573-341-6512. **E-Mail:** mleu@umr.edu

LEU, RICHARD WILLIAM, MICROBIOLOGY, IMMUNOLOGY. **Personal Data:** b Argonia, Kans, January 5, 1935; m 1960, c 2. **Education:** Northwestern State Col, Okla, BS, 1960; Univ Okla, MS, 1963, PhD (microbiol, immunol), 1970. **Professional Experience:** CHMN MICROBIOL, OKLA ACAD SCI, as of 2002; HEAD IMMUNOL SECT, NOBLE FOUND, 1976-; MEM STAFF, NOBLE FOUND, 1974-; USPHS res training fel pediat & path, Med Sch, Univ Minn, Minneapolis, 1970-1974. **Research Statement & Publications:** Cellular immunity; effector molecules associated with macrophage inhibition, proliferation and activation; role of cytophilic antibody in cellular immunity; localized immunity in the lung. **Mailing Address:** Okla Acad Sci, Campus Box 90, Edmond, OK 73034.

LEUBNER, GERHARD WALTER, ORGANIC CHEMISTRY. **Personal Data:** b Walton, NY, August 31, 1921; m 1944, c 3. **Education:** Union Col, BS, 1943; Univ Ill, PhD (chem), 1949. **Professional Experience:** RETIRED; res assoc, Eastman Kodak Co, beginning 1948; asst, Univ Ill, 1945-1946; chemist, Winthrop Chem Co, 1943-1945. **Memberships:** Am Chem Soc. **Research Statement & Publications:** Patent information storage and retrieval systems. **Mailing Address:** 151 Upland Dr, Rochester, NY 14617.

LEUBNER, INGO HERWIG, CRYSTALLIZATION, ASTROPHYSICS. **Personal Data:** b Prittlbach, Ger, April 9, 1938; American citizen; m 2002, Helga; c Ursula & Eapen. **Education:** Munich Tech Univ, Dipl, 1963, PhD (phys chem), 1966. **Honors & Awards:** Lieven Gevaert Medal, Soc Imaging Sci & Technol, 1995. **Professional Experience:** SR SCI, CRYSTALLIZATION CONSULTING, 1998-; Sr Res Chemist, Res Labs, Eastman Kodak Co, 1969- 1998; Welch Found fel & lectr photochem, Tex Christian Univ, 1968-1969; Ger Res Asn res fel phys chem, Munich Tech Univ, 1966-1968. **Memberships:** AAAS; Fel Soc Imaging Sci & Technol; Am Chem Soc; Sigma Xi; AGU. **Research Statement & Publications:** crystal formation (nucleation, modeling, experimets); photographic and imaging science; photochemistry; astrophysics; physics. **Mailing Address:** Crystallization Consulting, 35 Hillcrest Dr, Penfield, NY 14526-2411. **E-Mail:** ileubner@crystallizationcon.co

LEUCHTAG, H RICHARD, MEMBRANE BIOPHYSICS, ION CHANNEL THEORY. **Personal Data:** b Breslau, Ger, June 2, 1927; American citizen; m 1955, Alice; c Clyde R. **Education:** Univ Calif, Los Angeles, BA, 1950, MA, 1955; Ind Univ, PhD (physics), 1974. **Professional Experience:** PROF BIOL, TEX SOUTHERN UNIV, 1991-; vis scientist, Mat Res Lab, Pa State Univ, 1990; from asst prof to assoc prof, Tex Southern Univ, 1982-1991; secy, Int Conf Struct & Function Excitable Cells, 1981; res scientist, Dept Physiol & Biophys, Univ Tex Med Br, 1978-1982; consult, Dept Physiol & Biophys, NY Univ Med Ctr, 1978; assoc ed, Physics Today, Am Inst Physics, 1974-1978; res assoc, Biophys Lab, Phys Dept, NY Univ, 1972-1974; Physicist, Western Elec Co, 1966; Ind Univ-Purdue Univ, Indianapolis, 1965-1970; San Diego State Col, 1963-1965; instr, Univ San Diego Col Men, 1962-1963; instr, Don Bosco Tech High Sch, 1961-1962. **Memberships:** Am Phys Soc; Biophys Soc; Sigma Xi. **Research Statement & Publications:** Physical basis of excitability in channels and membranes; ferroelectric transition hypothesis; measurement of noise, admittance and impedance in axons; monitored retrievable disposal of high-level radioactive waste; electrostatics, instability, effects of tilt and chirality and transitions in electrically charged segments of channels. **Mailing Address:** Dept Biol, Tex Southern Univ, 3100 Cleburne Ave, Houston, TX 77006-6010. **Fax:** 713-313-7932. **E-Mail:** leuchtag@tsu.edu

LEUCK, EDWINE E, II, PLANT SYSTEMATICS. **Personal Data:** b June 21, 1951; m 1973, Beth; c Nicholas E & Victor R. **Education:** Mich State Univ, BS, 1973; Univ Okla, MS, 1975, PhD (bot), 1980. **Professional Experience:** CHMN, DEPT BIOL, CENTENARY COL, LA, as of 2004; PROF BIOL, CENTENARY COL, LA, 1980-. **Memberships:** Sigma Xi. **Research Statement & Publications:** Floristic studies in northwest Louisiana and on the Beaver Island archipelago in northeast lake Michigan. **Mailing Address:** Dept Biol, Centenary Col, PO Box 41188, 2911 Centenary Blvd, Shreveport, LA 71134. **Fax:** 318-869-5722. **E-Mail:** eleuck@centenary.edu

LEUNG, ALBERT YUK-SING, PHARMACOGNOSY, BIOMEDICAL INFORMATION SERVICES. **Personal Data:** b Hong Kong, May 24, 1938; American citizen; m 1968, c 2. **Education:** Nat Taiwan Univ, BS, 1961; Univ Mich, Ann Arbor, MS, 1965, PhD (pharmacog), 1967. **Professional Experience:** PRES, PHYTO-TECHNOLOGIES INC, as of 2006; consult natural prods, beginning 1977; dir res & develop, Dr Madis Labs Inc, 1974-1977; tech dir chem & microbiol consult, Sci Res Info Serv Inc, 1971-1974; res supvr microbial protein prod, Bohna Eng & Res Inc, 1969-1971; NIH res chemist, Med Ctr, Univ Calif, 1967-1969; Lily Found fel, 1963-1967. **Memberships:** Am Chem Soc; Am Soc Pharmacog; NY Acad Sci; Sigma Xi. **Research Statement & Publications:** isolation of active principles from plants and microorganisms; retrieval and dissemination of biomedical information, especially from Chinese sources. **Mailing Address:** Phyto-Technologies Inc, 107 Enterprise Dr, Woodbine, ID 51579. **Fax:** 712-647-2885.

LEUNG, ALEXANDER KWOK-CHU, GENERAL PEDIATRICS. **Personal Data:** b Hong Kong, October 1, 1948; Canadian citizen; m 1975, Rita; c 5. **Education:** Univ Hong Kong, MBBS, 1973; Royal Col Physicians London, DCH, 1777; Royal Col Surgeons Eng, DCH, 1977; Royal Col Physicians & Surgeons Ireland, DCH, 1979, MRCPI, 1978; MRCP(UK), 1980; FRCP (C), 1979, FAAP, 1980, Am Bd Pediat Endocrinol & Pediat, dipl, 1986. **Honors & Awards:** Gold Medal Award, ABI, 1987; Physician Recognition Award, AMA, 1987, 1990 & 1993; Prep Fel Award, Am Acad Pediat, 1987 & 1990. **Professional Experience:** CLIN ASSOC PEDIAT, UNIV CALGARY, 1990-; clin asst prof, Foothills Prov Hosp & Alta Childrens Hosp, 1982-1990; CONSULT PEDIAT, FOOTHILLS PROV HOSP & ALTA CHILDRENS HOSP, 1980-; consult pediat, Calgary Gen Hosp, 1980-1981; consult pediat, Grace Hosp, 1980-1982; endocrine fel, Univ Calgary, 1978-1980; lectr pediat, Univ Queensland, 1977; lectr surg, Univ Hong Kong, 1974; intern, Univ Hong Kong, 1973-1974. **Memberships:** Fel Royal Soc Med; fel Royal Soc Health; fel Can Pediat Soc; fel Am Acad Pediat; fel Royal Col Physicians Can; fel Royal Col Physicians Ireland; fel Royal Col Physicians Edinburgh; fel Royal Col Physicians Glasgow; fel Royal Acad Med. **Research Statement & Publications:** General pediatrics; author of over 350 publications in various fields of pediatrics. **Mailing Address:** Alta Childrens Hosp, Univ Calgary, Sutie 200 233-16th Ave NW, Calgary, AB T2M 0H5, Can. **Fax:** 403-242-6734. **E-Mail:** aleung@ucalgary.ca

LEUNG, BENJAMIN XERJEN, CELL BIOLOGY, ONCOLOGY. **Personal Data:** b Hong Kong, June 30, 1938; American citizen; m 1964, Helen Hsu; c Kay, Titus & Steven. **Education:** Seattle Pac Univ, BS, 1963; Colo State Univ, PhD (biochem), 1969. **Professional Experience:** Dir, grad studies, Div Cel Biol, 1990-1996; PROF, DEPT OBSTET & GYNEC, UNIV MINN, 1984-; chief, Div Cel Biol, 1984-1995; from assoc prof to prof, Dept Animal Physiol, Univ Minn, 1982-; assoc prof & dir, Hormone Res Lab, 1978-1983; sr res scientist, Dept Surg, Cedars-Sinai Med Ctr, Los Angeles, 1976-1978; assoc oncologist, Div Surg Oncol, Univ Calif, Los Angeles, 1976-1978; asst prof to assoc prof; dir, Dept. Surg, Univ Ore Health Sci Ct; Hormone Receptor Lab, Clin Res Ctr Lab, 1971-1976; NIH & Ford Found res fel reprod endocrinol, Med Sch, Vanderbilt Univ, 1969-1971; Res asst steroid hormones, Pacific Northwest Res Found, 1963-1966. **Memberships:** Am Soc Cell biol; Am Asn Cancer Res; Soc Chinese Bioscientists Am. **Research Statement & Publications:** Growth factors, oncogenes steroid hormone & ubignitin-proteasome protelysis in regulating fetal and cancer growth; cell biology; recipient of over 45 grants. **Mailing Address:** Dept Obstet & Gynec & Women's Health, Mayo Box 395 UMHC, Minneapolis, MN 55455. **Fax:** 612-626-0665. **E-Mail:** leung001@umn.edu

LEUNG, CHARLES CHEUNG-WAN, SEMICONDUCTOR PROCESSING, DEVICE PHYSICS. **Personal Data:** b Hong Kong, June 27, 1946; American citizen; m 1973, c 1. **Education:** Univ Hong Kong, BSc, 1969; Univ Chicago, MS, 1971, PhD (physics), 1976. **Professional Experience:** PRES & CHMN, BIPOLARICS, 1988-; sr mem tech staff, Avantek, 1981-1988; sr staff engr, Motorola, 1980-1981; Sr scientist, Corning Glass Works, 1976-1980. **Memberships:** Am Phys Soc; Am Chem Soc; Am Vacuum Soc; Soc Info Display. **Research Statement & Publications:** Electro-optic materials; glassification; carbon; vacuum deposition; thin film; surface science. **Mailing Address:** Bipolarics, 46766 Lakeview Blvd, Fremont, CA 94538-6529. **Fax:** 510-226-6765.

LEUNG, CHRISTOPHER CHUNG-KIT, EMBRYOLOGY, IMMUNOLOGY. **Personal Data:** b Hong Kong, January 3, 1939; American citizen. **Education:** Howard Univ, BS, 1964; Jefferson Med Col, PhD (anat, embryol), 1969. **Professional Experience:** DEPT SURG, UNIV MED & DENT NJ, as of 2004; Assoc prof, NJ Med Sch, 1985-2001; mem Ad Hoc Study Sect, NIH, 1985; NIH res grant, 1979-1989; assoc prof anat, Sch Med, La State Univ, 1979-1985; asst prof anat, Univ Kans Med Ctr, 1975-1979; res assoc prof pediat, Col Allied Health Sci, 1974-1975; instr, Col Allied Health Sci, 1970-1975; instr anat, Jefferson Med Col, Thomas Jefferson Univ, 1969-1975; from instr to assoc prof pediat, Jefferson Med Col, Thomas Jefferson Univ, 1969-1974; NIH fel, Stein Res Ctr, Thomas Jefferson Univ, 1965-1969; res asst, Sch Med, Univ Rochester, 1964-1965. **Memberships:** Teratol Soc; Am Asn Anatomists; Am Asn Immunologists; Am Soc Cell Biol. **Research Statement & Publications:** Teratology; immunopathology; cell biology; anatomy. **Mailing Address:** Dept Surg, Univ Med & Dent NJ, 185 S Orange Ave Rm 683, Newark, NJ 07103. **Fax:** 973-982-7489. **E-Mail:** leunjch@umdnj.edu

LEUNG, CHUNG NGOC, THEORETICAL PHYSICS, ELEMENTARY PARTICLE PHYSICS. **Personal Data:** b Macao, May 12, 1956. **Education:** Univ Minn, BS, 1977, PhD (physics), 1983. **Professional Experience:** PROF, UNIV DEL, 2000-; assoc prof, Univ Del, 1995-2000; asst prof, Univ Del, 1989-1995; vis prof, Purdue Univ, 1987-1989, vis prof, Max Planck Inst Physics & Astrophys, 1986-1987; vis prof, Purdue Univ, 1985-1986; res assoc, Fermi Nat Accelerator Lab, 1983-1985. **Memberships:** Am Phys Soc. **Research Statement & Publications:** Elementary particle theory; dynamical symmetry breaking in gauge theories; fermion mass problem; neutrino physics; phenomenology of elementary particles. **Mailing Address:** Dept Physics & Astron, Univ Del, Newark, DE 19716. **Fax:** 302-831-1637.

LEUNG, DONALD YAP MAN, KAWASAKI DISEASE, ATOPIC DERMATITIS. **Personal Data:** b New York, NY, October 1, 1949; m 1978, c 2. **Education:** Johns Hopkins Univ, BA, 1970; Univ Chicago, PhD (biochem), 1975, MD, 1977. **Professional Experience:** PROF PEDIAT, UNIV COLO, as of 2003; HEAD, DIV ALLERGY-IMMUNOL, NAT JEWISH CTR IMMUNOL & RESPIRATORY MED, 1989-; assoc prof pediat, Univ Colo, beginning 1989; dir allergy, Children's Hosp, 1987-1989; from asst prof to assoc prof pediat, Harvard Med Sch, 1983-1989; instr pediat, Harvard Med Sch, 1981-1985; fel allergy-immunol, Children's Hosp, Boston, 1979-1981; resident pediat, Children's Hosp, Boston, 1978-1979; clin fel pediat, Harvard Med Sch, 1977-1979; intern pediat, Children's Hosp, Boston, 1977-1978. **Memberships:** Am Fedn Clin Res; Am Acad Allergy & Immunol; Am Asn Immunologists; Soc Pediat Res; AAAS. **Research Statement & Publications:** Mechanisms of allergic diseases including atopic dermatitis, asthma and food allergy, IgE responses; immunopathogenesis of Kawasaki disease; use of immunomodulatory agents in the treatment of allergic disorders. **Mailing Address:** Dept Pediat K926, Nat Jewish Ctr Immunol & Resp Med 1400 Jackson St, Denver, CO 80206-2762.

LEUNG, FREDERICK C, MOLECULAR BIOLOGY, ZOOLOGY. **Personal Data:** b Hong Kong, December 1, 1952; American citizen; m 1978, c 2. **Education:** Univ Calif, Berkeley, BA, 1974, PhD (endocrinol), 1978. **Professional Experience:** DEAN, FAC SCI, UNIV HONG KONG, 2000-; ASSOC PROF, DEPT ZOOL, UNIV ONG KONG, 1994-; adj assoc prof, dept animal sci, Wash State Univ, 1986-1994; sr res scientist cell biol, Dept Biol & Chem, Battelle, Pac Northwest Labs, 1985-1994; res fel, Merck, Sharp & Dohme Res Labs, 1984-1985; Adj prof, dept animal sci, Rutgers Univ, 1982-1985; sr res biochemist animal physiol, Merck, Sharp & Dohme Res Labs, 1980-1984; Fel neuroendocrinol, dept physiol, Mich State Univ, 1978-1980. **Memberships:** Endocrinol Soc; Am Physiol Soc; NY Acad Sci; Am Soc Zool. **Research Statement & Publications:** Hormonal regulation of growth; hypothalamic regulation of anterior pituitary function; structure & function of growth hormone and its receptor; eukaryotic cell expression and gene insertion. **Mailing Address:** Univ Hong Kong, Pokfulam Rd, Hong Kong, China. **Fax:** 852-2858-4620. **E-Mail:** fcleung@hkucc.hku.hk

LEUNG, HELEN O, PHYSICS. **Education:** Calif State Univ, BS, 1982, BA, 1983; Harvard Univ, MA, 1985, PhD (chem), 1988. **Professional Experience:** PROF, DEPT CHEM, AAHERST COL, as of 2006. **Mailing Address:** Dept of Chem, Amherst Col, Amherst, MA 01075. **Fax:** 413-542-2660.

LEUNG, IRENE SHEUNG-YING, MINERALOGY. **Personal Data:** b Hong Kong, July 10, 1934. **Education:** Univ Hong Kong, BA, 1957; Ohio State Univ, MA, 1963; Univ Calif, Berkeley, PhD (geol), 1969. **Professional Experience:** PROF GEOL, LEHMAN COL, as of 2000; assoc prof geol, Lehman Col, beginning 1977; asst prof, Lehman Col, 1971-1977; res staff geologist, Yale Univ, 1969-1971. **Memberships:** Sigma Xi; Mineral Soc Am; Am Geophys Union; Geochem Soc; Asian Environ Soc. **Research Statement & Publications:** X-ray investigation of mineral inclusions in natural diamonds; magmatic crystallization and sector-zoning in crystals; deformation structures and glide mechanisms in deformed minerals. **Mailing Address:** Dept Geol & Geog, City Univ NY Lehman Col, G-318, 250 Bedford Park W, Bronx, NY 10468-1589. **E-Mail:** leung@lehman.cuny.edu

LEUNG, JOSEPH YUK-TONG, SCHEDULING THEORY, COMPLEXITY THEORY. **Personal Data:** b Hong Kong, June 25, 1950; m 1973, Maria; c Jonathan. **Education:** Southern Ill Univ, Carbondale, BA, 1972; Pa State Univ, PhD (comput sci), 1977. **Professional Experience:** DISTINGUISHED PROF COMPUT SCI, NJ INST TECHNOL, as of 2006; prof dept comput sci & eng, Univ Nebr, Lincoln, beginning 1990; chmn dept comput sci & eng, Univ Nebr, Lincoln, 1990-1996; assoc prog head, Univ Tex, Dallas, 1987-1990; prof comput sci prog, Univ Tex, Dallas, 1985-1990; assoc prof, Northwestern Univ, Evanston, 1981-1985; asst prof elec eng & comput sci, Northwestern Univ, Evanston, 1977-1981; asst prof comput sci, Va Polytech Inst & State Univ, 1976-1977. **Memberships:** Asn Comput Mach; Inst Elec & Electronics Engrs; AAAS; NY Acad Sci. **Research Statement & Publications:** Operating systems; scheduling theory; analysis of algorithms; real-time systems; computational complexity. **Mailing Address:** Dept Comput Sci & Eng, NJ Inst Technol, Newark, NJ 07102. **Fax:** 973-596-5777. **E-Mail:** leung@cis.njit.edu

LEUNG, JULIA PAULINE, MONOCLONAL ANTIBODY, CANCER BIOLOGY. **Education:** Univ Wash, PhD (cell biol), 1974. **Professional Experience:** DENGUE VACCINE PROJ DIR, HAWAII BIOTECH INC, 1999-; asst dir sci admn, Cancer Res Ctr Hawaii, Univ Hawaii, 1990-1999; sr res mgr, Dept Cell Biol, Hybritech Inc, 1981-1990. **Mailing Address:** Hawaii Biotech Inc, 99-193 Aiea Heights Dr, Ste 200, Aiea, HI 96701. **Fax:** 808-487-7341.

LEUNG, KAM-CHING, ASTRONOMY, ASTROPHYSICS. **Personal Data:** b Hong Kong, June 16, 1935; m 1963, c 2. **Education:** Queen's Univ, Ont, BSc, 1961; Univ Western

Ont, MA, 1963; Univ Pa, PhD (astron), 1967. **Professional Experience:** NSF res grant, NASA grant, 1986-1987; PROF PHYSICS & ASTRON, UNIV NEBR, LINCOLN, 1978-; mgt specialist, Off Nuclear Energy, ERDA, 1977; staff assoc astron sect, NSF, 1975; assoc prof, Univ Nebr, Lincoln, 1972-1978; dir observ, Univ Nebr, Lincoln, 1972-1975; asst prof physics, Univ Nebr, Lincoln, 1970-1972; NSF res grant, Univ Nebr, Lincoln, 1970-1971, 1975, 1981-1982, 1985-1987 & 1987-1989; Nat Acad Sci-Nat Res Coun res fel astron, Inst Space Studies, NASA, 1968-1970; sr assoc, Off Energy Res, Dept Energy. **Memberships:** Fel AAAS; Int Astron Union; Am Astron Soc. **Research Statement & Publications:** Stellar photometry and spectroscopy; intrinsic variable stars; binary stars. **Mailing Address:** Dept Physics & Astron, Univ Nebr, Lincoln, NE 68502. **E-Mail:** kleung@unlserve.unl.edu

LEUNG, KA-NGO, ELECTRICAL ENGINEERING, SYSTEMS DESIGN. **Personal Data:** b Canton, China. **Education:** Chinese Univ Hong Kong, BS, 1968; Univ Akron, MS, 1971; Univ Calif, Los Angeles, PhD (physics), 1975. **Professional Experience:** PROF IN RESIDENCE & HEAD PLASMA & ION SOURCE TECHNOL GROUP, LAWRENCE BERKELEY NAT LAB, as of 2006; sr staff physicist, Lawrence Berkeley Nat Lab, beginning 1988; staff physicist, Lawrence Berkeley Nat Lab, 1978-1988; asst prof physics, James Madison Univ, Va, 1975-1978. **Memberships:** Fel Am Phys Soc; Sigma Xi. **Research Statement & Publications:** Development of positiveand negative ion sources for neutral beam heating in fusion reactors and particle acceleratorsl recently published more than 10 books. **Mailing Address:** Lawrence Berkeley Nat Lab, Dept 9174 50135 Mailstop 5R0121, Berkeley, CA 94720. **Fax:** 510-486-5105. **E-Mail:** knleung@lbl.gov

LEUNG, LAI-WO STAN, NEUROPHYSIOLOGY, BEHAVIOR & NEURAL ACTIVITY. **Personal Data:** b Macau, July 21, 1952; m 1979, c 1. **Education:** Calif State Univ, Northridge, BS (Physics), 1973; Univ Calif, Berkeley, PhD (Biophys), 1978. **Honors & Awards:** Summa Cum Laude and Gold Medal, Dept Physics, Cal State Univ Northridge. **Professional Experience:** PROF, PHYSIOL & PHARMACOL, UNIV WESTERN ONT, LONDON, CAN, 1994-; Dir, Neurosci Grad Prog, Univ Western Ont, London, 2000-2004; Mem, Can Inst Health Res Behav Sci A review panel 2003-2006; Mem, Biopsychol Study Sect, NIH, 1987-1991; Assoc Prof to Prof, Clin Neurol Sci, 1986-2005; Asst Prof to Assoc Prof, Physiol & Psychol, 1980-1994; Res Fel, Inst Med Physics, Utrecht, Holland, 1979-1980; Fel Physiol Psychol, Univ Western Ont, London, Can, 1978-1979; teaching assoc Physiol & Biophys, Univ Calif, Berkeley, 1977-1978. **Memberships:** Soc Neuroscience; Can League Against Epilepsy. **Research Statement & Publications:** Analyses of normal and abnormal neuronal activities in the cerebral cortex in vivo and in vitro; neural plasticity after seizures, brain rhythms; experimental epilepsy, neural plasticity. **Mailing Address:** Dept Physiology & Pharmacology, Univ Western Ont, Medical Sci Bldg, London, ON N6A 5C1, Can. **Fax:** 519-661-3827. **E-Mail:** sleung@uwo.ca

LEUNG, MING-YING, MATHEMATICS & STATISTICS. **Education:** Univ Hong Kong, BS (Math), 1980; Stanford Univ, MS 1988, PhD (Math) 1989. **Professional Experience:** PROF MATH SCI & DIR BIOINFORMATICS PROG, UNIV TEX, EL PASO, 2003-; assoc prof, Dept Math & Mgt Sci, Univ Tex, San Antonio, 2002-2003. **Mailing Address:** Dept Math Sci, Univ Tex, 500 W Univ Ave, El Paso, TX 79968. **Fax:** 915-747-6502. **E-Mail:** mleung@utep.edu

LEUNG, PAK SANG, COLLOID CHEMISTRY. **Personal Data:** b Shanghai, China, June 8, 1935. **Education:** Nat Taiwan Univ, BS, 1957; Columbia Univ, MA, 1962, PhD (phys chem), 1967. **Professional Experience:** ASSOC PROF, ORANGE CO COL, MIDDLETOWN, NY, 1993-; Mem chem adv bd, Harriman Col, 1974-; sr res scientist, Union Carbide Corp, Tarrytown, 1967-1993; res scientist, Brookhaven Nat Lab-Columbia Univ, 1966-1967; demonstr chem, Hong Kong Baptist Col, 1959-1961; Dyes lab asst, Imp Chem Industs, 1957-1959. **Memberships:** Sigma Xi; Am Chem Soc. **Research Statement & Publications:** Surface and collidal chemistry; polymer composite; polymer processing; clinical chemistry. **Mailing Address:** 22 Woodland Rd, Highland Mills, NY 10930. **E-Mail:** pleung@mail.sunyorange.edu

LEUNG, PETER, DRUG METABOLISM, PHARMACOKINETICS. **Personal Data:** b New York, NY, April 12, 1955; m 1992, Bernice. **Education:** Johns Hopkins Univ, BA, 1977; State Univ NY, PhD (pharmacol), 1983; Am Bd Toxicol, dipl, 1987. **Honors & Awards:** Travel Award, Am Soc Pharmacol & Exp Therapeut, 1984. **Professional Experience:** SUPVR, DIV REGIST & HEALTH EVAL, MED TOXICOL BR, CALIF ENVIRON PROTECTION AGENCY, as of 2003; SR TOXICOLOGIST, DEPT PESTICIDE REGULATION, MED TOXICOL BR, CALIF ENVIRON PROTECTION AGENCY, 1996-; staff toxicologist, Dept Pesticide Regulation, Med Toxicol Br, Calif Environ Protection Agency, 1991-1996; staff toxicologist, Med Toxicol Br, Calif Dept Food & Agr, 1989-1996; sr scientist, Schering-Plough Corp, 1986-1989; Fel, Col Med, Tex A&M Univ, 1983-1986. **Memberships:** Soc Toxicol; Am Col Toxicol; Am Soc Pharmacol & Exp Therapeut. **Research Statement & Publications:** Metabolism and disposition of cyanide in the presence and absence of cyanide antagonists; new prophylactic and therapeutic treatments for cyanide intoxication; erythrocytes as drug carriers for purified enzymes. **Mailing Address:** Div Regist & Health Eval, Med Toxicol Br, Calif Environ Protection Agency, Sacramento, CA 95814. **E-Mail:** pleung@cdpr.ca.gov

LEUNG, PHILIP MAN KIT, MEDICAL PHYSICS, BIOPHYSICS. **Personal Data:** b Hong Kong, June 22, 1933; Canadian citizen; m 1959, c 2. **Education:** Univ Toronto, BASc, 1960; McMaster Univ, MSc, 1961; Univ Toronto, PhD (biophys), 1967. **Professional Experience:** Lectr, Dept Med Biophys, Univ Toronto, 1979-; investr, Children's Cancer Study Group, Nat Cancer Inst, USPHS, 1976-1977 & 1977-1978; ed, Physics Med & Biol, 1972-1975; consult physicist, Orillia Soldier Mem Hosp, Can, 1969-1970 & Can Soc Radiol Technicians, 1969-1978; SR PHYSICIST, ONT CANCER INST, 1968-; physicist, BC Cancer Inst, Can, 1967-1968; Fel, Univ BC, 1967-1968; Lectr, Ryerson Inst Technol, Can, 1961-1962. **Research Statement & Publications:** Radiation dosimetry; radiotherapy treatment techniques and new equipment associated with radiation oncology. **Mailing Address:** Ont Cancer Inst, 610 University Ave 1B738, Toronto, ON M5G 2M9, Can.

LEUNG, SO WAH, DENTISTRY, PHYSIOLOGY. **Personal Data:** b China, November 2, 1918; American citizen; m 1957, c 1. **Education:** McGill Univ, DDS, 1943, BSc, 1945; Univ Rochester, PhD (physiol), 1950; FRCDent(C). **Professional Experience:** Pres, Asn Can Fac Dent, 1970-1972; chmn res comt, Asn Can Fac Dent, 1968-1970; chmn exam comt, Nat Dent Exam Bd Can, 1967-1971; exec comt, Nat Res Coun Can, 1965-1968; mem, Nat Dent Exam Bd Can, 1965-1967; mem assoc comt dent res, Nat Res Coun Can, 1963-1968; consult, Nat Bd Dent Exam, 1960-1966 & Lever Bros, 1963-1965; PROF ORAL BIOL, UNIV BC, 1962-; dean sch dent, Univ Bc, 1962-1977; prof oral biol, Sch Dent & lectr physiol, Sch Med, Univ Calif, Los Angeles, 1961-1962; mem dent study sect, NIH, 1959-1963; consult, Colgate-Palmolive Co, 1958-1962; prof dent res & dir grad educ, Sch Dent, Univ Pittsburgh, 1957-1961; Mem comt dent, Nat Acad Sci-Nat Res Coun, 1957-1961; head dept, Sch Dent, Univ Pittsburgh, 1952-1961; from assoc prof to prof physiol, Sch Dent, Univ Pittsburgh, 1950-1961; Intern dent, Royal Victoria Hosp, Montreal, 1943-1944. **Memberships:** Am Dent Asn; fel Am Col Dent; fel Int Col Dent; NY Acad Sci; Sigma Xi. **Research Statement & Publications:** Salivary chemistry; oral calculus formation; physiology of salivary glands. **Mailing Address:** 4510 NW Marine Drive, Vancouver, BC V6R 1B8, Can.

LEUNG, WAI CHOI, MOLECULAR BIOLOGY. **Personal Data:** b Hong Kong, China, May 23, 1948. **Education:** Chinese Univ, Hong Kong, BS, 1970; Baylor Col Med, PhD (virol), 1974. **Professional Experience:** PROF, COURSE DIR & CHIEF MOLECULAR PATH, TULANE UNIV, as of 2003; fac mem, Dept Path, Tulane Univ Sch Med, beginning 1992; fac, Dept Med, Univ Ark Sch Med Sci, 1989-1992. **Memberships:** Am Chem Soc; Am Phys Soc. **Mailing Address:** Dept Path, Tulane Univ, 1430 Tulane Ave, Box SL-79, New Orleans, LA 70112-2699. **Fax:** 504-587-7389. **E-Mail:** wleung@tulane.edu

LEUNG, WAI YAN, PHYSICS. **Professional Experience:** ASST SCIENTIST, AMES LAB, IOWA STATE UNIV, as of 2003; ASSOC PROF, DEPT CHEM, AMES LAB, IOWA STATE UNIV, 1991-; asst prof, Dept Chem, Fla Int Univ, 1989-1991. **Memberships:** Am Phys Soc. **Research Statement & Publications:** Service structures. **Mailing Address:** Ames Lab, Iowa State Univ, 213 Asc one, Ames, IA 50011. **E-Mail:** wleung@iastate.edu

LEUNG, WING HAI, SURFACE CHEMISTRY & ADSORPTION, CYSTAL GROWTH. **Personal Data:** b Hong Kong, July 29, 1937; American citizen; m 1965, Lai-Yan; c Bill, Michael & Patrick. **Education:** Univ Hong Kong, BSc, 1963; Univ Miami, MS, 1970, PhD (phys chem), 1974. **Professional Experience:** ASSOC PROF CHEM, HAMPTON UNIV, 1982-; asst prof, Hampton Inst, 1978-1982; res scientist, Clinton Corn Corp, Iowa, 1977-1978; sr chemist res, GAF Corp, Binghamton, NY, 1976-1977; res assoc, State Univ NY, Buffalo, 1974-1976. **Memberships:** Am Chem Soc; Sigma Xi; Am Geophys Union. **Research Statement & Publications:** Surface phenomena and kinetic studies of crystal growth; the structure and interaction at solid solution interfaces. **Mailing Address:** Dept chem, Hampton Univ, Hampton, VA 23668.

LEUNG, WOON FONG (WALLACE), FLUID DYNAMICS & SOLID-LIQUID SEPARATION, ROTATING FLOW & CENTRIFUGATION. **Personal Data:** b Hong Kong, January 25, 1954; m 1978, Stella; c Jessica W & Jeffrey K. **Education:** Cornell Univ, BS, 1977; Mass Inst Technol, MS, 1978, ScD (mech eng), 1981. **Honors & Awards:** Cedric Ferguson Medal, Soc Petrol Engrs, 1987; Eng Merit Award, Am Filtration & Separation Soc, 1991; Baker Hughes Tech Achievement Award, 1992; Sr Scientist Tech Award, Am Filt & Separation Soc, 2002. **Professional Experience:** PRES, ADVANTECH, as of 2005; chmn, Int Delegates Filtration & 9th World Filtration Cong, 2000-2004; plenary speaker, Nordic Filtration Soc, 2000; sci comt, 8th World Filtration Cong, 2000, UK; plenary speaker, Eng Found Conf, 1999, 2001; chmn, Awards Comt, 1995-; dir, Am Filtration & Separation Soc, 1995; dir process technol, Bird Mach Co, beginning 1993; dir & conf chmn, Am Filtration & Separation Soc Ann meetings, 1993; tech session chmn, Am Filtration & Separation Soc Ann meetings, 1990, 1991; sr res scientist centrifuge dynamics & fluid/particle separation, Bird Mach Co, 1986-1993; proj leader flow near well-bore & transient testing, Schlumberger, 1984-1986; res engr flow porous media, Gulf Res & Develop Co, 1981-1984; course dir, Ctr prof advan, NJ; Chmn, Centrifuge Network. **Memberships:** Soc Mech Engrs; Soc Petrol Engrs; Am Filtration & Separation Soc; Am Inst Aeronaut & Astronaut; Soc Rheology, Soc Mining Engrs. **Research Statement & Publications:** Physical-chemical hydrodynamics for industrial applications, solid-liquid separation in industrial centrifuges, suspension and dense cake rheology, membrane filtration and inclined lamella settlers; fluid flow and compaction-consolidation in porous media; oil and gas production through wellbore perforations; petroleum reservoir engineering; develop and use computer models and experimental test rigs in research and developmental study; develop innovative dynamic balancing methods for rotating machinery under process condition; thirty published technical papers and over 800 inhouse technicalreports; author of one publication; granted over 34 US patents. **Mailing Address:** AdvanTech, PO Box 758, Sherborn, MA 01770. **E-Mail:** wallace.leung@advantechcompany.com

LEUNG, YIU M, PARALLEL PROCESSING, PROGRAMMING LANGUAGES. **Personal Data:** b Canton, China, July 29, 1951; American citizen. **Education:** Chinese Univ Hong Kong, BS, 1974; Syracuse Univ, MS, 1983, PhD (comput eng), 1992. **Professional Experience:** MEM TECH STAFF, LUCENT TECHNOL, 1996-; Adj fac parallel prog, State Univ NY, Binghamton, 1993-; res staff, IBM Corp, 1992-1996; Lead programmer, IBM Corp, 1979-1992. **Research Statement & Publications:** Parallel processing, in particular, parallel programming languages, parallel programming environment, communications, parallel computer architecture. **Mailing Address:** 23 Yellowbrook Rd, Marlboro, NJ 07746. **E-Mail:** leungym@unet.ibm.com

LEUPOLD, HERBERT AUGUST, PHYSICS, MAGNETIC DESIGN. **Personal Data:** b Brooklyn, NY, January 6, 1931. **Education:** Queens Col, NY, BS, 1953; Columbia Univ, AM, 1958, PhD (physics), 1964. **Honors & Awards:** Commendation, Inst for Explor Res, US Army, 1969 & Electronics Technol & Devices Lab, US Army, 1972; Harold Jacobs Award, 1987. **Professional Experience:** GEN TECH SERV, 2001-; Sr technol, US army res lab, 1995-2000; Lectr physics, Univ Dayton 1984, 1986, 1988; lectr chem, Trenton State Col, 1983; res physicist, Electronics Res Develop Command, US Army, 1967-1995; Lectr physics, Monmouth Col, 1967-1970; Fel physics, Lawrence Radiation Lab, Livermore, Calif, 1964-1967; Lectr physics, Queens Col, NY, 1957. **Memberships:** Am Phys Soc; Sigma Xi; fel Inst Elec & Electronics Engrs; Inst Elec & Electronics Engrs Magnetics Soc. **Research Statement & Publications:** Magnetism; semiconductors; superconductivity; thermodynamics; cryogenics; magnetic circuit design; magnetic materials. **Mailing Address:** 26 B Stony Hill Gardens, Eatontown, NJ 07724.

LEUSCHEN, M PATRICIA, PERINATOLOGY, NEUROENDOCRINOLOGY. **Personal Data:** b Iowa, June 3, 1943; m 1963, c 4. **Education:** Creighton Univ, BS, 1965, MS, 1967; Univ Nebr Med Ctr, Omaha, MS, 1974, PhD (anat), 1976. **Professional Experience:** ASSOC PROF, MED CTR, UNIV NEBR, OMAHA, 1991-; exec, Grad Comt, Univ Nebr Syst, 1990-1991; chmn, Med Sci Interdepartmental Area Grad Prog, Univ Nebr Med Ctr, 1989-; CLIN ASSOC PROF, CREIGHTON UNIV, OMAHA, 1989-; asst prof pediat & res dir, Div Newborn Med, 1982-1991; res asst pediat, Med Ctr, Univ Nebr, Omaha, 1980-1982. **Memberships:** Am Asn Anatomists; Am Soc Cell Biol; Soc Neuroscience; International Brain Res; Nat Multiple Sclerosis Soc; Am Soc Anat. **Research Statement & Publications:** Cerebral microvasculature and intracranial hemorrhage in premature infants; endorphin and related neurohormones and stress in neonates, ultrastructural studies including morphometry; association with perinatal asphyxia and apnea; interaction between prostaglandin synthesis and neuroendocrine axis; chloride changes and astrocyte swelling. **Mailing Address:** Dept Genetics Cell Biol Anat & Pediat, Univ Nebr Med Ctr, UH 3144A, Omaha, NE 68198-1205. **Fax:** 402-559-7328. **E-Mail:** pleusche@unmc.edu

LEUTENEGGER, WALTER, BIOLOGICAL ANTHROPOLOGY, PRIMATOLOGY. **Personal Data:** b Winterthur, Switz, October 18, 1941; American citizen. **Education:** Univ Zurich,

PhD (biol anthrop), 1969. **Professional Experience:** Prof biol anthrop, Univ Wis, Madison, beginning 1983; affil scientist, Wis Regional Primate Res Ctr, beginning 1971; from asst prof to assoc prof, Univ Wis-madison, 1971-1983; sci res asst biol anthrop, Univ Zurich, 1969-1971; anthropologist, Bern Natural Mus Hist, Switz, 1967-1969. **Memberships:** Am Asn Phys Anthropologists; Am Soc Naturalists; Am Soc Primatologists; Soc Vert Paleont. **Research Statement & Publications:** Functional anatomy of the primate locomotor apparatus; determinants of behavioral and morphological sexual dimorphism; reconstruction of early hominid social organization and behavior. **Mailing Address:** Dept Anthrop, Univ Wis Madison, 1180 Observatory Dr, Madison, WI 53706-1393. **E-Mail:** leuteneg@macc.wisc.edu

LEUTHEUSSER, H(ANS) J(OACHIM), FLUID MECHANICS, TRIBOLOGY. **Personal Data:** b Eisenach, Ger, February 1, 1927; Canadian citizen; m 1955, Gudrun; c Michael J, Doris E & Suzanne M. **Education:** Karlsruhe Univ, Dipl Ing, 1952; Univ Toronto, MASc, 1957, PhD (mech eng), 1961. **Professional Experience:** PROF EMER, DEPT MECH ENG, UNIV TORONTO, 1992-; Univ Victoria, Univ Shanghai & Tokyo, 1990; Univ Victoria, BC, 1989; assoc chmn dept & coordr grad studies, Dept Mech Eng, Univ Toronto, 1984-1988; Univ Santiago & Aristotle Univ, Thessaloniki, 1983; assoc chmn dept, Dept Mech Eng, Univ Toronto, 1977-1979; Inst Hydromech, Karlsruhe Univ, 1975-1976; sabbatical leaves, Inst Mech Statist Turbulence, Univ Aix Marseille, 1966-1967; from asst prof to prof fluid mech, Dept Mech Eng, Univ Toronto, 1963-1992; consult engr, beginning 1957; lectr, Dept Mech Eng, Univ Toronto, 1957-1962; instr fluid mech, Dept Mech Eng, Univ Toronto, 1955-1957; sr engr, Friedrich Buchner, Wuerzburg, Ger, 1953-1954; field engr, Oulujoki Oy, Helsinki, Finland, 1952-1953; asst hydraul eng, Theodor-Rehbock Lab, Karlsruhe Univ, 1951-1952. **Memberships:** Am Soc Civil Engrs; Int Asn Hydraul Res; Gesellschaff fuer angewandle Math & Mech (GAMM). **Research Statement & Publications:** Fundamental fluid mechanics and applications; turbulence; fluid elasticity and transients; biomechanics; building aerodynamics; tribology. **Mailing Address:** Dept Mech & Indust Eng, Univ Toronto, Toronto, ON M5S 3G8, Can. **Fax:** 416-978-7753. **E-Mail:** leutheu@mie.utoronto.ca

LEUTZINGER, RUDOLPH L(ESLIE), MECHANICAL ENGINEERING, AEROSPACE ENGINEERING. **Personal Data:** b Dallas Center, Iowa, June 17, 1922; m 1950, c 6. **Education:** Iowa State Univ, BS, 1943; Univ Mich, MS, 1952; Univ Iowa, PhD (mech eng), 1976. **Professional Experience:** PROF EMER MECH ENG, UNIV MO, KANS CITY, as of 2003; PROF EMER MECH ENG, UNIV MO-COLUMBIA, 1979-; DIR, AERO TURB MFG, 1979-; CONSULT ENGR, LEUTZINGER CONSULT ASSOCS, 1979-; assoc prof mech eng, Leutzinger Consult Assocs, 1976-1979; NASA fel propulsion, 1973 & 1977; vis lectr, Col Eng, Univ Iowa, 1969-; Kans City Regional Coun Higher Educ grant, 1964-1965; assoc prof eng & chmn dept, Univ Mo-Kans City, 1962-1976; NSF inst res grants, 1961, 1962 & 1964; mem grad fac, Univ Mo, 1959; assoc prof thermodyn, Univ Mo-Rolla, 1958-1960; assoc mem grad fac & eng admin coun, Agr & Mech Col Tex, 1958; Consult, Boeing Airplane Co, 1957; Gas Turbine Div, Westinghouse Elec Corp, 1956 & McDonnell Aircraft Corp, 1958, 1959 & 1962; assoc prof aerodyn, Agr & Mech Col Tex, 1956-1958; asst prof aeronaut eng & appl mech, Univ Kans, 1954-1956; res engr, Midwest Res Inst, Mo, 1951-1953; res assoc dynamics, Aeronaut Res Ctr, Univ Mich, 1951; instr aeronaut eng, Iowa State Univ, 1947-1950; Stress analyst, Douglas Airplane Co, 1944-1946 & McDonnell Airplane Co, 1946 & 1947. **Memberships:** Soc Eng Sci; Am Inst Aeronaut & Astronaut (secy-treas 1942 & 1975-1978); Am Soc Eng Educ; Nat Soc Prof Engrs; Am Soc Mech Engrs; Sigma Xi. **Research Statement & Publications:** Structural mechanics and dynamics; gas dynamics; flow fields in turbomachinery, especially three-dimensional and boundary layers; vehicle design and analysis; internal and external aerodynamics of ducts and bodies; granted 2 patents. **Mailing Address:** Div Civil & Mech Eng, Univ Mo, 352 Flarsheim Hall, 5100 Rockhill Rd, Kansas City, MO 64110-2499. **Fax:** 816-235-1260.

LEUZE, REX ERNEST, RADIOCHEMICAL PROCESS DEVELOPMENT, RADIOCHEMICAL PLANT OPERATION & SAFETY. **Personal Data:** b Sabetha, Kans, March 7, 1922; m 1948, Ruth; c Michael R, Robert M & Thomas E. **Education:** Kans State Univ, BS, 1944; Univ Tenn, Knoxville, MS, 1956. **Honors & Awards:** IR-100 Award Indust Res Fabrication Process for Nuclear Fuel (Gel-Sphere-Pac Process). **Professional Experience:** RETIRED; consult, radiochem opers safety, 1989-1994; head, Pilot Plant, 1981-1987; sect head, Exp Eng Sect, 1976-1981; asst chief, Pilot Plant Sect, 1972-1976; asst chief, Chem Develop Sect, 1963-1972; develop group leader transuranium element chem, Chem Tech Div, 1954-1963; develop group leader inorg fluorides, Chem Tech Div, 1949-1954; chem engr, Tech Div, Oak Ridge Nat Lab, 1947-1949; anal chemist, Clinton Labs, 1945-1947; anal chemist, Monsanto Chem Co, Ill, 1944-1945. **Memberships:** Am Nuclear Soc; Am Chem Soc; fel Am Inst Chem; Sigma Xi; AAAS. **Research Statement & Publications:** Ion exchange and solvent extraction, especially of the transuranium elements, neptunium through fermium; preparation and properties of concentrated colloids of metal oxides and hydroxides; nuclear fuel reprocessing and waste treatment. **Mailing Address:** 517 W Fifth Ave, Lenoir City, TN 37771.

LEV, OVADIA E, ENGINEERING. **Professional Experience:** Sr Project Engr, TRW Inc, as of 1987. **Memberships:** Am Soc Civil Engrs. **Mailing Address:** TRW Inc, 1180 Town Center Dr, Las Vegas, NV 89134-6363. **Fax:** 702-295-3933.

LEVA, JAMES ROBERT, ELECTRIC UTILITIES. **Personal Data:** b Boonton, NJ, May 10, 1932. **Education:** Fairleigh Dickinson Univ, BSEE, 1960; Seton Hall Law Sch, JD, 1980. **Professional Experience:** BD DIR, BALLARD POWER SYST INC, 1997-; chmn & chief exec officer & bd dirs, Gen pub Utilities, 1992-1997; pres & chief oper officer, Jersey Cent Power & Light, 1986-1992; pres& chief oper officer & dir, Pa Elec Co, Johnstown, 1982-1986; vpres consumer affairs, JerseyCent Power & Light, 1979-1982; dir, Jersey Cent Power & Light, 1976-1982; vpres personnel &serv, Jersey Cent Power & Light, 1969-1979; mgr employee rels, Jersey Cent Power & Light, 1968-1969; personnel rep, Jersey Cent Power & Light, 1962-1968; elec engr, Jersey Cent Power& Light, 1960-1962; chmn, pres, chief exec officer & bd dirs, GPU Serv Corp; chmn & bd dirs, GPU Nuclear Corp; chmn, chief exec officer & bd dirs, Met Edison Co, Pa Elec Co, Utilities Mutual Ins Co, NJ Utilities Asn; chmn, St Clares Health Care Found; bd overseers, NJ Inst Technol; trustee, Tri-County Scholar Fund, Fairleigh Dickinson Univ; chmn, Sch Planning & Pub Policy, Rutgers Univ. **Mailing Address:** Ballard Power Syst Inc, 9000 Glenlyon Pkwy, Burnaby, BC V5J 5J9, Can.

LEVAN, MARIJO O'CONNOR, MATHEMATICS. **Personal Data:** b Detroit, Mich, October 27, 1936. **Education:** Spring Hill Col, BS, 1959; Univ Ala, MA, 1961; Univ Fla, PhD (math), 1965. **Professional Experience:** RETIRED; prof emer, Dept Math & Statist, Eastern Ky Univ, as of 2003; actg assoc, Eastern Ky Univ, beginning 1996; vpres, Eastern Ky Univ, 1995-1996; chmn, Eastern Ky Univ, 1979-1984; actg chmn, Eastern Ky Univ, 1978-1979; prof math, Eastern Ky Univ, 1974-1993; assoc prof, Eastern Ky Univ, 1969-1974; asst prof, SoutheastMo State Col, 1967-1969; from instr to asst prof math, Univ Fla, 1962-1967. **Memberships:** Am Math Soc. **Research Statement & Publications:** Number theory; partition functions; translated geometric progressions; pseudo perfect numbers; additive distributive functions. **Mailing Address:** Dept Math & Statist, Eastern Ky Univ, Wallace 407, Richmond, KY 40475. **Fax:** 859-622-3051. **E-Mail:** marijo.levan@eku.edu

LEVAN, MARTIN DOUGLAS, ADSORPTION, FLUID MECHANICS. **Personal Data:** b Chattanooga, Tenn, August 30, 1949; m 1977, Barbara; c Theodore & Gregory. **Education:** Univ Va, BS, 1971; Univ Calif, Berkeley, PhD (chem eng), 1976. **Professional Experience:** CENTENNIAL PROF AND CHAIR CHEM ENG, VANDERBILT UNIV, 1997-; Fulbright sr scholar, LIMSI, Nat Ctr Sci Res, France, 1993-1994; dir, Int Absorption Soc, 1992-; prof chem eng, Univ Va, 1989-1996; chmn, Group I, Eng Sci & Fundamentals, 1989-1991; Fulbright sr scholar, Portugal, 1985-1986; chmn, Nat Prog Comt Adsorption & Ion Exchange, AM Inst Chem Engrs, 1985-1987; vchmn, Nat Prog Comt Adsorption & Ion Exchange, AM Inst Chem Engrs, 1983-1985; mem, Nat Prog Comt Interfacial Phenomena, 1982-; mem, Nat Prog Comt Adsorption & Ion Exchange, AM Inst Chem Engrs, 1980-; from asst prof to assoc prof, Univ VA, 1978-1989; Sr res engr, Amoco Prod Co, Stand Oil Co, 1976-1978. **Memberships:** Am Inst Chem Engrs; Am Chem Soc; Int Adsorption Soc, Am soc eng educ. **Research Statement & Publications:** Adsorption and fluid mechanics; fixed-bed adsorption; adsorption equilibria; low Reynolds number hydrodynamics; free surface flows; computer applications in chemical engineering. **Mailing Address:** Dept Chem Eng, Vanderbilt Univ Ru Station B, Box 351604, Nashville, TN 37235.

LEVAN, NHAN, ELECTRICAL ENGINEERING. **Personal Data:** b Quang Yen, Vietnam, November 6, 1936; m 1960, c 2. **Education:** Univ New Eng, Australia, BS, 1960; Univ New S Wales, Australia, MS, 1962; Monash Univ, Australia, PhD (elec eng), 1966. **Honors & Awards:** Excellence Eng Educ, Am Soc Eng Educ Award, 1979. **Professional Experience:** PROF ELEC ENG, SCH ENG & APPL SCI, UNIV CALIF, LOS ANGELES, 1979-; from asst prof to prof syst sci, Sch Eng & Appl Sci, Univ Calif, Los Angeles, 1967-1979; lectr elec eng, Monash Univ, Australia, 1965-1966. **Memberships:** AAAS; Inst Elec & Electronics Engrs; Sigma Xi. **Research Statement & Publications:** System theory; signal processing; distributed parameter systems; applied functional analysis and wavelet theory, control theory and applications. **Mailing Address:** Dept Elec Eng, Univ Calif, 56-125B, Los Angeles, CA 90024-1594. **Fax:** 310-206-8495. **E-Mail:** levan@ee.ucla.edu

LEVAND, OSCAR, ORGANIC CHEMISTRY, BIOCHEMISTRY. **Personal Data:** b Parnu, Estonia, November 3, 1927; American citizen; div, c Erika Helani Levand. **Education:** Miss State Col, BS, 1954; Purdue Univ, MS, 1958; Univ Hawaii, PhD (org chem), 1963; Univ Minn, Minneapolis, MPH, 1970. **Professional Experience:** RETIRED; assoc prof chem, Univ Guam, 1980-1994; asst prof, Univ Guam, 1974-1980; consult, Air Pollution Control Prog, Govt of Guam, 1970-1974; res chemist, Dole Co, Hawaii, 1963-1968; fel, NIH, 1962-1963; res chemist, Knoll Pharmaceut Co, NJ, 1958-1959; jr res chemist, Mead Johnson Co, Ind, 1954-1956. **Research Statement & Publications:** Air and water chemistry. **Mailing Address:** 3809 Fishing Trail, Sarasota, FL 34235.

LEVANDER, ORVILLE ARVID, NUTRITION. **Personal Data:** b Waukegan, Ill, April 6, 1940; m 1981, c 2. **Education:** Cornell Univ, BA, 1961; Univ Wis Madison, MS, 1963, PhD (biochem), 1965. **Honors & Awards:** Osborne & Mendel Award, Am Inst Nutrit, 1986; Klaus Schwarz Medal, 1995. **Professional Experience:** RES CHEMIST, USDA NUTRIT, RES CTR, 2000-; mem, comn Mil Nutrit Res, Inst Med, 1994-2000; res leader, USDA Human Nutrit Res Ctr, 1994-2000; mem WHO/FAO consult trace elements human nutrit, 1988-1993; travel fel, Danish Med Res Coun, 1987; Burroughs Wellcome vis prof nutrit, Ore State Univ, Corvallis, 1987; mem, US Nat Comt Int Union Nutrit Sci, 1985-1990; William Evans vis fel, Univ Otago, Dunedin, NZ, 1982; Comt Dietary Allowances, Food & Nutrit Bd, 1980-1985; mem, Comt Animal Nutrit, Agr Bd, Nat Res Coun, 1979-1983; temp adv, Environ Health Criteria Doc onSelenium, WHO, 1977-1987; mem subcomt nutrit, Safe Drinking Water Comt, 1977-1979; mem, Nat Res Coun Comt Biol Effects Environ Pollutants, 1974-1977; res chemist, USDA Human Nutrit Res Ctr, 1969-1994; res chemist, Food & Drug Admin, 1967-1969; res assoc, Sch Public Health, Harvard Univ, 1966-1967; res fel biochem, Col Physicians & Surgeons, Columbia Univ, 1965-1966. **Memberships:** AAAS; Am Soc Nutrit Sci; Am Chem Soc; Am Soc Clin Nutrit. **Research Statement & Publications:** Toxicology and nutrition of selenium; pharmacology of heavy metals; trace mineral nutrition; vitamin E; drug metabolism; lead poisoning; tropical parasitic diseases; malaria; coxsackie virus; influenza; nitric oxide; oxidative stress. **Mailing Address:** Nutrient Requirements & Functions Lab, USDA, Rm No 229 10300 Baltimore Ave Bldg 307-C Barc-E, Beltsville, MD 20705. **Fax:** 301-504-9062. **E-Mail:** levander@307.bhnrc.usda.gov

LEVANDOWSKY, MICHAEL, BEHAVIOR, MICROBIAL ECOLOGY. **Personal Data:** b Knoxville, Tenn, August 15, 1935. **Education:** Antioch Col, AB, 1961; Columbia Univ, MA, 1965, PhD (biol), 1970; NY Univ, MS, 1973. **Professional Experience:** ADJ PROF, DEPT BIOL & CHEM, PACE UNIV, as of 2000; ADJ ASSOC PROF, DEPT MICROBIOL, NYU DENT SCH, as of 2000; prof bol Haskins Labs, Pace Univ, 1990-; b dir, River Proj, 1989; secy, Environ Scientists Global Survival, 1988-1991; distinguished lectr, Northeast Algal Soc, 1986; mem citizens' adv comt on resource recovery for borough Brooklyn, 1981-1989; asst prof biol, York Col, NY, 1973-1974; Nat Sci Found sci fac fel, Courant Inst Math Sci, NY Univ, 1971-1972; RES SCIENTIST, HASKINS LABS, PACE UNIV, 1970-; asst prof biol, Haskins Labs, Pace Univ, 1970-1971; instr, Bronx Community Col, 1969-1970; instr biol, Bard Col, 1967-1969. **Memberships:** Soc Protozool; Phycol Soc Am; Am Soc Limnol & Oceanog; Am Soc Microbiol; Am Chem Soc; US Soc Ecol Econ. **Research Statement & Publications:** Mathematical models in ecology; microbial ecology; marine biology; sensory physiology and behavior of Protista; environmental problems and bioremediation; environmental education. **Mailing Address:** Dept Bio Sci, Pace Univ, 41 Park Row, New York, NY 10038.

LEVASSEUR, KENNETH M, GRAPH THEORY, ALGEBRA. **Education:** St Anselm Col, BA, 1971; Univ RI, MS, 1973, PhD (math), 1980. **Professional Experience:** PROF MATH, UNIV MASS, LOWELL, as of 2004; lectr math, Rivier Col, 1990-; vis lectr math, AT & T Bell Labs, 1989; assoc prof math, Univ Mass, Lowell, beginning 1985; asst prof, Univ Mass, Lowell, 1980-1985. **Memberships:** Math Asn Am; Sigma Xi. **Research Statement & Publications:** Interplay between graph theory and algebra. **Mailing Address:** Univ Mass, Dept Math Sci, One Univ Ave, Lowell, MA 01854. **E-Mail:** kenneth_levasseur@uml.edu

LEVASSEUR, MAURICE EDGAR, OCEANOGRAPHY. **Personal Data:** b Riviere-du-Loop, Que, June 30, 1953. **Education:** Univ Laval, Can, BS, 1979, MS, 1984; Univ BC, PhD (oceanog), 1990. **Professional Experience:** RESEARCHER, FISHERIES & OCEANS, CAN, 1990-; Biologist, 1985-1990. **Memberships:** Am Soc Limnol & Oceanog. **Research Statement & Publications:** Ecological and physiological aspects of marine algae; physiological effects of different N sources upon microalgae. **Mailing Address:** Maurice Lamontagne Inst, Fisheries & Oceans, PO Box 1000, 850 de la Mer Rd, Mont-Joli, PQ G5H 3Z4, Can. **Fax:** 418-775-0546. **E-Mail:** levasseurm@dfo-mpo.gc.ca

LEVCHUK, JOHN W, PARENTERAL TECHNOLOGY, HOSPITAL PHARMACY. **Personal Data:** b Hudson, NY, January 13, 1942. **Education:** Philadelphia Col Pharm & Sci, BS, 1963, MS, 1968; Univ Ariz, MEd, 1973, PhD (pharm), 1977. **Professional Experience:** DIR REGULATORY, FOOD & DRUG ADMIN, as of 2004; COMPLIANCE OFFICER, CTR DEVICES & RADIOLOGICAL HEALTH, FOOD & DRUG ADMIN, as of 2003; CONSUMER SAFETY OFFICER, OFF COMPLIANCE, DIV MFG PRODQUAL, STERILE DRUGS BR, US FOOD & DRUG ADMIN, 1987-; mem, Training Comt, Parenteral Drug Asn, 1983-; assoc prof sterile prod, Univ Tenn, 1983-1987; assoc prof sterileprod & hosp pharm, Univ Alta, 1979-1983; regional coordr residency progs, Can Soc HospPharmacists, 1979-1983; from asst prof to assoc prof hosp pharm & sterile prod, Univ Nmex, 1969-1979; dir, Poison Control & Drug Info Ctr, Buffalo Children's Hosp, 1967-1969; asst profdrug info & poison control, State Univ NY, Buffalo, 1967-1969; pharmacist, USPHS IndianHosp, Gallup, NMex, 1964-1966; comn officer, USPHS, 1964. **Memberships:** Parenteral Drug Asn; Am Soc Hosp Pharmacists. **Research Statement & Publications:** Microbiological quality of pharmaceutical processing facilities, activities and dosage forms; experimental aerobiology; packaging of sterile dosage forms. **Mailing Address:** Nicholson Lane Res Ctr, Food & Drug Admin, HFM-670, Rm A244, 5516 Nicholson Lane, Kensington, MD 20895. **Fax:** 301-827-3536. **E-Mail:** jwl@cdrh.fda.gov

LEVEAU, BARNEY FRANCIS, PHYSICAL MEDICINE, BIOMECHANICS. **Personal Data:** b Denver, Colo, October 2, 1939. **Education:** Univ Colo, BS, 1961, MS, 1966; Mayo Clin, RPT, 1965; Pa State Univ, PhD (physeduc), 1973. **Professional Experience:** CHMN, DEPT PHYS THER, GA STATE UNIV, as of 2004; PROF, DEPT PHYS THER, GA STATE UNIV, 1992-; chmn, Dept Phys Ther, GA State Univ, 1992-1996; prof & chmn, Dept Phys Ther, Southwestern Med Ctr, Dallas, 1985-1992; from asst prof to assoc prof phys ther, Sch Med, Univ NC, Chapel Hill, 1972-1985; from asst prof to assoc prof phys educ, WChester State Col, 1966-1970; teacher math & sci, Colorado Springs Sch Dist, 1961-1963. **Memberships:** Am Phys Ther Asn; Am Col Sports Med; Int Soc Biomech. **Research Statement & Publications:** Biomechanics as it applies to physical therapy and physical education; sports medicine. **Mailing Address:** Dept Phys Ther, Ga State Univ, Univ Plaza, Atlanta, GA 30303. **Fax:** 404-651-1584.

LEVEILLE, GILBERT ANTONIO, NUTRITION, BIOCHEMISTRY. **Personal Data:** b Fall River, Mass, June 3, 1934. **Education:** Univ Mass, BVA, 1956; Rutgers Univ, MS, 1958, PhD (nutrit), 1960. **Honors & Awards:** Res Award, Poultry Sci Asn, 1965; Mead Johnson Res Award, Am Inst nutrit, 1971. **Professional Experience:** VPRES, FOOD SYS DESIGN, CARGILL INC, 2002-; vpres, McNeil Nutrit, beginning 1999; pres, Am Inst Nutrit, beginning 1988; vpres res & tech serv, Nabisco Biscuit Co, 1986-1996; pres, Inst Food Technol, 1984-1985; dir nutrit &health sci, Gen Foods Corp, 1980-1986; prof food sci & human nutrit & chmn dept, Mich StateUniv, 1971-1980; prof, Univ Ill, Urbana, 1969-1971; assoc prof nutrit biochem, Univ Ill, Urbana, 1966-1969; biochemist, US Army Med Res & Nutrit Lab Colo, 1960-1966. **Memberships:** AAAS; Am Inst Nutrit; Am Soc Clin Nutrit; Am Chem Soc; Poultry Sci Asn; InstFood Technologists. **Research Statement & Publications:** Lipid metabolism; protein and amino acid nutrition and metabolism; atherosclerosis; obesity. **Mailing Address:** Food Sys Design, Cargill Inc, PO Box 9300, Minneapolis, MN 55440-9300. **E-Mail:** gilbert_leveille@cargill.com

LEVELTON, B(RUCE) HARDING, CHEMICAL ENGINEERING. **Personal Data:** b Bella Coola, BC, June 18, 1925; m 1950, c 3. **Education:** Univ BC, BASc, 1947, MASc, 1948; Tex A&M Univ, PhD (chem eng), 1951. **Professional Experience:** VPRES, CHATTERTON PETROCHEM CORP, 1984-; prin, B H Levelton & Assocs Ltd, 1966-; pres, B H Levelton & Assocs Ltd, 1966-; assoc head div appl chem, BC Res Coun, 1964-1966; res engr, BC Res Coun, 1958-1964; Spec lectr, Univ BC, 1957-1965; assoc res engr, BC Res Coun, 1954-1958; Asst res engr, BC Res Coun, 1951-1954. **Memberships:** Am Inst Chem Engrs; Nat Asn Corrosion Engrs; Air Pollution Control Asn; Chem Inst Can; Forest Prod Res Soc; Am Water Works Asn. **Research Statement & Publications:** Treatment and beneficiation of industrial minerals; utilization of wood wastes by carbonization; corrosion of metals in chemical industry and in marine service; corrosion of copper in potable waters; environmental technology; solid waste disposal; toxic and hazardous waste disposal. **Mailing Address:** 5531 Cornwall Dr No 48, Richmond, BC V7C 5N7, Can.

LEVEN, ROBERT MAYNARD, CELL BIOLOGY, HEMATOLOGY. **Personal Data:** b Chicago, Ill, November 7, 1955; m 1982, c 2. **Education:** Wash Univ, BA, 1977; Univ Pa, PhD (anat), 1982. **Professional Experience:** DIR DISABILITY SERVS, RUSH MED COL, CHICAGO, ILL, 1996-; prin investr, Am Cancer Soc, 1994-1997; ASST PROF ANAT & MED, RUSH MED COL, CHICAGO, ILL, 1990-; consult, Amgen, Inc, 1989-1990; prin investr, Nat Heart Lung & Blood Inst, NIH, 1988-1994; Instr anat, Univ Calif, San Francisco, 1986; staff scientist res med, Lawrence Berkeley Lab, 1984-1990; Postdoctoral fel thrombosis, Med Sch, Temple Univ, 1982-1984. **Research Statement & Publications:** Gene therapy & tissue eng appl to tissue regeneration in bone & nerve. **Mailing Address:** Dept Anat Rush Presby-St Luke's Med Col, 1653 W Congress Pkwy, Chicago, IL 60612-3833. **E-Mail:** rleven@rush.edu

LEVENBERG, MILTON IRWIN, MASS SPECTROMETRY, COMPUTER SCIENCE. **Personal Data:** b Chicago, Ill, November 5, 1937; div. **Education:** Ill Inst Technol, BS, 1958; Calif Inst Technol, PhD (chem), 1965. **Professional Experience:** MGR, ABBOTT LABS, 1990-; sect head, Abbott Labs, 1984-1990; assoc res fel, Abbott Labs, 1973-1984; sr chem physicist, Abbott Labs, 1965-1973. **Memberships:** Am Chem Soc; Sigma Xi; Am Soc Mass Spectrometry. **Research Statement & Publications:** Computer applications to instrumentation; instrumentation; electronics; mass spectrometry; nuclear magnetic resonance spectroscopy. **Mailing Address:** Abbott Labs D-418 AP-9, Abbott Park, IL 60064-3500.

LEVENBOOK, LEO, biochemistry; deceased, see previous edition for last biography

LEVENE, CYRIL, ANATOMY. **Personal Data:** b Gateshead, Eng, May 27, 1926. **Education:** Queen's Univ Belfast, MB, BCh & BAO, 1948, MD, 1960. **Professional Experience:** PROF EMER ANAT, FAC MED, UNIV CALGARY, 1988-; prof anat, div morphol sci, Univ Calgary, 1974-1988; assoc prof, dept anat, fac med, Univ Calgary, 1969-1974; assoc prof, Univ Western Ont, 1967-1969, WHO fel human genetics, 1966; sr lectr anat, Univ Col Wis, 1965-1967; lectr human anat, Univ Col Wis, 1954-1965; asst lectr, Queen's Univ Belfast, 1952-1954; demonstr anat, Queen's Univ Belfast, 1951-1952. **Memberships:** Hon mem Can Asn Anat. **Research Statement & Publications:** Medical education. **Mailing Address:** Dept Cell Biol & Anat, Fac Med, Univ Calgary, 6124 34th St SW, Calgary, AB T3E 5L6, Can. **E-Mail:** clevene@ucalgary.ca

LEVENE, HOWARD, mathematical statistics; deceased, see previous edition for last biography

LEVENE, RALPH ZALMAN, OPHTHALMOLOGY. **Personal Data:** b Winnipeg, Man, May 17, 1927. **Education:** Univ Man, MD, 1949; NY Univ, DSc(ophthal), 1957; Am Bd Ophthal, dipl, 1955. **Professional Experience:** CLIN PROF OPHTHAL, UNIV ALA, BIRMINGHAM, as of 2003; prof ophthal, Univ Ala, Birmingham, beginning 1973; from instr to assoc prof, Med Sch, NY Univ, 1955-1973; resident ophthal, Winnipeg Gen Hosp, Can, 1951-1955; intern, Winnipeg Gen Hosp, Can, 1949-1950. **Memberships:** AMA; Asn Res Vision & Ophthal; Am Acad Ophthal & Otolaryngol; NY AcadMed; Sigma Xi; Am Ophthal Soc. **Research Statement & Publications:** Clinical and basic science aspects of glaucoma. **Mailing Address:** Dept Ophthal Univ Ala, 2008 Brookwood Med Ctr Dr Ste 209, Birmingham, AL 35209. **Fax:** 205-877-2958.

LEVENSON, ALAN IRA, PSYCHIATRY. **Personal Data:** b Boston, Mass, July 25, 1935. **Education:** Harvard Univ, AB, 1957, MD, 1961, MPH, 1965; Am Bd Psychiat & Neurol, dipl, 1967. **Professional Experience:** PROF EMER, PSYCHIAT, HEALTH SCI CTR, UNIV ARIZ, 2000-; chief med officer, Palo Verde Ment Health Serv, 1991-1993; chief exec officer, Palo Verde Ment Health Serv, 1971-1991; prof psychiat, Col Med, Univ Ariz, 1969-2000; head dept, Col Med, Univ Ariz, 1969-1989; dir servs div, NIMH, 1967-1969; staff psychiatrist, NIMH, 1965-1966; resident psychiat, Mass Ment Health Ctr, Boston, 1962-1965; intern, Univ Hosp, Ann Arbor, 1961-1962. **Memberships:** Fel Am Psychiat Asn; fel Am Col Psychiat; Group Advan Psychiat; fel Am Col Mental Health Admin. **Research Statement & Publications:** Organization and delivery of mental health services; malpractice issues in psychiatry. **Mailing Address:** Health Sci Ctr, Univ Ariz, 75 N Calle Resplendor, Tucson, AZ 85716-4937. **Fax:** 520-327-6172. **E-Mail:** levenson@email.arizona.edu

LEVENSON, HAROLD SAMUEL, food science; deceased, see previous edition for last biography

LEVENSON, JAMES B, PLANT ECOLOGY, GEOGRAPHIC INFORMATION SYSTEMS. **Personal Data:** b San Francisco, Calif, August 22, 1944; c Lori, Brian & David. **Education:** Ind State Univ, Terre Haute, BS, 1971, MA, 1973; Univ Wis-Milwaukee, PhD (bot), 1976. **Professional Experience:** ECOLOGIST, ARGONNE NAT LAB, 1984-; asst environ sci, Argonne Nat Lab, 1979-1984; co-investr, NSF grant, 1978-1980; asst prof ecol, Saginaw Valley State Col, 1977-1979; res assoc, Univ Wis-Milwaukee, 1976-1977. **Memberships:** Ecol Soc Am. **Research Statement & Publications:** Interactions and resultant impacts of man-dominated systems on remnant ecosystem patches; identification, description and quantification of natural areas; application of ecological concepts to regional assessments. **Mailing Address:** 22136 S Eastcliff Dr, Joliet, IL 60436-9684. **Fax:** 630-252-6090. **E-Mail:** levenson@anl.gov

LEVENSON, MARC D, PHYSICS. **Education:** Stanford Univ, PhD, 1971. **Professional Experience:** PROPRIETOR, MD LEVENSON CONSULT, as of 2005. **Mailing Address:** 19868 Bonnie Ridge Way, Saratoga, CA 95070. **Fax:** 408-867-5846. **E-Mail:** muddle@aol.com

LEVENSON, MARC DAVID, LASERS, QUANTUM ELECTRONICS, MICROLIYHOGRAPHY. **Personal Data:** b Philadelphia, Pa, May 28, 1945; m 1971. **Education:** Mass Inst Technol, BS, 1967; Stanford Univ, MS, 1968, PhD (physics), 1972. **Honors & Awards:** Adolph Lomb Award, Optical Soc Am, 1976; Bacus Prize, SPIE, 1991. **Professional Experience:** RETIRED; head mgr optical storage, IBM Res Lab, 1987-1988; mem res staff, IBM Res Lab, 1979-1984; vis fel, Joint Inst Lab Astrophys, Univ Colo, 1978-1979; assoc prof physics & elec eng, Univ Southern Calif, 1977-1979; Alfred P Sloan fel, 1975-1977; asst prof physics, Univ Southern Calif, 1974-1977; res fel non-linear optics, Gordon McKay Lab, Harvard Univ, 1971-1974. **Memberships:** Am Phys Soc; Inst Elec & Electronics Engrs; Optical Soc Am, SPIE. **Research Statement & Publications:** Development and application of new techniques of laser spectroscopy to problems in atomic, molecular and condensed matter physics; application of optical and laser techniques to electronics manufacturing; quantum optics; optical memories; photolithography. **Mailing Address:** 19868 Bonnie Ridge Way, Saratoga, CA 95070.

LEVENSON, MARK S, STATISTICS. **Education:** Cornell Univ, BA, 1987; Univ Chicago, PhD (Statist), 1993. **Professional Experience:** MATH STATISTICIAN, STATISTICAL ENG DIV, NAT INST STAND & TECHNOL, as of 2000. **Memberships:** Inst Math Statist; Sigma Xi. **Research Statement & Publications:** Image and signal processing; statistical computation and graphics; and computational metrology. **Mailing Address:** Statistical Eng Div, Nat Inst Stand & Technol, NIST N Rm 341, Gaithersburg, MD 20899. **Fax:** 301-990-4127. **E-Mail:** mark.levenson@nist.gov

LEVENSON, MILTON, CHEMICAL ENGINEERING. **Personal Data:** b St Paul, Minn, January 4, 1923; wid Mary Novick (deceased); c James, Barbara, Richard, Scott & Janet. **Education:** Univ Minn, BChE, 1943. **Honors & Awards:** Robert E Wilson Award, Am Inst Chem Engrs, 1975; Source Term Award, Am Nuclear Soc, 1988. **Professional Experience:** CONSULT, 1990-; Nuclear Soc Int (past pres); vpres, Bechtel Int, 1983-1990; exec eng, Bechtel Power Corp, San Francisco, 1981-1990; dir nuclear power, Elec Power Res Inst, 1973-1981; from assoc engr to assoc lab dir energy & environ, Argonne Nat Lab, 1948-1973; asst engr, Oak Ridge Nat Labs, 1944-1948; Jr engr, Houdaille-Hershey Corp, 1944. **Memberships:** Nat Acad Eng; fel Am Inst Chem Engrs; fel Am Nuclear Soc (pres); AAAS. **Research Statement & Publications:** Water reactor technology; fuel cycle technology; breeder reactor development; nuclear safety. **Mailing Address:** 2319 Sharon Rd, Menlo Park, CA 94025.

LEVENSON, MORRIS E, MATHEMATICS. **Personal Data:** b New York, NY, November 13, 1914. **Education:** NY Univ, PhD (math), 1948. **Professional Experience:** PROF EMER MATH, BROOKLYN COL, as of 2001; prof math, Brooklyn Col, beginning 1971; from instr to assoc prof, BrooklynCol, 1949-1971; instr math, Cooper Union, 1946-1949; mathematician, David Taylor ModelBasin, 1944-1946; instr math, NY Univ, 1943-1944; asst, Duke Univ, 1937-1938. **Memberships:** Am Math Soc; Math Asn Am; Sigma Xi. **Research Statement & Publications:** Nonlinear vibrations. **Mailing Address:** Dept Math, Brooklyn Col, 1156 Ingersoll Hall, 2900 Bedford Ave, Brooklyn, NY 11210-2889. **Fax:** 718-951-4674.

LEVENSON, ROBERT, CELL BIOLOGY. **Personal Data:** b New York, NY. **Professional Experience:** ASSOC PROF CELL BIOL, SCH MED, YALE UNIV, beginning 1989. **Mailing Address:** Cell Biol Dept Sch Med, Yale Univ 333 Cedar St, New Haven, CT 06510-3219.

LEVENSON, STANLEY MELVIN, SURGERY, SURGICAL RESEARCH. **Personal Data:** b Dorchester, Mass, May 25, 1916. **Education:** Harvard Univ, AB, 1937, MD, 1941; Am Bd Nutrit, dipl, 1952; Am Bd Surg, dipl, 1957. **Honors & Awards:** Jonathan E Rhoads lectr, Am Soc Parenteral & Enteral Nutrit, 1978; Arnold MSeligman Mem, Sinai Hosp Baltimore, 1979; McCollum Award, Am Soc Clin Nutrit, 1983. **Professional Experience:** DISTINGUISHED UNIV PROF EMER SURG, ALBERT EINSTEIN COL MED, as of 2003; Am Surg Asn rep, Nat res Coun-Nat Acad Sci, 1971-1975; dep dir ressurg, Col Med, beginning 1967; NIH res career award, beginning 1962; consult, Walter Reed Army inst res, 1961-1963; dir div basic surg res, Walter Reed Army inst res, 1961; prof surg, Albert

Einstein Col Med, beginning 1961; dir surg metab lab & clin assoc prof, Georgetown Univ, 1959-1961; comt on trauma, Food & Nutrit Bd, Nat res Coun, beginning 1956; from assoc dir to dir deptgermfree res, Walter Reed Army inst res, 1956-1961; chief dept surg metab & physiol, WalterReed Army inst res, 1956-1961; from asst resident to sr asst resident surg, Med Col Va, 1950-1952; chmn subcomt burns & radiation injury, Food & Nutrit Bd, Nat res Coun, 1949-1950; surg scientist, Med Nutrit lab, Univ Chicago, 1947-1949; res fel med, Thorndike mem lab, Harvard Univ, 1944-1947; resident burn serv & res assoc surg, Boston City Hosp, 1942-1943; res assoc physiol, Sch Pub Health, Harvard Univ, beginning 1941; Surg house officer, BethIsrael Hosp, Boston, Mass, 1941-1942. **Memberships:** Am Surg Asn; Am Burn Asn; Am Inst Nutrit; Am Soc Clin Nutrit; Am ColSurgeons; Am Soc Parenteral & Enteral Nutrit. **Research Statement & Publications:** Metabolic and clinical response to trauma; wound healing; germfree life; infection; burns; neoplasia; nutrition; radiation. **Mailing Address:** Jacobi Med Ctr, Albert Einstein Col Med, 1400 Pelham Pkwy S, Rm 506, Bronx, NY 10461.

LEVENSPIEL, OCTAVE, CHEMICAL ENGINEERING. **Personal Data:** b Shanghai, China, July 6, 1926; American citizen; m 1952, Mary; c Bekki, Barney & Morris. **Education:** Univ Calif, BS, 1947; Ore State Col, MS, 1949, PhD (chem eng), 1952. **Honorary Degrees:** Dr, ENSIC, Nancy, France, 1987; Dr, Colo Sch Mines, 1997. **Honors & Awards:** 3M Lectureship Award, Am Soc Eng Educ, 1966; Wilhelm Award, Am Inst Chem Engrs, 1979; Danckwerts Award, London, 1988; W K Lewis Award, Am Inst Chem Engrs. **Professional Experience:** PROF EMER CHEM ENG, ORE STATE UNIV, 1991-; Univ Sydney, Australia, 1985; Univ Groningen, Neth, 1984; vis prof, Denmarks Tech Univ, 1977; vis prof, Univ NSW, Australia, 1976; prof, Ore State Univ, 1968-1991; NSF sr fel, Fulbright fel, 1968-1969; NSF sr fel, Cambridge Univ, 1963-1964; assoc & prof, Ill Inst Technol, 1958-1968; asst & assoc prof, Bucknell Univ, 1954-1958; asst prof chem eng, Ore State Col, 1952-1954; jr res engr, Inst Eng Res, Univ Calif, 1951-1952. **Memberships:** Am Chem Soc; Am Inst Chem Engrs; Nat Acad Eng. **Research Statement & Publications:** Chemical reactor design; fluidization. **Mailing Address:** Dept Chem Eng, Ore State Univ, Gleason Hall, Corvallis, OR 97331. **Fax:** 541-737-4600. **E-Mail:** levenspo@peak.org

LEVENTHAL, CARL M, NEUROLOGY, NEUROPATHOLOGY. **Personal Data:** b New York, NY, July 28, 1933; m 1962, c 4. **Education:** Harvard Univ, AB, 1954; Univ Rochester, MD, 1959. **Professional Experience:** RETIRED; dir, Div Demyelinating Atrophic & Dementing Dis, Nat Inst Neurol Dis & Stroke, 1981-1996; dep dir, Nat Inst Arthritis, Metab & Digest Dis, 1977-1981; dep dir, Bur Drugs, Food & Drug Admin, 1974-1977; actg dep dir sci, NIH, 1973-1974; asst to dep dir sci, NIH, 1968-1974; asst prof, Georgetown Univ, 1967-1974; neurologist, Nat Cancer Inst, 1966-1968; med officer, USPHS, 1964-1996; instr, Georgetown Univ, 1964-1966; assoc neuropathologist, Nat Inst Neurol Dis & Blindness, 1964-1966; resident, Mass Gen Hosp, 1963-1964; fel neuropath, Mass Gen Hosp, 1962-1963; fel, Harvard Univ, 1961-1964; asst resident neurol, Mass Gen Hosp, 1961-1962; asst res physician, Johns Hopkins Hosp, 1960-1961; fel, Johns Hopkins Univ, 1959-1961; Johns Hopkins Hosp, 1959-1960. **Memberships:** Am Acad Neurol; Am Asn Neuropath; Am Neurol Asn; Asn Res Nervous & Ment Dis. **Research Statement & Publications:** Government research administration; clinical neuropathology. **Mailing Address:** 10924 Brewer House Rd, Rockville, MD 20852-3422.

LEVENTHAL, EDWIN ALFRED, SOLID STATE PHYSICS. **Personal Data:** b Brooklyn, NY, January 26, 1934. **Education:** Cornell Univ, BEng Phys, 1956; Polytech Inst Brooklyn, MS, 1959; NY Univ, PhD (physics), 1963. **Professional Experience:** DIR, MKT INFO SYSTS, AM MED INT, 1984-; dir, systs planning, FriesenInt, 1974-1984; ed & publ, Med Instrument Reports, 1970-1974; Sr physicist, Philips Labs Div, NAm Philips Co, 1961-1970. **Memberships:** Am Phys Soc; Asn Advan Med Instrumentation; NY Acad Sci. **Research Statement & Publications:** Materials handling and information processing in hospital management and design; medical equipment planning. **Mailing Address:** 3 Woodfield Rd, Pomona, NY 10970.

LEVENTHAL, HOWARD, HUMAN EMOTION, HEALTH PSYCHOLOGY. **Personal Data:** b Brooklyn, NY, December 7, 1931; m 1954, Elaine A Silverman; c Edith (Burns) & Sharan. **Education:** City Univ New York Queens Col, BS, 1952; Univ NC Chapel Hill, MS, 1954, PhD (psychol), 1956. **Honors & Awards:** Outstanding Contrib to Health Psychol Award, Div Health Psychol, Am Psychol Asn, 1987; Outstanding Contrub to Develop Health Psychol, Div Health Psychol Div, Develop Psychol, Amer Psychol Assoc, 2001. **Professional Experience:** PROF PSYCHOL, RUTGERS UNIV, 1988-; chmn, Dept Psychol, Univ Wis-Madison, 1987-1988; mem, chmn Behav Med Study Sect, NIH, 1986-1991; assoc, Clin Cancer Ctr, 1980-; Prof sociol, Univ Wis-Madison, 1974-; prof psychol, Univ Wis-Madison, 1967-1988; assoc prof psychol, Yale Univ, 1964-1967; asst prof psychol, Yale Univ, 1958-1964; Sr asst sci psychol, USPHS, 1956-1958; Board Governors. **Memberships:** Inst Med-Nat Acad Sci; fel Am Psychol Asn; Acad Behav Med Res; fel Am Psychol Soc; Am Psychosom Asn; fel AAAS. **Research Statement & Publications:** Focus on common sense views of illness and how these representations affect health and illness behaviors and emotional reactions to health crises; effects of stress on immune function in elderly persons. **Mailing Address:** Inst Health Policy & Aging, Rutgers Univ, 30 Col Ave, New Brunswick, NJ 08903. **Fax:** 732-932-1945. **E-Mail:** hleventhal@ihhcpar.rutgers.edu

LEVENTHAL, JACOB J, ATOMIC PHYSICS, MOLECULAR PHYSICS. **Personal Data:** b Brooklyn, NY, December 18, 1937. **Education:** Wash Univ, BS, 1960; Univ Fla, PhD (physics), 1965. **Professional Experience:** CURATOR'S PROF PHYSICS, UNIV MO, ST LOUIS, 1987-; prof physics, Univ Mo, St Louis, 1976-1987; from asst prof to assoc prof, Univ Mo, St Louis, 1968-1976; assoc chemist, Brookhaven Nat Lab, 1967-1968; res assoc physics & chem, Brookhaven Nat Lab, 1965-1967; teaching asst, Univ Fla, 1960-1965; NSF fel, 1964. **Memberships:** fel Am Phys Soc; Optical Soc Am. **Research Statement & Publications:** Interactions of positive ions with neutral molecules; spectroscopic observations of excited state production in low energy atomic and molecular collision processes; published over 5 articles. **Mailing Address:** Dept Physics & Astron, Univ Mo, B508 Benton Hall, St Louis, MO 63121. **Fax:** 314-516-6152. **E-Mail:** jake@umsl.edu

LEVENTHAL, JOEL STEPHEN, GEOCHEMISTRY. **Personal Data:** b Saginaw, Mich, November 23, 1941; m 1984, c 4. **Education:** Calif State Univ, Los Angeles, BS, 1968; Univ Ariz, Tucson, MS, 1970, PhD (geochem), 1972. **Professional Experience:** Prin investr, Civilian Res & Develop Found, 1996-1998; co-prin investr collab res travel grant, NATO, 1990 & 1991; GS-15 PROJ CHIEF, MINERALS BR, US GEOL SURV, 1988-; GS-14 proj chief, Minerals Br, 1981-1987; GS-13 sect leader, Energy Br, 1978-1981; res chemist, GS-12 Energy Br, US Geol Surv, 1974-1977; asst res biogeologist fel, Univ Calif, Santa Barbara, 1972-1974; res asst, WF libby, Ucelep LosAngeles, 1963-1967. **Memberships:** AAAS; Geochem Soc; Am Geophys Union; fel Soc Econ Geologists; Colorado Sci Soc. **Research Statement & Publications:** Organic and inorganic geochemistry of metalliferous black shales and sedimentary ore deposits; environmental radioactivity, natural nuclear reactors and tritium hydrology; environmental arsenic related to mining and coal ash; global change in coastal wetlands and methane emissions. **Mailing Address:** US Geol Surv Fed Ctr, MS 973, Denver, CO 80225. **Fax:** 303-236-3200. **E-Mail:** jleventh@usgs.gov

LEVENTHAL, MARVIN, ASTROPHYSICS, ATOMIC PHYSICS. **Personal Data:** b New York, NY, December 4, 1937; m 1961, Alice; c Liza & Tama. **Education:** City Col NY, BS, 1958; Brown Univ, PhD (physics), 1964. **Professional Experience:** PROF ASTRON & CHMN, DEPT ASTRON, UNIV MD, 1993; Nat Res Coun fel, 1992-1993; exec comt, high energy astrophys div, Am Astron Soc; 1985-1986; mem tech staff, Bell Labs, 1968-1992; asst prof physics, Yale Univ, 1966-1968; res assoc physics, Yale Univ, 1964-1966. **Memberships:** AAAS; fel Am Phys Soc; Am Astron Soc; Sigma Xi. **Research Statement & Publications:** Precision measurements of atomic physics quantities which have bearing on quantum electrodynamics; experimental and theoretical gamma ray astronomy; laboratory astrophysics. **Mailing Address:** Dept Astron, Univ Md, Space Sci Bldg Stadium Dr, College Park, MD 20742-2421. **Fax:** 301-314-9067. **E-Mail:** ml@astro.umd.edu

LEVENTHAL, STEPHEN HENRY, NUMERICAL ANALYSIS, RESERVOIR SIMULATION. **Personal Data:** b New York, NY, April 2, 1949; m 1971, Ellen Warach; c Daniel & Seth. **Education:** Rutgers Univ, BA, 1969; Univ Md, MA, 1971; PhD (math), 1973. **Professional Experience:** SR STAFF RES MATH, SHELL DEVELOP, SHELL OIL CO, 1989-; staff res, Shell Develop CO, Shell Oil, 1985-1989; dir reservoir simulation, Gulf Res & Develop Co, Gulf Oil, 1983-1985; supvr math, Gulf Res & Develop Co, Gulf Oil, 1981-1983; sr res math, Gulf Res & Develop Co, Gulf Oil, 1979-1981; res math, Gulf Res & Develop Co, Gulf Oil, 1977-1979; Res math, Naval Surface Weapons Ctr, 1973-1977. **Memberships:** Soc Indust & Appl Math; Soc Petrol Engrs. **Research Statement & Publications:** Development of high order numerical methods and state of the art reservoir simulation; founder of OCI method; principal developer of Gulf Oil's Black Oil Simulator; one of the principal developers of Shell Oil's multi-purpose simulator. **Mailing Address:** Div Math Res, Shell Oil Co, PO Box 481, Houston, TX 77001. **Fax:** 713-245-7990. **E-Mail:** stephen.leventhal@shell.com

LEVENTIS, NICHOLAS, ELECTROCHEMISTRY OF CONDUCTING POLYMERS, MICROELECTROCHEMICAL DEVICES & ELECTROCHROMICS. **Personal Data:** b Athens, Greece, November 12, 1957. **Education:** Univ Athens, Greece, BS, 1980; Mich State Univ, PhD (org chem), 1985. **Honors & Awards:** Arthur K Doolittle Award, Am Chem Soc, 1993. **Professional Experience:** ASSOC PROF CHEM, UNIV MO-ROLLA, as of 2001; Hyperion Catalysis, Delta F Corp, 1992-1993; Hyperion Catalysis, Inc, 1989-1993; vpres res, Molecular Displays, Inc, 1988-1993; consult, Igen, Inc, 1987-1993; res assoc, Mass Inst Technol, 1985-1988. **Memberships:** Am Chem Soc; Electrochem Soc; Int Union Pure & Appl Chem. **Research Statement & Publications:** Development of electrode surface confined electrochromic polymers for large area transmittance control for application in smart windows; new concepts in the area of microelectrochemical immunochemical sensors based on conducting polymers synthetically modified at the monomer level to introduce specificity. **Mailing Address:** NASA Glenn Res Ctr, Cleveland, OH 65401. **Fax:** 573-341-6033. **E-Mail:** nicholas.leventis@grc.nasa.gov

LEVEQUE, RANDALL J, MATHEMATICS, APPLIED MATHEMATICS. **Personal Data:** b Ann Arbor, Mich, September 30, 1955. **Education:** Univ Calif, BA, 1977; Stanford Univ, PhD (comput sci), 1982. **Professional Experience:** PROF, MATH & APPL MATH, UNIV WASH, 1990-; prof, Inst Math, ETH Zurich, 1990-1991; vis mem, Courant Inst, NY Univ, 1990; vis lectr, Inst Math, ETH Zurich, 1989; consult, Inst Comput Appln Sci & Eng, NASA Langley Res Ctr, 1986-; from asst prof to assoc prof, Math & Appl Math, Univ Wash, 1985-1990; Hedrick asst prof math, Univ Calif, Los Angeles, 1983-1985; vis scientist, Inst Comput Appln Sci & Eng, NASA Langley Res Ctr, 1983, 1984, 1986; NSF fel, Courant Inst Math Sci, NY Univ, 1982-1983; Hertz Found grad fel, 1980-1982; NSF Grad fel, 1977-1980. **Research Statement & Publications:** Author of book, 28 journal publications and 15 conference proceedings. **Mailing Address:** Dept Appl Math Univ Wash, Box 352420, Seattle, WA 98195-2420. **Fax:** 206-685-1440. **E-Mail:** rjl@amath.washington.edu

LEVEQUE, WILLIAM JUDSON, MATHEMATICS. **Personal Data:** b Boulder, Colo, August 9, 1923; m 1970, c 1. **Education:** Univ Colo, BA, 1944; Cornell Univ, MA, 1945, PhD (math), 1947. **Professional Experience:** RETIRED; exec dir, Am Math Soc, 1977-1988; chmn, Conf Bd Math Sci, 1973-1974; prof math, Claremont Grad Sch, 1970-1977; chmn dept, Univ Mich, Ann Arbor, 1967-1970; exec ed, Math Rev, 1965-1966; Sloan res fel, 1957-1960; Fulbright res scholar, 1951-1952; from instr to prof, Univ Mich, Ann Arbor, 1949-1970; Benjamin Peirce instr math, Harvard Univ, 1947-1949. **Memberships:** Am Math Soc; Math Asn Am; fel AAAS. **Research Statement & Publications:** Theory of numbers. **Mailing Address:** 12684 Sunrise Dr, Bainbridge Island, WA 98110.

LEVER, ALFRED B P, INORGANIC CHEMISTRY. **Personal Data:** b London, Eng, February 21, 1936. **Education:** Univ London, BSc & ARCS, 1957, dipl, Imp Col & PhD (chem), 1960. **Honors & Awards:** Alcan Lecture Award, 1981; Gerhard Herzberg Award for Outstanding Achievements to Spectroscopy, awarded by the Spectroscopy Society of Canada, 1996; Killam Research Fellow, 2000/2002; Linstead Award for Career Achievements in Phthalocyanine Chemistry awarded by the 2nd International Conference on Porphyrin and Phthalocyanine Chemistry, Kyoto, 2002. **Professional Experience:** DISTINGUISHED RES PROF EMER CHEM, YORK UNIV, as of 2004; Univ Calabria, 1983 & Univ Pavia, 1989; vis prof, Sydney Univ, 1978; vis prof, Calif Inst Technol, 1976-1977; prof chem, York Univ, beginning 1972; prog chmn, XIVth Int ConfCoord Chem, Toronto, 1972; assoc prof, York Univ, 1967-1972; vis lectr, Ohio State Univ, 1967; Ed, Coord Chem Rev, 1966-; lectr chem, Inst Sci & Tech, Univ Manchester, 1962-1966; hon res assoc, Univ Col, London, 1961-1962; Hon res asst, Univ Col, London, 1960-1961. **Memberships:** Am Chem Soc; Chem Inst Can; Royal Soc Chem; fel Jan Prom Sci. **Research Statement & Publications:** Inorganic electronic spectroscopy; solar energy conversion; phthalocyanine chemistry; electrochemistry; alternate energy; electronic structure; chemical sensors. **Mailing Address:** Dept Chem, York Univ, 140 Campus Walk, 4700 Keele St, North York, ON M3J 1P3, Can. **Fax:** 416-736-5936. **E-Mail:** blever@yorku.ca

LEVER, ALVIN, ARCHITECTURE, PSYCHOLOGY. **Personal Data:** b St Louis, Mo, January 29, 1939. **Education:** Wash Univ, BS, 1961, BArch, 1963; Univ Santa Monica, MA, 1992. **Professional Experience:** EXEC VPRES & CHIEF EXEC OFFICER, AM COL CHEST PHYSICIANS, 1995-; exec dir, Am Col Chest Physicians, 1992-1995; dir membership & fin, Am Col Chest Physicians, 1990-1992; vpres & gen mgr, Apelco Int Ltd, 1974-1990; vpres facil develop, Michael Reese Med Ctr, 1972-1974; sr proj designer, 1965-1968, Hellmuth, Obata & Kassabaum, St Louis, vpres proj mgr, 1965-1968; proj designer, Sir Basil Spence Archits, Edinburgh, Scotland, 1963-1965. **Memberships:** Am Soc Med Soc Execs. **Mailing Address:** Am Col Chest Physicians, 3300 Dundee Rd, Northbrook, IL 60062-2303.

LEVER, CYRIL JR, ORGANIC CHEMISTRY. **Personal Data:** b Abington, Pa, June 5, 1929; m 1961, Norma; c Scott & Ruth. **Education:** Pa Mil Col, BS, 1953. **Professional Experience:** PRES & CHIEF EXEC OFFICER, C LEVER CO, INC, 1990-; pres & dir res,

C Lever Co, Inc, 1957-1990; asst treas & asst dir res, C Lever Co, Inc, 1953-1957. **Memberships:** Am Asn Textile Chemist & Colorist; Tech Asn Pulp & Paper Indust; Am Chem Soc. **Research Statement & Publications:** Dyes and colors for paper. **Mailing Address:** C Lever Co Inc, Lever Bldg 736 Dunks Ferry Rd, Bensalem, PA 19020-6575.

LEVER, JOHN, CHEMISTRY, NEUROSCIENCE. **Personal Data:** b Owensboro, Ky, November 7, 1953. **Education:** Univ SC, BS, 1975; NC State Univ, PhD (chem), 1981. **Professional Experience:** CHEMIST, DEPT ENVIRON HEALTH SCI, SCH HYG, JOHNS HOPKINS UNIV, 1983-. **Memberships:** Am Chem Soc; Soc Nuclear Med. **Mailing Address:** Dept Environ Health Sci Sch Hyg, John Hopkins Univ, Baltimore, MD 21205.

LEVER, JULIA ELIZABETH, BIOCHEMISTRY, MOLECULAR BIOLOGY. **Personal Data:** b Montreal, Que, November 23, 1945. **Education:** McGill Univ, BS, 1966; Univ Calif, PhD (biochem), 1971. **Professional Experience:** PROF, DEPT BIOCHEM & MOLECULAR BIOL, MED SCH, UNIV TEX, 1986-; mem fac, Grad Sch Biomed Sci, Univ Tex, 1979-; from asst prof to assoc prof, Dept Biochem & Molecular Biol, Med Sch, Univ Tex, 1979-1986; asst res prof, Salk Inst Biol Studies, 1977-1979; prin investr, Nat Cancer Inst, 1976-1977; vis scientist staff, Dept Cell Regulation, Imp Cancer Res Fund Lab, 1974-1977; vis res scientist, Roche Inst Molecular Biol, 1974. **Memberships:** Soc Biol Chemists; Am Physiol Soc. **Research Statement & Publications:** Biochemistry; molecular biology; numerous publications in the area of cell and molecular biology of membrane transport. **Mailing Address:** Dept Biochem & Molecular Biol, Univ Tex, PO Box 20708, Houston, TX 77225-0708. **Fax:** 713-500-0652. **E-Mail:** julia.e.lever@uth.tmc.edu

LEVERANT, GERALD ROBERT, MATERIALS SCIENCE ENGINEERING. **Personal Data:** b Hartford, Conn, June 18, 1940; m 1962, Michele; c Debra & Lori. **Education:** Rensselaer Polytech Inst, BMetE, 1962, PhD (metall), 1966. **Honors & Awards:** Henry Marion Howe Gold Medal, Am Soc Metals, 1970; Res & Develop 100 Award, Res & Develop Magazine, 2000. **Professional Experience:** DIR POWER GENERATION MAT, SOUTHWEST RES INST, 1994-; dir mat & mech, Southwest Res Inst, 1990-1994; dir mat sci, Southwest Res Inst, 1985-1990; asst dir, Southwest Res Inst, 1981-1985; mgr metall, Southwest Res Inst, 1977-1981; group leader, Mat Eng & Res Lab, Pratt & Whitney Aircraft Div, 1974-1977; sr res assoc, Mat Eng & Res Lab, Pratt & Whitney Aircraft Div, 1968-1974; res assoc, Mat Eng & Res Lab, Pratt & Whitney Aircraft Div, 1966-1968; sr res scientist, Res Lab, United Aircraft Corp, 1966. **Memberships:** Fel Am Soc Metals Int. **Research Statement & Publications:** Mechamical behavior and metacllurg of gas turbine materels and coatings, incheding life preduction and failure analysis. **Mailing Address:** Southwest Res Inst, PO Drawer 28510, San Antonio, TX 78228-0510. **Fax:** 210-522-6965. **E-Mail:** gleverant@swri.org

LEVERE, RICHARD DAVID, INTERNAL MEDICINE & HEMATOLOGY. **Personal Data:** b Brooklyn, NY, December 13, 1931; m 1978, c Scott M, Elyssa C & Colinne G. **Education:** State Univ NY, MD, 1956. **Professional Experience:** PROF MED & ASSOC DEAN, NY UNIV SCH MED, 1994-; sr vpres med affairs, Brooklyn Hosp Ctr, beginning 1994; dir med serv, Westchester Co Med Ctr, 1978-1993; prof med & chmn dept, NY Med Col, 1977-1993; adj prof, Rockefeller Univ, beginning 1973; chief hemat sect, State Univ NY Downstate Med Ctr, 1970-1977; NIH grant, 1965-1982; from asst prof to prof med, State Univ NY Downstate Med Ctr, 1965-1977; asst prof, Rockefeller Inst, 1964-1965; res assoc biochem, Rockefeller Inst, 1962-1963; instr med, State Univ NY, 1962-1963; Fel hemat, State Univ NY, 1961-1962; resident, Kings Co Hosp, 1960-1961; from intern to asst resident med, Bellevue Hosp, 1956-1958. **Memberships:** AAAS; Am Soc Clin Invest; Am Fedn Clin Res; Am Soc Hemat; Am Col Physicians; Sigma Xi. **Research Statement & Publications:** Control mechanisms in heme and porphyrin synthesis; metabolism of normal and abnormal hemoglobins; diseases of porphyrin metabolism. **Mailing Address:** Dept Her, NY Univ Sch Med, 550 First Ave, New York, NY 10016.

LEVERE, TREVOR HARVEY, HISTORY OF CHEMISTRY, SCIENCE & ARCTIC EXPLORATION. **Personal Data:** b London, Eng, March 21, 1944; Canadian & British citizen. **Education:** Oxford Univ, BA, 1966, MA, 1969, DPhil(mod hist &hist sci), 1969. **Professional Experience:** Resident fel, Dibner Inst, Mass Inst Technol, 1995; DIR, INST HIST & PHILOS SCI, 1993-; vis fel, Clare Hall & vis scholar, Scott Polar Res Inst, Cambridge Univ, 1983-1984, John Simon Guggenheim Found fel, 1983; PROF HIST SCI, UNIV TORONTO, 1981-; dir, Inst Hist & Philos Sci, 1981-1986; Killam fel, Can Coun, 1975-1977; from asst prof to assoc prof, Univ Toronto, 1969-1981; Lectr, Univ Toronto, 1968-1969. **Memberships:** Foreign mem Dutch Soc Sci; Can Soc Hist & Philos Sci; coresp mem Int AcadHist Sci; fel Royal Soc Can; Hist Sci Soc. **Research Statement & Publications:** History of chemistry; social and cultural contexts; science and Romanticism; science and Arctic exploration; history of sciences from eighteenth to twentieth centuries. **Mailing Address:** Inst Hist & Philos Sci & Tech, Univ Toronto, 91 Charles St W Rm 316 Victoria Col, Toronto, ON M5S 1K7, Can. **Fax:** 416-978-3003. **E-Mail:** tlevere@chass.utoronto.ca

LEVERENZ, CHRISTINE R, MATHEMATICS. **Education:** Butler Univ, BS, 1974; Univ Ky, MA, 1976, PhD, 1982, MS, 1998. **Professional Experience:** PROF, DEPT MATHS, GEORGETOWN COL, KY, as of 2006. **Mailing Address:** Dept Math, Georgetown Col, 400 E Col St Ste 1, Georgetown, KY 40324. **Fax:** 502-868-7744. **E-Mail:** cleveren@georgetowncollege.edu

LEVERENZ, HUMBOLDT WALTER, solid state science, luminescence, magnetics; deceased, see previous edition for last biography

LEVERT, FRANCIS EDWARD, NUCLEAR REACTOR NOISE ANALYSIS, RADIATION DETECTION. **Personal Data:** b Tuscaloosa, Ala, March 28, 1939; m 1965, Faye; c Francis, Gerald & Lisa. **Education:** Tuskegee Inst, BS, 1964; Univ Mich, MS, 1966; Pa State Univ, PhD (nuclear eng), 1971. **Honors & Awards:** Am Soc Eng Educ Indust fel, Ford Found, 1971. **Professional Experience:** VPRES, KEMP CORP, 1985-; radiation safety officer, Technol Energy Corp, 1985-1996; chief scientist, Technol Energy Corp, 1979-1985; nuclear engr, Appl Physics Div, Argonne Nat Lab, 1974-1979; indust fel reactor anal, Commonwealth Edison Elec Co, 1973-1974; Ford Found fel Am Soc Eng Educ, Commonwealth Edison Co, 1973-1974; mem, Am Nuclear Soc-Nuclear Educ & Comt Disadvantaged Youth, 1972-1974; head, Mech Eng Dept, 1972-1973; mem, Currie Comt Eng Educ Disadvantaged, Pa State Univ, 1969-1971; from asst prof to assoc prof nuclear eng & mech eng, Tuskegee Inst, 1966-1972. **Memberships:** Am Soc Mech Engrs; Nat Soc Prof Engrs; Am Nuclear Soc; Am Soc Mech Engrs. **Research Statement & Publications:** Nuclear reactor noise analysis, neutron and gamma ray detector development; thermionic converters and instrumentation development for the fossil power fuel power industry; author of 77 technical papers and two books; granted thirty one patents. **Mailing Address:** 1725 E Magnolia Ave, Knoxville, TN 37917-7827. **Fax:** 865-544-0840. **E-Mail:** fel@levertco.com

LEVERTON, WALTER FREDERICK, SOLID STATE PHYSICS, MATERIALS SCIENCE. **Personal Data:** b Imperial, Sask, December 24, 1922; m 1948, c 2. **Education:** Univ Sask, BS, 1946, MS, 1948; Univ BC, PhD (physics), 1950. **Professional Experience:** CONSULT, 1979-; mem, Defence Commun Agency Sci Adv Group, 1974-1979; group vpres develop, Aerospace Corp, 1960-1979; asst div mgr semiconductors, Res Div, Raytheon Co, 1951-1960; asst prof elec eng, Univ Minn, 1950-1951. **Memberships:** Am Phys Soc; fel Inst Elec & Electronics Engrs. **Research Statement & Publications:** Cathode materials; semiconductors; 1061 Glenhaven Dr. **Mailing Address:** 1061 Glenhaven Dr, Pacific Palisades, CA 90272.

LEVESON, NANCY, COMPUTER SCIENCE. **Education:** Univ Calif, Los Angeles, PhD, 1980. **Professional Experience:** PROF AERONAUT & ASTRONAUT, MASS INST TECHNOL, as of 2005; prof comput Sci & eng, Univ Wash, beginning 1993; ed-in-chief, Inst Elec & Electronic Engrs Transactions Software Eng; bd dirs, Comput Res Asn, Int Coun Systs Eng; mem, Comn Eng Tech Systs, Nat Res Coun, Comt Comput Pub Policy, Asn Comput Mach; chmn, Nat Res Coun. **Memberships:** Fel Asn Comput Mach. **Research Statement & Publications:** Demonstration of a safety assessment on part of the US Air Traffic Control System. **Mailing Address:** Mass Inst Technol, Dept Aeronaut & Astronaut, 33-334 77 Mass Ave, Cambridge, MA 02139. **Fax:** 617-253-4196. **E-Mail:** leveson@mit.edu

LEVESQUE, ALLEN HENRY, COMMUNICATION THEORY, COMMUNICATION SYSTEMS DEVELOPMENT. **Personal Data:** b Jewett City, Conn, November 1, 1936. **Education:** Worcester Polytech Inst, BSEE, 1959; Yale Univ, MEEE, 1960, PhD, 1965. **Professional Experience:** Sr scientist, GTE Govt Systs Corp, 1988-1999; ADJ PROF, ELECTRICAL AND COMPUTER ENG, CTR WIRELESS INFO NETWORK STUDIES, as of 2003; ADV, CTR WIRELESS INFO NETWORK STUDIES, as of 2003; PRIN, GPL COMMUN INC, as of 2003; assoc ed, Trans Commun, Inst Elec & Electronics Engrs, 1986-1990 & Int JWireless Info Networks, 1993-; sr scientist, Commun Systs Div, GTE Sylvania Inc, 1984-1988; sr eng specialist commun res & develop, Eastern Div, 1981-1984; adj prof elec eng, Northeastern Univ, 1978-1981; sr eng specialist, Eastern Div, 1974-1981; sr mem tech staff, GTE Labs, Inc, 1969-1974; eng specialist, SylvaniaCommun Systs Lab, 1966-1969; eng specialist commun res & develop, Sylvania Appl Res Lab, 1965-1966; res asst elec eng, Sch Eng, Yale Univ, 1963-1965; sr engr commun, Sylvania Appl Res Lab, 1960-1962. **Memberships:** Sr mem Inst Elec & Electronics Engrs; Sigma Xi. **Research Statement & Publications:** Information theory; algebraic coding theory; communication systems development; computer communications; digital signal processing; communication networks; authored articles and books on error-control coding and wireless information networks. **Mailing Address:** Elec Def Systs Div, Worcester Polytech Inst, 100 Inst Rd, Worcester, MA 01609-2280. **Fax:** 781-466-3720. **E-Mail:** levesque@rocky.tntn.gtegsc.com

LEVESQUE, CHARLES LOUIS, ORGANIC CHEMISTRY. **Personal Data:** b Manchester, NH, February 16, 1913. **Education:** Dartmouth Col, AB, 1934, AM, 1936; Univ Ill, PhD (org chem), 1939. **Professional Experience:** RETIRED; dean continuing educ, Eve Sch, Ursinus Col, 1979-1981; prof applsci & dir, Eve Sch, Ursinus Col, 1971-1979; asst dir res, Rohm & Haas Co, 1969-1971; ressupvr, Rohm & Haas Co, 1948-1969; lab head, Resinous Prod & Chem Co, 1945-1948; groupleader, Resinous Prod & Chem Co, 1941-1945; sr chemist, Resinous Prod & Chem Co, 1939-1941; Instr anal chem, Dartmouth Col, 1934-1936. **Memberships:** Am Chem Soc; Sigma Xi. **Research Statement & Publications:** Structures of vinyl polymers; polyester resins and raw materials; new organic synthesis; surface active agents; pharmaceuticals. **Mailing Address:** Normandy Farms Estates, Box 1108 Apt F-304, Blue Bell, PA 19422.

LEVESQUE, RENE J A, NUCLEAR PHYSICS. **Personal Data:** b St-Alexis, Que, October 30, 1926; div. **Education:** Sir George Williams Col, BSc, 1952; Northwestern Univ, PhD (physics), 1957. **Professional Experience:** RETIRED; pres, Atomic Energy Control Bd, 1987-1993; emer prof, Dept Physics, 1987; vpres res & planning, Dept Physics, 1985-1987; pres, Can-France-Hawaii Telescope Corp, 1980; pres, Asn Sci, Eng & Technol Community Can, 1980; vpres, Can-France-Hawaii Telescope Corp, 1979; vpres res, Dept Physics, 1978-1985; dean fac arts & sci, Dept Physics, 1975-1978; vdean res fac arts & sci, Dept Physics, 1973-1975; asst ed, Can J Physics, 1973-1975; dir, Dept Physics, 1968-1973; prof physics, Lab Nuclear Physics, 1967-1987; dir, Lab Nuclear Physics, 1965-1969; from asst prof to assoc prof, Univ Montreal, 1959-1967; res assoc physics, Univ Md, 1957-1959. **Memberships:** Can Asn Physicists (pres, 1976-1977); Natural Sci & Eng Res Coun Can (vpres, 1981-1986). **Research Statement & Publications:** Nuclear spectroscopy; nuclear reactions at low energy. **Mailing Address:** 190 Willowdale PH One, Outremont, PQ H3T 1G2, Can.

LEVETIN, MARTIN, ELECTRICAL ENGINEERING. **Education:** Pace Univ, MS; Northeastern Univ, BS, PhD (elec eng). **Professional Experience:** VPRES, Mobilepro Corp, as of 2006. **Mailing Address:** Ram Mobile Data, 10 Woodbridge Ctr Suite 950, Woodbridge, NJ 07869. **Fax:** 732-602-5285.

LEVETIN AVERY, ESTELLE, MYCOLOGY, BOTANY. **Personal Data:** b Boston, Mass, March 24, 1945. **Education:** State Col Boston, BS, 1966; Univ RI, PhD (bot & mycol), 1971. **Professional Experience:** PROF BOT, UNIV TULSA, as of 2004; assoc prof bot, Univ Tulsa, beginning 1978; consult, joint res prog, allergy clin tulsa inc, 1975-1976; asst prof, Univ Tulsa, 1972-1978; asst prof physiol, Mt St Joseph Col, 1972; fel res assoc, dept plant path, 1971-1972; asst prof, exten div, 1971-1972; lab instr & teaching asst bot, Univ RI, 1969-1971. **Memberships:** Mycol Soc Am; Bot Soc Am; Int Asn Aerobiol; Brit Mycol Soc; Pan Am Aerobiol Asn. **Research Statement & Publications:** Fungal allergens; distribution of fleshy fungi in Oklahoma; distribution of air-borne fungi and pollen in Tulsa County; allergenic spores and pollen; indoor air bioaerosols. **Mailing Address:** Dept Biol Sci, Univ Tulsa, 600 S Col, Tulsa, OK 74104. **Fax:** 918-631-2764. **E-Mail:** biol_el@utulsa.edu

LEVEY, DOUGLAS J, ECOLOGY, BEHAVIOR-ETHOLOGY. **Personal Data:** b Boston, Mass, September 20, 1957. **Education:** Earlham Col, BA, 1979; Univ Wis, MS, 1982, PhD (zoology), 1986. **Professional Experience:** PROF ORNITH, DEPT ZOOLOGY, UNIV FLA, as of 2005; asst prof ornith, Univ Fla, 1988; Archie Carr fel zoology, 1987-1988. **Memberships:** Ecol Soc Am; Am Ornithologists Union; Asn Trop Biol; Animal Behav Soc. **Research Statement & Publications:** Community structure and co-evolution of fruit eating birds and fruiting plants in the tropics; digestive physiology of frugivores; seed dispersal systems. **Mailing Address:** Dept Zoology, Univ Fla, 621 Carr PO Box 118525, Gainesville, FL 32611-8525. **Fax:** 352-392-3704. **E-Mail:** dlevey@zoo.ufl.edu

LEVEY, GERALD SAUL, INTERNAL MEDICINE, ENDOCRINOLOGY. **Personal Data:** b Jersey City, NJ, January 9, 1937. **Education:** Cornell Univ, AB, 1957; NJ Col Med, MD, 1961. **Professional Experience:** VICE CHANCELLOR & DEAN, MED SCI & DAVID GEFFEN SCH MED, UNIV CALIF, as of 2004; chmn, dept med, sch med, Univ Pa, Philadelphia, as of 2002; prof, sch med, Univ Miami, Fla, beginning 1973; investr, Howard Hughes Med Inst, beginning 1971; consult med, Vet Admin Hosp, Miami, Fla, 1970-, assoc prof med, 1970-1973, sr investr endocrinol, Nat Heart & Lung Inst, 1969-1970; clin assoc endocrinol, Nat Inst Arthritis & Metab Dis, 1966-1968; resident, Mass Gen Hosp, Boston, 1965-1966; NIH fel biochem, Med Sch, Harvard Univ, 1963-1965; resident, Jersey City Med Ctr, 1962-1963; intern med, Jersey City Med Ctr, 1961-1962. **Memberships:** Am Soc Clin Invest; Am Col Physicians; Am Thyroid Asn; Am Fedn Clin Res; Soc Exp Biol & Med. **Research Statement & Publications:** Mechanism of hormone action; cyclic adenosine monophosphate. **Mailing Address:** David Geffen Sch Med, 12-138 Ctr Health Sci, Los Angeles, CA 90095-1722. **Fax:** 310-825-4955. **E-Mail:** glevey@mednet.ucla.edu

LEVEY, HAROLD ABRAM, ENDOCRINE PHYSIOLOGY. **Personal Data:** b Boston, Mass, August 14, 1924. **Education:** Harvard Univ, AB, 1947; Univ Calif, Los Angeles, PhD (zoology), 1953. **Professional Experience:** China Med Bd vis prof physiol, Fac Med, Univ Singapore, 1966-1967; ASSOC PROF PHYSIOL, COL MED, STATE UNIV NY DOWNSTATE MED CTR, 1964-; from instr to asst prof, Col Med, State Univ NY Downstate Med Ctr, 1956-1964; USPHS fel, 1953-, Jr & asst res physiol chemist, Univ Calif, Los Angeles, 1953-1956. **Memberships:** AAAS; Am Physiol Soc; Endocrine Soc; NY Acad Sci; Harvey Soc. **Research Statement & Publications:** Pituitary chemistry and physiology; pituitary-thyroid interrelationships; factors influencing metabolism of endocrine organs; electrophysiology of thyroid. **Mailing Address:** Dept Physiol Box 31, 160 Columbia Hts Apt 9B, Brooklyn, NY 11201.

LEVI, ANTHONY FREDERIC JOHN, ELECTRONIC & OPTO-ELECTRONIC DEVELOPMENT. **Personal Data:** b London, Eng, February 3, 1959. **Education:** Univ Sussex, England, BS, 1980; Univ Cambridge, England, PhD (physics), 1983. **Professional Experience:** PROF ELEC ENG, PHYS & ASTRON, UNIV S CALIF, 1993-; distinguished mem technol staff physics, AT&T Bell Labs, beginning 1988; mem technol staff physics, AT&T Bell Labs, 1984-1988. **Memberships:** Am Physical Soc. **Research Statement & Publications:** Experimental and theoretical study of nonequilibrium electron transport in unipolar and bipolar semiconductor transistor structures; electron dynamics in quantized systems; exploration of new materials for electronic and opto-electronic device applications. **Mailing Address:** Dept Physics & Astron, Univ S Calif, KAP 132, Los Angeles, CA 90089-2533. **Fax:** 213-740-9280. **E-Mail:** alevi@usc.edu

LEVI, BARBARA GOSS, ARMS CONTROL, ENERGY & ENVIRONMENT. **Personal Data:** b Washington, DC, May 5, 1943; m 1966, Ilan; c Daniel S & Sharon R. **Education:** Carleton Col, BA, 1965; Stanford Univ, MS, 1967, PhD (physics), 1971. **Professional Experience:** JOURNALIST RESIDENCE, JOURNALIST FEL PROG KAVLI INST THEORETICAL PHYSICS, UNIV CALIF, SANTA BARBARA, as of 2004; CONTRIBUTING ED, PHYSICS TODAY, 2003-; mem exec bd, Forum Physics & Soc, Am Phys Soc, 1994-1996; sr ed, Physics Today, 1993-2003; counr, ForumPhysics & Soc, Am Phys Soc, 1992-1995; mem educ comt, Forum Physics & Soc, Am Phys Soc, 1989-1991; vis prof, Rutgers Univ, 1988-1989; chmn, Forum Physics & Soc, Am Phys Soc, 1988-1989; from assoc ed to sr assoc ed, Physics Today, 1987-1993; mem tech staff, Bell Labs, 1981-1982; mem res staff, Ctr Energy & Environ Studies, Princeton Univ, 1980-1982 & 1983-1987; consult, Off Technol Assessment, US Cong, 1976-1995; lectr, Ga Inst Technol, 1976-1980; mem task force energy, Am Asn Univ Women, 1975-1977; consult eed, Physics Today, 1970-1987 & 1988-1989; lectr physics, Fairleigh Dickinson Univ, 1970-1976. **Memberships:** fel Am Phys Soc; Am Asn Physics Teachers; fel AAAS. **Research Statement & Publications:** Writing news of current physics research; problems of science and society; arms control; global warming. **Mailing Address:** Kavli Inst Theoretical Physics, Univ Calif, Kohn Hall, Santa Barbara, CA 93106. **Fax:** 805-893-2431. **E-Mail:** bgl@physics.ucsb.edu

LEVI, DAVID WINTERTON, POLYMER CHEMISTRY. **Personal Data:** b Berryville, Va, September 2, 1921. **Education:** Randolph-Macon Col, BS, 1943; Va Polytech Inst, MS, 1951, PhD (chem), 1954. **Professional Experience:** SUPVRY CHEMIST, PICATINNY ARSENAL, DOVER, 1959-; From instrto assoc prof chem, Va Polytech Inst, 1946-1959. **Memberships:** Am Chem Soc. **Research Statement & Publications:** Solution properties of high polymers; polymer-energetic compatibility; adhesives; thermal degradation of polymers. **Mailing Address:** 17533 Victory Blvd, Van Nuys, CA 91406.

LEVI, ELLIOTT J, ORGANIC CHEMISTRY, PHYSICAL CHEMISTRY. **Personal Data:** b Brooklyn, NY, June 12, 1940. **Education:** City Col NY, BS, 1961; Univ Cincinnati, PhD (chem), 1966. **Professional Experience:** RETIRED; dir res planning, Ashland Chem Corp, 1985-1987; dir res &develop, Drew Chem Corp, 1981-1987; res mgr chem, Drew Chem Corp, 1970-1980; group leader, Chem Systs Inc, 1968-1970; adj asst prof, Upsala Col, 1967-1971; chief chemist, ApolloChem Corp, 1966-1968. **Memberships:** Sigma Xi. **Mailing Address:** 1307 Mercedes St, Teaneck, NJ 07666-2130.

LEVI, HERBERT WALTER, ARACHNOLOGY, SYSTEMATICS. **Personal Data:** b Frankfurt am Main, Ger, January 3, 1921; American citizen; m 1949, Lorna Rose; c Frances. **Education:** Univ Conn, BS, 1946; Univ Wis, MS, 1947, PhD (zool), 1949. **Honorary Degrees:** AM, Harvard Univ, 1970. **Honors & Awards:** Hon cur, Univ Panama Mus Inver. **Professional Experience:** PROF EMER BIOL, HARVARD UNIV, 1991-; pres, Ctr Int Document Arachnology, 1980-1983; vis prof, Hebrew Univ Jerusalem, 1975; Agassiz prof zool, Harvard Univ, 1972-1991; prof biol, Harvard Univ, 1970-1972; cur Arachnology, Mus Comp Zool, 1966-1991; vpres, Ctr Int Document Arachnology, 1965-1968; lectr biol, Harvard Univ, 1964-1970; mem fac educ, Harvard Univ, 1964-1966; secy, Rocky Mountain Biol Lab, 1959-1965; from asst cur to assoc cur, Mus, 1955-1966; from instr to assoc prof bot & zool, Exten Div, Univ Wis, 1949-1956. **Memberships:** Fel AAAS; Am Arachnol Soc (pres 1979-1981); Soc Syst Zool; Am Ecol Soc; Am Inst Biol Sci; Am Micros Soc; Soc Study Evolution; Soc Syst Biol; Am Soc Zool; Int Soc Arachnology. **Research Statement & Publications:** Evolution; systematic zoology; spiders and other arachnids; animal transplantation; systematic studies of orb-weaving spiders in the family Araneidae and Tetragnathidae. **Mailing Address:** Mus Comp Zool, Harvard Univ, 26 Oxford St, Cambridge, MA 02138-2902. **E-Mail:** herblevi@mac.com

LEVI, IRVING, MEDICINAL CHEMISTRY. **Personal Data:** b Winnipeg, Man, December 15, 1914. **Education:** Univ Man, BSc, 1938, MSc, 1939; McGill Univ, PhD (chem), 1942. **Professional Experience:** PRES, ALMEDIC DIV, RHOING LTD, 1968-; sr res chemist, Charles EFrosst & Co, 1948-1968; lectr, McGill Univ, 1946-1947; res assoc, McGill Univ, 1944-1946; Carnegie Corp res fel, McGill Univ, 1942-1943; Civilian with Can Govt, 1940-1944. **Memberships:** Am Chem Soc; fel Chem Inst Can. **Research Statement & Publications:** Organic synthesis; carbohydrates; synthetic analgesics and sedatives; antibiotic and cancer chemotherapy; amino acids and derivatives; steroids and hormones; medicinal applications of natural products and derivatives. **Mailing Address:** 22 Glenmore Rd, Hampstead, PQ H3X 3M6, Can.

LEVI, MICHAEL PHILLIP, FOREST PRODUCTS. **Personal Data:** b Leeds, Eng, February 5, 1941. **Education:** Univ Leeds, BS, 1961, PhD (biophys), 1964. **Professional Experience:** PROF WOOD PAPER SCI, NC STATE UNIV, 1977-; assoc prof forestry, NC State Univ, 1971-1977; head res wood preservation, Timber Res & Develop Lab, Hickson &Welch Eng, 1968-1971; sr biologist, Timber Res & Develop Lab, Hickson & Welch Eng, 1967-1968; Sci Res Coun-NATO res fel, Univ Leeds, 1966-1967; res fel, NC State Univ, 1965-1966; Fulbright travel scholar & res fel wood prod path, Sch Forestry, Yale Univ, 1965. **Memberships:** Forest Prod Res Soc; Royal Soc Chem; Am Phytopath Soc. **Research Statement & Publications:** Wood preservation; mode of action of fungicides; wood deterioration by fungi; wood as fuel. **Mailing Address:** 4909 Lites Rd, Raleigh, NC 27606.

LEVI, ROBERTO, PHARMACOLOGY, CARDIOVASCULAR IMMUNOPHARMACOLOGY. **Personal Data:** b Milano, Italy, March 2, 1934. **Education:** Univ Florence, MD, 1960. **Honors & Awards:** Pfizer Lect, Clin Pharmacol, Univ Minn Med Sch, 1987; Geoffrey B WestMem Lect, Europ Histamine Res Soc, 1993. **Professional Experience:** Vis prof, Dept Anesthesiol, Sch Med, Emory Univ, 1990; conf co-chmn, BiolLeukotrienes, NY Acad Sci, 1987; Sterling Drug vis prof, Med Sch, Ore Health Sci Univ, 1987; PROF PHARMACOL, MED COL, CORNELL UNIV, 1977-; vis prof pharmacol, ColPhysicians & Surgeons, Columbia Univ, 1977-1978, Nat Inst Gen Med Sci grant, 1974-1981, prin investr, NY Heart Asn grant, 1968-1971, 1971-1973 & 1974-1976, co-investr, NIHgrant, 1967-1969; prin investr, USPHS grant, 1967-1968; from asst prof to assoc prof, Med Col, Cornell Univ, 1966-1977; sr res fel electrophysiol, Univ Florence, 1963-1966; Fulbright travel fel pharmacol & exp therapeut, Sch Med, Johns Hopkins Univ, 1961-1963; asst pharmacol, Univ Florence, 1960-1961. **Memberships:** Am Soc Pharmacol & Exp Therapeut; Am Asn Immunologists; Am AsnPathologists; Int Soc Heart Res. **Research Statement & Publications:** Cardiovascular pharmacology; heart electrophysiology; neuropharmacology; immunopharmacology; autonomic pharmacology; pharmacology of mediators of immediate hypersensitivity; role of histamine in cardiac function and dysfunction; synthesis, release, actions of EDRF/nitric oxide in the heart and vasculature. **Mailing Address:** Dept Pharmacol, Cornell Univ Med Col 1300 York Ave, New York, NY 10021-4896. **Fax:** 212-746-8835. **E-Mail:** rlevi@cumc.cornell.edu

LEVIALDI, STEFANO, PARALLEL PROCESSING, MULTICOMPUTER ARCHITECTURES. **Personal Data:** b Rome, Italy, November 6, 1936. **Education:** Marconi Col, cert advan electronics, 1961. **Professional Experience:** Co-ed, J Visual Lang & Comput, 1989-; Image & Vision Comput, 1983- & JParallel & Distrib Comput, 1984-; PROF COMPUT SCI, UNIV ROME, 1983-; Assoc ed, Pattern Recognition Lett, 1982-; prof comput sci, Univ Bari, Italy, 1981-1983; Assoc ed, PatternRecognition, 1980-; Assoc ed, Computer Vision, Graphics & Image Processing & SignalProcessing, 1979-; sr researcher image processing, Ital Nat Coun Res, 1968-1981; Lectrelectronics, Univ Genoa, 1961-1965 & Univ Naples, 1966-1968. **Memberships:** Fel Inst Elec & Electronics Engrs; Int Asn Pattern Recognition (vpres, 1990-). **Research Statement & Publications:** Image analysis and understanding, algorithms, languages, architectures; visual languages; iconic interfaces; scientific visualization; computational metaphors. **Mailing Address:** Scienze Dell' Informazione, Univ Di Roma La Sapienza via Salaria 113, Rome 00198, Italy.

LEVICH, CALMAN, RADIATION BIOPHYSICS, AUTOMOBILE ACCIDENT ANALYSIS. **Personal Data:** b Iowa City, Iowa, May 26, 1921. **Education:** Morningside Col, BS, 1949; Cath Univ Am, PhD (physics), 1966. **Professional Experience:** Mem, Mich Indoor Radon Task Force, 1987-1990; PRES, CALEB ASSOCS, 1983-; PROF EMER PHYSICS, CENT MICH UNIV, 1983-; governor's task force on high levelradiation waste, legislative off sci adv, State Mich, 1983-1986; radiation adv bd, legislative off sci adv, State Mich, 1982-1990; Mem, legislative off sci adv, State Mich, 1980-1981; chmndept, Caleb Assocs, 1975-1983; prof, Caleb Assocs, 1970-1983; chmn dept, Seton Hall Univ, 1968-1970; assoc prof physics, Cent Mich Univ, 1967-1968; proj dir, Armed Forces Radiobiol Res Inst, 1961-1967; Biophysicist, Naval Med Res Inst, 1950-1961. **Memberships:** AAAS; Biophys Soc; Radiation Res Soc; Am Asn Physics Teachers; Sigma Xi. **Research Statement & Publications:** Radiation biophysics; reactor operator education; radiation safety and transport of radioactive materials. **Mailing Address:** Dept Physics, Cent Mich Univ, Mt Pleasant, MI 48859. **E-Mail:** clevich@aol.com

LEVIE, HAROLD WALTER, SURFACE PHYSICS. **Personal Data:** b Augusta, Ga, January 17, 1949. **Education:** William Marsh Rice Univ, BA, 1971, MS, 1973, PhD (mat sci), 1976. **Professional Experience:** MAT SCIENTIST SURFACE TECHNOL, INORG MAT DIV, LAWRENCE LIVERMORE LAB, 1975-; instr corrosion eng, Nat Asn Corrosion Engrs, 1975; physicist, PhysSci Lab, US Army Missile Command, 1971. **Memberships:** Nat Asn Corrosion Engrs; Sigma Xi. **Research Statement & Publications:** Analysis and characterization of solid surfaces; kinetics of surface reactions and interface formation. **Mailing Address:** 4279 Amherst Way, Livermore, CA 94550-4901. **E-Mail:** levie@llnl.gov

LEVIEN, LOUISE, PETROPHYSICS, CRYSTALLOGRAPHY. **Personal Data:** b New York, NY, March 23, 1952. **Education:** Brown Univ, ScB, 1974; State Univ NY, Stony Brook, MS, 1975, PhD (geochem), 1979. **Professional Experience:** RES SUPVR, EXXON PROD RES CO, 1994-; sr planning asst, Exxon ProdRes Co, 1992-1994; sr res specialist, Exxon Prod Res Co, 1991-1992; res specialist, Exxon ProdRes Co, 1984-1991; res geologist, Exxon Prod Res Co, 1981-1984; mem educ & humanresources comt, Am Geophys Union, 1980-1984; chmn, Am Geol Inst Women GeoscientistsComt, 1980; Weizmann fel, Calif Inst Technol, 1979-1981; Mem, Am Geol Inst WomenGeoscientists Comt, 1978-1980. **Memberships:** Am Asn Petrol Geologists; Am Geophys Union; Mineral Soc Am; Soc Prof WellLog Analysts; Soc Petrol Engrs. **Research Statement & Publications:** Geochemistry and geophysics of hydrocarbon reservoirs; relationship of elastic properties and crystal chemistry of minerals. **Mailing Address:** Exxon Prod Res Co, PO Box 2189, Houston, TX 77252-2189.

LEVIEN, ROGER ELI, INFORMATION SCIENCE, TECHNOLOGY STRATEGY. **Personal Data:** b Brooklyn, NY, April 16, 1935; m 1960, Carla; c Roy & Alisa. **Education:** Swarthmore Col, BS, 1956; Harvard Univ, MS, 1958, PhD (appl math), 1962. **Honors & Awards:** Austrian Ehrenkreuz First Class, Sci & Art. **Professional Experience:** PRES, STRATEGY & INNOVATION CONSULT, 1997-; vpres, Strat & Innovation, Xerox Corp, 1995-1997; vpres, Technol & Market Develop, Xerox Corp, 1992-1995; vpres, Strategy Off, Xerox Corp, 1985-1992; dir strategicsysts anal, Xerox Corp, 1982-1985; dir, Int Inst Appl Systs Anal, Austria, 1975-1981; proj leader, Int Inst Appl Systs Anal, Austria, 1974-1975; mgr, Wash Domestic Progs, 1971-1974; adj prof, Univ Calif, Los Angeles, 1970-1974; head, Syst Sci Dept, 1967-1971; mem, res staff, RandCorp, 1960-1967; vpres, Xerox 2005, Xerox Corp, 1996-1997. **Memberships:** Asn Comput Mach; Inst Elec & Electronics Engrs; AAAS; Asn Pub Policy Anal& Mgt. **Research Statement & Publications:** Policy analysis; research and development management; information sciences; strategic planning; tehnology strategy; document processing technology. **Mailing Address:** Strategy & Innovation Consult, 2 River Lane, Westport, CT 06880. **Fax:** 203-222-7150. **E-Mail:** rlevien@aol.com

LEVI-MONTALCINI, RITA, GROWTH FACTORS. **Personal Data:** b Torino, Italy, April 22, 1909; Italian & American citizen. **Education:** Univ Turin, MD, 1940. **Honorary Degrees:** Dr, Univ Uppsala, Sweden, 1977, St Mary's & Notre Dame's Col, 1980; PhD, Wash Univ Med Sch, St Louis, Mo, 1982, Univ London, Eng, 1987, Univ Buenos Aires, 1987, Loyola Univ, Chicago, 1987 & Biophys Inst, Univ Brazil, 1987, Harvard Univ, 1989 & UnivUrbino.

Honors & Awards: Nobel Prize Med/Physiol, 1986; Max Weinstein Award, Cerebral Palsy Found, 1962; Harvey Lectr, 1965; Feltrinelli Int Prize Med, 1969; Golden Plate Award, Am AcadAchievement, 1970; Ibico-Reggino Award Biol Sci, 1970; Int St Vincent Award, 1979; Knightsof Humanity Award, Int Philanthrop Soc, 1979; Gold Medal Sci, Rome, 1986; Albert LaskerMed Res Award, 1986; Thudicum Award & Lectr, Eng, 1987; US Nat Medal Sci, 1987; GoldMedal, Ministry Pub Health, Rome, 1988. **Professional Experience:** Mem, Int Sci Adv Bd, Int Acad Biomed & Drug Res, Belgium, 1990; NatComt Bioethics, Italy, & Nat Comn Unesco, Italy, 1990; FAC MEM, INST NEUROBIOL, DEPT BIOL, COMN NATURAL RESOURCES, NAT RES COUN, ROME, 1989-, guest prof, Inst Neurobiol, 1989; researcher/guest prof, Cellular Biol Lab, 1979-1989; Fogarty scholar, Washington, DC, 1978; EMER PROF NEUROBIOL, INST BIOL, WASH UNIV, 1977-; dir, Cellular Biol Lab, 1969-1979; Dir, Neurobiol Res Ctr, Comn Natural Resources, Nat Res Coun, 1961-1969; from assoc prof to prof, Inst Biol, 1951-1981; res assoc, Inst Zool, 1947-1951; Asstprof anat, Univ Turin, 1945-1947. **Memberships:** Nat Acad Sci; AAAS; Soc Develop Biol; Am Asn Anatomists; hon mem TissueCult Asn; Sigma Xi; Am Acad Arts & Sci; Am Philos Soc; hon mem Am Soc Zoologists; honmem Am Med Women's Asn; Nat Acad Sci Italy; Belg Royal Acad Med; Europ Acad Sci; AcadArts & Sci Florence; Nat Acad die Lineei; Pontifical Acad. **Research Statement & Publications:** Experimental neurology; effect of a nerve growth factor isolated from the mouse salivary gland on the sympathetic nervous system and of an antiserum to the nerve growth factor; specific growth factors. **Mailing Address:** Inst Neurobiol, Nat Res Coun Viale Marx 15, Rome 00156, Italy.

LEVIN, AARON R, PEDIATRICS, CARDIOLOGY. **Personal Data:** b Johannesburg, SAfrica, March 19, 1929; m 1955, Lenore; c 3. **Education:** Univ Witwatersrand, BSc, 1948, MBBCh, 1953, MD, 1968; Royal Col Physicians & Surgeons, dipl child health, 1960; FRCP, 1981. **Professional Experience:** PROF PEDIAT, NY MED COL, 1994-; from asst prof to prof pediat, Med Ctr, Cornell Univ, 1966-1994; instr pediat, Med Ctr, Duke Univ, 1964-1966; NIH fel cardiol, Med Ctr, Duke Univ, 1964-1966; gen pract, 1962-1963; pediat registr, Charing Cross Hosp, Eng, 1961; pediat registr, 1956-1960; pediat intern, Coronation Hosp, 1955-1956; sr intern, Johannesburg Fever Hosp, 1955; intern, Edenvale Hosp, SAfrica, 1954-1955; attend physician, Pediat Intensive Care Unit, NY Hosp-Cornell Med Ctr. **Memberships:** Fel Royal Col Physicians; Soc Pediat Res; Am Pediat Soc; Am Heart Asn; Am Col Cardiol. **Research Statement & Publications:** Pediatric cardiology, specifically related to studies of pressure-flow dynamics in various forms of congenital heart disease; extra cardiac factors in congenital heart disease; right ventricular hypertrophy at cellular level. **Mailing Address:** Pediat Cardiol Sect, NY Med Col, 618 Munger Pavilion, Valhalla, NY 10595. **Fax:** 914-594-4513.

LEVIN, ALAN EDWARD, FISSION REACTOR THERMAL-HYDRAULICS, NUCLEAR REACTOR SAFETY. **Personal Data:** b Baltimore, Md, May 17, 1953; m 1988, Bonnie; c Ariel L & Jonathan M. **Education:** Mass Inst Technol, SB (mech eng), 1975, ScD(fission reactor eng), 1980. **Honors & Awards:** Fellow, American Nuclear Society, 2003. **Professional Experience:** Technical Consultant, Framatome ANP, 2005-; Sr. Tech. Advsr. to Dir. of Research, US Nuclear Regulatory Comn, 2003-2005; Sr Asst for Reactors, Off of the Chmn, US Nuclear Regulatory Comn, 1999-2003; sr reactor engr, US Nuclear Regulatory Comn, 1992-1999; reactor engr, US Nuclear Regulatory Comn, 1990-1992; summer fac fel, Oak Ridge Assoc Univs, 1989; assoc prof nuclear eng, Ga Inst Technol, 1986-1990; professional engr, 1983-; staff mem, Oak Ridge Nat Lab, 1980-1986. **Memberships:** Am Nuclear Soc; Wash Interships for Students of Eng, Steering Comt, 1999-. **Research Statement & Publications:** Regulatory analysis of nuclear reactor technology; nuclear reactor thermal-hydraulics and safety; testing related to advanced power reactor designs. **Mailing Address:** 12410 Rousseau Terr, North Potomac, MD 20878. **E-Mail:** alevin@alum.mit.edu

LEVIN, ALFRED A, RESEARCH ADMINISTRATION, AGRICULTURAL & FOOD CHEMISTRY. **Personal Data:** b Chicago, Ill, May 18, 1928. **Education:** Univ Ill, Urbana, BS, 1951; Loyola Univ, Chicago, MS, 1962. **Professional Experience:** RETIRED; dir toxic substances control, labels & petitions, 1980-; dir staff &support progs, labels & petitions, 1978-1980; dir govt compliance, labels & petitions, 1976-1978; mgr, labels & petitions, 1970-1975; res chemist, Velsicol Chem Corp, 1955-1970; Chemist, Leaf Brands Inc, 1951-1953 & Wallace A Erickson & Co, 1953-1955. **Memberships:** Am Chem Soc; Am Inst Chemists. **Research Statement & Publications:** Synthesis of chemicals with intended pesticidal properties. **Mailing Address:** 8242 Ridgeway, Skokie, IL 60076.

LEVIN, ALLAN B, NEUROSURGERY. **Professional Experience:** UNIV WIS HOSP & CLIN, as of 1995. **Mailing Address:** Univ Wis Hosp & Clin, 600 Highland Ave, Madison, WI 53792.

LEVIN, ANDREW ELIOT, EXPERIMENTAL BIOLOGY. **Personal Data:** b Newton, Mass, March 9, 1954. **Education:** Princeton Univ, BA, 1976; Univ Wis-Madison, 1984. **Professional Experience:** CHIEF EXEC OFFICER & SCI DIR, IMMUNETICS INC, as of 2004; FOUNDER & PRES, IMMUNETICS INC, 1987-; fel, Dept Cellular & Develop Biol, Harvard Univ, 1984-1987; res technician, Genetics Unit, Mass Gen Hosp, 1976-1977; consult ed, Encycl Sci Instruments; adv bd mem, Am Chem Soc; consult, Soviet biotechnol & biomed res technol. **Memberships:** Am Soc Cell Biol. **Research Statement & Publications:** Immunochemistry and immunoassays; protein purification and characterization; cell culture; monoclonal antibodies and hybridoma production; immunofluorescence microscopy; four patents. **Mailing Address:** Immunetics Inc, 380 Green St, Cambridge, MA 02139. **Fax:** 617-868-7879.

LEVIN, ARTHUR A, TOXICOLOGY. **Education:** Univ Rochester Sch Med & Dent, PhD (Toxicol). **Professional Experience:** VPRES TOXICOL & PHARMACOKINETICS, ISIS PHARMCEUT INC, CALIF, 1995-. **Mailing Address:** Hoffmann LaRoche Inc, 340 Kingsland St, Nutley, NJ 07110-1199.

LEVIN, BARBARA CHERNOV, MICROBIOLOGY. **Personal Data:** b Providence, RI, May 5, 1939; m. **Education:** Brown Univ, BA, 1961; Georgetown Univ, PhD (microbial genetics), 1973. **Professional Experience:** PRIN INVEST MITOCHONDRIAL RES & GEN TOXICOL, as of 2004; RES BIOLOGIST BIOTECHNOL, NAT INST STAND & TECHNOL, 1993-2000; consult, Fire Toxicol & Inhalation Toxicol, 1992-1993; adj prof, Fire Protection Eng Dept, Univ Md, College Park, 1991-; counr, Am Col Toxicol, 1989-1991; proj leader fire toxicol, Nat Inst Stand & Technol, 1985-1992; chmn, Tech Adv Group, Int Standards Orgn, 1984-1994; mem & comt toxicity complex mixtures, Nat Acad Sci, 1984-1988; lectr environ toxicol, Grad Sch, NIH, 1983-1991; group leader, Nat Bur Stand, 1981-1985; sci officer, Extramural Res, 1978-1992; res biologist, Nat Bur Stand, 1978-1981; mem, comt develop toxicity, Nat Bur Stand, 1978-1982; staff fel, NIH, 1975-1978; fel molecular biol, NIH, 1973-1975; teaching asst biol, Georgetown Univ, 1968-1973; res asst endocrinol, Sch Med, Johns Hopkins Univ, 1962-1963; mem, Comt Improved Fire & Smoke Resistant Mat. **Memberships:** Soc Toxicol; Am Chem Soc; Sigma Xi; Am Col Toxicol; Asn Govt Toxicologists; Am Soc Testing & Mat. **Research Statement & Publications:** Toxicology of combustion products; assessment of acute inhalation toxicity; development of model to predict toxicity; mutagenesis and repair of DNA; DNA technology. **Mailing Address:** Nat Inst Stand & Technol, Bldg 227 Rm B224 100 Bureau Dr, Gaithersburg, MD 20899-8312. **Fax:** 301-330-3447. **E-Mail:** barbara.levin@nist.gov

LEVIN, BARRY EDWARD, NEUROBIOLOGY, NEUROLOGY. **Personal Data:** b Brooklyn, NY, May 1, 1942. **Education:** Emory Univ, MD, 1967; Am Bd Psychiat & Neurol, dipl. **Professional Experience:** ATTEND NEUROLOGIST, MARTLAND HOSP, COL MED NJ, 1978-; staff neurologist, Vet Admin Hosp, E Orange, NJ, 1977-; dir lab neuropharmacol & dept Neurosci, Col Med NJ, 1977-; PROF NEUROSCI, NJ MED SCH, UNIV MED & DENT NJ, 1977-; assoc prof Neurosci, Col Med NJ, beginning 1977; grantee, Vet Admin Res & Educ grant, 1974-; asst prof neurol & psychiat, Dartmouth Med Sch, 1974-1977; clin assoc, Nat Inst Neurol Dis & Blindness, 1972-1974; instr & chief resident neurol, Cornell Med Sch, 1971-1972. **Memberships:** Soc Neuroscience; Am Acad Neurol. **Research Statement & Publications:** Metabolism, axonal transport and rhythms of catecholamines in health and disease. **Mailing Address:** Dept Neuro Sci, NJ Med Sch, Univ Med & Dent NJ, Neurol Serv 127C VA Med Ctr E, Orange, NJ 07019. **Fax:** 973-972-5059, 973-395-7112. **E-Mail:** levin@umdnj.edu

LEVIN, BRUCE, MATHEMATICAL STATISTICS. **Personal Data:** b New York, NY, March 14, 1948. **Education:** Columbia Univ, BA, 1968; Harvard Univ, MA, 1972, PhD (appl math), 1974. **Professional Experience:** HEAD, DIV BIOSTATISTICS, COLUMBIA UNIV, as of 2006; chair, div biostatistics, Columbia Univ, 2000-; PROF PUB HEALTH BIOSTATISTICS, COLUMBIA UNIV, 1994-; dep head, div biostatistics, Columbia Univ, 1993-1998; assoc prof pub health biostatistics, Columbia Univ, 1992-1994; assoc prof clin pub health biostatistics, Columbia Univ, 1983-1985; asst prof clin pub health biostatistics, Columbia Univ, 1982-1983; statistician, Gertrude H Sergievsky Ctr Columbia Univ, NY, 1979-; sr res scientist, NY State Psychiat Inst, NY, 1979-1997; asst prof pub health biostatistics, Columbia Univ, 1979-1982; consult, Statistica Inc, 1978-; asst prof math statist & pub health biostatistics, Columbia Univ, 1976-1979; asst prof math statist, Columbia Univ, 1974-1979; res asst, Harvard Univ, 1973-1974; data analyst & comput programmer, Albert Einstein Col Med, 1967-1972; teaching asst, Columbia Univ, 1967-1968; consult ed, Am J Pub Health. **Memberships:** fel Am Statist Asn; Inst Math Statist; Sigma Xi. **Research Statement & Publications:** Statistical inference and data analysis; categorical data analysis; conditional likelihood analysis; clinical trials; sequential experimentation; statistics in law; reproductive epidemiology; astronomy; published over 50 articles. **Mailing Address:** Dept Biostatistics, Columbia Univ, 722 W 168th St Rm 626A, New York, NY 10032. **Fax:** 212-305-9408. **E-Mail:** bruce.levin@columbia.edu

LEVIN, DONALD A, BOTANY. **Education:** Univ IIL, BS, 1960, MS, 1962, PhD, 1964. **Honors & Awards:** Charles Lamb Award, Univ Nebr, Lincoln, 1983. **Professional Experience:** PROF, DEPT INTEGRATIVE BIOL, UNIV TEX, AUSTIN, as of 2006. **Mailing Address:** Dept Bot, Univ Tex, Austin, TX 78713. **E-Mail:** dlevin@uts.cc.utexas.edu

LEVIN, EDWIN ROY, SOLID STATE SCIENCE. **Personal Data:** b Philadelphia, Pa, November 4, 1927. **Education:** Temple Univ, AB, 1949, MA, 1951, PhD (physics), 1959. **Professional Experience:** RETIRED; consult, Electron Micros Applications, 1987-1992; guide prof, World Univ, beginning 1973; mem tech staff, RCA Labs, 1963-1987; secy army res & study fel, Cavendish Lab, Cambridge Univ, 1961-1962; physicist, Frankford Arsenal, US Army, 1951-1963; asst physics, Temple Univ, 1949-1951. **Memberships:** AAAS; Am Phys Soc; Electron Micros Soc Am. **Research Statement & Publications:** Solid state physics; theory of dielectrics; photoconductivity; quantum electronics; analysis of solid materials for electronics, including electron microscopy and related methodologies. **Mailing Address:** 37 Pineknoll Dr, PO Box 3263, Trenton, NJ 08648-3143.

LEVIN, EUGENE G, BIOCHEMISTRY. **Personal Data:** b Philadelphia, Pa, May 29, 1948. **Education:** Pa State Univ, BS, 1969; Univ Calif, Irvine, PhD (biochem), 1977. **Professional Experience:** PROF, VASCULAR & CANCER BIOL DIVISIONS, LA JOLLA INST MOLECULAR MED, 1999-; assoc prof, dept molecular & exp med, Scripps & Res Inst, Calif, 1990-1999; asst mem, 1984-1990, Felplasminogen activators, 1978-1983. **Memberships:** Am Heart Asn; Am Soc Cell Biol; Int Soc Fibrinolysis. **Mailing Address:** Dept Vascular & Cancer Biol, La Jolla Inst Molecular Med, 4570 Exec Dr, Ste 100, San Diego, CA 92121. **Fax:** 858-587-6742. **E-Mail:** glevin@ljimm.org

LEVIN, EUGENE (MANUEL), PHYSICS. **Personal Data:** b New York, NY, August 14, 1934; m 1960, c 3. **Education:** Univ Vt, BA, 1956; Columbia Univ, MA, 1959; NY Univ, PhD (physics), 1967. **Professional Experience:** PROF PHYSICS, YORK COL, NY, 1967-. **Research Statement & Publications:** Excited states and fluorescence properties of organic molecules; applications of fluorescence techniques to charged particle dosimetry. **Mailing Address:** York Col City Univ NY, Dept Physics, Jamaica, NY 11451. **E-Mail:** levin@york.cuny.edu

LEVIN, FRANK S, NUCLEAR PHYSICS, FEW-BODY PHYSICS SCATTERING THEORY. **Personal Data:** b Bronx, NY, April 14, 1933; m 1973, c 4. **Education:** Johns Hopkins Univ, AB, 1955; Univ Md, PhD (physics), 1961. **Honors & Awards:** Alexander von Humboldt Sr US Scientist Award, 1979-1980. **Professional Experience:** PROF EMER PHYSICS, BROWN UNIV, as of 2005; prof physics, Brown Univ, 1977-1998; sr vis fel, UK Sci Res Coun, 1974; exchange scientist, US-India Exchange Scientists Prog, 1973; assoc prof, Brown Univ, 1967-1977; temp res assoc, Atomic Energy Res Estab, Eng, 1965-1967; res assoc physics, Brookhaven Nat Lab, 1963-1965 & Rice Univ, 1961-1963; founder, Topical Group Few Body Systs & Multiparticle Dynamics, Am Phys Soc. **Memberships:** Fel Am Phys Soc. **Research Statement & Publications:** Nuclear reaction theory; scattering theory; few-body problems; molecular structure; published over 4 articles. **Mailing Address:** Dept Physics Brown Univ, Barus & Holley Rm 647, Providence, RI 02912. **E-Mail:** fsl@brownvm.brown.edu

LEVIN, FRANKLYN KUSSEL, EXPLORATION GEOPHYSICS. **Personal Data:** b Terre Haute, Ind, June 28, 1922. **Education:** Purdue Univ, BS, 1943; Univ Wis, PhD (physics), 1949. **Honors & Awards:** Robert Earll McConnell Award, 1981; Reginald Fessenden Award, Soc ExplorGeophys, 1984; Maurice Ewing Medal, Soc Explor Geophys, 1988. **Professional Experience:** CONSULT, GEOPHYSICAL CO, as of 2006; ASST ED, GEOPHYSICS, as of 2006; consult, 1987-; sr res scientist, Exxon Prod Res Co, 1973-1986; ed, Geophys, 1969-1971; res scientist, Esso Prod Res Co, 1967-1973; sr res assoc, Esso Prod ResCo, 1965-1967; sr res assoc, Jersey Prod Res Co, Standard Oil Co, 1963-1964; res assoc, JerseyProd Res Co, Standard Oil Co, 1959-1963; Lectr, Univ Tulsa, 1958-1963; physicist, Jersey ProdRes Co, Standard Oil Co, 1958-1959; physicist, Carter Oil Co, 1954-1958; asst dir, Hudson Labs, Columbia Univ, 1953-1954; physicist, Carter Oil Co, 1949-1953; asst physics, Univ Wis, 1946-1947; Physicist, Carbide & Carbon Chem Corp, 1944-1946; Physicist, Sam Labs, Columbia Univ, 1943-1944. **Memberships:** AAAS; Seismol Soc Am; Am Geophys Union; Acoust Soc Am; Soc ExplorGeophys; Europ Asn Explor Geophys; Inst Elec & Electronics Engrs. **Mailing Address:** 802 W Forest Dr, Houston, TX 77079.

LEVIN, GEOFFREY ARTHUR, PLANT SYSTEMATICS. **Personal Data:** b Los Alamos, NMex, December 7, 1955; m 2001, Lori; c Tobias & Madeline. **Education:** Pomona Col, BA, 1977; Univ Calif, Davis, MS, 1980, PhD (bot), 1984. **Honors & Awards:** Jesse M Greenman Award, 1987. **Professional Experience:** DIR, CTR BIODIVERSITY, 1996-; ASSOC PROF SCIENTIST, ILL NATURAL HIST SURV, 1996-2001; PROF SCIENTIST, ILL NATURAL HIST SURV, 2001-; adj prof, Univ Ill, 1995-; res assoc, Mo Bot Garden, 1994-; asst prof scientist, Ctr Biodiversity, 1994-1996; dir res & collections, San Diego Natural Hist Mus, 1993; vis prof biol, Univ San Diego, 1987, 1989-1990; Adj prof bot, San Diego State Univ, 1985-1993; cur bot, San Diego Natural Hist Mus, 1984-1993; Asst prof bot, Ripon Col, 1982-1984. **Memberships:** Bot Soc Am; Am Soc Plant Taxonomists; Sigma Xi; Am Inst Biol Sci; Soc Syst Biol. **Research Statement & Publications:** Systematics of Euphorbiaceae; Mexican flora; midwestern flora. **Mailing Address:** Ctr Biodiversity Ill Natural Hist Surv, 1816 S Oak St, Champaign, IL 61820. **Fax:** 217-244-0729. **E-Mail:** levin1@uiuc.edu

LEVIN, GERSON, MATHEMATICS. **Personal Data:** b Philadelphia, Pa, October 27, 1939. **Education:** Univ Pa, AB, 1961; Univ Chicago, MS, 1962, PhD (math), 1965. **Professional Experience:** STAFF MEM, PRUDENTIAL INS CO, 1985-; assoc prof math, Brooklyn Col, 1976-1985; asst prof, Brooklyn Col, 1974-1976; asst prof, NY Univ, 1967-1974; vis asst prof math, Univ Ore, 1966-1967; NSF fel, Univ Ore, 1966. **Research Statement & Publications:** Commutative rings and homological algebra. **Mailing Address:** 470 First St, Brooklyn, NY 11215.

LEVIN, GIDEON, PHYSICAL ORGANIC CHEMISTRY, PHOTOCHEMISTRY. **Personal Data:** b Mazkeret Ratia, Israel, April 6, 1936. **Education:** Israel Inst Technol, BSc, 1960; Purdue Univ, West Lafayette, MSc, 1965; State UnivNY Col Environ Sci & Forestry, PhD (chem), 1971. **Professional Experience:** AT DEPT MAT RES, WEIZMANN INST SCI, as of 2002; vis scientist, Weizmann Inst Sci, beginnig 1978; SR RES ASSOC, COL ENVIRON SCI & FORESTRY, STATE UNIV NY, 1975-; res assocphotochem, Col Environ Sci & Forestry, State Univ NY, 1972-1975; res assoc photochem, Upsala Univ, 1972; Chemist polymers, Dow Corning Corp, 1965-1967. **Memberships:** Am Chem Soc. **Research Statement & Publications:** Mechanism of photochemical reaction initiated by flash of light which includes conversion of light energy to chemical energy and photo-oxidation and photoreduction of organic and organo metallic molecules which have biological significance. **Mailing Address:** Dept Mat Res, Weizmann Inst Sci, Rehovot 76100, Israel.

LEVIN, GILBERT VICTOR, ENVIRONMENTAL HEALTH, ENGINEERING. **Personal Data:** b Baltimore, Md, April 23, 1924. **Education:** Johns Hopkins Univ, BE, 1947, MS, 1948, PhD (sanit eng), 1963. **Honors & Awards:** IR-100 Indust Res Mag, 1975; Necomb Cleveland Prize, AAAS, 1977. **Professional Experience:** FOUND, SPHERIX INCORP, as of 2001; trustee, Johns Hopkins Univ, 1982-1985; Viking Mission to Mars, 1976; NASA experimenter, Mariner 9, 1971; NASA planetary quarantine adv, 1965-1974; dir, Life Systs Div, 1965-1967; consult, Dept Interior, 1963-1971; dir spec res, Hazleton Labs, Inc, 1963-1965; biochemist, Dept Sanit Eng, DC, 1962-1963; vpres, Resources Res, Inc, 1956-1963; clin asst prof, Schs Med & Dent, Georgetown Univ, 1953-1960; res asst biochem, Schs Med & Dent, Georgetown Univ, 1952-1961; pub health engr, DC, 1951-1956; asst sanit engr, Dept Pub Health, Calif, 1950-1951; jr asst sanit engr, State Dept Health, Md, 1948-1950. **Memberships:** Am Soc Civil Eng; fel Am Pub Health Asn; Water Pollution Control Fedn; NYAcad Sci; Am Inst Biol Sci; AAAS; Am Water Works Asn. **Research Statement & Publications:** Inventor PhoStrip process for wastewater phosphorus removal; Lev-o-cal L-sugar noncaloric sweetener; D-tegatose nonfattening sweetener; life sciences; applied biology; water supply; waste disposal; sanitary biology; environmental sanitation; life detection techniques; public health and medical microbiology; low caloric sweeteners instrumentation; space biology. **Mailing Address:** Spherix Inc, 12051 Indian Creek Ct, Beltsville, MD 20705. **Fax:** 301-210-4909.

LEVIN, HAROLD LEONARD, GEOLOGY, PALEONTOLOGY. **Personal Data:** b St Louis, Mo, March 11, 1929. **Education:** Univ Mo, AB, 1951, MA, 1952; Wash Univ, PhD (paleont), 1956. **Professional Experience:** RETIRED; assoc dean, Col Arts & Sci, 1976-1994; chmn, dept earth & planetary sci, 1973-1976; consult ecol serv, Mo Bot Garden, 1973-1975; prof paleont, Wash Univ, beginning 1971; res grants, Wash Univ, 1961-1972; from asst prof to assoc prof, Wash Univ, 1961-1971; res geologist, Stand Oil Co Calif, 1956-1961. **Memberships:** AAAS; Soc Econ Paleont & Mineral; Paleont Soc; Geol Soc Am. **Research Statement & Publications:** Foraminifera, Coccolithophoridae and related microfossils; biostratigraphy of microorganisms; geological education; author of physical and historical geology and paleontology textbooks. **Mailing Address:** Dept Earth & Planetary Sci, Wash Univ, Campus Box 1169, One Brookings Dr, St Louis, MO 63130. **Fax:** 314-935-7361. **E-Mail:** levin@levee.wustl.edu

LEVIN, HARVEY STEVEN, NEUROPSYCHOLOGY. **Personal Data:** b New York, NY, December 12, 1946. **Education:** City Col, Univ NY, BA, 1967; Univ Iowa, MA, 1971, PhD (clin psychol), 1972. **Honors & Awards:** Caveness Award, Nat Head Injury Found, 1985. **Professional Experience:** Mem, med prof adv bd, Nat Head Injury Found, 1985-; ed, Brain Injury, 1985-; ed, Develop Neuropsychol, 1984-; mem, Vet Admin Merit Rev Bd, 1984-; PROF NEURO PSYCHOLOGY, BAYLOR COL MED, UNIV TEX MED BR, 1984-; Jacob K Javits Neuroscience Investr Award, 1984; ed, J Clin & Exp Neuropsychol, 1983-; vis prof, dept neurosurg, Univ PA, 1981-; ed, Cortex, 1981-; vis lectr, dept psychol, Univ Mo, Columbia, 1981; investr, int study group pharmacol memory, 1978-; prin investr, neuropsychol sect, Nat Inst Neurol & Commun Dis & Stroke Prog Proj, 1975-; from asst prof to assoc prof, Univ Tex Med Br, 1974-1984; intern clin psychol, Ill Masonic Med Ctr, 1973-1974; consult, Dept Neurol, Univ Hosps, Iowa, 1973-1974; Fel, Dept Neurol, Univ Iowa, 1972-1973. **Memberships:** AAAS; fel Am Psychol Asn; Soc Neuroscience; Acad Aphasia. **Research Statement & Publications:** Recovery from brain injury in children and adults; cholinergic augmentation in dementia of the Alzheimer type; visual perception in patients with focal brain lesions. **Mailing Address:** Cognitive Neuroscience Lab, 6560 Fannin, Suite 1144, Houston, TX 77030. **Fax:** 713-798-6898. **E-Mail:** hlevin@bcm.tmc.edu

LEVIN, IRA WILLIAM, BIOPHYSICS, CHEMICAL PHYSICS. **Personal Data:** b Washington, DC, September 20, 1935. **Education:** Univ Va, BS, 1957; Brown Univ, PhD (chem), 1961. **Honors & Awards:** Lippincott Award, 1985; Meggers Award, 1993; Iddles lectr, 1993. **Professional Experience:** Dep chief, lab chem physics, Nih, beginning 1987; actg chief, Lab Chem physics, 1984-1985; CHIEF, SECT MOLECULAR BIOPHYS, NIH, 1979-; assoc mem grad facchem, Georgetown Univ, 1974-1975; res chemist, lab chem physics, NIH, beginning 1972; reschem, phys biol lab, 1966-1972; staff fel, NIH, 1965-1966; lectr, Georgetown Univ, 1964-1965; guest worker, NIH, 1963-1965; res instr chem, Univ Wash, 1961-1962. **Memberships:** Coblentz Soc (pres, 1977-1978); fel Am Phys Soc; Biophys Soc; Am Soc Biol Chemists. **Research Statement & Publications:** Vibrational spectroscopy; absolute intensities; molecular dynamics and structure; spectra; spectroscopy of biomembranes. **Mailing Address:** Lab Chem Phys, Nat Inst Diabetes & Digestive & Kidney Dis, NIH, Bldg 5 B1-32, Bethesda, MD 20892-0510. **E-Mail:** iwl@helix.nih.gov

LEVIN, JACK, INTERNAL MEDICINE, HEMATOLOGY. **Personal Data:** b Newark, NJ, October 11, 1932; m 1975. **Education:** Yale Univ, BA, 1953, MD, 1957; Am Bd Internal Med, dipl, 1965, recert, 1974. **Honors & Awards:** Frederik B Bang Award, 1986; fel foundation for med res, paris, france, 1998; visition prof, biogontrum, univ of basel, basd, suritzadand, 1998. **Professional Experience:** Editor-in-chief, J Endoloxim res ch, 1998-; dir anticoagulation chmic, va hosp, 1996; mem, bd trustees, Marine Biol Lab, Woods Hole, Mass, 1988-1993; dir, Flow Cytometry Facil, Vet Admin Med Ctr, San Francisco, 1987-1990; atten physician Lab Med & Internal Med, Univ Calif Med Ctr, San Francisco, 1986-; ATTEND PHYSICIAN, LAB MED & INTERNAL MED, MED CTR, 1986-; PROF LAB MED & MED, UNIV CALIF SCH MED, SAN FRANCISCO, 1982-; dir, Hemat Lab & Blood Bank, Vet Admin Med Ctr, San Francisco, 1982-1993; prof med, div hemat, 1978-1982; res career develop award, USPHS, 1970-1975; consult, Vet Admin Hosp, Baltimore, Md, 1968-1982; Markle scholar acad med, 1968-1973; physician chg hemat out-patient clin, Johns Hopkins Hosp, 1967-1971, 1976-1982; mem corp, Marine Biol Lab, 1965-; from instr to assoc prof, Johns Hopkins Univ, 1965-1978; Chief resident & instr, Yale Univ, 1964-1965; Fel med, Sch Med, Johns Hopkins Univ, 1962-1964. **Memberships:** Int endotowin soc; Int Soc Hemat; Int Soc Exp Hemat; fel Am Col Physicians; Am Soc Hemat; Am Soc Clin Invest; Sigma Xi. **Research Statement & Publications:** Blood coagulation, platelets; thrombopoiesis; endotoxin and endotoxemia; thrombocytosis; invertebrate blood coagulation; megakaryocytopoiesis; transfusion medicine. **Mailing Address:** Hemat 111H2, Vet Admin Hosp 4150, Clement St, San Francisco, CA 94121-1598. **Fax:** 415-221-7542.

LEVIN, JACOB JOSEPH, MATHEMATICAL ANALYSIS. **Personal Data:** b New York, NY, December 21, 1926. **Education:** City Col NY, BEE, 1949; Mass Inst Technol, PhD, 1953. **Professional Experience:** PROF EMER MATH, UNIV WIS, MADISON, as of 2006; vis prof, Univ BC, 1977-1978; NSF sr fel, Univ Calif, Los Angeles, 1970-1971; prof Math, Univ Wis, Madison 1966-1970; assoc prof, Univ Wis-Madison, 1963-1966; staff mem, Lincoln Lab, 1956-1963; vis lectr, Mass Inst Technol, 1955-1956; instr, Purdue Univ, 1953-1955; instr math, Mass Inst Technol, 1952-1953. **Memberships:** Am Math Soc; Soc Indust & Appl Math. **Research Statement & Publications:** Differential equations; integral equations. **Mailing Address:** Dept Math, Univ Wis, 707 Van Vleck Hall E B 480 Lincoln Dr, Madison, WI 53706.

LEVIN, JEROME ALLEN, MEDICAL INFORMATICS. **Personal Data:** b Washington, DC, August 25, 1939. **Education:** Philadelphia Col Pharm & Sci, BSc, 1961; Univ Mich, PhD (pharmacol), 1966. **Professional Experience:** PROF EMER PHARMACOL, MEDCOL OHIO, 1997-; DIR COMPUTER LEARNING RESOURCE CTR, MED COL OHIO, 1988-; ASSOC DEAN ACAD RESOURCES, MED COL OHIO, 1987-; prof pharmacol, Medcol Ohio, beginning 1979; assoc prof pharmacol, Med Col Ohio, 1974-1979; interim chmn, Med ColOhio, 1973-1975; Am Heart Asn res grant, USPHS res grant, 1970-1976; Am Heart Asn res grant, Med Col Ohio, 1969-1975; asst prof, Med Col Ohio, 1968-1974; USPHS fel, State UnivNY Downstate Med Ctr, 1966-1968; res assoc pharmacol, State Univ NY Downstate Med Ctr, 1966-1968. **Memberships:** AAAS; Am Heart Asn; Am Soc Pharmacol & Exp Therapeut. **Research Statement & Publications:** Computer applications in medicine. **Mailing Address:** Dept Pharmacol, Med Col Ohio, CS 10008, Toledo, OH 43699-0008.

LEVIN, JOSEPH DAVID, industrial microbiology, biology; deceased, see previous edition for last biography

LEVIN, JOSHUA Z, MATHEMATICS. **Professional Experience:** SCIENTIST, SYNGENTA BIOTECHNOL INC, as of 2001. **Memberships:** Am Math Soc. **Mailing Address:** Syngenta Biotechnol Inc, 3054 Cornwallis Rd, Research Triangle Park, NC 27709. **Fax:** 919-541-8585. **E-Mail:** joshua.levin@syngenta.com

LEVIN, JUDITH GOLDSTEIN, VIROLOGY, MOLECULAR GENETICS. **Personal Data:** b Brooklyn, NY, November 8, 1934; m, c 2. **Education:** Barnard Col, Columbia Univ, BA, 1955; Harvard Univ, MA, 1957; Columbia Univ, PhD (biochem), 1962. **Professional Experience:** CHIEF, SEC VIRAL GENE REGULATION, LAB MOLECULAR GENETICS, NAT INST CHILD HEALTH& HUMAN DEVELOP, 1992- Chief, UNIT VIRAL GENE REGULATION, NAT INST CHILD HEALTH& HUMAN DEVELOP, 1984-1992; sr scientist, Lab Molecular Genetics, 1973-1992; estab investr, Am Heart Asn, 1969-1974; Sr scientist molecular biol viruses, Nat Cancer Inst, 1969-1973; consult lab path, Nat Cancer Inst, 1969, Am Heart Asn advan res fel, 1966-1968; USPHS fel, 1963-1965; Nat Heart Inst res fel biochem genetics, 1962-1969. **Memberships:** AAAS; Am Soc Biochem & Molecular Biol; Am Chem Soc; Am Soc Microbiol; Am Soc Virol. **Research Statement & Publications:** Molecular genetics of retrovirus (e.g. HIV) replication: correlation of gene structure with functional activity; reverse transcription and role of viral and host accessory proteins; regulated expression of viral genetic information. **Mailing Address:** Lab Molecular Genetics, Nat Inst Child Health & Human Develop, Rm 216, Bldg 6B, 9000 Rockville Pike, Bethesda, MD 20892-2780. **Fax:** 301-496-0243. **E-Mail:** levinju@mail.nih.gov

LEVIN, KATHRYN J, SOLID STATE PHYSICS THEORY. **Personal Data:** b Lawrence, Kans, February 25, 1944. **Education:** Univ Calif, Berkeley, BA, 1966; Harvard Univ, PhD (physics), 1970. **Professional Experience:** PROF PHYSICS, UNIV CHICAGO, 1985-; asst prof, Univ Chicago, 1975-1985; asst res physicist, Univ Calif, Irvine, 1972-1975; res assoc physics, Univ Rochester, 1970-1972. **Memberships:** Fel Am Phys Soc. **Research Statement & Publications:** Exotic superconductivity disordered systems. **Mailing Address:** James Franck Inst, Univ Chicago, 5640 Ellis Ave, Chicago, IL 60637. **E-Mail:** k-levin@uchicago.edu

LEVIN, LEONID A, ALGORITHMIC COMPLEXITY. **Personal Data:** b USSR, November 2, 1948. **Education:** Moscow Univ, PhD, 1972; Mass Inst Technol, PhD (math), 1979. **Professional Experience:** Vis prof, Univ London, 1999-; vis prof, Calif Inst Technol, 1987; vis MacKey prof, Univ Calif, Berkeley, 1986; PROF MATH & COMPUT SCI, BOSTON UNIV, 1980-; vis scientist comput sci, Mass Inst Technol, 1978-1980. **Research Statement & Publications:** Foundations of mathematics, statistics and computer science; algorithmic complexity with applications to randomness and information theories, inductive inference, functional analysis, combinatorics and graph theory, mathematical logic, theory of computations; randomness and information. **Mailing Address:** Dept Comput Sci, Boston Univ, 111 Cummington St, Boston, MA 02215-2411. **E-Mail:** lnd@bu.edu

LEVIN, LISA, OCEANOGRAPHY. **Education:** Scripps Inst Oceanog, PhD (Biol Oceanog). **Professional Experience:** PROF & PRIN INVESTR, SCRIPPS INST OCEANOG, as of 2005. **Research Statement & Publications:** Population and community ecology of soft-sediment habitats wetlands ecology and restoration; animal-sediment-plant-geochemical interactions; ecosystem-level consequences of species invasion; larval dispersal and the influence of life histories on population dynamics; ecology of deep-sea reducing environments (oxygen minimum zones; methane seeps). **Mailing Address:** Integrative Oceanog Div, Scripps Inst Oceanog, 9500 Gilman Dr, La Jolla, CA 92093-0218. **Fax:** 858-822-0562. **E-Mail:** llevin@ucsd.edu

LEVIN, MARTIN ALLEN, ELECTRON MICROSPY, CELL ULTRASTRUCTURE. **Personal Data:** b Philadelphia, Pa, August 14, 1949. **Education:** Rutgers Univ, BA, 1971, MS, 1973; Ohio Univ, PhD (zoology), 1977. **Professional Experience:** EXEC DIR, CTR EDUC EXCELLENCE, as of 2004; SECY, AM ASN UNIV PROF, EASTERN CONN STATE COL, as of 2003; PROF BIOL, EASTERN CONN STATE COL, 1988-; from asst prof to assoc prof, Eastern Conn State Col, 1978-1988; teaching assoc biol, Ohio Univ, 1974-1977; teaching asst biol, Rutgers Univ, 1971-1973; news-ed, Micros Soc Conn Newsletter. **Memberships:** Micros Soc Am. **Research Statement & Publications:** Ultrastructural studies of the abdominal muscles of terrestrial and semiterrestrial amphipods: correlating structure to locomotory function; ultrastructural and histochemical studies of the walking legs of brachyuran crabs. **Mailing Address:** Dept Biol, Eastern Conn State Univ, Ste Planetarium EM 83 Windham St, Willimantic, CT 06226. **Fax:** 860-465-5213. **E-Mail:** levin@easternct.edu

LEVIN, MICHAEL H(OWARD), ENVIRONMENTAL SCIENCES & ENGINEERING, ECOLOGY. **Personal Data:** b New York, NY, September 25, 1936. **Education:** Univ Vt, BS, 1958; Rutgers Univ, MS, 1960, PhD (bot), 1964. **Professional Experience:** Adj prof agr & natural resources, Del State Col, 1979-; DIR RES, ENVIRON RES ASSOCS INC, 1973-; PRES, ENVIRON RES ASSOCS INC, 1970-; asst prof landscape archit & regional planning, Univ Pa, 1968-1973; asst prof bot & cur herbarium, Univ Man, 1966-1968; cur, Greene-Nieuwland Herbarium & asst prof biol, Univ Notre Dame, 1964-1966; res assoc taxon, NY Bot Garden, 1964. **Memberships:** Fel AAAS; Ecol Soc Am; Sigma Xi. **Research Statement & Publications:** Environmental sciences and geotechnical investigations; ecology of altered communities and ecosystems; ecological management; application of gradient analysis to terrestrial communities; wetlands ecology; hydrobiology, hydrology and water resources; wood science; research and testing of natural and man made materials; health and safety evaluations; environmental studies and surveys; testing and laboratory services; engineering and planning. **Mailing Address:** Environ Res Assocs Inc, 414 Mill Rd, Havertown, PA 19083-3740.

LEVIN, MORRIS A, MICROBIOLOGY. **Personal Data:** b New York, NY, May 15, 1934. **Education:** Univ Chicago, BS, 1959; Univ RI, PhD (microbiol), 1970. **Professional Experience:** RES SCIENTIST, UNIV MD, as of 2004; Adj prof civil eng & microbiol, Univ RI, 1975; MICROBIOLOGIST HEALTHEFFECTS, ENVIRON PROTECTION AGENCY, 1970-; microbiologist marine microbiol, DeptHealth Educ & Welfare, 1966-1970; Microbiologist aerobiol, Dept Defense, 1957-1966. **Memberships:** Sigma Xi. **Research Statement & Publications:** Quantitating of microorganisms in the environment, dose-response relationships and epidemiological considerations correlating the public health effects of exposure to microbial populations under natural conditions; forecasting, trend analysis of environmental problems, genetic engineering. **Mailing Address:** 14405 Woodcrest Dr, Rockville, MD 20853.

LEVIN, MURRAY LAURENCE, INTERNAL MEDICINE, NEPHROLOGY. **Personal Data:** b Boston, Mass, November 14, 1935; m 1961, Joan E Solomon; c Russell J & Cynthia A. **Education:** Harvard Col, AB, 1957; Tufts Univ, MD, 1961 (Com laude). **Honors & Awards:** Distinguished Ser Award, Central Soc for clin Res 1994, Distinguished Ser Award, Dept of Med, Northwestern Univ Med Soc, 1994. **Professional Experience:** Chief, Patterson Teaching Firm, 1990-1999; chief, Sect Nephrology/Hypertension, Northwestern Univ Med Ctr, 1986-1991; secy-treas, Cent Soc Clin Res, 1982-1987; pres, Cent Soc Clin Res, 1992-1993; attending physician, Northwestern Mem Hosp, 1980-; PROF MED, MED SCH, NORTHWESTERN UNIV, CHICAGO, 1980-; chief med serv, Vet Admin Lakeside Hosp, Chicago, Ill, 1976-1985; assoc attend physician, Passavant Mem Hosp, 1975-1980; chief renal sect, Vet Admin Lakeside Hosp, Chicago, Ill, 1972-1976; from asst prof to assoc prof, Northwestern Univ, 1969-1980; adj staff, Passavant Mem Hosp, 1968-; Nat Inst Arthritis & Metab Dis res grant, 1967-1970; attend physician, Vet Admin Lakeside Hosp, Chicago, Ill, 1966-; Chicago Heart Asn res grants, 1966-1970 & 1973-1975; assoc, Northwestern Univ, 1966-1969; NIH res fel, 1965-1966; res fel renal dis, Univ Tex Southwestern Med Sch Dallas, 1964-1966; resident, Beth Israel Hosp, Boston, Mass, 1962-1964; intern med, Beth Israel Hosp, Boston, Mass, 1961-1962. **Memberships:** Am Fedn (pres, midwest section, 1974-1975); Int Soc Nephrol; Am Soc Nephrol; Cent Soc Clin rec (pres, 1982-1987, 1992-1993); Nat Kidney Found. **Research Statement & Publications:** Salt and water metabolism; uremia; membrane transport; calcium and phosphorus metabolism. **Mailing Address:** 210 E Pearson 57, 13-B, Chicago, IL 60611. **E-Mail:** m_levih@horthwestern.edu

LEVIN, NORMAN LEWIS, ZOOLOGY, PARASITOLOGY. **Personal Data:** b Hartford, Conn, March 31, 1924. **Education:** Univ Conn, BS, 1948, MS, 1949; Univ Ill, PhD (zool, parasitol), 1956. **Professional Experience:** PROF EMER BIOL, BROOKLYN COL, 1996-; dep chmn, Brooklyn Col, beginning 1982; from instr to prof, Brooklyn Col, 1960-1996; fel trop med, Sch Med, La State Univ, 1959; asst prof biol, Westminster Col, Mo, 1957-1960; instr, Univ Ill, 1956-1957; asst zoologist, Univ Ill, 1953-1956. **Memberships:** Fel AAAS; Am Soc Zool; Am Soc Parasitol; Am Soc Trop Med & Hyg; AmMicros Soc; Am Inst Biol Sci. **Research Statement & Publications:** General taxonomy; morphology; life cycles; interrelationship of larval trematodes and marine snails. **Mailing Address:** Dept Biol, Brooklyn Col, 2900 Bedford Ave, Brooklyn, NY 11210.

LEVIN, RACHEL N, ANIMAL SCIENCE. **Education:** Antioch Col, BS; Cornell Univ, PhD. **Professional Experience:** ASSOC PROF BIOL, POMANA COL, CALIF, as of 2006. **Research Statement & Publications:** Biology; Behavioral Ecology; Animal Behavior; Behavioral Endocrinology; Evolution of Communication Signals and Mating Systems; Origin of Sex Differences in Behavior; Evolution of Communication Signals and Mating Strategies; Evolution of Life History Traits; Animal Communication; Mating Systems & Strategies. **Mailing Address:** Dept Biol, Pomona Col, Seaver W 139 Lab 124, Claremont, CA 91711. **E-Mail:** Rachel_Levin@pomona.edu

LEVIN, ROBERT AARON, CLINICAL CHEMISTRY. **Personal Data:** b New York, NY, July 25, 1929. **Education:** St John's Univ, NY, BS, 1951, MS, 1955. **Professional Experience:** MGR PATH, ANATOMIC & CLIN PATH SECT, NORWICH-EATON PHARMACEUT, 1990-; unit leader clin path, Norwich Pharmacal Co, 1962-1980 & 1980-1989; sr researcher clin path & toxicol, Norwich Pharmacal Co, 1958-1962; Res toxicologist, Norwich Pharmacal Co, 1955-1958; Sci adv, Med Technol Dept, State Univ NY Agr & Tech Col Morrisville, Broome Tech Col, State Univ NY, Canton; adj prof, State Univ NY, Utica. **Memberships:** Am Chem Soc; Am Asn Clin Chem; Am Soc Vet Clin Pathologists. **Research Statement & Publications:** Automation and computerization of chemical technics; drug safety assessment; establishing effects on clinical pathology parameters; veterinary hematology. **Mailing Address:** 25 Hillview Dr, Norwich, NY 13815.

LEVIN, ROBERT E, MICROBIOLOGY, FOOD SCIENCE. **Personal Data:** b Boston, Mass, December 1, 1930. **Education:** Los Angeles State Col, BS, 1952; Univ Southern Calif, MS, 1954; Univ Calif, Davis, PhD (microbiol), 1963. **Professional Experience:** PROF FOOD SCI, UNIV MASS, AMHERST, 1977-; NIH res grant, 1965-1968; from asst prof to assoc prof, Univ Mass, Amherst, Cheenowth Lab, 1964-1977; asst prof microbiol, Ore State Univ, 1963-1964. **Memberships:** Am Soc Microbiol; Inst Food Technologists; Soc Cryobiology. **Research Statement & Publications:** Microbiological sulfate reduction; yeast cytology; psychophilic bacteria; enzymology; molecular taxonomy. **Mailing Address:** Dept Food Sci, Univ Mass, Chenoweth Lab Rm 346, Amherst, MA 01003-0002. **E-Mail:** relevin@foodsci.umass.edu

LEVIN, ROBERT EDMOND, LIGHT & RADIOMETRIC OPTICS. **Personal Data:** b Orange, Calif, October 11, 1931; m Karen; c Kristen & Erik. **Education:** Stanford Univ, BS, 1953, MS, 1954, Engr, 1956, PhD (elec eng), 1960. **Honors & Awards:** Illuminating Eng Soc N Am Medal, 1995. **Professional Experience:** Corporate Scientist, OSRAM SYLVANIA, 1963-; adj assoc prof archit, Rensselaer Polytech Inst, 1990-; adj prof elec eng, Univ NH, 1983-2000; contrib ed, McGraw-Hill, 1971-1975; instr continuing educ, Northeastern Univ, 1968-1982; consult engr, 1958-1963; assoc prof elec eng, Calif State Univ, San Jose, 1958-1963. **Memberships:** Optical Soc Am; sr mem Inst Elec & Electronics Engrs; fel Illum Eng Soc; Am Soc Photobiol; Soc Motion Picture & TV Engrs; Sigma Xi; Tau Beta Pi. **Research Statement & Publications:** Control and application of non-ionizing radiation in photobiological, photochemical and visual systems; radiometric optics. **Mailing Address:** Osram Sylvania Inc, 71 Cherry Hill Dr, Beverly, MA 01915. **Fax:** 978-750-1794. **E-Mail:** robert.levin@sylvania.com

LEVIN, ROBERT HAROLD, ORGANIC CHEMISTRY. **Personal Data:** b Chicago, Ill, November 1, 1915. **Education:** Univ Ill, AB, 1937; Univ Wis, PhD (org chem), 1941. **Professional Experience:** RES/MGT CONSULT, 1978-, vpres res, Richardson-Merrell, Inc, 1968-1978; asst dir res, Upjohn Co, Mich, 1958-1968; head dept chem, Upjohn Co, Mich, 1952-1958; Mem subcomt steroid nomenclature, Nat Res Coun, 1950-1955; group leader chem res, Upjohn Co, Mich, 1946-1952; res chemist, Upjohn Co, Mich, 1941-1946; asst chem, Univ Wis, 1937-1941; Chem libr asst, Univ Ill, 1934-1936; mem coun, Gordon Res Conf. **Memberships:** AAAS; Am Chem Soc; Sigma Xi. **Research Statement & Publications:** Chemistry of steroids, especially the cortical hormones; biomedical research and new drug development long range planning for pharmaceutical research; international pharmaceutical product licensing. **Mailing Address:** 11127 Jardin Pl, Cincinnati, OH 45241-6629.

LEVIN, ROBERT MARTIN, PHARMACOLOGY. **Personal Data:** b New York, NY, April 6, 1945. **Education:** Albright Col, BS, 1967; Univ Pa, MS, 1969, PhD (pharmacol), 1974. **Professional Experience:** DIR, OFF RES ADMIN, ALBANY COL PHARM, as of 2004; PROF PHARMACOL, ALBANY COL PHARM, 1996-; dir res, dept biol sci, Albany Col Pharm, beginning 1996; pharmacologist term appt, Vet Admin Med Ctr beginning 1984; from res assoc prof tores prof pharmacol & urol, Div Urol, Univ Pa, 1983-1996; res asst prof, Div Urol, Univ Pa, 1979-1983; dir urol res, Univ Pa, beginning 1978; res assoc, Div Urol, Univ Pa, 1978-1979; instr pharmacol, Dept Pharmacol, Med Col Pa, 1976-1978; fel, Dept Pharmacol, Med Col Pa, 1974-1976. **Memberships:** Int Continence Soc; Am Urol Asn; Am Soc Pharmacol & Exp Therapeut; Basic Urol Res Soc; Urodynamics Soc; Urol Res Soc; Int Soc Impotence Res. **Research Statement & Publications:** Smooth muscle plasticity in response to pathological situations. **Mailing Address:** Dept Basic & Pharmaceut Sci, Albany Col Pharm, 106 New Scotland Ave, Albany, NY 12208-3492. **Fax:** 518-445-7202. **E-Mail:** levinr@acp.edu

LEVIN, ROGER L(EE), MATERIALS SCIENCE. **Personal Data:** b Clearfield, Pa, March 21, 1936. **Education:** Pa State Univ, BS, 1958; Yale Univ, MS, 1961; Northwestern Univ, PhD (mat sci), 1963. **Professional Experience:** RETIRED; tech dir, Mar Inc, 1977-1992; pres, Mar Inc, 1972-1992; mgr undersea warfare progs, Hydrospace Res Corp, 1970-1972; anal officer, sonal opers anal, Naval Test & Eval Detachment, Fla, 1963-1965; sonar proj officer, USN, 1958-1970; sonar proj officer, Accoust Warfare Proj Off, Naval Ship Systs Command, DC, 1956-1970. **Memberships:** Am Soc Naval Engrs; Am Oceanic Orgn; Am Defense Preparedness Asn; US Naval Inst. **Research Statement & Publications:** Underwater acoustics. **Mailing Address:** 81 Black Angus Dr, Oakland, MD 21550.

LEVIN, RONALD HAROLD, ORGANIC CHEMISTRY. **Personal Data:** b San Francisco, Calif, September 26, 1945. **Education:** Case Western Res Univ, BS, 1967; Princeton Univ, PhD (chem), 1970. **Professional Experience:** MEM STAFF, IBM CORP, 1978-; asst prof chem, Harvard Univ, 1972-1977; fel chem, Univ Freiburg, 1970-1971 & Calif Inst Technol, 1971-1972. **Memberships:** Am Chem Soc; Chem Soc London; Sigma Xi. **Research Statement & Publications:** Reactive intermediates; thermal and photochemical transformations; applications of magnetic resonance; electrophotography. **Mailing Address:** Lexmark Int Inc, 6555 Monarch Rd PO Box 9042, Boulder, CO 80301.

LEVIN, RONALD L, BIOENGINEERING. **Education:** Mass Inst Tech, SB, 1973, Sm, 1973, ScD, 1976. **Professional Experience:** BIOMED ENGR, NATL INST HEALTH, 1980-. **Mailing Address:** Natl Inst Health, Bldg 13 Rm 3W13, Bethesda, MD 20892. **Fax:** 301-496-6608. **E-Mail:** levin@helix.nih.gov

LEVIN, ROY, PROGRAMMING ENVIRONMENT, DISTRIBUTED SYSTEMS & OPERATING SYSTEMS. **Personal Data:** b New York, NY, 1948. **Education:** Yale Univ, BS, 1970; Carnegie Mellon Univ, PhD (computer Sci), 1977. **Professional Experience:** DIR, MICROSOFT RES, SILLICON RES LAB, 2001-; SR CONSULT ENGR, SYSTS RES CTR, DIGITAL EQUIP CORP, 1988-; Chmn, Spec Interest Group Oper Systs, Asn Comput Mach, 1987-1991; Mem tech staff, SystsRes Ctr, Digital Equip Corp, 1984-1988. **Memberships:** Asn Comput Mach; Inst Elec & Electronics Engrs. **Mailing Address:** Microsoft Res, Sillicon Res Lab, 1065 La Avenida, Mountain View, CA 94043. **E-Mail:** roylevin@microsoft.com

LEVIN, SAMUEL JOSEPH, BIOCHEMISTRY. **Personal Data:** b Detroit, Mich, September 19, 1935. **Education:** Wayne State Univ, BA, 1958, PhD (chem), 1961; Am Bd Clin Chem, dipl. **Professional Experience:** ASST PROF, PATH, UNIV ILL, CHICAGO, COL MED, 1989-; ASSOC DIR, CLIN PATH, 1983-; dir, div biochem, Michael Reese Hosp, 1977-; mem, Michael Reese Inst, 1974-1976; asst dir clin path, Michael Reese Hosp, 1974-1976; from asst prof to assoc prof, SchMed, 1968-1974; from asst prof to assoc prof biochem, Sch Dent, Univ Mo-Kansas City, 1967-1974; chief biochemist, Dept Path, Kansas City Gen Hosp, 1966-1974; from instr to asstprof biochem, Div Grad Studies, Med Col, Cornell Univ, 1963-1966; assoc, Sloan-Kettering Inst, 1963-1966; asst attend biochemist, Mem Hosp Cancer & Allied Dis, 1962-1966; scientist, Warner Lambert Pharmaceut Co, 1961-1962; res assoc chem, Col Med, Wayne State Univ, 1955-1961. **Memberships:** AAAS; Am Asn Clin Chem; Clin Lab Mgt Asn; Sigma Xi. **Research Statement & Publications:** Clinical biochemistry. **Mailing Address:** Pathol M/C 847 Univ Ill Col Med, 1819 W Polk St, Chicago, IL 60612-7331. **Fax:** 312-413-0156. **E-Mail:** slevin@uic.edu

LEVIN, SBENEDICT, REMOTE SENSING, TECHNOLOGY TRANSFER. **Personal Data:** b New Orleans, La, July 9, 1910. **Education:** Columbia Univ, AB, 1931, BS, 1932, EM, 1933, PhD (geol), 1948. **Honors & Awards:** Medal, Antarctic Serv, NSF, 1965. **Profes-**

sional Experience: RETIRED; consult, earth resources, beginning 1979; adv coun, Technol Transfer, NASA, 1978-1980; prof eng & appl sci, George Wash Univ, 1976-1979; chmn Panel, Space Info, Nat Acad Eng, 1974-1975; execvpres, Earth Satellite Corp, 1970-1976; chmn, Defense Ctr Res, 1969-1970; mem, Fed Coun Sci & Technol, Acad Sci & Eng, 1969-1970; asst dir res, Off Secy Defense, 1968-1970; dir, Inst Explor Res, 1960-1968; mem, Solid State Sci Panel, Nat Acad Sci, 1949-1968; res dir, US Army Electronics Command, 1945-1960; geol engr mineral explor, USBur Mines, 1942-1945; instr geol, Hunter Col, 1937-1942; mining geologist, Central Am Mines, 1934-1937. **Memberships:** Fel Geol Soc Am; fel Am Geophys Union; Sigma Xi; fel Am Soc Photogram & Remote Sensing; fel Mineral Soc Am. **Research Statement & Publications:** Application of remote sensing from earth satellites and aircraft to resource exploration and development; solid state physics. **Mailing Address:** Lake Waramaug, New Preston, CT 06777.

LEVIN, SEYMOUR ARTHUR, CHEMICAL ENGINEERING. **Personal Data:** b Newark, NJ, September 16, 1922. **Education:** Johns Hopkins Univ, BE, 1943. **Professional Experience:** RETIRED; head long range planning, Nuclear Div, 1968-1989; dept head, Union Carbide Nuclear Co Div, Uniion Carbide Corp, 1945-1968; res asst, Columbia Univ, 1943-1945. **Memberships:** Am Chem Soc; AAAS; Nat Soc Prof Engrs. **Research Statement & Publications:** Design and analysis of isotope separation process. **Mailing Address:** 956 W Outer Dr, Oak Ridge, TN 37830.

LEVIN, SEYMOUR R, INTERNAL MEDICINE. **Personal Data:** b Chicago, Ill, April 27, 1934; m 1957, c 3. **Education:** Univ Ill, BS, 1956, MD, 1961; Am Bd Internal Med, dipl internal med, 1970 & endocrinol, 1973. **Professional Experience:** Grants, Vet Admin, 1973-1991 & NIH Tug grant assoc inv, 1983-1992; PROF MED, UNIV CALIF, LOS ANGELES, 1981-; assoc prof med, Univ Calif, Los Angeles, 1975-1981; dir diabetes clin & chief metab unit, Wadsworth Vet Admin Hosp, 1973-; Endocrine Div, Univ Calif, Los Angeles, 1973-; asst res physician, Univ Calif, San Francisco, 1969-1973; res fel endocrinol, Univ Calif, San Francisco, 1967-1969; physician, US Army Hosp, Ft Carson, 1965-1967; resident, Wadsworth Vet Admin Hosp, Los Angeles, 1962-1965; Intern, Cook Co Hosp, Chicago, 1961-1962. **Memberships:** Fel Am Col Physicians; Am Fedn Clin Res; Am Diabetes Asn; Endocrine Soc. **Research Statement & Publications:** Studies of insulin secretion and mechanisms of secretion by the endocrine pancreas. **Mailing Address:** Wadsworth Vet Admin Hosp, 691/111K, Los Angeles, CA 90073.

LEVIN, SIDNEY SEAMORE, PHYSIOLOGY, PHARMACOLOGY. **Personal Data:** b Philadelphia, Pa, March 29, 1929. **Education:** Univ Pittsburgh, BS, 1951, MS, 1953, PhD (biol sci), 1955. **Honorary Degrees:** MA, Univ Pa, 1971. **Professional Experience:** PROF EMER SURG, UNIV PA, as of 2004; res assoc, Harrison Surg res, Sch Med, Univ PA, beginning 1958. **Memberships:** AAAS; NY Acad Sci. **Research Statement & Publications:** Adrenal output in shock; effect of hypertension on adrenal cortical steroids; cytochrome P-450. **Mailing Address:** Dept Surg, Univ Pa, 3400 Spruce St, Philadelphia, PA 19104-6070.

LEVIN, SIMON ASHER, MATHEMATICS, BIOLOGY. **Personal Data:** b Baltimore, Md, April 22, 1941; m 1964, Carole Levin; c Jacob E & Rachel S Klopfer. **Education:** Johns Hopkins Univ, BA, 1961; Univ Md, PhD (math), 1964. **Honorary Degrees:** DSC, Eastern Mich Univ, 1990. **Honors & Awards:** Most cited paper ecol & environ 1990s, inst sci info, 2002; Okubo lifetime achievement award, soc math biol & Japanese Soc Theoret Biol, 2001; distinguished serv citation, Ecol Soc Am, 1998; distinguished statist ecol award, Int Asn Ecol, 1994; lansdowne lectr, Univ Victoria, BC, 1981; Grace Kimball Mem lectr, Wilkes Col, Pa, 1986; H J Oosting Mem lectr, Duke Univ, 1987; MacArthur Award, Ecol Soc Am, 1988. **Professional Experience:** Vis Miller Res Prof, Univ Calif, Berkeley, 2003; tech adv bd, Brit Petrol, 2002-; DIR, CTR BIOCOMPLEXITY, PRINCETON UNIV, 2001-; sci comn, Smithsonian Inst, 2001-; ed bd, Nat Acad of Sci, 2000-; Recovery sci review panel, Nat Marine Fisheries Serv, 2000-; ed-in-chief, Princeton series in theoret & computational biol, 2000-; vis prof, Inst Advanced Study, Spring, Tex, 1999; ed bd, Philos Trans Royal Soc, 1998-; ASSOC FAC, PRINCETON ENVIRON INST, PRINCETON UNIV, 1993-; dir, Princeton Environ Inst, Princeton Univ, 1993-1998; US Nat Comt for Man & Biosphere prog, 1993-1994; GEORGE M MOFFETT PROF BIOL, PRINCETON UNIV, 1992-; adj prof, Cornell Univ, 1992-; dir environ initiatives, Princeton Univ, 1992-; assoc fac, Appl & Computational Math, Princeton Univ, 1992-; sci bd, Santa Fe Inst, 1991-1999, 2001-; Charles A Alexander prof biol sci, 1985-1992; chmn, Hudson River Found, 1985-1986; mem, ed adv coun, Nat Res Modeling, 1984-; mem, Comn Life Sci, Nat Res Coun, Nat Acad Sci, 1983-1989; bd biol, Comn Life Sci, Nat Res Coun, Nat Acad Sci, 1983-1989; sci panel, Hudson River Found, 1982-; co-dir, autumn course ecol, Inter Atomic Energy Agency, UNESCO, Trieste, Italy, 1982, 1992; dir, Ecosysts Res Ctr, 1980-1987; chair, comt Human Rights Math Scientist, 1980-1983; vice chmn math, Comt Concerned Scientists, 1979-; managing ed, J Math Biol, 1979-; Math & Comput Modelling, 1979-; Guggenheim fel, 1979-1980; Vancouver, Univ BC, 1979-1980; mem adv comt, Environ Sci Div, Oak Ridge Nat Lab, 1978-1981; prof appl math & ecol, Ctr Environ Res, 1977-1992; Math intelligencer, 1977-1984; Weizmann Inst, Rehovot, Israel, 1977, 1980; consult ed, Evolutionary Theory, 1976-; adv ed, J Theoret Biol, 1976-; J Appl Math Biomathematics, Soc Indust & Appl Math 1976-; assoc ed, Theoret Pop Biol, 1976-1984; ed, J Math Biol, 1976-1979; mem US comt, Israel Environ, 1975-; J Appl Math, Soc Indust & Appl Math, 1975-1979; ed, Ecol & Ecol Monographs, Ecol Soc Am, 1975-1977; ed, Lect Math Life Sci, 1974-1979; chmn, Sect Ecol & Systs, Cornell Univ, 1974-1979; managing ed, Lecture Notes Biomath, 1973-; adv ed, J Math Biol, 1973-1976; assoc ed, Ecol & Ecol Monographs, Ecol Soc Am, 1973-1975; Univ Wash, Seattle, 1973- 1974; assoc prof, Ecol & Systs & Theoret & Appl Math, Cornell Univ, 1972-1977; assoc prof, Appl Math, Cornell Univ, 1971-1977; chmn, Theoret Biol & Biomath, Gordon Res Conf, 1971; co-chmn Biomathematics, Gordon Res Conf, 1970; vis prof, Univ Md, Col Park, 1968; asst prof math, Cornell Univ, 1965-1970; NSF fel biomath, Univ Calif, Berkeley, 1964-1965; res assoc, Univ Md, Col Park, 1964; asst math, Univ Md, 1961-1962. **Memberships:** Soc Math Biol (pres, 1987-1989, vpres, 1989-1991); Am Math Soc; Am Soc Naturalists; Ecol Soc Am (pres-elect, 1989-1990, pres, 1990-1991); Soc Indust & Appl Math; Brit Ecol Soc; Am Acad Arts & Sci; Am Inst Biol Sci. **Research Statement & Publications:** Theoretical ecology; mathematical and computational models of ecological and evolutionary processes; biological growth and spread; landscape models in relation to disturbance and global change; terrestrial, intertidal and marine ecosystems. **Mailing Address:** Dept Ecol & Evolutionary Biol, Princeton Univ, 203 Eno Hall, Princeton, NJ 08544-1003. **Fax:** 609-258-6819. **E-Mail:** slevin@princeton.edu

LEVIN, SIMON EUGENE, toxicology, industrial hygiene; deceased, see previous edition for last biography

LEVIN, VICTOR ALAN, NEURO-ONCOLOGY, CANCER. **Personal Data:** b Milwaukee, Wis, November 22, 1941; m 1963, Ellen; c Lisa M Katz & Jason D Levin. **Education:** Univ Wis-Madison, BS, 1963, MD, 1966. **Honors & Awards:** Fac Res Award, Am Cancer Soc, 1977-1981; Ann & Jason Faber Award, 1988; David A Frommer Mem Lectr Neuro-Oncol, Harvard Med Sch, 1990; Fred Plum Lectr, Sch Med, Univ Wash, 1991; Heath Mem Award Cancer Ctr, 1997; Gerry Pencer Mem Lect, ON Cancer Inst, 2000; Bukhart Vist Lect, Brain umer & Neu-Oncol Ctr, Cleveland Clin, 2001; Anne C Brooks Award, Dept Neurosurg, Univ TX, MD Anderson Cancer Ctr, 2001; Gold Medal Soc Neuro-Oncol, 2002. **Professional Experience:** BERNARD W BIEDENHARN CHAIR CANCER RES, UNIV TEX, as of 2004; PROF NEURO-ONCOL, M D CANCER CTR, UNIV TEX, 1988-; chmn, Dept Neuro-Oncol, Univ Tex, beginning 1988; prof neuro-oncol & pharmacol, 1981-1988 & chem, 1981-1988; from instr to assoc prof neurol, Univ Calif, San Francisco, 1972-1981; resident neurol, Nat Inst Neurol Dis & Stroke fel, 1971-1972; resident neurol, Mass Gen Hosp, 1969-1971; staff assoc chem pharm, Nat Cancer Inst, 1967-1969; intern med, St Louis City Hosp, Wash Univ, 1966-1967. **Memberships:** Am Acad Neurol; Am Asn Cancer Res; Am Soc Clin Oncol; AAAS; Soc Neuro-Oncol; AANS. **Research Statement & Publications:** Development of new therapeutic approaches for the treatment of brain tumors; preclinical pharmacology and design of therapeutic strategies for treating cancer in the nervous system. **Mailing Address:** Dept Neuro-Oncol, The Univ Tex M D Anderson Cancer Ctr, 1515 Holcombe Blvd Unit 431, Houston, TX 77030. **E-Mail:** vlevin@mdanderson.org

LEVIN, WAYNE, PROTEIN CHEMISTRY. **Personal Data:** b New York, NY, February 29, 1940; m Rosemary; c Kira & Darryl. **Education:** Ithaca Col, BA, 1962; Univ Ill, MS, 1964. **Honorary Degrees:** DSc, Rutgers Univ, 1993, Ithaca Col, 1995. **Honors & Awards:** Achievement Award, Acad Pharmaceut Sci, 1979; Bernard B Brodie Award, Am Soc Pharmacol & Exp Therapeut, 1988. **Professional Experience:** SR RES DIR, HOFFMANN-LAROCHE INC, 2002-; distinguished res leader, Dept Inflammation & Autoimmune Dis, Hoffmann-La Roche Inc, 1992-2002; dir, Dept Protein Biochem, Hoffmann-La Roche Inc, 1990-1992; adj prof, Rutgers Univ, 1989-; vis prof, Univ BC, 1989-1990; distinguished res leader, Dept Protein Biochem, Hoffmann-La Roche Inc, 1987-1990; mem, Roche Inst Molecular Biol, 1985-1987; distinguished lectr, Col Vet Med, Tex A&M Univ, 1985-1986; sect head, Dept Biochem, Hoffmann-La Roche Inc, 1978-1985; mem, Study Sect Chem Path, NIH, 1977-1979; group chief, Dept Biochem, Hoffmann-La Roche Inc, 1974-1978; sr scientist, Dept Biochem, Hoffmann-La Roche Inc, 1971-1974; biochemist, Dept Biochem, Hoffmann-La Roche Inc, 1970-1971; biochemist, Burroughs Wellcome & Co, 1965-1970. **Memberships:** Am Soc Biochem & Molecular Biol; Am Soc Pharmacol & Exp Therapeut; Am Asn Cancer Res; Soc Toxicol; NY Acad Sci; AAAS. **Research Statement & Publications:** Purification and characterization of soluble and membrane-bound proteins, structure-activity relationships and immunochemical characterization of proteins. **Mailing Address:** Roche Discovery Technologies, Hoffmann-La Roche, Inc, Bldg 123/1, 340 Kingsland St, Nutley, NJ 07110-1199. **Fax:** 973-235-5091. **E-Mail:** wayne.levin@roche.com

LEVIN, WILLIAM COHN, INTERNAL MEDICINE, HEMATOLOGY. **Personal Data:** b Waco, Tex, March 2, 1917. **Education:** Univ Tex, BA, 1938, MD, 1941. **Honorary Degrees:** Dr, Univ Montpellier, 1980. **Professional Experience:** PRES EMER, UNIV TEX MED BR, GALVESTON, as of 2005; pres, Univ Tex Med Br, Galveston, as of 2003; pres, Hemat Res Lab & Blood Bank, 1974-1987; PROF INTERNAL MED, UNIV TEX MED BR, GALVESTON, 1965-; dir, Hemat Res Lab & Blood Bank, 1946-1974; from instr to assoc prof internal med, Univ Tex Med Br, Galveston, 1944-1965. **Memberships:** Am Fedn Clin Res; Am Soc Hemat; AMA; fel Am Col Physicians; fel Int SocHemat. **Research Statement & Publications:** Hematology; immunology; oncology. **Mailing Address:** Dept Internal Med, Univ Tex Med Br, Galveston, TX 77553. **Fax:** 409-766-4662.

LEVIN, ZEV, ATMOSPHERIC SCIENCES, CLOUD PHYSICS. **Personal Data:** b Haifa, Israel, December 17, 1940; American & Israeli citizen; m 1965, Susan M Warshaw; c Rami & Tamar. **Education:** Calif State Univ, Los Angeles, BS, (Physics), (Honors), 1966; Univ Wash, PhD (atmospheric sci), 1970. **Honors & Awards:** Sigma Pi Sigma (Physics Honor soc) 1965 The Goldenberg Chair In atmospheric Physics at Tel Aviv univ 1994. **Professional Experience:** Head, the Porter Sch of Environmental Studies 2000-; fac fel, 1985 & Goddard Space Flight Ctr, 1992-1993; vpres res & develop & dean res, Dept Geophys & Planetary Sci, 1987-1992; head, Dept Geophys & Planetary Sci, 1985-1987; sr res assoc, Nat Res Coun, Ames Res Ctr, NASA, 1981; Vis sr scientist atmospheric sci, Nat Ctr Atmospheric Res, 1976-1977; PROF ATMOSPHERIC SCI, TEL AVIV UNIV, ISRAEL, 1971-; Res meteorologist, Univ Calif, Los Angeles, 1970-1971. **Memberships:** Am Meteorol Soc; Am Geophys Union; Sigma Xi; Europ Geophys Soc; Israel Aerosol Orgn. **Research Statement & Publications:** Formation of clouds and precipitation; cloud electrifications; atmospheric aerosols; ice nucleation; pi of meidex-The mediter Israeli dust exp- a proj under an agreement between NASA and the Israeli space agency, ISA. **Mailing Address:** Dept Geophys & Planetary Sci, Tel Aviv Univ, Ramat Aviv 69978, Israel. **Fax:** 972-364-08274; 972-364-09282. **E-Mail:** zev@hail.tau.ac.il

LEVINE, AARON WILLIAM, PHYSICAL CHEMISTRY, POLYMER CHEMISTRY. **Personal Data:** b New York, NY, July 14, 1943. **Education:** Yeshiva Univ, BA, 1963; City Col NY, MA, 1966; Seton Hall Univ, PhD (orgchem), 1970. **Professional Experience:** CONSULT, MAT & PROCESS COUNSULT SERV, as of 1998; sr mem tech staff, David Sarnoff Res Ctr, Subsid Sri Int, beginning 1996; mem tech staff, RCA Labs, 1992-1996; & Advan Mat Res, RCALabs, 1990-1992; head thin film & org mat res, RCA Labs, 1987-1989; head org mat & lithography res, RCA Labs, 1984-1987; mem tech staff, David Sarnoff Res Ctr, Subsid SRI Int, 1969-1984; res chemist, M&T Chem, Inc, 1966-1969; teacher, High Schs, NY, 1963-1966. **Memberships:** Am Chem Soc; fel Am Inst Chemists. **Research Statement & Publications:** Materials science and processing, materials selection, characterization and specification; polymers/plastics degradation and stabilization. **Mailing Address:** Mat & Process Consult Serv, PO Box 6764, Lawrenceville, NJ 08648. **Fax:** 609-896-0041.

LEVINE, ALAN E, TUMOR BIOLOGY, CELL BIOLOGY. **Personal Data:** b Los Angeles, Calif, May 5, 1952. **Education:** Univ Calif, Irvine, BA, 1974; Univ Wash, PhD (biochem), 1979. **Professional Experience:** ASSOC PROF BIOCHEM, HEALTH SCI CTR, UNIV TEX, 1991-; from asstprof to assoc prof pharmacol & growth factors, Baylor Col Med, 1982-1991; fel, Dept Neurobiology, Stanford Univ Med Sch, 1979-1982. **Memberships:** Am Soc Cell Biol; Am Asn Cancer Res; AAAS. **Research Statement & Publications:** Tumor biology; cell biology. **Mailing Address:** Dept Basic Sci, Univ Tex Health Sci Ctr, 6516 John Freeman Ave, Houston, TX 77030. **Fax:** 713-500-4500. **E-Mail:** alan.e.levine@uth.tmc.edu

LEVINE, ALAN L, MATHEMATICS. **Education:** State Univ NY, BS, 1976, MS, 1981, PhD, 1981; Hofstra Univ, MA, 1979. **Professional Experience:** ASSOC PROF, DEPT MATHS, FRANKLIN & MARSHALL COL, PA, as of 2006. **Mailing Address:** Dept Math, Franklin & Marshall col, 2330 Spring Valley Rd, Lancaster, PA 17604. **Fax:** 717-358-4507. **E-Mail:** alevine@fandm.edu

LEVINE, ALAN STEWART, HEMATOLOGY, BIOCHEMISTRY. **Personal Data:** b New York, NY, August 11, 1944. **Education:** Monmouth Col, NJ, BS, 1966; Univ Del, PhD (chem), 1971. **Professional Experience:** DIR, DR ALAN LEVINE & ASSOC, beginning

1997; dir, Blood Dis Prog, Nat Heart Lung Blood Inst, NIH, 1994-1997; chief, Cellular Hemat Br, 1991-1994; chief, Blood Dis Br, 1986-1991; health scientist adminr &dep br chief, NIH, 1977-1986; from staff fel to sr staff fel, NIH, 1972-1977; res assoc, SchPharm, Univ Kans, 1971-1972; teaching asst chem, Univ Del, 1966-1971. **Memberships:** Am Soc Hemat; AAAS; NY Acad Sci; Int Soc Exp Hemat. **Research Statement & Publications:** Molecular mechanism of human red blood cell sickling; diseases of the red blood cell; thalassemia; hematopoietic stem cell biology and transplantation; in utero stem cell therapy; gene therapy. **Mailing Address:** Dr Alan Levine & Assoc, 9535 Crescent View Dr N, Boynton Beach, FL 33437. **Fax:** 561-733-3878.

LEVINE, ALFRED MARTIN, QUANTUM OPTICS & DISSAPATIVE SYSTEMS. **Personal Data:** b Brooklyn, NY, April 5, 1941. **Education:** Cooper Union, BEE, 1961; Princeton Univ, MA, 1964, PhD (elec eng), 1966. **Professional Experience:** Vis scientist, Weizmann Inst, Israel, 1986; MEM DOCTORAL FAC PHYSICS, CITY UNIV, 1971-; PROF ENG SCI, COL STATEN ISLAND, CITY UNIV NY, 1970-; mem tech staff, Bell Labs, 1968-1970; scientist, Gas Lab, Ionizatti, Frascati, Italy, 1966-1968; mem res staff, Plasma Physics Lab, Princeton Univ, 1966. **Memberships:** Am Phys Soc; Inst Elec & Electronics Engrs; Optical Soc Am. **Research Statement & Publications:** noise in laser systems; quantum optics; four wave mixing; computer modelling of environmental systems; dissipation in quantum mechanical systems. **Mailing Address:** Dept Appl Sci & Physics, Col Staten Island, 2800 Victory Blvd, Staten Island, NY 10314.

LEVINE, ALLEN STUART, FOOD INTAKE, NUTRIENT ABSORPTION. **Personal Data:** b Newark, NJ, August 1, 1949. **Education:** Rutgers Univ, BA, 1970; Univ Minn, MS, 1973, PhD (nutrit), 1977. **Honors & Awards:** Mead Johnson Award, Am Inst Nutrit, 1985. **Professional Experience:** PROF PSYCHIAT, UNIV MINN, as of 2005; DIR, MINN OBESITY CTR, VA MED CTR, as of 2004; prof surg, Univ Minn, 1987-; ASSOC DIR RES, VET ADMIN MED CTR, 1987-; prof food sci & nutrit, Univ Minn, 1986-, from asst prof to assoc prof, 1981-1986; res chemist, Vet Admin Med Ctr, 1978-1987. **Memberships:** Am Inst Nutrit; Soc Neuroscience. **Research Statement & Publications:** Regulation of food intake; investigation of the interactions of neuropeptides and monoamines in the control of feeding; emphasis on the role of the endogenous opioids in the initiation of feeding; importance of specific opiate receptors; role of regulatory peptides in energy expenditure. **Mailing Address:** Vet Admin Med Ctr Neuroendocrine Res Lab, 151 One Veterans Dr, Minneapolis, MN 55417-2399. **E-Mail:** allenl@umn.edu

LEVINE, ALVIN SAUL, VIROLOGY. **Personal Data:** b Hamlet, NC, August 29, 1925. **Education:** Wake Forest Col, BS, 1948; Univ NC, MSPH, 1950; Rutgers Univ, PhD (microbiol), 1954. **Professional Experience:** PROF EMER MICROBIOL & IMMUNOL, SCH MED, IND UNIV, 1992-; asst dean, Sch Med, Ind Univ, beginning 1980; prof life sci & dir, Terre Haute Ctr Med Educ, IndState Univ, Terre Haute, 1971-1980; Fulbright vis prof, Univ Wis, 1967-1968; prof microbiol & immunol, Sch Med, Ind Univ, Indianapolis, 1964-1971; from asst prof to assoc prof microbiol, Sch Med, Ind Univ, Indianapolis, 1958-1964; instr bact & immunol, Harvard Med Sch, 1956-1958; teaching fel bact & immunol, Harvard Med Sch, 1954-1956; res fel microbiol, Rutgers Univ, 1951-1954; res asst biochem, Duke Univ, 1950-1951. **Memberships:** Fel Am Soc Microbiol; Am Asn Path; Am Asn Immunol; Am Asn Cancer Res. **Research Statement & Publications:** Infectious diseases; viral oncology; RNA viruses; biochemical, biophysical and immunological studies. **Mailing Address:** Dept Microbiol & Immunol, Ind Univ, 1120 S Dr, Fesler Hall, Indianapolis, IN 46202-5114.

LEVINE, ARNOLD DAVID, THEORETICAL PHYSICS. **Personal Data:** b Brooklyn, NY, October 24, 1925. **Education:** Columbia Univ, PhD (physics), 1958. **Professional Experience:** PROF EMER PHYSICS, WVA UNIV, as of 2001; prof physics, Wva Univ, beginning 1971; Consult, Columbia Liquified Natural Gas Corp, 1971-1973; from asst prof to assoc prof, Wva Univ, 1962-1971; asst prof, Wayne State Univ, 1960-1962; Asst prof physics, WVa Univ, 1957-1960; consult, Am Gas Asn, currently. **Memberships:** Combustion Inst; Am Phys Soc; Am Asn Physics Teachers; Sigma Xi. **Research Statement & Publications:** Meson physics; quantum field theory; non-equilibrium thermodynamics; fluid dynamics; combustion. **Mailing Address:** Dept Physics WVa Univ, PO Box 6315, Morgantown, WV 26506.

LEVINE, ARNOLD J, BIOLOGY. **Personal Data:** b Brooklyn, NY, July 30, 1939. **Education:** State Univ NY, BA, 1961; Univ Pa, PhD (microbiol), 1966. **Honors & Awards:** Merit Award, Nat Cancer Inst, 1989; Susan Swerling Lectr, Harvard Med Sch, 1990; Solomon Berson Mem Lectr, Mt Sinai Sch Med, 1992; Lila Gruber Cancer Res Award, Am Acad Dermat, 1992. **Professional Experience:** PROF, INST ADVAN STUDY, SCH NATURAL SCI, 2004-; vis prof, Inst Advan Study, 2003-2004; PROF, CANCER INST NY, 2003-; prof & head, Rockefeller Univ, 2002; pres & chief exec officer, Rockefeller Univ, 1998-2002; Robert Harriet Heilbrunn prof cancer biol, Rockefeller Univ, 1998-2002; Harry C Wiess prof life sci, Princeton Univ, 1984-1998; chair, Dept Molecular Biol, Princeton Univ, 1984-1996; chmn & prof, State Univ NY, 1979-1983; prof biochem, Princeton Univ, 1976-1979; from asst prof to assoc prof, Princeton Univ, 1968-1976. **Memberships:** Nat Acad Sci; Inst Med-Nat Acad Sci; Fedn Am Socs Exp Biol; Am Soc BiolChemists; Sigma Xi; Am Soc Microbiol; AAAS; NY Acad Sci. **Research Statement & Publications:** DNA replication; animal virology; tissue culture systems for the study of gene expression and the regulation of the cell cycle; genetics of higher organisms; viral oncogenesis; testicular teratomas. **Mailing Address:** Inst Advan Study Sch Natural Sci, Einstein Dr, Princeton, NJ 08540. **Fax:** 609-924-7592. **E-Mail:** alevine@ias.edu

LEVINE, ARNOLD MILTON, communication engineering; deceased, see previous edition for last biography

LEVINE, ARTHUR SAMUEL, MOLECULAR VIROLOGY, ONCOLOGY. **Personal Data:** b Cleveland, Ohio, November 1, 1936; m Ruth; c Amy, Raleigh & Jennifer. **Education:** Columbia Univ, AB, 1958; Chicago Med Sch, MD, 1964; Am Bd Pediat, dipl, 1970; Am Bd Hemat-Oncol, dipl, 1976. **Professional Experience:** PROF MED, MOLECULAR GENETICS & BIOCHEMISTRY, UNIV PITTSBURGH, 1998-; SR VICE CHANCELLOR HEALTH SCI, UNIV PITTSBURGH, 1998-; DEAN, SCH MED, UNIV PITTSBURGH, 1998-; Univ Bologna, Italy, 1989; Univ Calabria, Italy, 1990; ed-in-chief, New Biologist, 1988-; prof pediat, Uniformed Servs Univ Health Sci, 1983-; Karon Mem lectr, Univ Southern Calif, Los Angeles, 1983; Seham lectr, UnivMinn, Minneapolis, 1983; sci dir, Nat Inst Child Health & Human Develop, NIH, 1982-1998; Hebrew Univ, Israel, 1981; prof med & pediat, Georgetown Univ, beginning 1975; chief, Pediat Oncol Br, 1975-1982; vis prof, Benares Hindu Univ, India, 1974; Univ Minn, Minneapolis, 1974; vis lectr, Cold Spring Harbor Lab, NY, 1973; sr investr molecular virol & oncol, Div Cancer Treatment, Nat Cancer Inst, NIH, 1970-1975; clin assoc, Div Cancer Treatment, Nat Cancer Inst, NIH, 1967-1970; USPHS fel hemat & genetics, Univ Minn, Minneapolis, 1966-1967. **Memberships:** Am Soc Clin Invest; Soc Pediat Res; Am Asn Cancer Res; Am Soc Hemat; AAAS; Am Soc Microbiol. **Research Statement & Publications:** Molecular genetics of Simian Virus 40 and adenovirus-Simian Virus 40 hybrids; mechanism of viral oncogenesis; DNA repair and mutagenesis; oncology; authored or co-authored more than 240 scientific publications. **Mailing Address:** Sch Health Rehab Sci, Univ Pittsburgh, 4020 Forbes Tower, Pittsburgh, PA 15260. **Fax:** 412-383-6529.

LEVINE, BARRY FRANKLIN, LASERS. **Personal Data:** b Brooklyn, NY, September 5, 1942. **Education:** Polytech Inst Brooklyn, BS, 1963; Harvard Univ, PhD (physics), 1969. **Professional Experience:** Dept head, Bell Labs, beginning 1977; physicist, Bell Labs, beginning 1968. **Memberships:** Am Phys Soc. **Research Statement & Publications:** Experimental and theoretical nonlinear optics of crystals and liquids; coherent Raman scattering; optical picosecond spectroscopy of surfaces; novel high speed semiconductor devices (phototransistors, functional element tests, lasers, photodetectors). **Mailing Address:** AT&T Bell Labs, 600 Mountain Ave, Murray Hill, NJ 07974.

LEVINE, BERNARD BENJAMIN, IMMUNOLOGY & MEDICINE. **Personal Data:** b New York, NY, November 8, 1928. **Education:** City Col NY, BS, 1950; NY Univ, MD, 1954. **Professional Experience:** PROF MED, MED CTR, NY UNIV, 1970-; dir allergy, Med Ctr, Nyuniv, beginning 1962; from asst prof to assoc prof, Med Ctr, NY Univ, 1962-1970; res fel path, MedCtr, NY Univ, 1960-1962. **Memberships:** Am Asn Immunol; Soc Exp Biol & Med; Am Soc Clin Invest; Am Acad Allergy. **Research Statement & Publications:** Immunopathology; hypersensitivity; antigenicity; immune response; allergy. **Mailing Address:** Dept Inf Dis & Immun, NY Univ Sch Med, 566 First Ave, New York, NY 10016. **E-Mail:** levinb03@popmail.med.nyu.edu

LEVINE, BRUCE MARTIN, STATISTICAL OPTICS, ADAPTIVE OPTICS. **Personal Data:** b Lakewood, NJ, March 26, 1950. **Education:** Rochester Inst Technol, BS, 1972; Colo State Univ, MS, 1976; Univ Rochester, PhD (optics), 1986. **Professional Experience:** AT, JET PROPULSION LAB, NASA, as of 2003; Mem tech staff, Spatial Interferometry Group, Jet Propulsion Lab, 1990-1994; vis fac investr, Air Force Phillips Lab, 1988 & 1989, Fulbright travel fel, 1988; tech staff, Riverside Res Inst, 1986-1990; scanned imaging, Xerox Corp, 1984; Consult imaging sci, XeroxCorp, 1980-1981; Tech specialist, Xerox Corp, 1976-1980. **Memberships:** Optical Eng Soc; Optical Soc Am. **Research Statement & Publications:** Analysis of imaging optical systems such as adaptive optics andother forms of wavefront reconstruction; data analysis and theoretical analysis of laser beam propagation experiments. **Mailing Address:** Jet Propulsion Lab, NASA, 4800 Oak Grove Dr, Pasadena, CA 91109. **Fax:** 626-447-2402. **E-Mail:** marty@huey.jpl.nasa.gov

LEVINE, CHARLES (ARTHUR), PHYSICAL CHEMISTRY, ELECTROCHEMISTRY. **Personal Data:** b Des Moines, Iowa, December 25, 1922; m 1948, Beverly Damlos; c Alice & Dan. **Education:** Iowa State Col, BS, 1947; Univ Calif, PhD (chem), 1951. **Professional Experience:** VPres Techology, Carbon assoc Inc, as of 2002; SR SCIENTIST, OMNI-TECH, INT, 1986-; assoc scientist, Dow Chem Co, 1965-1986; res chemist, Dow Chem Co, 1951-1965; asst, Radiation Lab, 1949-1951; Asst, Univ Calif, 1948-1949. **Memberships:** AAAS; Electrochem Soc; Am Chem Soc; Am Phys Soc. **Research Statement & Publications:** Nuclear chemistry; radiation chemistry; electrochemistry. **Mailing Address:** 124 Buena Vista Ave, Santa Cruz, CA 95062. **E-Mail:** charlesl8671@aol.com

LEVINE, DANIEL, ELECTRICAL ENGINEERING. **Personal Data:** b New York, NY, July 21, 1920. **Education:** Univ Mich, BS, 1941, MS, 1942; Ohio State Univ, MSc, 1948, PhD (elec eng), 1955. **Professional Experience:** CONSULT SCIENTIST, LOCKHEED MISSILES & SPACE CO, 1961-; consult engr, 1956-1961; sr engr, Goodyear Aircraft Corp, Ariz, 1954-1956; br tech consult, Aerial Reconnaissance Lab, 1953-1954; Electronics engr, Aircraft Radiation Lab, Wright-Patterson AFB, Ohio, 1946-1951. **Memberships:** Optical Soc Am; Am Soc Photogram; Inst Elec & Electronics Engrs. **Research Statement & Publications:** System design of aerospace reconnaissance and mapping equipments; instrumentation for photographic and radar stereoanalysis; analogue simulators for radar trainers and guidance equipments; digital simulators for radar detection and tracking systems. **Mailing Address:** 1043 Enderby Way, Sunnyvale, CA 94087.

LEVINE, DAVID MORRIS, BEHAVIORAL SCIENCES, HEALTH EDUCATION. **Personal Data:** b Boston, Mass, December 15, 1937. **Education:** Brandeis Univ, AB, 1959; Univ Vt, MD, 1964; Johns Hopkins Univ, MPH, 1969, SCD, 1972; Nat Bd Med Examr, dipl, 1965; Am Col Prev Med, dipl, 1971; Pan Am Med Assoc, dipl. **Professional Experience:** PROF & ASSOC CHAIR DEPT MED, SCH MED, JOHNS HOPKINS UNIV, as of 2005; PROF, DEPT HEALTH POLICY MANAGEMENT, JOHNS HOPKINS SCH PUB HEALTH, as of 2003; prof behac sci, Health educ, Johns Hopkins Univ, beginning 1981; memstudy sect, Vet Admin Mert Rev, 1980-; mem study sect, Nat Heart-Lung Inst, NIH, 1975-; consult, Nat Ctr Health Serv Res, 1972- & Am Asn Med Col, 1973-; dir man power studies, Ctr health serv res & develop, beginning 1972; assoc prof pub health, med educ & internal med, 1972-1981; fel pub health serv, Sch Hyg & Pub Health, Johns Hopkins Univ, 1968-1971; resident prev med, Ctr Health Serv Res & Develop, 1968-1970, US Army MedCorp, 1966-1968, resident, Waltham Hosp, Mass, 1965-1966; intern, Montefiore Hosp, Pittsburgh, 1964-1965. **Memberships:** AAAS; Am Pub Health Asn; Am Fedn Clin Res; Am Col Prev Med; Pan Am Med Asn. **Research Statement & Publications:** Health behavior, health education and health promotion; health care manpower-services, health education strategies in managing chronic disease process and outcome of medical education. **Mailing Address:** Ross Res Bldg, Johns Hopkins Sch Med, 720 Rutland Ave, Baltimore, MD 21205. **Fax:** 410-614-5593. **E-Mail:** dlevine@jhmi.edu

LEVINE, D(ONALD) J(AY), ELECTRICAL ENGINEERING, TELECOMMUNICATIONS. **Personal Data:** b Brooklyn, NY, October 10, 1921. **Education:** City Col NY, BEE, 1943; Polytech Inst Brooklyn, MEE, 1952. **Honors & Awards:** Scott Helt Mem Award, Outstanding Contrib Inst Elec & Electronics Engrs Broadcast Tech Trans, 1989. **Professional Experience:** Vol, Adv Technol Prog, Nat Inst Space Technol, 1994; CONSULT, USN TELCOM, 1990-; electronics engr, Usn Telcom, 1989-1990; res vol, Nat Air & Space Mus, Smithsonian Inst, 1988-1994; consult, Int Broadcast Syst, Inc, 1988-1989; pres, Int Broadcast Systs, Inc, 1988; consult indust & govt, 1986-1993; consult, USIA/Voice Am (SES-4), Wash, DC, 1986-1988; chief, Broadcast Syst Eng Div, USIA/Voice Am (SES-4), Wash, DC, 1984-1986; Am Nucleonics Corp, Westlake Village, Calif, 1982-1983; vpres eng, Kings Electronics Co Inc, Tuckahoe, NY, 1976-1982; dir commun eng, Aerospace Corp, Wash, DC, 1975-1976; dir commun systs, Litton-Amecom, College Park, 1974-1975; dir systs eng, Page Commun Eng, Vienna, Va, 1973-1974; dept head, Network Eng & Anal Dept, Commun Div, Mitre Corp, 1967-1973; vpres & mgr, Transmission Systs Div, Commun Systs Inc, Comput Sci Corp, 1965-1967; dir, Radio Transmission & Anti-Submarine Warfare Lab, Int Tel & Tel Corp, 1948-1965; sr asst, Microwave Res Inst, Polytech Inst Brooklyn, 1946-1948. **Memberships:** Nat Soc Prof Engrs; sr mem Inst Elec & Electronics Engrs; Armed Forces Commun & Electronics Asn; AAAS; Asn of Old Crows. **Research Statement & Publications:** Microwave components, systems, antennas and antenna systems; radio communications; line of sight and troposcatter systems; switched telecommunications systems; network management planning and analysis; systems engineering for fixed, mobile, surface, air, space and submarine environments; operations analysis; shortwave/mediumwave broadcast systems engineering; avionics. **Mailing Address:** 7155 Summer Tree Dr, Boynton Beach, FL 33437. **Fax:** 561-737-3288. **E-Mail:** djlinfl@ieee.org

LEVINE, DONALD MARTIN, ZOOLOGY, PARASITOLOGY. **Personal Data:** b Boston, Mass, October 17, 1929. **Education:** Univ Vt, BA, 1951; Univ RI, MS, 1953; Univ Pa, PhD (zool), 1958. **Professional Experience:** PROF BIOL SCI, WILLIAM PATERSON COL NJ, 1974-; assoc prof, William Paterson Col NJ, 1962-1974; helminthologist, Liberian Inst, Am Found Trop Med, 1960-1962, USPHS fel, 1958-1960. **Memberships:** Am Soc Trop Med & Hyg; Am Inst Biol Sci. **Research Statement & Publications:** Immunology and ecology of parasitic infections. **Mailing Address:** Dept Biol Sci, William Paterson Col, 300 Pompton Rd, Wayne, NJ 07470-2103.

LEVINE, DOV I, PHYSICS. **Education:** Univ Pa, PhD, 1986. **Professional Experience:** ASSOC PROF & ADV, DEPT PHYSICS, TECHNION, ISRAEL INST TECHNOL, as of 2006; vis mem, & assoc prof, Inst Theoretical Physics, Univ Calif, Santa Barbara, 1997-1998; sr lectr physics, Technion, Israel Inst Technol, 1990; vis scientist, Dept Physics, Weizmann Inst Sci, 1988-1989; asst prof physics, univ fla, 1988-1991; mem, Inst Theoretical Physics, Univ Calif, Santa Barbara, 1986-1988. **Research Statement & Publications:** Statics and flow of granular materials; properties of densely packed systems; elasticity of foam. **Mailing Address:** Dept Physics, Technion-Israel Inst Technol, Haifa, 32000, Israel. **Fax:** 972-4-829-5755. **E-Mail:** levine@tx.technion.ac.il

LEVINE, DUANE GILBERT, CHEMISTRY, PHYSICS. **Personal Data:** b Baltimore, Md, July 5, 1933. **Education:** Johns Hopkins Univ, BES, 1956, MS, 1958. **Professional Experience:** MGR SCI & STRATEGY DEVELOP, EXXON CORP, 1989-; chmn, Forum Global Urbanization, 1988; chmn, Rene Dubos Int Forum Managing Hazardous Mat, New York, 1987; participant UN/Indust-Sponsored Conf Environ Mgt, Versailles, France, 1984; exec dir, CorpRes-Sci Labs, 1978-1989; gen mgr synthetic fuels res & develop, Baytown Res & Develop Div, 1976-1978; mgr petrol process eng, Gasoline & Lubes Process Eng Div, 1974-1976; mgr petrolfuels res & develop, Fuels Prod Qual Res Lab, Exxon Res& Eng Co, 1971-1974; mem, Air Pollution Res Adv Comt, joint comt US Govt, Petrol Indust & Automotive Indust, 1971-1974; mem, Eng & Tech Res Comt, Am Petrol Inst, 1971-1974; adv logistics, Exxon Corp, 1970-1971; head air pollution control res & develop, Automotive Emission Res Sect, 1968-1970; combustion, electrochem & petrol researcher, Exxon Res & Eng Co, 1959-1968; mem, Adv Comt, Calif Inst Technol, Johns Hopkins Univ, Rene Dubos Ctr. **Memberships:** AAAS; fel Am Inst Chemists; Am Inst Chem Engrs; Am Chem Soc; IntCombustion Inst; Sigma Xi; NY Acad Sci. **Research Statement & Publications:** Solid state sciences; surface sciences; optics; catalysis; materials; theoretical and mathematical sciences; biosci; engineering sciences; laser chemistry; polymer sciences; emulsion chemistry; chemical physics. **Mailing Address:** Exxon Corp, 5959 Las Colinas Blvd, Irving, TX 75039-2298. **Fax:** 214-444-1633.

LEVINE, ELISSA ROBIN, SOIL PROCESS MODELING. **Personal Data:** b New York, NY, December 10, 1952. **Education:** Kans State Univ, BS, 1978; Pa State Univ, MS, 1981, PhD (soil genesis), 1984. **Professional Experience:** INSTR, ENVIRON SCI & POLICY, JOHNS HOPKINS UNIV, 1996-; Vis prof, NC Agr & Tech Univ, 1992-; mem, Soil Subcomt, Fed Geog DataComt, 1992-; lectr, Am Women Geoscientists, 1990-; RES SCIENTIST, BIOSPHERIC SCI BR, NASA-GODDARD SPACE FLIGHT CTR, 1986-; fel, Nat Res Coun, 1986; RESIDENT RES ASSOC, GODDARD SPACE FLIGHT CTR, NASA, 1986-; fel, Univ Conn, 1985-1986; Soil consult, pvt firm, 1984-1986; SOIL SCIENTIST, USDA, CLEARFIELD, 1980-. **Memberships:** Am Soc Agron; Soil Sci Soc Am; Asn Women Soil Scientists. **Research Statement & Publications:** Modelling of processes related to the genesis of soils in response to environmental conditions using simulation models, artificial intelligence, techniques and remote sensing. **Mailing Address:** NASA Goddard Space Flight Ctr, Code 923, Greenbelt, MD 20771. **Fax:** 301-286-1757. **E-Mail:** elissa@lichen.gsfc.nasa.gov

LEVINE, ELLIOT MYRON, CELL BIOL, CELL CULTURE. **Personal Data:** b Brooklyn, NY, June 16, 1937; m 1959, Marian; c Bruce L, Eric S & Carolyn J. **Education:** Queens Col, NY, BS, 1957; Yale Univ, PhD (biochem), 1961. **Professional Experience:** PROF, WISTAR INST, 1984-; ASSOC FACULTY, PROF MED, WISTAR INST, UNIV PENN, 1996-; chmn, Am Type Cult Collection, 2000-; Wistar Inst, assoc dir, Sci Admin, 1994-1996; chmn, Cell Biol Study Sect, NIH, 1980-1982; mem, Cell Biol Study Sect, NIH, 1978-1982; staff mycoplasma detection course, W Alton Jones Cell Sci Ctr, 1977-; Lung Cell Comt, Am Type Cult Col, 1976-; mem grad groups cell biol, genetics & pathol, Univ Pa, 1975-; coordr res training, Wistar Inst, 1974-1980; NIH res grants, Wistar Inst, 1972-; from asst prof to assoc prof, Wistar Inst, 1972-1984; NSF res grants, Albert Einstein Col Med & Wistar Inst, 1970-; NIH fel, NIH career develop award, 1968-1972; NIH fel, NIH spec res fel, 1964-1965; from assoc to asst prof cell biol, Albert Einstein Col Med, 1963-1972; NIH fel, Albert Einstein Col Med, 1963-1964; sr asst scientist biochem, Nat Inst Arthritis, Metab & Digestive Dis, 1961-1963; mem bil dirs, Am Type Cult Collection. **Memberships:** Fel AAAS; Tissue Cult Asn (pres, 1990-1992); Sigma Xi; Soc In Vitro Biol. **Research Statement & Publications:** Proliferation and differentiation in cultured cells, especially vascular endothelial and smooth muscle cells; as well as osteoblast-like cells. **Mailing Address:** Wistar Inst, 3601 Spruce St, Philadelphia, PA 19104-4268. **Fax:** 215-898-0847. **E-Mail:** levine@wista.wistar.upenn.edu

LEVINE, EUGENE, ANALYTICAL STATISTICS, OPERATIONS RESEARCH. **Personal Data:** b Brooklyn, NY, January 11, 1925; m Barbara; c Gary M, Jeffrey H & Douglas E. **Education:** City Col NY, BBA, 1948; NY Univ, MPA, 1950; Am Univ, PhD (pub admin), 1960. **Honors & Awards:** Honorary Member, Sigma Theta Tau, Honor Society of Nursing, 2002. **Professional Experience:** PROF, GRAD SCH NURSING, UNIFORMED SERV UNIV HEALTH SCI, 1993-; Res consult, Sch Nursing, Georgetown Univ, 1984-; assoc, Levine Assoc, 1980-1993; dep dir, Div Health Prof Anal, 1978-1980; chief, Manpower Anal & Resources Br, Div Nursing, USPHS, 1950-1978; Statistician, New York City Dept Health, 1947-1950. **Memberships:** Am Pub Health Asn; Nat League Nursing; Am Statist Asn; Am Asn Health Serv Res: Academy of Medicine of D.C. **Research Statement & Publications:** Health manpower analysis; problems of health services organization and delivery; psychometric analysis into problems of job satisfaction; career choice and motivation; evaluation of health care programs; nursing research. **Mailing Address:** 8135 Inverness Ridge Rd, Potomac, MD 20854. **Fax:** 301-295-1707. **E-Mail:** elevine666@aol.com

LEVINE, FRED, GENETICS. **Education:** Univ Wash, PhD. **Professional Experience:** PROF, REBECCA & JOHN MOORES CANCER CTR, as of 2006; ASST PROF, CTR MOLECULAR GENETICS, UNIV CALIF, as of 2005. **Mailing Address:** Ctr Molecular Genetics Univ Calif, 122 CMG 9500 Gillman Dr, La Jolla, CA 92093-0634. **Fax:** 619-534-1422. **E-Mail:** flevine@ucsd.edu

LEVINE, FREDERIC M, PAIN MANAGEMENT & RESEARCH. **Personal Data:** b New York, NY, May 20, 1937. **Education:** City Col NY, BA, 1961; Northwestern Univ, MA, 1963, PhD (psychol), 1965. **Professional Experience:** PVT PRACTICE, 2002-; ASSOC PROF PSYCHOL, STATE UNIV NY, STONYBROOK, 1973-; asst prof, State Univ NY, Stony Brook, 1967-1973; res assoc psychol, Harvard Med Sch, 1965-1967. **Memberships:** Am Psychol Asn; Am Pain Asn. **Research Statement & Publications:** Social and psychological factors that influence pain report; models of psychotherapeutic intervention. **Mailing Address:** Dept Psychol, State Univ NY, Port Jefferson, NY 11777. **Fax:** 516-473-6622.

LEVINE, GEOFFREY, NUCLEAR PHARMACY, HEALTH PHYSICS. **Personal Data:** b Washington, DC, September 2, 1942. **Education:** Temple Univ, BS, 1965, MS, 1967; Northwestern Univ, PhD (civil eng & environhealth), 1978. **Professional Experience:** CLIN DIR, MONOCLONAL ANTIBODY CTR, PITTSBURGH CANCER INST, 1993-; consult, Mallinckrodt-NeoRxMonoclonal Antibody Develop Prog, 1988-1990; assoc mem, Pittsburgh Cancer Inst, 1987-; consult, Am Pharm Asn, 1986-; nuclear med res comt, Univ Health Ctr, Presby-Univ Hosp, 1985-; mem, Radioactive Drug Res Comt, 1985-; mem, Human Use Subcomt Radiation SafetyComt, Univ Pittsburgh, 1985-; dir nuclear pharm, Cent Imaging Serv, Inc, 1985-1991; assoc prof, Sch Pharm, 1985; assoc med staff, Univ Health Ctr, Presby-Univ Hosp, 1984-; PROF NUCLEAR MED, ALLEGHENY CO COMMUNITY COL, 1984-; consult, NEN-DupontRadiopharm Div, 1984; assoc prof radiol, Sch Med, Univ Pittsburgh, beginning 1983; consult, Charleston Area Med Ctr, 1979-1980; radiation res comt, Montefiore Hosp, 1978-; radiation safety comt, Univ Health Ctr, Presby-Univ Hosp, 1975-; pharm staff, Montefiore Hosp, 1975-; consult, Ames Labs, 1975; Grants, Am Cancer Soc, Union Carbide Corp, Soc NuclearMed & others, 1974-; consult, Shadyside Hosp, 1974-1975; clin asst med staff, Univ Health Ctr, Presby-Univ Hosp, 1973-1983; radiopharmacist, Univ Health Ctr, Presby-Univ Hosp, 1972-; radiopharm adv nuclear pharm, Univ Health Ctr, Presby-Univ Hosp, 1972-; dir nuclear pharm, Univ Health Ctr, Presby-Univ Hosp, 1972-1987; coord, prog radiopharm, 1972-1983; asst profradiol, prog radiopharm, 1972-1983; clin asst prof pharmaceut, Univ Pittsburgh, 1972-1980; at Abbott Lab, NChicago, 1966-1968; Pharmacist, 1965-1967. **Memberships:** Health Physics Soc; Soc Nuclear Med (secy-treas 1974); Sigma Xi; AmPharmaceut Asn; AAAS; Am Soc Hosp Pharmacists. **Research Statement & Publications:** Drug interactions; radioactive pharmaceuticals and radioactive monoclonal antibodies for tumor detection; author of numerous publications; cost-benefit risk analysis; inventory control modeling of radiopharmaceuticals; radiopharmacology. **Mailing Address:** Univ Pittsburgh Cancer Inst, 5150 Ctr Ave, Pittsburgh, PA 15232.

LEVINE, GILBERT, IRRIGATION ENGINEERING. **Education:** Cornell Univ, PhD. **Professional Experience:** PROF EMER, CORNELL UNIV, as of 2006; actg dir, Mario Einaudi Ctr Int Studies, 2002-2003; dir, Mario Einaudi Ctr Int Studies, 1994-1996. **Mailing Address:** Einaudi Ctr Int Studies, 170 Uris Hall Cornell Univ, Ithaca, NY 14853. **Fax:** 607-254-5000. **E-Mail:** gl14@cornell.edu

LEVINE, H, CONDENSED MATTER PHYSICS. **Education:** Princeton Univ, PhD, 1979. **Professional Experience:** PROF, DEPT PHYSICS, UNIV CALIF, SAN DIEGO, as of 2006. **Mailing Address:** Dept Physics 0319, Univ Calif San Diego, La Jolla, CA 92093-0319. **Fax:** 858-534-7664. **E-Mail:** levine@herbie.ucsd.edu

LEVINE, HAROLD, APPLIED MATHEMATICS. **Personal Data:** b New York, NY, March 24, 1922. **Education:** City Col NY, BS, 1941; Cornell Univ, PhD (physics), 1944. **Professional Experience:** PROF EMER MATH, STANDARD UNIV, as of 2004; prof, Stanford Univ, 1970-1992; assoc prof math, Stanford Univ, 1955-1970; lectr, Harvard Univ, 1952-1954; res fel physics, Harvard Univ, 1945-1954; consult, Lawrence Radiation Lab, Univ Calif. **Memberships:** Am Phys Soc. **Research Statement & Publications:** Boundary value problems of classical field theories, particularly acoustics, electrodynamics and hydrodynamics. **Mailing Address:** Dept Math, Stanford Univ, Stanford, CA 94305-2125.

LEVINE, HAROLD, MATHEMATICS. **Personal Data:** b Lynn, Mass, December 14, 1928. **Education:** Univ Chicago, PhD (math), 1957. **Professional Experience:** PROF MATH, BRANDEIS UNIV, 1970-; from asst prof to assoc prof, Brandeis Univ, 1960-1970; instr math, Yale Univ, 1959-1960; Fulbright fel & Ger Res Asngrant, Univ Bonn, 1957-1959. **Memberships:** Am Math Soc; Math Asn Am. **Research Statement & Publications:** Differential topology. **Mailing Address:** 32 Grande Rue 45360, Chatillon-Sur-Loire, France.

LEVINE, HARRY, POLYMER SCIENCE OF FOODS. **Personal Data:** b New York, NY, December 16, 1947. **Education:** Rensselaer Polytech Inst, BS, 1968, PhD (polymer chem), 1975. **Professional Experience:** FOOD POLYMER SCIENTIST, KRAFT FOODS INC, NABISCO RES & DEVELOP, as of 2002; res fel, Nabisco Foods Group, beginning 1991; course dir, Ctr Prof Advan, Am Asn Cereal Chem & Am Chem Soc, beginning 1987; sr prin scientist, Nabisco Brands, 1987-1991; srpolymer chemist, Gen Foods Corp, 1976-1987; Fel, Roswell Park Mem Inst, 1974-1976. **Memberships:** Fel Am Inst Chemists; Am Chem Soc; Am Asn Cereal Chemists; Sigma Xi. **Research Statement & Publications:** Polymer science approach to foods; glasses and glass transitions in foods; water relations in foods; water as plasticizer. **Mailing Address:** Kraft Foods Inc, Nabisco Res & Develop, PO Box 1944, East Hanover, NJ 07936-1944. **E-Mail:** harry.levine@kraft.com

LEVINE, HARRY III, ALZHEIMERS DISEASE, MEMBRANE BIOLOGY, PROTEIN MISFOLDING. **Personal Data:** b Utica, NY, July 12, 1949. **Education:** Cornell Univ, BS, 1971; Johns Hopkins Univ, PhD (physiol chem), 1975. **Professional Experience:** ASSOC PROF, SANDERS-BROWN CTR AGING & DEPT MOLECULAR & CELLULAR BIOCHEM, UNIV KY, 2003-; adj asst res Scientist, Dept Biol, Univ Mich, 1993-2001; res fel, Pfizer Inc, 1991-; adj asst prof, Dept Neurobiology, Duke Univ, 1989-1991; res investr, Glaxo Res Labs, 1987-1991; Postdoctoral Wellcome Res Labs, 1975-1977; res scientist, 1972-1987. **Research Statement & Publications:** Development of strategies to treat neurodegenerative diseases such as Alzheimer's disease; study of signal transduction mechanisms and the relationship of protein structure/function to pathophysiology. **Mailing Address:** Dept Molecular & Cellular Biochem, Univ Ky, 800 S Limestone St, Lexington, KY 40536-0230. **Fax:** 859-323-2866. **E-Mail:** hlevine@email.uky.edu

LEVINE, HARVEY ROBERT, PARASITOLOGY, MEDICAL ENTOMOLOGY. **Personal Data:** b New York, NY, September 15, 1931. **Education:** City Col New York, BS, 1953; Univ Mass, MS, 1955, PhD (entom), 1958. **Professional Experience:** Dir Title II Math, SciInst, 1989-1992; bd trustees, Quinnipiac Col, 1984-1993; asst dean Acad Affairs, Sch Sci, 1971-1972; PROF BIOL, QUINNIPIAC COL, 1968-; chmn Dept Biol, Quinnipiac Col, 1968-1976; from asst prof to prof biol, Bemidji State Col, 1958-1968; Instr entom, Univ Mass, 1955; Consult, Trout Unlimited; mem, Mus Natural Hist. **Memberships:** Am Inst Biol Sci; Am Asn Lab Animal Sci; Soc Vector Ecol; Entom Soc Am; Sigma Xi; Am Fedn Teachers. **Research Statement & Publications:** Acaptatious of freshwater insects; medical entomology (aquatic vectors); lyme disease diagnosis. **Mailing Address:** Dept Biol Sci, Quinnipiac Col, 275 Mt Carmel Ave, Hamden, CT 06518-1961.

LEVINE, HERBERT, PHYSICS. **Education:** Princeton Univ, PhD, 1979. **Professional Experience:** PROF, DEPT PHYSICS, UNIV CALIF, SAN DIEGO, as of 2005. **Mailing Address:** Dept Physics, Univ Calif, San Diego, B 019, La Jolla, CA 92093-0319. **Fax:** 858-534-7664. **E-Mail:** levine@herbie.ucsd.edu

LEVINE, HERBERT JEROME, CARDIOLOGY. **Personal Data:** b Boston, Mass, July 22, 1928. **Education:** Harvard Univ, AB, 1950; Johns Hopkins Univ, MD, 1954; Am Bd Internal Med, dipl, 1963. **Professional Experience:** PROF MED SCH MED, TUFTSUNIV, 1970-; lectr, US Naval Hosp, Mass, 1967-; consult, Vet Admin Hosp, Mass, 1966-; from asst prof to assoc prof, Tuftsuniv, 1963-1970; chief cardiol serv, New Eng Med Ctr Hosps, 1961-1988; sr instr, Tuftsuniv, 1961-1963; res fel, Harvard Med Sch, 1959-1961; sr resident, Peter Bent Brigham Hosp, 1958-1959; resident, Mass Gen Hosp, 1957-1958; Res fel cardiol, Peter Bent Brigham Hosp, 1956-1961; Intern med, Peter Bent Brigham Hosp, 1954-1955. **Memberships:** Fel Am Fedn Clin Res; fel Asn Univ Cardiol; fel Am Col Cardiol; fel Am SocClin Invest; Asn Am Physicians. **Research Statement & Publications:** Clinical cardiology; physiology of congestive heart failure; muscle mechanics and energetics in the intact heart. **Mailing Address:** New Eng Med Ctr Hosp, 750 Washington St, Boston, MA 02111.

LEVINE, HERMAN SAUL, PHYSICAL CHEMISTRY, HIGH TEMPERATURE CHEMISTRY, X-RAY SPECTROSCOPY. **Personal Data:** b Jeannette, Pa, February 11, 1922; m 1947, Leora (Remarried); c 3. **Education:** Univ Pittsburgh, BS, 1943; Univ Ill, PhD (phys chem), 1948. **Professional Experience:** RETIRED; mem tech staff, Sandia Labs, 1957-1989; staff mem, NY State Col Ceramics, Alfred Univ, 1948-1951 & USPHS, R A Taft Sanit Eng Ctr, 1951-1957; Res asst, Ill State Geol Surv, 1944-1946. **Memberships:** Am Chem Soc. **Research Statement & Publications:** X-ray spectroscopy. **Mailing Address:** 9128 Quail Terrace Way, Elk Grove, CA 95624.

LEVINE, HOWARD ALLEN, MATHEMATICS, MATHEMATICS BIOLOGY. **Personal Data:** b St Paul, Minn, January 15, 1942; m Elyse. **Education:** Univ Minn, Duluth, BA, 1964; Cornell Univ, MA, 1967, PhD (math), 1969. **Professional Experience:** Mem ed bd, Cancer Informatics, 2005-; assoc ed, Math Biosciences & Eng, 2002-; DISTINGUISHED PROF MATH, IOWA STATE UNIV, 1999-; assoc ed, J Math Anal & Applns, 1995-; assoc ed, Commun Appl Anal, 1994-; dept chmn, Iowa State Univ, 1989-1992; assoc prof, Consiglio Nazionale delle Recerche, Italy & Math Sci Res Inst, 1983; staff, Chem Eng Div, Ames Lab, Iowa, 1981; from assoc prof to prof math, Iowa State Univ, 1978-1999; NSF res grant, 1978-1979; part-time res consult, Naval Underwater Systs Ctr, 1977-1978; NSF res grant, 1974-1977; from asst prof to assoc prof, Univ RI, 1973-1978; vis asst prof, State Univ NY, Binghamton, 1973; Sci Res Coun Gt Brit grant, Univ Dundee, 1972; vis scientist, Battelle Advan Studies Ctr, Switz, 1971 & 1972; asst prof math, Univ Minn, Minneapolis, 1969-1973. **Memberships:** Am Math Soc; Sigma Xi; Soc Math Biol; Soc Indust & Appl Math. **Research Statement & Publications:** Partial differential equations; numerical analysis; modeling of angiogenesis and other branching processes in biology. **Mailing Address:** Dept Math, Iowa State Univ, Ames, IA 50011. **Fax:** 515-294-5454. **E-Mail:** halevine@iastate.edu

LEVINE, HOWARD BERNARD, COMPUTER LANGUAGES, SCIENTIFIC SOFTWARE. **Personal Data:** b Brooklyn, NY, April 15, 1928; m 1967, Helene; c Stefanie & Jessica. **Education:** Univ Ill, BS, 1950; Univ Chicago, MS, 1952, PhD (chem), 1955. **Professional Experience:** Principal Software Engr, Cobic Defent Applications Group, 1995; sr software engr, Teledyne Ryan Aeronaut, 1989-1995; pres, 21st Century Data, Inc, 1982-1989; prin scientist, Jaycor, 1976-1982; prog mgr chem systs, Systs, Sci & Software, 1973-1976; prof chem eng, Va Polytech Inst & State Univ, 1971-1973; proj assoc, Theoret Chem Inst & Space Sci & Eng Ctr, Univ Wis, 1970-1971; mem tech staff, NAm Aviation Sci Ctr, 1962-1970; chemist, Lawrence Radiation Lab, Univ Calif, 1956-1962; res fel chem, Inst Atomic Res, Iowa State Univ, 1955-1956; consult, Tech Adv Bd Supersonic Transport, Dept Com; mem ad hoc comt ozone & environ studies bd, Nat Acad Sci. **Memberships:** Am Chem Soc; fel Am Phys Soc; Am Inst Chem Eng. **Research Statement & Publications:** Thermodynamics; embedded real time computer systems; spectroscopy; atmospheric chemistry; molecular physics; applied mathematics; chemical kinetics; computer languages. **Mailing Address:** 2817 Luciernaga St, Carlsbad, CA 92009-5927. **Fax:** 858-505-1516. **E-Mail:** howard.levine@cubic.com

LEVINE, IRA NOEL, PHYSICAL CHEMISTRY. **Personal Data:** b Brooklyn, NY, 1937. **Education:** Carnegie Inst Technol, BS, 1958; Harvard Univ, AM, 1959, PhD (chem), 1963. **Professional Experience:** PROF CHEM, BROOKLYN COL, 1978-; Am Chem Soc Petrol Res Fund starter grant, 1965-1966; from instr to assoc prof, Brooklyn Col, 1964-1977; Res assoc chem, Univ Pa, 1963-1964. **Memberships:** Am Chem Soc. **Research Statement & Publications:** Quantum chemistry. **Mailing Address:** Chem Dept, Brooklyn Col, Brooklyn, NY 11210. **E-Mail:** inlevine@brooklyn.cuny.edu

LEVINE, JACK, mathematics; deceased, see previous edition for last biography

LEVINE, JEFFREY, MATHEMATICS. **Personal Data:** b Brooklyn, NY, February 7, 1945; m 1966. **Education:** State Univ NY Stony Brook, BS, 1966; Rutgers Univ, New Brunswick, PhD (math), 1970. **Professional Experience:** MEM STAFF, MCDONNELL DOUGLAS CORP, 1980-; asst prof math, State Univ NY Col Geneseo, 1971-1980; asst prof math, Monmouth Col, NJ, 1969-1971. **Memberships:** Am Math Soc; Math Asn Am. **Research Statement & Publications:** Ring theory. **Mailing Address:** 761 La Feil Dr, Ballwin, MO 63021.

LEVINE, JEFFREY R, GEOLOGY. **Professional Experience:** CONSULT GEOLOGIST, as of 2004. **Mailing Address:** 2077 N Collins Blvd, Suite 109, Richardson, TX 75080. **E-Mail:** jeffrey@levineonline.com

LEVINE, JEROME PAUL, TOPOLOGY. **Personal Data:** b New York, NY, May 4, 1937. **Education:** Mass Inst Technol, BS, 1958; Princeton Univ, PhD (math), 1962. **Honors & Awards:** Humboldt Prize, Ger. **Professional Experience:** Chmn dept, Brandeis Univ, 1974-1976, 1988-1990; PROF MATH, BRANDEIS UNIV, 1969-; assoc prof, Brandeis Univ, 1966-1969, Sloan Found fel, 1966-1968, from asst prof to assoc prof math, Univ Calif, Berkeley, 1964-1966, NSF fel, 1963-1964; instr math, Mass Inst Technol, 1961-1963. **Memberships:** Am Math Soc. **Research Statement & Publications:** Differential topology; knot theory. **Mailing Address:** Dept Math, Brandeis Univ, Waltham, MA 02254-9110.

LEVINE, JERRY DAVID, ENVIRONMENTAL PROTECTION, OCCUPATIONAL SAFETY. **Personal Data:** b Mount Vernon, NY, June 27, 1952; m 1977, Ronnie; c Audrey. **Education:** State Univ NY, Stony Brook, BS, 1974; Polytech Inst NY, MS, 1976. **Honors & Awards:** Nat Environ Policy Act Compliance Officer Award, USDept Energy, 1995. **Professional Experience:** Mem, Radiation Safety Comt, 1995-; CHMN, SAFETY REV COMT, PLASMA PHYSICS LAB, 1995-; HEAD, ENVIRON, SAFETY & HEALTH DIV, PLASMA PHYSICS LAB, 1997- HEAD, ENVIRON & SAFETY DIV, PRINCETON UNIV, 1995-1997; chmn environ rev comt, Plasma Physics Lab, Princeton Univ, 1992-1996; head, Environ & Health Br, 1991-1995; nuclear-environ engr, Plasma Physics Lab, 1987-1991; prin engr, Envirosphere Co, 1984-1987; sr engr, Ebasco Ser, Inc, 1980-1984; engr, Ebasco Ser, Inc, 1978-1980; assoc engr, Ebasco Ser, Inc, 1977-1978; Asst engr, Ebasco Ser, Inc, 1976-1977. **Memberships:** Am Nuclear Soc. **Research Statement & Publications:** Nuclear fusion safety studies; review nuclear safety and environmental aspects of design and operation of fusion experimental devices, including TFTR, NSTX, NCSX and ITER; develop national standard for fusion safety. **Mailing Address:** One Ivy Way, Dayton, NJ 08810-1420. **E-Mail:** jlevine@pppl.gov

LEVINE, JOEL S, ATMOSPHERIC SCIENCE, PLANETARY SCIENCE. **Personal Data:** b Brooklyn, NY, May 14, 1942; m 1968, Arlene Spielholz; c Lisa K. **Education:** Brooklyn Col, BS, 1964; NY Univ, MS (metcology), 1967; Univ Mich, MS (acronomy, planctory atmospheres), 1973, PhD, (atmospheric sci), 1977. **Honors & Awards:** Halpern Award Photochem, NY Acad Sci, 1982; Medal Except Sci Achievement, NASA, 1983; Virginia's outstanding scientist, 1987. **Professional Experience:** Proj scientist, NASA Mars airplane 2003; mem, Sci Team, Chesapeake Bay Impact Crater Core Drilling Proj at NASA Langley, 2000; micromission, 1999; lead auth, UN environ on wildland fires & environ, 1998-1999; leader, Langley Charters Freedom res team, 1998-; co-chair, WHO workshop health guidelines veg fire events, 1998; prin investr, Proj NOVA, 1995-1996; prin investr, firesat proj, 1994-; co-prin investr, Boreal Forest Res Exp, 1993-; dir, Atmospheric Sci Prog, Col William & Mary, Williamsburg, Va, 1992-; adj prof appl sci & physics, Atmospheric Sci Prog, Col William & Mary, Williamsburg, Va, 1992-; ed, Global Biomass Burning: Atmospheric, Climate & Biospheric Implications, 1991; prin investr, SAfrica Fire-Atmosphere Res Initiative, 1990-; mem, Burning Exp, 1990-; mem, Biosphere-Atmosphere Trace Gas Exp, 1990-; prin investr, search preindustrial air lead coffins, St Marys City Md, 1990-1992; co-dir, Global Emissions Inventory Biomass Burning, Int Global Atmospheric Chem Proj, 1990-; Sci Steering comt, Ctr Explor Prog Sci, 1988-1992; Sci Steering Comt, Space Sci & Appln Adv Comt, 1988-1990; prin investr, Atmospheric Chem Exp, Global Biomass Burning, 1987-; Sci Steering Comt, Origins Solar Systs Prog, 1987-1990; ed, Space Opportunities for Tropospheric Chem Res, 1987; mem, Va Dept Ed Sci Dir, 1985-; mem, NASA Life Sci Adv Comt, 1985-1988; adj assoc prof, Dept Geol Sci, 1985-1988; ed, Photochem Atmospheres Earth, Other Planets & Comets, 1985; prin investr, Photochem & Geochem Early Earth, 1983-1993; lectr, Tidewater Ctr, Univ Va, 1982-1985; prin guest investr, Int Ultraviolet Explorer, 1981-1983; Comt Planetary Biol & Chem Evolution, Space Sci Bd, Nat Res Coun-Nat Acad Sci, 1978-1981; prin investr, Global Troposheric Chem Photochem Processes, 1977-1989; res adv, Sch Eng, Old Dominion Univ, 1977-1981; lectr, Col William & Mary, 1976-1992; prin guest investr, Orbiting Astron Observ-Copernicus, 1974-1976; consult, Mars Aeronomy, Viking Proj NASA, 1972-1976; SR RES SCIENTIST, ATMOSPHERIC SCI DIV, LANGLEY RES CTR, NASA, 1970-; res scientist atmospheric sci, Geophys Sci Lab, NY Univ, 1964-1970; res scientist atmospheric sci, Goddard Inst Space Studies, 1964-1970; instr physics & dir astron observ, Brooklyn Col, 1964-1970. **Memberships:** Am Geophys Union; Int Soc Study Origin Life. **Research Statement & Publications:** Origin, evolution, physics and chemistry of planetary atmospheres; atmospheric photochemistry; biogeochemical cycling; global climate change; origin & evolution of life. **Mailing Address:** Chem & Dynamics Br, Sci Directorate, NASA Langley Res Ctr, Hampton, VA 23681-0001. **Fax:** 757-864-6326. **E-Mail:** j.s.levine@lare.nasa.gov

LEVINE, JON DAVID, MEDICAL SCIENCES, INTERNAL MEDICINE. **Personal Data:** b New York, NY, March 20, 1945. **Education:** Univ Mich, BS, 1966; Yale Univ, PhD (neurobiol), 1972; Univ Calif, San Francisco, MD, 1978. **Professional Experience:** PROF ORAL & MAXILLOFACIAL SURG MED, UNIV CALIF, SAN FRANCISCO, as of 2004; asst prof med, Univ Calif, San Francisco, beginning 1984; fel clin pharmacol & therapeut, Univ Calif, San Francisco, beginning 1982; fel rheumatol & clin immunol, Univ Calif, San Francisco, beginning 1981; Hartford Found fel. **Memberships:** Am Soc Clin Invest. **Research Statement & Publications:** Mechanisms of pain and anlagesia and application of research in this area to the diagnosis and mangement of clinical pain; pathophyisology of inflammatory joint disease; rheumatology; neurobiology; clinical pharmacology. **Mailing Address:** Dept Med & NeuroSci, Univ Calif, C-522 Box 0440 512 Parnassus Ave, San Francisco, CA 94143-0440. **Fax:** 415-476-6305. **E-Mail:** levine@itsa.ucsf.edu

LEVINE, JON HOWARD, ENDOCRINOLOGY. **Personal Data:** b Toronto, Ont, July 13, 1941. **Education:** Univ Toronto, MD, 1965, MSc, 1969; Royal Col Physicians & Surgeons Can, FRCP (C), 1971; Am Bd Internal Med, cert endocrinol, 1977. **Professional Experience:** PROF MED, MEHARRY MED COL, NASHVILLE, TENN & CHEIF ENDOCRINIL, METROPOLITAN NASHVILLE GEN HOSP, as of 2006; prof med, Med Unic SC, beginning 1982; from asst prof to assoc prof endocrinol, Med Univ SC, 1973-1982; instr, Vanderbilt Univ, 1971-1973; fel, Med Res Coun Can, 1971-1973. **Memberships:** Am Fedn Clin Res; Endocrine Soc; Can Soc Endocrin & Metab. **Research Statement & Publications:** Medical education; pituitary regulation of adrenal steroidogenesis; clinical problem solving techniques by physicians. **Mailing Address:** 2222 State St, Nashville, TN 37203.

LEVINE, JOSEPH H, RISK MANAGEMENT, PRODUCT ASSURANCE. **Personal Data:** b Mineral Wells, Tex, April 16, 1926; m 1950, c Edward. **Education:** Southern Methodist Univ, BS, 1950, MS, 1958. **Honors & Awards:** NASA Certs Commendation Apollo Skylab Programs Outstanding Techn & Mgt control. **Professional Experience:** OWNER, ENG CONSULT SERV, 1986-; mem, Nuclear Regulation Comn Invest Group, 1986; chief, Reliability Div, Johnson Space Ctr, NASA, 1962-1986; proj engr, Gen Dynamics Corp, 1956-1962. **Memberships:** Assoc fel Am Inst Aeronaut & Astronaut; Nat Asn Consults. **Research Statement & Publications:** Manufacturing processes relative to risk; process failure modes and effects analysis technique applied to solid propulsion improvement program and advanced solid propulsion program. **Mailing Address:** 3722 Montvale, Houston, TX 77059.

LEVINE, JOSEPH SAMUEL, PETROLEUM ENGINEERING. **Personal Data:** b San Antonio, Tex, September 14, 1915; m 1955, Doris; c Susan & Charles J. **Education:** Univ Tex, BS, 1936; Pa State Col, MS, 1938, PhD (petrol eng), 1941. **Professional Experience:** RETIRED; staff res engr, Shell Develop Co Div, Shell Oil Co, 1965-1983; staff engr, Shell Develop Co Div, Shell Oil Co, 1964-1965; sr exploitation engr, Shell Develop Co Div, Shell Oil Co, 1960-1964; sr chemist fluid flow res, Shell Develop Co Div, Shell Oil Co, 1946-1960; asst & instr petrol eng, Pa State Col, 1936-1942. **Memberships:** Am Inst Mining, Metall & Petrol Engrs; Soc Petrol Engrs. **Research Statement & Publications:** Fluid flow; hydrodynamics; fluid flow through porous media; mechanism of displacement of oil by water; secondary recovery of oil. **Mailing Address:** 5614 Jackwood St, Houston, TX 77096-1106.

LEVINE, JUDAH, PHYSICS. **Personal Data:** b New York, NY, November 17, 1940. **Education:** Yeshiva Col, BA, 1960; NY Univ, MS, 1963, PhD (physics), 1966. **Honors & Awards:** Bronze Medal, Dept Com, 1980; Gold Medal, Dept Com, 1983. **Professional Experience:** PHYSICIST, TIME & FREQUENCY DIV, NIST, as of 2000; fel, Joint inst lab Astrophys, 1976-; physicist, Time & Frequency div, Nat InstStand & technol, 1974-; prof, dept Physics, Univ Colo, beginning 1974; mem, Joint inst LabAstrophys, 1969-1975; physicist, Quantum Electronics div, Nat inst Stand & Technol, 1969-1973; NATO fel, Claredon lab, Oxford Univ, Eng, 1966-1967; fel, NSF, 1963-1966; resasst, Physics dept,

New York Univ, 1962-1963; Teaching asst, Physics dept, New York Univ, 1960-1962. **Memberships:** Fel Am Phys Soc; Am Asn Physics Teachers; Am Geophys Union. **Research Statement & Publications:** Physics. **Mailing Address:** S460, JILA Bldg, Univ Colo, Campus Box 440, Boulder, CO 80309-0440. **Fax:** 303-492-5235. **E-Mail:** judah.levine@colorado.edu

LEVINE, JULES DAVID, MATERIALS SCIENCE ENGINEERING. **Personal Data:** b New York, NY, June 24, 1937; m 1966, c 2. **Education:** Columbia Univ, BS, 1959; Mass Inst Technol, PhD (physics, nuclear eng), 1963. **Professional Experience:** BR MGR SOLAR CELL DEVELOP, TEX INSTRUMENTS, 1979-; proj mgr cathode res & develop, David Sarnoff Res Ctr, RCA Labs, 1976-1979; mem tech staff surface & mat res, proj mgr flat panel TV, 1973-1976; vis lectr elec eng, Princeton Univ, 1971-1972 & 1974-1975; mem tech staff surface & mat res, David Sarnoff Res Ctr, RCA Labs, 1963-1973. **Memberships:** Fel Inst Elec & Electronics Engrs; sr mem Am Vacuum Soc. **Research Statement & Publications:** Physical processes and engineering of surfaces; thin films; semiconductors; electron emitters; display and power tubes; thermionic energy conversion; high voltage phenomena; electron beams; varistors; vacuum science and technology; fabricates novel solar cells made from miniature single crystal silicon spheres mounted in a planar matrix. **Mailing Address:** Tex Instruments, MS 8207 PO Box 655303, Dallas, TX 75265.

LEVINE, JULES IVAN, HEALTH SCIENCES, MEDICAL ADMINISTRATION. **Personal Data:** b Brooklyn, NY, April 17, 1938. **Education:** Univ Va, BEE, 1960, PhD (biomed eng), 1972; Johns Hopkins Univ, MS, 1968. **Professional Experience:** INT PRES, ALPHA EPSILON PI FRATENITY, as of 2003; prof health affairs, Univ Va, beginning 1986; ASSOC VPRES HEALTH SCI, UNIV VA, 1986-; asst vpres health affairs, Univ Va, 1978-1986; assoc dean, Sch Med, Univ Va, 1974-1978; from asst prof to assoc prof pediat, Univ Va, 1972-1986; sr engr aerospace electronics, Westinghouse Elec Corp, 1963-1968; consult, NIH. **Memberships:** Soc Col & Univ Planning; Am Asn Med Cols. **Research Statement & Publications:** Planning and evaluation of health resources and the health care delivery system. **Mailing Address:** Alpha Epsilon Pi Fraternity, 8815 Wesleyan Rd, Indianapolis, IN 46268. **Fax:** 434-924-9967. **E-Mail:** jil@virginia.edu

LEVINE, LAWRENCE, IMMUNOCHEMISTRY. **Personal Data:** b Hartford, Conn, July 18, 1924. **Education:** Univ Conn, BA, 1948; Univ Mich, MS, 1950; Johns Hopkins Univ, DSc(microbiol), 1953. **Professional Experience:** PROF EMER BIOCHEM, BRANDEIS UNIV, as of 2005; prof biochem, Brandeis Univ, beginning 1970; from asst prof to assoc prof, Brandeis Univ, 1957-1970; res scientist, Div Labs & Res, State Dept Health, NY, 1954-1957; instr microbiol, Johns Hopkins Univ, 1953-1954. **Research Statement & Publications:** Blood proteins and their immunol properties. **Mailing Address:** Brandeis Univ, Dept Biochem, Waltham, MA 02254-2700. **Fax:** 781-736-2349. **E-Mail:** llevine@brandeis.edu

LEVINE, LAWRENCE ELLIOTT, APPLIED MATHEMATICS. **Personal Data:** b Chelsea, Mass, June 23, 1941. **Education:** Rensselaer Polytech Inst, BS, 1963; Univ Md, PhD (appl math), 1968, Stevens Inst Technol, MEng, 1977. **Honorary Degrees:** M Eng, Stevens Inst Technol, 1979. **Professional Experience:** Writer of column dealing with American Jewish history and other articles related to Judaism. COMMENTATOR, ARAB-WEST REPORT, 2003-; consult, Mcnair Academic High Sch, 2002-2003; head, Dept Pure & Appl Math, 1991-1996; prof math, Stevens Insttechnol, 1977, from asst prof to assoc prof, 1968-1977. **Memberships:** Am Math Asn. **Research Statement & Publications:** Fluid dynamics; partial differential equations; perturbation methods; CAI in mathematics; computer education. **Mailing Address:** Dept Math Sci, Stevens Inst Technol, Hoboken, NJ 07030. **Fax:** 201-216-8321. **E-Mail:** llevine@stevens.edu

LEVINE, LEO MEYER, MATHEMATICS. **Personal Data:** b Brooklyn, NY, May 26, 1922. **Education:** City Col New York, BS, 1942; NY Univ, PhD (math), 1960. **Professional Experience:** PROF EMER MATH, QUEENSBOROUGH COL, as of 2004; prof math, Queenborough Community Col, beginning 1981; assoc prof, Queensborough Community Col, 1970-1981; from asst prof to assoc prof, Courant Inst Math Sci, NY Univ, 1963-1970; Consult, Radio Corp Am, 1961-1962; from asst res scientist to assoc resscientist, Courant Inst Math Sci, NY Univ, 1959-1963; sr physicist, Mat Lab, NY NavalShipyard, 1947-1959; asst physicist, Signal Corps Labs, Eatontown, NJ, 1942-1943. **Memberships:** Am Math Soc; Math Asn Am. **Research Statement & Publications:** Applied mathematics; ordinary and partial differential equations; acoustics; electromagnetic theory. **Mailing Address:** 138-21 77th Ave, Flushing, NY 11367.

LEVINE, LEONARD, NEUROPHYSIOLOGY. **Personal Data:** b Atlantic City, NJ, January 28, 1929. **Education:** Rutgers Univ, BS, 1950; Columbia Univ, PhD (physiol), 1959. **Professional Experience:** TECH LEADER, EPRI, PALO ALTO, Calif, as of 2003; Res grant proposal evaluator, Regulatory Biol Prog, NSF, 1978-; prof pharmacol, Pac Univ, beginning 1976; USPHS res grants, 1967-1968 & 1970-1972; prof physiol, Pac Univ, beginning 1966; USPHS res grants, 1962-1965; from asst prof to assoc prof, Univ Va, 1961-1966; fel biophys, Univ Col, Univ London, 1960-1961; USPHS fel physiol, Columbia Univ, 1959-1960; Instr physiol, Columbia Univ, 1957-1960. **Memberships:** AAAS; Am Physiol Soc; Biophys Soc; Am Soc Zool; Am Soc Pharmacol & ExpTherapeut; Sigma Xi. **Research Statement & Publications:** Electrophysiology and pharmacology of ocular tissues; trophic interrelations between nerve and muscle tissues. **Mailing Address:** EPRI, Palo Alto, CA 94304.

LEVINE, LEONARD P, HUMAN-COMPUTER INTERFACING. **Personal Data:** b Newark, NJ, July 24, 1932; m 1954, Marilyn; c David. **Education:** Queens Col, NY, BS, 1954; Syracuse Univ, MS, 1956, PhD (physics), 1960. **Professional Experience:** PROF EMER ELEC ENG & COMPUT SCI, UNIV WIS-MILWAUKEE, as of 2006; dir comput ctr, Univ Wis-milwaukee, 1967-1970; prof elec eng & comput sci, Univ Wis-Milwaukee, beginning 1966; prin res scientist, Honeywell Res Ctr, 1964-1966; sr scientist, Honeywell Res Ctr, 1960-1964; engr, Sperry-Gyroscope Co, 1959-1960. **Memberships:** Asn Comput Mach. **Research Statement & Publications:** Human and machine interfacing; system to system interfacing; small machine system design; computer teaching techniques. **Mailing Address:** Dept Elec Eng & Comput Sci, Univ Wis, Milwaukee, WI 53201. **Fax:** 414-229-6958. **E-Mail:** levine@cs.uwm.edu

LEVINE, LOUIS, POPULATION & FORENSIC GENETICS. **Personal Data:** b New York, NY, May 14, 1921. **Education:** City Col NY, BS, 1942, MS, 1947; Columbia Univ, MA, 1949, PhD (zoology), 1955. **Professional Experience:** PROF EMER BIOL, CITY COL NY, as of 2005; prof biol, City Col NY, beginning 1968; AEC grant, 1963; NSF grants, 1960; from instr to assoc prof, City Col NY, 1955-1967. **Memberships:** Fel AAAS; Animal Behav Soc; Am Genetic Asn; Genetics Soc Am; Am Soc Naturalists. **Research Statement & Publications:** Population genetics of both humans and drosophila. **Mailing Address:** Dept Biol, City Col NY, MR 803, New York, NY 10031. **Fax:** 212-650-8585. **E-Mail:** llevine@ccny.cuny.edu

LEVINE, LOUIS DAVID, ARCHAEOLOGY. **Personal Data:** b New York, NY, June 4, 1940; div. **Education:** Univ Pa, BA, 1962, PhD, 1969. **Professional Experience:** ASST COMNR & DIR, NY STATE MUS, ALBANY, 1990-; assoc dir, RoyalOnt Mus, Toronto, Can, 1987-1990; vis prof, Univ Copenhagen, 1985; cur, Royal Ont Mus, Toronto, Can, 1981; assoc cur, Royal Ont Mus, Toronto, Can, 1975-1980; Mahidasht Proj, 1975-1979; dir, Seh Gabi Explor, Western Iran, 1971-1973; vis sr lectr, Hebrew Univ, Jerusalem, 1975-1976; from asst prof to prof, Univ Toronto, 1969-1990; asst cur, Royal Ont Mus, Toronto, Can, 1969-1975; instr, Hebrew Univ, Pa, 1966-1969. **Memberships:** Fel Inst Advan Studies; Brit Inst Persian Studies; Am Asn Mus; Am Oriental Soc. **Research Statement & Publications:** Archaeology. **Mailing Address:** NY State Mus, 3099 Cult Educ Ctr, Albany, NY 12230. **Fax:** 518-473-8496.

LEVINE, MAITA FAYE, MATHEMATICS. **Personal Data:** b Cincinnati, Ohio, October 17, 1930. **Education:** Univ Cincinnati, BA, 1952, BE, 1953, MAT, 1966; Ohio State Univ, PhD (math educ), 1970. **Honors & Awards:** Marilyn Sternbery Award, Am Assoc Univ Prof, 1996; Georgina Smith Award, Am Assoc Univ Prof, 2000. **Professional Experience:** PROF EMER MATH, UNIV CINCINNATI, 1996-; prof math, Univ Cincinnati, beginning 1985; NSF res grant, 1974, 1985, 1993; from instr to assoc prof, Univ Cincinnati, 1963-1985; teacher, High Sch, Ohio, 1953-1963. **Memberships:** Math Asn Am; Am Educ Res Asn; Nat Coun Teachers Math; Asn Women Math; Am Asn Univ Prof (vpres 1986-1988); Sigma Xi. **Research Statement & Publications:** Relationship between mathematical competence and mathematical confidence; mathematical modeling; reasons why qualified women do not pursue mathematical careers; applications of computers and graphics calculators in the undergraduate curriculum; applications of mathematics to politics. **Mailing Address:** Dept Math Sci, Univ Cincinnati, 820 A Old Chem PO Box 210025, Cincinnati, OH 45221-0025. **Fax:** 513-556-3417. **E-Mail:** maita.levine@uc.edu

LEVINE, MARK DAVID, ENERGY ANALYSIS. **Personal Data:** b Cleveland, Ohio, May 26, 1944. **Education:** Princeton Univ, BA, 1966; Univ Calif, Berkeley, PhD (chem), 1975. **Professional Experience:** DIV DIR, LAWRENCE BERKELEY LAB, 1997-; prog leader, Lawrence Berkeley Lab, 1978-1997; sr policy analyst, Stanford Res Inst, 1974-1978; Staff scientist, Ford Found EnergyPolicy Proj, 1972-1973; Fulbright scholar; Woodrow Wilson Found scholar; mem bd dirs, Ctr Clean Air Policy Adv Bd, Int Inst Energy Conserv; bd dirs, Am Coun Energy Efficient Econ. **Memberships:** Int Asn Energy Economists; Am Soc Heating Refrig & Air Conditioning Engrs; AAAS. **Research Statement & Publications:** Comprehensive analysis of energy efficiency and energy policy options for the People's Republic of China; analysis of energy efficiency standards and guidelines for commericial buildings with application in developing countries; development of techniques to improve energy demand forecasting in the US, particularly for the building sector; analysis of energy issues related to global climate change. **Mailing Address:** Lawrence Berkeley Lab, 1 Cyclotron Rd, MS 90-3026, Berkeley, CA 94720. **Fax:** 510-486-5454. **E-Mail:** mdlevine@lbl.gov

LEVINE, MARTIN, ENGINEERING, EDUCATION. **Personal Data:** b Brooklyn, NY, October 27, 1925; m 1960, c 2. **Education:** City Col NY, BSEE, 1950; Univ Pittsburgh, MLitt, 1950, MEd, 1960; Univ Mich, PhD (higher educ), 1969. **Professional Experience:** RETIRED; prof elec technol, Va West Community Col, 1968-1996; mem fac, Harrisburg Area Community Col, 1965-1968; mem fac, Pa State Univ, 1953-1963; proj engr, Air Res & Develop, 1950-1953. **Memberships:** Inst Elec & Electronics Engrs; Am Soc Eng Educ. **Research Statement & Publications:** Student-work interface. **Mailing Address:** 2269 Maiden Ln SW, Roanoke, VA 24015.

LEVINE, MARTIN DAVID, COMPUTER VISION. **Personal Data:** b Montreal, Que, March 30, 1938. **Education:** McGill Univ, BEng, 1960, MEng, 1963; Univ London, DIC & PhD (control theory), 1965. **Professional Experience:** Dir, Ctr Intelligent Mach, 1986-1998; vis prof comput sci, Hebrew Univ, Jerusalem, Israel, 1979-1980; PROF ELEC ENG, MCGILL UNIV, 1977-; tech staff mem, Image Processing & Jet Propulsion Labs, Pasadena, Calif, 1972-1973, Am Soc Eng Educ-Ford Found fel, 1972; from asst prof to assoc prof, McGill Univ, 1965-1977; assoc ed, Comput Vision, Graphics & Image Processing; assoc ed, Trans Pattern Anal & Mach Intel, Inst Elec & Electronics Engrs. **Memberships:** Fel Inst Elec & Electronics Engrs; Pattern Recognition Soc; Int Asn Pattern Recognition. **Research Statement & Publications:** Computer vision; biomedical image processing; artificial intelligence; intelligent robotics. **Mailing Address:** Dept Elec Eng, McGill Univ, 3480 Univ St Rm 410, Montreal, PQ H3A 2A7, Can. **Fax:** 514-398-7348. **E-Mail:** levine@cim.mcgill.ca

LEVINE, MELVIN MORDECAI, NUCLEAR ENGINEERING & REACTOR PHYSICS. **Personal Data:** b Richmond, Va, November 20, 1925; m 1950, Lilo; c Susan (Fox), Wendy (Dunn) & David. **Education:** Mass Inst Technol, BS, 1946; Univ Va, PhD (physics), 1955. **Professional Experience:** RETIRED; physicist, Brookhaven Nat Lab, 1959-1988; physicist, Babcock & Wilcox Co, 1955-1959; instr physics, Pa State Univ, 1946-1948. **Memberships:** Fel Am Nuclear Soc. **Research Statement & Publications:** Nuclear reactor safety research and applications, including neutronics and thermal hydraulic phenomena; computational methods for reactor physics and engineering problems. **Mailing Address:** Two Meadow Lane, Saranac Lake, NY 12983. **E-Mail:** mlevine@northnet.org

LEVINE, MICHAEL J, PHYSICS. **Education:** Calif Inst Technol, PhD. **Professional Experience:** PROF, DEPT PHYSICS, CARNEGIE MELLON UNIV, as of 2006. **Mailing Address:** 5822 Marlborough Ave, Pittsburgh, PA 15217. **Fax:** 412-268-5832. **E-Mail:** levine@psc.edu

LEVINE, MICHAEL S, ANIMAL PHYSIOLOGY. **Personal Data:** b Brooklyn, NY, September 22, 1944. **Education:** Queens Col, BA, 1966; Univ Rochester, PhD (physiol psychol), 1970. **Professional Experience:** PROF PSYCHIAT, UNIV CALIF, LOS ANGELES, 1985-; from asst prof to assoc prof psychiat, Brain Res Inst, 1976-1985; lectr psychol, Brain Res Inst, 1975-1976; consult, neurophysiologist, Hereditary dis Found, 1975; asst res neurophysiologist, Brain Res Inst, 1972-1976; fel neurophysiol, Brain Res Inst, 1970-1972. **Memberships:** Soc Neuroscience; Am Psychol Asn; Am Asn Anatomists; Sigma Xi. **Research Statement & Publications:** Neurophysiology and neuroanatomy of basal ganglia in mature, developing and aging animals; role of basal ganglia in regulation of behavior; development and prediction of learning ability in developing animals. **Mailing Address:** Ment Retardation Res Ctr, Dept Psychiat Univ Calif 760 Westwood Plaza, Los Angeles, CA 90024. **E-Mail:** mlevine@mednet.ucla.edu

LEVINE, MICHAEL STEVEN, DEVELOPMENTAL BIOLOGY. **Personal Data:** b Los Angeles, Calif, March 5, 1955; m 1985, Lily; c Eli & Aaron. **Education:** Univ Calif, Berkeley, BA, 1976; Yale Univ, PhD (molecular biol), 1981. **Honors & Awards:** Monsanto Prize in Molecular Biology, National Academy of Sciences, 1996 Singer Medal, Society of Developmentl Biology, 2004. **Professional Experience:** PROF GENETICS DEVELOP, UNIV CALIF, BERKELEY, as of 2005; prof biol, Univ Calif, San Diego, 1991-1996, Sloan fel, 1985; asst prof, Columbia Univ, beginning 1984; Fel, Univ Basel, Switz, 1982-1983 & Univ Calif, Berkeley, 1983-1984. **Memberships:** Fellow, Am Academy of Arts & Sciences,

1996 Member, National Academy of Sciences, 1998. **Research Statement & Publications:** Control of gene expression during early embryonic development; morphogen gradients; gene networks for gastrulation in Drosophila and heart formation in the ascidian, Ciona intestinalis; evolutionary origins of the chordate body plan. **Mailing Address:** Dept Genetics, Univ Calif, 401 Barker Hall, Berkeley, CA 94720. **E-Mail:** mlevine@uclink4.berkeley.edu

LEVINE, MICHAEL W, VISUAL SCIENCE, PSCHOPHYSICS. **Personal Data:** b New York, NY, March 10, 1943; m 1969, Jane; c Matthew & Andrea. **Education:** Mass Inst Technol, BS, 1965, MS, 1967; Rockefeller Univ, PhD (biophysics), 1972. **Honors & Awards:** Sr Int fel, Fogarty Ctr NIH, 1987; Teaching Recognition Prog Award, 1997. **Professional Experience:** Vis prof, Univ Sydney, Australia, 1987-1988; PROF PSYCHOL, UNIV ILL, CHICAGO, 1985-; assoc prof Bioengineering, Univ Ill Chicago, 1981-1984; vis scholar, Northwestern Univ, 1981; grad fel biophysics, Rockefeller Univ, 1967-1972; proj engr, Lion Res Corp, Newton, Mass, 1967; Res asst mech eng, Mass Inst Technol, 1965-1967. **Memberships:** AAAS; Sigma Xi; Soc Neuroscience; Vision Sci Soc. **Research Statement & Publications:** Visual processing in the action and cognition pathways; visual cognition. **Mailing Address:** Dept Psychol, Univ Ill, 1007 W Harrison St, Chicago, IL 60607-7137. **E-Mail:** mikel@uic.edu

LEVINE, MICHEAL JOSEPH, PHYSICS, DATA ACQUISITION. **Personal Data:** b Oak Park, Ill, December 1, 1940; m 1969, Dreania; c Dana N. **Education:** Yale Univ, BS, 1962, MS, 1964, PhD (physics), 1968. **Professional Experience:** SCI ASSOC, CERN, GENEVA, SWITZ, 2000-; guest physicist, Max Planck Inst Nuclear Physics, Heidelberg, Ger, 1975 & Ctr d'Etudes Nucleaires, Saclay, France, 1980-1981; consult, High Voltage Eng Corp, 1972-1975; SR PHYSICIST NUCLEAR PHYSICS, BROOKHAVEN NAT LAB, 1968-; sci assoc, CERN, Geneva, Switz. **Memberships:** Am Phys Soc; Inst Elec & Electronics Engrs. **Research Statement & Publications:** Study of nuclear reactions induced by relativistic heavy ions; development of magnetic spectrometers and associated focal plane detectors; development of data acquisition architectures; study of networking technol appl to data acquisition in high energy physics experiments. **Mailing Address:** Brookhaven Nat Lab, Bldg 510A, Upton, NY 11973-5000. **Fax:** 631-344-4206. **E-Mail:** levine@bnl.gov

LEVINE, MYRON, GENETICS, VIROLOGY. **Personal Data:** b Brooklyn, NY, July 28, 1926; m 1950, Barbara; c Sura &Peter. **Education:** Brooklyn Col, BA, 1947; Ind Univ, PhD (zoology), 1952. **Professional Experience:** PROF EMER HUMAN GENETICS, SCH MED, UNIV MICH, ANN ARBOR, 1996-; chmn, educ comt, Genetics Soc Am, 1986-1989; vis prof, Biol Dept, Harbin Normal Univ, Harbin, People's Repub China, 1986; vis scientist, Weizmann Inst Sci, Israel, 1983; Inst Sci Res Cancer, France, 1983; Clare Hall life fel, Cambridge Univ, 1982-; sr fel, Soc Fels, Univ Mich, 1982-1985; vis scientist, Imp Cancer Res Fund, London, 1973-1974; Cambridge Univ, 1982; mem & chmn genetic basis of dis rev comt, Nat Inst Gen Med Sci, NIH, 1975-1979; chmn grad prog cell & molecular biol in health sci, Univ Mich, 1974-1990; ed, J Virol, 1972-1976; Commonwealth Fund fel, Univ Geneva, 1966-1967; from assoc prof to prof, Sch Med, Univ Mich, Ann Arbor, 1961-1996; asst to assoc biologist, Brookhaven Nat Lab, 1956-1961; res assoc microbiol, Univ Ill, 1954-1956; Am Cancer Soc fel, Johns Hopkins Univ, 1953-1954. **Memberships:** Genetics Soc Am; Am Soc Microbiol; Am Soc Virol; AAAS; Amer Soc Gene Thepry. **Research Statement & Publications:** Genetics and regulation of gene expression of animal viruses; herpesvirus genetics, latency and biology; gene therapy for the central nervous system; molecular genetics. **Mailing Address:** Univ Mich, Sch Med, Dept Human Genetics, 4807 MSII, Ann Arbor, MI 48109-0618. **Fax:** 734-763-3784. **E-Mail:** mylevine@umich.edu

LEVINE, MYRON MAX, TROPICAL PEDIATRICS. **Personal Data:** b Riverdale, NY, February 11, 1944. **Education:** City Col NY, BS, 1963; Med Col Va, MD, 1967; London Sch Hyg & Trop Med, DTPH, 1974. **Honors & Awards:** Howard Fiorey Mem Lectr, Univ Adelaide, SAustralia, 1987; Bazely Oration, Australian Soc Microbiol, 1992; Colonel George W Hunter III Award, Walter Reed Army InstRes, 1995. **Professional Experience:** PROF MED, UNIV MD as of 2003; fel, Sackler Inst Adv Studies, Tel Aviv Univ, 1987-1988; sr assoc, Dept Epidemiol, Johns Hopkins Univ Sch Hyg & Pub Health, 1985-; head, Div Infectious Dis & Trop Pediat, beginning 1985; HEAD, DIV GEOG MED, 1984-; act head, Div Infectious Dis, 1984-1985; vis prof, Fac Med, Univ Peruana Cayetano Heredia, Peru, 1980-; dir, Ctr Vaccine Develop, Univ Md Sch Med, beginning 1974; from asst prof to prof, Dept Pediat, Univ Md Sch Med, 1972-1983; instr, Dept Pediat, Univ Md Sch Med, 1971-1972; fel, Div Pediat Infectious Dis Immunol, 1970-1972; from asst resident to sr resident, Bronx Munic Hosp Ctr, Albert Einstein Col Med, 1968-1970; internpediat, Bronx Munic Hosp Ctr, Albert Einstein Col Med, 1967-1968; Lederle-Praxis vis prof vaccinology, Oxford Univ. **Memberships:** Inst Med-Nat Acad Sci; fel Am Col Prev Med; fel Infectious Dis Soc Am; AmSoc Trop Med & Hyg; Am Epidemiol Soc; Royal Soc Trop Med & Hyg; Am Soc Microbiol; SocEpidemiol Res; Soc Intestinal Microbiol Ecol & Dis; Asn Am Physicians; fel Am Acad Pediat. **Mailing Address:** Univ Md, Ctr Vaccine Develop, 685 W Baltimore St Rm480, Baltimore, MD 21201. **Fax:** 410-706-6205. **E-Mail:** mlevine@umppa1.ab.umd.edu

LEVINE, NATHAN, communications engineering; deceased, see previous edition for last biography

LEVINE, O ROBERT, EXPERIMENTAL BIOLOGY. **Professional Experience:** CLIN PROF PEDIAT, UNIV MED & DENT NJ, 1972-. **Mailing Address:** Dept Pediat, Univ Med & Dent NJ, Med Sch, Newark, NJ 07103.

LEVINE, OSCAR, physical chemistry; deceased, see previous edition for last biography

LEVINE, PAUL HOWARD, VIRAL ONCOLOGY, INTERNAL MEDICINE. **Personal Data:** b New York, NY, September 11, 1937. **Education:** Cornell Univ, BA, 1959; Univ Rochester, MD, 1963. **Professional Experience:** RES PROF, DEPT EPIDEMIOL & BIOSTATIST, SCH PUB HEALTH & HEALTH SERV, GEORGE WASH UNIV, as of 2004; CLIN PROF, DEPT MED, SCH PUB HEALTH & HEALTH SERV, GEORGE WASH UNIV, as of 2004; sr investr, Epidemiol & Biostatists, 1982-; clin asst prof med, George Wash Univ, Med Ctr, 1978-; head clin studies sect, Lab Viral Carcinogenesis, 1978-1982; chmn clin adv group, Div Cancer Cause & Prev, 1976-1981; head clin studies sect, Viral Leukemia & Lymphoma Br, 1974-1975; chmn immunol-epidemiol segment, Virus Cancer Prog, 1972-1975; co-chmn immunol group, Nat Cancer Inst, 1971-1972; RES INVESTR VIRAL ONCOL, NAT CANCER INST, 1968-; resident internal med, Univ Colo, 1966-1968; resident fel oncol, Roswell Park Mem Inst, 1964-1966; intern internal med, Strong Mem Hosp, 1963-1964. **Memberships:** Am Asn Cancer Res; Am Col Physicians; Am Col Epidemiol; AAAS. **Research Statement & Publications:** Epidemiology of oncogenic viruses, particularly Epstein-Barr virus and HTLV-I; viral immunology, application of assays to cancer etiology, diagnosis, treatment. **Mailing Address:** Dept Epidemiol & Biostatist, Sch Pub Health & Health Serv, George Wash Univ, 2300 Eye St, NW, Ross Hall 106, Washington, DC 20037. **E-Mail:** paulhlevine@earthlink.net

LEVINE, PHILLIP J, PHARMACY. **Personal Data:** b Providence, RI, January 7, 1934. **Education:** Univ RI, BS, 1955; Univ Md, MS, 1957, PhD (pharm), 1963. **Professional Experience:** COORDR CONTINUING EDUC PROG PHARM, COL PHARM, DRAKE UNIV, 1977-; PROF PHARM, COL PHARM, DRAKE UNIV, 1970-; consult, Gov, State ofIowa, 1970-1972; chmn, Mayor's Task Force on Drugs, Des Moines, Iowa, 1969-1970; dir, CoopIV Additive Proj, 1967-1969; Consult, Dr Salsbury's Labs, Charles City, Iowa, 1965-1970; fromasst prof to assoc prof, Col Pharm, Drake Univ, 1963-1970; Instr pharm, Sch Pharm, Univ Md, 1957-1963. **Memberships:** Am Pharmaceut Asn. **Research Statement & Publications:** Development of topical anesthetic suspensions to test their applicability to long duration of anesthesia in dental patients; product development in area of suspension and formulations. **Mailing Address:** Dept Pharm, Drake Univ 2507 University Ave, Des Moines, IA 50311.

LEVINE, RANDOLPH HERBERT, ASTROPHYSICS, SOLAR PHYSICS. **Personal Data:** b Denver, Colo, November 20, 1946. **Education:** Univ Calif, Berkeley, BA, 1968; Harvard Univ, MA, 1969, PhD (physics), 1972. **Professional Experience:** PRES & CHIEF EXEC OFF, ZETTACORE INC, 1999-; mkt exec, Digital Equip Corp, beginning 1985; mgr software eng, atmospheric& environ res, 1982-1985; sr scientist & dir comput, atmospheric & environ res, 1981-1982; lectr astron, Ctr Astrophys, Harvard Col Observ, 1977-1981; res assoc solar physics, Ctr Astrophys, Harvard Col Observ, 1975-1981; res fel solar physics, Ctr Astrophys, Harvard Col Observ, 1974-1975; vis scientist solar physics, High Altitude Observ, Nat Ctr Atmospheric Res, Boulder, Colo, 1972-1974. **Memberships:** Am Astron Soc; Am Geophys Union; Int Astron Union; Am Phys Soc; Inst Elec& Electronics Engrs. **Research Statement & Publications:** Scientific computing; design and development of products. **Mailing Address:** ZettaCore, Inc, 2000 S Colo Blvd Ste 10000, Denver, CO 80222. **Fax:** 303-300-0977.

LEVINE, RAPHAEL DAVID, MOLECULAR REACTION DYNAMICS. **Personal Data:** b Alexandria, Egypt, March 29, 1938; Israeli citizen; m 1962, Gillian; c Ornah T. **Education:** Hebrew Univ, Jerusalem, MSc, 1959; Nottingham Univ, Eng, PhD (math), 1964; Oxford Univ, Eng, DPhil, 1966. **Honorary Degrees:** PhD, Univ Liege, Belg, 1991, Tech Univ Munich, 1996. **Honors & Awards:** Ann Award, Int Acad Quantum Molecular Sci, 1968; Landau Prize, 1972; Israel Prize Exact Sci, 1974; Weizman Prize, 1979; Wolf Prize, 1988; Rothschild Prize, 1992; Max Planck Prize for Int Cooperation, Humboldt Found, 1996. **Professional Experience:** A D White prof at large, Cornell Univ, 1989-; Univ Calif, Los Angeles, 1989; Miller res prof, Univ Calif, Berkeley, 1989; MAX BORN PROF, NATURAL PHILOS, 1985-; CHMN, RES CTR MOLECULAR DYNAMICS, 1981-; adj prof, Mass Inst Technol, 1980-1988; adj prof, Univ Tex, 1974-1980; Brittingham vis prof, Univ Wis, 1973; Battelle prof chem & math, Ohio State Univ, 1970-1974; Alfred P Sloan fel, 1970-1972; PROF THEORET CHEM, HEBREW UNIV, JERUSALEM, 1969-; vis asst prof, Univ Wis, 1966-1968; Ramsay mem fel, 1964-1966. **Memberships:** Fel Am Phys Soc; Am Philos Soc; Israel Acad Sci; Max Planck Soc; Acad Europe; Am Acad Arts & Sci; US Nat Acad of Sci. **Research Statement & Publications:** Author of various articles and books. **Mailing Address:** Dept Chem & Biochem, Univ Calif, Los Angeles, CA 90095-1569. **E-Mail:** rafi@fh.huji.ac.il

LEVINE, RICHARD JOSEPH, OCCUPATIONAL MEDICINE. **Personal Data:** b New York, NY, November 12, 1939; m 1969, c 2. **Education:** Princeton Univ, AB, 1960; Calif Inst Technol, MS, 1964, St Louis Univ, MD, 1971; Harvard Univ MPH, 1976. **Honors & Awards:** NIH Merit Award, 1997. **Professional Experience:** RES MED OFFICER, NIH, 1994-; expert, NIH, 1991-1994; adj assoc prof, dept epidemiol, Univ NC Sch pub health, 1984-1994; assoc prof, dept family Commun Med, Div Occup med, Duke Univ, 1983-1994; adj asst prof, dept family commun med, div occup med, Duke Univ, 1978-1982; chief epidemiol, chem Indust Inst Toxicol, 1977-1992; partic, Working Group Asbestos, int agency cancer res, 1977; sr med scientist, Ctr Occup & Environ Health, Stanford res inst, 1976-1977; epidemiologist, Cholera res lab, Dacca, Bangladesh, 1973-1975; epidemiologist, Ctr Dis Control, epidemic intell serv, 1972-1975; asst state epidemiologist, Ala State Health dept, 1972-1973; intern med, Grady mem Hosp, 1971-1972. **Memberships:** Soc Epidemiol res; fel Am Col occup environ med; Inst Soc Study Hypertension prog. **Research Statement & Publications:** Epidemiology of cholera and mass hysteria; environmental effects on male reproduction; preeclampsia. **Mailing Address:** Nat Inst Child Health & Develop, NIH, Rm 7B03 Bldg 6100, Bethesda, MD 20892. **E-Mail:** levinerj@exchange.nih.gov

LEVINE, RICHARD S, CORROSION CONTROL & WATER TREATMENT, ENVIRONMENTAL TESTING. **Personal Data:** b Pittsburgh, Pa, January 14, 1947. **Education:** Carnegie-Mellon Univ, BS, 1968; Univ Ill, MS, 1971. **Professional Experience:** PRES, INDUST CORROSION MGT, INC, 1973-; Chemist, Univ Ill, 1971-1973. **Memberships:** Am Chem Soc; Am Soc Testing & Mat; Am Water Works Asn; Asn Off AnalChemists. **Research Statement & Publications:** Corrosion control and water treatment in central air conditioning and heating systems; environmental testing; author of numerous publications. **Mailing Address:** Indust Corrosion Mgt Inc, 1152 Rte 10, Randolph, NJ 07869.

LEVINE, ROBERT, PEDIATRIC CARDIOLOGY. **Personal Data:** b New York, NY, November 10, 1926; m 1954, c 2. **Education:** City Col New York, BS, 1948; Western Res Univ, MD, 1954. **Professional Experience:** PROF PEDIAT & DIR PEDIAT CARDIOL, NJ MED SCH, COL MED & DENT NJ, 1972-; responsible investr, Nat Heart & Lung InstSCOR, Col Physicians & Surgeons, 1971-1972; prin investr, NIH Grad Training Prog Pediat Cardiol, Columbia Univ, 1970-1972; John Polachek Found fel, 1968-1969; NY City Health Res Coun career scientist award, 1962-1972; from instr to assoc prof, Col Physicians & Surgeons, Columbia Univ, 1962-1972; NIH trainee pediat cardiol, Col physicians & Surgeons, Columbia Univ, 1959-1961 & NIH fel cardiorespiratory physiol, 1961-1962; From intern to resident pediat, State Univ NY Upstate Med Ctr, 1954-1957. **Memberships:** Am Acad Pediat; Am Pediat Soc; Am Physiol Soc. **Research Statement & Publications:** Cardiorespiratory physiology. **Mailing Address:** Univ Med & Dent NJ Med Sch Rm F 576, Newark, NJ 07130-2714.

LEVINE, ROBERT ALAN, MEDICINE, PHARMACOLOGY. **Personal Data:** b New York, NY, June 12, 1932. **Education:** Cornell Univ, AB, 1954, MD, 1958; Cert, Am Bd Gastroenterol. **Professional Experience:** PROF MED, STATE UNIV NY UPSTATE MED CTR, 1971-; CHIEF DIV GASTRO ENTEROL, STATE UNIV HOSP, 1971-; assoc prof med, Brooklyn-Cumberland MedCtr, 1969-1971; chief div gastroenterol, Brooklyn-Cumberland Med Ctr, 1965-1971; from asst chief to chief metab div, Army Med Res & Nutrit Lab, Fitzsimons Gen Hosp, 1963-1965; res fel, Liver Study Unit, Sch Med, Yale Univ, 1962-1963; clin fel med, Liver Study Unit, Sch Med, Yale Univ, 1961-1962; clin fel gastroenterol, NY Hosp-Cornell Med Ctr, 1960-1961; asst resident, NY Hosp-Cornell Med Ctr, 1959-1960; Intern med, NY Hosp-Cornell Med Ctr, 1958-1959. **Memberships:** Am Soc Pharmacol & Exp Therapeut; Am Fedn Clin Res; Am Gastroenterol Asn; Am Asn Study Liver Dis. **Research Statement & Publications:** Basic and clinical research in gastroenterology, metabolism and pharmacology; cyclic adenosine 3', 5'-monophosphate in vivo and in vitro; isolated perfused rat liver; chronic hepatitis; hormone regulation of gastrointestinal function. **Mailing Address:** Dept Med, State Med Univ, 6823 Univ Hosp, Syracuse, NY 13210. **E-Mail:** kushnerk@upstate.edu

LEVINE, ROBERT JOHN, INTERNAL MEDICINE, MEDICAL ETHICS. **Personal Data:** b New York, NY, December 29, 1934. **Education:** George Wash Univ, MD, 1958; Am Bd Internal Med, dipl, 1965. **Professional Experience:** DIR, LAW, POLICY & ETHICS CORE, YALE UNIV, as of 2002; PROF INTERNAL MED & LECTR PHARMACOL, SCH MED, YALE UNIV, as of 2000; mem, Adv Comt Acquired Immune Deficiency Syndrome Prog, US Dept Health & Human Serv, 1989-1995; vchmn, Comn Fed Drug Approval Process, 1981-1982; ed, IRB: Rev Human Subjects Res, 1979-; mem lipid metab adv comt, Nat Heart, Lung & Blood Inst, 1977-1979; consult, Nat Comn Protection Human Subj Biomed & Behav Res, 1974-1978; dir, Physician's Assoc Prog, 1973-1975; ed, Clin Res, Am Fedn Clin Res, 1971-1976; mem myocardial infarction comt, Nat Heart & Lung Inst, 1969-1972; attend physician, Yale-New Haven Hosp, 1968-; attend physician, Vet Admin Hosp, West Haven, Conn, 1966-; chief, Sect Clin Pharmacol, 1966-1974; asst attend physician, Yale-New Haven Hosp, 1965-1968; from instr to assoc prof internal med & pharmacol, Yale Univ, 1964-1973; clin investr, Vet Admin Hosp, West Haven, Conn, 1964-1966; Clin asst, Yale-New Haven Hosp, 1964-1965; investr clin pharmacol, Nat Heart Inst, 1963-1964; resident internal med, Vet Admin Hosp, West Haven, Conn, 1962-1963; clin assoc clin pharmacol, Nat Heart Inst, 1960-1962; asst resident, Peter Bent Brigham Hosp, Boston, Mass, 1959-1960; intern internal med, Peter Bent Brigham Hosp, Boston, Mass, 1958-1959. **Memberships:** Am Soc Pharmacol; Am Soc Clin Invest; fel Am Col Physicians; Am Soc Law Med & Ethics (pres 1989-1990 & 1994-1995); fel Hastings Ctr; fel AAAS. **Research Statement & Publications:** Writing, teaching and consulting in the field of medical ethics; concentrating on research involving human subjects; the doctor-patient relationship and care of the dying patient. **Mailing Address:** Dept Internal Med, Yale Univ, Sch Med, New Haven, CT 06520. **Fax:** 203-785-2847. **E-Mail:** robert.levine@yale.edu

LEVINE, ROBERT PAUL, GENETICS. **Personal Data:** b Brooklyn, NY, December 18, 1926. **Education:** Univ Calif, Los Angeles, AB, 1949, PhD (genetics), 1951. **Honorary Degrees:** AM, Harvard Univ, 1957. **Professional Experience:** PROF GENETICS, MED SCH, WASH UNIV, 1978-; chmn dept, Harvard Univ, 1967-1970; NSF sr fel, 1963-1964; from asst prof to prof, Harvard Univ, 1953-1978; Instr biol, Amherst Col, 1951-1953. **Memberships:** AAAS; Genetics Soc Am; Sigma Xi; Soc Gen Physiol; Am Soc Cell Biol. **Research Statement & Publications:** Genetic specification of membrane structure. **Mailing Address:** Hopkins Marine Sta, Oceanview Blvd, Pacific Grove, CA 93950.

LEVINE, ROBERT S(IDNEY), FIRE RESEARCH, COMBUSTION. **Personal Data:** b Des Moines, Iowa, June 4, 1921; m 1970, Sharon; c Michelle, James, George & Gail. **Education:** Iowa State Col, BS, 1943; Mass Inst Technol, SM, 1946, ScD(chem eng), 1949. **Professional Experience:** RETIRED; sr engr, Nat Inst Sci & Technol, beginning 1980; prof combustion, George Wash Univ, 1977-1978; chief, Fire Res Resources Div, Nat Inst Sci & Technol, 1974-1980; asst prof heat & mass transfer, Univ Calif, Los Angeles, 1970-1974; chief liquid rocket res & technol, Off Advan Res & Technol, NASA, 1966-1974; mem subcomt combustion, Nat Adv Comt Aeronaut, 1958; assoc res dir, Rocketdyne Div, Rockwell Int, 1949-1966. **Memberships:** Am Chem Soc; Am Inst Aeronaut & Astronaut; Nat Fire Protection Asn; Combustion Inst (vpres, 1970, pres, 1974-1978); Soc Fire Protection Engrs. **Research Statement & Publications:** Combustion and combustion stability in liquid rocket engines; combustion phenomena and heat transfer in liquid rocket engines; mathematical modeling of growth of unwanted fire in buildings. **Mailing Address:** 19017 Threshing Pl, Gaithersburg, MD 20879-3143.

LEVINE, RUTH R, PHARMACOLOGY. **Personal Data:** b New York, NY. **Education:** Hunter Col, BA, 1938; Columbia Univ, MA, 1939; Tufts Univ, PhD (pharmacol), 1955. **Professional Experience:** ASSOC DEAN EMER, BOSTON UNIV, as of 2005; CHMN, PROGR MED SCI, BOSTON UNIV, as of 2005; dir, Med Sci Degree Prog, Div Grad Med Sci, Sch Med, Boston Univ, as of 2004; assoc dean, Boston Univ, beginning 1996; PROF EMER PHARMACOL & EXP THERAPEUT, BOSTON UNIV, 1996-; assoc dean, SchMed, 1981-1989; Univ prof pharmacol, Sch Med, 1972-1996; chmn, Div Med & Dent Sci, GradSch, 1964-1969; from asst prof to prof, Boston Univ, 1958-1965; from instr to asst prof pharmacol, Sch Med, Tufts Univ, 1955-1958. **Memberships:** Am Soc Pharmacol & Exp Therapeut (secy-treas 1975); Biophys Soc; AcadPharmaceut Sci; Am Chem Soc; fel AAAS; Sigma Xi. **Research Statement & Publications:** Pharmacokinetics mechanisms of transport of drugs across biological barriers, particularly the intestinal epithelium; biochemical, histological and physiological factors influencing intestinal absorption; environmental toxicology. **Mailing Address:** Boston Univ, Sch Med, Div Grad Med Sci, 715 Albany St, Boston, MA 02118-2394. **Fax:** 617-638-4248.

LEVINE, SAMUEL GALE, organic chemistry; deceased, see previous edition for last biography

LEVINE, SAMUEL HAROLD, NUCLEAR ENGINEERING & REACTOR PHYSICS, NEUTRON RADIOGRAPHY & RADIATION DETECTION. **Personal Data:** b Hazlehurst, Ga, November 30, 1925. **Education:** Va Polytech Inst, BS, 1947; Univ Ill, MS, 1948; Univ Pittsburgh, PhD (physics), 1954. **Honors & Awards:** Invention Award, NASA, 1973. **Professional Experience:** PROF EMER NUCLEAR ENG, PA STATE UNIV, 1991-; consult, PP&L, 1988-; consult, Int Atomic Energy Agency, 1977-; prof, Pa State Univ, Univ Park, 1968-1991; dir nuclear reactor facil, Pa State Univ, Univ Park, 1968; Lectr, Univ Calif, Los Angeles, 1964-1968; lab head nuclear sci, Northrop Space Labs, 1962-1968; group physicist, Rocketdyne Div, NAm Aviation, Inc, 1961-1962; physicist incharge, Gen Atomic Div, Gen Dynamics Corp, 1959-1961; mgr, Bettis Atomic Power Lab, Westinghouse Elec Corp, 1957-1959; supv scientist, Bettis Atomic Power Lab, Westinghouse Elec Corp, 1955-1957; sr scientist, Bettis Atomic Power Lab, Westinghouse Elec Corp, 1954-1955; instr physics, Va Polytech Inst, 1949-1950. **Memberships:** Am Phys Soc; fel Am Nuclear Soc. **Research Statement & Publications:** In-core fuel management; neutron detection; experimental reactor physics; neutron radiography; nuclear reactor fuel management; dosimetry. **Mailing Address:** Dept Nuclear Eng, Pa State Univ, 323 Reber Bldg, Univ Park, PA 16802. **Fax:** 814-865-8499. **E-Mail:** shl@psu.edu

LEVINE, SEYMOUR, BEHAVIOR. **Personal Data:** b Brooklyn, NY, January 23, 1925. **Education:** Univ Denver, BA, 1948; NY Univ, MA, 1950, PhD (psychol), 1952. **Honors & Awards:** Hoffheimer Res Award, 1961; Res Career Develop Award, NIMH, 1962, ResScientist Award, 1967. **Professional Experience:** ADJ PROF PSYCHIAT, UNIV CALIF, DAVIS, 1999-; dir, Neuroscience Prog, Univ, Newark, 1995-2000; res prof psychol, Univ Delaware, Newark, 1995-2000; dir, Stanford Primate Facil, beginning 1976; consult, Found Human Develop, Dublin, Ireland, beginning 1973; dir, Biol Sci Res Training Prog, Stanford Univ, beginning 1971; prof psychiatry, Sch Med, Stanforduniv, 1969-1995; assoc prof, Stanford Univ, 1962-1969; asst prof, Ohio State Univ, 1956-1960; asst prof, Boston Univ, 1952-1953. **Memberships:** Fel Am Psychol Asn; fel AAAS; Int Soc Develop Psychobiol (pres 1975-1976); IntSoc Psychoneuroendocrinol (pres 1990-1993); Am Soc Primatologists; Int Primatology Soc. **Mailing Address:** Dept Psychiat, Univ Calif, 2230 Stockton Blvd, Sacramento, CA 95817-1419. **E-Mail:** slevine@ucdavis.edu

LEVINE, SEYMOUR, PATHOLOGY, NEUROPATHOLOGY. **Personal Data:** b New York, NY, March 13, 1925; m 1945, Lillian; c Linda & Sandra. **Education:** NY Univ, BA, 1946; Chicago Med Sch, MB, 1947, MD, 1948. **Professional Experience:** Sr staff scientist, Nathan Kline Inst Psychiatric Res, 1990-; chief neuropath, Westchester Co Med Ctr, 1977-1987; consult, Vet Admin Hosp, Montrose, NY, 1977-1987; pathologist & chief labs, Ctr Chronic Dis, Bird S Coler Hosp, 1964-1977; PROF EMER PATH, NY MED COL, 1956-; pathologist, St Francis Hosp, Jersey City, NJ, 1956-1964. **Memberships:** Am Asn Neuropath (pres, 1968-1969). **Research Statement & Publications:** Demyelinating diseases; mechanisms of lithium action; muscle pathology; uremia. **Mailing Address:** Dept Path, NY Med Col, 140 Old Orangeburg Rd, Orangeburg, NY 10962.

LEVINE, SEYMOUR, VIROLOGY. **Personal Data:** b Chicago, Ill, April 30, 1922; wid, c 2. **Education:** Univ Chicago, BS, 1943; Univ Ill, MS, 1945, PhD (bact), 1949. **Professional Experience:** EMER PROF MICROBIOL, SCH MED, WAYNE STATE UNIV, 1989-; from assoc prof to prof, Sch Med, Wayne State Univ, 1971-1989; sr res scientist, Upjohn Co, Mich, 1965-1971; res biologist, Lederle Labs, Am Cyanamid Co, 1956-1965; from instr to asst prof biophys, Univ Colo, 1951-1956; Univ of Colo, 1949-1950; Western Res Univ, 1950-1951; Nat Res Coun AEC fel, Univ Colo, 1949-1950; Asst bact, Med Sch, Univ Ill, 1945-1949. **Memberships:** Am Soc Microbiol; Am Acad Microbiol; Am Soc Virol; soc for Invitrobiol; soc general Microbioe. **Research Statement & Publications:** Viral-host cell interactions; tissue culture; viral replication; viral interference and interferon. **Mailing Address:** 34223 Hillside Dr, Paw Paw, MI 49079-9555.

LEVINE, SIMON P, PHYSICAL MEDICINE & REHABILITATION. **Personal Data:** b Los Angeles, Calif, February 7, 1952. **Education:** Univ Calif, Los Angeles, BA, 1973; Univ Mich, MA, 1975, MS, 1976, PhD (bioeng), 1983. **Professional Experience:** PROF PHYSMED & REHAB & BIOMED ENG, UNIV MICH, as of 2004; DIR, REHAB ENG PROG & REHAB TECHNOL SERV, UMHS, as of 2004; Robert Wood Johnson Found, 1987-1990 & Nat Inst Disability & Rehab Res, 1993-; Prin investr, NIH, 1991-; Prin investr, Univ Mich, 1991-1992; assoc prof phys med & rehab, Rehab Eng Prog, dept Phys Med & Rehab, Univ Mich, beginning 1990; Nat Inst Handicapped res, 1981-1983 & WHO, 1989-1990; Prin investr, Mich Consortium EnablingTechnol, 1988-1989; dir, Rehab Technol Servs, Univ Mich, 1987-; consult, NIMH, 1987-1988; co-investr, Univ Mich, 1986-1987 & 1988-1989; chmn, Rehab Eng Comt, inst Elec &Electronics Engrs Eng Med & Biol Soc, 1986-1988; co-chmn, Elec Stimulation Spec InterestGroup, Rehab Eng Soc Nam, 1986-1987; Prin investr, Univ Space res Asn, 1986-1987; biomedengr, Res Servs, 1985-; Prin investr, Vet Admin, 1985-; clin consult, Rehab Med Servs, AnnArbor Vet Admin Med Ctr, 1984-; DIR, REHAB ENG PROG, DEPT PHYS MED & REHAB, UNIV MICH, 1983-; asst prof, Univ Mich, 1983-1990; co-investr, Kenny Mich Found, 1983-1985; sr res assoc & actg dir rehab eng, Univ Mich, 1980-1983; Prin investr, Kenny MichFound, 1979-1982 & 1987-1988; Prin investr, NIMH, 1979-1985; proj dir, Nat Inst Occup Safety& Health, 1979-1981; res assoc, Univ Mich, 1978-1980. **Memberships:** Rehab Eng Soc NAm; Am Cong Rehab Med; Inst Elec & Electronics Engrs; InstElec & Electronics Engrs Eng Med & Biol Sci; AAAS; Am Asn Univ Profs; Math Asn Am. **Research Statement & Publications:** Computerized and robotic assistive technology systems; etiology and prevention of pressure sores; specialized needs of people with disability. **Mailing Address:** Univ Mich Med Ctr, 1500 E Med Ctr Dr 1C335, Ann Arbor, MI 48109-0032. **Fax:** 734-936-7515. **E-Mail:** silevine@umich.edu

LEVINE, SIMON ROCK, MEMBRANE TRANSPORT PHENOMENA, BIOELECTRIC PHENOMENA. **Personal Data:** b Buffalo, NY, December 2, 1946; m 1969, c 2. **Education:** Calif Inst Technol, BS, 1968; Univ Cambridge, PhD (physiol), 1975. **Professional Experience:** ASSOC PROF PHYSIOL, UNIV COLO HEALTH SCI CTR, 1984-; asst prof, Univ Colo Health Sci Ctr, 1979-1984; fel chem, Calif Inst Technol, 1976-1979. **Memberships:** Biophys Soc; Soc Gen Physiologists; Soc Neuroscience. **Research Statement & Publications:** Molecular mechanisms which underlie electrical excitation phenomena in nerve and muscle cells; mechanisms of the voltage-sensitive sodium channel and the molecular structures which mediate its complex function. **Mailing Address:** Dept Physiol C240, Med Sch Univ Colo, Denver, CO 80262.

LEVINE, SOLOMON LEON, ELECTRODEPOSITION. **Personal Data:** b Schenectady, NY, January 7, 1940. **Education:** Rensselaer Polytech Inst, BS, 1961; Univ RI, PhD (anal chem), 1966. **Professional Experience:** PROF EMER CHEM, NC INST TECHNOL, as of 2004; prof, NC Inst Technol, beginning 1994; adj fac, Durham Tech Community Col, 1994-; sr chemist, Components Div, IBM Corp, 1979-1993; adv chemist, Components Div, IBMCorp, 1974-1979; develop chemist, Components Div, IBM Corp, 1972-1974; proj chemist, Components Div, IBM Corp, 1969-1972; staff chemist, Components Div, IBM Corp, 1968-1969; sr assoc chemist, Components Div, IBM Corp, 1966-1968; sr assoc engr, Components Div, IBMCorp, 1965-1966. **Memberships:** Sigma Xi; Soc Electroanal Chem; Am Chem Soc. **Research Statement & Publications:** Spectroscopy, absorption and emission; electroanalytical chemistry; electrodeposition. **Mailing Address:** Dept Chem, NC State Univ, 110 Skylark Way, Raleigh, NC 27615. **Fax:** 919-515-5079. **E-Mail:** slevine@pams.ncsu.edu

LEVINE, STEPHEN ALAN, ORGANIC CHEMISTRY, INFORMATION SYSTEMS. **Personal Data:** b Brooklyn, NY, December 24, 1938. **Education:** City Col NY, BS, 1961; Purdue Univ, PhD (org chem), 1966; Marist Col, MS (info systs), 1987. **Professional Experience:** ADJ PROF, MARIST COL, 1988-; SR RES CHEMIST, TEXACO RES CTR, 1979-; res chemist, Texaco Res Ctr, 1973-1979; sr chemist, Texaco Res Ctr, 1967-1973; chemist, Texaco Res Ctr, 1966-1967; res chemist, Acme Shellac Prod Co, 1961. **Memberships:** Fel Am Inst Chem; Sigma Xi; NY Acad Sci. **Research Statement & Publications:** Polymer chemistry; computer information system design and development; process research; lubricant additive synthesis. **Mailing Address:** 2274 Sierra Blvd Apt A, Sacramento, CA 95825-4710.

LEVINE, STEVEN RICHARD, STROKE, ANTIPHOSPHOLIPID ANTIBODIES. **Education:** Univ Mich, BS, 1977; Med Col Wis, MD, 1981. **Honors & Awards:** Co-recipient, Harold G Wolff Award Headache Res, 1989 & 1991. **Professional Experience:** Adj prof, Inst Int Health, Mich State Univ, as of 2004; PROF EMER ENVIRON SCI, UNIV MICH, SCH PUB HEALTH, as of 2003; Prin investr, Antiphospholipid Antibodies & Stroke Study, 1993-; chmn, Stroke Comt, Am Heart Asn Mich, 1992-; prin investr, NIH-Nat Inst Neurol Dis & Stroke, 1990-; Course dir, Am Acad Neurol, 1989-; clin assoc prof neurol, Univ Mich Med Sch, beginning 1989; DIR CLIN STROKE SERV & ACUTE STROKE UNIT, CTR STROKE RES, HENRY FORD HOSP, 1987-; Fel cerebrovascular dis, Univ Mich Med Sch, 1985-1987. **Memberships:** Assoc Am Acad Neurol; fel Am Heart Asn; AMA. **Research Statement & Publications:** Antiphospholipid antibodies and their significance in cerebrovascular disease; cocaine associated stroke; thrombolytic therapy for acute stroke; magnetic resonance in stroke. **Mailing Address:** Dept Environ Health Sci, Univ Mich, Ann Arbor, MI 48109-2029. **Fax:** 734-876-3014. **E-Mail:** slih@umich.edu

LEVINE, SUMNER NORTON, PHYSICAL CHEMISTRY. **Personal Data:** b Boston, September 5, 1923. **Education:** Brown Univ, BS, 1946; Univ Wis, PhD (phys chem), 1949. **Honors & Awards:** Dan Forth Lectureship, Am ResCol, 1964; Clemson Award, Soc Biol Mats Res, 1973. **Professional Experience:** Vis prof & dir urban res, Grad Ctr, City Univ New York, 1967-1968; PROF MAT SCI, STATE UNIV NY STONY BROOK, 1961-; chmn dept, State Univ NY Stony Brook, 1961-1967; sr staff scientist, head Solid State Devices & Electronics, 1960-1961; instr, Grad Div, Brooklyn Col, 1960 & City Col New York, 1960; sr staff scientist, Surface Commun Div, Radio Corp Am, 1958-1960; Albert Einstein Med Col, 1957 & Grad Div, Univ Conn, 1957-1958; mgr chem & physics lab, Gen Eng Labs, Am Mach & Foundry Co, 1956-1958; lectr, Atomic Indust Forum, 1956; dir res labs, US Vet Admin Hosp, East Orange, NJ, 1954-1956; Runyan fel, Columbia Univ, 1952; sr res fel, Columbia Univ, 1950-1954; Instr phys chem, Univ Chicago, 1949-1950; Childs fel, Univ Chicago, 1949; ed-in-chief, Advan Biomed Eng & Med Physics, J Socio-Econ Planning Sci & J Biomed Mat Res; NSF guest lectr, Berlin Acad Sci. **Memberships:** Am Chem Soc; Electrochem Soc; Sigma Xi; sr mem Inst Elec & ElectronicsEngrs; Inst Mgt Sci. **Research Statement & Publications:** Biophysical investigation of reaction mechanisms and isotopes; semiconductor physics; solid state high frequency devices; thermoelectric materials and devices; energy conversion techniques; superconductors. **Mailing Address:** PO Box 2118, Setauket, NY 11733-0883.

LEVINE, WALTER (GERALD), PHARMACOLOGY. **Personal Data:** b Detroit, Mich, December 18, 1930. **Education:** Wayne State Univ, BS, 1952, MS, 1954, PhD (physiol, pharmacol), 1958. **Professional Experience:** PROF EMER PHARMACOL, ALBERT EINSTEINCOL MED, as of 2005; prof pharmacol, albert einsteincol med, beginning 1976; from asst prof to assoc prof, Albert Einstein Col Med, 1961-1976; fel pharmacol, Albert Einstein Col Med, 1958-1961; asst, Wayne State Univ, 1956-1957; res assocphysiol & pharmacol, Wayne State Univ, 1954-1956 & 1957-1958; USPHS career develop award. **Memberships:** Am Soc Pharmacol & Exp Therapeut; NY Acad Sci; AAAS; Int Soc StudyX-enobiotics. **Research Statement & Publications:** Biochemical pharmacology; drug metabolism and disposition; regulation of the hepatic metabolism of azo dye carcinogens. **Mailing Address:** Dept Molecular Pharmacol, Albert Eisnstein Col Med, 1300 Morris Park Ave, Bronx, NY 10461-1975. **E-Mail:** wlevine@aecom.yu.edu

LEVINE, WILLIAM SILVER, ELECTRICAL ENGINEERING. **Personal Data:** b Brooklyn, NY, November 19, 1941; m 1963, c 2. **Education:** Mass Inst Technol, SB, 1962, SM, 1965, PhD (elec eng), 1969. **Honors & Awards:** Distinguished Mem, Inst Elec & Electronics Engrs Control Systs Soc, 1990. **Professional Experience:** Vis researcher, Univ Newcastle, Australia, 1992; vis scientist, Nat Inst Res Informatics & Automation, France, 1985-1986 & 1993; consult, BTS Inc, 1982-; PROF ELEC & COMP ENG, UNIV MD, COLLEGE PARK, 1981-; from asst prof to assoc prof, Univ MD, College Park, 1969-1981; asst, Mass Inst Technol, 1965-1969; res engr, Data Technol Inc, Mass, 1962-1964. **Memberships:** Fel Inst Elec & Electronics Engrs; Soc Ind & Appl Math. **Research Statement & Publications:** Optimal controls and systems with special emphasis on the theories of optimal feedback control and system identification and the application of this theory to biological and transportation systems; published over 100 articles. **Mailing Address:** Dept Elec & Comp Eng, Univ MD, 2369 AV Williams Bldg, College Park, MD 20742. **Fax:** 301-314-9281. **E-Mail:** wsl@eng.umd.edu

LEVINE, ZACHARY H, NONLINEAR OPTICS, SUBMICRON TOMOGRAPHY, ELECTRON MICROSCOPY. **Education:** Univ Pa, PhD (physics), 1983; Mass Inst Technol, BS, 1976. **Honors & Awards:** Bronze Medal, Dept Com, 1999; Silver Medal, Dept Com, 2002. **Professional Experience:** PHYSICIST, NAT INST STAND & TESHNOL, 1994-; res assoc, Ohio State Univ, 1989-1994; vis scientist, Cornell Univ, 1987-1989; sr/mem tech staff, AT&T Engineering Res Ctr, 1983-1987. **Memberships:** Am Phys Soc fel. **Research Statement & Publications:** Calculations of nonlinear optical properties of semiconductors; novel electron and x-ray tomography; showed importance of spatial dispersion of birefringence for CaF2 lenses for 157 nm lithography. **Mailing Address:** Nat Inst Stand & Technol STOP 8410, 100 Bureau Dr, Gaithersburg, MD 20899-8410. **Fax:** 301-208-6937. **E-Mail:** zlevine@nist.gov

LEVINGER, BERNARD WERNER, MATHEMATICS. **Personal Data:** b Berlin, Ger, September 3, 1928. **Education:** Lehigh Univ, BS, 1948; Mass Inst Technol, MS, 1950; NY Univ, PhD (math), 1960. **Professional Experience:** ASSOC PROF MATH, COLO STATE UNIV, 1968-; asst prof math, CaseWestern Res Univ, 1962-1968; res engr, Labs, Gen Tel & Electronics Corp, 1957-1962; resmetallurgist, Tung-Sol Elec, Inc, 1952-1957; Asst metallurgist, Armour Res Found, Ill InstTechnol, 1951-1952. **Memberships:** Am Math Soc; Math Asn Am; Soc Indust & Appl Math. **Research Statement & Publications:** Matrix theory; numerical analysis; group theory. **Mailing Address:** Math & Statist Dept, Colo State Univ, Ft Collins, CO 80523-0001.

LEVINGER, JOSEPH S, FEW-BODY SYSTEMS. **Personal Data:** b New York, NY, November 14, 1921; m 1998, Hedi; c Sam, Laurie, Louis & Joe. **Education:** Univ Chicago, BS, 1941, MS, 1944; Cornell Univ, PhD (physics), 1948. **Professional Experience:** PROF EMER PHYSICS, RENSSELAER POLYTECH INST, 1992-; Fulbright travel grant, 1972-1973, assoc prof, Univ Paris, 1972-1973; prof, Rensselaer Polytech Inst, 1964-1992; Avco vis prof, Cornell Univ, 1961-1964; Guggenheim fel, 1957-1958; from asst prof to prof, La State Univ, 1951-1961; instr physics, Conell Univ, 1948-1951; asst, 1946-1948; physicist, Franklin Inst, 1945-1946; jr physicist, Metall Lab, Univ Chicago, 1942-1944. **Memberships:** Fel Am Phys Soc. **Research Statement & Publications:** Theoretical physics: specialities, the few-nucleon problem and nuclear photoeffect. **Mailing Address:** Dept Physics, Rensselaer Polytech Inst, Troy, NY 12180. **Fax:** 518-276-6680. **E-Mail:** levinj@rpi.edu

LEVINGS, CHARLES SANDFORD, III, GENETICS. **Personal Data:** b Madison, Wis, December 1, 1930. **Education:** Univ Ill, BS, 1953, MS, 1956, PhD (agron), 1963. **Professional Experience:** DISTINGUISHED UNIV & WILLIAM NEAL REYNOLDS EMER PROF GENETICS, NC STATE UNIV, 2002-; assoc ed, Sci, 1988-1992; assoc ed, Plant Molecular Biol, 1986; assoc ed, Current Genetics, 1980-; assoc ed, Plant Physiol, 1980-1987; assoc ed, Maydica, 1980-1986; assoc ed, Develop Genetics, 1980-1985, prof, 1972-, from asst prof to assoc prof, 1964-1972, res instr, 1962-1964. **Memberships:** Nat Acad Sci; Am Genetic Asn; Genetics Soc Am; Am Soc Plant Physiologists; Am Soc Agron; AAAS; Int Soc Molecular Biol; Crop Sci Soc Am. **Research Statement & Publications:** Autotetraploid genetics; maize biochemical genetics; higher plants; extrachromosomal inheritance; mitochondria and mitochondrial genomes; molecular genetics. **Mailing Address:** 3726 Swift Dr, Raleigh, NC 27606. **E-Mail:** cs_levings@ncsu.edu

LEVINGS, COLIN DAVID, BIOLOGICAL OCEANOGRAPHY, FISHERIES ECOLOGY. **Personal Data:** b Victoria, BC, May 23, 1942. **Education:** Univ BC, BS Hons, 1965, MS, 1967; Dalhousie Univ, PhD (oceanog), 1972. **Professional Experience:** Vis scientist, Norweg Inst Nature Res, Trondheim, Norway, 1992; vis lectr, Univ Tsukuba, Japan, 1990; assoc ed, Can J Fish Aquat Sci, 1989-; vis scientist, Inst Marine Res, Bergen, Norway, 1989; SECT HEAD, SCI BR, COASTAL & MARINE HABITAT SCI, 1983-; res scientist & prog head, Sci Br, Coastal & Marine Habitat Sci, 1972-1983; scientist, Fisheries Res Bd Can, Pac Biol Sta, Nanaimo, BC, 1967-1968; field biologist technician marine fish ecol, Int Pac Halibut Comn, Seattle, Wash, 1962-1963; res assoc, Dept Zool, Univ BC. **Memberships:** Can Soc Zoologists; Pac Estuarine Res Soc (pres, 1988-); Estuarine Res Fedn. **Research Statement & Publications:** Ecology of marine and estuarine benthos; community structure at disrupted habitats; ocean dumping and dredging; coastal fish habitats and food webs; ecology of fjords; juvenile salmonid ecology; river habitats of fishes; aquaculture siting in coastal areas. **Mailing Address:** Dept Fisheries & Oceans, Can Coastal & Marine Habitat Sci Sect, W Vancouver Lab 4160 Marine Dr, West Vancouver, BC V7V 1N6, Can.

LEVINS, RICHARD, POPULATION BIOLOGY, MATHEMATICAL BIOLOGY. **Personal Data:** b Brooklyn, NY, June 1, 1930; m Rosario; c Aurora, Ricardo Manuel & Alejandro. **Education:** Cornell Univ, AB, 1951; Columbia Univ, PhD (zoology), 1965. **Honorary Degrees:** MPh, Harvard Univ, 1975; PhD, Univ Havana, 2003. **Honors & Awards:** Edinburgh Sci Medal, 1996. **Professional Experience:** FOREIGN SCI COLLABR, CUBAN INST ECOL & SYST, 2004-; JOHN ROCK PROF POP SCI, SCH PUB HEALTH, HARVARD UNIV, 1975-; from assoc prof to prof math biol, Univ Chicago, 1967-1975, NSF res grant, 1964-1966, consult agr ecol prog, Cuban Acad Sci, 1964-1965; NIH res grant, 1963-1966, assoc prof biol, Univ PR, 1961-1966; res assoc pop genetics, Univ Rochester, 1960-1961; farmer, 1951-1956. **Memberships:** Am Acad Arts & Sci; Am Soc Naturalists; Int Soc Ecosyst Health. **Research Statement & Publications:** Ecology and genetics; complex systems; agriculture; epidemiological ecology and evolution. **Mailing Address:** Dept Pop & Int Health, Harvard Sch Pub Health, Bldg I Rm 1109 665 Huntington Ave, Boston, MA 02115. **Fax:** 617-566-0365. **E-Mail:** humaneco@hsph.harvard.edu

LEVINSKAS, GEORGE JOSEPH, toxicology, industrial agricultural chemicals & food additives environmental health; deceased, see previous edition for last biography

LEVINSKY, WALTER JOHN, medicine; deceased, see previous edition for last biography

LEVINSON, ALFRED ABRAHAM, exploration geochemistry; deceased, see previous edition for last biography

LEVINSON, ALFRED STANLEY, ORGANIC CHEMISTRY. **Personal Data:** b Portland, Ore, August 27, 1932; wid Amy Perlstein (deceased); c Ellen E, Mark R & Rebecca Anne (deceased). **Education:** Reed Col, BA, 1954; Wesleyan Univ, MA, 1957; Ind Univ, PhD (org chem), 1963. **Professional Experience:** EMER PROF CHEM, PORTLAND STATE UNIV, 1994-; from asst prof to prof, Portland State Univ, 1963-1994; Res assoc chem, Ind Univ, 1962-1963. **Memberships:** AAAS; Am Chem Soc. **Mailing Address:** Portland State Univ, 2705 Sunset Blvd Box 751, Portland, OR 97201-1222.

LEVINSON, ARTHUR DAVID, MOLECULAR BIOLOGY. **Personal Data:** b Seattle, Wash, March 31, 1950. **Education:** Univ Wash, BS, 1972; Princeton Univ, PhD (biochem), 1977. **Honors & Awards:** Corp Leadership Award Sci, Irvington Inst, 1999; Corp Leadership Award, Nat Breast Cancer Coalition, 1999. **Professional Experience:** PRES & CHIEF EXEC OFFICER, GENENTECH INC, 1995-; sr vpres, Dept Cell Genetics, 1993-1995; vpres res, Dept Cell Genetics, 1990-1993; vpres res technol, Dept CellGenetics, 1989-1990; dir, Dept Cell Genetics, 1987-1989; staff scientist, Genentech, Inc, 1983-1983; sr scientist, Genentech, Inc, 1980-1983; sr res fel, Am Cancer Soc, 1978-1980; NIH res fel, Univ Calif, San Francisco, 1977-1978. **Memberships:** AAAS; Am Soc Microbiol; Am Soc Biochem & Molecular Biol. **Research Statement & Publications:** Role of cellular genes in tumor development; regulation of mammalian gene expression; molecular genetics. **Mailing Address:** Genentech Inc, 460 Pt San Bruno Blvd, South San Francisco, CA 94080.

LEVINSON, BARRY L, CENTRAL NERVOUS SYSTEM DISORDERS, ENDOCRINOLOGY & FERTILITY CONTROL. **Personal Data:** b Camden, NJ, July 2, 1955. **Education:** Princeton Univ, AB, 1977; Yale Univ, MPhil, 1980, PhD (molecular biol, biophys &biochem), 1983. **Professional Experience:** MGR, PRECLIN TECHNOL DEVELOP, BERLEX LABS, INC, 1994-; sranalyst, Preclin Technol Develop, Berlex Labs, Inc, 1992-1994; scientist, Preclin TechnolDevelop, Berlex Labs, Inc, 1989-1992; sr res scientist, Ecogen Inc, 1989; res scientist, EcogenInc, 1985-1989; fel, Univ Southampton, UK, 1983-1985; vis scientist, Weizmann Inst, Israel, 1977-1978; Res asst, Fox Chase Inst Cancer Res, 1976-1977. **Memberships:** AAAS; Am Chem Soc; Am Soc Biochem & Molecular Biol; Asn Univ TechnolMgrs; NY Acad Sci. **Research Statement & Publications:** Identify and develop new technologies and pharmaceuticals in central nervous system, autoimmune disease and female healthcare; author of 8 publications; granted 1 US patent. **Mailing Address:** Off Technol, 300 Faurfield Rd, Wayne, NJ 07470-7358. **Fax:** 973-292-8770. **E-Mail:** barry_levinson@berlex.com

LEVINSON, CHARLES, CELL PHYSIOLOGY. **Personal Data:** b San Antonio, Tex, December 31, 1936. **Education:** Univ Tex, BA, 1958; Trinity Univ, MA, 1960; Rutgers Univ, PhD (physiol), 1964. **Professional Experience:** RETIRED; dep chmn, Med Sch, Univ Tex, San Antonio, 1992-2000; prof physiol, Med Sch, Univ Tex, San Antonio, 1972-2000; assocprof, Med Sch, Univ Tex, San Antonio, 1968-1972; sr cancer res scientist, Roswell Park MemInst, 1966-1968; Nat Cancer Inst fel, Med Col, Cornell Univ, 1965-1966. **Memberships:** Biophys Soc; Soc Gen Physiol; Am Physiol Soc; Sigma Xi. **Research Statement & Publications:** Membrane phenomena; ion transport in tumor cells. **Mailing Address:** Dept Physiol, Univ Tex Health Sci Ctr, 7703 Floyd Curl Dr, San Antonio, TX 78229-3900. **Fax:** 210-567-4410.

LEVINSON, DAVID ALAN, SPACECRAFT ATTITUDE DYNAMICS, DYNAMICS OF MULTIBODY SYSTEMS. **Personal Data:** b Meadville, Pa, April 6, 1950. **Education:** Cornell Univ, BS, 1972; Stanford Univ, MS, 1973. **Honors & Awards:** Engr Yr Award, 1989 & 1997. **Professional Experience:** STAFF AEROSPACE ENGR, ADVAN TECHNOL CTR, LOCKHEED MARTIN MISSILES & SPACE, 1996-; lectr dynamics & spacecraft dynamics, Dept Mech Eng, Stanford Univ, 1993-1994; chmn, Discover E Eng Outreach Prog, Silicon Valley Eng Coun, 1993-1994; mem, Astrodyn Tech Comt Stand, 1992-1994; staff engr, Lockheed Missiles & Space Co, 1991-1996; staff scientist, Lockheed Missiles & Space Co, 1989-1991; lectr dynamics & spacecraft dynamics, Dept Mech Eng, Stanford Univ, 1988; res scientist, Lockheed Missiles & Space Co, 1985-1989; sr scientist, Lockheed Missiles & Space Co, 1982-1985; mem, Astrodyn Tech Comt, Am Inst Aeronaut & Astronaut, 1981-1984; Lectr dynamics & spacecraft dynamics, Dept Mech Eng, Stanford Univ, 1981; scientist, Lockheed Missiles & Space Co, 1979-1982; sr assoc scientist, Lockheed Missiles & Space Co, 1977-1979; lectr dynamics & spacecraft dynamics, Dept Mech Eng, Stanford Univ. **Memberships:** Fel Am Astronaut Soc; fel Am Soc Mech Engrs; assoc fel Am Inst Aeronaut & Astronaut; Am Acad Mech. **Research Statement & Publications:** Apply computerized symbol manipulation to the formulation of exact, explicit equations of motion of complex multibody systems, such as spacecraft, mechanisms and robots. **Mailing Address:** Missiles & Sapce Advan Technol Ctr Lockheed Martin Corp, EH-13 B/205 3251 Hanover St, Palo Alto, CA 94304-1191.

LEVINSON, DAVID W, PHYSICAL METALLURGY, FAILURE ANALYSIS. **Personal Data:** b Chicago, Ill, February 24, 1925; m 1949, Betty; c Louis E, Joseph P & Jeanne L. **Education:** Ill Inst Technol, BS, 1948, MS, 1949, PhD (metall eng), 1953. **Professional Experience:** ADJ PROF, UNIV ARIZ, as of 2000; adj prof, Univ Ariz, Tucson, 1990-; PROF EMER MAT SCI & ENG, UNIV ILL, CHICAGO CIRCLE, 1987-; consult, Triodyne Inc, 1987-; actg dean col eng, Dept Mat Eng, Univ Ill, Chicago Circle, 1967-1969; prof, Dept Mat Eng, Univ Ill, Chicago Circle, 1964-1987; assoc head, Dept Mat Eng, Univ Ill, Chicago Circle, 1964-1967; sci adv, Metals & Ceramics Div, IIT Res Inst, 1962-1964; asst dir metals res, Armour Res Found, 1959-1962; supvr non-ferrous metall res, Armour Res Found, 1957-1959; res metallurgist, Armour Res Found, 1953-1957. **Memberships:** Am Soc Mat Int; Am Inst Mining Metall & Petrol Engrs; Am Soc Eng Educ; Sigma Xi. **Research Statement & Publications:** High temperature alloy development; coatings for thermal control of surfaces; metallurgical transformations in alloys in thin film form; binary and ternary phase equilibria in metallic systems; stress relaxation in high carbon steels, fatigue and fracture toughness of resulfurized steels. **Mailing Address:** Dept Mat Sci & Eng Univ Ariz, Mines Bldg Rm 143, Tucson, AZ 85721. **Fax:** 520-621-8059. **E-Mail:** mandm13@juno.com

LEVINSON, HERBERT S, TRANSPORTATION. **Personal Data:** b September 25, 1924; m 1977, Sally. **Education:** Ill Inst Technol, BS, 1949. **Honors & Awards:** Presidential Design Award; Theordore M Matson Award, Inst Transp Engrs. **Professional Experience:** Res prof, Polytech Univ, 1988-1990; prof transp eng, Polytech Univ, 1986-1988; PRIN, HERBERT S LEVINSON, TRANSP CONSULT, 1980-; prof civil eng, Univ Ct, 1980-1986; vis lectr city planning, Yale Univ, 1961-1980; from assoc, prin assoc & vpres to sr vpres, Wilbur Smith & Assoc, 1952-1980; jr traffic engr, Chicago Park Dist, 1949-1951. **Memberships:** Nat Acad Eng; Am Soc Civil Engrs; Inst Transp Engrs; Am Inst Planners; Transp Res Bd. **Research Statement & Publications:** Public transportation; transportation, engineering and planning; parking; transportation policy. **Mailing Address:** 40 Hemlock Rd, New Haven, CT 06515. **E-Mail:** hslevmron@alu.com

LEVINSON, LIONEL MONTY, ELECTRONIC MATERIALS, CERAMIC ENGINEERING. **Personal Data:** b Johannesburg, SAfrica, March 12, 1943. **Education:** Univ Witwatersrand, BSc, 1965, MSc, 1966; Weizmann Inst Sci, PhD (solid statephysics), 1970. **Honors & Awards:** IR 100 Award; Dashman Award. **Professional Experience:** PRIN & OWNER, VARTEK ASSOC LLC, as of 2004; consult, Vertek Assoc LLC, 2002-2003; adj prof physics, Rensselaer Polytech Inst, 2000-2002; mgr, Electronic & Optical Mat, Ge Corp Res, 1980-2002; physicist, Gen Elec Corp Res & Develop, 1970-1979. **Memberships:** Nat Res Soc; fel Am Ceramic Soc (vpres). **Research Statement & Publications:** Electronic ceramics; varistors; electronic packaging; thermoelectrics transparent ceramics; current limiters; voltage limiters; scintillators; phyosphors. **Mailing Address:** Vartek Assoc LLC, PO Box 9227, Schenectady, NY 12309. **Fax:** 518-869-5192. **E-Mail:** lionel@lionellevinson.com

LEVINSON, MARK, HISTORY OF TECHNOLOGY, MECHANICS. **Personal Data:** b Brooklyn, NY, June 12, 1929. **Education:** Polytech Inst Brooklyn, BAeroE, 1951, MS, 1960; Calif Inst Technol, PhD, 1964. **Professional Experience:** PVT RES, 2002-; VIS PROF AERONAUT & ASTRONAUT, UNIV WASH, 1991-; sr fel, NSF, 1988-1989; dir, Technol & Soc Proj, 1985-1990, A W Mellon fel, 1984-1985, A O Willey prof mech eng, Univ Maine, Orono, 1980-1985; prof eng mech, McMaster Univ, 1967-1980; assoc prof theoret & appl mech, WVa Univ, 1966-1967; assoc prof, Clarkson Col Technol, 1964-1966; asst prof mech eng, Ore State Col, 1960-1961; sr asst appl mech, Polytech Inst Brooklyn, 1959; stress analyst, Foster-Wheeler Corp, 1957-1958; instr math, Polytech Inst Brooklyn, 1956; Asst appl mech, Polytech Inst Brooklyn, 1951-1952. **Memberships:** AAAS; Am Soc Mech Engrs; Am Inst Aeronaut & Astronaut; Soc Indust & ApplMath; Soc Hist Technol. **Research Statement & Publications:** Theory of elasticity; continuum mechanics; elastic stability; structural dynamics; theory of plates; history of early aviation. **Mailing Address:** 630 Giltner Lane, Edmonds, WA 98020.

LEVINSON, RACHEL E, BIOCHEMISTRY, SCIENCE POLICY. **Personal Data:** b Hornell, NY, April 16, 1952. **Education:** Univ Md, BS, 1975; George Washington Univ, MA, 1985. **Professional Experience:** ASST DIR, LIFE SCI, OFFICE SCI & TECHNOL POLICY, 1993-. **Memberships:** AAAS. **Mailing Address:** Off Sci & Technol Policy, Old Exec Off Bldg NW Rm 436, Washington, DC 20502. **Fax:** 202-456-6130. **E-Mail:** levinson@ostp.eop.gov

LEVINSON, SIDNEY BERNARD, chemistry, chemical engineering; deceased, see previous edition for last biography

LEVINSON, STANLEY S, PATHOLOGY. **Education:** Boston Univ, BA, 1964; Univ Calif, MS, 1967, PhD (physiol), 1970; Am Bd ClinChem, cert. **Professional Experience:** PROF PATH & LAB MED, UNIV LOUISVILLE, as of 2004; DIR CLIN CHEM & IMMUNOL, LAB SERV, VET ADMIN MED CTR, UNIV LOUISVILLE, 1989-; asst prof path, Univ Louisville, beginning 1989; adj assoc prof, Dept Path &assoc, Dept Biochem, 1988-1989; adj asst prof, Dept Path & assoc, Dept Biochem, Sch Med, Wayne State Univ, 1981-1986; lectr clin chem, Grad Sch Pharm & Health, Northeastern Univ, 1978-1980; dir clin lab, Joslin Found Diabetic Unit, Brookline Hosp, 1974-1980; res fel med, Clin Chem Lab, Mass Gen Hosp, 1973-1974; res assoc, Dept Nutrit, Mass Inst Technol, 1970-1973. **Memberships:** Clin Ligand Assay Soc; AAAS; AmAsn Clin Chem; Soc Complex Carbohydrates; Am Asn Immunol; Nat Acad Clin Biochem. **Research Statement & Publications:** Methods of assay of antigens via immunochemical techniques; methods of assaying circulating immune complexes, rheumatoid factors and idiotypic antibodies; regulation of the immune response through molecules that stimulate and inhibit the synthesis of circulating immune complexes and rheumatoid factors by affecting lymphocytes; clinical correlates with measurement of circulating immune complexes and complement function tests; testing for apolipoproteins and clinical studies related to lipid metabolism as risk factors for cardiovascular disease; numerous publications. **Mailing Address:** Vet Admin Med Ctr, Univ Louisville, 800 Zorn Ave, Louisville, KY 40206. **Fax:** 502-894-6265. **E-Mail:** levinson@louisville.edu

LEVINSON, STEPHEN, SPEECH PROCESSING, AUTOMATIC SPEECH. **Personal Data:** b New York, NY, September 27, 1944. **Education:** Harvard Univ, BA, 1966; Univ RI, MS, 1972, PhD (elec eng), 1974. **Honors & Awards:** Sigma Xi Res Prize, 1974. **Professional Experience:** FAC MEM, ARTFICIAL INTELLIGENCE GROUP, BECKMAN INST, as of 2004; PROF, ELEC & COMPUT ENG, UNIV ILL, as of 2000; head, Linguistic & Res Dept, AT&T Bell Lab, 1990-1997; distinguished mem technical staff, AT&T Bell Lab, 1990; Inst Elec & Electronic Engrs Signal Processing Soc Distinguished lectr, 1986; elec engr, Bell Lab, 1976-1997; instr comput sci, Yale Univ, 1974-1976. **Memberships:** Fel Inst Elec & Electronics Engrs; fel Acoust Soc Am. **Research Statement & Publications:** Speech synthesis, speech recognition, automatic natural language understanding, cognitive science, and artificial intelligence; publications on semantics and language acquisition. **Mailing Address:** Dept Elec & Comput Eng, Univ Ill, 2009 Beckman Inst Adv Sci & Technol 405 N Mathews, Urbana, IL 61801. **Fax:** 217-244-7075. **E-Mail:** sel@ifp.uiuc.edu

LEVINSON, STEVEN R, ANALYTICAL CHEMISTRY, PHOTOGRAPHY. **Personal Data:** b Brooklyn, NY, October 13, 1947. **Education:** Rensselaer Polytech Inst, BS, 1968, PhD (anal chem), 1973. **Professional Experience:** Instr, Rochester Inst Technol, 1976-; SR RES CHEMIST, PHOTOG RES DIV, KODAK RES LABS, EASTMAN KODAK CO, 1973-. **Memberships:** Am Chem Soc; Sigma Xi; Soc Photog Scientists & Engrs. **Research Statement & Publications:** Research and development of photographic materials. **Mailing Address:** 102 Mountain Rd, Rochester, NY 14625-1819.

LEVINSON, STUART ALAN, PALEONTOLOGY, GEOLOGY. **Personal Data:** b Detroit, Mich, October 29, 1920. **Education:** Wayne State Univ, BS, 1947; Wash Univ, AM, 1949, PhD (geol), 1951. **Professional Experience:** PRES, GULF COAST SEC SEPM INC, 2002-; res assoc, Esso Prod Res Co, 1966-1990; res supvr, Esso Prod Res Co, 1964-1966; sr geologist, Humble Oil & Refining Co, 1951-1964; instr, Wash Univ, 1950-1951; asst geol, Wash Univ, 1947-1951. **Memberships:** AAAS; Paleont Soc; Soc Econ Paleontologists & Mineralogists (vpres, 1957); Geol Soc Am; Am Asn Petrol Geologists. **Research Statement & Publications:** Invertebrate paleontology, micropaleontology and zoology. **Mailing Address:** 5050 Woodway Dr No 5G, Houston, TX 77056-0806.

LEVINSON, WARREN E, MICROBIOLOGY, IMMUNOLOGY. **Personal Data:** b Brooklyn, NY, September 28, 1933. **Education:** Cornell Univ, BS, 1953; Univ Buffalo, MD, 1957; Univ Calif, Berkeley, PhD (virol), 1965. **Professional Experience:** R W Johnson Health Policy fel, 1980-1981; PROF MICROBIOL, MED CTR, UNIV CALIF, SAN FRANCISCO, 1970-; assoc prof, Med Ctr, Univ Calif, San Francisco, 1965-1970; Am Cancer Soc fel tumor viruses, Univ Col, Univ London, 1965-1967. **Research Statement & Publications:** Tumor viruses. **Mailing Address:** Dept Microbiol, Univ Calif Med Ctr, PO Box 0414, San Francisco, CA 94143. **E-Mail:** warlev@itsa.ucsf.edu

LEVINTHAL, CHARLES F, NEUROSCIENCES. **Personal Data:** b Cincinnati, Ohio, July 6, 1945. **Education:** Univ Cincinnati, AB, 1967; Univ Mich, MA, 1968, PhD (exp psychol), 1971. **Professional Experience:** PRES HOFSTRA CHAP PHI BETA KAPPA, HOFSTRA UNIV, as of 2000; PROF PSYCHOL & DEPT CHMN, DEPT PSYCHOL, HOFSTRA UNIV, 1987-; from asst prof to assoc prof, 1971-1987. **Memberships:** Am Psychol Asn; Soc Neuroscience; Soc Psychophysiol Res; NY Acad Sci. **Research Statement & Publications:** Studies of hemisphere specialization among bilingual individuals; author of various articles. **Mailing Address:** Dept Psychol, 135 Hofstra Univ, Hauser Hall Rm 222, Hempstead, NY 11550-1091. **Fax:** 516-463-6052. **E-Mail:** charles.f.levinthal@hofstra.edu

LEVINTHAL, ELLIOTT CHARLES, PHYSICS. **Personal Data:** b Brooklyn, NY, April 13, 1922; m 1944, Rhoda Arons; c David, Judith, Michael & Daniel. **Education:** Columbia Univ, BA, 1942; Mass Inst Technol, MS, 1943; Stanford Univ, PhD (physics), 1949. **Professional Experience:** EMER PROF MECH ENG, SCH ENG, STANFORD UNIV, 1991-; prof & assoc dean res, Sch Eng, Stanford Univ, 1983-1990; dir, Sch Eng, Inst Mfg & Automation, 1983-1990; dir, defense sci off, Defense Advan Res Agency, Dept Defense, 1981-1983; prin investr & dep team leader, Viking Lunar Imaging Sci Team, 1975; adj prof genetics, Sch Med 1974-1980; assoc dean res affairs, Sch Med, Stanford Univ, 1971-1974; Co-investr, Mariner Mars Photo Interpretation Team, 1970; assoc dean res affairs, dir Instrumentation Res Lab, 1961-1981; pres, Levinthal Electronic Prod, Inc, 1953-1961; chief engr, Century Electronics & Instruments, Inc, 1952-1953; res dir, Varian Assocs, 1950-1952; res physicist, Varian Assocs, 1949-1950; res assoc nuclear physics, Stanford Univ, 1946-1948; Proj engr, Sperry Gyroscope Co, NY, 1943-1946. **Memberships:** AAAS; fel Am Phys Soc; sr mem Inst Elec & Electronics Eng; Optical Soc Am; Biomed Eng Soc; Sigma Xi. **Research Statement & Publications:** Measurements of nuclear moments; applications of computers to image processing and medical instrumentation; exobiology and planetary sciences; manufacturing and automation systems. **Mailing Address:** 59 Sutherland Dr, Atherton, CA 94027-6430. **Fax:** 650-854-6342.

LEVINTHAL, MARK, MICROBIAL GENETICS, MOLECULAR EVOLUTION. **Personal Data:** b Brooklyn, NY, March 3, 1941; m 1990, Donna; c Peter S & Sarita. **Education:** Brooklyn Col, BS, 1962; Brandeis Univ, PhD (biol), 1966. **Professional Experience:** ASSOC PROF BIOL, PURDUE UNIV, 1972-; staff fel genetics lab molecular biol, Nat Inst Arthritis & Metal Dis, 1968-1972; NIH fel, 1966-1968 & 1972-1977; fel genetics, Johns Hopkins Univ, 1966-1968. **Memberships:** Am Soc Microbiol; Sigma Xi; Genetics Soc Am; AAAS; Italian Molecular Biol Soc; Soc Study Evolution. **Research Statement & Publications:** Regulation of enzyme synthesis of biosynthetic pathways and its relationship to general metabolic controls in bacteria; regulatory mechanisms-their evolution and contribution to general evolutionary theory. **Mailing Address:** Dept Biol Sci, Purdue Univ, LILY 1-232, West Lafayette, IN 47907. **Fax:** 765-474-0876. **E-Mail:** marklev@purdue.edu

LEVINTON, JEFFREY SHELDON, ECOLOGY, PALEONTOLOGY. **Personal Data:** b New York, NY, March 20, 1946. **Education:** City Col NY, BS, 1966; Yale Univ, MPhil, 1969, PhD (Geol & Geophysics), 1971. **Professional Experience:** DISTINGUISHED PROF, DEPT ECOL & EVOLUTION, STATE UNIV NY, STONY BROOK, as of 2003; head, dept ecol & evolution, state Univ NY, Stony Brook, 1990-1993; vis prof, Dept Ecol & Evolution, UnivWash, 1990-1991; chmn, assoc ed Ecol Appln, 1990-1993; chmn, Panel Hudson River Found, 1986-1990; chmn, assoc ed Ecol, 1986-1989; chmn, Dept Ecol & Evolution, Univ Wash, 1985-1993, Guggenheim fel, 1984-1985, vis prof, Uppsala Univ, Sweden, 1981 & Univ Cambridge, 1984; PROF ECOL & EVOLUTION, STATE UNIV NY, STONY BROOK, 1983-; assoc prof ecol & evolution, State Univ NY, Stony Brook, 1975-1983; managing ed, Am Naturalist, 1974-1975; State Univ NY, Stony Brook Res Found fel & grant-in-aid, 1971; from instr to assoc prof paleoecol, State Univ NY, Stony Brook, 1970-1983; nat sci found fel, 1968-1970; NSF fel, 1968-1970. **Memberships:** Ecol Soc Am; Am Soc Naturalists; Soc Study Evolution; AAAS. **Research Statement & Publications:** Marine benthic ecology; paleoecology; fossil population dynamics; benthic deposit feeder-detritus-microbial interactions; evolutionary biology of marine invertebrates. **Mailing Address:** Dept Ecol & Evolution, State Univ NY, 680 Life Sci Bldg Sixth Floor, Stony Brook, NY 11794-5245. **Fax:** 631-632-7626. **E-Mail:** levinton@life.bio.sunysb.com

LEVINTOW, LEON, BIOCHEMISTRY, VIROLOGY. **Personal Data:** b Philadelphia, Pa, November 10, 1921. **Education:** Haverford Col, AB, 1943; Jefferson Med Col, MD, 1946. **Professional Experience:** PROF EMER MICROBIOL, SCH MED, UNIV CALIF, SAN FRANCISCO, as of 2005; CHMN, DEPT MICROBIOL & IMMUNOL, 1980-; prof microbiol, Sch Med, Univ Calif, San Francisco, beginning 1965; asst chief lab biol viruses, Nat InstAllergy & Infectious Dis, 1961-1965; asst chief lab cell biol, Nat Inst Allergy & Infectious Dis, 1956-1961; res fel, Biochem Res Lab, Mass Gen Hosp, Boston, 1951-1952; biochemist, NatCancer Inst, 1949-1956; chief lab, US Army Hepatitis Res Ctr, Ger, 1947-1949; intern, Jefferson Hosp, Philadelphia, Pa, 1946-1947. **Memberships:** Am Soc Microbiol; Am Chem Soc; Am Soc Biol Chemists. **Research Statement & Publications:**

Biochemistry of viruses. **Mailing Address:** Dept Microbiol & Immunol, Univ Calif Sch Med, Rm HSW 1542 Box 0552, San Francisco, CA 94143-0552.

LEVIS, ALEXANDER HENRY, COMMAND & CONTROL. **Personal Data:** b Yannina, Greece, October 3, 1940; American citizen; m 2001, Margaret; c Livia & Philip. **Education:** Ripon Col, BA, 1963; Mass Inst Technol, BS & MS, 1965, ME, 1967. **Honorary Degrees:** ScD, Mass Inst Technol, 1968. **Honors & Awards:** Except Civilian Serv Medal, US Air Force, 1994, 2001; Third Millennium Medal, Inst Elec & ELectronics Engrs. **Professional Experience:** Chief Scientist, US Air Force, 2001-2003; PROF ELEC, COMPUT & SYST ENG, GEORGE MASON UNIV, 1990-; sr res scientist, Mass Inst Technol, 1979-1990; from sr engr to dept mgr, Systs Control Inc, 1973-1979; from asst prof to assoc prof elec eng, Polytech Inst NY, 1968-1973; res asst, Electronics Systs Lab, 1965-1968; engr, Christina Lab, E I du Pont Del Nemours & Co Inc, 1965; res asst control systs, Eng Projs Lab, Mass Inst Technol, 1963-1965. **Memberships:** Fel Inst Elec & Electronics Engrs; Fel AAAS; Sigma Xi; Assoc Fel Am Inst Aeronaut & Astronaut; distinguished mem Control Systs Soc; Armed Forces Commun & Electronics Asn; INCOSE. **Research Statement & Publications:** Mathematical organization theory, distributed intelligence systems, command and control. **Mailing Address:** Dept Elec & Comput Eng, George Mason Univ, Fairfax, VA 22030. **Fax:** 703-759-5328. **E-Mail:** alevis@gmu.edu

LEVIS, C(URT) A(LBERT), RADIOWAVE PROPAGATION & ANTENNAS. **Personal Data:** b Ger, April 16, 1926; American citizen; m 1958, Katharine; c Alan P, Linda K (Volkovitsch) & Susan I (Groseclose). **Education:** Case Inst Technol, BS, 1949; Harvard Univ, AM, 1950; Ohio State Univ, PhD (elec eng), 1956. **Professional Experience:** EMER PROF, OHIO STATE UNIV, 1985-; guest vis, Inst Telecommun Sci, 1985-1986; sr fel, Nat Ctr Atmospheric Res, 1976-1977; dir, ElectroScience Lab 1961-1969; from asst prof to prof elec eng, Antenna Lab, Ohio State Univ, 1956-1985; assoc supvr, Antenna Lab, Ohio State Univ, 1956-1961; res assoc, Antenna Lab, Ohio State Univ, 1950-1956; studio engr, Radio Sta WSRS, Inc, 1948-1949. **Memberships:** Fel Inst Elec & Electronics Engrs. **Research Statement & Publications:** Radiowave propagation; antennas; electromagnetic theory; satellite communications. **Mailing Address:** Dept Elec Eng, Ohio State Univ, 2015 Neil Ave, Columbus, OH 43210-1272. **E-Mail:** levis.i@osu.edu

LEVIS, DONALD J, CLINICAL PSYCHOLOGY, BEHAVIORAL THERAPY. **Personal Data:** b Cleveland, Ohio, September 19, 1936. **Education:** John Carroll Univ, BSS, 1958; Kent State Univ, MA, 1960; Emory Univ, PhD (psychol), 1964. **Professional Experience:** PROF PSYCHOL, STATE UNIV NY, BINGHAMTON, as of 2004; adj prof, Col Med, Upstate Med Ctr, Syracuse, 1979-; dir & developer psycholres & training clin, State Univ NY, Binghamton, 1973-1976; prof clin psychol, State Univ Ny, Binghamton, beginning 1972; dir & developer clin psychol training prog, State Univ NY, Binghamton, 1972-1981; dir res & training clin, Univ Iowa, 1970-1972; from asst prof to assocprof clin psychol, State Univ NY, Binghamton, 1965-1972; res psychologist psychobiol, Lafayette Clin, Detroit, 1965-1966; adj asst prof, Wayne State Univ, 1965-1966; USPHS fel clinpsychol, Lafayette Clin, Detroit, 1964-1965; lectr, Emory Univ, 1963-1964. **Memberships:** Fel Am Psychol Asn; Psychonomic Soc; Asn Advan Behavior Ther; SocPsychophysiol Res; Sigma Xi. **Research Statement & Publications:** Developing the theoretical model and applied therapeutic behavioral technique of implosive (flooding) therapy; decoding of traumatic memories motivating psychopathology; author of over 80 scientific articles. **Mailing Address:** Dept Psychol, Binghamton Univ, Sci IV, Rm 206, Binghamton, NY 13902-0600.

LEVIS, WILLIAM WALTER, ORGANIC CHEMISTRY. **Personal Data:** b Chicago, Ill, May 14, 1918. **Education:** Univ Fla, BS, 1941. **Professional Experience:** RETIRED; sr res assoc, BASF Wyandotte Corp, 1984-1986; res supvr, BASF Wyandotte Corp, 1956-1984; sect head, BASF Wyandotte Corp, 1955-1956; sr res chemist, BASF Wyandotte Corp, 1952-1955; sr res chemist, Sharples Chem Inc, 1942-1952; res chemist, Fla Chem Indust, 1941-1942. **Memberships:** Am Chem Soc. **Research Statement & Publications:** Organic synthesis; catalysis; hydrogenation; amination; oxyalkyation. **Mailing Address:** 2069 SE 37th Ct Circle, Ocala, FL 34471.

LEVI-SETTI, RICCARDO, ION MICROSCOPY, SECONDARY ION MASS SPECTROMETRY. **Personal Data:** b Milan, Itlay, July 11, 1927. **Education:** Univ Pavia, Dr(physics), 1949; Univ Rome, Libera Docenza(physics), 1955. **Professional Experience:** PROF EMER PHYSICS, UNIV CHICAGO, as of 2002; dir, Enrico Fermi Inst, 1992-1998; hon res assoc, Field Mus Natural Hist, Chicago, 1976; prof physics, Univ Chicago, beginning 1965; John Simon Guggengheim fel, Europ Orgn Nuclear Res, Geneva, 1963; assoc prof, Enrico Fermi Inst, 1962-1965; Asst prof, Univ Pavia, Italy, 1949-1951 & Univ Milan, 1957-1964; asst prof, Enrico Fermi Inst, 1957-1962; resassoc, Enrico Fermi Inst, Univ Chicago, 1956-1957; Angelo della Riccia fel, Ital Phys Soc, 1954; res mem, Nat Inst Nuclear Res, Univ Milan, 1951-1956. **Memberships:** Fel Am Phys Soc. **Research Statement & Publications:** Imaging microanalysis of material by secondary ion mass spectrometry at high lateral resolution; studies of metal alloys, ceramics, minerals, biomaterials; development of new microanalytical instrumentatiom. **Mailing Address:** Enrico Fermi Inst, 5640 S Ellis Ave, Chicago, IL 60637-1433.

LEVISON, MATTHEW EDMUND, MEDICAL SCIENCE, HEALTH SCIENCES. **Personal Data:** b New York, NY, May 18, 1937. **Education:** Columbia Univ, BA, 1958; State Univ NY, MD, 1962. **Professional Experience:** PROF MED & CHIEF INFECTIOUS DIS DIV, ALLEGHANY UNIV HEALTH SCI, MCP HAHEMANN SCH MED, 1995-; prof med & chief infectious dis div, MedCol Pa, 1977-1995; attend staff, Philadelphia Vet Admin Hosp, beginning 1970; from asst prof to assocprof med & chief, Alleghany Univ Health Sci, Mcp Hahemann Sch Med, 1970-1977; clin instr, Downstate Med Ctr, State Univ, NY, 1969-1970; attend physician & chief infectious dis unit, Queens Hosp Ctr, Long Island Jewish Med Ctr affil, 1969-1970; instr, Med Col, Cornell Univ, 1968-1969; asst physician, NY Hosp, 1967-1969; asst instr med, Downstate Med Ctr, State UnivNY, 1965-1967. **Memberships:** Am Soc Microbiol; Am Fedn Clin Res; Infectious Dis Soc Am; fel Am Col Clin Pharmacol; fel Am Col Physicians; Soc Healthcare Epidemiol Am. **Research Statement & Publications:** Anaerobic bacteria, the pathogenesis of the renal concentrating defect in experimental pylonephritis and the pathogenesis of experimental endocarditis; antimicrobial pharmacodynamics. **Mailing Address:** Allegheny Univ Health Sci MCP Hahnemann Sch Med, 3300 Henry Ave, Philadelphia, PA 19129. **Fax:** 215-843-3515. **E-Mail:** levison@auhs.edu

LEVISON, SANDRA PELTZ, INTERNAL MEDICINE, NEPHROLOGY. **Personal Data:** b New York, NY, April 20, 1941. **Education:** Hunter Col, NY, BA; NY Univ, MD. **Honors & Awards:** Master ACP/SCIM; Laureate Pennsylvania College of Medicine; Reader's Digest American Health Hero; Local Legend - AMWA & National Library of Medicine; Physician Honoree Delaware Chapter National Kidney Foundation. **Professional Experience:** PROF & CHIEF, DIV NEPHROLOGY, DREXEL UNIV, as of 2004; SR CONSULT, INST WOMEN'S HEALTH, as of 1993; Clinical Service Chief, MED COL PA HOSP, 1993-2002; DIR NEPHROLOGY FEL PROG, HAHNEMANN; DIR WOMEN'S HEALTH EDUC PROG, 1993-2000; PROF MED, MED COL PA, 1981-1993; from instr to assoc prof med, Med Col Pa, 1970-1981; asst instr med, Med Ctr, NY Univ, 1967-1968; Asst instr med, State Univ NY, Downstate, 1966-1967 & 1968-1970; Bd mem, Am Diabetes Asn; consult, Food & Drug Admin; co-chair, Nat Acad Women's Health Med Educ; chief, Div Nephrology, Hahnenann Univ & MCP Hosps; clin serv chief, Dept Med, MCP Hosps. **Memberships:** Am Soc Nephrology; Master Am Col Physicians; Women In Neophrology; Am Soc of Hypertension. **Research Statement & Publications:** Elucidation of the renal concentrating defect in experimental infective Pyelonephritis; effects of exercise on blood pressure of adolescents; comparing blood pressures in infants and children of toxemic, hypertensive and normal mothers; geriatric renal disease; women's health; health and human rights. **Mailing Address:** Drexel Univ Col Med, 245 N 15th St, Philadelphia, PA 19102-1192. **Fax:** 215-762-8366. **E-Mail:** slevison@drexelmed.edu

LEVISON, WILLIAM H(ENRY), ENGINEERING PSYCHOLOGY, MAN-MACHINE SYSTEMS. **Personal Data:** b Cincinnati, Ohio, March 21, 1936. **Education:** Mass Inst Technol, BS, 1958, MS, 1960. **Honorary Degrees:** ScD, Mass Inst Technol, 1964. **Professional Experience:** CONSULT, 1996-, div scientist, BBN Corp, 1988-1996; sr scientist, BoltBeranek & Newman Inc, 1964-1988. **Memberships:** Inst Elec & Electronics Engrs; Transp Res Bd; Human Factors & Ergonomics Soc. **Research Statement & Publications:** Modeling and measurement of human operator performance. **Mailing Address:** 19 Phinney Rd, Lexington, MA 02421. **E-Mail:** levinson@tiac.net

LEVIT, EDITHE J, MEDICINE, MEDICAL ADMINISTRATION. **Personal Data:** b Wilkes-Barre, Pa, November 29, 1926. **Education:** Bucknell Univ, BS, 1946; Woman's Med Col Pa, MD, 1951. **Honorary Degrees:** DMS, Med Col Pa, 1978; DSc, Wilkes Univ, 1990. **Honors & Awards:** Commonwealth Comt Woman's Med Col Award, 1970; Distinguished Serv Award, Fedn State Med Bds, 1987. **Professional Experience:** Adv coun Inst Nuclear Power Opers, Atlanta, beginning 1988; PRES EMER, NAT MED ASN, 1987-; mem sci coun, Nat Lib Med Bd, beginning 1981; bd dirs, Philadelphia Elec Co, beginning 1980; Germantown Savings Bank, Philadelphia, beginning 1979; Off Technol Assessment, US Cong, 1978-1979; pres & chief exec officer, Nat Bd Med Examr, 1977-1986; Comt Pract Fed Conn, US Judiciary, 1977; vpres & secy, Nat Bd Med Examr, 1975-1977; secy & assoc dir, Nat Bd Med Examr, 1967-1975; consult, women med, Josiah Macy Jr Found, 1966-1976; asst dir, Nat Bd Med Examr, 1961-1967; dir med educ, Philadelphia Gen Hosp, 1957-1961; clin instr, Philadelphia Gen Hosp, 1953-1957; fel endocrinol, Philadelphia Gen Hosp, 1952-1953; intern med, Philadelphia Gen Hosp, 1951-1952. **Memberships:** Inst Med-Nat Acad Sci; AMA; master Am Col Physicians; Asn Am Med Cols. **Research Statement & Publications:** Evaluation of professional competence in medicine. **Mailing Address:** Nat Med Asn, 1012 Tenth St NW, Washington, DC 20001. **Fax:** 202-898-2510.

LEVIT, LAWRENCE BRUCE, PHYSICS. **Personal Data:** b Cleveland, Ohio, September 24, 1942. **Education:** Case Inst Technol, BS, 1964; Case Western Res Univ, PhD (physics), 1971. **Professional Experience:** CHIEF SCIENTIST, ION SYST INC, as of 2006; mkt mgr, Div High Energy Physics, Lecroy Res Syst Corp, beginning 1974; asst prof, La State Univ, Baton Rouge, 1969-1974; res assoc physics, Case Western Res Univ, 1966-1969. **Memberships:** Am Phys Soc; Am Inst Physics. **Research Statement & Publications:** Ultrahigh energy physics research using cosmic rays as a particle source. **Mailing Address:** Ion Syst, Inc, 107 Miss Ave, Crystal City, MO 63019. **Fax:** 636-937-1828.

LEVIT, ROBERT JULES, LOGIC, COMPUTER SCIENCE. **Personal Data:** b San Francisco, Calif, August 17, 1916; m 1955, Jean Bernasconi; c Lin d a Manette, Arthur Frank & Miles Theodore. **Education:** Calif Inst Technol, BS, 1938, MS, 1939; Univ Calif, PhD (math), 1941. **Professional Experience:** EMER PROF MATH, SAN FRANCISCO STATE UNIV, 1972-; from asst prof to prof, San Francisco State Univ, 1957-1972; mem staff, Appl Sci Div, Int Bus Mach Corp, 1955-1957; vis asst prof, Mass Inst Technol, 1954-1955; from asst prof to assoc prof, Univ Ga, 1946-1953; Asst math, Univ Calif, 1940-1941. **Memberships:** Am Math Soc; Math Asn Am; Asn Symbolic Logic. **Research Statement & Publications:** Foundations of mathematics; algebra; number theory, analysis. **Mailing Address:** 100 Bay Pl No 1902, Oakland, CA 94610.

LEVITAN, ALEXANDER ALLEN, MEDICAL ONCOLOGY, MEDICAL HYPNOSIS. **Personal Data:** b Boston, Mass, October 19, 1939; m 1967, Lucy; c Lara, Denise & Karen. **Education:** Cornell Univ, BA, 1959; Univ Rochester, MD, 1963; Univ Minn, MPH, 1970; Am Bd Internal Med, dipl, 1971 & 1977, dipl oncol, 1973. **Professional Experience:** PVT PRACT, INTERNAL MED & ONCOL, MINNEAPOLIS & FRIDLEY, MINN; clin assoc prof, Dept Family Pract, 1975-1989; instr microbiol, Univ Minn, Minneapolis, 1968-1970; med br, Nat Cancer Inst, NIH, Bethesda, MD, 1965-1967; med resident, Harvard Med Serv, Boston City Hosp, 1964-1965. **Memberships:** Am Fedn Clin Res; fel Am Soc Clin Hypnosis; fel Am Col Physicians; Am Soc Prev Oncol; fel Soc Clin & Exp Hypnosis; AAAS. **Research Statement & Publications:** Hypnosis and pain control for use in surgery with anesthesia. **Mailing Address:** 2051 Long Lake Rd, New Brighton, MN 55112. **Fax:** 651-633-6498.

LEVITAN, HERBERT, NEUROBIOLOGY, MEMBRANE BIOPHYSICS. **Personal Data:** b Brooklyn, NY, April 25, 1939. **Education:** Cornell Univ, BEE, 1962, PhD (elec eng), 1965. **Professional Experience:** SEC HEAD, DIV UNDERGRAD EDUC, NSF, 1993-; prog dir, NSF, Wash, DC, 1990-1992; Fulbright Hayes Fel, 1987-1988; prof, Dept Zool, Univ Md, Col Park, beginning 1983; neurophysiologist, Lab Neuroscience Geront Res Ctr, Nat Inst Aging, 1979-1982; instr neurobiology, Marine Biol Lab, WoodsHole, 1974; assoc prof, Dept Zool, Univ MD, Col Park, 1972-1983; Lab Neurobiology, Nat Inst Child Health & Human Develop, 1970-1972; Lab Neurophysiology, NIMH, 1970; NIH fel, Lab Neurophysiology Cellulaire Ctr Etude Physiol Nerveuse, Paris, France, 1968-1970; anatomist, Anat Dept, 1967; NIH fel neurophysiol, Brain Res Inst, Univ Calif, Los Angeles, 1965-1967. **Memberships:** Soc Neuroscience; Am Physiol Soc; Soc Gen Physiologists; Am Soc Cell Biol. **Research Statement & Publications:** Physico-chemical and biophysical mechanisms underlying the effects of drugs on the physiology of nerves and muscles. **Mailing Address:** Div Undergrad Educ, NSF, Rm 835 4201 Wilson Blvd, Arlington, VA 22203. **E-Mail:** hlevitan@nsf.gov

LEVITAN, MAX, GENETICS, ANATOMY. **Personal Data:** b Tverai, Lithuania, March 1, 1921. **Education:** Univ Chicago, AB, 1944; Univ Mich, MA, 1946; Columbia Univ, PhD (zoology), 1951. **Honors & Awards:** Res Career Develop Award, USPHS, 1963; Just Lectr, Howard Univ, 1968. **Professional Experience:** PROF HUMAN GENETICS, MT SINAI SCH MED, CITY UNIV NY, beginning 1995; auth & assoc ed, Evolution, 1977-1979; PROF ANAT & FUNCTIONAL MORPHOL, MT SINAI SCH MED, CITY UNIV NY, beginning 1970; assoc prof, MT Sinai Sch Med, City Univ NY, 1968-1970; prof biol & chmn dept, George Mason Col, Univ Va, 1966-1968; adj prof anat & genetics, George Wash Univ & Sch Med, Univ Va, 1966-1968; prof anat & med genetics, Woman's Med Col Pa, 1962-1966; spec lectr, Univ Pa, 1962-1963; Seminar assoc, Columbia Univ, 1958-; from asst prof to assoc prof anat, Woman's Med Col Pa, 1955-1962; assoc prof genetics, Va Polytech Inst, 1949-1955; asst zool, Columbia Univ, 1946-1949; Statistician, USPHS, 1944-1945. **Memberships:** Am Asn Anatomists; Am Soc Human Genetics; Genetics Soc Am; Soc Study Evolution; AAAS; Sigma Xi (secy vpres pres elect VPI chap; secy-treas Mt Sinai chap). **Research Statement & Publications:** Cytogenetics; population genetics of linked loci; chromosome breakage; cytoplasmic inheritance; medical genetics; author of textbook. **Mailing Address:** Mt Sinai Sch Med, City Univ NY, One Gustave L Levy Pl, PO Box 1007, New York, NY 10029. **Fax:** 212-241-7268. **E-Mail:** max.levitan@mssm.edu

LEVITAN, MICHAEL LEONARD, MATHEMATICS. **Personal Data:** b Brooklyn, NY, September 12, 1941. **Education:** Rensselaer Polytech Inst, BS, 1962; Univ Minn, MS, 1966, PhD (math), 1967. **Professional Experience:** ASSOC PROF MATH SCI, VILLANOVA UNIV, 1974-; asst prof, Villanova Univ, 1970-1974; asst prof math, Drexel Univ, 1967-1970. **Memberships:** Am Math Soc; Math Asn Am; Am Asn Univ Professors. **Research Statement & Publications:** Probability theory; Markov processes; operations research; statistics; math anxiety. **Mailing Address:** Dept Math Sci, Villanova Univ, St Augustine Ctr 376, Villanova, PA 19085-1699. **Fax:** 610-519-6928. **E-Mail:** michael.levitan@villanova.edu

LEVITAN, RUVEN, INTERNAL MEDICINE, GASTROENTEROLOGY. **Personal Data:** b Kaunas, Lithuania, March 12, 1927. **Education:** Hebrew Univ, Israel, MD, 1953; Am Bd Internal Med, dipl & cert gastroenterol. **Professional Experience:** PHYSICIAN, N SHORE GASTROENTEROLOGY SC, as of 2003; PROF MED, ABRAHAM LINCOLN SCH MED, UNIV ILL MED CTR, 1970-; chief gastroenterol sect, Vet Admin West Side Hosp, 1968-1977; assoc prof, Abraham Lincoln Sch Med, Univ Ill Med Ctr, 1968-1970; lectr, Sch Med, Boston Univ, 1965-1968; from asst prof to assoc prof, Sch Med, Tufts Univ, 1964-1969; dir gastroenterol res, New Eng Med Ctr Hosps, 1964-1968; sr res fel, Mass Mem Hosps, 1961-1962; fel gastroenterol & res fel med, Mass Mem Hosps & Sch Med, Boston Univ, 1959-1961; resident, Beth Israel Hosp, Boston, 1958-1959; Spec fel med neoplasia, Mem Ctr Cancer & Allied Dis, NY, 1957-1958; Resident, Mt Sinai Hosp, NY, 1956-1957; pres, Chicago Soc Gastroenterol. **Memberships:** Fel Am Col Physicians; Am Physiol Soc; Am Gastroenterol Asn; Am Asn StudyLiver Dis; Am Soc Clin Invest. **Research Statement & Publications:** Water electrolyte absorption from the intestine; hormonal influences on absorption; lymphomas, including involvement of liver and gastrointestinal tract. **Mailing Address:** Am Gastroenterol Assoc, Scokie, IL 60076. **Fax:** 847-677-1233.

LEVITAS, ALFRED DAVE, PHYSICS. **Personal Data:** b New York, NY, March 27, 1920. **Education:** Syracuse Univ, BA, 1947, MS, 1950, PhD (physics), 1958. **Professional Experience:** PROF EMER, DEPT PHYSICS, ALBANY UNIV, as of 1998; consult, Naval Res Lab, 1960-1963; prof physics, State Univ NY, Albany, beginning 1958; physicist, Honeywell Res Ctr, 1956-1958; res engr solid state physics, Sprague Elec Corp, 1955-1956; res engr solid state physics, Sylvania Elec Corp, 1953-1955. **Memberships:** Am Phys Soc. **Research Statement & Publications:** Solid state and statistical physics; thermodynamics. **Mailing Address:** Dept Physics, Albany Univ, Albany, NY 12205.

LEVITICUS, LOUIS I, TRACTOR-OFF ROAD VEHICLE DEVELOPMENT, ENGINE DEVELOPMENT. **Personal Data:** b Aalten, Neth, July 4, 1931; American citizen; m 1982, Rose; c Melanie & Joanna. **Education:** Technion, Israel Inst Technol, BSc, 1960, MSc, 1963; Purdue Univ, PhD (agr eng), 1969. **Professional Experience:** RETIRED; supv test & develop, Nebr Power lab, beginning 1990; assoc dir, Ctr Agr Equip, 1987-1990; PROF AGR ENG, UNIV NEBR, 1975-; chief engr, Tractor Test Lab, 1975-1987; consult & instr agr eng, Technion, Israel Inst Technol & Israel Defense Forces, 1971-1975; Sr res engr, Stevens Inst Technol, 1969-1971. **Memberships:** Int Soc Terrain Vehicle Systs; Soc Automotive Engrs; Am Soc Agr Engrs; Asian Asn Agr Engrs. **Research Statement & Publications:** Off-road locomotion, oriented on agricultural and military soil-wheel interaction; alternate fuel use in diesel engines, alcohol, ethanol, ETBE, natural gas, vegetable oils; instrumentation for handicapped farmers; renewable energy; safety on farm. **Mailing Address:** Rm 207 L W Chase Hall, Univ Nebr, Lincoln, NE 68583-0726. **Fax:** 402-472-8367. **E-Mail:** lleviticus1@unl.edu

LEVITIN, LEV BEROVICH, ENGINEERING SCIENCE. **Personal Data:** b Moscow, September 25, 1935; div. **Education:** Acad Sci USSR, PhD, 1969; Moscow Univ, MS, 1960. **Professional Experience:** DISTINGUISHED PROF, DEPT ELEC & COMPUT ENG, COL ENG, BOSTON UNIV, 1986-; prof, BostonUniv, 1982-1986; vis prof, Bielefeld Univ, 1980-1981 & Syracuse Univ, 1981-1982; vis scientist, Heinrich-Hertz Inst, 1980; Inst Optoelektronik, 1981; consult, Vishay Israel Ltd, 1979; sr lectr, Tel Aviv Univ, 1974-1980; ed, Prin Cybern, 1967; sr res scientist, Inst Transmission Prob, USSR Acad Sci, 1961-1973. **Memberships:** Fel Inst Elec & Electronics Engrs; Am Asn Univ Prof; Am Math Soc; AsnComput Mach; Soc Indust & Appl Math; Am Soc Eng Educ; Math Asn Am; AAAS; NY AcadSci. **Mailing Address:** Boston Univ, Col Eng, Dept Elec & Comput Eng, 44 Cummington St, Boston, MA 02215-2407. **Fax:** 617-353-6440. **E-Mail:** levitin@enga.bu.edu

LEVITON, ALAN, PUBLIC HEALTH, EPIDEMIOLOGY. **Personal Data:** b Brooklyn, NY, June 17, 1938. **Education:** NY Univ, AB, 1959; State Univ NY, MD, 1963; Harvard Univ, MS, 1971. **Professional Experience:** DIR, NEUROEPIDEMIOL UNIT, CHILDREN'S HOSP, BOSTON, as of 2005; PROF NEUROL, HARVARD MED SCH, 1996-; from instr to assoc prof, Sch Pub Health, 1971-1996; teaching fel epidemiol, Sch Pub Health, 1970-1971; resident neurol, Wash Univ, St Louis, 1967-1970; officer epidemiol, Epidemic Intel Serv, Ctr Dis Control, USPHS, 1965-1967; resident, Kings Co Hosp, Brooklyn, 1964-1965; intern, Kings Co Hosp, Brooklyn, 1963-1964. **Memberships:** Soc Epidemiol Res; Am Pub Health Asn; Am Neurol Asn; Child Neurol Soc; AmCol Epidemiol. **Research Statement & Publications:** Using epidemiological techniques to search for antecedents of neurologic disabilities in children. **Mailing Address:** Dept Neurol, Children's Hosp, Carnegie Two 300 Longwood Ave, Boston, MA 02115. **Fax:** 617-730-0880.

LEVITON, ALAN EDWARD, SYSTEMATIC ZOOLOGY, BIOGEOGRAPHY. **Personal Data:** b Brooklyn, NY, January 11, 1930; m Gladys; c 2. **Education:** Stanford Univ, AB, 1949, AM, 1953, PhD, 1960. **Honors & Awards:** Fellows Medal, California Acad of Science, 1999. **Professional Experience:** RES PROF BIOL SCI, SAN FRANCISCO STATE UNIV, 2001-; CUR & CHMN HERPET & ED, SCI PUBL, CALIF ACAD SCI, 1993-; cur herpet & chmn comput serv, Calif Acad Sci, 1983-1992; exec dir, Pac Div AAAS, 1979-1997; adj prof biol sci, San Francisco State Univ, 1967-2000; chmn dept, Calif Acad Sci, 1962-1983, 1988-1992, 2001-; lectr, Stanford Univ, 1962-1970; assoc cur div syst biol Stanford Univ, 1962-1963; from asst cur to cur, Calif Acad Sci, 1957-1962. **Memberships:** Fel AAAS; Soc Study Amphibians & Reptiles; Am Soc Ichthyol & Herpet; Fel Geol Soc Am; Hist Sci Soc; Hist Earth Sci Soc; pres AAAS Pacific Div 1999-2001; Fel Calif Acad Sci. **Research Statement & Publications:** Herpetology of Asia; Mesozoic-Tertiary paleogeography and biogeography of Asia; Phylogeny and taxonomy of reptiles; 19th century history of geology, exploration, and institutions of natural history. **Mailing Address:** Dept Herpet, Calif Acad Sci, 875 Howard St, San Francisco, CA 94103. **E-Mail:** aleviton@calacademy.org

LEVITSKY, DAVID A, CONTROL OF BODY WEIGHT, EFFECTS OF NUTRITION IN DEVELOPMENT. **Personal Data:** b Philadelphia, Pa, October 15, 1942. **Education:** Rutgers Univ, BA, 1964, MS, 1966, PhD (feeding behav), 1968. **Honors & Awards:** Outstanding Res Award, Soc Nutrit Educ, 1994. **Professional Experience:** PROF NUTRIT & PSYCHOL, DIV NUTRIT SCI, CORNELL UNIV, 1988-; traveling fel, NY State Col Agr & Life Sci, Israel, 1980 & France, 1988; assoc prof, Cornell Univ, 1976-1986; Career Develop Award, Nat Inst Child Health & Human Develop, 1974-1979; asst prof nutrit & psychol, Cornell Univ, 1970-1976; NIMH fel nutrit, Cornell Univ, 1968-1970. **Memberships:** Am Inst Nutrit; Am Psychol Asn; Am Asn Univ Professors. **Research Statement & Publications:** Control of food intake; techniques for changing food preference; role of drugs to control energy intake and energy expenditure; role of macronutrients in the control of energy intake. **Mailing Address:** Div Nutrit Sci, Col Human Ecol, Cornell Univ, 112 Savage Hall, Ithaca, NY 14853-0001. **Fax:** 607-255-1033. **E-Mail:** dal4@cornell.edu

LEVITSKY, LYNNE LIPTON, ENDOCRINOLOGY, PEDIATRICS. **Personal Data:** b Columbia, SC, May 14, 1942. **Education:** Bryn Mawr Col, BA, 1962; Yale Univ, MD, 1966. **Professional Experience:** CHIEF, PEDIATC ENDOCRINE UNIT, MASS GEN HOSP C, BOSTON, as of 2006; ASSOC PROF PEDIAT, HARVARD MED SCH, as of 2006; dir, div pediat endocrinol, Michael Reese Hosp Med Ctr, 1973-1986; from asst prof to assoc prof, Pediat Pritzker Sch Med, Univ Chicago, 1973-1985; asst prof pediat, Sch Med, Univ Ill, 1970-1973; fel endocrinol & metab, Sch Med, Univ Md, 1968-1970; resident, Childrens Hosp Philadelphia, 1967-1968; intern pediat, Bronx Munic Hosp Ctr, 1966-1967; prof, pediat pritzker, Sch Med, Univ Chicago, beginning 1955. **Memberships:** Soc Pediat Res; Endocrine Soc; Lawson Wilkins Pediat Endocrine Soc. **Research Statement & Publications:** Carbohydrate metabolism; diabetes; fetal and neonatal metabolism and endocrinology. **Mailing Address:** Mass Gen Hosp C, 55 Fruit St, Boston, MA 02114.

LEVITSKY, MYRON, MECHANICAL ENGINEERING. **Personal Data:** b New York, NY, June 22, 1930. **Education:** Cooper Union, BME, 1951; NY Univ, MS, 1964, PhD (mech eng), 1969. **Professional Experience:** RETIRED; vis mem, Courant Inst, 1977-1978; NSF res grant, City Col NewYork, 1971-1972; lectr & assoc prof mech eng, City Col New York, 1965-1991; assoc res scientist, NY Univ, 1965-1970; proj engr, Consumer's Union, 1962-1963; instr mech eng, NY Univ, 1953-1954; res engr, Heat & Mass Flow Analyzer Lab, Columbia Univ, 1951-1953. **Memberships:** AAAS; Am Soc Mech Engrs; Am Phys Soc; Am Soc Eng Educ; Am Acad Mech. **Research Statement & Publications:** Elasticity theory; heat transfer; thermal stresses in chemically hardening media; applications to concrete and plastic molding. **Mailing Address:** 392 Cent Park W, New York, NY 10025.

LEVITSKY, SIDNEY, CARDIOVASCULAR SURGERY, SURGERY. **Personal Data:** b New York, NY, March 3, 1936. **Education:** Albert Einstein Col Med, MD, 1960; Am Bd Surg & Bd Thoracic Surg, dipl, 1968. **Professional Experience:** DIR, CARDIOTHORACIC SURG, CAREGROUP, BOSTON & PROF, HARVARD MED SCH, as of 2003; sr consult, W Side Vet Hosp, 1975-; prof surg & pharmacol, Col Med, Univ Ill, beginning 1975; chief, Div Cardiothoracic Surg, Med Ctr, beginning 1974; attend surgeon, Cook Co Hosp, 1973-; Estab investr, Am Heart Asn, 1971; lectr surg, Cook Co, Grad Sch, 1970-1989; assoc prof surg, Col Med, Univ Ill, 1970-1975; sr investr cardiac surg, Nat Heart Inst, NIH, 1968-1970; thoracic surgeon, Valley Forge Army Hosp, 1967-1968; chief surg, Third Surg Hosp, Vietnam, 1966-1967; instr surg, Sch Med, Yale Univ, 1964-1966. **Memberships:** Soc Univ Surgeons; Am Physiol Soc; Soc Thoracic Surgeons; Am Asn ThoracicSurg; Asn Acad Surg; Sigma Xi; Am Surg Asn. **Research Statement & Publications:** Thoracic surgery; non-invasive methods of monitoring myocardial contractility; intra-operative protection of myocardium; myocardial ischemia and metabolism. **Mailing Address:** Harvard Med Sch, 25 Shattuck St, Boston, MA 02115.

LEVITT, BARRIE, PHARMACOLOGY, INTERNAL MEDICINE. **Personal Data:** b Brooklyn, NY, August 19, 1935. **Education:** State Univ NY Downstate Med Ctr, MD, 1959. **Professional Experience:** CARDIOLOGIST PVT PRACT, as of 2002; prof med & cardiol, Albert Einstein Col Med, beginning 1980; CONSULT, BUR DRUGS, US FOOD & DRUG ADMIN, 1971-; assoc prof med & pharmacol & dir, div Clin Pharmacol, 1970-1980; asst prof med, NY Med Col, 1969-1970; NY Heart Asn sr investr, Med Col, Cornell Univ, 1966-1969; from instr to asst prof pharmacol, Med Col, Cornell Univ, 1965-1969; fel, Med Col, Cornell Univ, 1964-1965; fel pharmacol, Downstate Med Ctr, State Univ NY, 1963-1964; resident med, Mt Sinai Hosp, NY, 1960-1963; Rotating intern, Mt Sinai Hosp, NY, 1959-1960; clin prof med, Albert Einstein Col Med. **Memberships:** Am Soc Pharmacol & Exp Therapeut; Am Heart Asn; Sigma Xi. **Research Statement & Publications:** Clinical and cardiovascular pharmacology; cardiology. **Mailing Address:** 1199 Park Ave, New York, NY 10128.

LEVITT, DAVID GEORGE, PHYSIOLOGY. **Personal Data:** b Minneapolis, Minn, May 9, 1942. **Education:** Univ Minn, BS, 1966, MD & PhD (physiol), 1968. **Professional Experience:** PROF PHYSIOL, UNIV MINN, MINNEAPOLIS, 1977-; assoc prof, 1968-1977. **Research Statement & Publications:** Theoretical transport processes across membranes and in capillary beds; intestinal absorption; microcirculation in skeletal muscle; published over 15 articles. **Mailing Address:** Dept Physiol, Sch Med, Univ Minn, 6-125 Jackson Hall 321 Church St SE, Minneapolis, MN 55455. **E-Mail:** levit001@umn.edu

LEVITT, GEORGE, ORGANIC CHEMISTRY, PESTICIDES. **Personal Data:** b Newburg, NY, February 19, 1925. **Education:** Duquesne Univ, BS, 1950, MS, 1952; Mich State Univ, PhD, 1957. **Honors & Awards:** Quadrennial Award Pesticide Res, Swiss Soc Chem Industs, 1982; Nat Agr Award Excellence, Nat Agr Mkt Asn, 1987, 1988; Am Chem Soc Award Creative Invention, Corp Assocs Am Chem Soc, 1989; Kenneth Spencer Award, Am Chem Soc, 1991; Nat Medal Technol, 1993. **Professional Experience:** RETIRED; res assoc, Exp Sta, E I du Pont de Nemours & Co Inc, 1981-1986; instr, Del Tech & Community Col, 1975-1980; sr res chemist, Exp Sta, E I du Pont de Nemours & Co Inc, 1968-1980; res chemist, Exp Sta, 1966-1968; res chemist, Stine Lab, 1963-1966; res chemist, Exp Sta, E I du Pont de Nemours & Co Inc, 1956-1963. **Memberships:** Am Chem Soc; Int Union Pure & Appl Chem; AAAS; Sigma Xi. **Research Statement & Publications:** Organic synthesis; herbicides, fungicides, medicinals; pesticides; heterocyclic compounds; synthesis, characterization and identification of novel organic compounds for biological evaluation; developed programs to define and optimize chemical structure- biological activity relationships; sulfonylurea herbicides; heterocyclics; exploratory process research. **Mailing Address:** 110 Downs Dr, Greenville, DE 19807-2556.

LEVITT, ISRAEL MONROE, astronomy; deceased, see previous edition for last biography

LEVITT, MICHAEL D, GASTROENTEROLOGY. **Personal Data:** b Chicago, Ill, May 10, 1935; m Shirley. **Education:** Univ Minn, BS, 1958, MD, 1950. **Professional Experience:** Consult med, Minneapolis Vet Admin Hosp, beginning 1974; PROF MED, MED SCH, UNIV MINN, 1974-; counr, Am Fedn Clin Res, 1974-1976; guest lectr, Gastroenterol Res-Group, 1972; from asst prof to assoc prof, Med Sch, Univ Minn, 1968-1974; fel gastroenterol, Boston City Hosp, 1965-1968; resident, Beth Israel Hosp, Boston, 1964-1965; resident, BostonUniv Hosp, 1961-1964; intern, Univ Minn Hosp, 1960-1961. **Member-**

ships: Am Fedn Clin Res; Am Soc Clin Invest; Am Gastroenterol Soc. **Research Statement & Publications:** Studies employing gas to investigate gastrointestinal physiology and studies of serum and urinary isoamylases. **Mailing Address:** VA Med Ctr, Univ Minn, One Veterans Dr, Minneapolis, MN 55417. **E-Mail:** levit015@umn.edu

LEVITT, MORTON, NEUROCHEMISTRY. **Professional Experience:** SR RES ASSOC, NY STATE PSYCHIAT INST, 1981-. **Mailing Address:** 32 Fenimore Rd, Scarsdale, NY 10583.

LEVITT, SEYMOUR H, RADIOTHERAPY. **Personal Data:** b Chicago, Ill, July 18, 1928; div. **Education:** Univ Colo, BA, 1950, MD, 1954. **Professional Experience:** ADJ PROF, KAROLINSKA INST, STOCKHOLM, 2002-; mem bd dirs, Soc Chmn Acad Radiol Oncol Prog, 1976-1978; pres, Soc Chmn Acad Radiol Oncol Prog, 1974-1976; PROF THERAPEUT RADIOL & HEADDEPT, UNIV MINN, MINNEAPOLIS, 1970-; prof radiol & chmn div radiation ther, Med ColVa, 1966-1970; assoc prof radiation ther & chief div, Sch Med, UnivOkla, 1963-1966; asstradiotherapist, Sch Med & Dent, Univ Rochester, 1962-1963; instr radiation ther & radiol, MedSch, Univ Mich, 1961-1962; consult radiother, Vet Admin Hosp, Minneapolis; trustee, Am Bd Radiol; mem, Am Joint Comt. **Memberships:** Fel Am Col Radiol; Am Radium Soc (pres, 1983); Soc Nuclear Med; Radiol SocNAm; Am Soc Therapeut Radiol (pres, 1978-1979). **Research Statement & Publications:** Experimental and clinical radiation therapy; radiation biology. **Mailing Address:** Dept Therapeut Radiol, Univ Minn, Minneapolis, MN 55455. **E-Mail:** levit002@tc.umn.edu

LEVITT, TOD S, MATHEMATICS. **Education:** Univ Minn, PhD (Maths), 1981. **Professional Experience:** CEO, INFO EXTRACTION & TRANSP INC, NY, as of 2006. **Memberships:** Inst Elec & Electronics Eng. **Mailing Address:** 14 Res Way Suite 3, PO Box 808, East Setauket, NY 11733. **Fax:** 703-841-3501. **E-Mail:** levitt@iet.com

LEVITZ, HILBERT, MATHEMATICS, COMPUTER SCIENCE. **Personal Data:** b Lebanon, Pa, November 13, 1931; m 1980, c David Maxamilian. **Education:** Univ NC, BA, 1953; Pa State Univ, PhD (math), 1965. **Professional Experience:** PROF EMER COMPUT SCI, FLA STATE UNIV, beginning 1985; courtesy prof philos, Fla State Univ, beginning 1985; assoc prof math, Fla State Univ, 1969-1984; asst prof, NY Univ, 1965-1969; Instr math, Williams Col, 1965. **Memberships:** Asn Symbolic Logic. **Research Statement & Publications:** Mathematical logic; concrete systems of ordinal notations. **Mailing Address:** Dept Comput Sci, Fla State Univ, 600 W Col Ave, Tallahassee, FL 32306-1096. **E-Mail:** levitz@cs.fsu.edu

LEVITZ, MORTIMER, BIOCHEMISTRY & ENDOCRINOLOGY. **Personal Data:** b New York, NY, May 11, 1921. **Education:** City Col NY, BS, 1941; Columbia Univ, MA, 1947, PhD (org chem), 1951. **Professional Experience:** Assoc ed-in-chief, Endocrinol, 1986-1987; ed, Endocrinol, 1983-1987; chmn, Endocrine Study Sect, NIH, 1983-1985; consult, Clin Sci Study Sect, 1981-1985; PROF OBSTET & GYNEC, MED CTR, NY UNIV, 1967-; consult, Endocrine Study Sect, NIH, 1966-1970 & 1973-1975; NIH res career award, 1962-1972; from asst prof to assoc prof, MedCtr, NY Univ, 1956-1967; res assoc, Med Ctr, NY Univ, 1952-1956; res assoc steroid biochem, Col Physicians & Surgeons, Columbia Univ, 1951-1952. **Memberships:** Am Chem Soc; Am Soc Biol Chemists; Endocrine Soc; Soc Gynec Invest. **Research Statement & Publications:** Estrogen metabolism and mechanisms of action in pregnancy and cancer. **Mailing Address:** Dept Obs & Gyne, NY Univ Med Ctr, TCH Five 528-532, 550 First Ave, New York, NY 10016-6402. **Fax:** 212-263-5742. **E-Mail:** levitm01@popmail.med.nyu.edu

LEVITZKY, MICHAEL GORDON, PULMONARY PHYSIOLOGY, CARDIOVASCULAR PHYSIOLOGY. **Personal Data:** b Elizabeth, NJ, January 3, 1947; m 1985, Elizabeth; c Edward B & Sarah E. **Education:** Univ Pa, BA, 1969; Albany Med Col, Union Univ, PhD (physiol), 1975. **Professional Experience:** Dir of Basic Sci Curriculum, La State Univ Sch of Med Health Sci, 1994-; adj prof pediat & physiol, Tulane Univ Med Ctr, 1990-; PROF PHYSIOL, MED CTR, LA STATE UNIV, 1985-; chmn, curric evaluation comt 1999-; chmn, Curric Comt, 1982-1988; chmn, Acad Studies Comt, La State Univ, 1981-1989; prin investr, NIH grants, 1976-1981 & 1982-1986; from asst prof to assoc prof, Med Ctr, LA State Univ, 1975-1985; Consult, NIH grants, 1974-1976 & 1979-1980; Instr physiol, Albany Med Col, Union Univ, 1974-1975. **Memberships:** Am Physiol Soc; Sigma Xi; Soc Exp Biol & Med; NY Acad Sci; Am Thoracic Soc. **Research Statement & Publications:** Cardiopulmonary physiology, particularly in those factors that control pulmonary blood flow. **Mailing Address:** La State Univ Health Sci Ctr, 1901 Perdido St Box P7-3, Dept Physiology, New Orleans, LA 70112-1393. **Fax:** 504-568-6158. **E-Mail:** mlevit@lsuhsc.edu

LEVKOV, JEROME STEPHEN, PHYSICAL CHEMISTRY, FORENSIC SCIENCES. **Personal Data:** b New York, NY, June 12, 1939. **Education:** City Col NY, BS, 1961; Univ Pa, PhD (phys chem), 1967. **Professional Experience:** PROF GEN & PHYS CHEM, IONA COL, 1980-; asst prof, Iona Col, 1970-1980; asst prof gen & phys chem, Drexel Univ, 1968-1969; Swiss Copper Inst fel, Swiss Fed Inst Technol, 1967-1968. **Memberships:** Am Chem Soc; AAAS. **Research Statement & Publications:** Forensic chemistry; computers in chemistry education. **Mailing Address:** 715 N Ave, New Rochelle, NY 10801. **Fax:** 914-633-2240. **E-Mail:** jlevkov@iona.edu

LEVOW, ROY BRUCE, COMPUTER SCIENCE. **Personal Data:** b Richmond, Va, June 3, 1943; m 1962, Esther; c Gina-Anne & Zachary S Levow. **Education:** Univ Pa, AB, 1964, PhD (appl math), 1969. **Professional Experience:** PRES, UNIV FAC SENATE, FLA ATLANTIC UNIV, as of 2006; MEM, BD TRUSTEES, FLA ATLANTIC UNIV, as of 2006; ASSOC CHAIR, FLA ATLANTIC UNIV, DAVIE, as of 2006; PROF COMPUT SCI & ENG, FLA ATLANTIC UNIV, 1993-; chmn dept, Fla Atlantic univ, 2002-2002; assoc prof comput sci, Fla Atlantic Univ, 1987-1993; spec asst comput & commun planning, Fla Atlantic Univ, 1985-1986; assoc prof comput & info syst, Fla Atlantic Univ, 1980-1987; consult comput aids, classification & retrieval, 1975- & prof develop & comput personnel, 1979-; chmn dept, Fla Atlantic Univ, 1974-1978; from asst prof to assoc prof math, Fla Atlantic Univ, 1970-1980; asst prof math, Univ Hawaii, 1969-1970; sci programmer, Atlantic-Richfield Co, 1964-1965. **Memberships:** Asn Comput Mach; Inst Elec & Electronics Engrs. **Research Statement & Publications:** Program lan and program environment; object-oriented system; data communication; operating system; computer science education. **Mailing Address:** Dept Comput Sci & Eng, Fla Atlantic Univ, 777 Glades Rd, Boca Raton, FL 33431. **Fax:** 561-297-2800. **E-Mail:** roy@cse.fau.edu

LEV-RAN, ARYE, DIABETES, INTERNAL MEDICINE. **Personal Data:** b Leningrad, USSR, June 7, 1930; American citizen; m 1968, c 4. **Education:** First Leningrad Med Sch, MD, 1953; Cand Sci, Inst Physiol, Acad Sci, Leningrad, 1959, DSci, 1964. **Professional Experience:** Clin prof med, Univ Southern Calif, 1982-; RES SCIENTIST, DEPT DIABETES & ENDOCRINOL, CITY HOPE MED CTR, DUARTE, CALIF, 1981-; staff physician, Scripps Clin, La Jolla, Calif, 1977-1981; sr lectr, Tel Aviv Univ Sch Med, 1969-1975; dir Central Endocrinol Lab Sick Fiend, Tel Aviv, Israel, 1967-1975; sr res scientist endocrinol, Dept Gen Endocrinol, Inst Ob/Gyn, Acad Med Sci, Leningrad, USSR, 1964-1967; Jr res scientist, 1956-1964. **Memberships:** Am Diabetes Asn; Endocrine Soc; Europ Asn Study Diabetes; fel Am Col Physicians; AAAS. **Research Statement & Publications:** Pathogenesis of diabetes; epidemial growth factor in pathology; EGF receptors in carcinogenosis. **Mailing Address:** 1500 Duarte Rd, Duarte, CA 91010.

LEVY, ALAN B, ORGANOMETALLIC CHEMISTRY. **Personal Data:** b San Francisco, Calif, April 12, 1945. **Education:** Univ Calif, Berkeley, BS, 1967; Univ Colo, Boulder, PhD (chem), 1971. **Professional Experience:** RES SCIENTIST, ALLIED-SIGNAL CORP, 1991-; res assoc, Allied Corp, 1985-1990; sr res chemist, Allied Corp, 1980-1985; asst prof chem, State Univ NY Stony Brook, 1974-1980; fel chem, Purdue Univ, 1971-1974. **Memberships:** Am Chem Soc; Sigma Xi; AAAS. **Research Statement & Publications:** The use of organoboranes and organocopper reagents for the development of new synthetic methods; the total synthesis of natural products; homogenous and heterogenous catalysis in organic synthesis; process control and the modeling of chemical processes. **Mailing Address:** Nine Southview Rd, Randolph, NJ 07869-4812.

LEVY, ALAN C, PHYSIOLOGY, TOXICOLOGY. **Personal Data:** b Baltimore, Md, February 24, 1930. **Education:** Univ Md, BS, 1952; George Washington Univ, MS, 1956; Georgetown Univ, PhD (physiol), 1958. **Professional Experience:** AT MICROBIOL ASSOCS INC, 2002-; SECT HEAD, DEPT TOXICOL & PATH, 1974-; group chief, Hoffmann-La Roche Inc, 1969-1974; dir labs, Woodard Res Corp, 1967-1969; sect head, Dept Endocrinol, William S Merrell Co, 1960-1967; Instr physiol, Sch Med, Howard Univ, 1958-1960. **Memberships:** Am Physiol Soc; Reticuloendothelial Soc; Endocrine Soc; NY Acad Sci; SocToxicol; Sigma Xi. **Research Statement & Publications:** Inflammation; anti-inflammation; adrenal cortex; neuroendocrinology; lipid metabolism; acute and chronic toxicology; teratology. **Mailing Address:** US EPA 7509C 401 M St SW, Washington, DC 20460-0001.

LEVY, ALAN JOSEPH, ELASTICITY & MICROMECHANICS, MECHANICAL BEHAVIOR OF MATERIALS. **Personal Data:** b New York, NY, October 30, 1955; m 1991, Janice; c Samantha. **Education:** State Univ, NY, BS, 1977; Columbia Univ, MS, 1979, MPhil, 1981, PhD (eng mech), 1982. **Professional Experience:** PROF, SYRACUSE UNIV, 2000-; assoc dept chair, Syracuse Univ, 1995-1996; assoc prof mech, Syracuse Univ, 1988-2000; Fac res fel mech, Mat Technol lab, US Army, 1987 & 1988; asst prof, Syracuse Univ, 1982-1988. **Memberships:** Am Soc Mech Eng; Soc Indust & Appl Math; Am Acad Mech; Sigma Xi. **Research Statement & Publications:** Micromechanics of cavity formation in solid media; effective properties of composites; phenomenological and physically Ok based constitutive modelling. **Mailing Address:** Syracuse Univ, 127 Link Hall Dept Mech Aerospace & Mfg Eng, Syracuse, NY 13244. **E-Mail:** ajlevy@syr.edu

LEVY, ALLAN HENRY, COMPUTER SCIENCES, MEDICAL EDUCATION. **Personal Data:** b New York, NY, November 2, 1929; m 1961, c 2. **Education:** Columbia Univ, AB, 1949; Harvard Med Sch, MD, 1953. **Professional Experience:** RETIRED; actg head, dept med info sci, Col Meed, beginning 2000; head, Dept Med Info Sci, Col Med, 1983-1995; prof clin sci, Univ Ill, beginning 1975; prof virol & epidemiol, Baylor Col Med, 1973-1975; prof comput sci, Baylor Col Med, 1971-1973; assoc prof virol & comput sci, Baylor Col Med, 1965-1971; consult div hosp & med facil, Bur State Serv, USPHS, 1965-1970; USPHS res career develop award, 1960-1965; from instr to asst prof microbiol, Johns Hopkins Univ, 1959-1965; res fel, Sch Med, Johns Hopkins Univ, 1957-1959; clin assoc, Nat Cancer Inst, 1955-1957; from intern to asst resident, Harvard Med Serv, Boston City Hosp, 1953-1955. **Memberships:** Am Fedn Clin Res; Am Med Info Asn; Am Col Med Informatics. **Research Statement & Publications:** Artificial intelligence in medicine; hospital information systems; general applications of digital computers to medicine and biology; hypertext and information retrieval techniques in medicine; uses of computers in medical student education and in biomedical research. **Mailing Address:** Univ Ill, 190 Med Sci Bldg, Urbana, IL 61801. **Fax:** 217-333-8868. **E-Mail:** a_levy@uiuc.edu

LEVY, ARTHUR, COMBUSTION KINETICS, ATOMOSPHERIC CHEMISTRY. **Personal Data:** b New York, NY, September 29, 1921. **Education:** Queen's Col, BS, 1943; Univ Minn, MS, 1948. **Professional Experience:** RETIRED; Ohio Coal Develop Off, 1992-; Consult, 1985-, res leader, Columbus Labs, Battelle Mem Inst, 1979-1985; mgr combustion, Columbus Labs, Battelle MemInst, 1976-1979; sr res leader, Columbus Labs, Battelle Mem Inst, 1973-1976; sr fel, ColumbusLabs, Battelle Mem Inst, 1971-1973; fel, Columbus Labs, Battelle Mem Inst, 1969-1971; asstchief, Columbus Labs, Battelle Mem Inst, 1956-1969; prin phys chemist, Columbus Labs, Battelle Mem Inst, 1951-1959; phys chemist, Brookhaven Nat Lab, 1950-1951; aeronaut resscientist, Nat Adv Comt Aeronaut, 1948-1950; Chemist, Los Alamos Nat Lab, 1944-1946. **Memberships:** Am Chem Soc; Combustion Inst; Air Pollution Control Asn. **Research Statement & Publications:** Kinetics of hydrogen and hydrocarbon oxidation; combustion chemistry; kinetics of radiation and ionic reactions; boron hydride chemistry; induced reactions; flame structure; air pollution kinetics; coal-oil combustion and environmental assessments; synthetic fuel combustion; clean coal technology. **Mailing Address:** 614 Farrington Dr, Worthington, OH 43085. **Fax:** 614-466-6532. **E-Mail:** alevy929@aol.com

LEVY, ARTHUR MAURICE, CARDIOLOGY. **Personal Data:** b New York, NY, November 20, 1930. **Education:** Harvard Univ, BA, 1952; Cornell Univ, MD, 1956; Am Bd Internal Med, dipl, 1966. **Professional Experience:** MED DIR, ALLEN HEALTH CARES DEPT NETWORK DEVELOP, COL MED, UNIV VT, as of 2004; PROF PEDIAT, COL MED, UNIV VT, 1977-; PROF MED, COL MED, UNIV VT, 1976-; fel coun clin cardiol, Am Heart Asn, beginning 1969; asoc prof pediat, Col Med, 1969-1977; teaching scholar, Am Heart Asn, 1966-1971; from instr to assoc prof med, Col Med, 1963-1976; trainee cardiol, Harvard Med Sch, Boston Children's Hosp, 1962-1963; Nat Heart Inst res fel, 1959-1960, NIH fel cardiol, Col Med, Univ Vt, 1959-1960; resident, Col Med, Univ MT, 1958-1959; resident med, Cornell Med Div, Bellevue Hosp, 1957-1958; intern, Cornell Med Div, Bellevue Hosp, 1956-1957. **Memberships:** Am Fedn Clin Res; fel Am Col Physicians; fel Am Col Cardiol. **Research Statement & Publications:** Clinical electrophysiology. **Mailing Address:** Dept Cardiol, Col Med, Univ VT, Burlington, VT 05401. **E-Mail:** Arthur.Levy@uvm.edu

LEVY, BERNARD C, STATISTICAL SIGNAL PROCESSING, MULTIDIMENSIONAL SIGNAL PROCESSING. **Personal Data:** b Princeton, NJ, July 31, 1951. **Education:** Nat Sch Advan Mines, Paris, ingenieur civil, 1974; Stanford Univ, PhD (elec eng), 1979. **Professional Experience:** Vis researcher, Nat Inst Info & Automat Res, France, 1993; PROF, DEPT ELEC & COMPUT ENG, UNIV CALIF, DAVIS, 1987-; consult, Draper Lab, 1986-1989; from asst prof to assoc prof eleceng, Mass Inst Technol, 1979-1987. **Memberships:** Fel Inst Elec & Electronics Engrs; Soc Indust & Appl Math; Acoust Soc Am. **Research Statement & Publications:** Signal estimation and detection, image analysis and processing and acoustic imaging. **Mailing Address:** Dept Elec & Comput Eng, Univ Calif, 3183 Kemper Hall, Davis, CA 95616. **Fax:** 530-752-8428. **E-Mail:** levy@ece.ucdavis.edu

LEVY, BORIS, PHOTOGRAPHIC CHEMISTRY, PHOTOCATALYSIS. **Personal Data:** b New York, NY, November 24, 1927; m 1956, Ann; c Michael, Daniel & Jennifer. **Educa-**

tion: NY Univ, BA, 1948, MS, 1950, PhD (phys chem), 1955. **Honors & Awards:** Journal Award Best Imaging Sci paper, J Imaging Sci, 1996. **Professional Experience:** RETIRED; res prof chem, Boston Univ, beginning 1989; assoc ed, Photog Sci & Eng, 1975; mgr, Imaging Mat Res & Develop, Polaroid Corp, 1965-1989; assoc prof, Trenton Jr Col, 1962-1965; sr res chemist, Socony Mobil Oil Co, 1960-1965; sr scientist, Westinghouse Elec Corp, 1956-1960; sr res chemist, Radio Corp Am, 1955-1956; res chemist, Sylvania Elec Co, 1950-1951. **Memberships:** Am Chem Soc; fel Soc Photog Scientists & Engrs. **Research Statement & Publications:** Radiotracers; surface chemistry; electrokinetics; photoconductivity; photoelectron emission from semiconductors; spectral sensitization; energy and electron transfer reactions across phase boundaries; photographic emulsion preparation and characterization; preparation of novel image receptor layers in diffusion transfer photography; kinetics of photo-induced processes; photovoltaic solar energy conversion. **Mailing Address:** Dept Chem, Boston Univ, Rm 299, 590 Commonwealth Ave, Boston, MA 02215-2521. **Fax:** 617-353-6466. **E-Mail:** blevy@bu.edu

LEVY, CHARLES KINGSLEY, RADIATION ECOLOGY. **Personal Data:** b Boston, Mass, December 25, 1924; div, c 3. **Education:** George Washington Univ, BSc, 1948, MSc, 1951; Univ NC, Chapel Hill, PhD (physiol), 1956. **Professional Experience:** Proj dir avian radioecol nuclear reactor site, AEC, Dept Energy, 1973-1978; PROF BIOL, BOSTON UNIV, 1970-; Fulbright prof zool, Univ Nairobi, 1969-1970; consult bioinstrumentation, NASA, 1967-; consult, Mass Gen Hosp, 1962-; assoc prof radiol & biol, Boston Univ, 1962-1970; staff scientist, Worcester Found Exp Biol, 1958-1962; staff scientist, Worcester Found Exp Biol, 1958-1962; Am Physiol Soc fel, Boston Univ, 1958; Res collabr, Brookhaven Nat Lab, 1957-1961; Instr physiol, Vassar Col, 1956-1958. **Memberships:** Am Physiol Soc; Radiation Res Soc; Soc Gen Physiol. **Research Statement & Publications:** Effect of high energy particulate radiation mammalian systems; dose-rate phenomena and responses of sensory and neural tissues to ionizing radiation; biological impact of reactor effluents on free ranging populations of wild birds; kinship in voles by radionuclide tagging and whole-body gamma spectroscopy. **Mailing Address:** Boston Univ, 10 Greenough circle, Brookline, MA 02445. **E-Mail:** junebug@qis.net

LEVY, DANIEL, BIOCHEMISTRY, MEMBRANES. **Personal Data:** b New York, NY, November 27, 1940. **Education:** City Col NY, BS, 1961; Brandeis Univ, MS, 1963, PhD (chem), 1965. **Professional Experience:** PROF BIOCHEM, SCH MED, UNIV SOUTHERN CALIF, 1980-; vis profbiochem, Univ Basel, Switzerland, 1977-1978; assoc prof, Sch Med, Univ Southern Calif, 1974-1980; NIH res grant, 1973-; Res biochemist, Univ Calif, Berkeley, 1967-1968; NIH fel biochem, Univ Calif, Berkeley, 1965-1967. **Memberships:** AAAS; Am Soc Biol Chem; Am Chem Soc. **Research Statement & Publications:** Membrane structure and function; mechanism of hormone action. **Mailing Address:** Dept Biochem & Molecular Biol, Univ Southern Calif, Los Angeles, CA 90033.

LEVY, DAVID ALFRED, ALLERGY. **Personal Data:** b Washington, DC, August 27, 1930. **Education:** Univ Md, BS, 1952, MD, 1954; Am Bd Internal Med, cert, 1962; Am Bd Allergy &Immunol, cert, 1974. **Professional Experience:** SCI ADV, CENTRE D'ALLERGIE HOSP, ROTHSCHILD, PARIS, 1991-; CONSULT, PHARMACEUT INDUST, 1990-; adj dir, Centre d'Immunologie et de BalogiePierre Fabre, 1985-1990; vis scientists, Inst Pasteur, Paris, 1984-1985; prof immunol &infectious dis, Sch Hyg & Pub Health, 1980-1985; Fogarty Sr Int fel, Col de France, Paris, 1976; prof biochem & epidemiol, Sch Hyg & Pub Health, 1973-1985; from assoc prof to prof radiol sci& epidemiol, Sch Med, Johns Hopkins Univ, 1968-1973; asst prof radiol sci, Sch Med, JohnsHopkins Univ, 1966-1968; USPHS fel, Sch Med, Johns Hopkins Univ, 1962-1966; staffphysician, Chest Serv, Vet Admin Hosp, Baltimore, 1961-1962; physician, Pulmonary Dis Serv, Fitzsimons Gen Hosp, Denver, 1959-1961; From intern to chief resident med, Univ Hosp, Baltimore, Md, 1954-1959. **Memberships:** Am Asn Immunol; fel Am Acad Allergy; Fr Soc Allergy & Clin Immunol; EuropAcad Allergol & Clin Immunol. **Research Statement & Publications:** Mechanisms of allergic reactions; mechanisms of immunotherapy for allergic diseases; allergy to latex. **Mailing Address:** 11 Quai Saint Michel, 75005, Paris, France. **Fax:** 330-140-193364.

LEVY, DAVID EDWARD, NEUROLOGY. **Personal Data:** b Washington, DC, May 10, 1941. **Education:** Harvard Univ, BA, 1963; Harvard Med Sch, MD, 1968; Am Bd Internal Med, dipl, 1972; Am Bd Psychiat & Neurol, dipl, 1975. **Honors & Awards:** Teacher-Scientist Award, Andrew W Mellon Found, 1975. **Professional Experience:** ADJ ASSOC PROF NEUROL, JOAN & SANFORD I WEILL MED COL, CORNELL UNIV, as of 2003; assoc attend neurologist, NY Hosp, 1980-; estab investr, Am Heart Asn, 1978; asst prof, Med Col, Cornell Univ, 1975-1980; asst attend neurologist, NY Hosp, 1975-1980; fel & instr, Med Col, Cornell Univ, 1972-1975; from intern to resident, NY Hosp, 1968-1972. **Memberships:** Soc Neuroscience; fel Am Col Physicians; Am Acad Neurol; Am Neurol Asn; fel AmHeart Asn. **Research Statement & Publications:** Brain carbohydrate and energy metabolism in cerebral ischemia; prediction of outcome from stroke and coma. **Mailing Address:** Dept Neurol & Neurosci, Joan Sanford I Weill Med Col, Cornell Univ, 1300 York Ave, New York, NY 10021.

LEVY, DEBORAH LOUISE, PSYCHOLOGY. **Personal Data:** b Minneapolis, Minn, November 3, 1950. **Education:** Univ Chicago, BA, 1972, PhD (psychol), 1976. **Honors & Awards:** Karl Menninger Sci Day Award, Menninger Found, 1979. **Professional Experience:** ASSOC PROF, DEPT PSYCHIAT, HARVARD MED SCH, 1994-; co-dir, Psychol Lab, Mclean Hosp, beginning 1990; dir psychophysiol, Hillside Hosp, Glen Oaks, NY, 1987-1990; prin investr, Res Scientist Develop Award, 1981-1986; res assoc, Dept Psychiat, UnivChicago, 1980-1987; res scientist & supvr clin teaching, Ill State Psychiat Inst, 1979-1987; asst unit chief, Ill State Psychiat Inst, 1979-1981; fel, Menninger Found, 1977-1979; intern clin psychol, NY Hosp, Cornell Med Ctr, 1976-1977; res assoc, Univ Chicago, 1972-1976. **Memberships:** AAAS; Am Psychol Asn; NY Acad Sci; Am Psychopath Asn; Soc Neuroscience; Sigma Xi. **Research Statement & Publications:** Genetics of the major psychoses. **Mailing Address:** Dept Psychiat, McLean Hosp, 115 Mill St, Belmont, MA 02478. **Fax:** 617-855-2778. **E-Mail:** levy@wjh.harvard.edu

LEVY, DONALD HARRIS, CHEMICAL PHYSICS, SPECTROSCOPY. **Personal Data:** b Youngstown, Ohio, June 30, 1939; m 1964, Susan; c Jonathan, Michael & Alexander. **Education:** Harvard Univ, BA, 1961; Univ Calif, Berkeley, PhD (chem), 1965. **Honors & Awards:** Jeremy Musher Mem Lectr, Hebrew Univ, 2002; Elly R Lippeneco Award, Optical Soc Am, 2000; Plyler Prize, Am Phys Soc, 1987; Albert Noyes Lectr, Rochester Univ; H H King Lectr, Kans State; Bourke Lectr, Royal Soc Chem; Frontiers in Chemical Research Lecturer, Texas A&M; Conference Universitaire de Suisse Occidentale lecture series; Powell Lecture, University of Richmond; American Chemical Society E Bright Wilson Award 2006. **Professional Experience:** Ed, J Chem Physics, 1998-; ALBERT A MICHELSON DISTINGUISHED SERVICE PROF, UNIV CHICAGO, 1997-; Lady Davis vis prof, Technion, 1997; mem, BESEC Comn on DOE Synchrotrons (Birgeneau Comn), 1997; mem vis comn, chem dept, Brookhaven National Lab, 1994-1999; Ralph and Mary Otis Isham prof, Univ Chicago, 1994-1997; chmn, NAS/NRC Comn on the Study of Free Electron Lasers, 1993-1995; mem, Coun Midwest Ctr, Am Acad Arts & Sci, 1992-1995; chmn, Molecular Electronic Spectros Gordon Conf, 1991; assoc ed, J Chem Physics, 1983-1998; mem ed comn, Ann Rev Phys Chem, 1983-1986; chmn, Dept Chem & Phys Sci, Univ Chicago, 1983-1985; mem rev panel chem physics, Nat Bur Stand, 1981-1984; mem chem adv comt, NSF, 1982-1985; chmn molecular spectros tech group, Optical Soc Am, 1982-1984; Sigma Xi Nat lectr, 1982-1983; prof chem, Univ Chicago, 1978-1994; Guggenheim fel 1975-1976; Dupont fac fel, 1969-1970; from asst prof to assoc prof, Dept Chem, Univ Chicago, 1967-1978; member, Advisory Council of the Chemistry Dept., Princeton Univ. 1995-1999; member, BESAC Panel on 4th Generation Light Sources (Leone committee) 1999; member, Committee to Review the national Nanotechnology Initiative, NAS/NRC, 2005-6; chair, American Institute of Physcis Editors' Panel, 2000-2002. **Memberships:** Nat Acad Sci; fel AAAS; fel Am Phys Soc; fel Am Acad Arts & Sci; fel Optical Soc of America. **Research Statement & Publications:** Optical spectroscopy in supersonic molecular beams; spectroscopy and photochemistry of van der Waals molecules; energy transfer; spectroscopy of porphyrin and related molecules; spectroscopy of gas phase amino acids and peptides. **Mailing Address:** James Franck Inst, Univ Chicago, 5640 S Ellis Ave, Chicago, IL 60637. **Fax:** 773-702-5863. **E-Mail:** levy@dilly.uchicago.edu

LEVY, DONALD M(ARC), DIGITAL SIGNAL PROCESSING, COMMUNICATION SYSTEMS. **Personal Data:** b Lynbrook, NY, March 27, 1935. **Education:** Univ Wis, BS, 1956, PhD (elec eng), 1965; Mass Inst Technol, MS, 1958. **Professional Experience:** SR STAFF ENGR, LOCKHEAD MISSLES & SPACE CORP, 1990-; supvr signal processing syst, Western Develop Labs, Ford Aerospace & Commun Corp, 1979-1987; from asst prof to assoc prof info eng, Univ Iowa, 1965-1979; instr elec eng, Univ Wis, 1963-1965; staff engr, Commun Systs Dept, IBM Corp, 1961-1963; instr elec eng, Univ Wis, 1959-1961; res asst & staff mem, Instrumentation Lab, Mass Inst Technol, 1957-1958; mem tech staff, Hycon Eastern, Inc, 1956-1957. **Memberships:** Inst Elec & Electronics Engrs. **Research Statement & Publications:** Statistical communication theory; topological network theory; bioengineering; digital signal processing. **Mailing Address:** 755 Newell Rd, Palo Alto, CA 94303.

LEVY, EDWARD KENNETH, ENERGY CONVERSION, POWER GENERATION. **Education:** Univ Md, BS, 1963; Mass Inst Technol, SM, 1964, ScD, 1967. **Honors & Awards:** Lindback Award, Lehigh Univ, 1972. **Professional Experience:** DIR, ENERGY RES CTR, 1973-; assoc Prof, Nat Acad Eng, 1973; mem tech staff, Bell Tel Lab, 1969; PROF MECH ENG, LEHIGH UNIV, 1967-; engr, Thermo Electron Corp, 1967-1968; engr, US Naval Ordinance Lab, 1965. **Memberships:** Am Soc Mech Engrs; Am Inst Chem Engrs; Am Nuclear Soc. **Research Statement & Publications:** Fluid mechanics, heat transfer and applied thermodynamic aspects of energy with emphasis on power generation systems. **Mailing Address:** Dept Mech Eng & Mech, Packard Lab, Lehigh Univ, 19 Mem Dr W, Bethlehem, PA 18015. **Fax:** 610-758-5959.

LEVY, EDWARD ROBERT, organic chemistry; deceased, see previous edition for last biography

LEVY, ELINOR MILLER, IMMUNE REGULATION, PSYCHONEUROIMMUNOLOGY. **Personal Data:** b New York, NY, March 18, 1942; m 1962, Charles; c Benjamin & Rebecca. **Education:** Brandeis Univ, BA, 1963; Emory Univ, PhD (biophysics), 1972. **Professional Experience:** Study sect mem, Nat Inst Alcohol Abuse & Alcoholism, 1990-1993; ASSOC PROF IMMUNOL, SCH MED, BOSTON UNIV, 1984-; from instr to asst prof, Sch Med, Boston Univ, 1976-1984; res assoc, Sch Med, Boston Univ, 1975-1976; res asst biophys, Univ BC, 1973-1975. **Memberships:** Am Asn Immunologists; AAAS; Psychoneuroimmunology Res Soc. **Research Statement & Publications:** Immune suppression and T-cell differentiation defects in the acquired immunodeficiency syndrome; psychosocial and neuroendocrine modulation of the immune response in humans. **Mailing Address:** Sch Med Boston Univ, 80 E Concord St, Boston, MA 02118. **Fax:** 617-638-4286. **E-Mail:** emlevy@bu.edu

LEVY, EUGENE HOWARD, ASTROPHYSICS, PLANETARY GEOPHYSICS. **Personal Data:** b New York, NY, May 6, 1944. **Education:** Rutgers Univ, AB, 1966; Univ Chicago, PhD (physics), 1971. **Honors & Awards:** Distinguished Pub Serv Medal, NASA, 1983; Alexander von Humboldt-Stiftung Sr Scientist Award, Fed Repub Ger, 1989. **Professional Experience:** HOWARD R HUGHES PROVOST & PROF PHYSICS & ASTRON, RICE UNIV, 2000-; prof physics, Col Sci, Univ Ariz, beginning 1995; mem, Comt Pub Educ, Am Astron Soc, 1994-; dean, Col Sci, Univ Ariz, 1993-2000; mem, Study Panel Robotic Explor Moon & Mars, Off Technol Assessment, US Cong, 1991; mem, Origins Solar Systs Progs Rev Panel, 1990-1991; mem, Astron & Astrophys Surv Comt, Sci Opportunities Panel, 1989-1990; mem, Lunar & Planetary Geophys Rev Panel, 1988-1990; mem, Comt Coop USSR Planetary Sci, 1988-1989; mem, Planetary Systs Sci Working Group, 1988-; mem, Lunar & Planetary Geophys Rev Panel, 1988-1990; mem, Mars Rover Sample Return Sci Working Group, 1987-1989; chmn, Adv Comt Int Coop Mars Sample Return, Space Sci Bd, Nat Acad Sci, 1986-1988; chmn, Comet Rendezvous & Asteroid Flyby Rev Panel, NASA, 1986; mem, Mars Explor Strategy Advan Group, NASA, 1986; mem, NASA-LPI Comt Future Space-Sta Sci Projs, 1985-; mem, Ariz Theoret Astrophys Prog, 1985-; distinguished vis scientist, Jet Propulsion Lab, Calif Inst Technol, 1985-1991; mem, NASA Space-Sta Sci User's Working Group, 1985-1988; mem, Space & Earth Sci Adv Comt, 1985-1988; mem, Study Panel Renewing US-Soviet Coop Space Sci, 1984; mem, Solar Syst Explor Div Mgt Coun, 1983-1985; head, Dept Planetary Sci, Univ Ariz, 1983-1994; dir, Lunar & Planetary Lab, Univ Ariz, 1983-1994; mem exec comt, Univs Space Sci Working Group, Asn Am Univs, 1982-; mem adv bd, Int Conf Cometry Explor, Budapest, 1982; head, US deleg, Nat Acad Sci-Europ Sci Found Joint Working Group, Coop Planetary Explor, 1982-1984; mem fac, Appl Math, Univ Ariz, 1981-; mem, Joint Working Group Near-Earth Space, Moon & Planets, USSR, 1981; mem, NASA deleg, Int Coop Invest Halley's Comet, Italy, 1981; assoc dept head, Univ Ariz, 1981-1983; sci consult, Rockwell Corp, 1980; chmn, Fields & Particles Panel, Int Comet Mission Rev Comt, NASA, 1980; mem, Theory Panel & Rev Panel Origins Plasmas Earth's Neighborhood, 1980; mem, Solar Syst Explor Comt, 1980-1983; mem, Comprehensive & Coord Sci Prog Int Tech Panel on Comets, 1980-1982; mem, chmn Comt Planetary & Lunar Explor, 1979-1982; mem, Space Sci Bd, 1979-1982; chmn, Comt Planetary & Lunar Explor, Nat Acad Sci, 1978-1982; co-chmn bd study, Explor Primitive Solar Syst Bodies, Nat Acad Sci, 1978; partic, Comet Halley Sci Working Group, NASA, 1977-1978; mem, Comt Planetary & Lunar Explor, Nat Acad Sci, 1976-1979; from asst prof to prof planetary sci, Univ Ariz, 1975-1994; asst prof, Bartol Res Found, Franklin Inst, 1973-1975; Ctr Theoret Physics fac fel, Univ Md, 1971-1973; fel physics & astron, Univ Md, 1971-1973. **Memberships:** Am Astron Soc; Int Astron Union; Sigma Xi; AAAS. **Research Statement & Publications:** Theoretical astrophysics and solar system studies; magnetohydrodynamics; space and solar physics; planetary and geophysics; magnetic field generation; physical processes associated with the origin of the solar system; techniques for the observational discovery and study of other planetary systems. **Mailing Address:** Physics & Astron Dept, Rice Univ, 430 Allen Ctr Mail Stop Two 6100 Main St, Houston, TX 77005. **Fax:** 713-348-5971. **E-Mail:** provost@rice.edu

LEVY, GEORGE CHARLES, COMPUTER METHODS. **Personal Data:** b Brooklyn, NY, June 4, 1944. **Education:** Syracuse Univ, AB, 1965; Univ Calif, Los Angeles, PhD (chem), 1968. **Honors & Awards:** Thomas L Saaty Prize, 1990. **Professional Experience:** PROF SCI & TECHNOL, SYRACUSE UNIV, 1985-; adj prof radiol, State Univ NY Upstate Med Ctr, 1984-; founder & chmn, New Methods Res Inc, 1983-1991; ed, Comput Enhanced Spectros J, 1982-1987; PROF CHEM, SYRACUSE UNIV, 1981-; dir res, Nuclear Magnetic Resonance & Data Processing, NIH, 1981-1990; Johnvan Geuns prof, Univ Amsterdam, 1979; Camille & Henry Dreyfus teacher-scholar, 1976-1981, Alfred P Sloan res fel, 1975-1977; from assoc prof to prof chem, Fla State Univ, 1973-1981; mem res staff, Gen Elec Corp, 1968-1973. **Memberships:** Am Chem Soc; Sigma Xi. **Research Statement & Publications:** Nuclear magnetic resonance spectroscopy and computer methods in chemistry; chemical and biophysical applications of carbon-13, nitrogen-15, and other nuclei nuclear magnetic resonance; statistical expert systems. **Mailing Address:** Syracuse Univ, Syracuse, NY 13244. **Fax:** 315-443-1022. **E-Mail:** glevy@cat.syr.edu

LEVY, GERALD FRANK, ECOLOGY. **Personal Data:** b Paterson, NJ, June 20, 1938. **Education:** Bowling Green State Univ, BS, 1960, MA, 1961; Univ Wis, PhD (bot), 1966. **Honors & Awards:** Pres Award, Va Wildlife Fedn, 1979. **Professional Experience:** RETIRED; mem sci adv bd, va mus nat hist, 1985-1987; chmn bd, environ consult, inc, 1981-1982; prof biol sci, Old Dom Univ, beginning 1978; vpres, environ consult, inc, 1973-1981; bot consult, animal ecol proj, 1968-1969; from asst prof to assoc prof biol & ecol, Old Dom Univ, 1967-1977; asst prof bot & zool, Univ Wis, marinette campus, 1965-1967; tech asst, Univ Wis, 1963-1965; secy & bd mem, Norfolk Bot Garden Soc. **Research Statement & Publications:** Phytosociology; longleaf pine regeneration; fire ecology; history and natural history; great dismal swamp. **Mailing Address:** Dept Biol Sci, Old Dom Univ, Rm 110 Alfriend Chem Bldg, Norfolk, VA 23529-0266. **Fax:** 757-683-5283. **E-Mail:** glevy@odu.edu

LEVY, GERHARD, PHARMACOLOGY. **Personal Data:** b Wollin, Ger, February 12, 1928. **Education:** Univ Calif, BS, 1955, PharmD, 1957. **Honorary Degrees:** Dr, Univ Uppsala, 1975; Dr, Phila Col Pharm & Sci, 1979; Dr, Long Island Univ, 1981; DSc, Univ Ill, 1986; DSc, Hoshi Univ, Tokyo, 1996. **Honors & Awards:** Richardson Pharm Award, 1957; McKeen Cattell Distinguished Achievement Award Clin Pharmacol, Am Col Clin Pharmacol, 1978; Host-Madsen Medal, Int Pharmaceut Fedn, 1978; Oscar B Hunter Mem Award, Am Soc Clin Pharmacol & Therapeut, 1982; Volwiler Res Achievement Award, Am Asn Col Pharm, 1982; Am Col Clin Pharm Therapeut Frontiers Lectr Award, 1983; Takeru Higuchi Res Prize, Acad Pharmaceut Sci, 1983; Sidney Riegelman Lectr, Univ Calif, San Francisco, 1983; Lifetime Achievement Award, Int Pharmaceut Fedn, 1994. **Professional Experience:** DISTINGUISHED PROF EMER PHARMACEUT, SCH PHARM, STATE UNIV NY, BUFFALO, as of 2004; vis prof, Basic Med Sci, 1985-1986; grad prof, Victorian Col Pharm, Melbourne, Australia, 1973-; Distinguished prof Pharmaceut, Sch Pharm, State Univ NY, Buffalo, beginning 1972; vis prof, Univ Rochester, 1972-1973; mem, Comt Probs Drug Safety, Nat Acad Sci-Nat res Coun, 1971-1975; consult, Bur Drugs, Food & Drug Admin, 1971-1973; chmn, Med Ctr, Univ Calif, 1966-1970; vis prof, Hebrew Univ, Jerusalem, 1966-; prof biopharmaceut, Med Ctr, Univ Calif, 1964-1972; actg chmn dept, Med Ctr, Univ Calif, 1959-1960; from asst prof to assoc prof pharm, Med Ctr, Univ Calif, 1958-1964; res pharmacist, Med Ctr, Univ Calif, 1957-1958. **Memberships:** Inst Med-Nat Acad Sci; Am Chem Soc; fel Am Pharmaceut Asn; Am Soc Pharmacol & Exp Therapeut; fel AAAS. **Research Statement & Publications:** Biopharmaceutics; clinical pharmacology; pharmacokinetics. **Mailing Address:** Dept Pharmaceut, State Univ NY Sch Pharm, 547 Hochstetter Hall N Campus, Amherst, NY 14260. **Fax:** 716-645-3693. **E-Mail:** glevy@acsu.buffalo.edu

LEVY, HANS RICHARD, ENZYMOLOGY. **Personal Data:** b Leipzig, Ger, October 22, 1929; m 1960, Betty; c Karen. **Education:** Rutgers Univ, BS, 1950; Univ Chicago, PhD (biochem), 1956. **Professional Experience:** PROF EMER, DEPT BIOL, SYRACUSE UNIV, 1999-; chmn, Dept Biol, Syracuse Univ, 1993-1999; prof biochem, Syracuse Univ, 1971-1999; from asst prof to assoc prof, Dept Biol, Syracuse Univ, 1963-1971; from instr to asst prof biochem, Ben May Lab, Univ Chicago, 1959-1963; USPHS fel, Hammersmith Hosp, London, Eng, 1958-1959; USPHS fel, Ben May Lab, Univ Chicago, 1956-1958. **Memberships:** AAAS; Am Soc Biol Chem; Am Chem Soc; Am Asn Univ Prof; emer mem, Protein Soc. **Research Statement & Publications:** Mechanisms of action and regulation of enzymes; protein structural features that determine pyridine nucleotide dehydrogenase coenzyme specificity, especially for various glucose 6-phosphate dehydrogenases. **Mailing Address:** Dept Biol, Syracuse Univ, Syracuse, NY 13244-1220.

LEVY, HARVEY LOUIS, BIOCHEMICAL GENETICS, PEDIATRICS. **Personal Data:** b Augusta, Ga, October 3, 1935; wid Barbara (Deceased); c Larni & Vicki. **Education:** Med Col Ga, MD, 1960. **Honors & Awards:** Robert Guthrie Award for Advances in Biochem & Molecular Genetics, Am Asn Ment Retardation, 1996; Robert Guthrie Award for World-Wide Recognition of Outstanding Contrib to Newborn Screening, Int Soc Neonatal Screening, 1997. **Professional Experience:** ASSOC PROF PEDIAT, HARVARD MED SCH, 1995-; sr assoc med & genetics & dir, Inborn Errors of Metab-Phenylketonuria Prog, Children's Hosp Med Ctr, 1978-; assoc neurologist & pediatrician, Mass Gen Hosp, beginning 1977; assoc prof neurol, Harvard Med Sch, beginning 1977; dir, Mass Metab Dis Prog, 1975-; assoc, Ctr Human Genetics, Harvard Med Sch, 1971-; prin investr, Mass Dept Pub Health, 1969-1975; lectr, Grad Sch Dent, Boston Univ, 1968-; from instr to asst prof, Harvard Med Sch, 1968-1977; consult, Walter E Fernald Sch Ment Retardation, 1967-; NIH fel neurol, Harvard Med Sch, 1966-1968; chief resident, Boston City Hosp, 1965-1966; asst resident pediat, Johns Hopkins Hosp, 1964-1965; asst resident path, Columbia-Presby Med Ctr, 1961-1962; intern pediat, Boston City Hosp, 1960-1961. **Memberships:** Fel Am Acad Pediat; Soc Pediat Res; Am Pediat Soc; pres, Soc Inherited Metab Disorders, (pres, 1983-1984); Am Soc Human Genetics. **Research Statement & Publications:** Inborn errors of metabolism; biochemical and genetic disorders; pathogenesis of inborn errors of metabolism. **Mailing Address:** Children's Hosp Boston, 300 Longwood Ave IC-106, Boston, MA 02115. **Fax:** 617-734-2652. **E-Mail:** harvey.levy@tch.harvard.edu

LEVY, HENRY N, COMPUTER SCIENCE. **Education:** PhD. **Professional Experience:** PROF & WISSNER SLIVKA CHAIR, DEPT COMPUT SCI & ENG, UNIV WASH, as of 2005. **Memberships:** Asn Comput Mach. **Mailing Address:** Dept Comput Sci & Eng, Univ Wash, Seattle, WA 98195. **E-Mail:** levy@cs.washington.edu

LEVY, HIRAM II, METEOROLOGY. **Education:** Harvard Univ, PhD, 1966. **Professional Experience:** VIS LECTR, DEPT GEOPHYS SCI & PROG ATMOSPHERIC & OCEANIC SCI, PRINCETON UNIV & SR RES SCIENTIST, GEOPHYS FLUID DYNAMICS LAB, NAT OCEANIC & ATMOSPHERIC ADMIN, as of 2004. **Mailing Address:** Natl Oceanic & Atmospheric Admin, 259 GFDL, Princeton, NJ 08540. **Fax:** 609-987-5063. **E-Mail:** Hiram.Levy@noaa.gov

LEVY, JACK BENJAMIN, ORGANIC CHEMISTRY. **Personal Data:** b Savannah, Ga, January 17, 1941. **Education:** Duke Univ, BA, 1962, NC State Univ, MS, 1964, PhD (chem), 1967. **Professional Experience:** PROF CHEM, UNIV NC, WILMINGTON, 1991-; ADJ PROF, UNIV NC, WILMILGTON, 1986-; Will S Deloach prof chem, Univ NC, 1986-1991; chmn dept, Univ NC, 1975-1992; from asst prof to prof, Univ NC, 1968-1973. **Memberships:** Am Chem Soc; Sigma Xi. **Research Statement & Publications:** Synthesis and spectral properties of new phenoxaposphine derivatives and related compounds. **Mailing Address:** Dept Chem, Univ NC Wilmington, Wilmington, NC 28403-3297. **Fax:** 910-962-3013. **E-Mail:** levyjb@uncwil.edu

LEVY, JERRE MARIE, PSYCHOBIOLOGY, COGNITIVE NEUROSCIENCE. **Personal Data:** b Birmingham, Ala, April 7, 1938; m 1958, c Marie Basch-Brown & Todd Basch. **Education:** Univ Miami, BA, 1962, MS, 1966; Calif Inst Technol, PhD (psychobiol), 1970. **Professional Experience:** PROF EMER NEUROSCI, UNIV CHICAGO, as of 2002; bd assoc eds, J Neurosci, 1990-; bd assoc eds, Neuropsychol, 1988-; bd assoc eds, Brain & Cognition, 1982-; prof biopsychol, Univ Chicago, beginning 1982; prin investr, NSF grant, 1975-1977 & NIH grant, 1977-1979 & Spencer Found grant, 1979-1988; assoc prof, Univ Chicago, 1977-1982; consult ed, J Exp Psychol: Human Perception & Performance, 1975-1984; from asst prof to assoc prof psychol, Univ Pa, 1972-1977; fel biochem, Ore State Univ, 1971-1972; fel psychol, Univ Colo, 1970-1971; res tech neuropsychol, Vet Admin Hosp, Denver, 1969-1970. **Memberships:** Soc Exp Psychologists; Int Neuropsychol Symp. **Research Statement & Publications:** Cerebral asymmetry and cognitive function; evolution and genetics of human brain, especially hemispheric lateralization and correlated behaviors; variations in human lateralization patterns. **Mailing Address:** Dept Psychol, Univ Chicago, 5848 S Univ Ave, Chicago, IL 60637-1515. **E-Mail:** jerre@uchicago.edu

LEVY, JOSEPH VICTOR, PHYSIOLOGY, PHARMACOLOGY. **Personal Data:** b Los Angeles, Calif, April 7, 1928. **Education:** Stanford Univ, BA, 1950; Univ Calif, Los Angeles, MS, 1956; Univ Wash, PhD (pharmacol), 1959. **Honors & Awards:** Lucien Szymd Mem Award, Univ Pac, 1994; Eberhardt Teacher-Scholar Award, Univ Pac, 1997. **Professional Experience:** PROF & CHMN PHYSIOL, SCH DENT, UNIV PAC, 1991-; mem expert adv panel geriat drugs, US Pharmacopea, 1985-1995; clin prof physiol & pharmacol, Sch Dent 1985-1991; PHARMACOL COURSE DIR, SCH DENT UNIV PAC, 1981-; consult, WHO & UN Develop Prog, 1981; mem, Hypertension Task Force, Nat Heart Inst, NIH, 1976-1977; mem res comt, Calif Heart Asn, 1975-1977; mem drug interaction panel, Am Pharmaceut Asn, 1973-1985; mem, Pharmacol & Therapeut Comt, Calif, Pac Med Ctr, beginning 1972; assoc prof, Sch Dent, Univ Pac, 1972-1985; assoc prof, Sch Med Sci, Univ Pac, 1969-1977; res career prog scientist, Nat Heart Inst, 1965-1970; dir, Lab Pharmacol & Exp Therapeut, Pac Presby Med Ctr, 1961-1989; sr res pharmacologist, Res Labs, Presby Med Ctr, 1960-1965; pharmacologist, Surg Res Labs, Presby Hosp, 1960; res fel, Am Heart Asn, 1959-1960; NIH res trainee pharmacol, 1957-1958 & anesthesiol, 1958-1959; asst, Univ Wash, 1956-1957; asst pharmacol, Stanford Univ, 1954-1956; asst physiol, Stanford Univ, 1951-1953; mem, Coun Basic Res, Am Heart Asn. **Memberships:** Soc Exp Biol & Med; Cardiac Muscle Soc; Am Soc Clin Pharmacol & Therapeut; Am Soc Pharmacol & Therapeut; Am Chem Soc; Am Physiol Soc. **Research Statement & Publications:** Physiology and pharmacology; hypertension; central nervous systems prostaglandins; inflammation; vascular; analgesia; thrombosis; platelets. **Mailing Address:** Dept Physiol & Pharmacol, Sch Dent, Univ Pac, 2155 Webster St, San Francisco, CA 94115. **Fax:** 415-929-6654. **E-Mail:** jlevy@pacific.edu

LEVY, JULIA GERWING, MICROBIOLOGY. **Personal Data:** b Singapore, May 15, 1934. **Education:** Univ BC, BA, 1955; Univ London, PhD (bact), 1958. **Honorary Degrees:** Dr, Univ Ottawa, 1989; Dr, Mt St Vincents Univ, 1990. **Honors & Awards:** Biely Sci Award; Killiam Sci Prize. **Professional Experience:** PROF EMER MICROBIAL, as of 2006; MEM CANCER RES UNIT, UNIV BC, 1977-; prof microbiol, Univ BC, beginning 1974; from instr to assoc prof, Univ BC, 1958-1974; vpres, Res & Develop, Quadralogic Technol Inc. **Memberships:** Am Asn Immunologists; fel Royal Soc Can. **Research Statement & Publications:** Characterization of antigenic determinants on natural antigens and the effect of these determinants on the cellular immune response; photoimmunotherapy; a study of immunotoxins to which photosensitizers have been conjugated. **Mailing Address:** QLT Photo Therapeut Inc, 520 W Sixth Ave Ste 200, Vancouver, BC V5Z 4H5, Can.

LEVY, LAURENE, PHYTOPATHOLOY. **Education:** Univ Calif, MS, PhD (plant path). **Professional Experience:** LAB DIR, NAT PLANT GERMPLASM & BIOTECHONOLGY LAB, USDA, as of 2005. **Mailing Address:** USDA Nat Germplasm Res Lab, BARC E Bldg 580, Beltsville, MD 20705. **Fax:** 301-504-8539. **E-Mail:** laurene.e.levy@usda.gov

LEVY, LAWRENCE S, ALGEBRA. **Personal Data:** b Cleveland, Ohio, October 2, 1933. **Education:** Juilliard Sch Music, BS, 1954, MS, 1956; Univ Ill, MA, 1958, PhD (math), 1961. **Professional Experience:** PROF EMER MATH, UNIV WIS, MADISON, as of 2005; adj prof math, Univ Nebraska, as of 2005; prof Math, Univ Wis, Madison, beginning 1971; from asst prof to assoc prof, Univ Wis-Madison, 1961-1971; instr math, Univ Ill, 1961. **Memberships:** Am Math Soc. **Research Statement & Publications:** Structure of associated rings and their modules. **Mailing Address:** Dept Math, Univ Wis, 2528 Van Hise Ave 480 Lincoln Dr, Madison, WI 53705-3850. **Fax:** 608-263-8891. **E-Mail:** levy@math.wisc.edu

LEVY, LEO, PSYCHOLOGY, PREVENTIVE MEDICINE. **Personal Data:** b New York, NY, July 11, 1928; m 1957, Annika Ameen; c Stephanie & Anna. **Education:** City Col New York, BS, 1950, MA, 1951; Univ Wash, PhD (psychol), 1958; Harvard Univ, SMHyg, 1964. **Professional Experience:** Clin fac psychiat, Univ NMex, 1994-; EMER PROF PUB HEALTH, UNIV ILL MED CTR, 1989-; vis prof, St George's Hosp Med Sch, London, 1979-1980; Fogerty Sr Int fel, Inst Psychiat, London, 1979-1980; prof pub health & prev med res, Univ Ill Med Ctr, 1975-1989; Fulbright Hays res grant, State Univ Leiden, 1972-1973; assoc prof prev med, Univ Ill Med Ctr, 1969-1975; vis assoc prof psychiat, McMaster Univ, 1969-1971; asst prof psychiat, Univ Ill Med Ctr, 1965-1969; dir planning & eval, Ill Dept Ment Health, 1964-1969; NIMH fels, Univ Mich, 1958-1960 & Harvard Univ, 1963-1964; adminr & chief psychologist, Pueblo Guid Ctr, Pueblo, Colo, 1960-1963; Instr psychol, Univ Mich, 1958-1960. **Memberships:** Emer fel Am Psychol Asn. **Research Statement & Publications:** Promotion and maintenance of mental health; social planning; drug abuse; social ecology; psychosocial epidemiology; problems of urban mental health. **Mailing Address:** 4804 Mariah Rd NW, Albuquerque, NM 87107.

LEVY, LEON BRUCE, INDUSTRIAL ORGANIC CHEMISTRY. **Personal Data:** b New York, NY, July 20, 1937. **Education:** NY Univ, BA, 1958; Harvard Univ, MA, 1959, PhD (chem), 1962. **Professional Experience:** RETIRED; sr res assoc, Tech Ctr, Hoechst Celanese Corp, beginning 1990; res assoc, Tech Ctr, 1972-1990; sr res chemist, Tech Ctr, 1965-1971; res chemist, Clarkwood Res Lab, Celanese Chem Co, 1962-1965. **Memberships:** Catalysis Soc. **Research Statement & Publications:** Kinetics and mechanisms of homolytic organic reactions; vapor phase oxidations of hydrocarbons; heterogeneous catalysis; monomer stability. **Mailing Address:** 6130 Coralridge Dr, Corpus Christi, TX 78413. **Fax:** 512-242-4087.

LEVY, LEONARD ALVIN, PODIATRIC DERMATOLOGY, AGING. **Personal Data:** b New York, NY, August 19, 1935. **Education:** NY Univ, BA, 1956; NY Col Podiat Med, DPM, 1961; Columbia Univ Sch Pub Health, MPH, 1967. **Professional Experience:** PROF FAMILY MED & PUB HEALTH, COL OSTEOP MED, NOVA SOUTHEASTERN UNIV, as of 2003; ASSOC DEAN, EDUC, PLANNING & RES, COL OSTEOP MED, NOVA SOUTHEASTERN UNIV, as of 2003; Interim vpres planning & res, Univ Tex Health Sci Ctr, 1993; mem spec med adv group, Dept Vet Admin, 1990-; mem test comt dermat, Nat Bd Podiat Med Examrs, 1981-; dean podiat med, Univ Osteopath Med & Health Sci, 1981-1993; governing coun mem, Am Pub Health Asn, 1978-1980 & 1984-1986; chmn & mem test comt, Nat Bd Podiat Med examrs, 1977-; consult podiat med, Univ Tex Health Sci Ctr, 1976-1981; dean podiat med, State Univ NY, Stony Brook, 1974-1976; clin assoc prof, Dept Dermat, Stanford Univ Sch Med, 1970-1974; mem rev comt, USPHS Adv Comt, 1968-1972; dean & vpres podiat med, Calif Col Podiat Med, 1967-1974. **Memberships:** Am Podiat Med Asn; Am Pub Health Asn; Am Acad Dermat; Am Asn Col Podiat Med; Asn Am Med Col; Nat Rural Health Asn. **Research Statement & Publications:** Podriatic medical education; public health dermatological problems of the foot and ankle; health promotion and prevention; geriatrics; rural health primary care. **Mailing Address:** Col Osteop Med, Nova SouthEastern Univ, 3200 S Univ Dr, Ft Lauderdale, FL 33328. **Fax:** 954-262-3536. **E-Mail:** levyleon@nova.edu

LEVY, LOUIS A, ORGANIC CHEMISTRY. **Personal Data:** b New York, NY, March 6, 1941. **Education:** City Col NY, BS, 1961; Univ Colo, PhD (chem), 1966. **Professional Experience:** RES CHEMIST, NAT INST ENVIRON HEALTH SCI, 2002-; SCIENTIST, LAB ENVIRON CHEM, 1967-; scientist, Nat Air Pollution Control Admin, USPHS, 1966-1967; proj leader synthesis, Int Flavors & Fragrances, Inc, 1965-1966. **Memberships:** Am Chem Soc; Chem Soc. **Research Statement & Publications:** Chemistry and synthesis of chemicals of environmental concern; Nuclear Magnetic Resonance spectroscopy. **Mailing Address:** Nat Inst Environ Health Sci, Lab Struct Biol PO Box 12233, Res Triangle Park, NC 27709.

LEVY, MARILYN, PHOTOGRAPHIC ENGINEERING, CHEMISTRY. **Personal Data:** b New York, NY, April 3, 1922. **Education:** Hunter Col, AB, 1942. **Professional Experience:** CONSULT, 1980-; US ARMY ADV, NATO PHOTOG STANDARDS COMT & AIR STANDARDIZATION COORD COMT, 1978-; chief photog optics div, Photog Eng, US Army Combat & Surveillance Lab, 1975-1980; chmn, Processing Sect, Soc Photog Scientists & Engrs, 1973-1974; Mem & US Army rep, Am Nat Standards Inst, 1962-; res chemist photog process, US Army Electronics Command, 1953-1974; inspector chem, NY Quartermaster Proc Agency, 1951-1952; chemist lacquer mfg, Valspar Corp, 1946-1948; chemist lacquer formulation, Roxalin Flexible Finishes, 1943-1946; Chemist anal-drugs, NY Quinine & Chem Co, 1942-1943. **Memberships:** Fel Soc Photog Scientists & Engrs; Am Chem Soc. **Research Statement & Publications:** Photographic processing; nonconventional photographic systems; aerial photography; photographic sensitometry; color photography; rapid processing; 26 patents and 20 papers in photo science field. **Mailing Address:** 1640 Anderson Ave, Ft Lee, NJ 07024.

LEVY, MARK B, mathematics; deceased, see previous edition for last biography

LEVY, MARTIN J LINDEN, MEDICAL SCIENCES, RESEARCH ADMINISTRATION. **Personal Data:** b Philadelphia, Pa, June 19, 1925. **Education:** Pa State Univ, BS, 1947; NJ Inst Technol, MS, 1956; Stevens Inst Technol, DrSci, 1963. **Professional Experience:** Med staff affil, St Barnabas Med Ctr, NJ & bd dir, Southern Inst Biomed Sci, 1980-1982; Adj prof, NJ Med Sch, Univ Med & Dent, 1980-1982; PROF ENG, NJ INSTTECHNOL, 1958-; Specialist engr, Jet Engine Div, Gen Elec, 1956-1958. **Memberships:** Am Col Cryosurg; NY Acad Sci; Int Soc Cryosurg. **Research Statement & Publications:** Biomedical sciences; application of engineering and technical methods to instrumentation for diagnosis and therapy. **Mailing Address:** NJ Inst Technol, 323 High St, Newark, NJ 07102.

LEVY, MATTHEW NATHAN, PHYSIOLOGY, BIOMEDICAL ENGINEERING. **Personal Data:** b New York, NY, December 2, 1922; m 1946, Ruth Joseph; c Donald J, Garry E & James R. **Education:** Western Res Univ, BS, 1943, MD, 1945. **Honors & Awards:** Lederle Med Fac Award, 1955-1957; Shanes Mem Lectureship, 1972; Wiggers Award, Am Physiol Soc, 1983; Merit Award, NIH, 1986; Distinguished Scientist Award, 1988; Mikamo Lectr, Kyoto, 1991; Gordon Moe Lectr, 1994. **Professional Experience:** Ed, Am J Physiol, Heart & Circulatory Physiol, 1976-1981; sect ed, Am J Physiol, 1975-; assoc ed, Circulation Res, 1970-1974; prof, physiol & biomed eng, Case Western Res Univ, 1968-; CHIEF DEPT INVESTIGATIVE MED, MT SINAI HOSP, 1967-; assoc prof, Case Inst Technol, 1963-1967; assoc prof, Case Western Reserve Univ, 1961-1968; dir res, St Vincent Charity Hosp, Cleveland, Ohio, 1957-1967; from asst prof to assoc prof, Albany Med Col, 1953-1957; From instr to asst prof physiol, Western Res Univ, 1949-1953; Res fel, Western Res Univ, 1948-1949. **Memberships:** Am Physiol Soc; Am Heart Asn. **Research Statement & Publications:** Cardiovascular physiology. **Mailing Address:** Rammelkamp Inst, Metro Health Medical cent, Cleveland, OH 44109. **Fax:** 216-297-1336. **E-Mail:** mnl@po.cwru.edu

LEVY, MATTHYS P, STRUCTURAL DESIGN IN ARCHITECTURE. **Personal Data:** b Basle, Switz. **Education:** City Col NY, BSCE, 1951; Columbia Univ, MSCE, 1956, CE, 1962. **Honors & Awards:** Lincoln Arc Welding Award, 1961, 1981 & 1991; Prestressed Concrete InstAward, 1963, 1971 & 1992; Medal of Excellence, Eng News Record, 1992; Innovation in CivilEng Award, Am Soc Civil Engrs, 1994. **Professional Experience:** EXEC VPRES & DIR STRUCT DIV, WEIDLINGER ASSOCS, 1986-; distinguished prof, Pratt Inst, NY, 1980-1981; prin, Weidlinger Assocs, 1964-1986; adj prof, Sch Archit, Columbia Univ, 1962-1980; vis critic archit, Yale Univ, 1960-1965; staff, Weidlinger Assocs, 1956-1964; asst opers officers, 453rd Eng Construct Battalion, US Army, Korea, 1952-1954; struct consult, New York, NY & Chicago, Ill, 1951-1955; lectr, Univ Idaho, Rutgers Univ, Princeton Univ, Harvard Univ, Cath Univ & Univ Fla. **Memberships:** Nat Acad Eng; fel Inst Civil Engrs; Am Concrete Inst; Nat Acad Forensic Engrs; Int Asn Shell & Spatial Struct; Int Asn Bridge & Struct Eng; fel Am Soc Civil Engrs; Am Inst Architects. **Mailing Address:** Weidlinger Assocs, 333 Seventh Ave, New York, NY 10001. **Fax:** 212-564-2279.

LEVY, MOISES, LOW TEMPERATURE SOLID STATE PHYSICS, PHYSICAL ACOUSTICS. **Personal Data:** b Panama, April 8, 1930. **Education:** Calif Inst Technol, BS, 1952, MS, 1955; Univ Calif, Los Angeles, PhD (physics), 1963. **Professional Experience:** PROF EMER PHYSICS, UNIV WIS-MILWAUKEE, as of 2005; Lady Doris fel, 1985-1986, vis prof, Techmon Univ, 1985-1986; chmn, Ultrasonics Symp, 1983 & 1974; prog comt mem, Ultrasonics Symp, 1982; vis prof, Univ Sao Paolo, 1983 & 1979, prog comt mem, Ultrasonics Symp, 1976, chmn dept, Univ Wis-Milwaukee, 1975-1978; prof physics, Univ Wis-Milwaukee, beginning 1973; prog comt mem, Ultrasonics Symp, 1972-; vis prof, Int Vis Info Serv, 1972; assoc prof, Univ Wis-Milwaukee, 1971-1973; asst prof ultrasonic invest solid state, Univ Calif, Los Angeles, 1965-1970; asst prof solid state physics, Univ Pa, 1964-1965, NATO postdoc fel, 1963-1964; mem tech staff, Semiconductor Div, Hughes Aircraft Co, 1956-1958; res chemist, Speciality Resins, Inc, 1953-1954. **Memberships:** Fel Am Phys Soc; Acoustical Soc Am; Ultrasonic Ferroelec & Frequency Control Soc. **Research Statement & Publications:** Experimental investigation of electron phonon interaction in superconductors and normal metals; spin phonon in magnetic superconductors and rare earth metals; surface wave investigation of superconducting films and magnetic films. **Mailing Address:** Dept Physics, Univ Wis, Milwaukee, WI 53201.

LEVY, MORRIS, BIOSYSTEMATICS. **Personal Data:** b Chicago, Ill, May 22, 1944; m 1974, c 1. **Education:** Univ Ill, Chicago Circle, 1967; Yale Univ, MPh, 1972, PhD (ecol, evolution), 1973. **Professional Experience:** PROF BIOL SCI, PURDUE UNIV, as of 2003; assoc prof biol sci, Purdue Univ, beginning 1979; NSF grant, 1978 & 1979; NSF grant, Res Prog Biomed Sci, 1975; dir, Kriebel Herbarium, Purdue Univ, 1973-; asst prof, Purdue Univ, 1973-1979. **Memberships:** Bot Soc Am; Soc Study Evolution; Soc Am Naturalists; AAAS. **Research Statement & Publications:** Systematics and biochemical ecology of plants; evolution of hybrid and polyploid species; population biology of weeds; host plant-fungal pathogen co-evolution; pollinetion ecology. **Mailing Address:** Dept Biol Sci, Purdue Univ, 915 W State St, W Lafayette, IN 47907-2054. **E-Mail:** levym@bilbo.bio.purdue.edu

LEVY, MORTIMER, RESEARCH ADMINISTRATION. **Personal Data:** b Rochester, NY, July 7, 1924. **Education:** Cornell Univ, BSEE, 1949; Columbia Univ, MA, 1951. **Professional Experience:** RETIRED; mgr mat, Processes & Corp Staff, 1978-; mgr, Process ElementSect, 1975-1978; mgr process sect, Xerox Corp, 1973-1975; mgr explor res, Xerox Corp, 1967-1973; sr scientist, Xerox Corp, 1964-1967; res scientist, Xerox Corp, 1963-1964; dir applres, Mat Res Corp, 1961-1963; sect leader, Xerox Corp, 1958-1961; Physicist, Xerox Corp, 1954-1957. **Memberships:** Soc Photog Sci & Eng. **Research Statement & Publications:** Electrostatic photography. **Mailing Address:** 105 Towpath Lane, Rochester, NY 14618.

LEVY, M(ORTON) FRANK, ORGANIC CHEMISTRY. **Personal Data:** b New York, NY, May 31, 1925; m 1990, c Brooke (Greene), Drew (Perry) & Alisa (Grandy). **Education:** Queens Col, NY, BS, 1950; Columbia Univ, MA, 1951; Yale Univ, PhD (chem), 1956. **Professional Experience:** RETIRED; res assoc, Univ Calif, Berkeley, 1975-1976; sr chemist, Mat Sci Lab, IBM Corp, San Jose, 1964-1990; group leader org synthesis, Harchem Div, Wallace & Tiernan, NJ, 1960-1964; group leader org synthesis & anal develop, Argus Chem Co, 1955-1960. **Memberships:** Am Chem Soc. **Research Statement & Publications:** Utilization of new raw materials in organic synthesis; photosensitive materials; dibasic acids; dye chemistry; preparation of radiolabeled compounds; new polymers; application of computers to chemistry. **Mailing Address:** 101 Pinta Ct, Los Gatos, CA 95032-6331. **E-Mail:** 73112, 611@compuserve.com

LEVY, NELSON LOUIS, PHARMACEUTICAL RESEARCH & DEVELOPMENT. **Personal Data:** b Somerville, NJ, June 19, 1941; m 1974, Louisa; c Scott, Erik, Jonathan, Michael, Andrew & David. **Education:** Yale Univ, BA & BS, 1963; Columbia Univ, MD, 1967; Duke Univ, PhD (immunol), 1973. **Professional Experience:** DIR, TARGETED GENETICS CORP, 1999-; chief exec officer, Ill Tech Develop Corp, 1993-1994; CHIEF EXEC OFFICER & CHMN, CORETECHS CORP, 1993-; pres, Fujisawa Pharmaceut Co, 1992-1993; chief exec officer, Coretechs Corp, 1984-1992; vpres, Pharmaceut Res, Abbott Labs, 1981-1984; from asst prof to assoc prof immunol, Duke Univ Med Ctr, 1976-1980; study sects, NIH, Nat Mult Sclerosis Soc, 1975-1980; resident neurol, Duke Univ Med Ctr, 1971-1972; res assoc virol & immunol, NIH, 1968-1970; intern surg, Univ Colo Med Ctr, 1967-1968; bd dir, Bionica Pty Ltd, Intek Diagnostics, SASHA Inc, Heybach Enterprises, MedVac Inc, Quantum Group Inc, Anthra Pharmaceut Inc, Myotech Corp, Chem Bridge Corp, Mei-Rui Pharma Ltd, Horizon Quest Inc, Ligand Pharmaceut. **Memberships:** Am Asn Cancer Res; Am Asn Immunologists; Soc Neuroscience; Pharmaceut Mfrs Asn; Drug Info Asn; Licensing Execs Soc. **Research Statement & Publications:** Immunologic and non-immunologic defenses against human cancer; pathogenesis and etiology of multiple sclerosis; neurologic control of the immune system; molecular modeling of pharmaceuticals. **Mailing Address:** Targeted Genetics Corp, 1100 Olive Way Ste 100, Seattle, WA 98101. **Fax:** 206-223-0288.

LEVY, NEWTON JR, INORGANIC CHEMISTRY, TECHNICAL MANAGEMENT. **Personal Data:** b Tampa, Fla, October 10, 1935; m 1961, c 2. **Education:** Univ Fla, BSCh, 1961, PhD (kinetics), 1964. **Professional Experience:** RETIRED; vpres sales-chem, Refractories Div, 1981-1991; mgr prod develop, Refractories Div, 1977-1981; mgr fuel additives, Refractories Div, 1974-1976; sect head refractories, Martin Marietta Labs, Martin Marietta Chem, 1972-1974; res supvr, Wash Res Ctr Div, W R Grace & Co, 1969-1972; sr chemist, Wash Res Ctr Div, W R Grace & Co, 1967-1969; res chemist, Wash Res Ctr Div, W R Grace & Co, 1964-1967. **Research Statement & Publications:** Preparation, fabrication, characterization and applications of reactive, fine sized ceramic oxide powders; properties and uses of magnesium oxide; chemical treatment of oils for combustion; chemical market studies; marketing specialty chemicals. **Mailing Address:** 23 Skye Dr, Brevard, NC 28712.

LEVY, NORMAN B, PSYCHIATRY, PSYCHOSOMATIC MEDICINE. **Personal Data:** b New York, NY, May 28, 1931; m 1970, Carol; c Karen, Susan, Joanne & Robert B. **Education:** NY Univ, BA, 1952; State Univ NY Downstate Med Ctr, MD, 1956. **Honors & Awards:** Wm A Console MD, Master Teach Awd in Psychiat, Alumi Soc, SUNY, Downstate Med Ctr, 1991; Thomas P Hackett MD Awd fpr Contrub to the field of Psychosom Med, Acad of Psychosom Med, 1993. **Professional Experience:** Vis prof psychiat & med, Univ Hawaii, 1981; PROF PSYCHIAT, MED & SURG, NY MED COL & DIR, LIAISON PSYCHIAT DIV, WESTCHESTER CO MED CTR & NY MED COL, 1980-; assoc ed, General Hosp Pschiat & ed sect, Liaison Rounds, 1979-; prof psychiat, Col Med, 1979-1980; assoc ed, Int J Psychiat Med, 1977-1978; presiding officer fac, Col Med, 1975-1976; examr psychiat, Am Bd psychiat & Neurol, 1974-; consult psychiat educ, Nat Inst Mental Health, 1974-; dir continuing educ psychiat, State Univ NY Downstate Med Ctr, 1974-1976; assoc prof, Col Med, 1973-1979; assoc dir, Med Psychiat Liaison Serv, 1972-1980; NIMH career teacher award, 1966; from instr to asst prof med & psychiat, State Univ NY Downstate Med Ctr, 1963-1973; resident psychiat, Kings Co Hosp Ctr, Brooklyn, NY, 1960-1963; dir med serv, USAF Hosp, Ashiya, Japan, 1958-1960; res physician & teaching fel med, Sch Med, Univ Pittsburgh, 1957-1958. **Memberships:** Fel Am Col Physicians; fel Am Psychiat Asn; fel Int Col Psychosom Med; Sigma Xi; fel Am Col Psychiatrists; Am Psychosom Soc. **Research Statement & Publications:** Effects of psychological stresses on kidney transplant rejections; psychological adaptation to hemodialysis; psychiatry and the changing role of males in society; attitudes of students and physicians on informing patients of their fatal diagnosis; use of fluoxetine in renal failure; use of fluoxetine in depressed patients with medical illnesses. **Mailing Address:** Dept Psychiat, NY Med Col, Brooklyn, NY 11218. **E-Mail:** nep4ropsyc@aol.com

LEVY, NORMAN STUART, OPHTHALMOLOGY, GLAUCOMA. **Personal Data:** b Detroit, Mich, July 17, 1940. **Education:** Case Western Res, MD, 1965; Univ Chicago, PhD (ophthal), 1975. **Honors & Awards:** Paleologos Award, 1995. **Professional Experience:** CO-CLIN ASSOC PROF FAMILY MED, UNIV FLA, 1981-; dir, KeratoRefractive Soc, 1980-1994; Chief ophthal, Vet Admin Hosp, Gainesville, 1973-1975 & Vet AdminMed Ctr, Lake City, 1976-1989; Asst prof ophthal & pediat, Univ Fla, 1972-1975. **Memberships:** Am Acad Ophthal; Asn Res Vision & Ophthal; Am Col Surgeons; KeratoRefractive Soc; Contemp Soc Ophthal (pres 1992-1994). **Research Statement & Publications:** Mechanism of damage in the disease, glaucoma, and method of diagnosis and early treatment; pharmaceutical glaucoma research. **Mailing Address:** 7106 NW 11th Pl, Gainesville, FL 32605-3157.

LEVY, PAUL, APPLIED MATHEMATICS. **Personal Data:** b New York, NY, May 25, 1941. **Education:** Rensselaer Polytech Inst, BS, 1963, MS, 1965, PhD (math), 1968. **Professional Experience:** ASST PROF MATH, STATE UNIV NY MARITIME COL, 1977-; asst prof math, NY Inst Technol, 1974-1977; asst prof math, NY Univ, 1967-1974. **Memberships:** Am Math Soc; Soc Indust & Appl Math. **Research Statement & Publications:** Investigation of problems in wave propagation and elasticity. **Mailing Address:** Brookhaven Nat Lab, Bldg 480 PO Box 5000, Upton, NY 11973-5000.

LEVY, PAUL F, ANALYTICAL CHEMISTRY, INSTRUMENTATION. **Personal Data:** b New York, NY, December 9, 1934. **Education:** City Col New York, BS, 1959; Columbia Univ, MA, 1961, PhD (anal chem), 1965. **Professional Experience:** MKT DEVELOP MGR, BIOMED PROD DEPT, E I DU PONT DENEMOURS & CO, 1985-; develop mgr, E I DuPont Del Nemours & Co, 1978-1985; prod mgrliquid chromatog, E I DuPont Del Nemours & Co, 1975-1978; prod mgr thermal anal, E I DuPontDe Nemours & Co, 1973-1975; supvr appln lab, E I DuPont Del Nemours & Co, 1969-1973; srproj engr, E I DuPont Del Nemours & Co, 1968-1969; proj engr, E I DuPont Del Nemours & Co, 1965-1968; Lectr chem, City Col New York, 1959-1965. **Memberships:** Am Chem Soc; Am Asn Clin Chemists. **Research Statement & Publications:** Theory, applications, design and development of thermal analysis and other material characterization instrumentation; coulostatic impulse-chain and other forms of polarography; electrochemical instrumentation; clinical and biomedical instrumentation; development management. **Mailing Address:** 4818 Hogan Dr 20381, Wilmington, DE 19808-1715.

LEVY, PAUL W(ARREN), solid state physics; deceased, see previous edition for last biography

LEVY, PETER MICHAEL, ELECTRON TRANSPORT IN MAGNETIC METALS. **Personal Data:** b Frankfurt, Ger, January 10, 1936; American citizen; m 1965, Darline; c Erik & Serge. **Education:** City Col NY, BME, 1958; Harvard Univ, MA, 1960, PhD (appl physics), 1963. **Honors & Awards:** Vermeil Medal, Soc Advan Progress, Paris, 1978. **Professional Experience:** Chmn dept, NY Univ, 1976-1982, 1991-1997; PROF PHYSICS, NY UNIV, 1975-; res exchange scientist, NSF-Nat Ctr Sci Res, France, 1975-1976, 1983-1984; Fulbright-Hays res scholar, France, 1975-1976; NSF grants, NY Univ, 1972-1975, 1975-1979, 1979-1982, 1982-1986, 1987; assoc prof, NY Univ, 1970-1975; Air Force Off Sci Res grant, Yale Univ & NY Univ, 1967-1972; asst prof, Yale Univ, 1966-1970; res assoc, Univ Pa, 1964-1966; fel, Nat Ctr Sci Res, France, 1963-1964; res assoc physics, Lab Electrostatics & Physics Metals, Grenoble, France, 1963-1964; NSF fel, 1958-1962. **Memberships:** Fel Am Phys Soc; Mat Res Soc. **Research Statement & Publications:** The magneto-transport properties of metallic multilayered structures (superlattices); magnetoresistivity of rare earth metallic compounds; orbital effects in rare earth compounds; anisotropy in disordered magnetic systems; spin glasses; long range interactions between local movements in metals; spin-dependent tunneling in ferromagnetic tunnel junctions; More than 15 publications. **Mailing Address:** Dept Physics, 4 Wash Pl, New York, NY 10003. **E-Mail:** levy@nyu.edu

LEVY, RALPH, MICROWAVE THEORY, CIRCUIT THEORY. **Personal Data:** b London, Eng, April 12, 1932; American citizen; m Barbara; c Mark S & Sharon E (Armao). **Education:** Cambridge Univ, MA, 1953; Univ London, PhD (appl sci), 1966. **Honors & Awards:** Microwave Career Award, Inst Elec & Electronics Engrs, Microwave Theory & Techniques Soc, 1997. **Professional Experience:** INDEPENDENT CONSULT, 1989-; vpres eng, Microwave Develop Labs, KW Microwave Inc, 1984-1989; vpres res microwave eng, Microwave Develop Labs, KW Microwave Inc, 1967-1984; consult, Weinschel Eng, 1965-1966; lectr elec eng, Univ Leeds, 1964-1967; consult, Decca Radar Ltd & Gen Elec Co, 1964-1967; mem sci staff microwave eng, Mullard Res Labs, Redhill, 1959-1964; mem sci staff microwave eng, Gen Elec Co, Stanmore, Eng, 1953-1959. **Memberships:** Fel Inst Elec & Electronics Engrs Mem Inst Elec Engineering (London). **Research Statement & Publications:** Microwave passive components; distributed circuit theory; military microwave systems; author of over 70 papers and 5 books and book chapters; granted 12 US patents. **Mailing Address:** R Levy Assoc, 1897 Caminito Velasco, La Jolla, CA 92037. **Fax:** 858-459-6752. **E-Mail:** r.levy@ieee.org

LEVY, RAM LEON, SEPARATION SCIENCE, CHEMICAL INTRUMENTATION. **Personal Data:** b Samokov, Bulgaria, October 7, 1933. **Education:** Israel Inst Technol, BSc, 1961, MSc, 1963; Univ Man, PhD (anal chem), 1967. **Professional Experience:** Vis lectr, Chem Dept, St Louis Univ, 1975; affil dir, Sch Continuing ProfEduc, Wash Univ, 1970-1972; SCIENTIST, POLYMER CHEMISTRY, MCDONNELL DOUGLAS RES LABS, MCDONNELL DOUGLAS CORP, 1968-; assoc chemist, Midwest ResLabs, Kansas City, 1967-1968; res assoc, Dept Plant Sci, Univ Man, 1963-1967. **Memberships:** Am Chem Soc; Am Soc Mass Spectrometry. **Research Statement & Publications:** Chemical mechanisms of polymer aging; detection of stress and fatigue induced molecular phenomena in polymers by infrared spectroscopy; chemluminescence of polymers; chromatographic characterization of oligimers; incorporation of molecular probes in polymer networks; thermal degradation of polymers. **Mailing Address:** Mcdonnell Douglas Res Lab, St Louis, MO 63166-0516.

LEVY, RENE HANANIA, PHARMACODYNAMICS. **Personal Data:** b Casa Blanca, Morocco, September 30, 1942. **Education:** Univ Bordeaux, Baccalaureat, 1960; Univ Paris, Pharm, 1965; Univ Calif, SanFrancisco, PhD (pharm, pharmaceut chem), 1970. **Professional Experience:** CHAIR PHARMACEUT, UNIV WASH, as of 2004; PROF PHARMACEUT, SCH PHARM, UNIV WASH, 1977-; PROF NEUROL SURG, SCH MED, UNIV WASH, 1977-; assoc prof, Col Pharm, 1974-1977; asst prof pharm, Col Pharm, 1970-1974; intern, Hosps Paris, Hopital Corentin Celton, 1964-1966. **Memberships:** Am Epilepsy Soc; Fedn Int Pharmaceut; Am Pharmaceut Asn; Acad Pharmaceut Sci. **Research Statement & Publications:** Pharmacokinetic evaluation of anticonvulsants prior to efficacy testing in primates; clinical pharmacology of new antiepileptic drugs; kinetics of drug metabolites; published over 20 articles. **Mailing Address:** Dept Pharm, Univ Wash, PO Box 357610, Seattle, WA 98195-7610. **E-Mail:** rhlevy@u.washington.edu

LEVY, RICARDO BENJAMIN, SURFACE CHEMISTRY, CHEMICAL ENGINEERING. **Personal Data:** b Quito, Ecuador, January 11, 1945; American citizen; m 1967, c 2. **Education:** Stanford Univ, BS, 1966, PhD (chem eng), 1972; Princeton Univ, MA, 1967. **Professional Experience:** CHMN & DIR, BD CATALYTICA ENERGY SYSTS INC, as of 2004; exec vpres consult res & develop, Catalytica Assocs, Inc, beginning 1977; vpres, Catalytica Assocs, Inc, 1974-1977; FOUNDER, CATALYTICA INC, 1974-; res eng chem physics, Exxon Res & Eng Co, 1972-1974; prof chem eng, Inst Politecnico Nac, Quito, Ecuador, 1967-1969; gen mgr mfg, Sudam Cia Ltda, 1967-1969. **Memberships:** Am Inst Chem Engrs; Am Chem Soc; Faraday Soc; Catalysis Soc. **Research Statement & Publications:** Reactivity of solid surfaces in catalytic reactions; new materials for catalysis; chemical vapor transport. **Mailing Address:** Catalytica, Inc, 430 Ferguson Dr, Mtain View, CA 94043. **Fax:** 415-960-0127.

LEVY, RICHARD, MEDICAL ENTOMOLOGY, CONTROLLED RELEASE TECHNOLOGY. **Personal Data:** b Brooklyn, NY, June 29, 1944. **Education:** Univ Fla, BS, 1967 & BS, 1968, MS, 1969, PhD (entom), 1971. **Professional Experience:** RES ENTOMOLOGIST MED ENTOM COORDR, LEE CO MOSQUITO CONTROL DIST, 1975-; res entomologist med entom, WFla Arthropod Res Lab, 1974-1975; tech & training consult pest control, Orkin Exterminating Co, 1974; res asst med entom, Dept Entom & Nematol, Univ Fla, 1971-1974; consult, US & overseas. **Memberships:** Am Registry Prof Entomologists; Entom Soc Am; Am Mosquito Control Asn; Am Chem Soc; Soc Invert Path; Controlled Release Soc; AAAS; Am Soc Testing Mats. **Research Statement & Publications:** Biological and chemical control of insects of medical and veterinary importance; US patents; overseas patents. **Mailing Address:** Lee Co Mosquito Control Dist, PO Box 06005, Ft Myers, FL 33906.

LEVY, RICHARD ALLEN, MEDICATION MANAGEMENT. **Education:** Univ Del, PhD (pharmacol), 1970. **Professional Experience:** VPRES SCI AFFAIRS, NAT PHARMACEUT COUN, 1981-. **Mailing Address:** Nat Pharmaceut Coun, 1894 Preston White Dr, Reston, VA 20191.

LEVY, RICHARD PHILIP, DIABETES, THROID DISEASE. **Personal Data:** b Hempstead, NY, November 3, 1923. **Education:** Yale Univ, BS, 1944, MD, 1947; Am Bd Internal Med, cert internal med, 1955, certendocrinol & metab, 1972. **Professional Experience:** ADJ PROF & INSTR, NORRIS COTTON CANCER CTR, DARTMOUTH HITCHCOCK MED CTR, as of 2001; RES PROF INTERNAL MED, NORTHEASTERN OHIO UNIVS COL MED, as of 2001; chmn, Dept Endocrinol, Med Ctr, St Thomas Hosp, beginning 1985; dir, chmn Inst Rev Bd, 1985-1989; dir, chmn Internal Med, 1983-1989; CLIN PROF MED, CASE WESTERN RESUNIV SCH MED, 1979-; PROF INTERNAL MED, NORTHEASTERN OHIO UNIVS COL MED, 1978-; prog dir, Internal Med, Canton Med Educ Found, 1978-1985; dir, Div Med, Northeastern Ohio Univs Col Med, 1978-1985; dir, Thyroid Ctr, Dept Med, Univ Hosps, 1975-1978; assoc prof, Case Western Res Univ, 1975-1978; from assoc prof to prof, Northeastern Ohio Univs Col Med, 1968-1978; asst prof radiol, Case Western Res Univ, 1968-1975; asst prof, Western Med Univ, 1961-1968; sr instr, Western Med Univ, 1958-1961; instr med, Western Med Univ, 1956-1958; teaching fel med, Zakraschefska fel med, 1955-1956, teaching fel med, Western Res Univ, 1954-1955, dir health serv, Univ Hosps, Cleveland, Ohio, 1953-1960; med consult, Cleveland State Hosp, 1953-1955; teaching fel med, Western Res Univ, 1953-1954; teaching fel, Univ Hosps, Cleveland, Ohio, 1952-1952. **Memberships:** Am Col Physicians; Am Diabetes Asn; Am Fedn Clin Res; Am Thyroid Asn; Endocrine Soc. **Research Statement & Publications:** Novel approaches to the treatment of insulin-requiring patients with diabetes; author of numerous scientific publications. **Mailing Address:** Norris Cotton Cancer Ctr, Dartmouth Hitchcock Med Ctr, One Med Ctr Dr, Lebanon, NH 03756. **Fax:** 603-650-2240.

LEVY, ROBERT, BIOCHEMISTRY, CLINICAL CHEMISTRY. **Personal Data:** b Montreal, Que, April 12, 1938. **Education:** McGill Univ, BS, 1959, PhD (biochem), 1965, Am Bd Clin Chem, dipl, 1980. **Professional Experience:** DIR LAB SERV, PATH DEPT, CHURCH HOSP CORP, 1971-; guest lectr, Towson State Col, 1969; asst prof neurobiol, Psychiat Inst, Univ Md, Baltimore City, 1967-1971; chief chemist, Vet Admin Hosp, Wash, DC, 1966-1967; asst prof, George Wash Univ, 1966-1967; NIH fel, Vet Admin Hosp, Univ Mo, Kansas City, 1964-1966. **Memberships:** AAAS; Am Asn Clin Chem. **Research Statement & Publications:** Neurochemistry of membranes; neurotransmitters; neuroenzymology; clinical enzymology. **Mailing Address:** 4010 Carthage Rd, Randallstown, MD 21133.

LEVY, ROBERT AARON, SOLID STATE PHYSICS, ACCIDENT RECONSTRUCTION. **Personal Data:** b El Paso, Tex, November 15, 1926. **Education:** Univ Tex, BS, 1947, MA, 1948; Univ Calif, Berkeley, MA, 1950, PhD (physics), 1955. **Professional Experience:** CONSULT PHYS PROB ENERGY & ENVIRON, 1969-, assoc prof, UnivCincinnati, 1963-1969; fel, Israel AEC, 1962-1963; physicists, Nat Co, 1961-1962; Assoc facmem, Ariz State Univ, 1958-1959 & Univ Southern Calif, 1960-1961; mem tech staff, HughesAircraft Co, 1959-1960; consult, US Naval Radiol Defense Lab, 1959; proj engr, Motorola, Inc, 1957-1959; physicist, Tex Instruments, Inc, 1955-1957; asst physics, Univ Calif, 1953-1955; Physicist, US Naval Radiol Defense Lab, 1950-1953. **Memberships:** AAAS; fel Am Phys Soc; Am Asn Univ Prof. **Research Statement & Publications:** Magnetic resonance spectroscopy; quantum electronics; solar energy. **Mailing Address:** 1617-D N Mesa St, El Paso, TX 79902-3527. **Fax:** 915-533-4327.

LEVY, ROBERT EDWARD, TECHNOLOGY PLANNING, ADVANCED PROCESS CONTROL. **Personal Data:** b Cincinnati, Ohio, May 23, 1939; m 1970, Candace; c Brian & Jessica. **Education:** Cornell Univ, BChE, 1962; Univ Calif, Berkeley, PhD (chem eng), 1967. **Professional Experience:** SR VPRES, UNIPURE CORP, 2000-; sr vpres, A F Dow & Assoc, 1998-1999; consult, 1997-; vpres govt & regulatory affairs, Energy Biosysts Corp, 1993-1997; vpres & dir technol develop, M W Kellogg Co, 1987-1993; independent consult, 1986-1987; engr & mgr, Exxon Corp, 1967-1986; actg instr process control, Univ Calif, Berkeley, 1965-1966. **Memberships:** Am Inst Chem Engrs; Sigma Xi; Indust Res Inst. **Research Statement & Publications:** Manage the scaleup and commercialization of breakthrough processes for; Desulfurization and upgrading of oil. **Mailing Address:** Unipure Corp, 12 Greenway Plaza Ste 1380, Houston, TX 77046. **Fax:** 713-850-7776. **E-Mail:** bob@unipurecorp.com

LEVY, ROBERT I, MEDICINE, BIOCHEMISTRY. **Personal Data:** b Bronx, NY, May 3, 1937. **Education:** Cornell Univ, BA, 1957; Yale Univ, MD, 1961. **Honors & Awards:** Arthur S Flemming Award, 1975; Humanitarian Award, Assoc Health Found, 1976; Am Asn Clin Chem Award, 1979; Donald D Van Slyke Award Clin Chem, 1980; AlbertLasker Spec Pub Health Award, 1980; Roger J Williams Award Prev Nutrit, 1985; HumanaHeart Found Award, 1988. **Professional Experience:** PRES, WYETH-AYERST RES, 1992-; adj prof med, Col Physicians & Surgeons, Columbia Univ, 1989-; pres, Sandoz Res Inst, 1988-1992; prof med, sr adv to Univ, 1984-1987; prof med, Col Physicians & Surgeons, 1983-1987; vpres health sci, Columbia Univ, 1983-1984; prof med, dean & vpres, Sch Med, Tufts Univ, 1981-1983; head, Sect Lipoproteins, 1975-1981; coordr, Cardiovasc Portion, US-USSR Agreement Health & Med Sci, 1975-1981; spec consult anti-lipid drugs, Food & Drug Admin, 1973-1983; dir, Div Heart & Vascular Dis, 1973-1975; mem & chmn numerous comts, councils & bd, 1970-; chief, Lipid Metab Br, 1970-1974; chief clin serv, Molecular Dis Br, 1969-1973; dep clin dir, Nat Heart Lung & Blood Inst, 1968-1969; inst dir, Nat Heart Lung & Blood Inst, 1966-1981; chief resident med, Nat Heart Lung & Blood Inst, 1965-1966; surgeon, USPHS, 1963-1966; clin asst med res, Nat Heart Lung & Blood Inst, 1963-1965; resident, Yale-New Haven Med Ctr, 1962-1963; intern med, Yale-New Haven Med Ctr, 1961-1962; mem, Coun Arteriosclerosis, Am Heart Asn. **Memberships:** Inst Med-Nat Acad Sci; fel NY Acad Sci; Am Soc Clin Invest; fel Am ColCardiol; Am Fedn Clin Res; fel Soc Behav Med; Am Inst Nutrit; Am Soc Clin Pharmacol &Therapeut; Asn Am Physicians; Int Soc Cardiol; Asn Univ Cardiologists; Int Soc Hypertension; Am Heart Asn; Am Soc Clin Nutrit. **Research Statement & Publications:** Lipid metabolism; lipid transport; atherosclerosis; hyperlipoproteinemia; lipoproteins; preventive cardiology; clinical nutrition; nutrition education. **Mailing Address:** Wyeth-Ayerst Res, PO Box 8299, Philadelphia, PA 19101. **Fax:** 610-995-4884.

LEVY, ROBERT SIGMUND, BIOCHEMISTRY, BIOLOGICAL PSYCHIATRY. **Personal Data:** b Fresno, Calif, November 3, 1921. **Education:** Univ Calif, Berkeley, AB, 1948, AM, 1952; Univ Southern Calif, PhD (biochem, nutrit), 1957. **Professional Experience:** EMER PROF, UNIV LOUISVILLE, AS OF AS OF 2004; dir, Lab-Biol Psychiat, beginning 1978; from asst prof to prof biochem, Sch Med, Univ Louisville, 1957-1972; asst biochem & nutrit, Sch Med, Univ Southern Calif, 1955-1957; asst zool, Univ Calif, Berkeley, 1949-1952; assoc psychiat & emergency med, Sch Med, Univ Louisville; fel, Coun Arteriosclerosis, Am Heart Asn. **Memberships:** Asn Multidiscipline Educ Health Sci; Sigma Xi; Am Chem Soc; Am Soc BiolChem; Soc Neuroscience. **Research Statement & Publications:** Isolation of unusual peptides from blood and hemodialysates of schizophrenic patients; detection of enkephalins and endorphins in biological fluids by radioimmunoassay and radioreceptor assay; biochemistry of brain function and role of neuropeptides; reversal of atherosclerosis by lipoproteins in cell culture. **Mailing Address:** Dept Psychiat, Univ Louisville Health Sci Ctr, Louisville, KY 40292. **Fax:** 502-588-6222.

LEVY, RONALD, MEDICINE. **Personal Data:** b Carmel, Calif. **Education:** Harvard Univ, BS; Stanford Univ, MD, 1968; Am Bd Internal Med, dipl. **Professional Experience:** CHIEF & PROF DIVI ONCOL, STANFORD UNIV, SCH MED, as of 2006; ASSOC PROF, DEPT MED-ONCOL, 2002-; MEM FAC, STANFORD UNIV, CALIF, 1975-; Helen Hay Whhitney Found fel, Dept Chem Immunol, Weizmann Inst Sci, Rehovot, Israel, 1973-1975; res, Mass Gen Hosp, Boston, 1969-1970; Intern, Mass GenHosp, Boston, 1968-1969. **Memberships:** Am Col Physicians; Am Soc Clin Oncol. **Research Statement & Publications:** Cancer research; oncology; medicine. **Mailing Address:** Dept Med-Oncol, Stanford Univ, 269 Campus Dr CCSR 1126, Stanford, CA 94305-5306. **Fax:** 650-725-1420. **E-Mail:** levy@stanford.edu

LEVY, RONALD FRED, TOPOLOGY. **Personal Data:** b St Louis, Mo, December 11, 1944; m 1966, c 1. **Education:** Wash Univ, BA, 1966, AM, 1970, PhD (math), 1974. **Professional Experience:** PROF MATH, GEORGE MASON UNIV, as of 2005; assoc prof math, George Mason Univ, beginning 1981; asst prof, George Mason Univ, 1976-1981; instr math, Wash Univ, 1975-1976; asst prof math, Goucher Col, 1974-1975. **Memberships:** Am Math Soc; Math Asn Am. **Research Statement & Publications:** Compact Hausdorff spaces; almost-P-spaces; linearly ordered topological spaces; Settheoretic Topology. **Mailing Address:** Dept Math, George Mason Univ, Rm 201B Sci & Technol Bldg I, Fairfax, VA 22030. **Fax:** 703-993-1491. **E-Mail:** rlevy@gmu.edu

LEVY, SALOMON, MECHANICAL ENGINEERING. **Personal Data:** b Jerusalem, April 4, 1926; American citizen; m 1951, Eileen; c Marshall & Linda. **Education:** Univ Calif, Berkeley, BS, 1949, MS, 1951, PhD (mech eng), 1953. **Honors & Awards:** Heat Transfer Mem Award, Am Soc Mech Engrs, 1966; Thermal Hydraul Div Tech Achievement Award, Am Nuclear Soc, 1987, Walter H Zinn Award, 1989; Donald Q Kern Award, Am Inst Chem Engrs, 1993. **Professional Experience:** CONSULT, LEVY & ASSOCS, 1994-; dir, Iowa Elec, 1985-; pres, S Levy Inc, Eng Consult, 1977-1994; mem, Brookhaven Nat Lab, 1977-; mem, Elec Power Res Inst, 1977-1985; consult, Assoc Midwestern Univ, 1976-1981; gen mgr boiling water reactor opers, Gen Elec Co, 1975-1977; gen mgr boiling water reactor systs dept, Gen Elec Co, 1973-1975; gen mgr nuclear fuel dept, Gen Elec Co, 1971-1973; mgr design eng dept, Gen Elec Co, 1968-1971; mgr systs eng, Gen Elec Co, 1966-1968. **Memberships:** Nat Acad Eng; fel Am Soc Mech Engrs; fel Am Nuclear Soc; Honorary Mem ASHE. **Research Statement & Publications:** Heat transfer and fluid flow, particularly two-phase flow and boiling heat transfer; nuclear reactor power plant design and analysis; authored over 50 publications. **Mailing Address:** Levy & Assocs, 3880 S Bascom Ave Ste 112, San Jose, CA 95124. **Fax:** 408-377-2846.

LEVY, SAMUEL C, ELECTROCHEMISTRY, ELECTROANALYTICAL CHEMISTRY. **Personal Data:** b Far Rockaway, NY, January 5, 1937. **Education:** Hofstra Col, BA, 1958; Iowa State Univ, PhD (inorg chem), 1962. **Professional Experience:** RETIRED; distinguished mem tech staff, Sandia Nat Labs, 1993-1996; vchmn, Battery Div, Electrochem Soc, 1992-1994; treas, Battery Div, Electrochem Soc, 1990-1992; staff mem, Sandia Nat Labs, 1962-1993. **Memberships:** Am Chem Soc; Electrochem Soc. **Research Statement & Publications:** Chemical to electrical energy conversion; mechanism of electrochemical reactions; lithium and lithium-ion battery research and development. **Mailing Address:** Sandia Labs, Div 2223 PO Box 5800, Albuquerque, NM 87185-0614.

LEVY, SAMUEL WOLFE, CLINICAL CHEMISTRY. **Personal Data:** b Montreal, Que, February 26, 1922. **Education:** McGill Univ, BSc, 1949, PhD (physiol), 1954; Univ Sask, MSc, 1951. **Honors & Awards:** Ames Award, Can Soc Clin Chem, 1975. **Professional Experience:** CONSULT, ST ANNE D'BELLEVUE HOSP, 1996-; dir, Dept Biochem, Queen Elizabeth Hosp, Montreal, 1979-1996; Dept Vet Affairs grant, 1964-1971; dir, DeptBiochem, Queen Mary Vet Hosp, Montreal, 1961-1979; Dom-Prov Health grant, 1956-1961; res assoc, Hotel-Dieu Hosp, Montreal, 1956-1961; Multiple Sclerosis Soc Can res fel biochem, McGill-Montreal Gen Hosp Res Inst, 1954-1956. **Memberships:** Chem Inst Can; Can Soc Clin Chem (pres, 1970-1971); Am Asn Clin Chem. **Research Statement & Publications:** Lysosomal enzymes in blood in inflammation disease; effects of heparin in vivo on enzymes and lipid in blood; serum ribonuclease; assay, properties and alterations in disease. **Mailing Address:** 5629 W Lake Ave, Cote St Luc, PQ H4W 2N3, Can.

LEVY, SANDER ALVIN, METALLURGY. **Education:** Lehigh Univ, BS & BA, 1962, PhD (elec eng), 1965. **Professional Experience:** PRES, ALUBEST CONSULT LLC, RICHMOND, VA, as of 2001; sr metallurgist, Metall Lab, Reynolds Metals Co, beginning 1990; tech specialist, Dept Mfg Technol, 1987-1990; mgr, Dept Mfg Technol, 1982-1986; mgr, DeptIngot Casting Technol & Metall Serv, 1978-1982; supvr, Ingot Casting Technol Sect, 1970-1978; res scientist, Metall Lab, Reynolds Metals Co, 1968-1970; casting res, Pittman Dun Res Labs, Frankford Arsenal, US Army & teacher welding metall, Drexel Inst Technol, 1966-1968; Mem tech staff, Bell Tel Labs, Murray Hill, NJ, 1965-1966. **Research Statement & Publications:** Metallurgy; ingot casting technology; molten metal quality for aluminum alloys; diamond machine of aluminum. **Mailing Address:** AluBest Consult LLC, Richmond, VA 23233.

LEVY, STUART B, MOLECULAR BIOLOGY, MICROBIOLOGY. **Personal Data:** b Wilmington, Del, November 21, 1938. **Education:** Williams Col, AB, 1960; Univ Pa, MD, 1965. **Honorary Degrees:** Biology, Wesleyan Univ, 1998, Des Moines Univ, 2001. **Honors & Awards:** Hoechst-Roussel Award, Am Soc Microbiol. **Professional Experience:** DIR, CTR ADAPTATION GENETICS & DRUG RESISTANCE, MED SCH, TUFTS UNIV, BOSTON, 1992-; lectr, Australian Soc Microbiol, 1990-; mem, Sci Eval Comt, Pasteur Inst, Paris, 1990; mem, Comt Environ Microbiol, Am Soc Microbiol, 1989-; lectr, Am Soc Microbiol Found, 1989-1990; mem, Subcomt Health & Antibiotic Resistance, Environ Protection Agency, 1988-; mem, Subcomt on Plasmid Ref Ctr Collection, Comt on Genetic & Molecular Microbiol, Am Soc Microbiol, 1986; mem, subcomt, Gram-Negative Facultatively Anaerobic Rods, Am Soc Metals, 1985-1988; consult, Food & Drug Admin, Wash, DC, 1985-1987; pres, Boston Blood Club, 1984; gen chmn, Int Task Forces on Use Antibiotics Worldwide, Fogarty Int Ctr, NIH, 1983-1986; overseas vis, Bd Postgrad Med Educ, Royal Melbourne Hosp, Australia, 1983-1984; pres, Alliance for Prudent Use Antibiotics, 1981-; adv, Fate Earth, Inc, 1981-; PROF MED, MOLECULAR BIOL & MICROBIOL, MED SCH, TUFTS UNIV, BOSTON, 1980-; consult, Food & Drug Admin, Wash, DC, 1978-1980; sci adv, Biomed Res Ctr, Univ Nat Pedro Henriquez Urena, Santo Domingo, Dominion Republic, 1977-1983; staff scientist, Cancer Res Ctr, Med Sch, Tufts Univ, 1976-; staff physician, Northeast Med Ctr Hosp, Boston, Mass, 1976-; Pasteur Inst, Paris, France, 1976; res career develop award, 1972-1977; from asst prof to assoc prof, Ctr Adaptation Genetics & Drug Resistance, 1971-1980; collabr, EAfrican Viral Inst, Entebbe, Uganda, 1971; fel hemat, New Eng Med Ctr, Boston, Mass, 1970-1971, vis prof, Dept Path, Univ Padua, Italy, 1970; staff assoc, Nat Inst Arthritis & Metab Dis, NIH, Bethesda, Md, 1967-1970; res fel, Dept Cellular Biol, 1966-1967; intern & med resident, Mt Sinai Hosp, NY, 1965-1967; publiker nutrit fel, Kenyatta Nat Hosp, Nairobi, 1964; res fel, Dept Microbiol, Keio Univ, Tokyo, 1964, res fel, Dept Microbiol, Univ Milan, Italy, 1962; President ASM 1998-1999. **Memberships:** Am Asn Cancer Res; Am Soc Biochem & Molecular Biol; Am Soc Clin Invest; Am Soc Hemat; Am Soc Microbiol; Infectious Dis Soc Am. **Research Statement & Publications:** Resistance to antibiotics and anticancer drugs. **Mailing Address:** Dept Molecular Biol & Microbiol, Sch Med, Tufts Univ, 136 Harrison Ave, Boston, MA 02111. **Fax:** 617-636-0458. **E-Mail:** stuart.levy@tufts.edu

LEW, CHEL WING, CHEMISTRY. **Personal Data:** b San Antonio, Tex, December 9, 1935. **Education:** Tex A&M Univ, BS, 1960. **Professional Experience:** RETIRED; from asst res chemist to sr res chemist, Southwest Res Inst, 1961-1994; technician chem, Southwest Res Inst, 1960-1961. **Memberships:** Sigma Xi. **Research Statement & Publications:** Microencapsulation. **Mailing Address:** 9218 Old Homestead, San Antonio, TX 78230.

LEW, GLORIA MARIA, BIOCHEMISTRY & NEUROCHEMISTRY, PHARMACOLOGY. **Personal Data:** b Kingston, Jamaica, March 7, 1934. **Education:** Mt St Vincent Col, BA, 1956; Boston Col, MS, 1958; Univ Calif, Berkeley, PhD (zoology), 1972. **Professional Experience:** RETIRED; prof anat, Mich State Univ, beginning 1992; from asst prof to assoc prof, Mich State Univ, 1972-1992; asst prof, Cardinal Cushing Col, 1968-1969; instr biol, Cardinal Cushing Col, 1966-1968; chmn, Sci Dept, Alpha Jr Col, 1964-1966. **Memberships:** Am Soc Zoologists; Am Soc Neuroscience; Am Physiol Soc; Int Soc Chronobiol; Am Asn Anatomists; Am Soc Neurochem. **Research Statement & Publications:** Circadian rhythms in catecholamine metabolism; effects of estrogen on catecholamine metabolism in genetic hypertension; biochemistry and ultrastructure of pineal gland effects of cocaine and PCP on neurochemistry of developing rats; molecular effects of drugs and hormones on neuroblastomas. **Mailing Address:** 746 Beech St, East Lansing, MI 48823. **E-Mail:** lew@msu.edu

LEW, HIN, PHYSICS. **Personal Data:** b Vancouver, BC, April 18, 1921. **Education:** Univ BC, BA, 1940; Univ Toronto, MA, 1942; Mass Inst Technol, PhD (physics), 1948. **Professional Experience:** GUEST SCIENTIST, NAT RES COUN CAN, 1985-; assoc & sr res officeratomic beams & molecular spectros, Nat Res Coun Can, 1949-1985; res assoc atomic beams, Mass Inst Technol, 1948-1949; Jr res physicist acoust, Nat Res Coun Can, 1942-1945. **Memberships:** Am Phys Soc; Can Asn Physicists. **Research Statement & Publications:** Hyperfine structure of atoms and molecules by the atomic beam magnetic resonance method; spectra and structure of molecular ions. **Mailing Address:** 28 Parkridge Crescent, Gloucester, ON K1B 3E7, Can.

LEW, JOHN S, APPLIED MATHEMATICS. **Personal Data:** b New York, NY, September 9, 1934. **Education:** Yale Univ, BS, 1955; Princeton Univ, PhD (physics), 1960. **Professional Experience:** RES STAFF MEM MATH SCI, T J WATSON RES CTR, IBM CORP, 1970-; asst prof appl math, Brown Univ, 1964-1970; C L E Moore instr math, Mass Inst Technol, 1962-1964. **Memberships:** Math Asn Am; Soc Indust & Appl Math; Sigma Xi. **Research Statement & Publications:** Applied analysis, especially asymptotic expansions; lattice points. **Mailing Address:** 122 Morningside Dr, Ossining, NY 10562-3010.

LEW, VEE MING, MATHEMATICS. **Education:** Cornell Univ, PhD, 1993. **Professional Experience:** ASSOC PROF MATH & COMPUT SCI, WILKES UNIV, as of 2005. **Mailing Address:** Math Dept, Wilkes Univ, 418 Stark Learning Ctr, Wilkes-Barre, PA 18766. **Fax:** 570-408-7871. **E-Mail:** veeming.lew@wilkes.edu

LEWANDOS, GLENN S, ORGANIC CHEMISTRY. **Personal Data:** b Dallas, Tex, February 23, 1945. **Education:** Southern Methodist Univ, BS, 1967; Univ Tex, Austin, PhD (chem), 1972. **Professional Experience:** Am Chem Soc Grant, 1988-1991; PROF CHEM, CENT MICH UNIV, 1985-; Am Chem Soc Grant, 1981-1984; Res Corp Grant, 1978-1980; from asst prof to assoc prof, Cent Mich Univ, 1977-1985, vis asst prof, Univ Tex, Austin, 1976-1977; asst prof chem, Sul Ross State Univ, 1972-1976. **Memberships:** Am Chem Soc; Royal Soc Chem. **Research Statement & Publications:** Synthesis and reactivity of organometallic pi complexes; catalysis by transition metals; crown ethers. **Mailing Address:** Dept Chem, Cent Mich Univ, Dow 361, Mt Pleasant, MI 48859. **Fax:** 989-774-3883. **E-Mail:** lewan1gs@mail.cmich.edu

LEWANDOWSKI, DOUGLAS E, MEDICAL RESEARCH. **Education:** Univ Chicago, AB, 1979. **Professional Experience:** ASSOC PROF RADIOL, HARVARD MED SCH, as of 1996; DIR, NUCLEAR MAGNETIC RESONANCE CTR BIOCHEM LAB, MASS GEN HOSP, as of 1996. **Mailing Address:** Nuclear Magnetic Resonance Ctr, Mass Gen Hosp, 13th St Bldg 149, Charlestown, MA 02129. **E-Mail:** doug@nmr.mgh.harvard.edu

LEWANDOWSKI, GORDON A, BIOLOGICAL TREATMENT OF HAZARDOUS WASTE. **Personal Data:** b Brooklyn, NY, February 3, 1945. **Education:** Polytech Inst Brooklyn, BS, 1965, MS, 1966; Columbia Univ, DEngSci, 1970. **Professional Experience:** DISTINGUISHED PROF, DEPT CHEM ENG, NJ INST TECHNOL, as of 2003; dept chmn chemeng, chem & environ sci, 1988-1993; prof chem eng, NJ Inst Technol, beginning

1986; from asst prof to assoc prof, NJ Inst Technol, 1977-1986; sr proj engr, Jacobs Eng Co, 1976-1977; proj engr, Exxon Res & Eng Co, 1973-1976; Res engr, FMC Corp, 1970-1973. **Memberships:** Am Inst Chem Engrs; Am Chem Soc. **Research Statement & Publications:** Biological treatment of hazardous waste (theoretical and experimental); in-situ treatment; sequencing batch reactors; reactor engineering. **Mailing Address:** Dept Chem Eng, NJ Inst Technol, 323 High St, Newark, NJ 07102. **E-Mail:** lewandow@adm.njit.edu

LEWANDOWSKI, JOHN JOSEPH, STRUCTURE PROPERTY RELATIONSHIPS & MECHANICAL BEHAVIOR OF METALS, COMPOSITES & BIOMEDICAL MATERIALS & DEFORMATION PROCESSING. **Personal Data:** b Pittsburgh, Pa, December 17, 1956; m 1983, Amy; c John R & Mark E. **Education:** Carnegie Mellon Univ, BS, 1979, ME, 1981, PhD (metall eng & mat sci), 1983. **Honors & Awards:** Overseas Fellow - Churchill College, Cambridge University, 2003; Highly Cited Researcher, ISI, 2003-present; Leonard Case Professorship, CWRU, 2000-present; CTSC Tech Educr Award, Cleveland Tech Soc, 2000; Charles Hatchett Award, Inst of Metals, UK, 1999; Res Silver Medal, Am Soc Metals Int, 1997; Bradley Stoughton Award, Am Soc Metals Int, 1989; Ralph R Teetor Educ Award, Soc Automotive Engrs, 1992; NSF Presidential Investigator Award, NSF, 1989-1994; NATO/NSF Postdoctoral Fellowship, NATO/NSF, 1984-1986. **Professional Experience:** Overseas Fellow, Churchill College - Cambridge University, 2003-2004; Chmn, TMS/ASM Composites Comt, 2001-2003; LEONARD CASE PROF ENG, CASE WESTERN RES UNIV, 2000-present; chmn, Gordon Conf on Phys Metall, Gordon Res Confs, 2000; mem, NRC fel panel, 1997-2003; prof mat sci & eng, Case Western Res Univ, 1994-2000; mem, Long Term Aging Effects Panel, 1994-1996; AFSTB Comt Hypersonics, 1997-1998; NSF Presidential Young Investr Award, NSF, 1989-1994; mem, Star-Bast Nat Comt, Nat Acad Sci, 1989-1991; vis scientist, Wright Patterson AFB, 1987; Director - Mechanical Characterization Facility, CWRU, 1987-present; vis scientist, Univ Cambridge, UK, 1986; from asst prof to prof, Case Western Res Univ, 1986-1993; NATO fel, Univ Cambridge, UK, 1984-1986; Hertz Found fel, Carnegie Mellon Univ, 1981-1983; Allegheny Int fel metall eng & mat sci, Carnegie Mellon Univ, 1979-1981; co-op metall engr, Chevron, USA, 1976-1979. **Memberships:** Minerals, Metals & Math Soc; fel Am Soc Metals Int; Math Res Soc; Soc Advan Mat & Process Eng; Soc Automotive Engrs; Sigma Xi. **Research Statement & Publications:** Effects of microstructure on deformation and fracture of materials, including crystalline and amorphous metals, intermetallics, ceramics, biomaterials and composites; effects of high pressure on deformation and fracture, including deformation processing, failure analysis, environmental effects, fracture and fatigue; blast resistant materials; bulk metallic glasses and composites. **Mailing Address:** Dept Materials Sci & Eng, Case Western Reserve Univ, Cleveland, OH 44106. **Fax:** 216-368-8618. **E-Mail:** JJL3@case.edu

LEWANDOWSKI, MELVIN A, CHEMICAL ENGINEERING. **Personal Data:** b Chicago, Ill, December 8, 1930. **Education:** Northwestern Univ, BS, 1954; Univ Chicago, MBA, 1974. **Professional Experience:** RETIRED; vpres & gen mgr, Richmond Lox, 1986-1988; consult, Lindsay Int Sales, 1985-1986; develop fertilizer group, Int Minerals & Chem Corp, 1983-1985; vpres chem group, Int Minerals & Chem Corp, 1980-1983; corp staff vpres res & develop, Int Minerals & Chem Corp, 1978-1980; exec vpres, Chinhae Chem Co, Seoul, Korea, 1975-1978; mgr eng & distrib, Int Minerals & Chem Corp, 1965-1974; purchasing agt, Int Minerals & Chem Corp, 1961-1965; Res engr, Int Minerals & Chem Corp, 1957-1961. **Memberships:** Am Inst Chem Engrs; Am Chem Soc. **Research Statement & Publications:** Administration. **Mailing Address:** 9917 N Calle Loma Linda, Oro Valley, AZ 85737. **Fax:** 520-544-7715.

LEWARS, ERROL GEORGE, ORGANIC CHEMISTRY. **Education:** London Univ, BSc, 1964; Univ Toronto, PhD (chem), 1968. **Professional Experience:** Adj prof chem, Queen's Univ, as of 2006; PROF CHEM, TRENT UNIV, 1986-; from asst prof to assoc prof, Trent Univ, 1973-1985; fel, Trent Univ, 1972-1973; Fel chem, Univ Western Ont, 1970-1972; Fel chem, Harvard Univ, 1968-1970. **Memberships:** Am Chem Soc. **Research Statement & Publications:** Synthetic organic chemistry; compounds of theoretical interest. **Mailing Address:** Dept Chem, Trent Univ, CSB E106, Peterborough, ON K9J 7B8, Can. **E-Mail:** elewars@trentu.ca

LEWBART, MARVIN LOUIS, BIOCHEMISTRY. **Personal Data:** b Philadelphia, Pa, May 28, 1929. **Education:** Philadelphia Col Pharm & Sci, BSc, 1951, MSc, 1953; Jefferson Med Col, MD, 1957; Univ Minn, PhD (biochem), 1961. **Professional Experience:** RETIRED; dir, Steroid Lab, Crozer-Chester Med Ctr, 1975-1990; clin assocprof med, Hahnemann Med Col, 1975-1990; assoc med dir, Franklin Mint Corp, 1974-1982; from asst prof to assoc prof med, Jefferson Med Col, 1967-1975; res assoc, Jefferson Med Col, 1962-1967; USPHS spec res fel, Univ Basel, 1961-1962, USPHS res fel, 1959-1961, felbiochem, Mayo Found, Univ Minn, 1958-1961; intern med, Lankenau Hosp, 1957-1958; resassoc biochem, Jefferson Med Col, 1953-1957; Intern pharm, Jefferson Med Col, 1951-1952. **Memberships:** AMA; Am Chem Soc; AAAS. **Research Statement & Publications:** Steroid chemistry and metabolism. **Mailing Address:** 333 Lancaster Ave, Malvern, PA 19355.

LEWELLEN, ROBERT THOMAS, GENETICS, PLANT BREEDING. **Personal Data:** b Nyssa, Ore, April 27, 1940; m 1962, Priscilla. **Education:** Ore State Univ, BS, 1962; Mont State Univ, PhD (genetics), 1966. **Honors & Awards:** Meritorious Award, Am Soc Sugar Beet Technol. **Professional Experience:** RES GENETICIST, AGR RES SERV, USDA, 1966-; asst agronomist, Mont State Univ, 1965-1966; appointment, Exp Sta, Univ Calif, Davis. **Memberships:** Fel Am Soc Agron; Crop Sci Soc Am; Am Phytopath Soc; Am Soc Sugar Beet Technol. **Research Statement & Publications:** Genetics of disease resistance in sugar beet, Beta vulgaris, and development of resistant lines; germplasm enhancement of beta genetic resources. **Mailing Address:** Agr Res Sta, USDA Agr Res Serv, 1636 E Alisal St, Salinas, CA 93905. **Fax:** 831-755-2814. **E-Mail:** rlewellen@pw.ars.usda.gov

LEWELLEN, WILLIAM STEPHEN, FLUID DYNAMICS. **Personal Data:** b Reedy, WVa, August 7, 1933. **Education:** WVa Univ, BS, 1957; Cornell Univ, MAeroE, 1959; Univ Calif, Los Angeles, PhD (eng), 1964. **Professional Experience:** RES PROF, WVA UNIV, 1993-; sr consult, CRT Inc, 1987-1993; sr vpres, Aeronaut Res Assoc Princeton, Inc, 1982-1986; adv comt, Mech & Aerospace Eng, WVa Univ, beginning 1981; vpres fluid mech, Aeronaut Res Assoc Princeton, Inc, 1979-1982; assoc ed, Am InstAeronaut & Astronaut J, 1978-1979; sr consult, Aeronaut Res Assoc Princeton, Inc, 1972-1979; consult, Aerojet Gen Corp, 1968-1970; assoc prof, Mass Inst Technol, 1967-1972; vis assoc profaeronaut & astronaut, Mass Inst Technol, 1966-1967; mgr fluid dynamics sect, Aerospace Corp, 1964-1966; mem tech staff, Aerospace Corp, 1960-1964; mem tech staff, Space Tech Labs, Inc, 1959-1960. **Memberships:** AAAS; Am Inst Aeronaut & Astronaut; Am Meteorol Soc. **Research Statement & Publications:** Energy conversion; fluid dynamics of vortex flows; micrometeorology; computer modeling of turbulent transport; pollutant dispersal. **Mailing Address:** Dept Mech & Aerospace Eng, WVa Univ, PO Box 6106, Morgantown, WV 26506-6106. **Fax:** 304-293-6689. **E-Mail:** william.lewellen@mail.wvu.edu

LEWENZ, GEORGE F, ORGANIC CHEMISTRY. **Personal Data:** b Berlin, Ger, August 29, 1920. **Education:** Western Res Univ, BS, 1947, MS, 1952. **Professional Experience:** RETIRED; res specialist, Dow Chem Co, 1973-1986; sr info chemist, 1971-1973; res logician, 1968-1971, chemist, Esso Res & Eng Co, NJ, 1959-1968; chemist, Texaco Inc, 1953-1958; aeronaut res scientist, NASA, 1948-1953. **Memberships:** Am Chem Soc; fel Am Inst Chemists. **Research Statement & Publications:** Organic synthesis; abstracting, indexing and information science. **Mailing Address:** 2305 Burlington Dr, Midland, MI 48642.

LEWERT, ROBERT MURDOCH, medical parasitology, immunology; deceased, see previous edition for last biography

LEWETT, GEORGE P, SYSTEMS DESIGN & SYSTEMS SCIENCE, OPERATIONS RESEARCH. **Personal Data:** b June 5, 1926. **Education:** Syracuse Univ, BS, 1950; Rutgers Univ, MA, 55. **Professional Experience:** DIR, OFF TECH INNOVATION, NAT INST STAND & TECHNOL, 1976-; prog mgr opers res, Off Tech Innovation, Nat Inst Stand & Technol, 1973-1976; CRU Inc, 1972-1973; Matrix Res Corp, 1965-1978; prog mgr, Tech Oprs Inc, 1963-1968; dept chief opers resmfg & eng, Western Elec, 1951-1963. **Memberships:** Technol Transfer Soc; Am Inst Indust Engrs. **Research Statement & Publications:** Manage an evaluation service providing assessments of technical and commercial feasibility of inventions and new technological applications. **Mailing Address:** Nat Inst Stand & Technol, Bldg 820 Rm 264, Gaithersburg, MD 20899-0001. **E-Mail:** george.lewett@nist.gov

LEWIN, ALFRED S, RNA CATALYSIS, GENE THERAPY & MITOCHONDRIA. **Personal Data:** b Chicago, Ill, April 25, 1951; m 1972, c 3. **Education:** Univ Chicago, AB, 1973, PhD (biol), 1978. **Honors & Awards:** Jr Fac Res Award, Am Cancer Soc, 1982; Estab Investr, Am Heart Asn, 1987. **Professional Experience:** PROF MOLECULAR GENETICS & MICROBIOL, UNIV FLA, 1995-; assoc prof immunol & med microbiol, Univ Fla, 1987-1995; vis prof, Univ Paris-South, 1985; jr fac res award, Am Cancer Soc, 1982; asst prof chem, Ind Univ, 1981-1987; Europ Molecular Biol Orgn fel, 1978-; acad asst biochem, Biocenter Univ, Basel, 1978-1981. **Memberships:** Am Soc Microbiol; Soc Am; AAAS; ARVO, ASBMB, ASGT. **Research Statement & Publications:** RNA catalysis-mechanisms and applications; Gene therapy for retinal, diseases and neurodegenerative diseases, gene therapy for cardio vascular diseases. **Mailing Address:** Dept Molecular Genetics & Microbiol, Univ Fla Col Med, PO Box 100266, Gainesville, FL 32610-0266. **E-Mail:** lewin@ufl.edu

LEWIN, ANITA HANA, PHYSICAL ORGANIC CHEMISTRY, MOLECULAR MODELLING. **Personal Data:** b Bucarest, Rumania, October 27, 1935; m 1956, Arie; c Tal M & Oren C. **Education:** Univ Calif, Los Angeles, BS, 1959, PhD (phys org chem), 1963. **Professional Experience:** SR RES CHEMIST, RES TRIANGLE INST, 1975-; fel, Res Triangle Inst, 1974-1975; from asst prof to assoc prof, Polytech Inst Brooklyn, 1966-1974; res asst prof chem, Univ Pittsburgh, 1964-1966. **Memberships:** Am Chem Soc. **Research Statement & Publications:** Reaction mechanisms; conformational analysis; retinoids-synthesis and properties; organic synthesis; synthesis of radiolabeled compounds; molecular modeling; receptor binding; alkaloid synthesis; structure activity correlations; peptide synthesis; glutamatergic system; Dopamine transporter. **Mailing Address:** Chem & Life Sci Group, PO Box 12194, Research Triangle Park, NC 27709-2194. **Fax:** 919-541-8868.

LEWIN, JONATHAN W, MATHEMATICS. **Education:** Univ Wis-Mad, PhD. **Professional Experience:** PROF, DEPT MATHS, KENNESAW STATE COL, as of 2006. **Mailing Address:** Dept Math, Kennesaw State Col, 1000 Chastain Rd NW, Kennesaw, GA 30144. **Fax:** 770-423-6629. **E-Mail:** jlewin@kennesaw.edu

LEWIN, JOYCE CHISMORE, MICROBIOLOGY. **Personal Data:** b Ilion, NY, November 13, 1926. **Education:** Cornell Univ, BS, 1948; Yale Univ, MS, 1950, PhD (bot, microbiol), 1953. **Professional Experience:** RETIRED; res prof oceanog, Univ Wash, 1974-; fromasst prof to prof, UnivWash, 1965-1974; asst res biologist, Scripps Inst, Univ Calif, San Diego, 1960-1965; res assocmarine biol, Woods Hole Oceanog Inst, 1956-1960; Guest res worker, Biol Lab, Nat Res CounCan, 1952-1955. **Memberships:** Am Soc Limnol & Oceanog; Phycol Soc Am; Am Inst Biol Sci; Marine Biol AsnUK; Int Phycol Soc. **Research Statement & Publications:** Culture of marine microalgae, especially diatoms; physiology and nutrition of marine diatoms; physiology and ecology of surf diatom blooms. **Mailing Address:** Sch Oceanog WB-10, Univ Wash, Seattle, WA 98195.

LEWIN, KLAUS J, PATHOLOGY, GASTROENTEROLOGY. **Personal Data:** b Jerusalem, Israel, August 10, 1936; American citizen. **Education:** Westminster Med Sch, London, Eng, MB & BS, 1959; Univ London, MD, 1966; Am Bd Path, dipl; FRC Path (Fel, Royal Col Path, England). **Honors & Awards:** Arris & Gale lectr, Royal Col Surgeons, 1968; Class Prize Surgery resident Teaching Award, Pathology UCLA 1998, Schwabe-Walsh Award UCLA_Gi Division 2002, President of the Gastro Pathology Soc 1985-1986 Chesterfield Medal, Inst Dermat, 1966. **Professional Experience:** PROF DEPT MED, DIV GASTENTEROL, 1986-; pres, Los Angeles Soc Pathologists Inc, 1985-1986; PROF PATH, MED SCH, UNIV CALIF, LOS ANGELES, 1980-; vchmn path, Los Angeles, 1979-1986; Mem, Curric Comt, Univ Calif, Riverside, 1977-1984; assoc prof, Dept Med, Div Gastenterol, 1977-1980; asst prof, Stanford Univ Med Sch, 1970-1976; vis asst prof path, Stanford Univ Med Sch, 1968-1970; rotating sr registr morbid anat, Royal Devon Exeter Hosp, 1964-1968; registr, Dept Morbid Anat, 1962-1964; Resident pathologist clin chem, bact, hemat, blood transfusion & serology, Westminster Hosp, Med Sch, 1961-1962; consult, Wadsworth Vet Affairs Hosp, Nat Cancer Inst, Sepulveda Vet Affairs Hosp. **Memberships:** Fel Royal Col Pathologists; Path Soc Gt Brit; Am Gastenterol Soc; Gastrointestinal Path Soc (pres 1985-1986); US Acad Path; Can Acad Path; Asn Clin Pathologists; Path & Bact Soc Gt Brit; Int Acad Path; Cal Soc of Path; Los Angeles Path Soc. **Research Statement & Publications:** Gastrointestinal pathology; cancer research; bacteriology; hematology; structure, function and pathologic disorders of gastrointestinal tract and liver. **Mailing Address:** Dept Path, Univ Calif Sch Med, 10833 Le Conte Ave, Los Angeles, CA 90024. **Fax:** 310-206-5178. **E-Mail:** klewin@pathlogy.medsch.ucla.edu

LEWIN, LEONARD, ELECTRICAL ENGINEERING, MATHEMATICS & EDUCATION. **Personal Data:** b Southend, Eng, July 22, 1919. **Honorary Degrees:** DSc, Univ Colo, 1967. **Honors & Awards:** Premium Awards, Brit Inst Elec Engrs, 1952 & 1960; Microwave Prize & W GBaker Award, Inst Elec & Electronics Engrs, 1962; Prestige Lectr, Nat Inst Elec Eng, NZ, 1987; MicrowaveCareer Award, Microwave Theory & Techniques Soc, 1993. **Professional Experience:** PROF EMER ELEC ENG, UNIV COLO, BOULDER, 1987-; Consult, MassInst Technol Lincoln Labs, 1985-1993; Fulbright fel, 1982; consult, Nat Bur Stand, 1978-1990; coordr telecommun prog, Univ Colo, Boulder, 1974-1986; Sci Res Coun Grants, UK, 1973 & 1975; consult, Westinghouse Corp, 1971; consult, Medion Ltd, 1970-1990; Consult, Stand Telecommun Labs, 1968-1990; prof, Univ Colo, Boulder, 1968-1986; sr prin reselectromagnetic theory, Stand Telecommun Labs, 1967-1968; asst mgr transmissions, StandTelecommun Labs, 1960-1966; dept head, Stand Telecommun Labs, 1950-1960; sr engrmicrowaves, Stand Telecommun Labs, 1946-1950; Sci officer radar, Brit Admiralty, 1941-1945. **Memberships:** Fel Brit Interplanetary Soc; Brit Inst Elec Engrs; fel Inst Elec & Electronics Engrs. **Research Statement & Publications:** Electromagnetic theory; wave propagation; waveguides and antennas; mathematics; mathematical applications to engineering; history and properties of the polylogarithmic functions. **Mailing Address:** Dept Elec Eng Campus, PO Box 425, Univ Colo, Boulder, CO 80309.

LEWIN, RALPH ARNOLD, PHYCOLOGY. **Personal Data:** b London, Eng, April 30, m 1969, Lanna. **Education:** Cambridge Univ, BA, 1942, MA, 1946, ScD, 1972; Yale Univ, MS, 1949, PhD, 1950. **Honors & Awards:** Darbaker Prize, Bot Soc Am, 1958. **Professional Experience:** PROF EXP PHYCOL, SCRIPPS INST OCEANOG, UNIV CALIF, 1967-; assoc prof marine biol, Scripps Inst Oceanog, Univ Calif, 1959-1967; investr phycol, NIH grant, Marine Biol Lab, Woods Hole, 1955-1959; asst res off biol, Maritime Regional Lab, Nat Res Coun Can, 1952-1955; instr bot, Yale Univ, 1951-1952; Spec lectr phycol, 1950-1951; mem, Corp Marine Biol Lab, Woods Hole. **Memberships:** Int Phycol Soc; Marine Biol Asn UK; Brit Phycol Soc; Phycol Soc Am (pres, 1970); Sigma Xi; Am Soc Limnol Oceanogr; International Soc Applied Phycology. **Research Statement & Publications:** Experimental phycology; marine microbiology. **Mailing Address:** Scripps Inst Oceanog, Univ Calif, La Jolla, CA 92093-0202. **Fax:** 858-534-7313. **E-Mail:** rlewin@ucsd.edu

LEWIN, SEYMOUR Z, PHYSICAL & ANALYTICAL CHEMISTRY. **Personal Data:** b New York, NY, August 16, 1921. **Education:** City Col NY, BS, 1941; Univ Mich, MS, 1942, PhD (chem), 1950. **Honors & Awards:** A Cressy Morrison Prize, NY Acad Sci, 1956; Kasimir Fajans Prize, 1958. **Professional Experience:** PROF EMER CHEM, COL ARTS & SCI, NY UNIV, 1991-; ed, Art & Archeol Tech Abstr, 1966-1969; Belg Am Educ Found fel, 1962; hon prof, Chem Inst, Inst Quimico Sarria, Barcelona, Spain, 1962; instrumentation ed, J Chem Educ, 1960-1968; from instr to prof chem, NY Univ, 1951-1991; lectr chem, Univ Mich, 1947; consult, US Army Chem Corp, Smithsonian Inst, Food & Drug Admin & Warner Lambert Co. **Memberships:** AAAS; Am Chem Soc; Soc Appl Spectros; Am Inst Chemists; fel NY Acad Sci; fel Am Inst Chemists. **Research Statement & Publications:** Crystal growth; spectroscopy; instrumentation; materials of art and archaeology; polymorphism; solid state chemistry; stone decay and preservation; food chemistry. **Mailing Address:** Dept Chem, Col Arts & Sci, NY Univ, Silver Ctr 100 Wash Square E Rm 910, New York, NY 10003-6688. **E-Mail:** seymourlewin@hotmail.com

LEWIN, VICTOR, ECOLOGY. **Personal Data:** b San Francisco, Calif, September 8, 1930. **Education:** Univ Calif, AB, 1953, PhD (zool), 1958. **Honors & Awards:** Painton Award, Cooper Ornith Soc, 1965. **Professional Experience:** PROF EMER ZOOL, UNIV ALTA, 1985-; prof zool, Univ Alta, ending 1985; cur herpet, Mus Zool, 1980-1987; asst prof, Univ Alta, beginning 1958; dir, Univ Alta, 1958-1980; asst cur, Mus Vert Zool, Univ Calif, 1955-1956; asst zoologist, Univ Calif, 1954-1958. **Memberships:** Wildlife Soc; Am Soc Mammalogists; Cooper Ornith Soc; Am OrnithologistsUnion; Can Soc Wildlife & Fishery Biol. **Research Statement & Publications:** Wildlife ecology; ecology of game birds and mammals, particularly reproductive anatomy and physiology of gallinaceous birds; effects of chlorinated hydrocarbon residues on birds; ecology of exotic game bird species. **Mailing Address:** Dept Zool, Univ Alta, Rm Z1011, Bio Sci Bldg, Edmonton, AB T6G 2H5, Can. **Fax:** 780-492-4924.

LEWIN, WALTER H G, HIGH ENERGY ASTROPHYSICS. **Personal Data:** b The Hague, Neth, January 29, 1936; c Paulien, Emanuel, Emma & Jakob. **Education:** Univ Delft, Ir, 1960, Dr(physics), 1965. **Honors & Awards:** Outstanding Sci Achievement Award, NASA, 1978; Alexander von Humboldt Award, 1984 & 1991; Prize for Outstanding Contrib to the physics Dept, MIT, 1988; Group Achievement Award for the Discovery of the Bursting Pulsar, NASA, 1997. **Professional Experience:** Distinguished spring lectr, Princeton Univ, 1986; Alexander von Humboldt award, 1984 & 1991; Recipient Guggenheim Fel, 1984; PROF PHYSICS, MASS INST TECHNOL, 1974-; assoc prof, Mass Inst Technol, 1968-1974; fel space res & asst prof, Mass Inst Technol, 1966; res assoc physics, Univ Delft, 1959-1966. **Memberships:** Int Astron Union; Am Astron Soc; Am Phys Soc; Royal Dutch Acad Sci; corresp mem Neth Nat Royal Acad Sci. **Research Statement & Publications:** Radioactive isotope applications; nuclear and atomic physics; x-ray astronomy; high-altitude ballooning; satellite observations, orbital solar observatory-7, small astronomy satellite-3, high energy astronomy observatory-1; astrophysics; ginga, rosat and gro; Ginga; RXTE, Chandra, XMM-Newton; published over 20 articles. **Mailing Address:** Dept Physics, Mass Inst Technol, Rm 37-627, Cambridge, MA 02139. **Fax:** 617-253-0861. **E-Mail:** lewin@space.mit.edu

LEWINSON, VICTOR A, OPERATIONS RESEARCH. **Personal Data:** b New York, NY, 1918. **Education:** Harvard Col, AB, 1939; Columbia Univ, MA, 1945, PhD (chem), 1950. **Professional Experience:** RETIRED; mem prof staff, Arthur D Little, Inc, 1961-1986; analyst opers res, Nat Acad Sci, 1954-1961; fel, Mellon Inst, 1951-1954; res fel chem, Calif Inst Technol, 1950-1951; res scientist & sect leader, Manhattan Proj, 1942-1945; Asst chem, Columbia Univ, 1939-1942. **Research Statement & Publications:** Freight transportation, especially maritime and railroad. **Mailing Address:** Arthur D Little Inc, 25 Acorn Park, Cambridge, MA 02140-2390.

LEWIS, AARON, BIOPHYSICS. **Personal Data:** b Calcutta, India, October 14, 1945. **Education:** Univ Mo, BS, 1966; Case Western Reserve Univ, PhD (phys chem), 1970. **Professional Experience:** Guggenheim fel, 1979-1980, vis prof, Calif Inst Technol, 1977 & HebrewUniv, 1979-1980; ASSOC PROF BIOPHYS, CORNELL UNIV, 1976-, Sloan fel, 1974-1976, asst prof, Cornell Univ, 1972-1976; instr, Cornell Univ, 1971-1972; NIH fel, Cornell Univ, 1970-1972; Instr phys chem, Case Western Reserve Univ, 1970. **Memberships:** AAAS; Am Chem Soc; Biophys Soc; Asn Res Vision & Ophthal; Am PhotobiolSoc. **Research Statement & Publications:** Molecular mechanism of ion gates and pumps, specifically bacteriorhodopsin and rhodopsin. **Mailing Address:** Dept Appl Physics Sch Appl Sci Bergmann Bldg, Hebrew Univ, Jerusalem, Israel.

LEWIS, ALAN ERVIN, MEDICINE. **Personal Data:** b Milwaukee, Wis, February 1, 1936. **Education:** Univ Wis-Madison, BS, 1957; Marquette Univ, MD, 1960. **Professional Experience:** CONSULT, 1987-, from asst prof to assoc prof med, Hahnemann Med Col & Hosp, 1971-1987; from instr to sr instr internal med, Hahnemann Med Col & Hosp, 1967-1971; fel endocrinol, Sch Med, Tufts Univ, 1965-1967; resident, Med Ctr, Univ Mich, 1961 & 1963-1965; intern, Hosp Univ Pa, 1960-1961. **Memberships:** Am Diabetes Asn; Am Fedn Clin Res; Am Col Physicians; Endocrine Soc. **Mailing Address:** 1450 S Dobson Rd, Mesa, AZ 85202.

LEWIS, ALAN GRAHAM, BIOLOGICAL OCEANOGRAPHY, ZOOLOGY. **Personal Data:** b Pasadena, Calif, March 14, 1934. **Education:** Univ Miami, BSc, 1956, MSc, 1958; Univ Hawaii, PhD (zool), 1961. **Professional Experience:** PROF OCEANOG & ZOOL, UNIV BC, 1976-; from asst prof to assoc prof, Univ Bc, 1964-1976; Asst prof zool, Univ NH, 1961-1964. **Memberships:** Am Geophys Union; Sigma Xi. **Research Statement & Publications:** Ecology of marine plankton. **Mailing Address:** Dept Earth & Ocean Sci, Univ BC 6270 Univ Blvd, Vancouver, BC V6T 1Z4, Can.

LEWIS, ALAN JAMES, PHARMACOLOGY. **Personal Data:** b Newport, Gwent, UK. **Education:** Southampton Univ, Hampshire, BSc, 1967; Univ Wales, Cardiff, PhD (pharmacol), 1970. **Professional Experience:** PRES, CELGENE SIGNAL RES, as of 2006; DIR, BIOMARIN PHARMACEUT INC, 2005-; DIR, CYTOCHROMA INC, 2001-; DIR, DISCOVERY PARTNERS INTERNATIONAL, 2000-; chief exec officer & chief opers officer, Signal Pharmaceut Inc, San Diego, beginning 1996; pres, Signal Pharmaceut Inc, San Diego, beginning 1994; vpres res, Am Home Prod, 1990-1994; asst vpres exp therapeut, Wyeth-Ayerst Res, 1987-1989; dir exp therapeut, Wyeth-Ayerst Res, 1985-1987; assoc dir exp therapeut, Wyeth-Ayerst Res, 1982-1985; res mgr immuno inflammation, Wyeth-Ayerst Res, 1979-1982; sr pharmacologist, Organon Labs Ltd, Lanarkshire, Scotland, 1973-1979; res assoc, Lung Res Ctr, Yale Univ, 1972-1973; fel biomed sci, Univ Guelph, Ont, Can, 1970-1972; ed, Allergy Sect, Agents & Actions; ed, Int Arch Pharmacodyn Ther; reviewer, J Petrol Technol; reviewer; Biochem Pharmacol; reviewer, Can J Physiol Pharmacol; reviewer, Europ J Pharmacol; reviewer, J Pharmaceut Sci. **Memberships:** Pulmonary Res Asn; Inflammation Res Asn (pres, 1986-1988); Am Soc Pharmacol& Exp Therapeut; Pharmaceut Mfrs Asn; Am Rheumatism Asn; Mid-Atlantic Pharmacol Soc (Pres, 1993-); Int Asn Inflammation Soc. **Research Statement & Publications:** Mechanisms and treatment of inflammatory diseases including arthritis and asthma; cardiovascular pharmacology; metabolic disorders; central nervous system pharmacology; osteoporosis. **Mailing Address:** 4550 Towne Ctr Ct, San Diego, CA 92121. **Fax:** 858-552-8775. **E-Mail:** alewis@celgene.com

LEWIS, ALAN JAMES, ISLAND BIOGEOGRAPHY, FLORISTIC BIOGEOGRAPHY. **Personal Data:** b Green Bay, Wis, June 2, 1943. **Education:** Wis State Univ-Eau Claire, BS, 1968; Rutgers Univ, PhD (plant ecol), 1971. **Professional Experience:** Fulbright scholar, Univ Papua, New Guinea, 1985; PROF ECOL, UNIV MAINE, MACHIAS, 1978-; asst prof, Mercyhurst Col, 1976-1978; vis prof, Swarthmore Col, 1975-1976; res assoc, Univ Houston, 1972; asst prof biol, Kean Col NJ, 1971-1974; teaching asst gen biol & plant ecol, Rutgers Univ, New Brunswick, 1970-1971; teaching asst gen biol, NSF fel, 1969-1970; NSF fel, Rutgers Univ, 1969; teaching asst gen biol, Rutgers Univ, NewBrunswick, 1968-1969. **Memberships:** AAAS; Am Inst Biol Sci; Ecol Soc Am; Sigma Xi. **Research Statement & Publications:** Floristic distributions of Maine; island biogeography of Maine. **Mailing Address:** Div Sci & Math, Univ Maine, 125 Sci Bldg, 9 OBrien Ave, Machias, ME 04654-1397. **E-Mail:** ajlewis@maine.edu

LEWIS, ALAN LAIRD, OPTOMETRY. **Personal Data:** b Holyoke, Mass, September 1, 1942. **Education:** Mass Col Optom, BSc, 1965, OD, 1970; Ohio State Univ, MSc, 1971, PhD (physioloptics), 1971. **Professional Experience:** PRES, NEW ENG COL OPTOM, 1999-; vpres, US Nat Comt, Comn Int L'Eclairage, beginning 1991; dean, Col Optom, Ferris State Univ, 1991-1999; pres, Ophthalmic Res Inst, 1985-1990; from asst prof to prof physiol optics, Col Optom, State Univ NY, 1972-1991; Optometrist, USN, 1965-1968. **Memberships:** fel Am Acad Optom; fel Illum Eng Soc; Asn Res Vision & Opthal; Optical Soc Am; Am Optom Asn. **Research Statement & Publications:** Visual performance; color vision; environmental effects on vision. **Mailing Address:** New Eng Col Optom, 424 Beacon St 7248 Mineral Pt Rd, Boston, MA 02115. **Fax:** 617-424-9202. **E-Mail:** lewisa@ne-optometry.edu

LEWIS, A(LBERT) D(ALE) M(ILTON), CIVIL ENGINEERING, STRUCTURAL ENGINEERING. **Personal Data:** b Paoli, Ind, May 20, 1920. **Education:** Purdue Univ, BS, 1941, MS, 1951. **Professional Experience:** PROF EMER STRUCT ENG, PURDUE UNIV, WEST LAFAYETTE, 1985-; vis assoc prof struct eng, Univ Calif, Los Angeles, 1971; assoc prof, Purdue Univ, West Lafayette, 1954-1985; design engr, Stand Oil Co, Calif, 1952-1954; instr struct eng, Purdue Univ, 1951-1952; Field engr oil refinery construct, 1946-1947 & Gulf Oil Corp, 1947-1949; field engr oil refinery construct, M W Kellogg Co, 1941-1944; consult, Truss Bridge Res Proj, Northwestern Univ. **Memberships:** Am Soc Civil Engrs; Am Soc Eng Educ; Am Concrete Inst; Am Rwy Eng Asn; Asn Comput Mach; Soc Exp Mech; Nat Soc Prof Engrs. **Research Statement & Publications:** Structural analysis; structural design; design optimization; digital computers; experimental mechanics. **Mailing Address:** Dept Civil Eng, Purdue Univ, West Lafayette, IN 47907.

LEWIS, ALLEN ROGERS, BEHAVIORAL ECOLOGY. **Personal Data:** b Ithaca, NY, August 11, 1947. **Education:** Cornell Univ, BS, 1969; Univ Del, MS, 1971; Univ Rochester, MS, 1977, PhD (biol), 1979. **Professional Experience:** Dir, Res & Develop Ctr, 2000-2001; dir, Minority Biomed Res Support Prog, NIH, 1995-2001; assoc dean res & external funding, Univ PR, 1991-1995; vis prof, Cornell Univ, Ithaca, 1988-1989; PROFBIOL, UNIV PR, 1986-; ed, Carribean J Sci, 1981-1990; from asst prof to assoc prof, Univ PR, 1978-1986; asst prof, Dept Biol, 1978-1981; PROF, UNIV PR, 1978-; lectr, Nazereth Col Rochester, 1977-1978; grad teaching asst, Univ Rochester, 1974-1978; marine exten specialist, Col Marine Studies, Univ Del, 1971-1974. **Memberships:** AAAS; Asn Trop Biol; Ecol Soc Am; Soc Study Amphibians & Reptiles; Animal Behav Soc; Am Soc Naturalists. **Research Statement & Publications:** Analysis of social behavior and ecology of tropical lizards. **Mailing Address:** Dept Biol, Col Arts & Sci, Univ PR, Mayaguez, PR 00681-9012. **Fax:** 787-265-2205. **E-Mail:** alewis@uprm.edu

LEWIS, ALVIN EDWARD, BIOSTATISTICS, PHYSIOLOGY. **Personal Data:** b New York, NY, November 21, 1921. **Education:** Univ Calif, Los Angeles, AB, 1938; Stanford Univ, AM, 1939, MD, 1944. **Professional Experience:** RETIRED; emer prof path, Univ Calif, 1974-1987; prof path & chmn dept, Med Sch, Univ S Ala, 1972-1974; prof path, Mich State Univ, 1966-1972; asst clin prof, Med Ctr, Univ Calif, San Francisco, 1959-1966; dir labs, Mt Zion Hosp, 1953-1966; attend physician, Wadsworth Gen Hosp, 1950-1953; vis physician, Los Angeles County Harbor Hosp, 1949-1953; clin instr & chief path sect, AEC Proj, Univ Calif, Los Angeles, 1949-1953; fel, Am Cancer Soc, Stanford Univ, 1948-1949; asst path, Stanford Univ, 1947-1948. **Memberships:** AAAS; Am Physiol Soc; AMA; fel Col Am Path. **Research Statement & Publications:** Hepatic function tests; plasma volume and distribution. **Mailing Address:** 21 Woodgreen Ct, Santa Rosa, CA 95409.

LEWIS, ARMAND FRANCIS, PHYSICAL CHEMISTRY, MATERIALS SCIENCE. **Personal Data:** b Fairhaven, Mass, May 22, 1932. **Education:** Southeastern Mass Univ, BS, 1953; Okla State Univ, MS, 1955; Lehigh Univ, PhD (chem), 1958. **Honors & Awards:** Union Carbide Award, Am Chem Soc, 1963. **Professional Experience:** PROF, TEXTILE SCI DEPT, UNIV MASS DARTMOUTH, as of 2005; vis lectr, Textile Sci Dept, Univ Mass Dartmouth, beginning 1993; resassoc, Kendall Co, 1984-1989; sr mat scientist, Lord Corp, 1973-1981; sr res assoc, Lord Corp, 1971-1973; proj leader noise control mat, Plastics & Resins Div, 1970-1971; group leader polymer Physics & adhesion, Plastics & Resins Div, 1964-1969; sr res chemist, Plastics & Resins Div, 1963-1964; res chemist, Cent Res Div, Am Cyanamid Co, 1959-1963; res asst rheology, Lehigh Univ, 1958-1959. **Memberships:** Am Chem Soc; Soc Rheology (treas, 1966-). **Research Statement & Publications:** Polymer physics; rheology; surface chemistry and adhesion; dynamic mechnical properties of polymers; glass transition phenomena in polymeric systems; polymer to metal adhesion and fracture of adhesive joints; vibration and noise control materials; rubber chemicals; engineering composites; marine materials. **Mailing Address:** Univ Mass Dartmouth, Textile Sci Dept, North Dartmouth, MA 02747. **E-Mail:** alewis@umassd.edu

LEWIS, ARNOLD D, ANALYTICAL CHEMISTRY. **Personal Data:** b Philadelphia, Pa, May 6, 1920. **Education:** Philadelphia Col Pharm, BS, 1940; Polytech Inst Brooklyn, MS, 1947. **Professional Experience:** RETIRED; dir tech affairs, SST Corp, 1981-1986, consult, 1978-1981; diranal & phys chem, Prof Prod Group, 1964-1977; sr res assoc, Chem Res Div, 1963-1964; sr scientist, Dept Org Chem, Warner-Lambert Co, 1954-1963; scientist, Dept Org Chem, Warner-Lambert Co, 1947-1954; jr scientist, G D Res Inst, 1944-1947, asst scientist to Dr E AH Friedheim, 1943-1944, pilot plant chemist, United Gas Improv Corp, 1941-1943; control chemist, Hance Bros & White, 1940-1941. **Memberships:** Am Chem Soc. **Research Statement & Publications:** Organic synthesis of heterocycles; infrared and ultraviolet absorption spectrophotometry; microanalysis; gas, paper, thin-layer and column chromatography; chemical safety; proton magnetic resonance spectroscopy. **Mailing Address:** 42 Intervale Rd, Livingston, NJ 07039-2756.

LEWIS, ARNOLD LEROY, II, INSTRUMENTATION, SPECTROSCOPY. **Personal Data:** b Portland, Ore, September 24, 1952. **Education:** Pac Lutheran Univ, BA, 1975; Ore State Univ, PhD (anal chem), 1981. **Professional Experience:** SR SCIENTIST, WESTINGHOUSE IDAHO NUCLEAR CO INC, 1981-; srchemist, Exxon Nuclear Idaho Co, Inc, 1981; res asst, Ore State Univ, 1978-1981; Teaching asstchem, Ore State Univ, 1975-1978. **Memberships:** Am Chem Soc. **Research Statement & Publications:** Laser atomic fluorescence studies of laser microprobe plumes; microcomputer interfacing to analytical instrumentation; methods development of analytical techniques in the nuclear industry. **Mailing Address:** No 195552, c/o Aramco Box 6011, Dhahran 31311, Saudi Arabia.

LEWIS, AUSTIN JAMES, ANIMAL NUTRITION. **Personal Data:** b Poole, Eng, November 29, 1945. **Education:** Univ Reading, BSc, 1967; Univ Nottingham, PhD (nutrit), 1971. **Honors & Awards:** ASAS fel Award, 2002; Gamma Sigma Delta Res Award, Nebr Chap; Am Feed Indust Asn Nutrit Award, Am Soc Animal Sci. **Professional Experience:** PROF, UNIV NEBR, as of 2006; prof emer animal nutrit, Univ NEBR, as of 2002; prof animal nutrit, Univ Nebr, 1985-2001; from asst prof to assoc prof, Univ Nebr, 1977-1985; asst prof, Univ Alta, 1975-1977; res assoc, Univ Nebr, 1974-1975; Assocanimal nutrit, Iowa State Univ, 1971-1974. **Memberships:** Am Soc Animal Sci; Am Inst Nutrit; ARPAS. **Research Statement & Publications:** Nutritional requirements of swine, especially proteins and amino acids. **Mailing Address:** Dept Animal Sci, Univ Nebr, 4507 E Eden Dr, Lincoln, NE 68583-0908. **E-Mail:** alewis2@unl.edu

LEWIS, BARBARA-ANN GAMBOA, ENVIRONMENTAL RADIOACTIVITY, CLAY CHEMISTRY. **Personal Data:** b Manila, Philippines, January 9, 1934; American citizen; m 1966, Roy; c Gilita (Star), Marya (Curie) & Stephen Berkeley. **Education:** Philippine Women's Univ, BS, 1953; Univ Calif, Berkeley, MS, 1963, PhD (soil sci), 1971. **Honors & Awards:** Palladium Medal, Nat Asn Eng Soc & Nat Audubon Soc, 1984. **Professional Experience:** ASSOC PROF ENVIRON ENG, NORTHWESTERN UNIV, 1979-; environ scientist, Argonne Nat Lab, 1973-1979; postdoctoral, Argonne Nat Lab, 1972-1973; staff res assoc soils, Dept Forestry, Univ Calif, Berkeley, 1971-1972. **Memberships:** Soil Sci Soc Am; Am Soc Agron; Am Chem Soc; Sigma Xi. **Research Statement & Publications:** Soil-contaminant-vegetation interactions; reclamation of distrubed land; soil-clay chemistry; radon and radium in soils; transport of contaminants in soil. **Mailing Address:** 923 Asbury Ave, Evanston, IL 60202. **E-Mail:** b-lewis@northwestern.edu

LEWIS, BERTHA ANN (BETTY), CARBOHYDRATE CHEMISTRY, FOOD CHEMISTRY. **Personal Data:** b Lewisville, Minn, October 21, 1927. **Education:** Univ Minn, BChem, 1949, MS, 1954, PhD (biochem), 1957. **Honors & Awards:** Highly Cited Res, ISI thomson Scientific, 2002. **Professional Experience:** Vis prof, Dept Chem, Univ BC, 1984 & 1985; mem, & Nat Agr Res Comt, 1980-1985; mem, US Dept Agr Comt Regional Res & Home Econ Sub-Comt Agr Exp Stas Comt on Policy, 1976-1979; assoc dean, Col Human Ecol & asst dir, Cornell Agr Exp Sta, 1974-1980; prin investr, NIH, 1971-1974 & 1980-1982; ASSOC PROF, DIV NUTRIT SCI, CORNELL UNIV, 1970-; assoc prof design & environ anal, Div Nutrit Sci, Cornell Univ, 1967-1970; res assoc, Univ Minn, St Paul, 1965-1967; res fel biochem, Univ Minn, St Paul, 1957-1965. **Memberships:** Am Chem Soc; Inst Food Technologists; Soc Glycobiol; Am Asn Cereal Chemists; AAAS. **Research Statement & Publications:** Carbohydrate chemistry and biochemistry; chemistry of glycoproteins; dietary fiber; anti-nutrients in food; phytochemicals. **Mailing Address:** Div Nutrit Sci, Cornell Univ 116 Savage Hall, Ithaca, NY 14853-6301. **Fax:** 607-255-1033. **E-Mail:** bal4@cornell.edu

LEWIS, BRIAN KREGLOW, HUMAN PHYSIOLOGY, TECHNOLOGY WRITING COMPUTER. **Personal Data:** b Durban, SAfrica, September 2, 1932; American citizen; m 1953, Helen Kidwell; c Brian E, James A, Charles A, Carol J, Robert E & Sharon H. **Education:** Ohio State Univ, BS, 1954; Tufts Univ, PhD (physiol), 1971. **Professional Experience:** Instr, Sarasota Co Tech Inst, 1995-1997; prof & chmn, Dept Physiol & dir comput sci, 1987-1991; OWNER, LEWIS & ASSOCS, 1984-; assoc prof physiol, Ponce Sch Med, 1981-1984; from asst prof to assoc prof health sci, Grand Valley State Col, 1975-1981; May Inst Med Res, Jewish Hosp Cincinnati, 1971-1974 & Col Med, Univ Cincinnati, 1974-1975; Adj asst prof physiol, Col Med, UnivCincinnati, 1972-1975; res assoc physiol, Sch Med, Tufts Univ, 1971. **Memberships:** emer mem Endocrine Soc; emer mem Sigma Xi. **Research Statement & Publications:** Publ of former res in metabo dis, ie Stroke, obesity, diabetes currently doing comput ser instr hard wave/software rev; technical writing. **Mailing Address:** 6423 Caracara St, Sarasota, FL 34241-9104. **E-Mail:** brian_klewis@hotmail.com

LEWIS, BRIAN MURRAY, GALAXIES, RADIO ASTRONOMY MEASUREMENTS. **Personal Data:** b Oxford, Eng, June 20, 1943; British & New Zealander citizen. **Education:** Adelaide Univ, Australia, BS, 1965; Australian Nat Univ, PhD (astron), 1970. **Professional Experience:** SR RES ASSOC, ARECIBO OBSERV, PR, as of 2004; vis prof, Cornell Univ, 1984, 1987; STAFF SCIENTIST RES, ARECIBO OBSERV, PR, 1982-; vis fel, Nat Radio Astron Observ, 1979-1980; dir teaching-pub rels-res, Carter Observ, Wellington, NZ, 1973-1981; secy, Nat Comt Astron, NZ, 1973-1980; res asst astron, Jodrell Bank, Univ Manchester, UK, 1969-1971. **Memberships:** Australian Astron Soc; Am Astron Soc; Int Astron Union. **Research Statement & Publications:** Properties of galaxies, the precision of velocity estimates and their use in Tully-Fisher relation; missing mass in galaxies; identification of OH IR stars; properties of circumstellar envelopes. **Mailing Address:** Arecibo Observ, PO Box 995, Arecibo, PR 00613. **E-Mail:** blewis@naic.edu

LEWIS, C S, JR, INTERNAL MEDICINE. **Personal Data:** b Muskogee, Okla, July 19, 1920. **Professional Experience:** DIR INT STUDIES INTERNAL MED, MED COL, UNIV OKLA, TULSA, as of 2002. **Memberships:** Inst Med-Nat Acad Sci. **Mailing Address:** Dept Internal Med, Univ Okla Med Col, Tulsa, OK 74129.

LEWIS, CARMIE PERROTTA, HISTOLOGY. **Personal Data:** b New Castle, Pa, June 9, 1929; m 1965, Angelica; c Angelica. **Education:** Thiel Col, BS, 1951; Univ NH, MS, 1953; Univ Wis, PhD (anat, zool), 1956. **Honors & Awards:** Prof emrit, suffolk com col, 1999 chancellors Award for exellence in teaching, state univ, NY, 1996, Board of trustees Award for faculty mem who made a difference, suffolk co com col, 1991, outstanding scientists of twentieth century, 2000, international biographical ctr of cambridge, 1999. **Professional Experience:** Mellon fel, Ctr Univ NY-Community Col Proj, 1988; PROF BIOL, SUFFOLK CO COMMUNITY COL, 1974-; assoc prof, Suffolk CO Community Col, 1967-1974; res collabr, Brookhaven Nat lab, 1964-1967; asst prof, Queens Col, NY, 1964-1967; USPHS res fel, 1961-1964; asst radiobiologist, Brookhaven Nat lab, 1961-1964; instr anat, Sch Med, Yale Univ, 1958-1961; lectr embryol & histol, Fac Med, Queen's Univ, Ont, 1957-1958; Am Asn Univ Women res fel, Cambridge Univ, 1956-1957; res asst, Univ Wis, 1953-1956. **Memberships:** Am Asn Anat. **Research Statement & Publications:** Radiobiology; endocrines of reproduction. **Mailing Address:** 107 Alden Dr, Port Jefferson, NY 11777.

LEWIS, CHARLES E, MEDICINE, PREVENTIVE MEDICINE. **Personal Data:** b Kansas City, Mo, December 28, 1928. **Education:** Harvard Med Sch, MD, 1953; Univ Cincinnati, MS, 1957, ScD (prev med), 1959. **Honors & Awards:** Ginsberg Prize, 1954; Glasier Award, 1988. **Professional Experience:** PROF EMER HEALTH SERV, FAMILY MED & NURSING, as of 2004; dir, Ctr Health Prom & Dis Prev, 1991-; head, Div Pres & Occup Med, Med Sch & dir, Health Servs Res Ctr, 1991-1993; comnr, Joint Comn Accreditation Health Care Orgn, 1990-; mem, Regent Am Col Physicians, 1988-; prof nursing, Univ Calif, Los Angeles, 1974-; prof med, Univ Calif, Los Angeles, 1972-; prof pub health, Univ Calif, Los Angeles, 1970-; prof social med, Harvard Med Sch, 1969-1970; dir, Kans Regional Med Prog, 1967-1969; prof prev med, Med Ctr, Univ Kans, 1962-1969; assoc prof med, Med Ctr, Univ Kans, 1961-1962; asst prof epidemiol, Col Med, Baylor Univ, 1960-1961; plant physician, Tex Div, 1959-1960; resident occup med, Eastman Kodak Co, 1958-1959, USPHS trainee, 1957-1958; fel prev med, Kettering Lab, Univ Cincinnati, 1956-1958; house officer med, Univ Kans Hosps, 1953-1954. **Memberships:** Am Pub Health Asn; Asn Am Physicians; Am Col Physicians. **Research Statement & Publications:** Medical care and education. **Mailing Address:** Sch Public Health, Univ Calif, Box 951772, Los Angeles, CA 90094-1772. **Fax:** 310-206-5717. **E-Mail:** lewis@admin.ph.ucla.edu

LEWIS, CHARLES J, ANIMAL SCIENCE MANAGER OF RESEARCH & DEVELOPMENT. **Personal Data:** b Park River, NDak, May 20, 1927; m 1950, Norma; c Patrick J & Susan L. **Education:** Utah State Univ, BS, 1952; Iowa State Univ, MS, 1954, PhD (animal nutrit), 1956 As No Dak sch Fonestry. **Professional Experience:** RETIRED; dir exec vpres, Grain Processing Corp & Kent Feeds, Inc, 1968-1993; prof animal sci & head dept, SDak State Univ, 1967-1968; mem, Bd Dirs, 1960-1967; vpres & nutritionist, Kent Feeds, Inc, 1958-1967; dir nutrit, Kent Feeds, Inc, 1956-1958; pres & dir, Friend Agr &Iowa State Univ Res Found. **Memberships:** AAAS; Am Inst Biol Sci; Am Soc Animal Sci; Inst Food Technologists; Poultry Sci Asn Am. **Research Statement & Publications:** Animal nutrition and research. **Mailing Address:** 7 Colony Dr, Muscatine, IA 52761.

LEWIS, CLARK HOUSTON, FLUID MECHANICS, GAS DYNAMICS. **Personal Data:** b McMinnville, Tenn, November 6, 1929. **Education:** Univ Tenn, BSME, 1951, MS, 1959, PhD (viscous flow), 1968. **Professional Experience:** PRES, VRA INC, 1984-; prof aerospace eng, Va Polytech Inst & State Univ, 1968-1984; supvr theoret gas dynamics, Aerophys Div, Aro Inc, Arnold Eng Develop Ctr, Tenn, 1951-1968. **Memberships:** Assoc fel Am Inst Aeronaut & Astronaut; Am Phys Soc; Am Soc Mech Engrs. **Research Statement & Publications:** Physical gas dynamics; high-speed viscous flows; chemically reacting flows; thermophysical gas properties; numerical methods in engineering. **Mailing Address:** VRA Inc, PO Box 60, Blacksburg, VA 24060.

LEWIS, CLAUDE IRENIUS, ANALYTICAL CHEMISTRY. **Personal Data:** b Stanley, NC, April 21, 1935. **Education:** Duke Univ, BS, 1957; Va Polytech Inst, MS, 1959, PhD (chem), 1962. **Professional Experience:** DIR QUAL ASSURANCE, LORILLARD CORP, 1970-; supvr anal develop, Lorillard Corp, 1970-1976; Instr, Guilford Col, 1967-1970; sr res chemist, Lorillard Corp, 1966-1970; res chemist, Lorillard Corp, 1965-1966; Res chemist, Texaco, Inc, 1961-1962 & E I duPont Del Nemours & Co, 1962-1965. **Memberships:** AAAS; Am Chem Soc; Am Inst Chem Eng; Am Soc Qual Control; Sigma Xi. **Research Statement & Publications:** Cigarette tobacco technology; tobacco smoke chemistry; polyester fiber technology; alkyl benzene synthesis; synthesis of polycyclic aromatic compounds. **Mailing Address:** 3001 Shadylawn Dr, Greensboro, NC 27408-2620.

LEWIS, CORNELIUS CRAWFORD, agronomy, soil science; deceased, see previous edition for last biography

LEWIS, CRISTINA T, ENZYMOLOGY. **Personal Data:** b West Palm Beach, Fla, November 11, 1962. **Education:** Univ SFla, BS, 1983; Univ Tenn, PhD (biochem), 1989. **Professional Experience:** SR SCIENTIST, AGOURON PHARMACEUT, 1996-; res scientist, Agouron Pharmaceut, 1993-1996; Jane Coffin Childs fel, Scripps Res Inst, 1990-1993. **Memberships:** Am Chem Soc; Am Soc Biochem & Molecular Biol. **Research Statement & Publications:** Enzymological characterization and purification of pharmaceutically relevant proteins; application of structure based drug design; detailed characterization of enzyme structure-function relationships. **Mailing Address:** Agouron Pharmaceut, 3565 Gen Atomics Ct, San Diego, CA 92121-1121. **Fax:** 619-622-7999. **E-Mail:** clewis@agouron.com

LEWIS, CYNTHIA LUCILLE, INVERTEBRATE BIOLOGY, DEVELOPMENTAL BIOLOGY. **Personal Data:** b Los Angeles, Calif, November 26, 1948. **Education:** Calif Polytech State Univ, BS, 1970; Univ Alta, PhD (zoology), 1975. **Honors & Awards:** Outstanding Instnl Advising Pro Award, Acad Advising Asn, 1990. **Professional Experience:** FOUNDER, LEWIS ASSOC, as of 2004; asst prof, biol dept, Point Loma Col, beginning 1982; res assoc, Scripps Inst Oceanog, 1979-1981; asst prof biol & chem, Point Loma Col, 1978-1979; asst prof zool & biol, San Diego State Univ, 1977-1978; fel develop biol & anomalies, Dent Inst, NIH, 1975-1977; fel, Smithsonian Inst, Wash, DC, 1973-1975; lab instr invert zool, marine biol & gen biol, Univ Alta, 1971-1975; lab instr physiol & invert embryol, Ore State Univ, 1970-1971. **Memberships:** Sigma Xi; Am Soc Zoologists; Grad Women Sci. **Research Statement & Publications:** Physiological mechanisms, morphological changes and morphogenetic movements involved in invertebrate development; larval development, physiological ecology and settlement of invertebrate larvae; editor and author for medicinal publications. **Mailing Address:** Lewis Assoc, 2727 Camino del Rio S Ste 156, San Diego, CA 92108. **Fax:** 619-308-4244. **E-Mail:** drlewis@lewisassoc.com

LEWIS, DANIEL MOORE, ALLERGIES & HYPERSENSITIVITY DISEASES, PULMONARY IMMUNOLOGY. **Personal Data:** b Barnesville, Ohio, October 1, 1945. **Education:** Ohio State Univ, BS, 1967; WVa Univ, MS, 1969, PhD (microbiol), 1974. **Professional Experience:** Chief, Immunol Sect, NIOSH, Morgantown, WVa, 1991-2003; adj prof, WVa

Univ, Morgantown, beginning 1989; from adj asst prof to adj assoc prof microbiol, WVa Univ, Morgantown, 1982-1989; immunologist, USPHS, Morgantown, 1980-1991; res asst prof immunol, Ohio State Univ, Columbus, 1976-1980; Res fel immunol, Mayo Clin & Found, Rochester, Minn, 1974-1976. **Research Statement & Publications:** Immunologic aspects of occupational lung diseases with special interest in allergy and occupational asthma; development of assays to evaluate the inflammatory potential of organic dusts found in agricultural work sites and development of assays for the measurement of airborne allergens in the worksite. **Mailing Address:** Immunol Sect, Nat Inst Occup Safety & Health, 1095 Willowdale Rd, Morgantown, WV 26505.

LEWIS, DANIEL RALPH, MATHEMATICS. **Personal Data:** b Camden, Ark, October 31, 1944. **Education:** La State Univ, Baton Rouge, 1966, MS, 1968, PhD (math), 1970. **Professional Experience:** PROF MATH, DEPT MATH, TEX A&M UNIV, 2001-; assocprof math, Ohio State Univ, 1977-2001; asst prof math, Univ Fla, 1972-1977; asst prof math, Va Polytech Inst & State Univ, 1970-1972. **Memberships:** Am Math Soc. **Research Statement & Publications:** Functional analysis. **Mailing Address:** Dept Math, Tex A&M Univ, Milner 319, Bryan, TX 77801. **Fax:** 979-845-6028.

LEWIS, DANNY HARVE, POLYMER CHEMISTRY. **Personal Data:** b Decatur, Ala, April 9, 1948; m 1968, c 2. **Education:** Univ NAla, BS, 1969; Univ Ala, PhD (chem), 1973. **Professional Experience:** DIR & CHMN SCI ADV BD, PR PHARMACEUT INC, 1998-; vpres new prod develop, Stolle Res & Develop Corp, 1982-1996; head, Biosysts Div, 1980-1982; head, Biomat Sect, 1977-1980; sr chemist polymer chem, Southern Res Inst, 1975-1977; res chemist textile fibers, E I du Pont Del Nemours & Co Inc, 1973-1975; consult, NIH. **Memberships:** Sigma Xi; Controlled Release Soc (pres-elect). **Research Statement & Publications:** Controlled-release delivery systems; biomaterials for dental and orthopedic use; synthesis and characterization of new polymers; physical properties of polymers; polymers for fiber spinning, polymers as adhesives and membranes. **Mailing Address:** PR Pharmaceut, Inc, PO Box 2126 1716 Heath Pkwy, Ft Collins, CO 80522-2126. **Fax:** 970-482-6184.

LEWIS, DAVID EDWIN, DEVELOPMENT OF SYNTHETIC METHODOLOGY, SYNTHESIS OF FLUORESCENT PROBES. **Personal Data:** b Tailem Bend, Australia, November 21, 1951; m 1978, Deborah; c Graeme & Vveronica. **Education:** Univ Adelaide, BSc, 1972, PhD (org chem), 1980. **Professional Experience:** PROF, UNIV WIS, EAU CLAIRE, 1997-; chmn, 1997-1999; dir res, Chem Div, Micro Bio Med Corp, 1993-1997; from assoc prof to prof, SDak State Univ, 1989-1997; vis distinguished scholar, Univ Adelaide, 1988; from asst prof to assoc prof, Baylor Univ, 1981-1988; vis asst prof, Univ Ill, Urbana-Champaign, 1980-1981; lectr, Univ Ark, 1979-1980; Res assoc chem, Univ Ark, 1977-1978. **Memberships:** Royal Australian Chem Inst Fel; Am Chem Soc. **Research Statement & Publications:** Development of new synthethic methods based on reactions in formic acid; development of site-specific fluorescent labels and probes; synthesis of biologically active natural products. **Mailing Address:** Univ Wis, Eau Claire, WI 54702-4004. **Fax:** 715-836-4979. **E-Mail:** lewisd@uwec.edu

LEWIS, DAVID HAROLD, CARDIOLOGY. **Personal Data:** b New York, NY, December 22, 1925. **Education:** Columbia Univ, AB, 1944, MD, 1947. **Professional Experience:** CHIEF CLIN RES, CLIN RES CTR, UNIV HOSP, LINKOPING UNIV, 1980-; guest investr, Clin Res Ctr, Univ Hosp, Linkoping Univ, 1978-1980; guest investr, FirstSurg Dept, Univ Goteborg, 1963-1978; estab investr, Am Heart Asn, 1957-1962; assoc cardiol, Grad Sch Med, 1955-1963; Chief hemodynamics sect, Div Cardiol, Philadelphia Gen Hosp, 1955-1963; from instr to asst prof physiol, Sch Med, Univ Pa, 1950-1957; resident, KingsCounty Hosp, 1949-1950; intern, Kings County Hosp, 1948-1949; Intern med, Bellevue Hosp, New York, 1947-1948. **Memberships:** Am Physiol Soc; Am Fedn Clin Res; Am Heart Asn. **Research Statement & Publications:** Cardiovascular physiology. **Mailing Address:** Clin Res Ctr Univ Hosp, Linkoping Univ Grangatan 7, S-58245 Linkoping, Sweden. **Fax:** 461-312-7465.

LEWIS, DAVID KENNETH, PHYSICAL CHEMISTRY. **Personal Data:** b Poughkeepsie, NY, February 11, 1943. **Education:** Amherst Col, AB, 1964; Cornell Univ, PhD (phys chem), 1970. **Professional Experience:** Interim pres, Conn Col, 2000-2001; provost & dean fac, Conn Col, 1997-2000; MARGARET W KELLY PROF CHEM, CONN COL, 1996-; prof chem, Conn Col, beginning 1995; Charles A Dana prof chem, Colgate Univ, beginning 1988; chmn chem, Colgate Univ, 1987-1988; vis prof chem, Univ NC, 1987; vis prof chem, Syracuse Univ, 1986; assoc dean fac, Colgate Univ, 1985-1986; DIR, DIV NAT SCI & MATH, 1982-1985 & 1988-; mem Cent NY Task Force Hazardous & Toxic Waste, 1982-1984; environ mgt coun, Madison County, NY, 1981-1986; vis sr res fel, Univ Colo, Nat Oceanic & Atmospheric Admin, 1977-1978; from asst prof to prof chem, Colgate Univ, 1969-1988. **Memberships:** Am Chem Soc; Sigma Xi. **Research Statement & Publications:** Chemical kinetics and energy transfer in gases at high temperatures; ultra-high resolution molecular spectroscopy; atmospheric chemistry and physics; innovative teaching methods. **Mailing Address:** Dept Chem, Hale Lab, Conn Col, PO Box 2485 270 Mohegan Ave, New London, CT 06320-4196. **E-Mail:** dklew@conncoll.edu

LEWIS, DAVID KENT, FOREST MANAGEMENT, FOREST ECONOMICS. **Personal Data:** b Madison, Wis, June 11, 1938. **Education:** Univ Minn, BS, 1960; Yale Univ, MF, 1966; Univ Oxford, D Phil, 1976. **Professional Experience:** Dir, Environ Sci Undergrad Prog, Okla State Univ, 2002-2005; ADJ ASSOC PROF FORESTRY, OKLA STATE UNIV, 1990-; ASSOC PROF FORESTERY, OKLA STATE UNIV, 1982-; forest economist, Res & Develop, Weyerhaeuser Co, Wash, 1976-1982; silviculturist, Forestry Res Ctr, 1967-1976; res asst, Yale Univ, 1965-1967; forester, Ore, 1963-1965. **Memberships:** Soc Am Foresters; Am Econ Asn. **Research Statement & Publications:** Economics of producing timber crops; economic of global climate change; impact of forest resources on reginal economics. **Mailing Address:** Dept Forestry, Okla State Univ, 022 Agr Hall, Stillwater, OK 74078. **Fax:** 405-744-3530. **E-Mail:** dklewis@okstate.edu

LEWIS, DAVID S(LOAN), JR, AERONAUTICAL ENGINEERING. **Personal Data:** b North Augusta, SC, July 6, 1917. **Education:** Ga Tech Univ, BS, 1939. **Honorary Degrees:** DSc, Clarkson Col Technol, 1971; LLD, St Louis Univ. **Honors & Awards:** Collier Trophy, Pres Ford, 1976; Wright Bros Trophy; Sands of Time Award, 1977; Distinguished Achievement Award, Wings Club, 1983. **Professional Experience:** RETIRED; dir, Gen Dynamics Corp, 1986-1992; chmn bd & chief execofficer, Gen Dynamics Corp, 1970-1986; pres, McDonnell Douglas Corp, 1967-1970; pres, McDonnell Aircraft Corp, 1962-1967; exec vpres, McDonnell Aircraft Corp, 1961-1962; sr vpresopers, McDonnell Aircraft Corp, 1960-1961; sr vpres, McDonnell Aircraft Corp, 1959-1961; vpres, McDonnell Aircraft Corp, 1957-1959; mgr all projs, McDonnell Aircraft Corp, 1956-1957; mgr sales, McDonnell Aircraft Corp, 1955-1956; chief preliminary design, McDonnell Aircraft Corp, 1952-1955; Mem, Subcomt Highspeed Aerodyn & Subcomt Stability& Control, Nat Adv Comt Aeronaut, 1951-1957; chief aerodyn, McDonnell Aircraft Corp, 1946-1952; Aerodynamicist, Martin Co, 1939-1946. **Memberships:** Nat Acad Eng; fel Am Inst Aeronaut & Astronaut. **Research Statement & Publications:** Aerodynamics; high speed flight characteristics; space mechanics. **Mailing Address:** 1 Gadsden Way Apt 239, Charleston, SC 29412. **Fax:** 803-577-9634.

LEWIS, DAVID THOMAS, AGRONOMY, SOIL MORPHOLOGY. **Personal Data:** b Downing, Mo, September 27, 1935; m 1968, c 1. **Education:** Univ Maine, BS, 1960, MS, 1962; Univ Nebr, PhD (agron), 1971. **Professional Experience:** PROF SOIL CLASSIFICATION, DEPT AGRON, UNIV NEBR, 1980-; from asst prof to assoc prof, Dept Agron, Univ Nebr, 1975-1980; instr agron, Dept Agron, Univ Nebr, 1967-1971; soil scientist, Soil Conserv Serv, USDA, 1962-1967; Instr soil sci, Dept Agron, Univ Maine, 1960-1962. **Memberships:** Soil Sci Soc Am; Soil Conserv Soc Am; Sigma Xi. **Research Statement & Publications:** Studies relating to the genesis and classification of soils and to the solution of problems that relate to proper correlation of survey mapping units. **Mailing Address:** Dept Agron E Campus, Univ Nebr 279 Plant Sci PO Box 830915, Lincoln, NE 68583-0915.

LEWIS, DAVID W(ARREN), MECHANICS. **Personal Data:** b Salem, Ohio, June 16, 1930. **Education:** Rice Univ, BA, 1952, BS, 1953, MS, 1955; Northwestern Univ, PhD (mech), 1958. **Professional Experience:** PROF EMER MECH ENG & BIOMED ENG, UNIV VA, as of 2004; prof Mech Eng & Biomed Eng, Univ Va, beginning 1971; assoc prof mecheng, Univ VA, 1963-1971; staff engr, IBM Corp, 1960-1963; asst prof, US Naval Postgrad Sch, 1958-1960; instr mech eng, Northwestern Univ, 1955-1957. **Memberships:** Am Soc Eng Educ; Am Soc Mech Engrs. **Research Statement & Publications:** Mechanics, especially elasticity and kinematics. **Mailing Address:** Dept Mech & Aerospace Eng, Univ Va, 122 Engrs Way PO Box 400746, Charlottesville, VA 22904-4746. **Fax:** 434-982-2037. **E-Mail:** dwl@virginia.edu

LEWIS, DEBRA A, CARDIOVASCULAR PHYSIOLOGY & PHARMACOLOGY, VASCULAR INJURY. **Personal Data:** b Burlington, Vt, November 13, 1953. **Education:** Univ NH, BS, 1975; Pa State Univ, MS, 1982, PhD, 1988. **Professional Experience:** ASST PROF & RES ASSOC, MAYO CLIN, 1994-; Minn affil res fel, Am Heart Asn, 1993-2004; Fel Cardiovasc Physiol & Pharmacol, Mayo Clin, 1988-1990; Dept Radiol, Mayo Clin. **Memberships:** Am Heart Asn; NAVBO. **Research Statement & Publications:** Vascular injury and the mechanisms that promote medial growth; transplant acclerated atherosclerosis in a porcine model. **Mailing Address:** Dept Radiol, St Marys Hosp, 1216 Second St, SW, Alfred Bldg Rm 6-460, Rochester, MN 55902. **Fax:** 507-255-4068. **E-Mail:** lewis.debra@mayo.edu

LEWIS, DENNIS ALLEN, ORGANIC CHEMISTRY. **Personal Data:** b Morristown, NJ, December 25, 1942. **Education:** St Peters Col, BS, 1964; Univ Conn, PhD (org chem), 1972. **Professional Experience:** PROF CHEM, ROSE-HULMAN INST TECHNOL, as of 2004; assoc prof chem, Rose-Hulman Inst Technol, beginning 1976; instr, US Army Reserve Sch, Ft Benjamin Harrison, Ind, 1973-; asst prof, Rose-hulman Inst Technol, 1972-1976; instr & sr instr, Nuclear Weapons Employ Div, Ft Sill, Okla, 1970-1971. **Memberships:** Am Chem Soc; Sigma Xi. **Research Statement & Publications:** Synthesis of small-ring compounds via photochemical reactions involving carbene and nitrene intermediates; investigation of chemiluminescent systems. **Mailing Address:** Dept Chem, Rose-Hulman Inst Technol, 5500 Wabash Ave, Terre Haute, IN 47803-3999. **E-Mail:** dennis.lewis@rose-hulman.edu

LEWIS, DONALD EVERETT, BIOCHEMISTRY, SCIENCE EDUCATION. **Personal Data:** b Paducah, Tex, July 3, 1931. **Education:** Abilene Christian Col, BS, 1952; Fla State Univ, MS, 1954, PhD (biochem), 1957. **Professional Experience:** RETIRED, 1997; vis prof chem, Univ Tex, Austin, 1980-1981; prof chem, Abilene Christian Col, 1968-1997; assoc prof, Abilene Christian Col, 1966-1968; vis assoc prof, Abilene Christian Col, 1963-1964; from assoc prof to prof chem, Queen's Col, NC, 1957-1966. **Memberships:** Am Chem Soc. **Research Statement & Publications:** Synthesis and biological assay of amino acid analogues. **Mailing Address:** 2541 Campus Courts, Abilene, TX 79601. **Fax:** 325-674-6988.

LEWIS, DONALD HOWARD, FISH PATHOLOGY, MICROBIOLOGY. **Personal Data:** b Stamford, Tex, May 31, 1936. **Education:** Univ Tex, Austin, BA, 1959; Southwest Tex State Univ, MA, 1964; Tex A&M Univ, PhD (vet microbiol), 1967. **Professional Experience:** PROF EMER, VET MED, TEX A&M UNIV, as of 2003; actg head, Vet Microbiol & Parasitol, Tex A&M Univ, beginning 1981; prof microbiol, Tex A&M Univ, beginning 1979; assoc prof, Tex A&M Univ, 1975-1979; Consult, TerEco Corp, 1975; asst prof, Tex A&M Univ, 1969-1975; Res assoc, Tex A&M Univ, 1966-1968. **Memberships:** AAAS; Am Soc Microbiol; Am Fisheries Soc; Soc Invert Path; World MaricultSoc. **Research Statement & Publications:** Microbial diseases and immune mechanisms of aquatic animals; role of microflora upon host welfare; antibiotic resistance; molecular biology. **Mailing Address:** Col Vet Med Tex A&M Univ, Col Sta, TX 77843-4467.

LEWIS, DONALD JOHN, MATHEMATICS, NUMBER THEORY. **Personal Data:** b Adrian, Minn, January 25, 1926; m Carolyn. **Education:** Col St Thomas, BS, 1946; Univ Mich, MS, 1949, PhD (math), 1950. **Honors & Awards:** Humboldt Stiftung Sr Award, 1980 & 1982 Amer Math Soc Distinguished Public Service Award, 1995. **Professional Experience:** PROF EMER MATH, UNIV MICH, ANN ARBOR, 2000-; dir, div math sci, NSF, 1995-1999; chmn, div math sci, NSF, 1984-1985; guest prof, Heidelberg Univ, 1979-1980 & 1983; vis fel, Brasenose Col, Oxford, 1969; sr vis fel, Trinity Col Cambridge Univ, 1965, 1969; prof math, Univ Mich, Ann Arbor, 1961-2000; NSF sr fel, Manchester & Cambridge Univs, 1959-1961; from asst prof to assoc prof, Univ Notre Dame, 1953-1961; NSF fel, Inst Adv Study, 1952-1953; Instr math, Ohio State Univ. **Memberships:** emer Am Math Soc; Soc Indust & Applied Math; trustee Am Math Soc 1994-1995. **Research Statement & Publications:** Diophantine equations; finite fields; algebraic number theory. **Mailing Address:** Dept Math, Univ Mich, Rm 4062, E Hall, Church St, Ann Arbor, MI 48109-1003. **Fax:** 734-763-0937. **E-Mail:** djlewis@umich.edu

LEWIS, DOUGLAS SCOTT, ANIMAL PHYSIOLOGY. **Personal Data:** b Dayton, Ohio, August 10, 1951. **Education:** Univ Ga, BS, 1973; Mich State Univ, PhD (biochem), 1978. **Professional Experience:** PROF & CHMN, HUMAN NUTRIT & FOOD SCI, CALIF STATE POLYTECH UNIV, POMONA, as of 2002; assoc prof food sci, Southwest Found Biomed Res, beginning 1992; assoc res scientist, Southwest Found Biomed Res, 1987-1992; asst prof, Dept Physiol, Univ Tex Health Sci Ctr, San Antonio, beginning 1984; asst res scientist, Southwest Found Biomed Res, 1980-1986; Postdoctoral physiol, Univ Tex Health Sci Ctr, San Antonio, 1978-1980. **Memberships:** Am Physiol Soc; Am Heart Asn; Am Soc Nutrit Sci. **Research Statement & Publications:** Mechanisms by which nutritional factors regulate lipid metabolism during growth and development; investigate endocrine regulation of fat cell and hepatic metabolism in preweaning infants using a non-human primate. **Mailing Address:** Dept Food Sci & Human Nutrit, Calif State Polytech Univ, Pomona, CA 91768. **Fax:** 909-869-5078. **E-Mail:** dslewis@csupomona.edu

LEWIS, EDWARD B, genetics; deceased, see previous edition for last biography

LEWIS, EDWARD LYN, OCEANOGRAPHY. **Personal Data:** b Aberystwyth, UK, October 9, 1930. **Education:** Univ London, BSc, 1951, MSc, 1958, PhD (physics), 1962. **Professional Experience:** EMER SCIENTIST, OCEAN SCI & SURV, DEPT FISHERIES & OCEANOG, CAN, 1995-; res scientist, Ocean Sci & Surv, Dept Fisheries & Oceanog, Can, 1962-1995; res assoc microwave electronics, Univ BC, 1959-1962; Harwell res fel, Univ London, 1956-1959; Physicist, Mullard Res Labs, 1952-1956. **Memberships:** Am Geophys Union; Glaciol Soc. **Research Statement & Publications:** Arctic oceanography; ice physics; energy exchange ocean-atmosphere; arctic instrument development. **Mailing Address:** 3904 Bedford Rd, Victoria, BC V8N 4K5, Can.

LEWIS, EDWARD SHELDON, CHEMISTRY, CHEMICAL DYNAMICS. **Personal Data:** b Berkeley, Calif, May 7, 1920; m 1955, Fofo Catsinas; c Richard & Gregory. **Education:** Univ Calif, BS, 1940; Harvard Univ, MA, 1947, PhD (chem), 1947. **Honors & Awards:** Southwest Regional Award, Am Chem Soc. **Professional Experience:** EMER PROF CHEM, RICE UNIV, 1990-; chmn dept, Rice Univ, 1980-1985; Univ Col, Dublin, 1978; vis prof, Phys Chem Lab, Oxford Univ, 1967-1968; Guggenheim fel, 1967; chmn, Dept Chem, Rice Univ, 1965-1967; Vis prof, Univ Southampton, 1957; from asst prof to prof, Rice Univ, 1948-1990; Nat Res Coun fel, Univ Calif, Los Angeles, 1947-1948. **Memberships:** Am Chem Soc; Royal Soc Chem; AAAS. **Research Statement & Publications:** Mechanism of reactions of organic compounds, especially diazonium salts, hydrogen isotope effects, methyl transfers and organo-phosphorus chemistry. **Mailing Address:** Dept Chem MS 60, Rice Univ 6100 Main St, Houston, TX 77005-1892. **Fax:** 713-285-5155.

LEWIS, EDWIN REYNOLDS, BIOENGINEERING, NEUROETHOLOGY. **Personal Data:** b Los Angeles, Calif, July 14, 1934. **Education:** Stanford Univ, AB, 1956, MS, 1957, PhD (elec eng), 1962. **Professional Experience:** PROF EMER, Electrical Engrng & Comp Sci, UNIV CALIF, BERKELEY, as of 2004; Mem faculty, EECS, UNIV CALIF BERKELEY, 1967-present; Mem res staff neuralmodeling, Lab Automata Res, Gen Precision, 1961-1967. **Memberships:** Fel Inst Elec & Electronics Engrs; Fel Acoust Soc Am; Soc Neuroscience; AAAS; AsnRes Otolaryngol; Sigma Xi. **Research Statement & Publications:** Applications of engineering analytical tools to problems in neurobiology; network models of dynamical biological systems; morphology and physiology of vestibular and auditory systems. **Mailing Address:** EECS, Univ Calif, 297 Cory, Berkeley, CA 94720-1770. **E-Mail:** lewis@eecs.berkeley.edu

LEWIS, FORBES DOWNER, COMPUTER SCIENCE. **Personal Data:** b New Haven, Conn, April 15, 1942. **Education:** Cornell Univ, BS, 1967, MS, 1969, PhD (comput sci), 1970. **Professional Experience:** PROF EMER COMPUT SCI, UNIV KY, as of 2004; prof comput sci, Univ KY, beginning 1983; assoc prof comput sci & chmn dept, Univ KY, 1978-1982; assoc prof, State Univ NY, Albany, 1975-1978; asst prof, Harvard Univ, 1970-1975. **Memberships:** Asn Comput Mach; Soc Indust & Appl Math; Inst Elec & Electronics Engrs. **Research Statement & Publications:** CAD algorithms for very-large-scale integration; computational complexity. **Mailing Address:** Dept Comput Sci, Univ KY, 971 Patterson Off Tower, Lexington, KY 40506. **E-Mail:** lewis@cs.engr.uky.edu

LEWIS, FRANK HARLAN, BOTANY. **Personal Data:** b Redlands, Calif, January 8, 1919; m 1984, Margaret; c Donald A & Frank M. **Education:** Univ Calif, Los Angeles, BA, 1941, MA, 1942, PhD (bot), 1946. **Honors & Awards:** Award of Merit, Bot Soc Am, 1972. **Professional Experience:** PROF EMER BOT, UNIV CALIF, LOS ANGELES, 1982-; ed, Evolution, 1972-1974; pres, Int Orgn Biosyst, 1969-1975; vpres, Int Orgn Biosyst, 1964-1969; dean, Div Life Sci, 1962-1982; chmn, Dept Bot, Univ Calif, Los Angeles, 1959-1962; consult, NSF, 1958-1969; Guggenheim fel, 1954-1955; from asst prof to prof, Univ Calif, Los Angeles, 1948-1982; Nat Res Coun fel, John Innes Hort Inst, London, 1947-1948; instr, Univ Calif, Los Angeles, 1946-1947; teaching fel, Calif Inst Technol, 1943-1944; asst instr bot, Univ Calif, Los Angeles, 1942-1944. **Memberships:** Fel AAAS; Am Inst Biol Sci; Am Soc Naturalists (pres, 1971); Am Soc Plant Taxonomists (pres, 1969); Soc Study Evolution (secy, 1953-1958, vpres, 1959, pres, 1961); Bot Soc Am; Genetics Soc Am. **Research Statement & Publications:** Mechanisms of evolution; systematics of flowering plants. **Mailing Address:** Dept Biol, Univ Calif, Los Angeles, CA 90095.

LEWIS, FRANK LEROY, ELECTRICAL ENGINEERING. **Personal Data:** b Wurzburg, Ger, May 11, 1949. **Education:** Rice Univ, BA & ME, 1971; Univ W Fla, MS, 1977; Ga Inst Technol, PhD (eleceng), 1981. **Honors & Awards:** Monie A Ferst Award for Outstanding Doctoral Res in Eng, Sigma Xi, 1981; Sigma Xi res award, 1981; Sigma Xi res award, 1984; Frederick E Terman Award, Am Soc Eng Educ, 1989; NASA Comt Space Sta, 1995. **Professional Experience:** Bd govs, Inst Elec & Electronics Engrs Control Systs Soc, 1995; invitedconsult-lectr, UN Umbrella Proj, Warsaw, Poland, 1991; adj prof, Ga Inst Technol, Atlanta, 1990-; PROF & MONCRIEF-O'DONNELL CHMN ELEC ENG, AUTOMATION & ROBOTICS RES INST, UNIV TEX, ARLINGTON, 1990-; Sigma Xi res award, 1990, Fulbright res award, 1988; assoc ed, J Circuits, Systs, Signal Processing, 1986; From asst prof to prof, Ga Inst Technol, Atlanta, 1981-1990. **Memberships:** Fel Inst Elec & Electronics Engrs Control Systs Soc; Soc Indust & Appl Math; AAAS; Sigma Xi; sr mem Inst Elec & Electronics Engrs. **Research Statement & Publications:** Intelligent control; nonlinear control; robotics; discrete event systems; manufacturing control; optimal control systems; neural networks and fuzzy logic; author of various publications; manufacturing. **Mailing Address:** UTA Automation & Robotics Res Inst, 7300 Jack Newell Blvd S, Ft Worth, TX 76118. **Fax:** 817-272-5989. **E-Mail:** lewis@uta.edu

LEWIS, FRANK M, ORTHOPEDICS, BIOMEDICAL ENGINEERING. **Education:** Univ Fla, BS, 1973, MS, 1974. **Professional Experience:** Consult, Holomedica Inc, beginning 1996; vpres Corp Develop, Bugeye Inc, beginning 1994; vpres develop spine & arthroscopy, Wright Med Technol Inc, 1994-1995; PRES & CHIEF EXEC OFFICER, INNERVISION INC, 1992-; vpres corp develop, K Plus A Med Int, 1991-1992; vpres res & develop, Danek Med Inc, 1988-1991; vis prof, Univ Philippines, 1986; dir eng, Richards Med Co Inc, 1982-1988; tech dir, Dow Corning Wright, 1976-1982; proj engr, Codman & Shurtleff Inc, 1975-1976; proprietor, Gainsville Bicycle Distribrs, 1970-1972; adj assoc prof mech eng, Memphis State Univ; instr biomech, Campbell Clin, Memphis; lectr total knee prosthesis, Univ Wash, Seattle & Univ Ky, Lexington. **Memberships:** Soc Biomat; Am Soc Testing & Mat; Orthop Surg Mfrs Asn (secy-treas, 1976-1986); Am Soc Artificial Internal Organs; Orthop Res Soc; Knee Soc; Scoliosis Res Soc. **Research Statement & Publications:** Gustilo metal base tibial prosthesis. **Mailing Address:** 6258 Shady Grove Rd E, Memphis, TN 38120.

LEWIS, FRED A, SCHISTOSOMIASIS, MICROBIOLOGY. **Personal Data:** b Atlanta, Tex, December 9, 1944. **Education:** La Tech Univ, BS, 1966; Northwestern State Univ, MS, 1971, PhD (microbiol), 1975. **Professional Experience:** SR SCIENTIST, BIOMED RES INST, 1977-. **Memberships:** Am Soc parasitologists; Am Soc Trop Med & Hyg; Am Asn Immunologists. **Research Statement & Publications:** Disease schistosomiasis; parasitology. **Mailing Address:** Biomed Res Inst, 12111 Parklawn Dr, Rockville, MD 20852-1784. **Fax:** 301-881-7640. **E-Mail:** flewis@afbr-bri.com

LEWIS, FRED P, METEOROLOGY. **Personal Data:** b Cottonwood, Ariz, March 2, 1949. **Education:** Univ Ariz, BS, 1972; Univ Utah, PhD (meteorol), 1979. **Professional Experience:** MEM SR EXEC SERV, DEP DIR DISTRIB PORTFOLIO MGT, COMMAND, CONTROL, COMMUN & COMPUT SYSTS DIRECTORATE, US, TRANSP COMMAND, SCOTT AFB, ILL, as of 2006; dir weather, Off Dep Chief Staff Air Space & Opers, Aerospace Corp, Wash, Dc, 1996-2000; Brigadier Gen, USAF, 1996-2000; dir, Joint Transp Corp Info Mgt Ctr, US Transp Command, Scott AFB, ILL, 1994-1996; chief, Weather Div, US Transp Command, Scott AFB, Ill, 1992-1994; dep chief staff automation support, Airlift Commun Div, 1990; comdr 26th Weather Squadron, Barksdale AFB, La, 1987-1989; vice comdr, Environ Tech Appln Ctr, Scott AFB, 1986-1987; asst chief Environ Servs Br, Hq Military Airlift Command, Scott AFB, Ill, 1984-1986; 30th Weather Squadron, Suwon AFB, S Korea, 1983-1989; officer in-chg, Weather Forecasts Models Unit, 1981-1982; asst chief Numerical Forecast Sect, Global Weather Ctr, Offutt AFB, Nebr, 1979-1981; automated prog designer, Global Weather Ctr, Offutt AFB, Nebr, 1973-1976; USAF, beginning 1972; officer in-chg operating location B, Detachment 1915; comdr, 1500th Comput Systs Group, Scott AFB, Ill, 1990-1992. **Research Statement & Publications:** Developing doctrine, policy, requirements and standards for weather support to the Air Force and Army. **Mailing Address:** Off Dept Chief Staff Air & Space Oper, USAF, 1490 Air Force Pentagon, Washington, DC 20330-1490.

LEWIS, FREDERICK D, PHOTOCHEMISTRY. **Personal Data:** b Boston, Mass, August 12, 1943; m 1968, Susan; c Gordon & Katherine. **Education:** Amherst Col, BA, 1965; Rochester Univ, PhD (chem), 1968. **Honors & Awards:** Photochemistry Award, Inter-Am Photochemical Soc, 2003; Cope Senior Scholar Award, Am Chem Soc, 2005. **Professional Experience:** Assoc ed, J, Am Chem Soc, 1995-; assoc ed, Int Union Pure & Appl Chem Comm Photochem, 1990-1996; assoc dean, Northwestern Univ, 1989-1992; assoc ed, J Phys Org Chem, 1987-1995; PROF, NORTHWESTERN UNIV, 1979-; fel, Sloan Found, 1975-1977; fel, Dreyfus Found, 1973-1978; from asst prof to assoc prof, Northwestern Univ, 1969-1979; USPHS res fel chem, Columbia Univ, 1968-1969; consult, 3M Corp. **Memberships:** Am Chem Soc; Inter Am Photochem Soc; Europ Photochem Asn; fel AAAS. **Research Statement & Publications:** Organic photochemistry; radical ions; free radicals; cycloaddition reactions; exciplexes; nucleic acids. **Mailing Address:** Dept Chem, Northwestern Univ, Tech K348, Evanston, IL 60208-3113. **Fax:** 847-467-2184. **E-Mail:** lewis@chem.chmnorthwestern.edu

LEWIS, GEORGE CAMPBELL, JR, OBSTETRICS & GYNECOLOGY, ONCOLOGY. **Personal Data:** b Williamsburg, Ky, March 25, 1919. **Education:** Haverford Col, BS, 1942; Univ Pa, MD, 1944; Am Bd Obstet & Gynec, dipl, 1953; Gyn Oncol, 1980. **Professional Experience:** CO FOUNDER, GYNEC ONCOL GROUP, JEFFERSON MED COL, as of 1996-; Chmn, Gynec Oncol Grp, 1975-1989; PROF GYNEC ONCOL & DIR DIV, JEFFERSON MED COL, 1973-; dir div gynec oncol, Hahnemann Med Col & Hosp, 1971-1973; Am Oncol Hosp, beginning 1963 & Magee Mem Hosp Rehab Ctr, beginning 1968; consult, Lankenau Hosp & Philadelphia Gen Hosp, beginning 1962; prof obstet & gynec & chmn dept, Hahnemann Med Col & Hosp, 1962-1973; consult lectr, US Naval HospPhiladelphia, 1956-1977; asst prof obstet & gynec, Sch Med, Univ Pa, 1956-1963; res asst, SchMed, Univ Pa, 1953-1956; instr radium ther, Sch Med, Univ Pa, 1951-1963; instr, Sch Med, Univ Pa, 1950-1953; Am Cancer Soc fel gynec oncol, Hosp Univ Pa, 1950-1952; resident obstet& gynec, Hosp Univ Pa, 1947-1950; Intern med, Hosp Univ Pa, 1944-1945; mem div gynec oncol, Am Bd Obstet & Gynec. **Memberships:** Am Cancer Soc; Soc Gynec Oncol (pres) 1969; Am Gynec Soc; Am Asn Obstet& Gynec; Am Col Obstet & Gynec. **Research Statement & Publications:** Etiology, early diagnosis and evaluation of modes of therapy of gynecologic oncology. **Mailing Address:** Gynec Oncol Group, Thomas Jefferson Univ, 1025 Walnut St, Philadelphia, PA 19107-5001.

LEWIS, GEORGE EDWIN, ORGANIC CHEMISTRY. **Personal Data:** b Decatur, Ga, January 6, 1933. **Education:** Emory Univ, AB, 1952, MS, 1953; Fla State Univ, PhD (chem), 1958. **Professional Experience:** PROF CHEM, JACKSONVILLE UNIV, 1980-; assoc prof, Jacksonville Univ, 1966-1980; asst prof chem, La State Univ, 1959-1966; Res asst, Ga Inst Technol, 1958-1959. **Memberships:** Am Chem Soc; The Chem Soc. **Research Statement & Publications:** Mechanisms of organic reactions. **Mailing Address:** Div Sci & Math, Jacksonville Univ, Jacksonville, FL 32211-3393.

LEWIS, GEORGE MCCORMICK, GEOMETRY. **Personal Data:** b Los Angeles, Calif, September 14, 1940; m Louise; c Melanie Lewis, Heather Lewis & Alice Gray Lewis. **Education:** Stanford Univ, BA, 1961; Univ Southern Calif, MA, 1964, PhD (math), 1970. **Professional Experience:** PROF MATH, CALIF POLYTECH STATE UNIV, SAN LUIS OBISPO, 1979-; assoc prof, Calif Polytech State Univ, San Luis Obispo, 1972-1979; Asst prof, Calif Polytech State Univ, San Luis Obispo 1967-1972. **Memberships:** Am Math Soc; Math Asn Am. **Research Statement & Publications:** Synthetic differential geometry. **Mailing Address:** Mathematics Dept, Calif State Polytech Univ, San Luis Obispo, CA 93407. **Fax:** 805-756-6537. **E-Mail:** glewis@calpoly.edu

LEWIS, GEORGE R(OBERT), CHEMICAL ENGINEERING. **Personal Data:** b Kansas City, Mo, June 26, 1924; m 1954, c 3. **Education:** Ohio State Univ, BChE, 1948, MSc, 1949, PhD (chem eng), 1951. **Professional Experience:** CONSULT, 1988-; tech dir, Paperboard Prod Div, 1969-1988; prod mgr, Paperboard Res Labs, Mead Corp, Dayton, 1964-1969; staff consult, Paperboard Res Labs, Mead Corp, Dayton, 1960-1964; res engr, Paperboard Res Labs, Mead Corp, Dayton, 1955-1960; chem develop supvr, Film Dept, 1953-1955; Res engr cellophane process, E I du Pont de Nemours & Co, 1951-1953. **Memberships:** Tech Asn Pulp & Paper Indust; Am Inst Chem Engrs. **Research Statement & Publications:** Industrial wastes; cellophane process; pulp and paper; recycled paperboard; paperboard products. **Mailing Address:** 9450 Sugar Bend Trail, Dayton, OH 45458-3863.

LEWIS, GILBERT N, MATHEMATICS. **Education:** Univ Wis-Milwaukee, PhD. **Professional Experience:** ASSOC PROF, DEPT MATHS, MICH TECH UNIV, as of 2006. **Mailing Address:** Math Dept, Mich Tech Univ, 1400 Townsend Dr, Houghton, MI 49931-1295. **Fax:** 906-487-3133. **E-Mail:** lewis@mtu.edu

LEWIS, GLENN C, SOIL CHEMISTRY. **Personal Data:** b Oakley, Idaho, July 13, 1920; m 1956, Norma; c Reed, Ann, Amy, Wallace, Rand & Camille. **Education:** Univ Idaho, BS, 1946, MS, 1949; Purdue Univ, PhD (soils), 1962. **Professional Experience:** PROF EMER, UNIV IDAHO, 1985-; from asst prof agr chem to prof soils, Univ Idaho, 1952-1985; anal agr chem, Univ Idaho, 1947-1952. **Memberships:** Soil Sci Soc Am; Int Soc Soil Sci; AAAS (pres, pacific div, 1979). **Research Statement & Publications:** Chemical and mineralogical studies on slick spot soils; water quality, including effects of irrigation water quality on soil characteristics; phosphorus reactions in calcareous soils; mineralogical studies on loess. **Mailing Address:** 1012 S Howard St, Moscow, ID 83843.

LEWIS, GORDON, CERAMIC ENGINEERING. **Personal Data:** b Cincinnati, Ohio, April 7, 1933. **Education:** Alfred Univ, BS, 1956, PhD (ceramics), 1963. **Professional Experience:** PROF CERAMIC ENG, UNIV MO, ROLLA, 1973-; assoc prof ceramic eng, Univ

MO, Rolla, 1964-1973; res assoc chem, Univ Kans, 1962-1964; Ceramic engr, Carborundum Co, NY, 1957-1958. **Memberships:** Am Ceramic Soc; Nat Inst Ceramic Engrs; Am Soc Eng Educ. **Research Statement & Publications:** High temperature chemistry; phase equilibria and vaporization behavior in oxide systems; thermogravimetric behavior and phase identification of high alumina refractory cements. **Mailing Address:** Dept Ceramic Eng, Clemson Univ 110 Olin Hall, Clemson, SC 29632-0001.

LEWIS, GORDON DEPEW, FOREST ECONOMICS, POLICY. **Personal Data:** b Charlottesville, Va, July 22, 1929. **Education:** Va Polytech Inst, BS, 1951; Duke Univ, MFor, 1957; Mich State Univ, PhD (forestecon), 1961. **Professional Experience:** RETIRED; asst dir, western environ forestry res, Rocky Mountain Forest ExpSta, 1981-1992; prog mgr, western environ forestry res, Rocky Mountain Forest Exp Sta, 1977-1981; proj leader, Rocky Mountain Forest Exp Sta, 1971-1977; br chief, Washington, DC, 1968-1971; economist, Washington, DC, 1966-1967; proj leader, Southeastern Forest Exp Sta, US Forest Serv, 1962-1966; Asst prof forest econ, Univ Mont, 1959-1962. **Memberships:** Soc Am Foresters; Am Econ Asn. **Research Statement & Publications:** Economic evaluations of alternative methods of exploiting natural resources for regional development consistent with the maintenance of the quality of rural and wildlife environments. **Mailing Address:** Three Weston Heights Dr, Asheville, NC 28803-8518.

LEWIS, GWYNNE DAVID, PLANT PATHOLOGY. **Personal Data:** b Hackensack, NJ, June 12, 1928. **Education:** Rutgers Univ, BS, 1951; Purdue Univ, MS, 1953; Cornell Univ, PhD, 1958. **Honors & Awards:** Bronze Medal, Am Rhododendron Soc, 1975. **Professional Experience:** PROF PLANT PATH, RUTGERS UNIV, NEW BRUNSWICK, 1970-; fromasst prof to assoc prof, Rutgers Univ, New Brunswick, 1958-1970; Asst plant path, Purdue Univ, 1951-1953 & Cornell Univ, 1953-1958. **Memberships:** Am Phytopath Soc. **Research Statement & Publications:** Diseases of vegetable crops; plant nematology; control of plant and vegetable diseases. **Mailing Address:** Dept Plant Path, Rutgers Univ, New Brunswick, NJ 08903.

LEWIS, H(AROLD) RALPH, PHYSICS, PLASMA & COMPUTATIONAL PHYSICS. **Personal Data:** b Chicago, Ill, June 7, 1931. **Education:** Univ Chicago, AB, 1951, SB, 1953; Univ Ill, MS, 1955, PhD (physics), 1958; Dartmouth Col, MA, 1993. **Professional Experience:** PROF PHYSICS, DARTMOUTH COL, 1991-; lab fel, Los Alamos Nat Lab, 1983-1991; dep group leader, Los Alamos Nat Lab, 1981-1983; assoc group leader, Los Alamos Nat Lab, 1975-1981; mem staff, Los Alamos Nat Lab, 1963-1975; instr, Princeton Univ, 1960-1963; res assoc physics, Univ Heidelberg, 1958-1960; fel, Ger Acad Exchange Serv, Univ Heidelberg, 1958-1959. **Memberships:** Fel Am Phys Soc. **Research Statement & Publications:** Plasma physics; nulcear spectroscopy; superconductivity; computational physics. **Mailing Address:** Dept Physics & Astron, Dartmouth Col, Hanover, NH 03755-3528. **E-Mail:** ralph.lewis@dartmouth.edu

LEWIS, HAROLD WARREN, PHYSICS. **Personal Data:** b New York, NY, October 1, 1923; m 1947, c 2. **Education:** NY Univ, AB, 1943; Univ Calif, AM, 1944, PhD (physics), 1948. **Professional Experience:** PROF EMER, PHYSICS, UNIV CALIF, SANTA BARBARA, 1991-; dir, Quantum Inst, Univ Calif, Santa Barbara, 1969-1973; prof physics, Univ Calif, Santa Barbara, beginning 1964; from assoc prof to prof physics, Univ Wis, 1956-1964; mem tech staff, Bell Tel Labs, NJ, 1951-1956; asst prof physics, Univ Calif, 1948-1953; mem staff, Inst Advan Study, 1947-1948 & 1950-1951. **Memberships:** Am Phys Soc; Sigma Xi. **Research Statement & Publications:** Theoretical physics. **Mailing Address:** Dept Physics, Univ Calif Santa Barbara, Santa Barbara, CA 93106. **E-Mail:** hlewis@physics.ucsb.edu

LEWIS, HENRY RAFALSKY, PHYSICS. **Personal Data:** b Yonkers, NY, November 19, 1925; m 1957, c 3. **Education:** Harvard Univ, AB, 1948, MA, 1949, PhD (physics), 1956. **Professional Experience:** RETIRED; dir, Oyax Corp, beginning 1996; Genzyme Corp, Cambridge, Mass, 1987-2000; vice chmn & dir, Dennison Mfg Corp, 1986-1991; sr vpres & dir, Dennison Mfg Corp, 1982-1985; dir, Delphan Syst, Randolph, Mass, 1980; group vpres & dir, Dennison Mfg Corp, 1974-1982; pres, Optel Corp, 1973-1974; vpres res & develop, Itek Corp, 1970-1973; dir, electronic res lab, 1966-1970; group head quantum electronics, David Sarnoff Res Ctr, RCA Corp, 1957-1966; mem staff opers res, Opers Eval Group, Mass Inst Technol, 1951-1953, 1956. **Memberships:** Am Phys Soc; Inst Elec & Electronics Engrs; NY Acad Sci; Sigma Xi. **Research Statement & Publications:** Paramagnetic resonance; quantum electronics; operations research; molecular beams. **Mailing Address:** 35 Clover St, Belmont, MA 02178. **E-Mail:** hhrrlewis@aol.com

LEWIS, H(ERBERT) CLAY, CHEMICAL ENGINEERING. **Personal Data:** b Newton, Mass, August 7, 1913. **Education:** Bowdoin Col, AB, 1934; Mass Inst Technol, MS, 1937; Carnegie Inst Technol, ScD (chem eng), 1942. **Professional Experience:** RETIRED; fel, Ctr Advan Eng Study, Mass Inst Technol, 1971-1972; vis prof, Imp Col, Univ London, 1960-1961; prof, Ga Inst Technol, 1953-1980; from asst prof to assoc prof chem eng, Ga Inst Technol, 1946-1953; res assoc, Mass Inst Technol, 1945-1946; from instr to asst prof chem eng, Univ Ill, 1942-1945; res assoc, Nat Defense Res Comt, 1941-1942; chem engr, Humble Oil & Ref Co, Tex, 1937-1940. **Memberships:** Am Chem Soc; Am Inst Chem Engrs. **Research Statement & Publications:** Chemical technology. **Mailing Address:** 212 Winnona Dr, Decatur, GA 30030.

LEWIS, HERMAN WILLIAM, GENETICS, ZOOLOGY. **Personal Data:** b Chicago, Ill, July 10, 1923; m 1942, Lewis, Helen; c Lewis, David N, Miriam Gerstenblith. **Education:** Univ Ill, BS, 1947, MS, 1949; Univ Calif, PhD (genetics), 1953. **Honors & Awards:** Mendel Medal, Govt of Czech., 1965. **Professional Experience:** RETIRED; dep exec dir, US-Israel Binat Sci Found, 1986-1989; dep dir, Div Molecular Biosci, 1984-1986; sr scientist, Cellular Biol Sect, 1977-1984; head, Cellular Biol Sect, 1966-1977; prog dir genetic biol, NSF, 1962-1966; prof life sci & chmn dept, Mich State Univ, 1961-1962; asst prof biol, Mass Inst Technol, 1954-1961; USPHS res fel, Univ Calif, 1952-1954. **Memberships:** AAAS; Biophys Soc; Genetics Soc Am; Am Soc Cell Biol; Am Soc Human Genetics. **Research Statement & Publications:** Biochemical, physiological and molecular genetics; biophysics and cytology of genetic material; human cell biology. **Mailing Address:** One Gristmill Ct Apt 204, Baltimore, MD 21208.

LEWIS, HOMER DICK, METALLURGY, NUCLEAR ENGINEERING. **Personal Data:** b Covington, Ky, October 4, 1926. **Education:** Univ Cincinnati, MetE, 1952; Univ NMex, MS, 1964, MSc, 1971. **Professional Experience:** RETIRED; sect leader, Solidification Tech, 1981-1986; mem, Nat Task Group, Los Alamos Lab Rep, 1977-1981; Co-prin investr, Liquid Metal Fast Breeder Reactor FuelsProperties, 1975-1978; staff mem, Los Alamos Sci Lab, Univ Calif, 1958-1986; res engr, BoeingAirplane Co, 1957-1958; Staff mem uranium casting, Los Alamos Sci Lab, Univ Calif, 1952-1957. **Memberships:** Am Soc Metals. **Research Statement & Publications:** Packing behavior of particulate solids; small particle statistics; physics of particulate systems; powder metallurgy; carbon and graphite research and development; electrical and thermal transport properties of plutonium and plutomium alloys and compounds; solidification process; thermochemistry of uranium, plutonium compounds; solidification processes. **Mailing Address:** PO Box 644, Bayfield, CO 81122.

LEWIS, IRA WAYNE, CONTINUUM THEORY, GEOMETRIC TOPOLOGY. **Personal Data:** b Hillsboro, Tex, September 22, 1950. **Education:** Univ Houston, BS, 1972; Tex A&M Univ, MS, 1974; Univ Tex, Austin, PhD (math), 1977. **Professional Experience:** PROF MATH, TEX TECH UNIV, 1989-; invited lectr, Inst Math, Hanoi, Vietnam, 1986; vis assoc prof, Auburn Univ, 1984-1985; Nat Acad Sci exchange scientist, Stephan Banach Ctr, 1984-1985; vis asst prof, Univ Ky, 1982; Nat Acad Sci exchange scientist, Inst Math, Polish Acad Sci, 1981; vis asst prof, Univ Ala, Birmingham, 1981; vis asst prof, Univ Tex, Austin, 1980; from asst prof to assoc prof, Tex Tech Univ, 1979-1989; vis asst prof, Tulane Univ, 1979-1980; vis lectr, Tex Tech Univ, 1977-1979. **Memberships:** Am Math Soc; Am Inst Aeronaut & Astronaut; Astron Soc Pac; AAAS; SigmaXi; Am Math Asn. **Research Statement & Publications:** Continuum theory and geometric topology including indecomposable continua, classification of homogeneous continua, embeddings of tree-like continua, continuous decompositions and homogeneous embeddings of continua in manifolds. **Mailing Address:** Dept Math, Tex Tech Univ, Mail Stop 1042, Lubbock, TX 79409-0001. **Fax:** 806-742-1112. **E-Mail:** wlewis@math.ttu.edu

LEWIS, IRWIN C, PYROLYSIS CHEMISTRY, CARBON & GRAPHITE. **Personal Data:** b New York, NY. **Education:** City Col NY, BS, 1953; Univ Kans, PhD (org chem), 1957. **Honors & Awards:** Charles Pettinos Int Award in Carbon Sci, Am Carbon Soc, 1987, Graffin Lectr, 1986. **Professional Experience:** SR CORP FEL, UCAR CARBON CO, as of 2002; corp fel, Union Carbidecorp, beginning 1960; assoc phys-org, Pa State Univ, 1958-1960. **Memberships:** Am Chem Soc; Sigma Xi; Am Carbon Soc. **Research Statement & Publications:** Studies of pyrolysis of aromatic hydrocarbons, characterization and reactions of carbonaceos materials, coal and petroleum chemistry, electron spin resonance of aromatic radicals, liquid crystal and polymerization in pitch, carbon fibers. **Mailing Address:** Parma Tech Ctr, UCAR Carbon Corp, PO Box 6116, Cleveland, OH 44136. **Fax:** 216-676-2423.

LEWIS, J(ACK) R(OCKLEY), METALLURGY. **Personal Data:** b Eureka, Kans, July 30, 1920. **Education:** Stanford Univ, BS, 1947, PhD (metall), 1951. **Professional Experience:** CONSULT ADVAN MAT TECHNOL, 1985-; mgr advan mat, RocketdyneDiv, Rockwell Int, 1967-1985; group leader mat develop, Atomics Int Div, NAm Aviation, Inc, 1961-1967; consult engr, Gen Elec Co, 1960-1961; supvr fuel element develop, Gen Elec Co, 1957-1960; engr, Gen Elec Co, 1951-1957; metallurgist, Fairchild Engine & Airplane Corp, 1950-1951; Res assoc metall, Stanford Univ, 1947-1950. **Memberships:** Am Inst Mining Metall & Petrol Engrs; Am Nuclear Soc; fel Am Soc Metals; AmInst Chem Engrs; Am Ceramics Soc. **Research Statement & Publications:** Nuclear reactorand radioisotope materials; liquid metals; high-temperature materials; intermetallic compounds and cermets; rocket engine materials and processes; composite materials; structrual ceramics. **Mailing Address:** 11300 Yarmouth Ave, Granada Hills, CA 91344.

LEWIS, JAMES, SYSTEM ENGINEERING, PROJECT MANAGEMENT. **Personal Data:** b Nashville, Tenn, September 17, 1942. **Education:** Vanderbilt Univ, BE, 1963; Princeton Univ, MSE, 1965; Purdue Univ, PhD (elec eng), 1969. **Professional Experience:** SPACE SYST MGR, TRW DEFENSE & SPACE SYSTS GROUP, 1978-; lectr, Loyola Marymount Univ, 1977-1981; head, Signal Design Sect, TRW Defense & Space Systs Group, 1975-1977; Japan Soc Prom Sci fel, Kyoto Univ, 1971-1972; mem tech staff, TRW Systs Group, 1969-1975; instr elec eng, Purdue Univ, 1966-1967. **Memberships:** Inst Elec & Electronics Engrs; Inst Math Statist. **Research Statement & Publications:** Systems engineering; communication theory; stochastic processes; optical communications. **Mailing Address:** TRW SPACE & ELECTRONICS GROUP, One Space Park, Redondo Beach, CA 90278. **E-Mail:** jim.lewis@trw.com

LEWIS, JAMES CHESTER, WILDLIFE ECOLOGY. **Personal Data:** b Kalamazoo, Mich, January 31, 1936. **Education:** Univ Mich, BS, 1957; Mich State Univ, MS, 1963; Okla State Univ, PhD (wildlife ecol), 1974. **Professional Experience:** RETIRED; consult, Nat Audubon Soc, 1980; tech ed, US Fish & Wildlife Serv, Colo State Univ, 1977-1997; from asst prof to assoc prof life sci, Sch Biophys Sci, 1967-1977; asst unit leader, Okla Coop Wildlife Res Unit, 1967-1977; res supvr, Tenn Game Div, 1964-1967; res proj leader game mgt, Tenn Game Div, 1960-1964; dist biologist, Tenn Game Div, 1959-1960; biologist aide, Mich Game Div, 1957-1959. **Memberships:** Wildlife Soc. **Research Statement & Publications:** Endangered species research; deer and turkey management; ecology of wildlife rabies; mourning dove and sandhill crane behavior and ecology. **Mailing Address:** 7712 Midge NE, Albuquerque, NM 87109.

LEWIS, JAMES KELLEY, RANGE SCIENCE. **Personal Data:** b Waco, Tex, October 24, 1924. **Education:** Colo State Univ, BS, 1948; Mont State Univ, MS, 1951. **Professional Experience:** Assoc prof, S Dak State Univ, 1958-1985; asst prof animal sci, S Dak State Univ, 1950-1958; PROF EMER, S DAK STATE UNIV. **Memberships:** Soc Range Mgt; Am Soc Animal Sci; Ecol Soc Am; Wildlife Soc; Brit Grassland Soc. **Research Statement & Publications:** Structure, function, measurement, manipulation, uses and systems analysis of range ecosystems; range animal nutrition and management; coupling of range and agronomic ecosystems. **Mailing Address:** S Dak State Univ, Brookings, SD 57007.

LEWIS, JAMES PETTIS, LIQUEFIED NATURAL GAS & CRYOGENIC TECHNOLOGY, FACILITY SAFETY FOR HAZARDOUS MATERIALS. **Personal Data:** b Omaha, Nebr, April 21, 1933. **Education:** Calif Inst Technol, BSME, 1955. **Professional Experience:** CHMN, PROJ TECH LIAISON ASSOC INC, as of 2003; PRES, PROJ TECH LIAISON ASSOCS, 1978-; proj mgr, Transco Energy Co, 1972-1978; tech dir, Distrigas Corp, 1969-1972; asst chief engr, Cosmodyne Corp, 1962-1969; dist engr, Richfield Oil Corp, 1955-1962. **Memberships:** Am Soc Mech Engrs; Am Inst Chem Engrs; Seismol Soc Am; Earthquake EngRes Inst; Nat Fire Protection Asn; NY Acad Sci. **Research Statement & Publications:** Life limiting mechanisms and life extension measures for hazardous facilities; non destructive composite material testing; failure mechanisms in brittle insulating materials; liquefied natural gas as vehicle fuel. **Mailing Address:** Proj Tech Liaison Assoc, 206 S Masonic St, Bellville, TX 77418. **Fax:** 281-251-5625. **E-Mail:** ptla@mail.net

LEWIS, JAMES VERNON, ENVIRONMENTAL SCIENCES. **Personal Data:** b Neligh, Nebr, May 2, 1915; div, c Alfred Bruce, Aleta & Lance Eric. **Education:** Univ Calif, AB, 1937, MA, 1939, PhD (math), 1942; Univ NMex, MCRP, 1984. **Professional Experience:** PROF EMER MATH, UNIV NMEX, 1980-; assoc prof, Univ Nmex, 1953-1980; asst prof, Univ Nev, 1946-1947; mathematician, Aberdeen Proving Ground, 1945-1953; mathematician, Radiation Lab, Univ Calif, 1943-1945; jr physicist, USN, Calif, 1942-1943; asst, Univ Calif, 1939-1942. **Memberships:** Am Planning Asn; Math Asn Am; Sigma Xi; Fedn Am Scientists. **Research Statement & Publications:** Urban planning; iterative methods for decision making in urban planning; calculuc of variations. **Mailing Address:** Dept Math & Statist, Univ Nmex, MSC03 2150 1, Albuquerque, NM 87131-0001. **Fax:** 505-277-5505.

LEWIS, JAMES W L, MOLECULAR PHYSICS, FLUID PHYSICS. **Personal Data:** b Natchez, Miss, May 3, 1938; m 1961, c 3. **Education:** Univ Miss, BS, 1960, MS, 1964, PhD (physics), 1966. **Professional Experience:** PHYSICIST, CALSPAN INC, 1981-; PROF PHYSICS, SPACE INST, UNIV TENN, 1977-; physicist, Aro, Inc, 1969-1980; UK Sci Res Coun fel physics, Queen's Univ, Belfast, 1968-1969; assoc prof physics, Space Inst, Univ Tenn, 1966-1977; physicist, US Naval Weapons Lab, 1961-1962 & ARO Inc, 1966-1968. **Memberships:** Am Inst Aeronaut & Astronaut; Am Phys Soc. **Research Statement & Publications:** Vibrational relaxation processes in gases; molecular processes in hypersonic flow phenomena; molecular and atomic beam collision processes using high temperature shock tube source; raman-rayleigh scattering in gases; condensation processes in gases; nonlinear optics. **Mailing Address:** Dept Physics, Univ Tenn Space Inst, 411 B H Goethert Pkwy, Tullahoma, TN 37388. **E-Mail:** jlewis@utsi.edu

LEWIS, JEFFREY KENNETH, PHYSICS. **Education:** Augustana Col, BA; Univ Md, PhD (pub policy). **Professional Experience:** EXEC DIR, MANAGING THE ATOM PROJ, ARMS CONTROL WORK, as of 2005. **Mailing Address:** 8101 Camino Media Apt 38, Bakersfield, CA 93311. **Fax:** 805-664-3158. **E-Mail:** ameyandjeff@mac.com

LEWIS, JERRY PARKER, MEDICINE. **Personal Data:** b Terre Haute, Ind, September 20, 1931. **Education:** James Millikin Univ, 1952; Univ Ill, BS, 1953, MD, 1956. **Professional Experience:** PROF EMER MED, UNIV CALIF, DAVIS, as of 2000; CHIEF DIV HEMAT & ONCOL, UNIV CALIF, DAVIS, 1982-; actg chmn, Dept Int Med, 1980-1982; chief staff, Med Ctr, 1979-1980; PROF PATH, UNIV CALIF, DAVIS, 1978-; consult, David Grant Hosp, Travis, AFB, Calif, 1968-; lectr clin path & vet med, Univ Calif, Davis, 1968-1974; chief div hemat & oncol, Univ Calif, Davis, 1967-1980; assoc prof, Univ Calif, Davis, 1967-1969; actg chief clinhemat & chief spec hemat, Presby-St Luke's Hosp, Chicago, 1965-1967; Asst prof med, Univ Ill, 1964-1967; res fel, Presby-St Luke's Hosp, Chicago, 1963-1965; NIH fel hemat, Presby-St Luke'sHosp, Chicago, 1961-1963. **Memberships:** Am Soc Hemat; Am Soc Clin Oncol; fel Am Col Physicians; Soc Exp Hemat; Am Soc Human Genetics. **Research Statement & Publications:** Leukemia; cytogenetics; toxicity of laetrile; molecular biology of oncogenes. **Mailing Address:** Sch Med, Univ Calif, 1508 Alhambra Blvd, Davis, CA 95616-6510.

LEWIS, JESSE C, MATHEMATICS, COMPUTER SCIENCES. **Personal Data:** b Vaughan, Miss, June 26, 1929. **Education:** Univ Ill, MS, 1955, MA, 1959; Syracuse Univ, PhD (math), 1966. **Professional Experience:** VPRES ACAD AFFAIRS, NORFOLK STATE UNIV, 1984-; deleg leader, Korea & Hong Kong, 1984; deleg leader, People to People Citizen Ambassador Prog, Western Europ & Russia, 1982; assoc dean comput serv & prof comput sci, Comput Ctr & chmn, Dept Comput Sci, Jackson State Univ, 1980-1984; mem eval panel sci comput, Nat Bur Stands, 1980-1983; dir, prof math & chmn Div Natural Sci, 1967-1980; dir, Comput Ctr & chmn, Dept Comput Sci, Jackson State Univ, 1966-1980; res asst, Comput Ctr, Syracuse Univ, 1963-1966; asst prof, Jackson State Col, 1959-1961; instr math, Southern Univ, 1955-1957 & Prairie View Agr & Mech Col, 1957-1958; consult, Comt Undergrad Prog Math, Jackson State Col. **Memberships:** Math Asn Am; Am Math Soc; Asn Comput Mach; Asn Educ Data Systs. **Research Statement & Publications:** Computer study of permanents of n-square (0, 1)-matrices with k l's in each row and column. **Mailing Address:** Norfolk State Univ, 2401 Corprew Ave, Norfolk, VA 23504. **Fax:** 757-683-9435.

LEWIS, JESSICA HELEN, MEDICINE, HEMATOLOGY. **Personal Data:** b Harpswell, Maine, October 26, 1917. **Education:** Goucher Col, AB, 1938; Johns Hopkins Univ, MD, 1942. **Professional Experience:** PROF EMER MED, UNIV PITTSBURGH, as of 2002; DIR EMER SCI, UNIV PITTSBURGH & CENT BLOOD BANK, 1992-; sci dir, Cent Blood Bank, 1987-1992; sr vpres, Cent Blood Bank, 1985-1992; med dir, Cent Blood Bank, 1985-1990; vpres, Cent Blood Bank Pittsburgh, beginning 1975; vpres, Cent Blood Bank, 1975-1985; prof med, Univ Pittsburgh, 1975-1985; res prof med, Univ Pittsburgh, 1970-1977; dir res, Cent Blood Bank Pittsburgh, 1969-1975; res assoc prof, Univ Pittsburgh, 1958-1970; staff mem, Presby-Univ Hosp, beginning 1955; res assoc med, Univ Pittsburgh, 1955-1958; assoc med, Med Sch, Duke Univ, 1951-1955; res assoc physiol, Univ NC, 1948-1955; res fel, USPHS, Univ NC, 1947-1948; res assoc, Med Sch, Emory Univ, 1946-1947; res fel, Thorndike Mem Lab & Harvard Univ, 1944-1946; asst med, Boston City Hosp, 1944-1946; asst resident, Univ Calif Hosp, 1943-1944; intern, Hosp Women, Baltimore, Md, 1942-1943. **Memberships:** Am Soc Hemat; World Fedn Hemophilia; Am Physiol Soc; Am Soc Clin Invest; Am Fedn Clin Res; Am Asn Blood Banks. **Research Statement & Publications:** Blood coagulation; enzyme and protein chemistry; comparative hematology in vertebrates. **Mailing Address:** Dept Med, Univ Pittsburgh, Pittsburgh, PA 15213.

LEWIS, JOHN BRADLEY, MARINE BIOLOGY. **Personal Data:** b Ottawa, Ont, January 12, 1925. **Education:** McGill Univ, BSc, 1940, MSc, 1950, PhD (zoology), 1954. **Professional Experience:** PROF EMER GEOG, DEPT GEOG, MCGILL UNIV, as of 2004; Dept Geog, McGill Univ, as of 1998; dir, Inst Oceanog, beginning 1983; dir, Pedpath Mus, 1971-1983; prof Marine Sci, McGill Univ, 1969-1983; assoc prof, Bellairs Res Inst, 1961-1969; dir, BellairsRes Inst, 1954-1971; asst marine biol, Inst Marine Sci, Univ Miami, 1951-1954. **Memberships:** Can Soc Zool; Int Soc Reef Studies. **Research Statement & Publications:** Tropical marine ecology and physiology; tropical marine organisms and coral reef ecology. **Mailing Address:** Dept Geog, McGill Univ, Rm 624, Burnside Hall, 805 Sherbrooke St W, Montreal, PQ H3A 2K6, Can. **Fax:** 514-398-7437. **E-Mail:** lewis@felix.geog.mcgill.ca

LEWIS, JOHN E, AUTOMATIC TEST. **Personal Data:** b Riverside, Calif, March 30, 1939. **Education:** Calif State Univ, BS, 1964; Univ Southern Calif, MS, 1975. **Professional Experience:** CONSULT, 1990-; sr engr, USN, 1967-1990; Qual mgr, Interstate Electronics, 1965-1967. **Memberships:** Sr mem Inst Elec & Electronics Engrs; fel Inst Automotive Engrs. **Research Statement & Publications:** Automatic test and test software. **Mailing Address:** Nine Alcoba, Irvine, CA 92714.

LEWIS, J(OHN) E(UGENE), ELECTRICAL ENGINEERING. **Personal Data:** b St John, NB, April 11, 1941. **Education:** Univ NB, Fredericton, BS, 1964; Univ BC, PhD (elec eng), 1968. **Professional Experience:** CHMN & DIR ELEC ENG, UNIV NB, FREDERICTON, as of 2004; dir, Cadmi Microelectronics, Inc, beginning 1986; prof elec eng, Univ Nb, Fredericton, beginning 1980; chmn dept, Univ Nb, Fredericton, 1980-1989; from asst prof to assocprof, Univ Nb, Fredericton, 1974-1980; nat res coun can fel, Univ Southampton, 1968-1969. **Memberships:** Inst Elec & Electronics Engrs; Brit Inst Elec Engrs; Int Microwave Power Inst. **Research Statement & Publications:** Industrial applications of microwaves to materials processing and process control; microwave measurement of nonelectrical quantities; low-loss waveguides. **Mailing Address:** Dept Elec Eng, Univ NB, Rm H-105 Head Hall, Fredericton, NB E3B 5A3, Can. **Fax:** 506-453-3589. **E-Mail:** jelewis@unb.ca

LEWIS, JOHN G, MATHEMATICS. **Education:** Stanford Univ, PhD, 1976. **Professional Experience:** OFF, CRAY INC, as of 2006. **Memberships:** Soc Indust & Appl Math. **Mailing Address:** Cray Inc, 411 First Ave S, Ste 600, Seattle, WA 98124-0346. **Fax:** 206-701-2500. **E-Mail:** jglewis@cray.com

LEWIS, JOHN HUBBARD, GEOLOGY. **Personal Data:** b Jamestown, NY, April 13, 1929; m 1983, c Patricia, Mark, David & Timothy. **Education:** Allegheny Col, BS, 1956; Univ Colo, PhD (geol), 1965. **Professional Experience:** CONSULT, 1980-; prof, Colo Col, 1974-1981; chmn dept, Colo Col, 1970-1978; US Antarctic res partic, Tex Tech Col, 1967-1968; dir, NSF Sec Sci Training Prog, Colo Col, 1965-1967; from instr to assoc prof geol, Colo Col, 1958-1974; lectr, Exten Div, Univ Colo, 1958-1966. **Research Statement & Publications:** Sedimentary petrology; petrology and diagenesis of upper Cambrian rocks of Colorado; structural geology. **Mailing Address:** 918 N Royer St, Colorado Springs, CO 80903. **E-Mail:** jhlrkdk@aol.com

LEWIS, JOHN L, OBSTETRICS & GYNECOLOGY. **Personal Data:** b San Antonio, Tex, June 5, 1929. **Education:** Harvard Univ, BA, 1952, MD, 1957; Am Bd Obstet & Gynec, dipl, 1967, cert, 1979. **Professional Experience:** ATTEND SURGEON, GYNEC SERV, MEM HOSP CANCER & ALLIED DIS & JAMES EWING HOSP, 1990-; mem, Sloan-Kettering inst Cancer res, 1973-; attend obstetrician & gynecologist, New York Lying-in Hosp, 1971-; PROF OBSTET & GYNEC, MED COL, CORNELL UNIV, 1971-; dir, Am Bd Obstet & Gynec, 1970-1976 & div Gynec Oncol, 1970-1976; lectr, Col Physicians& Surgeons, Columbia Univ, 1968-; attend surgeon, mem Hosp Cancer & Allied Dis, 1968-; chief gynec serv, mem Hosp Cancer & Allied Dis, 1968-1990; assoc, Sloan-Kettering Inst-Cancer res, 1968-1973; assoc prof, Gynec Serv, mem Hosp Cancer & Allied Dis & James Ewing Hosp, 1968-1971; assoc attend obstetrician & gynecologist, New York Lying-in Hosp, 1968-1971; assoc prof, Col Physicians & Surgeons, Columbia Univ, 1967; assoc attend obstetrician & gynecologist, Presby Hosp, NY, 1967; assoc attend gynecologist, Francis Delafield Hosp, 1967; sr investr surg br, Nat Cancer inst, 1965-1967; Sr investr clin ctr, NIH, 1965-1967; Clin assoc endocrinol br, Nat Cancer inst, 1959-1961; consult Am joint comt cancer staging & end result reporting. **Memberships:** Soc Gynec Invest; AMA; Soc Surg Oncol; Am Radium Soc; Am Asn Cancer Educ. **Research Statement & Publications:** Gynecological cancer; hormonal, immunologic and therapeutic aspects of gestational trophoblastic neoplasms. **Mailing Address:** Mem Sloan-Kettering Cancer Ctr, 1275 York Ave, New York, NY 10021-6007.

LEWIS, JOHN MORGAN, ANIMAL HUSBANDRY, ANIMAL SCIENCE & NUTRITION. **Personal Data:** b Joliet, Ill, June 5, 1920. **Education:** Univ Ill, BS, 1943. **Professional Experience:** RETIRED; assoc prof animal sci, Dixon Springs Exp Sta, 1962-1981; actg-supt, Univ Ill, Urbana, 1959-1962; Asst supt, Univ Ill, Urbana, 1943-1959. **Memberships:** Am Soc Animal Sci. **Research Statement & Publications:** Sheep breeding, feeding and management. **Mailing Address:** RR 2 Box 305, Metropolis, IL 62960-9655.

LEWIS, JOHN RAYMOND, POLYMER CHEMISTRY, ACQUISITION & MERGERS. **Personal Data:** b Philadelphia, Pa, July 25, 1918; m 1942, Rachel E Brinard; c Sondra L (Sperati). **Education:** Franklin & Marshall Col, BS, 1942. **Professional Experience:** RETIRED; Consult, 1983-1985; mgr corp acquisitions, New Enterprise Dept, 1977-1983; mgr planning & acquisitions, New Enterprise Dept, 1975-1977; venture projs, New Enterprise Dept, 1969-1975; mgr develop, Res Dept, 1964-1969; res assoc, Cent Res Div, 1964; res mgr, Plastics & Elastomers Div, 1959-1964; res supvr, Naval Stores Div, 1955-1959; res chemist, Naval Stores Div, 1949-1955; chemist, Naval Stores Div, 1945-1949; shift supvr, Explosives Dept, Sunflower Ord Works, Kans, 1944-1945; Chemist, Naval Stores Div, Res Ctr, Hercules Inc, 1942-1944. **Memberships:** Am Chem Soc; Financial Analysts Asn; Sigma Xi; Com Develop Asn. **Research Statement & Publications:** Commercial development; polymers, energy and raw materials; acquisitions. **Mailing Address:** 118 Dickinson Lane, West Park, Wilmington, DE 19807-3138.

LEWIS, JOHN REED, PHARMACOLOGY. **Personal Data:** b Ottawa, Kans, December 27, 1915. **Education:** Ottawa Univ, AB, 1937; Mich State Col, MS, 1940; Univ Mich, PhD, 1949. **Professional Experience:** RETIRED; consult, div drugs, 1981-1982; sr scientist, dept drugs, 1972-1981; assoc dir, AMA, 1964-1972; asst secy coun drugs, AMA, 1960-1964; assoc dir sect coord & integration, Sterling-Winthrop Res Inst, 1953-1960; sr biologist, Sterling-Winthrop Res Inst, 1947-1953; supvr biol control, Frederick Stearns & Co, 1941-1945; asst chem exp sta, Mich State Col, 1939-1941. **Memberships:** Am Soc Pharmacol & Exp Therapeut; Soc Toxicol; Am Soc Clin Pharmacol Therapeut; NY Acad Sci; Drug Info Asn. **Research Statement & Publications:** Vitamin assays; pharmacology of sympathomimetics and analgesics; diuretics; anticholinesterases; coordination of research projects in development of new drugs; medical writing. **Mailing Address:** 6337 Ravenwood Dr, Sarasota, FL 34243.

LEWIS, JOHN SIMPSON, GEOCHEMISTRY, METEORITICS. **Personal Data:** b Trenton, NJ, June 27, 1941. **Education:** Princeton Univ, AB, 1962; Dartmouth Col, MA, 1964; Univ Calif, San Diego, PhD, 1968. **Honors & Awards:** J B Macelwayne Award, Am Geophys Union, 1976; NASA Medal Exceptional Sci Achievement, 1981. **Professional Experience:** CO-DIR, UA/NASA SPACE ENG RES CTR, 1986-; PROF PLANETARY SCI, UNIV ARIZ, 1982-; prof planetary sci, earth & planetary sci, Mass Inst Technol, 1980-1982; space Sci Bd, Nat Acad Sci, 1980-1982; prof Planetary Sci, MIT, 1980-1982; mem, Phys Sci Comt, 1975-1978; mem, NASA Phys Sci Comt, 1975-1978; mem, Working Group Outer Planet Probe Sci, Ames Res Ctr, NASA, 1974-; mem, Working Group Outer Planet Probe Sci, NASA-Ames Res Ctr, 1974-; chmn, Uranus Sci Adv Comt, NASA-Jet Propulsion Lab, 1974-1975; sci lectr, Div Planetary Sci, Am Astron Soc, 1974; guggenheim lectr, Nat Air & Space Mus, Smithsonian Inst, 1973; from asst prof to assoc prof chem, earth & planetary sci, Mass Inst Technol, 1968-1980; mem, Sci Adv Group Outer Solar Syst; Space Sci Bd Spec Panels Outer Solar Syst & explor Venus, Nat Acad Sci-Nat Res Coun. **Memberships:** AAAS; Am Chem Soc; Int Astron Union; Am Astron Soc. **Research Statement & Publications:** Composition, structure and origin of planetary atmospheres; atmosphere-lithosphere interactions; application of thermodynamics to problems of composition and origin of meteorites; exploitation of extraterrestrial resources. **Mailing Address:** Dept Planetary Sci, Univ Ariz, Tucson, AZ 85721. **Fax:** 520-621-4933. **E-Mail:** jsl@u.arizona.edu

LEWIS, JOHNNYE L, TOXICOLOGY. **Education:** Miami Univ, BA, 1970; Univ Victoria, MA, 1976; Univ Man, PhD (Toxicol), 1989. **Professional Experience:** PROF, COL PHARM, UNIV NM, 2004-; MEM, CANCER RES & TREATMENT CTR, UNIV NM, 2003-; ADJ SR SCIENTIST, LOVELACE RESPIRATORY RES INST, 2002-; DIR, COMMUNITY OUTREACH & EDUC PROG, NM CTR NVIRON HEALTH SCI, UNIV NM, 2002-; res prof, Dept Internal Med Univ NM Health Sci Ctr, 2002-2004 fel, Inhalation Toxicol Res Inst, 1989-1992. **Mailing Address:** Col Phram, Univ NM, One Univ NM, Albuquerque, NM 87131. **Fax:** 505-272-4186. **E-Mail:** jlewis@cybermesa.com

LEWIS, JON C, CELLULAR BIOLOGY, ELECTRON MICROSCOPY. **Professional Experience:** PROF PATH, BOWMAN GREY SCH MED, WAKE FOREST UNIV, 1990-. **Research Statement & Publications:** Cellular and chemical aspects of athrosclorosis platelette membrane receptors; hemostasis and thrombosis; cell biology; electron microscopy. **Mailing Address:** Dept Pathol, Bowman Gray Sch Med, Wake Forest Univ, Med Ctr Blvd, Winston-Salem, NC 27157.

LEWIS, JONATHAN JOSEPH, GROWTH FACTOR SIGNAL TRANSDUCTION. **Personal Data:** b Johannesburg, SAfrica, May 23, 1958. **Education:** Witwatersrand Univ, MB Bch, 1982, PhD (cell biol), 1990; FRCS(E), 1987. **Professional Experience:** CHIEF MED OFFICER & CHMN, MED BOARD ANTIGENICS INC, as of 2003; CHIEF RESIDENT SURG, YALE UNIV SCH MED, 1990-; postdoctoralassoc surg & cell biol, Yale Univ Sch Med, 1987-1990; Resident surg, Witwatersrand Univ SchMed, 1983-1987. **Memberships:** Am Soc Cell Biol; Am Asn Cancer Res; AAAS; AMA; NY Acad Sci. **Research Statement & Publications:** Growth factor signal transduction; parietal cell signal transduction. **Mailing Address:** Antigenics, Chief Med Officer, 630 Fifth Ave, New York, NY 10111.

LEWIS, KATHERINE, CARCINOGENESIS, INTERMEDIARY METABOLISM. **Education:** Temple Univ, PhD (biochem), 1951. **Professional Experience:** ASST DEAN EDUC, UNIV MED & DENT NJ, 1959-. **Mailing Address:** Dept Biochem, Univ Med & Dent NJ 185 S Orange Ave, Newark, NJ 07103.

LEWIS, L GAUNCE, MATHEMATICS, ALBEBRAIC TOPOLOGY. **Personal Data:** b Boston, Mass, September 14, 1949. **Education:** Harvard Col, BA, 1971; Univ Chicago, MS, 1976, PhD (math), 1978. **Professional Experience:** PROF MATH, SYRACUSE UNIV, NY, 1993-; Alexander von Humboldt fel, 1989-1990; from asst prof to assoc prof, Syracuse Univ, NY, 1981-1993; asst prof, Univ Mich, Ann Arbor, 1978-1981. **Memberships:** Am Math Soc; Math Asn Am; Sigma Xi. **Research Statement & Publications:** Equivariant homotopy theory; generalized cohomology theories; stable category; group actions on rings; representation theory. **Mailing Address:** Dept Math, Syracuse Univ, 304D Carnegie, Syracuse, NY 13244-1200. **Fax:** 315-443-1475. **E-Mail:** lglewis@mailbox.syr.edu

LEWIS, LARY W, MATHEMATICS. **Education:** Univ Louisville, PhD, 1981. **Professional Experience:** ASSOC PROF MATH, SCH NAT SCI, SPALDING UNIV, as of 2005. **Mailing Address:** Spalding Univ, 851 S Fourth Ave Teilhard Hall 209, Louisville, KY 40203. **Fax:** 502-585-7104. **E-Mail:** llewis@spalding.edu

LEWIS, LAURENCE A, HUMAN ECOLOGY, LAND DEGRADATION. **Personal Data:** b 1939. **Education:** Antioch Co, BA, 1961; Northwestern Univ, MS, 1963, PhD (geog), 1965. **Honors & Awards:** Honor Award, Soil & Water Conserv Soc, 1989. **Professional Experience:** PROF PHYS GEOG, CLARK UNIV, 1970-. **Research Statement & Publications:** Environmental sciences; author of publications; relations between the human and physical environments with regard to sustainability. **Mailing Address:** Clark Univ, Dept Geog, Jefferson Acad Ctr Rm 103, Worcester, MA 01610. **Fax:** 508-793-8881. **E-Mail:** llewis@clarku.edu

LEWIS, LAWRENCE GUY, MATHEMATICS, INFORMATION SCIENCE. **Personal Data:** b Logan, Utah, July 28, 1941. **Education:** Univ Utah, BA, 1965; Ind Univ, PhD (math), 1969. **Professional Experience:** VPRES, INFO TECHNOL PARTNERS, 1991-; ADJ ASSOC PROF MATH, UNIV UTAH, 1986-; PRES, SOFTWARE FIRST INC, 1983-; dir, Mgt Info Serv, 1978-1982; mgr licensees, Ireco Chem, 1973-1978; asst prof math, Univ Utah, 1970-1973; fel math, Grad Ctr, City Univ New York, 1969-1970. **Memberships:** AAAS; Data Processing Mgt Asn; Planning Exec Group. **Research Statement & Publications:** Ideal boundaries and information systems. **Mailing Address:** Dept Math, Univ Utah, 214 JWB, Salt Lake City, UT 84112. **Fax:** 801-581-4148. **E-Mail:** llewis@math.utah.edu

LEWIS, LEROY CRAWFORD, PROCESS ANALYTICAL CHEMISTRY, PROCESS CHEMISTRY & ENGINEERING. **Personal Data:** b Pocatello, Idaho, March 18, 1940; m 1962, Catherine; c David & Elizabeth. **Education:** Col Idaho, BS, 1962; Ore State Univ, PhD (phys chem), 1968. **Professional Experience:** RETIRED; mgr analytical chem, 1996; eng& sci fel, 1996-2001; BR MGR, WESTINGHOUSE IDAHO NUCLEAR CO, 1984-; br mgr, Exxon Nuclear Idaho Co, 1979-1984; br mgr, Allied Chem Corp, 1976-1979; sect leader, Allied Chem Corp, 1974-1976; group supvr, Allied Chem Corp, 1972-1974; sr res chemist, Allied Chem Corp, 1971-1972; sr res chemist, Idaho Nuclear Corp, 1968-1971. **Memberships:** Sr mem, Am Chem Soc; Sr mem, Sigma Xi. **Research Statement & Publications:** Nuclear fuel reprocessing chemistry; chemical waste handling chemistry; actinide chemistry; electrochemistry; analytical chemistry. **Mailing Address:** 3774 S Fifth W, Idaho Falls, ID 83404-7983. **E-Mail:** llewisz@srv.net

LEWIS, LESLIE ARTHUR, GENETICS, MICROBIOLOGY. **Personal Data:** b Castries, St Lucia, WI, May 17, 1940. **Education:** Univ Toronto, BSA, 1963, MSA, 1964; Columbia Univ, PhD (genetics), 1968. **Professional Experience:** PROF BIOL, YORK COL, NY, 1985-; chmn, dept nat sci, York Col, NY, 1979-1985; Univ Paris, France, 1972-1973; from lectr to assoc prof, York Col, NY, 1969-1985; NIH fel, Mich State Univ, 1968-1969. **Memberships:** Genetics Soc Am; AAAS; Am Soc Microbiol. **Research Statement & Publications:** Non-reciprocal recombination in the fungus Sordaria; genetic basis of resistance to aminoglycoside antibiotics. **Mailing Address:** Dept Nat Sci, York Col, 94-20 Guy R Brewer Blvd, Jamaica, NY 11433-1101. **Fax:** 718-262-2369. **E-Mail:** lal@mbrs.york.cuny.edu

LEWIS, MARC SIMON, BIOPHYSICS, BIOCHEMISTRY. **Personal Data:** b Cleveland, Ohio, October 30, 1926; m 1992, Anne; c 6. **Education:** Western Res Univ, BS (chem), 1946, MS, Physics) 1947; Georgetown Univ, PhD (chem), 1955. **Honors & Awards:** NIH Dir Award, nat inst of Health, 1997. **Professional Experience:** CHIEF, MOLECULAR INTERACTIONS RES, DIV OF BIOENGINEERING AND PHYSICAL SCI, OFFICE OF RES SERV, OFFICE OF DIR, NIH, 1998-; dir, Analytical Ultracentrifugation res, Biomed eng& inst prog, NCRR, NIH, 1996-1996; adj prof, dept of biochem& mol biol, Georgetown Univ, 1996-1998; sr res investr, Lab Vision Res, nat eye inst, 1970-1978; Head, Sect Ophthal chem, Nat inst Neurol dis & blindness, 1962-1970; biochemist, nat inst dent res, 1958-1962; biochemist nat inst arthritis & metab dis, 1957-1958; USPHS fel, nat inst Arthritis & Metab dis NIH, 1955-1957; guest scientist, Nat Inst Arthritis & Metab Dis, 1952-195; biophysicist biomed eng & instrumentation, Biomed Eng & Inst Prog, Nat Ctr Res Resources, NIH, 1978-1996; sr res investr, Lab Vision Res, Nat Eye Inst, 1970-1978; head, Sect Ophthal Chem, Nat Inst Neurol Dis & Blindness, 1962-1970; biochemist, Nat Inst Dent Res, 1958-1962; biochemist, Nat Inst Arthritis & Metab Dis, 1957-1958; USPHS fel, 1955-1957; guest scientist, Nat Inst Arthritis & Metab Dis, 1952-1955. **Memberships:** Am Chem Soc; Biophys Soc; Am Soc Biochem & Molecular Biol; protein soc. **Research Statement & Publications:** Applications of analytical ultracentrifugation to physical biochemistry and biophysics, particularly to the thermodynamics of the interactions of molecules of biological interest; mathematical modeling for the study of such systems. **Mailing Address:** Molecular Interactions Resource, DBEPS, ORS, OD, NIH, Bethesda, MD 20892. **Fax:** 301-496-6608. **E-Mail:** mslewis@helix.nih.gov

LEWIS, MARGARET NAST, PHYSICS. **Personal Data:** b Baltimore, Md, August 20, 1911. **Education:** Goucher Col, AB, 1931; Johns Hopkins Univ, PhD (physics), 1937. **Professional Experience:** ASST PRIN, BROWN INTERMEDIATE CTR, BROWN UNIV, as of 2004; assoc, Harvard Col Observ, beginning 1970; res fel, Harvard Col Observ, 1961-1970; assoc prof, Univ Mass, 1958-1961; asst prof res, Brown Univ, 1954-1958; assoc physics res, Univ Pa, 1953-1954; radioisotopes res, Haverford Col, 1952-1954; physicist, Nat Bur Stands, 1950-1952; lectr, Boston Univ, 1948-1950; radioisotopes res, Mass Mem Hosp, 1948-1949; instr physics, Univ Pa, 1943-1948; instr, Vassar Col, 1942-1943; fel, Howell fel, 1940-1942; fel, Crocker Radiation Lab, 1939-1940; Am Asn Univ Women Berliner fel, Univ Calif, 1938-1939; asst physics, Vassar Col, 1937-1938; nat consult, Schlesinger Libr, Radcliffe Col. **Memberships:** Am Phys Soc; Sigma Xi. **Research Statement & Publications:** Spectroscopy; atomic structure. **Mailing Address:** Brown Intermediate Ctr, Brown Univ, Providence, RI 02912-1982.

LEWIS, MARIAN L MOORE, EXPERIMENTAL BIOLOGY. **Personal Data:** b Decatur, Ga, March 5, 1937. **Education:** Ga State Col Women, BA, 1959; Univ Ariz, MS, 1968; Univ Houston, PhD (biophys sci), 1979. **Professional Experience:** ADJ PROF BIOL SCI, UNIV ALA, 1991-; DIR, BIOREACTOR & MICROGRAVITY BIOTECHNOL LAB, KENNETH E JOHNSON RES CTR, UNIV ALA, 1991-; dir, Bioreactor Lab, Kenneth E Johnson Res Ctr, 1989-1991; res analyst, Dept Virol, Northrop Serv, Inc, 1971-1973; res asst, Dept Virol, M DAnderson Hosp & Tumor Inst, 1968-1971; res scientist, Dept Virol & Epidemiol, Col Med, Baylor Univ, Tex Med Ctr, 1964-1966; technician & res asst, Commun Dis Ctr, 1959-1964. **Memberships:** Assoc fel Am Inst Aeronaut & Astronaut; Am Soc Microbiol; NY Acad Sci; AAAS; Sigma Xi; Int Soc Thrombosis & Haemostasis; Am Heart Asn; Am Soc Cell Biol; AmSoc Space & Gravitational Biol; Inst Advan Studies Life Support. **Research Statement & Publications:** Experimental biology; numerous publications. **Mailing Address:** Dept Biol Sci Univ Ala, Rm 360 Wilson Hall, Huntsville, AL 35899. **Fax:** 256-824-6376. **E-Mail:** lewisml@email.uah.edu

LEWIS, MARILYN WARE, PUBLIC UTILITIES. **Personal Data:** b 1943. **Professional Experience:** BD DIRS & CHMN, AM WATER WORKS CO, INC, 2002-; pres, Solano Publ Co; bd dirs, Pa Fuel Gas Co, Cigna Corp. **Mailing Address:** 125 Lancaster Ave B, Strasburg, PA 17579.

LEWIS, MARION JEAN, IMMUNO-HAEMATOLOGY, MAPPING THE HUMAN GENOME. **Personal Data:** b Windsor, Ont, September 21, 1925. **Education:** Univ Man, BA, 1960. **Honorary Degrees:** DSc, Univ Winnipeg, 1986. **Honors & Awards:** Karl Landsteiner Mem Award, Am Asn Blood Banks, 1971; La Medaille de laVille de Paris, Paris, France, 1987. **Professional Experience:** PROF EMER, DEPT HUMAN GENETICS, UNIV MAN, 1996-; Prof immunogenetics, Dept Human Genetics, Univ Man, 1986-; profimmunohemat, Dept Pediat, 1984-1993; chmn, Int Soc Blood Transfusion, Working PartyTerminol Red Cell Surface Antigens, 1983-1990; Mem, Med Adv Comt, Children's HospWinnipeg Res Found, 1982-; From asst prof to assoc prof, Rh Lab, Dept Pediat, Univ Man, 1973-1984; SCIENTIST IMMUNOHEMAT, RH LAB, DEPT PEDIAT, UNIV MAN, 1944-. **Memberships:** Human Genome Orgn; hon fel Can Col Med Geneticists; Int Soc BloodTransfusion; fel Royal Soc Can Acad Sci. **Research Statement & Publications:** Description, distribution, expression, inheritance of red cell antigens; genetic linkage and mapping of blood group genes; red cell immunization in haemolytic disease of the newborn; international reference laboratory; author of 160 publications. **Mailing Address:** Dept Human Genetics, Univ Man, Winnipeg, MB R3T 2N2, Can. **Fax:** 204-474-7913.

LEWIS, MARK A, MATHEMATICS. **Professional Experience:** PROF, DEPT MATH, UNIV UTAH, as of 2006. **Memberships:** Am Math Soc; Ecol Soc Am; Can Appl Math Soc. **Mailing Address:** Math Dept, Univ Utah, Rm 306 INSCC, 155 S 1400 E 233 JWB, Salt Lake City, UT 84112. **Fax:** 801-585-1640. **E-Mail:** mlewis@math.utah.edu

LEWIS, MARK HENRY, PSYCHOPHARMACOLOGY. **Personal Data:** b Boston, Mass, February 5, 1950. **Education:** Bowdoin Col, BA, 1972; Western Mich Univ, MA, 1975; Vanderbilt Univ, PhD (psychol), 1980. **Professional Experience:** PROF PSYCHIAT & ASSOC CHMN RES, UNIV FLA, as of 2003; staff mem, Univ Fla, beginning 1985; fel, Biol Sci Res Ctr, Med Sch, Univ NC, 1980-1985. **Memberships:** Sigma Xi; Soc Neuroscience. **Research Statement & Publications:** Neuropharmacology of oxidative metabolitics of pherothiazine anti-psychotic drugs both in vivo and in vitro; dopamine receptor supersensitivity; function ascorbic acid in brain. **Mailing Address:** Dept Psychiat Univ Fla, 1600 SW Archer Rd PO Box 100256, Gainesville, FL 32610-0256. **E-Mail:** mlewis@psychiatry.ufl.edu

LEWIS, MICHAEL EDWARD, NEUROPHARMACOLOGY, HISTOCHEMISTRY. **Personal Data:** b Chicago, Ill, November 9, 1951. **Education:** George Wash Univ, BA, 1973; Clark Univ, MA, 1975, PhD (psychol), 1977. **Professional Experience:** COFOUNDER, CEPHALON INC & ADOLOR CORP & ARENA PHARMACEUT, as of 2002; PRES, BIODILIGENCE PARTNERS, 1996-; vpres res, Symphony Pharmaceut Inc, 1993-1996; dir pharmacol, Cephalon Inc, 1988-1993; VIS ASSOC PROF PHARMACOL, COL PA, 1986-; prin scientist, E I Dupont Co, 1985-1987; res investr, Ment Health Res Inst, Univ Mich, 1981-1985; John G Searle clin pharmacol fel, 1981; res psychologist, Sect Biochem & Pharmacol, Biol Psychiat Br, NIMH & Nat Inst Drug Abuse, 1980-1981; Twinning grant, Europ Training Prog Brain & Behav Res, Europ Sci Found, Strasbourg, 1979-; instr, Europ Div, Univ Col, Univ Md, 1979; Wellcome res fel, Wellcome Trust, London, 1979; fel behav neurochem, Psychol Lab, Cambridge Univ, 1977-1979; Felix & Elizabeth Brunner fel, Ment Health Found, London, 1977-1979; guest worker neurochem, Sect Intermediary Metab, Lab Develop Neurobiology, Nat Inst Child Health & Human Develop, NIH, 1977. **Memberships:** Soc Neuroscience; Div Med Chem, Am Chem Soc. **Research Statement & Publications:** Histochemical and biochemical analysis of receptors and endogenous ligands; pharmacology of neuropeptides and psychoactive drugs; recovery of function after brain damage; neuropsychology. **Mailing Address:** Biodiligence Partners, 1007 Saber Rd, Westchester, PA 19382.

LEWIS, MORTON, ORGANIC CHEMISTRY, ADHESIVES & COATINGS. **Personal Data:** b Oak Park, Ill, June 28, 1936. **Education:** Purdue Univ, BS, 1958; Univ Chicago, PhD (org chem), 1962. **Professional Experience:** PRIN CHEMIST, WILSON SPORTING GOODS CO, 1981-; head, Tech Prod Div, Unitech Chem, Inc Div, Esmark Inc, 1976-1981; head, Specialty Chem Res Div, Swift & Co Div, 1974-1976; res chemist, Swift & Co, 1962-1974. **Memberships:** Am Chem Soc; Sigma Xi; Royal Soc Chem; NY Acad Sci. **Research Statement & Publications:** Synthesis and reactions of steroid derivatives; products of fats and oils; surface active agents; quaternary ammonium salts and organophosphorous compounds; flame retardants; plastics adhesives and coatings; specialty chemicals; ultraviolet cured monomers oligomers and coatings; epoxidized oils and epoxy resins. **Mailing Address:** Wilson Sporting Goods Co, 2233 W St, River Grove, IL 60171.

LEWIS, NATHAN SAUL, ELECTROCHEMISTRY, PHOTOELECTROCHEMISTRY. **Personal Data:** b Los Angeles, Calif, October 20, 1955. **Education:** Calif Inst Technol, BS, 1977, MS, 1977, Mass Inst Technol, PhD (inorg chem), 1981. **Honors & Awards:** Am Chem Soc Award Pure Chem, 1990; Fresenius Award, 1990. **Professional Experience:** GEORGE L ARGYROS PROF, CALIF INST TECHNOL, as of 2004; PROF CHEM, CALIF INST TECHNOL, 1991-; assoc prof, Calif Inst Technol, 1988-1990; consult, Inst Defense Anal, 1985-1990; Alfred P Sloan Found fel, 1985-1987; div ed, J Electrochem Soc, 1984-1990; from asst prof to assoc prof, Stanford Univ, 1981-1988; res asst chem, Mass Inst

Technol, 1977-1981. **Memberships:** Am Chem Soc; Electrochem Soc; Int Soc Electrochem. **Research Statement & Publications:** Electrochemistry of semiconductor surfaces; scanning tunneling microscopy in electrochemistry; inorganic complexes use as electrocatalyst. **Mailing Address:** Dept Chem Calif Inst Technol, 210 Beckman Inst, Pasadena, CA 91125. **E-Mail:** nslewis@caltech.edu

LEWIS, NEIL JEFFREY, MEDICINAL CHEMISTRY, ORGANIC CHEMISTRY. **Personal Data:** b New York, NY, February 10, 1945. **Education:** City Col NY, BS, 1966; Univ Kans, PhD (medchem), 1972. **Professional Experience:** Mem, NJ Munic Environ Adv Comt, beginning 1991; adj prof, Bur Biol Res, Rutgers Univ, beginning 1989; VPRES RES, JACOBUS PHARMACEUT CO, 1988-; dir resdevelop, Muscular Dystrophy Asn, 1987-1988; mem, Int Comt Neuromuscular Dis Drug Develop, 1984-1988; dir drug develop & assoc dir res, Muscular Dystrophy Asn, 1982-1987; mem, US Environ Protection Agency Human Health Effects Study Sect, 1981-1985; Lady Davis vis prof, 1979-1980; dir, Environ Chem Anal Lab, 1977-1982; from asst prof to assoc prof med chem, Div Med Chem, Col Pharm, 1972-1982; NIH res assoc, Ohio State Univ, 1972. **Memberships:** Am Chem Soc; Am Pharmaceut Asn; Sigma Xi; NY Acad Sci; Soc Clin Trials; AAAS. **Research Statement & Publications:** Chemotherapeutics; environmental carcinogenesis and toxicology; immunochemotherapy; antiviral agents; drug development; neuromuscular diseases; clinical trials. **Mailing Address:** Jacobus Pharmaceut Co, Inc, 37 Cleveland Lane, Princeton, NJ 08540.

LEWIS, NINA ALISSA, COMPUTER SECURITY. **Personal Data:** b Princeton, NJ, October 5, 1954. **Education:** Univ Calif, Santa Barbara, BS, 1975, MS, 1985. **Professional Experience:** SR TECH STAFF, ORACLE CORP, 1992-; prin software engr, UnisysDefense Systs, Inc, 1985-1992. **Memberships:** Asn Comput Mach; Inst Elec & Electronics Engrs; Inst Elec & Electronics EngrsComput Soc. **Research Statement & Publications:** Computer penetration analysis; network security; database security. **Mailing Address:** Oracle Corp, 500 Oracle Pkwy, Redwood Shores, CA 94065. **Fax:** 650-573-0804. **E-Mail:** nlewis@oracle.com

LEWIS, NITA ARIES, HIGH PRESSURE SOLUTION REACTIONS, ELECTRON TRANSFER CHEMISTRY. **Personal Data:** b Guelph, Ont, April 14, 1949. **Education:** Univ Waterloo, BSc, 1972; Univ Guelph, PhD (chem), 1977. **Professional Experience:** Vis scientist, Toronto Sick Childrens Hosp, 1993-1994; nat sci & eng res coun, NSF, 1990-1991; alexander von humboldt fel, Univ Frankfurt, 1986-1987; Nat Sci &Eng Res Coun, Sigma Xi, 1986; vis assoc, Calif Inst Technol, 1985; nat sci & eng res coun, NIH, 1983-1989; ASSOC PROF CHEM, UNIV MIAMI, 1982-; nat sci & eng res coun, Can, 1980-1985; prin investr, Res Corp, 1980; from asst prof to assoc prof, Univ New Brunswick, 1979-1985; nat res coun fel, Stanford Univ, 1977-1979. **Memberships:** Am Chem Soc; fel Am Inst Chemists; Can Inst Chemists; Royal Soc Chem; Sigma Xi; NY Acad Sci. **Research Statement & Publications:** High pressure solution chemistry; chemistry in supercritical fluids; long distance electron transfer reactions; metobolic errors in epileptic children; cytochrome P450 chemistry; inorganic complexes and proteins. **Mailing Address:** Dept Chem, Univ Miami, 1301 Mem Dr, Coral Gables, FL 33146-0431. **Fax:** 305-284-4571. **E-Mail:** nlewis@umiami.ir.miami.edu

LEWIS, NORMAN G, PLANT CELL WALL SYNTHESIS, PHENYLPROPANOID METABOLISM. **Personal Data:** b September 16, 1949; div, c Fiona, Kathryn & Sebastien. **Education:** Univ Strathclyde, Glasgow, Scotland, BSc, 1973; Univ BC, Vancouver, PhD (chem), 1977. **Honors & Awards:** Biotechnol; Physiol, Animal, Phsiol, plant; Biochem; Syn Organic & Natural Product. **Professional Experience:** DIR, INST BIOL CHEM, WASH STATE UNIV, 1990-; EISIG-TODE DISTINGUISHED PROF, INST BIOL CHEM, WASH STATE UNIV, 1990-; mem, US-Russia Shuttle-MIR Collab, 1993-; consult, Am Soc Gravitational & Space Biol, 1993-; chair, grad prog plant physiol, Wash State Univ, 1993-; assoc ed, Phytochem, NAm ed, 1993-; chmn, Plant Biol Group, Gravitational Biol Facil for Space Sta Freedom, 1992-; consult, Am Inst Biol Sci, 1990-; assoc prof, Va Polytech Inst & State Univ, 1985-1990; group leader, Pulp & Paper Res Inst Can, 1982-1985; asst scientist, Pulp & Paper Res Inst Can, 1980-1982; res assoc, Nat Res Coun Can, 1980; Nat Res Coun fel, Univ Cambridge, Eng, 1978-1980; res chemist, Imp Chem Industs, 1969-1973. **Memberships:** Hon mem Russ Asn Space & Mankind; Phytochem Soc NAm; Am Chem Soc; Am Soc Plant Physiologists; Chem Inst Can; Can Pulp & Paper Asn; Am Soc Gravitational & Space Biol. **Research Statement & Publications:** Defining biochemical pathways to the phenylpropanoid metabolites, the lignins, lignans, and neolignans as well as phenylpropanoid-acetate products, the suberins; define how microgravity effects plant growth and development; biochemical pathway to antitumor alkaloids (taxol) and the lignans (podophyllotoxin); lignin and lignan biosynthesis and function. **Mailing Address:** Wash State Univ Inst Biol Chem, 467 Clark Hall, Pullman, WA 99164-6340. **Fax:** 509-335-7643. **E-Mail:** lewisn@wsu.edu

LEWIS, PAUL HERBERT, PHYSICAL CHEMISTRY. **Personal Data:** b New York, NY, January 19, 1924. **Education:** Columbia Univ, AB, 1947, MA, 1948; IA State Col, PhD (chem), 1952. **Professional Experience:** RETIRED; petrol chemist, Texaco Inc, 1952-1985; chemist paints, E I du Pontde Nemours & Co Inc, 1948. **Memberships:** Am Chem Soc. **Research Statement & Publications:** X-ray analysis; catalysts. **Mailing Address:** 1600 Tawakoni Lane, Plano, TX 75075-6728.

LEWIS, PAUL KERMITH, MEAT SCIENCE. **Personal Data:** b Monticello, Ark, January 24, 1931. **Education:** Okla State Univ, BS, 1953; Univ Wis, MS, 1955, PhD, 1958. **Professional Experience:** PROF EMER ANIMAL SCI, UNIV ARK, FAYETTEVILLE, 1995-; from asst prof to prof animal sci, Univ Ark, Fayetteville, 1957-1995; res asst animal husb & biochem, Univ Wis, 1953-1957. **Memberships:** AAAS; Am Soc Animal Sci; Am Meat Sci Asn; Inst Food Technologists; CounAgr Sci & Technol. **Research Statement & Publications:** Pre-slaughter stress and storage life of beef and pork; sensory characteristics of beef and pork; cholesterol comparatives of beef. **Mailing Address:** Dept Animal Sci, Univ Ark, Fayetteville, Arkansas, AR 72701.

LEWIS, PAUL OLLIN, POPULATION GENETICS, PLANT SYSTEMATICS & PHYLOGENETICS. **Personal Data:** b Louisville, Ky, December 29, 1961. **Education:** Georgetown Col, Ky, BS, 1982; Memphis State Univ, MS, 1984; Ohio State Univ, PhD (plant sci), 1991. **Professional Experience:** ASST PROF BIOL, UNIV CONN, as of 2003; molecular evolution fel, Smithsonian Inst, 1994-1995; res assoc, NC State Univ, 1991-1994. **Memberships:** Soc Study Evolution; Soc Syst Biologists; Bot Soc Am; Am Soc PlantTaxonomists. **Research Statement & Publications:** Analysis of population structure, plant systematics and biogeography, statistical genetics and phylogeny reconstruction. **Mailing Address:** Dept Biol, Univ Conn, Storris, CT 06269-3043. **E-Mail:** plewis@uconnvm.uconn.edu

LEWIS, PAUL WELDON, MATHEMATICS. **Personal Data:** b Dallas, Tex, January 31, 1943. **Education:** NTex State Univ, BA, 1965, MS, 1966; Univ Utah, PhD (math), 1970. **Professional Experience:** PROF MATH, UNIV NTEX, as of 2006; assoc prof math, Univ NTex, beginning 1974; asst prof, Univ NTex, 1970-1974. **Memberships:** Am Math Soc. **Research Statement & Publications:** Vector measures; functional analysis; operators on function space; structure of Banach spaces. **Mailing Address:** Dept Math, Univ NTex, Gen Acad Bldg 471AA, Denton, TX 76203-6737. **Fax:** 940-565-4805. **E-Mail:** lewis@unt.edu

LEWIS, PERNELL, MARINE ECOLOGY. **Professional Experience:** LECTR, LIVING MARINE RESOURCE COOP SCI CTR, UNIV MD, EASTERN SHORE, as of 2005; dir, Living Marine Resource Coop Sci Ctr, Univ Md, Eastern Shore, as of 2004. **Mailing Address:** Univ Md Eastern Shore, One Backbone Rd, Princess Anne, MD 21853. **E-Mail:** vplewis@mail.umes.edu

LEWIS, PETER A, ELECTRICAL ENGINEERING. **Professional Experience:** DIR, EDUC ACTIV, INST ELECT & ELECTRONICS INC, as of 2000. **Mailing Address:** Inst Elect & Electronics Eng Inc, 445 Hoes Lane, Piscataway, NJ 08854. **Fax:** 732-981-1721.

LEWIS, PETER A, ELECTRICAL ENGINEERING, ELECTRONICS ENGINEERING. **Personal Data:** b Somerville, NJ, February 18, 1938. **Education:** Lehigh Univ, BSEE, 1959; Newark Col Eng, MS, 1969. **Professional Experience:** MANAGING DIR EDUC ACTIV, INST ELEC & ELECTRONICS ENGRS, 1992-; consult, Gas Res Inst Chicago, 1988-; mgr res & develop planning, Pub Serv Elec Gas Co, 1988-1992; vchmn, Comn Tech Educ NJ, 1987-1995; chmn tech comt, Fuel Cell Users Group, 1979-1987; mgr energy utilization res & develop, Pub Serv Elec Gas Co, 1978-1988; consult, Elec Power Res Inst, 1973-1986; asst mgr res & develop, Pub Serv Elec Gas Co, 1971-1978; srengr, Pub Serv Elec Gas Co, 1971; Engr, Pub Serv Elec Gas Co, 1963-1971. **Memberships:** Fel Inst Elec & Electronics Engrs; Electrochem Soc; Nat Soc Prof Engrs. **Mailing Address:** Inst Elec & Electronics Engrs, PO Box 1331, Piscataway, NJ 08855-1331. **E-Mail:** p.lewis@ieee.org

LEWIS, PETER ADRIAN WALTER, STATISTICS. **Personal Data:** b Johannesburg, SAfrica, October 3, 1932. **Education:** Columbia Univ, BA, 1954, BS, 1955, MS, 1957; Univ London, PhD (statist), 1964. **Professional Experience:** DISTINGUISHED PROF STATIST & OPERS RES, NAVAL POSTGRAD SCH, as of 2002; prof statist & opers res, Naval Postgrad Sch, beginning 1971; NIHspec fel, Imp Col, Univ London, 1969-1970; res staff mem statist, Int Bus Mach Res Labs, 1955-1971. **Memberships:** Inst Math Statist; Royal Statist Soc; Am Statist Asn. **Research Statement & Publications:** Stochastic process; applications of statistics in computer applications. **Mailing Address:** DeptOper Res, Naval Postgrad Sch Code OR/LW, Monterey, CA 93943-5000.

LEWIS, PHILIP M, COMPUTER SCIENCE. **Personal Data:** b New York, NY, May 30, 1931. **Education:** Rensselaer Polytech Inst, BS, 1952; Mass Inst Technol, MS, 1954, PhD (Elec Eng), 1956. **Professional Experience:** PROF COMPUT SCI, STATE UNIV NY, STONYBROOK, 1987-; mgr, Comput Sci Br, 1978-1987; Coolidge fel, Gen Elec Res & Develop Corp, 1977-; managing ed, J Comput, Soc Indust & Appl Math, 1971-; mgr, Gen Elec Res & DevelopCtr, 1969-1978; adj prof, Rensselaer Polytech Inst, 1960-; mem tech staff, Gen Elec Res &Develop Ctr, 1959-1969; consult automata theory & software design, Gen Elec Res & DevelopCtr, 1959; Hycon Eastern Inc, 1956-1957 & Sanders assocs, Inc, 1958; Lincoln Labs, Mass InstTechnol, 1955-1956; consult, Epsco, Inc, 1955; from instr to asst prof elec eng, Mass InstTechnol, 1954-1959. **Memberships:** Asn Comput Mach; Soc Indust & Appl Math; fel Inst Elec & Electronics Engrs. **Research Statement & Publications:** Theory of information processing, including compiler design, retrieval and self organization; automata theory; abstract languages. **Mailing Address:** Dept Comput Sci, State Univ NY, Stony Brook, NY 11794-4400. **Fax:** 516-632-8334. **E-Mail:** pml@cs.sunysb.edu

LEWIS, RANDOLPH VANCE, PROTEIN STRUCTURE, PROTEIN FUNCTION. **Personal Data:** b Powell, Wyo, April 8, 1950; m 1972, Lorrie; c Brian & Karren. **Education:** Calif Inst Technol, BS, 1972; Univ Calif, San Diego, MS, 1974, PhD (biochem), 1978. **Professional Experience:** PROF MOLECULAR BIOL, UNIV WYO, 1989-; head molecular biol, Univ Wyo, 1986-1991; from asst prof to assoc prof biochem, Univ Wyo, 1980-1989; asst, Roche Inst Molecular Biol, 1978-1980. **Memberships:** Am Chem Soc; Am Soc Biol Chemists; Protein Soc. **Research Statement & Publications:** Peptide hormones of adrenal medulla; protein sequencing; chemical structures of spider silks; protein and peptide purification methods. **Mailing Address:** Dept Molecular Biol, Univ Wyo, 203 Animal Sci Molecular Biol Complex, Laramie, WY 82071-3944. **Fax:** 307-766-5098. **E-Mail:** silk@uwyo.edu

LEWIS, RICHARD THOMAS, CARBON CHEMISTRY, THERMAL ANALYSIS. **Personal Data:** b East Cleveland, Ohio, January 9, 1943; div. **Education:** Case Western Res Univ, BS, 1964; Univ Chicago, PhD (phys chem), 1970. **Professional Experience:** SR RES ASSOC, UCAR CARBON CO, 1996-; res assoc, Carbon Prod Div, Union Carbide Corp, 1982-1996; sr res scientist, Carbon Prod Div, Union Carbide Corp, 1980-1982; res scientist, Carbon Prod Div, Union Carbide Corp, 1978-1980; group leader, Carbon Prod Div, Union Carbide Corp, 1974-1978; staff scientist chem, Carbon Prod Div, Union Carbide Corp, 1970-1974; SR RES ASSOC, UCAR CARBON CO, 1996-; res assoc, Carbon Prod Div, Union Carbide Corp, 1982-1996; from res scientist to sr res scientist, Carbon Prod Div, Union Carbide Corp, 1978-1982; group leader, Carbon Prod Div, Union Carbide Corp, 1974-1978; staff scientist chem, Carbon Prod Div, Union Carbide Corp, 1970-1974. **Memberships:** Am Chem Soc; NAm Thermal Anal Soc. **Research Statement & Publications:** Surface chemistry; physical chemistry and chemistry of carbonization. **Mailing Address:** UCAR Carbon Co, 12900 Snow Rd, Parma, OH 44130. **Fax:** 216-676-2423. **E-Mail:** rick.lewis@ucar.com

LEWIS, ROBERT ALLEN, ORGANIC CHEMISTRY. **Personal Data:** b Dunkirk, NY, July 27, 1943. **Education:** Carnegie Inst Technol, BS, 1965; Princeton Univ, MS, 1967, PhD (org chem), 1969. **Professional Experience:** UNIT MGR, CHEVRON RES & TECHNOL CTR, CHEVRON CORP, RICHMOND, CALIF, 1990-; tech mgr, Orogil, Nevilly-Seine, France, 1986-1990; prod developmgr, Chevron Cent Labs, Rotterdam, Neth, 1982-1986; res assoc, Chevron Res Co, Richmond, 1970-1982; Postdoctoral, Mass Inst Technol, 1969-1970. **Memberships:** Am Chem Soc; Soc Automotive Engrs. **Research Statement & Publications:** Synthesis, evaluation and chemical process definition of fuel and lubricant additives. **Mailing Address:** 1298 Grizzly Peak Blvd, Berkeley, CA 94708-2128.

LEWIS, ROBERT ALLEN, EXPERIMENTALBIOLOGY. **Personal Data:** b New York, NY, February 2, 1945. **Education:** Yale Univ, BA, 1967; Univ Rochester, MD, 1971. **Professional Experience:** SR VPRES & HEAD, US DRUG INNOVATION & APPROVAL, AVENTIS PHARMACEUT, 2000-; exec vpres & dir, Basic Res & Drug Eval, Syntex Res, beginning 1989; adj prof med, Univ Calif, San Francisco, 1986-; assoc Clin prof Med, Stanford Univ, beginning 1986; sr vpres & dir, Basic Res, Syntex Res, 1986-1989; rheumatologist &immunologist, Brigham & Women's Hosp, 1982-1986; Allergic Dis Acad Award, NIH, 1980-1985; Robert B Brigham Div & jr assoc med, Peter B Brigham Div, Brigham & Women'sHosp, 1980-1982; from asst prof to assoc prof med, Harvard Med Sch, 1979-1987; asstphysician, Robert B Brigham Hosp, 1977-1979; Instr med, Harvard Med Sch,

1977-1979; Rheumatologist & allergist, Med & Pediat Serv, USAF Med Ctr, 1974-1976. **Memberships:** Am Fedn Clin Res; Am Asn Immunologists; Am Acad Allergy & Immunol; Collegium Int Allergologicum. **Research Statement & Publications:** Leukotriene structure, function and metabolism; regulation of prostagland in D2 Synthesis from mast cells; regulation of the mast cell secretory response. **Mailing Address:** Aventis Pharmaceut Inc, 300 Somerset Corporate Blvd, Bridgewater, NJ 08807-2854.

LEWIS, ROBERT E, MEDICAL RESEARCH. **Education:** Univ Calif, BS; Univ Fla, PhD (phsyiol). **Professional Experience:** PROF & MENTOR, UNIV NEBR MED CTR, as of 2005. **Mailing Address:** Eppley Cancer Ctr Univ Neb Med Ctr, 600 S 42nd St ESH 7008, Omaha, NE 68198-6805. **Fax:** 402-559-8270. **E-Mail:** rlewis@unmc.edu

LEWIS, ROBERT E, AERONAUTICS. **Education:** Univ Ill, PhD, 1959. **Professional Experience:** PROF EMER, IOWA STATE UNIV, as of 2006. **Mailing Address:** Iowa State Univ, Ames, IA 50011-3140. **Fax:** 515-294-5957.

LEWIS, ROBERT EARL, ENTOMOLOGY, VERTEBRATE ZOOLOGY. **Personal Data:** b Richmond, Ind, December 1, 1929; m 1994, Nancy A Bailie. **Education:** Earlham Col, AB, 1952; Univ Ill, MS, 1956, PhD (entom), 1959. **Professional Experience:** EMER PROF ENTOM, IOWA STATE UNIV, 1997-; ARS, 1967-1996; from assoc prof to prof, Iowa State Univ, 1967-1996; grants, Off Naval Res, 1966-1971; grants, NIH, 1964-1967; consult, US Naval Med Res Unit, Egypt, 1963-; from asst prof to assoc prof zoology, Am Univ, Beirut, 1959-1967. **Memberships:** Am Entom Soc; Am Soc Mammal; Royal Entom Soc London. **Research Statement & Publications:** Siphonaptera of the world, their host relationships and zoogeography. **Mailing Address:** 3906 Stone Brook Circle, Ames, IA 50010-4174. **Fax:** 515-233-1851. **E-Mail:** relewis@iastate.edu

LEWIS, ROBERT EDWIN, IMMUNOPATHOLOGY, PATERNITY TESTING. **Personal Data:** b Meridian, Miss, March 11, 1947. **Education:** Univ Miss, Oxford, BA, 1969, MS, 1973; Univ Miss, Jackson, PhD (immunol & path), 1976. **Professional Experience:** CO DIR, IMMUNOPATHOLOGY & TRANSPLANTATION SECT, UNIV MISS MED CTR, as of 2005; PROF PATH, TISSUE TYPING LAB & CLIN IMMUNOPATH LAB, UNIV MISS MED CTR, 1991-; DIR, PATERNITY TESTING LAB, UNIV MISS MED CTR, 1991-; assoc prof path, Univ Miss Med Ctr, 1984-1991; CO-DIR, TISSUE TYPING LAB & CLIN IMMUNOPATH LAB, UNIV MISS MED CTR, 1981-; DIR, PATERNITY TESTING LAB, UNIV MISS MED CTR, 1981-; asst prof anesthesiol, Univ MissMed Ctr, 1977-1985; asst prof, Univ Miss Med Ctr, 1977-1984; instr path & anesthesiol, Univ Miss Med Ctr, 1976-1977; sr ed, Path & Immunopath Res & Immunol Res & Transgene; dep ed-in-chief, Pathobiology. **Memberships:** Fel Royal Soc Health (UK); Am Asn Pathologists; Am Asn Immunologists; Can Soc Immunol; Reticuloendothelial Soc; Am Soc Microbiol. **Research Statement & Publications:** Cellular immunology; natural killer cell morphology, levels and function in human patients with leukemias, lymphomas and in renal allotransplant recipients; mechanisms of Natural Killer and natural cytotoxicity cell actions in allograft rejection and antitumor immunity; Interleukin-2 in immunomodulation of tumors in man and animals; author of various articles. **Mailing Address:** Dept Path, Univ Miss Med Ctr, R213, Jackson, MS 39216. **Fax:** 601-984-1531. **E-Mail:** rlewis@pathology.umsmed.edu

LEWIS, ROBERT GLENN, ENVIRONMENTAL CHEMISTRY & PHYSICS. **Personal Data:** b Morehead City, NC, November 11, 1937; m 1960, Sue; c Michael R, David G & Steven J. **Education:** Univ NC, BS, 1960; Univ Wis, PhD (org chem), 1964. **Honors & Awards:** Quintessence Award Excellence Environ Jour, Scipress, 1994; Merit Award, Am Soc Testing & Mat; EPA Bronze Medal Commendable Serv, 1979 & 1992. **Professional Experience:** SCIENTIST, SEEP, NCBA, ENVIRON PROTECTION AGENCY, 2001-; VCMN, ASTM COMT D22 ATMOSPHERES, 1996-; US REP ISO INDOOR AIR, 1994-; sr sci adv, Environ Protection Agency, 1994-2001; chief, Methods Develop Br, 1979-1994; sect chief, Environ Protection Agency, 1971-1979; group leader & res specialist, Chemstrand Res Ctr Inc, 1969-1971; res chemist, Chemstrand Res Ctr Inc, 1964-1969; NIH fel, 1961-1964; NSF fel, 1961. **Memberships:** Am Chem Soc; Sigma Xi; AAAS; fel Am Soc Testing & Mat; Air & Waste Mgt Asn. **Research Statement & Publications:** Environmental chemistry; environmental toxicology; air pollution analysis; human exposure assessment; organic photochemistry; ultraviolet-visible absorption and luminescence spectroscopy; organic analyses; pesticide chemistry and analysis; mass spectrometry; published over 250 books. **Mailing Address:** Nat Exposure Res Lab, US Environ Protection Agency, Triangle Park, NC 27711. **Fax:** 919-541-0339. **E-Mail:** lewis.bob-dr@epamail.epa.gov

LEWIS, ROBERT MILLER, IMMUNOLOGY. **Personal Data:** b Flushing, NY, May 20, 1937. **Education:** Wash State Univ, DVM, 1961. **Honors & Awards:** Mary Mitchell Award Outstanding Res, 1961. **Professional Experience:** PROF EMER PATH, NY STATE COL VET MED, CORNELL UNIV, as of 2005; prof path, Ny State Col Vet Med, Cornell Univ, beginning 1975; chief vet serv, New Eng Med Ctr Hosp, 1970-1975; dir, Lab Animal Sci, 1969-1975; clin asst, Harvard Med Sch, 1968-1976; affil med, Angell Mem Animal Hosp, 1968-1975; from asst prof to assoc prof, Sch Med, Tufts Univ, 1967-1975; mem spec sci staff, New Eng Med Ctr Hosp, 1966-1975; asst path, Harvard Med Sch, 1965-1968; from instr to sr instr surg, Sch Med, Tufts Univ, 1965-1967; assoc pathologist, Angell Mem Animal Hosp, 1965-1967; res fel, Harvard Med Sch, 1962-1965; consult surg res, New Eng Med Ctr Hosp, 1962-1965; res assoc path, Angell Mem Animal Hosp, 1962-1963; Intern, Angell Mem Animal Hosp, 1961-1962. **Memberships:** Am Vet Med Asn; Am Col Vet Pathologists; Int Acad Path; Am Asn Lab Animal Sci; Am Soc Vet Clin Pathologists; Sigma Xi. **Research Statement & Publications:** Investigations on the etiology and pathogenesis of spontaneous immunologic diseases of animals which mimic human diseases. **Mailing Address:** Dept Path, Col Vet Med Cornell Univ, T4-018 Vet Res Tower, Ithaca, NY 14853-6401.

LEWIS, ROBERT RICHARDS, THEORETICAL PHYSICS. **Personal Data:** b New Haven, Conn, March 7, 1927. **Education:** Univ Mich, BS, 1950, MS, 1953, PhD (physics), 1954. **Professional Experience:** PROF EMER PHYSICS, UNIV MICH, ANN ARBOR, 1993-; from asst prof to prof, Univ Mich, Ann Arbor, 1958-1992; mem, Inst Advan Study, 1956-1958; asst prof physics, Univ Notre Dame, 1954-1958. **Memberships:** Fel Am Phys Soc. **Research Statement & Publications:** Quantum theory; angular correlation theory; parity nonconservation in atoms; partial coherence theory. **Mailing Address:** Dept Physics, Univ Mich, 450 Church St, Ann Arbor, MI 48109-1040. **E-Mail:** boblewis@umich.edu

LEWIS, ROBERT WARREN, ELECTRICAL ENGINEERING, OPTICS. **Personal Data:** b Mansfield, Ohio, February 4, 1943; c Timothy j & Krista b. **Education:** Univ Cincinnati, BS, 1966; Univ Mich, MS, 1968, MA, 1969, PhD (elec eng), 1973. **Professional Experience:** ADJ PROF, OAKLAND COMMUNITY COL, 1990-; assoc sr res scientist optics & computerized tomography, Gen Motors Res Labs, 1978-1987; res assoc radar, Environ Res Inst Mich, 1972-1973; res asst coherent optics, Willow Run Labs, Univ Mich, 1969-1972; educ consult & imaging consult. **Memberships:** Inst Elec & Electronics Engrs. **Research Statement & Publications:** Optics and electrical engineering; computerized tomographic mapping of temperature induced refractive index fields in combusting mixtures. **Mailing Address:** McComb Comm Col Math Dept, 44575 Garfield Rd, Clinton Township, MI 48038.

LEWIS, ROGER ALLEN, BIOCHEMISTRY. **Personal Data:** b Wellington, Kans, June 1, 1941. **Education:** Phillips Univ, BA, 1963; Ore State Univ, PhD (biochem), 1968. **Professional Experience:** PROF EMER BIOCHEM, UNIV NEV, RENO, as of 2006; prof biochem, Univ Nev, Reno, beginning 1982; from asst prof to assoc prof, Univ Nev, Reno, 1969-1982; Res assoc pyrimidine nucleotide metab, Stanford Univ, 1968-1969. **Memberships:** Am Chem Soc; Sigma Xi; AAAS; Am Soc Pharmacol & Exp Therapeut; Am Soc Biochem Molecular Biol. **Research Statement & Publications:** Purine deoxynucleotide biosynthesis and its control; toxicology of pesticides with respect to nucleotide metabolism and DNA and/or RNA synthesis. **Mailing Address:** Dept Biochem, Univ Nev, Mail stop 222 1660 N Virgina St, Reno, NV 89557-0042. **E-Mail:** lewis@cabnr.unr.edu

LEWIS, ROY STEPHEN, METEORITICS. **Personal Data:** b Oakland, Calif, August 10, 1944. **Education:** Univ Calif, Berkeley, AB, 1967, PhD (atmospheric & space sci), 1973. **Honors & Awards:** Except Sci Achievement Medal, NASA. **Professional Experience:** SR SCIENTIST, ENRICO FERMI INST, UNIV CHICAGO, as of 2005; SR RES ASSOC METEORITICS, DEPT CHEM, UNIV CHICAGO, 1973-. **Memberships:** Meteoritical Soc; fel AAAS. **Research Statement & Publications:** Isotopic composition and elemental abundances of noble gases in meteorites and other samples. **Mailing Address:** Enrico Fermi Inst, Univ Chicago, 5630 S Ellis Ave, Chicago, IL 60637.

LEWIS, RUSSELL M(ACLEAN), TRAFFIC ENGINEERING, HIGHWAY SAFETY. **Personal Data:** b New York, NY, June 20, 1930; m 1957, Nancy; c Jeffrey, Cynthia, Roger & Susan. **Education:** Trinity Col, Conn, BS, 1952; Rensselaer Polytech Inst, BCE, 1953, MCE, 1959; Purdue Univ, PhD, 1962. **Professional Experience:** CONSULT ENGR, 1980-; mem, Construct & Maintenance Subcomt, Nat Comt Uniform Traffic Control Devices, 1979-; sr assoc, Byrd, Tallamy, MacDonald & Lewis, Div Wilbur Smith & Assocs, 1972-1980; partner, Byrd, Tallamy, MacDonald & Lewis, Div Wilbur Smith & Assocs, 1971-1972; assoc, Byrd, Tallamy, MacDonald & Lewis, Div Wilbur Smith & Assocs, 1968-1970; Ford Found fel, Purdue Univ, 1960-1962; from instr to assoc prof civil eng, Rensselaer Polytech Inst, 1957-1968; affil, Transp Res Bd, Nat Res Coun-Nat Acad Sci. **Memberships:** Am Soc Civil Engrs fel; Inst Traffic Engrs. **Research Statement & Publications:** Highway accident analysis; highway safety research; traffic and parking studies; expert witness testimony in accident cases; training programs for transportation agencies. **Mailing Address:** Old Farm Ln, Cazenovia, NY 13035. **Fax:** 315-655-4560. **E-Mail:** RMLewis@alum.rpi.edu

LEWIS, SARA M, ECOLOGY. **Education:** Harvard Col, Ab, 1976; Duke Univ, PhD (Zoology), 1984. **Professional Experience:** ASSOC PROF, EVOLUTIONARY & BAHAVIORAL ECOL, DEPT BIOL, TUFTS UNIV, 1997-; ADJ PROF, SCH PUB HEALTH, TUFTS UNIV, 1996-; asst prof, Dept Biol, Tufts Univ, 1991-1997; fel, Org & evolutionary Biol & Bunting Inst, Harvard Univ, 1987-1990. **Mailing Address:** Dept Bio, Tufts Univ, Barnum 103A 163 Packard Ave, Medford, MA 02155. **Fax:** 617-627-3805. **E-Mail:** sara.lewis@tufts.edu

LEWIS, SHELDON NOAH, PHYSICAL CHEMISTRY, ORGANIC CHEMISTRY. **Personal Data:** b Chicago, Ill, July 1, 1934; m 1957, Suzanne Goldberg; c Sara, Matthew & Rachel. **Education:** Northwestern Univ, BA & MS, 1956; Univ Calif, Los Angeles, PhD (phys & org chem), 1959. **Professional Experience:** PRES, SNL INC, TECHNOL CONSULT INDUST, 1991-; exec vpres & dir, Clorox Co, 1984-1991; group vpres & dir, Clorox Co, 1978-1984; vpres res & develop, Clorox Co, 1978; corp dir res polymers, resins & monomers worldwide, 1976-1978; dir, Europ Labs, France, 1975-1976; gen mgr, DCL Lab AG, Switz, 1974-1975; dir specialty chem res, Rohm & Haas Co, 1973-1974; res supvr, Rohm & Haas Co, 1968-1973; lab head, Rohm & Haas Co, 1963-1968; group leader org chem, Rohm & Haas Co, 1961-1963; sr chemist, Rohm & Haas Co, 1960-1961; NSF fel, Univ Basel, 1959-1960. **Memberships:** Am Chem Soc; Indust Res Inst; Soc Chem Indust. **Research Statement & Publications:** Reaction mechanisms; organic synthesis; process development; agricultural chemicals; polymers and surface coatings; leather, paper, textile, cosmetic and petroleum chemicals; plastics and modifiers; ion exchange resins; adhesives; building products; biocides, detergents, bleaches and household cleaning products. **Mailing Address:** 3711 Rose Ct, Lafayette, CA 94549. **Fax:** 510-283-6465. **E-Mail:** shel@aol.com

LEWIS, SHERRY M, NUTRITION, NUTRITIONAL BIOCHEMISTRY. **Personal Data:** b June 12, 1944. **Education:** Southern Ill Univ, BSc, 1977, MSc, 1979; Ohio State Univ, PhD, 1983. **Professional Experience:** MGR, APPL NUTRIT, NAT CTR TOXICOL RES, BIONETICS CORP, as of 2004; diet prep proj mgr, Nat Ctr Toxicol Res, 1992-1993; dep contract mgr, Nat CtrToxicol Res, 1990-1993; ANALYTICAL NUTRITIONIST, NAT CTR TOXICOL RES, 1987-; res instr, Univ Ill, 1985-1987; researcher, Ohio State Univ & Eli Lilly Corp, 1984. **Memberships:** Am Asn Lab Animal Sci; Am Inst Nutrit; Am Registry Prof Animal Sci. **Research Statement & Publications:** Scientific research and development to improve data bases, standards, methods and technologies; adjunct researcher program on nurtritional modulation of risk and toxicity; technol dietary process development. **Mailing Address:** Nat Ctr Toxicol Res, Bionetics Corp, 3900 NCTR Rd, Jefferson, AR 72079. **Fax:** 870-543-7065. **E-Mail:** slewis@fdant.nctr.fda.gov

LEWIS, SILAS DAVIS, ORGANIC CHEMISTRY. **Personal Data:** b Gastonia, NC, June 26, 1930. **Education:** Wake Forest Col, BS, 1952; Ga Inst Technol, PhD (org chem), 1959. **Professional Experience:** RETIRED; assoc prof chem, Augusta Col, 1966-1988; assoc prof chem, DelValley Col, 1963-1966; Sr chemist, Atlast Chem Industs, Inc, 1959-1963. **Memberships:** Am Chem Soc; Sigma Xi. **Research Statement & Publications:** Polyphenyls; Ullmann reaction; nitro and nitrato compounds and explosives. **Mailing Address:** 1760 Kissing Bower Rd, Augusta, GA 30904.

LEWIS, SIMON ANDREW, EPITHELIAL TRANSPORT, ELECTROPHYIOLOGY. **Personal Data:** b Welling Kent, Eng, April 18, 1948. **Education:** Univ BC, BSc, 1970, MSc, 1971; Univ Calif, Los Angeles, PhD (physiol), 1975. **Professional Experience:** PROF PHYSIOL & BIOPHYS, UNIV TEX, 1987-; from asst prof to assoc prof physiol, Yale Med Sch, 1977-1987; res assoc physiol, Med Br, Univ Tex, 1976-1977; Res assoc physiol, Univ Calif, Los Angeles, 1975-1976. **Memberships:** Biophys Soc; Am Physiol Soc. **Research Statement & Publications:** Mechanisms of salt and water transport across epithelial cells membranes using electrophysiological methods; Published numerous articles. **Mailing Address:** Dept Physiol & Biophys Univ Tex Med Br, 301 Univ Blvd, Galveston, TX 77555-0641. **E-Mail:** slewis@utmb.edu

LEWIS, STANDLEY EUGENE, ENTOMOLOGY, PALEONTOLOGY. **Personal Data:** b Twin Falls, Idaho, November 15, 1940. **Education:** Univ Nebr, Omaha, BA, 1962, MA, 1964; Wash State Univ, PhD (entom), 1968. **Professional Experience:** Sigma Xi, Geol Soc Am & St Cloud instnl grants, 1983 & 1985; PROF BIOL, ST CLOUD STATE COL,

1978-; Sigma Xi, Geol Soc Am & St Cloud instnl grants, 1977, res consult, N States Power Co, 1975-1977; Sigma Xi, Geol Soc Am & St Cloud instnl grants, 1975, Sigma Xi, Geol Soc Am & St Cloud instnl grants, 1970; from asst prof to assoc prof biol, St Cloud State Col, 1968-1978; Sigma Xi, Geol Soc Am & St Cloud instnl grants, 1968; res asst mosquito control, Adams County Abate Dist, beginning 1965; teaching asst zool-entom, Wash State Univ, 1964-1968; teaching asst biol, Univ Nebr, Omaha, 1963-1964; res assoc, Sci Mus Minn. **Memberships:** Sigma Xi; Paleont Soc Am; Entom Soc Am. **Research Statement & Publications:** Paleobiology, specifically paleoentomology; tertiary insect site in US; fossil insect studies, Miocene sites: Wash And Idaho, Oligocene sites: Mont, Cretaceous sites: Minn; fossil bison kill site in Central Minn. **Mailing Address:** St Cloud State Col, Biol Sci Bldg MS 262, St Cloud, MN 56304. **Fax:** 320-255-4166. **E-Mail:** selewis@stcloudstate.edu

LEWIS, STEPHEN ALBERT, PLANT NEMATOLOGY. **Personal Data:** b Sodus, NY, September 9, 1942. **Education:** Pa State Univ, BS, 1964; Rutgers Univ, MS, 1969; Univ Ariz, PhD (plant path), 1973. **Professional Experience:** CHMN & PROF NEMATOL, DEPT PLANT PATH & PHYSIOL, CLEMSON UNIV, as of 2006; assoc prof nematol, dept plant path & physiol, Clemson Univ, beginning 1977; asst prof, dept plant path & physiol, Clemson Univ, 1973-1977; sales rep, StandOil Calif, 1965-1966. **Memberships:** Soc Nematologists; Sigma Xi. **Research Statement & Publications:** Host-parasite relations of the phytoparasitic nematodes, Hoplolaimus columbus and Criconemoides xenoplax on field crops and peach trees, respectively; nematode-mycorrhizae-rhizobium relationships; gnotobiotic culture of nematodes; published recently more than 5 books; Involved in more than 3 research projects. **Mailing Address:** Dept Entom, Soils & Plant Sci, Clemson Univ, 206 Long Hall Box 340315, Clemson, SC 29634-0315. **Fax:** 864-656-0274. **E-Mail:** slewis@clemson.edu

LEWIS, STEPHEN B, ENVIRONMENTAL MEDICINE. **Personal Data:** b Berkeley, Calif, March 9, 1940. **Education:** Univ Calif, Berkeley, BA, 1962; Wash Univ, MD, 1966. **Professional Experience:** CAPT, US NAVAL MED CORPS, 1979-; Dep dir, Environ Med Dept, 1986-1990; clin asst prof med, Univ Calif, San Francisco, 1977-1983 & Tissue Bank Stem Cell Res, Naval Med Res Inst, 1983-1986; dir, Clin Invest Ctr & head, Endocrinol Br, 1978-1983; endocrinologist & asst dir, Clin Invest Ctr & head, Endocrinol & Metab Br, Med Serv, Naval RegionalMed Ctr, Oakland, Calif, 1972-1978; instr, Dept Med & res assoc, Dept Physiol, 1971-1972; Spec res fel, NIH, 1971-1972; fel, Dept Physiol, Sch Med, Vanderbilt Univ, 1969-1972; asst resident med, Dept Med, Michael Reese Hosp, Chicago, 1967-1969; Intern med serv & chmn, Dept Med, Michael Reese Hosp, Chicago, 1966-1967. **Memberships:** Am Diabetes Asn (pres 1981-1983); Am Fed Clin Res; Soc Exp Biol & Med; Endocrine Soc; AAAS; Am Physiol Soc; Europ Asn Study Diabetes. **Research Statement & Publications:** Blood and blood substitutes; wounds, sepsis and shock; hypothermia and non-freezing cold injury; readiness planning and material; post injury enhancement. **Mailing Address:** 2550 Almond Ave Ste 4-3, Concord, CA 94520.

LEWIS, STEVEN CRAIG, CHEMICAL CARCINOGENESIS, RISK ASSESSMENT & COMMUNICATION. **Personal Data:** b Anderson, Ind, December 30, 1943. **Education:** Ind Univ, BA, 1970, PhD (toxicol), 1975; Am Bd Toxicol, dipl, 1980, recert, 1985 &1990. **Professional Experience:** Chair sci policy, Am Indust Health Coun, 1996-; SR TOXICOL ASSOC, EXXON BIOMED SCI, INC, 1996-; consult, US Environ Protection Agency Sci Adv Bd, 1989-1992; mem sci rev group, NY Dept Environ Conserv, 1985-; vchmn & chmn, ToxicolComt, Am Petrol Inst, 1983-; toxicol assoc, Exxon Biomed Sci, Inc, 1982-1996; Mem bd dir, Toxicol Forum, 1982-1984; sr toxicologist & unit head, Exxon Biomed Sci, Inc, 1979-1982; toxicologist, Exxon Biomed Sci, Inc, 1975-1979; supvr, Statist Cancer Res Unit, 1972-1975; resfel toxicol, Med Sch, Ind Univ, 1971-1975; Res asst biochem, Med Sch, Ind Univ, 1965-1971. **Memberships:** Soc Risk Anal; Inter Soc Regulatory Toxicol & Pharmacol; Soc Toxicol. **Research Statement & Publications:** Chemical carcinogenesis; biostatistics; risk analysis; neurotoxicology; toxicology; product safety; noncancer risk assessment; risk communication. **Mailing Address:** Toxicol & Environ Scis Div, Rm LG-348, PO Box 971, 1545 Route 22 E, Annandale, NJ 08801-0971. **Fax:** 908-30-1151. **E-Mail:** steven.c.lewis@exxonmobil.com

LEWIS, STEVEN M, RESPIRATORY PHYSIOLOGY, SIMULATION. **Personal Data:** b Washington, DC, June 9, 1948. **Education:** Calif Inst Technol, BS, 1969; Univ Wash, PhD (biophys), 1974. **Professional Experience:** INDEPENDENT CONSULT, 1998-; mem tech staff, aerospace corp, beginning 1989; from asst prof to assocprof biomed eng, Univ Southern Calif, Univ Park, 1976-1989. **Memberships:** Biomed Eng Soc; Am Physiol Soc; Inst Elec & Electronics Engrs; Asn ComputMach. **Mailing Address:** 2350 E El Segundo Blvd, El Segundo, CA 90245.

LEWIS, SUSAN ERSKINE, IN VIVO MUTOGENESIS, DEVELOPMENTAL GENETICS. **Personal Data:** b Philadelphia, Pa, March 10, 1941. **Education:** Bryn Mawr Col, AB, 1963; NY Univ, MS, 1967; Albert Einstein Col Med, PhD (genetics), 1975. **Professional Experience:** SR PROG DIR, RES TRIANGLE INST, 1990-; sr res geneticist, Res Trianglelnst, 1979-1990; fel, Univ Mich, 1976-1979; Res assoc, Albert Einstein Col Med, 1975-1976. **Memberships:** Genetics Soc Am; Environ Mutagen Soc; Am Soc Human Genetics. **Research Statement & Publications:** Explore mechanism of action of toxic chemicals on the germ line; genetic control of mammalian development; in particular genes acting in the early embryo. **Mailing Address:** Rte 1 PO Box 12194, Research Triangle Park, NC 27709-2194. **Fax:** 919-541-7237.

LEWIS, SUSANNA MAXWELL, GENETICS. **Personal Data:** b Boston, Mass. **Education:** Tufts Univ, BS, 1976; Mass Inst Technol, PhD (biol), 1985. **Professional Experience:** SR SCIENTIST, HOSP FOR SICK CHILDREN RES INST, as of 2004; ASSOCPROF IMMUNOL, UNIV TORONTO, 1995-; scientist, hosp for sick children res inst, 1995-; res grant, Am Cancer Soc, 1990-; sr res fel biol, Calif Inst Technol, 1988-1995; staff fel, Lab Molecular Biol, NIH, 1986-1988, Helen HayWhitney fel, 1985-1988, Postdoctoral fel biochem, Stanford Univ, 1985-1986. **Memberships:** Am Asn Immunologists. **Research Statement & Publications:** Mechanism of immunoglobulin and T cell receptor gene rearrangement. **Mailing Address:** Hosp Sick Children, 555 University Ave, Toronto, ON M5G 1X8, Can. **Fax:** 416-813-8883. **E-Mail:** susanna@sickkids.ca

LEWIS, THEODORE, CHEMICAL ENGINEERING, POLYMER CHEMISTRY. **Personal Data:** b New York, NY, April 9, 1924. **Education:** Rensselaer Polytech Inst, BChE, 1946, MChE, 1948; Princeton Univ, PhD (chem eng), 1955; NY Univ, MBA, 1971. **Professional Experience:** INDUST, GOVT & UNIV CONSULT, 1974-; Adj fac, Fairleigh Dickinson Univ & Adelphi Univ, 1974-; assoc prof, Col Bus, Fairleig Dickinson Univ, Rutherford, pharmaceut/chem prog & admin asst to dean, 1971-1974; assoc synthetic elastomers dept, Enjay Chem Co, 1965-1971; sr mkt develop engr, Enjay Chem Co, 1959-1965; Res engr chem & chem eng, Esso Res Eng Co, Stand Oil Co, NJ, 1954-1959. **Memberships:** Am Chem Soc; Am Inst Chem Engrs. **Research Statement & Publications:** Textile fibers; synthetic elastomers; petrochemicals; products and process research; market development of thermosets, synthetic elastomers and special industries; granted 25 patents. **Mailing Address:** PO Box 486, Toms River, NJ 08754-0486.

LEWIS, T(HOMAS) SKIPWITH, ELECTRICAL ENGINEERING. **Personal Data:** b Bluefield, WVa, November 21, 1936. **Education:** Va Polytech Inst, BS, 1959; Univ Va, MS, 1964. **Honorary Degrees:** DSc (elec eng), Univ Va, 1967. **Professional Experience:** RETIRED; sr vpres eng, Hartford Steam Boiler, beginning 1994; sr vpres, Hartford Steam Boiler, 1985-1994; from asst vpres to vpres, Hartford Steam Boiler, 1981-1985; dean, Col Eng, 1971-1981; assoc prof, Univ Hartford, 1970-1981; sr res engr, United Aircraft Res Labs, 1967-1970; adj asst prof elec eng, Univ Hartford, 1967-1970; instr elec eng, Univ Va, 1964-1967; engr, Air Arm Div, Westinghouse Elec Corp, 1959-1962. **Memberships:** Inst Elec & Electronics Engrs. **Research Statement & Publications:** Microwave engineering and antennas; microwave properties of materials. **Mailing Address:** 96 Wheatland Rd, Lewisberry, PA 17339.

LEWIS, TREVOR JOHN, GEOPHYSICS. **Personal Data:** b Vancouver, BC, January 19, 1940. **Education:** Univ BC, BASc, 1963, MSc, 1964; Univ Western Ont, PhD (geophys), 1975. **Professional Experience:** EMER GEOTHERMICS, GEOL SURV CAN, as of 2005; res scientist geothermal studies, dept energy mines & resources, Geol Surv Can, beginning 1964. **Memberships:** Geol Asn Can; Can Geophys Union; Am Geophys Soc; Can Geothermal EnergyAsn; Int Heat Flow Comt. **Research Statement & Publications:** Geothermal studies, thermal structure of the earth. **Mailing Address:** Pac Geosci Ctr, PO Box 6000, Sidney, BC V8L 4B2, Can. **Fax:** 250-363-6565.

LEWIS, URBAN JAMES, ENDOCRINOLOGY. **Personal Data:** b Flagstaff, Ariz, April 28, 1923; m 1950, Loraine J Chambers; c Geoffrey P & Wayne K. **Education:** San Diego State Col, BA, 1948; Univ Wis, MS, 1950, PhD (biochem), 1952. **Professional Experience:** RETIRED; mem, Whittier Inst, 1982-1993; mem, Scripps Clin & Res Found, 1961-1982; sr biochemist, Merck & Co, Inc, 1954-1961; instr biochem & biochemist, Am Meat Found, Univ Chicago, 1953-1954; NIH fel, Med Nobel Inst, Stockholm, 1952-1953. **Memberships:** Am Soc Biol Chem; Am Chem Soc; Endocrine Soc. **Research Statement & Publications:** Proteolytic enzymes; pituitary hormones. **Mailing Address:** 5733 Skylark Pl, La Jolla, CA 92037-7742. **E-Mail:** lorjor@aol.com

LEWIS, VICTOR L, PLASTIC & RECONSTRUCTIVE SURGERY. **Personal Data:** b Evanston, Ill, September 22, 1942. **Education:** Yale Univ, BA, 1964; Northwestern Univ, MD, 1968. **Professional Experience:** PROF PLASTIC SURG, NORTHWESTERN UNIV MED SCH, as of 2004; assoc prof clin surg, Northwestern Univ Med Sch, beginning 1977. **Memberships:** Am Soc Maxillofacial Surgeons (pres 1992-1993); Am Soc Plastic & Reconstructive Surgeons; Am Col Surgeons; Am Asn Plastic Surgeons; Am Asn Surg Trauma. **Research Statement & Publications:** Role of nerves in wound healing; healing of soft tissue complications of chronic spine trauma. **Mailing Address:** Dept Surgery, Northwestern Univ Feinberg Sch Med, 210 E Huron St, Chicago, IL 60611. **Fax:** 312-926-3727.

LEWIS, W DAVID, HISTORY OF TECHNOLOGY. **Personal Data:** b Towanda, Pa, June 24, 1931. **Education:** Pa State Univ, BA, 1952, MA, 1954; Cornell Univ, PhD (hist), 1961. **Professional Experience:** DISTINGUISHED UNIV PROF, AUBURN UNIV, as of 2005; fel, Nat Humanities Inst, Univ Chicago, beginning 1978; dir, Nat Endowment Humanities Proj Technol, Human Values & Southern Future, Auburn Univ, beginning 1974; Hudson prof hist & eng, beginning 1971, from assoc prof to prof, State Univ NY, Buffalo, 1965-1971; fel coordr, Eleutherian Mills-Hagley Found, Inc, Wilmington & lectr hist, Univ Del, 1959-1965; instr pub speaking, Hamilton Col, 1954-1957; grants, State Univ NY, Auburn Univ, Eleutherian Mills Hist Libr, Nat Endowment Humanities & Delta Airlines Found. **Memberships:** Soc Hist Technol. **Research Statement & Publications:** History of technology, particularly history of iron and steel industry and aerospace history. **Mailing Address:** Dept Hist, Auburn Univ, Thach 308-A, Auburn, AL 36849. **Fax:** 334-844-6673. **E-Mail:** lewiswd@auburn.edu

LEWIS, WALLACE JOE, ENTOMOLOGY. **Personal Data:** b Smithdale, Miss, October 30, 1942. **Education:** Miss State Univ, BS, 1964, MS, 1965, PhD (entom), 1968. **Professional Experience:** SUPVY RES ENTOMOLOGIST, USDA, as of 2006; asst prof, Univ Fla, beginning 1970; entomologist, Southern Graininsects Res lab, Entom Res Div, Agr Res Serv, USDA, beginning 1967. **Memberships:** Entom Soc Am; Sigma Xi. **Research Statement & Publications:** Ecological and physiological relationships between parasitic insects and their hosts; development of methods for the use of parasitic insects for control of insect pests; more than 12 publications and involved in several projects. **Mailing Address:** USDA Agr Res Serv IBPMRL, 2747 Davis Rd Bldg 1, Tifton, GA 31793-0748. **Fax:** 229-387-2321. **E-Mail:** wjl@tifton.usda.gov

LEWIS, WALTER HEPWORTH, BOTANY. **Personal Data:** b Carleton Place, Ont, June 26, 1930. **Education:** Univ BC, BA, 1951, MA, 1954; Univ Va, PhD (bot), 1957. **Honors & Awards:** Horsley Res Award, Va Acad Sci, 1957. **Professional Experience:** PROF EMER BIOL, WASH UNIV, as of 2003; Sr botanist, Mo Bot Garden, 1972-; prof biol, Wash Univ, beginning 1969; dirherbarium, Mo Bot Garden, 1964-1972; assoc prof, Wash Univ, 1964-1969, Guggenheim fel, 1963-1964, assoc prof biol, Stephen F Austin State Col, 1961-1964; asst prof biol & dirherbarium, Stephen F Austin State Col, 1957-1961. **Memberships:** Bot Soc Am; Am Soc Plant Taxon; Asn Trop Biol; Int Asn Plant Taxon; Int OrgnBiosyst; fel Linnean Soc London. **Research Statement & Publications:** Cytotaxonomy of Rosa, the Rubiaceae, palynotaxonomy of angiosperms and southern flora; medical plants; allergy. **Mailing Address:** Dept Biol, Wash Univ, Campus Box 1137, One Brookings Dr, St Louis, MO 63130-4862. **E-Mail:** lewis@biology.wustl.edu

LEWIS, WILLIAM E(RVIN), COMPUTER PERFORMANCE EVALUATION, ANALYTICAL MODELING. **Personal Data:** b Hagerstown, Md, September 10, 1940. **Education:** Johns Hopkins Univ, BS, 1962; Northwestern Univ, Evanston, MS, 1964, PhD (indust eng), 1966. **Professional Experience:** VICE PROVOST INFO TECHNOL, ARIZ STATE UNIV, 1993-; staff mem, Ariz Dept Health Serv, 1987-; ASST DEAN ENG, ARIZ STATEUNIV, 1985-; PROF COMPUT SCI, ARIZ STATE UNIV, 1980-; chmn dept, Ariz State Univ, 1980-1985; staff mem, Intel, 1979-1980; consult, Honeywell Info Systs, 1971-1979; evalanalyst, Phoenix Alcohol Safety Action Proj, 1971-1973; consult, Gen Elec Info Systs, 1969-1971; consult, Good Samaritan Hosp, 1966-1968; assoc prof, Ariz State Univ, 1965-1980. **Memberships:** Am Inst Indust Engrs; Asn Comput Mach. **Research Statement & Publications:** Application of operations research and computer techniques to industrial problems; computer systems design. **Mailing Address:** Ariz State Univ, PO Box 870101, AZ 85287-0101. **Fax:** 602-965-7933. **E-Mail:** william.lewis@asu.edu

LEWIS, WILLIAM JAMES, MATHEMATICS. **Personal Data:** b Talahassee, Fla, February 11, 1945; m 1982, Doris; c Michael, Tanya & Steven. **Education:** La State Univ, Baton Rouge, BS, 1966, PhD (math), 1971. **Professional Experience:** PROF MATH, UNIV NEBR-LINCOLN, 1993-; CHAIR, UNIV NEBR-LINCOLN, 1988-; vice chmn dept, Univ Nebr-lincoln, 1980-1983; from asst prof to assoc prof, Univ Nebr-lincoln, 1971-1993; instr math, La State Univ, 1971. **Memberships:** Am Math Soc; Math Asn Am; Am Asn Univ Prof. **Research Statement & Publications:** Commutative algebra; mathematics education. **Mailing Address:** Dept Math, Univ Nebr, 808 Oldfather Hall 0323, Lincoln, NE 68588-0323. **Fax:** 402-472-8466. **E-Mail:** jlewis@math.unl.edu

LEWIS, WILLIAM MADISON, FISHERIES. **Personal Data:** b Faison, NC, November 26, 1922. **Education:** NC State Col, BS, 1943; Iowa State Col, MS, 1948, PhD (zool), 1949. **Professional Experience:** RETIRED; chmn, Dept Zool, 1972-; prof zool, Coop Fisheries Lab, 1960-; dir, Coop Fisheries Lab, 1949-; asst prof, Southern Ill Univ, 1949-1960; Sci bact aide, USDA, 1942. **Memberships:** Am Fisheries Soc. **Research Statement & Publications:** Aquaculture and fish management. **Mailing Address:** 7500 Pine Ridge, Faison, NC 78341.

LEWIS, WILLIAM MASON, WEED SCIENCE. **Personal Data:** b Ithaca, NY, August 13, 1929. **Education:** Tex A&M Univ, BS, 1952; Univ Minn, MS, 1956, PhD (plant genetics), 1957. **Honors & Awards:** Outstanding Exten Worker Award, Weed Sci Soc Am, 1988. **Professional Experience:** RETIRED; Vis prof, Univ Ill, 1974; prof crop sci & weed sci ext specialist, NC State Univ, 1969-; from instr to assoc prof, NC State Univ, 1956-1969; Asst agron & plantgenetics, Univ Minn, 1952-1956. **Memberships:** Am Soc Agron; Crop Sci Soc Am; Weed Sci Soc Am; Int Turf Grass Soc; Southern Weed Sci Soc. **Research Statement & Publications:** Agronomy; turf weed control. **Mailing Address:** Dept Crop Sci, NC State Univ, Raleigh, NC 27695-7620. **Fax:** 919-515-5315. **E-Mail:** wlewis@wolf.ces.ncsu.edu

LEWIS, WILLIAM P, MEDICAL MICROBIOLOGY. **Personal Data:** b Swatow, China, August 12, 1929; American citizen; m 1951, Phyllis; c Roberta (Daulton) & Michael. **Education:** Univ Redlands, BS, 1951; Univ Calif, Los Angeles, PhD (infectious dis), 1962. **Professional Experience:** EMER ASSOC PROF CLIN, DEPT PATH, KECK SCH MED, UNIV SOUTHERN CALIF, as of 2002; assoc prof path, Sch Med, Univ Southern Calif, beginning 1969; chief med microbiologist, Southern Calif Med Ctr, 1969-1994; asst res parasitologist & instr parasitol, Sch Pub Health, Univ Calif, Los Angeles, 1962-1969. **Memberships:** AAAS; Am Soc Trop Med & Hyg; Am Soc Microbiol; Am Soc Parasitol. **Research Statement & Publications:** Immunology of parasitic diseases, especially toxoplasmosis, amebiasis and filariasis; diagnostic bacteriology, parasitology and immunology. **Mailing Address:** Keck Sch Med, Univ Southern Calif, Los Angeles, CA 90089.

LEWONTIN, RICHARD CHARLES, GENETICS, POPULATION BIOLOGY. **Personal Data:** b New York, NY, March 29, 1929; m 1947, Mary; c 4. **Education:** Harvard Univ, AB, 1951; Columbia Univ, MA, 1952, PhD (zoology), 1954. **Professional Experience:** ALEXANDER AGASSIZ RES PROF, HARVARD UNIV, as 0f 2003; prof biol, Harvard Univ, 1973-1998; co-ed, Am Naturalist, Am Soc Nat, 1965; prof biol, Univ Chicago, 1964-1973; Fulbright fel, 1961-1962; sem assoc, Columbia Univ, 1959-1961; lectr, Columbia Univ, 1959; from asst prof to prof biol, Univ Rochester, 1958-1964; asst prof genetics, NC State Col, 1954-1958; NSF fel, 1954-1955, NSF, sr fel, 1961-1962 & 1971-1972; reader biomet, Columbia Univ, 1953-1954. **Memberships:** AAAS; fel Am Acad Arts & Sci; Genetics Soc Am; Soc Study Evolution (pres, 1970). **Research Statement & Publications:** Population genetics, ecology and evolution. **Mailing Address:** Mus Comp Zool, Harvard Univ, Cambridge, MA 02138. **Fax:** 617-495-5667.

LEWY, ALFRED JAMES, PSYCHIATRY, NEUROSCIENCE. **Personal Data:** b Chicago, Ill, October 12, 1945; m Colleen. **Education:** Univ Chicago, MD, 1973, PhD (pharmacol), 1973. **Professional Experience:** SR VICE CHMN, DEPT PSYCHIAT, ORE HEALTH SCI UNIV, as of 2005; DIR, SLEEP & MOOD DIS LAB, ORE HEALTH SCI UNIV, as of 2005; RICHARD H PHILLIPS PROF BIOL PSYCHIAT, ORE HEALTH SCI UNIV, as of 2005; PROF PHYSIOL, ORE HEALTH SCI UNIV, 1996-; PROF PHARMACOL, ORE HEALTH SCI UNIV, 1988-; PROF PSYCHIAT & OPHTHAL, ORE HEALTH SCI UNIV, 1986-. **Memberships:** Sigma Xi; Am Psychiat Asn; fel Am Col Neuropsychopharmacol; Sleep Res Soc; Soc Biol Rhythm. **Research Statement & Publications:** Chronobiology research in psychiatry; bright light treatment of sleep and mood disorders; clinical and basic pineal melatonin research. **Mailing Address:** Dept Psychiat, Ore Health Sci Univ, Mail Code L-469, Portland, OR 97201. **Fax:** 503-494-5329. **E-Mail:** lewy@ohsu.edu

LEX, R(OWLAND) G(ARBER), ELECTRICAL ENGINEERING. **Personal Data:** b Philadelphia, Pa, December 29, 1924. **Education:** Univ Pa, BS, 1949, MS, 1950. **Professional Experience:** RETIRED; vpres res develop & eng, Develop & Eng Dept, Instrument Group, 1987-1990; dir, Develop & Eng Dept, Instrument Group, 1976-1987; gen mgr, Recorder & Test Instrument Div, 1972-1976; mgr, Eng Coord & Serv Dept, 1969-1972; gen mgr, Digital Equip Div, 1968-1969; mgr, Develop Div, 1962-1968; sect head, Leeds & Northrup Co, 1958-1962; group chief, Leeds & Northrup Co, 1955-1958; elec engr, Leeds & Northrup Co, 1949-1955. **Memberships:** Inst Elec & Electronics Engrs; fel Instrument Soc Am. **Research Statement & Publications:** Application of digital techniques including computers to measurement and control of processes. **Mailing Address:** 914 Remington Rd, Wynnewood, PA 19096.

LEY, ALLYN BRYSON, MEDICINE. **Personal Data:** b Springfield, Mass, December 5, 1918; m 1967, Barbara; c 6. **Education:** Dartmouth Col, AB, 1939; Columbia Univ, MD, 1942; Am Bd Internal Med, dipl. **Professional Experience:** RETIRED; attend physician, Tompkins Community Hosp, 1971-1990; clin dir, Univ Health Serv, 1971-1987; Hosp Spec Surg, 1958-1971, Mem Sloan Kettering Cancer Ctr, 1971-1987; chief staff, SS Hope, 1969-1970; prof med, Sloan-Kettering Div, 1963-1993; attend physician & dir ambulatory serv, NY Hosp, 1963-1969; assoc vis physician, Bellevue Hosp, 1960-1967; consult, Manhattan Vet Admin Hosp, 1958-1960; dir hemat labs, Mem Hosp, 1955-1963; from asst prof to assoc prof, Sloan-Kettering Div, 1954-1963; cancer coord, Sloan-Kettering Div, 1954-1963; asst attend physician, NY Hosp, 1954-1963; asst dir, Sloan-Kettering Div, 1954-1955; dir blood bank, Mem Hosp, 1951-1963; instr, Med Col, Cornell Univ, 1951-1952; asst, Boston City Hosp, 1949-1951; asst med, Med Col, Cornell Univ, 1947-1949. **Memberships:** AAAS; Am Soc Hemat; Am Col Physicians. **Research Statement & Publications:** Immunohematology; erythrocyte biochemistry; medical education and care. **Mailing Address:** Cornell Univ Health Serv, Ten Central Ave, Ithaca, NY 14853.

LEY, HERBERT L, JR, experimental biology; deceased, see previous edition for last biography

LEY, KENNETH D, BIOMEDICAL RESEARCH. **Personal Data:** b Gallop, NMex, July 28, 1941. **Education:** NMex State Univ, BS, 1965; Wash State Univ, PhD (microbiol), 1969. **Professional Experience:** RES SCIENTIST, LOVELACE INST, 1986-; mem tech staff, Sandia NatLabs, 1977-1980; asst prof vet sci, Univ Fla, 1971-1977; Fel cell biol, Univ Calif, Los Angeles, 1969-1971. **Memberships:** Am Soc Biochem & Molecular Biol; AAAS. **Mailing Address:** PO Box 241, Torreon, NM 87061.

LEYBOURNE, A(LLEN) E(DWARD), III, CHEMICAL ENGINEERING. **Personal Data:** b Jacksonville, Fla, August 26, 1934. **Education:** Univ Fla, BS, 1956, PhD (chem eng), 1961; Pa State Univ, MS, 1958. **Professional Experience:** PROF ENG, SCH ENG TECHNOL, UNIV SOUTHERN MISS, as of 2003; dir eng, Interpine Lumber Co, beginning 1980; dir prod eng, Texfi Industs, Inc, 1977-1980; plant mgr, Texfi Industs, Inc, 1971-1977; supvr textile develop, Textile Div, Monsanto Co, 1963-1971; sr engr, Am Oil Co, 1961-1962; reschemist, Atlantic Refining Co, 1960; instr chem, Univ Fla, 1958-1959; Res Assoc petrol res, PaState Univ, 1956-1958. **Memberships:** Am Inst Chem Eng; Soc Mfg Engrs; Am Asn Eng Educ. **Research Statement & Publications:** Polymer textiles, ocean acoustics and signal processing. **Mailing Address:** Sch Eng Technol, Univ Southern Miss, PO Box 5173, Hattiesburg, MS 39406-5137. **E-Mail:** allen.leybourne@usm.edu

LEYDA, JAMES PERKINS, PHARMACY, PHARMACEUTICAL CHEMISTRY, TECHNOLOGY COMMERCIALIZATION. **Personal Data:** b Youngstown, Ohio, October 2, 1935; m 1967, Barbara; c Jason, Jeffrey & Justin. **Education:** Ohio Northern Univ, BS, 1957; Ohio State Univ, MS, 1959, PhD (pharm), 1962. **Honors & Awards:** Lunsford Richardson Award, 1960. **Professional Experience:** PRES, EMERGING CONCEPTS INC, 1998-; mgr, Strategic Res Alliance, Marion Merrell Dow Pharm, 1992-1998; assoc dir drug reg affairs, US area, Merrell Dow Res Inst, 1990-1992; dir com develop, US area, Merrell Dow Res Inst, 1984-1989; head, Dept Pharm Res & Develop, Merrell Dow Res Inst, 1981-1984; dir, Merrell Int Div, Richardson-Merrell, 1976-1981; mgr new prod develop, Merrell Int Div, Richardson-Merrell, 1969-1976; mgr prod develop, Int Med Res & Develop, 1966-1969; develop chemist, Lederle Labs Div, Am Cyanamid Co, 1962-1966; operating chmn, Sci Affairs Comt, Nat Pharmaceut Coun. **Memberships:** AAAS; Am Pharmaceut Asn; NY Acad Sci; Am Asn Pharm Scientist; Sigma Xi; Am Soc Hosp Pharmacists; Am Soc Microbiol. **Research Statement & Publications:** Drug delivery systems; product development; commercialization of pharmaceuticals; biotechnology. **Mailing Address:** Emerging Concepts Inc, 3130 Highland Ave, 3rd Floor, Cincinnati, OH 45219-2374. **Fax:** 513-221-1891. **E-Mail:** jleyda.eci@biostart.org

LEYDEN, DONALD E, ANALYTICAL CHEMISTRY. **Personal Data:** b Gadsden, Ala, June 26, 1938. **Education:** Ky State Univ, BS, 1960; Emory Univ, MS, 1961, PhD, 1964. **Professional Experience:** RETIRED; assoc prin scientist, Philip Morris, beginning 1988; prof chem, Colo State Univ, 1982-1988; Phillipson prof chem, Univ Denver, 1976-1981; from asst prof to assoc prof chem, Univ Ga, 1965-1976; res assoc, Univ NC, 1964-1965. **Memberships:** Am Chem Soc; Soc Appl Spectros; Mat Res Soc. **Research Statement & Publications:** Chemically modified surfaces; ion-exchange; applications of nuclear magnetic resonance to the study of chemical systems of analytical importance. **Mailing Address:** Res & Develop, Philip Morris, PO Box 26583, Richmond, VA 23261-6583.

LEYDEN, RICHARD NOEL, ORGANOMETALLIC CHEMISTRY, POLYMER CHEMISTRY. **Personal Data:** b Santa Monica, Calif, November 14, 1948. **Education:** Univ Calif, Los Angeles, BS, 1971, PhD (chem), 1975. **Professional Experience:** SCIENTIST, as of 2002; TECH STAFF POLYMER RES, HUGHES AIRCRAFT CO, 1977-; res asst inorg chem, Calif Inst Technol, 1976-1977; res asst polymer res, Univ Witwatersrand, 1975-1976. **Memberships:** Am Chem Soc; Sigma Xi. **Research Statement & Publications:** Polymers, especially with semiconducting or electrical properties; organometallic polymers; organic metals; ultra high pressure chemistry. **Mailing Address:** 22024 Alta Dr, Topanga, CA 90290-9755. **E-Mail:** av680@lafn.org

LEYH, GEORGE FRANCIS, CIVIL ENGINEERING. **Personal Data:** b Utica, NY, October 1, 1931. **Education:** Cornell Univ, BCE, 1954, MS, 1956. **Honors & Awards:** Bloem Distinguished Serv Award, Am Concrete Inst, 1972. **Professional Experience:** RETIRED; Bd dirs, Am Nat Stand Inst, beginning 1986; Am Soc Concrete Construct, beginning 1984; ed jour, Am Concrete Inst, beginning 1975; exec vpres, Am Concrete Inst, 1975-1998; dir mkt, Concrete Reinforcing Steel Inst, 1967-1975; struct engr, Portland Cement Asn, 1963-1967; assoc dir eng, Martin Marietta Corp, 1959-1963; struct engr, Eckerlin & Klepper, 1956-1959. **Memberships:** Am Soc Civil Engrs; Nat Inst Bldg Scientists; Am Rwy Eng Asn; Am Nat Stand Inst; Am Soc Concrete Construct. **Mailing Address:** 30405 Oakview Way, Bingham Farms, MI 48025.

LEYON, ROBERT EDWARD, ANALYTICAL CHEMISTRY, SPECTROSCOPY. **Personal Data:** b Newton, Mass, July 28, 1936; m 1962, c 2. **Education:** Williams Col, BA, 1958; Princeton Univ, MA, 1960, PhD (chem), 1962. **Professional Experience:** RETIRED; prof chem, Dickinson Col, 1992-1998; res assoc, Univ Tex, Austin, 1983-1984; chmn dept, Dickinson Col, 1979-1983, 1988-1990, 1994-1997; res assoc, Colo State Univ, 1975-1976; from asst prof to assoc prof, Dickinson Col, 1969-1992; res assoc, Univ NC, 1967-1968; from instr to asst prof, Swarthmore Col, 1962-1969; instr chem, Princeton Univ, 1961-1962. **Memberships:** Soc Appl Spectros. **Research Statement & Publications:** Graphite furnace spectroscopy; trace metal analysis by atomic absorption. **Mailing Address:** Dept Chem, Dickinson Col, PO Box 1773, Carlisle, PA 17013-2846. **E-Mail:** leyon@dickinson.edu

LEYSE, CARL F(ERDINAND), space nuclear propulsion & power, nuclear reactor technology & design; deceased, see previous edition for last biography

LEYSIEFFER, FREDERICK WALTER, MATHEMATICS, PROBABILITY. **Personal Data:** b Milwaukee, Wis, January 30, 1933; m 1964, Annelise; c Kirsten, Suzanne & Beth. **Education:** Univ Wis-Madison, BA, 1955, MA, 1956; Univ Mich, PhD (math), 1964. **Professional Experience:** PROF STATIST, FLA STATE UNIV, as of 2005; assoc vpres for Acad Affairs, 1997-; assoc dean, col arts & sci, 1994-1997; actg dean, Col Arts & Sci, 1994-1995; chmn dept, Dept of statist 1981-1987 & 1990-1993; vis lectr, Sheffield Univ, Sheffield, Eng, 1973-1974; vis lectr, Leverhulme Commonwealth-Am fel, 1973; assoc head dept, Dept of statist 1969-1976; from asst prof to assoc prof, Col Arts & Sci, 1964-1982. **Memberships:** Am Math Soc; Am Statist Asn; Math Asn Am; Inst Math Statist; AAAS; Sigma Xi. **Research Statement & Publications:** Probability theory; stochastic processes; sampling theory; environmental statistics. **Mailing Address:** Dept Statist, Fla State Univ, Tallahassee, FL 32306-3033. **E-Mail:** fleysief@mailer.fsu.edu

LEYSON, JOSE FLORANTE JUSTININANE, HUMAN SEXUALITY, URODYNAMICS. **Personal Data:** b Philippines, August 17, 1946. **Education:** Cebu Inst Technol, BS, 1965, MD, 1970; Am Bd Urol, dipl, 1979. **Honorary Degrees:** MS, US Army Comdr & Gen Staff Col, Kans, 1992. **Professional Experience:** ASSOC PROF UROL, NJ MED SCH, 1988-; fel sex educ &parenthood, Am Univ, Wash, DC, 1981; Sexual Dysfunction Ctr, Newark, NJ, 1980-; profsexuality, Fairleigh Dickinson Univ, NJ, 1980-1985, dir, Urodynamics & Sex Clin, Vet Admin Hosp, NJ, 1979-, consult, Urodynamics, Bronx Vet Admin Hosp, NY, 1979; Vis prof urodynamics, Yale Univ Hosp, 1979; Forum, Essence & Miss Quarterly Mag, 1978-; Fel urodynamics, Yale Univ Hosp, 1978; clin chief, spinal cord injury unit, vetadmin hosp, Orange, NJ, 1977-; fel spinal cord, NJ Med Sch, 1976-1977; fel sexuality, Johns Hopkins Hosp, 1976; Felentom, US Agency Int Develop, 1970-1971; AMA Archives Internal Med; chief, Urol Hosp Ctr Essex Co, Cedar Groves, NJ. **Memberships:** Philippines Asn Sexologists Am (pres, 1980-1982); Philippine Med Asn Am; AmUrol Asn Inc; Am Col Surg; Laser Soc; Am Col Clin Sexologists. **Research Statement & Publications:** Sexuality for both abled-bodied and disabled persons; drugs or electrical stimulations to produce erection in impotent patients; ways to produce urination in patients with paralysis and spinal defects due to injury or birth defects; laser erectiometer; erection pacemaker; author of two books; ointment for erection or orgasm. **Mailing Address:** Newport Medi Assoc, 562 W Side Ave, Jersey City, NJ 07304-1618.

LEZNOFF, CLIFFORD CLARK, ORGANIC CHEMISTRY, PHTHALOCYANINES. **Personal Data:** b Montreal, Que, May 30, 1940; m 1963, Judith; c Daniel, Michael & Benjamin. **Education:** McGill Univ, BSc, 1961, PhD (org chem), 1965. **Honors & Awards:** The Alfred Bader Award in organic chem, The Canadian soc for chem 1999. **Professional Experience:** PROF ORG CHEM, YORK UNIV, 1980-; chair chem, York Univ, 1990- 1993; Australian Nat Univ, 1980-1981 & Univ BC, 1987-1988; Vis prof, Weizmann Inst Sci, 1973-1974; from asst prof to assoc prof, York Univ, 1967-1979; Nat Res Coun Can overseas fel, Cambridge Univ, 1965-1967; Fel org chem, Northwestern Univ, 1964-1965. **Memberships:** Am Chem Soc 1967-; Chem Inst Can 1967-. **Research Statement & Publications:** Polymer supports in organic synthesis; synthesis of chiral compounds, pheromones, phthalocyanines and fluorinated heterocyclic compounds; phthalocyanines in photodynamic therapy of cancer, multinuclear phthalocyanines. **Mailing Address:** Dept Chem, York Univ, Toronto, ON M3J 1P3, Can. **Fax:** 416-736-5936. **E-Mail:** leznoff@yorku.ca

L'HERNAULT, STEVEN W, BIOLOGY. **Education:** Hofstra Univ, BA, 1976; Yale Univ, PhD, 1984. **Professional Experience:** PROF BIOL, EMORY UNIV, as of 2005. **Mailing Address:** Dept Biol Emory Univ O. Wayne Rollins Res Ctr, 1510 Clifton Rd NE Rm 2011, Atlanta, GA 30322. **Fax:** 404-727-2880. **E-Mail:** bioslh@emory.edu

L'HEUREUX, JACQUES (JEAN), COSMIC RAY PHYSICS, ASTROPHYSICS. **Personal Data:** b Trois-Rivieres, Que, December 20, 1939; div, c 3. **Education:** Univ Montreal, BS, 1961; Univ Chicago, MS, 1962, PhD (physics), 1966. **Professional Experience:** RETIRED; dir, Universities Space Res Assoc, Columbia, 1999-2004; sr res scientist, Bartol Res Inst, Univ Delaware, NY, 1990-1999; sr res assoc, Univ Chicago, beginning 1978; asst prof physics, Univ Ariz, 1969-1977; res assoc physics, Univ Chicago, 1966-1969. **Memberships:** fel Am Phys Soc; Am Geophys Union. **Research Statement & Publications:** Primary cosmic ray electrons; solar modulation of cosmic rays; primary heavy nuclei at high energies. **Mailing Address:** Univ Space Res Asn, 10221 Wincopin Circle, Ste 500, Columbia, MD 21044-3423. **Fax:** 410-730-3496. **E-Mail:** jlheureuxathq.usra.edu

L'HEUREUX, MAURICE VICTOR, BIOCHEMISTRY. **Personal Data:** b Lewiston, Maine, May 23, 1914; m 1946, Patricia; c Victor, Pierre, David, Paul & Claude. **Education:** Col Holy Cross, BS, 1936, MS, 1937; Yale Univ, PhD (biochem), 1944. **Professional Experience:** PROF EMER BIOCHEM, STRITCH SCH MED, LOYOLA UNIV CHICAGO, 1979-; from asst prof to prof, Stritch Sch Med, Loyola Univ Chicago, 1949-1979; assoc, Stritch Sch Med, Loyola Univ Chicago, 1946-1949; control chemist, Stokely Bros-Van Camp, Inc, Ind, 1940-1941. **Memberships:** Am Soc Biochem & Molecular Biol. **Research Statement & Publications:** Lipid metabolism; modifying and regulatory effects of parathyroid hormone, calcitonin and vitamin D upon calcium metabolism. **Mailing Address:** Dept Molecular & Cellular Biochem, 6525 N Sheridan Rd, Chicago, IL 60626.

LHILA, RAMESH CHAND, PRESSURE SENSITIVE ADHESIVES, POLYMER BLENDS. **Personal Data:** b Rangoon, Burma, India. **Education:** Calcutta Univ, BS, 1972, BTech, 1975; Univ Akron, PhD (polymer sci), 1983. **Professional Experience:** DIR RES, TESA TUCK INC, ROCHELLE, NY, 1988-; tech dir gen prod, Tuck Industs, New Rochelle, NY, 1987-1988; asst dir res & develop, Tuck Industs, NewRochelle, NY, 1983-1987; group leader res & develop, Tuck Industs, New Rochelle, NY, 1982-1983; Res chemist, Tuck Industs, New Rochelle, NY, 1982; Hon instr, St Xavier's Col, Calcutta, India, 1972. **Memberships:** Am Chem Soc; Am Chem Soc Polymer Chem Div; Am Chem Soc Rubber Div; fel Plastics & Rubber Inst; Soc Plastics Engrs. **Research Statement & Publications:** Pressure sensitive adhesive tapes based on rubber, acrylics and silicones by various methods including solution, hot melt and water-based coatings; coating technology; emulsion and solution polymerisation; polymer blends and rubber-modified high impact plastics. **Mailing Address:** 1780 Evergreen Ave, Akron, OH 44301.

LI, BAI-LIAN LARRY, ECOLOGICAL MODELLING. **Education:** Hubei Agr Univ, BSC, 1981; Wuhan Univ, DSc, 1986. **Professional Experience:** PROF ECOL, DEPT BOT & PLANT SCI, UNIV CALIF-RIVERSIDE, as of 2005. **Research Statement & Publications:** Mathematical and theoretical ecology; plant ecology; ecological modeling; ecological complexity; landscape ecology; and computational biology. **Mailing Address:** Dept Bot & plant Sci, Univ Calif-Riverside, Batchelor Hall 4133, Riverside, CA 92521. **E-Mail:** bai-lian.li@ucr.edu

LI, CHANG-YANG, NUCLEAR POWER. **Professional Experience:** STAFF, OFF NUCLEAR REACTOR REGULATION, as of 2006. **Memberships:** Inst Elec & Electronics Engrs. **Mailing Address:** US Nuclear Regulatory Comn, Off Nuclear Reactor Regulation, P O Box 11A11, Washington, DC 20555. **Fax:** 301-492-0875.

LI, CHE-YU, MATERIALS SCIENCE & ENGINEERING. **Personal Data:** b Honan, China, November 15, 1934; m 1961, c 3. **Education:** Nat Taiwan Univ, BSE, 1954; Cornell Univ, PhD (chem eng), 1960. **Professional Experience:** PROF EMER MAT SCI & ENG, CORNELL UNIV, as of 2006; dir, dept mat sci & eng, Cornell Univ, beginning 1993; dir, electronic packing prog, beginning 1990; prof mat sci & eng, cornell univ, beginning 1972; mem staff, Argonne Nat Lab, 1969-1971; mem staff, US Steel Res Ctr, 1965-1966; from asst prof to assoc prof, Dept Mat Sci & Eng, 1962-1972; res assoc, Dept Mat Sci & Eng, 1960-1962; consult, Nuclear Mat, Electronic Packaging. **Memberships:** Am Phys Soc; Am Inst Mining Metall & Petrol Engrs. **Research Statement & Publications:** Mechanical behavior; radiation damage; surface and interface; development of a state variable description of mechanical properties of crystalline solids; micro-mechanical testing; nuclear materials, electronic packaging, high-temperature engineering alloys. **Mailing Address:** Dept Mat Sci & Eng, Cornell Univ, 310 Bard Hall, Ithaca, NY 14853. **Fax:** 607-255-6575. **E-Mail:** alliance@msc.cornell.edu

LI, CHI, POLYMER PHYSICS, MULTIPHASE POLYMER SYSTEMS. **Personal Data:** b May 18, 1956. **Education:** City Col City Univ, NY, BE, 1984; Univ Wis-Madison, PhD (chem eng), 1988. **Professional Experience:** CHIEF PROD DEVELOP ENG, VEHICLE OPER, INT OPERS, FORDMOTOR CO, 1994-; Adj assoc prof, Wayne State Univ, 1993-; prin res scientist, Ford Res Labs, 1990-1994; sr res scientist, Vehicle Oper, Int Opers, Ford Motor CO, 1988-1990. **Memberships:** Am Chem Soc; Sigma Xi; Am Phys Soc; Am Inst Chem Engrs. **Research Statement & Publications:** Polymer processing research including structure property relationship; rheology; physical property characterization; adhesives research including mechanism of adhesion mechanical properties and adhesive processing. **Mailing Address:** PO Box 2053, MD 3198, Dearborn, MI 48121. **Fax:** 313-337-5581. **E-Mail:** cli@smail.srl.ford.com

LI, CHIA-CHUAN, OPTOELECTRONICS MATERIALS SCIENCE, MICROELECTRONICS. **Personal Data:** b Taipei, Taiwan, December 29, 1946; American citizen; m 1983, Clemencia Vasquez; c Angie & Andrew. **Education:** Nat Taiwan Univ, BS, 1969; Rutgers Univ, MS, 1974; Univ Mich, PhD (mat eng), 1977; Pepperdine Univ, MBA, 1986. **Professional Experience:** PRODUCT MGR SENSORS & TARGETING SYSTEMS, DRS TECHNOLOGIES, 2001-; product mgr, Boeing, 1996-2001; prog mgr, Electro-optical Ctr, Rockwell Int Corp, 1985-1996; syst engr, Electro-Optical & Data Systs, Hughes Aircraft Co, 1984-1985; lectr, San Diego City Col, 1980-1983; sr engr, Gen Atomic Co, 1977-1984. **Memberships:** Metall Soc; Sigma Xi; Am Soc Metals. **Research Statement & Publications:** Metallurgy, friction and wear; high temperature materials and coatings; infrared focal plane array materials; signal processing electronics; electro-optical systems. **Mailing Address:** 1 Raeburn Ln, Trabuco Cyn, CA 92679.

LI, CHIA-YU, electroanalytical chemistry; deceased, see previous edition for last biography

LI, C(HING) C(HUNG), PATTERN RECOGNITION & IMAGE PROCESSING, BIOCYBERNETICS. **Personal Data:** b Changshu, China, March 30, 1932; m 1961, Hanna; c William Wei-Lin & Vincent Wei-Tsin. **Education:** Nat Taiwan Univ, BS, 1954; Northwestern Univ, MS, 1956, PhD (elec eng), 1961. **Professional Experience:** Health Res & Serv Found, 1985-1986; sabbatical leave, Lab Info & Decision Systs, Mass Inst Technol, 1988; chmn, Int Asn Pattern Recognition, 1987-1990; assoc ed, Pattern Recognition, 1985-; Biomed Pattern Recognition Tech Comt, Int Asn Pattern Recognition, 1983-; Commonwealth Pa, Western Pa Advan Technol Ctr, 1983-1984, 1986-1988; fac res partic, Dept Energy, Pittsburgh Energy Technol Ctr, 1982, 1983, 1985, 1988, 1989; exec comt, Pattern Anal & Mach Intel Tech Comt, Inst Elec & Electronics Engrs, Comput Soc, 1981-1984; consult, Westinghouse Res Develop Ctr, 1981; Chmn, Cybernetics Standing Comt, 1979-1993; PROF COMPUT SCI, UNIV PITTSBURGH, 1977-; admin comt, Biocybernetics Tech Comt, Inst Elec & Electronics Engrs Systs, Man & Cybernetics Soc, 1977-1979; Commonwealth Pa, Dept Health, 1977-1979; prin investr, NSF Res Grants, 1975-1981, 1985-1987; chmn, Biocybernetics Tech Comt, Inst Elec & Electronics Engrs Systs, Man & Cybernetics Soc, 1972-1979; vis prin scientist, Alza Corp, Palo Alto, Calif, 1970; PROF ELEC ENG, UNIV PITTSBURGH, 1967-; vis assoc prof, Univ Calif, Berkeley, 1964; assoc prof, Univ Pittsburgh, 1962-1967; asst prof, Univ Pittsburgh, 1959-1960, 1961-1962. **Memberships:** AAAS; fel Inst Elec & Electronics Engrs; Pattern Recognition Soc; Biomed Eng Soc; NY Acad Sci; Sigma Xi. **Research Statement & Publications:** Application of wavelet transform to image processing; computer vision; biomedical pattern recognition; artificial neural networks and intelligent systems; biocybernetics. **Mailing Address:** Dept Elec Eng, Univ Pittsburgh, Pittsburgh, PA 15261. **Fax:** 412-624-8003. **E-Mail:** ccl@vms.cis.pitt.edu

LI, CHIN-HSIU, ENGINEERING MECHANICS, THERMAL TECHNOLOGY. **Personal Data:** b Taiwan, China, January 3, 1938. **Education:** Nat Cheng Kung Univ, BS, 1961; Nat Cent Univ, MS, 1964; Brigham Young Univ, MS, 1966; Univ Mich, PhD (eng mech), 1968. **Honors & Awards:** McCuen Award, Gen Motors Labs, 1984. **Professional Experience:** PRIN RES ENGR & SECT MGR, ENGINE RES DEPT, RES & DEVELOP CTR, GEN MOTORS RES LABS, 1994-; Engine Res Dept, Eng Mech Dept, 1988-1994; sr staff res engr, Eng Mech Dept, 1985-1988; staff res engr, Mech Res Dept, 1981-1985; sr res engr, eng mech, 1976-1981; assoc sr res engr, Gen Motors Res Labs, 1972-1976; res assoc, Univ Mich, 1972; vis assoc prof, Nat Cheng Kung Univ, 1971-1972; res assoc fluid mech, Case Western Res Univ, 1969-1971. **Memberships:** Soc Automotive Engrs; Am Soc Mech Engrs. **Research Statement & Publications:** Hydrodynamic stability; fluid flow and heat transfer; lubrication theory; rotor dynamics; mechanics of automotive components; computer-aided engine design, ceramic engines; engine thermostructure. **Mailing Address:** Engine Res Dept, Gen Motors Res Labs, Warren, MI 48090.

LI, CHI-TANG, PHYSICAL CHEMISTRY, CRYSTALLOGRAPHY. **Personal Data:** b Ningtu, Kiangsi, China, October 16, 1934; m 1962, Yen L Lee; c Mary, Florence, Albert & Thomas. **Education:** Nat Taiwan Univ, BS, 1955; Univ Louisville, MS, 1959; MontState Univ, PhD (chem), 1964. **Professional Experience:** SR ANALYTICAL SPECIALIST, ANALYTICAL SCI, DOW CORNING, 1983-; prin engr, Inst Gas Technol, 1980-1982; supvr fuel-cell mat res, Inst Gas Technol, 1978-1980; sr scientist, Adv Mat Res Sect, Owens-Ill Tech Ctr, 1967-1978; Scientist, Adv Mat Res Sect, Owens-Ill Tech Ctr, 1964-1967. **Memberships:** Am Chem Soc; Am Crystallog Asn; Am Ceramic Soc. **Research Statement & Publications:** Crystal structure and chemistry; studies of glass ceramic materials, research on high temperature materials; fuel cell research; fiber and composite development; x-ray diffraction of silicone materials. **Mailing Address:** Mat Res, 1510 Timber Dr, Midland, MI 48642.

LI, CHOU H(SIUNG), PHYSICAL METALLURGY, STATISTICS. **Personal Data:** b Haining, China, June 8, 1923; American citizen; m 1953, c 2. **Education:** Chiao Tung Univ, BS, 1944; Purdue Univ, MS, 1949, PhD (phys metall), 1951. **Honors & Awards:** David Gessner Prize, Am Soc Eng Educ, 1955 & 1956; NASA New Technol Innovation Award, 1977. **Professional Experience:** PRES, LMI TECHNOLOGIES LLC, as of 2004; prin investr, 1984-1991; pres, Lintel Technol, Inc, beginning 1981; dir, Res & Develop, Semi-Alloys, 1980-1981; staff technologist, Singer Co, 1978-1979; adj prof mat sci, State Univ NY, Stony Brook, 1977-1985; consult, 1977-1982; NASA Skylab consult specialist, 1972-1975; ed, Chinese Inst Engrs J, 1965-1968; sr res scientist, Grumman Aerospace Corp, 1962-1977; mgr semiconductors, Gen Instrument Corp, 1960-1962; sr scientist, Shockley Transistor Corp, 1959-1960; metallurgist, RCA, 1951-1959. **Memberships:** Sr mem Inst Elec & Electronics Engrs; sr mem Am Soc Qual Control; Am Inst Mining Metall & Petrol Engrs; Am Phys Soc; Chinese Inst Engrs. **Research Statement & Publications:** self-optimizing automation; ceramic bonding and coating; very large scale integrationand ultralarge scale integration microcircuits; intelligent manufacturing, servicing, training and education; automatic generation of optimized knowledge bases, expert systems and computer software; friction; physics of failures; reliability; computer programming; artificial intelligence. **Mailing Address:** LMI Technologies LLC, 240 Martin L King Blvd, Newark, NJ 11576. **Fax:** 973-643-5839. **E-Mail:** chou.li@njit.edu

LI, CHUNG-HSIUNG, HEAT TRANSFER, FLUID MECHANICS. **Personal Data:** b Chia-Yi, Taiwan, China, May 10, 1939; American citizen; m 1976, c 2. **Education:** Tunghai Univ, BS, 1964; Univ NH, MS, 1969; Univ Ill, Chicago, PhD (eng), 1976. **Professional Experience:** VPRES, CHINESE AM OCEANIC & ATMOSPHERIC ASSOC, as of 2004; PROF, TUNGHAI UNIV, 1989-; sr engr, C-E Air Preheater Co, 1979-1989; specialist eng, Sargent & Lundy Engrs, 1974-1979. **Memberships:** Nat Soc Prof Engrs; Am Inst Chem Engrs; Am Soc Mech Engrs; Soc Indust & Appl Math; Soc Eng Sci; Combustion Inst. **Research Statement & Publications:** Development of new technologies; heat transfer and fluid mechanics. **Mailing Address:** Dept Chem Eng, Tunghai Univ, PO Box 833, Taichung, 40704, Taiwan. **E-Mail:** chl@mail.thu.edu.tw

LI, CHUNG-SHENG, DIGITAL LIBRARY, MULTIMEDIA DATABASE. **Personal Data:** b Nantou, Taiwan, September 26, 1962; American citizen. **Education:** Nat Taiwan Univ,

BSEE, 1984; Univ Calif, Berkeley, MS, 1989, PhD (elec eng & comput sci), 1991. **Professional Experience:** MGR, IBM T J WATSON RES CTR, 1996-; RES STAFF MEM, IBM T J WATSON RES CTR, 1991-; researcher, IBM T J Watson Res Ctr, 1990-1991; researcher, Univ Calif, Berkeley, Elec Res Lab, 1987-1990; instr spectrum anal, Dept Elec Eng & Comput Sci Univ Calif, 1986-1987; instr electronics & commun theory, Air Force Comm & Electronics Acad, Taiwan, 1985-1986; teaching asst, Dept Elec Eng, Nat Taiwan Univ, 1983-1984; Programmer, Data Processing Ctr, Ministry Finance, Taiwan, 1982. **Memberships:** Inst Elec & Electronics Engrs. **Research Statement & Publications:** Development of protocols, system architectures and innovative devices for high-bandwidth hybrid- and all-optical networks for local area networks, metropolitan area networks and wide area network applications; development of optical interconnects for short-distance computer applications. **Mailing Address:** Thomas J Watson Res Ctr, IBM, PO Box 704, Yorktown Heights, NY 10598. **Fax:** 914-784-7455. **E-Mail:** csli@watson.ibm.com

LI, CONGMING, MATHEMATICS. **Education:** Courant Inst, PhD (math), 1989. **Professional Experience:** ASSOC PROF MATH, UNIV COLO, 1999-. **Mailing Address:** Prog Appl Math, Univ Colo, Boulder, CO 80309-0526. **Fax:** 303-494-9649. **E-Mail:** Cli@colorado.edu

LI, ELDON Y, COMPUTER SCIENCE. **Education:** Natl Chengchi Univ, BC; Texas Tech Univ, MSBA, PhD. **Professional Experience:** PROF, CALIF POLYTECH STATE UNIV, as of 2006. **Mailing Address:** Calif Polytech State Univ, Col Bus, San Luis Obispo, CA 93407. **Fax:** 805-756-1473. **E-Mail:** eli@calpoly.edu

LI, FREDERICK P, CANCER ETHOLOGY. **Personal Data:** b China, May 7, 1940. **Education:** Univ NY, Rochester, BA, 1960, MD, 1965; Georgetown Univ, MA, 1969. **Honorary Degrees:** MA, Harvard Univ. **Honors & Awards:** Mott Prize, Gen Motors Cancer Res Found, 1995. **Professional Experience:** VICE CHAIR, POP SCI, DANA-FARBER CANCER INST, as of 2004; PROF MED, HARVARD MED SCH, 2002-; PROF CLIN CANCER EPIDEMIOL, HARVARD SCH PUB HEALTH, 1980-; epidemiologist, Nat Cancer Inst, 1967-1980. **Memberships:** Am Soc Clin Oncol; Am Asn Cancer Res. **Research Statement & Publications:** Identification of persons at high risk of cancer; genetic and environmental causes of cancer susceptability. **Mailing Address:** Dana Farber Cancer Inst, Smith 201 44 Binney St, Boston, MA 02115. **Fax:** 617-632-3161. **E-Mail:** frederick_li@dfci.harvard.edu

LI, G P, ELECTRICAL ENGINEERING. **Education:** Nat Cheng Kung Univ, Taiwan, BS, 1978; Univ Calif, MS, 1982, PhD (elec eng), 1983. **Professional Experience:** PROF, ELEC ENG & COMPUT SCI, UNIV CALIF, as of 2006; PROF, BIOMED ENG, UNIV CALIF, as of 2006; DIR, INTEGRATED NANOSYSTEMS RES FACIL, UNIV CALIF, as of 2006. **Mailing Address:** Dept Elec & Computer Eng, Henry Samueli Sch Eng, Univ Calif, EG 2230, Irvine, CA 92697-2660. **Fax:** 949-824-3732. **E-Mail:** gpli@uci.edu

LI, GANG, MEDICINE. **Education:** MB, DPhil, PGCHET. **Professional Experience:** SR LECTR, DEPT TRAUMA & ORTHOPAEDICS, SCH MED, MUSGRAVE PARK HOSP, QUEEN'S UNIV BELFAST, UK, as of 2006. **Mailing Address:** Queen's Univ Belfast, Musgrave Park Hosp, Lisburn Rd Belfast City Hosp, Belfast, BT9 7JB, Ireland. **E-Mail:** g.li@qub.ac.uk

LI, GEORGE SU-HSIANG, ORGANIC CHEMISTRY. **Personal Data:** b Chunking, China, October 24, 1943; m 1971, Tung-Chia; c Kenneth C. **Education:** Cheng Kung Univ, BS, 1965; Purdue Univ, PhD (org chem), 1971. **Professional Experience:** RES SCIENTIST II, POLYMER RES, BP CO, OHIO, 1987-; res assoc, Polymer Res, BP Co, Ohio, 1977-1986; sr res chem, Polymer Res, BP Co, Ohio, 1974-1977; res assoc, Med Chem Dept, Purdue Univ, 1971-1973. **Memberships:** Am Chem Soc. **Research Statement & Publications:** Synthesis of latex based polymers; exploration of novel polymers with high heat resistance and barrier characteristics; polymer modification and alloying; granted 50 patents. **Mailing Address:** 4440 Warrensville Ctr Rd, Cleveland, OH 44128-2837.

LI, GUANG CHAO, SOIL CHEMISTRY, SURFACE ANALYSIS. **Personal Data:** b Lintong, Shaanixi, China, November 30, 1961. **Education:** Northwestern Agr Univ, BS, 1983; Univ Idaho, MS, 1989, PhD (soil sci), 1992. **Professional Experience:** SCI AID, UNIV IDAHO, 1993-; assoc, Univ Idaho, 1992; grad asst, UnivIdaho, 1987-1992; Instr soil sci, Northwestern Agr Univ, China, 1983-1987. **Memberships:** Soil Sci Soc China; Soil Sci Soc Am; Am Soc Agron. **Research Statement & Publications:** Soil nutrient availability in soils; effects of soil and environmental factors on soil nutrients in soils; the use of statistic analysis method in soil fertility research. **Mailing Address:** Soil Sci Div, Univ Idaho, Moscow, ID 83844. **E-Mail:** guangcha@idui1.csrv.uidaho.edu

LI, GUANGYE, MATHEMATICS. **Education:** Rice Univ, PhD, 1986. **Professional Experience:** STAFF, DEPT MATH, NDAK STATE UNIV, as of 2005. **Mailing Address:** Cray Res, 655 F Lone Oak Dr, Eagan, MN 55121. **Fax:** 612-683-5307. **E-Mail:** gli@cray.com

LI, HAIZHANG, OPTOELECTRONICAL INSTRUMENTS, PRECISION ENGINEERING. **Personal Data:** b Shanghai, China, February 10, 1946; m 1990, Xiaodan; c Ying. **Education:** Nanjing Univ Sci & Technol, BS, 1978; Beijing Univ Sci & Technol, MS, 1982; Univ Minn, MS, 1989, PhD (cad/cae), 1993. **Professional Experience:** Prin investr, Marshall Space Flight Ctr, NASA, 1994-1995 & 1996-; SR ENGR, CONTINENTAL OPTICAL CORP, 1993-; res asst, Univ Minn, 1985-1993; hon fel, Univ Minn, 1984-1985; instr optics, Nanjing Univ Sci & Technol, 1982-1984. **Memberships:** Soc Photo-Optical Instrumentation Engrs. **Research Statement & Publications:** X-ray mirror metrology; SR mirror metrology; pencil laser beam interferometry; laser beam focusing and steering drives; fiber optics; polarization optics; digital image processing; holographic interferometry; acoustic imaging. **Mailing Address:** Continental Optical Corp, 15 Power Dr, Hauppauge, NY 11788. **Fax:** 516-582-1054. **E-Mail:** haizhang@mindspring.com

LI, HENG-CHUN (DAVID), BIOCHEMISTRY. **Personal Data:** b Canton, China, October 22, 1938. **Education:** Nat Taiwan Univ, BS, 1962; Cornell Univ, PhD (biochem), 1968. **Professional Experience:** PROF BIOCHEM, MT SINAI MED CTR, 1986-; from asst prof to assoc prof, 1971-1981. **Memberships:** AAAS; Am Soc Biochem & Molecular Biol. **Research Statement & Publications:** Structure, function and regulation of phosphoprotein phosphatases. **Mailing Address:** Dept Biochem, Mt Sinai Sch Med, PO Box 1020 5 th Av, New York, NY 10029. **E-Mail:** heng-chun.li@mssm.edu

LI, HONG, SURFACE SCIENCE, THIN FILMS. **Personal Data:** b China, February 25, 1962. **Education:** Zhejiang Univ, China, BS, 1982; Univ Wis, MS, 1984, PhD (physics), 1988. **Professional Experience:** SR SCIENTIST, GROUP TECH CTR, BOC GROUP, INC, 1991-; res assoc, Dept Math Sci & Eng, State Univ NY, Stony Brook, 1988-1991; Res asst surface sci, Lab Surface Studies, Univ Wis, 1984-1988. **Memberships:** Am Phys Soc; Am Vacuum Soc. **Research Statement & Publications:** Surface science; structure of surfaces, interfaces and thin films; processing and characterization of epitaxially grown thin films on metals, semiconductors and polymers; development and application of surface analytical spectroscopies and microscopies. **Mailing Address:** Geoscience Res Lab, Toriumi Bldg 2F, 1794 Kamiwada Yamato, Kanagawa, Japan. **E-Mail:** li@geolab.jp

LI, HSUEH MING, POLYMER CHEMISTRY. **Personal Data:** b Taiwan, China, October 25, 1939. **Education:** Tunghai Univ, Taiwan, BS, 1962; Southern Methodist Univ, MS, 1966; Polytech Inst Brooklyn, PhD (polymer chem), 1971. **Professional Experience:** RES ASSOC, ETHYL CORP, 1985-; sr res chemist, Ethyl Corp, 1979-1985; res chemist polymer res, Ethyl Corp, 1973-1979; res assoc polymer chem, Midland Macromolecular Inst, 1972-1973; fel x-ray diffraction, Polytech Inst Brooklyn, 1970-1972. **Memberships:** Am Chem Soc. **Research Statement & Publications:** Opacifying plastic pigment; polymeric flame retardants based on phosphazene-synthesis and evaluation; synthesis, characterization and mechanism of linear and cyclic phosphonitrillic chloride oligomers; advanced composites, specialty glasses, high-tech ceramics. **Mailing Address:** Albemarie Corp, 8000 GSRI Ave, Baton Rouge, LA 70820-7497.

LI, HUA, SEMICONDUCTOR LASERS, NONLINEAR DYNAMICS IN OPTICAL SYSTEMS. **Personal Data:** b Xiam, China, September 28, 1945; div, c Jie L. **Education:** Beijing Univ, MS, 1981; Hannover Univ, PhD, 1990. **Professional Experience:** RES SCIENTIST, CTR HIGH TECHNOL MAT, UNIV NMEX, 1997-; instr optoelectronics, Ctr High Technol Mat, Univ Nmex, 1995; sr res engr, Ctr High Technol Mat, Univ Nmex, 1990-1996; vis scholar, Phys Tech Inst Ger, 1985-1990; instr optics, Physics Dept, Northwestern Univ, China, 1981-1988. **Memberships:** Optical Soc Am; Inst Elec & Electronics Engrs. **Research Statement & Publications:** Semiconductor laser systems including noise properties, modulation characteristics, mode structure and polization properties; different routes to chaos in edge emitting laser diodes; vertical cavity surface emitting lasers; unstable resonator high power laser diodes; optical feedback on external injections. **Mailing Address:** 13015 Sandia Point Rd Ne, Albuquerque, NM 87111. **Fax:** 505-277-6433. **E-Mail:** huali@chtm.unm.edu

LI, HUNG CHIANG, STATISTICS, ANALYTICAL MATHEMATICS. **Personal Data:** b Kinhwa, China, December 10, 1921. **Education:** Univ Chekiang, BS, 1946; Mich State Univ, MS, 1964; Purdue Univ, PhD (statist), 1969. **Professional Experience:** PROF EMER STATIST, UNIV SOUTHERN COLO, 1990-; Consult, UnivSouthern Colo, beginning 1969; prof, Univ Southern Colo, 1969-1990; assoc prof, Tunghai Univ, 1955-1962; asst prof, Taiwan Inst Technol, 1952-1955; instr, Nat Taiwan Univ, 1950-1952; Asst math, Taiwan Normal Univ, 1947-1950. **Memberships:** Inst Math Statist; Am Math Soc; Math Asn Am; Sigma Xi. **Research Statement & Publications:** Multivariate analysis, particularly interested in normal distributions and the asymptotic expansions for distributions of characteristic roots of normal populations. **Mailing Address:** 8911 S Atlantic Ave, Southgate, CA 90280.

LI, JACK H, PHARMACOLOGY. **Personal Data:** b Shanghai, China, August 27, 1942. **Education:** Univ Calif, Berkeley, BS, 1967; Tufts Univ, PhD (physiol), 1973. **Professional Experience:** GROUP LEADER, ZENECA PHARMACEUT CORP, 1990-; PRIN PHARMACOLOGIST, ZENECA PHARMACEUT CORP, 1988-; res pharmacologist, ZenecaPharmaceut Corp, 1982-1988; res assoc, Univ Hamburg, Ger, 1977-1982; med asst prof, Univ-Geneva, Switz, 1974-1977; researcher membrane physiol, Boston Med Sch, 1973-1974. **Memberships:** Am Soc Pharmacol & Exp Therapeut; Biophys Soc; NY Acad Sci. **Mailing Address:** Zeneca Pharmaceut Corp, 1800 Concord Pike, Wilmington, DE 19850-5437.

LI, JAMES CC, MEDICINE. **Education:** Nat Taiwan Univ, BS, 1961, MS, 1963; Boston Univ Sch Med, PhD (biochem), 1971. **Professional Experience:** ASST PROF & PHYSICIAN EMER MED, AUBURN HOSP, HARVARD MED SCH, as of 2006; PRIN ASSOC, DEPT MED, HARVARD MED SCH, 1984-; assoc dir, Med Res, Hebrew Rehab Ctr Aged, beginning 1982; clin chemists, Dept Path, New Eng Deaconess Hosp, 1980-1982; prin assoc, Dept Microbiol & Molecular Genetics, Harvard Med Sch, 1976-1979; res assoc, Dept Microbiol & Molecular Genetics, Harvard Med Sch, 1974-1976; res assoc exp biol, Worcester Found, 1972-1974; res fel microbiol & molecular genetics, Harvard Med Sch, 1970-1972; asst res fel, Academia Sinica, Taiwan, China, 1963-1967. **Research Statement & Publications:** Biochemistry and cell biology in medical research; all types cell culture including cultivation of cells from primary and secondary cultures; experienced in cell culture techniques such as growing cells in monolayer; roller bottle or spinner bottle; semisolid agar colonizing; cell volume determination. **Mailing Address:** Mt Auburn Hosp, Harvard Med Sch, 330 Mt Auburn St, Cambridge, MA 02238. **Fax:** 801-697-8794. **E-Mail:** jamesli@hms.harvard.edu

LI, J(AMES) C(HEN) M(IN), MATERIALS SCIENCE, MECHANICAL ENGINEERING. **Personal Data:** b Nanking, China, April 12, 1925; m 1950, c 3. **Education:** Nat Cent Univ, China, BS, 1947; Univ Wash, MS, 1951, PhD, 1953. **Honors & Awards:** Mathewson Gold Medal, Metall Soc, 1972; Robert Mehl Gold Medal, Am Inst Mining, Metall & Petrol Engrs & Inst Metals lectr, 1978. **Professional Experience:** Acta Metallurgica Gold Medal, Am Soc Metals Int, 1990; Lu Tse-Hon Medal, Chinese Soc Mat Sci, 1988; vis scientist, Naval Res Lab, 1984-1985, 1988; Alexander von Humboldt sr award, 1978-1979; vis prof, Ruhr Universitat Bochum, Ger, 1978-1979; NSF, 1975-1977 & US Steel Corp, 1976; ALBERT ARENDT HOPEMAN PROF ENG, UNIV ROCHESTER, 1971-; consult, Mat Res Ctr, Allied Chem Corp, 1971-1979; mgr strength physics dept, Mat Res Ctr, Allied Chem Corp, 1969-1971; adj prof, Columbia Univ, 1965-1971; staff scientist, Fundamental Res Lab, US Steel Corp, 1964-1969; Vis prof, Columbia Univ, 1964-1965; sr scientist, Fundamental Res Lab, US Steel Corp, 1960-1964; scientist, Fundamental Res Lab, US Steel Corp, 1957-1960; phys chemist, Res Labs, Westinghouse Elec Corp, 1956-1957; supvr res proj, Mfg Chemists Asn, Carnegie Inst Technol, 1955-1956; res chemist & fel, Univ Calif, Berkeley, 1953-1955; Res chemist, Sch Med, Univ Wash, 1951-1953. **Memberships:** Fel Am Phys Soc; fel Am Inst Mining Metall & Petrol Engrs; fel Am Soc Metals; Mat Res Soc; Am Soc Mech Engrs. **Research Statement & Publications:** Dislocations and defects; plastic deformation; amorphous and polymeric materials; microstructural interactions; equilibirum and non-equilibrium phenomena. **Mailing Address:** Dept Mech Eng, Univ Rochester, Rochester, NY 14627. **E-Mail:** li@me.rochester.edu

LI, JANE CHIAO, APPLIED STATISTICS. **Personal Data:** b Shanghai, China, May 1, 1939. **Education:** Hunter Col, BS, 1963; Rutgers Univ, MS, 1965, PhD (statist), 1971. **Professional Experience:** SR MGR STATIST & COMPUT APPLNS, UOP INC, 1995-; co-chair, Am Inst Chem Engrs Symposium 1987 & 1988; course dir, Ctr Prof Achievement, 1986-; sr mgr data anal & processing, Uop Inc, 1986-1995; mgr, Uop Inc, 1981-1986; sect head world-wide product testing, Paramins Div, Exxon Chem Co, 1979-1981; sr statistician, Paramins Div, Exxon Chem Co, 1978-1979; statist consult comput sci & statist, Rutgers Univ, 1974-1978; res chemist, Endo Labs, Long Island, NY, 1961-1963. **Memberships:** Sigma Xi; Am Statist Asn; Inst Math Statist; Am Soc Qual Control. **Research Statement & Publications:** Design and analysis of mixture experiments with process variables; statistical design of experiments and analysis of data for research and manufacturing; statistical process control for continuous and batch chemical processes;

database management for petroleum and chemical processes; total quality management. **Mailing Address:** 620 Rolling Lane, Arlington Heights, IL 60004.

LI, JEANNE B, ANALYTICAL CHEMISTRY, BIOCHEMISTRY. **Personal Data:** b New York, NY, April 15, 1944. **Education:** Vassar Col, BA, 1966; Harvard Univ, PhD (biochem), 1971. **Professional Experience:** PRIN SCIENTIST, WATERS CORP, MILFORD, MA as of 1999; sr appl chemist, waters Div, Hershey Med Ctr, Pa State Univ, beginning 1993; res assoc pediat, Waters Div, Hershey Med Ctr, PA State Univ, 1979-1995; Am Diabetes Asn grant, Hershey Med Ctr, Pa State Univ, 1974-1976; asst prof physiol, Waters Div, Hershey Med Ctr, PA State Univ, 1973-1979; res fel physiol, Harvard Med Sch, 1971-1973; Nat Cancer Inst & Muscular Dystrophy Asn fels, Harvard Med Sch, 1971-1973. **Memberships:** Am Physiol Soc; AAAS. **Research Statement & Publications:** Applied research instrumentation. **Mailing Address:** Waters Corp, 34 Maple St, Milford, MA 01757-2437.

LI, JOHN KONG-JIANN, CARDIOVASCULAR DYNAMICS & INSTRUMENTATION. **Personal Data:** b Taiwan, China, August 28, 1950; American citizen; m 1974, Evangeline Sim; c Michael & Christopher. **Education:** Univ Manchester, BSc, 1972; Univ Pa, MSEng, 1974, PhD (bioeng), 1978. **Professional Experience:** PROF BIOMED ENG, RUTGERS UNIV, 1989-; dir biomed eng, Rutgers Univ, 1986; chmn, Eng Med & Biol, Princeton Sect, Inst Elec & Electronics Engrs, 1985-; vis scientist, Fedn Am Soc Exp Biol, 1981-; adj prof surg & Bioengineering, Univ Med & Dent NJ, Rutgers Med Sch, 1981-; prin investr, Rutgers Univ, NSF, 1980-; from asst prof to assoc prof, Rutgers Univ, 1979-1989; thesis supvr, Univ Pa, 1978-1979; Chief biomed engr cardiol, Presby Univ Pa Med Ctr, 1977-1979; res fel Bioengineering, Univ Pa, 1973-1977; Instr physics, Cent Found High Sch, London, 1972. **Memberships:** Inst Elec & Electronics Engrs; Am Physiol Soc; Am Heart Asn; fel Am Col Angiol; Am Soc Hypertension; Biomed Eng Soc. **Research Statement & Publications:** Cardiovascular dynamics; biomedical instrumentation; diagnostic cardiology; comparative physiology; physiological controls; hypertension and myocardial ischemia; controlled drug delivery. **Mailing Address:** Dept Biomed Eng, Rutgers Univ, 110, Biomed Eng Bldg, 617 Bowser Rd, Piscataway, NJ 08854. **Fax:** 732-932-3753. **E-Mail:** jli@biomed.rutgers.edu

LI, JONATHAN J, HORMONAL CARCINOGENESIS, PHARMACOLOGY & TOXICOLOGY. **Personal Data:** b New York, NY. **Education:** Brown Univ, BA, 1962; State Univ NY, PhD (pharmacol & biochem), 1971. **Professional Experience:** Chmn, Int Symp Hormonal Carcanogenesis, Seattle, Wash, 1998 & Stockholm, Sweden, 1994; DIR, BREAST TUMOR, SERUM RESPOSITORY & CORE FACIL, KANS CANCER INST, UNIV KANS MED CTR, 1994-; PROF, DEPT PHARMACOL, TOXICOL & THERAPEUTICS, SCH MED, UNIV KANS, 1993-; DIR, DIV ETIOLOGY & PREV HORMONAL CANCERS, CANCER CTR, MED CTR, UNIV KANS, 1993-; dir, Cancer Prev Res Ctr, 1992-1993; chmn, Int Symp Hormonal Carcanogenesis, Cancun, Mex, 1991-; assoc, Prog Genetics & Cell Biol, 1991-1993; dir, Hormonal Carcinogenesis Lab, 1990-1993; dorothy Otto Kennedy distinguished prof pharmaceut sci, Sch Pharm, Wash State Univ, 1990-1993; sr lectr, Dept Pharmacol, Univ Minn, Minneapolis, 1989-1990; vis prof, Inst Pharmacol & Toxicol, Univ Wurzburg, Ger, 1989; chmn, Second Bienniel Gordon Res Conf, 1987; co-founder & co-chmn, First Biennial Gordon Res Conf Hormonal Carcinogenesis, New Hampton Sch, NH, 1985; dir, Hormonal Carcinogenesis Lab, 1983-1990; sr res scientist, Vet Admin Med Ctr, Minneapolis, 1976-1990; asst dir, SDTU, Med Res Labs, Res & Endocrine Sect, Vet Admin Med Ctr, Minneapolis, 1974-1976; res fel, Dept Biol Chem, Lab Human Reproduction & Reproductive Biol, Harvard Med Sch, 1971-1974. **Memberships:** Histochem Soc; AAAS; Am Asn Cancer Res; Am Soc Biochem & Molecular Biol; Endocrine Soc; Soc Toxicol; NY Acad Sci. **Research Statement & Publications:** Etiology and prevention of hormonal cancers; pharmacology, toxicology and therapeutics; education of the biologic, cellular and molecular processes involved in hormonal carcinogenesis of the kidney, liver, breast and prostate; cell cycle and cell proliferation, aneuploidy, genomic instability, photo-oncogene and supressor gene expression. **Mailing Address:** Hormonal Carcinogenesis Lab, Dept Pharmacol, Toxicol & Therapeut, Univ Kans Med Ctr, 3901 Rainbow Blvd, Kansas City, KS 66160. **Fax:** 913-588-4740. **E-Mail:** jli1@kumc.edu

LI, JORGE P, CHEMISTRY. **Professional Experience:** SANDOZ AGRO INC, RES DIV, CALIF, as of 1994. **Memberships:** Am Chem Soc. **Mailing Address:** Sandoz Agro Inc, Res Div, 975 California Ave, Palo Alto, CA 94304-1104.

LI, KAM W(U), MECHANICAL ENGINEERING. **Personal Data:** b China, February 16, 1934; m 1956, Margaret; c Christopher & Charles. **Education:** Chu Hai Col, Hong Kong, BSME, 1957; Colo State Univ, MSME, 1961; Okla State Univ, PhD, 1965. **Professional Experience:** RETIRED; prof mech eng, Ndak State Univ, 1973-2000; interim chmn mech eng dept, Ndak State Univ, beginning 1993; assoc dean, Eng Col, 1989-1991; consult, ctr prof Advan, NJ, 1982-1983; USDA res grants, 1974-1978 & 1976-1978; eng consult, Chas T Main Inc, Boston, 1973-1980; Am Soc Eng Educ-Ford Found resident fel, Northern States Power Co, Minneapolis, Minn, 1971-1972; dept defense grant, 1969; from asst prof to assoc prof mech eng, Ndak State Univ, 1967-1973; NSF inst fund grants, NDak State Univ, 1967-1968 & 1971; consult engr, Scott Eng Sci Corp, 1967-1968; asst prof, Tex A&I Univ, 1965-1967. **Memberships:** Am Soc Mech Engrs; NY Acad Sci. **Research Statement & Publications:** Heat transfer; fluid dynamics; thermodynamics; power generation; thermal system design; applied mathematics; energy models; new power generation systems. **Mailing Address:** Dept Mech Eng, NDak State Univ, Fargo, ND 58102.

LI, KELVIN K, PHYSICS. **Personal Data:** b Kwantung, China, March 25, 1934; m 1965, c 4. **Education:** McGill Univ, BEng, 1958; Mass Inst Technol, PhD (physics), 1964. **Professional Experience:** PHYSICIST, BROOKHAVEN NAT LAB, 1965-. **Memberships:** Am Phys Soc. **Research Statement & Publications:** Elementary particle interactions. **Mailing Address:** Dept Physics, Brookhaven Nat Lab, Upton, NY 11973.

LI, KUANG-PANG, ANALYTICAL CHEMISTRY. **Personal Data:** b Kwang-tung, China, October 11, 1938. **Education:** Nat Taiwan Univ, BS, 1961; Univ Ill, MS, 1968, PhD (anal chem), 1970. **Professional Experience:** ASSOC PROF, DEPT CHEM, UNIV MASS, LOWELL, 1980-; asst prof chem, UnivFla, 1973-1980; res assoc, Univ Ill, 1972-1973; res assoc, Ariz State Univ, 1970-1972; lectr chem, Kaohsiung Prov Inst Technol, Taiwan, 1964-1965. **Memberships:** Am Chem Soc; NY Acad Sci; AAAS. **Research Statement & Publications:** Metallic ion transport in biomembranes; membrane interactions of carcinogenic polynuclear aromatics; theoretical and practical developments of chromatographic methods; excitation mechanism in inductively coupled plasma (ICP). **Mailing Address:** Dept Chem, Univ Mass Lowell, Rm 318b Olney Hall One Univ Ave, Lowell, MA 01854. **Fax:** 978-934-3013. **E-Mail:** kuang_li@uml.edu

LI, KUN, CHEMICAL ENGINEERING. **Personal Data:** b Kunming, China, November 20, 1923; m 1951, c 2. **Education:** Nat Southwest Assoc Univ, China, BS, 1945; Carnegie Inst Technol, MS, 1949. **Honorary Degrees:** DSc, Carnegie Inst Technol, 1952. **Professional Experience:** PROF EMER CHEM ENG, CARNEGIE-MELLON UNIV, as of 2006; prof chem eng, carnegie-mellon univ, beginning 1964-1988; assoc prof chem eng, Carnegie-mellon Univ, 1962-1964; res assoc, Jones & Laughlin Steel Corp, 1958-1962; sr res engr, Jones & Laughlin Steel Corp, 1956-1958; supvr & sr res chemist, Petrol Res Lab, Carnegie Inst Technol, 1955-1956; res chemist, Petrol Res Lab, Carnegie Inst Technol, 1952-1955; consult, Jones & Laughlin Steel Corp. **Memberships:** Am Chem Soc; Am Inst Chem Engrs; Am Inst Mining Metall & Petrol Engrs. **Research Statement & Publications:** Fluid flow; kinetics of high-temperature processes. **Mailing Address:** Dept Chem Eng, Carnegie-Mellon Univ, Pittsburgh, PA 15213. **Fax:** 412-268-7139.

LI, LI-HSIENG, BIOCHEMISTRY. **Personal Data:** b Peking, China, December 31, 1933; m 1960, c 2. **Education:** Nat Taiwan Univ, BS, 1955; Va Polytech Inst, MS, 1962, PhD (biochem), 1964. **Professional Experience:** SR SCIENTIST, UPJOHN CO, 1988-; sr res scientist, Upjohn CO, 1965-1973; res assoc, Ind Univ, 1964-1965. **Memberships:** Am Asn Cancer Res; Am Asn Biol Chemists. **Research Statement & Publications:** mechanism of action of anticancer agent; immmunity and cancer; cell biology; experimental therapeutic and pharmacology. **Mailing Address:** Upjohn Co, 7000 Portage Rd, Kalamazoo, MI 49001.

LI, LING-FONG, THEORETICAL HIGH ENERGY PHYSICS. **Personal Data:** b Fukien, China, April 17, 1944; m 1977, Chi-Chuang; c Victor W & Herman W. **Education:** Nat Taiwan Univ, BS, 1965; Univ Pa, MS, 1967, PhD (physics), 1970. **Professional Experience:** PROF PHYSICS, CARNEGIE-MELLON UNIV, 1983-; from asst prof to assoc prof, Carnegie-mellon Univ, 1974-1983; res assoc, Stanford Linear Accelerator Ctr, Stanford Univ, 1972-1974; res assoc physics, Rockefeller Univ, 1970-1972. **Memberships:** Fel Am Phys Soc; Sigma Xi. **Research Statement & Publications:** Unified theories of weak and electromagnetic interactions in relation to the fundamental structure o. **Mailing Address:** Dept Physics, Carnegie-Mellon Univ, Pittsburgh, PA 15213. **Fax:** 412-681-0648. **E-Mail:** lfli@andrew.cmu.edu

LI, LU KU, BIOCHEMISTRY, PROTEIN CHEMISTRY. **Personal Data:** b Honan, China, April 26, 1936; m 1961, c 1. **Education:** Nat Taiwan Univ, BS, 1958; Princeton Univ, PhD (biol), 1964. **Professional Experience:** ASSOC RES SCIENTIST OPHTHAL, COLUMBIA UNIV, 1974-; asst prof, Columbia Univ, 1969-1974; assoc, Columbia Univ, 1968-1969; instr ophthal, Columbia Univ, 1966-1968; res assoc chem, Cornell Univ, 1964-1966; res asst biol, Princeton Univ, 1963-1964. **Memberships:** Sigma Xi; Am Chem Soc; Am Soc Biol Chemists. **Research Statement & Publications:** Maturation of lens fiber cells and its relation to cataractogenesis; the subunits interactions of lens proteins; vision and opthalmology. **Mailing Address:** 635 W 165th St, New York, NY 10032.

LI, LUYUAN, ENZYMATIC REACTION MECHANISMS, PROTEIN STRUCTURE-FUNCTION RELATIONSHIPS. **Personal Data:** b Hezhe, Shandong Prov, China, March 5, 1954; m 1982, c 2. **Education:** Sichuan Univ, China, BS, 1982; Cornell Univ, PhD (biochem), 1988. **Professional Experience:** ASSOC PROF, CELLULAR & MOLECULAR PATH, SCH MED, UNIV PITTSBURGH, as of 2004; consult, Peking Univ, China, 1993; sr scientist, Am Cyanamid Co, beginning 1991; fel, Pa State Univ, 1988-1991; res asst, Cornell Univ Med Col, 1982-1988. **Memberships:** Am Soc Biochem & Molecular Biol; AAAS; Soc Chinese Bioscientists Am. **Research Statement & Publications:** Regulation of angiogenesis; structure-function relationship of angiogenic factors; differential gene expression in endothelial cells; extracellular matrix remodeling. **Mailing Address:** Dept Cellular & Molecular Path, Sch Med, Univ Pittsburgh, 5117 Centre Ave G12C, Pittsburgh, PA 15213. **Fax:** 412-623-1119. **E-Mail:** lil@msx.upmc.edu

LI, MING, MATHEMATICS. **Education:** Hohai Univ, BE, 1983; Univ Oxford, PhD (Geophys), 1991. **Professional Experience:** ASSOC PROF, UNIV MD CTR ENVIRON SCI, HORN POINT LAB, 2001-. **Mailing Address:** Univ Md Ctr Environ Sci, Horn Point Lab, Cambridge, MD 21613. **Fax:** 410-221-8490. **E-Mail:** mingli@hpl.umces.edu

LI, MING CHIANG, PHYSICS, MATHEMATICS. **Personal Data:** b Ningpo, China, June 18, 1935. **Education:** Peking Univ, BS, 1958; Univ Md, PhD (physics, math), 1965. **Professional Experience:** Group leader, Naval Res Lab, 1988-, sr physicist, 1983-1988, Sr tech staff, Mitre Coop, 1982-1983; ASSOC PROF PHYSICS, VA POLYTECH INST & STATE UNIV, 1972-; asst prof, VA Polytech Inst & State Univ, 1968-1972; fel & mem sci, Inst Advan Study, 1965-1967; res asst, Univ Md, 1964-1965; Lectr physics, Norm Col Inner Mongolia, China, 1958-1961. **Memberships:** Am Phys Soc; Inst Elec & Electronics Engrs. **Research Statement & Publications:** Atomic and molecular physics; interferometry; laser optics; electronics counter measures radar development. **Mailing Address:** 11415 Bayard Dr, Bowie, MD 20721.

LI, NORMAN N, MATERIALS SCIENCE & POLYMER ENGINEERING. **Personal Data:** b Shanghai, China, January 14, 1933; American citizen; m 1963, Jane C; c Rebecca H & David H. **Education:** Taiwan Nat Univ, BS, 1954; Wayne State Univ, MS, 1957; Stevens Inst Technol, ScD (chem eng), 1963. **Honors & Awards:** Am Chem Soc Award in Separation Sci & Technol, 1988; Res Award, Am Inst Chem Eng Award, 1988, Ernest Thiele Award, 1995; Perkin Medal, Soc Chem Ind, 2000; Chem Eng Pract Award, Am Inst Chem Engr, 2000; Lifetime Achievement Award, World Cong Chem Engr, 2001. **Professional Experience:** CHIEF EXEC OFFICER, NL CHEM TECHNOL, INC, 1995-; dir res & technol, Allied Signal Inc, 1992-1995; chmn, Int Cong Membranes & Membrane Processes, 1990; dir eng prod & process technol, Allied Signal Inc, 1988-1992; dir separation sci & technol, Allied Signal Inc, 1984-1988; chmn, Eng Found Int Conf Separations, 1984 & 1987; dir separations res, UOP Inc, 1981-1984; sr res assoc, Exxon Res & Eng Co, 1977-1981; head, Separation Sci Group, 1976-1981; chmn, Gordon Res Conf Transport Phenomena Membranes, 1975; chmn, Gordon Res Conf Separations & Purification, 1973; res assoc, Exxon Res & Eng Co, 1970-1977; consult, Bell Aerosysts Co, 1967; sr res engr, Exxon Res & Eng Co, 1966-1970; vis lectr, Newark Col Eng, 1963-1967; res engr, Exxon Res & Eng Co, 1963-1966; instr chem, Newark Col Eng, 1961-1963; chem engr, Parke-Davis & Co, 1956, chem engr, Shinlin Paper & Pulp Co, 1953. **Memberships:** Nat Acad Eng; fel Am Inst Chem Engrs; Am Chem Soc; NAm Membrane Soc (pres, 1991-1993); Nat Acad Sci, China. **Research Statement & Publications:** Mass transfer; surface chemistry; interfacial phenomena; transport through membranes; separation techniques; catalysis; material engineering. **Mailing Address:** NL Chem Technol Inc, 479 Bus Ctr Dr Suite 100, Mt Prospect, IL 60056. **Fax:** 847-824-2898. **E-Mail:** nlchem@aol.com

LI, PEI-CHING, CHEMICAL ENGINEERING. **Personal Data:** b Yanghang, Kiangsu, China, November 2, 1919; m 1945, Al-Juel; c Robert Y, Lilian & Richard. **Education:** Nat Southwest Assoc Univ, China, BE, 1945; Univ Rochester, MS, 1955, PhD (chem eng), 1959. **Professional Experience:** RETIRED; adv engr, IBM Corp, 1968-1990; res scientist ceramics div, IIT Res Inst, 1965-1968; res scientist, Am Stand Corp, 1964-1965; mem res staff, Raytheon Co, 1959-1964; res assoc glass, Univ Rochester, 1958-1959; asst chem eng, Univ Rochester, 1954-1957; chemist & engr, Taiwan Sugar Corp, 1947-1953; teacher sci, Chungking Women's Norm Sch, 1946-1947; asst chem eng, Nat Southwest Assoc Univ, China, 1944-1946. **Memberships:** Sigma Xi. **Research Statement & Publications:**

Physical properties of molten glass, particularly enamel glass and binary system of borates; solid state reactions of ferrites; pyrolytic high temperature materials; chemical vapor deposition and plasma enhanced chemical vapor deposition of dielectric films. **Mailing Address:** 12466 Beechgrove Ct, Moorpark, CA 93021-3108. **E-Mail:** beijing@prodigy.net

LI, PEN H (PAUL), HORTICULTURE, PLANT PHYSIOLOGY. **Personal Data:** b China, May 4, 1933; American citizen; m 1963, c 2. **Education:** Ore State Univ, PhD (hort & plant physiol), 1963. **Honors & Awards:** Dow Chem Co Award, Am Soc Hort Sci, 1965, Alex Laurie Award, 1966. **Professional Experience:** Peking Agr Univ, 1980 & Inst Plant Physiol, USSR Acad Sci, 1987; Inst Low Temperature Sci, Hookkaido Univ, 1976; vis prof, Int Potato Ctr, 1973; PROF HORT & PLANT PHYSIOL, UNIV MINN, 1963-. **Memberships:** Fel Am Soc Hort Sci; Am Soc Plant Physiologists; Potato Asn Am; Soc Cryobiol; Am Soc Agron. **Research Statement & Publications:** Plant hardiness and stress physiology. **Mailing Address:** Dept Hort Sci, Univ Minn, 286 Alderman Hall, 1970 Folwell Ave, St Paul, MN 55108. **Fax:** 612-624-4941. **E-Mail:** lixxx008@umn.edu

LI, PETER WAI-KWONG, GEOMETRIC ANALYSIS, PARTIAL DIFFERENTIAL EQUATION. **Personal Data:** b Hong Kong, April 18, 1952; American citizen; m 1982, Glenna Seaver; c 3. **Education:** Calif State Univ, BA, 1974; Univ Calif, Berkeley, MA, 1977, PhD (math), 1979. **Professional Experience:** CHAIR, UNIV CALIF, IRVINE, 1993-; ED-IN-CHIEF, COMMUN ANAL & GEOM, 1992-; ED, PROC AM MATH SOC, 1991-; PROF MATH, UNIV CALIF, IRVINE, 1991-; ed, Rocky Mountain J Math, 1989-1991; prof, Univ Ariz, 1989-1991; prof, Univ Utah, 1985-1989; Guggenheim fel, John Simon Guggenheim Found, 1989; assoc prof, Purdue Univ, 1983-1985; res mem, Math Sci Res Inst, 1983; Sloan fel, Alfred P Sloan Found, 1982; prin investr, NSF, 1980-; asst prof math, Stanford Univ, 1980-1983; vis asst prof, Univ Calif, San Diego, 1980 & 1981; res mem, Inst Advan Study, 1979-1980. **Memberships:** Am Math Soc. **Research Statement & Publications:** Interplay between the geometry, topology and the analysis of geometrical objects. **Mailing Address:** Dept Math, Univ Calif, Irvine, CA 92697-3875. **Fax:** 949-824-7993. **E-Mail:** pli@math.uci.edu

LI, ROUNAN, BIO-MATERIAL IMPLANTS. **Education:** Univ Fla, PhD (mat sci), 1991. **Professional Experience:** SR RES ENGR, NORTON CO, as of 2002. **Memberships:** Am Ceramic Soc. **Research Statement & Publications:** Suprabrasive vitrified products and process research and development in order to improve performance, product consistency and grinding efficiency. **Mailing Address:** 32 Monroe St, Shrewsbury, MA 01545.

LI, SAN, MOLECULAR SPECTROSCOPY, ANALYTICAL-PHYSICAL CHEMISTRY. **Personal Data:** b Chengdu, China, September 28, 1962; m 1987, Mei; c Hansen. **Education:** Nankai Univ, China, BS, 1983; Memphis State Univ, PhD (phys chem), 1991. **Professional Experience:** RES SCIENTIST, BLACKLIGHT POWER CORP, MALVERN, PA, 1997-; postdoctoral fel, Pac Northwest Nat Lab, 1996-1997; res assoc, Univ Fla, 1991-1996; Asst lectr chem, Chengdu Univ Sci & Technol, 1983-1986. **Memberships:** Am Chem Soc; Coblentz Soc Spectros. **Research Statement & Publications:** Molecular spectroscopy studies of molecular structure, magnetic properties and photochemical reactions; new material designs, syntheses and characterizations. **Mailing Address:** 2500 George Washington Way No 209, Richland, WA 99352. **E-Mail:** li@pine.circa.ufl.edu

LI, SARA ANTONIA, HORMONAL CARCINOGENESIS, GENE EXPRESSION. **Personal Data:** b Monterrey, Mex, August 28, 1942. **Education:** Univ Labastida, Mex, BS, 1963; State Univ NY, PhD (pharmacol), 1969. **Professional Experience:** RES ASSOC PROF PHARMACOL, TOXICOL & THERAPEUT, KANS UNIV MED CTR, 1993-; assoc prof pharmacol sci, Wash State Univ, 1990-1993; res asst prof, Dept Pharmacol, UnivMinn, 1977-1990. **Memberships:** Am Asn Cancer Res; Endocrine Soc. **Research Statement & Publications:** Estrogen and its role in cancer; estrogen-induced kidney tumor of the Syrian hamster as a model system. **Mailing Address:** Dept Pharmacol, Toxicol & Therapuet, Med Ctr, Univ Kans, G034 Breidenthal Bldg 3901 Rainbow Blvd, Kansas City, KS 66160-7417. **Fax:** 913-588-4740. **E-Mail:** sli@kumc.edu

LI, SHENG SAN, ELECTRICAL ENGINEERING. **Personal Data:** b Hsin-Chu, Taiwan, December 10, 1938; m Julie; c Jim, Grace & Jeanette. **Education:** Natioanl Cheng Kung Univ, Taiwan, BS, 1962; Rice Univ, MS, 1966, PhD (elec eng), 1968. **Honors & Awards:** Prof Excellent Prog Award, Univ Fla, 1996; Univ Fla Res Prof, Univ Fla Res Found 2001-2003. **Professional Experience:** Consult, Advan Device Technol Inc, 1999-2003; vis prof, Nat Chiao-Tung Univ, Taiwan, 1995; consult, Hughes Res Labs, 1985-; consult, Battelle Columbus Labs, Ohio, 1975-1977 & Harris Semiconductors Inc, Fla, 1978-; PROF ELEC ENG, UNIV FLA, 1978-; Electronic engr, Nat Bur Stands, 1975-1976; from asst prof to assoc prof, Univ Fla, 1968-1973; teaching asst elec eng, Rice Univ, 1964-1967; engr, China Elec Mfg Co, Taiwan, 1963-1964. **Memberships:** Inst Elec & Electronics Engrs. **Research Statement & Publications:** Areas of specialty include defect characterization in semiconductors and SOI materials. **Mailing Address:** Dept Elec Eng, Univ Fla, 561 EB-33, Gainesville, FL 32611. **Fax:** 352-392-8381. **E-Mail:** shengli@eng.ufl.edu

LI, SHIN-HWA, CHEMICAL VAPOR DEPOSITION, III-V & GROUP IV SEMICONDUCTORS. **Personal Data:** b Taipei, Taiwan, April 8, 1958. **Education:** Nat Cent Univ, Taiwan, BS, 1980; Univ SWLa, Lafayette, MS, 1985; Univ Utah, SaltLake City, ME, 1987, PhD (mat sci eng), 1991. **Professional Experience:** ENGR, SGS-THOMSON MICROELECTRONICS, 1994-; res scientist, UnivMich, Ann Arbor, 1991-1994; res fel, Air Force Off Sci Res, 1991-1994; res assoc, Univ Utah, Salt Lake City, 1990-1991; res asst, Univ Utah, Salt Lake City, 1985-1990; res asst, Univ SWLa, Lafayette, 1983-1985; qual control engr, Ko-sheng Enterprises, Ltd, Taiwan, 1982-1983; Liaisonofficer, Repub China Marine Corps, 1980-1982. **Memberships:** Inst Elec & Electronics Engrs; Minerals Metals & Mat Soc; Mat Res Soc. **Research Statement & Publications:** Organometallic vapor-phase epitaxy reaction mechanisms; decomposition of the precursors for epitaxy of many three to five materials; mass spectrometric methods used to analyze the reaction mechanisms; gas-source molecular beam epitaxy of group four semiconductors, materials characterization, devices fabrication; chemical-mechanical polishing; photoluminescence; phase diagrams; velocity-field measurement. **Mailing Address:** SGS Thomson Microelectronics, 1000 E Bell Rd, Phoenix, AZ 85022-2649. **Fax:** 520-485-2955. **E-Mail:** shinhwa.li-phx@st.com

LI, SHU, CATALYSIS CHEMISTRY, ELECTROCHEMISTRY. **Personal Data:** b Changchun, China, March 11, 1958. **Education:** Jilin Univ, China, BS, 1982, MS, 1985; Rutgers Univ, PhD (solid state chem), 1990. **Professional Experience:** RES & DEVELOP MGR, POLYTRONIX, INC, 1993-; sr res scientist, Polytronix, Inc, 1992-1993; Res fel, Calif Inst Technol, 1991-1992. **Memberships:** Am Chem Soc; Mat Res Soc; Soc Info Displays. **Research Statement & Publications:** Materials issues related to liquid crystal displays; correlations between liquid crystal physical properties and performance of liquid crystal displays; developing new types of liquid crystal displays. **Mailing Address:** 595 Bernal Cmn, Fremont, CA 94539. **Fax:** 972-644-0805.

LI, STEVEN SHOEI-LUNG, GENETICS, BIOCHEMISTRY. **Personal Data:** b Taiwan, China, October 20, 1938; m 1967, Pearl; c Michael & Nancy. **Education:** Nat Taiwan Univ, BS, 1961, MS, 1963; Univ Mo, PhD (genetics), 1968. **Professional Experience:** Adj prof biochem & chem, Univ NC, Chapel Hill, beginning 1987; RES GENETICIST, NAT INST ENVIRON HEALTH SCI, NIH, 1977-; assoc prof, Mt Sinai Sch Med, 1974-1977; res assoc, Stanford Univ, 1970-1974; res assoc, Univ Tex, Austin, 1968-1970. **Memberships:** AAAS; Am Soc Biochem & Molecular Biol; Genetics Soc Am. **Research Statement & Publications:** Biochemical genetics; structure, regulation and evolution of eukayotic genes and proteins. **Mailing Address:** Nat Inst Environ Health Sci, NIH, Research Triangle Park, NC 27709.

LI, SU-CHEN, BIOCHEMISTRY. **Personal Data:** b Taipei, Taiwan, June 8, 1935. **Education:** Nat Taiwan Univ, BS, 1958; Univ Okla, PhD (biochem), 1966. **Professional Experience:** RES PROF BIOCHEM, SCH MED, TULANE UNIV, as of 2001; prof biochem, Sch Med, Tulane Univ, beginning 1980; Career Develop Award, NIH, 1975-1980; from asst prof to assoc prof, Sch Med, Tulane Univ, 1972-1980. **Memberships:** Am Soc Biol Chemists; AAAS; Soc Complex Carbohydrates. **Research Statement & Publications:** Biochemical studies of glycoconjugates and glycosidases. **Mailing Address:** Dept Biochem Med Sch, Tulane Univ, 1430 Tulane Ave, New Orleans, LA 70112-2699. **Fax:** 504-584-2739. **E-Mail:** sli4@tulane.edu

LI, TAO PING, ORGANIC CHEMISTRY. **Personal Data:** b Szechwan, China, November 16, 1920; m 1948, Grace; c William, Kenneth & Linda. **Education:** Nat Szechwan Univ, China, BS, 1941; Univ Tex, Austin, MA, 1959, PhD (org chem), 1960. **Professional Experience:** RETIRED; sci fellow, Monsanto Co, 1982-1987; from group leader to sr group leader, Monsanto Co, 1966-1982; res specialist, Monsanto Co, 1964-1966; sr proj chemist, Am Oil Co, Ind, 1961-1964; fel, Univ Tex, Austin, 1960-1961. **Memberships:** AAAS; Am Chem Soc; Catalysis Soc; NY Acad Sci. **Research Statement & Publications:** Chemical kinetics, heterogeneous catalysis and chemistry of metal organic compounds. **Mailing Address:** 293 Heather Crest Dr, Chesterfield, MO 63017-2855.

LI, THOMAS M, EXPERIMENTAL BIOLOGY. **Education:** Univ Ill, BS, 1972, PhD (biophys chem), 1976. **Professional Experience:** VPRES, RES & DEVELOP, HYCOR BIOMED INC, 1995-; sr develop mgr, Syva Co, 1991-1995; develop mgr, Syva CO, 1986-1988; develop mgr, Syntex Med Diag, 1984-1986; res & develop dir, 3M Diag, 1983-1984; res & develop mgr, Miles Labs, Inc, 1978-1983; res fel, Inst Cancer Res, Philadelphia, 1976-1978. **Memberships:** Sigma Xi; NY Acad Sci; Am Chem Soc; Biophys Soc; Protein Soc; Am Asn ClinChem; Am Soc Biochem & Molecular Biol; fel Am Inst Chemists; fel Nat Acad Clin Biochem. **Research Statement & Publications:** Experimental biology; numerous publications. **Mailing Address:** Develop Dept MS E1-130 Syva Co, 3403 Yerba Buena Rd PO Box 49013, San Jose, CA 95161-9013.

LI, TIEN-YIEN, MATHEMATICS. **Personal Data:** b Hunan, China, June 28, 1945; American citizen; c Edward. **Education:** Nat Tsing-Hua Univ, BS, 1968; Univ Md, PhD (math), 1974. **Professional Experience:** DISTINGUISHED PROF MATH, MICH STATE UNIV, 1998-; Guggenheim fel, 1995-1996; vis prof, Res Inst Math Sci, Kyoto Univ, Japan, 1987-1988; PROF MATH, MICH STATE UNIV, 1983-; vis assoc prof math, Res Ctr, Univ Wis, 1978-1979; from asst prof to assoc prof, Mich State Univ, 1976-1983; instr math, Univ Utah, 1974-1976; hon prof, Tsing-Hua Univ & Jilin Univ, People's Repub China. **Memberships:** Am Math Soc; Soc Indust & Appl Math. **Research Statement & Publications:** Differential equations, dynamical systems and numerical analysis. **Mailing Address:** Dept Math, Mich State Univ, 6439 E Island Lake Dr, East Lansing, MI 48824. **Fax:** 517-432-1562. **E-Mail:** li@math.msu.edu

LI, TING KAI, MEDICINE, BIOCHEMISTRY. **Personal Data:** b Nanking, China, November 13, 1934. **Education:** Northwestern Univ, AB, 1955; Harvard Med Sch, MD, 1959; Mass Inst Technol, 1961. **Honors & Awards:** Res Excellence Award, Res Soc on Alcoholism; Jellinck Award; James Blsaacson Award, Res Substance Abuse. **Professional Experience:** DISTINGUISHED PROF EMER, MED & BIOCHEM, IND UNIV, INDIANAPOLIS, as of 2006; distinguished prof med & biochem, Sch Med, Ind Univ, Indianapolis, beginning 1985; John B Hickam prof, Sch Med, Ind Univ, Indianapolis, 1980-1985; prof, Sch Med, Ind Univ, Indianapolis, 1971-1980; dep dir div biochem, Walter Reed Army Inst Res, 1969-1971; guest scientist, Nobel Med Inst, Sweden, 1968; Markle scholar acad med, 1967-1973; assoc, Harvard Med Sch, 1967-1969; instr med, Harvard Med Sch, 1965-1967; chief med resident, Peter Bent Brigham Hosp, 1965-1966; Med Found Boston fel, 1964-1968; res assoc biochem, Harvard Med Ach, 1963-1965; jr assoc, Peter Bent Brigham Hosp, 1963-1965; Helen Hay Whitney Found fel, 1960-1964; asst med, Peter Bent Brigham Hosp, 1960-1963; asst med, Harvard Med Ach, 1960-1963; house officer, Peter Bent Brigham Hosp, 1959-1960. **Memberships:** Am Chem Soc; Am Soc Clin Invest; Endocrine Soc; Am Soc Biol Chem; Am Inst Nutrit; Asn Am Physicians. **Research Statement & Publications:** Enzymology; metabolism; chemical basis of biological specificity; alcohol metabolism. **Mailing Address:** Dept Med, Ind Univ Sch Med, Emerson Hall 421 545 Barnhill Dr, Indianapolis, IN 46202-5124. **Fax:** 317-274-4311. **E-Mail:** tkli@iupui.edu

LI, TINGYE, ELECTRICAL ENGINEERING, OPTOELECTRONICS. **Personal Data:** b Nanjing, China, July 7, 1931; m 1956, Edith; c Deborah (Chunroh) & Kathryn (Dairoh). **Education:** Univ Witwatersrand, BSc, 1953; Northwestern Univ, MS, 1955, PhD (elec eng), 1958. **Honorary Degrees:** DEng, Nat Chiao Tung Univ, Hsinchu, Taiwan, 1991. **Honors & Awards:** W R G Baker Prize, Inst Elec & Electronics Engrs, 1975, David Sarnoff Award, 1979, John Tyndall Award, 1995; Achievement Award, Chinese Inst Engrs-USA, 1978; Achievement Award, ChineseAm Acad & Prof Asn, 1983. **Professional Experience:** CONSULT LIGHTWAVE COMMUN, as of 1999; mgr div, Commun Infrastructure Res Lab, AT&T Lab, ending 1998; head, Lightwave Networks Res Dept, At&T Labs, beginning 1996; head, Lightwave Systs Res Dept, 1984-1996; head, Lightwave Media Res Dept, 1976-1984; head, Repeater Tech Res Dept, 1967-1976; mem tech staff, AT&T Bell Labs, 1957-1967. **Memberships:** Nat Acad Eng; fel Optical Soc Am; fel AAAS; Chinese Inst Engrs-USA; fel Inst Elec & Electronics Engrs; fel Photonic Soc Chinese Americans; Chinese Acad Eng. **Research Statement & Publications:** Optical communications; lasers and coherent-wave optics; electromagnetic field theory; antennas and propagation; microwave theory and techniques; high-speed techniques and systems for lightwave transmission and networking; commercial application of optical fiber communications; author of over 90 publications; granted 16 patents. **Mailing Address:** 563 Locust Pl, Boulder, CO 80304-0575. **Fax:** 303-443-9116. **E-Mail:** tli@research.att.com

LI, TONGCHUAN, RESEARCH & DEVELOPMENT OF NEW ANTIBIOTICS, PRECLINICAL PHARMACOLOGY & TOXICOLOGY STUDIES OF ANTIMICROBIALS. **Personal Data:** b Yongtai, China, October 11, 1955; American citizen; m 1982, Xingxian; c Bing, Scion, Louisa & Mark. **Education:** Zhangzhou Health Sch, China, dipl, 1975; Fujian Med Col, China, MD, 1982; Univ Minn, PhD (pharmacol), 1990. **Professional Experience:** PROJ MGR, CUBIST PHARMACEUT INC, 1995-; sr scientist, Cyto Med Inc, 1993-1994;

postdoctoral Scientist, Boehringer Ingelheim Pharmaceut, 1990-1993. **Memberships:** Am Soc Pharmacol & Exp Therapeut; AAAS; NY Acad Sci. **Research Statement & Publications:** Preclinical studies in vivo pharmacology, toxicology and pharmacokinetics of new antimicrobiol agents effective against resistant pathology. **Mailing Address:** Cubist Pharmaceut, 24 Emily St, Cambridge, MA 02139. **Fax:** 781-861-0566. **E-Mail:** tcli@cubist.com

LI, WEN-CH'ING WINNIE, COMBINATURICS & FINITE MATHEMATICS, NUMBER THEORY. **Personal Data:** b Taiwan, December 25, 1948; c Jaline & Ylaine. **Education:** Nat Taiwan Univ, BS, 1970; Univ Calif, Berkeley, PhD (math), 1974. **Professional Experience:** Nat Ctr theoret sci, Hsinchu, Taiwan, 1999-2000; Nat Taiwan Univ, Taipei, Taiwan, 1992-1993; vis prof, Univ Pa, 1991-1992; vis prof, Univ Paris, Orsay, 1985-1986; PROF MATH, PA STATE UNIV, 1984-; Alfred Sloan fel, 1981-1983; assoc prof, PA State Univ, 1979-1984; mem, Inst Advan Study, Princeton, 1978, 1984 & 2000; asst prof math, Harvard Univ, 1974-1978 & Univ Ill, Chicago, 1978-1979; consult, AT & T Labs. **Memberships:** Am Math Soc. **Research Statement & Publications:** Automorphic forms; representation theory; number theory; combinatorics. **Mailing Address:** Dept Math, Pa State Univ, Univ Park, PA 16802. **Fax:** 814-865-3735. **E-Mail:** wli@math.psu.edu

LI, WEN-HSIUNG, EVOLUTIONARY GENETICS, MOLECULAR EVOLUTION. **Personal Data:** b Ping-Tung, Taiwan, September 22, 1942; American citizen; m 1975, Sue-Jean; c Vivian, Herman & Joyce. **Education:** Chung-Yuang Col Sci & Eng, Taiwan, BE, 1965; Nat Cent Univ, Taiwan, MS, 1968; Brown Univ, PhD (appl math), 1972. **Professional Experience:** JAMES WATSON PROF, DEPT ECOL & EVOLUTION, UNIV CHICAGO, as of 2000; George Wells Beadle Distinguished Serv Prof, Dept Ecol & Evolution, Univ Chicago, beginning 1999; assoc ed, J Molecular Evolution, 1998-; Betty Wheless Trotter prof, Univ Tex, Houston, 1996-1998; assoc, Can Inst Advan Res, Prog Evolutionary Biol, 1992-1997; assoc ed, Genetics, 1986-; prof pop genetics, Univ Tex, Houston, 1984-1998; from asst prof to assoc prof, Univ Tex, Houston, 1973-1984; proj assoc, Univ Wis-Madison, 1972-1973. **Memberships:** Nat Acad Sci; fel Am Acad Arts & Sci; Soc Syst Biol; Soc Molecular Biol & Evolution (pres, 2000); AAAS; Am Soc Human Genetics; Soc Study Evolution. **Research Statement & Publications:** Molecular evolution; biomathematics; human population genetics; evolution of DNA sequences, duplicate genes and pseudogenes; mathematical theory of population genetics; molecular evolutionary genetics of color vision. **Mailing Address:** Dept Ecol & Evolution, Univ Chicago, 5801 S Ellis, Chicago, IL 60637. **Fax:** 773-702-9740. **E-Mail:** whli@uchicago.edu

LI, WU, SCIENTIFIC COMPUTING, NUMERICAL SIMULATION OF ENGINEERING DESIGN. **Personal Data:** b Wenzhou, Zhejiang, China, November 8, 1958; American citizen; m 1985, Wan; c Maryann M & Victoria M. **Education:** Zhejiang Norm Univ, BA, 1982; Hangzhou Univ, MS, 1984; Pa State Univ, MS, 1990, PhD (math), 1990. **Professional Experience:** PROF MATH, OLD DOM UNIV, as of 2002; consult, ICASE, 2000-; assoc prof math, Old Dom Univ, 1996-2002; asst prof math, Old Dom Univ, 1990-1996. **Memberships:** affil Soc Indust Appl Math. **Research Statement & Publications:** published over sixty papers in the leading journals of applied and industrial mathematics, on topics including approximation theory, numerical optimization, scientific computing, and industrial applications of mathematics. **Mailing Address:** Dept Math & Statist, Old Dominion Univ, BAL 507, Norfolk, VA 23529-0077. **Fax:** 757-683-3885. **E-Mail:** wli@odu.edu

LI, WU-SHYONG, PHYSICAL ORGANIC CHEMISTRY. **Personal Data:** b Taipei, Taiwan, August 20, 1943; m 1975, c 2. **Education:** Nat Taiwan Univ, BS, 1966; Kent State Univ, MS, 1969; Univ Minn, PhD (org chem), 1973. **Professional Experience:** SR RES SPECIALIST, 3M CO, 1989-; res specialist, 3M Co, 1980-1988; sr chemist, 3M Co, 1978-1980; sr chemist plastic, Rohm & Haas Co, 1975-1978; fel, Ohio State Univ, 1973-1975. **Memberships:** Am Chem Soc. **Research Statement & Publications:** Reaction mechanism, kinetics, polymers and UV curing. **Mailing Address:** 3M Co, 3M Ctr Bldg 201-1C-18, St Paul, MN 55144.

LI, XIAO FENG, REPRODUCTIVE MEDICINE, GYNECOLOGICAL ENDOCRINOLOGY. **Personal Data:** b Zhejiang, China, October 17, 1957; m 1985, Xian; c Yao He. **Education:** Wenzhou Med Col, BMed, 1980, MD, 1984, MS, 1987; Birmingham Univ, PhD (human reproductive med), 1994. **Professional Experience:** SR RES FEL, MED COL WIS, 1996-; mem steering comt, Human Reproductive Prog, WHO, 1990-1996; fel, Birmingham Univ, UK, 1989-1991 & 1994-1996; prin investr, Zhejiang Acad Med, China, 1987-1989. **Research Statement & Publications:** Human reproductive biology including mechanism of menstruation, conception, contraception and placental physiology. **Mailing Address:** Dept Physiol, Med Col Wis, Milwaukee, WI 53226. **E-Mail:** lixteng@its.post.mcw.edu

LI, XIAO JIAN, BONE HISTOMORPHOMETRY, ANIMAL MODEL DEVELOPMENT. **Personal Data:** b Guangdong, China, June 18, 1954. **Education:** Guangdong Med Col, China, MD, 1982. **Professional Experience:** PRIN SCIENTIST & HEAD, HISTOPATHOL LAB, GENETICS INST, 1995-; scientist bone histomorphometrist, Proctor & Gamble Pharmacol, 1990-1995; dir, Bone BiolLab, Radiobiol Div, Univ Utah, 1987-1990; res fel, Radiobiol Div, 1984-1987. **Memberships:** Am Soc Bone & Mineral Res; Int Chinese Hard Tissue Soc (secy, 1994-1996). **Research Statement & Publications:** Conducting in vivo preclinical research which employ/develop appropriate animal models and histological methodologies to discover and develop therapeutic agents for the prevention and treatment of osteoporosis or for enhancing fracture healing. **Mailing Address:** Genetics Inst, One Burtt Rd, Andover, MA 01810. **Fax:** 978-623-1389. **E-Mail:** jli@genetics.com

LI, XIAOLIN, MATHEMATICS. **Education:** Columbia Univ, MS, 1985, PhD (appl math), 1987. **Professional Experience:** PROF & DIR, GRAD PROG, DEPT APPL MATH & STATIST, STATE UNIV NY, as of 2006. **Mailing Address:** Dept Appl Math & Statist, State Univ NY, Stony Brook, NY 11794-3600. **Fax:** 631-632-8490. **E-Mail:** xiaolin@ams.sunysb.edu

LI, XIEZHANG, ITERATIVE METHOD, EIGEN VALVE PROBLEMS FOR TOEPLITE & QUASITOEPLITE MATRICES. **Personal Data:** b October 20, 1942. **Education:** Shanghai Normal Univ, BS, 1966, MS, 1981; Kent State Univ, PhD (numerical anal), 1990. **Professional Experience:** PROF MATH, GA SOUTHERN UNIV, as of 2003; assoc prof math & comput sci, GA Southern Univ, beginning 1995; asst prof, GA Southern Univ, 1990-1995; vis prof, Kent State Univ, 1984-1985; instr math, Shanghai Normal Univ, 1981-1984. **Memberships:** Soc Indust & Appl Math. **Research Statement & Publications:** Develop near optimal iterative methods for solving a large system of linear equations; determine or estimate an upper bound of errors by function theory; approximation theory and conformat mapping theory. **Mailing Address:** Dept Math Sci, Ga Southern Univ, MP 3008, Rm 3008, 0203 Georgia Ave, Statesboro, GA 30460-8093. **Fax:** 912-681-0654. **E-Mail:** xli@georgiasouthern.edu

LI, YAO TZU, SCIENCE EDUCATION. **Personal Data:** b Beijing, China, February 1, 1914. **Education:** Mass Inst Technol, ScD, 1939. **Professional Experience:** HON CHMN & TREAS, SETRA SYSTS INC, 1996-; CHMN, Y T LEE ENG, 1982-; dir, Innovation Ctr, 1972-1979; prof control & guidance, Mass Inst Technol, 1970-1979; chmn & treas, Y T Lee Eng, 1968-1996. **Memberships:** Fel Nat Acad Eng. **Mailing Address:** Setra Systs Inc, 159 Swanson Rd, Boxborough, MA 01719.

LI, YAO-EN, HETEROGENOUS CATALYSIS, GAS PURIFICATION. **Personal Data:** b Shanghai, China, October 24, 1958. **Education:** Univ Ill, Chicago, BS, 1984, MS, 1986, PhD (chem eng), 1988. **Professional Experience:** SR ENGR, GLOBAL PHARMACEUT RES & DEVELOP, ABBOTT LAB, as of 2003; SR SCIENTIST, AIR LIQUIDE AM CORP, 1990-; scientist, Air Liquide AmCorp, 1988-1990; Student res award, Am Inst Chemists, 1984. **Memberships:** Am Chem Soc; Am Inst Chem Engrs. **Research Statement & Publications:** Research on gas separation, purification technologies; characterize noble metal supported catalysts; develop new process for chemical industry; contamination-free manufacture processes. **Mailing Address:** Air Liquide Am Corp, 5230 S E Ave, Countryside, IL 60525. **Fax:** 708-579-7833. **E-Mail:** david.li@airliquide.com

LI, YI, PLANT MOLECULAR BIOLOGY & PHYSIOLOGY. **Personal Data:** b Sichuan, China, April 27, 1958. **Education:** Beijing Forestry Col, BS, 1982; State Univ NY, Syracuse, PhD (plant physiol), 1989. **Professional Experience:** PROJ LEADER, NASA BIOSERVE CTR, 1996-; asst prof, Div Biol, Kans State Univ, 1994-1998; res asst prof, DeptBiochem, Univ Mo, 1991-1993; fel, Dept Biochem, Univ Mo, 1989-1991. **Memberships:** Am Soc Plant Physiologists; Am Soc Gravitional & Space Biol; Int Soc PlantMolecular Biol. **Research Statement & Publications:** Mechanisms of hormone action and gravitropism in higher plants using molecular, physiological and biochemical approaches. **Mailing Address:** Transgenic Plant Facil, Univ Conn, U-82, Storrs, CT 06269. **Fax:** 860-486-6777. **E-Mail:** yi.li@uconn.edu

LI, YING SING, STRUCTURAL CHEMISTRY, MOLECULAR SPECTROSCOPY & MATERIALS SCIENCES. **Personal Data:** b Kwangtung, China, July 26, 1936; American citizen; m 1968, Jackie; c Lawrence, Leon, Caroline & Jason. **Education:** Cheng Kung Univ, BS, 1960; Univ Kansas, PhD (chem), 1968. **Professional Experience:** PROF CHEM, UNIV of Memphis, as of 2006; Oak Ridge Nat Lab, 1990-1991; assoc prof chem, Memphis State Univ, beginning 1982; assoc prof, Benedict Col, 1978-1982; res assoc, Princeton Univ, 1968-1970 & Univ SC, 1970-1975 & 1976-1982; res asst, Taiwan Sugar Exp Sta, 1961-1963. **Memberships:** Am Chem Soc; Sigma Xi; Phi Lambda Upsilon. **Research Statement & Publications:** Microwave, infrared and Raman spectra conformations; structures of cyclic, fluoro, and organometalic compounds; chemical bonding; intermolecular interactions; matrix isolations infrared; surface-enhanced Raman scattering; corrosion protection. **Mailing Address:** Dept Chem, Memphis State Univ, Memphis, TN 38152. **Fax:** 901-678-3447. **E-Mail:** yingli@memphis.edu

LI, YONG-GANG FRANK, SEISMOLOGY. **Personal Data:** b Shanghai, China, January 23, 1945; American citizen; m 1973, Yungyung Nancy Wang; c Thomas. **Education:** Univ Southern Calif, PhD (geophys), 1987; Fudan Univ, China, BS, 1967. **Professional Experience:** RES SCIENTIST, RES PROF & RES FAC MEM, DEPT EARTH SCI, UNIV SOUTHERN CALIF, 1991-; res fel, Univ Southern Calif, 1985-1991; vis scholar, Univ Southern Calif, 1982-1984; res geophysicist, PI, Marine Geol & Geophys Inst, China, 1968-1981. **Memberships:** Am Geophys Union assoc; Seismol Soc Am assoc; Soc Exploration Geolphysicists assoc. **Research Statement & Publications:** Characterization of earthquake faults includes pioneering works in discovery and use of fault-zone t; authored 35 papers. **Mailing Address:** Dept Earth Sci, Univ Southern Calif, Los Angeles, CA 90089-0740. **Fax:** 213-740-8801. **E-Mail:** ygli@terra.usc.edu

LI, YUAN, SOLID STATE PHYSICS, HIGH ENERGY PHYSICS. **Personal Data:** b Ningpo, China, September 15, 1936. **Education:** Nat Taiwan Univ, BS, 1958; Ind Univ, PhD (physics), 1966. **Professional Experience:** PROF EMER PHYSICS, RUTGERS STATE UNIV NJ, NEWARK, as of 2002; assoc prof physics, Rutgers Univ State Univ NJ, beginning 1977; NSF res grant, 1976-1977; assoc prof, Tuskegee Inst, 1975-1977; asst prof, Rutgers State Univ NJ, 1965-1977; res assoc physics, Rutgers Univ State Univ NJ, 1965-1968. **Memberships:** Am Phys Soc; Am Asn Physics Teachers. **Research Statement & Publications:** Crystallography and lattice dynamics. **Mailing Address:** Dept Physics, Rutgers State Univ NJ, 211 Smith Hall 101 Warren St, Newark, NJ 07102. **Fax:** 973-353-1434.

LI, YUANJING, ELECTRONMICROSCOPIES, LASER TRIM OF THIN FILMS. **Personal Data:** b Nanjing, China, May 31, 1960. **Education:** Nanjing Inst Technol, BS, 1982; Univ Calif, Santa Barbara, MS, 1989, PhD (eleceng), 1992. **Professional Experience:** PROCESS RELIABILITY ENGR, ANALOG DEVICES INC, 1995-; Sr staffengr, Motorola Corp, 1994-1995. **Research Statement & Publications:** Process optimization for effective laser trim of thin film resistors. **Mailing Address:** 20094 Merritt Dr, Cupertino, CA 95014. **E-Mail:** yuanjing.li@analog.com

LI, YU-TEH, BIOCHEMISTRY. **Personal Data:** b Hsin-Chu City, Formosa, April 1, 1934. **Education:** Nat Taiwan Univ, BS, 1957, MS, 1960; Univ Okla, PhD (biochem), 1963. **Professional Experience:** VIS CHAIR BIOCHEM, SCH MED, TULANE UNIV, 1990-; Javits Neuroscience Investr Award, 1984-1991, 1991-1998; head biochem, Sch Med, Tulane Univ, 1975-1985; PROF BIOCHEM, SCH MED, TULANE UNIV, 1974-; NIH grant, 1971-, USPHS res careerdevelop award, 1971-1976; assoc prof biochem, Sch Med, Tulane Univ, 1971-1974; NSF grant, 1968-; chief, Delta Regional Primate Res Ctr, 1966-1985, Nat Cancer Inst grant, 1964-1966, From instr to asst prof biochem, Sch Med, UnivOkla, 1963-1966; asst prof biochem, Sch Med, Tulane Univ, 1966-1971; Asst Prof, Dept Biochem, Univ. Oklahoma, Sch Med, 1964-1966; Fel biochem, Sch Med, Univ Okla, 1963-1964. **Memberships:** Am Soc Neurochem; Am Soc Biol Chem. **Research Statement & Publications:** Biochemical studies on glycoconjugates and various glycosidases. **Mailing Address:** Dept Biochem, Tulane Univ Sch Med, 430 Tulane Ave, Box SL-43, New Orleans, LA 70112-2699. **Fax:** 504-584-2739. **E-Mail:** yli1@tulane.edu

LI, YUYING, SCIENTIFIC COMPUTING OPTIMIZATION. **Personal Data:** m 1992, Thomas; c Lena V. **Education:** Sichuan Univ, China, BS, 1982; Univ Waterloo, Can, MS, 1985, PhD (comput sci), 1988. **Honors & Awards:** Six Fox Prize, Oxford Univ. **Professional Experience:** SR RES ASSOC, CORNELL UNIV, 1995-; lectr, Cornell Univ, 1990, 1992, 1993 & 1995; res assoc, Cornell Univ, 1989-1995. **Memberships:** Soc Indust & Appl Math. **Research Statement & Publications:** Numerical optimization and scientific computing applying optimization techniques to many application problems, such as medical imaging and financial optimization. **Mailing Address:** 635 Rhodes Hall, Cornell Univ Upson, Ithaca, NY 14850. **Fax:** 607-255-4428. **E-Mail:** yuying@cs.cornell.edu

LI, ZHENG, SEMICONDUCTOR HIGH ENERGY PARTICLE DETECTORS, RADIATION DAMAGE & HARDNESS OF SEMICONDUCTOR DETECTORS. **Personal Data:** b Xiangtan, China, November 10, 1958; m Yan-Xia; c Michael & Katie. **Education:** Beijing Univ, BS, 1981; Pa State Univ, PhD (physics), 1986. **Professional Experience:** CO-CHMN, ORGANIZING COMT, BNL, as of 2001; ASSOC PHYSICIST, BROOKHAVEN NAT LAB,

1989-; asst physicist, 1986-1988. **Memberships:** Inst Elec & Electronics Engrs. **Research Statement & Publications:** Designing, developing and processing of silicon position sensitive particle detectors; radiation damage effects and radiation hardness study on silicon detectors. **Mailing Address:** Brookhaven Nat Lab, Bldg 535B BOX 5000, Upton, NY 11973-5000. **Fax:** 631-344-5773. **E-Mail:** zhengl@bnl.gov

LI, ZHONGSHAN, COMBINATORIAL MATRIX ANALYSIS, SIGN PATTERN MATRICES & THEIR GENERALIZATIONS. **Personal Data:** b Lanzhou, China, April 22, 1963; American citizen; m 1988, Joan; c Angela C & Andrew T. **Education:** Lanzhou Univ, China, BSc, 1983; Beijing Normal Univ, China, MSc, 1986; NC State Univ, PhD (math), 1990. **Professional Experience:** ASSOC PROF MATH, GA STATE UNIV, 1998-; asst prof math, Ga State Univ, 1992-1998; instr, GA State Univ, 1991-1992; instr, NC State Univ, 1990-1991; asst prof math, Hebei Normal Col, China, 1986. **Memberships:** Am Math Soc; Int Linear Algebra Soc. **Research Statement & Publications:** Matrix theory, especially combinatorial matrix theory and qualitative matrix theory, in which sign patterns and graphs are used extensively. **Mailing Address:** Dept Math & Stat, Ga State Univ, Atlanta, GA 30303-3083. **Fax:** 404-651-2246. **E-Mail:** matzli@panther.gsu.edu

LI, ZI-CAI, NUMERICAL METHODS, IMAGE TRANSFORMATION. **Personal Data:** b Sichnam, China, March 14, 1939; Canadian citizen; c 2. **Education:** Qing-Hua Univ, China, BA, 1963; Univ Toronto, PhD (appl math), 1986. **Professional Experience:** PROF MATH, NATIONAL SUN YAT-SEN UNIV, as of 1999; assoc res prof computer sci, Concordia Univ & ctr info, Montreal, beginning 1987; Assoc prof, Shanghai Inst Comput Technol, China, 1972-1980. **Memberships:** Soc Indust & Appl Math; Inst Elec & Electronics Engrs. **Research Statement & Publications:** Numerical methods for partial differential equations, in particular the combined methods and applied them into pattern recognitions and image processing; over 70 publications and two monographs. **Mailing Address:** Dept Math, Nat Sun Yat-Sen Univ, 70 Lien-hai Rd, Kaohsiung, Taiwan. **E-Mail:** zcli@math.nsysu.edu.tw

LIAN, BONG H. Professional Experience: John Simon Guggenheim Mem Found fel, 2003-2004; PROF, DEPT MATH, BRANDEIS UNIV, 2001-; chair, Dept Math, Brandeis Univ, beginning 2001. **Mailing Address:** Brandeis Univ, Dept Math, 415 S St Goldsmith Bldg Rm 314 MS 050, Waltham, MA 02454-9110. **Fax:** 781-736-3085. **E-Mail:** lian@brandeis.edu

LIAN, ERIC CHUN-YET, HEMATOLOGY. **Personal Data:** b Tainan Hsien, Taiwan, November 11, 1938; American citizen; m 1973, Maria; c Elizabeth & Alexander. **Education:** Nat Taiwan Univ, MD, 1964. **Professional Experience:** PROF MED, SCH MED, 1987-; Prin investr biochem, immunol & physiol of antihemophilic factor, 1976- & pathogenesis of thrombotic thrombocytopenic purpura, 1978-; assoc prof med, Sch Med, 1978-1987; DIR HEMOSTASIS LAB, UNIV MIAMI, 1976-1999; COMPREHENSIVE HEMOPHILIA CTR, UNIV MIAMI, 1976-1992; asst prof med, Sch Med, 1973-1976; res assoc hemostasis, Harvard Med Sch, 1971-1973; Res fel hemat, Univ Miami, 1969-1971. **Memberships:** Fel Am Col Physicians; Am Fedn Clin Res; Am Soc Hemat; Int Soc Thrombosis & Hemostasis. **Research Statement & Publications:** Thrombosis and hemostasis; hematology; thrombotic thrombocytopanic purpura; acquired factor VIII inhibitor; myelodysplatic syndrome, multiple myeloma. **Mailing Address:** Univ Miami hosp, 1475 NW 12th Ave (D8-4), Miami, FL 33136. **Fax:** 305-243-5239. **E-Mail:** elian@med.miami.edu

LIAN, JANE B, CELL BIOLOGY. **Education:** Boston Univ, PhD (biochem), 1972. **Professional Experience:** PROF CELL BIOL, UNIV MASS, MED CTR, 1988-. **Research Statement & Publications:** Cellular biology. **Mailing Address:** Dept Cell Biol Univ Mass Med Ctr, 55 Lake Ave N, Worcester, MA 01655-0001. **E-Mail:** jane.lian@umassmed.edu

LIAN, SHAWN, MATERIALS SCIENCE ENGINEERING. **Personal Data:** b Taipei, Taiwan, March 2, 1958. **Education:** Nat Taiwan Univ, BS, 1982. **Professional Experience:** RES ASSOC, UNIV TEX AUSTIN, 1987-; Res assoc, Chung Sun Acad Res Ctr, 1984-1987. **Memberships:** Am Phys Soc; Electrochem Soc. **Research Statement & Publications:** Photo-enhanced chemical vapor deposition to investigatelow temperature processing which is the main trend for future ultralarge-scale integration and heterostructure devices. **Mailing Address:** 2501 Lake Austin Blvd No A104, Austin, TX 78703.

LIANG, CHANG-SENG, CARDIOLOGY. **Personal Data:** b Fukien, China, January 6, 1941; American citizen; m 1968, c 3. **Education:** Nat Taiwan Univ, MD, 1965; BostonUniv, PhD (pharmacol), 1971. **Professional Experience:** DIR, CARDIAC FUNCTION SERV, UNIV ROCHESTER MED CTR, as of 2004; PROF MED, UNIV ROCHESTER MED CTR, 1986-; assoc prof med, Univ Rochester Med Ctr, 1982-1986; study sect reviewer, NIH, 1981-1985; prin investr, NIH res grants, 1977-; from asst prof to assoc prof med & pharmacol, Boston Univ Sch Med, 1973-1982; Instr med, Boston Univ Sch Med, 1973-1974. **Memberships:** Am Physiol Soc; Am Soc Pharmacol & Exp Therapeut; Am Heart Asn; Am Soc Clin Invest; Am Fedn Clin Res. **Research Statement & Publications:** Circulatory control and neurohumoral regulation of the cardiovascular system in heart failure; receptor pharmacology; changes of membrane signal transduction; hemodynamic measurements. **Mailing Address:** Cardiol Unit, 601 Elmwood Ave Box 679, Rochester, NY 14642. **Fax:** 585-271-2184.

LIANG, CHARLES SHIH-TUNG, AERONAUTICAL & ASTRONAUTICAL ENGINEERING. **Personal Data:** b Peking, China, December 10, 1940; American citizen; m 1965, Mary; c Philip & Sandy. **Education:** Univ Ill, BS, 1962, PhD (elec eng), 1968; Harvard Univ, MS, 1963. **Professional Experience:** SR TECHNICAL FEL, LOCKHEED MARTIN AERONAUTIC CO, as of 2003; co spec, Lockheed Martin Tactical Aircraft Co, 1993-2001; div specialist, Gen Dynamics, Ft Worth, 1989-1993; eng staff specialist, Ft Worth Div, Gen Dynamics Corp, 1969-1989; asst elec eng, Univ Ill, 1963-1968. **Memberships:** Inst Elec & Electronics Engrs; Am Inst Aeronautics & Astronaut; Int Union Radio Sci. **Research Statement & Publications:** Electromagnetic scattering research as related to low observables aircraft designs; radar antenna design and development; advanced technology aircraft design and development; radar cross-section measurement techniques. **Mailing Address:** Lockheed Martin Aeronaut Co, MZ 2890 PO Box 748, Ft Worth, TX 76101.

LIANG, EDISON PARK-TAK, ASTROPHYSICS, PLASMA RADIATION. **Personal Data:** b Canton, China, July 22, 1947; American citizen; m 1971, Lily; c Olivia, James & Justin. **Education:** Univ Calif, Berkeley, BA, 1967, PhD (physics), 1971. **Professional Experience:** ANDREW HAYS BUCHANAN CHAIR ASTROPHY, RICE UNIV, 2001-; PROF PHYSICS & ASTRON, RICE UNIV, 1991-; assoc div leader, Physics Dept, Lawrence Livermore Nat Lab, 1988-1990; group leader, Physics Dept, Lawrence Livermore Nat Lab, 1983-1990; physicist, Physics Dept, Lawrence Livermore Nat Lab, 1980-1993; lectr & vis scholar, Ctr Space Sci & Astrophys, Stanford Univ, 1980-1990; asst prof physics, Stanford Univ, 1976-1979; asst prof astrophys, Mich State Univ, 1975-1976; res assoc & assoc instr astrophys & relativity, Univ Utah, 1973-1975; res assoc, Univ Tex, Austin, 1971-1973. **Memberships:** Sigma Xi; Am Astronom Soc; fel Am Phys Soc; Int Astron Union. **Research Statement & Publications:** Plasma radiation; astrophysics of compact objects (x-ray and gamma ray sources); laser-plasma interactions; relativity and cosmology; supernova remnants. **Mailing Address:** Dept Physics & Astron, Rice Univ, MS 108, Houston, TX 77005-1892. **Fax:** 713-348-5143. **E-Mail:** liang@spacsun.rice.edu

LIANG, GEORGE H, PLANT GENETICS, SOMATIC CELL GENETICS, PLANT TRANSFORMATION. **Personal Data:** b Beijing, China, October 1, 1934; American citizen; m 1963, Yun-Teh; c J May & Roy C. **Education:** Taiwan Prov Col Agr, BS, 1956; Univ Wyo, MS, 1961; Univ Wis, PhD (agron), 1965. **Honors & Awards:** Int Agr Coop Award, Ministry Agr, 1993. **Professional Experience:** Germplasm Resources, Chinese Acad Agr Sci, 1993; tech consult, UN Develop Prog, 1991 & 1993; consult, World Bank, 1983; CHMN, GENETICS PROG, 1982-; Sabbatical, Univ Calif-Davis, 1981; PROF PLANT GENETICS & CYTOGENETICIST, KANS STATE UNIV, 1977-; from asst prof to assoc prof, Genetics Prog, 1964-1976; agronomist, Taiwan Prov Res Inst Agr, 1958-1959; distinguished prof, Chinese Acad Agr Sci, Jiangsu Agr Univ & Henan Agr Univ. **Memberships:** Am Soc Agron; Crop Sci Soc Am; Am Genetic Asn; Sigma Xi; Genetics Soc Can. **Research Statement & Publications:** Quantitative genetics in plant species; cytogenetics and breeding aspects in cultivated crops; somatic cell genetics; biotechnology: plant transformation. **Mailing Address:** Dept Agron, Kans State Univ 2004 Throckmorton, Manhattan, KS 66506. **Fax:** 785-532-6094. **E-Mail:** gliang@bear.agron.ksu.edu

LIANG, ISABELLA Y S, CARDIAC VASCULAR DISEASES. **Personal Data:** b Kwellin, China, American citizen. **Education:** Hong Kong Chinese Univ, BS, 1966; Hong Kong Univ, PhD (physiol), 1979. **Professional Experience:** HEALTH SCI ADMINR, NIH, 1990-. **Memberships:** Am Heart Asn; Sigma Xi; Am Physiol Soc; Am Soc Molecular Biol & Med. **Mailing Address:** NHLBI, Two Rockledge Ctr, Ste 9204, 6701 Rockledge Dr, MSC 7940, Bethesda, MD 20892-7940. **Fax:** 301-480-1454. **E-Mail:** liangi@mail.nih.gov

LIANG, JACK N, PROTEIN CHEMISTRY. **Personal Data:** b Taiwan, China, February 4, 1942. **Education:** Taiwan Normal Univ, BS, 1968; McMaster Univ, PhD (biophys chem), 1977. **Professional Experience:** BIOCHEMIST, BRIGHAM & WOMEN'S HOSP, 1982-; res assoc, Mass Eye & Ear Infirmary, 1981-1982; fel, Brown Univ, 1979-1981. **Memberships:** Biophys Soc; Am Chem Soc. **Research Statement & Publications:** Conformation of polypeptides and polysaccharides. **Mailing Address:** Dept Ophthal, Brigham & Women's Hosp, Harvard Med Sch, 221 Longwood Ave, Boston, MA 02115-5817. **Fax:** 617-278-0556. **E-Mail:** jliang@rics.bwh.harvard.edu

LIANG, JOSEPH JEN-YIN, MATHEMATICS. **Personal Data:** b China, American citizen; m 1965, c 2. **Education:** Nat Taiwan Univ, BA, 1958; Univ Detroit, MA, 1962; Ohio State Univ, PhD (math), 1969. **Professional Experience:** PROF EMER MATH, UNIV SFLA, as of 2003; Vis res prof, Nat Tsing Hua Univ, Taipei, Taiwan, Repub China, 1983; prof math, Univ Sfla, beginning 1978; vis assoc, Calif Inst Technol, 1975 & 1977; Vis asst prof, Ohio State Univ, 1972; From asst prof to assoc prof, Univ Sfla, 1970-1977; Res fel math, Calif Inst Technol, 1969-1970. **Memberships:** Am Math Soc; Math Asn Am. **Research Statement & Publications:** Number theory; coding theory; algorithms. **Mailing Address:** Dept Math Phys 114, Univ SFla 4202 Fowler Ave, Tampa, FL 33620-9951.

LIANG, KENG-SAN, MATERIALS SCIENCE, SOLID STATE PHYSICS. **Personal Data:** b Tainan, Taiwan, December 17, 1943; m 1969, c 2. **Education:** Nat Taiwan Univ, BS, 1966; Stanford Univ, MS, 1970, PhD (appl physics), 1973. **Professional Experience:** EXXON RES & ENG CO, as of 1999; STAFF PHYSICIST MAT SCI, CORP RES LABS, EXXON RES & ENG CO, 1978-; from assoc scientist to scientist mat sci, Xerox Corp, 1973-1978. **Memberships:** Am Phys Soc; Am Vacuum Soc. **Research Statement & Publications:** Amorphous solids, x-ray diffraction, x-ray photoelectron spectroscopy, electronic structure, thin films. **Mailing Address:** Exxon Corp Res, Rte 22 E, Annandale, NJ 08801.

LIANG, LIYUAN, ENVIRONMENTAL ENGINEERING SCIENCE. **Education:** NEastern Univ, BS, 1982; Calif Inst Technol, Pasadena, MS, 1983 & PhD (Environ Eng), 1988. **Professional Experience:** SCI LEADER, ENVIRON SCI DIV, OAK RIDGE NAT LAB, 1999-; STAFF SCIENTIST, ENVIRON SCI DIV, OAK RIDGE NAT LAB, 1990-; group leader, Environ Eng, Environ Sci Div, Oak Ridge Nat Lab, 1995-1997; sr lectr, Dept Earth Sci, Univ Wales, UK, 1997-1999; asst prof, Sch Pub Health, Univ SC, 1988-1990. **Research Statement & Publications:** Laboratory and field research on processes affecting colloidal particles in natural water environments: colloidal stability; deposition; and transport; chemical processes governing mineral precipitation and dissolution in water; aqueous chemical speciation and surface chemical reactions controlling fate of toxic metals and organic contaminants in environment. **Mailing Address:** Environ Sci Div, Oak Ridge Nat Lab, PO Box 2008, Oak Ridge, TN 37831-6038. **Fax:** 865-576-8646. **E-Mail:** liangl@ornl.gov

LIANG, SHOU CHU, CHEMISTRY. **Personal Data:** b Foochow, China, May 14, 1920; m 1950, Chi-Chan Woo; c Pitur & Maurice. **Education:** Cent Univ, China, BS, 1942; Princeton Univ, MA, 1946, PhD (chem), 1947. **Professional Experience:** PVT RES, COMINCO ELECTRONIC MAT INC, 1988-; consult, Cominco Electronic Mat Inc, 1985-1988; gen mgr, Cominco Electronic Mat Inc, 1970-1985; head gen metall res, Consol Mining & Smelting Co Can, Ltd, 1964-1970; res engr, Consol Mining & Smelting Co Can, Ltd, 1956-1964; group leader, Res Lab, Dom Tar & Chem Co, 1953-1956; fel, asst res officer II, 1951-1953; fel, Nat Res Coun Can, 1949-1951; res chemist, Merck & Co, NJ, 1948-1949; asst, Int Nickel Co fel, 1947-1948; asst, Princeton Univ, 1945-1947; anal chemist, China Match Raw Mat Mfg Co, 1942-1944; Instr, Teacher High Sch, China, 1942. **Memberships:** Am Chem Soc; NY Acad Sci; Chem Inst Can; AAAS. **Research Statement & Publications:** Flotation of ores; preperation of inorganic reagents; chemical method of analysis; surface catalysis; heterogeneity of catalyst surfaces for chemisorption; fast drying paint; metallurgy; semiconductors. **Mailing Address:** S 4206 Helena St, Spokane, WA 99203.

LIANG, SHOUDAN, CORRELATED CONDENSED MATTER SYSTEMS, COMPUTATIONAL PHYSICS. **Personal Data:** b Fuzhou, China, February 10, 1961. **Education:** Peking Univ, BS, 1982; Univ Chicago, PhD (physics), 1986. **Professional Experience:** MEM, NASA AMES RES CTR, UNIV CALIF, SANTA CRUZ, as of 2004; asst prof Physics, Pa State Univ, beginning 1990; res assoc physics, Princeton Univ, 1986-1988 & Univ Ill, Urbana-Champaign, 1988-1990. **Memberships:** Am Phys Soc. **Research Statement & Publications:** Theoretical condensed matter physics include quantum antiferromagnets, new algorithms for overcoming slow dynamics in spin glasses and simulated annealing, random growth and computational physics. **Mailing Address:** Dept Physics, Univ Calif, 1156 High St, Santa Cruz, CA 95064. **E-Mail:** liang@phys.psu.edu

LIANG, SHOUDENG, VACUUM TECHNOLOGY & APPLICATIONS, SURFACE CHARACTERIZATIONS & PROPERTY ANALYSIS. **Personal Data:** b Yantai, China, March 9, 1959. **Education:** Qufu Normal Univ, China, BS, 1981; Univ Ill-Chicago, MS, 1987; Univ Wis-Madison, MS, 1990. **Professional Experience:** RES SCI, NAT STANDARD TECH, as of 2004; RES ASST X-RAY LITHOGRAPHY, CTR X-RAY LITHOGRAPHY, UNIV WIS,

1990-; proj asst, Chem Dept, 1989-1990; res asst surface sci, Chem Dept, 1989; res asst surface chem, Chem Dept, Univ Ill, Chicago, 1986-1988; researcher catalysis & phys chem, Dalian Inst Chem Physics, China, 1982-1985. **Memberships:** Am Vacuum Soc; Mat Res Soc. **Research Statement & Publications:** Surface chemistry of thin films and interfaces of metals/semiconductors and gas/metals; application of synchrotron radiation to materials research and scanning x-ray spectromicroscopy; x-ray lithography from synchrotron radiation sources. **Mailing Address:** Nat Inst Stand & Technol, 221 Bldg, Gaithersburg, MD 20899. **E-Mail:** liang@enh.nist.gov

LIANG, SHU-MEI, CYTOKINE RESEARCH, STRUCTURE-FUNCTION STUDIES. **Personal Data:** b Taiwan, February 4, 1949; American citizen; c 1. **Education:** Nat Taiwan Univ, BS, 1971; Univ Ark, PhD (biochem), 1978. **Professional Experience:** Adj prof, Univ Ark, as of 2003; AT ACADEMIA SINICA, TAIWAN, as of 2003; dir & sr scientist, Dept Protein Chem, N Am Vaccine, Inc, 1993-1997; mgr, Protein Chem & Molecular Biol, Amvax Inc, 1992-1993; div cytokine biol, CBER, 1988-1992; res chemist, Div Virol, Food & Drug Admin, 1986-1988; res chemist res & regulatory work, Div Virol, CBER, 1986-1988; scientist res & develop, Dept Protein Chem, Biogen, SAm, 1983-1985; staff fel, Div Biochem & Biophysics, 1980-1983; vis fel res, Div Bact Prod, BOB, Food & Drug Admin, 1977-1980. **Memberships:** Am Soc Biochem & Molecular Biol; Protein Soc; Chinese Biochem Soc. **Research Statement & Publications:** Structure-function relationships of cytokines especially interleukin-2 and the regulation of immune response by thiol compounds; purification and characterization of proteins especially membrane proteins and recombinant DNA derived proteins; expression of bacterial membrane proteins in E coli. **Mailing Address:** Univ Ark, Fayetteville, AR 72701. **E-Mail:** smyang@gate.sinica.edu.tw

LIANG, TEHMING, BIOCHEMISTRY. **Personal Data:** b Taiwan, April 14, 1945; c 1. **Education:** Nat Taiwan Univ, BS, 1968; Univ Chicago, PhD (biochem), 1973; Univ Miami, MD, 1987. **Professional Experience:** BD CERT DERMATOLOGIST, BOLINGBROOK, ILL, 1995-; assoc prof, Dept Dermat, wright State Univ Sch MEd, 1992-1995; assoc prof, Dept Dermat, Vet Admin Med Ctr, Dayton, Ohio, 1992-1995; resident dermat, Robert Wood Johnson Med Sch, Univ Chicago, 1989-1991; resident internal med, Robert Wood Johnson Med Sch, Univ Chicago, 1987-1988; res fel, Merck Inst Therapeut Res, 1981-1987; sr res biochem, Merck Inst Therapeut Res, 1977-1981; res asst prof, Ben May Lab Cancer Res, Univ Chicago, 1976-1977; res assoc biochem, Ben May Lab Cancer Res, Univ Chicago, 1973-1976. **Memberships:** Am Soc Biol Chemists; Endocrine Soc; Soc Neuroscience; Am Med Asn; Am Acad Dermat; Soc Investigative Dermat. **Research Statement & Publications:** Molecular mechanism of hormone action. **Mailing Address:** 580 E Boughton Rd, Bolingbrook, IL 60440. **Fax:** 630-972-2604. **E-Mail:** Tehming_Liang@yahoo.com

LIANG, TUNG, OPERATIONS RESEARCH, AGRICULTURAL ENGINEERING. **Personal Data:** b Peking, China, June 7, 1932; m 1958, c 2. **Education:** Nat Taiwan Univ, BS, 1956; Mich State Univ, MS, 1963; NC State Univ, PhD (biol & agr eng), 1968. **Professional Experience:** PROF, DEPT MOLECULAR BIOSCIENCES & BIOENGINEERING, UNIV HAWAII, 1976-; From asst prof to assoc prof, 1967-1976. **Memberships:** Am Soc Agr Engrs. **Research Statement & Publications:** Agricultural system modeling and optimization; development of natural resource information system. **Mailing Address:** Dept Molecular Biosciences & Bioengineering, Univ Hawaii, 1955 EW Rd, Ag Sci 218, Honolulu, HI 96822-2270. **Fax:** 808-956-8867. **E-Mail:** tliang@hawaii.edu

LIANG, WEI CHUAN, ORGANIC CHEMISTRY, PROCESS DEVELOPMENT SAFETY. **Personal Data:** b Shanghai, China, November 23, 1936; m 1970, Yu-Lan; c Elan & Emay. **Education:** Kalamazoo Col, BA, 1961; Case Western Res Univ, MS, 1966; Ohio State Univ, PhD (org chem), 1972. **Professional Experience:** SR PRIN SCIENTIST, RHONE POULENC INC, 1987-; res scientist, Union Carbide Corp, 1982-1987; group leader process develop, Union Carbide Corp, 1977-1987; res chemist, Union Carbide Corp, 1974-1977; fel org chem res, Ga Inst Technol, 1972-1974; res chemist, Lubrizol Corp, 1961-1967. **Memberships:** Am Chem Soc; Am Inst Chem Engrs. **Research Statement & Publications:** Exploratory syntheses; pesticide process research; process research and development; process safety. **Mailing Address:** Rhone Poulenc Inc, CN 7500, Cranbury, NJ 08512. **Fax:** 609-860-0218.

LIANG, YOLA YUEH-O, ANALYTICAL CHEMISTRY, GOOD LABORATORY PRACTICE. **Personal Data:** b Taiwan, February 12, 1947; m 1975, c 2. **Education:** Nat Taiwan Normal Univ, BS, 1970; Univ Kans, PhD (chem), 1978. **Professional Experience:** RETIRED; res assoc, Anal Chem, Dow Chem Co, 1981-. **Memberships:** Am Chem Soc; Asn Women Sci. **Research Statement & Publications:** Analytical chemistry; organic electrochemistry; neurochemistry; enzyme kinetics; analytical separations using gas chromatography and liquid chromatography. **Mailing Address:** 386 Mt Sequoia Pl, Clayton, CA 94517. **E-Mail:** yolaliang@hotmail.com

LIANG, YUN-TEH S, CHEMISTRY. **Education:** SDak Univ, BS, 1959; Univ Wis, MS, 1961, PhD, 1965. **Professional Experience:** RES ASSOC EMER, GRAIN SCI & INDUST, KANS STATE UNIV, as of 2006. **Mailing Address:** Dept Grain Sci & Indust, Kans State Univ, Manhattan, KS 66506.

LIANG, ZHI-PEI, ELECTRICAL ENGINEERING, INTELLIGENT SYSTEMS. **Personal Data:** b Guangdong, China, December 25, 1961; m 1986, Bo Liu; c Annie Han. **Education:** SChina Inst Technol, BS, 1982; Case Western Res Univ, MS, 1985, PhD, 1989. **Honors & Awards:** RIA Award, NSF, 1994, Career Award, 1995. **Professional Experience:** PROF, DEPT ELEC & COMP SCI, UNIV ILL, URBANA, as of 2000; Reviewer, NIH, 1995, 1996 & 1997; reviewer, NSF, 1994; res asst prof, Biomed Magnetic Resonance Lab, 1991-1993; Whitaker biomed eng res grantee, 1991; postdoctoral fel, Nat Ctr Supercomput Appln, 1989-1991; Asst prof, dept elec & comput eng, Beckman inst advan sci & technol, coord sci lab, Bioengineering prog & Del; assoc ed, Trans on Med Imaging, Inst Elec & Electronics Engrs. **Memberships:** NY Acad Sci; Inst Elec & Electronics Engrs; Int Soc Magnetic Resonance Med. **Research Statement & Publications:** Magnetic resonance imaging; superresolution image reconstruction using a priori constraints; statistical, scale-space, and neural network approaches to image analysis; multimodality image registration and fusion. **Mailing Address:** Beckman Inst, Urbana, IL 61801. **Fax:** 217-244-0105. **E-Mail:** z-liang@uiuc.edu

LIANIDES, SYLVIA PANAGOS, PHYSIOLOGY, BIOCHEMISTRY. **Personal Data:** b Lynn, Mass, September 2, 1931; div, c 3. **Education:** Tufts Univ, BS, 1953, PhD (physiol), 1959. **Professional Experience:** RETIRED; chmn, Biol Dept, 1981-1983; prof anat & physiol, W Valley Col, Calif, 1975-1996; instr ecol, Chabot Col, 1973-1975; instr biol sci, De Anza Col, 1971-1973; lectr biol, Col Notre Dame, Calif, 1962-1971; res biologist, US Naval Radiol Defense Lab, 1959-1960. **Memberships:** AAAS; Sigma Xi; Nat Asn Biol Teachers; Nat Sci Teachers Asn. **Research Statement & Publications:** Hormonal and environmental influences upon mitochondrial oxidative phosphorylation; effects of environmental cold on lipid and carbohydrate metabolism; radiation physiology; anatomy. **Mailing Address:** PO Box 2334, Saratoga, CA 95070.

LIAO, HSUEH-LIANG, ANALYTICAL CHEMISTRY. **Personal Data:** b Silo, Taiwan, January 24, 1941; American citizen; m 1952, c 2. **Education:** Cheng Kong Univ, BS, 1965; Drexel Univ, MS, 1969; Georgetown Univ, PhD (chem), 1972. **Professional Experience:** GROUP LEADER & SCIENTIST, LEDERLE LABS, AM CYANAMID CO, 1977-; sr res scientist, Bristol Myers Co, 1976-1977; sr res chemist, Norwich Pharmacal Co, Morton-Norwich Prod Inc, 1974-1976; sr res assoc chem, Northeastern Univ, 1972-1974. **Memberships:** Am Chem Soc; Am Inst Chem Eng. **Research Statement & Publications:** Analytical methods development; chromatographic methods of separation (High Performance Liquid Chromatography, Gas Chromatography and TLC) and quantitation; analytical and physical chemistry of drug compounds; solution thermodynamics. **Mailing Address:** 83 Ridge Rd, New City, NY 10956-6824.

LIAO, JAMES C, CHEMICAL ENGINEERING. **Education:** Nat Taiwan Univ, BS; Univ Wis-Madison, PhD. **Professional Experience:** PROF, DEPT CHEM ENG, UNIV CALIF, as of 2006. **Mailing Address:** Dept Chem & Biomolecular Eng, Univ Calif, 5531 Boelter Hall 420 Westwood Plaza, Los Angeles, CA 90095. **Fax:** 310-206-4107. **E-Mail:** liaoj@seas.ucla.edu

LIAO, LUBY, MATHEMATICS. **Education:** Univ Calif San Diego, MS, 1989; Wash Univ, PhD (Maths), 1978. **Professional Experience:** PROF, MATH & COMPUT SCI DEPT, UNIV SAN DIEGO, as of 2005. **Mailing Address:** Dept Math & Comput Sci, Univ San Diego, San Diego, CA 92110. **Fax:** 619-452-7762. **E-Mail:** liao@SanDiego.edu

LIAO, MARTHA, SOMATIC CELL GENETICS, RECOMBINANT DNA. **Personal Data:** b Leeds, Eng, February 9, 1948; m 1991. **Education:** Bryn Mawr Col, BA, 1970; Univ Pa, PhD (chem), 1974. **Professional Experience:** Sr fel genetics, Health Sci Ctr, Eleanor Roosevelt Inst Cancer Res, Univ Colo, 1986-; assoc prof, Dept Pediat, Univ Colo Health Sci Ctr, 1986-; Am res scholar, Comt Scholarly Commun with People's Republic China, Nat Acad Sci, 1981-1982; inst fel, Health Sci Ctr, Eleanor Roosevelt Inst Cancer Res, Univ Colo, 1979-1986; NIH fel, 1976-1979; fel, Health Sci Ctr, Eleanor Roosevelt Inst Cancer Res, Univ Colo, 1975-1979; fel chem, Univ Denver, 1974-1975; AT DEPT MOLECULAR GENETICS, ALBERT EINSTEIN COL MED. **Memberships:** Am Cell Biol; Am Soc Human Genetics; AAAS. **Research Statement & Publications:** Human gene mapping using chinese hamster/human cell hybrids; using recombinant DNA techniques to obtain DNA markers from specific human chromosome. **Mailing Address:** Dept Molecular Genetics, Albert Einstein Col Med, 1300 Morris Park Ave, Bronx, NY 10461-1975.

LIAO, MEI-JUNE, INTERFERON SCIENCE. **Education:** Nat Tsing-Hua Univ, BS, 1973; Yale Univ, MPh, 1977, PhD (phys biochem), 1980. **Professional Experience:** DIR, RES & DEVELOP, INTERFERON SCI, INC, 1987-; dir cell biol, Cellular Immunol Group, 1985-1986; head, Cellular Immunol Group, 1984-1985; sr scientist, Bioresponse Modifier Group, Interferon Sci, Inc, 1983-1984; Assoc biochem & biophys, Mass Inst Technol, 1980-1983. **Memberships:** Am Soc Biochem & Molecular Biol; Int Soc Inteferon & Cytokine Res; Soc Chinese Bioscientists Am. **Research Statement & Publications:** Purification and characterization of natural and recombinant human interferon proteins; natural interferon induction systems; mechanism of interferon action; interferon receptor purification and characterization; production of monoclonal and polyclonal antibodies; development of immunochemical assay techniques; state of the art protein chemistrytechniques and cytokine assays and cDNA cloning and expression of human cytokines; preparation of PLA and response to the Food and Drug Administration for the approval of natural and recombinant interferon product. **Mailing Address:** Interferon Sci Inc, 783 Jersey Ave, New Brunswick, NJ 08901-3660.

LIAO, PAUL FOO-HUNG, ENGINEERING PHYSICS. **Personal Data:** b Philadelphia, Pa, November 10, 1944; m 1968, c 2. **Education:** Mass Inst Technol, BS, 1966; Columbia Univ, PhD (physics), 1973. **Professional Experience:** CHIEF TECHNOL OFFICER & PRES, PANASONIC TECHNOL INC, as of 2004; gen mgr, Network Foundations, Archit & Planning, Network Systs Res, Bellcore, beginning 1993; asst vpres, Bellcore, 1990-1993; asst vpres solid state sci & tech, Bellcore, 1989-1990; ed, J Optical Soc Am, 1988; div mgr photonic sci & tech res, Bellcore, 1987-1989; div mgr physics & optical sci res, Bellcore, 1984-1987; mem tech staff physics, head Quantum Electronics Res Dept, 1980-1983; mem tech staff physics, Bell Labs, 1973-1980; res assoc, Radiation Lab, Columbia Univ, 1972-1973; chmn, Joint Coun Quantum Electronics, 1966; ed, Acad Press, Quantum Electronics. **Memberships:** fel Am Phys Soc; fel Optical Soc Am; fel Inst Elec & Electronics Engrs. **Research Statement & Publications:** Communications systems; nonlinear optics. **Mailing Address:** Panasonic Technol, Inc, 3888 State St Ste 202, Santa Barbara, CA 93105. **E-Mail:** pliao@research.panasonic.com

LIAO, PING-HUANG, SANITARY & ENVIRONMENTAL ENGINEERING, OTHER ENVIRONMENTAL EARTH & MARINE SCIENCES. **Personal Data:** b Taipei, Taiwan, January 16, 1946; Canadian citizen; m 1971, Hsiu-mei; c Marrin, Perry & Justin. **Education:** Tunghai Univ, BS, 1969; Univ Neb, MS, 1973 & PhD (chem), 1976. **Professional Experience:** Instr, Columbia Col, 1981; RES SCIENTIST, UNIV BC, 1978-; fel, Univ BC, 1975-1978. **Memberships:** Int Asn Water Qual. **Research Statement & Publications:** Fermentation biotechnology, biomass utilization and bioenergy production from renewable resources; waste management; biological treatment; composting technology. **Mailing Address:** Dept Bio-Resource Eng, Univ BC, 2357 Main Hall, Vancouver, BC V6T 1Z4, Can. **Fax:** 604-822-5704. **E-Mail:** phliao@interchange.ubc.ca

LIAO, SHUEN-KUEI, CANCER, IMMUNOLOGY. **Personal Data:** b Morioka, Japan, June 27, 1940; Canadian citizen; m 1972, c 2. **Education:** Tunghai Univ, Taiwan, BSc, 1964; McMaster Univ, PhD (immunol), 1971. **Professional Experience:** Assoc prof path & pediat, Sch Med, McMaster Univ, beginning 1980; asst prof, Dept Pediat, 1976-1980; res grants, Med Res Coun Can, Ont Cancer Treatment & Res Found, 1974 & Nat Cancer Inst Can, 1981-; mem staff lab med, Henderson Gen Hosp, Hamilton, 1974-; Ont Cancer Fund res associateship, 1974-1984; lectr, Dept Pediat, 1974-1976; prof asst cancer, Hamilton Clin, Ont Cancer Found, 1973-1974; demonstr, fel histol, Univ Toronto, 1970-1973. **Memberships:** AAAS; Can Soc Cell Biol; Am Asn Cancer Res; Can Soc Immunol; NY Acad Sci; Int Soc Pigment Cell. **Research Statement & Publications:** Cancer immunology; cell biology. **Mailing Address:** 36 Mountain Brow Blvd, Hamilton, ON L8T 1A3, Can.

LIAO, SHUTSUNG, BIOCHEMISTRY, ENDOCRINOLOGY, BIOTECHNOL. **Personal Data:** b Tainan, Taiwan, January 1, 1931; m 1960, Shuching; c Jane, Tzufen, Tzuming & May. **Education:** Nat Taiwan Univ, BSc, 1954, MSc, 1956; Univ Chicago, PhD (biochem), 1961. **Honors & Awards:** Sci Achievement Award, Taiwanese-Am Found, 1983; Pfizer Lectr Award, Clin Res Inst Montreal, 1972; Gregory Pincus Medal & Award, Worcester Found, 1992; Tsung Ming Tu Award, Formosan Med Asn, 1993; Fellow Am Acad of Arts &

Sci, 1997. **Professional Experience:** DIR, TANG CTR FOR HERB MED RES, UNIV CHICAGO, 2000-; prof dept biochem & molecular biol, Ben May Inst, Univ Chicago, 1972; from asst prof to assoc prof, Ben May Inst, Univ Chicago, 1964-1971; NIH res grant, 1963-. **Memberships:** Am Soc Biol Chem; Endocrine Soc; Am Asn Cancer Res; NAm Taiwanese Prof Asn (pres, 1980-1981). **Research Statement & Publications:** Mechanism of hormone action; control of gene expression; nuclear receptors enzymology; prevention and suppresion of cancers. **Mailing Address:** Ben May Inst, MC 6027 Univ Chicago 5841 S Md, Chicago, IL 60637. **Fax:** 773-834-1770.

LIAO, SUNG JUI, PHYSICAL MEDICINE, ACUPUNCTURE. **Personal Data:** b Changsha, China, November 15, 1917; American citizen; wid Karin Agren (deceased); c Thomas, Elizabeth, Margaret & John. **Education:** Hsiang Ya Med Col, China, MD, 1942; Nat Cent Univ, China, MPH, 1944; London Sch Hyg & Trop Med, Univ London, DPH, 1946, dipl bact, 1947; Am Bd Phys Med & Rehab, dipl, 1958. **Honors & Awards:** British council scholar 1945-1949, Milbanle memorial fund fel-1947-49. **Professional Experience:** CLIN PROF SURG SCI, NY UNIV COL DENT, 1992-; hon physiatrist, Waterbury Hosp, 1991-; consult, Rhode Island State Bd Acupuncture, 1980-1984; clin prof oral & maxillo facial surg, NY Univ Col Dent, 1978-1992; lectr rehab med, Boston Univ Sch Med, 1973-1993; St Raphael Hosp, New Haven, Conn, 1972-1982; clin assoc prof rehab med, NY Univ Col Dent, 1971-1982; hon consult biomech, NY Univ Inst Rehab Med, 1969-1976; chief admin med consult, Waterbury & Danbury, Conn State Div Voc Rehab, 1969-1973; assoc clin prof, Sch Med, Boston Univ, 1967-1973; med consult, Waterbury & Danbury, Conn State Div Voc Rehab, 1963-1972; attend physiatrist, Waterbury Hosp, 1957-1990; dir phys med & rehab, Waterbury Hosp, 1957-1973; dir phys med & rehab, St Mary's Hosp, 1957-1967 & Danbury Hosp, 1957-1969; med dir, Waterbury Area Rehab Ctr, 1957-1962; consult physiatrist, Middlesex Mem Hosp, Middletown, Conn, 1957-1960; clin fel phys med, Mass Gen Hosp, Boston, 1955-1957; Asst prof prev med, Sch Med, Yale Univ, 1950-1954; res assoc & assoc res prof bact, Col Med, Univ Utah, 1949-1950; Milbank Mem fel prev med, Sch Med, Yale Univ, 1947-1949; secy, Am Acad Acupuncture, Inc; pres, Res Inst Acupuncture & Chinese Med; chmn, ad hoc comt acupuncture, Conn State Med Soc. **Memberships:** Sr fel Am Col Physicians; sr fel Royal Soc Med; sr fel Am Acad Phys Med & Rehab; sr mem Sigma Xi; chairman, Am col of Acupencture, Inc. **Research Statement & Publications:** Excitability and conduction nerve and muscle; biomedical engineering; acupuncture; themography; pain. **Mailing Address:** 10 Longwood Dr Apt 552, Westwood, MA 02090.

LIAO, TA-HSIU, PROTEIN CHEMISTRY, ENZYMOLOGY. **Personal Data:** b Taipei, Taiwan, February 22, 1942; c 2. **Education:** Nat Taiwan Univ, BS, 1964; Univ Calif, Los Angeles, PhD (biol chem), 1969. **Professional Experience:** PROF BIOCHEM, INST BIOCHEM, NAT TAIWAN UNIV, 1985-; Vis prof, A Kornberg's Lab, Stanford Univ, 1981; from asst prof to prof biochem, Biochem Dept, Okla State Univ, 1974-1985; asst prof biochem, Moore-Stein Lab, Rockefeller Univ, 1973-1974; Postdoctoral biochem, Moore-Stein Lab, Rockefeller Univ, 1972-1973. **Memberships:** Am Soc Biochem & Molecular Biol. **Research Statement & Publications:** Protein chemistry; enzymology; deoxyribonuclease; structure and function relationships of proteins; physical methods of characterization of biological macromolecules. **Mailing Address:** Biochem Dept, Nat Taiwan Univ Col Med No 1 Jen Ai Rd 1st Sect, Taipei, Taiwan. **Fax:** 886-239-15295; 886-239-38354.

LIAO, TSUNG-KAI, ORGANIC CHEMISTRY, PHARMACEUTICAL CHEMISTRY. **Personal Data:** b Chiayi, Taiwan, August 1, 1923; m 1963, c 3. **Education:** Nat Taiwan Univ, BS, 1952; Wesleyan Univ, MA, 1957; Univ Kans, PhD (chem), 1960. **Professional Experience:** SR CHEMIST, MIDWEST RES INST, 1987-; CHEM CONSULT, MIDWEST RES INST, 1987-; mem, Contract Develop Therapeut Comt, Nat Cancer Inst, 1985-1987; dir, molecular electronics, Carnegie-Mellon Inst Res, Carnegie-Mellon Univ, 1978-1987; vis prof, Midwest Res Inst, vis specialist Nat Sci Coun, Repub China & Lectr Sixth Tamkang Chair, Tamkang Col, 1976; sr chemist, Midwest Res Inst, 1961-1977; assoc chemist, Midwest Res Inst, 1961; res assoc, Univ Mich, 1960-1961; Fel, Res Inst, Univ Mich, 1960-1961; asst, Univ Kans, 1957-1960; fel, Wesleyan Univ, 1955-1957; Asst chem, Nat Taiwan Univ, 1953-1955. **Memberships:** Am Chem Soc; Sigma Xi. **Research Statement & Publications:** Synthesis of biologically active organic compounds; organic semiconductors; chemistry of nitrogen heterocyclic compounds; polymer chemistry, reverse osmosis composite membranes; high temperature lubricants; zeroshrink thermosetting polymers; polymer chemistry. **Mailing Address:** 1317 E 101 Terr, Kansas City, MO 64131.

LIAU, GENE, VASCULAR BIOLOGY. **Personal Data:** b Hsing-Chu, Taiwan, November 28, 1954. **Education:** Univ NC, BS, 1977; Vanderbilt Univ, PhD (biochem), 1982. **Honors & Awards:** Res career develop award, NIH, 1990. **Professional Experience:** SR SCIENTIST, DEPT MOLECULAR BIOL, HOLLAND LAB, AM RED CROSS, as of 2004; ADJ PROF GENETICS, GEORGE WASH UNIV, as of 2004; res scientist Ii, Dept Molecular Biol, Am Red Cross, beginning 1992; res scientist I, Dept Molecular Biol, Am Red Cross, 1987-1992; assoc mem, Dept Cell Biol, Revlon Biotechnol Res Ctr, 1985-1987; fel collagen gene regulation, NIH, 1982-1985; established investr, Am Heart Asn. **Memberships:** Am Soc Biochem & Molecular Biol; AAAS; Soc Chinese Biochemists. **Research Statement & Publications:** Vascular biology. **Mailing Address:** Dept Molecular Biol, Am Red Cross, Holland Lab, 15601 Crabbs Br Way, Rockville, MD 20855. **E-Mail:** liau@usa.redcross.org

LIAU, ZONG-LONG, SEMICONDUCTOR LASERS & MATERIALS, INTEGRATED OPTOELECTRONICS. **Personal Data:** b Taipei, Taiwan, August 25, 1950; American citizen; m 1979, Jane; c Albert & Brian. **Education:** Nat Taiwan Univ, BS, 1972; Calif Inst Technol, PhD (appl physics), 1979. **Professional Experience:** STAFF MEM, LINCOLN LAB, MASS INST TECHNOL, 1978-; vis scientist, Bell Labs, 1977-1978. **Memberships:** Optical Soc Am; Bohmische Phys Soc. **Research Statement & Publications:** Physics and technology of semiconductor devices; materials science and engineering; atomic phenomena in compound semiconductor surfaces; fabrication of diode lasers, miniature mirrors, microlenses, integrated micro-optical and optoelectronic systems; issued 9 patents. **Mailing Address:** Lincoln Lab, Mass Inst Technol, Lexington, MA 02420. **Fax:** 781-981-5793. **E-Mail:** liau@ll.mit.edu

LIAUW, KOEI-LIANG, ORGANIC CHEMISTRY. **Personal Data:** b Indonesia, May 4, 1935; American citizen; m 1961, c 1. **Education:** Nanyang Univ, Singapore, BSc, 1960; Univ Calif, Berkeley, MS, 1962, PhD (chem), 1964. **Professional Experience:** PROJ LEADER CENT RES, TECH CTR, WITCO CHEM CORP, 1969-; sr res chemist, Mobil Chem Co, Div Mobil Oil Corp, 1966-1968; Res chemist, Gen Chem Div, Allied Chem Corp, 1964-1966. **Memberships:** Sigma Xi; Am Chem Soc. **Research Statement & Publications:** Textile treating agents; paper sizings; process development; synthetic organic chemistry; organotin chemistry; stabilizers for polyvinyl chloride and polyolefins; flame retardants; vapor phase catalysis. **Mailing Address:** 285 W Steven Ave, Wyckoff, NJ 07481.

LIAW, HANG MING, MATERIALS SCIENCE ENGINEERING, ELECTRONICS ENGINEERING. **Personal Data:** b Taichung, Taiwan, February 1, 1936; American citizen; m Chau; c Tsui, Lucy & Sally. **Education:** Cheng Kung Univ, BS, 1959; Pa State Univ, MS, 1967, PhD (solid state sci), 1970. **Professional Experience:** SR MEM TECH STAFF, MOTOROLA INC, 1984-, mem tech staff, 1981-1984, prin staff engr, 1978-1981. **Memberships:** Inst Elec & Electronics Engrs. **Research Statement & Publications:** Deposition of thin films incl epitexial senicond actors S; Sige G, N; piezoelecttric films, (AIN); and electrodeposition of Noble metals, (An and pd). **Mailing Address:** 11540 N 104th St, Scottsdale, AZ 85260. **Fax:** 480-391-2021. **E-Mail:** mingliaw@aol.com

LIAW, JYE REN, NUCLEAR ENGINEERING, RADIATION PHYSICS. **Personal Data:** b Hsin-Chu, Taiwan, May 12, 1946; m 1972, c 2. **Education:** Nat Tsing Hua Univ, Taiwan, BS, 1968; Univ Ore, Eugene, MS, 1971; Ore State Univ, PhD (nuclear eng), 1975. **Professional Experience:** MEM STAFF, REACTOR ANAL DIV, ARGONNE NAT LAB, 1990-; mem staff, Appl Physics Div, 1980-1989; consult, Los Alamos Sci Lab, 1977-1980; asst prof nuclear eng, Univ Okla, 1975-1980; res asst nuclear eng, Ore State Univ, 1973-1975; res asst physics, Univ Ore, Eugene, 1971-1973. **Memberships:** Am Phys Soc; Am Nuclear Soc; Sigma Xi; Nat Soc Prof Engrs. **Research Statement & Publications:** Nuclear reactor design and analysis; radiation transport and dosimetry; nuclear fission product data evaluation; Van de Graff accelerator and nuclear reactor experiments; high vacuum technology; nuclear fuel reprocessing. **Mailing Address:** 1502 Terrance Dr, Naperville, IL 60565.

LIBAN, ERIC, APPLIED MATHEMATICS. **Personal Data:** b Vienna, Austria, June 20, 1921; American citizen; m 1954, c 3. **Education:** NY Univ, BA, 1948, MS, 1949, PhD (math), 1957. **Professional Experience:** CHMN MATH DEPT, YORK COL, 1975-; PROF MATH, YORK COL, 1971-; assoc prof, York Col, 1967-1971; adj assoc prof, Queens Col, 1967-1968; adj prof, Adelphi Univ, 1966-1967; adj lectr, Polytech Inst Brooklyn, 1962-1965; res scientist, Grumman Aircraft Eng Corp, 1961-1967; consult, Avco Res & Develop Corp, Mass, 1959-1960 & Comput Systs, Inc, NJ, 1959-1961; assoc prof eng sci, Pratt Inst, 1958-1961; staff mem analog comput & consult ctr, Dian Labs, Inc, 1955-1958; sr dynamics engr, Repub Aviation Corp, 1952-1955; assoc mathematician, Proj Cyclone, Reeves Instrument Corp, NY, 1952; mathematician, Naval Res Lab, 1951-1952; asst, Ind Univ, 1950-1951; lectr, Univ Md, 1950; instr math, Long Island Univ, 1949 & NY Univ, 1949-1950. **Memberships:** Am Math Soc; Asn Comput Mach. **Research Statement & Publications:** Applications and methods of simulation on analog computers; logical design of computing systems; automata studies; theory of servo and feedback systems; information and communication theory; operations research. **Mailing Address:** Dept Math, CUNY York Col 94-20 Guy Brewer Blvd, Jamaica, NY 11452-0001.

LIBBEY, LEONARD MORTON, FOOD SCIENCE. **Personal Data:** b Boston, Mass, April 17, 1930; m 1971. **Education:** Univ Mass, BVA, 1953; Univ Wis, MS, 1954; Wash State Univ, PhD (food technol), 1961. **Professional Experience:** PROF EMER FOOD SCI & TECHNOL, ORE STATE UNIV, as of 2003; prof food sci & technol, Ore State Univ, 1981-; From asst prof to assoc prof, 1961-1981. **Memberships:** AAAS; Inst Food Technologists; Am Chem Soc; Am Oil Chemists Soc; Sigma Xi; Am Soc Mass Spectrometry. **Research Statement & Publications:** Food chemistry; chromatographic and spectrometric analysis, especially gas chromatography and mass spectrometry. **Mailing Address:** Dept Food Sci & Technol, Ore State Univ, 100 Wiegand Hall, Corvallis, OR 97331-6602. **Fax:** 541-737-1877. **E-Mail:** libbeyl@bcc.orst.edu

LIBBEY, WILLIAM JERRY, POLYOLEFINS, ENGINEERING PLASTICS. **Personal Data:** b Grand Rapids, Minn, March 18, 1942; m 1964, June; c William B & Daniel. **Education:** Carleton Col, BA, 1964; Univ Wis, PhD (org chem), 1969. **Professional Experience:** RETIRED; res fel, E I Du Pont De Nemours & Co Inc, 1992-1996; sr res assoc, E I Du Pont De Nemours & Co Inc, 1985-1992; sect dir, Conoco, Inc, 1982-1985; res group leader, Conoco, Inc, 1977-1981; sr res chemist, Continental Oil Co, 1972-1976; res chemist, Continental Oil Co, 1968-1972. **Memberships:** Am Chem Soc. **Research Statement & Publications:** Carbonium ion chemistry; thermal rearrangements; alkyl halide chemistry; fischer-tropsch chemistry; polyolefins; ziegler-natta catalysis; hydrocarbon pyrolysis; high density polyethylene; engineering plastics. **Mailing Address:** 837 Baltimore Pike, Chadds Ford, PA 19317. **Fax:** 302-695-1513.

LIBBRECHT, KENNETH G, ASTRONOMY. **Personal Data:** b Fargo, NDak, June 9, 1958; m Rachel; c 2. **Education:** Caltech, BS, Phy, 1980; Univ Princeton, PhD, Phy, 1984. **Honors & Awards:** Newton Lacy Pierce Prize, Am Astron Soc, 1991. **Professional Experience:** CHAIR, DEPT PHYSICS, CALIF INST TECHNOL, as of 2004; EXEC OFFICER, DEPT PHYSICS, CALIF INST TECHNOL, 1997-; PROF PHYSICS, CALIF INST TECHNOL, 1995-; from asst prof to assoc prof, Calif Inst Technol, 1984-1995. **Memberships:** Am Astron Soc. **Research Statement & Publications:** Astronomy. **Mailing Address:** Dep Physics Calif Inst Technol, 264-33, Pasadena, CA 91125. **Fax:** 626-395-3814. **E-Mail:** kgl@caltech.edu

LIBBY, PAUL A(NDREWS), AERONAUTICAL ENGINEERING. **Personal Data:** b Mineola, NY, September 4, 1921; m 1955, c 2. **Education:** Polytech Inst Brooklyn, BAE, 1942, MS, 1947, PhD, 1949. **Honors & Awards:** Royal Soc Guest Fel, 1982-1983. **Professional Experience:** PROF EMER FLUID MECH, UNIV CALIF, SAN DIEGO, as of 2003; consult, Avco, 1976 & Systs Sci & Software, 1976-; Guggenheim fel, 1972-1973; assoc dean grad studies, Univ Calif, San Diego, 1967-1972; corresp mem, Eng Sci Sect, Int Acad Astronaut, Int Astronaut Fedn, 1966-; mem, Air Force Systs Command Scramjet Panel, 1964-1965 & Nat Acad Sci Adv Comn on Scramjet, 1965-; prof fluid mech, Univ Calif, San Diego, beginning 1964; mem, Fluid Mech Adv Comn, NASA, 1963-1969; mem, Fluid Dynamics Panel, Adv Group Aerospace Res & Develop, NATO, 1960-1972; asst dir aerodyn lab, Polytech Inst Brooklyn, 1959-1964; Gen Appl Sci Labs, Inc, 1956-1972; consult, NAm Aviation, Gen Elec Co, 1956; NAm Aviation, Inc, 1955; from asst prof to prof, Polytech Inst Brooklyn, 1949-1964; consult, Gen Bronze Corp, 1948; instr aeronaut eng, Polytech Inst Brooklyn, 1943-1944, 1946-1949; design engr, Chance Vought Aircraft Co, Conn, 1942-1943. **Memberships:** Fel Am Inst Aeronaut & Astronaut; Am Phys Soc. **Research Statement & Publications:** Combustion theory; turbulent flow; turbulent combustion. **Mailing Address:** Dept AMES, Univ Calif San Diego, La Jolla, CA 92093. **Fax:** 858-534-5354. **E-Mail:** libby @ mae.ucsd.edu

LIBBY, PAUL ROBERT, BIOCHEMISTRY, ENZYMOLOGY & ENDOCRINOLOGY. **Personal Data:** b Torrington, Conn, September 2, 1934; m 1968, Barbara; c 3. **Education:** Yale Univ, BS, 1956; Univ Chicago, PhD (biochem), 1962. **Professional Experience:** RETIRED; assoc res prof, Dept Pharmacol, 1980-1991; res prof, Niagara Univ, NY, beginning 1978; assoc cancer res scientist, Roswell Park Mem Inst, 1972-1991; from asst to assoc res prof, Dept Physiol, State Univ NY, 1971-1980; sr cancer res scientist, Roswell Park Mem Inst, 1963-1972; Fel biochem, Univ Calif, Davis, 1962-1963. **Memberships:** AAAS; Am Asn Cancer Res; Endocrine Soc; Am Chem Soc; Am Soc Cell Biol. **Research Statement & Publications:** Biochemical mechanisms of chemical carcinogenesis. **Mailing Address:** 93 Melody Lane, Tonawanda, NY 14150. **E-Mail:** libby@att.net

LIBBY, PETER, CELL BIOLOGY, CARDIOVASCULAR MEDICINE. **Personal Data:** b Berkeley, Calif, February 13, 1947; m 1975, c 2. **Education:** Univ Calif, Berkeley, BA, 1969; Univ Calif, San Diego, MD, 1973. **Honorary Degrees:** MA, Harvard Univ, 1996. **Honors & Awards:** Merit Award, Nat Heart, Lung & Blood Inst. **Professional Experience:** MALLINCKRODT PROF MED, HARVARD MED SCH, 1998-; CHIEF, CARDIOVASC MED, BRIGHAM & WOMEN'S HOSP, BOSTON, 1996-; PHYSICIAN & DIR, VASCULAR MED & ATHEROSCLEROSIS UNIT, CARDIOVASC DIV, DEPT MED BRIGHAM & WOMEN'S HOSP, 1990-; assoc prof physiol, Sch Med, Tufts Univ, 1988-1990; from asst prof to assoc prof med, Sch Med, Tufts Univ, 1980-1990; fel, Med Found, 1980-1982; cardiol fel, Brigham & Women's Hosp, 1979-1980; res fel physiol, Med Sch, Harvard Univ, 1976-1979; nat res serv award, Nat Heart, Lung & Blood Inst, 1976-1977; S A Levine fel, Am Heart Asn, 1976-1977; res physician, Peter Bent Brigham Hosp, 1973-1976; estab investr, Am Heart Asn; assoc prof med, Harvard Med Sch. **Memberships:** Am Heart Asn; Am Soc Cell Biol; AAAS; Am Fedn Clin Res; Am Soc Physiol; Am Soc Clin Invest; Am Col Cardiol; Am Asn Pathologists; Am Asn Immunologists; Asn Am Physicians. **Research Statement & Publications:** Cellular, molecular, and inflammatory aspects of cardiovascular diseases; atherogenesis; arterial wall biology. **Mailing Address:** Vascular Med Unit, Brigham & Women's Hosp, 75 Francis St, Boston, MA 02115. **Fax:** 617-732-6961. **E-Mail:** plibby@rics.bwh.harvard.edu

LIBBY, R DANIEL, ENZYMOLOGY, BIO-ORGANIC CHEMISTRY. **Personal Data:** b Waterville, Maine, February 5, 1946; m 1969, Carol Baker; c Lisa K. **Education:** Colby Col, AB, 1968; Pa State Univ, PhD (chem), 1974. **Professional Experience:** ASSOC PROF & CHAIR CHEM, MORAVIAN COL, 1992-; asst prof chem, Colby Col, 1985-1992; asst prof chem, Barnard Col, 1982-1985; res assoc biochem, Univ Ill, 1980-1982; asst prof chem, Skidmore Col, 1977-1980; vis asst prof chem, Kenyan Col, 1975-1977; vis asst prof chem, Oberlin Col, 1974-1975. **Memberships:** Am Chem Soc; Nat Col Sci Teachers Asn. **Research Statement & Publications:** Develop an understanding of the interplay among the pathways of the many reactions catalyzed by the enzyme chloroperoxidase. **Mailing Address:** Dept Chem Moravian Col, 1200 Main St, Bethlehem, PA 18018-6650. **Fax:** 610-625-7918. **E-Mail:** rdlibby@cs.moravian.edu

LIBBY, WILLIAM JOHN, FORESTRY, GENETICS. **Personal Data:** b Oak Park, Ill, September 10, 1932; m 1991, Iris; c Lisa (Albert), Eric L & Sara (Wampler). **Education:** Univ Mich, BS, 1954; Univ Calif, Berkeley, MS, 1959, PhD (genetics), 1961. **Professional Experience:** CONSULT, CTR ADVAN FOREST BIOTECHNOL, TE TEKO, NZ, 1994-; vis scientist, NZ Forest Res Inst, 1992-1993; HR MacMillan lectr, Univ BC, 1987; lectr, Swed Agr Univ, Garpenberg, Umea, 1985; sr fel, Norweg Forest Res Inst, 1980; Fulbright res scholar, Univ Zagreb, 1979; prof forestry & genetics, Univ Calif, Berkeley, 1972-1994; Fulbright res scholar, NZ Forest Res Inst, Univ Canterbury, Australian Forest Res Inst, 1971; L T Murray distinguished vis lectr forest resources, Univ Wash, 1968; assoc prof forestry & genetics, Univ Calif, Berkeley, 1967-1972; Pack lectr, Yale Univ, 1967; asst prof forestry, Univ Calif, Berkeley, 1962-1967; NSF fel genetics, NC State Col, 1961-1962. **Memberships:** Soc Am Foresters. **Research Statement & Publications:** Quantitative genetics of forest trees; genetic conservation; vegetative propagation of conifers; maturation of woody plant meristems; clonal forestry. **Mailing Address:** Ctr Forestry, 9A Eruini St, 28 Valencia Rd, Orinda, CA 94563. **Fax:** 510-376-7928. **E-Mail:** 100232.213@compuserve.com

LIBCHABER, ALBERT JOSEPH, PHYSICS GENERAL, FLUIDS MOLECULAR BIOLOGY. **Personal Data:** b Paris, France, October 23, 1934; American citizen; m 1955, Irene; c Jacques, Remy & David. **Education:** Univ Paris, BS, 1956; Univ Ill, MS, 1959; Sch Normale Super, Paris, PhD, 1965. **Honors & Awards:** Silver Medal, Fr Phys Soc, 1971, Prix Richard, 1979; Wolf Prize, Wolf Found, 1986. **Professional Experience:** DETLEV W BRONK PROF, ROCKEFELLER UNIV, 1995-; fel, NEC res inst, Princeton, 1991-; prof, dept Physics, Princeton Univ, NY, 1991-1994; ed, J nonlinearity, 1987-1993; prof, Paul Snowden distinguished serv prof physics, 1987-1991; MacArthur Found fel, 1986-1991, prof, Univ Chicago, 1983-1991; dir, Nat Ctr Sci res, Sch Normale, Paris, 1974-1983; Master res, Nat Ctr Sci res, Sch Normale, Paris, 1967-1974. **Memberships:** Am Phys Soc; Fr Phys Soc; Am Acad Arts & Sci; NY Acad Sci; corresp mem French Acad Sci. **Research Statement & Publications:** Physics; implications of nonlinear dynamics on the physical world, including the biological sciences; the evolution of fluids from laminar states, with emphasis on plate tectonics-like problems, coexistence of convections and solidification. **Mailing Address:** Rockefeller Univ, Box No 265 1230 York Ave, New York, NY 10021-6399. **Fax:** 212-327-7406. **E-Mail:** libchbr@rockvax.rockefeller.edu

LIBELO, LOUIS FRANCIS, THEORETICAL PHYSICS. **Personal Data:** b Brooklyn, NY, October 12, 1930. **Education:** Brooklyn Col, BS, 1953; Univ Md, MS, 1956; Rensselaer Polytech Inst, PhD (physics), 1964. **Honors & Awards:** Hinman Award, 1987; Inst Elec & Electronics Engrs Technol Achievement 1987. **Professional Experience:** Sr Sci, Sachs Freeman Assoc/Consultant & NRL 1998-; delegate, Nat Asn Acad Sci, 1997; vis scholar, Rensselaer Polytech Inst, 1996- 1998; guest res, US Naval Res Lab, 1996- 1998; fel-elect, Summa Found 1996; RES PHYSICIST, HARRY DIAMOND LAB, ARMY RES LAB, 1980-; consult physicist, Entron Inc & Lutech Inc, 1978-1981; consult physicist, L & L Assocs, 1976-; adj prof, State Univ NY, Albany, 1973-1979; adj prof, Am Univ, 1968-1973; asst prof physics, Am Univ, 1965-1968; Res physicist, US Naval Surface Weapons Ctr, 1964-1980; physicist, Opers Res Off, Johns Hopkins Univ, 1957-1958; proj engr, Ahrendt Instrument Co, 1955; Engr physics, Md Electronics Co, 1954. **Memberships:** Inst Elec & Electronic Engrs; Am Phys Soc; Electromagnetic Soc; Sigma Xi; NY Acad Sci. **Research Statement & Publications:** Scattering theory for finite size targets and by apertures; theory of cooperative phenomena in solids; theory of nonlinear phenomena in insulators; microwaves and electromagnet theory; interaction, coupling and generation; nonlinear optics. **Mailing Address:** L&L Assocs, 9413 Bulls Run Pkwy, Bethesda, MD 20817.

LIBERA, RICHARD JOSEPH, MATHEMATICS. **Personal Data:** b Thorndike, Mass, August 26, 1929; m 1954, c 2. **Education:** Am Int Col, BA, 1956; Univ Mass, MA, 1958; Rutgers Univ, PhD (math), 1962. **Professional Experience:** PROF EMER MATH, UNIV DEL, as of 2004; prof math, Univ Del, beginning 1973; from asst prof to assoc prof, Univ Del, 1962-1973; instr math, Rutgers Univ, 1960-1962. **Memberships:** Am Math Soc; Math Asn Am; Polish Math Soc. **Research Statement & Publications:** Geometric function theory. **Mailing Address:** Dept Math, Univ Del, 535 Ewing Hall, Newark, DE 19716. **Fax:** 302-831-4511. **E-Mail:** libera@math.udel.edu

LIBERATORE, FREDERICK ANTHONY, PROTEIN BIOCHEMISTRY. **Personal Data:** b Framingham, Mass, December 11, 1944; m 1968, Jeannine; c 4. **Education:** Mass State Col Framingham, BA, 1970; Univ NH, PhD (biochem), 1974. **Professional Experience:** Mem staff, DuPont, New Eng Nuclear Corp, 1978-2001; mem staff, Sigma Chem Co, 1976-1978; fel, Ohio State Univ, 1974-1976. **Memberships:** Sigma Xi; Am Chem Soc mem. **Research Statement & Publications:** Labeling proteins with radioactive isotopes including iodine; protein cross-linking; bifunctional chelators; protein purification and characterization; enzyme-linked immunosorbent assay and radio isotopic assay; protein purification; industrial scale-up. **Mailing Address:** 49 Liberty Dr, North Billerica, MA 01862-3276. **E-Mail:** liberafa@aol.com

LIBERMAN, ALLEN HARVEY, ELECTRICAL ENGINEERING. **Personal Data:** b Memphis, Tenn, September 15, 1943. **Education:** Rensselaer Polytech Inst, BS, 1965; Carnegie Inst Technol, MS, 1966; Univ Detroit, DEng (elec eng), 1968. **Professional Experience:** PARTNER, TRADE QUOTES INC, 1981-; vpres finance, DBX Inc, Newton, 1974-1981; vpres & dir comput res & develop, Nat Info Serv, Inc, 1969-1974; vpres comput res & develop, Mgt Sci Inc, 1969-1970; adj prof & grant, Univ Detroit, 1969-1970; assoc dir comput eng, Univ Detroit, 1969; consult, Burroughs Corp, 1968-1969; asst prof comput design, Univ Detroit, 1967-1969; engr, Fairchild Camera & Instrument Corp, 1964-1967 & Hell Corp, 1965; technician, Digital Electronics Inc, 1962-1963. **Memberships:** Am Soc Eng Educ; Inst Elec & Electronics Engrs. **Research Statement & Publications:** Digital computer applications in personal identification and high density photographic memories; multi-user, multi-task minicomputer operating systems. **Mailing Address:** Trade Quotes Inc, 675 Mass Ave, Cambridge, MA 02139. **Fax:** 617-354-3355.

LIBERMAN, ARTHUR DAVID, HIGH ENERGY PHYSICS, NUCLEAR WELL LOGGING. **Personal Data:** b Newark, NJ, October 13, 1940; m 1968, c 2. **Education:** Dartmouth Col, BA, 1962; Harvard Univ, MA, 1963, PhD (physics), 1969. **Professional Experience:** SR SCIENTIST, SCHLUMBERGER DOLL RES, as of 2001; staff mem, Schlumberger-Doll Res Ctr, beginning 1980; res physicist, High Energy Physics Lab, Stanford Univ, 1974-1980; adj asst prof particle physics, Univ Calif, Los Angeles, 1970-1974; res assoc high energy physics, Linear Accelerator Lab, Univ Paris, 1969-1970. **Memberships:** Am Phys Soc. **Research Statement & Publications:** The study of gamma rays and entirely neutral final states in the annihilation interactions at electron-positron storage rings by utilizing the crystal ball, a large solid angle, good energy resolution, highly modularized NaI(Tl) detector. **Mailing Address:** Schlumberger-Doll Res Ctr, Old Quarry Rd, Ridgefield, CT 06877. **Fax:** 203-438-3819. **E-Mail:** liberman@sdr.slb.com

LIBERMAN, IRVING, LASERS, OPTICAL PROCESSING & DEVICES. **Personal Data:** b New York, NY, June 24, 1937. **Education:** City Col New York, BEE, 1958; Northwestern Univ, MSEE, 1960, PhD (elec eng), 1965. **Professional Experience:** Indust staff mem, Los Alamos Nat Lab, 1974-1980; MGR MICROSYSTS, NORTHROP GRUMMAN SCI & TECHNOL CTR, 1963-. **Memberships:** Am Phys Soc; Optical Soc Am; Sigma Xi. **Research Statement & Publications:** Development of optically pumped solid state lasers and transverse electrically excited gas lasers; design, installation, alignment, and evaluation of optical systems; development of miniature atomic clocks; development of electro-optical components and devices. **Mailing Address:** 1501 Ardmore Blvd, Pittsburgh, PA 15221. **Fax:** 412-256-1661.

LIBERMAN, MARTIN HENRY, ANALYTICAL & POLYMER CHEMISTRY. **Personal Data:** b Los Angeles, Calif, October 5, 1936; m 1967, c 1. **Education:** Univ Calif, Los Angeles, BS, 1958; Fla State Univ, PhD (phys chem), 1968. **Professional Experience:** CUSTOM OFFICER, US CUSTOMS LAB & BORDER PROTECTION, as of 2004; CHEMIST, US CUSTOMS SERV, 1974-; res assoc, Stanford Univ, 1968-1972; asst, US Army Med Res & Nutrit Lab, Denver, Colo, 1960-1962. **Memberships:** Am Chem Soc; Royal Soc Chem; AAAS. **Research Statement & Publications:** Analytical chemistry; polymer chemistry. **Mailing Address:** US Customs Lab & Border Protection, 630 Sansome St Rm 1407, San Francisco, CA 94111. **E-Mail:** martin.h.liberman@treas.gov

LIBERMAN, ROBERT PAUL, PSYCHIATRY, CLINICAL PSYCHOLOGY. **Personal Data:** b Newark, NJ, August 16, 1937; m 1973, c 5. **Education:** Dartmouth Col, AB, 1959; Dartmouth Med Sch, dipl med, 1960; Univ Calif, MS, 1961; Johns Hopkins Univ, MD, 1963. **Honors & Awards:** First Prize, Int Rehab Film Festival, 1983; Silvano Arieti Award, Am Acad Psychoanal, 1986; Samuel Hibbs Award Innovations Treat, Am Psychiat Asn, 1988, Arnold Van Ameringen Award, Psychiat Rehab, 1989; Howard Davis Mem Award, Knowledge Transfer Soc, 1989. **Professional Experience:** Co-prin investr, Ctr Improving Ment Health Servs, 1991-1996; pres, Psychiat Rehab Consults, 1985-; consult, Charter Pac Hosp, 1984-1987; assoc ed, Schizophrenia Bull, 1980-1986; proj dir, Rehab Res & Training Ctr, 1980-1985; chief rehab med serv, Brentwood VA Med Ctr, 1980; mem, Res Rev Comt, NIMH, 1979-1981; prof psychiat, Sch Med, Univ Calif, Los Angeles, 1977-; prin investr, Mental Health Clin Res Ctr, 1977-; PROF PSYCHIAT RESIDENCE, SCH MED, UNIV CALIF, LOS ANGELES, 1977-; assoc ed, J Appl Behav Anal, 1976-1977; Fogarty sr res int fel, NIH, 1975-1976; consult, Ventura Co, Los Angeles Co Ment Health Dept & Calif State Dept Ment Health, 1972-; consult various insts & govt, 1970-; mem med staff, var hosps, 1970-; dir, prog clin res, Camarillo-Neuropsychiat Inst Res Prog, 1970-; from asst prof to assoc prof, 1970-1976; res scientist, NIMH, 1968-1970; NIMH res grants, 1967-; intern internal med, Bronx Munic Hosp Ctr, Albert Einstein Col Med, 1963-1964; PRIN INVESTR & DIR, MENT HEALTH CLIN RES CTR SCHIZOPHRENIA & PSYCHIAT REHAB. **Memberships:** Fel Am Psychiat Asn; Asn Advan Behav Ther; Physicians Social Responsibility; Int Physicians Against Nuclear War. **Research Statement & Publications:** Experimental analysis of behavior in clinical psychiatry and psychology; interactions between drug effects and behavior modification; community mental health; behavior therapy; schizophrenia; author of numerouus publications. **Mailing Address:** Community & Rehab Psychiat, W Los Angeles VA Med Ctr 11301 Wilshire Blvd, Los Angeles, CA 90073. **E-Mail:** rliberman@mednet.ucla.edu

LIBERSON, GARY, MATHEMATICAL STATISTICS. **Education:** PhD (statist). **Professional Experience:** SR MGT, PA LIFE SCI, as of 2005. **Memberships:** Agr & Nat Resources Comt. **Mailing Address:** 4601 N Fairfax Dr Ste 600, Arlington, VA 22203. **Fax:** 571-227-9001. **E-Mail:** info@paconsulting.com

LIBERTA, ANTHONY E, MYCOLOGY. **Personal Data:** b La Salle, Ill, May 17, 1933; m 1960, Susan; c Marc R & Valerie S. **Education:** Knox Col, Ill, AB, 1955; Univ Ill, Urbana, MS, 1959, PhD (bot), 1961. **Professional Experience:** EMER PROF, ILL STATE UNIV, 1993-; distinguished prof, Ill State Univ, 1990-1993; NSF grants, 1963-1971 & 1981-1987; from assoc prof to prof mycol, Ill State Univ, 1961-1990; res mycologist, Ill State Natural Hist Surv, 1961. **Memberships:** Mycol Soc Am. **Research Statement & Publications:** Effects of soil disturbance and surface-mining on endomycorrhizae; ecological relationships of prairie plants and endomycorrhizae; antifungal/antitumor activity of thiosemicarbazones; taxonomy of basidiomycetes fungi. **Mailing Address:** 905 Ruston Ave, Normal, IL 61761-2817.

LIBERTI, FRANK NUNZIO, POLYMER CHEMISTRY, PHYSICAL CHEMISTRY. **Personal Data:** b Warsaw, NY, November 2, 1939; m 1966, Margaret; c Patricia & Michael. **Education:** Rensselaer Polytech Inst, BChE, 1961, PhD (phys chem), 1967. **Professional Experience:** SITE RAW MAT PROGS LEADER, GEN ELEC PLASTICS, 1993-; prog commercialization leader, Lexan Core Prod Technol, 1990-1993; mgr, Lexan Core Prod Technol, 1988-1990; mgr prod develop progs, Plastics Bus Group, 1985-1988; mgr process technol, Gen Elec Co, 1979-1985; specialist prod develop, Gen Elec Co, 1976-

1979; specialist advan develop, Gen Elec Co, 1975-1976; mgr qual assurance, Gen Elec Co, 1973-1975; specialist prod develop, Gen Elec Co, 1969-1973; Develop chemist, Gen Elec Co, 1967-1969. **Memberships:** Soc Plastics Engrs. **Research Statement & Publications:** Stabilization of polymers; flame retardant polymers; solid state of polymers; polymer crystallinity; thermal analysis of polymers. **Mailing Address:** Gen Elec Plastics, One Lexan Lane, Mt Vernon, IN 47620. **Fax:** 812-831-7189. **E-Mail:** frank.liberti@gep.ge.com

LIBERTI, JOSEPH POLLARA, CELL BIOLOGY. **Personal Data:** b Passaic, NJ, November 2, 1937. **Education:** Fairleigh Dickinson Univ, BS, 1959; Loyola Univ, MS, 1962, PhD (biochem), 1964. **Professional Experience:** Vis scientist, Sloan-Kettering Cancer Inst, 1983-1984; vis prof, Oxford Univ, 1977-1978; PROF BIOCHEM, MED COL VA, RICHMOND, 1975-; from asst prof to assoc prof, Med Col VA, Richmond, 1967-1975; res assoc, Mem Sloan-Kettering Cancer Inst, 1966-1967; Instr biochem, Cornell Univ Med Ctr, 1966-1967; res fel endocrinol, Mem Sloan-Kettering Cancer Inst, 1965-1966; Res fel biochem, Univ Minn, 1964-1965. **Memberships:** Endocrine Soc; Am Chem Soc; Am Soc Biochem & Molecular Biol. **Research Statement & Publications:** Regulation of cell growth and proliferation: molecular actions of lactogenic hormones, particularly post-receptor signalling events. **Mailing Address:** Dept Biochem Box 614, Med Col Va Sta Med Col Va, Richmond, VA 23298.

LIBERTI, PAUL A, MAGNETIC LIQUIDS. **Personal Data:** b Lyndhurst, NJ, March 18, 1936; m 1996, Rae; c Paul P, Theodore, Roseanne & Joseph. **Education:** Columbia Col, BA, 1959; Loyola Univ, Ill, MS, 1961; Stevens Inst Technol, PhD (phys chem), 1966. **Honors & Awards:** Ottens Res Award, 1969; Nat Inst Allergy & Infectious Dis res career develop award, 1973. **Professional Experience:** CONSULT & MEM, IMMUNICON SCIENTIFIC ADV BD, 2004-; chief tech officer, Immunicon Corp, ending 2004; founder & chief exec officer, Immunicon Corp, 1986-1999; adj prof biochem, Jefferson Med Col, 1984-; pres & chief scientist, 1983-1994; from instr to prof biochem, Jefferson Med Col, 1967-1984; res fel phys chem, Stevens Inst Technol, 1966; lectr, Fairleigh Dickenson Univ, 1964-1967 & Temple Univ, 1967-. **Memberships:** Am Asn Immunol; Am Asn Biol Chem; Am Soc Hemat. **Research Statement & Publications:** Discovery and development of magnetic liquids and their application to tumor cell detection, cell ethergy and immuno assay. **Mailing Address:** Immunicon Corp, 3401 Masons Mill Rd Ste 100, Huntingdon Valley, PA 19006. **Fax:** 215-830-0751.

LIBERTINY, GEORGE ZOLTAN, MECHANICAL ENGINEERING, MATERIALS SCIENCE. **Personal Data:** b Szolnok, Hungary, June 14, 1934; American citizen; m 1956, Anna; c Thomas & Karen. **Education:** Univ Strathclyde, BS, 1959; Bristol Univ, PhD (mech eng), 1964. **Honors & Awards:** R R Teetor Award, Soc Automotive Engrs, 1967; Forest R McFarland Award, 1983; Outstanding Engr Award, Mich Soc Professional Engrs, 1984; Triodyne Safety Award, Am Soc Mech Eng, 1997. **Professional Experience:** Adj prof mech eng, Univ Mich, 1983-2001; assoc ed, J Vibration, Stress & Reliability Design, 1982-1986; prin res eng assoc, Automotive Safety Off, Ford Motor Co, 1978-1996; Eng Educ Comt, Am Soc Mech Engrs, 1974-; eng educ comt, Soc Automotive Engrs, 1973-1986; prin res eng assoc, Advan Testing Methods Dept, 1973-1978; sr res engr, Automotive Safety Off, Ford Motor Cc, 1971-1973; assoc prof, Ill Inst Technol, 1968-1971; mem, US Adv Comt, Int Stand Orgn Fluid Power, 1968-1971; FOUNDER & PRIN CONSULT, DESIGN & MFG DEFECT CONSULT, 1964-; from asst prof to assoc prof mech eng, Univ Miami, 1963-1968; res & develop engr, English Elec Co Ltd, Eng, 1959-1960. **Memberships:** Life fel Am Soc Mech Engrs; Soc Automotive Engrs. **Research Statement & Publications:** Fatigue of metals; static and dynamic fractures due to multiaxial stress-strain systems; nondestructive testing; experimental stress analysis; high pressure engineering; design; safety risk analysis; special transducer; US Patent no 387995. **Mailing Address:** Design & Mfg Defect Consult, 24637 Rockford St, Dearborn, MI 48124.

LIBESKIND, SHLOMO, MATHEMATICS. **Professional Experience:** PROF, DEPT MATH, UNIV ORE, as of 2004. **Mailing Address:** Dept Math, Univ Ore, Eugene, OR 97403. **Fax:** 541-346-0987. **E-Mail:** shlomo@darkwing.uoregon.edu

LIBESKIND-HADAS, RAN, COMPUTER SCIENCE. **Education:** Harvard Univ, BA, 1987; Univ Ill, Urbana-Champaign, MS, 1989 & PhD (Comput Sci), 1993. **Professional Experience:** PROF, DEPT COMPUT SCI, HARVEY MUDD COL, 2003-; from asst prof to assoc prof, Dept Comput Sci, Harvey Mudd Col, 1994-2003; asst prof, Dept Math, Harvey Mudd Col, 1993-1994. **Research Statement & Publications:** Routing algorithms for optical networks; collective communication in parallel computers and networks of workstations; algorithm design and analysis and complexity theory. **Mailing Address:** Dept Comput Sci, Harvey Mudd Col, 1250 N Dartmouth Ave, Claremont, CA 91711. **E-Mail:** hadas@cs.hmc.edu

LIBET, BENJAMIN, PHYSIOLOGY. **Personal Data:** b Chicago, Ill, April 12, 1916; m 1939, Fay; c Julian, Moreen, Ralph & Gayla. **Education:** Univ Chicago, BS, 1936, PhD (physiol), 1939. **Professional Experience:** EMER PROF PHYSIOL, MED SCH, UNIV CALIF, SAN FRANCISCO, 1984-; vis scientist, Japan Soc for Promotion Sci, 1979; scholar, Bellagio Study, Ctr Rockfeller Found, 1977; from asst to prof physiol, Med Sch, Univ Calif, San Francisco, 1962-1984; consult, Mt Zion Neurol Inst, 1956-; fel, Commonwealth Fund, 1956-1957 & 1964; staff physiologist, Kabat-Kaiser Inst, 1948-1949; from instr to asst prof physiol, Univ Chicago, 1945-1948; mat engr, Personal Equip Lab, USAF, Ohio, 1944-1945; instr physiol, Sch Med, Univ Pa, 1943-1944; res assoc physiol & biochem, Inst Pa Hosp, 1940-1943; instr, Albany Med Col, 1939-1940; asst physiol, Univ Chicago, 1937-1939. **Memberships:** Fel AAAS; Am Physiol Soc; Soc Neuroscience; Int Brain Res Orgn. **Research Statement & Publications:** Neurophysiology; electrical and metabolic aspects of neural function; synaptic mechanisms; cerebral mechanisms in conscious experience. **Mailing Address:** Dept Physiol, Sch Med Univ Calif, San Francisco, CA 94143-0444.

LIBOFF, ABRAHAM R, MEDICAL PHYSICS, BIOPHYSICS. **Personal Data:** b Paterson, NJ, August 27, 1927; m 1952, Mildred; c Margery. **Education:** Brooklyn Col, BS, 1948; NY Univ, MS, 1952, PhD (physics), 1964. **Professional Experience:** PROF EMER PHYSICS, OAKLAND UNIV, as of 2001; ed, Electromagnetic Biol & Med, beginning 2002; res prof Fla Atlantic Univ, 2002; dir med physics prog, Oakland Univ, 1973-1997; prof physics & chmn dept, Oakland Univ, 1972-2001; sr res scientist & proj coordr, Biophys Res Lab, 1969-1972; adj assoc prof physics, Hunter Col, NY, 1968-1972; assoc dir environ radiation lab, NY Univ, 1968-1969; assoc res scientist, NY Univ, 1964-1968; res asst cosmic ray lab, NY Univ, 1959-1964; sr physicist, Metall Res Lab, Sylvania Elec Prod, Inc, 1951-1958; jr physicist, Naval Ord Lab, Md, 1948-1950. **Memberships:** Am Phys Soc; Biophys Soc; Am Geophys Union; Am Asn Physicists in Med; Bioelec Repair & Growth Soc (secy, 1981) Bioelectromagnetics Soc. **Research Statement & Publications:** Electromagnetic Interactions with tissul, Physics of collagenous tissues; biophysics of growth and development; electrically induced osteogenesis; sea-level cosmic ray ionization; environmental radiation; acoustic detection of nucleonic cascades; pyroelectric properties of bone. **Mailing Address:** Dept Physics, Oakland Univ, Rochester, MI 48309-4401. **E-Mail:** arliboff@aol.com

LIBOFF, RICHARD L, THEORETICAL PHYSICS. **Personal Data:** b New York, NY, December 30, 1931; m 1954, c 2. **Education:** Brooklyn Col, AB, 1953; NY Univ, PhD (physics), 1961. **Professional Experience:** PROF EMER ELEC & COMPUT ENG, CORNELL UNIV, as of 2006; Fulbright scholar, 1984; consult, Battelle Columbus Lab, 1983 & 1985; Vis prof physics, Univ Paris, Orsay, 1979 & Tel Aviv Univ, 1984 & 1985; Air Force Off Sci Res, 1977-1981 & Army Res Off, 1983-; Solvay fel, Univ Brussels, 1971; prof elec eng & appl physics, Cornell Univ, beginning 1969; prin investr, Off Naval Res contract, 1966-1976; assoc prof, Cornell Univ, 1964-1969; chief consult, NRA, Inc, 1963-1965; asst prof physics, NY Univ, 1962-1964; res asst appl math, Courant Inst Math Sci, NY Univ, 1956-1961. **Memberships:** Sigma Xi; fel Am Phys Soc; sr mem Inst Elec & Electronics Engrs. **Research Statement & Publications:** Kinetic theory; quantum mechanics; short wavelength lasing; fusion physics; dense recombining plasma; strongly coupled plasmas and fluids; condensed-matter theory; semiconductor transport and superlattice theory; applied mathematics with emphasis on classical and quantum chaos; author of 3 technical books. **Mailing Address:** Dept Elec Eng, Cornell Univ, 117 Phillips Hall, Ithaca, NY 14850. **E-Mail:** richard@ece.cornell.edu

LIBONATI, JOSEPH PETER, CLINICAL MICROBIOLOGY. **Personal Data:** b Philadelphia, Pa, November 16, 1941; m 1969, c 3. **Education:** St Joseph's Col, Pa, BS, 1963; Duquesne Univ, MS, 1965; Univ Md, Baltimore, PhD (microbiol), 1968. **Professional Experience:** CHIEF, DIV MICROBIOL, LABS ADMIN, MD STATE DEPT HEALTH & MENT HYG, 1977-; SPEC LECTR MICROBIOL, SCH DENT, UNIV MD, BALTIMORE, 1969-; from instr to asst prof med clin microbiol, Sch Med, 1968-1977. **Memberships:** AAAS; Am Soc Microbiol. **Research Statement & Publications:** Enteric bacterial diseases; pathophysiology; immunologic response and vaccine development. **Mailing Address:** 3801 Juniper Rd, Baltimore, MD 21218.

LIBOW, LESLIE S, GERIATRICS, INTERNAL MEDICINE. **Personal Data:** b New York, NY, m 1973, Linda; c Adam & Alama. **Education:** Brooklyn Col, BA, 1954; Chicago Med Sch, MD, 1958. **Honors & Awards:** Kent Award, Geront Soc Am, 1981; Mascher-Manning Award, Am Geriat Soc, 1987. **Professional Experience:** PROF MED, MT SINAI SCH MED, as of 2004; SR VICE PRES, MED AFFAIRS, JEWISH HOME & HOSP NY, as of 2004; prof med, State Univ NY Stony Brook, beginning 1978; consult to dir, Nat inst Aging, Bethesda, beginning 1976; consult, NIH, beginning 1975; chief geriat med, Long Island Jewish Hillside Med Ctr, NY, 1975-; assoc prof, State Univ NY Stony Brook, 1975-1978; from asst prof to assoc prof med, Mt Sinai Sch Med, NY, 1967-1975; chief geriat med, Mt Sinai City Hosp Ctr, Elmhurst, NY, 1964-1975; resident, Mt Sinai Hosp New York, 1963-1964; res assoc, NIH, 1962-1963; clin assoc bio-med psychiat, NIH, 1960-1962; resident, Bronx Vet Admin Hosp, 1959-1960; intern, Mt Sinai Hosp New York, 1958-1959; CLIN DIR LONG TERM CARE DEPT, GERIAT & ADULT DEVELOP, MT SINAI SCH MED & CHIEF MED SERV, JEWISH HOME & HOSP AGED, NY; med dir, Jewish inst Geriat Care, New Hyde Park, NY. **Memberships:** Geront Soc; Am Geriat Soc; Am Col Physicians; AAAS. **Research Statement & Publications:** Diseases of late life; brain and behavioral changes; human aging; thyroid disease; health care delivery. **Mailing Address:** Dept Geriat & Adult Develop, Mt Sinai Sch Med, 120 W 106th St, New York, NY 10029. **Fax:** 212-870-4905.

LIBOWITZ, GEORGE GOTTHART, solid state chemistry, materials science; deceased, see previous edition for last biography

LIBURDY, ROBERT P, EXPERIMENTAL BIOLOGY. **Personal Data:** b Detroit, Mich, October 23, 1947. **Education:** Brown Univ, PhD (biochem), 1975; Univ Northern Colo, MBA, 1980. **Professional Experience:** Prin investr, Dept Energy Proj, 1988- & NIH Proj, High-Field NMR Bioeffects, 1991-; co-prin investr, Dept Energy Proj, Off Health & Environ Res, 1988-; adj prof mech eng, Col Eng, Clemson Univ, SC, 1987-; prin investr, Liposome Technol Inc, Menlo Park, Calif, 1986-; RES STAFF SCIENTIST, LAWRENCE BERKELEY LAB, RES MED & RADIATION BIOPHYS DIV, BIOELECTROMAGNETIC RES FACIL, 1984-; prin investr, Div Res Resources, NIH, 1984-1985; course instr, Health Effects Nonionizing Electromagnetic Radiation, Prog Environ Health Sci & Grad Sch Arts & Sci, NY Univ, Wash Sq, New York, 1983-1984; prin investr, Off Naval Res Proj, 1981-1987; prog environ health sci, Grad Sch Arts & Sci, NY Univ, Wash Sq, New York, 1981-1984; asst prof environ med, Inst Environ Med, NY Univ Med Ctr, New York, NY, 1981-1984; chief, Environ Health Serv, USAF Clin, Electronic Syst Div, Hanscom AFB, Mass, 1980-1981; prin investr, USAF Proj, 1975-1980; prin investr, Electromagnetic Radiation Bioeffects Res Prog, Radiation Sci Div, USAF Sch Aerospace Med, Brooks AFB, 1975-1980; grad teaching fel introductory biol, molecular biophysics & biochem pharmacol, Dept Biol & Med Sci, Brown Univ, 1969-1974. **Memberships:** Am Asn Immunologists; Am Chem Soc; Am HeartAsn; Am Soc Biochem & Molecular Biol; Bioelectromagnetics Soc; Biophys Soc; Inst Elec & Electronics Engrs; NY Acad Sci; Radiation Res Soc; Sigma Xi. **Research Statement & Publications:** Electromagnetic field interactions with biological systems; liposome drug delivery; response of cellular systems to hyperthermia; atherogenesis. **Mailing Address:** Lawrence Berkeley Lab, Lbl-Bldg 934 One Cyclotron Rd, Berkeley, CA 94720.

LICARI, JAMES JOHN, ORGANIC CHEMISTRY. **Personal Data:** b Norwalk, Conn, July 22, 1930; m 1948. **Education:** Fordham Univ, BS, 1952; Princeton Univ, PhD, 1955. **Professional Experience:** PRES, AVAN TECO, as of 2006; lectr, Calif State Univ, Fullerton; mgr, Microcircuit Eng Labs, Rockwell Int Corp, Anaheim, 1972-1988; supvr chem lab, Res & Eng Div, NAm Rockwell Corp, 1970-1972; group scientist, Res & Eng Div, NAm Rockwell Corp, 1967-1970; supvr org chem, NAm Aviation, Inc, 1961-1967; sr res engr, NAm Aviation Inc, 1959-1961; res proj chemist, Am Potash & Chem Corp, 1957-1959; res chemist, Am Cyanamid Co, 1955-1957; asst prof, FordhamUniv, 1955-1956. **Memberships:** Am Chem Soc; Int Soc Hybrid Microelec. **Research Statement & Publications:** Materials and processes for microelectronics. **Mailing Address:** 15711 Arbela Dr, Whittier, CA 90603.

LICEAGA, CARLOS ARTURO, RELIABILITY MODELING, FAULT-TOLERANT COMPUTING. **Personal Data:** b San Juan, PR, November 20, 1958; m 1980, Marisol; c Juan, Camil & Mariel. **Education:** Univ PR, BS, 1981; Col William & Mary, MS, 1984; Carnegie-Mellon Univ, PhD, 1992. **Professional Experience:** EXPLORER ACQUISITION MGR, EARTH & SPACE SCI NASA, 2001-; asst prof comput sci, Col William A Mary, 1993 & comput eng, Old Dominion, 1993; consult comput engr, Compass Consults Corp, 1990; comput sci instr, Thomas Nelson Community Col, 1987-1988; asst instr comput eng, Carnegie-Mellon Univ, 1985; instr, Electronics Col & Comput Prog, 1981; res comput engr, Langley Res Ctr, NASA, beginning 1979. **Memberships:** Inst Elec & Electronics Engrs; Digital Equip Comput Users Soc. **Research Statement & Publications:** Automation of reliability and availability modeling of life-critical fault-tolerant computer systems; software reliability engineering and modeling; fault-tolerant hardware and software research and design. **Mailing Address:** Langley Res Ctr, NASA, MS 160, Hampton, VA 23681-0001. **Fax:** 757-864-8894. **E-Mail:** carlos.a.liceaga@nasa.gov

LI-CHAN, EUNICE, FOOD PROTEIN CHEMISTRY, CHEMICAL MODIFICATION. **Personal Data:** b Hong Kong, October 23, 1953; Canadian citizen; m 1976, Michael; c

Timothy & Nicholas. **Education:** Univ BC, BSc, 1975, PhD (food sci), 1981; Univ Alta, MSc, 1977. **Professional Experience:** PROF, DEPT FOOD SCI, UNIV BC, 1999-; assoc prof, Univ BC, 1994-1999; asst prof, Dept Food Sci, 1992-1994; res assoc food chem, Dept Food Sci, 1983-1991; res asst, Univ BC, 1982-1983; Killam fel food chem, Can Coun, 1980-1982. **Memberships:** Am Chem Soc; Inst Food Technologists; Can Inst Food Sci & Technol; Int AOAC. **Research Statement & Publications:** Properties of food proteins, including the relationship of molecular structure to function; improvement in nutritional and functional properties by chemical or enzymatic modification; utilization of yolk antibodies; raman spectroscopy of food proteins. **Mailing Address:** Dept Food Sci, Univ BC, 6650 NW Marine Dr FNH 212, Vancouver, BC V6T 1Z4, Can. **Fax:** 604-822-3959. **E-Mail:** eunice.li-chan@ubc.ca

LICHENS-PARK, ANN ELIZABETH, RISK ASSESSMENT OF ENVIRONMENTAL INTRODUCTIONS OF BIOTECHNOLOGY PRODUCTS, DEVELOPER OF BIOMONITORING DATABASE ON CD-ROM. **Personal Data:** b Oakland, Calif, September 7, 1958; m 1987, Samuel; c Shirley & Christina. **Education:** Pomona Col, BA, 1980; Harvard Univ, PhD (microbiol & molecular genetics), 1988. **Professional Experience:** NAT PROG LEADER, COOP STATE EDUC & EXTEN SERV, USDA, as of 2005; PROG DIR PLANT PATH MOLECULAR GENETICS MICROBES, COOP STATE EDUC & EXTEN SERV, USDA, 1992-; fel, Harvard Univ, 1988-1989; fel, Dartmouth Med Sch, 1989-1990; res technician, Vet Admin, 1980-1981. **Memberships:** AAAS. **Research Statement & Publications:** Developed a database on CD-ROM containing information pertaining to the safety/risk of field testing biotechnology products. **Mailing Address:** Coop State Educ & Exten Serv, USDA, Stop 2241 1400 Independence Ave SW, Washington, DC 20250-2201. **Fax:** 202-401-4888. **E-Mail:** apark@csrees.usda.gov

LICHT, ARTHUR LEWIS, PHYSICS. **Personal Data:** b Hartford, Conn, December 18, 1934; m 1958. **Education:** Brown Univ, BSc, 1957; Univ Md, PhD (physics), 1963. **Professional Experience:** PROF EMER, UNIV ILL, as of 2006; assoc prof, Univ Ill, beginning 1970; mem sch math, Inst Adv Study, 1965-1966; asst prof, Univ Md, 1963-1965; res physicist, NASA, 1959-1961 & US Naval Ord Lab, 1961-1970; physicist, Nat Bur Stands, 1957-1959. **Memberships:** Am Phys Soc. **Research Statement & Publications:** Space physics; quantum field theory. **Mailing Address:** Dept Physics Univ Ill, 2154 SES, Chicago, IL 60612. **E-Mail:** licht@uic.edu

LICHT, PAUL, ZOOLOGY, ENDOCRINOLOGY. **Personal Data:** b St Louis, Mo, March 12, 1938. **Education:** Wash Univ (Mo), BA, 1959; Univ Mich, MS, 1961, PhD (zoology), 1964. **Honors & Awards:** Grace Pickford Award. **Professional Experience:** PROF EMER, DEPT INTEGRATIVE BIOL, COL LETTERS & SCI, UNIV CALIF, BERKELEY, as of 2005; DIR, ZOOL & CHMN DEPT, UNIV CALIF, BERKELEY as of 2005; dean biological sci, chair deans, Letters & Sci, Univ Calif Berkeley, 1994-2002; prof zool & chmn dept, Univ Calif, Berkeley, beginning 1973; consult ed, Col Div, McGraw-Hill Book Co, 1968-; Lalor Found grant, 1967-1968; USF grants, 1964-1990; from asst prof to assoc prof, Univ Calif, Berkeley, 1964-1973; chmn, Comp Endocrinol Div, Am Soc Zoologists. **Memberships:** fel AAAS; Soc Study Reproduction; Soc Integrative Comp Biol; Am Soc Ichthyologists & Herpetologists. **Research Statement & Publications:** Comparative physiology and evolution of pituitary hormones with special reference to reproduction; endocrinology of thyroid hormone bindings and sexual development in hyenas. **Mailing Address:** Botl Garden, Univ Calif, 200 Centennial Dr, Berkeley, CA 94720-5045. **Fax:** 510-642-3012. **E-Mail:** licht@socrates.berkeley.edu

LICHT, STUART LAWRENCE, SOLAR ENERGY & ENERGY STORAGE, ELECTROCHEMISTRY & ANALYTICAL CHEMISTRY. **Personal Data:** b Boston, Mass, July 24, 1954. **Education:** Wesleyan Univ, BA (chem) & BA (physics), 1976, MA, 1980; The Weizmann Inst Sci, PhD (chem), 1986. **Honors & Awards:** Delek Energy Award, Delek Corp, 1983; Elad Res Excellence Award, Weizmann Inst, 1985; Weizmann-Bantrell Award, Bantrell Found of Israel, 1986. **Professional Experience:** CARLSON CHAIR & ASSOC PROF CHEM, CLARK UNIV, 1988-; vis scientist & fel chem, Mass Inst Technol, 1985-1986; Vis asst prof chem, Northeastern Univ, 1985-1986. **Memberships:** Am Chem Soc; Electro Chem Soc; Sigma Xi; Mat Res Soc. **Research Statement & Publications:** Highest efficiency photoelectrochemical solar cells, novel materials for electrochemical energy storage, sulfur chemistry, analytical and environmental methods, and fundamental studies in the structure of electrolytes (pH, conductivity, and microelectrochemistry) and in electron correlation. **Mailing Address:** Dept Chem, Technion Israel Inst Technol, Haifa 32000, Israel.

LICHT, W(ILLIAM) JR, CHEMICAL ENGINEERING. **Personal Data:** b Cincinnati, Ohio, September 29, 1915; m 1942. **Education:** Univ Cincinnati, ChE, 1937, MS, 1939, PhD (chem eng), 1950. **Honors & Awards:** Award, Am Inst Chem Engrs, 1972. **Professional Experience:** RETIRED; emer prof chem eng, Univ Cincinnati, 1985-1986; vis prof, Univ Minn, 1968 & 1972; head dept, Univ Cincinnati, 1954-1968; consult govt & var indust concerns, 1942-; from instr to prof, Univ Cincinnati, 1939-1985; asst, Univ Cincinnati, 1937-1939. **Memberships:** Am Soc Eng Educ; fel Am Inst Chem Engrs; Air Pollution Control Asn. **Research Statement & Publications:** Properties of azeotropic mixtures; drying of gases and refrigerants; adsorption in dessicant beds; dewpoint indicators; mechanics of drops; air pollution control; dust collection; design of systems; mathematical modelling particulate collection; fuel ethanol production. **Mailing Address:** 3580 Shaw Ave, Cincinnati, OH 45208.

LICHTBLAU, IRWIN MILTON, CHEMICAL ENGINEERING. **Personal Data:** b Woodmere, NY, May 11, 1936; m 1965. **Education:** Princeton Univ, BSE, 1958; Yale Univ, MEng, 1960, DEng, 1963. **Professional Experience:** CONSULT, CORP DEVELOP, STAND OIL CALIF, 1980-; sr eng assoc, Chevron Res Corp, sr staff econ analyst, Anal Div, 1976-1980; mgr comput opers, Comput Serv Dept, 1971-1974; asst mgr systs develop & appln, Western Opers Inc, 1969-1971; sr res engr, Chevron Res Corp, 1963-1969. **Memberships:** Am Inst Chem Engrs; Sigma Xi. **Research Statement & Publications:** Petroleum process design; high pressure technology; compressibility of gas mixtures at high pressures and temperatures. **Mailing Address:** 1096 Upper Happy Vly Rd, Lafayette, CA 94549.

LICHTEN, MICHAEL, GENETICS. **Education:** Mass Inst Technol, PhD, 1982. **Professional Experience:** HEAD, DNA RECOMBINATION YEAST SECT, NAT CANCER INST, as of 2005; LAB CHIEF, LAB BIOCHEM, NAT CANCER INST, as of 2005. **Mailing Address:** Lab Biochem Nat Cancer Inst NIH, Bldg 37 Rm 6124 MSC 4255 37 Convent Dr, Bethesda, MD 20892-4255. **Fax:** 301-402-3095. **E-Mail:** lichten@helix.nih.gov

LICHTEN, WILLIAM LEWIS, PHYSICS, INTELLIGENCE TESTING. **Personal Data:** b Philadelphia, Pa, March 5, 1928; m 1950, Susan Lurie; c Michael, Stephen & Julia. **Education:** Swarthmore Col, BA, 1949; Univ Chicago, MS, 1953, PhD (physics), 1956. **Professional Experience:** PROF EMER PHYSICS & ENG & APPL SCI, YALE UNIV, 1999-; prof physics, 1975-1999; dir undergrad studies, Yale Univ, 1969-1971; prof physics, Yale Univ, 1964-1975; from asst prof to assoc prof physics, Univ Chicago, 1958-1964; res physicist, Radiation Lab, Columbia Univ, 1957-1958; NSF fel, 1956-1957; mem bd dirs, Nat Asn Metric Edu. **Memberships:** Emer mem Fel Am Phys Soc; Am Psychol Soc; Amer Asn Physics Teachers. **Research Statement & Publications:** Psychology of perception; chemical physics; optics; laser spectroscopy; atomic physics; science education; educational research; research on mental testing. **Mailing Address:** Dept Physics, Yale Univ, PO Box 208120, New Haven, CT 06520-8120. **Fax:** 203-432-6175. **E-Mail:** william.lichten@yale.edu

LICHTENBAUM, STEPHEN, ARTHMETIC ALGEBRAIC GEOMETRY. **Personal Data:** b Brooklyn, NY, August 24, 1939. **Education:** Harvard Univ, AB, 1960, AM, 1961, PhD (math), 1964. **Professional Experience:** Chmn, Dept Math 1994-1997; PROF MATH, BROWN UNIV, 1990-; chmn, Dept Math, 1979-1982; prof math, Dept Math, 1973-1990; Guggenheim fel, John Simon Guggenheim Mem Found, 1973-1974; from asst prof to assoc prof, Cornell Univ, 1967-1973; lectr math, Princeton Univ, 1964-1967. **Memberships:** Am Math Soc. **Research Statement & Publications:** Algebraic number theory and algebraic geometry, particularly the study of the values of zeta and L-functions. **Mailing Address:** Dept Math, Brown Univ, 211 Kassar-Gould House PO Box 1917, Providence, RI 02912. **Fax:** 401-863-9013. **E-Mail:** slicht@math.brown.edu

LICHTENBERG, ALLAN J, NON-LINEAR DYNAMICS. **Personal Data:** b Passaic, NJ, m 1959, Elizabeth. **Education:** Harvard Univ, AB, 1952; Mass Inst Technol, MS, 1954; Oxford, DPhil, 1961. **Professional Experience:** PROF EMER ELEC ENG & COMP SCI, UNIV CALIF, BERKELEY, as of 2004; PROF, GRAD SCH, UNIV CALIF, BERKELEY, as of 2004; NSF fel, 1984; prof Elec Eng & Comp Sci, Univ Calif, Berkeley, beginning 1972; Gugenheim fel, 1965; from asst prof to assoc prof, Univ Calif, Berkeley, 1961-1972; chmn energy & resources group, Univ Calif, Berkeley. **Memberships:** Fel Am Phys Soc. **Research Statement & Publications:** Plasma physics and engineering; non-linear dynamics; energy conservation and related problems. **Mailing Address:** Dept Elec Eng & Comput Sci, Univ Calif, 185M Cory Hall 1770, Berkeley, CA 94720-1770. **Fax:** 510-642-6330. **E-Mail:** ajl@eecs.berkeley.edu

LICHTENBERG, BYRON KURT, BIOENGINEERING, BIOMEDICAL ENGINEERING. **Personal Data:** b Stroudsburg, Pa, February 19, 1948; m 1970, c 7. **Education:** Brown Univ, ScB, 1969; Mass Inst Technol, MS, 1975, ScD, 1979. **Honorary Degrees:** DSc, Westminster Univ, 1993. **Honors & Awards:** Spaceflight Award, NASA, 1983 & 1992; Komarov Award, Int Aeronaut Fedn, 1984; Haley Spaceflight Award, Aerospace Indust Asn Am. **Professional Experience:** CAPT, as of 2003; PRES, ZERO GRAVITY CORP, as of 2002; pres, Omega Aerospace, Inc, beginning 1991; chief scientist, Payload Syst, 1989-1991; pres, Payload Syst, 1984-1989; res scientist, Mass Inst Technol, 1978-1984; res afil, Mass Inst Technol. **Memberships:** Sigma Xi; Asn Space Explorers. **Research Statement & Publications:** Human adaptation to spaceflight particularly in the field of the inner ear system; human-machine interface, performance and habitation in spaceflight. **Mailing Address:** Zero Gravity Corp, 2708 3 St St 5, Santa Monica, CA 90405. **Fax:** 775-942-3544.

LICHTENBERG, DON BERNETT, THEORETICAL PHYSICS. **Personal Data:** b Passaic, NJ, July 2, 1928; m 1954, Rita; c Naomi & Rebecca. **Education:** NY Univ, BA, 1950; Univ Ill, MS, 1951, PhD (physics), 1955. **Professional Experience:** PROF EMER PHYSICS, IND UNIV, BLOOMINGTON, 1994-; Imp Col, Univ Turin, 1987-1988; Fulbright travel grant, Italy, 1987-1988; Imp Col, Univ Wash, 1986-1987; sr fel, Sci Res Coun, UK, 1979-1980; Oxford Univ, 1979-1980; Imp Col, Univ London, 1971; vis prof, Tel-Aviv Univ, 1967-1968; from assoc prof to prof, Ind Univ, Bloomington, 1963-1993; physicist, Linear Accelerator Ctr, Stanford Univ, 1962-1963; from asst prof to assoc prof, Mich State Univ, 1958-1963; guest prof, Univ Hamburg, 1957-1958; res assoc physics, Ind Univ, 1955-1957. **Memberships:** Fel Am Phys Soc. **Research Statement & Publications:** Physics of the elementary particles. **Mailing Address:** Dept Physics, Ind Univ, 727 E Third St, Bloomington, IN 47405-7105. **Fax:** 812-855-5533. **E-Mail:** lichten@indiana.edu

LICHTENBERGER, DENNIS LEE, SURFACE SCIENCE, CATALYSIS. **Personal Data:** b Elkhart, Ind, September 30, 1947; m 1968, Mina; c Jeffifer A & Kathryn D. **Education:** Ind Univ, BS, 1969; Univ Wis-Madison, PhD (chem), 1974. **Honors & Awards:** Sci Award, Eastman Kodak, 1974. **Professional Experience:** Counr, Am Chem Soc, 1989-; PROF CHEM, UNIV ARIZ, TUCSON, 1987-; fel, Alfred P Sloan, 1979; from asst prof to assoc prof, Univ Ariz, Tucson, 1976-1987; fel, Univ Ill, Champaign-Urbana, 1974-1976. **Memberships:** AAAS; Am Chem Soc; NY Acad Sci; Am Vacuum Soc; Am Phys Soc. **Research Statement & Publications:** Study of the behavior of organometallic molecules, molecules on surfaces, and catalysts through the development of high resolution gas phase photoelectron spectroscopy, ultra high vacuum surface spectroscopy and scanning tunneling microscopy, published over 6 articles. **Mailing Address:** Dept Chem, Univ Ariz, Tucson, AZ 85721. **Fax:** 520-621-8407. **E-Mail:** dlichten@arizona.edu

LICHTENBERGER, GERALD BURTON, MEDICAL DEVICE TECHNOLOGIES, MEDICAL IMAGING. **Personal Data:** b St Louis, Mo, January 14, 1945; m 1973, c 3. **Education:** Mass Inst Technol, BS, 1966, MS, 1967; Yale Univ, PhD (elec eng), 1972. **Professional Experience:** VPRES, BUSINESS DEVELOP & DIR, VISION SCI INC, 1998-; pres & chief exec officer, Isight, Inc, 1990-1997; vpres, strategic planning, Pentax, 1986-1990; pres & founder, Systs Future, Inc, 1979-1986; prin scientist, dir & co-founder comput systs, Xybion Corp, 1975-1979; mem tech staff ocean systs res, Bell Labs, 1972-1975; consult appln statist, IBM Res, 1970-1972. **Memberships:** Inst Elec & Electronics Engrs. **Research Statement & Publications:** Application of state of the art computer technology to diverse disciplines such as interactive data management and analysis in medical research; signal and information processing; array processing; random process modeling, electronic imaging. **Mailing Address:** 11 Heather Hill Way, Mendham, NJ 07945-1233.

LICHTENBERGER, LENARD MICHAEL, PATHOGENESIS OF PEPTIC ULCERS. **Personal Data:** b New York, NY, April 26, 1947. **Education:** Wash Univ, St Louis, BS, 1968; Rutgers Univ, MS, 1970; Univ Okla Med Sch, PhD (endocrinol), 1972. **Professional Experience:** PROF INTEGRATIVE BIOL & PHARMACOLOGY, UNIV TEX MED SCH, 1987-; from asst prof to assoc prof, Univ Tex Med Sch, 1976-1987; fel gastrointestinal cell biol, Harvard Univ, 1974-1976; fel gastrointestinal endocrinol, Univ Calif, Los Angeles, 1972-1974. **Memberships:** Am Physiol Soc; Am Gastroenterol Soc. **Research Statement & Publications:** Currently investigation the pathogenesis of peptic ulceration induced on steroidal anti inflammatory drugs (NSAIDS) and drug discovery. **Mailing Address:** Dept Physiol & Cell Biol, Univ Tex Med Sch, MSMB 4-402 PO Box 20708, Houston, TX 77225-0708. **Fax:** 713-500-7444. **E-Mail:** lenardm.lichtenberger@uth.tmc.edu

LICHTENFELS, JAMES RALPH, PARASITOLOGY, TAXONOMY. **Personal Data:** b Robinson, Pa, February 14, 1939; m 1961, c 2. **Education:** Ind Univ Pa, BS, 1962; Univ Md, MS, 1966, PhD (zoology), 1968. **Professional Experience:** MICROBIOLOGIST, AGR RES SERV, USDA, as of 2004; chair, Fed Soc Parasitol, 1995-1996; asst ed, Systematic Parasitol, 1987-; ed, Proc Helm Soc Wash, 1983-1987; mem coun resources, Asn Syst Collections, 1975-1977; res assoc, Div Worms, Mus Natural Hist, Smithsonian Inst, Wash,

DC, 1972-; res affil, Div Parasitol, State Mus, Univ Nebr, Lincoln, 1972-; CUR NAT PARASITE COLLECTION, ANIMAL PARASITOL INST, AGR RES SERV, USDA, 1971-; instr, USDA Grad Sch, 1971-1977; ZOOLOGIST, ANIMAL PARASITOL INST, AGR RES SERV, USDA, 1967-. **Memberships:** Am Soc Parasitol (vpres, 1987); Wildlife Dis Asn; Am Micros Soc; Sigma Xi; Am Asn Zool Nomenclature (pres, 1986). **Research Statement & Publications:** Intra and interspecific variation in parasitic nematodes; effects of host on morphology of parasitic nematodes; identification, classification and description of parasitic nematodes of vertebrates especially of domestic animals. **Mailing Address:** Agr Res Serv, USDA, 4B Rm 1180 Bldg, Beltsville, MD 20705-2350. **Fax:** 301-504-6273. **E-Mail:** rlichten@anri.barc.usda.gov

LICHTENSTEIN, ALICE HINDA, LIPO PROTEIN METABOLISM, LIPO PROTEIN KINETICS. **Personal Data:** m Barry; c 2. **Education:** Cornell Univ, BS, 1971; Pa State Univ, MS, 1973; Harvard Univ, MS, 1975, DSc (nutrit), 1979. **Honors & Awards:** Special Recognition Award Council, 2001; Chem Basis & Vascular Biol Am Heart Asn, 1998; R Pike Lecturership Penn State, 1996; Outstanding Award Tufts Univ. **Professional Experience:** STANLEY N GERSHOFF PROF NUTRIT SCI & POLICY, FRIEDMAN SCH NUTRIT SCI & POLICY, as of 2006; PROF PUB HEALTH & FAMILY MED, TUFTS UNIV SCH MED, as of 2006; SR SCIENTIST, DIR, CARDIOVASC NUTRIT LAB, JEAN MAYER USDA HUMAN NUTRIT RES CTR AGING, 1995-; assoc prof, Dept Family Med & Community Health, beginning 1995; assoc prof, Sch Nutrit, Tufts Univ, beginning 1994; asst prof, Dept Family Med & Community Health, 1988-1994; asst prof med & biochem, Sch Med, Boston Univ, 1982-1988; fel, Sch Med, Boston Univ, 1979-1982; lectr, Tufts Univ, 1978-1982; instr, Queens Col, 1973-1974; teaching asst, Pa State Univ, 1971-1973. **Memberships:** Am Heart Asn; Am Inst Nutrit; Am Soc Clin Nutrit. **Research Statement & Publications:** Kinetic behavior of lipo protein particles in order to elucidate mechanisms responsible for changes in blood lipid levels induced by alterations in dietary fat and cholesterol intake. **Mailing Address:** Jean Mayer USDA Human Nutrit Res Ctr, Tufts Univ, 711 Wash St, Boston, MA 02111. **Fax:** 617-556-3103. **E-Mail:** alice.lichtenstein@tufts.edu

LICHTENSTEIN, HARRIS ARNOLD, ANALYTICAL CHEMISTRY, MOLECULAR BIOLOGY & BIOTECHNOLOGY. **Personal Data:** b Houston, Tex, May 7, 1941; div, c Jill & Gregg. **Education:** Tulane Univ, BA, 1963; Univ Houston, BS, 1966, MS, 1967, PhD (biol), 1970. **Professional Experience:** PRES & CHIEF EXEC OFFICER, OMNIMMUNE CORP, as of 2005; vpres, Keystone Environ Inc, Subsid Koppers Co Inc, 1986-1988; pres, Spectrix Corp, 1969-1986; chief exec officer & chmn, Intrepid Technol Inc; chief exec officer & chmn, Omnimmune Corp. **Mailing Address:** 4600 Post Oak Pl Dr Ste 152, Houston, TX 77057. **Fax:** 713-626-7566.

LICHTENSTEIN, LAWRENCE M, MEDICINE, IMMUNOLOGY. **Personal Data:** b Washington, DC, May 31, 1934; m 1956, c 3. **Education:** Univ Chicago, BA, 1954, MD, 1960; Johns Hopkins Univ, PhD (immunol), 1965. **Professional Experience:** DIR, JOHN HOPKINS ASTHMA & ALLERGY CTR, as of 2004; PROF MED, SCH MED, JOHNS HOPKINS UNIV, 1975-; from asst prof to assoc prof, 1966-1975; resident, 1965-1966; fel microbiol, 1961-1965; intern med, 1960-1961. **Memberships:** Am Acad Allergy; Am Asn Immunol; Am Fedn Clin Res; Am Soc Clin Invest; Am Asn Physicians. **Research Statement & Publications:** Mechanisms of reactions of immediate hypersensitivity and relationship to clinical problems. **Mailing Address:** Johns Hopkins Asthma & Allergy Ctr, 5501 Hopkins Bayview Circle, Baltimore, MD 21224-6801. **Fax:** 410-550-1733.

LICHTENWALNER, HART K, CHEMICAL ENGINEERING. **Personal Data:** b Easton, Pa, October 1, 1923; m 1945, c 3. **Education:** Lafayette Col, BS, 1943; Lehigh Univ, MS, 1949, PhD (chem eng), 1950. **Professional Experience:** RETIRED; mgr strategic planning & venture develop, Gen Elec Silicones-Europe, 1980-1987; managing dir, Gen Elec Silicones-Europe, 1977-1980; mgr var prod sect, Silicone Prod Dept, Gen Elec Co, 1970-1977; mgr res & develop, Silicone Prod Dept, Gen Elec Co, 1968-1970; mgr room temp vulcanising rubber develop, Silicone Prod Dept, Gen Elec Co, 1966-1968; mgr process develop, Silicone Prod Dept, Gen Elec Co, 1962-1966; eng leader, Silicone Prod Dept, Gen Elec Co, 1961-1962; chem engr, Silicone Prod Dept, Gen Elec Co, 1950-1961; org chemist, Res Labs, Gen Motors Corp, 1943-1948. **Memberships:** Am Chem Soc; fel Am Inst Chem Engrs; NY Acad Sci. **Research Statement & Publications:** Chemical process technology of organosilanes and siloxanes. **Mailing Address:** 24 Via Da Vinci, Clifton Park, NY 12065-2097.

LICHTER, BARRY D(AVID), MATERIALS SCIENCE, CORROSION & STRESS-CORROSION. **Personal Data:** b Boston, Mass, November 29, 1931. **Education:** Mass Inst Technol, SB, 1953, SM, 1955, ScD(metall), 1958. **Professional Experience:** Vis prof, Fac Chem Eng & Mat Sci, Delft Univ Technol, Neth, 1991-; consult, Off Technol Assessment, 1976-1978 & Oak Ridge Nat Lab, 1978-1979; NSF fac fel, 1975-1976; centennial fel, Vanderbilt Univ, 1974-1975; PROF MAT SCI & MGT TECHNOL, VANDERBILT UNIV, 1972-; assoc prof mat sci, Vanderbilt Univ, 1968-1972; tech consult, Boeing Co, 1966; assoc prof metall eng, Univ Wash, 1964-1968; fel, Lawrence Radiation Lab, Univ Calif, Berkeley, 1962-1964; metallurgist, Air Force Cambridge Res Ctr, 1958-1961 & Oak Ridge Nat Lab, 1961-1962; asst, Mass Inst Technol, 1952-1958. **Memberships:** Minerals Metals & Mat Soc; NY Acad Sci; Nat Asn Corrosion Engrs; Electrochem Soc; Am Soc Metals. **Research Statement & Publications:** Corrosion; oxidation & alloys; technology and human values; philosophy and engineering ethics; thermodynamics of alloys; stress-corrosion cracking. **Mailing Address:** Mat, Vanderbilt Univ 2201 W End Ave, Nashville, TN 37240-0001. **Fax:** 615-343-8730. **E-Mail:** lichter@vuse.vanderbilt.edu

LICHTER, EDWARD A, preventive medicine, community health; deceased, see previous edition for last biography

LICHTER, JAMES JOSEPH, ECONOMIC ANALYSIS OF ENVIRONMENTAL REGULATIONS. **Personal Data:** b Algona, Iowa, April 29, 1939. **Education:** Loras Col, BS, 1961; Fordham Univ, MS, 1963; Duke Univ, PhD (physics), 1969; Univ Calif, Santa Barbara, MA (economics) MBE, 1986. **Professional Experience:** ANALYST, CALIF TECHNOL TRADE & COM AGENCY, 1995-; energy specialist, Calif Energy Comn, 1987-1995; software specialist, ITT Fed Elec Corp, 1977-1983; assoc scientist, ITT Fed Elec Corp, 1969-1977; res asst, Duke Univ, 1965-1969; from physicist to res physicist, US Naval Ord Lab, Md, 1960-1965. **Memberships:** Am Phys Soc. **Research Statement & Publications:** Economic research to support economics development activities. **Mailing Address:** 2348 Am River Dr No 206, Sacramento, CA 95825. **E-Mail:** jlichter@commerce.ca.gov

LICHTER, PAUL RICHARD, OPHTHALMOLOGY. **Personal Data:** b Detroit, March 7, 1939; m 1960, Carolyn; c Laurie & Susan. **Education:** Univ Mich, BA, 1960, MD, 1964, MS, 1968; Am Bd Ophthal, dipl. **Professional Experience:** F BRUCE FRALICK PROF OPHTHAL, UNIV MICH, ANN ARBOR, as of 2003; DIR, UNIV MICH KELLOGG EYE CTR, as of 2003; pres, Mich Ophthal Soc, beginning 1993; bd dirs, Pan Am Asn Ophthal, beginning 1988; ed-in-chief, Ophthal J, beginning 1986; bd dirs, Am Acad Ophthal, beginning 1981; PROF & CHMN, DEPT OPHTHAL, UNIV MICH, ANN ARBOR, 1978-; from asst prof to assoc prof, Dept Ophthal, Univ Mich, Ann Arbor, 1971-1978; mem, Mich State Med Soc, Washtenaw Co Med Soc & Mich Ophthal Soc. **Memberships:** AMA; Pan Am Asn Ophthal; Asn Univ Profs Ophthal (pres 1991-1992). **Research Statement & Publications:** Ophthalmology; medicine. **Mailing Address:** Dept Opthal, Univ Mich Med Sch, Kellogg Eye Ctr 1000 Wall St, Ann Arbor, MI 48105-1912. **Fax:** 734-647-0247. **E-Mail:** plichter@umich.edu

LICHTER, ROBERT (LOUIS), ORGANIC CHEMISTRY, EDUCATION ADMINISTRATOR. **Personal Data:** b Cambridge, Mass, October 26, 1941; m 1991, c 2. **Education:** Harvard Univ, BA, 1962; Univ Wis-Madison, PhD (chem), 1967. **Professional Experience:** EXEC DIR, CAMILLE & HENRY DREYFUS FOUND INC, 1989-; vprovost res & grad studies, State Univ NY Stony Brook, 1986-1989; regional dir grants, Res Corp, 1983-1986; vis scientist, Exxon Res & Eng Co, 1982; vis scientist, Sandoz Res Lab, 1981; chmn dept, Hunter Col, 1977-1982; from asst prof to prof chem, Hunter Col, 1970-1983; res fel chem, Calif Inst Technol, 1968-1970; USPHS fel, Brunswick Tech Univ, 1967-1968. **Memberships:** Am Chem Soc; Sigma Xi; fel AAAS. **Research Statement & Publications:** Organonitrogen chemistry; nuclear magnetic resonance spectroscopy; application of carbon and nitrogen nuclear magnetic resonance to organic chemistry. **Mailing Address:** Camille & Henry Dreyfus Found Inc, 555 Madison Ave, New York, NY 10022. **E-Mail:** rlichter@panix.com

LICHTI, ROGER L, EXPERIMENTAL SOLID STATE PHYSICS, MAGNETIC RESONANCE. **Personal Data:** b Milford, Nebr, August 27, 1945; m 1970, c 2. **Education:** Ottawa Univ, BSc, 1967; Univ Ill, MS, 1969, PhD (physics), 1972. **Professional Experience:** PROF PHYSICS, TEX TECH UNIV, 1992-; from asst prof to assoc prof, Tex Tech Univ, 1979-1992; vis asst prof, Univ Mass, 1978-1979; res assoc, Univ Mass, 1974-1977; res assoc, Univ Kans, 1973-1974; vis asst prof, Univ Kans, 1972-1973. **Memberships:** Am Phys Soc; Math Res Soc. **Research Statement & Publications:** Magnetic resonance of dilute paramagnetic systems; muonium/hydrogen in semiconductors; muon spin rotation/resonance. **Mailing Address:** Dept Physics, Tex Tech Univ, Lubbock, TX 79409. **Fax:** 806-742-1182. **E-Mail:** roger.lichti@ttu.edu

LICHTIG, LEO KENNETH, CLINICAL & FINANCIAL INFORMATION SYSTEMS, HEALTH SERVICES RESEARCH. **Personal Data:** b Brooklyn, NY, October 20, 1953; m 1977, Susan; c Brielle J & Danica J. **Education:** Rensselaer Polytech Inst, BS & MS, 1974, PhD (commun res), 1976. **Professional Experience:** VP, AON CONSULT, LIFE SCIENCES, 2002-; appointee to NYS Dept of Health Data Protection Review Board, 2003-; mem, NYS Uniform Billing Comt, 2002-; sr vpres & chief info officer, Network Inc, 1995-2002; vpres res & develop, Network Inc, 1992-1995; adj fac, Union Col, 1991-1992; case mix economist, Network Inc, 1990-1992; subcomt Qual & Productivity Measures in Health Care, Am Statist Asn, 1988-1990; mem, Tech Adv Group, Health Info Reporting Co, 1987-1990; adj fac, Grad Prog Health Admin, Russell Sage Col, 1986-1994; mem, Tech Adv Comt, NY State Off Mental Health Case Mix Classification Proj Steering, 1986-1989; mem, Tech Adv Comt, Health Care Financing, 1985-1987; mem, tech rev comt & reimbursement adv group, NY State Long Term Care Case Mix Reimbursement Proj, 1984-1986; dir, Utilization Econ & Res, Empire Blue Cross Blue Shield, 1983-1990 chairperson, Inst Rev Bd, Health Care Res Found, 1983-1990; mem, Tech Adv Comt, NY Statewide Planning & Res Coop Syst, 1982-; vpres, Health Care Res Found, 1982-1990; contrib ed, Nat Report Comput & Health, 1982-1985; policy res specialist, Blue Cross Northeastern, NY, 1982-1983; assoc proj mgr, NJ State Dept Health, 1982; mem, Comt Privacy & Confidentiality, Am Statist Asn, 1981-1984; mem, Ad-hoc Comt, US Dept Health, Educ & Welfare, 1979-1981; asst proj mgr, NJ State Dept Health, 1977-1982; asst prof commun, State Univ NY Albany, 1976-1977; res asst commun res, Rensselaer Polytech Inst, 1974-1976. **Memberships:** Acad Health Serv Res; Healthcare Financial Mgt Asn; International Soc for Pharmacoeconomics and Outcomes Research. **Research Statement & Publications:** Integration of clinical and financial information to address issues affecting the cost and management of health services and public health policy; development of case mix classification systems for specialized patient populations. **Mailing Address:** 7 Sable Terrace, Latham, NY 12110. **Fax:** 518-782-1848. **E-Mail:** lichtl@rpi.edu

LICHTIN, J LEON, PHARMACEUTICAL CHEMISTRY, COSMETIC CHEMISTRY. **Personal Data:** b Philadelphia, Pa, March 5, 1924; m Beverly; c Benjamin Lloyd & Alan Eli. **Education:** Philadelphia Col Pharm, BS, 1944, MS, 1947; Ohio State Univ, PhD (pharmaceut chem), 1950. **Honors & Awards:** Lifetime Serv Award of the Soc of Cosmetic Chem 1991. **Professional Experience:** Emer Prof of Pharm, Andrew Jergens, 1991-; RETIRED; from assoc prof to prof, Andrew Jergens prof pharm, 1972-1992; from assoc prof to prof, Univ Cincinnati, 1955-1971; from asst prof to assoc prof pharm, Cincinnati Col Pharm, 1950-1955. **Memberships:** AAAS; fel Soc Cosmetic Chem. **Research Statement & Publications:** Dermatologicals; formulation of pharmaceutical products; cosmetics. **Mailing Address:** 801 Cloverview Ave, Cincinnati, OH 45231.

LICHTIN, NORMAN NAHUM, PHOTO CHEMISTRY, CATALYTIC CHEMISTRY. **Personal Data:** b Newark, NJ, August 10, 1922; m 1947, Phyllis Wasserman; c Harold H, Sara M (Boyd) & Daniel A. **Education:** Antioch Col, BS (chem), 1944; Purdue Univ, MS (chem), 1945; Harvard Univ, PhD (phys org chem), 1948. **Honors & Awards:** Coochbehar lectr, Soc Cult Sci, India, 1980. **Professional Experience:** Chief scientist, Nanotek, Inc, 1998-; consult, Zentox Corp, 1997- 1999; consult, Photox Corp, 1994-1996; EMER PROF CHEM, BOSTON UNIV, 1993-; consult, Clearflow Inc, 1993-1994; chief scientist, Proj Sunrise, Inc, 1987-1993; dir, Div Eng & Appl Sci, Boston Univ Grad Schl, 1983-1987; consult, Arco Solar, Inc, 1980-1988; vis prof, Inst Physics & Chem Res, Wako, Saitama, Japan, 1980; sabbatical vis, Solar Energy Res Inst, Golden, Colo, 1980; univ prof, Boston Univ, 1973-1993; chmn dept, Boston Univ, 1973-1984; consult, Solar Energy Conv Unit, Exxon Res & Eng Co, 1971-1978; NSF sr fel, 1962-1963; vis prof, Hebrew Univ Jerusalem, 1962-1963, 1970-1971, 1972, 1973, 1976 & 1980; guest scientist, Weizmann Inst, 1962-1963; resident consult, Atomics Int, 1961; res collab, Brookhaven Nat Lab, 1958-1970; Vis chemist, Brookhaven Nat Lab, 1957-1958; from instr to prof, Boston Univ, 1948-1993; lectr, Boston Univ, 1947; Teaching fel, Harvard Univ, 1945-1947. **Memberships:** Fel AAAS; Am Chem Soc; Sigma Xi. **Research Statement & Publications:** Radiation chemistry; atomic nitrogen chemistry; photochemical conversion of solar energy; physical photochemistry; photo-assisted solid catalysis; chemical reaction mechanism; electrolyte chemistry. **Mailing Address:** 195 Morton St, Newton Centre, MA 02159-1522. **E-Mail:** norlichtin@aol.com

LICHTMAN, ANDREW, MEDICAL RESEARCH. **Education:** Univ Rochester Sch Med, MD, PhD, 1981. **Professional Experience:** PATHOLOGIST, BRIGHAM & WOMEN'S HOSP, as of 2005; ASSOC PROF PATH, HARVARD MED SCH, as of 2005. **Mailing Address:** Dept Path Brigham & Women's Hosp, 221 Longwood Ave, Boston, MA 02115. **Fax:** 617-732-5795. **E-Mail:** alichtman@rics.bwh.harvard.edu

LICHTMAN, IRWIN A, SURFACE CHEMISTRY, SCIENCE EDUCATION. **Personal Data:** b New York, NY, November 3, 1920; m 1948, c 1. **Education:** City Col NY, BS, 1943; NY

Univ, MS, 1948, PhD (phys chem), 1951. **Professional Experience:** RETIRED; consult surface chem, beginning 1984; vis prof, NJ Inst Technol, Chem Eng Dept, 1982-1984; group mgr res & develop, process chem div, Diamond Shamrock Chem Co, Morristown, 1977-1982; mgr phys chem lab, 1964-1977; sr res chemist, Shell Chem Co, 1960-1964; group leader phosphates & detergents, Food Mach & Chem Co, 1955-1960; sr res chemist, Lever Bros Res Ctr, 1952-1955; asst prof, Community Col, NY, 1948-1952; instr chem, Seton Hall Col, 1947-1948. **Memberships:** Am Chem Soc; Am Inst Chem. **Research Statement & Publications:** Surface and colloid chemistry; defoamers; insecticide decomposition mechanisms; reaction kinetics; mechanism of defoamer action, particularly role of hydrophobic particles; volatile insecticides in polymeric matrix; phosphate glasses. **Mailing Address:** 24 Wenzel Lane, Stony Point, NY 10980-2310.

LICHTMAN, MARSHALL A, HEMATOLOGY, BIOPHYSICS. **Personal Data:** b New York, NY, June 23, 1934; m 1957, Alice; c Susan, Joanne & Pamela. **Education:** Cornell Univ, AB, 1955; Univ Buffalo, MD, 1960; Am Bd Internal Med, dipl, 1967. **Professional Experience:** PROF, MED M&D-HEMAT/ONCOL, UNIV ROCHESTER, as of 1999; exec vpres, res & Med Affairs, Leukemia Soc Am, 1996-; cochief, hemato unit, 1977-1989; chief hematol unit, radiation biol & biophys, 1975-1977; sr physician, Strong mem Hosp, 1974-; from asst prof to assoc prof med, radiation biol & biophys, 1971-1974; Leukemia Soc scholar, 1969-1974; USPHS res fel, Univ Rochester, 1967-1969; sr instr med, Sch Med, 1966-1967; from asst physician to sr assoc physician, Strong mem Hosp, 1965-1971; instr med, Sch Med & chief resident, Med Ctr, Univ Rochester, 1965-1966; res assoc epidemiol, Sch Pub Health, Univ NC, 1963-1965; resident internal med, Med Ctr, Univ Rochester, 1960-1963; ASSOC DEAN, UNIV ROCHESTER. **Memberships:** Master Am Col Physicians; Am Soc Hemat (vpres, 1987, pres, 1989); Am Soc Clin Invest; Asn Am Physicians; Am Physiol Soc; Am Soc Cell Biol. **Research Statement & Publications:** Biochemical and biophysical studies of human erythrocytes and leukocytes. **Mailing Address:** Dept Hematol Univ Rochester Med Ctr, PO Box 610 610 Elmwood Ave, RM 4-6311, Rochester, NY 14642. **Fax:** 585-276-1876. **E-Mail:** mal@medicine.rochester.edu

LICHTON, IRA JAY, NUTRITION. **Personal Data:** b Chicago, Ill, September 18, 1928; m 1949, Marilyn Mendel; c Alex I. **Education:** Univ Chicago, PhB, 1947; Univ Ill, BS, 1950, MS, 1951, PhD (physiol), 1954. **Professional Experience:** EMER PROF NUTRIT, UNIV HAWAII, 1992-; Vis prof, Hebrew Univ, 1988-1989; from assoc prof to prof, Univ Hawaii, 1962-1992; instr physiol, Stanford Univ, 1958-1962; Am Heart Asn res fel cardiovasc physiol, Med Res Inst, Michael Reese Hosp, Chicago, Ill, 1956-1958; Res assoc obstet & gynec, Univ Chicago, 1954-1956. **Memberships:** felAAAS; emer Am Physiol Soc. **Research Statement & Publications:** Water and electrolyte metabolism in pregnancy; growth; nutritional status. **Mailing Address:** 9 Kaapuni Dr, Univ Hawaii, Kailua, HI 96734-2323. **E-Mail:** lichton@hawaii.edu

LICHTWARDT, ROBERT WILLIAM, MYCOLOGY. **Personal Data:** b Rio de Janeiro, Brazil, November 27, 1924; American citizen; m 1951, Elizabeth Thomas; c Ruth E & Robert T. **Education:** Oberlin Col, AB, 1949; Univ Ill, MS, 1951, PhD (bot), 1954. **Honors & Awards:** Distinguished Mycologist Award, Mycol Soc Am, 1991. **Professional Experience:** EMER PROF BOT, UNIV KANS, 1995-; chmn, Dept Bot, Univ Kans, 1971-1974 & 1981-1984; ed-in-chief, Mycologia, 1965-1970; NSF sr fel, 1963-1964; from asst prof to prof, Univ Kans, 1957-1995; res assoc bot, Iowa State Univ, 1955-1957; Fel, NSF, 1954-1955. **Memberships:** AAAS; Bot Soc Am; Mycol Soc Am (pres, 1972-1973); Mycol Soc Japan; Brit Mycol Soc. **Research Statement & Publications:** Fungi association with arthropods, particularly those inhabiting their guts. **Mailing Address:** Dept Ecol & Evolutionary Biol, Univ Kans, Lawrence, KS 66045-2106. **Fax:** 785-864-5321. **E-Mail:** licht@ku.edu

LICHTY, MAYNARD E, ORGANIC CHEMISTRY. **Education:** Dickinson Col, BS; Villanova Univ, MS. **Professional Experience:** VPRES, VOYAGER PHARMACEUT CORP, NC, 2005-. **Mailing Address:** Voyager Pharmaceut Corp, 8540 Colonnade Ctr Dr, Raleigh, NC 27615. **Fax:** 919-846-4881.

LICINI, JEROME CARL, QUANTUM TRANSPORT, SEMICONDUCTOR DEVICES. **Personal Data:** b 1958; m 1985. **Education:** Princeton Univ, AB, 1980; Mass Inst Technol, PhD (condensed matter physics), 1987. **Professional Experience:** CONSULT, LEHIGHTON ELECTRONICS INC, 1996-; ASSOC PROF PHYSICS, LEHIGH UNIV, 1993-; consult, Valley Technol, Inc, 1991-1993; asst prof, Lehigh Univ, 1987-1993; assoc, Mass Inst Technol, 1987; vis researcher, AT&T Bell Labs, 1984-1985; res asst, IBM Corp, Tucson, 1981. **Memberships:** Am Phys Soc; Sigma Xi. **Research Statement & Publications:** New quantum phenomena in ultra-small semiconductor devices; fabrication of submicron silicon and gallium-arsenide sub- micron devices; measurement of quantum transport phenomena at ultra-low temperatures. **Mailing Address:** Dept Physics, Lehigh Univ, 16 Memorial Dr E, Bethlehem, PA 18015-3182. **Fax:** 610-758-5730. **E-Mail:** jcl3@lehigh.edu

LICK, DALE W, PURE MATHEMATICS, APPLIED MATHEMATICS. **Personal Data:** b Marlette, Mich, January 7, 1938; m Marilyn; c Lyn, Kitty, Diana & Ronald. **Education:** Mich State Univ, BS, 1958, MS, 1959; Univ Calif, Riverside, PhD (math, partial differential equations), 1965. **Honors & Awards:** National Science Foundation Summer Research Fellowship, University of California, Riverside, 1965 Phi Kappa Phi (National Honors Society) Beta Gamma Sigma (National Business Honors Society) "President's Award"; "In Recognition of Outstanding Contribution to Amateur Baseball in the United States of America, " United States Baseball Federation, January 4, 1985 Certificate of Appreciation for "Significant Contributions to the Progress of Education in the United States of America, " US Department of Education, September 26, 1985 "Medallion of Merit, " the national award presented to an individual who has made significant contributions toward the goals of the US Government Printing Office, September 29, 1988 Mortar Board, Inc (National College Honors Society) Golden Key (National Honor Society) Alpha Phi Omega (National Service Fraternity). **Professional Experience:** UNIV PROF, EDUC LADERSHIP & LEARNING SYST INST, FLA STATE UNIV, 1993-; prof math & pres, Fla State Univ, 1991-1993; prof math & pres, Univ Maine, 1986-1991; prof math & comput sci & pres, Ga Southern Col, 1978-1986; prof math & dean, Sch Sci & Health Professions, Old Dom Univ, 1974-1978; vpres acad affairs, Russell Sage Col, 1972-1974; assoc prof & head dept, Drexel Univ, 1969-1972; asst res mathematician, Dept Appl Math, Brookhaven Nat Lab, 1967-1968; consult, Union Carbide Corp, AEC, Oak Ridge Nat Lab, 1966-1972; from asst prof to assoc prof math, Univ Tenn, 1965-1969; from instr to asst prof math, Univ Redlands, 1961-1963; asst to comptroller, Mich Bell Tel Co, 1960-1961; instr math & chmn dept, Port Huron Jr Col, 1959-1960; adj assoc prof, Med Sch, Temple Univ, 1969-1972. **Memberships:** AAAS; Am Math Soc; Asn Comput Mach; Math Asn Am; Soc Indust & Appl Math; Sigma Xi. **Research Statement & Publications:** Singular non-linear hyperbolic second order partial differential equations; non-linearDirichlet problems; systems of non-linear boundary and initial value problems; partial differential equations and their numerical solution; leadershipand change; school improvement and school reform; learning teams and learning communities; and new learning systems. **Mailing Address:** Fla State Univ, 4600-C Univ Ctr, Tallahassee, FL 32306-2540. **Fax:** 850-553-4081. **E-Mail:** dlick@lsi.fsu.edu

LICK, DON R, MATHEMATICS. **Personal Data:** b Marlette, Mich, September 3, 1934; m 1961, c Ellyn & John. **Education:** Mich State Univ, BS, 1956, MS, 1957, PhD (math), 1961. **Honors & Awards:** Distinguished serv, Award, Michigan Section, Math Assoc of America Certificae of Meritorius serv, Matg Assic if Ameruca pres Award for Distinguished serv MIchigan Conference, Am Assoc of univ Prof. **Professional Experience:** PROF MATH, EASTERN MICH UNIV, 2001-; prof & head math, Eastern Mich Univ, 1985-2001; from assoc prof to prof math, Western Mich Univ, 1972-1985; vis prof, Univ Calif, Irvine, 1972-1973 & Calif State Univ, Los Angeles, 1972-1973; US Army Res Off Conf grant, 1971-1972; NSF res grant, 1969-1970; vis assoc prof, Western Mich Univ, 1965-1966; Asst prof math, Purdue Univ, 1961-1963 & NMex State Univ, 1963-1966. **Memberships:** Math Asn Am; Am Math Soc; Am Asn Univ Prof. **Research Statement & Publications:** Complex analysis; sets of convergence of series; representation of measurable functions by series; graph theory; connectivity; structural problems; coloring problems. **Mailing Address:** Dept Math, Eastern Mich Univ, Ypsilanti, MI 48197. **Fax:** 313-487-2489. **E-Mail:** don.lick@emich.edu

LICK, THOMAS ARTZ, PHYSICS. **Personal Data:** b Stillwater, Okla, September 22, 1940; m 1966, Miriam Ruble; c Deborah Lynn (Chiders) & Rodney Artz. **Education:** Muhlenberg Col, BS, 1962; Ohio Univ, PhD (physics), 1969. **Professional Experience:** PROF PHYSICS, STETSON UNIV, 1983-; chmn, Physics Dept, 1982-1995; vis res prof, Univ NC, Chapel Hill, 1981-1982; From asst prof to assoc prof, Stetson Univ, 1968-1983. **Memberships:** Sigma Xi; Am Phys Soc. **Research Statement & Publications:** Investigation of electric field effects using an electron spin echo spectrometer; thermoluminescence and x-ray stimulated luminescence in insulating crystals; computerized data acquisition and analysis in introductory physics laboratories. **Mailing Address:** Unit Physics, Stetson Univ, 211 Sage Hall, 421 N Woodland Blvd, Unit 8267, DeLand, FL 32723. **Fax:** 386-740-3600. **E-Mail:** tlick@stetson.edu

LICK, WILBERT JAMES, ENVIRONMENTAL ENGINEERING, MARINE SCIENCES. **Personal Data:** b Cleveland, Ohio, June 12, 1933; c James & Sarah. **Education:** Rensselaer Polytech Inst, BA, 1955, MA, 1957, PhD (aeronaut eng), 1958. **Professional Experience:** Chmn dept, Univ Calif, Santa Barbara, 1982-1984; PROF MECH & ENVIRON ENG, UNIV CALIF, SANTA BARBARA, 1979-; Fulbright fel, 1978; chmn dept earth sci, Case Western Res Univ, 1973-1976; prof geophys & eng, Case Western Res Univ, 1969-1979; assoc prof eng, Case Western Res Univ, 1966-1969; sr res fel aeronaut, Calif Inst Technol, 1966; Guggenheim fel, 1965; asst prof, Harvard Univ, 1961-1966; res fel & lectr mech eng, Harvard Univ, 1959-1961. **Memberships:** Am Geophys Union; Am Soc Mech Eng; Int Asn Great Lakes Res; Soc Indust Appl Math; Int Asn Sediment Water Sci. **Research Statement & Publications:** Environmental engineering and applied mathematics. **Mailing Address:** Dept Mech & Environ Eng, Univ Calif, Rm 2335 Eng II Bldg, Santa Barbara, CA 93106-5070. **Fax:** 805-893-8651. **E-Mail:** willy@erode.ucsb.edu

LICKO, VOJTECH, MATHEMATICAL BIOLOGY. **Personal Data:** b Banska Stiavnica, Czech, August 30, 1932; American citizen; m 1959, c 1. **Education:** Slovak Univ Bratislava, MS, 1954; Czech Acad Sci, CSc, 1963; Univ Chicago, PhD (math biol), 1966. **Professional Experience:** CONSULT, 1992-; adj prof biomath, Dept Biochem & Biophys, Cardiovasc Inst, Univ Calif, San Francisco, 1990-1992; dir, Biomath Core Fac, Liver Ctr, 1980-1992; assoc adj prof biomath, Dept Med, Univ Calif, San Francisco, 1980-1990; assoc adj prof, Dept Biochem & Biophys, Cardiovasc Inst, Univ Calif, San Francisco, 1978-1990; res asst biomath, Dept Biochem & Biophys, Cardiovasc Inst, Univ Calif, San Francisco, 1974-1978; res asst, Dept Biochem & Biophys, Cardiovasc Inst, Univ Calif, San Francisco, 1973-1974; res fel biomath, Dept Biochem & Biophys, Cardiovasc Inst, Univ Calif, San Francisco, 1968-1971; scientist & assoc prof biophys, Inst Physics, Comenius Univ, Bratislava, 1966-1968; fel math biol, Univ Chicago, 1963-1966; chief radioisotope lab, Inst Endocrinol, Slovak Acad Sci, Bratislava, 1954-1963. **Memberships:** Biophys Soc; AAAS; Soc Math Biol; NY Acad Sci. **Research Statement & Publications:** Pharmacokinetics and pharmacodynamics; mathematical modeling of biochemical and physiological processes; theory of secretory mechanisms; dynamics of glucose-insulin control in man; kinetics of transport of substances through epithelia. **Mailing Address:** 1786 Fell St, San Francisco, CA 94117-2027.

LIDDELL, CRAIG MASON, EPIDEMIOLOGY OF PLANT DISEASE, ECOLOGY OF SOIL FUNGI. **Personal Data:** b Sydney, NSW, Australia, June 10, 1958; c Scott & Alexandra. **Education:** Univ Sydney, BS, 1979, Dipl plant path, 1981, PhD (plant path), 1986. **Professional Experience:** Chmn, Regional Res Proj, USDA, 1993-1994; FAC MEM, MOLECULAR BIOL GRAD PROG, 1992-; PRIN INVESTR, COMPUT RES LAB, 1990-; asst prof plant path, Nmex State Univ, beginning 1989; res asst path, Univ Wis-Madison, 1988-1989; res asst plant path, Univ Calif, Davis, 1986-1987; sr ed, J Phytopath. **Memberships:** Am Phytopath Soc; Mycol Soc Am; Australian Plant Path Soc; Brit Mycol Soc; AAAS; Ecol Soc Australia. **Research Statement & Publications:** Physical ecology of soil fungi; computer modelling of fungal growth and development; computer modelling of plant disease epidemiology; biological control of soilborne diseases of crop plants. **Mailing Address:** Dept Entom & Weed Sci, NMex State Univ, Las Cruces, NM 88003. **Fax:** 505-646-8087. **E-Mail:** craig@taipan.nmsu.edu

LIDDELL, ROBERT WILLIAM, JR, ORGANIC CHEMISTRY, BIOCHEMISTRY. **Personal Data:** b Pittsburgh, Pa, September 11, 1913; m 1990, Mary M Moore; c 3. **Education:** Univ Pittsburgh, BS, 1934, PhD (chem), 1940. **Professional Experience:** Secy, Bd dirs, 2000-; Community Water Co, 1990-; CONSULT, 1978-; mgr pilot res & develop, Calgon Corp, 1970-1978; mgr prod eng, Calgon Corp, 1963-1970; asst res mgr, Hagan Chem & Controls, Inc, 1955-1963; res chemist, Hagan Chem & Controls, Inc, 1940-1955; chemist, Hall Labs, 1935-1936; Chem engr, Swindell-Dressler Corp, 1934-1935. **Memberships:** Am Chem Soc. **Research Statement & Publications:** Water treatment; phosphate chemicals; Natural plant chem. **Mailing Address:** 20 Calle Lecho, Green Valley, AZ 85614-1999.

LIDDELL, WILLIAM DAVID, PALEOECOLOGY. **Personal Data:** b Dayton, Ohio, September 17, 1951; m 1977. **Education:** Miami Univ, BA, 1973; Univ Mich, MS, 1975, PhD (geol), 1980. **Professional Experience:** ASST PROF GEOL & PALEONT, GEOL DEPT, UTAH STATE UNIV, 1981-; Asst prof geol & paleont, Earth Sci Dept, Univ New Orleans, 1979-1981. **Memberships:** AAAS; Ecol Soc Am; Int Palaeont Asn. **Research Statement & Publications:** Paleoecology of ancient, primarily Paleozoic, communities; geology and ecology of modern coral reefs. **Mailing Address:** 5080 W 3400 S, Logan, UT 84321.

LIDDICOAT, RICHARD THOMAS, JR, gemology, mineralogy; deceased, see previous edition for last biography

LIDDLE, CHARLES GEORGE, VETERINARY MEDICINE, RADIATION BIOLOGY. **Personal Data:** b Detroit, Mich, March 22, 1936; m 1960, c 4. **Education:** Mich State Univ, BS, 1958, DVM, 1960; Univ Rochester, MS, 1963. **Professional Experience:** RETIRED; res vet, Exp Biol Div, Health Effects Res Lab, Environ Res Ctr, 1973-1992; chief biophys unit, Twinbrook Res Lab, Environ Protection Agency, 1970-1973; vet, Pvt Pract, Mich, 1960-1961. **Memberships:** Am Vet Med Asn. **Research Statement & Publications:** The effects of microwaves on the immunologic competence of laboratory animals. **Mailing Address:** 21870 Hancock Lane, Nathrop, CO 81236.

LIDE, DAVID REYNOLDS, CHEMICAL PHYSICS, SCIENCE INFORMATION. **Personal Data:** b Gainesville, Ga, May 25, 1928; m 1988, Bettijoyce; c David A, Vanessa G (Whitcomb), James H & Quentin R. **Education:** Carnegie Inst Technol, BS, 1949; Harvard Univ, AM, 1951, PhD (chem physics), 1952. **Honors & Awards:** Silver Medal, US Dept Com, 1965, Gold Medal, 1968; Stratton Award, Nat Bur Stand, 1968; Presidential Rank Award Meritorious Fed Exec, 1986; Herman Skolnik Award, Am Chem Soc, 1988; Patterson-Crane Award, Am Chem Soc, 1991. **Professional Experience:** Chmn, US Nat Comt, CODATA, 1994-1997; CO-ED, HANDBOOK DATA ORG COMPOUNDS, 1992-; vchmn, Joint Comt Atomic & Molecular Phys Data, 1989-1993; guest scientist, Nat Inst Stands & Technol, 1989-1993; bd gov, Mat Properties Data Network, Inc, 1989-1993; ED-IN-CHIEF, CRC HANDBOOK CHEM & PHYSICS, 1988-; US Adv Comt Int Coun Sci Unions, 1987-1989; pres, Comt Data Sci & Technol, Int Coun Sci Unions, 1986-1990; adv comt, Eng Info, Inc, 1984-1988; pres, Phys Chem Div, 1983-1987 & Comt Chem Databases, 1985-1989; secy gen, Comt Data Sci & Technol, Int Coun Sci Unions, 1982-1986; mem, Petrol Res Fund, 1982-1984; comt on Atomic & Molecular Sci, NAS, Nat Res Coun, 1980-1984; mem adv bd, Chem Abstracts Serv, 1978-1983; chmn, Am Inst Physics Publ Bd, 1978-1980; chmn, Comn Symbols, Terminology & Units, Int Union Pure & Appl Chem, 1977-1981; counr, Am Phys Soc, 1976-1983; US nat deleg, Comt Data Sci & Technol, Int Coun Sci Unions, 1973-1981; ed, J Phys & Chem Ref Data, 1972-1992; dir, Off Stand Ref Data, 1968-1988; NSF sr fel, Univ Bologna, 1967-1968; chief, Infrared & Microwave Spectros Sect, 1963-1968; NSF sr fel, Univ London, 1959-1960; lectr, Univ Md, 1956-1966; physicist, Nat Bur Stands, 1954-1963; res fel, Harvard Univ, 1953-1954; Fulbright scholar & Ramsay mem fel, Oxford Univ, 1952-1953. **Memberships:** Am Chem Soc; fel Am Phys Soc; AAAS. **Research Statement & Publications:** Free radicals, high temperature, microwave and infrared spectroscopy; molecular structure and spectroscopy; critical data evaluation in the physical sciences; molecular lasers; scientific databases; thermodynamics. **Mailing Address:** CRC Handbook Chem & Physics, 13901 Riding Loop Dr, Gaithersburg, MD 20878. **Fax:** 301-738-7147. **E-Mail:** dlide@earthlink.net

LIDEN, NORMAN, MATHEMATICS. **Education:** Wash Univ, PhD, 1973. **Honors & Awards:** Edyth May Sliffe Award, 1994. **Professional Experience:** PROF MATH, CHERRY CREEK HIGH SCH, ENGLEWOOD, as of 1994. **Mailing Address:** Cherry Creek High Sch, 9300 E Union Ave, Greenwood Village, CO 80111. **Fax:** 303-762-8697.

LIDGARD, GRAHAM PETER, CANCER DIAGNOSTICS. **Personal Data:** b Hull, Eng, December 23, 1948. **Education:** Univ Manchester, Eng, BA, 1970, PhD (biol chem), 1974. **Professional Experience:** SR VICE PRES, RES & DEVELOP, NANOGEN, 2003-; vpres prod & develop, Dept Res & Develop, Maritech, Inc, beginning 1988; Dept Gen Probe Biotec, Dept Res & Develop, Maritech, Inc, beginning 1988; prog mgr, Cieba-Corning, 1984-1988; prod mgr, Cieba-Corning, 1977-1984; leader, Protein Chem Lab, Regional Hormone Lab, Univ Edenboro, Scotland, 1973-1977. **Memberships:** AAAS. **Research Statement & Publications:** Cancer diagnostics. **Mailing Address:** Nanogen Inc, La Jolla, CA 92037.

LIDIAK, EDWARD GEORGE, GEOLOGY. **Personal Data:** b La Grange, Tex, March 14, 1934. **Education:** Rice Univ, BA, 1956, MA, 1960, PhD (geol), 1963. **Professional Experience:** PROF EMER GEOL & PLANETARY SCI, UNIV PITTSBURGH, as of 2004; prof geol & planetary sci, Univ Pittsburgh, beginning 1976; chmn, dept geol, Univ Pittsburgh, beginning 1971; geologist, US Geol Surv, Pa, beginning 1965; from asst prof to assoc prof geol, Univ Pittsburgh, 1964-1980; res scientist, Univ Tex, 1962-1964. **Memberships:** AAAS; Geochem Soc; Geol Soc Am. **Research Statement & Publications:** Petrology of island are volcanic rocks; geology of buried Precambrian rocks of United States; phase equilibria in mineral systems. **Mailing Address:** Dept Geol, Univ Pittsburgh, 321 Old Engineering, Pittsburgh, PA 15260-3303. **E-Mail:** egl@pitt.edu

LIDICKER, WILLIAM ZANDER, ECOLOGY, VERTEBRATE BIOLOGY. **Personal Data:** b Evanston, Ill, August 19, 1932; m 1989, Louise; c Jeffrey R & Kenneth P. **Education:** Cornell Univ, BS, 1953; Univ Ill, MS, 1954, PhD (zoology), 1957. **Honors & Awards:** AAAS, fel, 1968; C Hart Marriam Award, Am Soc Mammalogists, 1986; Hon mem Am Soc Mammalogists, 1995; Polish Acad of Sci, Foreign mem, 2000, 50th anniv medal, 2004; Calif Acad of Sci, fel, 1969; Explorers Club, fel, 1979. **Professional Experience:** EMER PROF INTEGRATIVE BIOL CUR MAMMALS, UNIV CALIF, BERKELEY, 1994-; div zool, Univ Oslo, Norway, 1990; prof integrative biol, Mus Vert Zool, 1989-1994; vis scholar, Savannah River Ecol Lab, Univ Ga, 1989-1990; adjunct res. sci, Inst of Ecology, Univ. Ga, 1989 -; Bd of Trustees, BIOSIS (Biol AbstactsInc), 1987-1992, chr 1992; co-chmn, rodent specialist group, Species Survival Comn, Int Union Conserv Nature & Natural Resources, 1980-1984 & chmn, 1984-1989; NAm rep steering comt, Int Theriological/Mammalogical Congress, 1978-1989; actg dir, Mus Vert Zool, 1974-1975; hon res fel, Dept Animal Genetics, Univ Col London, 1971-1972; hon lectr, Dept Biol, Royal Free Hosp Sch Med, London, 1971-1972; cur mammals, Mus Vert Zool, 1969-1994; prof zool, Mus Vert Zool, 1969-1989; assoc dir, Mus Vert Zool, 1968-1981; assoc res prof, Miller Inst Basic Res Sci, 1967-1968; vchmn, Dept Zool, 1966-1967 & 1981-1983; Vis scholar, Dept Zool, Sydney Univ & Div Animal Genetics, CSIRO, Sydney, Australia, 1963-1964; from asst cur to assoc cur, Mus Vert Zool, 1957-1969; from instr to assoc prof zool, Univ Calif, 1957-1969. **Memberships:** Am Soc Mammal (2nd vpres, 1974-1976, pres, 1976-1978, bd of directors, 1967 -); Ecol Soc Am; Soc Study Evolution; Am Soc Naturalists; Soc Integrative & Comp Biol; Soc Conser Biol. **Research Statement & Publications:** Ecology and evolution of mammals; population dynamics; landscape ecology; conservation; social behavior; population genetics. **Mailing Address:** Mus Vert Zool, Univ Calif, Berkeley, CA 94720-0001. **Fax:** 510-643-8238. **E-Mail:** wlidicker@berkeley.edu

LIDIN, BODIL INGER MARIA, MICROBIOLOGY. **Personal Data:** b Malmo, Sweden, May 31, 1939; m 1973, c 1. **Education:** Univ Stockholm, MS, 1974; Univ Ala, Birmingham, PhD (microbiol), 1979. **Professional Experience:** RES FEL, DEPT SURG, UNIV ALA, BIRMINGHAM, as of 2003; res assoc surg, Univ Ala, Birmingham, 1984-1994; res assoc dept microbiol, Univ Ala, Birmingham, 1981-1983; fel, Dept Pediat & Infectious Dis, Univ Ala, Birmingham, 1979-1980 & Wallenberg Lab, Uppsala Univ, 1980-1981; res asst, Karolinska Inst, Stockholm, 1970-1973; sr technologist, Univ Fla, 1968-1969; sr technologist, Inst Gustove-Rossy, Paris, 1967-1968. **Memberships:** Am Soc Microbiol. **Research Statement & Publications:** Epstine-Barr virus. **Mailing Address:** Dept Clin Virol Univ Ala, Birmingham, AL 35294.

LIDMAN, WILLIAM G, METALLURGY, CERAMICS. **Personal Data:** b Rochester, NY, November 22, 1921; m 1943, Sheila Gluck; c Bonnie (Fox), Edward & Debra (Steinfeld). **Education:** Univ Mich, BS, 1943. **Professional Experience:** DIR, PROD MGT, KB ALLOYS, CABOT CORP, READING, PA, 1986-; prod mgr, Aluminum Master Alloys, 1984-1986; tech sales mgr develop prods, KBI Div, 1980-1984; group mgr metall res & develop, Kawecki Berylco Industs, 1974-1980; mgr Hazleton, Pa Plant & Yonkers NY Div, Cabot Corp, 1971-1974; tech dir beryllium mfg, Gen Astrometals Corp, 1961-1971; proj mgr nuclear fuel elements, Sylcor Div, Gen Tel & Electronics Corp, 1960-1961; eng dept head, Sylcor Div, Gen Tel & Electronics Corp, 1957-1960; eng sect head, Sylcor Div, Gen Tel & Electronics Corp, 1952-1957; Res scientist, NASA, Ohio, 1943-1952. **Memberships:** Sigma Xi; Am Soc Metals (treas, 1955-1957); Am Inst Metall Engrs. **Research Statement & Publications:** Sintering mechanism of powder metallurgy products; production methods for manufacturing fuel elements for nuclear reactors and beryllium products; chemical specialty metals and beryllium; non-ferrous materials; refractory metals and ceramics; special aluminum alloy additives. **Mailing Address:** 354 Pennsylvania Ave, Shillington, PA 19607. **E-Mail:** wslid@uno.com

LIDOFSKY, LEON JULIAN, NUCLEAR ENGINEERING, COMPUTER SCIENCE. **Personal Data:** b Norwich, Conn, November 8, 1924; m 1948, c 2. **Education:** Tufts Univ, BS, 1945; Columbia Univ, MA, 1947, PhD (physics), 1952. **Professional Experience:** PROF EMER & SPEC LECT APPL PHYSICS & NUCLEAR ENG, COLUMBIA UNIV, as of 2005; consult, Am Phys Soc Study Group, 1976-1977 & Mt Sinai Sch Med, 1970-1977; res scholar, Inst Nuclear Physics, Amsterdam, 1968-1969; prof appl physics & nuclear eng, columbia univ, beginning 1964; from asst prof to assoc prof nuclear sci & eng, Columbia Univ, 1959-1964; res assoc, Columbia Univ, 1952-1959; res asst, Columbia Univ, 1949-1952; instr physics, NY State Maritime Col, 1948-1949. **Memberships:** Am Nuclear Soc; Am Phys Soc. **Research Statement & Publications:** Radiation transport; nuclear physics. **Mailing Address:** Appl Physics, Columbia Univ, 2960 Broadway, New York, NY 10027-6902. **Fax:** 212-854-8257. **E-Mail:** lidofsky@columbia.edu

LIDOW, ERIC, ELECTRICAL ENGINEERING, SOLID STATE PHYSICS. **Personal Data:** b Vilnius, Lithuania, December 9, 1912; American citizen; m 1952, c 4. **Education:** Tech Univ, Berlin, MS, 1937. **Professional Experience:** PRES & CHMN BD, INT RECTIFIER CORP, 1947-; DIR, INT RECTIFIER CORP, 1947-; vpres charge res & eng, Selenium Corp Am, 1944-1946; Chief engr, Selenium Corp Am, 1941-1944. **Memberships:** Sr mem Inst Elec & Electronics Engrs. **Research Statement & Publications:** Photoelectric phenomena; selenium photocells; selenium rectifiers; silicone power devices. **Mailing Address:** Int Rectifier Corp, 233 Kansas St, El Segundo, CA 90245.

LIDTKE, DORIS KEEFE, COMPUTER SCIENCE EDUCATION, SOCIAL & ETHICAL ISSUES IN COMPUTING. **Personal Data:** b Bottineau Co, NDak, December 6, 1929; m 1951, Vernon. **Education:** Univ Ore, BS, 1952, PhD (comput sci educ), 1979; Johns Hopkins Univ, MEd, 1974. **Honors & Awards:** Golden Core, Inst Elec & ELectronics Engr Comput Soc, 1996. **Professional Experience:** Adj accreditation dir for comput, ABET, beginning 1999; prog dir, NSF, 1992-1993; PROF COMPUT SCI, TOWSON UNIV, 1990-; Software Productivity Consortium, 1987-1988; assoc prog dir, NSF, 1984; assoc prof, Towson State Univ, 1981-1990; vis assoc prof, Univ Ore, 1981-1983, 1985; asst prof comput sci & math, Towson State Univ, 1968-1981; educ specialist, Johns Hopkins Univ, 1968; asst prof comput, Lansing Community Col, 1963-1967; programmer, Univ Calif, Berkeley, 1960-1962; jr mathematician, Shell Develop Co, 1955-1959. **Memberships:** Asn Comput Mach; Inst Elec & Electronics Engrs Comput oc; Nat Educ Comput Conf; Comput Sci Accredation Bd; Asn Coput Mach Coun. **Research Statement & Publications:** Impact of computer on society; computer literacy and computer awareness; computers and education; computer and information sciences curriculiam. **Mailing Address:** Dept Comput & Info Sci, Towson State Univ, Baltimore, MD 21204.

LIE, WEN-RONG, MOLECULAR IMMUNOLOGY, IMMUNOGENETICS. **Personal Data:** b Taiwan, China, September 27, 1957; m 1986, Jen S Chan; c Jonathan C. **Education:** Tunghai Univ, BS, 1979; Iowa State Univ, PhD (immunobiol), 1987. **Professional Experience:** RES SCIENTIST, SEARLE, ST LOUIS, 1994-; sr res biologist, Monsanto, St Louis, 1992-1994; Am Asn Immunologists travel award, 1989; fel, Sch Med, Wash Univ, St Louis, 1987-1992. **Memberships:** Am Asn Immunologists. **Research Statement & Publications:** Molecular biology of class I major histocompatibility complex molecules. **Mailing Address:** Dept Immunol AA4G Searle Res & Develop Seaarle Monsanto, 700 Chesterfield Pkwy N, St Louis, MO 63198-0001.

LIEB, CARL SEARS, HERPETOLOGY. **Personal Data:** b San Antonio, Tex, May 27, 1949; m 1980, Joyce; c David, Eric & Joseph. **Education:** Tex A&M Univ, BS, 1971, MS, 1973; Univ Calif, Los Angeles, PhD (biol), 1981. **Professional Experience:** ASSOC CUR, LEB HERPET COLLECTIONS, as of 2004; ASST CHMN, DEPT BIOL SCI, UNIV TEX, EL PASO, as of 2004; ASSOC PROF & MEM GRAD FAC BIO SCI, UNIV TEX, EL PASO, as of 2004; dir, Indio Mountains Res Sta, 1991-1996; assoc prof & coordr, Introd Biol Labs, 1990-1992; interim dir, Centennial Mus, 1989-1990; herpetology ed, Southwestern Naturalist, 1987-1989; assoc cur, Lab Environ Biol, Univ Tex, El Paso, 1987-1989; vis fac, Brigham Young Univ, 1984-1985; mem, gred fac, Lab Environ Biol, Univ Tex, El Paso, beginning 1983; res assoc, Natural Hist Mus Los Angeles Co, 1982-; asst cur, Lab Environ Biol, Univ Tex, El Paso, 1981-1987; Mus assoc, Natural Hist Mus Los Angeles Co, 1973-1982. **Memberships:** Am Soc Ichthyologists & Herpetologists; Herpetologists' League; Soc Study Amphibians & Reptiles; Southwestern Asn Naturalists; Sigma Xi; Soc Molecular Biol & Evolution. **Research Statement & Publications:** Taxonomy, biosystematics and evolutionary genetics of amphibians and reptiles. **Mailing Address:** Dept Biol Sci, Univ Tex, 500 W Univ Ave Rm 202, El Paso, TX 79968-0519. **Fax:** 915-747-5808. **E-Mail:** elieb@mail.utep.edu

LIEB, ELLIOTT HERSHEL, MATHEMATICAL PHYSICS. **Personal Data:** b Boston, Mass, July 31, 1932; m 1975, Christiane Fellbaum; c Alexander & Gregory. **Education:** Mass Inst Technol, BSc, 1953; Univ Birmingham, U.K PhD (physics), 1956. **Honorary Degrees:** DSc, Univ Copenhagen, 1979, Fed Polytech Inst, Lausanne, 1995. **Honors & Awards:** Boris Pregel Award, NY Acad Sci, 1970; Heineman Prize, Am Phys Soc & Am Inst Physics, 1978; Sci Prize, UAP, 1985; Birkhoff Prize, Am Math Soc & Soc Indust Appl Math, 1988; Max-Planck Medal, Ger Phys Soc, 1992. **Professional Experience:** Coun mem, Am Math Soc, 1992-; mem bd trustees, Math Sci Res Inst, 1985-1989; mem bd gov, Inst Math & Applns, 1983-1987; vis prof, Inst Advan Study, NJ, 1982; PROF MATH & PHYSICS, PRINCETON UNIV, 1975-; Guggenheim Found fel, 1972 & 1978; guest prof, Inst Advan Sci Studies, France, 1972-1973; prof math, Mass Inst Technol, 1968-1975; prof, Northeastern Univ, 1966-1968; assoc prof physics, Belfer Grad Sch Sci, Yeshiva Univ, 1963-1966; consult, IBM Corp, 1963-1965; Sr lectr, Univ Col Sierra Leone, 1961-1962; staff physicist, Res Lab, IBM Corp, 1960-1963; lab nuclear studies, Cornell Univ, 1958-1960; res assoc, Univ Ill, 1957-1958; Fulbright fel physics, Kyoto Univ, 1956-1957; ed, Commun Math Phys, Studies Appl Math, Lett Math Phys & Rev Mod Phys. **Memberships:** Nat Acad Sci; fel Am Phys Soc; Austrian Acad Sci; Int Asn Math Physics (pres, 1982-1984 & 1997-1999); Royal Danish Acad Sci & Letts; Am Acad Arts & Sci. **Research Statement & Publications:** Statistical mechanics; field theory; solid state physics; atomic physics; analysis; mathematical physics. **Mailing Address:** Dept Physics Princeton Univ, PO Box 708 Jadwin Hall, Princeton, NJ 08544-0708. **Fax:** 609-258-6360.

LIEB, MARGARET, GENETICS. **Personal Data:** b Bronxville, NY, November 28, 1923. **Education:** Smith Col, BA, 1945; Ind Univ, MA, 1946; Columbia Univ, PhD, 1950. **Professional Experience:** Prog dir genetic biol, NSF, 1972-1973; PROF MICROBIOL, SCH MED, UNIV SOUTHERN CALIF, 1967-; NIH res career award, 1962-1972; assoc prof, Sch Med, Univ Southern Calif, 1962-1967; vis assoc prof, Sch Med, Univ Southern Calif, 1960-1962; Asst prof biol, Brandeis Univ, 1955-1960; French Govt fel, Inst Radium, 1954-1955; fel, Inst Pasteur, 1953-1954; USPHS fel, Nat Found Infantile Paralysis fel, 1952-1953; USPHS fel, Calif Inst Technol, 1950-1952. **Memberships:** Fel AAAS; Genetics Soc Am; emer mem Am Soc Microbiol. **Research Statement & Publications:** Bacteriophage genetics; DNA repair; spontaneous mutation. **Mailing Address:** Dept Molecular Microbiol & Immunol, Keck Sch Med, Univ Southern Calif, Los Angeles, CA 90089-0010. **Fax:** 323-442-1721. **E-Mail:** mlieb@hsc.usc.edu

LIEBE, RICHARD MILTON, GEOLOGY. **Personal Data:** b Norwalk, Conn, May 26, 1932; m 1955, c 3. **Education:** Bates Col, BS, 1954; Univ Houston, MS, 1959; Univ Iowa, PhD (geol), 1962. **Professional Experience:** PROF EMER GEOL, STATE UNIV NY, BROCKPORT, as of 2004; prof geol, State Univ NY, brockport, beginning 1967; assoc prof geol, Col Wooster, 1961-1967. **Memberships:** Paleont Soc; Nat Asn Geol Teachers. **Research Statement & Publications:** Stratigraphic paleontology of the Paleozoic era using conodonts; shallow water sedimentology and coral reef ecology. **Mailing Address:** Dept Earth Sci, State Univ NY, Brockport, NY 14420-2915. **E-Mail:** rmliebe@juno.com

LIEBECK, ROBERT H, AERONAUTICS. **Education:** Univ Ill, PhD (aeronaut & astronaut eng), 1968. **Honors & Awards:** Spirit St. Louis Medal, 2005. **Professional Experience:** SR FEL, BOEING CO, as of 2006; adj prof mech & aerospace eng, Univ Calif, Irvine, as of 2006. **Memberships:** Nat Acad Eng. **Mailing Address:** Univ Calif, Irvine, 305 Rockwell Eng Ctr, Irvine, CA 92697-3975. **Fax:** 949-824-8585. **E-Mail:** rliebeck@uci.edu

LIEBELT, ANNABEL GLOCKLER, MICROSCOPIC ANATOMY, CANCER. **Personal Data:** b Washington, DC, June 27, 1926; div, c Ralph A, Laurie A, Erica L & Nancy L (Guthrie). **Education:** Western Md Col, BA, 1948; Univ Ill, Col Med, MS, 1955; Baylor Col Med, PhD (anat), 1960. **Professional Experience:** SPEC VOL, NAT CANCER INST, 1992-; vis prof, Univ Tokushima Med Sch, Japan, 1990; fel expert, Nat Cancer Inst, 1987-1992; bd dirs, Portage Co Children's Serv Ctr, 1979-1982; chmn, Micros Anat Teaching Prog, 1979-1981; dir, Micros Anat Teaching Prog, 1978-1979; pres, Am Cancer Soc, Portage Co Unit, 1977-1978; coordr, Micros Anat Teaching Prog, 1977; consult, Breast Cancer Task Force, Nat Cancer Inst, NIH, 1976-1980; vpres, Am Cancer Soc, Portage Co Unit, 1976-1977; prof anat, Neastern Ohio Univs Col Med, 1974-1986; bd dirs, Am Cancer Soc, Portage Co Unit, 1974-1982; chair, Prof Educ Comt, 1974-1978; bd dirs, Augusta Radiation Ctr, 1972-1974; assoc prof cell & molecular biol, Med Col Ga, 1971-1974; dir, Kirschbaum Mem Lab, Col Med, Baylor Univ, 1962-1971; from instr to assoc prof, Col Med, Baylor Univ, 1958-1971; asst, Col Med, Baylor Univ, 1954-1958; asst anat, Col Med, Univ Ill, 1952-1954; biologist, Path Sect, Nat Cancer Inst, 1949-1952. **Memberships:** NY Acad Sci; life mem Am Cancer Soc; Am Asn Path; Am Asn Lab Animal Sci; Soc Toxicol Path; Am Asn Cancer Res; Sigma Xi; Am Asn Women Sci; Am Asn Anatomists; US & Can Acad Path. **Research Statement & Publications:** Carcinogenesis, aging and pathology in inbred mice of several organ systems, especially the endocrine and reproductive (emphasis on mammary gland); biology histopathology; etiology; metastasis, environmental influences; animal models; educational materials or study sets of microscopic slides and accompanying syllabi. **Mailing Address:** Registry Exp Cancers, Nat Cancer Inst, 830 Quince Orchard Blvd #202, Gaithersburg, MD 20878-0736. **Fax:** 301-402-1829.

LIEBELT, ROBERT ARTHUR, ANATOMY, ALCOHOLISM. **Personal Data:** b Chicago, Ill, February 3, 1927; m 1980, c 5. **Education:** Loyola Univ, Ill, BS, 1950; Wash State Univ, MS, 1952; Baylor Univ, PhD (anat), 1957, MD, 1958. **Professional Experience:** Dir med educ, St Thomas Hosp, Akron, Ohio, 1982; DIR, IGNATIA HALL ACUTE ALCOHOL TREAT CTR, AKRON, OHIO, 1982-; provost/dean, Northeastern Ohio Univ Col Med, 1979-1982; prof anat, Northeastern Ohio Univ Col Med, beginning 1974; charter dean, Northeastern Ohio Univ Col Med, 1974-1979; provost, Med Col Ga, 1972-1974; prof cell & molecular biol & exp med & assoc dean curriculum, Med Col Ga, 1971-1972; Vis prof, Okayama Univ, 1961; from instr to prof anat & chmn dept, Col Med, Baylor Univ, 1957-1971; asst, Col Med, Baylor Univ, 1954-1957; Asst, Wash State Univ, 1950-1952. **Memberships:** AAAS; Soc Exp Biol & Med; Am Asn Anat; Am Asn Cancer Res; NY Acad Sci. **Research Statement & Publications:** Adipose tissue in obesity; relationship between nutrition and neoplasia; hypothalamus and appetite control; hypothalmic-pituitary relationships in experimental neoplasia; effects of pressure on food intake and body composition; biostereometric analysis for breast cancer; medical education; alcoholism. **Mailing Address:** Summa Health Syst, 525 E Market St, PO Box 2090, Akron, OH 44309-2090.

LIEBENAUER, PAUL (HENRY), EXPERIMENTAL NUCLEAR PHYSICS. **Personal Data:** b Cleveland, Ohio, September 21, 1935; m 1962, c 2. **Education:** Case Western Reserve Univ, BS, 1957, MS, 1960, PhD (physics), 1971. **Professional Experience:** PROF EMER PHYSICS, STATE UNIV NY, OSWEGO, as of 2003; NSF grant, 1972; consult, NASA, 1971-; assoc prof physics, State Univ NY, Oswego, beginning 1970; asst prof, State Univ NY Col Oswego, 1968-1970; instr physics, Clarkson Col Technol, 1960-1962. **Memberships:** Am Phys Soc; Am Asn Physics Teachers; Sigma Xi. **Research Statement & Publications:** Low energy nuclear physics. **Mailing Address:** Dept Physics, State Univ Col, Oswego, NY 13126.

LIEBENBERG, DONALD HENRY, LOW TEMPERATURE PHYSICS, HIGH PRESSURES & SUPERCONDUCTIVITY. **Personal Data:** b Madison, Wis, July 10, 1932; m 1957, Norma; c Karl H & Kira J. **Education:** Univ Wis, BS, 1954, MS, 1956, PhD, 1971. **Professional Experience:** ADJ PROF PHYSICS, CLEMSON UNIV, 1996-; staff mem & sci officer condensed matter physics, Off Naval Res, 1988-1995; staff mem, NSF, 1981-1988; coordr, Solar Eclipse 1970; res prog dir, Solar-terrestrial, NSF, 1967-1968; staff mem physics, Los Alamos Nat Lab, 1961-1987; asst, Univ Wis, 1954-1961; adj prof physics; app liaison, Geophys Res Bd, Nat Acad Sci. **Memberships:** AAAS; Am Astron Soc; fel Am Phys Soc; Am Geophys Union. **Research Statement & Publications:** Low temperature physics, especially superfluidity and helium films; solar physics; magneto optics; high pressure physical measurements; high pressure physics, superconductivity. **Mailing Address:** Dept Physics & Astron, Clemson Univ, Clemson, SC 29634-0978.

LIEBER, ALBERT J, PHYSICS. **Education:** Cal Tech, BS; Univ Wash, PhD (Nuclear Physics). **Professional Experience:** RETIRED; scientist, Ames Res Ctr, NASA, ending 1998. **Mailing Address:** 13751 Nogales Dr, Southern California, CA 92014. **Fax:** 650-604-1592.

LIEBER, BARUCH B, BIOMEDICAL ENGINEERING. **Personal Data:** b Tel Aviv, Israel, August 6, 1952. **Education:** Tel Aviv Univ, BS, 1979; Ga Inst Technol, MS, 1983, PhD (biomed), 1985. **Professional Experience:** PROF, DEPT BIOMED ENG, UNIV MIAMI, 2001-; prof, Dept Mech, State Univ NY, 1998-2001; adj res prof, Roswell park Cancer Inst, 1996-2001; from asst prof to assoc prof, Dept mech, State Univ NY, 1987-1998; researcher, 1985-1987. **Memberships:** Biomed Eng Soc; Am Inst Aeronaut & Astronaut; Sigma Xi; Am Soc Med Eng. **Mailing Address:** Dept Biomed Eng, Univ Miami, PO Box 248294, Coral Gables, FL 33124-0621. **Fax:** 305-284-6494. **E-Mail:** blieber@miami.edu

LIEBER, CHARLES SAUL, INTERNAL MEDICINE, NUTRITION. **Personal Data:** b Antwerp, Belg, February 13, 1931; American citizen; m 1974, c 3. **Education:** Univ Brussels, MD, 1955. **Honors & Awards:** Laureate, Belg Govt, 1956; McCollum Award, Am Soc Clin Nutrit, 1973, Herman Award, 1993; Distinguished Achievement Award, Am Gastroent Asn, 1973, Hugh R Butt Award Liver/Nutrit, 1992; E M Jellinek Mem Award, 1977; W S Middleton Award, US Vet Admin, 1977; Sci Excellence Award, Res Soc Alcoholism, 1980, Distinguished Serv Award, 1992; Achievement Award, Am Soc Addictive Med, 1989; Outstanding Achievement Award, Am Col Nutrit, 1990. **Professional Experience:** DIR, ALCOHOLISM RES & TREAT CTR, 1977-; PROF MED & PATHOL, MT SINAI SCH MED, 1969-; CHIEF SECT LIVER DIS & NUTRIT, VET ADMIN HOSP, 1968-; assoc prof, Alcoholism res & Treat Ctr, 1968-1969; NIH res career develop award, 1964-1968; dir liver dis & nutrit unit, Bellevue Hosp, 1963-1968; assoc prof, Med Col, Cornell Univ, 1963-1968; assoc, Harvard Med Sch, 1962-1963; mem fat comt, Food & Nutrit Bd, Nat Acad Sci-Nat res Coun, 1961-1967; instr med, Harvard Med Sch, 1961-1962; Belg-Am Found res fel med, Harvard Med Sch, 1958-1960; Belg Coun Sci res fel internal med, Med Found Queen Elizabeth, 1956-1958; asst resident med, Univ Hosp Brugmann Brussels, Belg, 1955-1956. **Memberships:** Am Soc Clin Invest; Am Med Soc Alcoholism (pres, 1975); Am Soc Clin Nutrit (pres, 1975); Asn Am Physicians; Res Soc Alcoholism (pres, 1979). **Research Statement & Publications:** Diseases of the liver; nutrition and intermediary metabolism, especially alcoholic cirrhosis, fatty liver, hyperlipemia, hyperuricemia, pathogenesis and treatment of hepatic coma and ascites, and pathophysiology of liver regeneration and drug abuse. **Mailing Address:** Dept Path, Mt Sinai Sch Med, Annenberg Bldg, Bronx, NY 10468-3904. **Fax:** 718-733-6257.

LIEBER, MICHAEL, THEORETICAL PHYSICS. **Personal Data:** b Brooklyn, NY, December 28, 1936; m 1964, Eileen; c Kenneth, Laura & Deborah. **Education:** Cornell Univ, AB, 1957; Harvard Univ, AM, 1958, PhD (physics), 1967. **Professional Experience:** Vis mem, Inst Theoret Physics, Univ Calif, Santa Barbara, 1988; PROF PHYSICS, UNIV ARK, 1983-; chmn dept, Univ Ark, 1983-1986; prin investr, Dept Energy, 1980-1985; dir, Reach Kit Proj, 1974-1978; planetarium lectr, Univ Ark, 1972-1983; from asst prof to assoc prof, Univ Ark, 1970-1983; assoc res scientist & adj asst prof physics, NY Univ, 1967-1970; chief sci probs, Res & Advan Develop Div, Avco Corp, 1966-1967; sr scientist, Res & Advan Develop Div, Avco Corp, 1963-1966. **Memberships:** Am Phys Soc; Am Asn Physics Teachers; Sigma Xi (pres local chapter, 1998-1999). **Research Statement & Publications:** Quantum scattering theory; few body problems; quantum electrodynamics and field theory; mathematical methods; atomic collisions; cosmic rays; elementary particles; general relativity and cosmology. **Mailing Address:** Dept Physics, Univ Ark, PHYS 223, Fayetteville, AR 72701. **Fax:** 479-575-4580. **E-Mail:** mlieber@comp.uark.edu

LIEBER, RICHARD L, MUSCLE MECHANICS & REHABILITATION. **Personal Data:** b Walnut Creek, Calif, December 14, 1956; m 2004, Dina; c Katelyn & Kristin. **Education:** Univ Calif, Davis, BS, 1978, PhD, 1982. **Honors & Awards:** Talbot Award, Biophys Soc, 1981; Excellence in Free Paper Presentations, Intn'l Fed for Hand Surgery, 1998, 1995, Kappa Delta Award, Amer Academy of Orthopaedic Surgery, 1994; Nicolas Andry Award, Amer Bone & Joint Surgeons, 2002. **Professional Experience:** PROF ORTHOP SURG & BIOENGINEERING, UNIV CALIF, SAN DEIGO, as of 2004; Career Scientist, Veterans Affairs Med Center, San Diego, 2000-present; Assoc. Profeesor, University California, San Diego 1990-1994; Assist. Professor, University California, San Diego, Calif 1985-1990; Biomedical Engineer, Veterans Affairs Med Center, San Diego 1983-2000; Postgraduate Researcher, Physiologist, University California, San Diego 1982-1985. **Memberships:** Biophysics Soc; Am Physiological Soc; Orthopaedic Research Soc; Am Soc of Biomechanics; Am College of Sports Medicine. **Research Statement & Publications:** Characterize skeletal muscle adaptation to altered use; elucidate mechanisms of torque generation during normal movement. **Mailing Address:** Univ Calif, San Diego, 9500 Gilman Dr, La Jolla, CA 92093. **Fax:** 858-552-4381. **E-Mail:** rlieber@ucsd.edu

LIEBERBURG, IVAN M, NEUROSCIENCE, ENDOCRINOLOGY. **Personal Data:** b June 18, 1949. **Education:** Cornell Univ, BA, 1971; Rockefeller Univ, PhD (neurobiol), 1976; Univ Miami, MD, 1980; Am Bd Internal Med, cert, 1983, cert endocrinol & metab, 1985. **Professional Experience:** EXEC VPRES & CHIEF SCI & MED OFFICER, ELAN CORP, as of 2002; vpres res, Athena Neuroscience, Inc, beginning 1994; clin prof med, Univ Calif Hosps, San Francisco, beginning 1994; vpres Alzheimer's res, Dept Molecular Biol, Athena Neuroscience, Inc, 1990-1994; assoc clin prof med, Univ Calif Hosps, San Francisco, 1990-1994; sr scientist, Dept Molecular Biol, Athena Neuroscience, Inc, 1988-1990; staff scientist, Dept Cell Biol, Athena Neuroscience, Inc, 1987-1988; assoc prof neurobiology & psychiat, Mt Sinai Sch Med, 1987; asst prof endocrinol & med, Albert Einstein Col Med, 1984-1987; res fel endocrine, Univ, 1982-1984; med resident, Univ Calif Hosps, San Francisco, 1980-1982. **Memberships:** Fel Orgn Trop Studies; Endocrine Soc; Soc Neuroscience; Am Asn Cancer Researchers; Am Soc Cell Biol; Am Asn Neuropathologists. **Research Statement & Publications:** Neuroscience; endocrinology. **Mailing Address:** Elan Corp, Lincoln House, Lincoln Pl, Dublin, Ireland.

LIEBERMAN, ABRAHAM N, NEUROLOGY. **Personal Data:** b Brooklyn, NY, July 8, 1938; c 4. **Education:** Univ Cornell, AB, 1959; NY Univ Med Sch, MD, 1963. **Professional Experience:** MED DIR, NAT PARKINSON FOUND, as of 2003; prof neurol, NY Univ Med Ctr, 1980-; consult, AMA Drug Evaluations, Chicago, Ill, 1979-; dir, Neurol Clin, Bellevue Hosp, 1973-; grants & contracts, Univ var, cols & insts, 1971-1985; from asst prof to assoc prof, NY Univ Med Ctr, 1971-1980; attend physician, Univ Hosp, NY Univ Sch Med, 1970-; asst chief neurol, Manhattan Vet Admin Hosp, 1970-1972; instr, NY Univ Med Ctr, 1970-1971; staff neurologist, US Air Force Hosp, Tachikawa, Japan, 1967-1969. **Memberships:** Asn Res Nervous & Ment Dis; Am EEG Soc; Am Soc Clin Pharmacol & Therapeut; fel Am Col Clin Pharmacol; Am Neurol Asn. **Research Statement & Publications:** Published over 200 articles. **Mailing Address:** 500 W Thomas Rd Ste 300, Phoenix, AZ 85013.

LIEBERMAN, ALVIN, chemical engineering; deceased, see previous edition for last biography

LIEBERMAN, ARTHUR STUART, REGIONAL LANDSCAPE PLANNING & LANDSCAPE ECOLOGY. **Personal Data:** b Brooklyn, NY, February 24, 1931; m 1956, c 3. **Education:** Cornell Univ, BS, 1952, MS/LD, 1958. **Professional Experience:** STAFF MEM, DEPT OVERSEAS STUD PROGS, UNIV HAIFA; res dir, Cornell (Abroad) Prog Israel, 1987-; emer prof, Cornell Univ, 1986-; consult, UN Food & Agr Orgn, Bangalore, India, 1985; res fel, Lady Davis vis prof award, 1980-1981; prof, Technion, 1980-1981; res proj coordr, Multidisciplinary Int Land-Use Planning Prog, 1979-1986; chmn & coordr, Cornell Tree Crops, Cornell Univ, 1978-1986; res fel, Technion Israel Inst Technol, Haifa, 1975-1976; Adv, Nature Reserves Authority & Ministry Agr, Israel, 1971-1972; from instr to prof environ qual, Cornell Univ, 1958-1986; Teacher high sch, NY, 1952-1953. **Memberships:** Int Asn Landscape Ecol; Israel Soc Ecol & Environ Qual Sci. **Research Statement & Publications:** Physical environmental quality; ecology-based regional land-use planning; regional landscape inventories and information systems for physical planning; analysis and use of vegetation in comprehensive land planning; tree crops (agroforestry) for food and forage on rough marginal lands. **Mailing Address:** Dept Overseas Stud Progs, Univ Haifa, Mt Carmel Haifa 31905, Israel. **Fax:** 972-482-40391.

LIEBERMAN, BURTON BARNET, MATHEMATICS. **Personal Data:** b Boston, Mass, September 28, 1938; m 1963, Miriam; c Bruce S & Jenny M. **Education:** Harvard Univ, BA, 1960; NY Univ, MS, 1962, PhD (math), 1967. **Professional Experience:** PROF MATH, POLYTECH UNIV, 1994-; chair, Comput Sci Dept, Polytech Univ, 1995-1996; admin officer, Math Dept, 1991-; actg chmn, Math Dept, 1990; prin investr & consult, US Golf Asn, 1979-; assoc prof math, Polytech Univ, 1969-1993; asst prof, Math Dept, 1965-1969. **Memberships:** Am Math Soc; Sigma Xi; Inst Math Stat; Am Stat Asn; Math Asn Am. **Research Statement & Publications:** Ordinary differential equations; robust statistical methods; sports science; mathematical model of the impact and aerodynamics of the golf club and ball, respectively. **Mailing Address:** Dept Math, Polytech Univ, 6 Metrotech Ctr, Brooklyn, NY 11201. **E-Mail:** blieber@duke.ploy.edu

LIEBERMAN, DANIEL, PSYCHIATRY. **Personal Data:** b Gunnison, Utah, February 21, 1919; c Janine (Vogel). **Education:** Univ Calif, BA, 1942, MD, 1946. **Professional Experience:** Med dir, Medco Corp, 1991-1994; PROF EMER, DEPT PSYCHIAT & HUMAN BEHAV, JEFFERSON MED COL, THOMAS JEFFERSON UNIV, 1989-; prof & chmn, Psychosom Serv, 1983-1989; prof & dir, Psychosom Serv, 1976-1983; prof & actg chmn, Dept Psychiat & Human Behav, 1974-1976; consult, Nat Coun Community Health Ctrs, 1972-1973; consult, Vet Admin Hosp, Coatesville, Pa, 1967-1989; dir, Jefferson Community Ment Health-Ment Retardation Ctr, Thomas Jefferson Univ, 1967-1974; consult, Alcohol Rev Comt, 1967-1970; consult state ment progs, NIMH, 1965-1968; comnr ment health, Del Dept Ment Health, 1964-1967; pvt pract, 1963-1964; consult, Ment Health Res Inst, Palo Alto, Calif, Nat Inst Alcohol Abuse & Acoholism, 1963-1964; consult forensic psychiat, US Fed Court, 1961-; from chief dep dir to dir, State Dept Ment Health, 1960-1963; consult ment hosp serv, Am Psychiat Asn, 1960-1962; consult forensic psychiat, Calif Superior Courts, 1954-1963; supt & med dir, Mendocino State Hosp, 1954-1960; chief hosp serv, Sonoma State Hosp, Calif, 1949-1954. **Memberships:** fel AAAS; Am Col Psychiat; fel Am Asn Ment Deficiency; fel Acad Psychosom Med; fel Am Psychiat Asn; fel Am Asn Social Psych; Sigma Xi. **Research Statement & Publications:** Chronic pain; psychosomatic medicine; treatment of stress disorders. **Mailing Address:** Thomas Jefferson Univ, Curtis Bldg Rm 327F 11th & Walnut St, Philadelphia, PA 19107. **Fax:** 215-923-8219.

LIEBERMAN, DIANA DALE, POPULATION BIOLOGY, TROPICAL FOREST ECOLOGY. **Personal Data:** b Los Angeles, Calif, January 19, 1949; m 1968, Milton; c Sarah. **Education:** Univ Ghana, Legon, BSc, 1976, PhD (bot), 1979. **Professional Experience:** RESIDENT DIR, SAN LUIS BIOL STA, COSTA RICA, 1995-; Mellon Found res grant, 1994-1996; PROF BIOL, DEPT BIOL, UNIV NDAK, 1992-; NASA, res grant, 1987-1990; from asst prof to assoc prof, San Luis Biol Sta, Costa Rica, 1981-1992; NSF res grants, 1981-1986, 1992-; vis scholar forest ecol & trop biol, Dept Environ Sci, Univ Va, 1980-1981; demonstr plant ecol, Dept Bot, Univ Ghana, 1976-1979. **Memberships:** Ecol Soc Am; Sigma Xi; Asn Trop Biologists; Int Soc Trop Foresters. **Research Statement & Publications:** Tree growth rates, age-size relationships and tropical forest dynamics; plant population biology, phenology and seed dispersal; community ecology; tropical forest conservation and restoration. **Mailing Address:** Apdo 35, Santa Elena Monteverde, Punts, Costa Rica. **Fax:** 506-645-5277; 506-380-3255.

LIEBERMAN, EDWARD MARVIN, PHYSIOLOGY. **Personal Data:** b Lowell, Mass, February 10, 1938; m 1960, c 3. **Education:** Tufts Univ, BS, 1959; Univ Mass, MS, 1961; Univ Fla, PhD (physiol), 1965. **Professional Experience:** DIR, NEUROSCIENCE PROG, SCH MED, E CAROLINA UNIV, as of 2004; PROF PHYSIOL, SCH MED, E CAROLINA UNIV, 1978-; assoc prof, 1976-1978; assoc prof, Bowman Gray Sch Med, 1972-1976; asst prof, 1968-1972; Swed Med Res Coun fel, Col Med, Univ Uppsala, 1966-1968; res assoc physiol, Col Med, Univ Fla, 1966; fel, Univ Uppsala, Sweden, 1966-1968. **Memberships:** Soc Neuroscience; Biophys Soc; Am Heart Asn; Am Physiol Soc; NY Acad Sci. **Research Statement & Publications:** Cellular nerve physiology; membrane ion and water transport and metabolism; ultraviolet radiation effects on membranes; Schwann cell axon interactions. **Mailing Address:** Dept Physiol, Sch Med, E Carolina Univ, 6N51 Brody Bldg 600 Moye Blvd, Greenville, NC 27858-4354. **Fax:** 252-816-3460. **E-Mail:** liebermane@mail.ecu.edu

LIEBERMAN, EDWIN JAMES, PSYCHIATRY, SCIENCE COMMUNICATIONS. **Personal Data:** b Milwaukee, Wis, November 21, 1934; m 1988, Carol; c Karen L (Troccoli) & Daniel. **Education:** Univ Calif, Berkeley, AB, 1955; Univ Calif, San Francisco, MD, 1958; Harvard Univ, MPH, 1963; Am Bd Psychiat & Neurol, dipl, 1966. **Honors & Awards:** Life fel, Am Psychiat Asn. **Professional Experience:** PVT PRACTICE ADULT & FAMILY PSYCHIAT, FAMILY INST, as of 2005; CLIN PROF PSYCHIAT, SCH MED, GEORGE WASH UNIV, 1990-; adj prof, Family & Community Develop, Univ Md, 1987-1990; clin assoc prof psychiat, Sch Med, George Wash Univ, 1977-1987; dir family planning proj, Am Pub Health Asn, 1975-1977; dir ment health proj, Hillcrest Children's Ctr, DC, 1972-1975; dir family ther, Hillcrest Children's Ctr, DC, 1971-1974; vis lectr maternal & child health, Harvard Sch Pub Health, 1969-1973; mem bd dirs, Nat Coun Family Rels, 1969-1973; clin asst prof psychiat, Sch Med, Howard Univ, 1967-1976; mem bd dirs, Sex Info & Educ Coun US, 1966-1969 & 1973-1976; Child psychiat fel, Hillcrest Children's Ctr, DC, 1965-1966; psychiatrist & chief, Ctr Child & Family Ment Health, NIMH, 1963-1970; child psychiat fel, Putnam's Children Ctr, Boston, 1961-1962; Psychiat fel, Mass Ment Health Ctr, Boston, 1959-1961. **Memberships:** AAAS; fel Am Psychiat Asn; fel Am Pub Health Asn; fel Am Asn Marriage & Family Therapists; Esperanto League NAm (pres, 1972-1975). **Research Statement & Publications:** Mental health; preventive psychiatry; family planning; nonviolence; Esperantic studies; international language planning; Otto Rank (1884-1939); evolution of psycho therapy. **Mailing Address:** Pvt Practice Adult & Family Psychiat, Family Inst, 5410 Conn Ave NW, Washington, DC 20015. **E-Mail:** ejl@gwu.edu

LIEBERMAN, HERBERT A, PHARMACEUTICAL CHEMISTRY. **Personal Data:** b New York, NY, August 6, 1921; m 1949, Helen Oken; c Bruce Alan & Robert Adam. **Education:** Univ Ark, BS, 1940; Columbia Univ, AM, 1948, BS, 1951, Pharmacy MS, 1952; Purdue Univ, PhD (pharmaceut chem), 1955. **Honors & Awards:** Pres Sigma Xi, 1952; Phi lamda uepsilon, 1953; Rho chi soc, 1954; fel acad of pharmaceut sci, 1972; alumini federation medal, Columbia univ, 1973; distinguished service award, Columbia univ col of pharmaceut sci, 1975, 1976; Distinguished Am award, Purdue univ, 1984; fel Am asn of pharmaceut sci, 1986; fel Am found for pharmaceut educ, 1997. **Professional Experience:** RETIRED; pres, Lieberman Assocs Inc, Livingston, NJ, 1985-1994; dir develop consumer prods, Personal Prods Div, 1977-1985; vpres, Personal Prods Div, 1972-1977; dir pharmaceut res & develop, Warner Lambert Co, Inc, 1963-1972; sr res assoc, Warner Lambert Co, Inc, 1961-1963; mgr pharmaceut prod develop, Isodine Pharmacal Co, 1957-1961; res pharmacist, Res Inst, Wyeth Labs, 1954-1957; instr & assoc anal chem, Col Pharm, Columbia Univ, 1946-1952; chemist, Pine Bluff Arsenal, Ark, 1941-1943; Res fel biochem, Beth Israel Hosp, New York, 1940-1941; Ed, var pharmaceut journals. **Memberships:** Am Chem Soc; Am pharmaceut asn; Am Asn Pharmaceut Scientists; fel, 1972; fel Am Asn Pharmaceut Scientists, 1986. **Research Statement & Publications:** Industrial pharmacy; pharmaceutical technology, particularly process and product development; analytical methods development for pharmaceutical products. **Mailing Address:** 4 Browning Dr, Livingston, NJ 07039.

LIEBERMAN, HILLEL, ORGANIC CHEMISTRY, MICROBIAL BIOCHEMISTRY. **Personal Data:** b Philadelphia, Pa, January 24, 1942; m 1966, c 2. **Education:** Temple Univ, BS, 1963, MS, 1965, PhD (med org chem), 1970. **Professional Experience:** SR VPRES, BETZ INC, TREVOSE, 1987-; CHMN, BETZ INC, TREVOSE, 1986-; vpres res & develop, Betz Inc, 1982-1986; vpres res, Betz Inc, 1979-1982; asst vpres res, Betz Inc, 1976-1979; var admin & sci asst dir res, Betz Inc, 1973-1976. **Memberships:** Am Soc Microbiol; Am Chem Soc; Sigma Xi; Tech Asn Pulp & Paper Indust. **Research Statement & Publications:** Development of chemical agents of an antimicrobial and/or antipollution nature to be employed in industrial water systems; development of conceptual information to aid in application of the aforementioned. **Mailing Address:** 3782 Midvale Lane, Huntingdon Valley, PA 19006.

LIEBERMAN, JACK, PULMONARY DISEASES, ENZYMOLOGY. **Personal Data:** b Chicago, Ill, January 4, 1926; m 1955, c 4. **Education:** Univ Calif, Los Angeles, BA, 1949; Univ Southern Calif, MD, 1954; Am Bd Internal Med, dipl, 1962. **Professional Experience:** RETIRED; prof med, Univ Calif, Los Angeles, 1977-1994; chief, Respiratory Dis Div, Sepulveda Vet Admin Hosp, 1976-1988; assoc dir, Dept Respiratory Dis, City Hope Med Ctr, 1971-1976; assoc clin prof med, Sch Med, Univ Calif, Irvine, 1971-1976; assoc clin prof med, Sch Med, Univ Calif, Los Angeles, 1968-1971; sect chief internal med, Vet Admin Hosp, Long Beach, Calif, 1963-1968; clin investr, Vet Admin Hosp, Long Beach, Calif, 1960-1963; Long Beach Heart Asn res fel, Harbor Gen Hosp, 1958-1960; resident internal med, Harbor Gen Hosp, 1955-1958; Intern, Harbor Gen Hosp, 1954-1955. **Memberships:** AAAS; fel Am Col Physicians; fel Am Col Chest Physicians; Am Fedn Clin Res. **Research Statement & Publications:** Cystic fibrosis; emphysema; antitrypsin deficiency; blood test for sarcoidosis. **Mailing Address:** 17813 Lemarsh St, Northridge, CA 91325. **Fax:** 818-349-2512. **E-Mail:** jlieberman@prodigy.net

LIEBERMAN, JAMES S, NEUROLOGY, PHYSICAL MEDICINE & REHABILITATION. **Personal Data:** b Minneapolis, Minn, April 24, 1938; m 1975, Carolyn; c Alan & Rachel. **Education:** Univ Calif SF, BS, 1960, MD, 1963 Stanford Univ 1956-1959. **Professional Experience:** CHAIR, REHAB MED & Sr ASSOC DEAN CLIN SERV COLUMBIA UNIV COLL of PHYS & SURG as of 2004; SR ASSOC DEAN, CLIN SERV, COLUMBIA UNIV, 1996-; asst vpres health sci, Columbia Univ, beginning 1996; prof & chmn phys med & Rehab, Univ Calif, Davis, 1982-1991; from asst prof to prof, Univ Calif, Davis, 1972-1991; vis asst prof Neurol Columbia Univ, 1970-1972; Instr & asst prof Neurol, NY State Univ Downstate, 1967-1971. **Memberships:** Inst Med-Nat Acad Sci; Am Acad Clin Neurophysiol; Am Acad Neurol; Am Acad Phys Med & Rehab; Amer Coll of Phys; AAAS; Amer Cong of Rehab Med; Amer Physiol Soc, Sigma Xi. **Research Statement & Publications:** Physiology of muscle diseases, exercise physiology. **Mailing Address:** Dept Rehab Med Box 38 Columbia Univ Coll Phys & Surg, 630 W 168th St, New York, NY 10032. **Fax:** 212-305-3916. **E-Mail:** jsl12@columbia.edu

LIEBERMAN, LESLIE SUE, MEDICINE. **Professional Experience:** ASSOC PROF, DEPT ANTHROP, as of 2006. **Memberships:** Sigma Xi; Nat Asn Academies Sci. **Mailing Address:** Dept Anthrop, Univ Fla, 1350 TUR, Gainesville, FL 32611. **Fax:** 407-823-0890. **E-Mail:** llieberm@mail.ucf.edu

LIEBERMAN, LESLIE SUE, BIOLOGICAL ANTHROPOLOGY. **Personal Data:** b Rockville Ctr, NY, June 23, 1944; c 1. **Education:** Univ Colo, BA, 1965; Univ Ariz, MA, 1971; Univ Conn, PhD (biobehav sci), 1975. **Professional Experience:** PROF ANTHROP, UNIV CENT FLA, as of 2004; FOUNDING DIR, WOMENS RES CTR, UNIV CENT FLA, as of 2004; pres, Coun Nutrit Anthrop, 1996-; bd dirs, Nat Asn Acad Sci, 1996-; Univ Zagreb, Yugoslavia, 1988; exec comt, Am Anthrop Asn, 1987-1988; Fla State Univ, London, 1985; assoc prof anthrop & pediat, Univ Fla, beginning 1981; prin investr, NSF grant, 1981-1983; vis lectr, Am Anthrop Asn, 1981; mem, Coun Nutrit Anthrop, vpres, 1980-1982; RES EPIDEMIOLOGIST, DIABETES RES, EDUC & TREAT CTR, 1979-; grad coordr, Ctr Geront Studies, 1979-1982; asst prof anthrop, Diabetes Res, Educ & Treat Ctr, 1976-1981; proj assoc body composition, Human Performance Res Lab, Pa State Univ, Univ Park, 1975-1976; fel, Nat Inst Gen Med Sci Human Performance Res Lab & Dept Anthrop, Pa State Univ, 1974-1975. **Memberships:** AAAS; Am Anthrop Asn; Am Asn Phys Anthropologists; Human Biol Asn; Sigma Xi. **Research Statement & Publications:** Study of body composition and the effects of nutritional behavior and diet on adaptation and microevolution in human populations; epidemiology of diabetes mellitus especially in US minority populations. **Mailing Address:** Womens Res Ctr, Univ Cent Fla, PO Box 161990, Orlando, FL 32816-1990. **E-Mail:** llieberm@mail.ucf.edu

LIEBERMAN, MAURY L, OCCUPATIONAL MENTAL HEALTH, COMMUNITY DEVELOPMENT. **Personal Data:** b Chicago, Ill, April 29, 1942. **Education:** Univ Wis, BS, 1960; Rutgers Univ, MSW, 1966; Univ Pittsburgh, MURP, 1970. **Professional Experience:** CHIEF, SPEC PROGS, SUBSTANCE ABUSE & MENT HEALTH ADMIN, 1994-. **Mailing Address:** Ctr Ment Health Servs, 18C-07 5600 Fishers Lane Rm 16C-17, Rockville, MD 20857. **Fax:** 301-443-7912. **E-Mail:** nlieberman@samhsa.gov

LIEBERMAN, MICHAEL A, MOLECULAR GENETICS. **Personal Data:** b New York, NY, August 22, 1950; c 2. **Education:** Mass Inst Technol, SB, 1972; Brandeis Univ, PhD (biochem), 1978. **Professional Experience:** Mem, Study Sect Cellular Biol & Physiol II, NIH, 1986-1989; ASSOC PROF, DEPT MOLECULAR GENETICS, BIOCHEM & MICROBIOL, COL MED, UNIV CINCINNATI, 1983-; Jr fac award, Am Cancer Soc, 1981-1984; asst prof biochem, Dept Nutrit, Harvard Sch Pub Health, 1981-1983; res assoc, Dept Biol Chem, Sch Med, Wash Univ, 1979-1980; Fel, Dept Biol Chem, Sch Med, Wash Univ, 1977-1979. **Memberships:** Am Soc Biochem & Molecular Biol; Am Soc Cell Biol. **Research Statement & Publications:** Numerous publications; molecular genetics. **Mailing Address:** Molecular Genetics Biochem & Microbiol Dept, Univ Cincinnati Col Med 231 Bethesda Ave, Cincinnati, OH 45267-0524. **Fax:** 510-642-6330. **E-Mail:** lieber@eecs.berkeley.edu

LIEBERMAN, MICHAEL A, PLASMA PHYSICS. **Personal Data:** b October 3, 1940. **Education:** Mass Inst Technol, BS, 1962, PhD (physics), 1966. **Professional Experience:** PROF, UNIV CALIF, BERKELY, as of 2005; FAC MEM, DEPT ELEC ENG & COMPUT SCI, UNIV CALIF, BERKELEY, 1966-. **Memberships:** AAAS; fel Inst Elec & Electronics Engrs; fel Am Phys Soc. **Mailing Address:** Dept Elec Eng & Comput Sci Univ Calif, Rm 467 Cory Hall, Berkeley, CA 94720-1770. **Fax:** 510-643-7846. **E-Mail:** lieber@eecs.berkeley.edu

LIEBERMAN, MICHAEL MERRIL, CELLULAR IMMUNOLOGY, HUMORAL IMMUNOLOGY. **Personal Data:** b Chicago, Ill, June 10, 1944; div, c Ted. **Education:** Univ Chicago, BS, 1966, PhD (microbiol), 1969; Am Bd Med Lab Immunol, dipl. **Professional Experience:** RES ASSOC, DEPT CHEM, UNIV HAWAII, MANOA, 1996-; chief immunol serv, Fitzsimons Army Med Ctr, 1991-1996; chief microbiol & immunol, dept path, Wm Beaumont Army Med Ctr, El Paso, Tex, 1987-1991; chief microbiol serv, Dept Clin Invest, Tripler Army Med Ctr, Hawaii, 1983-1987; sr res microbiologist, Cutter Labs, Inc, 1971-1975 & Brooke Army Med Ctr, Tex, 1976-1983; Nat Res Coun res assoc, Ames Res Ctr, Calif, NASA, 1969-1971. **Memberships:** Am Soc Microbiol; Am Asn Immunol; Clin Cytometry Soc; fel Asn Med Lab Immunologists. **Research Statement & Publications:** Bacterial vaccine development; enzymology of halophilic bacteria; biochemical genetics and metabolic regulation; bacterial antigen and toxin purification; clinical and diagnostic immunology. **Mailing Address:** Dept Chem 2545 The Mall, Univ Hawaii Manoa, Honolulu, HI 96822. **Fax:** 808-956-5908. **E-Mail:** michaell@gold.chem.hawaii.edu

LIEBERMAN, MICHAEL WILLIAMS, EXPERIMENTAL PATHOLOGY, MOLECULAR BIOLOGY. **Personal Data:** b Pittsburgh, Pa, April 20, 1941; m 1968, c 2. **Education:** Yale Univ, BA, 1963; Univ Pittsburgh, MD, 1967, PhD (biochem), 1972; Am Bd Path, cert anat path, 1972. **Honors & Awards:** Warner-Lambert & Parke-Davis Award, Am Asn Pathologists, 1981. **Professional Experience:** DIR, BAYLOR COL MED CANCER CTR, HOUSTON, TEX, as of 2003; counr, Am Asn Pathologists, 1988-1990; vchmn, US Nat Comt Int Coun Soc Path, 1987-1990; chmn, dept path, Fox Chase Cancer Ctr, Philadelphia, PA, 1984-1988; prof, dept path & dir grad studies, div biol & biomed sci, 1980-1984; mem, Bd Toxicol, & Environ Health Hazards, Nat Res Coun, 1980-1984; mem, Chem Path Study Sect, NIH, 1978-; assoc pathologist, Barnes Hosp, St Louis, 1976-1984; assoc prof, Sch Med, Wash Univ, 1976-1980; res assoc, Fels Inst, Temple Health Sci Ctr, 1970-1972 & Exp Path Br, Nat Cancer Inst, 1974-1976; head, Somatic Cell Genetics Sect, Nat Inst Environ Health Sci, 1974-1976; adj asst & assoc prof, dept path, Med Sch, Univ NC, 1974-1976; Sarah Mellon Scaife fel, 1969-1970. **Memberships:** Am Asn Cancer Res; AAAS; Am Asn Pathologists; Environ Mutagen Soc; Am Soc Biochemists & Molecular Biologists. **Research Statement & Publications:** Molecular analysis of disease; molecular biology and gene expression, especially the role of oncogenes in the modulation of cellular gene expression in vitro and in carcinogenesis; chemical carcinogenesis. **Mailing Address:** Dept Path, Baylor Col Med, One Baylor Plaza Rm T203, Houston, TX 77030-3498. **Fax:** 713-798-5555. **E-Mail:** mikel@bcm.tmc.edu

LIEBERMAN, MILTON EUGENE, TROPICAL & QUANTITATIVE ECOLOGY. **Personal Data:** b Chicago, Ill, August 30, 1934; m 1968, Diana D Smith; c Sarah. **Education:** Univ Calif, Berkeley, AB, 1962; Ariz State Univ, MS, 1966; Univ Calif, Irvine, PhD (biol scis), 1969. **Professional Experience:** RESIDENT DIR, SAN LUIS BIOL STA, COSTA RICA, 1995-; Mellon Found res grant, 1994-1996; res grant, NASA, 1987-1990; sr res assoc, Nat Res Coun, 1985-1986; RES PROF, DEPT BIOL, UNIV NDAK, 1981-; NSF res grants, 1981-1986, 1992-; res assoc, Mo Bot Garden, St Louis, 1980-; vis prof, Dept Environ Sci, Univ Va, 1980-1981; sr lectr ecol, Dept Zool, Univ Ghana, 1974-1979. **Memberships:** Ecol Soc Am; Sigma Xi; Asn Trop Biologists; Int Soc Trop Foresters. **Research Statement & Publications:** Ecology of new world tropical forests, tropical marine benthic algal assemblages; reproductive phenology of temperate and tropical fleshy-fruited plants; plant-animal interactions; tropical forest conservation and restoration. **Mailing Address:** Apdo 35, Santa Elena Monteverde, Punts, Costa Rica. **Fax:** 506-645-5277; 506-380-3255.

LIEBERMAN, MORTON LEONARD, PHYSICAL CHEMISTRY. **Personal Data:** b Chicago, Ill, November 22, 1937; m 1962, Elaine; c Laura Amy & Neal Reid. **Education:** Ill Inst Technol, BS, 1959, MS, 1963, PhD (phys chem), 1965. **Professional Experience:** CONSULT, 2000-; staff mem tech res, Sandia Labs, 1968-2000; sr chemist, Res & Develop Labs, Corning Glass Works, 1965-1968. **Memberships:** Am Chem Soc. **Research Statement & Publications:** High-temperature chemistry, thermodynamics; phase transitions; thin films; optical properties; fossil fuels; pyrotechnics and explosives; carbon research. **Mailing Address:** 1316 Paisano NE St, Albuquerque, NM 87112-4524. **E-Mail:** mllieberman@yahoo.com

LIEBERMAN, RICHARD BARRY, OLEFIN POLYMERIZATION PROCESS DEVELOPMENT & CATALYSIS. **Personal Data:** b New York, NY, July 18, 1950. **Education:** Cooper Union, BE, 1970; Princeton Univ, PhD (chem eng), 1976. **Professional Experience:** DIR MFG TECHNOL, MONTELL, DEL, 1995-; dir technol strategy, Rev Develop Ctr, Himont USA Inc, 1992-1995; assoc dir, Rev Develop Ctr, Himont USA Inc, 1989-1992; mgr res, Rev Develop Ctr, Himont USA Inc, 1987-1989; res scientist, Rev Develop Ctr, Himont USA Inc, 1984-1987; sr res engr, Res Ctr, Hercules Inc, 1975-1984. **Memberships:** Am Chem Soc; Indust Res Inst. **Research Statement & Publications:** Direction of process and product development activities for the production of polyolefins, including research involving Ziegler-Natta catalysts. **Mailing Address:** Montell NAm 3 Little Falls Ctr, 2801 Centerville Rd PO Box 5437, Wilmington, DE 19850. **Fax:** 410-996-1805.

LIEBERMAN, ROBERT, RADIOCHEMISTRY. **Personal Data:** b Columbus, Ohio, April 9, 1924; m 1962, c 3. **Education:** Ohio State Univ, BA, 1948, MSc, 1952. **Professional Experience:** RES & DEVELOP CHEMIST, EASTERN ENVIRON RADIATION FACIL, ENVIRON PROTECTION AGENCY, 1974-; chief qual assurance sect, Eastern Environ Radiation Lab, 1974-1979; chief phys sci br, Eastern Environ Radiation Lab, 1971-1974; chief chem & biol, Southeastern Radiol Health Lab, USPHS, 1969-1971; chief bioassay sect, Southeastern Radiol Health Lab, USPHS, 1967-1969; sr chemist, Chem Physics Div, 1964-1967; res scientist, Chem Physics Div, 1958-1964; Chemist, Plastics Div, Battelle Mem Inst, 1955-1958. **Research Statement & Publications:** Polyurethane foams; fission gas release; neutron dosimetry; radiation effects on plastics; use of radiotracers on wear studies; measurement of radionuclides in environmental samples. **Mailing Address:** Eastern Environ Radiation, Montgomery, AL 36111.

LIEBERMAN, ROBERT ARTHUR, OPTICAL SENSORS-PHYSICAL & CHEMICAL, GUIDED WAVE OPTICAL DEVICES. **Personal Data:** b Grand Rapids, Mich, May 22, 1950; m 1988, Jaye C; c Sam & Lee. **Education:** Rensselaer Polytech Inst, BS, 1971, MS, 1973; Univ Mich, PhD (physics), 1981. **Honors & Awards:** Exceptional Contribution Award, AT&T Bell Labs, 1985, 1987 1988. **Professional Experience:** CTO, OPTECH VENTURES, LLC, 2001-; sr vpres & CTO, Intelligent Optical systems, Inc, 1998-2001; vpres & gen mgr, res & develop, Phys Optics Corp, 1996-1998; prin investr, NIH, 1994-; vpres res & develop sensor systs, Phys Optics Corp, 1994-1995; print investr, Navy, 1992-; print investr, NASA, 1992-; print investr, Defense Advan Res Prog Agency, 1992-; prin investr, DOE, 1992-; prin investr, USAF, 1991-; prin investr, NSF, 1991-; dir adv fiber optics, Phys Optics Corp, 1991-1994; chair, fibersensors conf, 2001; bd dirs, Int Soc Optical Engrs, 2002-; mem tech staff, AT&T Bell Labs, 1981-1991; fel, Univ Mich, 1981. **Memberships:** AAAS; Am Phys Soc; Am Stand Testing Mat; sr mem Inst Elec & Electronics Engrs; Optical Soc Am; fellow, SPIE Int Soc Optical Engrs. **Research Statement & Publications:** Fiberoptic sensors for gases, liquids and physical properties; development of distributed and multiplexed sensor configuration; planar-waveguide and surface plasmon devices; protein biophysics research; scientific project management; Corporate Start-up an management biosensors; environmental sensors; biological spectroscopy. **Mailing Address:** Op Tech Ventures, LLC, 2522 W 237th St, Torrance, CA 90505-5217. **Fax:** 310-530-7417. **E-Mail:** rlieberman@aol.com

LIEBERMAN, SAMUEL VICTOR, CHEMISTRY. **Personal Data:** b Philadelphia, Pa, November 3, 1914; m 1938, c 2. **Education:** Univ Pa, BS, 1936, MS, 1937, PhD (chem), 1948. **Professional Experience:** RETIRED; consult pharmaceut prod, 1961-1979; dir develop & phys sci, Phys Analysis Dept, Prod Div, Bristol-Myers Co, 1957-1960; scientist in charge, Phys Analysis Dept, Prod Div, Bristol-Myers Co, 1955-1957; sr res chemist, Wyeth Inst Med Res, 1948-1955; res chemist, Wyeth Inst Med Res, 1945-1947; asst, Sharp & Dohme, Inc, 1941-1942. **Memberships:** AAAS; Sigma Xi. **Research Statement & Publications:** Research, development and testing of pharmaceutical products. **Mailing Address:** 3400 N Ocean Dr No 508, Singer Island, FL 33404.

LIEBERMAN, SEYMOUR, BIOCHEMISTRY. **Personal Data:** b New York, NY, December 1, 1916; m 1944, c Paul B. **Education:** Brooklyn Col, BA, 1936; Univ Ill, MS, 1937; Stanford Univ, PhD (chem), 1941. **Honors & Awards:** Ciba Award, Endocrine Soc, 1952 & Koch Award, 1970, Roussel Prize, 1984, Dale Medal, 1986. **Professional Experience:** ASSOC DIR, OFF SCI & TECHNOL, COLUMBIA COL PHYSICIANS & SURGEONS, 1991-; PROF EMER BIOCHEM, COLUMBIA COL PHYSICIANS & SURGEONS, 1987-; assoc vprovost, Col Physicians & Surgeons, Columbia Univ, 1987-1990; assoc dean, Col Physicians & Surgeons, Columbia Univ, 1984-1990; pres, St Luke's-Roosevelt inst Health Sci, beginning 1981; prog officer, Ford Found, 1974-1975; mem, Gen Clin res Ctrs Comn, 1967-1970; assoc ed, J Clin Endocrinol & Metab, 1963-1967; chmn, Insts, 1963-1965; mem, Med Adv Comt, Pop Coun, 1961-1974; mem, Insts, 1959-1965; mem, Endocrinol Study Sect, NIH, 1958-1963; mem, Panel Steroids, Comt Growth, Nat res Coun, 1946-1950 & Panel Endocrinol, 1955-1956; from asst prof to emer prof biochem, Col Physicians & Surgeons, Columbia Univ, 1950-1987; traveling fel from mem Hosp, NY to Basel, Switz, 1946-1947; assoc, Sloan-Kettering inst, 1945-1950; spec res assoc, Harvard Univ, 1941-1945; Rockefeller Found asst, Stanford Univ, 1939-1941; chemist, Schering Corp, 1938-1939; DIR, BIOCHEM & STEROID HORMONES LAB, ST LUKE'S-ROOSEVELT INST HEALTH SCI. **Memberships:** Nat Acad Sci; Am Chem Soc; Am Soc Biol Chem; fel NY Acad Sci; Endocrine Soc (vpres 1967 pres 1974). **Research Statement & Publications:** Steroid chemistry and biochemistry; biogenesis and metabolism of steroid hormones; steroid hormone-protein conjugates; steroid sulfates and lipoidal derivatives of steroids. **Mailing Address:** St Luke's Roosevelt Hosp Ctr, New York, NY 10021. **Fax:** 212-523-6019.

LIEBERMANN, HOWARD HORST, THERMODYNAMICS & MATERIAL PROPERTIES, ELECTROMAGNETISM. **Personal Data:** b Ger, November 27, 1949; m 1979, Lynda; c Daniel & Amanda. **Education:** Polytech Inst NY, BS, 1972; Univ Pa, MS, 1975, PhD (metall & mat sci), 1977. **Professional Experience:** MGR RES & DEVELOP, ALLIED SIGNAL AMORPHOUS METALS, 1985-; sr metallurgist, Allied Corp Metals Prod, 1982-1984; staff metallurgist, Corp Res & Develop, Gen Elec Co, 1977-1981. **Memberships:** Sigma Xi; Inst Elec & Electronics Engrs Magnetics Soc; Am Soc Metals; Am Inst Mining, Metall & Petrol Engrs; Iron & Steel Soc. **Research Statement & Publications:** Materials processing; amorphous alloys; magnetic materials; electronic soldering alloys. **Mailing Address:** 11 Cynthia Dr, Succasunna, NJ 07876.

LIEBERMANN, LEONARD NORMAN, PHYSICS. **Personal Data:** b Ironwood, Mich, May 14, 1915; m 1941, Miller; c 3. **Education:** Univ Chicago, BS, 1937, MS, 1938, PhD (physics), 1940. **Professional Experience:** EMER PROF PHYSICS, UNIV CALIF SAN DIEGO, 1959-; vis prof, Imp Col, 1969-1970; vis prof, Yale Univ, 1952-1953; US sci rep, NATO, Italy, 1962-1963; dir, Proj Sorrento, 1959; prof physics, Univ Calif, 1954-1982; Guggenheim Found fel, 1952-1953; assoc prof geophys, Univ Calif, 1948-1954; res assoc, Univ Calif, 1946-1948; prin physicist, Bur Ships, Woods Hole Oceanog Inst, MA, 1944-1946; asst prof, Univ Kans, 1943-1944; instr, Univ Kans, 1941-1943; instr physics, Wash Univ, 1940-1941. **Memberships:** Fel Am Phys Soc; fel Acoust Soc Am. **Research Statement & Publications:** Ultrasonics; underwater sound; hydrodynamics; properties of liquids; electromagnetic propagation; solid state. **Mailing Address:** 2644 Ellentown Rd, La Jolla, CA 92093-0319.

LIEBERMANN, ROBERT C, GEOPHYSICS. **Personal Data:** b Ellwood City, Pa, February 6, 1942; m 1964, Barbara; c 3. **Education:** Calif Inst Technol, BS, 1964; Columbia Univ, PhD (geophys), 1969. **Honorary Degrees:** Dr Honoris Causa, Universite Paul Sabatier, Toulouse, France, 2004. **Professional Experience:** PROF, Stony Brook University, as of 1981; assoc prof, State Univ NY, Stony Brook, beginning 1976; assoc ed, J Geophys Res, 1973-1976; mem fac, Australian Nat Univ, 1970-1976; res fel geophys, Calif Inst Technol, 1970; res scientist, Lamont-Doherty Geol Observ, 1969-1970. **Memberships:** Fel Royal Astron Soc; Am Geophys Union; Seismol Soc Am. **Research Statement & Publications:** Relative excitation of seismic waves by earthquakes and underground explosions; elastic properties of minerals and rocks as a function of pressure and temperature; composition and mineralogy of earth's mantle. **Mailing Address:** Dept GeoScis, Stony Brook Univ, Stony Brook, NY 11794-2100. **Fax:** 631-632-8140. **E-Mail:** Robert.Liebermann@stonybrook.edu

LIEBERT, JAMES WILLIAM, ASTRONOMY, ASTROPHYSICS. **Personal Data:** b Coffeyville, Kans, June 19, 1946. **Education:** Univ Kans, BA, 1968; Univ Calif, Berkeley, MA, 1970, PhD (astron), 1977. **Honors & Awards:** Trumpler Prize, Astron Soc Pac, 1977. **Professional Experience:** PROF ASTRON, STEWARDV OBSERV, UNIV ARIZ, 1986-; asst prof, Steward Observ, Univ Ariz, 1979-1986; prin investr, NSF grant, Univ Ariz, 1978-1980; res assoc, Steward Observ, Univ Ariz, 1976-1979. **Memberships:** Am Astron Soc; Int Astron Union; Astron Soc Pac. **Research Statement & Publications:** Observational stellar astronomy and astrophysics; white dwarf stars. **Mailing Address:** Dept Astron, Univ Ariz, Tucson, AZ 85719. **Fax:** 520-621-1532. **E-Mail:** jliebert@as.arizona.edu

LIEBES, SIDNEY, PHYSICS. **Personal Data:** b San Francisco, Calif, December 13, 1929; m 1958, c 2. **Education:** Princeton Univ, BSE, 1952; Stanford Univ, PhD (physics), 1958. **Professional Experience:** MEM STAFF, DEPT COMPUT SCI, STANFORD UNIV, 1980-; res assoc-physicist, dept genetics, Med Ctr, 1964-1980; asst prof, Princeton Univ, 1961-1964; instr physics, Princeton Univ, 1957-1961; AT HEWLETT-PACKARD CO. **Memberships:** Am Phys Soc; Am Asn Physics Teachers. **Research Statement & Publications:** Experimental atomic and electron physics; gravitation experiments; mass spectrometry; physical microanalysis; techniques applied to bio-medical research;

computer imagery processing; Martian Lander imagery. **Mailing Address:** Hewlett-Packard Co, 1501 Page Mill Rd 4 U 1, Palo Alto, CA 94304.

LIEBESKIND, LANNY STEVEN, ORGANIC CHEMISTRY, ORGANOMETALLIC CHEMISTRY. **Personal Data:** b Buffalo, NY, September 5, 1950. **Education:** State Univ NY, Buffalo, BS, 1972; Univ Rochester, MS, 1974, PhD (chem), 1976. **Professional Experience:** SAMUEL CANDLER DOBBS PROF ORG CHEM, EMORY UNIV, as of 2004; SR ASS DEAN, EMORY COL OFF RES, EMORY UNIV, as of 2004; asst prof chem, Fla State Univ, 1978-; NIH fel, Stanford Univ, 1977-1978; NSF fel chem, Mass Inst Technol, 1976-1977. **Memberships:** Am Chem Soc. **Research Statement & Publications:** Application of organotransition metal chemistry to the solution of problems in synthetic organic chemistry. **Mailing Address:** Dept Chem, Emory Univ, Atlanta, GA 30322-0001. **E-Mail:** chemll1@emory.edu

LIEBHARDT, WILLIAM C, SOILS, SUSTAINABLE AGRICULTURE. **Personal Data:** b Duluth, Minn, February 16, 1936; m 1961, c 4. **Education:** Univ Wis-Madison, BS, 1958, MS, 1964, PhD (soils), 1966. **Professional Experience:** LECTR EMER, DEPT AGRON & RANGE SCI, UNIC CALIF, DAVIS, as of 2004; dir, Sustainable Agr Res & Educ Prog, Dept Agr & Range Sci, Univ Calif, Davis, beginning 1987; from assoc dir to dir res, Rodale Res Ctr, 1981-1987; from asst prof to assoc prof plant sci, Univ Del, 1970-1981; sr agronomist, Allied Chem Corp, 1968-1969; agronomist, Stand Fruit Co, 1966-1968. **Research Statement & Publications:** Soil fertility; plant nutrition; sustainable agriculture; farming systems. **Mailing Address:** Dept Agr & Range Sci, Univ Calif, One Shields Ave, Davis, CA 95616-8515. **Fax:** 530-752-4361. **E-Mail:** wcliebhardt@ucdavis.edu

LIEBLEIN, SEYMOUR, AEROSPACE ENGINEERING. **Personal Data:** b New York, NY, June 17, 1923. **Education:** City Col NY, BS, 1944; Case Inst Technol, MS, 1952. **Honors & Awards:** Gas Turbine Award, Am Soc Mech Engrs, 1961; Goddard Award, Am Inst Aeronaut & Astronaut, 1967. **Professional Experience:** RETIRED; mgr & owner, Tech Report Serv, beginning 1977; div tech asst, Short Takeoff, Landing & Noise Div, 1970-1974; chief, Vertical Takeoff & Landing Propulsion Br, 1965-1970; chief, Flow Anal Br, 1957-1965; researcher, Nat AdvComt Aeronauts, Lewis Res Ctr, NASA, 1944-1957. **Memberships:** Am Soc Mech Engrs; assoc fel Am Inst Aeronaut & Astronaut. **Research Statement & Publications:** Fluid flow and design in axial flow compressors; aerodynamic performance and design of vertical takeoff and landing propulsion systems; waste-heat systems, space power; technical report writing; wind turbine blades and flow. **Mailing Address:** 3400 Wooster Rd, Rocky River, OH 44116-4108.

LIEBLING, RICHARD STEPHEN, MINERALOGY. **Personal Data:** b Brooklyn, NY, August 31, 1938; m 1970. **Education:** Columbia Univ, BA, 1960, MA, 1961, PhD (mineral), 1963. **Professional Experience:** ASSOC PROF GEOL, HUNTER COL, 1973-; asst prof, Hunter Col, 1968-1973; sr ceramist, Carborundum Co, 1963-1968. **Memberships:** Mineral Soc Am; Sigma Xi. **Research Statement & Publications:** Clay mineralogy of sediments. **Mailing Address:** Dept Geol, CUNY Hunter Col, 695 Park Ave, New York, NY 10021-5024.

LIEBMAN, ARNOLD ALVIN, ORGANIC CHEMISTRY, RADIOCHEMISTRY. **Personal Data:** b St Paul, Minn, March 5, 1931; m 1977, c 4. **Education:** Univ Minn, BS, 1956, PhD (pharmaceut chem), 1961. **Professional Experience:** RETIRED; res investr, Hoffman LaRoche Inc, 1985-1993; res sect chief, Hoffman LaRoche Inc, 1982-1985; sr res group chief, Hoffman LaRoche Inc, 1980-1981; res group chief, Hoffman LaRoche Inc, 1972-1980; sr chemist, Hoffman LaRoche Inc, 1968-1972; asst prof chem, Sch Pharm, Univ Md, 1966-1968; Nat Inst Gen Med Sci res fel chem, Univ Calif, Berkeley, 1963-1966; asst prof biochem, Loyola Univ, La, 1961-1963. **Memberships:** AAAS; Am Chem Soc; Int Isotope Soc. **Research Statement & Publications:** Heterocyclic chemistry of natural products; isotopic synthesis, heterocyclic chemistry. **Mailing Address:** 144 Red Cedar Lane, Johns Island, SC 29455.

LIEBMAN, FREDERICK MELVIN, physiology; deceased, see previous edition for last biography

LIEBMAN, JEFFREY MARK, CELL BIOLOGY, OSTEOARTHRITIS. **Personal Data:** b Milwaukee, Wis, November 7, 1946; m 1974, Anita; c 3. **Education:** Oberlin Col, BA, 1968; Univ Calif, Los Angeles, PhD (psychol), 1973. **Professional Experience:** SR FEL, NOVARTIS PHARMACEUT, as of 2004; vis scientist, NIH, 1989-1991; sr res fel, Ciba-Ceigy Pharmaceut, beginning 1988; mgr behav neuroscience, Ciba-geigy Pharmaceut, 1983-1987; sr staff scientist psychopharmacol, Ciba-geigy Pharmaceut, 1976-1983; res fels, Sloan Found, 1973-1974 & Alcoholism, Drug Abuse & Ment Health Admin, 1974-1976; res assoc fel psychopharmacol, Sch Med, Univ Calif, San Diego, 1973-1976. **Memberships:** Soc Neuroscience; Sigma Xi; Am Soc Pharmacol & Exp Therapeut. **Research Statement & Publications:** Molecular biological aspects of osteoarthritis and inflammation. **Mailing Address:** Novartis Pharmaceut, One Health Plaza Dr 435-4117, E Hanover, NJ 07901-1330. **Fax:** 908-277-4739. **E-Mail:** jeffrey.liebman@pharma.novartis.com

LIEBMAN, JOEL FREDRIC, THEORETICAL CHEMISTRY, INORGANIC CHEMISTRY, ORGANIC CHEMISTRY. **Personal Data:** b Brooklyn, NY, May 6, 1947; 1970. **Education:** Brooklyn Col, BS (chemistry), 1967; Princeton Univ, MA, 1968, PhD (chemistry), 1970. **Honors & Awards:** USM (University System of Maryland) "Regents' Award for Excellence in Research, Scholarship and Creative Activity, " 2002; Maryland Section of the American Chemical Society, "Maryland Chemist of the Year, " 1998. **Professional Experience:** Norwegian Marshall Fund Fac Travel grantee, 1992 & 1994; Luro-Am Fund Luso Develop (Portugal), Faculty Travel Grantee, 1992; co-ed, struct, Energetics & Reactivity Chem, 1991- 1998; consult ed, Struct Chem, 1990-; mem ed adv bd, Methods Stereochem Anal, 1985-; co-ed, Molecular Struct & Energetics, 1984-1991; PROF, DEPT CHEM, UNIV MD, BALTIMORE CO, 1982-; German Acad Exchange Serv Fac fel, 1976; guest scientist, Argonne Nat Lab, 1975-1982; consult & contractor, Nat Bur Stand, 1972-; from asst prof to assoc prof, Dept Chem, Univ MD, Baltimore CO, 1972-1982; unofficial consult, Argonne Nat Lab, 1972-1975; Nat Res Coun & Nat Bur Stand fel, Inorg Chem Sect, Nat Bur Stand, 1971-1972; NATO fel, Depts Phys & Theoret Chem, Cambridge Univ, 1970-1971; Ramsay hon fel, Ramsay Mem Fel Trust, 1970. **Memberships:** Am Chem Soc; Am Phys Soc; Sigma Xi. **Research Statement & Publications:** Chemical bonding theory, rules and regularities of molecular geometry and energetics; strain and resonance energy of alicyclic and aromatic hydrocarbons; noble gas and fluorine compounds; thermochemistry of molecular ions; mathematical chemistry; structural chemistry; quantum chemistry. **Mailing Address:** Dept Chem & Biochem 1000 Hilltop Circle, Univ Md, Baltimore County, Baltimore, MD 21250. **Fax:** 410-455-2608. **E-Mail:** jliebman@umbc.edu

LIEBMAN, JON C(HARLES), ENVIRONMENTAL SYSTEMS ANALYSIS. **Personal Data:** b Cincinnati, Ohio, September 10, 1934; m 1958, Judith; c Christopher Brian, Rebecca Ann Knight & Michael Jon. **Education:** Univ Colo, BS, 1956; Cornell Univ, MS, 1963, PhD (sanit eng), 1965. **Professional Experience:** EMER PROF ENVIRON ENG, UNIV ILL URBANA-CHAMPAIGN, 1996-; head, Dept Civil Eng, 1978-1984; assoc head dept civil eng, Univ Ill Urbana-champaign, 1976-1978; prof environ eng, Dept Civil Eng, 1972-1996; From asst prof to assoc prof environ eng, Johns Hopkins Univ, 1965-1972. **Memberships:** Fel AAAS. **Research Statement & Publications:** Applications of operations research to the field of environmental engineering. **Mailing Address:** 110 Whitehall Court, Urbana, IL 61801-6664. **E-Mail:** jcl@uiuc.edu

LIEBMAN, JUDITH STENZEL, ENGINEERING OPTIMIZATION. **Personal Data:** b Denver, Colo, July 2, 1936; m, c 3. **Education:** Univ Colo, BA, 1958; Johns Hopkins Univ, PhD (opers res), 1971. **Honors & Awards:** George E Kimball Medal, Inst Opers Res & Mgt Sci Fellow, Inst Opers Res & Mgt Sci. **Professional Experience:** PROF EMER OPERS RES, UNIV ILL, URBANA, 1996-; vchancellor, Res & Dean Grad Col, 1987-1992; pres, bd dir, E Cent Ill Health Systs Agency, 1980-1982; from asst prof to prof, opers res, 1972-1996; asst prof & health serv res scholar, Johns Hopkins Univ, 1971-1972; res asst opers res, Johns Hopkins Univ, 1965-1971; programmer chem, Cornell Univ, 1964-1965; programmer eng systs, Gen Elec Co, 1963-1964; Engr data anal, Convair Astronaut, Gen Dynamics, 1958-1959. **Memberships:** Opers Res Soc Am (pres 1987-1988); Sigma Xi; Am Asn Univ Profs; AAAS; Inst Opers Res & Mgt Sci. **Research Statement & Publications:** Mathematical optimization; model building; applications of operations research in civil and military infrastructure management. **Mailing Address:** Dept Mech & Indust Eng, Univ Ill, 140 Mech Eng Bldg, 1206 W Green St, Urbana, IL 61801. **Fax:** 217-244-6534. **E-Mail:** jliebman@uiuc.edu

LIEBMAN, PAUL ARNO, BIOPHYSICS, PHYSIOLOGY. **Personal Data:** b Pittsburgh, Pa, August 1, 1933; c 1. **Education:** Univ Pittsburgh, BS, 1954; Johns Hopkins Univ, MD, 1958. **Professional Experience:** PROF BIOCHEM & BIOPHYS, UNIV PA, 1977-; PROF ANAT, UNIV PA, 1976-; assoc prof, Univ PA, 1969-1976; asst prof, Univ PA, 1965-1969; res assoc physiol, Univ PA, 1963-1965; fel biophys, Univ Pa, 1959-1963; Intern internal med, Barnes Hosp, St Louis, Mo, 1958-1959. **Memberships:** Biophys Soc; Asn Res Vision & Ophthal; Am Soc Neuroscience. **Research Statement & Publications:** Vision; microspectrophotometry of single visual receptors; transducer mechanism of photoreceptors in vision. **Mailing Address:** Dept Biochem & Biophys, Univ Pa, 143 Anat Chem Bldg, Philadelphia, PA 19104-6058. **Fax:** 215-898-4217. **E-Mail:** liebmanp@mail.med.upenn.edu

LIEBMAN, SUSAN WEISS, MOLECULAR GENETICS. **Personal Data:** b New York, NY, December 2, 1947; m 1969, Alan; c Judith & Michael. **Education:** Mass Inst Technol, BS, 1968; Harvard Univ, MA, 1969; Univ Rochester, PhD (biophys), 1974. **Professional Experience:** PROF BIOL, UNIV ILL, CHICAGO CIRCLE, 1987-; from asst prof to assoc prof, Univ Ill, Chicago Circle, 1977-1987; Am Cancer Soc fel, Sch Med & Dent, Univ Rochester, 1974-1976; USPHS career develop award. **Memberships:** AAAS; Genetics Soc Am; Am Soc Microbiol. **Research Statement & Publications:** Molecular genetics of yeast, including nonsense suppression, mutators, transposable elements; ribosomal RNA; prions; published over 19 articles. **Mailing Address:** Dept Biol Sci, Univ Ill, Rm 4070 900 S Ashland Ave, Chicago, IL 60607. **Fax:** 312-413-2691. **E-Mail:** suel@uic.edu

LIEBMANN, JEFFREY MITCHELL, GLAUCOMA. **Personal Data:** b New York, NY, March 10, 1958; m 1985, Cindy; c 3. **Education:** Boston Univ, BA, 1979, MD, 1984. **Professional Experience:** CLINICAL PROF OPHTHAL, NY UNIV SCH MED, 2000-; PRIN INVSTR, OCULAR HYPERTENSON TREAT STUDY, NAT EYE INST, NY, as of 2000; assoc clin prof ophthal, Ny Med Col, 1993-1999; asst clin prof, NY Med Col, 1989-1992; assoc dir glaucoma serv, Ny Eye & Ear Infirmary, 1988-1991; Clin instr, NY Med Col, 1987-1988. **Memberships:** AMA; Am Acad Ophthal; Asn Res Vision & Ophthal; Am Glaucoma Soc. **Research Statement & Publications:** Evaluation of new ophthalmic laser technologies and ocular imaging modalities such as ultrasound biomicroscopy. **Mailing Address:** NY Glaucoma Res Inst, NY Eye & Ear Infirmary, 310 E 14th St, New York, NY 10003. **Fax:** 212-420-8743. **E-Mail:** jml18@earthlink.net

LIEBNER, EDWIN J, RADIOLOGY, CHEST DISEASES. **Personal Data:** b Chicago, Ill, July 12, 1921; m Mary; c Mary Ann, Jena Marie & Ellen Marie. **Education:** Univ Ill, BS, 1944, MD, 1946. **Professional Experience:** ACTG CHMN, UNIV ILL COL MED, as of 2004; ACTG HEAD DEPT RADIOL, UNIV ILL COL MED, 1971-; PROF RADIOL, UNIV ILL HOSP, 1966-; consult radiol, Vet Admin Hosp, Hines, 1964-; DIR RADIOTHER DIV, ILL RES & EDUC HOSPS, 1961-; from asst prof to assoc prof, Univ Ill Hosp, 1956-1966; resident radiol, Ill Res Hosps, 1953-1956. **Memberships:** Am Radium Soc; Roentgen Ray Soc; Am Soc Therapeut Radiol; Radiol Soc NAm. **Research Statement & Publications:** Therapeutic lymphography; refrigeration and irradiation; therapeutic pediatric radiology. **Mailing Address:** Univ Ill, River Forest, IL 60305-1419.

LIEBNITZ, PAUL W, MATHEMATICS. **Personal Data:** b Kansas City, Mo, January 18, 1935; m 1961, Jennifer; c Philip, Karl, John, David & Kathryn. **Education:** Rockhurst Col, BS, 1955; Univ Kans, MA, 1957, PhD (math), 1964. **Professional Experience:** ASSOC PROF EMER MATH, UNIV MO, KANSAS CITY, as of 2004; assoc prof Math, Univ Mo, Kansas City, beginning 1967; asst prof, Univ Mo, Kansas City, 1961-1967. **Memberships:** Math Asn Am. **Research Statement & Publications:** Topology, theory of retracts. **Mailing Address:** Dept Math, Univ Mo, 5100 Rockhill Rd, Kansas City, MO 64110-2499.

LIEBOVITCH, LARRY S, FRACTALS, CHAOS. **Personal Data:** b New York, NY. **Education:** City Col NY, BS, 1972; Harvard Univ, MA, 1973, PhD (astron), 1978. **Professional Experience:** INTERIM DIR, CTR COMPLEX SYSTEM BRAIN SCI, FLA ATLANTIC UNIV, 2004-; PROF PSYCHOL, FLA ATLANTIC UNIV, 1998-; chair, Biophys Sect, NY Acad Sci, 1991-1992; from asst prof to assoc prof psychol, Fla Atlantic Univ, 1985-1998; postdoctoral asst prof, Columbia Col Physicians & Surgeons, 1979-1993; postdoctoral, Mt Sinai Sch Med, NY, 1978-1979. **Memberships:** AAAS; fel Am Phys Soc; Asn Acads Sci; Asn Res Vision & Ophthal; Math Asn Am; Am Acad Allergy & Immunol. **Research Statement & Publications:** Applying ideas from mathematics and physics to analysis, model and understand biomedical systems. **Mailing Address:** Ctr Complex Systs & Brain Sci, Fla Atlantic Univ, 777 Glades Rd, Boca Raton, FL 33431. **Fax:** 561-297-2223. **E-Mail:** liebovitch@walt.ccs.fau.edu

LIEBOW, CHARLES, ONCOLOGY, LASER SURGERY. **Personal Data:** b Brooklyn, NY, June 17, 1944; m 1968, Roslyn; c Bradley, Adam & Lisa. **Education:** NY Univ, AB, 1966; Harvard Univ, DMD, 1970; Univ Calif, San Francisco, PhD (physiol), 1973. **Professional Experience:** PROF, DEPT ORAL & MAXILLOFACIAL SURG, SCH DENT MED, STATE UNIV NY, BUFFALO, 1998; PROF, DEPT PHYSIOL, as of 1998; DIR, LASER SURG CTR, 1992-; PROF, DEPT OTOLARYNGOL, beginning 1991; assoc sci dir, Roswell Park Cancer Inst, 1984-1986; assoc sci dir, Nat Pancreatic Cancer Proj, Div Nat Cancer Inst, 1980-1984; assoc prof surg & physiol, La State Univ Med Sch, 1980-1984; assoc sci dir, Nat Pancreatic Cancer Proj, La State Univ, 1980-1984; asst prof physiol, Cornell Univ Med Sch, 1973-1980. **Research Statement & Publications:** How cells regulate intracellular functions; studied why cancer cells grow more rapidly than normal cells; how receptors can activate tyrosine phosphatase to slow growth; used hormone analogues activating these phosphatases to treat cancer; lasers and photodynamic therapy to treat cancers;

Author of over 51 articles and chapters. **Mailing Address:** Dept Oral & Maxillofacial Surg, State Univ NY, Buffalo, NY 14214. **Fax:** 716-829-3019. **E-Mail:** charles_liebow@sdm.buffalo.edu

LIEBOWITZ, JAY, MANAGEMENT SCIENCE. **Education:** George Wash Univ, BBA, 1979, MBA, 1980. **Honorary Degrees:** DSc, George Wash Univ, 1984. **Professional Experience:** PROF INFO TECHNOL, GRAD DIV BUS & MGT, JOHNS HOPKINS UNIV, ROBERT W. DEUTSCH DISTINGUISHED PROF INFO SYSTS, UNIV MD, BALTIMORE & PROF MGT SCI, GEORGE WASH UNIV, as of 2006. **Mailing Address:** Dept Info Technol, Johns Hopkins Univ, 9601 Med Ctr Dr, Rockville, MD 20850. **Fax:** 301-315-2892. **E-Mail:** jliebow1@jhu.edu

LIEBOWITZ, STEPHEN MARC, PHARMACEUTICAL CHEMISTRY. **Education:** State Univ NY, Buffalo, BS, 1974; Va Commonwealth Univ, PhD (med chem), 1980. **Professional Experience:** Prin investr, Robert A Welch Found, 1982-; ASST PROF ANALYSIS PHARMACEUT CHEM, UNIV TEX, AUSTIN, 1981-; fel, Adria Labs, 1980-1981; Fel, Ohio State Univ, 1980 & Adria Labs, 1980-1981. **Memberships:** Am Chem Soc; NY Acad Sci; AAAS. **Research Statement & Publications:** Synthesis of organic molecules to aid in a basic understanding of biochemical processes on a molecular level; new synthetic methodology. **Mailing Address:** Schering Plough K-2-1 F31A, 2000 Galloping Hill Rd, Kenilworth, NJ 07033-1310.

LIEBSON, SIDNEY HAROLD, PHYSICS. **Personal Data:** b New York, NY, July 9, 1920; m 1947, Jeannette Burman; c Alice R & Gail A. **Education:** City Col New York, BS, 1939; Univ Mich, MS, 1940; Univ Md, PhD (physics), 1947. **Professional Experience:** CONSULT, 1983-; mgr xerographic technol, mgr mfg Res & Develop, 1974-1983; sr corp planner, Xerox Corp, 1969-1974; mgr xerographic technol, Xerox Corp, 1966-1969; mgr phys res, Nat Cash Register Co, 1960-1966; asst dir physics, Armour Res Found, Ill Inst Technol, 1959-1960; mgr res & develop, Nuclear Develop Corp Am, 1955-1959; head electromagnetics br, Naval Res Lab, 1949-1955; physicist, Naval Res Lab, 1940-1949. **Memberships:** Fel Am Phys Soc; Inst Elec & Electronics Engrs. **Research Statement & Publications:** Solid state phenomena; Geiger counters; electronic circuit analysis and design; discharge mechanism of self-quenching Geiger-Miller counters; scintillation and fluorescence of organics; photoconductivity; manufacturing technologies; research administration. **Mailing Address:** 15 Forestwood Dr, Stamford, CT 06903.

LIECHTY, RICHARD DALE, ENDOCRINE SURGERY. **Personal Data:** b Lake Geneva, Wis, October 20, 1925; m 1952, Valerie; c Robert, Ann, Richard & Cameron. **Education:** Yale Univ, BA, 1950; Northwestern Univ, MD, 1954. **Professional Experience:** Assoc dean grad med educ, Med Sch, Univ Colo, 1984-1988; PROF SURG, MED SCH, UNIV COLO, 1971-; Assoc prof surg, Med Sch, Univ Iowa, 1961-1971. **Memberships:** Fel Am Col Surgeons; Am Thyroid Asn; Am Asn Endocrine Surgeons; Western Surg Asn (pres, 1986). **Research Statement & Publications:** Endocrinology; surgery of Grave's disease; anatomy of parathyroid glands. **Mailing Address:** 4900 E Mansfield Ave, B-192, Denver, CO 80237.

LIEDL, GERALD L(EROY), MATERIALS SCIENCE, METALLURGICAL ENGINEERING. **Personal Data:** b Fergus Falls, Minn, March 2, 1933; m 1957, c 2. **Education:** Purdue Univ, BS, 1955, PhD (metall eng), 1960. **Professional Experience:** RETIRED; prof, Purdue Univ, 1978-1999; head dept, Purdue Univ, W beginning 1978; prof metall eng, Purdue Univ, W Lafayette, beginning 1973; asst head dept, 1969-1978; from instr to assoc prof, 1958-1973. **Memberships:** Am Soc Eng Educ; fel Am Soc Metals; Metals Soc; Mat Res Soc; Am Ceramics Soc. **Research Statement & Publications:** Diffraction; electron microscopy; correlations among structure, texture, and properties of crystalline solids and thin films. **Mailing Address:** Sch Mat Eng, Purdue Univ, MSEE Bldg, W Lafayette, IN 47907-1968. **Fax:** 765-494-1204. **E-Mail:** liedl@ecn.purdue.edu

LIEDTKE, CAROLE M, CELLULAR BIOLOGY. **Personal Data:** b Cleveland, Ohio, 1944. **Education:** Case Western Res Univ, PhD (anat), 1980. **Professional Experience:** PROF PEDIAT, CHILDRENS HOSP, CASE WESTERN RES UNIV, 2000-; vis prof, James Chmn, Dept Bio, St Francis Xavier Univ, Antigonish, Nova Scotia, 1994; assoc prof cell physiol, Dept Pediat, Childrens Hosp, Case Western Res Univ, 1991-2000; grant, Canadian Cystic Fibrosis Foundation, 1989; asst prof, Dept Pediat& Physiol & Biophys, Case Western Reserve Univ, 1988-1991; asst prof, Dept Pediat & Develop Genetics, Case Western Univ, 1983-1988; instr, Dept Pedi, Case Western Res Univ, 1981-1983. **Research Statement & Publications:** Cellular biology. **Mailing Address:** Dept Pediat Rainbow Babies & Children's Hosp, Case Western Res Univ, 10900 Euclid Ave, Cleveland, OH 44106-4948. **E-Mail:** cxl7@po.cwru.edu

LIEF, HAROLD ISAIAH, MARITAL & SEX THERAPY & RESEARCH. **Personal Data:** b New York, NY, December 29, 1917; m 1961, c 5. **Education:** Univ Mich, BA, 1938; NY Univ, MD, 1942; Columbia Univ, cert psychoanal, 1950. **Honorary Degrees:** MA, Univ Pa, 1971. **Honors & Awards:** Ann Award Soc Sci, Am Asn Sex Educrs, Counrs & Therapists, 1980 & 1990. **Professional Experience:** CLIN PROF PYSCHIAT, THOMAS JEFFERSON UNIV, as of 2003; PROF EMER PSYCHIAT, PA HOSP, 1987-; psychiatrist, Pa Hosp, 1983-1987; PROF EMER PSYCHIAT, SCH MED, UNIV PA, 1982-; assoc psychiatrist, Pa Hosp, 1981-1983; hon co-pres, World Cong Sexology, 1981; consult, Psychiat Educ Br, NIMH, 1974-1975; consult, WHO, 1971 & 1974; consult, AMA, 1970-1978; consult, HEW, 1969-1976; dir, Marriage Coun Philadelphia & Ctr Study Sex Educ Med, Univ Pa, 1968-1981; pres, Sex Info & Educ Coun US, 1968-1970; prof, Univ Pa, 1967-1982; dir, Div Family Study, Univ Pa, 1967-1981; vis prof, Sch Med, Univ Va, 1958; from asst prof to prof psychiat, Sch Med, Tulane Univ, 1951-1967; res asst, Col Physicians & Surgeons, Columbia Univ, 1949-1951; resident psychiat, Long Island Med Col, 1946-1948; intern, Queens Gen Hosp, Jamaica, NY, 1942-1943. **Memberships:** fel Am Acad Psychoanal (pres, 1967-1968); fel Am Psychiat Asn; fel Am Col Psychiat; fel Am Col Psychoanal; Am Psychosomatic Soc; Soc Sex Therapists & Researchers; World Asn Sexology (secy, 1981-1985, vpres, 1985-1989). **Research Statement & Publications:** Marital and sexual relations; sex education in medicine; adult development; psycho-endocrinological-pharmacologic aspects human sexuality; adolescent sexuality. **Mailing Address:** Ctr Sexuality & Relig, 700 Spruce St Ste 503, Philadelphia, PA 19106. **Fax:** 610-995-0364. **E-Mail:** halief@aol.com

LIEFELD, ROBERT J, PHYSICS. **Education:** Ohio State Univ, PhD, 1959. **Professional Experience:** PROF EMER, DEPT PHYSICS, NMEX STATE UNIV, 2001-; prof, Dept Physics, Nmex State Univ, 1961-2001. **Mailing Address:** Dept of Phys New Mexico State Univ, PO Box 3D, Las Cruces, NM 88003. **Fax:** 505-646-1934. **E-Mail:** rliefeld@nmsu.edu

LIEGEY, FRANCIS WILLIAM, MICROBIOLOGY. **Personal Data:** b Frenchville, Pa, January 4, 1923; m 1947, c 6. **Education:** St Bonaventure Univ, BS, 1947, MS, 1950, PhD (microbiol), 1959. **Professional Experience:** RETIRED; chmn dept, Ind Univ Pa, 1972-1990; prof biol, Ind Univ Pa, beginning 1964; from instr to assoc prof biol, St Bonaventure Univ, 1948-1964. **Memberships:** Am Soc Microbiol. **Research Statement & Publications:** Microbial ecology of acid mine streams. **Mailing Address:** 23 Elm St, Indiana, PA 15701.

LIELMEZS, JANIS, CHEMICAL ENGINEERING. **Personal Data:** b Riga, Latvia, June 1, 1926; American citizen; m 1970, Alna. **Education:** Univ Denver, BS, 1954; Northwestern Univ, MS, 1956. **Honors & Awards:** Sci & Technol Award, World Fedn Free Latvians, 1981. **Professional Experience:** RETIRED; prof emer chem & biol eng, Univ Bc, 1991-2003; ed sci & technol, Latvian Encycl, 1976-; ed chem, Tech Rev, Latvian Engrs Asn, 1974-; from asst prof to prof, Univ Bc, 1963-1991; asst prof chem eng, Inst Mineral Res, Mich Col Mining & Technol, 1962-1963; res engr, Inst Mineral Res, Mich Col Mining & Technol, 1960-1963; consult chem eng, Shell Develop Co, 1958-1959; engr, Shell Develop Co, 1957-1958, 1959; engr, Snow, Ice & Permafrost Res Estab, US Army CEngrs, 1956. **Memberships:** Fel NY Acad Sci; fel Chem Inst Can. **Research Statement & Publications:** Applied and theoretical thermodynamics; applied mathematics; fluid flow; magnetism and phase transformations; magnetocatalytic effect in chemical reactions; transport properties of fluids. **Mailing Address:** Dept Chem Eng, Univ BC, Vancouver, BC V6T 1W5, Can. **Fax:** 604-822-6003.

LIEM, KAREL F, VERTEBRATE MORPHOLOGY. **Personal Data:** b Java, Indonesia, November 24, 1935; m 1965. **Education:** Indonesia Univ, BSc, 1957, MSc, 1958; Univ Ill, PhD (zoology), 1961. **Professional Experience:** Trustee, Cohosset Marine Biol Sta, 1974-; mem vis comt, New Eng Aquarium, 1974-; ed, Copeia & assoc ed, J Morphol, 1974-; HENRY BRYANT BIGELOW PROF & CUR ICHTHYOL, HARVARD UNIV, 1972-; Guggenheim fel, 1970-1971; mem comt Latimeria, Nat Acad Sci, 1967; head, Div Vert Anat, Chicago Natural Hist Mus, Ill, 1965-1972; from asst prof to assoc prof anat, Univ Ill Col Med, 1964-1972; asst prof zool, Leiden Univ, 1962-1964. **Memberships:** Am Soc Zool; Am Soc Ichthyol & Herpet; Soc Syst Zool; fel Zool Soc London; Neth Royal Zool Soc. **Research Statement & Publications:** Evolution of chordate structure; functional anatomy of teleosts; morphology and hydrodynamics of air-breathing teleost blood circulations; sex reversal in teleosts; functional anatomy and evolution of African cichlid fishes. **Mailing Address:** Organ Evol Biol Harvard Univ, 26 Oxford St, Cambridge, MA 02138-2902. **Fax:** 617-495-5667. **E-Mail:** csouza@oeb.harvard.edu

LIEM, RONALD KIAN HONG, NEUROBIOLOGY. **Personal Data:** b Lombok, Indonesia, February 8, 1946; American citizen. **Education:** Amherst Col, BA, 1967; Cornell Univ, MSc, 1969, PhD (chem). **Professional Experience:** PROF PATH, ANAT & CELL BIOL, COL PHYSICIANS & SURGEONS, COLUMBIA UNIV, 1991-; assoc prof, Anat & Cell Biol, Col Physicians & Surgeons, Columbia Univ, 1987-1990; assoc prof pharmacol, NY Univ Sch Med, 1978-1987. **Memberships:** Am Soc Cell Biol; Am Soc Neuroscience; Am Soc Neurochemistry. **Research Statement & Publications:** Biochemical studies on the neuronal cytoskeleton, especially with regard to the assembly of neurofilaments and their interactions with other cytoskeletal elements, both in vivo and in vitro. **Mailing Address:** Dept Path, Columbia Univ, 630 W 168th St, New York, NY 10032-3702. **Fax:** 212-305-5498. **E-Mail:** rk12@columbia.edu

LIEMOHN, HAROLD BENJAMIN, SPACECRAFT-ENVIRONMENT INTERACTIONS, SPACE-PLASMA WAVES. **Personal Data:** b Minneapolis, Minn, February 2, 1935; m 1957, Clarice Johnson; c Kimberley, Jeffrey, Thomas, Michael & Michelle. **Education:** Univ Minn, BA, 1956, MS, 1959; Univ Wash, PhD (physics), 1962. **Professional Experience:** MGR, SPACE STA ENVIRON, BOEING DEFENSE & SPACE GROUP, 1991-; MGR SPACE PHYSICS, ENG TECHNOL, BOEING AEROSPACE CO, 1977-; res staff math-physics, Pac Northwest, Battelle Mem Inst, 1972-1977; reporter particle-wave interactions, Comn V, Int Asn Geomag & Aeronomy, 1971-1973; chmn & secy local arrangements, Ann Meeting, Comt Space Res, Seattle, 1971; affil assoc prof, Univ Wash, 1968-; staff mem, Geo-Astrophys Sci Res Labs, Boeing Co, 1966-1972; Adj asst prof, Southern Methodist Univ, 1964-1965; asst prof atmospheric & space sci, Southwest Ctr Advan Studies, 1963-1966; staff mem geo-astrophys, Sci Res Labs, Boeing Co, 1959-1963; Teaching asst physics, Univ Minn, 1956-1959. **Research Statement & Publications:** Theoretical research in radiation belt physics, electromagnetic waves in magnetoplasma, hydromagnetic waves in magnetosphere, and spacecraft charging and contamination; ionizing radiation effects; sunlight reflections from space craft. **Mailing Address:** 2320 Fairwind Rd, Houston, TX 77062.

LIEN, ERIC JUNG-CHI, PHARMACEUTICAL CHEMISTRY. **Personal Data:** b Kaohsiung, Taiwan, November 30, 1937; American citizen; m 1965, Linda; c Raymond & Andrew Y. **Education:** Taiwan Univ, BS, 1960; Univ Calif, San Francisco, PhD (pharmaceut chem), 1966. **Professional Experience:** Sci adv, Nat Lab Food & Drugs, Dept Health, exed, Yuam, Taipei, Taiwan, Repub China, 1992-1994; consult, Ariz Dis Control Res Comn, Phoenix, Ariz, 1986-; mem comt, Develop Therapeut Contract Rev, Nat Cancer Inst, 1983-1987; coordr, Sch Pharm, Univ Southern Calif, 1978-1984; PROF PHARMACEUT & BIOMED CHEM, SCH PHARM, UNIV SOUTHERN CALIF, 1976-; from asst prof to assoc prof, Sch Pharm, Univ Southern Calif, 1968-1976; res assoc bio-org chem, Pomona Col, 1967-1968; teaching fel, Univ Calif, San Francisco Med Ctr, 1966-1967. **Memberships:** Fel AAAS; Am Pharmaceut Asn; Am Chem Soc; Am Asn Cols Pharm; Am Asn Cancer Res; fel Am Asn Pharmaceut Sci. **Research Statement & Publications:** Structure-activity relationship and bioorganic chemistry; physical organic chemistry; natural products; antiviral and antitumor agents. **Mailing Address:** Sch Pharm, Univ Calif, 1985 Zonal Ave PSC 600, Los Angeles, CA 90089. **Fax:** 323-442-1390. **E-Mail:** elien@usc.edu

LIEN, ERIC LOUIS, NUTRITIONAL BIOCHEMISTRY. **Personal Data:** b Hammond, Ind, April 9, 1946; m 1987, Winifred; c Steven, Janet, Elizabeth, Jeffrey, Alison & Caroline. **Education:** Col Wooster, BA, 1968; Univ Ill, Urbana-Champaign, MS, 1971, PhD (biochem), 1972. **Professional Experience:** VPRES, RES & DEVELOP, WYETH NUTRIT, as of 2002; sr dir nutrit res, Wyeth-Ayerst Labs, beginning 1993; dir, nutrit res & develop, 1990-1993; assoc dir, nutrit res & develop, 1987-1990; mgr, Metab Disorders Sect, 1983-1987; sr biochemist, Wyeth-Ayerst Labs, 1975-1983; fel biochem, Sch Med, Univ Pa, 1972-1975. **Memberships:** AAAS; Am Inst Nutrit; Am Soc Parenteral & Enternal Nutrit. **Research Statement & Publications:** Infant nutrition; triglyceride absorption; amino acid analysis. **Mailing Address:** Dept Nutrit Res, Wyeth-Ayerst Labs, PO Box 8299, Philadelphia, PA 19101. **Fax:** 215-989-4586. **E-Mail:** liene@war.wyeth.com

LIEN, HWACHII, TURBULENT FLOWS, ENGINEERING INSTRUMENTATION. **Personal Data:** b Taipei, Taiwan, November 10, 1930; American citizen; m 1964, Mei-shien; c Lyndon, Leslie & Lester. **Education:** Nat Taiwan Univ, BS, 1953; Kans State Univ, MS, 1956; Univ Pa, PhD (appl mech), 1962. **Professional Experience:** PRES & CHMN, FINANCIAL SCI INC, as of 2003; consult, Anathon Corp, 1979-; chmn, Liberty Bank & Trust Co, 1977-; pres, Financial Sci Inc, 1974-; gen mgr admin, Hopax Co, beginning 1974; prin scientist, Avco Syst Div, 1971-1974; tech dir, Yuen Foong Yu Paper Mfg Co, 1970-1971; vis prof, Nat Taiwan Univ, 1970-1971; asst mgr, Avco Syst Div, 1968-1970; tech supvr, Gen Appl Sci Lab, 1967-1968; staff scientist, Avco Missile Syst Div, 1962-1967. **Member-**

ships: Am Inst Aeronaut & Astronaut. **Research Statement & Publications:** Fluid dynamics and its related diagnostic instrumentation in general; turbulence; chemically reacting flows; magnetohydrodynamics; mechanics of multiphase fluids; electrostatic probes. **Mailing Address:** Financial Sci Inc, 21 Milk S, Boston, MA 02109.

LIENER, IRVIN ERNEST, BIOCHEMISTRY, NUTRITION. **Personal Data:** b Pittsburgh, Pa, June 27, 1919; m 1945, Dorothy; c Sally Anne Liener & Wendy Roberta Quammen. **Education:** Mass Inst Technol, BS, 1941; Univ Southern Calif, PhD (biochem, nutrit), 1949. **Honors & Awards:** Spencer Award Outstanding Achievement Agr & Food Chem, Am Chem Soc, 1977 & 1982; Fulbright Award, 1990; Stering B Hendricks Awd, 2002. **Professional Experience:** PROF EMER BIOCHEM, UNIV MINN, ST PAUL, 1989-; pres, Int Lectin Soc, 1987-1992; ed, J Agr & Food Univ, 1982-1999; vis prof nutrit, 1979; guggenheim fel, Carlsberg Lab, Copenhagen, Denmark, 1957; from instr asst prof to prof, Univ Minn, St Paul, 1949-1959. **Memberships:** Fel Venezuelan Asn Advan Sci; Am Chem Soc; Am Soc Biol Chem; Am Inst Nutrit; Sigma Xi. **Research Statement & Publications:** Isolation and characterization of antinutritional factors in legumes; structure and mechanism of action of proteolytic enzymes and their naturally-occurring inhibitors. **Mailing Address:** Dept Biochem, Molecular Biol, Biophys, Univ Minn, 1479 Gortner Ave, St Paul, MN 55108. **Fax:** 612-625-5780. **E-Mail:** liene001@umn.edu

LIENHARD, GUSTAV E, BIOCHEMISTRY. **Personal Data:** b Plainfield, NJ, June 21, 1938; m 1960, c 2. **Education:** Amherst Col, BA, 1959; Yale Univ, PhD (biochem), 1964. **Professional Experience:** PROF BIOCHEM, DARTMOUTH MED SCH, 1975-; assoc prof, Dartmouth Med Sch, 1972-1975; from asst prof to assoc prof biochem & molecular biol, Harvard Univ, 1965-1972; res fel biochem, Brandeis Univ, 1963-1965. **Memberships:** Am Soc Biochem & Molecular Biol. **Research Statement & Publications:** Mechanisms of insulin action; regulation of transport by hormones. **Mailing Address:** Dept Biochem, Dartmouth Med Sch, Hanover, NH 03755-3844. **E-Mail:** gus.lienhard@dartmouth.edu

LIENHARD, JOHN H, MECHANICAL ENGINEERING. **Education:** Univ Calif, Los Angeles, BS, 1982, MS, 1984; Univ Calif, San Diego, PhD. **Professional Experience:** PROF MECH ENG, ROHSENOW HEAT & MASS TRNSFER LAB, DEPT MECH ENG, MASS INST TECHNOL, as of 2006; UNDERGRAD OFFICER, DEPT MECH ENG, 2005-. **Mailing Address:** Mass Inst Technol, Dept Mech Eng, 77 Massachusetts Ave, Cambridge, MA 02139-4307. **E-Mail:** lienhard@mit.edu

LIENHARD, JOHN H(ENRY), HISTORY, MECHANICAL ENGINEERING. **Personal Data:** b St Paul, Minn, August 17, 1930; m Carol; c John H, V & Andrew J. **Education:** Ore State Col, BS, 1951; Univ Wash, Seattle, MS, 1953; Univ Calif, Berkeley, PhD (mech eng), 1961. **Honorary Degrees:** LHD, Univ Hooston, 2002, LHD, Sacred Heart Univ, 2002. **Honors & Awards:** Charles Russ Richards Mem Award, Am Soc Mech Engrs, 1980, Heat Transfer Mem Award, 1981, ASME Ralph Coats Roe Medal, 1989, Engr Historian award, 1998, Esther Farfel award, Univ Houston, 1991, ASEE Ralph Coats Roe award, 1994, ASME Edwin F Church Medal, 2000, Crystal Microphone Award, 2005. **Professional Experience:** Prof Emer. Mech. Engr. Univ Houston, 2000-; Prof Mech. Engr. Univ Houston, 1980-2000 prof mech eng, Univ KY, 1967-1980; assoc prof, Wash State Univ, 1961-1967; assoc, Univ Calif, Berkeley, 1956-1961; instr mech eng, Univ Wash, Seattle, 1955-1956; Design engr, Boeing Airplane Co, 1951-1952. **Memberships:** Hon mem Am Soc Mech Engrs; Am Soc Eng Educ; fel AAAS; Soc Hist Technol. **Research Statement & Publications:** Statistical mechanical modeling of macroscopic systems; thermal systems with emphasis on boiling and other two-phase problems; nuclear thermohydraulics; equations of state; history of technology. **Mailing Address:** Dept Mech Eng, Univ Houston, Houston, TX 77204-4006. **Fax:** 713-743-4503. **E-Mail:** jhl@uh.edu

LIENTZ, BENNET PRICE, INFORMATION SYSTEMS, REENGINEERING. **Personal Data:** b Hollywood, Calif, October 24, 1942. **Education:** Claremont Men's Col, BA, 1964; Univ Wash, MS, 1966, PhD (math), 1968. **Professional Experience:** ADV, UNIV CALIF, LOS ANGELES, as of 2004; dir, Off Admin Info Serv, 1978-1981; PROF GRAD SCH MGT, UNIV CALIF, LOS ANGELES, 1977-; assoc prof indust eng & Air Force Off Sci Res grant, Univ Southern Calif, 1970-1972; sr res scientist, Syst Develop Corp, 1968-1970; instr math, Univ Wash, 1965-1968. **Memberships:** Opers Res Soc Am (secy-treas 1971); Inst Math Statist; Am Statist Asn; Am Math Soc; Asn Comput Mach; Inst Elec & Electronics Engrs. **Research Statement & Publications:** Communication and network analysis; computers and systems analysis; computer security networks; re-engineering; distributed systems; published over 20 articles. **Mailing Address:** Grad Sch Mgt, Univ Calif, Cornell Hall Rm D509, Los Angeles, CA 90024. **Fax:** 310-794-4257. **E-Mail:** bennet.lientz@anderson.ucla.edu

LIEPA, GEORGE ULDIS, LIPID & PROTEIN METABOLISM. **Personal Data:** b Oldenburg, Ger, October 4, 1946; American citizen; m 1979, Candice; c Arlanne & Marisa. **Education:** Drake Univ, BA, 1968, MA, 1970; Iowa State Univ, PhD (molecular biol), 1976. **Professional Experience:** PROF, SCH HEALTH SCI, EASTERN MICH UNIV, as of 2005; assoc ed, Nutrit Clin Pract; prof nutrit, Tex Woman's Univ, beginning 1979; asst instr med & grad physiol, NIH fel, 1977-1978; asst instr med & grad physiol, Univ Tex Health Sci Ctr, San Antonio, 1976-1977. **Memberships:** Sigma Xi; Am Oil Chemists Soc; Am Inst Nutrit; Latvian-Am Asn Univ Profs & Scientists; Am Soc Clin Nutrit; Am Soc Parent & Ent Nutrit. **Research Statement & Publications:** Lipid and protein metabolism; dietary care of trauma patient; metabolism during trauma; diet and cancer; diet and kidney disease. **Mailing Address:** Sch Health Sci Eastern Mich Univ, 339 Marshall Bldg, Ypsilanti, MI 48197. **Fax:** 734-487-4095. **E-Mail:** george.liepa@emich.edu

LIEPINS, ATIS AIVARS, STRUCTURAL ENGINEERING, APPLIED MECHANICS. **Personal Data:** b Aloja, Latvia, April 17, 1935; m 1960, c 2. **Education:** Mass Inst Technol, SB, 1957, SM, 1960, Engr, 1960. **Professional Experience:** PARTNER CHARGE, METROP DIST COMMISSION, SIMPSON GUMPERTZ & HEGER INC, as of 2002; assoc, Simpson Gumpertz & Heger Inc, beginning 1977; sr staff engr, Littleton Res & Eng Corp, 1968-1977; prin engr, Dynatech Corp, 1961-1968; res engr appl mech, Res Labs, United Aircraft Corp, 1960-1961. **Memberships:** Am Inst Aeronaut & Astronaut; Am Soc Mech Engrs; Am Soc Civil Engrs. **Research Statement & Publications:** Static and dynamic response of thin shell structures; propeller induced ship vibration; soil-structure interaction. **Mailing Address:** Simpson Gumpertz & Heger Inc, 297 Broadway, Arlington, MA 02174. **E-Mail:** aaliepins@sgh.com

LIEPINS, RAIMOND, POLYMER ENGINEERING, SUPERCONDUCTORS. **Personal Data:** b Plavinas, Latvia, May 19, 1930; American citizen; m 1961, Leila Zayas; c Elsa, Ilze, Rebecca & Otto. **Education:** Southern Ill Univ, BA, 1954; Univ Minn, MS, 1956; Kans State Univ, PhD (org chem), 1960. **Honors & Awards:** Distinguished Serv Award, Los Alamos Nat Lab, 1983. **Professional Experience:** TECH COORDR, LOS ALAMOS NAT LAB, 1987-; assoc group leader, Los Alamos Nat Lab, 1986-1987; consult, 1985-; lectr, Brookhaven Nat Lab, 1985; lectr, State Univ NY, New Paltz, 1977; sect leader mat sci & technol, Los Alamos Nat Lab, 1977-1991; prin investr, Indust Org Chem Indust, Res Triangle Inst, Environ Protection Agency, 1976-1977; lectr, NC State Univ, 1976; lectr, Clemson Univ, 1976; sr chemist, Res Triangle Inst, 1966-1977; res assoc polymer res, Univ Ariz, 1964-1966; res chemist, B F Goodrich Co, 1960-1964. **Memberships:** Emer mem Am Chem Soc; fel Am Inst Chem. **Research Statement & Publications:** Coatings for laser fusion targets; gas phase coating techniques; flame retardance; low pressure plasma applications; high temperature polymers; piezoelectric polymers; organometallic polymers; conducting polymers; liquid crystal polymers; tamper proof packages; magnetic processing; super conductors. **Mailing Address:** 2303 North Ct, Santa Fe, NM 87505. **Fax:** 505-473-5898.

LIEPMANN, DORIAN, FLUID MECHANICS. **Education:** Univ Calif, San Diego, PhD (Appl Mech), 1990. **Professional Experience:** CHAIR, DEPT BIOENG, UNIV CALIF, BERKELEY, 2004-; PROF DEPT BIOENG & MECH ENG & VICE CHAIR UNDERGRAD AFFAIRS, DEPT BIOENG, UNIV CALIF, BERKELEY, 2003-; LESTER JOHN & LYNNE DEWAR LLOYD DISTINGUISHED PROF BIOENG, UNIV CALIF, BERKELEY, 2001-; assod prof, Depr Bioeng & Mech Eng, Univ Calif, Berkeley, 1998-2003; DIR, BERKELEY SENSOR & ACTUATOR CTR, UNIV CALIF, BERKELEY, 1998-; FAC MEM, JOINT UNIV CALIF, SAN FRANCISCO/UNIV CALIF, BERKELEY, BIOENG GRAD GROUP, 1992-; asst prof, Mech Eng, Univ Calif, Berkeley, 1992-1998; res eng, Inst Non-Linear Sci, Univ Calif, San diego, 1986-19992; res scientist, Sci Appln Int Corp, Tech Res Group, 1984-1992; tech staff, Jet Propulsion lab, Pasadena, 1983-1984. **Research Statement & Publications:** BioMEMS; microfluid dynamics; experimental biofluid dynamics; hemodynamics associated with valvular heart disease and other cardiac and arterial flows. **Mailing Address:** Dept Mech Eng, Univ Calif, 455 Evans Hall No 1762, Berkeley, CA 94720. **Fax:** 510-642-5835. **E-Mail:** liepmann@me.berkeley.edu

LIEPMANN, H(ANS) WOLFGANG, AERONAUTICS. **Personal Data:** b Berlin, Ger, July 3, 1914; American citizen; m 1954, c 2. **Education:** Univ Zurich, PhD (physics), 1938. **Honorary Degrees:** DEng, Tech Univ, Aachen, 1985. **Honors & Awards:** Ludwig-Prandtl-Ring, Ger Soc Aeronaut & Astronaut, 1968; Worcester Reed Warner Medal, Am Soc Mech Engrs, 1969; Monie A Ferst Award, Sigma Xi, 1978; Fluid Dynamics Prize, Am Phys Soc, 1980 & Otto Laporte Award, 1985; Fluids Eng Award, Am Soc Mech Engrs, 1984; Nat Medal Sci, 1986; Guggenheim Medal, 1986; Nat Medal Technol, 1993. **Professional Experience:** Foreign fel, Max-Planck Inst, 1988; THEODORE VON KARMAN PROF EMER AERONAUT, CALIF INST TECHNOL, 1985-; Theodore von Karman prof aeronaut, Calif Inst Technol, 1983-1985; Charles Lee Powell prof fluid mech & thermodyn, Calif Inst Technol, 1976-1983; dir, Grad Aeronaut Labs, 1972-1985; from asst prof to prof, Calif Inst Technol, 1945-1976; fel aeronaut, Calif Inst Technol, 1939-1945; Fel physics, Univ Zurich, 1938-1939. **Memberships:** Nat Acad Sci; Nat Acad Eng; AAAS; hon fel Am Inst Aeronaut & Astronaut; fel Am Acad Arts & Sci; hon fel Indian Acad Sci; hon mem Am Soc Mech Engrs. **Research Statement & Publications:** Laminar instability, transition and turbulence; shock wave boundary layer interaction; transonic flow; aerodynamic noise; fluid mechanics of Helium II. **Mailing Address:** Dept Aeronaut, Calif Inst Technol, 1200 E California Blvd, Pasadena, CA 91125. **Fax:** 626-449-2677.

LIEPSCH, DIETER W, BIOFLUID MECHANICS, FLUID MECHANICS. **Personal Data:** m 1982, c Stephen & Eva. **Education:** Tech Univ, Munchen, dipl-Ing, 1966, Dr-Ing, 1974, Dr-habil, 1986. **Professional Experience:** HEAD, LAB BIO FLUID MECH, 1989-; dir cardiovasc res, Hal B Wallis Res Facil, Eisenhower Med Ctr, 1987-1989; Adj prof, Univ Southern Calif, San Diego, 1987-1989; sr scientist, Hal B Wallis Res Facil, Eisenhower Med Ctr, 1986-1987; Guest prof, Univ Houston, 1983-1984; PROF FLUID MECH, HEAT TRANSFER, FACHHOCHSCHULE MUNCHEN & TECH UNIV, 1972-. **Memberships:** Am Soc Mech Engrs; Biomed Eng Soc; Europ Soc Biorheology; Europ Soc Microcirculation; Soc Ger Engrs; Soc App Math & Mech; Int Soc Optical Eng; Am Phys Soc. **Research Statement & Publications:** Flow visualization and laser doppler ancinometer studies in models of human blood vessels to find out specifically causes for athero clerosis and aging; blood flow studies coagulation, cell-cell and cell-vessel wall interactions; air conditioning and air flow in buildings. **Mailing Address:** Am Buchen Wald 29, 82340 Feldafing, Ger.

LIER, FRANK GEORGE, botany, ecology; deceased, see previous edition for last biography

LIER, JOHN, REGIONAL CLIMATOLOGY, TROPOSPHERIC METEOROLOGY. **Personal Data:** b Amsterdam, Neth, February 23, 1924; American citizen; m 1950, c 2. **Education:** Clark Univ, MA, 1963; Univ Calif, Berkeley, PhD (geog), 1968. **Professional Experience:** EMER PROF GEOG & ENVIRON STUDIES, CALIF STATE UNIV, HAYWARD, 1991-; prof, Calif State Univ, Hayward, 1968-1991; Asst prof geog, San Fransisco State Univ, 1965-1966 & Univ Hawaii, Hilo, 1966-1967; Instr geog, Univ Sask, Saskatoon, 1963. **Memberships:** Am Geog Soc; Am Meteorol Soc; Asn Am Geogr. **Research Statement & Publications:** Meteorology and regional climatology; coastal winds; climate classification; precipitation regimes; agroclimatology; agrometeorology; man-atmosphere interaction; 19th century weather observation; environmental aesthetics and ethics. **Mailing Address:** Dept Geog & Environ Studies, Calif State Univ, Hayward, CA 94542.

LIES, THOMAS ANDREW, organic chemistry; deceased, see previous edition for last biography

LIESCH, JERROLD MICHAEL, NATURAL PRODUCTS STRUCTURE DETERMINATION, MASS SPECTROMETRY. **Personal Data:** b Chicago, Ill, December 12, 1949. **Education:** Ill Inst Technol, BS, 1971; Univ Ill, MS, 1973, PhD (org chem), 1975. **Professional Experience:** SR INVESTR, MERCK & CO INC, 1977-; NIH fel org chem, Mass Inst Technol, 1976-1977. **Memberships:** Am Chem Soc; Am Soc Mass Spectrometry. **Research Statement & Publications:** Structure elucidation; mass spectrometry; proton and carbon magnetic resonance spectrometry. **Mailing Address:** Merck Res Labs, PO Box 2000 R50-105, Rahway, NJ 07065-0900. **E-Mail:** jerry_liesch@merck.com

LIESE, HOMER C, MINERALOGY, PETROLOGY. **Personal Data:** b New York, NY, October 25, 1931; m 1955. **Education:** Syracuse Univ, BS, 1953; Univ Utah, MS, 1957, PhD (mineral), 1962. **Professional Experience:** ASSOC PROF EMER GEOL, UNIV CONN, as of 1998; assoc prof geol, Univ Conn, beginning 1962; X-ray technician, Kennecott Copper Inc, 1960-1961. **Memberships:** Geol Soc Am; Mineral Soc Am; Soc Appl Spectros. **Research Statement & Publications:** Spectroscopy of minerals. **Mailing Address:** Dept Geol, Univ Conn, U-45 354 Mansfield, Storrs, CT 06269-0002.

LIESKE, JAY HENRY, ASTRONOMY. **Professional Experience:** STAFF, JET PROPULSION LAB, CALIF INST TECHNOL, as of 2005. **Memberships:** Int Astron Union. **Mailing Address:** Jet Propulsion Lab, 4800 Oak Grove Dr, Pasadena, CA 91109. **Fax:** 818-393-3800. **E-Mail:** jay.h.lieske@jpl.nasa.gov

LIETH, HELMUT HEINRICH FRIEDRICH, GEOECOLOGY, ECOLOGICAL MODELLING. **Personal Data:** b Kuerten-Steeg, Ger, December 16, 1925; m 1952, c 4. **Education:**

Univ Cologne, DrPhil, 1953; Univ Stuttgart-Hohenheim, PD, 1960. **Honors & Awards:** Biometerol Res Found Award, 1982; Biometeorol Award, Am Meteorol Soc, 1987. **Professional Experience:** Adv Hum Univ Irkutsk, 1994-; EMER PROF BIOL & ECOL, UNIV OSNABRUECK, 1991-; ed-in-chief, Vegetatio, 1990-1992; guest prof, Waseda Univ, Tokyo, 1988- & United Arab Emirates, Univ AC Ain, 1990; ed-in-chief, Int J Biometeorol, 1987-1993; ed-in-chief, Task for Veg Sci, 1981-; adj prof ecol, Univ NC, Chapel Hill, 1977-; prof, Univ Osnabrueck, 1977-1991; govt adv ecol, Portugal, 1974; guest scientist ecol & biophys, Nuclear Res Lab, Julich, Ger, 1973-1974; from assoc prof to prof bot & ecol, Univ NC, Chapel Hill, 1967-1977; prof, Univ Hawaii, 1966-1967; guest prof bot, Univ Tolima, Ibague, Colombia, 1963; guest prof bot, Cent Univ, Caracas, Venezuela, 1961; Nat Res fel bot & ecol, Univ Montreal, 1960-1961; asst bot, Agr Univ, Stuttgart-Hohenheim, 1955-1966; asst bot, Univ Cologne, 1954-1955. **Memberships:** Int Biometeorol Soc (pres, 1979-1984); Int Soc Trop Ecol (pres, 1985-1991); Inst Asn Ecol (treas, 1986-1990); Ecol Soc Am. **Research Statement & Publications:** Systems ecology, geoecology; interdisciplinary modelling ecology, economy, sociology, climate and atmosphere, plant relations, net primary productivity, phenology and seasonality; high salinity ecosystems. **Mailing Address:** AG Systs, Univ Osnabrueck, 49069 Osnabrueck, Ger. **Fax:** 495-496-92570.

LIETMAN, PAUL STANLEY, CLINICAL PHARMACOLOGY, PEDIATRICS & MOLECULAR SCIENCE. **Personal Data:** b Chicago, Ill, March 24, 1934; m 1956, c 3. **Education:** Western Reserve Univ, AB, 1955; Columbia Univ, MD, 1959; Johns Hopkins Univ, PhD (physiol chem), 1968. **Professional Experience:** WELLCOME PROF & DIR CLIN PHARMACOL & PROF MED, PEDIAT & PHARMACOL DEPT, JOHNS HOPKINS UNIV, 1980-; assoc prof med, Pediat & Pharmacol Dept, Johns Hopkins Univ, 1972-1980; asst prof pharmacol, Pediat & Pharmacol Dept, Johns Hopkins Univ, 1969-1972; investr, Howard Med Inst, 1968-1972; asst prof pediat, Pediat & Pharmacol Dept, Johns Hopkins Univ, 1968-1972. **Memberships:** Am Soc Pharmacol & Exp Therapeut; Soc Microbiol; Am Pediat Soc; Soc Pediat Res; Am Acad Pediat. **Research Statement & Publications:** Developmental pharmacology; antibiotics; antiviral agents. **Mailing Address:** Johns Hopkins Univ, Med Sch, 830 E Monument St, Ste 7100, Baltimore, MD 21287-5554. **E-Mail:** plietman@jhmi.edu

LIETZ, GERARD PAUL, NUCLEAR PHYSICS. **Personal Data:** b Chicago, Ill, December 10, 1937; m 1964, c 5. **Education:** DePaul Univ, BS, 1959; Univ Notre Dame, PhD (nuclear physics), 1964. **Professional Experience:** PROF EMER PHYSICS, DEPAUL UNIV, as of 2003; assoc prof physics, Depaul Univ, beginning 1977; asst prof, Depaul Univ, 1967-1977; exchange asst nuclear physics, Univ Basel, 1966-1967. **Memberships:** Am Phys Soc; Am Asn Physics Teachers; Sigma Xi. **Research Statement & Publications:** Energy levels in nuclei. **Mailing Address:** Dept Physics, DePaul Univ, 2219 N Kenmore, Chicago, IL 60614. **Fax:** 773-325-7334. **E-Mail:** glietz@depaul.edu

LIETZKE, DAVID ALBERT, PEDOLOGY, CLAY MINERALOGY. **Personal Data:** b Pontiac, Mich, April 20, 1940; m Elaine; c 2. **Education:** Mich State Univ, BS, 1962, MS, 1968, PhD (clay mineral geomorphol), 1972. **Professional Experience:** INDEPENDENT SOIL CONSULT, 1986-as of today; consult, soil mapping, soil invests, 1985; assoc prof soils, Univ Tenn, Knoxville, 1979-1986; asst prof & urban soils specialist, Va Polytech Inst & State Univ, 1973-1979; soil scientist, Mich Agr Exp Sta, 1968-1971; soil scientist, Soil Conserv Serv, Mich, 1962-1968 & 1971-1973. **Memberships:** Nat Soc Consult Soil Scientists (secy-treas, 1988-1990; pres-elect, 1993). **Research Statement & Publications:** Processes of soil formation, soil-geomorphic relationships, soil-climatic relationships and fundamental weathering processes of earth materials to form soil parent materials. **Mailing Address:** Lietzke Soil Serv & Cattleman, Rr 3, PO Box 607, Rutledge, TN 37861. **Fax:** 865-828-5336. **E-Mail:** elietzke@mindspring.com

LIEUX, MEREDITH HOAG, PALYNOLOGY, BOTANY. **Personal Data:** b Morgan City, La, November 9, 1939; m 1968. **Education:** La State Univ, Baton Rouge, BS, 1960, PhD (bot), 1969, JD, 1986; Univ Miss, MS, 1964. **Professional Experience:** ATTY, OFF LEGAL AFFAIRS & ENFORCEMENT, LA DEPT ENVIRON QUAL, 1991-; asst atty gen, Dept Justice, 1987-1990; law clerk, 19th Juducial Dist Conn, La, 1986-1987; from instr to assoc prof bot, La State Univ, Baton Rouge, 1972-1982; fel geol, La State Univ, Baton Rouge, 1971-1972; teacher pub schs, Lake Charles & Monroe, La, 1960-1971. **Memberships:** Am Asn Stratig Palynologists; Int Bee Res Asn; Bot Soc Am; Sigma Xi; Asn Women Sci; Am Bar Asn. **Research Statement & Publications:** Holocene spore and pollen studies in the gulf of mexico region; pollen morphology involving light, scanning electron and transmission electron microscopy; applied insect-pollen related studies, or melissopalynology. **Mailing Address:** 1627 Louvay Dr, Baton Rouge, LA 70808.

LIEW, CHOONG-CHIN, MOLECULAR BIOLOGY & PROTEIN CHEMISTRY OF CARDIOVASCULAR SYSTEM. **Personal Data:** b Malaysia, September 2, 1937; Canadian citizen; m 1964, Gik; c Gailina J, Allan S & Victor S. **Education:** Univ Toronto, MA, 1964, PhD (path chem), 1967; Nanyang Univ, Singapore, BS, 1960. **Honors & Awards:** Hoffman Mem Prize, 1967. **Professional Experience:** PROF LAB MED & PATH BIOL, UNIV TORONTO, as of 2004; assoc prof med, Univ Toronto, 1978-1979; from asst prof to assoc prof biochem, Univ Toronto, 1970-1978; guest investr, Rockefeller Univ, 1969-1970; hon prof biochem, Peking Union Med Col, Zhongshan Med Col, W China Med Univ, Zheijiang Med Univ, Shanghai Second Med Col, Xian Med Univ, Harabin Med Sci Univ, Shihezi Med Col, Xinjiang Med Col, Chinese Univ Hong Kong. **Memberships:** Can Biochem Soc; Biochem Soc; Am Soc Cell Biol; Am Heart Asn. **Research Statement & Publications:** Gene regulation in eukaryotes; chromosomal proteins; structure and function of cardiac myosin heavy chain genes; correlation of chromatin proteins and genetically determined heart diseases; catalogue of genes in the cardiovascular system. **Mailing Address:** Dept Clin Biochem, Univ Toronto, 100 Col St Rm 418 Banting Inst, Toronto, ON M5G 1L5, Can. **Fax:** 416-978-5650. **E-Mail:** liewcc@tcgu.med.utoronto.ca

LIEWER, PAULETT CREYKE, PHYSICS. **Education:** Cornell Univ, BS, 1967; Univ Md, PhD (Plasma Physics), 1972. **Professional Experience:** PRINCIPAL SCIENTIST & ASSOC CHIEF SCIENTIST, NASA JET PROPULSION LAB, as of 2006. **Mailing Address:** NASA Jet Propulsion Lab, M/S 169-506 4800 Oak Grove Dr, Pasadena, CA 91109. **Fax:** 818-354-8895. **E-Mail:** Paulett.C.Liewer@jpl.nasa.gov

LIFKA, BERNARD WILLIAM, METALLURGICAL ENGINEERING. **Personal Data:** b Chicago, Ill, April 8, 1931; m 1956, c 4. **Education:** Purdue Univ, BS, 1958. **Honors & Awards:** IR 100 Award, 1987; Arthur Vining Davis Award, 1988. **Professional Experience:** RETIRED; tech consult, Alcoa Labs, 1985-1993; tech supvr, Alcoa Labs, 1981-1985; staff engr, Alcoa Labs, 1980-1981; sr engr alloy develop, Alcoa Labs, 1977-1979; sr engr, Alcoa Labs, 1963-1977; engr corrosion, Alcoa Labs, 1958-1962. **Memberships:** Am Soc Metals; Nat Asn Corrosion Engrs; Sigma Xi; Am Soc Testing & Mat. **Research Statement & Publications:** Alloy development, increased plant production and resistance to corrosion of high-strength, heat-treatable aluminum alloys for aerospace and automotive applications. **Mailing Address:** 2750 Iowa Dr, New Kensington, PA 15068.

LIFSCHITZ, MEYER DAVID, NEPHROLOGY, EICOSINOID PHYSIOLOGY. **Personal Data:** b Patchogue, NY, January 9, 1942; m 1970, c 3. **Education:** Mass Inst Technol, BS, 1963; Boston Univ, MS, 1966, MD, 1967. **Professional Experience:** Mem, Kidney & Hypertension Coun, Am Heart Asn; actg chief, Div Nephrology, Univ Tex Health Sci Ctr, San Antonio, 1989-1991; consult, Brooke Army Med Ctr, 1979- & St Lukes Lutheran Hosp, 1984-; assoc chief staff res & develop, SDTU, 1984-; PROF MED, UNIV TEX HEALTH SCI CTR, SAN ANTONIO, 1984-; actg chief, SDTU, 1978-1981; chief, Renal Sect, Audie Murphy Vet Admin Hosp, 1976-1985; NIH, Vet Admin & NASA res grants, 1973-; From asst prof to assoc prof, Univ Tex Health Sci Ctr, San Antonio, 1973-1984; NIH fel, 1971; mem, Kidney & Hypertension Coun, Am Heart Asn. **Memberships:** Am Soc Nephrology; Am Physiol Soc; Am Soc Clin Invest; Am Heart Asn. **Research Statement & Publications:** Inter-relationships of hormones and kidney function. **Mailing Address:** Dept Med, Audie Murphy Vet Admin Hosp 7703 Floyd Curl Dr, San Antonio, TX 78284. **Fax:** 210-567-6550. **E-Mail:** lifschitz@uthscsa.edu

LIFSHITZ, KENNETH, NEUROPSYCHIATRY, PSYCHOBIOLOGY. **Personal Data:** b New York, NY, August 16, 1930. **Education:** Syracuse Univ, AB, 1951; State Univ NY, MD, 1955. **Professional Experience:** RES PROF PSYCHIAT, NY UNIV MED CTR, 1987-; HEAD NEUROPHYSIOL DIV, NATHAN S KLINE INST PSYCHIAT RES, 1986-; res assoc prof, Nathan S Kline inst Psychiat res, 1979-1987; chief psychiat res, Rockland res inst, 1976-1981; consult psychiat, Good Samaritan Hosp, Suffern, 1961-1987; chief investr psychobiol, Nathan S Kline inst, 1958-1986; capt, USAF Med Corp, 1956-1958. **Memberships:** Fel Am Psychiat Asn; fel Am EEG Asn; AAAS; Soc Biol Psychiat; Int Pharmaco-EEG Group. **Research Statement & Publications:** Major psychopathologies, their treatment, differential diagnostic issues, the effect of psychotropic medications; usefulness of computer analyzed electroencephalographs and non-human primate models. **Mailing Address:** Nathan Kline Inst, Orangeburg, NY 10962.

LIFSON, WILLIAM E(UGENE), CHEMICAL ENGINEERING. **Personal Data:** b Newark, NJ, April 17, 1921; m 1946, c 2. **Education:** Mass Inst Technol, BS, 1941, MS, 1942. **Professional Experience:** RETIRED; new facil proj exec, Exxon Eng Technol Dept, 1981-1984; relocation mgr, Exxon Eng Technol Dept, 1980-1981; asst gen mgr, Exxon Eng Technol Dept, 1969-1980; mgr chem planning & coord, Enjay Chem Labs, 1966-1969; dir, Enjay Chem Labs, 1965-1966; dir, Chem Res Div, 1964-1965; dir, Prod Res Div, 1962-1964; asst dir, Exxon Res & Eng Co, 1956-1962; sect head, Exxon Res & Eng Co, 1954-1956; group head, Exxon Res & Eng Co, 1951-1954; res engr petrol prod res, Exxon Res & Eng Co, 1946-1951. **Memberships:** Am Chem Soc; Soc Automotive Engrs. **Research Statement & Publications:** Petroleum products and petrochemicals; engineering research and development process industries. **Mailing Address:** 365 Long Hill Dr, Short Hills, NJ 07078-3399.

LIGGERO, SAMUEL HENRY, PHYSICAL ORGANIC CHEMISTRY. **Personal Data:** b Amsterdam, NY, April 17, 1942; m 1966, c 2. **Education:** Fordham Univ, BS, 1964; Georgetown Univ, PhD (chem), 1969. **Honors & Awards:** Chuck Hall Award, 1987. **Professional Experience:** LECTR, GORDON INST TUFTS UNIV, MEDFORD, as of 2006; CHIEF TECH OFFICER, & CO-FOUNDER, AIRPORT NETWORKS, as of 2006; vpres, Media Res & Develop, Polaroid Corp, ending 2001; dir, Imaging Appln, Polaroid Corp, beginning 1987; mktg dir, Polaroid Corp, 1985-1987; plant mgr, Polaroid Corp, 1982-1985; sr tech mgr, Polaroid Corp, 1979-1982; mgr process eng, Polaroid Corp, 1977-1978; res group leader film develop, Polaroid Corp, 1972-1976; sr lab supvr film develop, Polaroid Corp, 1970-1971; NIH fel, Princeton Univ, 1969-1970. **Memberships:** The Chem Soc; AAAS; Soc Photog Scientists & Engrs; Am Chem Soc; Sigma Xi. **Research Statement & Publications:** Application of physical organic chemistry principles to the development of instant color photographic transparencies employing diffusion transfer processes; application of chemistry, physics and engineering to the manufacture and development of the polaroid 35mm instant slide system. **Mailing Address:** Gordon Inst Tufts Univ, Four Colby St, Medford, MA 02155. **Fax:** 617-627-3180.

LIGGETT, JAMES ALEXANDER, CIVIL ENGINEERING. **Personal Data:** b Los Angeles, Calif, June 29, 1934; m 1960, Carole. **Education:** Tex Tech Col, BS, 1956; Stanford Univ, MS, 1957, PhD (civil eng), 1959. **Honors & Awards:** Rouse Award & Torrens Award, Am Soc Civil Engrs. **Professional Experience:** PROF EMER CIVIL & ENVIRON ENG, CORNELL UNIV, as of 2005; prof civil & environ eng, Cornell Univ, beginning 1961; asst prof hydraul, Univ Wis, 1960-1961; engr, Chance Vought Aircraft Corp, 1959-1960. **Memberships:** Am Soc Civil Engrs; Int Asn Hydraul Res. **Research Statement & Publications:** Hydraulics; fluid mechanics; free surface flow; circulation and temperature distribution in lakes; groundwater flow; numerical methods. **Mailing Address:** Sch Civil & Environ Eng, Cornell Univ, 220 Hillister Hall, Ithaca, NY 14853-3501. **E-Mail:** jal8@cornell.edu

LIGGETT, LAWRENCE MELVIN, ANALYTICAL CHEMISTRY, ORGANIC CHEMISTRY. **Personal Data:** b Denver, Colo, June 22, 1917; m 1943, Edith; c Pamela J (Schwartz) & Betty S (El Gammal). **Education:** Cent Col, Iowa, AB, 1938; Iowa State Col, PhD (chem), 1943. **Professional Experience:** RETIRED; bus & tech consult, beginning 1982; pres, Vacuum Equip & Systs, Airco Temescal Div, Airco Inc, 1975-1982; pres, Airco Speer Electronics Div, 1970-1975; vpres & gen mgr, Airco Speer Electronics, 1967-1970; vpres & tech dir, Speer Carbon Co, 1965-1967; dir res, Speer Carbon Co, 1955-1964; supvr inorg res, Wyandotte Chems Corp, 1948-1955; plant supt, Alkali Chlorates & Perchlorates Cardox Corp, 1943-1948; res chemist, Nat Defense Res Comt, Iowa State Col, 1941-1943. **Memberships:** Am Chem Soc; Electrochem Soc. **Research Statement & Publications:** Alkali perchlorate production; nonblack pigments for rubber and paper; carbon and graphite technology; resistors; capacitors and electronic components; technical management. **Mailing Address:** 1856 Piedras Circle, Danville, CA 94526-1329.

LIGGETT, THOMAS MILTON, INTERACTING PARTICLE SYSTEMS. **Personal Data:** b Danville, Ky, March 29, 1944; m 1972, Christina; c Timothy & Amy. **Education:** Oberlin Col, AB, 1965; Stanford Univ, MS, 1966, PhD (math), 1969. **Honors & Awards:** Wald Memorial Lecturer, Institute of Mathematical Statistics, 1996 Invited Lecturer, International Congress of Mathematicians, 1986 Fellow of the Institute of Mathematical Statistics, 1976. **Professional Experience:** Fel, Guggenheim Foud, 1997-1998; ed, Annals Probability, 1985-1987; PROF MATH, UNIV CALIF, LOS ANGELES, 1976-; sloan fel, 1973; from asst prof to assoc prof, Univ Calif, Los Angeles, 1969-1976. **Memberships:** Am Math Soc; Math Asn Am; Inst Math Statist. **Research Statement & Publications:** In interacting Particle Systems, we study rigorously the long time behavior of certain models that arise in Physics, Biology and other areas. An important phenomenon is multiplicity of equilibria. **Mailing Address:** Dept Math, Univ Calif, 405 Hilgard Ave, Los Angeles, CA 90095-1555. **E-Mail:** tml@math.ucla.edu

LIGGETT, WALTER STEWART, EXPERIMENTAL DESIGN, APPLIED STATISTICS. **Personal Data:** b Abington, Pa, August 27, 1940; m 1962, c 3. **Education:** Rensselaer Polytech Inst, BS, 1961, MS, 1964, PhD (math), 1967. **Professional Experience:** Mem, Am Statist Asn, Comt Statist & Environ, 1980-; MATH STATISTICIAN, STATIST ENG DIV,

NAT INST STAND & TECHNOL, 1979-; statistician, Div Environ Planning, Tenn Valley Authority, 1975-1979; mathematician, Rand Inst, New York, 1973-1975; prin engr, Submarine Signal Div, Raytheon Co, Portsmouth, 1965-1973. **Memberships:** Inst Math Statist; Soc Indust & Appl Math; Am Statist Asn. **Research Statement & Publications:** Statisticial planning of studies that involve physical mesaurements having non-standard error properties such as multiple components, a non constant variance, a non-normal distribution, or serial correlation. **Mailing Address:** Statist Eng Div, Nat Inst Stand & Technol, Nat Inst Stand & Technol N Rm 353, Gaithersburg, MD 20899. **Fax:** 301-990-4127. **E-Mail:** walter.liggett@nist.gov

LIGGITT, H DENNY, PATHOLOGY. **Personal Data:** b Denver, Colo, February 19, 1948. **Education:** Colo State Univ, BS, 1970, DVM, 1972, PhD (path), 1979. **Professional Experience:** PROF, DEPT COMP MED, SCH MED, UNIV WASH, 1989-; assoc dir & sr exp pathologist & head, Path Sect, 1987-1989; actg assoc dir, Dept Pharmacol Sci, Pathobiology Res Lab, Genentech Inc, 1985-1986; assoc prof, Dept Vet Microbiol & Path, Col Vet Med, Wash State Univ, 1984-1987; asst prof, Dept Vet Microbiol & Path, Col Vet Med, Wash State Univ, 1979-1984; res asst, Dept Path, Colo State Univ, 1976-1979; teaching assoc, Dept Path & Hyg, Univ Ill, Urbana, 1975-1976; assoc vet, Anchorage & Denver, 1972-1975. **Research Statement & Publications:** Pathogenesis of disease. **Mailing Address:** Dept Comp Med Sch Med, Univ Wash, Magnuson Health Sci Bldg Rm T-142, Seattle, WA 98368. **E-Mail:** dliggitt@u.washington.edu

LIGH, STEVE, MATHEMATICS. **Personal Data:** b Canton, China, November 12, 1937; American citizen. **Education:** Univ Houston, BS, 1961; Univ Mo-Columbia, MA, 1962; Tex A&M Univ, PhD (math), 1969. **Professional Experience:** PROF MATH, SOUTHEASTERN LA UNIV, 1990-; from assoc prof to prof math, Univ Southwestern La, 1972-1990; asst prof, Univ Fla, 1969-1970; Houston Baptist Col, 1965-1966 & Tex A&M Univ, 1968-1969; instr math, Ohio Univ, 1962-1964. **Memberships:** Math Asn Am; Am Math Soc. **Research Statement & Publications:** Algebra; generalizations of rings; near rings. **Mailing Address:** Dept Math, Southeastern La Univ, SLU 687, Hammond, LA 70402. **Fax:** 504-549-3396. **E-Mail:** ligh@selu.edu

LIGHT, ALBERT, BIOCHEMISTRY. **Personal Data:** b Brooklyn, NY, June 19, 1927; m 1952, c 2. **Education:** City Col New York, BS, 1948; Yale Univ, PhD (biochem), 1955. **Professional Experience:** PROF EMER, PURDUE UNIV, 1992-; head, Div Biochem, 1978-1982; from assoc prof to prof, Purdue Univ, 1965-1992; assoc prof, Univ Calif, Los Angeles, 1963-1965; asst res prof, Univ Utah, 1957-1963; Fel biochem, Cornell Univ, 1955-1957. **Memberships:** AAAS; Am Chem Soc; Am Soc Biochem & Molecular Biol. **Research Statement & Publications:** Protein chemistry and enzymology; protein folding; relationship of structure to function of biologically active proteins. **Mailing Address:** Dept Chem, Purdue Univ, Lafayette, IN 47907-1393.

LIGHT, DONALD W, SOCIAL & BEHAVIORAL MEDICINE, SOCIOLOGY. **Personal Data:** m Nancy; c Holly & Peter. **Education:** Stanford Univ, BA, 1963; Univ Chicago, MA, 1967; Brandeis Univ, PhD (sociol), 1970. **Professional Experience:** Vis prof, Ctr Bioethics, as of 2004; vis prof, Univ Pa, as of 2004; DeCamp fel, Princeton Univ, 1992-1993; sr consult, Carnegie Found, 1991-; vis fel, Oxford Univ, 1990 & 1992; Sr fel, Leonard Davis Inst Health Econs, 1984-; PROF COMP HEALTH CARE & DIR, DIV SOC BEHAV MED, UNIV MED & DENT NJ, 1980-; assoc prof, City Col NY, 1975-1980; asst prof, Princeton Univ, 1969-1975. **Memberships:** Fel Royal Soc Med. **Research Statement & Publications:** Comparative analysis and design of health care systems; social aspects of economic and professional behavior. **Mailing Address:** Div Soc & Behav Med, Univ Med & Dent, One Med Ctr Dr, Stratford, NJ 08084. **E-Mail:** dlight@princeton.edu

LIGHT, DOUGLAS B, ION CHANNEL REGULATION, OVERWINTERING ADAPTATIONS. **Personal Data:** b New York, NY, April 9, 1956; m 1977, c 3. **Education:** Colby Col, BA, 1978; Univ Minn, MS, 1986, PhD (physiol), 1986. **Honors & Awards:** Award for Res Excellence, Am Physiol Soc, 1987, Caroline tum Suden Award, 1988. **Professional Experience:** PROF BIOL, LAKE FOREST COL, 2003-; prof biol, Ripon Col, 2002-2003; assoc prof biol, Ripon Col, 1994-2002; asst prof biol, Ripon Col, 1989-1994; res assoc, Dartmouth Med Sch, 1988-1989; instr biol, Sch Life Long Learning, 1988; postdoctoral fel physiol, Dartmouth Med Sch, 1986-1988; res asst physiol, Univ Minn, 1984-1986; teaching asst physiol, Univ Minn, 1981-1984; biol teacher, Winslow High Sch, 1978-1981. **Memberships:** Sigma Xi; Biophys Soc; Am Soc Zoologists; Am Physiol Soc; Soc Gen Physiol & Cryobiol. **Research Statement & Publications:** Ion channel regulation, cell volume regulation and overwintering adaptations of invertebrates. **Mailing Address:** Dept Biol Lake Forest Col, 555 N Sheridan Rd, Lake Forest, IL 60045. **Fax:** 847-735-7243. **E-Mail:** light@lakeforest.edu

LIGHT, IRWIN JOSEPH, PEDIATRICS. **Personal Data:** b Montreal, Que, July 21, 1934; m 1972, c 2. **Education:** McGill Univ, BS, 1955, MD, 1959. **Professional Experience:** FIELD SERV EMER PROF, UNIV CINNATI, 2004-; chmn, Inst Rev Bd, Children's Hosp Med Ctr, beginning 1984; prof pediat, obstet & gynec, Univ Cincinnati, beginning 1973; dir newborn clin serv, Obstet & Gynec, Univ Cincinnati, 1973-1983; from asst prof to assoc prof obstet & gynec, Obstet & Gynec, Univ Cincinnati, 1968-1973; from asst prof to assoc prof pediat, Obstet & Gynec, Univ Cincinnati, 1965-1973; res assoc pediat, Children's Hosp Res Found, beginning 1963; clin fel pediat, Cincinnati Gen Hosp & res fel, Univ Cincinnati, 1963-1965; resident pediat, Montreal Children's Hosp, 1961-1963; resident, Royal Victoria Hosp, 1960-1961; intern med, Royal Victoria Hosp, 1959-1960. **Memberships:** AAAS; Am Acad Pediat; Soc Pediat Res; Am Pediat Soc; Am Fedn Clin Res. **Research Statement & Publications:** Neonatal infectious diseases; newborn metabolism. **Mailing Address:** Cincinnati Children's Hosp Med Ctr, 3333 Burnet Ave, Cincinnati, OH 45229-3039.

LIGHT, JOHN CALDWELL, CHEMICAL PHYSICS. **Personal Data:** b Mt Vernon, NY, November 24, 1934; m 1978, Phyllis; c 3. **Education:** Oberlin Col, BA, 1956; Harvard Univ, PhD (chem), 1960. **Professional Experience:** PROF CHEM, UNIV CHICAGO, as of 2005; ed, J Chem Phys, 1982-; chmn, Dept Chem, 1980-1982; vis fel, Joint Inst Lab Astrophys, Univ Colo, 1976-1977; prof chem, Univ Chicago, beginning 1970; dir, Mat Res Lab, 1970-1973; Sloan fel, 1966; from instr to assoc prof chem, Univ Chicago, 1961-1970; NSF fel, Brussels, 1959-1961. **Memberships:** fel AAAS; fel Am Phys Soc; Am Chem Soc; Int Acad Quantum Molecular Sci. **Research Statement & Publications:** Theoretical studies of elementary gas phase reactions; quantum mechanics and chemical kinetics; scattering theory; computational methods for theoretical chemistry; theoretical spectroscopy. **Mailing Address:** Dept Chem, Univ Chicago, Chicago, IL 60637. **E-Mail:** j-light@uchicago.edu

LIGHT, JOHN HENRY, MATHEMATICS. **Personal Data:** b Annville, Pa, December 15, 1924; m 1950, c 3. **Education:** Lebanon Valley Col, BS, 1948; Pa State Univ, MS, 1950 & 1957. **Professional Experience:** RETIRED; prof math, Dickinson Col, 1959-1987; consult, Naval Supply Depot, Mechanicsburg, Pa, 1959-1962; eng mech, Ord Res Lab, Pa State Univ, 1958-1959; res assoc, Ord Res Lab, Pa State Univ, 1951-1958. **Memberships:** Am Math Soc. **Research Statement & Publications:** Spectroscopy; environmental testing. **Mailing Address:** 619 Belvedre St, Carlisle, PA 17013.

LIGHT, KENNETH FREEMAN, mechanical engineering; deceased, see previous edition for last biography

LIGHT, KIM EDWARD, BIOGENIC AMINES, RECEPTORS. **Personal Data:** b Indianapolis, Ind, September 21, 1951; m 1975, c 1. **Education:** Ind State Univ, Terre Haute, BS, 1973; Ind Univ, Bloomington, MS, 1975, PhD (pharmacol), 1977. **Professional Experience:** DIR, RES & GRAD STUDIES, UNIV ARK MED SCI, as of 2006; PROF PHARMACOL, UNIV ARK MED SCI, as of 2005; CHMN, UNIV ARK MED SCI GRAD COUN, as of 2004; VICE CHMN, DEPT PHARMACEUT SCI, UNIV ARK MED SCI, as of 2004; asst prof, interdisciplinary toxicol, Univ Ark Med Sci, beginning 1980; collabr, Col Med, Tex Tech Univ Health Sci, 1979-; asst prof pharmacol, Univ Ark med sci, beginning 1979; fel, physiol, Sch Med, Tex Tech Univ, 1979. **Memberships:** Soc Neuroscience; Am Physiol Soc; Sigma Xi. **Research Statement & Publications:** Investigations into the functions and interactions of membrane receptors for biogenic amines; functional aspects and regulation of H1 and H2 histamine receptors in various tissues; Published over 5 articles. **Mailing Address:** Dept pharmaceut Sci, Med Sch, Univ Ark, 4301 W Markham, Little Rock, AR 72205. **Fax:** 501-686-6057. **E-Mail:** lightkime@uams.edu

LIGHT, ROBLEY JASPER, BIOCHEMISTRY, ORGANIC CHEMISTRY. **Personal Data:** b Roanoke, Va, November 8, 1935; m 1960, D Jeanne Kosko; c George E. **Education:** Va Polytech Inst, BS, 1957; Duke Univ, PhD (org chem), 1961. **Honors & Awards:** Alexander von Humboldt US Sr Scientist Award, 1977. **Professional Experience:** Prog dir biol instrumentation, NSF, 1990-1991; chmn, Fla State Univ, 1983-1990; PROF BIOCHEM, FLA STATE UNIV, 1972-; USPHS res career develop award, 1967-1972; from asst prof to assoc prof, Fla State Univ, 1962-1972; instr, Fla State Univ, 1962-1963; NSF fel biochem, Harvard Univ, 1960-1962. **Memberships:** Am Chem Soc; Am Soc Biochem & Molecular Biol. **Research Statement & Publications:** Lipid metabolism, structure, and function; polyketides and other secondary metabolites of microorganisms. **Mailing Address:** Dept Chem, Fla State Univ, Tallahassee, FL 32306. **Fax:** 850-644-8281. **E-Mail:** rlight@sb.fsu.edu

LIGHT, THOMAS BURWELL, PRINTER TECHNOLOGY, MATERIALS SCIENCE. **Personal Data:** b Dayton, Ohio, July 9, 1928; m 1951, c 4. **Education:** Antioch Col, BS, 1951; Ill Inst Technol, MS, 1954; Yale Univ, PhD (mat sci), 1966. **Professional Experience:** DEVELOP CONSULT, IBM US DEVELOP STAFF, IBM CORP, 1981-; mem res staff, Thomas J Watson Res Ctr, 1965-1981; Mem tech staff, Bell Tel Labs, 1953-1962. **Memberships:** AAAS; Am Phys Soc; Inst Elec & Electronics Engrs. **Research Statement & Publications:** Deposition, structure and properties of thin films; structure of and crystallization in amorphous materials; structure of oxide layers and interface reactions. **Mailing Address:** 94 Eastwood Dr, Portsmouth, NH 03801.

LIGHT, TRUMAN S, ANALYTICAL CHEMISTRY, ELECTRO-ANALYTICAL METHODS. **Personal Data:** b Hartford, Conn, December 16, 1922; m 1980, Arlene Wick; c Edward N, Stuart L (Licht) & Joel M. **Education:** Harvard Univ, SB, 1943; Univ Minn, MS, 1949; Univ Rome, DrChem, 1961 Chemistry. **Honors & Awards:** James L Waters, Award, 1996; Henry Hill Award 1993. **Professional Experience:** ADJ PROF CHEM, AQUINAS COL, 1994-; adj prof chem, Suffolk Univ, 1991-1992; CONSULT, Thornton, Ind, 1990 Aquinas Col, 1988-; adj prof chem, Boston Col, 1987-1988; prin res scientist, Chem Anal & Mat Lab, 1980-1988; mgr, Chem Anal & Mat Lab, 1972-1980; sr res chemist, Foxboro Co, 1964-1972; NSF fel, Chem Inst, Univ Rome, Italy, 1960-1961; staff scientist, Res & Adv Develop Div, Avco Corp, 1959-1964; consult, Children's Med Ctr, Boston, Mass, 1956-1960 & Watertown Arsenal, 1951-1955; Asst prof chem, Boston Col, 1949-1959. **Memberships:** Am Chem Soc (chair); Electrochem Soc; Soc Appl Spectros; Instrument Soc Am; Sigma Xi; Soc Elecroanal Chem. **Research Statement & Publications:** Instrumental methods of analysis; electrochemistry; physical chemistry; materials sciences, water quality and pollution controls. **Mailing Address:** 4 Webster Rd, Lexington, MA 02173-8222. **E-Mail:** tslight@aol.com

LIGHTBODY, JAMES JAMES, IMMUNOLOGY, BIOCHEMISTRY. **Personal Data:** b Detroit, Mich, March 1, 1939; m 1964, c 2. **Education:** Wayne State Univ, BA, 1961, BS, 1964, PhD (biochem), 1966. **Professional Experience:** Clin assoc prof internal med, sch med, Wayne State Univ, beginning 1976; ASSOC PROF BIOCHEM, SCH MED, WAYNE STATE UNIV, 1976-; lectr, Cancer Inst, Cairo Univ, 1974; assoc immunol, Sch Med, Wayne State Univ, beginning 1973; vis prof, Mem Sloan-Kettering Cancer Ctr, 1973; asst prof, Sch Med, Wayne State Univ, 1972-1976; res assoc, Univ Wis, 1971-1972; sr res assoc immunol, Basel Inst Immunol, 1970-1971; instr pediat & Swiss Nat Sci Found grant, Univ Bern, 1969-1970; res assoc biochem & NIH trainee, Brandeis Univ, 1967-1969. **Memberships:** AAAS; Am Asn Immunol; Transplantation Soc. **Mailing Address:** Dept Biochem, Wayne State Univ Sch Med, 540 E Canfield, Detroit, MI 48201.

LIGHTERMAN, MARK S, COMPUTER PROGRAMMING. **Personal Data:** b New York, NY, January 17, 1960. **Education:** Syracuse Univ, BS & BA, 1982; Univ Miami, MS, 1985. **Professional Experience:** PRES, HMMM CORP, as of 2004; Pres, Fla Alliance Technol Educ, 1991-; Mem bd, Fla Alliance Technol Educ, 1989-1991; vpres, Hmmm Corp, beginning 1982. **Memberships:** NY Acad Sci; Asn Comput Mach; Am Math Soc; Inst Elec & Electronics Engrs; Am Med Info Asn; Soc Motion Picture & TV Engrs. **Research Statement & Publications:** Curriculum enhancement by bringing technology back into the classroom. **Mailing Address:** Hmmm Corp, 9230 SW 59th St, Miami, FL 33173-1660.

LIGHTFOOT, DONALD RICHARD, BIOCHEMICAL GENETICS. **Personal Data:** b Los Angeles, Calif, August 8, 1940; m 1972. **Education:** Univ Redlands, BA, 1962; Univ Ariz, MS, 1967, PhD (biochem), 1972. **Professional Experience:** CONSULT, BIOSTAR TECHNOL, CA, 1996-; ASSOC PROF BIOL & DIR BIOCHEM & BIOTECHNOL, EASTERN WASH UNIV, 1980-; asst prof biochem & nutrit, Va Polytech Inst & State Univ, 1974-1979; fel, Univ Calif, Riverside, 1971-1974; res trainee biochem, Med Sch, Univ Ore, 1969-1971; teacher, Philippine High Sch, Peace Corps, 1962-1964; DNA diagnostics consult, Sacred Heart Med Ctr. **Memberships:** AAAS; Am Chem Soc; Soc Exp Biol & Med; Sigma Xi. **Research Statement & Publications:** Plant virology; tobacco mosaic virus infection process; gene titration in tobacco species; minor nucleosides; transfer RNA, messenger RNA 5.85 ribosomal RNA and viral RNA NMR structure and function; biotechnology education, turnip yellow mosaic virus structure/function; polymerase chain reaction applications. **Mailing Address:** Dept Biol, Eastern Wash Univ, 526 5th St, Cheney, WA 99004. **Fax:** 509-359-6867. **E-Mail:** dlightfoot@mail.ewu.edu

LIGHTFOOT, E(DWIN) N(IBLOCK), SEPARATIONS, BIOTECHNOLOGY. **Personal Data:** b Milwaukee, Wis, September 25, 1925; m 1949, c 5. **Education:** Cornell Univ, BS, 1947, PhD (chem eng), 1951. **Honorary Degrees:** Dr, Tech Univ Norway. **Honors & Awards:** William H Walker Award, Am Inst Chem Engrs, 1975; Food, Pharm & Bioeng Award, 1979; Van Winkle lectr, Univ Tex, 1984; Lacey lectr, Calif Inst Technol, 1984; Stanley Katz lectr, City Col, City Univ NY, 1986; Kloor Mem lectr, Indian Inst Sci, Bangalore, 1987; Goff Smith lectr, Univ Mich, 1987; Reilly lectr, Univ Notre Dame, 1988; Benjamin Smith Reynolds Award, Univ Wis Col Eng, 1988; Kelly lectr, Purdue Univ, 1989; Warren K Lewis Award, 1991; Harry G Fair lectr, Univ Okla, 1991; Hilldale Award, Univ Wis, 1992; E V Murphree Award, Am Chem Soc, 1992. **Professional Experience:** HILLDALE PROF EMER CHEM ENG, UNIV WIS, MADISON, 1995-; Hilldale prof chem eng, Univ Wis-Madison, 1980-1995; Univ Canterbury, NZ, 1972; Erskine fel, Univ Canterbury, NZ, 1972; vis prof, Stanford Univ & Tech Univ Denmark, 1971; vis prof, Tech Univ Norway, 1962; tech consult, 1953-1988; from asst prof to prof biochem eng, Univ Wis-Madison, 1953-1980; chem engr, Chas Pfizer & Co, 1950-1953. **Memberships:** Nat Acad Sci; Nat Acad Eng; Royal Norweg Soc Sci & Lett; Am Inst Chem Engr; Am Chem Soc. **Research Statement & Publications:** Physical separation techniques; mass transfer; biomedical engineering; author of 14 books and technical articles. **Mailing Address:** Dept Chem Eng, Univ Wis, 1415 Eng Dr 3018 Eng Hall, Madison, WI 53706. **Fax:** 608-262-5434. **E-Mail:** lightfoo@engr.wisc.edu

LIGHTMAN, ALAN PAIGE, THEORETICAL ASTROPHYSICS, THEORETICAL PHYSICS. **Personal Data:** b Memphis, Tenn, November 28, 1948; m 1976, Jean; c Elyse & Kara. **Education:** Princeton Univ, AB, 1970; Calif Inst Technol, MA, 1973, PhD (physics), 1974. **Honors & Awards:** Andrew Gemant Prize, Am Inst Physics, 1996. **Professional Experience:** JOHN E BURCHARD PROF SCI & WRITING, MASS INST TECHNOL, 1995-; prof sci & writing, Mass Inst Technol, beginning 1988; lectr astron & phys, Harvard Univ, 1979-1988; asst prof astron, Harvard Univ, 1976-1979; res assoc astrophysics, Cornell Univ, 1974-1976; res assoc physics, Calif Inst Technol, 1974. **Memberships:** Fel Am Phys Soc; Am Astron Soc; fel AAAS; Soc Lit & Sci; fel Am Acad Arts & Sci. **Research Statement & Publications:** Theoretical frameworks for analyzing modern gravitation theories; relativistic astrophysics, x-ray astronomy; stellar dynamics; radiation processes; philosophy of science. **Mailing Address:** Dept Physics, Mass Inst Technol, Cambridge, MA 02139.

LIGHTNER, DAVID A, BIOORGANIC CHEMISTRY, STEREOCHEMISTRY. **Personal Data:** b Los Angeles, Calif, March 25, 1939; m 1974, Renne; c Mikah & Derek. **Education:** Univ Calif, Berkeley, AB, 1960; Stanford Univ, PhD, 1963. **Professional Experience:** Counr, Am Soc Photobiol, 1990-1993; found prof, Univ Nev, Reno, 1987-1990; dept chmn, Univ Nev, Reno, 1985-1988; adj prof biochem, Univ Nev, Reno, 1984-; RC FUSON PROF CHEM, UNIV NEV, RENO, 1984-; assoc ed, Photochem Photobiol, 1983-1986; prof chem, Univ Nev, Reno, beginning 1976; assoc prof, Univ Nev, Reno, 1974-1976; assoc prof, Tex Tech Univ, 1972-1974; asst prof chem, Univ Calif, Los Angeles, 1965-1972; NSF fel, Univ Minn, 1964-1965; NSF fel, Stanford Univ, 1963-1964; fel, Ctr Advan Study, Univ Nev. **Memberships:** fel AAAS; Am Chem Soc; Royal Soc Chem; Am Soc Photobiol; Inter-Am Photochem Soc. **Research Statement & Publications:** Photochemistry of biological materials; molecular recognition; synthesis and stereochemistry; circular dichroism and optical rotatory dispersion; phototherapy and jaundice. **Mailing Address:** Dept Chem, Univ Nev, Reno, NV 89557-0020. **Fax:** 775-784-6804. **E-Mail:** lightner@chem.unr.edu

LIGHTNER, JAMES EDWARD, MATHEMATICS, EDUCATION. **Personal Data:** b Frederick, Md, August 29, 1937. **Education:** Western Md Col, AB, 1958; Northwestern Univ, AM, 1962; Ohio State Univ, PhD (math, educ), 1968. **Honors & Awards:** Distinguished Service Award, Kappa Mu Epsilon (national mathematics honor society) 1993. **Professional Experience:** PROF Emeritus, MATH, MCDANIEL COL, as of 1998; fac asst admin, Western Md Col, beginning 1995; exec secy, Md Coun Teachers Math, 1988-2003; dir math proficiency, Western Md Col, 1983-1995; coordr int studies, Western Md Col, 1980-1983; prof math & educ, Western Md Col, 1977-1998; fed Liaison Rep, Western Md Col, 1973-1978; dir Jan term, Western Md Col, 1969-1983; chmn dept, Western Md Col, 1968-1973; from instr to assoc prof math, Western Md Col, 1962-1977; Teacher, Frederick County Bd Educ, Md, 1958-1962; consult sch systs & Md State Dept Educ. **Memberships:** Nat Coun Teachers Math; Math Asn Am; Sigma Xi. **Research Statement & Publications:** Undergraduate mathematics curricula; secondary mathematics curricula and methodology; secondary school geometry; history of mathematics. **Mailing Address:** Dept Math, McDaniel Col, Lewis Hall Sci, Westminster, MD 21157. **Fax:** 410-857-2729. **E-Mail:** jlightne@mcdaniel.edu

LIGHTON, JOHN RB, ECOLOGICAL PHYSIOLOGY, WATER RELATIONS. **Personal Data:** b Johannesburg, SAfrica, August 25, 1952. **Education:** Univ Cape Town, BA, 1975, BSc, 1981, MSc, 1984; Univ Calif, Los Angeles, PhD (physiol), 1987. **Honors & Awards:** David & Lucille Packard Award. **Professional Experience:** ASST PROF ECOPHYSIOL, UNIV UTAH, 1991-; Guest prof ecophysiol, Univ Zurich, 1990; adj asst prof, Univ Calif, Los Angeles, 1989-1990; Hollaender distinguished postdoctoral fel ecophysiol, Univ Calif, Los Angeles, 1987-1989. **Memberships:** AAAS; Am Soc Zoologists. **Research Statement & Publications:** Ecological physiology of animals, concentrating on insects, their respiratory and ventilatory physiology. **Mailing Address:** Biol Dept, Univ Utah, 201 S Biol Bldg, Salt Lake City, UT 84112-1196. **Fax:** 801-581-4668. **E-Mail:** lighton@bioSci.utah.edu

LIGHTSEY, PAUL ALDEN, AERONAUTICAL & ASTRONAUTICAL ENGINEERING, ATMOSPHERIC CHEMISTRY & PHYSICS. **Personal Data:** b Wray, Colo, August 25, 1944; m 1965, c 1. **Education:** Colo State Univ, BS, 1966; Cornell Univ, MS, 1969, PhD (physics), 1972. **Professional Experience:** TELESCOPE CHIEF SYS ENG, BALL AEROSPACE & TECHNOL CORP, as of 2005; staff consult, Ball Aerospace Systs Group, beginning 1995; scientist, Nat Ctr Atmospheric Res, beginning 1986; prin systs engr, Ball Aerospace Systs Group, 1986-1994; physicist, Nat Oceanic & Atmospheric Admin, 1982-1984; instr, Frontiers Sci Inst, Univ Northern Colo, 1980-1982; assoc prof & chmn dept physics, Univ Northern Colo, 1977-1986; assoc prof physics & math, Colo Mountain Col, 1976-1977; electrician, Great Western Sugar Co, 1975-1976; asst prof physics & math, Univ Dallas, 1973-1975; lectr physics, Beloit Col, 1972-1973; res asst solid state physics, Cornell Univ, 1966-1972; physicist, surface physics, Dow Chem-Rocky Flats Div, 1966; res aide atmospheric physics, Colo State Univ, 1962-1966. **Memberships:** Am Asn Physics Teachers; Sigma Xi; Int Soc Biomechanics in Sports; Soc Photo Instrumentation Engrs; Optical Soc Am; Nat Sci Teachers Asn. **Research Statement & Publications:** Use of laser radar for remote sensing characteristics of atmosphere; biomechanical analysis of sports; optical propagation through atmospheric turbulence; electro-optical systems engineering; atmospheric optics; Hubble space telescope instrumentation. **Mailing Address:** Ball Aerospace & Technol Corp, PO Box 1062, Boulder, CO 80301. **E-Mail:** plightse@ball.com

LIGHTY, JOANN SLAMA, WASTE REMEDIATION, INCINERATION. **Personal Data:** b Weehawken, NJ, January 5, 1960. **Education:** Univ Utah, BS, 1982, PhD (chem eng), 1988. **Professional Experience:** DIR, INST COMBUSTION & ENERGY STUDIES, 2004-; PROF CHEM ENG, UNIV UTAH, 1999-; interim dean, Col Eng, Univ Utah, 1998; asooc dean, Col Eng, Univ Utah, 1997-2004; asst dean, Univ Utah, ending 1997; asst prof to assoc prof chem & fuels eng, 1994-1999; sr scientist, Reaction Eng Int, 1990-; asst prof chem eng, Univ Utah, beginning 1988; proj engr, Northwest Pipeline Corp, 1982-1984. **Memberships:** Am Inst Chem Eng; Soc Women Engrs; Combustion Inst; Air & Waste Mgt Asn. **Research Statement & Publications:** Remediation of contaminated solids by thermal treatment; MSW incineration; fate of metals during incineration; circulating fluidized bed combustion. **Mailing Address:** Dept Chem Eng, Univ Utah, 50 S Cent Campus Dr Rm 3290 2296 MEB, Salt Lake City, UT 84112-1114. **Fax:** 801-581-9291. **E-Mail:** djones@park.admin.utah.edu

LIGHTY, RICHARD WILLIAM, PLANT GENETICS, HORTICULTURE. **Personal Data:** b Freeport, Ill, November 8, 1933; m 1955, c 2. **Education:** Pa State Univ, BS, 1955; Cornell Univ, MS, 1958, PhD (genetics), 1960. **Honors & Awards:** A H Scott Medal & Award; Silver Medal, Mass Hort Soc; Eloise Payne Lequer Medal, Garden Club Am. **Professional Experience:** PROF EMER, DEPT PLANT & SOIL SCI, UNIV DEL, as of 2005; dir, Mt Cuba Ctr Study Piedmont Flora, Univ Del, 1983-1998; assoc prof plant sci & coordr Longwood prog ornamental hort, Univ Del, 1967-1982; geneticist, Longwood Gardens, Pa, 1960-1967. **Memberships:** AAAS; Am Asn Bot Gardens & Arboretums. **Research Statement & Publications:** Plant breeding; cytotaxonomy; horticultural taxonomy; floriculture. **Mailing Address:** Dept Plant & Soil Sci, Univ Del, 501 Ewing Hall, Newark, DE 19716-2553.

LIGLER, FRANCES SMITH, BIOSENSORS, BIOMATERIALS. **Personal Data:** b Louisville, Ky, June 11, 1951; m 1972, George T; c Amy E & Adam G. **Education:** Furman Univ, BS, 1972; Oxford Univ, Eng, Dphil (biochem), DSc (biosensors). **Honorary Degrees:** DSc, Oxford Univ, 2000. **Honors & Awards:** Am Asn Med Instrumentation Ann Meeting Manuscript Award, 3M; Policy Technol Transfer Award, Nat Drug Control; NRL Outstanding Performance Award, 1986, 1988, 1990-1999; Berman Award, Superior Tech Publ, 1988, 1993, 1995, 1996, 1998, 1999; Special Act Award, USN, 1991; NRL Technol Transfer Award for LEH Technol, 1991; Technol Transfer Award, Nat Drug Control, 1992; Edison Award for Most Outstanding NRL Patent, 1992 & 1994; NRL Technol Transfer Award for Drug Detection Technol, 1993; Hillebrand Award, Am Chem Soc, 1994; Sci Achievement Award, US Women Sci & Eng, 1995; Most Outstanding Innovations in the History of NRL Award, 1998; Outstanding Civilian Service Award, USN, 2000. **Professional Experience:** Opening plenary lectr, Int Cong Biosensors, 2002; fel SPIE, 2000; elected mem, Permanent Org Committee, Europ Conf Optical Biosensors, 2000; co-chmn, SPIE Conf on Micro- and Nanofabricated Electro-Optical Mech Systs, 1997, 1998; deleg head, Automated Biosensors, NATO Panel 33, 1996-2000; chair-elect, Gordon Conf on Bio/Anal Sensors, 1994; US rep, New Detection Technol, Intl Task Force 24, 1994-1995; US rep, Automated Biosensors, NATO Panel 33, 1994-1995; head, Biosensors & Biomat Lab, 1993-2001; co-chmn, SPIE Conf on Fluorescence Sensing, 1993, 1995, 1997, 2000; co-chmn, SPIE Conf on Environ Chem Sensors, 1992, 1993, 1995, 1997; SR SCIENTIST, NAVAL RES LAB, 1985-; group leader cellular immunol, E I du Pont de Nemours & Co, Inc, 1984-1985; from adj asst prof to adj assoc prof, Hahnemann Univ, 1981-1985; primary scientist immunol, E I du Pont de Nemours & Co, Inc, 1980-1984; instr, Southwestern Med Sch, 1978-1980; asst instr immunol, Southwestern Med Sch, 1976-1978; fel biochem, Univ Tex Health Sci Ctr, San Antonio, 1975-1976. **Memberships:** Am Asn Immunologists; AAAS; Am Asn Pathologists; Am Chem Soc; fel Soc Photooptical & Instrumentation Engrs. **Research Statement & Publications:** Biosensors; immunoassay development; fluorescence; non-medical biomaterials, microfluids. **Mailing Address:** Naval Res Lab, Code 6900, Washington, DC 20375-5348.

LIGOMENIDES, PANOS ARISTIDES, SYNERGETIC & NEURAL COMPUTERS, EXPERIMENTAL KNOWLEDGE ENGINEERING. **Personal Data:** b Pireus, Greece, April 3, 1928; American citizen; m 1973, c 2. **Education:** Univ Athens, Greece, dipl physics, 1951, MSc, 1952; Stanford Univ, MSc, 1956, PhD (elec eng & physics), 1958. **Professional Experience:** RETIRED; vpres res, Caelum Res Corp, 1987-1993; vis prof, Univ Athens, Greece, 1968-1969 & Polit Univ Madrid, Spain, 1982-1984; pres & owner, Comput Eng Consults, 1975-1981; prof comput eng, Elec Eng Dept, Univ MdD, 1971-1993; distinguished prof, Elec Eng Dept, Univ Md, 1971-1972; Salzburg Sem fel, Salzburg Sem Am Studies, 1971; Fulbright prof univs in Greece, 1970-1971; adjprof, Stanford Univ, 1969-1970; prin investr grants & contracts from indust & govt, 1968-; vis prof, Stanford Univ, 1967; Ford Found fel, SAm, 1966 & 1968; vis prof, Univ Ceara, Brazil, 1966; Orgn Econ Coop & Develop fel, Greece, 1965 & 1974; tech consult indust & govt, 1964-; asst prof elec eng, Univ Calif, Los Angeles, 1964-1969; res & staff engr elec eng & comput, IBM, 1958-1964; radio engr radiotel, Greek Tel & Tel Co, 1954-1955. **Memberships:** Sr mem Inst Elec & Electronics Engrs; Int Soc Optical Eng. **Research Statement & Publications:** Applied artificial intelligence; neural networks; decisions support technologies; pattern recognition; computer architectures; microcomputer-based systems; synergetic computer applications. **Mailing Address:** 8802 Magnolia Dr, Lanham, MD 20742.

LIGON, JAMES DAVID, ZOOLOGY. **Personal Data:** b Wewoka, Okla, February 2, 1939; m 1967, c 1. **Education:** Univ Okla, BS, 1961; Univ Fla, MS, 1963; Univ Mich, PhD (zoology), 1967. **Professional Experience:** CUR, DIV BIRDS, MUS SOUTHWESTERN BIOL, as of 2003; PROF BIOL, UNIV NMEX, 1977-; from asst prof to assoc prof, Univ NMex, 1968-1977; asst prof biol, Idaho State Univ, 1967-1968. **Memberships:** Am Ornith Union; Cooper Ornith Soc. **Research Statement & Publications:** Avian ecology and behavior. **Mailing Address:** Dept Biol, Univ NMex, Main Campus One Univ Campus, Albuquerque, NM 87131-0001. **E-Mail:** jdligon@unm.edu

LIGON, JAMES T(EDDIE), SOILS & SOIL SCIENCE. **Personal Data:** b Easley, SC, February 20, 1936; m 1958, Martha; c Melissa Grace, James Mark & Polly Claire. **Education:** Clemson Univ, BS, 1957; Iowa State Univ, MS, 1959, PhD (agr eng, soil physics), 1961. **Professional Experience:** ROCKY RETREAT BED & BREAKFAST, as of 2003; actg head, Agr Eng Dept, 1984-1985; chmn directorate, Water Resources Res Inst, 1975-1978; prof agr eng, Clemson Univ, beginning 1971; assoc prof, Clemson Univ, 1966-1971; asst prof agr eng, Univ Ky, 1961-1966. **Memberships:** Am Soc Agr Engrs; Am Geophys Union; Sigma Xi; Am Soc Eng Educ. **Research Statement & Publications:** Soil drainage and physics; soil, water and plant relationships; hydrologic modeling. **Mailing Address:** Rocky Retreat Bed & Breakfast, 1000 Millwee Creek Rd, Pendleton, SC 29670. **E-Mail:** jtligon@aol.com

LIGON, WOODFIN VAUGHAN, ORGANIC MASS SPECTROMETRY & CHEMISTRY. **Personal Data:** b Farmville, Va, April 24, 1944. **Education:** Longwood Col, BS, 1966; Univ Va, PhD (org chem), 1970. **Professional Experience:** STAFF SCIENTIST, ORG MASS SPECTROMETRY, GEN ELEC CORP RES & DEVELOP, 1973-; vis asst prof org chem, Univ Ill, 1972-1973; NIH fel, Univ Ill, Urbana, 1971-1972. **Memberships:** Am Soc Mass Spectrometry. **Research Statement & Publications:** New modes of ionization for mass spectrometry; secondary ion mass spectrometry; multidimensional gas chromatography. **Mailing Address:** 2251 Van Antwerp Rd, Schenectady, NY 12309.

LIGUORI, FRED, MAINTENANCE TESTING, WEAPON SYSTEMS SUPPORT. **Personal Data:** b Somerville, Mass, December 21, 1930; m 1957, Ebba L Knudson; c Victor &

Carol. **Education:** Tufts Univ, BSEE, 1957; Hofstra Univ, MB, 1960. **Honors & Awards:** Distinguished Serv Award, Inst Elec & Electronics Engrs, 1985. **Professional Experience:** HEAD, SYSTS SUPPORTABILITY BR, NAVAL AIR ENG CTR, 1995-; chair testing tech comt, Comput Soc Inst Elec & Electronics Engrs, 1995-1996; chair tech meetings, Comput Soc Inst Elec & Electronics Engrs, 1993-1994; sr technologist, Advan Develop Res & Develop Lab, 1991-1995; dir, Advan Develop Res & Develop Lab, 1988-1991; Ed, Trans Instrumentation Soc Elec & Electronics Engrs, 1981-1985; head, Automatic Test Equip Br, Naval Air Eng Ctr, 1971-1988; mgr, Automatic Test Equip Lab, Emerson Elec Co, 1968-1971; sr proj engr, RCA, 1961-1968; asst tech dir, Gen Commun Co, 1961; proposal mgr, Epsco Inc, 1960; Sr engr, Sperry Gyroscope Co, 1957-1960. **Memberships:** Fel Inst Elec & Electronics Engrs; Soc Logistics Engrs; Inst Elec & Electronics Engrs Instrument & Measurement Soc (pres 1985); Inst Elec & Electronics Engrs Comput Soc. **Research Statement & Publications:** Automatic test equipment; authored 45 technical papers on automatic testing. **Mailing Address:** 38 Clubhouse Rd, Browns Mills, NJ 08015-3207.

LIGUORI, RALPH A, MATHEMATICS. **Education:** Univ Ill, MA; Univ NMex, PhD. **Professional Experience:** ASSOC PROF MATH SCI, UNIV TEX, EL PASO, as of 2006. **Mailing Address:** Dept Math, Univ Tex El Paso, El Paso, TX 79968-0001. **Fax:** 915-747-5411. **E-Mail:** rliguori@utep.edu

LIGUORI, VINCENT ROBERT, MARINE MICROBIOLOGY. **Personal Data:** b Brooklyn, NY, December 15, 1928; m 1952, c 5. **Education:** St Francis Col, NY, BS, 1951; Long Island Univ, MS, 1958; NY Univ, PhD (microbiol), 1967. **Professional Experience:** RETIRED; mem, Bermuda Biol Sta Res, 1975-1978; mem bd dir, Mid Atlantic Natural Sci Coun, Inc, 1975-1978; prof biol, Dept Biol Sci, 1973-1995; assoc prof biol & dep chmn, Dept Biol Sci, 1971-1973; Queens Col, 1968-1969; Richmond Col, 1967-1970; res assoc microbiol, Osborn Labs Marine Sci, NY Aquarium, 1966-1971; lectr, Kingsborough Community Col, City Univ NY, 1966-1968; lectr, Nassau Co Mus Natural Hist, 1965-1968; asst prof biol & marine sci, Long Island Univ, 1965-1966; staff scientist microbiol, NY Aquarium, 1962-1965; supvr, Oncol Lab, Vet Admin Hosp, NY, 1956-1962; res asst cancer chemother, Sloan-Kettering Inst Cancer Res, 1955-1956. **Memberships:** Am Soc Microbiol; Sigma Xi. **Research Statement & Publications:** Biological effects of natural products and the mechanism of adhesion in marine invertebrates; role of marine microorganisms in the diseaseprocesses of marine animals; aquaculture; invertebrates. **Mailing Address:** 173 Edgewood Ave, PO Box 359, Oakdale, NY 11769.

LIH, MARSHALL MIN-SHING, CHEMICAL ENGINEERING. **Personal Data:** b Nanking, China, September 15, 1936; m 1962, c 3. **Education:** Nat Taiwan Univ, BS, 1958; Univ Wis-Madison, MS, 1960, PhD (chem eng), 1962. **Professional Experience:** Dir, div Engr Ed & Ctrs, beginning 1992; dir cross disciplinary res, Eng Chem & Energetics, 1987-1992; adj lectr, Georgetown Univ Med Sch, 1983-; US SR EXEC SERV, ENG CTRS, NSF, 1979-; div dir chem & process eng, Eng Chem & Energetics, 1979-1987; sect head, Eng Chem & Energetics, 1976-1979; prog dir, Thermodyn & Mass Transfer, NSF, 1973-1976; NSF vis prof & chmn, Dept Chem Eng, Nat Taiwan Univ, 1970-1971; dir, Inst Creative Eng Methodology, 1968-1970; sr res scientist, Nat Biomed Res Found, 1966-1976; mem fac chem eng, Cath Univ Am, 1964-1974; res engr, E I du Pont Del Nemours & Co, 1962-1964. **Memberships:** Fel Am Inst Chem Engrs; Sigma Xi. **Research Statement & Publications:** Kinetics and catalysis; transport processes; color technology; application of mathematics in chemical engineering; biomedical engineering. **Mailing Address:** NSF Ste 585, 4201 Willson Blvd, Arlington, VA 22230. **Fax:** 703-292-9098. **E-Mail:** mlih@nsf.gov

LIIMATAINEN, T(OIVO) M(ATTHEW), ENGINEERING PHYSICS, MATHEMATICS. **Personal Data:** b Gloucester, Mass, November 14, 1910; m 1950. **Professional Experience:** RETIRED; consult, 1971-1980; gen engr, Transp Systs Ctr, Dept Transp, Mass, 1970-1971; aerospace engr, Electronics Res Ctr, Cambridge, 1966-1970; aerospace engr, Goddard Space Flight Ctr, NASA, Md, 1963-1966; br chief microelectronics, Diamond Ord Fuze Labs, US Dept Army, 1959-1963; asst br chief electron devices, Diamond Ord Fuze Labs, US Dept Army, 1953-1959; proj engr, Nat Bur Stand, 1948-1953; engr, Sylvania Elec Prod Co, 1946-1948; engr, Gen Elec Co, 1941-1946. **Memberships:** AAAS; Inst Elec & Electronics Engrs; NY Acad Sci. **Research Statement & Publications:** Semiconductor devices; integrated circuits; microelectronics; high vacuum and gas discharge devices. **Mailing Address:** 1004 Union St, Schenectady, NY 12308.

LIIMATTA, ERIC WILHO, BIOCIDES, FORMULATION. **Personal Data:** b Two Harbors, Minn, July 25, 1962; m 1990, Willing; c Kalle & Kara. **Education:** Macalester Col, BA, 1984; Northwestern Univ, PhD (inorg chem), 1988. **Professional Experience:** RES & DEVELOP ADVISOR, ALBEMARLE CORP, 1989-; Postdoctoral fel, Univ Calif, Los Angeles, 1988-1989. **Memberships:** Am Chem Soc. **Research Statement & Publications:** Formulation and efficacy testing of biocidal cleaning products and applications research for oxidizing biocides. **Mailing Address:** PO Box 341, Baton Rouge, LA 70821. **Fax:** 225-359-2498. **E-Mail:** eric_liimatta@albemarle.com

LIITTSCHWAGER, JOHN M(ILTON), OPERATIONS RESEARCH, INDUSTRIAL ENGINEERING. **Personal Data:** b Alden, Iowa, October 24, 1934; m 1955, Virginia; c Jeffrey S, Fonda L (Weber), Robert J & Jean C (Matteson). **Education:** Iowa State Univ, BS, 1955; Northwestern Univ, MS, 1961. **Professional Experience:** PROF EMER INDUST & MGT ENG, UNIV IOWA, as of 2005; chmn dept, Univ Iowa, 1974-1981; prof Indust & Mgt Eng, Univ Iowa, beginning 1961; consult pub utility, Mid West Serv Co, 1956-1960; engr, foods div, Anderson Clayton & Co, 1955-1956. **Memberships:** Am Soc Qual Control; Int Ref Orgn Forensic Med & Sci; Inst Indust Eng. **Research Statement & Publications:** Legislative districting by computer; mathematical programming; reliability theory. **Mailing Address:** 4104 Eng Bldg, Univ Iowa, Iowa City, IA 52242. **Fax:** 319-335-5669.

LIJEWSKI, LAWRENCE EDWARD, MISSILE AERODYNAMICS, COMPUTATIONAL FLUID DYNAMICS. **Personal Data:** b Milwaukee, Wis, March 12, 1948; m 1975, c 2. **Education:** Univ Notre Dame, BSAE, 1970, MSAE, 1972, PhD (aerospace), 1974. **Professional Experience:** CHMN, PLANNING SUBCOMMITTEE, APA TC, as of 2002; AEROSPACE ENGR, AIR FORCE ARMAMENT LAB, 1977-; Mech engr, Army Aviation Systs Command, 1974-1977. **Memberships:** Am Inst Aeronaut & Astronaut. **Research Statement & Publications:** Aerodynamics of aircraft and missiles; computational fluid dynamics and experimental methods to obtain aerodynamic characteristics and fundamental understanding of basic aerodynamic phenomena. **Mailing Address:** USAF Armament Lab, 59 Country Club Rd, Shalimar, FL 32579. **Fax:** 850-882-2201. **E-Mail:** lijewski@eglin.af.mil

LI KAM WA, PATRICK, ULTRASHORT PULSE GENERATION FROM SOLID STATE LASERS & SEMICONDUCTOR OPTOELECTRONIC & ALL-OPTICAL DEVICES, INTEGRATED OPTICS DEVICES & SEMICONDUCTOR QUANTUM WELL & QUANTUM DOT OPTOELECTRONICS. **Personal Data:** b Mauritius, October 22, 1958; m 1982, Micheline; c Wendy K & Robert P. **Education:** Univ Sheffield, Eng, B Eng, 1982, PhD (electronic eng), 1987. **Professional Experience:** ASSOCIATE PROFESSOR, COLLEGE OF OPTICS: CREOL-UNIV CENT FLA, 1993-; res scientist, Creol-univ Cent Fla, 1989-1993; res assoc, Univ Sheffield, Eng, 1987-1989; Res asst, Univ Sheffield, Eng, 1985-1987. **Memberships:** Optical Soc Am; Inst Elec & Electronics Engrs. **Research Statement & Publications:** Design and implement optical switching devices and integrate monolithically on single chips. **Mailing Address:** Col Optics, CREOL & FPCE, Univ Cent Fla, PO Box 162700, Orlando, FL 32816-2700. **Fax:** 407-658-6880. **E-Mail:** plikamwa@creol.ucf.edu

LIKE, ARTHUR A, PATHOLOGY. **Personal Data:** b New York, NY. **Education:** Univ Columbia, MD, 1954. **Professional Experience:** PROF EMER PATH, MED SCH, UNIV MASS, as of 2004; prof path, Med Sch, Univ Mass, beginning 1975. **Mailing Address:** Dept Path, Univ Mass Med Sch, 55 Lake Ave N, Worcester, MA 01655-0125. **E-Mail:** arthur.like@umassmed.edu

LIKENS, GENE ELDEN, AQUATIC ECOLOGY, LIMNOLOGY. **Personal Data:** b Pierceton, Ind, January 6, 1935; m 1983, Phyllis; c Kathy S, Gregory G & Leslie D. **Education:** Manchester Col, BS, 1957; Univ Wis, MS, 1959, PhD (zoology), 1962. **Honorary Degrees:** DSc, Manchester Univ, 1979, Rutgers Univ, 1985, Plymouth State Col, 1989, Miami Univ, 1990, Marist Col, 1993; LHD, Union Col, 1991; Dr, Inst Bodenkultur, Vienna, Austria, 1992; Dr, Wageningen Ag univ, Netherlands, 1998. **Honors & Awards:** Am Motors Conserv Award, 1969; First G E Hutchinson Award, Am Soc Limnol & Oceanog, 1982; NY Acad Sci Award, 1986; Int ECI Prize, Limnetic Ecol, 1988; Distinguished Serv Award, Am Inst Biol Sci, 1990; Tyler Prize, 1993; Naumann-Thienemann Medal, Int Soc Limnol, 1995; Einar Naumann-Augustus Thienemann medal, Soc Int limnologiae, Brazil, 1995; Eminent Ecologist, Ecolog Soc Am, 1995; Distinguished Service Award, Hudson River Environ soc, Inc, 1997; R A vollenweider Award & Lectureship in Aquatic sci, nat Water Res Inst & canada center Inland Waters, Burlington, Ontario, Canada, 1998; Storm King Award, Scenic Hudson, 1998; Award of excellence, Nat coun state garden clubs, 1999; Lifetime achievement Award, AIBS, 2000; G Evelyn Hutchinson Chair ecol, Inst ecosyst studies, 2000; Huxley medal, Inst Biol, UK, 2001. **Professional Experience:** Walker-Ames prof, depts ocean& fishery sci, zool, forest resources, & civil eng, Univ Wash Seattle, 2001; PRES, INST ECOSYST STUDIES, 1993-; prof, Grad Field Ecol, Rutgers Univ, 1985-; adv, White House, Spec Envoy for Acid Rain to Pres, 1985; prof, dept Biol, Yale Univ, 1984-; mem, US Environ Protection Agency Steering Comt, State Univ NY, Albany, 1984-1985; adj prof, Sect Ecol & Syst, Cornell Univ, 1983-; DIR, INST ECOSYST STUDIES, 1983-; vpres, NY Bot Garden & dir, Mary Flagler Cary Arboretum, 1983-1993; sr adv, Ctr Energy & Environ Res, Univ PR, 1983-1988; assoc ed, Am Water Resources Asn, 1983-1988; vis prof, Ctr Advan Sci, dept Environ Sci, Univ Va, 1978-1979; mem, Assembly Life Sci, 1977-1982; mem, Biol Res Comt, Edmund Niles Huyck Preserves & resource adv, NY State dept Environ Conserv, 1974-1979; mem, Ecol Adv Comt & Sci Adv Bd, Environ Protection Agency, 1974-1978; mem, Comt Water Qual Policy, Nat Acad Sci, 1973-1976; chmn, Cornell Univ, 1973-1974; Guggenheim fel, 1972-1973; US Nat Rep, Int Asn Theoret & Appl Limnol, 1970-; mem adv panel, US Senate Comt Pub Works, 1970-1973; from assoc prof to prof ecol & syst, Cornell Univ, 1969-1983; NATO sr fel, Eng & Sweden, 1969; vis assoc ecologist, Brookhaven Nat lab, 1968; mem, US Nat Comt Int Hydrol Decade, 1966-1970; vis lectr, Univ Wis, 1963; res assoc meteorol, Univ Wis, 1962-1963; from proj asst to res assoc, Univ Wis, 1962; from instr to assoc prof biol sci, Dartmouth Col, 1961-1969; asst zool, Univ Wis, 1957-1961. **Memberships:** Nat Acad Sci; Am Polar Soc; Am Soc Limnol & Oceanog (vpres, 1975-1976, pres, 1976-1977); Ecol Soc Am (vpres, 1978-1979, pres, 1981-1982); Int Asn Theoret & Appl Limnol(pres, 2001-2004); hon mem Am Water Resource Asn; Am Acad Arts & Sci; Int Water Resource Asn; fel AAAS; Am Inst Biol Sci (pres, 2002); foreign mem Royal Danish Acad Sci & Lett; foreign mem Royal Swed Acad Sci; hon mem Brit Ecol Soc; Austrian acad sci. **Research Statement & Publications:** Circulation in lakes using radioactive tracers; meromictic lakes; biogeochemistry and analysis of ecosystems; Antarctic and Arctic limnology; precipitation chemistry; acid rain. **Mailing Address:** Inst Ecosyst Studies, PO Box AB, Millbrook, NY 12545. **Fax:** 845-677-5976. **E-Mail:** likensg@ecostudies.org

LIKHAREV, KONSTANTIN K, SUPERCONDUCTOR & LOW-TEMPERATURE ELECTRONICS. **Personal Data:** b Moscow, Russia, November 6, 1943; m 1963, Lioudmila; c Sergei & Natasha. **Education:** Moscow State Univ, MS, 1966, PhD (sci), 1969 & Dr Sci, 1979. **Professional Experience:** PROF PHYSICS, STATE UNIV NY, STONY BROOK, as of 2006; ADJ MAJ SCIENTIST, MOSCOW UNIV, beginning 1991; mem sci adv bd, Hypes Inc, beginning 1991; head, Lab Cryoelectronics, 1988-1991; sr scientist, Moscow Univ, 1973-1987; jr scientist, Moscow Univ, 1969-1973. **Memberships:** Am Phys Soc; Res & Develop Asn Future Electronic Devices (Japan); Inst Elec & Electronics Engrs. **Research Statement & Publications:** Josephson effect physics; Josephson junction dynamics, superconductor electronics (analog and digital), nonlinear dynamics (classical and quantum), correlated single-electron tunneling and its applications. **Mailing Address:** Dept Physics, State Univ NY, Stony Brook, NY 11794-3800. **Fax:** 613-632-8774. **E-Mail:** klikharev@notes.cg.sunysb.edu

LIKINS, PETER WILLIAM, DYNAMICS, CONTROL SYSTEMS. **Personal Data:** b Tracy, Calif, July 4, 1936; m 1955, c 6. **Education:** Stanford Univ, BS, 1957, PhD (eng mech), 1965; Mass Inst Technol, MS, 1958. **Professional Experience:** PRES, UNIV ARIZ, 1997-; pres, Lehigh Univ, 1982-1997; from prof & dean to provost, Columbia Univ, 1976-1982; from asst dean to assoc dean, Univ Calif, Los Angeles, 1974-1976; consult var industs & govt res agencies, 1966-; from asst prof to prof eng, Univ Calif, Los Angeles, 1964-1976; develop engr, Jet Propulsion Lab, Calif Inst Technol, 1958-1960; mem, US Pres Coun Adv Sci & Technol; mem, Adv Comt Health Univ, White House; mem bd, Comsat Corp, Consol Edison Co, Dynacs Eng Co, Parker-Hannifin Inc, St Lukes Hosp & Safeguard Sci Inc; Baker scholar. **Memberships:** Nat Acad Eng; fel Am Inst Aeronaut & Astronaut. **Research Statement & Publications:** Problems of space vehicle dynamics, stability and control; author of numerous articles and texts. **Mailing Address:** Univ Ariz, PO Box 210066, Tucson, AZ 85721. **E-Mail:** plikins@arizona.edu

LIKUSKI, ROBERT KEITH, BIOMEDICAL ENGINEERING, LIQUID CHROMATOGRAPHY. **Personal Data:** b Hillcrest, Alta, October 16, 1937; m 1971, Ines; c David & Andrew. **Education:** Univ Alta, BS, 1959; Univ Ill, MS, 1961, PhD (elec eng), 1964. **Professional Experience:** GROUP LEADER, BIO-RAD LABS, 1992-; adv develop mgr, Beckman Instr, 1981-1992; dir res & develop, Berkeley Bio-Eng, Inc, 1980-1981; chief engr biomed eng, Berkeley Bio-Eng, Inc, 1976-1980; staff engr comput memories, Micro-Bit Corp, 1970-1976; asst prof elec eng, Univ Tex, Austin, 1965-1970. **Memberships:** Inst Elec & Electronics Engrs; Sigma Xi. **Research Statement & Publications:** Development of instrumentation for analytical and medical use; capillary electrophorisis. **Mailing Address:** 4430 Sch Way, Castro Valley, CA 94546. **E-Mail:** bob_likuski@bio_rad.com

LILENFELD, HARVEY VICTOR, PHYSICAL CHEMISTRY. **Personal Data:** b Brooklyn, NY, August 25, 1945. **Education:** Polytech Inst Brooklyn, BS, 1966; Mass Inst Technol,

PhD (phys chem), 1971. **Professional Experience:** CONSULT, 1980-; scientist chem, McDonnell Douglas Corp, 1972-1980; res assoc, Brookhaven Nat Lab, 1971-1972. **Memberships:** Am Chem Soc; Sigma Xi. **Research Statement & Publications:** Laser chemistry; kinetics of gas phase reactions. **Mailing Address:** 2340 Driftwood Pl, St Louis, MO 63146. **Fax:** 314-777-1328, 314-878-5276.

LILES, SAMUEL LEE, PHYSIOLOGY. **Personal Data:** b Texas City, Tex, June 24, 1942; m 1986, c 1. **Education:** McNeese State Col, BS, 1964; La State Univ Med Ctr, New Orleans, PhD (physiol), 1968. **Professional Experience:** PROF PHYSIOL, LA STATE UNIV MED CTR, NEW ORLEANS, as of 2004; assoc prof physiol, La State Univ Med Ctr, New Orleans, beginning 1975; nat Inst Neurol Dis & Stroke grant, La State Univ Med Ctr, New Orleans, 1970-; asst prof, LA State Univ Med Ctr, New Orleans, 1970-1975; instr, LA State Univ Med Ctr, New Orleans, 1968-1970. **Memberships:** AAAS; Am Physiol Soc; NY Acad Sci; Soc Neuroscience; Sigma Xi. **Research Statement & Publications:** Regional neurophysiology; electrophysiological correlates between brain neuronal activity and voluntary motor and sensory function. **Mailing Address:** Dept Physiol, La State Univ, Health Sci Ctr, 1100 Fla Ave, New Orleans, LA 70119-2799. **Fax:** 504-619-8617. **E-Mail:** sliles@lsuhsc.edu

LILEY, NICHOLAS ROBIN, ZOOLOGY. **Personal Data:** b Halifax, Eng, December 17, 1936; m 1961. **Education:** Oxford Univ, BA, 1959, DPhil (zoology), 1964. **Professional Experience:** PROF EMER ZOOL, UNIV BC, as of 2004; Prof Zool, Univ Bc, beginning 1978; from asst prof to assoc prof, Univ BC, 1965-1978; Nat Res Coun Can fel zool, 1963-1965. **Memberships:** Animal Behav Soc; Can Soc Zool. **Research Statement & Publications:** Comparative ethology and the evolution of behavior; endocrine mechanisms in control of behavior. **Mailing Address:** Dept Zool, Univ BC, 6270 Univ Blvd, Vancouver, BC V6T 1Z4, Can. **E-Mail:** iley@zoology.ubc.ca

LILEY, PETER EDWARD, PHYSICS, CHEMICAL ENGINEERING. **Personal Data:** b Barnstaple, Eng, April 22, 1927; m 1963, Elaine E Kull; c Elizabeth E & Rebecca A. **Education:** Univ London, BSc, 1951, PhD (physics), 1957; Imp Col, Univ London, dipl, 1957. **Professional Experience:** PROF MECH ENG, PURDUE UNIV, WEST LAFAYETTE, 1972-; Mem, Thermophysical Properties comt, Am Soc Mech Engrs, 1960-1987 & chmn, 1971-1973; from asst prof to assoc prof, Purdue Univ, West Lafayette, 1957-1972; chem engr, Brit Oxygen Eng, Ltd, 1955-1957. **Research Statement & Publications:** Thermodynamic and transport properties of matter, principally fluids; cryogenic engineering; high pressure. **Mailing Address:** Sch Mech Eng, Purdue Univ, 585 Purdue Mall, West Lafayette, IN 47907-2088. **Fax:** 765-494-0539.

LILIEHOLM, ROBERT JOHN, LAND USE PLANNING, RISK & UNCERTAINTY. **Personal Data:** b Morristown, NJ, April 9, 1960; m 1985, c 2. **Education:** Utah State Univ, BS, 1983; La State Univ, MS 1984; Univ Calif, Berkeley, PhD (forestry), 1988. **Professional Experience:** ASSOC PROF, NATURAL RES. ECON, UTAH STATE UNIV, 1994-PRESENT; honors prof; fac assoc Lincoln Inst Land Policy, vis fellow, 1994-1995; vis fac, Org Trop Studies, 1990; asst prof forest mgt & econs, Forest Mgt & Econs, Utah State Univ, 1988-1994; baker-Bidwell res fel Univ Calif, Berkeley, 1986 & 1987; consult bus govt; expert witness US Dept Justice. **Memberships:** Soc Am Foresters; Opers Res Soc Am; Int Soc Trop Foresters; Am Econ Asn. **Research Statement & Publications:** Integrate economic and ecological approaches to resource management to meet diverse management objectives on a landscape level. **Mailing Address:** Dept Environment & Society, Utah State Univ, Logan, UT 84322-5215. **Fax:** 435-797-4048. **E-Mail:** rjl@cc.usu.edu

LILIEN, OTTO MICHAEL, GENITOURINARY SURGERY. **Personal Data:** b New York, NY, April 26, 1924; c 6. **Education:** Jefferson Med Col, MD, 1949; Columbia Univ, MA, 1960. **Professional Experience:** RETIRED; chmn dept, Upstate Med Ctr, State Univ NY, 1963-1988; from asst prof to prof urol, Upstate Med Ctr, State Univ NY, 1961-1988; Nat Cancer Inst trainee, 1956-1958; lectr zoology, Columbia Univ, 1956-1958. **Memberships:** AMA; Am Urol Asn; fel Am Col Surg. **Research Statement & Publications:** Renal and cell physiology. **Mailing Address:** 5164 N W 26th Circle, Boca Raton, FL 33496.

LILIENFIELD, LAWRENCE SPENCER, MEDICINE, PHYSIOLOGY. **Personal Data:** b New York, NY, May 5, 1927; m 1950, Eleanor Russ; c Jan, Adele S & Lisa. **Education:** Villanova Col, BS, 1945; Georgetown Univ, MD, 1949, MS, 1954, PhD, 1956; Am Bd Internal Med, dipl, 1957, 1974. **Professional Experience:** Assoc, Comt Int Exchange Persons, 1971-1976; vis prof, Univ Tel-Aviv, 1967-1968; consult, USPHS, 1965-1972; PROF PHYSIOL & BIOPHYS, SCHS MED & DENT, GEORGETOWN UNIV, 1964-; chmn, physiol & biophys, 1963-1993; USPHS sr res fel, 1959 & res career award, 1963; estab investr, Am Heart Asn, 1958; from asst prof to assoc prof med, physiol & biophys, 1957-1964; Am Heart Asn res fel, 1957; attend physician, DC Gen Hosp, 1956 & Vet Admin Hosp, 1957; instr physiol, Med Sch, Georgetown Univ, 1956-1957; asst chief cardiovasc res lab & attend physician, Georgetown Univ Hosp, 1956; instr med, Med Sch, Georgetown Univ, 1955-1957; base surgeon, USAF, 1951-1952; from jr asst resident to sr asst resident, Georgetown Univ Hosp, 1950-1953; intern med, Georgetown Univ Hosp, 1949-1950; vis prof, Univ Saigon. **Memberships:** AAAS; Biophys Soc; Am Physiol Soc; Soc Exp Biol & Med; Am Soc Clin Invest. **Research Statement & Publications:** Transcapillary exchange; hemodynamics; blood distribution in organs; renal concentrating mechanisms; medical education. **Mailing Address:** Dept Physiol Sch Med, Georgetown Univ, Washington, DC 20007-2187.

LILJESTRAND, CHERYL, GENETICS. **Education:** Tex A&M Univ, BS, 1978, PhD (microbiol), 1983; George Wash Univ, JD, 1997. **Professional Experience:** ASSOC/ ATTY, TANOX INC, as of 2002. **Mailing Address:** Tanox, Inc., 10301 Sella Link, Suite 110, Houston, TX 77025.

LILL, PATSY HENRY, IMMUNOLOGY, PATHOLOGY. **Personal Data:** b Mesa, Ariz, July 6, 1943. **Education:** Northwestern Univ, BS, 1966; Univ Wis, MST, 1972; Chicago Med Sch-Univ Health Sci, PhD (path), 1975. **Professional Experience:** ASSOC PROF PATH & MICROBIOL, SCH MED, UNIV SC, as of 2003; prin investr, Univ SC Res & Prod Scholarship grant, 1979 & Nat Cancer Inst grant, 1979-1982; fel tumor immunology & cancer biol, Frederick Cancer Res Ctr, 1975-1977; lab supvr cancer res, Dept Exp Path, Mt Sinai Hosp Med Ctr, 1970-1975; teacher biol, Highland Park High Sch, Ill, 1966-1970; asst prof path, Sch Med, Univ Sc, beginning; mem, Charles Louis Davis Doctor Vet Med Found. **Memberships:** AAAS; Am Asn Pathologists; Am Asn Cancer Res. **Research Statement & Publications:** Tumor immunology; effect of physical and chemical carcinogens on syngeneic tumor growth. **Mailing Address:** Dept Path, Univ SC Sch Med, Columbia, SC 29208-0001. **Fax:** 803-733-3192. **E-Mail:** lill@med.sc.edu

LILLARD, DORRIS ALTON, FOOD CHEMISTRY, BIOCHEMISTRY. **Personal Data:** b Thompson Station, Tenn, July 17, 1936. **Education:** Middle Tenn State Univ, BS, 1958; Ore State Univ, MS, 1961, PhD (food sci), 1964. **Professional Experience:** PROF EMER FOOD SCI, UNIV GA, as of 1998; prof food sci, Univ GA, beginning 1980; assoc prof, Univ GA, 1968-1980; asst prof food flavor chem, Iowa State Univ, 1964-1968; res fel lipid autoxidation, Ore State Univ, 1958-1964. **Memberships:** AAAS; Am Chem Soc; Am Oil Chem Soc; Inst Food Technol; Am Meat Sci Asn. **Research Statement & Publications:** Flavor chemistry of foods; autoxidation of lipids; mycotoxins in foods; food microbiology. **Mailing Address:** Dept Food Sci, Univ Ga, Athens, GA 30602.

LILLEGRAVEN, JASON ARTHUR, PALEONTOLOGY, PALEOGEOGRAPHY. **Personal Data:** b Mankato, Minn, October 11, 1938; m 1983, Linda; c Ture A & Brita A (Crowe). **Education:** Calif State Col Long Beach, BA (biol), 1962; SDak Sch Mines & Technol, MS (paleo & geol), 1964; Univ Kans, PhD (zoology), 1968. **Honors & Awards:** Honorary Mbrshp, Soc Vert Paleo, 2004; Distinguished Emeritus Professor Award Coll Arts & Sci, Univ Wyo; Alexander von Humboldt Sr US Scientist Award, 1988 & 1989 George Duke Humphrey Distinguished fac Award, 1987. **Professional Experience:** RETIRED PROF GEOL, UNIV WYO, 1978-2004; co-ed, Rocky Mountain Geol, 1996-; assoc ed, J Vert Paleo, 1993-1998; Bd Trustees The Nature Conservancy Wyoming Chapter, 2004-; assoc ed, Palaios, 2003-; ed bd, Cretaceous Research, 1998-2002; ed bd, J Mammal Evol, 1991-2001; ed bd, Res & Explor Nation Geogr Soc, 1986-1995; assoc dean, Col Arts & Sci, Univ Wyo, 1984-1985; Prog dir, syst biol prog, NSF, 1977-1978; co-ed, Contrib to Geol, 1976-1988; assoc prof, Univ Wyo, 1976-1978; from asst prof to prof zool, San Diego State Univ, 1969-1975; NSF fel paleont, Univ Calif, Berkeley, 1968-1969; Instr zool, Calif State Col Long Beach, summer, 1964. **Memberships:** Paleont Soc; Soc Vert Paleont (vpres & pres, 1984-1986); Am Soc Mammal; Soc Study Mammalian Evolution; Sigma Xi; Soc Study Evolution; National Center Sci Educ. **Research Statement & Publications:** Paleogeography; Mesozoic and early Cenozoic mammalian paleontology, comparative anatomy and evolution of mammalian reproduction; stratigraphy and structural geology. **Mailing Address:** Dept Geol & Geophys (emeritus status), Univ Wyo, Laramie, WY 82071-3006. **Fax:** 303-766-6679. **E-Mail:** bagpipe@uwyo.edu

LILLEHOJ, EIVIND B, PLANT PHYSIOLOGY, BIOCHEMISTRY. **Personal Data:** b Kimballton, Iowa, August 11, 1928; m 1948, c 4. **Education:** Iowa State Univ, BS, 1960, MS, 1962, PhD (plant physiol), 1964. **Professional Experience:** RETIRED; Southern Res Lab, Dept Agr New Orleans, 1989-1990; dir, Cancer Res Ctr, 1981-1989; microbiol, Northern Regional Res Lab, USDA, 1965-1979 & Southern Regional Res Lab, 1979-1989; pres, La Jolla Cancer Res Found, 1976-1989; NIH fel, Carlsberg Lab, Copenhagen, Denmark, 1964-1965. **Memberships:** Fel AAAS; Am Soc Microbiol. **Research Statement & Publications:** Fungal physiology; mycotoxins; fermentation; microbial products. **Mailing Address:** PO Box 22, Kimballton, IA 51543-0022.

LILLEHOJ, HYUN SOON, IMMUNOGENETICS, IMMUNOPARASITOLOGY. **Personal Data:** b Seoul, Korea, March 1, 1949; m 1979, c 2. **Education:** Univ Hartford, BS, 1974; Univ Conn, MS, 1976; Wayne State Univ, PhD (immunol), 1979. **Professional Experience:** Adj prof, Univ Del, 1989; assoc ed, Poultry Sci, 1988; RES IMMUNOLOGIST, BELTSVILLE AREA AGR RES SERV, USDA, 1984-; staff fel, Nat Inst Allergy & Infectious Dis, NIH, 1981-1984. **Memberships:** Am Asn Immunologists; Poultry Sci Asn; Am Asn Avian Vet Pathologists. **Research Statement & Publications:** Vaccine against Eimeria; monoclonal antibodies detecting avian lymphocytes and lymphokines; immunopathology and immunogenetics of avian coccidiosis; molecular cloning of avian lymphokines. **Mailing Address:** USDA, E Bldg 1040, Beltsville, MD 20705. **Fax:** 301-504-6170. **E-Mail:** hlilleho@anri.barc.usda.gov

LILLELEHT, L(EMBIT) U(NO), THERMAL SCIENCES, ENERGY CONVERSION. **Personal Data:** b Parnu, Estonia, March 9, 1930; American citizen; m 1960, Karen; c Erica & Mark L. **Education:** Univ Del, BS, 1953; Princeton Univ, MS, 1955; Univ Ill, PhD (chem eng), 1962. **Professional Experience:** EMER PROF CHEM ENG, UNIV VA, 1995-; vis sr scientist, Goddard Space Flight Ctr, NASA, 1991-1992; vis assoc prof, Solar Energy Res Inst, 1978-1979; lectr solar energy, US Int Comn Agency, 1978-1979; partner, Assoc Environ Consults, 1972-; from assoc prof to prof chem eng, Univ VA, 1966-1995; from asst prof to assoc prof chem eng, Univ Alta, 1960-1966; engr process develop & res, E I du Pont de Nemours & Co, Inc, 1954-1957. **Memberships:** Am Inst Chem Engrs; Am Chem Soc; Int Solar Energy Soc; Sigma Xi; Am Solar Energy Soc. **Research Statement & Publications:** Multiphase flows; air pollution control; nucleation and condensation of refractory vapors in microgravity environment; heat transfer; utilization of solar and other alternative energy resources. **Mailing Address:** Dept Chem Eng, Univ Va, Charlottesville, VA 22903-2442. **Fax:** 434-982-2658. **E-Mail:** lul@virginia.edu

LILLER, WILLIAM, ARCHAEOASTRONOMY. **Personal Data:** b Philadelphia, Pa, April 1, 1927; m 1985, c 3. **Education:** Harvard Univ, AB, 1949; Univ Mich, AM, 1950, PhD (astron), 1953. **Professional Experience:** Sr res fel, Isaac Newton Inst, Santiago, Chile, 1981-; head tutor, astron dept, 1977-1980; chmn, Bartol Found, 1976-1979; ROBERT WHEELER WILLSON PROF APPL ASTRON, HARVARD UNIV, 1970-; vis comnr, Bartol Found, 1968-; master, Adams House, Harvard Univ, 1968-1973; Guggenheim fel, 1964-1965; prof, dept astron, 1960-1970; chmn, dept astron, 1960-1966; from instr to assoc prof astron, McMath-Hulbert Observ, Univ Mich, 1953-1960; supt, Harvard Univ, 1952-1953; asst, McMath-Hulbert Observ, Univ Mich, 1952; mem meteor exped, Harvard Univ, 1947-1948. **Memberships:** Am Astron Soc; Royal Astron Soc Can; fel AAAS; Am Acad Arts & Sci; Int Astron Union; Brit Astron Asn. **Research Statement & Publications:** Photoelectric photometry of planetary nebulae and hot stars; investigation of x-ray sources; spectrophotometry; globular clusters; archaeoastronomy (easter I). **Mailing Address:** Vina del Mar, Casilla 5022 Renaca, Chile.

LILLESAND, THOMAS MARTIN, REMOTE SENSING. **Personal Data:** b Laurium, Mich, October 1, 1946; m 1968, Theresa; c Mark, Kari & Michael. **Education:** Univ Wis-Madison, BS, 1969, MS, 1970, PhD (civil eng), 1973. **Honors & Awards:** Alan Gordon Award, Am Soc Photogram & Remote Sensing, 1979; Talbert Abrams Award, 1984; Fennell Award, 1988. **Professional Experience:** PROF REMOTE SENSING, UNIV WIS-MADISON, 1982-; prof remote sensing, Univ Minn, 1978-1982; prof remote sensing, State Univ NY, Syracuse, 1973-1978; consult, 1973-. **Memberships:** Fel Am Soc Photogram & Remote Sensing (pres, 1998-1989); Am Soc Civil Engrs. **Research Statement & Publications:** Remote sensing and image processing of satellite data for application in agriculture, forestry, water resources and environmental monitoring; space policy; image interpretation; commercial applications of remote sensing. **Mailing Address:** Atmospheric Oceanic & Space Sci, 1225 W Dayton St Rm 1239, Madison, WI 53706. **E-Mail:** tmlilles@facstaff.wisc.edu

LILLEVIK, HANS ANDREAS, BIOCHEMISTRY. **Personal Data:** b Sherman, SDak, February 4, 1916; m 1946, c 4. **Education:** St Olaf Col, BA, 1938; Univ Minn, MS, 1940, PhD (biochem), 1946. **Professional Experience:** PROF BIOCHEM, MICH STATE UNIV, 1970-; Am Scand Found fel, Carlsberg Lab, Denmark, 1947-1948; from instr to assoc prof chem & biochem, Mich State Univ, 1946-1970; res chemist, Minn Mining & Mfg Co, 1944-1945; Instr biochem, Univ Minn, 1942-1944. **Memberships:** AAAS; Am Chem Soc; Am

Soc Biol Chemists; Am Dairy Sci Asn. **Research Statement & Publications:** Chemical properties and biological function of proteins and enzymes. **Mailing Address:** 708 Knoll Rd, East Lansing, MI 48823-2826.

LILLEY, ARTHUR EDWARD, ASTRONOMY. **Personal Data:** b Mobile, Ala, May 29, 1928. **Education:** Univ Ala, BS, 1950, MS, 1951; Harvard Univ, PhD (radio astron), 1954. **Honors & Awards:** Bok Prize, Harvard Univ, 1958. **Professional Experience:** Assoc dir, Harvard-Smithsonian Ctr Astrophys, 1972-1989; ASTRONOMER-IN-CHARGE, SMITHSONIAN OBSERV, 1965-; PROF RADIO ASTRON, HARVARD UNIV, 1963-; assoc prof, Harvard Univ, 1959-1963; Sloan res fel, 1958-1960; res Corp grant, 1957-1959; asst prof radio astron, Yale Univ, 1957-1959; physicist, Naval Res Lab, 1954-1957. **Memberships:** AAAS; Int Union Radio Sci; Int Astron Union; Am Astron Soc; Am Phys Soc. **Research Statement & Publications:** Spectral line and satellite radio astronomy; radio astronomical navigation techniques. **Mailing Address:** Harvard Univ Ctr Astrophys, 60 Garden St, Cambridge, MA 02138.

LILLEY, DAVID GRANTHAM, COMBUSTION AERODYNAMICS, FIRE MODELING. **Personal Data:** b Shipley, Eng, American citizen. **Education:** Sheffield Univ, Eng, BSc, 1966, MSc, 1967, PhD (chem eng), 1970. **Professional Experience:** PROF MECH ENG, OKLA STATE UNIV, 1982-; assoc prof, Okla State Univ, 1978-1982; assoc prof mech eng, Concordia Univ, Montreal, 1976-1978; vis assoc prof combustion, Univ Ariz, 1975-1976; sr res assoc, Cranfield Inst Technol, Eng, 1973-1975; lectr math, Sheffield Polytech, Eng, 1970-1973. **Memberships:** Assoc fel Am Inst Aeronaut & Astronaut; Am Soc Mech Engrs; Inst Fuel; assoc fel Inst Math & Applns. **Research Statement & Publications:** Theoretical combustion aerodynamics; computational fluid dynamics; swirling flows; combustor design; numerical methods; finite difference methods; turbulent reacting flows; heat transfer, fires, flames, and computer simulation. **Mailing Address:** Sch Mech & Aerospace Eng, Okla State Univ Main Campus, Stillwater, OK 74078-5016. **Fax:** 405-744-7873. **E-Mail:** lilley@okstate.edu

LILLICH, THOMAS TYLER, BACTERIAL PHYSIOLOGY, HOST PARASITE RELATIONS. **Personal Data:** b Cincinnati, Ohio, September 8, 1943; m 1965, c 2. **Education:** Miami Univ, BA, 1965; NC State Univ, MS, 1968, PhD (microbiol), 1970. **Professional Experience:** RETIRED; comt, SIll Univ Grad Sch, 1991; comt, Dent Accreditation, Am Dent Asn, 1990-1991; actg chair, Dept Oral Health Sci, Univ Ky, 1988-2003; Univ Tex Dent Br San Antonio, Ohio State Univ Col Dent, 1987; prof oral & maxillofacial Surg, Univ Ky, 1981-2003; chmn, dept oral biol, 1980-1988; vis prof, Roy Dent Col, Arhus Denmark, 1978; consult, Div Educ Res Prog, Am Asn Med Sch, 1977-1985; bd Educ Training, Am Soc Microbiol, 1977-1979; assoc prof oral biol & microbiol & immunol, Univ Ky, 1975-1981; act chmn oral biol, Univ Ky, 1975; mem microbiol grad fac, Univ Ky, 1974-2003; NIH res fel, & Agr Res Serv contractee, 1973-1976; asst prof oral & cell biol, Univ Ky, 1972-1975; NIH res fel, Univ Ky, 1970-1972. **Memberships:** Am Soc Microbiol; Am Asn Dent Sch (chair elect, 1975-1976 1988-1989; chair, 1976-1977 1989-1990); Int Asn Dent Res; Sigma Xi; Am Asn Dent Res. **Research Statement & Publications:** Effects of antimicrobials on the oral microflora; emphasis on oral microflora of medically comprised patients; identification and ratios of organisms; control with tropical antimicrobials to reduce systematic disease; host response to microbial challenge. **Mailing Address:** Dept Oral Health Sci Col Dent, Univ Ky, Lexington, KY 40536-0084.

LILLIE, CHARLES FREDERICK, AERONAUTICAL ENGINEERING, ASTRONAUTICAL ENGINEERING. **Personal Data:** b Indianola, Iowa, February 20, 1936; wid, c 3. **Education:** Iowa State Univ, BS, 1957; Univ Wis, Madison, PhD (astrophys), 1968. **Professional Experience:** PROJ MGR ADVAN PROG, CIVIL & INT SYSTS DIV, DIV SPACE & LASER PROD, TRW, as of 2001; sr systs engr, Fed Systs Div, 1979-; assoc prof astrogeophys, Attendant Rank & fel Lab Atmospheric & Space Physics, 1977-1979; team mem, Large Space Telescope Inst Definition Team High Resol Spectrograph, 1973-1975; prin investr, Voyager Photopolarimeter Exp, 1972-1979; co-investr, Apollo 17 Ultraviolet Spectrometer Exp, 1972-1974; from asst prof to assoc prof physics & astrophys, Univ Colo, 1970-1977; proj assoc, Space Astrophys Lab, 1968-1970; res asst, Washburn Observ, 1964-1968; teaching asst, Dept Astron, Univ Wis, 1962-1964; instr eng, NASA Flight Res Ctr, Edwards, Calif, 1960-1962. **Memberships:** Am Astron Soc; AAAS; Soc Photo-Optical Instrumentation Engrs; Int Astron Union; Am Inst Aeronaut & Astronaut; Air Force Asn. **Research Statement & Publications:** Surface brightness of the night sky, zodiacal light, diffuse galactic light, interstellar radiation density, extragalactic light; cometary physics, ultraviolet spectroscopy of stars and nebulae; spacecraft design, RF environment, contamination; spacecraft operations and on orbit servicing; optics. **Mailing Address:** Div Space & Laser Prod, TRW, One Space Park MS-2978, Redondo Beach, CA 90278. **E-Mail:** chuck.lillie@trw.com

LILLIE, JOHN HOWARD, ANATOMY, DENTISTRY. **Personal Data:** b Oak Park, Ill, December 16, 1940; m 1963, c 2. **Education:** Univ Mich, DDS, 1966, PhD (anat), 1972. **Professional Experience:** RETIRED; staff mem, Dent Res Inst, beginning 1972; prof anat & cell biol, sch med, Univ Mich, Ann Arbor, beginning 1972; admin, Sch Dent. **Memberships:** Am Soc Cell Biol; Am Asn Anat. **Research Statement & Publications:** Cellular control mechanisms in exocrine secretion and epithelia-connective tissue interactions; features of synthesis and control in the production of basal lamina constituents. **Mailing Address:** Dept Anat & Cell Biol, Univ Mich, Ann Arbor, MI 48109.

LILLIE, ROBERT JONES, POULTRY NUTRITION. **Personal Data:** b Rochester, Minn, April 15, 1921; m 1946, Mary; c Elizabeth & Kathryn. **Education:** Pa State Col, BS, 1944; Univ Md, MS, 1946, PhD (poultry nutrit), 1949. **Honors & Awards:** Am Poultry Sci Asn Award, 1950; Commission Award, US Civil Serv, 1976. **Professional Experience:** RETIRED; res animal scientist, Non ruminant Animal Nutrit Lab, Nutrit Inst, Sci & Educ Admin Agr Res, 1972-1978; mem stand diet subcomt, Nat Res Coun, 1954; poultry husbandman, Animal & Poultry Husb Res Br, USDA, 1947-1972; asst, Poultry Dept, Univ Md, 1945-1947. **Memberships:** Am Poultry Sci Asn; Am Inst Nutrit; Worlds Poultry Cong. **Research Statement & Publications:** Vitamins, antibiotics, surfactants, arsenicals, unidentified factors, proteins and amino acids; pesticides; reproductive efficiency; air pollutants affecting poultry; trace minerals in swine. **Mailing Address:** 7020 Tretp Circle, Cornwall, PA 17016-0125.

LILLIEFORS, HUBERT W, STATISTICS. **Personal Data:** b Reading, Pa, June 14, 1928; m 1980, c 2. **Education:** George Washington Univ, BA, 1952, PhD (statist), 1964; Mich State Univ, MA, 1953. **Professional Experience:** PROF STATIST, GEORGE Wash UNIV, 1967-; from instr to assoc prof, George Wash Univ, 1962-1967; mathematician opers res, Appl Physics Lab, Johns Hopkins Univ, 1957-1964; opers analyst, Opers Eval Group, 1956-1957; sr scientist opers res, Lockheed Missile Systs Div, 1955-1956; Mathematician, Diamond Ord Fuze Labs, 1953-1955. **Memberships:** Am Statist Asn; Inst Math Statist. **Research Statement & Publications:** Nonparametric statistics; statistical inference. **Mailing Address:** Dept Statist, George Washington Univ 2201 G St NW, Washington, DC 20052-4211. **Fax:** 202-994-6917. **E-Mail:** hlill@gwu.edu

LILLIEN, IRVING, ORGANIC CHEMISTRY, COMPUTER SCIENCES. **Personal Data:** b New York, NY, February 2, 1929. **Education:** Univ Denver, BS, 1950; Purdue Univ, MS, 1952; Polytech Inst NY, PhD (org chem), 1959. **Professional Experience:** RETIRED; from assoc prof to prof org chem, Miami-Dade Community Col, 1969-1996; assoc prof, Marshall Univ, 1967-1969; asst prof, Sch Med, 1965-1967; Air Force Off Sci & Res grant, 1963-1965; asst prof, Univ Miami, 1962-1965; asst prof, Georgetown Univ, 1961-1962; fel org chem, Wayne State Univ, 1959-1961. **Memberships:** AAAS; Am Chem Soc; Royal Soc Chem; Inst Elec & Electronics Engrs. **Research Statement & Publications:** Physical-organic chemistry; mechanisms of organic reactions; chemistry and conformation of small and medium size rings; science education and administration. **Mailing Address:** Dept Chem, Miami-Dade Community Col, 11011 SW 104 St, Miami, FL 33176. **E-Mail:** irvlillien@worldnet.att.net

LILLINGTON, GLEN ALAN, PULMONARY MEDICINE, CONTINUING MEDICAL EDUCATION. **Personal Data:** b Winnipeg, Man, October 20, 1926; m 1957, c Karlin, Peter & Barry. **Education:** Univ Man, BS, 1946, MD, 1951; Univ Minn, MS, 1957, FRCP, 1959, FACP, 1967. **Professional Experience:** PROF EMER MED, SCH MED, UNIV CALIF, DAVIS, as of 2005; dir residency med, Med Ctr, 1979-1980; chief staff, Dept Med, Med Sch, Univ Calif, Davis, 1979-1980; actg chmn, Dept Med, Med Sch, Univ Calif, Davis, 1979-1980; chief pulmonary, critical care div, 1975-1987; prof med, Med Ctr, 1975-1981; prof med, Sch Med, Univ Calif, Davis, beginning 1973; travelling fel, Webb-Waring Inst, Denver, 1973-1974; med dir respiratory therapy, Sch Respiratory Therapy, Foothill Col, 1972-1973; consult, Rand Corp, Santa Monica, 1969-1970; res assoc, Palo Alto Med Res Found, 1965-1973; asst clin prof, Sch Med, Stanford Univ, 1960-1973; lectr, Univ Manitoba Fac Med, 1958-1960; asst staff med, Mayo Clin & Found, 1957-1958. **Memberships:** Am Col Physicians. **Research Statement & Publications:** Experimental emphysema; pulmonary mechanics; differential diagnosis of pulmonary diseases based on roentgenographic patterns; decision analysis in medicine. **Mailing Address:** Dept Internal Med, Sch Med, Univ Calif, 4150 V St Ste 3400, Sacramento, CA 95817. **Fax:** 916-734-7924.

LILLWITZ, LAWRENCE DALE, INDUSTRIAL ORGANIC CHEMISTRY, INDUSTRIAL PROCESS CHEMISTRY. **Personal Data:** b Hinsdale, Ill, June 1, 1944; m 1968, c 5. **Education:** Ill Benedictine Col, BS, 1966; Univ Notre Dame, PhD (org chem), 1970. **Professional Experience:** ASSOC RES CHEMIST, AMOCO CHEM CO, 1986-; sr res chemist, Amoco Chem Co, 1981-1986; staff res chemist, Amoco Chem Co, 1979-1981; res chemist, Amoco Chem Co, 1977-1979; group leader, Chem Div, Quaker Oats Co, 1970-1977. **Memberships:** Am Chem Soc. **Research Statement & Publications:** Monomer synthesis; organic reaction mechanisms; homogeneous and heterogeneous catalysis. **Mailing Address:** 39 Cotswold Dr, Yorkville, IL 60560.

LILLY, ARNYS CLIFTON, JR, PHYSICS. **Personal Data:** b Beckley, WVa, June 3, 1934; m 1956, Agnes Micou; c Greg, Diane & Jim. **Education:** Va Polytech Inst, BS, 1957, PhD, 1989; Carnegie Inst Technol, MS, 1963. **Professional Experience:** VPRES & TECHNOL ASSESSMENT DIR, PHILLIP MORRIS RES CTR, 1996-; res fel, Phillip Morris Res Ctr, 1984-1996; prin scientist, Phillip Morris Res Ctr, 1981-1984; assoc prin scientist, Phillip Morris Res Ctr, 1974-1981; sr scientist, Physics Div, Phillip Morris Res Ctr, 1967-1974; res physicist, Phillip Morris Res Ctr, 1965-1967; res physicist, Gulf Res & Develop Co, Pa, 1957-1965. **Memberships:** Am Phys Soc; Sigma Xi. **Research Statement & Publications:** Ion & electron optics; dielectric theory and experiment; electrostatics and organic conduction; space charge in insulators; thermal physics; combustion; laser processing; fluid mechanics; quantum chemistry; theoretical physics; theory of liquids. **Mailing Address:** Philip Morris Res Ctr, PO Box 26583, Richmond, VA 23261.

LILLY, DOUGLAS KEITH, MESOSCALE DYNAMICS. **Personal Data:** b San Francisco, Calif, June 16, 1929; m 1954, Judith; c Kathryn L Dunbar, Donald R Lily & Carol S Lily. **Education:** Stanford Univ, BS, 1950; Fla State Univ, MS, 1954, PhD (meteorol), 1959. **Honors & Awards:** member, National Academy of Sciences, 2000; Rossby Medal, Am Meteorol Soc, 1986; Symons Mem Medal, Royal Meteorol Soc, UK, 1993. **Professional Experience:** PROF EMER METEOROL, UNIV OKLA, AS OF 2005; dir, Robert Lowrey Prof Meteorol, 1992-1995; dir, Ctr Anal & Prediction Storms, Univ Okla, 1989-1994; sr scientist, Nat Ctr Atmospheric Res, 1973-1982; prog scientist, Nat Ctr Atmospheric Res, 1965-1973; res meteorologist, US Weather Bur, 1958-1965. **Memberships:** Fel Am & honorary member Meteorol Soc; Royal Meteorol Soc. **Research Statement & Publications:** Atmospheric convection, turbulence and gravity waves; numerical simulation of meteorological flows. **Mailing Address:** Sch Meteorol, Univ Okla Main Campus, Norman, OK 73019. **Fax:** 405-325-7689. **E-Mail:** dlilly6@aol.com

LILLY, PERCY LANE, PLANT TAXONOMY. **Personal Data:** b Spanishburg, WVa, July 14, 1927; m 1951, c 4. **Education:** Concord Col, BS, 1950; Univ WVa, MS, 1951; Pa State Univ, PhD, 1957. **Professional Experience:** E R Kuch PROF EMER MICROBIOLOGY, HEIDELBERG COL, AS OF 2005; Spec field staff mem, Rockefeller Found, Colombia, 1968-1969; chmn dept, Heidelberg Col, beginning 1965; from asst prof to prof biol, Heidelberg Col, beginning 1956; instr biol, Salem Col, WVa, 1951-1953. **Memberships:** AAAS; Bot Soc Am. **Research Statement & Publications:** Plant genetics and microbiology; nitrogen fixation in Azotobacter; tropical botany. **Mailing Address:** 110 Mohawk St, Tiffin, OH 44883.

LILLYA, CLIFFORD PETER, ORGANIC CHEMISTRY. **Personal Data:** b Chicago, Ill, May 23, 1937; m 1962, Maija; c 2. **Education:** Kalamazoo Col, AB, 1959; Harvard Univ, PhD (chem), 1964. **Professional Experience:** PROF EMERCHEM, UNIV MASS, AMHERST, as of 2005; vis Scholor, Johannes Guterberg univ, Mainz, 1992; vis scholar, Stanford Univ, 1978; prof chem, Univ Mass, Amherst, beginning 1973; vis scholar, Univ Calif, Los Angles, 1970-1971; fel, Alfred P Sloan Found, 1969-1971; from asst prof to assoc prof, Univ Mass, Amherst, 1964-1973; staff assoc, Univ Mass, Amherst, 1963-1964; fel, NSF, 1959-1963; fel, Woodrow Wilson, 1959. **Memberships:** Am Chem Soc; AAAS; Fel Alfred P Sloan Found; Fel, NSF; Fel Woodrow Wilson. **Research Statement & Publications:** Web-delivered learning software. **Mailing Address:** Dept Chem, Univ Mass, 403F Tower A Box 34510, Amherst, MA 01003-4510. **E-Mail:** lillya@chem.umass.edu

LILLYWHITE, HARVEY B, COMPARATIVE PYHSIOLOGY, PHYSIOLOGICAL ECOLOGY. **Personal Data:** b Nogales, Ariz, December 1, 1943; m 1967, Jamie; c Steven M & Shauna R. **Education:** Univ Calif, Riverside, BA, 1966; Univ Calif, Los Angeles, MA, 1967, PhD (zoology), 1970. **Professional Experience:** Sr res assoc, NASA-Ames Res Ctr, 1992-1997; Fulbright fel, India, 1992-1993; res fel, Univ New Eng, Armidale, NSW, Australia, 1991; PROF ZOOL, UNIV FLA, GAINESVILLE, 1984-; sect ed, Ecol & Ecol Monographs, 1982-1986; mem publ policy comt, Am Soc Ichthyologists & Herpetologists, 1980-1982; vis scientist, Scripps Inst Oceanog, La Jolla, Calif, 1979-1980; res fel, San Diego Zoo & Wild Animal Park, 1979-1980; sect ed, Copeia, 1978-1982; secy nominating comt, Ecol Soc Am, 1978-1979; vis lectr, Monash Univ, Clayton, Victoria, Australia, 1975-

1976; from asst prof to prof physiol, Univ Kans, Lawrence, 1971-1984; fel zool, Univ Calif, Berkeley, 1970-1971. **Memberships:** Soc Integrative & Comp Biol; Am Physiol Soc; Ecol Soc Am; Am Soc Ichthyologists & Herpetologists; Soc Study Amphibians & Reptiles; AAAS. **Research Statement & Publications:** Comparative and ecological physiology of vertebrates, especially amphibians and reptiles; cardiovascular adaptations of reptiles; functional morphology of vertebrate integument; water and thermal relations; ecology of fire disturbance and animal coloration. **Mailing Address:** Dept Zool Univ Fla, Bartram Hall, Gainesville, FL 32611. **Fax:** 352-392-3704. **E-Mail:** hbl@zoo.ufl.edu

LIM, ALEXANDER TE, HEAT TRANSFER & THERMAL SCIENCES, AIR CONDITIONING & REFRIGERATION. **Personal Data:** b Manila, Philippines, June 17, 1942; American citizen; m 1971, c Gregory & Karen. **Education:** Univ St Thomas, BS, 1964; Duke Univ, MS, 1969. **Professional Experience:** Chmn, Air Conditioning & Refrig Inst Packaged Terminal Air- Conditioning Eng Comt, 1993-; DIR QUAL ASSURANCE & TECHNOL, INTER CITY PROD CORP, 1993-; mem, Res & Technol Comt, 1989-1991; DIR TECHNOL, Inter City Prod Corp, 1987-1993; vpres, ICG Keeprite Corp, 1986-1987; comt mem, Air Conditioning & Refrig Inst Packaged Terminal Air Conditioning Eng Comt, 1985-1991; dir res & develop, ICG Keeprite Corp, 1985-1986; dir eng, Light Residential Div, 1980-1985; comt mem, Am Home Appliance Mfrs Eng Comt, 1978-1983 & 1988-1991; mgr develop eng, Room Air Opers, 1976-1980; comt mem, Am Soc Heating, Refrig & Air Conditioning Engrs, Comt, 1974-1979; sr engr, Res & Develop Div, Carrier Corp, 1969-1976; teaching asst undergrad eng, Mech Eng Dept, Duke Univ, 1966-1969; Instr, Col Eng, Ateneo Del Manila Univ, 1964-1966. **Memberships:** Am Soc Mech Engrs; Am Soc Heating Refrig & Air Conditioning Engrs; Air Conditioning & Refrig Inst. **Research Statement & Publications:** Air-side and refrigerant-side heat and mass transfer as applied to air-conditioning and refrigeration; new concepts and cycles for air-conditioning application; granted four patents. **Mailing Address:** 1214 Choctaw Trail, Brentwood, TN 37027.

LIM, DANIEL V, PATHOGENIC MICROBIOLOGY, ENVIRONMENTALMICROBIOLOGY. **Personal Data:** b Houston, Tex, April 15, 1948; m 1973, Carol. **Education:** Rice Univ, BA, 1970; Tex A&M Univ, PhD (microbiol), 1973. **Honors & Awards:** Searle/Donald Richardson Mem Award, Am Col Obstet & Gynec, 1987; Fla Gov's Award Outstanding Contrib Sci & Technol, 1990; P R Edwards Award, southeastern, Branch Am Soc Microbiol, 2001. **Professional Experience:** NIH study sections, 2000-; council, Am Soc Microbiol, 2000-; career develop comt, Am Soc Microbiol, 1999-; Tilly & Graves, PA, 1990-1992; pres, Southeastern BR, Am Soc Microbiol, 1990-1991; grad fel panel, Nat Res Coun NSF, 1989-1992; dir, Inst Biomolecular Sci, 1988-1993; PROF MICROBIOL, UNIV SFLA, 1987-; pres, Micro Concepts Res Corp, 1986-; actg chmn biol, Univ SFla, 1983-1985; assoc fac mem, Tampa Gen Hosp, 1982-1988; Life Technols Inc-Gibco Labs, 1982-1986; Life Technols, Conservancy, 1980-1984; consult, Pharmacia Diag-Pharmacia AB, 1979-1986; from asst prof to assoc prof microbiol, Univ SFla, 1976-1987; fel, Baylor Col Med, 1973-1976. **Memberships:** Am Soc Microbiol; Inter-Am Soc Chemother (vpres, 1983-1988); AAAS; Sigma Xi; fel Am Acad Microbiol; Southeastern Branch Am Soc Microbio; Int Asn Food Protection. **Research Statement & Publications:** The virulence of bacteria and rapid diagnosis of bacterial diseases; group B streptococci, Biosensors and microarrays; author of two books. **Mailing Address:** Dept Biol Univ S Fla, SCA 110, Tampa, FL 33620-5200. **Fax:** 813-974-3263. **E-Mail:** lim@chuma1.cas.usf.edu

LIM, DAVID J, OTOLARYNGOLOGY, ELECTRON MICROSCOPY. **Personal Data:** b Seoul, Korea, November 27, 1935; American citizen; m 1966, c 2. **Education:** Yonsei Univ, Korea, AB, 1955, MD, 1960. **Honors & Awards:** First Award Scientific Exhibit, Am Acad Ophthal & Otolaryngal, 1972. **Professional Experience:** EXEC VICE PRES & RES HEAD CELL & MOLECULAR BIOL, HOUSE EAR INST, 2001-; SEC CHIEF PATHOGENESIS, HOUSE EAR INST, 2001-; fogarty sr Int & vis scientist, Swed Med Res Coun, Karolinska Inst, 1982; mem bd dir, Deafness Res Found, beginning 1980; adv-at-large, Comt Hearing, Bioacoust & Biomech, Nat Res Coun, beginnig 1980; mem, Nat Adv Neurol & Commun Disorders & Stroke Coun, NIH, 1979-1983; mem commun sci study sect, NIH, 1979; prof otolaryngol, 1976- & emer prof anat, beginning 1977; consult comt res otolaryngol, Am Acad Ophthal & Otolaryngol, beginning 1977; mem sci rev comt, Deafness Res Found, 1977-1980; mem ad hoc adv comt, Commun Disorders Prog, Nat Inst Neurol & Commun Disorders & Stroke, 1976-1979; prin investr, various grants & contracts, beginning 1969; mem task force, Am Acad Ophthal & Otolaryngol & Am Bd Otolaryngol, 1969-1972; dir, Otol Res Labs, Ohio State Univ, beginning 1967; from asst prof to assoc prof, Col Med, Ohio State Univ, 1967-1976; res assoc, Col Med, Ohio State Univ, 1966-1967; spec fel otol res, Mass Eye & Ear Infirmary & Harvard Med Sch, 1965-1966; resident otolaryngol, Nat Med Ctr, Seoul, Korea, 1961-1964; intern, Nat Med Ctr, Seoul, Korea, 1960-1961; chief otolaryngol biol, Nidcd, Nih, Rockville, Md. **Memberships:** Am Acad Otolaryngol; Soc Neuroscience; Am Otol Soc; Asn Res Otolaryngol (secy-treas, 1973-1975, pres, 1976-1977, past pres & prog chair, 1977-1978, ed hist, 1980-); Barany Soc; Histochem Soc; Am Soc Cell Biol; Soc Mucosal Immunol. **Research Statement & Publications:** Investigation of the ear as to the normal function and disorders of hearing and balance with the use of light and electron microscopy; immunocytochemistry; immunochemistry and microbiology. **Mailing Address:** Dept Cell & Molecular Biol, House Ear Inst, 2100 W 3rd St, Los Angeles, CA 90057. **Fax:** 213-413-6739. **E-Mail:** lim@hei.org

LIM, EDWARD C, PHYSICAL CHEMISTRY. **Personal Data:** b Seoul, Korea, November 17, 1932; American citizen; m 1958, Bee Tuan Uy; c Diane M & Janice C. **Education:** St Procopius Col, BS, 1954; Okla State Univ, MS, 1957, PhD (chem), 1959. **Professional Experience:** Ed-in-charge, Lasers Chem, 1992-; GOODYEAR PROF CHEM, UNIV AKRON, 1989-; ed, Excited States, 1974-; prof chem, Wayne State Univ, 1968-1989; from asst prof to prof, Loyola Univ, Ill, 1960-1968; instr phys chem, Loyola Univ, Ill, 1958-1960. **Memberships:** Fel Am Phys Soc; Am Chem Soc. **Research Statement & Publications:** Molecular electronic spectrosocpy; molecular photophysics. **Mailing Address:** Dept Chem, Univ Akron, KNCL 319a, Akron, OH 44325-3601. **Fax:** 330-972-6407. **E-Mail:** elim@uakron.edu

LIM, H(ENRY) C(HOL), CHEMICAL & BIOCHEMICAL ENGINEERING. **Personal Data:** b Seoul, Korea, October 24, 1935; American citizen; m Sun; c David, Carol & Michael. **Education:** Okla State Univ, BS, 1957; Univ Mich, MSE, 1959; Northwestern Univ, PhD (chem eng), 1967. **Honors & Awards:** Food Pharmaceut & Bioeng Award, Am Inst Chem Eng, 1987. **Professional Experience:** PROF CHEM & BIOCHEM ENG & PROF MICROBIOL & MOLECULAR GENETICS, UNIV CALIF, IRVINE, 1987-; Vis scholar, Calif Inst Technol, 1977; from asst prof to prof chem eng, Purdue Univ, 1966-1987; Process develop engr, Pfizer, Inc, 1959-1963. **Memberships:** Am Inst Chem Engrs; Am Soc Microbiol; Am Chem Soc. **Research Statement & Publications:** Modelling, optimization and control of chemical and biochemical processes; biological reactor engineering; cellular growth kenetics; optimal operating strategies for and on-line optimization of fed-batch bioreactors; engineering of recombinant cell product expression and secretion. **Mailing Address:** Chem Eng & Materials Sci, 816F Eng Tower, Univ Calif, Irvine, CA 92697-2575. **Fax:** 949-824-2541. **E-Mail:** hclim@uci.edu

LIM, HONG SEH, IMAGE PROCESSING, COMPUTER VISION. **Personal Data:** b Hong Kong, August 5, 1958; m 1984, c 3. **Education:** Univ Hong Kong, BSc, 1981; Stanford Univ, MS (elec eng) & MS (opers res), 1983, MS & PhD (elec eng), 1987. **Professional Experience:** PRES, MIL KERED INC, 1992-; lang mgr, Calera Recognition Systs, 1991-1992; staff mem, Los Angeles Sci Ctr, IBM, 1987-1990 & Palo Alto Sci Ctr, 1990-1991; consult, Univ Calif, San Francisco, 1990-1991; lectr, Univ Calif, Los Angeles, 1989; prin investr, AKM Assocs, 1985-1987; res asst, Stanford Univ, 1982-1987. **Memberships:** Sr mem Inst Elec & Electronics Engrs; Asn Comput Mach; Optical Soc Am; Opers Res Soc Am; Inst Mgt Sci. **Research Statement & Publications:** Application of image processing and computer vision to target identification, object recognition, industrial parts identification and manufacturing inspection; character recognition; multimedia, video compression. **Mailing Address:** Mil Kered Inc, 101 First St Ste 552, Los Altos, CA 94022. **E-Mail:** lim@btr.com

LIM, JAMES KHAI-JIN, PHARMACEUTICS. **Personal Data:** b Batavia, Java, March 11, 1933; American citizen; m 1962, c 3. **Education:** Univ Malaya, Singapore, BPharm, 1958; Univ NC, MS, 1962, PhD (pharmaceut), 1965. **Professional Experience:** RETIRED; prof pharm, sch pharm, WVa Univ, beginning 1976; dent res, inst Advan Educ Dent Res, 1971; from asst prof to assoc prof, Sch Pharm, Wva Univ, 1966-1976; vis scientist, Lipid Dept, Med Div, Oak Ridge, 1965-1966; res fel, Biochem Dept, Univ NC, 1965-1966. **Memberships:** Am Pharmaceut Asn; Am Asn Pharmaceut Sci; Am Asn Col Pharm; Am Asn Dent Res; Malayan Pharmaceut Asn; Soc Cosmetic Chemists. **Research Statement & Publications:** Pharmaceutical formulations for solubilization and stability of drugs; caries research involving in vitro pellicle and streptococci plaque; blood cholesterol and triglyceride levels with fiber diets; viscosity measurements of semisolids; tableting formulations. **Mailing Address:** Sch Pharm, Health Sci Ctr, WVa Univ, Morgantown, WV 26506.

LIM, JOHNG KI, GENETICS. **Personal Data:** b Seoul, Korea, February 12, 1930. **Education:** Univ Minn, BS, 1958, MS, 1960, PhD (genetics), 1964. **Professional Experience:** Vis prof, Dept Med Genetics, Univ Wis-Madison, 1977-1978; PROF BIOL, UNIV WIS-EAU CLAIRE, 1969-; from asst prof to assoc prof, Univ Wis-eau Claire, 1963-1969. **Memberships:** AAAS; Genetics Soc Am; Environ Mutagen Soc; Sigma Xi. **Research Statement & Publications:** Chemical mutagenesis; cytogenetics. **Mailing Address:** Dept Biol, Univ Wis, Eau Claire, WI 54701.

LIM, RAMON (KHE SIONG), NEUROCHEMISTRY. **Personal Data:** b Cebu, Philippines, February 5, 1933; m 1961, Victoria; c Jennifer, Wendell & Caroline. **Education:** Univ Santo Tomas, Manila, MD, 1958; Univ Pa, PhD (biochem), 1966. **Professional Experience:** EMER PROF NEUROL, UNIV IOWA, as of 2006; Nat Yang-Ming Med Col, Taipei, 1987; Int Soc Neurochem lectureship, China, 1986; prof & dir Neurol & Neurochem, Univ Iow, beginning 1981; Cent Univ Venezuela, Caracas, 1978; assoc prof neurochem, Brain Res Inst & Sect Neurosurg, Univ Chicago, 1976-1981; vis prof, Univ Santo Tomas, Manila, 1974; asst prof neurosurg & biochem, Brain Res Inst & Sect Neurosurg, Univ Chicago, 1969-1976; NIMH spec res fel, 1968-1969; asst res biochemist, Ment Health Res Inst, Univ Mich, 1966-1969; USPHS trainee & fel, Univ Pa, 1960-1966; intern, Long Island Col Hosp, NY, 1959-1960. **Memberships:** AAAS; Am Soc Neurochem; Int Soc Neurochem; Am Soc Biochem & Molecular Biol; Soc Neuroscience; Am Soc Cell Biol; Int Soc Develop Neursci. **Research Statement & Publications:** Brain proteins and peptides; tissue culture; growth and maturation of brain cells; signal transduction; molecular biology. **Mailing Address:** 118 Richards St, Iowa City, IA 52246-3516. **Fax:** 319-335-8528. **E-Mail:** ramon-lim@uiowa.edu

LIM, SOON-SIK, GAS LASERS, NUCLEAR PUMPED GAS LASERS. **Personal Data:** b Kaesung, Korea, March 2, 1944; American citizen; m 1973, Jae; c Steve & Anna. **Education:** Yonsei Univ, BS, 1971; Wayne State Univ, MS, 1975, PhD (chem eng), 1981. **Professional Experience:** PROF CHEM ENG, YOUNGSTOWN STATE UNIV, 1991-; from asst prof to assoc prof, Youngstown State Univ, 1981-1991; res engr, Pac Chem Co, 1970-1973. **Memberships:** Am Inst Chem Engrs; Am Chem Soc; Am Soc Eng Educ; Sigma Xi. **Research Statement & Publications:** Hazardous waste incineration calculation. **Mailing Address:** Dept Chem Eng, Youngstown State Univ, 2064 Moser Hall, Youngstown, OH 44514. **E-Mail:** slim@ysu.edu

LIM, SUNG MAN, PLANT PATHOLOGY. **Personal Data:** American citizen; m 1968, c 2. **Education:** Seoul Univ, Korea, MS, 1959; Miss State Univ, MS, 1963; Mich State Univ, PhD (crop sci & plant path), 1966. **Honors & Awards:** Soybean Researcher's Award, Am Soybean Asn; Distinguished Sci Award, Minist Sci & Technol, Korea. **Professional Experience:** FAC & HEAD, DEPT PLANT PATH, UNIV ARK, as of 2004; PROF, PLANT PATH, 1983-; PLANT PATHOLOGIST, USDA, 1977-; from asst prof to assoc prof, plant path, 1971-1983; res assoc, Univ Ill, 1967-1971; res asst, Mich State Univ, 1963-1966; res asst, Miss State Univ, 1961-1963; Agronomist, Crop Exp Sta, Suwon, Korea, 1960-1961; assoc ed, Plant Dis; assoc ed & sr ed, Phytopath; mem, Soybean Germplasm Adv Comt, USDA. **Memberships:** Fel Am Phytopath Soc; Am Genetic Asn; Am Soc Agron; Crop Sci Soc Am; fel AAAS. **Research Statement & Publications:** Epidemics of plant diseases; genetics of host-pathogen interactions. **Mailing Address:** Dept Plant Path, Univ Ark, 217 Plant Sci Bldg, Fayetteville, AR 72701. **Fax:** 479-575-7601. **E-Mail:** smlim@uark.edu

LIM, TECK-KAH, THEORETICAL NUCLEAR PHYSICS, THEORETICAL ATOMIC & MOLECULAR PHYSICS. **Personal Data:** b Malacca, Malaysia, December 1, 1942; m 1966, Nyok-Kheng; c Kian-Tat & Ai-Li. **Education:** Univ Adelaide, BS, 1964, PhD (nuclear physics), 1968. **Professional Experience:** Associate Vice Provost for Graduate Studies, DREXEL UNIVERSITY, 2005-; PROF PHYSICS & ATMOSPHERIC SCI, DREXEL UNIV, 1982-; assoc prof, Drexel Univ, 1975-1982; Humboldt Fellow, 1980-1981; asst prof physics, Drexel Univ, 1970-1975; res assoc nuclear physics, Fla State Univ, 1968-1970; lectr math, Univ Malaya, 1968; Consultant, UN Develop Prog, 1985; secy-treas, Topical Group, few-body systs, Am Phys Soc, 1986-1992. **Memberships:** fel Am Phys Soc. **Research Statement & Publications:** Few-nucleon problem; spin-polarized quantum systems; chemical physics; molecular physics; computers in education. **Mailing Address:** Dept Physics, Drexel Univ, Philadelphia, PA 19104. **Fax:** 215-895-5934. **E-Mail:** limtk@drexel.edu

LIM, TEONG CHENG, APPLIED PHYSICS, ELECTRICAL ENGINEERING. **Personal Data:** b Penang, Malaysia, October 4, 1939; m 1966. **Education:** Nat Taiwan Univ, BS, 1963; Ottawa Univ, MS, 1964; McGill Univ, PhD (elec eng), 1968. **Professional Experience:** DIR CORP DEVELOP & ACTG CHIEF EXEC OFFICER, ELECTRONIC SENSOR TECHNOL, CA, as of 2005; PRES, AMERASIA TECHNOL INC, 1984-; mgr, Sci Ctr, Rockwell Int, beginning 1980; group leader, Sci Ctr, NAm Rockwell Corp, 1975-1980; mem tech staff, Sci Ctr, NAm Rockwell Corp, 1970-1974; Nat Res Coun Can fel, Imp Col, Univ London, 1968-1970; res asst elec eng, McGill Univ, 1965-1968; electronic engr, Can Marconi Co, Montreal, 1965; res asst elec eng, Ottawa Univ, 1963-1964; elec engr, Malayan Racing Asn, 1962-1963. **Memberships:** Sr mem Inst Elec & Electronics Engrs; Brit Inst Elec Engrs. **Research Statement & Publications:** Physics of ferroelectric and display materials and devices. **Mailing Address:** Amerasia Technol Inc, 2307 Townsgate Rd, Westlake Village, CA 91361. **E-Mail:** tclim@estcal.com

LIM, YOUNG WOON (PETER), SURFACE CHEMISTRY, COLLOID CHEMISTRY. **Personal Data:** b Seoul, Korea, October 25, 1935; m 1968, c 3. **Education:** Ohio Wesleyan Univ, AB, 1957; Univ Dayton, MS, 1963; State Univ NY Col Forestry, Syracuse, PhD (polymer chem), 1969. **Professional Experience:** UNION CAMP, FRANKLIN, 1992-; proj leader, Boise Cascade, 1982-1992; proj leader, Crown Zellerbach Cent Res, Camas, Wash, 1977-1982; res assoc chem, Tissue & Towel Res & Develop, Am Consumer Prod, Am Can Co, Neenah, Wis, 1974-1977; group leader analytical chem, Appleton Papers Div, 1971-1974; res chemist, Paper Res Dept, NCR Corp, 1969-1971. **Memberships:** Am Chem Soc; Tech Asn Pulp & Paper Indust. **Research Statement & Publications:** Application of surface and colloid chemistry to pulp and paper research and development; morphology of cellulose and synthetic fibers; functional coatings; microencapsulation. **Mailing Address:** 1318 Meade Dr, Suffolk, VA 23434.

LIMA, GAIL M, INVERTEBRATE ZOOLOGY. **Personal Data:** b Cambridge, Mass, July 2, 1957. **Education:** Wash Univ, St Louis, AB, 1979; Tufts Univ, Medford, Mass, MS, 1983; Rutgers Univ, New Brunswick, PhD (zoology), 1987. **Professional Experience:** Res assoc, Boshe Inst, 1991-; ASST PROF BIOL, ILL WESLEYAN UNIV, 1987-. **Memberships:** Am Soc Zoologists; Am Malacological Union; Sigma Xi; Nat Asn Biol Teachers; Asn Biol Lab Educ. **Research Statement & Publications:** Invertebrate reproduction and development; larval biology; ecological and developmental implications of molluscan shell morphology; zebra mussel biology. **Mailing Address:** 68 Lincoln St, Dover Foxcroft, ME 04426. **Fax:** 309-556-3411. **E-Mail:** limag@vmd.cso.uiuc.edu

LIMA, JOHN J, CLINICAL PHARMACOKINETICS. **Personal Data:** b New Bedford, Mass, June 19, 1940; c 2. **Education:** Bridgewater State Col, BSEd, 1962; Mass Col Pharm, BS, 1967; Univ Mich, PharmD, 1977. **Professional Experience:** RETIRED; assoc prof pharm, Ohio State Univ, 1979-1993; res assoc, State Univ NY, Buffalo, 1977-1978; fel, State Univ NY, Buffalo, 1976-1977; pharm dir, Al Jordan Health Ctr, 1972-1975. **Memberships:** Am Asn Pharmaceut Scientist; Am Col Clin Pharm; Am Asn Cols Pharm. **Research Statement & Publications:** Modelling time course; extent and mechanisms associated with drug/hormone induced adaptations, specifically hypersensitivity to adrenergic stimulation folling chronic treatment with certain drugs. **Mailing Address:** 1525 Bethel Rd Apt 100, Columbus, OH 43220.

LIMB, JOHN ORMOND, COMMUNICATIONS, ELECTRICAL ENGINEERING. **Personal Data:** b Pinjarra, Australia. **Education:** Univ Western Australia, BEE, 1963, PhD (elec eng), 1967. **Honors & Awards:** Leonard G Abraham Award, Inst Elec & Electronics Engrs, 1973, Alexander Graham Bell Medal, 1991. **Professional Experience:** Lab dir, media technol lab, Hewlett-Packard Labs, 1992-1994; lab mgr, technol anal, Hewlett-Packard Labs, 1989-1992; lab dir, Hewlett-Packard Labs, 1986-1989; ed-in-chief, J Selected Areas Commun, Inst Elec & Electronics Engrs, 1984-1988; div mgr, Bell Commun Res, 1983-1985; dept head commun, Bell Tel Labs, 1971-1983; mem tech staff, Bell Tel Labs, 1967-1971; engr, res labs, Australian Post Off, 1966-1967; ed, Treas on Commun, Inst Elec & Electronics Engrs. **Memberships:** Optical Soc Am; fel Inst Elec & Electronics Engrs; Asn Comput Mach. **Research Statement & Publications:** Visual communications; efficient coding of picture signals; human visual perception; high-speed communications; interactive video systems. **Mailing Address:** Hewlett-Packard Labs, 1501 Page Mill Rd, Palo Alto, CA 94304. **Fax:** 650-813-3706. **E-Mail:** limb@hpl.hp.com

LIMBERT, DAVID EDWIN, DYNAMIC SYSTEMS MODELING & SIMULATION, CONTROL SYSTEMS ENGINEERING. **Personal Data:** b Omaha, Nebr, October 21, 1942; m 1972, Norma; c Sarah & Jarrod. **Education:** Iowa State Univ, BS-ME, 1964; Case Inst Technol, MS, 1965; Case Western Res Univ, PhD (control eng), 1969. **Honors & Awards:** Rail Transp Award, Am Soc Mech Engrs, 1991. **Professional Experience:** Senior Consultant/Owner, DEL Engineering, 1998-present; Retired from Univ of New Hampshire 1998: Prof Mech Eng 1983-1998, Assoc Prof 1974-1983, Assist Prof 1969-1974. **Memberships:** Am Soc Mech Engrs; Air Brake Assn; Sigma Xi. **Research Statement & Publications:** Modeling and computer simulation of freight train air brake systems including piping and valves; boundary element simulation of electric fields for electroplating; communication aids for handicapped; electric wheel chair controller design. **Mailing Address:** DEL Eng, 282 Notch Rd, Hiram, ME 04041-3431. **E-Mail:** contact_us@delEng.com

LIMBERT, DOUGLAS A(LAN), INSTRUMENTED SYSTEM & COMPONENT TESTING, SYSTEM DYNAMICS. **Personal Data:** b Council Bluffs, Iowa, February 6, 1948. **Education:** Mass Inst Technol, SB & SM, 1970, ScD, 1977. **Professional Experience:** PRIN ENGR & ASSOC DIR, FAILURE ANAL ASSOCS, EXPONENTS TEST & ENG CTR, PHOENIX, as of 2006; sr managing engr, Failure Analysis Assocs, Inc, beginning 1990; managing engr, Failure Analysis Assocs, Inc, 1984-1990; Assoc ed, Am Soc Mech Engrs Trans: J Dynamic Systs & Control, 1984-1987; asst prof mech eng, Ariz State Univ, 1977-1984; Instr mech eng, Mass Inst Technol, 1974-1976. **Memberships:** Sigma Xi; Am Soc Mech Engrs; Inst Elec & Electronic Engrs; Soc Automotive Engrs. **Research Statement & Publications:** Modeling, dynamics and control of physical systems; advanced ground transportation suspensions; test engineering; instrumentation; automotive engineering; failure analysis. **Mailing Address:** Failure Anal Assocs, Exponents Test & Eng, Phoenix, AZ 85027.

LIMBIRD, LEE EBERHARDT, SIGNAL TRANSDUCTION, MOLECULAR BASIS HORMONE & DRUG ACTION. **Personal Data:** b Philadelphia, Pa, November 27, 1948; m 1970, Thomas; c Eric & Jessica. **Education:** Col Wooster, BA, 1970; Univ NC, Chapel Hill, PhD (biochem), 1973. **Honors & Awards:** John Jacob Abel Award. **Professional Experience:** ASSOC VICE CHANCELLOR RES, VANDERBILT UNIV, as of 2004; PROF & CHAIR, DEPT PHARMACOL, VANDERBILT UNIV, 1983-. **Research Statement & Publications:** alpha-adrenergic receptors as a model system for understanding signal transduction via G-protein coupled receptors; structure function relationships of individual receptors; evaluating mechanisms for receptor targeting to partial or microdomains in cells; homologous recombination to introduce intentionally modified alpha receptor structures into the mouse genome. **Mailing Address:** Vanderbilt Univ Med Ctr, 417B PRB, Nashville, TN 37232-6600. **Fax:** 615-343-7286. **E-Mail:** llimbird@mmc.edu

LIMBURG, WILLIAM W, ORGANIC POLYMER CHEMISTRY. **Personal Data:** b Buffalo, NY, November 9, 1935; m 1966. **Education:** Univ Buffalo, BA, 1959, MA, 1962; Univ Toronto, PhD (organosilicon chem), 1965. **Professional Experience:** RETIRED; prin scientist, Supplies Delivery Unit, ending 2001; tech specialist & proj mgr, Xerox Corp, beginning 1980; sr scientist, 1973-1980; scientist, 1967-1973; from sr chemist to assoc scientist, 1965-1966. **Memberships:** Am Chem Soc; Royal Soc Chem; Soc Photog Scientists & Engrs. **Research Statement & Publications:** Synthesis of organometallic compounds; mechanistic and stereochemical studies of molecular rearrangements of carbon-functional silicon-containing compounds; non-silver halide imaging methods; synthesis of organic photoconductive materials; synthesis of novel polysiloxanes. **Mailing Address:** 66 Clearview Dr, Penfield, NY 14526-2433.

LIMERICK, JACK MCKENZIE, SR, CHEMISTRY. **Personal Data:** b Fredericton, NB, July 16, 1910; m 1937. **Education:** Univ NB, BSc, 1931, MSc, 1934. **Honors & Awards:** Award, Tech Asn Pulp & Paper Indust, 1959, 1982 & 1990. **Professional Experience:** CONSULT, PULP, PAPER & CONTAINER INDUST, BRAZIL, 1973- & US & CAN, 1980-; consult, Iran, 1972-1978; assoc dir res & develop, Consol-Bathurst Ltd, 1967-1971; Lectr, Royal Tech Inst, Sweden, 1952; tech & res dir, Bathurst Paper Co Ltd, 1944-1967; supt, Control Dept, 1941-1944; chief chemist, Bathurst Paper Co, 1937-1941; res chemist, Fraser Co, 1934-1937. **Memberships:** Fel Tech Asn Pulp & Paper Indust; Can Pulp & Paper Asn; fel Chem Inst Can; Pulp & Paper Res Inst Can. **Research Statement & Publications:** Pulp; paper; containers; author of over 100 publications. **Mailing Address:** 36 E St PH4, Oakville, ON L6L 5K2, Can.

LIMPERT, FREDERICK ARTHUR, HYDROLOGY. **Personal Data:** b Frankfort, NY, February 4, 1921; m 1944, Patricia Cheney. **Education:** Wash State Univ, BSCE, 1943. **Honors & Awards:** Meritorious Serv Award, US Dept Interior. **Professional Experience:** RETIRED; Mem, Interagency Adv Comt Water Data, 1972- & Coord Coun Water Data Acquisition Methods, 1974-; head hydrol sect & chief hydrologist, Bonneville Power Admin, 1961-1977; Civil engr, Columbia Basin Proj, Wash Bur Reclamation, 1946-1961. **Memberships:** Fel Am Soc Civil Engrs; Nat Soc Prof Engrs; Western Snow Conf. **Research Statement & Publications:** Use of satellite data for determining areal snow cover and cloud classification for areal precipitation. **Mailing Address:** 10701 Pinion Lane, Sun City, AZ 85373-1831. **E-Mail:** fritzlimpert@juno.com

LIMPERT, RUDOLF, MECHANICAL ENGINEERING. **Personal Data:** b Neuhaldensleben, Ger, March 19, 1936; American citizen; m 1962, c 6. **Education:** Wolfenbuettel Univ, Ger, Ing, 1958; Brigham Young Univ, BES & MS, 1968; Univ Mich, Ann Arbor, PhD (mech eng), 1972. **Professional Experience:** CONSULT, MOTOR VEHICLE SAFETY, 1981-; res prof, Univ Utah, 1973-1981; safety stand engr, Nat Hwy Traffic Safety Admin, Dept Transp, 1972-1973; res asst, Hwy Safety Res Inst, Univ Mich, Ann Arbor, 1969-1972; proj engr, Alfred Teves Corp, Ger, 1963-1965. **Memberships:** Soc Automotive Engrs. **Research Statement & Publications:** Motor vehicle accident reconstruction and cause analysis; product liability research; automotive systems design. **Mailing Address:** 1071 Tollgate Rd, Park City, UT 84098.

LIN, ALICE LEE LAN, SPACE PHYSICS, ELECTRO-OPTICS & ACOUSTO-OPTICS, NON DESTRUCTIVE TESTING OF MATERIALS. **Personal Data:** b Shanghai, China, October 28, 1937; American citizen; m 1962, c Peter A. **Education:** Univ Calif, Berkeley, AB, 1963; George Wash Univ, MA, 1974. **Honors & Awards:** Mencius Educ Award. **Professional Experience:** PHYSICIST, MECH MAT DIV, US ARMY MAT TECHNOL LAB, WATERTOWN, MASS, 1982-; physicist, Nondestructive Eval Br, 1980-1982; physicist, Goddard Space Flight Ctr, NASA, Univ Greenbelt, Md, 1975-1980; teaching fel physics, George Wash Univ, Wash, DC, 1972-1974; info anal specialist, Nat Acad Sci, Wash, DC, 1970-1971; res asst physics, Cavendish Lab, Cambridge, Eng, 1965-1966; physicist & instr, physics instr mat technol sch, Nondestructive Testing Sch, Army Res Lab, Watertown, Mass. **Memberships:** Am Phys Soc; Am Soc Nondestructive Testing; Soc Exp Stress Anal; Am Ceramic Soc; NY Acad Sci; AAAS. **Research Statement & Publications:** Nondestructive methods to detect flaws in materials. **Mailing Address:** 28 Hallett Hill Rd, 02493, MA 02193. **Fax:** 781-899-6751. **E-Mail:** plinmarcus@gis.net

LIN, ANTHONY T, PLASMA PHYSICS. **Personal Data:** b Taiwan, June 25, 1941. **Education:** Nat Taiwan Univ, BS, 1963; ETenn State Univ, MS, 1966; Univ Mich, PhD (elec eng), 1970. **Professional Experience:** FAC MEM, DEPT PHYSICS, UNIV CALIF, LOS ANGELES, 1973-. **Memberships:** Fel Am Phys Soc. **Mailing Address:** Dept Physics, Univ Calif, 1-130R Knudsen, Los Angeles, CA 90024. **E-Mail:** lin@physics.ucla.edu

LIN, BENJAMIN MING-REN, COMPUTER NETWORKING, REAL-TIME SYSTEMS. **Personal Data:** American citizen; m 1970, c 2. **Education:** Taipei Inst Technol, dipl, 1961; Univ Wyo, MS, 1967; Univ Iowa, PhD (elec eng), 1973. **Professional Experience:** Vis prof, Shandong Inst Mining & Technol, China, 1988; Dir, Grad Sch Info Eng, Tamkang Univ, Taiwan, 1980-1981; PROF COMPUT SCI, MOORHEAD STATE UNIV, 1973-; engr, Addressograph Multigraph Corp, 1968-1969; design & develop engr, Collins Radio Co, 1967-1968; Engr, Radio Wave Res Labs, 1962-1965. **Memberships:** Sigma Xi; Asn Comput Mach; Inst Elec & Electronics Engrs; Comput Soc. **Research Statement & Publications:** Application of microprocessors in consumer products and data communications; fault-tolerant computing systems design; computer architecture in artificial intelligence; real-time signature verification. **Mailing Address:** Moorhead State Univ, Moorhead, MN 56560.

LIN, BOR-LUH, MATHEMATICS. **Personal Data:** b Fukien, China, March 4, 1935; m 1963, Hsin; c David, Michael & James. **Education:** Nat Taiwan Univ, BS, 1956; Univ Notre Dame, MS, 1960; Northwestern Univ, PhD (math), 1963. **Professional Experience:** PROF MATH, UNIV IOWA, 1972-; vis prof, Univ Calif, Santa Barbara; vis assoc prof, Ohio State Univ, 1970-1971; from asst prof to assoc prof, Univ Iowa, 1963-1972. **Memberships:** Am Math Soc. **Research Statement & Publications:** Functional analysis, Banach spare theory; minimax theorems. **Mailing Address:** Univ Iowa, Iowa City, IA 52242-0001. **Fax:** 319-335-0627. **E-Mail:** bllin@math.uiowa.edu

LIN, CHARLES C L, MATHEMATICS. **Education:** NC State Univ, BSc. **Professional Experience:** STAFF, SAS INST, as of 2006. **Mailing Address:** SAS Inst PO Box 8000, Cary, NC 27513. **Fax:** 919-677-4444. **E-Mail:** clin@eng.umd.edu

LIN, CHENTAO, PLANT DEVELOPMENT BIOLOGY, PHOTOSENSORY SIGNAL TRANSDUCTION. **Personal Data:** m 1987, Hongyun; c Marysa D & Sophia D. **Education:** Iowa State Univ, MS, 1988; Mich State Univ, PhD (genetics), 1992. **Professional Experience:** PROF, MOLECULAR, CELL & DEVELOPMENTAL BIOLOGY, UNIV CALIF, LOS ANGELES, as of 2006; assoc prof, Univ Calif, Los Angeles, beginning 2001; asst prof, Univ Calif, Los Angeles, 1996-2001; asst prof, Univ Calif, Los Angeles, 1996-; NIH fel, Univ Pa, 1992-1996. **Memberships:** AAAS; Am Soc Plant Physiologists. **Research Statement & Publications:** Molecular mechanism of the function and signal transduction of photosensory receptors in higher plants. **Mailing Address:** Dept Molecular Cell Develop Biol, Univ Calif, 3317 Life Sci Bldg, Los Angeles, CA 90095-1606. **Fax:** 310-206-3987. **E-Mail:** clin@mcdb.ucla.edu

LIN, CHIA CHIAO, APPLIED MATHEMATICS. **Personal Data:** b Foochow, China, July 7, 1916; American citizen. **Education:** Nat Tsing Hua Univ, China, BSc, 1937; Univ Toronto, MA, 1941; Calif Inst Technol, PhD (aeronaut), 1944. **Honorary Degrees:** LLD, Chinese Univ Hong Kong, 1973. **Honors & Awards:** John Von Neumann lectr, Soc Indust & Appl Math-Am Math Soc, 1967; Otto Laporte Mem lectr, Am Phys Soc, 1973, DSD Prize, 1979; Timoshenko Medal, Am Soc Mech Engrs, 1975; Award Appl Math & Numerical Anal, Nat

Acad Sci, 1977; Fluid Dynamics Prize, Am Phys Soc & US Off Naval Res, 1979. **Professional Experience:** INST PROF EMER MATH, MASS INST TECHNOL, 1987-; mem, Comt on Support Res Math Sci, Nat Acad Sci, 1966-1968; mem, Inst Advan Study, Princeton, NJ, 1959-1960, 1965-1966; Guggenheim fels, 1953 & 1960; from assoc prof to inst prof, Mass Inst Technol, 1947-1987; from asst prof to assoc prof appl math, Brown Univ, 1945-1947; from asst to res engr, Calif Inst Technol, 1943-1945; asst, Tsing Hua Univ, China, 1937-1939. **Memberships:** Nat Acad Sci; Am Astron Soc; Soc Indust & Appl Math (pres, 1972-1974); Am Math Soc; fel Am Acad Arts & Sci; Am Philos Soc; Am Phys Soc; fel Inst Aerospace Sci. **Research Statement & Publications:** Hydrodynamics; stellar dynamics; astrophysical problems; spiral structure of galaxies; density wave theory developed in great mathematical detail with predictions checked against various astronomical observations. **Mailing Address:** Mass Inst Technol, Dept Math, Rm 2-330, Cambridge, MA 02139. **E-Mail:** cclin@math.mit.edu

LIN, CHII-DONG, ATOMIC PHYSICS. **Personal Data:** b Taiwan. **Education:** Nat Taiwan Univ, BS, 1969; Univ Chicago, MS, 1973, PhD (physics), 1974. **Professional Experience:** DISTINGUISHED PROF, KANS STATE UNIV, as of 2004; prof, kans state univ, beginning 1984; Sloan fel, 1979-1983; from asst prof to assoc prof, Kans State Univ, 1976-1980; fel astrophys, Ctr Astrophys, Harvard Col Observ, 1974-1976. **Memberships:** fel Am Phys Soc. **Mailing Address:** Dept Physics, Kans State Univ Cardwell Hall, Manhattan, KS 66506. **Fax:** 785-532-6806. **E-Mail:** cdlin@phys.ksu.edu

LIN, CHIN-CHUNG, BIOCHEMICAL PHARMACOLOGY. **Personal Data:** b Taipei, Taiwan, October 8, 1937; c 2. **Education:** Chung Hsing Univ, Taiwan, BS, 1960; Tuskegee Inst, MS, 1965; Northwestern Univ, PhD (biochem), 1969. **Professional Experience:** VPRES DRUG DEVELOP, VALEANT PHARMACEUT INT, 2002-; assoc dir, Schering Corp, beginning 1983; res fel, Schering Corp, 1979-1982; prin scientist, Schering Corp, 1975-1979; sr scientist, Schering Corp, 1969-1975; res fel biochem, Med Sch, Northwestern Univ, 1969. **Memberships:** AAAS; Am Chem Soc; Am Soc Pharmacol & Exp Therapeut; NY Acad Sci Res; Drug Metab & Mechanism Enzymatic Hydroxylation. **Mailing Address:** Valeant Pharmaceut Int, Valeant Plaza 3300 Hyland Ave, Costa Mesa, CA 92626. **Fax:** 714-556-0131.

LIN, CHING Y, ANIMAL BREEDING, QUANTITATIVE GENETICS. **Personal Data:** b Taiwan, May 22, 1940; Canadian citizen; m 1965, c 2. **Education:** Nat Chung-Hsing Univ, Taiwan, BS, 1963; Iowa State Univ, MS, 1971; Ohio State Univ, PhD (dairy sci), 1976. **Professional Experience:** Adj prof, Univ Guelph, Can, as of 2003; vis res fel, Japan, 1989-1990; RES SCIENTIST, AGR CAN, 1980-; res assoc poultry breeding, Dept Animal Sci, Univ Guelph, Can, 1976-1980; Jr specialist agr exten, Taiwan Prov Dept Agr & Forestry, 1964-1968. **Memberships:** Am Soc Animal Sci; Am Dairy Sci Asn; Can Soc Animal Sci. **Research Statement & Publications:** Dairy cattle breeding; quantitative genetics; statistical analysis as applied to animal breeding. **Mailing Address:** Dept Animal & Poultry Sci, Ctr Genetic Improv Livestock, Univ Guelph, Guelph, ON N1G 2W1, Can. **Fax:** 519-767-0573. **E-Mail:** clin@aps.uoguelph.ca

LIN, CHING-FANG, AERONAUTICS. **Education:** Univ Mich, Phd, (comput Info & control eng), 1980. **Professional Experience:** PRES & CHIEF EXEC OFFICER, AM GNC CORP, 1986-. **Mailing Address:** Am GNC Corp, PO Box 10987, Canoga Park, CA 91309-1987. **Fax:** 818-407-0093. **E-Mail:** cflin@americangnc.com

LIN, CHINLON, BROADBAND OPTICAL FIBER COMMUNICATIONS, CABLE TELEVISION & DIGITAL VIDEO DISTRIBUTION SYSTEMS. **Personal Data:** b Taiwan, China, January 19, 1945; m 1969, Helen Chou; c Thomas Yichiao & Daniel Yibin. **Education:** Nat Taiwan Univ, BS, 1967; Univ Ill, MS, 1970; Univ Calif, Berkeley, PhD (elec eng), 1974. **Professional Experience:** PROF PHOTONICS, CHINESE UNIV HONG KONG, as of 2003; DIR, INST OPTICAL SCI & TECHNOL, as of 2003; J Lightwave Technol Inst Elec & Electronics Engrs, 1991-1994; dir, Broadband Lightwave Systs, Bell Commun Res, beginning 1986; vis guest prof, Tech Univ Denmark, 1984; assoc ed, J Appl Optics, Optical Soc Am, 1982-1984; Mem tech staff, Laser Sci Res, Bell Labs, Holmdel, 1974-1985. **Memberships:** fel Inst Elec & Electronics Engrs; fel Optical Soc Am; fel Photonics Soc Chinese Am. **Research Statement & Publications:** Lasers and quantum electronics; optical fibers and lightwave communications; advanced photonics technologies and applications to broadband optical fiber telecommunications; high-capacity video distribution systems. **Mailing Address:** Dept Electronic eng, Chinese Univ Hong Kong, Rm 404, Ho Sin Hang eng Bldg, Shatin N T, China.

LIN, CHIN-TARNG, CELL BIOLOGY, NEUROBIOLOGY. **Personal Data:** b Chu-Nan, Taiwan, December 11, 1938; American citizen; m 1983, c 1. **Education:** Nat Taiwan Univ, DDS, 1963; Med Br, Univ Tex, Galveston, PhD (cell biol), 1975. **Professional Experience:** PROF PATHOL, COL MED, NAT TAIWAN UNIV, 1989-; RES FEL, INST BIOMED SCI, ACAD SINICA, TAIPEI, TAIWAN, ROC, 1987-; vis prof, dept pathol, 1987-1989; asst prof, Dept Physiol, Col Med, Pa State Univ, 1983-1987; res instr, Dept Cell Biol, Baylor Col Med, 1980-1983; res assoc, Dept Cell Biol, Baylor Col Med, 1978-1980; assoc prof path, Dept Path, Col Med, Nat Taiwan Univ, 1975-1978; teaching asst, Div Cell Biol, Med Br, Univ Tex, Galveston, 1971-1975; instr, Dept Path, Col Med, Nat Taiwan Univ, 1969-1975; Doctor & teaching asst path, Dept Path, Col Med, Nat Taiwan Univ, 1964-1969. **Memberships:** Histochem Soc; AAAS; Am Soc Cell Biol; Soc Neurosci. **Research Statement & Publications:** Immunochemical approaches to protein synthesis and transport in normal and cancer cells; cell biology; neurobiology; neurotransmitter synthesizing enzymes; immunohistochemistry; immunoelectron microscopy; in situ nucleic acid hybridization; monoclonal hybridoma technique; nasopharyngeal carcinoma tumor biology; stroke animal model. **Mailing Address:** Nat Taiwan Univ Hosp, Taipei 10007, Taiwan.

LIN, CHI-WEI, CANCER, BIOCHEMISTRY. **Personal Data:** b Hong Kong, May 16, 1937; m 1965, c 1. **Education:** Nat Taiwan Univ, BS, 1961; Univ Wis-Madison, MS, 1965, PhD (biochem), 1969. **Professional Experience:** RETIRED; dir, Urol Res Lab & Staff Mem, Dept Urol, Mass Gen Hosp, 1979-1997; asst prof path, Sch Med, Tufts Univ, 1972-1980; res assoc, Sch Med, Tufts Univ, 1971-1972; fel cancer res, Sch Med, Tufts Univ, 1969-1971. **Memberships:** Biochem Soc; AAAS; Histochem Soc; Am Asn Cancer Res; Sigma Xi. **Research Statement & Publications:** Biochemical characteristics of cancer, specifically, the studies of tumor-associated enzymes and isozymes, including histaminase, acid phosphatase and alkaline phosphatase; processes of synthesis and distribution of acid hydrolases and the biogenesis of lysosomes. **Mailing Address:** Dept Urol, Mass Gen Hosp, Fruit St, Boston, MA 02114. **E-Mail:** cwlin@humboldt1.com

LIN, CHUN CHIA, ATOMIC & MOLECULAR COLLISIONS, ELECTRONIC ENERGIES OF SOLIDS. **Personal Data:** b Canton, China, March 7, 1930; American citizen. **Education:** Univ Calif, Berkeley, BS, 1951, BA, 1952; Harvard Univ, PhD (chem), 1955. **Honors & Awards:** Will Allis Prize, Am Phys Soc, 1996. **Professional Experience:** Chmn, Div Atomic Molecular & Optical Physics, Am Phys Soc, 1994-1995; chmn elect, Div Atomic Molecular & Optical Physics, Am Phys Soc, 1993-1994; vchmn, Div Atomic Molecular & Optical Physics, Am Phys Soc, 1992-1993; JOHN & ABIGAIL VAN VLECK PROF PHYSICS, UNIV WIS, MADISON, 1991-; chmn, Gaseous Electronics Conf, 1990-1992; consult, Sandia Labs, 1976-1981; secy-treas, Div Electron & Atomic Physics, Am Phys Soc, 1974-1977; secy, Gaseous Electronics Conf, 1973; PROF PHYSICS, UNIV WIS, 1968-; Alfred P Sloan fel, 1962-1966; consult & univ retainee, Tex Instruments, Inc, 1960-1968; from asst prof to prof physics, Univ Okla, 1955-1968. **Memberships:** Am Phys Soc. **Research Statement & Publications:** Atomic and molecular collision processes; radiation of atoms and molecules excited by electron impact and laser irradiation; electronic energy band theory of crystalline solids, impurity atoms in solids, amorphous solids. **Mailing Address:** Dept Physics, Univ Wis, 1318 Chamberlin Hall Thomas C 1150 Univ Ave, Madison, WI 53706. **E-Mail:** cclin@facstaff.wisc.edu

LIN, CHUN-WEL, NEUROSCIENCE. **Personal Data:** b Taipei, Taiwan, December 30, 1953. **Education:** City Col NY, BS, 1976; Mt Sinai Med Ctr, MS, 1979, PhD (neuropharmacol), 1981. **Professional Experience:** GROUP LEADER, ABBOTT LABS, 1992-; assoc res fel, Abbott Labs, 1990-1992; res investr, Abbott Labs, 1987-1990; sr pharmacologist, Abbott Labs, 1984-1987; pharmacologist, Abbott Labs, 1982-1984; researcher, New York Med Sch, 1981-1982. **Memberships:** Soc Neuroscience; Am Soc Pharmacol & Exp Therapeut. **Research Statement & Publications:** Nuero peptide receptors. **Mailing Address:** NeuroSci Area, Abbott Labs, 100 Abbott Park Rd, R4CB, AP9A, Abbott Park, IL 60064-3500. **Fax:** 847-935-3585. **E-Mail:** chun.lin@abbott.com

LIN, DENIS CHUNG KAM, ANALYTICAL CHEMISTRY, MASS SPECTROMETRY. **Personal Data:** b Hong Kong, July 7, 1944; Canadian citizen; m 1969, c 1. **Education:** Univ Man, BS, 1968, MS, 1970, PhD (chem), 1972. **Professional Experience:** ETC CORP, 1980-; staff chemist, Battelle Mem Inst, 1974-1980; fel, Univ Montreal, 1972-1974. **Memberships:** Am Chem Soc; Am Soc Mass Spectrometry; Int Asn Forensic Toxicologists. **Research Statement & Publications:** Identification and quantification of low levels of drugs and their metabolites in biological samples by mass spectrometry and other techniques; nucleic acid and protein sequencing; pyrolytic reactions. **Mailing Address:** 214 Deepdale Dr, Middletown, NJ 07748-3057.

LIN, DIANE CHANG, CELL BIOLOGY, CELL MOTILITY. **Personal Data:** b China, August 6, 1944; American citizen; m 1969, Shin; c Howe & Payton. **Education:** Nat Taiwan Univ, BS, 1966; Univ Calif, Los Angeles, PhD (biol), 1971. **Professional Experience:** RETIRED; prin investr, Johns Hopkins Univ, 1978-1994; res scientist biophys, Johns Hopkins Univ, 1974-1994; Asst res scientist pharmacol, Univ Calif, San Francisco, 1971-1974. **Memberships:** Am Soc Biochem & Molecular Biol; Am Soc Cell Biol. **Research Statement & Publications:** Actin-binding proteins from chicken muscles. **Mailing Address:** Dept Biophys, Johns Hopkins Univ, 3400 N Charles St, Baltimore, MD 21218-2699. **Fax:** 410-516-5170.

LIN, DONG LIANG, PHYSICS, ELECTRICAL ENGINEERING. **Personal Data:** b Taiwan, China, March 5, 1947; m 1971, c 3. **Education:** Nat Taiwan Univ, BS, 1969; Columbia Univ, MS, 1972, PhD (physics), 1975. **Professional Experience:** MEM STAFF, BELL LABS, MURRAY HILLS, NJ, 1980-; staff scientist physics, Sci Appln Inc, 1977-1980; res fel physics, Johns Hopkins Univ, 1975-1977. **Memberships:** Am Phys Soc; Nat Soc Prof Engrs. **Research Statement & Publications:** Atomic physics; plasma physics; solid state physics. **Mailing Address:** Lucent Technol, Bell Labs, Rm 2C-553 600 Mountain Ave, Murray Hill, NJ 07974-0636. **Fax:** 908-582-5857. **E-Mail:** dong@research.bell-labs.com

LIN, DUO-LIANG, THEORETICAL PHYSICS & CONDENSED MATTER PHYSICS, ATOMIC & MOLECULAR & OPTICAL PHYSICS. **Personal Data:** b Ruian, China, May 16, 1930; American citizen; m 1963, Sharon; c Jennifer & Kenneth. **Education:** National Taiwan Norm Univ, BSc, 1956; National Tsing Hua Univ, China, MSc, 1958; Ohio State Univ, PhD (physics), 1961. **Professional Experience:** Profeaaor Emeritus, University at Buffalo, State University of New York, 2003- Assistant Professor, Associate Professor, Professor, University at Buffalo, State University of New York, Buggalo, New York, 1964-2002; Sr vis, Univ, of Oxford 1970-1971; Res Assoc Physics, Yale Univ, 1961-1964; Visiting Professor, Hong Kong University of Science and Technology, Hong Kong, 1993; Lanzhou University, Lanzhou, 1991; Sichuan Univ, Chengdu, 1990-; Shandong Univ, Jinan, 1988-; adj prof, Univ Sci & Technol China, Hefei, 1987-; Southwestern Jiao, Tong Univ, Chengdu, 1987-; adv prof, Chengdu Univ Sci & Technol, 1986-; Tokten consult, UN Develop Prog, 1986-1992; hon prof, Neimonggu Univ, China, 1985-; Southwestern Jiao, Chongqing Univ, 1985-; Liao Ning Univ, Shen Yang, 1981 & Jiaotong Univ, Shanghai, 1985; Tsing Hua Univ, Peking, 1978; Vis Prof, Nat Taiwan Univ, 1971. **Memberships:** Am Phys Soc. **Research Statement & Publications:** Quantum transport theory; electronic and optical properties of semiconductor nanostructures; nonlinear optical response and ultrafast processes in polymers photonics materials; critical phenomena and phase transitions in magnetic films. **Mailing Address:** Dept Physics, State Univ NY, Buffalo, NY 14260-1500. **Fax:** 716-645-2507. **E-Mail:** dllin@buffalo.edu

LIN, EDMUND CHI CHIEN, BIOCHEMISTRY. **Personal Data:** b Peking, China, October 28, 1928; American citizen. **Education:** Univ Rochester, AB, 1952; Harvard Univ, PhD, 1957. **Professional Experience:** PROF EMER MICROBIOL & MOLECULAR GENETICS, HARVARD MED SCH, as of 2004; vis prof biol, Univ Konstanz, Ger, 1981; hon res prof, Inst Plant Physiol, Academia Sinica, Shanghai, beginning 1980; Fogarty Sr Int fel, Univ Paris, VI, 1977-1978; prof chmn dept, Harvard Med Sch, 1973-1975; vis prof, Univ Calif, Berkeley, 1972; prof microbiol & molecular genetics, Harvard Med Sch, beginning 1969; Guggenheim fel, Pasteur Inst Paris, 1969; from asst prof to assoc prof, Harvard Med Sch, 1963-1969; assoc, Harvard Med Sch, 1960-1963; instr biochem, Harvard Med Sch, 1957-1960. **Memberships:** Am Soc Microbiol; Am Soc Biol Chem. **Research Statement & Publications:** Bacterial physiology and genetics and biochemical evolution. **Mailing Address:** Harvard Med Sch, Dept Microbiol & Molecular Genetics, 200 Longwood Ave, Boston, MA 02115. **Fax:** 617-738-7664. **E-Mail:** edmund_lin@hms.harvard.edu

LIN, FENG BOR, ENGINEERING. **Education:** Nat Taiwan Univ, BS, 1968; Univ Pittsburgh, MS, 1971; Carnegie-Mellon Univ, PhD (civil eng), 1975. **Professional Experience:** PROF, DEPT CIVIL & ENVIRON ENG, CLARKSON UNIV, NY, as of 2005. **Mailing Address:** Clarkson Univ Dept Civil & Environ Eng, 228 Rowley Lab PO Box 5710, Potsdam, NY 13699-5710. **Fax:** 315-268-7985. **E-Mail:** iu00@clarkson.edu

LIN, FREDDIE, OPTOELECTRONICS. **Education:** Tex Tech Univ, M.S, 1985, PhD (elec eng), 1987. **Professional Experience:** PRES & CHIEF EXEC OFFICER, BROADATA COMMUN INC, as of 2003; prin invest, Phys Optics Corp, 1987-1996. **Mailing Address:** Broadata Commun Inc, 2545 W 237th St Suite K, Torrance, CA 90505-5229. **Fax:** 310-530-5958. **E-Mail:** flin@broadatacom.com

LIN, FU HAI, MOLECULAR BIOLOGY, NEUROSCIENCES. **Personal Data:** b Fukien, China, February 15, 1928; American citizen; m 1956, Ruth Chen; c Nancy, Alan, Boris, Calvin & David. **Education:** Nat Taiwan Univ, BS, 1953; Univ WVa, MS, 1959; Rutgers Univ, PhD (bact), 1965. **Professional Experience:** RES SCIENTIST V & HEAD LAB VIRAL BIOCHEM, INST BASIC RES DEVELOP DISABILITY, 1976-; assoc res scientist,

Inst Basic Res Develop Disability, 1970-1976; sr res scientist, Inst Basic Res Develop Disability, 1969-1970; asst mem biochem, Albert Einstein Med Ctr, 1965-1969; res asst, Rutgers Univ, 1961-1965; tech asst biochem, Boyce Thompson Inst, 1959-1961; Asst, Univ WVa, 1958-1959. **Memberships:** AAAS; Am Soc Microbiol; Am Chem Soc; Sigma Xi; NY Acad Sci. **Research Statement & Publications:** Mitochondrial mutation in Alzheimer disease and related neurodegenerative syndromes; gene expression of animal RNA viruses of slow infection; biochemistry and function of proteins of slow viruses. **Mailing Address:** Inst Basic Res Developmental Disability, 1050 Forest Hill Rd, Staten Island, NY 10314. **Fax:** 718-698-3803.

LIN, GEORGE HUNG-YIN, GENERAL TOXICOLOGY & ENVIRONMENTAL TOXICOLOGY. **Personal Data:** b Shantung, China, March 9, 1938; m 1969, Margaret; c Benjamin. **Education:** Tunghai Univ, Taiwan, BS, 1960; Univ Nev, MS, 1965; Univ Calif, Davis, PhD (chem), 1969; Am Bd Toxicol, dipl, 1982-1987, 1987-1992, 1992. **Professional Experience:** PRIN SCIENTIST, XEROX CORP, 1991-; sr scientist, Xerox Corp, 1984-1991; adj fac toxicol, Univ Rochester, 1980-1982; staff toxicologist, Xerox Corp, 1974-1984; prog specialist, Xerox Corp, 1974-1976; Rockefeller fel chem, Univ Calif, Riverside, 1971-1974; NSF fel biochem, Univ Wis-Madison, 1969-1971. **Memberships:** Soc Toxicol; Environ Mutagen Soc. **Research Statement & Publications:** Industrial toxicology; inhalation toxicology; biometrics; chemical carcinogenesis; x-ray crystallography; general toxicology; carcinogen risk assessment; structure-activity relationships; environmental toxicology; environmental mutagenesis. **Mailing Address:** Xerox Corp, PUID Bldg 843, Webster, NY 14580. **Fax:** 716-422-6449.

LIN, GLORIA C, BIOCHEMISTRY. **Education:** Univ Hawaii, BS, 1986; Univ Calif, Los Angeles, PhD (phys chem), 1992. **Professional Experience:** NIH FEL, WELLMAN LABS, HARVARD MED SCH, 1993-; fel appln transient spectros, Harvard Med Sch, 1992-1993. **Memberships:** Am Chem Soc; Biophys Soc; Am Soc Photobiol & Photochem. **Research Statement & Publications:** Biochemistry. **Mailing Address:** Wellman Labs PhotoMed, Mass Gen Hosp, 50 Blossom St, Boston, MA 02114.

LIN, GRACE WOAN-JUNG, NUTRITIONAL BIOCHEMISTRY. **Personal Data:** b Taipei, Taiwan, American citizen. **Education:** Nat Taiwan Univ, BS, 1959; Tex Woman's Univ, MS, 1964; Univ Calif, Berkeley, PhD (nutrit), 1971. **Professional Experience:** ASSOC RES SPECIALIST, RUTGERS UNIV, 1983-; asst res specialist, Rutgers Univ, 1974-1983; res fel, Columbia Univ, 1969-1970; Res asst, US Naval Med Res Unit 2, 1959-1962 & Thorndike Mem Lab, Med Sch, Harvard Univ, 1964. **Memberships:** Res Soc Alcoholism; Am Inst Nutrit; Int Soc Biomed Res Alcoholism. **Research Statement & Publications:** Effects of ethanol on absorption and metabolism of nutrients (amino acids and water soluble vitamins) and on fetal development. **Mailing Address:** 9365 Wickham Way, Orlando, FL 32836-5518.

LIN, HO-MU, SUPERCRITICAL FLUID TECHNOLOGIES, FUEL TECHNOLOGIES. **Personal Data:** b Kaohsiung, Taiwan, July 12, 1938; m 1972, Su-Jung Wang; c Eugene T & Jeffrey E. **Education:** Nat Taiwan Univ, BS, 1962; Tokyo Inst Technol, 1966; Okla State Univ, PhD (chem eng), 1970. **Professional Experience:** PROF, DEPT CHEM ENG, NAT TAIWAN UNIV SCI & TECHNOL as of 2003; sr res fel, Purdue Univ, beginning 1988; sr sci adv, Bios Int, beginning 1987; co-prin investr, US Dept Energy, 1985-1987; Consult, Biotechnol Serv Int, 1984-1985; co-prin investr, Am Inst Chem Engrs, 1982-1987; Consult, Exxon, 1982; Consult, Great Lakes Chem, 1980; tech dir & sr engr, Thermodynamics Res Lab, 1979-1987; co-prin investr, Elec Power Res Inst, 1975-1986; res engr, Bios Int, 1975-1979; staff researcher, Rice Univ, 1974-1975; sr lectr & res assoc, Okla State Univ, 1970-1973; grad teaching & res asst, Okla State Univ, 1967-1970; lectr, Nat Taiwan Univ, 1966-1967; UNESCO fel, Tokyo Inst Technol, 1965-1966; Teaching & res asst, Nat Taiwan Univ, 1963-1965. **Memberships:** Am Inst ChemEngrs; Am Chem Soc; Sigma Xi; AAAS; fel Int Biog Asn. **Research Statement & Publications:** Explosion pretreatment of cellulosic materials for enhanced glucose production and supercritical fluid in utilization of cellulosic materials; author of over 100 technical publications. **Mailing Address:** Chem Eng Dept, Nat Taiwan Univ Sci & Technol, 43 Keelung Rd, Sect 4, Taipei, Taiwan. **E-Mail:** hml@ch.ntust.edu.tw

LIN, HSIU-SAN, RADIATION ONCOLOGY, MICROBIOLOGY. **Personal Data:** b Nagoya, Japan, March 15, 1935; American citizen; m 1962, Su-chiung; c Kenneth, Bertha & Michael. **Education:** Nat Taiwan Univ, MD, 1960; Univ Chicago, PhD (microbiol), 1968. **Honors & Awards:** Res Career Develop Award, Nat Cancer Inst, 1974. **Professional Experience:** Vis scientist, Harvard Med Sch, 1993; ASSOC PROF MICROBIOL, WASH UNIV, ST LOUIS, 1985-; PROF RADIOL, WASH UNIV, ST LOUIS, 1984-; vis scientist, Univ Oxford, Eng, 1977-1978; from asst prof to assoc prof, Wash Univ, St Louis, 1971-1984; consult ed, JLeukocyte Biol. **Memberships:** Am Soc Microbiologists; Am Soc Therapeut Radiol & Oncol; Am Asn Cancer Res; Reticuloendothelial Soc; Sigma Xi; fel, Am Col Radiol. **Research Statement & Publications:** Differentiation of monocytes and macrophages; radiobiology of mononuclear phagocytes. **Mailing Address:** Ctr Advan Med, Lower Level, Wash Univ Sch Med, St Louis, MO 63110. **Fax:** 314-362-8521. **E-Mail:** lin@radonc.wustl.edu

LIN, HUNG CHANG, ELECTRONICS. **Personal Data:** b Shanghai, China, August 8, 1919; American citizen; m 1959, c 2. **Education:** Chiao Tung Univ, BSEE, 1941; Univ Mich, MS, 1948; Polytech Inst Brooklyn, DEE(elec eng), 1956. **Honors & Awards:** Ebers Award, Inst Elec & Electronics Engrs Electron Device Soc, 1978. **Professional Experience:** PROF EMER, UNIV MD, COL PARK, 1990-; prof elec eng, Univ Md, Col Park, 1971-1990; SR ADV ENGR, AEROSPACE DIV, BALTIMORE, 1969-; vis prof elec eng, Univ Md, College Park, 1969-1971; lectr, Univ Md, Col Park, 1966-1969; vis lectr, Univ Calif, Berkeley, 1965-1966; mgr advan develop, Div Molecular Electronics, Westinghouse Corp, Linthicum Heights, 1963-1969; adv engr, Res Lab, Westinghouse Corp, Baltimore, 1959-1963; adj prof, Univ Pittsburgh, 1959-1963; mgr appln, CBS Semiconductor Opers, 1956-1959; res engr, RCA, 1948-1956; Engr, Cent Radio Works China, 1941-1944; Cent Broadcasting Admin China, 1944-1947. **Memberships:** Fel Inst Elec & Electronics Engrs; Sigma Xi. **Research Statement & Publications:** Semiconductor and integrated circuits. **Mailing Address:** Univ Md, Dept Elec Eng, College Park, MD 20742. **E-Mail:** hclin@eng.umd.edu

LIN, JAMES C H, GENETICS, CELL PHYSIOLOGY. **Personal Data:** b Macao, August 12, 1932; American citizen; wid, c David, Gilbert & Bruce. **Education:** Taiwan Prov Norm Univ, BS, 1954; Rice Univ, MA, 1960, NC State Univ, PhD (genetics), 1965. **Professional Experience:** Vis prof, Univ Tex, M D Anderson Hosp & Tumor Inst, 1980-1981; PROF BIOL, NORTHWESTERN STATE UNIV, 1975-; from asst prof to assoc prof, Northwestern State Univ, 1965-1975; res asst nuclear med, Methodist Hosp, Houston, Tex, 1959-1960 & Hermann Hosp, 1960; lab instr zool, Nat Taiwan Univ, 1955-1957. **Memberships:** Genetics Soc Am; Sigma Xi; Tissue Cult Asn. **Research Statement & Publications:** Chemical mutagenesis; cholinesterase in fire ants; crossing over in Drosophila; nucleolar organizing regions of Chinese hamster ovary cells; DNA methylation in drosophila. **Mailing Address:** Dept Biol Sci, Northwestern State Univ, Natchitoches, LA 71497. **Fax:** 318-357-4518. **E-Mail:** ling@cp=tel.net

LIN, JAMES CHIH-I, BIOENGINEERING, ELECTRICAL ENGINEERING. **Personal Data:** b Seoul, Korea, December 29, 1943; American citizen; m 1970, Mei Fei; c Janet, Theodore & Erik. **Education:** Univ Wash, Seattle, BS, 1966, MS, 1968, PhD (elec eng), 1971. **Honors & Awards:** Transactions Prize Paper Award 1975; Distinguished Ser Award, 1989; Distinguished Lect, Inst elec & electronics eng, Eng Med Bio Soc, 1991; Inst elec & electronics eng, Comt Man Radiation Spec Recognition Award 1991; Pres Comt Nat Medal Sci, 1992-1993; Outstanding Leadership Award, 1993; Chinese Acad & Prof Assoc Mid-Am; Adv Award, UIC Prof Eng Soc Coun, 1993; res Chair, 1993-1997. **Professional Experience:** Adv, Chung-Yuan Univ, Taiwan, 2001; Int Adv Com Electromag Fields, WHO, 2000-; Long Range Planning Comt, Int Union Radio Sci, 1999-; Standing Comt, Young Sci, 1999; Sci Comt, Gulglielmo Marconi Found, Italy, 1998-; vchair comn K, Int Union Radio, Sci, 1996-1999; mem Nat Res Coun, Nat Acad Sci Comt ELF Monitoring, 1995-1996; ed adv, Electromag Fields Living Sys, 1994-; dir spec proj eng, Univ Ill, Chicago, 1992-; fel comt, Whitaker Found, 1992; Distinguished Lect Bio & Med IEEE, 1991-; Luxtron Inc, 1990-; Stand Coord Comt SCC-28, IEEE, 1990-; chair, US Am Comn Man & Radiation, Inst Elec & Electronic Engrs, 1990-1991; chair, IEEE Comt Man & Radiation, 1990-1991; chair, Nat Coun Radio Protection & Measurement, 1988-1989; Shangdong Univ, China, 1988; ANSI C-95.4 Sub Comt Radiation Hazards Respect Personnel, Am Nat Stand Inst Chair, Peak Power Limit Group, 1987-; Arthur D Little, URS Corp, 1986-1987; Chung Yuan Univ, Univ Rome, 1985, 1988; Presidential Young Investr Award Panel, NSF, 1984-1989; mem, Ga Tech Res Inst, 1984-1986; dir robotics & automation lab, Univ Ill, Chicago, 1982-1989; vis prof, Chung Yuan Univ, Taiwan, 1981, 1988; appointee, Diag Radiol Study Sect, NIH, 1981-1985; Sec, Diagnostic Radiology Study, Nat Inst Health 1981-1985; vis prof, Nat Yang Ming Med Col, Taipei, 1981; prof elec eng & head bioeng, Univ Ill, Chicago, 1980-1992; Arthur D Little Inc, 1980-1982; appointee, Nat Acad Sci & Int Union Radio Sci, 1980-1982; PROF ELEC, BIOENG, PHYSIOL & BIOPHYS ENG, UNIV ILL, 1980-; consult, SRI Int, 1978-1979; consult, Battelle Mem Inst, 1976-1980; prof elec eng, Wayne State Univ, Detroit, 1974-1980; asst dir, Bioelectromagnetic Res Lab, 1974; consult, Walter Reed Army Inst Res, 1973-1975; asst prof rehab med, Univ Wash, Seattle, 1971-1974; teaching & res asst elec eng, Univ Wash, Seattle, 1967-1971; elec engr, Crown Zellerbach Corp, 1966-1967. **Memberships:** Fel Inst Elec & Electronics Engrs; Pres Bioelectromagnetic Soc; Biomed Eng Soc; fel AAAS; Nat Coun Radiation Protection & Measurements; founding fel, Am Inst of Med and Biolog Eng; Pres Chinese Am Acad & Prof Convection; Chair, Int Union of Radio Sci (URSI) Comn Electromag Biol & Med. **Research Statement & Publications:** Biological effects and medical applications of electromagnetic fields; hyperthermia for cancer therapy; visual and nonvisual robotic sensing; microwave technology for minimally invasive surgery; bioelectromagnetics; telemedicine. **Mailing Address:** Col Eng, Univ Ill, 851 S Morgan St MC154, Chicago, IL 60607-7053. **Fax:** 312-996-6465. **E-Mail:** lin@ece.uic.edu

LIN, JAMES PEICHENG, ALGEBRAIC TOPOLOGY. **Personal Data:** b New York, NY, September 30, 1949; m 1990, Julie; c Kelly & Krish. **Education:** Univ Calif, Berkeley, BS, 1970; Princeton Univ, PhD (math), 1974. **Professional Experience:** PROF MATH, UNIV CALIF, SAN DIEGO, 1986-; vis scholar, Mass Inst Technol, 1983-1984 & Univ Neuchatel, Switz, 1984; vis scholar, Univ Calif, Berkeley, 1982; mem, Inst Advan Studies, Hebrew Univ, Jerusalem, Israel, 1981-1982; Sloan Found fel, 1977-1978; vis prof math, Princeton Univ, 1976-1977; from asst prof to assoc prof, Univ Calif, San Diego, 1974-1986; prin invest, NSF grant. **Memberships:** Am Math Soc. **Research Statement & Publications:** Algebraic topology, concentrating on finite H-spaces. **Mailing Address:** Dept Math, Univ Calif, 9500 Gilman Dr Dept 0112, La Jolla, CA 92093-0112. **Fax:** 858-534-5273. **E-Mail:** jimlin@ucsd.edu

LIN, JANE HUEY-CHAI, ATHEROSCLEROSIS, ENDOTHELIA ACTIVATION. **Personal Data:** b Taipei, Taiwan. **Education:** Univ Ill, PhD (microbiol), 1986. **Professional Experience:** ASST PROF PATH, NY MED COL, 1993-; res asst prof, NY Med Col, 1990-1993; res assoc, NY Med Col, 1986-1990. **Research Statement & Publications:** Molecular mechanisms for endothelial activation by native low density lipo protein at atherogenic levels. **Mailing Address:** Dept Path, NY Med Col, Basic Sci Bldg, Valhalla, NY 10595. **Fax:** 914-594-4453. **E-Mail:** jane_lin@nymc.edu

LIN, JIA DING, FLUID MECHANICS, HYDROLOGY AND WATER RESOURCES. **Personal Data:** b Fuzhou, China, December 24, 1931; American citizen; m 1958, c 3. **Education:** Nat Univ Taiwan, BS, 1953, Univ Ill, MS, 1956; Mass Inst Technol, ScD(hydromech), 1961. **Professional Experience:** PROF EMER CIVIL ENG, UNIV CONN, as of 1998; prof civil eng, Univ Conn, beginning 1981; Vis prof, Taiwan Univ, 1979-1980; assoc prof, Univ Conn, 1964-1981; asst prof, Univ Conn, 1962-1964; Res scientist, Hydronautics Inc, 1960-1962. **Memberships:** Asn Hydrol Res; Am Geophys Union. **Research Statement & Publications:** hydrodynamics; hydrology. **Mailing Address:** Dept Civil Eng & Environ, Univ Conn, Main Campus U-37, 261 Glenbrook Rd, Storrs, CT 06269-2037.

LIN, JIAN, MARINE GEOPHYSICS, TECTONOPHYSICS. **Personal Data:** b Fuzhou, Fujian. **Education:** Univ Sci & Technol, China, BS, 1982; Brown Univ, MS, 1984, PhD (geophys), 1988. **Professional Experience:** Panelist, NSF US Geol Surv Ocean Drilling Prog, 1993-1997; mem, Earthquake Geol & Crustal Deformation Working Group, Southern Calif Earthquake Ctr, 1992-; ASSOC SCIENTIST GEOPHYS, WOODS HOLE OCEANOG INST, 1992-1996; assoc ed, J Geophys Res, 1992-1994; prog chmn, Tectonophysics Sect, Am Geophys Union, 1992-1993; vis fel, Southern Calif Earthquake Ctr, NSF, 1991-1992; Mem, Steering Comt & Crustal Accretion Variables Working Group, US Ridge Prog, 1989-1997; asst scientist, Woods Hole Oceanog Inst, 1988-1992; Vis scientist res geophys, US Geol Surv, Menlo Park, Calif, 1988; Assoc Scientist with Tenure, Woods Hole Oceanog Inst, 1996-, mem, Steering Comt & Chmn 4D Architecture of Oceanic Lithosphere & Hotspot-Ridge Interaction Working Groups, InterRidge Prog, 1999- Visiting Scientist, CNRS, Paris, France, 1999. **Memberships:** Am Geophys Union; Sigma Xi; Geol Soc Am; AAAS Seismological soc of Am. **Research Statement & Publications:** Mid-ocean ridge dynamics; thermal evolution of the lithosphere; mantle hotspots; crustal deformation; earthquake mechanisms. **Mailing Address:** Dept Geol & Geophys, Woods Hole Oceanog Inst, Woods Hole, MA 02543. **Fax:** 508-457-2187.

LIN, JIANN-TSYH, PLANT LIPID ANALYSIS & METABOLISM STUDY. **Personal Data:** b Taoyuan, Taiwan, January 15, 1940; American citizen; m 1969, Cheng-Ling; c Robert C & Jeffrey C. **Education:** Chung-Hsing Univ, Taiwan, BS, 1963; Univ Miss, MS, 1967; Drexel Univ, Philadelphia, PhD (biochem), 1971. **Professional Experience:** RES CHEMIST, USDA, ALBANY, CA, 1977-; res assoc, Harborview Med Ctr, Univ of Wash, Seattle, WA, 1976-1977; res assoc, Hormel Inst, Univ of Minn, 1972-1976; res assoc, Univ Tenn Med Ctr, Memphis, Tenn, 1971-1972. **Memberships:** Am Chem Soc; Am Oil Chemists Soc. **Research Statement & Publications:** Biochemistry and analytical chemistry of seed oil;

HPLC of acyl lipids (LC-MS); Biosynthetic pathway of Castor Oil. **Mailing Address:** USDA Western Regional Res Ctr, 800 Buchanan St, Albany, CA 94710. **Fax:** 510-559-5768. **E-Mail:** jtlin@pw.usda.gov

LIN, JIUNN H, DRUG METABOLISM. **Personal Data:** b Taiwan, 1943. **Professional Experience:** EXEC DIR & DEPT HEAD PRECLIN DRUG, MERCK RES LABS, as of 2004; assoc dir, merck sharp & dohme, beginning 1988. **Mailing Address:** Merck Res Labs, WP 44-B100, West Point, PA 19486.

LIN, KUANG-FARN, POLYMER SCIENCE. **Personal Data:** b Taiwan, China, February 25, 1936; m 1958, Grace; c 2. **Education:** Cheng Kung Univ, Taiwan, BSc, 1957; NDak State Univ, MS, 1963, PhD (polymers, coatings), 1969. **Professional Experience:** BUSINESS DEVELOP MGR, HERCULES RES CTR, 1995-; venture mgr, Hercules Res Ctr, 1989-1994; RES ASSOC, HERCULES RES CTR, 1984-; TECH MGR, HERCULES RES CTR, 1979-; RES SCIENTIST, HERCULES RES CTR, 1978-; sr res chemist, Hercules Res Ctr, 1974-1978; proj leader, Hercules Res Ctr, 1973-1975; res chemist, Hercules Res Ctr, 1969-1973; chemist, Hercules Res Ctr, 1963-1967; asst, NDak State Univ, 1963 & 1967; supt synthetic resins, Yung Koo Paint & Varnish Mfg Co, 1959-1961; asst instr chem, Chinese Naval Acad, 1957-1959. **Memberships:** Am Chem Soc; Sigma Xi; Tech Asn Pulp & Paper Indust; fel Am Inst Chemists; Am Inst Mining Metall & Petrol Engrs. **Research Statement & Publications:** Structure-property relationship; mineral processing; adhesion, coatings and polymer synthesis; elastomers. **Mailing Address:** Hercules Inc, Wilmington, DE 19894. **Fax:** 302-995-4448. **E-Mail:** klin@herc.com

LIN, KUANG-TZU DAVIS, BIOCHEMISTRY, BIOCHEMICAL GENETICS. **Personal Data:** b Nantou, Taiwan, August 12, 1940; m 1968, c 2. **Education:** Nat Taiwan Univ, BM, 1966; Univ Wis-Madison, PhD (physiol chem), 1971. **Professional Experience:** ASSOC PROF PEDIAT, MEHARRY, 1988-; med staff, Dept Pediat, William Beaumont Hosp, 1985-1986; assoc prof med biol, mem res ctr, Univ Tenn, 1982-1986; asst prof, Univ Tenn, 1974-1982; proj assoc, Univ Wis-Madison, 1971-1974; res asst physiol chem, Univ Wis-Madison, 1967-1971; surg officer, Tainan Air Force Hosp, 1966-1967; dir, Biochem Genetic Lab, Meharry Hubbard Hosp; med staff, Meharry Hubbard Hosp. **Memberships:** Soc Exp Biol Med; Am Soc Biochem & Molecular Biol; Am Bd Med Genetics. **Research Statement & Publications:** Structure and function, especially carbonic anhydrase, hemoglobin, protease inhibitors and erythropoietin; amino acid metabolic disorder; pediatrics; genetic disorder. **Mailing Address:** Dept Pediat Meharry Med Col, 1005 D B Todd Jr Blvd, Nashville, TN 37208-3599. **Fax:** 615-327-5989. **E-Mail:** linkut45@ccvax.mmc.edu

LIN, KWAN-CHOW, BIOLOGICAL WASTEWATER TREATMENT, WATER QUALITY STUDIES. **Personal Data:** b Hong Kong, Canadian citizen; m 1969, Kwok Yee. **Education:** Chu Hai Col Hong Kong, BSc, 1966; Univ NB, MScE, 1969; Univ Toronto, PhD (environ eng), 1974. **Professional Experience:** RETIRED; prof dept civil eng, Univ NB, 1983-2000; lectr, Univ Hong Kong, 1980; consult, var eng firms & munic Can, beginning 1978; consult, WHO, Copenhagen, 1976; from asst prof to assoc prof, Univ NB, 1974-1983; lectr, Univ NB, 1974; res assoc, Univ NB, 1969-1970; design engr, Environ Resources Consult Ltd, 1969-1970; civil engr, Domtar Newsprint Ltd, 1966-1967. **Memberships:** Can Soc Civil Eng; Eng Inst Can; Water Environ Fedn; Can Asn Water Qual; Overseas Chinese Environ Engrs & Scientists Asn. **Research Statement & Publications:** Aerobic, anoxic and anaerobic biological wastewater treatment; field and laboratory water quality studies; mathematical modelling of biological processes and surface and ground water quality and transport. **Mailing Address:** Dept Civil Eng, Univ NB, PO Box 4400, Fredericton, NB E3B 5A3, Can. **Fax:** 506-453-3568. **E-Mail:** lin@unb.ca

LIN, LARRY Y H, CIVIL ENGINEERING. **Personal Data:** b China. **Education:** Nat Taiwan Univ, BS, 1957; WVa Univ, MS, 1963, PhD (civil eng), 1966; Am Acad Environ Engrs, dipl. **Professional Experience:** MEM STAFF, ROY WESTON INC, 1966-; res asst assoc, WVa Univ, 1961-1964; Teaching asst, Nat Taiwan Univ, 1959-1961. **Memberships:** Water Pollution Control Fedn. **Research Statement & Publications:** Process design of industrial and municipal wastewater treatment facilities; physical, chemical and biological aspects of water pollution; air and solid waste problems; data analysis and computer programming; energy conservation. **Mailing Address:** 19 Montbard Dr, Chadds Ford, PA 19317.

LIN, LAWRENCE I-KUEI, STATISTICS, DATA MANAGEMENT. **Personal Data:** b Fuchou, China, May 21, 1948; m 1971, Sha-Li; c Juintu, Buortau & Shintau. **Education:** Nat Chengchi Univ, Taiwan, BC, 1970; Univ Iowa, MS, 1973, PhD (statist), 1979. **Professional Experience:** SR RES SCIENTIST STATIST, BAXTER HEALTHCARE CORP, 1995-; sr res statistician, Baxter Healthcare Corp, 1987-1995; res statistician, Baxter Healthcare Corp, 1979-1987; statistician, Iowa Epidemiol Study Pesticides, 1973-1979; res asst, Dept Prev Med, Univ Iowa, 1973. **Memberships:** Am Statist Asn; Biomet Soc; Drug Info Asn. **Research Statement & Publications:** Discriminant analysis; risk assessment; M-estimator; pharmacokinetics; generalized Linean model. **Mailing Address:** Baxter Healthcare Corp, Rte 120 & Wilson, Round Lake, IL 60073. **Fax:** 847-270-5449.

LIN, LEEWEN, MOLECULAR BIOLOGY, PROTEIN CHEMISTRY. **Personal Data:** b Taipei, Taiwan, m 1984, Fang-Jen; c Alice & Albert. **Education:** BS, Nat Taiwan Univ, 1980, MS, 1982; PhD, NC State Univ, 1987. **Professional Experience:** SR STAFF FEL, CBER FOOD & DRUG ADMIN, 1992-; staff fel, Cber Food & Drug Admin, 1990-1992; res Fel, Mass Gen Hosp, 1987-1990. **Memberships:** Am Soc Biochem & Molecular Biol. **Research Statement & Publications:** Molecular biology and genetics of parasites; vaccines against parasitic diseases. **Mailing Address:** CBER, Food & Drug Admin, Rm 511, Bldg 29, 8800 Rockville Pike, Bethesda, MD 20892. **Fax:** 301-496-4681.

LIN, LEU-FEN HOU, PROTEIN CHEMISTRY, NEUROTROPHIC FACTOR. **Personal Data:** b Kwangtung, China, American citizen; m 1972, Jiguan; c Cynthia & Elaine. **Education:** Nat Taiwan Univ, BS, 1967; Univ Minn, PhD (biochem), 1972. **Professional Experience:** LAB DIR, CYTOTHERAPEUTICS, INC, as of 2004; neuro scientist, Synergen, beginning 1988; asst neurol, Mass Gen Hosp, 1981-1988; scientist biochem, E K Shriver Ctr Ment Retardation, Harvard Med Sch, 1979-1988; res fel, Harvard Univ, 1976-1979; Instr biochem, Mt Sinai Sch Med, 1972-1976. **Memberships:** Soc Neurosci; Int Soc Neurochem. **Research Statement & Publications:** Neurotrophic factor. **Mailing Address:** CytoTherapeutics, Inc, 701 George Wash Hwy, Lincoln, RI 02865-4257.

LIN, MAO-SHIU, ELECTRICAL ENGINEERING. **Personal Data:** b Tainan, Taiwan, June 20, 1931. **Education:** Nat Taiwan Univ, BSE, 1955; Univ Mich, MSE, 1958, PhD (elec eng), 1964. **Professional Experience:** Chmn, elec & comput eng dept, 1976-1987; PROF ELEC ENG, SAN DIEGO STATE UNIV, 1972-; from asst prof to assoc prof elec eng, San Diego State Univ, 1966-1972; assoc res engr, Electron Physics Lab, Univ Mich, 1964-1966; Asst engr elec mach, Ta-Tung Elec Mfg Co, Taiwan, 1955-1956. **Memberships:** Inst Elec & Electronics Engrs; Am Soc Eng Educ. **Research Statement & Publications:** Material science; solid state electronics; quantum electronics; power engineering. **Mailing Address:** Dept Elec Eng, San Diego State Univ, 5402 College Ave, San Diego, CA 92182-0190. **E-Mail:** mao.lin@sdsu.edu

LIN, MICHAEL C, HORMONE REGULATION, CELLULAR DIFFERENTIATION. **Personal Data:** b 1938. **Education:** Med Col Ga, PhD (biochem), 1966. **Professional Experience:** HEALTH SCIENTIST ADMINR, NIH, as of 2002; RES CHEMIST, NIH, 1975-. **Memberships:** Am Soc Biochem & Molecular Biol; Am Chem Soc. **Mailing Address:** Nat Heart, Lung & Blood Inst, NIH, Two Rockledge Ctr 6701 Rockledge Dr Ste 10193, Bethesda, MD 20892-7956. **Fax:** 301-480-2849. **E-Mail:** michael_lin@nih.gov

LIN, MING CHANG, CHEMICAL KINETICS, LASER APPLICATIONS. **Personal Data:** b Hsinpu, Hsinchu, Taiwan, October 24, 1936; American citizen; m 1965, J H Chern; c Karen, L Hsinjih & Ellena J. **Education:** Taiwan Normal Univ, BSc, 1959; Univ Ottawa, Can, PhD (phys chem), 1965. **Honors & Awards:** Alexander von Humboldt Award, 1982. **Professional Experience:** Distinguished vis prof, Inst Atomic & Molecular Sci, Taipei, Taiwan, 1994; prize sci & technol, Taiwanese Am Found, 1989-; ROBERT W WOODRUFF PROF PHYS CHEM, DEPT CHEM, EMORY UNIV, 1988-; sr scientist, Naval Res Lab, 1982-1988; Guggenheim fel, 1982-1983; adj prof, Dept Chem, Catholic Univ, Wash, DC, 1981-1988; supvry res chemist, Naval Res Lab, 1974-1982; res chemist, Naval Res Lab, 1970-1974; res assoc, Cornell Univ, 1967-1969; res fel, Univ Ottawa, 1965-1967. **Memberships:** Am Chem Soc; Combustion Inst; Sigma Xi; Am Vacuum Soc; Mat Res Soc. **Research Statement & Publications:** Kinetics of chemical reactions are studies with modern diagnostic tools such as lasers with special emphasis on the elucidation of mechanisms of combustion and planetary reactions, heterogeneous catalytic processes and microelectronic processing chemistry. **Mailing Address:** Dept Chem, Emory Univ, Chem Bldg, Atlanta, GA 30322. **Fax:** 404-727-6586. **E-Mail:** chemmcl@emory.edu

LIN, MING-FONG, CANCER RESEARCH, SIGNAL TRANSDUCTION IN CELL GROWTH REGULATION & DIFFERENTIATION. **Personal Data:** b Taiwan, October 9, 1951; American citizen; m 1978, Fen-Fen; c Frank & Jamie. **Education:** Kaoshiung Med Col, Taiwan, BS (Pharmacy), 1974; Nat Tsing Hua Univ, Taiwan, MS (Molecular Biology), 1976; Roswell Park Mem Inst, Univ NY at Buffalo, Buffalo, NY, PhD (exp pathol/Cancer Biology), 1983. **Honors & Awards:** Best Proj Award, Nat Cancer Inst Organ System Program, 1989. **Professional Experience:** Prof, Biochem & Mol Biol, UNMC, 2000-present; Asso Prof, Biochem & Mol Biol, UNMC, 1995-2000; asst prof, Urol & Cancer Ctr, Uni S Calif Med Ctr, 1988-1995; res asst prof, Ore Health Sci Univ, 1987-8; res asst prof, La State Univ, Med Ctr, 1986; Fellow, La State Univ, Med Ctr, 1983-1986. **Memberships:** Am Asn Cancer Res; Am Soc Cell Biol; Am Soc Microbiol; AAAS; NY Acad Sci; Sigma Xi. **Research Statement & Publications:** Cell growth regulation, the approach is to delineate the regulation of tyrosine phosphorylation in cells; dephosphorylation by a protein tyrosine phosphatase, a tissue-specific differentiation antigen, the results will provide clues to understand the carcinogenesis of male prostate cancer it will also lead us to understand the biological significance of differentiation-associated phosphatases in cell growth regulation. **Mailing Address:** Dept Biochem & Molecular Biol, Univ Nebr Med Center, 985870 Nebr Medical Center, Omaha, NE 68198. **Fax:** 402-559-6650. **E-Mail:** mlin@unmc.edu

LIN, OTTO CHUI CHAU, POLYMER CHEMISTRY, RHEOLOGY. **Personal Data:** b Kwongtang, China, August 8, 1938; m 1963, c 3. **Education:** Nat Taiwan Univ, BS, 1960; Columbia Univ, MA, 1963, PhD (phys chem), 1967. **Professional Experience:** Bd dir, Feng Chia Univ, 1986-; VPRES, MAT RES LAB, ITRI, 1985-; bd dir, China Tech Consult, Inc, 1984-; DIR GENERAL, MAT RES LAB, ITRI, 1983-; Vis prof, Inst Polymer Sci & actg dean, Col of Eng, Nat Tsing Hua Univ, 1978-1980; res assoc, Marshall Res Lab, Fabrics & Finishes Dept, 1971-; staff chemist, E I Dupont de Nemours & Co, Inc, 1969-1971; Res chemist, E I Dupont de Nemours & Co, Inc, 1967-1969. **Memberships:** AAAS; Am Chem Soc; Am Inst Chem Engrs; NY Acad Sci; Soc Rheol; Chinese Soc Mat Sci (pres, 1986-). **Research Statement & Publications:** Physical chemical characterization of polymers; rheological properties of polymers; sedimentation; viscometry; organic coatings; ecological impacts of polymer applications; polymers for electronics applications. **Mailing Address:** 103 Clementi Rd, Singapore 129788, Singapore.

LIN, PAUL C S, HILBERT & BANACH SPACES, OPERATOR THEORY & INEQUALITIES, NUMERICAL RANGES, SPECTRAL THEORY. **Personal Data:** b Taiwan, October 3, Canadian citizen; m 1976, Margaret P M Aw; c Angela W Lin. **Education:** Nat Taiwan Norm Univ, BS, 1963; McMaster Univ, MS, 1965; Univ NB, PhD (math), 1973. **Honors & Awards:** Res Award, Nat Res Coun Can & Natural Sci & Eng Res Coun Can. **Professional Experience:** PROF MATH, BISHOP'S UNIV, 1988-; Dept Math, Univ New Brunwick, 1973-1976, St Thomas Univ, 1976-1979, UBC, 1979-1981 & Bishop's Univ, 1981-. **Memberships:** Am Math Asn; Math Asn Am; Can Math Soc. **Research Statement & Publications:** Normed linear spaces; Hilbert and Banach spaces; operators on Hilbert spaces. **Mailing Address:** Bishops Univ, Lennoxville, PQ J1M 1Z7, Can. **Fax:** 819-822-9661. **E-Mail:** plin@hera.ubishops.ca

LIN, PAUL KUANG-HSIEN, EXPERIMENTAL DESIGN, QUALITY ENGINEERING. **Personal Data:** b Tung-Shih, Taiwan, November 12, 1946; m 1978, Cathy; c Elizabeth & John. **Education:** Fu-Jen Univ, Taiwan, BS, 1970; Brigham Young Univ, MS, 1975; Wayne State Univ, PhD (statist), 1980. **Professional Experience:** ASSOC PROF STATIST, UNIV MICH, DEARBORN, 1987-; asst prof, Univ Mich, Dearborn, 1984-1987; asst prof statist, Western Mich Univ, 1982-1984; asst prof statist, Oakland Univ, 1980-1982; consult, Qual Improv. **Memberships:** Am Statist Asn; Inst Math Statist; Am Soc Quality Control; Sigma Xi. **Research Statement & Publications:** Experimental design; interval estimation and hypothesis testing; Taguchi's methods for quality improvement. **Mailing Address:** Dept Math Statist, Univ Mich, Dearborn, MI 48128-1491. **E-Mail:** plin@umd.umich.edu

LIN, P(EN) M(IN), ELECTRICAL ENGINEERING. **Personal Data:** b China, October 17, 1928; American citizen; m 1962, Louise S; c Marian, Margaret & Janice. **Education:** Taiwan Univ, BSEE, 1950; NC State Univ, MSEE, 1956; Purdue Univ, PhD (elec eng), 1960. **Professional Experience:** EMER PROF ELEC ENG, PURDUE UNIV, 1994-; from asst prof to prof, Purdue Univ, 1961-1994; mem tech staff, Bell Tel Labs, NJ, 1960-1961; From instr to asst prof elec eng, Purdue Univ, 1956-1960. **Memberships:** Life fel Inst Elec & Electronics Engrs. **Research Statement & Publications:** Circuit theory; computer-aided circuit analysis; author & coauthor three graduate and undergraduate textbooks on the anal of electronic circuits. **Mailing Address:** Sch Elec Eng, Purdue Univ, Lafayette, IN 47907.

LIN, PI-ERH, MATHEMATICAL STATISTICS. **Personal Data:** b Taiwan, China, January 8, 1938; m 1963, c 3. **Education:** Taiwan Norm Univ, BSc, 1961; Columbia Univ, PhD (math statist), 1968. **Professional Experience:** RETIRED; prof statist, Fla State Univ, 1980-2003; statist consult, Fla Dept Environ protection, 1998-2002; assoc prof, Fla State Univ, 1974-1980; Fla State Univ fac res grant, 1971-1972; asst prof, Fla State Univ, 1968-1974; consult med ctr, Columbia Univ, 1967-1968. **Memberships:** Inst Math Statist; Am Statist Asn; Bernoulii Soc. **Research Statement & Publications:** Multivariate analysis; statistical inference. **Mailing Address:** Dept Statist, Fla State Univ, 600 Col Ave W, Tallahassee, FL 32306-1096. **Fax:** 850-644-5271. **E-Mail:** lin@stat.fsu.edu

LIN, PING-WHA, ENVIRONMENTAL ENGINEERING. **Personal Data:** b Canton, China, July 11, 1925; American citizen; m 1960, c 2. **Education:** Jiao Tong Univ, BS, 1947; Purdue Univ, MS, 1949, PhD (sanit eng), 1951. **Honors & Awards:** Achievement Award, United Inventors & Scientists of Am, 1974. **Professional Experience:** PROF EMER CIVIL & ENVIRON ENG, TRI-STATE UNIV, 1995-; PRES, LIN TECHNOLOGIES INC, 1988-; consult, WHO, 1986; dept energy indiv grant, 1982; prof & Dresser chair prof, Lin Technologies, Inc, 1981-1995; proj mgr, WHO, 1979-1981; fel, NSF workshop, Mass Inst Technol, 1969; prof, Lin Technologies, Inc, 1966-1979; consult, World Health Orgn, 1962-1966; engr, John Graham & Co, NY, 1960-1961; engr, World Health Orgn, 1959-1960; engr, Lockwood Greene Engrs, 1957-1959; engr, Parsons, Brinkerhoff, Hall & MacDonald, 1955-1957; engr, Ebesco, 1954-1955; engr, Amman & Whitney, NY, 1951-1954. **Memberships:** Fel Am Soc Civil Engrs; Am Water Works Asn; Sigma Xi; Am Chem Soc. **Research Statement & Publications:** Acid neutralization; metal waste treatment; fly ash utilization; soil stabilization; quenching process; flue gas desulfurization; energy development; gas kinetics; Lin's theory of flux. **Mailing Address:** Dept Civil & Environ Eng, Tri-State Univ, 1 Univ Ave, Angola, IN 46703.

LIN, RAY Y, COATING & THIN FILM TECHNOLOGY. **Personal Data:** m 1956, Alice; c Andrew R. **Education:** Nat Taiwan Univ, BS, 1971; Univ Wis, MS, 1976; Mas Inst Technol, DSc, 1980. **Honorary Degrees:** DSc, Mass Inst Technol, 1991. **Professional Experience:** Sr tech adv, UN World Develop Prog, 1991; vis prof, Tohoku Univ, 1990-1991 & 1994-1995; consult appl sci, beginning 1984; vchair, Thermodyn Activity & Phase Equilibra Comt, Am Soc Metals Int, beginning 1983; PROF MAT SCI & ENG, UNIV CINCINNATI, 1983-; chair, ProcessFundamentals Comt, Minerals, Metals & Mat Soc, 1983; res scientist, Energy Lab, Mass Inst Technol, 1982-1983; mem tech staff, GTE Lab, 1980-1982; Metall engr, Kennecott Lab, 1979-1980. **Memberships:** Minerals, Metals & Mat Soc; Am Soc Metals Int; Am Ceramic Soc; Mat Res Soc; Am Composite Soc; Iron & Steel Soc. **Research Statement & Publications:** Coatings and thin film processing with sputter deposition; chemical vapor deposition and electroplating; infrared processing of materials; composite materials processing; metal matrix composites; composite interfaces; infrared joining of metals; superalloys and intermetallic compounds; engineering interlayer material development; functionally gradient materials. **Mailing Address:** Univ Cincinnati, ML No 12, Cincinnati, OH 45221-0012. **Fax:** 513-556-2569. **E-Mail:** Ray.Lin@UC.Edu

LIN, RENEE C, LIPID METABOLISM, CULTURE HEPATOCYTES. **Education:** Univ Wis, Madison, PhD (biochem), 1969. **Professional Experience:** ADJ PROF, SCH MED, IND UNIV, as of 2001; asst prof med, Sch Med, Ind Univ, beginning 1985; ASSOC SCIENTIST MED RES, VET ADMIN MED CTR, 1974-. **Mailing Address:** Dept Med, Ind Univ Sch Med, 975 W Walnut St-1B 424, Indianapolis, IN 46202-5121.

LIN, REN-LANG, TOXICOLOGY, PSYCHOPHARMACOLOGY. **Personal Data:** b Hsin-Chu, Taiwan, February 28, 1937; m 1965, c 2. **Education:** Nat Taiwan Univ, BS, 1959, MS, 1963; Okla State Univ, PhD (biochem), 1969. **Professional Experience:** CHIEF TOXICOLOGIST, NJ STATE MED EXAMR OFF, 1983-; asst chief toxicologist, Off Med Examiner, Cook County, 1978-1983; res scientist, Ill State Psychiat Inst, 1975-1978; res scientist, Galesburg State Hosp, Ill, 1971-1975; Fel, Univ Wis-Madison, 1969-1971. **Memberships:** Am Chem Soc; AAAS. **Research Statement & Publications:** Forensic toxicology; biochemistry of mental illness; biosynthesis and metabolism of biogenic amines; biochemistry and pharmacology of psychoactive drugs. **Mailing Address:** Dept Molecular Biochem, Beckman Res Inst 1450 E Duarte Rd, Duarte, CA 91010-3000.

LIN, ROBERT I-SAN, SCIENCE ADMINISTRATION, NUTRITION & DEGENERATIVE DISEASES. **Personal Data:** b Fukien, China, 1942; m 1971, Cecile; c Sylvia H, Alva H, Rose H & David H. **Education:** Nat Taiwan Univ, BS, 1961; Univ Calif, Los Angeles, MS, 1965, PhD (biophy & nuclear med), 1968. **Professional Experience:** Chmn, First World Cong on Health Significance Garlic, 1990; EXEC VPRES, NUTRIT INT, 1989-; sr vpres, Makers Kal, 1986-1987 & Weider Health & Fitness, 1988-1990; vpres, Natural Prod Div, Richardson Vicks, 1982-1985; vis distinguished prof nutrit & food sci, Tex Woman's Univ, 1981-; chief scientist, Frito-Lay Inc, 1975-1982; vpres technol diag prod, RIA Inc, 1974-1975; dir enzyme prod, Worthington Biochem Corp, 1973-1974; life sci mgr, Gen Tel & Electronic Corp, 1971-1973; trainee biotechnol & nutrit, Mass Inst Technol, 1971; clin trainee metab dis, Med Ctr, Univ Calif, 1970-1971; vis prof biochem & molecular biol, Pepperdine Univ, 1969-1970; res fel chem, Calif Inst Technol, 1968-1970. **Memberships:** NY Acad Sci; Sigma Xi; Am Photobiol Soc; Soc Appl Nutrit; Am Agr Econ Asn; Am Mgt Asn; Am Col Nutrit; Am Col Sport Med; Inst Food Technol; Am Chem Soc. **Research Statement & Publications:** Diet, nutrition, aging and degenerative diseases; biotechnology and genetic engineering: recombiant DNA-hybridoma and subcellular organelle transfer; chemistry and rheology of natural and synthetic polymers; physical chemistry of surfactants and viscosity modifiers; sport nutrition, herbal sciences and pharmacognosy; management of technological development and industrialization; operation research and econometrics. **Mailing Address:** Nutrit Int Co, PO Box 50632, Irvine, CA 92619-0632. **Fax:** 949-854-6170. **E-Mail:** drrlin@hotmail.com

LIN, ROBERT PEICHUNG, SOLAR & SPACE PLASMA PHYSICS, HIGH ENERGY ASTROPHYSICS. **Personal Data:** b China, January 24, 1942; American citizen; m 1983. **Education:** Calif Inst Technol, BS, 1962; Univ Calif, Berkeley, PhD (physics), 1967. **Professional Experience:** DIR, SPACE SCI LAB, UNIV CALIF, BERKELEY, 1998-; mem, Hiregs Antarctica, 1994; assoc dir, Space Sci Lab, 1992-1998; PROF PHYSICS, UNIV CALIF, BERKELEY, 1991-; mem, Max 91 Balloon, beginning 1989; adj prof astron, Univ Calif, 1988-1990; prin investr, Mars Observer, beginning 1987; prin investr, ISTP/GGS Wind, 1981-; sr fel, Univ Calif, 1980-1988; prin investr, NASA & ESA GiottoMission, beginning 1979; res physicist, Univ Calif, 1979-1988; from asst res physicist to assoc res physicist, Univ Calif, 1967-1979. **Memberships:** Am Geophys Union; Am Astron Soc. **Research Statement & Publications:** Solar flares, radio bursts and cosmic rays; interplanetary particles; magnetospheric processes; lunar magnetism; astrophysical x-ray and gamma ray spectroscopy; comets. **Mailing Address:** Dept Physics, Univ Calif, Berkeley, CA 94720-7300. **Fax:** 510-643-8302. **E-Mail:** boblin@ssl.berkeley.edu

LIN, RUEY Y, CHEMISTRY. **Education:** Nat Taiwan Univ, BS, 1955; WVa Univ, MS, 1959, PhD (chem), 1962. **Professional Experience:** ASST DIR, HOWMEDICA, INC, 1990-; prin res scientist, Howmedica, Inc, 1987-1990; sr mat res engr, Howmedica, Inc, 1984-1987; res assoc, Eastern Res Ctr, Stauffer Chem Co, 1977-1984; proj mgr nonwoven prod develop, Am Kynol, Inc, 1975-1976; sr develop assoc, Res Br, Res & Develop Div, Carborundum Co, 1974-1977; proj mgr, Res Br, Res & Develop Div, Carborundum Co, 1971-1973; sr res assoc, Res Br, Res & Develop Div, Carborundum Co, 1970-1971; res assoc, Res Br, Res & Develop Div, Carborundum Co, 1967-1969; sr chemist, Res Br, Res & Develop Div, Carborundum Co, 1963-1967; Res fel, State Univ NY, Buffalo, 1962-1963. **Memberships:** Am Chem Soc; Sigma Xi. **Research Statement & Publications:** Development of composite materials for orthopaedic applications; engineering thermoplastics; reaction injection molding technology; flame retarding area; high performance composites; refractory fibers; author of 15 publications; granted 13 US patents. **Mailing Address:** Howmedica Inc, 359 Veterans Blvd, Rutherford, NJ 07070-2584.

LIN, SHAO-CHI, AEROSPACE ENGINEERING. **Personal Data:** b Canton, China, January 5, 1925; American citizen; m 1955. **Education:** Nat Cent Univ, China, BSc, 1946; Cornell Univ, PhD (aeronaut eng), 1952. **Honors & Awards:** Res Award, Am Inst Aeronaut & Astronaut, 1966. **Professional Experience:** PROF EMER ENG PHYSICS, UNIV CALIF, SAN DIEGO, as of 2005; prof eng physics, Univ Calif, San Diego, beginning 1964; prin res scientist, Avco-Everett Res Lab, Mass, 1955-1964; actg asst prof, Cornell Univ, 1954; res assoc, Cornell Univ, 1952-1954; actg instr, Cornell Univ, 1952; asst, Cornell Univ, 1948-1951; engr, Bur Aircraft Indust, China, 1947-1948; panel mem re-entry physics, Nat Acad Sci-Nat Res Coun; consult, Aerospace Corp, Avco-Everett Res Lab, Inst Defense Anal & Rand Corp. **Memberships:** Am Inst Aeronaut & Astronaut; Am Phys Soc; Am Astronaut Soc; Am Geophys Union. **Research Statement & Publications:** Physical gas dynamics; hypersonic flight; reentry physics; laser physics and interaction. **Mailing Address:** Univ Calif, 9500 Gilman Dr, La Jolla, CA 92093-0411.

LIN, SHENG HSIEN, CHEMICAL KINETICS, CHEMICAL PHYSICS. **Personal Data:** b September 17, 1937; American citizen; m 1970, Pearl H Pi. **Education:** Nat Taiwan Univ, BS, 1959, MS, 1961; Univ Utah, PhD (chem), 1964. **Honors & Awards:** Marino lectr, 2001; Eminent Scientist Award, RIKEN, 1995; Taiwanese Am Found Prize, 1995. **Professional Experience:** Distinguished res fel, Acad Sinica, 1993-; dir, Inst Atomic & Molecular Sci, 1993-2001; hon prof, Xiamen Univ, 1990-; REGENT PROF, ARIZ STATE UNIV, 1988-; hon prof, Nanjing Univ, 1988-; Humboldt Sr US scientist awardee, 1979-1980 & 1988-1989; PROF CHEM, ARIZ STATE UNIV, 1972-; Guggenheim fel, 1971-1973; Alfred P Sloan fel, 1967-1969; from asst to assoc prof, Ariz State Univ, 1965-1972; fel chem, Columbia Univ, 1964-1965. **Memberships:** Am Chem Soc; Acad Sinica; Am Phys Soc. **Research Statement & Publications:** Energy transfer; femtosecond processes; optical rotations and the Faraday effect; reaction kinetics; electron transfer; magnetic properties of molecules; multi-photon processes; molecular relaxation processes; theory of time-resolved x-ray diffraction. **Mailing Address:** Dept Chem, Ariz State Univ, Tempe, AZ 85281. **Fax:** 602-965-2747.

LIN, SHENG-XIANG, ENZYMOLOGY, STRUCTURAL BIOLOGY. **Personal Data:** b Shanghai, China, August 27, 1945; m 1985, Ming Zhou. **Education:** Fudan Univ, Shanghai, BS, 1968; Shanghai Inst Biochem, MS, 1979; Nat Ctr Sci Res, France, Dr, 1982; Univ Louis Pasteur, DSc, 1984. **Honors & Awards:** Commemorative Medal, Gov-Gen Can, 1993. **Professional Experience:** PROF PHYSIOL, CHUL RES CTR, LAVAL UNIV, as of 2003; prin investr, Laval Univ Med Ctr, beginning 1990; sr scientist & assoc prof, Dept Physiol, Laval Univ Med Ctr, beginning 1989; vis prof, Dept Biochem, Laval Univ Med Ctr, 1988-1989; vis assoc prof, Dept Biochem, Case Western Res Univ, 1987-1988; from asst prof to assoc prof, Shanghai Inst Biochem, Acad Sinica, 1984-1987. **Memberships:** Am Soc Exp Biol; Protein Soc; Can Physiol Soc; Chinese Asn Biochem; Fr-Chinese Asn Res Biol & Med. **Research Statement & Publications:** Protein chemistry, enzymology and enzyme structure studies, especially for aminoacyl-tRNA synthetases and steroid dehydrogenases. **Mailing Address:** Dept Physiol, Laval Univ, CHUL Res Ctr 2705, Sts-Foy, PQ G1V 4G2, Can. **Fax:** 418-654-2761. **E-Mail:** sheng-xiang.lin@crchul.ulaval.ca

LIN, SHIN, BIOCHEMISTRY, BIOPHYSICS. **Personal Data:** b Hong Kong, February 14, 1945; American citizen; m 1969, c 2. **Education:** Univ Calif, Davis, BS, 1965; San Diego State Univ, MS, 1967; Univ Calif, Los Angeles, PhD (biol chem), 1971. **Professional Experience:** PROF DEVELOP & CELL BIOL, UNIV CALIF, IRVINE, as of 2004; prof biol, Johns Hopkins Univ, beginning 1985; chmn biophys, Johns Hopkins Univ, 1983-1996; prof biophys, Johns Hopkins Univ, beginning 1982; NIH res career develop award, 1976-1981; from asst prof to assoc prof, Johns Hopkins Univ, 1974-1982; fel, Univ Calif, San Francisco, 1971-1974. **Memberships:** AAAS; Am Soc Biol Chemists; Am Soc Cell Biol; Biophys Soc. **Research Statement & Publications:** Biochemical and biophysical studies on cytoskeletal and motile functions of eukaryotic cells, with emphasis on drugs and cellular proteins affecting the assembly and interactions of actin filaments in vivo and in vitro. **Mailing Address:** Off biomed Initiatives, Univ calif, 4230 McGaugh Hall, Irvine, CA 92697-2300. **Fax:** 949-824-4709. **E-Mail:** shinlin@uci.edu

LIN, SHU, ELECTRICAL ENGINEERING, INFORMATION SCIENCES. **Personal Data:** b Nanking, China, May 20, 1936; m 1963, c 3. **Education:** Nat Taiwan Univ, BS, 1959; Rice Univ, MS, 1964, PhD (elec eng), 1965. **Professional Experience:** PROF EMER ELEC ENG, UNIV HAWAII, as of 2004; vis prof, tech Univ Munich, Germany; chmn, dept elec eng, Univ Hawaii, 1989-1995; Irma Runyon chair prof, Tex A&M Univ, 1986-1987; prof elec eng, Univ Hawaii, 1986-1988; NASA grants, 1983-1991; prof elec eng, 1982-1988; vis scientist, IBM Watson Res Ctr, 1978-1979; prof, Univ Hawaii, 1973-1981; vis scholar, Univ Utah, 1971-1972; Air Force Cambridge Res Lab grant, 1970-1971; NSF grants, 1967-1992; prof, Univ Hawaii, beginning 1973; from asst prof to assoc prof elec eng, Univ Hawaii, 1965-1973. **Memberships:** fel Inst Elec & Electronics Engrs; Sigma Xi. **Research Statement & Publications:** Coding theory and error control in data transmission systems; coding theory and multi-access communications. **Mailing Address:** Dept Elec eng, Univ Hawaii, 2540 Dole St, Honolulu, HI 96822-2270. **Fax:** 808-956-3427. **E-Mail:** slin@spectra.eng.hawaii.edu

LIN, SHWU-YENG TZEN, TOPOLOGY. **Personal Data:** b Tainan, Formosa, May 11, 1934; m 1960, c 3. **Education:** Nat Taiwan Normal Univ, BSc, 1958; Tulane Univ, MS, 1962; Univ Fla, PhD (math), 1965. **Professional Experience:** ASSOC PROF MATH, UNIV SFLA, 1971-; Zentralblatt fur Mathmatik, 1970-; reviewer, Math Rev, Am Math Soc, 1968-; asst prof, Univ Sfla, 1965-1971; lectr, Univ Sfla, 1964-1965; instr, Tulane Univ, 1961-1963; asst math, Inst Math, Academia Sinica, 1958-1960. **Memberships:** Math Asn Am. **Research Statement & Publications:** Topology and relation-theory. **Mailing Address:** Dept Math Phy 114, Univ SFla 4202 E Fowler Ave, Tampa, FL 33620.

LIN, SIN-SHONG, HIGH TEMPERATURE CHEMISTRY. **Personal Data:** b Taiwan, October 24, 1933; m 1964, c 3. **Education:** Nat Taiwan Univ, BS, 1956; Nat Tsing-Hua Univ, Taiwan, MS, 1958; Univ Kans, PhD (chem), 1966. **Professional Experience:** Fel, Northwestern Univ, Evanston, 1966-1967; RES CHEMIST, ARMY RES LAB MAT DIRECTORATE. **Memberships:** Am Chem Soc; Am Vacuum Soc; Electrochem Soc; Am Carbon Soc; Soc Advancement Mat & Process Eng. **Research Statement & Publications:** Thermodynamics of vaporization processes; material research and development; atmospheric sampling of gases; carbon fiber processing and characterization; electron spectroscopy for chemical analysis & auger electron spectroscopy. **Mailing Address:** 40 Lyons Rd, Westwood, MA 02090-2230. **Fax:** 617-923-5385.

LIN, SPING, NEUROCHEMISTRY, PHYSIOLOGY. **Personal Data:** b Canton, China, September 8, 1918; American citizen; m 1946, Ying-hgsh; c James Tseuming & Judy Tsemei. **Education:** Sun Yat-Sen Univ, BA, 1940; Univ Minn, MS, 1950, PhD (entom), 1952.

Professional Experience: RETIRED; prof emer neurol, Med Sch, Univ Minn, beginning 1986; from asst prof to assoc prof, Med Sch, Univ Minn, Minneapolis, 1963-1986; res assoc, Med Sch, Univ Minn, Minneapolis, 1961-1963; res Fel, Med Sch, Univ Minn, Minneapolis, 1954-1961; instr, Sun Yat-Sen Univ, 1944-1947; asst entomologist, Sun Yat-Sen Univ, 1940-1944. **Memberships:** Int Soc Neurochem; AAAS; Am Soc Neurochem; Sigma Xi. **Research Statement & Publications:** Neurobiology; neurochemistry. **Mailing Address:** Dept Neurol, Univ Minn, St Paul, MN 55113. **E-Mail:** linxx024@maroon.tc.umn.edu

LIN, STEPHEN FANG-MAW, PHYSICAL CHEMISTRY, PROFESSOR. **Personal Data:** b Nantou, Taiwan, August 21, 1937; m 1966, Chun-Mei; c Jeffrey & David. **Education:** Nat Taiwan Univ, BS, chem engr 1960; Univ Ill, Urbana, MS, 196 7, PhD (phys chem), 1970. **Professional Experience:** ASSOC PROF CHEM, NC CENT UNIV, 1970-. **Memberships:** AAAS; Sigma Xi; Am Chem Soc. **Research Statement & Publications:** Conformation and stability of sulfur ring compounds; molecular spectroscopy. **Mailing Address:** 1801 Fayetteville Rd, Durham, NC 27707. **Fax:** 919-530-5135. **E-Mail:** SteveFLin@aol.com

LIN, STEPHEN Y, LIGNIN CHEMISTRY, ORGANIC CHEMISTRY. **Personal Data:** b Pingtung, Taiwan, April 23, 1939; American citizen; m 1972, Ilona; c Stephen S & Eva M. **Education:** Nat Taiwan Univ, Taipei, BS, 1962; Univ Wash, Seattle, MS, 1967; NC State Univ, Raleigh, PhD (chem), 1970. **Honors & Awards:** George Olmsted Award, Am Paper Inst, 1971. **Professional Experience:** RES MGR, LIGNOTECH US INC, 1991-; res mgr, Reed Lignin Inc, 1983-1988; res mgr, Daishowa Chemicals Inc, 1989-1991; sr supv res, Lignin Chem Res, Am Can Co, 1981-1982; supvr res, Lignin Chem Res, Am Can Co, 1980-1981; res assoc, Lignin Chem Res, Am Can Co, 1979-1980; sr res chemist, Westvaco Corp, 1976-1979; res chemist, Westvaco Corp, 1972-1976; adj prof, NC State Univ. **Memberships:** Tech Asn Pulp & Paper Indust; Am Chem Soc. **Research Statement & Publications:** Lignin organic-physical chemistry; modification and application of industrial lignins, including kraft and sulfite lignins; dispersants. **Mailing Address:** LignoTech USA Inc, 100 Hwy 51 S, Rothschild, WI 54474-1198. **Fax:** 715-355-3648.

LIN, SUE CHIN, MATHEMATICS. **Personal Data:** b Taipei, China, November 8, 1936; m 1962, c 2. **Education:** Univ Calif, Berkeley, MA, 1964, PhD (math), 1967. **Professional Experience:** DIR GRAD STUDIES, UNIV ILL, CHICAGO CIRCLE, 1986-; assoc prof math, Univ Ill, Chicago Circle, 1971-1986; mem, Inst Advan Study, 1969-1971; Asst prof math, Univ Miami, 1967-1969. **Memberships:** Am Math Soc. **Research Statement & Publications:** Functional analysis. **Mailing Address:** Dept Math, Univ Ill, Chicago, IL 60680.

LIN, SUI, HEAT & MASS TRANSFER, FLUID MECHANICS. **Personal Data:** b Wenlin, Zhejiang, China, 1929; Canadian citizen; c 2. **Education:** Ord Eng Col, Taiwan, BS, 1953; Univ Karlsruhe, WGer, Dipl-Ing 1962, Dr-Ing(mech eng), 1964. **Professional Experience:** PROF EMER HEAT TRANSFER & FLUID MECHANICS, DEPT MECH ENG, CONCORDIA UNIV, MONTREAL, as of 2004; sr vis scientist, QIT-Fer et Titane Inc, Sorel, Que, 1984-1985; prof heat transfer & fluid mechanics, Dept Mech Eng, Concordia Univ, Montreal, beginning 1981; assoc prof, Dept Mech Eng, Concordia Univ, Montreal, 1975-1981; asst prof thermodyn & fluid mech, Dept Mech Eng, Concordia Univ, Montreal, 1970-1975; fel sonic boom, Inst Aerospace studies, Univ Toronto, Ont, 1969-1970; res assoc refrig, Inst Refrig Eng, Univ Karlsruhe, WGer, 1962-1965; gas dynamics, Inst Fluid Mech & Fluid Mach, 1965-1969. **Memberships:** Eng Inst Can; Can Soc Mech Eng; Am Soc Heating Refrig & Air Conditioning Engrs; Deutsche Gesellschaft fuer Luft-und Raum-fahrt. **Research Statement & Publications:** Heat and mass transfer with phase changes; confined vortex flows; heat pump systems for cold climates; freezing preservation of biological cells; similarity and modelling processes. **Mailing Address:** Dept Mech Eng, Concordia Univ 1455 de Maisonneuve Blvd W, Montreal, PQ H3G 1M8, Can. **Fax:** 514-848-3175.

LIN, SUNG P, FLUID MECHANICS, APPLIED MATHEMATICS. **Personal Data:** b Taipei, Taiwan, April 18, 1937; American citizen; m 1966, Charlotte; c Anna & Martin. **Education:** Taiwan Univ, BS, 1958; Univ Utah, MS, 1961; Univ Mich, PhD (eng mech), 1965. **Professional Experience:** Mem, J of Atomization & Sprays, 2004-; vice chmn to Chmn, Am Phys Soc, 1995-1998; Chmn, Dept Mech & Aeronat Eng, 1994-1995; grantee, ARO, 1985-; grantee, NASA, 1984-1986 & 1993-; NASA fel, 1983 & 1984; CHMN APPL MECH PROG, CLARKSON UNIV, 1981-; Bausch & Lomb grant, 1980-1981; vis prof, Rochester Univ & Stanford Univ, 1980-1981; consult, Eastman Kodak Co, 1977-1981; Kodak grant, 1974-1976; NSF res grants, 1970-1972, 1974-1976, 1978-1980, 1980-1985 & 1988-1991; NSF initiation grant, 1967-1969; PROF, CLARKSON UNIV, beginning 1974; from asst prof to assoc prof mech eng, Clarkson Col Technol, 1966-1972; lectr eng mech, Univ Mich, 1965-1966; fel teaching, Univ Mich, 1964-1965; res asst, Univ Mich, 1961-1964; Engr, Ministry Econ, China, 1958-1960. **Memberships:** Fel Am Phys Soc; Am Soc Mech Engrs; assoc fel Am Inst Aeronaut & Astronaut. **Research Statement & Publications:** Theory and application of mechanics; fluid and biofluid mechanics; hydrodynamic stability; flow separation; heat transfer; transieut phenomena; film coating technology; aerosol dynamics; atomization. **Mailing Address:** Dept Mech & Aeronaut Eng, Clarkson Univ, 357 Camp Bldg, PO Box 5725, Potsdam, NY 13699-5725. **E-Mail:** gw02@clarkson.edu

LIN, TIEN-SUNG TOM, PHYSICAL CHEMISTRY & SPECTROSCOPY, BIOLOGICAL CHEMISTRY & MAGNETIC RESONANCE. **Personal Data:** b Taiwan, China, January 9, 1938; m 1966, Loretta; c Robin, Irvin & Natatia. **Education:** Tunghai Univ, BA, 1960; Syracuse Univ, MS, 1966; Univ Pa, PhD (phys chem), 1969. **Professional Experience:** Vis prof, Leiden Univ, Neth 1990 & Inst Atomic & Molecular Sci, Academia Sinica, Taiwan, 1995; PROF CHEM, WASH UNIV, 1986-; Scientist-in-Res, Argonne Nat Lab, 1980; from asst prof to assoc prof, Wash Univ, 1976-1986; postdoctoral res assoc, Harvard Univ, 1970. **Memberships:** Am Chem Soc. **Research Statement & Publications:** Molecular spectroscopy; photophysical and photochemical processes; structural aspects of organic free radicals; free radical pathology and anti-oxidants; characteristics of pentacene in zero-field magnetic resonance; dynamics of organic triplets. **Mailing Address:** Dept Chem, Wash Univ, McMillen 405, St Louis, MO 63130. **Fax:** 314-935-4481. **E-Mail:** lin@wuchem.wustl.edu

LIN, TSAU-YEN, ENZYMOLOGY. **Personal Data:** b Taiwan, China, July 18, 1932; m 1967, Woan-Jung. **Education:** Nat Taiwan Univ, BS, 1955, MS, 1957; Univ Calif, Berkeley, PhD (biochem), 1965. **Professional Experience:** MEM, LIN & ASSOCS, 1992-; scientist, Cal-Test Diagnostic, 1991-1992; biochemist, Merck Sharp & Dohme Res Labs, 1969-1991; asst res biochemist, Univ Calif, Berkeley, 1967-1968; res assoc, Univ Calif, Berkeley, 1965-1967; res asst biochem, US Naval Med Res Unit Number 2, Taiwan, 1959-1961; res chemist, China Chem & Pharmaceut Co, 1958-1959; instr clin chem, Kaohsiung Med Col, Taiwan, 1957-1958. **Memberships:** AAAS; Am Chem Soc; Am Soc Biol Chemists; Sigma Xi. **Research Statement & Publications:** Biosynthesis and function of complex carbohydrates; mechanism and active site structure of enzymes; biochemical characterization of complement. **Mailing Address:** Lin & Assocs, 9365 Wickham Way, Orlando, FL 32836-5518. **E-Mail:** tsauyen@aol.com

LIN, TSUE-MING, IMMUNOLOGY, MICROBIOLOGY. **Personal Data:** b Ping-tung, Taiwan, June 10, 1935; American citizen; m 1964, c 3. **Education:** Nat Taiwan Univ, DVM, 1958, dipl pub health, 1960; Tulane Univ, MS, 1964; Univ Tex Med Br, PhD (microbiol), 1968. **Professional Experience:** VPRES, RES & DEVELOP, DIAMEDIX CORP, 1990-; dir res, Res & Develop, Diamedix Corp, 1986-1990; res assoc prof pediat, Med Sch, Univ Miami, 1980-1986; sr staff immunologist to asst dir res & develop, 1977-1986; consult, Cordis Labs, 1972-1974; from instr to assoc prof pediat, 1969-1980; res assoc, 1968-1969; teaching asst & lab instr, Taipei Med Col, 1961-1962; teaching asst & lab instr med parasitol, Col Med, Nat Taiwan Univ, 1960-1962. **Memberships:** AAAS; Am Soc Microbiol; Am Asn Immunol. **Research Statement & Publications:** Host-parasite relationship; enzyme-linked immunoassays for infectious and immunological diseases; immunology; human heart autoimmune system; trichinosis; amebiasis; toxoplasmasis; human pregnancy-associated plasma proteins. **Mailing Address:** Hyperion Inc, 14100 SW 136th St, Miami, FL 33186.

LIN, TSUNG-MIN, PHYSIOLOGY, PHARMACOLOGY. **Personal Data:** b Chefoo, China, October 8, 1916; American citizen; m 1942, Hsia; c 2. **Education:** Nat Tsing Hua Univ, China, BS, 1938; Univ Ill, MS, 1952, PhD, 1954. **Professional Experience:** Adj prof physiol, Ind Univ Sch Med, 1987-1988; CONSULT, MED RES METHODIST HOSP, INDIANAPOLIS, IND, 1986-; sr res scientist, Res Labs, Eli Lilly & Co, 1964-1985; res scientist, Res Labs, Eli Lilly & Co, 1959-1963; pharmacologist, Res Labs, Eli Lilly & Co, 1956-1959; asst prof clin sci, Col Med, Univ Ill, 1954-1956; sr instr, Peking Union Med Col, 1948-1951; asst prof, Nat Kweiyang Med Col, 1946-1948; lectr, Nat Kweiyang Med Col, 1943-1946; lectr physiol, Nat Chung Cheng Med Col, 1941-1943; asst, Nat Chung Cheng Med Col, 1940-1941; asst physiol, Nat Tsing Hua Univ, China, 1939-1940; consult med res, Methodist Hosp, Indianapolis, Ind. **Memberships:** Am Physiol Soc; Am Soc Pharmacol & Exp Therapeut; Am Gastroenterol Asn; Am Pancreatic Asn. **Research Statement & Publications:** Gastrointestinal physiology and pharmacology. **Mailing Address:** 15 Kingspark Ct, Little Rock, AR 72227. **Fax:** 317-846-1250.

LIN, TU, INTERNAL MEDICINE, ENDOCRINOLOGY & METABOLISM. **Personal Data:** b Fukien, China, January 18, 1941; American citizen; m 1967, c 3. **Education:** Nat Taiwan Univ, Taipei, MD, 1966. **Professional Experience:** DIR, DIV ENDOCRINOL, DIABETES & METAB, SCH MED, UNIV SC, as of 2005; PROF ENDOCRINOL, SCH MED, UNIV SC, 1984-; physician, Richland Mem Hosp, Columbia, SC, 1977-; from asst prof to assoc prof, Univ SC, 1976-1984; CHIEF, ENDOCRINE SECT, WILLIAM JENNINGS BRYAN DORN VET HOSP, 1975-; staff physician, Vet Admin Hosp, Salisbury, 1973-1975; fel, Roger Williams Gen Hosp, Brown Univ, 1971-1973; fel endocrinol, Lahey Clin, Boston, 1970-1971; resident med, Berkshire Med Ctr, Union Univ, 1968-1970; intern, Episcopal Hosp, Temple Univ, 1967-1968. **Memberships:** Endocrine Soc; Am Fedn Clin Res; Am Soc Andrology; fel Am Col Physicians. **Research Statement & Publications:** Male reproductive endocrinology; Leydig cell function including cell membrane receptors, cyclic AMP metabolism, steroid receptors, steroidogenesis, phospholipid turnover and long term cell culture; insulin receptors, insulin-like growth factors I and II receptors of Leydig cells. **Mailing Address:** Dept Endocrinol, Sch Med, Univ SC, Two Medical Park Ste 502, Columbia, SC 29203. **Fax:** 803-540-1075. **E-Mail:** lin@gw.mp.sc.edu

LIN, TUNG HUA, MECHANICS. **Personal Data:** b Chungking, China, May 26, 1911; American citizen; m 1939, c 3. **Education:** Tangshan Col Eng, BS, 1933; Mass Inst Technol, SM, 1936; Univ Mich, DSc(eng mech), 1953. **Honors & Awards:** Theodore Van Karman Award, Am Soc Civil Engrs, 1988. **Professional Experience:** Prin investr res projs, NSF, 1961-1978 & US Off Naval Res, 1985-1993; EMER PROF, UNIV CALIF, LOS ANGELES, 1978-; consult, NAm Aviation Inc, 1962-1968 & ARA Inc, 1966-1994; Consult, Off Ord Res, 1958; prof eng, Univ Calif, Los Angeles, 1956-1978; prin investr res projs, Off Sci Res, USAF, 1955-1959, 1988-; Consult, Continental Motor Corp, Mich, 1954-1955; from assoc prof to prof aeronaut eng, Univ Detroit, 1949-1956; mem, Chinese Tech Mission in Eng, 1945-1949; from designer to chief engr & prod mgr, Chinese Aircraft Mfg Plant, 1939-1945; From assoc prof to prof aeronaut eng, Tsing Hua Univ, China, 1937-1939. **Memberships:** Nat Acad Eng; acad sinicai Soc Eng Sci; fel Am Acad Mech; Am Soc Civil Engrs; fel Am Soc Mech Engrs. **Research Statement & Publications:** Micromechanics; multiaxial stress-strain relations based on microstress fields in polycrystals; fatigue crack initiation mechanism based microstresses; inelastic structures; el astoplastic analysis of beams, columns and plates; creep analysis of columns and plates. **Mailing Address:** 906 Las Palgas Rd, Pacific Palisades, CA 90272. **Fax:** 310-206-2222.

LIN, TUNG-PO, MATHEMATICS. **Personal Data:** b Fukien, China, December 31, 1926; American citizen; m 1956, c 4. **Education:** Nat Cent Univ, China, BSc, 1949; Mass Inst Technol, PhD (phys chem), 1958. **Professional Experience:** EMER PROF MATH, CALIF STATE UNIV, NORTHRIDGE, as of 2006; prof math, Calif State Univ, Northridge, beginning 1969; from asst prof to assoc prof math, Calif State Univ, Northridge, 1961-1969; Consult, IBM Corp, 1961-1968; Res chemist, E I du Pont Del Nemours & Co, Del, 1958-1961. **Memberships:** Am Math Soc; Math Asn Am. **Research Statement & Publications:** Functional analysis; applied mathematics. **Mailing Address:** Calif State Univ, Northridge, CA 91330-0001. **E-Mail:** tungpo.lin@csun.edu

LIN, TZ-HONG, ORGANIC CHEMISTRY, RADIOPHARMACEUTICAL RESEARCH. **Personal Data:** b Taiwan, January 30, 1934; m 1969, KY; c Alan & Brian. **Education:** Nat Taiwan Univ, BS, 1956; NMex Highlands Univ, MS, 1964; Univ Calif, Berkeley, PhD, 1969. **Professional Experience:** GUEST SCIENTIST, LAWRENCE BERKELEY LAB, BERKELEY, CALIF, 1992-; vpres, IMP Inc, 1990-1992; consult, Photon Diag Inc, 1985-1987; assoc dir, Res & Develop, 1983-1985; proj mgr, Medi-Physics, Inc, 1978-1983; res group leader, Medi-Physics, Inc, 1974-1978; dir res chem, Medi-Physics, Inc, 1971-1974; vis asst prof, Dept Chem, La State Univ, 1969-1971; res asst, Biodynamics Lab, Lawrence Radiation Lab, 1964-1969; teaching asst, Dept Chem, Univ Calif, Berkeley, 1963-1964; teaching & res asst, Dept Chem, NMex Highlands Univ, 1961-1963. **Memberships:** Soc Nuclear Med; Am Chem Soc; AAAS. **Research Statement & Publications:** Research and development of new radiopharmaceuticals; hot atom chemistry; free radical chemistry; antibody research. **Mailing Address:** THL Res, 1765 Ondina Dr, Fremont, CA 94539-3784.

LIN, WEI, WATER & WASTEWATER TREATMENT, HAZARDOUS WASTE MANAGEMENT. **Personal Data:** m Xing-guang Wang; c Jack & Patrick. **Education:** Beijing Inst Civil Eng & Archit, BS, 1982; State Univ NY, Buffalo, MS, 1989, PhD (environ eng), 1992. **Professional Experience:** ASST PROF CIVIL ENG, NDAK STATE, as of 1999; asst res prof civil & environ eng, W Va Univ, beginning 1996; sr engr, Ecol & Environ, Inc, 1992-1995; asst lectr, Beijing Inst Civil Eng & Archit, 1982-1985. **Memberships:** Water Environ Fedn. **Research Statement & Publications:** Experimental studies and mathematical model analyses of physico-chemical and biological unit processes for water and wastewater treatment; kinetic studies of biological growth and organic pollutant degradation in natural environment and in wastewater treatment systems. **Mailing Address:** Dept Civil & Construct Eng, NDak State Univ, CIE 201N, Fargo, ND 58105. **E-Mail:** wei.lin@ndsu.nodak.edu

LIN, WEI-CHING, SPACE PHYSICS. **Personal Data:** b Taipei, China, December 31, 1930; m 1959. **Education:** Nat Taiwan Univ, BSc, 1954; Univ Iowa, MSc, 1961, PhD (physics), 1965. **Professional Experience:** RETIRED; assoc prof space physics, Univ PEI, beginning 1968; asst prof, Dalhousie Univ, 1964-1968; res assoc spacephysics, Univ Iowa, 1963-1964. **Memberships:** Am Geophys Union; Am Asn Physics Teachers. **Research Statement & Publications:** Galactic and solar cosmic rays. **Mailing Address:** 56 Maplewood Crescent, Charlottetown, PE C1A 2X5, Can.

LIN, WEN-C(HUN), ELECTRICAL & COMPUTER ENGINEERING. **Personal Data:** b Kutien, China, February 22, 1926; American citizen; m 1956, c 3. **Education:** Taiwan Univ, BS, 1950; Purdue Univ, MS, 1956, PhD (elec eng), 1965. **Professional Experience:** PROF EMER ELEC ENGR & COMP, UNIV CALIF, DAVIS, as of 2005; prof elec engr & comp, Univ Calif, Davis, beginning 1978; from asst prof to prof syst eng, Case Western Reserve Univ, 1965-1978; instr, Purdue Univ, 1961-1965; sr engr, electronic data processing div, Honeywell Inc, 1959-1961; engr high voltage lab, Gen Elec Co, 1956-1959; engr, elec lab, Taiwan Power Co, 1950-1954; Autonomous Mobile Robot Syst. **Memberships:** Inst Elec & Electronics Engrs. **Research Statement & Publications:** Special electronic instrumentation; signal processing; pattern recognition; microcomputers; artificial neuron network. **Mailing Address:** Dept Elec & Comput Eng, Univ Calif, 2064 Eng R II, Davis, CA 95616-5294.

LIN, WILLY, PLANT PHYSIOLOGY, PLANT MOLECULAR BIOLOGY. **Personal Data:** b Taiwan, China, July 2, 1944; m 1971, c 2. **Education:** Nat Taiwan Norm Univ, BS, 1967; Ill State Univ, MS, 1972; Univ Ill, Urbana, PhD (biol), 1976. **Professional Experience:** BUS MGR & CONSULT, DUPONT CROP PROTECTION PROD as of 2005; staff scientist, Agr Prod Dept, E I Du Pont de Nemours & Co, 1987-; staff scientist, Cent Res & Develop Exp Sta, 1977-1986; Res assoc, Dept Biol, Brookhaven Nat Lab, 1976-1977. **Memberships:** Am Soc Plant Physiologists; Am Inst Biol Sci; Sigma Xi; NY Acad Sci; Int Asn Plant Tissue Culture; AAAS. **Research Statement & Publications:** Ion transport mechanism in plant tissues; plant tissue culture and genetic transformation. **Mailing Address:** DuPont Crop Protection Prod, WM4-270, PO Box 80038, Wilmington, DE 19880-0038. **Fax:** 302-992-6051. **E-Mail:** willy.lin@usa.dupont.com

LIN, WOEI, MATHEMATICS. **Education:** Univ Md, PhD (Appl Math), 1984. **Professional Experience:** FAC, DEPT MATHS, MORGAN STATE UNIV, as of 2005. **Mailing Address:** 6609 Gleaming Sand Chase, MORGAN STATE UNIV, Columbia, MD 21044. **Fax:** 443.885.8200.

LIN, WUNAN, GEOPHYSICS, ROCK MECHANICS. **Personal Data:** b Tainan, Taiwan, August 1, 1942; American citizen; m 1971, Doris. **Education:** Cheng-Kung Univ, BSE, 1964; Univ Calif, Berkeley, MS, 1969, PhD (geophys), 1977. **Professional Experience:** TASK LEADER, YUCCA MOUNTAIN PROJ, 1990-; GEOPHYSICIST, LAWRENCE LIVERMORE NAT LAB, UNIV CALIF, 1977-; Jane Lewis fel, 1968-1970; res asst, Univ Calif, Berkeley, 1967-1968 & 1971-1977; prof asst mining eng, Cheng-Kung Univ, 1965-1967; Chou Kai-Chi fel, 1962-1964. **Memberships:** Am Geophys Union; Int Soc Rock Mech; Inst Elec & Electronic Engrs. **Research Statement & Publications:** Solid earth geophysics; physical properties of rocks at high pressure and high temperature. **Mailing Address:** Lawrence Livermore Nat Lab, Univ Ca, L-201, 7000 E Ave, PO Box 808, Livermore, CA 94551. **Fax:** 510-424-6401.

LIN, XI-WEI, SUBMICRON INTEGRATED CIRCUIT PROCESS TECHNOLOGY, MULTI LEVEL INTERCONNECT INTEGRATION. **Personal Data:** b Gejiu, China, December 18, 1961; m 1989, Jiawen. **Education:** Beijing Univ, BS, 1982; Univ Paris, MS, 1984, PhD (solid state physics), 1987. **Professional Experience:** PRIN DESIGN ENGR, MICRON TECHNOL INC, as of 2006; staff engr, Vlsi Technol Inc, beginning 1995; vis scholar, Univ Fed Rio Grande Do Sul, Brazil, 1994; staff scientist, Lawrence Berkeley Lab, 1991-1995; res assoc, Northwestern Univ, 1987-1991; vis scientist, Univ Que, 1985. **Memberships:** Mat Res Soc; Inst Elec & Electronics Engrs. **Research Statement & Publications:** Interconnect, metallization, ion implantation, process integration, device engineering, materials defects; interfacial reactions, phase transformation, molecular beam epitaxy, metal hydrogenation, superconductivity and computer simulations; author of over 50 publications in field; patentee in field. **Mailing Address:** Microchip Technol Inc, 2355 W Chandler Blvd, Chandler, AZ 85224-6199. **Fax:** 480-899-9210. **E-Mail:** xi-wei.lin@sanjose.vlsi.com

LIN, YEONG-JER, METEOROLOGY, ATMOSPHERIC SCIENCES. **Personal Data:** b Taiwan, China, November 11, 1936; m 1966, Chiung-Chen; c Kathleen & Diana. **Education:** Nat Taiwan Univ, BS, 1959; Univ Wis-Madison, MS, 1964; NY Univ, PhD (meteorol), 1969. **Professional Experience:** PROF METEOROL, ST LOUIS UNIV, 1976-; NSF res grants, St Louis Univ, 1970-1993; from asst prof to assoc prof, St Louis Univ, 1969-1976; assoc res scientist, NY Univ, 1969; asst res scientist, NY Univ, 1965-1969; res asst meteorol, Univ Wis-Madison, 1962-1964. **Memberships:** Am Meteorol Soc; Am Geophys Union. **Research Statement & Publications:** Dynamical and observational studies of severe local storms; numerical modelling of meso-scale circulation. **Mailing Address:** Dept Earth & Atmospheric Sci, St Louis Univ, 3507 Laclede Ave, St Louis, MO 63103. **Fax:** 314-977-3117. **E-Mail:** lin@eas.slu.edu

LIN, YI-JONG, DRUG METABOLISM, TOXICOLOGY. **Personal Data:** b Feng Yuan, Taiwan, June 19, 1944; American citizen; c 2. **Education:** Univ Tokyo, BS, 1967, MS, 1971, PhD (pharmaceut), 1975. **Professional Experience:** ASSOC DIR, EISAI INC, as of 2006; sect leader pharmacol, Colgate-Palmolive Co, 1990-1999; Prin, CACA Mid-Jersey Chinese Sch, 1987-1988; group leader, Colgate-palmolive CO, 1984-1990; sr res pharmacologist, Colgate-palmolive CO, 1979-1984; res fel pharmacol, Univ Mo, Kansas City, 1977-1979; res assoc pharmaceut, State Univ NY, Buffalo, 1976; Postdoctoral fel pharmacol, Univ Mich, 1975-1976. **Memberships:** Am Pharmaceut Soc; Am Soc Pharmacol & Exp Therapeut. **Research Statement & Publications:** Plan and execute projects on pharmacokinetics, drug metabolism, drug delivery, bucal absorption and drug safety evaluation; plan and monitor acute, chronic toxicity, carcinogenicity, clinical pharmacokinetics, mutagenicity and reproductive toxicology studies. **Mailing Address:** Eisai Inc, 7 Argyle Way, West Windsor, NJ 08550. **Fax:** 201-462-9349. **E-Mail:** yi-jong_lin@eisai.com

LIN, YI-LING, MICROBIOLOGY. **Education:** Univ Calif, Los Angeles, PhD. **Professional Experience:** ASSOC RES FEL, DEPT MICROBIOL & IMMUNOL, INST PREV MED, INST BIOMED SCI, ACADEMIA SINICA, as of 2002. **Mailing Address:** Dept Microbiol & Immunol, Inst Prev Med, Inst Biomed Sci, Academia Sinica, Taipei, Taiwan. **E-Mail:** yll@ibms.sinica.edu.tw

LIN, YONG YENG, BIO-ORGANIC CHEMISTRY. **Personal Data:** b February 2, 1933; Taiwanese citizen; m 1961, c 2. **Education:** Nat Taiwan Univ, BSc, 1956; Tokyo Kyoiku Univ, MSc, 1963; Tohoku Univ, Japan, PhD (org chem), 1966. **Professional Experience:** RES SCIENTIST CHEM, INST BASIC RES, UNIV TEX MED BR, 1982-; Fogarty sr int fel, 1981; res scientist chem, Inst Basic Res, Univ Tex Med Br, 1972-1981; res assoc chem, Univ Toronto, 1970-1972; res assoc biochem, Univ Tex Med Br, Galveston, 1968-1970; res assoc chem, Fla State Univ, 1966-1968. **Memberships:** AAAS; Am Chem Soc; Sigma Xi. **Research Statement & Publications:** Mechanisms of biological oxidation; enzyme models; application of enzymes and enzyme models to preparative organic chemistry; organic synthesis. **Mailing Address:** Inst Basic Res, Univ Tex Med Br, Staten Island, NY 10314. **Fax:** 718-494-1080.

LIN, YOU-FENG, TOPOLOGY. **Personal Data:** b Feng-Shan, Taiwan, July 31, 1932; m 1960, c 3. **Education:** Nat Taiwan Normal Univ, BS, 1957; Univ Fla, PhD (math), 1964. **Professional Experience:** PROF MATH, UNIV SFLA, 1969-; Reviewer, Math Rev, Am Math Soc, 1965-; res asst prof, Univ Sfla, 1965-1966; from asst to assoc prof, Univ Sfla, 1964-1969; asst math, Inst Math, Chinese Acad Sci, 1956-1959. **Memberships:** Am Math Soc; Math Asn Am. **Research Statement & Publications:** Topological algebra; structure of topological semigroups; semigroup of measures; topology and relation-theory. **Mailing Address:** Dept Math Phy, Univ SFla, 114 4202 E Fowler Ave, Tampa, FL 33620.

LIN, YU, SPACE PLASMA PHYSICS, MAGNETOSPHERIC PHYSICS. **Education:** Peking Univ, BS, 1985; Inst Geophys, MS, 1988; Univ Alaska, PhD (space physics), 1993. **Professional Experience:** PROF PHYSICS, AUBURN UNIV, as of 2005; asst prof physics, Auburn Univ, beginning 1994. **Memberships:** Am Geophys Union. **Research Statement & Publications:** Theoretical and simulation studies of the magnetic reconnection processes in the Earth's magnetosphere; interaction of interplanetary discontinuities with the Earth's magnetosphere; structure and ion heating of collisionless shocks. **Mailing Address:** Physics Dept Auburn Univ, 203 Allison Lab, Auburn, AL 36849-5311. **E-Mail:** linyu01@auburn.edu

LIN, Y(U) K(WENG), STRUCTURAL ENGINEERING, APPLIED PROBABILITY. **Personal Data:** b Foochow, China, October 30, 1923. **Education:** Amoy Univ, BS, 1946; Stanford Univ, MS, 1955, PhD (struct eng), 1957. **Honorary Degrees:** DEng, Univ Waterloo, Can, 1994. **Honors & Awards:** Alfred M Freudenthal Medal, Am Soc Civil Engrs, 1984; Stochastic Dynamics Res Award, Int Asn Struct Safety & Reliability, 1993; Theodore von Karman medal, Am Soc Cir Engrs, 1998; Alexander von Humboldt awd for Sr US Scientists, 2000, J P Den Hartog awd, Am Soc Mech Engrs, 2001. **Professional Experience:** Brookhaven Nat Lab, 1990-; TRW defense & space systs, 1978-; PROF & DIR, CHARLES E SCHMIDT EMINENT SCHOLAR ENG, FLA ATLANTIC UNIV, 1983-; sr vis fel, Inst Sound & Vibration Res, Univ Southampton, Eng, 1976; res Labs, Gen Motors Corp, 1975-; US Army Weapons Command, Ill, 1972-1977; NSF sr fel, 1967-1968; vis prof, Mass Inst Technol, 1967-1968; consult, Gen Dynamics/Convair, 1967; from assoc prof aeronaut & asstronaut eng to prof, Univ Ill, Urbana, 1962-1983; consult, Wichita Div, 1962; consult, transport div, Boeing Co, 1961; asst prof aeronaut eng, Univ Ill, Urbana, 1960-1962; res engr, Boeing Co, 1958-1960; prof eng, Imp Col Eng, Ethiopia, 1957-1958; stress engr, Vertol Aircraft Corp, Pa, 1956-1957. **Memberships:** Am Inst Aeronaut & Astronaut; Acoust Soc Am; Am Acad Mech; Am Soc Civil Engrs; Int Asn Struct Safety & Reliability; Am Asn Wind Eng; Earthquake Eng Res Inst; U.S. Natl Acad of Enginr Russian Acad of Engr (foreign mem). **Research Statement & Publications:** Structural dynamics; random vibrations; systems reliability. **Mailing Address:** Ctr Appl Stochastics Res, Fla Atlantic Univ, Rm 204, Bldg 36, Boca Raton, FL 33431-0991. **E-Mail:** linyk@casr.fau.edu

LIN, YU-CHONG, PHYSIOLOGY. **Personal Data:** b Taiwan, China, April 24, 1935; American citizen; m 1960, Dora; c Mimi & Betty. **Education:** Taiwan Norm Univ, BS, 1959; Univ NMex, MS, 1964; Rutgers Univ, PhD (physiol), 1968. **Professional Experience:** Nat Defense Med Col, Taipei, Taiwan, 1989-; vis prof, Nat Yang Ming Med Col, Taipei, Taiwan, 1983-; Kosin Med Col, Basan, Korea, 1983-; Physiologist consult, Tripler Army Med Ctr, 1979-; PROF PHYSIOL, SCH MED, UNIV HAWAII, MANOA, 1976-; sr res fel, Ames Res Ctr, Moffett Field, NASA, 1975-1976; from asst prof to assoc prof, Sch Med, Univ Hawaii, Manoa, 1969-1976; res assoc, Univ Calif, Santa Barbara, 1968-1969; Teaching asst biol, Taiwan Norm Univ, 1960-1962. **Memberships:** AAAS; Am Physiol Soc; Fedn Am Socs Exp Biol; Undersea & Hyperbaric Med Soc. **Research Statement & Publications:** Cardiovascular research in the area of diving, exercise, and effect of environmental factors. **Mailing Address:** Dept Physiol Sch Med, Univ Hawaii 1906 E-W Rd, Honolulu, HI 96822. **Fax:** 808-956-9722. **E-Mail:** yclin@hawaii.edu

LIN, YUE JEE, CYTOGENETICS. **Personal Data:** b Canton, China, October 8, 1945; m 1972, Chen; c 2. **Education:** Nat Taiwan Univ, BS, 1967; Ohio State Univ, MS, 1972, PhD (genetics), 1976. **Professional Experience:** Mem bd dirs, Chinese Am Acad & Prof Soc, 1987-1992; ASSOC PROF GENETICS & CYTOGENETICS, ST JOHN'S UNIV, 1982-; asst prof, St John's Univ, 1976-1982; teaching assoc genetics & biol, Ohio State Univ, 1970-1976; res asst, Taiwan Agr Res Inst, 1969-1970; res asst, Nat Taiwan Univ, 1968-1969. **Memberships:** Am Soc Cell Biol; Genetics Soc Am; Am Genetic Asn; Sigma Xi. **Research Statement & Publications:** Cytogenetics of complex heterozygotes, Rhoeo spathacea; cytogenetics of polyploids; cytogenetic effects of mutagens and environmental chemicals. **Mailing Address:** Dept Biol Sci, St John's Univ, Jamaica, NY 11439. **E-Mail:** liny@stjohns.edu

LIN, YUH LANG, ATMOSPHERIC SCIENCES. **Education:** Fu Jen Catholic Univ, BS, 1976; Yale Univ, PhD (metrol & geophys fluid dynamics), 1984; SDakota Sch Mines & Technol, MS, 1979; Fordham Univ, MS, 1978. **Professional Experience:** PROF, DEPT MARINE, EARTH & ATMOSPHERIC SCI, NC STATE UNIV, 1998-; asst prof to assoc prof, Dept Marine, Earth & Atmospheric Sci, NC State Univ, 1987-1998. **Memberships:** Am Metrol Soc; Sigma Xi. **Mailing Address:** Dept Marine, Earth & Atmospheric Sci, NC State Univ, Raleigh, NC 27695-8208. **E-Mail:** yl_lin@ncsu.edu

LINAM, JAY H, ENTOMOLOGY. **Personal Data:** b Carey, Idaho, March 9, 1931; m 1965, c 2. **Education:** Univ Idaho, BS, 1953; Univ Utah, MS, 1957, PhD (entom, zool), 1965. **Professional Experience:** PROF EMER BIOL, COLO STATE UNIV, PEUBLO, as of 2004; chmn dept life sci, Univ Southern Colo, 1987-1988; prof biol, Univ Southern Colo, beginning 1975; from instr to assoc prof, Univ Southern Colo, 1965-1975; mgr, Magna Mosquito Abatement Dist, Utah, 1960-1962; Asst entomologist, Ecol Res Lab, Univ Utah, 1958-1959. **Memberships:** Entom Soc Am; Am Mosquito Control Asn. **Research Statement & Publications:** Taxonomy and biology of mosquitoes of Western United States. **Mailing Address:** 2791 Country Farm Rd, Pueblo, CO 81006.

LINARES, OLGA F, AGRARIAN SYSTEMS, TROPICAL FOREST SOCIETIES. **Personal Data:** b November 10, 1936; m Martin. **Education:** Vassar Col, BA, 1958; Harvard Univ, PhD (anthrop), 1964. **Professional Experience:** St John's overseas vis fel, Cambridge Univ, UK, 1986-1987; vis prof anthrop, Stanford Univ, 1982; fel, Ctr Advan Study Behav

Sci, Stanford Univ, Calif, 1979-1980; res cur Cent Am archaeol, Peabody Mus, Harvard Univ, 1974-; SR SCIENTIST, SMITHSONIAN TROP RES INST, 1974-; vis prof anthrop, Univ Tex, Austin, 1974; lectr anthrop, Univ Pa, 1966-1971. **Memberships:** Nat Acad Sci; Am Anthrop Asn; African Studies Asn; Royal Anthrop Asn; Latin Am Studies Asn; fel AAAS. **Research Statement & Publications:** Agrarian practices and political economy of West African and Central American rural populations. **Mailing Address:** Smithsonian Trop Res Inst, Unit 948, APO, AA 34002-0948. **Fax:** 507-212-8148. **E-Mail:** linareso@si.edu

LINASK, KERSTI KATRIN, CELL ADHESION, SIGNAL TRANSDUCTION. **Personal Data:** b Zittau, Ger, February 10, 1945; American citizen; m 1967, Juri; c 2. **Education:** Russell Sage Col, BA, 1967; Univ Calif, Los Angeles, MA, 1968; Univ Pa, PhD (develop biol), 1986. **Professional Experience:** Assoc prof, univ med dent of nj; amer assoc of anatomists; soc for dcvclop biol, 1995-; Asst prof, Children's Hosp Philadelphia, 1990-; ASST PROF PEDIAT, UNIV PA, 1990-; fel develop biol, Thomas Jefferson Univ, 1986-1989; Instr biol, Holy Family Col, 1970-1980; mem, Basic Sci Coun, Am Heart Asn Coun Cardiovasc Dis of the Young. **Memberships:** Soc Develop Biol; Am Soc Cell Biol; Int Soc Develop Biol; Am Heart Asn; AAAS. **Research Statement & Publications:** Mechanisms underlying cell adhesion systems, growth factor signalling and signal transduction during early avian and mammalian heart development. **Mailing Address:** Dept Cell Biol, Univ Med & Dent NJ 2 Medical Center Dr, Stratford, NJ 08084. **Fax:** 856-566-6017. **E-Mail:** linaskkk@umdrj.edu

LINAWEAVER, FRANK PIERCE, ENVIRONMENTAL ENGINEERING, CIVIL ENGINEERING. **Personal Data:** b Woodstock, Va, August 22, 1934; m 1968, c 2. **Education:** Johns Hopkins Univ, BES, 1955, PhD (water resources, sanit eng), 1965; Am Acad Environ Engrs, dipl. **Professional Experience:** RETIRED; pres, E A Eng Inc, 1986-1993; trustee, Johns Hopkins Univ, 1980-1986, 1987-; dir, T Rowe Price Mutual Funds, 1979-; partner, Rummel, Klepper & Kahl, Consult Engrs, 1978-1986; vis comt, Sch Archit, Univ Md, 1975-1978; consult environ & civil eng, 1974-1978; consult rev panel, URS, Inc, 1970-1972; dir, Dept Pub Works, City of Baltimore, 1969-1974; mem, President's Air Qual Adv Bd, 1968-1971; dep dir, Dept Pub Works, City of Baltimore, 1968-1969; assoc prof environ sci, Dept Environ Eng & Geog, 1967-1968; White House fel, US Govt, 1966-1967; res staff mem, water resources group, Resources for Future, Inc, DC, 1966; res assoc, Dept Environ Eng Sci, 1965-1966; res staff asst, Dept Sanit Eng & Water Resources, Johns Hopkins Univ, 1961-1965; from jr civil engr to sr civil engr, Bur Water Supply, Baltimore, 1955 & 1958-1961. **Memberships:** Fel Am Soc Civil Engrs; Am Acad Environ Eng; fel AAAS; Nat Soc Prof Engrs; Am Water Works Asn; Am Consult Engrs Coun. **Research Statement & Publications:** Residential and commercial water use and their impact on urban water systems; urban water management and water resources; street cleaning relation to water pollution control; public works; sanitary environmental engineering; hydrology. **Mailing Address:** 224 Wendover Rd, Baltimore, MD 21218.

LINBERG, STEVEN E, BIOLOGY. **Education:** Univ Del, BA, 1973; Pa State Univ, MS, 1975, PhD (physiol), 1978. **Professional Experience:** Pres & founder, Res Fund Inc, 1992-; PRES & CONSULT, LINBERG RES INC, 1992-; dir clin res, Univax Biologics, Inc, 1992; assoc dir clin res & proj leader, Boehringer Mannheim Pharmaceut, 1986-1992; vis res assoc, Inst Emergency Med Serv Syst, Univ Md, 1985-1991; proj leader & clin res scientist, Med Div, Burroughs Wellcome Co, 1985-1986; founder, exec dir & mem bd dir, Shock Trauma Res Fund, 1983-1992; asst prof path, Grad Fac, Univ Md, 1980-1984; res assoc clin physiol, Inst Emergency Med Serv Syst, Univ Md, 1978-1984. **Memberships:** Am Physiol Soc; Am Soc Microbiol; Am Col Cardiol; Am Soc Nephrology; Am Heart Asn; Regulatory Affairs Prof Soc. **Research Statement & Publications:** Physiology; biology. **Mailing Address:** Clin Prod Develop, 22401 Rolling Hill Lane, Gaithersburg, MD 20882-2345.

LIN-CHUNG, PAY-JUNE, SEMICOUNDUCTOR PHYSICS, THEORETICAL SOLID STATE PHYSICS. **Personal Data:** b Tienjin, China, nat American citizen; m 1967, c 2. **Education:** Nat Taiwan Univ, China, BS, 1958; Univ Penn, MS, 1961, PhD (physics), 1965. **Professional Experience:** AT NAVAL RES LAB, as of 2004; Cambridge Univ, England, 1978-1979; vis lectr, Univ Durham, England, 1973-1974; vis scientist, Argonne Nat Lab, 1971; RES PHYSICIST, NAVAL RES LAB, 1967-; asst prof physics, State Univ Northridge Calif, 1966-1967; res physicist, Univ Calif, Berkeley, 1965-1966; Res Physicist, Inst Metals, Univ Chicago, 1964-1965. **Memberships:** Am Phys Soc; Mat Res Soc. **Research Statement & Publications:** Theoretical investigations of the electronic and lattice vibrational structure and of electro-optical effects in solids; defects, surfaces and superlattices on semiconductors. **Mailing Address:** Code 6877, Naval Res Lab, Bldg 208, Rm 343, 4555 Overlook Ave SW, Washington, DC 20375-5347. **E-Mail:** linchung@nrlfs1.nrl.navy.mil

LINCICOME, DAVID RICHARD, PARASITOLOGY, PHYSIOLOGY. **Personal Data:** b Champaign, Ill, January 17, 1914; m 1953, Margaret Stirewalt; c Judith A & David. **Education:** Univ Ill, BS & MS, 1937; Tulane Univ, PhD (parasitol), 1941; Am Bd Med Microbiol, dipl, 1965. **Honors & Awards:** Anniversary Award, Helminthological Soc, 1976. **Professional Experience:** RETIRED; founder & ed, Int Goat & Sheep Res; dir & registrar, Jacob Sheep Conservancy; dir, Am Goat Soc, 1991-; dist dir, Natural Colored Wool Growers Asn, 1990-; vis scholar, Nat Agr Libr, 1990-1992; guest scientist, USDA Exp Sta, Beltsville, Md, 1978-; dir res, Am Dairy Goat Asn, mem bd dirs, 1973-1979; chmn comt exam & cert, Am Bd Med Microbiol, 1972-; dir, Am Dairy Goat Asn, 1972-1988 & Nat Pygmy Goat Asn; ed, Trans, Am Micros Soc, 1970-1971; vis scientist, Lab Phys Biol, Nat Inst Arthritis & Metab Dis, 1964-1965; ed, Int Rev Trop Med, 1960-; USPHS res grants, 1958-1968; from asst prof to prof zool, Howard Univ, 1955-1970; guest scientist, Naval Med Res Inst, 1955-1961; ed & founder Exp Parasitol, 1949- & chmn ed bd, 1950-1976; sr res parasitologist, E I du Pont de Nemours & Co, 1949-1954; asst prof parasitol, Univ Wis, 1947-1949; from instr to asst prof zool, Univ Ky, 1941-1947; asst zool, Univ Ill, 1937; asst trop med, Sch Med, Tulane Univ, 1934-1941. **Memberships:** Fel AAAS; Am Soc Parasitol; Helminth Soc (secy, 1960, vpres, 1961, pres, 1968); fel NY Acad Sci; Am Dairy Goat Asn; Nat Pygmy Goat Asn (pres, 1979); Natural Colored Wool Growers Asn. **Research Statement & Publications:** Diagnosis of protozoan and helminthic diseases; amebiasis; taxonomy and systematics of Acanthocephala, Nematoda and Cestoda; epidemiology of tropical diseases; molecular biology of parasitism; nutritional exchange between parasite and host. **Mailing Address:** 3032 Courtney School House Rd, Midland, VA 22728.

LINCK, ALBERT JOHN, PLANT PHYSIOLOGY. **Personal Data:** b Portsmouth, Ohio, August 18, 1926; m 1957, c 2. **Education:** Ohio State Univ, BSc, 1950, MSc, 1951, PhD (plant physiol), 1955. **Professional Experience:** RETIRED; provost & acad vpres, Colo State Univ, 1984-1988; assoc vpres acad admin, Col Agr, 1973-1984; dean, Col Agr, 1971-1973; asst dir, Minn Agr Exp Sta, 1966-1971; From instr to prof plant physiol, Univ Minn, St Paul, 1955-1984. **Memberships:** AAAS; Am Soc Plant Physiol; Bot Soc Am; Scand Soc Plant Physiol; Am Inst Biol Sci. **Research Statement & Publications:** Translocation of inorganic and organic compounds; mechanism of action of growth regulators. **Mailing Address:** 1710 Grandview Ave, Portsmouth, OH 45662.

LINCK, RICHARD WAYNE, BIOCHEMISTRY, CELL & MOLECULAR BIOLOGY. **Personal Data:** b Los Angeles, Calif, April 9, 1945; m 1972, Madeleine; c Guthrie, Peter, Theodor & Anna. **Education:** Stanford Univ, BA, 1967; Brandeis Univ, PhD (biol), 1972. **Professional Experience:** PROF, DEPT GENETICS, CELL BIOL & DEVELOP, UNIV MINN, 1987-; assoc prof, Dept Cell Biol & Neuroanat, Univ Minn, 1984-1987; assoc prof, Harvard Med Sch, 1981-1984; asst prof, Harvard Med Sch, 1975-1981; instr, Harvard Med Sch, 1974-1975; fel, Lab Molecular Biol, Med Res Coun, Cambridge, Eng, 1971-1973. **Memberships:** Am Soc Cell Biol; Biophys Soc; AAAS. **Research Statement & Publications:** Function of microtubule cystoskeleton in motility, development and morphogenesis, using biochemistry, molecular biology and structural studies; cytology; published over 15 articles. **Mailing Address:** Dept Genetics, Cell Biol & Develop, Univ Minn, 6-160 Jackson, 321 Church St SE, Minneapolis, MN 55455. **Fax:** 612-624-8118. **E-Mail:** linck@mail.ahc.umn.edu

LINCK, ROBERT GEORGE, INORGANIC CHEMISTRY. **Personal Data:** b St Louis, Mo, November 18, 1938; m 1962. **Education:** Case Inst Technol, BS, 1960; Univ Chicago, PhD (inorg chem), 1963. **Honors & Awards:** Catalyst Award, Chem Mfrs Asn. **Professional Experience:** Assoc prof, US Naval Acad, 1986-1988; PROF CHEM, SMITH COL, 1985-; from asst prof to assoc prof, Smith Col, 1981-1985; from asst prof to assoc prof, Univ Calif, 1966-1981. **Memberships:** AAAS; Am Chem Soc. **Research Statement & Publications:** Rates of inorganic reactions, especially electron-transfer reactions; electronic structure and photochemistry of complex ions; bond lengths; space charge and dipolar effects in ethanes; charge variation. **Mailing Address:** Dept Chem, Smith Col, Sabin-Reed 429, Northampton, MA 01063-0048. **Fax:** 413-585-3786. **E-Mail:** rlinck@email.smith.edu

LINCOLN, CHARLES ALBERT, THEORETICAL PHYSICS. **Personal Data:** b Rudyard, Mont, May 13, 1939; m 1963, c 3. **Education:** Mont State Univ, BS, 1962, MS, 1964; Univ Va, DSc(eng physics), 1969. **Professional Experience:** RETIRED; consult electroacoust, noise control & archit acoust; adj res assoc physics, Whitman Col, 1984-; adj instr, Walla Walla Community Col, 1981-; Fulbright exchange prof, Newcastle upon Tyne Polytech, Newcastle/Tyne, Eng, 1973-1974; Inst Statist Mech & Theoret Thermodyn, Univ Tex, 1970; NDEA fel, Univ Va, 1966-1969; NSF assistantship, Theoret Inst Physics, Boulder, 1968; from instr to assoc prof physics, State Univ NY Col Fredonia, 1964-1979. **Memberships:** Am Phys Soc; Am Asn Physics Teachers; Inst Elec & Electronic Eng; Am Sci Affil; Audio Eng Soc; Am Astron Soc; Astron Soc Pac; Int Soc Optical Eng. **Research Statement & Publications:** Field theoretic methods in statistical mechanics and fluids; a generalized dynamical formalism of statistical mechanics; information theory and electroacoustics; astrophysics. **Mailing Address:** 2163 Granite Dr, Walla Walla, WA 99362.

LINCOLN, DAVID ERWIN, CHEMICAL ECOLOGY. **Personal Data:** b Detroit, Mich, October 8, 1944; m 1970. **Education:** Kalamazoo Col, BA, 1971; Univ Calif, Santa Cruz, PhD (biol), 1978. **Professional Experience:** PROF BIOL SCI, UNIV SC, as of 2005; assoc prof biol, Univ Sc, beginning 1987; asst prof, Univ SC, 1980-1986; fel, Stanford Univ, 1978-1980. **Memberships:** Ecol Soc Am; Bot Soc Am; AAAS; Entom Soc Am; Int Soc Chem Ecol; Phytochem Soc NAm. **Research Statement & Publications:** Environmental and genetic control of secondary chemical production by plants and the roles of these chemicals in plant-herbivore coevolution; effects of rising atmospheric carbon dioxide on plant-herbivore interactions. **Mailing Address:** Dept Biol Sci, Univ SC, Columbia, SC 92908. **Fax:** 803-777-4002. **E-Mail:** lincoln@sc.edu

LINCOLN, JEANNETTE VIRGINIA, GEOPHYSICS, SOLAR PHYSICS. **Personal Data:** b Ames, Iowa, September 7, 1915. **Education:** Wellesley Col, BA, 1936; Iowa State Univ, MS, 1938. **Honors & Awards:** Gold Medal, Dept of Com, 1973. **Professional Experience:** RETIRED; mem comn 40, Int Astron Union, beginning 1976; US Nat Comt, Int Union Geodesy & Geophys, 1976-1979; chmn working group V6, Geophys Indices, 1973-1981; vchmn, Ionospheric Network Adv Group, 1972-1981; chief data serv & dir, World Data Ctr, Solar-Terrestrial Physics, Nat Geophys & Solar Terrestrial Data Ctr, Environ Data & Info Serv, Nat Oceanic & Atmospheric Admin, 1970-1981; Am Geophys Union mem, Am Geophys Union-Int Sci Radio Union Bd of Radio Sci, 1969-1974; secy, Ionospheric Network Adv Group, 1969-1972; mem working groups 3 & 5, Inter-Union Comn on Solar-Terrestrial Physics, 1969-1972; forecasting reporter, mem comns IV & V, 1967-1973; dep chief data serv & chief, Upper Atmosphere Geophys, 1966-1970; dep chief data serv, Inst Telecommun Sci & Aeronomy, Environ Sci Serv Admin, 1965-1966; mem, US Comn G, Int Sci Radio Union, beginning 1963; forecasting reporter, Int Asn Geomagnetism & Aeronomy, 1963-1967; secy, Int Ursigram & World Days Serv, 1961-1981; mem US preparatory comt study group ionospheric propagation, Int Radio Consult Comt, 1959-1980; sect chief, Radio Warning Serv, Colo, 1959-1965; physicist, Nat Bur Stands, DC, 1942-1954; instr, Iowa State Univ, 1938-1942; asst household equip, Iowa State Univ, 1937-1938. **Memberships:** Fel AAAS; Sigma Xi; fel Am Geophys Union; Am Astron Soc; fel Soc Women Engrs. **Research Statement & Publications:** Radio propagation disturbances and forecasts; solar-terrestrial relationships; publication of solar and geophysical data; prediction of solar indices; data center management. **Mailing Address:** 2005 Alpine Dr, Boulder, CO 80304-3607.

LINCOLN, KENNETH ARNOLD, HIGH TEMPERATURE CHEMISTRY, MASS SPECTROMETRY. **Personal Data:** b Oakland, Calif, October 1, 1922; m 1956, Shirley Simpson; c 4. **Education:** Stanford Univ, AB, 1944, MS, 1948, PhD (phys chem), 1957. **Professional Experience:** ELORET INST, PALO ALTO, CALIF, 1986-; res scientist, NASA-Ames Res Ctr, 1970-1986; Phys chemist, US Naval Radio Defense Lab, 1958-1969. **Memberships:** Am Chem Soc; Am Soc Mass Spectrometry; Am Sci Affil; Combustion Inst. **Research Statement & Publications:** Thermochemistry of the vaporization of refractory materials; thermokinetics of pulsed energy deposition; development of instrumentation combining lasers and high-speed mass spectrometry for in-situ analyses of short-lived chemical species; space flight spectrometric instrumentation. **Mailing Address:** 2016 Stockbridge Ave, Redwood City, CA 94061-4131.

LINCOLN, LEWIS LAUREN, PHOTOGRAPHIC CHEMISTRY. **Personal Data:** b Canandaigua, NY, October 9, 1926; m 1949, c 6. **Professional Experience:** RES ASSOC CHEM, RES LABS, EASTMAN KODAK, 1970-; sr res chemist, 1965-1970; res chemist, 1960-1965; lab technician, 1946-1960. **Memberships:** Am Chem Soc. **Research Statement & Publications:** The study and synthesis of photographic sensitizing dyes and addenda. **Mailing Address:** 426 Mount Airy Dr, Rochester, NY 14617-2164.

LINCOLN, RICHARD CRIDDLE, APPLIED PHYSICS. **Personal Data:** b Boston, Mass, November 25, 1942; c 2. **Education:** Cornell Univ, BEP, 1966, MS, 1968, PhD (mat sci), 1971. **Professional Experience:** SR MEM TECH STAFF, SANDIA NAT LABS, as of 1998; tech staff mem appl physics, Sandia Labs, beginning 1971; Instr & res assoc mat sci, Cornell Univ, 1970-1971; SUPVR, APPL TECHNOL DIV. **Research Statement & Publications:** High pressure and high temperature experimental techniques; analysis of nuclear waste management systems. **Mailing Address:** Sandia Nat Labs, PO Box 5800, Albuquerque, NM 87185.

LINCOLN, THOMAS M, MOLECULAR BIOLOGY, CELLULAR BIOLOGY. **Personal Data:** b Orange, NJ, September 21, 1948. **Education:** Univ Tenn, PhD (zoology), 1974. **Professional Experience:** PROF PATH, UNIV ALA, BIRMINGHAM, 1992-; DIR GRAD PROG PATH, UNIV ALA, BIRMINGHAM, 1992-. **Research Statement & Publications:** Molecular biology; cellular biology; signal transduction. **Mailing Address:** Dept Path Univ Ala, Volker Hall G038 1670 Univ Blvd, Birmingham, AL 35294-0019. **E-Mail:** lincoln@path.uab.edu

LIND, ARTHUR CHARLES, NUCLEAR MAGNETIC RESONANCE, MATERIALS CHARACTERIZATION. **Personal Data:** b Chicago, Ill, May 28, 1932; m 1957, Barbara Collins; c Julie (Northrip), Catherine (Lind-Kern) & Charles. **Education:** Univ Ill, Urbana, BS, 1955; Rensselaer Polytech Inst, PhD (physics), 1966. **Professional Experience:** PRES, LIND SCIENTIFIC, 1998-; MDC Fel, McDonnell Douglas Aerospace, 1998-; Mgr, McDonnell Douglas Res Labs, 1994-; Dir Res, McDonnell Douglas Res Labs, 1993-; Chief Scientist, McDonnell Douglas Res Labs, 1989-; Prin Scientist, McDonnell Douglas Res Labs, 1988-; Sr Scientist, McDonnell Douglas Res Labs, 1983-; Scientist, McDonnell Douglas Res Labs, 1979-; Assoc Scientist, McDonnell Douglas Res Labs, 1976-; Sr Engr, McDonnell Douglas Aerospace, 1971-; Scientist, Watervliet Arsenal, 1966-; Engr, Knolls Atomic Power Lab, 1958-1961. **Memberships:** Am Phys Soc; Sigma Xi; American Chemical Society. **Research Statement & Publications:** Invent, design and characterize materials having tailored electromagnetic properties; electromagnetic processing of composite materials; nuclear magnetic resonance studies of polymers; theoretical and experimental studies of electromagnetic scattering; propagation of electromagnetic waves in turbulent media. **Mailing Address:** 15450 Country Mill Ct, Chesterfield, MO 63017. **E-Mail:** art@lindscientific.com

LIND, CAROL JOHNSON, MINERAL IDENTIFICATION, CHEMICAL ANALYSIS. **Personal Data:** b Minneapolis, Minn, December 8, 1926; div, c Karen & John. **Education:** Univ Minn, BS, 1949. **Professional Experience:** Res chemist, US Geol Surv, 1967-1998; phys sci tech chem res, US Geol Surv, 1966-1967; phys sci tech pollen identification, US Geol Surv, 1963-1966; jr chemist org res, Julius Hyman Co, 1950-1952; Anal chemist coal anal, Twin City Testing Co, 1949-1950. **Memberships:** Am Chem Soc; Am Geophys Union; Int Union Pure & Appl Chem. **Research Statement & Publications:** Natural-water chemistry of aluminum, aluminum-silicon, trace metals and manganese and their corresponding natural-organic influences. **Mailing Address:** 3727 Hamilton Way, Redwood City, CA 94062.

LIND, DAVID ARTHUR, NUCLEAR PHYSICS & PHYSICS OF SNOW & AVALANCHE PHENOMENA. **Personal Data:** b Seattle, Wash, September 12, 1918; m 1948, Mary; c 4. **Education:** Univ Wash, Seattle, BS, 1940; Calif Inst Technol, MS, 1943, PhD (physics), 1948. **Professional Experience:** PROF EMER PHYSICS, UNIV COLO, BOULDER, as of 2005; consult, Los Alamos Nat Lab, 1983-; chmn users group, Los Alamos Meson Facil, 1975-1976; chmn dept physics & astrophys, Univ Colo, Boulder, 1974-1978; mem prog adv comn, Los Alamos Meson Facil, 1971-1974; physicist div res, US AEC, 1969-1970; consult off instnl prog, NSF, 1963-1966; from assoc prof to prof, Univ Colo, Boulder, 1956-1983; asst prof, Univ Wis, 1951-1956; Guggenheim fel, Nobel Inst Physics, Stockholm, 1950-1951; res fel physics, Calif Inst Technol, 1948-1950; physicist, Appl Physics Lab, Univ Wash, Seattle, 1943-1945; jr aerodynamicist, Boeing Airplane Co, Wash, 1942-1943. **Memberships:** Fel Am Phys Soc; Sigma Xi. **Research Statement & Publications:** X-rays; crystal diffraction; nuclear spectroscopy; sector focused cyclotron design; charged particle scattering; reaction studies; fast neutron spectroscopy; particle beam optics; physics of snow and avalanche phenomena; physics of skiing. **Mailing Address:** Dept Phys, Univ Colo, NPL 214, Boulder, CO 80309. **E-Mail:** lind@spectr.Colorado.EDU

LIND, DAVID MELVIN, SURFACE PHYSICS, MAGNETIC ORDERING IN OXIDE LAYERED & OTHER NOVEL MATERIALS. **Personal Data:** m 1981, Celeste; c Christa, Eric, Jennifer, Kyle & Wesley. **Education:** Brigham Young Univ, BS, 1981; W M Rice Univ, MA, 1985, PhD (physics), 1987. **Professional Experience:** ASSOC PROF PHYSICS, FLA STATE UNIV, 1993-; prin investr, US Off Naval Res, 1992-; prin investr, NSF, 1992-; asst prof, Fla State Univ, 1988-1993; Off Naval Training/Am Soc Eng Educ fel, US Naval Res Lab, 1986-1988. **Memberships:** Am Vacuum Soc; Am Phys Soc; AAAS. **Research Statement & Publications:** Structural and magnetic ordering in heteroepitaxial oxide and metallic single-crystalline thin-films; superlattice and ultrathin-film synthesis by molecular beam epitaxy; spin-resolved electron spectroscopies, magnetometry and diffaction based probes of magnetocrystalline properties. **Mailing Address:** Dept Physics, Fla State Univ, Tallahassee, FL 32306-3016. **Fax:** 850-644-6504. **E-Mail:** lind@magnet.fsu.edu

LIND, DOUGLAS A, MATHEMATICS. **Personal Data:** b Arlington, Va, August 11, 1946. **Education:** Univ Va, BS, 1968; Stanford Univ, MA, 1971, PhD (math), 1973. **Professional Experience:** Consult, Heath Tecna Aerospace Co, 1989-1990; vis fac, IBM Watson Res Ctr, 1984; PROF MATH, UNIV WASH, 1983-; mem, math sci res inst Berkely, Calif, 1983-1984; asst to assoc prof math, Univ Wash, 1976-1983; fel, Inst Advan studies, Hebrew Univ, Jerusalem, Israel, 1975-1976; Miller res fel, Univ Calif, 1973-1975. **Memberships:** Am Math Soc. **Research Statement & Publications:** Researches the interplay between symbol dynamics; smooth dynamical systems and data storage and transmission. **Mailing Address:** Dept Math, Univ Wash, Seattle, WA 98195. **Fax:** 206-322-1443. **E-Mail:** lind@math.washington.edu

LIND, MAURICE DAVID, PHYSICAL CHEMISTRY, X-RAY CRYSTALLOGRAPHY. **Personal Data:** b Jamestown, NY, July 25, 1934; m 1962, c 1. **Education:** Otterbein Col, BS, 1957; Cornell Univ, PhD (phys chem), 1962. **Professional Experience:** Vis prof appl physics, Tech Univ Denmark, 1985; MEM TECH STAFF, SCI CTR, ROCKWELL INT, 1966-; res chemist phys chem, Union Oil Co, Calif, 1963-1966; NSF fel, 1962-1963. **Memberships:** Am Phys Soc; Am Crystallog Asn; Sigma Xi; Am Asn Crystal Growth. **Research Statement & Publications:** X-ray crystal mography; crystal growth. **Mailing Address:** 4501 Amberwood Rd, Haw River, NC 27258.

LIND, NIELS CHRISTIAN, APPLIED MECHANICS, RISK ASSESSMENT. **Personal Data:** b Copenhagen, Denmark, March 10, 1930; Canadian citizen; m 1984, c Julie W (Robbins), Peter C, Adam C & Andreas M. **Education:** Royal Tech Univ Denmark, MSc, 1953; Univ Ill, PhD (theoret & appl mech), 1959. **Honors & Awards:** A Ostenfeld Gold Metal. **Professional Experience:** Adj prof, Univ Victoria, 1993-1996; DISTINGUISHED PROF EMER CIVIL ENG, UNIV WATERLOO, 1992-; dir, Inst Risk Res, 1982-1987; Adv Comt Nuclear Safety, Atomic Energy Control Bd, 1981-1995; Inst Eng, Nat Univ Mex, 1975 & 1981 & Tech UnivDenmark, 1977-1978; vis prof, Univ Laval, 1969; mem, Can Nat Study Group Math Higher Educ, Orgn Econ Coop & Develop, 1963-1965; from assoc prof to prof, Univ Waterloo, 1960-1991; asst prof theoret & appl mech, Univ Ill, 1959-1960; res assoc, Univ Ill, 1958-1959; instr, Univ Ill, 1957-1958; asst stress anal, Univ Ill, 1956-1957; design engr, Fenco, Que, 1956; field engr, Drake & Merritt Co, Labrador, 1955-1956; engr, Bell Tel Co, Can, 1954-1955; design engr, Dominia Ltd, Denmark, 1953-1954. **Memberships:** Fel Am Acad Mech (pres 1971-1972); fel Royal Soc Can. **Research Statement & Publications:** Structural mechanics; theory of design; structural reliability and optimization; risk assessment. **Mailing Address:** Dept Civil Eng, Univ Waterloo, Waterloo, ON N2L 3G1, Can. **E-Mail:** nlind@hamilton.uvic.ca

LIND, OWEN THOMAS, LIMNOLOGY, WATER RESOURCES. **Personal Data:** b Emporia, Kans, June 2, 1934; m 1990, Laura; c Thomas & Richard. **Education:** William Jewell Col, AB, 1956; Univ Mich, MS, 1960; Univ Mo, PhD (zoology), 1966. **Professional Experience:** Prin investr, NSF, 1988; prin investr, NSF, 1983; consult, State Tex, 1982; consult, USAID, 1981-1983; PROF LIMNOL & MICROBIOL ECOL, BAYLOR UNIV, 1979-; consult, Corps Engrs, 1979; Chair, Exec. Com., Tyler Prize Environ. Achiev, 1974-; consult, US Nat Park Serv, 1974-1976; dir, Inst Environ Studies, 1971-1976; prin investr, Off Water Resource & Technol, 1971, 1973, 1976; consult, US Nat Park Serv, 1969; from asst prof to assoc prof, Baylor Univ, 1966-1979; res assoc limnol, Univ Mo, 1966; asst prof biol, William Jewell Col, 1960-1962; biologist, Parke Davis & Co, Mich, 1956-1960. **Memberships:** Am Soc Limnol & Oceanog; Sigma Xi; Int Asn Theoret & Appl Limnol; Brit Freshwater Biol Asn; NAm Lake Mgt Soc, Mex. Asn. Limnol. **Research Statement & Publications:** Factors governing production of lakes and reservoirs; tropical limnology; algal-bacterial interaction. **Mailing Address:** Dept Biol, Coll Arts & Sci, Baylor Univ, Box 97388, Waco, TX 76798-7388. **Fax:** 254-710-2969. **E-Mail:** owen_lind@baylor.edu

LIND, R BRUCE, MATHEMATICS. **Education:** Wis State Univ, BS, 1962; Univ Wis, MS, 1964, PhD (math), 1972. **Professional Experience:** PROF MATH, UNIV PUGET SOUND, as of 2004. **Mailing Address:** Dept Math & Comput Sci, Univ Puget Sound, Thompson 601, 1500 N Warner, Tacoma, WA 98416. **Fax:** 206-756-3352. **E-Mail:** lind@ups.edu

LIND, ROBERT WAYNE, THEORETICAL PHYSICS, ENGINEERING PHYSICS. **Personal Data:** b Ishpeming, Mich, August 25, 1939; m 1964, Eugenia; c Ingrid & Erik. **Education:** Mich Technol Univ, BS, 1961; Univ Pittsburgh, PhD (physics), 1970. **Professional Experience:** Res physicist, Naval Res Lab, 1987-1988; PROF EMERITUS, UNIV WIS-PLATTEVILLE, 2003-PROF PHYSICS & ELECT ENG, UNIV WIS-PLATTEVILLE, 1983-2003; assoc prof, Univ Wis-platteville, 1978-1983; chmn dept & assoc prof, WVa Inst Technol, 1976-1978; asst prof physics, WVa Inst Technol, 1974-1976; res assoc, Fla State Univ, 1973-1974; sr res assoc, Temple Univ, 1972-1973; res assoc physics, Syracuse Univ, 1970-1972; Engr, Ford Motor Co, 1963-1966. **Memberships:** Am Asn Physics Teachers; Int Soc Gen Relativity & Gravitation; AAAS. **Research Statement & Publications:** General relativity and electromagnetism; analysis of high frequency radio wave probing of the ionosphere; elementary and middle school science education. **Mailing Address:** Dept Physics, Univ Wis, One Univ Plaza, Platteville, WI 53818-3099. **Fax:** 608-342-1559. **E-Mail:** lindr@uwplatt.edu

LIND, VANCE GORDON, PHYSICS, ASTROPHYSICS. **Personal Data:** b Brigham City, Utah, February 12, 1935; m 1964, c Bretton R, Mark G, Kimara S (Thompson), Cherise D, Justin A, Zachary L, Rixa E, Vanessa A, Marilyse L & Lisette C & Tyson F. **Education:** Utah State Univ, BS, 1959; Univ Wis, MS, 1961, PhD (elem particles), 1964. **Professional Experience:** PROF PHYSICS, UTAH STATE UNIV, 1975-; CAZIER PROF, UTAH STATE UNIV, 1995-; investr, Dept Energy res grant, 1986-; dept head, Utah State Univ, 1981-1988; investr, NSF res grant, Utah State Univ, 1966-1971, 1978-1980 & 1980-1985; from asst prof to assoc prof, Utah State Univ, 1964-1975; Utah State Univ Res Found grant, 1964-1966, 1972-1976 & 1978-1979; res assoc, Univ Mich, 1964; res asst, Edgerton, Germeshausen & Grier, Inc, summer, 1960; Woodrow Wilson fel, 1959-1964; eng asst, Edgerton, Germeshausen & Grier, Inc, summer, 1959. **Memberships:** Am Asn Physics Teachers; Am Phys Soc; Sigma Xi; Am Solar Energy Soc; Int Solar Energy Soc. **Research Statement & Publications:** Basic interactions; elementary particle interactions, meson and nucleon interactions with nuclei, nuclear mass measurements, astronomy and astrophysics; solar energy technology; beta delayed nuclear particle decay; physics education. **Mailing Address:** Dept Physics, Utah State Univ, Logan, UT 84322-4415. **Fax:** 435-750-2492. **E-Mail:** glind@usu.edu

LIND, WILTON H(OWARD), CHEMICAL ENGINEERING. **Personal Data:** b Oakland, Calif, February 14, 1927; m 1951, Audrey; c Howard & Barbara. **Education:** Univ Calif, Berkeley, BS, 1950, MS, 1952; JD, Empire, Col, 1977. **Professional Experience:** RETIRED; mgr legal process & secy dept, Chevron Corp, 1985-1986; asst secy, Finance Dept, 1980-1985; analyst, Chevron Res Co, 1978-1980; from asst res engr to sr res engr, Chevron Res Co, 1951-1978. **Memberships:** Am Chem Soc; Am Inst Chem Engrs. **Research Statement & Publications:** Petrochemical research and development; aromatics chemistry; pilot plant design and operation. **Mailing Address:** 121 Northcreek Circle, Walnut Creek, CA 94598.

LINDAHL, LASSE ALLAN, MOLECULAR GENETICS, RNA. **Personal Data:** b Copenhagen, Denmark, September 9, 1944; m 1978, c 3. **Education:** Univ Copenhagen, MSc, 1969, PhD (microbiol), 1973. **Professional Experience:** PROF & CHAIR BIOL SCI, UNIV MD, BALTIMORE CO, 1994-; from asst prof to prof biol, Univ Rochester, 1978-1994; asst prof, Univ Aarhus, Denmark, 1976-1978; fel molecular biol, Univ Wis-Madison, 1973-1976. **Memberships:** Am Soc Microbiol; AAAS. **Research Statement & Publications:** Molecular basis for the regulation of ribosome synthesis; ribosomal RNA processing; assembly of ribosomes. **Mailing Address:** Univ Md, Dept Biosci, 1000 Hilltop Circle, Baltimore, MD 21250. **Fax:** 410-455-3875. **E-Mail:** lindahl@umbc.edu

LINDAHL, ROBERT J, MATHEMATICS. **Education:** Univ Ore, PhD, 1964. **Professional Experience:** RETIRED; assoc prof, Morehead State Univ, as of 2000. **Mailing Address:** Dept Math, Morehead State Univ, UPO 829, Morehead, KY 40351.

LINDAHL, RONALD GUNNAR, MOLECULAR BIOLOGY, BIOCHEMISTRY. **Personal Data:** b Detroit, Mich, August 11, 1948; m 1970, Diane; c Jared & Melissa. **Education:** Wayne State Univ, BA, 1970, PhD (biol), 1973. **Professional Experience:** CHAIR, DEPT BIOCHEM & MOLECULAR BIOL, SCH MED, UNIV SDAK, 1989-; reviewer, NSF, 1987-1990 & NIH, 1989-1990; PROF & DEAN, DEPT CELLULAR & MOLECULAR BIOL, SCH MED, UNIV SDAK, 1989-; co-prin investr, Nat Inst Alcohol Abuse & Alcoholism, 1987-; univ res prof, Univ Ala, 1984-1989; prin investr, Nat Cancer Inst grant, beginning 1979; prof biol, Univ Ala, 1975-1989; fel, Argonne Nat Lab, 1974-1975. **Memberships:** Am Soc Biochem & Molecular Biol; Am Asn Cancer Res; AAAS; Int Soc Biomed Res Alcoholism; Sigma Xi. **Research Statement & Publications:** Molecular biology of gene expression; aldehyde dehydrogenases; genetic changes in carcinogenesis, transplacental and perinatal; Biochemical changes during neoplasia; Genetic regulation of enzyme activity. **Mailing Address:** Dept Biochem & Molecular Biol, Univ SDak Sch Med, 414 E Clark St 145 Lee Med Bldg, Vermillion, SD 57069. **Fax:** 605-677-5124.

LINDAHL, ROY LAWRENCE, DENTISTRY. **Personal Data:** b Los Angeles, Calif, August 22, 1925; m 1976, c 7. **Education:** Univ Southern Calif, BS & DDS, 1950; Univ Mich, MS, 1952; Am Bd Pedodontics, dipl, 1956. **Professional Experience:** RETIRED; emer prof pediat dent, Sch Dent, Univ NC, Chapel Hill, beginning 1985; pres, Delta Dent Plan of

NC, 1985-1997; dir continuing educ & dent demonstr pract, Sch Dent, Univ NC, Chapel Hill, 1970-1983; chmn, Am Bd Pedodontics, 1967; consult, Womack Army Hosp, Ft Bragg, NC, 1960-1978; examr, Am Bd Pedodontics, 1960-1967; mem bd trustees, NC Cerebral Palsy Hosp, 1957-1963; from asst prof to prof, Sch Dent, Univ NC, Chapel Hill, 1952-1985. **Memberships:** AAAS; Am Soc Dent; Am Dent Asn; Am Acad Pedodontics (vpres, 1962-1963, pres-elect, 1963-1964, pres, 1964-1965); Int Asn Dent Res. **Research Statement & Publications:** Pedodontics; effective utilization of dental auxiliary personnel; problems of the handicapped patient; pre-payment dental care programs; health services research-quality assurance. **Mailing Address:** 305 Clayton Rd, Chapel Hill, NC 27514.

LINDAMOOD, JOHN BENFORD, DAIRY TECHNOLOGY. **Personal Data:** b Galax, Va, August 6, 1929; m 1953, c 1. **Education:** Va Polytech Inst & State Univ, BS, 1953, MS, 1955; Ohio State Univ, PhD (educ), 1974. **Professional Experience:** PROF EMER, DEPT FOOD SCI & TECHNOL, OHIO STATE UNIV, as of 2006; from asst prof to assoc prof, Dept Food Sci & Nutrit, Ohio State Univ, 1974-1992; prod mgr, Evaporated Milk Div, Carnation Co, 1956-1961. **Memberships:** Inst Food Technologists; Am Dairy Sci Asn; Int Asn Milk, Food & Environ Sanitarians. **Research Statement & Publications:** Milk and milk products. **Mailing Address:** Dept Food Sci & Technol, Ohio State Univ, Main Campus 2121 Fyffe Rd, Columbus, OH 43210.

LINDAU, EVERT INGOLF, SOLID STATE PHYSICS. **Personal Data:** b Vaxjo, Sweden, October 4, 1942. **Education:** Chalmers Univ Technol, Sweden, Civilingenjor, 1968, Technol Licentiat, 1970, PhD (physics), 1971, DrTechnol, 1972. **Professional Experience:** PROF PHYSICS, STANFORD UNIV, 1974-; res assoc physics, Stanford Univ, 1972-1974; res scientist, Varian Assocs, 1971-1972; Res asst physics, Chalmers Univ Technol, Sweden, 1968-1971. **Memberships:** Am Phys Soc; Am Vacuum Soc; Swed Soc Technol. **Research Statement & Publications:** Optical and photoemission studies of the electronic structure of materials using synchrotron radiation with emphasis on surface properties; surface states, surface photoemission, physisorbtion, chemisorbtion, surface composition and catalytic activities. **Mailing Address:** Stanford Electronics Lab, Stanford Univ, Stanford, CA 94305.

LINDAUER, GEORGE CONRAD, NUCLEAR ENGINEERING, INFORMATION SCIENCE. **Personal Data:** b Queens, NY, November 5, 1935; m 1959, c 3. **Education:** Cooper Union, BS, 1956; Mass Inst Technol, ScM, 1957; Univ Pittsburgh, PhD (mech eng), 1962; Long Island Univ, MS, 1971. **Professional Experience:** PROF EMER MECH ENG, SPEED SCI SCH, UNIV LOUISVILLE, 1998-; prof mech eng, Speed Sci Sch, Univ Louisville, 1979-1998; prof nuclear sci & librn, Speed Sci Sch, Univ Louisville, 1978-1992; from asst chem engr to chem engr, Brookhaven Nat Lab, 1964-1971; From jr engr to sr engr, Bettis Atomic Power Lab, Westinghouse Elec Corp, 1957-1964. **Memberships:** Am Soc Mech Engrs; Sigma Xi. **Research Statement & Publications:** heat transfer; fluid dynamics. **Mailing Address:** Dept Mech Eng, Univ Louisville, 102 Sackett Hall, Louisville, KY 40292.

LINDAUER, IVO EUGENE, PLANT ECOLOGY, SCIENCE EDUCATION. **Personal Data:** b Grand Valley, Colo, April 7, 1931; m 1957, Betty J Barstow; c Julia A & Sarah D. **Education:** Colo State Univ, BS, 1953, PhD (bot), 1970; Univ Northern Colo, MA, 1960. **Professional Experience:** Sci educ Evaluator, 1996-2004; prog dir, NSF, 1992-1994; Colo Div Wildlife grant, 1984-1985; northwest Colo wildlife consortium grant, 1981-1983; asst dean, Col Arts & Sci, 1976-1981; prof Bot, Univ Northern Colo 1975-1996; US Bur Reclamation grant, 1970-1972, 1972-1975; Tri-Univ Proj grant, NY Univ, 1970; from asst prof to assoc prof, Univ Northern Colo, 1967-1975; res assoc & teaching asst bot, Colo State Univ, 1965-1967; pres, Nat Asn Biol Teachers, 1963; asst prof sci, Univ Northern Colo, 1960-1965; instr biol, Univ Northern Colo, 1960-1964; mem, vpres & pres bd trustees, Colo Nature Conservancy. **Memberships:** Nat Asn Res Sci Teaching; life & hon mem Nat Asn Biol Teacher; Southwestern Asn Naturalists; Sigma Xi; Nature Conservancy. **Research Statement & Publications:** Analysis of vegetational communities found along floodplains; ecological studies of river bottom ecosystems; ecosystem modeling and assessment of remote sensing vegetation data bases; use of analogies in teaching science; profiles of biology teachers. **Mailing Address:** 269 Lodgepole Circle, Parachute, CO 81635. **Fax:** 970-285-1114. **E-Mail:** ivo38@aol.com

LINDAUER, MAURICE WILLIAM, ANALYTICAL CHEMISTRY, PHYSICAL CHEMISTRY. **Personal Data:** b Millstadt, Ill, September 25, 1924; m 1946, J Ruth Shiver; c Jane (Elder), Rosemary (Brannen) & Jack. **Education:** Wash Univ, AB, 1949, AM, 1953; Harvard Univ, MEd, 1962; Fla State Univ, PhD, 1970. **Professional Experience:** RETIRED; head dept, Valdosta State Col, 1981-1984; prof chem, Valdosta State Col, 1971-1984; assoc prof anal & phys chem, Valdosta State Col, 1957-1971; res chemist, Nitrogen Div, Allied Chem & Dye Corp, 1956-1957; Res chemist, Mallinckrodt Chem Works, 1952-1955 & Am Zinc, Ill, 1955-1956. **Memberships:** Am Chem Soc; Sigma Xi. **Research Statement & Publications:** Mossbauer spectroscopy; history of chemistry; thermodynamics and chemical equilibrium. **Mailing Address:** 1401 Miramar St, Valdosta, GA 31601-3616.

LINDBERG, CRAIG ROBERT, STATISTICS & SIGNAL PROCESSING, WAVE PROPAGATION. **Personal Data:** b Edmonton, Alta. **Education:** Univ Alta, BSc, 1979; Univ Calif, San Diego, PhD (earth sci), 1986. **Professional Experience:** CLIMATOLOGIST, PRINCETON UNIV, as of 2004; VIS RES SCIENTIST, PRINCETON UNIV, 1991-; resident visitor, AT&T Bell Labs, 1991-1992; assoc ed, Am Geophys Union, 1990-; postdoctoral mem tech staff, AT&T Bell Labs, 1988-1990; consult, AT&T Bell Labs, 1987; postgrad geophysicist, Univ Calif, San Diego, 1986-1988; assoc prin investr, Univ Calif, San Diego, 1984-1988; res asst geophys, Univ Calif, San Diego, 1980-1986; res asst physics, Mass Inst Technol, 1979-1980; Researcher geophys, Esso Resources Ltd, 1979. **Memberships:** Soc Indust & Appl Math; Am Statist Asn; Inst Elec & Electronic Engrs; Am Geophys Union. **Research Statement & Publications:** Statistical signal processing and application to physical problems; robust regression methods; climate change; seismic and speech data analysis; group theory solution of pdes. **Mailing Address:** Princeton Univ, Princeton, NJ 08544.

LINDBERG, DAVID ROBERT, PALEOBIOLOGY, EVOLUTIONARY ECOLOGY. **Personal Data:** b Elgin, Ill, February 7, 1948; m 1968, Dixie; c Jason D. **Education:** San Francisco State Univ, BA, 1977; Univ Calif, Santa Cruz, PhD (biol), 1983. **Professional Experience:** PROF & CHAIR IB & RES PALEONTOLOGIST, UNIV CALIF, as of 2004; asst dir, dept integrative biol, beginning 1991; adj assoc prof, dept integrative biol, beginning 1989; Willi Hennig Soc, Stockholm, 1988; res assoc, Dept Invert Paleont, Nat Hist Mus Los Angeles, Calif, 1986-; fel, Calif Acad Sci, 1985-; assoc res paleontologist, Mus Paleont, Univ Calif, Berkeley, beginning 1984; asst res paleontologist, Dept Integrative Biol, 1984-1986; sr mus sci, Dept Integrative Biol, 1982-1984; co-investr, res prog, US Fish & Wildlife Serv, Univ Calif, Santa Cruz, 1979-1991; res assoc, Dept Invert Zool, Calif Acad Sci, San Francisco, 1977-; res biologist, Dept Invert Zool, Calif Acad Sci, 1975-1977; dir res, Farallon Res Group, Oceanic Soc, 1973-1977. **Memberships:** Am Soc Zoologists; Am Malacological Union; Paleont Res Inst; Paleont Soc; Soc Systematic Zoologists. **Research Statement & Publications:** The evolution and biology of patellaean limpets; the evolution of brooding and hermaphroditism in molluscs; rocky intertidal community structure; molluscan evolution; author of various articles. **Mailing Address:** Dept Integrative Biol, Univ Calif, 3060 Valley life Sci Bldg, Berkeley, CA 94720-3140. **Fax:** 510-642-1822. **E-Mail:** drl@Berkeley.Edu

LINDBERG, DONALD ALLAN BROR, PATHOLOGY, COMPUTER SCIENCE. **Personal Data:** b Brooklyn, NY, September 21, 1933. **Education:** Amherst Col, AB, 1954; Columbia Univ, MD, 1958; Am Bd Path, dipl, 1963. **Honorary Degrees:** ScD, Amherst Col, 1979 & State Univ NY, Syracuse, 1987; LLD, Univ Mo, 1990. **Honors & Awards:** Silver Core Award, Int Fedn Info Processing, 1986; Surgeon General's Medallion, USPHS, 1989; Nathan Davis Award, AMA, 1989; Presidential Sr Exec Rank Award, 1990; Outstanding Service Medal, Uniformed Serv Univ Health Sci, 1992; Computers in Healthcare Pioneer Award, Computers in Healthcare Publ, 1993; Silver Award, US Nat Comn Libr & Info Sci, 1996. **Professional Experience:** Dir, Nat Coord Off High Performance Comput & Commun, 1992-1995; mem coun, Inst Med-Nat Acad Sci, 1990-; adj prof path, Sch Med, Univ Md, 1984-; DIR NAT LIBR MED, NIH, 1984-; mem, Biomed Rev Libr Comt, Nat Libr Med, 1979-1980; consult & mem, Peer Rev Group, TRIMIS, Dept Defense, 1977-1984; dir, Health Serv Res Ctr & Health Care Technol Ctr, Univ Mo, Columbia, 1976-1980; mem, Joint CBX Comt, Nat Bd Med Examrs & Am Bd Internal Med, 1974-1981; dir info sci group, Sch Med, 1971-1984; chmn, CBX Adv Comt, Nat Bd Med Examrs, 1971-1974; mem, Comput Res & Biomath Study Sect, NIH, 1967-1971 & Comput Sci & Eng Bd, Nat Acad Sci, 1971-1973; prof & chmn, Dept Info Sci, Sch Libr & Info Sci, 1969-1971; markle scholar, 1964-1969; from instr to prof path, Sch Med, 1962-1984; us rep, Comt Comput Med, Int Fedn Info Processing. **Memberships:** Inst Med-Nat Acad Sci; Am Med Informatics Asn; Col Am Pathologists; Am Asn Artificial Intel; fel Am Inst Med & Biol Eng; fel Am Col Med Informatics; Sigma Xi; fel AAAS. **Research Statement & Publications:** Information processing; computers in medicine; infectious diseases; author of 4 books and over 100 technical articles. **Mailing Address:** Nat Libr Med, NIH, Rm 2E-17 Bldg 38 8600 Rockville Pike, Bethesda, MD 20892. **Fax:** 301-496-4450. **E-Mail:** lindberg@nlm.nih.gov

LINDBERG, EDWARD E, MECHANICAL ENGINEERING. **Personal Data:** b Boston, Mass, August 16, 1938; m 1958, c 2. **Education:** Worcester Polytech Inst, BSME, 1960, MSME, 1963. **Professional Experience:** DIR COMPUT SERV, WESTERN NEW ENG COL, 1968-; ASSOC PROF MECH ENG, WESTERN NEW ENG COL, 1967-; asst prof mech eng, Western New Eng Col, 1963-1967; engr, Alden Res Labs, Worcester Polytech Inst, 1961-1963; Test engr, Scintilla Div, Bendix Corp, 1960-1961. **Memberships:** Am Soc Mech Engrs; Am Soc Eng Educ; Instrument Soc Am; Sigma Xi. **Research Statement & Publications:** Automatic controls; fluid mechanics; thermodynamics; computer sciences. **Mailing Address:** 76 Craiwell Ave, West Springfield, MA 01089-2916.

LINDBERG, GEORGE DONALD, PLANT PATHOLOGY. **Personal Data:** b Salt Lake City, Utah, February 9, 1925; m 1955, Jean; c Susan, Donald & Ann. **Education:** Ariz State Univ, BS, 1950; Okla State Univ, MS, 1952; Univ Wis, PhD (plant path), 1955. **Professional Experience:** RETIRED; from asst prof to prof plant path, La State Univ, Baton Rouge, 1955-1994. **Memberships:** Am Phytopath Soc. **Research Statement & Publications:** Plant virology; diseases of forage crops; abnormalities in the fungi. **Mailing Address:** 2074 Cambridge Circle, Pensacola, FL 32514-5465.

LINDBERG, JAMES GEORGE, ORGANIC CHEMISTRY. **Personal Data:** b Grand Rapids, Mich, September 19, 1940; c 3. **Education:** Kalamazoo Col, BA, 1962; Baylor Univ, PhD (org chem), 1969. **Professional Experience:** Vis Prof Chem, Grinnell Col, 2002-2004; PROF EMER CHEM, DRAKE UNIV, 2002-; vis Prof & Vis Sci, Stanford Univ, 1998-1999; vis Prof Chem, Univ Ore, 1990-1991; vis scholar, Stanford Univ, 1983-1984; prof chem, Drake Univ, 1978-2002; from asst prof to assoc prof, Drake Univ, 1967-1978. **Memberships:** Am Chem Soc; Royal Soc Chem. **Research Statement & Publications:** Nuclear magnetic resonance spectroscopic studies of steric effects; conformational analysis of cyclohexanones. **Mailing Address:** Dept Chem, Drake Univ, Des Moines, IA 50311-4516. **E-Mail:** james.lindberg@drake.edu

LINDBERG, JOHN ALBERT, MATHEMATICAL ANALYSIS. **Personal Data:** b New York, NY, April 19, 1934; m 1964, c 2. **Education:** Wagner Col, BA, 1954; Univ Minn, MA, 1957, PhD (math), 1964. **Professional Experience:** PROF MATH, SYRACUSE UNIV, 1972-; res fel math, Yale Univ, 1968-1969; from asst to assoc prof, Syracuse Univ, 1962-1972; instr math, Yale Univ, 1960-1962; instr math, Univ Minn, 1958-1959. **Memberships:** AAAS; Am Math Soc; Math Asn Am; Sigma Xi. **Research Statement & Publications:** Theory of algebraic extensions of Banach algebras and factorization of polynomials over such algebras; inverse producing normed extensions. **Mailing Address:** Dept Math, Syracuse Univ, 317B Carnegie, Syracuse, NY 13244-1200. **Fax:** 315-443-1475. **E-Mail:** jalindbe@syr.edu

LINDBERG, LOIS HELEN, MEDICAL MICROBIOLOGY. **Personal Data:** b Scott Air Force Base, Ill, September 1, 1932. **Education:** San Jose State Col, BA, 1952; Univ Calif, MPH, 1958; Stanford Univ, PhD, 1967. **Professional Experience:** PROF EMER MICROBIOL, SAN JOSE STATE UNIV, 1988-; prof microbiol, San Jose State Univ, beginning 1980; assoc dean fac, San Jose State Univ, 1978-1979; prof biol, San Jose State Univ, 1970-1980; NSF fel, 1966 & 1967; assoc prof biol, San Jose State Univ, 1965-1970; NSF sci teachers fel, 1962; asst prof bact, San Jose State Univ, 1958-1965; assoc pub health, Pub Health Lab, Univ Calif, 1955-1958; instr bact, San Jose State Col, 1954-1955; jr microbiologist, State Dept Pub Health, Calif, 1953-1954; res assoc, Stanford Univ Med Sch. **Memberships:** AAAS; Am Pub Health Asn; Am Soc Microbiol. **Research Statement & Publications:** Medical microbiologyas related with the pathology and immunology of streptococcal infections. **Mailing Address:** Dept Microbiol, San Jose State Univ, One Wash Square, San Jose, CA 95192.

LINDBERG, R(OBERT) G(ENE), ZOOLOGY. **Personal Data:** b Los Angeles, Calif, June 9, 1924; m 1947, c 4. **Education:** Univ Calif, Los Angeles, BA, 1948, PhD (zoology), 1952. **Professional Experience:** RES BIOLOGIST, LAB NUCLEAR MED & RADIATION BIOL, 1975-; mem, Space Biol Adv Panel, Am Inst Biol Sci/NASA, 1975-1980; LECTR ENVIRON SCI ENG, UNIV CALIF, LOS ANGELES, 1974-; secy, Bd Trustees, BIOSIS, 1974-1979; mem sr tech staff, Labs, 1967-1974; consult, Sch Med, Univ Calif, Los Angeles, 1959-1965 & Am Inst Biol Sci, 1967-1970; head bio astronaut lab, Northrop Corp, 1959-1967; asst res biologist, Atomic Energy Proj, 1955-1959; jr res biologist radiation ecol, Atomic Energy Proj, 1952-1955; Pauley fel, Univ Hawaii, 1952; instr, Art Ctr Col Design, 1951-; asst zoology, Univ Calif, Los Angeles, 1950. **Memberships:** AAAS; Ecol Soc Am; Am Soc Zoologists. **Research Statement & Publications:** Radiobiology; circadian rhythms; chronobiology; environmental effects of alternative energy systems. **Mailing Address:** Environ Sci & Eng, Univ Calif, Los Angeles, CA 90024.

LINDBERG, STEVEN EDWARD, ORGANIC CHEMISTRY, POLYMER CHEMISTRY. **Personal Data:** b St Paul, Minn, October 17, 1942; c 2. **Education:** Gustavus Adolphus Col,

BS, 1964; Univ Minn, Minneapolis, PhD (org chem), 1969. **Professional Experience:** RES SUPVR, RES & DEVELOP DEPT, AMOCO CHEM CO, 1975-; res chemist, Amoco Chem Co, 1969-1975. **Memberships:** Am Chem Soc; Am Soc Testing & Mat. **Research Statement & Publications:** Petroleum additives, lubricant formulation; polymers; tertiary oil recovery; plastics. **Mailing Address:** Amoco Chem Co, PO Box 3011, Naperville, IL 60566-7011.

LINDBERG, STEVEN ERIC, GEOCHEMISTRY, ENVIRONMENTAL SCIENCES. **Personal Data:** b Waukegan, Ill, May 9, 1947; m 1969, Kay Caulk; c Kristina. **Education:** Duke Univ, BS, 1969; Fla State Univ, MS, 1973, PhD (oceanog), 1979. **Honors & Awards:** Environ Sci Achievement Award, Oak Ridge Nat Lab, 1984; Martin Marietta Tech Achievement Award, 1987. **Professional Experience:** CORP RES FEL, ENVIRON SCI DIV, OAK RIDGE NAT LAB, 2000-; Adj prof, Univ Mich, 1996-; adj res prof, Sch Agr, Univ Tenn, 1991-; vis prof, Inst Bioclimat, Univ Gottingen, Ger, 1988; Alexander von Humboldt fel, 1987; sr res staff, Environ Sci Div, Oak Ridge Nat Lab, beginning 1985; res staff, Environ Sci Div, Oak Ridge Nat Lab, 1979-1984; res assoc, Environ Sci Div, Oak Ridge Nat Lab, 1974-1978; fel chem oceanog, Fla State Univ, 1971-1974; Teacher & adv, Antioch Upper Grade Ctr, 1969-1971; chmn, Int Conf Heavy Metals Environ; chmn, Nat Atmosphere Deposition Prog. **Memberships:** AAAS; Am Geophys Union. **Research Statement & Publications:** Influence of fossil fuel utilization on geochemical cycles, especially the role of atmosphere/surface exchange in the biogeochemistry of forests. **Mailing Address:** Environ Sci Div, Oak Ridge Nat Lab, PO Box 2008, Bethel Valley Rd, Oak Ridge, TN 37831-6038. **Fax:** 865-576-8646. **E-Mail:** lindbergse@ornl.gov

LINDBERG, VERN WILTON, SOLID STATE PHYSICS, PHYSICAL VAPOR DEPOSITION. **Personal Data:** b Rimbey, Alta, May 5, 1949; m 1973, Joan; c David & Daniel. **Education:** Univ Alta, BSc, 1969; Case Western res Univ, MS, 1972, PhD (physics), 1976. **Professional Experience:** Fac fel, Ctr Interfacial Eng, Univ Minn, 1993-1994; vis res scientist, Kodak res labs, 1984-1985; ASSOC PROF PHYSICS, ROCHESTER INST TECHNOL, 1979-; asst prof physics, Hartwick Col, 1976-1979; vis researcher, Case Western res Univ, 1976 & 1978. **Memberships:** Am Asn Physics Teachers; Am Vacuum Soc. **Research Statement & Publications:** Vacuum deposition of thin films by evaporation and sputtering; adhesion of thin films to polymers, surface morphology, resistivity of thin films; use of glow discharge and ion beam to modify substrate; optical thin films. **Mailing Address:** Dept Physics, Rochester Inst Technol, Rochester, NY 14623-0887. **E-Mail:** vwlsps@rit.edu

LINDBLAD, WILLIAM JOHN, WOUND HEALING, COLLAGEN BIOCHEMISTRY. **Personal Data:** b Glen Head, NY, October 14, 1954; m 1985, c 2. **Education:** Univ Maine, BS, 1976; Cleveland State Univ, MS, 1977; Univ RI, PhD (pharmacol), 1980. **Professional Experience:** ASSOC PROF, DEPT PHARMACEUT SCI, WAYNE STATE UNIV, 1990-; from asst prof to assoc prof, Dept Surg, Med Col Va, 1989-1990; res assoc, Dept Surg, Med Col Va, 1981-1983; fel, Dept Surg, Med Col Va, 1980-1981. **Memberships:** Am Asn Study Liver Dis; NY Acad Sci; Am Soc Pharmacol & Exp Therapeut; Wound Healing Soc. **Research Statement & Publications:** Fibrogenic response to tissue injury; developing pharmacologic approaches to control fibrogenesis in pathologic conditions; determine the ability of extracellular matrices to control cellular phenotype. **Mailing Address:** Dept Pharmaceut Sci, Wayne State Univ, Rm 3116, Detroit, MI 48202. **Fax:** 313-577-2033. **E-Mail:** wlindbl@wayne.edu

LINDBURG, DONALD GILSON, ANIMAL BEHAVIOR. **Personal Data:** b Wagner, SDak, November 6, 1932; m 1954, c 3. **Education:** Houghton Col, BA, 1956; Univ Chicago, MA, 1962; Univ Calif, Berkeley, PhD (anthrop), 1967. **Honors & Awards:** Nat Zoo Centennial Award for Excellence in Zoo Res, 1990. **Professional Experience:** AT OFF GIANT PANDA CONSERV, ZOOL SOC SAN DIEGO, as of 2004; Mem, Res Adv Bd, Int Soc Endangered Cats, 1988-; ed, Zoo Biol, 1988-; vis prof, Univ Calif, San Diego, 1985; exec bd, Int Primatol Soc, 1984-1986; prin investr, Conserv Lion-tailed Macaque, Inst Mus Serv grant, 1984-1985; RES BEHAVIORIST, SAN DIEGO ZOO, 1979-; assoc prof anthrop, Univ Calif, Los Angeles, 1975-1979; chmn & assoc prof, Ga State Univ, 1973-1975; NSF fel, Univ Calif, Davis, 1972-1975; vis lectr, Univ Calif, Berkeley, 1972; res anthropologist, Sch Med, Univ Calif, Davis, 1969-1972; asst prof anthrop, Univ Calif, Davis, 1967-1973; res anthropologist, Nat Ctr Primate Biol, 1966-1969; res asst primatol, Nat Ctr Primate Biol, 1964-1966. **Memberships:** Am Soc Primatology (pres 1984-1986); Animal Behav Soc; Int Primatol Soc; Am Asn Phys Anthrop Int Primatol Soc. **Research Statement & Publications:** Captive reproduction of exotic mammals; behavioral correlates of steroid hormone excretions during different phases of the reproductive cycle in primates and carnivores. **Mailing Address:** Off Giant Panda Conserv, Zool Soc San Diego, PO Box 120551, San Diego, CA 92112-0551. **Fax:** 619-744-3346. **E-Mail:** dlindburg@sandiegozoo.org

LINDE, ALAN TREVOR, GEOPHYSICS. **Personal Data:** b Lowood, Australia, February 13, 1938; m 1960, c 3. **Education:** Univ Queensland, BSc, 1959, PhD (physics), 1972. **Professional Experience:** GEOPHYSICST, DEPT MAGNETISM, CARNEGIE INST, as of 2004; Staff Scientist, Dept Magnetism, Carneigie Inst, 1972-; Lectr physics, Univ Queensland, 1962-1972. **Memberships:** Am Geophys Union; Seismol Soc Am; fel Japan Soc Prom Sci. **Research Statement & Publications:** Theoretical and observational studies of earthquake source mechanisms to determine properties of the earth's interior and hence to understand the earth's tectonic engine. **Mailing Address:** Carnegie Inst, 5241 Broad Br Rd NW, Washington, DC 20015. **E-Mail:** dtm-linde@dtm.ciw.edu

LINDE, ANDREI, COSMOLOGY, THEORY OF PHASE TRANSITIONS. **Personal Data:** b Moscow, Russia, March 2, 1948; m 1975, Renata; c Dmitri & Alexander. **Education:** Lebedeu Phys Inst, Moscow, PhD (physics), 1975. **Honors & Awards:** Lomonosov Award, Acad Sci, USSR, 1978. **Professional Experience:** PROF PHYSICS, STANFORD UNIV, as of 1996; staff mem, Europ Org Nuclear Res, Switz, 1989-1990; prof physics, Lebedev Phys Inst, Moscow, 1984-1989. **Research Statement & Publications:** Co-author of theory of cosmological phase transitions and of inflationary cosmology; author of two books and 140 papers. **Mailing Address:** Dept Physics, Stanford Univ, Varian Physics Bldg, 382 Via Pueblo Mall, Stanford, CA 94305-4060. **Fax:** 650-723-9389, 650-725-6544. **E-Mail:** alinde@stanford.edu

LINDE, HARRY WIGHT, ANESTHESIOLOGY. **Personal Data:** b Woodbridge, NJ, January 1, 1926; m 1956, c 2. **Education:** Tufts Col, BS, 1950; Mass Inst Technol, PhD (chem), 1953. **Professional Experience:** RETIRED; emer prof anesthesia, Med Sch, 1991-; chair, 1970-1976 & res comt, 1987-1988; gen fac comt, 1970-1976 & res comt, 1985-1988; vchmn res, Anesthesia Res Ctr, 1977-1991; assoc dean hons prog med educ, Anesthesia Res Ctr, 1976-1991; assoc staff mem, Chicago Wesley Mem Hosp, 1969-1972 & Northwestern Mem Hosp, 1972-; human subj rev, 1970-1976 & res comt, 1971-1976; coordr res res & sponsored progs, Anesthesia Res Ctr, 1971-1976; from assoc prof to prof, Anesthesia Res Ctr, 1970-1991; assoc ed, Yearbk Anesthesia, 1970-1981; consult, US Naval Hosp, Great Lakes, 1969-1978; consult res anesthesia, Vet Admin Lakeside Med Ctr, Chicago, 1968-1991; mem, Comt Admis, Northwestern Univ, 1967-1972; asst dir, Anesthesia Res Ctr, 1967-1971; asst prof, Northwestern Univ, 1965-1970; group leader, Air Prod & Chem, Inc, 1963-1965; res assoc anesthesia, Med Sch, Univ Pa, 1956-1963; Res assoc, Col Med, Univ Ill, 1955-1956; Sr chemist, Res Labs, Air Reduction Co, Inc, 1953-1956. **Memberships:** Fel AAAS; Am Chem Soc; Int Anesthesia Res Soc; Am Soc Anesthesiol; Sigma Xi. **Research Statement & Publications:** Pharmacology of anesthesia; gas analysis; bioanalytical chemistry. **Mailing Address:** 89 Metedeconk Rd, Brick, NJ 08723.

LINDE, LEONARD M, cardiology, physiology; deceased, see previous edition for last biography

LINDE, PETER FRANZ, PHYSICAL CHEMISTRY, ELECTROCHEMISTRY. **Personal Data:** b Berlin, Ger, June 9, 1926; American citizen; m 1953, c 4. **Education:** Reed Col, BA, 1946; Univ Ore, MA, 1949; Wash State Univ, PhD (chem), 1954. **Professional Experience:** PROF EMER CHEM, SAN FRANCISCO STATE UNIV, 1995-; ed, Gmelin, Frankfurt, Ger, 1981-1982; prof chem, San Francisco State Univ, beginning 1966; from asst prof to assoc prof, San Francisco State Univ, 1957-1966; Phys chemist, Sandia Corp, 1953-1957. **Memberships:** Am Chem Soc; Sigma Xi. **Research Statement & Publications:** Electrochemistry of quaternary ammonium compounds; supporting electrolytes in polarography; shock tube measurements; chemometrics. **Mailing Address:** Dept Chem & Biochem San Francisco State Univ, 1600 Holloway Ave, San Francisco, CA 94132-4163. **Fax:** 415-338-3024.

LINDE, RONALD K(EITH), PHYSICS OF SOLIDS, ENVIRONMENTAL SCIENCE. **Personal Data:** b Los Angeles, Calif, January 31, 1940; m 1960, Maxine. **Education:** Univ Calif, Los Angeles, BS, 1961; Calif Inst Technol, MS, 1962, PhD (mat sci), 1964. **Professional Experience:** VICE CHMN EMER, HARVEY MUDD COL, 1998-, vice chmn bd trustees, 1993-1998; co-chmn, Titan Financial Group, 1994-1998; mem law & bus adv coun, Stanford Univ Law Sch, 1991-1994; chmn bd, Ronald& Maxine Linde Found, 1989-; trustee, Calif Inst Technol, 1989-; chmn bd & chief exec officer, Envirodyne Industs Inc, 1969-1989; dir phys sci, Stanford res inst, 1968-1969; chief exec, Poulter Labs, 1967-1968; chmn shock & high pressure physics dept & mgr tech serv, Poulter Labs, 1967; head solid state res, Poulter Labs, SRI, 1965-1967; mat scientist, Poulter labs, SRI Int, 1964-1967; res asst, Calif Inst Technol, 1961-1964; Engr& consult, Litton Systs, Inc, 1961-1963. **Research Statement & Publications:** solid state physics; properties of materials; physical chemistry; crystallographic phase transformations; shock wave propagation in solids; physics of soilds; Environmental engineering; pollution control. **Mailing Address:** Harvey Mudd Col, 301 Platt Blvd, Claremont, CA 91711.

LINDEBERG, GEORGE KLINE, SOLID STATE PHYSICS. **Personal Data:** b Spencer, Iowa, June 6, 1930; m 1954, c 2. **Education:** St Olaf Col, BA, 1952; Princeton Univ, PhD (exp physics), 1957. **Professional Experience:** PHYSICIST, MINN MINING & MFG CO, 1957-; Asst physics, Princeton Univ, 1956-1957. **Memberships:** Am Phys Soc. **Research Statement & Publications:** Non-equilibrium electronic processes in solids; thermodynamics; physics operations research. **Mailing Address:** 276 W Grove Rd, Hudson, WI 54016.

LINDELL, ISMO VEIKKO, ELECTROMAGNETIC THEORY. **Personal Data:** b Viipuri, Finland, November 23, 1939; m 1964, Liisa Nop o la; c Riina & Antti. **Education:** Helsinki Univ Technol, dipl eng, 1963, LicTech, 1967, DrTech(radio eng), 1971. **Honors & Awards:** SA Schelkunoff Prize, Inst Elec & Electronics Engrs, Antennas & Propagation Soc, 1987 Maxwell premium of inst elec engrs (IEE, London) 1997 and 1998, fel of IEEE, 1990, Honorary prof at southeast univ, Nanjing china, 2002. **Professional Experience:** ACAD PROF ELECTRONMAGNETICS ACAD FINLAND, HELSINKI UNIV TECHNOL, 1996-; prof electromagnetics, Helsinki Univ Technol, 1989-1996; vis scientist, Mass Inst Technol, 1986-1987; Vis prof, Univ Ill, 1972-1973; From asst prof to assoc prof radio eng, Helsinki Univ Technol, 1962-1989. **Memberships:** Fel Inst Elec & Electronics Engrs Antennas & Propagation Soc; Int Union Radio Sci. **Research Statement & Publications:** Electromagnetic theory; author of 2 books. **Mailing Address:** Elec Eng Dept, Helsinki Univ Technol, Espoo, Finland. **E-Mail:** ismo.lindell@hut.fi

LINDELL, THOMAS JAY, MOLECULAR & CELLULAR BIOLOGY. **Personal Data:** b Red Wing, Minn, July 22, 1941; div, c 2. **Education:** Gustavus Adolphus Col, BS, 1963; Univ Iowa, PhD (biochem), 1969. **Professional Experience:** ASSOC PROF, DEPT MOLECULAR & CELL BIOL, UNIV ARIZ, as of 2005; ACTG HEAD MOLECULAR & CELLULAR BIOL, UNIV ARIZ, 1983-; assoc prof pharmacol, Health Sci Ctr, 1970-1983; USPHS fel biochem, Univ Wash, 1968-1969 & biochem, biophys & develop biol, Univ Calif, San Francisco, 1969-1970; assoc ed, J Life Sci. **Memberships:** AAAS; Sigma Xi; Am Soc Biol Chemists; Am Soc Microbiol. **Research Statement & Publications:** Control of eukaryotic transcription. **Mailing Address:** Dept Molecular Cellular Biol, Univ Ariz, Rm 254 Life Sci S, 1007 E Lowell St, Tucson, AZ 85721-0106. **E-Mail:** tlindell@u.arizona.edu

LINDEMAN, ROBERT D, INTERNAL MEDICINE, NEPHROLOGY, GEROATROC MED. **Personal Data:** b Ft Dodge, Iowa, July 19, 1930; m 1982, Lynn; c William Douglas, Ann Denise (Hendrix), James Lawrence, Peter Verlus, David Matthew, Laurel (Lisinski), Lisa (Ringhoff), Kristine (Cannaday) & Robert M Lind. **Education:** State Univ NY Col Forestry, Syracuse Univ, BS, 1952; State Univ NY, MD, 1956. **Professional Experience:** PROF EMER, DEPT INTERNAL MED, UNIV NMEX, 1999-. **Memberships:** emer mem Cent Soc Clin Res; emer mem Int Soc Nephrology; emer mem Southern Soc Clin Invest; fel Am Col Physicians; Master Am Col Nutrition; fel Am Geriat Soc; emer mem Geront Soc Am; emer mem West Assoc Phys; emer mem Am Soc Nephrology. **Research Statement & Publications:** Renal and electrolyte problems; hypertension; renal and cardiovascular physiology; aging; trace metal metabolism and nutrition. **Mailing Address:** Dept Med, Univ NMex, 1404 Fla St, NE, Albuquerque, NM 87110. **Fax:** 505-272-9135. **E-Mail:** rlindeman@salud.unm.edu

LINDEMANN, CHARLES BENARD, CELL PHYSIOLOGY, BIOPHYSICS. **Personal Data:** b Staten Island, NY, December 17, 1946; m Linda; c Jessie (Haglund), Christopher & Laurel. **Education:** State Univ NY Albany, BS, 1968, PhD (biol), 1972. **Professional Experience:** PROF PHYSIOL, OAKLAND UNIV, 1974-; res assoc biophys, State Univ NY Albany, 1973-1974; Res assoc cell physiol, Pac Biomed Res Ctr, Univ Hawaii, 1972-1973. **Memberships:** Biophys Soc; Am Soc Cell Biol; Soc Study Reprod. **Research Statement & Publications:** Flagellar motility; the mechanisms of force production and the factors which control motility onset are under investigation in mammalian sperm; author of the "Geometric Clutch" hypothesis to explain flagellar beating. **Mailing Address:** Dept Biol Sci, Oakland Univ, 330 Dodge Eng Hall, Rochester, MI 48309-4476. **Fax:** 248-370-2286. **E-Mail:** lindeman@oakland.edu

LINDEMANN, MARTIN K, CHEMISTRY OF POLYVINYL ACETATE & POLYVINYL ALCOHOL, EMULSION POLYMERIZATION. **Education:** Tech Univ Hanover, Ger, BS, 1951; Polytech Inst NY, MS, 1962. **Honors & Awards:** Olney Medal Achievements Polymer & Textile Chem, Am Asn Textile Chemists & Colorists, 1988. **Professional**

Experience: CHEM CONSULT, SEQUA CHEM INC, CHESTER, SC, 1981-; vpres & tech dir, C S Tanner Co, Subsid Ciba-Geigy Corp, Greenville, SC, 1968-1980; mgr resin res, Mobil Chem Corp, Edison, NJ, 1966-1968; polymer develop supvr, Air Reduction Co, Inc, Bound Brook, NJ, 1955-1966; res chemist, Onyx Oil & Chem Corp, Jersey City, NJ, 1951-1954. **Memberships:** Am Chem Soc; Tech Asn Pulp & Paper Indust; Fedn Paint Socs; Am Asn Textile Chemists & Colorists. **Research Statement & Publications:** Polymer and organic chemistry; author of numerous publications and granted several patents. **Mailing Address:** 102 Independence Dr, Greenville, SC 29615.

LINDEMANN, WILLIAM CONRAD, SOIL MICROBIOLOGY. **Personal Data:** b East St Louis, Ill, August 31, 1948; m 1978. **Education:** Southern Ill Univ, BS, 1970; Univ Minn, MS, 1974, PhD (soil sci), 1978. **Professional Experience:** PROF AGRON & HORT, NMEX STATE UNIV, as of 2003; asst prof soil microbiol, NMex State Univ, beginning 1978; tech asst, Res Seeds Inc, 1974-1975; res asst, Univ Minn, 1972-1974, 1975-1977. **Memberships:** AAAS; Am Soc Microbiol; Am Soc Agron; Soil Sci Soc Am; Sigma Xi. **Research Statement & Publications:** Soil nitrogen fixation; rhizobiology; legume innoculation; legume nutrition; iron characterization; decomposition of pecan wood chips; waste management. **Mailing Address:** Dept Agron & Hort, NMex State Univ, PO Box 30003, MSC 3Q, Las Cruces, NM 88003-8003. **E-Mail:** wlindema@nmsu.edu

LINDEMER, TERRENCE BRADFORD, HIGH TEMPERATURE CHEMISTRY, NUCLEAR CHEMISTRY. **Personal Data:** b Gary, Ind, February 17, 1936; m 1962, c 2. **Education:** Purdue Univ, BS, 1958; Univ Fla, PhD (metall eng), 1966. **Professional Experience:** MEM RES STAFF, CHEM TECHNOL DIV, OAK RIDGE NAT LAB, 1966-; Mem res staff, Inland Steel Co, 1958-1961 & Solar Aircraft Co, 1961-1963. **Memberships:** Fel Am Ceramic Soc; Mat Res Soc. **Research Statement & Publications:** Thermodynamic and kinetic factors affecting reactor performance of nuclear fuels and fission products; ceramic superconductors; structural ceramics. **Mailing Address:** 10931 Sallings Rd, Knoxville, TN 37922.

LINDEMEYER, ROCHELLE G, PEDIATRIC DENTISTRY. **Personal Data:** b Philadelphia, Pa, 1952. **Education:** West Chester State Col, BA, 1972; Univ Pittsburgh, DMD, 1977. **Honors & Awards:** Am Acad Gen Dent Award, 1977. **Professional Experience:** DIR, PEDIAT DENT RESIDENCY PROG, CHILDRENS HOSP, PHILADELPHIA, as of 2004; ASST PROF, DEPT PEDIAT DENT, SCH DENT MED, UNIV PA, as of 2004; dipl & fel, Am Bd Pediat Dent, 1989-; assoc prof oral pediat, Sch Dent, Temple Univ, beginning 1981; clin affil, Children's Hosp Philadelphia, 1979- & St Christopher's Hosp Children, 1982-; asst prof oper dent, Sch Dent, Temple Univ, 1979-1981; pvt pract pedodontics, 1977-; residency pedodontics, Children's Hosp Philadelphia, 1977-1979. **Memberships:** Int Asn Dent Res; Sigma Xi; Am Acad Pediat Dent; Am Dent Asn; Am Soc Dent Children; Int Col Dentists. **Research Statement & Publications:** Hormone receptors; periodontitis in the pediatric dental patient. **Mailing Address:** Dept Pediat Dent, Robert Schattner Ctr, Sch Dent Med, Univ Penn, 240 S 40th st, Philadelphia, PA 19104.

LINDEMUTH, IRVIN R, MATHEMATICS. **Education:** Lehigh Univ, BS, 1965; Univ Calif, MS, 1967, PhD, 1971. **Professional Experience:** STAFF, INERTIAL FUSION & PLASMA THEORY GROUP APPL THEORET PHYSICS DIV, LOS ALAMOS NAT LAB, as of 1990. **Mailing Address:** Los Alamos Nat Lab, PO Box 1663, Los Alamos, NM 87544-2842. **Fax:** 505-667-7844. **E-Mail:** irvl@att.net

LINDEN, CAROL D, CELL MEMBRANE, ENDOCYTOSIS. **Personal Data:** b Philadelphia, Pa, October 1, 1949; c 2. **Education:** Univ Calif, Los Angeles, PhD (molecular biol), 1974. **Professional Experience:** DIR, MED CHEM & BIOL DEFENSE RES PROG US ARMY MED RES INST, 2000-; BIOLOGIST, US ARMY MED RES INST, 1979-. **Memberships:** Am Soc Cell Biol; AAAS; Am Women Sci. **Mailing Address:** Prog Anal Off, US Army Med Res Inst Infectious Dis, 1425 Porter St, Frederick, MD 21701. **Fax:** 301-619-7667.

LINDEN, DENNIS ROBERT, SOIL SCIENCE, HYDROLOGY. **Personal Data:** b Greeley, Colo, June 22, 1942; m 1966, c 2. **Education:** Colo State Univ, MS, 1968, MS, 1970; Univ Minn, PhD (soil), 1979. **Honors & Awards:** Emil Truog Soil Sci Award. **Professional Experience:** ASSOC PROF EMER, DEPT SOIL & WATER & CLIMATE, UNIV MINN, as of 2004; SOIL SCIENTIST, AGR RES, USDA, 1970-. **Memberships:** Am Soc Agron; Soil Sci Soc Am; Int Soil Sci; Int Soil & Tillage Res Org. **Research Statement & Publications:** Soil physics and hydrology; water and energy transport within soil and exchange with the atmosphere at the soil-atmosphere interface; earthworm ecology and impact in agricultural systems. **Mailing Address:** Dept Soil & Water & Climate, Univ Minn, 439 Borlaug Hall, 1991 Upper Burford Circle, St Paul, MN 55108. **Fax:** 612-649-5175. **E-Mail:** dlinden@soils.umn.edu

LINDEN, DUANE B, PLANT GENETICS, CELL BIOLOGY. **Personal Data:** b Toledo, Ohio, June 1, 1930; m 1967, c 3. **Education:** Hiram Col, AB, 1952; Univ Minn, PhD (plant genetics), 1956. **Professional Experience:** CHMN DEPT, KEAN COL NJ, 1973-; PROF BIOL, KEAN COL NJ, 1969-; assoc prof biol, Kean Col NJ, 1965-1969; assoc scientist, PR Nuclear Ctr, 1961-1965; asst prof genetics, Univ Fla, 1957-1961; Res assoc plant genetics, Univ Minn, 1956-1957. **Memberships:** AAAS; Am Inst Biol Sci; Genetics Soc Am; Nat Asn Biol Teachers; Inst Soc Ethics & Life Sci. **Research Statement & Publications:** Effects of radiation on biological systems; study of paramutagenic systems in maize. **Mailing Address:** 1238 Medinah Dr, Ft Myers, FL 33919.

LINDEN, HENRY R(OBERT), RESEARCH ADMINISTRATION, ENERGY POLICY & ECONOMICS. **Personal Data:** b Vienna, Austria, February 21, 1922; American citizen; m 1967, Natalie; c Robert S & Debra J (Thomas). **Education:** Ga Inst Technol, BS, 1944; Polytech Inst Brooklyn, MChE, 1947; Ill Inst Technol, PhD (chem eng), 1952. **Honors & Awards:** Oper Sect Award, Am Gas Asn, 1956; Coal Res Awards, Am Chem Soc, 1959 & 1962, Henry H Storch Award, 1967; Walton Clark Medal, Franklin Inst, 1972; Bunsen Pettenkofer Ehrentafel Award, Deut Ver des Gas und Wasserfaches, 1978; Gas Indust Res Award, Am Gas Asn, 1982; Nat Energy Resources Orgn Res Award, 1986; Homer H Lowry Award, US Dept Energy, 1991; US Energy Award, US Energy Asn, 1993. **Professional Experience:** Sr adv, Putnam, Hayes & Bartlett Inc, 1996-; actg dir, Ctr Excellence Polyner Sci & Eng, 1995-; DIR, IIT ENERGY & POWER CTR, 1990-; MAX MCGRAW PROF ENERGY & POWER ENG & MGT, ILL INST TECHNOL, 1990-; interim pres & chief exec officer, Ill Inst Technol, 1989-1990; frank w gunsaulus distinguished prof chem eng, Ill Inst Technol, 1987-1990; res prof chem eng, Ill Inst Tech, 1978-1987; prof gas eng, Ill Inst Tech, 1978-1985; pres & mem bd dirs, Inst Gas Technol, 1976-1987; pres & mem bd dirs, Gas Res Inst, 1976-1987; pres & trustee, Inst Gas Technol, 1974-1978; consult, Energy Res & Develop Off, Fed Energy Admin, 1974-1975; chief exec officer, Gas Develop Corp, subsid Inst Gas Technol, 1973-1978; dep dir, Supply Tech Adv Task Force, Nat Power Survey, Fed Power Comn, 1972-1975; exec vpres, Inst Gas Technol, 1969-1974; chmn, Div Fuel Chem, Am Chem Soc, 1967; dir, Gas Develop Corp, subsid Inst Gas Technol, 1965-1978; chief operating officer, Gas Develop Corp, subsid Inst Gas Technol, 1965-1973; chmn, Gordon Res Conf Coal Sci, 1965; from adj assoc prof to adj prof, Ill Inst Tech, 1954-1978; from asst res dir to dir, Inst Gas Technol, 1952-1969; supvr oil gasification, Inst Gas Technol, 1947-1952; chem engr, petrol fuel res, Socony-Vacuum Labs, 1944-1947. **Memberships:** Nat Acad Eng; Am Chem Soc; Am Gas Asn; fel Am Inst Chem Engrs; fel Brit Inst Fuel; Sigma Xi; fel Inst Energy. **Research Statement & Publications:** Petroleum properties; petrochemicals; fossil fuel combustion and gasification; synthetic fuels; coal and petroleum pyrolysis and hydrogenolysis; energy economics; energy policy; hydrocarbon resource economics; sustainable energy systems; global climate change; author and co-author of over 200 publications; granted 27 patents. **Mailing Address:** Dept Chem & Environ Eng, Ill Inst Technol, Rm 135 Perlstein Hall, Chicago, IL 60616-3793. **Fax:** 312-567-3967. **E-Mail:** linden@iit.edu

LINDEN, JAMES CARL, PLANT BIOCHEMISTRY, INDUSTRIAL MICROBIOLOGY. **Personal Data:** b Greeley, Colo, September 12, 1942; m 1968, Susan; c Diana & Christina. **Education:** Colo State Univ, BS (chem), 1964; Iowa State Univ, PhD (biochem), 1969. **Professional Experience:** PROF, DEPT CHEM, BIORESOURCE ENG & MICROBIOL, COLO STATE UNIV, 1997-; vis scientist, Univ Regensburg, 1994; Prin investr, Colo Res Develop Corp, 1984-1985; consult, Dept Biotechnol, Swiss Fed Inst Technol, 1980; assoc prof, Dept Agr, Chem Eng & Microbiol, 1978-1997; sr chemist, Adolph Coors Co, 1977-1978; biochemist, Great Western Sugar Co, 1972-1976; fel mammalian cell cult, Dept Microbiol, St Louis Univ, 1971-1972; fel plant biochem, Bot Inst, Univ Munich, 1971; Alexander von Humboldt stipend, Bot Inst, Univ Munich, 1969. **Memberships:** Am Chem Soc; Soc Indust Microbiol; Am Soc Plant Biol. **Research Statement & Publications:** Fuels from biomass, lignocellulose pretreatment, cellulase enzymology; membrane biochemistry; microbial fermentations; plant cell culture; plant signal transduction; plant secondary metabolite production; plant defense responses; shear stress effects on taxus cuspidata; paclitaxel production. **Mailing Address:** Colo State Univ, 100 Glover Bldg, Ft Collins, CO 80523-1370. **Fax:** 970-491-1815. **E-Mail:** jlinden@colostate.edu

LINDEN, JOEL MORRIS, PHARMACOLOGY, CARDIOLOGY. **Personal Data:** b Boston, Mass, May 30, 1952. **Education:** Brown Univ, BS, 1974; Univ Va, PhD (pharmacol), 1978. **Professional Experience:** PROF CARDIOVASCULAR MED & MOLECULAR PHYSIOL & BIOL PHYSICS, UNIV VA, 1996-; assoc prof Internal Med, Univ Va, beginning 1989; asst prof physiol, Dept Pharmacol, 1986-1989; asst mem, Okla Med Res Found, 1982-1986; res asst prof Physiol & Pharmacol, Univ Va, 1978-1979; res assoc, Dept Pharmacol, 1978-1980. **Memberships:** Am Soc Pharmacol & Exp Therapeut; Am Physiol Soc. **Research Statement & Publications:** Molecular cloning and characterization of adenosine receptors. **Mailing Address:** Div Cardiovascular Med, Univ Va, MR5, Rm 1312, Box 801394, Charlottesville, VA 22908-0001. **Fax:** 434-982-2828. **E-Mail:** jlinden@virginia.edu

LINDEN, KURT JOSEPH, OPTOELECTRONICS, SOLID STATE PHYSICS. **Personal Data:** b Berlin, Ger, December 27, 1936; American citizen; m 1962, Alpert; c Judith, Philip & Benjamin. **Education:** Univ Utah, BS, 1959; Mass Inst Technol, MS, 1961; Mass Inst technol, EE, 1964 Purdue Univ, PhD (elec eng), 1966. **Professional Experience:** SR SCIENTIST, BIOMEDICAL DIV, SPIRE CORP, 2002-; dir of operations, Axcel Photonics, 2000-2001; mgr, Laser Prof Develop, Spire Corp, 1993-2000; dir, Electronic Mat Div, 1989-1992; mgr, Laser Prof Develop, Spire Corp, 1984-1988; guest lectr, Mass Inst Technol, 1979-; SR LECTR, NORTHEASTERN UNIV, 1977-; mgr diode laser activ, laser anal inc, 1976-1984; from sr engr to group leader, Raytheon Co, 1966-1976; instr, NSF fel, 1965; instr, Purdue Univ, 1963-1966; Engr physics, Air Force Cambridge Res Lab, 1963; teaching asst, Mass Inst Technol, 1961-1963; Res asst elec eng, Mass Inst Technol, 1959-1961. **Memberships:** Sr mem Inst Elec & Electronic Engrs; Am Phys Soc; Int, Optical soc of Am Soc Optical Engrs. **Research Statement & Publications:** Optoelectronic semiconductor materials and devices; infrared detectors and emitters; low energy detectors and diode lasers of gallium arsenide, gallium aluminum arsenide Ind phosphide and lead salts; management of research and development and manufacturing activities. **Mailing Address:** Spire Corp, One Patriots Pk, Bedford, MA 01730-2396. **Fax:** 781-275-7470. **E-Mail:** klinden@spirecorp.com

LINDENAUER, S MARTIN, SURGERY. **Personal Data:** b New York, NY, December 10, 1932; m 1956, c 4. **Education:** Tufts Univ, MD, 1957. **Professional Experience:** PROF EMER SURG, UNIV MICH, ANN ARBOR, as of 2001; chief staff, Vet Admin Hosp, 1974-1981; asst dean, Med Sch, 1974-1981; prof surg, Univ Mich, Ann Arbor, beginning 1972; chief surg serv, Vet Admin Hosp, 1968-1974; from instr to assoc prof, Univ Mich, Ann Arbor, 1964-1972. **Memberships:** Am Col Surg; Asn Acad Surg; Soc Vascular Surg; Int Cardiovasc Soc; Soc Surg Alimentary Tract. **Research Statement & Publications:** Vascular surgery; biliary tract surgery. **Mailing Address:** Dept Surg, Univ Mich, Ann Arbor, MI 48105. **Fax:** 734-998-0173. **E-Mail:** smartinl@umich.edu

LINDENBAUM, S(EYMOUR) J(OSEPH), PHYSICS. **Personal Data:** b New York, NY, February 3, 1925; m 1958. **Education:** Princeton Univ, AB, 1945; Columbia Univ, MA, 1948, PhD (physics), 1951. **Professional Experience:** PROF EMER PHYSICS, CITY COL NY, as of 2002; Dep sci affairs, High Energy Prog, Div Phys Res, Energy Res & Develop Agency, 1976-1977; mark w zemansky chair physics, City Col New York, beginning 1970; SR PHYSICIST, BROOKHAVEN NAT LAB, 1963-; vis prof, Univ Rochester, 1958-1959; Group leader high energy counter res group, Brookhaven Nat Lab, 1954-1988; physicist, City Col New York, 1954-1963; assoc physicist, City Col New York, 1951-1954; res assoc, Nevis Cyclotron Lab, Columbia Univ, 1947-1951; vis, Europ Orgn Nuclear Res; consult, Saclay Nuclear Res Ctr. **Memberships:** AAAS; fel Am Phys Soc; NY Acad Sci. **Research Statement & Publications:** High energy elementary particle interactions; high energy experimental techniques; heavy ion physics search for a quark gluon plasma; search for and probable discovery of glueballs of quantum chromodynamics (with collaborators). **Mailing Address:** Physics Dept, City Col NY, 138th St, Convent Ave, New York, NY 10031. **Fax:** 212-650-6940.

LINDENBERG, KATJA, CHEMICAL PHYSICS, NONLINEAR PHYSICAL & CHEMICAL SYSTEMS, STATISTICAL MECHANICS. **Personal Data:** b Quito, Ecuador, November 2, 1941; American citizen; m 1990, Theodore; c Misha & Dania. **Education:** Alfred Univ, BA, 1962; Cornell Univ, PhD (theoret physics), 1967. **Professional Experience:** Chmn, Dept Chem, Inst Nonlinear Sci, 1992-1996; ASSOC DIR, INST NONLINEAR SCI, 1987-; PROF CHEM, UNIV CALIF, SAN DIEGO, 1981-; assoc, La Jolla Inst, 1979-1988; consult, Chem Div, Oak Ridge Nat Lab, 1975; from asst prof to assoc prof, Univ Calif, 1973-1981; asst prof chem residence, Univ Calif, 1972-1973; researcher, Oak Ridge Summer Inst Theoret Biophys, 1969-1975; lectr chem & res chemist, Univ Calif, 1969-1972; Res physicist, Univ Calif, San Diego, 1969-1971; Univ Rochester, 1967-1969. **Memberships:** Fel Am Phys Soc; Am Chem Soc; AAUP; Am Women Sci. **Research Statement & Publications:** Theory of stochastic processes with applications to physical and chemical systems; nonequilibrium statistical mechanics; soft condensed matter theory; nonlinear systems; pulse dynamics; phase transitions; self-similarity in random collision processes; diffusion on crystalline surfaces; diffusion in liquids. **Mailing Address:** Dept Chem & Biochem, Univ Calif, 3202 Urey Hall, 9500 Gilman Dr, MC 0332, La Jolla, CA 92093-0332. **Fax:** 619-534-7244. **E-Mail:** klindenberg@ucsd.edu

LINDENBLAD, IRVING WERNER, ASTROMETRY, GEODETIC ASTRONOMY. **Personal Data:** b Port Jefferson, NY, July 31, 1929; m 1994, Joyce Waters; c Werner & Nils. **Education:** Wesleyan Univ, BA, 1950; Colgate Rochester Divinity Sch, MDiv, 1956; George Washington Univ, MA, 1963. **Professional Experience:** ASTRONR, US NAVAL OBSERV, 1953-. **Memberships:** Fel Royal Astron Soc; Emer mem Am Astron Soc. **Research Statement & Publications:** Photographic visual binary stars; motion and magnitude difference of the components of sirius; variation of latitude; rotation and polar motion of the earth; sunspots. **Mailing Address:** US Naval Observ, Washington, DC 20007-4201.

LINDENFELD, PETER, LOW TEMPERATURE PHYSICS. **Personal Data:** b Vienna, Austria, March 10, 1925; American citizen; m 1953, Lore Kadden; c Thomas & Naomi. **Education:** Univ BC, BASc, 1946, MASc, 1948; Columbia Univ, PhD (physics), 1954. **Honors & Awards:** Warren Sasman Award, patgus univ, 1988, hon mem, N J Section, Am Assn Physics Teachers Robert A Millikan Medal, Am Asn Physics Teachers, 1989. **Professional Experience:** EMER PROF, MBR OF GRADUATE SCHOOL, KYOTO UNIV, 1999-, guest scholar, 1982; Rutgers Res Coun fel & guest scientist fac sci, Univ Paris-South, 1970-1971; prof physics, Rutgers Univ, 1966-1996 & 1999; dir, NSF, in-serv insts for high sch teachers, 1964-1966; regional counr NJ, Am Inst Physics, 1963-1971; from instr to assoc prof, Rutgers Univ, 1953-1966; res scientist, Columbia Univ, 1953; vis lectr, Drew Univ, 1952-1953; asst, Columbia Univ, 1948-1952; Asst physics, Univ BC, 1946-1947. **Memberships:** Fel Am Phys Soc; Am Asn Physics Teachers; Am Asn Univ Prof. **Research Statement & Publications:** Metal-insulator transition and its relation to superconductivity; thin superconducting films; electric, magnetic, and thermal properties of materials. **Mailing Address:** Dept Physics and Astronomy, Rutgers Univ, Piscataway, NJ 08854-8019. **E-Mail:** lindenf@physics.rutgers.edu

LINDENLAUB, JOHN CHARLES, ELECTRICAL ENGINEERING, COMPUTER ENGINEERING. **Personal Data:** b Milwaukee, Wis, September 10, 1933; m 1957, Deborah; c Brian, Mark, Anne & David. **Education:** Mass Inst Technol, BS, 1955, MS, 1957; Purdue Univ, PhD (elec eng), 1961. **Honors & Awards:** Helen Plants Award, Frontiers in Educ Conf, 1980, 1987 & 1993; Educ Soc Achievement Award, Inst Elec & Electronics Engrs, 1984; Chester F Carlson Award, Am Soc Eng Educ, 1988. **Professional Experience:** PROF EMER ELEC ENG, PURDUE UNIV, as of 2004; dir instrnl develop, Elec Eng Sch, 1984-1996; dir, Ctr Instrnl Develop Eng, 1977-1981; prog leader technol transfer, Lab Appln Remote Sensing, Purdue Univ, 1974-1979; prof elec eng, Purdue Univ, beginning 1972; mem tech staff, Bell Tel Labs, Inc, 1968-1969; Danforth Assoc, Danforth Found, 1966; from asst prof to assoc prof, Purdue Univ, 1961-1972. **Memberships:** Fel Inst Elec & Electronics Engrs (sec/treas, 1973-1974, vpres, 1975-1976, pres, 1977); fel Am Soc Eng Educ. **Research Statement & Publications:** Computer engineering; engineering education; author of numerous publications. **Mailing Address:** Sch Elec & Comput Eng, Purdue Univ, EE 342, 465 NWestern Ave, West Lafayette, IN 47907-2035. **E-Mail:** linden@ecn.purdue.edu

LINDENMAYER, GEORGE EARL, BIOCHEMICAL PHARMACOLOGY. **Personal Data:** b Port Arthur, Tex, August 22, 1940; m 1963, c 2. **Education:** Baylor Univ, BS, 1962; Baylor Col Med, MD & MS, 1967, PhD (pharmacol), 1970. **Professional Experience:** RETIRED; interim chmn cell, Med Univ SC, ending 2004; prof pharmacol & assoc prof med, Med Univ SC, beginning 1977; assoc prof pharmacol & med, Med Univ SC, 1975-1977; assoc prof cell biophys & med, Baylor Col Med, 1974-1975; Estab investr, Am Heart Asn, 1973-1978; asst prof pharmacol & med, Baylor Col Med, 1972-1974; staff assoc cardiol, Nat Heart & Lung Inst, 1970-1972; Instr pharmacol, Baylor Col Med, 1969-1970. **Memberships:** Am Soc Pharmacol & Exp Therapeut; Int Study Group Res Cardiac Metab; Am Chem Soc; Biophys Soc; Am Heart Asn; Sigma Xi. **Research Statement & Publications:** Information transfer between extracellular and intracellular environments of myocardial cells; immunoblotting and immunofluorescence microscopy. **Mailing Address:** 686 Fort Sumter Dr, Charleston, SC 29412.

LINDENMEIER, CHARLES WILLIAM, THEORETICAL PHYSICS, NUCLEAR PHYSICS. **Personal Data:** b Ft Collins, Colo, December 2, 1930; m 1958, JO; c Charlene & Clark. **Education:** Colo State Univ, BS, 1952; Cornell Univ, PhD (theoret physics), 1960. **Professional Experience:** RETIRED; sr staff engr, neutron & fuel mgt, 1990-1994; mgr neutron develop, neutron & fuel mgt, 1981-1990; mgr design anal, Laser Enrichment Dept, Advan Nuclear Fuels Corp, 1974-1981; mgr math & physics res, Pac Northwest Labs, Battelle Mem Inst, 1970-1973; mgr, Pac Northwest Labs, Battelle Mem Inst, 1965-1970; mgr theoret physics, Hanford Labs, Gen Elec Co, 1963-1964; sr physicist, Hanford Labs, Gen Elec Co, 1960-1963. **Memberships:** Am Phys Soc; Am Nuclear Soc. **Research Statement & Publications:** Reactor physics; neutron thermalization; nuclear reactions; computer applications; laser isotope separation. **Mailing Address:** 1307 Canyon Ave, Richland, WA 99352. **E-Mail:** retphys@att.net

LINDER, ALLAN DAVID, VERTEBRATE ZOOLOGY. **Personal Data:** b Grand Island, Nebr, September 27, 1925; m 1949, Mary; c JoAnne. **Education:** Univ Nebr, BSc, 1951; Okla State Univ, MSc, 1952, PhD (zoology), 1956. **Professional Experience:** RETIRED; assoc dean, Col Lib Arts, 1966-1969 & 1976-1978; prof zoology, Col Lib Arts, 1960-1987; chmn dept, Idaho State Univ, 1960-1975; asst prof zoology, Southern Ill Univ, 1959-1960; asst prof zoology, Univ Wichita, 1956-1959. **Memberships:** Audubon; Nature Conservency; ID Acad Sci. **Research Statement & Publications:** Ichthyology, paleo-ichthyology and herpetology. **Mailing Address:** 14 Tower Bridge Ct, Pueblo, CO 81001-1360.

LINDER, BRUNO, THEORETICAL CHEMISTRY, CHEMICAL PHYSICS. **Personal Data:** b Sniatyn, Poland, September 3, 1924; American citizen; m 1953, Cecelia Fahn; c William, Diane, Richard, Nancy & Carolyn. **Education:** Upsala Col, BS, 1948; Univ Ohio, MS, 1950; Univ Calif, Los Angeles, PhD (chem), 1955. **Professional Experience:** PROF EMER CHEM, FLA STATE UNIV, 1998-; assoc chmn dept, Fla State Univ, 1980-1983; vis prof, Hebrew Univ, Jerusalem, 1973; chmn chem physics prog, Fla State Univ, 1971-1973 & 1975-; prof phys chem, Fla State Univ, 1965-1998; Guggenheim fel, Inst Theoret Physics, Univ Amsterdam, 1964-1965; from asst prof to assoc prof, Fla State Univ, 1957-1965; proj assoc theoret chem, Naval Res Lab, Wis, 1955-1957; asst res chemist, Univ Calif, Los Angeles, 1955; asst chem, Univ Calif, Los Angeles, 1950-1955; Asst chem, Univ Ohio, 1948-1949. **Memberships:** Am Phys Soc; Sigma Xi. **Research Statement & Publications:** Intermolecular forces; van der Waals dipoles; liquid crystal theory; solvent effects on infrared and Raman intensities; statistical mechanical approach to unfolding of biomolecules. **Mailing Address:** Dept Chem, Fla State Univ, Tallahassee, FL 32306. **Fax:** 352-644-8281.

LINDER, DONALD ERNST, LIQUID CHROMATOGRAPHY, GEL PERMEATION CHROMATOGRAPHY. **Personal Data:** b Yoakum, Tex, October 4, 1938; m 1961, c 3. **Education:** Sul Ross State Univ, BS, 1961; Tex A&M Univ, MS, 1964, PhD (anal chem), 1967. **Professional Experience:** CONSULT, as of 2005; VPRES & CONSERV DIR, OKLA FEDN, as of 2005; mgr, environ serv div, Conoco Inc, beginning 1966. **Memberships:** Am Chem Soc. **Research Statement & Publications:** Liquid chromatography, adsorption, liquid-liquid, ion exchange and gel permeation; large scale preparative gas-liquid chromatography; analytical distillations; environmental sampling and testing; EPA protocol groundwater monitoring. **Mailing Address:** 2409 Cardinal Rd, Ponca City, OK 74604-2806. **E-Mail:** linderde@sbcglobal.net

LINDER, HARRIS JOSEPH, ZOOLOGY. **Personal Data:** b Brooklyn, NY, January 3, 1928; m 1952, c 4. **Education:** Long Island Univ, BS, 1951; Cornell Univ, MS, 1955, PhD (zoology), 1958. **Professional Experience:** Contrib ed, Instrnl Media, J Col Sci Teaching, 1976-1979; ASSOC PROF ZOOL, UNIV MD, COL PARK, 1963-; asst prof, Univ MD, Col Park, 1958-1963; resident res assoc, Div Biol & Med, Argonne Nat Lab, 1957-1958; asst zool, Cornell Univ, 1952-1957. **Memberships:** AAAS; Am Soc Zool; Am Micros Soc; Am Inst Biol Sci; Soc Study Reproduction; Sigma Xi. **Research Statement & Publications:** Comparative invertebrate endocrinology; neurosecretion; experimental studies on earthworm reproduction. **Mailing Address:** Univ Md, Dept Zool, College Park, MD 20742-0001.

LINDER, JAMES, PATHOLOGY, MICROBIOLOGY. **Personal Data:** b Omaha, Nebr, October 21, 1954. **Education:** Iowa State Univ, BS, 1976; Univ Nebr, MD, 1980; Am Bd Path, cert anat & clin path, 1983, cert cytopath, 1989. **Professional Experience:** DEAN ADMIN, MED CTR, UNIV NEBR, 1998-; PROF PATH & MICROBIOL, MED CTR, UNIV NEBR, 1989-; dir regional lab, Univ Nebr, 1989-1990; DIR SURG PATH, DEPT PATH & LAB MED, MED CTR, UNIV NEBR, 1985-; mem grad fac, Med Ctr, Univ Nebr, 1984-1987; DIR CYTOPATH, DEPT PATH & LAB MED, MED CTR, UNIV NEBR, 1983-; from asst prof to assoc prof path, Univ Nebr, 1983-1989; dir path residency prog, Univ Nebr, 1983-1989; path resident, Univ Nebr, 1982-1983; clin path fel, Duke Univ/Caberras Hosp, 1981-1982; med examr, Durham, NC, 1981-1982; path resident, Med Ctr, Duke Univ, 1980-1982; teaching asst, Univ Minn, 1976-1977; teaching asst, Dept Biochem, Iowa State Univ, 1975-1976; consult. **Memberships:** Am Fedn Clin Res; Am Soc Cytol; Am Asn Pathologists; fel Col Am Pathologists; fel Am Soc Clin Pathologists; AMA; Sigma Xi. **Research Statement & Publications:** Immune disorders; hematologic disorders. **Mailing Address:** Dept Path & Microbiol, Med Ctr, Univ Nebr, 42nd & Emile, Omaha, NE 68198.

LINDER, JOHN SCOTT, MICROELECTRONICS, SOLID STATE PHYSICS. **Personal Data:** b Baton Rouge, La, May 3, 1935. **Education:** La State Univ, BS, 1956, MS, 1960; Univ Ariz, PhD (elec eng), 1967. **Professional Experience:** Teledyne 1979-; PROF ELEC ENG, TEX A&M UNIV, 1979-; missiles & space div, LTV Aerospace Corp & Consoltec Inc, 1969-; assoc prof, Tex A&M Univ, 1968-1979; consult, Burr Brown Corp, 1967-1968; asst prof elec eng, Tex A&M Univ, 1967-1968; mem tech staff, Sandia Corp, 1966; instr elec eng, Univ Ariz, 1963-1967; instr, La State Univ, 1962-1963; sr engr, comput div, Bendix Corp & Control Data Corp, 1960-1962; assoc elec eng, La State Univ, 1958-1960; tech investr chem processing, E I du Pont Del Nemours & Co, 1956-1958. **Memberships:** Inst Elec & Electronics Engrs; Am Soc Eng Educ; Am Phys Soc. **Research Statement & Publications:** Solid state devices; semiconductor technology; solid state materials; active and distributed synthesis. **Mailing Address:** Dept Elec Eng & Comput Sci, Tex A&M Univ, Kingsville, TX 78363. **E-Mail:** j-linder3985@tamu.edu

LINDER, LOUIS JACOB, ANALYTICAL CHEMISTRY & OPTICAL EMISSION SPECTROSCOPY. **Personal Data:** b East St Louis, Ill, May 10, 1916; m 1948, Elizabeth Schaeffer; c Harriett, Louis III & Mark. **Education:** Wash Univ, AB, 1941. **Professional Experience:** RETIRED; lab mgr Sch Sci, Southern Ill Univ, Edwardsville, 1972-1986; res chemist, Alumina & Chem Div, Res Labs, Aluminum Co Am, 1950-1972; anal chemist, Alumina & Chem Div, Res Labs, Aluminum Co Am, 1946-1950; Chemist, Eagle-Picher Lead Co, 1941-1944 & US Army Chem Warfare Serv, 1944-1946. **Memberships:** non mem, Soc Appl Spectros. **Research Statement & Publications:** Analytical procedures on aluminous materials; application of optical emission spectroscopy to analysis of alumina, aluminous ores and sodium aluminate liquors; spectrographic analysis of gallium oxide and metal. **Mailing Address:** 7907 W Washington St, Belleville, IL 62223-2317.

LINDER, MARIA C, CHEMISTRY, GENERAL BIOCHEMISTRY. **Personal Data:** b New York, NY. **Education:** Harvard Univ, Cambridge, MA, Ph.d, 1966; Vassar Col, Poughkeepsie, NY, BSc, 1960. **Professional Experience:** PROF BIOCHEM, CALIF STATE UNIV, FULLERTON, 1978-; postdoctoral, MIT, cambridge, MA, 1968-1970; postdoctoral, Harvard Med School, Boston, MA, 1966-1968. **Mailing Address:** Chem & Biochem Dept, Calif State Univ, Fullerton, CA 92634. **Fax:** 714-449-5316. **E-Mail:** mlinder@fullerton.edu

LINDER, MAURINE E, BIOCHEMISTRY. **Personal Data:** b Dagget, Mich, January 18, 1955. **Education:** Mich State Univ, BS, 1976; Univ Tex, Dallas, PhD (cell biol), 1987. **Professional Experience:** ASSOC PROF CELL BIOL & PHYSIOL, DIV BIOL & BIOMED SCI, WASH UNIV, as of 2004; asst prof cell biol, Med Sch, Wash Univ, beginning 1993; instr, Univ Tex, 1991-1993; asst instr pharmacol, Univ Tex, 1989-1991; fel signal transduction, Univ Tex, 1987-1989. **Memberships:** Am Soc Biochem & Molecular Biol; AAAS; Am Soc Cell Biol. **Mailing Address:** Dept Cell Biol & Physiol, Sch Med, Wash Univ, 5517 Cancer Res Bldg, Box 8228, St Louis, MO 63110-1093. **Fax:** 314-362-7463. **E-Mail:** mlinder@cellbio.wustl.edu

LINDER, REGINA, MICROBIOLOGY, BIOCHEMISTRY. **Personal Data:** b New York, NY, June 21, 1945. **Education:** City Col NY, BS, 1967; Univ Mass, MS, 1969; NY Univ, PhD (microbiol), 1975. **Professional Experience:** PROF, MED LAB SCI PROG, HUNTER COL, CITY UNIV NEW YORK, as of 2005; adj assoc prof microbiol, Sch Med, NY Univ, as of 2005; DIR, MED LAB SCI PROG, HUNTER COL, CITY UNIV NEW YORK, 1989-; assoc prof, Health Sci, Hunter Col, City Univ New York, beginning 1987; asst prof, Hunter Col, City Univ New York, 1982-1987; asst prof microbiol, Sch Med, NY Univ, 1978-1982; Asst res scientist, Sch Med, NY Univ, 1975-1978. **Memberships:** Am Soc Microbiol; Sigma Xi. **Research Statement & Publications:** Investigation of the mechanism of action of bacterial and animal toxins which specifically interact with membrane lipids; pathogenesis of rhodococcus equi; tissue destructive toxins. **Mailing Address:** Sch Health Sci, Hunter Col, 425 E 25th St, New York, NY 10010. **Fax:** 212-420-9135. **E-Mail:** regina.linder@hunter.cuny.edu

LINDER, SEYMOUR MARTIN, ORGANIC ANALYTICAL CHEMISTRY, INDUSTRIAL ORGANIC CHEMISTRY. **Personal Data:** b New York, NY, December 17, 1925; m 1955, Elise; c Bonnie & Karen (Staubs). **Education:** City Col NY, BS, 1946; Polytech Inst Brooklyn, MS, 1949, PhD (chem), 1953. **Professional Experience:** RETIRED; prin chemist & shift leader, Patapsco & Back River Wastewater Treatment Plants, Balto City, 1981-1990; dir synthesis res, Alcolac Inc, 1972-1980; proj leader, Org Chem Div, 1958-1972; proj leader, Becco Chem Div, FMC Corp, 1953-1958; jr chemist, Hoffmann-La Roche Inc, 1946-1951. **Memberships:** Am Chem Soc; fel Am Inst Chemists. **Research Statement & Publications:** Chemistry of hydrogen peroxide and peroxy acids; epoxidations; epoxyresins; process development; terpene and medicinal chemistry; insecticides; gas chromatography; specialty organic chemicals; functional monomers; (meth)acrylate esters; organometallic compounds; quaternary salts; copolymerizable surfactants; analysis of wastewater and sludge; determination of primary pollutants by GC and GC/MS; toxicity studies on wastewater treatment plant biomass. **Mailing Address:** 1902 Tadcaster Rd, Baltimore, MD 21228.

LINDER, SOLOMON LEON, INFRARED SYSTEMS, LASER SYSTEMS. **Personal Data:** b Brooklyn, NY, March 13, 1929; m 1953, c 3. **Education:** Rutgers Univ, BS, 1950; Wash Univ, PhD (physics), 1955. **Professional Experience:** Adj prof, Wash Univ, as of 2003; INSTR, SOUTHERN ILL UNIV, EDWARDSVILLE, 1974-1975 & UNIV COL, WASH UNIV, 1975-; Univ Col, Fla Technol Univ, 1970-1971; SR GROUP ENGR & TECH SPECIALIST, MCDONNELL DOUGLAS ASTRONAUT CO, 1967-; Univ Col, Wash Univ, 1963-1967; sr group engr, McDonnell Aircraft Corp, 1962-1967; Eve instr, Fairleigh Dickinson Univ, 1959-1962; Mem tech staff, Bell Tel Labs, Inc, 1955-1962. **Memberships:** Optical Soc Am; sr mem Inst Elec & Electronics Engrs. **Research Statement & Publications:** Nuclear magnetic resonance; military systems; electrooptics. **Mailing Address:** 14571 Coeur Dalene Ct, Chesterfield, MO 63017.

LINDERMAN, ROBERT G, PLANT PATHOLOGY. **Personal Data:** b Crescent City, Calif, February 2, 1939; m 1961, Lynne; c Matthew, Stacey & Tami. **Education:** Fresno State Col, BA, 1960; Univ Calif, Berkeley, PhD (plant path), 1967. **Professional Experience:** RES PLANT PATHOLGIST, USDA AGRI RES SERV, ORE, as of 2005; COURTESY PROF BOT & PLANT PATH, ORE STATE UNIV, 1973-; res plant pathologist, Agr Res Serv, USDA, 1967-1973; asst res plant pathologist, Univ Calif, Berkeley, 1967; Lab technician plant path, Univ Calif, Berkeley, 1964-1967. **Memberships:** Am Phytopath Soc. **Research Statement & Publications:** Ecology of soil-borne fungus plant pathogens; biological control; biological effects of plant residue decomposition in soil; ornamental plant diseases; mycorrhizal fungi; phytophthora ramorum; managing rhizosphere microbial communities; oregon blueberry survey. **Mailing Address:** Hort Crops Res Unit, USDA-ARS, 3420 NW Orchard Ave, Corvallis, OR 97330. **Fax:** 541-738-4025. **E-Mail:** lindermr@Sci.oregonstate.edu

LINDERS, JAMES GUS, COMPUTER SCIENCE, MATHEMATICS. **Personal Data:** b St Catharines, Ont, June 27, 1936; m 1965, Jean; c John, Donald & Heather. **Education:** Univ Toronto, BASc, 1960, MASc, 1961; Univ London, DIC & PhD (comput sci), 1969. **Professional Experience:** PROF EMER, UNIV GUELPH, as of 2006; prof, Dept Comput & Info Sci, Univ Guelph, 1977-2001; chmn, Dept Comput & Info Sci, Univ Guelph, 1996-2001; consult, Ministry Natural Resources, Ont, beginning 1977; chmn, Dept Comput & Info Sci, 1977-1982; asst prof, Univ Waterloo, 1969-1977; consult, dept energy, Mines & Resources, Can, beginning 1967; lectr, Imp Col, Univ London, 1965-1969; lectr comput sci, Ryerson Polytech Inst, 1962-1965; teaching fel math, St Michael's Col, Univ Toronto, 1961-1963; pres, Georef Systs Ltd, Waterloo, Can. **Memberships:** Fel Brit Comput Soc; fel Royal Geog Soc; Asn Comput Mach; Inst Elec & Electronics Engrs; Am Asn Artificial Intel. **Research Statement & Publications:** Computer-aided design; data base design; knowledge base engineering; remote sensing and data fusion; geo referenced data systems. **Mailing Address:** Dept Comput & Info Sci, Univ Guelph, Guelph, ON N1G 2W1, Can. **Fax:** 519-885-4946. **E-Mail:** jgl@snowhite.cis.uoguelph.ca

LINDFORS, KARL RUSSELL, PHYSICAL CHEMISTRY. **Personal Data:** b Saginaw, Mich, July 10, 1937; m 1958, c 2. **Education:** Univ Mich, BS, 1959; Univ Wis, PhD (phys chem), 1963. **Professional Experience:** PROF EMER CHEM, CENT MICH UNIV, as of 2005; chmn dept, Cent Mich Univ, beginning 1978; prof chem, Cent Mich Univ, beginning 1964; spectroscopist, Tracerlab, 1963-1964. **Memberships:** Am Chem Soc. **Research Statement & Publications:** Molecular spectroscopy; species in solution; determination of the regiosequence distribution; heteronuclear NMR techniques. **Mailing Address:** Dept Chem, Cent Mich Univ, Dow 268, Mt Pleasant, MI 48859-0002. **Fax:** 989-774-3883. **E-Mail:** lindf1kr@mail.cmich.edu

LINDGREN, ALICE MARILYN LINDELL, RADIATION BIOLOGY, CELL BIOLOGY. **Personal Data:** b Minneapolis, Mich, January 31, 1937; m 1959, Gordon; c Carmy, Kyle & Tim. **Education:** Augsburg Col, BA, 1958; Univ Minn Minneapolis, MS, 1961; Univ Iowa, PhD (radiation biol), 1970. **Professional Experience:** Vis prof radiol, Univ Iowa, 1984-1985; PROF BIOL, BEMIDJI STATE UNIV, 1981-; vis asst prof radiation biol, Univ Iowa, 1975; consult, agassiz nursing educ consortium, 1972-; consult, Itasca Nursing Educ Consortium, 1981-; from instr to assoc prof, Bemidji State Univ, 1963-1981. **Memberships:** Sr mem Sigma Xi; sr mem Radiation Res Soc. **Research Statement & Publications:** Cell cycle kinetics; effect of radiation on the cell cycle; control of the cell cycle; response of rat lens epithelial cells to a wound stimulus; perturbation by drugs and radiation; differential gone expression. **Mailing Address:** Dept Biol, Bemidji State Univ, Bemidji, MN 56601. **Fax:** 218-755-4107. **E-Mail:** alindgren@bemidjistate.edu

LINDGREN, BERNARD WILLIAM, MATHEMATICS. **Personal Data:** b Minneapolis, Minn, May 13, 1924; m 1945, c 3. **Education:** Univ Minn, PhD (math), 1949. **Professional Experience:** PROF EMER STATIST, UNIV MINN, MINNEAPOLIS, as of 2003; prof statist, Univ Minn, Minneapolis, beginning 1969; chmn dept, Univ Minn, Minneapolis, 1963-1973; from instr to assoc prof, Univ Minn, Minneapolis, 1953-1969; res mathematician, Minn-Honeywell Regulator Co, 1951-1953; instr math, 1946-1949; instr math, Mass Inst Technol, 1949-1951; instr math, Univ Minn, 1943-1944. **Memberships:** Fel Am Statist Asn; Int Statist Inst; Sigma Xi. **Research Statement & Publications:** Analysis; probability; statistics. **Mailing Address:** Dept Statist, Sch Statist, Univ Minn, 392 Ford Hall, 224 Church St SE, Minneapolis, MN 55455-0488. **Fax:** 612-624-8868. **E-Mail:** bernie@stat.umn.edu

LINDGREN, BO STAFFAN, PEST MANAGEMENT, CHEMICAL ECOLOGY. **Personal Data:** b Norrkoping, Sweden, July 18, 1950; Canadian citizen; m 1985, Laurie; c Mitchell O & Jordan M. **Education:** Uppsala Univ, Sweden, Filosofie Kandidat, 1975; Simon Fraser Univ, MS, 1980, PhD (biol), 1982. **Professional Experience:** PROF, NATURAL RESOURCES & ENVIRON STUDIES, UNIV NORTHERN BC, as of 2005; vis scientist, Swed Univ Agr Sci, 1993; RES DIR, PHERO TECH INC, 1984-; indust fel, Phero Tech Inc, 1984-1986; fel, Univ BC, 1982-1984; asst prof, Forestry Prog, Univ Northern BC; lectr, Simon Fraser Univ. **Memberships:** Entom Soc Can; Entom Soc Am. **Research Statement & Publications:** Chemical ecology of bark beetles, particularly the application of sermiochemicals for pest management purposes; chemical ecology of other insect groups. **Mailing Address:** Forestry Prog, Univ Northern BC, 3333 Univ Way, Prince George, BC V2N 4Z9, Can. **Fax:** 250-960-5791.

LINDGREN, CLARK ALLEN, SYNAPTIC PHYSIOLOGY, NEUROMUSCULAR PHYSIOLOGY. **Personal Data:** b Green Bay, Wis, August 31, 1958; c 2. **Education:** Wheaton Col, BS, 1980; Univ Wis-Madison, MS, 1982, PhD (physiol), 1985. **Professional Experience:** ASSOC PROF BIOL, GRINNELL COL, as of 2004; asst prof biol, Allegheny Col, beginning 1989; vis lectr, Univ NC, Chapel Hill, 1988-1989; res assoc neurobiology, Dept Neurobiology, Duke Univ Med Ctr, 1985-1989. **Memberships:** Soc Neuroscience; AAAS. **Research Statement & Publications:** Presynaptic mechanisms at the chemical synapse; role of calcium in activating neurotransmitter release; modulation of release by hormones and co-transmitters; disturbance of neuromuscular transmission in Lambert-Eaton myasthenic syndrome. **Mailing Address:** Dept Biol, Grinnell Col, Sci 2010, Grinnell, IA 50112-1690. **Fax:** 641-269-4285. **E-Mail:** lindgren@grinnell.edu

LINDGREN, E(RIK) RUNE, THEORETICAL & EXPERIMENTAL FLUID MECHANICS, DYNAMICS. **Personal Data:** b Sodertlje, Sweden, August 15, 1919; m 1963, Joan; c Eva, Jan E, Lisa L & Maja B. **Education:** Tech Col Stockholm, BS, 1943; Royal Inst Technol, Sweden, MS, 1947, Tekn lic, 1956, DSc, 1957. **Professional Experience:** PROF EMER ENG SCI, UNIV FLA, as of 2005; res grants, Off Naval Res, 1975-1980; vis prof mech, Roy Inst Technol, Sweden, 1972-; grants, NSF, 1966-1980; prof eng sci, Univ Fla, beginning 1965; assoc prof mech & fluid mech, Okla State Univ, 1963-1965; consult, David Taylor Model Basin, US Bur Ships, 1962-1965; consult, Res Lab, Presby Hosp, 1962-1963; vis asst prof mech, Johns Hopkins Univ, 1961-1963; Docent Fluid Dynamics, Royal Inst Technol, Sweden, 1959-; lectr, Royal Inst Technol, Sweden, 1959-1961; Air Res & Develop Command, US Air Force, 1956-1959; res grants, Swed State Coun Tech Res, 1953-1956; res fel fluid mech, Royal Inst Technol, Sweden, 1951-1959; consult, Kockums Shipyard & Royal Swed Naval Bd, 1951-1959; lectr physics & mech, Tech Col Stockholm, 1949-1951; Aeronaut Lab, Royal Inst Technol, Sweden, 1947-1949; resident assoc, Lumalampan Inc, Sweden, 1945-1947. **Memberships:** Am Phys Soc; Swed Math Soc. **Research Statement & Publications:** Experimental mechanics; cavitation; turbulent transition; structure of shear in flows of Newtonian and non-Newtonian systems, specifically liquid crystals; dynamics of immersed bodies; Theory of inviscid, imcompressible fluid dynamics; non-linear mechanics; Classical dynamics. **Mailing Address:** Dept AeMES Univ Fla, Aero Bldg, Gainesville, FL 32611. **Fax:** 352-392-7303. **E-Mail:** erl@aero.ufl.edu

LINDGREN, FRANK TYCKO, BIOPHYSICS. **Personal Data:** b San Francisco, Calif, April 14, 1924; m 1953. **Education:** Univ Calif, Berkeley, BA, 1947, PhD (biophys), 1955. **Professional Experience:** MEM EMER, LIFE SCI DIV, LAWRENCE BERKELEY NAT LAB, as of 1997; res biophysicist, Donner Lab, Univ Calif, Berkeley, beginning 1967; assoc ed, Lipids, Am Oil Chemists Soc, 1966-1976; from res asst to res assoc biophysicist, Donner Lab, Univ Calif, Berkeley, 1955-1967; reviewer, NIH, NSF grants; fel, coun arteriosclerosis, Am Heart Asn. **Memberships:** Am Oil Chemists Soc; Sigma Xi; AAAS; Am Heart Asn. **Research Statement & Publications:** Physical chemistry and biochemistry of blood lipids and lipo-proteins as they occur in states of health and diseases; instrumentation and engineering necessary to facilitate such investigations. **Mailing Address:** Life Sci Div, Lawrence Berkeley Nat Lab, One Cyclotron Rd, Berkeley, CA 94720.

LINDGREN, GORDON EDWARD, PHYSICS, MATH. **Personal Data:** b Minneapolis, Minn, April 29, 1936; m 1959, c 3. **Education:** Augsburg Col, BA, 1959; Univ SDak, MA, 1963; Univ Iowa, PhD (sci educ), 1970. **Professional Experience:** PROF EMERITUS PHYSICS, BEMIDNI STATE UNIV, as of 2005; prof physics, Bemidji State Univ, beginning 1977; dean sci & math, Bemidji State Univ, 1972-1980; from instr to assoc prof, Bemidji State Univ, 1963-1977; Teacher physics & math, Minnetonk High Sch, Excelsior, Minn, 1959-1961. **Memberships:** Am Asn Physics Teachers; Am Asn Univ Prof; Radiation Res Soc. **Research Statement & Publications:** Electron spin resonance; radiation physics. **Mailing Address:** Dept Physics, Bemidji State Univ, Sattgast 319 1500 Birchmont Dr, Bemidji, MN 56601. **E-Mail:** glind@bemidjistate.edu

LINDGREN, RICHARD ARTHUR, NUCLEAR PHYSICS. **Personal Data:** b Providence, RI, June 2, 1940; m 1963, c 4. **Education:** Univ RI, BA, 1962; Wesleyan Univ, MA, 1964; Yale Univ, PhD (nuclear physics), 1969. **Professional Experience:** RES PROF, PHYSICS, UNIV VA, as of 2005; consult, Naval Res Lab, 1977-; consult, Lawrence Livermore Nat Lab, 1981-; assoc prof, Nuclear Physics Group, Univ Mass, Amherst, beginning 1977; assoc prof, Cath Univ Am, 1975-1976; res physicist nuclear physics, Naval Res Lab, Wash, DC, 1973-1977; instr, George Mason Univ, 1973-1975; res assoc, Nat Res Coun, Nat Acad Sci, 1970-1971; res assoc, Univ Rochester, 1971-1973; res assoc nuclear physics, Univ Md, Col Park, 1969-1970. **Memberships:** Sigma Xi; Am Phys Soc. **Research Statement & Publications:** Nuclear structure studies using inelastic electron scattering, particularly those nuclear states excited strongly via nuclear magnetization currents; comparison of inelastic proton and electron scattering for high spin stretched states. **Mailing Address:** Dept Physics, Univ Va, Rm 302 Physics Bldg, Charlottesville, VA 22904-4714. **Fax:** 434-924-4576. **E-Mail:** rlindgren@virginia.edu

LINDGREN, VALERIE, OBSTETRICS. **Education:** Univ Chicago, BA, 1973, PhD (genetics), 1982. **Professional Experience:** ASSOC PROF PATH, UNIV ILL, as of 2002; DIR CYTOGENETICS, UNIV ILL, as of 2002. **Mailing Address:** Dept Path Univ Ill, 211A CSN MC 750, Chicago, IL 60612. **Fax:** 312-413-0156. **E-Mail:** lindgren@uic.edu

LINDGREN, WILLIAM FREDERICK, MATHEMATICS. **Personal Data:** b San Mateo, Calif, December 23, 1942; c 1. **Education:** SDak Sch Mines & Technol, BS, 1964, MS, 1966; Southern Ill Univ, PhD (math), 1971. **Professional Experience:** PROF MATH, SLIPPERY ROCK UNIV, PA, 1980-; vis prof math, Va Polytech Inst, 1978-1979; assoc prof, Slippery Rock State Col, 1971-1980; mathematician & analyst, Atomic Energy Div, Phillips Petrol Co, 1966-1967. **Memberships:** Am Math Soc; Sigma Xi. **Research Statement & Publications:** General topology; Quasi-uniform spaces. **Mailing Address:** Slippery Rock Univ Pa, 229 Vincent Sci Hall, Slippery Rock, PA 16057-9989. **E-Mail:** william.lindgren@sru.edu

LINDH, ALLAN GODDARD, SEISMOLOGY, EARTHQUAKE PREDICTION. **Personal Data:** b Mason City, Wash, March 18, 1943; m 1971, c 2. **Education:** Univ Calif, BA, 1972; Stanford Univ, PhD (geophys), 1980. **Professional Experience:** Chief, Br Seismol, US Geol Surv, 1990-1994; GEOPHYSICIST, US GEOL SURV, 1973-. **Memberships:** Am Geophys Union; Seis Soc Amer; Int Soc Study Origin & Life. **Research Statement & Publications:** Earthquake prediction and estimation of probabilities of earthquake occurrence; quantification of earthquake characteristics; published over 20 articles. **Mailing Address:** US Geol Surv MS 977, 345 Middlefield Rd, Menlo Park, CA 94025-3561. **E-Mail:** lindh@usgs.gov

LINDHEIMER, MARSHALL D, INTERNAL MEDICINE, NEPHROLOGY. **Personal Data:** b Brooklyn, NY, June 28, 1932; m Jaqueline; c Daniele, Joel, Philippe, Robin & Claire. **Education:** Cornell Univ, AB, 1952; Univ Geneva, BSM, 1957, MD, 1961. **Honors & Awards:** Chesley Award, 1988. **Professional Experience:** PROF EMER MED, OBSTET & GYNEC, UNIV CHICAGO, as of 2003; Fel, Asn Am Physicians, 1985; fel, High Blood Pressure Res Coun, Am Heart Asn, 1980; Prin investr grants, NIH, 1972-; from asst to assoc prof, Obstet & Gynec, Univ Chicago, 1970-1976; asst prof, Northwestern Univ, 1969-1970; sr instr med, Case Western Res Univ, 1966-1969; US Pub Health Serv fel, Boston Univ, 1964-1966; resident & chief resident, Brookdale Hosp, Brooklyn, 1963-1964; resident, Brooklyn Vet Admin Hosp, 1962-1963; intern, Rochester Gen Hosp, 1961-1962. **Memberships:** Am Physiol Soc; Soc Gynec Invest; fel Am Col Physicians; Int Soc Study Hypertension Pregnancy (secy-treas 1981-1987 pres elect 1988); Asn Am Physicians. **Research Statement & Publications:** Salt and water physiology and renal disease;

renal physiology and hypertension in pregnancy; volume homeostasis and vasopressin in gravid animal models. **Mailing Address:** Chicago Hosp & Clins, MC 5100, 5841 S Md Ave, Chicago, IL 60637. **E-Mail:** mlindhei@medicine.bsd.uchicago.edu

LINDHOLM, FREDRIK ARTHUR, ELECTRICAL ENGINEERING. **Personal Data:** b Tacoma, Wash, February 26, 1936; m 1969. **Education:** Stanford Univ, BS, 1958, MS, 1960; Univ Ariz, PhD (elec eng), 1963. **Honors & Awards:** Awards, Inst Elec & Electronics Engrs, 1963 & 1965. **Professional Experience:** PROF EMER, DEPT ELEC & COMPUT ENG, UNIV FLA, as of 2005; consult, Los Alamos Nat Lab, 1981-; consult, Motorola Bipolar Technol Ctr, Mesa, Ariz, 1984-; consult, Jet Propulsion Lab, Pasadena, Calif, 1978-; vis prof elec eng, Univ Leuven, Belg, 1973-1974; mem res adv comt electronics, NASA, 1968-1970; prof elec eng, Univ Fla, beginning 1966; sr engr, Motorola Semiconductor Prods, Phoenix, Ariz, 1963-1966; from instr to assoc prof elec eng, Univ Ariz, 1960-1966; assoc scientist, Lockheed Corp, 1960. **Memberships:** Fel Inst Elec & Electronics Engrs; Am Phys Soc; Am Asn Physics Teachers. **Research Statement & Publications:** Semiconductor device physics, including transistors, diodes, integrated circuits, photovoltaics, photoconductivity and equivalent circuit representations; solar cells. **Mailing Address:** Dept Elec & Comput Eng, Univ Fla, 427 EB PO Box 116200, Gainesville, FL 32611-6200. **E-Mail:** lindholm@ece.ufl.edu

LINDHOLM, JOHN C, MACHINE DESIGN, DYNAMICS. **Personal Data:** b Wichita, Kans, November 3, 1923; m 1947, Mildred; c Martha (Milleson), Susan (Harrington), John C Jr & Barbara (Angell). **Education:** Kans State Univ, BS (mech eng) & BS (bus admin), 1949; Univ Kans, MS, 1956; Purdue Univ, PhD (mach design), 1961. **Professional Experience:** PROF EMER, KANS STATE UNIV, as of 2004; Fulbright prof, Univ Assiut, Egypt, 1992-1993; Fulbright prof, Univ S Pac, 1987-1988; prof mech eng, Kans State Univ, 1987-1989; prof eng tech & head dept, Kans State Univ, 1980-1987; prof mech eng, Kans State Univ, 1974-1980; vis prof, Univ Assiut, 1964-1966; assoc prof, Kans State Univ, 1960-1974; instr, Purdue Univ, 1957-1959; instr mech eng, Univ Kans, 1954-1957; sr engr, Midwest Res Inst, 1952-1954; design engr, Gen Elec Co, 1949-1952. **Memberships:** Am Soc Mech Engrs; Am Soc Eng Educ; Soc Exp Mech. **Research Statement & Publications:** Three-dimensional photoelastic stress analysis; mechanical properties materials at intermediate strain rates; kinematic synthesis of mechanisms. **Mailing Address:** 744 Elling Dr, Manhattan, KS 66502-3636. **Fax:** 785-532-7057. **E-Mail:** lindholm@ksume.me.ksu.edu

LINDHOLM, ROBERT D, PHYSICAL CHEMISTRY. **Personal Data:** b Rockford, Ill, June 17, 1940; m 1962, c 2. **Education:** Northern Ill Univ, BS, 1963, MS, 1964; Univ Southern Calif, PhD (phys chem), 1969. **Professional Experience:** RES ASSOC, EASTMAN KODAK CO, 1973-; sr res chemist, 1968-1973. **Memberships:** Am Chem Soc. **Research Statement & Publications:** Photochemistry of transition-metal complexes; silver halide photochemistry and microelectronics fabrication. **Mailing Address:** Res Lab, Eastman Kodak Co, Rochester, NY 14650.

LINDHOLM, ROY CHARLES, SEDIMENTOLOGY. **Personal Data:** b Washington, DC, March 8, 1937; m 1965, c 2. **Education:** Univ Mich, BS, 1959; Univ Tex, MA, 1963; Johns Hopkins Univ, PhD (geol), 1967. **Professional Experience:** PROF EMER GEOL, GEORGE WASH UNIV, as of 2005; chmn geol, George Wash Univ, 1986-1989; prof, George Wash Univ, 1986-1989; from asst prof to assoc prof, George Wash Univ, 1967-1977; instr, Johns Hopkins Univ, 1965-1966. **Memberships:** Nat Asn Geol Teachers; Soc Econ Paleont & Mineral; NC Bluebird Soc. **Research Statement & Publications:** Paleozoic carbonate rocks of eastern United States; sequences of carbonate cements; geology of Triassic-Jurassic rocks in Virginia; lacustrine deposits; sedimentology of Cretaceous sandstones in northern Virginia. **Mailing Address:** 97517 Franklin Ridge, Chapel Hill, NC 27514-8319.

LINDHOLM, ULRIC S, MATERIALS SCIENCE, APPLIED MECHANICS. **Personal Data:** b Washington, DC, September 11, 1931; m 1962, c 4. **Education:** Mich State Univ, BS, 1953, MS, 1955, PhD (appl mech), 1960. **Professional Experience:** VPRES DIV ENG & MAT SCI, SOUTHWEST RES INST, 1985-; dir, Dept Mat Sci, 1973-1985; asst dir, Dept Mech Sci, 1971-1973; mgr eng mech, Southwest Res Inst, 1964-1971; Sr res engr, Southwest Res Inst, 1960-1964. **Memberships:** Fel Am Soc Mech Engrs; Sigma Xi; Am Soc Metals; fel AAAS. **Research Statement & Publications:** Applied mechanics, structural dynamics and vibrations; wave propagation; material properties. **Mailing Address:** 110 Honey Bee Lane, San Antonio, TX 78231.

LINDL, JOHN D, INERTIAL CONFINEMENT FUSION. **Personal Data:** b Toledo, Ohio, July 27, 1946; m Anne; c 2. **Education:** Cornell Univ, Bs, 1968; Princeton Univ, MA, 1970; PhD (astrophys), 1972. **Professional Experience:** LEADER, FUSION ENERGY PROG, LAWRENCE LIVERMORE NAT LAB, as of 2005; actg inertial confinement fusion, Lawrence Livermore Nat Lab, beginning 1994; dep prog leader, Inertial Confinement Fusion, Lawrence Livermore Nat Lab, 1990-1994; dep prog leader, Inertial Confinement Fusion, Lawrence Livermore Nat Lab, 1989-1990; div leader, Inertial Confinement Fusion, Lawrence Livermore Nat Lab, 1983-1990; Assoc prog leader, Inertial Confinement Fusion, Lawrence Livermore Nat Lab, 1983-1989; assoc div leader, Inertial Confinement Fusion, Lawrence Livermore Nat Lab, 1981-1983; group leader, Inertial Confinement Fusion, Lawrence Livermore Nat Lab, 1978-1981; physicist, Inertial Confinement Fusion, Lawrence Livermore Nat Lab, 1972-1978. **Memberships:** Fel Am Phys Soc. **Research Statement & Publications:** Theory and target design. **Mailing Address:** Lawrence Livermore Nat Lab, PO Box 808, 7000 E Ave, Livermore, CA 94551. **Fax:** 510-424-6401. **E-Mail:** lindl1@llnl.gov

LINDLEY, BARRY DREW, PHYSIOLOGY, BIOPHYSICS. **Personal Data:** b Orleans, Ind, January 25, 1939; m 1982, Elizabeth; c Theodore, Matthew & Sarah. **Education:** DePauw Univ, BA, 1960; Case Western Res Univ, PhD (physiol), 1964. **Professional Experience:** RETIRED; dean, Grad Sch, beginning 1996; prof physiol & biophysics, Univ Ark Med Sci, beginning 1993; vchancellor acad affairs, Univ Ark Med Sci, beginning 1993; assoc dean med educ, Sch Med, Case Western Res Univ, 1985-1993; mem, Physiol Study Sect, NIH, 1975-1979; USPHS res career develop award, 1971-1976; Lederle med fac award, 1967-1970; from asst prof to prof, Sch Med, Case Western Res Univ, 1965-1993; NSF fel neurophysiol, Nobel Inst Neurophysiol, Karolinska Inst, Sweden, 1964-1965; prof & actg chmn anat. **Memberships:** Am Physiol Soc; Soc Gen Physiologists; Biophys Soc. **Research Statement & Publications:** Muscle biophysics; ion and water transport; membrane permeability; irreversible thermodynamics; electrophysiology of nerve, muscle and glandular tissue. **Mailing Address:** Univ Ark Med Sci, 4301 W Markham MS 541, Little Rock, AR 72205.

LINDLEY, CHARLES A(LEXANDER), AEROSPACE SYSTEMS ENGINEERING, ALTERNATIVE ENERGY SYSTEMS. **Personal Data:** b Union City, Ind, May 12, 1924; m 1946, c 2. **Education:** Ohio State Univ, BAeroEng & MS, 1949; Calif Inst Technol, PhD (aeronaut), 1956. **Professional Experience:** Sr staff engr, Threat Anal off, 1978-1991; assoc dir advan systs off, Energy Systs Group, Aerospace Corp, 1974-1978; res assoc, Environ Qual Lab, Calif Inst Technol, 1973-1974; dir vehicle design, Satellite Systs Div, 1965-1973; sr staff engr, Appl Mech Div, Aerospace Corp, 1963-1965; chief res consult, Marquardt Corp, 1961-1963; res consult, Marquardt Corp, 1959-1961; mgr engine res, Marquardt Corp, 1957-1959; eng specialist, Marquardt Corp, 1955-1957; consult, Thompson Aircraft Prod, Inc, 1952-1955; compressor design engr, Thompson Aircraft Prod, Inc, 1949-1952; eng aid, Nat Adv Comt Aeronaut, 1948; instr, Ohio State Univ, 1947-1948; CONSULT; lectr & consult wind power & wind resources, Univ Calif, Santa Barbara. **Memberships:** AAAS; assoc fel Am Inst Aeronaut & Astronaut; Sigma Xi. **Research Statement & Publications:** Aeronautical and space propulsion; air breathing and recoverable boosters; physics and chemistry of the upper atmosphere; satellite systems engineering; wind and solar energy; manned and unmanned space vehicle systems engineering; energy conversion devices; meteorology. **Mailing Address:** 18900 Pasadero Dr, Tarzana, CA 91356.

LINDLEY, KENNETH EUGENE, ELECTRICAL ENGINEERING, MATHEMATICS. **Personal Data:** b Stratton, Colo, March 16, 1924; m 1948, Katherine Walberger; c Lois, Margaret, Eileen & Mark. **Education:** Univ Wis, BS, 1948, MS, 1949; State Univ Iowa, PhD (elec eng), 1953. **Professional Experience:** RETIRED; Develop consult, Acme Elec Corp, 1966-; prof physics & math & chmn, Sci & Math Div, Houghton Col, 1963-1989; From instr to prof elec eng, SDak State Col, 1949-1963. **Memberships:** Inst Elec & Electronics Engrs; Am Soc Eng Educ. **Research Statement & Publications:** Electrical power supplies. **Mailing Address:** 7343 Park Dr, Houghton, NY 14744-8728. **E-Mail:** kennethlindley@hotmail.com

LINDMAN, ERICK LEROY, FUSION ENERGY, COMPUTATIONAL PLASMA PHYSICS. **Personal Data:** b Seattle, Wash, March 20, 1938; m 1963, Joy; c Barbara, Susan, Melissa, Jennifer & Allison. **Education:** Calif Inst Technol, BS (physics), 1960; Univ Calif, Los Angeles, MS (physics), 1963, PhD (physics), 1964. **Professional Experience:** Staff mem Thermonuclear Appl, Los Alamos Nat Lab, 1995-; staff mem inertial fusion, Los Alamos Nat Lab, 1992-1995; sr scientist, Mission Res Corp, 1997-1982; staff mem inertial fusion, Los Alamos Nat Lab, 1986-1987; group leader advan concepts & plasma appl, Los Alamos Nat Lab, 1983-1986; vis prof, Imperial Col, London, 1982-1983; assoc group leader inertial fusion, Los Alamos Nat Lab, 1979-1980; staff mem inertial fusion, Los Alamos Nat Lab, 1974-1979; staff mem high altitude nuclear effects, 1971-1974; physicist, Austin Res Assoc, 1968-1971; asst prof physics, Univ Tex, Austin, 1965-1968; res scientist, Univ Tex, Austin, 1964-1965; staff mem, Inertial Fusion, 1992-; SR SCIENTIST, MISSION RES CORP, 1987-; sr scientist, Mission Res Corp, 1987-1992; group leader, staff mem Inertia Fusion, 1986-1987; group leader, advan concept & Plasma applns, 1983-1986; Eng Res Coun, Blackett Lab, Imp Col, London UK, 1982-1983; assoc group leader inertial fusion supporting physics, Los Alamos Nat Lab, 1980-1982; assoc group leader laser fusion target design, Los Alamos Nat Lab, 1978-1980; staff mem, Los Alamos Nat Lab, 1971-1978; physicist, Austin Res Assocs, 1968-1971; asst prof physics, Univ Tex, Austin, 1965-1968; res scientist, Univ Tex, Austin, 1964-1965; vis prof, sr vis fel, UK Sci. **Memberships:** Am Phys Soc. **Research Statement & Publications:** High-energy-density physics, inertial fusion, computational plasma physics with appln to weapons and fusion energy. **Mailing Address:** Los Alamos Nat Lab, Group X-2 MS T085, Los Alamos, NM 87545. **Fax:** 505-662-2227. **E-Mail:** ell@lanl.gov

LINDNER, DUANE LEE, PHYSICAL CHEMISTRY, THERMODYNAMICS. **Personal Data:** b Ft Dodge, Iowa, May 7, 1950; m 1977, Deborah; c John, Nathaniel & Elizabeth. **Education:** Mass Inst Tehnol, SB, 1972; Univ Calif, Berkeley, PhD (chem), 1977. **Professional Experience:** PROG DIR, CHEM & BIOL NAT SECURITY PROG, SANDIA NAT LAB, as of 2006; DEP DIR, DEPT CHEM & BIOL, SANDIA NAT LABS, as of 2003; MGR, ADVAN DESIGN & MFG PROG, SANDIA NAT LABS, 1993-; mgr mat sci & technol, Chem Div, 1989-1992; supvr, Chem Div, 1986-1989; mem tech staff, 1977-1986. **Memberships:** Am Chem Soc; Mat Res Soc; Sigma Xi. **Research Statement & Publications:** Chemical kinetics and reaction mechanisms of solid-solid and gas-solid systems, particularly metal-hydrogen reactions; materials engineering; advance product realization, systems development. **Mailing Address:** Dept Chem & Biol, Sandia Nat Labs, PO Box 969, Livermore, CA 94551-0969. **Fax:** 510-294-3410. **E-Mail:** dllindu@sandia.gov

LINDNER, ELEK, ANALYTICAL BIOCHEMISTRY, MARINE BIOLOGY. **Personal Data:** b Budapest, Hungary, June 3, 1924; American citizen; m 1960, c 1. **Education:** Budapest Tech Univ, Dipl Chem Eng, 1946, PhD (biochem), 1974. **Professional Experience:** SUPVRY RES CHEMIST, NAVAL OCEAN SYSTS CTR, 1973-; res chemist, Naval Ship Res & Develop Ctr, Annapolis, Md, 1973; res chemist, Paint Lab, Mare Island Naval Shipyard, 1965-1973; prod mgr, Sawyer Tanning Co, Calif, 1964-1965; Res & Develop Div, Lever Bros Co, NJ, 1957-1961 & Chevron Res Corp, Calif, 1961-1964; res chemist, Res Inst, Fatty Oil Chem Indust, 1951-1956; chief chemist, Anal & Res Lab, Elida Cosmetic Factory, 1950-1951; Prof asst agr chem, Budapest Tech Univ, 1947-1948 & food chem, 1948-1950. **Memberships:** Am Chem Soc. **Research Statement & Publications:** Chemistry and biochemistry of food and agricultural products; analytical methods; chemistry of fatty oils; detergents and surfactants; biochemistry of marine organisms. **Mailing Address:** PO Box 82148, San Diego, CA 92138-2148.

LINDNER, LUTHER EDWARD, PATHOLOGY. **Personal Data:** b Toledo, Ohio, August 6, 1942; m 1969, Elizabeth; c 3. **Education:** Univ Toledo, BS, 1964; Western Res Univ, MD, 1967, Case Western Res Univ, PhD (exp path), 1974. **Professional Experience:** ASSOC PROF PATH, LAB MED, TEX A&M UNIV, 1982-; SR LECTR, DEPART SYSTS BIOL & TRANSLATIONAL MED, TEX A&M UNIV, as of 2005; asst prof lab med, Univ Nev, 1975-1982; chief, Anatomic Path, 1974-1975; staff pathologist, William Beaumont Army Med Ctr, 1972-1974; fel path, Case Western Res Univ, 1969-1972; From intern to resident, Univ Hosp, Cleveland, 1967-1972; vpres, Pac Biotech Int Inc, Houston; dir lab, Path Consult Serv, Tex A & M Univ; Consult path, Cent Tex Veterans Health Care Syst, St Joseph's Hosp, Bryan, Tex; Col Sta Med Ctr, Col Sta, Tex. **Memberships:** Am Soc Cytol; Am Soc Clin Path; Col Am Pathologists; US-Can Acad Path. **Research Statement & Publications:** Studies of anatomic changes in disease with histochemical correlations and application to diagnosis; Modern Pathology; sexually transmitted diseases; other infectious diseases. **Mailing Address:** Dept Path & Lab Med, Tex A&M Univ, Col Sta, TX 77843-1114. **Fax:** 979-862-1299. **E-Mail:** lindner@tamu.edu

LINDNER, MANFRED, NUCLEAR CHEMISTRY, RADIOCHEMISTRY. **Personal Data:** b Chicago, Ill, October 21, 1919; m 1946, c Mark J & Roger B. **Education:** Northwestern Univ, Ill, BS, 1940; Univ Calif, Berkeley, PhD (nuclear chem), 1948. **Professional Experience:** RETIRED; fel, Weizmann Inst Sci, 1962-1963; sr chemist, Radiochem Div, Lawrence Livermore Lab, 1953-1988; chemist, Calif Res & Develop Co, 1951-1953; asst prof chem, Wash State Col, 1948-1951; res asst, Univ Calif, Berkeley, 1946-1948; chemist, Hanford Eng Works, Wash, 1944-1946. **Memberships:** AAAS; Am Phys Soc; Sigma Xi. **Research Statement & Publications:** Neutron capture cross-sections; nuclear structure; fission yield distribution; half life determination. **Mailing Address:** 32 Corte Nogal, Danville, CA 94526.

LINDORFF, DAVID EVERETT, HYDROGEOLOGY. **Personal Data:** b Moline, Ill, August 25, 1945; m 1972, Ruth; c Paul & Tim. **Education:** Augustana Col, BA, geology, 1967; Univ Wis-Madison, MA, geology, 1969, MS, water resources management, 1971. **Honors & Awards:** Distinguished Serv Award, Wis Section of Am Water Res Assoc, 2002. **Professional Experience:** HYDROGEOLOGIST PROGRAM COORDINATOR, WIS DEPT OF NAT RESOURCES, 1997-; hydrogeologist supvr, Wis Dept Nat Resources, 1993-1997; hydrogeologist, Wis Dept Nat Resources, 1980-1993; asst geologist, Ill State Geol Surv, 1975-1980; Geologist, Pa Dept Environ Resources, 1971-1975. **Memberships:** Mem of Wisconsin Ground Water Asn; mem of Am Water Res Assoc Wis Section. **Research Statement & Publications:** Groundwater contamination; hydrogeology of strip mines; siting of sanitary landfills; groundwater standards; groundwater sampling procedures; wellhead protection; groundwater education. **Mailing Address:** Dept Natural Resources, PO Box 7921, Madison, WI 53707. **Fax:** 608-267-7650. **E-Mail:** lindod@dnr.state.wi.us

LINDOW, DONALD FRANK, AGRICULTURE & FINE CHEMICAL INTERMEDIATE SYTHESIS RESEARCH & DEVELOPMENT, QUALITY CONTROL & ASSURANCE. **Personal Data:** b Cleveland, Ohio, November 2, 1938; c Erica L (Butler) & Susan E. **Education:** Case Inst Technol, BS, 1960, PhD (org chem), 1968. **Professional Experience:** VPRES TECH OPERS, LOBECO PROD INC, 1990-; res & develop mgr, Mobay Chem Corp, 1974-1986 & Rm Engineered Prod, 1986-1990; asst prof, Ben May Lab Cancer Res, Univ Chicago, 1968-1973; Asst prof chem, State Univ, NY, Buffalo, 1965-1968. **Research Statement & Publications:** Research, development and batch industrial custom organic synthesis of fine chemical intermediates for dyestuff, pigment, agricultural and pharmaceutical industries. **Mailing Address:** Lobeco Prod Inc, PO Box 630, Lobeco, SC 29931. **Fax:** 803-846-4777.

LINDOWER, JOHN OLIVER, SCIENCE EDUCATION. **Personal Data:** b Ashland, Ohio, March 15, 1929; m 1951, c 3. **Education:** Ashland Col, AB, 1950; Ohio State Univ, MD, 1955, PhD (pharmacol), 1968. **Professional Experience:** PROF EMER, DEPT PHARMACOL & TOXICOL, WRIGHT STATE UNIV, 1995-; interim dean, Wright State Univ, beginning 1987; mem, Drug Info Adv Panel Geriat, US Pharmacopoieia, Inc, 1985-; proj dir, Area Health Educ Ctr, Region IV, Ohio, 1982-1987; prof pharmacol & toxicol, Wright State Univ, 1982-1995; assoc dean Acad Affairs, Wright State Univ, 1981-1987; mem, NCent Res Rev & Adv Comn, Am Heart Asn, 1979-1981; mem, Comn Accrediting, Asn Theol Schs US & Can, 1978-1980; from asst dean to assoc dean Curric Affairs, Wright State Univ, 1976-1981; prof & chmn pharmacol, Wright State Univ, 1975-1982; coordr curric affairs, Sch Med, Wright State Univ, 1975-1976; from instr to assoc prof, Col Med, Ohio State Univ, 1968-1975; fel pharmacol, Col Med, Ohio State Univ, 1965-1968; gen med pract, Dayton, Ohio, 1959-1965; asst surg resident, Miami Valley Hosp, Dayton, Ohio, 1958-1959; gen med officer, US Army, 1956-1958; Gen rotating internship, Miami Valley Hosp, Dayton, Ohio, 1955-1956. **Memberships:** AMA. **Research Statement & Publications:** Clinical pharmacology; cardiovascular research; subcellular and ultrastructural pharmacology. **Mailing Address:** Dept Pharmacol, Sch Med, Wright State Univ, PO Box 927, Dayton, OH 45401-0927.

LINDQUIST, ANDERS GUNNAR, SYSTEMS AND CONTROL. **Personal Data:** b Lund, Sweden, November 21, 1942; m 1986, Galina Degtyareva; c Johan, Martin & Max. **Education:** Royal Inst Technol, Sweden, MS, 1967, TeknL, 1968, TeknD(optimization & systs theory), 1972. **Professional Experience:** Affil prof, Washington Univ, St Louis, 1989-; PROF OPTIMIZATION & SYSTS THEORY, ROYAL INST TECHNOL, 1982-; prof, Univ Ky, 1980-1983; assoc prof, Univ Ky, 1974-1980; assoc prof, Brown Univ, 1973; vis asst prof math, Univ Fla, 1972-1973; docent, Royal Inst Technol, Sweden, 1972; Res assoc optimization, Royal Inst Technol, Sweden, 1969-1972. **Memberships:** Soc Indust & Appl Math; fel Inst Elec & Electronics Engrs; Royal Swed Acad Eng Sci; Hungarian Oper Res Soc. **Research Statement & Publications:** Stochastic systems theory, control theory and estimation. **Mailing Address:** Dept Math, Royal Inst Technol, Stockholm 10044, Sweden. **E-Mail:** alq@math.kth.se

LINDQUIST, EVERT E, ACAROLOGY, SYSTEMATIC ENTOMOLOGY. **Personal Data:** b Susanville, Calif, June 26, 1935; m 1957, Maxine; c Evert A, Catherine A, Adele M & Leah F. **Education:** Univ Calif, Berkeley, BS, 1957, MS, 1959, PhD (entom), 1963. **Honors & Awards:** Acarology Award, Ohio State Univ, 1974, Agr Acarology Award, 1988. **Professional Experience:** HON RES ASSOC, SYST ENTOM, EASTERN CEREAL & OILSEED RES CTR, AGR & AGRI-FOOD CAN, 2000-; prin res scientist, Biosyst Res Ctr, Agr Can, 1995-2000; collabr & vis instr, Arthropods La Selva project, Costa Rica, 1992-1999; mem, Exec Comt, Int Cong Acarology, 1990-1998; vis lectr, Inst Polytech Nat Mex, 1987; vis lectr, Col Postgrad Mex, 1987; vis lectr, Univ Nat Auton Mex, 1983 & 1987; sr res scientist, Biosyst Res Ctr, Agr Can, 1975-1995; vis lectr, Summer Acarology Prog, Ohio State Univ, 1972-1988; adj prof, Carleton Univ, 1971-1983; res scientist, Biosyst Res Ctr, Agr Can, 1962-1975. **Memberships:** Fel Entom Soc Can; Acarological Soc Am; Sigma Xi; Europ Asn Acarologists; Latin Am Soc Acarology. **Research Statement & Publications:** Systematics, cladistics and classification of Acari diversi; symbiotic relationships between mites, insects, namatodes and fungi; homology of acarine external structures; biodiversity of targeted mite taxa in selected ecosystems; predatory mites as bio-indicators in environmental monitoring. **Mailing Address:** Eastern Cereal & Oilseed Res Ctr, Agr & Agri-food Can, 960, Carling Ave, KW Neatby Bldg, Ottawa, ON K1A 0C6, Can. **Fax:** 613-759-1927. **E-Mail:** lindquiste@agr.gc.ca

LINDQUIST, H D ALAN, PARASITOLOGY, DIAGNOSTIC TESTS FOR WATER SUPPLY. **Personal Data:** b New York, NY, August 1961; m 1991, Wantana. **Education:** Miami Univ, Ohio, BA, 1983, MEn, 1986; Uniformed Serv Univ, PhD (parasitol), 1995. **Professional Experience:** MICROBIOLOGIST, BIOHAZARD ASSESSMENT BR, NAT EXPOSURE RES LAB, US ENVIRON PROTECTION AGENCY, 1996-; postgrad fel parasitol, Oak Ridge Inst Sci & Educ, 1995-1996; postdoctoral asst parasitol, Uniformed Serv Univ Health Sci, 1995; vol malaria control, US Peace Corps, 1986-1989; biologist, Environ Monitoring & Support Lab, US Environ Protection Agency, 1986. **Memberships:** Am Soc Parasitologists; Am Soc Microbiologists; Sigma Xi; Maleria Asn Thailand. **Research Statement & Publications:** Develop molecular and immunological protocols for use in water to detect and identify protozoan parasites of significance in causing human disease. **Mailing Address:** US Environ Protection Agency, 26 W Martin Luther King Dr, Cincinnati, OH 45268-1320. **Fax:** 513-569-7117. **E-Mail:** lindquist.alan@epamail.epa.gov

LINDQUIST, NORMAN F, MATHEMATICS. **Professional Experience:** ASSOC PROF, DEPT MATH, WESTERN WASH UNIV, as of 2003. **Memberships:** Math Asn Am. **Mailing Address:** Dept Math, Western Wash Univ, Bellingham, WA 98225-9063. **Fax:** 360-650-7788. **E-Mail:** lnorm@cc.wwu.edu

LINDQUIST, RICHARD KENNETH, ENTOMOLOGY. **Personal Data:** b Minneapolis, Minn, October 2, 1942; m 1969. **Education:** Gustavus Adolphus Col, BA, 1964; Kans State Univ, MS, 1967, PhD (entom), 1969. **Professional Experience:** SR TECH SERV MANAGER & WESTERN REGIONAL SALES MANAGER, OLYMPIC HORTICULTURAL PRODUCTS, as of 2006; assoc prof entom, Ohio Agr Res & Develop Ctr, beginning 1974; asst prof, Ohio Agr Res & Develop Ctr, 1969-1974; instr entom, Kans State Univ, 1968-1969. **Memberships:** Entom Soc Am. **Research Statement & Publications:** Biology, ecology and control of insect and mite pests of floral and greenhouse vegetable crops. **Mailing Address:** Olympic Hort Products, 1594 Sunset Lane, Wooster, OH 44691. **Fax:** 330-345-1311. **E-Mail:** rlindquist@olympichort.com

LINDQUIST, RICHARD WALLACE, PHYSICS. **Personal Data:** b Worcester, Mass, May 6, 1933; m 1957, Jane Tandy; c Peter & David. **Education:** Worcester Polytech Inst, BS, 1954; Princeton Univ, AM, 1957, PhD (physics), 1962. **Professional Experience:** Chair, Math, Sci & Technol, Charter Oak State Col, 1995-1997; chair, Wesleyan Univ, 1978-1984 & 1986-1989; emer prof physics, Wesleyan Univ, 1998; prof physics, Wesleyan Univ, 1977-1998; assoc prof, Wesleyan Univ, 1965-1977; res assoc, Univ Tex, 1964-1965; asst prof, Adelphi Univ, 1960-1964; Instr physics, Princeton Univ, 1958-1960. **Memberships:** Am Phys Soc; Am Asn Physics Teachers emer mem. **Research Statement & Publications:** General relativity; geometrodynamics; gravitational collapse. **Mailing Address:** 34 west woods, Yarmouth Port, MA 02675.

LINDQUIST, ROBERT HENRY, PHYSICAL CHEMISTRY. **Personal Data:** b Minneapolis, Minn, February 27, 1928; m 1950, c 2. **Education:** Univ Minn, BS, 1949, MS, 1950; Univ Calif, PhD (chem), 1955. **Professional Experience:** PRES, LINDQUIST CONSULT, 1988-; mgr corp res planning dept, Chevron Res Co. 1986-1988; consult corp develop, Chevron Corp, 1980-1986; mgr solar, Chevron Res Co, 1978-1980; asst to pres, Chevron Res Co, 1975-1978; sr res assoc, Chevron Res Co, 1964-1975; sr res chemist, Chevron Res Co, 1960-1964; Res chemist, Chevron Res Co, 1955-1960; consult, high tech bus profitability. **Memberships:** Am Chem Soc; Am Phys Soc. **Research Statement & Publications:** Solid state physics; magnetic resonance; physics of ultra-fine particles; heterogeneous catalysis; reaction kinetics; synthetic fuels; alternate energy sources. **Mailing Address:** Lindquist Consult, PO Box 8355, Berkeley, CA 94707. **Fax:** 510-527-6604.

LINDQUIST, ROBERT MARION, ORGANIC CHEMISTRY, PHOTOGRAPHIC CHEMISTRY. **Personal Data:** b Cumberland, Wis, December 4, 1923; c 3. **Education:** Univ Wis, BS, 1944; Univ Minn, PhD, 1950. **Honors & Awards:** First Level Invention Award, IBM Corp, 1962, Outstanding Contrib Award, 1974. **Professional Experience:** SR CHEMIST, IBM CORP, 1965-; develop chemist, IBM Corp, 1963-1965; adv chemist, IBM Corp, 1962-1963; staff chemist, IBM Corp, 1957-1962; assoc chemist photog processes, IBM Corp, 1956-1957; Res chemist photog res, Gen Aniline & Film Corp, 1950-1956. **Memberships:** Sr mem Am Chem Soc; Sigma Xi; fel Am Inst Chemists; sr mem Soc Photog Scientists & Engrs. **Research Statement & Publications:** Electrophotographic processes. **Mailing Address:** 4788 Briar Ridge Trail, Boulder, CO 80301.

LINDQUIST, ROBERT NELS, BIOCHEMISTRY, ORGANIC CHEMISTRY. **Personal Data:** b Bakersfield, Calif, September 29, 1942; m 1968. **Education:** Occidental Col, BA, 1965; Ind Univ, PhD (chem), 1968. **Professional Experience:** PROF EMER CHEM, SAN FRANCISCO STATE UNIV, 2000-; prof chem, San Francisco State Univ, beginning 1980; from asst prof to assoc prof, San Francisco State Univ, 1971-1980; res chemist, Shell Develop Co, 1968-1971; chemist, Shankman Labs, 1965-1966; fel, Harvard Univ. **Memberships:** AAAS; Am Chem Soc. **Research Statement & Publications:** Enzyme and enzyme model reaction kinetics and mechanisms. **Mailing Address:** Dept Chem & Biochem, San Francisco State Univ, 1600 Holloway Ave, San Francisco, CA 94102. **Fax:** 415-338-2384.

LINDQUIST, SUSAN LEE, STRUCTURE & FUNCTION OF CHAPERONE PROTEINS, ABNORMAL PROTEINS & PRIONS. **Personal Data:** b Chicago, Ill, June 5, 1949; m Edward; c Eleanora & Alana. **Education:** Univ Ill, Champaign-Urbana, BA, 1971; Harvard Univ, PhD (biol), 1976. **Honors & Awards:** Berlin lectr, Northwestern Univ, 1995; Boyce Thompson lectr, Cornell Univ, 1995. **Professional Experience:** Dir, Whitehead Inst, Mass Inst Technol, beginning 2001; PROF BIO, MASS INST TECHNOL, 2001-; prof, Dept Molecular Genetics & Biol, Univ Chicago, 1988-2001; INVESTR, HOWARD HUGHES MED INST, 1988-; mem, Biomed Sci Study Sect, 1988-1990; consult, Mus Sci & Indust, Chicago, 1983-1987; vis scholar, Cambridge Univ, Eng, 1983; mem, Genetic Basis Dis Study Sect, NIH, 1982; from asst prof to assoc prof, Howard Hughes Med Inst, 1978-1988; Am Cancer Soc postdoctoral fel, Howard Hughes Med Inst, 1976-1978. **Memberships:** Nat Acad Sci; Am Acad Arts & Sci; Molecular Med Soc; Am Soc Cellular biol; Genetics Soc Am; Am Soc Microbiol; Fedn Am Scientists Exp Biol. **Research Statement & Publications:** Mechanisms that organisms employ to protect themselves from environmental stresses, such as high temperatures, ethanol and toxic metal ions; problems of protein folding related to human disease. **Mailing Address:** Whitehead Inst, Nine Cambridge Ctr, Cambridge, MA 02142-1479. **E-Mail:** lindquist_admin@wi.mit.edu

LINDQUIST, WILLIAM BRENT, NUMERICAL SOLUTION OF PDES, RIEMANN PROBLEMS. **Personal Data:** b Ft Frances, Ont, June 23, 1953; m 1989, Carol; c Lars I. **Education:** Univ Man, BS, 1975; Cornell Univ, PhD (physics), 1981. **Professional Experience:** ASSOC CHAIR, DEPT MATH & STATIST, STATE UNIV NY, STONY BROOK, 1999-; PROF APPL MATH, STATE UNIV NY, STONY BROOK, 1994-; assoc prof appl math, State Univ NY, Stony Brook, 1989-1994; from res asst prof to res assoc prof, Courant Inst Math Sci, NY Univ, 1985-1989; consult, Inst Energy Technol, Kjeller, Norway, 1985-1988; assoc res scientist, Courant Inst Math Sci, NY Univ, 1981-1985. **Memberships:** Am Phys Soc; Soc Indust & Appl Math; Am Math Soc; Soc Petrol Engrs; Am Geophys Union. **Research Statement & Publications:** Hyperbolic equations; numerical methods for PDE's; flow in porous media; anomalous magnetic moment of the electron. **Mailing Address:** State Univ NY, Dept Appl Math & Statist, Stony Brook, NY 11794-3600. **Fax:** 516-632-8490. **E-Mail:** lindquis@ams.sunysb.edu

LINDROOS, ARTHUR E(DWARD), CHEMICAL ENGINEERING. **Personal Data:** b Worcester, Mass, August 14, 1922; m 1944, c 4. **Education:** Worcester Polytech Inst, BS, 1943, MS, 1944; Yale Univ, DEng, 1949. **Professional Experience:** RETIRED; dir eng, Unit CPC Int, Penick Corp, 1986-1990; mgr eng, Unit CPC Int, Penick Corp, 1985-1986; assoc mgr eng, Unit CPC Int, Penick Corp, 1979-1985; div supvr, Unit CPC Int, Penick Corp, 1976-1979; vpres, Techni-Chem Co, 1971-1976; eng mgr, Airco Chem & Plastics Co, 1969-1971; mgr process eng, Airco Chem & Plastics Co, 1967-1969; mgr process eng, Air Reduction Chem & Carbide Co, 1962-1967; tech mgr, Cumberland Chem Corp, 1961-1962; mgr develop, Air Reduction Chem Co, NJ, 1959-1961; chem engr process develop, Air Reduction Chem Co, NJ, 1953-1959; Chem engr res & develop, Kellex Corp, 1949-1953. **Memberships:** Am Chem Soc; Am Inst Chem Engrs; Sigma Xi. **Research Statement & Publications:** Mass transfer; phase equilibria at elevated pressures; nuclear reactor fuel reprocessing; acetylenic chemistry; vinyl monomers; resins and emulsions; polyvinyl alcohol; calcium carbide; lime recovery; chlorinated hydrocarbons; narcotics; pharmaceuticals. **Mailing Address:** 40 Moon Compass Lane, Sandwich, MA 02563-2765.

LINDROTH, RICHARD L, BIOLOGICAL SCIENCES, ECOLOGY. **Personal Data:** b 1954; m 1978, Nancy; c Kristen L & Nicole R. **Education:** Iowa State Univ, BS, 1977; Univ Ill,

Urbana, PhD (ecol), 1984. **Professional Experience:** Fulbright sr scholar, AgRes Grassland Res Ctr, Palmerston, NZ, 1997; PROF, DEPT ENTOM, UNIV WIS-MADISON, 1996-; from asst prof to assoc prof, Dept Entom, Univ Wis-madison, 1988-1996. **Memberships:** Ecol Soc Am; Entom Soc Am; Int Soc Chem Ecol. **Research Statement & Publications:** Chemical ecology of plant-insect interactions; ecological effects of global environmental change. **Mailing Address:** Dept Entom, Univ Wis-Madison, 1630 Linden Dr, Madison, WI 53706. **Fax:** 608-262-3322. **E-Mail:** lindroth@entomology.wisc.edu

LINDSAY, BRUCE GEORGE, MIXTURE MODELS, HIGH DIMENSIONAL INFERENCE. **Personal Data:** b The Dalles, Ore, March 7, 1947; m 1997, Laura; c Dylan, Camden & Maia. **Education:** Univ Ore, BA (math), 1969; Univ Wash, PhD (biomath), 1978. **Honors & Awards:** Humboldt Sr Scientist Award, Humboldt Found, Ger, 1990; GUGGENHEIM FELLOW, 1996-7; Landsdowne Lectr, Univ Victoria, Can, 1997. **Professional Experience:** WILLAMAN PROF STATIST, PA STATE UNIV, 2004-; DISTINGUISHED PROF STATIST, PA STATE UNIV, 1991-2004; Cornell Univ, 1988 & Yale Univ, 1990; vis prof, Johns Hopkins Univ, 1987; Prin investr, NSF, 1979-; From asst prof to prof, PA State Univ, 1979-1991. **Memberships:** Fel Inst Math Statist; FEL Am Statist Asn; fel Int Statist Inst. **Research Statement & Publications:** Statistical methods in semiparametric models, with emphasis on maximum likelihood and minimum distance methods in mixture models and THEIR computation. **Mailing Address:** 422 Thomas Bldg, Univ Park, PA 16802. **Fax:** 814-863-7114. **E-Mail:** bgl@psu.edu

LINDSAY, DAVID TAYLOR, DEVELOPMENTAL BIOLOGY. **Personal Data:** b Philadelphia, Pa, March 22, 1935; m 1959, c 1. **Education:** Amherst Col, BA, 1957; Johns Hopkins Univ, PhD (biol), 1962. **Professional Experience:** ASSOC PROF EMER, DEPT CELLULAR BIOL, UNIV GA, 1998-; MEM FAC, UNIV GA, 1977-; Nat Sci Found res grant develop biol, 1963-1966; from asst prof to assoc prof zool, Univ GA, 1962-1977. **Memberships:** AAAS; Soc Develop Biol; Am Soc Zoologists; NY Acad Sci. **Research Statement & Publications:** Mechanisms of cellular differentiation; regulation of protein synthesis in differentiation; biological role of histone proteins; bilateral symmetry. **Mailing Address:** Dept Cellular Biol Univ Ga, 701 Biological Scis, Athens, GA 30601-3040. **E-Mail:** lindsay@cellmate.cb.uga.edu

LINDSAY, EVERETT HAROLD, VERTEBRATE PALEONTOLOGY. **Personal Data:** b La Junta, Colo, July 2, 1931; div, c 3. **Education:** Chico State Col, AB, 1953, MA, 1957; Cornell Univ, MST, 1962; Univ Calif, Berkeley, PhD (paleont), 1967. **Professional Experience:** PROF EMER, DEPT GEOL, UNIV ARIZ, as of 2004; prof geol, Univ Ariz, beginning 1980; from asst prof to assoc prof, Univ Ariz, 1967-1980. **Memberships:** AAAS; Soc Vert Paleont; Geol Soc Am; Paleont Soc. **Research Statement & Publications:** Biostratigraphy; magnetostratigraphy; taxonomy and evolution of small mammal fossils. **Mailing Address:** Dept Geosci Univ Ariz, Gould-Simpson Bldg 1040 E 4th St, Tucson, AZ 85721-0077. **E-Mail:** ehlind@dakotacom.net

LINDSAY, GEORGE EDMUND, plant taxonomy; deceased, see previous edition for last biography

LINDSAY, GLENN FRANK, INDUSTRIAL ENGINEERING, OPERATIONS RESEARCH. **Personal Data:** b Portland, Ore, June 13, 1935; m 1965. **Education:** Ore State Univ, BSc, 1960; Ohio State Univ, MSc, 1962, PhD (indust eng), 1968. **Professional Experience:** ASSOC PROF OPERS RES, NAVAL POSTGRAD SCH, 1969-; asst prof opers res, Naval Postgrad Sch, 1965-1969; Res assoc, Systs Res Group, Ohio State Univ, 1961-1965. **Memberships:** Opers Res Soc Am; Inst Mgt Sci; Am Soc Eng Educ. **Research Statement & Publications:** Counter-insurgency small-unit military operations; industrial inspection systems. **Mailing Address:** Dept Opers, Naval Postgrad Sch Res, Monterey, CA 93943-5000.

LINDSAY, HAGUE LELAND, VERTEBRATE ZOOLOGY. **Personal Data:** b Ft Worth, Tex, January 24, 1929; m 1956, c John, Robert, Carol & Dana. **Education:** Tex Christian Univ, BA, 1949; Univ Tex, MA, 1951, PhD (zoology), 1958. **Professional Experience:** RETIRED; prof zoology, Univ Tulsa, 1956-1957; res scientist, Univ Tex, 1954. **Memberships:** AAAS; Am Fisheries Soc; Am Soc Ichthyol & Herpet. **Research Statement & Publications:** Vertebrate speciation, especially with amphibians; fish distribution and ecology, especially with darters. **Mailing Address:** 5145 S Vandalia Ave, Tulsa, OK 74135.

LINDSAY, HUGH ALEXANDER, PHYSIOLOGY. **Personal Data:** b Moose Jaw, Sask, March 5, 1926; m 1956, c 3. **Education:** Univ Western Ont, BSc, 1949, MSc, 1952; Univ Toronto, PhD (pharmacol), 1955; WVa Univ, MD, 1973. **Professional Experience:** PROF PHYSIOL, SCH MED, WVA UNIV, 1970-; from asst prof to assoc prof, Sch Med, Wva Univ, 1955-1970; asst pharmacol, Univ Toronto, 1952-1955. **Memberships:** AAAS; NY Acad Sci; Am Physiol Soc; Pharmacol Soc Can. **Research Statement & Publications:** Growth in congenital cardiovascular disease; osteoporosis. **Mailing Address:** 1133 Van Voorhis Rd, Morgantown, WV 26505-3431.

LINDSAY, JAMES EDWARD, JR, ELECTRICAL ENGINEERING. **Personal Data:** b Denver, Colo, February 26, 1928; m 1949, c 5. **Education:** Univ Denver, BS, 1953; Univ Colo, Boulder, MS, 1958, PhD (elec eng), 1960. **Professional Experience:** PROF ELEC ENG, UNIV WYO, 1980-; assoc prof, Univ Wyo, 1976-1980; res engr, Denver Res Inst, Univ Denver, 1970-1976; assoc prof geophys & basic eng, Colo Sch Mines, 1967-1970; res engr, Martin Marietta Co, 1966-1967; from asst prof toassoc prof elec eng, Univ Denver, 1962-1965; from instr to assoc prof appl math & elec eng, Univ Colo, 1958-1962; res engr, Denver Res Inst, 1957-1958; instr elec eng, Univ Denver, 1955-1956; Res engr, RCA Labs, 1953-1955. **Memberships:** Soc Indust & Appl Math; Inst Elec & Electronics Engrs; Sigma Xi. **Research Statement & Publications:** Electromagnetic field theory; antennas and propagation; teaching of graduate and undergraduate courses in electrical engineering, geophysics and applied mathematics. **Mailing Address:** 1938 Riverwood Trails Dr, Florissant, MO 63031-7438.

LINDSAY, KENNETH LAWSON, ORGANIC CHEMISTRY. **Personal Data:** b Springfield, Ill, August 26, 1925; m 1949, c 1. **Education:** Univ Ill, BS, 1948; Univ Minn, PhD (chem), 1952. **Professional Experience:** AUTOMATED PUBLISHING CONSULT, 1985-; sr res assoc, Ethyl Corp, 1978-1982; process res supvr, Ethyl Corp, 1963-1978; develop assoc, Ethyl Corp, 1961-1963; develop chemist, Ethyl Corp, 1955-1961; res chemist, Ethyl Corp, 1952-1955. **Memberships:** Am Chem Soc; Am Inst Chem. **Research Statement & Publications:** Applied kinetics; organometallic chemistry; chlorine chemistry. **Mailing Address:** 55-130 Naupaka St, Laie, HI 96762.

LINDSAY, RAYMOND H, BIOCHEMISTRY, PHARMACOLOGY. **Personal Data:** b Perry, Ga, December 9, 1928; m 1985, c 5. **Education:** Jacksonville State Col, BS, 1948; Univ Ala, MS, 1957, PhD (pharmacol), 1961. **Professional Experience:** RETIRED; prof med, Med Ctr, 1972-1990; prof pharmacol, Med Ctr, 1971-1990; dir pharmacol res unit, Vet Admin Hosp, 1971-1990; dir metab res, Vet Admin Hosp, Birmingham, 1965-1967; asst chief radioisotope serv, Vet Admin Hosp, Birmingham, 1964-1972; from asst prof to assoc prof med, Univ Ala, Birmingham, 1963-1972; From asst prof to assoc prof pharmacol, Univ Ala, Birmingham, 1963-1971; univ fel, Univ Wis, 1962-1963; NIH fel physiol chem, Univ Wis, 1960-1962. **Memberships:** AAAS; Endocrine Soc; Am Thyroid Asn; Am Chem Soc; Am Physiol Soc; Am Soc Pharmacol & Exp Therapeut. **Research Statement & Publications:** Biochemistry, pharmacology and physiology of thyroid function; antithyroid drugs; environmental goitrogens. **Mailing Address:** PO Box 5189, Navarre, FL 32566.

LINDSAY, RICHARD H, NUCLEAR PHYSICS. **Personal Data:** b Portland, Ore, September 24, 1934; m 1958, c 6. **Education:** Univ Portland, BS, 1956; Stanford Univ, MS, 1958; Wash State Univ, PhD (nuclear physics), 1961. **Professional Experience:** PROF EMER PHYSICS, WESTERN WASH UNIV, as of 2006; prof physics, Western Wash Univ, beginning 1966; assoc prof, Western Wash Univ, 1961-1966; teaching assoc physics, Wash State Univ, 1960-1961. **Memberships:** Am Phys Soc; Am Asn Physics Teachers. **Research Statement & Publications:** Nuclear reactions with 30 to 65 million electron volts alpha particles; reactions with 14 million electron volts neutrons; theoretical nuclear physics; instrument design. **Mailing Address:** Dept Physics, Western Wash Univ, BH 166, Bellingham, WA 98225.

LINDSAY, ROBERT CLARENCE, FOOD SCIENCE, FOOD CHEMISTRY. **Personal Data:** b Montrose, Colo, November 30, 1936; m 1957, Glenda; c Alison & Kellie. **Education:** Colo State Univ, BS, 1958, MS, 1960; Ore State Univ, PhD (food sci), 1965. **Honors & Awards:** Dairy Res Found Award, 1986; Stephen S Chang Award, Inst Food technologist, 1998. **Professional Experience:** PROF FOOD SCI, UNIV WIS, MADISON, 1974-; assoc prof, Univ Wis-madison, 1969-1974; asst prof food sci, Ore State Univ, 1964-1969. **Memberships:** Am Chem Soc; fel Inst Food Technologists; Am Dairy Sci Asn; Am Soc Microbiol. **Research Statement & Publications:** Flavor chemistry; sensory evaluation of food; enzymic generation of flavor chemicals and biotechnological applications. **Mailing Address:** Dept Food Sci, Univ Wis-Madison, 7 Babcock Hall, Madison, WI 53706. **Fax:** 608-262-6872. **E-Mail:** rlindsay@facstaff.wisc.edu

LINDSAY, ROBERT KENDALL, ARTIFICIAL INTELLIGENCE, COGNITIVE THEORY. **Personal Data:** b Cleveland, Ohio, August 13, 1934; m 1970, c 2. **Education:** Carnegie-Mellon Univ, BS, 1956, PhD (admin), 1961; Columbia Univ, MA, 1957. **Professional Experience:** RES PROF EMER, MENTAL HEALTH RES INST, UNIV MICH, as of 2005; PROF EMER PSYCHOL, UNIV MICH, as of 2005; prof psychol, Univ Mich, as of 2003; res scientist, Mental Health Res Inst, Univ Mich, beginning 1965; from asst prof to assoc prof psychol, Univ Tex, Austin, 1960-1965. **Memberships:** Am Asn Artificial Intel; AAAS. **Research Statement & Publications:** Artificial intelligence and cognitive science, especially verbal and spatial reasoning and their interactions; expert systems; methodological and philosophical aspects of psychological theory and computation. **Mailing Address:** Univ Mich, Mental Health Res Inst, 205 Zina Pitcher Pl, Ann Arbor, MI 48109-0720. **Fax:** 734-647-4130. **E-Mail:** lindsay@umich.edu

LINDSAY, STUART, BIOPHYSICS. **Personal Data:** b London, Eng, July 3, 1951. **Education:** Univ Manchester, BS, 1972, PhD (physics), 1976. **Professional Experience:** PROF, BIOPHYS & SCANNING TUNNELING MICROS, ARIZ STATE UNIV, as of 2000; fac mem, dept physics, ariz state univ, beginning, beginning 1979; Res scientist, Philips Industs, 1977-1979. **Memberships:** Am Phys Soc. **Mailing Address:** Dept Physics & Astron, Ariz State Univ, PSB 351, PO Box 851504, Tempe, AZ 85287-1504. **Fax:** 480-965-7954. **E-Mail:** stuart.lindsay@asu.edu

LINDSAY, WILLARD LYMAN, SOILS, SOIL SCIENCE. **Personal Data:** b Dingle, Idaho, April 7, 1926; m 1951, Lorna Lance; c 4. **Education:** Utah State Univ, BS, 1952, MS, 1953; Cornell Univ, PhD (soil sci), 1956. **Professional Experience:** PROF AGRON, COLO STATE UNIV, 1974-; vis prof, State Agr Univ, Wageningen, Neth, 1972; centennial prof, Colo State Univ, 1970-1978; from assoc prof to prof, Colo State Univ, 1962-1970; asst prof agron, Colo State Univ, 1960-1962; soil chemist, Soils & Fertilizer Res Br, Tenn Valley Authority, 1956-1960; Res asst Utah State Univ, 1952-1953 & Cornell Univ, 1953-1956. **Memberships:** Soil Sci Soc Am; fel Am Soc Agron; Int Soc Soil Sci; Sigma Xi. **Research Statement & Publications:** Chemical reactions of phosphate in soils; physicochemical equilibria of plant nutrients in soils; chemistry and availability of micronutrients to plants; equilibrium of metal chelates in soils; solubility of heavy metals in soils. **Mailing Address:** Dept Agron, Colo State Univ, 2407 Agron Hall, Ames, IA 50011-1010.

LINDSAY, WILLIAM GERMER, PHYSIOLOGY. **Personal Data:** b Cleveland, Ohio, November 22, 1928; m 1956, Barbara; c 3. **Education:** Oberlin Col, AB, 1951; Univ Pa, MS, 1957, PhD (zoology), 1962. **Professional Experience:** RETIRED; prof biol, Elmira Col, 1975-1996; from asst prof to assoc prof, Elmira Col, 1966-1975; instr physiol, Albany Med Col, 1962-1966. **Memberships:** AAAS; Soc Study Reproduction. **Research Statement & Publications:** Spermatozoa metabolism; biological limnology; marine ecology. **Mailing Address:** 505 Euclid Ave, Elmira, NY 14915.

LINDSAY, WILLIAM TENNEY, JR, CHEMICAL ENGINEERING. **Personal Data:** b Scranton, Pa, April 4, 1924; m 1951, c 2. **Education:** Rensselaer Polytech Inst, BChE, 1948; Mass Inst Technol, PhD (phys chem), 1952. **Professional Experience:** CONSULT, LINDSAY & ASSOC, 1983-; consult, Res & Develop Ctr, Westinghouse Elec Corp, 1977-1983; mgr phys & inorg chem dept, Res Labs, 1973-1977; mgr phys chem dept, Res Labs, 1964-1973; fel engr, Res Labs, 1959-1964; supv engr, Atomic Power Div, Westinghouse Elec Corp, 1955-1959; sr scientist, Atomic Power Div, Westinghouse Elec Corp, 1953-1954; res assoc, Mass Inst Technol, 1952-1953; asst, Mass Inst Technol, 1949-1951; Engr, Procter & Gamble Co, 1948. **Memberships:** Fel AAAS; Am Chem Soc; Am Phys Soc; Electrochem Soc; NY Acad Sci; Am Soc Testing & Mat; Am Inst Chem Engrs. **Research Statement & Publications:** Electrolytic solutions; nuclear reactor coolant technology. **Mailing Address:** 47 E Main St, Hopkinton, MA 01748-1238.

LINDSETH, ROY O, SCIENCE. **Education:** Kauffman Gold Medal, Soc Explor Geophysicists, 1970. **Professional Experience:** CONSULT. **Mailing Address:** 273296 Alberta Ltd, 1023 Cameron Ave SW, Calgary, AB T2T 0K2, Can.

LINDSEY, BRUCE GILBERT, NEUROPHYSIOLOGY, NEUROANATOMY. **Education:** Williams Col, BA, 1971; Univ Pa, PhD (neuroanat), 1974. **Honors & Awards:** Javits Neuroscience Investigator Award, NINDS, 2004. **Professional Experience:** CHAIR, UNIV SFLA MED CTR, 1996-; FROM ASST PROF TO PROF PHYSIOL & BIOPHYS, UNIV SFLA MED CTR, 1977-; Fel neurophysiol, Univ Pa, 1974-1977. **Memberships:** Soc Neuroscience; AAAS; Am Physiol Soc. **Research Statement & Publications:** Parallel information processing in the nervous system; sensory-motor intergration; brain stem control of breathing. **Mailing Address:** Dept oft Physiology, USF Health, 12901 Bruce B Downs Blvd, Tampa, FL 33612. **Fax:** 813-974-3079. **E-Mail:** blindsey@hsc.usf.edu

LINDSEY, CASIMIR CHARLES, ICHTHYOLOGY. **Personal Data:** b Toronto, Ont, March 22, 1923; m 1948. **Education:** Univ Toronto, BA, 1948; Univ BC, MA, 1950; Cambridge

Univ, PhD (zoology), 1952. **Professional Experience:** PROF EMER ZOOL, UNIV BC, VANCOUVER, 1989-; dir, Inst Animal Resource Ecol, 1980-1988; Can Deleg Pac Sci, Khabarovsk USSR, 1979; prof Zool, Univ Bc, Vancouver, 1979-1989; Can Deleg Pac Sci, Vancouver, 1975; Univ S Pac, Can Int Develop Agency, 1971-1972; Can Deleg Pac Sci, Australia, 1971; prof zool, Univ Man, 1966-1979; Can Deleg Pac Sci, Japan, 1966; fisheries consult, Pakistan, 1964; vis prof, Wallace mem lectr, 1963; vis prof, Univ Singapore, 1962-1963; from asst prof to assoc prof zool, Univ BC, 1957-1966; Can Deleg Pac Sci, Cong, Thailand, 1957; cur fishes, Inst Fisheries, 1952-1966; res biologist, BC Dept Game, 1952-1957. **Memberships:** Fel Royal Soc Can; Can Soc Zoologists (pres, 1977-1978). **Research Statement & Publications:** Meristic variation; taxonomy; zoogeography of northern freshwater fishes; comparison of tropical and temperate fisheries. **Mailing Address:** Dept Zool, Univ BC, 6270 Univ Blvd, Vancouver, BC V6T 1Z4, Can. **Fax:** 604-822-2416.

LINDSEY, CHARLES E, MATHEMATICS. **Professional Experience:** ASSOC PROF MATH, COL ARTS & SCI, FLA GULF COAST UNIV, as of 2005. **Memberships:** Am Math Soc; Math Asn Am; Can Soc Hist & Philos Math. **Mailing Address:** Dept Math, Fla Gulf Coast Univ, Modular Bldg 2 Rm 35, Ft Myers, FL 33919. **Fax:** 941-590-7200. **E-Mail:** clindsey@fgcu.edu

LINDSEY, DAVID ALLEN, GEOLOGY. **Personal Data:** b Nebraska City, Nebr, May 26, 1942; m 1966, Barbara; c 2. **Education:** Univ Nebr, BS, 1963; Johns Hopkins Univ, PhD (geol), 1967. **Honors & Awards:** Meritorious Serv Award, Dept Interior. **Professional Experience:** GEOLOGIST, US GEOL SURV, COLO, 1992-; chief, Br Cent Mineral Resources, 1987-1991; geologist, US Geol Surv, Colo, 1976-1986 & 1967-1974; staff geologist mineral resources, Va, 1974-1975; Geol Soc Am res grant, 1965-1966. **Memberships:** Geol Soc Am; Am Asn Petrol Geol. **Research Statement & Publications:** Glacial deposits, alluvial conglomerates and sandstones; beryllium deposits and volcanic rocks in Utah; intrusive complexes in central Montana; copper in sedimentary rocks; laramide and tertiary tectonics; stream gravels for aggregate. **Mailing Address:** Denver Fed Ctr, US Geol Surv, MS 905 P O Box 25286, Denver, CO 80225. **Fax:** 303-202-4693.

LINDSEY, DONALD L, PLANT PATHOLOGY. **Personal Data:** b Stockton, Kans, May 25, 1937; m 1961, c 3. **Education:** Ft Hays Kans State Col, BS, 1959; Colo State Univ, MS, 1962, PhD (plant path), 1965. **Professional Experience:** ACTG ASSOC DEAN & DIR EMER, COL AGR & HOME ECONOMICS, as of 2003; PROF EMER ENTOM, PLANT PATH & WEED SCI, NMEX STATE UNIV, as of 2003; prof plant path, NMex State Univ, 1981-; from asst prof to assoc prof, Nmex State Univ, 1969-1981; asst plant pathologist, Colo State Univ, 1966-1969; instr bot, Colo State Col, 1966; Jr plant pathologist, Colo State Univ, 1961-1965. **Memberships:** Am Phytopath Soc; Sigma Xi; Soc Nematologist. **Research Statement & Publications:** Biological control of plant pathogens; ecology of soil fungi; mine spoil revegetation. **Mailing Address:** Dept Entom, Plant Path & Weed Sci, NMex State Univ, MSC 3BE, Skeen Hall Bldg, Las Cruces, NM 88003.

LINDSEY, DORTHA RUTH, THERAPEUTIC EXERCISE, GEROKINESIATRICS. **Personal Data:** b Kingfisher, Okla, October 26, 1926. **Education:** Okla State Univ, BS, 1948; Univ Wis, MS, 1956; Ind Univ, PED, 1963. **Honors & Awards:** Julian Vogel Mem Award, Am Kinesiotherapy Asn, 1988. **Professional Experience:** RETIRED; ed, Perspectives J Western Soc, Phys Ed Col Women, 1987-1995; consult fitness & exercise, Ask the Profs, beginning 1982; prof, Calif State Univ, Long Beach, 1976-1988; vis prof, Utah Univ, 1975-1976; vis prof, Univ Utah, 1975-1976; author & lectr, phys fitness & wellness, beginning 1968; consult, Payne Co Guid Ctr, 1966-1971; ed, Fencing Guide, Am Asn Health, Phys Educ & Recreation, 1961-1962; prof health, phys educ & recreation, Okla State Univ, 1956-1975; instr, DePauw Univ, 1954-1956; instr, Monticello Col, 1951-1954; instr health, phys educ & recreation, Okla State Univ, 1948-1950; mem, Coun on Aging & Adult Develop. **Memberships:** Am Alliance Health, Phys Ed, Recreation & Dance; Am Kinesiotherapy Asn; Nat Coun Against Health Fraud. **Research Statement & Publications:** Physical education; kinesiotherapy; electromyographical and kinesiological analyses of muscle action; quackery in physical fitness and reducing; therapeutic exercise; gerokinesiatrics; proprioceptive neuromuscular facilitation exercise effect on range of neck motion; physical fitness and wellness. **Mailing Address:** 9332 Ambassador Dr, Westminster, CA 92683.

LINDSEY, EDWARD STORMONT, MEDICINE. **Personal Data:** b West Palm Beach, Fla, June 3, 1930; m 1953, c 2. **Education:** Tulane Univ, BS, 1951, MD, 1958, MMedSci, 1968. **Professional Experience:** ADJ PROF, DEPT STRUCT & CELLULAR BIOL, TULANE UNIV, as of 2004; CLIN ASSOC PROF SURG, TULANE UNIV, 1976-; DIR TRANSPLANTATION RES UNIT, TULANE UNIV, 1966-; mem adv comt, Nat Transplant Registry, 1966-1967; consult surg, Charity Hosp La & Keesler Air Force Hosp, 1965-; Nat Heart Inst spec fel, Univ Edinburgh, 1964-1965; from instr to assoc prof, Tulane Univ, 1963-1976; resident surg, Southern Baptist Hosp, 1961-1962; resident surg, 1959-1961 & thoracic surg, 1963-1964; Intern, Charity Hosp, La, 1958-1959. **Memberships:** Transplantation Soc; Am Col Surg; NY Acad Sci; Asn Advan Med Instrumentation; Am Soc Artificial Internal Organs. **Research Statement & Publications:** Thoracic and vascular surgery; transplantation biology. **Mailing Address:** Dept Med, Tulane Univ, Sch Med, 1415 Tulane Ave, New Orleans, LA 70112. **E-Mail:** elindsey@tulane.edu

LINDSEY, GEORGE ROY, MILITARY STRATEGIC ANALYSIS, SYSTEMS ANALYSIS. **Personal Data:** b Toronto, Ont, June 2, 1920; m 1951, June; c Robin & Jane. **Education:** Univ Toronto, BA, 1942; Queen's Univ Ont, MA, 1946; Cambridge Univ, PhD (physics), 1950. **Honors & Awards:** Award of Merit, Can Opers Res Soc, 1984; Officer of the Order of Can, 1989. **Professional Experience:** COORDR, BALLISTIC MISSILE DEFENCE & HOMELAND SECURITY, CAN INST INT AFFAIRS, as of 2003; mem bd dirs, Can Inst Strategic Studies, beginning 1992; dir, Int Inst Strategic Studies, beginning 1992; vis fel, Can Inst Int Peace & Security, 1990-1992; SR RES FEL, CAN INST STRATEGIC STUDIES, 1987-; chmn, TTCP Panel, Undersea Warfare, 1981-1986; head, Can deleg NATO High Level Group Nuclear Planning, 1977-1987; consult, Inst Res Pub Policy, 1975-1978; mem, Can Comt Int Inst Appl Systs Anal, 1973-1979; mem, Can Govt Bicult Develop Prog, 1970-1971; chief oper res anal estab, Dept Nat Defense, 1967-1987; sr oper res scientist, Dept Nat Defense, 1964-1967; oper res group leader, Antisubmarine Warfare Res Ctr, Supreme Allied Comdr, Atlantic, Italy, 1961-1964; dir, Defense Systs Anal Group, Can Dept Nat Defense, 1959-1961; sr oper res officer, Air Defense Command, Royal Can Air Force, 1954-1959; defense sci officer oper res, Can Defense Res Bd, 1950-1953. **Memberships:** Opers Res Soc Am; Can Inst Strategic Studies; Int Inst Strategic Studies; Can Oper Res Soc (pres 1961); Can Inst Int Affairs; Royal Can Astron Soc. **Research Statement & Publications:** Arms control; advancing military technology and security analysis of strategic problems related to the attainment and preservation of a stable military balance. **Mailing Address:** Can Inst Strategic Studies, 55 Westward Way, Rockcliffe, ON K1L 5A8, Can. **Fax:** 613-745-3161. **E-Mail:** georgelindsey@sympatico.ca

LINDSEY, GERALD HERBERT, MECHANICAL & AERONAUTICAL ENGINEERING. **Personal Data:** b Marshall, Mo, August 3, 1934; m 1958, Beth; c Stuart P, Greg A, Kristine, Bryan S, Bradley P & Karen D. **Education:** Brigham Young Univ, BES, 1960, MS, 1962; Calif Inst Technol, PhD (aeronaut eng), 1966. **Professional Experience:** EMER PROF, DEPT AERONAUT ENG, NAVAL POSTGRAD SCH, as of 2004; chmn, Dept Aeronaut Eng, Naval Postgrad Sch, beginning 1997; assoc dean eng, Naval Postgrad Sch, 1990-1993; dean acad admin, Naval Postgrad Sch, 1982-1989; prof aeronaut eng, Naval Postgrad Sch, 1966-1997; consult, chem systs div, United Technol, 1966-1972. **Memberships:** Am Inst Aeronaut & Astronaut; Am Soc Eng Educ. **Research Statement & Publications:** Fracture, aircraft fatigue and design; viscoelastic stress and fracture. **Mailing Address:** Dept Aeronaut, Naval Postgrad Sch, Monterey, CA 94943. **Fax:** 408-656-2313. **E-Mail:** lindsey@aa.nps.navy.mil

LINDSEY, JAMES RUSSELL, PATHOLOGY. **Personal Data:** b Tifton, Ga, December 6, 1933; m 1958, c 4. **Education:** Univ Ga, BS, 1956, DVM, 1957; Auburn Univ, MS, 1961; Am Col Lab Animal Med, dipl, 1967; Am Col Vet Pathologists, dipl, 1967. **Honors & Awards:** Charles River Prize Lab Animal Med, Am Vet Med Asn, 1979; T S Williams lectr, Tuskegee Inst, 1982; Nathan R Brewer Award, Am Asn Lab Animal Sci, 1997. **Professional Experience:** PROF GENETICS, UNIV ALA, BIRMINGHAM, as of 2005; prof & chmn comp med, Sch Med & Dent, beginning 1986; prof path, Univ Ala, Birmingham, beginnning 1985; adj prof, Sch Vet Med, Auburn Univ, 1980-; vis scientist & consult lab animal dis, Orgn Health Res, Inst Exp Geront & Radiobiol, Rijswijk, Neth & Cent Lab Animal Breeding Fac, Zeist, Neth, 1978-1979; assoc prof path, Sch Med & Dent, 1969-1985; chief, RILAMSAT, Birmingham Vet Admin Hosp, 1968-; prof, Sch Med & Dent, 1967-1986; chmn dept com med, Sch Med & Dent, 1967-1975; from instr to asst prof, lab animal med & path, Johns Hopkins Univ Sch Med, 1961-1967; fel path, Johns Hopkins Univ, 1961-1963; from instr to asst prof, Sch Vet Med, Auburn Univ, 1957-1961. **Memberships:** Am Vet Med Asn; Sigma Xi; Int Acad Path; Am Asn Pathologists; Am Thoracic Soc; Am Soc Microbiol; Int Orgn Mycoplasmologists. **Research Statement & Publications:** Comparative pathology; mycoplasmal respiratory disease; laboratory animal diseases complicating research. **Mailing Address:** Dept Genetics, Volker Hall, Rm 402 1670 Univ Blvd, Birmingham, AL 35294-0019. **Fax:** 205-975-4418. **E-Mail:** rlindsey@uab.edu

LINDSEY, JULIA PAGE, MYCOLOGY, PLANT PATHOLOGY. **Personal Data:** b Pine Bluff, Ark, December 9, 1948. **Education:** Hendrix Col, BA, 1970; Univ Ariz, MS, 1972, PhD (plant path), 1975. **Professional Experience:** PROF BIOL, FT LEWIS COL, as of 2005; asst prof biol, Ft Lewis Col, beginning 1978; seed analyst seed cert, Ark State Plant Bd, 1975-1978; teaching asst plant path, Univ Ariz, 1972-1975; teaching asst biol, Univ Ariz, 1970-1972. **Memberships:** Mycol Soc Am. **Research Statement & Publications:** A compilation of descriptive, cultural and taxonomic data concerning woodrotting basidiomycetes that decay aspen in North America; identification and taxonomy of plant pathogenic fungi. **Mailing Address:** Dept Biol & Agr, Ft Lewis Col, 1000 Rim Dr, Durango, CO 81301. **E-Mail:** lindsey_p@fortlewis.edu

LINDSEY, LEANN L, FERTILIZATION. **Personal Data:** b Palo Alto, Calif, January 25, 1950. **Education:** Calif Polytech State Univ, BS, 1983; Univ Calif, Davis, PhD (biochem), 1988. **Professional Experience:** ASST RES BIOLOGIST, BODEGA MARINE LAB, UNIV CALIF, 1992-; fel fertilization, Univ Calif, 1989-1992. **Memberships:** AAAS; Sigma Xi. **Mailing Address:** Bodega Marine Lab Univ Calif, PO Box 247, Bodega Bay, CA 94923-0247.

LINDSEY, MARVIN FREDERICK, PLANT BREEDING. **Personal Data:** b Stockville, Nebr. **Education:** Univ Nebr, BSc, 1953, MSc, 1955; NC State Univ, PhD (genetics), 1960. **Professional Experience:** RETIRED; area dir, Dekalb-Pfizer Genetics, 1970-1990; asst prof agron, Univ Wis, 1966-1969; geneticist, Rockefeller Found, 1964-1966; Asst prof agron, Univ Nebr, 1960-1963. **Memberships:** Am Soc Agron; Crop Sci Soc Am. **Research Statement & Publications:** Maize breeding and genetics. **Mailing Address:** 520 Q St, Beaver City, NE 68926.

LINDSEY, NORMA JACK, CLINICAL MICROBIOLOGY. **Personal Data:** b Canton, Tex, June 16, 1929. **Education:** Tex Woman's Univ, BA & BS, 1951; Univ Calif, MPH, 1964; Colo State Univ, PhD (microbiol), 1969. **Professional Experience:** RETIRED; asst prof path & actg head, Microbiol Sect, Clin Labs, Med Ctr, Univ Kans, 1973-1992; res microbiologist, HEW, 1970-1973; chief, N Mex Health Labs, 1969-1970; teaching asst microbiol, Colo State Univ, 1966-1967; microbiologist, Ariz Health Dept Labs, Tucson, 1956-1965; bacteriologist, Dallas Health Dept Lab, Tex, 1951-1954. **Memberships:** NY Acad Sci; Am Soc Microbiol; Am Pub Health Asn; AAAS; Sigma Xi. **Research Statement & Publications:** Clinical and applied microbiology. **Mailing Address:** 9931 Cedar Dr, Overland Park, KS 66207.

LINDSEY, ROLAND GRAY, chemical engineering; deceased, see previous edition for last biography

LINDSEY, WILLIAM C, ELECTRICAL ENGINEERING. **Education:** Univ Ark, BS, 1958; Purdue Univ, MS, 1959, PhD (elec eng), 1962. **Professional Experience:** PROF ELEC ENG, UNIV SOUTHERN CALIF, 1968-; First vchmn & second chmn, Commun Theory Comt; vpres tech affairs, Inst Elec & Electronics Engrs; mem, Commun C, Signals & Systs Int Sci Union & Commun Change Initiation Request Stands Comt. **Memberships:** Nat Acad Eng; fel Inst Elec & Electronics Engrs. **Research Statement & Publications:** Channel characterization, measurement, synchronization and communication techniques as applied to global mobile communication and navigation systems; satellite communications and personal communication networks. **Mailing Address:** Elec Eng Dept EEB510, Univ Southern Calif, Los Angeles, CA 90089. **Fax:** 213-740-8729. **E-Mail:** wcl@usc.edu

LINDSLEY, DAN LESLIE, DROSOPHILA CYTOGENETICS. **Personal Data:** b Evanston, Ill, October 13, 1925; m 1947, c 4. **Education:** Univ Mo, AB, 1947, MA, 1949; Calif Inst Technol, PhD (genetics), 1952. **Honors & Awards:** T H Morgan Medal, Genetics Soc Am, 1989. **Professional Experience:** Vis scientist, Inst Molecular Biol, Univ Rome, Italy, 1992; RES PROF BIOL, UNIV CALIF, SAN DIEGO, 1991-; Fogarty Int fel, Dept Develop Genetics, Ctr Molecular Biol, Autonomous Univ Madrid, Spain, 1980-1981; chmn dept, Univ Calif, San Diego, 1977-1979; USPHS spec fel, Dept Genetics, Div Plant Indust, Commonwealth Sci & Indust Res Orgn, Canberra, Australia, 1972-1973; prof, Univ Calif, San Diego, 1967-1991; NSF sr fels, Univ Sao Paulo, 1960-1961 & Inst Genetics, Univ Rome, 1965-1966; from assoc biologist to biologist, Oak Ridge Nat Lab, 1954-1967; NSF fel, Univ Mo, 1953-1954; Nat Res Coun fel biol, Princeton Univ, 1952-1953. **Memberships:** Nat Acad Sci; Genetics Soc Am (treas, 1975-1978, vpres, 1985, pres, 1986); Am Acad Arts & Sci; Lepidopterists Soc. **Research Statement & Publications:** Cytogenetics of Drosophila. **Mailing Address:** Dept Biol, Univ Calif San Diego, 9500 Gilman Dr, La Jolla, CA 92093-0346. **E-Mail:** dlindsley@ucsd.edu

LINDSLEY, DAVID FORD, NEUROPHYSIOLOGY. **Personal Data:** b Cleveland, Ohio, May 18, 1936; m 1960, Elizabeth; c Eric, Karen & Victoria. **Education:** Stanford Univ, BA, 1957; Univ Calif, Los Angeles, PhD (anat, neurophysiol), 1961. **Professional Experience:** Guggenheim fel, 1974-1975; visitor, Max Planck Inst Psychiat, Munich, 1971 &

1974-1975; assoc prof physiol, Med Sch, Univ Southern Calif, beginning 1967; Lederle med fac award, 1964-1967; asst prof physiol, Med Sch, Stanford Univ, 1963-1967; USPHS fels, Moscow State Univ, 1961-1962 & Cambridge Univ, 1962-1963. **Memberships:** AAAS; Am Physiol Soc; Am Asn Anatomists; Soc Neuroscience; Int Brain Res Orgn. **Research Statement & Publications:** Central nervous system neurophysiology; behavioral neurophysiology; brain mechanics of attention and perception, using single neurons of central visual system of primates with particular interest in where in the brain and how incoming sensory stimuli become tagged as significant. **Mailing Address:** Dept Physiol, Univ SC Med Sch, 1333 San Pablo St, Los Angeles, CA 90033-4526. **Fax:** 213-342-2283.

LINDSLEY, DONALD HALE, PHASE EQUILIBRIA, GEOTHERMOMETRY. **Personal Data:** b Princeton, NJ, May 22, 1934; m 1959, Carol; c Glenn, Janet & Bruce. **Education:** Princeton Univ, AB, 1956; Johns Hopkins Univ, PhD (geol), 1961. **Honors & Awards:** Roebling Medal, Mineral Soc Am, 1996; Ktenas Award Mineral, Acad Athens, 1998. **Professional Experience:** DISTINGUISHED PROF, DEPT GEOSCIENCES, STONY BROOK UNIV, beginning 2001; adj prof, Univ Wyo, 1990-2000; vis scientist, Univ BC, 1976-1977; vis assoc prof, Calif Inst Technol, 1969; petrologist, Geophys Lab, Carnegie Inst, Wash, 1962-1970; fel, Geophys Lab, Carnegie Inst, Wash, 1960-1962; prof petrol, Dept Geosciences, State Univ NY, Stony Brook. **Memberships:** Mineral Soc Am (vpres, 1981, pres 1982); fel Geol Soc Am; Geochem Soc (vpres, 1989-1991, pres, 1991-1993); fel Am Geophys Union; fel AAAS. **Research Statement & Publications:** High-pressure and high-temperature phase relations and thermodynamic solution models of mineral syst; redox reactions in earth; origin of anorthosites and related rocks; origin of lunar magmas; Fractional crystallization processes on Earth, Moon, and Mars. **Mailing Address:** Dept GeoScis, State Univ NY, 100 Nicolls Rd, Stony Brook, NY 11794-2100. **Fax:** 631-632-8240. **E-Mail:** donald.lindsley@stonybrook.edu

LINDSLEY, JANET E, BIOCHEMISTRY. **Education:** Davidson Col, BA; Univ Wismadison, PhD. **Professional Experience:** ASSOC PROF BIOCHEM, UNIV UTAH, as of 2006. **Mailing Address:** Dept Biochem, Univ Utah, 15 N 2030 E Rm 1400, Salt Lake City, UT 84112-5330. **E-Mail:** janet.lindsley@hsc.utah.edu

LINDSTEDT-SIVA, K JUNE, BIOLOGY. **Personal Data:** b Minneapolis, Minn, September 24, 1941; m 1969, Ernest. **Education:** Univ Southern Calif, AB, 1963, MS, 1967, PhD (biol), 1971. **Honors & Awards:** Trident Award Marine Sci, Int Rev Underwater Activities, Ustica, Italy, 1970; Award Merit, Am Soc Testing & Mat, 1990. **Professional Experience:** RETIRED; sr consult, ENSR Consult & Eng, beginning 1996; Alaska OCS Panel, Polar Res Bd, 1993-1996; Alaska OCS Panel, Nat Acad Sci, 1992-; adv coun, Nat Inst Environ, 1992-1995; mem panel oil spill res & develop, Nat Acad Sci, 1990-; pres, Southern Calif Acad Sci, 1990-1992; mem panel ecol risk reduction, Environ Protection Agency, 1990; Sci Indications, 1989 & Biodiversity, 1989-1990; chmn, Int Oil Spill Conf, 1989; Nat Sci Bd Comt, Int Sci, 1988-; Nat Sci Bd Comt, Polar Regions, 1987-1990; res subcomt, Bermuda Biol Sta Res, beginning 1986; mgr, Environ Protection, ARCO, Los Angeles, 1986-1996; mem adv bd, Cabrillo Marine Museum, 1985-; Nat Sci Bd Comt, Educ & Human Resources, 1985-1990; mgr, Environ Protection, Atlantic Richfield Co, 1984-1990; mem bd dir, Southern Calif Acad Sci, 1984-1993; mem, Nat Sci Bd, 1984-1990; chmn, Spills Technol Comt, 1983-1985; chmn, Dispersant Use Guidelines Task Force, Am Soc Testing & Mat, 1982-; mem, Nat Acad Sci Ecol Panel, Outer Continental Shelf Environ Studies Prog Rev, 1982-1984; biol adv coun, Calif State Univ, Long Beach, beginning 1981; mgr, environ sci, 1981-1986; chmn, Environ Subcomt, Marine Indust Group, 1981-1982; mem bd trustees, Bermuda Biol Sta Res, 1979-; sr sci adv, Atlantic Richfield Co, 1977-1981; mem task force, Fate & Effects Oil, Am Petrol Inst, 1973-1980; sci adv, Atlantic Richfield Co, 1973-1977; asst prof biol, Calif Lutheran Col, 1972-1973; Consult, Jacques Cousteau, Metromedia Producers Co, 1970 & Southern Calif Edison Co, 1972; environ specialist, Southern Calif Edison Co, 1971-1972; Asst coordr sea grant progs, Univ Southern Calif, 1971; mem, Univ Southern Calif; chmn biol res subcomt. **Memberships:** Soc Petrol Indust Biologists (pres); Marine Technol Soc; AAAS; Sigma Xi; Am Inst Biol Sci; fel Am Soc Testing & Mat. **Research Statement & Publications:** Effects of oil on marine organisms; oil spill response planning; oil spill cleanup and control; environmental planning and management in industry; use of dispersants in oil spill response. **Mailing Address:** ENSR Consult & Eng, 1716 Heath Pkwy, Ft Collins, CO 80524. **Fax:** 303-493-0213. **E-Mail:** jsiva@isdis.net

LINDSTROM, DAVID JOHN, GEOCHEMISTRY. **Personal Data:** b Ashland, Wis, March 1, 1945; m 1971. **Education:** Univ Wis-Madison, BS, 1966; Univ Chicago, SM, 1968; Univ Ore, PhD (chem), 1976. **Professional Experience:** SPACE SCIENTIST, JOHNSON SPACE CTR, as of 2003; res assoc lunar sci, Goddard Space Flight Ctr, NASA, 1975-1977; RES SCIENTIST GEOCHEM, DEPT EARTH & PLANETARY SCI, WASH UNIV, 1971-. **Research Statement & Publications:** Experimental trace element geochemistry; experimental petrology; properties of silicate liquids; extraterrestrial materials processing. **Mailing Address:** Johnson Space Ctr, NASA, Mail Stop ST, Houston, TX 77058. **E-Mail:** david.j.lindstrom1@jsc.nasa.gov

LINDSTROM, DUAINE GERALD, MECHANICAL ENGINEERING. **Personal Data:** b Raymond, Wash, January 18, 1937; m 1967, Vieno. **Education:** Univ Wash, BS, 1959, PhD (nuclear eng), 1968; Univ Mich, MS, 1960. **Professional Experience:** RETIRED; assoc prof & prog coordr nuclear & chem eng, Wash State Univ, Richland, Wash, 1982-1999; assoc prof nuclear eng, Univ Okla, 1975-1982; lectr nuclear technol, Imperial Col, London, 1971-1975; lectr, Calif State Univ, Sacramento, 1969-1970; physics specialist, Aerojet Nuclear Systs Co, Sacramento, 1968-1971. **Memberships:** Am Nuclear Soc; Brit Nuclear Energy Soc; Health Physics Soc; Sigma Xi; Am Inst Chem Engrs. **Research Statement & Publications:** Radiation transport, radiation shielding and protection; nuclear fuel cycle; reactor operations; power systems and incineration. **Mailing Address:** 16 River Rock Rd, Winthrop, WA 98862. **E-Mail:** lindstro@beta.tricity.wsu.edu

LINDSTROM, ERIC JON, PHYSICAL OCEANOGRAPHY. **Personal Data:** b Long Beach, Calif, June 22, 1956. **Education:** Mas Inst Technol, BS, 1977; Univ Wash, MS, 1979, PhD (oceanog), 1983. **Professional Experience:** PRIN, SHULLER FERRIS LINDSTROM & ASSOC, as of 2004; RES SCIENTIST, TEX A&M UNIV, 1992-; assoc dir, Toga Coare Proj Off, 1990-1991; PROG SCIENTIST, US WORLD OCEAN CIRCULATION EXP INTERAGENCY OFF, 1989-; dir, Tex A&M Univ, 1988-1989; sr res scientist, Commonwealth Sci & Indust Res Orgn, Australia, 1983-1990. **Memberships:** Am Meteorol Soc; Am Geophys Union; Oceanog Soc; Australian Marine Sci Asn; Australian Meteorol & Oceanog Soc. **Research Statement & Publications:** General circulation of the oceans; western tropical Pacific circulation. **Mailing Address:** SFLA Archit, 214 Burgess St, Fayetteville, NC 28301. **Fax:** 910-484-1466. **E-Mail:** elindstrom@sfla-architects.com

LINDSTROM, EUGENE SHIPMAN, BACTERIOLOGY. **Personal Data:** b Ames, Iowa, January 12, 1923; m 1949, c 4. **Education:** Univ Wis, BA, 1947, MS, 1948, PhD (bact), 1951. **Professional Experience:** PROF EMER BACT, PA STATE UNIV, as of 2001; from asst prof to assoc prof, 1977-1988; head, Dept Biol, 1977-1988; from asst dean to assoc dean col sci, Pa State Univ, 1966-1977; prof bact, Pa State Univ, 1964-1968; NSF fel, Univ Minn, 1961; from asst prof to assoc prof, Pa State Univ, 1952-1964; AEC fel enzyme chem, 1951-1952; asst bact, Univ Wis, 1946-1951. **Memberships:** Am Soc Microbiol; Am Acad Microbiol; Am Soc Biol Chem & Molecular Biol; AAAS. **Research Statement & Publications:** Bacterial physiology; physiology of Athiorhodaceae; physiology and ecology of photosynthetic bacteria. **Mailing Address:** Dept Biol, Pa State Univ, Univ Park, PA 16802-5301. **E-Mail:** esl2@psu.edu

LINDSTROM, FREDRICK THOMAS, APPLIED MATHEMATICS. **Personal Data:** b Astoria, Ore, July 30, 1940; m 1964, c 2. **Education:** Ore State Univ, BS, 1963, MS, 1965, PhD (appl math), 1969. **Professional Experience:** ASSOC PROF STATIST & MATH, ORE STATE UNIV, 1974-; asst prof, Ore State Univ, 1969-1974; res asst, Ore State Univ, 1964-1969. **Memberships:** Soc Indust & Appl Math; Am Math Soc; Am Statist Asn; Sigma Xi. **Research Statement & Publications:** Mass transport phenomenon, especially in porous and permeable mediums; compartmental analysis andthe mathematical modeling of drug distributions in mammalian tissue systems. **Mailing Address:** 429 NE 89th Ave, Portland, OR 97220.

LINDSTROM, GARY J, SEMICONDUCTOR PROCESS ENGINEERING, PROCUREMENT ENGINEERING. **Personal Data:** b Beacon, NY, August 4, 1939; m 1963, Catherine. **Education:** Dutchess Community Col, AAS, 1960; Marist Col, BA, 1969. **Professional Experience:** PRES, HUDSON VALLEY CHAP, as of 2001; FIELD APPLN ENGR, GASONICS INC, 1996-; substitute teacher math & sci, Beacon City Sch Dist & Wappingers Cent Sch Dist, 1990-1993; adv engr, IBM Corp, 1964-1990. **Research Statement & Publications:** Science education; field applications engineering. **Mailing Address:** Hudson Valley Chapter, Wappingers Falls, NY 12590-3845.

LINDSTROM, IVAR E, JR, PHYSICS. **Personal Data:** b Milligan, Nebr, October 15, 1929; m 1952, c 2. **Education:** Nebr Wesleyan Univ, AB, 1950; Univ Ore, MA, 1952, PhD (physics), 1959. **Professional Experience:** RETIRED; MEM STAFF PHYSICS, LOS ALAMOS NAT LAB, UNIV CALIF, 1958-. **Memberships:** Am Phys Soc; Sigma Xi. **Research Statement & Publications:** Explosives, particularly initiation by shock waves; nuclear spectroscopy; solid state physics. **Mailing Address:** 327 Venado St, Los Alamos, NM 87544.

LINDSTROM, JON MARTIN, AUTOIMMUNITY. **Personal Data:** b Moline, Ill, October 9, 1945; m 1977, Suzanne; c Laurel A, Kara M & Jon K. **Education:** Univ Ill, BA, 1967; Univ Calif, San Diego, PhD (biol), 1971. **Honors & Awards:** McKnight Neuroscience Develop Award; Jacob Javits Award. **Professional Experience:** TRUSTEE PROF NEUROL SCI & PHARMACOL, MED SCH, UNIV PA, 1990-; adj prof neurosci, Univ Calif, San Diego, 1987-1990; assoc prof neurosci & mem, Salk Inst Biol Studies, 1983-1990; from asst res prof to assoc res prof, Salk Inst Biol Studies, 1973-1983; Muscular Dystrophy Asn fel, Salk Inst Biol Studies, 1971-1973; mem sci adv comt, MDA, Los Angeles & Calif chap MG Found; Sloan fel. **Memberships:** Soc Neuroscience. **Research Statement & Publications:** Acetylcholine receptor structure and function; pathological mechanisms in myasthenia gravis; effects of niedine on nicalinic receptors. **Mailing Address:** Dept Neurosci, Med Sch, Univ Pa, 217 Stemmler Hall/ 6074, Philadelphia, PA 19104-6074. **Fax:** 215-573-2858. **E-Mail:** jslkk@mail.med.upenn.edu

LINDSTROM, MARILYN MARTIN, GEOCHEMISTRY & COSMOCHEMISTRY, IGNEOUS PETROLOGY. **Personal Data:** b Jacksonville, Fla, November 28, 1946; m 1971, David; c Peter & Ingrid. **Education:** Univ Calif, San Diego, BA, 1969; Univ Ore, PhD (geochem), 1976. **Professional Experience:** PLANETARY SCIENTIST, JOHNSON SPACE CTR, NASA, 1986-; sr res scientist geochem, Dept Earth & Planetary Sci, Wash Univ, 1979-1986; res scientist, Dept Earth & Planetary Sci, Wash Univ, 1977-1979; res assoc, Univ Md, 1975-1977; technician geochem, Geol Dept, Univ Ore, 1968-1969; prin investr, NSF & NASA grants; assoc ed, Proc Lunar & Planetary Sci Conf & Geochim Cosmochim Acta; GSA Penrose grants. **Memberships:** Geochem Soc; Am Geophys Union; Meteoritical Soc; Asn Women Geoscientists; Am Asn Univ Women. **Research Statement & Publications:** Geochemistry and petrology of igneous rocks and extraterrestrial materials; oceanic volcanic rocks, lunar samples and meteorites; trace element geochemistry; instrumental neutron activation analysis. **Mailing Address:** Johnson Space Ctr, NASA, Mail Code SN2, Houston, TX 77058. **Fax:** 713-483-5347. **E-Mail:** mlindstr@ems.jsc.nasa.gov

LINDSTROM, MERLIN RAY, COATINGS CHEMISTRY, POLYMER CHEMISTRY. **Personal Data:** b New Rockford, NDak, October 28, 1951; m 1972, c 3. **Education:** NDak State Univ, BS, 1973, PhD (chem), 1978. **Professional Experience:** CHEMIST, PHILLIPS PETROL CO, beginning 1978. **Memberships:** Fedn Coatings Technol; Soc Mfg Engrs. **Research Statement & Publications:** Coatings; sulfur chemicals; metal cleaners; adhesives; water soluble resins; electroplating; sealants. **Mailing Address:** 919 Kings Circle, Bartlesville, OK 74006.

LINDSTROM, RICHARD EDWARD, PHYSICAL PHARMACY. **Personal Data:** b Bristol, Conn, June 15, 1932; m 1952, c 3. **Education:** Univ Conn, BS, 1955; Syracuse Univ, MS, 1962, PhD (phys chem), 1967. **Professional Experience:** PROF PHARMACEUT SCI, NOVA SOUTHEASTERN UNIV, 2002-; consult, USAF, beginning 1981; consult, US, beginning 1980; consult, Vick Chem Co, beginning 1974; from assoc prof to prof pharmaceut, Univ Conn, beginning 1968; asst prof chem, USFA, 1962-1966 & Salem State Col, 1966-1968. **Memberships:** Am Chem Soc; Am Pharmaceut Asn; Acad Pharmaceut Sci. **Research Statement & Publications:** Thermodynamics of solution phenomena via molar volume and solubility data. **Mailing Address:** One Club Circle, Tequesta, FL 33469.

LINDSTROM, TERRY DONALD, DRUG METABOLISM, PHARMACOKINETICS. **Personal Data:** b Minneapolis, Minn, September 23, 1951; m 1976, c 2. **Education:** Augsburg Col, BA, 1973; Univ Minn, PhD (pharmacol), 1977. **Professional Experience:** RES ADV, LILLY RES LABS, 1994-; head CNS Res, Lilly Res Labs, 1987-1988; from res scientist to sr res scientist, Lilly Res Labs, 1985-1994; ASST PROF, DEPT PHARMACOL, MED SCH, IND UNIV, 1982-; sr pharmacologist, Lilly Res Labs, 1979-1985; fel biochem, Mich State Univ, 1977-1979; Mem, Ind drug Utilization Rev Bd. **Memberships:** Am Soc Pharmacol & Exp Therapeut; Int Soc Study Xenobiotics; Int Union Pharmacol; Soc Toxicol. **Research Statement & Publications:** Oxidative and reductive metabolism of various drugs in subcellular, cellular and in vivo metabolism models; pharmacokinetics and toxicokinetic relationships with efficacy and toxicity. **Mailing Address:** Drug Metab & Disposition, Lilly Res Labs, Eli Lilly & Co Lilly Corp Ctr, Indianapolis, IN 46285-0001. **Fax:** 317-276-4218. **E-Mail:** lindstrom_terry@lilly.com

LINDT, JAN THOMAS, POLYMER ENGINEERING, CHEMICAL ENGINEERING. **Personal Data:** b Amsterdam, Holland, July 8, 1942; m 1977, c 3. **Education:** Delft Univ Technol, MSc, 1964, PhD (chem eng), 1971. **Professional Experience:** PROF POLYMER ENG, UNIV PITTSBURGH, 1985-; fel, Nat Ctr Sci Res, 1983 & 1987; assoc prof, Univ

Pittsburgh, 1978-1985; scientist polymer eng, Shell Res Ltd, 1972-1977; asst prof chem eng, Delft Univ Technol, 1969-1971. **Memberships:** Soc Rheology; Soc Plastics Engrs; Polymer Proc Soc. **Research Statement & Publications:** Plasticating extrusion; reaction injection molding; reactive extrusion of polymers; devolatilization of polymer solutions; polyurethane foaming processes; polymer composites; polymer blends. **Mailing Address:** Dept Chem Eng 1234 Benedum Hall, Univ Pittsburgh Main Campus, Pittsburgh, PA 15260. **Fax:** 412-624-9639. **E-Mail:** jtlindt@pitt.edu

LINDZEN, RICHARD SIEGMUND, DYNAMIC METEOROLOGY, APPLIED MATHEMATICS. **Personal Data:** b Webster, Mass, February 8, 1940; m 1965, Nadine; c Eric & Nathaniel. **Education:** Harvard Univ, AB, 1960, SM, 1961, PhD (appl math), 1964. **Honors & Awards:** Meisinger Award, Am Meteorol Asn, 1968; Charney Award, 1985 & Bernhard Haurwitz Mem Lectr, 1996; Macelwane Award, Am Geophys Union, 1969; Landsdowne Lectr, Univ Victoria, 1993. **Professional Experience:** ALFRED P SLOAN PROF METEOROL, DEPT EARTH, ATMOSPHERIC & PLANETARY SCI, MASS INST TECHNOL, as of 2004; sackler vis prof, Tel Aviv Univ, 1992; Space Studies Bd, 1988- & NRS Bd Atmospheric Sci & Climate, beginning 1990; DISTINGUISHED VIS SCIENTIST, JET PROPULSION LAB, 1988-; mem staff, Woods Hole Oceanog Inst Corp, beginning 1987; mem, Nat Resource Coun Math Sci Educ Bd, 1987-1990; fel, Japanese Soc Prom Sci, 1986-1987; dir, Ctr Earth & Planetary Physics, 1980-1983; mem, Nat Acad Assembly Math & Phys Sci, 1978-1981; Control Data Corp, 1977 & NASA, 1977-1985; prof meteorol, Harvard Univ, 1972-1983; consult, Naval Res Lab, 1972-1983; Alfred P Sloan fel, 1970-1976; exec mem, Nat Acad Comt Global Atmospheric Res Prog, 1968-1979; prof, Univ Chicago, 1968-1972; res scientist, Nat Ctr Atmospheric Res, 1965-1968; res fel meteorol, Univ Wash, 1964 & Univ Oslo, 1964-1965; vis scientist, Jet Propulsion Lab. **Memberships:** Nat Acad Sci; fel Am Acad Arts & Sci; fel Am Meteorol Soc; fel Am Geophys Union; fel AAAS; Sigma Xi; Norweg Acad Sci & Lett. **Research Statement & Publications:** Hydrodynamic stability; climatology; upper atmosphere dynamics; general atmospheric circulation; tides. **Mailing Address:** Dept Earth & Atmospheric & Planetary Sci, Mass Inst Technol, Bldg 54 1720, Cambridge, MA 02139-4307. **Fax:** 617-964-3953. **E-Mail:** lindzen@wind.mit.edu

LINE, JOHN PAUL, MATHEMATICS, APPLIED MATHEMATICS. **Personal Data:** b Pontiac, Mich, March 2, 1929; m 1957, Frances; c Paul, Carl, Mark & John. **Education:** Univ Mich, BS, 1950, MS, 1951. **Professional Experience:** PROF EMER MATH, GA INST TECHNOL, as of 2004; assoc prof math, Ga Inst Technol, beginning 1962; asst prof, GA Inst Technol, 1956-1962; Instr math, Oberlin Col, 1955 & Univ Rochester, 1955-1956. **Memberships:** Am Math Soc; Math Asn Am. **Research Statement & Publications:** Integral transformations as applied to solution of boundary value problems in partial differential equations. **Mailing Address:** Sch Math, Ga Inst Technol, 686 Cherry St, Atlanta, GA 30332-0160. **Fax:** 404-894-4409.

LINEBACK, DAVID R(AY), Starch science, food science/safety. **Personal Data:** b Russellville, Ind, June 7, 1934; m Patricia; c Linda Lee Lineback, D Scott & Karen Louise Merchant. **Education:** Purdue Univ, BS, 1956; Ohio State Univ, PhD (org chem), 1962. **Honors & Awards:** Fellow, Institute of Food Technologists, 1982; Spec Award Merit, Japanese Soc Starch Sci, 1985; Purdue University "Old Master, " 1986; William F Geddes Mem Lecturship, 1988; Carl R Fellers Award, Phi Tau Sigma/Inst Food Sci & Technol, 1991; Geddes Mem Award, Am Asn Cereal Chemists, 1998; Fellow, International Academy of Food Science and Technology, 1999; Fellow, Institute of Food Science and Technology (UK), 2000; Fellow, American Association for the Advancement of Sciencer, 2001. **Professional Experience:** DIR (Retired), JOINT INST FOOD SAFETY & APPL NUTRIT, UNIV MD, 1998-; dean Col Agr, Univ Idaho, 1993-1998; prof food sci & dept head, NC State Univ, 1980-1993; prof food sci & head dept, Pa State Univ, 1976-1980; from assoc prof to prof grain sci & indust, Kans State Univ, 1969-1976; from instr to asst prof biochem, Univ Nebr, Lincoln, 1964-1969; fel, Univ Alta, 1962-1964; res chemist, Monsanto Chem Co, 1956-1957. **Memberships:** Am Asn Cereal Chem (pres-elect 1982-1983 pres 1983-1986); Inst Food Sci & Technol (pres-elect 1992 pres 1993); Am Chem Soc; Am Soc Nutrit Sci; Japanese Soc Appl Glycoscience; International Union of Food Science and Technology (pres-elect 2003 - 2006). **Research Statement & Publications:** Reaction and structure of carbohydrates; characterization of enzymes of starch hydrolysis and synthesis; cereal chemistry; structure of starch and functionality in food products. **Mailing Address:** 4414 Gauntlet Dr SE, Southport, NC 28461. **Fax:** 910-253-6888. **E-Mail:** lineback@umd.edu

LINEBACK, JERRY A(LVIN), REGIONAL GEOLOGY. **Personal Data:** b Ottawa, Kans, October 25, 1938; m 1969, Mary; c Nathan, Benjamin & Daniel. **Education:** Univ Kans, BS, 1960, MS, 1961; Ind Univ, PhD (geol), 1964. **Professional Experience:** RETIRED; asst state geologist & regulatory support prog mgr, Ga Geol Surv, 1987-1995; sr geologist, Robertson Res, 1981-1986; from asst geologist to geologist, Stratig & Areal Geol Sect, Ill State Geol Surv, 1964-1981. **Memberships:** Fel Geol Soc Am. **Research Statement & Publications:** Ground water quality and protection; ground water resource development and management; Mississippian stratigraphy; regional geology. **Mailing Address:** 22 W 3 St, Garnett, KS 66032. **Fax:** 404-657-8379.

LINEBERGER, ROBERT DANIEL, HORTICULTURE, PLANT PHYSIOLOGY. **Personal Data:** b Dallas, NC, November 9, 1948; m 1971, c 3. **Education:** NC State Univ, BS, 1971; Cornell Univ, MS, 1974, PhD (hort), 1978. **Professional Experience:** ASSOC PROF HORT, OHIO STATE UNIV, 1977-; L H Bailey res asst, Dept Floricult, Cornell Univ, 1971-1977. **Memberships:** Tissue Cult Asn; Am Soc Hort Sci; Am Soc Plant Physiologists; Bot Soc Am. **Research Statement & Publications:** Plant cell and tissue culture; freeze preservation of germ plasm; freezing injury to plant cells; plant cell ultrastructure. **Mailing Address:** Dept Hort, Tex A&M Univ, College Station, TX 77843-2133. **Fax:** 979-845-0627. **E-Mail:** dan-lineberger@tamu.edu

LINEBERGER, WILLIAM CARL, CHEMICAL PHYSICS. **Personal Data:** b Hamlet, NC, December 5, 1939; m 1979, Katherine. **Education:** Ga Inst Technol, BEE, 1961, MSEE, 1963, PhD, 1965. **Honors & Awards:** Hanon Rosenthal lectr, Yale & Columbia Univ, 1977; Herbert P Broida Prize, Am Phys Soc, 1981; Fred M Garland Mem lectr, Tex A&M Univ, 1987; Bomem Michelson Prize, 1987; William F Meggers Prize, Optical Soc Am, 1988; Jonathan Rohrig Distinguished lectr, Carleton Col, 1988; Davidson lectr, Univ Kans, 1990; George B Kistiakowsky lectr, Harvard Univ, 1992; Earle K Plyler Prize, 1992; George C Pimentel lectr, Univ Calif, Berkeley, 1993; Reilly lectr, Notre Dame Univ, 1994; Irving langmuir Prize, Am Chem Soc, 1995; Peter Debye Award, Am Chem Soc, 2003-2004. **Professional Experience:** PROF CHEM, UNIV COLO, as of 2006; chair, Sect Chem, beginning 1993; vchair & chair elect, Topical Group Laser Sci, 1992-1995; chair, Basic Energy Sci Adv Comt, Dept Energy, 1990-1995; mem, Bd Chem Sci & Technol, 1989-1995; chmn, Div Atomic, Molecular & Optical Physics, 1987; vchmn, Div Atomic, Molecular & Optical Physics, 1986; CONDON DISTINGUISHED PROF CHEM, UNIV COLO, BOULDER, 1985-; chmn, Joint Inst Lab Astrophys, Univ Colo, 1985-1986; NDak State Univ, 1985 & Northwestern Univ, 1985; mem, Bd Physics & Astron, Nat Res Coun, 1983-1988; assoc ed, Atomic Data & Nuclear Data Tables, 1974-1982 & Chem Physics Lett, 1982-; distinguished vis prof, Univ Fla, 1982 & 1993; chmn, Div Chem Physics, Am Phys Soc, 1982-1983; vis prof, Stanford Univ & Univ Chicago, 1982; J S Guggenheim mem fel, 1981-1982; vchmn, Div Chem Physics, Am Phys Soc, 1981-1982; distinguished vis prof, Univ Rochester, 1981; distinguished vis prof, Univ Calif, Irvine, 1980; mem, Comt Atomic & Molecular Sci, Nat Acad Sci, 1979-1982; Alfred P Sloan Res Fel, 1972-1975; fel physics, Joint Inst Lab Astrophys, beginning 1971; from asst prof to prof, Joint Inst Lab Astrophys, Univ Colo, 1970-1985; mem, Joint Inst Lab Astrophys, Univ Colo, 1970-1971; res assoc physics, Joint Inst Lab Astrophys, Univ Colo, 1968-1970; res physicist atmospheric physics, US Army Ballistic Res Lab, Aberdeen Proving Ground, Md, 1965-1968; asst prof elec eng, Ga Inst Technol, 1965; chair, comn phys sci, math, Nat Res Coord. **Memberships:** Nat Acad Sci; fel AAAS; Am Chem Soc; fel Am Phys Soc; Optical Soc Am. **Research Statement & Publications:** Negative ion structure; molecular fluorescence; ion molecule reactions; tunable lasers; ultrafort processes; photophysics and dynamics of cluster ions. **Mailing Address:** Dept Chem & Biochem, Univ Colo, Joint Inst Lab Astrophys A810, Boulder, CO 80309-0440. **Fax:** 303-492-8994. **E-Mail:** william.lineberger@colorado.edu

LINEHAN, JOHN HENRY, MECHANICAL & BIOMEDICAL ENGINEERING. **Personal Data:** b Chicago, Ill, July 8, 1938; m 1960, c 5. **Education:** Marquette Univ, BSME, 1960; Rensselaer Polytech Inst, MSME, 1962; Univ Wis-Madison, PhD (mech eng), 1968. **Professional Experience:** CONSULT PROF BIOENGINEERING, STANFORD UNIV, as of 2005; vpres, Whitaker Found, 1998-2005; adj prof physiol & med, Univ Wis, ending 1998; ROSE EANNELLI BAGOZZI PROF BIOMED ENG & CHMN, DEPT BIOMED ENG, MARQUETTE UNIV, 1989-; prof physiol, Med Col Wis, beginning 1979; from asst prof mech & biomed eng to prof, Med Col Wis, 1968-1989; instr mech eng, Med Col Wis, 1962-1964; engr, Knolls Atomic Power Lab, NY, 1960-1962. **Memberships:** Am Soc Mech Engrs; Am Physiol Soc; Biomed Eng Soc; Am Soc Eng Educ; Microcirculatory Soc; Am Thoracic Soc. **Research Statement & Publications:** Multiphase flow; heat and mass transfer; hemodynamics; lung physiology; fluid mechanics; biomedical instrumentation, medical imaging. **Mailing Address:** Dept Biomed Eng, Marquette Univ, PO Box 1881, Milwaukee, WI 53201-1881. **Fax:** 414-288-1578. **E-Mail:** linehanj@vms.csd.mu.edu

LINEHAN, URBAN JOSEPH, PHYSICAL GEOGRAPHY, HISTORY & PHILOSPHY OF SCIENCE. **Personal Data:** b Brockton, Mass, October 13, 1911; m 1950, Mary; c Mary A, Katherine A & Teresa M. **Education:** Bridgewater State Col, BS, 1933; Clark Univ, MA, 1946, PhD (geog), 1955. **Professional Experience:** RETIRED; analyst, US Govt, 1956-1973; asst prof, Cath Univ Am, 1948-1956; from instr to asst prof, Univ Pittsburgh, 1945-1948; instr geog, Univ Cincinnati, 1940-1945. **Research Statement & Publications:** Synoptic climatology of Pittsburgh, Pennsylvania; areal and temporal distribution of tornado deaths in the United States; landscapes and off-road recreation of southwestern United States. **Mailing Address:** 13921 Pinetree Dr, Sun City West, AZ 85375.

LINEHAN, WILLIAM MARSTON, CANCER RESEARCH, MOLECULAR BIOLOGY. **Personal Data:** b Tulsa, Okla, June 25, 1947; m 1979, Tracey; c Erin L & Emily P. **Education:** Brown Univ, BA, 1969; Univ Okla, MD, 1973. **Honors & Awards:** Gold Cysooscom Award, Am Urol Asn. **Professional Experience:** CHIEF, UROL & ONCOL SECT, SURG BR, NAT CANCER INST, as of 2006; sr investr, Nat Cancer Inst, NIH, 1982-. **Memberships:** Am Urol Asn; Soc Univ Surgeons; Am Col Surgeons. **Research Statement & Publications:** Co-discoverer of the gene for kidney cancer. **Mailing Address:** Nat Cancer Inst, Surg Br, Bldg 10 Rm 2B47, Bethesda, MD 20892. **Fax:** 301-402-0922. **E-Mail:** wml@helix.nih.gov

LINEMEYER, DAVID L, BIOCHEMISTRY REGULATION. **Personal Data:** b April 19, 1949. **Education:** Colo State Univ, BS, 1971; Univ Wash, MS, 1973, PhD (microbiol), 1977. **Professional Experience:** ASSOC DIR, DEPT BIOCHEM, MERCK RES LABS, RAHWAY, NJ, 1989-; Dept Molecular Pharmacol & Biochem, Dept Biochem Genetics, Merck Sharp & Dohme Res Labs, Rahway, NJ, 1986-1989; Dept Biochem Fundamental & Exp Res, Dept Biochem Genetics, Merck Sharp & Dohme Res Labs, Rahway, NJ, 1985-1986; res fel, Dept Biochem Genetics, Merck Sharp & Dohme Res Labs, Rahway, NJ, 1981-1985; sr staff fel, Lab Tumor Virus Genetics, Nat Cancer Inst, NIH, Bethesda, Md, 1980-1981; staff fel, Lab Tumor Virus Genetics, Nat Cancer Inst, NIH, Bethesda, Md, 1977-1980. **Memberships:** AAAS; Am Soc Biochem & Molecular Biol. **Research Statement & Publications:** Author of numerous scientific publications. **Mailing Address:** Synaptic Pharmaceut Corp, 215 Col Rd, Paramus, NJ 07652-1431. **E-Mail:** davidl@mbasis.com

LINES, MALCOLM ELLIS, THEORETICAL MATERIALS PHYSICS. **Personal Data:** b Banbury, Eng, April 26, 1936; m 1962, Kathleen Morse; c Richard & Stephen. **Education:** Oxford Univ, BA, 1959, MA & DPhil(physics), 1962. **Professional Experience:** DISTINGUISHED MEM TECH STAFF, AT&T BELL LABS, 1985-; consult, Atomic Energy Res Estab, Harwell, Eng, 1973; mem tech staff, AT&T Bell Labs, 1963-1965 & 1966-1985; fel physics, Magdalen Col, Oxford Univ, 1961-1963, 1965-1966. **Memberships:** Fel Brit Inst Physics; Am Ceramic Soc; fel Phys Soc Gt Brit; Soc Photo-Optical Instrumentation Engrs. **Research Statement & Publications:** Statistical mechanics; magnetism; ferroelectricity; structure of glasses; light scattering; author of four books on math and physics.

LINEVSKY, MILTON JOSHUA, PHYSICAL CHEMISTRY. **Personal Data:** b Glen Cove, NY, April 20, 1928; m 1958, Barbara; c Joanne & Richard. **Education:** Rensselaer Polytech Inst, BS, 1949; Pa State Univ, MS, 1950, PhD, 1953. **Professional Experience:** Adj prof mech emg, Penn State Univ, beginning 1998; consult, General Phy Corp, Columbia, Md, 1996-1998; staff mem, NSF, Wash, 1993-1996; physics chemist, Johns Hopkins Appl Physics Lab, Laurel, Md, 1979-1996; Gen Elec, King of Prussia, Pa, 1957-1979; phys chemist, US Army, 1955-1957; post doctor, Penn State Univ, 1953-1955. **Memberships:** Am Chem Soc. **Research Statement & Publications:** Invention and development of technique for matrix isolation applied to high temperature materials; development of first flam laser using chemical pumping reactions. **Mailing Address:** 700 Hermleigh Rd, Silver Spring, MD 20902-1697. **E-Mail:** mjl18@psu.edu

LINFOOT, JOHN ARDIS, MEDICINE, ENDOCRINOLOGY. **Personal Data:** b Grand Forks, NDak, May 16, 1931; m 1955, c 3. **Education:** Univ NDak, BA, 1953, BS & MS, 1955; Harvard Univ, MD, 1957; Am Bd Internal Med, dipl; Am Bd Endocrinol, dipl; Am Bd Nuclear Med, dipl. **Professional Experience:** AT DIABETES AND ENDOCRINOLOGY INST, OAK LAND, CALIF, as of 2006; clin prof med, Univ Calif, Davis, Sacramento Med Ctr, beginning 1981; dir endocrine & metab servs, Alta Bates Hosp, 1970; sr staff scientist, Donner Lab, Univ Calif, Berkeley, 1961-1981; sr staff scientist, Lawrence Berkeley Lab, 1961-1976; fel metab & endocrinol, Univ Utah Hosps, 1959-1960; dir, Diabetes & Endocrine Inst, Providence Hosp; consult, Martinez Vet Admin Hosp & Children's Hosp, East Bay. **Memberships:** AAAS; Am Fedn Clin Res; fel Am Col Physicians; Endocrine Soc; Am Diabetes Asn. **Research Statement & Publications:** Growth hormone; acromegaly; Cushing's syndrome; diabetic retinopathy; heavy particle pituitary irradiation. **Mailing Address:** Providence Hosp, 350 30th St Ste 208, Oakland, CA 94609-3425.

LINFORD, GARY JOE, LASER PHYSICS, NONLINEAR OPTICS. **Personal Data:** b Laramie, Wyo, June 13, 1940; m 1986, Shirley; c Alicia, Lara & Lawrence. **Education:** Mass Inst Technol, BS (physics), 1962; Univ Utah, PhD (physics), 1971. **Professional Experience:** RES DIR & SR SCIENTIST, PFEIFER SCI ASSOC, 1994-; area leader advan laser technol, Optics & Directed Energy Lab, 1990-1994; chief scientist, Optics & Directed Energy Lab, 1986-1990; chief scientist, Odel TRW, 1986-1990; mgr, Advan Technol Dept, TRW, 1984-1986; sect head, Appl Tech Div, 1983-1984; physicist laser res, Max Planck Inst Quantum Optics, WGer, 1982-1983; guest lectr, Dept Physics, Calif State Univ, 1981-1982; guest scientist, Max Planck Inst for Plasma Physics, 1978-1979; group head laser res, Laser Fusion Prog, Lawrence Livermore Nat Lab, Univ Calif, 1974-1982; sect head, Laser Div, Hughes Aircraft Co, 1971-1974; teaching asst physics & astron, Univ Utah, 1969-1971; group head, Laser Div, 1968-1969; mem tech staff laser physics, Laser Technol Dept, Aerospace Group, Hughes Aircraft Co, 1963-1968; res asst physics, Electronics Res Lab, Mass Inst Technol, 1961-1962. **Memberships:** Am Phys Soc; MIT Alumni Asn; Alramie Astronomical Soc & Space Observers. **Research Statement & Publications:** Inertial confinement laser fusion; harmonic conversion of infrared light to ultraviolet; design of laser amplifiers and high power propagation optics; target irradiation experiments and diagnostics; non-linear optics; excimer lasers; chemical lasers; free electron lasers; ramanlaser physics; phase conjugation; spacecraft telescopes; xenon lasers, xenon flashlamps; zeeman spectroscopy; remote sensing; long lasers; semiconductor laser diodes. **Mailing Address:** 1325 Whitman St, Laramie, WY 82070. **E-Mail:** lin4d@aol.com

LINFORD, RULON KESLER, MAGNETIC CONFINEMENT SYSTEMS FOR FUSION ENERGY. **Personal Data:** b Cambridge, Mass, January 31, 1943; m 1965, Cecile; c R Scott, Laura, Hilary & Philip L. **Education:** Univ Utah, BS, 1966; Mass Inst Technol, SM & EE, 1969, PhD (elec eng), 1973. **Honors & Awards:** E O Lawrence Award, Dept Energy, 1992. **Professional Experience:** ASSOC VICE PROVOST RES & LAB PROGS, LOS ALAMOS NAT LAB, as of 2001; COORDR SCI & TECHNOL, LOS ALAMOS NAT LAB, 1994-; staff mem, Los Alamos Nat Lab, 1993-1994; prog dir, Los Alamos Nat Lab, 1991-1993; mem, Int Thermonuclear Exp Reactor Steering Comt, 1990; div leader, Los Alamos Nat Lab, 1989-1991; mem var comts, Am Phys Soc Div Plasma Physics, 1987-1991; prog dir, Los Alamos Nat Lab, 1986-1989; mem, Ignition Tech Oversight: CIT Steering Comt, 1985-1990; mem, Magnetic Fusion Adv Comt, 1982-1986; assoc div leader, Los Alamos Nat Lab, 1981-1986; asst div leader, Los Alamos Nat Lab, 1980-1981; group leader, Los Alamos Nat Lab, 1977-1980; asst group leader, Los Alamos Nat Lab, 1975-1977; staff mem, Los Alamos Nat Lab, 1973-1975. **Memberships:** Fel Am Phys Soc; Sigma Xi. **Research Statement & Publications:** Fusion energy and accelerator transmution of radioactive waste. **Mailing Address:** Los Alamos Nat Lab, Univ Calif, PO Box 1663, Los Alamos, NM 87545. **Fax:** 505-665-3199. **E-Mail:** rlinford@lanl.gov

LIN-FU, JANE S, GENETICS. **Education:** Univ Santo Thomas, Phillippines, MD, 1955; Am Bd Pediat, dipl, 1962. **Honors & Awards:** H John Heinz III Nat Leadership Award, USPHS, 1993. **Professional Experience:** RETIRED; chief, Health Resources & Serv Admin, Dept Health & Human Servs, beginning 1990; Bur Maternal & Child Health & Resources Develop, childhood Lead Poisoning Prev Prog & Pediat & consult, Bur Health Care Delivery & Assistance, 1987-1990; coordr, Comt Women's Health, Food & Drug Admin, 1987; Task Force Women's Health Issues, Pub Health Serv, 1985; dir, childhood Lead Poisoning Prev Prog & Pediat & consult, Bur Health Care Delivery & Assistance, 1982-1987; Task Force Opportunities Women Pediat, Dept Health & Human Serv, 1982; mem, President's Comt Ment Retardation, 1972; mem, Task Force Surgeon General's Statement Childhood Lead Poisoning Prev, 1970; pediat consult, Maternal & Child Health Servs, 1969-1973; Pediat consult, Children's Bur, HEW, 1963-1969. **Memberships:** Fel Am Acad Pediat. **Research Statement & Publications:** Authored numerous papers in professional journals. **Mailing Address:** Genetics Serv Br, Health Resources & Serv Admin, Rm 18A-20, 5600 Fishers Lane, Rockville, MD 20857. **Fax:** 301-443-8604. **E-Mail:** jlin-fu@hrsa.ssw.dhhs.gov

LING, ALFRED SOY CHOU, clinical research, development; deceased, see previous edition for last biography

LING, CHUNG-MEI, BIOCHEMISTRY. **Personal Data:** b Chekiang, China, May 5, 1931; m 1957, Amy Hsieh; c 2. **Education:** Nat Taiwan Univ, BS, 1958; Ill Inst Technol, MS, 1962, PhD (biochem), 1965. **Professional Experience:** HON CHMN, GEN BIOL CORP, TAIWAN, ROC, 1991-; adj prof, Nat Tsing Hua Univ, Taiwan, 1991-1993; chief sci consult, Kangling Biotech, 1988-; CHIEF SCI OFFICER, GEN BIOL CORP, TAIWAN, ROC, 1988-; chmn bd, Gen Biol Corp, Taiwan, Roc, 1984-1987; mgr, Res & Develop Diag Div, 1982-1984; head, virol lab, 1977-1982; res fel, Dept Biochem, 1974-1984; head, Molecular Biol Lab, 1974-1977; assoc res fel virol, Abbott Labs, 1971-1974; molecular biologist, Abbott Labs, 1968-1971; Adj asst prof, Ill Inst Technol, 1968-1969; asst prof biochem, Ill Inst Technol, 1965-1968; res assoc biochem res, Michael Reese Res Found, Chicago, 1964-1965; Teaching asst biochem & physiol, Ill Inst Technol, 1960-1964. **Memberships:** AAAS; Sigma Xi; Am Soc Biol Chemists; Am Soc Clin Chem; fel Am Acad Microbiol. **Research Statement & Publications:** Research in areas of molecular biology, immunodiagnostics, and biofunctional and health products; more than 50 scientific publications and numerous US and other patents. **Mailing Address:** Gen Biol Corp No Six Innovation, First Rd Sci-Based Indust Pk, HsinChu 30077, Taiwan. **Fax:** 886-357-83158.

LING, DANIEL, AUDIOLOGY, COMMUNICATIONS. **Personal Data:** b Wetherden, Eng, March 16, 1926; Canadian citizen; m 1958, c 2. **Education:** St John's Col, Univ York, dipl, 1950; Victoria Univ, Manchester, dipl, 1951; McGill Univ, MS, 1966, PhD (human commun dis), 1968. **Professional Experience:** CONSULT, CHILDHOOD HEARING IMPAIRMENT, AVISRAEL, CAN, 1994-; prof aural habilitation & educ, Dept Commun Dis, 1974-1991; dir, Speech & Hearing Div, 1970-; dir, Speech & Hearing Div, Royal Victoria Hosp, 1970-1991; assoc prof & dir oral rehab, Sch Human Commun Dis, Univ Western Ont, 1970-1991; asst prof audiol, Sch Human Commun Dis, 1968-1970; hon dir, Coun Children's Audiol Rehab, Ctr Deaf Children, Mexico City, 1966-; Can Fed Prov Health grants, McGill Univ, 1966-; dir res deaf children, McGill Univ, 1966-1970; prin, Montreal Oral Sch Deaf, 1963-1966; Organizer educ deaf, Reading Educ Comt, 1955-1963; res assoc educ, Cambridge Univ, 1955-1958. **Memberships:** Am Speech & Hearing Asn; Can Speech & Hearing Asn; Am Audiol Soc; Acoust Soc Am. **Research Statement & Publications:** Communication development in deafchildren; speech production among hearing impaired children; speech recognition using linear and coding amplifiers; diagnostic procedure relative to deafness. **Mailing Address:** 956 Cherry Point Rd RR 3, Cobble Hill, BC V0R 7L0, Can.

LING, F(REDERICK) F(ONGSUN), TRIBOLOGY, MANUFACTURING. **Personal Data:** b Tsingtao, China, January 2, 1927; m 1954, Linda; c Erica H, Alfred F & Arthur T. **Education:** St John's Univ, China, BS, 1947; Bucknell Univ, BS, 1949; Carnegie Inst Technol, MS, 1951, DSc, 1954. **Honors & Awards:** Nat Award, Soc Triboligists & Lubrication Engrs, 1970; Mayo D Hersey Award, Am Soc Mech Engrs, 1984; Charles Russ Richards Mem Award, Am Soc Mech Engrs, 1991. **Professional Experience:** PROF EMER MECH ENG, UNIV TEX, AUSTIN, as of 2004; hon mem Acad Romania, 1994; Earnest F Gloyna Regents Chair Eng, Univ Tex, Austin, beginning 1992; ASSOC DIR ENG, MFG SYSTS CTR, 1992-; pres, Inst Productivity Res, 1990-1992; prof mech eng, Columbia Univ, 1987-1990; dir, Columbia Eng Prod Ctr, 1987-1990; Jacob Wallenburg Found grantee, Sweden, 1987; chmn, Dept Mech Eng, Aeronaut Eng & Mech, 1974-1986; Mech Tech Inc, 1962-1970 & Wear Sci Corp, 1971-; from asst prof to prof mech, William Howard Hart prof rational & tech mech, 1970-1988; vis prof, Univ Leeds, 1970-1971; NSF sr fel, 1970; consult, Mitre Corp, 1961-1963; Alco Prod, Inc, 1961-1962; consult, Gen Elec Co, 1960-1962; consult, Southwest Res Inst, 1959-1965; from asst prof to prof mech, Rensselaer Polytech Inst, 1955-1970; asst prof math, Carnegie Inst Technol, 1954-1956; proj mech engr, Carnegie Inst Technol, 1952-1954. **Memberships:** Nat Acad Eng; fel Am Soc Mech Engrs; fel Am Acad Mech; fel AAAS; fel Soc Tribologists & Lubrication Engrs; fel Am Soc Mfg Engrs. **Research Statement & Publications:** Gradual wear life prediction theory of lubricating surface films; questions of factories of the 21st century, including in-situ microsensors in the small scale and larger questions concerning the total systems. **Mailing Address:** Dept Mech Eng, Univ Tex, Austin, TX 78712-1063. **Fax:** 512-471-9155. **E-Mail:** fredling@mail.utexas.edu

LING, GILBERT NING, PHYSIOLOGY. **Personal Data:** b Nanking, China, December 26, 1919; m 1951, c 3. **Education:** Nat Cent Univ, China, BSc, 1943; Univ Chicago, PhD (physiol), 1948. **Professional Experience:** DIR DEPT MOLECULAR BIOL, PA HOSP, 1962-; sr staff scientist, Eastern Pa Psychiat Inst, 1957-1962; from asst prof to assoc prof neurophysiol, Univ Ill, 1953-1957; instr physiol optics, Sch Med, Johns Hopkins Univ, 1950-1953; Comen fel, Univ Chicago, 1948-1950; Mem, Woods Hole Marine Biol Corp. **Memberships:** Am Physiol Soc. **Research Statement & Publications:** Molecular mechanisms in cell function. **Mailing Address:** 307 Berkeley Rd, Merion, PA 19066.

LING, HAO, ELECTROMAGNETICS, ANTENNAS. **Personal Data:** b Taichung, Taiwan, September 26, 1959; American citizen; m 1984, Wei-Na; c Chloe & Calvin. **Education:** Mass Inst Technol, BS, 1982; Univ Ill, Urbana-Champaign, MS, 1983, PhD (elec eng), 1986. **Honors & Awards:** NSF Presidential Young Investr Award, 1987. **Professional Experience:** L B (PREACH) MEADERS PROFESSORSHIP, UNIV TEX, as of 2005; PROF ELEC ENG, DEPT ELEC & COMPUT ENG, UNIV TEX, 1995-; assoc prof elec eng, Dept Elec & Comput Eng, Univ Tex Austin, 1990-1995; air Force fel, Rome Air Develop Ctr, Hanscom AFB, 1990; vis fac mem, Lawrence Livermore Nat Lab, 1987; asst prof, Dept Elec & Comput Eng, Univ Tex Austin, 1986-1990; engr, IBM Res Lab, 1982. **Memberships:** Inst Elec & Electronics Engrs; Int Union Radio Sci; Appl Comput Electromagnetics Soc. **Research Statement & Publications:** Electromagnetic scattering; numerical methods; radar signature prediction; target identification. **Mailing Address:** Dept Elec & Comput Eng Univ Tex, One Univ Sta C0803, Austin, TX 78712-0240. **Fax:** 512-471-1856. **E-Mail:** ling@ece.utexas.edu

LING, HARRY WILSON, INORGANIC CHEMISTRY. **Personal Data:** b Painesville, Ohio, February 14, 1927; div. **Education:** Bowling Green State Univ, AB, 1950; Ohio State Univ, PhD (inorg chem), 1954. **Professional Experience:** MGR TECH SERV, E I DUPONT Del NEMOURS & CO, INC, 1974-; prod mgr, Sales Div, 1972-1974; supvr, Sales Div, 1969-1972; sr res chemist, Sales Div, 1967-1969; tech serv chemist, Sales Div, 1964-1967; Res chemist, Pigments Dept, Res Div, E I DuPont Del Nemours & Co, Inc, 1954-1964. **Memberships:** Am Chem Soc; Fedn Soc Paint Technol; Sigma Xi. **Research Statement & Publications:** Inorganic nitrogen chemistry; elemental silicon; anodic oxidation of metal substrates; electrolytic capacitors; titanium dioxide pigments; pigment colors. **Mailing Address:** 2410 Alister Dr, Wilmington, DE 19808.

LING, HSIN YI, MICROPALEONTOLOGY. **Personal Data:** b Taiwan, December 5, 1930; m 1958, c 2. **Education:** Nat Taiwan Univ, BS, 1953; Tohuku Univ, MS, 1958; Wash Univ, PhD (geol), 1963. **Professional Experience:** DISTINGUISHED RES PROF, DEPT GEOL, NORTHERN ILL UNIV, 1993-; PROF, GEOL DEPT, NORTHERN ILL UNIV, 1978-; res prof, Dept oceanog, Univ Wash, 1974-1978; from res asst prof to res assoc prof, Dept oceanog, Univ Wash, 1964-1974; res instr geol oceanog, Dept oceanog, Univ Wash, 1963-1964; res engr, Res Ctr, Pan Am Petrol Corp, Okla, 1960-1963; instr geol, Nat Taiwan Univ, 1954-1955. **Memberships:** Fel AAAS; Soc Econ Paleontologists & Mineralogists; Paleont Soc; Paleont Res Inst; Sigma Xi. **Research Statement & Publications:** Marine micropaleontology and palynology. **Mailing Address:** Dept Geol, Northern Ill Univ, De Kalb, IL 60115-2825.

LING, HUBERT, MICROBIAL GENETICS, PLANT TISSUE CULTURE. **Personal Data:** b Chungking, China, April 28, 1942; American citizen; m 1968, Mildred; c Jonathan & Matthew. **Education:** Queens Col, BS, 1963; Brown Univ, MS, 1966; Wayne State Univ, PhD (biol), 1969; Co Col Morris, RN, 1994. **Professional Experience:** Plant propagator, Native Plant Soc NJ, 1985-; ASSOC PROF BIOL, CO COL MORRIS, 1983-; plant scientist tissue cult, Samsen Lab, 1981; sterilization scientist, Johnson & Johnson, Ethicon, 1980-1981; res microbiologist, E I du Pont, 1977-1980; Consult, Morton Salt Co, 1972-1974 & Int Chem Co, 1974-1975; Assoc prof biol, Univ Del, 1969-1977. **Memberships:** Torrey Bot Club; assoc native plant Soc of NJ board mem, plant propagator, newsletter editor. **Research Statement & Publications:** Genetic control of asexual cell fusion in Myxomycetes; ultrastructure of Myxomycetes; control of sporulation in Myxomycetes; tissue culture propagation of North American terrestrial orchids: Platanthera, Cypripedium and Calopogon. **Mailing Address:** Biol Dept, County Col Morris Rte 10, Randolph, NJ 07869-2086. **Fax:** 973-328-5361. **E-Mail:** hling@ccm.edu

LING, HUEI, COMPUTER ARCHICTECTURE & LOGIC DESIGN. **Personal Data:** b Fukien, China, February 24, 1934; m 1964. **Education:** Nat Taiwan Univ, BSc, 1957; Univ NB, MSc, 1961; Univ Okla, PhD (elec eng), 1965. **Professional Experience:** DEPT MGR COMPUT ENG, IBM RES CTR, IBM CORP, 1980-; mgr logic design & exp eng, San Jose Res Lab, 1977-1980; adj prof, Fairleigh-Dickinson Univ, Teaneck Campus, 1968; Adj assoc prof, Fairleigh-Dickinson Univ, Teaneck Campus, 1967-1968; res staff mem, San Jose Res Lab, 1965-1977; asst prof, Fla State Univ, 1965; electronic engr, Sundstrand Aviation, 1962-1963; Method supvr, Bell Tel Can, 1961. **Memberships:** Asn Comput Mach; Inst Elec & Electronics Engrs. **Research Statement & Publications:** Computer design. **Mailing Address:** 5 Whippoorwill Rd, Chappaqua, NY 10514.

LING, HUNG CHI, MATERIALS SCIENCE & ELECTRONIC CERAMICS, FIBER OPTICS, INTELLECTUAL PROPERTY POLICY. **Personal Data:** b Wenchow, China, 1950; American citizen; m 1979, Gigi; c Maya, Alicia & Byron. **Education:** Mass Inst Technol, BS, 1972, ScD, 1978; State Univ NY, Stony Brook, MA, 1974. **Professional Experience:** SR MGR, STANDARDS, INTELLECTUAL PROPERTY & TECHNOL TRANSFER, LUCENT BELL LABS, 1998-; tech mgr & distinguished mem tech staff, AT&T Bell Labs

Eng Res Ctr, Princeton, NJ, 1981-1997; Res assoc mat sci, Dept Mat Sci & Eng, Mass Inst Technol, 1978-1981; Vis lectr, Shanghai Jiao Tong Univ, Peoples Repub China, 1982. **Memberships:** Metall Soc Am Inst Mech Engrs; fel Am Ceramic Soc; sr mem Inst Elec & Electronics Engrs; Optical Soc Am. **Research Statement & Publications:** Thin film materials; electronics ceramics; dielectrics and varistors; superconducting oxides; metal-ceramic interaction; fiber optics; optoelectronics packaging; technology and intellectual property policy and mgt. **Mailing Address:** Lucent Technol Bell Labs, Rm 4c-620A, 101 Crawfords Corner Rd, Holmdel, NJ 07733-3030. **Fax:** 732-949-1196. **E-Mail:** hling@lucent.com

LING, JOSEPH TSO-TI, AIR & WATER POLLUTION & HAZARDOUS WASTE TECHNOLOGY. **Personal Data:** b Peking, China, June 10, 1919; American citizen; m 1944, Rose S Hsu; c Lois, Rosa-mei, Louis & Lorraine. **Education:** Hangchow Christian Col, Shanghai, BS, 1944; Univ Minn, Minneapolis, MS, 1950, PhD (sanit eng, pub health), 1952. **Honors & Awards:** Edward Cleary Award, Am Acad Environ Engrs, 1981; First Gold Medal Int Corp Environ Award, World Environ Ctr, 1985; Queneau Palladium Medal, Nat Audubon Soc, 1990; Leadership Award, Nat Asn Photog Mfrs, 1990; Distinguished Award, Ministry Econ Affairs, Taiwan, 1993; UN Global 500 honor role, 1981, Outstanding Achivement Award, Univ Minn, 1982. **Professional Experience:** Selection committee of pres G. Bush's award on enveron enhacement & resource conser 1990-1992; Chairmen, Am Inst Pollution Prevention, 1988-1996; INDEPENDENT CONSULT, 1984-; mem, World Environ Ctr, 1984-; sci adv bd, US Environ Protection Agency, 1984-1988; exec consult, Community Serv Exec Prog, 1984-1987; mem environ health comt, President's Domestic Policy Rev, 1978-1980; bd mem, Freshwater Found, 1974-; vpres, environ eng & pollution control, 1974-1984; President's adv bd air qual, 1974-1978; Environ Pollution Panel, US Chamber of Com, 1967-1972 & Tech Contact, Nat Indust Pollution Control Coun, 1971-1984; dir, environ eng & pollution control, 1970-1974; mgr, sanit & civil eng, 1966-1969; Adv, Ohio River Water Sanit Comn, 1962-1970; mgr, water & sanit eng, 3M Co, 1960-1965; prof civil eng, Baptist Univ, Hong Kong, 1958-1959; dir, Nat Res Inst Munic Eng, Peking, China, 1956-1957; sr staff engr, Gen Mills, Inc, 1953-1955; res asst sanit eng, Univ Minn, 1948-1952; Dist engr, Nanking-Shanghai RR Syst, 1944-1947. **Memberships:** Nat Acad Eng; Am Soc Civil Engrs; Air Pollution Control Asn; Water Pollution Control Fedn; Am Water Works Asn; Am Acad Environ Engrs. **Research Statement & Publications:** Water filtration and related purification processes; biological oxidation and advanced treatment technology for water pollution control; thermo-oxidation, control techniques in air pollution and solid and hazardous waste disposal; waste minimization & pollution prevention technologies. **Mailing Address:** 2090 Arcade St, St Paul, MN 55109.

LING, NICHOLAS CHI-KWAN, PEPTIDE CHEMISTRY, PEPTIDE HORMONES. **Personal Data:** b Hong Kong, August 15, 1940; m 1971, Betty; c Aaron. **Education:** San Jose State Univ, BS, 1964; Stanford Univ, PhD (org chem), 1969. **Honors & Awards:** Sidney H Ingbar Distinguished Serv Award, Endocrine Soc, 1994. **Professional Experience:** RES FEL, NEUROCRINE BIOSCIENCE INC, as of 2003; SR DIR PEPTIDE CHEM, NEUROCRINE BIOSCIENCE INC, 1996-; dir peptide chem, Neurocrine Bioscience, Inc, 1994-1995; mem, Endocrinol Study Sect, NIH, 1990-1993; sr mem, Whittier Inst, 1989-1993; assoc res prof, Stalk Inst, 1979-1988; asst res prof, Stalk Inst, 1974-1978; res assoc biochem, Stalk Inst, 1970-1973; res assoc crystallog, Stanford Univ, 1969-1970. **Memberships:** Am Chem Soc; AAAS; Protein Soc; Endocrine Soc; Am Soc Biol Chem; Soc Neuroscience. **Research Statement & Publications:** Isolation and characterization of peptide hormones; synthesis of peptides by solid phase methodology; peptide sequence determination by mass spectrometry and Edman technique; biological function of peptide hormones. **Mailing Address:** Neurocrine Biosci Inc, 10555 Sci Ctr Dr, San Diego, CA 92121.

LING, ROBERT FRANCIS, STATISTICS. **Personal Data:** b Hong Kong, April 21, 1939; American citizen; m 1963, c 1. **Education:** Berea Col, BA, 1961; Univ Tenn, MA, 1963; Yale Univ, MPhil, 1968, PhD (statist), 1970. **Honors & Awards:** Frank Wilcoxon Prize, 1984. **Professional Experience:** PROF EMER, MATH SCI, CLEMSON UNIV, as of 2003; prof statist, Clemson Univ, beginning 1977; Grad Sch Bus, Harvard, 1990; Grad Sch Bus, Mass Inst Technol, 1989; bd dirs, Classification Soc NAm, 1988-1990; vis lectr, Comt Pres Statist Socs, 1983-1986; Grad Sch Bus, Univ Chicago, 1983; prog chmn, Classification Soc N Am, 1982 & 1989; vis prof, Owen Grad Sch Bus, 1982; assoc ed, J Am Statist Asn, 1977-1985; assoc prof, Clemson Univ, 1975-1976; mem coun, Classification Soc N Am, 1974-1977; from instr to asst prof statist, Univ Chicago, 1970-1975; asst prof math, E Tenn State Univ, 1964-1966. **Memberships:** Fel Am Statist Asn; Classification Soc N Am. **Research Statement & Publications:** Applied statistics; statistical computing; interactive data analysis; regression diagnostics. **Mailing Address:** Dept Math Sci, Clemson Univ, Clemson, SC 29632-0001. **Fax:** 864-654-4755. **E-Mail:** rfling@clemson.clemson.edu

LING, RUNG TAI, COMPUTATIONAL ELECTROMAGNETICS, COMPUTATIONAL FLUID DYNAMICS. **Personal Data:** b Taipei, Taiwan, July 28, 1943; American citizen; wid Carol; c Biabca & Fricka. **Education:** Nat Taiwan Univ, BS, 1965; Univ Mo, Columbia, MS, 1968; Univ Calif, San Diego, PhD (physics), 1972. **Professional Experience:** CHIEF SCIENTIST, HELMHOLT LAB, 2001-; vis prof, Technical Univ Hamburg, Ger, 1999-2001; mem, Electromagnetics Acad, 1990; SR TECH SPECIALIST, NORTHROP GRUMMAN CORP, 1984-; sr res specialist, Lockheed Corp, 1981-1984; sr res scientist, R & D Assoc, 1978-1981; sr res scientist, STD Res Corp, 1976-1978; res fel, Calif Inst Technol, 1973-1976; lectr physics, San Diego State Univ, 1972-1973. **Memberships:** Am Phys Soc. **Research Statement & Publications:** Computational physics including numerical solutions and modelling of atomic and molecular physics problems; electromagnetic and acoustic scattering phenomena; fluid dynamics including magnetohydrodynamics and radiation hydrodynamics. **Mailing Address:** 4715 Lasheart Dr, La Canada, CA 91011.

LING, TA-YUNG, ELEMENTARY PARTICLE PHYSICS. **Personal Data:** b Shianghai, China, February 2, 1943; American citizen; m 1969, Marjorie; c Benjamin, Alan & Theresa. **Education:** Tunghai Univ, Taiwan, BS, 1964; Univ Waterloo, Ont, MS, 1966; Univ Wis-Madison, PhD (physics), 1971. **Honors & Awards:** Outstanding Jr Investr, Dept Energy, 1977. **Professional Experience:** PROF PHYSICS, OHIO STATE UNIV, COLUMBUS, 1983-; from asst prof to assoc prof, Ohio State Univ, Columbus, 1977-1983; asst prof, Univ Pa, 1975-1977; res assoc physics, Univ Pa, 1972-1975; res asst, Univ Wis-Madison, 1967-1971; teaching asst physics, Univ Wis-Madison, 1966-1967; Teaching asst physics, Univ Waterloo, Can, 1965-1966. **Memberships:** Am Phys Soc. **Research Statement & Publications:** Experimental high energy physics: deep inelastic neutrino; nucleon scattering, neutrino masses and mixing, neutrino oscillations, deep inelastic electron-proton scattering, high energy proton-proton collisions. **Mailing Address:** Dept Physics, Smith Lab Ohio State Univ 174 W 18th Ave, Columbus, OH 43210. **Fax:** 614-292-8776. **E-Mail:** ling@mps.ohio-state.edu

LING, VICTOR, EXPERIMENTAL THERAPEUTICS. **Personal Data:** b March 16, 1943. **Education:** Univ Toronto, BS, 1966; Univ BC, PhD (biochem) 1969. **Honors & Awards:** Cancer Res Award, Milken Family Med Found, 1988; Kettering Prize, Gen Motors Cancer Res Found, 1991; Int Award, Gairdner Found, 1992; Bruce F Cain Mem Award, Am Asn Cancer Res, 1993. **Professional Experience:** VPRES RES, BC CANCER RES CTR, 1996-; PROF, DEPT PATH & BIOCHEM, UNIV BC, 1996-; bd dirs, Hosp Sick Children Found, Am Asn Cancer Res & Can Cancer Soc, beginning 1992; bd sci coun, Dir Cancer Treatment, beginning 1990; head, Div Molecular & Struct Biol, 1989-1996; vchmn, Coun Sch Grad Studies, Univ Toronto, beginning 1988; Scholar Comt, Med Res Coun, Can, beginning 1988; Bd govs, Wellesly Hosp Res Inst, 1988-1990; mem, Study Sect Exp Therapeut, NIH, beginning 1986; mem, Fac Med Res Comt, beginning 1985; mem, Coun Sch Grad Studies, Univ Toronto, 1984; prof med biophys, Univ Toronto, 1983-1996; staff scientist, Ont Cancer Inst, 1971-1996. **Memberships:** Fel Royal Soc Can; Am Asn Cancer Res; Am Soc Cell Biol; Can Cancer Soc; Can Soc Cell Biol; Can Biochem Soc. **Research Statement & Publications:** Cellular physiology; molecular pharmacology. **Mailing Address:** BC Cancer Res Ctr, 601 W Tenth Ave, Vancouver, BC V5Z 1L3, Can. **Fax:** 604-877-6150.

LINGANE, PETER JAMES, ELECTROCHEMISTRY, HYDROMETALLURGY. **Personal Data:** b Oakland, Calif, May 12, 1940; m 1967, c 2. **Education:** Harvard Univ, AB, 1962; Calif Inst Technol, PhD (chem), 1966. **Professional Experience:** FINANCIAL SECURITY DESIGN, as of 2005; SUPVR, STAND ALASKA PROD CO, 1984-; group leader, Prod Res Div, Conoco, 1977-1984; sr chemist, Ledgemont Lab, Kennecott Copper Corp, 1970-1977; asst prof chem, Univ Minn, Minneapolis, 1966-1970. **Memberships:** Am Chem Soc; Soc Petrol Engrs. **Research Statement & Publications:** Chemistry related to the solution mining of nonferrous ore minerals and to enhanced oil recovery, specifically carbon dioxide flooding; kinetics and mechanisms of solution reactions with particular emphasis upon the reactions which surround electrode processes; phase behavior of hydro carbon systems. **Mailing Address:** Financial Security Design, 852 Acampo Dr, Lafayette, CA 94549-5040. **Fax:** 925-299-0473. **E-Mail:** peter@lingane.com

LINGAPPA, BANADAKOPPA THIMMAPPA, MICROBIOLOGY. **Personal Data:** b Mysore, India, March 19, 1927; American citizen; m 1953, Yamuna; c Vishwanath, Jaisri & Jairam. **Education:** Benaras Hindu Univ, BS, 1950, MS, 1952; Purdue Univ, PhD, 1957. **Professional Experience:** PROF EMER BIOL, COL HOLY CROSS, 1996-; vis scientist, Harvard Univ, 1988; vis scientist, Worc Found Exp Biol, 1976-1977; fac fel, Col Holy Cross, 1970 & 1988; vis prof, Inst Gen Bot, Univ Geneva, 1969-1970; prof biol, Col Holy Cross, 1968-1996; vis scientist, Mass Inst Technol, 1968-1969; from asst prof to assoc prof, Col Holy Cross, 1962-1968; asst prof, Mich State Univ, 1961-1962; Nat Inst Sci India sr res fel, Bot Lab, Univ Madras, 1961; asst prof med mycol, Mich State Univ, 1960; res assoc, Mich State Univ, 1959-1960; res assoc, Univ Mich, 1957-1959; res asst, Purdue Univ, 1953-1957; lectr mycol, Benaras Hindu Univ, 1952-1953. **Memberships:** Mycol Soc Am; Am Soc Microbiol; Sigma Xi; AAAS; Am Phytopath Soc. **Research Statement & Publications:** Physiology of fungi; dormancy and germination of spores; methane production by anaerobic fermentation of solid waste; molecular biology. **Mailing Address:** Dept Biol, Col Holy Cross, One Col St, Worcester, MA 01610. **E-Mail:** blingapp@holycross.edu

LINGAPPA, JAIRAM R, MOLECULAR BIOLOGY. **Education:** MD, PhD. **Professional Experience:** MED DIR & ASST PROF, DEPT MED, UNIV WASH, WASH, as of 2006. **Mailing Address:** Univ Wash, Box 359927, Seattle, WA 98195-9927. **Fax:** 206-520-3831. **E-Mail:** lingappa@u.washington.edu

LINGAPPA, JAISRI RAO, INFECTIOUS DISEASES. **Personal Data:** b AnnArbor, Mich, June 11, 1959. **Education:** Swarthmore Col, BA, 1979; Harvard Univ, PhD (cell biol), 1985; Univ Mass, Worcester, MD, 1987. **Honors & Awards:** Am Med Women's Asn Award, 1987. **Professional Experience:** ASST PROF, DEPT PATHOBIOLOGY, UNIV WASH, 2002-; infectious dis fel, Dept Med, Univ Calif, San Francisco, 1990-2002; resident internal med, Dept Med, Univ Calif, San Francisco, 1987-1990. **Memberships:** Sigma Xi. **Mailing Address:** Dept Pathobiology, Univ Wash, Box 357238, Seattle, WA 98195-7238. **E-Mail:** jais@u.washington.edu

LINGAPPA, VISHWANATH R, CELL BIOLOGY, MEDICINE. **Education:** Swarthmore Col, BA (Biol), 1975; Univ Calif, CA, 1980-1982; Rockfeller Univ, PhD (Biol), 1979; Cornell Univ Med Col, MD(Cell Med), 1980. **Professional Experience:** PROF EMER PHYSIOL & MATH, UCSF MED CTR, 1991-; PRIN FOUND & MAIN INVENTOR, PROSETTA CORP, as of 2006; assoc prof physiol & math, Ucsf Med Ctr, 1987-1991; Med Resident, Unif Calif, 1981-1982; asst prof physiol & math, Ucsf Med Ctr, 1981-1987. **Mailing Address:** Dept Physiol, UCSF Med Ctr, Box 0444 UCSF, San Francisco, CA 94143-0444. **Fax:** 415-476-4929. **E-Mail:** vrl@itsa.ucsf.edu

LINGAPPA, VISWANATH R, CELL BIOLOGY. **Education:** Rockefeller Univ, PhD, 1979; Cornell Univ, MD, 1980. **Professional Experience:** PROF EMER, PHYSIOL & MED, UNIV CALIF, SAN FRANSICO, as of 2004-; CHIEF TECHNOL OFFICER, PROSETTA CORP, CA, 2004-. **Memberships:** AAAS. **Mailing Address:** Dept Physiol Univ Calif, Med Ctr Box 0444, San Francisco, CA 94143-0444. **Fax:** 415-476-4929. **E-Mail:** vrl@itsa.ucsf.edu

LINGAPPA, YAMUNA, MICROBIOLOGY. **Personal Data:** b Mysore, India, December 6, 1929; American citizen; m 1953, Banadakoppa T Lingappa; c Vishwanath, Jaisri & Jairam. **Education:** Mysore Univ, BSc, 1949; Madras Univ, BT, 1951; Purdue Univ, MS, 1955, PhD, 1958. **Professional Experience:** Fac adv, Undergrad Res Partic Proj Methane Generation, Col Holy Cross, vis lectr nutrit & world hunger, 1978; comnr, Gov Comn on Status of Women, Mass, 1977-1979; instr human nutrit, Clark Univ & Worcester State Col, 1974; Vis scientist, Inst Bot, Univ Geneva, 1969-1970; RES ASSOC BIOL, COL HOLY CROSS, 1963-; sci pool officer, Govt India, 1961; Res assoc, Univ Mich, 1957-1959 & Mich State Univ, 1959-1960; res consult, Dept Pub Health, City Worcester. **Memberships:** Mycol Soc Am; Am Soc Microbiol; Sigma Xi; Am Inst Biol Sci. **Research Statement & Publications:** Human nutrition; solid waste disposal; physiology of pathogenic fungi; microbial interactions. **Mailing Address:** 4 McGill St, Worcester, MA 01607.

LINGELBACH, D(ANIEL) D(EE), ELECTROMECHANICAL ENERGY CONVERSION. **Personal Data:** b Wilkinsburg, Pa, October 4, 1925; m 1949, Ruby; c Jean M, Dickey L & David G. **Education:** Kans State Col, BSEE, 1947, MS, 1948; Okla State Univ, PhD, 1960. **Honors & Awards:** Charles Schneider Award, Nat Asn Relay Mfrs, 1968. **Professional Experience:** PROF EMER ELEC & COMPUT ENG, OKLA STATE UNIV, 1986-; prof elec eng, Okla State Univ, 1979-1986; assoc prof, Okla State Univ, 1961-1979; asst prof, Okla State Univ, 1955-1961; from instr to asst prof elec eng, Univ Ark, 1948-1955. **Memberships:** Am Soc Eng Educ; Nat Soc Prof Engrs; Inst Elec & Electronics Engrs; Sigma Xi. **Research Statement & Publications:** Electric power system modeling and optimization; power systems analysis. **Mailing Address:** 1116 S Gray St, Stillwater, OK 74074. **Fax:** 405-744-7554.

LINGENFELTER, RICHARD EMERY, ASTROPHYSICS, COSMIC RAY PHYSICS. **Personal Data:** b Farmington, NMex, April 5, 1934; m 1957, Naomi; c Andrea & Kendale. **Education:** Univ Calif, Los Angeles, AB, Physics, 1956. **Professional Experience:** RES PHYSICIST, CTR ASTROPHYS & SPACE SCI, UNIV CALIF, SAN DIEGO, 1979-; prof residence, Dept Geophys & Space Physics, 1969-1979 & Dept Astron, 1974-1979; Fulbright res fel geophys & planetary physics, Tata Inst Fundamental Res, Bombay, India, 1968-1969; res geophysicist, Inst Geophys & Planetary Physics, 1966-1969; assoc res geophysicist, Univ Calif, Los Angeles, 1962-1966; physicist, Lawrence Radiation Lab, Univ Calif, 1957-1962. **Memberships:** Fel Am Phys Soc; Int Astron Union; Am Astron Soc; Am Geophys Union. **Research Statement & Publications:** Cosmic ray origins and interactions; gamma ray astronomy; solar flare particle interactions; planetology; radiocarbon variations. **Mailing Address:** Ctr Astrophys & Space Sci, Univ Calif San Diego, La Jolla, CA 92093-0424. **Fax:** 858-534-2294. **E-Mail:** rlingenfelter@ucsc.edu

LINGG, AL J, MICROBIOLOGY. **Personal Data:** b Mt Hope, Kans, March 26, 1938; m 1961, c 3. **Education:** Kans State Univ, BS, 1964, MS, 1966, PhD (microbiol), 1969. **Professional Experience:** PROF EMER MICROBIOL, UNIV IDAHO, 1998-; dir, Sch Family & Consumer Sci, 1992-1993; assoc dean & dir acad & int prog, Col Agr, 1987-1998; fulbright lectr, Nepal, 1979-1980; prof microbiol, Univ Idaho, beginning 1969; instr, Kans State Univ, 1966-1968. **Memberships:** Sigma Xi; Am Soc Microbiol. **Research Statement & Publications:** Environmental microbiology; water quality; fungal insect pathogens. **Mailing Address:** Dept Microbiol, Univ Idaho, PO Box 3052, Moscow, ID 83844-3052. **Fax:** 208-885-6518.

LINGLE, SARAH ELIZABETH, PHYSIOLOGY, BIOCHEMISTRY. **Personal Data:** b Woodland, Calif, July 22, 1955; m 1989, Thomas. **Education:** Univ Calif, Davis, BS, 1977; Univ Nebr, MS, 1978; Wash State Univ, PhD (agron), 1982. **Professional Experience:** Research Plant Physiologist, USDA, Agr. Res. Serv., New Orleans, LA, 1997- Actg res leader, Weslaco, 1991-1992; PLANT PHYSIOLOGIST, USDA, AGR RES SERV, WESLACO, TEX, 1984-1997; res assoc, Fargo, NDak, 1982-1984; res asst, Wash State Univ, 1979-1982; teaching asst plant breeding, Wash State Univ, 1979-1980; Res asst, Univ Nebr, 1977-1978. **Memberships:** Am Soc Agron; Crop Sci Soc Am; Am Soc Plant Physiologists; AAAS; Sigma Xi. **Research Statement & Publications:** Physiology and biochemistry of sucrose accumulation in sugarcane, specifically the transport and metabolism of sucrose and how it relates to the balance between growth and storage in the stalk. **Mailing Address:** USDA, Agr Res Serv, 1100 Robert E Lee Blvd, New Orleans, LA 70124. **Fax:** 504-286-4419. **E-Mail:** slingle@srrc.ars.usda.gov

LINGREL, JERRY B, MOLECULAR GENETICS. **Personal Data:** b Byhalia, Ohio, July 13, 1935; m 1958, c 2. **Education:** Otterbein Col, BS, 1957; Ohio State Univ, PhD (biochem), 1960. **Honors & Awards:** George Rieveschl Award. **Professional Experience:** PROF & CHMN MOLECULAR GENETICS, BIOCHEM & MICROBIOL, UNIV CINCINNATI, 1981-; from asst prof to prof biol chem, Biochem & Microbiol, Univ Cincinnati, 1962-1981; fel biol, Calif Inst Technol, 1960-1962. **Memberships:** Am Soc Biol Chemists; Am Soc Cell Biol. **Research Statement & Publications:** Regulation of gene expression in animal cells; hemoglobin biosynthesis; messenger RNA; gene structure. **Mailing Address:** Dept Micro & Molecular Genetics, Univ Cincinnati Col Med, PO Box 670524, Cincinnati, OH 45267-0524. **E-Mail:** lingrejb@ucmail.uc.edu

LINGREN, WESLEY EARL, PHYSICAL CHEMISTRY, OCEANOGRAPHY. **Personal Data:** b Pasadena, Calif, August 27, 1930; m 1961, c 2. **Education:** Seattle Pac Col, BS, 1952; Univ Wash, MS, 1954, PhD (electrochem), 1962. **Professional Experience:** DEAN SCH SCI, SEATTLE PAC UNIV, 1990-; NSF fel, Solar Energy Res Inst, 1984; DIR GEN HONORS, SEATTLE PAC UNIV, 1970-; prof chem, Seattle Pac Univ, beginning 1968; chmn dept, Seattle Pac Univ, 1968-1973; NSF fel, Yale Univ, 1967-1968; res assoc, US Naval Radiol Defense Lab, 1963-1969; from asst prof to assoc prof, Seattle Pac Univ, 1962-1968; instr phys sci, Pasadena Col, 1956-1958. **Memberships:** Am Chem Soc; Sigma Xi. **Research Statement & Publications:** Rates of electrode reactions; electroanalytical chemistry; oxidation states of elements in seawater oceanography. **Mailing Address:** Dept Chem, Seattle Pac Univ, 10628 NE 16th St, Bellevue, WA 98004.

LINGWOOD, CLIFFORD ALAN, PROTEIN-GLYCOLIPID INTERACTIONS. **Personal Data:** b Dorset, Eng, January 2, 1950; m 1974, c 3. **Education:** Univ Hull, BSc, 1971; Univ London, PhD (cell biol), 1975. **Professional Experience:** PROF, DEPT PEDIAT LAB MED, 1997-; PROF, DEPT BIOCHEM, UNIV TORONTO, 1997-; SR SCIENTIST, RES INST, DIV MICROBIOL, DEPT PEDIAT LAB MED & BIOCHEM, HOSP SICK C, 1989-; ASSOC PROF, DEPT CLIN BIOCHEM, BIOCHEM & MICROBIOL, UNIV TORONTO, 1989-; assoc prof, dept microbiol, 1987-; asst prof, Dept Microbiol, 1987-1989; asst prof, Dept Biochem, 1984-1989; asst prof, Dept Clin Biochem, 1983-1989; asst prof, Dept Biochem, Hospital Sick C, Toronto, 1982-1989; asst prof, dept biochem, Hosp Sick C, Toronto, 1981-; res fel, Med Res Coun scholar, 1981-1986; res fel, Hosp Sick C, Toronto, 1977-1981; res fel, Dept Biochem, Hosp Sick C, Toronto, 1977-1981; res fel, Dept Biochem, Univ Toronto, 1977-1980; vis scientist, Dept Biochem Oncol, Fred Hutchinson Cancer Res Ctr, Seattle, Wash, 1976-1977; Res fel, Dept Pathobiology, Univ Wash, Seattle, 1975-1977. **Memberships:** Am Soc Cell Biol; Soc Complex Carbohydrates; Am Soc Microbiol; Can Biochem Soc. **Research Statement & Publications:** Glycolipid receptors for microorganisms; glycolipid binding by verotoxin, glycolipids and HIV infection, glycolipids and cancer/MDR1; Glycolipid intracellular trafficking, lipid rafts. **Mailing Address:** Dept Pediat Lab Med Div Microbiol, Hosp Sick C 555 Univ Ave, Toronto, ON M5G 1X8, Can. **Fax:** 416-813-5993. **E-Mail:** cling@sickkids.ca

LINHARDT, ROBERT JOHN, BIOPOLYMER CARBOHYDRATE CHEMISTRY, APPLIED ENZYMOLOGY. **Personal Data:** b Passaic, NJ, October 18, 1953; m 1975, Kathryn; c Kelley & Barbara. **Education:** Marquette Univ, BS, 1975; Johns Hopkins Univ, MA, 1977, PhD (org chem), 1979. **Honors & Awards:** Horace S Isbell Award, Am Chem Soc, 1994; Volweiler Award, Am Asn Col Pharm, 2000; Claude S Hudson Award, Am Chem Soc, 2003. **Professional Experience:** ANN JOHN H BROADBENT SR CONSTELLATION CHAIR, BIOCATALYSIS & METABOLIC ENG, RENSSELAER POLYTECH INST, 2003-; PROF CHEM & CHEM BIOL, BIOL & CHEM BIOL ENG, RENSSELAER POLYTECH INST, 2003-; F Wendell Miller distinguished prof chem, Med & Natural Products Chem & prof chem & biochem eng, Col Pharm, Univ Iowa, 1999-2003; F Wendell Miller distinguished prof, Univ Iowa, 1996-2003; prof med chem & natural prods chem, Col Pharm, Univ Iowa, 1996-2003; ed bd, J Biol Chem, 1995-2000; vis prof, Univ Calif, San Diego, Cancer Ctr & La Jolla Cancer Res Found, 1992; from asst prof to assoc prof, Col Pharm, Univ Iowa, 1982-1990; Johnson & Johnson fel, Whitaker Col Health Sci, Technol & Mgt, 1981-1982; res assoc, Dept Appl Biol, Biochem Eng Labs, Mass Inst Technol, 1979-1982; res asst, Dept Chem, Johns Hopkins Univ, 1975-1979. **Memberships:** Am Chem Soc; AAAS; Soc Glycobiol; Am Acad Pediat; Am Asn Pharmaceut Scientists; Am Soc Biochem Molecular Biol; Am soc Matrix biol. **Research Statement & Publications:** Bio-organic chemistry and applied enzymology in the study of the structure-activity-relationship of complex polysaccharides; biopolymeric drugs and carbohydrate chemistry; published over 20 articles. **Mailing Address:** Rensselaer Polytech Inst, 4005C BioTechnol Bldg 110 Eighth St, Troy, NY 12180-3590. **Fax:** 518-276-3405. **E-Mail:** linhar@rpi.edu

LINHART, YAN BOHUMIL, EVOLUTION, ECOLOGY. **Personal Data:** b Prague, Czech, October 8, 1939; American citizen. **Education:** Rutgers Univ, New Brunswick, BS, 1961; Yale Univ, MF, 1963; Univ Calif, Berkeley, PhD (genetics), 1972. **Professional Experience:** USDA Grant 1995-2000; Nat Geog Soc grant, 1984-1985; PROF BIOL, UNIV COLO, BOULDER, 1983-; NSF grants, 1975-1994 & 2001-2004; Colo Energy Res Inst grant, 1975-1976; from asst prof to assoc prof, Univ Colo, Boulder, 1971-1983; res grant, Univ Colo, Boulder, 1971-1973; asst specialist, Univ Colo, Boulder, 1965-1966; jr specialist forest genetics, Sch Forestry, Univ Calif, Berkeley, 1963-1965. **Memberships:** AAAS; Am Inst Biol Sci; Brit Ecol Soc; Soc Study Evolution; Soc Am Foresters; Asn Trop Biol; Am Soc Naturalists; Bot Soc Am; Ecol Soc Am. **Research Statement & Publications:** Adaptation; population biology; reproductive biology of plants; pollination biology; forest biology; plant biogeography; plant-animal interactions- chemical ecology. **Mailing Address:** Dept Ecol & Eval Biol, Univ Colo, PO Box 334, Boulder, CO 80309-0334. **E-Mail:** yan.linhart@colorado.edu

LINHOLM, L W, ELECTRICAL ENGINEERING. **Personal Data:** b November 14, 1945. **Education:** Univ Md, MA, 1973. **Professional Experience:** GROUP LEADER, INTEGRATED CIRCUITS TECHNOL GROUP, NAT INST STAND & TECHNOL, 1978-. **Mailing Address:** Integrated Circuits Technol Group, Nat Inst Stand & Technol, B360 Technol Bldg, Gaithersburg, MD 20899. **Fax:** 301-948-4081. **E-Mail:** linholm@apollo.eeel.nist.gov

LININGER, LLOYD LESLEY, MATHEMATICS, MATHEMATICAL STATISTICS. **Personal Data:** b Iowa City, Iowa, March 13, 1939; m 1959, c 3. **Education:** Univ Iowa, PhD (math), 1964. **Professional Experience:** ASSOC PROF EMER MATH, STATE UNIV NY, ALBANY, as of 2005; statistician, Environ Protection Agency, 1985-1988; statistician, Biometry Sect, NIH, Bethesda, 1977-1978; assoc prof math, State Univ NT, Albany, beginning 1970; res instr, Univ Mich, 1967-1970; asst to Prof Montgomery, Inst Advan Study, Princeton Univ, 1965-1967; asst prof math, Univ Mo, 1964-1965. **Memberships:** Am Math Soc; Am Statist Asn; Am Pub Health Asn. **Research Statement & Publications:** Applications of statistics; biostatistics; survival distributions. **Mailing Address:** Dept Math, State Univ NY, Albany, NY 12222-1000.

LINK, BERNARD ALVIN, MEAT SCIENCE, FOOD SCIENCE. **Personal Data:** b Columbus, Wis, March 23, 1941. **Education:** Univ Wis-Madison, BS, 1962, MS, 1964, PhD (meat & animal sci), 1968. **Professional Experience:** INNKEEPER, VICTORIAN BED & BREAKFAST, as of 2003; MGR, PROTEIN RES, CARGILL INC, 1977-; res biochemist, Protein Res, Cargill Inc, 1973-1977; res assoc biochem & biophys, Tex A&M Univ, 1972-1973; res scientist meat chem, Tex A&M Univ, 1970-1972; Welch Found fel, Tex A&M Univ, 1968-1972; res asst meat sci, Univ Wis-Madison, 1962-1968. **Memberships:** Am Meat Sci Asn; Sigma Xi; Am Asn Cereal Chemists; Inst Food Technol. **Research Statement & Publications:** Soy protein products. **Mailing Address:** Victorian Bed & Breakfast, 620 S High St, Lake City, MN 55041. **Fax:** 888-345-2167.

LINK, CONRAD BARNETT, HORTICULTURE. **Personal Data:** b Dunkirk, NY, March 5, 1912. **Education:** Ohio State Univ, BS, 1933, MS, 1934, PhD (hort), 1940. **Honors & Awards:** Ware Award, Am Soc Hort Sci, L H Vaughan Award. **Professional Experience:** RETIRED; EMER PROF HORT, UNIV MD, COLLEGE PARK, 1982-; prof, Univ MD, College Park, 1948-1982; horticulturist, Brooklyn Bot Garden, 1945-1948; exten specialist, Ohio State Univ, 1939-1940; from instr to asst prof floricult, Pa State Univ, 1938-1945; asst hort, Ohio State Univ, 1935-1938; Hybridist, Good & Reese Co, Ohio, 1934-1935. **Memberships:** Fel AAAS; fel Am Soc Hort Sci; Bot Soc Am; Am Hort Soc (secy, 1948-1949); Int Soc Hort Sci; Soc Econ Bot. **Research Statement & Publications:** Photoperiodism; plant anatomy, nutrition and plant propagation of greenhouse and nursery crops. **Mailing Address:** 407 Russell Ave Apt A813, Gaithersburg, MD 20877. **Fax:** 301-314-9308.

LINK, GORDON LITTLEPAGE, PHYSICAL CHEMISTRY. **Personal Data:** b Charleston, WVa, February 9, 1932; m 1955, c 1. **Education:** Col William & Mary, BS, 1954; Univ Va, PhD (phys chem), 1958. **Professional Experience:** RETIRED; mem tech staff, Bell Labs Inc, 1958-1987. **Memberships:** Sigma Xi. **Research Statement & Publications:** Dielectrics. **Mailing Address:** 18 Tingley Rd, PO Box 87, Brookside, NJ 07926.

LINK, PETER K, GEOLOGY, METEOROLOGY. **Personal Data:** b Batavia, Java, November 7, 1930; American citizen; m 1990, c 2. **Education:** Univ Wis, BS, 1953, MS, 1955, PhD (stratig geol), 1965. **Professional Experience:** STAFF INSTR, OIL & GAS CONSULT INT, INC, TULSA, 1979-; found mem, Associated Resource Consult Inc, Tulsa, 1979; Adj prof geol, Univ Tulsa, 1974-1977; CONSULT, 1973-; sr res scientist, Amoco Prod Co, 1970-1973; sr res geophysicist, Atlantic Richfield Co, Dallas, 1968-1970; res geologist, Atlantic Richfield Co, Dallas, 1965-1968; regional geologist, Humble Oil & Refining Co, Okla, 1962-1963; regional geologist, Esso Stand Inc, Libya, 1960-1961; subsurface geologist, Esso Stand Inc, Libya, 1959-1960; party chief, Esso Stand Inc, Libya, 1958-1959; Geologist, Esso Stand Inc, Libya, 1957-1958. **Memberships:** Am Asn Petrol Geologists; fel Geol Soc Am. **Research Statement & Publications:** Stratigraphy; structure; tectonics; field, regional, well site, subsurface and petroleum geology; research operations; stratigraphic-seismic research exploration; exploration programs; sedimentation; photogeology; minerals and petroleum exploration; author one book. **Mailing Address:** 7637 S Centaur Dr, Evergreen, CO 80439.

LINK, WILLIAM B, ANALYTICAL CHEMISTRY, ORGANIC CHEMISTRY. **Personal Data:** b Darke, WVa, March 25, 1928; m 1956, Ruby; c Wesley B, Gregory C & David G. **Education:** Shepherd Col, BS, 1953. **Professional Experience:** RETIRED; supvy anal res chemist, US Food & Drug Admin, 1963-1985; supvy chemist, US Food & Drug Admin, 1962-1963; anal chemist, US Food & Drug Admin, 1957-1962; chemist, US Food & Drug Admin, 1955-1957; med technician, Baker Vet Ctr, Martinsburg, WVa, 1955. **Research Statement & Publications:** Chemistry of all color additives used in foods, drugs and cosmetics. **Mailing Address:** 4113 LaMarre Dr, Fairfax, VA 22030.

LINK, WILLIAM EDWARD, ANALYTICAL CHEMISTRY. **Personal Data:** b Ironwood, Mich, January 24, 1921; m 1947, c 2. **Education:** Northland Col, BA, 1942; Univ Wis, MS, 1951, PhD, 1954. **Professional Experience:** DIR RES & DEVELOP, SHEREX CHEM CO, 1979-; res mgr, Chem Prod Div, 1976-1978; Ed, Off & Tentative Methods, Am Oil Chemists Soc, 1971-; mgr, Anal Chem Res & Develop Div, Ashland Oil & Refining Co Ohio, 1971-1976; group leader, Res Ctr, Ashland Chem Co, 1969-1971; group leader, Res Lab, ADM Chem, 1954-1969; Asst prof chem, Northland Col, 1947-1952. **Memberships:** Am Chem Soc; Am Oil Chemists Soc (pres 1975-1976). **Research Statement & Publications:** Organic analytical research; fats and oils chemistry; industrial fatty derivatives; specialty chemicals; fatty nitrogen chemicals; industrial fatty derivatives analysis; resin analysis. **Mailing Address:** 6039 Sedgwick Rd, Columbus, OH 43235.

LINKE, HARALD ARTHUR BRUNO, MICROBIOLOGY. **Personal Data:** b Bautzen, Ger, August 18, 1936; m 1971, c 1. **Education:** Univ Berlin, BSc, 1961; Univ Gottingen, MSc, 1963, PhD (biochem, microbiol), 1967. **Professional Experience:** PROF EMER, DEPT MICROBIOL, NY UNIV DENT CTR, as of 2006; prof, Dept Microbiol, NY Univ Dent Ctr, beginning 1985; from asst prof to assoc prof, Dept Microbiol, NY Univ Dent Ctr, 1973-1985; res assoc, Inst Microbiol, Rutgers Univ, 1972-1973; res microbiologist, Allied Chem Corp, 1969-1972; fel biochem, Rutgers Univ New Brunswick, 1967-1969; referee, Zentralblatt Bakteriologie II, Abteilung, 1966-; res assoc enzym, Univ Gottingen, 1966-1967. **Memberships:** NY Acad Sci; Am Soc Microbiol; Ger Chem Soc; Am Asn Dental Res; Europ Orgn Caries Res. **Research Statement & Publications:** Isolation and characterization of enzymes; utilizing isotope techniques in the study of microorganisms; biosynthesis and biodegradation of chemical and natural compounds; taxonomy of streptococci; etiology of dental caries and periodontal disease; artificial sweeteners. **Mailing Address:** Dept Microbiol, NY Univ Dent Ctr, 421 First Ave, New York, NY 10010. **Fax:** 212-995-4087.

LINKE, RICHARD ALAN, HARDWARE SYSTEMS. **Personal Data:** b Plainfield, NJ, February 15, 1946; m 1967, c 2. **Education:** Columbia Col, BA, 1968, MS, 1970, PhD (physics), 1972. **Honors & Awards:** Traveling Lectr Award, Inst Elec & Electronic Engrs/Lazers & Electro-optics Soc. **Professional Experience:** DIR, SCI POLICY, OPTICAL SOC AM, 2003-; SR RES SCIENTIST, NEC RES INST, 1989-; head, Lightware Commun Res Dept, 1986-1989; mem tech staff radio physics res, AT&T Bell Labs, 1972-1986. **Memberships:** Fel Optical Soc Am; fel Inst Elec & Electronics Engrs. **Research Statement & Publications:** Application of optical communications techniques to computing; optical fiber communications systems; development of low noise millimeter wave receivers. **Mailing Address:** Optical Soc Am, 2010 Mass Ave NW, Washington, DC 20036-1023. **Fax:** 202-223-1096.

LINKE, SIMPSON, ELECTRICAL ENGINEERING EDUCATION. **Personal Data:** b Jellico, Tenn, August 10, 1917; American citizen; m 1946, Esther S; c Martha Ellen & Laura Miriam. **Education:** Univ Tenn, BS, 1941; Cornell Univ, MEE, 1949. **Professional Experience:** Ed elec & comput eng, Cornell Univ Newsletter Connections, 1992-2005; Attwood assoc, US Nat Comt, Int Conf Large Elec Systs, 1988-; PROF EMER ELEC ENG, CORNELL UNIV, 1986-; coordr Elec Eng Grad Studies, Cornell Univ, 1981-1984; Brookhaven Nat Labs, 1976-1980 & NMex Pub Serv Comn, 1980-1982; actg dir, Lab Plasma, Cornell Univ, 1975-1976; prog mgr, NSF, 1971-1972; asst dir lab plasma, Cornell Univ, 1967-1975; mem, US Nat Comt, Int Conf Large Elec Systs, 1963-1988; chief investr, NSF res grant, 1961-1964; consult, Philadelphia Elec Co, 1956-1957; from instr to prof, Cornell Univ, 1946-1986. **Memberships:** Life fel, Inst Elec & Electronics Engrs; Sigma Xi; Eta Kappa Nu. **Research Statement & Publications:** Transient stability of synchronous machines; energy conversion, electric energy systems; high voltage direct current transmission; electric power transmission. **Mailing Address:** Dept Elec & Comput Eng, Cornell Univ, 204 Phillips Hall, Ithaca, NY 14850. **Fax:** 607-254-3508. **E-Mail:** sl78@cornell.edu

LINKE, WILLIAM FINAN, PHYSICAL CHEMISTRY, PHASE EQUILIBRIA, CATALYSTS. **Personal Data:** b Ravena, NY, August 5, 1924; m 1949, Ruth A Renz; c William, Robert & Jennifer. **Education:** City Col New York, BS, 1945; NY Univ, MS, 1946, PhD (chem), 1948. **Professional Experience:** DIR, CHEM RES DIV, AM CYANAMID CO, 1986-; dir, technol assessment & licensing, 1980-1985; dir, Stamford Res Ctr, 1972-1979; dir res, Indust Chem & Plastics Div, 1971; tech dir paper chem dept, Am Cyanamid Co, 1967-1970; mgr res & develop paper & film chem, Am Cyanamid Co, 1965-1967; group leader paper chem, Am Cyanamid Co, 1959-1964; group leader phys chem, Am Cyanamid Co, 1957-1959; from instr to asst prof, NY Univ, 1948-1957; Asst chem, NY Univ, 1945-1948. **Memberships:** AAAS; emer mem Am Chem Soc; Tech Asn Pulp & Paper Indust; Soc Chem Indust; Indust Res Inst; CT Acad of Sci & Environ. **Research Statement & Publications:** Solubilities; phase equilibria; polyelectrolytes; stability of colloids; flocculation; adsorption; mining and paper chemicals; sizing; polymers; monomers; petrochemical processes; refinery catalysts; auto exhaust catalysts; research management and direction. **Mailing Address:** 75 Ridgecrest Rd, Stamford, CT 06903-3120.

LINKER, ALFRED, biochemistry, carbohydrate chemistry; deceased, see previous edition for last biography

LINKER-ISRAELI, MARIANA, AUTOIMMUNE DISEASE, CYTOKINES. **Personal Data:** b Bucharest, Romania, September 1, 1939; American citizen; m 1966, Leonard; c Dana & Sharon. **Education:** Hebrew Univ, Jerusalem, Israel, BS, 1962, MS, 1965; Weizman Inst, Rehovot, Israel, PhD (immunol), 1972. **Professional Experience:** RETIRED; assoc prof med, Univ Calif, Los Angeles, as of 2005; res scientist, Cedars Sinai Med Ctr, beginning 1989; from asst prof to assoc prof med, Univ Southern Calif, 1981-1989. **Memberships:** Am Asn Immunologists. **Research Statement & Publications:** Immune regulation; regulation of cytokine expression and other genes that contribute to dysregulated responses in autoimmune diseases. **Mailing Address:** 563 Tahquitz Pl, Palisades, CA 90272.

LINKINS, ARTHUR EDWARD, BIOLOGY. **Personal Data:** b Middletown, Ohio, January 13, 1945; m 1974, c 2. **Education:** Dartmouth Col, BA, 1967; Univ Mass, Amherst, PhD (bot), 1973. **Professional Experience:** VPRES & PROVOST, SALEM INT UNIV, as of 2003; EXEC VPRES, INST PROF DEVELOP, OSHKOSH, as of 2003; ACAD LEADER, SALEM INT UNIV, as of 2003; VPRES, ACAD AFFAIRS, SALEM INT UNIV, as of 2003; vpres, Acad Affairs, Lakeland Col, beginning 1993; dean, Sch Sci, Lakeland Col, beginning 1989; prof Biol, Clarkson Univ, Potsdam, NY, beginning 1985; chmn, Dept Biol, 1985-1992; adj assoc prof, Inst Arctic Biol, Univ Alaska, beginning 1980; sr res prof, Inst Arctic Biol, Univ Alaska, 1980-1991; from asst prof to assoc prof, Dept Biol Va Polytech Inst & State Univ, Blacksburg, Va, 1974-1985; fel plant physiol, Dept Plant Sci, Univ Calif, Riverside, 1972-1974; assoc Col Independent Scholar. **Memberships:** Am Soc Microbiol; Soil Sci Soc Am; Mycological Soc Am; AAAS; Am Inst Biol Sci. **Research Statement & Publications:** Fungal physiological ecology: role of temperature in regulation of physiology and role of temperature, oxygen, and substrate quality in regulation of fungal associated decomposition of organic matter. **Mailing Address:** Salem Int Univ, 223 W Main St PO Box 500, Salem, VA 26426-0500.

LINN, BRUCE OSCAR, MEDICINAL CHEMISTRY, BIOCHEMISTRY. **Personal Data:** b East Orange, NJ, December 12, 1929; m 1951, c 3. **Education:** Duke Univ, BS, 1952, PhD (org chem), 1956. **Professional Experience:** RETIRED; res fel, Merck Sharp & Dohme Res Lab, 1976-1993; sr chemist, Merck Sharp & Dohme Res Lab, 1956-1975; asst, Off Naval Res, 1953-1954; asst, Duke Univ, 1952-1954. **Memberships:** Am Chem Soc. **Research Statement & Publications:** Medicinal and synthetic organic chemistry in human and animal health. **Mailing Address:** 743 Wingate Dr, Bridgewater, NJ 08807-1608.

LINN, DEVON WAYNE, LIMNOLOGY. **Personal Data:** b Estherville, Iowa, October 9, 1929; m 1953, c 3. **Education:** Mankato State Col, BA, 1952; Ore State Univ, MS, 1955; Utah State Univ, PhD (fishery biol, statist), 1962. **Professional Experience:** Vis prof biol, Univ Swaziland, Kwaluseni, Africa, 1983-1985; PROF BIOL, SOUTHERN ORE STATE COL, 1973-; Peace Corps vol serving as Dep to Chief Fisheries Officer, Fisheries Dept Ministry Agr & Natural Resources, Lilongwe, Malawi, EAfrica, 1973-1975; chmn dept, Southern Ore State Col, 1969-1973; from asst prof to assoc prof, Southern Ore State Col, 1964-1973; Consult, Northwest Biol Consults, beginning 1962; asst prof biol, Dakota Wesleyan Univ, 1962-1964; res biologist, Fisheries Res Inst, Univ Wash, 1955-1958; Chemist, Mayo Clin, Minn, 1952-1953. **Memberships:** Am Sci Affil. **Research Statement & Publications:** Physiological effects of radiation; water pollution and abatement; environmental quality and resource management. **Mailing Address:** 899 Hillview Dr, Ashland, OR 97520.

LINN, JOHN CHARLES, COMPUTER SCIENCE, SYSTEMS THEORY. **Personal Data:** b Bellingham, Wash. **Education:** Univ Wash, BS, 1968; Stanford Univ, MS, 1969, PhD (elec eng), 1973. **Professional Experience:** DIR, SYSTS & SOFTWARE LAB, TEX INSTRUMENTS INC, as of 2001; MEM TECH STAFF COMPUT SCI, TEX INSTRUMENTS INC, 1973-; instr comput sci, Stanford Univ, 1972; Res engr laser commun, Honeywell Inc, 1968. **Memberships:** Inst Elec & Electronics Engrs; Asn Comput Mach. **Research Statement & Publications:** Computer architecture; algorithms, memory organization; human speech and language. **Mailing Address:** Tex Instruments Inc, 305 Mail Sta 8373 PO Box 655303, Dallas, TX 75265. **E-Mail:** linn@ti.com

LINN, STUART MICHAEL, MOLECULAR BIOLOGY, NUCLEIC ACIDS. **Personal Data:** b Chicago, Ill, December 16, 1940. **Education:** Calif Inst Technol, BS, 1962; Stanford Univ, PhD (biochem), 1966. **Professional Experience:** PROF & ASSOC DIR MOLECULAR & CELLULAR BIOL, UNIV CALIF, as of 2004; CONSULT, 1990-; head, div biochem & molecular biol, Univ Calif, Berkeley, 1987-1990; Guggenheim fel, 1974-1975; res grants, USPHS, Univ Calif, Berkeley, 1968- & Dept Energy, 1970-; from asst prof to prof biochem, Univ Calif, Berkeley, 1968-1987; Helen Hay Whitney fel, Univ Geneva, 1966-1968; mem, Grad Groups Biophys & Comparative Biochem. **Memberships:** AAAS; Am Soc Microbiol; Am Soc Biol Chemists; Am Acad Arts & Sci; Env Soc. **Research Statement & Publications:** Biochemistry of nucleic acids; nucleic acid enzymes. **Mailing Address:** Dept Molecular & Cell Biol, Univ Calif, 401 Barker Hall 3202, Berkeley, CA 94720-3202. **E-Mail:** slinn@socrates.berkeley.edu

LINN, WILLIAM JOSEPH, ORGANIC CHEMISTRY. **Personal Data:** b Crawfordsville, Ind, July 14, 1927; m 1991, Beverly; c 2. **Education:** Wabash Col, AB, 1950; Univ Rochester, PhD (chem), 1953. **Professional Experience:** RETIRED; res assoc, Northwestern Univ, 1969-1970; E I du Pont de Nemours & Co Inc. **Memberships:** Am Chem Soc; AAAS; Catalysis Soc N Am. **Research Statement & Publications:** Organometallic compounds; heterogeneous and homogeneous catalysis; catalytic oxidation; process chemistry. **Mailing Address:** 1311 Circle Dr, W Chester, PA 19382-8241. **E-Mail:** linn@voicenet.com

LINNA, TIMO JUHANI, CANCER, IMMUNOLOGY. **Personal Data:** b Tavastkyro, Finland, March 16, 1937; m 1961, c 3. **Education:** Univ Uppsala, BMed, 1959, MD, 1965, PhD (histol), 1967. **Professional Experience:** DIR RES, SYNTEX RES, 1990-; res prof microbiol & immunol, Sch Med, Temple Univ, 1980-; group leader, Immunol Control Res & Develop Dept, E I Dupont De Nemours & Co, Inc, Wilmington, 1980-1990; prof, Sch Med, Temple Univ, 1978-1980; consult immunol, UN Develop Prog/World Bank/WHO spec prog for res & training in tropical dis, WHO, Geneva, Switz, 1978-1979; adv clin immunol, Sch Med, Temple Univ, 1972-1980; from asst prof to assoc prof, Sch Med, Temple Univ, 1970-1978; USPHS int res fel, Univ Minn spec res fel, 1970; USPHS int res fel, Univ Minn, Minneapolis, 1968-1970; Asst prof histol, Med Sch, Univ Uppsala, 1967-1971. **Memberships:** Am Soc Exp Path; NY Acad Sci; Reticuloendothelial Soc; Swed Royal Lymphatic Soc; Am Asn Immunologists; Am Asn Cancer Res. **Research Statement & Publications:** Immunobiology; experimental pathology; tumor immunology; cell kinetics. **Mailing Address:** Roche Labs, 3401 Hillview Ave A3-208, Palo Alto, CA 94304-1397.

LINNARTZ, NORWIN EUGENE, forest soils, silviculture; deceased, see previous edition for last biography

LINNELL, ALBERT PAUL, ASTROPHYSICS. **Personal Data:** b Canby, Minn, June 30, m 1993, Ann; c Carol Anne, Paul Huston, John Andrew, Barbara Marie (Westerwick) & James Scott. **Education:** Col Wooster, AB, 1944; Harvard Univ, PhD (astron), 1950; Amherst Col, MA, 1962. **Honorary Degrees:** MA, Amherst Col, 1962. **Professional Experience:** AFFIL. PROF., UNIV. OF WASHINTON 2005- PROF EMER PHYSICS & ASTRON, MICH STATE UNIV, 1991-; prof, Astron Dept, 1966-1991; chmn, Astron Dept, 1966-1976; mem bd dirs, Asn Univs for Res Astron, 1962-1965; Mem adv comt, Comput Ctr, Mass Inst Technol, 1960-1963; From instr to prof astron, Amherst Col, 1949-1966. **Memberships:** Int Astron Union; AAAS; Am Astron Soc; Sigma Xi. **Research Statement & Publications:** Instrumentation for photoelectric photometry; photometry and theory of eclipsing binaries; computer modeling; binary stars including accretion disks; synthetic spectra. **Mailing Address:** Dept Astrophys & Astron, Mich state univ, East Lansing, MI 48824-1116. **Fax:** 206-522-8319. **E-Mail:** linnell@pa.msu.edu

LINNELL, J ANDREW, STORAGE SUBSYSTEMS, VIRTUAL REALITY & THE HUMAN FUTURE. **Personal Data:** b Northampton, Mass, January 18, 1950; div, c David, Nathan & Moriah. **Education:** Univ Mich, BSE, 1972, MSE, 1973. **Professional Experience:** ENG MGR, DIGITAL EQUIP CORP, 1990-; mgr, Digital Equip Corp, 1986-1990; sect mgr II, Wang Labs, 1980-1986; proj leader & engr, IBM, 1973-1980. **Memberships:** Asn Comput Mach; Inst Elec & Electronics Engrs Comput Soc. **Research Statement & Publications:** Network attached storage servers; effects of virtual reality on future culture, society. **Mailing Address:** 23 Blueberry Lane, Peterborough, NH 03458. **E-Mail:** linnell@mail.dec.com

LINNELL, RICHARD D(EAN), AERODYNAMICS. **Personal Data:** b Rapid River Twp, Mich, September 18, 1920; m 1958, c 1. **Education:** Univ NH, BS, 1946; Mass Inst Technol, SM, 1948, ScD(aerodyn eng), 1950. **Professional Experience:** RETIRED; engr, Tracor Inc, 1981-1985; analyst, Ctr Naval Anal, 1962-1979; Chance Vought prof aeronaut eng, Sch Eng, Southern Methodist Univ, 1960-1962; staff scientist aerodyn, Convair Div, Gen Dynamics Corp, 1956-1960; actg mgr aerothermodyn, Gen Elec Co, 1955-1956; aerodyn engr, Convair Div, Gen Dynamics Corp, 1952-1955; sr engr, Mass Inst Technol, 1950-1952; aerodyn engr, Mass Inst Technol, 1949; Aerodyn engr, United Aircraft Corp, 1948. **Memberships:** Am Phys Soc; Am Inst Aeronaut & Astronaut. **Research Statement & Publications:** Systems analysis; fluid mechanics; vehicle design. **Mailing Address:** 154 N Main St Apt 3A, Concord, NH 03301.

LINNELL, ROBERT HARTLEY, ACADEMIC ADMINISTRATION, INSTITUTIONAL RESEARCH. **Personal Data:** b Kalkaska, Mich, August 15, 1922; m 1950, Myrle; c Charlene, Lloyd, Randa & Dean. **Education:** Univ NH, BS, 1944, MS, 1947; Univ Rochester, PhD (chem), 1950. **Professional Experience:** CONSULT, ENVIRON HEALTH & SAFETY, as of 2002; pres, Cent Calif Chap, Am Lung Asn, 1991-1992; mem bd dirs, Cent Calif Chap, Am Lung Asn, 1986-; consult environ health & safety, 1985-; EMER PROF CHEM, UNIV SOUTHERN CALIF, 1985-; chmn, Dept Safety Sci, 1982-1985; Carnegie Corp, 1976-1977 & 1978-1980; Exxon Educ Found, 1974-1976 & 1978-1980; dir, Off Instl Studies, 1970-1982; prof chem, Col Lett, Arts & Sci, Univ Southern Calif, 1969-1985; dean, Col Lett, Arts & Sci, Univ Southern Calif, 1969-1970; dep dir, Dept Develop Prog, 1967-1969; staff assoc planning, NSF, 1965-1967; prog dir phys chem, NSF, 1962-1965; lab dir, Scott Res Labs, 1961-1962; grants, USPHS, 1961-1962; grants, Am Petrol Inst, 1961-1962; grants, NSF, 1959-1961; consult, Tizon Chem Co, 1958-1962; consult, Reheis Corp, 1958-1961; assoc prof chem, Univ Vt, 1958-1961; dir, Tizon Chem Co, 1955-1962; vpres, Tizon Chem Co, 1955-1958; assoc prof & chmn dept, Am Univ Beirut, 1952-1955; grants, Res Corp, 1950-1954 & 1958-1960; asst prof, Am Univ Beirut, 1950-1952; instr chem, Univ NH, 1947; Col Chem Consult Serv, Lake Erie Environ Studies Prog & Environ Protection Agency. **Memberships:** AAAS; Am Chem Soc; Asn Instnl Res; Am Soc Safety Engrs. **Research Statement & Publications:** Hydrogen bonds; air pollution energy planning; science and public policy; science manpower; faculty and staff personnel research (salaries, fringe benefits, policies for consulting, intellectual properties and adult education); student and faculty surveys; higher education evaluation and planning; indoor air pollution; asbestos; radon; environmental health and safety; drunk driving. **Mailing Address:** 82 Stagecoach Rd, White River Junction, VT 05001. **Fax:** 802-295-9575.

LINNEMANN, ROGER E, RADIOLOGY, NUCLEAR MEDICINE. **Personal Data:** b St Cloud, Minn, January 12, 1931; m 1951, c 5. **Education:** Univ Minn, Minneapolis, BA, 1952, BS & MD, 1956; Am Bd Radiol, cert, 1964; Am Bd Nuclear Med, cert, 1972. **Professional Experience:** Vis assoc prof clin radiol, Northwestern Univ Sch Med, 1977-; ASSOC PROF CLIN RADIOL, UNIV PA, 1974-; mem ad hoc comt med aspects radiation accidents, AEC, 1969-; PRES, RADIATION MGT CORP, 1969-; asst prof, Hosp, 1969-1974; nuclear med consult, Philadelphia Elec Co, 1968-; Nat Res Coun James Picker Found res grant radiol, 1968-1969; radiologist, Hosp, 1968-1969; asst prof radiol, Univ Minn, Minneapolis, 1968; cmndg officer, Nuclear Med Res Detachment, US Army, Europe, 1965-1968; US deleg radiation protection comt & panel experts med aspects nuclear biol & chem warfare, NATO, 1965-1968; resident radiol, Walter Reed Army Hosp, 1962-1965; res assoc radiobiol, Walter Reed Army Hosp, 1961-1962; physician, US Army, Europe, 1957-1961; Intern, Walter Reed Army Hosp, 1956-1957; res scholar, Univ Minn. **Memberships:** AMA; Am Col Radiol; Am Nuclear Soc; Am Pub Health Asn; Indust Med Asn. **Research Statement & Publications:** Medical aspects of nuclear industry accidents; kidney function studies using isotopes; radiological health. **Mailing Address:** Radiation Mgt Consult, Tacony St, Box 208, Philadelphia, PA 19137-2309.

LINNERUD, ARDELL CHESTER, EXPERIMENTAL STATISTICS. **Personal Data:** b Whitehall, Wis, April 9, 1931; m 1956. **Education:** Wis State Univ River Falls, BS, 1953; Univ Minn, MS, 1962, PhD (dairy husb), 1964. **Professional Experience:** EMER ASSOC PROF STATIST, NC STATE UNIV, 2002-; assoc prof statist, NC State Univ, 1975-2002; Statist consult, Inst for Aerobics Res, 1974-; asst prof statist, NC State Univ, 1967-1975; fel biomath, NC State Univ, 1964-1967; consult biomet, Univ Minn, 1964; Res asst dairy husb, Univ Minn, 1957-1963. **Memberships:** Am Dairy Sci Asn; Am Soc Animal Sci. **Research Statement & Publications:** Design of experiments and mathematical model building; animal science and exercise physiology. **Mailing Address:** 1309 DeBoy St, Raleigh, NC 27606.

LINNSTAEDTER, JERRY LEROY, MATHEMATICS. **Personal Data:** b Lindale, Tex, July 25, 1937; m 1962, Julie; c Jean, Joan & Jane. **Education:** Tex A&M Univ, BA, 1959, MS, 1961; Vanderbilt Univ, PhD (math), 1970. **Professional Experience:** PRES, INPAC LEARNING SYST INC, 1995-; ASSOC VICE CHANCELLOR, ARK STATE UNIV, 1997-; assoc dean arts & sci, Ark State Univ, 1995-1997; PROF MATH, ARK STATE UNIV, 1971-; res grant, Ark State Univ, 1969-1971; chmn, Dept Comput Sci, Math & Physics, 1968-1995; assoc prof, Ark State Univ, 1968-1971; instr, Vanderbilt Univ, 1967-1968; instr math, Northeast La Univ, 1961-1963; mem, Ark Comn Improving Pub Sch Basic Skill Opportunities; prin investr, NASA. **Memberships:** Am Math Soc; Math Asn Am; Sigma Xi. **Research Statement & Publications:** Multistage calculus of variations; classical analysis; multi stage bolza problems and related control problems; trajectory analysis; Zermelo flow problems. **Mailing Address:** Po box 877, State Univ, AR 72467. **Fax:** 870-972-3849. **E-Mail:** linnstaedter@astate.edu

LINOWSKI, JOHN WALTER, PHYSICAL CHEMISTRY, ANALYTICAL CHEMISTRY. **Personal Data:** b Boston, Mass, July 7, 1945; m 1972, Rosemary Bodo. **Education:** Boston Col, BS, 1967; Canisius Col, MS, 1970; Rutgers Univ, PhD (phys chem), 1974. **Honors & Awards:** Rieman Award 1976. **Professional Experience:** GLOBAL DIR CATALYSIS TECHNOL, DOW CHEM CO, 1992-; lab dir, Dow Chem Co, 1991-1992; sr res mgr, Dow Chem Co, 1991; res mgr, Dow Chem Co, 1987-1991; group leader, Dow Chem Co, 1982-1987; res leader, Dow Chem Co, 1981-1982; sr res chemist, Dow Chem Co, 1976-1981; Res assoc molecular dynamics, Univ Ill, 1974-1976. **Memberships:** Am Chem Soc; Sci Res Soc NAm; Sigma Xi. **Research Statement & Publications:** Dynamic nuclear polarization; molecular dynamics of liquids at high pressure and extreme temperatures; nuclear magnetic resonance; catalysis; process chemistry. **Mailing Address:** 702 Lake Rd, Lake Jackson, TX 77566.

LINS, THOMAS WESLEY, MARINE GEOLOGY, STRUCTURAL GEOLOGY. **Personal Data:** b November 24, 1923; American citizen; m 1969. **Education:** Cornell Univ, BS, 1948; Univ Kans, MS, 1959, PhD (geol), 1969. **Professional Experience:** RETIRED; from asst prof to assoc prof geol & geog, Miss State Univ, 1974-1989; asst prof geol, Lamar Univ, 1968-1974; res geologist, Monsanto Chem Co, 1961-1963; div geologist, Monsanto Chem Co, 1960-1961; asst div geologist, Monsanto Chem Co, 1957-1960; dist geologist, Monsanto Chem Co, 1951-1957; dist geologist, Sunray Oil Corp, 1950-1951. **Memberships:** AAAS; Geol Soc Am. **Research Statement & Publications:** Tectonics, structure of island arcs and trenches, recent sedimentation of the Gulf of Mexico. **Mailing Address:** PO Box 5167, Mississippi State, MS 39762.

LINSAY, ERNEST CHARLES, ORGANIC CHEMISTRY. **Personal Data:** b Cleveland, Ohio, May 3, 1942; m 1966, Jane; c 3. **Education:** Yale Univ, BS, 1963; Univ Wis-Madison, PhD (org chem), 1968. **Professional Experience:** MGR, HERCULES INC, as of 2003; RES SCIENTIST, COATINGS & ADDITIVES, HERCULES INC, 1987-; res & develop supt, Organics Dept, 1986-1987; tech supt, Organics Dept, 1983-1986; from res chemist to sr res chemist, Organics Dept, 1968-1983. **Memberships:** Am Chem Soc; Soc Automotive Engrs. **Research Statement & Publications:** Physical organic chemistry; rosin and fatty acids; dispersions and emulsions; rosin-, terpene- and hydrocarbon-based resins; coatings; nitrocellulose; jet engine lucricants; wood preservatives. **Mailing Address:** Hercules, Inc, 1313 N Market St, Wilmington, DE 19894-0001. **Fax:** 302-594-5400.

LINSCHITZ, HENRY, PHYSICAL CHEMISTRY. **Personal Data:** b New York, NY, August 18, 1919; m 1964, c 1. **Education:** City Col New York, BS, 1940; Duke Univ, MA, 1941, PhD (chem), 1946. **Professional Experience:** PROF EMER CHEM, BRANDEIS UNIV, 2002-; guggenheim fel, Weizmann Inst, 1971-1972; study sect comt photobiol, Nat Res Coun, 1964-1969; study sect biophys & biophys chem, NIH, 1962-1966; mem adv comt space biol, NASA, 1960-1961; Fulbright vis prof, Hebrew Univ, Israel, 1960; prof chem, Brandeis Univ, 1959-2002; chmn dept, Brandeis Univ, beginning 1958; assoc prof, Brandeis Univ, 1957-1959; vis scientist, Brookhaven Nat Lab, 1956-1957; from asst prof to assoc prof chem, Syracuse Univ, 1948-1957; fel, Inst Nuclear Studies, Univ Chicago, 1946-1948; sect leader, Los Alamos Sci Lab, 1943-1945; mem staff, explosives res lab, Nat Defense Res Comt, 1943. **Memberships:** AAAS; Am Chem Soc; Am Acad Arts & Sci; Fedn Am Scientists. **Research Statement & Publications:** Photochemistry; spectroscopy and luminescence of complex molecules; photobiology. **Mailing Address:** Dept Chem, Brandeis Univ, 415 S St, Waltham, MA 02454. **Fax:** 781-736-2516. **E-Mail:** linschitz@brandeis.edu

LINSCOTT, WILLIAM DEAN, IMMUNOLOGY. **Personal Data:** b Bakersfield, Calif, April 23, 1930; m 1955, c 3. **Education:** Univ Calif, Los Angeles, BA, 1951, PhD (infectious dis), 1960. **Professional Experience:** RETIRED; From asst prof to prof microbiol, Med Ctr, Univ Calif, San Francisco, 1964-1985; Div Exp Path, Scripps Clin & Res Found, Calif, 1962-1964; USPHS res fels, Labs Microbiol, Howard Hughes Med Inst, Fla, 1960-1962; publ, Linscott's Dir Immunol & Biol Reagents. **Research Statement & Publications:** Complement; immunologic unresponsiveness. **Mailing Address:** 4877 Grange Rd, Santa Rosa, CA 95404.

LINSENMEIER, ROBERT A, BIOMEDICAL ENGINEERING. **Education:** Northwestern Univ, PhD. **Professional Experience:** PROF, DEPT BIOMED ENG, NORTHWESTERN UNIV, ILL, as of 2005. **Mailing Address:** Biomed Eng Dept, Technol Inst Northwestern Univ, Evanston, IL 60208. **Fax:** 847-491-4928.

LINSHAW, MICHAEL A, PEDIATRICS. **Education:** Tufts Univ Sch Med, MD. **Professional Experience:** PEDIAT NEPHROLOGIST, MASS GEN HOSP C, BOSTON, as of 2005. **Mailing Address:** Mass Gen Hosp C, Po Box 11218, Boston, MA 02211. **Fax:** 617-724-0581.

LINSKY, CARY BRUCE, BIOLOGICAL CHEMISTRY. **Personal Data:** b Chicago, Ill, June 9, 1942; m 1968, c 2. **Education:** Univ Wis-Madison, BS, 1964; Loyola Univ, PhD (biochem), 1971. **Professional Experience:** RETIRED; prod dir, Ethicon Inc, beginning 2002; asst mgr, Johnson & Johnson, beginning 1980; res assoc, beginning 1971. **Memberships:** Am Chem Soc; Sigma Xi; Am Burn Asn. **Research Statement & Publications:** Role of inflammatory response and local environment in cutaneous wound healing; cellular components of inflammation; scar formation in surgical wounds; collagen biochemistry; hemostasis; prevention of post surgical adhesions. **Mailing Address:** 25 Beacon Hill Dr, East Brunswick, NJ 08816.

LINSKY, JEFFREY L, SPACE PHYSICS, SOLAR PHYSICS. **Personal Data:** b Buffalo, NY, June 27, 1941; m 1967, Lois; c 2. **Education:** Mass Inst Technol, BS, 1963; Harvard Univ, MS, 1965, PhD (astron), 1968. **Honors & Awards:** NASA Medal for Except Sci Achievement, NASA, 1988; NASA Group Achievement Award, 1991; NASA Goddard Except Achievement Award, 1994. **Professional Experience:** RES PROF, DEPT ASTROPHYS, PLANETARY & ATMOSPHERIC SCI, UNIV COLO 1996-; FEL, CTR ASTROPHYS & SPACE ASTRON, UNIV COLO 1986-; prof adjoint, Dept Astrophys, Planetary & Atmospheric Sci, 1979-1995; assoc prof adjoint, Dept Astrophys, Planetary & Atmospheric Sci, 1974-1979; consult, NASA, 1972-; fel, Joint Inst Lab Astrophys, 1971-; FEL, JOINT INST LAB ASTROPHYS, UNIV COLO 1971-; astronomer, Quantum Physics Div, Nat Inst Stand & Technol, 1969-1995; lectr, Dept Physics & Astrophys, & Dept Astrogeophys, Univ Colo, beginning 1969; mem, Joint Inst Lab Astrophys, 1968-1971; res assoc, Univ Colo, 1968-1969. **Memberships:** Am Astron Soc (counr, 1995-1998); Int Astron Union. **Research Statement & Publications:** Radiative transfer; formation of spectral lines in the solar and stellar chromospheres; atmospheres of latetype stars; stellar coronae; ultraviolet and x-ray astronomy from space. **Mailing Address:** Joint Inst Lab Astrophys, Univ Colo, Campus Box 440, Boulder, CO 80309-0440. **Fax:** 303-492-5235. **E-Mail:** jlinsky@jila.colorado.edu

LINSLEY, JOHN, PHYSICS, ASTRONOMY. **Personal Data:** b Minneapolis, Minn, March 12, 1925; m 1966, c 3. **Education:** Univ Minn, BPhys, 1947, PhD (physics), 1952. **Professional Experience:** RETIRED; res prof physics, Univ NMex, beginning 1977; adj prof, Univ NMex, 1972-1977; res assoc, Mass Inst Technol, 1958-1972; asst prof, Mass Inst Technol, 1955-1958; res assoc, Mass Inst Technol, 1954-1955; res fel, Univ Minn, 1952-1954; asst prof physics, Univ Va, 1951-1952. **Memberships:** Fel Am Phys Soc; Sigma Xi; Am Astron Soc. **Research Statement & Publications:** Origin and behavior of highest-energy cosmic rays by means of experimental and theoretical investigations of extensive air showers. **Mailing Address:** 1712 Old Town Rd NW, Albuquerque, NM 87104.

LINSLEY, PETER SEAN, GENERAL BIOLOGY. **Personal Data:** m Leslie; c Jeremy & Drew. **Education:** Univ Calif, Los Angeles, PhD (molecular biol), 1980. **Professional Experience:** VPRES & SENIOR DIR, RES & DEVLOP, ROSETTA INPHARMATICS, INC, 1997-; sr scientist & sr res fel, Bristol-Myers Squibb, 1983-1997. **Memberships:** AAAS; Am Asn Internists. **Research Statement & Publications:** T lymphocyte costimulatory receptors. **Mailing Address:** Rosetta Inpharmatics, Inc, 12040-115th Ave, NE, Kirkland, WA 98034. **E-Mail:** tadpole1@haleyon.com

LINSLEY, ROBERT MARTIN, INVERTEBRATE PALEONTOLOGY. **Personal Data:** b Chicago, Ill, February 19, 1930; div. **Education:** Univ Mich, BS, 1952, MS, 1953, PhD (geol), 1960. **Professional Experience:** HAROLD ORVILLE WHITNALL PROF EMER GEOL, COLGATE UNIV, 1992-; Harold Orville Whitnall prof, Colgate Univ, 1978-1992; chmn dept, Colgate Univ, 1964-1971; dir natural sci course, Colgate Univ, 1962-1970; phys sci course, Colgate Univ, 1959-1964; from instr to prof, Colgate Univ, 1955-1978; Ford intern Colgate Univ, Colgate Univ, 1954-1955; trustee emer, Paleont Res Inst. **Memberships:** AAAS; Geol Soc Am; Paleont Soc; Soc Study Evolution; Sigma Xi. **Research Statement & Publications:** Evolution, functional morphology; behavior and taxonomy of Gastropoda. **Mailing Address:** Dept Geol, Colgate Univ, 13 Oak Dr, Hamilton, NY 13346. **Fax:** 315-228-7187.

LINSTEDT, KERMIT DANIEL, WATER REUSE, WATER & WASTE WATER TREATMENT. **Personal Data:** b Portland, Ore, November 6, 1940; m 1964, Cynthia; c Jennifer E, Melissa L & Joseph P. **Education:** Ore State Univ, BS, 1962; Stanford Univ, MS, 1963, PhD (sanit eng), 1968. **Honors & Awards:** Dow Award, Am Soc Eng Educrs, 1972; Bedell Award, Water Pollution Control Fedn, 1973; Res Div Award, Am Water Works Asn, 1978. **Professional Experience:** RETIRED; sr partner, Black & Veatch, Denver, 1992-1994; partner, Black & Veatch, Denver, 1989-1992; regional off mgr, Black & Veatch, Denver, 1988-1994; proj mgr, Black & Veatch, Denver, 1981-1988; Consult, Denver Metro

Dist, 1969-1971 & Environ Protection Agency, 1978-1981; from asst prof to prof sanit eng, Dept Civil & Environ Eng, Univ Colo, 1967-1981; sanit engr asst, Los Angeles Dept Water & Power, 1961-1962. **Memberships:** Water Environ Fedn; Am Water Works Asn. **Research Statement & Publications:** Treatment methods for water reuse; characterization and treatment of oil shale retort water. **Mailing Address:** 1709 W Brookhaven Circle, Ft Collins, CO 80525.

LINSTONE, HAROLD A, CORPORATE PLANNING, FORECASTING. **Personal Data:** b Hamburg, Ger, June 15, 1924; m 1946, c Fred & Clark. **Education:** City Col NY, BS, 1944; Columbia Univ, MA, 1947; Univ Southern Calif, PhD (math), 1954. **Professional Experience:** Vis prof, Univ Kiel, 1989; UNIV PROF EMER, PORTLAND STATE UNIV, 1986-; Univ Calif, Riverside, 1985-1986; prof systs sci, Portland State Univ, 1977-1986; vis prof, Univ Wash, 1977; vis prof, Univ Rome, 1974; pres, Systs Forecasting Inc, 1970-; consult, IBM, Electric Power Resource Inst, Atlantic Richfield Co, Weyerhauser, Nero & Assocs, Inc, UN Asian-Pac Ctr Technol Transfer, 1970-; dir systs sci PhD prog, Portland State Univ, 1970-1977; Ed-in-chief, Technol Forecasting & Social Change, 1969-; assoc dir corp develop planning, Lockheed Aircraft Corp, 1963-1970; Sr scientist, Hughes Aircraft Co, 1949-1961 & Rand Corp, 1961-1963. **Memberships:** Opers Res Soc Am; Inst Mgt Sci; Int Soc Systs Sci (pres 1993-1994). **Research Statement & Publications:** Multiple perspectives for decision making; technological forecasting; futures research; corporate planning; risk analysis; systems science; policy analysis. **Mailing Address:** Dept Sys Sci, Portland State Univ, PO Box 751, Portland, OR 97207-0751. **Fax:** 503-725-4991. **E-Mail:** hwhl@pdx.edu

LINSTROMBERG, WALTER WILLIAM, ORGANIC CHEMISTRY. **Personal Data:** b Beaufort, Mo, October 30, 1912; m 1943, c 2. **Education:** Univ Mo, AB, 1937, MA, 1950, PhD (chem), 1955. **Professional Experience:** RETIRED; vis prof & res assoc, Univ Nebr, 1960; Vis prof, Utah State Univ, 1957; from asst prof to prof org chem, Univ Nebr, Omaha, 1955-1978; Instr chem, Univ Mo, 1952-1955. **Memberships:** Am Chem Soc; Sigma Xi. **Research Statement & Publications:** Pharmaceutical chemistry. **Mailing Address:** 630 S 90th St, Omaha, NE 68114-5114.

LINSTROMBERG, WILLIAM J, MECHANICAL ENGINEERING. **Professional Experience:** FEL, AM SOC HEATING & REFRIGERATING & AIR-CONDITIONING, as of 2003. **Mailing Address:** 1583 St Joseph Circle, St Joseph, MI 49085.

LINT, THOMAS F, IMMUNOLOGY. **Personal Data:** b Pittsburgh, Pa, December 22, 1946. **Education:** Univ Dayton, BS, 1968; Tulane Univ, PhD (biochem), 1973. **Professional Experience:** ASSOC CHMN, DEPT IMMUNOL, RUSH UNIV MED CTR, as of 2004; PROF IMMUNOL, RUSH UNIV MED CTR, 1990-; from asst prof to assoc prof, Rush Univ Med Ctr, 1975-1990; fel immunochem, Rush Univ Med Ctr, 1973-1975. **Memberships:** Am Asn Immunologists; Am Fedn Clin Res; Clin Immunol Soc. **Mailing Address:** Dept Immunol & Microbiol, Rush Univ Med Ctr, 1653 W Congress Pkwy, Chicago, IL 60612. **Fax:** 312-942-2808.

LINTNER, CARL JOHN, JR, PHARMACEUTICAL CHEMISTRY. **Personal Data:** b Louisville, Ky, July 15, 1917; m 1948, c Laura & Jack. **Education:** Univ Ky, BS, 1940; Univ Wis, PhD (pharmaceut chem), 1950. **Honors & Awards:** W E Upjohn Award Distinguished Kentuckian, Louisville Male High Hall of Fame. **Professional Experience:** CONSULT, 1982-; Adj prof, Fla A&M Univ, Col Pharm, 1975-; sect head, Upjohn Co, 1955-1982; Res chemist, Upjohn Co, 1950-1955. **Memberships:** AAAS; fel Acad Pharmaceut Sci; Am Pharmaceut Asn. **Research Statement & Publications:** Organic synthesis; determination of functional groups; essential oil determination; kinetic studies; chromatography and ion exchange resins; phytochemistry; tablet coatings; ointment bases; chemistry of antibiotics; instrumentation tablet compression; pharmaceutical product stability. **Mailing Address:** 2125 Aberdeen Dr, Kalamazoo, MI 49008.

LINTON, EVERETT PERCIVAL, PHYSICAL CHEMISTRY. **Personal Data:** b St John West, NB, December 30, 1906; m 1980, c 3. **Education:** Mt Allison Univ, BSc, 1928; McGill Univ, MSc, 1930, PhD (chem), 1932. **Honorary Degrees:** DSc, Acadia Univ, 1978. **Professional Experience:** RETIRED; head dept, Acadia Univ, 1966-1975; prof chem, Acadia Univ, 1944-1975; asst phys chemist, Fisheries Res Bd, Halifax, 1941-1944; instr chem, Acadia Univ, 1936-1941; chemist, Biol Bd Can, Halifax, NS, 1934-1936; Royal Soc Can fel, Univ Munich, 1932-1933; Instr chem, Mt Allison Univ, 1928-1929. **Memberships:** Am Chem Soc. **Research Statement & Publications:** Preparation of hydrogen peroxide; measurement of dielectric constants; interaction of neutral molecules; air-drying solids; smokes; colloidal chemistry; dipole moments of amine oxides; drying and smoke curing of fish. **Mailing Address:** 39 Highland Ave, Wolfville, NS B0P 1X0, Can.

LINTON, FRED E J, MATHEMATICS, CATEGORY THEORY. **Personal Data:** b Italy, April 8, 1938; American citizen; m 1990. **Education:** Yale Univ, BS, 1958; Columbia Univ, MA, 1959, PhD (math), 1963. **Honorary Degrees:** MA, Wesleyan Univ, 1972. **Honors & Awards:** Hon Gold Medal, Polytech Univ Blagoevgrad, Bulgaria, 1987. **Professional Experience:** Chmn dept, Wesleyan Univ, 1975; PROF MATH, WESLEYAN UNIV, 1972-; Izaak Walton Killam sr res fel, Dalhousie Univ, 1969-1970; Nat Res Coun res fel, Swiss Fed Inst Technol, 1966-1967; Res assoc, Univ Chicago, 1964-1965; From asst prof to assoc prof, Wesleyan Univ, 1963-1972. **Memberships:** Am Math Soc; Math Asn Am. **Research Statement & Publications:** Categorical algebra, a branch of positive speculative philosophy. **Mailing Address:** Dept Math, Wesleyan Univ, Wesleyan Sta, Middletown, CT 06459. **E-Mail:** flinton@wesleyan.edu

LINTON, RICHARD WILLIAM, SURFACE SPECTROSCOPY, MICROBEAM ANALYSIS. **Personal Data:** b Scranton, Pa, April 17, 1951. **Education:** Univ Del, BS, 1973; Univ Ill, MS, 1975, PhD (chem), 1977. **Honors & Awards:** Outstanding Young Scientist Award, Microbeam Anal Soc, 1990; Presidential Serv Award, 1995. **Professional Experience:** VPRES RES & GRAD STUDIES & DEAN, GRAD SCH, UNIV ORE, as of 2004; PROF CHEM, UNIV ORE, as of 2004; Consult, Monsanto, 1992-; assoc vpres res, Univ NC, Chapel Hill, beginning 1991; ed-in-chief, Microbeam Anal J, 1991-1996; vis scholar, Chem Res Prom Ctr, Nat Sci Coun, Taiwan, 1991; prof chem, Univ NC, Chapel Hill, beginning 1989; consult, Glaxo Inc, 1989-1991; asst vpres res, Univ NC, Chapel Hill, 1986-1991; vis prof, Univ Antwerp, Belg, 1986; From asst prof to assoc prof, Univ NC, Chapel Hill, 1977-1988; current prin investr, ARO, Environ Protection Agency, USDA. **Memberships:** Am Chem Soc; Microbeam Analysis Soc; Micros Soc Am; Am Soc Mass Spectrometry; Am Vacuum Soc; Nat Coun Univ Res Adminr. **Research Statement & Publications:** Surface and microprobe techniques for chemical analysis (dynamic and static SIMS, XPS); biological microanalysis; ion beam-surface interactions; environmental analytical chemistry; chemistry and characterization of polymer surfaces. **Mailing Address:** Dept Chem, Grad Sch, Univ Ore, 125 Chapman Hall, Eugene, OR 97403-1219. **Fax:** 541-346-2804. **E-Mail:** rlinton@uoregon.edu

LINTON, THOMAS LARUE, FISHERIES. **Personal Data:** b Carlisle, Tex, July 25, 1935; m 1961, c 2. **Education:** Lamar State Col, BS, 1959; Univ Okla, MS, 1961; Univ Mich, PhD (fisheries), 1965. **Professional Experience:** PROF, DEPT WILDLIFE & FISHERIES SCI, TEX A&M UNIV, 2002-; mem staff, NC Dept Natural & Econ Resources, 1973-1980; mem staff, Div Com Sports Fisheries, NC Dept Conserv & Develop, 1970-1973; asst prof, Univ Ga, 1967-1970; res grants, US Dept Interior, beginning 1966; res grants, Ga Game & Fish Comn, 1965-1968; res assoc, Univ Ga, 1965-1967; Ga rep biol comt, Atlantic State Marine Fisheries Comn, 1964-1966; res asst zool, Univ Ga, 1963-1965. **Memberships:** AAAS; Am Fisheries Soc. **Research Statement & Publications:** Physiology; commercial and sport fisheries; pollution ecology. **Mailing Address:** Dept Wildlife & Fisheries Sci, Tex A&M Univ, 210 Nagle Hall, College Station, TX 77843-0100. **Fax:** 979-845-7750. **E-Mail:** t-linton@tamu.edu

LINTVEDT, RICHARD LOWELL, PHYSICAL INORGANIC CHEMISTRY. **Personal Data:** b Edgerton, Wis, June 23, 1937; m 1959, c 3. **Education:** Lawrence Univ, BA, 1959; Univ Nebr, PhD (inorg chem), 1966. **Professional Experience:** Chmn dept, Wayne State Univ, beginning 1983; Dept energy grant, 1978-1983; PROF CHEM, WAYNE STATE UNIV, beginning 1976; NSF grant, 1976-1990; assoc prof, Wayne State Univ, 1971-1976; res Corp grant, 1969-1971; asst prof inorg chem, Wayne State Univ, 1966-1971; petrol res fund grant, 1966-1968, 1970-1973, 1976-1978 & 1984-1986; res chemist, chem div, Morton Int, 1959-1962. **Memberships:** Am Chem Soc; fel AAAS. **Research Statement & Publications:** Electronic structure and bonding in inorganic coordination and chelate compounds; electrochemistry; physical inorganic chemistry; magnetochemistry of transition metal complexes. **Mailing Address:** Dept Chem, Wayne State Univ, Rm 479 221 Chem Bldg, Detroit, MI 48202. **E-Mail:** rll@chem.wayne.edu

LINTZ, JOSEPH JR, GEOLOGY. **Personal Data:** b New York, NY, June 15, 1921; m 1944, c 3. **Education:** Williams Col, AB, 1942; Univ Okla, MS, 1947; Johns Hopkins Univ, PhD (geol), 1956. **Professional Experience:** PROF EMER GEOL, MACKAY SCH MINES, UNIV NEV, RENO, 1994-; actg dean, Univ Nev, Reno, 1981-1982; consult, Atomic Energy Comn, 1971-1979; consult, Econ Comm Asia & Far East, UN, 1971 & 1974; Nat Acad Sci-Nat Res Coun res assoc, Manned Spacecraft Ctr, Tex, 1966-1967; prof geol, Univ Nev, Reno, beginning 1965; vis prof, Bandung Tech Inst, 1959-1961; assoc geologist, Nev Bur Mines, beginning 1956; from asst prof to assoc prof, Univ Nev, Reno, 1951-1965; asst geologist, Nev Bur Mines, 1951-1956; instr, Mt Lake Biol Sta, Va, 1951; geologist, Pure Oil Co, 1949; Jr geologist, Gen Petrol Corp, 1947-1948. **Memberships:** Paleont Soc; Am Asn Petrol Geol; AAAS. **Research Statement & Publications:** Remote sensing of environment; petroleum possibilities and Pennsylvanian system of Nevada. **Mailing Address:** Geol Sci Dept, Mackay Sch Mines, Univ Nev, Reno, NV 89557.

LIN-VIEN, DAIMAY, INFRARED-SPECTROSCOPTIST, POLYMER SPECTROSCOPIST. **Personal Data:** Taiwanese citizen; c 1. **Education:** Kans State Univ, PhD (anal chem), 1988. **Professional Experience:** SR RES CHEMIST ANALYSIS CHEM, SHELL DEVELOP CO, 1997-; assoc res chemist, Shell Develop Co, 1988-1997. **Memberships:** Soc Appl Spectros; Coblenz Soc. **Research Statement & Publications:** Analytical applications of fourier transform infrared spectroscopy; fourier transform infrared microspectroscopy; raman spectroscopy; polymer characterization; polymer-polymer interaction; additive-polymer interaction. **Mailing Address:** 4415 Warwick Dr, Sugar Land, TX 77479.

LINVILL, JOHN G(RIMES), ELECTRICAL ENGINEERING, SOLID-STATE ELECTRONICS. **Personal Data:** b Kansas City, Mo, August 8, 1919. **Education:** William Jewell Col, AB, 1941; Mass Inst Technol, SB, 1943, SM, 1945, ScD(elec eng), 1949. **Honorary Degrees:** DApplSci, Cath Univ Louvain, 1966; DSc, William Jewell Col, 1992. **Honors & Awards:** Educ Medal, Inst Elec & Electronics Engrs, 1976; John Scott Award, 1980; Medal Achievement, Am Electronics Asn, 1983; Louis Braille Prize, Deutscher Blindenverband, 1984. **Professional Experience:** EMER PROF ELEC ENG, STANFORD UNIV, 1989-; prof integrated systs & dir, Ctr Integrated Systs, 1981-1991; assoc dean, Sch Eng, 1972-1980; Co-founder & dir, Telesensory Systs, Inc, 1971-; chmn dept, Stanford Univ, 1964-1980; prof elec eng, Sch Eng, 1957-1989; assoc prof elec eng, Stanford Univ, 1955-1957; mem tech staff, Bell Tel Labs, Inc, 1951-1955; Asst prof elec eng, Mass Inst Technol, 1949-1951. **Memberships:** Nat Acad Eng; fel Inst Elec & Electronics Engrs; fel AAAS; fel Am Acad Arts & Sci. **Research Statement & Publications:** Custom integrated circuits and systems as sensory aids for the blind. **Mailing Address:** Dept Elec Eng, Stanford Univ, Stanford, CA 94305-4070.

LINVILLE, RAYMOND NEAL, Speech Science. **Education:** Iowa Univ, PhD. **Professional Experience:** ASSOC DEAN, WALDRON COL HEALTH & HUMAN SERV, RADFORD UNIV, as of 2006; DIR, DEPT COMMUN SCI & DIS, RADFORD UNIV, as of 2006. **Mailing Address:** Dept Commun Sci & Dis, Radford Uni, POBox 6961, Radford, VA 24142. **Fax:** 540-831-7669. **E-Mail:** rlinvill@radford.edu

LINVILLE, T M, ELECTRICAL ENGINEERING. **Professional Experience:** PROF & DEAN, UNIV VA SCH ENG & APPL SCI, as of 2004. **Mailing Address:** Univ Va Sch Eng & Appl Sci, PO Box 400246, Charlottesville, VA 22904.

LINZ, PETER, COMPUTER SCIENCE. **Personal Data:** b Apatin, Yugoslavia, July 19, 1936; American citizen; m 1982, c 2. **Education:** McGill Univ, BSc, 1957; Univ Mich, MS, 1960; Univ Wis, PhD (comput sci), 1968. **Professional Experience:** PROF EMER COMPUT SCI, UNIV CALIF, DAVIS, 2002-; prof, comput sci, Univ Calif, Davis, 1983-2002; prof math, Davis, 1977-1983; from asst prof to assoc prof, Davis, 1970-1977; asst prof comput sci, NY Univ, 1968-1970; staff specialist numerical anal, Comput Ctr, Univ Wis, 1965-1968; assoc programmer, IBM Corp, 1963-1965; res engr, Dominion Eng Ltd, 1957-1959. **Research Statement & Publications:** Numerical analysis; quadrature methods; solution and applications of integral equations; numerical software. **Mailing Address:** Dept Comput Sci, Col Eng, Univ Calif, 3021 Kemper Hall, Davis, CA 95616. **Fax:** 530-752-4767. **E-Mail:** linz@cs.ucdavis.edu

LINZER, MELVIN, ULTRASOUND, PHYSICAL CHEMISTRY. **Personal Data:** b New York, NY, August 5, 1937; m 1964, c 4. **Education:** Brooklyn Col, BS, 1957; Princeton Univ, MA, 1959, PhD (chem), 1962. **Honors & Awards:** Ross Coffin Purdy Award, Am Ceramic Soc, 1975; US Dept Commerce Gold Medal Award, 1977; Nat Bur Stands Appl Res Award, 1978. **Professional Experience:** GROUP LEADER, FRACTURE & DEFORMATION DIV, 1981-; ed-in-Chief, Ultrasonic Imaging, 1979-; chmn, Int Symp on Ultrasonic Mat Characterization, 1978-; group leader signal processing & imaging, Fracture & Deformation Div, 1978-1981; co chair, Ultrasonic Tissue Signature Working Group, 1976-1978; chmn, Int Symp Ultrasonic Imaging & Tissue Characterization, 1975-; PHYSICAL CHEMIST, NAT BUR STANDS, 1963-; Nat Acad Sci-Nat Res Coun fel, Fracture & Deformation Div, 1961-1963; res assoc chem, Princeton Univ, 1961. **Memberships:** Am Phys Soc; Am Inst Ultrasound in Med; Sigma Xi. **Research Statement & Publications:** Nondestructive evaluation; ultrasound medical diagnosis; acoustic emission; laser spectroscopy; combustion diagnostics; magnetic resonance spectroscopy; measurement techniques for spectroscopic and materials applications; shock wave structure. **Mailing Address:** 2 Fulham Ct, Silver Spring, MD 20902.

LINZEY, ALICIA VOGT, POPULATION & COMMUNITY ECOLOGY OF MAMMALS, CONSERVATION BIOLOGY. **Personal Data:** b Bloomingburg, NY, January 27, 1943; m 2005, Arthur; c David W & Thomas A. **Education:** Cornell Univ, BS, 1964, MS, 1965; Va Polytech Inst & State Univ, Ph.D., 1981. **Professional Experience:** Emeritus Prof Biol, Ind Univ PA, 2004-; Interim Vice Provost for Research and Dean of Graduate Studies, Ind Univ PA, 2002-2004; Prof Biol Ind Univ Pa, 1988-2004; Fulbright fel, Sub-Saharan Africa Reg Res Prog, 1992-1993; Assoc Prof Ind Univ PA, 1985-1988; Asst Prof, Ind Univ PA, 1982-1985; Asst prof biol, Roanoke Col, 1981-1982. **Memberships:** Am Soc Mammalogists (bd dirs 1988-; 2nd v pres, 1993-1994; 1st v pres, 1994-1996; pres, 1996-1998); Ecol Soc Am; Soc Conserv Biol; Am Inst Biol Sci; Zool Soc Southern Africa. **Research Statement & Publications:** Population and community ecology of small mammals; related applied areas in conservation biology, including responses to habitat disturbance selection of sites for mammal conserv, species of special concern; ecology and distribution of sibling species of Aethomys in Southern Africa. **Mailing Address:** Dept Biol, Ind Univ Pa, Indiana, PA 15705-0001. **Fax:** 724-357-5700. **E-Mail:** avlinzey@iup.edu

LIOI, ANTHONY PASQUALE, FLUID MECHANICS. **Personal Data:** b Pittsburgh, Pa, May 15, 1949; m 1975, c 5. **Education:** Univ Pittsburgh, BS, 1971; Drexel Univ, MS, 1976, PhD (biomed eng), 1979. **Professional Experience:** CO-PRIN INVESTR, RES SCIENTIST & MGR, MED DEVICES, NU-TECH INDUST INC, 1986-; prin investr, Univ Utah Artificial Heart Res Lab, 1985-1986; co-prin investr, Univ Utah Artificial Heart Res Lab, 1982-1985; res instr surg, Univ Utah Artificial Heart Res Lab, 1979-1986. **Research Statement & Publications:** Artificial heart research; development of automatic physiolosic control methods and the design and development of a miniature hydraulic pump drive system for the artificial heart; blood pump design. **Mailing Address:** 1305 Round Rock, W Cove, Round Rock, TX 78681.

LIONETTI, FABIAN JOSEPH, BIOCHEMISTRY. **Personal Data:** b Jersey City, NJ, March 3, 1918; m 1943, c Karen, Fabian Jr & Donald. **Education:** NY Univ, AB, 1943, MS, 1945; Rensselaer Polytech Inst, PhD (phys chem), 1948. **Honors & Awards:** Mathewson Medal, Am Inst Metals, 1952. **Professional Experience:** SR INVESTR EMER, CTR BLOOD RES, as of 2000; sr investr, Ctr Blood Res, beginning 1968; assoc mem, Inst Health Sci, Brown Univ, 1965-1968; from instr to assoc prof biochem, Sch Med, Boston Univ, 1949-1965. **Memberships:** Am Soc Biol Chemists; Am Chem Soc. **Research Statement & Publications:** Metabolism and preservation of human blood cells. **Mailing Address:** Ctr Blood Res, 800 Huntington Ave, Boston, MA 02115-6399. **E-Mail:** lionetti@cbr.med.harvard.edu

LIONS, JACQUES LOUIS, PHYSICS. **Personal Data:** b Grassee, France, May 2, 1928; m 1950, Andree Oliver; c Pierre L. **Education:** Univ Paris, DSc, 1954. **Honorary Degrees:** Dr, Univ Liege, 1973, Univ Madrid, 1976, Univ Fudan, 1981 Goteborg Univ, 1984, Heriot Watt Univ, Edinburgh, 1982, Polytech Univ, Madrid, 1988, St Jacques de Compostella, 1993-1994, Univ Malaga, 1997, Univ Santingo, Chile, 1997. **Honors & Awards:** Japan Prize, 1991; Harvey Prize, 1991. **Professional Experience:** High sci adv, Dassault Indust, 1993-; pres, Nat Ctr Specialty Studies, 1984-1992; pres, Nat Inst Res Informatique & Automatique, 1980-1984; PROF MATH, COL FRANCE, PARIS, 1973-; Prof, Ecole Polytech, Paris, 1967-1986; Fac mem, Univ Paris, 1962-1973; Fac mem, Univ Nancy, France, 1954-1962; bd dir, St Gobain & Pechiney & Dassault Syst. **Memberships:** Foreign assoc Nat Acad Sci; French Acad Sci (pres, 1997-); Royal Acad Sci; Pontifical Acad Sci; Brasil Acad Sci; Royal Acad Belgium; Russ Acad Sci; Ukraine Acad Sci; Am Acad Arts & Sci; Int Acad Astronaut Chile Acad Sci. **Mailing Address:** Col France, 3 rue d'Ulm, Paris 75231 Cedex 05, France.

LIONS, PIERRE LOUIS, MATHEMATICS. **Personal Data:** b Grasse, France, August 11, 1956; m 1979, Lila Laurenti; c DorianC. **Education:** Univ Paris VI, DSc, 1979. **Honorary Degrees:** Dr, Heriot & Watt Univ, Edinburgh, 1995. **Honors & Awards:** Fields Medal, 1994. **Professional Experience:** Aerospatiable, Space Defense, Mureaux, 1996; Pechiney, St-Jean de Maurienne, 1995-; Ctr Dis Control, Paris, 1995-; CRS4, Cagliari, 1994-; dir, Ceremade, Paris, 1991-1996; Cognitech, Santa-Monica, 1990-; PROF, POLYTECH SCH, PALAISEAU, FRANCE, 1984-; Cea-Dam, Paris, 1982-; PROF, UNIV PARIS-DAUPHINE, FRANCE, 1979-; Consult, Cisi, Paris, 1979-. **Memberships:** Fr Acad Sci; Acad Europea. **Research Statement & Publications:** Published articles in professional journals. **Mailing Address:** 42 rue du Hameau, Paris 75015, France.

LIOR, NOAM, ENERGY CONVERSION, WATER DESALINATION. **Personal Data:** American citizen; c 3. **Education:** Technion, Israel, BS, 1962, MS, 1966; Univ Calif, Berkeley, PhD (mech eng), 1973. **Honorary Degrees:** MA, Univ PA, 1978. **Honors & Awards:** Ralph Teetor Award, SAE, 1986; Japan Soc for the Promo of Sci Sr Fellow Awd, 1991, Am Soc Mech Engrs Fellow; Am Inst Aero Astr Assoc Fellow, Am Soc Mech Engrs Adv Energy Sys Div Edward F Obert Best Paper Awd, 1992; Am Soc Mech Engrs Adv Energy Sys Div Best Paper Awd, 2004; Japan Heat Transfer Soc Sci Prizefor 1994; Inter'l Desalination Assoc Best Treatise Awd, 1995; Inter'l Desalinatuon Assoc Best Essay Awd, 1995. **Professional Experience:** Vis prof Royal Inst Tech Sweden, 1998-1999; Vis Prof Mitsubishi Electric Corp. Advanced Technology R&D Center, Japan, 1997, vis prof, Dept Mech Systs Eng, Tokyo Univ Agr & Technol, 1991-1992; sr fel, Japan Soc Prom Sci, 1991; chmn, Mech Eng Grad Group, 1986-1990; consult, Westinghouse Elec Corp, 1977-1978; Prin investr, NSF grants, Pa Sci & Eng Found grant, US HUD grant, 1975- & US Dept Energy grant, 1975-; mem, Solar Collector Stand Comt, Alm Soc Heating, Refrig & Air Conditioning Engr, 1975; PROF MECH ENG, DEPT MECH ENG & APPL MECH, UNIV PA, 1973-; res asst res eng water desalination, Seawater Conversion Lab, Univ Calif, Berkeley, 1966-1973; Instr, Dept Mech Eng, Technion, 1965-1966; consult, Solar Energy Res Inst; consult, Argonne Nat Lab; consult, Lawrence Livermore Labs Editorships: Editor-in-Chief, Energy, The International Journal, 1998- Technical Editor (OTEC, Solar Ponds, Desalination), ASME Journal of Solar Energy Engineering, 1983 1989. Board of Editors Member, Desalination, The International Journal of Desalting and Water Purification, 1988- Board of Editors Member, Russian Journal of Engineering Thermophysics, 1990- Regional Editor for North America and Europe, Energy Conversion and Management journal, 1994- Board of Editors Member, Encyclopedia of Life Support Systems, 1994- Board of Editors Member, The International Desalination & Water Reuse Quarterly, 1997-2002 Editor, Thermal Science and Engineering journal (Japan), 1999-. **Memberships:** Fel Am Soc Mech Engrs; Am Inst Aero Astr Assoc Fellow; Int Desalination Asn. **Research Statement & Publications:** Heat transfer, thermodynamics, and fluid mechanics as related to solar energy applications, water desalination, combustion and materials processing; thermo-fluid measurements. **Mailing Address:** Dept Mech Eng Univ Pa, 212 Towne Bldg, Philadelphia, PA 19104-6315. **Fax:** 215-573-6334. **E-Mail:** lior@seas.upenn.edu

LIOTTA, DENNIS C, DRUG DESIGN. **Personal Data:** b Brooklyn, NY, January 31, 1949; m Helene M Saxton; c John & Matthew. **Education:** Queens Col, City Univ New York, BA, 1970, PhD, 1974. **Professional Experience:** Alexander von Humboldt sr scientist fel, 1994-; CHMN DEPT, EMORY UNIV, 1993-; PROF CHEM, EMORY UNIV, 1988-; Camille & Henry Dreyfus teacher scholar fel, 1981-1986; Fel, Alfred P Sloan Found, 1980-1984; From asst prof to assoc prof, Emory Univ, 1976-1988. **Memberships:** Am Chem Soc; AAAS. **Research Statement & Publications:** Drug design and drug development; new synthetic methodology; molecular modeling. **Mailing Address:** Chem Bldg, Dept Chem Emory Univ, Atlanta, GA 30322. **E-Mail:** dliotta@emory.edu

LIOTTA, LANCE, PATHOLOGY. **Professional Experience:** CHIEF, LAB PATH, NAT CANCER INST, NIH, as of 2005; actg chief, Nat Cancer Inst, NIH, 1981-1982. **Mailing Address:** Lab Path, NCI NIH, Rm B1B41, Bldg Ten, Bethesda, MD 20892. **Fax:** 301-480-0853. **E-Mail:** lance@helix.nih.gov

LIOU, JUHN G, METAMORPHIC PETROLOGY, GEOCHEMISTRY. **Personal Data:** b Taiwan, December 28, 1939; m 1964, c 2. **Education:** Nat Taiwan Univ, BS, 1962; Univ Calif, Los Angeles, PhD (geol), 1969. **Honors & Awards:** Mineral Soc Am Award, 1977. **Professional Experience:** PROF EMER, STANFORD UNIV, as of 2005; nat chair vis prof, Nat Taiwan Univ, 2004; prof, Inst Geol, Academia Sinica, 1996; prof geol & environ sci, Stanford Univ, 1993-; prof, Chinese Acad Geol Sci, 1988; prof, Dept Geol, Stanford Univ, 1983-1993; Guggenheim fel, John Simon Guggenheim Found, 1978-1979; from asst prof geol to assoc prof geol, Stanford Univ, 1972-1983; res fel geochem, Nat Res Coun, NASA, Houston, 1970-1972; NSF fel, Univ Calif, 1970; teaching asst, Univ Calif, Los Angeles, 1965-1969; teaching & res asst geol, Nat Taiwan Univ, 1963-1964. **Memberships:** Geol Soc Am; Am Geophys Union; Mineral Soc Am. **Research Statement & Publications:** To understand, through hydrothermal experiments and field observations, the parageneses and compositions of metamorphic minerals zeolites, prehnite, pumpellites and epidote; their imposed physical conditions for low-grade metabasites. **Mailing Address:** Dept Geol & Environ Sci, Stanford Univ, Green Earth Sci Bldg 221, Stanford, CA 94305-2115. **Fax:** 650-725-0979. **E-Mail:** liou@pangea.stanford.edu

LIOU, KUO-NAN, ATMOSPHERIC PHYSICS, REMOTE SENSING. **Personal Data:** b Taipei, Taiwan, November 16, 1943; American citizen; m 1968, c Julia & Clifford. **Education:** Nat Taiwan Univ, BS, 1965; NY Univ, MS, 1968, PhD (atmospheric physics), 1970. **Honors & Awards:** Creativity Award, NSF, 1996. **Professional Experience:** DISTINGUISHED PROF ATMOSPHERIC SCI, UNIV CALIF LOS ANGELES, 2004-; distinguished vis scientist, Jet Propulsion Lab & Calif Inst Tech, 2003-2005; chair, Dept Atmospheric Sci, Univ Calif Los Angeles, 2000-2004; DIR, INST RADIATION & REMOTE SENSING, UNIV CALIF LOS ANGELES, 1997-; PROF ADMOSPHERIC SCI, UNIV CALIF LOS ANGELES, 1997-; adj prof meteorol, Univ Utah, 1997-; chmn, Dept Meteorol, Univ Utah, 1996-1997; vis prof, Univ Ariz, 1995; adj Prof Geophysics, Univ Utah, 1992-; RES PROF PHYSICS, UNIV UTAH, 1992-; vis prof, Peking Univ, China, 1989-; dir, Ctr Atmospheric & Remote Sounding Studies, 1987-1997; ed, Theoret & Appl Climat & Meterol & Atmosheric Physics, 1985-; vis scholar, Harvard Univ, 1985; mem adv panel, Int Satellite Cloud Climat Prog, Climate Res Comt, Nat Acad Sci, 1984-1987; consult, Ames Res Ctr, NASA, 1984; vis prof, Univ Calif, Los Angeles, 1981; prof meteorol, Univ Utah, 1980-1997; prin investr, NSF, NASA, Air Force, 1980; assoc prof, Dept Meteorol, 1975-1980; vis scientist, Nat Ctr Atmospheric Res, 1975; asst prof atmospheric sci, Univ Wash, 1972-1974; res assoc, Goddard Inst Space Studies, 1970-1972; res asst, NY Univ, 1966-1970. **Memberships:** Fel Optical Soc Am; fel Am Meteorol Soc; fel Am Geophys Union; AAAS; Nat Acad Eng. **Research Statement & Publications:** Cloud-radiation and radiative transfer in bonds; feedbacks in numerical models, remote sensing of cloud microphysics, light scattering by ice crystals; optics; published over 150 articles. **Mailing Address:** Dept Atmospheric Oceanic Sci, Univ Calif, 7127 Math Sci Bldg 405 Hilgard Ave, Los Angeles, CA 90095-1565. **Fax:** 310-267-2252. **E-Mail:** knliou@atmos.ucla.edu

LIOU, MENG-SING, COMPUTATIONAL FLUID DYNAMICS, AEROPROPULSION. **Personal Data:** b Taichung, Taiwan, November 20, 1947; American citizen; m May Fun; c Victoria, Yu-Ming & Deng-Yuan. **Education:** Nat Cheng Kung Univ, BS, 1969; Nat Taiwan Univ, MS, 1972; Univ Mich, MS, 1975, PhD (aerospace eng), 1977. **Honors & Awards:** Except sci Achievement Award, NASA, 1992. **Professional Experience:** Vis prof, Nat Cheng Kung Univ, 1997; SR SCIENTIST, LEWIS RES CTR, NASA, 1990-; mem, Nat Aerospace Plane Prog, 1990; br chief, Lewis Res Ctr, NASA, 1988-1990; scientist, Lewis Res Ctr, NASA, 1986-1988; vis assoc prof computational fluid dynamics, Univ Mich, 1984-1986; prof & chmn aerodynamics propulsion & combustion, Nat Cheng Kung Univ, 1981-1984; Consult, Aeronaut Indust Develop Ctr, 1981-1984; res scientist, McDonnell Douglas Corp, 1978-1981; Res investr, Univ Mich, 1977-1978. **Memberships:** Assoc fel Am Inst Aeronaut & Astronaut. **Research Statement & Publications:** Advanced numerical methods for computational fluid dynamics; solving problems with complex physics in practical applications; author of over 100 publications. **Mailing Address:** MS 5-11, NASA Glenn Res Ctr, Cleveland, OH 44135. **Fax:** 216-433-5802. **E-Mail:** fsmsl@lerc.nasa.gov

LIOU, MING-LEI, ELECTRICAL ENGINEERING. **Personal Data:** b Tinghai, China, January 6, 1935; American citizen; m Pearl B Shen; c Michael, Christopher & Derek. **Education:** Nat Taiwan Univ, BSEE, 1956; Drexel Univ, MSEE, 1961; Stanford Univ, PhD (elec eng), 1964. **Professional Experience:** DIR, HONG KONG TELECOM INST INFO TECH, 1993-; PROF, HONG KONG UNIV SCI & TECHNOL, 1992-; Ed, Trans Circuits & Systs Video Technol, 1991-1995; dir, Bell Commun Res, 1984-1992; Ed, Trans Circuits & Systs, Inst Elec & Electronics Engrs, 1979-1981; supvr, AT&T Bell Labs, 1966-1984; mem tech staff, Bell Labs, 1963-1966; res asst, Stanford Electronics Labs, Stanford Univ, 1961-1963; instr, Dept Elec Eng, Drexel Univ, 1958-1961; Commun engr, Chinese Govt Radio Admin, 1957-1958. **Memberships:** Fel Inst Elec & Electronics Engrs; fel Hong Kong Inst Engrs; Inst Elec & Electronics Engrs Circuits & Systs Soc; Sigma Xi. **Research Statement & Publications:** Contributed chapters to engineering books. **Mailing Address:** Dept Elec & Electronics Eng, Hong Kong Univ Sci & Technol Clearwater Bay, Kowloon Hong Kong, China.

LIOU, SY-HWANG, MAGNETIC MATERIALS, SUPERCONDUCTING MATERIALS. **Personal Data:** b Taiwan, China, March 13, 1951; American citizen; m 1977, Mei-Lan; c Jenny & Michael. **Education:** Soochow Univ, Taiwan, BS, 1974; Fla Inst Technol, MS, 1979; Johns Hopkins Univ, PhD (physics), 1985. **Professional Experience:** ASSOC PROF DEPT PHYSICS & ASTRON, UNIV NEBR, 1993-; Co-ed, Appl Physics Commun, 1990-; asst prof, Univ Nebr, 1988-1993; fel, AT&T Bell Labs, 1986-1988; fel, Johns Hopkins Univ, 1985-1986; Inst modern physics lab, Soochow Univ, 1976-1977. **Memberships:** Am Phys Soc; Mat Res Soc. **Research Statement & Publications:** M icrostructural characterization, using scanning probe microscopy; nanofabrication, using focused ion beam milling. **Mailing Address:** Physics/Astron, 260 Bel Univ NE Lincoln 364 Behlen, Lincoln, NE 68588-0111. **Fax:** 402-472-2879. **E-Mail:** sliou@unl.edu

LIOY, FRANCO, PHYSIOLOGY. **Personal Data:** b Gorizia, Italy, May 24, 1932; m 1966, c 1. **Education:** Univ Rome, MD, 1956, Univ.Rome, Cardiology, 1959, Univ Minn, Minneapolis, PhD (physiol), 1967. **Professional Experience:** PROF EMER PHYSIOL, UNIV BC, 2002-; prof physiol, Univ BC, 1975-2002; from asst prof to assoc prof, Univ BC, 1967-1975; instr physiol, Univ Minn, Minneapolis, 1966-1967; Instr med, Univ Rome,

1956-1961; Mem, Sci Subcomt, Can Heart Found. **Memberships:** Can Physiol Soc. **Research Statement & Publications:** Cardiovascular physiology; coronary circulation; effect of hyperthermia on circulatory system; sympathetic control of circulation. **Mailing Address:** Dept Physiol, Univ BC, 2146 Health Sci Mall, Vancouver, BC V6T 1Z3, Can. **Fax:** 604-822-6048. **E-Mail:** flioy@interchange.ubc.ca

LIOY, PAUL JAMES, ENVIRONMENTAL HEALTH & HUMAN EXPOSURE SCIENCES, AEROSOLS & HAZARDOUS WASTES & EMERGENCY RESPONSE & PREPARATION. **Personal Data:** b Passaic, NJ, May 27, 1947; m 1971, Mary; c Jason. **Education:** Montclair State Col, BA, 1969; Auburn Univ, MS, 1971; Rutgers Univ, MS, 1973, PhD (environ sci), 1975. **Honors & Awards:** Biomed researcher Award, UMDNJ-RWJMS, 1992; Wesolowski Award, Internat soc for Exposure Analysis, 1998; Chambers award, Air and Waste Managment Association, 2003, ISI Highly Cited, 2001 - Present, Category of Environment and Ecology. **Professional Experience:** DEP DIRector Environ & OCCUP HEALTH SCI INST; Prof of Environ and Comm med, Univ Med & Dent of NJ RWJMS, Prof School of public health, UMDNJ assoc ed, Environ Res, 1994-; NRC, mem, board of Toxicol and Environ studies 1989 - 1992; NRC, mem, comt Particulate matter research 1998 -2004, mem, comt on Dept Energy Site Remediation, 1993-1994; mem, US-Can Air Quality Bd, Int Joint Comn, 1992-; co-dir, Joint Grad Prog Exposure Assessment, 1990-1994; NRC, CHAIR mem, Comn Air Pollution Exposure Assessment, 1990; mem, Sci Adv Bd Comt Indoor Air & Total Human Exposure, Comt Clean Air compliance1989-2003, Mem Com on Homeland security, 2005- Environ Protection Agency; Vice Chair, WTC Expert Technical Panel, 2004-2005, US EPA; exed ed, Atmos Environ, 1989-1994; PROF ENVIRON & COMMUNITY MED, EXPOSURE SCIENCE DIV, UNIV MED & DENT NJ, 1988-; chmn, Comt Air Pollution epidemiol, Nat Acad Sci, 1987-1990; dir human exposure, Environ & Occup Health Sci Inst, Univ Med & Dent NJ, Rutgers Univ, 1986-; DIR, EXPOSURE, MEASUREMENT & ASSESSMENT DIV, UNIV MED & DENT NJ, 1986-; assoc prof environ & community med, Exposure, Measurement & Assessment Div, Univ Med & Dent NJ, 1985-1988; consult, US Environ Protection Agency Off Res & Develop, 1984-1991; mem, Comt Air Pollution epidemiol, Nat Acad Sci, 1984-1985; chmn, NJ Clean Air Coun, 1983-1985; mem, NJ Clean Air Coun, 1981-1994; indust orgn, State NJ, 1980-; consult, State NJ, 1978-1990; Acad Councilor NJ state Legislature; from asst prof to assoc prof environ med, Inst Environ Med, NY Univ Med Ctr, 1978-1985; Lectr, Dept Civil & Environ Eng, Polytech Inst NY, 1976-1978; Sr air pollution engr, Interstate Sanit Comn, NY, 1975-1978. **Memberships:** Air Pollution Control Asn; Ed review brd, (chair 1978-1984); fel NY Acad Sci; Int Soc Environ Epidemiol; Am Asn Aerosol Res; Air & Waste Mgt Asn; Int Soc Exposure Anal (treas, 1991-1993, pres, 1993-1994); Am Conf Govt Indust Hygienists. **Research Statement & Publications:** Theoretical and Experimental basis of Exposure Sciences, Environmental health, Atmospheric transport of pollutants; chemical characteristics of inorganic trace elements and organic species in multiple media; and exposure pathwaysaerosol and gaseous monitoring equipment and techniques; industrial and occupational hygiene; environmental health; human exposure to toxic pollutants and epidemiology; hazardous wastes and multimedia pollution issues; modeling of human exposure and dose response relationships; strategies for measuring industrial and community exposures and toxic substances; Strategies for Emergency Response and HLS author 216 peer reviewed publications; patentee in field. **Mailing Address:** Environ & Occup Health Sci Inst, Univ Med & Dent NJ Rutgers 170 Frelinghuysen Rd, Piscataway, NJ 08855. **Fax:** 732-445-0116. **E-Mail:** plioy@eohsi.rutgers.edu

LIPARI, NUNZIO OTTAVIO, SOLID STATE PHYSICS, MOLECULAR PHYSICS. **Personal Data:** b Ali' Terme, Italy, January 1, 1945; m Gloria. **Education:** Univ Messina, Laurea Physics, 1967; Lehigh Univ, PhD (physics), 1970. **Professional Experience:** PRES & CHIEF EXEC OFFICER, LIPARI INT CONSULT, 1995-; consult, CNRSM, Brindisi, 1993-1994; adj prof, Univ Lecce, 1993-1994; from res staff mem to sr tech consul, IBM Corp, 1977-1993; from assoc scientist to sr scientist, Xerox Corp, 1972-1977; res fel, Univ Ill, 1970-1972; Res asst solid state physics, Lehigh Univ, 1967-1970. **Memberships:** Fel Am Phys Soc. **Research Statement & Publications:** Optical properties of solids; electron-phonon interaction in molecular systems; excitation and impurity states in semiconductors. **Mailing Address:** Lipari Int Consult, 8702 Carpenter Rd, Baldwinsville, NY 13027. **Fax:** 315-638-9559. **E-Mail:** nunzio@dreamscape.com

LIPELES, MARTIN, INTERNET, DATA MIGRATION, DATABASE. **Personal Data:** b New York, NY, June 22, 1938; m 1968, Lois; c Aaron & Elliot. **Education:** Columbia Univ, AB, 1960, MA, 1962, PhD (physics), 1966. **Professional Experience:** COMPUTER CONSULT, 1988-; mgr systs eng, Alpharel Inc, 1983-1988; dir res & develop, Autologic Inc, 1978-1983; pres, Med Microcomputers Inc, 1977-1978; mem tech staff, Sci Ctr, Rockwell Int, 1966-1976; Part-time res physicist, Radiation Lab, Columbia Univ, 1962-1966. **Memberships:** AAAS; Sigma Xi; Asn Comput Mach. **Research Statement & Publications:** Data migration and databases, software for design of digital type and typesetter design; inelastic, ion-atom collisions at low energies; physics and chemistry of photochemical aerosol formation in the atmosphere. **Mailing Address:** Thousand Oaks, CA 91360. **E-Mail:** mlipeles@acm.org

LIPES, MYRA A, IMMUNOLOGY. **Education:** McGill Univ, Montreal, MD. **Honors & Awards:** Charles H Hood Found Child Health Res Award; Career Develop Award, Am Diabetes Asn. **Professional Experience:** INVESTR, SECT IMMUNOL & IMMUNOGENETICS & DIR, TRANSGENIC MOUSE CARE FACIL, JOSLIN RES LAB, HARVARD MED SCH, 1987-; ASST PROF MED, HARVARD MED SCH, 1987-. **Research Statement & Publications:** Cellular and molecular events that initiate beta cell autoimmunity; developing genetic strategies to prevent and treat type 1 diabetes. **Mailing Address:** Joslin Diabetes Ctr, Harvard Med Sch, One Joslin Pl, Boston, MA 02215.

LIPICKY, RAYMOND JOHN, INTERNAL MEDICINE, PHARMACOLOGY. **Personal Data:** b Cleveland, Ohio, May 3, 1933; m 1983, Freda; c Laura Lee, Josh Wesley, Ronald Lowell, Robert Boardwell & Elizabeth Dorenda. **Education:** Ohio Univ, AB, 1955; Univ Cincinnati, MD, 1960. **Professional Experience:** DIR, LIPICKY, LLC, 2002-; dir, division of carno-renel, prof products, Food & Drug Admin, 1984-2001; actg dir, Div Cardiorenal Drug Prods, 1981-1984; guest worker, Lab Biophysics, NIH, 1979-1984; med officer, Div Cardiorenal Drug Prods, 1979-1981; prof med & dir, Div Clin Pharmacol, 1973-1979; prof pharmacol, Col Med, Univ Cincinnati, 1972-1979; from asst prof to assoc prof med, Col Med, Univ Cincinnati, 1966-1973; from asst prof to assoc prof pharmacol, Col Med, Univ Cincinnati, 1966-1972; trainee cardiol, Strong Mem Hosp, Rochester, 1965-1966; resident, Strong Mem Hosp, Rochester, NY, 1964-1965; fel pharmacol, Univ Cincinnati, 1963-1964; fel pharmacol, Univ Pa, 1962-1963; from intern to resident med, Barnes Hosp, St Louis, Mo, 1960-1962. **Memberships:** Soc Neuroscience; Biophys Soc; Am Physiol Soc; Am Soc Pharmacol & Exp Therapeut; Am Soc Hypertension. **Research Statement & Publications:** Ion transport; clinical pharmacology; membrane permeability; bioelectric potentials; hemodynamics. **Mailing Address:** Lipicky, LLC, 15201 Apricot Lane, Gaithersburg, MD 20878. **Fax:** 301-216-9798.

LIPIN, BRUCE REED, PETROLOGY, ECONOMIC GEOLOGY. **Personal Data:** b New York, NY, November 27, 1947; m 1971, Cookie; c Adam & Jonah. **Education:** City Col NY, BS, 1970; Pa State Univ, PhD (mineral, petrol), 1975. **Professional Experience:** GEOLOGIST, US GEOL SURV, as of 2004; assoc chief, Off Mineral Resources, 1993-1996; consult res, George Wash Univ, 1993-1995; Nat Res Coun res assoc fel, Chief Eastern Mineral Resources, 1984-1989; geologist, US Geol Surv, 1975-1984 & 1989-1993; Nat Res Coun res assoc fel, US Geol Surv, 1974-1975; fel, Geophys Lab, Carnegie Inst Wash, 1973-1974. **Memberships:** Soc Econ Geol. **Research Statement & Publications:** Economic geology of ultramafic rocks including chromite, platinum, asbestos and talc; petrology and origin of ultramafic rocks. **Mailing Address:** US Geol Surv, 4C 208 MS 954 Nat Ctr 12201 Sunrise Valley Dr, Reston, VA 20192. **Fax:** 703-648-6338. **E-Mail:** blipin@usgs.gov

LIPINSKI, BOGUSLAW, BIOELECTRICITY. **Personal Data:** b Sochaczew, Poland, July 21, 1933; American citizen; m 1957, c 1. **Education:** Inst Nuclear Res, Warsaw, PhD (biochem), 1962; Univ Lodz, Poland, DSc, 1971. **Professional Experience:** RES FEL, JOSLIN DIABETES CTR, as of 2004; lectr, Soc Catholic Social Scientists, as of 2002; Dir, Bioelec Lab, St Elizabeth's Hosp, Tufts Univ Sch Med, beginning 1981; asst ed, J Bioelec, 1981-; assoc dir, Vascular Lab, 1976-1981; vis prof, Vascular Lab, Lemnel Shattuck Hosp, Sch Med, Tufts Univ, 1971-1976. **Memberships:** AAAS; Int Soc Thrombosis & Hemostosis; Fedn Am Scientists; Int Soc Bioelec (pres, 1980-). **Research Statement & Publications:** Mechanism of intravascular coagulation and fibrinolysis; effect of nutrition on thrombosis and atherosclerosis; effect of electricity on biological systems in relation to tissues regeneration and healing. **Mailing Address:** Joslin Diabetes Ctr, Harvard Sch Med, One Joslin Pl, Boston, MA 02215. **Fax:** 617-732-2667. **E-Mail:** boguslaw_lipinski@joslin.harvard.edu

LIPINSKI, CHRISTOPHER ANDREW, ORGANIC CHEMISTRY. **Personal Data:** b Dundee, Scotland, February 1, 1944; American citizen. **Education:** San Francisco State Col, BS, 1965; Univ Calif, Berkeley, PhD (phys org chem), 1968. **Honors & Awards:** Div Med Chem Award, Am Chem Soc, 2004; E B Hershberg Award, Am Chem Soc, 2005. **Professional Experience:** ADJ SR RES FEL, PFIZER GLOBAL RES & DEVELOP, 2003-; sr res fel, Pfizer Global Res & Develop, 1998-2002, res adv, Groton Labs, 1986-1998; prin res investr, Med Res Labs, Pfizer Cent Res, 1981-1986; sr res investr, Med Res Labs, Pfizer Cent Res, 1976-1981; sr res sci, Med Res Labs, Pfizer Cent Res, 1974-1976; res sci, Med Res Labs, Pfizer Cent Res, 1970-1974; Nat Inst Gen Med Sci fel, Calif Inst Technol, 1969-1970. **Memberships:** Am Chem Soc; Am Asn Pharm Sci. **Research Statement & Publications:** Medicinal chemistry of gastrointestinal and antidiabetic agents; histamine M2-receptor antagonists; aldose reductase inhibitors; bioisosteusm. **Mailing Address:** Pfizer Global R&D, Groton Lab, Eastern Point Rd MS8200-36, Groton, CT 06340-5196. **Fax:** 860-715-3149. **E-Mail:** lialbert@apScis.com

LIPINSKI, JOSEPH FLOYD, PSYCHOTIC DISORDERS, MOVEMENT DISORDERS. **Personal Data:** b New Kensington, Pa, January 22, 1940; m 1979, Edith; c Jed & Tom. **Education:** Jefferson Med Col, MD, 1966. **Professional Experience:** DIR, AFFECTIVE DIS PROG, MED UNIV SC, 2002-; ASSOC PROF PSYCHIAT, MED UNIV SC, 1993-; from asst prof to assoc prof, Harvard Med Sch-Mass Gen Hosp, 1973-1993; fel, Harvard Med Sch-Mass Gen Hosp, 1972-1973; fel, Harvard Med Sch, Mass Gen Hosp, 1972-1973; residency psychiat, Harvard Med Sch-Mass Gen Hosp, 1971; residency psychiat, Harvard Med Sch, Mass Gen Hosp, 1971; Internship med, Jefferson Med Hosp, 1967; dir, Clin Res Ctr Study Psychotic Disorder & chief, Psychopharmacol Lab, Maulman Res Ctr, McLean Hosp. **Memberships:** Am Col Neuropsychopharmacol; Psychiat Res Soc; Cong Int Neuropsychopharmacol; AAAS. **Research Statement & Publications:** Pathophysiology of the major psychiatric and neurological movement disorders. **Mailing Address:** Med Univ SC, 171 Ashley Ave, Charleston, SC 29425. **Fax:** 803-792-4394.

LIPINSKI, WALTER C(HARLES), ELECTRICAL ENGINEERING, NUCLEAR ENGINEERING. **Personal Data:** b Chicago, Ill, January 5, 1927; m 1951, Jo A Miller; c Marjorie. **Education:** Univ Ill, BSc, 1950; Ill Inst Technol, MSc, 1963, PhD (elec eng), 1969. **Professional Experience:** RETIRED; Consult, Adv Comt Reactor Safeguards, US Nuclear Regulatory Comn, 1964-1996; From asst elec engr to sr elec engr, Argonne Nat Lab, 1950-1996. **Research Statement & Publications:** Control engineering; instrumentation; nuclear reactor control and instrumentation; nuclear power plant development; nuclear reactor safety. **Mailing Address:** 9700 S Cass Ave Bldg 208, Argonne Nat Lab, Argonne, IL 60439.

LIPINSKY, EDWARD SOLOMON, SYSTEMS ANALYSIS COMMERCIAL DEVELOPMENT, DYNAMIC MODELING. **Personal Data:** b Asheville, NC, November 15, 1929; m 1954, Sherry; c Edward & Sarah. **Education:** Mass Inst Technol, BS, 1952; Harvard Univ, AM, 1954. **Honors & Awards:** Tech Achievement Award, US Dept Energy, 1994 & 1995. **Professional Experience:** PRES, INNOVATIVE THINKING INC, as of 2005; res leader org & polymer chem, Battelle Columbus Memorial Inst, 1985-1995; sr res leader res mgt, Battelle Columbus Memorial Inst, 1979-1985; res leader, Battelle Columbus Memorial Inst, 1975-1979; assoc div chief bus & tech planning, Battelle Columbus Memorial Inst, 1971-1974; prin res scientist, Battelle Columbus Memorial Inst, 1959-1971; res assoc, Ohio State Univ, 1957-1959. **Memberships:** Am Chem Soc; fel AAAS; Sigma Xi; Am Inst Chem Engrs; Tech Asn Pulp & Paper Indust. **Research Statement & Publications:** Chemicals and final from biomass; renewable resource technology; diffusion-controlled reactions; computer-aided idea generation; dynamic simulation modeling of chemical processes. **Mailing Address:** 6481 Bellbrook Pl, Worthington, OH 43085-2988. **E-Mail:** elipinsk@sprynet.com

LIPKA, BENJAMIN, ORGANIC CHEMISTRY. **Personal Data:** b New York, NY, February 5, 1929; m 1958, Loretta; c Leslie, Jane & Stephanie. **Education:** NY Univ, BA, 1949, PhD (org chem), 1958. **Professional Experience:** RETIRED; consult technol group, Stamford, Ct, 1992-2000; sr develop chemist, Upjohn Co, 1967-1992; sr chemist, Allied Chem Corp, 1960-1967; chemist, Geigy Chem Corp, 1959-1960. **Memberships:** Am Chem Soc. **Research Statement & Publications:** Laboratory synthesis and chemical plant production of organic compounds. **Mailing Address:** 19 Northrop Rd, Woodbridge, CT 06525-1722.

LIPKA, JAMES J, BIOINORGANIC CHEMISTRY. **Personal Data:** b Highland Park, Mich, August 1, 1954; m 1980. **Education:** Univ Mich, BS, 1976; Columbia Univ, MA, 1977, PhD (chem), 1982. **Professional Experience:** PATENT LIAISON, DEPT TECHNOL ASSESSMENT & ACQUISITIONS, ABBOTT LABS, ABBOTT PARK, ILL, 1994-; sr res biochemist, Dept Hepatitis Tech Prod Develop, 1993-1994; mgr diag prod develop, Genelabs, Inc, Redwood City, Calif, 1992-1993; Consult, Genelabs Asia Ltd, Singapore, 1991-1992; res assoc, Dept Path, Stanford Univ Blood Bank, Stanford Univ Med Sch, Palo Alto, Calif, 1987-1992; asst res chemist res serv, Vet Admin Med Ctr, San Francisco & Anesthesia Dept, Univ Calif, San Francisco, 1955-1987. **Memberships:** Am Chem Soc; Sigma Xi; AAAS; NY Acad Sci. **Research Statement & Publications:** Methods for labelling biological polymers and assemblies with heavy atoms for the purpose of increasing contrast in high-resolution electron microscopy. **Mailing Address:** Dept 7CE Bldg Ap 32sw-3, Abbott Labs Blds 200 Abbott Park Rd, Abbott Park, IL 60064-3537.

LIPKA, STEVEN, MARINCE SCIENCE. **Education:** Univ Va Charlottesville, PhD. **Professional Experience:** ASSOC PROF, DEPT OCEAN ENG, FLA ATLANTIC UNIV, as of 2005. **Mailing Address:** Ocean Eng Dept, Fla Atlantic Univ, Boca Raton, FL 33431.

LIPKE, PETER NATHAN, CELL ADHESION, CELL SURFACE DEVELOPMENT. **Personal Data:** b San Francisco, Calif, June 18, 1950; m 1971, Anne; c Jonathan, Maria, David, Nathan, Michael, Jermaine & Omar. **Education:** Univ Chicago, BS, 1971; Univ Calif, Berkeley, PhD (biochem), 1976. **Professional Experience:** PROF MOLECULAR CELL BIOL, DEPT BIOL SCI, HUNTER COL, 1990-; from asst prof to assoc prof, Dept Biol Sci, Hunter Col, 1976-1989; Fel, Dept Zool, Univ Wis-Madison, 1976-1978; Lectr, Fed Am Soc Exp Biol. **Memberships:** Am Soc Microbiol; fel AAAS; Am Soc Biochem & Molecular Biol; Glycobiology Soc. **Research Statement & Publications:** Molecular basis for cell-cell adhesion in eukaryotes, using mating in Saccharomyces cerevisiae as a model; developmental changes in cell surface structure; architecture and biosynthesis of fungal cell walls; fungal cell wall structure; Structure-function analyses of fungal adhesins. **Mailing Address:** Dept Biol, Hunter Col 695 Park Ave, New York, NY 10021. **Fax:** 212-772-5227. **E-Mail:** lipke@genectr.hunter.cuny.edu

LIPKE, WILLIAM G, PLANT PHYSIOLOGY, PLANT BIOCHEMISTRY. **Personal Data:** b Chesterton, Ind, December 19, 1936; m 1957, c 4. **Education:** Purdue Univ, BS, 1959; Univ Nebr, MS, 1962; Tex A&M Univ, PhD (plant physiol), 1966. **Professional Experience:** ASSOC PROF BIOL, NORTHERN ARIZ UNIV, 1974-; PLANT PHYSIOLOGIST, NORTHERN ARIZ UNIV, 1965-; from asst prof to assoc prof plant physiol, Northern Ariz Univ, 1965-1974. **Memberships:** AAAS; Am Soc Plant Physiol. **Research Statement & Publications:** Plant physiology, especially mineral nutrition; weed science, especially plant enzymes. **Mailing Address:** 452 W Spruce St, Camp Verde, AZ 86322.

LIPKIN, DAVID, nucleic acid chemistry, phosphorus chemistry; deceased, see previous edition for last biography

LIPKIN, EDWARD W, BIOCHEMISTRY & ENDOCRINOLOGY. **Education:** Case Western Reserve Univ, OH, MD, PhD (biochem). **Professional Experience:** ASSOC PROF MED, DIV METAB, ENDOCRINOL & NUTRIT, UNIV WASH MED CTR, as of 2005. **Mailing Address:** Div Metab & Endocrinol, Sch Med Univ Wash, 1959 NE Pac St Mail Box 356426, Seattle, WA 98195-6426.

LIPKIN, GEORGE, MEDICINE, DERMATOLOGY. **Personal Data:** b New York, NY, December 31, 1930; m 1957, Sari Berger; c Michael D & Lisa S. **Education:** Columbia Univ, AB, 1952; State Univ NY Downstate Med Ctr, MD, 1955. **Professional Experience:** Dir, Berger Found Cancer Res, 1978-; PROF DERMAT, MED SCH, NY UNIV, 1974-; vis scientist, Univ Zurich, 1972-1973; Prin investr, Nat Cancer Inst res grants, Dermat Found, Med Ctr, NY Univ, 1961-1997; From instr to assoc prof, Med Sch, NY Univ, 1961-1974. **Memberships:** Soc Invest Dermat; AAAS; Am Acad Dermat; Harvey Soc; Union Concerned Scientists. **Research Statement & Publications:** Biology of malignant melanoma; biologic transformation of malignant cells; endogenous inhibitors of growth. **Mailing Address:** 61 Virginia Ave, Clifton, NJ 07012. **Fax:** 212-263-6649.

LIPKIN, HARRY JEANNOT, NUCLEAR PHYSICS, PARTICLE PHYSICS. **Personal Data:** b New York, NY, June 16, 1921; m 1949, c 2. **Education:** Cornell Univ, BEE, 1942; Princeton Univ, AM, 1948, PhD (physics), 1950. **Honors & Awards:** Rothschild Prize, Jerusalem, 1980. **Professional Experience:** HERBERT H LEHMAN CHAIR THEORET PHYSICS, WEIZMANN INST SCI, ISRAEL, 1971-; vis scientist, Argonne Nat Lab & Nat Accelerator Lab, Ill, 1971-1972, 1976-1977, 1979-1981; vis prof, Princeton Univ, 1967-1968; vis prof, Univ Ill, 1962-1963 & Tel Aviv Univ, 1965-1966; actg head dept physics, Weizmann Inst Sci, 1960-1961; from assoc prof to prof, Weizmann Inst Sci, Israel, 1959-1971; vis assoc prof physics, Univ Ill, 1958-1959; vis lectr, Hebrew Univ, Israel, 1956-1958; consult, AEC, Israel, 1955-1958; vis res fel reactor physics, AEC, France, 1953-1954; Res physicist, Weizmann Inst Sci, 1952-1960; Mem staff, Radiation Lab, Mass Inst Technol, 1942-1946. **Memberships:** Am Phys Soc; Ital Phys Soc; Phys Soc Israel; Europ Phys Soc; Israel Acad Sci & Humanities. **Research Statement & Publications:** Elementary particle theory; theoretical and experimental nuclear structure; collective motion in many particle systems; Beta decay; Mossbauer effect; reactor and particle physics; theoretical physics. **Mailing Address:** Dept Physics, Weizmann Inst Sci, Rehovot 76100, Israel. **E-Mail:** harry.lipkin@weizmann.ac.il

LIPKIN, LEWIS EDWARD, NEUROPATHOLOGY, COMPUTER SCIENCES. **Personal Data:** b New York, NY, November 2, 1925; m 1952, c 2. **Education:** NY Univ, BA, 1944; Long Island Col Med, MD, 1949; Am Bd Path, dipl & cert anat path & neuropath, 1952. **Professional Experience:** FAC EMER, NAT CANCER INST, NIH, as of 2005; chief image processing sect, lab math biol, nat cancer inst, nih, beginning 1980; dir, Div Cancer Biol & Diagnosis, head, Image Processing Unit Off, 1972-1980; head neuropath, Path Sect, Perinatal Res Br, Nat Inst Neurol Dis & Stroke, 1962-1972; consult, Nat Inst Neurol Dis & Stroke, 1961-1962; USPHS res grant, 1959-1962; asst prof path & neuropath, State Univ NY Downstate Med Ctr, 1956-1962; asst pathologist, Kings County Hosp, 1956-1962; usphs sr res fel neuropath, Mt Sinai Hosp NY, 1955-1956; from intern med to resident path, Mt Sinai Hosp NY, 1949-1953. **Memberships:** Asn Res Nerv & Ment Dis; Int Acad Path; Am Asn Neuropath; Asn Comput Mach. **Research Statement & Publications:** Computer analysis of microscopic images, especially neuropathologic material; automation of analysis of two dimensional gel electrophoresis; analysis and synthesis of nucleic acid secondary structure. **Mailing Address:** Molecular Struct Sect, Lab Exp & Computational Biol, Nat Cancer Inst, Rm B109 Bldg 12B, Bethesda, MD 20892. **Fax:** 301-402-4724. **E-Mail:** llipkin@helix.nih.gov

LIPKIN, MARTIN, GASTROENTEROLOGY, ONCOLOGY. **Personal Data:** b New York, NY, April 30, 1926; m 1958, Joan; c Richard & Steven. **Education:** NY Univ, BA, 1946, MD, 1950. **Professional Experience:** PROF MED, WEILL MED COL, CORNELL UNIV, as of 2003; DIR CLIN RES, STRANG CANCER PREV CTR, ROCKEFELLER UNIV, 1996-; head, Irving Weinstein lab Gastrointestinal Cancer Prev, beginning 1990; mem & attend physician, Memorial Sloan-Kettering Cancer Ctr, beginning 1985; ann hon lectr, Israel Med Asn & Gastroenterol Soc, 1982; hon pres, Int Acad Pathol Conf colorectal cancer, 1981; PROF, WEILL GRAD SCH MED SCI, CORNELL UNIV, 1978-; chmn, Sci Prog Comt, 1973; vchmn, Sect Gastroenterol & Colon & Rectal Surg, 1972; assoc attend physician, New York Hosp, 1970- & mem Hosp, 1971-; assoc prof, Grad Sch Med Sci, Cornell Univ, 1971-1978; secy, Sect Gastroenterol & Colon & Rectal Surg, 1971; award lectr, Med Soc State NY, 1971; NIH res career prog award, 1961-1971; guest investr, Rockefeller inst, 1959-1960; from instr to assoc prof, Cornell Univ, 1958-1978; res collabr, Brookhaven Nat lab, 1958-1972; dir gastroenterol res unit, Cornell Med div, Bellevue Hosp, 1958-1968; fel med, Med Col, Cornell Univ, 1955-1958; USPHS res fel, 1955-1956; Instr physiol, Sch Med, Univ Pa, 1953-1954; fel physiol, Med Col, Cornell Univ, 1952-1953; vis physician, Rockefeller Univ Hosp. **Memberships:** Fel Am Col Physicians; Am Soc Clin Invest; Am Physiol Soc; Am Gastroenterol Asn; Am Asn Cancer Res. **Research Statement & Publications:** Cancer prevention, chemoprevention, natural compounds and pharmaceutical agents; proliferation and differentiation of premalignant and malignant gastrointestinal cells in man; application of intermediate biomarkers to human chemoprevention studies and analyses of chemopreventive properties of naturally occurring and pharmaceutical compounds. **Mailing Address:** Strang Cancer Res Lab, Rockefeller Univ, 1230 York Ave, New York, NY 10021. **Fax:** 212-570-6995. **E-Mail:** lipkin@rockvax.rockefeller.edu

LIPKOWITZ, KENNY BARRY, COMPUTATIONAL CHEMISTRY, PHYSICAL ORGANIC CHEMISTRY. **Personal Data:** b Bronx, NY, April 1, 1950; m 1978, c 2. **Education:** State Univ NY, Geneseo, BS, 1972; Mont State Univ, PhD (chem), 1975. **Professional Experience:** CHMN CHEM, PURDUE UNIV, as of 2003; PROF CHEM, PURDUE UNIV, 1990-; Univ Calif, San Francisco, 1989-1990; vis prof, Princeton Univ, 1981-1982; from asst prof to assoc prof, Purdue Univ, 1977-1990; asst chem, Ohio State Univ, 1976-1977. **Memberships:** Am Chem Soc. **Research Statement & Publications:** Theoretical studies of organic molecules using quantum mechanical and molecular mechanics methods. **Mailing Address:** Dept Chem, IUPUI, 402 N Blackford St, Indianapolis, IN 46202-3274. **Fax:** 701-231-8831. **E-Mail:** kenny.lipkowitz@ndsu.nodak.edu

LIPMAN, DAVID J, BIOTECHNOLOGY. **Education:** Brown Univ, BA, 1976; Univ NY, Buffalo, MD, 1980. **Professional Experience:** DIR, NAT CTR BIOTECHNOL INFO, NAT LIBR MED, NIH, 1988-. **Memberships:** Nat Acad Sci; fel Am Col Med Informatics. **Mailing Address:** Nat Libr Med, NIH, Rm 8N807 Bldg 38A 8600 Rockville Pike, Bethesda, MD 20894. **Fax:** 301-480-9241. **E-Mail:** lipman@ncbi.nlm.nih.gov

LIPMAN, JACK M, PATHOLOGY, CELLULAR TOXICOLOGY. **Personal Data:** b Huntington, NY, October 25, 1954. **Education:** State Univ NY, PhD (exp path), 1986. **Professional Experience:** ASSOC RES INVESTR, HOFFMAN-LA ROCHE, 1993-. **Research Statement & Publications:** Alternatives to animal research. **Mailing Address:** Dept Toxicol & Pathol Invest Toxicol, Hoffman-La Roche Inc, 340 Kingsland St Bldg 100/1, Nutley, NJ 07110-1199.

LIPMAN, JOSEPH, MATHEMATICS. **Personal Data:** b Toronto, Ont, June 15, 1938; American citizen; m 1962, c 2. **Education:** Univ Toronto, BA, 1960; Harvard Univ, MA, 1961, PhD (math), 1965. **Professional Experience:** Res prof, Math Sci Res Inst, 1989-1990; head, Dept Math, Purdue Univ, West Lafayette, 1987-1992; PROF, MATH DEPT, PURDUE UNIV, WEST LAFAYETTE, 1972-; from asst prof to assoc prof, Dept Math, Purdue Univ, West Lafayette, 1966-1972; vis asst prof, Columbia Univ, 1967-1968; asst prof math, Queen's Univ, Ont, 1965; teaching fel, Harvard Univ, 1963-1964. **Memberships:** Am Math Soc. **Research Statement & Publications:** Algebraic geometry; commutative algebra; singularities. **Mailing Address:** Dept Math, Purdue Univ, Math 750, West Lafayette, IN 47907-1968. **Fax:** 765-494-0548. **E-Mail:** jlipman@purdue.edu

LIPMAN, MARC JOSEPH, GRAPH THEORY. **Personal Data:** b Chicago, Ill, March 19, 1950; m 1981, c 3. **Education:** Lake Forest Col, BA, 1971; Dartmouth Col, AM, 1973, PhD (math), 1976. **Professional Experience:** DEAN, SCH ARTS & SCI, IND-PURDUE UNIV, FORT WAYNE, 2002-; chmn, Math Sci, Oakland Univ, Rochester, Mich, 1997-2002; assoc, Nat Res Coun, Naval Res Lab, 1980; from asst prof to assoc prof, Ind Univ/Purdue Univ, Ft Wayne, 1976-1989; lectr math, Dartmouth Col, 1973. **Memberships:** Math Asn Am; Sigma Xi; Inst Combinatorics & Its Appl. **Research Statement & Publications:** Graph theory; intelligent systems. **Mailing Address:** Sch Arts & Sci, Ind-Purdue Univ, Ft Wayne, IN 46805. **Fax:** 260-481-6985. **E-Mail:** lipmanm@ipfw.edu

LIPMAN, PETER WALDMAN, GEOLOGY. **Personal Data:** b New York, NY, April 21, 1935; m 1962, Beverly; c Ben & Tim. **Education:** Yale Univ, BS, 1958; Stanford Univ, MS, 1959, PhD (geol), 1962. **Honors & Awards:** Burwell Award, Geol Soc Am, 1983, Councilor, Geol soc Am, 2000-2002. **Professional Experience:** NSF fel, Geol Inst, Tokyo, 1964-1965; GEOLOGIST, US GEOL SURV, 1962-. **Memberships:** Geol Soc Am; Mineral Soc Am; Am Geophys Union. **Research Statement & Publications:** Petrology and structural geology; volcanology, especially geology of calderas and related ash flows. **Mailing Address:** US Geol Surv MS 910, 345 Middlefield Rd, Menlo Park, CA 94025. **E-Mail:** plipman@usgs.gov

LIPNER, HARRY JOEL, reproductive endocrinology; deceased, see previous edition for last biography

LIPNER, STEVEN BARNETT, SOFTWARE SYSTEMS, COMPUTER SECURITY. **Personal Data:** b Independence, Kans, September 30, 1943; m 1980. **Education:** Mass Inst Technol, SB, 1965, SM, 1966. **Professional Experience:** MGR, SECURITY RESPONSE CTR, MICROSOFT CORP, 1999-; dir, Mitretek Systs Inc, 1997-1999; vpres, Trusted Info Syst Inc, 1994-1997; dir, Ctr Info Syst, Mitre Corp, 1992-1994; Mem, Nat Computer Systs Security & Privacy Adv Bd, 1989-; mem, Nat Res Coun Comt Comput Security, Dept Energy, 1987-1988; Chmn comt security & privacy, Inst Elec & Electronics Engrs Comput Soc, 1983-1984; group mgr, Secure Systs, Digital Equip Corp, 1981-1992; Command & Control Systs, 1980-1981; Assoc dept head, Intel & Info Syst, Mitre Corp, 1977-1980. **Memberships:** Asn Comput Mach; Sigma Xi; Inst Elec & Electronics Engrs Comput Soc. **Research Statement & Publications:** Security controls for computer systems; theoretical and practical advances in network security and secure operating systems. **Mailing Address:** Security Response Ctr, Microsoft Corp, One Microsoft Way, Redmond, WA 98052-6399.

LIPNICK, ROBERT LOUIS, PREDICTIVE TOXICOLOGY, SCIENCE POLICY. **Personal Data:** b Baltimore, Md, September 9, 1941; m 1967, Anne; c Deborah E & David H. **Education:** Univ Md, Col Park, BS, 1963; Brandeis Univ, PhD (org chem), 1969. **Professional Experience:** US rep, NAm Comn Environ Coop, 2002-; mem exec comt, Environ Chem Div, Am Chem Soc, 2000-; Com Sci fel, Off Sci, Technol & Health, US State Dept's Bur Oceans, Environ & Sci Affairs, 1993-1994; mem ed bd, Quant Struct-Activ Relationships, 1991-2004; mem, Int Sci Comt, Fourth Int Workshop Quant Struct-Active Relationship Environ Toxicol & Chem, Veldhoven, Neth, 1990; invited lectr, Comn Europ Communities, Ispra, Italy, 1990; assoc ed, Soc Environ Toxicol, beginning 1989; vis scientist, Pharmacol Inst, Univ Lund, Sweden, 1989; co-organizer workshop, Environ Protection Agency, 1988; vis scientist, Borstel Res Inst, Fed Repub Ger, 1986; SR CHEMIST, US ENVIRON PROTECTION AGENCY, 1985-; leader struct activ group, US Environ Protection Agency, 1980-1985; chemist, US Environ Protection Agency, 1979-1980; res assoc, Sloan-Kettering Inst, 1974-1979; vis scientist, var African univs, 1973-1974; fel chem, Univ Minn, Minneapolis, 1968-1972. **Memberships:** Am Chem Soc; Am Gov Toxicologists; Soc Environ Toxicol & Chem; Int Group Correlation Anal Org Chem. **Research Statement & Publications:** Development of quantitative structure-activity relationships for predictive toxicology; estimation of physicochemical, conformational and reactive properties of molecules from chemical structure; quantitative structure activity relationship; edited four books and author or co-author of 72 articles in scientific journals and books. **Mailing Address:** Off Pollution Prev & Toxics 7403M, US Environ Protection Agency, 1200 Pa Ave NW, Washington, DC 20460. **Fax:** 202-564-7450. **E-Mail:** lipnick.robert@epa.gov

LIPO, THOMAS ANTHONY, POWER ELECTRONICS, ELECTRICAL MACHINES. **Personal Data:** b Milwaukee, Wis, February 1, 1938; American citizen; m 1964, Christine; c Carl, Emily, Patrick & Anna. **Education:** Marquette Univ, BEng, 1962, MS, 1964; Univ Wis-Madison, PhD, 1968. **Honors & Awards:** Outstanding Achievement Award, Inst Elec & Electronic Engrs, Indust Applications Soc, 1986; William E Newell Award, Inst Elec & Electronic Engrs, Power Electronics Soc, 1990. **Professional Experience:** GRAINGER PROF POWER ELECTRONICS & ELEC MACH, UNIV WIS-MADISON, 1990-; chmn, Indust Power Conversion Systs, Inst Elec & Electronic Engrs, Indust Appln Soc, 1989-; vis prof, Univ Sydney, 1989; DIR, WIS POWER ELECTRONICS RES CTR, 1987-; ed, Inst Elec & Electronic Engrs, Power Electronics Soc Trans, 1983-1990; co-dir, Wis Elec Mach & Power Electronics Consortium, beginning 1981; prof, Univ Wis-madison, 1981-1990; prof, Purdue Univ, 1979-1980; vis assoc prof, Purdue Univ, 1973-1974; elec engr, Gen Elec Co, Schenectady, 1969-1979; Nat Res Coun res fel, Univ Manchester Inst Sci & Technol, Eng, 1968-1969; instr, Univ Wis-Milwaukee, 1964-1966; eng analyst, Allis-Chalmers Mfg Co, Milwaukee, 1964; grad trainee, Allis-Chalmers Mfg Co, Milwaukee, 1962-1964. **Memberships:** Fel Inst Elec & Electronic Engrs; Inst Elec & Electronic Engrs Power Eng Soc; Inst Elec & Electronic Engrs Indust Applications Soc; Inst Elec & Electronic Engrs Power Electronics Soc. **Research Statement & Publications:** New power electronic circuits, controls and electrical machines for alternating current adjustable speed drives for industrial, commercial and utility applications. **Mailing Address:** Dept Elec & Comput Eng Univ Wis, 1415 Johnson Dr, Madison, WI 53706-1691. **Fax:** 608-262-5559. **E-Mail:** lipo@engr.wisc.edu

LIPOTI, JILL, ENVIRONMENTAL SCIENCE. **Education:** Cook Coll, BS, 1977; MS, Rutgers Univ, PhD, 1985. **Honors & Awards:** Gerald S Parker Award, 2001. **Professional Experience:** DIR, DIV ENVIRON SAFETY & HEALTH, NJ DEPT ENVIRON PROTECTION TRENTON, NJ, 2006-; asst dir, Div Environ Safety, NJ Dept Environ Protection, 1989-2006; asst adj prof, Environ & Occup Health, NJ Ctr Public Health Preparedness, Univ Med & Dent NJ. **Memberships:** Nat Coun Radiation Protection & Measurement. **Mailing Address:** NJ Dept Environ Protection, Div Environ Safety & Health, 729 Alexander Rd CN 415, Princeton, NJ 08625-0415. **Fax:** 609-987-6390. **E-Mail:** jill.lipoti@dep.state.nj.us

LIPOVSKI, GERALD JOHN (JACK), COMPUTER ENGINEERING, ELECTRICAL ENGINEERING. **Personal Data:** b Coleman, Alta, January 28, 1944; m 1968, c 3. **Education:** Univ Notre Dame, AB & BSEE, 1966; Univ Ill, Urbana, MS, 1967, PhD (elec eng), 1969. **Professional Experience:** Grace Hopper chair comput sci, Naval Postgrad Sch, Calif, 1988-1989; PROF ELEC ENG & COMPUT SCI, COL ENG, UNIV TEX, AUSTIN, 1982-; assoc prof, Univ Tex, Austin, 1976-1982; Consult, Harris Semiconductor, 1973-1974 & Sycor, 1976-1977; asst prof elec eng, Univ Fla, 1969-1976; asst comput archit, Coordinated Sci Lab, Univ Ill, Urbana, 1968-1969; asst electronics, Coordinated Sci Lab, Univ Ill, Urbana, 1967-1968; res fel automata theory, Coordinated Sci Lab, Univ Ill, Urbana, 1966-1968. **Memberships:** Asn Comput Mach; Comput Soc of Inst Elec & Electronics Engrs. **Research Statement & Publications:** Computer architecture; parallel and distributed computer architectures; data base processor architectures; microcomputer architectures and applications; hardware design languages; artificial intelligence. **Mailing Address:** Dept Elec Eng & Comput Sci, Col Eng, Univ Tex, ENS 515A, Austin, TX 78712. **E-Mail:** lipovski@ece.utexas.edu

LIPOWITZ, JONATHAN, ORGANOMETALLIC CHEMISTRY, MATERIALS SCIENCE & CERAMICS ENGINEERING. **Personal Data:** b Paterson, NJ, April 25, 1937; m 1960, Evelyn; c Robert A & Suzanne J. **Education:** Rutgers Univ, Newark, BS, 1958; Univ Pittsburgh, PhD (chem), 1964. **Professional Experience:** SCIENTIST, RES DEPT, DOW CORNING CORP, 1987-; assoc scientist, Dow Corning Corp, 1979-1987; sr res specialist, Dow Corning Corp, 1975-1979; res specialist, Dow Corning Corp, 1974-1975; res chemist, Dow Corning Corp, 1965-1974; fel, Pa State Univ, Univ Park, 1964-1965. **Memberships:** Am Chem Soc; Sigma Xi; Am Ceramic Soc; Mat Res Soc; AAAS; NY Acad Sci. **Research Statement & Publications:** Silicone flammability, mechanisms of effects of silicones on flammability of organic polymers; silicone chemistry and physical properties; characterization of advanced ceramics; preparation of ceramic fibers from polymers. **Mailing Address:** Dow Corning Corp, 2200 W Salzburg Rd P O Box 994, Midland, MI 48686-0995. **Fax:** 989-496-6109.

LIPP, STEVEN ALAN, INORGANIC CHEMISTRY. **Personal Data:** b Brooklyn, NY, January 25, 1944; c 2. **Education:** Brooklyn Col, BS, 1965; Univ Calif, Berkeley, PhD (inorg chem), 1970. **Honors & Awards:** Achievement Award, RCA Labs, 1974; David Sarnoff Award, RCA Corp, 1975. **Professional Experience:** MEM TECH STAFF, SARNOFF CORP, 1970-. **Memberships:** Electrochem Soc; Soc Info Display. **Research Statement & Publications:** Preparation and evaluation of new cathodoluminescent materials, as well as the design and testing of enhancements for chemical milling; fabrication of active liquid crystal display substrate involving all photolithography and processing. **Mailing Address:** Sarnoff Corp, Wash Rd, Princeton, NJ 08543-4300.

LIPPA, ERIK ALEXANDER, OPHTHALMOLOGY, CLINICAL RESEARCH. **Personal Data:** b November 1945; m Linda; c 2. **Education:** Calif Inst Technol, BS, 1967; Univ Mich, MS, 1968, PhD (math), 1971; Albert Einstein Col Med, MD, 1980. **Professional Experience:** VPRES, GLOBAL MED AFFAIR & CLINC SERV, ALLERGAN INC, IRVINE, CALIF, 1998-; sr med dirt, med affir, Allergan, 1997-1998; dir, Med Affairs, Allergan, Inc, Irvine, Calif, 1993-1997; asst surgeon, Wills Eye Hosp, Philadelphia, 1991-1993; clin assoc, Dept Ophthal, Univ Pa, Philadelphia, 1987-1993; instr, Wills Eye Hosp, Philadelphia, 1986-1991; adj clin asst prof, Jefferson Med Col, Philadelphia, Pa, 1986-1989, 1991-1996; from assoc dir to dir clin res, Merck Res Lab, Blue Bell, Pa, 1985-1993; ophthalmologist, St Paul, Minn, 1984-1985; ophthal resident, Ill Eye & Ear Infirmary, Chicago, Ill, 1981-1984; med intern, NY Univ & Manhattan Vet Admin Hosp, 1980-1981; asst prof math, Purdue Univ, W Lafayette, 1972-1978; NATO fel math, Oxford Univ, 1971-1972. **Memberships:** Am Acad Ophthal; Asn Res Vision & Ophthal; Int Soc Eye Res; Sigma Xi; Am Glaucoma Soc; Amer Acad Derm. **Research Statement & Publications:** Ophthalmology; clinical pharmacology and clinical research; drug development; applications of mathematics to medicine and pharmaceutical sciences; analytic number theory. **Mailing Address:** Allergan Inc, 2525 Dupont Dr PO Box 16517, Irvine, CA 92612. **Fax:** 714-246-5445. **E-Mail:** lippa_erik@allergan.com

LIPPA, LINDA SUSAN MOTTOW, OCULAR PATHOLOGY, MEDICAL OPHTHALMOLOGY. **Personal Data:** b Boston, Mass, April 9, 1951; m 1980, c 2. **Education:** Harvard Univ, AB, 1973; Columbia Univ, MD, 1977. **Professional Experience:** ASSOC CLIN PROF, UNIV CALIF, IRVINE, 1994-; clin asst prof, Jefferson Med Col, Philadelphia, Pa, 1986-1993; asst surgeon opthal, Wills Eye Hosp, 1985-1993; ocular path, Wills Eye Hosp, 1985-1986; vis lectr, Dept Ophthal, Univ Md, 1985; attend ophthalmologist, Wills Eye Hosp, 1985; clin asst prof ophthal, Univ Minn & attend opthalmologist & ocular pathologist, St Paul Ramsey Med Ctr, 1984-1985; clin asst prof, Loyola Univ Med Ctr, Chicago, Ill & Hines Vet Admin Hosp, 1983-1984; attend ophthalmologist & ocular pathologist, Cook Co Hosp, Chicago, Ill, 1982-1984; clin instr ophthal, Loyola Univ Med Ctr, Chicago, Ill & Hines Vet Admin Hosp, 1982-1983; clin attend & ocular pathologist, Hines, VA, 1981-1984; fel ophthalmic path, Eye & Ear Infirmary, Univ Ill, Chicago, 1981-1982; chmn, Ophthalmologists in Training Comt & Continuing Educ Comt, 1980-1981; chief resident, Montefiore Hosp & Med Ctr & Albert Einstein Col Med, Bronx, NY, 1980-1981; rep, Ophthalmologists in Training Comt, Am Acad Ophthal, 1978-1981; adv fac, Continuing Educ Comt, 1978-1981; resident ophthal, Montefiore Hosp & Med Ctr & Albert Einstein Col Med, Bronx, NY, 1978-1980; lab teaching asst, Harkness Eye Inst, 1974 & Albert Einstein Col Med, 1978; Intern internal med, St Luke's Hosp & Med Ctr, New York, NY, 1977-1978; org chem, Harvard Bur Study Coun, 1973; Josephine Murray traveling fel, Radcliffe Col Res London, 1972; mem, Path Curric Comt, Dept Ophthal, Montefiore Hosp & Med Ctr, Albert Einstein Col Med. **Memberships:** Am Acad Ophthal; AMA. **Research Statement & Publications:** Retinal embryonal development; inflammatory and neoplastic ocular and adnexal disease; glaucoma; development of pharmacologic models for new compound and vehicle assessment; ophthalmology; medical education. **Mailing Address:** PO Box 16517, Irvine, CA 92623-6517.

LIPPARD, STEPHEN J, INORGANIC CHEMISTRY, BIOCHEMISTRY. **Personal Data:** b Pittsburgh, Pa, October 12, 1940; m 1964, Judith; c Joshua & Alexander. **Education:** Haverford Col, BA, 1962; Mass Inst Technol, PhD (chem), 1965. **Honorary Degrees:** DSc, Tex A&M Univ, 1995 DSc, Haverford Col, 2000. **Honors & Awards:** Camille & Henry Dreyfus Teacher-Scholar Award, 1972; Henry J Albert Award, Int Precious Metals Inst, Eng, 1985; Inorg Chem Award, Am Chem Soc, 1987; Remson Award, Am Chem Soc, 1988; Alexander von Humboldt Sr US Scientist Award, 1988; Bailar Medal, 1993; Inorg Chem Award, Am Chem Soc, 1994; Nichols Medal, 1995; Richards Medal, 2002; Bader Award, Am Chem Soc 2004; National Medal of Science, 2004. **Professional Experience:** HEAD, CHEM DEPT, MASS INST TECHNOL, 1995-2005; ARTHUR AMOS NOYES PROF CHEM, MASS INST TECHNOL, 1988-; assoc ed, J Am Chem Soc, 1988-; prof chem, Mass Inst Technol, 1983-1988; from asst prof to prof chem, Columbia Univ, 1966-1982; NSF fel, Mass Inst Technol, 1965-1966. **Memberships:** Nat Acad Sci; Inst Med-Nat Acad Sci; Am Crystallog Asn; hon mem Ital Chem Soc; hon mem Royal Irish Acad; Am Acad Arts & Sci; fel AAAS; Am Chem Soc. **Research Statement & Publications:** Inorganic and bioinorganic chemistry, especially preparation, structural properties and reactions of transition metal complexes; ligand bridged bimetallic complexes and proteins; metal binding to nucleic acids; platinum antitumor drugs; methane monooxygenase; zinc and nitric oxide signaling in the central nervous system. **Mailing Address:** Mass Inst Technol Rm 18-498, Cambridge, MA 02139. **Fax:** 617-258-8150. **E-Mail:** lippard@mit.edu

LIPPEL, KENNETH, ATHEROSCLEROSIS LIPID METABOLISM. **Personal Data:** b New York, NY, February 21, 1929; m 1961, c 1. **Education:** City Col NY, BS, 1949, MBA, 1960; Univ Fla, PhD (biochem), 1966. **Professional Experience:** RETIRED; Fel, Coun Arteriosclerosis, Am Heart Asn, 1975-; health sci adminr, Lipid Metab Br, Div Heart & Vascular Dis, Nat Heart, Lung & Blood Inst, NIH, 1972-1993; res biochemist, Lipids Br, Human Nutrit Res Div, Agr Res Serv, USDA, 1970-1972; asst prof dermat & biochem, Sch Med, Univ Miami, 1968-1970; NIH fel biochem, Univ Calif, Los Angeles, 1966-1968. **Memberships:** AAAS; Am Soc Biol Chem; Am Heart Asn; Am Chem Soc; Fedn Am Socs Exp Biol; Sigma Xi; Am Asn Clin Chem. **Research Statement & Publications:** Regulation of fatty acid and lipid metabolism; relationship of lipoprotein metabolism to atherosclerosis; vitamin A metabolism. **Mailing Address:** 4400 East-West Hwy Apt 715, Bethesda, MD 20814.

LIPPERT, BRUCE J, ENZYME CHEMICALS. **Personal Data:** b New York, NY. **Professional Experience:** RETIRED; Sr res biochemist, Marion Dow Res Inst, 1981-1994. **Mailing Address:** 32 Fleming Rd, Cincinnati, OH 45215.

LIPPERT, BYRON E, PHYCOLOGY. **Personal Data:** b Los Angeles, Calif, July 1, 1929; m 1952, c 3. **Education:** Univ Ore, BS, 1954, MS, 1957; Ind Univ, PhD (bot), 1966. **Professional Experience:** PROF EMER BIOL, PORTLAND STATE UNIV, as of 2004; assoc prof biol, Portland State Univ, beginning 1969; asst prof, Portland State Univ, 1960-1969; instr biol, Eastern Ore Col, 1956-1959. **Memberships:** Phycol Soc Am; Brit Phycol Soc; Int Phycol Soc; Bot Soc Am; Sigma Xi. **Research Statement & Publications:** Morphology, life cycles and sexual reproduction in desmids. **Mailing Address:** Room 140W SB2, Dept Biol, Portland State Univ, 1719 SW 10th Ave, Portland, OR 97201. **E-Mail:** algae@gte.net

LIPPERT, ERNEST, CHEMISTRY. **Education:** Univ Ok, BS, 1953, MS, 1955. **Professional Experience:** OWNER, MONARCH ANAL LABS INC, as of 2002. **Mailing Address:** Monarch Anal Labs Inc, 2747 Tamarack Dr, Toledo, OH 43614-5544. **Fax:** 419-897-9111.

LIPPERT, LLOYD EDWARD, TRANSFUSION MEDICINE, IMMUNOGENETICS. **Personal Data:** b Hoven, SDak, March 31, 1944. **Education:** SDak State Univ, MS, 1970; Bowling Green State Univ, SAB, 1975, MS, 1975; Med Col Va, PhD (path), 1987. **Professional Experience:** PROJ MGR, BIONETICS CORP, 1995-; lab mgr, Walter Reed Army Med Ctr, 1993-1995; prof mgr, Off Asst Secy Health Affairs, Dept Defense, 1992-1993; chief res opers, Walter Reed Army Med Ctr, 1987-1992; lab mgr & chief blood bank, Tripler Army Med Ctr, 1980-1983. **Research Statement & Publications:** Extending the shelflife of liquid stored red blood cells beyond 42 days to 8 weeks and possibly longer; manufacture precision grade hemoglobin-based blood substitute for research. **Mailing Address:** 2575 Scott Mill Dr S, Jacksonville, FL 32223.

LIPPES, JACK, OBSTETRICS & GYNECOLOGY, REPRODUCTION. **Personal Data:** b Buffalo, NY, February 19, 1924; m 1947, c Howard, B Fredda & Harold. **Education:** Univ Buffalo, MD, 1947. **Professional Experience:** PROF EMER OBSTET & GYNEC, SCH MED, STATE UNIV NY, BUFFALO, as of 2000; clin chief, Erie Co Med Ctr, Buffalo, NY, 1981-1994; vis prof obstet & gynec, Charing Cross Hosp, Med Sch, London, 1981; World Neighbors Found, Syntex Res, 1978-1979; WHO Comt Studying Human Reprod, 1974-1978 & Sterling-Winthrop Pharmaceut Corp grant, 1977-1978; prof obstet & gynec, sch med, State Univ NY, buffalo, beginnning 1975; chmn, Dept Obstet & Gynec, Deaconess Hosp, Buffalo, 1975-1981; investr, Upjohn Pharmaceut Co, 1975-1978 & Prog Appl Res Fertil Regulation, 1975-1978; World Neighbors Found, Ortho Pharmaceut Corp, 1966-1978; World Neighbors Found, Okla, 1966-1978; assoc prof, State Univ NY, Buffalo, 1966-1975; Consult, Pop Coun, 1966-1970; consult, Birth Control Ministries Health, SKorea, Taiwan, Pakistan, India, Turkey & Tunisia, 1964-1966; clin assoc, State Univ NY, Buffalo, 1960-1966; consult, Rockefeller Univ, 1959-1975; Clin instr, State Univ NY, Buffalo,

1952-1960. **Memberships:** Asn Planned Parenthood Physicians; Planned Parenthood Fedn; Am Fertil Soc; Am Col Obstet & Gynec; Asn Health Reproductive Professionals. **Research Statement & Publications:** Human oviductal fluid; contraception, especially intrauterine contraception; inventor and researcher of intrauterine contraceptive device known as the Loop; immunology of the genital tract; immunosuppresive proteins in the female genital tract. **Mailing Address:** Dept Gynec & Obstet, State Univ NY, Buffalo, NY 14222.

LIPPINCOTT, BARBARA BARNES, MICROBIOLOGY, PLANT PHYSIOLOGY. **Personal Data:** b Raleigh, Ill, October 27, 1934; m 1956, James A; c Jeanne M, Thomas R & John J. **Education:** Washington Univ, St Louis, AB, 1955, MA, 1957, PhD (zool & molecular biol), 1959. **Professional Experience:** RETIRED; Sr res assoc biochem, molecular biol & cell biol, 1980-1995; vis scientist, Inst Bot, Univ Heidelberg, 1974; lectr, Northwestern Univ, 1972-1973 & 1981-1998; vis scholar, Univ Calif Berkeley, 1970-1971; res assoc biol sci, molecular biol & cell biol, 1960-1980; Jane Coffin Childs Mem Fund Med Res fel physiol genetics, Lab Physiol Genetics, Nat Ctr Sci Res, France, 1959-1960. **Memberships:** Emer mem Am Soc Microbiol; emer mem Sigma Xi. **Research Statement & Publications:** Electron spin resonance in biological systems; crown-gall tumor formation; control mechanisms in replication, growth and development. **Mailing Address:** 2815 Harrison St, Evanston, IL 60201.

LIPPINCOTT, EZRA PARVIN, NUCLEAR PHYSICS, SHIELDING. **Personal Data:** b Philadelphia, Pa, September 7, 1939. **Education:** Mass Inst Technol, BS, 1961, PhD (nuclear physics), 1966. **Professional Experience:** Consult, Self-Employed, 1994; SR SCIENTIST, NUCLEAR ENG, WESTINGHOUSE ELEC CORP, 1972-; sr scientist, Battelle-Northwest Labs, 1966-1972. **Memberships:** Am Nuclear Soc; Am Phys Soc; Am Soc Testing & Mat Fel. **Research Statement & Publications:** Experimental and theoretical reactor physics; passive and active neutron and gamma-ray dosimetry; data analysis; methods development; nuclear cross section measurement and data file evaluation; standards preparation. **Mailing Address:** 1776 McClure Rd, Monroeville, PA 15146.

LIPPINCOTT, JAMES ANDREW, PLANT PHYSIOLOGY. **Personal Data:** b Cumberland Co, Ill, September 13, 1930; m 1956, Barbara Barnes; c Jeanne M, Thomas R & John J. **Education:** Earlham Col, AB, 1954; Wash Univ, AM, 1956, PhD, 1958. **Honors & Awards:** Centennial lectr, Mich State Univ Agr Exp Sta, 1975; Tanner-Shaughnessy Merit Award, Ill Soc Microbiol, 1981. **Professional Experience:** EMER PROF BIOCHEM, MOLECULAR & CELL BIOL, NORTHWESTERN UNIV, 1995-; prof, Molecular & Cell Biol, Northwestern Univ, 1981-1995; assoc dean biol sci, Molecular & Cell Biol, Northwestern Univ, 1980-1983; vis prof, Univ Heidelberg, 1974; Vis assoc prof, Univ Calif, Berkeley, 1970-1971; from asst prof to prof biol sci, Molecular & Cell Biol, Northwestern Univ, 1960-1981; Jane Coffin Childs Mem Fund Med Res fel, Lab Phytotron, Nat Ctr Sci Res, France, 1959-1960; Res assoc plant physiol & lectr bot, Wash Univ, 1958-1959. **Memberships:** emer mem AAAS; emer mem Am Soc Plant Physiol; emer mem Bot Soc Am; emer mem Am Soc Microbiol; emer mem Am Phytopath Soc; emer mem Sigma Xi; emer mem Am Soc Biol Chemists. **Research Statement & Publications:** Crown-gall tumor formation; control mechanisms in replication, growth and development; tumor induction in plants by Agrobacterium tumefaciens. **Mailing Address:** 2815 Harrison St, Evanston, IL 60201.

LIPPINCOTT-SCHWARTZ, JENNIFER, MOLECULAR MEMBRANE BIOLOGY, INTRACELLULAR MEMBRANE TRAFFICKING. **Personal Data:** b Kans, October 19, 1952; m 1975, c 2. **Education:** Swarthmore Col, BA, 1974; Stanford Univ, MS, 1979; Johns Hopkins Univ, PhD (biol), 1986. **Professional Experience:** HEAD, ORGANELLE BIOL, CELL BIOL & METAB BR, NICHD, NIH, as of 2004; sr staff scientist, Nat Inst Child Health & Hum dev, NIH, beginning 1990; fel, Nat Res Serv Award Prog, 1988-1990; fel, Pharmacol Res Assoc, Nat Inst Gen Med Sci, 1986-1988. **Memberships:** Am Soc Cell Biologists; AAAS. **Research Statement & Publications:** Intracellular membrane transport pathways and the molecular basis for intracellular membrane sorting and the biogenesis of organelles. **Mailing Address:** Cell Biol & Metab Br, NICHD, NIH, Bldg 18T Rm 100, Bethesda, MD 20892. **E-Mail:** jl122w@nih.gov

LIPPKE, HAGEN, ANIMAL NUTRITION. **Personal Data:** b Yorktown, Tex, November 4, 1936; m 1958, c 3. **Education:** Tex A&M Univ, BS, 1959, MS, 1961; Iowa State Univ, PhD (animal nutrit), 1966. **Professional Experience:** ASSOC PROF ANIMAL SCI, TEX A&M UNIV, 1974-; from asst prof to assoc prof ruminant nutrit, Tex A&M Univ, 1966-1974. **Memberships:** Am Dairy Sci Asn; Am Soc Animal Sci; AAAS. **Research Statement & Publications:** Ruminant nutrition; forage utilization by cattle; forage characteristics influencing intake and digestibility. **Mailing Address:** Dept Animal Sci, Tex A&M Univ, Uvalde, TX 78801. **Fax:** 830-278-1570. **E-Mail:** h-lippke@tamu.edu

LIPPMAN, ABBY, WOMENS HEALTH, GENETIC SCREENING & TESTING. **Personal Data:** b Brooklyn, NY, c 2. **Education:** Cornell Univ, BA, 1960; McGill Univ, PhD (human genetics), 1979. **Honors & Awards:** Marion Porter Prize, Can Res Inst Advan Women. **Professional Experience:** PROF, DEPT HUMAN GENETICS, MCGILL UNIV, 1992-; assoc mem, Univ Que, Montreal, 1991-; res assoc social studies med, McGill Ctr Res & Teaching Women, McGill Univ, 1990-; adj prof, Dept Prev Social Med, Univ Montreal, beginning 1989; mem, McGill Ctr Res & Teaching Women, McGill Univ, 1988-; Nat health res scholar, Health & Welfare Can, 1981-1986 & 1986-1992. **Memberships:** Fel Can Col Med Geneticists; fel Am Col Epidemiol; Am Public Health Asn; Am Soc Human Genetics; fel AAAS; fel Can Soc Obstet & Gynecol. **Research Statement & Publications:** Women's health; social, ethical and political implications of genetic screening and testing; feminist critique of biomedicine. **Mailing Address:** Dept Epidemiol McGill Univ, 1020 Pine Ave W, Montreal, PQ H3A 1A2, Can. **Fax:** 514-398-4503. **E-Mail:** abby.lippman@mcgill.ca

LIPPMAN, GARY EDWIN, MATHEMATICAL ANALYSIS, COMPUTER SCIENCE. **Personal Data:** b Little Rock, Ark, c 2. **Education:** San Jose State Col, BA, 1963; Univ Calif, Riverside, MA, 1965, PhD (math), 1970; Univ San Francisco, JD, 1978. **Professional Experience:** PROF MATH, CALIF STATE UNIV, HAYWARD, 1971-; vis prof elec eng & computer sci, Univ Calif, Berkeley, 1983-1988; vis asst prof math, Univ Tenn, vis assoc prof comput sci & statist, Univ RI, 1978-1979; asst prof math, Kenyon Col, 1970-1971. **Memberships:** Am Math Soc; Math Asn Am; Comput Law Soc, ACM. **Research Statement & Publications:** Fourier analysis; patent law; Computer prog. **Mailing Address:** Dept Math & Comput Sci, Calif State Univ, 25800 Carlos Bee Blvd, Hayward, CA 94542-3092. **E-Mail:** gary.lippman@csueastbay.edu

LIPPMAN, MARC ESTES, BREAST CANCER. **Personal Data:** b Brooklyn, NY, January 15, 1945. **Education:** Cornell Univ, BA, 1964; Yale Med Sch, MD, 1968. **Honors & Awards:** Mallinckrodt Award, Clin Radioassay Soc, 1978; D R Edwards Lect & Medal, Tenovus Inst, Wales, 1985; Transatlantic Medal & Lect, Brit Endocrine Socs, 1989; Tiffany Award Distinction, Komen Found, 1989. **Professional Experience:** CHMN, INTERNAL MED, HEALTH SYST, UNIV MICH, 2001-; JOHN G SEARLE PROF INTERNAL MED, HEALTH SYST, UNIV MICH, 2001-; Hon dir, Y-ME, Nat Orgn Breast Cancer Info & Support, 1990-; Woodward vis prof, mem Sloan-Kettering, 1990; sci adv bd, Coord Coun Cancer Res, 1989-; bd trustees, Am Cancer Soc, Dist Columbia, 1989-1992; chmn, local organizing comt, Am Soc Clin Oncol, 1989-1990; dir, Lombardi Cancer Ctr, Wash, DC & prof med & pharmacol, Georgetown Univ Sch Med, 1988-2001; Am Soc Clin Oncol, 1987-1989 & Am Soc Clin Invest, 1988; chmn, Gordon Res Conf on Hormone Action, 1985; treas, Int Cong Hormones & Cancer, 1984-; co-chmn, Gordon Res Conf on Hormone Action, 1984; Endocrine Treatment Comt, Nat Surg Adjuvant Breast Proj, 1977-1986 & pub affairs comt, Endocrine Soc, 1980-1981; clin prof med & pharmacol, Uniformed Serv, Univ Health Sci, 1978-; consult, Dept Pharmacol, George Wash Sch Med, 1978-1989; mem, Merit Rev Bd Oncol, Vet Admin Med Res Serv, 1977-1981; head, Med Breast Cancer Sect, 1976-1988; sr investr, Med Br, 1974-1988; fel endocrinol, Yale Med Sch, New Haven, Conn, 1973-1974; clin assoc, Lab Biochem, 1971-1973; clin assoc, Leukemia Serv, Nat Cancer Inst, NIH, 1970-1971; asst resident, Osler Med Serv, Johns Hopkins Hosp, Baltimore, Md, 1969-1970; intern, Osler Med Serv, Johns Hopkins Hosp, Baltimore, Md, 1968-1969. **Memberships:** Asn Am Physicians; Am Soc Clin Invest; Am Soc Biol Chemists; fel Am Col Physicians; Am Fedn Clin Res; Endocrine Soc; Am Soc Cell Biol; Am Asn Cancer Res; Am Soc Clin Oncol; Metastasis Res Soc. **Research Statement & Publications:** Growth regulation of cancer; breast cancer; cancer endocrinology; growth factor receptors. **Mailing Address:** Dept Internal Med Univ Mich, Rm 3101 A Alfred Taubman Ctr 1500 E Med Ctr Dr Box 0368, Ann Arbor, MI 48109. **Fax:** 734-615-2645. **E-Mail:** lippmanm@umich.edu

LIPPMANN, DAVID ZANGWILL, CHEMICAL KINETICS, STATISTICAL MECHANICS. **Personal Data:** b Houston, Tex, July 6, 1925; m 1969, Jane. **Education:** Univ Tex, BSc, 1947, MA, 1949; Univ Calif, Berkeley, PhD (phys chem), 1953. **Professional Experience:** Vis scholar, Univ Tex, Austin, 1980-; ASSOC PROF CHEM, SW TEX STATE UNIV, 1969-; asst prof, SW Tex State Univ, 1963-1969; Proteus, Inc, 1961-1963; Fulton-Irgon Div, Lithium Corp Am, 1957-1961; chemist, Reaction Motors, Inc, 1954-1957. **Memberships:** Am Chem Soc; Sigma Xi; AAAS. **Research Statement & Publications:** Theoretical physical chemistry, especially thermodynamics and statistical mechanics; rocketry and ballistics; properties of gems. **Mailing Address:** Dept Chem, Sw Tex State Univ, San Marcos, TX 78666. **Fax:** 512-245-2374. **E-Mail:** lippmann@physics.utexas.edu

LIPPMANN, MARCELO JULIO, GEOTHERMICS, GROUNDWATER HYDROLOGY. **Personal Data:** b Buenos Aires, Arg, May 27, 1939; m 1965, Martha; c 1. **Education:** Univ Buenos Aires, MS, 1966; Univ Calif, Berkeley, MS, 1969, PhD (eng sci), 1974. **Professional Experience:** Assoc ed, Geothermics, 1991-1995; LEADER GEOTHERMAL GROUP, EARTH SCI DIV, LAWRENCE BERKELEY LAB, 1983-; US tech coordr, Dept Energy, Comn Federal Del Electricidad, 1977-; STAFF SCIENTIST, EARTH SCI DIV, LAWRENCE BERKELEY LAB, 1976-; asst res eng, Dept Civil Eng, Univ Calif, Berkeley, 1974-1976; Jane Lewis fel, Univ Calif, Berkeley, 1969-1971; consult hydrogeologist, Hidrosud SA, Buenos Aires, 1967; sedimentologist, Arg Geol Serv, 1966-1967; asst geologist, Arg Geol Serv, 1963-1966; pvt consult, Hydrogeol-Geothermal Energy. **Memberships:** Am Geophys Union; Soc Petrol Engrs. **Research Statement & Publications:** Geothermal and groundwater resources; physics and numerical modeling of processes in porous media. **Mailing Address:** Earth Sci Div, Lawrence Berkeley Nat Lab, Berkeley, CA 94720. **Fax:** 510-486-5686. **E-Mail:** mjlippmann@lbl.gov

LIPPMANN, MORTON, ENVIRONMENTAL SCIENCES HEALTH. **Personal Data:** b Brooklyn, NY, September 21, 1932; m 1956, Janet; c Amy, Stanley & David. **Education:** Cooper Union, BChE, 1954; Harvard Univ, SM, 1955; NY Univ, PhD (Environ Health Sci), 1967. **Honors & Awards:** David Sinclair Award, Am Asn Aerosol Res; Donald E Cummings Award, Am Indust Hyg Asn; Herbert E Stokinger Award, Am Conf Govt Indust Hygienists; Henry F Smyth Jr Award, Am Acad Indust Hyg. **Professional Experience:** Chmn, Environ Protection Agency Exec Comm, 2000-2001; mem & chmn, bd sci counr, Nat Inst Occup Safety & Health, 1988-1993; chmn, Environ Protection Agency Indoor Air & Total Human Exposure Adv Comt, 1987-1993; chmn, Environ Protection Agency Clean Air Sci Adv Comn, 1983-1987; PROF ENVIRON MED & DIR, HUMAN EXPOSURE & HEALTH EFFECTS PROG, INST ENVIRON MED, NY UNIV, 1977-; from asst prof to assoc prof, Human Exposure & Health Effects Prog, Inst Environ Med, NY Univ, 1967-1977; assoc res scientist aerosol physiol, Human Exposure & Health Effects Prog, Inst Environ Med, NY Univ, 1964-1967; sr res engr, Del Electronics Corp, 1962-1964; US AEC, NY, 1957-1962; indust hygienist, USPHS, Ohio, 1955-1957. **Memberships:** Am Conf Govt Indust Hygienists; Am Indust Hyg Asn; Int Soc Environ Epidemiol; Am Asn Aerosol Res; Int Soc Exposure Anal. **Research Statement & Publications:** Environmental hygiene; regional deposition and clearance of inhaled particles; sampling and analysis of atmospheric particles; aerodynamic behavior of respirable aerosols; field and laboratory studies of health effects of airborne toxicants. **Mailing Address:** NY Univ Nelson Inst Environ Med, SLF Two 266B, 57 Old Forge Rd, Tuxedo, NY 10987. **Fax:** 845-351-5472. **E-Mail:** lippmann@env.med.nyu.edu

LIPPMANN, SEYMOUR A, APPLIED PHYSICS. **Personal Data:** b Brooklyn, NY, November 23, 1919; m 1945, c Raymond Lippmann & Susan L Bennett. **Education:** Cooper Union, BChE, 1942. **Professional Experience:** RETIRED; mgr Tire-Vehicle Systs Labs, Uniroyal Tire Co, Uniroyal Inc, 1975-1985; res assoc, Res Dept, US Rubber Co, 1971-1975; dept mgr phys res, Res Dept, US Rubber Co, 1960-1971; group leader appl physics, Res Dept, US Rubber Co, 1947-1960; sem instr, Tire & Vehicle Dynamics, Soc Automotive Engrs. **Memberships:** Am Phys Soc; Fel Soc Automotive Eng; Inst Elec & Electronics Eng; Am Soc Testing & Mat; Sigma Xi. **Research Statement & Publications:** Physics of polymeric materials; transmission of noise and vibrations; design of electronic instrumentation for the study of dynamic systems and properties; perception of sound in the presence of background noise; dynamics of the human as a link in control systems; mechanics of laminates and tires. **Mailing Address:** 12767 Lincoln Dr, Huntington Woods, MI 48070.

LIPPMANN, WILBUR, BIOCHEMICAL PHARMACOLOGY. **Personal Data:** b Galveston, Tex, September 6, 1930. **Education:** Tex A&M Col, BS, 1951; Univ Tex, MA, 1956, PhD (biochem), 1961. **Professional Experience:** RETIRED; dir, Dept Biochem Pharmacol, 1969-1980; head biogenic amine lab, Ayerst Labs, Can, 1966-1969; res biochemist, Lederle Labs, Am Cyanamid Co, NY, 1962-1966; fel, Univ Tex, 1961-1962; res biochemist, Univ Tex, M D Anderson Hosp & Tumor Inst, 1958; res biochemist, Virus Inst, Univ Calif, Berkeley, 1956-1958; res biochemist, Biochem Inst, Univ Tex, 1954-1956, 1958-1962. **Memberships:** AAAS; Am Chem Soc; Am Soc Pharmacol & Exp Therapeut; Pharmacol Soc Can; NY Acad Sci. **Research Statement & Publications:** Biosynthesis and mode of action of the biogenic amines; biochemical mechanisms of action of drugs with respect to cardiovascular, central nervous and gastrointestinal systems; biochemical mechanisms involved with gonadotrophin secretion. **Mailing Address:** 2334 W Coventry Circle, Fullerton, CA 92633-1267.

LIPPOLD, HERBERT R, JR, ENGINEERING, GENERAL. **Personal Data:** b April 9, 1926. **Education:** New Eng Col, BS, 1949; Univ NH, BE, 1950. **Honors & Awards:** Environ Merit Award, US Environ Protection Agency, 2002. **Professional Experience:** PRES,

BIG ISLAND POND CORP, ATKINSON, NH, 1985-; dir, Nat Ocean Surv, Nat Oceanic & Atmospheric Admin, 1981-1984; at Coast & Geodetic Survey, Nat Oceanic & Atmospheric Admin, beginning 1951. **Mailing Address:** Nat Ocean Surv, Nat Oceanic & Atmospheric Admin, Rockville, MD 20852.

LIPPS, FREDERICK WIESSNER, theoretical physics, mathematics; deceased, see previous edition for last biography

LIPPS, JERE HENRY, GEOLOGY, INVERTEBRATE PALEONTOLOGY. **Personal Data:** b Los Angeles, Calif, August 28, 1939; m 1973, Susanna; c Jeremy C & Jamison W. **Education:** Univ Calif, Los Angeles, AB, 1962, PhD (geol), 1966. **Honors & Awards:** Lipps Island, Antarctica named in honor; W Storrs Cole Award, Geol Soc Am, 1993; Darwin Award, Nat Ctr Sci Educ, 1993. **Professional Experience:** Vis Scholar, Dept Hist Earth, Nat Mus Natural Hist, Paris, 2005-2006; guest lectr, Inst & Mus Geol & Paleont, Univ Tuebingen, Germany, 1997; chair, Dept Integrative Biol, Univ California, Berkeley, 1991-1994; PROF INTEGRATIVE BIOL & DIR MUS PALEONT, UNIV CALIF, BERKELEY, 1989-; vis scientist, Brit Mus (natural hist), London, 1989; dir, Mus Paleont, Univ Calif, Berkeley, 1989-1997; prof paleont, Univ Calif, Berkeley, 1988-1989; guest prof, Aarhus Univ, Denmark, 1977; chair, Dept Geol, Univ Calif, Davis, 1979-1984 & 1972-1974; guest prof, Geologisk Inst, Aarhus Univ, Aarhus, Denmark, 1977; vis scientist, Dept Geol, Oxford Univ, 1975; dir, Inst Ecol, Univ Calif, Davis, 1971; prin investr grants, NSF, 1968-2002, 1988 & Nat Park Serv, 1970-1973; from asst prof to prof geol, Univ Calif, Davis, 1967-1988; res geologist, Univ Calif, Los Angeles, 1965-1967; res assoc, Los Angeles Co Mus, 1963-; asst res geologist invert paleont, Calif Res Corp, 1963-1965; dir, Cushman Found Foraminiferal Res. **Memberships:** Fel AAAS; fel Geol Soc Am; Paleont Soc (pres, 1996-1997); Soc Econ Paleont & Mineral. **Research Statement & Publications:** Ecology of Foraminifera; evolutionary biology of protists; marine ecology and evolution; geology; Antarctica. **Mailing Address:** Dept Integrative Biol & Mus Paleont, Univ Calif, Berkeley, CA 94720. **Fax:** 510-642-1822. **E-Mail:** jlipps@berkeley.edu

LIPSCHULTZ, FREDERICK PHILLIP, PHYSICS. **Personal Data:** b Los Angeles, Calif, August 27, 1937. **Education:** Stanford Univ, BS, 1959; Cornell Univ, PhD (physics), 1966. **Professional Experience:** ASSOC PROF EMER PHYSICS, UNIV CONN, as of 2000; vis fel physics, Univ Nottingham, 1976-1977; assoc prof physics, Univ Conn, beginning 1972; asst prof, Univ Conn, 1967-1972; fel, Brookhaven Nat Lab, 1965-1967; res assoc physics, Cornell Univ, 1962-1965. **Memberships:** AAAS; Am Phys Soc; Inst Elec & Electronic Engrs. **Research Statement & Publications:** Thermal conductivity; low temperature physics; ultrasonics; use of thermal and acoustic properties of materials to investigate microscopic defects in solids; laboratory computer interfacing for research and teaching. **Mailing Address:** Dept Physics, Univ Conn, Storrs, CT 06269. **E-Mail:** lipschul@pacbell.net

LIPSCHUTZ, MICHAEL ELAZAR, RADIOCHEMISTRY, COSMOCHEMISTRY. **Personal Data:** b Philadelphia, Pa, May 24, 1937; m Linda; c Joshua H, Mark D & Jonathan M. **Education:** Pa State Univ, BS, 1958; Univ Chicago, SM, 1960, PhD (phys chem), 1962. **Honors & Awards:** Nininger Meteorite Res Award, 1962; Cert of Recognition for Creative Develop Technol, Cert of Spec Recognition, NASA, 1979; NASA Group Achievement Award, 1983; Cert of Appreciation, Nat Comn Space, 1986; Cert of Recognition for Cold War service, US Defense Dept, 2001; minor planet 2641 Lipschutz named by Int Astron Union. **Professional Experience:** Assoc head chem, 1993-2001; COSPAR/SAFISY Panel Space Sci Experts, 1990-; dir, Chem Opers, Primelab, 1990-2001; vis prof chem, Max-Planck Inst Chem, Mainz, Ger, 1987; consult, NASA, 1973-2002 & Lunar Planetary Inst, 1981-2002; PROF CHEM, PURDUE UNIV, 1973-; prof chem & Geoscience, Purdue Univ, 1973-1978; fulbright-hays scholar, Tel Aviv Univ, 1971-1972; assoc prof, Purdue Univ, 1968-1973; asst prof Geoscience, Purdue Univ, 1967-1968; asst prof chem, Purdue Univ, 1965-1968; NSF and NATO fel, Physics Inst, Berne, 1964-1965. **Memberships:** AAAS; Am Geophys Union; fel Meteoritical Soc; Am Chem Soc; Planetary Soc; Sigma Xi; Int Astron Union. **Research Statement & Publications:** Neutron activation, atomic absorption and inductively coupled plasma mass spectrometric methods for trace and ultratrace analysis; geochemistry; stable isotopes in lunar samples and meteorites; cosmogenic nuclear reactions; high pressure and temperature reactions; author or co-author of over 190scientific papers. **Mailing Address:** Dept Chem, Wetherill Lab, Purdue Univ, 560 Oval Dr, West Lafayette, IN 47907-2038. **Fax:** 765-494-0239. **E-Mail:** rnaapuml@purdue.edu

LIPSCOMB, DAVID M, FORENSIC AUDIOLOGY, HEARING CONSERVATION. **Personal Data:** b Morrill, Nebr, August 4, 1935; m 1995, JoAnn M Hoogstad; c Scott, Steven, Doris, Anthony, Shari, Clinton & Julia. **Education:** Univ Redlands, BA, 1957, MA, 1959; Univ Wash, PhD (audiol), 1966. **Professional Experience:** PRES, CORRECT SERV, INC, 1986-; prof audiol & speech path, Univ Tenn, Knoxville, 1972-1987; dir, Noise Res Lab, 1971-1987; assoc prof, Univ Tenn, Knoxville, 1969-1972; asst prof, Univ Tenn, Knoxville, 1962-1964 & 1966-1969; Asst prof audiol, WTex State Univ, 1960-1962; Consult, various industs & attorneys. **Memberships:** Fel Am Speech & Hearing Asn; Acoust Soc Am; Am Auditory Soc; Nat Hearing Conserv Asn; Am Acad Audiol. **Research Statement & Publications:** Effect of high intensity noise upon the peripheral auditory mechanism. **Mailing Address:** PO Box 1680, Stanwood, WA 98292-1680. **Fax:** 360-629-3755. **E-Mail:** dmlipscomb@worldnet.att.net

LIPSCOMB, JOHN DEWALD, SPECTROSCOPY ENZYMOLOGY. **Personal Data:** b Wilmington, Del, April 16, 1947; m 1972, c 1. **Education:** Amherst Col, BA, 1969; Univ Ill, MS, 1971, PhD (biochem), 1974. **Professional Experience:** PROF BIOCHEM, MOLECULAR BIOL & BIOPHYS, UNIV MINN, 1987-; prin investr, NIH res grant, 1978-; from asst to assoc prof, Freshwater Biol Inst, 1977-1987; fel, Freshwater Biol Inst, 1975-1977. **Memberships:** Am Chem Soc; Sigma Xi; Am Soc Biol Chemists. **Research Statement & Publications:** Enzyme mechanisms, in particular metalloenzymes such as dioxygenases, monooxygenases iron-sulfur proteins; resonance spectroscopy; chemical modification reactions; transient kinetics. **Mailing Address:** Dept Biochem, Molecular Biol & Biophys, Univ Minn, Off 5-112 BSBE 4-225 Millard Hall 435 Del St SE, Minneapolis, MN 55455. **Fax:** 612-624-5121. **E-Mail:** lipsc001@tc.umn.edu

LIPSCOMB, NATHAN THORNTON, POLYMER CHEMISTRY. **Personal Data:** b Winchester, Ky, January 16, 1934; m 1962, c 2. **Education:** Eastern Ky State Col, BS, 1956; Univ Louisville, PhD (phys chem), 1960. **Professional Experience:** PROF EMER CHEM, UNIV LOUISVILLE, as of 2005; Consult, ORGI, 1988-; prof chem, Univ Louisville, beginning 1975; From asst prof to assoc prof, Univ Louisville, 1960-1975. **Memberships:** Am Chem Soc; Sigma Xi. **Research Statement & Publications:** Kinetics of polymerization; radiation induced polymerization; polymer characterization; polymer properties. **Mailing Address:** Dept Chem, Univ Louisville, Bel Knap Campus, Louisville, KY 40292. **Fax:** 502-852-8149. **E-Mail:** ntlips01@athena.louisville.edu

LIPSCOMB, PAUL ROGERS, orthopedic surgery; deceased, see previous edition for last biography

LIPSCOMB, STEPHEN LEON, SYMMETRIC INVERSE SEMIGROUP, IMBEDDING FINITE DIMENSIONAL METRIC SPACES. **Personal Data:** b Junior, WVa, January 31, 1944; m 1962, Patrecia; c Stephen II & Darrin Joel. **Education:** Fairmont State Col, BA, 1965; WVa Univ, MA, 1967; Univ Va, PhD (math), 1973. **Professional Experience:** PROF EMER, DEPT MATH, MARY WASH COL, as of 2004; sr fel, USN-Am Soc Eng Educ, 1994 & 1995; prof math, Mary Wash Col, beginning 1990; chmn, Dept Math, 1990-1996; chmn, Dept Math Sci, 1984-1987; assoc prof math, Mary Wash Col, 1983-1989; adj prof math, Va Inst Technol, 1976-1992; sr mathematician, Naval Surface Warfare Ctr, 1967-1983. **Memberships:** Am Math Soc. **Research Statement & Publications:** Topology; dimension theory; semigroups; path notation; author of numerous research articles. **Mailing Address:** Dept Math, Mary Wash Col, 1301 Col Ave Trinkle Hall, Fredericksburg, VA 22401. **Fax:** 540-654-2445. **E-Mail:** slipscom@mwc.edu

LIPSCOMB, WILLIAM NUNN, PHYSICAL CHEMISTRY. **Personal Data:** b Cleveland, Ohio, December 9, 1919; m 1983, c 3. **Education:** Univ Ky, BS, 1941; Harvard Univ, MA, 1959; Calif Inst Technol, PhD (phys chem), 1946. **Honorary Degrees:** DSc, Univ Ky, 1963, Long Island Univ, 1977, Rutgers Univ, 1979, Gustavus Adolphus Col, 1980, Marietta Col, 1981, Miami Univ, 1983, Univ Denver, 1985 & Ohio State Univ, 1991; Dr, Univ Munich, 1976. **Honors & Awards:** Nobel Prize in Chem, 1976; Howe Award, Am Chem Soc, 1958, Peter Debye Award, 1973, Remsen Award, 1976; Welch Found lectr, Univ Tex, 1966; Phillips lectr, Univ Okla & Priestly lectr, Pa State Univ, 1967; William Pyle Phillips lectr, Haverford Col, 1968; Baker lectr, Cornell Univ & Coover lectr, Iowa State Univ, 1969; Centenary lectr, Chem Soc, 1972; Weizmann Lectr, Rehovoth, Israel, 1974; Van-tHoff centenary commemoration lectr, Univ Leiden & Gilbert Newton Lewis Mem lectr, Berkeley, 1974; Renaud lectr, Mich State Univ, 1975; Dreyfus distinguished scholar-lectr & John Strauffer Mem lectr, Univ Southern Calif, Los Angeles, 1980; Probst lectr, Souther Ill Univ-Edwardville, 1980. **Professional Experience:** ABBOTT & JAMES LAWRENCE PROF EMER CHEM, HARVARD UNIV, 1990-; Gensia Pharmaceut Inc, 1991-; Nova Pharmaceut Corp, 1985-; Daltex Med Sci Inc, 1984-; adv comt, Dow Chem Co, Inst Amorphous Studies, 1983-; bd dirs, Dow Chem Co, 1982-1989; mem sci adv bd, Robert A Welch Found, 1982-; speaker/session chmn, Conf Quantum Chem Biomed Sci, NY Acad Sci, 1980; probst lectr, Southern Ill Univ at Edwardsville, 1980; Dreyfus distinguished scholar, Univ Chicago, 1980; bd assocs, Linus Pauling Inst Sci & Med, 1977; Guggenheim fel, Oxford, 1954-1955 & Cambridge, 1972-1973; Harvard lectr, Yale, 1972; centenary lect, Chem Soc, 1972; Abbott & James Lawrence prof, Harvard Univ, 1971-1990; mem, adv comt, Ctr Struct Biochem, Brookhaven Nat Labs, 1970; distinguished lectr, Howard Univ, 1966; NSF sr fel, 1965-1966; chmn dept, Harvard Univ, 1962-1965; Upjohn Co, 1958 & Adv Res Projs Agency, 1961-1973; prof chem, Harvard Univ, 1959-1971; grants, NIH, 1958-; grants, Off Naval Res, 1958-1977; grants, Air Force Off Sci Res, 1958-1964; grants, NSF, 1956-1965 & 1977-1978; mem rev comt, Chem Div, Argonne Nat Lab, 1956-1965; chief, Univ Minn, 1954-1959; mem nat comt crystallog, Nat Res Coun, 1954-1958, 1960-1963 & 1965-1967; grants, Off Ord Res, 1954-1956; actg chief div, Univ Minn, 1952-1954; from asst prof to prof phys chem, Univ Minn, 1946-1959. **Memberships:** Nat Acad Sci; fel Am Phys Soc; Am Chem Soc; Am Crystallog Asn (pres, 1955); fel Am Acad Arts & Sci; Sigma Xi; hon mem Chem Soc London; hon fel Royal Soc Chem; Int Acad Quantum Mech Sci; Mineral Soc Am; hon mem Int Asn Bioinorg Scientists; foreign mem Neth Acad Arts & Sci. **Research Statement & Publications:** Diffraction studies of crystals and molecules of biochemical interest; relationship between structure and function, including the relationship of three-dimensional structure and mechanisms of enzymes and other proteins; relationship of geometric and electronic structures in theoretical inorganic and organic chemistry. **Mailing Address:** Dept Chem, Harvard Univ, 12 Oxford St, Cambridge, MA 02138. **Fax:** 617-495-3330. **E-Mail:** lipscomb@chemistry.harvard.edu

LIPSETT, FREDERICK ROY, FLUORESCENCE MEASUREMENTS, CRYSTAL GROWTH & MICROGRAVITY. **Personal Data:** b Vancouver, BC, September 26, 1925; m 1957, c 2. **Education:** Univ BC, BApSc, 1948, MApSc, 1951; Univ London, PhD (physics), 1954. **Professional Experience:** RETIRED; consult, Conf Quantum Chem Biomed Sci, Ny Acad Sci, beginning 1987; part time lectr, Carleton Univ, Can, 1962-1964; sr res officer elec eng div, Nat Res Coun Can, 1954-1987. **Memberships:** Catgut Acoustical Soc; Am Asn Crystal Growth; AAAS; Acoust Soc Am; World Forum Acoust Ecol. **Research Statement & Publications:** Luminescence; analysis and computer simulation of police patrol operations; floating zone crystal growth; science and music. **Mailing Address:** 37 Oriole Dr, Gloucester, ON K1J 7E8, Can.

LIPSEY, SALLY IRENE, MATHEMATICS EDUCATION. **Personal Data:** b December 31, 1926; American citizen; m 1948, Robert; c Marion, Carol & Eleanor. **Education:** Hunter Col, AB, 1947; Univ Wis, AM, 1948; Columbia Univ, DEduc, 1965. **Professional Experience:** RETIRED; from asst prof to assoc prof math, Brooklyn Col, 1970-1985; asst prof educ, Brooklyn Col, 1965-1970; asst prof, Bronx Community Col, 1959-1965; lectr, Barnard Col, 1953-1959; lectr, Hunter Col, 1949-1953; high sch teacher, Bd Educ, NY, 1948-1949; asst, Dept Math, Univ Wis, 1947-1948. **Memberships:** Nat Coun Teachers Math; Math Asn Am; Am Math Soc; Asn Women Math; NY Acad Sci; Women & Math Educ (pres, 1999-2001). **Research Statement & Publications:** Writer on the following subjects: the teaching of mathematics, mathematics in nursing science; women in mathematics; editor of articles on mathematics education; editor, "Encyclopedia of Mathematics Education" (with Louise Grinstein). **Mailing Address:** 70 E Tenth St, New York, NY 10003.

LIPSHITZ, HOWARD DAVID, DEVELOPMENTAL GENETICS, DEVELOPMENTAL BIOLOGY. **Personal Data:** b Durban, SAfrica, October 30, 1955; American citizen; m 1986, Susanna; c Sarah Starr Lipshitz-Lewis. **Education:** Univ Natal, Durban, SAfrica, BSc, 1976, BSc Hons, 1977; Yale Univ, New Haven, Conn, MPhil, 1980, PhD (biol), 1983. **Honors & Awards:** Canada Research Chair in Developmental Biology, Univ Toronto, 2001-present; Fellow, AAAS, 1990. **Professional Experience:** PROF since 1995 & CHAIR since 2005, DEPT MEDICAL GENETICS & MICROBIOLOGY, GRAD DEPT MOLECULAR & MEDICAL GENETICS, UNIV TORONTO; CANADA RES CHAIR IN DEV BIOL, UNIV TORONTO since 2001; SR SCIENTIST, DEVELOP BIO, HOSP SICK C, since 1995; Program Head, Develop Bio, Hosp Sick C, 2001-2005; Assoc Dir, Res Inst, Hosp Sick C, 1997-2001; assoc prof, Calif Inst Technol, Pasadena, 1992-1995; prin investr, Canadian Inst Health Res, 1995-present; prin investr, Natl Cancer Inst Canada, 1996-present; prin investr, Amer Cancer Soc, 1990-1992, prin investr, March Dimes Birth Defects Found, 1990-1992; Searle scholar, 1988-1991; prin investr, NIH, 1987-1993; asst prof, Div Biol, Calif Inst Technol, Pasadena, 1986-1992; Helen Hay Whitnet Foundation postdoc res fel, Dept Biochem, Stanford Univ, 1983-1986; South African Natl Scholarship, Yale Univ, 1978-1980. **Memberships:** AAAS; Genetics Soc Am; Am Soc Cell Biol; Soc Develop Biol; RNA Soc: Genetics Soc Canada. **Research Statement & Publications:** Molecular genetics of embryonic pattern formation and morphogenesis; localization and posttranscriptional control of RNA; life and work of Edward B. Lewis (book). **Mailing Address:** Dept Medical Genetics & Microbiology, Univ Toronto, 1 King's Col Circle, Toronto, ON M5S 1A8, Can. **Fax:** 416-971-2494. **E-Mail:** howard.lipshitz@utoronto.ca

LIPSHITZ, STANLEY PAUL, ELECTROACOUSTICS, SOUND RECORDING & REPRODUCTION. **Personal Data:** b Cape Town, SAfrica, November 25, 1943; Canadian citizen. **Education:** Univ Natal, BSc, 1964; Univ SAfrica, MSc, 1965; Univ Witwatersrand, PhD (math), 1970. **Honors & Awards:** AES Silver Medal Award, 1993. **Professional Experience:** PROF APPL MATH & PHYSICS, UNIV WATERLOO, 1988-; from asst prof to assoc prof, Univ Waterloo, 1970-1988; vis lectr math, Univ Ariz, 1967-1968. **Memberships:** Fel Audio Eng Soc (pres, 1988-1989); Acoust Soc Am; Inst Elec & Electronics Engrs. **Research Statement & Publications:** Mathematical, physical, and engineering problems of audio and electroacoustics; transducer design and measurement; digital audio signal processing; stereo and surround sound recording and reproduction. **Mailing Address:** Dept Appl Math, Univ Waterloo, Waterloo, ON N2L 3G1, Can. **Fax:** 519-746-4319. **E-Mail:** spl@audiolab.uwaterloo.ca

LIPSHULTZ, LARRY I, UROLOGY. **Personal Data:** b Philadelphia, Pa, April 24, 1942; m 1966, c 2. **Education:** Franklin & Marshall Col, BS, 1960; Univ Pa, MD, 1968. **Professional Experience:** DIR, DIV MALE REPRODUCTIVE MED & SURG, SCOTT DEPT UROL, BAYLOR COL MED, 1998-; PROF UROL, SCOTT DEPT UROL, BAYLOR COL MED, 1981-; prof urol, Med Sch, Univ Tex, Houston, 1980-1981; assoc prof, Med Br, Univ Tex, Houston, 1977-1980; adj asst prof urol, Baylor Col Med, 1976-1982; asst prof & clin fel reprod med, Med Br, Univ Tex, Houston, 1975-1977; res scholar, Am Urol Asn, 1975-1977; instr, Univ Pa, 1974-1975; asst instr urol, Univ Pa, 1973-1974. **Memberships:** Am Fertil Soc; Am Soc Andrology; Am Urol Asn; Soc Univ Urol. **Research Statement & Publications:** The evaluation and diagnosis of reproductive disorders in the male, especially in the field of infertility; androgen binding protein in the human testis and epididymis and evaluation of androgen binding protein as a possible marker of sertoli cell function. **Mailing Address:** Scott Dept Urol, Baylor Col Med, 6560 Fannin, Houston, TX 77030. **Fax:** 713-798-5553.

LIPSHUTZ, NELSON RICHARD, ECONOMICS. **Personal Data:** b Philadelphia, Pa, July 14, 1942; m 1964, c 3. **Education:** Univ Pa, BA, 1962, MBA, 1972; Univ Chicago, MS, 1963, PhD (physics), 1967; Wharton Sch Finance, MBA, 1972. **Professional Experience:** CONSULT, AM LAND TITLE ASSOC, as of 2003; Instr, Sch Bus, Northeastern Univ, 1986; PRES, REGULATORY RES CORP, 1977-; mgr consult, Arthur D Little, Inc, 1972-1977; mgt res analyst, Mgt & Behav Sci Ctr, Wharton Sch Finance & Commerce, Univ Pa, 1970-1972; from instr to asst prof, Duke Univ, 1967-1970; res assoc physics, Univ Chicago, 1967. **Memberships:** Am Phys Soc; Inst Mgt Sci; AAAS; NY Acad Sci; Nat Asn Forensic Econs. **Research Statement & Publications:** Theory of elementary particles; mathematical analysis of management decision problems; economic analysis of regulated industries; anti-trust economics; business valuation. **Mailing Address:** Am Land Title Assoc, 1828 L St, NW, Ste 705, Washington, DC 20036. **Fax:** 202-223-5843.

LIPSICH, H DAVID, MATHEMATICS. **Personal Data:** b Pittsburgh, Pa, February 20, 1920; m 1946, c 2. **Education:** Univ Cincinnati, MA, 1945, PhD (math), 1949; Princeton Univ, MA, 1946. **Professional Experience:** DEAN EMER MATH, MCMICKEN COL ARTS & SCI, as of 2006; dean, Mcmicken Col Arts & Sci, beginning 1977; provost undergrad studies, Mcmicken Col Arts & Sci, 1967-1977; vprovost, Mcmicken Col Arts & Sci, 1967; prof math, Univ Cincinnati, beginning 1961; head dept, Mcmicken Col Arts & Sci, 1961-1977; NSF fac fel, 1959-1960; from instr to assoc prof, Mcmicken Col Arts & Sci, 1946-1961. **Memberships:** Am Math Soc; Math Asn Am; Asn Symbolic Logic. **Research Statement & Publications:** Mathematical logic; set theory. **Mailing Address:** Dept Math, McMicken Col Arts & Sci, Univ Cincinatti, PO Box 210025, Cincinnati, OH 45221. **E-Mail:** david.lipsich@uc.edu

LIPSICK, JOSEPH STEVEN, MOLECULAR ONCOLOGY. **Personal Data:** b Sharon, Pa, January 6, 1955; m 1978, c 2. **Education:** Oberlin Col, BA, 1974; Univ Calif, San Diego, PhD (physiol, pharmacol), 1981, MD, 1982. **Professional Experience:** PROF DEPT PATH, STANFORD UNIV, as of 2006; assoc prof, dept path, Stanford Univ, beginning 1993; assoc prof, dept microbiol, State Univ NY, Stony Brook, 1989-1993; asst prof residence molecular path, Univ Calif, San Diego, 1986-1989. **Memberships:** Am Soc Microbiol; AAAS. **Research Statement & Publications:** To understand the molecular mechanisms by which nuclear protein products of oncogenes cause leukemia, particulary the myb oncogene, which is highly conserved in evolution. **Mailing Address:** Dept Path, Stanford Univ, Sch Med, Stanford, CA 94305-9991. **E-Mail:** joseph.lipsick@forsythe.stanford.edu

LIPSIG, JOSEPH, PHYSICAL CHEMISTRY. **Personal Data:** b Brooklyn, NY, December 13, 1930; m 1960, c 1. **Education:** Brooklyn Col, BA, 1950; Polytech Inst Brooklyn, PhD (phys chem), 1961. **Professional Experience:** PROF EMER CHEM, STATE UNIV NY COL OSWEGO, as of 2005; assoc prof chem, State Univ Ny Col Oswego, beginning 1968; asst prof, State Univ NY Col Oswego, 1966-1968; sr res chemist, Atlantic Ref Co, 1962-1966; res assoc, Cornell Univ, 1960-1962. **Memberships:** Am Chem Soc. **Research Statement & Publications:** Catalysis; geochemistry. **Mailing Address:** State Univ NY, Dept Chem, Oswego, NY 13126. **E-Mail:** lipsig@oswego.edu

LIPSITT, DON RICHARD, PSYCHIATRY, PSYCHOANALYSIS. **Personal Data:** b Boston, Mass, November 24, 1927; m 1953, Merna; c Eric D & Steven D. **Education:** NY Univ, BA, 1949; Boston Univ, MA, 1950; Univ Vt, MD, 1956; Boston Psychoanal Soc & Inst, cert, 1969. **Honorary Degrees:** MA, Harvard Univ, 1990. **Honors & Awards:** Soc Liaison Psychiat Award, 1994. **Professional Experience:** Pres, Mass Psychiat Soc, 1996-1997; CLIN PROF, HARVARD MED SCH, 1990-; ed, Gen Hosp Psychiat, 1979-; fac div primary care & family med, Harvard Med Sch, 1977-; from instr to assoc prof psychiat, Harvard Med Sch, 1974-1990; consult, Dept Psychiat, Cambridge Hosp, 1971- & NIMH, 1974-1980; consult psychiatrist, McLean Hosp, 1971-; mem fac, Boston Psychoanal Soc & Inst, Simmons Col, 1971-1972, 1981; adj prof, Sch Social Work, 1971-1980; ed, Int J Psychiat Med, 1970-1979; consult behav sci, Lincoln Lab, Mass Inst Technol, 1969-1973; dir med psychol liaison serv, Beth Israel Hosp, Boston, 1966-1969; Dept Health, Educ & Welfare res grant, 1966-1968; assoc, Beth Israel Hosp, Boston, 1964-1966; head integration clin, Beth Israel Hosp, Boston, 1962-1969; asst, Harvard Med Sch, 1962-1965; asst psychiat, Beth Israel Hosp, Boston, 1962-1964; Teaching fel psychiat, Harvard Med Sch, 1960-1962. **Memberships:** Am Psychiat Asn; Am Psychosom Soc; Asn Acad Psychiat; fel Am Col Psychiat; Am Asn Gen Hosp Psychiat; Acad Psychosom Med; Int Col Psychosom Med (pres elect). **Research Statement & Publications:** Application of medical psychology to health problems in hospital and community; relationshipof varieties of doctor-patient interaction to invalidism and chronicity; psychiatry and primary care; hypochondriasis; factitious illness. **Mailing Address:** Mt Auburn Hosp, Dept Psychiat, 330 Mt Auburn St, Cambridge, MA 02138-5597. **Fax:** 617-499-5498. **E-Mail:** dlipsitt@warren.med.harvard.edu

LIPSITT, LEWIS PAEFF, INFANT BEHAVIOR & DEVELOPMENT. **Personal Data:** b New Bedford, Mass, June 28, 1929; American citizen; m 1952, Edna Duchin Lipsitt; c Mark S & Ann D. **Education:** Univ Chicago, BA, 1950; Univ Mass, MS, 1952; Univ Iowa, PhD (child psychol), 1957. **Honorary Degrees:** MS (honoris causa), Brown Univ, 1966. **Honors & Awards:** Sauer Lectr, Northwestern Univ, 1980. **Professional Experience:** RES PROF PSYCHOL, BROWN UNIV, 1996-; emer prof psychol, med sci & human develop, 1996; consult, Behav Sci Panel, NIMH, 1987-1988; mem bd adv, Archives Hist Am Psychol, 1986-; mem bd sci counr, Nat Inst Child Health & Human Develop, 1984-1988; fel, Ctr Advan Study Behav Sci, Stanford Univ, 1979-1980; Guggenheim fel behav develop, Res Unit, St Mary's Hosp, London 1972-1973; USPHS fel, 1971; dir, Child Study Ctr, 1967-1991; dir child training, Brown Univ, 1960-1980; from instr to prof med sci, Brown Univ, 1957-1996; clin psychologist, USAF, 1952-1954. **Memberships:** Am Psychol Asn; AAAS; Soc Res Child Develop; Am Asn Univ Prof; Psychonomic Soc; Int Soc Infant Studies. **Research Statement & Publications:** Infant behavior and development, particularly sensory and learning processes of babies; crib death; adolescent suicide; studyof behavioral misadventures or hazards; lifespan consequences of early experience; Long-term consequences of early adversity. **Mailing Address:** Dept Psychology, Box 1853, Brown Univ, Providence, RI 02912. **Fax:** 401-863-1300. **E-Mail:** Lewis_Lipsitt@brown.edu

LIPSITZ, PAUL, ORGANIC CHEMISTRY. **Personal Data:** b York, Pa, April 23, 1923; m 1948, c 4. **Education:** Lebanon Valley Col, BS, 1944; Univ Cincinnati, MS, 1948, PhD (chem), 1950. **Professional Experience:** RETIRED; Patent & Licences Dept, Sun Ventures Inc, 1969-1983; sr patent agent, Pennsalt Chems Corp, 1959-1969; chemist, E I du Pont de Nemours & Co, 1950-1959. **Memberships:** Am Chem Soc; Am Inst Chem. **Mailing Address:** 1001 Easton Rd, Willow Grove, PA 19090-2028.

LIPSITZ, PHILIP JOSEPH, PEDIATRICS, NEONATAL-PERINATAL. **Personal Data:** b Piketberg, SAfrica, May 17, 1928; American citizen. **Education:** MRCP Royal Col Physician Edinburgh Univ Cape Town, MB, ChB, 1952; Royal Col Physicians & Surgeons, dipl child health, 1956; Am Bd Pediat, dipl, neonatal-perinatal med, cert. **Professional Experience:** PROF PEDIAT, ALBERT EINSTEIN COL MED, 1990-; CHIEF NEONATAL-PERINATAL MED, SCHNEIDER CHILDREN'S HOSP, LONG ISLAND JEWISH-HILLSIDE MED CTR, NEW HYDE PARK, 1974-; prof pediat, Health Sci Ctr, State Univ NY, Stony Brook, 1973-1990; dir pediat, South Shore div, Long Island Jewish-Hillside Med Ctr, Far Rockaway, 1973-1974; assoc prof, Beth Israel Med Ctr & Mt Sinai Sch Med, 1968-1973; assoc prof, Med Col Ga, 1967-1968; asst prof pediat, Med Col Ga, 1965-1967; with hosp appointments, Southwest Africa, 1962-1965; clin & res fel pediat & med, Children's Hosp Med Ctr, Harvard Med Sch, 1960-1961; fel pediat, Sch Med, Western Reserve Univ, 1958-1960; resident med officer, Red Cross War mem Children's Hosp, Univ Cape Town, 1958; registr, prof Unit, Children's Hosp, Sheffield, Eng, 1957-1958; resident med officer, Banstead Br, Queen Elizabeth Hosp for Children, 1956; house physician, Royal Hosp Sick Children, Edinburgh, Scotland, 1956; Charles' house physician, St Hosp, London, Eng, 1955; resident surg house officer, Gen Hosp, Salisbury, SRhodesia, 1953; house physician, Somerset Hosp, Cape Town, SAfrica, 1953; House surgeon, Univ Cape Town, 1952. **Memberships:** Royal Col Physicians & Surgeons; Soc Pediat Res; NY Acad Sci; Am Acad Pediat. **Research Statement & Publications:** Resp. physiology- pulmonary function tests in newborn. Effects of material adminiatration on the newborn. **Mailing Address:** LI Jewish-Hillside Med Ctr, Schneider Children's Hosp, 270-05, 76th Ave, New Hyde Park, NY 11040. **E-Mail:** lippylipsitz@msn.com

LIPSIUS, STEPHEN LLOYD, PHYSIOLOGY. **Personal Data:** b New York, NY, September 25, 1947. **Education:** State Univ NY, BA, 1969, PhD (physiol), 1975. **Professional Experience:** PROF CELLULAR & MOLECULAR PHYSIOL, LOYOLA UNIV, as of 2004; asst prof physiol, Loyola Univ, beginning 1978; NIH fel, Univ Vt, 1976-1978; res fel, 1975-1978; teaching asst, Downstate Med Ctr, 1970-1975. **Memberships:** Int Study Group Res Cardiac Metab; Cardiac Electrophysiolic Soc. **Research Statement & Publications:** Electrophysiological mechanisms responsible for latent atrial pacemaker function; antiarrhythmic agents. **Mailing Address:** Dept Physiol, Loyola Univ, Rm 4630 Bldg 102 6525 N Sheridan Rd, Chicago, IL 60626. **Fax:** 708-216-2606. **E-Mail:** slipsiu@lumc.edu

LIPSKY, JOSEPH ALBIN, PHYSIOLOGY. **Personal Data:** b Glen Lyon, Pa, March 31, 1930; m 1957, c 2. **Education:** Pa State Univ, BSc, 1951; Ohio State Univ, MSc, 1959, PhD (physiol), 1961. **Professional Experience:** PROF EMER PHYSIOL, COL MRD, OHIO STATE UNIV, as of 2003; rof Physiol, Col Med, Ohio State Univ, beginning 1977; Consult to coun, Nat Bd Dent Exam, 1967-; From asst prof to assoc prof, Col Med, Ohio State Univ, 1961-1977. **Memberships:** AAAS; Fedn Am Socs Exp Biol; Am Physiol Soc; Sigma Xi. **Research Statement & Publications:** Carbon dioxide transients and stores; hyperventilation. **Mailing Address:** Dept Physiol, Ohio State Univ Col Med 302 Hamilton 1645 Neil Ave, Columbus, OH 43210.

LIPSKY, ROBERT H, MOLECULAR BIOLOGY. **Personal Data:** b Washington, DC, October 27, 1955. **Education:** Va Polytech Inst & State Univ, BS, 1977; Med Col Va, MS, 1979; Cornell Univ, PhD (genetics), 1983. **Professional Experience:** CHIEF MOLECULAR GENETICS, LAB NEUROGENETICS, NIAAA, NIH, as of 2004; scientist I, Am Red Cross, beginning 1988; NIH sr staff fel develop neurol biol, Molecular Biol Lab, Nat Inst Neurol Dis & Stroke, 1983-1987. **Memberships:** Am Soc Cell Biol; Am Soc Biochem & Molecular Biol. **Mailing Address:** Lab Neurogenetics, Nat Inst Alcoholism & Alcohol Abuse, NIH, 5635 Fishers Lane, MSC 9304, Bethesda, MD 20892-9304. **Fax:** 301-443-8579. **E-Mail:** rlipsky@mail.nih.gov

LIPSKY, STEPHEN E, SIGNAL PROCESSING, ARTIFICAL INTELLIGENCE. **Personal Data:** b New York, NY, January 18, 1932; m 1979, c 3. **Education:** NY Univ, Col Eng, BEE, 1953, MEE, 1962. **Honors & Awards:** Bronze Medal, Armed Forces Commun & Electronics Asn, 1953. **Professional Experience:** Adj univ prof microwaves, Drexel Univ Grad Sch, beginning 1987; mem, Comt 1986 Symp, Inst Elec & Electronics Engrs Ant/Microwave Prop Soc, 1985-1987; ed consult, 1985-; sr vpres eng & chief tech officer, Ael Defense Corp, beginning1979; dir adv systs, Govt Systs Div, Gen Instrument Corp. 1970-1979; eng consult, Radiometric Div Polarad, 1970-1977; corp vpres eng, Polarad Elec Corp, 1963-1970; proj leader eng, Fisher Radio Corp, 1958-1963; eng consult, Electro Acoust Res Labs, 1958-1960; design eng microwaves, Prod Res Corp, 1955-1958; eng officer, TV eng, US Army Pictorial Ctr, 1953-1955. **Memberships:** Fel Inst Elec & Electronic Engrs; Armed Forces Commun & Electronics Asn; British Inst Elec Engrs. **Research Statement & Publications:** Monopulse passive direction finding and receiving methods for detection and identification of radar and communications signals; microwave analytic design techniques for antenna systems and associated feed networks; author of publication on Microwave Passive Direction Finding. **Mailing Address:** PO Box 404, Barnegat Lgt, NJ 08006.

LIPSON, EDWARD DAVID, PHOTOBIOLOGY, SENSORY TRANSDUCTION. **Personal Data:** b Winnipeg, Man, October 27, 1944; m 1966, c 2. **Education:** Univ Man, BSc, 1966; Calif Inst Technol, PhD (physics), 1971. **Professional Experience:** CHMN, DEPT PHYSICS, SYRACUSE UNIV, 2003-; adj prof, dept Elec Eng & Comput Sci, Syracuse Univ, 2002-; adj prof, dept Radiol, Upstate Med Univ, Syracuse, 1999-; PROF, DEPT PHYSICS, SYRACUSE UNIV, 1985-; dir, grad biophysics prog, Syracuse Univ, 1983-

1989; res fel, Alfred P Sloan Found, 1979-1983; from asst prof to assoc, Syracuse Univ, 1976-1985; sr res fel, Calif inst Technol, 1974-1976; res fel biol, Calif inst Technol, 1971-1974. **Memberships:** Biophys Soc; AAAS; Am Soc Photobiol; Am Phys Soc. **Research Statement & Publications:** Light-growth responses of the microorganism, Phycomyces, with approaches from genetics, biochemistry and nonlinear systems theory, to elucidate the cellular and molecular mechanisms of sensory transduction and adaptation. **Mailing Address:** Dept Physics, Syracuse Univ, Syracuse, NY 13244. **Fax:** 315-443-9103. **E-Mail:** edlipson@syr.edu

LIPSON, HERBERT GEORGE, SOLID STATE PHYSICS. **Personal Data:** b Boston, Mass, July 4, 1925; m 1951, Gloria Freedman; c Neil, Jerold & Elayne. **Education:** Mass Inst Technol, BS, 1948; Northeastern Univ, MS, 1964. **Professional Experience:** RETIRED; Dept Electronic Technol, Rome Air Develop Ctr, Hanscom AFB, 1958-1990; Lincoln Lab, Mass Inst Technol, 1955-1958; physicist, Naval Res Lab, 1951-1955; physicist, Brookhaven Nat Lab, 1951; Jr physicist metall physics, Sylvania Elec Prods, Inc, 1948-1950. **Memberships:** Am Phys Soc; Mat Res Soc. **Research Statement & Publications:** Optical properties of solids; lattice vibrations, impurities and plasma effects in semiconductors; laser and laser window material properties; infrared optical properties of impurities in quartz, radiation effects on quartz for radiation hardened oscillators. **Mailing Address:** 68 Aldrich Rd, Wakefield, MA 01880.

LIPSON, MELVIN ALAN, ORGANIC CHEMISTRY. **Personal Data:** b Providence, RI, June 1, 1936; m 1961, Jacqueline; c Donna, Robert, Michelle & Judith. **Education:** Univ RI, BS, 1957; Syracuse Univ, PhD (org chem), 1963. **Professional Experience:** Pivotech, Inc, 1996-; chief exec officer, Avrelon, 1994-; PRES, LIPSON ASSOC, 1992-; vpres, Morton Int, 1989-1992; pres, Dynachem Div, 1986-1989; exec vpres, Tech Opers, 1985-1986; sr vpres, Tech Opers, 1982-1985; vpres, Morton Thiokol Inc, 1972-1982; tech dir, Morton Thiokol Inc, 1969-1972; res mgr, Wayland Chem Div, Philip A Hunt Chem Corp, RI, 1967-1969; res supvr org synthesis, Wayland Chem Div, Philip A Hunt Chem Corp, RI, 1964-1967; res chemist, Eltex Res Corp, 1963-1964; res chemist, I C I (Organics) Inc, 1963. **Memberships:** AAAS; Am Chem Soc; Chem Soc. **Research Statement & Publications:** Amino acids and peptides; chelating agents; photographic chemicals; surface active compounds; polymers; dyestuffs; carbohydrates; photopolymers; photoresists; electroless plating; corrosion inhibitors; coatings; adhesives; inks. **Mailing Address:** 1715 Plaza Del Sur, Newport Beach, CA 92661-1417. **Fax:** 714-675-3621.

LIPSON, STEVEN MARK, ENVIRONMENTAL MICROBIOLOGY & IMMUNOLOGY. **Personal Data:** b New York, NY, May 25, 1945; m 1971, c 2. **Education:** Long Island Univ, BS, 1967; C W Post Col, MS, 1972; NY Univ, PhD (microbiol), 1982. **Professional Experience:** ASST PROF, DEPT PHYS & BIOL SCI, NY CITY COL TECHNOL, CITY UNIV NY, as of 2003; asst prof microbiol med, Cornell Univ Med Col, as of 2002; dir, diag virol lab, div infectious dis, North Shore Univ Hosp, Cornell Univ Med Col, beginning 1990; adj prof, biol, C W Post Col, 1987-; chief, Virol lab, Nassau County Med Ctr, NY, 1984-1990; adj asst prof, Fiorello H LaGuardia Community Col & Manhattan Community Col, 1983-1985; supvr, Hemat/Oncol Lab, Brooklyn Hosp/Caledonian Hosp, 1983-1984; res assoc, dept Neoplastic Dis, Mt Sinai Med Ctr, 1981-1983; adj instr biol, Fordham Univ, 1981-1982; vis lectr microbiol, Adelphi Univ, 1976; technologist microbiol, mem Hosp, 1975-1976; res assoc biol, NY Univ, 1974-1980; teaching fel biol, NY Univ, 1974-1975; teacher biol, Erasmus Hall & Prospect Heights High Schs, 1967-1972. **Memberships:** Am Soc Microbiol. **Research Statement & Publications:** Epidemiology and rapid identification medically relevant viruses; surface interactions between viruses, cells, polymers, and particulates; polymerase chain reaction in the identification of viruses; antiviral susceptibility; testing flow cytometry. **Mailing Address:** Dept Phys & Biol Sci, NY City Col Technol, 812, Namm Hall, Manhasset, NY 11030. **E-Mail:** slipson@citytech.cuny.edu

LIPTAY, ALBERT, HORTICULTURE, PLANT PHYSIOLOGY. **Personal Data:** b Hampton, Ont, November 9, 1941; m 1967, c 3. **Education:** Univ Guelph Hort, BSA, 1966, MSc, 1967; McMaster Univ, PhD (biol), 1972. **Professional Experience:** RES SCIENTIST, PHYSIOL VEG CROP PROD, GREENHOUSE & PROCESSING CROPS RES CTR, AGR & AGRI FOOD CAN, 1974-; asst prof biol, Camrose Lutheran Col, 1973-1974; lectr life sci, Conestoga Col, 1972-1973. **Memberships:** Am Soc Hort Sci; Int Soc Hort Sci; Can Soc Hort Sci; Agr Inst Can; Inst Elec & Electronics Engrs. **Research Statement & Publications:** Vegetable management and physiology; seed germination; seed vigour; plant establishment; growth factors. **Mailing Address:** Greenhouse & Process Crops Res Ctr, Agr & Agri-Food Can, 2585 County Rd 20, Harrow, ON N0R 1G0, Can. **Fax:** 519-738-3756. **E-Mail:** liptaya@agr.gc.ca

LIPTON, ALLAN, INTERNAL MEDICINE, ONCOLOGY. **Personal Data:** b New York, NY, December 29, 1938; m 1965, c 3. **Education:** Amherst Col, BA, 1959; NY Univ, MD, 1963; Am Bd Internal Med, dipl, 1970. **Professional Experience:** PROF, MED CTR, PA STATE UNIV, 1980-; chief, Div Oncol, Dept Med, beginning 1974; from asst prof to assoc prof, Div Oncol, Dept Med, 1971-1980; Dernham fel, Salk Inst Biol Studies, 1969-1971; fel oncol, Mem Hosp, NY, 1968-1969; fel hemat, Mem Hosp, New York, 1967-1968; resident, Bellevue Hosp, NY, 1964-1965; intern med, Bellevue Hosp, NY, 1963-1964. **Memberships:** AAAS; Am Asn Cancer Res; Am Fedn Clin Res. **Research Statement & Publications:** Control of growth of normal and malignant cells by serum factors. **Mailing Address:** Dept Med, Hershey Med Ctr, Pa State Univ, Hershey, PA 17033. **Fax:** 717-531-5076.

LIPTON, JAMES MATTHEW, NEUROSCIENCES. **Personal Data:** b 1938. **Education:** Univ Colo, PhD, 1964. **Professional Experience:** PROF PHYSIOL, SOUTHWESTERN MED CTR, UNIV TEX, DALLAS, as of 2002; mem, Neurol Study Sect, 1986-1990; MEM STAFF, ANESTHESIOL DEPT, SOUTHWESTERN MED SCH, SOUTHWESTERN MED CTR, UNIV TEX, DALLAS, 1981-; consult neurol, Vet Admin Hosp, Dallas, 1974-1980; USPHS sr fel, Inst Animal Physiol, UK, 1970-1971; USPHS fel, Neuropath Lab, Med Sch, Univ Mich, 1964-1966. **Memberships:** AAAS; Soc Neuroscience; Am Physiol Soc. **Research Statement & Publications:** Inflammation and antiinflammatory peptides; central nervous system and peripheral modulation of inflammation. **Mailing Address:** Dept Physiol, Southwester Med Ctr, Univ Tex, 5323 Harry Hines Blvd, Dallas, TX 75235-9040. **Fax:** 214-648-4703. **E-Mail:** lipton@utsw.swmed.edu

LIPTON, MICHAEL FORRESTER, PROCESS DEVELOPMENT. **Personal Data:** b Huntington, WVa, October 28, 1950; m 1985, Kathy O'Falahee; c Grayson B, Logan M & Todd M Schip. **Education:** Purdue Univ, BS, 1972; Univ Colo, PhD (chem), 1976. **Honors & Awards:** charman, organic reaction & processe gordon res conffrence, 2001. **Professional Experience:** MEM STAFF, UPJOHN CO, 1980-; Res assoc, Dept Entom, USDA, Mich State Univ, 1979-1980; asst prof, Mich State Univ, 1978-1980; Res assoc chem, Fordham Univ, 1976-1978. **Memberships:** editorial advisory borad of "organic process res and develop"; Am Chem Soc. **Research Statement & Publications:** Process development in the pharmaceutical industry; rapid scale-up and design of chemical routes of synthesis of biologically active molecules. **Mailing Address:** Pharmacia & Upjohn Inc, 7171 Portage Rd, Kalamazoo, MI 49001-0199. **Fax:** 269-833-9158. **E-Mail:** michae.f.lipton@pharmacia.com

LIPTON, STUART ARTHUR, CELLULAR & MOLECULAR NEUROSCIENCE. **Personal Data:** b Danbury, Conn, January 11, 1950; m 1980, Elisabeth; c Jennifer Ann & Jeffrey Harris. **Education:** Cornell Univ, BA, 1971; Univ Pa, MD, 1977, PhD (Biophys & Biochem), 1977; Am Bd Psychiat & Neurol, dipl, 1982. **Honors & Awards:** Nobel Lectr, Karolinska Inst, 1994; San Diego Health Hero Award, Am Parkinson's Dis Assoc, 2002. **Professional Experience:** PROF & SCI DIR, CTR NEUROSCIENCE & AGING, BURNHAM INST, CALIF, 1999-; ATTEND NEUROLOGIST, USCD MED CTR, 1999-; chief, ctr Nervous Syst Res Inst, Brigham & Women's Hosp, 1997-1999; investr, Am Heart Asn, 1988-1993; dir, NIH Develop Neurol Training Prog, Children's Hosp, Boston, 1988-1994; assoc neurol, Brigham & Women's hosp, Boston, 1988-1997; assoc prof neurol & Neuroscience, Harvard Med Sch, 1987-1997; dir, Lab Cellular & Molecular Neuroscience, Children's Hosp, Boston, 1987-1997; assoc neurol, Beth Israel Hosp, Boston, 1986-1993; NIH fel, 1984-1989; asst prof neurol & Neuroscience, Cent Nervous Syst Res Inst, Brigham & Women's Hosp, 1983-1987; fel, Hartford Found, 1981-1984; instr neurol, Harvard Med Sch, 1981-1983; asst neurol, Children's Hosp, Boston, 1981-1988; asst neurol, Beth Israel Hosp, Boston, 1981-1986; res fel neurbiol, Harvard Med Sch, 1980-1983; chief neurol resident, Beth Israel, Brigham Hosp, Women's Hosp, Boston & Children's Hosp, Boston, 1980-1981; esident neurol, Beth Israel, Brigham Hosp, Women's Hosp, Boston & Children's Hosp, Boston, 1978-1980; neurologist, Mass Gen Hosp, Brigham Hosp, Women's Hosp, Beth Israel Hosp & Children's Hosp; dir cellular & molecular Neuroscience, Children's Hosp & Harvard Med Sch. **Memberships:** AAAS; Am Acad Neurol; Am Neurol Asn; Soc Neuroscience; Asn Res Vision & Ophthal; Biophys Soc. **Research Statement & Publications:** Contributed articles to professional journals; patentee. **Mailing Address:** Ctr Neuro Sci & Aging, Burnham Inst, 10901 N Torrey Pines Rd, La Jolla, CA 92037. **E-Mail:** slipton@burnham-inst.org

LIPTON, WERNER JACOB, FOOD SCIENCE & TECHNOLOGY, PLANT PHYSIOLOGY. **Personal Data:** b Ger, October 16, 1928; American citizen; m 1952, c 4. **Education:** Mich State Univ, BS, 1951, MS, 1953; Univ Calif, PhD (plant physiol), 1957. **Professional Experience:** Sci ed, W Sect, 1988-; CONSULT, 1987-; vpres, W Sect, 1981-1982; chmn postharvest hort sect, Am Soc Hort Sci, 1976-1977; assoc ed, Am Soc Hort Sci, 1972-1976, 1978-; sr plant physiologist, Hort Field Sta, USDA, 1957-1987; asst, Univ Calif, 1953-1957. **Memberships:** AAAS; fel Am Soc Hort Sci; Sigma Xi. **Research Statement & Publications:** Postharvest physiology of vegetables; emphasis on effects of modified atmospheres and preharvest environmental factors. **Mailing Address:** 4550 E Redlands Ave, Fresno, CA 93726.

LIRA, EMIL PATRICK, ORGANIC CHEMISTRY. **Personal Data:** b Chicago, Ill, March 17, 1934; m 1958, c 4. **Education:** Elmhurst Col, BS, 1956; Rutgers Univ, PhD (org chem), 1963. **Professional Experience:** RETIRED; dir process technol, Sandoz, 1986-1997; dir agr-chem res, Northwest Ind Inc, Chicago Lab, 1976-1986; dir res, Velsicol Chem Corp, 1974-1976; mgr org chem, Int Mineral & Chem Corp, 1973-1974; supvr org synthesis, Int Mineral & Chem Corp, 1969-1973; res chemist, Int Mineral & Chem Corp, 1963-1969; chemist, Corn Prod Co, 1958-1959; chemist, Swift & Co, 1956. **Memberships:** Am Chem Soc; Indust Res Inst. **Research Statement & Publications:** Organic research and development with plasticizers, adhesives, polymer additives; plant growth regulators; pesticides; animal health products; synthetic sweeteners; organic processes. **Mailing Address:** 8129 Manchester Lane No 25, Lake Mills, WI 53551-9733.

LIS, ELAINE WALKER, NUTRITION, BIOCHEMISTRY. **Personal Data:** b Denver, Colo, April 25, 1924; m 1958, c 3. **Education:** Mills Col, AB, 1945; Univ Calif, Berkeley, PhD (nutrit), 1960. **Professional Experience:** RETIRED; from assoc prof to prof, Crippled Children's Div, Ore Health Sci Univ, 1968-1987; lectr, Portland State Univ, 1964-1968; Consult, Crippled Children's Div, Med Sch, Univ Ore, 1964-1968; Asst nutrit, USPHS fel, 1960-1962; Asst nutrit, Univ Calif, Berkeley, 1956-1960. **Memberships:** Am Asn Univ Prof; Am Asn Ment Deficiency; Soc Nutrit Educ; Am Home Econ Asn. **Research Statement & Publications:** Metabolic approach to possible causes of retardation, emotional disturbances or other handicapping conditions with emphasis on inborn errors of metabolism such as phenylketonuria. **Mailing Address:** 7950 SW Crestline Dr, Portland, OR 97219.

LIS, JOHN THOMAS, MOLECULAR GENETICS. **Personal Data:** b Willimantic, Conn, June 15, 1948; c 1. **Education:** Fairfield Univ, BS, 1970; Brandeis Univ, PhD (biochem), 1975. **Professional Experience:** BARBARA MCCLINTOCK PROF MOLECULAR BIOL & GENETICS, CORNELL UNIV, as of 2005; assoc prof biochem, Cornell Univ, beginning 1984; asst prof, Cornell Univ, 1978-1984; fel, Dept Biochem, Stanford Univ, 1975-1978. **Research Statement & Publications:** Relationship between genome structure and gene regulation using the heat shock genes of Drosophila melanogaster and yeast as model systems. **Mailing Address:** Dept Molecular Biol & Genetics, Cornell Univ, 416, Biotechnol Bldg, Ithaca, NY 14853-0001. **Fax:** 607-255-2428. **E-Mail:** jtl10@cornell.edu

LIS, STEVEN ANDREW, OPTICAL COMPUTING, MATERIALS RESEARCH. **Personal Data:** b Dunkirk, NY, October 13, 1950; m 1976, c 2. **Education:** Fredonia State Univ Col, NY, BS, 1972; Princeton Univ, PhD (chem), 1977. **Professional Experience:** SR SCIENTIST & MARKET DEVELOP SPECIALIST, ELECTROCHEM INC, as of 2004; PRIN INVESTR, SPARTA INC, 1988-; Sr prin develop engr, Honewell Electro-Optics Div, 1988; Sr scientist, Radiation Monitoring Devices, 1977-1981 & GCA Corp, 1981-1988. **Memberships:** Am Phys Soc; Electro-Chem Soc. **Research Statement & Publications:** Optical computing systems; holography; materials and device; integrated circuit process development; advanced lithographic equipment. **Mailing Address:** Electrochem Inc, 400 W Cummings Park, Woburn, MA 01801. **Fax:** 781-935-6966.

LISACK, JOHN JR, SURVEYING & MAPPING. **Personal Data:** b May 22, 1945; m 1972, c 3. **Education:** Univ Mass, BSCE, 1968, MBA, 1970. **Professional Experience:** ASSOC DIR, AM ASSOC PHARMACEUT SCIENTISTS, 2003-; exec dir, Am Cong Surv & Mapping, 1990-1998; exec vpres, Nat Asn Personnel Consult, 1986-1990; dep dir, Am Soc Eng Educ, 1975-1986; financial anaylst, Co Fairfax, 1974-1975; exec dir property admin, Real Equity Investments Inc, 1973-1974; mgr land develop & planning, Foxvale Construct Co Inc, 1972-1973; Asst adminr, Prince William Co, 1971-1972; Chmn, Coun Eng & Sci Soc Execs Comts. **Mailing Address:** Am Assoc Pharmaceut Scientists, 2107 Wilson Blvd, Suite 700, Arlington, VA 22201-3042.

LISAK, ROBERT PHILIP, NEUROLOGY, IMMUNOLOGY. **Personal Data:** b Brooklyn, NY, March 17, 1941; m 1964, Deana; c Ilene & Michael. **Education:** NY Univ, BA, 1961; Columbia Univ, MD, 1965. **Honors & Awards:** Physician's Award, Myasthenia Gravis Found, 1991. **Professional Experience:** PROF IMMUNOL & MICROBIOL, 2002-; PROF NEUROL & CHMN DEPT, SCH MED, WAYNE STATE UNIV, 1987-; spec consult, Nat Multiple Sclerosis Soc, 1975 & Swiss Acad Med, 1981; res assoc, Univ Col London & Nat

Inst Neurologic Dis, London, 1978-1979; fulbright Hays sr res scholar, UK, 1978-1979; mem immunol grad group, Hosp, Sch Med, Univ Pa, 1975-1987; from asst prof to prof neurol, Hosp, Sch Med, Univ Pa, 1972-1987; Consult neurol, Vet Admin Hosp, Philadelphia, 1972-1982; trainee allergy & immunol, Hosp Univ Pa, 1971-1972; resident neurol, Hosp, Sch Med, Univ Pa, 1969-1972; jr resident med, Bronx Munic Med Ctr, Albert Einstein Col Med, 1968-1969; res assoc immunol, Lab Clin Sci, NIMH, 1966-1968; intern med, Montefiore Hosp & Med Ctr, 1965-1966; Med Adv Bd. **Memberships:** Am Asn Immunologists; Am Acad Neurol; AAAS; Soc Neuroscience; Am Neurol Asn; Int Soc Neuroimmunol (secy, treas); Res Prog Award Commt, Nat Mult Sclerosis Soc. **Research Statement & Publications:** Humoral and cell-mediated immunologic mechanisms involved in clinical and experimental diseases of the central and peripheral nervous system and muscle. **Mailing Address:** Dept Neurol, Sch Med, Wayne State Univ, 8A Univ Health Ctr 6E 4201 St Antoine, Detroit, MI 48201. **E-Mail:** rlisak@med.wayne.edu

LISANO, MICHAEL EDWARD, REPRODUCTIVE PHYSIOLOGY, ENDOCRINOLOGY. **Personal Data:** b Houston, Tex, October 6, 1942; c 2. **Education:** Sam Houston State Univ, BS, 1964, MS, 1966; Tex A&M Univ, PhD (physiol), 1970. **Professional Experience:** ASSOC PROF PHYSIOL, AUBURN UNIV, 1977-; asst prof, Auburn Univ, 1970-1977; instr biol, Hardin-Simmons Univ, 1966-1967. **Memberships:** Wildlife Soc; Southeastern Asn Fish & Wildlife Agencies. **Research Statement & Publications:** Reproductive physiology and endocrinology of economically important game species. **Mailing Address:** Dept Biol, Auburn Univ, 116 Cary Hall, Auburn, AL 36849-3501. **E-Mail:** lisanme@mail.auburn.edu

LISCHER, LUDWIG F, engineering; deceased, see previous edition for last biography

LI-SCHOLZ, ANGELA, ATOMIC PHYSICS, NUCLEAR PHYSICS. **Personal Data:** b Hong Kong, August 15, 1936; American citizen; m 1966, c 2. **Education:** Manhattanville Col, BA, 1956; NY Univ, MS, 1957, PhD (physics), 1963. **Professional Experience:** MENTOR EMER, EMPIRE STATE COL, STATE UNIV NY, ALBANY, as of 2006; ed, Atomic Data & Nuclear Data Tables, 1982-; res prof, Dept Physics, State Univ NY, Albany, 1978-; prof sci, Empire State Col, State Univ NY, 1977-; assoc prof, 1972-1977; res assoc nuclear chem, Rensselaer Polytech Inst, 1970-1972; res assoc solid state physics, Univ Pa, 1967-1970; asst prof physics, City Col New York, 1965-1966; res assoc nuclear physics, Yale Univ, 1963-1965; res assoc high energy physics, NY Univ, 1963; jr res assoc nuclear physics, Brookhaven Nat Lab, 1960-1963. **Memberships:** Am Phys Soc. **Research Statement & Publications:** Atomic inner shell ionization; microbeam analysis; interaction of nuclei with electromagnetic fields in solids. **Mailing Address:** Dept Physics, State Univ NY, Albany, NY 12222. **Fax:** 518-442-5260. **E-Mail:** lischolz@albany.edu

LISCUM, LAURA, PHYSIOLOGY. **Personal Data:** b Boston, Mass, September 1, 1954. **Education:** Hunter Col, BA, 1976; Columbia Univ, MA, 1978, PhD, 1982. **Honors & Awards:** John S Newberry Prize, 1982. **Professional Experience:** PROF PHYSIOL, SCH MED, TUFTS UNIV, as of 2005; DIR CELLULAR & MOLECULAR PHYSIOL PROG, TUFTS UNIV, as of 2005; Am Heart Asn estab investr, 1987-1992; asst prof physiol, Sch Med, Tufts Univ, beginning 1985; postdoctoral fel, Dept Molecular Genetics, Health Sci Ctr, Univ Tex, Dallas, 1982-1985; fac fel, Dept Biol Sci, Columbia Univ, 1976-1982. **Research Statement & Publications:** Author of numerous publications. **Mailing Address:** Tufts Univ, Dept Physiol Sch Med, 136 Harrison Ave, Boston, MA 02111-1800. **Fax:** 617-636-0445. **E-Mail:** laura.liscum@tufts.edu

LISELLA, FRANK SCOTT, PUBLIC HEALTH. **Personal Data:** b Lancaster, Pa, August 11, 1936; m 1990, Lynn; c Brad & Michael. **Education:** Millersville State Univ, 1957; Tulane Univ, MPH, 1961; Univ Iowa, PhD (prev med), 1970. **Professional Experience:** RETIRED; dir, Environ Health & Safety Off, Emory Univ, 1988-1998; head biosafety off & leader, Hazardous Mat Group, Ga Tech Res Inst, 1987-1988; dir, Off Biosafety, Ctr Dis Control, Ga, 1984-1987; asst dir, Chronic Dis Div, 1981-1984; adj clin assoc prof, Emory Sch Pub Health, 1978-; chief, Prog Develop Br, Environ Health Servs Div, Ctr Dis Control, 1973-1981; health sci adv, Nat Med Audiovisual Ctr, 1972-1973; adj prof, Dekalb Col, 1970-1975; asst dir, Div Pesticide Community Studies, Environ Protection Agency, 1970-1972; asst to dir, Div Community Studies, Food & Drug Admin, Ga, 1969-1970; chief training & consult, Pesticides Prog, Nat Commun Dis Ctr, 1966-1968; coordr, Commun Dis Control Proj, USPHS, Fla, 1964-1966; sanitarian, Pa Dept Health, 1957-1964. **Memberships:** Nat Environ Health Asn; Am Pub Health Asn; Am Biol Safety Asn; Can Asn Biol Safety. **Research Statement & Publications:** Epidemiology of acute intoxications involving chemical agents of various types; etiology of self-induced intoxications involving medicants, pesticides and other chemical compounds and measures for prevention of repetitive episodes; control/containment of hazardous chemicals and biologicals. **Mailing Address:** Environ Health & Safety Off, Med Sch Info, Emory Univ, Atlanta, GA 30322. **E-Mail:** flisell@emory.edu

LISENBEE, ALVIS LEE, STRUCTURAL GEOLOGY. **Personal Data:** b Lamesa, Tex, December 3, 1940; m 1968, c 2. **Education:** Univ NMex, BS, 1964, MS, 1967; Pa State Univ, PhD (geol), 1972. **Professional Experience:** Homestabe Mining Co, beginning 1994; Fulbright prof, Turkey, 1983 & Yates Petrol Co, beginning 1991; consult, Turkish Nat Petrol Co, 1985-1989; consult, SDak Geol Surv, 1982; consult, Exxon Mineral Co, 1982; consult, Gulf Oil Corp, 1981-1982; consult, Armco Steel Corp, 1979-1981; dept head, Dept Geol Eng, Sdak Sch Mines, 1978-1985; chief geologist, Posora Mining Co, Esfahan, Iran, 1973-1976; PROF GEOL, DEPT GEOL ENG, SDAK SCH MINES, 1972-; asst geologist, Ark & La Gas Co, 1964. **Memberships:** Geol Soc Am; Sigma Xi. **Research Statement & Publications:** The evolution of mountain systems, specifically the timing and types of geological features which evolved in the northern Rocky Mountains and the Basin and Range of the US. **Mailing Address:** Dept Geol Eng, SDak Sch Mines, MI 302 GEOL, Rapid City, SD 57701. **Fax:** 605-394-6703. **E-Mail:** alvis.lisenbee@sdsmt.edu

LISK, DONALD J, OCCUPATIONAL EPIDEMIOLOGY, EFFECTS OF SOLID WASTES IN AGRICULTURE & DIETARY CONTROL OF CANCER. **Personal Data:** b Buffalo, NY, May 12, 1930; American citizen; m 1959, Nanette L; c 4. **Education:** Univ Buffalo, BA, 1952; Cornell Univ, MS, 1954, PhD (soil chem), 1956. **Professional Experience:** PROF EMER TOXICOL, CORNELL UNIV, 1995-; prof toxicol & dir, toxic chemicals lab, ny state col agr, cornell univ, beginning 1956; past reviewer, Nat Insts Health, Nat Inst Environ Health Sci. **Memberships:** Soc Toxicol; Am Chem Soc; Sigma Xi. **Research Statement & Publications:** Fate of toxicants in agriculture and environmental systems; heavy metals; pesticides; industrial toxicants; over 480 publications. **Mailing Address:** Toxic Chemicals Lab NY State Col Agr, Cornell Univ Tower Rd, Ithaca, NY 14853-7401. **E-Mail:** djl22@cornell.edu

LISKA, KENNETH J, CHEMISTRY, PHARMACOLOGY. **Personal Data:** b Hinsdale, Ill, June 4, 1929; m 1957, Paula; c 3. **Education:** Univ Ill, BS, 1951, MS, 1953, PhD (med chem), 1956. **Professional Experience:** PROF EMER, MESA COL, 1993-; prof chem, Mesa Col, 1975-1993; chmn, San Diego Sect, Am Chem Soc, 1975-1976; assoc prof chem, US Int Univ, 1969-1975; assoc prof pharmaceut chem, Univ Pittsburgh, 1961-1969; assoc prof pharmaceut chem, Duquesne Univ, 1956-1961. **Memberships:** Am Chem Soc; AAAS; Former chairman, San Diego CA, sect ACS. **Research Statement & Publications:** Synthetic organic medicinal chemistry; author of eight books. **Mailing Address:** 2947 Honors Ct, San Diego, CA 92122.

LISKAY, ROBERT MICHAEL, GENETIC RECOMBINATION, SOMATIC CELL GENETICS. **Personal Data:** b April 16, 1948; American citizen. **Education:** Univ Calif, Irvine, BS, 1970; Univ Wash, Seattle, PhD (genetics), 1974. **Professional Experience:** PROF MOLECULAR & MED GENETICS, ORE HEALTH & SCI UNIV, as of 2001; scholar, Leukemia Soc Am, 1984-; ASSOC PROF THERAPEUT RADIOL GENETICS, SCH MED, YALE UNIV, 1984-; asst prof, Sch Med, Yale Univ, 1980-1984; res assoc, Univ Colo, 1977-1980. **Memberships:** Genetics Soc Am. **Research Statement & Publications:** Homologous recombination in mammalian cells, its mode of action and cellular processes that it influences; X-chromosome inactivation in mammals. **Mailing Address:** Dept Molecular & Med Genetics, Ore Health & Sci Univ, L103 3181 S W Sam Jackson Park Rd, Portland, OR 97239-3098. **Fax:** 503-494-6886. **E-Mail:** liskaym@ohsu.edu

LISKEY, NATHAN EUGENE, HEALTH SCIENCE. **Personal Data:** b Live Oak, Calif, April 26, 1937; m 1957, c 2. **Education:** La Verne Col, BA, 1959; Ind Univ, Bloomington, MS, 1961, HSD(health safety), 1969. **Professional Experience:** PROF HEALTH SCI, CALIF STATE UNIV, FRESNO, 1975-; sex therapist, Ctr Coun & Ther, 1973-; USPHS grant, HEW, 1968-1969; from asst prof to assoc prof, Calif State Univ, Fresno, 1965-1975; teacher pub schs, Calif, 1959-1965. **Memberships:** Soc Sci Study Sex; Am Asn Sex Educ & Coun; Nat Coun Int Health. **Research Statement & Publications:** Physical and emotional aspects of behavior relating to accident prevention; human sexuality; sexual behavior of the aged. **Mailing Address:** 27931 Calle Casal, Mission Viejo, CA 92692.

LISKOV, BARBARA H, Software Systems, Distributed Computing. **Personal Data:** b Los Angeles, Calif, November 7, 1939; m 1970, c 1. **Education:** Univ Calif, Berkeley, BA, 1961; Stanford Univ, MS, 1965, PhD (Computer Science), 1968. **Honorary Degrees:** (Hon) Doctorate, ETH Zuich, 2005. **Honors & Awards:** John von Neumann Medal, IEEE, 2004 1996 Achievement Award, Soc of Women Engineers. **Professional Experience:** PROF COMPUT SCI, MASS INST TECHNOL, 1972-; tech staff, Mitre Corp, 1968-1972; res asst, Stanford Univ, 1963-1968; programmer, Harvard Univ, 1962-1963; programmer, Mitre Corp, 1961-1962. **Memberships:** Member Nat Acad Eng, 1989; Member, Inst Elec & Electronics Engrs; Fellow Am Acad Arts & Sci; Fellow Assn for Comput Mach. **Research Statement & Publications:** Programming methodology; distributed computing; programming languages; operating systems; numerous articles, papers and publications; more than 100 technical papers. **Mailing Address:** Dept Elec Eng & Comput Sci, Mass Inst Technol, 32 Vassar St, Cambridge, MA 02139. **Fax:** 617-253-8460. **E-Mail:** liskov@csail.mit.edu

LISMAN, FREDERICK LOUIS, nuclear chemistry; deceased, see previous edition for last biography

LISMAN, PERRY HALL, research administration, systems development & electronics systems; deceased, see previous edition for last biography

LISONBEE, LORENZO KENNETH, BIOLOGY, SCIENCE EDUCATION. **Personal Data:** b Mesa, Ariz, November 25, 1914; m 1938, c 8. **Education:** Ariz State Univ, BA, 1937, MA, 1940, EdD, 1963. **Professional Experience:** RETIRED; chmn, Ariz Comt Corresp, 1984-1986; fac assoc, Ariz State Univ, 1963-1985; pres, Ariz Acad Sci, 1963-1964; contribr, Encyclopedia Britannica, 1962, 1974; sci supvr, Phoenix High Schs, 1958-1985; vis prof, San Jose State Univ, 1956; pres, Ariz Sci Teachers Asn, 1956; teacher sci & dept chmn high schs, Ariz, 1940-1958; summer fac, San Jose State Univ; consult, Am Geol Inst. **Memberships:** Fel AAAS; Nat Asn Res Sci Teaching; Nat Sci Teachers Asn; Nat Asn Biol Teachers. **Research Statement & Publications:** Research in science teaching; desert biology. **Mailing Address:** 4844 W Commonwealth Pl, Chandler, AZ 85226.

LISOWSKI, RONALD L, AERONAUTICS. **Professional Experience:** MODERATOR, DEPT ASTRONAUT, US AIR FORCE ACAD, as of 2000. **Memberships:** Am Inst Aeronaut & Astronaut. **Mailing Address:** Dept Astronaut, US Airforce Acad, 2354 Fairchild Dr 6J71, Colorado Springs, CO 80840. **Fax:** 719-333-3723. **E-Mail:** ron.lisowski@usafa.af.mil

LISS, ALAN, MICROBIOLOGY, BIOPHARMACEUTICALS. **Personal Data:** b Pittsburgh, Pa, September 14, 1947; m 1971, Connie; c Brian Z, Gordon D & Jonathan S. **Education:** Univ Calif, Berkeley, BS, 1969; Univ Rochester, PhD (microbiol), 1973. **Honors & Awards:** Sigrid Juselius Found Award, 1975. **Professional Experience:** SR DIR, BARR LAB, as of 2005; DIR, WORLDWIDE QUAL SYSTS, CENTEON LLC, 1996-; gen mgr, Aeropharm, Inc, 1996; dir qual assurance & control, Inst Molecular Biol, Inc, 1994-1996; dir, Qual Systs & Technol Develop, Adams Sci, 1991-1993; res dir, Ecol Eng Assocs, 1989-1991; asst prof biol, State Univ NY, Binghampton, 1982-1989; expert-consult, Nat Inst Allergy & Infectious Dis, Rocky Mountain Labs, 1979-1982; sr staff fel, NIH, 1977-1979; asst prof biol, Univ Conn, 1975-1977; Nat Cancer Inst fel, Scripps Clin & Res Found, 1974-1975; Fel microbiol, York Univ, 1973-1974; pres, IOEA Consult. **Memberships:** Am Soc Qual Control; Int Soc Pharmaceut Engrs. **Research Statement & Publications:** Develop quality systems for continuous improvement of biotechnology and pharmaceuticals. **Mailing Address:** 102 Summit Lane, Bala Cynwyd, PA 19004. **Fax:** 610-668-0378. **E-Mail:** lissnest@aol.com

LISS, IVAN BARRY, COMPUTER SCIENCE EDUCATION, DATA STRUCTURES. **Personal Data:** b Lebanon, Ky, June 21, 1938; m 1977, Frances; c Barry & David. **Education:** Georgetown Col, BA, 1960; Univ Ky, MA, 1963; Univ Louisville, PhD (chem), 1973; Univ Ill, 1985. **Professional Experience:** DEAN, COL ARTS & SCI, RADFORD UNIV, 1997-; interim dean, Col Arts & Sci, Radford Univ, 1996-1997; assoc dean, Radford Univ, 1993-1996; chair, Radford Univ, 1991-1993; DIr acad comput, Radford Univ, 1988-1991; prof comput sci, Radford Univ, 1985-1991; prof chem, Blackburn Col, Ill, 1974-1985; fel, Univ Mo, Columbia, 1973-1974; instr chem, Univ Louisville, 1971-1973; NDEA fel, Univ Louisville, 1968-1971; chemist, Reliance Universal, Inc, 1965-1967; Teacher chem, Shelby Co High Sch, Ky, 1960-1965. **Memberships:** Sigma Xi; Asn for Computing Machinery (ACM); Am Asn of Higher Edu. **Research Statement & Publications:** Methods and approaches for computer science education at the university level. **Mailing Address:** Col Arts & Sci, Radford Univ, PO Box 6940, Radford, VA 24141. **Fax:** 540-831-5970. **E-Mail:** iliss@radford.edu

LISS, LEOPOLD, NEUROPATHOLOGY. **Personal Data:** b Lwow, Poland, November 19, 1923; American citizen; m 1948, c 2. **Education:** Lwow Gramar Sch, Poland, BA, 1941; Univ Heidelberg, MD, 1950; Univ Mich, MS, 1955. **Professional Experience:** CO-DIR OFF GERIAT MED, COL MED, 1977-; PROF NEUROPATH, OHIO STATE UNIV, 1964-; assoc prof, Col Med, 1960-1964; from instr to asst prof neuropath, Univ Mich, 1951-1960. **Memberships:** Am Asn Neuropath; Soc Neuroscience; Int Acad Path; Am Geriat Soc; Asn Res Nerv & Ment Dis; Sigma Xi. **Research Statement & Publications:** Clinical and experimental neuropathology; aging brain; Dementia; Alzheimer's disease; alcoholic encephalopathies; aluminum neurotoxicity. **Mailing Address:** 2124 Chardon Rd, Columbus, OH 43220-4461.

LISS, MAURICE, biochemistry, biology; deceased, see previous edition for last biography

LISS, WILLIAM JOHN, FISHERIES ECOLOGY, LIMNOLOGY. **Personal Data:** b Pittsburgh, Pa, June 18, 1947. **Education:** Pa State Univ, BS, 1969; Ore State Univ, MS, 1974, PhD (fisheries), 1977. **Professional Experience:** PROF EMER FISHERIES, ORE STATE UNIV, as of 2003; assoc prof Fisheries, Ore State Univ, beginning 1985; asst prof, Ore State Univ, 1978-1985; Res assoc, Ore State Univ, 1977-1978; prof fisheries, Ore State Univ. **Memberships:** Am fisheries Society. **Research Statement & Publications:** Population and community ecology of aquatic organisms with emphasis on habitat relationships at multiple spatial scales. **Mailing Address:** Dept Wildlife & Fisheries, Ore State Univ, 104 Nash Hall, Corvallis, OR 97331-3803. **Fax:** 541-737-3590. **E-Mail:** william.liss@orst.edu

LISSAMAN, PETER BARRY STUART, AERODYNAMICS. **Personal Data:** b Durban, SAfrica, April 10, 1931; American citizen; m 1980, Garbilla; c 4. **Education:** Univ Natal, BS, 1951; Cambridge Univ, MA, 1954; Calif Inst Technol, MS, 1955, PhD (aeronaut), 1966. **Honorary Degrees:** Dr, Natal Univ, 1990. **Honors & Awards:** Longstreth Medal, Franklin Inst, 1979; Kremer Medal, Royal Aeronaut Soc, 1979. **Professional Experience:** PROF, AEROSPACE ENG, UNIV SOUTHERN CALIF, as of 2000; prof, Southern Calif Inst Archit, beginning 1992; adj prof, Aerospace Eng, Univ Southern Calif, beginning 1991; nat lectr, Sigma Xi Soc, 1986-1989; prof, Art Ctr Design, 1976-; vpres, Aerovironment Inc, 1972-1991; distinguished lectr, Am Inst Aeronaut & Astronaut, 1972-1979; dir continuum mech lab, Northrop Corp, 1969-1971; Calif Inst Technol, 1962-1969 & Jet Propulsion Lab, 1968-1969; consult, McDonnell Douglas Corp, 1965-1968; asst prof aeronaut, US Naval Postgrad Sch, 1958-1962; res aerodynamicist, Handley-Page Aircraft, Eng, 1956-1958; designer & struct analyst, Bristol Aircraft Co, Eng, 1955-1956. **Memberships:** Fel Am Inst Aeronaut & Astronaut; Soc Exp Test Pilots. **Research Statement & Publications:** Aerodynamics, hydrodynamics, structure and dynamics of aircraft; marine and ground vehicles; wind and marine turbines; automotive aerodynamics; wing, rotor theory; turbulence, diffusion, plume modelling; energy systems; bird flight; engineering education. **Mailing Address:** Aerospace Dept, Univ Southern Calif, Los Angeles, CA 90089-1191. **Fax:** 213-740-7774. **E-Mail:** lissaman@spock.usc.edu

LISSANT, ELLEN KERN, PHYCOLOGY, ENVIRONMENTAL SCIENCE. **Personal Data:** b St Louis, Mo, November 4, 1922; m 1947, Kenneth; c Joyce E, Keith J & Nathan K. **Education:** Wash Univ, St Louis, AB, 1944, AM, 1946, PhD (bot), 1968. **Professional Experience:** RETIRED; instr, St Louis Community Col, Meramec, 1981-1985; fac assoc, Wash Univ, 1979-1981; from lectr to prof biol, Fontbonne Col, 1960-1978; asst herbarium, Stanford Univ, 1947; asst bot, Wash Univ, St Louis, 1946-1947; bot artist, 1945-; teacher, Webster Groves High Sch, 1945-1946; lab instr bot, Wash Univ, St Louis, 1943-1945. **Memberships:** Bot Soc Am; Phycol Soc Am; Sigma Xi. **Research Statement & Publications:** Palaeobotany; genetics; morphogenetic studies in the genus Erythrocladia Rosenvinge. **Mailing Address:** 851 Carob Rd, Clever, MO 65631.

LISSANT, KENNETH JORDAN, colloid chemistry, emulsions; deceased, see previous edition for last biography

LISSAUER, DAVID ARIE, ELEMENTARY PARTICLE PHYSICS. **Personal Data:** b Haifa, Israel, March 23, 1945; m 1968, Elaine; c Ariella, Michal & Jonathan. **Education:** Univ Calif, Berkeley, BA, 1966, MA, 1968, PhD (physics), 1971. **Professional Experience:** GROUP LEADER, BROOKHAVEN NAT LAB, as of 2005; sr Physicist, Brookhaven Nat Lab, 1998-; prof, Tel-Aviv Univ, 1987-1993; PHYSICIST, BROOKHAVEN NAT LAB, 1985-; assoc prof, Tel Aviv Univ, 1979-1981; res assoc, European Nuclear Res Orgn (CERN), 1977-1978, 1981-1982; sr lectr, Tel Aviv Univ, 1975-1977; res assoc, Argonne Nat Lab, 1974-1975; lectr physics, Tel Aviv Univ, 1972-1974. **Memberships:** Am Phys Soc. **Research Statement & Publications:** Lepton production in high energy interactions. **Mailing Address:** Brookhaven Nat Lab, 510 A Rm 1-73, Upton, NY 11973. **Fax:** 631-282-5568. **E-Mail:** lissauer@bnl.gov

LISSAUER, JACK JONATHAN, PLANETARY SCIENCE, PLANET FORMATION. **Personal Data:** b San Franciso, Calif, March 25, 1957. **Education:** Mass Inst Technol, SB, 1978; Univ Calif, Berkeley, PhD (appl math), 1982. **Honors & Awards:** Harold C Urey Prize, Div Planetary Sci, Am Astron Soc, 1992. **Professional Experience:** Consult prof, Geol Environ Sci, Stanford Univ, 2002 adj assoc prof, Astron Group, State Univ NY, Stony Brook, 1996-2002; SPACE SCIENTIST, AMES RES CTR, NASA, 1996-; Astron Dept, Univ Calif, Berkeley, 1994-1995; assoc researcher, Inst Astrophys, Paris, 1993; vis asst res physicist, Inst Theoret Physics, Univ Calif, Santa Barbara, 1992; invited prof, Dept Physics, Paris Observ, Univ Paris VII, 1990; vis scholar, Dept Planetary Sci & Lunar & Planetary Lab, Univ Ariz, Tucson, 1990; vis researcher, Univ Calif, Santa Barbara, 1985-1987; asst res astronr, Univ Calif, Berkeley, 1985; resident res assoc, Ames Res Ctr, NASA, Calif, 1983-1985. **Memberships:** Am Astron Soc; Int Astron Union; Am Geophys Union. **Research Statement & Publications:** Modelling the formation of planetary systems with particular emphasis on the dynamical processes involved in the final stages of planetary growth and the consequences for time scales of planetary growth and the origin of planetary rotation. **Mailing Address:** Space Sci 245-3, Ames Res Ctr NASA, Moffett Field, CA 94035. **E-Mail:** jlissauer@ringside.arc.nasa.gov

LISSNER, DAVID, MATHEMATICS. **Personal Data:** b Rochester, NY, July 25, 1931. **Education:** Mass Inst Technol, BS, 1953; Cornell Univ, PhD (math), 1959. **Professional Experience:** PROF EMER MATH, SYRACUSE UNIV, as of 2004; prof math, Syracuse Univ, beginning 1971; from asst prof to assoc prof, Syracuse Univ, 1962-1977; instr, Yale Univ, 1960-1962; off Naval Res fel math, Northwestern Univ, 1959-1960; design engr, NAm Aviation, Inc, 1953-1955. **Memberships:** Am Math Soc. **Research Statement & Publications:** Ring theory; linear, commutative and homological algebra; algebraic geometry. **Mailing Address:** Dept Math, Syracuse Univ, 100 Univ Pl, Syracuse, NY 13244-1200. **Fax:** 315-443-1475.

LIST, ALBERT JR, plant physiology; deceased, see previous edition for last biography

LIST, HARVEY L(AWRENCE), PROCESS HAZARDS ANALYSIS, INCIDENT INVESTIGATION. **Personal Data:** b Brooklyn, NY, September 5, 1924; m 1946, Anita; c Eric & Ian. **Education:** Polytech Inst Brooklyn, BChE, 1950, DChE, 1958; Univ Rochester, MS, 1950. **Professional Experience:** Pres, Rickian Inc, Forensic Chem Engrs, 1982-1994; PROF EMER CHEM ENG, CITY COL NY, 1980-; ed, Int Petrochem Develop 1980-1989; PRES, LIST ASSOCS INC, 1969-; Fulbright prof, Tunghai Univ, 1963-1964; private consult, beginning 1955; from assoc prof to prof, List Assocs, Inc, 1955-1980; Process engr chem eng, Esso res & Eng Co, 1950-1955; tech coordr, Adhesive & Sealant Coun, Ill. **Memberships:** Am Chem Soc; Am Soc Eng Educ; Am Inst Chem Engrs. **Research Statement & Publications:** Fluidization of solids; petroleum refining; chemical process economics; international relations; risk analysis; hazard and operability studies; accident investigation. **Mailing Address:** Dept Chem Eng, City Col NY, Rm T-322, Steinman Hall, 140th St, New York, NY 10031. **Fax:** 212-650-6660.

LIST, JAMES CARL, HERPETOLOGY. **Personal Data:** b Paducah, Ky, July 6, 1926; m 1947, c 2. **Education:** Notre Dame Univ, BS, 1948, MS, 1949; Univ Ill, PhD (zool), 1956. **Professional Experience:** EMER PROF BIOL, BALL STATE UNIV, 1988-; from instr to prof biol, Ball State Univ, 1957-1988; From instr to asst prof biol, Loyola Univ, Ill, 1952-1957. **Memberships:** Am Soc Ichthyol & Herpet; Herpetologists League; Soc Study Amphibians & Reptiles; Sigma Xi. **Research Statement & Publications:** Anatomy and ecology of amphibians and reptiles. **Mailing Address:** 7522 W Bethel Ave, Muncie, IN 47304.

LIST, ROLAND, ATMOSPHERIC PHYSICS. **Personal Data:** b Frauenfeld, Switz, February 21, 1929; Canadian & Swiss citizen; wid Gertrud K Egli (deceased); c Beat R & Claudia G. **Education:** Swiss Fed Inst Technol, Dipl phys sc nat, 1952; Swiss Fed Inst Technol, DSc, 1960. **Honors & Awards:** Medal, Univ Leningrad, 1970; Patterson Medal, 1979. **Professional Experience:** Mem, 2 US acad of sci comt on weather modif, 2001 & 2002; chmn, committee on weather modification, Am meteor soc, 1999-2002; Secy_gen, Int asn meteor atm sci IAMAS, 1995-; organizer, biennial IAMAS assemblies; rep, Int union Geodesy & Geophys with world meteorol orgn, WMO, 1995-; consultant, governments & private sector; vis prof, swiss fed inst technol, 1998 & 1974; chmn evaluation comt faculty environmental sciences, swiss fed inst technol, 1995; chmn WMO comm experts hail suppression, south africa 1995; rep, Int Union Geol & Geophys, World Meteorol Orgn, 1995-; EMER PROF PHYSICS, UNIV TORONTO, 1995-; chmn, Ital Sci Comt Rain Enhancement, Techagro, Rome, 1990-; prof, Univ Toronto, 1984-1995; dep secy-gen, World Meteorol Orgn, Geneva, Switz, 1982-1984; mem, Shuttle Sci Coun, Univ Space Res Asn, 1978-1981; bd dir, US Nat Ctr Atmospheric Res, Univ Corp Atmospheric Res, 1975-1978; vis prof, Swiss Fed Inst Technol, 1974; Chmn working groups cloud physics & weather modifications, World Meteorol Orgn, 1969-1982; assoc chmn, Dept Physics, 1969-1973; prof physics, Univ Toronto, 1963-1982; Sect head atmospheric ice formation, Swiss Fed Inst Snow & Avalanche Res, 1952-1963; chmn, Comt Meteorol & Atmospheric Sci, Nat Res Coun. **Memberships:** Fel Am Meteorol Soc; Am Geophys Union; fel Royal Meteorol Soc; Can Meteorol Soc; Swiss Acad Natural Sci; Can Acad Sci; fel Royal Soc Can. **Research Statement & Publications:** Precipitation physics; cloud dynamics; weather modification; heat and mass transfer; aerodynamics; all activities experimental, theoretical numerical and field. **Mailing Address:** Dept Physics, Univ Toronto, Toronto, ON M5S 1A7, Can. **Fax:** 416-978-8905. **E-Mail:** list@atmosp.physics.utoronto.ca

LISTER, CHARLES ALLAN, ELECTRICAL ENGINEERING, ELECTRONICS ENGINEERING. **Personal Data:** b Trenton, NJ, November 15, 1918; m 1946, Janet A Dressler; c Joan, Judith & Robert. **Education:** Tufts Univ, BS, 1940; Case Western Reserve Univ, MS, 1951. **Professional Experience:** CONSULT ENGR, 1984-; sr staff engr, Square D Co, Columbia, SC, 1983-1984; mgr eng serv, Res & Develop, Otis Elevator Co, 1976-1983; mgr proj admin, Res & Develop, Otis Elevator Co, 1974-1975; asst to vpres, Res & Develop, Otis Elevator Co, 1972-1974; mgr prod eng, Res & Develop, Otis Elevator Co, 1967-1972; dept head, Res & Develop, Otis Elevator Co, 1965-1967; mgr spec devices eng, Lockheed Aircraft Serv Co, 1964-1965; mgr test equip eng, Lockheed Missiles & Space Co, Calif, 1963-1964; design specialist, Lockheed Missiles & Space Co, Calif, 1962-1963; supvr new prod develop, Elec Controller & Mfg Div, Square D Co, Cleveland, 1956-1962; asst supvr, Elec Controller & Mfg Div, Square D Co, Cleveland, 1954-1956; develop engr, Elec Controller & Mfg Div, Square D Co, Cleveland, 1949-1954; asst prof elec eng, Swarthmore Col, 1947-1949; appln engr, Gen Elec Co, NY, 1946-1947; design engr, Gen Elec Co, NY, 1941-1943; Test engr, Gen Elec Co, NY, 1940-1941. **Memberships:** Inst Elec & Electronics Engrs; Sigma Xi. **Research Statement & Publications:** Electromechanical and electronic systems and devices; high-voltage contactors; electric brakes; lifting magnets; elevator dispatching computer systems; elevator control systems; arc interruption; standards for industrial controls. **Mailing Address:** 3215 Gulf Shore Blvd N, Apt 511, Naples, FL 34103-3915. **Fax:** 239-262-3575.

LISTER, EARL EDWARD, RUMINANT NUTRITION. **Personal Data:** b Harvey, NB, April 14, 1934; m 1983, c 3. **Education:** McGill Univ, BS, 1955, MS, 1957; Cornell Univ, PhD (nutrit), 1960. **Professional Experience:** Dir, Animal Res Ctr, 1987-1992; dir gen, Pesticides Directorate, Food Prod & Inspection Br, 1985-1987; dir gen, Atlantic Region Res Br, 1980-1985; prog specialist, Cent Region, Ottawa, 1978-1980; ed, Can J Animal Sci, 1975-1978; dep dir, Animal Res Inst, 1975-1978; assoc ed, Can J Animal Sci, 1973-1975; res scientist, Ottawa, Agr Can, 1965-1975; Feed nutritionist, Ogilvie Flour Mills Ltd, 1960-1965. **Memberships:** Can Soc Animal Sci; Am Dairy Sci Asn; Am Soc Animal Sci; Agr Inst Can; Asn Advan Sci Can. **Research Statement & Publications:** Nutritional requirements of immature ruminants; feeding and management systems for beef cows and calves; production of beef from dairy breeds of cattle. **Mailing Address:** 390 Hinton Ave, Ottawa, ON K1Y 1B1, Can.

LISTER, FREDERICK MONIE, MATHEMATICS. **Personal Data:** b Trenton, NJ, May 9, 1923; m 1954, c 3. **Education:** Tufts Univ, BS, 1947; Univ Mich, MA, 1951; Univ Utah, PhD (math), 1966. **Professional Experience:** RETIRED; prof, Cent Wash State Col, 1969-1988; assoc prof math, Cent Wash State Col, 1968-1969; prof, Southern Ore Col, 1967-1968; from asst prof to assoc prof, Western Wash Col Educ, 1958-1967; asst prof, Chico State Col, 1957-1958; instr, Western Wash Col Educ, 1954-1956; instr math, Phillips Acad, Mass, 1947-1949. **Memberships:** Am Math Soc; Math Asn Am. **Research Statement & Publications:** Geometric topology; embeddings of 2-spheres in Euclidean 3-space. **Mailing Address:** Cent Wash Univ, Ellensburg, WA 98926.

LISTER, MARK DAVID, EXPERIMENTAL BIOLOGY. **Personal Data:** b Kansas City, Mo, August 12, 1953; m Deborah Adams; c Hannah. **Education:** William Jewell Col, BA, 1975; Univ Mo, PhD (chem), 1985. **Professional Experience:** MGR, GLOBAL SAMPLE MGT, LILLY RES LABS, as of 2004; SCIENTIST II, SPHINX PHARMACEUT CO, 1992-; scientist I, Sphinx Pharmaceut CO, 1989-1992; Fel lipid enzymol, Univ Calif, San Diego, 1985-1989. **Memberships:** Am Chem Soc; AAAS; Am Soc Biochem & Molecular Biol. **Research Statement & Publications:** Protein purification; enzymatic characterization; kinetics; inhibitor studies; chemical and enzymatic synthesis; study of second messengers in cell signal transduction; development of high through-put assays for drug screening programs. **Mailing Address:** Lilly Res Labs, Indianapolis, IN 46285. **Fax:** 919-489-1308.

LISTER, MAURICE WOLFENDEN, INORGANIC CHEMISTRY. **Personal Data:** b Tunbridge Wells, Eng, March 27, 1914; Canadian citizen; m 1940, c 5. **Education:** Oxford Univ, PhD, 1938, MA, 1947. **Professional Experience:** RETIRED; from assoc prof to prof chem, Univ Toronto, beginning 1953. **Research Statement & Publications:** Complex inorganic compounds; mechanisms of inorganic reactions; magnetic susceptibilities; thermodynamics of solids. **Mailing Address:** 20 Burnham Rd, Toronto, ON M4G 1C1, Can.

LISTERMAN, THOMAS WALTER, SOLID STATE SCIENCE. **Personal Data:** b Cincinnati, Ohio, December 21, 1938; m 1969, c 2. **Education:** Xavier Univ, BS, 1959; Ohio Univ, PhD (solid state physics), 1965. **Professional Experience:** EMER PROF, WRIGHT STATE UNIV, 2000-; vis res assoc prof elec eng, Univ Cincinnati, 1987-1988; assoc prof physics, Wright State Univ, 1972-2000; asst provost, Wright State Univ, 1971-1973; asst dean sci & eng, Wright State Univ, 1970-1971; asst prof, Wright State Univ, 1967-1972; sr res physicist, Mound Lab, Monsanto Res Corp, 1965-1967. **Research Statement & Publications:** Electronic properties of materials; cryogenics; semiconductor device physics. **Mailing Address:** Dept Physics & Eng Physics Prog, Wright State Univ, 248 Fawcett Hall, Dayton, OH 45435. **Fax:** 937-775-2222. **E-Mail:** thomas.listerman@wright.edu

LISTGARTEN, MAX A, DENTISTRY, PERIODONTOLOGY. **Personal Data:** b Paris, France, May 14, 1935; Canadian citizen; m 1963, Eileen; c Karen, Sheralyn & Michael. **Education:** Univ Toronto, DDS, 1959; FRCD(C), 1969. **Honorary Degrees:** MA, Univ Pa, 1971; PhD, Univ Athens, Greece, 1993. **Honors & Awards:** Award Basic Res Periodont Dis, Int Asn Dent Res, 1973; William J Gies Periodont Award, Am Acad Periodont, 1981, Clin Res Award, 1987. **Professional Experience:** PROF EMER PERIODONT, UNIV PA, 2001-; VIS PROF PERIODONT, UNIV CALIF, SAN FRANCISCO, 2001-; prof Periodont & dir Periodont res, Sch Dent Med, Univ Pa, 1994-2001; pres, Am Asn Dent res, 1991-1992; Chmn Periodont, Univ PA, 1984-1992; oral biol & med study sect, NIH, 1980-1984; US ed, J Biol Buccale, 1972-1992; assoc prof, Univ PA, 1968-1971; from asst prof to assoc prof, fac Dent, Univ Toronto, 1964-1967; res assoc periodont, Harvard Med Sch, 1963-1964; Nat res Coun Can fel periodont, Harvard Med Sch, 1960-1963; Intern dent, Hosp for Sick Children, Toronto, 1959-1960. **Memberships:** Fel AAAS; Am Dent Asn; fel Am Acad Periodont; Int Asn Dent Res; Am Asn Dent Res. **Research Statement & Publications:** Ultrastructural investigations of the supporting structures of teeth and associated microbial flora in health and disease; microbiological diagnosis in the treatment of periodontal diseases. **Mailing Address:** Dept Periodont Sch Dent Med, Univ Pa 4001 Spruce St, Philadelphia, PA 19104. **Fax:** 215-573-2117. **E-Mail:** maxl@biochem.dental.upenn.edu

LISTON, AARON IRVING, BOTANY. **Personal Data:** b Cleveland, Ohio, December 2, 1959; m 1990, Sara. **Education:** Hebrew Univ, BSc, 1982, MSc, 1984; Claremont Grad Sch, PhD (bot), 1990. **Professional Experience:** DIR HERBARIUM, DEPT BOT & PLANT PATH, ORE STATE UNIV, CORVALLIS, as of 2005; Nature Conservancy, 1994; Nat Acad Sci/Nat Res Coun, 1993; prin investr, Hardman Found & Hoover Trust, 1993 & 1994; ASST PROF, DEPT BOT & PLANT PATH, ORE STATE UNIV, CORVALLIS, 1991-; prin investr, M J Murdock Charitable Trust, 1991-1992; prin investr, Ore Dept Agr, 1991; fel researcher, Dept Genetics, Univ Calif, Davis, 1990; prin investr, Sigma Xi, 1988; prin investr, NSF, 1988, 1993 & 1994; res asst, Rancho Santa Ana Bot Garden, Calif, 1987-1989; prin investr, Claremont Grad Sch, 1986, 1987 & 1989; Herbarium asst, Hebrew Univ, 1982-1986. **Memberships:** AAAS; Am Soc Plant Taxonomists; Asn Systs Collections; Bot Soc Am; Soc Molecular & Biol Evolution; Soc Syst Biologists. **Research Statement & Publications:** Botany; plant conservation genetics; molecular systematics; author of numerous publications. **Mailing Address:** Ore State Univ, 4086 Cordley Hall, Corvallis, OR 97331-2902. **E-Mail:** listona@bcc.orst.edu

LISTON, RONALD ARGYLE, MECHANICAL ENGINEERING, ENGINEERING MECHANICS. **Personal Data:** b Buffalo, NY, April 11, 1926; m 1981, Nancy; c 9. **Education:** Univ Vt, BS, 1949; Univ Mich, MS (mech eng), 1958 & MS (eng mech), 1961; Mich Technol Univ, PhD (eng mech), 1973. **Professional Experience:** GEN SECY, APPL RES DIV, US ARMY COLD REGIONS RES & ENG LAB, as of 2001; SUPVR RES GEN ENGR, US ARMY COLD REGIONS RES & ENG LAB, 1975-; res ctr dir, Mich Technol Univ, 1974-1975; res mech engr, Cold Regions Res & Eng Lab, 1970-1974; supvr automotive res engr, Tank-Automotive Command, 1958-1970; proof officer ballistics & automotive, US Army, 1950-1956; secy, Army Res; study fel. **Memberships:** Fel Int Soc Terrain-Vehicle Systs; Sigma Xi; Am Soc Mech Engrs. **Research Statement & Publications:** Off road vehicles; over snow vehicles; simulation of engineer activities in combat operations; rapid stabilization of soils. **Mailing Address:** Div Appl Res, US Army Cold Regions Res Lab, 72 Lyme Rd, Hanover, NH 03755-1290. **Fax:** 603-646-4640. **E-Mail:** rliston@crrel.usace.army.mil

LISTOWSKY, IRVING, BIOCHEMISTRY. **Personal Data:** b Vilna, Poland, December 21, 1935; m 1963, c 3. **Education:** Yeshiva Univ, BA, 1957; Polytech Inst Brooklyn, PhD (org chem), 1963. **Honors & Awards:** NIH career develop award, 1971-1976. **Professional Experience:** PROF BIOCHEM, ALBERT EINSTEIN COL MED, 1979-; sr investr, NY Heart Asn, 1967-1970; from instr to assoc prof, Albert Einstein Col Med, 1965-1978. **Memberships:** Am Soc Biol Chemists. **Research Statement & Publications:** Structure-function relationships of biological substances; iron metabolism, intracellular transport and detoxification mechanisms. **Mailing Address:** Albert Einstein Col Med, 1300 Morris Park Ave, Bronx, NY 10461. **E-Mail:** irving@aecom.yu.edu

LISY, JAMES MICHAEL, SPECTROSCOPY, MOLECULAR BEAMS. **Personal Data:** b Cleveland, Ohio, August 5, 1952; m 1976, c 2. **Education:** Iowa State Univ, BS, 1974; Harvard Univ, MA, 1977, PhD (chem physics), 1979. **Professional Experience:** PROF CHEM, UNIV ILL, as of 2003; assoc prof chem, Univ Ill, beginning 1987; Alfred P Sloan Res fel, 1987-1991; asst prof, Univ Ill, 1981-1987; Res assoc, Lawrence Berkeley Lab, 1979-1981. **Memberships:** Am Chem Soc; Am Phys Soc. **Research Statement & Publications:** Structure, bonding and intramolecular energy transfer of small molecular and ion clusters are studied using molecular beam techniques and laser spectroscopy. **Mailing Address:** Dept Chem, Univ Ill, A224 Chem & Life Sci Lab, 600 S Mathews Ave, Urbana, IL 61801. **Fax:** 217-244-3186. **E-Mail:** j-lisy@uiuc.edu

LISZT, HARVEY STEVEN, RADIO ASTRONOMY, SPECTRUM MANAGEMENT. **Personal Data:** b Newark, NJ, December 5, 1945; m 1973, Mehrak; c Jeffrey & Gregory. **Education:** Univ Mass, BS, 1967; Princeton Univ, MA, 1969, PhD (astron), 1974. **Professional Experience:** NRAO Spectrum Manager 2003-present; GBT proj scientist, 1995-1997; res prof, Univ Va, beginning 1981; SCIENTIST ASTRON, NAT RADIO ASTRON OBSERV, 1979-; assoc scientist, Nat Radio Astron Observ, 1976-1979; asst prof physics, Univ Pittsburgh, 1975-1976; res assoc, Nat Radio Astron Observ, 1973-1975; Res assoc spectros, Princeton Univ Observ, 1969-1971. **Memberships:** Int Astron Union. **Research Statement & Publications:** Structure and evolution of interstellar clouds; radiation transport in simple interstellar molecules; structure of the galactic nucleus, interstellar chemistry. **Mailing Address:** Nat Radio Astron Observ, 520 Edgemont Rd, Charlottesville, VA 22903-2475. **Fax:** 434-296-0278. **E-Mail:** hliszt@nrao.edu

LIT, JOHN WAI-YU, OPTICS. **Personal Data:** b Canton, China, August 31, 1937; Canadian citizen; m Chi; c Wilson & Eugene. **Education:** Univ Hong Kong, BSc, 1958, dipl Ed, 1961; Univ Laval, PhD (optics), 1969. **Professional Experience:** PROF EMER PHYSICS, WILFRID LAURIER UNIV, as of 2006; founding pres, southwestern ont sect, Opt Soc Am, 1994-1995; mem exec comt, bd dirs, Nat Optics Inst, 1988-1991; adj prof elec eng & elec comput eng, Univ Waterloo, 1987-1993; adj prof physics, Univ Waterloo, 1980-; prof physics, Wilfrid Laurier Univ, beginning 1980; chmn physics dept, Wilfrid Laurier Univ, 1980-1986 & beginning 1992; chmn, div optical physics, Can Asn Physicists, 1977-1978 & 1988-1989; assoc prof, Wilfrid Laurier Univ, 1977-1980; assoc ed, optical soc am, 1974-1979; from asst prof to assoc prof optics, Univ Laval, 1971-1977; res assoc, Univ Laval, 1969-1971; fel optics, Univ Western Ont, 1968-1969; teacher sci, quebec high sch, 1964-1965; head physics, diocesan boys sch, 1961-1964; consult, various indust & govt labs; chair gen physics, Grants Selection Comt, Natural Sci & Eng Res Coun Can. **Memberships:** Can Asn Physicists; fel Optical Soc Am; Inst Elec & Electronics Engrs. **Research Statement & Publications:** Fiber and integrated optics; optical sensing; optical instrumentation. **Mailing Address:** Dept Physics & Comput, Wilfrid Laurier Univ, Waterloo, ON N2L 3C5, Can. **E-Mail:** jlit@mach1.wlu.ca

LITCHFIELD, CARTER, BIOCHEMISTRY. **Personal Data:** b Pasadena, Calif, February 18, 1932; m 1960. **Education:** Rensselaer Polytech Inst, BS, 1953; Am Inst Foreign Trade, BFT, 1957; Tex A&M Univ, PhD (chem), 1966. **Honors & Awards:** Bond Award, Am Oil Chem Soc, 1963, 1966 & 1978. **Professional Experience:** WRITER & PUBL, OLEARIUS ED, 1979-; Vis scientist, Fisheries Res Bd Can, 1967 & Univ Trondheim, 1975 & 1979; from assoc prof to prof biochem, Rutgers Univ, 1973-1979; assoc prof lipid biochem, Rutgers Univ, 1969-1973; from asst prof to assoc prof lipid biochem, Tex A&M Univ, 1960-1969; Chemist, Procter & Gamble Co, 1953-1960. **Memberships:** Soc Hist Technol; Am Oil Chem Soc; Soc Indust Archeol. **Research Statement & Publications:** Biochemistry of lipids of marine organisms; analysis of natural fat triglyceride mixtures; gas liquid chromatography of lipids; biochemical systematics of lipids; history of lipid biochemistry; history of fats & oils technology. **Mailing Address:** 28 White Oak Rd, Kemblesville, PA 19347.

LITCHFIELD, JOHN HYLAND, FOOD SCIENCE, INDUSTRIAL MICROBIOLOGY. **Personal Data:** b Scituate, Mass, February 13, 1929; wid. **Education:** Mass Inst Technol, SB, 1950; Univ Ill, MS, 1954, PhD (food technol), 1956. **Honors & Awards:** Charles Porter Award, Soc Indust Microbiol, 1977; Carl R Fellers Award, Inst food Technol, 1994. **Professional Experience:** ADJ PROF, DEPT FOOD SCI & TECHNOL, OHIO STATE UNIV, COLUMBUS, OHIO, 1990-; RES LEADER BIOTECHNOL, COLUMBUS LABS, BATTELLE MEM INST, 1981-; prog mgr biol sci, Columbus Labs, 1980-1981; adj assoc prof human nutrit & food mgt, Ohio State Univ, Columbus, Ohio, 1977-1978; mgr Bioengineering & Health Sci Sect, Columbus Labs, 1976-1980; sr tech adv, Columbus Labs, 1973-1976; mgr biol & med sci sect, Columbus Labs, 1970-1972; assoc mgr life sci, Dept Chem Eng, 1968-1970; chief biochem & microbiol res, 1964-1967 & microbiol & environ biol res, 1967-1968; asst chief Bioscience res, Battelle Mem Inst, 1962-1964; proj leader Bioscience, Battelle Mem Inst, 1961-1962; sr food technologist, Battelle Mem Inst, 1960-1961; Consult to food indust, 1957-1960; asst prof food eng, Ill Inst Technol, 1957-1960; res food technologist, Swift & Co, Ill, 1956-1957; Chief chemist, Searle Food Corp, Fla, 1950-1951. **Memberships:** Fel AAAS; Am Inst Chemists; fel Am Acad Microbiol; fel Soc Indust Microbiol (pres 1970-1971); fel Inst Food Technologists (pres 1991-1992; fel Inst. Food Sci Techology U.K.; fel Inst. Biology, U.K. **Research Statement & Publications:** Food processing and preservation; fermentation technology, food, industrial, sanitary and public health microbiology; microbial biochemistry; mass cultivation of microorganisms. **Mailing Address:** Battelle Mem Inst 505 King Ave, Columbus, OH 43201-2693. **E-Mail:** litchfield.3@osu.edu

LITCHFIELD, WILLIAM JOHN, BIOCHEMISTRY, CLINICAL CHEMISTRY. **Personal Data:** b Waukegan, Ill, February 28, 1950; m 1972, Marilyn; c 2. **Education:** Univ Ill, BS, 1972, MS, 1973; Mich State Univ, PhD (biochem), 1976. **Professional Experience:** METHODS MGR, E I DUPONT DEL NEMOURS & CO INC, 1996-; QUAL ASSURANCE MGR, E I DUPONT DEL NEMOURS & CO INC, 1993-; prod & res mgr, Instrument Prod Div, E I DuPont Del Nemours & Co, Inc, 1990-1993; new bus develop mgr, Instrument Prod Div, E I DuPont Del Nemours & Co, Inc, 1978-1990; res biochemist, Instrument Prod Div, E I DuPont Del Nemours & Co, Inc, 1976-1978; NIH fel, 1976-1977; fel biophys, Johnson Res Found, Sch Med, Univ Pa, 1976-1977. **Memberships:** Am Chem Soc; Am Asn Clin Chem; Biophys Soc; Am Asn Immunologists; Soc Qual Assurance. **Research Statement & Publications:** Biophysics; solid state biochemical reactions; free-radical reactions in leukocytes, mitochondria and photosystems; immunology, enzymology, lipid chemistry; immunochemistry; immunodiagnostics. **Mailing Address:** 23 Covered Bridge Lane, Newark, DE 19711-2062. **E-Mail:** litchfwj@esvax.dnet.dupont.com

LITCHFORD, GEORGE B, ELECTRONICS. **Personal Data:** b Long Beach, Calif, August 12, 1918; m 1942, c 2. **Education:** Reed Col, BA, 1941. **Honors & Awards:** Wright Bros Lect Medal & Citation, Am Inst Aeronaut & Astronaut, 1978; Lamme Medal, Inst Elec & Electronics Engrs, 1981. **Professional Experience:** GEN PARTNER, LITCHSTREET CO, as of 2002; PRES & HEAD DEPT AVIATION SYSTS CONSULT BUS, LITCHFORD SYSTS, 1965-; head, Dept Aviation Systs Res, 1957-1965; asst supvr Navig Dept, Litchford Systs, 1951-1955; head eng sect, Aircraft Radio Dept, Sperry Gyroscope Co, 1941-1951; consult, Dept Transp, Dept Defense, NASA & indust, mem, Radio Tech Comn Aeronaut. **Memberships:** Fel Inst Elec & Electronics Engrs; fel Am Inst Aeronaut & Astronaut. **Research Statement & Publications:** Inventor of many systems including precision omniranges, navy and shuttle landing systems, secondary radar systems; developed collision avoidance systems, now in production; holder of over 70 patents; development of Passur, passive ground range. **Mailing Address:** Litchstreet Co, 32 Cherry Lawn Lane, Northport, NY 11768.

LITHERLAND, ALBERT EDWARD, PHYSICS, ACCELERATOR MASS SPECTROMETRY RADIOCARBON DATING. **Personal Data:** b Wallasey, Eng, March 12, 1928; Canadian citizen; m 1956, Anne Allen; c Jane E & Rosamund M. **Education:** Univ Liverpool, BSc, 1949, PhD, 1955. **Honors & Awards:** Gold Medal Physics, Can Asn Physicists, 1971; Rutherford Medal, Inst Physics, London, 1974; Henry Marshall Tory Medal, Royal Soc Can, 1993. **Professional Experience:** EMER UNIV PROF PHYSICS, UNIV TORONTO, 1993-; Guggenheim fel, 1986-1987; Killam fel, 1980-1981; from prof to univ prof, Univ Toronto, 1966-1993; sci officer, Atomic Energy Can, 1955-1966; Rutherford scholar, Atomic Energy Can, 1953-1955. **Memberships:** Fel Royal Soc Can; Can Asn Physicists; fel AAAS; fel Am Phys Soc. **Research Statement & Publications:** Radiocarbon dating for art/archaeology/geophysics using accelerator mass spectrometry; iodine-129 tracing for oceanography; fundamentals of accelerator mass spectrometry. **Mailing Address:** 3 Hawthorn Gardens, Toronto, ON M4W 1P4, Can.

LITKE, JOHN DAVID, COMPUTER SCIENCE, PHYSICS. **Personal Data:** b Winchester, Mass, May 30, 1944; m 1966. **Education:** Mass Inst Technol, BS, 1965; Johns Hopkins Univ, PhD (physics), 1976. **Professional Experience:** CONSULT, as of 2004; DIR, FUTURE TECHNOL, ABC BROADCASTING, 1996-; COORDR, LUTHERAN THEOL CTR, NY, 1993-; consult, Off Automation Technol, 1986-; dir res, Northrop Grumman, 1985-1996; prin scientist photociruits, Bell Lab, 1980-1984; Bell Lab, 1976-1980; Instr physics, Johns Hopkins Univ, 1967-1975. **Memberships:** Sigma Xi; Am Phys Soc; Inst

Elec & Electronics Engrs; Asn Comput Mach; Soc Motion Picture & Television Engrs. **Research Statement & Publications:** Sofware engineering; distributed and fault tolerant systems; real time multi-media systems. **Mailing Address:** Future Technol, ABC Inc, 47 W 66th St 11th Floor, New York, NY 10023. **E-Mail:** litkej@abc.com

LITMAN, BERNARD, ELECTRICAL ENGINEERING. **Personal Data:** b New York, NY, October 26, 1920; m 1949, Ellen; c Barbara & Richard. **Education:** Columbia Univ, BS, 1941, PhD (elec eng), 1949; Univ Pittsburgh, MS, 1943. **Professional Experience:** RETIRED; sci consult, 1993-1995; prin scientist, Avionics Systs, Cull Inc, 1983-1993; chief engr, Ambac Industs, Div United Technologies Corp, 1963-1983; res, Ambac Industs, Div United Technologies Corp, 1959-1961; mgr airborne equip, Ambac Industs, Div United Technologies Corp, 1956-1958; engr fire control & guid, Ambac Industs, Div United Technologies Corp, 1948-1953; instr elec eng, Univ Pittsburgh, 1947; engr mach design, Westinghouse Elec Corp, 1941-1947. **Memberships:** Inst Elec & Electronics Engrs; Am Inst Aeronaut & Astronaut. **Research Statement & Publications:** Electromechanical control and computing equipment; weapon control and navigation; inertial guidance; data management systems for aircraft and scientific instruments. **Mailing Address:** 228 Wagon Wheel Lane, Columbus, NJ 08022.

LITMAN, BURTON JOSEPH, BIOCHEMISTRY, BIOPHYSICS. **Personal Data:** b Boston, Mass, May 8, 1935; m 1958, Elaine; c Deborah & Daniel. **Education:** Boston Univ, BA, 1958; Univ Ore, PhD (biophys chem), 1966. **Professional Experience:** CHIEF & INVESTR FLUORESCENCE STUDIES, NIH, 1993-; vis prof, Dept Biochem, Univ Va, 1993-1994; chmn, Dept Biochem, 1984-1993; asst dean, Sch Med, 1981-1983; from asst prof to prof biochem, NIH, Dept Biochem, Univ Va, 1968-1993; fel, NIH, Dept Biochem, Univ Va, 1966-1968. **Memberships:** Biophys Soc; Am Soc Biochem & Molecular Biol; Res Soc Alcoholism. **Research Statement & Publications:** Structure-function relationships in biological membranes with particular emphasis on the molecular mechanism of vision; signal transduction in vision; role of lipid composition in modulating membrane protein function; mechanism of action of ethanol and general anesthetics. **Mailing Address:** Lab Membrane Biochem & Biophys, Nat Inst Alcohol Abuse & Alcoholism, Nat Inst Health, Rm 114 Park 5 12420 Parklawn Dr, Rockville, MD 20852. **Fax:** 301-594-0035. **E-Mail:** litman@helix.nih.gov

LITMAN, DIANE JUDITH, COMPUTATIONAL LINGUISTICS, KNOWLEDGE REPRESENTATION & REASONING. **Personal Data:** b New York, NY, March 5, 1958. **Education:** Col William & Mary, BA, 1980; Univ Rochester, MS, 1982, PhD (comput sci), 1986. **Professional Experience:** ASSOC PROF COMP SCI, UNIV PITTSBURGH, 2001-; RES SCIENTIST, UNIV PITTSBURG, LEARNING RES AND DEVELOP CTR, 2001-; asst prof comput sci, Columbia Univ, 1990-1992; prin tech staff mem, AT & T Labs Res, 1985-2001. **Memberships:** Asn Computational Ling; Am Asn Artificial Intel. **Research Statement & Publications:** Artificial intelligence, particularly computational linguistics, knowledge representation and reasoning, plan recognition, spoken dialogue agents, user modeling and applications of machine learning. **Mailing Address:** Dept Comput Sci, Univ Pittsburg, 5105 Sennott Sq 210 S Bouquet St, Pittsburgh, PA 15260. **Fax:** 412-624-8854. **E-Mail:** litman@cs.pitt.edu

LITMAN, GARY WILLIAM, IMMUNOLOGY, MOLECULAR GENETICS. **Personal Data:** b Shoemaker, Calif, June 26, 1945; m 1970, Ronda; c Matthew & Eryn. **Education:** Univ Minn, BA 1967, PhD (microbiol)1972. **Honors & Awards:** University of South Florida Distinguished University Professor 2004; University of South Florida Outstanding Faculty Research Achievement Award 2002; The Henry Kunkel Society 2001; NIH MERIT Award 1995. **Professional Experience:** HINES PROF, DEPT PEDIATRICS, COL MED, UNIV S FLA, as of 1990; CHMN, DEPT MOLECULAR GENETICS, TAMPAY BAY RES INST, 1985-1990; assoc prof immunol, Sloan-Kettering Div, Grad Sch Med Sci, Cornell Univ, 1980; chmn biol unit, Sloan-Kettering Div, Grad Sch Med Sci, Cornell Univ, 1978-1980; ASSOC PROF GENETICS, SLOAN-KETTERING DIV, GRAD SCH MED SCI, CORNELL UNIV, 1976-; ASSOC PROF BIOL, SLOAN-KETTERING DIV, GRAD SCH MED SCI, CORNELL UNIV, 1973-; assoc mem, Dept Macromolecular Biochem, Sloan-Kettering Inst, 1972-; asst prof path, Univ Minn, 1972; instr pediat & path, Univ Minn, 1970-1972; teaching specialist microbiol & pediat, Univ Minn, 1968-1970; Res asst microbiol, Univ Minn, 1967-1968. **Memberships:** AAI; ASBMB; ASHG; FASEB; HENRY KUNKEL SOCIETY. **Research Statement & Publications:** Evolution of immunoglobulin structure; a typical solubility characteristics of proteins; chemical carcinogenesis; chromosomal proteins. **Mailing Address:** Dept Pediatics, Univ S Fla, 830 First St S CRI 3008, St Petersburg, FL 33701. **Fax:** 727-553-3610. **E-Mail:** litmang@allkids.org

LITMAN, GEORGE H, MATHEMATICS. **Education:** Cornell Univ, PhD. **Professional Experience:** DEP PROVOST, NAT LOUIS UNIV, as of 2006. **Mailing Address:** Nat Louis Univ, 2840 Sheridan Rd, Evanston, IL 60201. **Fax:** 312-261-3247.

LITMAN, IRVING IRA, FOOD TECHNOLOGY. **Personal Data:** b Chelsea, Mass, November 16, 1925; c 6. **Education:** Univ Mass, BA, 1949, MS, 1951; Wash State Univ, PhD (food technol), 1956. **Professional Experience:** PRES, LITMAN TECHNOL CORP, 1987-; Globe Fla Corp, 1981-1983 & Manheimer Corp, 1984-1986; RES DIR, STEPAN FLAVORS & FRAGRANCES, INC, 1966-; dir res, Stepan Chem Corp, 1966-1981; sect head, Durkee Famous Foods, 1964-1965; flavor chemist, Givaudan Corp, 1962-1964; proj leader, Res Ctr, Gen Foods Corp, 1956-1962; jr res chemist, Univ Calif, 1955-1956; asst dairy technologist, Wash State Univ, 1953-1955; food technologist, Gen Prod Div, Qm Food & Container Inst, US Armed Forces, 1951-1953; Processed food inspector, Prod & Mkt Admin, USDA, 1950-1951. **Memberships:** Royal Soc Chem; Inst Food Technologists; AAAS; Sigma Xi; Flavor Chemists Soc. **Research Statement & Publications:** Development of synthetic and natural flavorings for food, tobacco and pharmaceuticals. **Mailing Address:** 447-B New Haven Way, Jamesburg, NJ 08831-1824.

LITMAN, NATHAN, PEDIATRICS, INFECTIOUS DISEASES. **Personal Data:** b New York, NY, November 22, 1946; m 1969, Norma; c Levi, Matthew & Sarah. **Education:** Brooklyn Col, BS, 1967; Albert Einstein Col Med, MD, 1971. **Honors & Awards:** Alpha omega alpha, albert einstein col of med, 1971. **Professional Experience:** PROF PEDIAT, MONTEFIORE MED CTR, as of 2005; CHIEF, SECT INFECTIOUS DIS, DEPT PEDIAT, as of 2005; dir pediat & pediat infectious dis montefiore med ctr, 1998-; prof of pediat, Albert Einstein Col Med, 1997-; attend pediat & infectious dis, Montefiore Med Ctr, beginning 1978; fel infectious dis, Albert Einstein Col Med, 1976-1978; lieutenant comdr pediat, USPHS, 1974-1976; intern, resident & chief resident pediat, Montefiore Hosp & Med Ctr, 1971-1974. **Memberships:** Fel Am Acad Pediat; Infectious Dis Soc Am; Pediat infectious dis soc. **Research Statement & Publications:** Infectious etiologies of pediatric diarrhea. **Mailing Address:** Montefiore med center, 111 E 210 St Rosenthal Pavilion, Bronx, NY 10467. **Fax:** 718-654-6692.

LITOSCH, IRENE, PHYSIOLOGICAL CHEMISTRY. **Personal Data:** b New York, NY, June 7, 1952. **Education:** NY Univ, Univ Arts & Sci, BA, 1974; State Univ NY, Downstate Med Ctr, PhD (pharmacol), 1979. **Professional Experience:** ASSOC PROF MOLECULAR & CELLULAR PHARMACOL, MIAMI UNIV, as of 2004; asst prof molecular & cellular pharmacol, Univ Miami, 1985-1991; fel res, Sect Physiol Chem, Brown Univ, 1979-1982. **Memberships:** NY Acad Sci. **Research Statement & Publications:** Mechanism of regulation of intiacularlur calcium. **Mailing Address:** Dept Molecular & Cellular Pharmacol, Univ Miami Med Sch, 6088 Rosenstiel Med Sci Bldg, Miami, FL 33101. **Fax:** 305-243-4555. **E-Mail:** ilitosch@chroma.med.miami.edu

LITOV, RICHARD EMIL, CLINICAL NUTRITION. **Personal Data:** b New York, NY, 1953; m Davis. **Education:** Univ Calif, Davis, BS, 1975, PhD (nutrit), 1980. **Professional Experience:** DIR RES & DEVELOP, NUTRATEC, 1993-; pediat, beginning 1990; USDA Competitive Grants Prog, beginning 1990; bd trustees, Evansville Mus Arts & Sci, beginning 1987; reviewer, Am J Clin Nutrit, 1986-; sr scientist res, Bristol-Myers Squibb, 1985-1993; scientist, Bristol-Myers Squibb, 1981-1985; res asst, UnivCalif, Med Sch & Primate Res Ctr, Davis, 1976-1980; staff res assoc, UnivCalif, Med Sch & Primate Res Ctr, Davis, 1975-1976. **Memberships:** Inst Food Technologists; Am Soc Clin Nutrit; Am Inst Nutrit. **Research Statement & Publications:** Functional foods; infant and enteral formulas; therapeutic biologics; oral rehydration solutions; antiinfections; mineral bioavailability; burn injury; selenium bioavailability and aluminum status. **Mailing Address:** NutraTec, LLC, 10340 Schaeffer Rd, Evansville, IN 47720. **Fax:** 812-963-9588. **E-Mail:** relitov@nutratec.com

LITOVITZ, THEODORE AARON, PHYSICS. **Personal Data:** b New York, NY, October 14, 1923; m 1946, c 2. **Education:** Cath Univ, AB, 1946, PhD, 1950. **Professional Experience:** PROF EMER PHYSICS, CATH UNIV AM, as of 2004; CO-DIR, VITREOUS STATE LAB, 1968-; prof physics, Cath Univ Am, beginning 1959; from asst prof to assoc prof, Vitreous State Lab, 1950-1959; Consult, Univ Hosp, Georgetown, 1950-1957. **Memberships:** Fel Am Phys Soc; fel Acoust Soc Am; Am Philos Soc. **Research Statement & Publications:** Ultrasonic propagation and light scattering in studies of molecular motions in liquids and glasses; development of glasses with unique technical applications. **Mailing Address:** Vitreous State Lab, Cath Univ Am, 620 Michigan Ave, NE, Washington, DC 20064. **E-Mail:** litovitz@cua.edu

LITSEY, LINUS R, GEOLOGY. **Education:** Univ Mich, BS, 1947; Univ Colo, PhD (geol), 1955. **Professional Experience:** RETIRED; sr consult, Sci Software-Intercomp, 1980-1996; formation eval geologist, Chevron Oil Co, Denver, Colo, 1976-1980; supvr reservoir description unit, Aramco, Arabia, 1974-1976; well log analyst, Aramco, Arabia, 1972-1974; digital well log processing, Houston, Tex, 1969-1972; dipmeter analyst, Chevron Oil Co, New Orleans, 1965-1969; dipmeter res, Chevron Res Co, La Habra, Calif, 1963-1965; geologist, Chevron Oil Co, New Orleans, La, 1957-1963; uranium geologist, US Geol Surv, 1954-1957. **Memberships:** Am Asn Petrol Geologists; Geol Soc Am; Soc Prof Well Log Analysts; Sigma Xi. **Mailing Address:** 5098 Ndcbu, Taos, NM 87571.

LITSKY, BERTHA YANIS, microbiology, hospital administration; deceased, see previous edition for last biography

LITSTER, JAMES DAVID, SOLID STATE PHYSICS, SCATTERING SPECTROSCOPY. **Personal Data:** b Toronto, Ont, June 19, 1938; m 1965, Cheryl; c Robin & Heather. **Education:** McMaster Univ, BEng, 1961; Mass Inst Tech, PhD (physics), 1965. **Honorary Degrees:** DSc, McMaster Univ, 1992. **Honors & Awards:** Irving Langmuir Prize, Chem Physics, 1993. **Professional Experience:** Dean grad edu, Mass Inst Technol, 1996-1999; dean & vpres & dean res, Francis Bitter Nat Magnet Lab, 1991-2001; dir, Francis Bitter Nat Magnet Lab, 1988-1991; regional ed, Molecular Crystals & Liquid Crystals, 1986-; mem, Solid State Sci Panel, Nat Res Coun, 1986-; dir, Ctr Mat Sci & Eng, Mass Inst Technol, 1983-1988; chmn, Condensed Matter Sci Subcomt, 1980-1981; head, Div Atomic, Condensed Matter & Plasma Physics, Dept Physics, 1979-1983; mem Mat Res Adv Comt, NSF, 1978-1981; vis scientist, Riso Nat Lab, Denmark, 1978; PROF PHYSICS, MASS INST TECHNOL, 1975-; lectr physics, Harvard Med Sch, 1974-1985; vis prof, Univ Paris, Orsay, 1971-1972; fel, John Simon Guggenheim Mem Found, 1971-1972; from instr to assoc prof, Mass Inst Technol, 1965-1975. **Memberships:** Fel AAAS; fel Am Phys Soc; fel Am Acad Arts & Sci. **Research Statement & Publications:** Magnetism; light scattering; liquid crystals; x-ray scattering using synchrotron radiation. **Mailing Address:** Dept Physics, Mass Inst Technol, Rm 13-2030 77 Mass Ave, Cambridge, MA 02139. **Fax:** 617-253-8554. **E-Mail:** litster@mit.edu

LITT, IRIS F, MEDICINE. **Personal Data:** b December 25, 1940. **Education:** Cornell Univ, BA, 1961; State Univ NY, MD, 1965, Am Bd Pediat, cert, 1993. **Honors & Awards:** Sect Adolescent Health Award, Am Acad Pediat, 1982; Eli & Edith Friedman Mem Lectr, Boston Univ Sch Med, 1988; Outstanding Achievement Award Adolescent Med, Soc Adolescent Med, 1992; Ellen Soefer Lectr, Temple Univ Sch Med, 1992. **Professional Experience:** Mem, Comt Youth Develop, 1995-1996; ed-in-chief, J Adolescent Med, beginning 1990; DIR, INST RES WOMEN & GENDER, 1990-; Wyeth vis prof, Soc Adolescent Med, 1990; PROF PEDIAT, DIV ADOLESCENT MED, STANFORD UNIV SCH MED, 1987-; fel, Ctr Adv Study Behav Sci, Stanford, 1984-1985; J Pediat vis prof, State Univ NY Downstate Med Ctr, 1982 & Tulane Univ Sch Med, 1983; assoc prof, Stanford Univ Sch Med, 1982-1987; mem, Comt Toxic Shock Syndrome, Inst Med-Nat Acad Sci, 1981-1982; DIR, DIV ADOLESCENT MED, STANFORD UNIV SCH MED, 1976-; fel, Stanford Ctr Study Youth Develop, Stanford Univ, 1976-1995; assoc prof pediat, Stanford Univ Sch Med, 1976-1982; assoc prof, Albert Einstein Col Med, NY, beginning 1976; med dir, Adolescent Reception & Detention Ctr, Rikers Island Prison Health Serv, 1974-1976; asst prof, Albert Einstein Col Med, NY, 1970-1976; asst dir adolescent med, Juv Ctr Serv Div Adolescent Med, Montefiore Hosp & Med Ctr NY, 1968-1976; dir, Juv Ctr Serv Div Adolescent Med, Montefiore Hosp & Med Ctr NY, 1968-1973; instr pediat, Albert Einstein Col Med, NY, 1968-1970; asst chief resident, NY Hosp, 1967-1968; teaching fel, Cornell Univ Med Col, New York, 1967-1968; jr resident, NY Hosp, 1966-1967; intern, NY Hosp, 1965-1966. **Memberships:** Inst Med-Nat Acad Sci; Soc Adolescent Med (pres 1981-1982); Ambulatory Pediatric Asn; Am Acad Pediat; Soc Pediat Res; Am Pediat Soc; Soc Res Child Develop. **Mailing Address:** Dept Pediat, Stanford Univ Sch Med, 750 Welch Rd Ste 325, Palo Alto, CA 94304. **Fax:** 650-725-8347. **E-Mail:** irislitt@stanford.edu

LITT, LAWRENCE, MEDICAL PHYSICS, NEUROSCIENCES. **Personal Data:** b Brooklyn, NY, October 31, 1941; m 1967, c Natalya E & Jonathan Z. **Education:** Columbia Univ, AB, 1963; Harvard Univ, AM, 1964, PhD (physics), 1971; Univ Miami, MD, 1979. **Professional Experience:** PROF ANESTHESIA & RADIOL, UNIV CALIF, SAN FRANCISCO, 1992-; mem, Neurol A Study Sect, NIH, 1991-; prin investr, NIH, 1985-1988 & 1989-; from asst prof to assoc prof, Univ Calif, San Francisco, 1983-1992; asst prof anesthesia, Stanford Univ, 1982-1983; asst prof physics, Mich State Univ, 1974-1977; Vis res physicist, CERN, Geneva, Switz, 1971-1974; Fel, Rockefeller Univ, 1971-1974. **Memberships:** Fel Am Phys Soc; fel Am Col Physicians; Int Soc Cerebral Blood Flow & Metab; Soc Magnetic Resonance Med; Int Soc Magnetic Resonance. **Research Statement & Publications:** Studies of cerebral metabolic protection during oxygen deprivation;

provide new insights for stroke protection and treatment. **Mailing Address:** Anesthesia Dept, 521 Parnassus Ave, rm C455, San Francisco, CA 94143. **Fax:** 415-476-9516. **E-Mail:** llitt@itsa.ucsf.edu

LITT, MICHAEL, GENETICS. **Personal Data:** b New York, NY, April 17, 1933; m 1970, Ruth; c Barbara, David & Fred. **Education:** Oberlin Col, BA, 1954; Harvard Univ, PhD (chem), 1958. **Professional Experience:** PROF EMER, MOLECULAR & MED GENETICS, ORE HEALTH & SCI UNIV, as of 2006; prof, molecular & med genetics, Med Sch, Univ Ore, beginning 1996; vis prof cellular, viral & molecular biol, Univ Utah Med Sch, 1981-1982; prof biochem & med genetics, Med Sch, Univ Ore, beginning 1971; assoc prof biochem, Med Sch, Univ Ore, 1967-1971; NSF fel, Auckland Univ, 1966-1967; assoc prof, Reed Col, 1964-1967; NIH spec fel, Mass Inst Technol, 1962-1963; instr chem, Reed Col, 1958-1962. **Memberships:** Am Soc Human Genetics. **Research Statement & Publications:** Human gene mapping with DNA polymorphisms. **Mailing Address:** Dept Molecular & Med Genetics, Ore Health & Sci Univ, L103A, Portland, OR 97201-3098. **Fax:** 503-494-4411. **E-Mail:** litt@ohsu.edu

LITT, MITCHELL, BIOENGINEERING, CHEMICAL ENGINEERING. **Personal Data:** b Brooklyn, NY, October 11, 1932; m 1955, Zelda; c Ellen Beth & Steven Eric. **Education:** Columbia Univ, AB, 1953, BS, 1954, MS, 1956, DEngSc(chem eng), 1961. **Professional Experience:** DIR DENT BIOENGINEERING INST, UNIV PA, as of 1999; chmn Bioengineering, 1981-1990; vis prof, Weizmann Inst, 1979; PROF BIOENGINEERING, UNIV PA, 1973-; PROF CHEM ENG, UNIV PA, 1971-; from asst prof to assoc prof, Univ PA, 1961-1971; res engr, Esso Res & Eng Co, NJ, 1958-1961. **Memberships:** Am Inst Chem Engrs; Am Soc Eng Educ; Biomed Eng Soc; Am Chem Soc; Int Soc Biorheology; Eng Med Biol Soc; Soc Rheology. **Research Statement & Publications:** Application of chemical engineering techniques to biomedical problems; biorheology, with applications to blood and epithelial secretions. **Mailing Address:** Dept BioEng, Sch Eng & Appl Sci, Univ Pa, 120 Hayden Hall, 3320 Smith Walk, Philadelphia, PA 19104. **Fax:** 215-573-2071. **E-Mail:** litt@seas.upenn.edu

LITT, MORTIMER, IMMUNOLOGY. **Personal Data:** b Brooklyn, NY, September 28, 1925; m 1954, c 3. **Education:** Columbia Univ, BA, 1947; Univ Rochester, MD, 1952. **Professional Experience:** ASSOC DEAN EDUC PROGS, HARVARD MED SCH, 1979-; asst dean teaching resources, Harvard Med Sch, 1973-1978; ASSOC PROF MICROBIOL & MOLECULAR GENETICS, HARVARD MED SCH, 1971-; asst dir, Dept Bact, Boston City Hosp, 1969-1977; asst prof, Harvard Med Sch, 1965-1971; estab investr, Am Heart Asn, 1963-1968; assoc, Harvard Med Sch, 1960-1965; Helen Hay Whitney Found fel, 1959-1963; instr, Harvard Med Sch, 1956-1959; Res fel, Harvard Med Sch, 1954-1956 & 1956-1959; med house officer & asst resident physician, Peter Bent Brigham Hosp, 1952-1954. **Research Statement & Publications:** Eosinophil leukocyte. **Mailing Address:** Harvard Med Sch, 25 Shattuck St Gordon Hall, Boston, MA 02115. **Fax:** 617-432-0566. **E-Mail:** mortimer_litt@hms.harvard.edu

LITT, MORTON HERBERT, POLYMER CHEMISTRY, STRUCTURE/PROPERTY RELATIONSHIPS. **Personal Data:** b Brooklyn, NY, April 10, 1926; m 1957, Lola Abrahamson; c Jonathan & Jennifer. **Education:** City Col New York, BS, 1947; Polytech Inst Brooklyn, MS, 1953, PhD (polymer chem), 1956. **Professional Experience:** PROF POLYMER SCI, CASE WESTERN RESERVE UNIV, 1976-; assoc prof, Case Western Reserve Univ, 1967-1976; assoc dir res, Cent Res Lab, Allied Chem Corp, 1965-1967; sr scientist, Cent Res Lab, Allied Chem Corp, 1960-1964; res assoc, State Univ NY Col Forestry, Syracuse, 1958-1960; Turner & Newall res fel, Manchester Univ, 1956-1957. **Memberships:** Fel AAAS; emer mem Am Chem Soc; Chem Soc; Electrochemical Soc; Mat Res Soc. **Research Statement & Publications:** Ionic and free radical polymerization mechanisms; organo-fluorine chemistry; polymer mechanical properties; polymer electrical properties; emulsion polymerization; solid polymer electrolytes; fuel cell membranes. **Mailing Address:** Case Western Res Univ, K H Smith Bldg, Cleveland, OH 44106-7202. **Fax:** 216-368-4202. **E-Mail:** mhl2@po.cwru.edu

LITTAUER, ERNEST LUCIUS, ELECTROCHEMISTRY, METALLURGY. **Personal Data:** b London, Eng, March 8, 1936; American citizen; m 1969, Deveda. **Education:** Univ London, BSc, 1958, PhD (electrometall), 1961. **Honorary Degrees:** Dr, Univ Surrey, UK. **Honors & Awards:** Silver Knight Award, Nat Mgt Asn. **Professional Experience:** CONSULT, RES & DEVELOP/TECHNOL MGT, 1997-; vpres, Adv Technol Ctr, Lockheed Martin Missiles & Space, 1995-1996; bd mem, Planning Systs Inc, McClean, Va, 1991-; vpres & asst gen mgr, Lockheed Missile & Space Co, 1990-1995; dir mat sci, Res & Develop Div, 1984-1990; lectr electrochem, Univ Santa Clara, 1974-1976; mgr, Chem Dept, 1972-1984; mgr, Electrochem Dept, 1967-1972; chmn, Res Coun Corrosion Comt, Lockheed Aircraft Corp, 1966-; sr scientist, Lockheed Aircraft Serv Co, 1963-1967; lectr, Sir John Cass Col & Enfield Col, London, 1962-1963; Res scientist, Derby Luminescents Div, Derby Metals, London, 1962-1963; Fel corrosion, Battersea Col Technol, 1961-1962. **Memberships:** Electrochem Soc; assoc fel Am Inst Aeronaut & Astronaut; Mat Res Soc. **Research Statement & Publications:** Electrochemistry; energy conversion; process chemistry; analytical, inorganic and plasma chemistry; materials evaluation; chemical and chemical engineering development and design; metallurgy; materials science engineering; nondestructive test technology. **Mailing Address:** 27305 Deer Springs Way, Los Altos Hills, CA 94022. **E-Mail:** ellittauer@aol.com

LITTAUER, RAPHAEL MAX, HIGH ENERGY PHYSICS, ELECTRONICS. **Personal Data:** b Leipzig, Ger, November 28, 1925; American citizen; m 1950, c 2. **Education:** Cambridge Univ, MA & PhD (physics), 1950. **Professional Experience:** PROF EMER PHYSICS & NUCLEAR STUDIES, CORNELL UNIV, as of 2005; chmn dept, Cornell Univ, 1974-1977; prof physics & nuclear studies, Cornell Univ, beginning 1965; res prof, Cornell Univ, 1963-1965; res assoc prof physics, Cornell Univ, 1955-1963; res assoc nuclear physics, Synchrotron Lab, Gen Elec Co, 1954-1955 & Cornell Univ, 1950-1954; asst physics, Cambridge Univ, 1947-1950. **Memberships:** Am Phys Soc fel. **Mailing Address:** Cornell Univ, 210 Newman Lab, Ithaca, NY 14853. **Fax:** 607-254-4552. **E-Mail:** rml6@cornell.edu

LITTELL, RAMON CLARENCE, AGRICULTURAL STATISTICS, MATHEMATICAL STATISTICS. **Personal Data:** b Rolla, Kans, November 18, 1942; m 1966, c 2. **Education:** Emporia State Univ, BS, 1964; Okla State Univ, MS, 1966, PhD (statist), 1970. **Professional Experience:** PROF STATIST, INST FOOD & AGR SCI, UNIV FLA, GAINESVILLE, 2002-; consult; assoc ed, J Agricultural, Biol & Environ Statist. **Memberships:** Am Statist Asn; Biomet Soc; fel Am Statist Asn. **Research Statement & Publications:** Combining tests of significance; mixed linear models; experimental design; repeated measures. **Mailing Address:** Dept Statist, Inst Food & Agr Sci, Univ Fla, PO Box 110339, Gainesville, FL 32611-0339. **Fax:** 352-392-5175. **E-Mail:** littell@stat.ufl.edu

LITTEN, RAYE Z, III, PHYSIOLOGY. **Education:** Bridgewater Col, BA, 1969; Med Col Va, MS, 1972, PhD (physiol), 1976. **Professional Experience:** Instr, Wash Area Coun Alcoholism & Drug Abuse, beginning 1991; PHYSIOLOGIST & PROG OFFICER, TREAT RES BR, DIV CLIN & PREVENTION RES, NAT INST ALCOHOL ABUSE & ALCOHOLISM, ROCKVILLE, MD, 1989-; res physiologist, Armed Forces Radiobiol Res Inst, Bethesda, Md, 1985-1989; vis res assoc, dept surg res, Naval Med Res Inst, Bethesda, 1985-1987; res asst prof, Dept Physiol & Biophys, Univ Vt, 1978-1985; numerous grants, univs & asns, 1976-1990; postdoctoral fel, Dept Physiol, Med Col Va, 1976-1978; instr, dept physiol, Med Col Va, 1976. **Memberships:** Am Physiol Soc; Sigma Xi. **Research Statement & Publications:** Biochemistry of contractile proteins from vascular smooth muscle; biochemistry of contractile proteins from hypertrophied hearts; cardiovascular alterations from whole-body irradiation, myosin isoenzymes and pituitary-thyroid function; biochemical markers of alcoholism, nutrition and alcohol-induced pathophysiology; numerous scientific publications. **Mailing Address:** Div Clin & Prev Res, NIAAA Willco Bldg, Ste 505 6000 Exec Blvd MSC-7003, Bethesda, MD 20892-7003.

LITTENBERG, LAURENCE STEPHEN, EXPERIMENTAL K DECAY. **Personal Data:** b Brooklyn, NY, October 30, 1941; m 1970, Marcia; c Jeffrey. **Education:** Cornell Univ, AB, 1963; Univ Calif, San Diego, PhD (physics), 1969. **Professional Experience:** Mem, High Energy Physics Adv Panel, Dept Energy, 1990-1993; SR PHYSICIST, BROOKHAVEN NAT LAB, 1989-; Prin investr high energy physics, Physics Dept, Brookhaven Nat Lab, 1989-; from assoc physicist to physicist, Brookhaven Nat Lab, 1974-1989; Sr res assoc, Davesbury Lab, 1970-1974. **Memberships:** Fel Am Phys Soc. **Research Statement & Publications:** Rare decays of charged and neutral kaons; new interactions and new forms of hadronic matter; neutrino oscillations. **Mailing Address:** Physics S10E, Brookhaven Nat Lab, Upton, NY 11973. **Fax:** 631-344-4741. **E-Mail:** littenbe@bnl.gov

LITTERIA, MARILYN, NEUROENDOCRINOLOGY. **Personal Data:** b Cleveland, Ohio, August 9, 1931. **Education:** Case Western Res Univ, BS, 1955; Univ Calif, Berkeley, PhD (physiol), 1967. **Professional Experience:** RES PHYSIOLOGIST & PRIN INVESTR, VET ADMIN MED CTR, NORTH CHICAGO, ILL, 1972-; instr anat & Sloan fel, Northwestern Univ, 1971-1972; res assoc reproductive biol, Univ NC, 1970-1971; res fel endocrinol, Scripps Clin & Res Found & Develop Neuroendocrinol Lab, Vet Admin Hosp, San Fernando, 1967-1969; lab technician, Case Western Res Univ, 1955-1960. **Memberships:** Endocrine Soc; Soc Neuroscience. **Research Statement & Publications:** The role of sex steroids in central nervous system development. **Mailing Address:** Vet Admin Med Ctr, North Chicago, IL 60064.

LITTERST, CHARLES LAWRENCE, PHARMACOLOGY. **Personal Data:** b Cleveland, Ohio, 1944; c 2. **Education:** Purdue Univ, BS, 1966; Univ Wis, MS, 1968, PhD (toxicol), 1970. **Professional Experience:** CHIEF, DRUG DEVELOP SECT, DDCSB, DAIDS, NIAID, as of 1997; Mem, Occup Safety Health Comt, NIH, beginning 1996; TOXICOLOGIST, NIAID, BETHESDA, MD, 1987-; Fac FAES-NIH (Toxicology), beginning 1974; mem, Toxicol Info subcomt HEW comt to coord toxicol & related progs, 1974-1979; toxicologist, Nat Cancer Inst, 1972-1987; Pharmacologist, Food & Drug Admin, Wash, DC, 1970-1972. **Memberships:** Am Soc Pharmacol & Exp Therapeut; Soc Toxicol; Sigma Xi; Am Asn Cancer Res. **Research Statement & Publications:** Factors altering hepatic microsomal drug metabolism; toxicology and pharmacology of platinum; toxicology of antineoplastic and antiviral drugs. **Mailing Address:** Drug Develop & Clin Sci Br AIDS Div NIAID, 6003 Exec Blvd, Bethesda, MD 20892. **E-Mail:** cl30x@nih.gov

LITTLE, A BRIAN, OBSTETRICS & GYNECOLOGY. **Personal Data:** b Montreal, Que, March 11, 1925; American citizen; m 1984, Bitten; c Michael (deceased), Deborah, Susan, Catherine, Jane & Lucinda. **Education:** McGill Univ, BA, 1948, MD, CM, 1950; Royal Col Physicians & Surgeons, Can, cert obstet & gynec, 1955, FRCS(C), 1957; Am Bd Obstet & Gynec, dipl, 1959. **Professional Experience:** Clin prof obstet & gynec, NJ Med Sch, 1994-; PROF OBSTET & GYNEC, MCGILL UNIV, 1983-; prof & chmn, Mcgill Univ, 1983-1994; chief obstet & gynec, Royal Victoria Hosp, Montreal, 1983-1994; Arthur H Bill prof & dir, Dept Reproductive Biol, 1972-1983; assoc obstetrician & gynecologist, dir Dept Obstet & Gynec, 1972-1982; prof obstet & gynec, Sch Med, Case Western Res Univ, 1966-1972; dir, Dept Obstet & Gynec, Cleveland Metrop Hosp, Ohio, 1966-1972; assoc obstetrician & gynecologist, Univ Hosps, Cleveland, 1966-1972; vis surgeon, Boston City Hosp, 1965; mem courtesy staff, Free Hosp Women, 1964-1965; mem consult staff, Elliott Community Hosp, Keene, NH, 1963-1965; dir, Boston City Hosp, 1963-1965; asst prof, Harvard Med Sch, 1963-1965; chief consult, Hunt Mem Hosp, Danvers, 1962-1965; mem consult staff, Sturdy Mem Hosp, Attleboro, 1961-1965; obstetrician & gynecologist, Boston Lying-in-Hosp, 1959-1965; asst surgeon, Free Hosp Women, 1958-1964; assoc obstet & gynec, Harvard Med Sch, 1958-1963; assoc dir dept obstet & gynec, Boston City Hosp, 1958-1963; assoc, Boston Lying-in-Hosp, 1958-1959; tutor med sci, Harvard Med Sch, 1957-1965; instr obstet & gynec, Harvard Med Sch, 1956-1958; asst obstetrician, Boston Lying-in-Hosp, 1956-1958; assoc vis surgeon, Boston City Hosp, 1955-1964; sr obstetrician prenatal metab div, USPHS, 1955-1956; asst obstetrician outpatients, Boston Lying-in-Hosp, 1955-1956; asst obstet, Harvard Med Sch, 1955-1956; Teaching fel obstet & gynec, Harvard Med Sch, 1952-1954; instr, Sch Nursing, Boston Univ, 1951 & 1955-1957; asst resident & resident, Boston Lying-in-Hosp & Free Hosp Women, Boston, 1951-1954; intern, Montreal Gen Hosp, 1950-1951. **Memberships:** Fel Am Col Obstet & Gynec; Am Gynec & Obstet Soc; Soc Gynec Invest; fel Am Col Surgeons; Endocrine Soc. **Research Statement & Publications:** Steroid mechanism in vivo, in vitro, primarily in reproduction. **Mailing Address:** Dept Obstet & Gynec Royal Victoria Hosp, McGill Univ Sch Med 687 Pine Ave W, Montreal, PQ H3A 1A1, Can. **Fax:** 514-843-1678. **E-Mail:** brian@rvhob2lan.mcgill.ca

LITTLE, ALEX G, THORACIC SURGERY. **Personal Data:** b Atlanta, Ga, August 24, 1943; m 1975, c 2. **Education:** Univ NC, BA, 1965; Johns Hopkins Univ, MD, 1974. **Professional Experience:** ELIZABETH BERRY GRAY CHAIR & PROF, DEPT SURG, WRIGHT STATE UNIV BOONSHOFT SCH MED, as of 2005; prof & chmn surg, Univ Nev, 1988; from asst prof to assoc prof surg, Univ Chicago, 1981-1988. **Memberships:** Am Col Surgeons; Am Assoc Thoracic Surg; Soc Thoracic Surgeons; Soc Univ Surgeons; Am Surg Asn. **Research Statement & Publications:** Pathophysiology of benign esophageol diseases; research in basic mechanisms of esophageal and lung cancer. **Mailing Address:** Dept Surg, Sch Med, Wright State Univ, One Wyo St Ste 7000 WCHE PO Box 927, Dayton, OH 45409. **Fax:** 937-208-6154. **E-Mail:** alex.little@wright.edu

LITTLE, ANGELA C, HISTORY OF MEDICINE & HEALTH REGIMENS. **Personal Data:** b San Francisco, Calif, January 12, 1920; m 1947, George G; c Judith K. **Education:** Univ Calif, AB, 1940, MS, 1954, PhD (agr chem), 1969. **Professional Experience:** Fac, Fromm Inst, Univ San Francisco, 1993- 1997; EMER PROF, UNIV CALIF, BERKELEY, 1985-; from assoc prof to prof, Univ Calif, Berkeley, 1979-1982; Vis scholar, Univ Wash, Seattle, 1976-1977; assoc food scientist, Univ Calif, Berkeley, 1971-1979; lectr food sci, Univ Calif, Berkeley, 1969-1979; asst food scientist, Univ Calif, Berkeley, 1969-1971; from asst specialist to assoc specialist, Univ Calif, Berkeley, 1958-1969; jr specialist, Univ Calif, Berkeley, 1956-1958; Res asst food sci, Univ Calif, Berkeley, 1953-1956. **Memberships:** NY Acad Sci; Sigma Xi. **Research Statement & Publications:** Taste perception related to changes in physiological state; determinants of human food practices-historical, cultural, ecological, religious, etc; history of medical systems. **Mailing Address:** 85 Cleary Ct No 3, San Francisco, CA 94109.

LITTLE, BRENDA JOYCE, MICROBIOLOGICALLY INFLUENCED CORROSION, COLLOID & INTERFACE CHEMISTRY. **Personal Data:** b Akron, Ohio. **Education:** Baylor Univ, BS, 1967; Tulane Univ, PhD (chem), 1983. **Professional Experience:** Br head, Naval Ocean Res & Develop Activ, 1985-1986; RES CHEMIST, NAVAL RES LAB, 1976-; microbiologist, Nat Park Serv, 1974-1976. **Memberships:** Am Chem Soc; Int Humic Substances Soc; Nat Asn Corrosion Engrs; Adhesion Soc; Sigma Xi. **Research Statement & Publications:** Factors influencing the absorption of dissolved organic material from natural waters and their impact on adhesion of microorganisms; elucidation of mechanisms for biodeterioration of metals in marine environments. **Mailing Address:** 6528 Alakoko Dr, Diamondhead, MS 39525-3421. **Fax:** 228-688-5379.

LITTLE, BRIAN WOODS, NEUROPATHOLOGY & NEUROMUSCULAR PATHOLOGY. **Personal Data:** b Boston, Mass, December 15, 1945. **Education:** Cornell Univ, BA, 1967; Univ Vt, MD, 1973, PhD (biochem), 1977. **Professional Experience:** CHAIR, ACCREDATION COUN CONTINUING MED EDU, as of 2006-; VPRES ACAD AFFAIRS & RES CHRISTIANA CARE HEALTH SERV, as of 2000; attend pathologist, Lehigh V Alley Hosp Ctr, beginning 1987; asst prof path, State Univ NY, Stony Brook, 1984-1987; asst prof biochem, Univ Vt, 1980-1984; attend pathologist, Med Ctr Hosp Vt, 1976-1984; asst prof path, Univ Vt, 1976-1984; resident pathologist, Med Ctr Hosp Vt, 1973-1976; vet Admin Med Ctr, Northport, NY. **Memberships:** Am Soc Clin Pathologists; Col Am Pathologists. **Research Statement & Publications:** Mammalian nucleic acid metabolism; muscle disease; histochemistry; epidemiology of CNS disorders; pediatric, anatomic and clinical pathology. **Mailing Address:** Off Acad Affairs & Res, Christiana Care Health Serv, 4755 Ogletown-Stanton Rd, Newark, DE 19718. **Fax:** 302-733-1068. **E-Mail:** brlittle@christianacare.org

LITTLE, CHARLES DURWOOD, ANATOMY, CELL BIOLOGY. **Personal Data:** b Denver, Colo, December 28, 1946. **Education:** Calif State Polytech Univ, Pomona, BS, 1973; Univ Pittsburgh, PhD (anat & cell biol), 1977. **Professional Experience:** PROF, ANAT & CELL BIOL, UNIV KANS, as of 2005; assoc prof anat, Univ VA, 1987-2005; asst prof, Univ VA, 1981-1987; fel, Biol Dept, Univ Calif, San Diego, 1979-1981; Res fel, Develop Biol Lab, Mass Gen Hosp, Harvard Med Sch, 1977-1979; mem, PBC Study Sect, NIH; bd trustees, Soc Develop Biol; Adv panel develop biol, NSF; postdoc fel, Harv Med Sch, Boston, 1979; postdoc fel, Univ Calif, San Diego, 1981. **Memberships:** Develop Biol Soc; Am Soc Cell Biol. **Research Statement & Publications:** Developmental biology of the extracellular matrix; cell surface matrix interactions; double immunolabeling techniques for use in fluorescence and electron microscopy. **Mailing Address:** Dept Anat & Cell Biol, Univ Kans Medl Ctr, 3901 Rainbow Boulevard, 2008 Wahl Hall E, Kansas City, KS 66160. **Fax:** 913-588-2710. **E-Mail:** clittle@kumc.edu

LITTLE, CHARLES EDWARD, MATHEMATICS. **Personal Data:** b Kansas City, Kans, April 18, 1926; m 1947, c 3. **Education:** Univ Kans, AB, 1948; Kans State Col, Ft Hyas, MS, 1955; Colo State Col, EdD(math educ), 1964. **Professional Experience:** PROF EMER MATH EDUC, NORTHERN ARIZ UNIV, as of 1997; Dean, Col Arts & Sci, 1974-1984; prof math educ, Northern Ariz Univ, beginning 1968; chmn dept math, Northern Ariz Univ, 1967-1970; from asst prof to assoc prof, Northern Ariz Univ, 1964-1968; instr math, Colo State Col, 1961-1963; supt, Kans, 1960-1961; Instr pub sch, Kans, 1951-1960; Nat Coun Teachers Math. **Memberships:** Math Asn Am. **Research Statement & Publications:** Training of elementary and secondary mathematics teachers; methods of instruction in mathematics at college level, particularly educational media and techniques for handling large groups; mathematics for the social and behavioral sciences; linear models and statistics. **Mailing Address:** Dept Math Educ, N Arizona Univ, S San Francisco St, Flagstaff, AZ 86001.

LITTLE, CHARLES GORDON, ATMOSPHERIC PHYSICS, REMOTE SENSING. **Personal Data:** b Hunan, China, November 4, 1924; m 1954, Mary; c Deane, Joan, Katherine, Margaret & Patricia. **Education:** Univ Manchester, BSc, 1948, PhD (radio astron), 1952. **Honors & Awards:** Cleveland Abbe Award, Am Meteorol Soc, 1984; R M Losey Amos Sci Award, Am Inst Aeronaut & Astronaut, 1992. **Professional Experience:** RETIRED; George Haltiner res prof, Navad Postgrad Sch, 1989-1990; sr fel, Univ Corp Atmospheric Res, Naval Environ Res Prediction Fac, 1987-1989; dir, Wave Propagation Lab, Nat Ocean & Atmospheric Admin, 1967-1986; dir, Inst Telecommun Sci & Aeronomy, Nat Ocean & Atmospheric Admin, 1965-1967; dir, Cent Radio Propagation Lab, Nat Bur Stand, 1962-1965; dir, Upper Atmosphere & Space Physics Div, Nat Bur Stand, 1960-1962; chief, Radio Astron & Arctic Propagation Sect, Nat Bur Stand, 1958-1962; prof geophys & dep dir, Geophys Inst, Univ Alaska, 1954-1958; asst lectr physics, Univ Manchester, Eng, 1952-1953; jr physicist, Ferranti Ltd, Manchester, 1946-1947; jr engr, Cosmoe Mfg Co, Enfield, Eng, 1944-1946. **Memberships:** Nat Acad Engr; AAAS; fel Inst Elec & Electronics Engrs; fel Am Meterol Soc. **Research Statement & Publications:** Radiostar scintillation, auroral ionosphere, development of remote sensors of atmosphere and ocean, using electromagnetic and acoustic waves. **Mailing Address:** 4907 Country Club Way, Boulder, CO 80301. **E-Mail:** cglitt@aol.com

LITTLE, CHARLES ORAN, ANIMAL NUTRITION, AGRICULTURE. **Personal Data:** b Schulenburg, Tex, July 21, 1935; m 1955, c 3. **Education:** Univ Houston, BS, 1957; Iowa State Univ, MS, 1959, PhD (animal nutrit), 1960. **Honors & Awards:** Distinguished Nutritionist Award, Nat Distillers Feed Res Coun, 1964; Outstanding Res Awards, Thomas Poe Cooper & Ky Res Founds, 1967. **Professional Experience:** RETIRED; dean, Col Agr, Univ Ky, 1988-2000; dir agr exp station & dir coop exten, La State Univ, beginning 1988; vice chancellor res & dir, Exp Sta, 1985-1988; mem, Exp Sta Comt Policy, beginning 1978; chmn, Southern Asn Agr Exp Sta Dirs, 1976-1977; mem, Southern Res Planning Comt, 1973-1975; mem & chmn, Southern Regional Res Comt, 1972-1975; assoc dir, Ky Agr Exp Sta, beginning 1969; assoc dean res, Col Agr, Univ Ky, 1969-1985; prof animal sci, Col Agr, Univ Ky, 1967-1985; from asst prof to assoc prof, Agr Res Serv grant, 1964-1967; indust res grants, Col Agr, Univ Ky, 1961-1972; from asst prof to assoc prof, Col Agr, Univ Ky, 1960-1967; res asst animal nutrit, Iowa State Univ, 1957-1960. **Memberships:** AAAS; Am Soc Animal Sci; Am Inst Nutrit. **Mailing Address:** 2357 Woods Lane, Lexington, KY 40502. **E-Mail:** olittle@uky.edu

LITTLE, EDWARD E, AQUATIC TOXICOLOGY. **Education:** State Univ NY, Stony Brook, PhD, 1974. **Professional Experience:** RES BIOLOGIST, COLUMBIA ENVIRON RES CTR, US GEOL SURV, as of 2004. **Mailing Address:** Columbia Environ Res Ctr US Geol Surv, 4200 New Haven Rd, Columbia, MO 65201. **E-Mail:** edward_little@nbs.gov

LITTLE, EDWIN DEMETRIUS, organic chemistry; deceased, see previous edition for last biography

LITTLE, ELBERT L(UTHER), JR, BOTANY, DENDROLOGY. **Personal Data:** b Ft Smith, Ark, October 15, 1907; m 1943, Ruby R Rice Little; c Gordon R, Melvin W & Alice Stroud. **Education:** Univ Okla, BA, 1927, BS, 1932; Univ Chicago, MS & PhD (bot), 1929. **Honors & Awards:** Barringtom Moore Award, Soc Am Foresters, 1986. **Professional Experience:** Consult, Okla Forestry Div 30, 1977-1978; res assoc, Dept Bot, US Nat Mus Natural Hist, Smithsonian Inst, Wash, DC, 1976-2001; consult, UN mission, Nicaragua, 1971; Vis prof, Va Polytech Inst & State Univ, 1966-1967 & Univ DC, 1979; collabr, US Nat Mus Nat Hist, Smithsonian Inst, Wash, DC, 1965-1976; consult, UN mission, Ecuador, 1965 & 1975; consult, UN mission, Costa Rica, 1964-1965 & 1967; botanist from Univ Md, Guyana, 1955; vis prof, Univ Andes, Venzuela, 1953-1954 & 1960; prod specialist, US Com Co, Mexico City, 1945; Botanist, Econ Admin, Bogota, 1943-1945; dendrologist, US Forest Serv, Wash, DC, 1942-1976; from asst forest ecologist to assoc forest ecologist, Ariz, 1934-1942; asst prof biol, Southwestern Okla State Univ, 1930-1933. **Memberships:** fel Soc Am Foresters; Bot Soc Am; Am Soc Plant Taxon; Am Inst Biol Sci; Ecol Soc Am. **Research Statement & Publications:** Trees of United States and tropical America, their identification, classification, nomenclature, and distribution; pinyons; conifers; ecology; author of tree identification books in English & Spanish. **Mailing Address:** 375 E 32nd Ave, Eugene, OR 97405.

LITTLE, GORDON R, OPTICS. **Professional Experience:** ASSOC PROF ELECTRO-OPTICS, UNIV DAYTON, as of 1995; RES OPTICAL PHYSICIST, UNIV DAYTON, as of 1995. **Memberships:** Ohio State Univ BS 1966 MS 1970 PhD (physics) 1973. **Mailing Address:** Univ Dayton, 2637 Oak Park Ave, Kettering, OH 45419.

LITTLE, GWYNNE H, BIOCHEMISTRY OF DEVELOPMENT, PROGRAMMED CELL DEATH. **Personal Data:** b Birmingham, Ala, June 25, 1941; m 1966, Donnie; c Mary E (Carol) & Sally L (Ball). **Education:** Med Col Ga, PhD (biochem), 1970. **Professional Experience:** ASSOC PROF CELL BIOL & BIOCHEM, HEALTH SCI CTR, TEX TECH UNIV, 1980-. **Memberships:** Am Soc Biol Chem. **Mailing Address:** Dept Biochem, Sch Med, Tex Tech Univ Health Sci Ctr, Lubbock, TX 79430-0001. **E-Mail:** gwynne.little@ttmc.ttuhsc.edu

LITTLE, HAROLD FRANKLIN, ENTOMOLOGY, FUNCTIONAL MORPHOLOGY. **Personal Data:** b Williamsport, Pa, June 18, 1932; m 1959, c 1. **Education:** Lycoming Col, AB, 1954; Pa State Univ, MS, 1956, PhD (zool), 1959. **Professional Experience:** CHMN DEPT, UNIV HAWAII, HILO, 1986-; chmn, Biol Dept, 1973-1978; PROF BIOL, UNIV HAWAII, HILO, 1971-; chmn, Div Nat Sci, 1968-1971 & 1973-1979; from asst prof to assoc prof, Univ Hawaii, Hilo, 1963-1971; Asst prof biol, WVa Wesleyan Col, 1959-1963. **Memberships:** Entom Soc Am. **Research Statement & Publications:** Damage to Medfly pupal flight mucles; histology and ultrastructure of tephritid fruit fly pheromone glands. **Mailing Address:** Div Nat Sci Univ Hawaii Hilo, 200 W Kawili St, Hilo, HI 96720-4075. **Fax:** 808-933-3693.

LITTLE, JACK EDWARD, PETROLEUM ENGINEERING. **Personal Data:** b Dallas, Tex, September 9, 1938. **Education:** Tex A&M Univ, BS, 1960, MS, 1961, PhD, 1966. **Professional Experience:** DIR, TXU CORP, as of 2001-; pres & chief exec officer, Shell Explor & Prod Co, 1995-1998; exec vpres explor & prod, Shell Oil Co, Houston, 1986-1995; sr vpres admin, Pac Div, 1985-1986; head, Southeast Asia Div, Shell Int Petrol Co, London, 1982-1985; vpres corp planning, Pac Div, 1981-1982; gen mgr, Pac Div, 1980-1981; gen mgr prod, Western Explor & Prod Region, Houston, 1979-1980; div prod mgr, Onshore Div, SRegion Shell Oil Co, New Orleans, 1978-1979; nat bd dirs, Houston Sect, 1977-1978; dir prod res & explor res, Bellaire Res Ctr, Shell Develop Co, Houston, 1977; bd dirs, Bakersfield Sect, 1970; bd dirs, Houston Sect, 1969; Chmn nat comts career guid, investments & mgt, Soc Petrol Engrs, 1967-1981; dir, Nat Ocean Indust Asn; vchmn & dir, Gas Res Inst. **Memberships:** Nat Acad Eng; Soc Petrol Engrs; Mid-Continent Oil & Gas Asn; Nat Ocean Indust Asn. **Research Statement & Publications:** Petroleumengineering; exploration and production. **Mailing Address:** TXU Corp, 1601 Bryan St, Dallas, TX 75201. **Fax:** 214-812-7077.

LITTLE, JAMES ALEXANDER, METABOLISM, LIPIDS & DIABETES. **Personal Data:** b Detroit, Mich, December 8, 1922; Canadian citizen; m 1985, Barbara Bradt; c Ann & Roger. **Education:** Univ Toronto, MD, 1946, MA, 1950; FRCP (C), 1952. **Professional Experience:** Pres, Can Lipoprotein Conf, 1989-1990; Pfizer Travelling fel, Clin Res Inst Montreal, 1984; PROF MED, ST MICHAEL'S HOSP, UNIV TORONTO, 1974-; mem, Exec Comt, Coun Atherosclerosis, Am Heart Asn, 1974-1977; mem, Comt Nutrit & Cardiovasc Dis, Health Protection Br, Med Comt, Govt Can, 1974-1976; proj dir, McMaster Lipid Res Ctr, Univ Toronto, 1972-1993; mem, Can Nat Comn, Int Union Nutrit Sci, 1971-1975; dir, Div Endocrinol, Metab & Nephrol, Lipid Clin, St Michael's Hosp, 1970-1973; dir, Lipid Clin, 1966-1990; from asst prof to assoc prof, Res Soc, 1966-1974; res coordr & secy, Res Soc, 1964-1992; dir, Clin Invest Unit, 1964-1972; assoc, Diabetic Clin, 1963-1966; dir, Diabetic Clin, 1954-1970; clin teacher, St Michael's Hosp, Univ Toronto, 1954-1963; res & assoc dir, Artherosclerosis Proj, 1952-1967; Resassoc med, St Michael's Hosp, Univ Toronto, 1952-1967; Res & dir, Atherosclerosis Proj, 1952-1967; Can Red Cross fel arthritis, Sunnybrook Dept Vet Affairs Hosp, 1951-1952; Nat Res Coun Can fel biochem, Univ Toronto, 1947-1949. **Memberships:** Am Heart Asn; Can Cardiovasc Soc; Am Diabetes Asn; Nutrit Soc Can; Can Soc Clin Invest; Can Atherosclerosis Soc (pres, 1987-1988). **Research Statement & Publications:** Relation between human atherosclerosis, plasma lipoproteins, nutrition and genetic factors; effect of insulin antibodies on diabetic complications. **Mailing Address:** RR No 1, Nobel, ON P0G 1G0, Can. **E-Mail:** alick@zeuter.com

LITTLE, JAMES NOEL, ANALYTICAL CHEMISTRY. **Personal Data:** b Kansas City, Mo, July 3, 1940; m 1991, Barbara; c David, Matthew & Sarah. **Education:** Univ Kans, BS, 1962, Mass Inst Technol, PhD (anal chem), 1966. **Professional Experience:** PRES, CETEK CORP, 2001-; sr vpres, Cetek Corp, 1998-2001; sr vpres, Zymark Corp, 1983-1998; dir, Rhenometrics, 1982-1985; dir, Cyborg Corp, 1982-1987; vpres, Zymark Corp, 1981-1982; vpres, Waters Assocs, Inc, 1971-1981; mgr chromatography res, Waters Assocs, Inc, 1969-1971; sr res chemist, Waters Assocs, Inc, 1968-1969; res chemist, Hercules, Inc, Del, 1966-1967; dir, Microfluidics Corp. **Memberships:** Am Chem Soc. **Research Statement & Publications:** Separations; chromatography; polymer characterization; analytical methods development; spectroscopy; robotics. **Mailing Address:** Cetek Corp, 260 Cedar Hill St, Marlborough, MA 01752-3017. **Fax:** 508-229-2344. **E-Mail:** j.little@cetek.com

LITTLE, JOHN BERTRAM, CANCER BIOLOGY, RADIATION BIOLOGY. **Personal Data:** b Boston, Mass, October 5, 1929; m Francoise; c Jean B & Frederic. **Education:** Harvard Univ, AB, 1951; Boston Univ, MD, 1955; Am Bd Radiol, dipl, 1961, cert nuclear med, 1961. **Honors & Awards:** Failla Award, Radiation Res Soc NAm, 1994; Kaplan Award, Int Asn Radiation Res, 1999; Lauriston Taylor Award, Nat Coun Radiation Protection, 2005; Outstanding Investigator grant, Nat Cancer Inst, 1988-2001. **Professional Experience:** JAMES STEVENS SIMMONS PROF EMER, HARVARD SCH PUB HEALTH, as of 2006; chmn, dept cancer biol, Harvard, 1997-2001; mem coun, Int Asn Radiation Res, 1995-

1999; sci coun, Radiation Effects Res Found, Hiroshima, Japan, 1992-1999; mem coun, Nat Coun Radiation Protection, 1992-; chmn, Bd Radiation Effects Res, Nat Acad Sci, 1992-1998; coun deleg med sci, Coun Affairs Comt, 1989-1991, AAAS: Bd sci counselors, Nat Toxicol Prog, Nat Cancer Inst, 1987-1991; chmn, Bd Sci Counr, Nat Inst Environ Health Sci, 1982-1984; dir, Kresge Ctr Environ Health, 1981-1998 Harvard Univ; chmn dept Physiol, Harvard Sch Pub Health, 1980-1983; prof radiobiol, Harvard Sch Pub Health, beginning 1975; Consult. Brigham and Women's Hosp, 1968-1990; Consult in Radiology, Mass General Hosp, 1965- lecturer Med Sch, 1968-; Consult, Mass Gen Hosp, 1965-; from asst prof to assoc prof, Harvard Sch Pub Health, 1965-1975; instr physiol, Harvard Sch Pub Health, 1963-1965; USPHS res fel, Harvard Sch Pub Health, 1961-1963; resident radiol, Mass Gen Hosp, 1958-1961; intern med, Johns Hopkins Hosp, 1955-1956. **Memberships:** AAAS; Am Physiol Soc; Health Physics Soc; Am Asn Cancer Res; Radiation Res Soc (pres-elect 1985 pres 1986-1987); Am Soc Photobiol. **Research Statement & Publications:** Cellular and molecular radiation biology with emphasis on mutagenesis; experimental carcinogenesis; genomic instability; bystander effects. **Mailing Address:** Dept Genetics & Complex Dis, Harvard Univ, Rm 505, 665 Huntington Ave, Boston, MA 02115. **Fax:** 617-432-0107. **E-Mail:** jlittle@hsph.harvard.edu

LITTLE, JOHN C, ENVIRONMENTAL ENGINEERING. **Personal Data:** b Cape Town, SAfrica, August 11, 1956. **Education:** Univ Capetown, MSc, 1984, BSc, 1985; Univ Calif, Berkeley, MS, 1988, PhD (environ eng), 1990. **Honors & Awards:** NSF Career Award, 1996. **Professional Experience:** PROF ENVIRON ENG, VA POLYTECH INST & STATE UNIV, as of 2005; asst prof environ eng, Va Polytech Inst & State Univ, beginning 1993; postdoctoral fel, Lawrence Berkeley Nat Labs, Calif, 1990-1993. **Mailing Address:** Environ Eng, Va Polytech Inst & State Univ, 405 Durham Hall, Blacksburg, VA 24061. **E-Mail:** jcl@vt.edu

LITTLE, JOHN CLAYTON, ORGANIC CHEMISTRY, PROCESS DEVELOPMENT. **Personal Data:** b Battle Creek, Mich, January 1, 1933; m 1987, Marianne; c Michael, Susan, Linda & Martin. **Education:** Univ Calif, BS, 1954; Univ Ill, PhD (org chem), 1957. **Professional Experience:** RETIRED; facil prog mgr, Western Div Res & Develop, 1989-1992; mgr chem technol, Agr Prod Dept, 1981-1989; res mgr, Dow Chem USA, 1971-1981; group leader, Dow Chem USA, 1964-1971; sect ed, Chem Abstracts, 1964-1968; proj leader, Dow Chem USA, 1962-1964; res chemist, Dow Chem USA, 1957-1962; mem, Mich Found Advan Res. **Memberships:** Am Chem Soc; Sigma Xi; The Chem Soc. **Research Statement & Publications:** Pilot plant and process development studies; organic syntheses and structure-biological activity relationships; chemical manufacturing, environmental studies; petrochemical processing; chlorination; catalytic oxidation and reduction; Diels-Alder reactions and synthetic methods; fluorination processes; research facilities design and management. **Mailing Address:** 2524 Pebble Beach Loop, Lafayette, CA 94549. **E-Mail:** jackandmarianne@aol.com

LITTLE, JOHN DUTTON CONANT, MARKETING, MANAGEMENT SCIENCE. **Personal Data:** b Boston, Mass, February 1, 1928; American citizen; m 1953, Elizabeth; c John N, Sarah A, Thomas D C & Ruel D. **Education:** Mass Inst Technol, SB, 1948, PhD (physics), 1955. **Honorary Degrees:** Dr, Univ Liege, Belg, 1992; Dr, Catholic Univ Mons, Belgium, 1997; Dr, London Business sch, Univ London, UK, 2002. **Honors & Awards:** Charles Coolidge Parlin Award, 1978; Kimball Medal, Opers Res Soc Am, 1987; Converse Award, Am Mkt Asn, 1992. **Professional Experience:** INST PROF, MASS INST TECHNOL, 1989-; Philip McCord Morse lectr, Opers Res Soc Am, 1989-1990; vis prof, Europ Inst Bus Admin, Fontainebleau, France, 1989; adv panel decision, Risk & Mgt Sci Prog, Nat Sci Found, 1986-1989; dir, Info Resources Inc, 1985-; head behav & policy sci area, Mass Inst Technol, 1982-1988; George M Bunker prof mgt sci, Sloan Sch, 1978-1989; head, Mgt Sci Group, Mass Inst Technol, 1972-1982; dir, Opers Res Ctr, Mass Inst Technol, 1969-1975; chmn, Mgt Decision Systs, Inc, 1967-1985; pres, Mgt Decision Systs, Inc, 1967-1980; prof opers res & mgt, Mass Inst Technol, 1967-1968; assoc prof opers res, Mass Inst Technol, 1962-1967; from asst prof to assoc prof opers res, Case Inst Technol, 1957-1962; asst physics, Mass Inst Technol, 1951-1954; engr tube develop, Gen Elec Co, 1949-1950. **Memberships:** Nat Acad Eng; fel AAAS; Opers Res Soc Am (pres, 1979-1980); Inst Mgt Sci (vpres, 1976-1979, pres, 1984-1985); Am Mkt Asn; Inst Opers Res & Mgt Sci (pres, 1995). **Research Statement & Publications:** Research on marketing, decision support systems, traffic control, optimization, queing. **Mailing Address:** Mass Inst Technol Sloan Sch, 38 Memorial Dr Rm E56-308, Cambridge, MA 02142. **Fax:** 781-259-0709. **E-Mail:** jlittle@mit.edu

LITTLE, JOHN RUSSELL, JR, IMMUNOLOGY INFECTIOUS DISEASES. **Personal Data:** b Cheyenne, Wyo, October 23, 1930; m 1955, Katharine; c Nancy, Susan & Bryn. **Education:** Cornell Univ, AB, 1952; Univ Rochester, MD, 1956. **Professional Experience:** PROF MED & MICROBIOL, SCH MED, WASHINGTON UNIV, 1973-; from asst prof to assoc prof med & microbiol, Sch Med, Washington, 1969-1973; Fel microbiol, 1962-1964. **Memberships:** fel infectious dis soc of Am; Am soc for clinical invest; Am asn for the advan of sci. **Research Statement & Publications:** Infectious diss. **Mailing Address:** Washington U School of Med, 660 S Euclio Ave Box 8051, St Louis, MO 63110-1092.

LITTLE, JOHN STANLEY, ORGANIC CHEMISTRY. **Personal Data:** b Fredericton, NB, July 27, 1931; m 1957, c 1. **Education:** Univ NB, BS, 1952, PhD (org chem), 1955. **Professional Experience:** MANAGING DIR, ASSOC OCTEL CO LTD, 1989-; vpres corp technol, Great Lakes Chem Corp, 1981-1989; dir int indust markets, Celanese Corp, NY, 1978-1981; dir textile prod develop, Celanese Fibers Mkt Co, 1973-1978; dir spec prod develop, Celanese Fibers Mkt Co, 1971-1973; mgr indust prod develop, Celanese Fibers Mkt Co, 1970-1971; mgr appln res, Celanese Corp, Can, 1967-1970; sect leader all process & prod res, Celanese Corp, Can, 1965-1967; group leader fiber res & develop, Can Industs, Ltd, 1962-1965; res chemist, Can Industs, Ltd, 1956-1962; Lord Beaverbrook Overseas Scholar, Univ London, 1955-1956. **Memberships:** Fel Chem Inst Can. **Research Statement & Publications:** Synthetic fibers; alkaloids and steroids. **Mailing Address:** Assoc Octel Co Ltd PO Box 17, Ellesmere Port Oil Sites Rd, South Wirral L65 4HF, UK.

LITTLE, JOHN WESLEY, BIOCHEMISTRY. **Personal Data:** b Washington, DC, June 24, 1941; m 1969, Meredith; c Christopher & Bernice. **Education:** Stanford Univ, BS, 1962, PhD (biochem), 1967. **Professional Experience:** PROF BIOCHEM, UNIV ARIZ, 1991-; assoc prof, Univ Ariz, 1985-1991; asst prof biochem, Univ Ariz, 1982-1985; adj assoc prof molecular & med microbiol, Univ Ariz, 1980-1981; adj asst prof microbiol, Univ Ariz, 1978-1980; res assoc, Univ Ariz, 1977-1978; res fel, Stanford Univ, 1973-1976; sr staff fel, NIH, 1969-1972; sr asst scientist, NIH, 1967-1969. **Memberships:** AAAS; Am Soc Biol Chemists; Am Soc Microbiol. **Research Statement & Publications:** Regulatory system that controls E coli's response to conditions, which damage DNA, including the biochemistry of the proteins controlling this response. **Mailing Address:** Dept Biochem, Univ Ariz, 1007 E Lowell St, Life Sci S 548A, Tucson, AZ 85721-0106. **Fax:** 520-621-3709. **E-Mail:** jlittle@u.arizona.edu

LITTLE, JOSEPH ALEXANDER, MEDICINE. **Personal Data:** b Bessemer, Ala, March 16, 1918; m 1941, c 3. **Education:** Vanderbilt Univ, BA, 1940, MD, 1943. **Professional Experience:** PROF EMER, INTERDISCIPLINARY HUMAN STUDIES, LA STATE UNIV, 2002-; prof pediat & head dept, Sch Med, La State Univ, Shreveport, 1970-2002; assoc prof, Sch Med, Vanderbilt Univ, 1962-1970; PHYSICIAN CHIEF, CHILDRENS HOSP, 1956-; med dir, State Crippled Children Comn, Ky, 1951-1954; from asst prof to prof, Sch Med, Univ Louisville, 1949-1962; consult, State Dept Health, Ky, 1949-1951; instr pediat, Col Med, Univ, 1948-1949; Dir outpatient dept, Childrens Hosp, 1948-1949; resident, Childrens Hosp, Univ Cincinnati, 1947-1948; Intern, Vanderbilt Univ Hosp, 1943 & 1946-1947. **Memberships:** AAAS; Am Pediat Soc; Am Acad Pediat; NY Acad Sci. **Research Statement & Publications:** Pediatric cardiology. **Mailing Address:** 185 Turning Point Lane, Sewanee, TN 27275-9706.

LITTLE, JOYCE CURRIE, COMPUTER ETHICS, SOFTWARE ENGINEERING. **Personal Data:** b Pioneer, La, 1934. **Education:** Northeast La State Col, BS, 1957; San Diego State Col, MS, 1963; Univ Md, Col Park, PhD (educ admin & comput sci), 1984. **Professional Experience:** PROF, DEPT COMPUT & INFO SCI, TOWSON STATE UNIV, 1991-; consult, Univ Md, College Park, beginning 1986; CHAIR, DEPT COMPUT & INFO SCI, TOWSON STATE UNIV, 1984-. **Memberships:** Asn Comput Mach; Inst Elec & Electronics Engrs Computer Soc; Am Asn Univ Professors; Sigma Xi. **Research Statement & Publications:** Computer personnel research. **Mailing Address:** Dept Comput & Info Sci, Towson State Univ, Towson, MD 21252. **Fax:** 410-830-3868. **E-Mail:** jclittle@saber.towson.edu

LITTLE, MAURICE DALE, MEDICAL PARASITOLOGY. **Personal Data:** b North Grove, Ind, April 13, 1928; m 1955, Marcella; c Julie, Randall & Linda. **Education:** Purdue Univ, BS, 1950; Tulane Univ, MS, 1958, PhD (parasitol), 1961. **Professional Experience:** PROF EMER, TULANE UNIV, 1998-; prof parasitol, Sch Pub Health & Trop Med, Tulane Univ, 1976-1998; assoc ed, Am Soc Trop Med & Hyg, 1975-1984; assoc prof, Sch Med, 1968-1976; from instr to asst prof, Sch Med, 1963-1968; NIH fel, Tulane Univ, 1961-1963; microbiologist, Ind State Bd Health, 1953-1956. **Memberships:** AAAS; Am Micros Soc; Am Soc Parasitologists (secy-treas 1980-1981); Am Soc Trop Med & Hyg; Wildlife Dis Asn. **Research Statement & Publications:** Morphology, biology and epidemiology of strongyloides species; zoonotic helminthiases; soil-transmitted helminths; parasites in sewage sludges. **Mailing Address:** Pub Health Tulane Univ Sch Pub Health, 1430 Tulane Ave, New Orleans, LA 70112-2699. **E-Mail:** dlittle@tulane.edu

LITTLE, MICHAEL ALAN, PHYSICAL ANTHROPOLOGY, HUMAN BIOLOGY. **Personal Data:** b Abington, Pa, March 24, 1937; m 1965, Adrienne; c Jason P & Diana A. **Education:** Pa State Univ, BA, 1962, MA, 1965, PhD (anthrop), 1968. **Honors & Awards:** National Geographic Society Research Grant (with Michael A DeLuca and Kenneth L Campbell) Pregnancy Loss and Reproduction in Settled Turkana, 1993-1994 Wenner-Gren Foundation for Anthropological Research and International Union of Biological Sciences (Paris) conference support "Human Biodiversity in Anthropological and Ecological Perspectives, Human Biology Association, 1996 National Associate of the National Academies, National Research Council (NRC), National Academy of Sciences (NAS), Washington, DC, 2001-lifetime (this is not an elected member, but rather a service associate membership) Franz Boas Distinguished Achievement Award, Human Biology Association, April 2005. **Professional Experience:** Mem, US Nat Committee, Int Union Biol Sci 1988-1994, chair 1995-1997; mem, US Nat Committee Man & the Biosphere Prog, 1983-1994; vice-chair 1987-1995; Distinguished prof Anthrop 1998-; PROF ANTHROP, STATE UNIV NY, BINGHAMTON, 1981-; NSF sci equip grants, 1974 & 1980 & res grant, 1978, 1980, 1982, 1985, 1987, 1988-1990; vis assoc prof anthrop & sci coordr, US Int Biol Prog, Human Adaptability Component, Pa State Univ, 1972-1973; State Univ NY Binghamton res fel & grant, Nunoa, 1972; from asst prof to assoc prof, State Univ NY, Binghamton, 1971-1981; Ohio State Univ res fel, Nunoa, Peru, 1968; Asst prof anthrop, Ohio State Univ, 1967-1970. **Memberships:** Fel AAAS; fel Am Asn Phys Anthrop (vpres, 1988-1990, pres 1991-1994); Soc Study Human Biol fel; Human Biol Asn (secy-treas, 1973-1975, exec comt, 1987-1991, pres elect 1995-1996, pres 1996-1998; past pres 1998-1999); Am Anthrop Asn. **Research Statement & Publications:** Biocultural adaptations; human biology; environmental stress; heat and cold adaptation; circadian rhythms; human populations at high altitude; child growth and development; ecology of savanna pastoralists; history of biological anthropology. **Mailing Address:** Dept Anthrop, State Univ NY, Binghamton, NY 13902-6000. **Fax:** 607-777-2477. **E-Mail:** mlittle@binghamton.edu

LITTLE, PATRICK JOSEPH, PSYCHIATRY. **Personal Data:** b Washington, DC, October 6, 1958. **Education:** Col William & Mary, BS, 1981; Va Commonwealth Univ, PhD (pharmacol & toxicol), 1989. **Professional Experience:** SR RES FEL, ADOLOR CORP, as of 2006; postdoctoral fel, Dept Pharmacol, Med Ctr, Duke Univ, beginning 1990; postdoctoral fel, Dept Psychiat, Sch Med, Wash Univ, St Louis, 1989-1990; lab specialist, Dept Pharmacol & Toxicol, Med Col Va, 1981-1985. **Memberships:** Am Soc Pharmacol & Exp Therapeut; Soc Neuroscience. **Research Statement & Publications:** Drug dependence. **Mailing Address:** Adolor Corp, 700 Pa Dr, Exton, PA 19341. **Fax:** 484-595-1551. **E-Mail:** plittle@adolor.com

LITTLE, PERRY L, NUTRITION, PHYSIOLOGY. **Personal Data:** b Ball Ground, Ga, August 3, 1928; m 1951, c 1. **Education:** Berry Col, BS, 1950; Auburn Univ, MS, 1957, PhD (path, nutrit, physiol), 1966. **Professional Experience:** PROF POULTRY SCI, SAM HOUSTON STATE UNIV, 1980-; assoc prof, Sam Houston State Univ, 1962-1980; res asst poultry sci, Auburn Univ, 1955-1962; High sch teacher, Ala, 1950-1952 & 1953-1955. **Memberships:** Poultry Sci Asn; World Poultry Sci Asn. **Research Statement & Publications:** Nutrition of parasites which involve poultry, currently doing alligator nutrition. **Mailing Address:** Dept Agr, Sam Houston State Univ, Huntsville, TX 77341-1001.

LITTLE, RANDEL QUINCY, ORGANIC CHEMISTRY. **Personal Data:** b Richmond, Va, August 14, 1927; m 1949, Ann; c 3. **Education:** Univ Richmond, BS, 1948; Univ Mich, MS, 1949, PhD (org chem), 1954. **Professional Experience:** RETIRED; dir fuels res, Amoco Oil Co, 1983-1987; dir lubricants & agr prod res, Am Oil Co, Stand Oil Co, Ind, 1974-1983; asst dir lubricants res, Am Oil Co, Stand Oil Co, Ind, 1968-1974; res supvr, Am Oil Co, Stand Oil Co, Ind, 1962-1968; group leader motor oil additives, Am Oil Co, Stand Oil Co, Ind, 1960-1962; res chemist, Am Oil Co, Stand Oil Co, Ind, 1953-1960. **Memberships:** Am Chem Soc; Sigma Xi; Soc Automotive Engrs. **Research Statement & Publications:** Organic reactions; motor oil additives; lubricants; fuels. **Mailing Address:** 860 W Dr way, Glen Ellyn, IL 60137-6155.

LITTLE, RAYMOND DANIEL, ORGANIC CHEMISTRY. **Personal Data:** b Superior, Wis, September 12, 1947; m 1972, c 3. **Education:** Univ Wis-Superior, BS, 1969; Univ Wis-Madison, PhD (org chem), 1974. **Professional Experience:** Vis prof, Univ British Columbia, Vancouver, Can, 1987; PROF ORG CHEM, UNIV CALIF, SANTA BARBARA, 1986-; from asst prof to assoc prof, Univ Calif, Santa Barbara, 1975-1986; fel, Yale Univ, 1974-1975. **Memberships:** Am Chem Soc; Sigma Xi. **Research Statement & Publica-**

tions: Development of new synthetic methods, especially diyl trapping and electroreductive cyclization; total synthesis of pharmacologically active molecules; mechanistic organic chemistry of thermal, electro and photochemical reactions. **Mailing Address:** Dept Chem, Univ Calif, Santa Barbara, CA 93106. **Fax:** 805-893-4120. **E-Mail:** little@chem.ucsb.edu

LITTLE, RICHARD ALLEN, GENERAL MATHEMATICS, GENERAL COMPUTER SCIENCES. **Personal Data:** b Coshocton, Ohio, January 12, 1939; m Laura. **Education:** Wittenburg Univ, BSc, 1960; Johns Hopkins Univ, MA, 1961; Harvard Univ, EdM, 1965; Kent State Univ, PhD (math educ), 1971. **Honors & Awards:** Christofferson-Fawcett Award, Long & Dedicated Serv Maths & Maths Teaching Ohio, Ohio Coun Teachers Maths, 1990. **Professional Experience:** Strosacker Award For Excellance Teaching, Baldwin-Wallace, 1999; vis prof maths & maths educr, Ohio State Univ, 1992-1996; mathematician educr, Initiative Proj Discovery, Ohio State Univ, NSF, 1992-1996; vis prof math, Ohio State Univ, Columbus, 1987-1988; chmn, Math Dept, 1978-1983; PROF MATH & COMPUT SCI, BALDWIN-WALLACE COL, OHIO, 1975-; from instr to assoc prof math, Kent State Univ, Stark, 1967-1975; curric consult math, India Inst Proj, NSF, 1967; instr & curric consult math, Nigerian Proj, Harvard Univ, 1965-1967; Ford Found, Johns Hopkins Univ, 1960-1961 & NSF, Harvard Univ, 1963-1964; Teacher & coach math, Culver Acad, Ind, 1961-1965; Scholarship, Gen Motors Corp, Wittenburg, 1957-1960; Fac Excellance Award by Student Senate Baldwin-Wallace; Visiting Prof of Math, Bowling Green St. Univ, 2004-2005. **Memberships:** Math Asn Am; Nat Coun Teachers Math; Ohio Council Teachers Math. **Research Statement & Publications:** Mathematics and computer science education; computer applications in small to medium size businesses. **Mailing Address:** Dept Math, Baldwin-Wallace Col, 275 Eastland Rd, Berea, OH 44017. **Fax:** 440-826-6973. **E-Mail:** rlittle@bw.edu

LITTLE, ROBERT, PLASMA PHYSICS. **Personal Data:** b Jedburgh, Scotland, March 3, 1939; m 1962, c 3. **Education:** Univ Glasgow, BSc, 1961, PhD (physics), 1964. **Professional Experience:** PROF STAFF PHYSICS, PRINCETON PLASMA PHYSICS LAB, PRINCETON UNIV, 1975-; res assoc physics, Mass Inst Technol, 1973-1975 & Cambridge Electron Accelerator, Harvard Univ, 1964-1973. **Research Statement & Publications:** Development of large tokomaks for controlled thermonuclear research. **Mailing Address:** Princeton Plasma Phys Lab, Princeton Univ, Princeton, NJ 08544.

LITTLE, ROBERT COLBY, PHYSIOLOGY, MEDICINE. **Personal Data:** b Norwalk, Ohio, June 2, 1920; m 1945, c 2. **Education:** Denison Univ, AB, 1942; Western Res Univ, MD, 1944, MS, 1948. **Professional Experience:** CHMN TECH PROG, LOS ALAMOS LAB, as of 2002; PROF EMER PHYSIOL & ENDOCRINOL, MED COL GA, 1989-; chmn emer, Dept Physiol & Endocrinol, beginning 1987; prof physiol, Dept Physiol & Endocrinol, 1973-1989; chmn, Dept Physiol, 1973-1986; prof physiol, chmn dept & asst prof med, Col Med, Ohio State Univ, 1964-1973; asst prof med, Seton Hall Col Med, 1959-1964; prof physiol, Seton Hall Col Med, 1958-1964; dir, Cardio-Pulmonary Labs, Scott & White Clin, Tex, 1957-1958; dir clin res, Mead Johnson & Co, 1954-1957; assoc prof med, Univ Tenn, 1953-1954; from asst prof to assoc prof physiol, Univ Tenn, 1950-1954; resident med, Crile Vet Hosp, Cleveland, 1949-1950; USPHS res fel, Western Res Univ, 1948-1949; Intern, Grace Hosp, Detroit, Mich, 1944-1945. **Memberships:** Am Physiol Soc; Soc Exp Biol & Med; Am Heart Asn; Am Fedn Clin Res; AMA; Sigma Xi. **Research Statement & Publications:** Cardiovascular dynamics; heart sounds; clinical physiology; muscle dynamics. **Mailing Address:** Los Alamos Lab, PO Box 1663, MS F663, Los Alamos, NM 87545. **Fax:** 505-665-3046. **E-Mail:** rcl@lanl.gov

LITTLE, ROBERT E(UGENE), MECHANICAL DESIGN, MECHANICAL METALLURGY. **Personal Data:** b Enfield, Ill, May 24, 1933; m 1961, Barbara; c Susan, James, Richard & John. **Education:** Ohio State Univ, MSME, 1960; Univ Mich, PhD (mech eng), 1963. **Professional Experience:** PROF MECH ENG, UNIV MICH, DEARBORN, 1968-; assoc prof, Univ Mich, Dearborn, 1965-1968; asst prof mech eng, Okla State Univ, 1963-1965. **Memberships:** Am Soc Testing & Mat. **Research Statement & Publications:** Modes of failure; fatigue; reliability; planned experiments; composites. **Mailing Address:** Univ Mich, Dept Mech Eng, 4901 Evergreen Rd, Dearborn, MI 48128-1491. **Fax:** 313-593-3851. **E-Mail:** relittle@umich.edu

LITTLE, ROBERT LEWIS, GEOLOGY. **Personal Data:** b Monticello, Miss, July 1, 1929; m 1953, c 2. **Education:** Univ Miss, BA, 1951, MS, 1959; Univ Tenn, Knoxville, PhD (geol), 1969. **Professional Experience:** RETIRED; prof geol & dept head physics, astron & geol, 1981-1985; head dept, Valdosta State Col, 1969-1981; from asst prof to assoc prof, Valdosta State Col, 1969-1981; Instr geol, Univ Miss, 1958-1959 & Univ Tenn, Knoxville, 1959-1969. **Memberships:** Geol Soc Am; Am Asn Univ Prof; Nat Asn Geol Teachers. **Research Statement & Publications:** Areal geology; stratigraphy and structural geology. **Mailing Address:** 711 Northside Dr, Valdosta, GA 31602.

LITTLE, SARAH ALDEN, EXPERIMENTAL JET FLOW, CONVECTION. **Personal Data:** b Cleveland, Ohio, April 27, 1959. **Education:** Stanford Univ, BS, 1981; Mass Inst Technol, PhD (marine geophys), 1988. **Professional Experience:** FINANCE ENGR, LEWTON TECHOL, 1995-; vis investr, Woods Hole Oceanog Inst, 1990-1995; consult, Mackie Martin & Assoc, 1989-1990; Hon postdoctoral, Dept Math, Univ Western Australia, 1989-1990; postdoctoral fel, Ctr Water Res, Univ Western Australia, 1988-1989. **Memberships:** Am Geophys Union; Am Women Sci. **Research Statement & Publications:** Developing techniques and applications of dynamical systems analysis to natural systems such as fluid flow, ecology and earthquakes. **Mailing Address:** 14 Montvale Rd, Wellesley, MA 02181.

LITTLE, STEPHEN JAMES, ASTRONOMY, ASTROPHYSICS. **Personal Data:** b Akron, Ohio, July 5, 1939. **Education:** Univ Kans, BA, 1961, MA, 1963; Univ Calif, Los Angeles, PhD (astron), 1971. **Professional Experience:** Res assoc, CASA, Univ Colo, 1990-1997; sci tech staff, Gen Res Co, 1986-1990; asst prof, Bentley Col, 1985-1990; sr fel, Nat Res Coun, 1983-1985; consult scientist, Solar Physics Div, Am Sci & Eng, Cambridge, 1976-1977; asst prof astron, Wellesley Col, 1975-1983; VIS PROF ASTRON, UNIV COLO, 1971-; asst prof, Ferris State Col, Big Rapids, Mich, 1970-1975; fac assoc astron, Univ Tex, Austin, 1968-1970. **Memberships:** Am Astron Soc; Sigma Xi. **Research Statement & Publications:** Astronomical spectroscopy and photometry of red giant stars, Ap stars, and planets; solar x-ray physics. **Mailing Address:** CASA, Univ Colo, PO Box 389, Boulder, CO 80309. **E-Mail:** slittle@casa.colorado.edu

LITTLE, WILLIAM ARTHUR, PHYSICS. **Personal Data:** b Adelaide, SAfrica, November 17, 1930; American citizen; m 1955, c 3. **Education:** Univ SAfrica, BSc, 1950; Rhodes Univ, SAfrica, PhD, 1955; Univ Glasgow, PhD, 1957. **Professional Experience:** PROF EMER PHYSICS, STANFORD UNIV, as of 2004; NSF sr fel, 1971-1972; Prof Physics, Stanford Univ, 1965-1994; Guggenheim fel, 1964-1965; invited prof, Univ Geneva, 1964-1965; Alfred P Sloan fel, 1959-1962; from asst prof to assoc prof, Stanford Univ, 1958-1965; Nat Res Coun Can fel, Univ BC, 1956-1958; chmn, MMR Technol Inc. **Memberships:** Fel Am Phys Soc. **Research Statement & Publications:** Organic fluorescence; magnetic resonance; low temperature physics; superconductivity; phase transition; chemical physics; neural network theory. **Mailing Address:** Dept Physics, Stanford Univ, Stanford, CA 94305.

LITTLE, WILLIAM C, CARDIOLOGY, CARDIAC PHYSIOLOGY. **Personal Data:** b Cleveland, Ohio, May 1, 1950; m 1975, c 2. **Education:** Oberlin Col, Ohio, BA, 1972; Ohio State Univ, MD, 1975. **Honors & Awards:** Harrison Award, Southern Soc Clin Invest, 1993. **Professional Experience:** SECT HEAD & PROF CARDIOL, BAPTIST MED CTR, WAKE FOREST UNIV, as of 1995; CHIEF, CARDIOL SECT, 1990-; mem, Study Sect, 1989-1990; prin investr, NIH, 1986-1992 & 1989-1994; assoc prof, Cardiol Sect, 1986-1989; from asst prof to assoc prof med, Univ Tex Health Sci Ctr, 1981-1986; Instr, Univ Ala Sch Med, 1980-1981. **Memberships:** Am Soc Clin Invest; Am Physiol Soc; Cardiac Syst Dynamics Soc; Asn Univ Cardiologists; Asn Professors Cardiol. **Research Statement & Publications:** Cardiac dynamics and pathophysiology of myocardial infarction. **Mailing Address:** Sect Cardiol, Med Ctr Blvd, Wake Forest Univ Sch Med, Winston-Salem, NC 27157-1045. **Fax:** 336-716-5324.

LITTLE, WILLIAM FREDERICK, ORGANIC CHEMISTRY, INORGANIC CHEMISTRY. **Personal Data:** b Morganton, NC, November 11, 1929; m 1958, Dell; c 1. **Education:** Lenoir Rhyne Col, BS, 1950; Univ NC, MA, 1952, PhD (org chem), 1955. **Honorary Degrees:** DSc, Lenoir Rhyne Col, 1984. **Honors & Awards:** Thomas Jefferson Award, 1980. **Professional Experience:** RETIRED; interim provost, Univ NC, Chapel Hill, 1991-1992; corp secy & chmn exec comt, Res Triangle Found, beginning 1986; pres, Triangle Univ Ctr Adv Studies Inc, 1982-1986; univ distinguished prof, Univ NC, Chapel Hill, 1977-1996; vchancellor develop & pub serv, Univ NC, Chapel Hill, 1973-1978; prof chem & chmn dept, Univ NC, Chapel Hill, 1965-1970; asst to dean, Grad Sch Res Admin, Univ NC, Chapel Hill, 1959-1962; consult, Res Triangle Inst, 1956-1969; from instr to assoc prof, Univ NC, Chapel Hill, 1956-1965; instr chem, Reed Col, 1955-1956; vpres acad affairs & vpres, Univ NC Syst. **Memberships:** Am Chem Soc; Sigma Xi. **Research Statement & Publications:** Organometallic compounds, especially metallocenes, and group VIII metals. **Mailing Address:** 201 Markham Dr, Chapel Hill, NC 27514.

LITTLE, WINSTON WOODARD, NUCLEAR ENGINEERING. **Personal Data:** b Gainesville, Fla, September 4, 1938. **Education:** Mass Inst Technol, BS, 1960, MS, 1962, ScD(nuclear eng), 1964. **Professional Experience:** STAFF SCIENTIST, BATTELLE NW LABS, 1982-; consult scientist, Westinghouse Hanford Co, 1977-1982; mgr fast flux test facil, Nuclear Design & Anal Unit, Pac NW Labs, Battelle Mem Inst, 1966-1977. **Memberships:** Am Nuclear Soc. **Research Statement & Publications:** Nuclear design of the fast flux test facility. **Mailing Address:** Battelle NW Labs, 3230 Q Ave, Richland, WA 99352.

LITTLEDIKE, ERNEST TRAVIS, ENDOCRINOLOGY, MINERAL METABOLISM. **Personal Data:** b Logan, Utah, February 25, 1935; m 1960, c 4. **Education:** Utah State Univ, BS, 1958; Wash State Univ, DVM, 1960; Univ Ill, PhD (physiol), 1965. **Professional Experience:** DIR, VET TECH PROG, USDA, 1994-; vet Sci, Univ Nebr, 1989-1996; res leader, Agr Res Serv, 1989-1994; nat prog leader, USDA, 1985-1988; vis scientist endocrinol, Mayo Clinic, 1975-1976; adj prof, Col Vet Med, Iowa State Univ, 1970-1985; vet med officer physiol, Nat Animal Dis Ctr, 1965-1985; res leader, USDA, 1965-1985; fel endocrinol, Univ Wis, 1964-1965; instr anat, NIH fel physiol, 1962-1964; instr anat, Univ Ill, 1960-1962; Cong Res Workers Am Dis. **Memberships:** Endocrine Soc; Am Soc Bone & Marine Res; World Vet Anatomists Asn; World Vet Physiologists & Pharmacologists Asn; Animal Sci Asn. **Research Statement & Publications:** Mineral metabolism in domestic amimals and the diseases that result from mineral imbalances; factors that effect mineral metabolism and the pathogenesis of diseases of mineral metabolism in domestic animals; respiratory diseases of cattle and sheep and food safety research in cattle and sheep; copper metabolism in cattle and sheep. **Mailing Address:** Omaha Col Health Careers, 10845 Harney St, Omaha, NE 68154.

LITTLEFIELD, JOHN WALLEY, GENETICS, PEDIATRICS. **Personal Data:** b Providence, RI, December 3, 1925; m 1950, Elizabeth; c Peter, John Jr & Elizabeth. **Education:** Harvard Med Sch, MD, 1947; Johns Hopkins Univ, Sch Hyg & Pub Health, MHS, 1992. **Professional Experience:** PROF EMER PHYSIOL & PEDIAT, JOHNS HOPKINS UNIV, 1992-; prof physiol & chmn dept, Johns Hopkins Univ, 1985-1992; Josiah Macy scholar, 1979; prof pediat & chmn dept, Johns Hopkins Univ, 1974-1985; prof, Harvard Med Sch, 1970-1973; asst prof pediat, Harvard Med Sch, 1966-1969; Guggenheim fel, 1965-1966; tutor, Harvard Univ, 1959-1965; tutor, Harvard Med Sch, 1959-1965; Am Cancer Soc scholar, 1956-1959; from clin & res fel to asst prof med, Harvard Med Sch, 1954-1966; USPHS fel, Inst Enzyme Res, Univ Wis, 1951; from intern to resident med, Mass Gen Hosp, 1947-1950. **Memberships:** Nat Acad Sci; Am Soc Human Genetics; Am Soc Clin Invest; Am Pediat Soc; Am Soc Biol Chemists; Soc Pediat Res; Asn Am Physicians. **Research Statement & Publications:** Human, somatic cell and molecular genetics; developmental biology. **Mailing Address:** Sch Med, Johns Hopkins Univ, 1830 Bldg Ste 501, Baltimore, MD 21205. **Fax:** 410-955-1561. **E-Mail:** jlittlef@jhmi.edu

LITTLEFIELD, LARRY JAMES, PLANT PATHOLOGY. **Personal Data:** b Ft Smith, Ark, February 7, 1938; m 1963, Julianne; c 3. **Education:** Cornell Univ, BS, 1960; Univ Minn, MS, 1962, PhD (plant path), 1964. **Professional Experience:** PROF EMER, DEPT PLANT PATH, OKLA STATE UNIV, as of 2005; sabbatical, Univ Ga, 1997; prof, Dept Entom & Plant Pathol, Okla State Univ, 1996-; sabbatical, Mich State Univ, 1993; prof & head, Dept Plant Pathol, Okla State Univ, 1985-1996; sabbatical, US Dept Agr, Wash, DC, 1980-1982; sabbatical, Oxford Univ, 1973-1974; sabbatical, Purdue Univ, 1969-1970; from asst prof to prof plant path, NDak State Univ, 1965-1985; NSF res fel, Univ Uppsala, 1964-1965. **Memberships:** Mycol Soc Am; Brit Mycol Soc; Am Phytopath Soc. **Research Statement & Publications:** Histology of host-parasite relations; fungus physiology; electron microscopy of fungi and diseased plants; lasmodiophorioid vectors of plant viruses. **Mailing Address:** Dept Entom & Plant Path, Okla State Univ, Stillwater, OK 74078. **Fax:** 405-744-6039. **E-Mail:** ljlplpa@okstate.edu

LITTLEFIELD, NEIL ADAIR, TOXICOLOGY. **Personal Data:** b Santa Fe, NMex, April 25, 1935; m 1960, c 5. **Education:** Brigham Young Univ, BS, 1961; Utah StateUniv, MS, 1964, PhD (toxicol), 1968. **Professional Experience:** DIR, DIV CHEM TOXICOL, NAT CTR TOXICOL RES, FOOD & DRUG ADMIN, 1979-; mem, Food & Drug Admin Task Force Aerosol Prod, 1975-; Chmn, Interagency Task Force Inhalation Chronic Toxicity & Carcinogenesis, 1974-1975; toxicologist, Div Chem Toxicol, Nat Ctr Toxicol Res, Food & Drug Admin, 1972-1979; pharmacologist pesticide regulation, Environ Protection Agency, 1971-1972; staff scientist inhalation toxicol, Hazleton Lab, Inc, 1967-1970; Res assoc air pollution, Univ Utah, 1966-1967. **Memberships:** Sigma Xi. **Research Statement & Publications:** Investigations in concepts of long-term, low-dose exposures; extrapolation of animal toxicology data to risk-benefit in man; carcinogenesis. **Mailing Address:** 3404 Millbrook Rd, Little Rock, AR 72227.

LITTLEJOHN, OLIVER MARSILIUS, PHARMACY. **Personal Data:** b Cowpens, SC, September 29, 1924; m 1948, c 2. **Education:** Univ SC, BS, 1948 & 1949; Univ Fla, MS,

1951, PhD (pharm), 1953. **Professional Experience:** DEAN EMER, SOUTHERN SCH PHARM, MERCER UNIV, as of 2006; dean, Southern Sch Pharm, Mercer Univ, 1957-1987; prof & head dept, Univ Ky, 1956-1957; asst prof pharm & head dept, Southern Col Pharm, 1953-1956. **Memberships:** Fel Am Found Pharmaceut Educ; Sigma Xi. **Research Statement & Publications:** Pharmaceutical preservatives. **Mailing Address:** Southern Sch Pharm, Mercer Univ, 3001 Mercer Univ Dr, Atlanta, GA 30341-4415.

LITTLE-MARENIN, IRENE RENATE, ASTROPHYSICS. **Personal Data:** b Pilsen, Czech, May 4, 1941; American citizen; m 1973, Stephen; c Erika & Kevin. **Education:** Vassar Col, AB, 1964; Ind Univ, MA, 1966, PhD (astrophys), 1970. **Professional Experience:** PRIN INVESTR, UNIV COLO, as of 2004; NSF vis prof women, Univ Colo, 1990-1991; assoc prof astron, Wellesley Col, beginning 1989; Univ resident res fel, Air Force Geophys Lab, 1986-1988; res fel, JILA, 1983-1984; vis scientist, Univ Colo, 1980-1981; Vis asst prof, Dennison Univ & Ohio State, 1980-1981; asst prof, Wellesley Col, 1977-1989; res asst solar x-rays, Am Sci & Eng, 1976-1977; teaching fel, Ferris State Col, 1974; asst prof, Univ Western Ont, 1972-1973; fel astron, Ohio State Univ, 1970-1972. **Memberships:** Am Astron Soc; Sigma Xi. **Research Statement & Publications:** A search for the radioactive element technetium in long-period variable stars; analysis of infrared absorption spectroscopy; low resolution spectra of circumstellar dust in evolved stars; correlation of water maser emission and optical light curves for long period variable stars. **Mailing Address:** Univ Colo, CASA CB 389, Boulder, CO 80309. **E-Mail:** irene.little@casa.colorado.edu

LITTLEPAGE, JACK LEROY, BIOLOGICAL OCEANOGRAPHY. **Personal Data:** b San Diego, Calif, April 14, 1935; m 1960. **Education:** San Diego State Col, BA, 1957; Stanford Univ, PhD (biol), 1966. **Professional Experience:** ASSOC PROF EMER, DEPT BIOL, UNIV VICTORIA, as of 2006; oceanog consult mining industs, beginning 1971; assoc prof biol, Univ Victoria, beginning 1971; asst prof, Univ Victoria, 1965-1971. **Memberships:** AAAS; Am Soc Limnol & Oceanog. **Research Statement & Publications:** Physiologyand ecology of marine zooplankton, especially copepods and euphausids; pollution monitoring; salmonid IHN virus; geothermal aguaculture. **Mailing Address:** Dept Biol, Univ Victoria, PO Box 1700, Victoria, BC V8W 2Y2, Can. **E-Mail:** littlepg@uvvm.uvic.ca

LITTLER, DIANE SCULLION, EXPERIMENTAL TAXONOMY, NATURAL HISTORY OF MARINE PLANTS. **Personal Data:** b Salem, Ohio, August 26, 1945; m 1966, Mark M. **Education:** Univ Hawaii, BS, 1968; Pac Western Univ, PhD (marine bot), 1985. **Professional Experience:** SR SCIENTIST, HARBOR BR OCEANOG INST, 1994-; RES ASSOC, SMITHSONIAN INST, 1982-; Univ Calif, Irvine, 1970-1982; Res assoc, Univ Hawaii, 1969-1970. **Memberships:** Phycol Soc Am; Int Phycol Soc; Int Soc Reef Studies; Europ Phycol Soc; Soc Women Geogrs. **Research Statement & Publications:** Experimental taxonomy, functional morphology biodiversity and natural history of marine plants; effects of disturbance on the structure and function of marine ecosystems. **Mailing Address:** Dept Bot No 166, Smithsonian Inst, Washington, DC 20560.

LITTLER, MARK MASTERTON, TAXONOMY, FUNCTIONAL MORPHOLOGY. **Personal Data:** b Athens, Ohio, September 24, 1939; m 1966. **Education:** Ohio Univ, BS, 1961, MS, 1966; Univ Hawaii, PhD (marine bot), 1971. **Honors & Awards:** Earle C Anthony Innovative Res Award, 1973; Durbaker Prize, Bot Soc Am, 1984; Lifetime Achievement Award, Am Acad Underwater Sci, 2003. **Professional Experience:** Rep, Int Univ Biol Sci, Biol Monitoring Proj, Int Phycol Soc, 1985-; SR SCIENTIST, SMITHSONIAN INST, 1985-; mem bd vis, Ohio Univ Col Arts & Sci, 1985-1988; adj prof, George Mason Univ, 1984-; ed, Smithsonian Contrib to Bot, 1982-1987; chmn cur bot res, Smithsonian Inst, 1982-1987; assoc ed, J Psychol 1982-1986; assoc ed, Phycolog Soc Am, 1982-1986; assoc ed, Aquatic Bd, 1982-1985; distinguished vis scientist, Univ Nebr, Lincoln, 1981; distinguished vis scientist, Northwestern Univ, 1981; mem bd, S Calif Acad Sci, 1980-1982; vis prof, Univ S Calif, 1973 & 1975; vis prof, Stanford Univ, 1973 & 1974; from asst prof to prof biol res, Univ Calif, Irvine, 1970-1982; chemist, Testing Lab, Ohio State Hwy Dept, 1961-1964. **Memberships:** Ecol Soc Am; Int Phycol Soc; Phycol Soc Am; Int Soc Reef Studies; Am Soc Limnol & Oceanog. **Research Statement & Publications:** Man's effect on marine ecosystems; taxonomy, developmental morphology and seasonal cycles of marine benthos and phytoplankton; standing stock, productivity and the physiological ecology of temperate and reef-building benthic organisms. **Mailing Address:** Dept Bot, Nat Mus Natural Hist, Smithsonian Inst, PO Box 37012 MRC 166, Washington, DC 20560-0166. **Fax:** 202-786-2563. **E-Mail:** littler.mark@nmnh.si.edu

LITTLETON, H(AROLD) T(HOMAS) J(ACKSON), CHEMICAL ENGINEERING. **Personal Data:** b Parksley, Va, June 28, 1921; m 1948, Marian Mote; c Thomas J. **Education:** Univ Va, BChE, 1943. **Professional Experience:** RETIRED; lab adminr, Platics Prod & Resins Dept, 1974-1982; res assoc, Plastic Dept, 1969-1973; sr res engr, Plastic Dept, 1962-1969; res supvr, E I Du Pont de Nemour Co, Inc, 1953-1962; chem engr, Res Div, Polychem Dept, Exp Sta, E I Du Pont de Nemour Co, Inc, 1946-1953; chem engr, Naval Res Lab, 1943-1946. **Memberships:** Am Chem Soc. **Research Statement & Publications:** Process development on nylon intermediates; high pressure processes; new plastics and plastics processing methods. **Mailing Address:** 320 Walden Rd, Sharpley, Wilmington, DE 19803.

LITTLETON, JOHN EDWARD, STELLAR EVOLUTION, MOLECULAR SPECTROSCOPY. **Personal Data:** b Ballston Spa, NY, July 28, 1943; m 1988, Rebecca. **Education:** Cornell Univ, BS, 1965; Univ Rochester, PhD (astrophys), 1972. **Professional Experience:** PROF PHYSICS, WVA UNIV, 1988-; vis scientist, Ind Univ, 1984; vis assoc res astron, Univ Calif Berkeley, 1984, 1985, 1993-1994; vis assoc prof, Univ Ill, 1982; from asst prof to assoc prof, Wva Univ, 1975-1988; res assoc, Harvard Col Observ, 1974-1975; res fel, Harvard Col Observ, 1973-1974; Res assoc astrophys, Belfer Grad Sch Sci, Yeshiva Univ, 1972-1973. **Memberships:** Am Astron Soc; Am Asn Physics Teachers; Astron Soc Pac. **Research Statement & Publications:** enery balance in the solar wind. **Mailing Address:** Dept Physics, WVa Univ, PO Box 6315, Morgantown, WV 26506-6315. **E-Mail:** john.littleton@mail.wvu.edu

LITTLETON, PRESTON A, JR, DENTAL RESEARCH. **Professional Experience:** EXEC DIR, AM ASN DENT SCHS, 1990-. **Mailing Address:** Am Asn Dent Schs, SW N502, 1625 Massachusetts Ave NW, Washington, DC 20036.

LITTLETON, ROBERT T, engineering geology; deceased, see previous edition for last biography

LITTLEWOOD, BARBARA SHAFFER, BIOCHEMISTRY, GENETICS. **Personal Data:** b Buffalo, NY, October 8, 1941; m 1970. **Education:** Univ Rochester, BA, 1963; Univ Pa, PhD (biochem), 1968. **Professional Experience:** RES ASSOC BIOCHEM, UNIV WISMADISON, 1976-; res assoc physiol chem, Univ Wis-madison, 1973-1976; Lectr, Dept Genetics, Cornell Univ, 1970 & Dept Biochem, Univ Wis-Madison, 1972; res assoc biochem, Univ Wis-madison, 1970-1973; NIH trainee, Cornell Univ, 1968-1970. **Memberships:** Genetics Soc Am; Am Soc Microbiol. **Research Statement & Publications:** Yeast genetics and biochemistry. **Mailing Address:** 5109 Coney Weston Pl, Madison, WI 53711-1105.

LITTLEWOOD, PETER B, CONDENSED MATTER PHYSICS. **Personal Data:** b May 18, 1955. **Education:** Univ Cambridge, Eng, BA, 1976, PhD (physics), 1980. **Professional Experience:** Head, Theoret Physics Dept, AT & T Bell Labs, beginning 1991; mem tech staff, Theoret Physics Dept, AT&T Bell Labs, 1980-1981 & 1982-1991; kennedy scholar, Mass Inst Technol, 1976-1977. **Memberships:** Fel Am Phys Soc. **Research Statement & Publications:** Dynamics of sliding charge density; nucleation at a first order phase transition; electron gas in high magnetic fields; high temperature superconductivity; flux lattice in type II superconductors. **Mailing Address:** Cavendish Lab, Univ Cambridge, Madingley Rd, Cambridge, CB3 0HE, UK. **E-Mail:** pbl21@phy.cam.ac.uk

LITTLEWOOD, ROLAND KAY, COMPUTER SCIENCE, MOLECULAR BIOLOGY. **Personal Data:** b Mendota, Ill, November 26, 1942; m 1970, Barbara; c David & Peter. **Education:** Univ Ill, Urbana, BS, 1964; Cornell Univ, PhD (genetics), 1970. **Professional Experience:** DISTINGUISHED EMER INFO PROCESSING CONSULT, INST MOLECULAR VIROL, UNIV WIS, MADISON, as of 2002; Distinguished Info Processing consult, Inst Molecular Virol, Univ Wis, Madison 1993-1997; sr info processing consult, Biophys Lab, 1986-1993; asst scientist, Lab Molecular Biol, Univ Wis-Madison, 1978-1986; Proprietor, Digital Comput Appl, beginning 1974; res assoc, Lab Molecular Biol, Univ Wis-Madison, 1972-1978; NIH fel, Lab Molecular Biol, Univ Wis-Madison, 1970-1972. **Research Statement & Publications:** Application of computers in the biological sciences. **Mailing Address:** Inst Molecular Virol, 1525 Linden Dr Univ Wis, Madison, WI 53706. **E-Mail:** rklittle@wisc.edu

LITTMAN, ARMAND, MEDICINE. **Personal Data:** b Chicago, Ill, April 4, 1921; m 1952, c 3. **Education:** Univ Ill, Chicago, BS, 1942, MD, 1943, MS, 1948, PhD (physiol), 1951. **Professional Experience:** PROF MED, COL MED, UNIV ILL, 1964-; CHIEF MED SERV, HINES VET ADMIN HOSP, 1959-; prof, Cook County Grad Sch Med, 1958-; US AEC travel award, 1958; Raymond B Allen instructorship award, Univ Ill, 1957; attend physician, Res & Educ Hosps, 1955-; pvt pract, 1952-1959; resident, Cook County Hosp, Chicago, 1948-1950; from clin asst to assoc prof, Hines Vet Admin Hosp, 1946-1964; Intern, Cook Co Hosp, Chicago, 1944. **Memberships:** AMA; Am Col Physicians; Am Fedn Clin Res; Am Gastroenterol Asn; Sigma Xi. **Research Statement & Publications:** Gastroenterology; physiology. **Mailing Address:** Vet Admin Hosp, Hines, IL 60141.

LITTMAN, BRUCE H, EXPERIMENTAL MEDICINE. **Personal Data:** b New York, NY, November 18, 1944; c 1. **Education:** Univ Wis, BS, 1966; State Univ NY, MD, 1970; Am Bd Internal Med, dipl, 1975, dipl rheumatology, 1978. **Professional Experience:** EXEC DIR EXP MED, PFIZER GLOBAL RES & DEVELOP, CONN, as of 2006; sr assoc dir exp med, Pfizer Centres, Pfizer Inc, Groton, Conn, beginning 1989; mem, Immunol Sci Study Sect, Div Res Grants, NIH, 1983-1987; chief, Rheumatology Sect, Med Serv, McGuire Vet Admin Med Ctr, Richmond, 1982-1989; Vis scientist, Metab Br, Nat Cancer Inst, Bethesda, Md, 1981-1982; from asst prof to assoc prof med & microbiol, Med Col Va, 1976-1989; res fel, Robert B Brigham Hosp, Harvard Med Sch, 1974-1976; postdoctoral fel, Am Cancer Soc, Mass Div, Boston, 1974-1976; asst med, Peter Bent Brigham Hosp, 1974-1976; resident, Tufts New Eng Med Ctr, 1973-1974; staff assoc tumor & immunol res, Nat Cancer Inst, NIH, Bethesda, Md, 1971-1973; Intern med, Tufts New Eng Med Ctr, Boston, 1970-1971. **Memberships:** Fel Am Col Rheumatology; Am Fedn Clin Res; Am Asn Immunologists; fel Am Col Physicians; Sigma Xi. **Research Statement & Publications:** Transplantation immunity in dogs; cellular immunology; immunogenetics; nucleotide biochemistry; author of numerous articles, chapters and books. **Mailing Address:** Pfizer Cent Res, 445 Eastern Pt Rd, Groton, CT 06340-5196.

LITTMAN, HOWARD, FLUID-PARTICLE SYSTEMS. **Personal Data:** b Brooklyn, NY, April 22, 1927. **Education:** Cornell Univ, BChE, 1951; Yale Univ, PhD (chem eng), 1956. **Professional Experience:** PROF EMER CHEM ENG, RENSSELAER POLYTECH INST, as of 2003; Irex grantee, Univ Belgrade, 1973; Fulbright-Hays lectr, Univ Belgrade, 1972; vis prof, Imperial Col, London, 1971-1972; prof chem eng, Rensselaer Polytech Inst, beginning 1967; assoc prof, Rensselaer Polytech Inst, 1965-1967; Resident res assoc, Argonne Nat Lab, 1957-1959; res asst chem eng, Brookhaven Nat Lab, NY, 1957; from asst prof to assoc prof chem eng, Syracuse Univ, 1956-1965; vis prof, Chonnam Nat Univ, Kwangju, Korea. **Memberships:** Am Chem Soc; Am Inst Chem Engrs. **Research Statement & Publications:** Fluidization and fluid-particle systems; research on fluid mechanics and transport phenomena, in spouted, fluidized and packed beds. **Mailing Address:** Dept Chem Eng, Rensselaer Polytech Inst, 110 Eighth St, Troy, NY 12180-3590. **Fax:** 518-276-4030. **E-Mail:** littmh@rpi.edu

LITTMAN, MICHAEL GEIST, TUNABLE LASER DESIGN, ADAPTIVE OPTICS. **Personal Data:** b Washington, DC, March 29, 1950; m 1971, L Marion Katz; c Emily & Eric. **Education:** Brandeis Univ, AB, 1972; Mass Inst Technol, PhD (physics), 1977. **Professional Experience:** PROF MECH & AEROSPACE ENG, PRINCETON UNIV, 2000-; assoc prof, Mech & Aerospace Eng, Princeton Univ, 1985-2000; founding topical ed, J Optical Soc Am, 1980-1983; asst prof, Mech & Aerospace Eng, Princeton Univ, 1979-1985; mem, Comt Line Spectra Elements, Nat Res Coun, 1979-1983; Vis scientist, TJ Watson Lab, IBM, 1979. **Memberships:** Optical Soc Am; Sigma Xi; Am Astron Soc; Phi Beta Kappa. **Research Statement & Publications:** Design of Tunable Laser Cavities; Coronagraph Design for Terrestrial Planet Finder. **Mailing Address:** Princeton Univ, D202 Eng Quadrangle, Princeton, NJ 08544. **E-Mail:** mlittman@princeton.edu

LITTMAN, WALTER, MATHEMATICAL ANALYSIS. **Personal Data:** b Vienna, Austria, September 17, 1929; American citizen; m 1960, c 3. **Education:** Univ NY, BA, 1952, PhD (math), 1956. **Professional Experience:** Hebrew Univ, Jerusalem, Israel, 1981-1982 & 1989; Chalmers Technol Univ, Gothenburg, Sweden, 1975; vis prof, Mittag-Leffler Inst, Djursholm, Sweden, 1974; vis mem, Courant Inst Math Sci, NY Univ, 1967-1968; PROF MATH, UNIV MINN, MINNEAPOLIS, 1966-; from asst prof to assoc prof, Univ Minn, Minneapolis, 1960-1966; asst prof, Univ Wis, 1959-1960; lectr, Univ Calif, Berkeley, 1958-1959; instr math, Univ Calif, Berkeley, 1956-1958. **Memberships:** Am Math Soc. **Research Statement & Publications:** Partial differential equations; functional analysis; mathematical physics. **Mailing Address:** Dept Math, Inst Technol, Univ Minn, 105 Walter Libr, Minneapolis, MN 55455. **E-Mail:** littman@math.umn.edu

LITTMANN, MARTIN F(REDERICK), METALLURGY & PHYSICAL METALLURGICAL ENGINEERING. **Personal Data:** b Brazil, Ind, February 9, 1919; m 1944, Anne; c Carol & Daniel. **Education:** Univ Cincinnati, ChemE, 1941, MS, 1943. **Professional Experience:** RETIRED; consult, 1983-1994; prin res engr, Armco Inc, 1975-1983; prin res engr, Armco Inc, 1968-1975; prin res assoc, Armco Inc, 1968-1975; from jr res engr to sr res engr, Armco Inc, 1943-1968. **Memberships:** Inst Elec & Electronics Engrs; Am Inst Mining, Metall & Petrol Engrs; Sigma Xi; Am Soc Affil. **Research Statement & Publications:**

Deformation and recrystallization orientations in soft magnetic materials; studies of magnetic properties in relation to metallurgy of soft magnetic materials. **Mailing Address:** 137 Marisa Dr, Middletown, OH 45042.

LITTMANN, WALTER E, METALLURGY. **Education:** Mass Inst Technol, PhD (metall). **Professional Experience:** RETIRED. **Memberships:** Fel Am Soc Metals. **Mailing Address:** Failure Anal Assocs Inc, 2100 E Maple Rd, Detroit, MI 48009.

LITVAK, AUSTIN S, urology; deceased, see previous edition for last biography

LITVAK, MARVIN MARK, QUANTUM ELECTRONICS, MOLECULAR PHYSICS. **Personal Data:** b Newark, NJ, October 20, 1933; m 1963, Marilyn Canney; c Stephanie & David. **Education:** Cornell Univ, BEngPhys, 1955, PhD (theoret physics), 1960. **Professional Experience:** CHIEF SCIENTIST, TECHNOL RES ASSOCS, 1992-; sr staff scientist, TRW, 1985-1992; mem tech staff, Jet Propulsion Lab, Calif Inst Technol, 1978-1985; consult, Lincoln Lab, Mass Inst Technol, 1977-1992 & Jet Propulsion Lab, Calif Inst Technol, 1993-; sr radio astronomer, Smithsonian Astrophys Observ, 1970-1978; lectr, Harvard Col Observ, 1970-1978; group leader, Lincoln Lab, Mass Inst Technol, 1963-1970; sr staff mem, Avco Res Lab, 1960-1963; consult, Avco Corp, 1955-1960. **Memberships:** Int Astron Union; fel & sr mem Am Phys Soc; Am Astron Soc. **Research Statement & Publications:** Non-linear propagation effects of lasers, molecules and masers; millimeter-wave radio astronomy and aeronomy; digital image correction. **Mailing Address:** 1525 Espinsoa Circle, Palos Verdes Estates, CA 90274.

LITVAN, GERARD GABRIEL, SURFACE CHEMISTRY. **Personal Data:** b Vienna, Austria, May 17, 1927; Canadian citizen; m 1964, c 1. **Education:** Eotovos Univ, Budapest, Dipl, 1952; Univ Toronto, PhD (surface chem), 1962. **Professional Experience:** MAT CONSULT, INST RES CONSTRUCT, NAT RES COUN CAN, 1993-; Can Stand Asn Subcomt chmn, 1978; Lectr, Chem Dept, Carleton Univ, 1966-1967; prin res officer, Inst Res Construct, Nat Res Coun Can, 1962-1993; res chemist phys polymer chem, Can Industs Ltd, 1957-1959; assoc phys chem, Cent Chem Res Inst, Hungarian Acad Sci, 1955-1956; Asst prof phys chem, Inst Phys Chem, Eotovos Univ, 1952-1955; First Int Conf Durability Bldg Mat & Components. **Memberships:** Fel Am Ceramic Soc; Am Concrete Inst; Am Chem Soc; fel Chem Inst Can; Am Soc Testing & Mat; Can Stand Asn. **Research Statement & Publications:** Phase transitions of substances adsorbed in porous solids; mechanism of cyroinjury and cyroprotection in plant and animal tissue; mechanism of frost action in porous building materials; materials science engineering; corrosion of reinforcing steel in concrete, rehabilitation of concrete structures. **Mailing Address:** Nat Res Coun, 1200 Montreal Rd, Ottawa, ON K1N 8J8, Can.

LITVIN, FAYDOR L, ANALYSIS & KINEMATICS OF MECHANISMS, COMPUTERIZED GENERATION. **Personal Data:** American citizen; m 1938, Shifra Gershenovich; c Boris & Julia. **Education:** Leningrad Polytech Inst, BSc, 1937; Tomsk Polytech Inst, PhD (mech eng), 1944. **Honorary Degrees:** Dr (Tech Sci), Leningrad Polytech Inst, 1954. **Honors & Awards:** Tech-Brief Awards, NASA, 1987-2004; Thomas Bernard Hall Prize, UK, 2001; Edison Best Patent Award, Am Soc Mech Engrs, 2004. **Professional Experience:** DIR, GEAR RES CTR, UNIV ILL, as of 2002; DISTINGUISHED EMER PROF, UNIV ILL, CHICAGO, 1993-; Nissan, Ford Motor Co, 1992-; Nissan, Japan, 1991-; Consult, Gleason Works, 1991-1994; Consult, Cone Drive, 1989-1990; Consult, Braun Eng Co, 1988-1990; Consult, Dana Corp, 1983-1993; Consult, Ingersol Milling Mach, 1981-1982; Consult, Clow Corp, 1980-1981; prof, Univ Ill, Chicago, 1979-1993; prof & dept head, Leningrad Inst Precision Mechs & Optics, 1964-1978; prof theory mech, Leningrad Polytech Inst, 1949-1964. **Memberships:** Fel Am Soc Mech Engrs; Am Gear Mfrs Asn. **Research Statement & Publications:** Theory of gearing and application; analysis and synthesis of mechanisms; meshing and contact of gears. **Mailing Address:** Dept Mech Eng, Eng & Res Facility, Univ Ill, 842 W Taylor St Rm 2039, Chicago, IL 60607-7022. **Fax:** 312-413-0447. **E-Mail:** Faydor.L.Litvin@uic.edu

LITWACK, GERALD, BIOCHEMISTRY & ENDOCRINOLOGY, CELL BIOLOGY & MOLECULAR BIOLOGY. **Personal Data:** b Boston, Mass, January 11, 1929; m 1973, Ellen J Schatz; c Katherine V, Geoffrey S & Claudia. **Education:** Hobart Col, BA, 1949; Univ Wis, MS, 1951, PhD (biochem), 1953. **Honors & Awards:** Lalor Found Award, 1956; Fac Res Award, Temple Univ, 1987; Laura H Carnell Prof Biochem, Temple Med Sch, 1988. **Professional Experience:** VIS SCHOLAR, DEPT BIOL CHEM, DAVID GEFFEN SCH MED, UNIV CALIF, as of 2005; vice dean res, Sci Affairs, 2001-; assoc dean, Sci Affairs, 2001-; PROF EMER & FORMER CHAIR, DEPT BIOCHEM & MOLECULAR PHARMACOL, THOMAS JEFFERSON UNIV MED COL, 1996-2005; Israel cancer res fund, US Army Breast Cancer Study Sect, 1994; mem adv bd, Oncol Reports, beginning 1993; ed-in-chief, Vitamins & Hormones, beginning 1993; assoc dir basic sci, Dept Pharmacol & dep dir, Jefferson Cancer Inst, Thomas Jefferson Univ, 1993-1997; mem adv bd, Oncol Res, beginning 1992; Israel cancer res fund, Study Sect, 1992-1993; ed-in-chief, receptor, beginning 1991; chmn, dept pharmacol & dep dir, Jefferson Cancer Inst, Thomas Jefferson Univ, 1991-1997; prof biochem, Laura H Carnell prof biochem, 1988-1991; spec study, Reproductive Endocrine Sect, NIH, 1985; counc, Soc Exp Biol & Med, beginning 1984; mem adv bd, Anticancer Res, beginning 1982; mem, Cell Physiol Panel, NSF, 1980-1983; mem adv bd, Endocrinol, 1980-1983; chmn, biochem & chem carcinogenesis, Am Cancer Soc, 1979; dep dir, sch med, Temple Univ, 1978-1991; mem adv bd, biochem & chem carcinogenesis, Am Cancer Soc, 1977-1980; vis scientist, Univ London, 1971 & Univ Calif, 1972; prof biochem, Sch Med, Temple Univ, 1964-1991; fels res inst, Sch Med, Temple Univ, 1964-1991; Nat inst arthritis & metab dis res career develop award, 1963-1969; res assoc prof, Grad Sch Med, Univ Pa & dir biochem, Div Cardiol, Philadelphia Gen Hosp, 1960-1964; hon prof, Rutgers Univ, 1960-1964; vis prof, Univ Calif, 1956; trainee, Oak Ridge Inst Nuclear Studies, 1955; from asst prof to prof biochem, Rutgers Univ, 1954-1964; Nat found infantile paralysis fel, Biochem Lab, Univ Sorbonne, 1953-1954. **Memberships:** Am Soc Biochem & Molecular Biol; Am Asn Cancer Res; Endocrine Soc; Am Chem Soc. **Research Statement & Publications:** Ligandin; hormonal control of enzyme formation and activity; glucocorticoid receptor; mineralocorticoidreceptor; immunophilins apoptosis modulator. **Mailing Address:** 4610 Ledge Ave, Toluca Lake, CA 91602. **E-Mail:** gerry.litwack@mail.tju.edu

LITWAK, EUGENE, SOCIOMEDICAL SCIENCE. **Education:** Wayne State Col, BA, 1948; Columbia Univ, PhD, 1958. **Professional Experience:** PROF SOCIOMEDICAL SCI, MAILMAN SCH PUB HEALTH, COLUMBIA UNIV, as of 2005. **Mailing Address:** Mailman Sch Pub Health Columbia Univ, 722 W 168th St Rm 1207B, New York, NY 10032. **Fax:** 212-305-0315. **E-Mail:** el12@columbia.edu

LITWAK, ROBERT SEYMOUR, SURGERY. **Personal Data:** b New York, NY, November 25, 1924; c 3. **Education:** Ursinus Col, BS, 1945; Hahnemann Med Col, MD, 1949; Am Bd Surg, dipl, 1956; Am Bd Thoracic Surg, dipl, 1958. **Professional Experience:** PROF, DEPT CARDIOTHORACIC SURG, MT SINAI SCH MED, 1971-; attend surgeon & chief div cardiothoracic surg, Mt Sinai Hosp, 1962-; Consult, Vet Admin Hosp, Coral Gables, Fla, 1957- & Variety Children's Hosp, 1959-; chief div thoracic & cardiovasc surg, Jackson Mem Hosp, 1959-1962; from instr to assoc prof surg, Med Sch, Univ Miami, 1956-1962; asst surg, Sch Med, Boston Univ, 1952. **Memberships:** Fel Am Col Surg; fel Am Col Chest Physicians; fel Am Col Cardiol; fel NY Acad Sci. **Research Statement & Publications:** Cardiovascular physiology; cardiac surgery. **Mailing Address:** Dept Cardiothoracic Surg, Mt Sinai Sch Med, PO Box 1028 One E 100th St, New York, NY 10029. **Fax:** 212-534-3357. **E-Mail:** litwak@earthlik.net

LITWHILER, DANIEL W, OPERATIONS RESEARCH. **Personal Data:** b Ringtown, Pa, February 28, 1942; m 1966, Peggy; c Daniel, Christopher, Kevin & Heather. **Education:** Fla State Univ, BS, 1963, MS, 1965; Univ Okla, PhD (indust eng), 1977. **Professional Experience:** CHMN, DIV BASIC SCI, USAF ACAD, 1994-; vdean fac, Dept Math Sci, 1992-1994; prof math & head, Dept Math Sci, 1986-1991; tenure prof, USAF Acad, 1983-1985; plans & issue analyst, staff group, Off Secy Air Force, 1982; assoc prof, USAF Acad, 1972-1974 & 1977-1981; Opers officer, mgt analyst, comptroller & progs officer, US Air Force, 1965-1972. **Memberships:** Opers Res Soc Am. **Research Statement & Publications:** Location theory, particularly large regions; military applications of operations research. **Mailing Address:** Dept Math Sci, US Air Force Acad, Colorado Springs, CO 80840. **E-Mail:** lithwhilerdw.dfms@usafa.af.mil

LITWILLER, BONNIE H, MATHEMATICS. **Education:** Ill State Univ, BS, MS. **Professional Experience:** PROF EMER, DEPT MATH, UNIV NOTHERN IOWA, 2003-. **Mailing Address:** Dept Math, Univ Northern Iowa, Cedar Falls, IA 50614. **Fax:** 319-266-8160. **E-Mail:** bonnie.litwiller@uni.edu

LITWIN, MARTIN STANLEY, SURGERY. **Personal Data:** b Florence, Ala, January 8, 1930; m 1985, Cheryl Mason; c Anna M, Rebecca, Benjamin & Martin. **Education:** Univ Ala, BS, 1951, MD, 1955; Am Bd Surg, dipl, 1963, MMM Tulane, 1998. **Honors & Awards:** Ralph McBurney Outstanding Med Serv Award. **Professional Experience:** ASSOC DEAN MED DIR FAC PRACT, ROBERT & VIOLA LOBRANO PROF SURG, SCH MED, TULANE UNIV, 1977-; Nat Heart Inst investr career develop award, 1968-1972; consult, Vet Admin Hosp, W Roxbury, 1966-; from asst prof to prof, Robert & Viola Lobrano Prof Surg, Sch Med, Tulane Univ, 1966-1977; instr, Harvard Med Sch, 1966; Spec Study Sect Laser & NIH session chmn, Gordon Conf Lasers Biol Med, 1965-1967; jr assoc surg, Peter Bent Brigham Hosp, Boston, 1965-1966; chief surg res, Peter Bent Brigham Hosp, Boston, 1965; adj prof biomed eng, Northeastern Univ, 1964-1967; clin invetr, Vet Admin Hosp, W Roxbury, 1964-1966; Am Cancer Soc clin fel, 1961-1962; sr resident, Peter Bent Brigham Hosp, Boston, 1961-1962; sr asst resident, Peter Bent Brigham Hosp, Boston, 1960-1961; surg registr, St Mary's Hosp & Med Sch, London, 1959-1960; regr to prof teaching unit, St Mary's Hosp, London, 1959-1960; George Gorham Peters fel, Peter Bent Brigham Hosp, Boston, 1959-1960; jr asst resident, Peter Bent Brigham Hosp, Boston, 1957 & 1958-1959; asst, Peter Bent Brigham Hosp, Boston, 1956-1958; surg res fel, Harvard Med Sch, 1956-1958; intern surg, Michael Reese Hosp, Chicago, 1955-1956; Instr med physiol, Sch Med, Univ Ala, 1953; sr vis surgeon, Charity Hosp of La, mem active staff, Tulane Hosp; mem, Surgeon-Gen Adv Comt Optical Lasers, Working Group Safety Stand Use Lasers, Armed Forces Nat Res Coun Comt Vision, Ad Hoc Initial Rev Group, Nat Ctr Radiol Health. **Memberships:** Fel Am Col Surgeons; Am Surg Asn; Am Asn Surg Trauma; Soc Univ Surgeons; Soc Surg Alimentary Tract; Int Surg Soc. **Research Statement & Publications:** Blood rheology; vascular and gastrointestinal surgery; surgical metabolism; blood transfusion and treatment of skin cancer. **Mailing Address:** Tulane Univ Med Sch, 1415 Tulane Ave, New Orleans, LA 70112-2600. **E-Mail:** mlitwin@tulane.edu

LITYNSKI, DANIEL MITCHELL, OPTICAL SIGNAL PROCESSING. **Personal Data:** b Amsterdam, NY, March 13, 1943; m 1963, c 3. **Education:** Rensselaer Polytech Inst, BS, 1965, PhD (physics), 1978; Univ Rochester, MS, 1971. **Professional Experience:** PROVOST & VPRES ACAD AFFAIRS, WESTERN MICH UNIV, 2002-; PROF, DEPT ELEC & COMPUT ENG, WESTERN MICH UNIV, 1999-; prof & head elec eng & comput sci, US Mil Acad, West Point, NY, 1990-1999; USMA fel, Indust Col Armed Forces, 1988-1989; adj res prof, Elec Comput & Syst Engr Dept, Rensselaer Polytech Inst, 1987-; prof, dep & actg head, Elec Engr, 1986-1989; prin investr, US Army Res Off, 1981-; assoc prof, 19th Maintenance Battalion, WGer, 1980-1986; lectr, Europ Div, Univ Md, 1980; exec officer, 19th Maintenance Battalion, WGer, 1978-1980; asst prof physics, US Mil Acad, 1974-1978; vis researcher, Harry Diamond Labs, 1974 & 1975; res physicist, Ballistics Res Labs, 1972-1973; commanding officer, 551st Lt Maint Co, Vietnam& H0 Co, US Ord Ctr, 1967-1968; exec officer B, 2/34 Armor Battalion, Vietnam, US Army, 1966-1967; dep & actg head, Elec Engr, US Army, beginning 1965. **Memberships:** Sigma Xi; Inst Elec & Electronics Engrs; Optical Soc Am; Soc Photo-Optical Instrumentation Engrs; Am Soc Eng Educ; NY Acad Sci; Armed Forces Commun & Electronics Asn. **Research Statement & Publications:** Optical signal processing using surface acoustic wave devices; optical matrix processing; optical computing. **Mailing Address:** Col Eng & Appl Sci, Western Mich Univ, 4601 Campus Dr B-236, Kalamazoo, MI 49008-5329. **Fax:** 269-276-3151. **E-Mail:** dan.litynski@wmich.edu

LITZ, CHARLES J, JR, MATHEMATICAL PHYSICS, SPACE ENVIRONMENT SIMULATION. **Personal Data:** b Philadelphia, Pa, November 5, 1928; m 1971, Ronalda C Kapczynski; c Stacey A & Mark C. **Education:** Univ Del, BME, 1951; Tex Western Univ, BS, 1955; LaSall Col, MS, 1959. **Honors & Awards:** Scientific paper; Anti Stall Aircraft w Hot gas boundary layer, US army @ West point 1986. **Professional Experience:** Prin investr, Am Soc Mech Engrs, 1996; SR ENG SCIENTIST, BOING CO, 1986-; sr design engr, Ford Motor & Aerospace, 1977-1986; air bag prin investr, Ford Motor Co, 1977-1981; ord prin investr, Duke Univ, 1961-1967; Minute Man Mark X & XII consult, USAF, 1959-1961; sr mech engr, Frankfort Arsenal, 1958-1977; electro-mech engr, Honeywell, 1956-1958; lectr electronic physics, US Army, Ft Bliss, 1954-1956; Lectr Nike missile systs, US Army, 1954-1956; Mech engr, US Navy, Pa, 1951-1954. **Memberships:** Am Soc Mech Engrs; Prof Engrs Asn. **Research Statement & Publications:** Design test electromechanical ordnance devices; aircraft life support and guided missile systems; design of experiments in statistical analysis of test data; aerospace simulation and testing of space station system; granted 11 patents; prepare processes & prodecures for testing in Boeing eng lab. **Mailing Address:** 29221 Tieree St, Laguna Niguel, CA 92677. **Fax:** 714-896-2439. **E-Mail:** litzm_charlie@mdaw.com

LITZ, LAWRENCE MARVIN, GAS LIQUID SOLID MIXING, MEMBRANE APPLICATIONS & ENGINEERING. **Personal Data:** b Chicago, Ill, October 22, 1921; m 1942, c Barbara, Heidi, Michelle & Lisa. **Education:** Univ Chicago, BS, 1942; Ohio State Univ, PhD (phys chem), 1948. **Honors & Awards:** Kirkpatrick Award, Chem Eng J, 1975. **Professional Experience:** PRES, LITZ GLOBAL CONSULT, 1992-; corp fel, Union Carbide Indust Gases, Inc, 1986-1992; mgr process chem, Linde Div, 1986-1990; sr develop assoc, Membrane Systs, 1977-1986; gen mgr, Membrane Systs, 1972-1977; sr group leader membrane technol, Corp Develop, 1966-1972; develop mgr fuel cells, Advan Develop Dept, 1962-1966; group leader high temperature mat, Carbon Div, Union Carbide Co, 1953-1962; group leader chem metal, Standard Oil Calif, 1951-1953; res chemist catalysis, Allied Chem Corp, 1947-1951; res metallurgist, Manhattan Proj, Los Alamos,

1943-1945; Res chemist, Tenn Valley Auth, 1942-1943. **Memberships:** Am Inst Chem Engrs; Am Chem Soc; Electrochem Soc; Soc Mining & Metall Engrs; Sigma Xi. **Research Statement & Publications:** Membrane technology; high temperature materials and processes; electrochemical and process engineering; fuel cells, nuclear chemistry; chemical and physical metallurgy; gas-liquid chemical processing; bioengineering. **Mailing Address:** 3925 Tarpon Pointe Circle, Palm Harbor, FL 34684. **Fax:** 727-789-1078.

LITZ, RICHARD EARLE, PLANT PATHOLOGY, HORTICULTURE. **Personal Data:** b Presque Isle, Maine, July 3, 1944; m 1969, c 2. **Education:** Dalhousie Univ, BSc, 1966, MSc, 1968; Univ Nottingham, PhD (plant virol), 1971. **Professional Experience:** PROF, DEPT HORT SCI, UNIV FLA, as of 2004; assoc ed, Am Soc Hort Sci, 1986-1989; assoc prof, Fruit Crops Dept, Univ Fla, 1984-1988; Rockefeller Found grants, 1979-1981 & 1981-1985; USDA grant, 1979-1984; asst prof, Fruit Crops Dept, Univ Fla, 1979-1984; Rare Fruits Coun Int grant, 1978-; res assoc plant path, Fruit Crops Dept, Univ Fla, 1977-1978; fel, Fruit Crops Dept, Univ Fla, 1976-1977; res officer plant path, Twyford Labs Ltd, 1973-1976; fel mycol, Univ Durham, 1971-1973. **Memberships:** Int Asn Plant Tissue Cult; Sigma Xi; Am Soc Hort Sci; Int Soc Plant Molecular Biol. **Research Statement & Publications:** Tissue culture of tropical fruits; disease resistance in tropical fruits. **Mailing Address:** Dept Tropical Res & Educ Ctr, Univ Fla, 18905 SW 280 St, Homestead, FL 33031-3314. **Fax:** 305-478-7001 Ext 310. **E-Mail:** rel@ifas.ufl.edu

LIU, ALICE YEE-CHANG, HEAT SHOCK GENES, CELL AGING. **Personal Data:** b Hunan, China, July 12, 1948; American citizen; m 1978, Kuang; c Andrew & Winston. **Education:** Chinese Univ Hong Kong, BSc Hons, 1969; City Univ NY, PhD (pharmacol), 1974. **Professional Experience:** PROF, DEPT BIOL SCI, RUTGERS STATE UNIV, 1989-; mem, Cell Biol Panel, NSF, 1989-1993; assoc prof, Dept Biol Sci, Rutgers State Univ, 1984-1989; mem, Pharm Sci Rev Comt, NIQMS, NIH, 1984-1988; Am Cancer Soc scholar award, 1982-1985; asst prof, pharmacol, Med Sch, Harvard Univ, 1977-1984; fel, Sch Med, Yale Univ, 1973-1977; instr, pharmacol, Mt Sinai Sch Med, 1973; chmn, Educ Policy Comt, Rutgers State Univ; DIR, GRAD PROG, CELL & DEVELOP BIOL. **Memberships:** Am Soc Biochem & Molecular Biol. **Research Statement & Publications:** Signal transduction and gene expression; transcriptional regulation of heat shock genes in cell aging and differentiation. **Mailing Address:** Dept cell biol & neuroSci Nelson Biol Bldg, Rutgers State Univ, Piscataway, NJ 08854-1059. **Fax:** 732-445-3694. **E-Mail:** liu@biology.rutgers.edu

LIU, ANDREW C F, MATHEMATICS. **Education:** Univ Alta PhD. **Honors & Awards:** Adrien Pouliot Award, Can Math Soc, 2003. **Professional Experience:** PROF, DEPT MATH & STATIST SCI, UNIV ALTA, as of 2006. **Mailing Address:** Dept Math & Statist Sci, Univ Alta, CAB 607 632 Cent Acad Bldg, Edmonton, AB T6G 2G1, Can. **Fax:** 780-492-6826. **E-Mail:** aliu@math.ualberta.ca

LIU, ANTONY A K, REMOTE SENSING, IMAGE PROCESSING. **Personal Data:** b Taipei, Taiwan, September 7, 1947; American citizen; m Linda; c Eileen & Eric. **Education:** Nat Chung-Hsiing Univ, BS, 1970; Johns Hopkins Univ, PhD (mech), 1976. **Honors & Awards:** Distinguished Authorship Award, Nat Oceanic & Atmospheric Admin, 1986; Award of Excellence, Fed Asian Pac Am Coun, 1995. **Professional Experience:** Vis prof, Ocean Univ Qingdao, China, 1994-1996; Nat Taiwan Ocean Univ, 1996; Const Watch Prog, Nat Oceanic & Atmospheric Admin, beginning 1996; Can Radar Sat Res Prog, 1996; consult, Taiwan Cent Weather Bur, 1995-1997; SR SCIENTIST, GODDARD SPACE FLIGHT CTR/NASA, 1993-; Satellite Verification Proj, Japan Earth Remote Sensing Satellite, 1993-1995; prin investr, Earth Resources Satellite Proj, Europ Space Agency, beginning 1991; sci officer, Off Naval Res, 1988-1989; oceanogr, Goddard Space Flight Ctr/nasa, 1986-1992; sect head ocean technol, Dynamics Technol Inc, 1981-1986; res scientist, Dynamics Technol Inc, 1976-1981. **Memberships:** Am Phys Soc; Am Geophys Union; Sigma Xi; Oceanog Soc. **Research Statement & Publications:** Remote sensing research in air-sea-ice interaction, ship wakes, ocean waves and data analysis with applications to climate study, fisheries, oceanography and ocean coastal monitoring using satellite data. **Mailing Address:** Goddard Space Flight Ctr, NASA, Code 971, Greenbelt, MD 20771-0001. **Fax:** 301-614-5644. **E-Mail:** liu@neptune.gsfc.nasa.gov

LIU, BEDE, ELECTRICAL ENGINEERING. **Personal Data:** b Shanghai, China, September 25, 1934; American citizen; m 1959, c Beatrice. **Education:** Nat Taiwan Univ, BSEE, 1954; Polytech Inst Brooklyn, MEE, 1956, DEE, 1960. **Honors & Awards:** Centennial Medal (1984), Millennium Medal (2000), Inst Elec & Electronic Engrs; Best paper award (1988), soc Award (2000), Signal Processing Soc, 1985; Mac Van Valkenburg Award (1997), Golden Jubilee Medal (2000), Best video technol paper award (1994 & 1996), Circuits Systs Soc; mem, National Academy of engr (2002) Honorary Prof, Academia Sinica, China (1988), Honorary Prof, Chinese Univ of Electronics Sc & Tech (1997). **Professional Experience:** PROF ELEC ENG, PRINCETON UNIV, 1969-; from asst prof to assoc prof, Princeton Univ, 1962-1969; mem tech staff commun systs, Bell Tel Labs, 1959-1962; Equipment engr, Western Elec Co, 1954-1956. **Memberships:** Mem bd dirs, Inst Elec & Electronic Engrs, 1984-1985; Fel Inst Elec & Electronic Engrs; Inst Elec & Electronic EngrsCircuit Systs Soc (pres, 1982). **Research Statement & Publications:** Signal and image processing. **Mailing Address:** Dept Elec Eng, Princeton Univ, Princeton, NJ 08544-1099. **E-Mail:** liu@ee.princeton.edu

LIU, BENJAMIN Y H, MECHANICAL ENGINEERING. **Personal Data:** b Shanghai, China, August 15, 1934; m 1958, c 1. **Education:** Univ Nebr, BSME, 1956; Univ Minn, Minneapolis, PhD (mech eng), 1960. **Honorary Degrees:** Dr, Univ Kupio, Finland, 1991. **Honors & Awards:** Fuchs' Prize, Aerosal Soc US, Japan & Ger, 1994. **Professional Experience:** REGENTS PROF EMER MECH ENG, UNIV MINN, as of 2004; PRES, MSP CORP, as of 2004; dir, Particle Technol Lab, 1973-; prof mech eng, Univ Minn, Minneapolis, beginning 1969; Guggenheim fel, 1968-1969; from asst prof to assoc prof, Univ Minn, Minneapolis, 1960-1969; sr US scientist award, Alexander von Humboldt Found, WGer. **Memberships:** Nat Acad Eng; Solar Energy Soc; Am Soc Heat Refrig & Air-Conditioning Engrs; Air Pollution Control Asn; fel AAAS. **Research Statement & Publications:** Terrestrial and space application of solar energy; aerosol science and technology; instrumentation and measurement. **Mailing Address:** Dept Mech Eng, Inst Technol, Univ Minn, 111 Church St SE, Minneapolis, MN 55455-0111. **E-Mail:** bliu@mailbox.mail.umn.edu

LIU, BING, COATINGS, INKS. **Personal Data:** b Linzhon, China, January 31, 1957; m 1985, Yubin; c Ronald & William. **Education:** SChina Univ Technol, BS, 1982; NY Univ, PhD (chem), 1996. **Professional Experience:** DIR TECHNOL, ELECTROCAL INC, 1996-; sr chemist, Pa Color Inc, 1994-1996; chemist, Polytex Environ Inks, 1992-1994. **Memberships:** Am Chem Soc; Soc Plastics Engrs. **Mailing Address:** Electrocal Inc, 78 Edwin Rd, South Windsor, CT 06074. **Fax:** 860-289-7847.

LIU, CHAIN T, CERAMICS ENGINEERING. **Education:** Nat Taiwan Univ, BS, 1960; Brown Univ, MS, 1964, PhD (Mat Sci & Eng), 1967. **Honors & Awards:** Pioneer/Jupiter Award, NASA, 1974, Pioneer II Saturn Mission Team Award, 1977, Spacecrafts Voyage I & II Team Award, 1984; IR 100 Award, 1979 & 1983; Henry J Albert Award, Int Precious Metals Inst, 1980; E O Lawrence Award, US Dept Energy, 1988; RD 100 Award, 1990; Outstanding Achievement Award to Galileo RTG Team, Dept Energy, 1990. **Professional Experience:** Prin ed, J Mat Res, 1990-; CORP FEL, MARTIN MARIETTA ENERGY SYSTS, INC, 1985-; mem, Adv Tech Awareness Coun, Am Soc Metals, 1984; group leader, alloying behav & design group, metals & ceramics div, 1983-; sr res staff mem, Oak Ridge Nat Lab, 1967-1982; Teaching asst, Brown Univ, 1962-1966. **Memberships:** Fel Am Soc Metals; hon platinum mem Int Precious Metals Inst. **Research Statement & Publications:** Mechanical behavior of metals, alloys and intermetallic compounds; phase transformation; gas-metal interactions; alloy design of high-temperature materials; metal-matrix composites; environmental effects on ductability and fracture in metals and alloys; 14 patents; numerous technical publications. **Mailing Address:** 122 Newell Lane, Oak Ridge, TN 37830.

LIU, CHAMOND, PERFORMANCE OF OPERATING SYSTEMS. **Personal Data:** b Waltham, Mass, September 28, 1948. **Education:** Univ Calif, Berkeley, AB, 1968; Cornell Univ, MS, 1971, PhD (math), 1973. **Professional Experience:** CLEARITY COMPUT, 1994-; CONSULT, 1994-; staff programmer, IBM Corp, 1981-1994; sr assoc programmer, IBM Corp, 1979-1981; NSF grant, 1975-1976; asst prof math, Fordham Univ, 1973-1979. **Memberships:** Am Math Soc; Math Asn Am; Asn Comput Mach. **Research Statement & Publications:** Performance and performance methodology of large operating systems including automatic work load characterization, automatic work load generation and architectural design. **Mailing Address:** 202 N Spooner St, Madison, WI 53705.

LIU, C(HANG) K(ENG), MECHANICAL ENGINEERING. **Personal Data:** b Soochow, China, March 28, 1921; American citizen; m 1951, c 2. **Education:** Nat Chiao-Tung Univ, China, BS, 1943; Univ Ill, MS, 1946, PhD (theoret & appl mech), 1950. **Professional Experience:** RETIRED; fallout shelter analyst, 1966-; from asst prof to prof mech eng, Univ Ala, Tuscaloosa, 1963-1986; Consult, Marshall Space Flight Ctr, NASA, 1960-1968; res assoc appl math, Brown Univ, 1952-1954; ammunition design engr, Picatinny Arsenal, 1952; Res assoc theoret & appl mech, Univ Ill, 1950-1952. **Memberships:** Am Soc Mech Engrs; Am Soc Eng Educ; Soc Eng Sci; Am Inst Aeronaut & Astronaut. **Research Statement & Publications:** Radiation safety; fluid mechanics; viscous fluid flow; stability of social and human behavior; heat conduction in solids. **Mailing Address:** 2236 Woodland Rd, Tuscaloosa, AL 35404-5086.

LIU, CHANGNONG, BIOLOGY. **Education:** Hunan Agr Univ, BS, MS, 1984; Univ Minn, PhD (genetics), 1990. **Professional Experience:** CO-FOUNDER, GRANGE BIOTECHNOL CO, as of 2005. **E-Mail:** cnliu@sbcglobal.net

LIU, CHAO-HAN, PHYSICS, ELECTRICAL ENGINEERING. **Personal Data:** b Kwangsi, China, January 3, 1939; m 1963, Tsuei-ChuMong; c Alice & Robert. **Education:** Nat Taiwan Univ, BS, 1960; Brown Univ, PhD (elec sci), 1965. **Professional Experience:** PROF & PRES, NAT CENT UNIV, CHUNG-LI, TAIWAN, 1990-; distinguished lectr, Nat Sci Coun, Taiwan, 1988; Chair prof, Nat Taiwan Univ, 1981; from asst prof to prof elec eng, Univ Ill, Urbana-Champaign, 1966-1994; Res assoc, Univ Ill, Urbana-Champaign, 1965-1966. **Memberships:** Am Phys Soc; Am Geophys Union; fel Inst Elec & Electronics Engrs. **Research Statement & Publications:** Ionosphere, plasma and atmospheric physics; wave propagation in plasma and random media; radar remote sensing. **Mailing Address:** Nat Cent Univ, Chungli, Taiwan. **E-Mail:** t341426@ncu865.ncu.edu.tw

LIU, CHAOQUN, MATHEMATICS. **Education:** Tsinghua Univ, BS (Fluid Mechanics), 1967; Tsinghua Univ, MS, 1981; Univ Colo, Denver, Phd (appl Math), 1989. **Professional Experience:** PROF & DIR, DEPT MATH, UNIV TEX, ARLINGTON, as of 2005. **Mailing Address:** Math Dept, Univ Tex, Mail Box 19408, Pickard Hall, Rm No. 456, Arlington, TX 76019. **Fax:** 817-272-5802.

LIU, CHEN YA, MECHANICAL ENGINEERING, APPLIED MATHEMATICS. **Personal Data:** b Shanghsien, China, September 21, 1924; American citizen; m 1956, Anita Go; c Leo, Isabel & Ursula. **Education:** Cent Univ, China, BS, 1948; NY Univ, MME, 1955, EngScD, 1959. **Honors & Awards:** Tech Award, NASA. **Professional Experience:** CONSULT, 1987-; fel, Columbus Labs, Battelle Mem Inst, 1972-1987; assoc fel, Columbus Labs, Battelle Mem Inst, 1969-1972; sr res engr, Columbus Labs, Battelle Mem Inst, 1965-1969; lectr, Univ Akron, 1962-1964; sr res engr, Res Ctr, B F Goodrich Co, 1961-1964; Consult, Budd Electronics, Inc, 1961; asst prof, Carnegie Inst Technol, 1959-1961; instr mech eng, NY Univ, 1955-1959; proj engr, Ord Serv, China, 1952-1954; Res engr, Ord Serv, China, 1948-1952. **Memberships:** Am Inst Aeronaut & Astronaut; Am Soc Mech Engrs. **Research Statement & Publications:** Fluid mechanics and heat transfer; elasticity of orthotropic materials. **Mailing Address:** 3139 Alameda, Menlo Park, CA 94025.

LIU, CHEN-CHING, ELECTRICAL ENGINEERING. **Personal Data:** b Taiwan, December 30, 1954. **Education:** Nat Taiwan Univ, BS, 1976, MS, 1978; Univ Calif, Berkeley, PhD (comput sci & elec eng), 1983. **Honors & Awards:** Presidental Young Investr Award, White House & Natl Sci Found, 1987. **Professional Experience:** DIR, ADVAN POWER TECHNOLOGIES CTR, as of 2005; DIR, ELEC ENERGY INDUST CONSORTIUM, as of 2005; PROF & ASSOC DEAN, ELEC ENG, UNIV WASH, as of 2005; mem exec bd, Power Eng Soc, Inst Elec & Electronics Engrs, 1992-; prof elec eng, Univ Wash, beginning 1991; chmn, Tech Comt Power Syst, 1989; chmn, Seattle Sec, 1987-1988; chmn, Expert Syst Task Force, Inst Elec & Electronics Engrs, 1987; from asst prof to assoc prof, Univ Wash, 1983-1991; instr elec, Army Signals & Electronic Sch, Taiwan, 1978-1980. **Memberships:** Fel Inst Elec & Electronics Engrs; Int Conf Large High Voltage Elec Systs. **Research Statement & Publications:** Application of expert systems to electric power systems; develop analytical and computer methods for power systems planning and operation; power electronic circuits analysis. **Mailing Address:** Dept Elec Eng, Univ Wash, PO Box 352500 215I EE/CSE Bldg, Seattle, WA 98195. **Fax:** 206-543-3842. **E-Mail:** liu@ee.washington.edu

LIU, CHEN-HUEI, AERONAUTICS. **Education:** NY Univ, PhD, (math) 1971. **Professional Experience:** SR SCIENTIST, NASA LANGLEY RES CTR, as of 2006. **Mailing Address:** NASA Langley Res Ctr, MS 128, Hampton, VA 23681. **Fax:** 804-864-2154.

LIU, CHIEN, INFECTIOUS DISEASES, VIROLOGY. **Personal Data:** b Canton, China, March 6, 1921; m 1947, c 4. **Education:** Yenching Univ, BS, 1942; WChina Union Univ, MD, 1947; Am Bd Pediat, dipl, 1964. **Professional Experience:** PROF EMER MED, SCH MED, UNIV KANS, as of 2003; vis prof, Nat Defense Med Ctr, Taiwan, 1966-1967; med consult, US Naval Med Res Unit 2, 1966-1967; USPHS res career award & Res Career Award, Nat Inst Allergy & Infectious Dis, 1963-; prof med & pediat, Sch Med, Univ Kans, beginning 1963; assoc prof pediat, Sch Med, Univ Kans, 1958-1963; asst prof, Harvard Med Sch, 1958; assoc, Harvard Med Sch, 1955-1958; res assoc bact & immunol, Harvard Med Sch, 1952-1955; asst med, Johns Hopkins Univ, 1951-1952; asst physician, Johns Hopkins Hosp, 1949-1952; Res fel med, Sch Med, Johns Hopkins Univ, 1949-1951; med intern, Garfield Mem Hosp, Wash, DC, 1947-1948; Intern, Ill Masonic Hosp, 1946-1947. **Memberships:** Soc Pediat Res; Am Soc Microbiol; Am Asn Immunologists; Am Acad Microbiol; Infectious Dis Soc Am. **Mailing Address:** Dept Med, Sch Med, Univ Kans, Mail Stop 1028, 6080 Delp Pavilion, 3901 Rainbow Blvd, Kansas City, KS 66160. **E-Mail:** cliu@kumc.edu

LIU, CHIH-RAY, MEDICAL PHYSICS. **Education:** Univ Nebr-Lincoln, MS, PhD (Physics). **Professional Experience:** ASSOC PROF & PHYSICIST, COL MED, UNIV FLA, as of 2006. **Memberships:** Am Asn Physicists Med. **Research Statement & Publications:** Clinical radiation physics; Enhanced dynamic wedge; Dynamic MLC Conformal therapy. **Mailing Address:** Dept Radiation Oncol, Health Sci Ctr Univ Fla, PO Box 100385, Gainesville, FL 32610-0385.

LIU, CHI-LI, BACTERIOLOGY, BIOCHEMISTRY. **Personal Data:** b Taiwan, August 20, 1952; American citizen. **Education:** Nat Taiwan Univ, BS, 1974; Univ Ga, MS, 1979, PhD (biochem), 1981. **Professional Experience:** MGR MICROBIOL, ENTOTECH INC, as of 2001; GROUP LEADER, ENTOTECH INC, 1990-; staff researcher, Novo Labs Inc, 1984-1990; assoc, Exxon Res & Eng Co, Annandale, NJ, 1982-1984; lab instr cell biol, Univ Ga, 1979. **Memberships:** Am Soc Microbiol. **Research Statement & Publications:** Industrial microbiology. **Mailing Address:** Novo Nordisk Entotech Inc, 1497 Drew Ave, Davis, CA 95616.

LIU, CHING SHI, AERONAUTICS, FLUID DYNAMICS. **Personal Data:** b Shanghai, China, July 23, 1935. **Education:** SDak Sch Mines & Technol, BS, 1957; Kans State Univ, MS, 1958; Nwestern Univ, PhD (mech eng), 1961. **Professional Experience:** ASSOC PROF ENG SCI, STATE UNIV NY, BUFFALO, 1968-; sr res fel, Calif Inst Technol, 1965-; res assoc, Argonne Nat Lab, 1963-1964; asst prof gas dynamics, Northwestern Technol Inst, 1961-1968; consult, Cook res Lab, Ill, 1961-1962; res engr, Bendix Corp, 1959-1960; design engr, Int Harvester Co, 1956-1957. **Memberships:** Am Inst Aeronaut & Astronaut; Am Soc Mech Engrs; Am Soc Eng Educ; Inst Elec & Electronics Engrs. **Research Statement & Publications:** Gas dynamics; magneto gas dynamics; plasma physics. **Mailing Address:** Dept Eng Sci, State Univ NY, 316 Jarvis Hall, Buffalo, NY 14260. **Fax:** 716-645-3875. **E-Mail:** chingliu@eng.buffalo.edu

LIU, CHING-TONG, PHYSIOLOGY, PHARMACOLOGY. **Personal Data:** b Tai-Shin, Kiangsu, China, October 19, 1931; American citizen; m 1970, In-May Hsin; c Rex, Grace, Jeannette & Christine. **Education:** Nat Taiwan Univ, BS, 1956; Univ Tenn, MS, 1959, PhD (physiol), 1963. **Professional Experience:** RETIRED; asst chief, Dept Physiol Pharmacol, beginning 1992; chief, Dept Clin & Exp Physiol, 1984-1992; Adj prof physiol, Baylor Col Med, 1980-; asst prof physiol, Baylor Col Med, 1966-1973; Assoc res biologist pharmacol, Sterling-Winthrop Res Inst, 1965-1966; USPHS trainee, 1963-1965; res physiologist, US Army Med Res Inst Infectious Dis. **Memberships:** Am Soc Pharmacol & Exp Therapeut; Am Physiol Soc; Soc Exp Biol & Med. **Research Statement & Publications:** Cardiovascular and renal physiology; water, electrolyte and lipid metabolism; mechanisms of infectious diseases and toxemias; effect of muscle trauma; dynamic functional changes and systematically integrated responses to certain viral infections and toxemias in animals. **Mailing Address:** 7915 W Seventh St, Frederick, MD 21702.

LIU, CHI-SHENG, PHYSICAL ELECTRONICS, MATHEMATICS. **Personal Data:** b Chinan, China, November 1, 1934; American citizen; m 1960, c 3. **Education:** Nat Taiwan Univ, BSEE, 1957; WVa Univ, MSEE, 1962; Univ Ill, Urbana, PhD (elec eng), 1968. **Professional Experience:** SR RES SCIENTIST GASEOUS DISCHARGE, WESTINGHOUSE RES LABS, 1969-; David Sarnoff fel, RCA, 1965-1968; mem eng staff TV, RCA Consumer Electronics Div, 1962-1969; Elec engr radio, Philco Corp, 1960-1961. **Memberships:** Am Phys Soc. **Research Statement & Publications:** Study of high pressure gas discharges; high efficiency arc lamps and gas lasers. **Mailing Address:** 11625 Caminito Magnifica, San Diego, CA 92131.

LIU, CHONG TAN, INORGANIC CHEMISTRY. **Personal Data:** b Shanghai, China, May 11, 1936; American citizen; m 1963, c 3. **Education:** Nat Taiwan Univ, BSc, 1956; Univ Pittsburgh, PhD (inorg chem), 1964. **Professional Experience:** GROUP SUPVR, STAUFFER CHEM CO, 1979-; sr res chemist, Stauffer Chem CO, 1972-1978; sr res chemist, Hooker Chem Corp, 1964-1971. **Memberships:** Am Chem Soc. **Research Statement & Publications:** Water treatment; industrial chemical processes; metal finishing; plating on plastics; corrosion controls; high temperature chemistry; coordination chemistry. **Mailing Address:** 3 Demarest Mill Ct, West Nyack, NY 10994-1502.

LIU, CHUAN SHENG, THEORETICAL SPACE PHYSICS, PLASMA PHYSICS. **Personal Data:** b Kwanhsi, China, January 9, 1939; m 1965, Jing; c Albert, Benjamine, Jennifer & Anna. **Education:** Tunghai Univ, BS, 1960; Univ Calif, Berkeley, MA, 1964, PhD (physics), 1968. **Professional Experience:** DIR, DEPT PHYSICS, UNIV MD, as of 2003; PROF PHYSICS, UNIV MD, 1990-; chmn, Dept Physics & Astron, 1985-1990; dir, Theoret Sci Div, GA Technololgies, 1981-1984; mem, Inst Advan Study, 1971-1974; vis scientist, Gulf Gen Atomic Inc, 1970-1971; asst prof residence physics, Univ Calif, Los Angeles, 1968-1970; chmn, Div Plasma Physics, Am Phys Soc. **Memberships:** Fel Am Phys Soc; AAAS. **Research Statement & Publications:** Fusion and plasma physics; space plasma physics. **Mailing Address:** Dept Physics, Univ Md, 2313 Comput & Space Sci Bldg, College Park, MD 20742-4111. **Fax:** 301-341-9525. **E-Mail:** chuan_sheng_liu@umail.umd.edu

LIU, CHUI HSUN, ANALYTICAL CHEMISTRY, INORGANIC CHEMISTRY. **Personal Data:** b China, November 5, 1931; American citizen; m 1962. **Education:** Univ Ill, BA, 1952, PhD (chem), 1957. **Professional Experience:** EMER PROF CHEM, ARIZ STATE UNIV, 1995-; prof, Ariz State Univ, 1965-1995; from asst prof to assoc prof chem, Polytech Inst Brooklyn, 1957-1965. **Memberships:** Am Chem Soc. **Research Statement & Publications:** Chemistry, electrochemistry and spectroscopy in molten salts and other nonaqueous solvents; chemistry of coordination compounds; chelating agents in chemical separations and analyses. **Mailing Address:** Dept Chem & Biochem, Ariz State Univ PO Box 871604, Tempe, AZ 85287-1604. **Fax:** 480-965-2747.

LIU, CHUNG LAUNG, COMPUTER SCIENCE. **Personal Data:** b Canton, China, October 25, 1934; American citizen; m 1960, c 1. **Education:** Cheng Kung Univ, Taiwan, BS, 1956; Mass Inst Technol, SM, 1960, ScD(elec eng), 1962. **Honors & Awards:** Karl V Karlstron Outstanding Educr Award, Asn Comput Mach, 1990. **Professional Experience:** PROF EMER COMPUT SCI, UNIV ILL, URBANA, as of 2000; prof comput sci, Univ Ill, Urbana, beginning 1973; from asst prof to assoc prof elec eng, Mass Inst Technol, 1962-1972. **Memberships:** Inst Elec & Electronics Engrs; Asn Comput Mach. **Research Statement & Publications:** Theory of computation; combinatorial mathematics. **Mailing Address:** Dept Comput Sci, Univ Ill, Urbana, IL 61801.

LIU, CHUNG-CHIUN, CHEMICAL ENGINEERING. **Personal Data:** b Canton, China, October 8, 1936; m Ann; c Peter. **Education:** Cheng Kung Univ, Taiwan, BS, 1959; Calif Inst Technol, MS, 1962; Case Western Reserve Univ, PhD (chem eng), 1968. **Professional Experience:** DIR ELECTRONICS DESIGN CTR, CASE WESTERN RESERVE UNIV, 1985-; PROF CHEM ENG, CASE WESTERN RESERVE UNIV, 1978-; prof chem eng, Univ Pittsburgh, 1968-1978; res assoc, Eng Design Ctr, Case Western Reserve Univ, 1968; Wallace R Persons Prof sensor technol & control. **Memberships:** Am Inst Chem Engrs; Electrochem Soc. **Research Statement & Publications:** Electrochemistry; biomedical engineering; material science. **Mailing Address:** Electronics Design Ctr, Case Western Reserve Univ, Rm 112 Bingham, Cleveland, OH 44118. **Fax:** 216-368-8738. **E-Mail:** cxl9@po.cwru.edu

LIU, CHUNG-YEN, AERONAUTICAL ENGINEERING. **Personal Data:** b Canton, China. **Education:** Nat Cheng-Kung Univ, BS, 1956; Brown Univ, MS, 1958; Calif Inst Technol, PhD (aeronaut), 1962. **Professional Experience:** EMER PROF CIVIL ENVORION ENG, UNIV CALIF, LOS ANGELES, 2002-; from asst prof to prof eng, Univ Calif, Los Angeles, beginning 1962. **Memberships:** Am Phys Soc; Am Inst Aeronaut & Astronaut. **Research Statement & Publications:** Fluid mechanics. **Mailing Address:** 860 Gregna Greenway, Los Angeles, CA 90049. **Fax:** 310-838-5654.

LIU, DAPHNE DER-FEN, MATHEMATICS. **Education:** Nat Cent Univ, Taiwan, BS, 1985; Univ SC, PhD (math), 1991. **Professional Experience:** PROF MATH, COL NAT & SOCIAL SCI, CALIF STATE UNIV, LOS ANGELES, as of 2005. **Mailing Address:** Dept Math & Comput Sci, Calif State Univ, Simpson Tower F201 Simpson Tower F201, Los Angeles, CA 90032. **Fax:** 323-343-5071. **E-Mail:** dliu@calstatela.edu

LIU, DARRELL T, BIOCHEMISTRY. **Personal Data:** b Taiwan, China, May 24, 1932; American citizen; c 3. **Education:** Nat Taiwan Univ, BS, 1955; Univ Pittsburgh, PhD, 1961. **Professional Experience:** Mem, Recombinant DNA Rev Comt, 1981-1989; DIR, DIV BIOCHEM & BIOPHYS, OFF BIOL RES, CTR BIOL, EVAL RES, FOOD & DRUG ADMIN, 1980-; Mem, Regulatory Sci Prom Comt, Food & Drug Admin, 1979-1980; dep dir, Div Bact Prod Chief, Biochem Br, Bur Biol, 1975-1980; sr chief biochem microbial struct, Develop Immunol Br, Nat Inst Child Health Develop, NIH, 1974; res chemist, Develop Immunol Br, Nat Inst Child Health Develop, NIH, 1973; sr biochemist, Brookhaven Nat Lab, 1969-1973; biochemist, Brookhaven Nat Lab, 1967-1969; asst prof, Rockefeller Univ, 1965-1967; Res assoc, Rockefeller Univ, 1961-1965. **Memberships:** Sigma Xi; Am Soc Biol Chemists. **Research Statement & Publications:** Human C-reactive protein; prototypic acute phase reactant; employing molecular cloning techniques to explore the mechanism of induction and control of the biosynthesis of this protein at the chromosomal level; technique of homologous gene transfection is being pursued to investigate the possible physiological function of CRP in xenopus; isolation and cloning of the genes coding for the enzymes and substrate proteins associated with a unique coagulation cascade system form Limulus. **Mailing Address:** Academia Sinica Nankang Taipei, Taipei 115, Taiwan.

LIU, DAVID SHIAO-KUNG, FLUID MECHANICS, NUMERICAL METHODS. **Personal Data:** b Chung-King, China, August 27, 1940; American citizen; m 1966, c 3. **Education:** Cheng-Kung Univ, Taiwan, BS, 1962; Univ Calif, Berkeley, MS, 1965; NY Univ, PhD (appl math & hydraul), 1973. **Professional Experience:** Sr consult, Va Inst Marine Sci, 1977-; PROF HYDRAUL, NAT CHENG-KUNG UNIV, 1977-; SR PHYS SCIENTIST, RAND CORP, 1976-; phys scientist fluid mech, Nat Cheng-kung Univ, 1972-1976; adv, Sci & Technol Adv Group, Taiwan. **Memberships:** Am Soc Civil Eng; Int Asn Water Resources. **Research Statement & Publications:** Numerical modeling of three-dimensional nonhomogeneous geophysical fluid systems; stochastic analysis and control theory of physical systems. **Mailing Address:** 3706 Oceanhill Way, Malibu, CA 90265.

LIU, DENNIS DONG, THIN FILM TECHNOLOGIES, SEMICONDUCTOR TECHNOLOGIES. **Personal Data:** m 1986, Shauna H Wang. **Education:** Xian Jiantong Univ, BSc, 1982; Univ Man, MSc, 1985, PhD (mat & devices), 1992. **Professional Experience:** SR ENGR, SILTEC SILICON, 1994-; Res assoc, Dept Elec Eng, Univ Alta, 1992-1994. **Memberships:** Mat Res Soc. **Research Statement & Publications:** Thin film technologies for the deposition and characterization of films; application of plasma technologies; semiconductor processes for electronic devices; vacuum and gas flow systems. **Mailing Address:** Siltec Silicon, 1351 Tandem Ave, Salem, OR 97302-0139. **Fax:** 541-540-2600.

LIU, DICKSON LEE SHEN, MICROBIOLOGY, WATER POLLUTION. **Personal Data:** b Shantung, China, April 6, 1935; Canadian citizen; m 1967, Alice; c Stanley K. **Education:** Nat Taiwan Chung Hsin Univ, BSc, 1962; Univ BC, MSc, 1966, PhD (microbiol), 1971. **Professional Experience:** Vis prof, Okayama Univ, Japan, 1993; Environ Toxicol Water Qual, Int J, 1991-; PROF, DEPT ENVIRON HEALTH SCI, TULANE MED CTR, NEW ORLEANS, LA, 1990-; co-ed, Toxicity Assessment: An Int J, 1986-1990; co-chmn, Int Symposia on Toxicity Assessment using Microbial Systs, 1983-; assoc prof, Nat Water Res Inst, 1981-1989; expert biodegradation, Can Nat Comt, Int Orgn Stand, 1977-; tech ed, Can Res, 1977-1983; mem, Assoc Comt Sci Criteria Environ Qual, Nat Res Coun Can, 1977-1980; adv, Wastewater Technol Ctr, 1975-; RES SCIENTIST TOXIC SUBSTANCES, NAT WATER RES INST, 1975-; res scientist wastewaters, Can Wastewater Technol Ctr, 1972-1975; res scientist eutrophication, Can Ctr Inland Waters, 1971-1972; Expert, Food Agr Orgn, UN, 1968-; Res scientist marine biochem, BC Res Coun, 1966-1968. **Research Statement & Publications:** Biodegradation of toxic substances; development of standard procedure for assessing the persistence of new substances in the natural environments; lake and river eutrophication; biological treatment of toxic industrial wastewaters; environmental toxicology; biotechnology. **Mailing Address:** Nat Water Res Inst, PO Box 5050, Burlington, ON L7R 4A6, Can. **Fax:** 905-336-4989. **E-Mail:** dickson.liu@cciw.ca

LIU, FRED WEI JUI, PHYSICAL CHEMISTRY. **Personal Data:** b Canton, China, January 29, 1926; American citizen; m 1961. **Education:** St John's Univ, China, BS, 1948; Temple Univ, MA, 1950; Lehigh Univ, PhD (chem), 1952. **Professional Experience:** PRES, CONTINENTAL TRADING CO, 1965-; DIR, CONTINENTAL CONSULTS, INC, 1964-; chief chemist, Lester Labs, Inc, 1953-1964; Res assoc, Lehigh Leather Inst, Pa, 1952-1953. **Memberships:** Am Chem Soc; Nat Asn Corrosion Engrs. **Research Statement & Publications:** Colloid or surface chemistry; detergents; cleaning and maintenance chemicals formulation; corrosion; water treatment; foreign trade; industrial chemicals. **Mailing Address:** 157 Lake Forest Lane NE, Atlanta, GA 30342-3209.

LIU, FREDERICK F, SYSTEMS DESIGN & SYSTEMS SCIENCE. **Personal Data:** b Chefoo, China, April 19, 1919; American citizen; m 1946, c 2. **Education:** Technische Hochschule, Berlin, dipl, 1939; Carnegie Inst Technol, BS, 1946; Princeton Univ, PhD (sci admin), 1951. **Honorary Degrees:** DSc, Polytech Univ Inst, China, various univ & insts, 1954. **Professional Experience:** Vis scientist & prof, Inst Mech, Chinese Acad Sci, beginning 1979; guest lectr, Technische Univ, Berlin, beginning 1970; vis scientist, Kyoto Univ, Japan, beginnning 1967; vis lectr, Cambridge Univ, Eng, 1964; vis lectr, Mass Inst Technol, 1956; SCI DIR & PRES, QUANTUM DYNAMICS INC, 1959-; exec vpres, Dresser Dynamics, Inc, 1957-1959; dir res, Dresser Dynamics, Inc, 1957; res eng specialist, Rockethyne & Atomics Int, NAm Aviation, Inc, 1955-1957; res assoc, Princeton Univ,

1952-1955; res asst, Princeton Univ, 1950-1952. **Memberships:** Sigma Xi; Am Phys Soc; Am Inst Aeronaut & Astronaut; assoc fel Int Inst Refrigeration; fel Am Inst Elec Eng. **Research Statement & Publications:** Extremely fast, dynamic and transient phenomena relating to propulsion, weapon, nuclear and space; low temperature physical phenomena, trans-regine viscosity effects on fluid flow theory, together with the development of a range of modern instrumentation and computing technologies. **Mailing Address:** Quantum Dynamics Co Inc, 6414 Independence Ave, Woodland Hills, CA 91367-2607. **Fax:** 818-719-0147.

LIU, FU-WEN (FRANK), POMOLOGY, POSTHARVEST HORTICULTURE. **Personal Data:** b Taiwan. **Education:** Taiwan Univ, BS, 1957; Cornell Univ, MS, 1969, PhD (pomol), 1974. **Professional Experience:** EMER PROF HORT, NAT TAIWAN UNIV, 1992-; FAO consult, 1987-1988; from asst prof to prof pomol, Cornell Univ, 1974-1991; Horticulturist, Sino-Am Joint Comn Rural Reconstruct, 1969-1971. **Memberships:** Am Soc Hort Sci; Sigma Xi. **Research Statement & Publications:** Postharvest physiology with emphasis on the control mechanism of maturation and ripening of fruits and storage methods of fruits. **Mailing Address:** Dept Hort Nat Taiwan Univ, Roosevelt Rd Sect 4, Taipei, Taiwan.

LIU, GANG-YU, CHEMISTRY. **Personal Data:** b Zhengzhou, China, April 19, 1964; m 1987, Xiaoyuan. **Education:** Peking Univ, China, BS, 1988; Princeton Univ, MS, 1990, PhD, 1992. **Professional Experience:** ASST PROF CHEM, WAYNE STATE UNIV, beginning 1994; Camille & Henry Dreyfus fel, 1994; Postdoctoral assoc, Univ Calif, Berkeley, 1992-1994; miller res fel, Miller Res Inst Basic Res Sci, 1992-1994. **Memberships:** AAAS; Am Chem Soc; Am Phys Soc; Am Vacuum Soc. **Research Statement & Publications:** Materials, development, modification; nondestructive evaluation. **Mailing Address:** Dept Chem, Wayne State Univ, 73 Chem 5101 Cass Ave, Detroit, MI 48202. **Fax:** 313-577-8822. **E-Mail:** gyl@chem.wayne.edu

LIU, HAIYING, MAGNETIC RESONANCE IMAGING, BIOMEDICAL ENGINEERING. **Personal Data:** b Shanghai, China, 1963. **Education:** Jilin Univ, BS, 1985; Univ Minn, PhD (solid state physics), 1991. **Professional Experience:** ASST PROF RADIOL, UNIV MINN, 1996-; Staff scientist, Picker Int Inc, 1991-1996. **Memberships:** Am Phys Soc. **Research Statement & Publications:** Develop a better magnetic resonance imaging system for clinical diagnosis and interventional procedure; reserch and develop new medical devices for minimally invasive surgical procedures; solid state device physics; fabrication and application in medicine. **Mailing Address:** Dept Radiol, Univ Minn, Box 292, 420 Delaware St SE, Minneapolis, MN 55455. **Fax:** 612-626-1951. **E-Mail:** liuxx105@tc.umn.edu

LIU, HAN-SHOU, EARTH PHYSICS, SPACE PHYSICS. **Personal Data:** b Hunan, China, March 9, 1930; American citizen; m 1957, c 2. **Education:** Cornell Univ, MS, 1962, PhD, 1963. **Honors & Awards:** Apollo Achievement Award, NASA, 1969. **Professional Experience:** GEOPHYSICIST, GEODYNAMICS BR, GODDARD SPACE FLIGHT CTR, NASA, as of 2001; SCIENTIST, GODDARD SPACE FLIGHT CTR, NASA, 1965-; res assoc, Nat Acad Sci, 1963-1964. **Memberships:** Fel AAAS; Am Astron Soc; Am Geophys Union; Am Inst Aeronaut & Astronaut; Planetary Soc. **Research Statement & Publications:** Physics of the earth; planetary interiors. **Mailing Address:** Goddard Space Flight Ctr, NASA, Code 921, Greenbelt, MD 20771. **E-Mail:** hanshou@denali.gsfc.nasa.gov

LIU, HAO-WEN, MECHANICS, MATERIALS SCIENCE. **Personal Data:** b China, August 20, 1926; American citizen; m 1955, c 5. **Education:** Univ Ill, BS, 1954, MS, 1956, PhD (appl mech), 1959. **Professional Experience:** RETIRED; prof mech & aeronaut eng, Syracuse Univ, 1984-1993; prof mat sci, Syracuse Univ, 1968-1984; assoc prof metall, Syracuse Univ, 1963-1968; sr res fel, Calif Inst Technol, 1961-1963; asst prof appl mech, Univ Ill, 1959-1961. **Memberships:** Am Soc Mech Engrs; Am Inst Mech Engrs; Am Soc Testing & Mat; Sigma Xi. **Research Statement & Publications:** Mechanical behavior and properties of materials and applied mechanics. **Mailing Address:** 1040 Continentals Way, Belmont, CA 94002.

LIU, HENRY, FLUID MECHANICS. **Personal Data:** b Peking, China, June 3, 1936; m 1964. **Education:** Nat Taiwan Univ, BS, 1959; Colo State Univ, MS, 1963, PhD (fluid mech), 1966. **Honors & Awards:** Aerospace Div Award, Am Soc Civil Engrs; Distinguished Lectr Award, Int Freight Pipeline Soc. **Professional Experience:** PROF EMER CIVIL ENG, UNIV MO-COLUMBIA, as of 2003; chmn, Exec Comt, Aerospace Div, Am Soc Civil Engrs, 1989-1990; endowed chair, James C Dowell, 1988-; bd dirs, US Wind Eng Res Coun, 1985-1989; prof, Natural Gas Pipeline Co, 1983-1987; Capsule Pipeline res grants, US Dept Energy, 1978-1981 & NSF grants, 1980-1986; vis prof, Univ Melbourne, Australia, 1980; prof civil eng, Univ Mo-Columbia, beginning 1977; prin investr water resources res grants, Dept Interior, 1966-1968; from asst prof to assoc prof, Univ Mo-columbia, 1965-1977. **Memberships:** Am Soc Civil Engrs; Am Wind Energy Asn; Sigma Xi; US Wind Eng Res Coun; Int Freight Pipeline Soc (pres, 1989-1993). **Research Statement & Publications:** Electrokinetics; exploration of the physics of streaming potential fluctuations and the utilization of this phenomenon to study turbulence characteristics in liquid flows; dispersion of pollutants in river; hydraulic capsule pipeline; wind pressure inside buildings; flow measurement; cherepnov water lifter; hydropower; wind damage mitigation; wind energy utilization. **Mailing Address:** Dept Civil Eng, Univ Mo-Columbia, E1511A Lafferre Hall, Columbia, MO 65211. **E-Mail:** liuh@missouri.edu

LIU, HOUNG-ZUNG, BIOCHEMICAL & PLANT PROTOPLAST GENETICS. **Personal Data:** b China, January 23, 1931; m 1969, c 2. **Education:** Taiwan Prov Col, BS, 1953; NDak State Col, MS, 1959; Cornell Univ, PhD (genetics, biochem, plant physiol), 1964. **Professional Experience:** FAC EMER, STATE UNIV NY, PLATTSBURGH, as of 2004; dean, fac arts & sci, State Univ NY Col, Plattsburgh, beginning 1983; actg dean, Fac Arts & Sci, 1981-1982; res collabr, Brookhaven Nat Lab, 1973-1974; prof genetics & chmn, Dept Biol Sci, 1969-1981; NIH spec res fel, Marquette Univ, 1967-1968; assoc prof genetics, Fac Arts & Sci, State Univ NY Col, Plattsburgh, 1964-1969; asst gen genetics, Cornell Univ, 1959-1964; asst cytol, Taiwan Agr Res Inst, Taipei, 1954-1956. **Memberships:** AAAS; Am Chem Soc; Genetics Soc Am; Int Plant Tissue Asn. **Research Statement & Publications:** Tryptophan operon mutants of Escherichia coli and indoleglycerolphosphate synthetase; plant protoplast fusion and culture; plantlet regeneration. **Mailing Address:** State Univ NY, Dept Bio Sci, 101 Broad St, Plattsburgh, NY 12901.

LIU, HSING-JANG, SYNTHETIC METHODS NATURAL PRODUCTS SYNTHESIS. **Personal Data:** b Kiang-Su, China, December 2, 1942; m 1966, Hsiao-Ku; c Richard, Jonathan & Mimi. **Education:** Nat Taiwan Norm Univ, BS, 1964; Univ NB, Fredericton, PhD (chem), 1968. **Honors & Awards:** Int Union Pure & Appl Chem Award, Can Nat Comt, 1984. **Professional Experience:** PROF EMER CHEM, UNIV ALTA, 1998-; natural prod ed, Can J Chem, 1995-; vis examr chem, Chinese Univ Hong Kong, 1991-1994; sci consult, Torcan Chem Ltd, Aurora, Can, 1984-; prof chem, Univ Alta, 1983-1998; from asst prof to assoc prof, Univ Alta, 1971-1983; teaching & res assoc, Univ NB, Fredericton, 1970-1971; res assoc, Columbia Univ, 1969-1970; fel chem, Univ NB, Fredericton, 1968-1969. **Memberships:** Am Chem Soc; fel Chem Inst Can. **Research Statement & Publications:** Natural products, isolation, identification and synthesis; development of novel synthetic methods. **Mailing Address:** Dept Chem, Univ Alta, Edmonton, AB T6G 2G2, Can. **Fax:** 780-492-8231. **E-Mail:** hsing-jang.liu@ualberta.ca

LIU, HUA-KUANG, LASER OPTICS, ELECTROOPTICS. **Personal Data:** b Kueilin, China, September 2, 1939; American citizen; m, c Tien-Wen Solomon & Ren-wen Lawrence. **Education:** Nat Taiwan Univ, BS, 1962; Univ Iowa, MS, 1965; Johns Hopkins Univ, PhD (elec eng), 1969. **Professional Experience:** PROF, NAT TAIWAN UNIV, 2002-; pres, Lumin Inc, 1998-2002; VIS SCIENTIST, OAK RIDGE NAT LAB, 1995-; prof, Univ South Ala, 1985-1998; sr res eng, Jet Propulsion Lab, Calif Inst Technol, 1984-1995; vis prof, Nat Taiwan Univ & Univ Wis-Madison, 1982-1983; vis assoc prof elec eng, Stanford Univ, 1975-1976; consult, NASA Marshall Space Flight Ctr, US Army Missile Command, 1973; res grants, NSF, 1971-1973 & 1975-1977 & NASA, 1973-1978; res grants, Univ Ala, Tuscaloosa, 1970-1971; consult, Optimal Data Corp, Ala, 1969-; from asst prof to prof elec eng, Univ Ala, 1969-1984; res asst, Johns Hopkins Univ & jr instr, Eve Col, 1965-1969; instr elec eng, Va Mil Inst, 1964-1965; res asst, Univ Iowa, 1963-1964; consult, Newport Res Corp, Rockwell Int. **Memberships:** Sr mem Inst Elec & Electronics Engrs; fel Optical Soc Am; fel Soc Photo-Instrumentation Engrs. **Research Statement & Publications:** Solid-state electronics; nonlinear optical image processing; optical pattern recognition, holography and holographic nondestructive testing; halftone contact screens for printing. **Mailing Address:** Oak Ridge Nat Lab, P O Box 2008, Oak Ridge, TN 37831. **E-Mail:** liuhk@aol.com

LIU, HUNG-KUNG, STATISTICS. **Education:** Nat Cent Univ, Taiwan, BS; Cornell UNiv, MS & PhD (Statist). **Professional Experience:** MATH STATISTICIAN, STATIST ENG DIV, NAT INST STAND TECHNOL, as of 2001. **Memberships:** Am Statistical Asn, Sigma Xi-Scientific Res Soc. **Research Statement & Publications:** Validity of computer intensive methods; prediction through empirical linear models; multivariate tolerance regions. **Mailing Address:** Statistical Eng Div, Nat Inst Stand & Technol, NIST N Rm 353, Gaithersburg, MD 20899. **Fax:** 301-990-4127. **E-Mail:** hung-kung.liu@nist.gov

LIU, HUNG-WEN, BIO-ORGANIC CHEMISTRY, MECHANISTIC ENZYMOLOGY. **Personal Data:** b Taipei, Taiwan, August 28, 1952. **Education:** Tang-hai Univ, Taiwan, BS, 1974; Columbia Univ, PhD (chem), 1981. **Honors & Awards:** Jr Fac Award, Am Chem Soc, 1985, Horace Isabelle Award, 1993; Res Career Develop Award, NIH, 1990. **Professional Experience:** GEORGE H. HITCHINGS REGENTS CHAIR DRUG DESIGN, UNIV TEX, as of 2003; PROF CHEM & BIOCHEM, UNIV TEX, as of 2001; PROF PHARM, UNIV TEX, as of 2001; distinguished McKnight Univ Prof, Univ Minn, 1999; prof bio-org chem, Univ Minn, beginning 1994; from asst prof to assoc prof, Univ Minn, 1984-1994; Distinguished New Fac Chem, Dryfuss Found, 1984; fel enzym, Univ Minn, 1981-1984. **Memberships:** Am Chem Soc; AAAS; Am Soc Biochem & Molecular Biol; Chinese Am Chem Soc. **Research Statement & Publications:** Bio-organic chemistry; mechanistic enzymology. **Mailing Address:** Org & Biochem Div, Univ Tex, PHR 3 206B WEL 5 235, Austin, TX 78712-0165. **Fax:** 512-471-2746. **E-Mail:** h.w.liu@mail.utexas.edu

LIU, JIA-MING, OPTICS, ELECTRICAL ENGINEERING. **Personal Data:** b Taichung, Taiwan, July 13, 1953; American citizen; m 1990, Vida; c Janelle J. **Education:** Nat Chiao Tung Univ, BS, 1975; Harvard Univ, SM, 1979, PhD (appl physics), 1982. **Honors & Awards:** Patent Award, Gen Tel & Electronics Corp, 1986, 1987, 1988, 1989. **Professional Experience:** PROF ELEC ENG, UNIV CALIF, LOS ANGELES, 1993-; mem, Battelle Columbus Div, US Army, 1989-1990; consult, Jaycor, 1987-; assoc prof, Univ Calif, Los Angeles, 1986-1993; sr mem tech staff, Gen Tel & Electronics Corp Labs, Inc, 1983-1986; asst prof elec eng, State Univ NY, Buffalo, 1982-1984. **Memberships:** Fel Optical Soc Am; Sr mem Inst Elec & Electronics Engrs Laser & Electro-Optics Soc; Am Phys Soc; Sigma Xi. **Research Statement & Publications:** Nonlinear Optics, ultrafast optics, laser chaos, ultrafast processes, and optical commun Ultrashort laser pulses and applications; nonlinear optics; optical wave propagation; semiconductor lasers optoelectronics and photonics, fiber optics. **Mailing Address:** Elec Eng Dept, Univ Calif, 56-147C Eng IV, Los Angeles, CA 90095-1594. **Fax:** 310-206-8495. **E-Mail:** liu@ee.ucla.edu

LIU, JIN-ZHOU, INFANT NUTRITION, PREVENTIVE MEDICINE. **Personal Data:** b Teng-Zhou, China, October 20, 1955; m 1984, Shen Pan; c Fang Yuan & Devin R. **Education:** Shandong Med Univ, China, MD, 1982, MS, 1985; Pa State Univ, PhD (nutrit), 1993. **Honors & Awards:** Nat Med Res Award, Chinese Ministry Pub Health, 1986; Young Outstanding Scientist Award, Chinese Nutrit Soc, 1988; Med Discoverer in 20th Century, Chinese Acad Med Sci, 1989. **Professional Experience:** AT, ROSS PROD DIV PD 98, ABBOTT LAB, as of 2002; adj asst prof & prin investr, Pa State Univ, 1995-1996; PROJ LEADER RES & DEVELOP, ABBOTT LABS, 1994-; res asst prof, Pa State Univ, 1993-1994; Asst prof nutrit, Shandong Med Univ, 1986-1987. **Memberships:** Am Soc Nutrit Sci; Am Soc Clin Nutrit; Asn Gnotobiotics; Chinese Nutrit Soc. **Research Statement & Publications:** Dietary factors for preventing cancer; nutritional factors for preventing infant diseases; novel approaches for preventing infectious diseases. **Mailing Address:** Ross Prod Div pd 98, Abbott Labs, 625 Cleveland Ave, Columbus, OH 43215. **Fax:** 614-624-3453.

LIU, JOHN, OPHTHALMIC PHARMACOLOGY. **Personal Data:** b Taiwan. **Professional Experience:** ASSOC PROF, DEPT OPHTHAL, UNIV CALIF LOS ANGELES, 1991-; Assoc scientist, Eye Res Inst, 1988-1991. **Mailing Address:** Dept Ophthal, Univ Calif Los Angeles San Diego, 9500 Gilman Dr, La Jolla, CA 92093-0946.

LIU, JOHN K(UNGFU), MECHANICS. **Personal Data:** b Hankow, China, August 22, 1930; American citizen; m 1957. **Education:** Univ Pa, BSME, 1952; Ill Inst Technol, MS, 1957. **Professional Experience:** VPRES, CLUTCH DIV, PHILADELPHIA GEAR CORP, 1968-; vpres, Force Control, Inc, 1962-1968; mgr marine tech lab, Stromberg Carlson Co Div, Gen Dynamics Co, 1960-1962; dir marine tech dept, Tech Ctr, 1959-1960; from sr proj engr to actg dir res & develop, Clearing Div, US Industs, 1957-1960; from design engr to proj engr, Int Harvester Co, 1952-1957; Struct engr, Shih & Assoc, 1948-1952. **Memberships:** Am Soc Mech Engrs; Sigma Xi; Am Soc Inventors. **Research Statement & Publications:** Oceanographic instruments and devices; solid and fluid mechanics; marine propulsion equipment; pressure vessel design and development; fluid shear power transmission devices; industrial electronics and transducers. **Mailing Address:** 2749 Paige St, Lower Burrell, PA 15068-3111.

LIU, JOSEPH JENG-FU, CELESTIAL & THEORETICAL MECHANICS, APPLIED MATHEMATICS. **Personal Data:** b Chiangsi, China, October 24, 1940; m 1971, c 3. **Education:** Cheng Kung Univ, Taiwan, BS, 1962; Auburn Univ, MS, 1966, PhD (celestial mech), 1971. **Honors & Awards:** P V H Weems Award, Inst Navig, 1988. **Professional Experience:** CHIEF, ASTRODYNAMICS DIV, HQ USSPACE COMMAND, 1986-; adj, asst prof appl math, Univ Colo, Colorado Springs, 1982-; mem tech staff, Astrodyn Aerospace Defense Command, 1977-1986; mem res staff astrodyn, Northrop Serv Inc, Huntsville, Ala, 1971-1977; teaching asst appl mech, Auburn Univ, 1966-1971 & Cheng Kung Univ, 1963-1964. **Memberships:** Assoc fel Am Inst Aeronaut & Astronaut; Am

Astronaut Soc; Am Astron Soc. **Research Statement & Publications:** General, special perturbation and semi-analytic theories, their applications for the orbital and attitude motions of an artificial satellite perturbed by conservative and nonconservative forces. **Mailing Address:** HQ US Space Command, DOJY Stop 7, Peterson AFB, CO 80914-3040. **Fax:** 719-380-3496.

LIU, JOSEPH T C, PHYSICS. **Education:** Calif Inst Technol, PhD. **Professional Experience:** PROF, DIV ENG BROWN UNIV, as of 2006. **Memberships:** ASME; Fel Am Phys Soc. **Mailing Address:** Div Eng, Brown Univ Box D, Providence, RI 02912. **Fax:** 401-863-3301. **E-Mail:** Joseph_Liu@brown.edu

LIU, J(OSEPH) T(SU) C(HIEH), FLUID MECHANICS. **Personal Data:** b Shanghai, China, November 9, 1934; American citizen; m 1964, c 3. **Education:** Univ Mich, BSE, 1957, MSE, 1958; Calif Inst Technol, PhD (aeronaut), 1964. **Honors & Awards:** Nat Award, Inst Aeronaut Sci, 1958. **Professional Experience:** PROF ENG, BROWN UNIV, 1973-; vis, Dept Math, Imperial Col, Univ London, 1972-1973 & 1979-1980; Consult, Systs Div, 1969-1970; from asst prof to assoc prof, Brown Univ, 1966-1973; consult, Space Systs Div, Avco Corp, Mass, 1966-1967; res assoc aerospace & mech sci, Gas Dynamics Lab, Princeton Univ, 1964-1966; propulsion engr aerothermodyn group, Gen Dynamics & Convair, 1958-1959. **Memberships:** Am Soc Mech Engrs; Am Phys Soc; Am Meteorol Soc; Am Inst Aeronaut & Astronaut. **Research Statement & Publications:** Coherent structures in turbulent shear flows, nonlinear hydrodynamic stability and transition; aeroacoustics; fluidized bed instabilities; published over 20 article. **Mailing Address:** Div Eng Brown Univ, Campus Box D, Providence, RI 02912-9127. **Fax:** 401-863-1157. **E-Mail:** joseph_liu@brown.edu

LIU, JUN S, MATHEMATICAL STATISTICS. **Personal Data:** b Beijing, China, April 26, 1965. **Education:** Beijieng Univ, BS, 1986; Univ Chicago, PhD (statist), 1991. **Professional Experience:** PROF STATIST, HARVARD UNIV, as of 2004; vis fac, Nat Ctr Biotechnol Info, NIH, 1993; asst prof statist, Harvard Univ, beginning 1991. **Memberships:** Am Statist Asn; Inst Math Statist. **Research Statement & Publications:** Bayesian methodology in statistical analysis, including theory, applications and computing, especially applications in molecular biology and genetics; Markov chain theory and missing data problems. **Mailing Address:** Dept Statist, Harvard Univ, Cambridge, MA 02138-2901. **E-Mail:** jliu@stat.harvard.edu

LIU, K J RAY, SIGNAL PROCESSING, COMMUNICATIONS. **Personal Data:** b Taiwan, February 11, 1961; American citizen. **Education:** Nat Taiwan Univ, BS, 1983; Univ Calif, Los Angeles, PhD (elec eng), 1990. **Honors & Awards:** Young Investr Award, NSF, 1994. **Professional Experience:** PROF ELEC COMPUT ENG, UNIV MD, as of 2005; chief scientist, Neo Paradigm Lab, 1996-1997; vis assoc prof, Stanford Univ, 1996-1997; assoc prof, Univ Md, beginning 1995; asst prof, Univ Md, 1990-1995. **Research Statement & Publications:** Signal processing with application to image video, wireless communication, networking and medical technology. **Mailing Address:** Univ Md, Dept Elec Eng, 2232 Kim Bldg, College Park, MD 20742. **E-Mail:** kjrliu@isr.umd.edu

LIU, KAI, CONTROL & SYSTEMS, MODELING & SIMULATION. **Personal Data:** b Beijing, China, June 20, 1948; m Hong Xu; c Julie. **Education:** Beijing Normal Univ, China, BS, 1980; Beijing Polytech Univ, China, MS, 1982; Ga Inst Technol, PhD (elec eng), 1990. **Professional Experience:** Specialist, Elec Eng Dept, Univ Tex Arlington, 1991-; SR RES ENGR, AUTOMATION & ROBOTICS RES INST, UNIV TEX, ARLINGTON, 1990-; Lectr, Elec Eng Dept, Beijing Polytech Univ, 1982-1986. **Memberships:** Sigma Xi; Inst Elec & Electronics Engrs; Inst Elect & Electronics Engrs Robotics & Automation Soc; Inst Elec & Electronics Engrs Control Systs Soc; Inst Elec & Electronics Engrs Neural Networks Coun. **Research Statement & Publications:** Theoretical issues about fuzzy logic control and neural nets and their applications in automatic control, material handling, system identification and signal processing; continuous robust techniques to various industrial applications. **Mailing Address:** 3325 Mason Dr, Plano, TX 75025. **Fax:** 817-794-5952. **E-Mail:** kliu@arri.uta.edu

LIU, LEROY FONG, DNA TOPOISOMERASES, CANCER PHARMACOLOGY. **Personal Data:** b Tao-yuan, Taiwan, July 28, 1949; American citizen; c 2. **Education:** Nat Taiwan Univ, Taiwan, BS, 1971; Univ Calif, Berkeley, PhD (biophys chem), 1977. **Professional Experience:** PROF BIOCHEM, JOHNS HOPKINS UNIV, 1988-; Vis prof, Inst Molecular Biol, Academia Sinica, Taiwan, 1986-1987; from asst prof to assoc prof, Johns Hopkins Univ, 1980-1988; Fel molecular biol, Harvard Univ, 1977-1978 & Univ Calif, San Francisco, 1978-1980. **Memberships:** Am Soc Biochem & Molecular Biol; Am Asn Cancer Res; Am Math Soc. **Research Statement & Publications:** Biological functions of multiple DNA topoisomerases; DNA topoisomerases as therapeutic targets. **Mailing Address:** Dept Pharmacol, UMDNJ-Robert Wood Johnson Med Sch 675 Hoes Lane, Piscataway, NJ 08854-5635. **Fax:** 732-235-4073. **E-Mail:** lliu@umdnj.edu

LIU, LIU, THEORY OF ELECTRONIC PROPERTIES OF SOLIDS. **Personal Data:** b Shanghai, China, August 12, 1930; m 1956, c 3. **Education:** Univ Taiwan, BS, 1954; Univ Chicago, MS, 1957, PhD (physics), 1961. **Professional Experience:** PROF EMER, DEPT PHYSICS, NORTHWESTERN UNIV, 2002-; Fulbright sr res scholar, France, 1975-1976; prof physics, Northwestern Univ, Ill, 1974-2002; from asst prof to assoc prof, Northwestern Univ, Ill, 1961-1974; consult, Argonne Nat Lab, 1961-1964. **Memberships:** Fel Am Phys Soc. **Research Statement & Publications:** Theory of narrow-gap and zero-gap semiconductors and magnetic semiconductors. **Mailing Address:** Dept Physics, Northwestern Univ 633 Clark St, Evanston, IL 60201.

LIU, LIXIN, MATHEMATICS. **Education:** Simon Fraser Univ, PhD, 1993. **Professional Experience:** STAFF, DEPT MATHS & STATIST, SIMON FRASER UNIV, as of 2006. **Mailing Address:** Dept Math & Statist, Simon Fraser Univ, Burnaby, BC V5A 1S8, Can. **Fax:** 604-291-5052. **E-Mail:** liu@math.sfu.ca

LIU, LON-CHANG, PHYSICS, NUCLEAR STRUCTURE. **Personal Data:** b China, American citizen. **Education:** Univ Neuchatel, PhD (physics), 1973. **Professional Experience:** TECH STAFF MEM, LOS ALAMOS NAT LAB, 1979-; asst prof physics, City Univ New York, 1975-1979; instr, City Univ New York, 1973-1975. **Memberships:** Am Phys Soc; Sigma Xi. **Research Statement & Publications:** Theoretical intermediate energy nuclear physics; meson nucleus interaction; neural network. **Mailing Address:** Los Alamos Nat Lab, T16, MS B243, PO Box 1663, Los Alamos, NM 87545. **Fax:** 505-667-9671. **E-Mail:** liu@lanl.gov

LIU, MAO-ZU, MATHEMATICAL MODELING OF PHYSIOLOGICAL SYSTEM & BIOMEDICAL ENGINEERING, TECHNICAL MANAGEMENT. **Personal Data:** b Sichuan, China, June 27, 1946; m 1989, Jane; c Rose D & Thomas Y. **Education:** Univ Sci & Technol China, BS, 1965; Temple Univ, MA, 1984; Drexel Univ, PhD (biomed eng), 1989. **Honors & Awards:** Award First Sci Convocation of Anhui Prov, State Coun Anhui Prov, China & State Coun, People's Repub China, 1978. **Professional Experience:** DIR DEPT BIOMED ENG, BRONX-LEBANON HOSP CTR, 1992-; res biomed engr, Westchester County Med Ctr, 1991-1992; asst prof, Univ Tenn, 1989-1992; researcher, Seismic Telecommun Network, Shanghai, China, 1980-1981; lectr physics, Univ Sci & Technol, Shanghai, China, 1979-1980; researcher & mgr, Anhui Inst Seismol, Anhui, China, 1972-1979. **Memberships:** Inst Elec & Electronics Engrs; Biomed Eng Soc. **Research Statement & Publications:** Mathematical modeling of the cardiovascular system and the application of computer techniques to cardiovascular dynamics and pharmacokinetics; the design and optimization of devices used in cardiovascular treatment and biomedical instrumentation. **Mailing Address:** 7 Belmont St, White Plains, NY 10605.

LIU, MATTHEW J P, MATHEMATICS. **Personal Data:** b Peking, China, July 19, 1935; American citizen; m 1961, c 2. **Education:** Lafayette Col, BS & BA, 1958; Ill Inst Technol, MS, 1961; Ind Univ, PhD (math), 1975. **Professional Experience:** PROF EMER MATH, UNIV WIS, STEVENS POINT, as of 2003; prof math, Univ Wis, Stevens Point, beginning 1976; NSF fel, Ind Univ, 1967-1968; from instr to assoc prof, Univ Wis, Stevens Point, 1961-1976. **Memberships:** Math Asn Am; Am Math Soc; Nat Coun Teachers Math. **Research Statement & Publications:** Mathematics, summability. **Mailing Address:** Dept Math, Univ Wis, 2100 Main St, Stevens Point, WI 54481-3871.

LIU, MAW-SHUNG, MEDICAL PHYSIOLOGY, SURGERY. **Personal Data:** b Taiwan, February 2, 1940; m 1966, Min-chan; c Chien-Ye. **Education:** Kaohsiung Med Col, Taiwan, DDS, 1964; Univ Ky, MSc, 1970; Univ Ottawa, PhD (physiol), 1976. **Professional Experience:** Vis prof, Kaohaiung Med Col & Chang Gung Med Col, 1989-; mem, Surg, Anesthesiol & Trauma Study Sect, NIH, 1988-1992; Hunan Med Univ, China, 1988; vis prof, Zhejiang Med Univ China, 1986, 1988; vis prof, Beijing Med Univ, 1984, 1986, 1992; hon prof, Nanjing Med Col, China, 1984; PROF PHARMACOL & PHYSIOL SCI, SCH MED, ST LOUIS UNIV, 1982-; assoc prof physiol, Bowman Gray Sch Med, Wake Forest Univ, Winston-Salem, NC, 1978-1982; asst prof physiol, Sch Med, La State Univ Med Ctr, New Orleans, 1976-1978; instr physiol, Sch Med, La State Univ Med Ctr, New Orleans, 1974-1976; Alcoholism & Drug Addiction Res Found Ont res scholar, 1973-1974; Med Res Coun Can fel, 1970-1973; intern path, Med Ctr, Univ Ky, 1968-1969; staff dent & lectr oral surg, Chinese Army Hosp, Kaohsiung Med Col Hosp, Taiwan, 1964-1968. **Memberships:** Int Soc Heart Res; Shock Soc; Am Physiol Soc. **Research Statement & Publications:** Myocardial and hepatic intermediary metabolism in endotoxic and septic shock; published over 60 papers and 60 abstracts. **Mailing Address:** Dept Pharmacol & Physiol Sci, Sch Med, St Louis Univ, 1402 S Grand Blvd Rm M 362, St Louis, MO 63104. **Fax:** 314-577-8233. **E-Mail:** lium@slu.edu

LIU, MIAN, TECTONO PHYSICS, NUMERICAL MODELLING. **Personal Data:** b Sichuan, China, October 15, 1960. **Education:** Nanjing Univ, People's Repub China, BSc, 1982; McGill Univ, MSc, 1985; Univ Ariz, PhD (geophysics), 1989. **Professional Experience:** PROF GEOL SCI, UNIV MO, as of 2002; Fel geophys, Minn Supercomputer Inst, 1989-1990 & Pa State Univ, 1990-1994. **Memberships:** Am Geophys Union. **Research Statement & Publications:** Geodynamics; mantle convection; deformation and evolution of lithosphere; numerical modelling. **Mailing Address:** Dept Geol Sci, Univ MO, 101 Geol Bldg, Columbia, MO 65211-1380. **Fax:** 573-882-5458. **E-Mail:** lium@missouri.edu

LIU, MICHAEL T H, PHYSICAL CHEMISTRY, PHYSICAL ORGANIC CHEMISTRY. **Personal Data:** b Hong Kong, China, March 1, 1939; Canadian citizen; m 1975, Betty; c David, Stephen & Peter. **Education:** St Dunstan's Univ, BSc, 1961; St Francis Xavier, MA, 1964; Univ Ottawa, PhD (phys chem), 1967. **Honors & Awards:** Haut Niveau Award, Ministry Educ, Paris, 1989; Int Collabr Award, Nat Sci & Eng Res Coun Can, 1991 & 1993. **Professional Experience:** Res chmn, Kyushu Univ, Japan, 1997-1998; PROF EMER, UNIV PRINCE EDWARD ISLAND, 1997-; vis prof, Univ Bordeaux, 1993 & 1995; adj prof, Univ Bordeaux, 1988-1989; ed, CRC Press, Boca Raton, Fla, 1987; sabbatical leave, Univ BC, 1975 & Univ Geneva, 1982; prof chem, Univ Prince Edward Island, 1980-1997; adj prof, Dalhousie Univ, 1979-1985; Def Res Bd Can grant-in-aid, 1974-1976; Nat Sci & Eng Res Coun Can grant-in-aid, 1968-; from asst prof to assoc prof, Univ Prince Edward Island, 1968-1980; nat res coun fel, Univ Reading, 1967-1968; group leader qual control, Chemcell Ltd, 1964; technician, Can Celanese Ltd, 1961-1962. **Memberships:** Fel Chem Inst Can; Inter-Am Photochem Soc. **Research Statement & Publications:** Carbene chemistry; synthesis of new diazirines and 1, 2-hydrogen migration; cyclopropanation of electrophilic and ambiphilic carbenes; thermolysis, photolysis and laser photolysis of diazirines; 1, 2-H shift in ammonium ylide; 1, 5 cyclization of pyridinium ylide; cycloaddition of carbenes to carbon 60. **Mailing Address:** Dept Chem, Univ PEI, Charlottetown, PE C1A 4P3, Can. **Fax:** 902-566-0632. **E-Mail:** liu@upei.ca

LIU, MING-BIANN, PHYSICAL CHEMISTRY, CHEMICAL ENGINEERING. **Personal Data:** b Chang-Hua, Taiwan, June 22, 1942; m 1975, Yola; c Jomay & Joy. **Education:** Cheng-Kung Univ, Taiwan, BS, 1968; Ill Inst Technol, PhD (chem), 1974, MS, 1980. **Professional Experience:** AM SKYNET ELECTRONIC CO, 1992-; Dow Chem Co, Pittsburg, 1988-1992; asst chemist, Dow Chem Co, Midland, 1981-1988; asst chemist, Chem Eng Div, 1978-1981; res, Chem Div, Argonne Nat Lab, 1976-1978; res & teaching, Univ Kans, 1974-1975. **Memberships:** Am Chem Soc; Electrochem Soc. **Research Statement & Publications:** High temperature materials and technology; plasma surface interaction; gas surface interaction; electrochemical processes and technology; flame retardants. **Mailing Address:** 386 Mount Sequoia Pl, Clayton, CA 94517.

LIU, MING-TSAN, COMPUTER SCIENCE, COMPUTER ENGINEERING. **Personal Data:** b Taiwan, China, August 30, 1934; American citizen; m 1966, c 3. **Education:** Cheng Kung Univ, BS, 1957; Univ Pa, MS, 1961, PhD (elec eng), 1964. **Professional Experience:** Ed, Inst Elec & Electronics Engrs Trans Comput, 1982-1986 & ed-in-chief, 1986-; consult, AT&T Bell Labs, Columbus, Ohio, 1982-1984; distinguished vis, Comput Soc, Inst Elec & Electronics Engrs, 1981-1984; PROF COMPUT SCI & ENG, OHIO STATE UNIV, 1978-; consult, Burroughs Corp, Paoli, Pa, 1977; assoc prof, Ohio State Univ, 1969-1978; asst prof, Moore Sch Elec Eng, Univ Pa, 1965-1969; Consult, Comput Command & Control Co, Philadelphia, Pa, 1964-1965; instr, Moore Sch Elec Eng, Univ Pa, 1962-1965; Asst elec eng, Cheng Kung Univ, 1959-1960. **Memberships:** Fel Inst Elec & Electronics Engrs; Asn Comput Mach; Sigma Xi. **Research Statement & Publications:** Computer architecture; computer networks; distributed processing; microcomputer systems; computer communication. **Mailing Address:** Dept Comput Sci & Eng, Ohio State Univ, 2015 Neil Ave, Columbus, OH 43210-1277. **Fax:** 614-292-9021. **E-Mail:** mike.liu@osu.edu

LIU, PAN-TAI, APPLIED MATHEMATICS. **Personal Data:** b Taipei, Taiwan, September 22, 1941; m 1966, c 1. **Education:** Nat Taiwan Univ, BS, 1963; State Univ NY, Stony Brook, PhD (appl math), 1968. **Professional Experience:** PROF MATH, UNIV RI, KINGSTON, 1980-; assoc prof, Univ RI, Kingston, 1974-1980; vis prof, Dept Elec Eng, Nat Taiwan Univ, Taipei, Taiwan, 1974-1975; asst prof, Univ RI, Kingston, 1968-1974. **Memberships:** Am Math Soc. **Research Statement & Publications:** Optimal controls; differential games; stochastic processes. **Mailing Address:** Dept Math, Univ RI, Kingston, RI 02881.

LIU, PAUL CHI, WIND WAVE DYNAMICS, PHYSICAL OCEANOGRAPHY & COASTAL ENGINEERING. **Personal Data:** b Chefoo, China, June 18, 1935; m 1965, Teresa; c Christina. **Education:** Nat Taiwan Univ, BS, 1956; Virginia Polytech Inst, MS, 1961; Univ Mich, PhD (oceanic sci), 1977. **Professional Experience:** Fel, Coop Inst Limnol & Ecosyst Res, 1990-; Vis scholar, Univ Mich, 1978-; OCEANOGR, GREAT LAKES ENVIRON RES LAB, NAT OCEANIC & ATMOSPHERIC ADMIN, 1974-; res phys scientist, Lake Surv Ctr, Nat Ocean Surv, 1971-1974; Res phys scientist, US Lake Surv, Army CEngr, 1965-1971. **Memberships:** Am Geophys Union; Am Meterol Soc; Am Soc Civil Engrs; Soc Indust & Appl Math; Phi Kappa Phi; Sigma Xi. **Research Statement & Publications:** Study of the evolution of wind waves as time-localized processes, e.g. wave grouping, breaking waves, and freak or rogue waves. Seek new conceptualizations and new generations of ocean wave measurement system. **Mailing Address:** 2205 Commonwealth Blvd, Ann Arbor, MI 48105. **Fax:** 734-741-2055. **E-Mail:** paul.c.liu@noaa.gov

LIU, PAUL ISHEN, CLINICAL PATHOLOGY. **Personal Data:** b Taiwan, November 23, 1932; American citizen; m 1963, Grace; c Spencer. **Education:** Nat Taiwan Univ, MD, 1960; St Louis Univ, PhD (path), 1969. **Professional Experience:** CHIEF PATH, OLIVE-VIEW MED CTR, 1992-; prof path & vchmn dept, Univ Sala, 1981-1992; prof & vchmn, Med Univ SC, 1976-1980; assoc dir lab med, Med Col Ga, 1974-1976; Assoc prof path, Med Ctr, Univ Kans, 1973-1974. **Memberships:** AMA; Col Am Path Fel; Am Soc Clin Path. **Research Statement & Publications:** Leukemia; immunology. **Mailing Address:** Dept Path/A116 Oliveview Med Ctr, 14445 Oliveview Dr, Sylmar, CA 91342. **Fax:** 818-364-4065.

LIU, PHILIP L-F, HYDRODYNAMICS, COASTAL ENGINEERING. **Personal Data:** b Fu-Chu, China, December 11, 1946; m Christine; c 2. **Education:** Nat Taiwan Univ, BS, 1968; Mass Inst Technol, SM, 1971, ScD(hydrodyn), 1974. **Honors & Awards:** Walter L Huber Prize, Am Soc Civil Engrs, 1978; John G Maffatt-Frank E Nichol Harbor & Coastol Eng Award, ASCE 1997. **Professional Experience:** Vis prod inst for advanced studies in mediteranian sea, Spain, 2002-; vis prof, Nat Taiwan Univ, 1995 & Tech Univ Denmark, 1988; Nat Sci Coun fel (Taiwan), 1994; Osaka city univ fel (Japan), 1993; vis scientist, Delft Hydraulics, 1987; assoc dean, Col Eng, 1986-1987; assoc dir, Sch Civil & Environ Eng, 1985-1986; PROF CIVIL & ENVIRON ENG, CORNELL UNIV, 1983-; vis assoc, Calif Tech, 1980-1981; J S Guggenheim fel, 1980; Eng Found fel, 1979; Justice asst prof, Justice Found, 1978-1979; from asst prof to assoc prof environ eng, Cornell Univ, 1974-1983; res asst civil eng, Mass Inst Technol, 1969-1974. **Memberships:** Am Soc Civil Engrs; Am Geophys Union; Int Asn Hydraulic Res. **Research Statement & Publications:** Wave hydrodynamics in coastal engineering; coastal currents and shoreline processes; numerical methods for nonlinear free surface problems; groundwater flow modeling. **Mailing Address:** Sch Civil & Environ Eng, Cornell Univ, 118 Hollister Hall, Ithaca, NY 14853.

LIU, PINGHUI VICTOR, MEDICAL MICROBIOLOGY. **Personal Data:** b Formosa, China, February 9, 1924; American citizen; m 1959, c 2. **Education:** Tokyo Jikel-kai Sch Med, MD, 1947; Tokyo Med Sch, PhD (microbiol), 1957; Am Bd Med Microbiol, dipl, 1962. **Honors & Awards:** res career develop award, 1962-. **Professional Experience:** PROF EMER MICROBIOL & IMMUNOL, SCH MED, UNIV LOUISVILLE, as of 2003; prof microbiol & immunol, Sch Med, Univ Louisville, beginning 1981; mem, Subcomt Pseudomonas & Related Organisms, Int Comt Bact Nomenclature, 1963-; USPHS sr res fel, 1959-; from instr to prof microbiol, Sch Med, Univ Louisville, 1957-1981; res fel microbiol, Sch Med, Univ Louisville, 1956-1957; intern internal med, Louisville Gen Hosp, 1955-1956; Intern, Mercy Hosp, Cedar Rapids, Iowa, 1954-1955. **Memberships:** AAAS; Am Soc Microbiol; Infectious Dis Soc Am; NY Acad Sci. **Research Statement & Publications:** Pathogenesis and taxonomy of pseudomonads and related organisms, such as aeromonads and vibrios; extracellular toxins, such as hemolysin, lecithinase and protease; immunities to infections. **Mailing Address:** Dept Microbiol & Immunol, Univ Louisville Sch Med, 2301 S Third St, Louisville, KY 40292-0001.

LIU, PU, HUMAN GENETICS, CANCER GENETICS. **Personal Data:** b Beijing, China, June 22, 1957; American citizen; m 1985, Yao-yao. **Education:** Beijing Second Med Col, China, MD, 1982; Univ Tex, Houston, PhD (genetics), 1991. **Professional Experience:** Tech sr investr, Nat Ctr Human Genome Res Inst, NIH, 2001-; SR STAFF FEL & INVESTR HUMAN GENOME RES, NAT CTR HUMAN GENOME RES, NIH, 1993-; res assoc, Howard Hughes Med Inst, Univ Mich, 1992-1993; proj investr, M D Anderson Cancer Ctr, Univ Tex, 1991-1992; resident internal med, Peking Union Med Col, China, 1983-1985. **Memberships:** Am soc clim invest; Am soc hemat; Am Soc Human Genetics. **Research Statement & Publications:** Studing genetic control of lenken orenecil and lematipoicsis in animal models. **Mailing Address:** 49 Convent Dr Rm 3A18, Bethesda, MD 20892.

LIU, QING HUO, WAVE PROPAGATION, NUMERICAL ANALYSIS. **Personal Data:** b Fujian, China, February 4, 1963; m 1987, Tong; c Winston & Austin. **Education:** Xiamen Univ, China, BSc, 1983, MSc, 1986; Univ Ill, Urbana-Champaign, PhD (elec eng), 1989. **Honors & Awards:** Presidential Early Career Award for Scientists and Engineers, 1996 EPA Career Research Award, 1996 NSF CAREER Award, 1997 Fellow of the IEEE, 2005 Fellow of the Acoustical Society of America, 2005. **Professional Experience:** PROF ELEC & COMPUT ENG, DUKE UNIV, 2004-; assoc prof elec & comput eng, Duke Univ, 1999-2003; res scientist electromagnetics, Schlumberger-Doll Res, 1990-1995; postdoctoral res assoc, Univ Ill, Urbana-Champaign, 1988-1990; res asst elec eng, Univ Ill, Urbana-Champaign, 1986-1988; teaching asst, Xiamen Univ, China, 1985-1986; Res asst physics, Xiamen Univ, China, 1984-1986; Mem Comn B, Int Union Radio Sci. **Memberships:** Inst Elec & Electronics Engrs Antennas & Propagation Soc; Inst Elec & Electronics Engrs Microwave Theory & Tech Soc; Inst Elec & Electronics Engrs Geosci & Remote Sensing Soc. **Research Statement & Publications:** Large scale computation for the foward and inverse modeling of electromagnetic wave propagation in inhomogeneous media. **Mailing Address:** Dept Elec & Comput Eng, Duke Univ, PO Box 90291, 130 Hudson Hall, Durham, NC 27708-0291. **Fax:** 919-660-5293. **E-Mail:** qhliu@ee.duke.edu

LIU, RAY HO, FORENSIC DRUG ANALYSIS, QUANTIFICATION IN MASS SPECTROMETRY. **Personal Data:** b Taiwan, April 3, 1942; American citizen; m 1965, Hsiu-Lan; c Yu-Ting, Eugene & Hubert. **Education:** Cent Police Col, Taiwan, LLB, 1965; Southern Ill Univ, PhD (chem), 1976. **Professional Experience:** PROFESSOR EMERITUS, UNIV ALA, BIRMINGHAM, 2005-; ed-in-chief, Forensic Sci Rev J, 1989-; lab inspector, Nat Inst Drug Abuses Nat Lab Cert Prog, 1988-; PROF FORENSIC SCI, UNIV ALA, BIRMINGHAM, 1984-2004; drug urinalysis expert witness & resource person, USCG, 1988-1993; tech dir, Environ Health Res & Testing, Inc, 1987-1991; assoc prof, Univ Ala, Birmingham, 1984-1989; ctr mass spectrometrist, USDA, 1982-1983; mass spectrometrist, US Environ Protection Agency, 1980-1982; Asst prof forensic sci, Univ Ill, Chicago, 1977-1980. **Memberships:** Fel Am Acad Forensic Sci; Am Chem Soc; Am Soc Mass Spectrometry. **Research Statement & Publications:** Application and development of new approaches for solving existing and emerging problems in forensic sciences, with special emphasis on analytical approaches that may be used for sample differentiation purposes. **Mailing Address:** Dept Justice Sci, Univ Ala, UBOB 210, 1201 Univ Blvd, Birmingham, AL 35294. **Fax:** 205-934-2067. **E-Mail:** rayliu@uab.edu

LIU, ROBERT SHING-HEI, ORGANIC CHEMISTRY. **Personal Data:** b Shanghai, China, August 1, 1938; m 1967, Regina; c 2. **Education:** Howard Payne Col, BS, 1961; Calif Inst Technol, PhD (chem), 1965. **Honors & Awards:** Creativity Award, NSF, 1987; Merit Award, NIH, 1989. **Professional Experience:** UH Fujio Matsuda Scholar, 1984-1985; John Simon Guggenheim Found fel, 1974-1975; PROF CHEM, UNIV HAWAII, 1972-; Alfred P Sloan fel, 1969-1971; assoc prof, Univ Hawaii, 1968-1972; res chemist, E I du Pont de Nemours & Co, Inc, 1964-1968. **Memberships:** Inter-Am Photochem Soc; Am Chem Soc; Am Soc Photobiol. **Research Statement & Publications:** Photochemistry of polyenes; energy transfer processes in solutions; bioorganic reaction mechanisms; new geometric isomers of vitamin A and carotenoids; visual pigments: primary processes, analogs and binding sites; bacteriorhodospin analogs; nuclear magnetic resonance of retinoid and carotenoid binding proteins. **Mailing Address:** Dept Chem, Univ Hawaii, 2545 McCarthy Mall, Honolulu, HI 96822-2275. **Fax:** 808-956-5908. **E-Mail:** rliu@gold.chem.hawaii.edu

LIU, RUEY-WEN, ELECTRICAL ENGINEERING. **Personal Data:** b Kiangsu, China, March 18, 1930; American citizen; m 1957, c 2. **Education:** Univ Ill, BS, 1954, MS, 1955, PhD (elec eng), 1960. **Professional Experience:** PROF EMER ELEC ENG, UNIV NOTRE DAME, as of 2003; vis prof, Nat Taiwan Univ, 1969 & Univ Calif, Berkeley, 1977-1978; prof elec eng, Univ Notre Dame, beginning 1966; vis assoc prof, Univ Calif, Berkeley, 1965-1966; NSF grants 1962-1963, 1964-1966 & 1971-1973; from asst prof to assoc prof, Univ Notre Dame, 1960-1966. **Memberships:** Am Math Soc; fel Inst Elec & Electronics Engrs. **Research Statement & Publications:** System and network theory; large-scale dynamical systems. **Mailing Address:** Dept Elec Eng, Univ Notre Dame, 203 Cushing Hall Eng, Notre Dame, IN 46556. **Fax:** 574-631-4393. **E-Mail:** rueywen.liu.1@nd.edu

LIU, SAMUEL HSI-PEH, theoretical solid state physics; deceased, see previous edition for last biography

LIU, SHIH-CHUN, HEMATOLOGY RESEARCH IN BIO-MEMBRANE. **Personal Data:** b Taipei, Taiwan, January 2, 1946. **Education:** Fu-Jen Catholic Univ, Taiwan, BS, 1969; Carnegie-Mellon Univ, PhD (biochem), 1975. **Professional Experience:** Prin investr, NIH, 1992-; assoc res prof, Tufts Univ, St Elizabeth Hosp, beginning 1992; asst res prof, Tufts Univ, St Elizabeth Hosp, 1978-1992; fel, Univ Mass Med Sch, St Vincent Hosp, 1975-1978. **Memberships:** Am Soc Cell Biol; Am Hemat Soc. **Research Statement & Publications:** Hematology in bio-membrane. **Mailing Address:** Div Cell Biol, Tufts Univ, St Elizabeth Hosp, 736 Cambridge St, Boston, MA 02135.

LIU, S(HING) G(ONG), ELECTRICAL ENGINEERING, APPLIED PHYSICS. **Personal Data:** b Soochow, China, October 24, 1933; m 1960, c 3. **Education:** Univ Taiwan, BS, 1954; NC State Col, MS 1958; Stanford Univ, PhD (elec eng), 1963. **Professional Experience:** RES SCIENTIST, RCA LABS, 1963-; asst microwave ferrites, Stanford Univ, 1959-1963; assoc engr, IBM Corp, 1959; Jr engr, IBM Corp, 1958-1959. **Memberships:** Am Phys Soc; Inst Elec & Electronics Engrs. **Research Statement & Publications:** Spin waves in ferrites; microwave and optical frequency devices using semiconductors; ion implantation in gallium arsenide and related III-V compound semiconductors. **Mailing Address:** MMTC Inc, Princeton, NJ 08540.

LIU, SHU Q, Biomedical Engineering. **Personal Data:** b Lian-cheng, China, December 22, 1956; m 1983, Wu; c Diana & Charley. **Education:** Med Sch NeiMongu, China, BS, 1980, MS, 1983; Univ Calif, San Diego, PhD, 1990. **Honors & Awards:** 1993 Best Journal Paper Award, Journal of Biomechanical Engineering, American Society of Mechanical Engineers 1994 Melville Medal, American Society of Mechanical Engineers 1999 Established Investigator Award, American Heart Association 2000 Richard Skalak Best Journal Paper Award, American Society of Mechanical Engineers 2003 Two papers (Liu et al, AJP 2003a and Liu et al, AJP 2003b) selected as featured articles by the Association for Eradication of Heart Attack. **Professional Experience:** ASSOC PROF BIOMED ENG DEPT, NORTHWESTERN UNIV, 2001-PRESENT; aSST PROF BIOMED ENG DEPT, NORTHWESTERN UNIV 1995-2001; ASST RESEARCH PROF, Univ Calif, San Diego, 1992-1995; Postdoctoral fel, Univ Calif, San Diego, 1990-1992. **Memberships:** 1995- Biomedical Engineering Society 1996- American Heart Association 2000- American Physiological Society 2005- American Soc for Biochemistry and Molecular Biology. **Mailing Address:** Biomed Eng Dept Northwestern Univ, 2145 Sheldon Rd, Evanston, IL 60208-3107. **Fax:** 847-491-4928. **E-Mail:** sliu@northwestern.edu

LIU, SI-KWANG, VETERINARY PATHOLOGY. **Personal Data:** b Kwangsi, China, December 1, 1925; m 1960, c David, Ernie, Diana & Phillip. **Education:** Vet Col Chinese Army, DVM, 1949; Univ Calif, Davis, PhD (vet path), 1964. **Honors & Awards:** Ralston Purina res Award Cardiovasc Path, 1982; Carnation res Awards Feline Dis & Nutrit, 1984; Beecham Award res Excellence, 1986; ROC Award Comp Path, Chinese Histopath Soc, 1989; Chinese Vet Med Asn res Awards, 1993 & 1995. **Professional Experience:** ASSOC DIR, MARGARET M CASPARY INST VET RES, ANIMAL MED CTR, 1998-; vis prof, dept Vet Med, Nat Taiwan Univ, Taiwan, Repub China, 1987-; SR RESEARCHER & CONSULT, PIG RES INST, TAIWAN, REPUB CHINA, 1983-; SR STAFF, DEPT PATH, ANIMAL MED CTR, 1980-; sci fel, NY Zool Soc, Bronx Zoo, 1979-; vis prof vet path, Nat Taiwan Univ & vis expert, Chinese Sci Coun, 1976-1977 & 1985-1986; SR STAFF MEM, ANIMAL MED CTR, 1973-; asst head, dept Path, 1969-1973; cardiopulmonary pathologist, Animal Med Ctr, 1966-1969; assoc pathologist, Animal Med Ctr, 1964-1966; res asst path & parasitol, Sch Vet Med, Univ Calif, Davis, 1959-1964; lectr vet path, Col Agr, Taiwan Univ, 1956-1959; chief, Path lab, Univ Vet Hosp, 1956-1959; sr vet res & diag, Provincial Taitung Agr Sta, China, 1950-1955; clin prof comp path, NY Med Col. **Memberships:** hon mem Am Vet Med Asn; Am Soc Parasitol; Sigma Xi; NY Acad Sci; Int Acad Path; Int Skeletal Soc; Int Cardiovasc Path Soc. **Research Statement & Publications:** Cardiovascular pathology in domestic animals as well as zoo animals; comparative pathology in cardiovascular and orthopedic diseases. **Mailing Address:** Animal Med Ctr, 510 E 62nd St, New York, NY 10021.

LIU, STEPHEN C Y, MICROBIOLOGY, IMMUNOLOGY. **Personal Data:** b Hunan, China, February 24, 1927; m 1954, c 4. **Education:** Taiwan Univ, BSc, 1951, MSc, 1954; Univ Minn, PhD, 1957. **Professional Experience:** PROF EMER MICROBIOL, EASTERN MICH UNIV, as of 2003; tech consult, People's Republic China, UN, 1980-1981; prof microbiol, Eastern Mich Univ, beginning 1974; from asst prof to assoc prof, Eastern Mich Univ, 1965-1974; asst mgr Chas Pfizer & Co, Inc, 1962-1965; res plant virologist, Nat Res Coun, 1958-1962; from res asst to res assoc, Univ Minn, 1954-1958; instr plant path, Taiwan Univ, 1951-1954. **Memberships:** AAAS; Am Phytopath Soc; Am Soc Microbiol; NY Acad Sci; Sigma Xi. **Research Statement & Publications:** Genetics of bacteria; immunology; virology; hydrobiology. **Mailing Address:** Dept Microbiol, Eastern Mich Univ, 202 Welch Hall, Ypsilanti, MI 48197. **E-Mail:** sliu1@emich.edu

LIU, TAI-PING, MATHEMATICAL ANALYSIS. **Personal Data:** b Taiwan, China, November 18, 1945; m 1973. **Education:** Nat Taiwan Univ, BS, 1968; Ore State Univ, MS, 1970; Univ Mich, PhD (math), 1973. **Professional Experience:** DISTINGUISHED RES FEL, INST MATH, ACADEMIA SINICA, as of 2003; PROF, STANFORD UNIV, 1990-; fac mem, NY Univ, 1988-1990; prof math, Univ Md, 1981-1988; from asst prof to assoc prof, Univ MD, College Park, 1973-1981; Sloan fel; Guggenheim fel. **Memberships:** Am Math Soc. **Research Statement & Publications:** Nonlinear partial differential equations and mechanics; qualitative behavior of solutions to physical systems such as compressible flow and elastic models; gas dynamics. **Mailing Address:** Dept Math, Stanford Univ, Bldg 382 V Rm 2125, Stanford, CA 94305-2060. **E-Mail:** liu@math.stanford.edu

LIU, TEH-YUNG, BIOCHEMISTRY. **Personal Data:** b Tainan, Taiwan, May 24, 1932; American citizen; m 1961, Sue C Chen; c Cornelia J, Rebecca & Daniel H. **Education:** Taiwan Nat Univ, BS, 1955; Univ Pittsburgh, PhD (biochem), 1961. **Professional Experience:** DIR, DIV ALLERGENIC PROD & PARISITOL, CTR BIOLOGICS EVAL & RES, FOOD & DRUG ADMIN, 1993-; dir, Div Biochem & Biophys, 1980-1993; dep dir, Div Bact Prod, 1974-1979; sect head biochem microbial struct, Nat Inst Child Health & Human Develop, 1973-1974; biochemist, Biol Dept, Brookhaven Nat Lab, 1967-1973; asst prof, Rockefeller Univ, 1965-1967; Res assoc biochem, Rockefeller Univ, 1961-1965; vis prof, Univ Peking, China, Kyoto Univ, Japan, Union Med Col, Peking, China; fel, St Johns Col, Cambridge, Eng; adj prof, Chem Dept, Cath Univ Am, Wash, DC. **Memberships:** Am Soc Biol Chem & Molecular Biol. **Research Statement & Publications:** Limulus lysate; protein chemistry; human C-reactive protein; Rubella virus. **Mailing Address:** Ctr & Biologics Eval & Res, FDA Bldg 29 Rm 516 NIH, Bethesda, MD 20892.

LIU, TING-TING Y, STARCHBIOSYNTHESIS. **Personal Data:** b Taipei, Taiwan, August 4, 1949; m 1975, c 1. **Education:** Nat Taiwan Univ, BS, 1971; Univ Hawaii, MS, 1974; Pa State Univ, PhD (hort), 1979. **Professional Experience:** Res assoc, Ohio Agr Res &Develop Ctr, 1985-1986; res asst, Dept Dairy Sci, Ohio State Univ, 1982-1985; tech asst, Dept Dairy Sci, Ohio State Univ, 1979-1982; res assoc, Dept Hort, Pa State Univ, 1979; grad asst, Dept Hort, Pa State Univ, 1974-1978; Res asst, Dept Agron, Nat Taiwan Univ, 1971-1972. **Memberships:** Am Soc Plant Physiologists; Sigma Xi. **Research Statement & Publications:** Isolate amyloplasts from corn endosperm to study sugar translocation and starch biosynthesis in plant, and the analysis of research data for animal toxicity studies statistically. **Mailing Address:** 1707 Wessel Dr, Worthington, OH 43085-4313.

LIU, TONY CHEN-YEH, STRUCTURAL ENGINEERING, CIVIL ENGINEERING. **Personal Data:** b Fu-Chien, China, July 27, 1943; American citizen; m 1969, c 2. **Education:** Nat Chung-Hsing Univ, Taiwan, BS, 1965; SDak Sch Mines & Technol, MS, 1968; Cornell Univ, PhD (civil eng), 1971. **Honors & Awards:** Wason Res Medal, Am Concrete Inst, 1974 & 1983. **Professional Experience:** CHIEF MAT ENG SECT, US ARMY CORPS ENGRS, 1981-; res engr, Waterways Exp Sta, 1976-1981; guide prof, World Open Univ, 1975; group leader nuclear eng, Gen Atomic Co, 1972-1976; struct engr civil eng, Ammann & Whitney Inc, 1971. **Memberships:** Fel Am Concrete Inst; Am Soc Civil Engrs; Sigma Xi; Am Soc Testing & Mat. **Research Statement & Publications:** Design of concrete hydraulic structures, precast concrete structures, repair and rehabilitation of deteriorated concrete structures and thermal stress analysis for mass concrete structures. **Mailing Address:** US Army Corps Engrs, HQUSACE(DAEN ECE D) 20 Mass Ave, Washington, DC 20314. **Fax:** 202-761-0907. **E-Mail:** tony.c.liu@usace.army.mil

LIU, TUNG, chemical engineering; deceased, see previous edition for last biography

LIU, VI-CHENG, AEROSPACE ENGINEERING. **Personal Data:** b China, September 1, 1917; American citizen; m 1947, Hsi-Yen. **Education:** Chiao Tung Univ, BS, 1940; Univ Mich, MS, 1947, PhD (aeronaut eng), 1951. **Professional Experience:** Hon prof, Nanjing Aeronaut Inst, China, 1991; vis chmn prof, Nanjing Aeronaut Inst, China, 1990; PROF EMER AEROSPACE ENG, UNIV MICH, ANN ARBOR, 1989-; vis prof, Inst Mech, Chinese Acad Sci, Beijing, 1980; prof, Res Inst, Univ Mich, Ann Arbor, 1959-1989; res engr, Res Inst, Univ Mich, Ann Arbor, 1950-1959; res assoc eng, Res Inst, Univ Mich, Ann Arbor, 1948-1950; res fel, Ministry Educ, 1946-1948; res instr, Aeronaut Res Inst, Tsing Hua Univ, China, 1944-1946; res asst aerodyn, Aeronaut Res Inst, Tsing Hua Univ, China, 1940-1944. **Memberships:** Am Phys Soc; assoc fel Am Inst Aeronaut & Astronaut. **Research Statement & Publications:** Upper atmosphere; rocket flight, rarefied gas and ionospheric gas dynamics; thermal diffusion; boundary layer flow; turbulent dispersion; plasma interaction; magnetospheric physics; geophysical Fluid Dynamics; ionospheric aerodynamics. **Mailing Address:** Univ Mich, Dept Aerospace Eng, Ann Arbor, MI 48104.

LIU, WEI, MODELING OF SHORT-ROTATION INTENSIVE SULTURE WOODY BIOMASS PRODUCTION, HARVESTING PROCESSING & TRANSPORTATION SYSTEMS. **Personal Data:** b Beijing, China, June 28, 1962; m 1988, Li. **Education:** Beijing Univ Posts & Telecommun, BEng, 1984; Univ Hawaiii, Manoa, MS, 1992. **Professional Experience:** JR RESEARCHER AGR ENG DEPT, UNIV HAWAII, 1992-; res asst, Univ Hawaii, 1989-1992; engr, Beijing Res Inst Postal Sci & Technol, 1984-1989. **Memberships:** Am Soc Agr Engrs. **Research Statement & Publications:** Developed a spatial model for the economic evaluation of short-rotation intensive-culture woody biomass plantation, harvesting, processing and transportation systems for energy production in Hawaii; resource assessment and possible alternative land use analysis in Hawaii. **Mailing Address:** Agr Eng Dept Univ Hawaii, 3050 Maile Way, Honolulu, HI 96822. **Fax:** 808-956-9269. **E-Mail:** wliu@uhunix.uhcc.hawaii.edu

LIU, WING KAM, WAVELETS, FINITE ELEMENTS & MULTIPLE SCALE ANALYSIS. **Personal Data:** b Hong Kong, May 19, 1952; American citizen; m 1986, Betty; c Melissa & Michael. **Education:** Univ Ill, Chicago, BS, 1976; Calif Inst Technol, MS, 1977, PhD (civil eng), 1981. **Honors & Awards:** Melville Medal, Am Soc Mech Engrs, 1979, Pi Tau Sigma Gold Medal, 1985; Ralph Teetor's Award, Soc Automotive Engrs, 1983; Thomas J Jaeger Prize, Int Asn Struct Mech Reactor Technol, 1989; Gustus L Larson Mem Award, Am Soc Mech Engrs, 1995; Most Highly Cited Res Eng, Inst Sci Info, 2001; Comput Struct Mech Award, US Asn Comput Mech, 2001; Gustus L Larson Mem Award, Am Soc Eng Educ, 1995. **Professional Experience:** DIR, NSF SUMMER INST NANO MECH & MAT, as of 2006; WALTER P MURPHY PROF MECH & CIVIL ENG, NORTHWESTERN UNIV, 1988-; consult, Reactor Anal & Safety Div, Argonne Nat Lab, 1981-; from asst prof to assoc prof, Northwestern Univ, 1980-1988; res asst, Univ Ill, Chicago, 1974-1976; res asst, Calif Inst Technol, 1976-1980; grants, NSF, Army Res Off, NASA, ONR; grants, Air Force Off Sci Res. **Memberships:** Fel Am Soc Mech Engrs (chair, applied mech div, 2005); fel Am Soc Civil Engrs; fel Am Acad Mech; fel USACM; fel IACM. **Research Statement & Publications:** Finite elements; computer simulations; fluid-structure interactions; non-linear and inelastic analysis; computer-aided engineering; liquid storage tanks; wavelets and reproducing kernel methods; virtual manufacturing prototyping. **Mailing Address:** Dept Mech Eng, Northwestern Univ, 2145 Sheridan Rd Rm A326, Evanston, IL 60208. **Fax:** 847-491-3915. **E-Mail:** w-liu@northwestern.edu

LIU, WING-KI, SURFACE SCIENCE. **Personal Data:** b Hong Kong, February 24, 1950. **Education:** Univ Ill, Urbana, BS, 1971, MS, 1972 & PhD (physics), 1975. **Professional Experience:** PROF PHYSICS, UNIV WATERLOO, as of 2005; ASSOC DEAN SCI GRAD STUDIES, DEPT PHYSICS, UNIV WATERLOO, as of 2005; assoc prof physics, Univ Waterloo, beginning 1986; res asst prof to assoc prof, Calif Inst Technol, 1981-1986; vis asst prof, Calif Inst Technol, 1980-1981; vis assoc, Calif Inst Technol, 1979-1980; res assoc, Calif Inst Technol, 1976-1979; fel, Calif Inst Technol, 1975-1976. **Memberships:** Am Phys Soc; Can Assoc Physicists. **Research Statement & Publications:** Classical and quantum chemical dynamics; theory of chemical physics of solid surfaces. **Mailing Address:** Dept Physics, Univ Waterloo, Waterloo, ON N2L 3G1, Can. **E-Mail:** wkliu@uwaterloo.ca

LIU, WINGYUEN TIMOTHY, REMOTE SENSING, AIR-SEA INTERACTION. **Personal Data:** b 1946; American citizen. **Education:** Ohio Univ, BS, 1971; Univ Wash, MS, 1974, PhD (atmospheric sci), 1978. **Honors & Awards:** Medal Except Sci Achievement, NASA, 1990; NASA Achievement Medal, 1998; Distinguished Sci Award, Pan Oceanic Remote Sensing Award Comt, 2002. **Professional Experience:** SR RES SCIENTIST, JET PROPULSION LAB, as of 2004; SR RES SCIENTIST SATELLITE OCEANOG, JET PROPULSION LAB, CALIF INST TECHNOL, 1993-; proj scientist, Jet Propulsion Lab, 1992-1993; team leader, Jet Propulsion Lab, 1989-; prin investr, Jet Propulsion Lab, 1979-; res assoc atmospheric sci, Univ Wash, 1978-1979; res asst, Univ Wash, 1971-1978. **Memberships:** Am Meteorol Soc; Am Geophys Union. **Research Statement & Publications:** Study of the boundary layers, the energy exchanges across the atmosphere-ocean interface and their effects on climate variability. **Mailing Address:** Jet Propulsion Lab, Code 300-323 4800 Oak Grove Dr, Pasadena, CA 91109-8099. **Fax:** 818-393-6720. **E-Mail:** liu@pacific.jpl.nasa.gov

LIU, XIAOHUA, LIGHT SCATTERING, ELECTRICAL TESTING & MEASUREMENT. **Personal Data:** m Ying; c Jennifer. **Education:** Nanjing Univ, China, BS, 1986; Ohio State Univ, MS, 1995, PhD (physics), 1996. **Professional Experience:** MEM TECH STAFF, LUCENT TECHNOL, 1996-; res asst, Narjing Univ, China, 1986-1990. **Research Statement & Publications:** Light scattering technique to study sound and magnetic waves in magnetic thin films. **Mailing Address:** Lucent Technol, 6200 E Broad St, Columbus, OH 43213.

LIU, XICHUN, SEMICONDUCTOR PHYSICS, MAGNETOSPECTROSCOPY. **Personal Data:** b Tianjin, China, September 5, 1959; m 1986, Lijing; c Alina C. **Education:** Tianjin Univ, China, BSc, 1982; State Univ NY, Buffalo, PhD (physics), 1990. **Professional Experience:** SPONSORED RES TECH STAFF, MASS INST TECHNOL, 1994-; fel res assoc, Univ Ill, Urbana-Champaign, 1990-1992; asst lectr, Tianjin Univ, China, 1982-1984. **Memberships:** Am Phys Soc; Mat Res Soc. **Research Statement & Publications:** Optical and magneto-optical studies and characterization of semiconductor compounds, optoelectronic materials, quantum wells, superlatives and diluted magnetic semiconductor; laser spectroscopy, raman scattering; high magnetic field effects on the properties of solid state materials and structures especially low temperatures. **Mailing Address:** Mass Inst Technol NW 14-4115, 170 Albany St, Cambridge, MA 02139. **Fax:** 617-253-5405. **E-Mail:** xcliu@slipknot.mit.edu

LIU, XUAN, TRANSCRIPTION, CANCER RESEARCH. **Personal Data:** b Beijing, China, April 8, 1959. **Education:** Beijing Med Univ, MD, 1983; WVa Univ, PhD (biochem), 1990. **Professional Experience:** ASSOC PROF BIOCHEM, UNIV CALIF, RIV as of 2004; DAMON RUNYON-WALTER WINCHELL FEL, UNIV CALIF, LOS ANGELES, 1990-. **Memberships:** Am Soc Cell Biologists; AAAS. **Research Statement & Publications:** Study tumor suppressor transcriptional regulation during cell cycle control. **Mailing Address:** Dept Biochem, Univ Calif, 1217 Grossmont Dr, Riverside, CA 92506. **Fax:** 909-787-4434. **E-Mail:** xuan.liu@ucr.edu

LIU, YI, AUTOMOTIVE ELECTRONICS, LASER MATERIAL INTERACTION. **Personal Data:** b Zhengjiang, Jiangsu, China, October 8, 1963; American citizen; m 1991, Liqun; c Jennifer Liu & Edward Lin. **Education:** Beijing Univ, China, BS, 1984; Ohio State Univ, MS, 1986, PhD (physics), 1991. **Professional Experience:** CUSTOMER QUALITY MGR, SIEMENS VDO, 2000-; dir res & develop & qual mgr, Utilase Inc 1993-2000; res scientist, Argonne Nat Lab, 1991-1993; res assoc, Ohio State Univ, 1986-1991; teaching asst gen physics, Ohio State Univ, 1984-1986. **Memberships:** Soc Mfg Engrs; Am Welding Soc; Int Soc Optical Eng; Soc Appl Spectros; Am Soc Qual Control; Soc of Auto Engr. **Research Statement & Publications:** Laser material interaction; laser application; develop on-line real time process monitoring systems; develop machine vision systems for quality control; Engine Management System Design; Electrical Components for Automotive. **Mailing Address:** 39394 Carrie Dr, Sterling Heights, MI 48313. **Fax:** 248-209-7357. **E-Mail:** yi.liu@at.siemens.com

LIU, YINONG, HEMATOLOGY, ONCOLOGY. **Education:** Shanghai Med Univ, Shanghai, China, MD, 1984; Am Bd Intl Med, cert, 2000. **Professional Experience:** PHYSICIAN, DANVILLE, KY, as of 2006; E Tenn State Univ, Johnson City, Tenn, 1997-2000. **Mailing Address:** 216 Southtown Dr, Danville, KY 40422. **Fax:** 859-236-9446.

LIU, YONG-BIAO, PESTICIDE RESISTANCE, CHEMICAL ECOLOGY. **Personal Data:** b Ningxia, China, May 15, 1960; m 1992, Min; c Yang. **Education:** Beijing Forestry Univ, BA, 1982; Univ BC, MS, 1987; Univ Maine, PhD (biol sci), 1990. **Honors & Awards:** Fred Griffee Mem Award, Maine Agr Exp Sta, 1990; George F Dow Award, 1990. **Professional Experience:** RES ENTOMOLOGIST, US AGR RES SERV, USDA, as of 2004; asst res scientist, Univ Ariz, beginning 1997; fel, Univ Hawaii, 1993-1997; scholar, Univ Ky, 1990-1993. **Memberships:** Entom Soc Am; Sigma Xi. **Research Statement & Publications:** Toxicology of limonoid insect antifeedants; sex pheromone-mediated insect behavior; pesticide resistance; granted 1 US patent. **Mailing Address:** Dept Entom US Agr Res Serv, 1636 E Alisal St, Salinas, CA 93905. **Fax:** 831-755-2814. **E-Mail:** yliu@pw.ars.usda.gov

LIU, YOUNG KING, BIOMECHANICS, BIOMEDICAL ENGINEERING. **Personal Data:** b Nanking, China, May 3, 1934; American citizen; div, c 2. **Education:** Bradley Univ, BS, 1955; Univ Wis-Madison, MS, 1959; Wayne State Univ, PhD (mech), 1963. **Professional Experience:** PRES, UNIV NORTHERN CALIF, 1994-; prof & dir, Biomech Lab, 1990-1994; adv at large, Nat Res Coun, Comt Hearing, Bioacoust & Biomech, NAS, beginning 1979; prof & dir, Ctr Mat Res, Univ Iowa, Iowa City, 1978-1990; biophys consult, US Army Aeromed Res Lab, beginning 1972; prof biomech, Tulane Univ, 1972-1978; NIH res career develop award, 1971-1976; assoc prof, Tulane Univ, 1969-1972; vis asst prof aeronaut & astronaut, Stanford Univ, 1968-1969; NIH spec res fel, Stanford Univ, 1968-1969; asst prof, Univ Mich, Ann Arbor, 1964-1968; lectr, Univ Mich, Ann Arbor, 1963-1964; instr mech, Wayne State Univ, 1960-1963. **Memberships:** Am Soc Eng Educ; Orthop Res

Soc; Sigma Xi; Am Acad Mech; Int Soc Study Lumbar Spine; Int Soc Study Pain. **Research Statement & Publications:** Biomechanics, biomaterials and physiologic basis of acupuncture. **Mailing Address:** Univ Northern Calif, 1304 Southpoint Blvd Ste 220, Petaluma, CA 94954.

LIU, YU, OPTICS, LASERS. **Personal Data:** b China, American citizen; m 1967, c 1. **Education:** Ga Inst Technol, PhD (physics), 1974. **Professional Experience:** PHYSICIST LASER, INFRARED & OPTICS, US ARMY AVIATION RES & DEVELOP COMMAND, 1979-; res physicist laser & optics, US Army Missile Res & Develop Command, 1976-1979; physicist optics & laser, US Army Missile Res & Develop Lab, 1974-1976; teaching asst physics, Ga Inst Technol, 1969-1974; instr physics, Tex Tech Univ, 1966-1969; Res asst physics, Rice Univ, 1962-1969. **Memberships:** Asn US Army. **Research Statement & Publications:** Research, design and development of laser guidance links; low temperature physics research. **Mailing Address:** 1865 Schoettler Valley Dr, Chesterfield, MO 63017.

LIU, YUNG SHENG, PHYSICS, LASERS. **Personal Data:** b China, September 23, 1944; m 1979, Ming Lee; c Alan & Jenny. **Education:** Nat Taiwan Univ, BS, 1966; Cornell Univ, PhD (appl physics), 1972. **Professional Experience:** VPRES & DIR, OPTO ELECTRONICS SYST LAB, as of 2004; CHMN, OPTICAL ENG SOC, 2001-; CHMN, TAIWAN OPTICAL COMMUN INDUST ALLIANCE, 2001-; ASST DIR, TAIWAN ELECT& ELECTRONICS MFR, 2001-; DIR, TAIWAN PHYSICAL SOC, 2000-; DIR, TAIWAN UNIV PHYSICS ALUMNI ASN, 2000-; Res prof Physics Rensellaer Polytech Inst, 1995-1997; prog mgr, Res & Develop Consortium, 1992-1996; prin investr, Res & Develop Consortium, 1992-1995; prin scientist, GE Med Systs, 1990-1992; lectr, Max Planck Soc, Ger, 1989 & 1992; mem, Comt Applns Physics, Am Phys Soc, 1988-1991; prin scientist, GE Res & Develop Ctr, 1987-1992; adj prof physics, State Univ NY, Albany, 1986-1992; adj prof, Dept Physics, State Univ NY, Albany, 1986-1992; consult, UN Develop Prog, China, 1986; PHYSICIST, GEN ELEC RES CTR, 1972-; Darpa Prog Mgr, Gen Electric Res Ctr, 1972-1994; prin investr & proj leader, GE Res & Develop Ctr, 1972-1986; res asst, Cornell Univ, 1970-1973; Avco fel, 1970; Cornell Univ, 1969; Vis scientist physics, Univ Calif, Los Angeles, 1968-; Teaching asst physics, Cornell Univ, 1968-1969; prin investr & major grantee, USAF, Off Naval Res, Advan Res Projs Agency. **Memberships:** Optical Soc Am; Am Phys Soc; Sigma Xi; AAAS; Inst Elec & Electronics Engrs; Am Vacuum Soc; Mat Res Soc. **Research Statement & Publications:** Laser physics; quantum electronics and optics; laser-matter interactions; semiconductor electronics; author or coauthor of over 60 publications; 20 patents. **Mailing Address:** Indust Technol Res Inst, 195 Chung Hsing Rd, Sec4 Chu Tung, Hsin Chu, Taiwan.

LIU, YUNG YUAN, AGING MANAGEMENT OF NUCLEAR POWER PLANTS, TRANSPORTATION OF RADIOACTIVE MATERIALS. **Personal Data:** b Taipei, Taiwan, March 20, 1950; American citizen; m 1975, Teresa; c Sharon & Alvin. **Education:** Nat Tsing-Hua Univ, Taiwan, BS, 1971; Mass Inst Technol, MS, 1976. **Honorary Degrees:** DSc (nuclear eng), Mass Inst Technol, 1978. **Professional Experience:** SECT MGR, ARGONNE NAT LAB, as of 2005; Mgr, Aging Mgt & Transp Hazardons Mat, Energy Technol Div, Argonne Nat Lab, 1997-; consult, Nordion Int, 1996-1997; staff engr irradiation performance, Mat & Components Technol Div, 1989-1993; staff engr high temperature corrosion-erosion, Tribology, 1986-1988; staff reviewer, Am Soc Mech Engrs, 1983-; staff reviewer, Nuclear Technol, 1982-; staff engr, theorist radiation effects & nuclear mat-casting-solidification, Mat Sci & Technol Div, 1982-1985; consult, Los Alamos Nat Lab, 1982-1983; prin investr, Mat Sci & Technol Div, Argonne Nat Lab, 1978-; assoc staff engr, Argonne Nat Lab, 1978-1982; mem, Fast Reactor Fuel Performance Code Comt, US Dept Energy & Fuel Performance Eval Task Force, 1978-1981; staff engr, Entropy Ltd, Lincoln, Mass, 1977-1978; res asst, Radiation Effects, 1976-1978; struct mech, Radiation Effects, 1975-1976; teaching asst phys metall, Dept Nuclear Eng, Mass Inst Technol, 1974-1975; res asst cogeneration, Dept Nuclear Eng, Mass Inst Technol, 1974. **Memberships:** Am Soc Metals; AAAS; Am Nuclear Soc. **Research Statement & Publications:** Radiation effects on materials and development of nuclear fuel and breeder materials for fission and fusion reactors; packaging and transportation of radioactive materials; foam explosives; aging management of nuclear power plants. **Mailing Address:** Argonne Nat Lab, 9700 S Cass Ave Bldg 308, Argonne, IL 60439. **Fax:** 630-252-3250. **E-Mail:** yyliu@anl.gov

LIU, YUNG-PIN, CARCINOGENESIS MECHANISMS. **Education:** Baylor Univ, PhD (biochem), 1969. **Professional Experience:** PROG DIR CARCINOGENESIS MECHANISMS, NAT CANCER INST, 1984-. **Research Statement & Publications:** Biochemical pharmacology. **Mailing Address:** Div Cancer Etiol, Nat Cancer Inst, Exec Plaza N Ste 700, Bethesda, MD 20892. **Fax:** 301-496-1040. **E-Mail:** y198v@nih.gov

LIU, YU-YING, SYNTHESIS OF LABELLED COMPOUND. **Personal Data:** b China, May 16, 1944; m Herbert; c Jeffrey Hu & Mindy Hu. **Education:** Taiwan Normal Univ, BS, 1967; Univ Minn, PhD (chem), 1972. **Professional Experience:** RES LEADER, HOFFMAN LAROCHE INC, 1995-; res investr, Hoffmann Laroche, Inc, 1986-1995; sr scientist, Hoffmann Laroche, Inc, 1974-1985; Fel, Am Health Found, 1971-1973. **Memberships:** Am Chem Soc int Isotope soci. **Research Statement & Publications:** Natural product isolation; metabolism; quantitative analysis; synthesis of labelled compound of pharmaceutical interest. **Mailing Address:** Hoffmann LaRoche Inc, 340 Kingsland St, Nutley, NJ 07110-1199. **E-Mail:** yu-ying.liu@roche.com

LIU, ZHENGYU, PHYSICAL OCEANOGRAPHY, CLIMATE DYNAMICS. **Personal Data:** m 1987, Huixia; c Neil & Diana. **Education:** Nanjing Inst Meterol, BA, 1982; Acad Sinica, MA, 1985; Mass Inst Technol, PhD (phys oceanog). **Professional Experience:** PROF ATMOS & OCEAN SCI & ENVIORN STUDIES, UNIV WIS-MADISON, as of 2005; DIR, CTR CLIMATIC RES, as of 2005; Asst Prof Phys Oceanog, Univ Wis-Madison, 1993-; Fel, Princeton Univ, 1991-1993. **Mailing Address:** 1225 W Dayton St, Madison, WI 53706. **E-Mail:** znl@meteor.wisc.edu

LIU, ZHUANGYI, CONTROL OF DISTRIBUTED PARAMETER SYSTEMS, PARTIAL DIFFERENTIAL EQUATIONS. **Personal Data:** b Shanghai, China, May 2, 1954; American citizen; m 1991, Junyi; c Jieming & Yiming. **Education:** Fudan Univ, BS, 1982; Va Polytech Inst, MS, 1986, PhD (math), 1989. **Professional Experience:** PROF MATH, UNIV MINN, DULUTH, 2000-; from asst prof to assoc prof, Univ Minn, Duluth, 1989-2000. **Memberships:** Soc Indust & Appl Math; Am Math Soc. **Research Statement & Publications:** Published 30+ papers in professional journals on stability and control of PDE systems. **Mailing Address:** Dept Math & Statist Univ Minn, CCTR140 10 Univ Dr, Duluth, MN 55812. **Fax:** 218-726-8399. **E-Mail:** zliu@d.umn.edu

LIU-GER, TSU-HUEI, THEORETICAL PHYSICS, SOFTWARE DEVELOPMENT. **Personal Data:** b Kwei-yang, Kwei-chow, China, March 10, 1943; American citizen; m 1971, Kai-Hwa; c Kwang-yi & Kwang-chien. **Education:** Nat Taiwan Univ, BS, 1964; Univ Ore, PhD (physics), 1969. **Professional Experience:** SUPVRY ENGR, BONNEVILLE POWER ADMIN, US DEPT ENERGY, 1982-; physicist, Bonneville Power Admin, US Dept Energy, 1975-1982; Asst prof physics, Portland State Univ, 1969-1975. **Research Statement & Publications:** Development of electromagnetic transient program of the power systems. **Mailing Address:** 3179 Oak Tree Ct, West Linn, OR 97068. **Fax:** 503-230-3212. **E-Mail:** 71203.736@compuserve.com

LIUIMA, FRANCIS ALOYSIUS, physics; deceased, see previous edition for last biography

LIUKKONEN, JOHN ROBIE, MATHEMATICAL ANALYSIS. **Personal Data:** b Oakland, Calif, October 23, 1942. **Education:** Harvard Univ, BA, 1965; Columbia Univ, PhD (math), 1970. **Professional Experience:** PROF MATH, TULANE UNIV, as of 2006; ASSOC PROF MATH, TULANE UNIV, beginning 1975; Asst prof, Tulane Univ, 1970-1975. **Research Statement & Publications:** Representations of locally compact groups; harmonic analysis on locally compact groups. **Mailing Address:** Dept Math, Tulane Univ, 6823 St Charles Ave, New Orleans, LA 70118-5665. **Fax:** 504-865-5063. **E-Mail:** jrl@math.tulane.edu

LIUZZI, MICHEL, VIROLOGY & RIBONUCLEOTIDE REDUCTASE, HELICASE-PRIMASE & DNA METABOLISM. **Personal Data:** b Noci, Italy, May 13, 1957; m 1987, Natalie; c Gabrielle A. **Education:** Univ Liege, Belg, BS, 1980, PhD (chem), 1984. **Professional Experience:** Group leader, Dept Biol Sci, Bio Mega/Boehringer Ingelheim Res Inc, beginning 1989; fel, Cross Cancer Inst, Alta, 1984-1989. **Memberships:** Antiviral Res Soc; Am Asn Cancer Res; Am Soc Biochem & Molecular Biol; AAAS. **Research Statement & Publications:** Investigate mechanism of inhibition of herpes simplex virus replication by helicase-primase inhibititors and ribonucleotide reductase subunit association inhibitions for the development of novel antiherpetic agents; DNA repair; enzymology; DNA replication. **Mailing Address:** Bio-Mega/Boehringer Ingelheim Res Inc, 2100 Cunard St, Laval, PQ H7S 2G5, Can. **Fax:** 514-689-8434.

LIUZZO, JOSEPH ANTHONY, FOOD SCIENCE. **Personal Data:** b Tampa, Fla, December 16, 1926; wid Elaine; c Paul A, Patricia J & Jolaine M. **Education:** Univ Fla, BS, 1950, MSA, 1955; Mich State Univ, PhD (nutrit, biochem), 1958. **Honors & Awards:** Prof Scientist Award, Southern Asn Agr Scientists, 1985 outstanding regional communicator, inst of food technol, 1987-1988; outstanding alumini award, mich state univ, 1994; 1991 inducted into Omicron Delta Kappa Honorary Leadership Society. **Professional Experience:** Prof emer of food sci, LSU, 1997-; prof of food sci, LSU, 1969-1997; PROF FOOD SCI, LA STATE UNIV, BATON ROUGE, 1969-; assoc prof food sci & technol, LA State Univ, Baton Rouge, 1962-1969; asst prof biochem, LA State Univ, Baton Rouge, 1958-1962; asst, Mich State Univ, 1955-1958; asst, Univ Fla, 1954-1955; asst to dir biol res, Nutrilite Prod, Inc, Calif, 1953-1954; dir microbiol, Nutrilite Prod, Inc, Calif, 1951-1953; Res microbiologist, Univ Fla, 1950-1951. **Memberships:** Sigma Xi; Am Inst Nutrit; fel Inst Food Technologists; Phi Tau Sigma. **Research Statement & Publications:** Improved utilization of brown ad milled rice; radiation preservation of foods; utilization of by-products from agricultural commodities. **Mailing Address:** Dept Food Sci, La State Univ, Baton Rouge, LA 70803-0001. **Fax:** 225-578-5300. **E-Mail:** jliuzzo@agcenter.lsu.edu

LIV, PENG TU, BIOMETRICS. **Personal Data:** b Taipei, Taiwan, December 23, 1939. **Education:** Nat Taiwan Univ, BS, 1962; Univ Philippines, MS, 1967; Johns Hopkins Univ, ScD, 1971. **Professional Experience:** BR CHIEF, BIOMETRICS & RISK ASSESSMENT BR, CTR FOOD SAFETY & APPL NUTRIT, 1981-; math statistician, Food & Drug Admin, 1977-1981; Asst prof, Johns Hopkins Sch Pub Health, 1971-1976. **Memberships:** Am Statist Asn. **Mailing Address:** Biomet & Risk Assessment Ctr Food Safety & Appl Nutrit, 200 C St SW, Washington, DC 20204. **Fax:** 202-205-5069.

LIVANT, PETER DAVID, PHYSICAL ORGANIC CHEMISTRY. **Personal Data:** b New York, NY, September 18, 1948. **Education:** City Col NY, BS, 1969; Brown Univ, PhD (chem), 1975. **Professional Experience:** ASSOC PROF CHEM, AUBURN UNIV, 1977-; res fel, Univ Guelph, 1976-1977; res fel, Univ Ill, Urbana-Champaign, 1975-1976; vis asst prof chem, Univ Ill, Urbana-Champaign, 1974-1975. **Memberships:** Am Chem Soc. **Research Statement & Publications:** Mechanisms of radical reactions; chemistry of hypervalent species; tetracoordinate tetracovalent sulfur compounds; chemically induced dynamic nuclear polarization dependence on magnetic field strength. **Mailing Address:** Dept Chem & Biochem, Auburn Univ, Auburn, AL 36849-5312. **E-Mail:** livanpd@auburn.edu

LIVDAHL, PHILIP V, PHYSICS. **Personal Data:** b Bismarck, NDak, February 1, 1923; m 1944, c 3. **Education:** St Olaf Col, BA, 1948; Univ Wash, MS, 1952. **Professional Experience:** RETIRED; assoc dir, Fermi Nat Accelerator Lab, beginning 1979; actg dir, Fermi Nat Accelerator Lab, 1978-1979; physicist, Fermi Nat Accelerator Lab, beginning 1967; assoc physicist, Argonne Nat Lab, 1957-1967; physicist, Lawrence Radiation Lab, Calif, 1954-1957; assoc physicist, Calif Res & Develop Corp, 1951-1954. **Research Statement & Publications:** High energy accelerators; linear accelerators and associated equipment forsynchrotron injectors; experimental planning and operation for the zero gradient synchrotron. **Mailing Address:** 137 Harleman Dr, Sequim, WA 98382.

LIVE, DAVID H, BIOPHYSICS, PHYSICAL CHEMISTRY. **Personal Data:** b Philadelphia, Pa, April 3, 1946. **Education:** Univ Pa, BA, 1967; Calif Inst Technol, PhD (chem), 1974. **Professional Experience:** SR RES ASSOC & MGR, DEPT BIOCHEM, MED SCH, UNIV MINN, 1997-; mem prof staff, Calif Inst Technol, 1991-1992; assoc prof chem, Emory Univ, 1986-1991; asst prof phys biochem, Rockefeller Univ, 1978-1985; consult, Jet Propulsion Lab, Calif Inst Technol, 1975-; res assoc biophys, Rockefeller Univ, 1974-1978; assoc lab mem, Mem Sloan Ketttering Cancer Ctr. **Memberships:** Am Chem Soc; AAAS; NY Acad Sci. **Research Statement & Publications:** Biophysical applications of magnetic resonance to studying molecular conformation, particularly in peptides and proteins; geochemical investigations by magnetic resonance of terrestrial and lunar samples. **Mailing Address:** Dept Biochem, Molecular Biol & Biophys, Med Sch, Univ Minn, Rm 6-155 Jackson Hall 321 Church St SE, Minneapolis, MN 55455. **Fax:** 612-625-2163. **E-Mail:** livex001@umn.edu

LIVENGOOD, DAVID ROBERT, BIOPHYSICS, ELECTROPHYSIOLOGY. **Personal Data:** b LaJunta, Colo, March 18, 1937; c 4. **Education:** Butler Univ, BS, 1960; Ind Univ, PhD (physiol), 1970. **Professional Experience:** CHMN, DEPT CELLULAR RADIOBIOL, ARMED FORCES RADIOBIOL RES INST, 1995-; adj staff, Dept Physiol & Biophys, Georgetown Univ Sch Med, 1984-; adj staff, Dept Physiol, Uniformed Serv Univ Health Sci, 1980-1990; chmn, Dept Physiol, 1980-1995; chief, Radiation Biophys Div, 1979-1980; res consult, Dept Physiol, George Wash Univ, 1978-1984; fel, Marine Biol Lab, STI, 1976; res physiologist, Dept Neurobiology, Armed Forces Radiobiol Res Inst, 1973-1979; Grass Found fel, Woods Hole Marine Biol Lab, 1971; res assoc, Dept Biophys, Sch Med, Univ Md, 1971-1973. **Memberships:** Biophys Soc; Soc Neuroscience; Soc Gen Physiologists; Oxygen Soc. **Research Statement & Publications:** Biophysical properties of the membranes of nerve and muscle cells; free radical damage; toxicology of depleated uranium. **Mailing Address:** Dept Cellular Radiobiol, Armed Forces Radiobiol Res Inst, 8901 Wis Ave, Bethesda, MD 20889-5603. **Fax:** 301-295-0313. **E-Mail:** livengood@usuhsb.vsons.mil

LIVENGOOD, JOHN R, PREVENTATIVE MEDICINE. **Personal Data:** b Cumberland, Md, March 25, 1954. **Education:** Columbia Univ, MPhil, 1990; Univ Md, MD, 1980. **Professional Experience:** DEP ASSOC DIR SCI, OFF SCI POLICY & TECHNOL TRANSFER, CTR DIS CONTROL & PREV, as of 2003; DIR, EPIDEMIOL & SURVEILLANCE DIV, NAT IMMUNIZATION & SURVEILLANCE DIV, CTR DIS CONTROL & PREV, as of 2003; assoc dir sci, Div Chronic Dis Control & Community Intervention, 1991-1996. **Memberships:** Am Pub Health Asn. **Mailing Address:** Off Sci Policy & Technol Transfer, Ctr Dis Control & Prev, MS D50, 1600 Clifton Rd, NE, Atlanta, GA 30333. **Fax:** 404-639-8616. **E-Mail:** jrl1@cdc.gov

LIVERMAN, JAMES LESLIE, PLANT PHYSIOLOGY, BIOCHEMISTRY. **Personal Data:** b Brady, Tex, August 17, 1921; m 1959, Mary; c Carol J, Barbara J, Robert J, James L Jr & Jean L. **Education:** Tex A&M Univ, BS, 1949; Calif Inst Technol, PhD (plant physiol, bio-org chem), 1952. **Professional Experience:** EXPERT, ENVIRON & RADIOL SAFETY, DEFENSE NUCLEAR FACIL SAFETY BD, 1992-; consult & dir tech trf database, Univ Sci Eng & Tech, Inc, 1988-1990; consult, Maxwell Commun Biomed Res & Develop Planning, 1987-1988; vpres prod develop, Organon Teknika Corp, 1985-1987; vpres bionetics res, Appl Sci Div, Litton Bionetics Inc, 1985-1987; sr vpres & gen mgr, Appl Sci Div, Litton Bionetics Inc, 1979-1985; dep asst secy, Dept Energy, 1978-1979; actg asst secy environ, Dept Energy, 1977-1978; dir, Div Biomed & Environ Res & asst adminr environ & safety, US Energy Res & Develop Admin, 1975-1977; asst gen mgr biomed & environ res & safety, Div Biomed & Environ Res, US AEC, 1973-1975; dir, Div Biomed & Environ Res, US AEC, 1972-1975; assoc dir biomed & environ sci, Oak Ridge Nat Lab, 1969-1972; asst dir life sci, Oak Ridge Nat Lab, 1967-1969; interim dir, Univ Tenn-Oak Ridge Grad Sch Biomed Sci, 1965-1966; assoc dir, Biol Div, Oak Ridge Nat Lab, 1964-1967; chmn, Gordon Conf Biochem & Agr, 1961; chief, Biol Br, AEC, 1960-1964; asst chief, Biol Br, AEC, 1959-1960; biochemist, AEC, 1958-1959; Consult agr chemist, 1956-1958; from asst prof to prof biochem, Agr & Mech Col, Univ Tex, 1953-1960; fel plant physiol, Calif Inst Technol, 1952-1953. **Memberships:** Fel AAAS; Am Soc Plant Physiol; Am Chem Soc; Radiation Res Soc; Ecol Soc Am; Am Mgt Asn. **Research Statement & Publications:** Cell physiology; photoperiodism; radiation in biological systems; immunology; bioengineering; policy science. **Mailing Address:** 5308 Manor Lake Ct, Rockville, MD 20853.

LIVERMORE, JOHN S, METALLURGY. **Honors & Awards:** Daniel C Jackling Award, Soc Mining Metall Explor, 1995. **Mailing Address:** 1755 E Plumb St Suite 170, Reno, NV 89502.

LIVERSAGE, RICHARD ALBERT, DEVELOPMENTAL BIOLOGY, REGENERATION. **Personal Data:** b Fitchburg, Mass, July 8, 1925; m 1954, June; c John W, Robert R, James K & Ross A. **Education:** Marlboro Col, BA, 1951; Amherst Col, AM, 1953; Princeton Univ, AM, 1957, PhD (biol), 1958. **Professional Experience:** EMER PROF ZOOL, UNIV TORONTO, as of 2004; Actg chmn, Univ Toronto, 1980-1981; assoc chmn grad affairs, Univ Toronto, 1978-1984; grad secy dept, Univ Toronto, 1975-1977; vis prof, Dept Biophys, Strangeways Res Lab, Cambridge, Eng, 1972; prof zool, Univ Toronto, beginning 1969; Vis investr, Huntsman Marine Lab, NB, Can, 1968-1971; from asst prof to assoc prof, Univ Toronto, 1960-1969; instr biol, Princeton Univ, 1958-1960; Lab instr biol, Amherst Col, 1954-1955; Lab instr biol, Bowdoin Col, 1953-1954. **Memberships:** Can Soc Zool; Soc Develop Biol; Royal Can Inst; Sigma Xi. **Research Statement & Publications:** Regulation of appendage regeneration in amphibians: role of hormones and nerves; determination and fate of the progenitor cell source(s) via gene expression; author of 87 publications. **Mailing Address:** Ramsay Wright Zool Labs, Univ Toronto, Toronto, ON M5S 3G5, Can. **Fax:** 416-978-8532. **E-Mail:** liversag@zoo.utoronto.ca

LIVESAY, GEORGE ROGER, MATHEMATICS. **Personal Data:** b Ashley, Ill, December 9, 1924. **Education:** Univ Ill, BS & MS, 1948, PhD, 1952. **Professional Experience:** PROF EMER MATH, CORNELL UNIV, as of 2004; from asst prof to assoc prof, Cornell Univ, 1958-1969; res assoc, Cornell Univ, 1956-1958; instr math, Univ Mich, 1950-1956. **Research Statement & Publications:** Topology. **Mailing Address:** Dept Math, Cornell Univ, Rm 7901, 530 Malott Hall, Ithaca, NY 14853. **Fax:** 607-255-7149. **E-Mail:** grl30@earthlink.net

LIVESEY, STEVEN J, HISTORY & PHILOSOPHY OF SCIENCE, MEDIEVAL SCIENCE & HISTORY OF SCIENTIFIC METHODOLOGIES. **Personal Data:** b San Fernando, Calif, September 25, 1951; m 1978, Nina; c Daniel A & Elizabeth F. **Education:** Univ Calif, Los Angeles, MA, 1977, PhD (hist), 1982; Stanford Univ, BS & BA, 1974. **Professional Experience:** CHMN, DEPT HIST SCI, UNIV OKLA, 1999-; PROF, HIST SCI, UNIV OKLA, 1995-; chmn, Dept Hist Sci, Univ Okla, 1994-1997; assoc dir res, Univ Paris & CNRS, 1993-1994; fulbright fel, 1987-1988 (U.K.) and 2005 (France); NEH Fellowship 1998-1999; from asst to assoc prof, hist sci, Univ Okla, 1982-1995. **Memberships:** Hist Sci Soc; Medieval Acad Am; Soc Intl Etude Philos Medievale. **Research Statement & Publications:** Investigation of scientific methodologies in antiquity and the middle ages; editions of related texts; relationship between science and religion; prosopographical and institutional aspects of medieval science. **Mailing Address:** Dept Hist Sci, Univ Okla, 601 Elm, Rm 625, Norman, OK 73019-0315. **Fax:** 405-325-2363. **E-Mail:** slivesey@ou.edu

LIVETT, BRUCE G, NEUROSCIENCES, BIOCHEMICAL PHARMACOLOGY. **Personal Data:** b Melbourne, Australia, August 27, 1943; m 1976, Dianne Whelan; c Andrew & Erica. **Education:** Monash Univ, BSc, 1965, PhD (biochem), 1968. **Professional Experience:** Coun mem, Int Soc Neurochem, 1987-1992 & Australian Neurosci Soc, 1987-1994; READER & DEP HEAD, DEPT BIOCHEM, UNIV MELBOURNE, AUSTRALIA, 1983-; prin investr & mem adv bd, Muscular Dystrophy Asn Can, 1978-1982; prin investr, McMaster Univ, 1977-; from assoc prof to prof med & biochem, Montreal Gen Hosp, McGill Univ, 1977-1983; Med Res Coun fel neurosci, McMaster Univ, 1975-1976; asst prof, Monash Univ, 1973-1977; Queen Elizabeth II res fel biochem, Monash Univ, 1971-1973; jr res fel, Wolfson Col, 1970-1971; Nuffield Dominions demonstr pharmacol, Oxford Univ, 1969-1971. **Memberships:** Int Brain Res Orgn; Int Soc Neurochem; Soc Neurosci; Australian Neurosci Soc; Australian Soc Biochem Molecular Biol; Australian Physiol & Pharmacol Soc; Australian Soc Comput Learning Tertiary Educ. **Research Statement & Publications:** Investigation into the role of neuropeptides as neuromodulators of catecholamine secretion in the endocrine adrenal medulla and nervous system; structure-function studies of marine neurotoxins. **Mailing Address:** Dept Biochem, Univ Melbourne, Parkville Victoria 3052, Australia. **Fax:** 613-934-77730. **E-Mail:** brucegl@unimelb.edu.au

LIVIGNI, RUSSELL ANTHONY, POLYMER CHEMISTRY. **Personal Data:** b Akron, Ohio, July 20, 1934. **Education:** Univ Akron, BS, 1956, PhD (polymer chem), 1960. **Professional Experience:** CONSULT, as of 2002; vpres, corp technol, 1995-1996; mem, NSF Indust Panel Sci & Technol, 1990-; vpres & dir, corp technol, GenCorp, 1988-1995; trustee & mem bd dirs, Edison Polymer Innovation Corp, beginning 1986; assoc dir, Ford Sci Lab, Gen Tire & Rubber Co, 1980-1987; chmn, Gordon Res Conf Elastomers, 1978; mgr, Ford Sci Lab, Gen Tire & Rubber Co, 1975-1980; sec head, Ford Sci Lab, Gen Tire & Rubber Co, 1963-1975; group leader, Ford Sci Lab, Gen Tire & Rubber Co, 1962-1963; sr res chemist, Ford Sci Lab, Gen Tire & Rubber Co, 1961-1962; res scientist polymer chem, Ford Sci Lab, Gen Tire & Rubber Co, 1960-1961. **Memberships:** Am Chem Soc; AAAS. **Research Statement & Publications:** Technical programs resulting in advanced and improved products and processes, especially related to polymer based technology; granted 32 patents; author of several publications. **Mailing Address:** 2291 Manchester Rd, Akron, OH 44314-3602. **Fax:** 216-794-6375.

LIVINGOOD, JOHN N B, mathematics; deceased, see previous edition for last biography

LIVINGSTON, ALBERT EDWARD, MATHEMATICAL ANALYSIS. **Personal Data:** b Hartford, Conn, February 28, 1936. **Education:** Boston Col, BA, 1958, MA, 1960; Rutgers Univ, MS, 1962, PhD (math), 1963. **Professional Experience:** PROF EMER MATH, UNIV DEL, as of 2004; prof math, Univ Del, beginning 1975; from asst prof to assoc prof, Univ Del, 1967-1975; asst prof math, Lafayette Col, 1963-1967. **Memberships:** Math Asn Am; Am Math Soc; Sigma Xi. **Research Statement & Publications:** Univalent and multivalent functions, particularly the application of methods of extreme point theory and subordination chains to extremal problems in multivalent function theory. **Mailing Address:** Dept Math, Univ Del, 535 Ewing Hall, Newark, DE 19716. **Fax:** 302-831-4511. **E-Mail:** livingst@math.udel.edu

LIVINGSTON, DANIEL ISADORE, POLYMER PHYSICS, RUBBER TECHNOLOGY. **Personal Data:** b New York, NY, October 15, 1919; m 1956, Helen Porritt; c 2. **Education:** City Col New York, BS, 1941; Polytech Inst Brooklyn, PhD (phys chem), 1950. **Professional Experience:** PRES LIVINGSTON ASSOC CONSULTS, 1986-; res & develop assoc, Polymer Physics Sect, Goodyear Tire & Rubber Co, 1985-1986; ed, Tire Sci & Technol, 1973-1982; Assoc ed, Rubber Chem & Technol, 1969-1972; head, Polymer Physics Sect, Goodyear Tire & Rubber Co, 1959-1984; sr res chemist, Continental Can Co, Ill, 1957-1959; sr res engr, Ford Motor Co, 1955-1957; scientist, Polaroid Corp, 1951-1955; Dir polymer chem, Gen Latex & Chem Corp, 1950-1951. **Memberships:** Am Chem Soc; Am Phys Soc; Tire Soc (pres 1986-1988); Am Soc Testing & Mat. **Research Statement & Publications:** Physical chemistry of polymers; high polymer synthesis, research and development; radiation effects in polymer systems; polymer physics; tire physics; materials science; rubber technology.

LIVINGSTON, DAVID J, BIOTECHNOLOGY, BIOCHEMISTRY. **Professional Experience:** Pres & chief exec officer, Spherics Inc, ending 2002. **Mailing Address:** Spherics Inc, 300 Metro Ctr Blvd, Ste 150, Warwick, RI 02886. **Fax:** 401-734-9204.

LIVINGSTON, DAVID M, MEDICINE. **Personal Data:** b Cambridge, Mass, March 29, 1941; m 1986, Emily; c Catherine & Julie. **Education:** Harvard Univ, BA, 1961; Tufts Univ, MD, 1965; Am Bd Internal Med, cert, 1971. **Professional Experience:** EMIL FREI PROF MED & GENETICS, DANA FARBER CANCER INST, HARDVARD MED SCH, as of 2004; DEPUTY DIR, DANA FARBER CANCER INST, HARDVARD MED SCH, as of 2004; dir & physician-in-chief, Dana-Farber Cancer Inst, Boston, Mass, 1991-; CHMN, EXEC RES, DANA FARBER CANCER INST, 1991-; vpres, Dana-Farber Cancer Inst, 1989-1991; physician, Med Internship Selection Comt, 1982-; prof med, Harvard Med Sch, Boston, Mass, beginning 1982; mem, Virol Study Sect, Div Res Grants, NIH, 1979-1983, 1986-1988; assoc physician, Dana-Farber Cancer Inst, 1977-1983; sr assoc med, Brigham & Women's Hosp, Boston, Mass, 1976-1982; mem, Med Internship Selection Comt, 1975-; vis physician med serv, Brigham & Women's Hosp, 1974-1985; from asst prof to assoc prof med, Harvard Med Sch, 1973-1982; sr clin assoc, Dana-Farber Cancer Inst, 1973-1977; assoc med, Brigham & Women's Hosp, Boston, Mass, 1973-1977; sr investr, Nat Cancer Inst, NIH, 1972-1973; sr staff fel, Lab Biochem, Nat Cancer Inst, NIH, 1971-1972; res fel biol chem, Harvard Med Sch, Boston, Mass, 1969-1971; res assoc, Lab Biochem, Nat Cancer Inst, NIH, 1967-1969; jr resident, Peter Bent Brigham Hosp, Boston, Mass, 1966-1967; intern med, Peter Bent Brigham Hosp, Boston, Mass, 1965-1966. **Memberships:** Nat Acad Sci; Inst Med-Nat Acad Sci; Am Soc Microbiol; Am Soc Clin Invest; Am Soc Biol Chem & Molecular Biol; Asn Am Physicians; Am Soc Virol; Am Fedn Clin Res. **Research Statement & Publications:** Molecular biology of virus-induced neoplastic transformation; control of eukaryotic gene expression and DNA replication; author or co-author of over 90 publications. **Mailing Address:** Dana-Farber Cancer Inst, 44 Binney St Smith 870, Boston, MA 02115. **Fax:** 617-632-4381. **E-Mail:** david_livingston@dfci.harvard.edu

LIVINGSTON, DOUGLAS ALAN, PROCESS RESEARCH FOR ORGANIC SYNTHESES, MEDICINAL CHEMISTRY. **Personal Data:** b Nagoya, Japan, December 29, 1954; American citizen; m 1977, Elizabeth; c Andrew S. **Education:** Univ Wash, BS, 1977; Columbia Univ, MA, 1981, MPhil, 1982, PhD (org chem), 1982. **Professional Experience:** SR VPRES & GEN MGR, DISCOVERY PARTNERS INT, as of 2006; assoc dir Chem Opers, Lajolla Pharmaceut Co, beginning 1992; res scientist, Burroughs-Wellcome Co, 1990-1992; res scientist, Upjohn Co, 1983-1990; swiss NSF researcher, ETH-Zurich, 1982-1983. **Research Statement & Publications:** Design and synthesis of potential new pharmaceutical entities; development of new methodology for existing drugs including steroids, aminothioglycosides, alkaloids, nucleosides and oligonucleosides. **Mailing Address:** Discovery Partners Int, 9640 Towne Ctr Dr, San Diego, CA 92121. **Fax:** 858-546-3081.

LIVINGSTON, ELLEN S, MATHEMATICS. **Education:** Colo State Univ, BS, 1967, MS, 1970; Wash Univ, PhD (math), 1982. **Professional Experience:** STAFF, ACOUST DIV, NAVAL RES LAB, as of 2006. **Memberships:** Acoust Soc Am; Soc Indust & Appl Math; Am Math Soc. **Mailing Address:** Naval Res Lab, Code 7121, Washington, DC 20375-5000. **Fax:** 202-404-7813. **E-Mail:** ellen@wave.nrl.navy.mil

LIVINGSTON, G E, FOOD SCIENCE & NUTRITION. **Personal Data:** b Rotterdam, Neth, February 1, 1927; m 1991, Joan; c David J, Gary M & Nina J. **Education:** NY Univ, BA, 1948; Univ Mass, MS, 1951, PhD (food technol), 1952. **Honors & Awards:** Sigma Xi Res Award, 1957; Carl R Fellers Award, Inst Food Technol, 1993 & Food Serv Distinguished Achievement Award, 1996. **Professional Experience:** Ed-in-chief, Pioneers Food Sci, 1992-; vpres, Mithcell Lane Kitchens Inc, 1992-1993; CHMN, SIERRA SUNSET INC, 1988-; co-ed, J Food Serv Systs, 1980-1983; adj prof, NY Univ, 1978-; adj prof, Pratt Inst, 1973-1978; mem, Bd Govs, Food Update, Food & Drug Law Inst, 1971-1975; consult, US Army Natick Labs, 1971-1983 & numerous others; chmn, Panel VII, Nat Conf Food Protection, 1971; chmn, Food & Nutrit Coun, Am Health Found, 1969-1991; mem bd sci consults, Food & Nutrit Coun, Am Health Found, 1969-1980; invitee, White House Conf Food, Nutrit & Health, 1969; chmn, Comt Food Serv Systs, 1968-1971; dir, Food Sci Prog, Columbia Univ, 1966-1972; adj prof, Columbia Univ, 1966-1972; mgr, Instnl Prod Dept, Morton Frozen Foods Co, 1962-1965; mem, Adv Bd Mil Personnel Supplies, Nat Acad Sci-Nat Res Coun, 1961-1964; res supvr, Continental Baking Co, 1959-1962; vis lectr, City Col New York, 1959-1960; PRES FOOD SCI ASSOCS INC, 1956-; vis prof, Laval Univ, 1954; from asst prof to assoc prof food technol, Univ Mass, 1951-1959; chemist, Bur Chem, NY Produce Exchange, 1949; mem, Food Stability Comn. **Memberships:** Am

Chem Soc; Soc Food Serv Systs (pres, 1981-1983); Fel Inst Food Technologists; Res & Develop Assocs Mil Food & Packaging Systs; fel Am Col Nutrit; fel AAAS; NY Acad Sci. **Research Statement & Publications:** Food colorimetry; prepared foods; food service systems; nutritive value; fresh food safety; author of one hundred publications; granted two US patents. **Mailing Address:** Food Sci Assocs Inc, PO Box 330, Dobbs Ferry, NY 13522. **Fax:** 914-693-1869. **E-Mail:** fsagild@idt.net

LIVINGSTON, HUGH DUNCAN, RADIOCHEMISTRY, OCEANOGRAPHY. **Personal Data:** b Glasgow, Scotland, November 12, 1940; American citizen; m 1965. **Education:** Glasgow Univ, BSc, 1962, PhD (chem), 1966. **Professional Experience:** DIR, MARINE ENVIRON LAB, INT ATOMIC ENERGY AGENCY, as of 2003; sr res specialist chem, Woods Hole Oceanog Inst, beginning 1979; res specialist, Woods Hole Oceanog Inst, 1973-1979; res assoc, Woods Hole Oceanog Inst, 1971-1973; res fel, Bowman Gray Sch Med, 1969-1971; Res assoc chem, Woods Hole Oceanog Inst, 1967-1969. **Research Statement & Publications:** Studies of artificial radioisotopes in the marine environment. **Mailing Address:** Int Atomic Energy Agency, 4 Quai Antoine 1er BP 800, Monaco. **E-Mail:** h.d.livingston@iaea.org

LIVINGSTON, JAMES DUANE, SUPERCONDUCTIVITY, FERROMAGNETISM. **Personal Data:** b Brooklyn, NY, June 23, 1930; m 1985, Sherry; c Joan, Susan & Barbara. **Education:** Cornell Univ, BEP, 1952; Harvard Univ, MA, 1953, PhD (appl physics), 1956. **Professional Experience:** SR LECTR MAT SCI, DEPT MAT SCI & ENG, MASS INST TECHNOL, CAMBRIDGE, 1989-; vis prof, Rensselaer Polytech Inst, 1987-1988; guest prof, Univ Gottingen, 1970; physicist, Gen Elec Corp, Schenectady, NY, 1956-1989; gen elec Coolidge fel, distinguished career award, Am Inst Metall Eng. **Memberships:** Nat Acad Eng; fel Am Phys Soc; fel Am Soc Metals Int; AAAS; Metall Soc; Inst Elec & Electronics Engrs. **Research Statement & Publications:** Superconducting, ferromagnetic and mechanical properties of materials and their relation to microstructure and processing. **Mailing Address:** Mass Inst Technol, 13-4066, Cambridge, MA 02139. **Fax:** 781-848-1806. **E-Mail:** jdliv@mit.edu

LIVINGSTON, KNOX W, forestry; deceased, see previous edition for last biography

LIVINGSTON, MARILYN LAURENE, NUMBER THEORY. **Personal Data:** b High Prarie, Alta, March 3, 1940; wid. **Education:** Univ Alta, BSc, 1961, MSc, 1963, PhD (math), 1966. **Professional Experience:** Vis scholar, Univ Mich, Ann Arbor, 1986-1987; prof math, Southern Ill Univ, 1978-2002; mem, Sch Math, Inst Advan Study, Princeton, NJ, 1974-1975; from asst prof to assoc prof, Southern Ill Univ, 1969-1978; vis asst prof, Ore State Univ, 1967-1969; asst prof, Western Wash State Col, 1966-1967. **Memberships:** Asn Comput Mach; Soc Indust & Appl Math; Inst Elec & Electronic Engrs. **Research Statement & Publications:** Combinatorics; design and analysis of algorithms; parallel algorithms for distributed memory machines. **Mailing Address:** Dept Comput Sci, Southern Ill Univ, 6 Hairpin Dr, Edwardsville, IL 62026-0001.

LIVINGSTON, ROBERT J, HYDROLOGY & WATER RESOURCES. **Education:** Univ Miami, PhD, 1970. **Professional Experience:** PROF BIOL SCI, FLA STATE UNIV, as of 2004; DIR, CTR AQUATIC RES & RESOURCES MGT, FLA STATE UNIV, as of 2004. **Research Statement & Publications:** Published more than 30 articles. **Mailing Address:** Ctr Aquatic Res & Resource Mgt, Fla State Univ, MC 1100, Tallahassee, FL 32306. **Fax:** 850-644-9829. **E-Mail:** livingst@bio.fsu.edu

LIVINGSTON, WILLIAM CHARLES, ASTRONOMY. **Personal Data:** b Santa Ana, Calif, September 13, 1927; m 1957, Dorothy Newell; c Peter & Ann. **Education:** Univ Calif, Los Angeles, AB, 1953; Univ Calif, PhD (astron), 1959. **Professional Experience:** EMER ASTRONR, KITT PEAK NAT OBSERV, 1994-; ASTRONR, NAT OPTICAL ASTRON OBSERV, 1984-; from jr astronr to astronr, Nat Optical Astron Observ, 1959-1993; observer, Mt Wilson Observ, Carnegie Inst, 1951-1953. **Memberships:** Am Astron Soc; Int Astron Union; Astron Soc India; foreign mem Norweg Acad Sci. **Research Statement & Publications:** Solar spectroscopy; solar magnetism; solar cycle studies. **Mailing Address:** PO Box 26732, Tucson, AZ 85726. **Fax:** 520-318-8278. **E-Mail:** wcl@noao.edu

LIVINGSTONE, DANIEL ARCHIBALD, LIMNOLOGY, PALEOECOLOGY. **Personal Data:** b Detroit, Mich, August 3, 1927; American & Canadian citizen; m 1989, Patricia; c Laura, Mary, Malcolm, Christina & Elizabeth. **Education:** Dalhousie Univ, BSc, 1948, MSc, 1950; Yale Univ, PhD (zoology), 1953. **Honorary Degrees:** DSc, Waterloo, 2000. **Honors & Awards:** Hutchinson Medal, Am Soc Limnol & Oceanog. **Professional Experience:** JAMES B DUKE PROF EMER BIOL & GEOL & RES PROF, as of 2005; J B Duke prof biol, Duke Univ, beginning 2000; J B Duke prof earth & ocean sciences, Duke Univ, 1999; J B Duke prof geol, Duke Univ, 1989; J B Duke prof zool, Duke Univ, 1983; mem environ biol panel, consult NSF Polar Prog, 1974-1976; PROF ZOOL, DUKE UNIV, 1966-; mem environ biol panel, NSF, 1964-; Guggenheim fel, 1960-1961; from asst prof to assoc prof, Duke Univ, 1956-1966; limnologist, US Geol Surv, 1956-1963; asst prof zool, Univ Md, 1955-1956; spec lectr biogeog, Dalhousie Univ, 1954-1955; Nat Res Coun Can fels, Dalhousie Univ, 1954-1955; Nat Res Coun Can fels, Cambridge Univ, 1953-1954; asst zool, Yale Univ, 1950-1953; field collector, NS Mus Sci, summers & demonstr biol, Dalhousie Univ, winters, 1947-1950. **Memberships:** Ecol Soc Am (ed Ecol Monogr, 1962-1966); Am Soc Limnol & Oceanog; Am Geophys Union; Am Quaternary Asn; Sigma Xi; Amer Asn Adv Sci fel. **Research Statement & Publications:** Pollen analysis; history of lakes; Pleistocene geology of Alaska, Nova Scotia, West, East and Central Africa; geochemistry of hydrosphere; sodium cycle; coring technology; paleoecology; limnology; biogeography of African fishes; distribution of grasses and sedges. **Mailing Address:** Dept Biol, Duke Univ, Durham, NC 27708. **Fax:** 919-684-6168. **E-Mail:** livingst@duke.edu

LIVINGSTONE, FRANK BROWN, physical anthropology; deceased, see previous edition for last biography

LIVNE, ELI, AERONAUTICAL ENGINEERING. **Education:** Technion Israel Inst Technol, BSc, 1974, MSc (aeronaut eng & eng educ), 1982; Univ Calif Los Angeles, PhD (aerospace eng), 1990. **Honors & Awards:** ASME/Boeing Structures & Materials Award, 1997. **Professional Experience:** PROF AERONAUT & ASTRONAUT, DEPT ENG, UNIV WASH, 1991-; assoc ed, AIAA Jour. **Mailing Address:** Dept Aeronautics & Astronautics, Univ Wash, 309A Guggenheim PO Box 352400, Seattle, WA 98195-2400. **E-Mail:** eli@aa.washington.edu

LIVOLSI, VIRGINIA ANNE, ENDOCRINE PATHOLOGY, GYNECOLOGIC PATHOLOGY. **Personal Data:** b New York, NY, July 29, 1943. **Education:** Col Mt St Vincent, NY, BS, 1965; Columbia Univ, MD, 1969. **Honorary Degrees:** MA, Univ Pa, Philadelphia, 1983. **Honors & Awards:** Medal of Honor, Tokyo Univ, 1992. **Professional Experience:** PROF PATH, DEPT PATH & LAB MED UNIV PA, SCH MED, as of 2004; consult path, Chester Co Hosp, Pa, 1985- & Vet Admin Med Ctr, Philadelphia, 1988-1990; dir, lab Cytol, 1975-1977; from asst prof to assoc prof path, Yale Univ Sch Med, 1974-1983; attend pathologist, Yale-New Haven Hosp, Conn, 1974-1983; instr path, Columbia Univ, 1973-1974. **Memberships:** Am Acad Path; Can Acad Path; Am Thyroid Asn; Am Soc Clin Pathologists; Asn Dir Anat & Surg Path. **Research Statement & Publications:** Evaluation of thyroid nodules, benign and malignant; clinical behavior. **Mailing Address:** Dept Path & Lab Med, Univ Pa Sch Med, Philadelphia, PA 19104-4283.

LJUNGDAHL, LARS GERHARD, BIOCHEMISTRY, MICROBIOLOGY. **Personal Data:** b Stockholm, Sweden, August 5, 1926; m 1949, c 2. **Education:** Stockholm Tech Inst, BS, 1945; Western Reserve Univ, PhD (biochem), 1964. **Professional Experience:** GA POWER DISTINGUISHED PROF, BIOTECHNOL, UNIV GA, as of 2004; DIR, CTR BIOL RESOURCE RECOVERY, UNIV GA, as of 2004; PROF BIOCHEM & MOLECULAR BIOL, UNIV GA, 1975-; Alexander Von Humboldt Sr Scientist Award, 1974-; from mem fac to assoc prof, Univ GA, 1967-1975; asst prof, Case Western Reserve Univ, 1966-1967; sr instr, Case Western Reserve Univ, 1964-1966; technician biochem, Case Western Reserve Univ, 1958-1959; res chemist, Stockholm Brewery Co, 1947-1958; technician med chem, Karolinska Inst, Univ Sweden, 1943-1946. **Memberships:** Am Soc Microbiol; Am Chem Soc; Brit Biochem Soc; Swed Chem Soc; Am Soc Biochem; Sigma Xi. **Research Statement & Publications:** Carbohydrate metabolism, carbon dioxide fixation, and one carbon metabolism inanaerobic microorganism; role of corrinoids, tetrahydrofolate derivatives and properties of enzymes in these processes. **Mailing Address:** Dept Biochem Univ Ga, A214 Life Sci Bldg, Athens, GA 30602. **E-Mail:** larsljd@arches.uga.edu

LLAURADO, JOSEP G, NUCLEAR MEDICINE, BIOMEDICAL ENGINEERING. **Personal Data:** b Barcelona, Catalonia, Spain, February 6, 1927; American citizen; m 1966, Deirdre; c Thadd, Oleg, Montserrat, Raymund, Wilfred & Mireya. **Education:** Balmes Inst, Barcelona, BA & BS, 1944; Univ Barcelona, MD, 1950, PhD, 1960; Drexel Univ, MS, 1963. **Honors & Awards:** XII Batista-Roca Prize, inst Exterior projection of Catalam Culture, Barcelona 2000; Mem Royal acad med catalonia, Barcelona; Joan d'Alos Prite, Cardiovascular Center St Jordi, Barcelona 1999; Catalan Jocs Florals Prize, Amsterdam, 1974 & Caracas, 1975. **Professional Experience:** PROF RADIOL, UNIV LOMA LINDA SCH MED, as of 2006; hon ed, Int J Med Info, 1997-; dep ed, Environ Mgt & Health 1992-; ed, Int J Biomed Comput 1984-1997; consult, Kaiser Permanente, Riverside, Calif 1987-; CHIEF NUCLEAR MED SERV, VET ADMIN HOSP, LOMA LINDA, CALIF, 1983-; consult, Good Samaritan Hosp, Milwaukee, Wis & St Joseph Mem Hosp, West Bend, 1979-1982; vis prof, Univ Zulia, Venezuela, 1974 & 1975 & Univ Padua, Italy, 1975; US rep, Int Atomic Energy Agency Symp Dynamic Studies Radioisotopes Med, Rotterdam, 1970 & Knoxville, Tenn, 1974; vis prof, Polytech Univ, Barcelona, Spain, 1973 & 1975; physician, Vet Admin Hosp, Wood, Wis, 1967-; prof biomed engr & physiol, Marquette Univ & Med Col, Wis, 1967-1982; partic, Nat Colloquim Theoret Biol, NASA, Colo, 1965; assoc prof physiol, Sch Med, Univ Pa, 1963-1967; USPHS Found fel steroid biochem, Col Med Univ Utah, 1958-1959; Rockefeller vis prof, Univ Valle, Colombia, 1958; Hite Found fel exp med, Univ Tex M D Anderson Hosp & Tumor Inst, 1957-1958; asst prof exp surg, Med Sch, Univ Otago, NZ, 1954-1957; asst med res, Postgrad Med Sch, Univ London, 1952-1954; Brit Coun scholar, Postgrad Med Sch, Univ London, 1952-1954; fel, Coun Adv Sci Invests, Spain, 1950-1952; Inst med, Sch Med, Univ Barcelona, 1950-1952. **Memberships:** Soc Nuclear Med; Am Soc Pharmacol & Exp Therapeut; Catalan Soc Biol; Biomed Engr Soc charter; life mem Inst Elec & Electronics Engrs; Am Physiol Soc. **Research Statement & Publications:** Radionuclides in cardiology (thallium-201 and analogs); radionuclide (P-32) treatment of pulmonary cancer; computers in nuclear medicine; biomathematics; compartmental analysis of electrolytes. **Mailing Address:** Loma Linda Univ Sch Med VA Hosp, 115, Loma Linda, CA 92357-0001. **Fax:** 909-777-3204.

LLENADOL, RAMON, CHEMISTRY. **Education:** Univ Santo Tomas, Philippines, BS; State Univ NY, PhD (chem). **Professional Experience:** VPRES, CLOROX CO, 1991-; div vpres household prod res, dir prod develop & vpres res & develop, L&F Prod Inc, 1983-1991; Staff mem, Procter & Gamble Co, 1972-1983; bd dirs, Soap & Detergent Asn & Chem Specialties Mfg Asn. **Research Statement & Publications:** Chemistry; household products. **Mailing Address:** Clorox Co, 1221 Broadway, Oakland, CA 94612-1888. **Fax:** 510-832-1463.

LLEWELLYN, GERALD CECIL, BIONUCLEONICS. **Personal Data:** b Lonaconing, Md, February 8, 1940; m 1962, c 3. **Education:** Frostburg State Col, BS, 1962; Purdue Univ, MS, 1966, PhD (bionucleonics). 1970. **Professional Experience:** BR CHIEF, ENVIRON HEALTH EVALUATION & TOXICOL, VA COMMONWEALTH UNIV, as of 2004; ASSOC BIOL EDUC, VA COMMONWEALTH UNIV, 1977-; from asst prof to assoc prof, VA Commonwealth Univ, 1969-1977; lectr biol & microbiol, Frederick Community Col, 1966-1967; instr biol chem, Frederick County Bd Educ, Md, 1962-1966; dir, bur toxic substances, Va Commonwealth Univ. **Memberships:** Nat Sci Teachers Asn; Sigma Xi. **Research Statement & Publications:** Toxicological responses of hamsters to aflatoxin B. **Mailing Address:** Dept Toxicol & Pharmacol, Va Commonwealth Univ, PO Box 980613 12th Clay, Richmond, VA 23298.

LLEWELLYN, J(OHN) ANTHONY, ENGINEERING SCIENCE, CHEMICAL PHYSICS. **Personal Data:** b Cardiff, Wales, April 22, 1933; m 1957, c 3. **Education:** Univ Wales, BSc, 1955, PhD (chem), 1958. **Professional Experience:** ASSOC DEAN & DIR ENG COMPUT, as of 2002; DIR, ACAD COMPUT, UNIV S FLA, as of 2002; PROF DEPT CHEM & MECH ENG, UNIV S FLA, 1972-; scientist astronaut, NASA, 1967-1968; assoc prof eng sci, Sch Eng Sci, 1964-1972; asst prof chem, Inst Molecular Biophys, 1962-1964; res assoc chem, Inst Molecular Biophys, 1961-1962; res assoc chem, Fla State Univ, 1960-1961; Nat Res Coun Can fel, 1958-1960. **Memberships:** Am Chem Soc; Am Inst Aeronaut & Astronaut; Royal Inst Chemists; Am Soc Mass Spectrometry; Am Vacuum Soc. **Research Statement & Publications:** Computing applications in medical imaging; theories of reaction rates; computer applications in chemical engineering. **Mailing Address:** Dept Chem Eng, Univ S Fla, 4202 Fowler Ave, Tampa, FL 33620-9951. **Fax:** 813-974-3651. **E-Mail:** che@eng.usf.edu, tony@usf.edu

LLEWELLYN, RALPH A, NUCLEAR PHYSICS, ENVIRONMENTAL PHYSICS. **Personal Data:** b Detroit, Mich, June 27, 1933; m 1955, Laura D Alsop; c Mark, Rita, Lisa & Eric. **Education:** Rose-Hulman Inst Technol, BS, 1955; Purdue Univ, PhD (physics), 1962. **Professional Experience:** PROF PHYSICS, UNIV CENT FLA, 1980-; dean, Col Arts & Sci, 1980-1984; prof physics & chmn dept, Ind State Univ, Terre Haute, 1974-1980; exec secy, Bd on Energy Studies, Nat Acad Sci, Nat Res Coun, 1973-1974; prof & chmn dept, Ind State Univ, Terre Haute, 1970-1973; prof physics & acting chmn dept, St Mary-of-the-Woods Col, 1969-1970; chmn dept, Rose-Hulman Inst Technol, 1969-1970; prof, Rose-Hulman Inst Technol, 1968-1970; assoc prof, Rose-Hulman Inst Technol, 1964-1968; Mem, NSF Apparatus Develop Workshop, Rensselaer Polytech Inst, 1964-1965; Asst prof physics, Rose-Hulman Inst Technol, 1961-1964. **Memberships:** AAAS; Am Phys Soc; Am Asn Physics Teachers; NY Acad Sci; Sigma Xi; Nat Geog Soc. **Research Statement & Publications:** Environmental physics, particularly beta and gamma decay; low level radiation in the environment; energy resources, energy and public policy; world energy resources; aluminum-26 in meteorites and lunar materials. **Mailing Address:** Dept Physics, Univ Cent Fla, Orlando, FL 32816-2385. **Fax:** 407-823-5112. **E-Mail:** ral@physics.ucf.edu

LLINAS, MIGUEL, NUCLEAR MAGNETIC RESONANCE SPECTROSCOPY, MOLECULAR BIOPHYSICS. **Personal Data:** b Cordoba, Arg, October 16, 1938; div, c Laura D, Miguel Jr, Gabriel & Manuel. **Education:** Cordoba Nat Univ, Argentina, Licentiate, 1963; Univ Calif, Berkeley, PhD (biophys), 1971. **Professional Experience:** Vis prof, Catalonia Polytech Univ, 1990; vis prof, Univ Utrecht, 1989; PROF CHEM, CARNEGIE-MELLON UNIV, 1988-; dir grad studies, Dept Chem, 1987-1991; chmn grad prog biophys & biochem, Carnegie-Mellon Univ, 1987-1988; assoc prof, Carnegie-Mellon Univ, 1976-1988; asst, Swiss Fed Inst Technol, Zurich, 1974-1976; fel assoc, Univ Calif, Berkeley, 1971-1974. **Memberships:** Biophys Soc; Am Chem Soc; AAAS; Protein Soc; Am Heart Asn. **Research Statement & Publications:** Applications of nuclear magnetic resonance spectroscopy to the study of biological polypeptides; structure and function of antithrombotics; protein structure and dynamics; conformation of human plasminogen and its interaction with antifibrinolytics; domain structures in mosaic proteins. **Mailing Address:** Dept Chem, Carnegie-Mellon Univ, 4400 Fifth Ave, Pittsburgh, PA 15213-3890. **Fax:** 412-268-1061. **E-Mail:** llinas@andrew.cmu.edu

LLINAS, RODOLFO R, NEUROBIOLOGY, ELECTROPHYSIOLOGY. **Personal Data:** b Bogota, Colombia, December 16, 1934; American citizen; m 1965, Gillian Kimber; c Raphael & Alexander. **Education:** Pontificial Univ Javeriana, Colombia, MD, 1959; Australian Nat Univ, PhD (neurophysiol), 1965. **Honorary Degrees:** Dr, Univ Salamanca, 1985, Univ Barcelona, 1993 & Univ Nacional, Colombia, 1994. **Honors & Awards:** Bowditch Lectr, Am Physiol Soc, 1973; Lang Lectr, Marine Biol Lab, Woods Hole, 1982; McDowall Lectr, King's Col, London, 1984; Ulf von Euler Lectr, Karolinska Inst, 1987; Ralph Gerard Lectr, Univ Calif, Irvine, 1987; Luigi Galvani Lectr & Award, Georgetown Univ, 1988; Craythorne Lectr, Univ Miami, 1988; F O Schmitt Lectr & Award, Rockefeller Univ, 1989; Albert Einstein GoldMedal Award Sci, UNESCO, 1991. **Professional Experience:** THOMAS & SUZANNE MURPHY PROF NEUROSCIENCE, DEPT PHYSIOL & NEUROSCIENCE, SCH MED, NY UNIV, 1985-; chmn, USA Nat Comt IBRO, Nat Res Coun, 1983-1988; actg chmn, USA Nat Comt IBRO, Nat Res Coun, 1982; mem, USA Nat Comt IBRO, Nat Res Coun, 1978-1981; panel mem, Task Force Basic Sci, 1978; PROF & CHMN, DEPT PHYSIOL & NEUROSCIENCE, SCH MED, NY UNIV, 1976-; chief ed, Neuroscience, 1974-; assoc, Neuroscience Res Prog, Mass Inst Technol, 1974-1984; mem, Neurol A Study Sect, 1974-1978; consult, Sch Aerospace Med, USAF, 1972-1975; mem, Neurol Sci Res Training A Comt, NIH, 1971-1974; prof physiol & biophys & head, Div Neurobiology, Univ Iowa, 1970-1976; clin prof, Col Med, Univ Ill, 1968-1972; head, Dept Neurobiology, 1968-1970; guest prof, Wayne State Univ, 1967-1974; assoc prof, Med Sch, Northwestern Univ, 1967-1971; prof lectr, Col Med, Univ Ill, 1967-1968; mem, Inst Biomed Res, AMA Educ & Res Found, 1966-1967; assoc prof, Univ Minn, 1965-1966; res scholar, Australian Nat Univ, 1963-1965; fel physiol, Univ Minn, 1961-1963; res fel psychiat & neurosurg, Mass Gen Hosp, 1959-1961; instr neurophysiol, Nat Univ Colombia, 1959. **Memberships:** Nat Acad Sci; Am Soc Cell Biol; Soc Neurosci; Int Brain Res Orgn; Biophys Soc; Am Physiol Asn; Am Acad Arts & Sci; Am Philos Soc. **Research Statement & Publications:** Structural and functional studies of neuronal systems; synaptic transmission in vertebrate and invertebrate forms; evolution and development of the central nervous system; author of 8 publications. **Mailing Address:** Dept Physiol & Biophys, NY Univ Med Ctr, New York, NY 10016. **Fax:** 212-689-9060. **E-Mail:** llinar01@popmail.med.nyu.edu

LLOYD, CAROL JEAN, ENGINEERING GEOPHYSICS. **Personal Data:** b Pittsburgh, Pa, August 21, 1951; American citizen; m 2004, Ralph; c Michelle & Jason. **Education:** Rensselaer Polytech Inst, BS Physics, 1973; Univ Wis, (Oceanography & Limnology), MS 1976, PHD 1980. **Professional Experience:** Geophysical Associate, ExxonMobil Exploration Co., 2005-?; Geophys. Assoc., ExxonMobil Prod. Co., 2003-2005; Geophys. Assoc., ExxonMobil Develop. Co., 2002-2003; Geophys. Assoc., ExxonMobil Explor. Co., 1999-2002; Geophys. Assoc., Exxon Explor. Co., 1998-1999; Sr. Explor. Geophys., Exxon Explor. Co, 1991-1998; Research Specialist, Exxon Prod. Res. Co., 1980-1991; Teaching Asst., Univ. Wis-Madison, 1976-1977; Res. Asst., Univ Wis-Madison, 1974-1980. **Memberships:** Society of Exploration Geophysicists; Marine Technological Soc; Sigma Xi (sr mem). **Research Statement & Publications:** Evaluation and design of seismic source and receiver arrays for offshore oil exploration; development of exploration techniques and strategies for offshore placer exploration; design of exploration strategy for vertical seismic profiling; seismic interpretation; processing for direct hydrocarbon indicators; Depth Conversion; Attribute Analysis. **Mailing Address:** ExxonMobil Exploration Company, PO Box 4778, Houston, TX 77210-4778. **Fax:** 281-654-7818. **E-Mail:** carol.j.lloyd@exxonmobil.com

LLOYD, DOUGLAS ROY, MEMBRANE SCIENCE, POLYMER SCIENCE. **Personal Data:** b Kitchener, Ont, September 15, 1948; m 1974. **Education:** Univ Waterloo, BASc, 1973, MASc, 1974, PhD (chem eng), 1977. **Professional Experience:** HENRY BECKMAN PROF CHEM ENG, UNIV TEX, as of 2006; assoc prof chem eng, Univ Tex, beginning 1983; asst prof, Univ Tex, 1980-1983; asst prof chem eng, Va Polytech Inst & State Univ, 1978-1980; fel, Dept Chem Eng, Univ Waterloo, 1977-1978; res assoc, Angelstone Ltd, 1973; res assoc, Dept Chem Eng, Univ Waterloo, 1972; res engr, Crane Can Ltd, 1970-1971; res engr, Union Carbide Can, 1969-1970. **Memberships:** Am Chem Soc; Am Inst Chem Engrs; N Am Membrane Soc. **Research Statement & Publications:** Synthetic polymeric membranes; membrane separation processes; polymer physics; enzyme engineering. **Mailing Address:** Dept Chem Eng, Univ Tex, CPE 3422 One Univ Sta C0400, Austin, TX 78712-0231. **Fax:** 512-471-7060. **E-Mail:** lloyd@che.utexas.edu

LLOYD, DOUGLAS SEWARD, PUBLIC HEALTH. **Personal Data:** b Brooklyn, NY, October 16, 1939. **Education:** Duke Univ, AB, 1961, MD, 1971; Univ NC, MPH, 1971. **Professional Experience:** DIR, CTR PUBLIC HEALTH PRACT, HEALTH RESOURCES & SERV ADMIN, as of 2000; ASSOC ADMINR, HEALTH RESOURCES & SERV ADMIN, as of 1998; lectr, Sch Med, Yale Univ, 1973-; lectr, Univ Conn Health Ctr, 1973-; mem courtesy staff, Hartford Hosp, 1973-; COMNR, CONN STATE DEPT HEALTH SERV, 1973-; comdr & spec consult, Naval Med Command, US Naval Res; health commentator, WFSB-TV House-Call prog; chmn, Asn State & Territorial Health Off Found, McLean, Va; pres, Asn State & Territorial Health Officers. **Memberships:** Asn State & Territorial Health Off (past pres); US Interagency Comt Smoking & Health. **Mailing Address:** Health Resources & Serv Admin, 5600 Fishers Lane Rm 14-15, Rockville, MD 20857-0001. **Fax:** 202-296-1252. **E-Mail:** dsl@asph.org

LLOYD, EDWIN PHILLIPS, ENTOMOLOGY. **Personal Data:** b San Antonio, Tex, September 18, 1929; m 1954, c 1. **Education:** Tex A&M Univ, BS, 1951, MS, 1952, PhD (entom), 1958. **Honors & Awards:** Superior Serv Award, USDA, 1974; Res Award, Miss Entom Asn, 1974. **Professional Experience:** RETIRED; dir, Boll Weevil Res Lab, Agr Res Serv, USDA, 1982-1986; adj prof, Miss State Univ, 1971-1986; sci adv, pilot boll weevil eradication exp, 1971-1973; res entomologist, Boll Weevil Res Lab, Agr Res Serv, USDA, 1956-1986. **Memberships:** Entom Soc Am. **Research Statement & Publications:** Cotton insects, specifically the boll weevil. **Mailing Address:** PO Box 1143, Starkville, MS 39759.

LLOYD, ERROL L, MATHEMATICS. **Education:** Pa State Univ, BS, 1975; Mass Inst Technol, MS, 1977, PhD (Comput Sci), 1980. **Professional Experience:** PROF COMPUT & INFO SCI, UNIV DEL, 1994-. **Memberships:** Asn Comput Mach; Soc Indust & Appl Math; Inst Elec & Electronics Engrs. **Mailing Address:** Dept Comput & Info Sci, Univ Del, 454 Smith Hall, Reisterstown, MD 19716. **Fax:** 302-831-1958. **E-Mail:** elloyd@udel.edu

LLOYD, HARRIS HORTON, CANCER, CHEMOTHERAPY. **Personal Data:** b Conway, Ark, November 14, 1937; m 1960, Emily; c Beth, Dwight, Mark & John. **Education:** Ouachita Baptist Univ, BA & BS, 1959; Purdue Univ, PhD (phys chem), 1968. **Professional Experience:** ADJ PROF COMPUT SCI, UNIV ARK, LITTLE ROCK, 1987-; CHIEF, INFO RESOURCES MGT, VA MED CTR, NORTH LITTLE ROCK, ARK, 1983-; head, Math Biol & Data Anal Sect, Southern Res Inst, 1972-1983; res chemist, Math Biol & Data Anal Sect, Southern Res Inst, 1968-1972; chief, Dept Chem, 406th Med Lab, US Army Med Command, Japan, 1964-1967. **Memberships:** Cell Kinetics Soc; Am Sci Affil. **Research Statement & Publications:** Chemical kinetics; data analysis and mathematical simulation; pharmacokinetics; kinetics of tumor growth and cell killing; design of computer-based information management systems. **Mailing Address:** Vet Admin Med Ctr, 2200 Ft Roots Dr, North Little Rock, AR 72114.

LLOYD, JAMES EDWARD, INSECT BEHAVIORAL ECOLOGY BIOTAXONOMY, POPULATION BIOLOGY. **Personal Data:** b Oneida, NY, January 17, 1933; m 1958, Dorothy; c Robert Stanley & Kyle Anne. **Education:** State Univ NY Col Fredonia, BS, 1960; Univ Mich, MA, 1962; Cornell Univ, PhD (entom), 1966. **Honors & Awards:** Res Award, Sigma Xi, 1974 Elected Distinguished mem of nat soc of Collegiate scholars, 1999; EE Guyton Distinguished Lecturer, Auburn univ, 1994. **Professional Experience:** Nat Geog Soc res grant, 1980; PROF ENTOM & NEMATOL, UNIV FLA, 1974-; NSF res grant 1968, 1980; from asst prof biol sci & entom to assoc prof entom & nematol, Univ Fla, 1966-1974; NSF res assoc syst & evolutionary biol, 1966; teacher high sch, 1960. **Memberships:** nat assoc of scholars; Coleopterist's Soc Fla entom soc; nat Ctr for sci ed. **Research Statement & Publications:** Function of luminescence in insects; systematics, behavior and ecology of Lampyridae; Toward understanding species and speciation. **Mailing Address:** Dept Entom Univ Fla, PO Box 110620, Gainesville, FL 32611-0620. **Fax:** 352-392-0190. **E-Mail:** pjhowell@.ufl.edu

LLOYD, JAMES NEWELL, PHYSICS. **Personal Data:** b Orange, NJ, October 20, 1932; m 1959, c 2. **Education:** Colgate Univ, BA, 1954; Cornell Univ, PhD (physics), 1963. **Professional Experience:** PROF EMER PHYSICS, COLGATE UNIV, 1996-; prof physics, Colgate Univ, 1979-1996; chmn, Dept Physics & Astron, 1973-1976; from instr to assoc prof physics, Colgate Univ, 1961-1979. **Memberships:** Am Phys Soc; Am Asn Physics Teachers. **Research Statement & Publications:** Ferromagnetic resonance and transport properties in metals. **Mailing Address:** Dept Physics & Astron, Colgate Univ, 13 Oak Dr, Hamilton, NY 13346. **E-Mail:** jlloyd@mail.colgate.edu

LLOYD, JOHN EDWARD, VETERINARY & MEDICAL ENTOMOLOGY, ENTOMOLOGY EDUCATION. **Personal Data:** b Munhall, Pa, September 28, 1940; m 1962, Deanna; c Gwendolyn J (Johnson) & John E Jr. **Education:** Pa State Univ, BS, 1962; Cornell Univ, PhD (entom), 1967. **Professional Experience:** Actg head, Plant Sci Dept, 1985-1986; PROF ENTOM, UNIV WYO, 1976-; from asst prof to assoc prof, Univ Wyo, 1968-1976; Asst prof entom, Pa State Univ, 1967-1968. **Memberships:** Entom Soc Am; Am Mosquito Control Asn; World Asn Adv Vet Parasitol. **Research Statement & Publications:** Economic entomology; insects affecting livestock; insects affecting man; veterinary parasitology. **Mailing Address:** Dept 3354, Univ Wyo, Laramie, WY 82071. **Fax:** 307-766-5025. **E-Mail:** lloyd@uwyo.edu

LLOYD, JOHN RAYMOND, MECHANICAL ENGINEERING. **Personal Data:** b Minneapolis, Minn, August 1, 1942; m 1963, Mary; c Jay William & Stephanie Christine. **Education:** Univ Minn, BS, 1964, MSME, 1966, PhD (mech eng), 1971. **Honors & Awards:** Melville Medal, Am Soc Mfg Engrs, 1978; Ralph E Teetor Educ Award, Soc Automotive Engrs, 1986; Heat Transfer Mem Award, Am Soc Mfg Engrs, 1995. **Professional Experience:** Chmn, Midwest Energy Consortium, 1993-; DISTINGUISHED PROF, MICH STATE UNIV, 1991-; mem, Nat Bur Stand Assessment Panel, Nat Res Coun, 1987-1993; adv, NSF, 1987-1990; Azdel Inc, Shelby, NC, 1987-1990; mem, Sci Coun, Int Ctr Heat & Mass Transfer, Yugoslavia, 1986-; univ distinguished prof, Mich State Univ, 1983-1992; chmn, Dept Mech Eng, 1983-1991; Consult, LeRoy Troyer & Assoc, Mishawaka, Ind, 1980-1990; prof mech eng, Univ Notre Dame, 1970-1983; develop engr, Proctor & Gamble Co, 1966-1967. **Memberships:** Fel Am Soc Mech Engrs. **Research Statement & Publications:** Contributed over 90 articles to professional journals; contributed chapters to books. **Mailing Address:** Dept Mech Eng, Mich State Univ, East Lansing, MI 48824. **Fax:** 517-353-1750. **E-Mail:** lloyd@egr.msu.edu

LLOYD, JOHN WILLIE, III, ENDOCRINOLOGY, PHARMACOLOGY. **Personal Data:** b Winchester, Va, May 25, 1943; m 1965, c 2. **Education:** Shepherd Col, BS, 1966; WVa Univ, MS, 1969, PhD (endocrinol), 1973. **Professional Experience:** PROF, COMP SCI LAB, AUSTRALIAN NAT UNIV, as of 2006; assoc prof, endocrinol, howard univ, 1978-2005; dir, Endocrine Serv, Eastern Va Med Sch, 1976-1978; asst prof, endocrinol, Eastern Va Med Sch, 1974-1978; asst prof, pharmacol, WVa Univ, 1973-1974. **Memberships:** Sigma Xi; Soc Exp Biol & Med; Endocrine Soc; Am Physiol Soc. **Research Statement & Publications:** Endocrinology; Reproductive physiology; hormonal regulation of the adrenal gland and accessory sex organs; prostatic cancer. **Mailing Address:** Comput Sci Lab, Australian Nat Univ, Corner N & Daley Rd Bldg 115, Canberra, ACT 0200, Australia. **Fax:** 612-6125-8651. **E-Mail:** jwl@csl.anu.edu.au

LLOYD, KENNETH OLIVER, BIOCHEMISTRY, IMMUNOCHEMISTRY. **Personal Data:** b Denbigh, Wales, May 17, 1936; American citizen; m 1962, c 2. **Education:** Univ Wales, BSc, 1957, PhD (chem), 1960. **Honors & Awards:** Philip Levine Award, Am Asn Clin Pathologists, 1986. **Professional Experience:** HEAD, TUMOR ANTIGEN IMMUNOCHEM LAB, as of 2004; CHMN, IMMUNOL PROG, 1989-; MEM, MEM SLOAN-KETTERING CANCER CTR, 1987-; mem, Allergy & Immunol Study Sect, NIH, 1984-1988; assoc mem, Immunol Prog, 1978-1987; assoc, Immunol Prog, 1975-1978; assoc prof, Sch Med, Tex Tech Univ, 1974-1975; asst prof biochem, Columbia Univ, 1968-1974; USPHS res career develop award, 1968-1973; res assoc microbiol, Columbia Univ, 1963-1968; fel, Wash Univ, 1960-1963. **Memberships:** AAAS; Am Chem Soc; Am Asn Immunologists; Soc Complex Carbohydrates; Am Asn Cancer Res. **Research Statement & Publications:** Biochemistry, structure and immunochemistry of glycoproteins and glycolipids, particularly tumor antigens. **Mailing Address:** Mem Sloan Kettering Cancer Ctr, 1275 York Ave, New York, NY 10021. **Fax:** 212-717-3379. **E-Mail:** k-lloyd@ski.mskcc.org

LLOYD, L KEITH, UROLOGY. **Personal Data:** b 1941; m Karen; c Kristen, Keith & Kevin. **Education:** Centenary Col, BS, 1962; Tulane Univ Sch Med, MD, 1966. **Professional Experience:** DIR, DIV UROL, 1996-; bd dirs & comt educ, Am Spinal Injury Asn, 1986; PROF UROL, DEPT SURG, UNIV ALA MED CTR, 1981-; DIR UROL REHAB & RES CTR, SPAIN REHAB CTR, BIRMINGHAM, 1977-; from asst prof to assoc prof, Div Urol, 1974-1981; sr resident urol, Tulane Univ Sch Med, 1972-1974; resident instr, Tulane Univ Sch Med, 1972-1974; resident urol, Tulane Univ Sch Med, 1972-1973; res fel urol, Tulane Univ Sch Med, 1971-1972; asst resident instr, Tulane Univ Sch Med, 1970-1972; asst resident urol, Tulane Univ Sch Med, 1970-1971; med officer, US Pub Health Serv Hosp, Norfolk, Va, 1968-1970; jr asst resident, Gen Practice Prog, 1967-1968; intern, US Pub Health Serv Hosp, Norfolk, Va, 1966-1967. **Memberships:** Am Urol Asn; Am Med Asn; Am Col Surgeons; Am Spinal Injury Asn. **Research Statement & Publications:** Urodynamics and neurogenic bladder; urologic care in spinal cord injury; male sexual dysfunction; over 60 publications on urology, nuclear and physical medicine and rehabilitation; author of 6 books in urology. **Mailing Address:** Kirklin Clin, UAB Med Ctr, 2000 Sixth Ave S, Birmingham, AL 35249.

LLOYD, LAURANCE H(ENRY), operations research, electrical engineering; deceased, see previous edition for last biography

LLOYD, MICHAEL R, MATHEMATICS. **Education:** Kans State Univ, Manhattan, PhD (Maths). **Professional Experience:** ASSOC PROF, MATH DEPT, HENDERSON STATE UNIV, 1997-. **Mailing Address:** Math Dept, Henderson State Univ, 1100 Henderson St, Arkadelphia, AR 71999-0001. **Fax:** 870-230-5479.

LLOYD, MILTON HAROLD, INORGANIC CHEMISTRY. **Personal Data:** b Des Moines, Iowa, March 27, 1925; m 1944, c 3. **Education:** Creighton Univ, BS, 1950, MS, 1954. **Professional Experience:** RETIRED; sect mgr process res & develop, Oak Ridge Nat Lab, 1956-1986; chemist prod develop, Tidy House Prod Co, 1950-1956; sr res chemist, Oak Ridge Nat Lab. **Memberships:** Am Chem Soc; AAAS. **Research Statement & Publications:** Transuranium element isolation and purification; plutonia sol-gel processes for preparation of advanced reactor fuels; chemical studies of plutonium behavior in reactor fuel reprocessing and waste solutions. **Mailing Address:** 360 Lab Rd Apt 505, Oak Ridge, TN 37830.

LLOYD, NELSON ALBERT, ANALYTICAL CHEMISTRY. **Personal Data:** b Lorain, Ohio, October 12, 1926; m 1945, c 5. **Education:** Southern Methodist Univ, BS, 1950, MS, 1951; Okla State Univ, PhD (analytical chem), 1955. **Professional Experience:** RETIRED; chief, Geochem Div, Geol Surv Ala, Tuscaloosa, 1970-1992; chmn, Div Natural Sci, Mobile Col, 1967-1970; Consult, Tuscaloosa Metall Res Ctr, US Bur Mines, 1963-1967 & State Oil & Gas Bd, Ala, 1966-1967; assoc prof analytical chem, Northeastern La State Col, 1956-1961 & Univ Ala, Tuscaloosa, 1961-1967; Res chemist, Goodyear Atomic Corp, 1954-1956. **Memberships:** Am Chem Soc. **Research Statement & Publications:** Rock analysis, whole rock and trace metals in rock; trace substances in water, heavy metals, pesticides herbicides and various nitrogen species. **Mailing Address:** 209 32nd Ave E, Tuscaloosa, AL 35404.

LLOYD, NORMAN EDWARD, BIOCHEMISTRY, BIOTECHNOLOGY. **Personal Data:** b Oak Park, Ill, February 20, 1929; m 1951, c 8. **Education:** Rockjurst Col, BS, 1952; Kans State Col, MS, 1953; Purdue Univ, PhD (biochem), 1956. **Professional Experience:** RETIRED; group dir biotechnol, Clinton Corn Processing Co, 1983-1989; vpres tech, Clinton Corn Processing Co, 1979-1982; dir res & develop, Clinton Corn Processing Co, 1978-1979; supvr chem res, Clinton Corn Processing Co, 1970-1978; asst res dir, Clinton Corn Processing Co, 1969-1970; dir sci develop, Clinton Corn Processing Co, 1964-1969; supvr starch chem res, Clinton Corn Processing Co, 1960-1964; cereal chemist, Int Milling Co, 1958-1959; assoc chemist, Corn Prods Co, 1956-1958. **Memberships:** Am Chem Soc; Am Asn Cereal Chem. **Research Statement & Publications:** Production and characterization of starches, sweeteners and enzymes; enzyme kinetics and immobilization; food biotechnology. **Mailing Address:** Four Lincolnshire Ct, Durham, NC 27712-9456.

LLOYD, RAY DIX, RADIATION PHYSICS, RADIOBIOLOGY. **Personal Data:** b March 10, 1930; m 1954, Louise; c 5. **Education:** Univ Utah, PhD (biol), 1974; Am Bd Health Physics, cert, 1968. **Professional Experience:** Prin investr, Radiobiol Div, 1996-2002; RES PROF, RADIOBIOL DIV, SCH MED, UNIV UTAH, 1986-; res prof, Dept Radiobiol & pharmacol, 1984-1986; coun mem, Nat Coun Radiation Protection & Measurements, 1980-1992; res assoc prof, Radiobiol Div, Sch Med, Univ Utah, 1979-1984; res asst prof anat, Radiobiol Div, Dept Anat, Col Med, Univ Utah, 1961-1979. **Memberships:** Radiation Res Soc; fel Health Physics Soc; Int Radiation Protection Asn; Am Acad Health Physics. **Research Statement & Publications:** Biological effects of ionizing radiation; internal emitters; dose-response models; risk assessment; risk modification by chelation therapy; application of radioactivity to biomedical studies; health physics; reconstruction of radiation dose from Nevada nuclear testing. **Mailing Address:** Sch Med, Univ Utah, Radiobiol Div Bldg 586, Salt Lake City, UT 84112. **E-Mail:** ray.lloyd@hsc.utah.edu

LLOYD, RAYMOND CLARE, NUCLEAR REACTORS, CRITICALITY ANALYSIS. **Personal Data:** b Sioux Falls, SDak, July 22, 1927; m 1949, c 3. **Education:** Augustana Col, BA, 1949; SDak State Univ, MS, 1951. **Professional Experience:** STAFF SCIENTIST, BATTELLE PAC NORTHWEST LAB, 1965-; Scientist, Hanford Atomic Plant, Gen Elec Co, 1951-1965. **Memberships:** Am Nuclear Soc. **Research Statement & Publications:** Reactor physics and criticality analysis. **Mailing Address:** 2068 Hudson Ave, Richland, WA 99352.

LLOYD, THOMAS A, OBSTETRICS & GYNECOLOGY, PHARMACOLOGY. **Personal Data:** b Olney, Ill, September 4, 1942. **Education:** Antioch Col, BA, 1964; Harvard Univ, PhD (pharmacol), 1970. **Professional Experience:** DIR, PA STATE CLIN RES SCHOLARS PROG, PA STATE UNIV, as of 2005; PROF HEELTH EVAL SCI, OBSTET & GYNEC & PHARMACOL, COL MED, PA STATE UNIV, 1993-; estab investr, Am Heart Asn, 1978-1983; numerous res grants, 1976-; from asst prof to assoc prof, Dept Obstet & Gynec & Pharmacol, Col Med, PA State Univ, Hershey, 1975-1993; sr staff fel, Lab Neurochem, NIMH, 1974-1975; staff fel, Lab Neurochem, NIMH, 1972-1974; res fel, Lab Neurochem, NIMH, 1970-1972. **Memberships:** Am Soc Pharmacol & Exp Therapeut; Am Inst Nutrit; Am Soc Clin Nutrit; Am Soc Bone & Mineral Res. **Research Statement & Publications:** Obstetrics and gynecology; pharmacology. **Mailing Address:** Dept Obstet & Gynec & Pharmacol, Col Med, Pa State Univ, Hershey, PA 17033-0850. **Fax:** 717-531-3922. **E-Mail:** tal3@psu.edu

LLOYD, THOMAS BLAIR, INDUSTRIAL CHEMISTRY, INTERFACE SCIENCE. **Personal Data:** b Reedsville, WVa, August 29, m Barbara; c Thomas B Jr, Judith & Althea. **Education:** Wash & Jefferson Col, BS, 1942; Western Res Univ, MS, 1946, PhD (phys chem), 1948. **Professional Experience:** RES SCIENTIST EMER, LEHIGH UNIV, as of 2003; res scientist, Lehigh Univ, beginning 1983; investr, 1954-1966, res supvr, NJ Zinc Co, 1966-1983; asst prof chem, Muhlenberg Co, 1948-1954; consult surface sci. retired. **Memberships:** Pres.(1955)Lehigh Valley Section Am Chem Soc; Sigma Xi; Engineers Club of Lehigh Valley pres (1960). **Research Statement & Publications:** Industrial process research, particularly pigments, hydrometallurgy and pollution control; particle dispersion in various media; surface science; PTFE etching; coal; adhesives. **Mailing Address:** Lehigh Univ, 6 Packer Ave, Bethlehem, PA 18015. **E-Mail:** tbl0@lehigh.edu

LLOYD, WALLIS A(LLEN), CHEMICAL ENGINEERING. **Personal Data:** b Harrisburg, Pa, July 24, 1926; m 1955, c 4. **Education:** Pa State Univ, BS, 1949; Univ Minn, PhD (chem eng), 1954. **Professional Experience:** Adj prof chem eng, PA State Univ, as of 2004; RES DIR, CANNON INSTRUMENT CO, 1964-; asst prof chem eng, Pa State Univ, 1956-1964; design engr, Calif Res Corp Div, Standard Oil Co Calif, 1955-1956; Res assoc chem eng, Univ Minn, 1954-1955. **Memberships:** Am Inst Chem Engrs; Am Nuclear Soc; Am Soc Testing & Mat; Sigma Xi. **Research Statement & Publications:** Heat transfer; chemonuclear research; separation processes; viscometry. **Mailing Address:** Dept Chem Eng, Pa State Univ, 201 Shields Bldg, Box 3000, University Park, PA 16804-3000. **E-Mail:** wal3@psu.edu

LLOYD, WELDON S, CALCIUM & BONE METABOLISM. **Personal Data:** b Miami, Fla, July 26, 1939; m 1960, c 2. **Education:** Boston Univ, BA, 1966; Northeastern Univ, MS, 1971. **Honorary Degrees:** DSc, Boston Univ, 1978. **Professional Experience:** Sr lectr, Roxbury Community Col, 1980; ASSOC PROF NUTRIT, BOSTON UNIV, 1978-; assoc pharmacol res, Boston Univ, 1971-1978; instr oral pharmacol, Boston Univ, 1968-1971; assoc, Harvard Univ, 1963-1968. **Memberships:** AAAS. **Research Statement & Publications:** Bone disease and hormone related studies; calcium and bone metabolism related studies in health and disease. **Mailing Address:** Boston Univ, Admissions 305, 100 E Newton St, Boston, MA 02118. **E-Mail:** wlloyd@bu.edu

LLOYD, WILLIAM GILBERT, ORGANIC CHEMISTRY, COAL SCIENCE. **Personal Data:** b New York, NY, July 10, 1923; m 1947, Anne Henderson; c Susan (Schulz), David G & Peter H. **Education:** Kalamazoo Col, AB, 1947; Brown Univ, ScM, 1950; Mich State Univ, PhD (org chem), 1957. **Professional Experience:** EMER PROF CHEM, WESTERN KY UNIV, 1988-; prof, Ogden Col Sci, Technol & Health, 1980-1988; dean, Ogden Col Sci, Technol & Health, 1980-1985; assoc dir & mgr, Mat Div, 1977-1980; chief chemist, Inst Mining & Minerals Res, Univ Ky, 1975-1977; sr res scientist, Inst Mining & Minerals Res, Univ Ky, 1974-1975; Dir, Larox Res Corp, 1972-1992; prof chem, Western Ky Univ, 1967-1974; sr process res specialist, Lummus Co, NJ, 1962-1967; assoc scientist, Dow Chem Co, 1960-1962; Chemist, Dow Chem Co, 1950-1960. **Memberships:** Am Chem Soc. **Research Statement & Publications:** Chemistry of coal and coal-derived products; catalysis of organic reactions. **Mailing Address:** Dept Chem, Western Ky Univ, Bowling Green, KY 42101. **E-Mail:** wglloyd@mindspring.com

LLOYD, WINSTON DALE, ORGANIC CHEMISTRY. **Personal Data:** b Pensacola, Fla, September 9, 1929; wid Luella (Deceased); c Pamela D, Donald G & Craig W. **Education:** Fla State Univ, BS, 1951; Univ Wash, PhD (org chem), 1956. **Professional Experience:** EMER PROF CHEM, UNIV TEX, 1996-; res prof, Univ Tex, 1965-1966; assoc prof chem, Univ Tex, El Paso, 1962-1996; org chemist, USDA, 1959-1962; Naval Stores Res Lab, USDA, 1959-1962; org chemist, Dow Chem Co, 1956-1958. **Memberships:** Emer Am Chem Soc; emer Sigma Xi. **Research Statement & Publications:** Stereochemistry of cyclic dienes; mechanisms of organic chemical reactions; natural products; synthesis. **Mailing Address:** Dept Chem, Univ Tex, El Paso, TX 79968. **Fax:** 915-747-5748. **E-Mail:** lloyd@utep.edu

LLUBERES, ROSA P, BIOCHEMISTRY, IMMUNOLOGY. **Personal Data:** b Dominican Repub, August 19, 1934; American citizen; m Edmundo; c Maribel & Ed. **Education:** Univ Santo Domingo, Dominican Repub, Doctor, 1955; Univ PR, Sch Med, MT, 1956. **Professional Experience:** Dept Microbiol, Sagrado Corazon Univ, 1986-1987; Dept Microbiol, Sch Med Del Caribe, 1984-1986; Lectr sch med technol, Univ PR, Sch Med, 1972-1978; CHEMIST RES, DEPT VET AFFAIRS, 1967-; biochem, Univ PR, Sch Med, 1965-1967; res asst chem, Vet Admin Med Ctr, PR, 1961-1965; Chemist, Health Dept Dominican Repub, 1956-1961. **Memberships:** Am Soc Microbiol; PR Soc Microbiol (pres 1978-1979 1988-1989 & 1991-); Asn Women Sci; NY Acad Sci; Am Soc Chemists. **Research Statement & Publications:** Immunology; principal objective is immunodefficiency reacted to rheumatology and gastroenterology. **Mailing Address:** 662 Calle Miramar Apt 104, San Juan, PR 00907.

LLUCH, JOSE FRANCISCO, CONSTRUCTION MANAGEMENT, ENGINEERING EDUCATION. **Personal Data:** b San German, PR, January 30, 1954; m 1979, Maria N Mercad; c 2. **Education:** Univ PR, Mayaguez, BSCE, 1975; Ga Inst Technol, MSCE, 1976, PhD (construct mgt), 1981. **Professional Experience:** PROF CIVIL ENG, UNIV PR, MAYAGUEZ, 1989-; DEAN ENG, UNIV PR, MAYAGUEZ, 1988-; asst dean eng, Univ PR, Mayaguez, 1986-1988; actg dir grad studies, Univ PR, Mayaguez, 1985-1986; from asst prof to assoc prof, Univ PR, Mayaguez, 1981-1989; prin investr & co-prin investr, var externally funded res projs, NSF & others, 1981-1988; Construct mgt consult, var construct contractors, 1981-1988; Instr civil eng, Univ PR, Mayaguez, 1977-1979. **Memberships:** Am Soc Civil Engrs. **Research Statement & Publications:** Construction project planning and control; computer applications in construction management. **Mailing Address:** Dept Civil Eng, Univ PR, PO Box 9041, Mayaguez, PR 00681-9041. **E-Mail:** jlluch@caribe.net

LNENICKA, GREGORY ALLEN, ELECTROPHYSIOLOGY. **Personal Data:** b Cedar Rapids, Iowa, December 4, 1952; m 1983, Linda; c Emily & Katherine. **Education:** Univ Iowa, BA, 1976; Univ Va, PhD (biol), 1982. **Honors & Awards:** Ten research grants from National Science Foundation and National Institute of Health. **Professional Experience:** Professor, State Univ. NY, Albany, NY 2003-present; Associate Professor State Univ NY, Albany, NY 1994-2002; Assistant Professor, State Univ NY, Albany, NY 1987-1993; Fellow, Univ Toronto, 1982-1987. **Memberships:** Society for Neuroscience; Am Asn for the Advancement of Science; Am Physiological Society. **Research Statement & Publications:** Physiology and plasticity of neurons and synapses. **Mailing Address:** Biol Dept, Univ at Albany, 1400 Wash Ave, Albany, NY 12222. **Fax:** 418-442-4767. **E-Mail:** gregl@albany.edu

LNENICKA, WILLIAM J(OSEPH), structural engineering; deceased, see previous edition for last biography

LO, ANDREW W, FINANCIAL ECONOMICS. **Personal Data:** American citizen. **Education:** Yale Univ, BA, 1980; Harvard Univ, MA & PhD (econ), 1984. **Professional Experience:** HARRIS & HARRIS GROUP PROF & DIR, LAB FINANCIAL ENG, SLOAN SCH MGT, MASS INST TECHNOL, as of 2003; prof finance, Sloan Sch Mgt, Mass Inst Technol, beginning 1991; Batterymarch fel, Batterymarch Financial Mgt, 1989; res assoc, Nat Bur Econ Res, beginning 1988; assoc prof, Sloan Sch Mgt, Mass Inst Technol, 1988-1991; res assoc, Olin fel, 1988; assoc prof, Wharton Sch, Univ Pa, 1987-1988; asst prof finance, Wharton Sch, Univ Pa, 1984-1987. **Memberships:** Am Finance Asn; Am Statist

Asn; Am Econ Asn; Inst Math Statist; Econometric Soc; Soc Indust & Appl Math. **Research Statement & Publications:** Statistical analysis of financial asset pricing models for equities, fixed income securities and derivative products; numerical computation of economic systems for financial forecasting. **Mailing Address:** Mass Inst Technol, Sloan Sch Mgt, E52-437 50 Mem Dr, Cambridge, MA 02142-1347. **Fax:** 781-863-9695. **E-Mail:** alo@mit.edu

LO, ARTHUR W(UNIEN), COMPUTER SCIENCE. **Personal Data:** b Shanghai, China, May 21, 1916; American citizen. **Education:** Yenching Univ, China, BS, 1938; Oberlin Col, MA, 1946; Univ Ill, PhD (elec eng), 1949. **Professional Experience:** EMER PROF ELEC ENG & COMPUT SCI, PRINCETON UNIV, 1986-; prof, Princeton Univ, 1964-1986; mgr adv tech develop, Data Systs Div, Int Bus Mach Corp, 1960-1964; sr mem tech staff, RCA Labs, 1952-1960; res & develop engr, Victor Div, Radio Corp Am, 1951-1952; lectr, City Col New York, 1950-1951; Asst prof elec eng, Mich Col Mining & Technol, 1949-1950. **Memberships:** Fel Inst Elec & Electronics Engrs. **Research Statement & Publications:** Digital electronics and computer organization. **Mailing Address:** 102 Maclean Circle, Princeton, NJ 08540. **E-Mail:** eandalo@aol.com

LO, BERNARD, MEDICAL ETHICS. **Education:** Harvard Univ, BA, 1966, AM, 1970; Univ Sussex, MA, 1968; Stanford Univ, MD, 1975; Am Bd Internal Med, dipl, 1978. **Honors & Awards:** Walter Zuckerman Lectr, Harvard Univ, 1993; Robert S Boas Vis Lectr, Cornell Univ & N Shorte Univ Hosp, 1993. **Professional Experience:** Prog dir, Robert Wood Johnson Found Initiative on Patient-Provider Relationship Changing Health Care Environ, 1996; Univ Rochester, 1995 & Wash Univ, 1996; Div AIDS, Nat Inst Allergy & Infectious Dis, 1995-; mem bd dirs, Am Soc Law, Med & Ethics, 1994-; mem, Chiron, 1994-; Bd Health Sci Pol, Inst Med, 1994-; PROF MED, UNIV CALIF, SAN FRANCISCO, 1993-; mem, Data Safety Monitoring Bd, Genentech, 1993-; vis prof, Sch Med, Yale Univ, 1993; William Chambers vis prof, Dartmouth Med Sch, 1993; DIR PROG MED ETHICS, UNIV CALIF, SAN FRANCISCO, 1989-; actg chief, Div Med Ethics, 1987-1989; from asst prof to assoc prof, Univ Calif, San Francisco, 1980-1993; residency internal med, Robert Wood Johnson clin scholar, 1978-1980; residency internal med, Stanford Univ, 1977-1978; intern & residency internal med, Univ Calif, Los Angeles, 1975-1977. **Memberships:** Inst Med-Nat Acad Sci; fel Am Col Physicians; Western Soc Clin Invest; Western Asn Physicians. **Mailing Address:** Univ Calif, 521 Parnassus Ave Rm C126, San Francisco, CA 94143-0903.

LO, CHENG FAN, WOOD CHEMISTRY. **Personal Data:** b Taichung, Taiwan, December 14, 1937; m 1966, c 3. **Education:** Nat Taiwan Univ, BS, 1962; Auburn Univ, MS, 1966; Ore State Univ, PhD (wood chem), 1970. **Professional Experience:** RES CHEMIST, BOISE CASCADE CHEM RES LAB, 1969-; wood chemist, Forest Res Lab, Ore State Univ, 1966-1969; res asst, Dept Forestry, Auburn Univ, 1964-1966. **Memberships:** Am Chem Soc; Tech Asn Pulp & Paper Indust; Forest Prod Res Soc. **Research Statement & Publications:** By-products development in wood cellulose and lignin material; technical assistance to paper production. **Mailing Address:** 3817 SE 153rd Ct, Vancouver, WA 98683.

LO, CHI-CHANG, MATHEMATICS. **Education:** Tam-kang Univ, BS, 1977; Wayne State Univ, MA, 1982; Univ S Fla, PhD (math), 1989. **Professional Experience:** PROF MATH, CLEARWATER CHRISTIAN COL, as of 2000. **Mailing Address:** Clearwater Christian Col, 3400 Gulf to Bay Blvd, Clearwater, FL 34619. **Fax:** 727-712-5861. **E-Mail:** chichang@spcollege.edu

LO, CHU SHEK, ENDOCRINOLOGY, BIOCHEMISTRY & PHYSIOLOGY. **Personal Data:** b Hong Kong, American citizen; m 1969, c 1. **Education:** Nat Taiwan Univ, Taipei, Repub China, BS, 1962; Univ Notre Dame, Ind, MS, 1965; Ind Univ Med Sch, Indianapolis, PhD (physiol), 1972. **Honors & Awards:** Sidney C Wener lectr, Dept Med, Col Physicians & Surgeon, Columbia Univ, 1980. **Professional Experience:** Mem res comt & peer rev subcomt, Md Affil, Inc, Am Heart Asn, 1990-1992; mem Grad Affairs Comt, Grad Educ Comt, 1988-1990; mem Grad Affairs Comt, Dept Physiol, Uniformed Servs Univ Health Sci, 1985-; ASSOC PROF, DEPT PHYSIOL, UNIFORMED SERV UNIV HEALTH SCI, BETHESDA, MD, 1981-; asst prof, Dept Physiol, Uniformed Serv Univ Health Sci, Bethesda, MD, 1977-1981; guest worker, Metab Dis Br, NIH, 1976-1978; Collaborator, Roche Res Found, Sci Exchange & Biomed, Switz, 1976; asst prof Dept Physiol, Sch Med, Univ Md, Baltimore, 1975-1977; fel, Cardiovasc Res Inst, Sch Med, Univ Calif, San Francisco, 1972-1975; sr lab technician, Ind Univ, 1967-1968; sr lab technician, Dept Physiol, Sch Med, Univ Miami, 1965-1966. **Memberships:** Am Physiol Soc; Am Soc Cell Biol; Soc Chinese Bioscientists Am. **Research Statement & Publications:** Germ-free animal research; cellular aging including whole body electrolytes in young and old rats; effects of mucosal anaerobiosis on galactose transport across the apical membrane of the hamster small intestine; mode of action of thyroid hormone and corticosterone on sodium transport in rat kindney and small intestine; mechanism of action of catecholamine on sodium and potassium transport; molecular biological approches to study the mechanisms of action of hormone(thyroid and gluocorticoid) on membrane transport and membrane biochemistry; mechanisms of action of growth factors on phosphatidylinositol metabolism in smooth muscle cell; signal transduction in diabetics glomerulus. **Mailing Address:** Dept Physiol, Uniformed Serv Univ Health Sci, 4301 Jones Bridge Rd, Bethesda, MD 20814-4799.

LO, CLIFFORD W, PEDIATRICS. **Personal Data:** b Hempstead, NY, September 9, 1951; m 1984, c 1. **Education:** Stanford Univ, AB, 1972; Univ Hawaii, MD, 1977; Univ Calif, Los Angeles, MPH, 1981; Mass Inst Technol, ScD(nutrit biochem), 1986. **Honors & Awards:** Nat Osteoporosis Found Prize, 1990. **Professional Experience:** Adj assoc prof nutrit, Inst Health Prof, Mass Gen Hosp, 1990-; ASSOC DIR, NUTRIT SUPPORT SERV, 1990-; lectr nutrit, Inst Health Prof, Mass Gen Hosp, 1989-1990; Royal Soc guest fel, MRC Dunn Nutrit Unit, Cambridge, Eng, 1989; Fulbright scholar, Univ Cambridge, Eng, 1989; DIR, HOME TPN PROG, 1986-; ASST MED, CHILDREN'S HOSP, BOSTON, 1985-; CLINASSOC & INSTR PEDIAT, HARVARD MED SCH, MASS GEN HOSP, 1984-. **Memberships:** Am Gastroenterol Asn; NY Acad Sci; Hist Sci Soc; Am Soc Bone & Mineral Res. **Research Statement & Publications:** Vitamin D, parathyroid hormone and calcium metabolism; calcium nutrition and bone density in adolescents; total parenteral nutrition in pediatrics; international nutrition. **Mailing Address:** 28 Litchfield Rd, Cambridge, UK.

LO, DAVID S(HIH-FANG), COMPUTER MEMORY TECHNOLOGY, SWITCH-MODE POWER CONVERSION. **Personal Data:** b China, August 27, 1932; American citizen; m 1959, c 2. **Education:** Nat Taiwan Univ, BS, 1954; Univ Minn, MS, 1958, PhD (elec eng), 1962. **Professional Experience:** RETIRED; adj prof, Elec Eng, 1982-1999; sr staff scientist, Electronic & Info Systs Group, 1980-1990; staff physicist, Unisys Corp, 1972-1979; prin physicist, Unisys Corp, 1964-1971; lectr, Univ Minn, beginning 1962; sr res scientist, Honeywell Res Ctr, 1962-1964. **Memberships:** Inst Elec & Electronics Engrs. **Research Statement & Publications:** Electrical properties of ferric oxide semiconductors; ferromagnetic films; magnetic and optical memories; electroluminescent displays; optoelectronics; switch-mode power conversion. **Mailing Address:** 2313 Explorer Ct, Burnsville, MN 55337.

LO, ELIZABETH SHEN, ORGANIC CHEMISTRY, POLYMER CHEMISTRY, ADHESIVES, ELECTRONIC MATERIALS. **Personal Data:** b Shanghai, China, February 24, 1926; American citizen; m 1950, Arthur; c Katherine & James. **Education:** St John's Univ, Shanghai, BS with hon, 1945; Univ Ill, MS, 1947, PhD (chem), 1949. **Professional Experience:** RETIRED; mgr polymer mat, Electro-Sci Labs, Inc, Pa, 1982-1990; chief chemist, Optel Div, Refac Electronics Corp, 1979-1981; mem tech staff, David Sarnoff Res Ctr, RCA, 1976-1977; mgr mat & chem process, Fairchild-PMS Prod, 1974-1975; vis fel, Princeton Univ, 1971-1973; sr res chemist, Thiokol Chem Corp, 1965-1970; staff chemist, IBM Corp, 1960-1963; Permacel Div, Johnson& Johnson, 1957-1960; M W Kellogg Co, 1953-1957; J T Baker Chem Co Div, Vick Chem Co, 1951-1952; res chemist, Metalsalsts Corp, 1951; Fel, Univ Ill, 1949-1950. **Memberships:** Am Chem Soc; Int Soc Hybrid Microelectronics. **Research Statement & Publications:** Polymer, rubber and resin chemistry; fluorocarbon polymers; liquid crystals; polymer thick film for electronic industry. **Mailing Address:** 102 Maclean Circle, Princeton, NJ 08540. **E-Mail:** eandalo@aol.com

LO, GEORGE ALBERT, CHEMICAL PROPULSION, TECHNICAL MANAGEMENT. **Personal Data:** b Hong Kong, June 26, 1934; American citizen; m 1957, Jean; c Deborah, Jeffrey & Laura. **Education:** Univ Ore, BA, 1957, MA, 1960; Wash State Univ, PhD (chem), 1963. **Professional Experience:** MGR, CHEM DEPT, LOCKHEED PALO ALTO RES LAB, 1987-; sr staff scientist, Chem Dept, Lockheed Palo Alto Res Lab, 1977-1987; mem tech staff, Rocketdyne Div, Rockwell Int Corp, 1963-1977. **Memberships:** Am Chem Soc; Sigma Xi. **Research Statement & Publications:** Chemical kinetics and propulsion; chemistry of inorganic complexes; environment monitor and remediation; polymers and composites. **Mailing Address:** Lockheed-Martin Palo Alto Dept H1-32 Bldg 204, 3251 Hanover St, Palo Alto, CA 94304-1191.

LO, GRACE S, FIBER RESEARCH. **Professional Experience:** DIR FIBER RES, RALSTON PURINA CO, CHECKERBOARD SQ, 1976-. **Mailing Address:** Dept Fiber Res, Ralston Purina Co, Checkerboard Sq, St Louis, MO 63164-0001.

LO, HILDA K, SURGERY. **Education:** Nat Taiwan Univ, BS, 1964; Ill Inst Technol, MS, 1968, PhD (biol), 1974. **Professional Experience:** RES ASST PROF, DEPT SURG, UNIV MIAMI, 1989-; DEPT ORTHOP & REHAB, 1990-; res instr, Div Endocrinol & Metab, Univ Miami, Sch Med, 1981-1989; instr med, Div Endocrinol & Metab, Univ Miami, Sch Med, 1977-1980; postdoctoral fel, Div Endocrinol & Metab, Univ Miami, Sch Med, 1974-1977; fel lipid biochem & microbiol, Ill Inst Technol, 1970-1974; res assoc, Dept Microbiol, Chicago Med Sch, 1968-1970; microbiol & virol, Dept Biol, Ill Inst Technol, 1966-1968; res asst genetics, Dept Biol, Ill Inst Technol, 1964-1966. **Research Statement & Publications:** Author of numerous scientific articles, books and chapters. **Mailing Address:** Univ Miami, 1600 NW Tenth Ave R-2, Miami, FL 33136-1015.

LO, HOWARD H, GEOCHEMISTRY, PETROLOGY & ENVIRONMENTAL SCIENCES. **Personal Data:** b Hsinchu, Taiwan, September 3, 1937; American citizen; m 1965, Polly; c Wilbur & Gilbert. **Education:** Nat Taiwan Univ, BS, 1960; Univ Minn, MSc, 1964; Wash Univ, PhD (geochem), 1970. **Professional Experience:** PROF GEOL, CLEVELAND STATE UNIV, 1992-; vis prof, Nat Taiwan Univ, 1990; vis res prof, Purdue Univ, 1978; vis res prof, Ctr Volcanology, Univ Ore, 1974; from asst prof to assoc prof, Cleveland State Univ, 1970-1992. **Memberships:** Am Geophys Union; Geol Soc Am; Ohio Acad Sci Chinese Earth Sci Asn N Am; Overseas Chinese Environ Engrs & Sci Asn; Ohio Acad Sci (vice pres, 1991-1993); Overseas Chinese Engrs Sci Asn (assist exec dir, beginning 2000). **Research Statement & Publications:** Geochemical and petrological study of the volcanic rocks, igneous rocks and some metamorphic rocks, especially in the modern island arcs and canadian shield; geochemical study of lake and river waters; environmental quality study including treatment of municipal and industrial wastewater. **Mailing Address:** Dept Biol, Geol & Environ Sci, Cleveland State Univ, Cleveland, OH 44115. **Fax:** 216-687-9366. **E-Mail:** h.lo@csuohio.edu

LO, KWOK-YUNG, RADIO ASTRONOMY, ASTROPHYSICS. **Personal Data:** b Nanking, China, October 19, 1947; American citizen; m 1973, Helen; c Jan Hsin & Derek P Hsin. **Education:** Mass Inst Technol, SB, 1969, PhD (physics), 1974. **Honors & Awards:** Alexander von Humboldt Res Award, 1994-1995. **Professional Experience:** CHMN, ADV COMT, as of 2004; DIR, NAT RADIO ASTRON OBSERVATORY, 2002-; PROF PHYSICS, NAT TAIWAN UNIV, 1998-; DIR & DISTINGUISHED RES FEL, INST ASTRON & ASTROPHYS ACAD SINICA, TAIPEI, TAIWAN, REPUB CHINA, 1997-; chmn, Astron Dept, Univ Ill, 1995-1997; Alexander von Humboldt sr scientist, Max Planck Inst physics, 1994-; assoc, Ctr Advan Study, Univ Ill, 1991-1992; prof astron, Univ Ill, 1986-2000; vis lectr, Astron Dept, Univ Minn, 1985; vis astronr, Onsala Space Observ, Sweden, 1985; asst prof radio astron, Calif Inst Technol, 1980-1986; sr res fel, Calif Inst Technol, 1978-1980; asst res astronr, Radio Astron Lab, Univ Calif, Berkeley, 1978; Miller fel basic res sci, Univ Calif, Berkeley, 1976-1978; res fel radio astron, Owens Valley Radio Observ, Calif Inst Technol, 1974-1976. **Memberships:** Am Astron Soc; Int Astron Union; Int Union Radio Sci; AAAS. **Research Statement & Publications:** Microwave spectroscopy studies of phenomena associated with star formation; studies of the intergalactic medium in nearby groups of galaxies; high angular resolution studies of galactic and extragalactic radio sources by interferometry and very long baseline interferometry techniques; millimeter-wave interferometry; galactic center; dwarf galaxies; cosmic microwave background radiation. **Mailing Address:** Nat Radio Astron Observ, 520 Edgemont Rd Dir Fred Lo, Charlottesville, VA 22903-2475. **Fax:** 434-296-0385. **E-Mail:** flo@nrao.edu

LO, MIKE MEI-KUO, PHYSICAL CHEMISTRY. **Personal Data:** b Formosa, China, September 21, 1936; m 1967. **Education:** Nat Taiwan Univ, BS, 1959; Univ Ill, MS, 1965, PhD (chem), 1967. **Professional Experience:** SR RES CHEMIST, S C JOHNSON & SON INC, 1967-; res fel, Univ Ill. **Memberships:** Am Chem Soc; Fine Particle Soc; Am Indust Hyg Asn; Am Soc Testing & Mat. **Research Statement & Publications:** Microwave spectroscopy; ultrasonic impedometry; gas chromatography and mass spectroscopy; aerosol science and technology. **Mailing Address:** 3721 Spring Lake Dr, Racine, WI 53405.

LO, THEODORE CHING-YANG, MEMBRANE FUNCTIONS, SOMATIC CELL GENETICS. **Personal Data:** b Shanghai, China, December 22, 1943; Canadian citizen; m 1974, Mimi; c 2. **Education:** Univ Man, BSc, 1969; Univ Toronto, PhD (Med Biophys), 1973. **Professional Experience:** PROG DIR, BACHELOR MED SCI PROG, UNIV WESTERN ONT, 2000 - 2005; CHMN, DEPT BIOCHEM, UNIV WESTERN ONT, 1996-2005; PROF BIOCHEM, UNIV WESTERN ONT, 1987-; from asst prof to assoc prof, Univ Western Ont, 1975-1987; res fel biochem, Harvard Univ, 1973-1975. **Memberships:** Can Biochem Soc. **Research Statement & Publications:** Molecular mechanisms for hexose transport in rat myoblasts; human muscle cells. **Mailing Address:** Dept Biochem, Univ Western Ont, London, ON N6A 5C1, Can. **E-Mail:** tcylo@uwo.ca

LO, THERESA NONG, BIOCHEMISTRY. **Personal Data:** b Hai Pong, North Vietnam, March 16, 1945; American citizen; m 1969, Chu; c Francesca C. **Education:** Clarke Col, Dubuque, Iowa, BA, 1968; Ind Univ, PhD (biochem), 1974. **Professional Experience:** HEALTH SCI ADMINR, NAT INST ARTHRITIS & MUSCULOSKELETAL & SKIN DIS, NIH, 1991-1999; health sci adminr, Div Extramural Activ, Nat Cancer Inst, 1989-1991; health sci adminr, Div Blood Dis & Resources, 1988-1989; res chemist, Lab Chem Pharmacol, 1982-1988; res chemist, Lab Cellular Metab, Nat Heart, Lung & Blood Inst, 1979-1982; vis fel, Lab Immunobiol, Nat Cancer Inst, 1977-1978; vis fel, Pulmonary Br, NIH, 1975-1977; USPHS trainee, Cardiovasc Res Inst, Univ Calif, San Francisco, 1973-1975; res asst dept biochem, Ind Univ, 1968-1973; lab asst dept chem, Clarke Col, 1966-1968. **Memberships:** Am Soc Pharmacol & Exp Therapeut Retired; Inflammation Res Asn; emer mem Am Soc Biochem & Molecular Biol; Sigma Xi. **Research Statement & Publications:** Enzymology of blood constituents; mechanisms of action peptide cytotoxins; proteases and proteases inhibitors; mechanisms of action of nonsteroidal anti inflammatory drugs; chemotaxis; energy-linked transport processes; author and co-author of numerous articles. **Mailing Address:** 5304 Elsmere Ave, Bethesda, MD 20814-4799.

LO, W(ING) C(HEUK), CERAMICS, METALLURGY. **Personal Data:** b Macao, May 20, 1924; American citizen; m 1957, Mary S Huang; c David D, Cynthia S & Alan Y. **Education:** Lingnan Univ, BS, 1947; Mo Sch Mines, BS, 1954; Rutgers Univ, PhD (ceramic eng), 1960. **Professional Experience:** RETIRED; mem tech staff, Bell Tel Labs, 1959-1986; res asst ceramics, Rutgers Univ, 1955-1959; Assoc ceramic engr, Crane Co, Ill, 1954-1955. **Memberships:** emer mem Am Ceramic Soc; Nat Inst Ceramic Engrs. **Research Statement & Publications:** Evaluation and development of material and process for the fabrication of components for light wave communication. **Mailing Address:** 1466 Locksley Dr, Bethlehem, PA 18018.

LO, WOO-KUEN, LENS RESEARCH. **Personal Data:** b Hualien, Taiwan, December 20, 1945; m 1972, Ji-Hua; c Wayne, Cindy & Kevin. **Education:** Wayne State Univ, PhD (anat), 1978; Nat Taiwan Norm Univ, BS, 1969; State Univ NY, MA, 1974. **Professional Experience:** PROF ANAT & DIR, ELECTRON MICROS FACIL, MOREHOUSE SCH MED, 1992-; adj assoc prof Ophthalmol, Emory Univ Sch Med, 1989-; vis fel biol, Princeton Univ, 1988; assoc prof, Morehouse Sch Med, 1987-1992; from asst prof to assoc prof anat, Morehouse Sch Med, 1983-1992; dir electron micros facil, Morehouse Sch Med, 1983-1992; grad assist anat, Wayne State Univ, Detroit, Mich, 1974-1978; teaching res assist anat, Nat Taiwan Univ, Taipei, 1970-1972; dir, Electron Micros Facil. **Memberships:** Am Soc Cell Biol; Am Asn Anatomists; Asn Res Vision & Ophthal; Int Soc Eye Res; Electron Microscopy Soc Am; AAAS; Sigma XI. **Research Statement & Publications:** Cell biology of the ocular lens; focusing on structures and functions of intercellular junctions, cell membranes and cytoskeleton, as well as their changes during cataractogenesis; author of various articles. **Mailing Address:** Dept Anat, Morehouse Sch Med, 720 Westview Dr SW, Atlanta, GA 30310-1495. **Fax:** 404-752-1037. **E-Mail:** lowk@msm.edu

LO, Y(UEN) T(ZE), ELECTRICAL ENGINEERING. **Personal Data:** b China, January 31, 1920; American citizen; m 1953, c 2. **Education:** Nat Southwest Assoc Univ, BS, 1942; Univ Ill, MS, 1949, PhD (elec eng), 1952. **Honors & Awards:** John T Bolljahn Mem Award, Inst Elec & Electronics Engrs, 1964, Centennial Medal, 1984, Distinguished Achievement Award, 1996; HalliBurt Eng, Educ & Leadership Award, 1986. **Professional Experience:** PROF EMER ELEC ENG, UNIV ILL, URBANA, 1990-; consult, Lockheed, 1986; consult, Ford Aerospace, 1986; consult, TRW, 1985-1986; dir, Electromagnetics Lab, Univ Ill, Urbana, 1982-1990; consult, Jet Propulsion Lab, 1981-1985; consult, Raytheon, 1969-1973; consult, IBM Corp, 1969; consult, Emerson Elec, 1968-1969; consult, Am Electronics Lab, 1966; consult, Andrew Corp, 1963; consult, Westinghouse Elec Corp, 1957-1958; from asst prof to prof, Univ Ill, Urbana, 1956-1990; proj engr, Channel Master Corp, 1952-1956; instr, Tsinghua & Yenching Univs, 1946-1948; asst, Radio Res Inst, Tsinghua Univ, Peking, 1942-1946; hon prof, Northwest Telecommunications Eng Inst & Northwest Polytech Univ, People's Repub China. **Memberships:** Nat Acad Engr; Int Union Radio Sci; Sigma Xi. **Research Statement & Publications:** Antenna; electromagnetic theory; waves in plasma; radio astronomy. **Mailing Address:** Univ Ill, 1401 W Green St, Urbana, IL 61801.

LOACH, KENNETH WILLIAM, DATA ANALYSIS, TEACHING. **Personal Data:** b Portsmouth, Eng, September 5, 1934; American citizen; m 1966, Sandra K; c Matthew William & Catherine Genna. **Education:** Univ Auckland, BSc, 1956, MSc, 1958; Univ Wash, PhD (chem), 1969. **Professional Experience:** EMER PROF CHEM, PLATTSBURGH STATE UNIV, 1999-; vis assoc prof, Univ Del, 1985-1986; sr vis fel, Univ Leeds, 1977-1978; assoc prof, 1973-1999; NSF grants, State Univ NY Res Found fel, 1972-1973 & 1977-1978; NSF grants, State Univ NY Col Plattsburgh, 1972-1973; NSF grants, Tufts Univ, 1971; asst prof, State Univ NY Col Plattsburgh, 1963-1973; div plant indust, Commonwealth Sci & Indust Res Orgn, Australia, 1960-1963; chemist, Ruakura Animal Res Sta, NZ, 1958-1960. **Memberships:** AAAS; Am Chem Soc; United Univ Professions. **Research Statement & Publications:** Principles of analytical chemistry; chemical computing. **Mailing Address:** Plattsburgh State Univ, Dept Chem Hudson Hall, Plattsburgh, NY 12901-2681.

LOACH, PAUL A, BIOCHEMISTRY, PHYSICAL BIOCHEMISTRY. **Personal Data:** b Findlay, Ohio, July 18, 1934; m 1957, c 4. **Education:** Univ Akron, BS, 1957; Yale Univ, PhD (biochem), 1961. **Professional Experience:** PROF BIOCHEM & MOLECULAR BIOL, NORTHWESTERN UNIV, 1974-; PROF CHEM, NORTHWESTERN UNIV, 1973-; res career develop award, NIH, 1971-1976; from asst prof to assoc prof, Northwestern Univ, 1963-1973; Nat Acad Sci-Nat Res Coun fel photosynthesis, Univ Calif, Berkeley, 1961-1963. **Memberships:** AAAS; Am Chem Soc; Am Soc Biol Chem; Biophys Soc; Am Soc for Photobiology. **Research Statement & Publications:** Primary photochemistry of photosynthesis; chemistry of porphyrins and metalloporphyrins; biological oxidation and reduction; structure and function in bioenergetic membranes; photochemical models of photosynthesis; published numerous articles. **Mailing Address:** Dept Biochem & Molecular Biol, Northwestern Univ, Rm Tech D157, Evanston, IL 60208-3500. **E-Mail:** p-loach@northwestern.edu

LOADER, CLIVE ROLAND, MATHEMATICAL STATISTICS. **Personal Data:** b Saffron Walden, Eng, March 11, 1965; New Zealander citizen. **Education:** Univ Canterbury, NZ, BSc, 1986; Stanford Univ, PhD (statist), 1990. **Professional Experience:** MEM TECH STAFF, AT&T BELL LABS, 1990-; Biometrician, Ministry Agr & Fisheries, 1986. **Memberships:** Inst Math Statist; Am Statist Asn. **Research Statement & Publications:** Statistical applications of stochastic processes; boundary crossing problems; change points; sequential analysis; scan statistics; goodness of fit tests; confidence bands. **Mailing Address:** Bell Labs, Lucent Technol, 700 Mountain Ave, Murray Hill, NJ 07974-0636. **E-Mail:** clive@bell-labs.com

LOADHOLT, CLAUDE BOYD, BIOSTATISTICS. **Personal Data:** b Fairfax, SC, March 26, 1940; m 1963, c 2. **Education:** Clemson Univ, BS, 1962, MS, 1965; Va Polytech Inst, PhD (statist), 1969. **Professional Experience:** PRES & CHIEF EXEC OFFICER, AGENTOWNED REALTY CO/SERV GROUP INC, as of 2006; ASSOC PROF BIOMET, MED UNIV SC, 1970-; asst prof exp statist, Clemson Univ, 1968-1970; asst exp sta statistician, Clemson Univ, 1965-1966. **Memberships:** Biomet Soc. **Research Statement & Publications:** Statistical consultation in biological and medical research; design of experiments; statistical data processing. **Mailing Address:** AgentOwned Realty Co/Serv Group, Inc, 1341 Venning Rd, Mt Pleasant, SC 29464. **E-Mail:** boyd@agentowned.com

LOAN, LEONARD DONALD, POLYMER CHEMISTRY. **Personal Data:** b London, Eng, October 6, 1930; m 1955, c 3. **Education:** Univ Birmingham, BSc, 1951, PhD (polymer chem), 1954. **Professional Experience:** HEAD PLASTICS CHEM, RES & ENG, AT&T BELL LABS, 1974-; mem tech staff polymer chem, Res & Eng, AT&T Bell Labs, 1966-1974; prin sci off rubber chem, Rubber & Plastics Res Asn, 1959-1966; chemist, Arthur D Little Res Inst, 1957-1959; Sci off combustion chem, Royal Aircraft Estab, 1954-1957. **Memberships:** Am Chem Soc. **Research Statement & Publications:** Polymer crosslinking and aging. **Mailing Address:** 107 Central Ave, New Providence, NJ 07974.

LOAN, RAYMOND WALLACE, IMMUNOBIOLOGY. **Personal Data:** b Ephrata, Wash, April 24, 1931; m 1952, c 4. **Education:** Wash State Univ, BS, 1952, DVM, 1958; Purdue Univ, MS, 1960, PhD (animal path), 1961. **Professional Experience:** ASSOC DEAN RES & GRAD INSTR, COL VET MED, TEX A&M UNIV, 1978-; PROF VET MICROBIOL & PARASITOL, TEX A&M UNIV, 1978-; chmn dept, Univ Mo-Columbia, 1969-1978; from asst prof to prof vet microbiol, Univ Mo-Columbia, 1961-1978; instr vet microbiol, Purdue Univ, 1958-1961. **Memberships:** Am Vet Med Asn; Am Asn Immunol; Am Col Vet Microbiol; Am Soc Microbiol; Conf Res Workers Animal Dis. **Research Statement & Publications:** Cell mediated immunity; immunologic aspects of avian leukosis; Bovine Respiratory Disease. **Mailing Address:** Dept Vet Microbiol & Parasitol, Col Vet Med Sci, Tex A&M Univ, College Station, TX 77843-4467.

LOAR, JAMES M, AQUATIC ECOLOGY, FISHERIES BIOLOGY. **Personal Data:** b Lancaster, Pa, September 10, 1944. **Education:** Gettysburg Col, BA, 1966; Temple Univ, MEd, 1969; Univ Wyo, PhD (zool), 1975. **Professional Experience:** GROUP LEADER, ENVIRON ANAL GROUP, ENVIRON SCI DIV, OAK RIDGE NAT LAB, as of 2002; prin investr, Oak Ridge Nat Lab, beginning 1975; res assoc, Environ Sci Div, Oak Ridge Nat Lab, beginning 1975; Teacher biol, Cherry Hill High Sch W, NJ, 1966-1970. **Memberships:** AAAS; Am Fisheries Soc; Ecol Soc Am; Sigma Xi. **Research Statement & Publications:** Assessment of impact of nuclear, fossil and hydroelectric energy technologies; responses of aquatic biota to altered flow regimes below hydroelectric projects. **Mailing Address:** Environ Sci Div, Oak Ridge Nat Lab, Knoxville, TN 37831-6036. **Fax:** 865-576-8543. **E-Mail:** loarjm@ornl.gov

LOASE, JOHN F, MATHEMATICS. **Professional Experience:** STAFF, DEPT MATH, CONCORDIA COL, as of 2005. **Memberships:** Math Asn Am. **Mailing Address:** Concordia Col, 171 White Plains Rd, Bronxville, NY 10708. **Fax:** 914-395-4500. **E-Mail:** splurge47@aol.com

LOATMAN, ROBERT BRUCE, COMPUTATIONAL LINGUISTICS, KNOWLEDGE-BASED SYSTEMS. **Personal Data:** b Washington, DC, August 23, 1945; m 1996, Konthip; c Thomas, Cynthia, Ryan & Michael. **Education:** Fordham Col, BA, 1967; Fordham Univ, MA, 1971, PhD (math), 1976. **Honors & Awards:** Parallax Prize, Emhart Corp, 1988; Advan Technol Achievement Award, Litton Indust, 1996. **Professional Experience:** SR PRIN CONSULT KEANE INC 2001-; sr tech staff, Explore Reasoning Systs, 2001; Prin Arch Spaceworks Inc, 2000-2001; chief scientist, Prc Inc, 1990-2000; dir artificial intel develop, Prc Inc, 1984-1993; comput scientist, Prc Inc, 1980-1984; consult, Phonic Ear Inc, 1980; mem tech staff, Mitre Corp, 1978; tech dir, Killalea Assocs Inc, 1976-1980; instr math, Georgetown Univ, 1973-1976; programmer, Gen Elec Co, 1968-1969. **Memberships:** Am Asn Artificial Intel; Asn Computational Ling; AAAS; Am Math Soc. **Research Statement & Publications:** Computational linguistics research and development; natural language text understanding systems; knowledge-based systems; intelligent visual interface. **Mailing Address:** 10991 Clover Hunt Ct, Reston, VA 20194. **E-Mail:** loatman_rbloatman@comcast.net

LOATS, JAMES, MATHEMATICS. **Education:** Oklahoma State Univ, BA (math), 1964-1968; Ohio Univ, MS (math), 1970; Univ Colo, Phd (math), 1977. **Professional Experience:** PROF, DEPT MATH SCI, Metrop State Col, as of 2005. **Mailing Address:** Box 38, Metrop State Col Denver, PO Box 173362, Denver, CO 80217-3362. **Fax:** 303 556-5381. **E-Mail:** loatsj@mscd.edu

LOBAUGH, BRUCE, BONE & MINERAL METABOLISM, VITAMIN D METABOLISM. **Personal Data:** b Charleroi, Pa, November 4, 1953; m 1983, Leslie; c Trevor R & Stephanie M. **Education:** Clarion Univ Pa, BS, 1975, Pa State Univ, MS, 1978, PhD, 1981. **Professional Experience:** ASSOC CLIN PROF PATH, DUKE UNIV MED CTR, as of 2002; chairperson, Dept Labs, QA1Q1 Comt, Duke Univ Med Ctr, 1993-; ASSOC RES PROF MED & CELL BIOL, DIVS ENDOCRINOL & PHYSIOL, 1993-; DIR, ENDOCRINOL METAB LAB, DUKE UNIV MED CTR, 1992-; asst res prof, Div Physiol, 1990-1993; dir, Lipid Lab & Supvr, Bone & Mineral Lab, 1990-1992; supvr, Surg Endocrinol-Oncol Lab, 1983-1990; asst res prof physiol & surg, Duke Univ Med Ctr, 1983-1990; prin investr, NIH res grants, 1982-1985 & 1987-1990; res assoc, Duke Univ Med Ctr, 1980-1983. **Memberships:** Am Physiol Soc; Am Soc Bone & Mineral Res; Am Fed Clin Res; Adv Mineral Metabolism; AAAS; Am Asn Clin Chem; Clin Lab Mgt Asn. **Research Statement & Publications:** Characterization of the mechanisms underlying regulation of vitamin D metabolism in normal and disease states; changes in vitamin D metabolism which are attendant on the natural aging process. **Mailing Address:** Duke Univ Med Ctr, PO Box 3208, Durham, NC 27710. **E-Mail:** lobau003@mc.duke.edu

LOBB, BARRY LEE, COMPUTER SCIENCE, TOPOLOGY. **Personal Data:** b Easton, Pa, November 25, 1943; c Angela (Marie) & Steven L. **Education:** Lafayette Col, BS, 1965; Duke Univ, MA, 1968, PhD (math), 1969; Ind Univ-Purdue Univ, MS, 1985. **Professional Experience:** PROF COMPUT SCI, LYNCHBURG COL, 1985-; prof math, Butler Univ, 1969-1985. **Memberships:** Asn Comput Mach. **Research Statement & Publications:** Computer science. **Mailing Address:** Dept Compu Sci, Lynchburg Col, 1501 Lakeside Dr, Lynchburg, VA 24501. **E-Mail:** lobb@acavax.lynchburg.edu

LOBB, CHRISTOPHER J, MESOSCOPIC DEVICES, QUANTUM COMPUTING. **Personal Data:** b Tuxedo, NY, July 30, 1952; m 1998, Paola. **Education:** Harvard Univ, (appl physics), PhD, 1980; Harvard Univ, SM, 1976; Rutgers Univ, BA, 1974. **Professional Experience:** ASSOC DIR, CTR FOR SUPERCONDUCTIVITY RES, UNIV MD, 1996-; vis scholar, Univ Chicago, 1996; acting dir, Ctr for Superconductivity Res, Univ MD, 1996; guest scientist, NIST, Gaithersburg, MD, 1994-1996; PROF PHYSICS, UNIV MD, 1993-; assoc prof physics, Univ MD, 1990-1993; vis prof, Tech Univ Denmark, 1990; assoc prof physics, Harvard Univ, 1986-1990. **Memberships:** Am Physics Soc fel. **Research Statement & Publications:** Applications and properties of superconductors, Josephson junctions, Josephson-junction arrays, and single-electron transistors; quantum computing using Josephson devices. **Mailing Address:** Dept Physics, Univ MD, 1365 Physics Bldg, College Park, MD 20742. **Fax:** 301-405-3779. **E-Mail:** lobb@squid.umd.edu

LOBB, CRAIG J, IMMUNOLOGY. **Personal Data:** b Salt Lake City, Utah, April 15, 1949; c 3. **Education:** Lewis & Clark Col, BS, 1971; Utah State Univ, MS, 1976, PhD (immunol), 1980. **Professional Experience:** PROF, DEPT MICROBIOL, MED CTR, UNIV MISS, as of 2005; assoc prof, dept microbiol, med ctr, Univ Miss, beginning 1989; prin investr, Nat Inst Allergy & Infectious Dis, NIH, 1982-; asst prof, dept microbiol, med ctr, Univ Miss, 1982-1989; co-prin investr, USDA, 1982-1987; instr, dept microbiol, med ctr, Univ Miss, 1980-1982; adj asst, dept immunol & med microbiol, sch med, Univ Fla, 1978-1980. **Memberships:** Am Asn Immunologists; Int Soc Develop & Comp Immunol; Am Soc Microbiol; Am Fisheries Soc. **Research Statement & Publications:** Antibody structure and function in ectothermic vertebrates; organization and phylogeny of immunoglobulin genes; immunity to gram-negative bacterial infections, especially as applied to aquaculturally important teleost fish; co-author of numerous scientific publications. **Mailing Address:** Dept Microbiol, Univ Miss Med Ctr, 2500 N State St, Jackson, MS 39216-4505. **Fax:** 601-984-1708. **E-Mail:** clobb@microbio.umsmed.edu

LOBB, DONALD EDWARD, PHYSICS. **Personal Data:** b Saskatoon, Sask, April 25, 1940. **Education:** Univ Sask, BE, 1961, MSc, 1963, PhD (physics), 1966. **Professional Experience:** PROF EMER PHYSICS, UNIV VICTORIA, BC, as of 2000; prof physics, Univ Victoria, Bc, beginning 1987; assoc prof, Univ Victoria, BC, 1971-1987; asst prof, Univ Victoria, BC, 1967-1971; Nat Res Coun Can overseas fel, 1966-1967. **Memberships:** Inst Elec & Electronics Engrs; Can Asn Physicists. **Research Statement & Publications:** Beam optics and beam transport systems; computer aided design of magnets. **Mailing Address:** Dept Physics, Univ Victoria, Elliott 208 PO Box 3055, Sta CSC, Victoria, BC V8W 3P6, Can. **Fax:** 250-721-7715. **E-Mail:** lobb@uvphys.phys.uvic.ca

LOBDELL, DAVID HILL, SURGICAL PATHOLOGY. **Personal Data:** b Erie, Pa, July 9, 1930. **Education:** Kenyon Col, AB, 1952; Univ Mich, MD, 1956. **Professional Experience:** SR ATTENDING PATHOLOGIST, ST VINCENT'S MED CTR, 1996-; lectr histol, Fairfield Univ, 1964-1973; dir, Sch Med Technol, St Vincent's Med Ctr, 1963-1995; dir labs, St Vincent's Med Ctr, 1963-1995; asst clin prof path, Sch Med, NY Univ, 1961-1969; assoc pathologist, St Vincent's Med Ctr, 1960-1963; instr, Sch Med, NY Univ, 1959-1961; asst pathologist, Bellevue Hosp, NY, 1959-1960; from intern to resident pathologist, Bellevue Hosp, NY, 1956-1959. **Memberships:** fel Col Am Path; fel Am Soc Clin Path. **Research Statement & Publications:** Osmometry; myeloproliferative disorders. **Mailing Address:** St Vincent's Med Ctr, Bridgeport, CT 06606-4292.

LOBECK, CHARLES CHAMPLIN, PEDIATRICS. **Personal Data:** b New Rochelle, NY, May 20, 1926; m 1954, c 4. **Education:** Hobart Col, AB, 1948; Univ Rochester, MD, 1952. **Professional Experience:** PROF EMER, MED SCH, UNIV WIS-MADISON, as of 2003; dean, Sch Med, Univ Mo, Columbia, beginning 1975; assoc dean clin affairs, Sch Med, Univ Wis-Madison, 1974-1975; chmn dept, Sch Med, Univ Wis-Madison, 1964-1974; from asst prof to prof, Sch Med, Univ Wis-Madison, 1958-1975; from instr to sr instr pediat, Sch Med & Dent, Univ Rochester, 1955-1958. **Memberships:** Sigma Xi. **Research Statement & Publications:** Metabolic disease; membrane transport; cystic fibrosis. **Mailing Address:** 3420 Valley Creek Circle, Middleton, WI 53562-1990. **E-Mail:** cclobeck@facstaff.wisc.edu

LOBEL, STEVEN A, CLINICAL IMMUNOLOGY DIRECTOR, IMMUNOPATHOLOGY. **Personal Data:** b Brooklyn, NY, February 8, 1952; m 1978, c 3. **Education:** Univ Tex, Austin, BA, 1973; State Univ NY, Buffalo, MA, 1975, PhD (immunol), 1977; Am Bd Med Lab Immunol, dipl, 1987. **Professional Experience:** ADV, QUEST DIAG, as of 2002; STAFF, SMITH, KLINE BEECHAM, MD, 1993-; lab dir, Immunol, Dept Clin Path, Am Med Labs, 1988-1993; Dept Pathol, Med Col Ga, 1983-1988; asstprof immunol, Dept Pediat & Microbiol, Univ Ill, Chicago, 1980-1983; dept Pathol, Univ Pittsburgh, 1978-1980; Fel, immunol, HHH Ctr Cancer Res, Hadassah, Jerusalem, 1977-1978; fel, Lady Davis Found, 1977. **Memberships:** Am Asn Immunol; Am Asn Path; Am Soc Clin Path; Am Soc Microbiol; Am Asn Clin Chem; Clin Immunol Soc. **Research Statement & Publications:** Cellular immunology of human immunodeficiency virus infection. **Mailing Address:** Quest Diag, 1901 Sulphur Springs Rd, Baltimore, MD 21227. **Fax:** 410-737-1266. **E-Mail:** steven.lobel@questdiagnostics.com

LOBL, THOMAS JAY, PHARMACEUTICAL CHEMISTRY, REPRODUCTIVE PHYSIOLOGY. **Personal Data:** b Danville, Va, October 20, 1944; m 1968, c 2. **Education:** Univ NC, Chapel Hill, BS, 1966; Johns Hopkins Univ, PhD (org chem), 1970. **Honors & Awards:** President's Award, Am Soc Andrology. **Professional Experience:** VPRES RES & DEVELOP, ALLECURE CORP, 2002-; chmn, San Diego Sect, beginning 1992; dir, Chem Sci Dept, Tanabe Res Labs Usa, beginning 1990; dir, Peptide Res Lab, Immunetech Pharmaceut, 1988-1990; assoc ed, J Andrology & Arch Andrology, 1980-1984; chmn, Kalamazoo Sect, Am Chem Soc, 1979; sr res scientist chem & biochem, UpJohn Co, 1973-1988; res fel biochem, Calif Inst Technol, 1970-1973. **Memberships:** Am Chem Soc; AAAS; Sigma Xi; Am Soc Andrology (treas, 1981-1984); NY Acad Sci; Am Peptide Soc. **Research Statement & Publications:** Regulation of male reproduction; spermatogenesis; epididymal function; hormone transport and receptor proteins; male contraception; chemical and biological deaminations; heterocyclic and steroid synthesis; reproductive physiology; peptide synthesis and chemistry; peptide/protein chemistry and biochemistry; signal peptides; peptide secondary structure activity relationships; peptide transport and targeting; peptide membrane interaction, autoimmune diseases, immunology, rheumatoid arthritis, allergy, type I diabetes. **Mailing Address:** AlleCure Corp, 28903 Ave Paine, Valencia, CA 91355-4169.

LOBO, ANGELO PETER, BIO-ORGANIC CHEMISTRY. **Personal Data:** b Masindi, Uganda, May 19, 1939; m 1967, Victoria; c Stephen & Michael. **Education:** Univ Bombay, BSc, 1958; Ind Univ, Bloomington, PhD (org chem), 1966. **Professional Experience:** SR RES SCIENTIST, WADSWORTH CTR LABS & RES, NY STATE DEPT HEALTH, 1970-; res asst chem, Rensselaer Polytech Inst, 1968-1970; rockefeller found spec lectr org chem, Makerere Univ Col, Kampala, Uganda, 1966-1968. **Memberships:** Am Chem Soc. **Research Statement & Publications:** Synthesis of nucleotide/nucleoside substrates and inhibitors, oligonucleotide synthesis. **Mailing Address:** Wadsworth Ctr Labs & Res, NY State Dept Health, Corning Tower, Albany, NY 12201.

LOBO, CECIL T(HOMAS), ENGINEERING MECHANICS. **Personal Data:** b Mangalore, India, September 22, 1934; c 2. **Education:** Gujarat Univ, India, BE, 1955; Univ Notre Dame, MS, 1960; Purdue Univ, PhD (civil eng), 1966. **Professional Experience:** PROF CIVIL ENG, ROSE-HULMAN INST TECHNOL, 1971-; actg ch Minn dept, Rose-Hulman Inst Technol, 1971-1972; from instr to assoc prof, Rose-Hulman Inst Technol, 1963-1971; asst engr, Shah Construct Co, Ltd, India, 1956-1957; consult, Universal Tank & Iron Works, Inc, Ind. **Memberships:** Am Soc Civil Engrs; Am Soc Eng Educ; Sigma Xi; Am Concrete Inst; Prestressed Concrete Inst. **Research Statement & Publications:** Structural and soil mechanics. **Mailing Address:** 3561 N Limberlost Lane, Terre Haute, IN 47803-3999.

LOBO, FRANCIS X, MICROBIOLOGY. **Personal Data:** b Aden, UAR, October 8, 1925; American citizen; m 1960, c 3. **Education:** Univ Bombay, BS, 1947, MS, 1950; Inst Divi Thomae, PhD (exp med, biol), 1959; NatRegistry Microbiol, cert. **Professional Experience:** Mem eval team, Pa Dept Educ, 1971; PROF BIOL SCI, MARYWOOD COL, 1970-; chmn Dept Biol, Marywood Col, 1970-1974; fac res partic, Argonne Nat Lab, 1967 & St Jude Children Res Hosp, Memphis, Tenn, 1970; resident res assoc, Argonne Nat Lab, 1968-1969; NSF grant, Argonne Nat Lab, 1966; Consult, Radio Corp Am, 1965-; assoc prof sci, Marywood Col, 1960-1970; control & res microbiologist-chemist, Chemo Pharma Labs Ltd, Worli, Bombay, 1950-1957; Technician, Path Dept, Worli Gen Hosp, India, 1950. **Memberships:** Am Soc Microbiol; NY Acad Sci. **Research Statement & Publications:** Intestinal microorganisms by enrichment culture techniques; citric acid from a cane-sugar molasses; beef brain extract in controlling staphylococcus infections; etiology of sludge formation in industrial wastes. **Mailing Address:** Dept Sci, Marywood Col, 2300 Adams Ave, Scranton, PA 18509-1514.

LOBO, PAUL A(LLAN), CHEMICAL ENGINEERING, MERGER & ACQUISITION IN THE CHEMICAL INDUSTRY. **Personal Data:** b La Cumbre, Colombia, October 10, 1928. **Education:** Mass Inst Technol, SB, 1950, SM, 1951; Univ Mich, PhD (chem eng), 1955. **Professional Experience:** RETIRED; prin, Lobo & Assocs Inc, 1993-1994; sr vpres eng, Huls Am Inc, 1989-1993; vpres int, Nuodex Inc, 1983-1988; vpres planning, Saddle Brook, NJ, 1980-1983; dir corp planning, Saddle Brook, NJ, 1975-1980; dir, Tech Group, 1973-1975; dir bus develop & planning, Tenneco Chem Inc, Piscataway, 1971-1973; vpres & gen mgr, Pitt-Consol Chem Co, 1968-1970; mgr develop, Petrochem Dept, 1967-1968; exec asst to pres, NY, 1965-1967; petrolchem coord, Continental Oil Co, Ltd, Eng, 1964-1965; Europ rep, Res Dept, Holland, 1963-1964; lectr, Univ Okla, 1956-1963; supvr process develop sect, Petrochem Res Div, Continental Oil Co, Okla, 1955-1963. **Memberships:** Am Chem Soc; Am Inst Chem Engrs. **Research Statement & Publications:** High pressure; petrochemical process development; reaction kinetics. **Mailing Address:** 155 Nantwich Ct, Somerset, NJ 08873.

LOBO, ROGERIO A, ENDOCRINOLOGY. **Education:** Georgetoen Univ Sch Med, MD. **Professional Experience:** DIR REI FEL PROG, COLUMBIA UNIV MED CTR, as of 2004. **Research Statement & Publications:** Hyperandrogenic disorders and polycystic ovary syndrome; reproductive endocrinology and infertility including estrogen metabolism and menopause. **Mailing Address:** Dept Obstet & Gynec, Columbia Univ Med Ctr, 622 West 168th St 16th Floor, New York, NY 10032.

LOBODZINSKI, SLAWOMIR M, BIOENGINEERING, BIOMEDICAL ENGINEERING. **Personal Data:** b Lublin, Poland, April 26, 1948. **Education:** Tech Univ Warsaw, BS, 1971, MS, 1972; Tech Univ Vienna, Austria, PhD (biomed eng), 1978. **Professional Experience:** Fulbright scholar, Univ Auckland, NZ, 1995-1996; PROF ELEC ENG, CALIF STATE UNIV, 1986-; assoc prof elec eng, Calif State Polytech Univ, 1979-1983; res engr, Sch Med, Univ Vienna, 1975 & 1978. **Memberships:** Inst Elec & Electronics Engrs; Am Soc Echocardiography; Int Soc Optical Eng; Asn Comput Mach. **Mailing Address:** Dept Elec Eng, Calif State Univ, 1250 Bellflower Blvd, Long Beach, CA 90840. **Fax:** 562-985-7561. **E-Mail:** slobo@csulb.edu

LOBSTEIN, OTTO ERVIN, CLINICAL BIOCHEMISTRY. **Personal Data:** b Czech, April 12, 1922; American citizen; m 1952, Miriam; c Dennis D, Harvey R & Heidi M. **Education:** Univ London, BSc, 1945; SMAE Inst, Eng, MSF, 1945; Northwestern Univ, PhD (biochem), 1952; Am Bd Clin Chem, dipl, 1955. **Honors & Awards:** Sci Award, Cancer Fedn, 1979. **Professional Experience:** RETIRED; emer prof, Rush Presby St Lukes Med Ctr, Chicago, beginning 1993; biochemist, 1982-1993; prof biochem & path, Rush Presby St Lukes Med Ctr, Chicago, 1976-1993; dir clin chem, Mt Sinai Hosp Med Ctr, Cook Co Hosp, 1976-1982; vis assoc prof, Purdue Univ, 1968-1973; head, Biochem Dept, St Elizabeth Hosp Med Ctr, 1965-1976; adj prof, Purdue Univ, 1965-1976; asst prof chem, Loyola Univ, Calif, 1964-1965; biochemist-owner, Lobstein Biochem Lab, Calif, 1962-1964; secy-treas, Res Found Dis Eye, 1959-1965; vis res prof, Univ Redlands, 1959-1965; med dir res, Chemtech Labs, 1952-1962; res assoc zoology, Univ Southern Calif, 1952-1953; instr chem, Wesley & Passavant Mem Hosps, Ill, 1949-1951; biochemist, Elgin State Hosp, Ill, 1947-1948; asst res chemist, Howards & Sons, Ltd, Eng, 1942-1946. **Memberships:** Fel AAAS; Am Soc Microbiol; sr mem Am Chem Soc; fel Am Asn Clin Chem (secy, 1981-1983); Am Chem Soc; fel Nat Acad Clin Biochem. **Research Statement & Publications:** Biochemical investigation of the crystalline lens of the eye, protein structure and constitution in normal and in cataract lenses of the human and other species; changes in protein with a changed electrolyte environment; clinical investigation of lysozyme in carcinomatosis. **Mailing Address:** 2006 Maple Ave, Northbrook, IL 60062-5266.

LOBUE, JOSEPH, PHYSIOLOGY, HEMATOLOGY. **Personal Data:** b Union City, NJ, April 19, 1934; m 1959, Catherine; c Philip, Joseph & Ellen. **Education:** St Peter's Col, NJ, BS, 1955; Marquette Univ, MS, 1957; NY Univ, PhD (physiol), 1962. **Honors & Awards:** Christian R & Mary F Lindback Found Award, NY Univ, 1965. **Professional Experience:** Nat Leukemia Asn grant, 1974-1976; PROF BIOL, NY UNIV, 1971-; NatCancer Inst grant, 1971-1973, 1975-1978, 1979-1981; assoc, Danforth Found, 1968-; CO-DIR, A S GORDON LAB EXP HEMAT, NY UNIV, 1967-; co-dir, Hemat Training Prog, NIH, 1965-1975; Am Cancer Soc grant, 1965-1966; Sigma Xi grant-in-aid, 1964-1965; from asst prof to assoc prof, NY Univ, 1962-1971; NIH fel, 1962. **Memberships:** Int Soc Exp Hemat. **Research Statement & Publications:** Mechanisms controlling leukocyte and erythrocyte production and release; pathophysiology and cytokinetics of rodent and avian leukemias. **Mailing Address:** Dept Biol, New York Univ, 100 Wash Sq E, New York, NY 10003-6688.

LOBUGLIO, ALBERT FRANCIS, HEMATOLOGY, IMMUNOLOGY. **Personal Data:** b Buffalo, NY, February 1, 1938; m 1962, c 5. **Education:** Georgetown Univ, MD, 1962. **Professional Experience:** PROF, UNIV ALA, as of 2001; DIR, COMPREHENSIVE CANCER CTR, UNIV ALA, BIRMINGHAM, 1983-; prof med, Univ Mich, beginning 1978; prof, Ohio State Univ, 1973-1978; hemat consult, Dayton, Ohio, 1969-; assoc prof med, Ohio State Univ, 1969-1973; asst prof, State Univ NY Buffalo, 1968-1969; hemat consult, Vet Admin Hosp, Buffalo, 1967-1969; instr, State Univ NY Buffalo, 1967-1968; hemat fel, Thorndike Mem Lab, Boston City Hosp, 1965-1967; resident, Presby Univ Hosp, Pittsburgh, 1963-1965; intern med, Presby Univ Hosp, Pittsburgh, 1962-1963. **Memberships:** Am Fedn Clin Res; Am Soc Hemat; Am Soc Clin Invest. **Research Statement & Publications:** Tumor immunology; transplant immunology; human macrophage and lymphocyte functions. **Mailing Address:** Cancer Ctr & Div Hematol-Oncol Univ Ala, Univ Sta 1824 Sixth Ave S Rm 237, Birmingham, AL 35294-3300. **E-Mail:** lobuglio@uab.edu

LOBUNEZ, WALTER, INDUSTRIAL CHEMISTRY. **Personal Data:** b Ukraine, November 22, 1945; American citizen; m 1945, c 1. **Education:** Univ Pa, MS, 1952, PhD (chem), 1954. **Professional Experience:** RETIRED; res assoc, FMC Corp, 1980-1983; sr res chemist 1967-1980; res chemist, FMC Corp, 1960-1967; sr scientist chem, Textile Res Inst, 1959-1960; protein chem, Childrens Hosp, Univ Penn, 1955-1959; res assoc immunol, Jefferson Med Col, 1954-1955. **Research Statement & Publications:** Chemistry of hydrocarbons; protein chemistry; chemistry of cellulose; soda ash processes; bromine and strontium processes. **Mailing Address:** 562 Ewing St, Princeton, NJ 08540.

LOCASCIO, SALVADORE J, HORTICULTURE. **Personal Data:** b Hammond, La, October 29, 1933; m 1954, c 3. **Education:** Southeastern La Col, BS, 1955; La State Univ, MS, 1956; Purdue Univ, PhD (plant physiol), 1959. **Honors & Awards:** Pres Gold Medal Award, 1978. **Professional Experience:** PROF HORT, DEPT VEG CROPS, UNIV FLA, 1969-; assoc prof Hort, Dept Veg Crops, Univ Fla, beginning 1965; assoc horticulturist, Univ Fla, 1965-1969; asst prof, Univ Fla, 1959-1965. **Memberships:** Weed Sci Soc Am; Sigma Xi; fel Am Soc Hort Sci. **Research Statement & Publications:** Fertilizer and water requirements of vegetables; strawberry culture; chemical weed control for vegetables; teaching of commercial vegetable crops and nutrition of horticultural crops. **Mailing Address:** Dept Hort Univ Fla, 406 NW 32nd St, Gainesville, FL 32611. **E-Mail:** sil@mail.ifas.ufl.edu

LOCHHEAD, JOHN HUTCHISON, INVERTEBRATE ZOOLOGY. **Personal Data:** b Montreal, Que, August 7, 1909; American citizen; m 1938, c 2. **Education:** Univ St Andrew's, MA, 1930; Cambridge Univ, BA, 1932, Bachelor scholar, 1933, PhD (zool), 1937. **Professional Experience:** EMER PROF ZOOL, UNIV VT, 1975-; mem corp, Woods Hole Marine Biol Lab, 1944-; instr, Woods Hole Marine Biol Lab, 1943-1955; from instr to prof, Univ VT, 1942-1975; asst biologist, Va Fisheries Lab, 1941-1942; Lectr, Col William & Mary, 1941-1942; fel by courtesy, Johns Hopkins Univ, 1940; instr zool, Mus Zool, Cambridge Univ, 1936-1938; sr cur, Mus Zool, Cambridge Univ, 1935-1938; With Cambridge Univ Table, Marine Zool Sta, Naples, 1934-1935. **Memberships:** Am Soc Zool; Crustacean-Soc. **Research Statement & Publications:** Anatomy and physiology of Crustacea including their feeding mechanisms, locomotion, factors controlling swimming positions, responses to light, functions for the blood and related tissues, molting and reproduction. **Mailing Address:** 49 Woodlawn Rd, London SW6 6PS, UK.

LOCHMULLER, CHARLES HOWARD, ANALYTICAL CHEMISTRY. **Personal Data:** b New York, NY, May 4, 1940; m 1963, Patricia; c 3. **Education:** Manhattan Col, BS, 1962; Fordham Univ, MS, 1964, PhD (analytical chem), 1968. **Honors & Awards:** Chromatography Award, Am Chem Soc, 1987; N Carolina chemist Award, Am Int Col, 1988; Societal Medal Eesti Keemia Selts, Estonian Chem Soc, 1997. **Professional Experience:** Dir, Ctr Biochem Eng, 1991-1993; dir grad studies biochem eng, 1989-1990; PROF BIOCHEM ENG, DUKE UNIV, 1987-; chair, Analytical Div, Am Chem Soc, 1983-1984; chmn dept, Duke Univ, 1982-1987; PROF CHEM, DUKE UNIV, 1978-; from asst prof to assoc prof, Duke Univ, 1969-1978; res assoc, Purdue Univ, 1967-1969; fel Royal Soc Chem; fel, Am Int Col. **Memberships:** Am Chem Soc; fel Royal Soc Chem; fel Am Inst Chemists. **Research Statement & Publications:** Factors effecting separation processes; spectroscopy. **Mailing Address:** Dept Chem, Duke Univ, Durham, NC 27708. **Fax:** 919-660-1605. **E-Mail:** clochmul@chem.duke.edu

LOCHNER, JANIS ELIZABETH, MEMBRANE BIOCHEMISTRY, CELLULAR COMMUNICATION. **Personal Data:** b Bethesda, Md, November 27, 1954. **Education:** Allegheny Col, BS, 1976; Univ Ore, PhD (biochem), 1981. **Professional Experience:** DR ROBERT B PAMPLIN JR PROF BIOCHEM, LEWIS & CLARK COL, as of 2004; res fel biochem, Ore Health Sci Univ, 1981-; asst prof chem, Lewis & Clark Col, beginning 1981. **Memberships:** AAAS. **Research Statement & Publications:** Role of the plasma membrane in cellular communication; mechanisms of membrane transduction. **Mailing Address:** Dept Chem, Lewis & Clark Col, 223 Olin Ctr 0615 SW Palatine Hill Rd, Portland, OR 97219. **E-Mail:** lochner@lclark.edu

LOCHNER, ROBERT HERMAN, STATISTICS. **Personal Data:** b Madison, Wis, April 17, 1939; m 1962, Sarajane; c Ann, Susan, Mary K & Daniel. **Education:** Univ Wis-Madison, BS, 1961, MS, 1962 & 1966, PhD (statist), 1969. **Professional Experience:** QUAL CONSULT & PARTNER, QUAL RIGHT CONSULT, as of 2003; QUAL MEASUREMENT SPECIALIST, JOINT COMN ACCREDITATION HEALTH CARE ORGN, 1993-; lectr bus admin, Marquette Univ, 1991-1993; consult statist, & qual mgt, 1985-1993; from asst prof to assoc prof statist & math, Marquette Univ, 1968-1985; math analyst, A C Electronics Div, Gen Motors Corp, 1962-1965. **Memberships:** Am Statist Asn. **Research Statement & Publications:** Statistical methods in reliability, life testing and quality improvement. **Mailing Address:** Qual Right Consult, 2840 S Root River Pkwy, Milwaukee, WI 53227.

LOCHSTET, WILLIAM A, PHYSICS. **Personal Data:** b Port Jefferson, NY, December 5, 1936; m 1982, c 2. **Education:** Univ Rochester, BS, 1957, MA, 1960; Univ Pa, PhD (physics), 1965. **Professional Experience:** ASSOC PROF & HEAD, DEPT PHYSICS, UNIV PITTSBURGH, as of 1999; asst prof physics, Univ Pittsburgh, beginning 1986; asst prof physics, Pa State Univ, 1966-1986; instr, Pa State Univ, 1965-1966. **Memberships:** Am Phys Soc; AAAS; Sigma Xi; Am Asn Physics Teachers. **Mailing Address:** Dept Physics, Univ Pittsburgh, 450 Sch House Rd, Johnstown, PA 15904. **E-Mail:** lochstet@vms.cis.pitt.edu

LOCICERO, JOSEPH CASTELLI, ORGANIC CHEMISTRY. **Personal Data:** b Ontario Center, NY, 1914; m 1937, c 2. **Education:** Univ Rochester, BA, 1936; Pa State Univ, MS, 1947, PhD (biochem), 1948. **Professional Experience:** RETIRED; from asst prof to prof chem, Camden County Col, 1971-1984; sr scientist, Rohm& Haas Co, 1952-1971; res chemist, Rohm& Haas Co, 1948-1952; sr res chemist, Nuodex Prods Co, NJ, 1943-1945; chemist, Hooker Electrochem Co, NY, 1937-1943. **Memberships:** AAAS; Am Chem Soc. **Research Statement & Publications:** Plasticizers, fungicides and insecticides; high pressure reactions; detergents; process development; ion exchange; sugar technology; halogenation; plastics. **Mailing Address:** 2113 Fleet Landing Blvd, Atlantic Beach, FL 32233-7501.

LOCK, BRIAN EDWARD, SEDIMENTOLOGY. **Personal Data:** b Yeovil, Eng, March 21, 1944; m 1968, c 3. **Education:** Cambridge Univ, BA, 1966, PhD (geol), 1969, MA, 1970. **Honors & Awards:** Outstanding Educr Award, Gulf Coast Asn Geol Soc, 1991. **Professional Experience:** HEAD, DEPT GEOL, UNIV SOUTHWESTERN LA, as of 2004; PROF GEOL, UNIV SOUTHWESTERN LA, 1980-; assoc prof, Univ Southwestern La, 1977-1980; sr lectr, Rhodes Univ, SAfrica, 1975-1977; overseas res burser, Coun Sci & Indust Res, Pretoria, 1975-1976; sr res assoc, Exeter Univ, Eng, 1975-1976; lectr, Rhodes Univ, SAfrica, 1970-1974; consult, Fina Petrol Co, Belg, 1969-1970; consult basic appl geol, Superior Oil Co. **Memberships:** Am Asn Petrol Geologists; Soc Econ Paleontologists & Mineralogists; Geol Soc Am; Int Asn Volcanology & Chem Earth's Interior; Int Asn Sedimentologists. **Research Statement & Publications:** Sedimentology of carbonate rocks; other aspects of sedimentology and stratigraphy; field work in South Africa, Ireland, Spitsbergen, Reunion Island, Canada and United States. **Mailing Address:** Dept Geol, Univ Southwestern La, PO Box 44530, Lafayette, LA 70504-4530. **E-Mail:** belock@louisiana.edu

LOCK, G(ERALD) S(EYMOUR) H(UNTER), MECHANICAL ENGINEERING. **Personal Data:** b London, Eng, June 30, 1935; m 1959, c 3. **Education:** Univ Durham, BS, 1959, PhD (mech eng), 1962. **Honors & Awards:** Queen Elizabeth Silver Jubilee Medal, 1979. **Professional Experience:** PROF EMER MECH ENG, UNIV ALTA, as of 2000; prof mech eng, Univ Alta, beginning 1970; chmn comt heat transfer, Nat Res Coun Can, 1969-1971; from asst prof to assoc prof, Univ Alta, 1962-1970. **Memberships:** Am Soc Mech Engrs; fel Eng Inst Can; fel Can Soc Mech Engrs (pres 1977-1978). **Research Statement & Publications:** Thermodynamics and heat transfer, especially ice engineering; technology assessment. **Mailing Address:** Dept Mech Eng, Univ Alta, 4-9 Mech Eng Bldg, Edmonton, AB T6G 2G8, Can. **Fax:** 403-492-2208.

LOCK, JAMES ALBERT, LIGHT SCATTERING. **Personal Data:** b Cleveland, Ohio, February 12, 1948; m 1972. **Education:** Case Inst Technol, BS, 1970, MS, 1973; Case Western Reserve Univ, PhD (physics), 1974. **Professional Experience:** TOPICAL ED, J APPL OPTICS, 1994-; PROF PHYSICS, CLEVELAND STATE UNIV, 1990-; from asst prof to assoc prof, Cleveland State Univ, 1978-1990; res assoc physics, Case Western Reserve Univ, 1974-1978; lectr, Case Western Reserve Univ, 1970-1974. **Memberships:** Sigma Xi; Optical Soc Am. **Research Statement & Publications:** Light scattering; single scattering and multiple scattering by small particles, analysis of optical caustics and morpholoby-dependent resourances; atmospheric optics. **Mailing Address:** Dept Physics, Cleveland State Univ, Cleveland, OH 44115.

LOCK, KENNETH, ELECTRICAL ENGINEERING, COMPUTER SCIENCE. **Personal Data:** b Wushi, China, March 15, 1932; m 1954, c 4. **Education:** Battersea Polytech Inst, BSc, 1955; Univ London, MSc, 1957; Calif Inst Technol, PhD (elec eng, physics), 1962. **Professional Experience:** PRES, CYBERTEC, 1980-; dept mgr, MCO div, 1977-1980; mgr design automation, Burroughs Corp, 1971-1977; pres, Cyber Data Inc, Calif, 1969-1971; vis fel, Int Bus Mach Corp, 1967-1969; advan programmer, Int Bus Mach Corp, 1965-1967; consult, Jet Propulsion Lab, 1962-1965; from instr to asst prof elec eng, Calif Inst Technol, 1959-1965; PRES, ZYBEX. **Memberships:** Inst Elec & Electronics Engrs; Asn Comput Mach. **Research Statement & Publications:** Physical systems on computers; network analysis; switching theory; programming system research; computer design; interactive use of computers in engineering, science and business. **Mailing Address:** 5425 Calumet Ave, La Jolla, CA 92037.

LOCK, ROBIN H, MATHEMATICS. **Professional Experience:** PROF, DEPT MATH, ST LAWRENCE UNIV, as of 2006. **Memberships:** Am Statist Asn. **Mailing Address:** Dept Math, St Lawrence Univ, Canton, NY 13617-1455. **Fax:** 315-229-7413. **E-Mail:** rlock@vm.stlawu.edu

LOCKARD, ISABEL, ANATOMY. **Personal Data:** b Brandon, Man, June 27, 1915. **Education:** Northwestern Univ, BS, 1938; Univ Mich, MA, 1942, PhD (anat), 1946. **Professional Experience:** PROF EMER ANAT, MED UNIV SC, 1985-; from asst prof to prof, Med Univ SC, 1952-1985; asst prof, Sch Med Georgetown Univ, 1949-1952; instr, Sch Med Georgetown Univ, 1947-1949; instr, Univ Pittsburgh, 1944-1945; asst anat, Univ Mich, 1942-1944 & 1947; consult, Med Univ SC. **Memberships:** Am Asn Anatomists; Sigma Xi. **Research Statement & Publications:** Neuroanatomy; blood supply of central nervous system. **Mailing Address:** Dept Anat & Cell Biol, Med Univ SC, 171 Ashley Ave, Charleston, SC 29425.

LOCKARD, J DAVID, BOTANY, SCIENCE EDUCATION. **Personal Data:** b Renovo, Pa, December 20, 1929; m 1951, c 4. **Education:** Pa State Univ, BS, 1951, MEd, 1955; PhD (bot), 1962. **Professional Experience:** PROF EMER BOT & SCI EDUC, UNIV MD, COLLEGE PARK, as of 2005; DIR, INTERNATIONAL CLEARINGHOUSE ADVAN SCI, UNIV MD, as of 2003; rep, US Nat Comn to UNESCO, 1975-; dir, NSF Impact Study, 1974-1975; prof bot & sci educ, Univ MD, College Park, 1970-; NSF grants, acad year inst sci supvrs, 1969-1973; dir, NSF-AID Study Improvisation Sci Teaching Mat Worldwide, 1968-1972; dir off bio educ, Am Inst Biol Sci, 1966-1967; dir, Sci Teaching Ctr, Univ Md, Col Park, beginning 1962; NSF-AAAS grant, Develop & Maintain Int Clearinghouse Sci & Math Curric Develops, 1962-; from asst prof to assoc prof, Univ Md, Col Park, 1961-1970; asst bot, Pa State Univ, 1958-1961; consult, sci teaching improvement prog, AAAS, 1956-1958; dept chmn, Sci Dept High Sch, Pa, 1953-1956. **Memberships:** AAAS (vpres, 1971); Am Soc Plant Physiol; Int Coun Asn Sci Educ (pres, 1973-1976); Nat Asn Res Sci Teaching (pres, 1972-1973); Nat Sci Teachers Asn; Sigma Xi; Nat Asn Biol Teachers. **Research Statement & Publications:** Investigating medicinal and poisonous plants; improving science teaching techniques and equipment; studying science and math curriculum developments internationally; consulting in science education; science writing; studing use of computers in science instructions. **Mailing Address:** Univ Md, Dept Bot, College Park, MD 20742. **E-Mail:** jl51@umail.umd.edu

LOCKARD, RAYMOND G, HORTICULTURE. **Personal Data:** b Patricia, Alta, January 1, 1925; American citizen; m 1951, Joyce M Powers; c Dianne, David & Kathleen. **Education:** Univ BC, BSA, 1949; Univ Idaho, MSc, 1951; Univ London, PhD, 1956. **Honors & Awards:** CONSULT to Oman, 3 wks, 1985; consult to Sahah, 1 wk, 1974; consult, Papua, New Guinea, 3 wks, 1965. **Professional Experience:** RETIRED; horticulturist, Calif State Polytech Univ, Pomona, USAID Prog, Sanaa, Yemen Arab Repub, 1985-1988; prof crop sci & crop sci coordr, La State Univ, USAID Prog, Cent Agr Res Inst, Liberia, 1981-1984; from assoc prof to prof hort, Univ Ky, 1967-1981; tech expert, Food & Agr Orgn, Philippines, 1964-1967; Plant physiologist, Ghana, 1959-1964; Plant physiologist, Can For Aid, Malaysia, 1954-1959. **Memberships:** Int Soc Hort Sci; Am Soc Hort Sci. **Research Statement & Publications:** Chill requirements. **Mailing Address:** 18462 SW Kelly View Loop, Aloha, OR 97007-7600. **Fax:** 503-591-1754. **E-Mail:** rj.lockard@verizon.net

LOCKART, ROYCE ZENO, MOLECULAR BIOLOGY. **Personal Data:** b Marshfield, Ore, September 7, 1928; m 1951, c 3. **Education:** Whitman Col, AB, 1950; Univ Wash, MS, 1953, PhD (microbiol), 1957. **Professional Experience:** RETIRED; patent assoc, E I du Pont de Nemours & Co Inc, beginning 1983; biologist, E I du Pont de Nemours & Co Inc, 1980-1983; res supvr, E I du Pont de Nemours & Co Inc, 1966-1980; from asst prof to assoc prof microbiol, Univ Tex, 1960-1966; bacteriologist, Radiation Br, Nat Cancer Inst, 1958-1960; res fel, Nat Inst Allergy & Infectious Dis, 1957-1958. **Research Statement & Publications:** Virus cell interactions, particularly animal viruses and their control by natural means and by chemicals; image analysis of immunological cells; writing biotechnology patents. **Mailing Address:** 1418 Bucknell Rd Green Acres, Wilmington, DE 19803.

LOCKE, BEN ZION, APPLIED STATISTICS, EPIDEMIOLOGY. **Personal Data:** b New York, NY, September 8, 1921; m 1947, c 4. **Education:** Brooklyn Col, AB, 1947; Columbia Univ, MS, 1949. **Honors & Awards:** Rema Lapouse Award, Am Pub Health Asn, 1990. **Professional Experience:** CHIEF, EPIDEMIOL PSYCHOPATH BRANCH, NIMH, 1985-;

from asst chief to chief, Ctr Epidemiol Studies, 1967-1985; assoc prof eval & dir res & eval, Community Ment Health Ctr, Temple Univ, 1966-1967; chief consult sect, Biomet Br, NIMH, 1956-1966; Statistician, NY State Health Dept, 1947-1956. **Memberships:** AAAS; fel Am Pub Health Asn; Am Statist Asn; Soc Epidemiol Res; fel Am Col Epidemiol. **Research Statement & Publications:** Epidemiology of mental disorders; evaluation of programs designed to prevent and control mental disorders and promote mental health. **Mailing Address:** 11803 Saddlerock Rd, Silver Spring, MD 20902.

LOCKE, CARL EDWIN, CORROSION, POLYMER SCIENCE. **Personal Data:** b Palo Pinto Co, Tex, January 11, 1936; m 1956, Sammie; c Stephen & Carlene. **Education:** Univ Tex, Austin, BS, 1958, MS, 1960, PhD (chem eng), 1972. **Honors & Awards:** D Grant Mickle Award, Transp Res Bd, 1988; Eben Junkin Award, Nat Asn Corrosion Engrs, 1990. **Professional Experience:** DEAN EMER & PROF EMER, SCH ENG, UNIV KANS, as of 2006; prof chem & petrol eng, Univ Kans, as of 2003; dean eng, Univ Kans, 1986-2002; prof & dir chem eng & mat sci, Univ Okla, 1980-1986; Proj dir, Okla Dept Transp, 1975 & 1976-1979; from asst prof to assoc prof, Univ Okla, 1973-1980; instr & vis asst prof, Univ Tex, 1971-1973; prog res engr, Tracor Inc, 1966-1968; prod engr, R L Stone Co, 1965-1966; res engr, Continental Oil Co, 1959-1965. **Memberships:** Am Inst Chem Engrs; Nat Asn Corrosion Engrs; Am Soc Testing & Mat; Am Soc Eng Educ; Nat Soc Prof Engr; Am Soc Eng Educ. **Research Statement & Publications:** Corrosion; corrosion in concrete; electrochemistry of corrosion. **Mailing Address:** Dept Chem & Petrol Eng, Univ Kans, 4150D Learned Hall, Lawrence, KS 66045-0001. **Fax:** 785-864-4967. **E-Mail:** lok@ku.edu

LOCKE, DAVID CREIGHTON, CHEMICAL SEPARATIONS. **Personal Data:** b Garden City, NY, March 1, 1939; m 1962, Carol. **Education:** Lafayette Col, BS, 1961; Kans State Univ, PhD (chem), 1965. **Professional Experience:** PROF CHEM, QUEENS COL, NY, 1976-; from asst prof to assoc prof, Queens Col, NY, 1968-1976; NSF fel, Univ Col Swansea, Univ Wales, 1967-1968; res chemist, Esso Res & Eng Co, 1965-1967. **Memberships:** AAAS; Am Chem Soc; Int Inst Conserv Hist & Artistic Works; NY Acad Sci. **Research Statement & Publications:** Analytical chemistry; chemical separations; GC/MS; supercritical fluids; biosolids characterization; packaging recycling. **Mailing Address:** Dept Chem, Queens Col, SB B312, Flushing, NY 11367-0904. **Fax:** 718-997-3349. **E-Mail:** dlocke@qcunix1.qc.edu

LOCKE, HAROLD OGDEN, PHYSICAL CHEMISTRY, ANALYTICAL CHEMISTRY. **Personal Data:** b Camden, NJ, September 14, 1931; m 1959, Elizabeth Bellmer; c Bruce & David. **Education:** Wesleyan Univ, BA, 1953, MA, 1956; Rutgers Univ, PhD (chem), 1962. **Professional Experience:** ANALYTICAL CHEMIST, GAF CORP, 1965-; Res chemist, Armstrong Cork Co, 1961-1965. **Memberships:** Am Chem Soc. **Research Statement & Publications:** X-ray crystallography; polymer characterization; surfactants. **Mailing Address:** 816 Prince St, Palmer Twp, Easton, PA 18042-2435.

LOCKE, JACK LAMBOURNE, PHYSICS. **Personal Data:** b Brantford, Ont, May 1, 1921; m 1946, Joyce; c John A & M Jane (Green). **Education:** Univ Toronto, BA, 1946, MA, 1947, PhD (physics), 1949. **Honors & Awards:** Rumford Medal, AAAS, 1971. **Professional Experience:** RETIRED; dir, Herzberg Inst Astrophys, 1975-1985; assoc dir, Radio & Elec Eng Div & chief astrophys br, 1970-1975; radio astronr, Nat Res Coun Can, 1966-1970; chief, Stellar Physics Div, 1959-1966; officer in-chg, Dom Radio Astrophys Observ, 1959-1962; astrophysicist, Dom Observ, 1949-1959; demonstr physics, Univ Toronto, 1945-1947. **Memberships:** Am Astron Soc; Can Astron Soc; Int Astron Union. **Research Statement & Publications:** Astrophysics; radio astronomy; solar physics; molecular spectra; infrared spectrum of the atmosphere. **Mailing Address:** 2150 Braeside Ave, Ottawa, ON K1H 7J5, Can.

LOCKE, JOHN, GENETICS. **Education:** Univ Western Ont, BSc, 1980; Queen' s Univ, PhD, 1985. **Professional Experience:** PROF BIOL SCI, UNIV ALBERTA, as of 2005. **Mailing Address:** Dept Genetics Univ Alberta, Biol Sci Bldg Rm G319, Edmonton, AB T6G 2E9, Can. **Fax:** 780-492-9234. **E-Mail:** john.locke@ualberta.ca

LOCKE, JOHN LAUDERDALE, SPEECH PATHOLOGY, PSYCHOLINGUSITICS. **Personal Data:** b Oak Park, Ill, November 16, 1940; m 1977. **Education:** Ripon Col, BA, 1963; Ohio Univ, MA, 1965, PhD (speech path), 1968. **Professional Experience:** DIR & SR RES SCIENTIST, MASS GEN HOSP INST HEALTH, as of 2006; prof, Dept Hearing & Speech Sci, Univ Md, Col park, 1980-; res consult, Vet Admin Hosp, Ft Howard, Md, 1980-; res consult, Vet Admin Hosp, Danville, Ill, 1974-1980; res fel, Yale Univ, 1972-1973 & Oxford Univ, 1973-1974; prof, Univ Ill, Champaign, 1969-1980; speech pathologist, Vet Admin Ctr, 1968-1969. **Memberships:** Am Speech & Hearing Asn; Ling Soc Am; Am Asn Appl Ling. **Research Statement & Publications:** Language acquisition and impairment; child phonology; reading and cognition of the deaf; aphasia; speech perception. **Mailing Address:** Mass Gen Hosp Inst Health, 15 River St, Boston, MA 02108-3413.

LOCKE, KRYSTYNA KOPACZYK, BIOCHEMISTRY, ENZYMOLOGY. **Personal Data:** b Warsaw, Poland, December 2, 1926; m 1970. **Education:** Wayne State Univ, BS, 1953; Western Reserve Univ, MS, 1956; Univ Ill, Champaign-Urbana, PhD (lipid chem), 1962. **Professional Experience:** TOXICOLOGIST, TOXICOL BR, HAZARD EVAL DIV, OFF PESTICIDE PROGS, ENVIRON PROTECTION AGENCY, 1977-; res biochemist, Biochem Toxicol Br, Div Toxicol, Food & Drug Admin, 1969-1977; proj assoc, Univ Wis-Madison, 1966-1969; trainee, Inst Enzyme Res, Univ Wis-Madison, 1964-1966; Nat Inst Neurol Dis & Blindness fel biochem, Ment Health Res Inst, Univ Mich, Ann Arbor, 1962-1964; res nutritionist, Atherosclerosis Res Proj, Vet Admin Hosp, Downey, Ill, 1956-1958. **Memberships:** NY Acad Sci; Am Chem Soc. **Research Statement & Publications:** Effects of environmental agents on biochemistry and ultrastructure of mitochondria. **Mailing Address:** 1006 Featherston Ct, Fredericksbrg, VA 22401.

LOCKE, LOUIS NOAH, ANIMAL PATHOLOGY, AVIAN TOXICOLOGY. **Personal Data:** b Stockton, Calif, March 14, 1928. **Education:** Univ Calif, AB, 1950, DVM, 1956. **Honors & Awards:** Distinguished Serv Award, Wildlife Dis Asn, 1984; Merton Rosen Mem Lectr, 1985. **Professional Experience:** RETIRED; wildlife pathologist, Nat Wildlife Health Lab, US Fish & Wildlife Serv, 1975-1989; histopathologist, Patuxent Wildlife Res Ctr, US Dept Interior, 1961-1975; wildlife res biologist, Patuxent Wildlife Res Ctr, US Dept Interior, 1958-1960; vet, USPHS, 1956-1958. **Memberships:** Am Asn Avian Path; Am Vet Med Asn; emer mem Wildlife Dis Asn (secy, 1988-1991, pres, 1991-1993). **Research Statement & Publications:** Wildlife diseases, especially diseases and parasites of the mourning doves, waterfowl; effects of pollutants upon wild birds; lead poisoning in migratory birds. **Mailing Address:** Nat Wildlife Health Res Ctr, 6006 Schroeder Dr, Madison, WI 53711.

LOCKE, MICHAEL, INSECT PHYSIOLOGY, INSECT STRUCTURE & CELL BIOLOGY. **Personal Data:** b Nottingham, Eng, February 14, 1929; Canadian citizen; m 1980, Janet; c John, Timothy, Marius & Vanessa. **Education:** Cambridge Univ, BA, 1952, MA, 1955, PhD, 1956, DSc, 1976. **Honors & Awards:** Rockefeller Found Award, 1960; Carnegie Award, 1961; Gold Medal, Int Award Insect Morphol & Embryol, Wigglesworth Medal & Lecturer, 2000. **Professional Experience:** PROF EMER, DEPT BIOL, UNIV WESTERN ONT, 1994-; Killam res fel, 1988; prof, Dept Zool, Univ Western Ont, 1985-1994; vis dir res, Int Ctr Insect Physiol & Ecol, Nairobi, Kenya, 1977-1981; prof & chmn, Dept Zool, Univ Western Ont, 1971-1985; Raman prof, Univ Madras, 1969; ed, Soc Develop Biol, 1962-1969; from assoc prof to prof biol, Case Western Res Univ, 1961-1971; lectr zool, Univ West Indies, 1956. **Memberships:** Fel AAAS; Am Soc Cell Biol; fel Royal Soc Can; fel Royal Entom Soc; fel Entom Soc Am. **Research Statement & Publications:** Coordination of growth in insects; insect cell development; insect morphogenesis; structure of the epidermis and fat body; cuticle secretion, ferritin and iron metabolism; author of over 200 papers. **Mailing Address:** Dept Biol, Univ Western Ont, London, ON N6A 5B7, Can. **Fax:** 519-433-4166. **E-Mail:** mlocke@uwo.ca

LOCKE, PHILIP M, MATHEMATICS. **Personal Data:** b Rockford, Ill, July 12, 1937; m 1961, Helen; c 2. **Education:** Bluffton Col, BS, 1959; Univ NH, MS, 1964, PhD (math), 1967. **Professional Experience:** ASSOC PROF EMER MATH, UNIV MAINE, as of 2006; assoc prof math, Univ Maine, Orono, beginning 1974; asst prof, Univ Maine, Orono, 1968-1974; asst prof math, Mont State Univ, 1967-1968. **Memberships:** Math Asn Am. **Research Statement & Publications:** Ordinary differential equations; differential geometry. **Mailing Address:** Dept Math & Statist, Univ Maine, Orono, ME 04469. **E-Mail:** locke@math.umaine.edu

LOCKE, RAYMOND KENNETH, BIOCHEMISTRY, TOXICOLOGY. **Personal Data:** b Terre Haute, Ind, July 2, 1940; m 1970. **Education:** Wash Univ, BS, 1965. **Professional Experience:** TOXICOLOGIST, OFF TOXIC SUBSTANCES, US ENVIRONPROTECTION AGENCY, 1979-; chemist, Div Toxicol, Contaminants & Natural Toxicants Eval Br, 1977-1979; res chemist, Biochem Toxicol Br, 1973-1977; biochem & Metab Sect, Div Pesticides, 1969-1971 & Metab Br, Div Toxicol, 1971-1973; res chemist, Div Nutrit, Food & Drug Admin, 1968-1969; res asst biochem, Univ Tex, Dallas, 1966-1967. **Memberships:** AAAS; Am Chem Soc; NY Acad Sci. **Research Statement & Publications:** Biochemical studies of the comparative in vivo and in vitro metabolism of foreign compounds by animals, plants and man. **Mailing Address:** US Eviron Protection Agency, Ben Franklin Sta PO Box 7672, Washington, DC 20044.

LOCKE, STANLEY, MATHEMATICS, PHYSICS. **Personal Data:** b New York, NY, June 18, 1934; m 1958, Jane; c 3. **Education:** NY Univ, BME, 1955, MS, 1957, PhD (math), 1960. **Professional Experience:** RETIRED; consult engr, Teleco Oilfield Serv, 1988-1992; consult, Stanley Locke & Assoc, 1987-1988; mem sci staff, Schlumberger-Doll Res Ctr, 1965-1986; res mathematician, Repub Aviation Corp, 1959-1960. **Memberships:** Sigma Xi; sr mem Inst Elec & Electronics Engrs. **Research Statement & Publications:** Solution of mechanical, electro-magnetic, acoustic and nuclear problems arising in the development of new oil field services. **Mailing Address:** 17 Deerwood Ct, Norwalk, CT 06851.

LOCKE, STEPHEN CHARLES, GRAPH THEORY & ALGORITHMS. **Personal Data:** b London, Eng, May 30, 1953; British & Canadian citizen; m 1974, Katharine; c Geoffrey Charles & Daniel Richard. **Education:** Univ Waterloo, BMath, 1975, MMath, 1976, PhD (combinatorics & optimization), 1982. **Professional Experience:** PROF, DEPT MATH, FLA ATLANTIC UNIV, 1993-; preprof chmn, Dept Math, Fla Atlantic Univ, 1997-; asst chmn, Dept Math, Fla Atlantic Univ, 1992-; mem, Inst Comput Sci & Eng, 1985-1988; from asst prof to assoc prof, Dept Math, Fla Atlantic Univ, 1981-1993. **Memberships:** Am Math Soc; Math Asn Am; Can Math Soc. **Research Statement & Publications:** Graph theory; cycle space; cycles in graphs; dirac-type conditions; independent sets in triangle-free graphs. **Mailing Address:** Dept Math Sci, Fla Atlantic Univ, Boca Raton, FL 33431-0991. **E-Mail:** lockes@fau.edu

LOCKE, STEVEN ELLIOT, BEHAVIORAL MEDICINE, MEDICAL INFORMATICS. **Personal Data:** b Englewood, NJ, December 2, 1945; m 1984, c 2. **Education:** Cornell Univ, AB, 1968; Columbia Univ Col Physicians & Surgeons, MD, 1972. **Honors & Awards:** First Prize, Sci Exhib, Am Col Emergency Physicians. **Professional Experience:** ASSOC PROF HEALTH SCI & TECHNOL, MASS INST TECHNOL, 1996-; ASSOC PROF PSYCHIAT, HARVARD MED SCH, 1996-; chief behav med, Harvard Pilgrimhealth Care, 1995-1997; dir psychiat informatics, Ctr Clin Comput, Harvard Medsch, 1993-1994; med student educ psychiat, Comput Psychiat, 1989-; dir, Comput Psychiat, 1987-; asst prof psychiat, Harvard Med Sch, 1987-1996; instr, Harvard Med Sch, 1980-1987; assoc dir, Psychiat Consult Serv, Beth Israel Hosp, 1980-1987; lectr, Beth Israel Hosp, 1980-1982; fel, Boston Univ Sch Med, 1977-1979; clin instr, Harvard Med Sch, 1977-1979; resident, McLean Hosp, Belmont, MA, 1974-1977; fel psychiat, Harvard Med Sch, 1974-1977; intern, Mt Zion Hosp & Med Ctr, San Francisco, Calif, 1972-1973. **Memberships:** Biofeedback Soc Am; Am Med Informatics Asn; fel Am Psychiat Asn; Am Psychosom Soc; Soc Behav Med. **Research Statement & Publications:** Interactive computing in psychiatry and medicine; behavioral medicine; co-author of five books, 30 papers and book chapters; disease and demand management; behavioral health-primary care integration, health promotion/disease prevention; author of various articles. **Mailing Address:** Inst Cyber Med, Ten Deer Run, Wayland, MA 01778. **Fax:** 801-340-6828. **E-Mail:** steven_locke@hms.harvard.edu

LOCKE, WILLIAM, INTERNAL MEDICINE, ENDOCRINOLOGY. **Personal Data:** b Morden, Man, March 16, 1916; m 1945, Katherinee Acer. **Education:** Univ Man, MD, 1938; Univ Minn, MS, 1947; McGill Univ, DTM, 1945. **Professional Experience:** EMER CLIN PROF MED, SCH MED, TULANE UNIV, 1987-; TRUSTEE, ALTON OCHSNER MED FOUND, 1978-; emer head, Sect Endocrinol & Metab, Alton Ochsner Med Found, 1976-1986; partner, OchsnerClin, 1957-1981; pres staff, Alton Ochsner Med Found, 1954-1955; mem staff, Ochsner Clin & Found Hosp, 1950-1986; Nat Res Coun & Commonwealth Fund fel, Harvard Univ, 1948-1950; sr visphysician, Charity Hosp, New Orleans. **Memberships:** AAAS; Am Diabetes Asn; fel Am Col Physicians; Endocrine Soc; Sigma Xi. **Research Statement & Publications:** Metabolic diseases. **Mailing Address:** 150 Broadway St Apt 1104, New Orleans, LA 70118.

LOCKE, WILLIAM W, GEOLOGY. **Education:** Dartmouth Col, NH, BA, 1970; Univ Colo, MS, 1976, PhD (geol), 1980. **Professional Experience:** PROF GEOL, MONT STATE UNIV, as of 2003. **Mailing Address:** Dept Earth Sci, Montana State Univ, Traphagen Hall 223, Bozeman, MT 59717-3480. **Fax:** 406-994-6923. **E-Mail:** wlocke@montana.edu

LOCKENOUR, JERRY L, AERONAUTICS. **Education:** Purdue Univ, BS, 1967; Ohio State Univ, MS. **Professional Experience:** DIR TECHNOL INTEGRATION, NORTHROP GRUMMAN CORP, as of 2005. **Mailing Address:** Northrop Corp, One Northrop Ave, Hawthorne, CA 90250-3277. **Fax:** 310-212-0905. **E-Mail:** jerry.lockenour@ngc.com

LOCKER, JOHN L, mathematics; deceased, see previous edition for last biography

LOCKER, JOHN S, MATHEMATICS. **Education:** Calif State Univ, PhD. **Professional Experience:** PROF EMER, DEPT MATHS, COLO STATE UNIV, COLO, as of 2006. **Mailing Address:** Colo State Univ, Dept Maths, Ft Collins, CO 80523-1801. **E-Mail:** locker@math.colostate.edu

LOCKEY, RICHARD FUNK, ALLERGY & IMMUNOLOGY, INTERNAL MEDICINE. **Personal Data:** b Lancaster, Pa, January 15, 1940; m Carol; c Brian C & Keith E. **Education:** Haverford Col, BS, 1961; Univ Mich, Ann Arbor, MS, 1972; Temple Univ, MD, 1965. **Honors & Awards:** Claude P Brown Mem Lectr, Asn Clin Scientists Spring Meeting, 1981. **Professional Experience:** Dir, Am Bd Allergy & Immunol, 1993-; co-ed, J Invest Allergol & ClinImmunol, 1991-; co-ed, Allergol & Clin Immunol, 1984-1990; PROF MED, PEDIAT & PUB HEALTH, COL MED, UNIV SFLA, TAMPA, 1983-; CHIEF, SECT ALLERGY & IMMUNOL, VET ADMIN HOSP, TAMPA, FLA, 1983-; DIR, DIV ALLERGY & IMMUNOL, VET ADMIN HOSP, TAMPA, FLA, 1982-; chief, Allergy & Immunol Sect, James A Haley VetAdmin Hosp, Tampa, Fla, 1982-; asst dir, Div Allergy & Immunol, Vet Admin Hosp, Tampa, Fla, 1979-1982; from asst prof to assoc prof med, Col Med, Univ SFla, Tampa, 1973-1983; asst chief, Sect Allergy & Immunol, Vet Admin Hosp, Tampa, 1973-1982; chief, Allergy & Immunol Sect, Carswell AFB Hosp, USAF, Ft Worth, Tex, 1971-1973; fel allergy & immunol, Univ Hosp, Univ Mich, 1969-1970; resident, Univ Hosp, Univ Mich, 1966-1968; asst resident internal med, Univ Hosp, Univ Mich, 1966-1967. **Memberships:** Fel Am Acad Allergy & Immunol (secy, 1989-1990, treas 1990-1991, pres-elect 1991-1992, pres, 1992-1993); fel Am Col Physicians; fel Am Col Chest Physicians; Am Asn Cert Allergists; AAAS; Int Asn Aerobiol; hon fel Can Soc Allergy & Clin Immunol; AMA; Clin Immunol Soc. **Research Statement & Publications:** Hymenoptera hypersensitivity; imported fire ant; asthma; inflammatory mechanisms; important aeroallergens of Florida; immunity and the aged; allergy immunotherapy. **Mailing Address:** Vet Admin Hosp Div Allergy & Immunol, 13000 Bruce B Downs Blvd, Tampa, FL 33612. **Fax:** 813-910-4041. **E-Mail:** rlockey@hsc.usf.edu

LOCKHART, BENHAM EDWARD, PLANT PATHOLOGY, AGRICULTURE. **Personal Data:** b St Vincent, WI, January 18, 1945; American citizen; m 1970, c 2. **Education:** Univ WI, Trinidad, BSc, 1965; Univ Calif, Riverside, PhD (plant path), 1969. **Professional Experience:** PROF PLANT PATH, UNIV MINN, as of 2000; assoc prof plant path, Univ Minn, St Paul, beginning 1980; asst prof, Univ Minn, St Paul, 1976-1980; asst prof, Minn Proj, US AID, Rabat, Morocco, 1971-1976; res fel plant path, Univ Nebr, 1969-1970 & Univ Calif, Berkeley, 1970-1971. **Memberships:** Am Phytopath Soc; Am Soc Hort Sci; Int Soc Hort Sci. **Research Statement & Publications:** Identification properties and control of viruses of vegetable and ornamental crops. **Mailing Address:** Dept Plant Path, Univ Minn, 495 Borlaug Hall 1991 Upper Buford Circle, St Paul, MN 55108. **Fax:** 612-625-9728. **E-Mail:** plpa@puccini.crl.unn.edu

LOCKHART, DEBORAH F, MATHEMATICS. **Education:** NY Univ, BA; Rensselaer Polytech Inst, MS, PhD (math). **Professional Experience:** EXEC OFFICER, DIV MATH SCI NSF, VA, as of 2005; PROG DIR, APPL MATH PROG, NSF, VA, as of 2000. **Memberships:** Asn Women Math. **Mailing Address:** NSF, 201 Wilson Blvd Suite 1025, Arlington, Va 20550. **Fax:** 703-292-9032. **E-Mail:** dlockhart@nsf.gov

LOCKHART, HAINES BOOTS, NUTRITION, BIOCHEMISTRY. **Personal Data:** b Crawfordsville, Ind, October 29, 1920; m 1944, Ruth; c Haines Jr & Anne Elizabeth. **Education:** Wabash Col, AB, 1942; Univ Ill, PhD (biochem), 1945. **Professional Experience:** RETIRED; staff nutritionist, Quaker Oats Co, 1991-1995; sect head, New Foods Div, Swift & Co, 1966-1971; from res nutritionist chemist to head, Baby Foods Res Div, 1945-1966; mem tech adv group, Comt on Nutrit, Am Acad Pediat. **Memberships:** Am Chem Soc. **Research Statement & Publications:** Amino acids and proteins in nutrition; infant and geriatric nutrition. **Mailing Address:** 333 Sunset Dr, Village of Lakewood, IL 60014-5330.

LOCKHART, HAINES BOOTS, ENVIRONMENTAL CHEMISTRY, BIOCHEMISTRY. **Personal Data:** b Evergreen Park, Ill, February 4, 1946; m 1990, Janet; c Trey & Meegan. **Education:** Wabash Col, AB, 1967; Univ Nebr, Lincoln, MS, 1969, PhD (chem), 1973. **Professional Experience:** DIR, CORP HEALTH, SAFETY & ENVIRON PROG, EASTMAN KODAK CO, 1995-; dir, corp environ, 1991-1994; dir, Occup Health Lab, 1988-1991; dir, Environmental Tech Serv, 1986-1988; mgr, Health Regulations, 1985-1986; tech assoc, Health & Safety Lab, 1981-1985; sr res biochemist, Eastman Kodak Co, 1972-1981. **Memberships:** Am Chem Soc; Soc Environ Toxicol & Chem. **Research Statement & Publications:** Environmental impact of synthetic chemicals, their biodegradation, photodegradation and bioconcentration in aquatic organisms; risk assessment of chemical impacts on exposed populations. **Mailing Address:** Eastman Kodak Co, B 320 Kodak Park 1100 Ridgeway Ave, Rochester, NY 14652-6256. **E-Mail:** haines.lockhart@kodak.com

LOCKHART, JAMES MARCUS, LOW TEMPERATURE PHYSICS, SUPERCONDUCTING ELECTRONICS. **Personal Data:** b Portsmouth, Ohio, June 11, 1948; m 1981, c 2. **Education:** Univ Mich, BS, 1970; Stanford Univ, MS (physics), 1972 & MS (elec eng), 1975, PhD (physics), 1976. **Professional Experience:** PROF PHYSICS, SAN FRANCISCO STATE UNIV, 1987-; vis scholar, Stanford Univ, 1983-; assoc prof, San Francisco State Univ, 1983-1987; sr res assoc, Stanford Univ, 1982-1983; asst prof physics, Colo Sch Mines, 1980-1981; actg asst prof, Stanford Univ, 1977-1980; fel, Dept Physics, Stanford Univ, 1976-1978; actg instr physics, Stanford Univ, 1976-1977; res affil, Stanford Univ, 1976. **Memberships:** Am Phys Soc; Am Asn Physics Teachers; Sigma Xi. **Research Statement & Publications:** Low temperature electrical properties of solids; electron beams; superconductivity, superconducting detectors and electronics, Squids ultra-low; semiconductor device physics; musical acoustics; architectural acoustics; electroacoustics. **Mailing Address:** Dept Physics & Astron, San Francisco State Univ, 1600 Holloway Ave, San Francisco, CA 94132. **Fax:** 415-338-2178. **E-Mail:** lockhart@stars.sfsu.edu

LOCKHART, LILLIAN HOFFMAN, MEDICINE. **Personal Data:** b Columbus, Tex, October 23, 1930; m 1951, c 3. **Education:** Rice Univ, BA, 1951; Univ Tex Med Br, Galveston, MA, 1955, MD, 1957. **Professional Experience:** PROF PEDIAT & GENETICS, UNIV TEX MED BR, GALVESTON, 1983-; from asst prof to assoc prof, Univ Tex Med Br, Galveston, 1963-1983; fel hemat, Univ Tex Med Br, Galveston, 1962-1963. **Memberships:** Am Acad Pediat. **Research Statement & Publications:** Genetics; chromosome disorders. **Mailing Address:** Children's Hosp, 9th & Market St, Galveston, TX 77555. **Fax:** 409-772-9595.

LOCKHART, WILLIAM LAFAYETTE, INORGANIC CHEMISTRY. **Personal Data:** b Nashville, Tenn, October 15, 1936; m 1960, c 2. **Education:** Tenn Technol Univ, BS, 1958; Univ Miss, MS, 1961; Vanderbilt Univ, PhD (inorg chem), 1967. **Professional Experience:** Chmn dept, West GA Col, 1978-1982; PROF CHEM, WEST GA COL, 1977-; from asst prof to assoc prof, West GA Col, 1967-1977; Res biochemist, US Food & Drug Admin, 1960-1963. **Research Statement & Publications:** Kinetics and mechanisms of inorganic reactions. **Mailing Address:** W GA Tech Col, 303 Ft Dr, LaGrange, GA 30240.

LOCKHEAD, GREGORY ROGER, EXPERIMENTAL PSYCHOLOGY. **Personal Data:** b Boston, Mass, August 8, 1931; m 1964, Jeanne; c Diane, Elaine & John. **Education:** Tufts Univ, BS, 1958; Johns Hopkins PhD, 1965. **Professional Experience:** PROF PSYCHOLOGOCAL & BRAIN SCIENCES, DUKE UNIV as of 2003; chmn, Dept Exp psychol, Duke Univ, Durham, beginning 1991; prin investr, Air Force Off Sci Res, 1983-1991; fel, Wolfson Col, Oxford Univ, Eng, 1980-1981; vis prof, Stanford Univ, 1971-1972; res assoc, Univ Calif, Berkeley, 1971-1972; prin investr, NSF, 1966-1969, 1979-1984; from asst prof to prof psychol, Duke Univ, Durham, 1965-1991; prin investr, USPHS, 1963-1979; psychologist res staff, IBM Res, NY, 1958-1961; consult human eng. **Memberships:** Fel Am Psychol Asn; fel Am Psychol Soc; Psychonomic Soc; Int Soc Psychophys; Sigma Xi; Soc exp psychologists. **Research Statement & Publications:** Psychology; perception, cognition, human performance. **Mailing Address:** Dept Psychol Brain Sci, Duke Univ, Rm 242, Soc Psychol Bldg, Durham, NC 27708. **Fax:** 919-660-5726. **E-Mail:** greg@psych.duke.edu

LOCKLEY, MARTIN GAUDIN, VERTEBRATE ICHNOLOGY, MUSEUM SCIENCE & CONSERVATION. **Personal Data:** b St Helier, Jersey, UK, March 17, 1950; m Linda-Dale; c Peter, Katie, Lois F Jennings & Linda F Jennings. **Education:** Queens Univ, Northern Ireland, BS, 1974; Birmingham Univ, Eng, PhD (geol), 1977. **Professional Experience:** PROF GEOL, UNIV COLO, DENVER, 1993-; assoc ed, Ichnos int Trace Fossil J, 1992-; distinguished lectr, Am Asn Petrol Geologists, 1991-1992; prin investr, NSF, 1987-; assoc cur, Mus Western Colo, 1987-; assoc prof, Univ Colo, Denver, 1984-1993; asst prof geol, Univ Colo, Denver, 1980-1984; res assoc, Glasgow Univ, 1976-1980. **Memberships:** Paleont Soc; Paleont Asn; Soc Econ Paleontologists & Mineralogists; Am Asn Petrol Geologists. **Research Statement & Publications:** Dinosaur tracks and other fossil footprints of North America, Europe and East Asia; author of numerous publications. **Mailing Address:** Dept Geol, Campus Box 172, PO Box 173364, Denver, CO 80217-3364. **Fax:** 303-556-6197. **E-Mail:** mlockley@carbon.cudenver.edu

LOCKRIDGE, OKSANA, BIOCHEMICAL PHARMACOLOGY, Toxicology. **Personal Data:** b Czech, September 4, 1941; American citizen; m Lawrence; c Katherine. **Education:** Smith Col, BA, 1963; Northwestern Univ, Ill, PhD (chem), 1971. **Professional Experience:** PROF, UNIV NEBR MED CTR, 1990-; res scientist, Univ Mich, Ann Arbor, 1982-1990; Prin Investr, Univ Mich, Ann Arbor, 1979-1990; res assoc pharmacol, Univ Mich, Ann Arbor, 1974-1981; Fel human genetics, Univ Mich, Ann Arbor, 1972-1974. **Memberships:** Am Chem Soc; Asn Women Sci; AAAS; Am Soc Biol Chemists; Am Soc Human Genetics. **Research Statement & Publications:** Toxicology of organophosphorus agents as studied by mass spectroscopy. Genetic variants of human butyrylcholinesterase and mouse knockout models of deficiency in acetylcholinesterase and butyrylcholinesterase. **Mailing Address:** Univ Nebr Med Ctr, Eppley Inst 600 S 42nd St, Omaha, NE 68198-6805. **Fax:** 402-559-4651. **E-Mail:** olockrid@unmc.edu

LOCKSHIN, MICHAEL DAN, RHEUMATOLOGY, IMMUNOLOGY. **Personal Data:** b Columbus, Ohio, December 9, 1937; m 1965, c 1. **Education:** Harvard Col, AB, 1959; Harvard Med Sch, MD, 1963. **Professional Experience:** CO-DIR, MARY KIRKLAND CTR LUPUS RES, HOSP SPEC SURG, 2001-; DIR & PROF, BARBARA VOLCKER CTR WOMEN & RHEUMATIC DIS, 1997-; from sr adv to dir, Warren G Magnuson Clin Ctr, NIH, 1995-1997; actg dir, Nat Inst Arthritis & Musculoskeletal & Skin Dis, NIH, Bethesda, 1994-1995; dir extramural prog, Nat Inst Arthritis & Musculoskeletal & Skin Dis, NIH, 1989-1994; attending physician, Hosp Spec Surg, New York Hosp, 1982-; mem bd dirs, Arthritis Found, 1975-1989; consult rheumatol, Mem Hosp, New York, 1970-; from asst prof to prof med, Col Med, Cornell Univ, 1970-1989; assoc scientist & assoc attend physician, Hosp Spec Surg, New York Hosp, 1970-1982; fel rheumatol, Columbia Presby Med Ctr, 1968-1970; resident, Second (Cornell) Div Med, Bellevue & Mem Hosp, New York, 1966-1968; adj asst prof epidemiol, Sch Pub Health, Univ Pittsburgh, 1965-1966; epidemic intel serv officer, Epidemic Intel Serv, Commun Dis Ctr, 1964-1966; Intern, Second (Cornell) Div Med, Bellevue & Mem Hosp, New York, 1963-1964. **Memberships:** Am Col Rheumatism; Am Col Physicians. **Research Statement & Publications:** Cellular immunology; clinical rheumatology. **Mailing Address:** Barbara Volcker Ctr Women & Rheumatic Dis, Sutton Pl S 14BN Hosp Spec Surg 535 E 70th St, New York, NY 10021-4872. **Fax:** 212-774-2374. **E-Mail:** volkerctr@hss.edu

LOCKSHIN, RICHARD ANSEL, PHYSIOLOGY, DEVELOPMENTAL BIOLOGY. **Personal Data:** b Columbus, Ohio, December 9, 1937; m 1963, c 2. **Education:** Harvard Univ, AB, 1959, MS, 1961, PhD (biol), 1963. **Honors & Awards:** Presidential Award, Long Island Univ, 1987. **Professional Experience:** PROF, DEPT BIOL, ST JOHN'S UNIV, NY, as of 2004; bd dir, Am Aging Asn, 1993-1998; NIH grants 1985-1988, 1991-1996; chmn, dept biol sci, St John's Univ, NY, 1983-1992; from assoc prof to prof physiol, dept biol sci, St John's Univ, NY, 1975-1983; asst prof physiol, sch med, Univ Rochester, 1965-1975; NSF fel, NIH fel, 1964-1965; NSF grants, 1965-1978; NSF fel, inst animal genetics, Univ Edinburgh, 1963-1964. **Memberships:** AAAS; Soc Cell Biol; Soc Develop Biol; Gerontol Soc; Am Soc Entom; fel Gerontol Soc Am; Sigma Xi; Am Soc Cell Biol; NY Acad Sci; Am Physiol Soc; Am Zool Soc; Int Embryol Soc; Am Entom Soc; Call Death Soc(pres, 1997-2000); Geront Soc Am. **Research Statement & Publications:** Destruction of tissues during metamorphosis of insects; early developmental events in insect embryogenesis; cellular differentiation. **Mailing Address:** Dept Biol Sci, St John's Univ, Grand Cent Utopia Pkwy, Jamaica, NY 11439-0001. **E-Mail:** lockshir@stjohns.edu

LOCKWOOD, DAVID H, GENETICS. **Education:** Univ Tex, PhD (human & molecular genetics), 1986. **Professional Experience:** DENNIS JOHNSTON DIR LAB, GENZYME GENETICS, as of 2005. **Mailing Address:** Genzyme Genetics, 2000 Vivigen Way, Santa Fe, NM 87505-5600.

LOCKWOOD, DAVID JOHN, SOLID STATE PHYSICS, RAMAN SPECTROSCOPY. **Personal Data:** b Christchurch, NZ, January 7, 1942; Canadian citizen; m 1979, Eugenia; c Alisa N, Ilana E & Lilia R. **Education:** Univ Canterbury, BSc, 1964, MSc, 1966, PhD (physics), 1969, DSc(Physics) 2000; Univ Edinburgh, DSc, 1978. **Professional Experience:** Distinguished visitor, nat Univ Singapore, 2001; secy, Canadian nat IUPAP Liaison comm, 2000-; distinguished visitor, Chinese Acad Sci, Beijing, 1992; head, Thin Films Group, Phys Characterization Group, 1991-1992; mem Can adv group, NATO Sci Comt, 1990-1994; head, Phys Characterization Group, 1990-1992; chmn, NATO, 1989-1990; sect head surface & interface physics, Nat Res Coun Can, 1987-1990; mem sci panel, NATO, 1987-1988; distinguished vis prof, Ctr Sci Res France, 1987-1988; prog consult & reviewer, Nat Sci & Eng Res Coun Can, 1986-; vis prof, Essex Univ, England, 1981-1983; PRIN RES OFFICER PHYSICS, NAT RES COUN CAN, 1978-; consult vis, Univ Paul Sabatier, Toulouse, France, 1977-1992; tutor, Open Univ, UK, 1977-1978; res fel physics, Univ Edinburgh, 1972-1978; consult vis, Battelle Ctr de Res, Switz, 1972-1976; fel chem, Univ Waterloo, Can, 1970-1971; Univ bursaries, NZ Univ Grants Comt, 1966-1968; teaching fel physics, Univ Canterbury, NZ, 1965-1969. **Memberships:** Am Phys Soc; Royal Commonwealth Soc; World Fedn Scientists; Can Asn Physicists; Electrochem Soc(dir, 2001-2003); Mat Res Soc; Royal Soc Can. **Research Statement & Publications:** Light scattering studies of structural and magnetic phase transitions, electronic exitations, magnons and phonons in solids; optical properties of semiconductors and superlattices. **Mailing Address:** Inst Microstructural Sci, Nat Res Coun, 1191 Montreal Rd, Ottawa, ON K1A 0R6, Can. **Fax:** 613-993-6486. **E-Mail:** david.lockwood@nrc-cnrc.gc.ca

LOCKWOOD, DEAN H, biochemistry, medicine; deceased, see previous edition for last biography

LOCKWOOD, FRANCES ELLEN, LUBRICANT OXIDATION, TRIBOLOGICAL BEHAVIOR OF LIQUID CRYSTALS. **Personal Data:** b Passaic, NJ, m 1978, c 1. **Education:** Rensselaer Polytech Inst, BS, 1973, Pa State Univ, MS, 1976, PhD (chem eng), 1978. **Honors & Awards:** Martin/ Marietta Labs Invention Award, 1982 & 1983. **Professional Experience:** SR VPRES TECHNOL PROD DEVELOP, VALVOLINE CO, 2002-; vpres technol prod develop, Valvoline Co, 1994-2002; vpres phys sci, Pennzoil Prod Co, 1985-1994; dir, Pennzoil Prod Co, 1984-1985; sr scientist, Martin Marietta Lab, 1980-1984; assoc sr res engr, Gen Motors Res Labs, 1978-1980. **Memberships:** Soc Tribologists & Lubrication Engrs; Am Inst Chem Engrs; Soc Automotive Engrs; Am Soc Testing & Mat. **Research Statement & Publications:** Lubricant oxidation, tribological behavior of liquid crystals and lubrication of ceramic dry pressing; metal rolling and metal forging lubrication; the fluid state and hydrocarbon oxidation. **Mailing Address:** Valvoline Co, 3499 Blazer Pkwy, Lexington, KY 40509.

LOCKWOOD, GEORGE WESLEY, ASTRONOMY, PLANETARY SCIENCES. **Personal Data:** b Norfolk, Va, June 28, 1941; m 1992, Susan. **Education:** Duke Univ, BS, 1963; Univ Va, MA, 1965, PhD (astron), 1968. **Professional Experience:** SR RES ASTRONR, LOWELL OBSERV, as of 2005; astronr, Lowell Observ, beginning 1973; astronr, Kitt Peak Nat Observ, 1968-1973. **Memberships:** Am Astron Soc; Int Astron Union; Astron Soc Pac; Am Geophys Union; Sigma Xi. **Research Statement & Publications:** Planetary atmospheres; stellar/solar physics; solar-planetary relations; variable stars. **Mailing Address:** Lowell Observ, 1400 W Mars Hill Rd, Flagstaff, AZ 86001-4499. **Fax:** 520-774-6296. **E-Mail:** gwl@lowell.edu

LOCKWOOD, GRANT JOHN, ELECTRON PHYSICS, RADIATION PHYSICS. **Personal Data:** b Byram, Conn, October 28, 1931; m Margaret; c Steven, Jeffrey, Dale & Nancy. **Education:** Univ Conn, BA, 1954, MS, 1959, PhD (physics), 1963. **Professional Experience:** PRIN INVESTR, MAT RADIATION DIV, SANDIA NAT LABS, as of 1999; distinguished Mem Tech Staff, Sandia Labs, beginning 1963; Res asst physics, Univ Conn, 1960-1963. **Research Statement & Publications:** Electronic, atomic and molecular interactions to include ion-atom, ion-molecule, atom-atom and atom-molecule; interaction with surface and solids of ion beams. **Mailing Address:** Mat Radiation Sci MS 1159, Sandia Nat Labs, PO Box 5800, Albuquerque, NM 87185-1159. **Fax:** 505-845-0657. **E-Mail:** gjlockw@sandia.gov

LOCKWOOD, HARRY F, SEMICONDUCTOR DEVICES. **Personal Data:** b New York, NY, January 23, 1935. **Education:** St Johns Univ, BS, 1957; NY Univ, PhD, 1972. **Professional Experience:** STAFF, LOCKWOOD GROUP, NEWTON, MASS, as of 2003; PRIN, LOCKWOOD GROUP, NEWTON, 1992-; FOUNDER, LOCKWOOD GROUP, NEWTON, MASS, 1992-; prog dir, Advan Components Technol Ctr, 1989-1992; dir, Advan Components Technol Ctr, 1982-1989; Staff, GTE Inc, Waltham, Mass, 1979-1992; tech mgr, optoelectronic & high speed discrete & integrated devices, 1979-1982. **Memberships:** Fel Inst Elec & Electronics Engrs; Am Phys Soc. **Research Statement & Publications:** Awarded 17 patents; published over 50 articles. **Mailing Address:** Lockwood Group, PO Box 620132, Newton, MA 02462-0132. **Fax:** 617-965-4154. **E-Mail:** lockwood@world.std.com

LOCKWOOD, JEFFREY ALAN, ECOLOGY & PEST MANAGEMENT, ENVIRON ETHICS. **Personal Data:** b Manchester, Conn, March 9, 1960; m 1982, Nancy; c Erin K & Ethan J. **Education:** NMex Tech, BS, 1982; La State Univ, PhD (entom), 1985. **Honors & Awards:** Brown Medal, New Mexico Tech, 1982; R T Gast Award, Entom Soc Am, 1985; L D Newsom Award, La State Univ, 1986; Gamma Sigma Delta Award of Merit, Univ Wyo, 1991; Nat Award for Excellence in Teaching NASULGC, 1993; Albert Schweitzer Sermon Award, Unit Univ Assoc 1999; Award for Excellence in Internation Alization, Univ wyo, 2001. **Professional Experience:** Fel, Org Econ Coop & Develop, 1997; ADJ PROF NATURAL SCI, UNIV WYO, 1996-; PROF NATURAL SCI & HUMANITIES, UNIV WYO, 1996-; vis scientist, CSIRO Div Entom, Australia, 1993-1994; vis fel, Div Bot & Zool, Australian Nat Univ, 1993-1994; from asst prof to assoc prof, Univ Wyo, 1986-1996; postdoctoral res entom, La State Univ, 1985-1986. **Memberships:** Sigma Xi; Entom Soc Am; Orthopterists Soc (fmr exec dir); Assoc Appl Acridology Int (fmr dir). **Research Statement & Publications:** Insect ecology; conservation biology, population ecology of rangeland grasshoppers; nonlinear modeling of population dynamics; biological control and pest management; environmental ethics. **Mailing Address:** Col Agriculture (Renewable Resources), Dept 3354, 1000 E Univ Ave, Laramie, WY 82071-3354. **Fax:** 307-766-5025. **E-Mail:** lockwood@uwyo.edu

LOCKWOOD, JOHN ALEXANDER, physics; deceased, see previous edition for last biography

LOCKWOOD, JOHN LEBARON, PLANT PATHOLOGY. **Personal Data:** b Ann Arbor, Mich, May 28, 1924; m 1959, Jean E Springborg; c James L & Laura A. **Education:** Mich State Col, BA, 1948, MS, 1950; Univ Wis, PhD (plant path), 1953. **Professional Experience:** EMER PROF BOT & PLANT PATH, MICH STATE UNIV, 1990-; NSF sr fel, Cambridge Univ, 1970-1971; from asst prof to prof, Mich State Univ, 1955-1990; Asst prof bot & plant path, Ohio Agr Exp Sta, 1953-1955. **Memberships:** Fel Am Phytopath Soc (pres, 1984-1985). **Research Statement & Publications:** Ecology of root-infecting fungi; soybean diseases. **Mailing Address:** Dept Bot & Plant Path, Mich State Univ, East Lansing, MI 48824. **Fax:** 517-353-1926.

LOCKWOOD, JOHN PAUL, VOLCANOLOGY. **Personal Data:** b Bridgeport, Conn, October 26, 1939; m 1963, Martha; c Pamela & Glen. **Education:** Univ Calif, Riverside, AB, 1961; Princeton Univ, PhD (geol), 1966. **Professional Experience:** PRES, GEO-HAZARDS CONSULT INT INC, 1995-; res dir, Volcanol, Bandung, Indonesia, 1980-1982; geologist, US Geol Surv, 1966-1995; Partic, Sci Exchange Prog, Nat Res Coun-Nat Acad Sci, USSR, res, Geol Inst Scad Sci, Moscow, 1966; affil prof, Univ Hawaii. **Memberships:** Geol Soc Am; Am Geophys Union; Int Asn Volcanology; Asn Am Inst Prof Geologists. **Research Statement & Publications:** Petrology, mineralogy and structural features of serpentinites; general geology of the Sierra Nevada Mountains; circum-Pacific distribution of volcanic rocks; Caribbean geology; volcanic hazards; eruptive history and structure of Mauna Loa volcano, Hawaii; volcanic disaster assessments in Indonesia, Italy, Colombia, Cameroon, Northern Marianas Islands, Rwanda, Zaire and Philippines. **Mailing Address:** Geohazards Consult Int, PO Box 479, Volcano, HI 96785. **Fax:** 808-967-8525. **E-Mail:** geohaz@aloha.net

LOCKWOOD, LINDA GAIL, ENVIRONMENTAL BIOLOGY, SCIENCE EDUCATION. **Personal Data:** b New York, NY, May 25, 1936. **Education:** Columbia Univ, BS, 1960, MA, 1961 & 1965, PhD (bot), 1969. **Professional Experience:** RETIRED; assoc prof Environ Sci, Univ Mass, Amherst, ending 2000; grants, NSF, 1975-1979; co-dir, US Off Educ grant, 1974-1975; fac res grant, Univ Mass, 1974-1975; grant, Water Resources Res Ctr, 1974-1975; grant environ sci educ, Teachers Col, Columbia Univ, 1971-1973; asst prof bot & ecol, Teachers Col, Columbia Univ, 1969-1973. **Memberships:** Sigma Xi; AAAS; Scientist's Inst Pub Info; Nat Asn Biol Teachers; Audubon Soc. **Research Statement & Publications:** Influence of photoperiod and exogenous nitrogen-containing compounds on the reproductive cycles of the liverwort Cephalozia media Lindb; experimental morphology and physiological ecology; environmental biology, especially physiological ecology, aquatic systems; environmental science education, especially teacher training, history and philosophy of science. **Mailing Address:** 100 French Hall, Amherst, MA 01003. **Fax:** 413-545-3075.

LOCKWOOD, ROBERT GREENING, NATURAL & SYNTHETIC ELASTOMERS, SPECIAL ORGANIC COATINGS. **Personal Data:** b Faribault, Minn, January 12, 1928; m 1953, c 2. **Education:** Carleton Col, BA, 1949; Univ Minn, PhD (org chem), 1953. **Professional Experience:** RETIRED; sr res specialist, 3M Co, 1981-1992; res specialist, 3M Co, 1965-1981; sr chemist, 3M Co, 1954-1965; res chemist, New Prod Develop Lab, Chem Div, Gen Elec Co, 1953-1954; lab instr inorg & org chem, Univ Minn, 1949-1953. **Memberships:** Am Chem Soc; Sigma Xi. **Research Statement & Publications:** Organic synthesis; carboxylic acids and derivatives; condensation polymers; manufacture of alkylated aromatic hydrocarbons and polycarboxylic acids; pressure-sensitive adhesives; release agents. **Mailing Address:** 2 Hingham Circle, St Paul, MN 55118-1921.

LOCKWOOD, WILLIAM RUTLEDGE, PHYSICS, GENERAL OPTICS. **Personal Data:** b Memphis, Tenn, April 10, 1929; c 2. **Education:** Univ Miss, BA, 1949, MA, 1950; Univ Tenn, Memphis, MD, 1957. **Professional Experience:** RETIRED; assoc prof med, Med Ctr, Univ Miss, 1970-1991; asst dean res & assoc chief staff res, Vet Admin Ctr, 1969-1973; asst prof microbiol & path, Med Ctr, Univ Miss, 1966-1970; attend physician, Univ Miss Hosp, 1964-; grant, Med Ctr, Univ Miss, 1964-1967; vis instr, Wash Univ, 1964; from instr to asst prof, Med Ctr, Univ Miss, 1962-1970; USPHS fel, Med Ctr, Univ Miss, 1961-1964; resident med, Med Ctr, Univ Miss, 1959-1961; intern, Charity Hosp La, New Orleans, 1957-1958. **Memberships:** Fel Infectious Dis Soc Am; fel Am Col Chest Physicians; Am Soc Trop Med & Hyg; Am Soc Microbiol; fel Am Col Physicians. **Research Statement & Publications:** Pathogenesis of acute inflammation; pharmacology of antimicrobial agents. **Mailing Address:** 13501 Bay View Circle, Ocean Springs, MS 39564.

LOCKYER, NIGEL STUART, LIFETIME MEASUREMENT OF B-QUARKS, CHARGE-PARITY VIOLATION IN B-MESON DECAYS. **Personal Data:** b Annan, Scotland, November 5, 1952; m 1976, Ellen; c Geoffrey, Martin & Sara. **Education:** York Univ, BSc, 1975; Ohio State Univ, PhD (physics), 1980. **Professional Experience:** PROF PHYSICS, UNIV PA, 1998-; assoc prof physics, Univ Pa, 1990-1998; vis scientist, Fermilab, 1987 & 1988 & SSC lab, 1989-1990; asst prof, Univ PA, 1984-1990; postdoctoral fel, Stanford Linear Accelerator Ctr, 1980-1984. **Memberships:** Am Phys soc. **Research Statement & Publications:** Bottom quarks decay using collider detector; measured the branching ratio of several bottom decays and the bottom lifetime; charge-parity violation in B-decays. **Mailing Address:** Dept Physics, Univ Pa, Philadelphia, PA 19104-6396. **Fax:** 215-898-8512. **E-Mail:** lockyer@lockyer.hep.upenn.edu

LOCOCK, ROBERT A, PHARMACEUTICAL CHEMISTRY, PHARMACOGNOSY. **Personal Data:** b Toronto, Ont, August 14, 1935; m 1961. **Education:** Univ Toronto, BSc, 1959, MSc, 1961; Ohio State Univ, PhD (pharm), 1965. **Professional Experience:** ASSOC PROF PHARMACEUT SCI, UNIV ALTA, 1974-; ASSOC PROF PHARM, UNIV ALTA, 1970-; asst prof, Univ Alta, 1965-1970; asst pharm, Ohio State Univ, 1964-1965; lectr pharmaceut chem, Univ BC, 1961-1962. **Memberships:** AAAS; Am Chem Soc; Am Soc Pharmacog; Sigma Xi. **Research Statement & Publications:** Chemistry of natural products; phytochemistry; chemotaxonomy; alkaloids and terpenoids. **Mailing Address:** Dept Pharm Univ Alta, 13943 107A Ave, Edmonton, AB T5M 2A8, Can.

LOCY, ROBERT DONALD, ENIROMENTAL STRESS, PHYSIOLOGY. **Personal Data:** b Defiance, Ohio, January 12, 1947; m 1969, Marcia; c Michelle L, Ian D & Eric M. **Education:** Defiance Col, AB, 1969; Purdue Univ, PhD (plant biochem), 1974. **Professional Experience:** PROF, DEPT BIOL SCI, AUBURN UNIV, 1998-; dir cell sci ctr, Auburn Univ, 1991-; mgr, floral prod res, 1988-1990; sr res scientist, Nat Prevention Inst, Salt Lake City, Utah, 1983-1988; prof agr, Ind-Purdue, Ft Wayne, 1982-1983; asst prof hort, NC State Univ, 1978-1982; res fel, Dept Environ Res Lab, Mich State Univ, 1976-1978; res assoc biochem, McMaster Univ, 1974-1976. **Memberships:** Am Soc Plant Physiol; Tissue Cult Asn Am; Sigma Xi. **Research Statement & Publications:** Plant physiology, biochem, biophysiology and environmental stress tolerance. **Mailing Address:** Dept Biol Sci, Auburn Univ, 131 Carry Hall 328 Life Sci Bldg, Auburn, AL 36849. **Fax:** 334-844-1645. **E-Mail:** locyrob@auburn.edu

LODA, RICHARD THOMAS, SPECTROSCOPY. **Personal Data:** b Derby, Conn, May 19, 1948. **Education:** Waterburg State Tech Col, AAS, 1968; Univ Bridgeport, BA, 1971; Wesleyan Univ, PhD (phys chem), 1980. **Professional Experience:** VPRES & CHIEF TECH OFFICER, EHS INC, 1994-; Naval Res Lab, 1985-1993; chemist res dept, Instrumental Chem Analysis Br, Naval Weapons Ctr, 1981-1985; NIH fel, Chem Dept, Univ Ore, 1980-1981. **Memberships:** Am Chem Soc; Am Phys Soc. **Research Statement & Publications:** Application of lasers and spectroscopy to problems of physical and chemical interest; photochemistry; site selection and linewidth phenomena in condensed phase systems; coherent antistokes Raman scattering. **Mailing Address:** 8 Larkfield Lane, Laguna Niguel, CA 92677-5323.

LODATO, MICHAEL W, OPERATIONS RESEARCH. **Personal Data:** b Rochester, NY, June 17, 1932; m 1959, c 4. **Education:** Colgate Univ, BA, 1954; Univ Rochester, MS, 1959; Rutgers Univ, PhD (math), 1962. **Professional Experience:** ASSOC PROF BUS ADMIN, CALIIF LUTHERAN UNIV, as of 2004; PRES, MWL INC, 1980-; exec vpres, Spectrum Int, Inc, 1978-1980; vpres indust systs, Informatics, Inc, 1971-1978; prin bus planner, Xerox Data Systs, 1970-1971; pres, Macro Systs Assocs, Inc, 1968-1970; mgr, Info Technol Dept, McDonnell Douglas Corp, 1967-1968; srexec adv, Douglas Aircraft Corp, 1966-1967; head opers anal sub dept, Appl Math Dept, Mitre Corp, Mass, 1965-1966; mem tech staff, Appl Math Dept, Mitre Corp, Mass, 1963-1965; Scientist, LFE Monterey Lab, 1962-1963. **Memberships:** Opers Res Soc Am; Asn Data Process Serv Orgn. **Research Statement & Publications:** Topology; planning, scheduling and resource allocation; orbital mechanics; production and inventory control; strategic management; author of two books on computer sales and strategic management. **Mailing Address:** Dept Bus Admin, Calif Lutheran Univ, 60 West Olsen Rd, Thousand Oaks, CA 91360. **E-Mail:** lodato@clunet.edu

LODEN, MICHAEL SIMPSON, OLIGOCHAETA, WATER QUALITY. **Personal Data:** b Fayette, Ala, March 30, 1945; m 1968, Karen; c Jonathan M. **Education:** Univ Auburn, BS, 1967, MS, 1973; La State Univ, PhD (zoology), 1978. **Professional Experience:** DIR, ENVIRON RESOURCES, GULF ENG & CONSULTS INC, 1990-; environ dir, Jefferson Parish, La, 1981-1990; asst prof zool, La State Univ, 1978-1981; aquatic biologist, Aquatic Control Inc, 1973-1975. **Memberships:** Sigma Xi; NAm Benthol Soc; Am Micros Soc; Water Environ Fedn. **Research Statement & Publications:** Systematics, life histories, ecology and distribution of aquatic Oligochaeta; Published Over 30 articles. **Mailing Address:** 13546 Shady Ridge Ave, Baton Rouge, LA 70817. **E-Mail:** loden@communique.net

LODER, EDWIN ROBERT, CHEMISTRY. **Personal Data:** b Irvington, NJ, February 24, 1925; m 1945, Charlotte; c 4. **Education:** Syracuse Univ, BA, 1952; Mass Inst Technol, PhD, 1955. **Professional Experience:** RETIRED; pres, GRL & Assoc, 1990-1997; pres, Delray Chem Co, 1985-1990; group exec vpres, Du Bois Chem Div, Chemed Corp, 1974-1985; exec vpres, Du Bois Chem Div, Chemed Corp, 1973-1974; sr vpres corp affairs, Du Bois Chem Div, Chemed Corp, 1972-1973; dir res & vpres, Du Bois Chem Div, Chemed Corp, 1970-1972; from dep dir to dir res, Du Bois Chem Div, W R Grace & Co, 1966-1970; sect mgr & tech assoc, Gen Aniline & Film Co, NY, 1965-1966; dir res serv, Maumee Chem, 1962-1965; instr, Univ Toledo, 1961-1962; chief anal chemist, Maumee Chem, 1959-1962; chemist, Eastman Kodak Co, 1955-1959; asst org microanal, Mass Inst Technol, 1953-1955; asst chem, Mass Inst Technol, 1952-1953. **Memberships:** Fel AAAS; fel Am Inst Chem; Am Chem Soc; Soc Photog Sci & Eng; Am Soc Qual Control; Sigma Xi. **Research Statement & Publications:** Electrochemistry; spectroscopy; research management; statistics. **Mailing Address:** 12258 Eagles Landing Way, Boynton Beach, FL 33437.

LODEWIJK, ERIC, SYNTHETIC ORGANIC CHEMISTRY. **Personal Data:** b Hague, Neth, November 15, 1940. **Education:** Univ Amsterdam, BSc, 1965, PhD (org chem), 1968. **Professional Experience:** HEAD CHEM DEVELOP, F HOFFMANN & LA ROCHE LTD, 1995-; group dir, Process Res & Develop, 1991-1995; dir res & develop, Chem Div, 1986-1991; mgr process res, Chem Div, 1979-1986; group leader res org chem, Chem Div, 1977-1979; sr res chemist, Chem Div, 1973-1977; group leader process develop, Chem Div, 1970-1973; Res chemist org chem, Syntex Chem, Inc, Bahamas, 1969-1970. **Memberships:** Am Chem Soc. **Research Statement & Publications:** Process development and process research on fine organic chemicals and drugs; synthesis of fluorocorticosteroids and IG steroids; antiflammatory analgesies, beta blockers. **Mailing Address:** F Hoffmann & La Roche Ltd, Basel CH-4070, Switzerland.

LODGE, ARTHUR SCOTT, physics; deceased, see previous edition for last biography

LODGE, CHESTER RAY, ELECTRICAL ENGINEERING. **Personal Data:** b McCausland, Iowa, February 19, 1923; wid. **Education:** Iowa State Univ, BS, 1943, MS, 1949, PhD (eng), 1952. **Professional Experience:** PROF EMER, SAN DIEGO UNIV, 1988; prof eng, San Diego State Univ, 1958-1988; assoc prof, San Diego State Univ, 1954-1958; asst prof, Iowa State Univ, 1954; Fulbright lectr, Pakistan, 1952-1953; dean eng, Univ Peshawar, Pakistan, 1952-1953. **Memberships:** Am Soc Eng Educ; Inst Elec & Electronics Engrs. **Research Statement & Publications:** Automatic control systems; symmetrical components and applications. **Mailing Address:** 5492 Redding Rd, San Diego State Univ, San Diego, CA 92115.

LODGE, DAVID MICHAEL, LAKES, HERBIVORY. **Personal Data:** b Athens, Tenn, April 1, 1957; m 1985, Andrea; c 3. **Education:** Univ South, BS, 1979; Oxford Univ, DPhil(zoology), 1982. **Professional Experience:** PROF FRESHWATER ECOL & BIOL INVASIONS, UNIV NOTRE DAME, as of 2004; vis scientist, Inst Mar Sci, Univ NC, Chapel Hill, 1992-1993; assoc ed, J NAm Benthological Soc, 1990-1992; exec comn, Am Midland Naturalist, 1989-; asst prof invert zool & ecol, Univ Notre Dame, beginning 1985; asst scientist, Ctr Limnol, Univ Wis, 1982-1985. **Memberships:** Am Sci Affil; Am Soc Limnol & Oceanog; Ecol Soc Am; NAm Benthological Soc; Am Inst Biol Sci; Int Soc Limnol. **Research Statement & Publications:** Determining the relative importance of biotic and abiotic factors in determining the distribution and abundance of freshwater benthic organisms; predation and herbivory; impact of exotic species on freshwater ecosystems; comparative ecology of plant-animal interactions in freshwater, marine and terrestrial ecosystems; interaction of benthic and pelagic habitats in lakes; author of various articles. **Mailing Address:** Dept Biol Sci, Univ Notre Dame, Notre Dame, IN 46556. **E-Mail:** david.m.lodge.1@nd.edu

LODGE, JAMES ROBERT, REPRODUCTIVE PHYSIOLOGY. **Personal Data:** b Downey, Iowa, July 1, 1925; m 1947, c 2. **Education:** Iowa State Univ, BS, 1952, MS, 1954; Mich State Univ, PhD (dairy), 1957. **Professional Experience:** PROF EMER PHYSIOL, UNIV ILL, as of 2003; prof physiol, Univ Ill, beginning 1969; Res fel, Nat Inst Child Health & Human Develop, 1969-1970; from asst prof to assoc prof, Univ Ill, Urbana, 1960-1969; res assoc dairy sci, Univ Ill, Urbana, 1957-1960; asst dairy, Mich State Univ, 1954-1957. **Memberships:** AAAS; Am Physiol Soc; Soc Study Reproduction; Am Soc Animal Sci; Am Dairy Sci Asn. **Research Statement & Publications:** Physiology of reproduction and endocrinology. **Mailing Address:** 312 Animal Sci Lab, Univ Ill 1207 W Gregory Dr, Urbana, IL 61801.

LODGE, MALCOLM A, COMPUTER SCIENCE, ENGINEERING. **Personal Data:** b Borden, PEI, March 16, 1939; c 2. **Education:** NS Tech Col, BEng, 1962, MScEng, 1969. **Professional Experience:** PRES & GEN MGR, AOC WIND TURBINES, as of 2003; pres, Island Technol Inc, beginning 1986; tech progs officer, Inst Man & Resources, 1977-1986; res engr, Resource Ventures, Inc, 1977-1986; prof elec eng, Holland Col, 1969-1977; prod design engr, Can Westinghouse Co, Ltd, 1964-1969; nat Res Coun fel, 1964; sonar engr, Can Forces Dockyard, Halifax, 1962-1963. **Memberships:** Can Wind Energy Asn; Am Wind Energy Asn; Asn Prof Engrs. **Research Statement & Publications:** Wind turbine systems; process x-ray applications; biomedical computer applications; energy conservation and supply systems. **Mailing Address:** Atlantic Orient Corp, PO Box 832 49 Pownal St, Charlottetown, PE C1A 7L9, Can. **Fax:** 902-368-7139. **E-Mail:** aocadmin@aocwind.com

LODGE, NICHOLAS JOHN, CARDIOVASCULAR PHYSIOLOGY, ELECTROPHYSIOLOGY. **Personal Data:** b Nottingham, Eng, January 31, 1957. **Education:** Univ Lancaster, BSc, 1978, PhD (physiol), 1982. **Professional Experience:** AT, BRYSTOL-MEYERS SQUIBB PHARMACEUT RES INST, as of 2001; SR RES INVESTR II, BRYSTOL-MEYERS SQUIBB, 1991-; res scientist, Wyeth Ayerst, 1989-1992; sr scientist, Wyeth Ayerst, 1988-1989; Young investr award, Am Pediat Soc, 1985; Res asst prof, Univ Miami, Fla Sch Med, 1983-1988. **Memberships:** Biophys Soc; Physiol Soc. **Research Statement & Publications:** Cardiovascular physiology; electrophysiology; cellular physiology. **Mailing Address:** Bristol Myers Squibb Res Inst, Pennington, NJ 08534.

LODGE, TIMOTHY PATRICK, POLYMER SOLUTION DYNAMICS. **Personal Data:** b Sale, Eng, April 11, 1954; m 1988. **Education:** Harvard Univ, BA, 1975; Univ Wis, PhD (chem), 1980. **Professional Experience:** DISTINGUISHED MCKNIGHT UNIV PROF CHEM, UNIV MINN, TWIN CITIES, as of 2004; US Regional ed, Macromolecular Chem & Physics, 1994-; PROF CHEM, UNIV MINN, 1991-; from asst prof to assoc prof, Univ Minn, 1982-1991; Nat Res Coun assoc fel, Nat Bur Stand, 1981-1982. **Memberships:** Fel Am Chem Soc; Am Phys Soc; Soc Rheology; Sigma Xi. **Research Statement & Publications:** Conformation and dynamics of macromolecules in solutions and melts studied by means of oscillatory flow birefringence, quasi-elastic light scattering, small angle neutron scattering, and forud rayleigh scattering. **Mailing Address:** Dept Chem, Univ Minn, 235 Smith Hall 207 Pleasant St SE, Minneapolis, MN 55455-0431. **Fax:** 612-626-7541. **E-Mail:** lodge@chem.umn.edu

LODHI, MOHAMMAD ARFIN KHAN, NUCLEAR PHYSICS, RENEWABLE SOURCES OF ENERGY. **Personal Data:** b Agra, India, September 17, 1933; m 1965, Khalida; c 3. **Education:** Univ Karachi, BSc, Hons, 1952, MSc, 1956; Univ London, DIC, 1960, PhD (nuclear physics), 1963. **Honors & Awards:** Alkhwarzmi Award. **Professional Experience:** Vis prof, Univ Pertanian, Malaysia, 1989-1990; consult & expert, UN Nat Inst-Oceanog, Karachi, Pakistan, 1988; vis prof, Middle East Tech Univ, Ankara, Turkey, 1987; guest scientist, Ctr Solar Energy Hyderabad Sin Pakistan, 1986-1987; vis prof, Ctr Excellence Anal Chem, Sind Pakistan, 1986; NSF coordr, deleg Int NathiagaliSummer Col, Pakistan; vis prof, Bahauddin Zakariya Univ, Pakistan, 1984-1985; consult, Nat Inst Oceanog, Karachi, Pakistan, 1984 & 1985; UN expert & consult, var univs in Pakistan, 1981 & 1983; PROF PHYSICS, TEX TECH UNIV, 1973-; guest scientist, Pinstech, Pakistan, 1973 & 1976; vis assoc prof, Univ Wash, 1969-1970 & Univ Calif, San Diego, 1972; res assoc, State Univ NY, Buffalo, 1969; vis asst prof, Univ Fla, Gainesville, 1967 & Univ Wyo, Laramie, 1968; from asst prof to assoc prof, Tex Tech Univ, 1963-1973; vis res scholar, Bohr Inst Theoret Physics, Copenhagen, Denmark, 1962; lectr math, S M Col, Karachi, 1952-1959. **Memberships:** Brit Inst Physics; Pakistan Math Soc; fel Phys Soc UK; Sigma Xi; Am Phys Soc; Am Asn Univ Professors; Am Astronaut Soc; Pakistan Inst Physics; Solar Energy Soc Pakistan. **Research Statement & Publications:** High energy electron scattering by nuclei and electromagnetics transitions in nuclei and their role in elucidating nuclear structure; nuclear shell, cluster and resonating group models and their relationship; nuclear nonlocal potential and nuclear systematics; short-range nucleon-nucleon correlations; solar-hydrogen system collection, transduction; extraction of energy from renewable sources, including ocean currents and tides. **Mailing Address:** Dept Physics, Tex Tech Univ PO Box 41051, Lubbock, TX 79409. **Fax:** 806-742-1182. **E-Mail:** b5mak@ttacs.ttu.edu

LODISH, HARVEY FRANKLIN, BIOCHEMISTRY, CELL BIOLOGY. **Personal Data:** b Cleveland, Ohio, November 16, 1941; m 1963, Pamela; c Heidi, Martin & Stephanie. **Education:** Kenyon Col, AB, 1962; Rockefeller Univ, PhD (genetics), 1966. **Honorary Degrees:** DSc, Kenyon Col, 1982. **Honors & Awards:** Stadie Award, Am Diabetes Asn, 1989; Fellow, American Association for the Advancement of Science 1986; National Academy of Sciences 1987; Fellow, American Academy of Microbiology 1990; Associate Member, European Molecular Biology Organization 1996; Fellow, American Academy of Arts and Sciences 1999; President, American Society of Cell Biology 2004. **Professional Experience:** PROF BIO BIO ENG, MASS INST TECHNOL, as of 1999; MEM, WHITEHEAD INST, as of 1982; Assoc mem, Europ Molecular Biol Orgn, 1995-; Red Blood Cells, 1985 & Membrane Molecular Biol, 1989; mem, Whitehead Inst Biomed Res, 1982-; Guggenheim fel, 1977-1978; vis scientist, Imp Cancer Res Fund, 1977-1978; PROF BIOL, MASS INST TECHNOL, 1976-; chmn, Gordon Conf on Animal Cells, 1976; mem panel develop biol, NSF, 1972-; res career develop award, Nat Inst Gen Med Sci, 1971-1975; from asst prof to assoc prof, Mass Inst Technol, 1968-1976; Am Cancer Soc fel biol, Lab Molecular Biol, Med Res Coun, Eng, 1966-1968. **Memberships:** Nat Acad Sci; Am Soc Microbiol; Am Chem Soc; Am Soc Biol Chemists; Am Soc Cell Biol; fel AAAS; fel Am Acad Microbiol. **Research Statement & Publications:** Structure, function and assembly of plasma membrane proteins; erythropoetin receptor and erythropoiesis; adiponectin and its role in diabetes; hematopoietic stem cells. **Mailing Address:** Whitehead Inst Biomed Res, 9 Cambridge Ctr, Cambridge, MA 02142. **Fax:** 617-258-6768. **E-Mail:** lodish@wi.mit.edu

LODMELL, DONALD LOUIS, VIROLOGY. **Personal Data:** b Polson, Mont, August 27, 1939; m 1963. **Education:** Northwestern Univ, BA, 1961; Univ Mont, MS, 1963, PhD (microbiol), 1967. **Professional Experience:** CHIEF & SPEC EXPERT, LAB PERSISTENT VIRAL DIS, NIH, 1999-; sci dir virol, Rocky Mountain Lab, Nih, beginning 1981; fac affil, Dept Microbiol, Univ Mont, 1978-; sr scientist, Rocky Mountain Lab, NIH, 1972-1981; res assoc, Lab Oral Med, NIH, 1971-1972; scientist virol, Rocky Mountain Lab, NIH, 1967-1971. **Memberships:** Am Soc Microbiol; Am Asn Immunologists; Am Soc Virol. **Research Statement & Publications:** Immunological mechanisms of host defense against viral infections of the central nervous system; rabies. **Mailing Address:** Lab Persistent Viral Dis, Nat Inst Allergy & Infectious Dis, Nat Inst Health, 6610 Rockledge Dr MSC 6612, Bethesda, MD 20892. **E-Mail:** dlodmell@niaid.nih.gov

LODOEN, GARY ARTHUR, POLYMER CHEMISTRY. **Personal Data:** b Camp Rucker, Ala, May 3, 1943. **Education:** Univ NDak, BS, 1965; Cornell Univ, PhD (org chem), 1969. **Professional Experience:** RES ASSOC, TEXTILE FIBERS DEPT, E I DU PONT DEL NEMOURS & CO INC, 1983-; sr res chemist, E I Du Pont Del Nemours & Co, Inc, 1977-1982; process supvr, E I Du Pont Del Nemours & Co, Inc, 1975-1977; res & develop supvr, E I Du Pont Del Nemours & Co, Inc, 1973-1975; sr res chemist, E I Du Pont Del Nemours & Co, Inc, 1973; res chemist, E I Du Pont Del Nemours & Co Inc, 1970-1973; fel, Univ Iowa, 1969-1970. **Memberships:** Am Chem Soc. **Research Statement & Publications:** Spandex chemistry and structure; polyester glycol synthesis and properties; development of new and novel raw materials for spandex yarns. **Mailing Address:** 500 Pelham Dr, Waynesboro, VA 22980. **E-Mail:** galodoen@cfw.com

LODWICK, GWILYM SAVAGE, RADIOLOGY, BIOENGINEERING. **Personal Data:** b Mystic, Iowa, August 30, 1917; m 1970, Maria; c Gwilym S, Philip G, Malcolm K & Terry Ann. **Education:** Univ Iowa, BA, 1942, MD, 1943. **Honors & Awards:** Gold Medal, XIII Int Conf Radiol, Madrid, 1973; Sakari Mustakallio Medal, Finland, 1979; Founder's Gold Medal, Int Skeletal Soc, 1990; Med Tech Leadership Award, Nat Elec Mfrs Asn, 1995. **Professional Experience:** Hon radiologist, Mass Gen Hosp, 1992-; chmn bd sci coun, Nat Libr Med, 1987-1989; radiologist-in-chief, Spaulding Rehab Hosp, 1986-1992; distinguished practr, Nat Acad Pract Med, 1984; PROF EMER RADIOL, UNIV MO, COLUMBIA, beginning 1983; vis prof, Harvard Med Sch, 1983-1992; radiologist, Mass Gen Hosp, 1983-1992; chmn, Dept Radiol, Sch Med, Univ Mo, Columbia, 1981-1983; chmn, Radiation Study Sect, Div Res Grants, NIH, 1980-1982; interim chmn radiol, Sch Med, Univ Mo, Columbia, 1980-1981; mem, Study Sect Diag Radiol & Nuclear Med, NIH, 1979-1982; vis prof, Univ Turku, Finland, 1979; res prof, Dept Radiol, Sch Med, Univ Mo, Columbia, 1978-1983; mem, Radiation Study Sect, Div Res Grants, NIH, 1976-1979; vis prof, Sch Med, Keio Univ, Tokyo, 1974; Sigma Xires Award, Univ Mo-Columbia, 1972;

mem, Comt Radiol, Div Med Sci, Nat Res Coun, 1970-1975; consult, Jet Propulsion Lab, Calif Inst Technol, 1969-1973; Nat Inst Gen Med Sci spec fel, 1967-1968; mem radiol training comt, Nat Inst GenMed Sci, 1966-1970; consult, Ellis Fischel State Cancer Hosp, 1959-; assoc dean, Sch Med, Univ Mo, Columbia, 1959-1964; actg dean, Sch Med, Univ Mo, Columbia, 1959; prof radiol & chmn dept, Sch Med, Univ Mo, Columbia, 1956-1978; assoc prof, Col Med, Univ Iowa, 1955-1956; chief radiol serv, Vet Admin Hosp, Iowa City, 1952-1955; clin asst prof radiol, Univ Iowa, 1952-1955; fel, Armed Forces Inst Path, 1951; dir, Mid-Am Bone Diag Ctr & Registry; mem, Comt Radiol, Nat Acad Sci. **Memberships:** Sr mem Inst Med-Nat Acad Sci; AAAS; AMA; Radiol Soc NAm (3rd vpres 1974-1975); fel Am Col Radiol; fel Am Col Med Info. **Research Statement & Publications:** Diagnostic radiology; diagnosis and prognosis of bone disease, computer-aided medical diagnosis; automated image analysis and pattern recognition; information systems. **Mailing Address:** Dept Radiol, Univ Mo, Columbia, MO 65211.

LODWICK, WELDON A, MATHEMATICS. **Education:** Muskingum Col, BS, 1967; Univ Cincinnati, MA, 1969; Ore State Univ, PhD (maths), 1980. **Professional Experience:** FULL PROF, UNIV COLO, 2003-. **Mailing Address:** Math Dept Univ Colo, Campus Box 170 PO Box 173364, Denver, CO 80217-3364. **Fax:** 303 556-8550. **E-Mail:** weldon.lodwick@cudenver.edu

LOE, HARALD, PERIODONTICS. **Personal Data:** b Steinkjer, Norway, July 19, 1926; American citizen; c 2. **Education:** Thirteen from US & foreign univs, 1973-1990. **Honorary Degrees:** DSc, Univ Gothenburg, Sweden, 1973, Cath Univ Leuven, Belg, Univ Athens, Greece & Royal Dent Col, Aarhus, Denmark, 1980; Univ Lund, Malmo & Georgetown Univ Sch Dent, 1983, Univ Bergen, 1985, Univ Md, 1986 & Univ Med & Dent NJ, 1987. **Honors & Awards:** Peridont Award, William J Gies Found, 1978; Int Asn Dent Res Award, 1969; Ingv Stokke Prize, 1965; Erik Berg Found Prize, 1969; Aalborg Dent Soc Prize, 1969; Am Soc Prev Dent Int Award, 1972; Arthur Merritt Mem lectr, Baylor Univ, 1977; William J Gies Award, Am Acad Periodont, 1978; Lister Hill Mem lectr, Univ Ala, Birmingham, 1983; Goldstein lectr, Emory Univ, 1986; Exemplary Serv Award, Surgeon Gen, 1988; Swed Dent Soc Int Prize, 1988; Award Distinction, Acad Dent Int, 1990. **Professional Experience:** RETIRED; consult, Med Res Coun, 1987; consult, Naval Dent Sch, Naval Med Command, 1985-1988; search comt ed J Periodont, 1985, 1988; consult, appraisals comt, Ont Coun Grad Studies & Lord Robens Appeal, Brit Soc Dent Res, 1985; comt mission & goals, Orban Prize competition, 1984-1987; dir, Nat Inst Dent Res, NIH, Bethesda, Md, 1983-1994; consult, Coun Int Rel, Am Dent Asn, 1983-1988; hon mem comt, Int Asn Dent Res, 1981-1984; foreign rel comt, chmn, Orban Prize Competition 1981-1982; consult, Periodont DisClin Res Ctr, State Univ NY, Buffalo, 1980-1981; mem, int rel comt, Int Asn Dent Res, 1979-1982; hon mem comt, Orban Prize competition, 1979-1982; consult, J Am Dent Asn, 1979-1982; mem, gen prog comt, Int Asn Dent Res, 1978-1980; Orban Prize competition, beginning 1978; mem, Finance Comt, Int Asn-Dent Res, 1978-1980; mem, Organizing Comt, bd dirs, Int Asn Dent Res, Int Conf Periodont Res, Gothenburg, Sweden, 1977-1982; consult, Coun Dent Therapeut, Am Dent Asn, 1977-1982; secy, Jury Int Prev Dent Award, Int Dent Fed, 1976; mem, comt Orban Prize competition, 1976; mem, comt outreach activ, Univ Conn, dent sch res grant comt & periodont res prog comt, Int Asn Dent Res, 1976; foreign expert mem, J Indian Dent Asn, 1974-1982; dean & prof periodont, Sch Dent Med, Univ Conn, 1974-1982; comt res periodont, Am Asn Periodontologist, 1974-1979; mem, comt long range planning, Am Asn Periodontologist, 1974-1975; prof & dir, Dent Res Inst, Univ Mich, 1972-1974; chmn, Aarhus Br, 1972; from assoc dean to dean elect, Royal Dent Col, Aarhus, Denmark, 1971-1972; pres, Periodont Res Group, 1970-1971; consult, dir, Nat Inst Dent Res, beginning 1969; consult, Procter & Gamble Co, 1969-1976; chmn & mem, Basic Res Periodont Dis Award Comt, Int Asn Dent Res, 1969-1974; co-chmn, Scan Symp Prosthetics & Periodont, Aarhus, Denmark & IntConf Periodont Res, Rochester, NY, 1969; rapporteur, Conf Undergrad Dent Educ Europe, WHO, 1968; consult, Comt Foreign Rel, Am Asn Periodontologists, 1967-1971; vis prof, Hebrew Univ, Jerusalem, 1966-1967; vis prof periodont, Hebrew Univ, Jerusalem, 1966-1967; secy, World Workshop Periodont, Path Sect, Ann Arbor, 1966; ed, J Periodont Res, 1965-1985; bd dir, Scand Odontological Act, 1965-1972; chmn, Scand Symp Periodont, Aarhus, Denmark, 1965; prof & chmn periodont, Royal Dent Col, Aarhus, Denmark, 1962-1972; assoc ed, Scand J Dent Res Munksgaard, Copenhagen, Denmark, 1962; assoc prof periodont, Sch Dent, Oslo Univ, 1960-1961; univ res fel, Oslo Univ, 1959-1962; mem & chmn, Comt Postgrad Educ, Oslo Dent Soc, 1959-1961; fulbright res fel, res assoc oral path, Univ Ill, 1957-1958; res assoc, Norweg Inst Dent Res, 1956-1962; instr oper dent, Sch Dent, Oslo, 1952-1955. **Memberships:** Inst Med-Nat Acad Sci; Int Asn Dent Res (pres, 1979-1981); fel Int Col Dentists; fel Am Col Dentists; fel AAAS; corresp mem Swed Dent Asn; corresp mem Finnish Dent Soc; hon mem Scand Soc Periodont; hon mem Belg Periodont Soc; hon mem Norweg Dent Asn; Int Dent Fed; Int Col Dentists; Sigma Xi. **Research Statement & Publications:** Epidemiology, experimental pathology and prevention of peridontal disease; author or coauthor of over 200 scientific articles; author of over 275 publications. **Mailing Address:** One Redwood Lane, Farmington Hills, Avon, CT 06001.

LOEB, ALEX LEWIS, CARDIOVASCULAR PHARMACOLOGY, ENDOTHELIUM DEPENDENT RESPONSES. **Personal Data:** b Ithaca, NY, August 4, 1955; m 1983, Joan; c Orlando. **Education:** Beloit Col, BS, 1977; George Wash Univ, MS, 1981, PhD (pharmacol), 1984. **Professional Experience:** ASST PROF, DEPT ANESTHESIA & PHARMACOL, UNIV PA, 1992-; Res Asst Prof, Dept Pharmacol, Univ VA, 1987-1988; postdoctoral Fel, Univ Va, 1984-1987; teaching fel, George Wash Univ, 1981-1984; chemist, Nat Bur Stand, 1977; med dir, Complete Healthcare Commun; med dir, Ingenix Pharmaceut Serv. **Memberships:** AAAS; Am Heart Asn; Microcirulatory Soc. **Research Statement & Publications:** Characterization and properties of endothelium-derived relaxing factor from intact vessels and in cultured cells; interactions between endothelium, smooth muscle and platelets in microcirculation, in vivo; mechanisms of anesthetic action. **Mailing Address:** Complete Healthcare Commun, 203 Wilmington Pike Ste 300, Glen Mills, PA 19119. **E-Mail:** loeba@mail.med.upenn.edu

LOEB, GERALD ELI, NEUROPHYSIOLOGY, BIOMEDICAL ENGINEERING. **Personal Data:** b New Brunswick, NJ, June 26, 1948; m 1988, Frances; c Jason. **Education:** Johns Hopkins Univ, BA, 1969, MD, 1972. **Honors & Awards:** Commendation Medal, USPHS queen's nat scholar, queen's univ, 1988; fel of the Am Inst for med & biological eng, 2000. **Professional Experience:** PROF BIOMED ENG, UNIV SOUTHERN CALIF & DIR MED DEVICE DEVELOP FACILITY, AE MANN INST BIOMED ENG, as of 2005; dir biomed eng & prof physiol, Queen's Univ, 1988-1999; chief scientist, advanced bionics corp, 1994-1999; adj assoc prof bioengineering, 1985-1988; pres, Biomed Concepts Inc, 1981-1988; vis scientist, Univ Calif, San Francisco, 1979-1983; med officer & sect chief, Nat Inst Neurol & Commun Dis & Stroke, 1973-1988; resident surg, Univ Ariz, 1972-1973; fel, Seeing Eye, 1969-1972; guest res assoc, Artificial Eye Proj, Univ Utah, 1971. **Memberships:** Soc Neuroscience; Inst Elec & Electronics Engrs; International Functional Elect Stimulation Soc; Can Physiol Soc; Can Med Biol Eng Soc. **Research Statement & Publications:** Sensorimotor neurophysiology in mammals, neural prostheses; electromyography. **Mailing Address:** Univ Southern Calif, Denny Res Bldg B12 UPC MC 1112 1042 Downey way, Los Angeles, CA 90089-1112. **Fax:** 213-821-1120. **E-Mail:** gloeb@usc.edu

LOEB, JEROD M, CARDIOVASCULAR PHYSIOLOGY. **Personal Data:** b Brooklyn, NY, October 21, 1949; m 1986, Sherri; c Jennifer M & Rebecca E. **Education:** City Univ NY, BS, 1971; State Univ NY, PhD (physiol), 1976. **Honors & Awards:** Established Investr Award, Am Heart Asn, 1987. **Professional Experience:** VPRES, RES & PERFORMANCE MEASUREMENT, JOINT COMN ACCREDITATION HEALTHCARE ORGN, as of 2004; ASST VPRES SCI & TECHNOL & SECY COUN SCI AFFAIRS, AMA, 1991-; dir, Div Biomed Sci, AMA, 1988-1991; adj prof physiol, Northwestern Univ, beginning 1987; dir, Div Basic Sci, AMA, 1987-1988; prin investr, NIH Grant, beginning 1982; career develop award, Schweppe Found, Chicago, Ill, 1980-1983; prin investr, Am HeartAsn Grant-in-Aid, 1980-1982; from asst prof to assoc prof surg & physiol, Med Sch, Northwestern Univ, 1979-1987; res assoc physiol, Stritch Sch Med, Loyola Univ, Chicago, 1977-1979; res fel med, Harvard Med Sch, 1976-1977; teaching asst physiol, State Univ NY Downstate Med Ctr, 1972-1976; mem, Coun Basic Sci, Am HeartAsn. **Memberships:** Am Physiol Soc; Sigma Xi; NY Acad Sci; Soc Exp Biol & Med; Am Heart Asn; Am Pub Health Asn. **Research Statement & Publications:** Electrophysiologic analysis of normal and abnormal cardiac pacemaker activity; autonomic control of cardiac pacemakers; electrophysiologic mapping of human cardiac arrhythmias. **Mailing Address:** Joint Comn Accreditation Healthcare Orgn, One Renaissance Blvd, Oakbrook Terrace, IL 60181. **Fax:** 312-464-5841.

LOEB, JOHN NICHOLS, MECHANISMS OF HORMONE ACTION & CELLULAR TRANSPORT, ENERGY METABOLISM. **Personal Data:** b New York, NY, December 17, 1935. **Education:** Harvard Col, AB, 1957; Harvard Med Sch, MD, 1961; Am Bd Internal Med, Cert, 1968. **Honors & Awards:** MERIT award, NIH, 1988-1998. **Professional Experience:** PROF EMER MED & SPEC LECTR MED, COLUMBIA UNIV, as of 2005; vice chair acad affairs, Columbia Univ, beginning 2003; assoc chmn res, Dept Med, Columbia Univ, 1997-2003; dir, Royal Soc Med Found, 1984-1995; vis prof dept med Univ Cape Town Observ, Rep S Africa, 1982; attend physician, Presby Hosp, NY, beginning 1979; Praktikant, Friedrich Miescher inst, bil saintgerland 1986; prof med, Columbia Univ, beginning 1979; adj assoc prof, Rockefeller Univ, 1975-1981; vis prof, Dept Internal Med, Pahlavi Univ, Shiraz, Iran, 1974 & 1977; adj asst prof, Rockefeller Univ, 1970-1975; asst attend physician to assoc attend physician, Presby Hosp, NY, 1967-1979; NIH trainee metab, 1966-1967; from asst prof to assoc prof, 1967-1979; instr med, Columbia Univ, 1965-1966; chief resident, Presby Hosp, NY, 1965-1966; res assoc, Lab Molecular Biol, Nat Inst Arthritis & Metab Dis, NIH, 1963-1965; asst resident med, Presby Hosp, NY, 1962-1963; intern Med, Mass Gen Hosp, 1961-1962. **Memberships:** Fel Am Col Physicians; Am Soc Clin Invest; Asn Am Physicians; fel AAAS; Endocrin Soc Am Philos Soc. **Research Statement & Publications:** Mechanisms of glucocorticoid and thyroid hormone action; mechanisms of glucose and sodium transport; physical chemistry of hormone-receptor interactions. **Mailing Address:** Dept Med Columbia Univ, 630 W 168th St, New York, NY 10032. **Fax:** 212-305-8466. **E-Mail:** jnl1@columbia.edu

LOEB, LAWRENCE ARTHUR, CANCER, BIOCHEMISTRY, MOLECULAR BIOL. **Personal Data:** b Poughkeepsie, NY, December 25, 1936; m, c 3. **Education:** City Col NY, BS, 1957; NY Univ, MD, 1961; Univ Calif, Berkeley, PhD (biochem), 1967. **Honors & Awards:** pres, Am Asn for Cancer Res 1988-1989; pres, Evinron Mutagen Soc, 2002-2003; Outstanding Investr Award, NIH, 1985-1999, EMS Award 1998, Princess Takamatsu Lecturer 2005. **Professional Experience:** PROF DEPT PATH, SCH MED, UNIV WASH, 1978-; DIR, GOTTSTEIN MEM CANCER RES LABS, 1978-; PROF DEPT BIOCHEM, 1993-; mem, Fox Chase Inst Cancer Res, 1977-1978; assoc mem, Fox ChaseInst Cancer Res, 1971-1977; Res grants, NIH, 1969-2008; asst mem biochem, Fox Chase Inst Cancer Res, 1967-1969; Res grants, Am Cancer Soc, 1967-1969; assoc prof, Dept Path, Sch Med & mem biol & molecular biol grad groups, Univ Pa, 1967-1968; res assoc zool, Univ Calif, Berkeley, 1964-1967; res assoc biochem, Nat Cancer Inst, 1962-1964; Intern, Med Ctr, Stanford Univ, 1961-1962. **Memberships:** Am Asn Cancer Res (pres, 1988-1989); Fedn Am Socs Exp Biol; Am Soc Cell Biol; fel Am Col Physicians. **Research Statement & Publications:** Fidelity of DNA replication; environmental carcinogenesis; mechanism of catalysis by DNA polymerases; Werner syndrome; mutator phenotype in cancer, lethal mutageresis of HIV, mutations and aging. **Mailing Address:** Dept Path, Univ Wash Sch Med Box 357705, Seattle, WA 98195-7705. **Fax:** 206-543-3967. **E-Mail:** laloeb@u.washington.edu

LOEB, MARCIA JOAN, INVERTEBRATE PHYSIOLOGY. **Personal Data:** b New York, NY, March 26, 1933; m 1953, George; c 2. **Education:** Brooklyn Col, BA, 1953; Cornell Univ, MS, 1957; Univ Md, PhD (physiol), 1970. **Professional Experience:** Physiologist, USDA, beginning 1977; prof lectr physiol, Am Univ, 1975-1977; res assoc marine biol, Marine Sci Lab, Univ Col NWales, 1974; instr biol & physiol, Northern Va Community Col, 1973; Nat Res Coun res assoc physiol & endocrinol coelenterate develop, Naval Res Lab, 1970-1972. **Memberships:** Am Soc Zoologists; Entom Soc Am; Int Soc Invert Reproduction; Sigma Xi; Soc Invitro Biol. **Research Statement & Publications:** Environmental, physiological and endocrine control of strobilation in the Chesapeake Bay sea nettle, Chrysaora quinquecirrha; associated physiological phenomena in Chrysaora quinquecirrha; physiology of settlement in some marine bryzoan larvae; endocrinology and physiology of spermatogenesis in lepidoptera; hormones associated with the testis and reproductive tract of lepidoptera; insect midgut cell culture. **Mailing Address:** Insect Biocontrol Lab, Bldg 011A Rm 211 BARC West, Beltsville, MD 20705.

LOEB, MARILYN ROSENTHAL, BIOCHEMISTRY OF BACTERIAL CELL SURFACE. **Personal Data:** b New York, NY, February 26, 1930; m 1949, c 3. **Education:** Barnard Col, Columbia Univ, BA, 1951; Bryn Mawr Col, MA, 1955; Univ Pa, PhD (biochem), 1958. **Professional Experience:** SCIENTIST, MED SCH, UNIV ROCHESTER, 1989-; from asst prof to assoc prof pediat, Med Sch, Univ Rochester, 1978-1989; prog assoc cell biol prog, NSF, 1977-1978; asst res prof microbiol, Med Sch, George Wash Univ, 1975-1977; res assoc biochem, Inst Cancer Res, 1968-1975; res assoc, Med Col Pa, 1965-1968; res assoc biochem, Univ Pa, 1958-1959. **Memberships:** AAAS; Am Soc Microbiol; Sigma Xi. **Research Statement & Publications:** Role of outer membrane components in pathogenesis of gram negative bacteria. **Mailing Address:** Dept Pediiat, Univ Rochester Med Ctr, 601 Elmwood Ave PO Box 690, Rochester, NY 14642.

LOEB, PETER ALBERT, MATHEMATICS. **Personal Data:** b Berkeley, Calif, July 3, 1937; m 1958, Jane; c Eric, Gwen & Aaron. **Education:** Harvey Mudd Col, BS, 1959, Princeton Univ, MA, 1961; Stanford Univ, PhD (math), 1964. **Professional Experience:** PROF MATH, UNIV ILL, URBANA, 1975-; grant, Ctr Advan Studies, 1971; from asst prof to assoc prof, Univ Ill, Urbana, 1968-1975; asst prof math, Univ Calif, Los Angeles, 1964-1968. **Memberships:** Am Math Soc. **Research Statement & Publications:** Topology; potential theory; non-standard analysis; covering theorems. **Mailing Address:** Dept Math, Univ Ill, 1409 W Green St, Urbana, IL 61801-2975. **E-Mail:** loeb@math.uiuc.edu

LOEB, VIRGIL JR, oncology, hematology; deceased, see previous edition for last biography

LOEBBAKA, DAVID S, X-RAY IMAGING IN FLUIDS. **Personal Data:** b Gary, Ind, August 18, 1939; m 1979, c 3. **Education:** Calif Inst Technol, BS, 1961; Univ Md, PhD (physics), 1967. **Professional Experience:** Fluids Div, Nat Bur Stand, 1982-1985; PROF & CHMN PHYSICS, UNIV TENN, 1977-; assoc prof, Univ Tenn, 1972-1977; asst prof high energy physics, Vanderbilt Univ, 1968-1972; assoc res scientist, Univ Notre Dame, 1966-1968. **Memberships:** Sigma Xi; Am Asn Physics Teachers. **Research Statement & Publications:** X-ray imaging in fluid flow. **Mailing Address:** Dept Geol, Geosci & Physics, Univ Tenn, 222 EPS Bldg, Martin, TN 38238. **Fax:** 901-587-7443. **E-Mail:** dloebbaka@utm.edu

LOEBER, JOHN FREDERICK, MECHANICAL ENGINEERING, ENGINEERING MECHANICS. **Personal Data:** b White Plains, NY, October 5, 1942; m 1962, Linda; c Kenneth, Keith, Scott, Kimberly, Terrence, Russell & Victoria. **Education:** Lehigh Univ, BS, 1964, MS, 1965, PhD (appl mech), 1968; George Wash Univ, MEA, 1986. **Professional Experience:** MGR, NCSG MECH DESIGN, KNOLLS ATOMIC POWER LAB, 1990-; resident engr, Develop Apparatus Rep, 1984-1989; mgr AFC reactor equip design, Knolls Atomic Power Lab, 1981-1984; mgr methods develop, Knolls Atomic Power Lab, 1975-1981; lead engr, Knolls Atomic Power Lab, 1971-1973; Engr, Knolls Atomic Power Lab, 1967-1971; NASA fel, Lehigh Univ, 1964-1967. **Memberships:** Am Soc Mech Engrs. **Research Statement & Publications:** Finite element methods of structural analysis including computer program development and graphics; theoretical fracture mechanics. **Mailing Address:** 1659 Broadway, Schenectady, NY 12306.

LOEBL, ERNEST MOSHE, CHEMICAL PHYSICS, QUANTUM CHEMISTRY. **Personal Data:** b Vienna, Austria, July 30, 1923; m 1950, Suzanne; c Judith & David (deceased). **Education:** Hebrew Univ, MSc, 1946; Columbia Univ, PhD (chem), 1952. **Professional Experience:** PROF EMER, POLYTECH UNIV, BROOKLYN, 1990-; dep dept head chem, Polytech Univ, NY, 1988-1990; dean, Natural Sci & Math, Yeshiva Univ, Ny, 1980; Sheffield Univ, Eng, 1971 & Hebrew Univ, Jerusalem, 1973; head div, Polytech Univ, NY, 1965-1973; Oxford Univ, Eng, 1964; prof phys chem, Polytech Univ, NY, 1963-1990; NSF fel, 1963-1964; vis prof, Uppsala Univ, Sweden, 1963; from instr to assoc prof, Polytech Univ, NY, 1952-1963; instr, Rutgers Univ, 1950-1951; asst chemist, Columbia Univ, 1948-1950; res chemist, Olamith Cement Co, 1947; lectr, Esso Res. **Memberships:** AAAS; Am Chem Soc; Am Phys Soc; Sigma Xi; Am Asn Univ Professors. **Research Statement & Publications:** Theoretical chemistry; quantum theory; polyelectrolytes; solid state; catalysis. **Mailing Address:** 128 Willow St No 6A, Brooklyn, NY 11201. **Fax:** 718-875-2622. **E-Mail:** eloebl@aol.com

LOEBL, RICHARD IRA, MATHEMATICS. **Personal Data:** b Battle Creek, Mich, October 18, 1945; m 1976. **Education:** Harvard Univ, AB, 1967; Univ Calif, Berkeley, PhD (math), 1973. **Professional Experience:** ASSOC PROF MATH, WAYNE STATE UNIV, 1979-; fac res award, Wayne State Univ, 1975-1976; res assoc, Univ Calif, Berkeley, 1974; asst prof, Wayne State Univ, 1973-1979; actg instr, Univ Calif, Santa Cruz, 1972-1973; teaching assoc, Univ Calif, Berkeley, 1967-1972. **Memberships:** Am Math Soc; Math Asn Am. **Research Statement & Publications:** Functional analysis-operator theory. **Mailing Address:** 25319 Scotia Rd, Huntington Woods, MI 48070.

LOEBLICH, ALFRED RICHARD, III, PHYCOLOGY, MARINE BIOLOGY. **Personal Data:** b New Orleans, La, March 2, 1941; American citizen; m 1963, c 2. **Education:** Univ Calif, Berkeley, AB, 1963; Univ Calif, San Diego, PhD (marine biol), 1971. **Honors & Awards:** Darbaker Prize, Bot Soc Am, 1977. **Professional Experience:** Dir Marine Sci Prog, Univ Houston, Houston, TX, 1979-1983; ASSOC PROF BIOL, UNIV HOUSTON, 1978-; mem, Darbaker Prize Comt, Bot Soc Am, 1978-; mem, Comt Systs & Evolution, Soc Protozoologists, 1977-; assoc prof & assoc cur, Harvard Univ, 1976-1978; mem, Nomenclature Comt Algae, Int Asn Plant Taxon, 1975-; Mass Sci & Technol Found grant, 1975-1977; NSF grant, 1974-; NIH grant, 1972-1978; asst cur, Harvard Univ, 1972-1976; asst prof, Harvard Univ, 1971-1976; lab technician marine biol, Univ Calif, San Diego, 1970-1971; USPHS fel, Univ Calif, San Diego, 1964-1970; teaching asst, Dept Bot, 1963-1964; lab helper, Herbarium, Univ Calif, Berkeley, 1962-1963. **Memberships:** Phycol Soc Am; Soc Protozoologists; Int Phycological Soc; Am Soc Limnol Oceanog; Marine Biol Asn UK; Calif Bot Soc; Bot Soc Am; AAAS; Int Palm Soc; Am Fruit Explorers. **Research Statement & Publications:** Dinoflagellate genetics; characterization of DNA of primitive algae; ultrastructure and physiology of unicellular algae; algal evolution. **Mailing Address:** Dept Biol & Biochem, Univ Houston, 316 Sci Bldg, Houston, TX 77204-5001. **Fax:** 713-743-2699. **E-Mail:** aloeblich@uh.edu

LOEBLICH, HELEN NINA (TAPPAN), micropaleontology, paleoecology; deceased, see previous edition for last biography

LOEBLICH, KAREN ELIZABETH, ANIMAL BEHAVIOR, ENTOMOLOGY. **Personal Data:** b Ft Sill, Okla, October 10, 1944; m 1975. **Education:** Univ Calif, Los Angeles, AB, 1966, MA, 1967; Univ Calif, Davis, PhD (zoology), 1973. **Professional Experience:** FINE ARTS APPRAISER & WRITER, DEPT ENTOM, UNIV CALIF, DAVIS, 1980-; MEM STAFF, DEPT ENTOM, UNIV CALIF, DAVIS, 1978-; lectr ecol & behav, San Diego State Univ, 1977-1978; mem staff, Agr Div, Upjohn Co, 1975-1980; res scientist entomol, Agr Div, Upjohn Co, 1975-1976; res assoc, Univ Hawaii, 1974; lectr entomol & zoology, San Francisco State Univ, 1973-1975; res assoc, Univ Calif, Riverside, 1972-1973; res assoc entomol, Univ Calif, Davis, 1971-1972. **Memberships:** Asn Study Animal Behav; Entomol Soc Am; Ecol Soc Am; Sigma Xi; AAAS. **Research Statement & Publications:** Behavior and evolution of Diptera; Drosophilidae of Hawaii; insect grooming behavior; integrated pest management, especially of cotton. **Mailing Address:** Univ Calif, PO Box 1164, Davis, CA 95617.

LOECHELT, CECIL P(AUL), CHEMICAL ENGINEERING. **Personal Data:** b Elfers, Fla, November 4, 1935; m 1956, c 3. **Education:** Vanderbilt Univ, BE, 1956; La State Univ, MS, 1962, PhD (adsorption), 1964. **Professional Experience:** SR ECON EVAL ENGR, ETHYL CORP, 1970-; sr process design engr, Ethyl Corp, 1964-1970; Instr chem eng, La State Univ, 1963-1964. **Memberships:** Am Inst Chem Engrs. **Research Statement & Publications:** Mathematical simulation of physical processes; evaluation and design of chemical processes. **Mailing Address:** 1904 Stanford Ave, Baton Rouge, LA 70808.

LOEFFLER, ALBERT L, JR, turbulence; deceased, see previous edition for last biography

LOEFFLER, FRANK JOSEPH, PHYSICS. **Personal Data:** b Ballston Spa, NY, September 5, 1928; m 1951, Jane; c Peter, James, Margaret & Anne Marie. **Education:** Cornell Univ, BS, 1951, PhD (physics), 1957. **Professional Experience:** PROF EMER PHYSICS, PURDUE UNIV, as of 2004; Univ Hawaii, 1985-1986; Univ Heidelberg, 1971; prof physics, Purdue Univ, beginning 1967; vis prof, Univ Hamburg, 1963-1964; from asst prof to assoc prof, Purdue Univ, 1958-1967; mem staff, Princeton Univ, 1957-1958. **Memberships:** Fel Am Phys Soc; Sigma Xi. **Research Statement & Publications:** Elementary particle physics; experimental study of elementary particle interactions at high energy using electronic detection systems; atmospheric physics; investigation of high energy gamma rays and muons from point sources in space; experimental astrophysics using the Haleakala Gamma Ray Observatory and the South Pole GASP facility. **Mailing Address:** Dept Physics, Purdue Univ, 525 NWestern Ave, West Lafayette, IN 47907-2036. **Fax:** 765-494-0706.

LOEFFLER, ROBERT J, BOTANY. **Personal Data:** b Worcester, Mass, October 20, 1922; m 1956, c 4. **Education:** Syracuse Univ, BA, 1948; Univ Wis, MS, 1950, PhD (bot, zool), 1954. **Professional Experience:** EMER PROF BOT, CONCORDIA COL, MOORHEAD, MINN, 1973-; from asst prof to prof, Concordia Col, 1954-1973. **Memberships:** Bot Soc Am; Am Inst Biol Sci. **Research Statement & Publications:** Pollen analysis of Spiritwood Lake, North Dakota; phytoplankton; plant anatomy and morphology. **Mailing Address:** 704 Eighth St, Moorhead, MN 56560.

LOEGERING, DANIEL JOHN, PHYSIOLOGY. **Personal Data:** b Minn, March 11, 1943; m 1968, c 3. **Education:** St John's Univ, Minn, BS, 1965; Univ SDak, Vermillion, MA, 1967; Univ Western Ont, PhD (physiol), 1970. **Professional Experience:** PROF PHYSIOL, ALBANY MED COL, 1987-; from asst prof to assoc prof, Albany Med Col, 1973-1987; Wis Heart Asn fel, NIH spec res fel, 1972-1973; Wis Heart Asn fel, Med Col Wis, 1970-1972; instr physiol, Med Col Wis, 1969-1973. **Memberships:** Reticuloendothelial Soc; Am Physiol Soc. **Research Statement & Publications:** Mononuclear phagocyte system function as related to systemic host defense following injury and the cell biology of macrophages. **Mailing Address:** Dept Physiol, Albany Med Col, 43 New Scotland Ave, Albany, NY 12208. **E-Mail:** loegerd@mail.amc.edu

LOEHLE, CRAIG S, LIFE HISTORY THEORY, LANDSCAPE ECOLOGY. **Personal Data:** b Chicago, Ill, October 23, 1952; m 1980, Neda; c 3. **Education:** Univ Ga, BS, 1976; Univ Wash, MS, 1978; Colo State Univ, PhD (math ecol), 1982. **Professional Experience:** MATH ECOLOGIST, ENVIRON RES LAB, ARGONNE RES LAB, as of 2004; scientist, Argonne Nat Lab, beginning 1991; res ecologist, Westinghouse Savannah River Co, 1987-1991; postdoctoral ecol, Univ Ga, 1984-1987; sci programmer, SPSS, Inc, 1982-1984. **Memberships:** Ecol Soc Am; Int Soc Ecol Modeling. **Research Statement & Publications:** Application of mathematics and statistics to ecology, including landscape ecology; simulation modeling; expert systems and artificial intelligence; plant morphology and reproductive strategies; stability theory; author of 80 publications, one book of philosophy and one book on creativity. **Mailing Address:** Environl Res Div Argonne Nat Lab, 9700 S Cass Ave, Argonne, IL 60439. **Fax:** 630-252-5498. **E-Mail:** craig_loehle@qmgate.anl.gov

LOEHLIN, JAMES HERBERT, PHYSICAL CHEMISTRY, CRYSTALLOGRAPHY. **Personal Data:** b Mussoorie, UP, India, May 23, 1934; American citizen; m 1975, Alice; c Robert C & David W. **Education:** Col Wooster, BA, 1956; Mass Inst Technol, PhD (phys chem), 1960. **Professional Experience:** PROF EMER CHEM, WELLESLEY COL, 2001-; vis scholar, Brandeis Univ, 1997-; vis prof, Univ Minn, 1990-1991; vis scholar, Cambridge Univ, 1984; vis scholar, Brandeis Univ, 1983-1984; prof chem, Wellesley Col, 1977-2001; vis mem fac, Inst Chem, Univ Uppsala, 1976-1977; chmn, Wellesley Col, 1971-1974, 1981-1983 & 1986; res assoc, Univ Chicago, 1969-1970; from asst prof to assoc prof, Wellesley Col, 1966-1977; asst prof, Swarthmore Col, 1964-1966; from instr to asst prof, Col Wooster, 1961-1964; instr chem, Swarthmore Col, 1960-1961. **Memberships:** Am Crystallog Asn; AAAS; Sigma Xi; Int Solar Energy Soc; Am Chem Soc. **Research Statement & Publications:** Crystallography; molecular structure and solids; energy conversion; intermolecular hydrogen bonds in crystals; chemistry educ. **Mailing Address:** Wellesley Col, Dept Chem, Wellesley, MA 02481. **Fax:** 781-283-3642. **E-Mail:** jloehlin@lucy.wellesley.edu

LOEHMAN, RONALD ERNEST, CERAMICS, SOLID STATE CHEMISTRY. **Personal Data:** b San Antonio, Tex, February 22, 1943; m 1982, Ellen; c Rachel A & Matthew C. **Education:** Rice Univ, BA, 1964; Purdue Univ, PhD (chem), 1969. **Honors & Awards:** Snow Award, Am Ceramic Soc, 1984, Fulrath Award, 1988. **Professional Experience:** DISTINGUISHED PROF, UNIV NMEX, 1991-; Nat Defense Acad, Japan, 1988; DEPT MGR, SANDIA NAT LABS, 1987-; div supvr, Univ Nmex, 1986-1987; Vis scientist, Univ Rennes, France, 1984; staff mem, Univ NMex, 1982-1986; staff scientist, SRI Int, 1978-1982; staff mem, Sandia Labs, Albuquerque, 1977-1978; from asst prof to assoc prof mat eng, Univ Fla, 1970-1978; res fel mat res, Thermophys Properties Res Ctr, Purdue Univ, 1969-1970. **Memberships:** Fel Am Ceramic Soc; AAAS; Nat Inst Ceramic Engrs; Sigma Xi. **Research Statement & Publications:** Metal ceramic interfaces and ceramic joining; high temperature materials; electronic properties of materials; glass formation and crystallization; nitrogen ceramics. **Mailing Address:** Dept Nuclear Eng, Univ NMex, 1001 Univ Blvd SE, Albuquerque, NM 87131-1341. **Fax:** 505-272-7304. **E-Mail:** loehman@unm.edu

LOEHR, RAYMOND CHARLES, ENVIRONMENTAL ENGINEERING. **Personal Data:** b Cleveland, Ohio, May 17, 1931; m 1953, Joan. **Education:** Case Inst Technol, BS, 1953, MS 1956; Univ Wis, PhD (sanit eng), 1961. **Honors & Awards:** Water Conserv Award, Nat Wildlife Fedn, 1967; Rudolph Hering Medal, Am Soc Civil Engrs, 1969, G Brooks Earnest Lectr award, 1991; Thomas R Camp Lectr award, 1992; Billy & T H Feng Distinguished Lectr, Univ Mass, 1994; Rachel Carson Award, Soc Environ Toxicol & Chem, 1995; Gordon M Fair Award, Am Acad Environ Engrs, 1996; Thomas R Camp Medal, Water environ Fedn, 1997; Simon W Freese Award, Am Soc Civil Engrs, 1999. **Professional Experience:** HUSSEIN M ALHARTHY CENTENNIAL CHMN EMER CIVIL ENG, UNIV TEX, AUSTIN, as of 2004; mem bd, Environ Sci Toxicol, Nat Acad Sci, 1995-1998; head, Environ Solutions Prog, 1990-1999; chmn, Sci Adv Bd, USEPA, 1988-1994; H M Alharthy Centennial chmn & prof civil eng, Univ Tex, Austin, beginning 1985; chmn, & Environ Eng Comt, USEPA 1982-1988; dir, Liberty Hyde Bailey prof eng, 1981-1985; sr Fulbright scholar, NZ, 1979; chmn, Technol Assessment & Pollution Control Adv Comt, Sci Adv Bd, Environ Protection Agency, 1978-1980; dir, Environ Studies Prog, 1972-1980; prof agr eng & civil eng, Cornell Univ, 1968-1985; USPHS & Environ Protection Agency res grants, 1963-; from assoc prof civil & sanit eng to prof, Univ Kans, 1961-1968; from instr civil eng to asst prof, Case Inst Technol, 1954-1961. **Memberships:** Nat Acad Eng; AAAS; Am Soc Civil Engrs; Water Environ Fedn Soc Environ Toxicol & Chem. **Research Statement & Publications:** Environmental health engineering; water and wastewater treatment; hazardous waste treatment; industrial waste management; land treatment of wastes; use of hazardous waste management technologies for contaminated liquids, slurries, solids and soils; transformations, transport and fate of constituents when wastes are treated by hazardous and industrial waste management processes; over 250 technical publications. **Mailing Address:** Dept Civil Eng, Univ Tex, One Univ Sta C1786, Austin, TX 78712. **Fax:** 512-471-5870. **E-Mail:** r.loehr@mail.utexas.edu

LOEHR, THOMAS MICHAEL, INORGANIC CHEMISTRY, BIOCHEMISTRY. **Personal Data:** b Munich, Ger, October 2, 1939; American citizen; m 1965, Joann. **Education:** Univ Mich, Ann Arbor, BS, 1963; Cornell Univ, PhD (chem), 1967. **Professional Experience:** PROF EMER CHEM, OGI SCH SCI & ENG, ORE HEALTH & SCI UNIV, as of

2004; actg dept head, Ore Grad Inst, 1992-1993; chmn, Gordon Res Conf, 1987; actg dept chmn, Ore Grad Ctr, 1980-1981; prof chem, Ore Grad Ctr, beginning 1978; mem, NIH Metallobiochem Study Sect, 1978-1982; vis assoc chem, Calif Inst Technol, 1978-1979; res grant, NSF, 1974-1977; NIH res grant, Ore Grad Ctr, 1971-; vis lectr, Portland State Univ, 1971-1972; from asst prof to assoc prof, Ore Grad Ctr, 1968-1978; asst prof chem, Cornell Univ, 1967-1968. **Memberships:** Am Chem Soc; Soc Appl Spectros. **Research Statement & Publications:** Structural inorganic chemistry; infrared and Raman spectroscopy; metal ion complexes; metallobiochemistry; molecular and electronic structure of metalloproteins; resonance raman spectroscopy. **Mailing Address:** Dept Environ & Biomolecular Syst, OGI Sch Sci & Eng, 20000 N W Walker Rd, Beaverton, OR 97006-8921. **Fax:** 503-690-1464. **E-Mail:** loehr@admin.ogi.edu

LOEHRKE, RICHARD IRWIN, MECHANICAL ENGINEERING. **Personal Data:** b Milwaukee, Wis, May 11, 1935; m 1957, c 2. **Education:** Univ Wis, BS, 1957; Univ Colo, MS, 1965; Ill Inst Technol, PhD (mech eng), 1970. **Professional Experience:** PROF MECH ENG, COLO STATE UNIV, as of 2004; assoc prof mech eng, Colo State Univ, beginning 1976; asst prof, Colo State Univ, 1971-1976; asst prof mech eng, Ill Inst Technol, 1970-1971; res engr, Sundstrand Corp, 1961-1965; Tech engr aircraft nuclear propulsion dept, Gen Elec Co, 1957-1961. **Memberships:** Am Soc Mech Engrs; Am Inst Aeronaut & Astronaut; Sigma Xi. **Research Statement & Publications:** Heat transfer; fluid mechanics. **Mailing Address:** Dept Mech, Colorado State Univ, Ft Collins, CO 80523.

LOEKEN, MARY R, MOLECULAR BIOLOGY. **Education:** Univ Md, PhD (Reproductive Endocrinol). **Professional Experience:** ASST PROF MED, JOSLIN DIABETES CTR, HARVARD MED SCH, as of 2006; INVESTR, SEC MOLECULAR BIOL, HARVARD MED SCH, 1998-. **Research Statement & Publications:** Birth defects resulting from diabetic pregnancy. **Mailing Address:** Joslin Diabetes Ctr, Harvard Med Sch, One Joslin Pl, Boston, MA 02215. **Fax:** 617-732-2525. **E-Mail:** mary.loeken@joslin.harvard.edu

LOELIGER, DAVID A, COORDINATION CHEMISTRY, ARCHAEOLOGICAL SOILS. **Personal Data:** b Scranton, Pa, March 1, 1939; m 1960, c 4. **Education:** Col Wooster, BA, 1961; Univ Chicago, MS, 1962, PhD (chem), 1965. **Professional Experience:** Dir, Int Educ Exchange, 1981-1987; RES CONSULT, ARCHEOL RES CTR, 1975-; Missionary, Am Lutheran Church, 1972-; ASSOC PROF CHEM, INT CHRISTIAN UNIV, 1972-; sr res chemist, Eastman Kodak Co, 1967-1972; asst prof chem, Purdue Univ, 1964-1967. **Memberships:** Am Chem Soc; Japan Soc Sci Study Cult Properties. **Research Statement & Publications:** Oxidation-reduction and subtitution reactions of transition metal ions and complexes; application of chemical techniques to problems of archaeological interest; chemical analysis of archaeological artifacts and soils. **Mailing Address:** 920 Rockefeller Dr Apt 5B, Sunnyvale, CA 94087-2139.

LOEPPERT, RICHARD HENRY, SOIL CHEMISTRY. **Personal Data:** b Raleigh, NC, September 26, 1944; m 1989, Sara; c Anthony. **Education:** NC State Univ, BS, 1966; Univ Fla, MS, 1973, PhD (soil sci), 1976. **Honors & Awards:** fel soil sci soc Am, 1997 (chmn, soil chem div, 1990-1991); fel Am soc agr, 1998; fel American Association for the Advancement of Science, 2005 Marion L and Chrystie Jackson soil sci award, soil sci soc Am, 1999. **Professional Experience:** PROF SOIL CHEM, TEX A&M UNIV, 1991-; from asst prof to assoc prof, Tex A&M Univ, 1979-1991; Asst county agriculturalist, Agr Exten Serv, Univ Fla, 1966-1969. **Memberships:** Soil Sci Soc Am; Am Soc Agron; Am Chem Soc; Clay Minerals Soc; AAAS; Sigma Xi (pres Tex A&M chap, 1991-1992). **Research Statement & Publications:** soil chem; trace metal chem; phosphate chem; soil anal; arsenic chemistry; flooded soils; nutrient and toxic metal acquisition by plants; soil carbonate chem. **Mailing Address:** Dept Soil & Crop Sci, 2474-TAMU, Tex A&M Univ, College Station, TX 77843. **Fax:** 979-845-0456. **E-Mail:** r-loeppert@tamu.edu

LOEPPERT, RICHARD HENRY, ORGANIC CHEMISTRY. **Personal Data:** b Chicago, Ill, March 13, 1914; m 1940, Adeline Radtke; c Richard. **Education:** Northwestern Univ, BS, 1935; Univ Minn, PhD (phys chem), 1940. **Professional Experience:** EMER PROF CHEM, NC STATE UNIV, 1979-; prof, NC State Univ, 1959-1979; from instr to assoc prof, NC State Univ, 1940-1959; res chemist, Richardson Co, Ill, 1939-1940; Asst, Univ Minn, 1935-1939. **Memberships:** Am Chem Soc. **Mailing Address:** 1317 Rand Dr, Raleigh, NC 27608.

LOEPPKY, JACK ALBERT, RESPIRATORY & ENVIRONMENTAL PHYSIOLOGY. **Personal Data:** b Saskatoon, Sask, January 14, 1944; American citizen; m 2001, Robyn; c Kris & Ninya. **Education:** Univ Sask, BA, 1966; Univ NMex, MS, 1969, PhD (biol), 1973. **Honors & Awards:** prin investr grants; Am Heart Asn, 1982-1984 & 1988-1989; NSF, 1984; NASA, 1989-1995; US Army contract, 1996-2000. **Professional Experience:** HEALTH SCIENTIST, CARDIOLOGY DIV, VA MED CTR, ALBUQUERQUE, NM, 2002-; scientist, New Mexico Resonance, Albuquerque 2000-2002; assoc scientist and scientist, Lovelace Med Found, 1975-2000; vis scientist, Max Planck Inst Exp Med, Gottingen, Ger, 1983-1984; adj asst prof, Univ New Mex, 1982-; technologist, Physiol Dept, Wellington Hosp, NZ, 1975; res assoc, Physiol Dept, Lovelace Med Found, 1970-1975. **Memberships:** Int Soc Gravitational Physiol; Am Physiol Soc. **Research Statement & Publications:** Normal and pathological pulmonary physiology and gas exchange; effects of hypoxia and hypercapnia; pulmonary blood flow determinations from respiratory gases; changes in body gas stores in response to gravitational stress; pulmonary ventilation/perfusion distributions and their influence on non-steady state respiratory gas exchange; fluid balance changes with simulated microgravity and high altitude; pulmonary gas exchange at high altitude; change in human brain magnetic resonance images resulting from acute mountain sickness; training benefits of limb exercise with ischemia. **Mailing Address:** Cardiology Section, VA Medical Center, 1501 San Pedro Dr SE, Albuquerque, NM 87108. **Fax:** 505-256-5703. **E-Mail:** loeppky@unm.edu

LOEPPKY, RICHARD N, PHYSICAL ORGANIC CHEMISTRY, MECHANISTIC TOXICOLOGY, STRUCTURE ELUCIDATION. **Personal Data:** b Lewiston, Idaho, August 2, 1937; div, c 2. **Education:** Univ Idaho, BS, 1959; Univ Mich, MS, 1961, PhD (chem), 1963. **Honors & Awards:** Kasimir Fajans Award, 1965; Merit Award, Nat Cancer Inst, 1986, 1992; Fogarty Fellow, 1993-1994; U of Idaho Distinguisted Alumnus 2000; Prof Emeritus, 2003. **Professional Experience:** H. G. SCHLUNDT DISTINGUISHED PROF CHEM, UNIV MO-COLUMBIA, as of 2004; Fogarty sr fel, 1993-1994; guest prof, Univ Kaiserslautern, Ger, 1993-1994; prof chem, Univ Mo-Columbia, beginning 1980; resident vis, Bell Labs, 1971-1972; from asst prof to assoc prof, Univ MO-Columbia, 1964-1980; NIH fel org chem, Univ Ill, 1963-1964; instr chem, Univ Mich, 1963. **Memberships:** Am Chem Soc; fel AAAS; Am Asn Cancer Res; Sigma Xi. **Research Statement & Publications:** Chemical carcinogenesis and mechanistic organic chemistry; nitrosation chemistry and chemical/biochemical transformation of nitrosamines directed at understanding their environmental and biochemical formation, transformation and destruction. **Mailing Address:** Univ Mo, 125 Chem Bldg, Columbia, MO 65211-0001. **Fax:** 573-882-2754. **E-Mail:** loeppkyr@missouri.edu

LOESCH, HAROLD CARL, BIOLOGICAL OCEANOGRAPHY, MARINE SCIENCE. **Personal Data:** b Tex, October 3, 1926; m 1945, Mabel; c Stephen, Gretchen, Jonathon & Frederick. **Education:** Tex A & M Univ, BS, 1951, MS, 1954, PhD (biol oceanog), 1962. **Professional Experience:** RETIRED; consult, Shrimp Growers Asn Ecuador, 1985; proj mgr, UN Food & Agr Orgn, Bangladesh, 1981-1985; proj mgr & sr resource assessment surveyor, fisheries proj, Bangladesh, 1981-1985; consult, UNESCO, 1979-1980; expert marine biol, UN Develop Prog, 1976-1979; estuarine ecologist, UNESCO, Mexico, 1976-1979; vis prof, Org Am States Marine Sci prog, Ecuador, 1972; prof, Dept Marine Sci, Off Sea Grant Develop, 1970-1975; prof, dept zool & physiol, La State Univ, Baton Rouge, 1968-1969; fisheries officer, Food & Agr Orgn, UN, 1967-1968; fisheries biologist, Food & Agr Orgn, UN, 1962-1966; shrimp biologist, Food & Agr Orgn, UN, 1960-1962; assoc res scientist, Tex A & M Res Found, 1958-1960; prin marine biologist & actg lab dir, Dept Conservation, State Ala, 1952-1957. **Memberships:** Am Fisheries Soc; Am Soc Limnol & Oceanog; Am Soc Ichthyologists & Herpetologists; fel Int Acad Fishery Sci; Sigma Xi; AAAS. **Research Statement & Publications:** Estuarine hydrology and biology; shrimp, spiney lobster and inshore fishes ecology; fisheries statistics. **Mailing Address:** 2140 E Scott St, Pensacola, FL 32503.

LOESCH, JOSEPH G, MARINE BIOLOGY. **Personal Data:** b Middle Village, NY, May 5, 1930; m Marilyn; c 3. **Education:** Univ RI, BS, 1965; Univ Conn, MS, 1968, PhD, 1969. **Professional Experience:** PROF EMER MARINE SCI, COL WILLIAM & MARY, as of 2003; ANADROMOUS FISH STUDIES, VA, COL WILLIAM & MARY, 1976-; STATE-FED FISHERY MGT COMTS, 1976-; SHELLFISH POP STUDIES, COL WILLIAM & MARY, 1969-; prof marine sci, Col William & Mary, beginning 1969; asst proj leader, Conn River Herring Study, Col William & Mary, 1966-1969; res asst bluefish migrations, Col William & Mary, 1965-1966; sr marine scientist, Va Inst Marine Sci. **Memberships:** Am Fisheries Soc. **Research Statement & Publications:** Marine fisheries; life history studies of anadromous fishes; biometrics and population dynamics of commercially important fishes. **Mailing Address:** Va Inst Marine Sci, PO Box 1346, Gloucester Point, VA 23062. **Fax:** 804-642-7327. **E-Mail:** solo@vims.edu

LOESCHE, WALTER J, DENTAL DECAY, PERIODONTAL DISEASE. **Personal Data:** b New Haven, Conn, March 28, 1935; m 1958, c 3. **Education:** Yale Univ, BA, 1957; Harvard Sch DentMed, DMD, 1961; Mass Inst Technol, PhD (biochem), 1967. **Honorary Degrees:** Dr, Univ Goteborg, Sweden, Univ Ghent, Belg. **Honors & Awards:** Int Asn Dent Res Award, 1994. **Professional Experience:** PROF EMER MICROBIOL, MED SCH, UNIV MICH, as of 2005; PROF EMER DENT, DEPT BIOL & MAT SCI, SCH DENT, UNIV MICH, as of 2005; MARCUS WARD PROF EMER, UNIV MICH SCH DENT, as of 2005; Rosenstat vis prof, Univ Toronto, 1990; dir res, Univ Mich, Sch Dent, 1987-1989; mem, Nat Affairs Comt, Am Asn Dent Res, 1985-1988; bd dirs, Nat Affairs Comt, Am Asn Dent Res, 1985-1988; mem, Educ Affairs Comt, Univ Mich Sch Dent, 1983-1986; prof oral biol, Sch Dent, Univ Mich, 1974-; prof Microbiol, Sch Med, Univ Mich, beginning 1974; mem Grad Studies Comt, Univ Mich Sch Med, 1973-; assoc prof microbiol, Univ Mich, Sch Dent, 1971-1974; assoc prof oral biol, Univ Mich, Sch Dent, 1969-1974; mem staff, Forsyth Dent Ctr, 1967-1969; assoc nutrit, Mass Inst Technol, 1964-1966; res assoc microbiol, Harvard Sch Dent Med, 1961 & 1964; Marcus Ward prof, Univ Mich Sch Dent. **Memberships:** Am Soc Microbiol; Int Asn Dent Res; Am Asn Dent Res (pres 1987-1988); Am Dent Asn. **Research Statement & Publications:** Research intends to demonstrate dental decay is a specific S mutans infection and that advanced periodontal disease is a treatable anaerobic infection; clinical studies are used to document the role of the above bacteria in human decay and periodontal disease; relationship between dental disease and medical disease in older individuals. **Mailing Address:** Univ Mich, Sch Dent, Dept Biol & Mat Sci, 3209 Dent, Ann Arbor, MI 48109-1078. **Fax:** 734-647-2110. **E-Mail:** wloesche@umich.edu

LOESCHER, WAYNE HAROLD, PLANT PHYSIOLOGY & GROWTH & DEVELOPMENT, MOLECULAR BIOLOGY. **Personal Data:** b Lima, Ohio, November 6, 1942; m 1967, c 1. **Education:** Miami Univ, BA, 1964, MS, 1966; Iowa State Univ, PhD (plant physiol), 1972. **Professional Experience:** PROF PLANT PHYSIOL, MICH STATE UNIV, 2002-; assoc dean, Col Agr & Natural Resources, Mich State Univ, 2000-2002; chmn Hort, Mich State Univ, 1990-2000; prof & act chmn, Hort & Landscape Archit, Wash State Univ, 1988-1990; prof, Hort & Landscape Archit, Wash State Univ, 1987-1990; from asst to assoc prof Hort & Landscape Archit, Wash State Univ, 1975-1987. **Memberships:** Am Soc Plant Biologists; Bot Soc Am; Am Soc Hort Sci; Am Asn Advan Sci; Sigma Xi. **Research Statement & Publications:** Plant growth and development; plant tissue culture. **Mailing Address:** Dept Plant Physiol, Mich State Univ, A328 Plant & Soil Sci, East Lansing, MI 48824-1325. **Fax:** 517-353-0890. **E-Mail:** loescher@msu.edu

LOESCH-FRIES, SUE LORETTA, PLANT VIROLOGY. **Personal Data:** b Ventura, Calif, September 5, 1947; m 1976, Robert; c Michael & Matthew. **Education:** Wash State Univ, BS, 1969; Univ Wis, PhD (plant path), 1974. **Professional Experience:** Grants rev panel, NRICGP-plant genetic mechanisms program, 1998; ASSSOC PROF PLANTPATHOL, PURDUE UNIV, 1997-; grants rev panel, Tobacco & Health Res Inst, Kentucky, 1995-1996; asst prof, Purdue univ, 1991-1996; grants rev panel, Dept Energy, 1988; asst adj prof, Univ Wis, 1987-1991; grants rev panel, Coop State Res Serv, USDA, 1985 & 1986; sr res scientist & consult, Agrigenetics, 1981-1989; asst scientist, Dept Hort, Univ Wis, 1980-1981; res assoc, Dept Hort, Univ Wis, 1977-1980; res assoc, Dept Plant Path, Univ Fla, 1976-1977. **Memberships:** Am Phytopath Soc; Sigma Xi; AAAS; Am Soc Virol; Int Soc Plant Molecular Biol; Am Soc Plant Physiologist. **Research Statement & Publications:** Genome organization and replication of plant viruses; determination of the role of virus gene products in infection; how plant viruses cause disease and reduce crop yield; their role in disease develop; control of plant viruses; granted US patents. **Mailing Address:** Dept Bot & Plant Path, Purdue univ, Ernest C Young Hall Rm B80 302 Wood St, West Lafayette, IN 47907-1057. **Fax:** 765-494-5896. **E-Mail:** loeschfr@purdue.edu

LOESER, EUGENE WILLIAM, MEDICINE. **Personal Data:** b Buffalo, NY, November 5, 1926; m 1955, c 1. **Education:** Univ Buffalo, MD, 1952. **Professional Experience:** RETIRED; mem staff, Kirkwood Outpatient Ctr, formerly; clin assoc prof neurol, Rutgers Med Sch, 1971-1978; asst prof clin neurol, NY Univ, 1964-1971; asst prof, Univ NC, 1957-1961; asst neurol, Columbia Univ, 1956-1957. **Memberships:** AMA; Am Acad Neurol. **Research Statement & Publications:** Medical neurology. **Mailing Address:** 118 Palomino Dr, Jupiter, FL 33458.

LOESER, JOHN DAVID, NEUROLOGICAL SURGERY, PAIN MANAGEMENT. **Personal Data:** b Newark, NJ, December 14, 1935; m 1977, Karen; c Sarah A, Thomas E, Derek W & David W. **Education:** Harvard Univ, BA, 1957; NY Univ, MD, 1961. **Honors & Awards:** Phi Beta Kappa 1957 Alpha Omega Alpha 1961 University of Washington Medical School Award for Teaching Excellence 1985 Distinguished Service Award, American Pain Society 1986 Fulbright Senior Scholar, Australia 1989-1990 Pain Society of the Philippines, Honorary Member 1989 Fellow, American Association for the Advancement of Science 1994 Romanian Association for the Study of Pain, Honorary Member 1994 Israel Pain

Society, Honorary Member 1994 Honorary Fellow, Faculty of Physical Medicine and Rehabilitation, Royal College of Physicians, Australia 1995 American Society for Regional Anesthesia, Honorary Member 1995 International Association for the Study of Pain, Honorary Member 1999. **Professional Experience:** Fulbright sr scholar, Australia, 1989-1990; chief neurosurg, Children's Hosp, Seattle, 1985-1993; dir, Multidisciplinary Pain Ctr, 1983-1997; PROF NEUROSURG, UNIV WASH, 1981-; vis prof, Univ NSW, 1980; Asst dean curric, Univ Wash, 1977-1982; from asst prof to assoc prof, Univ Wash, 1969-1981; med corp, US Army, 1968-1969; Asst prof neurosurg, Univ Calif, Irvine, 1967-1968. **Memberships:** Am Pain Soc (treas, 1980-1985, pres, 1986-1987); Am Asn Neurol Surgeons; Int Asn Study Pain (secy, 1984-1990, pres, 1993-1996); AAAS; Soc Neuroscience; Am Acad Pain Med. **Research Statement & Publications:** Clinical and research aspects of chronic pain, pain associated with injuries to nervous system, epidemiology and etiology of low back pain, pediatric neurosurgery, especially congenital malformations. **Mailing Address:** Dept Neurol Surg, Univ Wash Box 356470, Seattle, WA 98195. **Fax:** 206-543-8315. **E-Mail:** jdloeser@u.washington.edu

LOEV, BERNARD, ORGANIC CHEMISTRY, MEDICINAL CHEMISTRY. **Personal Data:** b Philadelphia, Pa, February 26, 1928; m 1954, c 3. **Education:** Univ Pa, BSc, 1949; Columbia Univ, MA, 1950, PhD (org chem), 1952. **Honors & Awards:** Award Outstanding Contrib Med & Org Chem, Am Chem Soc, 1974. **Professional Experience:** CONSULT, PHARMACEUT, as of 2004; PRES, CHEM & PHARMACEUT CONSULT SERV INC, 1986-; exec vpres, Creative Licensing Int, beginning 1986; vpres sci affairs, Chem Res & Develop Div, USV Pharmaceut Corp, Revlon Health Care Group, 1983-1986; vpres tech affairs, Chem Res & Develop Div, USV Pharmaceut Corp, Revlon Health Care Group, 1983; vpres chem res & develop, Chem Res & Develop Div, USV Pharmaceut Corp, Revlon Health Care Group, 1980-1983; dir, Chem Res & Develop Div, USV Pharmaceut Corp, Revlon Health Care Group, 1975-1980; from asst dir to assoc dir chem, Smith Kline & French Labs, Pa, 1967-1975; sr investr, Smith Kline & French Labs, Pa, 1966-1967; group leader, Smith Kline & French Labs, Pa, 1958-1966; proj leader, Pennsalt Chem Co, 1952-1958; instr inorg & org chem, Columbia Univ, 1949-1951; mem bd dirs, Int Heterocyclic Cong; mem adv bd, Index Chemicus & Intra-Sci Res Found. **Memberships:** AAAS; Am Chem Soc; Am Inst Chem; NY Acad Sci. **Research Statement & Publications:** Organic synthesis; organic sulfur compounds; medicinal chemistry; nitrogen and sulfur heterocycles; natural products; central nervous system, cardiovascular, asthma, anti-arthritic, anti-ulcer areas; dermatology; patent, strategies and licensing. **Mailing Address:** CECON Consul Group, 242 N James St, Wilmington, DE 19804-3168. **Fax:** 302-994-8837.

LOEVINGER, ROBERT, dosimetry; deceased, see previous edition for last biography

LOEW, ELLIS ROGER, VISUAL PHYSIOLOGY, SENSORY BIOPHYSICS. **Personal Data:** b Los Angeles, Calif, January 18, 1947; c 2. **Education:** Univ Calif, Los Angeles, BA, 1968, MA, 1971, PhD (biol), 1973. **Professional Experience:** PROF PHYSIOL, CORNELL UNIV, as of 2004; assoc prof physiol, Cornell Univ, beginnig 1983; asst prof, Cornell Univ, 1977-1983; res fel, Cornell Univ, 1975-1977; vis fel, Vision Unit, Med Res Coun, 1974-1975; fel, Vision Unit, Med Res Coun, 1973-1974. **Memberships:** AAAS; Brit Photobiol Asn; Inst Elec & Electronic Engrs; Asn Res Vision & Ophthal. **Research Statement & Publications:** Physiology and biochemistry of visual photoreceptors; biochemistry and biophysics of visual pigments; sensory ecology. **Mailing Address:** Dept Biomed Sci, Cornell Univ, 445 E 69th St, Ithaca, NY 14853-6401. **Fax:** 607-253-3846. **E-Mail:** erl1@cornell.edu

LOEW, GILDA HARRIS, THEORETICAL BIOLOGY, BIOPHYSICS. **Personal Data:** b New York, NY, c 4. **Education:** NY Univ, BA, 1951; Columbia Univ, MA, 1952; Univ Calif, Berkeley, PhD (chem physics), 1957. **Professional Experience:** Prog dir molecular theory, Life Sci Div, Stanford Res Inst, beginning 1979; adj prof, Rockefeller Univ, beginning 1979; PRES & RES DIR, MOLECULAR RES INST, PALO ALTO, CALIF, 1979-; NASA, beginning 1969 & NIH, beginning 1974; adj prof genetics, Med Ctr, 1974-1979; res biophysicist & instr biophys, Med Sch, Stanford Univ, 1969-1979; Grants, NSF, beginning 1966; from asst prof to assoc prof physics, Pomona Col, 1966-1969; assoc quantum biophys, Biophys Lab, Stanford Univ, 1964-1966; res physicist, Lawrence Radiation Lab, Univ Calif, Berkeley, 1957-1962 & Lockheed Missiles & Space Co, 1962-1964. **Memberships:** Biophys Soc; fel Am Phys Soc; Int Soc Magnetic Resonance. **Research Statement & Publications:** Molecular orbital and crystal field quantum chemical calculations; models for protein active sites; mechanisms and requirements for specific drug action; theoretical studies related to chemical evolution of life. **Mailing Address:** Molecular Res Inst, 845 Page Mill Rd, Palo Alto, CA 94304. **Fax:** 415-4249501.

LOEW, LESLIE MAX, PHYSICAL ORGANIC CHEMISTRY, BIOPHYSICAL CHEMISTRY. **Personal Data:** b New York, NY, September 2, 1947; m 1970, Helen; c Daniel, Rena & Aviva. **Education:** City Col NY, BS, 1969; Cornell Univ, MS, 1972, PhD (chem), 1974. **Professional Experience:** PROF CELL BIOL & COMPUT SCI & ENG, UNIV CONN, 2003-; DIR, CTR CELL ANAL & MODELING, UNIV CONN HEALTH CTR, 1994-; adj prof physiol, Univ Mass, 1991-; prof physiol, Univ Conn, 1987-2003; assoc prof physiol, Univ Conn, 1984-1987; vis assoc prof, Cornell Univ, 1984; vis scientist, Weizmann Inst Sci, 1981-1982; career develop award, NIH, 1981; from asst prof to assoc prof chem, State Univ NY, Binghamton, 1974-1984; res assoc chem, Harvard Univ, 1973-1974. **Memberships:** Am Chem Soc; Biophys Soc; AAAS. **Research Statement & Publications:** Organic dye chemistry; biomembranes; theoretical organic chemistry; electrical, adhesive and chemical properties of biomembranes using spectroscopic techniques; microscopy; image processing, cellphysiology, cell biophysics. **Mailing Address:** Dept Cellbiol, Univ Conn, Farmington, CT 06030-3505. **Fax:** 860-679-1269. **E-Mail:** les@volt.uchc.edu

LOEWE, WILLIAM EDWARD, APPLIED PHYSICS. **Personal Data:** b Chicago, Ill, April 22, 1932; m 1953, Virginia; c Nancy Jean, Mary Ellen & William Edward. **Education:** Univ Chicago, AB, 1952; Univ Ill, BS, 1953; Ill Inst Technol, MS, 1959, PhD (physics), 1963. **Professional Experience:** RETIRED; consult, beginning 1991; sr physicist, Lawrence Livermore Nat Lab, Univ Calif, 1967-1990; adv Scientist, Nerva, Astro-nuclear Lab, Westinghouse Elec Corp, 1966-1967; mgr nuclear physics, IIT Res Inst, 1963-1966; res physicist group leader, IIT Res Inst, 1962-1963; res physicist, IIT Res Inst, 1959-1962; assoc physicist, IIT Res Inst, 1957-1959; reactor physicist, Savannah River Plant, 1954-1957; reactor physicist, Savannah River Lab, E I du Pont de Nemours & Co, 1953-1954. **Memberships:** Am Phys Soc. **Research Statement & Publications:** Physics of ionized media and radiation transport, applied hydrodynamics, and criticality safety. **Mailing Address:** 1072 Xavier Way, Livermore, CA 94550.

LOEWEN, ERWIN G, OPTICS. **Personal Data:** b Frankfurt am Maine, Ger, April 12, 1921; m 1952, Joanna; c Oliver F & Heidi R. **Education:** NY Univ, BME, 1941; Mass Inst Technol, SM, 1949, ME, 1950, ScD, 1952. **Honors & Awards:** David Richardson Medal, Optical Soc Am, 1984, Fraunhofer Medal, 1993; F W Taylor Medal, Soc Mfg Engrs, 1982. **Professional Experience:** RETIRED; emer prof, Univ Rochester, 1988-1997; vpres res, Develop & Eng, Milton Roy, 1985-1987; dir, Grating & Metrol Labs, 1967-1984; head dept metrol, Bausch & Lomb Co, 1960-1967; tech dir, Taft-Peirce Mfg Co, 1955-1960. **Memberships:** AAAS; Am Soc Mech Engrs; Soc Mfg Engrs; Optical Soc Am; Soc Photo Instr Engrs. **Research Statement & Publications:** Precision Engineering; metrology; diffraction; co-author of one publication. **Mailing Address:** 34A Brook Hill Lane, Rochester, NY 14625.

LOEWENFELD, IRENE ELIZABETH, PHYSIOLOGY. **Personal Data:** b Munich, Ger, June 2, 1921; American citizen. **Education:** Univ Bonn, PhD (zoology), 1956. **Professional Experience:** PROF OPHTHAL, SCH MED, WAYNE STATE UNIV, 1981-; from asst prof to assoc prof, Sch Med, Wayne State Univ, 1968-1981; res assoc, Columbia Univ, 1962-1968; instr, Columbia Univ, 1961-1962; asst ophthal, Columbia Univ, 1958-1961. **Memberships:** Asn Res Vision & Ophthal. **Research Statement & Publications:** Neurophysiology; neuroophthalmology; autonomic nervous system; pupil; visual physiology. **Mailing Address:** Dept Physiol, Wayne State Univ, Detroit, MI 48202.

LOEWENSON, RUTH BRANDENBURGER, BIOMETRICS. **Personal Data:** b Zurich, Switz, American citizen; c 2. **Education:** Univ Minn, Minneapolis, BA, 1959, MS, 1961, PhD (biomet), 1968. **Professional Experience:** CONSULT, 1990-; consult statistician, FDA Neurol Devices Panel, 1983-; assoc prof neurol & biomet, Sch Med, Univ Minn, Minneapolis, 1972-1990; consult statistician, Vet Admin Hosp, Minneapolis, 1971-1983; from instr to asst prof, Sch Med, Univ Minn, Minneapolis, 1965-1972. **Memberships:** Am Statist Asn; Biomet Soc; Soc Epidemiol Res; Soc Clin Trials. **Research Statement & Publications:** Clinical studies in neurology; clinical trials in neurology. **Mailing Address:** 3320 Louisiana Ave S, Minneapolis, MN 55426.

LOEWENSTEIN, ERNEST VICTOR, OPTICS, SPECTROSCOPY. **Personal Data:** b Offenbach am Main, Ger, September 3, 1931; American citizen; m 1961, c 2. **Education:** Cornell Univ, BA, 1953; Johns Hopkins Univ, PhD (physics), 1960. **Professional Experience:** PVT PRACT, OPTOMETRIST, as of 2005; ASSOC PROF, NEW ENG COL OPTOM, 1978-; Physicist, Optical Physics Lab, Air Force Cambridge Res Labs, 1962-1975. **Memberships:** Fel Optical Soc Am. **Research Statement & Publications:** Optical properties of far infrared materials; optical properties of the atmosphere; Fourier spectroscopy. **Mailing Address:** New Eng Col Optom, 471 Wash St, Newton, MA 02458. **E-Mail:** ernloew@attbi.com

LOEWENSTEIN, HOWARD, FORESTRY. **Personal Data:** b New York, NY, January 1, 1924; m 1958, c 2. **Education:** Colo State Univ, BS, 1952; Univ Wis, PhD (soils), 1955. **Professional Experience:** RETIRED; from asst prof to prof forest soils, Univ Idaho, 1958-1989; asst prof silvicult, Col Forestry, State univ NY, Syracuse, 1957-1958; Instr soils, Univ Wis, 1955-1956. **Memberships:** Soil Sci Soc Am. **Research Statement & Publications:** Forest soil-site relationships; forest fertilization; problems of tree seedling establishment; soil microbiology. **Mailing Address:** 1010 Valdal Rd, Moscow, ID 83843.

LOEWENSTEIN, JOSEPH EDWARD, ENDOCRINOLOGY, INTERNAL MEDICINE. **Personal Data:** b Crockett, Tex, November 25, 1937; m 1958, Marjorie; c Sarah F & Edward B. **Education:** Univ Tex, Austin, BA, 1959; Wash Univ, MD, 1963. **Professional Experience:** CONSULT STAFF, DEPT INTERNAL MED, MIDLAND MEM HOSP, as of 2004; PROF MED, SCH MED, TEX TECH HEALTH SCI CTR, 1999; assoc clin prof med, Case Western Res Univ, 1992-; chief, Div Endocrinol & Metab, Meridia Huron Hosp, 1991-; clin prof med, La State Univ, Shreveport, 1984-1991; chmn, Endocrine & Metab Drugs Adv Comt, US Food & Drug Admin, 1982-1984; mem, Endocrine & Metab Drugs Adv Comt, US Food & Drug Admin, 1980-1984; consult, US Vet Admin Hosp, Shreveport, 1970-; from asst prof to prof med, La State Univ, Shreveport, 1970-1984; chief sect endocrinol, La State Univ, Shreveport, 1970-1984; instr med, Wash Univ, 1970; Nat Inst Arthritis & Metab Dis fel metab, Wash Univ, 1969-1970; resident, Barnes Hosp, St Louis, 1967-1969; mem staff, Nat Cancer Inst, 1966-1967; res assoc, Nat Cancer Inst, 1964-1966; Intern internal med, Barnes Hosp, St Louis, 1963-1964. **Memberships:** Endocrine Soc; fel Am Col Physicians. **Research Statement & Publications:** Physiology of prolactin in humans; kinetics of iodine metabolism in thyroid; metabolic acidosis in diabetes. **Mailing Address:** Dept Med, Sch Med, Tex Tech Health Sci Ctr, Amarillo, TX 79106.

LOEWENSTEIN, MATTHEW SAMUEL, GASTROENTEROLOGY, FOOD POISONING, INTERNAL MEDICINE. **Personal Data:** b New York, NY, December 3, 1941; m 1965, Davida; c Andrew, Mara & Laura. **Education:** Union Col, BS, 1962; Harvard Med Sch, MD, 1967. **Professional Experience:** Asst clin prof, Harvard Univ, as of 2003; ACTIVE STAFF, MT AUBURN HOSP, 1978-; SR RES ASSOC, MALLORY GASTROENTEROL RES LAB, BOSTON CITY HOSP, 1976-; Asst prof med, Harvard Med Sch, 1975-; asst vis physician, instr & clin res assoc, 1975-1980; courtesy staff, Mt Auburn Hosp, 1975-1977; clin fel, instr & clin res assoc, 1973-1975; sr resident, Harvard Med Unit, Boston City Hosp, 1972-1973; chief, Enteric Dis Sect, USPHS, 1970-1972; dep chief, Salmonella Unit, Ctr Dis Control, 1969-1970; jr asst resident, Harvard Med Unit, Boston City Hosp, 1968-1969; intern, Harvard Med Unit, Boston City Hosp, 1967-1968. **Memberships:** Am Gastroenterol Asn; Am Soc Gastrointestinal Endoscopy. **Research Statement & Publications:** Clinical use of tumor markers, particularly carcinoembryonic antigen. **Mailing Address:** Mt Auburn Hosp, 300 Mt Auburn St 507, Cambridge, MA 02238.

LOEWENSTEIN, MORRISON, DAIRY CHEMISTRY, NUTRITION. **Personal Data:** b Kearney, Nebr, August 21, 1915; m 1939, Genevieve; c Kentley A, Roger E & Douglas B. **Education:** Univ Nebr, BS, 1938; Kans State Univ, MS, 1940; Ohio State Univ, PhD (dairy tech), 1954. **Professional Experience:** PROF EMER ANIMAL & DAIRY SCI, UNIV GA, 1981-; prof, Univ GA, 1966-1981; chmn bd, Sutton Crest Proteins Ltd, Can, 1964-1966; res dir, Crest Foods Co, Inc, 1955-1966; from asst prof to assoc prof dairy, Okla State Univ, 1947-1955; instr dairy, NMex State Col, 1940-1941; asst supt, Roberts Dairy Co, 1939-1940; asst dairy, Kans State Col, 1938-1939. **Memberships:** Am Dairy Sci Asn; Inst Food Technol; AAAS; Sigma Xi. **Research Statement & Publications:** Development, modification and compositional control of new and improved dairy products and milk protein concentrates and their application in special nutritional formulations. **Mailing Address:** Off Inst Res Univ Ga, 110 E Clayton St Ste 725, Athens, GA 30602. **Fax:** 706-425-3200.

LOEWENSTEIN, WALTER B, RESEARCH ADMINISTRATION, SAFETY MANAGEMENT. **Personal Data:** b Gensungen, Ger, December 23, 1926; American citizen; m 1959, Lenore; c Mark V & Marcia B. **Education:** Univ Puget Sound, BS, 1949; Ohio State Univ, PhD (physics), 1954. **Professional Experience:** CONSULT, ENERGY TECHNOLOGY, as of 2004; secy-treas, Am Asn Eng Soc, 1990; dep dir, Nuclear Power Div, 1981-1989; dir, Safety & Analysis Dept, Elec Power Res Inst, 1973-1981; dir, EBR-II Proj, 1972-1973; actg dir, EBR-II Proj, 1972; assoc dir, EBR-II Proj, 1968-1972; Europ-Am adv comt reactor physics, Atomic Energy Comn, 1966-1973 & adv comt reactor physics, 1966-1973; mgr physics sect, Liquid Metal Fast Breeder Reactor, prog off, 1966-1968; head, Fast Reactor Analysis Sect, Reactor Physics Div, 1963-1966; mem, Int Atomic Energy Agency Symp, Vienna, 1961; mem staff, UK Atomic Energy Authority, Dounreay, Scotland, 1959;

tech adv, US deleg, Int Conf Peaceful Uses Atomic Energy, Geneva, 1958; from asst physicist to sr physicist reactor physics, Argonne Nat Lab, 1954-1963. **Memberships:** Nat Acad Eng; fel Am Nuclear Soc (vpres 1988-1989 pres 1989-1990); fel Am Phys Soc. **Research Statement & Publications:** Fast reactor physics and related technology, including fast reactor design, analysis and planning of fast critical experiments, fast flux irradiation facilities and conceptual studies; reactor safety; research program development; space nuclear power; technology transfer; research management; safety management. **Mailing Address:** 515 Jefferson Dr, Palo Alto, CA 94303. **Fax:** 650-327-7128.

LOEWENSTEIN, WERNER RANDOLPH, BIOPHYSICS, CELL BIOLOGY. **Personal Data:** b Spangenberg, Ger, February 14, 1926; m 1971, c 4. **Education:** Univ Chile, BSc(physics) & BSc(biol), 1945, PhD (physiol), 1950. **Professional Experience:** DIR, LAB CELL COMMUN, MARINE BIOL LAB, WOODS HOLE, as of 2003; USAF sci adv bd, 1982-1986; mem, biochem, molecular genetics & cell biol sect, President's Biomed Res Adv Panel, 1977; USSR acad sci lectr, Leningrad, 1975; PROF PHYSIOL & BIOPHYS & CHMN DEPT, SCH MED, UNIV MIAMI, 1971-; ed, handbook sensory physiol, 12 vols, 1971-1977; fulbright distinguished prof, 1970; ed-in-chief, J Membrane Biol, beginning 1969; ed, biochem & biophys act, 1967-1973; lectr, royal swedish acad sci, 1966; block lectr, Univ Chicago, 1960; from asst prof to prof physiol, Col Physicians & Surgeons, Columbia Univ, 1957-1971; res zoologist, Univ Calif, Los Angeles, 1954-1955; fel neurophysiol, Kellogg Int fel physiol, 1953-1955; fel neurophysiol, sch med & hosp, Johns Hopkins Univ, 1953-1954; from instr to assoc prof physiol, Univ Chile, 1951-1957. **Memberships:** AAAS; Biophys Soc; Am Physiol Soc; Harvey Soc; fel NY Acad Sci. **Research Statement & Publications:** Mechanisms of nerve impulse production and energy conversion at sensory nerve endings; excitation of the nerve cells; biophysics of cellular membranes; intercellular communication. **Mailing Address:** Dept Physiol & Biophys, Sch Med, Univ Miami, PO Box 016430, R430, Miami, FL 33101-6430.

LOEWENTHAL, LOIS ANNE, DEVELOPMENTAL BIOLOGY, HISTOLOGY. **Personal Data:** b Middletown, Conn, October 31, 1926. **Education:** Mt Holyoke Col, AB, 1948; Brown Univ, AM, 1950, PhD, 1954. **Professional Experience:** ASSOC PROF EMER BIOL, UNIV MICH, ANN ARBOR, 1982-; prof, Univ Mich, Ann Arbor, 1974-1982; from instr to assoc prof zool, Univ Mich, Ann Arbor, 1957-1974; instr animal genetics, Univ Conn, 1954-1956; res assoc zool, Mt Holyoke Col, 1950-1951; asst biol, Brown Univ, 1948-1953. **Research Statement & Publications:** Histology and embryology; skin and hair growth. **Mailing Address:** Univ Mich, Dept Biol, 4126 Nat Sci, Ann Arbor, MI 48109-1048.

LOEWUS, FRANK A, BIOCHEMISTRY, PLANT PHYSIOLOGY. **Personal Data:** b Duluth, Minn, October 22, m Mary; c Rivkah R, David I & Daniel. **Education:** Univ Minn, BSc, 1942, MSc, 1950, PhD (biochem), 1952. **Honors & Awards:** Charles Reid Barnes Award, Am Soc Plant Physiologists, 1993. **Professional Experience:** PROF EMER BIOL CHEM, WASH STATE UNIV, 1990-; fel, Dept Agr Chem, Wash State Univ, 1980-1990; ed, Phytochem Soc NAm, 1976, 1980-1984; prof biochem, Dept Agr Chem, Wash State Univ, 1975-1989; agr chemist, Dept Agr Chem, Wash State Univ, 1975-1980; mem staff, Marine Biol Lab, Woods Hole, 1969-1974; prof cell & molecular biol, Dept Biol, State Univ NY, Buffalo, 1964-1975; chemist, USDA, 1955-1964; res assoc biochem, Univ Chicago, 1952-1955; Asst agr biochem, Univ Minn, 1947-1951. **Memberships:** Life mem Phytochem Soc NAm (pres 1975-1976); AAAS; Am Chem Soc; Am Soc Biochem & Molecular Biol; Am Soc Plant Physiol; NY Acad Sci. **Research Statement & Publications:** Intermediary metabolism in plants, mechanisms of enzyme action; biochemistry of natural products; pollen physiology and enzymology. **Mailing Address:** 1700 NE Upper Dr, Pullman, WA 99163-4624. **E-Mail:** loewus@wsu.edu

LOEWUS, MARY W, BIOCHEMISTRY, ENZYMOLOGY. **Personal Data:** b Duluth, Minn, February 15, 1923; m 1947, Frank; c Rivkah R, David I & Daniel. **Education:** Univ Minn, PhD (biochem), 1953. **Professional Experience:** RETIRED; Assoc scientist, Inst Biol Chem, Wash State Univ, 1976- 1986. **Memberships:** Emer mem Am Soc Biochem & Molecular Biol. **Mailing Address:** NE 1700 Upper Dr, Pullman, WA 99163-4624. **E-Mail:** loewus@mail.wsu.edu

LOEWY, ARTHUR D(ECOSTA), NEUROANATOMY. **Personal Data:** b Chicago, Ill, January 9, 1943; m 1971, c 1. **Education:** Lawrence Univ, BA, 1964; Univ Wis-Madison, PhD (anat), 1969. **Honors & Awards:** Merit Award, Nat Heart, Lung & Blood Inst, 1989. **Professional Experience:** PROF ANAT & NEUROBIOLOGY, SCH MED, WASH UNIV, 1985-; from asst prof to assoc prof, Sch Med, Wash Univ, 1975-1985; sr res fel neuroanat, Mayo Grad Sch Med, Univ Minn, 1974-1975; res assoc, Mayo Grad Sch Med, Univ Minn, 1971-1974; res assoc & instr neuroanat, Univ Chicago, 1969-1971; investr, Am Heart Asn. **Memberships:** Soc Neuroscience; Am Physiol Soc. **Research Statement & Publications:** Organization of central autonomic pathways; neural control of cardiovascular system. **Mailing Address:** Dept Anat & Neurobiology, Sch Med, Wash Univ, P O Box 8108 903 McDonnell Med Sci Bldg, St Louis, MO 63110. **Fax:** 314-362-3446. **E-Mail:** loewya@thalamus.wustl.edu

LOEWY, ROBERT G(USTAV), AERONAUTICAL & MECHANICAL ENGINEERING. **Personal Data:** b Philadelphia, Pa, February 12, 1926; m 1955, Lila Spinner; c Esther Elizabeth, Joanne Victoria & Raymond Matthe w. **Education:** Rensselaer Polytech Inst, BAE, 1947; Mass Inst Technol, MS, 1948; Univ Pa, PhD (eng mech), 1962. **Honors & Awards:** Lawrence Sperry Award, Am Inst Aeronaut & Astronaut, 1958; Except Civilian Serv Award, USAF, 1966, 1975 & 1985; Nikolsky Mem Lectr, Am Helicopter Soc, 1984; Spirit of St Louis Medal, Am Soc Mech Engrs, 1996; Doughan Lectr On Res, 1999, AIAA. **Professional Experience:** WM RT OAKES PROF & CHMN, SCH AEROSPACE ENG, GA INST TECHNOL, 1993-; dir, Rotorcraft Technol Ctr, 1982-1993; inst prof mech & aerospace sci, Rensselaer Polytech Inst, 1978-1993; chmn, Aeronaut Adv Comt, NASA, 1977-1983; vpres acad affairs & provost, Rensselaer Polytech Inst, 1974-1978; chmn, 1978-1984, USAF AERONAUT SYSTS ADV GROUP; mem, Aeronaut Comt, Res & Technol Adv Coun, NASA, vchmn, 1978-1983; Sci Adv Bd, 1971-1973; mem, Mil Aircraft Panel, President's Sci Adv Coun, 1968-1972; chmn, 7 3 -7 5, USAF Sci Adv Bd, 1967-1976 & 1978-1985; dean, Col Eng & Appl Sci, Univ Rochester, 1967-1974; mem, Res & Eng Adv Coun, US Post Off Dept, 1966-1968 & Aviation Sci Adv Group, US Army Aviation Mat Command, 1967-1971; mem, Div Adv Group, Aeronaut Systs Div, USAF, 1967-1969; dir, Space Sci Ctr, Univ Rochester, 1966-1971; chief scientist, Dept Air Force, 1965-1966; from assoc prof to prof mech & aerospace sci, Univ Rochester, 1962-1974; Consult, 1959-; chief tech engr, Vertol Aircraft Corp, Pa, 1958-1962; chief dynamics engr, Vertol Aircraft Corp, Pa, 1955-1958; prin engr, Cornell Aero Lab, Buffalo, 1953-1955; staff stress engr, Piasecki Helicopter Corp, Pa, 1952-1953; assoc res engr, Cornell Aero Lab, Buffalo, 1949-1952; sr vibration engr, Martin Co, Md, 1948-1949; Res asst, Mass Inst Technol, 1948. **Memberships:** Nat Acad Eng; hon fel Am Inst Aeronaut & Astronaut; hon fel Am Helicopter Soc, secy-treas, 2001-2002; Am Soc Eng Educ; fel AAAS. **Research Statement & Publications:** Structural dynamics and aeroelasticity; unsteady aerodynamics; rotorcraft technology. **Mailing Address:** 3420 Wood Valley Rd, Atlanta, GA 30327. **Fax:** 404-894-2760.

LOF, JOHN L(ARS) C(OLE), ELECTRICAL ENGINEERING. **Personal Data:** b Denver, Colo, December 11, 1915; m 1948, Ruth Addison; c Richard. **Education:** Univ Denver, BS, 1938; Mass Inst Technol, SM, 1941, EE, 1951. **Honors & Awards:** Inst Elec Eng Prize, Inst Elec & Electronics Engrs, 1958. **Professional Experience:** PROF EMER ELEC ENG, UNIV CONN, 1976-; dir, Comput Ctr, 1961-1976; from asst prof to prof, Univ Conn, 1952-1976; instr, Mass Inst Technol, 1949-1952; res assoc, Mass Inst Technol, 1945-1949; Asst elec eng, Mass Inst Technol, 1938-1945. **Memberships:** Am Soc Eng Educ; Inst Elec & Electronics Engrs; Sigma Xi. **Research Statement & Publications:** Electronic computing systems; analog and digital computers; digital differential analyzers. **Mailing Address:** Dept Elec Eng, Univ Conn, Storrs, CT 06268.

LOFGREEN, GLEN PEHR, animal nutrition; deceased, see previous edition for last biography

LOFGREN, CLIFFORD SWANSON, ENTOMOLOGY. **Personal Data:** b St James, Minn, July 29, 1925; m 1954, c 3. **Education:** Gustavus Adolphus Col, BA, 1950; Univ Minn, MS, 1954; Univ Fla, PhD (entom), 1968. **Professional Experience:** RETIRED; prof entom, Inst Food & Agr Sci, Univ Fla, beginning 1980; asst prof entom & asst entomologist, Univ Fla, 1974-1980; entomologist, Insects Affecting Man Res Lab, beginning 1963; entomologist, Plant Pest Control Div, 1957-1963; entomologist, Entom Res Div, Agr Res Serv, USDA, 1955-1957. **Memberships:** Entom Soc Am; Am Mosquito Control Asn; Int Union Study Social Insects. **Research Statement & Publications:** Methods of controlling mosquitoes, imported fire ants and other insects of medical importance, particularly insecticides and equipment evaluation; studies on resistance, chemosterilants, pheromones and biology. **Mailing Address:** Dept Entomol, Univ Fla, 1321 NW 31st Dr, Gainesville, FL 32611.

LOFGREN, EDWARD JOSEPH, PHYSICS, ACCELERATORS. **Personal Data:** b Chicago, Ill, January 18, 1918; m 1968, c Helen, Laurel (Phillipson) & Claire. **Education:** Univ Calif, AB, 1938, PhD (physics), 1946. **Professional Experience:** ASSOC DIR EMER, LAWRENCE BERKELEY NAT LAB, UNIV CALIF, 1982-; sr staff scientist, Lawrence Berkeley Nat Lab, Univ Calif, 1979-1981; assoc dir, Lawrence Berkeley Nat Lab, Univ Calif, 1973-1979; mem, High Energy Physics Adv panel, 1967-1970; with Europ Orgn Nuclear Res, 1959; group leader, Lawrence Berkeley Nat Lab, Univ Calif, 1948-1973; asst prof physics, Univ Minn, 1946-1948; group leader, Los Alamos Sci Lab, 1944-1945; physicist, Lawrence Berkeley Nat Lab, Univ Calif, 1940-1944 & 1945-1946; asst, Univ Calif, 1938-1940. **Memberships:** Fel AAAS; fel Am Phys Soc. **Research Statement & Publications:** Elementary particle physics; accelerators for particle and heavy-ion physics and for biomedical applications; separation of uranium isotopes; discovery of heavy component of cosmic rays. **Mailing Address:** Lawrence Berkeley Nat Lab, Univ Calif, Rm 113 Bldg 47, Berkeley, CA 94720-5230. **Fax:** 510-486-5392.

LOFGREN, GARY ERNEST, EXPERIMENTAL PETROLOGY, PLANETARY SCIENCES. **Personal Data:** b Los Angeles, Calif, April 17, 1941; m 1994, Patti. **Education:** Stanford Univ, BS, 1963, PhD (geol), 1969; Dartmouth Col, MA, 1965. **Honors & Awards:** Super Achievement Award, NASA, 1978; Spec Commendation, Geol Soc Am, 1973. **Professional Experience:** Planetary Scientist, Johnson Space Cent, 1968-; Lunar Curator, Johnson Space Cent, 1997-; adj prof, Univ Houston, 1976-1987; team leader, Basaltic Volcanism Study Proj, 1976-1981; convener, Penrose Conf, Geol Soc Am, 1976; Mem, Lunar Sample Preliminary Exam Team, 1969-1972; SPACE GEOSCIENTIST, JOHNSON SPACE CTR, NASA, 1968-; teaching asst, Stanford Univ, 1965-1968; res geologist, Cold Regions Res & Eng Lab, 1965; Res asst geol, Dartmouth Col, 1963-1965. **Memberships:** Fel Geol Soc Am; Fel Mineral Soc Am; Am Geophys Union; Fel Meteoritical Soc. **Research Statement & Publications:** Crystallization properties of silicate melts with emphasis on the kinetics of nucleation and crystal growth in chondrules; textures of igneous rocks and rock genesis. **Mailing Address:** KT/NASA Johnson Space Ctr, 2101 NASA Parkway, Houston, TX 77058. **Fax:** 281-483-5347. **E-Mail:** gary.e.lofgren@nasa.gov

LOFGREN, JAMES R, PLANT BREEDING, GENETICS. **Personal Data:** b West Point, Nebr, May 18, 1931; m 1962, c 3. **Education:** Univ Nebr, BS, 1960; NDak State Univ, MS, 1962; Kans State Univ, PhD (plant breeding, genetics), 1968. **Professional Experience:** STA MGR & PLANT BREEDER, PIONEER HAWAII-BRED INT, INC, 1993-; agronomist-plant breeder, Dahlgren & Co, Inc, 1971-1993; asst prof, Northwest Exp Sta, Univ Minn, 1967-1971; res asst, Kans State Univ, 1962-1967; Asst agron, NDak State Univ, 1960-1962. **Memberships:** Am Soc Agron; Crop Sci Soc Am. **Research Statement & Publications:** Breeding and genetics of sunflowers to improve productivity and quality. **Mailing Address:** RR 4, Moorhead, MN 56560.

LOFGREN, KARL ADOLPH, SURGERY. **Personal Data:** b Killeberg, Sweden, April 1, 1915; American citizen; m 1942, Jean Frances Taylor; c Karl Edward & Anne. **Education:** Harvard Med Sch, MD, 1941; Univ Minn, MS, 1947; Am Bd Surg, dipl, 1953. **Professional Experience:** Prof emer surg, Mayo Med Sch, 1982-; STAFF EMER MEM, MAYO CLIN, 1982-; sr consult, Mayo Clin, 1979-1981; from assoc prof to prof, Mayo Grad Sch Med, 1974-1981; Head sect peripheral vein surg, Mayo Clin, 1966-1979; from instr to asst prof, Mayo Grad Sch Med, 1951-1974; mem surg staff, Mayo Clin, 1950-1981; asst to staff, Mayo Clin, 1949-1950; resident, Royal Acad Hosp, Univ Uppsala, 1949; resident surg, Mayo Grad Sch Med, Univ Minn, 1942-1944 & 1946-1948; Intern, Univ Minn Hosp, 1941-1942. **Memberships:** Fel Am Col Surgeons; Int Cardiovasc Soc; Soc Vascular Surg; Swed Surg Soc; Sigma Xi; Midwestern Vascular Surg Soc. **Research Statement & Publications:** Peripheral venous disorders. **Mailing Address:** 1001 Seventh Ave NE, Rochester, MN 55906-7074.

LOFGREN, PHILIP ALLEN, NUTRITION, RESEARCH ADMINISTRATION. **Personal Data:** b Iowa, July 30, 1944; m 1977, Lousanne; c Kristofer A. **Education:** Iowa State Univ, BS, 1966; Cornell Univ, MS, 1969, PhD (nutrit), 1971. **Professional Experience:** NUTRIT RES CONSULT, NAT CATTLEMEN BEEF ASN, 1992-; dir grant serv, Nutrit Res, Nat Dairy Coun, 1985-1992; asst dir, Nutrit Res, Nat Dairy Coun, 1973-1985; fel nutrit, Univ Calif, Berkeley, 1972-1973; res asst animal nutrit, Cornell Univ, 1966-1971. **Memberships:** Am Dairy Sci Asn; Inst Food Technologists; Am Oil Chemists Soc; Am Inst Nutrit. **Research Statement & Publications:** Human and animal nutrition; unidentified growth factors; nutrient interactions; nutritional physiology of food intake regulation; research program management; food, nutrition and health issues; research interpretation; technical writing. **Mailing Address:** 922 N E Ave, Oak Park, IL 60302-1330.

LOFQUIST, GEORGE W, MATHEMATICS, COMPUTER SCIENCES. **Personal Data:** b Brookhaven, Miss, October 6, 1930; m 1955, c 2. **Education:** Univ NC, BS, 1952, MEd, 1959; La State Univ, Baton Rouge, MS, 1963, PhD (math), 1967; Univ SFla, MS, 1989. **Professional Experience:** PROF EMER MATH, ECKERD COL, 1993-; from asst prof to prof, Eckerd Col, 1967-1993; Instr math, La State Univ, New Orleans, 1959-1964 & Baton Rouge, 1966-1967. **Memberships:** Am Math Soc; Math Asn Am. **Research Statement & Publications:** Algebra; number theory. **Mailing Address:** 118 Col Circle, Swannanoa, NC 28778.

LOFQUIST, MARVIN JOHN, INORGANIC CHEMISTRY. **Personal Data:** b Chicago, Ill, October 19, 1943; m 1965, c 2. **Education:** Augustana Col, BA, 1965; Northwestern Univ, PhD (inorg chem), 1970. **Professional Experience:** ADMIN, FERRIS STATE UNIV, 1992-; prof & dept head, Phys Sci Dept, 1981-1992; mem fac, Ferris State Univ, 1973-1988; asst prof chem, Camrose Lutheran Col, 1969-1973. **Memberships:** Am Chem Soc. **Research Statement & Publications:** Kinetics and mechanisms of organometallic transition metal complexes. **Mailing Address:** 478 Sheridan Rd, Evanston, IL 60202.

LOFSTROM, JOHN GUSTAVE, analytical chemistry; deceased, see previous edition for last biography

LOFSVOLD, DAVID E, BIOLOGY. **Education:** Univ Wash, BA; Univ Chicago, MS, PhD (Evol Biol). **Professional Experience:** CAROL/TREVELYAN STRATEGY GROUP, DIV KINTERA INC, as of 2006. **Mailing Address:** Carol/Trevelyan Strategy Group, 1718 Conn AveNW 6th Floor, Washington, DC 20009.

LOFT, JOHN T, CHEMISTRY, ADHESIVES & SEALANTS. **Personal Data:** b Mankato, Minn, July 21, 1932. **Education:** Gustavus Adolphus Col, BA, 1954; State Univ Iowa, MS, 1956, PhD (chem), 1958. **Professional Experience:** CONSULT, 1996-; mgr com develop, new bus develop, 1986-1996; mgr com develop, Loctite Corp, 1983-1986; proj mgr mkt, Loctite Corp, 1979-1983; new bus coordr, Loctite Corp, 1977-1979; projs mgr, Microporus Div, Amerace Corp, 1972-1977; com develop, Celanese Plastics Co, 1968-1972; sr res chemist, Sundry Dix Oil Co, 1958-1965 & Celanese Corp, 1965-1968; chmn, Tulsa Sect, Am Chem Soc, 1963-1965; lectr, Chem Dept, Univ Tulsa, 1960. **Mailing Address:** 369 Crepe Myrtle Dr, Greer, SC 29651.

LOFTFIELD, ROBERT BERNER, ORGANIC CHEMISTRY, BIOCHEMISTRY. **Personal Data:** b Detroit, Mich, December 15, 1919; wid, c 10. **Education:** Harvard Univ, BS, 1941, MA, 1942, PhD (org chem), 1946. **Honors & Awards:** Warren Triennial Prize, 1953. **Professional Experience:** PROF EMER, BIOCHEM, MED SCH, UNIV NMEX, 1990-; Fulbright & Heinemann Stiftung fel, Med Univ, Hannover, Ger, 1983; mem, Fulbright Adv Comn, 1978-1981; Fulbright prof, Abo Akademi, Turku, Finland, 1977; mem adv comn proteins & nucleic acids, Am Cancer Soc, 1971-1974; USPHS sr res fel, Dunn Sch Path, Oxford Univ, 1971-1972; prof, Med Sch, Univ Nmex, 1964-1990; chmn dept, Med Sch, Univ Nmex, 1964-1971 & 1978-1990; mem biochem study sect, USPHS, 1964-1968; mem adv comn pathogenesis cancer, Am Cancer Soc, 1964-1967; Guggenheim fel, Med Res Coun, Cambridge, Eng, 1961-1962; asst prof org chem, Harvard Med Sch, 1960-1964; instr, Marine Biol Lab, Woods Hole, 1959-1962; assoc biochemist, Mass Gen Hosp, 1956-1964; assoc, Harvard Med Sch, 1956-1960; Runyon fel, Medinska Nobel Inst, Stockholm, 1952-1953; Fel, Brookhaven Nat Lab, 1950; tutor, Harvard Univ, 1948-1964; res assoc, Mass Gen Hosp, 1948-1956; res assoc, Mass Inst Technol, 1946-1948; chief spec asst div, Off Strategic Serv, 1946-1947; res assoc, Harvard Univ, 1944-1946; Asst chem, Harvard Univ, 1942-1944. **Memberships:** Am Chem Soc; Am Soc Biol Chem; Am Asn Cancer Res; Biophys Soc; Am Pub Health Asn. **Research Statement & Publications:** Radioactive carbon 14 techniques; organic synthesis; organic reaction mechanisms; protein biosynthesis; mechanism of enzymic catalysis. **Mailing Address:** Univ NMex Med Sch, Albuquerque, NM 87131. **Fax:** 505-272-8452.

LOFTIN, KARIN CHRISTIANE, AEROSPACE BIOMEDICINE, KNOWLEDGE-BASED SYSTEM IN MEDICINE. **Personal Data:** m 1972, Richard; c Elisabeth & Benjamin. **Education:** Oakland Univ, Mich, BA, 1970; Univ Tex, MS, 1973, PhD (biomed sci), 1979. **Professional Experience:** ASST PROF, MED LAB SCI COL HEALTH SCI, OLD DOMINION UNIV, as of 2003; SR SCIENTIST, KRUG, LIFE SCI INC, 1989-; sr res assoc dept obstet gynec, Univ Tex Med Sch, Houston, 1986-1989; instr microbiol prog infectious dis & clin microbiol, Univ Tex Med Sch, Houston, 1984-1986; Henry Holcomb fel, Dept Clin Immunol & Biol Ther, Univ Tex-M D Anderson Hosp, 1983-1984; res asst, Dept Pediat, Univ Tex Med Br, 1982; res assoc, Microbiol Dept, 1982; vis instr gen biol, Univ Houston, Univ Park, 1979-1981. **Memberships:** Sigma Xi; Nat Mgt Asn; Am Soc Microbiol; Am Asn Artificial Intel. **Research Statement & Publications:** Study man's immune response and host resistance to do adverse environmental conditions such as high altitude and microgravity and the application of new technology, such as artificial intelligence, to medical systems. **Mailing Address:** Med Lab Sci - Col Health Sci, Old Dominion Univ, 214 B Spong Hall, Norfolk, VA 23529-0286. **E-Mail:** kloftin@odu.edu

LOFTSGAARDEN, DON OWEN, MATHEMATICAL STATISTICS. **Personal Data:** b Big Timber, Mont, July 7, 1939; m 1962, Nenette; c Debra, Lisa & Meta. **Education:** Mont State Univ, BS, 1961, MS, 1963, PhD (math statist), 1964. **Professional Experience:** PROF EMER MATH, UNIV MONT, as of 2004; chmn dept math, Univ Mont, 1978-1979, 1992-1995; prof math, Univ Mont, beginning 1975; from asst prof to assoc prof, Univ Mont, 1967-1975; asst prof, Western Mich Univ, 1965-1967; instr statist, Mont State Univ, 1964-1965; statistician, Battelle Mem Inst, 1963; res engr, Autonetics Div, N Am Aviation Inc, 1962. **Memberships:** Am Statist Asn; Inst Math Statist; Math Asn Am. **Research Statement & Publications:** Applied statistical inference; mathematical statistics. **Mailing Address:** Dept Math, Univ Mont, Math Bldg, Missoula, MT 59812-0864. **Fax:** 406243-2674. **E-Mail:** dlofts@amerion.com

LOFTUS, JOSEPH P, JR, statistics, psychology; deceased, see previous edition for last biography

LOGAN, ALAN, PALEOECOLOGY. **Personal Data:** b Newcastle-on-Tyne, Eng, September 20, 1937; m 1962, c 2. **Education:** Univ Durham, BSc, 1959, PhD (paleont), 1962. **Professional Experience:** PROF EMER GEOL, UNIV NB, as of 2004; prof geol, Univ NB, St John, beginning 1976; assoc prof, Univ NB, St John, 1970-1976; asst prof, Univ NB, St John, 1967-1970; lectr paleont, Univ Leeds, 1964-1967; Nat Res Coun fel, McMaster Univ, 1962-1964; vis fel, Univ Calgary. **Memberships:** Int Soc Reef Studies. **Research Statement & Publications:** Paleontology, paleoecology and ecology of Permian, Triassic and Holocene bivalves and brachiopods; ecology of Holocene coral reefs. **Mailing Address:** Dept Phys Sci, Univ NB, Ganong Hall 200, St John, NB E2L 4L5, Can. **Fax:** 506-648-5650. **E-Mail:** logan@unbsj.ca

LOGAN, BRIAN ANTHONY, NUCLEAR PHYSICS. **Personal Data:** b Newcastle-upon-Tyne, Eng, December 22, 1939; m 1969, c 2. **Education:** Univ Birmingham, BSc, 1960, PhD (physics), 1964. **Professional Experience:** MEM, OTTAWA-CARLETON INST PHYSICS, as of 2003; PROF PHYSICS, UNIV OTTAWA, 1981-; from asst prof to assoc prof, Univ Ottawa, 1966-1981; lectr, Univ Ottawa, 1965-1966; res assoc physics, Univ Birmingham, 1964-1965. **Memberships:** Can Asn Physicists; Am Phys Soc. **Research Statement & Publications:** Nuclear physics. **Mailing Address:** Ottawa-Carleton Inst Physics, 10 Marie Curie St Rm 023, Ottawa, ON K1N 6N5, Can. **Fax:** 613-562-5190.

LOGAN, BRUCE E, ENVIRONMENTAL SCIENCES. **Education:** Rensselaer Polytech Inst, BS, 1979, MS, 1980; Univ Calif, PhD, (Environ Eng), 1986. **Professional Experience:** DIR & KAPPA PROF ENVIRON ENG, DEPT CIVIL & ENVIRON ENG, PA STATE UNIV, PA, 1997-. **Mailing Address:** Pa State Univ, 231Q Sackett Bldg Dept Civil & Environ Eng, University Park, PA 16802. **Fax:** 814-863-7304. **E-Mail:** blogan@psu.edu

LOGAN, CHARLES DONALD, WOOD CHEMISTRY. **Personal Data:** b St John, NB, May 15, 1924; wid, c 3. **Education:** Mt Allison Univ, BSc, 1945; McGill Univ, PhD (org chem), 1949. **Professional Experience:** RETIRED; dir chem res, Que & Ont Paper Co Ltd, 1974-1984; asst dir, Que & Ont Paper Co Ltd, 1965-1974; from res chemist to sr res chemist, Que & Ont Paper Co, Ltd, 1949-1965. **Memberships:** Am Chem Soc; Am Pulp & Paper Assoc; Brit Paper & Board Makers Asn; Can Res Mgt Asn; Chem Inst Can. **Research Statement & Publications:** Vanillin and lignin chemistry; ion exchange chemical recovery; pulp and paper by-product utilization; chemimech pulping. **Mailing Address:** 9 Marlene Dr, St Catharines, ON L2T 3E7, Can.

LOGAN, CHERYL ANN, ANIMAL BEHAVIOR, NEUROPSYCHOLOGY. **Personal Data:** b Syracuse, NY, April 1, 1945. **Education:** Southern Methodist Univ, BA, 1967; Univ Calif, San Diego, PhD, 1974. **Professional Experience:** PROF PSYCHOL, UNIV NC, GREENSBORO, as of 2004; ADJ PROF BIOL, UNIV NC, GREENSBORO, as of 2004; assoc psychol, Univ NC, Greensboro, beginning 1980; asst prof, Univ NC, 1974-1979; fulbright scholar, Univ Vienna. **Memberships:** Animal Behav Soc; Am Ornith Union; Sigma Xi. **Research Statement & Publications:** Animal communication; ecology and evolution of learning; structure and function of birdsong; territorial and reproductive function of mockingbird song. **Mailing Address:** Dept Psychol, Univ NC, 272 Eberhart, Greensboro, NC 27412. **E-Mail:** cheryllogan@uncg.edu

LOGAN, DARYL LEE, STRESS ANALYSIS USING FINITE ELEMENT METHOD, MACHINE DESIGN & ANALYSIS. **Personal Data:** b Goodman, Wis, November 12, 1948; m Diane; c Katherine, Daryl Jr & Paul. **Education:** Bucknell Univ, BS, 1978; Pa State Univ, BS, 1979, ME, 1980, PhD, 1987. **Professional Experience:** PROF MECH ENG, UNIV WIS-PLATTEVILLE, 1993-; chmn, Mech Eng Dept, 1993-1996; vis lectr, Univ Ill, Chicago, 1983; assoc prof, Rose Hulman Inst Technol, 1982-1993; asst prof, Rose Hulman Inst Technol, 1977-1982. **Memberships:** Am Soc Eng Educ; Am Soc Mech Engrs. **Research Statement & Publications:** Mechanics of materials and finite element method; author of several technical papers. **Mailing Address:** Dept Mech Eng, Univ Wis, 1 Univ Plaza, Platteville, WI 53818. **Fax:** 608-342-1566. **E-Mail:** logan@uwplatt.edu

LOGAN, DAVID ALEXANDER, MICROBIOLOGY. **Personal Data:** b Abingdon, Va, December 7, 1952; m 1976. **Education:** Knoxville Col, BS, 1975; Univ Tenn, MS, 1977, PhD (microbiol), 1981. **Professional Experience:** ASSOC PROF BIOL, CLARK ATLANTA UNIV, as of 2004; prof biol, clark atlanta univ, beginning 1995; asst prof biol, cell biol & microbiol, Drexel Univ, 1984-1995; lab asst med microbiol, Univ Calif, Irvine, 1982-1984; instr biol, Knoxville Col, 1980-1981; teaching asst microbiol, Univ Tenn, 1975-1980. **Memberships:** Am Soc Microbiol; Mycol Soc Am. **Research Statement & Publications:** Biochemistry of proteinases in fungi. **Mailing Address:** Dept Biol Sci Res Ctr Sci, Clark Atlanta Univ, Rm 4040 James P Brawley Dr SW, Atlanta, GA 30314. **Fax:** 404-880-8065. **E-Mail:** dlogan@cau.edu

LOGAN, DAVID MACKENZIE, MOLECULAR BIOLOGY, BIOCHEMISTRY. **Personal Data:** b Toronto, Ont, July 23, 1937; m 1960, Susan E Hanna; c Richard, Heather & Michael. **Education:** Univ Toronto, BA, 1960, MA, 1963, PhD (med biophys), 1965. **Professional Experience:** ASSOC DEAN PURE & APPL SCI, YORK UNIV, 1993-; PROF MOLECULAR BIOL, YORK UNIV, 1989-; from asst prof to assoc prof, York Univ, 1968-1988; Nat Res Coun Can fel, McMaster Univ, 1967-1968; Jane Coffin Childs Mem Fund fel med res, 1965-1967; res assoc biochem, NIH, 1965-1967. **Memberships:** AAAS; Biophys Soc; Can Biochem Soc; NY Acad Sci; Environ Mutagen Soc. **Research Statement & Publications:** Biochemical and biophysical aspects of nerve-muscle interactions; short term essays of biohazardous chemicals, in particular para-amino-hippuric and bioremediation of contaminated sites; toxicology. **Mailing Address:** Off Pure & Appl Sci 108 Steacie Sci Bldg, York Univ 4700 Keele St, North York, ON M3J 1P3, Can.

LOGAN, GEORGE BRYAN, PEDIATRICS. **Personal Data:** b Pittsburgh, Pa, August 1, 1909; m 1939, c 2. **Education:** Wash & Jefferson Col, BS, 1930; Harvard Univ, MD, 1934; Univ Minn, MS, 1940; Am Bd Pediat, dipl, 1941; Am Bd Allergy & Immunol, dipl, 1972. **Professional Experience:** EMER STAFF, MAYO CLIN, beginning 1975; prof pediat, Mayo Med Sch, 1973-1975; sr consult, sect pediat, Mayo Clin, 1968-1975; chmn sub-bd allergy, Am Bd Pediat, 1963-1966; from instr to prof pediat, Univ Minn, Mayo Grad Sch Med, 1940-1973; consult, sect pediat, Mayo Clin, 1940-1968. **Memberships:** AAAS; Am Pediat Soc; AMA; Am Acad Allergy & Immunol; Am Acad Pediat (pres 1967-1968). **Research Statement & Publications:** Allergic and liver diseases in children. **Mailing Address:** Minn Med Asn, 1300 Godward St NE, Ste 2500, Minneapolis, MN 55413.

LOGAN, JAMES COLUMBUS, BATTERY RESEARCH & DEVELOPMENT, CORPORATE MANAGEMENT. **Personal Data:** b Baltimore, Md. **Education:** Johns Hopkins Univ, BES, 1968; Harvard Univ, MS, 1969, PhD (appl physics), 1973. **Professional Experience:** VPRES, ALTUS CORP, 1979-; br head, Naval Ocean Systs Ctr, 1975-1979; Res fel, Calif Inst Technol, 1973-1975. **Memberships:** Am Phys Soc; Am Soc Metals; AAAS. **Research Statement & Publications:** Research and development of new batteries; lithium batteries and primary lithium batteries. **Mailing Address:** 2055 Yale St, Palo Alto, CA 94306.

LOGAN, JAMES EDWARD, CLINICAL CHEMISTRY, HEMATOLOGY. **Personal Data:** b Thorndale, Ont, January 14, 1920; m 1982, c 2. **Education:** Univ Western Ontario, BSc, 1949, PhD (biochem), 1952. **Honors & Awards:** Ames Award, Can Soc Clin Chem, 1981. **Professional Experience:** RETIRED; Chmn, Int Fedn Clin Chem Expert Panel, Evaluation Diag Reagent Sets, 1979-; chief clin chem, Lab Ctr Dis Control, 1979-1984; actg dir, Bur Med Biochem, 1977-1979; chief clin chem, Clin Labs, 1973-1977; sr biochemist, Clin Labs, 1959-1973; chemist, Biol Control Labs, Can Dept Nat Health & Welfare, 1954-1959; Sr res asst biochem, Univ Western Ont, 1952-1954. **Memberships:** Fel Nat Acad Clin Biochem; Can Soc Clin Chem; Am Asn Clin Chem; Can Biochem Soc. **Research Statement & Publications:** Chemistry of peripheral nervous system; radioisotope tracer studies; quality control and methodology; hemoglobin; evaluation of diagnostic kits and clinical laboratory instruments; radioimmunoassay; reference methods; trace element analyses. **Mailing Address:** 2005 Saville Row, Ottawa, ON K2A 1A3, Can.

LOGAN, JESSE ALAN, POPULATION ECOLOGY, ENTOMOLOGY. **Personal Data:** b Pueblo, Colo, June 11, 1944; m 1970, c 2. **Education:** Colo State Univ, BS, 1967, MS, 1969; Wash State Univ, PhD (entom), 1977. **Honors & Awards:** John I Davidson Pres Award, Am Soc Photogram & Remote Sensing, 1993. **Professional Experience:** PROJ LEADER, WESTERN BARK BEETLE PROJ, LOGAN FORESTRY SCI LAB, USDA, 2004-; res entomologist, Mountain Pine Beetle Proj, USDA, 1999-2004; PROF, DEPT FOREST RANGE & WILDLIFE, UTAH STATE UNIV, as of 2004; proj leader, Mountain Pine Beetle Proj, Logan Forestry Sci Lab, USDA, 1992-1999; assoc prof entom & forestry, Va Polytech Inst & State Univ, 1988-1992; sr res fel, Nat Res Adv Coun NZ, 1984-1985; asst prof zool & entom, Colo State Univ, 1978-1988; res fel, NC State Univ, 1976-1978;

grad res asst, Wash State Univ, 1973-1976; comput programmer, Dept Entom, Wash State Univ, 1972-1973; res assoc entom, Colo State Univ, 1971-1972; grad res asst, Colo State Univ, 1967-1969. **Memberships:** AAAS; Sigma Xi; Entom Soc Am; Am Inst Biol Sci; Int Union Forest Res Organisations. **Research Statement & Publications:** Systems analysis and population dynamics of invertebrate populations; relationship of these organisms to the efficient utilization of renewable natural resources. **Mailing Address:** Dept Forest Range & Wildlife Sci, Utah State Univ, 5230 Old Main Hill, Logan, UT 84322-5230. **Fax:** 435-797-3796. **E-Mail:** jalogan@fs.fed.us

LOGAN, JOHN MERLE, STRUCTURAL GEOLOGY, TECTONOPHYSICS. **Personal Data:** b Pittsburgh, Pa, July 7, 1934; m 1982, Lorna. **Education:** Mich State Univ, BS, 1956; Univ Okla, MS, 1962, PhD (geol), 1965. **Professional Experience:** PROF EMER EXP ROCKDEFORMATION, DEPT GEOPHYS & GEOL, TEX A&M UNIV, as of 2004; Dir, Ctr Tectonophys, Tex A&M Univ, 1984-1986; prof exp rockdeformation, dept geophys & geol, Tex A&M Univ, 1978-; consult, Los Alamos Nat Lab, 1978-1986; NSF grant, 1971-1986; US GeolSurv grant, 1971-1985; Advan Projs Res Agency, US Dept Defense res grant, 1971-1978; consult, Amoco Prod Co, 1967-1986; from asst prof to assoc prof geol & geophys, Dept Geophys & Geol, Tex A&M Univ, 1967-1978; geologist, Shell Develop Co, 1965-1967; consult, John MLogan & Assocs, Inc. **Memberships:** Assoc Geol Soc Am; assoc Am Geophys Union; AAAS. **Research Statement & Publications:** Experimental rock deformation as applied to structural geological problems and architectural and engineering of building exteriors. **Mailing Address:** Dept Geol, Tex A&M Univ, College Station, TX 77843-0100.

LOGAN, JOSEPH GRANVILLE, PHYSICS. **Personal Data:** b Washington, DC, June 8, 1920; m 1944, c 2. **Education:** DC Teachers Col, BS, 1941; Univ Buffalo, PhD (physics), 1955. **Professional Experience:** RETIRED; dir, Urban Univ Ctr, Univ Southern Calif, 1979-1989; dir physics dept, Calif Polytech Univ, Pomona, 1978-1979; pres, Appl Energy Sci Inc, 1974-1978; chief engr nuclear weapons effects, Western Div, 1972-1974; mgr vulnerability & hardening develop eng, Western Div, McDonnell Douglas Astronaut Co, 1969-1972; spec asst to dir res & develop, Western Div, McDonnell Douglas Astronaut Co, 1967-1969; dir aerodyn & propulsion lab, Aerospace Corp, 1960-1967; mgr propulsion res dept, Space Technol Labs Inc, 1959-1960; head aerophys lab, Space Technol Labs Inc, 1957-1959; physicist aerodyn propulsion, Cornell Aeronaut Lab Inc, 1947-1957; physicist aerodyn, Nat Bur Stand, 1943-1947. **Memberships:** Am Phys Soc; NY Acad Sci. **Research Statement & Publications:** New energy systems. **Mailing Address:** 3652 Olympiad Dr, Los Angeles, CA 90043.

LOGAN, JOSEPH SKINNER, INSULATORS, ELECTROSTATIC CHUCKS. **Personal Data:** b New York, NY, June 4, 1932; m Nancy; c Jennifer M (Haber), Susan, Annette (Miller) & Joseph S Jr. **Education:** Cornell Univ, BEE, 1955, MS, 1956; Stanford Univ, PhD (elec eng), 1961. **Professional Experience:** Pres consultant, 1993-; sr engr res, E Fishkill Facil, 1984-1992; sr engr, E Fishkill Facil, 1971-1983; Adv engr, IBM Corp, 1960-1971; sr engr, IBM Yorktown, 1984-1992; sr engr, IBM E Fishkill facil 1971-1983; Adv engr, IBM E Corp, 1960-1971; CONSULT. **Memberships:** mem inst elec & electronics engrs, (IEEE), life mem; Am vacuum soc; Inst Elec & Electronics Engrs; Am Vacuum Soc. **Research Statement & Publications:** Semiconductor surface physics and device development; radio frequency sputtering of thin insulator films; resputtering; plasma processing. **Mailing Address:** 149 Seaside Dr, Jamestown, RI 02835. **E-Mail:** jslogan@compuserve.com

LOGAN, KATHRYN VANCE, MATERIALS RESEARCH & DEVELOPMENT. **Personal Data:** b Atlanta, Ga, June 12, 1946; m 1967, WilliamS Sr; c Stephanie & William Jr. **Education:** Ga Inst Technol, BCerE, 1970, MSCerE, 1980, PhD (Civil eng), 1992. **Honors & Awards:** Monie A Ferst Award, 1970; Soc Women Engrs Award, 1980 James A Mueller award lecture engg ceramics Dir/Amer, cer, soc. **Professional Experience:** Prin, Resengremerita, 2001; PRIN RES ENGR, School of Materials Sci Engr, GA INST TECHNOL, 1992-; INTERM ASST VPRES, INTERDISCIPLINARY PROG, 1992-; res award, Ga Tech Res Inst, 1990; HEAD, CERAMIC BR, GA INST TECHNOL, 1989-; prin investr, 1982-; Consult, 1981-; From res engr I to sr res engr, Ga Inst Technol, 1970-1992. **Memberships:** Fel Am Ceramic Soc; Nat Inst Ceramic Fel Engrs; Ceramic Educ Coun; Sigma Xi; Mat Res Soc; Nat Soc Prof Engrs Pres-select Am cer soc 2002. **Research Statement & Publications:** Materials characterization via analytical instrumentation, advanced materials development, microwave ferrites, directionally solidified composites; crystal growth by directional solidification; clay mineralogy; thermite synthesis and forming of titanium diboride. **Mailing Address:** 295 Junction Track, Roswell, GA 30075. **Fax:** 770-993-7952. **E-Mail:** kathryn.logan@mse.gatech.edu

LOGAN, LOWELL ALVIN, ecology, plant taxonomy; deceased, see previous edition for last biography

LOGAN, RALPH ANDRE, MATERIALS SCIENCE ENGINEERING. **Personal Data:** b Cornwall, Ont, September 22, 1926; American citizen; m 1950, Ann; c Howard, Mary, Marguerite, Anthony, Enid, Alisa, Ruth, Thomas & John. **Education:** McGill Univ, BSc, 1947, MSc, 1948; Columbia Univ, PhD (physics), 1952. **Professional Experience:** RETIRED; distinguished mem tech staff, Bell Labs, 1982-1996; mem tech staff, Bell Labs, 1952-1982; asst physics, Columbia Univ, 1949-1952. **Memberships:** Nat Acad Eng; fel Inst Elec & Electronics Engrs; fel Am Phys Soc. **Research Statement & Publications:** Semiconductor research. **Mailing Address:** Seven Cindy Dr, Manahawkin, NJ 08050-4230. **E-Mail:** ralphlogan@aol.com

LOGAN, RICHARD SUTTON, CHEMICAL ENGINEERING, TECHNICAL MANAGEMENT. **Personal Data:** b Carthage, Mo, October 8, 1918; wid, c 1. **Education:** Univ Mo, BS, 1947; Okla Agr & Mech Col, MS, 1953. **Professional Experience:** RETIRED; mgr, Petrol & Petrochemical Processes Div, 1980-1984; dir petrol res, group leader uranium milling processes, 1957-1958 & lubricant additives, 1980; mgr refining & separation br, group leader uranium milling processes, 1957-1958 & lubricant additives, 1966-1980; mgr catalytic reactions sect, group leader uranium milling processes, 1957-1958 & lubricant additives, 1962-1966; mgr process develop sect, group leader uranium milling processes, 1957-1958 & lubricant additives, 1960-1962; Phillips Petrol Co, group leader uranium milling processes, 1957-1958 & lubricant additives, 1958-1960; mem staff lubricant & lubricant additives group, Res & Develop Dept, 1948-1957. **Memberships:** Am Inst Chem Engrs; Nat Soc Prof Engrs. **Research Statement & Publications:** Petroleum processing; uranium milling; lubricant oils and additives; sulfonation; halogenation; alkylation; catalytic cracking; research and development management. **Mailing Address:** 1808 Skyline Pl, Bartlesville, OK 74006.

LOGAN, ROBERT KALMAN, PHYSICS, COMMUNICATIONS. **Personal Data:** b New York, NY, August 31, 1939. **Education:** Mass Inst Technol, BS, 1961, PhD (physics), 1965. **Professional Experience:** ASSOC PROF PHYSICS, DEPT MEASUREMENT, EVAL & COMPUT APPLNS, 1984-; assoc prof physics, Univ Toronto, beginning 1975; asst prof, Dept Measurement, Eval & Comput Applns, Univ Toronto, 1968-1975; res assoc, Dept Measurement, Eval & Comput Applns, Univ Toronto, 1967-1968; res assoc physics, Univ Ill, 1965-1967. **Research Statement & Publications:** Computer applications in education; impact and effect of communication media on science and society. **Mailing Address:** Dept Physcis, Univ Toronto, MP306 60 St George St, Toronto, ON M5S 1A7, Can. **Fax:** 416-978-1547. **E-Mail:** logan@physics.utoronto.ca

LOGAN, ROWLAND ELIZABETH, PHYSIOLOGY. **Personal Data:** b Los Angeles, Calif, August 1, 1923. **Education:** Univ Calif, AB, 1945; Northwestern Univ, MS, 1951, PhD (physiol), 1954. **Professional Experience:** RETIRED; asst prof biol, Gettysburg Col, 1958-1988; instr biol, Bard Col, 1956-1958; Instr physiol, Sch Med, WVa Univ, 1954-1955. **Memberships:** AAAS. **Research Statement & Publications:** Cell metabolism; arthropod behavior. **Mailing Address:** 8C60 Box 302, Islesboro, ME 04848.

LOGAN, TED JOE, INDUSTRIAL CHEMISTRY, TECHNICAL RECRUITING. **Personal Data:** b Ft Wayne, Ind, June 22, 1931; m 1954, Ruthanne; c Thomas E & Patricia A. **Education:** Ind Univ, AB, 1953; Purdue Univ, MS, 1956, PhD (chem), 1958. **Professional Experience:** CONSULT, EMPLOY & CAREER, as of 2006; assoc dir & mgr tech recruiting, Procter & Gamble Co, 1991-1996; mgr recruiting, Procter & Gamble Co, beginning 1978; sect head, Procter & Gamble Co, 1963-1978; res chemist, Procter & Gamble Co, 1958-1963. **Memberships:** Am Chem Soc. **Research Statement & Publications:** Product development. **Mailing Address:** 8880 Livingston Rd, Cincinnati, OH 45251. **E-Mail:** tjlogancin@aol.com

LOGAN, TERRY JAMES, SOIL CHEMISTRY. **Personal Data:** b Georgetown, Guyana, February 6, 1943; American citizen; m 1973, c 2. **Education:** Calif Polytech State Univ, BS, 1966; Ohio State Univ, MS, 1969, PhD (soil sci), 1971. **Professional Experience:** Dir Environ Sci Grad Prog, Ohio State Univ, as of 1995; PROF SOIL CHEM, OHIO STATE UNIV, 1980-; from asst prof to assoc prof, Ohio State Univ, 1972-1980; asst prof soil chem, Ohio Agr Res & Develop Ctr, 1971-1972. **Memberships:** Fel Soil Sci Soc Am; fel Am Soc Agron; Int Soil Sci Soc; Soil Conserv Soc Am; Int Asn Great Lakes Res. **Research Statement & Publications:** Non-point sources of pollution; phosphate chemistry of soil and sediments; land disposal of sewage sludge; erosion and sedimentation of agricultural soils. **Mailing Address:** Dept Agron, Sch Nat Resources, Ohio State Univ, 412C Kottman Hall 2021 Coffey Rd, Columbus, OH 43210-1044. **Fax:** 614-292-7162. **E-Mail:** logan.4@osu.edu

LOGCHER, ROBERT DANIEL, CIVIL ENGINEERING, COMPUTER SCIENCE. **Personal Data:** b The Hague, Neth, December 27, 1935; American citizen; m 1963, c 3. **Education:** Mass Inst Technol, BS, 1958, MS, 1960, DSc (civil eng), 1962. **Professional Experience:** Consult, as of 1997; PROF EMER CIVIL & ENVIRON ENG, MASS INST TECHNOL, 1996-; MEM, BD ADV, KRI MGT INC, LEXINGTON, 1985-; from asst prof to prof, Mass Inst Technol, 1962-1996; Ford Found fel, 1962-1964; dir & sr consult, Eng Comput Int, Inc, Mass. **Memberships:** Am Soc Civil Engrs; Asn Comput Mach; Sigma Xi. **Research Statement & Publications:** Application of digital computer to structural design; development of computer-aided design techniques; design process; management of constructed facility projects; information systems. **Mailing Address:** Dept Civil & Environ Eng, Mass Inst Technol, Rm 1-376 77 Mass Ave, Cambridge, MA 02139. **Fax:** 617-253-6324. **E-Mail:** logcher@mit.edu

LOGDBERG, LENNART ERIK, CELLULAR BIOLOGY, CELL ADHESION. **Personal Data:** b Lund, Sweden, March 13, 1954; m 1987, Linda A Paul; c Optimus & Kristina. **Education:** Univ Lund, Swed, MD, 1982, PhD, 1982. **Professional Experience:** SR ASSOC FEL, SANDOZ RES INST, 1992-; assoc fel, Sandoz Res Inst, 1989-1991; head, Immunol Dept, BioCarb AB, Sweden, 1988; vis fel, Lab Immunol, Nat Inst Allergy & Infectious Dis, NIH, Bethesda, 1983-1984; Asst prof, Dept Anat, Univ Lund, Sweden, 1982-1988. **Memberships:** Clin Immunol Soc; Am Asn Immunologists; Swed Med Asn; Int Soc Develop & Comp Immunol. **Research Statement & Publications:** Cell adhesion/integrin biology and sepsis; therapeutic monoclonal antibodies; structure and function of T lymphocytes antigens; co-author of 40 scientific publications. **Mailing Address:** Sandoz Res Inst 59 Rte 10, Bldg 404, East Hanover, NJ 07936. **Fax:** 973-503-6870.

LOGEMANN, JERILYN ANN, SPEECH PATHOLOGY. **Personal Data:** b Berwyn, Ill, May 21, 1942. **Education:** Northwestern Univ, Chicago, BA, 1963, MS, 1964, PhD (speech path), 1968. **Honors & Awards:** Ill DiCarlo Award, Ill Speech-Lang-Hearing Asn, 1988; One Award, Except Lifetime Contrib Commun Dis, Vanderbilt Univ, 1990; Presidential Citation, Am Head & Neck Soc, 1999. **Professional Experience:** RALPH & JEAN SUNDIN PROF, DEPT COMMUN SCI & DIS, 1995-; chmn, Dept Commun Sci & Dis, Northwestern Univ, 1982-1996; PROF, DEPT OTOLARYNGOL-HEAD & NECK SUR & NEUROL, FEINBERG SCH MED, NORTHWESTERN UNIV, CHICAGO, 1983-; prof, Cleft Palate, Northwestern Univ Dent Sch, 1983-2001; from asst prof to assoc prof, Northwestern Univ, Chicago, 1974-1983; assoc attend staff, Northwestern Mem Hosp, 1973-; consult, Downey Vet Admin Hosp, 1973-1976; res assoc, Northwestern Univ, Chicago, 1970-1974; instr, Dept Communicative Dis, Mundelein Col, 1967-1971; NIH fel, Northwestern Univ, Chicago, 1968-1970; fel, Inst Med Chicago; instr, Speech & Audiol, DePaul Univ, 1964-1965; grad asst, Dept Communicative Dis, Northwestern Univ, 1963-1968. **Memberships:** Am Speech & Hearing Asn; Linguistic Soc Am; Sigma Xi; fel Am Speech Lang & Hearing Asn. **Research Statement & Publications:** Speech science; laryngeal physiology; voice disorders; swallowing physiology; dysphagia. **Mailing Address:** Dept Commun Sci & Dis, Northwestern Univ, Frances Searle Bldg Rm 3-358 2240 Campus Dr, Evanston, IL 60208-2952. **Fax:** 847-491-5692. **E-Mail:** j-logemann@northwestern.edu

LOGGINS, DONALD ANTHONY, HEAVY METAL DYNAMICS. **Personal Data:** b Brooklyn, NY, June 13, 1951. **Education:** City Univ NY, BA, 1974; C W Post Col, NY, MPA, 1976. **Honors & Awards:** US Environ Protection Agency Award, 1979. **Professional Experience:** HRA-MIS, TASK FORCE NY, 1981-; staff analyst environ protection & eng, Task Force NY, 1979-1981; vpres, G G Inc, 1977-1979; consult, NY Consult Group, 1976-; consult, urban design, Coun Environ NY, 1976-1977. **Memberships:** Nat Audubon Soc; Am Mgt Asn; Am Planning Asn. **Research Statement & Publications:** Effects of lead and cadmium in urban soils and flora; urban soil science; environmental design of urban spaces. **Mailing Address:** 723 E Tenth St, Brooklyn, NY 11230. **Fax:** 212-206-3652.

LOGGINS, PHILLIP EDWARDS, ANIMAL NUTRITION. **Personal Data:** b Yorkville, Tenn, February 12, 1921; m 1942, c 2. **Education:** Okla State Univ, BS, 1952, MS, 1953. **Professional Experience:** RETIRED; prof animal husb, Agr Exp Sta, 1974-1990; animal husbandman, Agr Exp Sta, 1955-1990; from asst prof to assoc prof, Univ Fla, 1955-1974; instr animal husb, Univ Fla, 1953-1955. **Memberships:** Am Soc Animal Sci. **Research Statement & Publications:** Animal nutrition; parasitic effect on nutritional requirements; feeding requirements of animals during reproduction. **Mailing Address:** 1625 NW 14th Ave, Gainesville, FL 32608.

LOGIN, ROBERT BERNARD, ORGANIC CHEMISTRY, POLYMER CHEMISTRY. **Personal Data:** b Brooklyn, NY, November 15, 1942; m 1971, Lisa; c Joshua & Jason. **Education:** Brooklyn Col, BA, 1966; Purdue Univ, PhD (org chem), 1970. **Professional Experience:** VPRES TECHNOL, SYBRON CHEM INC/TANATEX, 1996-; dir polymer sci & prin scientist, ISP Corp, 1993-1996; dir polymer sci res & develop, Gaf Chem Corp, 1988-1993; dir surfactants & specialties res & develop, Gaf Chem Corp, 1985-1988; tech dir, Jordan Chem Co, 1980-1985; supvr fiber specialities, BASF-Wyandotte Corp, 1975-1980; sect head, BASF-Wyandotte Corp, 1974-1975; sr chemist, BASF-Wyandotte Corp, 1973-1974; Chemist paper specialties, Spring House Lab, Rohm & Haas Co, 1970-1973. **Memberships:** Am Chem Soc; Am Asn Textile Chemists & Colorists; Soc Cosmetic Chemists. **Research Statement & Publications:** Synthesis and applications of polymers and specialties derived from acetylenic-based intermediates; specialty polymers and surfactants. **Mailing Address:** 30 Bark Ct, Travelers Rest, SC 29690.

LOGOTHETIS, ANESTIS LEONIDAS, POLYMER CHEMISTRY. **Personal Data:** b Thessaloniki, Greece, June 29, 1934; c 2. **Education:** Grinnell Col, BA, 1955; Mass Inst Technol, PhD (org chem), 1958. **Professional Experience:** RES FEL, E I DUPONT DEL NEMOURS & CO, INC, 1983-; div head fluoroelastomer res, Cent Res Dept, E I Du Pont Del Nemours & Co, Inc, 1976-1983; supvr develop, Cent Res Dept, E I Du Pont Del Nemours & Co, Inc, 1972-1976; Elastomers Dept, Cent Res Dept, E I Du Pont Del Nemours & Co, Inc, 1966-1972; Res chemist, Cent Res Dept, E I Du Pont Del Nemours & Co, Inc, 1958-1966. **Memberships:** Am Chem Soc. **Research Statement & Publications:** Fluoropolymers; development of new products. **Mailing Address:** 2816 Kennedy Rd, Wilmington, DE 19810-3430.

LOGOTHETIS, ELEFTHERIOS MILTIADIS, SOLID STATE DEVICES, ELECTRONIC PROPERTIES OF MATERIALS. **Personal Data:** b Almyros, Greece, American citizen; m 1966, c 2. **Education:** Univ Athens, BS, 1959; Cornell Univ, MS, 1965, PhD (physics), 1967. **Professional Experience:** SR STAFF SCIENTIST, FORD RES LAB, FORD MOTOR CO, 1992-; Adj prof physics, Wayne State Univ, 1982-; prin res scientist, Ford Motor Co, 1981-1992; staff scientist, Ford Motor Co, 1976-1981; prin res scientist assoc, Ford Motor Co, 1972-1976; Res scientist, Ford Motor Co, 1967-1972. **Memberships:** Fel Am Phys Soc; Mat Res Soc. **Research Statement & Publications:** Electrical and optical properties of semiconductors, metal oxides, layered compounds, ionic materials and high temperature superconductors; defect chemistry and gas/solid interactions; solid state devices such as gas, optical and general automotive sensors. **Mailing Address:** Ford Motor Co, MD 3028, PO Box 2053, Dearborn, MI 48121-2053. **Fax:** 313-322-7044. **E-Mail:** elogothe@ford.com

LOGOTHETOPOULOS, J, MEDICINE, PHYSIOLOGY. **Personal Data:** b Athens, Greece, March 12, 1918; Canadian citizen; m 1953, c 1. **Education:** Nat Univ Athens, MD, 1941; Univ Toronto, PhD (physiol), 1962. **Professional Experience:** EMER PROF, BANTING & BEST DEPT MED RES, UNIV TORONTO, 1988-; From asst prof to prof, Banting & Best Dept Med Res, Univ Toronto, 1959-1988; fel med res, Banting & Best Dept Med Res, Univ Toronto, 1956-1959; Res fel, Postgrad Med Sch, Univ London, 1952-1956. **Memberships:** Am Diabetes Asn; Am Soc Exp Path; Can Physiol Soc. **Research Statement & Publications:** Structure and function of the thyroid and the pituitary gland; experimental diabetes; structure and function of the islets of Langerhans. **Mailing Address:** Banting & Best Dept Med Res Univ Toronto, C H Best Inst Rm 410 112 College St, Toronto, ON M5G 1L6, Can.

LOGSDON, CHARLES ELDON, PLANT PATHOLOGY. **Personal Data:** b Mo, May 8, 1921; m 1948, Arloine; c Charles L, Onnalie M & John C. **Education:** Univ Kansas City, AB, 1942; Univ Minn, PhD, 1954. **Professional Experience:** Consult, Pleasant Green N, 1986-1992; EMER PROF PLANT PATH, UNIV ALASKA, 1978-; pres, Agresources Co, 1978-1985; assoc dir, Inst Agr Sci, 1971-1978; prof, Univ Alaska, 1968-1978; plant pathologist, Univ Alaska, 1953-1971; res prof plant path, Univ Alaska, 1953-1968. **Memberships:** Am Phytopath Soc. **Research Statement & Publications:** Potato and vegetable diseases. **Mailing Address:** PO Box 387, Palmer, AK 99645-0387.

LOGSDON, DONALD FRANCIS, JR, BIOLOGY, MEDICAL TECHNOLOGY. **Personal Data:** b Chicago, Ill, March 7, 1940; m 1963, Nancy Graham; c David, Christopher, Cynthia & Valory. **Education:** Northwestern Univ, BA, 1961; Trinity Univ, MS, 1970; LaSalle Exten Univ, LLB, 1972; Colo State Univ, PhD (zool), 1975; Thomas A Edison Col, BS, 1977; Chapman Col, MAEd, 1982, BA, 1983, ms, 1985, MA, 1987, MA, 1990; Nat Univ, MS, 1994, MA (Mgt), MBA (bus A. **Professional Experience:** Online instructor: nat Univ, Univ phoenix, union inst, Embry Riddle Univ, Franklin Univ, Southern New Hampshire Univ, 1996-; Sierra Col, Univ Phoenix, 1994-; Sierra Col, Nat Univ, 1993-; Sierra Col, Golden Gate Univ, 1993-; instr, English as Second Lang, Bach Viet Asn, 1992-; INSTR, ENG AS SECOND LANG, SACRAMENTO SCH DIST, 1990- & BACH VIET ASN, 1992-; Sierra Col, Cosumner River Col, 1990; mkt dir, educ prog coordr & prof, Sacramento Area Residence Educ Ctr, 1981-1990; Sierra Col, Embry-Riddle Aeronaut Univ, 1980; health sci coordr & asst prof, Chapman Col, 1978-1981; Sierra Col, Rocklin, Calif, 1977-1978; Instr life sci, Am River Col, Sacramento, Calif, 1975-1979; from asst chief to chief & staff biomed scientist, USAF Occup Environ Health Lab, 1975-1978; assoc prof, Dept Life Sci, USAF Acad, 1970-1975; chief, Radioisotope Lab, USAF Sch Aerospace Med, 1967-1970; Chief clin lab, 4510th USAF Hosp, Luke AFB, Ariz, 1966-1967. **Memberships:** AAAS; Sigma Xi; Am Indust Hyg Asn; Asn Off Anal Chemists; Am Soc Radiol Technologists. **Research Statement & Publications:** Effects of radiation on living methods for radiation detection; action of radioprotective drugs; comparison of routine plating versus fluorescent antibody methods for the detection of Beta Streptococcus; medical technology. **Mailing Address:** 7341 Spicer Dr, Citrus Heights, CA 95621. **E-Mail:** logsdond@hotmail.com

LOGSDON, JOHN MORTIMER, III, SPACE POLICY. **Personal Data:** b Cincinnati, Ohio, October 17, 1937. **Education:** Xavier Univ, BS, 1960; NY Univ, PhD, 1970. **Honors & Awards:** NASA Distinguished Pub Serv Medal, 2001. **Professional Experience:** PROF EMER POLIT SCI & INT AFFAIRS, GEORGE WASH UNIV, as of 2006; RES PROF, SPACE POLICY & INT AFFAIRS, as of 2006; dir, Ctr Int Sci & Technol Policy, 1989-2002; DIR, SPACE POLICY INST, 1987-; prof polit sci & int affairs, George Wash Univ, beginning 1970. **Memberships:** AAAS; fel Am Inst Aeronaut & Astronaut; Int Acad Astronaut. **Research Statement & Publications:** Evolution, current status and future prospects of the US civilian space program and its relationships with the space programs of other countries; issues of national science and technology policy. **Mailing Address:** Space Policy Inst, Elliott Sch Int Affairs, George Wash Univ, 1957 E St NW Ste 403, Washington, DC 20052. **Fax:** 202-994-1639. **E-Mail:** logsdon@gwu.edu

LOGSDON, SALLY D, SOIL PHYSICS. **Personal Data:** b Grand Rapids, Mich, 1957. **Education:** Cedarville Col, BA, 1979; Mich State Univ, MS, 1981; Va Tech Inst & State Univ, PhD (soil physics), 1985. **Professional Experience:** ASSOC PROF, IOWA STATE UNIV, as of 2006; SOIL SCIENTIST, NAT SOIL TILTH LAB, AGR RES SERV, USDA, 1990-; asst prof & collabr agron & water resources, Iowa State Univ, beginning 1990; res assoc, Soil & Water Group, St Paul, 1987-1990; vis asst prof biol, Wilmington Col, 1986-1987. **Memberships:** Soil Sci Soc Am; Am Soc Agron. **Research Statement & Publications:** Preserving soil quality and soil structure; soil water cycle and plant use. **Mailing Address:** Nat Soil Tilth Lab, 2150 Pammel Dr, Ames, IA 50011-3120. **Fax:** 515-294-8125. **E-Mail:** logsdon@nstl.gov

LOGUE, JAMES NICHOLAS, EPIDEMIOLOGY. **Personal Data:** b Pittston, Pa, June 18, 1946; m 1972, Mary; c Melissa, Jimmy & Jeffrey. **Education:** King's Col, BS, 1968; Univ Mich, MPH, 1971; Columbia Univ, DrPH(epidemiol), 1978. **Professional Experience:** DIR, DIV ENVIRON HEALTH EPIDOMIOLOGY, PA DEPT HEALTH, 1982-; chief, Epidemiol Sect, Epidemiol Studies Br, US Food & Drug Admin Bur Radiol Health, 1980-1982; sr environ epidemiologist mgt consult, Geomet, Inc, 1978-1980; sr med biostatistician, Ciba-Geigy Pharmaceut Co, 1973-1978; statistician pharmaceut res, Warner-Lambert Res Inst, 1971-1973. **Memberships:** Soc Epidemiol Res; fel Am Col Epidemiol; Am Pub Health Asn; AAAS. **Research Statement & Publications:** Chronic disease; epidemiology; environmental and occupational epidemiology; clinical trials research; mental health research; disaster research. **Mailing Address:** Pa Dept Health, Bur Epidemiol, Rm 933, Harrisburg, PA 17011. **Fax:** 717-772-6975. **E-Mail:** jlogue@state.pa.us

LOGUE, J(OSEPH) C(ARL), TECHNICAL CONSULTING. **Personal Data:** b Philadelphia, Pa, December 20, 1920; m 1943, c Raymond, Marilyn, Paul. **Education:** Cornell Univ, BEE, 1944, MEE, 1949. **Professional Experience:** Mem, Eval Comt, Nat Acad Eng Electronics, 1989-1992; CONSULT TO INDUST, 1986-; dir packaging technol & systs, Corp Tech Comt, 1986; fel, Eval Comt, Inst Elec & Electronics Engrs, 1984-1986; mgr technol & design systs, Corp Tech Comt, 1977-1985; dir, Corp Tech Comt, 1967-1977; mgr adv logic tech develop, IBM, 1964-1967; mgr adv tech systs, IBM, 1963-1964; mgr tech develop, IBM, 1959-1963; mgr explor eng, IBM, 1958-1959; mgr solid state circuit develop, IBM, 1957-1958; Secy, Int Solid State Circuits Conf, 1957; mgr mach develop, IBM, 1956-1957; develop engr, IBM, 1955-1956; proj engr, IBM, 1953-1955; tech engr, IBM, 1951-1953; asst prof spec assignment, Brookhaven Nat Lab, 1949-1951; Instr elec eng, Cornell Univ, 1944-1949. **Memberships:** Nat Acad Eng; fel AAAS; fel Inst Elec & Electronics Engrs; Sigma Xi. **Research Statement & Publications:** Development and application of new discoveries to advanced digital computers and systems; solid state devices and their applications; electronic aids to aircraft navigation. **Mailing Address:** 52 Boardman Rd, Poughkeepsie, NY 12603.

LOGUE, MARSHALL WOFORD, CHEMICAL SYNTHESIS. **Personal Data:** b Danville, Ky, June 4, 1942; m 1980, Joan; c Timothy & Lauren. **Education:** Centre Col Ky, AB, 1964; Ohio State Univ, PhD (chem), 1969. **Professional Experience:** Mem, Comt Nomenclature, Am Chem Soc, 1997-1999; chair, Org Exam Comt, ACS DIVCHED Exam Inst, 1988-1995; ASSOC PROF CHEM, MICH TECH UNIV, 1981-; mem, Org Exam Comt, ACS DIVCHED Exam Inst, 1978-1995; asst prof chem, NDak State Univ, 1977-1981; asst prof chem, Univ Md, Baltimore Co, 1971-1977; res assoc chem, Univ Ill, 1969-1971. **Memberships:** NY Acad Sci; AAAS; Am Chem Soc; Royal Soc Chem; Sigma Xi; Int Soc Nucleosides Nucleotides & Nucleic Acids. **Research Statement & Publications:** Synthetic organic chemistry; bio-organic chemistry; pyrimidines; nucleosides; synthesis of carbohydrates and nucleosides. **Mailing Address:** Dept Chem, Mich Tech Univ, 610 ChemSci 1400 Townsend Dr, Houghton, MI 49931-1295. **Fax:** 906-487-2061. **E-Mail:** mwlogue@mtu.edu

LOGULLO, FRANCIS MARK, ORGANIC POLYMER CHEMISTRY. **Personal Data:** b Wilmington, Del, December 19, 1939; m 1962, c 3. **Education:** Univ Del, BS, 1961; Case Inst Technol, PhD (org chem), 1965. **Professional Experience:** CONSULT, MSDS CONSULT, as of 2003; SR FORENSIC CONSUL, GLOBAL CHEM AFFAIRS, AM SOC ASSOC INC, 2000-; REGULATORY AFFAIRS CONSULT, 1993-; regulatory affairs consult, E I du Pont Del Nemours & Co Inc, 1990-1993; res assoc, E I du Pont Del Nemours & Co Inc, 1977-1990; sr res chemist, E I du Pont Del Nemours & Co Inc, 1970-1977; res chemist, E I du Pont Del Nemours & Co Inc, 1965-1970. **Memberships:** Am Chem Soc. **Research Statement & Publications:** Polymer chemistry; synthetic fibers; chemistry of arynes; regulatory affairs. **Mailing Address:** MSDS Consult, 5210 Wayland Dr, Hockessin, DE 19707-9724. **Fax:** 302-239-3172. **E-Mail:** frank.logullo@dol.net

LOH, EDWIN DIN, PHYSICS. **Personal Data:** b Suchow, China, January 21, 1948; American citizen; c 1. **Education:** Calif Inst Technol, BS, 1969; Princeton Univ, PhD (physics), 1977. **Professional Experience:** ASSOC PROF ASTRONOMY & ASTRO PHYSICS, MICH STATE UNIV, 1987-; from instr to asst prof physics, Princeton Univ, 1976-1987; physicist, US Army Missile Command, 1969-1971. **Research Statement & Publications:** Astrophysics; photometric redshifts of galaxies. **Mailing Address:** Mich State Univ, 1219 BMPS Bldg, E Lansing, MI 48824-1116. **E-Mail:** loh@pa.msu.edu

LOH, EUGENE C, cosmic ray, high energy; deceased, see previous edition for last biography

LOH, HORACE H, BIOCHEMISTRY, BIOCHEMICAL PHARMACOLOGY. **Personal Data:** b Canton, China, May 28, 1936; m 1962, c 2. **Education:** Nat Taiwan Univ, BS, 1958; Univ Iowa, PhD (biochem), 1965. **Honors & Awards:** Humboldt Award Sr US Scientists, 1977; Merit Award, Nat Inst Drug Abuse, 1988; Hamilton Davis Lectr in Neuroscience, Sch Med, Univ Calif, Davis, 1988; Pfizer Lectr, Med Col Wis, Milwaukee, 1988; Otto Krayer Award, Am Soc Pharmacol & Exp Therapeutics, 1999. **Professional Experience:** DIR MOLECULAR & CELL BIOL, BASIC RES CTR, UNIV MINN, MINNEAPOLIS, as of 2004; assoc ed, Annual Rev Pharmacol & Toxicol, 1990-; FREDERICK & ALICE STARK PROF NEUROSCIENCE, DEPT PHARMACOL, MED SCH, UNIV MINN, MINNEAPOLIS, 1990-; HEAD, DEPT PHARMACOL, MED SCH, UNIV MINN, MINNEAPOLIS, 1989-; chmn, Spec Rev Comt Drug Develop, 1989 & Drug Abuse AIDS Res Rev Comt, 1989-1993; assoc ed, CRC Critical Rev Pharmacol Sci, 1987-1988; chmn, Biochem Subcomt, Biomed Res Rev Comt, Nat Inst Drug Abuse, 1986-1988; chair, Biomed Res Rev Comt, Nat Inst Drug Abuse, 1986-1988; wellcome vis prof award pharmacol, Fedn Am Socs Exp Biol & Burroughs Wellcome Labs, 1985; mem, Biomed Res Rev Comt, Nat Inst Drug Abuse, 1984-1988; USPHS res scientist award, 1983-1988, 1989-1994; consult, US Army Res &Develop, Dept Defense, 1980-1984; mem, Preclin Psychopharmacol Study Sect, NIMH, 1977-1979 & Basic Psychopharmacol & Neuropsychopharmacol Res Rev Comt, 1980-1981; USPHS career develop award, 1973-1978 & 1978-1983; from assoc prof to prof, Dept Psychiat & Dept Pharmacol, Sch Med, Univ Calif, San Francisco, 1972-1988; chief, Drug Dependence Res Ctr, Mendocino State Hosp, Talmage, Calif, 1971-1972; res specialist, Langley Porte Neuropsychiat Inst, 1970-1972; assoc prof biochem pharmacol, Wayne State Univ, 1968-1970; asst res pharmacologist, Univ Calif, San Francisco, 1967-1968; lectr biochem pharmacol, Univ Calif, San Francisco, 1967; fel biochem, Univ Calif, San Francisco, 1965-1966. **Memberships:** Am Chem Soc; Am Soc Pharm Exp Therapeut; Am Col Neuropsychopharmacol; Soc Chinese Bioscientists Am; Western Pharmacol Soc. **Research Statement & Publications:** Opiate receptors; mechanisms of drug tolerance. **Mailing Address:** Dept Pharmacol, Univ Minn, 6-120 Jackson 321 Church St SE, Minneapolis, MN 55455-0217. **Fax:** 612-625-8408. **E-Mail:** lohxx001@umn.edu

LOH, IH-HOUNG, BIOMEDICAL ENGINEERING. **Honorary Degrees:** ScD. **Professional Experience:** PRES, BUS DEVELOP, ADVANCED SURFACE TECH INC, MASS, as of 2006. **Mailing Address:** Advanced Surface Tech Inc, 9 Linnell Cir, Billerica, MA 01821-3902. **E-Mail:** iloh@astp.com

LOH, PHILIP CHOO-SENG, ANIMAL VIROLOGY. **Personal Data:** b Singapore, September 14, 1925; American citizen; m 1955, Susie; c Valerie K H & Rhonda K H. **Education:** Morningside Col, BS, 1950; Univ Iowa, MS, 1953; Univ Mich, MPH, 1954, PhD, 1958; Am Bd Microbiol, dipl, 1963. **Professional Experience:** RETIRED; chmn, Univ Hawaii, 1985-1991; vis sr scientist, NIH, 1982; vis prof, Dept Pathol, Sch Med, Univ Bristol, UK, 1975; Eleanor Roosevelt int cancer fel, Int Union Against Cancer, Geneva, 1975; USPH spec res fel, NIH, 1967-1968; prof virol, Univ Hawaii, beginning 1966; assoc prof, Univ Hawaii, 1961-1966; asst prof, Virus Lab, Univ Mich, 1961; res assoc, Virus Lab, Univ Mich, 1958-1960. **Memberships:** Fel AAAS; Am Asn Immunol; Am Soc Microbiol; Soc Exp Biol & Med; Am Soc Virol; fel Am Acad Microbiol; Soc In Vitro Biol. **Research Statement & Publications:** Biosynthesis and pathobiology of animal viruses at the cellular level and environmental virology; viral diseases of marine animals and development of animal cell culture systems. **Mailing Address:** 2552 Peter St, Honolulu, HI 96822.

LOH, ROLAND RU-LOONG, HIGH TEMPERATURE SUPERCONDUCTING MATERIALS, STRUCTURAL & ELECTRONIC CERAMICS. **Personal Data:** b Shanghai, China, August 1, 1942; m 1973, Grace A; c Lucian X. **Education:** Shanghai Iron & Steel Inst, BS, 1963; Univ Calif, Berkeley, MS, 1985. **Professional Experience:** Prin investr, Dept Energy, 1989-1990 & NASA, 1991-; collabr, Los Alamos Nat Lab, 1991-1993; DIR RES & DEVELOP, ADVAN CERAMETRICS, INC, 1988-; sr engr, Lambertville Ceramic Mfg Co, 1986-1988; staff scientist, Lawrence Berkeley Nat Lab, 1983-1985; vis scholar, Univ Calif, Berkeley, 1982-1983; Consult, Shanghai Bao-Shan Iron & Steel Complex, 1978-1980; dir res & develop, Dept Ceramics, 1976-1981; engr, Shanghai Iron & Steel Co, 1966-1975; Lectr math, Iron & Steel Col, Shanghai, 1964-1965. **Memberships:** Am Ceramic Soc; Mat Res Soc. **Research Statement & Publications:** Transfering scientific concept and result into production implementation; advanced ceramics and composite materials; author of more than 40 publications; technology transfer and joint venture between United States companies and Far East countries' companies. **Mailing Address:** 1226 Pemeroke, Newark, OH 43055. **Fax:** 609-265-1718.

LOH, YOKE PENG, CELLULAR NEUROBIOL, MOLECULAR ENDOCRINOLOGY. **Personal Data:** b Singapore, July 27, 1947; American citizen; m 1987, c 1. **Education:** Univ Col Dublin, BSc, 1969; Univ Penn, PhD (molecular biol), 1973. **Honors & Awards:** Super Serv Award, Pub Health Serv. **Professional Experience:** Adj prof biochem, Uniform Serv Univ Health Sci, Bethesda, 1990-; SECT CHIEF, NIH, 1983-; res chemist, NIH, 1979-1983; sr staff fel, NIH, 1976-1979; vis fel, NIH, 1974-1976. **Memberships:** Am Soc Cell Biol; Soc Neuroscience; Endocrinol Soc; Soc Neurochem. **Research Statement & Publications:** Mechanisms involved in the intracellular trafficking and sorting of pro-hormones and pro-neuropeptides into regulated secretory granules for processing by unique proteolytic enzymes. **Mailing Address:** Sect Cellular Neurobiol, Lab Develop Neurobiol, Nat Inst Child Health Develop, NIH, Rm 5A38 Bldg 49 49 Convent Dr MSC 2280, Bethesda, MD 20892-4480. **Fax:** 301-496-9939.

LOHER, WERNER J, ZOOLOGY. **Personal Data:** b Landshut, Ger, June 27, 1929; m 1961, c 1. **Education:** Univ Munich, PhD (zoology), 1955; Univ London, PhD (entom) & DIC, 1959. **Honors & Awards:** A V Humboldt Sr Distinguished Sci Award. **Professional Experience:** PROF EMER, UNIV CALIF, BERKELEY, AS OF 2006; dir, Gump SPac Biol Res Sta, Moorea, French, Polynesia, beginning 1985; mem, Acad Sci & Lit, Mainz, 1983; prof entom, Univ Calif, Berkeley, beginning 1970; assoc prof, Univ Calif, Berkeley, 1967-1970; vis lectr, Glasgow Univ, 1967; pvt docent, Univ Tubingen, 1965-1967; asst prof zoophysiol, Univ Tubingen, 1960-1965; sr res award, Antilocust Res Ctr, Eng, 1956-1959. **Memberships:** AAAS; Animal Behav Soc; Brit Soc Exp Biol; Ger Zool Soc. **Research Statement & Publications:** Hormonal control of reproduction in insects. **Mailing Address:** Dept Entom, Univ Calif, Berkeley, CA 94720-0001.

LOHMAN, TIMOTHY GEORGE, BODY COMPOSITION. **Personal Data:** b Park Ridge, NJ, December 10, 1940; m 1961, c 4. **Education:** Univ Ill, Urbana, BS, 1962, MS, 1964, PhD (body compos), 1967. **Professional Experience:** DIR CTR PHYS ACTIV & NUTRIT, UNIV ARIZ, as of 2005; PROF, DEPT PHYSIOL, UNIV ARIZ, as of 2006; adj prof, Dept Physiol, Univ Ariz, as of 2002; prof, Dept Exercise & Sports Sci, Univ Ariz, beginning 1984; assoc prof phys educ, Univ Ill, Urbana, 1977-1983; asst prof body compos animals & man, Dept Animal Sci, Univ Ill, Urbana, 1969-1977; res assoc whole-body counting, Univ Ill, Urbana, 1967-1969. **Memberships:** AAAS; Am Col Sports Med; Soc Study Human Biol; Am Acad Phys Educ; Am Alliance Health Phys Educ & Recreation. **Research Statement & Publications:** Exercise physiology; human body composition; physical exercise and body compositional and nutrition. **Mailing Address:** Dept Health Phys Educ, Univ Ariz, PO Box 210093, 1600 E Univ Blvd, Tucson, AZ 85721-0001. **E-Mail:** lohman@email.arizona.edu

LOHMAN, TIMOTHY MICHAEL, BIOPHYSICAL CHEMISTRY, PROTEIN DNA INTERACTIONS. **Personal Data:** b Rockville Ctr, NY, June 2, 1951; m 1978, c 2. **Education:** Cornell Univ, Ithaca, AB, 1973; Univ Wis-Madison, PhD (phys chem), 1977. **Professional Experience:** MARVIN A BRENNECKE PROF BIOL CHEM, SCH MED WASH UNIV, as of 2005; PROF BIOCHEM & MOLECULAR BIOPHYS, WASH UNIV, 1990-; assoc prof biochem, biophys & chem, 1985-1990; asst prof biochem & biophys, Tex A&M Univ, 1981-1985; NIH fel, Univ Ore, 1979-1981; res asst biophys chem, Univ Calif, San Diego, 1977-1979. **Memberships:** Biophys Soc; Am Soc Biochem & Molecular Biol; AAAS. **Research Statement & Publications:** Thermodynamics and kinetics of macromolecular interactions; mechanisms of DNA helicases (motor proteins); protein-nucleic acid interactions involved in DNA replication, recombination and control of gene expressions. **Mailing Address:** Dept Biochem & Molecular Biophys, Sch Med, Wash Univ, Box 8231 2801 N Bldg, St Louis, MO 63110. **Fax:** 314-362-7183. **E-Mail:** lohman@biochem.wustl.edu

LOHNER, DONALD J, ORGANIC CHEMISTRY. **Personal Data:** b Brooklyn, NY, March 10, 1939. **Education:** Queens Col, BS, 1961; Adelphi Univ, PhD (org chem), 1966. **Professional Experience:** RETIRED; res fel, E I Du Pont De Nemours & Co Inc, 1989-1992; sr res assoc, E I Du Pont De Nemours & Co Inc, 1985-1989; res assoc, E I Du Pont De Nemours & Co Inc, 1976-1985; res chemist, E I Du Pont De Nemours & Co Inc, 1966-1976; instr chem, Adelphi Univ, 1964-1966. **Memberships:** Am Chem Soc. **Mailing Address:** 33 Willow Lane, Englishtown, NJ 07726.

LOHNES, ROBERT ALAN, GEOTECHNICAL ENGINEERING, GEOLOGY. **Personal Data:** b Springfield, Ohio, February 5, 1937; div, c 2. **Education:** Ohio State Univ, BSc, 1959; Iowa State Univ, MS, 1961, PhD (soil eng, geol), 1964. **Professional Experience:** PROF EMER CIVIL, CONSTRUCT & ENVIRON ENG, IOWA STATE UNIV, as of 2006; prof civil eng, beginning 1974; vis assoc prof civil eng, Middle E Tech Univ, Ankara, Turkey, 1973-1974; from asst prof to assoc prof, Iowa State Univ, 1965-1974; asst prof, Wis State Univ, River Falls, 1964-1965; instr, Iowa State Univ, 1962-1964; asst geol, Iowa State Univ, 1959-1962. **Memberships:** Am Soc Civil Engrs; Am Geophys Union; Geol Soc Am; Am Rwy Engr Asn; Int Soc Soil Mech & Found Engrs. **Research Statement & Publications:** Applied geomorphology; soil creep and shear strength; engineering properties of tropical soils; quantitative geomorphology; mechanics of bulk solids; loads on buried pipes; Landslides; Physical-chemistry Properties of Soil. **Mailing Address:** Dept Civil Eng, Iowa State Univ, 488 Town, Ames, IA 50011-9012. **Fax:** 515-294-8216. **E-Mail:** rlohnes@iastate.edu

LOHR, D(ELMAR) FREDERICK, POLYMER CHEMISTRY. **Personal Data:** b Madison Co, Va, September 9, 1934. **Education:** Va Polytech Inst, BS, 1962; Duke Univ, MA, 1963, PhD (chem), 1965. **Professional Experience:** RETIRED; res assoc, Bridgestone/Firestone, Inc, 1988-1994; res assoc, Firestone Tire & Rubber Co, 1984-1988; assoc scientist, Firestone Tire & Rubber Co, 1978-1983; sr res scientist, Firestone Tire & Rubber Co, 1970-1977; res org chemist, Firestone Tire & Rubber Co, 1965-1970. **Memberships:** Am Chem Soc; Sigma Xi. **Research Statement & Publications:** Synthesis and reactions of aromatic heterocycles, particularly those containing both nitrogen and sulfur; polymer synthesis and characterization. **Mailing Address:** 200 Casterton Ave, Akron, OH 44303-1517.

LOHR, DENNIS EVAN, PHYSICAL BIOCHEMISTRY, GENE EXPRESSION. **Personal Data:** b Waukegan, Ill, January 12, 1944. **Education:** Beloit Col, BA, 1965; Univ NC, Chapel Hill, PhD (biochem), 1969. **Professional Experience:** PROF BIOCHEM, COL LIB ARTS & SCI, ARIZ STATE UNIV, 1991-; from asst prof to prof, Ariz State Univ, 1979-1990; res assoc biochem, Ore State Univ, 1972-1979; teacher chem, Peace Corps, Kenya, E Africa, 1970-1971. **Research Statement & Publications:** Enzymatic investigation of the subunit structure of yeast chromatin the chromatin structure of enkaryotic promoters. **Mailing Address:** Dept Chem & Biochem, Col Lib Arts & Sci, Ariz State Univ, PSD-323, Tempe, AZ 85287-1604. **Fax:** 480-965-2747. **E-Mail:** dlohr@asu.edu

LOHR, JAMES E, CHEMISTRY. **Education:** Northwestern Univ, BA; Univ Nebr, PhD (phys chem). **Professional Experience:** CHMN, COLUMBUS MOLECULAR SOFTWARE INC, as of 2005. **Mailing Address:** Columbus Molecular Software Inc, 1275 Kinnear Rd, Columbus, OH 43210. **Fax:** 614-675-3732.

LOHR, JOHN MICHAEL, PLASMA PHYSICS. **Personal Data:** b Chicago, Ill, June 21, 1944. **Education:** Univ Tex, Austin, BS, 1966; Univ Wis-Madison, MS, 1967, PhD (nuclear physics), 1972. **Professional Experience:** PRIN SCIENTIST MGR, DIII D ECH OPERATIONS, GEN ATOMICS CO, as of 2003; STAFF PHYSICIST, GEN ATOMICS CO, SAN DIEGO, 1976-; res assoc plasma physics, Fusion Res Ctr, Univ Tex, Austin, 1972-1976. **Memberships:** Am Phys Soc. **Research Statement & Publications:** Tokamak and plasma physics research. **Mailing Address:** Gen Atomics, PO Box 85608, San Diego, CA 92186-9784. **Fax:** 858-455-4190. **E-Mail:** lohr@fusion.gat.com

LOHR, LAWRENCE LUTHER, THEORETICAL CHEMISTRY. **Personal Data:** b Charlotte, NC, May 29, 1937; m 1963, c 1. **Education:** Univ NC, BS, 1959; Harvard Univ, AM, 1962, PhD (chem), 1964. **Professional Experience:** PROF EMER CHEM, UNIV MICH, ANN ARBOR, as of 2002; prog officer, NSF, Wash, DC, 1996, 1992-1993 & 1988, Univ Nac Auto Mexico, Mex City, 1989; Univ Helsinki, Finland, 1984; vis scientist, Inst Molecular Sci, Okazaki, Japan, 1981; vis prof & scholar, Univ Calif, Berkeley, 1974-1975; prof chem, Univ Mich, Ann Arbor, beginning 1973; consult, Ford Motor Co, 1968-1971 & Bell Tel Labs, 1969 & 1972; res fel, Alfred P Sloan, 1969-1971; assoc prof, Univ Mich, Ann Arbor, 1968-1973; res scientist, Sci Lab, Ford Motor Co, 1965-1968; res assoc chem, Univ Chicago, 1963-1965. **Memberships:** Am Phys Soc; Am Chem Soc; AAAS. **Research Statement & Publications:** Theories of chemical bonding; interpretation of electronic spectra of molecules and solids; relativistic quantum chemistry; reaction mechanisms; rotational dynamics of molecules. **Mailing Address:** Dept Chem, Univ Mich, 1040 Chem Bldg, Ann Arbor, MI 48109. **E-Mail:** llohr@umich.edu

LOHRENGEL, CARL FREDERICK, II, GEOLOGY. **Personal Data:** b Kansas City, Mo, November 24, 1939; m 1971. **Education:** Univ Kansas City, BS, 1962; Univ Mo-Columbia, MA, 1964; Brigham Young Univ, PhD (geol), 1968. **Professional Experience:** PROF GEOL & MATH, SNOW COL, SOUTHERN UTAH UNIV, 1981-; from asst prof to assoc prof, Snow Col, 1969-1981; res assoc, Marine Inst, Univ Ga, 1968-1969. **Memberships:** Am Asn Petrol Geol; Am Inst Prof Geologists; Nat Asn Geol Teachers. **Research Statement & Publications:** Palynology of the Upper Cretaceous of Utah; Upper Cenozoic and modern dinoflagellates of the Georgia coastal plain; Cretaceous stratigraphy of Utah; Upper Cretaceous stratigraphy of Wyoming. **Mailing Address:** Dept Geol, Southern Utah Univ, 351 W Ctr St, Cedar City, UT 84720-2498.

LOHRMANN, ROLF, BIO-ORGANIC CHEMISTRY. **Personal Data:** b Bissingen-Enz, Ger, March 2, 1930; m 1960. **Education:** Stuttgart Tech Univ, dipl(chem), 1958, Dr rer nat(chem), 1960. **Professional Experience:** Assoc res prof, Salk Inst Biol Studies, beginning 1974; sr res assoc, Salk Inst Biol Studies, 1965-1974; Proj assoc, Inst Enzyme Res, Univ Wis, 1962-1965; INVENTOR, MOLECULAR BIOSYSTEMS, INC. **Memberships:** Ger Chem Soc; Am Chem Soc. **Research Statement & Publications:** Prebiotic chemistry; molecular evolution. **Mailing Address:** 3040 Science Park Rd, San Diego, CA 92121.

LOHSE, DAVID JOHN, POLYMER PHYSICS, NEUTRON SCATTERING. **Personal Data:** b New York, NY, September 14, 1952; m 1978, Marisa. **Education:** Mich State Univ, BS (physics) & BS (comput sci), 1974; Univ Ill, PhD (polymer sci), 1978. **Honors & Awards:** Fellow, American Physical Society, 2000; Fellow, American Chemical Society Division of Polymeric Materials; Science and Engineering, 2005. **Professional Experience:** SENIOR RES ASSOC, EXXONMOBIL RES & ENGR CO, 2000-; staff engr, Exxon Res & Engr Co, 1988-2000; sr engr, Exxon Chem Co, 1980-1987; res assoc, Nat Bur Standards, 1978-1980; res asst, Univ Ill, 1974-1978. **Memberships:** Am Phys Soc; Am Chem Soc, mem, councilor, polymeric materials; sci & Engr div, 2003 - present. **Research Statement & Publications:** Physics of polymer systems, especially the morphology and thermodynamics of polymer blends and solutions and their structure-property relations; polymer nanocomposites; effects of long chain branching. **Mailing Address:** 556 Stony Brook Dr, Bridgewater, NJ 08807. **Fax:** 262-313-4775. **E-Mail:** david.j.lohse@exxonmobil.com

LOHUIS, DELMONT JOHN, CHEMISTRY. **Personal Data:** b Oostburg, Wis, January 24, 1914; m 1937, Charlotte; c Ardyth, Arden & Daryl A. **Education:** Carroll Col, Wis, BA, 1934; Univ Wis, MS, 1936. **Professional Experience:** RETIRED; asst to pres, Tech Air Corp, 1975-1978; dir & vpres res & develop, Tech Air Corp, 1961-1964; dir corp res & develop staff, Tech Air Corp, 1970-1975; asst to corp vpres res & develop, Am Can Co, 1960-1961 & 1964-1970; res dept, Am Can Co, 1935-1978. **Memberships:** Am Chem

Soc; fel Am Inst Chem. **Research Statement & Publications:** Container construction materials; pyrolysis and gasification of ligno cellulosic materials; resource recovery from solid wastes; paper based consumer products; specialty chemicals. **Mailing Address:** 1000 Applewood Dr, Roswell, GA 30075.

LOIGMAN, HAROLD, CONSTRUCTION MANAGEMENT, GEOTECHNICAL ENGINEERING. **Personal Data:** b Philadelphia, Pa, January 25, 1930; m 1951, c 2. **Education:** Univ Pittsburgh, BS, 1951; Univ Pa, MS, 1963. **Professional Experience:** TECH SPECIALIST SAFETY, KMJ CONSULT INC, as of 2003; SR CONSULT, DAY & ZIMMERMANN, INC, 1990-; Grad Sch, Villanova Univ, 1988-1989 & Pa State Univ, 1990; adj prof eng, Temple Univ, 1975-1976; cmndg officer, 21st Reserve Construct Battalion, 1974-1976; pres, Site Engrs, Inc, 1972-1990; chief staff, 8th Reserve Naval Construct Regt, 1972-1974; vpres, Valley Forge Labs, Inc, 1968-1972; adj prof eng, Villanova Univ, 1968-1970; Supvry engr, US Army CEngr, 1955-1968; Active reserve officer, Naval Reserve Construct Forces, 1951-1982. **Memberships:** Am Soc Civil Engrs; Soc Am Mil Engrs; Nat Soc Prof Engrs; Am Soc Hwy Engrs; Int Soc Soil Mech & Found Engrs. **Mailing Address:** KMJ Consult, Inc, PO Box 157, 355D Lancaster Ave, Haverford, PA 19041-0157. **Fax:** 610-896-8002.

LOIRE, NORMAN PAUL, ORGANIC CHEMISTRY. **Personal Data:** b St Louis, Mo, May 7, 1927; m 1953, c 3. **Education:** Shurtleff Col, BS, 1951; NY Univ, PhD (chem), 1960. **Professional Experience:** SR RES CHEMIST, MORTON THIOKOL INC, WOODSTOCK, ILL, 1977-; lab mgr, Saber Labs, Wheeling, 1971-1977; sr res chemist, Chemplex Co, 1967-1971; sr res chemist, Narmco Res & Develop Div, Whittaker Corp, 1962-1967; res chemist, Benger Res Lab, TextileFibers Dept, E I du Pont Del Nemours & Co, 1958-1962; Chemist, Ciba Pharmaceut Prod Co, 1952-1954. **Memberships:** Am Chem Soc. **Research Statement & Publications:** Development of new products based on water-borne polymer systems. **Mailing Address:** 36113 Karcher Rd, Burlington, WI 53105.

LOIZZI, ROBERT FRANCIS, MILK SECRETION, CELL BIOLOGY. **Personal Data:** b Oak Park, Ill, October 18, 1935; m 1960, Charlotte M Nichols; c Robert G, Mary-Frances T (Zimmerman), Christopher M & John F. **Education:** Loyola Univ, Ill, BS, 1957; Marquette Univ, MS, 1960; Iowa State Univ, PhD (cell biol), 1966. **Professional Experience:** Prof emer, physiol & biophys, 1999 DIR, res RESOURCE S CTR WEST, 1997-; asst dir, Res Resources Ctr, 1986-1997; Assoc dean, Sch Basic Med Sci, Col Med, 1980-1981; PROF PHYSIOL, UNIV ILL, 1978-; from asst prof to assoc prof, Resource Ctr West Facil, 1966-1978; Instr physiol, Iowa State Univ, 1965-1966. **Memberships:** Non mem AAAS; Am Soc Cell Biol; Am Physiol Soc. **Research Statement & Publications:** Regulation and cell biology of mammary gland; cytoskeleton and milk secretion; hormonal regulation of microtubules; cyclic nucleotides and lactose synthesis; mammary tumor growth; fine structure of secretory processes. **Mailing Address:** 135 E View, Lombard, IL 60148.

LOK, ROGER, ORGANIC CHEMISTRY. **Personal Data:** b Macao, October 19, 1943; American citizen; m 1970, c 2. **Education:** Univ Calif, Berkeley, BS, 1966; Univ Wash, PhD (org chem), 1971. **Professional Experience:** RES CHEMIST, EASTMAN KODAK CO, 1974-; fel, Dept Pharmacol, Yale Univ, 1971-1974. **Memberships:** Am Chem Soc; Sigma Xi. **Research Statement & Publications:** Organic synthesis; preparation of dyes; enzyme immobilization; affinity chromatography; synthesis of photographically active compounds; study of photographically active compounds. **Mailing Address:** 204 Dorchester Rd, Rochester, NY 14610-1327.

LOKAY, JOSEPH DONALD, CHEMICAL ENGINEERING. **Personal Data:** b Chicago, Ill, December 17, 1929; m 1954, LaVerne; c Joe, William, Barbara & James. **Education:** Ill Inst Technol, BS, 1952, MS, 1953, PhD (chem eng), 1955. **Professional Experience:** PROF, UNIV PITTSBURGH, 1983-; staff engr res & develop, Gulf Oil Corp, 1966-1983; mgr res & develop, Continental Can Co, 1962-1966; engr, Westinghouse Elec Corp, 1955-1959 & Argonne Nat Lab, 1959-1962. **Memberships:** Am Inst Chem Engrs. **Research Statement & Publications:** Application of computers to teaching; research and development planning; the commercial evaluation of research and development projects related to petroleum processes and products including synthetic fuels and minerals. **Mailing Address:** Dept Natural Sci, Univ Pittsburgh, Smith Hall B-5, Greensburg, PA 15601-5860. **E-Mail:** lokay@pitt.edu

LOKEMOEN, JOHN THEODORE, RESEARCH OF NESTING WATERFOWL, WATERFOWL PHILOPATRY. **Personal Data:** b Merrill, Wis, December 12, 1936. **Education:** Univ Wis, Stevens Point, BS, 1959; Univ Mont, MS, 1962. **Professional Experience:** RETIRED; WILDLIFE RES BIOLOGIST, NAT BIOL SURV NORTHERN PRAIRIE SCI CTR, 1965-; Wildlife Res Biologist, US Fish & Wildlife Serv, Minn, 1962-1965. **Memberships:** Wildlife Soc; Am Ornith Union. **Research Statement & Publications:** Primarily studied breeding waterfowl populations in the Northern Great Plains in the Prairie Pothole Region; study raptors, neo-tropical migrants in agricultural environments and upland game birds; published over 45 articles. **Mailing Address:** 818 Seventh Ave SW, Jamestown, ND 58401. **Fax:** 701-252-4217. **E-Mail:** lokemoen@daktel.com

LOKEN, HALVAR YOUNG, ORGANIC & POLYMER CHEMISTRY. **Personal Data:** b Oslo, Norway, June 18, 1944; American citizen; m 1981, Sarah; c Kaia, Rolf, Erik & Trygue. **Education:** Clark Univ, AB, 1966; Brown Univ, PhD (chem), 1971. **Professional Experience:** MARKET DEVELOP MGR, DUPONT ADVAN FIBER SYSTS, as of 2000; NEW PROD DEVELOP MGR, E I DUPONT DEL NEMOURS & CO, 1992-; chmn, Honeycomb Core Task Force, Suppliers Advan Composites Mfrs Asn, 1985-1990; bus strategist & res assoc, E I DuPont Del Nemours & Co, 1984-1992; mkt rep, E I DuPont Del Nemours & Co, 1982-1984; carpet tech supvr, E I DuPont Del Nemours & Co, 1980-1981; sr res chemist, E I DuPont Del Nemours & Co, 1976-1980; res chemist, E I DuPont Del Nemours & Co, 1972-1976; fel trace org anal, Nat Inst Allergy & Infectious Dis, Baker Lab, Cornell Univ, 1970-1972. **Memberships:** Am Chem Soc; Soc Advan Mat & Process Eng; Am Soc Testing & Mat; Am Helicopter Soc. **Research Statement & Publications:** Chemistry and physics of composite materials. **Mailing Address:** DuPont Adv Fibers Systs, PO Box 27001 5401 Jefferson Davis Hwy, Richmond, VA 23234. **E-Mail:** hal.y.loken@usa.dupont.com

LOKEN, MERLE KENNETH, nuclear medicine, biophysics; deceased, see previous edition for last biography

LOKEN, STEWART CHRISTIAN, EXPERIMENTAL HIGH ENERGY PHYSICS. **Personal Data:** b Montreal, Que, February 16, 1943; American citizen; m 1970, c Kristen & Scott. **Education:** McMaster Univ, BSc, 1966; Calif Inst Technol, PhD (physics), 1971. **Professional Experience:** Dir info & comput sci div, Lawrence Berkeley Lab, Univ Calif, 1988-2000; PHYSICIST, LAWRENCE BERKELEY LAB, UNIV CALIF, 1974-; Res assoc physics lab nuclear studies, Cornell Univ, 1971-1974. **Memberships:** Fel Am Phys Soc. **Research Statement & Publications:** Study of high energy hadron collisions at the CERN Large Hadron Collider. **Mailing Address:** Bldg 50-4049 Lawrence Berkeley Lab, Univ Calif, Berkeley, CA 94720. **E-Mail:** scloken@lbl.gov

LOKENSGARD, JERROLD PAUL, ORGANIC CHEMISTRY. **Personal Data:** b Saskatoon, Sask, July 30, 1940; American citizen; m 1965, Elizabeth; c Michael & Ann-Marie. **Education:** Luther Col, Iowa, BA, 1962; Univ Wis, Madison, MA, 1964, PhD (org chem), 1967. **Professional Experience:** ROBERT MCMILLEN PROF CHEM, LAWRENCE UNIV, 1993-; CHMN DEPT, LAWRENCE UNIV, 1992-; vis assoc prof chem, Cornell Univ, 1980-1981; chmn dept, Lawrence Univ, 1976-1979 & 1987-1990; res assoc chem, Univ Toronto, 1973-1974; from asst prof to prof, Lawrence Univ, 1967-1993; NIH fel, 1967; res assoc chem, Iowa State Univ, 1967. **Memberships:** Am Chem Soc. **Research Statement & Publications:** Organic reaction mechanisms; applications of nuclear magnetic resonance spectroscopy; identification and synthesis of natural products; strain effects on organic reactions. **Mailing Address:** Dept Chem, Lawrence Univ, PO Box 599, Appleton, WI 54912. **Fax:** 920-832-6962. **E-Mail:** jerrold.p.lokensgard@lawrence.edu

LOKKEN, DONALD ARTHUR, INORGANIC CHEMISTRY, SOLID STATE CHEMISTRY. **Personal Data:** b Tomahawk, Wis, September 27, 1937; c 2. **Education:** Univ Wis-Madison, BA, 1963; Iowa State Univ, PhD (inorg chem), 1970. **Professional Experience:** DIR, UPWARD BOUND MATH/SCI REGIONAL CTR, UNIV ALASKA, FAIRBANKS, as of 2005; ASSOC PROF CHEM, UNIV ALASKA, FAIRBANKS, 1975-; teaching & res asst, Iowa State Univ, 1963-1970; pesticide chem, Wis Alumni Res Found, 1959-1963; chemist, Enzyme Inst, Univ Wis-Madison, 1957-1959. **Memberships:** Am Chem Soc; Am Crystallog Asn; Sigma Xi. **Research Statement & Publications:** Inorganic and solid state chemistry; x-ray crystallography; unusual oxidation states. **Mailing Address:** Dept Chem, Univ Alaska, PO Box 756160, Fairbanks, AK 99775.

LOLLE, SUSAN JANNE, PLANT DEVELOPMENT. **Personal Data:** b Copenhagen, Denmark, February 14, 1958; Canadian citizen. **Education:** Queen's Univ, BSc, 1981; McGill Univ, PhD (biol), 1987. **Professional Experience:** RES ASSOC, HARVARD UNIV, 1996-; adj asst prof biol, Reed Col, 1992-1996; Grantee, USDA, 1992-1994; McKnight fel, 1990-1992; fel, Nat Sci & Eng Res Coun Can, 1987-1989. **Research Statement & Publications:** Study cell-cell interactions in plant development using molecular and genetic approaches. **Mailing Address:** Biol Labs, Harvard Univ, 16 Divinity Ave, Cambridge, MA 02138. **Fax:** 503-777-7773. **E-Mail:** slolle@reed.edu

LOLY, PETER DOUGLAS, THEORETICAL PHYSICS, SOLID STATE PHYSICS. **Personal Data:** b Edmonton, Eng, March 7, 1941; Canadian citizen; div, c 2. **Education:** Univ London, BSc, 1963, PhD (physics) & DIC, 1966. **Professional Experience:** Assoc head, Univ Man, 1989-1991; physique, Imp Col, 1982; physique, Univ Sherbrooke, 1981-1982; PROF PHYSICS, UNIV MAN, 1980-; sabbatical leave, Lab Solid State Physics, Univ Paris-Sud, 1975-1976; travel fel, Nat Res Coun Can, 1975; from asst prof to assoc prof, Univ Man, 1968-1980; fel, Theoret Physics Inst, Alta, 1966-1968. **Memberships:** Am Phys Soc; Can Asn Physicists; Brit Inst Physics; Am Asn Physics Teachers. **Research Statement & Publications:** Spin waves; density of states; Brillouin zone sums; lattice green functions; real space rescaling; many-body problems; band structure modelling; crystals; physics pedagogy; mathematics, maple. **Mailing Address:** Dept Physics, Univ Man, 318 Allen Bldg, Winnipeg, MB R3T 2N2, Can. **Fax:** 204-269-8489. **E-Mail:** loly@cc.umanitoba.ca

LOMAN, JAMES MARK, RADIATION EFFECTS. **Personal Data:** b Waterbury, Conn, November 14, 1954; m 1975, c 3. **Education:** Villanova Univ, BS, 1975; Univ Notre Dame, MS, 1977; Univ Del, PhD (physics), 1980. **Professional Experience:** MGR, ADVAN ELECTRONICS & PHOTONICS LAB, GE CORP, as of 2003; STAFF ENGR, GEN ELEC CO, 1983-; eng specialist, Ford Aerospace & Commun Corp, 1981-1983; res assoc, Brookhaven Nat lab, 1980-1981. **Memberships:** Am Phys Soc. **Research Statement & Publications:** Experimental radiation effects in electronic devices and insulators; spacecraft charging; radiation effects in geological material for nuclear waste disposal applications. **Mailing Address:** GE Corp R&D Ctr, Rm KWC-1609, PO Box 8, Schenectady, NY 12301-0008. **E-Mail:** loman@crd.ge.com

LOMAN, M LAVERNE, MATHEMATICS. **Personal Data:** b Stratford, Okla, June 10, 1928; m 1944, Coy E; c S Leigh (Easton). **Education:** Univ Okla, BS, 1956, MA, 1957, PhD (math educ), 1961. **Professional Experience:** EMER PROF MATH, UNIV CENT OKLA, 1993-; from asst prof to prof, Univ Cent Okla, 1961-1993; From asst to instr math, Univ Okla, 1956-1961. **Memberships:** Math Asn Am; Nat Coun Teachers Math. **Research Statement & Publications:** Mathematics education. **Mailing Address:** 2201 Tall Oaks Trail, Edmond, OK 73003.

LOMANITZ, ROSS, theoretical physics; deceased, see previous edition for last biography

LOMAS, CHARLES GARDNER, FLUID FLOW INSTRUMENTATION. **Personal Data:** b Ft Peck, Mont, c 1. **Education:** Univ Md, BS, 1957, BS, 1964, MS, 1975. **Professional Experience:** FAC MEM, ORE INST TECHNOL, 1992-; assoc prof eng technol, Calif Polytech State Univ, 1988-1992; assoc prof fluid power technol, Northampton Community Col, 1986-1988; asst prof mech eng, Rochester Inst Technol, 1985-1986; instr eng sci, Lafayette Col, 1980-1982; engr, Dantec Electronics, 1977-1980; asst instr mech engr, Univ Md, 1971-1977; Engr, Miller Fluid Power, 1970-1971. **Memberships:** Am Soc Mech Engrs; Am Soc Eng Educ. **Mailing Address:** Ore Inst Technol, Klamath Falls, OR 97601. **Fax:** 541-885-1855. **E-Mail:** lomasc@oit.osshe.edu

LOMAS, LYLE WAYNE, BEEF CATTLE NUTRITION. **Personal Data:** b Monett, Mo, June 8, 1953; m 1976, Connie G Frey; c Amy L & Eric W. **Education:** Univ Mo, BS, 1975, MS, 1976; Mich State Univ, PhD, 1979. **Professional Experience:** PROF ANIMAL SCI, KANS STATE UNIV, Southeast AGR RES CTR, 1992-; Bd dirs, Parsons Rotary Club, 1992-; HEAD, KANS STATE UNIV, Southeast AGR RES CTR, 1985-. **Memberships:** Am Soc Animal Sci; Am Registry Prof Animal Scientists; Am Forage & Grassland Coun; Res Ctr Adminr Soc (secy 1999-2000; vpres 2001-2002; pres 2002-2003). **Research Statement & Publications:** Ruminant nutrition; forage utilization by grazing stocker cattle. **Mailing Address:** Southeast Agr Res Ctr, Kan State Univ, 114 Waters Hall, Manhattan, KS 67341. **E-Mail:** llomas@ksu.edu

LOMAX, MARGARET IRENE, MOLECULAR GENETICS, GENOME ORGANIZATION OF NUCLEAR GENES FOR CYTOCHROME C OXIDASE. **Personal Data:** b Roanoke, Va, November 13, 1938; m 1964, c 2. **Education:** Case Western Reserve Univ, BA, 1960; Univ Mich, PhD (biol chem), 1964. **Professional Experience:** RES PROF, CELL & DEVELOP BIOL, UNIV MICH, ANN ARBOR, as of 2005; RES PROF OTOLARYNGOL, UNIV MICH, ANN ARBOR, as of 2005; DIR, MOLECULAR BIOL LAB, KRESGE HEARING RES INST, as of 2005; DIR, DNA SEQUENCING FACIL, UNIV MICH, ANN ARBOR, 1990-; asst res sci, dept anat & cell biol, Univ Mich, Ann Arbor, beginning 1988; asst res sci, Dept Microbiol & Immunol, Univ Mich, Ann Arbor, 1985-1988 & Div Biol Sci, 1974-1985; instr, Univ Mich, Ann Arbor, 1967-1988; res assoc biol chem, Univ Mich, Ann Arbor, 1964-1967; Am Cancer Soc fel, 1964-1966. **Memberships:** AAAS; Am Soc Microbiol; Am Soc Biol Chemists; Asn Women Sci. **Research Statement & Publications:** Genome organization and molecular evolution of cytochromec oxidase in primates; tissue-specific expression of cytochrome C oxidace nuclear genes. **Mailing Address:** Dept Otolaryngol, Univ Mich Med Sch, Ann Arbor, MI 48109. **Fax:** 734-615-8111. **E-Mail:** mlomax@umich.edu

LOMAX, RONALD J(AMES), SOLID STATE DEVICES, COMPUTER SIMULATION. **Personal Data:** b Stockport, Eng, July 18, 1934; American citizen; m 1964, Margaret; c Catherine & Ian. **Education:** Cambridge Univ, England, BA, 1956, MA & PhD (appl math), 1960. **Professional Experience:** PROF EMER, ELEC ENG & COMPUT SCI, UNIV MICH, ANN ARBOR, 2000-; vis prof, Stanford Univ, 1977-1978; prof elec eng & comput sci, Univ Mich, Ann Arbor, 1973-2000; from vis asst prof to assoc prof, Univ Mich, Ann Arbor, 1961-1973; Bye fel Peterhouse, Univ Cambridge, Eng, 1959-1961. **Memberships:** Inst Elec & Electronics Engrs Sr mem; fel Cambridge Philos Soc. **Research Statement & Publications:** Solid-state devices; electron device modeling; finite element method; very large scale integrated circuit design. **Mailing Address:** Univ Mich, Dept Elec Eng & Comput Sci, Ann Arbor, MI 48109-2122. **Fax:** 734-763-1503. **E-Mail:** rjl@engin.umich.edu

LOMBARD, DAVID BISHOP, EXPERIMENTAL PHYSICS. **Personal Data:** b Lexington, Mass, June 10, 1930; m 1952, Josephine Cooper; c Suzanne, Jonathan, Robin, Patricia & Katherine. **Education:** Northeastern Univ, BA, 1953; Pa State Univ, MS, 1955, PhD (physics), 1959. **Professional Experience:** PRES, DBL CONSULTS, 1997-; team leader, geothermal res, 1987-1997; asst dir, off renewable technol, 1983-1987; br chief, geothermal & biomass progs, Dept Energy, 1977-1983; br chief, geothermal energy div, Energy Res Develop Admin, 1975-1977; prog mgr, NSF, 1974; vpres, Subcom, Inc, 1972-1974; pres, Geo-Resource Assocs, 1971-1972; mgr, Atcor, Inc, 1970-1971; Sr physicist, Lawrence Livermore Lab, Univ Calif, 1959-1970. **Memberships:** Sigma Xi; Am Phys Soc; Soc Petrol Engrs. **Research Statement & Publications:** Geopressured geothermal energy; neutron physics, fission-to-indium age of neutrons in water; strong shocks in solids; applications of nuclear explosions; oil shale; geothermal energy applications; geothermal drilling technology; geothermal energy conversion. **Mailing Address:** DBL Consults, 6640 Hazel Lane, McLean, VA 22101-5113. **Fax:** 703-821-1729. **E-Mail:** dlombard@mailaps.org

LOMBARD, JULIAN H, PHYSIOLOGY, ZOOLOGY. **Personal Data:** b El Paso, Tex, October 31, 1947. **Education:** Univ Tex-El Paso, BA, 1969; Ariz State Univ, MS, 1971; Med Col Wis, PhD (physiol), 1975. **Honors & Awards:** Nat Res Serv Award, NIH, 1975-1977. **Professional Experience:** PROF PHYSIOL, MED COL WIS, 1988-; estab investr, Am Heart Asn, 1985-; Young Investr res grant, Nat Heart, Lung & Blood Inst, 1978-1981; from asst prof to assoc prof, Med Col Wis, 1977-1988; mem, Coun High Blood Pressure Res, Am Heart Asn; mem coun, Microcirulatory Soc. **Memberships:** Am Physiol Soc; Soc Exp Biol & Med; Sigma Xi; Microcirculatory Soc; Shock Soc. **Research Statement & Publications:** Vascular smooth muscle physiology; physiology of the microcirculation; local regulation of blood flow and nervous control of small blood vessels during hemorrhage, low flow states, and hypertension. **Mailing Address:** Dept Physiol, Med Col Wis, 8701 Watertown Plank Rd, Milwaukee, WI 53226-0509. **Fax:** 414-456-6546. **E-Mail:** jlombard@mcw.edu

LOMBARD, PORTER BRONSON, HORTICULTURE. **Personal Data:** b Yakima, Wash, February 6, 1930; m 1955, c 3. **Education:** Pomona Col, BA, 1952; Wash State Univ, MS, 1955; Mich State Univ, PhD (hort), 1958. **Professional Experience:** PROF EMER HORT, ORE STATE UNIV, as of 2003; prof hort, Ore State Univ, beginning 1970; SUPT, SOUTHERN ORE EXP STA, 1963-; assoc prof, Southern Ore Exp Sta, 1963-1970; asst horticulturist, Citrus Exp Sta, Calif, 1958-1963. **Memberships:** AAAS; Am Soc Hort Sci. **Research Statement & Publications:** Pear varieties; rootstocks; nutrition, pear fruit bud hardiness and water requirements. **Mailing Address:** Dept Hort, Ore Univ, 4017 Ag & Life Science Bldg, Corvallis, OR 97331-7304. **Fax:** 541-772-5110.

LOMBARD, RICHARD ERIC, MORPHOLOGY. **Personal Data:** b Brooklyn, NY, May 16, 1943; m 1967, c 2. **Education:** Hanover Col, AB, 1965; Univ Chicago, PhD (anat), 1971. **Professional Experience:** PROF ANAT & ORGANISMAL BIOL, UNIV CHICAGO, as of 2004; RES ASSOC, DEPT GEOL, FIELD MUS NATURAL HIST, 1981-; assoc prof Anat & Evolutionary Biol, Univ Chicago, beginning 1978; asst prof, Field Mus Natural Hist, 1972-1978; res assoc, Univ Southern Calif, 1971-1972; res assoc, Mus Vert Zoology, Univ Calif, Berkeley, 1971. **Memberships:** AAAS; Am Soc Ichthyologists & Herpetologists; Am Soc Zoologists; Soc Study Amphibians & Reptiles; Soc Study Evolution. **Research Statement & Publications:** The evolutionary and functional morphology of major adaptive features of lower vertebrates including auditory periphery in frogs, feeding apparatus of frogs and salamanders and the vestibular system in salamanders. **Mailing Address:** Dept Anat, Univ Chicago, Anat 202 1025 E 57th St Culver Hall, Chicago, IL 60637. **Fax:** 773-702-0037. **E-Mail:** elombard@midway.uchicago.edu

LOMBARDI, GABRIEL GUSTAVO, LASERS, NON-LINEAR OPTICS. **Personal Data:** b Buenos Aires, Arg, September 5, 1954; American citizen. **Education:** Univ Chicago, BA, 1975; Harvard Univ, PhD (physics), 1981. **Professional Experience:** PHYSICIST, MISSION RES CORP, 1992-; mem res tech staff, Northrop Res & Tech Ctr, 1984-1992; mem tech staff, TRW Inc, 1983-1984; Res assoc, Nat Inst Standards & Tech, 1980-1982. **Memberships:** Optical Soc Am; Am Phys Soc. **Research Statement & Publications:** laser remote sensing; stimulated brillouin scattering; stimulated raman scattering; atomic spectroscopy; gas discharge lasers; turbulence. **Mailing Address:** 3625 Del Amo Blvd, Ste 260, Torrance, CA 90503. **Fax:** 310-793-1633. **E-Mail:** glombardi@mrcla.com

LOMBARDI, JOHN ROCCO, PHYSICAL CHEMISTRY. **Personal Data:** b Yonkers, New York, June 10, 1941; American citizen; c 1. **Education:** Cornell Univ, AB, 1963; Harvard Univ, AM, 1966, PhD (chem), 1967. **Professional Experience:** PROF CHEM, CITY COL, CITY UNIV NY, 1977-; assoc prof, City Col, City Univ NY, 1975-1977; vis scientist, Mass Inst Technol, 1973-1975; vis scientist, Univ Leiden, Neth, 1972-1973; asst prof chem, Univ Ill, 1967-1972; ed, Advan in Laser Spectros; sr ed, Asian J Spectros. **Memberships:** Int Photochem Soc; Sigma Xi. **Research Statement & Publications:** Laser spectroscopy; molecular structure; scattering; stark effects; transition metals. **Mailing Address:** Dept Chem, City Col, City Univ NY, 160 Convent Ave, New York, NY 10031-9101. **Fax:** 212-650-6848. **E-Mail:** lombardi@sci.ccny.cuny.edu

LOMBARDI, MAX H, RADIATION BIOLOGY, NUCLEAR MEDICINE. **Personal Data:** b Huanuco City, Peru, April 25, 1932; m 1961, c 3. **Education:** Univ Lima, BSc & DVM, 1958; Cornell Univ, MSc, 1961, Am Bd Sci Nuclear Med, cert, 1979. **Professional Experience:** PROF NUCLEAR MED, HILLSBOROUGH COMMUNITY COL, 1977-; asst dir vitro div, Tampa Gen Hosp, 1977-1979; sr scientist & coordr, Radiation Biol & Med Radioisotope Training Progs, Oak Ridge Assoc Univs, 1968-1977; scientist biomed appln & consult, lectr & overall coord progs Latin Am, Oak Ridge Assoc Univs, 1964-1968; from asst prof to assoc prof biochem & nutrit, Vet Col Peru, 1960-1964. **Memberships:** Soc Nuclear Med; Clin Ligand Assay Soc; World Fedn Nuclear Med & Biol. **Research Statement & Publications:** Author of 24 publications in three languages. **Mailing Address:** Allied Health, Hillsborough County Col PO Bopx 30030, Tampa, FL 33630-3030.

LOMBARDI, PAUL SCHOENFELD, MICROBIOLOGY, PHYSICAL SCIENCE EDUCATION. **Personal Data:** b Salt Lake City, Utah, November 13, 1940; m 1968, c 3. **Education:** Univ Utah, BA, 1963, MA, 1965; Univ Rochester, PhD (microbiol), 1969. **Professional Experience:** TEACHER S DAVIS JR HIGH SCH, 1985-; Am Cancer Soc fel, NIH grant, 1974-1976; asst prof microbiol, Col Med, Univ Utah, 1973-1978; Instr, Col Med, Univ Utah, 1971-1973; Am Cancer Soc fel, Univ Utah, 1971-1973; Damon Runyon Mem Fund fel, Swiss Inst Exp Cancer Res, 1969-1970. **Memberships:** Am Soc Microbiol; Nat Sci Teachers Asn. **Research Statement & Publications:** Cell-virus interactions of polyoma virus in permissive cells; structural proteins of polyoma virions; mycoplasma viruses and their interactions with mammalian cells. **Mailing Address:** S Davis Jr High Sch, 298 W 2600 S, Centerville, UT 84010. **Fax:** 801-402-6401. **E-Mail:** plombardi@admin.sdavjr.davis.k12.ut.us

LOMBARDINI, JOHN BARRY, PHARMACOLOGY. **Personal Data:** b San Francisco, Calif, July 2, 1941; m 1968, c 2. **Education:** St Mary's Col Calif, BS, 1963; Univ Calif, San Francisco, PhD (biochem), 1968. **Professional Experience:** PROF PHARMACOL, TEX TECH UNIV, HEALTH SCI CTR, as of 2003; assoc prof pharmacol, Tex Tech Univ, Health Sci Ctr, beginning 1977; asst prof, Tex Tech Univ, Health Sci Ctr, 1973-1977; res assoc pharmacol, Sch Med, Johns Hopkins Univ, 1972-1973; fel, Sch Med, Johns Hopkins Univ, 1968-1972. **Memberships:** Am Soc Pharmacol & Exp Therapeut. **Research Statement & Publications:** Function of taurine as a possible neurotransmitter or modulator of nerve impulses; role of taurine in cardiac and retinal tissues; formation, function and regulatory properties of S-adenosylmethionine synthetase. **Mailing Address:** Dept Pharmacol, Health Sci Ctr, Tex Tech Univ, PO Box 4569, Lubbock, TX 79430-0001. **Fax:** 806-743-2744. **E-Mail:** jbarry.lombardini@ttuhsc.edu

LOMBARDINO, JOSEPH GEORGE, RESEARCH ADMINISTRATION. **Personal Data:** b Brooklyn, NY, July 1, 1933; m 1960, Roberta; c Anna-Marie, George & Anthony. **Education:** Brooklyn Col, BS, 1954; Polytech Univ, PhD, 1958. **Honors & Awards:** Eli Whitney Award, Conn Patent Law Asn, 1989; distinguished alumnus, Polytechnic Univ. **Professional Experience:** RETIRED, 1999; sr dir oper planning, Pfizer Inc, 1994-; dir develop planning, Pfizer Inc, 1986-1994; res adv, Pfizer Inc, 1979-1986; sr res investr, Pfizer Inc, 1977-1979. **Memberships:** Am Chem Soc; Int Soc Heterocyclic Chem; Inflammation Res Asn; fel Am Inst Chemists; Proj Mgt Inst. **Research Statement & Publications:** Synthetic organic medicinals; nitrogen heterocycles; anti-inflammatory drugs; immunoregulatory drugs. **Mailing Address:** 13 Laurel Hill Dr, Niantic, CT 06357.

LOMBARDO, ANTHONY, ORGANICCHEMISTRY. **Personal Data:** b Brooklyn, NY, January 4, 1939. **Education:** Queens Col, NY, BS, 1961; Syracuse Univ, PhD (org chem), 1967. **Professional Experience:** INTERIM DEAN, UNDERGRAD STUDIES, FLA ATLANTIC UNIV, as of 2004; prof chem, Fla Atlantic Univ, beginning 1982 & chmn, beginning 1983; from asst prof to assoc prof, Fla Atlantic Univ, beginning 1982 & chmn, 1968-1982; fel, Univ Calif, Santa Barbara, 1967-1968. **Memberships:** Sigma Xi. **Research Statement & Publications:** Coenzyme models; donor-acceptor complexes; kinetics; spectroscopy. **Mailing Address:** Dept Chem & Biochem, Charles E schmidt Col Sci, Fla Atlantic Univ, SU 216, Boca Raton, FL 33431-0991. **Fax:** 561-297-4222. **E-Mail:** lombardo@fau.edu

LOMBARDO, R(OSARIO) J(OSEPH), CHEMICAL ENGINEERING. **Personal Data:** b Pawcatuck, Conn, October 17, 1921; c 3. **Education:** Univ RI, BS, 1943, MS, 1947; Pa State Univ, PhD (chem eng), 1951. **Professional Experience:** MGR MFT SERV, CHEM & PIGMENTS DEPT, E I DU PONT DENEMOURS & CO, INC, 1979-; prod mgr, Chem & Pigments Dept, 1968-1979; mgr plants tech sect, Pigments Dept, 1965-1968; asst dir tech serv lab, E I Du Pont Del Nemours & Co Inc, 1961-1964; asst plant mgr, E I Du Pont Del Nemours & Co Inc, 1961; tech supt, E I Du Pont Del Nemours & Co Inc, 1959-1960; tech supvr, E I Du Pont Del Nemours & Co Inc, 1956-1959; chem engr, E I Du Pont Del Nemours & Co Inc, 1951-1956; Engr, Hamilton Stand Div, United Aircraft Corp, 1943-1946. **Memberships:** Am Inst Chem Engrs; Sigma Xi. **Research Statement & Publications:** Engineering administration; production administration. **Mailing Address:** 1307 Copley Dr, Wilmington, DE 19803.

LOMBOS, BELA ANTHONY, MATERIALS SCIENCE, MICROELECTRONICS. **Personal Data:** b April 22, 1931; Canadian citizen; m 1956. **Education:** Univ Szeged, BSc, MSc, 1955; Univ Montreal, PhD (spectros), 1967. **Professional Experience:** Silonex, Inc, 1986-; PROF ENG, CONCORDIA UNIV, 1974-; assoc prof, Sir Georges Williams Univ, 1969-1974; fel Nat Ctr Sci Res, France, 1967-1969; Consult, Northern Elec Co, Ltd, 1964-1967; Battelle Mem Inst, 1956-1959 & Res & Develop, Northern Elec Co, 1959-1964; Sci staff, Cent Labs Construct Mat, 1955-1956. **Memberships:** Electrochem Soc; Am Soc Crystal Growth. **Research Statement & Publications:** Electronic materials sciences; low energy gap semiconductors for photovoltaic infrared detectors; technology of gallium arsenide: semi-insulating gallium arsenide for IC's; semi-magnetic semiconductors. **Mailing Address:** Dept Elec Eng, Concordia Univ Sir G Williams 1455 de Maisonneuve Blvd, Montreal, PQ H3G 1M8, Can.

LOMEDICO, PETER T, MOLECULAR BIOLOGY. **Personal Data:** b New York, NY, December 23, 1948; m 1974, Marcia; c Mark & Alexandra. **Education:** Villanova Univ, BS, 1970; Univ Tex, PhD (molecular biol), 1977. **Professional Experience:** VPRES, DISCOVERY RES, CURAGEN CORP, as of 1999; FOUNDER, CHMN & CHIEF EXEC OFFICER, CURAGEN CORP, as of 1999; CHIEF SCI OFFICER, MORPHOGENESIS, INC, 1994-; at Hoffmann-LaRoche Inc, 1980-1993; at Harvard Univ, 1977-1980. **Mailing Address:** CuraGen Corp, 555 Long Wharf Dr, New Haven, Ct 06511. **Fax:** 203-401-3331.

LOMEN, DAVID ORLANDO, APPLIED MATHEMATICS. **Personal Data:** b Decorah, Iowa, May 11, 1937; m 1961, Constance; c Catherine (Hoerth). **Education:** Luther Col, Iowa, BA, 1959; Iowa State Univ, MS, 1962, PhD, 1964. **Honors & Awards:** Marshall Fund Award, Norway-Am Found, 1980. **Professional Experience:** REGULAR FAC, UNIV ARIZ, as of 2004; distinguished prof, Univ Ariz, beginning 1996; prof, Harvard Univ Summer Sch, Cambridge, Mass, 1990; consult, Off Comput Based Instr, Univ Delaware, 1982-1983; consult, Control Data Corp, Minneapolis, Minn, 1981-1985; vis sr scientist, Norway, 1980, 1983; consul, Rand Corp, Santa Monica, Calif, 1975-1978; prof math, Univ Ariz, beginning 1974; consul, Gen Dynamics, Convair, San Diego, Calif, 1966-1975; from asst prof to assoc prof, Univ Ariz, 1966-1974; asst prof, San Diego State Col, 1964-1966; design specialist, Gen Dynamics & Astronaut, 1963-1966; consult var industs; teaching asst, Iowa State Univ, 1959-1963. **Memberships:** Soc Indust & Appl Math; Am Math Soc; Soil Sci Soc Am; Geophys Union; Europ Geophys Soc. **Research Statement & Publications:** Modeling water and solute flow in soils; curriculum and software development in mathematics. **Mailing Address:** Dept Math, Univ Ariz, 617 N Santa Rita Ave PO Box 210089, Tucson, AZ 85721-0089. **Fax:** 520-621-8322. **E-Mail:** lomen@math.arizona.edu

LOMMEL, J(AMES) M(YLES), TECHNICAL INFORMATION, COPYRIGHT ISSUES, METALLURGY. **Personal Data:** b Evanston, Ill, February 7, 1932; m MARAN; c JOAN MINTZ & PATRICIA BRUTTOMESSO. **Education:** Ill Inst Technol, BS, 1953, MS, 1954;

Harvard Univ, PhD (appl physics), 1958. **Professional Experience:** Mgr. Technical Publications 2004 -; MGR TECH INFO, GEN ELEC GLOBAL RES CTR, 1996-2004; mgr support serv, Info Ctr, 1991-1995; mgr, Info Ctr, 1988-1991; consult, Info Systs, 1983-1987; mgr info res oper, Electronics Sci & Eng, 1977-1983; mgr personnel & tech admin, Electronics Sci & Eng, 1969-1977; metallurgist, Gen Elec Res & Develop Ctr, 1957-1969; teaching asst, Tufts Univ, 1955 & Harvard Univ, 1955-1956; metallurgist, H M Harper Co, 1954-1956. **Memberships:** Inst Elec & Electronics Engrs; Am Inst Mining, Metall & Petrol Engrs; Industrial Technical Information Managers Group. **Research Statement & Publications:** Physical metallurgy; magnetic materials and recording; computer systems service; information retrieval; technical information. **Mailing Address:** GE GLOBAL RESEARCH, 1 Res Circle, Niskayuna, NY 12309. **E-Mail:** lommel@research.ge.com

LOMNITZ, CINNA, SEISMOLOGY. **Personal Data:** b Cologne, Ger, May 4, 1925; m 1988, c 4. **Education:** Univ Chile, CE, 1948; Harvard Univ, MS, 1950; Calif Inst Technol, PhD (geophys), 1955. **Honors & Awards:** Nat Sci Prize, Mex, 1995. **Professional Experience:** Vis assoc, Calif Inst Technol & Univ Calif, San Diego, 1969-; PROF SEISMOL, INST GEOPHYS, NAT UNIV MEX, 1968-; assoc res seismologist, Seismog Sta, Univ Calif, Berkeley, 1964-1968; Consult, Geol Surv, Chile, 1958-; dirinst geophys & seismol, Univ Chile, 1958-1964; prof geophys, Univ Chile, 1957-1964; Res fel seismol, Calif Inst Technol, 1955-1957. **Memberships:** Seismol Soc Am; Am Geophys Union; Sigma Xi. **Research Statement & Publications:** Earthquake hazard; creep properties of rocks; viscoelasticity and internal friction in solids; seismicity; structure of the Andes; origin of earthquakes and tsunamis. **Mailing Address:** Geophys Inst, Nat Univ Mex, Mexico 04510 DF, Mex. **Fax:** 525-550-2486. **E-Mail:** cinna@ollin.igeofcu.unam.mx

LOMON, EARLE LEONARD, PARTICLE & NUCLEAR THEORY. **Personal Data:** b Montreal, Que, November 15, 1930; American citizen; m 1951, Ruth; c M Glynis, C Dylan & Deirdre N. **Education:** McGill Univ, BSc, 1951; Mass Inst Technol, PhD (theoret physics), 1954. **Professional Experience:** PROF EMER PHYSICS, MASS INST TECHNOL, as of 2005; prof, Naning univ, Nanjing, 2002-; Lady Davis vis prof, Hebrew Univ, Jerusalem, 1993-1994; KFA, Julich, WGER, 1986-1990; Univ Calif, Los Angeles, 1983; Univ Wash, Seattle, 1985; res fel, Univ Col, London, 1980; adj prof, Louvain-la-Neuve, Belg, 1980; vis prof, Univ Paris, 1979-1980, 1986-1987; proj dir, Unified Sci & Math Elem Sch, 1971-1977; prof physics, Mass Inst Technol, beginning 1970; vis scientist, Los Alamos Nat Lab, 1968-; Guggenheim Mem Found fel, 1965-1966; vis scientist, Cern, Geneva, 1965-1966; assoc prof, Mass Inst Technol, 1960-1970; assoc prof theoret physics, McGill Univ, 1957-1960; res assoc, Lab Nuclear Studies, Cornell Univ, 1956-1957; fel, Weizmann Inst, 1955-1956; Nat Res Coun Can overseas res fel, Inst Theoret Physics, Denmark, 1954-1955; res physicist, Can Defence Res Bd, 1950-1951; Baird Assocs, Mass, 1952-1953. **Memberships:** Am Phys Soc; Can Asn Physicists. **Research Statement & Publications:** Nuclear and medium energy particle physics; field theory. **Mailing Address:** Mass Inst Technol, Dept Physics, Cambridge, MA 02139. **Fax:** 617-253-8674. **E-Mail:** lomon@mitlns.mit.edu

LOMONACO, SAMUEL JAMES, MATHEMATICS, COMPUTER SCIENCE. **Personal Data:** b Dallas, Tex, September 23, 1939; m 1968, c 1. **Education:** St Louis Univ, BS, 1961; Princeton Univ, PhD (math), 1964. **Professional Experience:** PROF, DEPT COMPUT SCI, UNIV MD, BALTIMORE CO, 1985-; vis lectr, Dept Math, Princeton Univ, 1975-1976; vis, Inst Defense Analysis, Princeton, NJ, 1974-1976; actg chmn, Dept Comput Sci, State Univ NY, Albany, 1973-1974; assoc prof comput sci & math, State Univ NY Albany, 1971-1980; res mathematician & comput scientist, Tex Instruments, Inc, 1969-1971; indust prof, Southern Methodist Univ, 1969-1971; asst prof math, St Louis Univ, 1964-1965 & Fla State Univ, 1965-1969. **Memberships:** Am Math Soc; Asn Comput Mach; Math Asn Am; Soc Indust & Appl Math; Sigma Xi. **Research Statement & Publications:** Algebraic topology, higher dimensional knot theory; algebraic coding theory; complexity theory. **Mailing Address:** Univ Md, Dept comput Sci & Elec Eng, 1000 Hilltop Circle, Baltimore, MD 21250. **Fax:** 410-455-3969. **E-Mail:** lomonaco@umbc.edu

LOMONT, JOHN S, MATHEMATICAL PHYSICS. **Personal Data:** b Ft Wayne, Ind, August 26, 1924. **Education:** Purdue Univ, MS, 1947, PhD (physics), 1951. **Professional Experience:** PROF EMER, UNIV ARIZ, as of 2004; sabbatical, Courant Inst Math Sci, NY Univ, 1971-1972; prof math, Univ Ariz, beginning 1965; prof math, Polytech Inst Brooklyn, 1962-1965; physicist, NY Univ, 1954-1957 & Int Bus Mach Corp, 1957-1960; physicist, Res Dept, Michelson Lab, Naval Ord Test Sta, 1952-1954; physicist theoret solid state physics, NAm Aviation, Inc, 1951-1952. **Memberships:** Am Phys Soc; Am Math Soc. **Research Statement & Publications:** Applied group theory; quantum field theory; functional analysis. **Mailing Address:** Univ Ariz, Bldg 89, Tucson, AZ 85721-0001.

LONADIER, FRANK DALTON, PHYSICAL CHEMISTRY, INORGANIC CHEMISTRY. **Personal Data:** b Clarence, La, May 6, 1932; m 1959, Janice Goodwin Lonadier; c Robert C & James D. **Education:** Northwestern State Col, La, BS, 1954; Univ Tex, PhD (phys chem), 1959. **Professional Experience:** PROF OF CHEM, SINCLAIR COM COLL, 1993-; mgr, Mfg Mound Lab, Monsanto Res Corp, 1987-1990; mgr advan devices prod, Monsanto Res Corp, 1976-1986; mgr explosive technol, Monsanto Res Corp, 1969-1976; mgr nuclear prod, Monsanto Res Corp, 1967-1969; sect mgr nuclear develop, Monsanto Res Corp, 1965-1967; sect mgr mat eval, Monsanto Res Corp, 1964-1965; group leader inorg & nuclear chem, Monsanto Res Corp, 1961-1964; sr res chemist, Monsanto Res Corp, 1959-1961; res asst, Los Alamos Sci Lab, Univ Calif, 1957-1958; tech Safety Appraisals for Radioactive Mfg. **Memberships:** Am Chem Soc; Am Soc Qual Control. **Research Statement & Publications:** Actinide elements, particularly uranium and plutonium; inorganic chemistry of polonium; behavior of secondary explosives; environmental pollutant abatement. **Mailing Address:** 221 Estates Dr, Dayton, OH 45459-2837. **Fax:** 937-512-2308. **E-Mail:** alumni@utexas.net

LONARD, ROBERT (IRVIN), PLANT TAXONOMY. **Personal Data:** b Valley Falls, Kans, June 5, 1942; m 1965, c 1. **Education:** Emporia State Univ, BSE, 1964, MS, 1966; Tex A&M Univ, PhD (plant taxon), 1970. **Honors & Awards:** Donovan Stewart Correll Mem Award, Native Plant Soc Tex, 1997. **Professional Experience:** RETIRED; prof chmn, Dept biol, 1992-1994; adj prof, Dept biol, SW Tex State Univ, 1988; wetland res assoc, Dept biol, Univ Tex-Pan Am, 1982-2003; from asst prof to assoc prof, Dept biol, Pan Am Univ, 1970-1982; asst Curator, Tracy Herbarium, Tex A & M Univ, 1970; grad teaching asst, Tex A & M Univ, 1966-1969; grad teaching asst, Emporia State Univ, 1964-1965; undergrad teaching asst, Emporia State Univ, 1963-1964. **Memberships:** AAAS; Am Soc Plant Taxonomists; Int Asn Plant Taxonomists; Bot Acad Sci; Bot Res Inst Tex. **Research Statement & Publications:** Flora of south Texas; grass systematics. **Mailing Address:** Dept Biol, Univ Tex Pan Am, SCIE 2332 1201 W Univ Dr, Edinburg, TX 78541. **Fax:** 956-381-3657. **E-Mail:** rlonard@panam.edu

LONBERG-HOLM, KNUD KARL, BIOCHEMISTRY. **Personal Data:** b New York, NY, September 22, 1931; m 1961, c 3. **Education:** Harvard Univ, BA, 1953; Univ Calif, Berkeley, PhD (biochem), 1962. **Professional Experience:** CONSULT, 1988-; adj prof, Hahnemann Univ, 1988-1992; vis prof microbiol & immunol, Hahnemann Univ, 1985-1988; assoc prof microbiol & immunol, Sch Med, Temple Univ, 1976-1977; USPHS fel, Univ Uppsala, 1967-1969; biochemist, Cent Res Dept, E I du Pont Del Nemours & Co, Inc, 1962-1985; chemist, Hyman Labs, Fundamental Res, Inc, 1959-1960. **Research Statement & Publications:** Biochemistry of plasma proteins; virus-cell interaction; biochemical virology. **Mailing Address:** PO Box 95, Lockwood, NY 14859. **E-Mail:** klonbergh@aol.com

LONDERGAN, JOHN TIMOTHY, NUCLEAR THEORY. **Personal Data:** b Niagara Falls, NY, March 13, 1943; m 1986, Gail; c 3. **Education:** Univ Rochester, BS, 1965; Oxford Univ, DPhil, 1969. **Professional Experience:** DIR WELLS SCHOLARS PROG, IND UNIV, as of 2004; chair, Dept Physics, Ind Univ, 1990-1997; vis prof, Univ Adelaide, Australia, 1989, 1995, 1999; consult, Los Alamos Nat Lab, 1988-1996; dir, Nuclear Theory Ctr, 1985-1987, 1997-2003; Assoc dean, Grad Sch, 1984-1988; GEORGE F GETZ JR PROF, WELLS SCHOLARS PROG, IND UNIV, 1983-; vis prof, Swiss Inst Nuclear Res, 1982-1983; from asst prof to assoc prof, Physics Dept, 1973-1982; Res assoc physics, Univ Wis, 1971-1973; Res assoc physics, Case Western Res Univ, 1969-1971. **Memberships:** Am Phys Soc; Sigma Xi. **Research Statement & Publications:** Intermediate-energy nuclear theory; structure of the nucleon; quark-nuclear physics; quark symmetries. **Mailing Address:** Dept Physics, Ind Univ, Swain Hall W Rm 117, Bloomington, IN 47405. **Fax:** 812-855-3780. **E-Mail:** tlonderg@indiana.edu

LONDON, A(LEXANDER) L(OUIS), MECHANICAL ENGINEERING. **Personal Data:** b Nairobi, Kenya, August 31, 1913; American citizen; m 1938, c 3. **Education:** Univ Calif, BS, 1935, MS, 1938. **Professional Experience:** EMER PROF MECH ENG, STANFORD UNIV, 1978-; Res assoc, Argonne Nat Lab, 1955-1956; from instr to prof, Stanford Univ, 1938-1978; instr, Univ Santa Clara, 1937-1938; Engr, Stand Oil Co Calif, 1936-1937. **Memberships:** Nat Acad Eng; Am Soc Mech Engrs; Am Soc Eng Educ; Soc Naval Eng. **Research Statement & Publications:** Heat transfer; thermodynamics; fluid mechanics. **Mailing Address:** Dept Mech Eng, Stanford Univ, Stanford, CA 94305.

LONDON, DAVID, METAMORPHIC PETROLOGY, FLUID INCLUSION ANALYSIS. **Personal Data:** b Ardmore, Okla, February 27, 1953. **Education:** Wesleyan Univ, BA, 1975; Ariz State Univ, Tempe, MS, 1979, PhD, 1981. **Honors & Awards:** Honorary namesale londonite, new mineral species, approved 1999 IMA. **Professional Experience:** PROF, SCH GEOL & GEOPHYS, UNIV OKLA, 1983-. **Memberships:** Am Geophys Union; Mineral Asn Can; Fel Mineral Soc Am. **Research Statement & Publications:** Internal evolution of fractionated granite-pegmatite systems; emphasis on crystallization sequences, melt-vapor equilibrium and trace element partitioning and formation of rare-element deposits. **Mailing Address:** Sch Geol & Geophys, Univ Okla, 810 Sarkeys Energy Ctr 100E Boyd, Norman, OK 73019-1009. **Fax:** 405-325-3140. **E-Mail:** dlondon@ou.edu

LONDON, DR RAY WILLIAM WILLIAM, STRESS-CRISIS-CONFLICT-CHANGE MANAGEMENT, POLICY-LEGAL-ETHICAL CONCERNS. **Personal Data:** b Burley, Idaho, May 29, 1943. **Education:** Weber State Col, BS, 1967; Univ Southern Calif, MSW, 1973, PhD (psychol), 1976, MBA, 1989; PtGradCert Dispute Resolution, Pepperdine Univ Sch Law; LLM Information Technol & Telecommunications Law, Univ Strathclyde Sch Law. **Honors & Awards:** SCEH, Morton Priance Award. **Professional Experience:** CHIEF EXEC OFFICER, HUMAN STUDIES CENTER, Ltd, as of 1987-; Dean, School of Business and Information Technology, Argosy Universityt Orange Campus, 2001-; res affil, Ctr Crisis Mgt, Univ Southern Calif, 1987-; adv ed, Int J Clin & Exp Hypn, 1981-; clin fac, Univ Calif Irvine Col Med, 1978-; fel, Inst Social Scientist Neurobiology & Mental Illness, 1978; pres, Human Factors Prog, 1976-; chief exec officer, London Assoc Int, 1976-; mem fac, Univ Calif, Los Angeles, Univ Southern Calif, Calif State Univ, 1976-1986; res assoc, Nat Comt Protection Human Subjects Biomed & Behav Res, 1976; Consult & pvt pract, st joseph hosp, 1973-; clin trainee & fel, Vet Admin & Children's Hosp, 1971-1974; mental health liasion, San Bernardino County Social Serv, 1968-1972; dir, Meaning Found, 1966-1969; res assoc, Bus Adv, Inc, 1965-1967; Erickson Scholar Dipl, Neuropsychology, Med Psychol, Family Psychol, Clin Forensic Psychol, Hypn, Certified Management Consultant, Certified Professional Consultant to Management, Certified Focus Group Director - Qualitative Research, Association for Conflict Resolution - Society of Professionals in Dispute Resolution, Section on Dispute Resolution - American Bar Association [Ethics and Technology Committees], Southern California Mediation Association, California Dispute Resolution Council, Professional Mediation Association, London Court of International Arbitration, and American Arbitration Association. American Registry of Arbitrators (Registered Arbitrator). **Memberships:** IntAcad Med & Psychol (pres 1980-); Soc Clin & Exp Hypn (treas 1987-1989); Int Psychosomatic Inst; Am Bd Psychol Hypn (pres 1989-); Am Bd Clin Hypn (pres 1990-); Int Consults Found. **Research Statement & Publications:** Scientific investigation, integration and application of behavioral science, managment, technology, law, Internet, to stress, change, conflict, crisis and human performance issues, problems and policy concerns. **Mailing Address:** Human Studies Center, 17995 Sky Park Circle, Ste E, Irvine, CA 92614-6374. **Fax:** 714-285-9197. **E-Mail:** rwl@humanstudiescenter.org

LONDON, EDYTHE D, NEUROCHEMISTRY, NEUROPHARMACOLOGY. **Personal Data:** b Rome, Italy, September 14, 1948; American citizen; c 2. **Education:** George Wash Univ, BS, 1969; Towson State Univ, MS, 1973; Univ Md, PhD (pharmacol), 1976. **Honors & Awards:** Mathilde Salowey Award, 1987. **Professional Experience:** PROF DEPT PSYCHIAT & BIOBEHAVIORAL SCI & MOLECULAR & MED PHARMACOL, DAVID GEFFEN SCH MED, as of 2005; DISTINGUISHED SCIENTIST, LONDON NEUROIMAGING RES GROUP, UNIV CALIF, as of 2000; DIR, LONDON NEUROIMAGING RES GROUP, UNIV CALIF, 1996-; actg chief, Neuroscience br 1995-; CHIEF, BRAIN IMAGING SECT, NAT INST DRUG ABUSE, 1992-; chief, Neuropharmacol Lab, 1985-1992; pharmacologist, Brain Imaging Ctr, 1984-1985; pharmacologist, Nat Inst on Aging, 1981-1982; staff fel, Nat Inst on Aging, 1979-1981; fel psychopharmacology, Sch Med, Johns Hopkins Univ, 1976-1978; adj prof pharmacol & exp therapeut, Univ Md Sch Med; assoc prof radiol, Johns Hopkins Sch Med. **Memberships:** Soc Neuroscience; Am Soc Pharmacol Exp Therapeut; Am Soc Neurochem; Int Soc Cerebral Blood Flow & Metab; Am Col Neuropsychopharmacol; Col Probs Drug Dependence. **Research Statement & Publications:** Regional cerebral metabolism and changes in neurotransmitter balance in the aging brain; localization of the actions of psychoactive drugs; developing methods for noninvasive imaging of brain function; positron emission tomography; studies on mechanisms of addiction and development of treatment. **Mailing Address:** Dept Psychiat & Biobehavioral Sci, Neuropsychiatric Inst, Univ Calif, Mail 175919 760 Westwood Plaza C8 532, Los Angeles, CA 90024. **Fax:** 310-825-0812. **E-Mail:** elondon@mednet.ucla.edu

LONDON, GILBERT J(ULIUS), MATERIALS SCIENCE, BERYLLIUM TECHNOLOGY. **Personal Data:** b Philadelphia, Pa, May 30, 1931; m 1976, c 4. **Education:** Drexel Inst Technol, BS, 1953; Univ Pa, MS, 1955, PhD (metall eng), 1959. **Professional Experience:** BR HEAD STRUCT MAT, NAVAL AIR DEVELOP CTR, 1975-; mgr metall res &

develop, Kawecki Berylcolndusts, 1970-1975; sr res metallurgist & mgr, Mech Metall Lab, Franklin Inst, Pa, 1959-1970; Metallurgist, Aerosci Lab, Gen ElecCo, 1956-1959; adj prof, Drexel Univ. **Memberships:** Am Inst Mining Metall & Petrol Engrs; Sigma Xi. **Research Statement & Publications:** Flow and fracture of iron; dispersed hard particle strengthening of metals; beryllium; purification; high purity alloys; micro-strain properties; slip analysis; coextruded composites; beryllium alloys. **Mailing Address:** Naval Air Warfare Ctr, Code 434P, Patuxent River, MD 20670.

LONDON, IRVING M, MEDICINE. **Personal Data:** b Malden, Mass, July 24, 1918; m 1955, Huguette; c Robert L J & David T D. **Education:** Harvard Univ, AB, 1939, MD, 1943. **Honorary Degrees:** ScD, Univ Chicago, 1966. **Honors & Awards:** Theobald Smith Award in Med Sci, AAAS, 1953; Jean Oliver Lectr, State Univ NY, 1957; Roger Morris Lectr, Univ Cincinnati, 1958; Stuart McGuire Lectr, Med Col Va, 1960; Eugene A Stead Jr Vis Lectr, Duke Univ Med Ctr, 1970; E Stanley Emery Jr Mem Staff Lectr, Peter Bent Brigham Hosp, 1971; Bloomfield Lectr & Bloomfield Medalist, Lady Davis Inst, Montreal, 1986. **Professional Experience:** GROVER M HERMANN PROF EMER HEALTH SCI & TECHNOL, MASS INST TECHNOL, 1989-; PROF EMER BIOL & MED, MASS INST TECHNOL, 1989-; sr consult med, Brigham & Women's Hosp, Boston, 1987-; mem bd dirs, Johnson & Johnson, 1982-1989; mem, Bd Sci Coun, Nat Inst Arthritis, Metab & Digestive Dis, 1979-1983; dir, Whitaker Col Health Sci Technol & Mgt, 1978-1982; Grover M Hermann prof health sci & technol, Mass Inst Technol, 1977-1989; dir, Div Health Sci & Technol, 1977-1985; vis prof med, Rockefeller Univ Hosp, 1975; Univ Rotterdam, Neth, 1975; prof, Harvard Med Sch, 1972-1989; prof med, Mass Inst Technol, 1972-1989; mem, Nat Cancer Adv Bd, 1972-1976; vis prof med, Albert Einstein Col Med, NY, 1970-; prof biol, Mass Inst Technol, 1969-1989; dir, Harvard-Mass Inst Technol Prog Health Sci & Technol, 1969-1977; vis prof med, Harvard Med Sch, 1969-1972; bd med, Panel Biol Sci & Advan Med, Nat Acad Sci, 1967-1970; mem adv comt to dir, NIH, 1966-1970; mem, Panel Biol Sci & Advan Med, Nat Acad Sci, 1966-1967; mem bd sci coun, Nat Heart Inst, 1964-1968; chmn, USPHS, 1961-1963; bd sci consult, Sloan-Kettering Inst Cancer Res, 1960-1972; metab study sect mem, USPHS, 1960-1963; res coun mem, Pub Health Res Inst, NY, 1958-1963; prof & chmn dept, Albert Einstein Col Med, 1955-1970; mem, Med Fel Bd & Subcomt Blood & Related Probs, Nat Acad Sci-Nat Res Coun, 1955-1963; from asst attend physician to assoc attend physician, Presby Hosp, NY, 1952-1954; from instr to assoc prof med, Columbia Univ, 1947-1955; asst physician, Presby Hosp, NY, 1947-1952; asst resident med serv, Presby Hosp NY, 1946-1947; physician, Peter Bent Brigham Hosp. **Memberships:** Nat Acad Sci; Am AcadArts & Sci; Asn Am Physicians; Am Soc Clin Invest (pres 1963-1964); Am Soc Biol Chemists; fel AAAS; Int Soc Hemat; Soc Develop Biol; Harvey Soc. **Research Statement & Publications:** Hemoglobin metabolism; metabolism of erythrocytes; eukaryotic protein synthesis; gene therapy; author of numerous publications. **Mailing Address:** Mass Inst Technol, Harvard-MIT, Div Health Sci & Technol, Bldg E25 Rm 551 77 Mass Ave, Cambridge, MA 02139. **Fax:** 617-253-3459. **E-Mail:** imlondon@mit.edu

LONDON, J PHILLIP, BUSINESS ADMINISTRATION. **Personal Data:** b Oklahoma City, Okla, April 30, 1937; c J Phillip Jr & Laura (McLain). **Education:** US Naval Acad, BSc, 1959; US Naval Postgrad Sch, MSc, 1967; George Wash Univ, Doctorate(bus admin), 1971. **Professional Experience:** PRES & CHIEF EXEC OFFICER, CACAI INC, as of 2003; CHMN BD, CACI INT INC, 1990-; pres & chief exec officer, CACI Int Inc, Arlington, Va, 1984-1990; pres operating div, CACI Int Inc, Arlington, Va, 1982-1984; exec vpres, CACI Int Inc, Arlington, Va, 1979-1982; sr vpres, CACI Int Inc, Arlington, Va, 1977-1979; vpres, CACI Int Inc, Arlington, Va, 1976-1977; mgr, CACI Int Inc, Arlington, Va, 1972-1976; Prog mgr, Challenger Res Inc, 1971-1972. **Memberships:** High Tech Entrepreneur Award KPMG Peat Marwick 1995. **Mailing Address:** CACI Int Inc, 1100 N Glebe Rd, Arlington, VA 22201-4798.

LONDON, JOHN R, III, AERONAUTICS. **Education:** Clemson Univ, BS; Florida Inst Tech, MS. **Professional Experience:** SR EXEC, MARSHALL SPACE FLIGHT CTR, NASA, as of 2000. **Mailing Address:** NASA, Marshall Space Flight Ctr, Mail Code VP62, Huntsville, AL 35812. **Fax:** 256-961-7523.

LONDON, JULIUS, METEOROLOGY. **Personal Data:** b Newark, NJ, March 26, 1917. **Education:** Brooklyn Col, BA, 1941; NY Univ, MS, 1948, PhD, 1951. **Honorary Degrees:** DSc, Fed Inst Technol, Zurich, Switz, 1991. **Professional Experience:** EMER PROF ASTROPHYS, PLANETARY & ATMOSPHERIC SCI, UNIV COLO, BOULDER, 1987-; lectr, Chinese Acad Sci, Inst Atmospheric Physics, 1980; chief US deleg, XVII Gen Assembly, Int Asn Meteorol & Atmospheric Physics, 1979; mem, Comt Human Resources, 1978-1981; vis prof, Swiss Fed Inst Technol, 1967, 1974-1976; chmn dept, Planetary & Atmospheric Sci, Univ Colo, Boulder, 1966-1969; chmn panel ozone, Nat Res Coun, Nat Acad Sci, 1964-1965; prof astro-geophys, Planetary & Atmospheric Sci, Univ Colo, Boulder, 1961-1987; vis res scientist, Nat Ctr Atmospheric Res, 1961-1966; mem, Int Ozone Comn, Int Asn Meteorol & Atmospheric Physics, 1960-; assoc prof, NY Univ, 1959-1961; Max Planck Inst Physics, Gottingen, 1958; res assoc prof, NY Univ, 1956-1959; vis prof, Pa State Univ, 1955; Lectr, Columbia Univ, 1954-1955; asst prof, NY Univ, 1952-1956; res assoc meteorol, NY Univ, 1948-1952; instr meteorol, USAF, 1942-1947; Meteorologist, US Weather Bur, 1942. **Memberships:** AAAS; Int Asn Metorol & Atmospheric physics; Sigma Xi; Am Geophys Union; Int Radiation Comn (secy 1963-1971 pres 1971-1979) American Meteorological Soc. **Research Statement & Publications:** Atmospheric radiation; physics of the atmosphere; ozone; observed and theoretical variations of atmospheric ozone; radiative, photochemical, and dynamical processes and their effect on responses of the stratosphere and mesosphere to solar perturbations or anthropogenic processes; Earth's radiation budget, its interaction with the large-scale motions of the atmosphere, and relation to climatic change. **Mailing Address:** Astrophys Plantetary & Atmospheric Sci Dept, Campus Box 391, Univ Colo, Boulder, CO 80309-0391. **Fax:** 303-492-6946. **E-Mail:** julius.london@colorado.edu

LONDON, MARK DAVID, IMPACT ASSESSMENT, MANAGEMENT. **Personal Data:** b Brooklyn, NY, May 24, 1947; m 1970, c 2. **Education:** C W Post Col, Long Island Univ, BS, 1970, MS, 1974. **Professional Experience:** VPRES, ENVIRON-SCI INC, as of 2004; dir, Environ Rev Div, NY Dept City Planning, 1988-1991; environ studies mgr, Pub Serv Elec & Gas Co, 1982-1988; chmn, Twp Denville, NJ Environ Comn, 1981-1987; sr biologist, Pub Serv Elec & Gas Co, 1980; mem, Twp Denville, NJ Environ Comn, 1980-1981; sr staff biologist, Pub Serv Elec & Gas Co, 1979-1980; lead biologist, Pub Serv Elec & Gas Co, 1977-1979; biologist, Pub Serv Elec & Gas Co, 1976-1977; environ scientist, Woodward-Clyde Consult, 1972-1976; biologist, Eng Sci, Inc, 1969-1972; asst vpres, Environ-Sci Inc. **Memberships:** Am Soc Testing & Mat; Soc Power Indust Biologists; Am Soc Limnol & Oceanog; Edison Elec Inst Biologist; Am Inst Biol Sci. **Research Statement & Publications:** Director and chief reviewer of New York City's City Environmental Quality Review Process reviewing all non-as-of- right-construction in New York City. **Mailing Address:** Environ-Sci Inc, Ste 108 111 Howard Blvd, Mt Arlington, NJ 07856. **Fax:** 201-798-8037.

LONDON, MORRIS, BIOCHEMISTRY, ENZYMOLOGY. **Education:** Ohio State Univ, PhD (physiol), 1950. **Professional Experience:** CHIEF CLIN CHEM, BROOKDALE MED CTR, 1971-. **Research Statement & Publications:** Clinical chemistry. **Mailing Address:** 141-36 73rd Terr, Flushing, NY 11367-2307.

LONDON, RICHARD A, PHYSICS. **Education:** Univ Colo, PhD (physics & astrophysics). **Professional Experience:** GROUP LEADER, ADVAN TECHNOL X DIV, DEFENSE NUCLEAR TECHNOLOGIES DIRECTORATE, as of 2006. **Mailing Address:** L-477 LLNL UCL, PO Box 808, Livermore, CA 94550. **Fax:** 510-423-9208.

LONDON, ROBERT ELLIOT, BIOPHYSICAL CHEMISTRY, NUCLEAR MAGNETIC RESONANCE. **Personal Data:** b Brooklyn, NY, October 25, 1946; m 1969, Phyllis; c Stephen, Jeffrey & Elise. **Education:** Brooklyn Col, BS, 1967; Univ Ill, MS, 1969, PhD (physics), 1973. **Professional Experience:** PRIN INVESTR, NUCLEAR MAGNETIC RESONANCE, NAT INST ENVIRON HEALTH SCI, as of 2006; NUCLEAR MAGNETIC RESONANCE GROUP LEADER, LAB STRUCT BIOL, NAT INST ENVIRON HEALTH SCI, 1984-; staff mem biophys chem, Los Alamos Nat Lab, 1975-1983; fel, Los Alamos Nat Lab, 1973-1975. **Memberships:** Am Soc Biochem & Molecular Biol; Biophys Soc. **Research Statement & Publications:** Nuclear magnetic resonance studies of biologically important molecules. **Mailing Address:** Nat Inst Environ Health Sci, 101 Bldg Rm MRI-08 Box 12233, Research Triangle Park, NC 27709-2233. **Fax:** 919-541-5707. **E-Mail:** london@niehs.nih.gov

LONDON, STEVEN D, MATHEMATICS. **Professional Experience:** PROF, DEPT APPL MATH SCI, UNIV HOUSTON DOWNTOWN, as of 2006. **Memberships:** Nat Coun Teachers Math. **Mailing Address:** Dept Appl Math Sci Univ Houston Downtown, One Main St, Houston, TX 77002. **Fax:** 713-221 8086. **E-Mail:** londons@zeus.dt.uh.edu

LONDON, WILLIAM THOMAS, INTERNAL MEDICINE, EPIDEMIOLOGY. **Personal Data:** b New York, NY, March 11, 1932; m 1957, Linda Greenman; c Barbara, Katharine, Emily & Nancy. **Education:** Oberlin Col, BA, 1953; Cornell Univ, MD, 1957. **Honors & Awards:** Med Excellente Award, Del Valley Cha, Am Liver Found, 1991, Distinguished Scientist Award, Hepatitis B Foundation, 1998; Distinguished Interdisciplinary Research Award, Am Cancer Society, Southeast Region 1999. **Professional Experience:** ADJ PROF EPIDEMIOL, SCH MED, UNIV PA, 1999-; SR MEM POP SCI DIV, FOX CHASE CANCER CTR, 1990-; sr res physician, Int Cancer Res, 1978-1989; from asst prof to assoc prof, Fox Chase Cancer Ctr, 1971-1978; Adj Prof Med, Sch Med, Univ Pa, beginning 1971; res physician, Inst Cancer Res, 1966-1978; assoc, Fox Chase Cancer Ctr, 1966-1971; instr, Sch Med, George Wash Univ, 1964-; res epidemiologist, Nat Inst Arthritis & Metab Dis, 1962-1966; asst, Med Col, Cornell Univ, 1960-1962; Fel endocrinol, Sloan-Kettering Inst, NY, 1960-1962; resident, Med Ctr, 1958-1960; Intern med, Bellevue Hosp, 1957-1958. **Memberships:** Am Asn Cancer Res; Am Soc Prev Oncol; Am Soc Virol; Soc Epidemiol Res; Am Col Physicians. **Research Statement & Publications:** Susceptibility factors to cancer; variations in host response to hepatitis B infection; molecular epidemiology of hepatocellular carcinoma. **Mailing Address:** Fox Chase Cancer Ctr, 7701 Burholme Ave, Philadelphia, PA 19111. **Fax:** 215-214-4053. **E-Mail:** wt_london@fccc.edu

LONE, M(UHAMMAD) ASLAM, EXPERIMENTAL NUCLEAR PHYSICS. **Personal Data:** b East Punjab, India, January 28, 1937; m 1970, c 3. **Education:** Punjab Univ, West Pakistan, BS, 1958, MS, 1960; State Univ NY Stony Brook, PhD (physics), 1967. **Professional Experience:** SR PHYSICIST, OFF CHIEF ENGR, ATOMIC ENERGY CAN LTD, as of 2002; SR RES SCIENTIST PHYSICS, CHALK RIVER LABS, ATOMIC ENERGY-CAN LTD, 1983-; from res officer physics to assoc res officer, Chalk River Labs, Atomic Energy Can Ltd, 1970-1983; Nat Res Coun Can fel, Chalk River Labs, Atomic Energy Can Ltd, 1968-1970; fel, Ind Univ, Bloomington, 1967-1968; lectr physics, Govt Col, Lahore, Pakistan, 1960-1962; mem, Int Atomic Energy Agency, Nuclear Data Comt. **Memberships:** Can Asn Physicists; Am Phys Soc; Can Radiol Prof Asn; Can Nuclear Soc. **Research Statement & Publications:** Nuclear spectroscopy by gamma ray, neutron, and charged particle induced reactions; investigation of nuclear reaction mechanism; radiation physics, utilization of nuclear radiation for industrial processing; industrial neutron sources. **Mailing Address:** Off Chief Engr, Atomic Energy Can Ltd, Sta E4, Chalk River, ON K0J 1J0, Can. **Fax:** 613-584-8047. **E-Mail:** lonea@aecl.ca

LONERGAN, DENNIS ARTHUR, FOOD SCIENCE, FOOD TECHNOLOGY. **Personal Data:** b West Bend, Ind, May 30, 1949; m 1980. **Education:** Univ Wis-Madison, BS, 1971, MS, 1975, PhD (food sci), 1978. **Professional Experience:** GOLDEN VALLEY MICRO, WARE FOOD INC, 1990-; scientist res, Pillsbury Co, 1983-1990; asst prof food analysis, Purdue Univ, 1980-1983; Scientist res, Pillsbury Co, 1978-1980. **Memberships:** Inst Food Technologists. **Research Statement & Publications:** Functionality of casein as a food ingredient; methods of determining water mobility in food; membrane processing of foods. **Mailing Address:** 1825 County Rd 24, Long Lake, MN 55356.

LONERGAN, THOMAS A, BIOLOGICAL SCIENCE. **Personal Data:** b Syracuse, NY. **Education:** Univ Ill, PhD, 1977. **Professional Experience:** PROF BIOL SCI, UNIV NEW ORLEANS, 1988-. **Mailing Address:** Dept Biol Sci, Univ New Orleans, Off CC 203, New Orleans, LA 70148-0001. **Fax:** 504-280-6121. **E-Mail:** tlonerga@uno.edu

LONEY, ROBERT AHLBERG, STRUCTURAL GEOLOGY, PETROLOGY. **Personal Data:** b Odebolt, Iowa, June 16, 1922; wid, c 3. **Education:** Univ Wash, BS, 1949, MS, 1951; Univ Calif, Berkeley, PhD (geol), 1961. **Professional Experience:** GEOLOGIST, US GEOL SURV, 1956-; Geologist, Superior Oil Co, Tex, 1951-1952 & Wyo, 1952-1954. **Memberships:** Am Geophys Union; Geol Soc Am; Mineral Soc Am; Ger Geol Asn. **Research Statement & Publications:** Structural petrology and petrology of mafic-ultramafic complexes and associated terranes; Pacific coastal region including Alaska. **Mailing Address:** 12112 Foothill Lane, Los Altos, CA 94022.

LONG, ADRIAN E, IN-SITU CONCRETE TESTING, CONCRETE DURABILITY. **Personal Data:** b Northern Ireland, April 15, 1941; British citizen; m 1967, Elaine; c Michael Andrew, Alison Elizabeth (Wallace). **Education:** Queen's Univ Belfast, (structural eng), PhD, 1967; Queen's Univ, Belfast, BS, 1963. **Honorary Degrees:** DSc, Queen's Univ Belfast, 1984. **Honors & Awards:** Irish Acad of Engineering Founder Fel, 1998; Am Concrete Inst Fel, 1996; Esso Energy Award (Gold Medal), Royal Soc, 1994; Royal Acad of Engineering(UK)Fel, 1989; Winner of various awards/medals for technical publications by Inst Civil Engrs, Inst Structural Engrs, Am Concrete Inst/Am Soc Civil Engrs. **Professional Experience:** DEAN, FAC OF ENGINEERING, QUEEN'S UNIV, BELFAST, 1998-; dir, Sch the Built Environ, Queen's Univ, Belfast, 1989-1998; dean, Fac of Engineering, Queen's Univ, Belfast, 1988-1991; head dept of civil eng, Dept of Civil Engineering, Queen's Univ, Belfast, 1977-1989; PROF CIVIL ENG, QUEEN'S UNIV, BELFAST, 1976-; lectr, Dept of Civil Engineering, Queen's Univ, Belfast, 1971-1976; asst prof, Dept of Civil Engineering, Queen's Univ, Kingston, Can, 1968-1971; bridge design engr, FENCO, Toronto, Can, 1967-1968. **Memberships:** Inst Civil Engs, London, emer mem, vpres, 1999-2002; pres, 2002-2003. **Research Statement & Publications:** Durability of structural materials and the design of reinforced and prestressed concrete structures, including buildings, bridges and offshore construction; research on wave energy conversion. **Mailing Address:** Sch Civil Engineering, David Keir Bldg, Queen's Univ, Belfast, BT7 1NN, Northern Ireland.

LONG, ALAN JACK, FOREST ECOLOGY, FOREST GENETICS. **Personal Data:** b Baton Rouge, La, October 17, 1944; m 1966, c 2. **Education:** Univ Calif, Berkeley, BS, 1967, MS, 1971; NC State Univ, PhD (forestry & genetics), 1973. **Honors & Awards:** C Hux Coulter Award, Soc Am Foresters, 2001. **Professional Experience:** ASSOC PROF FOREST OPERATIONS, FIRE & EXTEN, UNIV FLA, as of 2004; asst prof forestry, Univ Fla, beginning 1987; forestry res field sta mgr, Weyerhaeuser Co, 1980-1987; field sta mgr trop forestry res, Indonesia, 1979-1980; res scientist regeneration ecol, Weyerhaeuser Co, 1974-1979; asst prof forest genetics, Pa State Univ, 1973-1974. **Memberships:** Soc Am Foresters; Fla forestry Asn; Int Soc Trop Foresters. **Research Statement & Publications:** Technology requisite for plantation establishment and early growth of western conifers; use of clonal material in tree improvement and regeneration programs; root growth of conifer seedlings. **Mailing Address:** Sch Forest Resources & Conserv, Univ Fla, PO Box 110410 355 Newins-Ziegler Hall, Gainesville, FL 32611-0410. **Fax:** 352-846-1277. **E-Mail:** ajl2@ufl.edu

LONG, ALAN K, DESIGN OF SOFTWARE TOOLS FOR ORGANIC CHEMISTS. **Personal Data:** b Burlington, Vt, June 19, 1950; m 1984, Carol; c 2. **Education:** Yale Univ, BS, 1971; Harvard Univ, MA, 1976, PhD (chem), 1979. **Professional Experience:** LHASA PROJ DIR, DEPT CHEM, HARVARD UNIV, as of 2004; asst dean, res finances & systs, fac arts & sci, harvard univ, beginning 2000; lab dir, Depts Chem, Earth & Planetary Sci, Harvard Univ, 1992-2000; res assoc, Dept Chem, 1979-1992. **Memberships:** Am Chem Soc. **Research Statement & Publications:** Development of the LHASA computer program for computer-assisted analysis of problems in synthetic organic chemistry; coordination of database expansion for LHASA. **Mailing Address:** Dept Chem Harvard Univ, 12 Oxford St, Cambridge, MA 02138-2902. **Fax:** 617-496-5618. **E-Mail:** postdoc@lhasa.harvard.edu

LONG, ALEXANDER B, NUCLEAR ENGINEERING. **Personal Data:** b New York, NY, January 16, 1943; m 1966. **Education:** Williams Col, BA, 1964; Univ Ill, Urbana, MS, 1966, PhD (nuclear eng), 1969. **Professional Experience:** PRES & CO-FOUNDER, ENVIRON SOFTWARE PROVIDERS, as of 2003; pres, Expert Ease Systs, 1983-1990; mem staff elec power res, Nuclear Safety Anal, 1978-; prog mgr, Elec Power Res Inst, 1974-1983; asst nuclear engr, Argonne Nat Lab, 1969-1978. **Memberships:** Am Nuclear Soc; Inst Elec & Electronics Engrs. **Research Statement & Publications:** Reactor physics, especially experimental techniques for on line determination of reactor physics parameters; fission physics. **Mailing Address:** Environ Software Providers, 444 Castro St Ste 800, Mtain View, CA 94041.

LONG, ALEXIS BORIS, CLOUD PHYSICS, WEATHER MODIFICATION. **Personal Data:** b New York, NY, September 9, 1944; m 1974, c 3. **Education:** Reed Col, BA, 1965; Syracuse Univ, MS, 1966; Univ Ariz, PhD (atmospheric sci), 1972. **Professional Experience:** PRIN RES SCIENTIST, DIV ATMOSPHERIC RES, COMMONWEALTHSCI & INDUST RES ORGN, AUSTRALIA, 1987-; assoc ed, J Climate & Appl Meteorol, 1985-; consult meteorlogist, Am Meteorol Soc, 1984-; ASSOC RES PROF, ATMOSPHERIC SCI CTR, DESERT RES INST, RENO, NEV, 1981-; assoc res scientist, dept meteorol, Texas A & M Univ, 1979-1981; Mem comt cloud physics, Am Meteorol Soc, 1976-1982; scientist & head hail suppression group, Nat Hail Res Exp & Convective Storms Div, Nat Ctr Atmospheric Res, 1975-1979; res assoc cloud physics, Coop Inst Res Environ Sci, Univ Colo, 1973-1975; NSF fel & vis scientist, Div Cloud Physics, Commonwealth Sci & Indust Res Orgn, 1972-1973; Res asst cloud physics, Inst Atmospheric Physics, Univ Ariz, 1969-1972. **Memberships:** Am Meteorol Soc; Am Geophys Union; Royal Meteorol Soc; Sigma Xi. **Research Statement & Publications:** Cloud physics; precipitation processes in convective and orographic clouds; Doppler radar meteorology and microwave remote sensing; mesometeorological interactions with terrain; precipitation forecasting and modification in mountainous regions; hail measuring systems and methods. **Mailing Address:** 70 Glenelg Dr, Desert Res Inst, Mentone Victoria 3194, Australia.

LONG, ALTON LOS, JR, ELECTRONICS, MATERIALS TECHNOLOGY. **Personal Data:** b Liberty, Tex, September 25, 1932; m 1955, c 4. **Education:** Carnegie Inst Technol, BS, 1953, MS, 1955; Univ Penn, MS cand, 1988. **Professional Experience:** PROG MKT MGR, GOV PROG, COMPUTER SYSTS PROD GROUP, UNISYS DEFENSE SYSTS, 1990-; Mgr, Infusec Prod & Technols, 1987-1990; dir opers, Spec Devices Div, Systs Develop Corp, Burroughs Corp, 1982-1987; prog mgr advan technol, Components Eval, 1977-1981; dept mgr, Components Eval, 1973-1977; prog mgr, Illiac IV Syst, 1972-1973; prog mgr, Comput Microfilm Systs, 1970-1972; staff engr, Adv Develop Dept, 1965-1970; supvr testing & eval sect, Unisys Defense Systs, 1961-1965; develop engr lab, Unisys Defense Systs, 1960-1961; nuclear scientist, US Army Signal Res & Develop Labs, Ft Monmouth, 1960; Instr, Monmouth Col, 1958-1959; unit chief radiation effects, US Army Signal Res & Develop Labs, Ft Monmouth, 1957-1960; Jr res chemist radiochem, Carnegie Inst Technol, 1953-1954. **Memberships:** Armed Forces Commun & Electronics Asn; Inst Elec & Electronic Engrs; Sigma Xi; Nat Mgt Asn; Inst Cert Prof Mechs. **Research Statement & Publications:** Microelectronics; information science; radiation effects on materials; electronic materials; environmental science; physics of failure; radiocarbon dating; applied radiation technology; interconnection and packaging technology. **Mailing Address:** 87 Bismark Ave, Tiverton, RI 02878.

LONG, ANDREW FLEMING, JR, MATHEMATICS. **Personal Data:** b Amboy, WVa, December 20, 1938. **Education:** WVa Univ, BS, 1960, MS, 1961; Duke Univ, PhD (math), 1965. **Professional Experience:** Assoc prof emer 2001- ASSOC PROF MATH, UNIV NC, GREENSBORO, 1975-2001; asst prof, Univ NC, Greensboro, 1967-1975; Asst prof math, St Andrews Presby Col, 1965-1967. **Memberships:** Sigma Xi. **Research Statement & Publications:** Irreducible factorable polynomials over a finite field; number theory; computer software. **Mailing Address:** Dept Math, Univ NC, Greensboro, NC 27412. **E-Mail:** aflong@uncg.edu

LONG, AUSTIN, GEOCHEMISTRY. **Personal Data:** b Olney, Tex, December 12, 1936; m 1961, c 2. **Education:** Midwestern Univ, BS, 1957; Columbia Univ, MA, 1959; Univ Ariz, PhD (geochem), 1966. **Professional Experience:** PROF EMER, DEPT GEOSCIENCE, UNIV ARIZ, as of 2005; prof geoscience, hydrol & water resources & chief scientist, Lab Isotope Geochem, Univ Ariz, beginning 1987; assoc prof Geoscience, Hydrol & Water Resources & Chief Scientist, Lab Isotope Geochem, Univ Ariz, 1968-1987; geochemist, Smithsonian Inst, 1963-1968; res asst geochem, Geochronol Labs, Univ Ariz, 1959-1963. **Memberships:** Geochemistry Soc. **Research Statement & Publications:** Pleistocene paleoclimatology; radiocarbon dating; stable isotope geochemistry. **Mailing Address:** Dept Geosci, Univ Ariz, GS 136A Gould Simpson Bldg 1040 E 4 St, Tucson, AZ 85721-0001. **E-Mail:** along@geo.arizona.edu

LONG, AUSTIN RICHARD, ANIMAL DRUGS, METHODS DEVELOPMENT & ANALYTICAL. **Personal Data:** b Akron, Ohio, September 15, 1949. **Education:** Ohio State Univ, BS, 1980, MS, 1983, PhD (food sci), 1987. **Professional Experience:** DIR, PAC REGIONAL LAB NORTHWEST, as of 2004; dir, Atlanta Ctr Nutrient Analysis, beginning 1996; dir, Animal Drugs Res Ctr, Food & Drug Admin, 1990-1996; sr fel biochem, La State Univ, 1987-1990; res assoc, Ohio State Univ, 1985-1987; teaching asst food sci, Burgwald fel, 1984; teaching asst food sci, Ohio State Univ, 1982-1983. **Research Statement & Publications:** Veterinary drug residue in animal feed, edible animal tissue and aquaculture species; development of analytical methods for regulatory use; author and inventor. **Mailing Address:** Atlanta Ctr Nutrient Anal Food & Drug Admin, 60 Eight St NE, Atlanta, GA 30309. **Fax:** 303-236-3099. **E-Mail:** rlong@ora.fda.gov

LONG, BILLY WAYNE, PHYSIOLOGY. **Personal Data:** b Tupelo, Miss, April 5, 1948; m 1972, Rebecca; c Scott & David. **Education:** David Lipscomb Col, Nashville, BA, 1969; Univ Miss, MD, 1973. **Honors & Awards:** Mount Review Award, Vet Admin, 1979. **Professional Experience:** ASST PROF MED, UNIV MISS, 1981-; asst prof med, Univ Pa, 1979-1981; fel gastroenterol, Univ Pa, 1977-1979; clin assoc digestive dis, NIH, 1975-1977; intern & resident med, Univ Miss, 1973-1975. **Memberships:** Fel Am Col Gastroenterol; fel Am Col Physicians; Am Soc Gastrointestinal Endoscopy; AMA. **Research Statement & Publications:** Physiology of pancreatic exocrine secretion; physiology of gastrointestinal hormones. **Mailing Address:** Gastro Assocs PA, 1421 N State St Ste 203, Jackson, MS 39202-1658.

LONG, CALVIN H, ANALYTICAL CHEMISTRY. **Personal Data:** b Myerstown, Pa, February 16, 1927; m 1954, c 2. **Education:** Univ Miami, BS, 1950; Franklin & Marshall Col, MS, 1956; Stanford Univ, PhD (chem), 1963. **Professional Experience:** RETIRED; mgr, Kerr-McGee Corp, 1979-1988; sect mgr, Kerr-McGee Corp, 1969-1978; res group leader analytical chem, Kerr-McGee Corp, 1964-1968; res chemist, Chevron Res Co, 1963-1964; chemist, Armstrong Cork Co, 1950-1958. **Memberships:** Am Chem Soc. **Research Statement & Publications:** Chemical equilibria; mineral benefication. **Mailing Address:** 2779 Woodgate Lane, Sarasota, FL 34231.

LONG, CALVIN LEE, BIOCHEMISTRY. **Personal Data:** b NC, January 27, 1928; m 1951, c 3. **Education:** Wake Forest Col, BS, 1948; NC State Col, MS, 1951; Univ Ill, PhD, 1954. **Professional Experience:** DIR RES, BAPTIST MED CTR, 1984-; ADJ PROF NUTRIT SCI, UNIV ALA, BIRMINGHAM, 1984-; from assoc prof to prof Biochem & Surg, Med Col Ohio, 1975-1984; res assoc, Harvard Univ, 1963 & Col Physicians & Surgeons, Columbia Univ, 1964-1974; proj leader, Gen Food Corp, 1957-1962; assoc chemist biochem, Gen Food Corp, 1954-1957. **Memberships:** AAAS; Am Inst Nutrit; Am Chem Soc; NY Acad Sci; Am Soc Parenteral & Enteral Nutrit. **Research Statement & Publications:** Intermediary metabolism and nutritional biochemistry. **Mailing Address:** Dept Res Carraway Methodist Med Ctr, 1600 Carraway Blvd, Birmingham, AL 35234.

LONG, CALVIN THOMAS, ELEMENTARY NUMBER THEORY, COMBINATORIAL NUMBER THEORY. **Personal Data:** b Rupert, Idaho, October 10, 1927; m 1952, Jean; c Gregory T & Tracy J. **Education:** Univ Idaho, BS, 1950; Univ Ore, MS, 1952, PhD (math), 1955. **Honors & Awards:** Cert of meritorious Ser, MAA, 1991; Cert of Meritorious Ser Nw Sec, MAA, 1991; Pres Fac Excellence Award for Teaching Wash State Univ, 198. **Professional Experience:** RETIRED; pres, Fibonacci Assoc, 1985-1998; ad prof, Northen Ariz Univ, 1994-; William Clare, Prentice Hall Publ Co, 1987-; mem, Ad Hoc Comt Accreditation, 1986-1990; assoc ed, Math Mag, 1986-1990; mem, Bd of Gov, MAA, 1982-1985; mem, Task Force on Post Baccalaureate Educ of Teachers, Nat Coun Teachers of Math, 1986-1988; William Clare, NSF, 1985-1987; mem, Comt Math Educ of Teachers, 1983-1988; chair, Comt Adult Educ, 1983 & 1985; William Clare, Wash State Dept Educ, 1983, 1987-1988, 1989; mem, Comt Employment of Math, 1980-1988; mem, Bd of Gov, MAA, 1982-1985; Gov NW Sec MAA, 1982-1985; mem, Ad Hoc Comt NCATE Guidelines, 1979-1980; vis prof, Portland State Univ, 1979; mem, Coun Conf Bd Math Sci, 1978-1980; mem, Comt Rev Guidelines for the Accreditation of Col Math Progs, 1978-1980; mem, Comt Adult Educ, 1978-1980; vis prof, Clemson Univ, 1978-1979; educ consult, Rand McNally & Co, 1975-1977; consult, Educ Comn States, Nat Assessment Educ Progress, 1975; chair, Comt Rev Guidelines for the Accreditation of Col Math Progs, 1974-1978; William Clare, Ltd, 1973-1977; vis prof, Univ BC, 1972; chmn dept, Wash State Univ, 1970-; prof math, Wash State Univ, 1965-1993; vis prof, Univ Jabalpur, India, 1965; educ consult, Wash State Dept Educ, 1961-1967 & NSF, 1963-1983; from asst prof to assoc prof, Wash State Univ, 1956-1965; analyst, Nat Security Agency, 1955-1956. **Memberships:** Math Asn Am; Nat Coun Teachers Math; Asn Teachers Math; Fibonacci Asn; Am Math Soc. **Research Statement & Publications:** Probabilistic and combinatorial number theory and other combinatorial problems. **Mailing Address:** 2120 N Timberline Rd, Flagstaff, AZ 86004-7548.

LONG, CARL F(ERDINAND), REINFORCED CONCRETE DESIGN, MANAGEMENT OF WATER WORKS COMPANY. **Personal Data:** b New York, NY, August 6, 1928; m 1955, Joanna; c Carl F Jr & Barbara A. **Education:** Mass Inst Technol, SB, 1950, SM, 1952; Yale Univ, DEng, 1964. **Honorary Degrees:** MA, Dartmouth Col, 1971. **Honors & Awards:** Robert Fletcher Award, Thayer Sch Eng, 1985. **Professional Experience:** RETIRED; pres & dir, Hanover Water Works Inc, beginning 1990; pres & dir, Roan Thayer Inc, 1987-1993; dir, Micro-Weigh Systs Inc, 1987-1993; emer dean & dir, Cook Eng Design Ctr, 1984-1994; mem, vis comt, Mass Bd Regents Higher Educ, 1984-1993; dir, Micro-Tool Co Inc, Fitchburg, MA, 1984-1992; pres & dir, OS-Oxygen Processes, Portland, Maine, 1979-1984; vpres opers, Controlled Environ Corp, Grantham, NH, 1976-1981; trustee, Mt Wash Observ, 1975-; dir, Controlled Environ Corp, Grantham, NH, 1975-1981; mem bd overseers, Mary Hitchcock Mem Hosp, beginning 1973; mem, ad hoc vis comt, Eng Coun Prof Develop, 1973-1981; from assoc dean to dean, Thayer Sch Eng, Dartmouth Col, 1972-1984; prof eng, Thayer Sch Eng, Dartmouth Col, 1970-1994; consult, NH State Water Pollution Comn, 1958-1993; consult, Small Arms Systs Agency, US Army; from instr civil eng to assoc prof, Mass Inst Technol, 1954-1970; res engr, Mass Inst Technol, 1954; asst civil eng, Mass InstTechnol, 1952-1954. **Memberships:** AAAS; Am Soc Civil Engrs; Am Soc Eng Educ. **Research Statement & Publications:** Analytical and experimental investigations of structures and structural elements; planning and decision making for small towns and cities with time-sharing computers; maintenance, planning and funding modest size water distribution systems. **Mailing Address:** 25 Resevoir Rd, Hanover, NH 03755-1311. **Fax:** 603-646-3856.

LONG, CAROLE ANN, IMMUNOLOGY, PARASITOLOGY. **Personal Data:** b Baltimore, Md, October 2, 1944; m 1980, Walter; c 5. **Education:** Cornell Univ, AB, 1965; Univ Pa, PhD (microbiol & immunol), 1970. **Professional Experience:** PROF, DEPT MICROBIOL & IMMUNOL, ALLEGHENY UNIV, 1996-; chair, Adv Comn Parasitol, Burroughs-Wellcome Found, 1996-; from asst prof to prof, Hahnemann Univ, 1977-1996; asst mem, Inst Med Res, 1976-1977; sr res scientist, Wyeth Labs, Radnor, Pa, 1973-1975; fel, Univ Pa Sch Med, 1970-1973; res grants, NIH; res grants, WHO. **Memberships:** Am Asn Immunologists; Tissue Cult Asn (treas 1976); AAAS; Asn Women Sci; Sigma Xi; Am Soc Trop Med

& Hyg (pres, 1994-1995). **Research Statement & Publications:** Host-parasite relationships in malaria parasites; vaccine developement for malaria. **Mailing Address:** Depart MicrobioL & Immunol, Allegheny Univ, MS 410 Broad & Vine St, Philadelphia, PA 19102. **Fax:** 215-762-8509. **E-Mail:** longc@allegheny.edu

LONG, CEDRIC WILLIAM, BIOCHEMISTRY, VIROLOGY. **Personal Data:** b Minneapolis, Minn, March 4, 1937. **Education:** Univ Calif, Los Angeles, BA, 1960, MA, 1962; Princeton Univ, PhD (biochem), 1966. **Professional Experience:** SPEC ASST TO DIR, DIV EXTRAMURAL ACTIVITIES, Nat Cancer Inst, NIH, 1997-; gen mgr proj officer, Frederick Cancer Res & Develop Ctr, Nat Cancer Inst, 1986-1997; actg assoc dir, Biol Response Modifiers Prog, DCT, 1985; actg chief, Biol Resources Br, 1984-1985; chief, Preclin Trials Sect, 1980-1986; head, Biol Type C Viruses Sect, Litton Bionetics, Inc, Frederick Cancer Res Ctr, 1976-1980; head, Cell & Viral Biol Sect, 1972-1976; sr scientist, Flow Labs, Inc, 1970-1972; instr cell biol, Med Sch, NY Univ, 1969-1970; Nat Cancer Inst fel path, Med Sch, NY Univ, 1968-1969; Am Cancer Soc fel biochem, Univ Calif, Berkeley, 1966-1968. **Memberships:** Am Soc Biol Chem & Molecular Biol; Am Soc Biochem & Molecular Biol. **Research Statement & Publications:** Genetic and biochemical aspects of mammalian cell growth; expression of retroviruses; functional aspects of viral proteins; modification of host reponse to tumor cells. **Mailing Address:** Div Extramural Activities, Nat Cancer Inst, Nat Inst Health, Rm 600 Bldg 427 8 Exec Plaza N, Rockville, MD 20892-9903.

LONG, CHARLES ALAN, GENETICS, FISH & WILDLIFE. **Personal Data:** b Pittsburg, Kans, January 19, 1936; m 1960, Claudine; c Alan & John. **Education:** Pittsburg State Univ, BS, 1957, MS, 1958; Univ Kans, PhD (zoology), 1963. **Honors & Awards:** Sigma Xi Res Scholar Award, 1996; Pucci Award biol, 1996; Charles A Long Museum Mammal Collection, Univ Wis, named in honor, 2000. **Professional Experience:** PROF EMER BIOL, UNIV WIS, STEVENS POINT, 1996-; joint appt, Wildlife Mgt, 1994-; vis prof, St Olaf Col, 1991; fulbright scholar, 1977; consult, Lake Mich Proj, Argonne Nat Lab, 1974-1980 & Ojibway Tribe, Lac Del Flambeau, 1983-1985; Univ Adv Minor Mus Tech, 1974-; dir, Mus Natural Hist, 1968-1983; cur mammals, Mus Natural Hist, 1966-; from asst prof to prof, Univ Wis Stevens Point, 1966-1996; asst prof zool & life sci, Univ Ill Urbana, 1965-1966; fac fel, Univ Ill, 1964; instr, Univ Ill Urbana, 1963-1965; asst zool, Univ Kans, 1959-1963; fel, Pittsburg State Univ, 1957-1958. **Memberships:** Am Soc Mammal; Sigma Xi. **Research Statement & Publications:** Vertebrate zoology, systematics and zoogeography of mammals; morphology and ecology; variability of mammals; Wyoming and Wisconsin mammals; badgers; fractal geometry, tree branching and morphology; genetics in periodical cicadas; physics and flight. **Mailing Address:** Dept Biol, Univ Wis, Stevens Point, WI 54481. **E-Mail:** clong@uwsp.edu

LONG, CHARLES ANTHONY, CHEMICAL PHYSICS. **Personal Data:** b San Antonio, Tex, February 22, 1945. **Education:** Carleton Col, BA, 1967; Ind Univ, PhD (chem physics), 1972; Johns Hopkins Univ, BEE, 1982, MAS, 1992. **Honors & Awards:** Roseman Award, 1985. **Professional Experience:** INSTRUMENTATION SUPVR, JOHNS HOPKINS UNIV, 1979-; res assoc, Brookhaven Nat Lab, 1977-1979; NSF res grant, 1974; asst prof chem, Lake Forest Col, 1973-1977; fel chem physics, Univ Calif, Riverside, 1972-1973. **Memberships:** Am Phys Soc; Am Chem Soc; Inst Elec & Electronics Engrs. **Research Statement & Publications:** Applications of lasers to problems of the chemistry and physics of small molecules; chemical instrumentation of all forms. **Mailing Address:** Dept Chem, Johns Hopkins Univ 34th & Charles, Baltimore, MD 21218. **E-Mail:** selrahc@purcell400.chm.jhu.edu

LONG, CHARLES JOSEPH, NEUROPSYCHOLOGY. **Personal Data:** b Caruthersville, Mo, December 25, 1935; m 1958, Rosemary; c 8. **Education:** Memphis State Univ, BS, 1960, MA, 1962; Vanderbilt Univ, PhD (psychol), 1967. **Professional Experience:** PROF PSYCHOL, MEMPHIS STATE UNIV, 1974-; pres, Am Bd Prof Neuropsychol, 1993; Universal Trainer, Memphis State Univ, 1972-; dir, Neuropsychol Training Prog, 1972-; from asst prof to assoc prof, Memphis State Univ, 1967-1974. **Memberships:** Sigma Xi; Am Psychol Asn; Int Neuropsychol Asn; Nat Acad Neuropsychologists (treas, 1986). **Research Statement & Publications:** Neuropsychological assessment and cognitive retraining of head injured, learning and neurologically impaired; study of functional factors influencing chronic pain. **Mailing Address:** Dept Physiol, Memphis State Univ, Memphis, TN 38152. **Fax:** 901-678-2579. **E-Mail:** clong@memphis.edu

LONG, CLAUDINE FERN, CHEMISTRY. **Personal Data:** b Nevada, Mo, September 10, 1938; m 1960, c 2. **Education:** Pittsburg State Univ, BS, 1960; Univ Ill-Urbana, MS, 1964. **Professional Experience:** RETIRED; sr lectr chem, Univ Wis, Stevens Point, beginning 1985; Earthwatch researcher, Isle Rhum, Hebrides, Scotland, 1985; prin investr serol hyaluronidase, 1984-; prof, Univ Malaya, Kuala Lumpur, 1983; leader group nat res, Malaysia, 1982-1983; instr biol, Univ Wis, 1979-1982; teacher math & sci, PJ Jacobs Jr High Sch, Stevens Point, Wis, 1976-1979; univ coordr student teachers, Univ Wis, Stevens Point, 1971-1975; instr biol, Univ Wis, Stevens Point, 1969-1970; teacher sci, Ben Franklin Jr High Sch, Stevens Point, Wis, 1968; teacher sci, W Jr High Sch, Lawrence, Kans, 1960-1963. **Memberships:** Nat Wildlife Fedn. **Research Statement & Publications:** Insecticide resistant houseflies; natural history of birds and mammals; serological properties of hyaluronidase (trematoda); resources of Malaysia (tin, palm oil, pewter, etc); ecology of shore birds; Isle of Rhum, Hebrides, Scotland. **Mailing Address:** Dept chem, Univ Wis-Stevens Point, Stevens Point, WI 54481.

LONG, CLIFFORD A, mathematics; deceased, see previous edition for last biography

LONG, DALE DONALD, PHYSICS INSTRUCTION, EXPERIMENTAL PHYSICS. **Personal Data:** b Louisa, Va, January 30, 1935; m 1965, Lou; c Donald & Douglas. **Education:** Va Polytech Inst, BS, 1958, MS, 1962; Fla State Univ, PhD (physics), 1966. **Professional Experience:** PROF EMER RESIDENCE, VA POLYTECH INST & STATE UNIV, 2000-; prof physics, Va Polytech Inst & State Univ, 1992-2000; vis assoc prof, Davidson Col, 1988-1989; from asst prof to assoc prof, VA Polytech Inst & State Univ, 1967-1992; instr, Samford Univ, 1960-1962; instr physics, Va Polytech Inst, 1960. **Memberships:** Am Phys Soc; Am Asn Physics Teachers. **Research Statement & Publications:** Development of multimedia materials for physics instruction; enhancement of the effectiveness of physics instruction, author of introductory physics textbooks; experimental nuclear physics. **Mailing Address:** Dept Physics, Va Polytech Inst & State Univ, Robeson 301D, Blacksburg, VA 24061-0435. **Fax:** 540-231-7511. **E-Mail:** dale.long@vt.edu

LONG, DARREL GRAHAM FRANCIS, CLASTIC & CARBONATE SEDIMENTOLOGY, COAL GEOLOGY. **Personal Data:** b Yorkshire, Eng, September 6, 1947; m 1973, c 2. **Education:** Univ Leicester, Eng, BSc, 1969; Univ Western Ont, MSc, 1973, PhD (geol), 1976. **Professional Experience:** Chair, Dept Earth Sci, Laurentian Univ, 2003; PROF SEDIMENTOL, DEPT EARTH SCI, LAURENTIAN UNIV, SUDBURY, 1989-; from asst prof to assoc prof, Laurentian Univ, Sudbury, 1981-1989; res scientist coal geol, Geol Surv Can, 1977-1981; fel geol, Geol Surv Can, 1976-1977. **Memberships:** Geol Asn Can; Geol Soc Am; Int Asn Sedimentologists; Soc Econ Paleontologists & Mineralogists; Can Soc Petrol Geologists; Geol Soc Australia. **Research Statement & Publications:** Clastic sedimentology of Precambrian sequences in Ontario, Yukon and Northwest Territory Canada; sedimentology and coal bearing sequences in British Columbia, Yukon, Northwest Territory and Ontario; phanerozoic sedimentology and tectonics of the Arctic Islands and Quebec. **Mailing Address:** Dept Earth Sci, Laurentian Univ, Ramsey Lake Rd, Sudbury, ON P3E 2C6, Can. **E-Mail:** dlong@laurentian.ca

LONG, DARYL CLYDE, SOIL SCIENCE. **Personal Data:** b Mason City, Iowa, August 19, 1939; m 1960, Peggy; c Keith, Eric & Christy. **Education:** Iowa State Univ, BS, 1962, MS, 1964; Univ Nebr, Lincoln, PhD, 1967. **Professional Experience:** PROF SCI, PERU STATE COL, 1981-; from asst prof to assoc prof sci & math, Peru State Col, 1967-1981; instr soils, Univ Nebr, Lincoln, 1964-1967. **Memberships:** Am Soc Agron; Soil Sci Soc Am; Nat Coun Teachers Math; Sigma Xi. **Research Statement & Publications:** Mechanics of soil erosion and plant removal of nutrients from soil aggregates. **Mailing Address:** Dept Nat Sci, Peru State Col, Hoyt Sci Hall Rm 118 600 Hoyt St PO Box 10, Peru, NE 68421. **E-Mail:** dlong@oakmail.peru.edu

LONG, DAVID G, SCATTEROMETRY, RADAR. **Education:** Brigham Young Univ, BS, 1982, MS, 1983; Univ Southern Calif, PhD (elec eng), 1989. **Honors & Awards:** NASA Achievement Award, 1996, 2000. **Professional Experience:** PROF ELEC ENG, BRIGHAM YOUNG UNIV, 1990-; prin investr, NASA, beginning 1989; group leader, Jet Propulsion Lab, 1983-1990. **Memberships:** Inst Elec & Electronic Engrs; Am Geophys Union. **Research Statement & Publications:** Spaceborne scatterometry; radar; microwave remote sensing; mesoscale atmospheric dynamics; speech and signal processing; estimation theory. **Mailing Address:** Dept Elec & Comput Eng, 459 Clyde Bldg, Brigham Young Univ, Provo, UT 84602-1021. **Fax:** 801-378-6586, 801-422-0201. **E-Mail:** long@byu.edu

LONG, DAVID MICHAEL, CARDIOVASCULAR SURGERY, THORACIC SURGERY. **Personal Data:** b Shamokin, Pa, February 26, 1929; c 6. **Education:** Muhlenberg Col, BS, 1951; Hahnemann Med Col, MS, 1954, MD, 1956; Univ Minn, PhD (physiol), 1965; Am Bd Surg, dipl, 1966; Bd Thoracic Surg, dipl, 1967. **Honors & Awards:** First Prize Res, Am Urol Asn, 1966. **Professional Experience:** CHMN & CHIEF EXEC OFFICER, BIOFIELD INC, as of 2006; PRES, ABEL LABS INC, 1991-; chmn, Abel Labs Inc, beginning 1991; founder & chmn, Alliance Pharmaceut Corp, 1989-1991; pres & chmn, Fluoromed Pharmaceut Inc, 1985-1988; clin assoc prof radiol, Univ Calif, San Diego, 1973-1992; pvt pract, 1973-1985; from assoc prof to prof surg, Abraham Lincoln Sch Med, Univ Ill Med Ctr, 1969-1973; dir, Hektoen Inst Med Res, 1968-1973; attend staff & head div cardiovasc & thoracic surg, Hosp, 1967-1973; consult, Chicago State Tuberc Sanitarium, 1967-1972; attend staff, W Side Vet Admin Hosp, 1966-1973; assoc attend staff, Cook County Hosp, 1965-1973; assoc prof, Cook County Grad Sch Med, 1965-1973; asst dir dept surg res, Hektoen Inst Med Res, 1965-1968; from asst prof to assoc prof, Chicago Med Sch, 1965-1967; instr surg, Univ Minn, 1965. **Memberships:** AAAS; Am Asn Thoracic Surg; fel Am Col Cardiol; fel Am Col Chest Physicians; fel Am Col Surg. **Research Statement & Publications:** Surgical research; physiology and morphology; cancer chemotherapy; development of the radiopaque compound perfluorocarbon; development of fluorocarbon emulsions as blood substitutes; electropotential differential diagnosis of breast cancer. **Mailing Address:** Abel Labs Inc, 2727 Orange Way, Ste 108, Spring Valley, CA 91978-1745. **Fax:** 619-670-3175.

LONG, DIANA E, HISTORY OF MEDICINE & WOMENS STUDIES. **Personal Data:** b New Haven, Conn, May 11, 1938; m 1989, Thomas; c John Greenword, Jeffrey Drisko & Hugh Frenklin Hall. **Education:** Smith Col, BA, 1959; Yale Univ, MA, 1960, PhD (hist sci & med), 1966. **Professional Experience:** PROF HIST, UNIV SOUTHERN MAINE, 1995-; assoc prof hist, 1990-1995; dir, Women's Studies, 1990-1993; vis sr historian, Nat Libr Med, 1989-1990; dir, F C Wood Inst Hist Med, Col Physicians, Philadelphia, 1983-1989; NSF & NIH res grants, 1976-1978; fel, Radcliffe Inst, 1976-1977; asst prof biol & hist, Boston Univ, 1973-1983; lectr biol, Boston Univ, 1970-1973; res assoc, Yale Univ, 1967-1970. **Memberships:** AAAS (secy, 1977-1981); Hist Sci Soc; Am Asn Hist Med; Am Hist Asn; Org Am Hist. **Research Statement & Publications:** Biomedical research in twentieth century; eighteenth century medical science; sex research-scientific and social aspects; Am medicine in 20th century; medical language and classification; women in science. **Mailing Address:** Dept hist, Univ Southern Maine, PO Box 9300 96 Falmouth St, Portland, ME 04104-9300. **Fax:** 207-780-5311. **E-Mail:** dlong@usm.maine.edu

LONG, DONLIN MARTIN, NEUROSURGERY, ELECTRON MICROSCOPY. **Personal Data:** b Rolla, Mo, April 14, 1934; m 1959, Harriett; c Kimberley Page, Elisabeth Merchant & David Bradford. **Education:** Univ Mo, MD, 1959; Univ Minn, PhD (anat), 1964. **Honors & Awards:** Wakeman Award, Wakeman Foundation, 1990; Jamison Medal, Australian nsq soc, 1986; Beks Medal, Dutch nsq soc, 1998; qinde Medal, Indian nsq soc, 1999. **Professional Experience:** PROF NEUROL SURG & DIR DEPT, SCH MED, JOHNS HOPKINS UNIV, 1973-; consult neurosurgeon, Vet Admin Hosp, Minneapolis, 1967-; assoc prof neurosurg, Univ Minn Hosps, 1967-1973; clin assoc, Surg Neurol Bd, NIH, 1965-1967. **Memberships:** AAAS; Am Asn Neurol Surg; Cong Neurol Surg; AAAS; Soc Neuroscience. **Research Statement & Publications:** Outcomes of ther for Spinal Pain, neuropath of Brian Edema. **Mailing Address:** Dept Neurol Surg, Johns Hopkins Univ Sch Med, Baltimore, MD 21287-7709. **E-Mail:** dmlong@jhmi.edu

LONG, EARL ELLSWORTH, PUBLIC HEALTH LABORATORY ADMINISTRATION. **Personal Data:** b Akron, Ohio, March 27, 1919; m 1941, Eileen; c Robert E, Dan C, Jack C & James W. **Education:** Univ Akron, BSc, 1942; Univ Pa, MSc, 1947. **Professional Experience:** RETIRED; dir labs, Ga Dept Pub Health, 1961-1982; dir labs, Akron Health Dept, 1949-1961; asst prof bact, Univ Akron, 1948-1949; asst instr med bact, Sch Med, Univ Pa, 1945-1948. **Memberships:** Am Soc Microbiol; fel Am Pub Health Asn; Asn State & Territorial Pub Health Labs Dirs (pres, 1980); Sigma Xi. **Research Statement & Publications:** State public health laboratory administration with emphasis on implementation of rapidly changing concepts in service and research. **Mailing Address:** 25313 Plantation Dr, Atlanta, GA 30324-2946.

LONG, EDWARD B, WETLANDS ECOLOGY. **Personal Data:** b White Plains, NY, December 5, 1927; m 1970, c 3. **Education:** Hamilton Col, BA, 1952; Kent State Univ, MS, 1971, PhD (biol), 1975. **Professional Experience:** ENVIRON CONSULT, 1981-; tech mgr, Environ Prog, Northeast Ohio Areawide Coord Agency, 1975-1981; proj mgr, New Prod Mkt Develop, 1964-1969; mem staff mkt, Carbon Prod Div, Union Carbide Corp, 1952-1964. **Memberships:** Am Soc Limnol & Oceanog; AAAS. **Research Statement & Publications:** Environmental quality of Northeast Ohio. **Mailing Address:** 3140 N Martadale Dr, Akron, OH 44333.

LONG, EDWARD R, POLLUTANT-CAUSED BIOLOGICAL EFFECTS, ESTUARINE SEDIMENT TOXICOLOGY. **Personal Data:** b Washougal, Wash, 1942. **Education:** Ore State Univ, BS, 1965, MS, 1967. **Professional Experience:** RETIRED, 2000; marine biologist, Nat Oceanic & Atmospheric Admin, 1975-2000; res biologist, Wapora, Inc, 1973-1975; lectr, George Wash Univ, 1970-1975; biol oceanogr, Naval Oceanog Off, 1967-1973;

private consulting, ERL Environmental. **Memberships:** mem Soc of Environ Toxicol & Chem. **Research Statement & Publications:** Marine pollution research, focusing upon measures of biological effects in contaminated sediments. **Mailing Address:** 3691 Cole Rd So, Salem, OR 97306. **E-Mail:** elongna@earthlink.net

LONG, EDWARD RICHARDSON, MOLECULAR PHYSICS, MATERIALS SCIENCE. **Personal Data:** b Annapolis, Md, September 1, 1941; m 1968. **Education:** Col William & Mary, BS, 1963, MS, 1967; NC State Univ, PhD (molecular physics, nuclear magnetic resonance), 1974. **Professional Experience:** LONGHILL TECHNOLOGIES INC, as of 2004; RES SCIENTIST MAT SCI, MAT DIV, ENVIRON EFFECTS BR, LANGLEY RES CTR, NASA, 1980-; assoc prof, George Wash Univ, 1976-; res scientist mat sci, Mat Div, Mat Res Br, 1976-1980; res scientist org pollution, Environ & Space Sci Div, Laser & Molecular Physics Br, 1972-1976; res scientist solid state physics, Appl Math & Physics Div, Chem & Physics Br, 1969-1972; res scientist human factors, Aeronaut & Space Mech Div, Guid & Control Br, Langley Res Ctr, NASA, 1963-1967. **Memberships:** Am Phys Soc. **Research Statement & Publications:** Solid state physics and organic chemical physics as applied to pollution spectroscopy and materials science. **Mailing Address:** Langley Res Ctr, NASA, Waynesboro, VA 22980. **Fax:** 320-209-5288. **E-Mail:** e.r.long@larc.nasa.gov

LONG, ERIC CHARLES, DNA-DRUG INTERACTIONS, PEPTIDE CHEMISTRY. **Personal Data:** b Reading, Pa, November 20, 1962. **Education:** Albright Col, BS, 1984, Univ Va, PhD (chem), 1989. **Professional Experience:** PROF & ASSOC CHMN BIOL CHEM, IND UNIV-PURDUE UNIV, INDIANAPOLIS, as of 2002; mem, Molecular & Biophys Prog, Ind Univ Grad Sch, 1991-; asst prof chem, Ind Univ-Purdue Univ, Indianapolis, 1991; Jane Coffin Childs fel, Dept Chem, Calif Inst Technol & Columbia Univ, 1989-1991. **Memberships:** Am Chem Soc; Am Peptide Soc. **Research Statement & Publications:** Design, synthesis and testing of structured peptides and metallopeptides that target nucleic acids sequence-selectively. **Mailing Address:** Dept Chem Eng, Ind Univ-Purdue Univ, 402 N Blackford St, Indianapolis, IN 46202. **Fax:** 317-274-4701. **E-Mail:** long@chem.iupui.edu

LONG, F(RANCIS) M(ARK), MICROCIRCUITS. **Personal Data:** b Iowa City, Iowa, November 10, 1929; wid Mary A Coyne; c Ann (Brett), Mary (Bronwyn), Thomas M & Caitlin F. **Education:** Univ Iowa, BS, 1953, MS, 1956; Iowa State Univ, PhD (elec eng, biomed electronics), 1961. **Professional Experience:** Adj prof, Univ Colo-Denver, 1998; PROF EMER, ELEC ENG, UNIV WYO, 1998; PROF, ELEC ENG, UNIV WYO, 1995-; Naval Res Lab, Summers 1988, 1989, 1991; TEACHING & CONSULT SURFACE MOUNT TECHNOL, WYO BIOTELEMETRY INC, 1983-; cofounder, Wyo Biotelemetry Inc, 1978; head, Dept Elec Eng, 1977-1987; Globe Union Co, 1975; NIH spec fel, 1972-1973; dir bioeng, Univ Wyo, 1965-1974; from asst prof to prof, Dept Elec Eng, 1960-1995; instr, Univ Wyo, 1956-1958 & Iowa State Univ, 1958-1960; US Naval Air Missile Testing Ctr, Calif, 1956 & Good-All Elec Co, 1957; asst elec eng, Univ Iowa, 1955-1956; engr, Collins Radio Co, 1955. **Memberships:** Sr mem Inst Elec & Electronics Engrs; Am Soc Eng Educ (vpres, 1977-1979); Alliance for Eng in Med & Biol (pres, 1983-1984); Int Soc Hybrid Microelectronics. **Research Statement & Publications:** Instrumentation and system design; system modelling; microcircuit technology; animal biotelemetry; polymer thick film circuits; concurrent engineering/TQM, Design of Experiments. **Mailing Address:** 1888 S Jackson St No 701, Denver, CO 80210. **E-Mail:** flong3959@aol.com

LONG, GABRIELLE GIBBS, MICRO STRUCTURE CHARACTERIZATION, X-RAY OPTICS. **Personal Data:** m 1982, Knox; c Janet C (Cox) & Daniel. **Education:** Polytech Inst Brooklyn, PhD (physics), 1972. **Professional Experience:** GROUP LEADER, NAT INST STAND & TECHNOL, 1990-; Coun, Am Phys Soc, 1996; coun, Mat Res Soc, 1995-1997; asst prof physics, State Univ NY, Stony Brook, 1979; asst prof physics, Vassar Col, 1976-1978; res assoc physics, Columbia Univ, 1972-1976. **Memberships:** Fel Am Physics Soc; Am Ceramic Soc; Mat Res Soc; Am Crystallog Asn. **Research Statement & Publications:** Microstructure of characterization of materials; x-ray optics; x-ray ihelastic scattering; anomalous x-ray scattering; multiple-small-angle neutron scattering; x-ray dynamical diffraction by imperfect crystalls; surface x-ray absorbtion spectroscopy of ultrathin films. **Mailing Address:** Nat Inst Stand & Technol, 100 Bur Dr, Stop 8520, Gaithersburg, MD 20899. **Fax:** 301-975-5334. **E-Mail:** gabrielle.long@nist.gov

LONG, GARY JOHN, PHYSICAL INORGANIC CHEMISTRY, SOLID STATE CHEMISTRY. **Personal Data:** b Binghamton, NY, December 3, 1941; m Fernande; c Jeffrey Robert. **Education:** Carnegie-Mellon Univ, BS, 1964; Syracuse Univ, PhD (chem), 1968. **Professional Experience:** Int Found Francqui Chmn Belg, 2002-2003; J William Fulbright scholar, 1993-1994; vis prof physics, Univ Liege, 1992-1994; Univ Geneva, Switz, 1988; vis prof chem, Univ Padova, Italy, 1986-1988; sci & eng res coun fel, Univ Liverpool, 1983-1984; NATO vis prof chem, Univ Padova, Italy, 1983; PROF CHEM, UNIV MO, ROLLA, beginning 1982; res assoc, Atomic Energy Res Estab, Harwell, 1975-1981; res assoc, Inorg Chem Lab & St John's Col, Oxford Univ, 1974-1975; from asst prof to assoc prof, Univ MO, Rolla, 1968-1982. **Memberships:** Am Chem Soc; fel Royal Soc Chem; Sigma Xi; Am Phys Soc; Am Geophys Union; AAAS. **Research Statement & Publications:** Transition metal inorganic coordination chemistry and solid state chemistry; Mossbauer and electronic spectroscopy; high-pressure optical and infrared spectroscopy; magnetic studies of coupled systems and permanent magnetic materials; x-ray and neutron diffraction studies. **Mailing Address:** Dept Chem, Univ Mo, 335 Schrenk Hall, Rolla, MO 65409-0010. **Fax:** 573-341-6033. **E-Mail:** glong@umr.edu

LONG, GEORGE, CHEMICAL ENGINEERING. **Personal Data:** b Greenville, Miss, January 17, 1922; m 1951, c 1. **Education:** Univ Tulane, BE, 1944. **Professional Experience:** CONSULT, NATURAL GAS INDUST, 1987-; mgr dir res & develop, Northern Ill Gas Co, 1977-1987; dir, Northern Ill Gas Co, 1967-1977; gen coordr res & develop, Northern Ill Gas Co, 1962-1967; res engr, Aluminum Co Am, 1946-1962; chief chemist, USAAF, 1945-1946; res chemist, Div 8, Nat Defense Res Comt, Ohio, 1944-1945. **Memberships:** Am Gas Asn; Sigma Xi; fel Am Inst Chem; Chem Mkt Res Asn; Am Chem Soc. **Research Statement & Publications:** Process metallurgy of aluminum melting and smelting; aluminum-water explosions; high temperature refractory materials; natural gas utilization, materials and devices for distribution systems, substitute natural gas processes and natural gas combustion; synthetic fuel processes. **Mailing Address:** 24 Sylvia Lane, Naperville, IL 60540-8014.

LONG, GEORGE GILBERT, INORGANIC CHEMISTRY. **Personal Data:** b Cincinnati, Ohio, July 12, 1929; m 1952, c 3. **Education:** Ind Univ, AB, 1951; NC State Univ, MS, 1953; Univ Fla, PhD (chem), 1957. **Professional Experience:** RETIRED; prof chem, NC State Univ, 1970; chmn analytical inorg chem, NC State Univ, 1969-1977; from asst prof to assoc prof, NC State Univ, 1958-1970; Chemist, Ethyl Corp, 1957-1958. **Memberships:** Am Chem Soc Sigma Xi. **Research Statement & Publications:** Chemistry of group V metalloids-organometalloid compounds; 121-Sb Mossbauer spectroscopy, structure and syntheses; vibrational spectroscopy. **Mailing Address:** 2701 Kilgore Ave, Raleigh, NC 27607.

LONG, GEORGE LOUIS, BIOCHEMISTRY, MOLECULAR BIOLOGY. **Personal Data:** b Atkin, Minn, December 20, 1943; m 2000. **Education:** Pac Lutheran Univ, BA, 1966; Brandeis Univ, PhD (biochem), 1971. **Honors & Awards:** Intellectual Property Owners Association National Inventor of the Year, 2002; elected to the Vermon. **Professional Experience:** PROF BIOCHEM, UNIV VT, 1991-; assoc prof, Univ Vt, 1986-1991; scientist, Lilly Res Labs, 1982-1986; NIH sr fel biochem, Univ Wash, 1979-1982; asst prof chem, Pomona Col, 1973-1979; NIH trainee molecular endocrinol sch med, Univ Calif, San Diego, 1971-1973. **Memberships:** Am Soc Molecular & Biol Chem; Am Chem Soc; AAAS; International Soc on Thrombosis & Haemostasis. **Research Statement & Publications:** Comparative enzymology of glycolytic enzymes; molecular biology of hemostasis; bone biochemistry. **Mailing Address:** Dept Biochem, Sch Med, Univ Vt, C450A Given Bldg, Burlington, VT 05405. **E-Mail:** george.long@.uvm.edu

LONG, HOWARD CHARLES, ACOUSTICS, ATOMIC & MOLECULAR PHYSICS. **Personal Data:** b Seizholtzville, Pa, December 12, 1918; m 1945, Frances; c Howard C, David W & Carol (Boll). **Education:** Northwestern Univ, BS, 1941; Ohio State Univ, PhD (physics), 1948. **Professional Experience:** PROF EMER PHYSICS, DICKINSON COL, 1981-; NSF sci fac fel, 1967-1968; chmn dept, Dickinson Col, 1963-1974; prof, Dickinson Col, 1959-1981; consult, Naval Ord Lab, 1954-1973; prof & chmn dept, Gettysburg Col, 1953-1959; assoc prof physics & chmn dept, Am Univ, 1952-1953; physicist, Naval Ord Lab, 1951-1952; asst prof, Wash & Jefferson Col, 1948-1951; instr physics, Ohio State Univ, 1947-1948; physicist, Naval Ord Lab, 1942-1945. **Memberships:** Am Phys Soc; Am Asn Physics Teachers. **Research Statement & Publications:** Low period fluctuations in earth's magnetism; environmental noise reduction; air pollution by solid particulates; molecular structure and infrared spectroscopy; electromagnetism. **Mailing Address:** Dept Physics, Dickinson Col, PO Box 1773, Carlisle, PA 17013.

LONG, H(UGH) M(ONTGOMERY), ENHANCED OIL RECOVERY, SUPERCONDUCTING SYSTEMS. **Personal Data:** b Montgomery, Ala, June 28, 1924; m 1949, c 2. **Education:** Ala Polytech Inst, BS, 1947, MS, 1949; Oxford Univ, DPhil(physics), 1953. **Professional Experience:** STAFF EXEC, ENHANCED ENERGY SYSTS INC, 1981-; vpres mkt develop, Vedette Energy Res Inc, 1980-1981; mgr elec energy systs prog, Energy Div, 1976-1980; mem & chmn, US Delegation USSR Scientific & Technol Exchange Superconductivity Power Transmission, 1973-1979; assoc prof elec eng, Univ Tenn, Knoxville, 1971-1980; group leader eng sci, Thermonuclear Div, 1971-1976; US rep, Comt I, Int Inst Refrig, beginning 1964; cryogenics consult, Linde Div, Oak Ridge Nat Lab, Union Carbide Corp, 1961-1971; Mem, Nat Acad Sci-Nat Res Coun adv panel to Nat Bur Standards Cryogenic Eng Lab, 1961-1965; res physicist, Linde Div, Oak Ridge Nat Lab, Union Carbide Corp, 1954-1961; res asst, Auburn Univ, 1947-1949; instr math, Auburn Univ, 1947-1948. **Memberships:** AAAS; Am Phys Soc; sr mem Inst Elec & Electronics Engrs; NY Acad Sci; Soc Petrol Engrs. **Research Statement & Publications:** Low temperature physics; cryogenic engineering; gas liquefaction; low temperature phase equilibria; mechanical properties of materials at low temperatures; superconductivity; power system engineering; energy management. **Mailing Address:** 3551 Lilac Ave, Corona Del Mar, CA 92625.

LONG, JAMES A, EXPLORATION GEOPHYSICS, INTERPRETATIONS & OPERATIONS. **Personal Data:** b Porto Alegre, Brazil, July 13, 1917; American citizen; wid Sui; c Frank, David, Susan & Kathryn. **Education:** Univ Okla, BA, 1937. **Professional Experience:** RETIRED; geophys adv, Yacimientos Petroliferos Fiscales Bolivianos, Santa Cruz, Bolivia, 1974-1977; int consult geophysicist, Peru, US, Australia, Colombia, 1973-1984; sr geophysicist, Tetra Tech Inc, 1973-1974; special tech & res assignments, MB Dobrin, 1962-1967 regional mgr, Latin Am, 1967-1972; party chief supvr, area mgr & regional opers mgr, United Geophys Corp, South & Cent Am, 1946-1962; comput & party chief, Stanolind Oil & Gas Co, 1937-1946. **Memberships:** Soc Explorer Geophysicists; fel Explorers Club. **Research Statement & Publications:** Seismic surface sources; special seismic interpretation problems and supervision of operations particularly in South America and Australia. **Mailing Address:** 114 Moorings Park Dr, Naples, FL 34105.

LONG, JAMES DELBERT, AGRONOMY, HERBICIDE RESEARCH. **Personal Data:** b Dover, Okla, December 18, 1939; c 5. **Education:** Okla State Univ, BS, 1962; Univ Md, College Park, MS, 1967, PhD (hort), 1969. **Professional Experience:** RETIRED; res assoc, Agr Chem Dept, 1983-1992; prod develop mgr, E I DuPont de Nemours & Co Inc, Wilmington, Del, 1979-1983; res biologist agr chem, E I DuPont de Nemours & Co Inc, Wilmington, Del, 1968-1979; instr hort, Univ Md, College Park, 1967-1968; Res asst weed control, Univ Md, College Park, 1964-1967. **Memberships:** Southern Weed Sci Soc; Sigma Xi. **Research Statement & Publications:** Control and modification of plant growth through the use of chemicals; new herbicide discovery and development. **Mailing Address:** 213 Blake Rd, Elkton, MD 21921.

LONG, JAMES DUNCAN, ZOOLOGY. **Personal Data:** b Rusk, Tex, September 23, 1925. **Education:** Sam Houston State Col, BS, 1948, MA, 1951; Univ Tex, PhD, 1957. **Honors & Awards:** Pres Citation, Am Mosquito Control Asn. **Professional Experience:** PROF EMER BIOL, SAM HOUSTON STATE UNIV, 1999-; prof biol, Sam Houston State Univ, beginning 1963; dir dept, Sam Houston State Univ, 1963-1972; assoc prof, Sam Houston State Univ, 1959-1963; assoc prof biol & head dept, Ill Col, 1956-1959; asst, Univ Tex, 1953-1956; instr biol, Lamar State Col Technol, 1952-1953; teacher, High Sch, Tex, 1948-1949 & Pub Schs, 1951-1952; newsletter ed, Am Mosquito Control Asn. **Memberships:** Am Mosquito Control Asn; Entom Soc Am. **Research Statement & Publications:** Mosquito biology. **Mailing Address:** Dept Biol, Sam Houston State Univ, 300 Lee Drain Box 2116, Huntsville, TX 77341-1001. **Fax:** 409-294-1598. **E-Mail:** bio_jdl@shsu.edu

LONG, JAMES N, ENVIRONMENTAL SCIENCES. **Education:** Univ Wash, BS, 1968, MS, 1973, PhD (forest ecol & silviculture), 1976. **Professional Experience:** PROF, DEPT FOREST ECOL, & WILDLIFE SCI, UTAH STATE UNIV, UTAH, as of 2006. **Memberships:** Sigma Xi; Nat Sci Found. **Mailing Address:** Dept Forest Resources, Utah State Univ, Logan, UT 84322-5215. **Fax:** 435-797-4040. **E-Mail:** FAKPB@cc.usu.edu

LONG, JAMES WILLIAM, BIOCHEMISTRY. **Personal Data:** b Boise, Idaho, August 26, 1943; m 1965, Judith; c Gregory P & Jeffrey W. **Education:** Univ Wash, BS, 1965; Univ Calif, Berkeley, PhD (biochem), 1969. **Professional Experience:** SR INSTR EMER CHEM, UNIV ORE, as of 2004; sr instr chem, Univ Ore, beginning 1978; from asst prof to assoc prof chem, Col Great Falls, 1974-1978; res assoc, Univ Ore, 1973-1974; res assoc, Purdue Univ, West Lafayette, 1972-1973; Res assoc biochem, NIH res fel, 1971-1972; Res assoc biochem, Purdue Univ, West Lafayette, 1970-1971. **Memberships:** Am Chem Soc; AAAS. **Research Statement & Publications:** Computers in chemical education; structure-function relationships in enzymes; mechanisms of enzyme action; enzyme model systems; role of metal ions in enzyme catalysis. **Mailing Address:** Dept Chem, 1253 Univ Ore, Eugene, OR 97403-1253. **Fax:** 541-346-4643. **E-Mail:** jlong@uoregon.edu

LONG, JEROME R, MAGNETIC & TRANSPORT PHENOMENA. **Personal Data:** b Lafayette, La, May 17, 1935; m 1990, Peggy; c Christopher & Jeremy. **Education:** Univ Southwestern La, BS, 1956; La State Univ, MS, 1958, PhD (physics), 1965. **Professional Experience:** ASSOC PROF EMER RESIDENCE, VA POLYTECH INST & STATE UNIV, as of 2004; vis prof, Naval Res Lab, 1987; vis prof, Mont State Univ, 1986; vis prof, Simon Fraser Univ, 1978-1979; assoc prof physics, Va Polytech Inst & State Univ, beginning 1971; asst prof physics, VA Polytech Inst & State Univ, 1967-1971; fel metall, Univ Pa, 1965-1967; res engr, Gen Dynamics/Pomona, 1958-1959. **Memberships:** Am Phys Soc; Int Elec & Electronics Engrs. **Research Statement & Publications:** Transport and magnetic properties of metallic materials; cryophysics; squid susceptometry on layered and or film magnetic and or superconducting materials. **Mailing Address:** Dept Physics, Va Polytech Inst & State Univ, Robeson 303, Blacksburg, VA 24061-0435. **Fax:** 540-231-7511. **E-Mail:** jrlong@vt.edu

LONG, JIM T(HOMAS), ELECTRICAL ENGINEERING. **Personal Data:** b Central, SC, October 5, 1923; m 1946, c 1. **Education:** Clemson Col, BEE, 1943; Ga Inst Technol, MSEE, 1949, PhD (elec eng), 1964. **Professional Experience:** PROF ELEC ENG & COORDR UNDERGRAD PROG, CLEMSON UNIV, 1967-; asst prof, Ga Inst Technol, 1957-1964; Asst, Ga Inst Technol, 1948-1949; From instr to assoc prof, Clemson Univ, 1943-1967. **Memberships:** Am Soc Eng Educ; Inst Elec & Electronics Engrs; Sigma Xi. **Research Statement & Publications:** Electronics; network theory; solid state electronics. **Mailing Address:** 108 Mitchell Ave, Clemson, SC 29631.

LONG, JOHN A, AGRONOMY, RESOURCE MANAGEMENT. **Personal Data:** b Lewistown, Mont, September 1, 1927; m 1949, Jean Kirk; c Tim, Mark, Deborah & Christine. **Education:** Univ Idaho, BS, 1952; Wash State Univ, MS, 1954; Tex A&M Univ, PhD (agron), 1961. **Professional Experience:** CONSULT AGRON/HORT, 1996-; consult, O M Scott & Sons Co, 1990-1995; chmn, Turf & Garden Com Fertilizer Inst, 1987-1988; pres, Nat Coun Com Plant Breeders, 1979-1980; mem prog comt, Agr Res Inst, 1973-1974; chmn mem comt, Agr Res Inst, 1972-1973; from dir biochem res to dir prod develop, O M Scott & Sons Co, 1963-1990; turf sect, Weed Sci Soc Am, 1963-1964; proj leader agron, O M Scott & Sons Co, 1961-1963; Chmn student interest comt, Southern Weed Control Asn, 1959-1960; instr, Tex A&M Univ, 1956-1961; Asst agron, NMex State Univ, 1954-1956. **Research Statement & Publications:** Agronomy; horticulture. **Mailing Address:** 17 Scott Cir, Marysville, OH 43040. **Fax:** 937-642-2664.

LONG, JOHN KELLEY, NUCLEAR PHYSICS. **Personal Data:** b NY, December 12, 1921; m 1948, c 3. **Education:** Columbia Univ, BS, 1942; Ohio State Univ, PhD (physics), 1953. **Professional Experience:** RETIRED; consult, NUS Corp, 1991-; Reactor Engr, US Nuclear Regulatory Comm, 1974-1983; physicist, Idaho Div, Argonne Nat Lab, 1955-1974; physicist, Battelle Mem Inst, 1952-1955; engr, Wright Field, 1947-1950; Chemist plastics, Hercules Powder Co, 1942-1945. **Research Statement & Publications:** Fast reactor physics; critical experiments; reactor licensing; fast reactor safety test facilities; plutonium toxicity. **Mailing Address:** 227 S 35th West, Idaho Falls, ID 83402.

LONG, JOHN PAUL, PHARMACOLOGY. **Personal Data:** b Albia, Iowa, October 4, 1926; m 1950, c 3. **Education:** Univ Iowa, BS, 1950, MS, 1952, PhD (pharmacol), 1954. **Professional Experience:** RETIRED; PROF EMER, UNIV IOWA, as of 2003; CARVOR PROF PHARMACOL, COL MED, UNIV IOWA, 1985-; head dept, Col Med, Univ Iowa, 1970-1983; prof, Col Med, Univ Iowa, 1962-1970 & 1983-1985; from asst prof to assoc prof, Col Med, Univ Iowa, 1956-1962; res assoc, Sterling-Winthrop Res Inst, 1954-1956; From asst to instr pharmacol, Univ Iowa, 1950-1954. **Memberships:** Am Soc Pharmacol & Exp Therapeut; Soc Exp Biol & Med. **Research Statement & Publications:** Structure-activity relationships of autonomic and anesthetic agents. **Mailing Address:** Dept Pharmacol, Col Med, Univ Iowa, Iowa City, IA 52242-0001. **E-Mail:** john-long@uiowa.edu

LONG, JOHN REED, INDUSTRIAL ENGINEERING, MANUFACTURING ENGINEERING. **Personal Data:** b Chicago, Ill, October 2, 1922; wid, c Stephen K & J Craig. **Education:** Northwestern Univ, BS, 1947; Iowa State Univ, MS, 1948, PhD (chem eng), 1951. **Professional Experience:** RETIRED; supvr process engr, Hercules, Inc, 1980-1985; sr process engr, Hercules, Inc, 1966-1980; process engr, Hercules, Inc, 1961-1966; sr engr, Hercules, Inc, 1951-1960; AEC asst, Ames Lab, Iowa State Univ, 1948-1951. **Memberships:** Am Chem Soc; Am Inst Chem Engrs; Sigma Xi. **Research Statement & Publications:** Process design of chemical plants. **Mailing Address:** 5 Clyth Dr Perth, Wilmington, DE 19803.

LONG, JOHNFREDERICK, VETERINARY NEUROPATHOLOGY, COMPARATIVE PATHOLOGY. **Personal Data:** b Napoleon, Ohio, May 30, 1924; m 1948, Sarah E Brackney; c George L, Helen L (Corcoran), Harold R, Clara A (Lawrence) & Nancy C (Sieber). **Education:** Ohio State Univ, BA, 1947, MSc, 1948, DVM, 1955, PhD (comp neuropath), 1966. **Honors & Awards:** Distinguished Alumnus Asard, Col Vet Med, Ohio State Univ, 1999. **Professional Experience:** ASSOC PROF VET PATH, OHIO STATE UNIV, 1971-; asst prof vet path, Ohio State Univ, 1968-1971; NIH spec res fel comp neuropath, Ohio State Univ, 1967-1968; instr vet path, Ohio State Univ, 1966-1967; NIH res fel, Ohio State Univ, 1964-1966; res assoc comp neuropath, Ohio State Univ, 1963-1964; diag vet pathologist, Vet Diag Lab, State of Ohio, 1955-1963; res asst animal sci, Ohio Agr Exp Sta, 1949-1950; Asst, Dept Zool, Ohio State Univ, 1947-1949. **Memberships:** Am Vet Med Asn; Am Asn Avian Path; ohio vet med asn. **Research Statement & Publications:** Comparative neuropathology; use of brain explant culture and germ-free animals in the study of the effects of encephalitogenic agents; development of model to visualize reactive oxygen species generation within living cells; aging. **Mailing Address:** Dept Vet Biosci 124 Goss Lab, Ohio State Univ, Columbus, OH 43210-1358.

LONG, JOSEPH POTE, OBSTETRICS & GYNECOLOGY. **Personal Data:** b Baker Summit, Pa, February 26, 1913; m 1942, c 4. **Education:** Juniata Col, BS, 1934; Jefferson Med Col, MD, 1939; Univ Pa, MS, 1948. **Professional Experience:** RETIRED; hon clin prof, Jefferson Med Col, Thomas Jefferson Univ, 1978-1990; clin prof, Jefferson Med Col, Thomas Jefferson Univ, 1975-1978; from demonstr to assoc prof obstet & gynec, Jefferson Med Col, Thomas Jefferson Univ, 1948-1975. **Memberships:** AMA; Am Col Surg; Am Col Obstet & Gynec; Am Fertil Soc; NY Acad Sci. **Mailing Address:** 16 Strawberry Dr, Carlisle, PA 17013-4438.

LONG, KEITH ROYCE, ENVIRONMENTAL HEALTH. **Personal Data:** b Lincoln, Kans, March 17, 1922; m 1945, c 5. **Education:** Univ Kans, AB, 1951, MA, 1953; Univ Iowa, PhD, 1960. **Professional Experience:** RETIRED; dir, Inst Agr Med, 1974-1983; prof civil eng, Inst Agr Med & Environ Health, Col Med, 1970-1986; prof prev med, Inst Agr Med & Environ Health, Col Med, 1969-1986; assoc prof hyg & prev med, Inst Agr Med, 1960-1969; asst bact, Inst Agr Med, 1958-1960; instr, Inst Agr Med, 1957-1958; sr bacteriologist & virologist, State Hyg Lab, Col Med, Univ Iowa, 1956-1957; instr bact res, Med Ctr, 1953-1956; asst instr bact, Univ Kans, 1952-1953. **Memberships:** Am Pub Health Asn; NY Acad Sci. **Research Statement & Publications:** Environmental toxicology; epidemiology; pesticides. **Mailing Address:** 2717 Friendship St, Iowa City, IA 52245.

LONG, KENNETH MAYNARD, INORGANIC CHEMISTRY, SPELEOLOGY. **Personal Data:** b Nappanee, Ind, July 10, 1932; m 1952, Nancy Yoder; c Gregory, Steven, Jeffrey, Kristen & Kevin. **Education:** Goshen Col, BS, 1954; Mich State Univ, MA, 1960; Ohio State Univ, PhD (chem), 1967. **Professional Experience:** PROF EMER CHEM, SCHOLAR-IN-RESIDENCE, NORTHEAST UNIV, 2002-; Shenyang, Liaoning, Peoples Repub China, 1988-1989; chair, Westminster col, PA, 1983-1999; prof chem, Westminster Col, PA, 1979-2002; fel, Kent State Univ, 1979; asst dean, Westminster Col, PA, 1971-1975; NIH fel Ohio State, 1965-1967; from instr to assoc prof, Westminster Col, PA, 1962-1979; instr, High Sch, Mich, 1956-1961; Instr, Parochial Sch, Ark, 1954-1956. **Memberships:** Am Chem Soc; Nat Asn Geosci Teachers; Nat Speleol Soc; Sigma Xi. **Research Statement & Publications:** Macrocyclic complexes of transition metals; catalytic properties of transition metal complexes; kinetics; hydrology; geology and mapping of caves. **Mailing Address:** Dept Chem, Westminster Col, New Wilmington, PA 16172. **Fax:** 412-946-7158. **E-Mail:** longkm@westminster.edu

LONG, LAWRENCE WILLIAM, POLLUTION PREVENTION. **Personal Data:** b Akron, Ohio, November 6, 1942; m 1969, Catherine; c Anna & Susan. **Education:** Franklin & Marshall Col, AB, 1965; Wash Univ, MBA; Villanova Univ, PhD (chem), 1971. **Professional Experience:** PRES, ANHEUSER BUSCH INC, as of 2004; DIR SAFETY & ENVIRON INITIATIVES, ANHEUSER BUSCH INC, 1993-; mgr allied prod, Anheuser Busch, Inc, 1978-1993; proj leader chem, Anheuser Busch, Inc, 1974-1977; res scientist, Stevens Inst Technol, 1973-1974; instr biochem, Thomas Jefferson Univ, 1971-1973. **Research Statement & Publications:** Process optimization to reduce waste. **Mailing Address:** Anheuser Busch Co, Inc, 1 Bush Pl, St Louis, MO 63118. **Fax:** 314-577-3581. **E-Mail:** lawrence.long@anheuser-busch.com

LONG, LELAND TIMOTHY, GEOPHYSICS, SEISMOLOGY. **Personal Data:** b Auburn, NY, September 6, 1940; m 1970, Sarah Blackhard; c 3. **Education:** Univ Rochester, BS, 1962; NMex Inst Mining & Technol, MS, 1964; Ore State Univ, PhD (geophys), 1968. **Professional Experience:** PROF GEOPHYS, GA INST TECHNOL, 1981-, consult seismol, 1978-, from asst prof to assoc prof, GA Inst Technol, 1968-1980. **Memberships:** Am Geophys Union; Seismol Soc Am; Soc Explor Geophys; Sigma Xi. **Research Statement & Publications:** Seismic data acquisition and analysis; earthquake seismology; tectonophysics, vibrations from highways, gravity data acquisition and analysis. **Mailing Address:** Sch Earth & Atmospheric Sci, Ga Inst Technol, Atlanta, GA 30332. **Fax:** 404-894-5638. **E-Mail:** tim.long@eas.gatech.edu

LONG, LEON EUGENE, GEOCHEMISTRY. **Personal Data:** b Wanatah, Ind, May 4, 1933; m 1956, c 2. **Education:** Wheaton Col, BS, 1954; Columbia Univ, MA, 1958, PhD (geochem), 1959. **Professional Experience:** PROF GEOL, UNIV TEX, AUSTIN, 1975-; from asst prof to assoc prof, Univ Tex, Austin, 1962-1975; NSF fel, Oxford Univ, 1960-1962; geochemist, Lamont Geol Observ, Columbia Univ, 1959-1960. **Memberships:** Fel Geol Soc Am; Geochem Soc; Sigma Xi. **Research Statement & Publications:** Isotopic age methods. **Mailing Address:** Dept Geol Sci, Univ Tex, One Univ Sta C1100, Austin, TX 78712-1026. **Fax:** 512-471-9425. **E-Mail:** leonlong@mail.utexas.edu

LONG, LYLE NORMAN, COMPUTATIONAL PHYSICS, PARALLEL PROCESSING. **Personal Data:** b Fergus Fall, Minn, April 7, 1954; m 1981, Laura; c David A & Robert A. **Education:** Univ Minn, BME, 1976; Stanford Univ, MS, 1978; George Wash Univ, DSc, 1983. **Honors & Awards:** Gordon Bell Prize, Inst Elec & Electronics Engrs, 1993. **Professional Experience:** PROF COMPUT SCI & ENG, PA STATE UNIV, 2001-; vis scientist, NASA Langley Res Ctr, 1999-2000; PROF AEROSPACE ENG, PA STATE UNIV, 1998-; DIR, INST COMPUTATIONAL SCI, PA STATE UNIV, 1995-; asst prof to assoc prof Aerospace Eng, Pa State Univ, 1989-1998; sr res scientist, Lockheed Aero Systs Co, 1983-1989; res assoc, George Wash Univ, 1978-1983; res asst, Stanford Univ, 1977-1978; mem, AmInst Aeronaut & Astronaut. **Memberships:** Am Inst Aeronaut & Astronaut; Am Soc Eng Educ; Inst Elec & Electronics Engrs; Soc Indust & Appl Math. **Research Statement & Publications:** Computational physics; fluid dynamics; unsteady aerodynamics; hypersonic aerodynamics; electromagnetics; parallel processing. **Mailing Address:** Penn State Univ, 233 Hammond Bldg, Univ Park, PA 16802. **Fax:** 814-865-1172. **E-Mail:** lnl@psu.edu

LONG, MAURICE W(AYNE), ELECTRONICS, PHYSICS. **Personal Data:** b Madisonville, Ky, April 20, 1925; c Douglas Downing, Patricia Downing, Anne (Key), Elizabeth (Rice). **Education:** Ga Inst Technol, BS, 1946, MS, 1957, PhD (physics), 1959; Univ Ky, MS, 1948. **Professional Experience:** NASA Space Appln Adv Comt, 1983-1986; mem, Comt Remote Sensing Prog for Earth Resources Surv, Nat Acad Sci, 1977; CONSULT, 1975-; bd trustees, Ga Tech Res Inst, 1968-1982; dir res, Eng Exp Sta, Ga Tech Res Inst, 1968-1975; prof elec eng, Ga Inst Technol, 1968-1974; liaison scientist, Off Naval Res, London, 1966-1967; prin res physicist, Ga Inst Technol, 1965-1975; chief, Electronics Div, Ga Inst Technol, 1959-1968; head, Radar Br, Ga Inst Technol, 1955-1960; spec res engr, Eng Exp Sta, Ga Inst Technol, 1953-1965; asst prof, Eng Exp Sta, Ga Inst Technol, 1951-1953; res engr, Eng Exp Sta, Ga Inst Technol, 1950-1951; instr elec eng, Univ Ky, 1947-1949; asst, Eng Exp Sta, Ga Inst Technol, 1946-1947. **Memberships:** Fel Inst Elec & Electronics Engrs; Acad Electromagnetics. **Research Statement & Publications:** Antennas and propagation; radar; electromagnetic scattering from rough surfaces. **Mailing Address:** 1036 Somerset Dr NW, Atlanta, GA 30327.

LONG, MICHAEL EDGAR, PHYSICAL CHEMISTRY, TECHNICAL MANAGEMENT. **Personal Data:** b Canal Zone, June 22, 1946; m 1988, c 1. **Education:** Univ Toledo, BEd, 1968; Wayne State Univ, PhD (chem), 1973. **Professional Experience:** MGR PROCESS ENG, EASTMAN KODAK CO, as of 1998; PHOTOG SCI, EASTMAN KODAK CO, 1975-; NIH fel, Cornell Univ, 1974-1975; Fel chem, Cornell Univ, 1973-1975. **Research Statement & Publications:** Electronic photographic systems development. **Mailing Address:** Eastman KodakCo, Res Labs Bldg 69, Rochester, NY 14650.

LONG, NANCY CAROL, EFFECT OF EXPOSURE TO ENVIRONMENTAL AGENTS ON HOST DEFENSE MECHANISMS IN THE LUNG. **Personal Data:** b Columbus, Ohio, October 12, 1963. **Education:** Oberlin Col, BA, 1985; Univ Mich, PhD (physiol), 1989. **Professional Experience:** LECTR, PHYSIOL PROG, HARVARD SCH PUB HEALTH, as of 2005; adj asst prof, physiol prog, Harvard Sch Pub Health, beginning 1998; res assoc, physiol prog, Harvard Sch Pub Health, 1994-1998; asst prof, div sci & math, Boston Univ, 1994-1999; adj instr, Grad Nursing Prog, Simmons Col, 1993-; sect leader, Harvard Univ Col Arts & Sci, 1993; res fel, physiol prog, Harvard Sch Pub Health, 1991-1994; fel, Yamaguchi Med Sch, Japan, 1990-1991. **Memberships:** Sigma Xi; Am Soc Zoologists; Am Physiol Soc; Am Men & Women Sci. **Research Statement & Publications:** Physiology of host-defense systems; mechanisms of fever and stress-induced hyperthermia; mechanism of the inflammatory response in the lung. **Mailing Address:** Dept Environ Health, Harvard Sch Pub Health, Rm 1307 Bldg One 665 Huntington Ave, Boston, MA 02115. **Fax:** 617-432-3468. **E-Mail:** nlong@hsph.harvard.edu

LONG, PAUL EASTWOOD, METEOROLOGY, NUMERICAL ANALYSIS. **Personal Data:** b Philadelphia, Pa, October 9, 1942; div, c 2. **Education:** Drexel Univ, BS, 1965, MS, 1968, PhD (physics), 1970. **Professional Experience:** METEOROLOGIST, NAT WEATHER SERV, 1976-; res meteorologist, Savannah River Lab, E I du Pont Del Nemours & Co Inc, 1974-1976; res meteorologist, Nat Weather Serv, 1973-1974; assoc, Nat Weather Serv, 1971-1973; fel, Drexel Univ, 1970-1971; Mathematician, Philco-Ford Corp, 1964-1965. **Memberships:** Am Meteorol Soc; Am Inst Physics. **Research Statement & Publications:** Numerical planetary boundary layer modeling. **Mailing Address:** Nat Meteorol Ctr, W-N MC 23 Rm 204 WWB, Washington, DC 20233.

LONG, PHILIP LEE, INFORMATION SCIENCE. **Personal Data:** b Cleveland, Ohio, January 24, 1943; m 1982, LeAnn Boyack Edvalson; c Sarah J, Caitlin T, Philip Imants & Michael Oskar. **Education:** Ohio State Univ, BEE, 1968, MSc, 1970. **Professional Experience:** PRES, PHILIP LONG ASSOCS LTD, SOUTH ORANGE, NJ, 1993-; vpres, Telerate Systs Inc, 1983-1993; vpres, Novell Data Systs, 1981-1982; pres, PhilipLong Assocs Inc, Salt Lake City, 1975-1981; assoc comput systs develop, State Univ NY, Albany, 1974-1975; assoc dir, Ohio Col Libr Ctr, 1969-1973; consult, UNESCO, Bibliotheque Nat France, Lib Cong, Nat Commun Libr & Info Sci, Nat Res Coun &Nat Acad Sci; instr comp sci, Ohio State Univ; instr libr sci, State Univ NY; instr libr sci, CathUniv Am. **Memberships:** Am Soc Info Sci; Inst Elec & Electronics Engrs; Asn Comput Mach. **Research Statement & Publications:** Contributed articles to professional journals. **Mailing Address:** Phillip Long Assoc Ltd, 397 Thornden St, South Orange, NJ 07079.

LONG, RAYMOND CARL, AGRONOMY. **Personal Data:** b Shattuck, Okla, June 17, 1939; m 1959, Marie; c 4. **Education:** Kans State Univ, BS, 1961, MS, 1962; Univ Ill, Urbana, PhD (plant physiol), 1966. **Professional Experience:** PROF CROP SCI, NC STATE UNIV, 1982-; vis prof, Dept agron, Univ Wis, Madison, 1975-1976; from asst prof to assoc prof, Dept crop sci, NC State Univ, 1966-1982; chair & ed, Tobacco Sci. **Memberships:** Am Soc Plant Physiol; Am Soc Agron; Crop Sci Soc Am. **Research Statement & Publications:** Biochemistry of growth and senescence of higher plants; nitrogen metabolism; environmental stress and plant growth; production and bioprocessing of tobacco for engineered proteins and pharmaceuticals; precision application of agrichemicals. **Mailing Address:** Dept Crop Sci, Col Agr & Life Sci, NC State Univ, 3709 Hillsborough St Box 8604, Raleigh, NC 27695-8604. **Fax:** 919-515-7378. **E-Mail:** ray_long@ncsu.edu

LONG, RICHARD PAUL, SUBSURFACE DRAINAGE, FIELD BEHAVIOR OF CLAYS. **Personal Data:** b Allentown, Pa, November 29, 1934; m 1964, c Marybeth & Christopher. **Education:** Univ Cincinnati, CE, 1957; Rensselaer Polytech Inst, MSCE, 1963, PhD (civil eng), 1966. **Honors & Awards:** AT&T Award Excellence Eng Educ, Am Soc Eng Educ, 1988. **Professional Experience:** Chmn, Tech Comt, Transp Res Bd, Nat Acad Sci-Nat Res Ctr, 1987-1994; PROF CIVIL ENG, UNIV CONN, 1978-; dept head, Univ Conn, 1977-1990; vis assoc prof, Mass Inst Tech, 1975; Proj mgr, Storch Engrs, 1974; from asst prof to assoc prof, Univ Conn, 1967-1978; NSF fel res, Rensselaer Polytech Inst, 1966-1967; mgt trainee, Lehigh Struct Steel Co, 1957-1958. **Memberships:** Am Soc Civil Engrs; Am Soc Eng Educ; Transp Res Bd. **Research Statement & Publications:** Geotechnical engineering; invention of prefabricated underdrain for soils; development of techniques for analyzing field data for settlement of clay; investigation of the process of capping dredged material deposited at shallow ocean sites; investigation of corrosion of steel piles. **Mailing Address:** Dept Civil Eng, Univ Conn, PO Box U-37, Storrs, CT 06269-2037. **Fax:** 860-486-2298.

LONG, ROBERT ALLEN, PHARMACEUTICAL CHEMISTRY, MEDICAL SCIENCES. **Personal Data:** b Kingman, Ariz, August 17, 1941; m 1963, c 3. **Education:** Portland State Univ, BA, 1964; Univ Utah, PhD (org chem), 1970. **Professional Experience:** ASSOC DIR CLIN RES, CARDIOVASC/CRITICAL CARE, GLAXO WELLCOME, 1995-; sr clin res scientist, Cardiovasc Sect, Med Div, 1983-1995; clin res scientist, Cardiovasc Sect, Burroughs Wellcome Co, 1977-1983; Res chemist, ICN Pharmaceut Inc, Calif, 1970-1977. **Memberships:** Am Pharmaceut Asn; Acad Pharmaceut Sci; Am Soc Clin Pharmacol & Therapeut; Drug Info Asn. **Research Statement & Publications:** Heterocyclic chemistry; nucleic acid chemistry; antiviral and antitumor research; cardiovascular and respiratory research, clinical trials of new drugs; continued medical support for marketed products; project leader for new product development. **Mailing Address:** Glaxo Wellcome Inc, Five Moore Dr, Research Triangle Park, NC 27709.

LONG, ROBERT LEROY, TECHNICAL MANAGEMENT, INDUSTRIAL HEALTH & SAFETY, TEAM BUILDING & LEADERSHIP. **Personal Data:** b Renovo, Pa, September 9, 1936; m 1957, Ann E Gullborg; c Beth Ann, Jeffrey, Alan & Mark Andrew. **Education:** Bucknell Univ, BS, 1958; Purdue Univ, MSE, 1959, PhD (nuclear eng), 1962. **Honors & Awards:** distinguished engr alumnus, purdue univ, 1993; Pioneer nuclear training, am nuclear soc, 1999. **Professional Experience:** RETIRED; consult nuclear Stewardship, LLC, as of 2002; vpres Servs Div, 1994-1996; vpres, corp serv & TMI-Z, 1989-1994; vpres, vpres Planning & Nuclear Safety Div, 1987-1989; vpres, Nuclear Asn Div, 1982-1987; dir, training & educ, 1980-1982; dir Reliability Eng Dept, Gen Pub Utilities Serv Corp, 1979-1980; mgr, Generation Productivity Dept, GPU Nuclear Corp, 1978-1979; proj mgr nuclear eng & opers, Elec Power Res Inst, 1976-1977; chmn chem & nuclear eng dept, Univ NMex, 1974-1978; asst dean, Univ NMex, 1972-1974; assoc reactor engr, Con Edison, NY, 1970-1971; res assoc nuclear res div, Atomic Weapons Res Estab, Eng, 1966-1967; from asst prof to prof nuclear eng, Univ NMex, 1965-1978; consult, White Sands Missile Range Fast Burst Reactor Facil, 1965-1978; Res partic, Sandia Corp, 1965-1978; reactor specialist nuclear effects br, White Sands Missile Range, NMex, 1962-1965; Res assoc exp reactor physics, Argonne Nat Lab, 1960-1962. **Memberships:** Fel Am Nuclear Soc, (pres, 1991-1992); Nuclear Energy Inst. **Research Statement & Publications:** Reliability engineering data and applications; experimental reactor physics; fast burst reactors; power reactor technology; engineering teaching methods; leadership & team building. **Mailing Address:** 9615 Elena NE, Albuquerque, NM 87122.

LONG, ROBERT RADCLIFFE, METEOROLOGY. **Personal Data:** b Glen Ridge, NJ, October 24, 1919; m Cristina; c Robert & John. **Education:** Princeton Univ, AB, 1941; Univ Chicago, MS, 1949, PhD, 1950. **Professional Experience:** RETIRED; prof fluid mech, Johns Hopkins Univ, 1959-; from asst prof to assoc prof meteorol, Johns Hopkins Univ, 1951-1959; sr investr, Hydrodyn Lab, Univ Chicago, 1949-1951; Meteorologist, US Weather Bur, 1946-1947; Mem adv panel gen sci, US Secy Defense Res & Eng. **Memberships:** Am Meteorol Soc. **Research Statement & Publications:** Geophysical fluid mechanics; theoretical studies and laboratory models of geophysical phenomena; general circulation of the atmosphere; atmospheric and oceanic flow over barriers. **Mailing Address:** PO Box 10381, Sarasota, FL 34278.

LONG, RONALD KILLWORTH, ELECTRICAL ENGINEERING. **Personal Data:** b Steubenville, Ohio, December 5, 1932; m 1959. **Education:** Ohio Wesleyan Univ, BA, 1954; Harvard Univ, MS, 1956; Ohio State Univ, PhD, 1963. **Professional Experience:** RETIRED; prof elec eng, Antenna Lab, Ohio State Univ, 1969-1980; from asst prof to assoc prof, Antenna Lab, Ohio State Univ, 1963-1969; asst supvr, Antenna Lab, Ohio State Univ, 1958-1963; res engr, NAm Aviation Inc, 1956-1957; asst, Harvard Univ, 1955-1956; res engr labs, Radio Corp Am, 1955. **Research Statement & Publications:** Lasers; atmospheric propagation; infrared techniques; computer data acquisition. **Mailing Address:** 1516 Essex Rd, Columbus, OH 43221.

LONG, SALLY YATES, EMBRYOLOGY, TERATOLOGY. **Personal Data:** b Moyock, NC, November 8, 1941; m 1973, c 2. **Education:** Col William & Mary, BS, 1963; Univ Fla, PhD (anat), 1967. **Professional Experience:** ASSOC DEAN STUDENT AFFAIRS, MED COL WIS, 1981-; asst dean student affairs, Med Col Wis, 1978-1981; ASSOC PROF ANAT, MED COL WIS, 1976-; asst prof, Med Col Wis, 1971-1976; res assoc teratology, Karolinska Inst, Sweden, 1970-1971; NIH fel, McGill Univ, 1968-1970; lectr genetics, McGill Univ, 1968-1970. **Memberships:** Teratology Soc (secy, 1977-); Am Asn Anat; Europ Teratology Soc. **Research Statement & Publications:** Interactions of genetic and environmental factors in causing malformations, especially cleft palate and limb defects. **Mailing Address:** Univ Wis Milwaukee, 6186 Wash Circle, Milwaukee, WI 53213.

LONG, SHARON RUGEL, PLANT BIOLOGY. **Personal Data:** b San Marcos, Tex, March 2, 1951; div, c 2. **Education:** Calif Inst Technol, BS, 1973; Yale Univ PhD (biol), 1979. **Honors & Awards:** Presidential Young Investr, 1984; Charles Shull Award, 1989; Shell Res Found Award, 1989; MacArthur Prize, 1992; Outstanding Alumni Award, Caltech, 1998. **Professional Experience:** 2001 Dean, Humanities & Sciences, Stanford; investr, Howard Hughes Med Inst, 1994-2001; PROF, DEPT BIOL SCI, STANFORD UNIV, 1992-; from asst prof to assoc prof, Dept Biol Sci, Stanford Univ, 1982-1992; Res fel, Dept Biol, Harvard Univ, 1978-1981. **Memberships:** Nat Acad Sci; Genetics Soc Am; Am Soc Microbiol; Am Soc Plant Physiologists; Am Philosophical Society. **Research Statement & Publications:** Genetics and developmental biology of symbiotic nitrogen fixation in legumes; role of plasmids in symbiosis; plant cell biology; plant molecular biology. **Mailing Address:** Professor & Dean, Dept Biol Sci, Stanford Univ, Stanford, CA 94305-5020. **Fax:** 650-723-3235. **E-Mail:** srl@stanford.edu

LONG, STEPHEN INGALLS, INTEGRATED CIRCUIT DESIGN, HIGH SPEED SEMICONDUCTOR DEVICES. **Personal Data:** b Alameda, Calif, January 11, 1946; m 1966, Molly; c Christopher A & Betsy E. **Education:** Univ Calif, Berkeley, BS (eng phys), 1967; Cornell Univ, MS, 1969, PhD (elec eng), 1974. **Honors & Awards:** Microwave Applns Award, Inst Elec & Electronics Engrs, 1978. **Professional Experience:** VICE CHAIR ELEC & COMPUT ENG, UNIV CALIF, SANTA BARBARA, as of 2004; PROF ELEC & COMPUT ENG, UNIV CALIF, SANTA BARBARA, 1981-; vis res, Hewlett-Packard Co, 1999; vis prof, Tech Univ Denmark, 1994; fulbright res scholar, Tampere Univ Technol, Signal Processing Lab, Tampere, Finland, 1994; vis researcher, Gen Elec Co/Hirst Res Ctr, 1988; mem tech staff, Rockwell Int Sci Ctr, 1978-1981; sr engr, Varian Assocs, 1974-1977. **Memberships:** Sr mem Inst Elec & Electronics Engrs; Am Sci Affil. **Research Statement & Publications:** Fabrication and design of high performance integrated circuits using compound semiconductor devices. **Mailing Address:** 895 N Patterson Ave, Santa Barbara, CA 93111-1107. **Fax:** 805-893-3262. **E-Mail:** long@ece.ucsb.edu

LONG, STUART A, APPLIED ELECTROMAGNETICS & ANTENNAS, SUPERCONDUCTORS. **Personal Data:** b Philadelphia, Pa, March 6, 1945; m 1969, Judy; c Meredith, Garrett & Brittany. **Education:** Rice Univ, BA, 1967, MEE, 1968; Harvard Univ, PhD (appl physics), 1974. **Professional Experience:** ASSOC DEAN, UNIV HOUSTON, 1996-; PROF ELEC ENG, UNIV HOUSTON, 1985-; chmn dept, Univ Houston, 1981-1995; from asst prof to assoc prof 1974-1984. **Memberships:** Fel Inst Elec & Electronic Engrs; Antennas & Propagation Soc; Int Union Radio Sci. **Research Statement & Publications:** Applied electromagnetics: antennas; applications of high temperature superconductors; subsurface communications; millimeter waveguiding and radiating structures. **Mailing Address:** Dept Elec & Compute Eng, Univ Houston, N 308 Eng Bldg one, Houston, TX 77204-4005. **Fax:** 713-743-4440. **E-Mail:** long@uh.edu

LONG, TERRILL JEWETT, BOTANY. **Personal Data:** b Newark, Ohio, March 19, 1932; m 1955, c 4. **Education:** Ohio Univ, BSAg, 1956; Ohio State Univ, MSc, 1959, PhD (bot), 1961. **Professional Experience:** PROF EMER BIOL, CAPITAL UNIV, 1998-; prof biol, Capital Univ, 1983-1998; from asst prof to assoc prof, Capital Univ, 1967-1983; consult, C S Fred Mushroom Co, 1966-1970; res assoc biochem, Ohio State Univ, 1965-1967; asst prof biol, Vanderbilt Univ, 1964-1965; res assoc bot, Oak Ridge Nat Lab, 1963-1964; NIH fel, Oak Ridge Nat Lab, 1961-1963. **Memberships:** AAAS; Bot Soc Am; Mycol Soc Am. **Research Statement & Publications:** Physiology and biochemistry of irradiated wheat and mushrooms and related fungi. **Mailing Address:** Dept Biol, Capital Univ, 2199 E Main St, Columbus, OH 43209-2394.

LONG, WALTER KYLE, VIROLOGY. **Personal Data:** b Montgomery, Ala, December 5, 1944. **Education:** Univ Ga, BS, 1966; Univ Ill, PhD (microbiol), 1972. **Professional Experience:** RES ASSOC PROF, SOL SHERRY THROMBOSIS RES CTR, as of 2004; ASST PROF, FELS INST, as of 2004; ASSOC PROF MICROBIOL & IMMUNOL, SCH MED, TEMPLE UNIV, 1986-; from asst prof to assoc prof, Sch Dent, 1976-1986; res assoc, Dept Microbiol & Pediat, Univ Ala, Birmingham, 1975-1976; fel, Dept Microbiol & Pediat, Univ Ala, Birmingham, 1972-1975. **Memberships:** AAAS; Am Soc Microbiol; Sigma Xi. **Research Statement & Publications:** Effects of antiviral drugs on herpes viruses; oncogenicity of herpes viruses; latency and reactivation of herpes viruses; role of DNA methylation in gene expression. **Mailing Address:** Dept Microbiol & Immunol, Sch Med, Temple Univ, 3400 N Broad St, Philadelphia, PA 19140. **Fax:** 215-707-7788.

LONG, WILLIAM ELLIS, HYDROLOGY, GEOMORPHOLOGY. **Personal Data:** b Minot, NDak, August 18, 1930; m 1971, c 6. **Education:** Univ Nev, BS, 1957; Ohio State Univ, MS, 1961, PhD (geol), 1964. **Honors & Awards:** Long Hills, Antarctica named in honor. **Professional Experience:** ADJ PROF, MATANUSKA-SUSITNA COL, as of 2001; chief, Water Resources Sect, Alaska State Geol Surv, beginning 1978; consult, Forest Oil Co, 1974-1975; prof geol, Alaska Methodist Univ, beginning 1972; vis lectr, Univ Canterbury, 1972; consult, Shelf Explor Co, 1971; investr potential natural landmarks Alaska, Nat Park Serv, 1971; mem discharge prediction glacial melt-water, Off Water Res, 1968-1970; from asst prof to assoc prof, Alaska Methodist Univ, 1965-1972; explor geologist, Tenneco Oil Co, La, 1964-1965; mem, US Antarctic Res Prog, NSF Geol Invest, 1963-1964; instr geol, Ohio State Univ, 1963-1964. **Memberships:** Am Groundwater Asn; Am Asn Petrol Geol; Am Inst Prof Geol; Geol Soc Am; Glaciol Soc; Sigma Xi. **Research Statement & Publications:** Stratigraphic, geologic and glaciological exploration of Gondwana sequences of Antarctica during International Geophysical Year and following years; stratigraphic and glacial geology; water resources of Alaska. **Mailing Address:** Matanuska-Susitna Col, Palmer, AK 99645.

LONG, WILLIAM HENRY, AGRICULTURAL CROP & PEST MANAGEMENT. **Personal Data:** b Decatur, Ala, September 20, 1928; m 1953, Janice Rogers; c Janice F, Nancy A & Daniel H. **Education:** Univ Tenn, BA, 1952; NC State Col, MS, 1954; Iowa State Col,

PhD, 1957. **Professional Experience:** Distinguished serv prof biol sci, Nicholls State Univ, 1985-1994; entom expert, Int Atomic Energy Agency, 1975-1976; UN Food & Agr Orgn, United Arab Repub, 1973-1974; INDEPENDENT AGR CONSULT, 1965-; prof, Nicholls State Univ, 1965-1985; from asstentomologist to prof entom, La State Univ, 1957-1965. **Memberships:** Entom Soc Am; Am Soc Sugarcane Technologists; Nat Alliance Independent Crop Consult. **Research Statement & Publications:** Development and refinement of sugarcane pest management programs; study of insects and other factors which affect sugarcane. **Mailing Address:** PO Box 1193, Thibodaux, LA 70302. **Fax:** 504-446-3520. **E-Mail:** long@cajunnet.com

LONG, WILLIS FRANKLIN, ELECTRICAL ENGINEERING, ELECTRIC POWER SYSTEMS. **Personal Data:** b Lima, Ohio, January 30, 1934; wid, c Andrew, Kristin & David. **Education:** Univ Toledo, BS (engr phys), 1957, MS (elec eng), 1962; Univ Wis-Madison, PhD (elec eng), 1970. **Professional Experience:** Prof elec eng & eng prof develop, UnivWis-Madison, beginning1985; consult, ABB Power Syst, 1985-; dir, ASEA Power Systs Ctr, New Berlin, Wis, 1983-1985; chmn exten eng, Univ Wis-Madison, 1980-1983; spec adv comt, Wis Dept Indust, Labor & Human Rels, 1976-1977; consult, Hughes Aircraft Co, Los Angeles Dept Power & Water, 1973-; from asst prof to prof elec eng & exten eng, Univ Wis-Madison, 1973-1983; mem tech staff, Hughes Res Labs, 1969-1973; lectr, Univ Wis-Madison, 1969; NSF fel, Univ Wis-Madison, 1967-1968; instr elec eng, Univ Toledo, 1962-1966; asst, Univ Toledo, 1960-1962; proj engr, Doehler Jarvis, Nat Lead Co, 1957, 1959-1960; PROF EMER, UNIV WIS-MADISON. **Memberships:** Fel Inst Elec & Electronics Engrs; Int Council Large High Voltage Elec Systs. **Research Statement & Publications:** Analysis, simulation and testing of interconnected AC/DC electric power systems; power electronics switching techniques; continuing education, electric power systems. **Mailing Address:** Univ Wis-Madison, 432 N Lake St, Madison, WI 53706-1498.

LONG, WILMER NEWTON, JR, MEDICINE, OBSTETRICS & GYNECOLOGY. **Personal Data:** b Hagerstown, Md, April 24, 1918; m 1942, c 2. **Education:** Juniata Col, BS, 1940; Johns Hopkins Univ, MD, 1943. **Professional Experience:** PROF GYNEC & OBSTET, SCH MED, EMORY UNIV, 1967-; assoc prof, Sch Med, Emory Univ, 1965-1967; med officer chg obstet & gynec, Navajo Med Ctr, Ft Defiance, Ariz, 1953-1955; pvt pract obstet, 1948-1965; instr gynec & obstet, Sch Med, Johns Hopkins Univ, 1948-1965. **Memberships:** Am Col Obstet & Gynec; AMA. **Research Statement & Publications:** Diabetes in pregnancy. **Mailing Address:** 69 Bulter St SE, Atlanta, GA 30303-3056.

LONGACRE, RONALD SHELLEY, PARTICLE PHYSICS. **Personal Data:** b Lindsay, Calif, August 15, 1941; wid, c 4. **Education:** Calif Polytech State Univ, BS, 1964; Univ Calif, Berkeley, MA, 1968, PhD (physics), 1974. **Professional Experience:** PHYSICIST, BROOKHAVEN NAT LAB, 1980-; asst physicist, Brookhaven Nat Lab, 1978-1980; res asst, Northeastern Univ, Boston, 1975-1978; res asst, Dept Physics Elem Particles, Comn L'Etude des Nuages-SACLAY, 1974-1975. **Research Statement & Publications:** Determine Hadronic particle spectrum using three particle decay models; chief tool is the use of partial wave analyses via the Isobar model; model hadronic production in heavy ion collisions. **Mailing Address:** Dept Physics, Brookhaven Nat Lab, PO Box 5000 Bldg 510A, Upton, NY 11973-5000. **Fax:** 631-344-4206. **E-Mail:** longacre@bnl.gov

LONGACRE, SUSAN ANN BURTON, STRATIGRAPHY, SEDIMENTARY PETROLOGY & PETROLEUM GEOLOGY. **Personal Data:** b Los Angeles, Calif, May 26, 1941; m 1964, c 2. **Education:** Univ Tex, Austin, BS, 1964, PhD (geol), 1968. **Honors & Awards:** Distinguished Serv Award, Am Asn Petrol Geologists, 1994. **Professional Experience:** RETIRED; adv coun, Earth Sci, Nat Sci Found, 1993-; adv coun, Geol Found, Univ Tex, Austin, 1993-; hon fel, Texaco Houston Res Ctr, 1991-; sr scientist, Texaco Houston Res Ctr, 1990-; chmn, N Am Comm Stratig Nomenclature, 1986-1987; vchmn, N Am Comm Stratig Nomenclature, 1985-1986; sr res consult, Texaco Houston Res Ctr, 1984-1990; prof specialist, Texaco Houston Res Ctr, 1980-1984; comnr, N Am Comm Stratig Nomenclature, 1979-; geol specialist II, res scientist III explor & prod res, 1978-1980; geol specialist II, Offshore Dist, 1976-1978; res scientist I geol, Explor & Prod Res Lab, 1975-1976; res assoc III, res assoc IV, 1972-1975; res assoc III, Getty Oil Co, 1969-1972. **Memberships:** Am Asn Petrol Geologists; Geol Soc Am; Soc Econ Paleontologists & Mineralogists. **Research Statement & Publications:** Petrology and petrography of carbonate and clastic sediments, particularly those Permian, Jurassic and Cretaceous sediments that accumulated in shallow marine to continental depositional environments. **Mailing Address:** Texaco Houston Res Ctr, 3901 Briarpark, Houston, TX 77042. **Fax:** 713-954-6113.

LONGANBACH, JAMES ROBERT, PHYSICAL-ORGANIC CHEMISTRY, FUEL CHEMISTRY. **Personal Data:** b Akron, Ohio, July 4, 1942; m 1966, Mary; c Diane M & David M. **Education:** Univ Akron, BS, 1964; Yale Univ, MS, 1966, MPh, 1967, PhD (chem), 1969. **Professional Experience:** NAT ENERGY TECHNOL LAB, US DEPT ENERGY, as of 2000; Fuel div prog chmn, Am Chem Soc, 1993; PROJ MGR, MORGANTOWN ENERGY TECHNOL CTR, US ENERGY DEPT, 1987-; prin res chemist, Columbus Labs, Battelle Mem Inst, 1976-1987; sr chemist, Res Div, Occidental Petrol Corp, 1971-1976; chemist, E I du Pont Del Nemours & Co, Inc, 1969-1971. **Memberships:** Am Chem Soc. **Research Statement & Publications:** Physical-organic, energy and process development chemistry; coal gasification. **Mailing Address:** US Dept Energy, Nat Energy Technol Lab, 3610 Collins Ferry Rd, Morgantown, WV 26507-0880. **E-Mail:** james.longanbach@netl.doe.gov

LONGENECKER, BRYAN MICHAEL, IMMUNOLOGY, CELL BIOLOGY. **Personal Data:** b Dover, Del, September 1, 1942; m 1963, c 2. **Education:** Univ Mo, AB, 1964, PhD (zoology), 1968. **Professional Experience:** PROF EMER MICROBIOL & IMMUNOL, UNIV ALTA, as of 2003; SR VICE PRES, BIOMIRA INC, UNIV ALTA, as of 1999; asst prof immunol & mem, Nat Cancer Inst, Univ Alta, beginning 1977; Nat Cancer Inst Can res scholar immunol, Univ Alta, 1971-1977; Nat Cancer Inst Can res grant, Univ Alta, 1971-1973; Med Res Coun Can fel, Univ Alta, 1968-1971. **Memberships:** AAAS. **Research Statement & Publications:** Genetic control of allo-immunocompetence and resistance to virally induced neoplasms. **Mailing Address:** Univ Alta, Edmonton, AB T6N 1H1, Can.

LONGENECKER, HERBERT EUGENE, BIOLOGICAL CHEMISTRY. **Personal Data:** b Lititz, Pa, May 6, 1912; m 1936, Jane Segar; c Herbert E Jr, Marjorie (White), Geoffrey H & Stanton L. **Education:** Pa State Col, BS, 1933, MS, 1934, PhD (agr biol chem), 1936. **Honorary Degrees:** ScD, Duquesne Univ, 1951; LLD, Loyola Univ, 1963; LittD, Univ Miami, 1972; DSc, Loyola Univ & Univ Ill, 1976. **Professional Experience:** Mgr dir, Int Trade Mart, 1976-1979; dir, Fed Home Loan Bank Little Rock, 1976-1979; PRES EMER, TULANE UNIV, 1975-; dir, United Student Aid Funds, 1971-1984; mem panel sci & technol, US House Rep Comt Sci & Astronaut, 1970-1973; dir, A G Bush Found, 1969-1985; dir, Equitable Life Assurance Soc US, 1968-1984; dir, CPC Int, 1966-1985; chmn acad bd adv, US Naval Acad, 1966-1972; mem, Coun Financial Aid to Educ, 1964-1971; pres, Tulane Univ, 1960-1975; mem bd gov, Inst Med Chicago, 1957-1960; vpres charge, Univ Ill Med Ctr, 1955-1960; chmn, Western Europe Sect, Fulbright student awards, 1954-1955; memadv panel biol & chem warfare, Off Asst Secy Defense, 1953-1961; mem nat selection comn Fulbright student awards, 1953-1955; mem res coun, Chem Corps Adv Bd, 1949-1965; chmn comt food protection, Nat Res Coun, 1948-1953; dean grad sch, Univ Pittsburgh, 1946-1955; dean res natural sci, Univ Pittsburgh, 1944-1955; mem food & nutrit bd, Nat Res Coun, 1943-1953; from asst prof to prof, Univ Pittsburgh, 1938-1955; fac mem, Univ Pittsburgh, 1938-1955; Nat Res Coun fel, Queen's Univ, Ont, 1938; Nat Res Coun fel, Univ Cologne, 1937-1938; Nat Res Coun fel, Univ Liverpool, 1936-1937; instr, Pa State Col, 1935-1936; Asst agr & biochem, Pa State Col, 1933-1935. **Memberships:** Am Chem Soc; Inst Nutrit; fel Am Inst Chem; Sigma Xi. **Research Statement & Publications:** Nutrition; fat metabolism; research administration. **Mailing Address:** Tulane Univ, 6823 St Charles Ave, New Orleans, LA 70118.

LONGENECKER, JOHN BENDER, NUTRITION, BIOCHEMISTRY. **Personal Data:** b Salunga, Pa, July 8, 1930; m 1954, c 2. **Education:** Franklin & Marshall Col, BS, 1952; Univ Tex, MS, 1954, PhD (biochem), 1956. **Professional Experience:** PROF EMER, DEPT HUMAN ECOL COL NATURAL SCI, UNIV TEX, AUSTIN, as of 2004; Allied Health Fel grant, 1969-1974; prof nutrit sci & head div, Univ Tex, Austin, beginning 1964; USPHS grant, 1964-1971; group leader, Mead Johnson & Co Ind, 1961-1964; res biochemist, E I du Pont Del Nemours & Co Inc, Del, 1956-1961. **Memberships:** Am Chem Soc; Am Inst Nutrit; NY Acad Sci. **Research Statement & Publications:** In vivo plasma amino acid studies to evaluate protein and amino acid nutrition; interrelationships among nutrients; nutritional status studies. **Mailing Address:** Dept Human Ecol Col Natural Sci, Univ Tex, Austin, TX 78712. **Fax:** 512-471-6842.

LONGERICH, HENRY PERRY, ANALYTICAL CHEMISTRY, COMPUTER SCIENCE. **Personal Data:** b Du Quoin, Ill, June 20, 1940; m 1964, Linda; c Lora L. **Education:** Millikin Univ, BS, 1963; Ind Univ, PhD (chem), 1967. **Professional Experience:** PROF EMER, PROF EARTH SCI, MEM UNIV NFLD, 1993-; assoc prof, Mem Univ Nfld, 1984-1993; sessional comput sci, Mem Univ, 1979-1982; asst prof, Mem Univ Nfld, 1978-1984; res fel, Mem Univ Nfld, 1975-1978; res assoc, Mem Univ Nfld, 1974-1975; fel, Dalhousie Univ, 1972-1974; asst prof chem, Univ Alaska, 1967-1972. **Memberships:** Am Chem Soc; Spectros Soc Can; Soc Appl Spectros. **Research Statement & Publications:** Real-time on-line computer control and data acquisiton at analytical instrumentation, ICP-MS. **Mailing Address:** Dept Earth Sci, Mem Univ Nfld, ER 5030, St John's, NL A1B 3X5, Can. **Fax:** 709-737-2589. **E-Mail:** henry@esd.mun.ca

LONGEST, WILLIAM DOUGLAS, INVERTEBRATE ZOOLOGY. **Personal Data:** b Pontotoc, Miss, January 22, 1929; m 1960. **Education:** Baylor Univ, BSc, 1954, MSc, 1956; La State Univ, PhD (invert zool, ecol), 1966. **Professional Experience:** PROF EMER BIOL, UNIV MISS, as of 2004; prof biol, Univ Miss, beginning 1973; from asst prof to assoc prof, Univ Miss, 1966-1973; instr, La State Univ, 1965-1966; teaching asst zool, La State Univ, 1963-1965; instr biol, Memphis State Univ, 1962-1963; prof natural sci, Blue Mountain Col, 1959-1962; instr biol, Northwest Jr Col, 1956-1959; Teacher, Parma High Sch, 1955-1956. **Memberships:** Bot Soc Am; Am Soc Zool. **Research Statement & Publications:** Botanical research; foliar embryos of Kalanchoe studied in an explant medium; taxonomy of freshwater Tricladida; study of freshwater triclads in the Florida Parishes of Louisiana. **Mailing Address:** Dept Biol, Univ Miss, 188 County Road 198, Oxford, MS 38655-9803. **Fax:** 662-915-5144.

LONGFELLOW, DAVID G(ODWIN), MOLECULAR CARCINOGENESIS, BIOCHEMISTRY. **Personal Data:** b Akron, Ohio, November 16, 1942; m 1965, Bente; c Robyn M & Daniel G. **Education:** Lynchburg Col, BS, 1964; Johns Hopkins Univ, PhD (biol), 1972. **Professional Experience:** PROG DIR & SR COORDR, CANCER ETIOLOGY BR, NAT CANCER INST, as of 2004; chief chem & phys carcinogenesis br, div Canceretiology, Nat Cancer Inst, NIH, beginning 1984; asst chief, Chem & Phys Br, Div Cancer Etiology, 1979-1984; sect head, Molecular Carcinogenesis Sect, 1976-1979; res staff, Biol Lab, Div Cancer Biol, Nat Cancer Inst, NIH, 1975-1976; res fel, Biol Lab, Div Cancer Biol, Nat Cancer Inst, NIH, 1974-1975; damon runyon res fel breast cancer, Biol Lab, Div Cancer Biol, Nat Cancer Inst, NIH, 1972-1974. **Memberships:** Am Asn Cancer Res; Int Soc Polycyclic Aromatic Compounds (pres elect 1993). **Research Statement & Publications:** Chief of an extramural program awarding contracts and grants for research and resource support in the cause and prevention of chemical and physical carcinogenesis. **Mailing Address:** Cancer Etiology Br, Nat Cancer Inst, NIH, 6130 Exec Blvd EPN 5000 MSC 7398, Bethesda, MD 20892-7398. **Fax:** 301-496-1040. **E-Mail:** dl58s@nih.gov

LONGFIELD, JAMES EDGAR, PHYSICAL CHEMISTRY. **Personal Data:** b Mt Brydges, Ont, March 12, 1925; American citizen; m 1947, Mary; c Judianne Coster, Bradley & Jeryl Erickson. **Education:** Univ Western Ont, BSc, 1947, MSc, 1948; Univ Rochester, PhD (phys chem), 1951. **Professional Experience:** RETIRED; dir Process Technol Assessment & Lecturary, Am Cyanamid chem Res 1982-1987; dir, Bound Brook Labs, 1974-1982; dir, process eng dept, Chem Res Div, 1972-1974; mgr eng res, Res Div, Am Cyanamid Co, 1962-1972; group leader eng res, Res Div, Am Cyanamid Co, 1957-1962; res chemist, Res Div, Am Cyanamid Co, 1951-1957; asst, Univ Rochester, 1948-1950. **Memberships:** Emer Mem Am Chem Soc; Am Inst Chem Eng. **Research Statement & Publications:** Vapor phase reactions of organic compounds; reaction kinetics; catalysis; reactor design and mechanism studies. **Mailing Address:** Eight Honey Locust Circle, Hilton Head Island, SC 29926-2680. **E-Mail:** james1843@aol.com

LONGHI, JOHN, IGNEOUS PETROLOGY, PHYSICAL CHEMISTRY. **Personal Data:** b White Plains, NY, October 12, 1946; m 1970, c 1. **Education:** Univ Notre Dame, BS, 1968; Harvard Univ, PhD (geol), 1976. **Professional Experience:** SR RES SCIENTIST, LAMONT-DOHERTY GEOL OBSERV, 1988-; from asst prof to assoc prof, Yale Univ, 1980-1988; res assoc lunar petrol, Univ Ore, 1977-1980; res assoc, Mass Inst Technol, 1976-1977. **Memberships:** Am Geophys Union; Mineral Soc Am; Sigma Xi. **Research Statement & Publications:** Origin and evolution of the moon and planets; experimental petrology; physical chemistry of silicates. **Mailing Address:** Lamont-Doherty Earth Observ, 49 Geochem 61 Route 9W PO Box 1000, Palisades, NY 10964. **Fax:** 845-365-8155. **E-Mail:** longhi@ldeo.columbia.edu

LONGHI, RAYMOND, INORGANIC CHEMISTRY, ORGANIC CHEMISTRY. **Personal Data:** b Plymouth, Mass, November 14, 1935; m 1961, Betty H Johnson; c 3. **Education:** Univ Mass, BS, 1957; Dartmouth Col, MA, 1959; Univ Ill, PhD (inorg chem), 1962. **Professional Experience:** SR RESFEL, E I DU PONT DEL NEMOURS & CO INC, 1989-; res mgr, Int Technol Transfer, 1987-1989; mgr, Int Technol Transfer, 1985-1987; res & deveop site mgr, E I Du Pont Del Nemours & Co Inc, 1978-1985; tech supt, E I Du Pont Del Nemours & Co Inc, 1974-1978; sr supvr res & develop, E I Du Pont Del Nemours & Co Inc, 1971-1974; sr supvr tech, E I Du Pont Del Nemours & Co Inc, 1969-1971; res supvr, E I Du Pont Del Nemours & Co Inc, 1965-1969; sr res chemist, E I Du Pont Del Nemours & Co Inc, 1964-1965; Res chemist, E I Du Pont Del Nemours & Co Inc, 1962-1964. **Memberships:** Am Asn Textile Chemists & Colorists; Am Chem Soc; Sigma Xi. **Research**

Statement & Publications: Structures of transition metal complexes; reactions of nitrogen oxide; characterization of organic compounds; textile fibers; polymer chemistry. **Mailing Address:** E I du Pont de Nemours & Co Inc, 450 N Access Rd, Chattanooga, TN 37415.

LONGHURST, ALAN R, BIOLOGICAL OCEANOGRAPHY, MARINE ECOLOGY. **Personal Data:** b Plymouth, Eng, May 3, 1925; Canadian citizen; m 1963, c 2. **Education:** Univ London, BSc, 1952, PhD (zool), 1962, DSc, 1969. **Professional Experience:** RETIRED; res scientist, Ocean Sci & Surv, Atlantic, Can Dept Fisheries & Oceans, 1987-1996; secy, Sci Coun Oceanic Res, 1979-1986; dir gen, Ocean Sci & Surv, Atlantic, Can Dept Fisheries & Oceans, 1979-1986; dir, Marine Ecol Lab, Bedford Inst Oceanog, NS, 1977-1979; Dartmoor Nat Park Comt, UK Deleg UN Conf Law Sea, 1974-1977; Dartmoor Nat Park Comt, Devon Co Coun, 1974-1976; dep dir, Inst Marine Environ Res, Nat Environ Res Coun, Eng, 1971-1977; mem, Food & Agr Orgn Adv Comt Marine Res, 1969-1974; chmn, Continuous Monitoring Biol Oceanog, Sci Comt Oceanic Res/Adv Comt Marine Resources Res, 1969-1972; mem, Group Experts Ocean Variability Intergovt Oceanog Comn/Integrated Global Ocean Sta Syst, 1969-1971; dir, Fishery-Oceanog Ctr, Nat Oceanic & Atmospheric Admin, 1967-1971; Coordr, Eastern Trop Pac Oceanog Expeditions, 1967-1970; assoc res biologist, Scripps Inst Oceanog, 1963-1967; prin sci officer, Fed Fisheries Serv, Lagos, Nigeria, 1960-1963; sr sci officer, Fishery Develop & Res Unit, Sierra Leone, 1958-1960; marine biologist, Fisheries Lab, Wellington, NZ, 1957-1958; Sci officer, African Fisheries Res Inst, Sierra Leone, 1954-1957. **Research Statement & Publications:** Ecology of tropical benthos; population dynamics of tropical demersal fish; descriptive tropical physical oceanography; response to climate changes of marine biota; production and grazing relation in zooplankton in tropical, temperate and arctic oceans; formulation of large scale numerical ecological models; ecology of microplankton and sub-micron particles. **Mailing Address:** Place d l'Eglise, Cajarc, France. **Fax:** 902-426-7827.

LONGHURST, JOHN CHARLES, CARDIOVASCULAR PHYSIOLOGY, INTERNAL MEDICINE. **Personal Data:** b Napa, Calif, March 18, 1947; m 1969, c 3. **Education:** Univ Calif, Davis, BS, 1969, MD, 1973, PhD (physiol), 1974; Am Bd Internal Med, dipl, 1977. **Honors & Awards:** Loren D Carlson, Med Stud Res Award, 1973. **Professional Experience:** PROF & ASSOC DEAN, SCH MED, UNIV CALIF, IRVINE, as of 2005; prof & chmn, Dept Med, Univ Calif, Irvine, beginning 2003; asst prof, physiol, Health Sci Ctr, Univ Tex, Dallas, beginning 1981; estab investr, Am Heart Asn, 1981-1986; asst prof, internal med, Health Sci Ctr, Univ Tex, Dallas, beginning 1980; instr, internal med & physiol, Health Sci Ctr, Univ Tex, Dallas, 1979-1980; fac assoc, internal med, Health Sci Ctr, Univ Tex, Dallas, 1978-1979; assoc prof, dept med, Univ Calif, San Diego. **Memberships:** Am Fedn Clin Res; Am Physiol Soc; fel Am Col Cardiol; fel Am Col Physicians; Am Heart Asn; Soc Neuroscience. **Research Statement & Publications:** Neural control of the circulation; exercise physiology; physiology of the coronary circulation. **Mailing Address:** Dept Med, Univ Calif, Med Sci One C240, Davis, CA 92697. **Fax:** 949-824-2200. **E-Mail:** jcl@uci.edu

LONGINI, IRA MANN, EPIDEMIOLOGY. **Personal Data:** b Cincinnati, Ohio, October 2, 1948. **Education:** Univ Fla, BS, 1971, MS, 1973; Univ Minn, PhD (biomet), 1977. **Professional Experience:** PROF, DEPT BIOSTATIST, SCH PUB HEALTH, EMORY UNIV, as of 2004; assoc prof, Dept Epidemiol & Biostatist, Emory Univ, beginning 1984; scholar biomet & lectr epidemiol, Dept Epidemiol, Univ Mich, 1980-1984; vis prof biomath, Univ Del Valle, 1977-1979; assoc fel biomath, Int Ctr Med Res, 1977-1979. **Memberships:** Biomet Soc; Soc Math Biol. **Research Statement & Publications:** Development of mathmatical and statistical methods in epidemiology; geneticsand biology. **Mailing Address:** Dept Biostatist, Rollins Sch Pub Health, Emory Univ, 1518 Clifton Rd NE Rm 354, Atlanta, GA 30322. **Fax:** 404-727-1370. **E-Mail:** ilongin@sph.emory.edu

LONGINI, RICHARD LEON, physics, bioengineering; deceased, see previous edition for last biography

LONGLEY, B JACK, SURGERY. **Personal Data:** b Dousman, Wis, July 19, 1913; m 1948, c 3. **Education:** Univ Wis, BS, 1934, PhD (pharmacol), 1940, MD, 1942. **Professional Experience:** Asst Chief Surg Serv, Vet Admin Hosp, beginning 1950; Assoc Prof Surg, Sch Med Univ Wis, Madison, beginning 1949; Asst Dir Tumor Clin, Univ Wis-Madison, beginning 1949; instr, UnivWis-Madison, 1947-1949; PROF EMER, UNIV WIS, MADISON. **Research Statement & Publications:** Cardiovascular research. **Mailing Address:** 13065 N 99th Dr, Sun City, AZ 85351.

LONGLEY, GLENN, LIMNOLOGY, WATER QUALITY. **Personal Data:** b Del Rio, Tex, June 2, 1942; m 1961, Frances; c Kelly Frances, Kristy Lee, Katherine Camille & Glenn Campbell. **Education:** Southwest Tex State Univ, BS, 1964; Univ Utah, MS, 1966, PhD (environ biol), 1969. **Honors & Awards:** Eminent Tex Hydrologist Award, AIH & Tx Sect AWRA, 1993. **Professional Experience:** DIR, RES & DATA CTR, 1979-; PROF AQUATIC RESOURCES, TEX STATE UNIV, 1969-; res grants, US Fish & Wildlife Serv, Nat Resources Conserv Soc, US Environ Protection Agency, various water agencies. **Memberships:** Water Environ Fedn; Am Water Resources Asn.; Soc Environ Toxicol & Chem; Soil & Water Conserv Soc; Asn Groundwater Scientists & Engrs; Sigma Xi. **Research Statement & Publications:** Use of subterranean fauna as indicators of ground water quality; edwards aquifer studies; water quality investigations; toxicity testing; aquatic endangered species studies. **Mailing Address:** Edwards Aquifer Res & Data Ctr, Tex State Univ, 248 Freeman Bldg, San Marcos, TX 78666. **Fax:** 512-245-2669. **E-Mail:** gl01@txstate.edu

LONGLEY, H(ERBERT) JERRY, MATHEMATICS, THEORITICAL PHYSICS. **Personal Data:** b Tahoka, Tex, January 3, 1926; div, c Elizabeth, Bonnie, Jerry J, Lyn L & Lea L. **Education:** Univ Tex, BS, 1946, PhD (physics), 1952; Tex Tech Col, BS, 1948. **Professional Experience:** RETIRED; Fraunhoter-Int, Euskirchen, WGer, 1989-1992; Radiation Res Assocs, Inc, Ft Worth, 1982-1989; consult, Lawrence Livermore Lab, Calif, 1978-1982; consult, Mission Res Corp, 1978-1979; consult, Los Alamos Nuclear Corp, 1971-1988; prin physicist, Mission Res Corp, 1971-1978; res assoc, Los Alamos Nuclear Corp, 1970-1971; staff mem, Los Alamos Sci Lab, Univ Calif, 1954-1976; asst prof & res assoc physics, NMex Inst Mining & Technol, 1952-1954. **Memberships:** Am Phys Soc. **Research Statement & Publications:** Nuclear weapons and weapons testing; hydrodynamics, numerical solutions; radioactive waste storage; nuclear weapons effects; electromagnetic pulse; nuclear physics; linec design; fundamental particles; author of numerous publications. **Mailing Address:** 5808 Chaparral Circle, Farmington, NM 87402-4880.

LONGLEY, JAMES BAIRD, HISTOCHEMISTRY. **Personal Data:** b Baltimore, Md, June 27, 1920; m 1944, c 4. **Education:** Haverford Col, BSc, 1941; Cambridge Univ, PhD (zoology), 1950. **Professional Experience:** PROF EMER, UNIV LOUISVILLE, AS OF 2003; ed, Stain Technol, Biol Stain Comn, 1973-1987; actg ed, J Histochem & Cytochem, Histochem Soc, 1964-1965; prof anat & chmn dept, Sch Med, Univ Louisville, 1962-1986; USPHS sr res fel, 1960-1962; assoc prof anat, Sch Med, Georgetown Univ, 1960-1962; asst ed, J Histochem & Cytochem, Histochem Soc, 1957-1964; instr, Sch Med, Johns Hopkins Univ, 1951-1952; from asst scientist to scientist, Nat Inst Arthritis & Metab Dis, 1950-1960. **Memberships:** Histochem Soc; Am Asn Anat; Am Soc Cell Biol; Biol Stain Comn. **Research Statement & Publications:** Renal histochemistry, morphology and physiology. **Mailing Address:** Dept Anat, Univ Louisville, Health Sci Ctr Box 35260, Louisville, KY 40292.

LONGLEY, ROBERT W(ILLIAM), NUTRITION, BIOCHEMISTRY. **Personal Data:** b Baltimore, Md, July 7, 1925; m 1986, Maureen; c 5. **Education:** Loyola Col, Md, BS, 1945; George Wash Univ, MS, 1955, PhD (biochem), 1957. **Professional Experience:** RETIRED; dir regulatory affairs, Sandoz Nutrit Corp, 1982-1986; dir res, Delmark Co, Minneapolis, 1973-1986; pres, Grist Mill Co, Minn, 1972-1973; consult food indust, 1971-1972; mgr spec proj corp res & develop, Joseph Schlitz Brewing Co, Wis, 1971; dir food prod res, Mead Johnson Res Ctr, 1970-1971; mgr res & develop, Camargo Foods Div, Drackett Co, Bristol Myers Co, Ohio, 1969-1971; dir food res, Drackett Co, 1968-1970; dir food res, Nutrit Div, Mead Johnson Subsidiary, Bristol Myers Co, Ind, 1967-1968; res assoc, James F Bell Res Ctr, 1962-1967; biochemist, Cent Res Labs, Gen Mills Inc, 1960-1962; asst prof, Med Col Ala, 1958-1960; investr, Dorn Lab Med Res, 1956-1958; instr biochem, George Wash Univ, 1956; technician biochem, George Wash Univ, 1953-1955; res asst, Res Lab, Brady Urol Inst, 1947-1953. **Memberships:** Am Asn Cereal Chemists; Inst Food Technologists; Am Soc Parenteral & Enteral Nutrit; Enteral Nutrit Coun. **Research Statement & Publications:** Carbohydrate metabolism; diabetes; clinical nutrition. **Mailing Address:** 100 Sweetwater Dr, St Paul, MN 55124.

LONGLEY, ROSS E, IMMUNOLOGY. **Personal Data:** b Enid, Okla, July 17, 1952. **Education:** Univ Okla, BS, 1975, MS, 1977, PhD (immunol), 1981. **Professional Experience:** SR VPRES, TAXALOG INC, 2002-; group leader immunol, harbor br, Oceanog Inst, beginning 1987; asst prof immunol & microbiol, Univ Cent Fla, 1984-1987; fel immunol, Univ Okla, 1981-1984. **Research Statement & Publications:** Immunology; microbiology. **Mailing Address:** Taxalog Inc, 3216 Sessions Rd Ste 100, Tallahassee, FL 32303. **Fax:** 850-558-0362.

LONGLEY, WILLIAM JOSEPH, REPRODUCTIVE PHYSIOLOGY, ENDOCRINOLOGY. **Personal Data:** b Middleton, NS, May 25, 1938; American citizen; m 1963, Mary; c Jeffery & Michael. **Education:** Univ Toronto, BSA, 1961, MSA, 1963; Univ Mass, PhD (vet animal sci), 1967. **Professional Experience:** DIR RES DEVELOP, GREAT PLAINS LAB, 1999-; chemist, Marion Labs, 1984-1992; prod develop mgr, Corning Med & Sci, 1981-1984; qual control tech prod mgr, Corning Glass Works, 1980-1981; asst prof path, Med Sch, Dalhousie Univ, 1973-1980; Endrocrinologist, NS Dept Pub Health, 1973-1980; asst prof, Med Sch, Dalhousie Univ, 1968-1973; lectr physiol, Med Sch, Dalhousie Univ, 1967-1968. **Memberships:** Can Soc Clin Chem; Soc Study Reproduction; Sigma Xi. **Research Statement & Publications:** Endocrinology of the female, particularly fetal-placental function as related to steroid synthesis; clinical chemistry of various hormones including thyroid and adrenal. **Mailing Address:** 8935 Outlook Dr, Overland Park, KS 66207-2112.

LONGLEY, W(ILLIAM) WARREN, GEOLOGY. **Personal Data:** b Paradise, NS, April 8, 1909; American citizen; m 1957, c 3. **Education:** Acadia Univ, BS, 1931; Univ Minn, MS & PhD (geol), 1937. **Professional Experience:** EMER PROF GEOL, UNIV COLO, BOULDER, 1977-; prof, Univ Colo, Boulder, 1952-1977; Kennecott Copper Corp, 1945- & Kennco Explor Ltd, 1946-; from asst prof to assoc prof geol & geophys, Univ Colo, Boulder, 1940-1952; Consult, Que Dept Mines, 1936-1950; Instr geol, Dartmouth Col, 1935-1940. **Memberships:** Fel Geol Asn Can; fel Geol Soc Am; Soc Econ Geol; Am Asn Petrol Geol; Soc Explor Geophys. **Research Statement & Publications:** Photogeology; mineral deposits in pre-Cambrian shield of Canada. **Mailing Address:** 821 Spring Dr, Boulder, CO 80303.

LONGMAN, JOYCE F, MATHEMATICS. **Education:** Col William & Mary, BA, 1960, MA, 1965; Temple Univ, PhD, 1976. **Professional Experience:** ASSOC PROF MATH SCI, VILLANOVA UNIV, as of 2006. **Mailing Address:** Villanova Univ, Villanova, PA 19087. **Fax:** 610-519-6928.

LONGMAN, RICHARD WINSTON, CONTROL THEORY, ANALYTICAL DYNAMICS. **Personal Data:** b Iowa City, Iowa, September 2, 1943. **Education:** Univ Calif, Riverside, BA, 1965; Univ Calif, San Diego, MS, 1967, MA & PhD (aerospace eng), 1969. **Honors & Awards:** Dirk Brouwer Award, Am Astronaut Soc, 1989. **Professional Experience:** Sr fel, Nat Res Coun, 1990-1991; Alexander Von Humboldt res fel, Polytech Darmstadt, WGer, 1980 & 1977; PROF MECH ENG, COLUMBIA UNIV, 1979-; consult, Langley Res Ctr & Goddard Space Flight Ctr, NASA, Europ Space Opers Ctr, Lockheed Missiles & Space Co, Aerospace Systs Div, Naval Res Lab, Martin Marietta Corp, Gen Elec Co, XeroxRes Lab, Marine Environ Corp, Designatronics, Inc & Syst Develop Corp; vis fac, Mass Inst Technol, Univ Bonn & Polytech Darmstadt, Univ Augsburg, Univ Heidelberg, Ger, Univ Newcastle, Australia, Nat Cheng Kung Univ & Taiwan Nanjing Aeronaut Inst, China; managing ed, J Astronaut Sci, 1976-1984; from asst prof to assoc prof, Columbia Univ, 1970-1979; mem tech staff, Control Systs Res Dept, Bell Tel Labs, NJ, 1969-1970; consult, Rand Corp, 1966-1969. **Memberships:** Fel Am Astronaut Soc (vpres, 1978-1984); fel Am Inst Aeronaut & Astronaut; fel Brit Interplanetary Soc; Am Soc Mech Engrs. **Research Statement & Publications:** System dynamics and control: learning and repetitive control, system identification, robot optimal path planning, robotics in space, satelite dynamics, shape control of large flexible spacecraft, vibration control. **Mailing Address:** Dept Mech Eng, Columbia Univ, New York, NY 10027. **Fax:** 212-854-3304. **E-Mail:** rwl4@columbia.edu

LONGMIRE, MARTIN SHELLING, ENGINEERING PHYSICS, GENERAL PHYSICS. **Personal Data:** b Morristown, Tenn, March 6, 1931. **Education:** Univ Cincinnati, BS, 1953; Mass Inst Technol, PhD (phys chem), 1961. **Professional Experience:** RETIRED; res physicist, Nat Oceanic & Atmospheric Admin, 1972; res physicist, Naval Res Lab, 1971 & 1973-1988; assoc prof physics, Western Ky Univ, 1970-1988; physicist, Electronics Res Ctr, NASA, Cambridge, Mass, 1965-1970; res assoc, Mass Inst Technol, 1964-1965; res fel, Mellon Inst, 1962-1964; res assoc phys chem, Ohio State Univ, 1961-1962. **Memberships:** AAAS; Am Phys Soc; emer fel Am Inst Chem; Sigma Xi. **Research Statement & Publications:** Processing of signals from infrared sensors; development of infrared surveillance systems; absorption of solar ultraviolet light by atmospheric contaminants and minor constituents. **Mailing Address:** PO Box 105, Whitesburg, TN 37891-0105.

LONGMORE, WILLIAM JOSEPH, BIOCHEMISTRY. **Personal Data:** b La Jolla, Calif, October 7, 1931; m 1953, Martha Baxter; c David J, William B, Timothy S & Christopher D. **Education:** Univ Calif, Berkeley, AB, 1957; Univ Kans, PhD (biochem), 1961. **Professional Experience:** PROF EMER BIOCHEM, ST LOUIS UNIV, 1997-; PROF EMER INTERNAL MED, ST LOUIS UNIV, 1997-; Fogarty int sr fel, State Univ Utrecht, Neth, 1977-1978; prof biochem, Sch Med, St Louis Univ, beginning 1973; USPHS res career develop award, 1966-1976; from asst prof to assoc prof, Sch Med, St Louis Univ, 1966-1973; res assoc biochem, Scripps Clin & Res Found, 1963-1966; Nat Heart Inst fel metab res, Scripps Clin & Res Found, 1961-1963. **Memberships:** AAAS; Am Chem Soc; Am

Soc Biol Chemists; Sigma Xi. **Research Statement & Publications:** Phospholipid metabolism; control mechanisms for lipid metabolism, phospholipid trafficking, especially in lung tissue; pulmonary surfactant. **Mailing Address:** Dept Biochem, St Louis Univ, 1402 S Grand, St Louis, MO 63104. **Fax:** 314-577-8156.

LONGMUIR, ALANGORDON, CONTROL ENGINEERING. **Personal Data:** b Vancouver, BC, March 1, 1941; c 2. **Education:** Univ BC, BASc, 1964, PhD (elec eng), 1968. **Professional Experience:** VPRES RES DEVELOP, KAISER ALUMINUM & CHEM CORP, 1988-; dir mfg systs, Kaiser Aluminum & Chem Corp, 1984-1988; mgr metals automation, Kaiser Aluminum & Chem Corp, 1978-1984; assoc ed, Automatica, 1976-1983; Chem Corp, 1968-1978; control engr, Kaiser Aluminum & Chem Corp. **Memberships:** Indust Res Inst. **Research Statement & Publications:** Development of products and processes related to aluminum and its alloys. **Mailing Address:** PO Box 5009, San Ramon, CA 94583. **Fax:** 510-847-4400. **E-Mail:** alan_longmuir@kacc.com

LONGMUIR, IAN STEWART, BIOCHEMISTRY, PHYSIOLOGY. **Personal Data:** b Glasgow, Scotland, March 12, 1922; m 1949, c 4. **Education:** Cambridge Univ, BA, 1943, MA & MB, BChir, 1948. **Professional Experience:** PROF CHEM & BIOCHEM, NC STATE UNIV, 1965-; Isaac Ott fel, Univ Pa, 1962-1963; Ed jour, Brit Polarographic Soc, 1957-1962; sr lectr biochem, Univ London, 1954-1965; prin sci officer, Ministry Supply, Eng, 1951-1954; Res assoc colloid sci, Cambridge Univ, 1948-1951. **Memberships:** AAAS; Am Physiol Soc; Int Soc Oxygen Transport to Tissue; Am Soc Biol Chem; Aerospace Med Asn. **Research Statement & Publications:** Oxygen transport in blood and tissue; inert gas metabolism. **Mailing Address:** Dept Biochem, NC State Univ 2408 Tyson St, Raleigh, NC 27612-4729.

LONGNECKER, DANIEL SIDNEY, ANATOMIC PATHOLOGY. **Personal Data:** b Omaha, Nebr, June 8, 1931; m 1952, Louise; c Matthew, Daniel, Jane & Thomas. **Education:** Univ Iowa, AB, 1954, MD, 1956, MS, 1962. **Honorary Degrees:** MA, Dartmouth Col, 1974. **Professional Experience:** PROF PATH, DARTMOUTH MED SCH, 1972-; assoc prof, Sch Med, St Louis Univ, 1969-1972; Dartmouth Col, 1975-1996; St Louis Univ, 1969-1971; res grants, USPHS, Univ Iowa, 1967-1969; spec fel & vis asst prof, Dept Path, Univ Pittsburgh, 1965-1967; from asst to assoc prof path, Univ Iowa, 1961-1969. **Memberships:** Am Soc Clin Path; Int Acad Path; Am Pancreatic Asn Pres, 1987-1988; Am Asn Investigative Path; Am Asn Cancer Res; Int Asn Pancreatology. **Research Statement & Publications:** Biochemical mechanisms of cell injury; pancreatic carcinogenesis; pathology of pancreatic disease and experimental carcinogenesis in the pancreas; morphologic and molecular comparison of human and animal pancreatic carcinomas. **Mailing Address:** Dept Path, Dartmouth Med Sch, Lebanon, NH 03756. **Fax:** 603-650-6120.

LONGNECKER, DAVID EUGENE, ANESTHESIOLOGY. **Personal Data:** b Kendallville, Ind, May 29, 1939; m 1963, Charlene; c Ann, Mary & Andrew. **Education:** Ind Univ, AB, 1961, MD, 1964, MA 1968; Am Bd Anesthesiol, dipl, 1969. **Honors & Awards:** Van Bergen Lectr, Univ Minn, 1981; E M Papper Lectr, Univ Calif, Los Angeles, 1984; Louis R Orkin Lectr, NY Acad Med, 1993; Evan L Frederickson Res Lectr, Emory Univ, 1993; E A Rovenstine Mem Lectr, Am Soc Anesthesiologists, 1996. **Professional Experience:** ROBERT DUNNING DRIPPS PROF EMER, DEPT ANESTHESIA, UNIV PA & DIR DIV HEALTH CARE AFFAIRS ASSOC AM MED COL, as of 2006; sr vpres & chief med officer, Univ Pa, Health Syst, 2002-; vice dean prof serv, Univ Pa, Health Syst, 1999-2002; chair, dept anesthesia, Univ Pa, 1999-2002; pres, Am Bd Anesthesiol, 1994-; Robert Dunning Dripps Prof, Dept Anesthesia, Univ Pa, 1988-; chmn Anesthesiol, Univ Pa, 1988-2002; ed, Int J Microcirculation, 1986-; Harold Carron prof anathesiol, Univ Va, 1986-1988; distinguished prof anesthesiol, Univ Va, 1982-1985; prof anesthesiol, Univ Va, 1978-1982; res career develop award, Nat Heart & Lung Inst, 1975; from assoc prof to prof, Univ Va, 1972-1978; asst prof, Univ Mo, Columbia, 1970-1973; clin assoc, NIH, 1968-1970; NIH spec res fel, Ind Univ, 1967-1968; resident anesthesiol, Ind Univ, Indianapolis, 1965-1968; intern, Blodgett Mem Hosp, Grand Rapids, 1964-1965. **Memberships:** Inst Med-Nat Acad Sci; Inst Anesthesia Res Soc; Am Physiol Soc; Asn Univ Anesthetists (pres, 1992-1994); Am Soc Anesthesiologists; AMA; Microcirculatory Soc; Sigma Xi; Am Soc Critical Care Anesthesiologists; Europ Microcirculatory Soc; Int Soc Oxygen Transport to Tissue. **Research Statement & Publications:** Microcirculatory mechanisms during hemorrhagic shock; effect of anesthetics on the microcirculation during normovolemia and hypovolemia. **Mailing Address:** Dept Anesthesia, Univ Pa, Sch Med, HUP 3400 Spruce St 4N Dulles, Philadelphia, PA 19104-4283. **Fax:** 215-349-5341.

LONGO, DAN L, IMMUNOLOGY, MEDICAL ONCOLOGY. **Personal Data:** b St Louis, Mo, April 25, 1949; m 1971, Nancy; c Jennifer A, Adam D & Paul A. **Education:** Wash Univ, BA, 1970; Univ Mo, Columbia, MD, 1975. **Honors & Awards:** Tovi Comet-Wallerstein Award, 1992; Plenary Lect, 1989. **Professional Experience:** Distinguished vis prof, Dept Med, Duke Univ, 1996; SCIENTIFIC DIR, NAT INST AGING, NIH, BALTIMORE & BETHESDA, 1995-; assoc ed, J Immunotherapy, 1989-; assoc ed, Yr Bk Oncol & J Immunol, 1988-; assoc ed, Cancer Res & J Nat Cancer Inst, 1987-; ed, Clin Oncol Alert, 1985-1995; from assoc dir to dir, Biol Response Modifiers Prog, Div Cancer Treatment, Nat Cancer Inst, NIH, 1985-1995; asst ed, Am J Clin Nutrit, 1981-1991; sr investr, Biol Response Modifiers Prog, Med Br, Nat Cancer Inst, 1980-1982; clin assoc immunol, Lab Immunol, Nat Inst Allergy & Infectious Dis, 1978-1980; clin assoc med oncol, Med Br, Nat Cancer Inst, 1977-1978; fel med, Harvard Med Sch, 1975-1977; resident internal med, Peter Bent Brigham Hosp, 1975-1977; researcher, Dep Path, Columbia Univ Col Physicians & Surgeons, 1974-1975. **Memberships:** Am Asn Immunologists; Am Soc Clin Oncol; Am Fedn Clin Res; Am Asn Cancer Res; Am Soc Hemat; Am Soc Clin Invest; fel AAAS; Am Soc Cell Biol; fel Am Col Physicians; Sigma Xi; Am Soc Microbiol. **Research Statement & Publications:** Thymus function and control of lymphocyte proliferation and gene expression; treatment of lymphoproliferative diseases; biological therapy of human neoplastic infectious and immunological diseases; published over 690 articles. **Mailing Address:** Nat Inst Aging NIH, 5600 Nathan Shock Dr, Baltimore, MD 21224-6825. **Fax:** 410-558-8137. **E-Mail:** longod@grc.nia.nih.gov

LONGO, FRANK JOSEPH, DEVELOPMENTAL BIOLOGY. **Personal Data:** b Cleveland, Ohio, November 16, 1939; m 1962, c 6. **Education:** Loyola Univ, BS, 1962; Ore State Univ, MS, 1965, PhD (cell biol), 1967. **Honors & Awards:** NIH Careeer Devolp Awardee, NIH, 1971-1976. **Professional Experience:** PROF EMER ANAT, COL MED, UNIV IOWA, 2002-; from assoc prof to prof anat, Col Med, Univ Iowa, 1975-2002; asst prof, Col Med, Univ Iowa, 1970-1975; res fel, Univ Mass, 1968-1970. **Memberships:** AAAS; Am Soc Cell Biol; Am Asn Anat; Soc Study Reproduction. **Research Statement & Publications:** Cellular and developmental biology at the fine structural and biochemical levels; comparative pronuclear development and fusion; gametogenesis and fertilization; cell division and differentiation. **Mailing Address:** Dept Anat, Univ Iowa, Iowa City, IA 52442-0001. **Fax:** 319-335-7198. **E-Mail:** frank-longo@uiowa.edu

LONGO, FREDERICK R, PHYSICAL CHEMISTRY. **Personal Data:** b Trenton, NJ, May 4, 1930; c 6. **Education:** Villanova Col, BA, 1953; Drexel Inst, MS, 1958; Univ Pa, PhD (phys chem), 1962. **Professional Experience:** PROF EMER CHEM, DREXEL UNIV, as of 2003; Sr res assoc, Nat Res Coun, 1985-1986; head, Dept Chem & Chem Eng, Evening Col, 1973-1976; prof chem, Drexel Univ, beginning 1968; assoc prof, Drexel Univ, 1957-1968; Chemist, Am Biltrite Rubber Co, 1955-1957. **Memberships:** Am Chem Soc; Sigma Xi; NY Acad Sci. **Research Statement & Publications:** Synthesis and spectral properties of porphyrins; investigation of microemulsions as media for controlled chemical reactions. **Mailing Address:** Dept Chem, Drexel Univ, Philadelphia, PA 19129.

LONGO, JOHN M, SOLID STATE CHEMISTRY, MINERAL REACTIONS. **Personal Data:** b Hartford, Conn, November 6, 1939; wid Ligita; c Karen, Michael & Julie. **Education:** Univ Conn, BA, 1961, PhD (inorg chem), 1964; Post Doc Solid State Chem US Stockholm 1965. **Honors & Awards:** Best Paper Award, Petroleum Soc of CIM, 1994. **Professional Experience:** Baker Atlas 2005-, ExxonMobilUpstream Res, 1981-2004; chemist, Corp Res Labs, 1970-1981; chemist, Lincoln Lab, Mass Inst Technol, 1965-1970; Fel, Univ Stockholm, 1964-1965. **Memberships:** Am Chem Soc. **Research Statement & Publications:** Preparation and characterization of solid state inorganic materials. **Mailing Address:** Baker Atlas, 2001 Rankin Rd, Houston, TX 77073. **E-Mail:** jmlongo@swbell.net

LONGO, JOSEPH THOMAS, SOLID STATE PHYSICS. **Personal Data:** b Ferndale, Mich, January 13, 1942; m 1964, c 2. **Education:** Univ Detroit, BS, 1964; Mich State Univ, MS, 1966, PhD (solid state physics), 1968. **Professional Experience:** VPRES & GEN MANAGER, ROCKWELL SCI CTR as of 2004; DIR, N AM ROCKWELL SCI CTR, 1978-; asst dir, N Am Rockwell Sci Ctr, 1977-1978; mgr, N Am Rockwell Sci Ctr, 1972-1977; mem tech staff, N Am Rockwell Sci Ctr, 1969-1972; fel, N Am Rockwell Sci Ctr, 1968-1969; asst, Mich State Univ, 1964-1968. **Memberships:** Am Phys Soc. **Research Statement & Publications:** High field magnetoresistance and Hall effect in intermetallic compounds; crystal growth, optical and device properties of narrow gap semiconductors. **Mailing Address:** 24770 Outlook Dr, Carmel, CA 93923.

LONGO, LAWRENCE DANIEL, DEVELOPMENTAL NEUROBIOLOGY, FETAL PHYSIOLOGY. **Personal Data:** b Los Angeles, Calif, October 11, 1926; m Betty; c April Celeste, Lawrence Anthony, Elisabeth Lynn & Camilla Giselle. **Education:** Pac Union Col, BA, 1949; Loma Linda Univ, MD, 1954. **Professional Experience:** DIR, CTR PERINATAL BIOL, LOMA LINDA UNIV, as of 1998; consult, NatInst Child Health & Human Develop, 1971; HEAD, CTR PERINATAL BIOL, LOMA LINDAUNIV, 1970-; USPHS res career develop award, Loma Linda Univ, 1968- & grant, 1969-; PROF PHYSIOL, OBSTET & GYNEC, LOMA LINDA UNIV, 1968-; asst prof physiol, Univ Pa, 1966-1968; USPHS spec fel physiol, UnivPa, 1964-1966 & res career develop award, 1966-1968; lectr physiol, Univ Pa, 1964-1966; asst prof, Univ Calif, Los Angeles, 1962-1964; asst prof obstet & gynec, Univ Ibadan, 1959-1962; USPHS fel obstet & gynec, Univ Calif, Los Angeles, 1959; Ed, Classic Pages Obstet & Gynec Am, J Obstet & Gynec. **Memberships:** AAAS; NY Acad Sci; Am Physiol Soc; Soc Gynec Invest (secy-treas pres); Perinatal Res Soc; Am Col Obstet & Gynec; Soc Neuroscience; fel Royal Col Obstet & Gynec. **Research Statement & Publications:** Regulation of fetal growth and development; regulation of cerebral blood flow; fetal oxygenation; developmental neurobiology. **Mailing Address:** Ctr Perinatal Biol, Loma Linda Univ, Sch Med, Loma Linda, CA 92350. **Fax:** 909-558-4029. **E-Mail:** llongo@llu.edu

LONGO, MICHAEL JOSEPH, HIGH ENERGY PHYSICS, SCIENCE EDUCATION. **Personal Data:** b Philadelphia, Pa, April 7, 1935; c 3. **Education:** La Salle Col, BA, 1956; Univ Calif, Berkeley, PhD (physics), 1961. **Professional Experience:** PROF PHYSICS, UNIV MICH, ANN ARBOR, 1968-; from asst prof to assoc prof, Univ Mich, Ann Arbor, 1962-1968; NSF fel physics, Saclay Nuclear Res Ctr, France, 1961-1962. **Memberships:** Am Phys Soc; Sigma Xi. **Research Statement & Publications:** Nucleon-nucleon interaction at high energies; proportional chambers and scintillation counters; neutrino interactions; magnetic monopoles; science communications; software systems; medical imaging. **Mailing Address:** Univ Mich, Dept Physics, 354 W Hall, Ann Arbor, MI 48109-1120. **Fax:** 734-936-1817. **E-Mail:** mlongo@umich.edu

LONGOBARDO, ANNA KAZANJIAN, TECHNICAL MANAGEMENT. **Personal Data:** b New York, NY, m 1952, Guy; c Guy & Alicia. **Education:** Columbia Univ, BS, 1949, MS, 1952. **Professional Experience:** RETIRED; dir strategic initiatives, Unisys Corp, 1993-1996; mem bd dirs, Woodward Clyde Group Inc, beginning 1989; dir field eng, Unisys Corp, 1989-1993; dir tech serv, Unisys Corp, 1982-1989; mgr planning, Sperry Rand Corp, 1981-1982; mgr prog planning, Sperry Rand Corp, 1977-1981; mgr eng personnel utilization, Sperry Rand Corp, 1973-1977; res sect head, Sperry Rand Corp, 1965-1973; sr systs engr, Am Bosch Arma Corp, 1950-1965. **Memberships:** Am Soc Mech Engrs; Am Inst Aeronaut & Astronaut; fel Soc Women Engrs. **Research Statement & Publications:** Supervised the Independent Research and Development program and was the strategic planner of a large unit of the Sperry Corporation; supervised the activities of approximately 400 field engineers in sixty locations worldwide who are giving life cycle support to diverse equipments including weather radar systems, radar landing systems, sonar systems and combat systems. **Mailing Address:** 15 Crows Nest Rd, Bronxville, NY 10708. **Fax:** 914-779-2448.

LONGOBARDO, GUY S, MECHANICAL ENGINEERING, BIOENGINEERING. **Personal Data:** b New York, NY, October 23, 1928; m 1952, c 2. **Education:** Columbia Univ, BS, 1949, MS, 1950, EngScD, 1961. **Professional Experience:** CONSULT, CASE WESTERN UNIV, 1988-; sr forecaster, World Trade Corp, 1981-1988; mem corp staff, Med Info Systs, IBM Corp, 1977-1981; Consult, Am Mach & Foundry Co, 1961-1965 & Case Western Dept Med, 1975-; adv engr, Med Info Systs, IBM Corp, 1965-1977; dir, Fluid Mech Lab, 1963-1965; asst prof mech eng & Bioengineering, Sch Eng, Columbia Univ, 1961-1965; instr mech eng, Sch Eng, Columbia Univ, 1952-1961; develop engr, E I Du Pont Del Nemours & Co, 1950-1952. **Memberships:** Assoc Am Soc Mech Engrs. **Research Statement & Publications:** Medical information systems, clinical application of computer technology, operation of the respiratory control system and its unstable modes; medical information systems. **Mailing Address:** 15 Crows Nest Rd, Bronxville, NY 10708.

LONGONE, DANIEL THOMAS, ORGANIC CHEMISTRY. **Personal Data:** b Worcester, Mass, September 16, 1932; m 1954. **Education:** Worcester Polytech Inst, BS, 1954; Cornell Univ, PhD (org chem), 1958. **Professional Experience:** PROF EMER CHEM, UNIV MICH, ANN ARBOR, as of 2005; vis prof, Univ Calif, Los Angeles, 1976; prof org chem, Univ Mich, Ann Arbor, beginning 1971; Fulbright scholar, 1970-1971; vis prof, Univ Cologne, 1970-1971; Am Chem Soc-Petrol Res Fund int fel, 1967-1968; from instr to assoc prof, Univ Mich, Ann Arbor, 1959-1971; res assoc org chem, Univ Ill, 1958-1959. **Memberships:** Am Chem Soc. **Research Statement & Publications:** Synthetic and mechanistic organic chemistry; bridged aromatic compounds; cyclophane chemistry; monomer synthesis and polymerization. **Mailing Address:** Univ Mich, Dept Chem, 3537 Chem, Ann Arbor, MI 48109-1055. **E-Mail:** dtlong@umich.edu

LONGORIA, RAUL, MECHANICAL ENGINEERING. **Personal Data:** b Rio Grande Valley, 1962. **Education:** Univ Tex, Austin BSME, 1985 & PhD, 1989. **Professional Experi-**

ence: SITE DIR, NSF I/UCRC VIRTUAL PROVING GROUND SIMULATION, UNIV TEX, AUSTIN, 1998-; ASSOC PROF, DEPT MECH ENG, UNIV TEX, AUSTIN, 1997-; asst prof, Dept Mech Eng, Univ Tex, Austin, 1991-1997; fel, Offshore Technol res Ctr, 1990-1991. **Memberships:** Soc Automotive Engrs; Am soc Engr Educ; Am Soc Mech Engrs; Soc Comput Simulation. **Research Statement & Publications:** Multienergetic dynamic system modeling and simulation; vehicle system dynamics and controls; electromechanical system modeling and simulation. **Mailing Address:** Dept Mech Eng, Univ Tex, One Univ Sta C2200, Austin, TX 78712-0292. **Fax:** 512-471-0530. **E-Mail:** r.longoria@mail.utexas.edu

LONGPRE, EDWIN KEITH, SYSTEMATIC BOTANY. **Personal Data:** b Detroit, Mich, March 7, 1933; m 1965, c 1. **Education:** Univ Mich, BS, 1955, MS, 1956; Mich State Univ, PhD (bot), 1967. **Professional Experience:** EMER PROF CONSULT, WESTERN STATE COL COLO, 1997-; Pres-elect, Colo-Wyo Acad Sci, 1985-1986; prof bot, Western State Col Colo, 1980-1997; assoc prof bot & biol, Western State Col Colo, 1965-1980; Instr bot, Tex Tech Col, 1956-1957. **Memberships:** Am Soc Plant Taxon; AAAS; Sigma Xi. **Research Statement & Publications:** Systematical studies in the tribe Heliantheae of the family Compositae; general cytotaxonomical and floristic studies. **Mailing Address:** 1200 US Hwy 50 C-5, Gunnison, CO 81230.

LONGROY, ALLAN LEROY, ORGANIC CHEMISTRY. **Personal Data:** b Flint, Mich, May 28, 1936; m 1955, c 3. **Education:** Univ Mich, AB, 1958, MS, 1961, PhD (chem), 1963. **Professional Experience:** PROF EMER CHEM, PURDUE UNIV, as of 2005; assoc prof chem, Purdue Univ, beginning 1969; asst prof, Purdue Univ, 1967-1969; asst prof, Ind Univ, 1964-1967; res fel chem, Brandeis Univ, 1962-1964. **Memberships:** Am Chem Soc. **Research Statement & Publications:** Organic reaction mechanisms and kinetics; demonstrations in chemistry. **Mailing Address:** Dept Chem, Purdue Univ, 2101 Coliseum Blvd, Ft Wayne, IN 46805-1499. **E-Mail:** longroya@ipfw.edu

LONGSHORE, JOHN DAVID, PETROLOGY. **Personal Data:** b Birmingham, Ala, March 8, 1936; m 1964, c 2. **Education:** Emory Univ, BA, 1957; Rice Univ, MA, 1959, PhD (geol), 1965. **Professional Experience:** NASA res grant chem invest Med Lake Area, 1967-1969; PROF GEOL, HUMBOLDT STATE UNIV, 1965-; teacher, Westminster Schs, Ga, 1960-1962. **Research Statement & Publications:** Chemistry and petrology of igneous rocks. **Mailing Address:** Dept Geol, Humboldt State Univ, 6A Founders Hall, Arcata, CA 95521. **Fax:** 707-826-5241. **E-Mail:** jdl1@axe.humboldt.edu

LONGSTRETH, DAVID J, PLANT ECOPHYSIOLOGY. **Personal Data:** b Phoenix, Ariz, March 22, 1948. **Education:** Ariz State Univ, BS 1970, MS, 1972; Duke Univ, PhD (bot), 1976. **Professional Experience:** ASSOC PROF BOT, LA STATE UNIV, 1985-; asst prof, LA State Univ, 1979-1985; fel, Duke Univ & Univ Calif, Los Angeles, 1977-1979. **Memberships:** Am Soc Plant Physiologists; Ecol Soc Am; Sigma Xi; AAAS. **Research Statement & Publications:** Plant carbon balance in aquatic and semiaquatic environments; salinity effects on plant water relations and photosynthetic response. **Mailing Address:** Dept Biol Sci, La State Univ, 202 Life Sci Bldg, Baton Rouge, LA 70803. **E-Mail:** btlong@lsu.edu

LONGSWORTH, RALPH C, MECHANICAL ENGINEERING. **Personal Data:** b New York, NY, June 17, 1934; m 1958, Roberta; c Gordon & Margaret. **Education:** Columbia Univ, BA, 1956, BS, 1957; Syracuse Univ, MS, 1960, PhD (mech eng), 1966. **Professional Experience:** CHIEF SCIENTIST, APD CRYOG INC, 1992-; prin investr, NASA & APD Cryog, 1992-1996; sr res assoc, Apd Cryog, 1980-1992; mem bd, Cryog Eng Conf, 1976-1987; sr res engr, Apd Cryog, 1968-1980; gen mgr, Cryomech Inc, 1965-1967. **Memberships:** Am Soc Mech Engrs; Am Vacuum Soc. **Research Statement & Publications:** Small cryogenic refrigeration; Gifford McMahon refrigeration; pulse tube refrigeration; cryopumps; small helium liquifiers; fast cooldown; Joule Thomson; commercialized refrigerant technology in small 80K refrigerators. **Mailing Address:** APD Cryog Inc, 1833 Vultee St, Allentown, PA 18103. **Fax:** 610-791-0440.

LONGTIN, BRUCE, THERMODYNAMICS, NUCLEAR & RADIOCHEMISTRY. **Personal Data:** b North Fork, Calif, August 23, 1913; m 1953, Cecilia; c 6. **Education:** Univ Calif, BS, 1935, MS, 1937, PhD (chem), 1938. **Professional Experience:** RETIRED; teaching assoc, Univ SC, Salkehatchie, 1978-1981, 1983-1984; from chemist to staff chemist, E I du Pont de Nemours & Co Inc, 1951-1978; assoc chemist, Argonne Nat Labs, 1948-1949; from instr to assoc prof, Ill Inst Technol, 1939-1951; asst chem, Shell Oil Co fel, 1938-1939. **Memberships:** Am Chem Soc. **Research Statement & Publications:** Thermodynamics of industrial processes; thermodynamic properties of solutions; reactor water and water wastes; chemistry, radiolysis and control of impurities in water coolant and moderator of nuclear reactors; rheology and mechanical properties of polymers. **Mailing Address:** 1209 Summerhill Rd, North Augusta, SC 29841.

LONGUEMARE, R NOEL, ENGINEERING. **Personal Data:** b March 26, 1932. **Education:** Johns Hopkins Univ, MS, 1958. **Professional Experience:** PRIN DEP UNDER SECY DEFENSE ACQUISITION & TECHNOL, DEPT DEFENSE, 1993-. **Mailing Address:** Dept Defense, 3015 Defense Pentagon, Washington, DC 20301.

LONGUET-HIGGINS, MICHAEL SELWYN, OCEAN PHYSICS, PROJECTIVE GEOMETRY. **Personal Data:** b Lenhan, Eng, December 8, 1925. **Education:** Univ Cambridge, BA, 1945, MA, 1946, PhD (geophysics), 1951. **Honors & Awards:** Sberdrup Gold Medal, Am Meteorol Soc, 1983; Int Coastal Eng Award, Am Soc Civil Engrs, 1984; Oceanog Award, Soc Underwater Technol, 1990. **Professional Experience:** RES EMER, INST NON-LINEAR SCI, UNIV CALIF, SAN DIEGO, as of 2005; sr res physicist, Inst Non-Linear Sci, Univ Calif, San Diego, beginning 1988; adj prof, Scripps Inst Oceanog, 1988-; res emer fel, Trinity Col, 1969-1989; res prof, Royal Soc, Univ Cambridge, 1969-1989. **Memberships:** Foreign assoc Nat Acad Sci; fel Am Geophys Union; fel Royal Soc London. **Mailing Address:** Inst Non-Linear Sci, Univ Calif San Diego, 9500 Gilman Dr, La Jolla, CA 92093-0402. **E-Mail:** mlonguet@ucsd.edu

LONGUSKI, JAMES M, ASTRODYNAMICS, SPACE MISSION DESIGN. **Personal Data:** b Dearborn, Mich, July 3, 1951; m 1988, Holly. **Education:** Univ Mich, BSE, 1973; MSE, 1975, PhD (aerospace engr), 1979. **Honors & Awards:** NSF Initiation Award, Natl Sci Foundation, 1989-1992; AIAA Distinguished Lecturer, Am Inst of Aero&Astronautics, 1991-1993; Award for Galileo Systems Design, Jet Propulsion Lab, 1991; NOVA Award, Jet Propulsion Lab, 1999. **Professional Experience:** PROF ASTRONAUTICS, PURDUE UNIV, 1988-; mem, technical staff, Jet Propulsion Lab, Calif Inst Technol, 1979-1988. **Memberships:** assoc fel Am Inst of Aero&Astronautics; Am Astronaut Soc; assoc Com on Space Res. **Research Statement & Publications:** Spacecraft dynamics and control; reentry theory; mission design; space trajectory optimization; and a new test of general relativity; written over 100 papers in astrodynamics. **Mailing Address:** Dept Aeronautics & Astronautics, Purdue Univ, 315 N Grant St, West Lafayette, IN 47907-2023. **Fax:** 765-494-0307. **E-Mail:** james.m.longuski.1@purdue.edu

LONGWELL, ARLENE CROSBY (MAZZONE), genetics & cytogenetics, animal breeding; deceased, see previous edition for last biography

LONGWELL, JOHN PLOEGER, chemical engineering, combustion; deceased, see previous edition for last biography

LONGWELL, P(AUL) A(LAN), CHEMICAL ENGINEERING. **Personal Data:** b Santa Maria, Calif, August 4, 1919; m 1940, c 2. **Education:** Calif Inst Technol, BS, 1940, MS, 1941, PhD (chem eng), 1957. **Professional Experience:** CHIEF SCIENTIST, ENVIROGENICS CO, AEROJET-GEN CORP, 1970-; sr staff scientist, Aerojet-Gen Corp, 1964-1970; consult, Aerojet-Gen Corp, 1961-1964; from instr to assoc prof chem eng, Calif Inst Technol, 1955-1964; head, Explosives Dept, 1951-1954; head ord processing, US Naval Ord Test Sta, 1950-1951; chem engr, US Naval Ord Test Sta, 1945-1950; instr chem eng, Calif Inst Technol, 1941-1945; chemist, Shell Oil Co, Calif, 1941. **Memberships:** Am Chem Soc; Am Inst Chem Engrs. **Research Statement & Publications:** Applied mathematics in engineering problems; heat, mass and momentum transfer; cryogenic plant processes; desalting plant processes. **Mailing Address:** 1000 Crest Dr, Encinitas, CA 92024-4042.

LONGWORTH, JAMES W, BIOPHYSICS, CHEMICAL PHYSICS. **Personal Data:** b Stockton Heath, Eng, September 16, 1938; m 1965, c 2. **Education:** Univ Sheffield, BS, 1959, PhD (biochem), 1962. **Professional Experience:** ASSOC PROF PHYSICS, ILL INST TECHNOL, as of 2004; ed, Comments Molecular & Cellular Biophys, 1980-; prog comt, Int Congr Photobiol, 1980; assoc ed, Biophys J, 1979-1981; chmn, US Nat Comt Photobiol, 1976-1978; mem, US Nat Comt Photobiol, 1972-1976; mem staff, Biol Div, Oak Ridge Nat Lab, beginning 1965; mem staff, Bell Tel Labs, 1963-1965; USPHS fel phys chem, Univ Minn, 1962-1963. **Memberships:** Am Soc Photobiol (pres, 1978-1979); Biophys Soc; Brit Biochem Soc; Brit Biophys Soc; Am Soc Biol Chem. **Research Statement & Publications:** Photophysics and excited state chemistry of proteins, nucleic acids and their synthetic analogues, particularly their luminescent behavior; use of optical methods to study conformation and function of proteins and nucleic acids and their complexes. **Mailing Address:** Dept Physics, Ill Inst Technol, 156 Life Sci Bldg 3101 S Dearborn St, Chicago, IL 60616. **Fax:** 312-567-3494. **E-Mail:** longworth@iit.edu

LONGWORTH, RUSKIN, POLYMER CHEMISTRY, POLYMER PHYSICS. **Personal Data:** b Oldham, Eng, August 13, 1927; m 1957, Joyce Kettaneh; c Monica, Kim, Jennifer & Alys. **Education:** Univ London, BSc, 1950, PhD (chem), 1956. **Professional Experience:** RETIRED; sr res chemist, Polymer Prod Dept, Exp Sta, E I Du Pont de Nemours & Co, Inc, 1957-1985; chemist, Vauxhall Motors Ltd, Eng, 1956-1957; res fel, Univ Leiden, Holland, 1955-1956; Asst, Polytech Inst Brooklyn, 1952-1955. **Memberships:** Am Chem Soc; fel Royal Soc Chem; AAAS. **Research Statement & Publications:** Physical chemistry of polymers, especially rheology, solution properties, ionicpolymers, polyimides and polyolefines. **Mailing Address:** 10 Walnut Ridge Rd, Greenville, DE 19807. **E-Mail:** ruskin1@dca.net

LONIGRO, ANDREW JOSEPH, INTERNAL MEDICINE, PHARMACOLOGY. **Personal Data:** b St Louis, Mo, July 22, 1936; m 1968, c 3. **Education:** St Louis Univ, BS, 1958, MD, 1966. **Professional Experience:** PROF PHARMACOL & PHYSIOL SCI, ST LOUIS UNIV, 1984-; prog specialist clin pharmacol, Vet Admin, 1976-; DIR DIV CLIN PHARMACOL, SCH MED, ST LOUIS UNIV, 1976-; chief clin pharmacol, Vet Admin Hosp, St Louis, 1976-1987; assoc prof, St Louis Univ, 1976-1984; clin investr, Vet Admin, 1974-1976; res & educ assoc, Vet Admin, 1972-1974; from instr to asst prof pharmacol & internal med, Med Col Wis, 1971-1976; fel cardiol, St Louis Univ Hosps, 1969-1971; spec res fel, USPHS, 1969-1971; intern-resident, St Louis Univ Hosps, 1966-1969. **Memberships:** Am Fedn Clin Res; Am Soc Nephrology; Am Physiol Soc; Am Soc Pharmacol & Exp Therapeut. **Research Statement & Publications:** Circulatory control mechanisms; protaglandins, hypertension; renal function. **Mailing Address:** Dept Pharmacol & Physiol Sci, St Louis Univ, 1402 S Grand Blvd, St Louis, MO 63104. **Fax:** 314-977-6410. **E-Mail:** lonigro@slu.edu

LONKY, MARTIN LEONARD, ELECTRONIC PHYSICS, SOLID STATE PHYSICS. **Personal Data:** b New York, NY, January 5, 1944; m 1966. **Education:** Rensselaer Polytech Inst, BS, 1964; Univ Del, MS, 1967, PhD (physics), 1972. **Professional Experience:** PRES & CHIEF EXEC OFFICER, TRYLON CORP, as of 2005; MGR SOLID STATE TECHNOL, QUESTRON CORP, 1979-; fel engr physics, Westinghouse Elec Corp, 1976-1979; sr engr electronics, Westinghouse Elec Corp, 1973-1975; res analyst, US Army Land Warfare Lab, 1972-1973; presidential intern chem, US Army Land Warfare Lab, 1972; res fel, Univ Del, 1967-1972; teaching asst physics, Univ Del, 1964-1967. **Memberships:** Electrochem Soc; Inst Elec & Electronics Engrs. **Research Statement & Publications:** Electron device physics, with emphasis on memory field effect transistors and transparent gate metal-oxide-silicon technology; device fabrication technologies. **Mailing Address:** Trylon Corp, 27600 Alvesta Pl, Rancho Palos Verdes, CA 90732.

LONNERDAL, BO L, INFANT NUTRITION. **Personal Data:** b Linkoping, Sweden, March 5, 1948; m 1974, c 4. **Education:** Univ Uppsala, BS, 1969, MS, 1971, PhD (biochem), 1973. **Honors & Awards:** Henning Throne Holst's Award, 1977. **Professional Experience:** PROF NUTRIT & INTERNAL MED, UNIV CALIF, DAVIS, as of 2004; from asst prof to assoc prof, Univ Calif, Davis, 1981-1985; asst res nutritionist, Univ Calif, Davis, 1980-1981; vis asst res nutritionist, Univ Calif, Davis, 1978-1980; asst prof nutrit, Inst Nutrit, Univ Uppsula, beginning 1976; res assoc, Inst Nutrit, 1974-1976; res asst, Dept Biochem, Univ Uppsula, 1969-1974. **Memberships:** Am Inst Nutrit; Am Soc Clin Nutrit; Soc Exp Biol & Med. **Research Statement & Publications:** Composition of breast milk, cow's milk and formulas; trace element metabolism in the perinatal period. **Mailing Address:** Dept Nutrit, Univ Calif, 3109 Meyer Hall One Shields Ave, Davis, CA 95616-5270. **Fax:** 530-752-8966. **E-Mail:** blLonnerdal@ucdavis.edu

LONNES, PERRY BERT, ENVIRONMENTAL SCIENCE, ANALYTICAL CHEMISTRY. **Personal Data:** b St Paul, Minn, February 22, 1940; m 1965, c 1. **Education:** Univ Minn, St Paul, BS, 1963, MS, 1965, PhD (environ sci), 1972. **Professional Experience:** MGR & CHIEF EXEC OFFICER, ENVIRON MEASUREMENTS, INTERPOLL LAB INC, 1973-; mgr anal serv & contract res, Environ Res Corp, 1970-1973; instr air analysis, Univ Minn, St Paul, 1968-1970; treas, Interpoll Lab Inc. **Memberships:** Am Chem Soc; Air Pollution Control Asn. **Research Statement & Publications:** Characterization of adsorbents to predict gas sampling potentials; gas sampling methodology; gas chromatography; air pollution analytical instrumentation. **Mailing Address:** 4500 Ball Rd NE, Circle Pines, MN 55014.

LONNGREN, KARL E(RIK), PLASMA PHYSICS, ELECTRICAL ENGINEERING. **Personal Data:** b Milwaukee, Wis, August 8, 1938; m 1963, Vicki; c Sondra & Jon. **Education:** Univ Wis-Madison, BS, 1960, MS, 1962, PhD (elec eng), 1964. **Professional Experience:** Danish Atomic Energy Comn, 1982; Inst space & astronaut sci, Japan, 1981; los alamos nat labs, 1979, 1980; math res ctr, Univ Wis-Madison, 1976-1977;

PROF ELEC ENG, UNIV IOWA, 1972-; inst plasma physics, Japan, 1972; vis scientist, Univ Sask, 1971; vis scientist, Oak Ridge Nat Lab, 1967 & 1969; from asst prof to assoc prof, Univ Iowa, 1965-1972; royal inst technol, Sweden, 1964-1965; alumni res found res asst, Univ Wis, 1964. **Memberships:** Fel Am Phys Soc; fel Inst Elec & Electronics Engrs. **Research Statement & Publications:** Nonlinear plasma physics. **Mailing Address:** Dept Elec & Comput Eng, Univ Iowa, 4312 Seamans Ctr, Iowa City, IA 52242. **E-Mail:** karl-lonngren@uiowa.edu

LONSDALE, CAROL JEAN, INFRARED ASTRONOMY, GALAXY EVOLUTION. **Personal Data:** b Stockport, Eng, March 9, 1955; American citizen; m 1989, Harding; c Kimberley J (Persson) & Tamsyn E (Lonsdale-Smith). **Education:** Univ St Andrews, BSc, 1976; Univ Edinburgh, PhD (astron), 1980. **Professional Experience:** PRIN INVESTR, INFRARED PROCESSING & ANAL CTR, CALIF INST TECHNOL, as of 2005; mem user comt, High Energy Astrophys Res Ctr, 1992-1993; GROUP SUPVR, CALIF INST TECHNOL, 1990-; ed, conf proc, Calif Inst Technol, 1987; organizer, Astrophys Data Prof, NASA, 1985-1992; staff scientist, Calif Inst Technol, 1985-1990; fel, Jet Propulsion Lab, 1983-1985; SCI STAFF IPAC, CALIF INST TECHNOL, 1983-; asst prof astron, Univ Calif, Los Angeles, 1981-1983; res fel, Univ Hawaii, NATO, 1980-1981. **Memberships:** Int Astrophys Union; Am Astron Soc. **Research Statement & Publications:** Study of the connection between active galactic nuclei and starbursts using infrared and radio interferometry techniques and the evolution of galaxies since their origin to the present. **Mailing Address:** Infrared Processing & Anal Ctr, Calif Inst Technol, 1200 E Calif Blvd, Pasadena, CA 91125. **Fax:** 818-397-9600. **E-Mail:** cjl@ipac.caltech.edu

LONSDALE, EDWARD MIDDLEBROOK, electrical engineering; deceased, see previous edition for last biography

LONSDALE, HAROLD KENNETH, PHYSICAL CHEMISTRY, MEMBRANE SCIENCE & TECHNOLOGY. **Personal Data:** b Westfield, NJ, January 19, 1932; m 1993, Bryn Hazell; c Karen (Trachsel) & Harold K Jr. **Education:** Rutgers Univ, BS, 1953; Pa State Univ, PhD (chem), 1957. **Professional Experience:** RETIRED; chmn, Bend Res, Inc, 1987-1990; ed, J Membrane Sci, 1975-1990; pres, Bend Res, Inc, 1975-1987; vis prof, Weizmann Inst, 1974; vis scientist, Max Planck Inst Biophys, 1973; prin scientist, Alza Corp, 1970-1972; staff mem, Gen Atomic Co, 1959-1970. **Memberships:** Am Chem Soc. **Research Statement & Publications:** Transport in synthetic membranes, desalination by reverse osmosis; controlled release of biologically active agents. **Mailing Address:** 1420 NE Sharkey Terr, Bend, OR 97701.

LONSDALE-ECCLES, JOHN DAVID, PROTEIN BIOCHEMISTRY, CELL BIOLOGY. **Personal Data:** b Cheshire, Eng, January 14, 1946; m 1973, c 4. **Education:** Queen's Univ Belfast, BS Hons, 1970, PhD (biochem), 1974. **Professional Experience:** PROF, DEPT BIOCHEM, UNIV ALA, as of 2003; LAB COORDR, INT LAB RES ANIMAL DIS, NAIROBI, 1991-; consult, WHO, 1990-; external examr, Univ Nairobi, 1987-; SCIENTIST BIOCHEM, INT LAB RES ANIMAL DIS, NAIROBI, 1983-; res assoc, Dept Periodont, 1978-1982; lectr, Ctr Res Oral Biol, Seattle, 1978-1982; sr fel biochem, Univ Wash, Seattle, 1975-1978; res fel biochem, Queen's Univ Belfast, 1974-1975. **Memberships:** Royal Soc Chem; Biochem Soc; NY Acad Sci; Am Soc Cell Biol; Protein Soc; Biochem Soc Kenya. **Research Statement & Publications:** Disecting the biochemical aspects of endocytosis by African tryparosomes and their mechanisms of differentiation from one life cycle stage into another; protenses, protein binases and protein phosphates of the parasites. **Mailing Address:** Dept Biochem Univ Ala, 2128 Montreat Dr, Birmingham, AL 35294.

LONSKI, JOSEPH, DEVELOPMENTAL BIOLOGY. **Personal Data:** b Port Jefferson, NY, 1943; c 2. **Education:** Cornell Univ, BS, 1964; Univ Calif, Los Angeles, MA, 1966; Princeton Univ, PhD (biol), 1973. **Professional Experience:** CONSULT, 1983-; from asst prof to assoc prof biol, Bucknell Univ, 1972-1983; instr biol, Princeton Univ, 1971-1972; instr biol, Southampton Col, 1966; stockbroker. **Memberships:** Sigma Xi; Am Soc Plant Physiol; Soc Develop Biol. **Research Statement & Publications:** Chemotaxis in the myxobacteria and cellular slime molds. **Mailing Address:** 151 Mt Lucas Rd, Princeton, NJ 08540.

LONTZ, ROBERT JAN, PHYSICS. **Personal Data:** b Wilmington, Del, October 19, 1936; m 1962, c 2. **Education:** Yale Univ, BSc, 1958; Duke Univ, PhD (physics), 1962. **Professional Experience:** FOUNDER & PRES, MRPATH, as of 2004; interim pres, Magnetic Imaging Technol, Inc, 1998-1999; pres, Res & Develop Anal Inc, 1993-; CO-FOUNDER, MAGNETICIMAGING TECHNOL INC, 1993-; consult, res funding, Res Definition & Mgt, Tech Writing, 1988-1993; dep asst res, Off Undersecy Defense Res & Eng, 1978-1979; dir, Gen Physics Div, US Army Res Off, 1973-1988; assoc dir, Gen Physics Div, US Army Res Off, 1967-1973; chief, Gen Physics Div, US Army Res Off, 1964-1967; asst, Physics Div, US Army Res Off, 1962-1964. **Research Statement & Publications:** Paramagnetic resonance spectroscopy; lasers. **Mailing Address:** Mrpath Inc, 1415 W Nc Hwy, Durham, NC 27707.

LONZETTA, CHARLES MICHAEL, ORGANIC CHEMISTRY, PHYSICAL-ORGANIC CHEMISTRY. **Personal Data:** b Hazleton, Pa, January 28, 1950; m 1971, c 3. **Education:** Pa State Univ, BS, 1971; Harvard Univ, AM, 1974, PhD (org chem), 1977. **Professional Experience:** RES CHEMIST, ROHM & HAAS CO, 1978-; fel phys org chem, Brandeis Univ, 1976-1978; head teaching fel, Harvard Exten Sch, 1974-1978. **Memberships:** Am Chem Soc. **Research Statement & Publications:** Mechanistic organic chemistry: singlet oxygen formation and reactions; organophosphorus reaction kinetics; free radical reactions; pulsed megawatt infrared laser reaction kinetics; monomer process technology. **Mailing Address:** Rohm & Haas Co, PO Box 672 Tidal Rd, Philadelphia, PA 19106-2399.

LOO, BILLY WEI-YU, INSTRUMENT SCIENCE, X-RAY DETECTORS. **Personal Data:** b Chungking, China, October 26, 1939; American citizen; m 1965, c 2. **Education:** Univ Mich, Ann Arbor, BSE, 1963, MS, 1965, PhD (physics & nuclear eng), 1972. **Professional Experience:** SR ENG PHYSICIST, LAWRENCE BERKELEY LAB, UNIV CALIF, 1972-; asst res physicist high energy physics, Univ Mich, 1965-1969. **Memberships:** Am Phys Soc; AAAS. **Research Statement & Publications:** Research and development in medical instrumentation, lung and bone density measurements, and special Si(Li) x-ray detectors for space and nuclear science applications; sampling and analysis of atmospheric aerosols. **Mailing Address:** Lawrence Berkeley Lab, 1 Cyclotron Rd Mail Stop 7-222, Berkeley, CA 94720.

LOO, MELANIE WAI SUE, GENETICS. **Personal Data:** b Honolulu, Hawaii, November 24, 1948. **Education:** Univ Calif, BA, BS, 1970; Univ Wash, PhD (genetics), 1974. **Professional Experience:** ASST PROF BIOL & GENETICS, DEPT BIOL SCI, CALIF STATE UNIV, SACRAMENTO, 1977-; proj res assoc genetics, Dept Physiol Chem, Univ Wis, 1975-1977. **Memberships:** AAAS. **Research Statement & Publications:** Genetic regulation. **Mailing Address:** Calif State Univ, Col Nat Sci & Math, 414 Sequoia Hall, Sacramento, CA 95819-2605. **E-Mail:** mwloo@csus.edu

LOO, TI LI, CLINICAL PHARMACOLOGY, CANCER & AIDS CHEMOTHERAPY. **Personal Data:** b Changsha, China, January 7, 1918; American citizen; m 1951, Marie; c Michael, Agnes & Jonathan. **Education:** Tsing Hua Univ, China, BSc, 1940; Oxford Univ, DPhil, 1947 & DSc, 1985. **Honors & Awards:** Gottlieb Award, Univ Tex M D Anderson Cancer Ctr, 1987. **Professional Experience:** PART-TIME FAC, DEPT PHARMACOL & PHYSIOL, MED CTR, GEORGE WASH UNIV, as of 2003; res prof pharmacol, Med Ctr, George Wash Univ, beginning 1985; spec lectr, Japan Soc Clin Pharmacol, 1985; pharmacologist & prof, Ashbel Smith prof ther, 1981-1985; adj prof pharmacol, Univ Houston, 1977-1985; pharmacologist & prof, Dept Develop Therapeut, Univ Tex M D Anderson Hosp & Tumor Inst & prof pharmacol, Univ Tex Med Sch & Grad Biomed Sci, 1965-1985; supvry chemist, NIH, 1955-1965; res assoc, Christ Hosp Inst Med Res, 1951-1954; fel org chem, Univ Md, 1947-1951; asst pharmacol, Oxford Univ, 1946-1947. **Memberships:** Am Chem Soc; Am Asn Cancer Res; Royal Soc Chem; Am Soc Clin Oncol; Am Soc Clin Pharmacol & Therapeut; Sigma Xi; Am Soc Pharmacol Exp Therapeut. **Research Statement & Publications:** Pharmacology of anticancer and anti-AIDS drugs; cancer chemotherapy; metabolism of drugs; chemical structure and biological activities; pharmacokinetics; anti-AIDS chemotherapy. **Mailing Address:** Dept Pharmacol, Med Ctr, George Wash Univ, 2300 Eye St NW, Washington, DC 20037-2337. **Fax:** 202-994-2870.

LOOK, DAVID C, SOLID STATE PHYSICS. **Personal Data:** b St Paul, Minn, December 19, 1938; m 1968, Rita; c James & Christine. **Education:** Univ Minn, BPhys, 1960, MS, 1962; Univ Pittsburgh, PhD (physics), 1966; Univ Dayton, MS, 1978. **Honors & Awards:** Outstanding Scientist Award, Eng Coun, Dayton. **Professional Experience:** SR RES PHYSICIST & DIR SEMICONDUCTOR RES CTR, WRIGHT STATE UNIV, 1980-; sr res physicist, Univ Dayton, 1969-1980; res physicist, US Airforce, Dayton, 1966-1969. **Memberships:** Fel Am Phys Soc; Am Sci Affil. **Research Statement & Publications:** Transport properties in semiconductor materials and devices; nuclear magnetic resonance; ion implantation; radiation damage. **Mailing Address:** Semiconductor Res Ctr, Wright State Univ, 3640 Col Glenn Hwy, Dayton, OH 45435. **Fax:** 937-255-3374. **E-Mail:** david.look@wpafb.af.mil

LOOK, DWIGHT CHESTER, THERMAL RADIATIVE HEAT TRANSFER, THERMOPHYSICAL PROPERTIES. **Personal Data:** b Smith Center, Kans, August 25, 1938; m 1960, Wellbaum; c Dwight III & Douglas. **Education:** Cent Col, Fayette, Mo, BS, 1960; Univ Nebr, MS, 1962, Univ Okla, PhD (mech & aerosysts), 1969. **Honors & Awards:** R R Testor Award, Soc Automotive Engrs, 1978. **Professional Experience:** PROF EMER MECH ENG & AEROSPACE ENG, UNIV MO-ROLLO, as of 2000; prof mech eng, Univ Mo-Rollo, 1978-2000; co-prin investr, NSF grants, 1975-; from asst prof to assoc prof, Univ Mo-Rollo, 1969-1978; spec instr thermodyn, Univ Okla, 1969; adj instr ele maths, Tex Christian Univ, 1967; aerosysts engr, Ft Worth Div, Gen Dynamics, 1963-1967; teaching asst eng physics, Univ Nebr, 1960-1963. **Memberships:** Am Soc Mech Engrs; Am Inst Aeronaut & Astronaut; Am Soc Eng Educ; Int Soc Optical Eng. **Research Statement & Publications:** Experimental investigation of thermophysical properties, particularly the reflectance of light from solids and the electromagnetic scattering from small particles; thermodynamics. **Mailing Address:** Dept Mech eng, Univ Mo Rolla, 125 Mech Eng Annex 1870 Miner Circle, Rolla, MO 65409-0050. **Fax:** 573-341-4115. **E-Mail:** look@umr.edu

LOOKER, JEROME J, ORGANIC CHEMISTRY. **Personal Data:** b Columbus, Ohio, July 7, 1935; m 1957, c 3. **Education:** Kenyon Col, AB, 1958; Univ Ill, MS, 1960, PhD (org chem), 1961. **Professional Experience:** RES CHEMIST, EASTMAN KODAK CO, 1962-; Nat Sci Found fel, Cornell Univ, 1961-1962. **Memberships:** Am Chem Soc. **Research Statement & Publications:** Synthetic organic chemistry. **Mailing Address:** 333 Panorama Terr, Rochester, NY 14625-2315.

LOOKHART, GEORGE LEROY, ANALYTICAL CHEMISTRY & PHYSICAL BIOCHEMISTRY OF CEREAL PROTEINS. **Personal Data:** b North Platte, Nebr, August 25, 1943; m 1963, Judy; c Jeff, Jodii & Jill. **Education:** Univ Nebr, Kearney, BS, 1968; Univ Wyo, PhD (phys chem), 1973. **Professional Experience:** PROF & MEM GRAD FAC, KANS STATE UNIV, 2004-; group leader, Baking Sci & Grain Qual Groups, 1990-; adj prof, Grain Sci Dept, Kans State Univ, 1985-; adj asst prof, Grain Sci Dept, Kans State Univ, 1980-1985; sr res chemist & prog lead scientist, USDA, US Grain Mkt Res Lab, 1976-2004; fel biochem, Univ Mo, Columbia, 1974-1976; teaching internship fel, Dept Chem, Univ Ky, 1973-1974. **Memberships:** Am Chem Soc; Am Asn Cereal Chemists (Board of Directors, 2000-2002); fel Am Assoc Cereal Chem. **Research Statement & Publications:** Develop high pressure liquid chromatographic methods of analysis for protein, estrogens, amino acids and vitamins; development of new electrophoretic methods to cereal proteins for identifying cultivars and characterizing individual proteins; relationships of protein groups or individuals with quality. **Mailing Address:** US Grain Mkt Res Lab, 1515 Col Ave, Manhattan, KS 66502. **Fax:** 785-776-2792. **E-Mail:** george@usgmrl.ksu.edu

LOOMANS, MAURICE EDWARD, DERMATOLOGY. **Personal Data:** b Wisconsin Rapids, Wis, August 10, 1933; m 1957, c 3. **Education:** Hope Col, BA, 1957; Univ Wis, MS, 1959, PhD (biochem), 1962. **Professional Experience:** RETIRED; res chemist, Miami Valley Labs, Procter & Gamble Co, 1962-1993. **Memberships:** Soc Invest Dermat. **Research Statement & Publications:** Keratinization; epidermal cellular control; acne; percutaneous absorption; mediators of inflammation; animal models; rheumatology; arthritis. **Mailing Address:** 5231 Jessup Rd, Cincinnati, OH 45247.

LOOMIS, CARSON ROBERT, PROTEIN CHEMISTRY, DRUG DISCOVERY. **Personal Data:** b Syracuse, NY, February 17, 1945; m 1980, Mayre Mercer; c Nathan, Dawn & Duncan. **Education:** Univ Vt, BA, 1969; Boston Univ, PhD (chem), 1976. **Professional Experience:** SR VPRES, NORAK BIOSCIENCE, INC, 2004; SCI CO FOUNDER, NORAK BIOSCIENCE, INC, as of 2004; co founder, Xanthon Inc, beginning 1997; VPRES RES, SPHINX PHARMACEUT, 1991-; dep dir, Signal Transduction Div, Duke Univ Cancer Ctr, 1985-1987; res assoc, Duke Univ Med Ctr, 1976-1984. **Memberships:** Am Soc Biol Chemists. **Research Statement & Publications:** Signal transduction mechanisms and protein kinases and phosphatases. **Mailing Address:** Norak Biosciences Inc, PO Box 14769, Research Triangle Park, NC 27709-4769. **Fax:** 919-248-8033.

LOOMIS, EARL ALFRED, JR, CHILD DEVELOPMENT, SUBSTANCE DEPENDENCE. **Personal Data:** b Minneapolis, Minn, May 21, 1921; m 1969, Anita M; c Rebecca, Kathleen, Jennifer & Amy. **Education:** Univ Minn, BA, 1942, MD, 1945; Am Bd Psychiat & Neurol, cert, 1951 & 1958. **Professional Experience:** RETIRED; psychiat dir, Child Adolescent Prog, Ga Regional Hosp, Augusta, 1981-1982 & Eugene Talmadge Hosp, 1982-1984; prof psychiat, Dept Psychiat & Health Behav, Med Col Ga, 1981-1990; attend psychiatrist, Eastern Long Island Hosp, 1973-1981; psychiat dir child & adolescent psychiat, Blueberry Treatment Ctr Seriously Disturbed Children, 1963-1981; lectr, Herbert Holt Inst, 1963-1973; res fel in residence child develop, Univ Geneva, Switz, 1962-1963; prof psychiat & relig, Union Theol Sem, NY, 1956-1963; chief, Div Child Psychiat, St Luke's Hosp, NY, 1955-1962; assoc prof, Univ Pittsburgh, 1952-1956; Consult child psychiat, Gov Bacon Health Ctr, Del, 1949-1957; instr psychiat, Univ Pa, 1949-1952; fel psychiat & child psychiat, Hosp Univ Pa & Inst Pa Hosp, 1948-1950; resident psychiat, Western Psychiat Inst, Pittsburgh, 1946-1948; Intern internal med & pediat, Evans Mem & Mass Mem Hosp, 1945-1946. **Memberships:** Am Psychiat Asn; Am Psychoanal Asn; Am Acad Child Psychiat; Am Soc Addiction Med. **Research Statement & Publications:** Play patterns of non-verbal children as indices of ego function and dysfunction; conscience of condoners, abusers and abused in physical and sexual abuse; consequences of parallel and out of phase development of conscience and cognition. **Mailing Address:** PO Box 697, Greenport, NY 11944. **E-Mail:** amploomis@aol.com

LOOMIS, FREDERICK B, PETROLEUM & MINE GEOLOGY. **Personal Data:** b Amherst, Mass, February 10, 1915. **Education:** Amherst Univ, BA, 1937. **Professional Experience:** CONSULT GEOLOGIST, 1975-; mgr Can oper, Petro-Consult, Alta, Can, 1970-1975; geologist & mgr foreign oper, Clark Oil Refining, Milwaukee, Wis, 1960-1970; direct mgr, Clark Oil Refining, Milwaukee, Wis, 1939-1959. **Memberships:** Fel Geol Soc Am; Am Asn Petrol Geologists. **Mailing Address:** 9257 W Union Hills Dr, Peoria, AZ 85382.

LOOMIS, HAROLD GEORGE, NUMERICAL WAVE THEORIES. **Personal Data:** b Erie, Pa, August 22, 1925; m 1947, c 4. **Education:** Stanford Univ, BS, 1950; Pa State Univ, MS, 1952, PhD (math & physics), 57. **Professional Experience:** PROF OCEAN ENG, UNIV HAWAII, 1982-; Secy, Tsunami Comn, Int Union Geod & Geophys, 1976-1982; scientist, Nat Oceanic & Atmospheric Admin, 1966-1982; asst prof math, Univ Hawaii, 1963-1966; asst prof math, Amherst Col, 1957-1962; instr math, Pa State Univ, 1955-1957; Scientist, HRB Singer, 1952-1955. **Memberships:** Soc Indust & Appl Math. **Research Statement & Publications:** Numerical hydrodynamics; long and short water wave theories; time series analysis; statistics. **Mailing Address:** 9218 NE Bluefin, Bainbridge Island, WA 98110.

LOOMIS, HERSCHEL HARE, ELECTRICAL ENGINEERING, COMPUTER ENGINEERING. **Personal Data:** b Wilmington, Del, May 31, 1934; m 1957, c 2. **Education:** Cornell Univ, BEE, 1957; Univ Md, MS, 1959; Mass Inst Technol, PhD (elec eng), 1963. **Professional Experience:** PROF SPACE SYSTEM, NAVAL POSTGRAD SCH, MONTEREY, CALIF, as of 1999; PROF ELEC & COMPUT ENG, NAVAL POSTGRAD SCH, MONTEREY, CALIF, 1983-; consult, Signal Sci, Inc, Santa Clara, Calif, beginning 1981; chmn & prof, Navelex, 1981-1983; prof elec eng, Univ Calif, Davis, 1974-1983; chmn dept, Univ Calif, Davis, 1970-1975; consult, Lawrence Livermore Lab, Univ Calif, 1963-1988; from asst prof to assoc prof elec eng, Univ Calif, Davis, 1962-1974; staff engr, Lincoln Lab, Mass Inst Technol, 1960-1961. **Memberships:** Inst Elec & Electronics Engrs; Asn Comput Mach. **Research Statement & Publications:** Theory, design and applications of digital computers; digital design automation; digital signal processing systems; published more than 10 books. **Mailing Address:** Dept Elec Eng, Naval Postgrad Sch, Monterey, CA 93953-3019. **E-Mail:** loomis@ece.nps.navy.mil

LOOMIS, ROBERT MORGAN, FORESTRY. **Personal Data:** b Mauston, Wis, August 31, 1922; m 1948, Lucille; c 6. **Education:** Univ Mich, BS; Univ Mo, MS, 1965. **Professional Experience:** RETIRED; E Lansing, Mich, 1971-1980; N Cent Forest Exp Sta, Columbia, Mo, 1966-1971; res forester, Cent States Forest Exp Sta, Columbia, Mo, 1957-1966; adminr, Mo Nat Forests, 1956-1957; adminr, Ottawa Nat Forest, Mich, 1951-1956; forester, Ochoco Nat Forest, Ore, 1948-1951. **Memberships:** Soc Am Foresters. **Research Statement & Publications:** Forest fire effects, fuels and danger rating. **Mailing Address:** 104 Redwood Ct, Atlantic Beach, NC 28512.

LOOMIS, ROBERT SIMPSON, CROP ECOPHYSIOLOGY. **Personal Data:** b Ames, Iowa, October 11, 1928; m 1951, Ann; c 3. **Education:** Iowa State Univ, BS, 1949; Univ Wis, MS, 1951, PhD (bot), 1956. **Honorary Degrees:** Honarary Doctorate, tech univ of Lisbon (Portugal) 2001. **Professional Experience:** Emer prof 1991 vis prof, Melbourne Univ, 1985; vis scientist, Agr Univ, Wagenigen, 1979; NZ Nat Res Adv Coun res fel, 1971; assoc dean environ studies, Inst Ecol, 1970-1972; dir, Inst Ecol, 1969-1972; PROF AGRON & AGRONOMIST, UNIV CALIF, DAVIS, 1968-; 1991; emer prof 1991- NIH spec fel, Harvard Univ, 1963-1964; from asst prof & asst agronomist to assoc prof & assoc agronomist, Univ Calif, Davis, 1958-1968; Instr agron & jr agronomist, Univ Calif, Davis, 1956-1958. **Memberships:** emer mem agron Soc, Crop Sci Soc am, Fel AAAS; Am Soc Plant Physiol (secy, 1965-1967); fel Am Soc Agron; fel Crop Sci Soc am. **Research Statement & Publications:** Physiology and ecology of field crops including growth and development; integrative physiology with emphasis on system simulation. **Mailing Address:** 708 Elmwood Dr, Davis, CA 95616. **Fax:** 916-752-4361. **E-Mail:** rsloomis@ucdavis.edu

LOOMIS, STEPHEN HENRY, COMPARATIVE PHYSIOLOGY. **Personal Data:** b Flint, Mich, October 3, 1952; m 1980, c 2. **Education:** Univ Calif, Davis, BS, 1974, PhD (zoology), 1979. **Professional Experience:** JEAN C TEMPEL '65 PROF BIOL, CONN COL, as of 2004; assoc prof biol, Conn Col, beginning 1986; asst prof, Conn Col, 1980-1986; res assoc, Rice Univ, 1979-1980. **Memberships:** Am Soc Zoologists; AAAS; Soc Cryobiol; Sigma Xi. **Research Statement & Publications:** Freezing tolerance of intertidal invertebrates. **Mailing Address:** Dept Biol, Conn Col, Box 5496 270 Mohegan Ave, New London, CT 06320. **E-Mail:** shloo@conncoll.edu

LOOMIS, TED ALBERT, PHARMACOLOGY, TOXICOLOGY. **Personal Data:** b Spokane, Wash, April 24, 1917; c 2. **Education:** Univ Wash, BS, 1939; Univ Buffalo, MS, 1941, PhD (pharmacol), 1943; Yale Univ, MD, 1946. **Professional Experience:** PROF EMER, UNIV WASH, as of 2004; prof pharmacol & toxicol, Sch Med, Univ Wash, beginning 1959; State toxicologist, Wash, 1955-1977; assoc prof, Sch Med, Univ Wash, 1947-1959; Intern, US Marine Hosp, 1946-1947. **Research Statement & Publications:** Pesticide and insecticide toxicology; anticoagulant agents; alcohol research; toxicological methods; mechanisms of drug action and action of toxic chemicals. **Mailing Address:** 2707 E Becker Rd, Clinton, WA 98236-9003.

LOOMIS, TIMOTHY PATRICK, PETROLOGY, REACTION KINETICS. **Personal Data:** b Alhambra, Calif, May 25, 1946. **Education:** Univ Calif, Davis, BS, 1967; Princeton Univ, PhD (geol), 1971. **Professional Experience:** ASSOC PROF GEOL, UNIV ARIZ, 1976-; asst prof, Univ Ariz, 1974-1976; adj asst prof, Univ Calif, Los Angeles, 1973-1974; J W Gibbs instr geol, Yale Univ, 1971-1973. **Memberships:** Geol Soc Am; Am Geophys Union. **Research Statement & Publications:** Heat and mass transfer and reaction kinetics in chemical processes. **Mailing Address:** 1605 Alison Ave, Mtain View, CA 94040.

LOOMIS, WALTER DAVID, BIOCHEMISTRY. **Personal Data:** b Fayetteville, Ark, March 2, 1926; m 1952. **Education:** Iowa State Univ, BS, 1948; Univ Calif, PhD (comp biochem), 1953. **Professional Experience:** PROF EMER BIOPHYS & BIOCHEM, ORE STATE UNIV, as of 2003; prof biochem, Ore State Univ, beginning 1968; vis researcher, Univ Col Wales, 1965-1966; USPHS res career develop award, 1961-1967; from asst prof to assoc prof, Ore State Univ, 1954-1968; Instr biochem, Ore State Univ, 1953-1954. **Memberships:** Am Chem Soc; Am Soc Plant Physiol; Am Soc Biol Chem; Phytochem Soc NAm; Can Soc Plant Physiol. **Research Statement & Publications:** Plant enzymes and proteins; terpene metabolism. **Mailing Address:** Dept Biochem & Biophysics, Ore State Univ, 2011 Ag & Life Sci Bldg, Corvallis, OR 97331-7305. **Fax:** 541-737-0481. **E-Mail:** loomisw@ucs.orst.edu

LOOMIS, WILLIAM FARNSWORTH, DEVELOPMENTAL BIOLOGY. **Personal Data:** b Boston, Mass, September 17, 1940; c Catherine & Emily. **Education:** Harvard Univ, BS, 1962; Mass Inst Technol, PhD (microbiol), 1965. **Professional Experience:** PROF BIOL, UNIV CALIF, SAN DIEGO, 1979-; from asst prof to assoc prof, Univ Calif, San Diego, 1966-1979; NIH fel, Brandeis Univ, 1965-1966. **Memberships:** Soc Develop Biol (pres); Am Soc Biol Chemists. **Research Statement & Publications:** Cellular interactions involved in the biochemical differentiation in Dictyostelium discoideum; genetics of slime molds; complex processes of cellular interaction can be dissected by molecular genetics; concepts generated in one system can often be applied to others. **Mailing Address:** Dept Biol, Univ Calif, San Diego, 9500 Gillman Dr, La Jolla, CA 92093-0346. **E-Mail:** wloomis@ucsd.edu

LOONEY, CARL G, COMPUTER SCIENCE. **Personal Data:** m, c 2. **Education:** PhD (Comput Sci). **Professional Experience:** PROF, DEPT COMPUT SCI & ENG, UNIV NEV, as of 2006. **Research Statement & Publications:** Clustering algorithms, pattern recognition; Computational science and engineering; Digital image processing; Machine learning, automation and intelligent systems; Applications algorithms. **Mailing Address:** Dept Comput Sci & Eng, Univ Nevada, Reno, NV 89557. **Fax:** 775-784-1877. **E-Mail:** looney@cs.unr.edu

LOONEY, NORMAN E, POMOLOGY, PLANT GROWTH REGULATION. **Personal Data:** b Adrian, Ore, May 31, 1938; m 1983, Norah; c Pamela (Licopautis), Patricia (Braidwood) & Steven. **Education:** Wash State Univ, BS, 1960, PhD (hort), 1966. **Professional Experience:** PRES, PAC AGR-FOOD RES CTR, SUMMERLAND, as of 2006; RES SCIENTIST, AGR FOOD RES CTR, SUMMERLAND, as of 2004; E Malling Res Sta, Maidstone, Eng, 1981-1982 & Lincoln Univ, NZ, 1990-1991; head hort & basic studies, Pac Agr Food & Agr Res Sta, beginning 1987; vis scientist, CSIRO, Sydney, Australia, 1971-1972; pomologist & plant physiologist, Pac Agr Food & Agr Res Sta, beginning 1966; res asst post-harvest hort, Wash State Univ, 1962-1966; sr exp aid hort, Wash State Univ, 1960-1962. **Memberships:** Fel Am Soc Hort Sci; Can Soc Hort Sci; Int Soc Hort Sci. **Research Statement & Publications:** Physiology of growth, development and ripening of temperate zone fruits; investigations of flowering physiology and plant growth regulator effects. **Mailing Address:** Pac Agr Food Res Ctr, Summerland, BC V0H 1Z0, Can. **Fax:** 250-494-0755. **E-Mail:** looney@agr.gc.ca

LOONEY, STEPHEN WARWICK, MULTIVARIATE ANALYSIS, BIOSTATISTICS. **Personal Data:** b Atlanta, Ga, September 6, 1952; m 1980, Teresa McVeigh. **Education:** Univ Ga, BS, 1974, MS, 1976, PhD (statist), 1980. **Professional Experience:** PROF SCH MED, UNIV LOUISVILLE, 1995-; vis fel, Keele Univ, 1997-1998; ASSOC PROF, SCH MED, UNIV LOUISVILLE, 1991-1995; MBA dir, La State Univ, 1989-1991; vis biostatist, Upjohn Co, 1987-1988; assoc prof quant bus analysis, La State Univ, 1986-1991; asst prof, La State Univ, 1981-1986; vis fel, Health & Welfare Can, 1980-1981; chief statist analyst, Northeast Ga Health Dist, 1979-1980. **Memberships:** Fel Am statist assn; fel Royal statist soc; Am Soc Qual Control; Int Asn Statist Comput. **Research Statement & Publications:** Research in applied statistics and how it can be applied in medical res. **Mailing Address:** Dept Family & Commun Med, 530 S Jackson St Rm A1 HOS/ACB, Louisville, KY 40292.

LOOP, MICHAEL STUART, VISION, HERPETOLOGY. **Personal Data:** b Pittsburgh, Pa, February 28, 1946; c 4. **Education:** Fla State Univ, BS, 1968, MS, 1971, PhD (psychobiol), 1972. **Professional Experience:** SCIENTIST, VISION SCI RES CTR, as of 2005; ASSOC PROF PHYSIOL OPTICS & PSYCHOL & NEUROBIOLOGY, UNIV ALA, BIRMINGHAM, 1981-; asst prof, Univ Ala, Birmingham, 1978-1981; vis asst prof physiol & biophys, Univ Ill, 1975-1978; NIH fel neurol surg, Sloane Found fel physiol, 1974-1975; NIH fel neurol surg, Univ Va, 1972-1974. **Memberships:** Soc Neuroscience. **Research Statement & Publications:** Vertebrate visual system psychophysics; comparative animal behavior; color vision. **Mailing Address:** Dept Physiol Optics, Univ Ala, Birmingham, AL 35294-0001. **E-Mail:** loop@uab.edu

LOOP, ROSE-ANN, NUTRITION. **Personal Data:** b Cherokee, Okla, July 13, 1943; c Jeffrey & Jamie. **Education:** Emporia State Univ, BS, 1964; Univ Tex, Austin, PhD (chem), 1968. **Professional Experience:** PROF NUTRIT, UNIV TEX, AUSTIN, 1981-; res grantee, USDA & FDA. **Memberships:** Am Inst Nurtit; Am Soc Clin Nutrit; Am Dietetic Asn; Res Soc Alcoholism. **Research Statement & Publications:** Role of nutrients on cholesterol homeostasis in humans; animal models of alcoholism. **Mailing Address:** Dept Grad Nutrit, Univ Tex, GEA 117, Austin, TX 78712. **Fax:** 512-471-5630. **E-Mail:** zann@mail.utexas.edu

LOOS, HENDRICUS G, ENVIRONMENTAL PHYSICS, NEURAL NETWORKS. **Personal Data:** b Amsterdam, Neth, December 18, 1925; American citizen; m 1952, Jansje; c Charles & Ingrid. **Education:** Univ Amsterdam, Drs(math), 1951; Univ Delft, ScD, 1952. **Professional Experience:** DIR, LAGUNA RES LAB, 1974-; prof math, Cleveland State Univ, 1971-1974; adj prof, Univ Calif, Riverside, 1970-1976; sr staff scientist, McDonnell-Douglas Astronaut Co, 1970-1971; mem staff, Douglas Advan Res Lab, 1966-1970; assoc prof residence, Univ Calif, Riverside, 1964-1970; Lectr, Univ Calif, Riverside, 1963-1964; sr physicist, Giannini Sci Corp, 1957-1966; sr engr, Propulsion Res Corp, 1955-1957; res fel, Calif Inst Technol, 1952-1955. **Memberships:** Am Phys Soc. **Research Statement & Publications:** Gauge theory; atmospheric physics; fluid mechanics; general relativity; neural networks. **Mailing Address:** 3015 Rainbow Glen, Fallbrook, CA 92028-9765.

LOOS, JAMES STAVERT, HIGH-SPEED DIGITAL ELECTRONICS & ELECTRONIC PACKAGING. **Personal Data:** b Grafton, NDak, May 24, 1940; m 1961, Janet; c Rebecca (Palacios) & Michael W. **Education:** Univ NDak, BS, 1962; Univ Ill, MS, 1963, PhD (physics), 1968. **Professional Experience:** AT LUCENT TECHNOL INC, as of 2001; physics & eng res & develop, AT&T Bell Labs, beginning 1986; res physicist high energy physics, Argonne Nat Lab, 1977-1986; asst prof physics, Duke Univ, 1972-1977; res assoc high energy physics, Stanford Linear Accelerator Ctr, 1968-1972. **Memberships:** Am Phys Soc; Inst Elec & Electronics Engrs. **Research Statement & Publications:** Experimental high energy physics; high energy particle detectors and techniques; high-speed electronics; electronic packaging; system interconnect. **Mailing Address:** Lucent Technol, 2000 N Naperville Rd Rm 4F128, Naperville, IL 60563.

LOOS, KARL RUDOLF, PHYSICAL CHEMISTRY, ENVIRONMENTAL ANALYSIS. **Personal Data:** b New York, NY, July 10, 1939; m 1965, c 3. **Education:** Rensselaer Polytech Inst, BS, 1960; Mass Inst Technol, PhD (phys chem), 1965. **Professional Experience:** SR CONSULT, CRA INT CHEM PRACT, as of 2006; SR STAFF RES CHEMIST, SHELL DEVELOP CO, 2002-; staff res chemist, Shell Develop Co, 1967-; res assoc, Inst Phys Chem, Swiss Fed Inst Technol, 1965-1966. **Memberships:** Am Chem Soc. **Re-**

search Statement & Publications: Environmental air analysis; source emissions; ambient air; trace organic determinations. **Mailing Address:** Shell Global Solutions, PO Box 1380, Houston, TX 77251-1380. **Fax:** 281-544-7268. **E-Mail:** karl.loos@shell.com

LOOSE, LELAND DAVID, PHYSIOLOGY, IMMUNOLOGY. **Personal Data:** b Reading, Pa, January 25, 1940; m 1971, c 3. **Education:** Tenn Wesleyan Col, BS, 1963; ETenn State Univ, MA, 1965; Univ Mo, Columbia, PhD (physiol), 1970. **Professional Experience:** EXEC DIR CLIN DEVELOP, PFIZER GLOBAL & DEVELOP, as of 2004; assoc dir Clin Res, Pfizer Inc, beginning 1988; asst dir clin res, Pfizer Inc, 1985-1988; proj leader immunother, Pfizer Inc, 1980-1985; assoc prof, Dept Physiol & Inst Exp Path & Toxicol, Albany Med Col, 1975-1980; asst prof physiol, Dept Physiol & Inst Exp Path & Toxicol, Albany Med Col, 1974-1975; asst prof, Sch Med, Tulane Univ, 1970-1974; instr physiol, Lees-McRae Col, 1965-1967; clin mem, clin res & develop, Pfizer Inc. **Memberships:** Am Physiol Soc; Am Soc Trop Med & Hyg; NY Acad Sci; Am Soc Zool; Sigma Xi; Am Rheumatic Assoc; Am Soc Microbiol; Am Asn Immunol. **Research Statement & Publications:** Physiological control mechanisms of immune responses; influence of environmental chemicals on immune responses; differentiation of lymphoid tissue with special reference to hormonal effects; macrophage antigen processing; calcium alterations in shock; pharmacological control of inflammation. **Mailing Address:** Clin Res & Develop, Pfizer Global Res & Develop, 50 Pequot Ave B2237, New London, CT 06320. **Fax:** 860-715-8752.

LOOSLI, JOHN KASPER, animal nutrition; deceased, see previous edition for last biography

LOOV, ROBERT EDMUND, STRUCTURAL ENGINEERING. **Personal Data:** b Wetaskiwin, Alta, October 29, 1933; m 1979, Carrol; c 2. **Education:** Univ Alta, BSc, 1958; Stanford Univ, MS, 1959; Univ Cambridge, DPhil, 1973. **Honors & Awards:** Award Merit, Can Stand Asn Fellow, Engineering Institute of Canada, 2001 Fellow, Canadian Precast/Prestressed Concrete Institute, 2004. **Professional Experience:** PROF EMER CIVIL ENG, UNIV CALGARY, as of 2003; Prin investr concrete Can, Network Ctr Excellence High Performance Concrete, 1996-; head civil eng, Univ Calgary, 1984-1989; vis prof, Univ NSW, Australia, 1983; actg head civil eng, Univ Calgary, 1980-1981; prof civil eng, Univ Calgary, beginning 1974; asst to vpres, Univ Calgary, 1970-1973; on leave, Churchill Col, Eng, 1967-1969; Nat Res Coun Can res grants, 1964-1967 & 1969-; from asst prof to assoc prof, Univ Calgary, 1963-1974; chief engr, Con-Force Prod Ltd, 1961-1963; sales engr, Con-Force Prod Ltd, 1959-1961; comt mem, Can Stand Asn, comt chmn, 90-te Design & Construct. **Memberships:** Am Concrete Inst; fel Can Soc Civil Engrs; Prestressed Concrete Inst. **Research Statement & Publications:** Strength and behavior of precast connections; optimum design of reinforced and prestressed concrete; bond strength of reinforced and prestressed concrete; high strength concrete; generalized concrete stress-strain curves; shear of concrete. **Mailing Address:** Dept Civil Eng, Univ Calgary, 2500 Univ Dr NW, Calgary, AB T2N 1N4, Can. **Fax:** 403-286-0775. **E-Mail:** loov@ucalgary.ca

LOOYENGA, ROBERT WILLIAM, ANALYTICAL CHEMISTRY. **Personal Data:** b NDak, October 21, 1939. **Education:** Hope Col, BA, 1961; Wayne State Univ, PhD (analytical chem), 1969. **Professional Experience:** PROF EMER CHEM, S DAK SCH MINES & TECHNOL, as of 2006; prof chem, S Dak Sch Mines & Technol, beginning 1987; Chemist, S Dak Racing Comn, 1975-1978; from asst prof to assoc prof, S Dak Sch Mines & Technol, 1972-1987; res chemist, Printing Develop Inc, 1970-1972; fel chem, Univ Wis, Milwaukee, 1970; forensic chemist, Rapid City; expert witness, Pa Co States Atty; consult, S Dak Law Enforcement Agencies. **Research Statement & Publications:** Analytical research and analysis of trace metals and organics in municipal and natural waters, of new chemical deicers and of abused drugs; analytical separations and methods development. **Mailing Address:** 1107 Wildlife Rd, Rapid City, SD 57702.

LOPARDO, VINCENT JOSEPH, MECHANICAL ENGINEERING. **Personal Data:** b Pittsburgh, Pa, December 1, 1925; m 1950, Mary; c 4. **Education:** Univ Pittsburgh, BSME, 1948, MSME, 1951; Cath Univ Am, PhD (mech eng), 1968. **Professional Experience:** PROF EMER MECH ENG, US NAVAL ACAD, 1994-; nat Bur Stand grant, Naval Ship Res & Develop Ctr, 1981; chmn dept, US Naval Acad, 1976-1980; naval Acad Res Coun grant, US Naval Acad, 1968-1969; fac fel, NSF, 1966; sr assoc, Trident Eng Assocs, 1961-; from assoc prof to prof, US Naval Acad, 1960-1994; consult, Charles M Wellons Consult Engrs, 1955-1960; from instr to asst prof mech eng, Univ Pittsburgh, 1951-1960; design engr, Hunting, Larsen & Dunnells Engrs, 1951-1955; res prof eng res div, Univ Pittsburgh, 1951-1953; design engr, Peth & Reed Engrs, 1948-1949 & Hunting, Larsen & Dunnells Engrs, 1951. **Memberships:** Soc Exp Stress Analysis; Am Soc Eng Educ; Am Soc Mech Engr. **Research Statement & Publications:** Stress analysis; stress and strains in large deformations of polyurethanes using photoelasticity and moire; exergy and the second law analyses of power systems; computer simulation of gas turbine engines. **Mailing Address:** Dept Mech Eng, US Naval Acad, 590 Holloway Rd, Annapolis, MD 21402-5042.

LOPATA, EUGENE S, CHEMISTRY. **Education:** Univ Mich-Ann Arbor. **Professional Experience:** AMES RES CTR, CHEM RES PROJ OFF, NASA, as of 1975. **Mailing Address:** Ames Res Ctr, NASA, Moffett Field, CA 94035.

LOPATIN, DENNIS EDWARD, MICROBIOLOGY. **Personal Data:** b Chicago, Ill, October 26, 1948. **Education:** Univ Ill, PhD (microbiol), 1974. **Professional Experience:** SR ASSOC DEAN, SCH DENT, UNIV MICH, 2004-; PROF DENT, UNIV MICH, 1990-; res scientist, Univ Mich, 1986-1990; from asst prof to assoc prof dent, Univ Mich, 1976-1990. **Memberships:** Am Asn Immunologists; Am Asn Dent Res; Am Asn Microbiol. **Research Statement & Publications:** Studies host immunological response to members of the oral flora; primary interest in immunology of periodontal diseases. **Mailing Address:** Sch Dent, Univ Mich, 1216 Dent Bldg PO Box 1078, Ann Arbor, MI 48109-1078. **Fax:** 734-764-8046. **E-Mail:** lopatin@umich.edu

LOPATIN, WILLIAM, BIOCHEMISTRY, BIO-ORGANIC CHEMISTRY. **Personal Data:** b Brooklyn, NY, July 20, 1946; m 1967, c 2. **Education:** Univ Fla, BS, 1967; Univ S Fla, MA, 1971, PhD (chem), 1977. **Professional Experience:** DIR SCI & OFF SYST, BAYER CORP, 1990-; dir sci info systs, Bayer Corp, 1980-1990; res assoc biochem, Univ Tex, 1977-1980; chmn sci dept, Blake High Sch, Tampa, 1970-1971; teacher chem, Hillsborough Co, Fla Bd Pub Instr, 1969-1973. **Memberships:** Sigma Xi; AAAS; Am Chem Soc. **Research Statement & Publications:** Application of physical organic techniques to the study of enzyme reaction mechanisms. **Mailing Address:** 50900 Mercury Dr, Granger, IL 46530-9795.

LOPER, CARL R(ICHARD), METALLURGICAL ENGINEERING, ENVIRONMENTAL SCIENCE. **Personal Data:** b Wauwatosa, Wis, July 3, 1932; m 1956, Jane; c Cynthia L (Koch) & Anne E. **Education:** Univ Wis, BS, 1955, MS, 1958, PhD (metall eng), 1961. **Honors & Awards:** Foundry Hall Fame, 2001; Hall of Fame, ASM Milwaukee, 1995; Distinguished prof, Foundry educ found; Adams Mem Award, Am Welding Soc, 1964; H F Taylor Award, Am Foundrymen's Soc, 1967, John A Penton Gold Medal, 1972; EG Hoyt Lectr, 1992; Medal, Chinese Foundrymen's Soc, 1989. **Professional Experience:** RETIRED, as of 2004; adj prof materials, Univ Wisc Milwaukee, beginning 2001; Nat Sci Coun, Rep China, 1989; hon lectr, Univ Nacional de Colombia, 1984; hon lectr, Antioquia Univ, Medellin, Colombia, 1983; Zhejiang Univ, China, 1981; Brazilian Soc Metals, Santa Catarina, 1981; Waseda Univ, Japan, 1981; assoc dir, Univ-Indust Res Prog & assoc chmn, Dept Metall & Mineral Eng, 1979-1981; pres, Int Comn Compacted Graphite Cast Iron, beginning 1977; Sperry-New Holland, beginning 1974; Oil City Iron Works, beginning 1973; Kyushu Univ, Japan, 1974; Disamatic Conv, Korea Inst Sci & Technol & Korea Inst Advan Series, 1974; prof materials sci & eng, Univ Wis-Madison, 1969-2001; Disamatic Conv, Copenhagen, Denmark, 1969; invited lectr, Korea Foundry Soc & Korea Inst Sci & Technol, Seoul, 1968; consult, Gen Motors Corp & Brillion Iron Works, beginning 1966; consult, Gray & Ductile Iron Founders Soc, beginning 1962; res metallurgist, Allis Chalmers Mfg Co, beginning 1961; from asst prof to assoc prof, Univ Wis-Madison, 1961-1969; res metallurgist, Allis Chalmers, 1961; res proj asst, Univ Wis-Madison, 1958-1960; instr metall eng, Univ Wis-Madison, 1956-1958; metall engr, Pelton Steel Castings Co, 1955-1956. **Memberships:** Hon mem Am Foundrymen's Soc; Am Welding Soc; fel Am Soc Metals; Sigma Xi; Am Inst Metall Eng; Foundry Educ Found. **Research Statement & Publications:** Solidification and process control of cast irons; solidification and property relationships in aluminum and copper base alloys; fracture toughness of cast components; welding metallurgy; failure analysis; recycling of metallic solid wastes. **Mailing Address:** Dept Mat Sci & Eng, 1509 Univ Ave, Madison, WI 53706. **Fax:** 608-238-8353. **E-Mail:** loper@engr.wisc.edu

LOPER, DAVID ERIC, MAGNETOHYDRODYNAMICS, MATHEMATICAL GEOPHYSICS & KARST HYDROGEOLOGY. **Personal Data:** b Oswego, NY, February 14, 1940; m 1966, c 4. **Education:** Carnegie Inst Technol, BS, 1961; Case Inst Technol, MS, 1964, PhD (mech eng), 1965. **Honors & Awards:** Distinguished Res Prof, 1992; Fel, Am Geophys Union, 1997. **Professional Experience:** Prof geol sci, 1997-2003; vis fel, Univ Cambridge, 1990; prof math, Fla State Univ, 1977-1997; sr vis fel, Univ Newcastle-upon-Tyne, Eng, 1974-1975; from asst prof to assoc prof, Fla State Univ, 1968-1977; nat Ctr Atmospheric Res fel, 1967-1968; sr scientist, Douglas Aircraft Corp, 1965-1968; PROF EMER, GEOPHYS FLUID DYNAMICS. **Memberships:** Am Geophys Union; Sigma Xi. **Research Statement & Publications:** Dynamics of Earth's outer core; evolution of the earth's core including stratification, heat transfer and solidification; Structure, stability and convection of mushy layers; Flow and transport in karstic aquifers. **Mailing Address:** Fla State Univ, GFDI-4360, Tallahassee, FL 32306. **E-Mail:** loper@gfdi.fsu.edu

LOPER, GERALD D, NUCLEAR PHYSICS. **Personal Data:** b Brooklyn, NY, May 4, 1937; m 1960, c 1. **Education:** Univ Wichita, BA, 1959; Okla State Univ, MS, 1962, PhD (physics), 1964. **Professional Experience:** ASSOC VPRES RES, OFFICE RES ADMIN, WICHITA STATE UNIV, 1994-; interim exec dir, Nat Inst Aviation Res, ending 1999; DIR OFFICE RES ADMIN, WICHITA STATE UNIV, 1994-; actg dean liberal arts & sci, Wichita State Univ, 1992-1994; assoc dean liberal arts & sci, Wichita State Univ, 1987-1992; asst dean grad studies, Wichita State Univ, 1986-1987; ASSOC PROF PHYSICS, WICHITA STATE UNIV, 1967-; chmn dept, Wichita State Univ, 1966-1978; asst prof, Wichita State Univ, 1964-1967; vis scientist, Argonne Nat Lab. **Memberships:** Am Phys Soc; Sigma Xi. **Research Statement & Publications:** Measurement of positron lifetimes in solids; nuclear spectroscopy; internal conversion. **Mailing Address:** Off Res Admin, Wichita State Univ, 1845 Fairmount, Wichita, KS 67260-0007. **Fax:** 316-978-3750. **E-Mail:** gerald.loper@wichita.edu

LOPER, GERALD MILTON, AGRONOMY, BIOCHEMISTRY. **Personal Data:** b Sykesville, Md, January 7, 1936; m 1962, Peiffer; c David Milton & Timothy Paul. **Education:** Univ Md, Bsc, 1958; Univ Wis, MSc, 1960, PhD (agron), 1961. **Professional Experience:** RETIRED; from assoc prof to prof agron & plant genetics, Univ Ariz, 1974-1997; res plant physiologist, Fed Honeybee Lab, 1967-1996; res agronomist, USDA, SDak, 1962-1967. **Memberships:** Bot Soc Am; Am Soc Agron; Entom Soc Am. **Research Statement & Publications:** Effect of environment and infective organisms on the chemical composition of forages in relation to animal nutrition; attractiveness of forage legumes to honey bees; pollination physiology; seed production and crop physiology investigations of the genetics and mating biology of feral and Africanized honey bees. **Mailing Address:** Fed Honeybee Lab, Agr Res Serv, USDA, 2000 E Allen Rd, Tucson, AZ 85719.

LOPER, JOHN C, ENVIRONMENTAL TOXICOLOGY, BIODEGRADATION. **Personal Data:** b Hadley, Pa, June 21, 1931; m 1956, Dorothy; c John T, Robert D & Christopher L. **Education:** Western Md Col, BA, 1952; Emory Univ, MS, 1953; Johns Hopkins Univ, PhD (biol), 1960. **Professional Experience:** PROF EMER, DEPT MOLECULAR GENETICS, UNIV CINCINNATI, COL MED, as of 2004; prin investr, Nat Inst Environ Health Sci Superfund basic res prog grant, 1991-1998; assoc dir, Dept Molecular Genetics, Univ Cincinnati, 1988-1999; co-investr, Nat Inst Environ Health Sci Superfund basic res prog grant, 1988-1991; prof environ health, Col Med, Univ Cincinnati, 1979-1999; mem subcomt toxicol, Safe Drinking Water Comt, Nat Res Coun, 1978-1979; Environ Protection Agency grants, 1976-1986; prof microbiol, Col Med, Univ Cincinnati, beginning 1974; mem biol comt, Argonne Nat Lab-Argonne Univ Asn, 1970-1973; NIH spec vis fel genetics, Res Sch Biol Sci, Australian Nat Univ, 1970-1971; from asst prof to assoc prof, Col Med, Univ Cincinnati, 1963-1974; NIH res grants, 1962-1978; from instr to asst prof pharmacol, Sch Med, St Louis Univ, 1960-1963. **Memberships:** Am Soc Microbiol; Genetics Soc Am; Am Chem Soc; Am Soc Biochem Molecular Biol. **Research Statement & Publications:** Molecular genetics of cytochrome P450 systems in yeasts and fungi; microbial pathways of detoxication and degradation of xenobiotic compounds; genetics of antifungal resistance. **Mailing Address:** Dept Molecular Genetics Biochem & Microbiol, Univ Cincinnati Col Med, Cincinnati, OH 45267-0524. **E-Mail:** john.loper@uc.edu

LOPER, JOYCE E, PHYTOPATHOLOGY. **Personal Data:** b November 21, 1952; m Carl. **Education:** Univ Calif, Davis, BS, 1974, MS 1978; Univ Calif, Berkeley, PhD (plant path), 1983. **Honors & Awards:** Ciba-Geigy Award, Am Phytopath Soc, 1995. **Professional Experience:** RES PLANT PATHOLOGIST, AGR RES SERV, USDA, CORVALLIS, 1987-; PROF, DEPT BOT & PLANT PATH, ORE STATE UNIV, 1997-; res Leader, Agr Res Serv USDA Corvallis, 1997-2000; assoc ed, Molecular Plant-Microbe Interactions, 1996-; mem sci adv panel, NSF Ctr Microbial Ecol, Mich State Univ, 1992-1996; mem, Nat Res Coun Bd Agr, Nat Acad Sci, 1992-1995; sr ed, Am Phytopath Soc Press, 1990-1993; from asst prof to assoc prof, Agr Res Serv, USDA, Corvallis, 1988-1997; res plant pathologist, Agr Res Serv, USDA, Beltsville, 1985-1986; res scientist, Biol Control Prog, Biotechnol Group, Chevron Chem Co, 1983-1985. **Memberships:** Am Phytopath Soc; Am Soc Microbiol; Int Soc Molecular Plant-Microbe Interactions. **Research Statement & Publications:** Reaserch on biological control of plant disease. **Mailing Address:** USDA Agr Res Serv Hort Crops Lab, 3420 NW Orchard Ave, Corvallis, OR 97330.

LOPER, WILLARD H(EWITT), AGRICULTURAL ENGINEERING. **Personal Data:** b Alden, NY, April 30, 1926; m 1950, c 4. **Education:** Cornell Univ, BSA, 1953. **Professional**

Experience: Assoc prof agr eng, Calif Polytech State Univ, San Luis Obispo, beginning 1963; tech leader, Foreign Agr Serv, USDA, 1959; Civil engr, Bur Reclamation, US Dept Interior & State Div Hwys, 1957 & 1958; asst prof, Calif Polytech State Univ, San Luis Obispo, 1955-1963; design & prod engr, Cochran Equip Co, 1954-1955; Sales & serv rep, Holz Col, 1953-1954. **Memberships:** Am Soc Agr Engrs. **Research Statement & Publications:** Agricultural crop harvest mechanization. **Mailing Address:** 266 Luneta Dr, San Luis Obispo, CA 93405.

LOPES, ANIBAL, ANALYTICAL METHOD DEVELOPMENT, HIGH THROUGHPUT PURIFICATION. **Personal Data:** b Sao Paulo, Brazil, October 30, 1955; American citizen; m 1988, Theresa. **Education:** Fordham Univ, BS, 1976; Columbia Univ, MA, 1977, Univ Rochester, MS, 1979, PhD (org chem), 1981. **Professional Experience:** SR RES SCIENTIST, RHONE-POULENC AG CO, 1992-; scientist, Rhone-Poulenc Ag Co, 1981-1992; analytical chemistry manager, Scynexis, Inc. **Memberships:** Am Chem Soc. **Research Statement & Publications:** Dev high throughput Analytical methods using liquid chromatography and mass spectrometry; for combinatorial chemistry manage a high throughput purification system. **Mailing Address:** 8500 Paddle Wheel Dr, Raleigh, NC 27615-8018. **Fax:** 919-544-8697. **E-Mail:** anibal.lopes@scynexis.com

LOPES, EDISON REIS, PATHOLOGY. **Professional Experience:** AT COL MED MINING TRIANGLE, as of 2004. **Mailing Address:** Col Med Mining Triangle, FMTM St Getulio Sentry box, 130 Abbey, Uberaba, Brazil. **E-Mail:** rsbmt@mednet.com.br

LOPES, JOHN MANUEL, GENE EXPRESSION, TRANSCRIPTIONAL CONTROL. **Personal Data:** b Coimbra, Port, June 24, 1961; American citizen; m 1985, Teresa D Parton; c Sean V. **Education:** Univ RI, BS, 1982; Univ SC, PhD (biol), 1987. **Professional Experience:** ASST PROF BIOCHEM, LOYOLA UNIV, CHICAGO, 1991-; Fel, Carnegie Mellon Univ, 1987-1991. **Memberships:** Fel Genetics Soc Am; fel Am Soc Biochem & Molecular Biol; fel Am Soc Microbiol. **Research Statement & Publications:** Study how cellular membranes are synthesized in yeast in particular how transcription affects gene expression of phospholipid biosynthetic genes. **Mailing Address:** 2160 S First Ave, Maywood, IL 60153.

LOPES, LOUIS A, JR, MATHEMATICS. **Education:** Calif Inst Technol, PhD, 1964. **Professional Experience:** STAFF, UNIV MASS, as of 2004. **Mailing Address:** Univ Mass, 6665 Golfcrest Dr, San Diego, CA 92119-2416. **Fax:** 508-999-8901.

LOPES, VICENTE L, HYDROLOGY. **Education:** Fed Univ Ceara, BS, 1975; Fed Univ Paraiba, MS, 1980; Univ Ariz, PhD, 1987. **Professional Experience:** ASSOC PROF WATERSHED MGT & AGR & BIOSYSTS ENG, UNIV ARIZ, as of 2003. **Mailing Address:** Sch Natural Resources Univ Ariz, 310 Biosci E, Tucson, AZ 85721. **Fax:** 520-621-8801. **E-Mail:** vlopes@ag.arizona.edu

LOPES-GAUTIER, ROSALY, VOLCANOLOGY, PLANETARY SCIENCE. **Personal Data:** b Rio de Janeiro, Brazil, January 8, 1957; American citizen; c Thomas N IV. **Education:** Univ London, BSc, 1978, PhD (planetary sci), 1986. **Honors & Awards:** Woman of the Year sci & technol, gem TV, 1997. **Professional Experience:** DEP CHIEF COORDR, NIMS, as of 2005; Invest scientist, Cassini Radar Team, Jet Propulsion Lab, 2002; sci coordr, Galileo Proj, Jet Propulsion Lab, 1991-2002; Nat Res Coun, 1989-1991; Nat Res Coun res assoc, Galileo Proj, Jet Propulsion Lab, 1989-1991; res assoc, Observ Vesuviano, Italy, 1989; Cur astron, Old Royal Observ, Greenwich, UK, 1985-1989. **Memberships:** Int Astron Union; Am Geophys Soc; Am Astron Soc; Royal Astron Soc; Int Asn Volcanology & Chem Earth's Interior; Soc Hisp Prof Engrs. **Research Statement & Publications:** Planetary and terrestrial surface processes, with emphasis on volcanology; volcanism on IO using infra-red and other spacecraft data; volcanic hazards on earth. **Mailing Address:** MS 183-601, Jet Propulsion Lab, Pasadena, CA 91109. **Fax:** 818-393-4530. **E-Mail:** rlopes@issac.jpl.nasa.gov

LOPES-VIRELLA, MARIA FERNANDA LEAL, IMMUNE MECHANISMS OF ATHEROSCLEROSIS, LIPOPROTEIN METABOLISM & CORONARY HEART DISEASE. **Personal Data:** b Vila Nova De Foz Coa, Port, December 25, 1942; American citizen; m Gabriel Virella; c Sara & Isabel. **Education:** Univ Lisbon, Portugal, MD, 1967, ECFMG, 1975, FLEX, 1979, PhD (int med & biochem), 1990. **Professional Experience:** Nutrit Study Sect, NIH, 1991-1995; PROF MED & PATH, MED UNIV SC, 1989-; staff physician & chief, Nutrit Support Team, Vet Admin Med Ctr, Charleston, SC, 1987-; prin investr, Nat Heart Lung Blood Inst & NIH, 1987-1993; prin investr, Vet Admin Res Prog, 1985-; course dir & lectr, Clin Nutrit Med Students, Med Univ SC, 1985-; clin investr, Vet Admin Med Ctr, Charleston, SC, 1984-1986; from asst prof to assoc prof, Med Univ SC, 1979-1989; Spec Emphasis Res Career Award, Nat Heart Lung Blood Inst, Nat Inst Arthritis Metab & Digestive Dis, 1978-1983; mem, Coun Atherosclerosis, Am Heart Asn. **Memberships:** Fel Am Heart Asn; fel Am Col Nutrit; Am Diabetes Asn; Am Fedn Clin Res. **Research Statement & Publications:** Mechanisms leading to accelerated atherosclerosis in diabetes. **Mailing Address:** Med Univ SC, 171 Ashley Ave, Charleston, SC 29425. **Fax:** 843-876-5133. **E-Mail:** virellam@musc.edu

LOPEZ, A JAVIER, BIOLOGY. **Education:** Duke Univ, PhD. **Professional Experience:** ASSOC PROF, DEPT BOIL SCI, CARNEGIE MELLON UNIV, as of 2005. **Mailing Address:** Dept Biol Sci Carnegie Mellon Univ, 4400 Fifth Ave, Pittsburgh, PA 15213. **Fax:** 412-268-7129. **E-Mail:** jlaa@andrew.cmu.edu

LOPEZ, ANTHONY, FOOD SCIENCE. **Personal Data:** b Chile, SAm, May 13, 1919; American citizen; m 1947, c Martita, Anthony & Michael. **Education:** Catholic Univ, Chile, BS, 1942; Univ Mass, PhD (food tech), 1947. **Professional Experience:** RETIRED; UN Food & Agr Orgn, Arg, 1980, Chile, 1984, Mex 1989-1990, PR, 1990-1991; tech ed, Food Prod Mgt, 1971-1987; Orgn Am States in Mex, 1970-1974; consult food technol, UN Food & Agr Orgn, Chile, 1966 & Brazil, 1969, 1972, 1975, 1979; consult food processing, Govt Spain, 1962, 1963; lectr, Ministry Commerce, Spain, 1960; prof food sci & technol, Va Polytech Inst & State Univ, 1954-1988; assoc prof, Univ Ga, 1953-1954; assoc res prof food technol, Univ Mass, 1952-1953; instr, UN Latin Am Fisheries Training Ctr, Chile, 1952; tech dir, Indust de Productos Alimenticios, 1948-1952; chemist, SA Organa, Chile, 1942-1945. **Memberships:** Am Chem Soc; fel Inst Food Technologists; Chilean Soc Nutrit. **Research Statement & Publications:** Processing and nutritive value of fish; composition of fresh fruits and vegetables; processing of fruits and vegetables; chemical changes in processed foods during storage; food packaging; microwave irradiation of foods; effect of processing on nutritive value of foods. **Mailing Address:** 721 Hutcheson Dr, Blacksburg, VA 24060-3209. **E-Mail:** alopex721@aol.com

LOPEZ, ANTONIO VINCENT, PHARMACEUTICAL CHEMISTRY, PHARMACOGNOSY. **Personal Data:** b Montgomery, Ala, April 24, 1938. **Education:** Auburn Univ, BS, 1959, MS, 1961; Univ Miss, PhD (pharm chem), 1966. **Professional Experience:** PROF EMER, SOUTHERN SCH PHARM, MERCER UNIV, as of 2005; prof & assoc dean student affairs, Southern Sch Pharm, Mercer Univ, 1994-; chmn, Div Natural Sci, formerly, dir student affairs, 1985-1994; from asst dean to assoc dean, Dept Pharmaceut Chem, 1978-1985; chmn, Dept Pharmaceut Chem, 1966-1976. **Memberships:** AAAS; Am Col; Am Asn Col Pharm. **Research Statement & Publications:** Central nervous system drugs. **Mailing Address:** Southern Sch Pharm, Mercer Univ, 3001 Mercer Univ Dr, Atlanta, GA 30341.

LOPEZ, CARLOS, IMMUNOLOGY, VIROLOGY. **Personal Data:** b Ponce, PR, January 15, 1942; m 1970, c 1. **Education:** Univ Minn, BS, 1965, MS, 1966, PhD (pub health), 1970. **Professional Experience:** RETIRED; chmn, Sci Adv Bd, Ctr Regenerative Biol & Med, Ind Univ Purdue Univ, as of 2003; res fel, Infectious Dis, Eli Lilly, beginning 1996; exec dir infectious dis, Infectious Dis, Eli Lilly, 1993-1996; dir biol res, Infectious Dis, Eli Lilly, 1987-1993; assoc mem, Sloan- Kettering Cancer Ctr & asst prof biol, Sloan-Kettering Div, Cornell Univ Sch med, 1973-1987; asst prof path, Univ Minn, 1972-1973; fel, Nat Thoracic & Respiratory Dis Asn, 1971-1973; res fel, Univ Minn, 1970-1972; NIH fel, 1970-1971. **Memberships:** Am Asn Immunologists; Am Asn Exp Pathologists; Am Soc Microbiol; AAAS. **Research Statement & Publications:** Immunological resistance to virus infections; immunologic response to virus induced tumors. **Mailing Address:** Dept Biol, Ind Univ Purdue Univ, SL 306 723 W Mich St, Indianapolis, IN 46202-5191.

LOPEZ, DIANA MONTES DE OCA, MICROBIOLOGY, IMMUNOLOGY. **Personal Data:** b Havana, Cuba, August 26, 1937; American citizen; m 1958, c 3. **Education:** Univ Havana, BS, 1960; Univ Miami, MS, 1968, PhD (microbiol), 1970. **Professional Experience:** PROF MICROBIOL & IMMUNOL, SCH MED, UNIV MIAMI, 1983-; sect leader tumor immunol, Sylvester Comprehensive Cancer Ctr, State Fla, 1980-; from instr to assoc prof, Sch Med, Univ Miami, 1971-1983; res assoc, Sch Med, Univ Miami, 1970-1971. **Memberships:** Am Soc Microbiol; Tissue Cult Asn; Sigma Xi; Am Asn Immunologists; NY Acad Sci; Int Asn Breast Cancer Res (pres-elect, 1985 & pres, 1987-1989). **Research Statement & Publications:** Tumor immunology; viral oncogenesis; cell kinetics. **Mailing Address:** Dept Microbiol & Immunol, Sch Med, Univ Miami, Rm 210 Papanicolaou Bldg 1550 NW 10 Ave, Miami, FL 33101-6960. **Fax:** 305-243-4409. **E-Mail:** dlopez@med.miami.edu

LOPEZ, GENARO, ECONOMIC ENTOMOLOGY. **Personal Data:** b Brownsville, Tex, January 24, 1947; m 1972, Lee; c G Daniel & Adriana. **Education:** Tex Tech Univ, BS, 1970; Cornell Univ, PhD (econ entom), 1975. **Professional Experience:** PROF BIOL, UNIV TEX, BROWNSVILLE, 1995-; asst prof biol, Tex Southmost Col, beginning 1976; entomologist, Tex Agr Exten Serv, Tex A&M Univ, 1975-1976; res asst entom, Cornell Univ, 1970-1975. **Memberships:** Entom Soc Am; Acaralogical Soc Am. **Research Statement & Publications:** Bionomics, ecology and control of insects affecting man's home environment; teaching biology to the bicultural/bilingual student at the college level; methylmercury levels in fish at Port of Brownsville. **Mailing Address:** Dept Biol, Univ Tex, 11818A LHSB, Brownsville, TX 78520. **Fax:** 956-554-5043. **E-Mail:** gnrolpz@utb.edu

LOPEZ, GUIDO WILFRED, THERMOFLUIDS, COMPUTER SIMULATION OF ENGINEERING SYSTEMS. **Personal Data:** b Ibarra, Ecuador, July 31, 1954. **Education:** Nat Polytech Sch, ME, 1978; Northeastern Univ, MS, 1981 PhD (thermofluids), 1993. **Professional Experience:** CHMN, ENG & SCI DIV, DANIEL WEBSTER COL, 1993-; lectr thermodyn, heat transfer & instrumentation, Northeastern Univ, 1986-1993; Consult thermal systs, installation design & mfg, 1981-1986; Asst prof thermodyn, Nat Polytech Sch, 1981-1986. **Memberships:** Planetary Soc. **Research Statement & Publications:** Energy generation for aerospace propulsion, nuclear fusion and electromagnetic space drive. **Mailing Address:** Daniel Webster Col Dept Math & Eng, 20 Univ Dr, Nashua, NH 03063-1323.

LOPEZ, JAVIER A, MOLECULAR BIOLOGY. **Education:** Duke Univ, PhD. **Professional Experience:** ASSOC PROF, DEPT BIOL SCI, CARNEGIE MELLON INST, PA, as of 2005. **Mailing Address:** Dept Biol Sci Carnegie Mellon Univ, 4400 Fifth Ave 243B Mellon Inst, Pittsburgh, PA 15213. **Fax:** 412-268-7129. **E-Mail:** jlaa@andrew.cmu.edu

LOPEZ, JORGE ALBERTO, HEAVY ION REACTIONS, COMPUTATIONAL PHYSICS. **Personal Data:** b Monterrey, Mex, January 23, 1955; m 1979, c 2. **Education:** Tex A&M Univ, PhD (physics), 1986. **Professional Experience:** CHMN & SHUMAKER PROF, DEPT PHYSICS, UNIV TEX, EL PASO, as of 2004; assoc prof physics, Univ Tex, El Paso, beginning 1990; assoc prof, Calpoly State Univ, San Luis Obispo, 1989-1990; researcher, NielsBohr Inst, Denmark, 1985-1987 & Lawrence Berkeley Lab, 1987-1989. **Memberships:** Am Phys Soc. **Research Statement & Publications:** Nuclear physics; heavy ion physics; computational physics. **Mailing Address:** Dept Physics, Univ Tex, Phys Sci Bldg 209 A 500 W Univ Ave, El Paso, TX 79968. **Fax:** 915-747-6807. **E-Mail:** jorgelopez@utep.edu

LOPEZ, JOSE MANUEL, ENVIRONMENTAL CHEMISTRY, CHEMICAL OCEANOGRAPHY. **Personal Data:** b San Juan, PR, January 7, 1950; m 1973, c Sara, Christina, Yania & Kiani. **Education:** Univ PR, BS, 1971; Univ Wis, Madison, MS, 1973; Univ Tex, PhD (environ chem), 1976. **Professional Experience:** ASSOC PROF, DEPT MARINE SCI, UNIV PR, 1991-; sr scientist, Ctr Energy & Environ Res, 1985; head, Marine Ecol Div, Ctr Energy & Environ Res, 1979-1985; pres, Sci Teachers Asn, 1979-1980; res scientist marine chem, Res & Develop Ctr, Ctr Energy & Environ Res, 1978-1981; asst pof, Dept Chem, Univ PR, 1978-1979; consult, Dames & Moore, PR, 1978; lectr, Environ Studies Inst, Univ Tex, Dallas, 1974-1976; consult, EnviroQual Inc, 1973-1976; res scientist, Univ Tex, 1975; res asst, Univ Tex, 1974-1975; res asst, Tex A&M Univ, 1973-1974; teaching asst, Univ PR, 1969. **Memberships:** AAAS; Am Chem Soc; Am Soc Limnol & Oceanog; Am Bot Soc; Water Pollution Control Fedn. **Research Statement & Publications:** Sources, fate and significance of chemicals in aquatic ecosystems; biological availability of contaminants to aquatic organisms; nutrient dynamics; mangroves ecology; remote sensing of ocean color; biogeochemistry and primary production. **Mailing Address:** Dept Marine Sci, Univ PR, PO Box 5000, Mayaguez, PR 00681-9013. **Fax:** 787-834-8025. **E-Mail:** jo_lopez@rumac.upr.clu.edu

LOPEZ, LEONARD ANTHONY, ENGINEERING SOFTWARE SYSTEMS. **Personal Data:** b Waltham, Mass, December 27, 1940; m 1961, Ruth-Linda; c Marianne, Christopher & Michael. **Education:** Tufts Univ, BS, 1962; Univ Ill, MS, 1963, PhD (civil eng), 1966. **Professional Experience:** PROF EMER, UNIV ILL, URBANA, 1998-; von humboldt res fel, 1979-1980; prof civil eng, Univ Ill, Urbana, 1967-1998; asst prof civil eng, Lehigh Univ, 1966-1967. **Memberships:** mem, Am Soc Civil Engrs, beginning 1966. **Research Statement & Publications:** Digital simulation; numerical methods; mechanics of nonlinear solids; computer system and parallel processing. **Mailing Address:** Dept Civil & Environ Eng, Univ Ill, 205 N Mathews St, Urbana, IL 61801-2374.

LOPEZ, R C GERALD, AGRICULTURAL FORMULATIONS RESEARCH. **Personal Data:** b London, Eng, March 12, 1957; m 1980, c 3. **Education:** Oxford Univ, BA, 1980, PhD (org chem), 1982. **Professional Experience:** MGR AGRFORMULATIONS RES, ROHM & HAAS CO, 1988-; sr scientist, Rohm & Haas Co, 1982-1988; MGR AGR CHEM OP-

ERS, ROHM & HAAS CO. **Research Statement & Publications:** Discovery and optimization of formulations for new and existing agricultural chemicals, including fungicides, herbicides and insecticides. **Mailing Address:** 100 S Independence Mall W, Philadelphia, PA 19106.

LOPEZ, RAFAEL, PEDIATRICS, HEMATOLOGY. **Personal Data:** b Dominican Repub, December 15, 1929; m 1956, c 2. **Education:** Seton Hall Univ, BSc, 1952; Univ PR, MD, 1956. **Professional Experience:** RETIRED; spec asst to pres & chief exec officer, NY Med Col, Our Lady Mercy Med Ctr, 1994-1996; dir pediat, NY Med Col, Our Lady Mercy Med Ctr, 1985-1993; assoc prof pediat, NY Med Col, Our Lady Mercy Med Ctr, 1980-1996; Assoc prof pediat, Flower & Fifth Ave Hosp, 1965-1980. **Memberships:** Soc Study Blood; Int Soc Hemat; Am Soc Hemat; NY Acad Sci; Am Acad Pediat; Am Col Qual Assurance. **Research Statement & Publications:** Glutathione reductase as a tool for diagnosis of riboflavin deficiency in infants, children, adolescents; malabsorption syndromes and the effect of phototherapy upon this vitamin in the newborn. **Mailing Address:** 140 Cabrini Blvd, New York, NY 10033.

LOPEZ, ROBERT J, MATHEMATICS. **Education:** Marist Col, BA; Univ Mo, MS, Purdue Univ, PhD (math). **Professional Experience:** PROF EMER, ROSE-HULMAN INST TECHNOL, as of 2006. **Mailing Address:** Rose-Hulman Inst Technol, Terre Haute, IN 47803. **Fax:** 812 877-8883.

LOPEZ-BERESTEIN, GABRIEL, ONCOLOGY, IMMUNOLOGY. **Personal Data:** b La Habana, Cuba, August 13, 1947; American citizen; c 1. **Education:** Univ PR, San Juan, BA, 1970; Univ Navarre, Spain, MD, 1976. **Honors & Awards:** Stohlman Award, 1990. **Professional Experience:** PROF MED & INTERNIST, MD ANDERSON CANCER CTR, UNIV TEX, 1991-; mem, Biomed Sci Study Sect, NIH, 1988-; assoc prof biomed sci, Health Sci Ctr, Univ Tex, 1984-; assoc prof pharm, med sch, beginning 1984; from asst prof to assoc prof, Med Sch, 1981-1991; asst internist, Med Sch, 1981-1984. **Memberships:** Am Asn Cancer Res; AMA; Am Soc Clin Oncol; AAAS; Am Soc Immunologists. **Research Statement & Publications:** Oncology; immunology; tumor immunology; therapeutic drug targetting; macrophage biology. **Mailing Address:** MD Anderson Cancer Ctr Sect Immunobiol & Drug Carriers, Univ Tex PO Box 60 1515 Holcombe Blvd, Houston, TX 77030. **Fax:** 713-796-7731. **E-Mail:** gabriel_lopez@isqm.mdacc.tmc.edu

LOPEZ-ESCOBAR, EDGAR GEORGEKENNETH, MATHEMATICS. **Personal Data:** b Buenos Aires, Arg, January 7, 1937. **Education:** Cambridge Univ, BA, 1958, MA, 1971; Univ Calif, Berkeley, MA, 1961, PhD (math), 1965. **Professional Experience:** PROF MATH, UNIV MD, 1966-. **Memberships:** Asn Symbolic Logic; Soc Exact Philos; Am Math Soc. **Research Statement & Publications:** Computer application as applied to mathematical logic. **Mailing Address:** Dept Math, Univ Md, Rm 2209, Annapolis, MD 21403-4216. **Fax:** 301-314-0827. **E-Mail:** egkle@math.umd.edu

LOPEZ-MAJANO, VINCENT, NUCLEAR MEDICINE, PULMONARY MEDICINE. **Personal Data:** b Madrid, Spain, April 3, 1921; American citizen; m 1952, c 2. **Education:** Inst Cardenal Cisneros, BA & BS, 1939; Univ Madrid, MD, 1945, PhD, 1951. **Professional Experience:** Vis scholar, Nat Cancer Inst, 1985; Ed, Respiration, 1970-1971 & J Nuclear Med & Allied Sci, 1982; vis scientist, Nat Acad Sci, 1981-1984; assoc prof med, Chicago Med Sch, 1980-1987; CHMN NUCLEAR MED, COOK COUNTY HOSP, CHICAGO, 1977-; dir nuclear med, Gottlieb Mem Hosp, 1973-1977; vis prof, Nat Univ Mex, 1973; chief training sect nuclear med, Vet Admin Hosp, Hine, Ill, 1970-1974; clin assoc prof med, Loyola Stritch Sch Med, 1970-1973; asst prof environ med, Johns Hopkins Inst, Baltimore, 1968-1970; chief, Pulmonary Function Lab, Vet Admin Hosp, Baltimore, 1960-1970; physician, Sanatorium Carlos Duran, Costa Rica, 1951-1956 & Tuberc Sanatorium, Md, 1955-1960; Resident, Gen Hosp, Madrid, 1945-1951. **Memberships:** Nuclear Med Soc; Physiol Soc; Mex Nuclear Med Soc; Am Fed Clin Res. **Research Statement & Publications:** Inflammatory diseases of the lungs; regional lung function; staging of neoplasms; studies of cardiac function with radionuclides. **Mailing Address:** 3100 N Sheridan Rd, Chicago, IL 60657.

LOPEZ-SANTOLINO, ALFREDO, MEDICINE, BIOCHEMISTRY. **Personal Data:** b Salamanca, Spain, July 23, 1931; m 1962, c 2. **Education:** Inst Ensenanza Media, Salamanca, BS, 1949; Lit Univ Salamanca, MD, 1955, PhD (med sci), 1958; Tulane Univ, PhD (biochem), 1963. **Professional Experience:** FRED ALLISON JR PROF MED & VICE CHAIR, DEPT INTERN MED & CHIEF, SECT NUTRIT, LA STATE UNIV MED CTR, NEWORLEANS, as of 2006; prof intern med, Med Sch, La State Univ Med Ctr, Neworleans, beginning 1974; assoc prof, Med Sch, LA State Univ Med Ctr, New Orleans, 1967-1974; asst prof internal med, Col Med & biochemist, Clin Res Ctr, Univ Iowa, 1964-1967; instr biochem, Cali Univ Sch Med, 1958-1959; asst prof physiol med, Sch Med, Lit Univ Salamanca, 1956-1958. **Memberships:** AAAS; Am Oil Chem Soc; Soc Nutrit Educ; Am Inst Nutrit; Am Soc Clin Nutrit; Am Heart Asn. **Research Statement & Publications:** Nutrition and metabolic diseases; metabolism of lipids and steroid hormones; published 4 books recently. **Mailing Address:** Dept Med, La State Univ Sch Med, 1542 Tulane Ave Box T4M-Three, New Orleans, LA 70112. **Fax:** 504-568-2127. **E-Mail:** alopez@lsumc.edu

LOPINA, ROBERT F(ERGUSON), AERONAUTICAL ENGINEERING, AVIONICS. **Personal Data:** b Jamestown, NY, May 13, 1936; m 1958, c 3. **Education:** Purdue Univ, Lafayette, BS, 1957; Mass Inst Technol, MSc, 1965, ME, 1966, PhD (mech eng), 1967. **Professional Experience:** VPRES, ADVAN PROGS OFF, FORD AEROSPACE/LORAL AERONUTRONIC DIV, NEWPORT BEACH, CALIF, 1988-; dir, Advan Develop, Ford Aerospace Corp, Detroit, Mich, 1987-1988; dep, Aeronaut Systs Div, USAF, 1983-1987; vpres eng & prog dir T-46, Fairchild Repub Co, Farmingdale, NY, 1983-1987; dep reconnaissance strike & extreme width, USAF, 1982-1983; dep eng, Aeronaut Systs Div, USAF, 1980-1982; comdr & dir, Air Force Avionics Lab, USAF, 1978-1980; chief, Flight Control Div, Air Force Flight Dynamics Lab, USAF, 1977-1978; chief scientist, Europ Off Aerospace Res & Develop, USAF, 1974-1976; assoc prof aeronaut, USAF, 1967-1974; USAF, 1957-1983. **Memberships:** Am Inst Aeronaut & Astronaut; Am Soc Mech Engrs; Sigma Xi; Air Force Asn; Nat Mgt Asn; Asn Old Crows. **Research Statement & Publications:** Swirl flow heat transfer; computer applications in aeronautical education; night attack systems development; trainer aircraft development and production; integrated circuits for radio frequency applications. **Mailing Address:** Loral, 29947 Avenida de los Bard, Rancho Santa Margarita, CA 92688. **Fax:** 714-459-4425.

LO PINTO, RICHARD WILLIAM, MARINE BIOLOGY, BIOMONITORING & AQUATIC TOXICOLOGY. **Personal Data:** b New York City, November 7, 1942; m 1970, c 2. **Education:** Iona Col, BS, 1963; Fordham Univ, MS, 1965, PhD (physiol ecol), 1972. **Professional Experience:** Professor Fairleigh Dickinson University; Co-Chair Columbia University Seminar on Pollution and Water Resources; Supervisor Bio-monitoring/Aquatic Toxicology Laboratory of CFM Environmental Engineers Inc. Whippany, N.J.; Director Mid-Atlantic Region of Sigma Xi the Scientific Research Society; Environmental Commissioner, City of Hackensack, NJ; Research and Engineering Associate U.S. Army Biomedical Research & Development Laboratory Ft. Detrick MD; Head Biological Testing Program-Organization for Economic Cooperation & Development- Paris; Assistant to the Director, Office of Analysis and Evaluation (OAE)US Environmental Protection Agency- Washington D.C; Assoc Editor Bulletin NJ Academy of Sciences; Chair Technical Advisory Committee NJ Water Quality Program; Consultant to Hartz Mountain Industries on Residential Development in Hackensack Meadowlands; Assistant Director Meadowlands Regional Study Center; Director Marine Biology Program & Environmental Science Programs Fairleigh Dickinson University; Consultant to NJ State Hackensack Meadowlands Development Commission. **Memberships:** Sigma Xi. **Research Statement & Publications:** Bioassay Development for Marine and Fresh Water Organisms; Aquatic Toxicology; Phytoplankton Physiology; Pollution and Water Resources. **Mailing Address:** Sch Natural Scis, Fairleigh Dickinson Univ, 1000 River Rd, Teaneck, NJ 07666-1996. **E-Mail:** richard_lo_pinto@fdu.edu

LOPO, ALINA C, MEDICAL EDUCATION, DEVELOPMENT OF EXPERTISE. **Personal Data:** b Havana, Cuba, June 14, 1951; American citizen; m 1982, Stephen; c 1. **Education:** Univ Miami, Coral Gables, BS, 1972, MS, 1974; Univ Calif, Davis, PhD (cell biol), 1979; Univ Calif, Los Angeles, MD, 1994. **Professional Experience:** ASST CLIN PROF MED, SCH MED, UNIV CALIF, LOS ANGELES, as of 2004; resident, dept med, Univ Calif, Los Angeles Sch Med, beginning 1994; asst prof biomed sci, Univ calif, Riverside, 1985-1990; Univ Calif Sch Med, Davis, 1981-1985; lectr, Sch Optom, Univ Calif, Berkeley, 1981; fel, NIH, 1980-1981; fel, Rockefeller Found, Univ Calif, San Francisco, 1979-1980; res asst, Univ Calif, San Diego, 1978-1979; teaching asst, Am Asn Univ Women fel, 1977-1978; teaching asst, Univ Calif, Davis, 1975-1977; res asst, Univ Miami, Coral Gables, 1973-1975; instr gen biol, Miami-Dade Community Col, 1972-1975; teaching asst, Univ Miami, Coral Gables, 1972-1974. **Memberships:** AMA. **Research Statement & Publications:** Medical education; transition novice to expert in clinical problem-solving. **Mailing Address:** Dept Med, Sch Med, Univ Calif, Los Angeles, CA 90095-1361. **Fax:** 909-684-4655. **E-Mail:** alopo@ucla.edu

LOPPNOW, HARALD, CELLULAR IMMUNOLOGY, VASCULAR CYTOKINES. **Personal Data:** German citizen. **Education:** Kiel Univ, dipl microbiol, 1983, PhD (immunol), 1986. **Professional Experience:** Lectr, Kiel Univ, 1990; res assoc immunol, Sclavo Res Ctr, Siena I, 1987 & Tufts Univ, Boston, 1988-1990; travel award, IV Int Conf Immunopharmacol, 1988; RES ASSOC IMMUNOL, FORSCHUNGSINST, 1983-1988 & 1990-; lab instr microbiol, Forschungsinst 1981-1983. **Memberships:** Ger Soc Immunol; Am Asn Immunologists. **Research Statement & Publications:** Vascular and immune cell responses to pathophysiologically relevant stimuli such as bacterial lipopolysaccharide or cytokines; determine proliferation, cytokine production, or adhesion of cells; biochemical, cell biological, immunological and molecular biological methods. **Mailing Address:** Dept Biochem, Forschungsinst Borstel Parkallee 22, 23845 Borstel, Ger.

LOPREST, FRANK JAMES, PHYSICAL CHEMISTRY. **Personal Data:** b New York, NY, January 8, 1929; m 1960, c 5. **Education:** St John's Univ, NY, BS, 1950; NY Univ, MS, 1952, PhD, 1954. **Professional Experience:** RETIRED; Assoc dir basic res, Colgate-Palmolive Co, 1983-1994; dir basic sci, Princeton Res Ctr, Am Can Co, 1977-1983; mgr appl chem, Res & Develop & Res Serv, Indust Photog Div, 1969-1977; sect mgr new imaging processes res, Res & Develop Div, GAF Corp, 1967-1969; tech assoc, Res & Develop Div, GAF Corp, 1965-1967; sr res chemist & supvr adv res, Reaction Motors Div, Thiokol Chem Corp, 1956-1965; res chemist, Oak Ridge Nat Lab, 1954-1956. **Memberships:** Am Chem Soc; Sigma Xi. **Research Statement & Publications:** Heterogeneous equilibria; kinetics of liquid solid reactions; high temperature materials; physical chemistry of liquid and solid propellants; adhesion phenomena; cellulose and paper science; surface & colloid chem, detergency. **Mailing Address:** 590 Beverly Rd, Holland, PA 18966-2185.

LOPRESTI, PHILIP V(INCENT), ELECTRICAL ENGINEERING. **Personal Data:** b Johnstown, Pa, September 27, 1932; m 1959, Patricia; c Daniel P, David B & Amy P. **Education:** Univ Notre Dame, BSEE, 1954, MSEE, 1958; Purdue Univ, Lafayette, PhD (elec eng), 1963. **Professional Experience:** RETIRED; adj prof elec eng, Univ PA, 1997-2002; consult, Mem Res Staff, Eng Res Ctr, Lucent Technol 1970-1996; asst prof eng, Northwestern Univ, 1967-1970; asst prof elec eng, Ill Inst Technol, 1964-1967; consult, Ill Inst Technol, 1964-1970; instr, Purdue Univ, Lafayette, 1960-1963; instr, Univ Notre Dame, 1958-1960. **Memberships:** Inst Elec & Electronics Engrs; Sigma Xi; Eng Accrediation Bd; Circuit & Systs Soc. **Research Statement & Publications:** Automatic control theory; digital signal processing; analog integrated circuits; hybrid integrated circuits. **Mailing Address:** 327 Sked St, Pennington, NJ 08534.

LOPUSHINSKY, THEODORE, PEDAGOGY, GRANTS WRITING. **Personal Data:** b Brooklyn, NY, October 25, 1937; m Joanne; c Andrew & John. **Education:** PENN STATE UNIV, BS, 1959 (Zoology / Entomology); UNIV TENNESSEE, MS, 1961; (Parasitology/ Genetics); MICHIGAN STATE UNIV, PhD, 1969 (Wildlife Ecol, Pathology. **Honors & Awards:** Ohaus Award (College) for "Innovations in Science Teaching"; Natural Science Teachers Assn, 1982. **Professional Experience:** PROF EMERITUS, CTR INTEGRATIVE STUDIES SCI, MICH STATE UNIV, 2004; Prof, 1995-2004; DEPARTMENT NATURAL SCIENCE, MSU:Asoc Prof 1975-1995; Asst Prof 1969-1970; COLL HUMAN MEDICINE, MSU: Project Developer, 1973-1975; MICH ASSN REGIONAL MEDICAL PROGRAMS: Acting Director 1972; Dir Program Development, 1972-1973; Program Representative; 1970-1972. **Memberships:** SIGMA XI; NATIONAL SCIENCE TEACHERS ASSN; MICHIGAN SCIENCE TEACHERS ASSN; Soc FOR COLL SCI TEACHERS (President, 1989-1991); National Memembership Chmn, 1984-1987; Archivist, 1981-2004. **Research Statement & Publications:** general education science; applying "Bronowskian" humanities methodology in the science class; Parasitism and other pathologies in wildlife populations. **Mailing Address:** Rm 100 N Kedzie Lab, Mich State Univ, East Lansing, MI 48824. **E-Mail:** lopushin@msu.edu

LORANCE, ELMER DONALD, SCIENCE EDUCATION. **Personal Data:** b Tupelo, Okla, January 18, 1940; m 1969, Phyllis; c Edward D & Jonathan A. **Education:** Okla State Univ, BA, 1962; Kans State Univ, MS, 1967; Univ Okla, PhD (bioorg chem), 1977. **Professional Experience:** CHMN, DIV NATURAL SCI & MATH, VAGUARD UNIV 1993-; chmn, Div Natural Sci & Math, 1985-1989; PROF CHEM, SOUTHERN CALIF COL, 1980-; adj prof, Calif State Univ, Fullerton, 1977; from asst prof to assoc prof, Div Natural Sci & Math, 1970-1980; chmn, Dept Chem, 1999-. **Memberships:** Am Chem Soc; AAAS; Am Sci Affil. **Research Statement & Publications:** Isolation and structure elucidation of compounds from marine organisms; organic synthesis; chemical taxonomy of desert plants. **Mailing Address:** Div Natural Sci & Math, Southern Calif Col, 55 Fair Dr, Costa Mesa, CA 92626.

LORAND, JOHN PETER, PHYSICAL ORGANIC CHEMISTRY. **Personal Data:** b Wilmington, Del, December 6, 1936; m 1964, Priscilla; c Susan, Katherine & Wangden. **Education:** Brown Univ, ScB, 1958; Harvard Univ, PhD (org chem), 1964. **Professional Experience:** PROF EMER CHEM, CENT MICH UNIV, as of 2004; vis assoc prof, Rutgers State Univ NJ, 1986-1988; prof org chem, Cent Mich Univ, beginning 1977; vis scientist, Univ

Groningen, Neth, 1977-1978; from asst prof to assoc prof, Cent Mich Univ, 1971-1977; asst prof org chem, Boston Univ, 1965-1971; NSF scientist, Univ Calif, Los Angeles, 1964-1965. **Memberships:** Am Chem Soc; Sigma Xi. **Research Statement & Publications:** C-H and N-H hydrogen bonding; amine N-oxides; organic free radicals. **Mailing Address:** Dept Chem, Cent Mich Univ, Dow 364, Mt Pleasant, MI 48859. **Fax:** 989-774-3883. **E-Mail:** loran1jp@mail.cmich.edu

LORAND, LASZLO, BIOCHEMISTRY, PHYSIOLOGY. **Personal Data:** b Gyor, Hungary, March 23, 1923; American citizen; m 1953, c 1. **Education:** Budapest Univ, absolutorium med, 1948; Leeds Univ, PhD (biomolecular struct), 1951. **Honorary Degrees:** DSc, Univ Ill. **Honors & Awards:** James F Mitchell Found Int Award Heart & Vascular Res, 1973. **Professional Experience:** RES PROF, DEPT CELL & MOLECULAR BIOL, NORTHWESTERN UNIV, ILL, 1993-; DISTINGUISHED INVESTR, FEINBERG CARDIOVASC INST, MED SCH, NWESTERN UNIV, CHICAGO, ILL, 1993-; lectr, Japan Soc Prom Sci, beginning 1990; dep dir basic sci, Cancer Ctr, 1990-1991; prof biochem, molecular & cell biol, Northwestern Univ, Evanston, 1981-1993; prof biochem & molecular biol, Northwestern Univ, Evanston, 1974-1981; USPHS career award, 1962-1993; dir, Biochem Training Prog, Northwestern Univ, 1961-1966; Lalor fac award, 1957; from asst prof to prof chem, Northwestern Univ, Evanston, 1955-1974; asst prof, Wayne State Univ, 1953-1955; res assoc physiol & pharmacol, Wayne State Univ, 1952-1953; Beit mem fel, Eng, 1952; asst biomolecular struct, Leeds Univ, 1948-1952; demonstr biochem, Budapest Univ, 1946-1948; mem corp, Marine Biol Lab, Woods Hole, Mass. **Memberships:** Nat Acad Sci; AAAS; Am Soc Biol Chem; Soc Exp Biol & Med; Am Physiol Soc; Brit Biochem Soc; Am Chem Soc; foreign mem Hungarian Acad Sci; fel Int Soc Hemat; Biophys Soc; fel Japan Soc Prom Sci; Am Soc Biochem & Molecular Biol; Am Heart Asn; Am Soc Cell Biol; Int Soc Thrombosis & Haemostasis; Asn Res Vision & Ophthal. **Research Statement & Publications:** Blood proteins; coagulation of blood; muscle chemistry; protein and enzyme chemistry; author of numerous publications. **Mailing Address:** Dept Cell & Molecular Biol, NorthWestern Univ, Searle 4-555, 303 E Chicago Ave, Chicago, IL 60611-3008. **Fax:** 312-503-0590. **E-Mail:** l-lorand@northwestern.edu

LORBEER, JAMES W, PLANT PATHOLOGY, MYCOLOGY. **Personal Data:** b Oxnard, Calif, October 30, 1931; m 1964. **Education:** Pomona Col, BA, 1953; Univ Wash, MS, 1955; Univ Calif, Berkeley, PhD (plant path), 1960. **Professional Experience:** PROF PLANT PATH, CORNELL UNIV, 1972-; from asst prof to assoc prof, Cornell Univ, 1960-1972; res asst plant path, Univ Calif, Berkeley, 1955-1960; asst bot, Univ Wash, 1953-1955. **Memberships:** Mycol Soc Am; Am Phytopath Soc; NY Acad Sci; Brit Mycol Soc. **Research Statement & Publications:** Diseases of vegetable crops; epidemiology; plant disease control; biology of Botrytis; fungal genetics. **Mailing Address:** Dept Plant Path, Cornell Univ 334 Plant Sci Bldg, Ithaca, NY 14853-0001. **Fax:** 607-255-4471. **E-Mail:** jwl5@cornell.edu

LORBER, BENNETT, INFECTIOUS DISEASES. **Personal Data:** b Philadelphia, Pa, April 1, 1943; m 1964, Carol; c Samuel & Joshua Edward. **Education:** Swarthmore Col, BA, 1964; Univ Pa, MD, 1968. **Honorary Degrees:** DSc, Swarthmore Col, 1996. **Professional Experience:** PROF MED & SECT CHIEF INFECTIOUS DIS, TEMPLE UNIV HOSP, 1983-; from asst prof to assoc prof med, Med Sch, Temple Univ, 1974-1983. **Memberships:** Infectious Dis Soc Am; Am Col Physicians; Am Soc Microbiol; Am Fedn Clin Res; Physicians for Human Rights; Anerobe Soc Am. **Research Statement & Publications:** Listeriosis, anaerobic infections, impact of societal change on disease patterns. **Mailing Address:** Dept Infectious Dis, Temple Univ Hosp, Parkinson Pavilion Fifth FlRm 500 Broad & Tioga St, Philadelphia, PA 19140. **E-Mail:** blorber@astro.temple.edu

LORBER, HERBERT WILLIAM, ELECTRONIC WARFARE, DECISION ANALYSIS. **Personal Data:** b Indianapolis, Ind, July 12, 1929; m 1962, c 2. **Education:** Purdue Univ, BS, 1951; Rutgers Univ, MSc, 1955; Univ Pa, PhD (elec eng), 1962. **Professional Experience:** SR STAFF SPECIALIST, LOCKHEED AERONAUT SYSTS CO, 1982-; Consult, N J Damaskos, Inc, Los Alamos Tech Assocs, Inc & Convair Div Gen Dynamics, 1982; mem staff, Los Alamos Nat Lab, 1976-1982; electron res specialist, Teledyne Ryan Aeronaut, 1972-1976; sr sci specialist, Edgerton Germeshausen & Grier, Inc, 1962-1971; mem tech staff, RCA Labs, 1955-1962; Engr, Signal Corp Eng Labs, 1951 & 1953-1954. **Memberships:** Inst Elec & Electronic Engrs; Oper Res Soc Am; AAAS; Sigma Xi. **Research Statement & Publications:** Interaction of spacecraft and military vehicles with radar systems; quantitative space-system concept assessment; applications of utility theory to management decision-making; analysis of military and business operations. **Mailing Address:** 3205 Deer Creek Dr, Canton, GA 30114-8978.

LORBER, MORTIMER, PHYSIOLOGY, HEMATOLOGY. **Personal Data:** b New York, NY, August 30, 1926; m 1956, Eileen Segal; c Kenneth & Stephanie. **Education:** NY Univ, BS, 1945; Harvard Univ, DMD, 1950, MD, 1952. **Professional Experience:** RETIRED; ASSOC PROF PHYSIOL, SCH MED, GEORGETOWN UNIV, 1968-; Lederle Med Fac Award, USPHS res career develop award, 1963-1970; Lederle Med Fac Award, Georgetown Univ, 1960-1963; from instr to asst prof, Univ Hosp, 1959-1968; sr asst resident med, Univ Hosp, 1958; asst resident med, Mt Sinai Hosp, NY, 1957; med officer hemat res, Naval Med Res Inst, 1955-1956; med officer hemat res, USN Med Corps, 1954-1955; resident hemat, Mt Sinai Hosp, NY, 1953-1954; Rotating intern, Univ Chicago Clins, 1952-1953. **Memberships:** Am Soc Hemat; Int Soc Hemat; Am Soc Cell Biol; Int Asn Dent Res; Am Physiol Soc; Asn Res Vision Ophthal. **Research Statement & Publications:** Splenic function; iron metabolism in Gaucher's disease; organ regeneration, particularly of mammalian submandibular salivary glands following removal of parenchyma; exocrine gland structure and tension; mastication reflexly increases gastroduodenal motility. **Mailing Address:** 5823 Osceola Rd, Bethesda, MD 20816-2032. **Fax:** 202-687-7407.

LORCH, I JOAN, CELL BIOLOGY, PROTOZOOLOGY. **Personal Data:** b Offenbach, Ger, June 13, 1923; m 1952, c 2. **Education:** Univ Birmingham, BSc, 1945; Univ London, PhD (physiol), 1948. **Professional Experience:** PROF EMER BIOL, CANISIUS COL, as of 2004; prof biol, Canisus Col, beginning 1984; vis prof for women, NSF, 1984-1985; chair, Biol Dept, 1981-1984; from asst prof to assoc prof, Canisius Col, 1972-1984; lectr, Canisius Col, 1971-1972; res asst prof, Ctr Theoret Biol, State Univ NY Buffalo, 1968-1972; res assoc cell biol, Ctr Theoret Biol, State Univ NY Buffalo, 1963-1968; Nuffield fel, King's Col, Univ London, 1949-1952. **Research Statement & Publications:** Nuclear-cytoplasmic relationships; species specificity; protozoa; bio-ethics; symbiosis. **Mailing Address:** Dept Biol, Canisius Col, 2001 Main St, Buffalo, NY 14208-1098. **Fax:** 716-888-2525.

LORCH, LEE (ALEXANDER), MATHEMATICS. **Personal Data:** b New York, NY, September 20, 1915; wid, c Alice (Bartels). **Education:** Cornell Univ, BA, 1935; Univ Cincinnati, MA, 1936, PhD (math), 1941. **Honorary Degrees:** LHD, City Univ NY, 1990; LLD, York Univ, 1993, Fisk Univ, 1996. **Honors & Awards:** Lifetime Achivement Award, Nat Asn Mathematicians, 1995. **Professional Experience:** PROF EMER MATH, YORK UNIV, 1985-; prof, York Univ, 1968-1985; from assoc prof to prof, Univ Alta, 1959-1968; vis lectr, Wesleyan Univ, 1958-1969; prof & chmn dept, Philander Smith Col, 1955-1958; prof & chmn dept, Fisk Univ, 1953-1955; assoc prof & chmn dept, Fisk Univ, 1950-1953; asst prof, Pa State Univ, 1949-1950; instr math, City Col New York, 1946-1949; asst mathematician, Nat Adv Comt Aeronaut, 1942-1943. **Memberships:** Am Math Soc; Can Math Soc; Asn Women Math; Nat Asn Mathematicians; fel Royal Soc Can; Math Asn Am; fel AAAS. **Research Statement & Publications:** Fourier series; special functions; summability; ordinary differential equations. **Mailing Address:** Dept Math & Statist, York Univ, 4700 Keele St, Toronto, ON M3J 1P3, Can. **Fax:** 416-736-5757. **E-Mail:** lee.lorch@mathstat.yorku.ca

LORCH, STEVEN KALMAN, FORENSIC SCIENCE, MANAGEMENT. **Personal Data:** b New York, NY, August 21, 1944; m 1967, Harriet; c Jacob R, Elisar R & David P. **Education:** City Col NY, BS, 1966; State Univ NY Binghamton, MA, 1970; Univ Md, PhD (plant physiol), 1972. **Professional Experience:** RETIRED; guest lectr, Univ Detroit Mercy, beginning 1994; team leader, Disaster Asst Recovery Team, beginning 1988; Mich State Police Rep, Sci Adv Comn, Mich Bd Pharm, 1983-; asst lab dir, Northville Sci Lab, Forensic Sci Div, Mich State Police, beginning 1982; supvr, Narcotics & Dangerous Drug Unit, Madison Heights Sci Lab, 1978-1982; E Lansing Sci Lab, 1977-1978; chief drug identification unit, Div Crime Detection, Mich Dept Pub Health, 1975-1977; crime lab scientist, Div Crime Detection, Mich Dept Pub Healthm 1973-1975; res assoc, Mich State Univ-AEC Plant Res Lab, 1972-1973; dir, Mich State Police Crime Lab; pres, JSHED consult. **Memberships:** Am Chem Soc; Am Acad Forensic Sci. **Research Statement & Publications:** Identification of controlled and prescription drugs; gas chromatographic-mass spectrometry; forensic plant identification; crime scene investigation, clandestine laboratories; development of latent fingerprints; automated fingerprint identification systems; major disaster victim identification. **Mailing Address:** 15680 George Wash, Southfield, MI 48075. **E-Mail:** stevenkl@comcast.net

LORD, ARTHUR E, PHYSICS, GEOSYNTHETICS. **Personal Data:** b Buffalo, NY, April 7, 1935; m 1962, Rose; c Susan & Katherine. **Education:** Purdue Univ, BSc, 1957, MSc, 1959; Columbia Univ, PhD (metall), 1964. **Professional Experience:** PROF EMER, DEPT PHYSICS, DREXEL UNIV, as of 2006; consult, House Comt Kennedy & King Assasinations, 1978; mem, NASA Electromagnetic Containerless Processing Task Team, 1977; prof physics, Drexel Univ, beginning 1975; assoc prof, Drexel Univ, 1968-1975; asst res prof physics, Brown Univ, 1966-1968; res assoc appl math, Brown Univ, 1964-1966; fel, Columbia Univ, 1964. **Memberships:** Am Phys Soc; Acoustic Emission Working Group; Int Geotextile Soc. **Research Statement & Publications:** Nondestructive testing techniques in geotechnical problems; geomembranes and geotextiles; centrifuge modelling in geotechnical areas; removal of pollutants from soil by steam stripping techniques. **Mailing Address:** Dept Physics, Drexel Univ, 32nd Chestnut St, Philadelphia, PA 19104. **Fax:** 215-895-1437. **E-Mail:** lordae@dunx1.ocs.drexel.edu

LORD, ARTHUR N(ELSON), PHYSICAL METALLURGY. **Personal Data:** b Los Angeles, Calif, May 7, 1932; m 1961, c 2. **Education:** Stanford Univ, BS, 1953, MS, 1955, PhD (creep of aluminum), 1960. **Professional Experience:** METALLURGIST, KNOLLS ATOMIC POWER LAB, GEN ELEC CO, 1965-; Physical metallurgist, Adv Tech Labs, 1958-1965. **Memberships:** Am Inst Mining Metall & Petrol Engrs; Am Phys Soc; Am Soc Metals. **Research Statement & Publications:** Transport properties of solids; effects of radiation damage in metals. **Mailing Address:** Seven Spring Rd, Scotia, NY 12302-2614.

LORD, EDITH M, IMMUNOLOGY. **Personal Data:** b Kingman, Kans. **Education:** Univ Kans, BA, 1970; Univ Calif, PhD (biol), 1975. **Professional Experience:** PROF ONCOL, UNIV ROCHESTER, as of 2004; asst prof oncol, Univ Rochester, beginning 1977; sr instr, Univ Rochester, 1976-1977; res immunologist, Univ Calif, San Francisco, 1975-1976. **Memberships:** Am Asn Immunologists; Radiation Res Soc. **Research Statement & Publications:** Interaction between host immune cells and tumor cells; modulation of these interactions for therapeutic advantage. **Mailing Address:** Sch Med & Dent, Univ Rochester, 601 Elmwood Ave Box 704, Rochester, NY 14642. **Fax:** 585-473-9573. **E-Mail:** edith_lord@urmc.rochester.edu

LORD, ELIZABETH MARY, BOTANY, CELL BIOLOGY. **Personal Data:** b Baltimore, Md, July 2, 1949; m 1984, Barkin; c Matthew Lord Barkin. **Education:** Univ Mass, BA, 1972; Univ Calif, Berkeley, PhD (bot), 1978. **Honors & Awards:** Pelton Award, Bot Soc Am. **Professional Experience:** VICE PROVOST, ACAD PERSONNEL, UNIV CALIF, RIVERSIDE, as of 2005; dept chair bot, Univ Calif, Riverside, 1997-2001; PROF BOT, UNIV CALIF, RIVERSIDE, 1989-; mem, develop biol panel, NSF, 1983-1986; from asst prof to assoc prof, Univ Calif, Riverside, 1978-1989. **Memberships:** Am Soc Plant Physiologists; Sigma Xi; Asn Women Sci; Bot Soc Am. **Research Statement & Publications:** Use of comparative development data as a tool to elucidate sequence of events leading to a mature floral form; pollination processes in flowering plants; adhesive molecules in pollination; published over 50 articles. **Mailing Address:** Dept Bot & Plant Sci Univ Calif Riveside, Rm 3118 Batchelor Hall, Riverside, CA 92521-0101. **Fax:** 951-827-4437. **E-Mail:** elizabeth.lord@ucr.edu

LORD, HAROLD WILBUR, MEASUREMENT OF VOLTAGE TRANSIENTS. **Personal Data:** b Eureka, Calif, August 20, 1905; m 1928, c 4. **Education:** Calif Inst Technol, BS, 1926. **Honors & Awards:** Centennial Award, Inst Elec & Electronics Engrs, 1984. **Professional Experience:** CONSULT ELEC ENGR, 1966-; chmn, sci & electronic comt, Inst Elec & Electronics Engrs, 1962-1963; elec engr, Gen Elec Co, 1926-1966. **Memberships:** Inst Elec & Electronics Engrs (tech vpres, 1962). **Research Statement & Publications:** Development of and design procedures for electromagnetic devices in electronics circuits; voltage transients due to swithching. **Mailing Address:** 1565 Golf Course Dr, Rohnert Park, CA 94928.

LORD, HARRY CHESTER, III, PHYSICAL CHEMISTRY, ANALYTICAL CHEMISTRY. **Personal Data:** b Utica, NY, May 28, 1939; m 1989, Jessica; c 5. **Education:** Tufts Univ, BS, 1961; Univ Calif, San Diego, PhD (chem), 1967. **Honors & Awards:** Gold Medal, Am Inst Chemists, 1961. **Professional Experience:** Dir, Dosibi Environ Corp, 1989-1990; PRES, AIR INSTRUMENTS & MEASUREMENTS INC, 1988-; Chmn, Energy Technol & Control Ltd, 1986-1988; pres, Syconex Corp, 1980-1988; pres, Environ Data Corp, 1977-1981; vpres, Jet Propulsion Lab, 1969-1977; sr scientist, Jet Propulsion Lab, 1967-1969. **Memberships:** Am Chem Soc; Air Pollution Control Asn; Combustion Inst; Sigma Xi; Instrument Soc Am. **Research Statement & Publications:** Modification of combustion, improved control techniques; hardware to increase efficiency and to reduce pollutant emissions; development of state-of-the-art sensors to monitor environmental emissions of toxic and reactive gases. **Mailing Address:** Air Instruments & Measurements Inc, 13300 Brooks Dr St A, Baidwin Park, CA 91706. **Fax:** 626-338-2585. **E-Mail:** hlord@aimanalysis.com

LORD, JERE JOHNS, PHYSICS, HIGH ENERGY PHYSICS & COSMIC RAYS. **Personal Data:** b Portland, Ore, January 3, 1922; m 1947, c 3. **Education:** Reed Col, BA, 1943; Univ Chicago, MS, 1948, PhD (physics), 1950. **Professional Experience:** EMER PROF

PHYSICS, UNIV WASH, 1992-; prof, Univ Wash, 1962-1992; instr, Univ Wash, 1952-1962; res assoc physics, Univ Chicago, 1950-1952. **Memberships:** fel Am Phys Soc; Am Asn Phys Teachers; fel AAAS; Marine Technol Soc. **Research Statement & Publications:** Cosmic ray and high energy physics. **Mailing Address:** Dept Physics, Univ Wash, PO Box 351560, Seattle, WA 98195. **Fax:** 206-685-0635. **E-Mail:** lord@phys.washington.edu

LORD, PETER REEVES, TEXTILE ENGINEERING, TEXTILE TECHNOLOGY. **Personal Data:** b Ruckinge, Eng, February 10, 1923; m 1947, Mavis; c 3. **Education:** Battersea Polytech, Eng, BSc, 1950; Univ London, PhD (eng), 1966, DSc(eng), 1976. **Honors & Awards:** Harold DeWitt Smith Award, Am Soc Testing & Mat, 1979; Alexander von Humboldt US sr scientist award, 1980; Warner Medal Textile Inst 1991. **Professional Experience:** Pres, Raltex Inc, beginning 1990; ABEL C LINEBERGER PROF EMER TEXTILE, NC STATE UNIV, 1990-; Abel C Lineberger prof textiles, Raltex Inc, 1975-1990; from assoc prof to prof, Raltex Inc, 1969-1975; lectr textile technol, Univ Manchester, 1958-1969; sr test engr, Vickers Armstrongs Ltd, 1951-1958; sect leader eng, Vacuum Oil Co Ltd, 1947-1951; draughtsman, Fairey Aviation Co Ltd, 1946-1947; res asst heat transfer, Delaney-Gallay Ltd, Eng, 1945-1946. **Memberships:** Fel Brit Inst Mech Eng; fel Brit Textile Inst; Am Fiber Soc; Sigma Xi. **Research Statement & Publications:** Modern methods of yarn formation; open-end spinning; fabric forming systems; sliver and yarn monitoring systems; design of textile machinery; physics of fibrous assemblies. **Mailing Address:** 3116 Monticello Dr, Raleigh, NC 27612. **Fax:** 919-787-5720. **E-Mail:** sjlord@unity.ncsu.edu

LORD, SAMUEL SMITH, ANALYTICAL CHEMISTRY, POLYMER CHEMISTRY. **Personal Data:** b Rockland, Maine, April 10, 1927; m 1948, Evelyn; c Steven, Jonathan, Nathaniel, Victoria & William. **Education:** Tufts Col, BS, 1947; Mass Inst Technol, PhD (analytical chem), 1952. **Professional Experience:** RETIRED; managing dir, Maydown Works, Du Pont, Eng, 1986-1988; works dir, Maydown Works, Du Pont, Eng, 1984-1988; works mgr, Beaumont Works, 1975-1984; asst works dir, Maydown Works, Du Pont Co Ltd, 1971-1975; gen prod supt, Elastomer Chem Dept, 1970-1971; supt monomer area, Elastomer Chem Dept, 1967-1970; supt qual control, Elastomer Chem Dept, 1965-1967; div head, Elastomer Chem Dept, 1959-1965; res supvr, Elastomer Chem Dept, 1957-1959; res chemist, Org Chem Dept, 1952-1957; res chemist, Fabrics & Finishes Dept, E I du Pont de Nemours & Co Inc, 1947-1949. **Memberships:** emer mem AAAS; fel Am Chem Soc. **Research Statement & Publications:** Polarography; coulometry; infrared and ultraviolet spectrophotometry; urethane chemistry. **Mailing Address:** 1240 Nottingham Lane, Beaumont, TX 77706-4316.

LORD, WILLIAM B, POLICY ANALYSIS, INSTITUTIONAL ANALYSIS. **Personal Data:** b Omaha, Nebr, January 2, 1929; m 1951, c 3. **Education:** Univ Mich, BS, 1951, MF, 1958; Univ Wis, MS, 1959; Univ Mich, PhD (forestry), 1964. **Professional Experience:** PROF EMER AGR ECON, UNIV ARIZ, 1996-; prof agr econ, Univ Ariz, 1990-1996; dir, Water Resources Res Ctr, 1985-1990; vis prof econ, Univ Colo, 1981; & comt groundwater resources & coal mining, Task Force on Oil Shale & Tar Sands, Nat Res Coun, 1979-1981; vis sr scientist, Nat Ctr Atmospheric Res, 1979-1980; mem, Task Force on Oil Shale & Tar Sands, Nat Res Coun, 1978-1980; pres, Policy Sci Assocs, 1977-1985; tech asst expert, UN Develop Prog, 1976; res assoc, Inst Behav Sci, Univ Colo, 1974-1977; res Mex, Resources for Future, Inc, 1972-1974; dir, Ctr Res Policy Studies, 1967-1972; economist policy anal, Off Secy, US Dept Army, 1965-1967; asst prof res, dept agr econ, Univ Wis, 1959-1965; res forester, Lake States Forest Exp Sta US Forest Serv, 1954-1957. **Memberships:** Am Water Resources Asn; Am Agr Econ Asn; Asn Evolutionary Econ; Asn Environ & Resources Economists; Nat Asn Environ Profs. **Research Statement & Publications:** Natural resource policy and institutions; water conflict resolution; integrated water management. **Mailing Address:** Dept Agr Econ Univ Ariz, Econ Bldg 23, Tucson, AZ 85721.

LORD, WILLIAM JOHN, POMOLOGY. **Personal Data:** b Farmington, NH, November 3, 1921; m 1947, c 1. **Education:** Univ NH, BS, 1943, MS, 1953; Pa State Univ, PhD (hort), 1955. **Professional Experience:** RETIRED; exten prof pomol, Agr Exten Serv, Univ Mass, Amherst, 1955-1985. **Memberships:** Am Soc Hort Sci. **Research Statement & Publications:** Weed control; nutrition; growth regulators. **Mailing Address:** 238 Chancellor Gdns, E Longmeadow, MA 01028.

LORDI, JOHN A, AERONAUTICS. **Education:** Mass Inst Technol, BS, 1961, MS, 1961; State Univ NY, PhD (mech eng), 1968. **Professional Experience:** RES PROF, UNIV BUFFALO, as of 2006. **Memberships:** Sigma Xi. **Mailing Address:** Univ Buffalo, 17 Capen Hall, Buffalo, NY 14260-1660. **Fax:** 716-645-3875.

LORDI, NICHOLAS GEORGE, PHARMACEUTICS. **Personal Data:** b Orange, NJ, March 25, 1930; m 1961, Bertha Taylor; c Keith, Scott & Nicole. **Education:** Rutgers Univ, BSc, 1952 & MSc, 1953; Purdue Univ, PhD (pharmaceut chem), 1955. **Professional Experience:** PROF EMER PHARMACEUT, RUTGERS STATE UNIV NJ, NEW BRUNSWICK, as of 2003; DIR, PHARMACEUT COMPACTION RES, LAB & INFO CTR, SCH PHARMA, RUTGERS STATE UNIV NJ, as of 2003; asst dean, Rutgers State Univ NJ, 1981-1996; chmn dept, Rutgers State Univ NJ, 1977-1982; prof pharm, Rutgers State Univ NJ, beginning 1964; From asst prof to assoc prof, Rutgers State Univ NJ, 1957-1964. **Memberships:** Am Chem Soc; AAAS; fel Am Asn Pharmaceut Sci. **Research Statement & Publications:** Physical stability pharmaceutical systems; pharmaceutical technology; compaction thermal analysis. **Mailing Address:** Dept Pharmaceut, Rutgers State Univ NJ, New Brunswick, NJ 08855-0789. **Fax:** 732-445-5767. **E-Mail:** nlordi@rci.rutgers.edu

LORDS, JAMES LAFAYETTE, PHYSIOLOGY. **Personal Data:** b Salt Lake City, Utah, April 5, 1928; m 1955, Katherine; c Kevin & John. **Education:** Univ Utah, BS, 1950, MS, 1951, PhD (plant physiol), 1960. **Professional Experience:** PROF MOLECULAR & GENETIC BIOL, UNIV UTAH, 1975-; PROF BIOL, UNIV UTAH, 1975-; from asst prof to assoc prof, Univ Utah, 1962-1975; proj assoc plant path, Univ Wis, 1960-1962; instr biol, Univ Utah, 1958-1959; asst bot, Univ Utah, 1956-1958. **Memberships:** Am Physiol Soc. **Research Statement & Publications:** Microwave interactions with biological systems. **Mailing Address:** Dept Biol, Univ Utah, 200 S Univ St, Salt Lake City, UT 84112. **E-Mail:** lords@bioSci.utah.edu

LORE, JAMES A, AGRICULTURAL ENVIRONMENTAL ISSUES. **Education:** Univ Alta, BSc, 1954. **Professional Experience:** DIR, OLD COL FOUND, as of 2005; consult, Jim Lore & Assoc Ltd, beginning 1984. **Memberships:** Fel Agr Inst Can; Int Right Way Asn; fel Can Consult Agrologists Asn; Can Soc Animal Sci; Can Range Mgt; Can Soc Agr Econs & Farm Mgrs; Can Soc Agron. **Mailing Address:** Old Col Found, 4500 50th St, Olds, AB T4H 1R6, Can. **Fax:** 403-556-4754.

LORE, JOHN M, JR, otolaryngology, surgery; deceased, see previous edition for last biography

LORENCE, MATTHEW C, EXPERIMENTAL BIOLOGY. **Professional Experience:** PROD MGR MOLECULAR MICRO, APPL BIOSYST, as of 2002; ASSOC PROD LINE MGR, BIO-RAD LABS, 1990-. **Mailing Address:** Molecular Micro, Applsyst, 850 Lincoln Ctr, Foster City, CA 94404. **Fax:** 650-638-6333. **E-Mail:** lorencmc@appliedbiosystems.com

LORENS, STANLEY A, NEUROPHARMACOLOGY. **Personal Data:** b Galion, Ohio, July 19, 1936. **Education:** Univ Notre Dame, BA, 1965; Univ Chicago, PhD (biopsychol), 1968. **Professional Experience:** PROF PHARMACOL, LOYOLA UNIV MED CTR, 1984-; assoc prof, LoyolaUniv Med Ctr, 1977-1984; asst prof psychiat, IowaUniv, 1968-1972; fel psychopharmacol, Univ Ill, 1965-1968; first lectr pharmacol, Univ Bergen Norway. **Memberships:** Soc Neuroscience; Am Soc Pharmacol & Exp Therapeut. **Research Statement & Publications:** Neuropharmacology. **Mailing Address:** Dept Pharmacol, Loyola Univ, Rm 002, Bldg 54, Maywood, IL 60153-5589. **Fax:** 708-216-4118. **E-Mail:** slorens@lumc.edu

LORENSEN, LYMAN EDWARD, ORGANIC POLYMER CHEMISTRY. **Personal Data:** b Lincoln, Nebr, September 26, 1923; m 1950, c 3. **Education:** Univ Nebr, BS, 1947; Cornell Univ, PhD (chem), 1952. **Professional Experience:** RETIRED; consult, 1988-2000; mem staff, composites & polymer technol & actg technol leader, Lawrence Livermore Nat Lab, Univ Calif, 1964-1988; mem staff, Mfg Res Dept, Shell Oil Co, 1958-1960; chemist, Shell Develop Co, 1952-1958 & 1960-1964; asst org chem, Cornell Univ, 1950-1952; jr chemist, Bristol Labs, 1947-1948. **Memberships:** emer mem Am Chem Soc. **Research Statement & Publications:** High temperature polymers; polymers for geothermal applications; unsaturated glycols; possible precursors in biosynthesis of rubber; lubricating oil additives; silicone and epoxy polymers; filled polymers; foams; coatings. **Mailing Address:** 9 Broadview Terr, Orinda, CA 94563.

LORENTS, ALDEN C, DATABASE, COMPUTER AIDED SOFTWARE ENGINEERING. **Personal Data:** b Bagley, Minn, April 29, 1937; m 1960, c Heidi & Troy. **Education:** Concordia Col Minn, BSBA, 1960; Univ Minn, MBA, 1962, PhD (acct), 1971. **Professional Experience:** Sandia Labs, 1983 & Ariz Pub Serv, 1987-1989 & 1994-1995; internship, Lawrence Livermore Labs, 1981; consult, Ariz Guid Ctr, 1973-1983 & Univ Kuwait, 1983; PROF COMPUT INFO SYSTS, NORTHERN ARIZ UNIV, beginning 1971; asso dir, Minn Higher Educ Coord Comn, 1970-1971; dir comput, Bemidji State Univ, 1966-1971; programmer & analyst, Honeywell, 1960-1966. **Memberships:** Soc Info Mgt; Data Processing Mgt Asn; Decision Sci Inst. **Research Statement & Publications:** Software engineering; re-engineering; repository development; database development; computer aided software engineering. **Mailing Address:** Dept Compu Info Systs, Northern Ariz Univ, Flagstaff, AZ 86011. **Fax:** 928-523-7331. **E-Mail:** alden.lorents@nau.edu

LORENTS, DONALD C, LASER PHYSICS, ATOMIC CLUSTER PHYSICS. **Personal Data:** b Minn, March 26, 1929; m 1952, Doris; c Christine & Nancy. **Education:** Concordia Col, Moorhead, Minn, BA, 1951; Univ Nebr, MA, 1954, PhD (physics), 1958. **Professional Experience:** RETIRED; sci dir, Molecular Physics Lab, Stanford Res Inst Int, 1990-1994; dir, Chem Physics Lab, Stanford Res Inst Int, 1984-1990; dir, Molecular Physics Lab, Stanford Res Inst Int, 1980-1984; assoc dir, Atomic & Molecular Collisions Sect, Stanford Res Inst Int, 1975-1979; sr physicist, Atomic & Molecular Collisions Sect, Stanford Res Inst Int, 1970-1975; physicist, Atomic & Molecular Collisions Sect, Stanford Res Inst Int, 1969-1970; vis res physicist, Inst Physics, Aarhus Univ, 1968-1969, 1970, 1987; head, Atomic & Molecular Collisions Sect, Stanford Res Inst Int, 1967-1968; chmn, Dept Molecular Physics, Stanford Res Inst Int, 1963-1967; physicist, Stanford Res Inst Int, 1959-1963; res physicist, Westinghouse Res Labs, 1958-1959. **Memberships:** AAAS; fel Am Phys Soc. **Research Statement & Publications:** Atomic and molecular collision processes with emphasis on scattering, charge transfer and excitation in ion-atom or ion-molecule collisions; kinetic processes in electronically excited dense gases; molecular spectroscopy; cluster physics; fullerenes. **Mailing Address:** Stanford Res Inst Int, 333 Ravenswood, Menlo Park, CA 94025.

LORENTZ, GEORGE G, MATHEMATICAL ANALYSIS. **Personal Data:** b St Petersburg, Russia, February 25, 1910; m 1942, c 5. **Education:** Univ Leningrad, Cand, 1935; Univ Tuebingen, Dr rer nat (math), 1944. **Honorary Degrees:** Dr, Univ Tuebingen. **Honors & Awards:** Humboldt Prize, A von Humboldt Stiftung, 1973. **Professional Experience:** PROF EMER MATH, UNIV TEX AUSTIN, 1980-; prof, Univ Tex, Austin, 1969-1980; prof, Syracuse Univ, 1958-1969; prof, Wayne State Univ, 1953-1958; from asst to asst prof, Univ Toronto, 1949-1953; prof, Univ Tubingen, 1948-1949; lectr math, Univ Leningrad, 1936-1942 & Univ Frankfurt, 1946-1948; res grants, NSF & Off Sci Res. **Memberships:** Am Math Soc; Math Asn Am; Ger Math Soc. **Research Statement & Publications:** Mathematical analysis, especially approximations and expansions; summability; Birkhoff interpolation; functional analysis, especially Banach function spaces; interpolation theorems for operators; published several monographs on Approximation and Interpolation. **Mailing Address:** Dept Math, Univ Tex, One Univ Sta C1200, Austin, TX 78712-0257. **Fax:** 512-471-9038. **E-Mail:** combs@math.utex.edu

LORENTZEN, KEITH EDEN, PHYSICAL ORGANIC CHEMISTRY. **Personal Data:** b Heber City, Utah, April 13, 1921; m 1980, Evelyn; c Rebecca A, Frank M, Heidi J, Wendy S, John K & Mitzi K. **Education:** Univ Utah, BA, 1942, MS, 1947; Pa State Univ, PhD (chem), 1951. **Professional Experience:** ASSOC PROF EMER CHEM, DEPT CHEM, as of 2004; chmn, Dept Physics & Astron, 1977-1988; from asst chmn to chmn dept, Ind Univ NW, 1966-1988; from asst prof to assoc prof chem, Ind Univ NW, 1963-1988; chemist, Stand Oil Co, Ind, 1951-1962. **Memberships:** Am Chem Soc; fel Am Inst Chemists; Am Asn Univ Professors. **Research Statement & Publications:** Conductivity measurements; chemistry of lubricating oils and additives; organic analytical chemistry; chromatography; polarography; Friedel-Crafts methylation of xylenes; aromatic deuteration of methylbenzenes. **Mailing Address:** 8831 Harrison Ave Apt 101, Munster, IN 46321.

LORENZ, CARL EDWARD, ORGANIC CHEMISTRY. **Personal Data:** b New York, NY, August 22, 1933; m 1956, Mathilda M Lorenz; c Darryl Paul, Karin Dale Clark, Erin Dawn Irwin. **Education:** NY Univ, BA, 1953, PhD (chem), 1957. **Honors & Awards:** Award, Am Inst Chem, 1953. **Professional Experience:** RETIRED; vpres res & develop, Du Pont Chemicals, 1990-1993; dir, Chemicals & Pigments Dept, 1985-1990; dir, Ethylene Polymers Div, 1983-1985; dir res & develop, Polymer Prod Dept, 1981-1983; dir Res Div, Cent Res & Develop, 1979-1981; dir, Feedstocks Div, 1978-1979; prod mgr, Int Dept, 1976-1978; asst dir, Int Dept, 1974-1976; res mgr, Wilmington, 1972-1974; res lab mgr, Sabine River Works, 1970-1972; lab supt, Plastics Dept, Exp Sta, E I Du Pont de Nemours & Co, Inc, 1969-1970; from supvr to sr supvr, Plastics Dept, Exp Sta, E I Du Pont de Nemours & Co, Inc, 1968-1969; from chemist to sr res chemist, Plastics Dept, Exp Sta, E I Du Pont de Nemours & Co, Inc, 1957-1968; Asst chem, NY Univ, 1953-1957. **Memberships:** Am Chem Soc; Am Inst Chem; The Chem Soc; NY Acad Sci. **Research Statement & Publications:** Fluorocarbon monomer syntheses and polymerizations; high pressure hydrocarbon syntheses; heterogeneous catalysis; chemistry of anionic and radical polymerizations. **Mailing Address:** 103 Bellant Circle, Wilmington, DE 19807-2219. **E-Mail:** celorenz@aol.com

LORENZ, DONALD H, ORGANIC CHEMISTRY, POLYMER CHEMISTRY. **Personal Data:** b Brooklyn, NY, October 18, 1936; m 1962, Patricia; c Peter M & Jeanne C. **Education:** Polytech Inst Brooklyn, BS, 1958, PhD (org chem), 1963. **Professional Experience:** PRES, RIDGE SCI ENTPRISES INC, 1991-; exec vpres, Hydromer Inc, 1989-1991; dir res & develop, Hydromer Inc, 1980-1989; mgr vinyl polymer res, GAF Corp, 1974-1980; group leader polymer synthesis, GAF Corp, 1970-1974; explor polymer chemist, Gen Aniline & Film Co, 1965-1970; sr polymer chemist, Tex-US Chem Co, 1963-1965; asst scientist chem eng res div, NY Univ, 1962-1963; organometallics, Polytech Inst Brooklyn, 1959-1962; Asst org chem, Polytech Inst Brooklyn, 1958-1959. **Memberships:** Am Chem Soc; Asn Consult Chemists & Chem Engrs. **Research Statement & Publications:** Organometallic chemistry; elastomers; resins; adhesives; polymers of vinyl ethers and vinyl amides; polyurethanes; fire retardants; ultraviolet and electron beam curable resins; coatings for medical devices; drug delivery systems; wound dressings; hydrogels; conductive adhesives. **Mailing Address:** 12 Radel Pl, Basking Ridge, NJ 07920. **Fax:** 908-534-9034.

LORENZ, EDWARD NORTON, METEOROLOGY. **Personal Data:** b West Hartford, Conn, May 23, 1917; m 1948, Jane; c 3. **Education:** Dartmouth Col, AB, 1938; Harvard Univ, AM, 1940; Mass Inst Technol, SM, 1943, ScD, 1948. **Honorary Degrees:** DSc, McGill Univ, 1983, Univ Ariz, 1989, Rutgers Univ, 1990, Dartmouth Col, 1992. **Honors & Awards:** Clarence Leroy Meisinger Award, Am Meteorol Soc, 1963, Carl Gustaf Rossby Res Med, 1969; Symons Mem Gold Medal, Royal Meteorol Soc, 1973; Holger & Anna-Greta Crafoord Prize, Royal Swed Acad Sci, 1983; Elliott Creson Medal, Franklin Inst, 1989; Roger Revelle Medal, Am Geophys Union, 1992. **Professional Experience:** PROF EMER, DEPT EARTH, ATMOSPHERIC & PLANETARY SCI, MASS INST TECHNOL, 1987-; vis sr scientist, Univ Oslo, 1982; norweg Meteorol Inst, 1962 & Europ Ctr Medium Range Weather Forecasts, 1981-1982; head, Dept Meteorol & Phys Oceanog, 1977-1981; sr assoc, Nat Ctr Atmospheric Res, 1973-1974; from asst prof to prof, Mass Inst Technol, 1955-1987; vis assoc prof, Univ Calif, Los Angeles, 1954-1955; vis scientist, Lowell Observ, 1951; res staff, Mass Inst Technol, 1948-1954; mem staff, Mass Inst Technol, 1948-1954; asst meteorol, Mass Inst Technol, 1946-1948. **Memberships:** Fel Nat Acad Sci; fel Am Acad Arts & Sci; hon mem Am Meteorol Soc; hon mem Royal Meteorol Soc; hon fel Indian Acad Sci; Norweg Acad Sci & Lett; foreign mem USSR Acad Sci; foreign mem Royal Soc London. **Research Statement & Publications:** General circulation of the atmosphere; dynamical and statistical weather prediction; chaotic dynamical systems; author of numerous publications. **Mailing Address:** Mass Inst Technol, Dept Earth Atmospheric & Planetary Sci, 77 Mass Ave, Cambridge, MA 02139-4307. **Fax:** 617-253-8298. **E-Mail:** jmsloman@mit.edu

LORENZ, JOHN DOUGLAS, MANUFACTURING SYSTEMS DESIGN, ASSEMBLY SYSTEMS DESIGN. **Personal Data:** b Talmage, Nebr, July 2, 1942; m 1967, Alice Heutzen; c Christian. **Education:** Univ Nebr, Lincoln, BS, 1965, MS, 1967, PhD (indust eng), 1973. **Professional Experience:** Dir, Jr Eng Tech Soc, 1991-; Richard L Terrell prof acad leadership, GMI Eng & Mgt Inst, 1990-; VPRES ACAD AFFAIRS & PROVOST, GMI ENG & MGT INST, 1988-; asst dean res & grad studies, GMI Eng & Mgt Inst, 1987-1988; dept head indust eng, GMI Eng & Mgt Inst, 1984-1987; PROF INDUST ENG, GMI ENG & MGT INST, 1978-; From asst prof to assoc prof, GMI Eng & Mgt Inst, 1973-1978. **Memberships:** Soc Mfg Engrs; Soc Automotive Engrs; Nat Soc Prof Engrs; Am Soc Eng Educr. **Research Statement & Publications:** Manufacturing systems design; assembly systems design; computer assisted assembly line balancing. **Mailing Address:** GMI Eng & Mgt Inst, Provost's Off, 1700 W Third Ave, Flint, MI 48504. **Fax:** 810-762-7885. **E-Mail:** jlorenz@nova.gmi.edu

LORENZ, KLAUS J, CEREAL CHEMISTRY. **Personal Data:** b Berlin, Ger, June 22, 1936; American citizen; m 1960, c 3. **Education:** Northwestern Univ, Ill, PhB, 1968; Kans State Univ, MS, 1969, PhD (food sci), 1970. **Professional Experience:** PROF EMER FOOD SCI & NUTRIT, COLO STATE UNIV, as of 2005; prof food sci & nutrit, Colo State Univ, beginning 1978; assoc prof, Colo State Univ, 1974-1978; asst prof, Colo State Univ, 1970-1974; food technologist, Nat Dairy Prod Corp, 1965-1968; baking technologist, Am Inst Baking, 1961-1965. **Memberships:** Am Asn Cereal Chem; Inst Food Technologists; Switz Soc Food Sci & Technol. **Research Statement & Publications:** Cereal chemistry and technology; carbohydrate chemistry; baking science. **Mailing Address:** Dept Food Sci & Human Nutrit, Colo State Univ, Ft Collins, CO 80523-1571. **Fax:** 970-491-3875.

LORENZ, PATRICIA ANN, TECHNICAL & PATENT INFORMATION MANAGEMENT ANALYTICAL CHEMISTRY. **Personal Data:** b New York, NY, January 31, 1938; m 1962, Donald; c Peter & Jeanne. **Education:** Marymount Manhattan Col, BS, 1959; Polytech Inst Brooklyn, PhD (anal chem), 1965. **Honors & Awards:** NJ Tribute Women Indust, Twin Award, 1997. **Professional Experience:** RES ASSOC & TEAM LEADER, INFO RES & ANAL, EXXON MOBIL RES & ENG CO, as of 2005; SECT HEAD, INFO RES & ANAL, EXXON MOBIL RES & ENG CO, 2000-; res assoc corp res, Info Res & Analysis, Exxon Res & Eng Co, 1996-2000; sect head, info res analysis, 1992-1996; res assoc, Comput & Info Support Div, 1987-1992; sect head, Comput & Info Support Div, 1983-1987; info chemist, Exxon Res & Eng Co, 1965-1967; group head, Anal & Info Div, 1978-1983; consult info sci, 1967-1977. **Memberships:** Am Chem Soc; Am Petrol Inst; Patent Info Users Group. **Research Statement & Publications:** Mechanism of acid base reactions in benzene. **Mailing Address:** Exxon Mobil Res & Eng Co, 1545 Rte 22 East, Annandale, NJ 08801. **Fax:** 732-730-3230. **E-Mail:** patricia.a.lorenz@exxonmobil.com

LORENZ, PHILIP BOALT, PHYSICAL CHEMISTRY, PETROLEUM PRODUCTION. **Personal Data:** b Dayton, Ohio, August 14, 1920; m 1946, Irene; c Douglas, Eugene & David. **Education:** Swarthmore Col, AB, 1941; Harvard Univ, MA, 1946, PhD (chem), 1949. **Professional Experience:** RETIRED; consult, 1985-1993; sci adv, Nat Inst Petrol & Energy Res, 1983-1985; res chemist, Bartlesville Energy Technol Ctr, US Dept Energy, 1975-1983; res chemist, Petrol Prod & Environ Res, 1971-1975; phys chemist surface chem, Petrol Res Ctr, US Bur Mines, 1949-1971; asst phys chem, SAM Labs, Columbia Univ, 1944-1945; asst biol, Princeton Univ, 1942-1943. **Memberships:** Am Chem Soc; Soc Petrol Engrs. **Research Statement & Publications:** Surface chemistry; electrochemistry; petroleum engineering. **Mailing Address:** 1541 Keeler Ave, Bartlesville, OK 74003-5723.

LORENZ, ROMAN R, ORGANIC CHEMISTRY, MEDICINAL CHEMISTRY. **Personal Data:** b Breslau, Ger, July 15, 1935; American citizen; m 1960, Dana Rebmann; c Peter, Robert & Stephen. **Education:** Rensselaer Polytech Inst, BS, 1958; Univ Mich, MS, 1960, PhD (med chem), 1962. **Professional Experience:** EXEC DIR CHEM DEVELOP, STERLING RES GROUP, 1990-; DIR, NIKOMET, 1990-; dir chem develop, Sterling-Winthrop Res Inst, 1977-1990; sr res assoc & sect head, Sterling-Winthrop Res Inst, 1974-1976; sr res chemist & sect head, Sterling-Winthrop Res Inst, 1969-1974; Res org chemist, Sterling-Winthrop Res Inst, 1962-1969. **Memberships:** Am Chem Soc. **Research Statement & Publications:** Synthesis of organic and medicinal compounds. **Mailing Address:** 941 Evergreen Lane, Chester Springs, PA 19425.

LORENZEN, JANICE R, ENDOCRINOLOGY. **Personal Data:** b Chicago, Ill, May 29, 1950. **Education:** Valparaiso Univ, BS, 1972; Albany Med Col, PhD (physiol), 1976; Univ Ill, MD, 1986. **Professional Experience:** ENDOCRINOLOGIST, DETAR HEALTH CARE SYST, as of 2001; endocrinologist, Endocrine Clin Southeast Tex, beginning 1997; physician, Rockford Clin, Col Med, Univ Ill, 1986-1997; Asst prof, Dept Biol Sci, Western Mich Univ, 1981-1982. **Memberships:** Endocrine Soc; Am Col Physicians. **Mailing Address:** DeTar Health Care Syst, 2700 Citizens Plaza Suite 306, Victoria, TX 77901. **Fax:** 361-574-1789.

LORENZEN, JERRY ALAN, QUALITY IMPROVEMENT, APPLIED STATISTICS. **Personal Data:** b Grand Island, Nebr, October 3, 1944; m 1967, Barbara; c Jeffrey & Marc. **Education:** Midland Lutheran Col, BS, 1966; Okla State Univ, PhD (chem), 1970. **Professional Experience:** RETIRED; dir qual, Fair-Rite Prod Corp, beginning 1996; pres, Lorenzen Consult, 1992-1996; sr engr, IBM Corp, 1970-1992; instr chem, Okla State Univ, 1969-1970. **Memberships:** Am Chem Soc; Am Soc Qual Control; Am Productivity & Inventory Control Soc; Am Statist Asn. **Research Statement & Publications:** Environmental chemistry; quality improvement; engineering statistics; design of experiments. **Mailing Address:** 52 Spruce Valley Rd, Stone Ridge, NY 12484-9802.

LORENZETTI, OLE JOHN, PHARMACOLOGY, BIOCHEMISTRY. **Personal Data:** b Chicago, Ill, October 25, 1936; m 1961, Lorna; c Elizabeth A & Maria A & Darion. **Education:** Univ Ill, Chicago, BS, 1958; Ohio State Univ, MS, 1963, PhD (pharmacol & toxicol), 1965; Mass Inst Technol, MBA, 1989. **Professional Experience:** VPRES, THERAPEUT RES, ALCON LABS, as of 2005; pres Therapeut Res, Alcon Labs, Ft Worth, 1993-; SR DIR THERAPEUT RES/LICENSING, ALCON LABS, FT WORTH, 1992-; vis lectr, Univ Tex Med Schs, 1990-1996; sr dir surg, Alcon Labs, 1983-1992; dir ophthal, Alcon Labs, 1980-1983; assoc dir dermatol, Alcon Labs, 1975-1980; clin prof dermatol, Univ Tex Health Sci Ctr, Dallas, 1974-1980; vis lectr, therapeutic & drug res, Univ Ill, 1973-1980; adj prof, Tex Christian Univ, 1972-1982; mgr, Res & Develop Div, preclin sci, Alcon Labs, 1972-1975; assoc prof pharmacol, Univ Tex Health Sci Ctr, Dallas, 1970-1990; toxicologist consult, Tarrant County Tex, 1970-1973; scientist res & develop, Alcon Labs, Ft Worth, 1969-1972; toxicologist consult, South Bend, Ind, municipality, 1967-1969; sr scientist, Dome Labs Div, Miles Labs, 1967-1969; Kaufman-Lattimer lectr, Ohio State Univ, 1967, 1970, 1973, 1978; scientist, Miles Lab, Elkhardt, Ind, 1965-1967; JJ Able lectr pharmacol, Ohio N Univ, 1965, 1969; res fel, Ohio StateUniv, Columbus, 1964-1965; asst instr pharmacol, Ohio State Univ, 1959-1962; instr pharm, Univ Ill, Chicago, 1958-1959; asst chief pharmacist, W Suburban Hosp, 1958. **Memberships:** AAAS; Am Chem Soc; Soc Cosmetic Chem; Am Acad Clin Toxicol; Am Soc Pharmacol & Except Therapeut; Am Acad Ophthal; Am Intraocular Implant Soc; Am Pharmacol Asn; NY Acad Sci; Soc Investigative Dermatol; Am Col Toxicol; Inflamation Res Asn; Am Soc Clin Pharmacol; Asn Res & Vision & Opthal; Drug Info Asn; Sigma Xi. **Research Statement & Publications:** Pharmacodynamics; evaluations of analgesic, anti-inflammatory agents and antiglaucoma agents; development of drug screening programs; autonomic and biochemical pharmacology; topical pharmacology and toxicology of eye and skin; ophthalmology; ophthalmic surgical devices; toxicology; immunology; drug metabolism; pharmacokinetics. **Mailing Address:** Alcon Labs Inc, P O Box 6600 6201 S Freeway, Ft Worth, TX 76134-2099. **Fax:** 817-551-4584. **E-Mail:** ole.lorenzetti@alconlabs.com

LORENZO, ANTONIO V, NEUROPHARMACOLOGY, NEUROCHEMISTRY. **Personal Data:** b Vigo, Spain, July 23, 1928; American citizen; m 1958, c 2. **Education:** Univ Chicago, BA, 1956, BS, 1958, PhD (pharmacol), 1966. **Professional Experience:** Assoc prof pharmacol, Harvard Med Sch, beginning 1971; Nat Inst Neurol Dis & Stroke proj grant, 1971-1973; NIH career develop award, Harvard Med Sch, 1970-1975; asst prof, Harvard Med Sch, 1969-1971; DIR NEUROSURG, CHILDREN'S HOSP MED CTR, 1968-; instr pharmacol, Children's Hosp Med Ctr, 1966-1968; Epilepsy Found Am fel, Children's Hosp Med Ctr, 1965 & dir neurol res, 1969-1978; from asst to assoc neurol, Children's Hosp Med Ctr, 1964-1968. **Memberships:** AAAS; Am Soc Pharmacol & Exp Therapeut; NY Acad Sci; Am Soc Neurochemistry; Am Acad Neurol. **Research Statement & Publications:** Pathophysiology of the blood, role of brain barrier, putative transmitter seizures; cerebrospinal fluid transport phenomena; cerebrospinal fluid dynamics. **Mailing Address:** Dept Neurosurg, Children's Hosp Med Ctr, 300 Longwood Ave, Boston, MA 02115-5737.

LORENZO, MICHAEL, ENGINEERING. **Personal Data:** b Newton, NJ, 1920; m Anastasia; c 5. **Education:** Pa State Univ, BS, 1947, George Wash Univ, MEA, 1956. **Professional Experience:** FOUNDER & PRES, TECH PROTECTION ENG CO, 1982-; dep under-secy def, Wash, 1981-1982; dir environ qual control, Westinghouse Mgt Serv Inc, 1970-1973; mgr air resources, Westinghouse Mgt Serv Inc, 1966-1970; staff, Westinghouse Elec Corp, 1965-1981; Aerospace engr, Dept Defense, 1952-1965; field instrumentation engr, Fischer & Porter Co, Pa, 1947-1952. **Research Statement & Publications:** Patented stall surge sonic sensors; contributed articles to professional journals. **Mailing Address:** First Lady Realty Corp, 3126 Shadeland Dr, Falls Church, VA 22044-1726.

LORETZ, CHRISTOPHER ALAN, ENDOCRINOLOGY. **Personal Data:** b Santa Monica, Calif, April 28, 1951. **Education:** Univ Wash, BS, 1972; Univ Calif, Los Angeles, MA, 1974, PhD (comp physiol), 1978. **Professional Experience:** Dir, Nat Sci Found Tokyo Regional Off, 2002-2005; prog officer, Nat Sci Found, 1998-2000; vis res, Ocean Res Inst, Univ Tokyo, 1995-2002, 2005; ASSOC PROF, DEPT BIOL SCI, STATE UNIV NY BUFFALO, 1987-; fac mem, Aquavet Prog, Marine Biol Lab, Woods Hole, 1983-2001; asst prof, Dept Biol Sci, State Univ NY Buffalo, 1981-1987; postdoctoral fel, NIH, 1978-1981. **Memberships:** Am physiol soc. **Research Statement & Publications:** Osmoregulation in aquatic vertebrates; hormonal control of epithelial ion transport. **Mailing Address:** Dept Biol Sci, Univ Buffalo State Univ NY, 109 Cooke Hall Box 601300, Buffalo, NY 14260-1300. **Fax:** 716-645-2975. **E-Mail:** loretz@buffalo.edu

LORETZ, THOMAS J, FIBEROPTIC IMAGING & COMMUNICATION, COMPUTER AIDED MANUFACTURING. **Personal Data:** b Oceanside, NY, March 19, 1951; m 1983, c 2. **Education:** State Univ NY, BS, 1973, MS, 1978. **Professional Experience:** PRES, COMPUT ENG SERV, 1993-; secy bd, Bd Dirs, Charlton Credit Union, Mass, 1990-; consult, NIH Spec Comt Fiberoptics Med, 1986-1987; prin investr, NASA, SBIR Progs Advan Space Telescopy, 1985-; dir res & develop electro-optic glasses, Detector Technol, Brookfield, Mass, 1985-1993; sr scientist fiberoptic med develop, Johnson & Johnson, Southbridge, Mass, 1982-1985; dir res & develop mat & electro-optics, Galileo Electro-Optics, Sturbridge Mass, 1978-1982; consult & inventor, Buffalo Med Specialties, Fla, 1976-1990; proj engr glass res & develop, Schott Optical Glass, Duryea, Pa, 1974-1978. **Memberships:** Am Ceramic Soc; Nat Inst Ceramic Engrs; Soc Photog Instrumentation

Engrs. **Research Statement & Publications:** solid state, electron multiplication; glasses and geometries to enhance lifetime and characteristics of continuous dynode single channel and microchannel plate devices. **Mailing Address:** 33 Oak Ridge Dr, Charlton, MA 01507.

LORIA, EDWARD ALBERT, METALLURGY & PHYSICAL METALLURGICAL ENGINEERING. **Personal Data:** b Pittsburgh, Pa, April 29, 1917; m 1954, Helen Kerdys; c Elene, Diane & Corinne (Brody). **Education:** Carnegie Inst Technol, BS, 1944, MS, 1946. **Honors & Awards:** Charles H Herty Award, Am Inst Mining & Metall Engrs, 1967; Edgar C Bain Award, Am Soc Metals, 1982, Andrew Carnegie Lectr, 1984, William Hunt Eisenman Award, 1991. **Professional Experience:** RETIRED; consult, Niobium Prod Co, Subsid CBMM, Pittsburgh, Pa, 1984-1992; consult, Universal-Cyclops Specialty Steel Div, Cyclops Corp, Pittsburgh, Pa, 1984-1986; Subcomt Roll Res, Asn Iron & Steel Engrs-RMI, 1975-1977 & Comt Gen Res, Am Iron & Steel Inst, 1981-1984; div prod metallurgist, Universal-Cyclops Specialty Steel Div, Cyclops Corp, Pittsburgh, Pa, 1977-1984; tech dir, Roll Mfrs Inst, Pittsburgh, Pa, 1975-1977; Mem, Advan Res Medal Comt, Am Soc Metals, 1975-1977; supvr mat & processes, Res & Develop Eng Div, Nat Steel Corp, Weirton, WVa, 1964-1975; supv res metallurgist, Reno Metall Res Ctr, US Dept Interior, Bur Mines, 1963-1964; mgr alloy & stainless steels & superalloys develop, Climax Molybdenum Co, Div Am Metal Climax, Inc, NY, 1959-1963; prod metall engr titanium & superalloys, Cent Metall Dept, Crucible Steel Co Am, Pittsburgh, Pa, 1957-1959; staff metall engr alloy & stainless steels, Cent Metall Dept, Crucible Steel Co Am, Pittsburgh, Pa, 1953-1959; sr engr metall, Res & Eng Ctr, Carborundum Co, Niagara Falls, NY, 1950-1952; sr fel, Mellon Inst Indust Res, Pittsburgh, Pa, 1948-1950; fel, Mellon Inst Indust Res, Pittsburgh, Pa, 1946-1948; Asst metallurgist, Res Lab, Carnegie-Ill Steel Div, US Steel Corp, Pittsburgh, Pa, 1944-1946. **Memberships:** Minerals, Metals & Mat Soc; fel Am Soc Metals. **Research Statement & Publications:** Practical application of metallurgy for an unusually wide range of metals and alloys and transferred significant research results into commercial practice; author of over 150 publications. **Mailing Address:** 1828 Taper Dr, Pittsburgh, PA 15241.

LORIA, ROGER MOSHE, VIROLOGY, IMMUNOLOGY. **Personal Data:** b Antwerp, Belg, April 19, 1940; American citizen; m 1978, c 3. **Education:** Bar-Ilan Univ, Israel, BS, 1965; State Univ NY, Buffalo, MS, 1968; Boston Univ, PhD (microvirol), 1972. **Professional Experience:** PROF MICROBIOL & IMMUNOL, VA COMMAN WEALTH UNIV, 1991-; pres, Va Commonwealth Chap, Am Asn Univ Prof, 1990; vpres, Va Commonwealth Chap, Am Asn Univ Prof, 1989; adv, Consol Labs Commonwealth Va, 1982-1986; asst prof acad path, Sch Med, Harvard Univ, 1980-1982; instr pediat, Childrens Hosp, Boston, Mass, 1980-1981; young investr develop award, Am Diabetes Asn, 1975-1977; NIH res grants, Heart & Lung Div, 1975; from asst prof to assoc prof, Med Col Va, 1974-1991; res assoc, Sch Med, Boston Univ, 1974; NIH res grants, Arthritis & Metab Dis, 1974, 1978, 1979; Mass Heart Asn fel, 1972-1974; instr microbiol, Sch Med, Boston Univ, 1972-1974; asst prof biochem, Mass Col Optom, 1969-1970; asst virol, Sch Med, Boston Univ, 1968-1972. **Memberships:** Am Soc Microbiol; AAAS; Am Fedn Clin Res; Reticuloendothelial Syst Soc; Am Diabetes Asn; Am Soc Virol; Am Asn Univ Prof; Int Soc Anti-viral Res; Am Inst Nutrit; Am Soc Clin Nutrit; fel Am Acad Biol. **Research Statement & Publications:** Investigation on the role of group B coxsackieviruses in diabetes, atherosclerosis and cardiovascular disease in experimental animal models; general aspects of host-virus interaction; viral infection by the oral route; nutritional hypercholesteremia; effects on host resistance; rapid viral diagnosis; immune-up regulations; publication of 51 manuscripts and 64 abstracts, 2 US patents; pathogenic and immunological responses following virus infections; hormonal regulation of immune response to protect against infections, lethal infection by viruses or bacteria; viruses in diabetes; nutrition and lipids in infection. **Mailing Address:** Dept Microbiol & Immunol, Va Commonwealth Univ, PO Box 980678 1101 E Marshall St 7-068 Sanger Hall, Richmond, VA 23298-0678. **Fax:** 804-828-9946. **E-Mail:** loria@vcu.edu

LORIAUX, D LYNN, GROWTH & DEVELOPMENT. **Personal Data:** b Bartlesville, Okla, April 29, 1940; m 1986, c 4. **Education:** Baylor Med Sch, MD, 1967, PhD (biochem), 1968; Colo State Univ, BS, 1962. **Professional Experience:** CHMN, DEP MED, ORE HEALTH SCI UNIV, 1994-; HEAD, DIV ENDOCRINOL, DIABETES & CLIN NUTRIT, ORE HEALTH SCI UNIV, 1990-; ED-CHIEF, ENDOCRINOL, 1990-; clin dir, Nat Inst Child Health & Human Develop, NIH, 1981-1990; chief, develop endocrinol bd, 1980-1990; actg clin dir, Nat Inst Child Health & Human Develop, NIH, 1977-1981; head, endocrinol serv, Nat Inst Child Health & Human Develop, NIH, 1974-1980; actg head, endocrinol serv, Nat Inst Child Health & Human Develop, NIH, 1973-1974; USPHS fel, 1967-1968. **Memberships:** The Endocrine Soc. **Research Statement & Publications:** The endocrinology of growth and development. **Mailing Address:** Dep Med, Ore Health Sci Univ, 3181 S W Sam Jackson Park Rd, Portland, OR 97239-3098. **Fax:** 503-494-4348. **E-Mail:** loriauxl@ohsu.edu

LORIG, THOMAS W, MATHEMATICS. **Education:** Ariz State Univ, PhD, 1973. **Professional Experience:** ASSOC FAC, ARIZ STATE UNIV, as of 2006. **Mailing Address:** Ariz State Univ, 1417 E Colt Rd, Tempe, AZ 85284-2456. **Fax:** 480-965-5277. **E-Mail:** Thomas.Lorig@asu.edu

LORIMER, GEORGE HUNTLY, CARBON METABOLISM, ENZYMOLOGY. **Personal Data:** b Eng, October 14, 1942; m 1970, c 2. **Education:** Univ St Andrews, BSc, Scotland, 1965; Univ Ill, MS, 1968; Mich State Univ, PhD (biochem), 1972. **Honors & Awards:** Alexander von Humboldt Res Prize, 1997. **Professional Experience:** DISTINGUSHIED PROF CHEM & BIOCHEM, UNIV MD, as of 2002; res leader, cent res & develop dept, Ei Du Pont Del Nemours & Co, beginning 1978. **Memberships:** Nat Acad Sci; Am Soc Biol Chemists; Royal Soc. **Research Statement & Publications:** Identifying natural substrates for chaperonins using a sequence-based approach Annealing function of GroEL: structural and bioinformatic analysis Chaperonin-mediated protein folding. **Mailing Address:** Dept Chem & Biochem, Univ MD, 2121-Biomolecular Sci Bldg, College Park, MD 20742-2021. **Fax:** 301-314-9121. **E-Mail:** glorimer@umd.edu

LORIMER, JOHN WILLIAM, PHYSICAL CHEMISTRY. **Personal Data:** b Oshawa, Ont, April 16, 1929; m 1954, Shirley; c Charles CJ (deceased), Ian AJ & Nancy E. **Education:** Univ Toronto, BA, 1951, MA, 1952, PhD (phys chem), 1954. **Professional Experience:** Mem bur, Comn V-8, Int Union Pure & Appl Chem, 1994-; PROF EMER PHYS CHEM, UNIV WESTERN ONT, 1994-; chmn, Comn V-8, Int Union Pure & Appl Chem, 1987-1991; Murdoch Univ, Perth, Australia, 1983; Glasgow Univ, 1983-1984; mem, Comn V-8, Int Union Pure & Appl Chem, 1979-; vis prof, Univ Southampton, 1970-1971; from asst prof to prof, Univ Western Ont, 1961-1994; assoc res officer, Atlantic Regional Lab, Nat Res Coun Can, 1961; asst res officer, Atlantic Regional Lab, Nat Res Coun Can, 1956-1961; asst phys chem, Univ Leiden, Netherlands, 1954-1956. **Memberships:** Fel Chem Inst Can; Electrochem Soc. **Research Statement & Publications:** Thermodynamics of liquids; transport in membranes; irreversible thermodynamics; electrochemistry. **Mailing Address:** Dept Chem, Univ Western Ont, London, ON N6A 5B7, Can. **E-Mail:** lorimer@julian.uwo.ca

LORIMER, NANCY L, INSECT GENETICS. **Personal Data:** b Mishawaka, Ind, February 8, 1947; m 1972, c 3. **Education:** Ind Univ, AB, 1969; Univ Notre Dame, PhD (biol), 1975. **Professional Experience:** RETIRED; asst dir, N Cent Res Sta, USDA, ending 2003; prog coordr, Eastern Forest Hills, 2002-; staff entom, USDA FPM, 1992-; assoc ed, Am Midland Nat, 1980-; adj asst prof, Dept Entom, Fish Wildlife, Univ Minn, 1979-1992; res entomologist, N Cent Forest Exp Sta, Forest Serv, USDA, 1975-; fel genetic control, Int Centre Insect Ecol & Physiol, 1974-1975; consult, WHO, 1973. **Memberships:** Entom Soc Am; Asn Women Sci; AAAS; Genetics Soc Am; Sigma Xi. **Research Statement & Publications:** Assessment of genetic variation in forest insect populations and how these variations interact with other factors to influence population dynamics. **Mailing Address:** Forest Serv, USDA, 1992 Folwell Ave, St Paul, MN 55108. **Fax:** 651-649-5256. **E-Mail:** nlorimer@fs.fed.us

LORINCZ, ALLAN LEVENTE, DERMATOLOGY. **Personal Data:** b Chicago, Ill, October 31, 1924; m 1952, Lillian; c 3. **Education:** Univ Chicago, SB, 1945, MD, 1947. **Professional Experience:** Mem dermat adv comt, Food & Drug Admin, 1971-1972; PROF DERMAT, UNIV CHICAGO, 1967-; nat consult to Surgeon Gen, USAF, 1962-; mem comt cutaneous syst, Div Med Sci, Nat Res Coun, 1962-1965; mem dermat training grants comt, USPHS, 1961-1964; from instr to assoc prof, Cancer Clin, 1951-1967; res fel dermat, Cancer Clin, 1950-1951. **Memberships:** Soc Invest Dermat; Soc Exp Biol & Med; Am Soc Dermatopath; Am Dermat Asn; Am Fedn Clin Res; Sigma Xi. **Research Statement & Publications:** Psoriasis; cutaneous fungus infections; biochemistry and physiology of the skin, especially melanin chemistry and sebaceous gland control by endocrine factors; immunology; published numerous articles. **Mailing Address:** Univ Chicago, 5841 S Md Ave, MC 5067, Chicago, IL 60637. **Fax:** 773-702-8398. **E-Mail:** alorincz@medicine.bsd.uchicago.edu

LORINCZ, ANDREW ENDRE, PEDIATRICS, BIOCHEMISTRY. **Personal Data:** b Chicago, Ill, May 17, 1926; m 1965, Diane. **Education:** Univ Chicago, PhB, 1948, BS, 1950, MD, 1952. **Professional Experience:** PROF EMER PEDIAT, MED CTR, UNIV ALA, BIRMINGHAM, as of 2000; prof, Sch Pub Health, beginning 1984; sci adv comt, Nat Tay-Sachs & Allied Dis Asn, 1979-; prof pediat, Med Ctr, Univ Ala, Birmingham, beginning 1971; assoc prof biochem & dir Ctr Develop & Learning Disorders, Med Ctr, 1968-1980; from asst prof to assoc prof, Sch Med, Univ Fla, 1959-1968; instr, La Rabida Inst, 1957-1959; instr, Sch Med, 1956-1959; Res fel, Univ Chicago, 1954-1955 & Arthritis & Rheumatism Found res fel, 1955-1958; jr asst resident fel, Rosenthal Clin, 1954-1955; from intern to jr asst resident pediat, Univ Chicago Clin, 1952-1954. **Memberships:** Am Chem Soc; Soc Pediat Res; fel Am Acad Pediat; Soc Invest Dermat; fel Am Acad Cerebral Palsy & Develop Med; Asn Clin Scientists. **Research Statement & Publications:** Heritable disorders of connective tissue acid mucopolysaccharides; inborn errors of metabolism; mental retardation; biophysical cytochemistry; fluorescence microscopy. **Mailing Address:** Dept Pediat Univ Ala, 1825 Univ Blvd, Birmingham, AL 35294-2010. **Fax:** 205-975-9147. **E-Mail:** aelorincz@vprua.vprua.vab.edu

LORING, ARTHUR PAUL, GEOLOGY, ENVIRONMENTAL GEOLOGY. **Personal Data:** b New York, NY, May 22, 1936; m 1963, Carol; c Wendy (Slater), Karen S (Gemery) & David P. **Education:** Columbia Univ, BA, 1958; Pa State Univ, MS, 1961; NY Univ, PhD (geol), 1966. **Professional Experience:** PROF EMER, YORK COL, NY, as of 2003; prof, York Col, NY, beginning 1995; consult geol & environ, Rock Soil Water Int, Inc, 1985-1992; coordr geol, York Col, NY, 1973-; from asst prof to assoc prof, York Col, NY, 1967-1995; asst prof, Upsala Col, 1967; instr, Upsala Col, 1966-1967; lectr geol, Brooklyn Col, 1962-1965. **Memberships:** Fel Geol Soc Am; Asn Eng Geol; Sigma Xi. **Research Statement & Publications:** General geologic field mapping in areas of folded and faulted sediments; environmental geology and ground water hydrology. **Mailing Address:** Dept Geol, York Col, Rm 2E15 AC Bdlg 2F09, Jamaica, NY 11451. **E-Mail:** loring@york.cuny.edu

LORING, DAVID WILLIAM, NEUROPSYCHOLOGY. **Personal Data:** b Richmond, Ind, July 13, 1956; m 1988, Sherrill; c Jason Michael, Sarah Elizabeth, Rachel Erin & Leah Rebecca. **Education:** Wittenberg Univ, BA, 1978; Univ Houston, MA, 1980, PhD (clin neuropsychol), 1982. **Professional Experience:** PROF, DEPT NEUROL, MED COL GA, as of 2002; assoc prof, Dept Neurol, Med Col Ga, beginning 1989; asst prof, Dept Neurol, Med Col GA, 1985-1989; instr, Univ Tex Med Br, 1984-1985; res assoc, Univ Tex Med Br, 1983-1984; fel, Baylor Col Med, 1982-1983. **Memberships:** AAAS; NY Acad Sci; Int Neuropsychol Soc; Am Psychol Asn; Soc Psychol Res; Soc Philos & Psychol. **Research Statement & Publications:** Electrophysiological measures of human hippocampus; neurochemical manipulation of human hippocampal responses; memory function in patients with mesial temporal lobe damage. **Mailing Address:** Dept Neurol, Med Col Ga, 1120 15th St, Augusta, GA 30912-3275. **Fax:** 706-721-7588. **E-Mail:** dwloring@neuro.mcg.edu

LORING, DOUGLAS HOWARD, MARINE GEOCHEMISTRY. **Personal Data:** b Concord, NH, July 25, 1934; Canadian citizen; m 1961, c 3. **Education:** Acadia Univ, BSc, 1954, MSc, 1956; Univ Manchester, PhD (geochem), 1960. **Professional Experience:** Spec lectr, Dalhousie Univ, 1962-1968; RES SCIENTIST, BEDFORD INST, 1960-; res fel geochem, Univ Manchester, 1957-1960; tech officer, Geol Surv Can, 1954-1955. **Memberships:** Mineral Asn Can; fel Geol Asn Can; Geochem Soc. **Research Statement & Publications:** Geochemistry of ancient and modern marine sediments; development of analytical methods for the determination of trace metals in sediments and SPM. **Mailing Address:** Atlantic Oceanog Lab, Bedford Inst Box 1006, Dartmouth, NS B2Y 4A2, Can.

LORING, ROGER FREDERIC, NONEQUILIBRIUM STATISTICAL MECHANICS, THEORY OF MOLECULAR SPECTROSCOPY. **Personal Data:** b Berkeley, Calif, September 14, 1958; m 1990. **Education:** Univ Calif, Davis, BS, 1980; Stanford Univ, PhD (phys chem), 1984. **Professional Experience:** PROF CHEM & CHEM BIOL, CORNELL UNIV, as of 2005; assoc prof chem, Cornell Univ, beginning 1993; asst prof, Cornell Univ, 1987-1993; res assoc chem, Univ Rochester, 1984-1987; fel Alfred P Sloan Found. **Research Statement & Publications:** Dynamics of molecular electronic and vibrational excited states in condensed phases; solvation effects in electronic spectroscopy; theory of nonlinear spectroscopy; structure and dynamics of polymer fluids. **Mailing Address:** Dept Chem & Chem Biol, Cornell Univ, 208 Baker Lab, Ithaca, NY 14853-1301. **Fax:** 607-255-4137. **E-Mail:** rfl2@cornell.edu

LORING, STEPHEN H, RESPIRATORY PHYSIOLOGY. **Personal Data:** b Boston, Mass, July 9, 1946. **Education:** Amherst Col, BS, 1968; Dartmouth Med Sch, BMS, 1970; Harvard Med Sch, MD, 1973. **Honors & Awards:** Res Career Develop Award, NHLBI, 1981; mem, Respiratory & Appl Physiol, Respiratory Physiology Study Sect, National Heart, Lung & Blood Inst, 1998-2002; mem, Observ Study Monitoring Board, Heart Health Study, National Heart, Lung & Blood Inst, 2000. **Professional Experience:** ASSOC PROF, DEPT ENVIRON HEALTH, HARVARD SCH PUB HEALTH, 1993-; ASSOC PROF ANESTHESIA, HARVARD MED SCH, 1991-; SCIENTIFIC DIR, RESPIRATORY THERAPY, BETH ISRAEL HOSP, BOSTON, 1991-; assoc prof physiol, Dept Environ Health, Harvard Sch Pub Health, 1985-1991; asst prof, Dept Environ Health, Harvard Sch

Pub Health, 1974-1985; Intern med, Univ Hosp, Boston, 1973-1974. **Memberships:** Am Phys Soc; Am Thoracic Soc. **Mailing Address:** Dept Anesthesia & Critical Care, Beth Israel Deaconess Med Ctr, 330 Brookline Ave, Boston, MA 02215. **Fax:** 617-432-3468. **E-Mail:** sloring@caregroup.harvard.edu

LORIO, PETER LEONCE, FOREST SOILS, TREE PHYSIOLOGY. **Personal Data:** b New Orleans, La, April 10, 1927; m 1957, c 6. **Education:** La State Univ, BS, 1953; Duke Univ, MF, 1954; Iowa State Univ, PhD (forestry-soils), 1962. **Honors & Awards:** Superior Serv Award, USDA, 1984. **Professional Experience:** SCIENTIST EMER, SOUTHERN RES STA, USDA FOREST SERV, 2003-; supvry soil scientist, Forest Insect Res Proj, Southern Forest Exp Sta, US Forest Serv, beginning 1977; prin soil scientist, Forest Insect Res Proj, Southern Forest Exp Sta, US Forest Serv, 1968-1976; soil scientist, Forest Insect Res Proj, Southern Forest Exp Sta, US Forest Serv, 1962-1968; chief soil scientist, Stand Fruit & Steamship Co, 1958-1959; soil scientist, Stand Fruit & Steamship Co, 1954-1958. **Memberships:** Am Soc Agron; Int Soc Trop Foresters; Sigma Xi; Soil Sci Soc Am; Int Soc Soil Sci; Soc Am Foresters. **Research Statement & Publications:** Soil, tree, and stand factors affecting pine susceptibility to bark beetles; tree physiology; soil water; tree rooting; stand composition, age, density. **Mailing Address:** Southern Res Sta, USDA Forest Serv, 2500 Shreveport Hwy, Pineville, LA 71360. **Fax:** 318-473-7222. **E-Mail:** srs_pineville@fs.fed.us

LOROS, JENNIFER J, BIOCHEMISTRY. **Education:** Univ Calif, Santa Cruz, BA, 1979 & PhD (Biol), 1984. **Professional Experience:** PROF, DEPT BIOCHEM & GENETICS, DARMOUTH MED SCH, 2001; PROF, DEPT BIOCHEM, DARMOUTH MED SCH, 2000-; assoc prof, Markey Found, Dept Biochem, Darmouth Med Sch, 1996-2000; vis prof, Dept Human Pathol, Univ Rome, 1998; from res asst prof to res assoc prof, Dept Biochem, Darmouth Med Sch, 1988-1996; mem, Molecular Genetics Lab, Darmouth. **Memberships:** Genetics Soc Am; AAAS; Soc Res Biol Rhythms; Am Psysiol Soc. **Mailing Address:** Dept Biochem, Dartmouth Med Sch, 704 Remsen, Hanover, NH 03755. **Fax:** 603-650-1128. **E-Mail:** jennifer.loros@dartmouth.edu

LOROS, JENNIFER JANE, CIRCADIAN CLOCK BIOLOGY, CLASSICAL & MOLECULAR GENETICS OF FUNGAL DEVELOPMENT. **Personal Data:** b San Mateo, Calif, April 15, 1950; m 1984, Jay; c Marjorie E & Hayes M. **Education:** Univ Calif, Santa Cruz, BA, 1979, PhD (biol), 1984. **Professional Experience:** PROF, DEPT BIOCHEM & GENETICS, DARTMOUTH MED SCH, as of 2002; assoc prof biochem, Dartmouth Med Sch, 1996-2000; res assoc prof, Dartmouth Med Sch, 1994-1996; ad hoc reviewer, NIMH, 1994; mem, Neurospora Policy Comt, 1993-1997; sci prog reviewer, USAF Off Sci Res, 1992-1993; ad hoc reviewer, NSF, 1990-1993; prin investr, NSF, 1988-; res asst prof, Dartmouth Med Sch, 1988-1994; res assoc, Dartmouth Med Sch, 1984-1988; assoc ed, Genetics. **Memberships:** Genetics Soc Am; Soc Res Biol Rhythms; AAAS; Am Phys Soc. **Research Statement & Publications:** Isolation and dissection of genes involved in photo-entrainment of the clock and genes under control of the biological clock in order to understand how the circadian clock is reset by light information; how the clock transfers temporal information out into the cell organism to control metabolism and development. **Mailing Address:** Dept Biochem, Dartmouth Med Sch, 7400 Remsen, Hanover, NH 03755. **Fax:** 603-650-1128. **E-Mail:** jennifer.lorus@dartmouth.edu

LORRADINI, MICHAEL L, NUCLEAR ENGINEERING. **Education:** Marquette Univ, BS, 1975; Mass Inst Tech, MS, 1976, PhD (Nuclear Eng) 1978. **Professional Experience:** PROF, DEPT ENG PHYSICS, COL ENG, UNIV WIS-MADISON, as of 2006. **Mailing Address:** Dept Eng Physics, Col Eng, Univ Wis-Madison, 147 Eng Res Bldg, Madison, WI 53706. **Fax:** 608-263-7451. **E-Mail:** corradini@engr.wisc.edu

LORRAIN, PAUL, MAGNETOHYDRODYNAMICS OF NATURAL PHENOMENA. **Personal Data:** b Montreal, Que, September 8, 1916; m 1944, Dorothee; c Francois, Denis, Claire & Louis. **Education:** Univ Ottawa, BA, 1937; McGill Univ, BSc, 1940, MSc, 1941, PhD (physics), 1947. **Professional Experience:** VIS PROF EARTH & PLANETARY SCI, MCGILL UNIV, 1983-; visitor, Inst Astrophys Paris, 1991-1996; visitor, Inst Physics, Globe Paris, 1989 & 1990; vis prof, Univ Murcia, 1986-1988; vis prof, six Chinese univs, 1985; vis fel, Oxford Univ, 1981; vis prof fac sci, Univ Madrid, 1968-1969 & Univ Grenoble, France, 1961-1962; Mem, Nat Res Coun, 1960-1966; head dept, Univ Montreal, 1957-1966; prof physics, Univ Montreal, 1949-1982; res assoc, Lab Nuclear Studies, Cornell Univ, 1947-1949; mem, Inst Physics, Univ Montreal, 1946 & Univ Laval, 1943-1946; lectr physics, Sir George Williams Col, 1942-1943. **Memberships:** Royal Soc Can; Am Phys Soc; Can Asn Physicists (pres, 1964-1965). **Research Statement & Publications:** Magnetohydrodynamics of natural phenomena. **Mailing Address:** Dept Earth Sci, McGill Univ 3450 Univ, Montreal, PQ H3A 2A7, Can. **Fax:** 514-398-4680. **E-Mail:** paull@eps.mcgill.ca

LORSCHEIDER, FRITZ LOUIS, MEDICAL PHYSIOLOGY, ENDOCRINOLOGY. **Personal Data:** b Rochester, NY, August 27, 1939; m 1967, c 4. **Education:** Univ Wis, BS, 1963; Mich State Univ, MS, 1967, PhD (physiol, endocrinol), 1970. **Professional Experience:** PROF EMER PHYSIOL & BIOPHYSICS, UNIV CALGARY, as of 2005; prof med physiol, fac med, Univ Calgary, beginning 1980; from asst prof to assoc prof, Fac Med, Univ Calgary, 1970-1980; NIH fel, Mich State Univ, 1970; res asst endocrinol, Radioisotope Unit, Med Col Wis, 1963-1964. **Memberships:** Am Physiol Soc; Am Soc Biochem & Molecular Biol; Can Physiol Soc; Can Soc Clin Invest; AAAS; NY Acad Sci. **Research Statement & Publications:** Reproductive and fetal physiology; chemistry and physiology of onco-fetal proteins; fetal macroglobulin and steroid metabolism; metabolism of mercury released from dental amalgam fillings. **Mailing Address:** Dept Physiol & Biophys, Fac Med, Univ Calgary, 2500 Univ Dr NW, Calgary, AB T2N 4N1, Can. **Fax:** 403-283-4740. **E-Mail:** fllorsch@ucalgary.ca

LORTON, STEVEN PAUL, REPRODUCTIVE PHYSIOLOGY. **Personal Data:** b Brookline, Mass, October 9, 1950; m 1979, Lynn Conder. **Education:** Clark Univ, BA, 1972; Univ Wis-Madison, MS, 1975, PhD (endocrinol & reproductive physiol), 1978. **Professional Experience:** Vpres sci prog & tech serv, Minitube Int Inc, Verona Wis, 1994-2000; mgr physiol & animal prod res, Am Breeders Serv, 1993-1994; mgr biol res, Am Breeders Serv, 1989-1993; adj assoc prof, Dept Meat & Animal Sci, Univ Wis-Madison, 1984-; res scientist, Am Breeders Serv, 1984-1989; res assoc, Am Breeders Serv, 1980-1984; res assoc, Animal Sci Dept, Cornell Univ, 1978-1980. **Memberships:** Soc Study Reproduction; Sigma Xi; Int Embryo Transfer Soc; Am Soc Androl. **Research Statement & Publications:** Physiology and cryopreservation of spermatozoa for use in artifical insemination, with emphasis on the domestic species; development of improved techniques of cryopreservation and characteristics of semen quality versus fertility. **Mailing Address:** 913 Sauk Ridge Trail, Madison, WI 53717. **E-Mail:** splorton@wisc.edu

LORY, HENRY JAMES, ELECTRICAL ENGINEERING. **Personal Data:** b Baltimore, Md, March 3, 1936; m 1960, c 3. **Education:** Johns Hopkins Univ, BES, 1958, PhD (elec eng), 1963. **Professional Experience:** MEM TECH STAFF, BELL TEL LABS, 1963-; mem res staff, Radiation Lab, 1961-1963; asst, Air Res & Develop Command Contract Proj, Johns Hopkins Univ, 1957-1958. **Memberships:** Sigma Xi. **Research Statement & Publications:** Development of Schottky barrier devices, especially analysis of high temperature failure mechanisms; design of linear integrated circuits. **Mailing Address:** 3221 Stoudts Ferry Bridge Rd, Reading, PA 19605-1430.

LOS, MARINUS, CHEMISTRY, HERBICIDES & SCREENING FOR HERBICIDES. **Personal Data:** b Ridderkerk, Neth, September 18, 1933; m 1957, Lorraine; c Simon, Sija & Michael, Martin (deceased). **Education:** Univ Edinburgh, BSc, 1955, PhD (chem), 1957. **Honors & Awards:** Nat Medal Technol, 1993; Perkin Medal, 1994; Award Creative Invention, Am Chem Soc, 1995; Heroes Chem Award, Am Chem Soc, 1999; Int Award Res Agrochemicals, Am Chem Soc, 2002. **Professional Experience:** RETIRED; res dir, Crop Sci, 1992-1996; assoc dir, Crop Sci, 1988-1992; mgr, Crop Protection Chem Discovery, 1986-1988; res chemist, Herbicide Discovery, 1984-1986; group leader organic synthesis, Am Cynamid Co, 1971-1984; sr res fel, Dept Pharmacol, Univ Edinburgh, 1969-1970; res chemist, Am Cynamid Co, 1960-1971; res fel, Nat Res Coun Can, 1958-1960. **Memberships:** Am Chem Soc. **Research Statement & Publications:** Aliphatic and aromatic chemistry, especially nitrogen heterocycles; natural products, especially alkaloids and terpenes; screening for mode of action of and field testing of herbicides; synthesis of herbicides. **Mailing Address:** 107 Drummond Dr, Pennington, NJ 08534. **E-Mail:** losmar@aol.com

LOSCALZO, ANNE GRACE, MICROCHEMISTRY, ANALYTICAL CHEMISTRY. **Personal Data:** b New York, NY, September 2, 1917; m 1940, c 1. **Education:** NY Univ, BA, 1937, MS, 1941, PhD (chem), 1943. **Professional Experience:** RETIRED; prof chem, Long Island Univ, 1971; from asst prof to assoc prof, Long Island Univ, 1958-1971; lectr, City Col New York, 1953-1958; instr, Wash Square Col, NY Univ, 1943-1946; Asst instr chem, Wash Square Col, NY Univ, 1941-1943. **Memberships:** Am Chem Soc. **Research Statement & Publications:** Educational projects to improve learning abilities of students in chemistry. **Mailing Address:** 3078 38th St Apt 4A, Long Island City, NY 11103.

LOSCALZO, JOSEPH, THROMBOSIS, ATHEROSCLEROSIS. **Personal Data:** b Camden, NJ, October 26, 1951; m 1974, Anita; c Julia & Alexander. **Education:** Univ Pa, AB, 1972, PhD (biochem), 1977, MD, 1977. **Honors & Awards:** Clin Scientist Award, Am Heart Asn, 1983. **Professional Experience:** WADE PROF & CHMN MED, BOSTON UNIV, as of 2005; PROF BIOCHEM, BOSTON UNIV, as of 2005; DIR, WHITAKER CARDIOVASC INST, as of 2005; dir, Nat Heart Lung & Blood Inst Spec Ctr Res, Boston Univ, 1995-; assoc ed, NEng J Med, 1995-; distinguished prof, Whitaker Cardiovasc Inst, 1993-1996; Glaxo cardiovasc res award, 1989-1994; prin investr, NIH grants & Nat Heart, Lung, Blood Inst grants, 1988-1993; consult, Cardiol Dept, Children's Hosp, Boston, 1987-; chief, Cardiol Sect, Va Med Ctr, W Roxbury, 1987-; dir, Ctr Res Thrombolysis, 1987-; from asst prof to assoc prof med, Harvard Univ, 1985-1993; Sandoz med scholar, 1984-1990; assoc physician, 1983-; instr med, Harvard Univ, 1983-1985; chief resident physician, Brigham & Women's Hosp, 1983-1984; res fel med, Harvard Univ, 1981-1983; clin fel cardiol, Harvard Univ, 1981-1983; clin fel med, Harvard Univ, 1978-1981; resident physician, Brigham & Women's Hosp, 1978-1981; res fel biochem, Univ Pa, 1978; asst ed, J Vascular Med & Biol. **Memberships:** Fel Am Col Cardiol; fel Am Col Physicians; AAAS; Am Heart Asn; Biophys Soc; Am Soc Biol Chemists; Am Soc Hemat; Am Soc Clin Invest. **Research Statement & Publications:** The relationship of thrombosis to cardiovascular disease; the role of platelets and the fibrinolytic system in thrombotic events; the interactions between thrombosis and otherosclerosis; role of nitric oxide in the cardiovascular system. **Mailing Address:** Dept Med, Boston Univ, Boston, MA 02118. **E-Mail:** jloscalz@bu.edu

LOSCHER, ROBERT A, COMPUTERIZED MANAGEMENT OF INFORMATION, COMPUTER NETWORKING. **Personal Data:** b Philadelphia, Pa, May 2, 1930. **Education:** Univ Pa, BS, 1958, MS, 1960. **Professional Experience:** RETIRED; dir telecommun, Glassboro State Col, 1987-1992; dir data processing, dir MIS, 1975-1987; dir data processing, Glassboro State Col, 1971-1975; res & develop engr, Selas Corp Am, 1960-1963 & Dupont Co, Chambers Works, 1963-1971; Asst prof chem eng, Univ Pa, 1959-1960; adj prof, Glassboro State Col & Del Co Community Col. **Memberships:** Am Inst Chem Engrs; AAAS; Asn Comput Mach; NY Acad Sci. **Research Statement & Publications:** Computerization of gas chromatography and IR spectrometry; computer control of chemical manufacturing plants; digital process control; combustion control of lehrs and furnaces; computerization of information management; conversion from batch computer shops to on-line multi-station telecommunication systems. **Mailing Address:** 2607 SW 41st St, Cape Coral, FL 33914-5421.

LOSCHIAVO, SAMUEL RALPH, INSECT PHYSIOLOGY, NUTRITION. **Personal Data:** b Transcona, Man, June 28, 1924; m 1950, Hilda; c Larry (deceased) & Ken. **Education:** Univ Man, BSc, 1946, MSc, 1950, PhD, 1964. **Professional Experience:** RETIRED; vis prof, Univ Hawaii, 1976; res assoc, Univ Wis, 1961; res scientist, Can Dept Agr, 1949-1987; chemist, Man Sugar Co, 1948; Hon prof, Univ Man. **Memberships:** Fel Entom Soc Can; hon mem Entom Soc Can. **Research Statement & Publications:** Biology, behavior and control of insects associated with stored grain and milled cereal products; Canadian and US patents. **Mailing Address:** 112 Linacre Rd, Winnipeg, MB R3T 3G6, Can.

LOSECCO, JOHN M, WEAK INTERACTIONS, COLLIDER PHYSICS. **Personal Data:** b New York, NY, October 21, 1950; m 1986, Lynne; c Anna & Daniel. **Education:** Cooper Union, BS, 1972; Harvard, AM, 1973, PhD (physics), 1976. **Honors & Awards:** Bruno Rossi Prize, Am Astron Soc, 1989. **Professional Experience:** PROF PHYSICS, UNIV NOTRE DAME DU LAC, 1985-; jr investr, Dept Energy, 1982-1985; asst prof physics, Calif Inst Technol, 1981-1985; asst res scientist physics, Univ Mich, 1979-1981; res assoc physics, Harvard Univ, 1976-1979; res asst, Albert Einstein College Med, 1968-1972. **Memberships:** Am Phys Soc. **Research Statement & Publications:** Studying extensions to the standard model of elementary particle; applications of particle physics to astrophysics and cosmology. **Mailing Address:** Physics Dept, Univ Notre Dame, Notre Dame, IN 46556. **Fax:** 574-631-5952. **E-Mail:** losecco@nd.edu

LOSEE, DAVID LAWRENCE, SOLID STATE PHYSICS, SEMICONDUCTORS. **Personal Data:** b Mineola, NY, July 19, 1939; m 1963, c 2. **Education:** Cornell Univ, BEng, 1962, MS, 1963; Univ Ill, PhD (solid state physics), 1967. **Professional Experience:** RES ASSOC, EASTMAN KODAK CO, beginning 1967. **Memberships:** Am Phys Soc; Electrochem Soc; Sigma Xi. **Research Statement & Publications:** Physics of the noble gas solids; physics of semiconductors and semiconductor devices. **Mailing Address:** Eastman Kodak Co, 343 State St, Rochester, NY 14650.

LOSEE, FERRIL A, ELECTRICAL ENGINEERING. **Personal Data:** b Lehi, Utah, June 5, 1928; m 1953, c 9. **Education:** Univ Utah, BSEE, 1953; Univ Southern Calif, MSEE, 1957. **Professional Experience:** RETIRED; engr, EG&G SP, 1989-1993; engr, SRS Technologies, 1984-1989; prof elec eng & chmn dept, Brigham Young Univ, 1965-1983; elec engr, Hughes Aircraft Co, 1953-1959 & Aeronutronic Div, Philco Corp, 1959-1965;

consult. **Research Statement & Publications:** Communication; electronic countermeasures; systems engineering; radar engineering. **Mailing Address:** 3145 Bannock Dr, Provo, UT 84604.

LOSEKAMP, BERNARD FRANCIS, POLYMER & ORGANIC CHEMISTRY, INFORMATION SCIENCE. **Personal Data:** b Cincinnati, Ohio, July 16, 1936; wid, c 4. **Education:** Xavier Univ, Ohio, BS, 1958, MS, 1961; Univ Akron, PhD (polymer chem), 1966. **Honorary Degrees:** LLD, Univ Akron, 1990. **Professional Experience:** SR ED, CHEM ABSTR SERV, COLUMBUS, OHIO, 1972-; group leader, Chem Abstr Serv, 1971-1972; sr indexer, Chem Abstr Serv, 1969-1971; from asst ed to assoc ed, Chem Abstr Serv, 1964-1969; res chemist, Inst Polymer Sci, Univ Akron, 1961-1964; res asst, Wm S Merrell Co, Ohio, 1961. **Memberships:** Am Chem Soc. **Research Statement & Publications:** Acenaphthene arsenicals; synthesis and characterization of polymers; polymer nomenclature; thermal polymerization; information science. **Mailing Address:** 2011 Chelsea Rd, Columbus, OH 43212-1945.

LOSER, RONALD E, MATHEMATICS. **Education:** Adams State Col, BA, 1965; Univ Colo, MA, 1967; Univ Northern Colo, DA, 1977. **Professional Experience:** PROF, MATHS & COMPUT SCI, ADAMS STATE COL, CO, as of 2003. **Mailing Address:** Dept Math & Comput Sci, Adams State Col, Alamosa, CO 81102-0001. **E-Mail:** rloser@unm.edu

LOSEY, GEORGE SPAHR, MARINE ZOOLOGY, ETHOLOGY. **Personal Data:** b Louisville, Ky, June 30, 1942; m 1967, c 2. **Education:** Univ Miami, BS, 1964; Scripps Inst Oceanog, Univ Calif, PhD (marine biol), 1968. **Honors & Awards:** Stoye Award, Am Soc Ichthyol & Herpet, 1967. **Professional Experience:** ASSOC DIR, HAWAII INST MARINE BIOL, UNIV HAWAII, HONOLULU, as of 2004; RESEARCHER, HAWAII INST MARINE BIOL, UNIV HAWAII, HONOLULU, as of 2004; chmn, Univ Hawaii, 1990-1993; vis researcher, Univ Leiden, 1987-1988; PROF ZOOLOGY, HAWAII INST MARINE BIOL, UNIV HAWAII, 1980-; assoc dir, Univ Hawaii, 1980-1990; Res fel, Univ Calif, Berkeley, 1978; from asst prof to assoc prof zoology, Univ Hawaii, 1970-1980; NIH res fel fish behav, Hawaii Inst Marine Biol, 1968-1970. **Memberships:** Fel Animal Behav Soc; Am Soc Ichthyol & Herpet. **Research Statement & Publications:** Ethology and ecology of fish; symbiotic cleaner fish; behavioral ecology of herbivorous fish; development of aggression; computerized data acquisition; learning and modification of species-typical behavior; ultraviolet coloration in fishes. **Mailing Address:** Dept Zoology, Univ Hawaii, 2538 McCarthy Mall, Edmondson 152, Honolulu, HI 96822. **Fax:** 808-956-9812. **E-Mail:** losey@hawaii.edu

LOSICK, RICHARD MARC, MOLECULAR BIOLOGY. **Personal Data:** b Jersey City, NJ, July 27, 1943; m 1970. **Education:** Princeton Univ, AB, 1965; Mass Inst Technol, PhD (biochem), 1969. **Honors & Awards:** Camille & Henry Dreyfus Award, Camille & Henry Dreyfus Found, 1973. **Professional Experience:** MARIA MOORS COBAT PROF BIOL, HARVARD UNIV, as of 2003; PROF MOLECULAR & CELLULAR BIOL, HARVARD UNIV, 1977-; assoc prof, Harvard Univ, 1974-1977; asst prof, Harvard Univ, 1971-1974; Harvard Soc fels jr fel biochem, Harvard Univ, 1968-1971. **Memberships:** Nat Acad Sci; Am Soc Microbiol; Am Soc Biol Chemists. **Research Statement & Publications:** Bacterial sporulation; regulatory subunits of RNA polymers. **Mailing Address:** Dept Molecular & Cellular Biol, Harvard Univ, 16 Divinity Ave Rm 3023, Cambridge, MA 02138. **Fax:** 617-496-4642. **E-Mail:** losick@mcb.harvard.edu

LOSIN, EDWARD THOMAS, PHYSICAL ORGANIC CHEMISTRY, ENERGY CONVERSION. **Personal Data:** b Racine, Wis, July 9, 1923; m 1950, c 2. **Education:** Univ Ill, BS, 1948; Columbia Univ, AM, 1950, PhD (chem), 1954. **Professional Experience:** CHEM CONSULT, 1988-; sr res scientist, Allis-Chalmers Corp, 1973-1988; mgr non-metallic mat, Allis-Chalmers Corp, 1971-1973; sr res scientist, Allis-Chalmers Corp, 1963-1971; chem dept mgr, Isomet Corp, 1961-1963; res chemist, Union Carbide Corp, 1957-1961; Res assoc, Eng Res Inst, Univ Mich, 1954-1957. **Memberships:** Am Chem Soc; The Chem Soc; NY Acad Sci; AAAS; Sigma Xi. **Research Statement & Publications:** Reaction mechanisms of organic, stereospecific and free radical gas-phase reactions; electrical insulation materials and systems for various applications; epoxy technology; high temperature fuel gas cleanup; coal combustion of pulverized fuel in entrained-bed combustors; coal-fired cement and iron ore pelletizing systems; coal water slurry fuels technology. **Mailing Address:** 10000 N Sheridan Dr, Mequon, WI 53092.

LOSOS, JONATHAN B, EVOLUTIONARY DIVERSIFICATION. **Personal Data:** b December 7, 1961. **Education:** Harvard Univ, AB, 1984; Univ Calif, Berkeley, PhD (zoology), 1989. **Honors & Awards:** Dobzhansky Prize, Soc Study Evolution, 1991; david starr jordan prize, 1998. **Professional Experience:** Ed, the Am naturalist, beginning 2002; PROF BIOL, WASH UNIV, 2001-; dir, tyson res center, 2000; from asst to assoc prof, Wash Univ, 1992-2001; fel, Ctr Pop Biol, Univ Calif, Davis, 1990-1992. **Memberships:** Soc Study Evolution; Soc Study Amphibians & Reptiles; Am Soc Naturalists; Soc Conserv Biologists; Am Soc Ichthyologists & Herpetologists. **Research Statement & Publications:** Studies of evolutionary diversification, combining functional, behavioral, ecological, and evolutionary approaches (lizards of the genus Anolis used as a model system). **Mailing Address:** Dept Biol Wash Univ, Campus Box 1137, St Louis, MO 63130. **Fax:** 314-935-4432. **E-Mail:** losos@biodec.wustl.edu

LOSS, FRANK J, FRACTURE MECHANICS, FAILURE ANALYSIS. **Personal Data:** b Homestead, Pa, May 14, 1936; m 1966, c 2. **Education:** Carnegie Mellon Univ, BS, 1958, MS, 1959, PhD (mech eng), 1961. **Professional Experience:** EXEC VPRES, MAT ENG ASN, LANHAM, MD, 1982-; head, Mech Mat Br, US Naval Res Lab, Wash, DC, 1964-1982; first lt, US Army Corps Engrs, 1962-1964; Engr, Westinghouse Bettis Atomic Power Lab, Pittsburgh, Pa, 1961-1962. **Memberships:** Am Nuclear Soc; Am Soc Mech Engrs; Am Soc Testing & Mat. **Research Statement & Publications:** Structural technology development; fracture mechanics of structural steels; corrosion fatigue; failure analysis; radiation embrittlement of nuclear materials; materials characterization in hostile environments; nuclear power plant structural reliability; consulting in materials analysis. **Mailing Address:** Mat Eng Asn, 9700 M L King Jr Hwy, Lanham, MD 20706-1837. **Fax:** 301-577-4936.

LOSSING, FREDERICK PETTIT, CHEMICAL PHYSICS, ION CHEMISTRY. **Personal Data:** b Norwich, Ont, August 4, 1915; m 1938, c 3. **Education:** Univ Western Ont, BA, 1938, MA, 1940; McGill Univ, PhD (phys chem), 1942. **Professional Experience:** RETIRED; hon sr res prof, Dept Chem, Univ Ottawa, 1980-1994; asst dir, Div Chem, Nat Res Coun Can, 1969-1977; prin res officer, Div Chem, Nat Res Coun Can, 1946-1949 & 1977-1980; Res chemist, Shawinigan Chem, Ltd, 1942-1946. **Memberships:** Fel Royal Soc Can; Royal Astron Soc Can; Am Soc Mass Spectrometry. **Research Statement & Publications:** Mass spectrometry; chemical kinetics; photochemistry; heats of formation of organic cations and free radicals; ionization processes. **Mailing Address:** 95 Dorothea Dr, Univ Ottawa, Ottawa, ON K1Z 7C6, Can.

LOSSINSKY, ALBERT S, EXPERIMENTALNEUROPATHOLOGY, MICRO BLOOD VESSEL PATHOLOGY. **Personal Data:** b Passaic, NJ, May 17, 1946; m 1981, c 4. **Education:** Kans Wesleyan Univ, BA, 1969; Empire State Univ, MS, 1974; Polish Acad Sci, PhD (neurobiology), 1994. **Professional Experience:** DIR IMMUNOHISTOCHEMISTRY, HUNTINGTON MED RES INST, PASADENA, as of 2005; PRIN INVESTR, HUNTINGTON MED RES INST, PASADENA, as of 2004; EXP NEUROPATHOLOGIST, HUNTINGTON MED RES INST, PASADENA, 1996-; res scientist neuroviol, Inst Basic Res Develop Disablities, beginning 1986; asst supvr, Clin Electron Microscopy Lab, Inst Basic Res Develop Disabilities, 1983-; res scientist second neurobiology, Inst Basic Res Develop Disabilities, 1981-1985; res scientist path, Inst Basic Res Develop Disabilities, 1979-1981; assoc res neuropath, Univ Md Sch Med, 1976-1979; chief res immunolpathol, Johns Hopkins Univ, 1973-1976; sr lab technician, Johns Hopkins Univ, 1973-1976. **Memberships:** Am Soc Cell Biol; Soc Neuroscience; Am Asn Neuropathologists; NY Acad Sci. **Research Statement & Publications:** Investigation using animal modes of mechanisms of macromolecular and inflammatory cell transport acrossthe altered blood-brain barrier of mammals; electron microscopic analysis of human tissue biopsy material for clinical diagnosis. **Mailing Address:** Huntington Med Res Inst, Pasadena, CA 91105.

LOSURDO, ANTONIO, PHYSICAL CHEMISTRY, ORGANIC ANALYTICAL ENVIRONMENTAL CHEMISTRY/MASS SPECTROMETRY. **Personal Data:** b Spadafora, Italy, January 1, 1943; American citizen; m 1988, Claudia. **Education:** Syracuse Univ, BA, 1965, PhD (chem), 1970. **Professional Experience:** SR ORG ANAL CHEM, LOCKHEED MARTIN, 1999-; spec proj group leader/chief chemist, Roy F Weston Inc, 1991-1999; sr tech mgr, Roy F Weston Inc, 1988-1999; sect chief, Anal Sect, 1988-1991; chief chemist & gas chromatography/mass spectrometry & qual assurance/qual control group leader, O'Brien & Gere Engrs Inc, 1982-1987; res assoc prof, Univ Miami, 1979-1981; res asst prof chem oceanog, Univ Miami, 1977-1979; chief chemist, Cambridge Instrument Co, 1975-1976; res assoc chem, Clark Univ, 1974-1975; lectr chem, Ohio State Univ, 1973-1974; res assoc, Ohio State Univ, 1972-1973; mem vis fac chem, Syracuse Univ, 1971-1972; instr chem, Rutgers Univ, 1970-1971; NIH fel, Rutgers Univ, 1969-1970; res asst chem, Syracuse Univ, 1965-1969. **Memberships:** Am Chem Soc; NY Acad Sci; Sigma Xi; AAAS. **Research Statement & Publications:** Physical chemistry of multicomponent electrolyte solutions and seawater; thermochemistry and thermodynamics of solutions; solute-solvent and solute-solute interactions; transport properties of hydrophobic electrolytes; electroanalytical chemistry; trace organics analyses; gas chromatography and mass spectrometry of priority pollutants, polychlorinated dibenzo-p-dioxins and dibenzofurans; polynuclear aromatic hydrocarbons in several matrices of environmental concern. **Mailing Address:** 6 Chestnut Hill Rd, Howell, NJ 07731-1708. **Fax:** 732-494-4021. **E-Mail:** antonio.losurdo@lmco.com

LOTAN, JAMES E, SILVICULTURE, FIRE ECOLOGY. **Personal Data:** b Mich, March 20, 1931; m 1951, c Gloria (Stablein), Ellen (Hafner), Eric, Lei & Kari M. **Education:** La State Univ, BSF, 1959; Univ Mich, MF, 1961, PhD, 1970. **Professional Experience:** PROPRIETOR, LUTAN HORSE LOGGING, 1991-; adj prof, Dept Forest Resources, Univ Idaho, Moscow, 1987-1991; res forester, Forestry Sci Lab, 1984-1987; prog mgr, Northern Forest Fire Lab, 1979-1984; prog mgr, Fire Mgt Res & Develop Prog, 1974-1979; proj leader forest sci res, Forest Serv, USDA, 1965-1974; res forester, Forest Serv, USDA, 1961-1965; asst forest res, Univ Mich, 1960; fire control, Deerlodge Nat Forest, Mont, 1959; Forestry technician, Southern Forest Exp Sta, US Forest Serv, La, 1957-1959. **Memberships:** Am Forestry Asn; Soc Am Foresters; NAm Horse & MuLe Loggers Asn (vpres 1992-). **Research Statement & Publications:** Silviculture and ecology of Pinus contorta, Pinus ponderosa & Pseudotsuga menziesli; effects of fire on forests and rangelands of the northern Rocky Mountains; fire management RD & A program; fire effects research and development program; horse logging. **Mailing Address:** 1550 Mid Burnt Fork Rd, Stevensville, MT 59870. **E-Mail:** jimlotan@cyberhet1.com

LOTAN, REUBEN, BIOCHEMISTRY. **Personal Data:** b Sumarkand, USSR, March 19, 1946. **Education:** Tel Aviv Univ, MD, 1971; Weizmann Inst, PhD (physics), 1976. **Professional Experience:** PROF, DEPT THORACIC, HEAD & NECK MED ONCOL, UNIV TEX, as of 2005; IRVING & NADINE MANSFIELD & ROBERT DAVID LEVITT CANCER RES CHAIR, UNIV TEX, M D ANDERSON CANCER CTR, HOUSTON, as of 2005; assoc prof biophys, Weizmann Inst, 1980-1984; vis asst prof develop biol, Univ Calif, Irvine, 1978-1980. **Memberships:** Am Asn Cancer Res; Am Soc Cell Biol; Soc Complex Carbohydrates. **Mailing Address:** Dept Tumor Biol, MD Anderson Cancer Ctr, Univ Tex, 1515 Holcombe Blvd, Houston, TX 77030-4095. **Fax:** 713-794-0209. **E-Mail:** rlotan@notes.mdacc.tmc.edu

LOTH, JOHN LODEWYK, AERODYNAMICS, DESIGN. **Personal Data:** b Hague, Neth, September 14, 1933; m Harriet; c 3. **Education:** Univ Toronto, BASc, 1957, MASc, 1958, PhD (mech eng), 1962. **Honors & Awards:** Assoc fel, AM Inst Aeronau & Astrona, 1979. **Professional Experience:** Chmn, Allegheney Sect, Am Inst Aeronaut & Astronaut 1985-1995; consult, Dept Energy, 1973-; pres, Dynamic Flow Inc, 1972-; PROF AEROSPACE ENG, WVA UNIV, 1971-; consult, Off Naval Res, 1968-1972; assoc prof, WVa Univ, 1967-1971; consult, Air Force & ARO Inc, 1963-1966; asst prof aeronaut eng, Univ Ill, Urbana, 1962-1967; lectr mech eng, Univ Toronto, 1960-1962; French Govt fel aeronaut eng, Nat Ctr Sci Res, Ministry Ed, France, 1958-1959; consult, Ellard Wilson Assocs, Ont, 1957-1961; prin investr, Lockheed Ga & US Dept Energy. **Memberships:** Assoc fel Am Inst Aeronaut & Astronaut; Sigma Xi; Am Soc Engr Educ. **Research Statement & Publications:** Low speed aerodynamics; aerodynamic mixing and supersonics; combustion; aircraft design; propulsion. **Mailing Address:** Dept Mech & Aero Eng, WV Univ, PO Box 6106, Morgantown, WV 26506. **Fax:** 304-293-8829. **E-Mail:** jloth@wvu.edu

LOTHSTEIN, LEONARD, ANTI-CANCER DRUG RESISTANCE. **Personal Data:** b Newark, NJ, August 21, 1954; m 1982, Judith Soberman; c Katherine & Alexander. **Education:** Bowdin Col, BA, 1976; Vanderbilt Univ, MS, 1980, PhD (molecular biol), 1983. **Professional Experience:** ASSOC PROF, DEPT PHARMACOL, 1993-; MEM, CANCER CTR, UNIV TENN, 1991-; asst prof, Dept Pharmacol, 1988-1993; res assoc & fel, Albert Einstein Col Med, 1983-1988; Res assoc, Sloan Kettering Cancer Inst, 1982-1983. **Memberships:** Am Asn Cancer Res; NY Acad Sci; Sigma Xi; Am Soc Cell Biol. **Research Statement & Publications:** Structure and activity analyses of novel anthracyclines; anthracycline resistance in tumor cells. **Mailing Address:** Rm 411 Crowe Research Building, Dept Pharmacol, Col Med Univ Tenn, Memphis, TN 38163. **Fax:** 901-448-7206. **E-Mail:** llothstein@utmem.edu

LOTLIKAR, PRABHAKAR DATTARAM, BIOCHEMISTRY, PHARMACOLOGY. **Personal Data:** b Shirali, India, May 21, 1928; American citizen; m 1960, Faye; c Jeffrey. **Education:** Univ Bombay, BS, 1950, MS, 1954; Ore State Univ, PhD (biochem, pharmacol, bact), 1960. **Professional Experience:** PROF BIOCHEM, SCH MED, TEMPLE UNIV & FELS INST CANCER RES & MOLECULAR BIOL, 1993-; res career develop award, USPHS, Nat Cancer Inst, 1969-1973; from asst prof to assoc prof, Fels Res Inst, Sch Med, Temple Univ, 1968-1993; res instr, Fels Res Inst, Sch Med, Temple Univ, 1967-1968; instr, McArdle Lab Cancer Res, Univ Wis, 1965-1966; proj assoc, McArdle Lab Cancer Res,

Univ Wis, 1963-1965; res fel oncol, McArdle Lab Cancer Res, Univ Wis, 1960-1963; asst chemist, Raptakos Brett & Co, Ltd, India, 1950-1955. **Memberships:** AAAS; Am Chem Soc; Am Asn Cancer Res; Am Soc Biol Chem. **Research Statement & Publications:** Mechanisms of chemical carcinogenesis and cancer prevention. **Mailing Address:** Fels Res Inst, Temple Univ Sch Med, 3420 N Broad St, Philadelphia, PA 19140. **Fax:** 215-707-2102. **E-Mail:** lotlikar@unix.temple.edu

LOTRICH, VICTOR ARTHUR, POPULATION ECOLOGY. **Personal Data:** b Pueblo, Colo, July 10, 1934; m 1955, c 3. **Education:** Northern Colo Univ, BA, 1956, MA, 1960; Univ Ky, PhD (biol), 1969. **Professional Experience:** RETIRED; assoc prof ecol, Univ Del, beginning 1969. **Research Statement & Publications:** Population dynamics of tide marsh fish and tide marsh estuarine interactions. **Mailing Address:** Dept Ecol, Univ Del, Newark, DE 19713. **E-Mail:** 47902@udel.edu

LOTSPEICH, FREDERICK BENJAMIN, environmental land classification, geochemistry of biotic systems; deceased, see previous edition for last biography

LOTSPEICH, JAMES FULTON, OPTICS. **Personal Data:** b Cincinnati, Ohio, October 22, 1922; m 1960, Helen. **Education:** Princeton Univ, BA, 1943; Univ Cincinnati, MS, 1949; Columbia Univ, PhD (physics), 1958. **Professional Experience:** RETIRED; res physicist, Labs, Hughes Aricraft Co, 1956-1988; asst, Columbia Univ, 1951-1956; lab instr gen physics, Univ Cincinnati, 1947-1948. **Memberships:** AAAS; Am Phys Soc; Sigma Xi; fel Optical Soc Am. **Research Statement & Publications:** Microwave spectroscopy and molecular structure; electrooptic techniques; applied laser technology; photodetection techniques; integrated optics. **Mailing Address:** 25346 Malibu Rd, Malibu, CA 90265.

LOTT, JAMES ANTHONY, COMPOUND SEMICONDUCTORS. **Personal Data:** b San Jose, Calif, July 4, 1961. **Education:** Univ NMex, Albuquerque, PhD (elec eng), 1993. **Professional Experience:** PROF ELEC ENG, AIR FORCE INST TECHNOL, 1993-; mem tech staff, Sandia Nat Labs, 1988-1993. **Research Statement & Publications:** Visible photonic devices and gallium arsenide integrated circuits. **Mailing Address:** Air Force Inst Technol Eng, Bldg 640 2950 P St, Wright-Patterson AFB, OH 45433-7765. **Fax:** 937-476-4055. **E-Mail:** James.Lott@afit.edu

LOTT, JOHN ALFRED, CLINICAL CHEMISTRY. **Personal Data:** b Ger, October 30, 1936; American citizen; m 1963, Gerlinde; c Christopher. **Education:** Rutgers Univ, BS, 1959, MS, 1961, PhD (anal chem), 1965. **Honors & Awards:** Katchman Award, Am Asn Clin Chem, 1979, Outstanding Contrib Educ Award, 1987; Presidential Award, Nat Acad Biochemist, 1983. **Professional Experience:** PROF EMER PATH, OHIO STATE UNIV, 2000-; prof path, Ohio State Univ, beginning 1979; from asst prof to assoc prof, Ohio State Univ, ending 1979; dir, Clin Chem Lab, Ohio State Univ Hosp, 1968-1979; asst prof, Flint Col, Univ Mich, 1965-1968; Instr chem, Rutgers Univ, 1964-1965; expert witness, clin chem. **Memberships:** Am Assoc Clin Chem; Nat Acad Clin Biochemists, (treas, 1978-1979, pres, 1981-1982); Am Chem Soc; Asn Clin Scientists; Am Asn Univ Prof. **Research Statement & Publications:** Instrumentation; methodology development; enzymology; specific-ion electrodes. **Mailing Address:** Dept Path, Ohio State Univ Med Ctr, Starling Loving M-368, Columbus, OH 43210-1240. **Fax:** 614-292-7072. **E-Mail:** lott.1@osu.edu

LOTT, JOHN NORMAN ARTHUR, SEED PHYSIOLOGY, SEED ULTRASTRUCTURE. **Personal Data:** b Summerland, BC, January 20, 1943; m 1966, Daphne; c Steven & Alison. **Education:** Univ BC, BSc, 1965; Univ Calif, Davis, MSc, 1967, PhD (bot), 1969. **Professional Experience:** PROF BIOL, MCMASTER UNIV, 1981-; res asst bot, Univ Calif, Davis, 1965-1969; from asst prof to prof, McMaster Univ. **Memberships:** Can Bot Asn; Bot Soc Am; Micros Soc Can. **Research Statement & Publications:** Ultrastructure and physiological studies of developing and germinating seeds, with special emphasis on protein bodies; mineral nutrient storage in seeds. **Mailing Address:** Dept Biol, McMaster Univ, Hamilton, ON L8S 4K1, Can. **Fax:** 905-522-6066. **E-Mail:** lott@mcmaster.ca

LOTT, JOHNNY WARREN, MATHEMATICS EDUCATION, CURRICULUM DEVELOPMENT. **Personal Data:** b Selmer, Tenn, July 2, 1944; m 1966, Carolyn Jernigan; c Jon J. **Education:** Union Univ, BS, 1965; Emory Univ, MAT, 1969; Ga State Univ, PhD (math educ), 73. **Professional Experience:** PROF MATH, UNIV MONT, 1974-; from instr to asst prof, Ga State Univ, 1970-1974; teacher math, Westminister Schs, 1969-1970; teacher math, DeKalb Co Pub Schs, 1965-1969. **Memberships:** Math Asn Am; Nat Coun Teachers Math (pres 2002-2004). **Research Statement & Publications:** Curriculum development including geometry, logo, integrated math and math for elementary teachers. **Mailing Address:** Dept Math, Univ Mont, Math 204, Missoula, MT 59812-0864. **Fax:** 406-243-2674. **E-Mail:** jwlott@earthlink.net

LOTT, LAYMAN AUSTIN, PHYSICS. **Personal Data:** b Ft Collins, Colo, September 21, 1937; m 1958, c 4. **Education:** Colo State Univ, BS, 1959, MS, 1961; Iowa State Univ, PhD (physics), 1965. **Professional Experience:** SR ENG SPECIALIST, IDAHO NAT ENG LAB, 1973-; sr res physicist, Rocky Flats Div, Dow Chem USA, 1971-1973; res physicist, Rocky Flats Div, Dow Chem USA, 1965-1971. **Memberships:** Am Phys Soc; Am Soc Nondestructive Test; Sigma Xi. **Research Statement & Publications:** Solid state physics; physical properties of materials; nondestructive testing; development of advanced nondestructive testing methods. **Mailing Address:** Idaho Nat Eng Lab, PO Box 1625 701 9 St, Idaho Falls, ID 83415-2209.

LOTT, PETER F, PHYSICAL CHEMISTRY, ANALYTICAL CHEMISTRY. **Personal Data:** b Berlin, Ger, March 26, 1927; American citizen; m 1956, c 2. **Education:** St Lawrence Univ, BS, 1949, MS, 1950; Univ Conn, PhD (chem), 1956. **Honors & Awards:** Benedetti-Pichler Award, Am Microchem Soc. **Professional Experience:** LAB DIR, SPECIALIZED SCI SERV, LLC, 1993-; emer prof, Univ Mo, Kansas City, 1964-1993; assoc prof, St John's Univ, NY, 1960-1964; chemist, Pure Carbon Co, 1959-1960; assoc prof, Univ Mo, 1956-1959; res chemist, E I du Pont Del Nemours & Co, 1956; Asst instr chem, Univ Conn, 1954-1956. **Memberships:** Am Chem Soc; Am Microchem Soc; Am Indust Hyg Asn. **Research Statement & Publications:** Analytical methods development; trace and instrumental analysis; chemical kinetics; chemical microscopy; physical measurements; organic reagents; forensic chemistry; asbestos analysis. **Mailing Address:** Specialized Sci Serv LLC, Twin Oaks N Lobby, Box 151 500 Oak St, Kansas City, MO 64112. **Fax:** 816-756-2810.

LOTT, SAM HOUSTON, PHYSICS, HEALTH PHYSICS. **Personal Data:** b New Orleans, La, September 22, 1936; m 1959. **Education:** La State Univ, BS, 1958; Vanderbilt Univ, MS, 1960, PhD (physics), 1965. **Professional Experience:** RADIATION SAFETY OFFICER, GUIDANT CORP, as of 2000; head, Health Physics Dept, King Faisal Specialist Hosp & Res Ctr, 1976-1985; consult, Nat Cancer Inst, 1973-1976; consult, 1966-1976; dir radiation safety off, Vanderbilt Univ, 1966-1976; res assoc physics, Vanderbilt Unib, 1965-1966. **Memberships:** Am Phys Soc; Health Phys Soc; Am Asn Physicists Med. **Research Statement & Publications:** Three-color photometric study of variable stars; Zeeman and Faraday effects in high pulsed magnetic fields; calibration techniques fordiagnostic and therapeutic machines. **Mailing Address:** Guidant Corp, 8934 Kirby Dr, Houston, TX 77054.

LOTTES, P(AUL) A(LBERT), MECHANICAL ENGINEERING. **Personal Data:** b Wilkinsburg, Pa, August 2, 1926; m 1947, c 3. **Education:** Purdue Univ, PhD (mech eng), 1950. **Professional Experience:** RETIRED; sr mech engr, Argonne Nat Lab, 1960-1991; assoc mech engr, Argonne Nat Lab, 1950-1960. **Memberships:** Fel Am Soc Mech Engrs; fel Am Nuclear Soc. **Research Statement & Publications:** Heat transfer and pressure drop in boiling; nuclear reactor safety. **Mailing Address:** 101 Green Valley Dr, 9700 S Cass Ave, Naperville, IL 60540.

LOTTI, VICTOR J, NEUROPHARMACOLOGY. **Personal Data:** b Trenton, NJ, January 6, 1938. **Education:** Univ Conn, BS, 1959; Univ Mo, MS, 1961; Univ Calif, Los Angeles, PhD (pharmacol), 1965. **Professional Experience:** RETIRED; sr scientist, Dept Pharmacol, 1979-1993; sr dir, Dept Pharmacol, Chibret, France, 1977-1979; sr dir res coordr, Dept Pharmacol, Merck, Sharp & Dohme Res Labs, 1975-1977; dir neuropsychopharmacol, Dept Pharmacol, Merck, Sharp & Dohme Res Labs, 1973-1975; res fel neuropharmacol, Dept Pharmacol, Merck, Sharp & Dohme Res Labs, 1969-1973; sr res pharmacologist, Dept Pharmacol, Merck, Sharp & Dohme Res Labs, 1967-1969. **Memberships:** Am Soc Pharmacol & Exp Therapeut; Am Chem Soc. **Mailing Address:** 214 Brookside Circle, Harleysville, PA 19438.

LOTTMAN, ROBERT P(OWELL), CIVIL ENGINEERING. **Personal Data:** b Brooklyn, NY, September 24, 1933; m 1956. **Education:** Polytech Inst Brooklyn, BCE, 1954; Purdue Univ, MSCE, 1956; Ohio State Univ, PhD, 1965. **Professional Experience:** PROF EMER CIVIL ENG; as of 1995; prof civil eng, Univ Idaho, beginning 1966; asst prof civil eng, Transp Eng Ctr, Ohio State Univ, 1965-1966; instnl & comt mem, Hwy Res Bd, Nat Acad Sci-Nat Res Coun, 1960-; res supvr hwy mat, Transp Eng Ctr, Ohio State Univ, 1959-1965; supvr, Asphalt Tech Serv Lab, Stand Oil Co, Ohio, 1957-1959; proj engr, Struct Appln Sect, Grumman Aircraft Eng Corp, 1956-1957. **Memberships:** Asn Asphalt Paving Technol; Am Soc Testing & Math. **Research Statement & Publications:** Study and evaluation of physical and chemical properties of construction materials to determine mechanicalbehavior under various loading and environmental conditions. **Mailing Address:** 3728 S Gandy St, Spokane, WA 99203-2709.

LOTTS, ADOLPHUS LLOYD, NUCLEAR SAFETY, ISOTOPE SEPARATION. **Personal Data:** b Buchanan, Va, June 10, 1934; m 1954, c 4. **Education:** Va Polytech Inst, BS, 1955, MS, 1957. **Honors & Awards:** E O Lawrence Mem Award, US Dept Energy, 1976. **Professional Experience:** RETIRED CHMN, LEGISLATIVE COMT, COALITION OAK RIDGE RETIRED EMPLOYEES, as of 2003; CONSULT, 1989-; dir, Atomic Vapor Laser Isotope Separation Div, Martin Marietta Energy Systs, Inc, 1983-1990; dir, Nuclear Regulatory Comn Prog, 1981-1983; head Fuel Cycle Technol Oper, dir Nuclear Waste Prog, 1978-1981; head Fuel Cycle Technol Oper, assoc dir Gas-cooled Reactor & Thorium Utilization Progs, 1970-1978; chmn long range planning group, Nuclear Regulatory Comn Prog, 1969-1983; head Fuel Cycle Technol Oper, Metals & Ceramics Div, 1966-1970; assoc metallurgist, group leader Fuel Cycle Technol, 1961-1966; assoc metallurgist, Metals & Ceramics Div, Oak Ridge Nat Lab, 1959-1961; assoc mat scientist, Atomic Energy Div, Babcock & Wilcox Co, 1958-1959; Instr metall eng, Va Polytech Inst, 1956-1957; div dir res reactors, Oak Ridge Nat Lab. **Memberships:** Fel Am Nuclear Soc; Am Soc Metals. **Research Statement & Publications:** Nuclear fuel processing technology; economics and properties of nuclear fuel; materials for reactor systems; radioactive and toxic waste management; nuclear reactor and safety technology; laser isotope separation technology. **Mailing Address:** Coalition Oak Ridge Retired Employees, Knoxville, TN 37922.

LOTZ, MARGARET M, CELL BIOLOGY. **Personal Data:** b New York, NY, October 29, 1958. **Education:** State Univ NY, BS, 1982; Duke Univ, PhD (biol), 1989. **Professional Experience:** INSTR SURG, BETH ISRAEL-DEACONESS, HARVARD MED SCH, 1993-; NRSA fel cell biol, 1989-1993. **Memberships:** Am Soc Cell Biol. **Research Statement & Publications:** Cell biology. **Mailing Address:** Beth Israel-Deaconess, Dept Surg, 330 Mt Auburn St, Boston, MA 02138. **E-Mail:** mlotz@bidmc.harvard.edu

LOTZ, W GREGORY, ENDOCRINOLOGY, THERMAL PHYSIOLOGY. **Personal Data:** m 1972, Vicki; c 3. **Education:** Heidelberg Col, BS, 1972; Univ Rochester, MS, 1975, PhD (biophys), 1977. **Professional Experience:** ASSOC DIR SCI, DIV APPL RES & TECHNOL, 2002-; chief, Non-ionizing Radiation Sect, 2000-2004; chief, Phys Agents Effects Br, Nat Inst Occup Safety & Health, 1994-2000; chief, Radiation Sect, 1992-1994; chief, Environ Physiol Div, Naval Aerospace Med Res Lab, 1976-1992. **Memberships:** Am Physiol Soc; Bioelectromagnetics Soc; AAAS; ACGIH; Commissioned Officers Asn USPHS. **Research Statement & Publications:** Physiological affects of nonionizing radiation. **Mailing Address:** Div Appl Res & Technol, Nat Inst Occup Safety & Health, MS R-2, 5555 Ridge Rd, Cincinnati, OH 45213. **Fax:** 513-841-4508. **E-Mail:** wlotz@cdc.gov

LOTZE, MICHAEL T, LYMPHOKINE RESEARCH, T-CELL IMMUNOBIOLOGY. **Personal Data:** b Pasadena, Calif, July 11, 1952; m 1977, Joan; c Thomas, Anna, Michael & Jenette. **Education:** Northwestern Univ, BS, 1973, MD 1974. **Professional Experience:** DIR, CLIN & TRANSLATIONAL RES MOLECULAR MED INST, as of 2002; co-dir, Biologic Ther Div, Univ Pittsburgh Med Ctr, 1992-2000; PROF SURG, MOLECULAR GENETICS & BIOCHEM, UNIV PITTSBURGH, 1990-; asst prof surg, Uniformed Serv Univ Health Sci, 1983-1988; Sr investr surg, Nat Cancer Inst, 1982-1990; med officer, Nat Health Serv Corp, 1977-1978; from intern surg to sr & chief res surg, Univ Rochester, 1975-1982; jr med fel surg, Md Anderson Tumor Inst, 1975. **Memberships:** Am Col Surgeons; Am Asn Immunol; Am Soc Clin Oncol; Am Asn Cancer Res; Soc Surg Oncol; Soc Univ Surgeons. **Research Statement & Publications:** Tumor immunology and developmental therapeutics; lymphokine function and T-cell immunobiology; surgical treatment of primary and metastatic liver tumors and melanoma. **Mailing Address:** Dept Surg & Pittsburgh Cancer Inst, Univ Pittsburgh, Rm 411 BST W1146 300 Technol Dr, Pittsburgh, PA 15219. **Fax:** 412-648-2520. **E-Mail:** ltzmichaelt@aol.com

LOU, ALEX YIH-CHUNG, ENGINEERING MATERIALS, MECHANICS. **Personal Data:** b Chungking, China, November 10, 1938; American citizen; m 1969, c 2. **Education:** Nat Taiwan Univ, BS, 1960; Purdue Univ MS, 1965, PhD (solid mech), 1969. **Professional Experience:** PHILLIPS RES CTR, PHILLIPS PETROL CO, 1981-; sr res scientist mat, Firestone Tire & Rubber Co, 1976-1981; res scientist, Firestone Tire & Rubber Co, 1970-1976; sr engr composites, Boeing Co, 1969-1970. **Memberships:** Am Soc Mech Engr. **Research Statement & Publications:** Characterization and evolution of composite; polymer materials for engineering applications; tire mechanics such as rolling resistance. **Mailing Address:** 2564 Georgetown Dr, Bartlesville, OK 74006.

LOU, DAVID YEONG-SUEI, MECHANICAL ENGINEERING. **Personal Data:** b Yuncom, China, November 12, 1937; m 1964, Marjorie; c Eugene & Derek. **Education:** Taiwan Univ, BS, 1959; Mass Inst Technol, MS, 1963, ME, 1966, ScD (mech eng), 1967. **Professional Experience: Assoc ed, J Eng Gas Turbines & Power, 1995-2002; LUDWICKSON PROF & CHMN, DEPT MECH ENG, UNIV NEBR, LINCOLN, 1993-; prof & chmn mech & aerospace eng, Syracuse Univ, Syracuse, NY, 1990-1992; prof & chmn mech eng, Univ Tex, Arlington, 1979-1990; from asst prof to prof mech eng, Univ Del, 1967-1979; asst molecular beams, Mass Inst Technol, 1965-1967; asst mech eng, Mass Inst Technol, 1964-1965; asst thermionic energy conversion, Mass Inst Technol, 1963-1964; thermodyn engr, Jackson & Moreland Consult Co, 1963; res asst mech eng, Mass Inst Technol, 1961-1963. **Memberships:** Am Phys Soc; Am Inst Aeronaut & Astronaut; Am Soc Mech Engrs; Am Soc Elec Engrs. **Research Statement & Publications:** Solar energy; kinetic theory of gases; molecular beams; thermodynamics; fluid mechanics; heat transfer; biomedical engineering. **Mailing Address:** Dept Mech Eng, Univ Nebr, Lincoln, NE 68588. **Fax:** 402-472-1465. **E-Mail:** dlou1@unl.edu

LOU, JACK Y K, OFFSHORE STRUCTURES, FLUID-STRUCTURE INTERACTIONS. **Education:** Mass Inst Technol, SM, 1962; Polytech Inst, Brooklyn, PhD (appl mech), 1969. **Honors & Awards:** Golden Cert Award, Am Soc Mech Engrs, 1981, Bd Gov Award, 1982. **Professional Experience:** PROF EMER CIVIL & OCEAN ENG, TEX A&M UNIV, 1996-; from assoc prof to prof, Tex A&M Univ, 1974-1995; from asst prof to assoc prof ocean eng, Columbia Univ, 1968-1974; staff engr, Hydrosysts Inc, 1966-1968; Marine div, Litton Industs, 1965-1966; prin dynamics engr, Hydrospace Div, Repub Aviation Corp, 1963-1965; naval architect, George Sharp Co, 1962-1963; engr, Ingalls-Taiwan Shipbuilding & Dry Dock Co, 1958-1960. **Memberships:** Fel Am Soc Mech Engrs; Am Soc Civil Engrs; Soc Naval Architects & Marine Engrs. **Research Statement & Publications:** Dynamic analysis of offshore structures and fluid-structure interactions. **Mailing Address:** Dept Civil eng, Tex A&M Univ, College Station, TX 77843-3136. **Fax:** 979-845-6156.

LOU, KINGDON, MICROBIOLOGY. **Personal Data:** b Stockton, Calif, August 3, 1922; m 1945, c 2. **Education:** Stanford Univ, AB, 1952, AM, 1956; Am Bd Bioanal, dipl. **Professional Experience:** RETIRED; consult, Immunoassay Technol, Inc, 1981-1992; vpres & dir immunol res, ICL Sci, 1970-1981; dir immunol, Kallestad Labs, 1968-1969; sr immunochemist, Res Div, Hoffmann-La Roche, 1967-1968; Dir, Immunol Dept, Res Div, Hyland Labs, Baxter, 1957-1967. **Memberships:** Am Soc Microbiol; Am Asn Clin Chemists; NY Acad Sci; AAAS. **Research Statement & Publications:** Immunochemical diagnostic reagents; hybridoria and monoclonal antibodies; immunoassays. **Mailing Address:** PO Box 1849, Tustin, CA 92681-1849.

LOU, PETER LOUIS, MOLECULAR BIOLOGY, OPHTHALMOLOGY. **Personal Data:** b Shanghai, China, December 9, 1945; American citizen; m 1980, Vibeke; c Jared, Kristina & Elizabeth. **Education:** Univ Ottawa, BSc, 1967, MD, 1974; McMaster Univ, Can, MSc, 1970, Univ Toronto, dipl ophthal, 1977. **Professional Experience:** Surgeon, Mass Eye & Ear Infirmary, Boston, 1995-; Consult vitreo-retinal dis, 1982-; CLIN INSTR OPHTHAL, HARVARD MED SCH, 1979-; vitreo-retinal fel, Boston, 1978; fel, Mass Eye & Ear Infirmary, 1977-1979; resident ophthal, Univ Toronto, 1975-1977; intern, Univ Toronto, 1974-1975; instr biol, McMaster Univ, 1967-1970. **Memberships:** Asn Res Vision & Ophthal; fel Am Acad Ophthal; Vitreous Soc; AMA. **Research Statement & Publications:** Effect of near ultraviolet light on aphakic retina metabolism; diabetic retinopathy; pathophysiology of vitreous and retina; vitreo-retinal disorders. **Mailing Address:** Dept Opthal, Harvard Med Sch, 75 Blossom Ct, Boston, MA 02114.

LOUBSER, PAUL GERHARD, SPINALCORD INJURY, CARDIOVASCULAR ANESTHESIOLOGY. **Personal Data:** b Cape Town, SAfrica, July 19, 1953. **Education:** Univ Cape Town Sch Med, MB & ChB, 1977; Am Bol Anesthesiol, dipl, 1991. **Professional Experience:** MANAGING DIR, NAT CARDIAC ANESTHESIA CONSULT, PA, as of 2004; ASST PROF ANESTHESIOL, BAYLOR COL MED, 1993-; from clin instr to clin asst prof, Baylor Col Med, 1985-1992; dir anesthesiol serv & prin investr, Inst Rehab & Res, 1985-1992; Fel res, Tex Heart Inst, 1984-1985; Res assoc, Heart Dis Res Found, 1983-1984. **Memberships:** Am Soc Anesthesiol; Asn Appl Psychol Physiol & Bioffed Pain; Soc Cardiovasc Anesthesia; Int Soc Study Pain; Am Spinal Injury Asn. **Research Statement & Publications:** Spinal cord injury-management of chronic spasticity and pain using regional anesthetic and intrathecal pharmaco therapy; cardiopulmanary bypass-cellular, humoral and immune chances considered detrimental. **Mailing Address:** Nat Cardiac Anesthesia Consultants, Sugar Land, TX 77478. **Fax:** 713-798-7345. **E-Mail:** loubser@earthlink.net

LOUCK, JAMES DONALD, MATHEMATICAL PHYSICS. **Personal Data:** b Grand Rapids, Mich, December 13, 1928; m 1960, c 3. **Education:** Ala Polytech Inst, BS, 1950; Ohio State Univ, MS, 1952, PhD (physics), 1958. **Professional Experience:** STAFF MEM, LOS ALAMOS NAT LAB, UNIV CALIF, 1963-; assoc res prof physics, Auburn Univ, 1960-1963; Staff mem, Los Alamos Nat Lab, 1958-1960. **Memberships:** Am Phys Soc; AAAS; Int Asn Math Physicists. **Research Statement & Publications:** Application and development of group theoretical methods in physics. **Mailing Address:** Los Alamos Nat Lab, PO Box 1663, Los Alamos, NM 87545. **Fax:** 505-665-5757. **E-Mail:** u058141@lanl.gov

LOUCKS, DANIEL PETER, SYSTEMS ANALYSIS, WATER RES ENGINEERING. **Personal Data:** b Chambersburg, Pa, June 4, 1932; m 1967, Marjorie; c Jennifer L & Susan L. **Education:** Pa State Univ, BS, 1954; Yale Univ, MS, 1955; Cornell Univ, PhD (systs eng, econ), 1965. **Honors & Awards:** Res Awards, Am Soc Civil Engrs, 1970 & 1986; Alexander Von Humboldt Sr Scientist Award, 1992. **Professional Experience:** Aachen Univ Technol, 1993 & Delft Univ Technol, 1995; distinguished vis prof, Univ Colo, 1992; distinguished vis prof, Univ Adelaide, 1992; CONSULT, 1981-; res scholar, Int Inst Appl Systs Anal, Austria, 1981-1982; assoc dean res & grad study, Col Eng, Cornell Univ, 1980-1981; vis prof, Mass Inst Technol, 1977-1978; prof environ eng & chmn dept, Col Eng, Cornell Univ, 1976-1980; economist, World Bank, 1972-1973; assoc prof environ eng, Col Eng, Cornell Univ, 1970-1975; res fel, Harvard Univ, 1968; Visiting prof TU-Delft, TU-Aachen, Univ Colorado, Univ Adelaide; Res. scientist IIASA, 1981-1982; Prin investr, NSF, Environ Protection Agency, Nato, Ford Found, Resources for the Future & US Dept Interior Res Grants, 1967-; sem assoc, Columbia Univ, 1967-1980; Prof water resources eng, Col Eng, Cornell Univ, 1965-; consult, UN Develop Prog, WHO, Food & Agr Orgn, NATO, UN & IRBD. **Memberships:** Nat Acad Eng; AAAS; Opers Res Soc Am; Int Mgt Sci; fel Am Geophys Union; hon fel Am Soc Civil Engrs; Int Hydraul Res Asn; Am Water Resources Assn; Int Water Resources Assn. **Research Statement & Publications:** Applications of operations research to problems in environmental and water resources engineering; public policy analysis; interactive modelling and computer based decision support systems. **Mailing Address:** Hollister Hall, Cornell Univ, Ithaca, NY 14853. **Fax:** 607-255-9004. **E-Mail:** DPL3@cornell.edu

LOUCKS, ORIE LIPTON, BIOLOGY, ENVIRONMENTAL SCIENCE. **Personal Data:** b Minden, Ont, October 2, 1931. **Education:** Univ Toronto, BSc, 1953, MSc, 1955; Univ Wis, PhD (bot), 1960. **Honors & Awards:** George Mercer Award, Ecol Soc Am, 1964 Distinguished Service Award, Am Inst of Biological Science1994; Conservation Achievement Award in Sci, Nat'k Wildlife Fed, 2001. **Professional Experience:** PROF EMER ZOOL, MIAMI UNIV, as of 2002; dir, Ctr Sustainable Systems, beginning 1999; chmn, Nature Conservancy Bd Gov Sect, beginning 1990; pres, Asn Ecosyst Res Ctrs, 1990-1992; ohio eminent scholar & prof zool, Miami Univ, beginning 1989; co-chmn, Nat Res Coun/RSC comt Great Lakes Water Qual Agreement, 1984-1985; dir, Holcomb Res Inst, 1983-1989; sci dir, Inst Ecol, 1978-1982; coordr environ mgt progs, US/Int Biol Prog, Univ Tex, 1973; Univ Wis rep, State Bd Preserv Sci Areas, 1964-1978; from asst prof to prof bot, Univ Wis, Madison, 1962-1978; forest ecologist, Dept Forestry, Can Govt, 1955-1962. **Memberships:** Fel AAAS; Soc Am Foresters; Ecol Soc Am; Am Inst Biol Sci; Am Soc Limnol Oceanog; Int Ecol Asn; Soc for Conserv Biol. **Research Statement & Publications:** Business and science synthesis. **Mailing Address:** Zool Dept, Miami Univ, Oxford, OH 45056. **E-Mail:** oloucks@icvalue.com

LOUCKS, VERNON R, JR, RESEARCH ADMINISTRATION. **Personal Data:** b Evanston, Ill, October 24, 1934; m 1972, Linda Kay Olson; c 6. **Education:** Yale Univ, BA, 1957; Harvard Univ, MBA, 1963. **Professional Experience:** DIR, PAIN THERAPEUT INC, as of 2004; DIR, GENOME THERAPEUT CORP, as of 2004; DIR, EMERSON ELECTRIC CO, as of 2004; DIR, EDWARDS LIFESCIENCES CORP, as of 2004; DIR, AFFYMETRIX INC, as of 2004; chief exec officer, Segway LLC, 2003; CHMN BD, AETHENA GROUP LLC, 2001-; DIR, ANHEUSER-BUSCH COMPANIES, INC, 1988-; chief exec officer & chmn, Baxter Int Inc, 1987-1999; pres & chief oper officer, Baxter Travenol Labs Inc, 1980-1987; exec vpres & bd dirs, Baxter Travenol Labs Inc, 1976-1980; staff, Baxter Travenol Labs Inc, 1966-1976; Sr mgt consult, George Fry & Assocs, Chicago, 1963-1965; trustee, Rush-Presby-St Luke's Med Ctr; bd adv, Nestle USA; assoc, Northwestern Univ; bd dirs, Dun & Bradstreet Corp, Emerson Elec Co, Quaker Oats Co & Anheuser-Busch Co. **Memberships:** Health Indust Mfr Asn. **Mailing Address:** Anheuser-Busch Co, One Busch Pl, St Louis, MO 63118-1852.

LOUD, ALDEN VICKERY, CELL BIOLOGY, BIOPHYSICS. **Personal Data:** b Boston, Mass, April 6, 1925; m 1950, Ruth Moody; c Kenneth R, Jane A, Thomas W & Peter A. **Education:** Mass Inst Technol, BS & MS, 1951, PhD (biophys), 1955. **Professional Experience:** PROF EMER PATH, NY MED COL, 1990-; from assoc prof to prof, NY Med Col, 1968-1990; asst prof path, Col Physicians & Surgeons, Columbia Univ, 1965-1968; Res assoc, Detroit Inst Cancer Res & asst prof biophys, Col Med, Wayne State Univ, 1957-1965; Res fel med, Mass Gen Hosp, 1951-1957. **Memberships:** Electron Micros Soc Am; Am Soc Cell Biol; Int Soc Stereology; Royal Micros Soc; Am Heart Asn. **Research Statement & Publications:** Stereologic morphometry; quantitative electron microscopy and methods of ultrastructure research; correlation of cellular ultrastructure with metabolic function. **Mailing Address:** 205 Washington Ave, Tappan, NY 10983.

LOUD, WARREN SIMMS, MATHEMATICS. **Personal Data:** b Boston, Mass, September 13, 1921; m 1947, Mary L Strasburg; c Margaret (McCamant), Elizabeth (Liebman) & John. **Education:** Mass Inst Technol, SB, 1942, PhD (math), 1946. **Professional Experience:** EMER PROF MATH, UNIV MINN, MINNEAPOLIS, 1992-; vis prof, Kyoto Univ, Japan, 1974-1975 & Univ Florence & Univ Trento, Italy, 1981-1982; guest prof, Darmstadt Tech Univ, 1964-1965; vis fel, Mass Inst Technol, 1955-1956; from asst prof to prof, Univ Minn, Minneapolis, 1947-1992; Res engr, Mass Inst Technol, 1945-1947; Instr math, Mass Inst Technol, 1943-1947. **Memberships:** AAAS; Am Math Soc; Soc Indust & Appl Math; Math Asn Am. **Research Statement & Publications:** Theory of differential equations; numerical methods of solution of differential equations; stationary solutions of Van der Pol's equation with a forcing term; nonlinear mechanics. **Mailing Address:** Sch Math, Univ Minn 206 Church St SE, Minneapolis, MN 55455. **Fax:** 612-359-9858. **E-Mail:** loud@math.umn.edu

LOUDA, SVATA M, PLANT-INSECT INTERACTIONS, PLANT DEMOGRAPHY. **Personal Data:** b Prague, Czech, American citizen; m Rodney; c Dan L Griffigh. **Education:** Pomona Col, BA, 1965; Univ Wash, Seattle, BS, 1968; Univ Calif, Santa Barbara, MS, 1972; Univ Calif, Riverside & San Diego State Univ, PhD (ecol), 1978. **Honors & Awards:** George Mercer Award, Ecol Soc Am, 1982 Outstanding Scientist Award 1001 from sigma Xi Scientific res soc. **Professional Experience:** Besey prof, Univ Nebraska, 2002; panel mem ecol, NSF, 1993-1997; PROF BIOL, UNIV NEBR, LINCOLN, 1992-, assoc ed ecol & ecol monogaphs, 1992-1994; coun mem, Am Inst Biol Sci, 1991-1993; assoc ed, Oecologia, 1990-1992; RESEARCHER & PRIN INVESTR, CEDAR PT BIOL STA, 1983-; from asst prof to assoc prof, Univ Nebr, Lincoln, 1983-1992; res Scientist, Bot Dept& res asst prof, Marine Lab, Beaufort 1981-1983, Durham, Duke Univ, 1981-1983; sr Scientist, Rocky Mountain Biol Lab, 1979-1990; postdoctoral fel bot, Yale Univ, 1979-1981; asst economist, Pac Northwest Bell Tel, 1965-1966 & Syst Develop Corp, 1968-1969. **Memberships:** Ecol Soc Am; Am Inst Biol Sci; Entom Soc Am; Bot Soc Am; fel AAAS; Sigma Xi; Soc Conserv Biol. **Research Statement & Publications:** Plant population dynamics; community ecology; interaction of plants with insects; biological control of weeds; insect herbivory; nontarget host plant use; prairie ecology; insect seed predation. **Mailing Address:** Sch Biol Sci 410A Manter Hall, Univ Nebr, Lincoln, NE 68588-0118. **Fax:** 402-472-2083. **E-Mail:** slouda@unl.edu

LOUDEN, L RICHARD, GEOCHEMISTRY, SATELLITE COMMUNICATIONS. **Personal Data:** b Monroe, Wash, July 8, 1933; m 1963. **Education:** Univ Wurzburg, PhD (geochem), 1963. **Professional Experience:** Vpres environ, Ecco Inc, Anchorage, 1990-; vpres, satellite commun, Drilling Info Serv Co, 1981-1982; PRES, L-R RESOURCE DEVELOP CORP, 1980-; exec vpres res, eng, construct & mfg, Analysts Inc, 1978-1980; mkt mgr, Dresser-Swaco, 1976-1978; prod mgr, Dresser Pollution, Dresser Oilfield Prod Div, 1973-1976; develop mgr, Dresser Pollution, Dresser Oilfield Prod Div, 1972-1973; spec proj engr, X-ray Dept, 1971-1972; tech adv, X-ray Dept, 1969-1971; mgr anal sect, X-ray Dept, 1967-1969; supvr, X-ray Dept, 1965-1967; geologist, Magnet Cove Barium Corp, 1964-1965; Co-worker, NASA grant, Univ Houston, 1963-1964; Assoc prof geochem, Univ Houston, 1963-1964. **Memberships:** AAAS; Marine Tech Soc; Clay Minerals Soc; Ger Geol Asn; Nat Oilfield Equip Mfrs & Distribr Soc. **Research Statement & Publications:** Organic geochemistry, oceanography, clay mineralogy, and x-ray analysis; new and novel equipment and chemicals for oilwell and other drilling practices; geotechnical services; project management; geophysical analysis; glycol recycling; oil/water seperation. **Mailing Address:** 8011 Highmeadow Dr, Houston, TX 77063.

LOUDON, CATHERINE, PHYSIOLOGICAL ECOLOGY, INVERTEBRATE BIOMECHANICS. **Personal Data:** b Chanute, Kans, November 1, 1958; m 1984, Andrew; c Jedidiah E (Borovik). **Education:** Brown Univ, SB, 1980; Duke Univ, PhD (zoology), 1986. **Professional Experience:** ASSOC PROF, UNIV KANS, as of 2005; asst prof, Kans State Univ, beginning 1993; res asst, Univ Calif, Berkeley, 1990-1992; NSF fel, Cornell Univ, 1989-1990; asst prof, Ithaca Col, 1988-1990; res asst, Univ Minn, 1986-1988. **Memberships:** AAAS; Entom Soc Am; Am Soc Zoologists; Sigma Xi. **Research Statement & Publications:** Physiology; physiological ecology; invertebrate biomechanics. **Mailing Address:** Dept Ecol & Evolutionary Biol Univ Kans, 6002 Haworth Hall, Lawrence, KS 66045-7534. **Fax:** 785-864-5321. **E-Mail:** loudon@ku.edu

LOUDON, GORDON MARCUS, BIOCHEMISTRY, ORGANIC CHEMISTRY. **Personal Data:** b Baton Rouge, La, October 10, 1942. **Education:** La State Univ, Baton Rouge,

BS, 1964; Univ Calif, Berkeley, PhD (org chem), 1968. **Professional Experience:** GUSTAV E CWALINA DISTINGUISHED PROF MED CHEM, PURDUE UNIV, 1996-; SR ASSOC DEAN RES & GRAD PROGS, COL PHARM, NURSING & HEALTH SCI, PURDUE UNIV, 1987-; prof med chem, Purdue Univ, beginning 1983; assoc prof, Purdue Univ, 1977-1983; from asst prof to assoc prof chem, Cornell Univ, 1970-1977; lectr biochem, Univ Calif, Berkeley, 1970; USPHS fel, Univ Calif, Berkeley, 1968-1970. **Memberships:** Am Soc Biol Chemists; Am Chem Soc; AAAS; Am Asn Cols Pharm. **Research Statement & Publications:** Peptide chemistry; enzyme model systems; bioanalytical methods; textbook author. **Mailing Address:** Dept Med Chem, Purdue Univ, Heine Pharm Bldg 575 Stadium Mall Dr 1330 RHPH, West Lafayette, IN 47907-2091. **Fax:** 765-494-7880. **E-Mail:** marc.loudon.1@purdue.edu

LOUDON, ROBERT G, INTERNAL MEDICINE. **Personal Data:** b Edinburgh, Scotland, June 27, 1925; American citizen; m 1955, c 3. **Education:** Univ Edinburgh, MB & ChB, 1947. **Professional Experience:** PROF EMER MED, COL MED, UNIV CINCINNATI, as of 2003; prof internal med, med ctr & dir pulmonary dis div, Col Med, Univ Cincinnati, beginning 1971; chief res respiratory dis, Vet Admin Cent Off, Wash, DC, 1969-1971; assoc prof med, Sch Med, George Wash Univ, 1969-1971; staff physician, Woodlawn Hosp, Dallas, 1961-1969; from asst prof to assoc prof internal med, Univ Tex Southwestern Med Sch Dallas, 1961-1969; supt, South-East Kans Tuberc Hosp, Chanute, 1960-1961; assoc med, Univ Kans, 1957-1961; staff physician, South-East Kans Tuberc Hosp, Chanute, 1956-1960; clin tutor gen med, Royal Infirmary, Edinburgh, 1953-1954; house physician, Chest Hosp, Brompton Hosp, London, Eng, 1951-1952; asst med officer, Tor-na-Dee Sanatorium, Aberdeen, 1950-1951; sr house physician tuberc wards, City Hosp, 1949-1950; house physician gen med, Western Gen Hosp, Edinburgh, Scotland, 1947-1948. **Memberships:** Am Thoracic Soc; AMA. **Research Statement & Publications:** Chest diseases; tuberculosis; aerobiology. **Mailing Address:** Dept Med Pulmonary Dis, Col Med, Univ Cincinnati, 231 Bethesda Ave, Cincinnati, OH 45267-0001.

LOUDON, RODNEY, QUANTUM OPTICS. **Personal Data:** b Manchester, Eng, July 25, 1934; m 1960, Mary A Philips; c Anne Elizabeth & Peter Thomas. **Education:** Oxford Univ, MA, DPhil, 1959. **Honors & Awards:** Thomas Young Medal, Inst Physics, 1987; Max Born Award Optical Soc Am, 1992. **Professional Experience:** PROF PHYSICS, ESSEX UNIV, 1989-; Sch Polytech, Lausanne, 1985 & Univ Rome, 1987 & 1996; RCA, 1975 & Brit Telecommun Res Labs, 1984 & 1989-1995; prof, Essex Univ, 1984; Univ Calif, Irvine, 1980; Vis prof, Yale Univ, 1975; mem tech staff, Bell Labs, 1965-1966 & 1970; Sci civil servant, Radar Res Estab, 1960-1965. **Memberships:** Fel Royal Soc; Optical Soc Am; Inst Physics UK. **Research Statement & Publications:** Authored four books. **Mailing Address:** Physics Dept Univ Essex, Wivenhoe Pk, Colchester CO4 3SQ, UK. **E-Mail:** loudr@essex.ac.uk

LOUGEAY, RAY LEONARD, PHYSICAL GEOGRAPHY, REMOTE SENSING. **Personal Data:** b Medford, Ore, February 9, 1944; m 1968. **Education:** Rutgers Univ, AB, 1966; State Univ, MS, 1969; Univ Mich, PhD (phys geog), 1971. **Professional Experience:** PROF GEOG, STATE UNIV NY, GENESEO, as of 2002; adj prof geog, State Univ NY, Geneseo, 1993-; DIR ENVIRON STUDIES, STATE UNIV NY COL GENESEO, 1979-; assoc prof geog, State Univ NY, Geneseo, beginning 1979; asst prof, State Univ NY Col Geneseo, 1971-1979; lectr phys geog, Univ Mich, 1969-1970. **Memberships:** Asn Am Geogr; AAAS; Am Meteorol Soc; Am Soc Photogram. **Research Statement & Publications:** Remote sensing; applied climatology and environmental modification as a function of radiative energy balances and hydrologic water balances; Alpine periglacial environments. **Mailing Address:** Dept Geog, State Univ NY, Fraser 105A, Geneseo, NY 14454. **Fax:** 716-245-5180. **E-Mail:** raylou@uno.cc.geneseo.edu

LOUGH, JOHN WILLIAM, ANATOMY, CELL BIOLOGY. **Personal Data:** b St Louis, Mo, April 2, 1943; m 1968, c 3. **Education:** St Louis Univ, BS, 1965, MS, 1968; Wash Univ, St Louis, PhD (cell biol & anat), 1975. **Professional Experience:** PROF, DEPT CELL BIOL, ANAT & NEUROBIOL, MED COL WIS, as of 2004; assoc prof, Mass Inst Technol, beginning 1983; asst prof anat, Mass Inst Technol, 1977-1983; res assoc biol, Mass Inst Technol, 1975-1977; grad fac, prog cell & develop biol. **Memberships:** Am Soc Cell Biol; Am Asn Anatomists; Am Heart Asn. **Research Statement & Publications:** Muscle differentiation in cell culture; changes in chromosomal proteins during myoblast differentiation. **Mailing Address:** Dept Cell Biol, Neurobiol & Anat, Med Col Wis, 8701 Watertown Plank Rd, Milwaukee, WI 53226-0509. **Fax:** 414-456-6517. **E-Mail:** jlough@mcw.edu

LOUGHEED, EVERETT CHARLES, HORTICULTURE. **Personal Data:** b Thornbury, Ont, July 16, 1927; m 1959, Leslie; c Stephen, Katherine & Robert. **Education:** Ont Agr Col, BSc, 1958; Univ Toronto, MSc, 1960; Mich State Univ, PhD, 1964. **Professional Experience:** PROF EMER, DEPT PLANT AGR, UNIV GUELPH, ONT, as of 2004; assoc grad fac, Univ Guelph, ont, beginning 1992; mgr aid proj, Can Int Develop Agency, Arg, 1989-1992; consult, Food & Agr Orgn, 1985; from asst prof to prof, Univ Guelph, Ont, 1964-1992; lectr, Ont Agr Col, 1960-1962. **Memberships:** Fel Am Soc Hort Sci; Agr Inst Can; Can Soc Hort Sci (pres 1973-1974); Int Soc Hort Sci; Int Stands Orgn; Sigma Xi. **Research Statement & Publications:** Horticulture; agriculture. **Mailing Address:** Dept Plant Agr, Ont Agr Col, Univ Guelph, 50 Stone Rd W, Guelph, ON N1G 2W1, Can. **Fax:** 519-763-8933.

LOUGHLIN, KEVIN RAYMOND, UROLOGIC ONCOLOGY & RESEARCH, MALE INFERTILITY. **Personal Data:** b 1949; m 1994, Christine. **Education:** Princeton Univ, BA, 1971; NY Med Col, MD, 1975; Am Bd Urol, cert; Boston Univ, MBA, 2000. **Honorary Degrees:** MA, Harvard Univ, 2000. **Professional Experience:** Staff urologist, Brigham & Women's Hosp & Dana Farber Cancer Inst, Boston, 1991-; PROF SURG, HARVARD MED SCH, 1990-; DIR UROL RES, BRIGHAM & WOMEN'S HOSP, 1987-. **Memberships:** Soc Univ Urologists; fel Am Col Surgeons; Am Urol Asn; Soc Basic Urol Res. **Research Statement & Publications:** New and novel therapies for superficial and invasive bladder cancer. **Mailing Address:** Brigham & Womens Hosp, 75 Francis St, Boston, MA 02115-6195. **Fax:** 617-566-3475. **E-Mail:** kloughlin@partners.org

LOUGHLIN, THOMAS RICHARD, MARINE MAMMALOGY, BEHAVIORAL ECOLOGY. **Personal Data:** b Santa Monica, Calif, July 19, 1943; m 1971, c 2. **Education:** Univ Calif, Santa Barbara, BA, 1972; Humboldt State Univ, MA, 1974; Univ Calif, Los Angeles, PhD (biol), 1977. **Professional Experience:** Assoc prof, Ore State Univ, 1985-; MARINE MAMMAL RES SPECIALIST, NAT MARINE MAMMAL LAB, ALASKA FISHERIES SCI CTR, NOAA, 1977-; vis scientist, Smithsonian Inst & US Dept Com alt mem, US Endangered Species Sci Authority, 1977-1980; recipient res funds, Univ Calif, 1975 & US Marine Mammal Comn, 1975-1977; biol consult, TerraScan, Inc, Environ Consults, 1972-1974. **Memberships:** AAAS; Am Asn Biol Sci; Am Soc Mammalogists; Animal Behav Soc; Soc Marine Mammalogists. **Research Statement & Publications:** Natural history, including physiological and behavioral ecology of marine mammals and the impact of man caused perturbations on them; recovery of endangered species; phylogenetic relationship between marine mammals; general oceanography. **Mailing Address:** Nat Marine Mammal Lab, Alaska Fisheries Sci Ctr, NOAA, 7600 Sand Point Way NE, Seattle, WA 98115-6349. **Fax:** 206-526-6615. **E-Mail:** tom.loughlin@noaa.gov

LOUGHLIN, TIMOTHY ARTHUR, APPLIED MATHEMATICS. **Personal Data:** b Bay Shore, NY, November 16, 1942; m 1965, Carol; c Shelley, Shannon, Sheryl & Scott. **Education:** State Univ NY Stony Brook, BS, 1964; Rensselaer Polytech Inst, MS, 1966, PhD (math), 1969. **Professional Experience:** PROF MATH, NY INST TECHNOL, 1991-; CHMN DEPT MATH, NY INST TECHNOL, 1990-; assoc prof, NY Inst Technol, 1976-1991; asst prof math, Union Col, NY, 1969-1976. **Memberships:** Math Asn Am. **Research Statement & Publications:** Network theory; realization of matrices as impedance and admittance matrices. **Mailing Address:** Dept Math, NY Inst Technol, Harry Schure Hall Rm 114 PO Box 9029, Central Islip, NY 11722. **Fax:** 631-851-1077. **E-Mail:** tloughli@nyit.edu

LOUGHMAN, BARBARA ELLEN EVERS, IMMUNOBIOLOGY. **Personal Data:** b Frankford, Ind, October 26, 1940; m 1962, c 2. **Education:** Univ Ill, BS, 1962; Notre Dame Univ, PhD (microbiol & immunol), 1972. **Professional Experience:** PRES & CHIEF OPERATING OFFICER & GEN MGR, ENCOREPHARMA DEVELOP SERV, ENCOREPHARMA LAB LLC, 1998-; vpres, Develop Servs, Imtci-Pra, beginning 1995; dir global regulatory affairs, Marion Merrell Dow, 1991-1995; dir & consult proj mgt, Rorer Cent Res, 1988-1991; dir immunol res, Monsanto Co, 1985-1988; res mgr, Hypersensitivity Dis Res, Upjohn Co, 1984-1985; res head immunol, Hypersensitivity Dis Res, Upjohn Co, 1979-1984; res scientist, Hypersensitivity Dis Res, Upjohn Co, 1974-1979; staff fel immunol, Nat Inst Child Health & Human Develop, 1972-1974; res scientist immunol, Ames Res Lab, Miles Labs Inc, 1971-1972; from asst res microbiologist to assoc res microbiologist, Ames Res Lab, Miles Labs Inc, 1962-1971. **Memberships:** AAAS; Asn Women Sci; Am Asn Immunologists. **Research Statement & Publications:** Cellular immunology; regulatory mechanisms in cells using controlled in vitro and in vivo systems as models for specific intervention in an immune response; clinical research immunobiology of transplantation and blood dyscrasia; management; strategic planning; project and portfolio management. **Mailing Address:** EncorePharma Develop Serv, EncorePharma Lab LLC, Ste 400 1401 Res Park Dr, Riverside, CA 92507. **Fax:** 909-275-5888.

LOUGHMAN, WILLIAM D, CLINICAL CYTOGENETICS ESPECIALLY PRE-NATAL DIAGNOSIS & CANCER CYTOGENETICS. **Personal Data:** b Oklahoma City, Okla, July 10, 1932; m 1967, Katherine Hershey; c Paul O, Elizabeth L & Donald E. **Education:** Univ Calif, Berkeley, BS, 1960, MS, 1964, PhD (genetics), 1973; Am Bd Med Genetics, dipl, 1982. **Professional Experience:** RETIRED; dir cytogenetics lab, Childrens Hosp, Oakland, 1989-1996; spec cytogeneticist, Childrens Hosp, Oakland, 1982-1989; adj assoc prof, Univ Calif, San Francisco, 1980-1982; dir, Cytogenetics Lab, Univ Calif, San Francisco, 1975-1982; from asst res geneticist to assoc res geneticist, Univ Calif, San Francisco, 1975-1980; lectr, Univ Calif, Berkeley, 1974-1977; biophysicist, Lawrence Berkeley Lab, 1965-1974. **Memberships:** emer mem AAAS; Sigma Xi; Am Soc Human Genetics; fel Am Col Med Genetics. **Research Statement & Publications:** Cytogenetics; pre-natal diagnosis and cancer cytogenetics. **Mailing Address:** 393 Gravatt Dr, Berkeley, CA 94705-1503.

LOUGHRAN, EDWARD DAN, Physical Chemistry. **Personal Data:** b Canton, Ohio, June 2, 1928; wid, c Nancy (Wathen, deceased), Steven & Glenn. **Education:** Ohio State Univ, BS, 1950; MS, 1953, PhD (chem), 1955. **Professional Experience:** RETIRED; Lab assoc, Los Alamos Nat Lab, 1991-1998; sect leader, Los Alamos Nat Lab, 1986-1990; assoc group leader, Los Alamos Nat Lab, 1981-1986; mem staff, Los Alamos Nat Lab, 1955-1990; Asst chem, Res Found, Ohio State Univ, 1953-1955. **Research Statement & Publications:** Analytical mass spectrometry; surveillance and compatibility studies of plastic-bonded explosives; physical properties, modes of decomposition and radiation chemistry of organic explosives. **Mailing Address:** 5116 Timan Ave NW, Albuquerque, NM 87114. **E-Mail:** edanl@aol.com

LOUGHRIDGE, MICHAEL SAMUEL, MARINE GEOLOGY. **Personal Data:** b Jacksonville, Tex, August 27, 1936; m 1961, c 1. **Education:** Rice Univ, BA, 1958; Harvard Univ, MA, 1961, PhD (geol), 1967. **Professional Experience:** DIR, NAT GEOPHYS DATA CTR, as of 1997; supvry oceanogr, Nat Geophys & Solar Terrestrial Data Ctr, beginning 1978; sci staff asst, Oceanog Surv Dept, US Naval Oceanog Off, 1968-1978; asst res geologist, Marine Phys Lab, Scripps Inst, Calif, 1967-1968; grad res geologist II, postgrad res geologist III, 1964-1967; grad res geologist II, postgrad res geologist II, 1963-1964; grad res geologist II, Marine Phys Lab, Scripps Inst, Calif, 1961-1963. **Memberships:** AAAS; Geol Soc Am; Am Geophys Union; Soc Explor Geophys. **Research Statement & Publications:** Studies of specialized techniques of echo sounding and the microtopography of the sea floor; studies of fine scale magnetics of the sea floor; instrumentation for marine geology; seismic profiling; quantitative geomorphology; stream hydraulics; relationships between archaeology and geology. **Mailing Address:** Nat Geophys Data Ctr, NOAA/NESDIS, Code E/GC 325 Broadway, Boulder, CO 80303. **Fax:** 303-497-6386. **E-Mail:** michael.s.loughridge@noaa.gov

LOUGHRIN, JOHN HUDSON, PLANT-INSECT INTERACTIONS, NATURAL PRODUCTS CHEMISTRY. **Personal Data:** m 1985, Linda; c John James. **Education:** Univ Ky, BS, 1981, MS, 1989, PhD (plant physiol), 1991. **Professional Experience:** RETIRED; postdoctoral scholar, Community Res Serv, Ky State Univ, beginning 1997; postdoctoral scholar, Dept Entom, 1995-1997; res chemist, Insect Attractants, Behavior & Basic Biol Res Lab, 1992-1995; prin lab technician, Dept Hort, Univ Ky, 1984-1997. **Memberships:** Entom Soc Am. **Research Statement & Publications:** Feeding-induced odors in insect aggregation; biochemistry of host plant resistance, especially as regards biochemical changes induced in plants by insect feeding; circadian and diurnal rhythms. **Mailing Address:** Ky State Univ, 127 THRI, Lexington, KY 40546. **Fax:** 606-323-1077. **E-Mail:** j.loughrin@worldnet.att.net

LOUGHTON, ARTHUR, HORTICULTURE. **Personal Data:** b Wisbech, Eng, May 25, 1931; Canadian citizen; m 1955, Ruth; c Martin & Graham. **Education:** Univ Nottingham, Eng, BSc, 1954, MSc, 1960. **Professional Experience:** RETIRED; mgr transition crop team, Ont Ministry Agr & Food, Simcoe, 1986-1991; dir hort res, Hort Exp Sta, 1975-1996; res scientist veg res, Hort Res Inst Ont, Vineland Sta, 1967-1975; dep dir, Yorkshire, Eng, 1962-1967; hort officer res, Stockbridge House Exp Hort Sta, Ministry Agr, Fisheries & Food, Yorkshire, Eng, 1954-1962. **Memberships:** Can Soc Hort Sci; Agr Inst Can. **Research Statement & Publications:** Production of field vegetables, including integrated pest management, specialising cole crops, management of total station research programs in fruit and vegetables. **Mailing Address:** RR 1, Vittoria, ON N0E 1W0, Can.

LOUI, MICHAEL CONRAD, THEORETICAL COMPUTER SCIENCE. **Personal Data:** b Philadelphia, Pa, June 1, 1955; m 1983, Cynthia; c Eric & Jeremy. **Education:** Yale Univ, BS, 1975; Mass Inst Technol, MS, 1977, PhD (comput sci), 1980. **Professional Experience:** PROF ELEC & COMPUT ENG, UNIV ILL, as of 2006; bd govs, Soc Social Implications Technol, 2002-2004, 2005-2007; assoc dean, Grad Col, 1996-2000; RES PROF, COORD SCI LAB & PROF ELEC & COMPUT ENG, UNIV ILL, URBANA, 1991-; prog dir, NSF, 1990-1991; res assoc prof, Coord Sci Lab & assoc prof elec & comput eng, 1986-1991; res asst prof & asst prof elec eng, 1982-1986; vis res asst prof & vis asst prof elec eng, Univ Ill, Urbana, 1981-1982; adv Bd, Online Ethics Ctr Eng & Sci; exec Bd, Nat Inst Eng Ethics. **Memberships:** Asn Comput Mach; Am Soc Eng Educ; Soc Indust & Appl Math; Inst Elec & Electronics Engrs; Sigma Xi. **Research Statement & Publications:** Computational complexity theory; parallel and distributed computation; software reliability; engineering ethics. **Mailing Address:** Dept Elec & Comput Eng, Univ Ill, 212 Coord Sci Lab 1308 W Main St, Urbana, IL 61801. **E-Mail:** m-loui@uiuc.edu

LOUIE, DEXTER STEPHEN, GASTROENTEROLOGY. **Personal Data:** b San Francisco, Calif. **Education:** Univ Calif, Berkeley, AB, 1974, BS, 1976, PhD (nutrit), 1982. **Professional Experience:** Investr, Ctr Gastrointestinal Biol & Dis, 1991-; ASST PROF NUTRIT, UNIV NC, CHAPEL HILL, 1991-; asst res scientist, Univ Mich, Ann Arbor, 1990-1991; res investr, Univ Mich, Ann Arbor, 1987-1990; Res fel gastroenterol, Univ Mich, Ann Arbor, 1985-1987. **Memberships:** Am Gastroenterol Asn; Am Inst Nutrit; Am Pancreatic Asn; Am Physiol Soc. **Research Statement & Publications:** Neurohormonal control of exocrine pancreatic secretion; intracellular messenger mechanisms. **Mailing Address:** Dept Nutrit CB 2202 McGarran-Greenberg Hall No 7400, Univ NC, Chapel Hill, NC 27599-7400. **Fax:** 919-966-7216. **E-Mail:** dlouie@sphvax.sph.unc.edu

LOUIE, MING, POLYMER IN ELECTRONIC APPLICATION, ELECTROCHEMISTRY. **Personal Data:** b Canton, China, December 8, 1948; American citizen; c 1. **Education:** Univ Conn, BA, 1971; Pa State Univ, MS (polymer sci) & MS (phys chem), 1975. **Professional Experience:** TECH STAFF, ELASTOMERIC TECHNOLOGIES INC, 1989-; res chemist, West Co, 1985-1989; Chemist, Zapata Industs Inc, 1978-1985. **Memberships:** Am Chem Soc; Soc Plastics Engrs; Int Inst Connector & Interconnection Technol Inc; Int Soc Hybrid Microelectronics. **Research Statement & Publications:** Formulation of conductive silicone rubber for electronic application such as elastomeric connectors; conduct testing programs on the connectors for electronics applications; development of fine-line electronic connection technologies; granted one patent; author of several publications. **Mailing Address:** Elastomeric Technologies Inc, 2940 Turnpike Dr, Hatboro, PA 19040-4229.

LOUIE, RAYMOND, PLANT PATHOLOGY. **Personal Data:** b Canton, China, June 22, 1936; American citizen; m 1962, c 1. **Education:** Univ Calif, Berkeley, BS, 1959; Cornell Univ, MS, 1965, PhD (plant path), 1968. **Professional Experience:** Adj prof, Dept plant pathol, Ohio State Univ, as of 2005; assoc prof virol, Ohio State Univ & res plant pathologist, Ohio Agr Res & Develop Ctr, USDA, 1967-; scientist, USDA. **Memberships:** Am Phytopath Soc. **Research Statement & Publications:** Epiphytology of plant viruses; virus vector relationships; mechanical transmission of plant viruses. **Mailing Address:** Dept Plant Path & Environ Grad Studies, Ohio State Univ, 023 Selby Hall USDA/OARDC 1680 Madison Ave, Wooster, OH 44691-4096. **Fax:** 330-263-3841. **E-Mail:** louie.2@osu.edu

LOUIE, ROBERT EUGENE, VIROLOGY. **Personal Data:** b Oakland, Calif, August 2, 1929; m 1962, c 1. **Education:** Univ Calif, Berkeley, BA, 1951, MA, 1953, PhD (bacteriol), 1963. **Professional Experience:** MGR VIROL RES DEPT, CUTTER LABS, 1977-; res microbiologist virol, Cutter Labs, 1961-1977; Res asst virol, Ft Detrick, Md, 1954-1955. **Memberships:** Am Soc Microbiol; Sigma Xi. **Research Statement & Publications:** Development of viral vaccines for human use; viral chemotherapy; virus-cell relationships. **Mailing Address:** 1026 Cragmont Ave, Berkeley, CA 94708.

LOUIE, STEVEN GWON SHENG, THEORETICAL SOLID STATE PHYSICS. **Personal Data:** b Canton, China, March 26, 1949; American citizen. **Education:** Univ Calif, AB, 1972, PhD (physics), 1976. **Honors & Awards:** US Dept Energy Award, 1993; Aneesur Rahman Prize, Am Phys Soc, 1996; Davisson Germer Prize, Am Phys SOC, 1999. **Professional Experience:** Prof, Miller Inst Basic Res, 1995; sr fac scientist, Lawrence Berkeley Lab, 1993-; vis prof, Fourier Univ, Grenoble, France, 1990; J S Guggenheim fel, 1989-1990; vis scholar, Univ Tokyo, 1989; prof, Miller Inst Basic Res Sci, 1986-1987; PROF PHYSICS, UNIV CALIF, BERKELEY, 1984-; assoc prof, Univ Calif, Berkeley, 1980-1984; A P Sloan fel, 1980-1982; asst prof physics, Univ Pa, 1979-1980; fel theoret solid state physics, T J Watson Res Ctr, IBM Corp, 1977-1979; NSF fel, Dept Physics, Univ Calif, Berkeley, 1976-1977. **Memberships:** Fel Am Phys Soc; Mat Res Soc. **Research Statement & Publications:** Theoretical solid state physics; electronic properties of solids and of solid surfaces and interfaces; many-body effects in solids. **Mailing Address:** Dept Physics, Univ Calif, 545 Birge, Berkeley, CA 94720-7300. **Fax:** 510-643-9473. **E-Mail:** sglouie@uclink.berkeley.edu

LOUIS, ADRIAAN ANTHONY, PHYSICS. **Education:** Cornell Univ, PhD, 1998. **Professional Experience:** Res fel, Hughes Hall, 1998. **Mailing Address:** Dept Physics, Cornell Univ 117 Clark Hall, Ithaca, NY 14853. **Fax:** 607-255-6428.

LOUIS, JOHN, HEMATOLOGY, CLINICAL PHARMACOLOGY. **Personal Data:** b Chicago, Ill, June 21, 1924; div. **Education:** Univ Ill, BS, 1948, MS & MD, 1950. **Professional Experience:** Chief hematol sect, Vet Admin Hosp, Downey, Ill, 1975; assoc dir, Div Hematol & Oncol, Chicago Med Sch, 1975; Prof med, Chicago Med Sch, 1975; CONSULT HEMAT & ONCOL, 1970-; asst prof, Stritch Sch Med, Loyola Univ, Chicago, 1965-1970; chmn, Leukemia Task Force, 1962-1965; US deleg, Eighth Int Cancer Cong, 1962; chmn, Leukemia Criteria Comt, NIH, 1961-1965; chmn, Midwest Coop Chemother Group, 1959-1969; consult to various hosps & Chicago State TB Sanatorium, 1958-; instr med, Col Med, Univ Ill, 1951-1965; prin investr, Leukemia A Group, MCCG, Eastern Coop Oncol Group. **Memberships:** Am Soc Hemat; Am Soc Clin Oncol; Am Col Physicians; Am Soc Clin Path; emer mem Cent Soc Clin Res; Int Soc Hemat. **Research Statement & Publications:** Clinical pharmacology of drugs relating to hematology and cancer. **Mailing Address:** 347 Circle Lane, Lake Forest, IL 60045.

LOUIS, KWOK TOY, TEXTILE CHEMISTRY. **Personal Data:** b Shanghai, China, January 22, 1927; m 1954, Harriet Poon; c Arthur, Mark & Jeffrey. **Education:** Tex Tech Univ, BS, 1951. **Professional Experience:** VPRES, APEX CHEM CO, INC, 1978-; tech dir, Apex Chem CO, Inc, 1976-1977; dir tech dept, Dyes & Chem Div, Crompton & Knowles Corp, NJ, 1971-1976; mgr cent lab, Tech Appln Prod, 1968-1971; admin mgr res & appln, Tech Appln Prod, 1964-1968; group leader appln res & qual control, Ciba Chem & Dye Co, 1963-1964; applns chems, Ciba Chem & Dye Co, 1961-1962; chief chemist, United Piece Dye Works, SC, 1957-1961; develop chemist, Burlington Indust, Inc, NC, 1955-1956; Lab dir, Otto Goedecke, Inc, Tex, 1953-1954. **Memberships:** Am Asn Textile Chemists & Colorists; Nat Flaxseed Processors Asn. **Mailing Address:** 442 Ellis Place, Wyckoff, NJ 07481.

LOUIS, LAWRENCE HUA-HSIEN, biochemistry; deceased, see previous edition for last biography

LOUIS, THOMAS MICHAEL, REPRODUCTIVE ENDOCRINOLOGY. **Personal Data:** b Pensacola, Fla, December 27, 1946; m 1969, c 2. **Education:** Va Polytech Inst & State Univ, BS, 1968, MS, 1971; Mich State Univ, PhD (sci), 1975. **Honors & Awards:** Richard Hoyte Res Prize, Am Dairy Sci Asn, 1975. **Professional Experience:** PROF ANAT, SCH MED, E CAROLINA UNIV, 1985-; from asst prof to assoc prof, Sch Med, E Carolina Univ, 1976-1985; lalor res fel reproductive endocrinol, Univ Oxford, 1975-1976; vis res fel, Inst Pasteur. **Memberships:** AAAS; Soc Gynec Invest; Sigma Xi; Soc Study Endocrinol; Am Asn Anatomists. **Research Statement & Publications:** Chronic effects of alcohol, nicotine, and the nervous system on pregnancy and parturition; studies include endocrinology of parturition, fetal endocrinology, effects of fetal asphyxia on the neonate and endocrine control of the hypothalamus and pituitary. **Mailing Address:** Dept Anat, Sch Med, E Carolina Univ, Brody 8E 14 600 Moye Blvd, Greenville, NC 27834. **Fax:** 252-744-2850. **E-Mail:** louisth@mail.ecu.edu

LOUIS-FERDINAND, ROBERT T, PHARMACOLOGY. **Education:** Univ RI, PhD, 1970. **Professional Experience:** PROF, DEPT PHARMACOL, WAYNE STATE UNIV, as of 2004. **Mailing Address:** Pharmaceut Sci, Wayne State Univ Shapero Hall, Detroit, MI 48202. **Fax:** 313-577-2033.

LOULLIS, COSTAS CHRISTOU, NEUROBIOLOGY, NEUROCHEMISTRY. **Personal Data:** b Nicosia, Cyprus, January 5, 1950. **Education:** Fairfield Univ, BS, 1974; Syracuse Univ, MA, 1975, PhD (biopsychol), 1978. **Professional Experience:** FOUNDER & PRES, ANIXIS BIOMED CONSULT, as of 2005; exec vpres, Ancile Pharmaceut, 1998-2000; sr & group sr vpres, res, develop, clin & regulatory, PharmaPrint, 1996-1997; sr dir pre clin & clin res & vpres, Trega Biosci, 1992-1996; scientist, Med Res Div, Am Cyanamid Co, 1980-1992; NIMH fel neurochem & behavior, Dept Psychiat, Sch Med, Ind Univ, 1978-1980; teaching asst biopsychol, Dept Psychol, Syracuse Univ, 1974-1978. **Memberships:** Soc Neuroscience; NY Acad Sci; AAAS. **Research Statement & Publications:** Psychopharmacology; CNS lesions; limbic system; schedule induced polydipsia; taste aversion; operant behavior; eating and drinking behaviors; neurotransmitters; aging; calmedulin; calcium; cyclic neucleotides. **Mailing Address:** 454 Sierra Vista Lane, Valley Cottage, NY 10989.

LOULOU, RICHARD JACQUES, OPERATIONS RESEARCH, PROBABILITY. **Personal Data:** b Relizane, Algeria, April 19, 1944; Canadian citizen; m 1967, c 2. **Education:** Sch Polytech, Paris, BSc, 1966; Univ Calif, Berkeley, MSc, 1968, PhD (opers res), 1971. **Honorary Degrees:** DSc, Univ Grenoble, France, 1978. **Professional Experience:** ASSOC DEAN ACAD & DIR, FAC MGT, MCGILL UNIV, 1993-; dir group studies & res anal decisions, Res Ctr, Mcgill Univ, 1988-1992; PROF MGT SCI, MCGILL UNIV, 1984-; Children's Hosp, Can Ministry Energy, Mines & Resources, 1984-1985; Prof Opers Res, McGill Univ, beginning 1983; invited researcher, Dept Appl Math, Univ Grenoble, 1983-1984; tenured assoc prof mgt sci, McGill Univ, 1977-1984; sabbatical, Univ Grenoble, 1976-1977; invited prof, Univ Sherbrooke, 1972-1973; consult, Archer, Seaden & Assocs, 1972-1973; from asst prof to assoc prof, McGill Univ, 1970-1977. **Memberships:** Inst Mgt Sci; Opers Res Soc Am; Can Opers Res Soc; Soc Indust & Appl Math. **Research Statement & Publications:** Queueing theory; congested service systems; stochastic processes simulation; heuristics in optimization. **Mailing Address:** Dept Mgt, McGill Univ, 1001 Sherbrooke St W, Montreal, PQ H3A 1G5, Can. **Fax:** 514-398-3876. **E-Mail:** loulou@management.mcgill.ca

LOUNGE, JOHN M, AERONAUTICS. **Personal Data:** b June 28, 1946. **Education:** US Naval Acad, BS, 1969; Univ Colo, MS, 1970. **Professional Experience:** DIR, SPACEHAB INC, as of 2006. **Memberships:** Am Inst Aeronaut & Astronaut. **Mailing Address:** Spacehab Inc, 1215 Jefferson Davis Hwy, Arlington, VA 22202-4302. **Fax:** 202-488-8251.

LOUNIBOS, LEON PHILIP, INSECT ECOLOGY, INSECT BEHAVIOR. **Personal Data:** b Petaluma, Calif, August 19, 1947; div, c Andrea Lounibos & Andrew Pragnell. **Education:** Univ Notre Dame, BS, 1969; Harvard Univ MS, 1970, PhD (biol), 1974. **Professional Experience:** PROF ENTOM, UNIV FLA, 1993-; prin investr, Nat Inst Allergy & Infectious Dis, NIH, 1991-1997 & 1994-1997 & 1999-2001; assoc prof, Fla Med Entom Lab, 1983-1993; entomologist III, Fla Med Entom Lab, 1977-1983; res scientist & head, Int Ctr Insect Physiol & Ecol, Coastal Res Sta, 1974-1977; NIH fel, 1969-1977, 1988-1989. **Memberships:** AAAS; Sigma Xi; Entom Soc Am; Animal Behav Soc; Ecol Soc Am; Am Soc Trop Med & Hyg. **Research Statement & Publications:** Insect ecology: seasonality, diapause strategies, predator-prey relationships, community organization; insect behavior: building, predatory, oviposition behaviors; biosystematics. **Mailing Address:** Fla Med Entom Lab, 200 9 St SE, Vero Beach, FL 32962. **Fax:** 772-778-7205.

LOUNSBURY, JOHN BALDWIN, PHOTOLITHOGRAPHIC TECHNOLOGY, HIGH BANDWIDTH COMMUNICATION SYSTEMS. **Personal Data:** b Urbana, Ill, January 30, 1936; m 1963, c 3. **Education:** Univ Vt, BA, 1957; Columbia Univ, MA, 1958; Ill Inst Technol, PhD (phys chem), 1966. **Professional Experience:** Res assoc physics, Armour Res Found, Chicago, Ill, 1959-1962; SR ENGR & MGR, IBM CORP, ARMONK, NY, 1958-. **Research Statement & Publications:** Career research activities include quantum chemistry of molecular structure, plasma chemistry, physics and materials/processes of photolithography for semiconductor fabrication; one patent and 20 publications. **Mailing Address:** Sunset Hill Rd, Millbrook, NY 12569.

LOURENCO, RUY VALENTIM, MEDICINE, PHYSIOLOGY. **Personal Data:** b Lisbon, Port, March 25, 1929; American citizen; m 1960, c 2. **Education:** Univ Lisbon, BSc, 1946, MD, 1951. **Professional Experience:** PROF MED PHARMACOL & PHYSIOL, UNIV MED DENT, NJ, as of 2000; dean, Univ Med Dent, NJ, 1989-1999; comt int affairs, Am Col Chest Physicians, beginning 1984; comt smoking & health, Am Lung Asn, beginning 1981; foley prof med, Abraham Lincoln Sch Med, Col Med, Univ Ill, beginning 1978; physician-in-chief, Univ Ill Hosps, 1977-; mem, inhalation toxicol comt, Nat Ctr Toxicol Res, 1977-; mem, Asn Prog Dirs Internal Med, beginning 1977; chmn dept med, abraham lincoln sch med, col med, Univ Ill, beginning 1977; vis prof, cardiothoracic inst, brompton hosp, Univ London, 1975-1976; chmn sci assembly, Am Thoracic Soc, 1974-1975; consult, career develop prog, Vet Admin, beginning 1972; mem study sect, NIH, 1972-1976; mem task force sci basis respiratory therapeut, Nat Heart & Lung Inst, 1971-1972; dir pulmonary sect, Dept Med, 1970-1977; Pulmonary Sect & Labs, 1970-1977 & dept pulmonary med, Univ Ill Med Ctr, 1969-1970; prof med & physiol, Abraham Lincoln Sch Med, Univ Ill Col Med, beginning 1969; Univ Ill hosp, cock county hosp & Wside Va hosp, beginning 1967; respiratory res, Hektoen Inst Med Res, Chicago, 1967-1971; assoc prof, Abraham Lincoln Sch Med, Univ Ill Col Med, 1967-1969; respiratory physiol lab, Cook Co Hosp, 1967-1969; consult physician, Vet Admin Hosps, beginning 1965; from asst prof to assoc prof, NJ Col Med, 1963-1967; respiratory physiol, Dept Med, NJ Col Med, 1963-1967; Jersey city med ctr & Va hosp, NJ & Newark City Hosp, 1963-1967; polachek found fel, 1961-1963; lederle int fel, 1959-1960; fel med, Columbia-Presby Med Ctr, 1959-1963 & Cologne Univ, 1957; dir, respiratory physiol lab, Univ Lisbon Med Sch, Portugal, 1957-1961; attend physician, Lisbon Univ Hosp, 1956-1961; instr med, Sch Med, Lisbon, 1956-1959; attend physician, Nat Cancer Inst, Lisbon, Portugal, 1955-1961; resident internal med, Lisbon City Hosps, 1953-1955; intern, Lisbon City Hosps, 1952; reviewer, var physiol, respiratory & clin journals; mem cardio-pulmonary coun, Am Heart Asn; lectr, var univs US, Brazil, Portugal & Spain Cancer Inst, Lisbon, Portugal, 1955-1961; resident internal med, Lisbon City Hosps, 1953-1955; intern, Lisbon City Hosps, 1952; reviewer, var physiol, respiratory & clin journals; mem cardio-pulmonary coun, Am Heart Asn; lectr, var univs US, Brazil, Portugal & Spain. **Memberships:** Am Physiol Soc; Am Fedn Clin Res; Am Thoracic Soc; Am Soc Clin Invest; Soc Exp Biol & Med; Int Soc Aerosols Med; Asn Profs Med. **Research Statement & Publications:** Internal medicine; chest diseases; respiratory physiology and biochemistry; regulation of ventilation; muscles of breathing; pulmonary defense mechanisms. **Mailing Address:** Dept Pharmacol & Physiol, NJ Med Sch, Univ Med & Den NJ, 185 S Orange Ave, Newark, NJ 07103-2714. **Fax:** 973-982-7104.

LOURIA, DONALD BRUCE, INTERNAL MEDICINE, MICROBIOLOGY. **Personal Data:** b New York, NY, July 11, 1928; m 1955, c 3. **Education:** Harvard Univ, BS, 1949, MD, 1953. **Professional Experience:** CHMN EMER DEPT, NJ MED SCH, COL MED & DENT NJ, as of 2003; chmn dept, nj med sch, Col Med & Dent Nj, beginning 1969; PROF PREV MED & COMMUNITY HEALTH, NJ MED SCH, COL MED & DENT NJ, 1969-; pres, NY State Coun Drug Addiction, 1965-1973; from instr to assoc prof med, Col Med, Cornell Univ, 1958-1969. **Memberships:** Am Soc Clin Invest; Am Fedn Clin Res; Am Soc Microbiol; Am Col Physicians. **Research Statement & Publications:** Mycology, especially fungal toxins and the pathogenesis of Candida infections; prevention programs for adults; health education; health manpower; cancer epidemiology; health problems of the aging. **Mailing Address:** Dept prev med & community health, Univ Med & Dent, 30 Bergen St, ADMC 1605, Newark, NJ 07107. **E-Mail:** louriado@umdnj.edu

LOURIE, ALAN DAVID, ORGANIC CHEMISTRY. **Personal Data:** b Boston, Mass, January 13, 1935; m 1959, Elizabeth S; c 2. **Education:** Harvard Univ, AB, 1956; Univ Wis, MS, 1958; Univ Pa, PhD (org chem), 1965; Temple Univ, JD, 1970. **Honors & Awards:** jefferson medal for contributions, 1998. **Professional Experience:** JUDGE, COURT APPEALS, FED CIRCUIT, 2002-; vpres corp patents, Smithkline Corp, 1976-1990; asst dir, patent dept, 1974-1976; assoc patent coun, Smith Kline & French Labs, 1971-1974; patent atty, Smith Kline & French Labs, 1970-1971; patent agent chem, Smith Kline & French Labs, 1964-1970; patent chemist, Wyeth Labs, 1962-1964; lit chemist, Wyeth Labs, 1960-1962; res chemist, Wyeth Labs, 1959-1960; es chemist, Monsanto Co, 1957-1959. **Memberships:** Am Chem Soc. **Research Statement & Publications:** Synthesis of heterocyclic compounds; medicinal chemistry. **Mailing Address:** Court Appeals Fed Circuit, 717 Madison Pl NW Nat Court Bldg, Washington, DC 20439.

LOUTFY, RAFIK OMAR, PHOTOCHEMISTRY, PHYSICAL CHEMISTRY. **Personal Data:** b Cairo, Egypt, November 1943; Canadian citizen; m 1965, c 2. **Education:** Ain Shams Univ, Cairo, BSc, 1964, MSc, 1967; Univ Western Ont, PhD (photochem), 1972; Univ Toronto, MBA, 1985. **Professional Experience:** PROF CHEM ENG, MCMASTER UNIV, 2004-; bd ed mem Res & Technol Mgt J, 2000-; vpres, Xerox Res Ctr Can, 2000-2004; vpres, Corp Bus Strategy, Stamford Conn, 1999-2000; chief Tech Officer & sr vpres Xerox Bus Group Operations, Webster, NY, 1998-1999; vis prof, Stanford Univ, Palo Alto, 1997-1998; advi bd mem, Univ Windsor, Can, 1994-1998; vice pres, Xerox Res Ctr Can, 1994-1997; vpres, Strategy Planning & Innovation, 1991-1998; adj prof, Univ Western Ont, Can, 1985-1991; lab mgr, Xerox res Ctr Can, 1985-1991; area mgr, Xerox Res Ctr Can, 1980-1985; adj prof, Univ Western Ont, 1979-; mem res staff, Xerox Res Ctr Can, 1974-1980; fel photochem, Univ Toronto, 1974; fel laser flash photolysis, Nat Res Coun Can, 1972-1974; Walter Booth Chair Eng Entrepreneurship & Innovation. **Memberships:** Am Chem Soc; Chem Inst Can; Inter-Am Photochem Soc; Europ Photochem Soc; Soc Photog Scientists & Engrs. **Research Statement & Publications:** Photophysics of small molecules and polymers; solar energy conversion using organic semiconductors; dye sensitization of semiconductors; electrochemistry and spectroscopy of organic molecules and dyes; photo conductors. **Mailing Address:** Dept Chem Eng, McMaster Univ, ITC 108 Info Technol Ctr, 1280 Main St W, Hamilton, ON L8S 4L7, Can. **Fax:** 905-521-1350. **E-Mail:** loutfyr@mcmaster.ca

LOUTHAN, MCINTYRE R, JR, MATERIALS SCIENCE. **Education:** Va Polytech Inst, BS, 1960, MS; Univ Notre Dame, PhD. **Professional Experience:** SR ADV ENGR, SAVANNAH RIVER LAB, SC, as of 2006. **Memberships:** Am Soc Metals. **Mailing Address:** Mat Technol Sect Savannah River Lab, Westinghouse Savannah River Co, Aiken, SC 29808.

LOUTINSKY, KARL J, AERONAUTICS. **Professional Experience:** STAFF, NASA, as of 2005. **Memberships:** Am Inst Aeronaut & Astronaut. **Mailing Address:** NASA, 300 E St SW, Washington, DC 20546-0005. **Fax:** 202-358-4625. **E-Mail:** kloutins@mail.hq.nasa.gov

LOUTTIT, RICHARD TALCOTT, BEHAVIORAL SCIENCES, NEUROSCIENCE. **Personal Data:** b Bloomington, Ind, December 5, 1932; wid, c Robert & Cathy. **Education:** DePauw Univ, AB, 1954; Univ Mich, MA, 1959, PhD (psychol), 1961. **Professional Experience:** RETIRED; div dir, Div Behav & Neural Sci, NSF, 1975-1993; Staff dir, President's Biomed Res Panel, 1975; prof & head, Dept Psychol, Univ Mass, Amherst, 1970-1975; health sci adminr, NIH, 1964-1970; Asst prof psychol, Univ Pac, 1961-1964. **Memberships:** Fel AAAS; Am Psychol Soc. **Mailing Address:** 225 Three Oaks Dr, Gore, VA 22637.

LOUTTIT, ROBERT IRVING, EXPERIMENTAL HIGH ENERGY PHYSICS. **Personal Data:** b Honolulu, Hawaii, July 23, 1929; m 1986, Anne; c Eric, Laura & Kimberly. **Education:** Univ NH, BS, 1952; Wash Univ, PhD (physics), 1958. **Professional Experience:** RETIRED; sr physicist, Accelerator Develop Br, 1984-1986; head, Accelerator Develop Br, 1984-1986; physicist, Nuclear Res Ctr, Saclay, France, 1963-1964; from asst physicist to physicist, Brookhaven Nat Lab, 1958-1984. **Memberships:** AAAS; Am Phys Soc; Sigma Xi. **Research Statement & Publications:** Bubble chamber development; neutrino interactions. **Mailing Address:** 205 McTeer Dr, St Helena Island, SC 29920. **E-Mail:** louttit@islc.net

LOUX, MARK, WEED SCIENCE. **Education:** Univ Del, BS, 1981; Univ Ill, MS, 1985, PhD (agron), 1988. **Professional Experience:** PROF & EXTEN SPECIALIST, DEPT HORT & CROP SCI, OHIO STATE UNIV, as of 2005. **Mailing Address:** Dept Hort & Crop Sci, Ohio State Univ, 2021 Coffey Rd, Columbus, OH 43210. **E-Mail:** loux.1@osu.edu

LOVAGLIA, ANTHONY RICHARD, MATHEMATICS. **Personal Data:** b San Jose, Calif, January 25, 1923; m 1944, c 3. **Education:** Univ Calif, Los Angeles, AB, 1945, PhD (math), 1951; Stanford Univ, MA, 1948; Univ Calif, Berkeley, PhD (math), 1951. **Professional Experience:** PROF EMER MATH, SAN JOSE STATE UNIV, 1986-; prof math, San Jose State Univ, beginning 1960; from asst prof to assoc prof, San Jose State Univ, 1951-1960. **Memberships:** Math Asn Am. **Research Statement & Publications:** Analysis. **Mailing Address:** Dept Math, San Jose State Univ, 308 Macquarrie Hall, San Jose, CA 95192. **Fax:** 408-924-5080.

LOVALD, ROGER ALLEN, ORGANIC POLYMER CHEMISTRY. **Personal Data:** b Marshall, Minn, August 8, 1938; m 1957, c 2. **Education:** Univ Minn, BChem, 1960; Univ Wis, PhD (org chem), 1965. **Professional Experience:** RETIRED; tech dir resins, Gen Mills Chem Inc, 1975-1997; sect leader resin develop, Gen Mills Chem Inc, 1971-1975; cent res, Gen Mills Chem Inc, 1967-1971; chemist, Spring Res Lab, Rohm & Haas Co, 1965-1967. **Memberships:** Am Chem Soc. **Research Statement & Publications:** Heteroaliphatic and organic chemistry; addition and condensation polymerization; acrylics; polyamides; polyesters; polyurethanes. **Mailing Address:** 751 Pondhurst Circle, Amery, WI 54001.

LOVALLO, WILLIAM ROBERT, BEHAVIORAL MEDICINE, PSYCHOPHARMACOLOGY. **Personal Data:** b Newark, NJ, November 16, 1946. **Education:** Univ Calif, Los Angeles, BA, 1968; Univ Colo, MA, 1970; Univ Okla Health Sci Ctr, PhD (biol & psychol), 1978. **Professional Experience:** PROF, PSYCHIAT & BEHAV SCI, UNIV OKLA HEALTH SCI CTR, as of 2005; DIR, BEHAV SCI LABS, OKLA CITY VET ADMIN MED CTR, 1986-; NIH grant, Caffeine Effects, 1985-; assoc prof, Psychiat & Behav Sci, Univ Okla Health Sci Ctr, 1985-; asst prof, Psychiat & Behav Sci, Univ Okla Health Sci Ctr, 1980-1985; asst dir, Mind-Body Interactions, John D & Catherine T MacArthur Found Network. **Memberships:** AAAS; Am Psychol Asn; Soc Psychophysiol Res; Soc Behav Med; Psychosomatic Soc. **Research Statement & Publications:** Psychological and behavioral stress; the role of stress on the development of cardiovascular diseases; author of various articles. **Mailing Address:** Vet Admin Med Ctr 151A, 921 NE 13th St, Oklahoma City, OK 73104. **E-Mail:** bill@mindbody1.org

LOVAS, FRANCIS JOHN, MOLECULAR SPECTROSCOPY, RADIO ASTRONOMY & THERMAL RADIOMETRY. **Personal Data:** b Cleveland, Ohio, July 29, 1941; m 1999, Hong; c Daniel. **Education:** Univ Detroit, BS, 1963; Univ Calif, Berkeley, PhD (phys chem), 1967. **Honors & Awards:** Gold Medal, Dept Com, 1977; George vanBiesbroeck Prize, AAS 1998. **Professional Experience:** RETIRED; vis scientist, Nat Inst Stand & Technol, beginning 1972; assoc, Nat Res Coun-Nat Bur Stand, 1970-1972; NATO fel, Phys Inst, Free Univ Berlin, 1968-1970; res grant, Lawrence Radiation Lab, Univ Calif, Berkeley, 1967-1968. **Memberships:** Am Phys Soc. **Research Statement & Publications:** Properties of diatomic molecules by high temperature microwave adsorption and molecular beam electric resonance techniques; microwave spectroscopy of transient molecules and molecular radio astronomy; critical evaluation of microwave spectroscopic data. **Mailing Address:** Div Optical Technol, Nat Inst Stand & Technol, Gaithersburg, MD 20899. **Fax:** 301-869-5700. **E-Mail:** lovas@nist.gov

LOVASS-NAGY, VICTOR, APPLIED MATHEMATICS, ELECTRICAL ENGINEERING & CONTROL THEORY. **Personal Data:** b Debrecen, Hungary, April 25, 1923; m 1951, Klara; c Steven & Christine. **Education:** Budapest Tech Univ, dipl, 1947, PhD (math), 1949. **Professional Experience:** PROF EMER ELEC ENG & MATH, CLARKSON UNIV, as of 2004; prof elec eng & math, clarkson univ, beginning 1982; prof math, Clarkson Univ, 1966-1982; reader eng math, Univ Khartoum, 1964-1966; consult engr, Ganz Elec Works, Hungary, 1960-1964; from asst prof to assoc prof, Budapest Tech Univ, 1949-1958; instr math, Budapest Tech Univ, 1947-1949. **Memberships:** Sr mem Inst Elec & Electronics Engrs. **Research Statement & Publications:** Matrix theory; numerical analysis; control theory. **Mailing Address:** Dept Elec & Comp, Clarkson Univ, Box 5720, Potsdam, NY 13699-5820. **Fax:** 315-268-7600. **E-Mail:** lovass@clarkson.edu

LOVATT, CAROL JEAN, METABOLIC REGULATION. **Personal Data:** b Kansas City, Mo, May 14, 1947; div, c 2. **Education:** Univ Mass, BA, 1973; Univ RI, MS, 1976, PhD (bot), 1980. **Honors & Awards:** Fruit Publ Award, Am Soc Hort Sci, 1987, Cross Commodity Publ Award, 1988. **Professional Experience:** CHAIR, BIOL SCI, UNIV CALIF, RIVERSIDE, as of 2005; PROF PHYSIOL, UNIV CALIF, RIVERSIDE, as of 2004; PLANT PHYSIOLOGIST, DEPT BOT & PLANT SCI, UNIV CALIF, RIVERSIDE, as of 2004; assoc prof plant physiol, Dept Bot & Plant Sci, Univ Calif, Riverside, beginning 1987; assoc plant physiologist, Dept Bot & Plant Sci, Univ Calif, Riverside, beginning 1987; asst prof plant physiol & asst plant physiologist, Univ Calif, Riverside, 1980-1987; res assoc, Univ Calif, Riverside, 1980. **Memberships:** Am Soc Plant Physiologists; AAAS; Am Women Sci; Sigma Xi; Am Soc Hort Sci. **Research Statement & Publications:** Metabolic regulation of nucleotide metabolism and arginine biosynthesis urea cycle; citrus and avocado physiology: regulation of flowering, fruit set, and fruit growth; role of essential nutrient elements in plant metabolism. **Mailing Address:** Dept Bot & Plant Sci, Univ Calif, 4130 Batchelor Hall, Riverside, CA 92521-0124. **Fax:** 951-827-4437. **E-Mail:** carol.lovatt@ucr.edu

LOVE, ALLAN WALTER, ELECTROMAGNETISM, ANTENNAS & MICROWAVES. **Personal Data:** b Toronto, Ont, May 28, 1916; American citizen; wid Shirley D Corrigan (deceased); c Karen M, Peter J & Elizabeth M. **Education:** Univ Toronto, BA, 1938, MA, 1939, PhD (microwave physics), 1951. **Honors & Awards:** Leonard da Vinci Medallion, Rockwell Int, 1989; Millenium Medal, Inst Elec & Electronics Engrs, 2000. **Professional Experience:** RETIRED; prin scientist, Satellite Systs Div, Rockwell Int, 1976-1990; prog mgr, Space Div, NAm Rockwell Corp, 1973-1976; mem tech staff, Space Div, NAm Rockwell Corp, 1971-1973; group scientist theoret analysis, Antenna Lab, Autonetics Div, NAm Aviation Inc, 1965-1971; area mgr, Nat Eng Sci Co, 1963-1965; group scientist, Antenna Lab, Autonetics Div, NAm Aviation Inc, 1963; mgr, Physics Lab, Calif, 1962-1963; staff scientist, Giannini Res Lab, Wiley Electronics Co, Ariz, 1957-1962; chief instrumentation, Newmont Explor Ltd, Conn & Ariz, 1951-1957; demonstr asst, Physics Lab, Univ Toronto, 1948-1951; res officer, Radiophysics Lab, Commonwealth Sci & Indust Res Orgn, Australia, 1946-1948. **Memberships:** fel Inst Elec & Electronics Engrs; Inst Elec & Electronics Engrs Antenna & Propagalim Soc (pres, 1984). **Research Statement & Publications:** Microwave and millimeter wave physics; antenna theory and design; development of spacecraft antenna systems. **Mailing Address:** 518 Rockford Pl, Corona Del Mar, CA 92625-2721. **E-Mail:** awlove@att.net

LOVE, CALVIN MILES, PYROTECHNICS, EXPLOSIVES. **Personal Data:** b Chicago, Ill, March 2, 1937; m 1960, Sue; c Peggy (High), David M & Andrew I. **Education:** Ill Inst Technol, BS, 1959; Mich State Univ, PhD (inorg chem), 1964. **Professional Experience:** SR RES SPECIALIST, EG&G MOUND APPL TECHNOLOGIES INC, 1980-; res specialist, EG&G Mound Appl Technologies Inc, 1964-1980. **Memberships:** AAAS; Am Chem Soc; N Am Thermal Analysis Soc. **Research Statement & Publications:** Kinetics and mechanisms of inorganic oxidation-reduction reactions; plutonium separation and recovery; polonium process development; metal hydrides; radiation damage; thermal analysis; hydrides for hydrogen storage; chemistry of pyrotechnics; chemistry of explosives; calorimetry. **Mailing Address:** 7601 Eagle Creek Dr, Dayton, OH 45459. **Fax:** 513-865-3680.

LOVE, CARL G(EORGE), SYSTEMS ANALYSIS. **Personal Data:** b Warsaw, NY, September 20, 1940; m 1971, c 2. **Education:** Rochester Inst Technol, BS, 1963; Carnegie Inst Technol, MS, 1965, PhD (elec eng), 1967. **Professional Experience:** SR

SYSTS SCIENTIST, WESTINGHOUSE RES & DEVELOP CTR, 1991-; dir corp venture progs, Corp Planning, 1984-1991; sr consult corp planning, Westinghouse Elec Corp, 1982-1984; mgr syst planning & tech assessment, Westinghouse Res & Develop Ctr, 1972-1991; fel engr, Westinghouse Res & Develop Ctr, 1972; sr engr, Westinghouse Res & Develop Ctr, 1967-1971; proj engr, Delco Appl Div, Gen Motors Corp, 1963; coop student, Delco Appl Div, Gen Motors Corp, 1960-1963; coop student, Rochester Gas & Elec Corp, 1958-1960. **Memberships:** Inst Elec & Electronics Engrs; Inst Mgt Sci; Opers Res Soc Am. **Research Statement & Publications:** Technology forecasting; business analysis; energy analysis. **Mailing Address:** Sch Comput Sci, Carnegie-Mellon Univ, 500 Forbes Ave, Pittsburgh, PA 15213.

LOVE, DANIEL JOSEPH, ELECTRICAL POWER GENERATION & DISTRIBUTION, ELECTRICAL & FIRE PROTECTION. **Personal Data:** b Fall River, Mass, September 27, 1926; m 1989, Adeline; c Amy, Timothy, Terence, Kevin, Eric, Brian & Jason. **Education:** Ill Inst Technol, BSEE, 1951, MSEE, 1956; Calif State Univ, MBA, 1973. **Honors & Awards:** Outstanding Engr Award, Inst Adv Eng, 1986; Richard Harold Kaufmann Award, Inst Elec & Electronics Engrs, 1994. **Professional Experience:** RETIRED; chmn, Power Systs Comt, Indust Appln Soc, Inst Elec & Electronics Engrs, 1990-1991; consult engr, Calif, 1987-2005; eng specialist, Norwalk, Calif, 1983-1987; chief elec engr, Madrid, 1980-1983; eng specialist, Bechtel Co, Calif, 1968-1980; pres & gen mgr, McKee Automation Co, 1965-1968; mkt mgr & asst to pres, Emerson Elec Co, 1963-1965; mkt mgr, Control Data Co, 1961-1962; proj engr & opers mgr, Panellit Co, 1953-1960; designer, Pioneer Serv & Eng Co, 1952-1953; test engr, Int Harvester Co, 1951-1952. **Memberships:** Fel Inst Elec & Electronics Engrs; Soc Fire Protection Engrs; Nat Acad Forensic Engrs; Nat Soc Prof Engrs; Instrument Soc Am. **Research Statement & Publications:** Contributed articles to professional journals. **Mailing Address:** 16300 E Soriano Dr, Hacienda Heights, CA 91745. **Fax:** 818-918-5205. **E-Mail:** dan.love@ieee.org

LOVE, DAVID VAUGHAN, FOREST MANAGEMENT. **Personal Data:** b St John, NB, August 25, 1919; m 1943, c 3. **Education:** Univ Nebr BSc, 1941; Univ Mich, MF, 1946. **Professional Experience:** RETIRED; dean, Univ Toronto, 1984-1985; assoc dean, Univ Toronto, 1977-1983; vice chmn, Can Coun Rural Develop, 1975-1979; pres, Conserv Coun Ont, 1974-1975; rep, Can Forestry Asn, 1973; asst dean, Univ Toronto, 1972-1976; vpres, Conserv Coun Ont, 1959-1964; from lectr to prof, Univ Toronto, 1946-1972. **Memberships:** Soc Am Foresters; Can Pulp & Paper Asn; Can Inst Forestry (secy-mgr, 1948-1954, pres, 1965-1966); Ont Forestry Asn (vpres, 1970-1971, pres, 1972-1973); Can Forestry Asn (vpres, 1974 & 1975, pres, 1975). **Research Statement & Publications:** Land use; forests; acid precipitation. **Mailing Address:** 16 Marchwood Dr, North York, ON M3H 1J8, Can.

LOVE, DAVID WAXHAM, QUATERNARY STRATIGRAPHY. **Personal Data:** b Laramie, Wyo, November 1, 1946. **Education:** Beloit Col, BA, 1969; Univ NMex, MS, 1971, PhD (geol), 1980. **Professional Experience:** SR ENVIRON GEOLOGIST, NMEX BUR GEOL & MINERAL RESOURCES, 1980-; asst prof geol, Wash State Univ, 1976-1978. **Memberships:** Geol Soc Am; Sigma Xi; Soc Archeol Sci. **Research Statement & Publications:** Geomorphic processes and stratigraphy of surficial deposits in New Mexico and adjacent areas for assessing natural hazards and for determining stability of land forms for siting industrial plants or for storing hazardous materials. **Mailing Address:** NMex Bur Mines & Mineral Resources, 801 Leroy Pl, Socorro, NM 87801-4796. **E-Mail:** dave@gis.nmt.edu

LOVE, GEORGE M, ORGANIC CHEMISTRY. **Personal Data:** b Lima, Ohio, October 5, 1944; m 1972. **Education:** DePauw Univ, BA, 1966; Wake Forest Univ, MA, 1968; Mich State Univ, PhD (org chem), 1972. **Professional Experience:** ASSOC DIR CHEM PROCESS DEVELOP, SCHERING-PLOUGH, 1980-; res fel, Merck Inc, 1980; sr res chemist, Merck Inc, 1973-1980; fel org chem, Rutgers Univ, 1972-1973. **Memberships:** Sigma Xi; Am Chem Soc. **Research Statement & Publications:** Process research in organic chemistry. **Mailing Address:** Schering Plough Res U 1 1, 1011 Morris Ave, Union, NJ 07083.

LOVE, GORDON ROSS, MATERIALS SCIENCE. **Personal Data:** b Cleveland, Ohio, July 31, 1937; m 1962, c 1. **Education:** Case Western Reserve Univ, BS, 1958; Carnegie Mellon Univ, MS, 1960, PhD (metall), 1963. **Professional Experience:** BD MEM, CETEK TECHNOL INC, as of 2005; VPRES STRATEGIC PLANNING, TECH DIR & DIR, CETEK TECHNOL INC, 1993-; tech dir ceramic div, Alcoa Tech Ctr, Alcoa, 1987-1992; ed, Trans Comp Hyb Mfrs Tech, Inst Elec Electronics Engrs, 1981-1985; vpres, Sprague Elec Co, 1978-1987; asst mgr technol, Mat Syst Div, Union Carbide Corp, 1970-1978; lectr, Univ Tenn, 1966-1967; group leader superconducting mat, Oak Ridge Nat Lab, 1964-1970; metallurgist, Oak Ridge Nat Lab, 1962-1964. **Memberships:** Sigma Xi; Inst Elec & Electronics Engrs. **Research Statement & Publications:** Diffusion; superconductivity; statistical process control; powder technology; surface and interface properties; ceramic dielectric materials. **Mailing Address:** Cetek Technologies Inc, 19 Commerce St, Poughkeepsie, NY 12603-2608.

LOVE, HARRY SCHROEDER, JR, botany, ecology; deceased, see previous edition for last biography

LOVE, HUGH MORRISON, PHYSICS. **Personal Data:** b Northern Ireland, August 21, 1926. **Education:** Queen's Univ, Belfast, BSc & PhD (physics), 1950. **Professional Experience:** PROF EMER PHYSICS, QUEEN'S UNIV, ONT, 1992-; vprin, Queen's Univ, Ont, 1976-1992; from asst prof to prof, Queen's Univ, Ont, 1952-1992; lectr, Univ Toronto, 1950-1952; asst lectr, Queen's Univ, Belfast, 1946-1950. **Memberships:** Am Phys Soc. **Research Statement & Publications:** Solid state physics; surface physics. **Mailing Address:** Dept Physics, Queen's Univ, Stirling Hall, Kingston, ON K7I 3N6, Can.

LOVE, JIM, ORGANIC CHEMISTRY. **Personal Data:** b Bathgate, Scotland, October 21, 1938; m 1962, c 2. **Education:** Univ Edinburgh, BSc, 1960, PhD (carbohydrate chem), 1963. **Professional Experience:** BUS DEVELOP MGR, FERRO PERFORMANCE & FINE CHEM INC, as of 2005; global dir process res, Dow Elan Co Ind, beginning 1995; lab dir, Midland, Mich, 1988-1995; lab dir, Pittsburg, Calif, 1983-1988; res mgr, Dow Chem Co Mich, 1979-1983; group leader, Dow Chem Co Mich, 1977-1979; res specialist, Dow Chem Co Mich, 1974-1977; Western Div, Dow Chem Co Mich, 1967-1974; res chemist, Dow Chem Co Mich, 1965-1967; fel, Ohio State Univ, 1964-1965 & Scripps Inst, Univ Calif, 1963-1964. **Memberships:** Am Chem Soc; The Chem Soc. **Research Statement & Publications:** Carbohydrate chemistry, particularly polysaccharide and mucopolysaccharide structural determination and biological activity; synthesis and biological activityof heterocyclic compounds. **Mailing Address:** Ferro Performance & Fine Chems, Inc, 7061 E Pleasant Valley Rd, Cleveland, OH 44114-7000. **Fax:** 216-750-1416. **E-Mail:** lovejd@ferro.com

LOVE, JIMMY DWANE, ANALYTICAL CHEMISTRY, THERMODYNAMICS & MATERIAL PROPERTIES. **Personal Data:** b Plainview, Tex, February 2, 1946; m 1967, c 2. **Education:** Stephen F Austin State Univ, Nacogdoches, Tex, BS, 1969, MS, 1976. **Professional Experience:** COM DEVELOP MGR, GA-PAC CORP, 1988-; carbonless paper prod mgr, Moore Bus Forms, 1985-1988; qual assurance mgr, Moore Bus Forms, 1983-1985; tech serv mgr, Moore Bus Forms, 1980-1983; lab mgr, Moore Bus Forms, 1978-1983; sr chemist, Moore Bus Forms, 1974-1978; Bench chemist, Moore Bus Forms, 1970-1974. **Memberships:** Am Chem Soc; Am Soc Qual Control; Am Soc Testing & Mat; Tech Asn Pulp & Paper Indust; Paper Indust Mgt Asn. **Research Statement & Publications:** Micro encapsulation chemistry and techniques; coatings technology; papermaking chemistry; applied technology. **Mailing Address:** Ga Pac Corp, 55 Park Pl, Atlanta, GA 30374.

LOVE, JOHN DAVID, GEOLOGY. **Personal Data:** b Riverton, Wyo, April 17, 1913; m 1940, c 4. **Education:** Univ Wyo, BA, 1933, MA, 1934; Yale Univ, PhD (geol), 1938. **Honorary Degrees:** LLD, Univ Wyo, 1961. **Honors & Awards:** Meritorious Serv Award, US Dept Interior, 1977 & Distinguished Serv Award, 1987; Nat Pub Serv Award, Am Asn Petrol Geologists, 1991. **Professional Experience:** EMER SCIENTIST, US GEOL SURV, 1987-; affil, Univ Minn, 1981-1983; affil, Univ Wash, 1979-1983; exten instr geol, Univ Calif, Davis, 1977-; affil prof geol, Univ Idaho, 1974-; adj prof, Univ Wyo, 1969-; supvr, Laramie Off, Regional Geol Br, US Geol Surv, 1969-1987; supvr heavy metals, Jackson Proj, US Geol Surv, 1966-1968; instr & trustee, Teton Sci Sch, 1965-1985; distinguished lectr, Univ Wyo, 1965; supvr heavy metals, Northern Rocky Mts Br, US Geol Surv, 1964-1966, 1967-1969; STAFF GEOLOGIST, US GEOL SURV, 1956-; in charge Wyo basins fuels proj, US Geol Surv, 1943-1956; from assoc geologist to prin geologist, US Geol Surv, 1943-1956; asst geologist, US Geol Surv, 1942-1943; from asst geologist to geologist, Shell Oil Co Inc, 1938-1942; field asst, US Geol Surv, 1938; asst geologist, Geol Surv Wyo, 1933-1937; grad res adv, Univ Wash. **Memberships:** AAAS; fel Geol Soc Am; Am Asn Petrol Geol; Sigma Xi. **Research Statement & Publications:** Geology of fuels; uranium, vanadium and gold investigations; stratigraphic and structural geology; author or coauthor of about 220 scientific publications. **Mailing Address:** US Geol Surv, PO Box 3007 Univ Sta, Laramie, WY 82071-3007.

LOVE, JOSEPH E(UGENE), JR, CIVIL ENGINEERING. **Personal Data:** b Chicago, Ill, April 9, 1920; m 1942, Barbara Duncan; c 2. **Education:** Northwestern Univ, BS, 1942, MS, 1948, PhD (civil eng), 1951. **Professional Experience:** CONSULT, 1985-; mem, working group containment, Int Orgn Stand, 1984-1988; chmn working group containment, Int Orgn Stand, Technol Comt 85, subcomt 3, 1976-1984; mgr plant struct systs, nuclear energy div, 1975-1984; mgr advan eng, Atomic Power Equip Dept, 1972-1975; mgr arrangements & struct design, Atomic Power Equip Dept, 1966-1972; struct engr, Atomic Power Equip Dept, 1955-1966; struct engr, Hanford Atomic Prod Oper, Gen Elec Co, 1952-1955; from instr to asst prof civil eng, Northwestern Univ, 1946-1951; instr math & eng, Ripon Col, 1943-1945; struct analyst, Curtiss-Wright Corp, 1942-1943; contribr, 1st Int Conf Peaceful Uses Atomic Energy. **Memberships:** Am Soc Civil Engrs; Sigma Xi. **Research Statement & Publications:** Plasticity effects in flexure; nuclear power plant design. **Mailing Address:** 14799 Dove Rd, Grass Valley, CA 95949-7631. **E-Mail:** joslov@nccn.net

LOVE, L J CLINE, luminescence, micellar chemistry; deceased, see previous edition for last biography

LOVE, LEON, RADIOLOGY. **Personal Data:** b New York, NY, September 7, 1923; m 1956, c 3. **Education:** City Col New York, BS, 1943; Chicago Med Sch, MD, 1946; Am Bd Radiol, dipl, 1951. **Professional Experience:** PROF RADIOL & CHMN DEPT, MED CTR, LOYOLA UNIV CHICAGO, 1969-; clin prof, Chicago Med Sch, 1967-1969; consult, House Correction, Chicago, 1961- & WSide Vet Admin Hosp, 1962-; dir diag radiol, Cook Co Hosp, Chicago, 1961-1969; assoc prof radiol, Chicago Med Sch, 1958-1967; Consult, Dwight Vet Admin Hosp, 1956-1962; Radiologist, Cook Co Hosp, Chicago, 1956-1961. **Memberships:** Am Col Radiol; Radiol Soc NAm. **Research Statement & Publications:** Renal radiology; radiology of the gastro-intestinal tract. **Mailing Address:** Loyola Univ Stritch Sch Med, 2160 S First, Maywood, IL 60153-5500.

LOVE, NORMAN DUANE, LOW TEMPERATURE PHYSICS. **Personal Data:** b Howell, Mich, January 1, 1939; m 1962, Suzanne; c Aaron M, Heather A (Constantino), Nathan D & Amber S. **Education:** Albion Col, AB, 1960; Western Mich Univ, MA, 1962; Mich State Univ, PhD (physics), 1967. **Professional Experience:** NETWORK COMMUN CONSULT, DIGITAL EQUIP CORP, 1994-; commun consult, Digital Equip Corp, 1982-1994; software specialist, Digital Equip Corp, 1977-1982; dir comput serv, Maryville Col, 1971-1977; Nat Sci Found comput grant, 1968-1973; from asst prof to assoc prof, Maryville Col, 1967-1977. **Memberships:** Am Phys Soc; Am Asn Physics Teachers. **Research Statement & Publications:** Effect of magnons on transport of phonons; phase boundaries in an antiferro magnetic material using calorimetric techniques. **Mailing Address:** Digital Equip Corp, 430 Blockhouse Rd, Maryville, TN 37803. **E-Mail:** loven@mail.dec.com

LOVE, RAYMOND CHARLES, CLINICAL PHARMACY. **Personal Data:** b Washington, DC, July 30, 1953; m 1976. **Education:** Univ Md, Baltimore, DrPharm, 1977. **Professional Experience:** PROF & VICE CHAIR, CLIN PHARM, DEPT PHARM PRACT & SCI, UNIV MD SCH PHARM, as of 2005; DIR, MENTAL HEALTH PROG, DEPT PHARM PRACT & SCI, UNIV MD SCH PHARM, as of 2005; Mem adv coun, Md High Blood Pressure Coord Coun, 1978-; lectr, Squibb Pharmaceut, E R Squibb & Son, 1978-; consult, Mem Hosp, Cumberland, Md, Sacred Heart Hosp, Thomas B Finan Ctr & Memt Health Clin, Allegany Health Ctr, 1977-; asst prof clin pharm, Sch Pharm, Univ MD, 1977-; dir, Area Health Educ Ctr, Cumberland, 1977-1978. **Memberships:** Am Soc Hosp Pharmacists; Am Asn Cols Pharm. **Research Statement & Publications:** Tardive dyskinesia; psychotherapeutic agents; hypertension; geriatric health care. **Mailing Address:** Dept Pharm Pract & Sci, Univ MD Sch Pharm, 20 N Pine St Rm 440, Baltimore, MD 21201-1180. **Fax:** 410-706-0319. **E-Mail:** rlove@rx.umaryland.edu

LOVE, RICHARD HARRISON, UNDERWATER ACOUSTICS. **Personal Data:** b Brooklyn, NY, August 23, 1939; m 1963, c 2. **Education:** Univ Md, BS, 1961, MS, 1963; Cath Univ Am, PhD (mech eng), 1976. **Professional Experience:** OCEANOGR ACOUST, NAVAL RES LAB, 1976-; oceanogr acoust, Naval Oceanog Off, 1967-1976; mech engr, Naval Res Lab, 1965-1967; res scientist fluid mech, Hydronautics Inc, 1963-1965. **Memberships:** Acoust Soc Am. **Research Statement & Publications:** Scattering and reflection of underwater acoustic energy from marine organisms and ocean boundaries. **Mailing Address:** Naval Res Lab, Stennis Space Ctr, MS 39529.

LOVE, RUSSELL JACQUES, SPEECH PATHOLOGY. **Personal Data:** b Chicago, Ill, January 11, 1931; m 1961, Barbara Williams; c Steven & Gregory. **Education:** Northwestern Univ, Ill, BS, 1953, MA, 1954, PhD (speech path), 1962. **Professional Experience:** PROF EMER HEARING & SPEECH SCI, SCH MED, VANDERBILT UNIV, as of 2004; prof hearing & speech sci, sch med, vanderbilt univ, beginning 1978; mem, Nat Comt Accessible Environ, 1974-1978; consult & res speech pathologist, Bill Wilkerson Hearing & Speech Ctr, Tenn, 1971-; consult, Vet Admin Hosp, Murfreesboro, 1970-1989; from asst prof to assoc prof, Sch Med, Vanderbilt Univ, 1967-1978; chief speech pathologist, Bill Wilkerson Hearing & Speech Ctr, Tenn, 1967-1971; assoc prof speech path, De-

Paul Univ, 1964-1967; Consult speech pathologist, Michael Reese Hosp & Med Ctr, Chicago, Ill, 1964-1967; res speech pathologist, Vet Admin Hosp, Coral Gables, Fla, 1962-1964; audiologist, WSide Vet Admin Hosp, Chicago, Ill, 1961-1962; staff clinician, Cerebral Palsy Speech Clin, Northwestern Univ, Ill, 1958-1961; Speech & hearing therapist, Moody State Sch Cerebral Palsied Children, Tex, 1954-1956. **Memberships:** Am Speech Lang & Hearing Asn; Am Cleft Palate Asn; fel Am Speech Lang Hearing Asn. **Research Statement & Publications:** Aphasia; Dyspraxia of speech; Dysarthria; childhood motor speech disability; rights of the handicapped; cerebral palsy; neurology of speech and language. **Mailing Address:** Dept Hearing & Speech Sci, Sch Med, Vanderbilt Univ, 1114 19th Ave S, Nashville, TN 37240-5555. **Fax:** 615-936-5013.

LOVE, SYDNEY FRANCIS, MANAGEMENT SCIENCE, ELECTRONICS. **Personal Data:** b Winnipeg, Man, June 20, 1923. **Education:** Univ Toronto, BASc, 1947, MA, 1948; Univ Waterloo, MASc(systs design), 1970. **Professional Experience:** RETIRED; pres, Advan Prof Develop Inst, beginning 1974; consult, Xerox Corp, 1972-1974 & Govt of Can, 1974-1977; pres mgt sci, Designectics Int Inc, beginning 1970; fel, Cent Mortgage & Housing Corp, 1968-1970; fel, Imp Oil Ltd, 1967-1968; consult electronics, Sparton Can, 1966-1968; mgr TV & organ eng, Electrohome Ltd, 1959-1966; supvr appln, Can Gen Elec Co Ltd, 1952-1959. **Memberships:** Sr mem Inst Elec & Electronics Engrs; Proj Mgt Inst. **Mailing Address:** 23022 Maraleste Rd, Laguna Niguel, CA 92677-2917.

LOVE, TOM JAY, JR, HEAT TRANSFER, BIOMEDICAL ENGINEERING. **Personal Data:** b Jonesboro, Ark, October 2, 1923; wid Georgia Mathis (deceased); c Tom III, Deborah & Nancy. **Education:** Univ Okla, BS, 1948; Univ Kans, MS, 1956; Purdue Univ, PhD (mech eng), 1963. **Honors & Awards:** Thermophysics Award, Am Inst Aeronaut & Astronaut, 1984; Heat Transfer Mem Award, Am Soc Mech Engrs. **Professional Experience:** PROF EMER AEROSPACE & MECH ENG, UNIV OKLA, 1988-; interim dean, Col Eng, 1986-1987; mem, adv coun, Sverdrup Technol, Inc, 1977- 1990; mem bd dirs, Sverdrup-ARO, Inc, 1977-1981; George Lynn Gross Prof, Univ Okla, 1973-1988; Halliburton Prof Eng, Univ Okla, 1972-1988; prof aerospace & mech eng, Univ Okla, 1965-1972; dir sch, Univ Okla, 1963-1972; from asst prof to assoc prof mech eng, Univ Okla, 1956-1965; sr res engr, Midwest Res Inst, 1952-1956; proj engr, Colgate Palmolive Co, 1947-1952. **Memberships:** Am Inst Aeronaut & Astronaut; Am Soc Mech Engrs; Am Soc Eng Educ; Am Soc Testing & Mat; Am Acad Thermology. **Research Statement & Publications:** Physiological heat transfer; radiative heat transfer; thermography. **Mailing Address:** Sch Aerospace & Mech Eng, Univ Okla, Norman, OK 73072-6720.

LOVE, WARNER EDWARDS, BIOPHYSICS. **Personal Data:** b Philadelphia, Pa, December 1, 1922; m 1945, Lois J Hosbach; c Rebecca (Burton) & Michael W. **Education:** Swarthmore Col, BA, 1946; Univ Pa, PhD (physiol), 1951. **Honors & Awards:** Phillips Lectr, Haverford Col, 1955. **Professional Experience:** RETIRED; prof biophys, Johns Hopkins Univ, beginning 1965; Chmn dept, Johns Hopkins Univ, 1972-1975 & 1980-1983; from asst prof to assoc prof, Johns Hopkins Univ, 1957-1965; res assoc, Inst Cancer Res, 1956-1957; res asst physics, Inst Cancer Res, 1955-1956; assoc, Johnson Found, 1953-1955; fel biophys, Johnson Found, 1951-1953; Asst instr physiol, Univ Pa, 1948-1949. **Memberships:** Protein Soc; Biophys Soc; Am Crystallog Asn; Am Soc Biol Chemists; Sigma Xi. **Research Statement & Publications:** Biological ultrastructural basis of functions; x-ray crystallography of macromolecules, hemoglobins. **Mailing Address:** Johns Hopkins Univ, 3400 N Charles St, Baltimore, MD 21218. **Fax:** 410-516-4118.

LOVE, WILLIAM ALFRED, PHYSICS, ELEMENTARY PARTICLES. **Personal Data:** b Pittsburgh, Pa, August 4, 1932; m 1957, Jane; c Thomas, Daniel. **Education:** Carnegie Inst Technol, BS, 1954, MS, 1955, PhD (physics), 1958. **Professional Experience:** RETIRED; physicist, Brookhaven Nat Lab, 1966-1999; from asst physicist to assoc physicist, Brookhaven Nat Lab, 1960-1966; fel, Nat Sci Found, European Orgn Nuclear Res, Switzerland, 1959-1960; Res physicist, Carnegie Inst Technol, 1958-1959. **Memberships:** Fel Am Phys Soc. **Research Statement & Publications:** Particle physics. **Mailing Address:** Dept Physics, Brookhaven Nat Lab, Upton, NY 11973.

LOVE, WILLIAM GARY, NUCLEAR PHYSICS. **Personal Data:** b Meridian, Miss, August 16, 1941; m 1966, Janice; c Teresa & Cynthia. **Education:** Univ Tenn, BS, 1963, PhD (physics), 1968. **Professional Experience:** Assoc ed, Phys Rev C, as of 2002; REGENTS PROF PHYSICS, UNIV GA, as of 2005; PROF PHYSICS, UNIV GA, 1980-; from asst prof to assoc prof, Univ GA, 1970-1980; res assoc physics, Fla State Univ, 1968-1970. **Memberships:** Fel Am Phys Soc. **Research Statement & Publications:** Study of the properties of the nucleon-nucleon interaction as they are manifested in many nucleon systems, for example in scattering. **Mailing Address:** Dept Physics & Astron, Univ Ga, 207 Physics Bldg, Athens, GA 30602. **E-Mail:** wglove@physast.uga.edu

LOVEALL, CLELLON LEWIS, CIVIL ENGINEERING. **Personal Data:** b Carthage, Tenn, June 13, 1938; m 1960, Jane Ellen Johnson; c Lisa Renee, Sharon Kay & Angela Dawn. **Education:** Vanderbilt Univ, BEng, 1959. **Honors & Awards:** Govt Civil Engr Yr Award, Am Soc Civil Engrs, 1984. **Professional Experience:** ASST DIR PLANNING & DEVELOP, TENN DEPT TRANSP, 1986-; state bridge engr, Tenn Dept Transp, 1978-1986; asst state bridge engr, Tenn Dept Transp, 1969-1978; chief bridge design engr, Tenn Dept Transp, 1966-1969; sr bridge design engr, Tenn Dept Transp, 1963-1966; Bridge design engr, Tenn Dept Transp, 1959-1963; Mem, Transp Res Bd. **Memberships:** Am Soc Civil Engrs; Am Soc Testing & Mat; Am Concrete Inst; Am Iron & Steel Inst; Am Asn State Hwy & Transp Officials; Prestressed Concrete Inst; Post Tensioning Inst; Segmental Bridge Inst. **Mailing Address:** Tenn Dept Transp Bur Planning & Develop, James K Polk Bldg 505 Deaderick St Suite 700, Nashville, TN 37243.

LOVECCHIO, FRANK VITO, ANALYTICAL CHEMISTRY. **Personal Data:** b Syracuse, NY, April 30, 1943. **Education:** Syracuse Univ, AB, 1965, PhD (chem), 1970. **Professional Experience:** RES CHEMIST, EASTMAN KODAK CO, 1973-; fel, Ohio State Univ, 1970-1973. **Memberships:** Am Chem Soc; Soc Photog Scientists & Engrs. **Research Statement & Publications:** Reactions and mechanisms of coordination compounds, including electron transfer reactions. **Mailing Address:** Eastman Kodak Co, 343 State St, Rochester, NY 14650.

LOVEJOY, DAVID ARNOLD, SOUTHERN NEW ENGLAND FLORA. **Personal Data:** b Nashua, NH, December 12, 1943; m 2001, Deborah; c Carolyn & Catherine. **Education:** Univ Conn, BA, 1965, PhD (zool, ecol), 1970. **Professional Experience:** PROF BIOL, WESTFIELD STATE COL, 1985-; from asst prof to assoc prof, Westfield Col, 1970-1985. **Memberships:** Am Soc Mammalogists (emer mem); New Eng Bot Club. **Research Statement & Publications:** Flora of Massachusetts. **Mailing Address:** Dept Biol, Westfield State Col, C228 Wilson Col, Westfield, MA 01086. **Fax:** 413-562-3613. **E-Mail:** dlovejoy@wsc.ma.edu

LOVEJOY, DEREK R, ENERGY PHYSICS, SUSTAINABLE ENERGY PROGRAMS. **Personal Data:** b London, Eng, January 19, 1928; Canadian citizen; m 1953, Margot; c Shaun, Kristin & Megan. **Education:** Univ London, BS, 1950; Univ Toronto, MA, 1952, PhD (physics), 1954. **Professional Experience:** RETIRED; sr tech adv new sources energy, Tech Adv Div, 1978-1994; sr tech adv, Tech Adv Div, 1972-1978; proj officer, Res Div, UN Develop Prog, 1966-1972; Expert thermal metrol, Nat Phys Lab Metrol Proj, Cairo, United Arab Repub, UNESCO, 1964-1965; assoc res officer, Appl Physics Div, Nat Res Coun Can, 1954-1966. **Memberships:** AAAS; US Int Solar Energy Soc. **Research Statement & Publications:** Liquid helium physics; temperature scales and measurements from very low to very high temperatures. **Mailing Address:** 16604 81st Ave, Jamaica, NY 11432.

LOVEJOY, DONALD WALKER, GENERAL EARTH SCIENCES. **Personal Data:** b New York, NY, March 29, 1931. **Education:** Harvard Col, BA, 1953; Columbia Univ, AM, 1956 & PhD (geol), 1958. **Professional Experience:** ASSOC PROF OCEANOG, PALM BEACH ATLANTIC UNIV, 1979-; vpres, Nasson Col, Springvale, 1973-1975; fac dean, Mass Bay Community Col, 1969-1973; asst dean, Northeastern Univ, Boston, 1962-1969; dept chair geol, Rollins Col, Winter Park, 1959-1962; Asst prof geol, Univ Calif, Los Angeles, 1957-1958. **Memberships:** Fel Geol Soc Am. **Research Statement & Publications:** Florida pleistocene anastasia formation; karstification. **Mailing Address:** Dept Oceanog, Palm Beach Atlantic Univ, PO Box 24708, West Palm Beach, FL 33416-4708. **E-Mail:** lovejoyd@pbac.edu

LOVEJOY, JENNIFER CAROLE, DIABETES, OBESITY. **Personal Data:** b Seattle, Wash, March 30, 1961; m 1995, Robert; c Teresa S. **Education:** Duke Univ, BS, 1982; Emory Univ, MA, 1986, PhD (psychobiol), 1988. **Professional Experience:** ASSOC PROF, PENNINGTON BIOMED RES CTR, 1997-; asst prof, Pennington Biomed Res Ctr, 1991-1997; instr md, Dept Med, Emory Univ, 1989-1991; postdoctoral fel, Dept Med, Emory Univ, 1988-1989. **Memberships:** Am Soc Clin Nutrit; Am Diabetes Asn; NAm Asn Study Obesity. **Research Statement & Publications:** Role of diet and reproductive hormones in the etpology of obesity and type II diabetes in women; role of ethnic background in modulating risk for these chronic diseases. **Mailing Address:** Pennington Biomed Res Ctr, 6400 Perkins Rd, Baton Rouge, LA 70808-4124.

LOVEJOY, OWEN C, HUMAN BIOLOGY, BIOMECHANICS. **Personal Data:** b Paducah, Ky, February 11, 1943; m 1969. **Education:** Western Res Univ, BA, 1965; Case Inst Technol, MA, 1967; Univ Mass, Amherst, PhD (humanbiol), 1970. **Professional Experience:** DIR, MATHEW FERRINI IINST, as of 2003; bd ed, Am Anthropologist, 1990-1993; adj prof anat, Dept Human anat, Northeastern Ohio Univ Col Med, 1989-; sci asso, Inst Human Origins, Berkeley, 1982-1991; ASST CLIN PROF, DIV ORTHOP SURG, SCH MED, CASE WESTERN RES UNIV, SCH MED, 1980-; chmn, Biol Anthrop Area Comt, Div Biomed Sci, Kent State Univ, 1980-1991; tech adv biol, anthrop, Cuyahoga County Coroner Off, Cleveland, 1978-; sci assoc, Ctr Res Anthropologic Found Technol, Ind Univ, 1970-; prof social & anthrop, Kent State Univ, 1977-; assoc prof phys anthrop, Kent State Univ, 1969-1977; UNIV PROF, DEPT ANTHROP, KENT STATE UNIV, 1968-. **Memberships:** Brit Soc Study Human Biol; Am Asn Phys Anthrop; Am Eugenics Soc. **Research Statement & Publications:** Primate anatomy, biomechanics and taxonomy; human palaeontology and palaeodemography; skeletal biology. **Mailing Address:** Dept Anthrop, Kent State Univ, 239 Lowry Hall, Kent, OH 44242-0001. **E-Mail:** olovejoy@aol.com

LOVEJOY, SHAUN MACDONALD, Fractals, MULTIFRACTALS. **Personal Data:** b August 1960; m 1985, Helene; c Vanda & Miro. **Education:** Trinity Col, BA, 1976, MA, 1981; McGill Univ, PhD (physics), 1981. **Professional Experience:** Adv board Stochastic environ res & Risk Analysis 1997-; PROF PHYSICS, MCGILL UNIV, 1997-; co-ed, Nonlinear Processes Geophys, 1993-1996; from asst prof to assoc prof, Mcgill Univ, 1985-1997; Univ res fel, Natural Sci & Eng Res Coun Can, 1985-1995; Postdoctoral, Nat Meteorol, Paris, 1981-1985. **Memberships:** Europ Geophys Soc; Am Geophys Union. **Research Statement & Publications:** All aspects of scale invariance; applications in turbulence, geophysics, hydrology and climate. **Mailing Address:** Physics Dept, McGill Univ, Montreal, PQ H3A 2T8, Can. **Fax:** 514-398-8434. **E-Mail:** lovejoy@physics.mcgill.ca

LOVEJOY, THOMAS E, ECOLOGY. **Personal Data:** b New York, NY, August 22, 1941; div, c Elizabeth & Katherine. **Education:** Yale Col, BS, 1964; Univ Yale, PhD (biol), 1971. **Honorary Degrees:** DSC, Colo State Univ, 1989, Williams Col, 1990; Lynn Univ, LHD, 1991. **Honors & Awards:** Ronneberg Lectr, Denison Univ, 1987; David French Lectr, Claremont Col, 1983; Charles A Lindbergh Lectr, Woods Hole Marine Biol Lab, 1981; Manley Lectr, Univ Calif, Santa Barbara, 1981. **Professional Experience:** PRES, THE H JOHN HEINZ III, CTR SCI, ECON & ENVIRON; CHIEF BIODIVERSITY OFFICER, WORLD BANK, 1998-; coun secy biodiversity & environ affairs, Smithsonian Inst, 1994-2000; rep, US Deleg, UN Conf Environ & Develop, 1992; mem, Nat Coun, Environ Defense Fund, 1991-; mem, Nat Policy Coun, Nat Inst Global Environ Change, 1990-; mem, White House Sci Coun, Off Sci & Technol Policy, Exec Off Pres, 1988-1989; asst secy, external affairs, Smithsonian Inst, 1987-1994; mem, Panel Microlivetock, Nat Res Coun, Comt Biodiversity, 1987-1991; exec vpres, World Wildlife Fund-US, 1985-1987; res assoc, Int Ctr African, Near Eastern & Asian Cult, 1984-1987; vis lectr, trop ecol, Yale Sch Forestry & Environ Studies, 1982; vis lectr trop ecol, Ctr Environ Studies, Univ Wash, 1981; mem, Wildlife Panel, AAAS, 1981; vpres sci, World Wildlife Fund-US, 1978-1985; chmn, Wildlife Preserv Trust Int, 1974-; treas, Int Coun Bird Preserv, 1973-1984; prog dir, World Wildlife Fund-US, 1973-1978; exec asst to sci dir, resources & planning, Acad Natural Sci, 1972-1973; asst to vpres resources & planning, Acad Natural Sci, 1972-1973; Res assoc ornithol, Acad Natural Sci, 1971-1974; Res assoc biol, Univ Pa, 1971-1974. **Memberships:** Fel AAAS; Am Inst Biol Sci; fel Am Ornithologists Union; Soc Conserv Biol (pres 1989-1991). **Research Statement & Publications:** Tropical ecology; ornithology; problems of ecology theory relating to conservation and natural resource management; Published over 10 articles. **Mailing Address:** Smithsonian Inst, Castle Bldg Rm 320, Washington, DC 20560.

LOVELACE, ALAN MATHIESON, CHEMISTRY. **Personal Data:** b St Petersburg, Fla, September 4, 1929; m 1952, Kathryn; c William M & Denise T. **Education:** Univ Fla, BA, 1951, MA, 1952, PhD (chem), 1954. **Honors & Awards:** Von Karman Medal, 1984; Goddard Astronaut Award, Am Inst Aeronaut & Astronaut, 1989; George Low Award, 1991 Preudents Citizens Medal, 1981. **Professional Experience:** CHMN, COM LAUNCH SERV INC, 1993-; corp vpres, Space Syst Div, 1991-1993; corp vpres & gen mgr, Space Syst Div, 1985-1991; corp vpres prod & qual assurance, Gen Dynamics Corp, 1982-1985; vpres sci & eng, Gen Dynamics Corp, 1981-1982; Chmn, Adv Group Aerospace Res & Develop, NATO, 1979-1981; dep admin, NASA, 1976-1981; assoc admin, Aerospace Technol Off Aeronaut & Space Technol, 1974-1976; prin dep asst secy, Air Force Res & Develop, 1973-1974; dir sci & technol, Andrews AFB, Wash, DC, 1972-1973; Mem staff, Air Force Mat Lab, Wright Patterson AFB, 1954-1972. **Memberships:** Nat Acad Eng; fel Past Chmn Am Inst Aeronaut & Astronaut; res Am Astronaut Soc; Sigma Xi; Int Aeronaut Fedn. **Research Statement & Publications:** High performance macromolecular materials; aliphatic fluorine chemistry; advance composite materials; space launch vehicles. **Mailing Address:** 10960 S Tropical Trail, Merritt Island, FL 32952. **Fax:** 619-974-3717.

LOVELACE, C JAMES, PLANT PHYSIOLOGY, BIOCHEMISTRY. **Personal Data:** b Holdenville, Okla, September 26, 1934; div, c 3. **Education:** Harding Col, BS, 1961; Utah State Univ, MS, 1964, PhD (plant physiol), 1966. **Professional Experience:** PROF BOT, HUMBOLDT STATE UNIV, as of 2006; summer res assoc, Utah State Univ, Justus-Liebig Univ, Inst Plant Nutrit, Giessen, Ger, 1987-1988. **Memberships:** Am Soc Plant Physiol; Int Soc Fluoride Res sr mem; adv ed bd. **Research Statement & Publications:** Plant mineral nutrition; fluoride research in relation to enzyme reactions within plants; heavy metal toxicants; iron metabolism in plants; chlorophyl biosynthesis. **Mailing Address:** Dept Biol, Humboldt State Univ One Harps St, Arcata, CA 95521-8299. **Fax:** 707-826-3201. **E-Mail:** cjl2@axe.humboldt.edu

LOVELACE, CLAUD WILLIAM VENTON, THEORETICAL PHYSICS. **Personal Data:** b London, Eng, January 16, 1934. **Education:** Univ Capetown, BS, 1954. **Professional Experience:** PROF PHYSICS, RUTGERS STATE UNIV NJ, NEW BRUNSWICK, 1970-; sr physicist, Europ Orgn Nuclear Res, Geneva, 1965-1971; lectr physics, Imp Col, Univ London, 1962-1965; Dept Sci & Indust Res res fel, Imp Col, Univ London, 1961-1962. **Research Statement & Publications:** Theoretical particle physics; strong interactions; high energy phenomenology. **Mailing Address:** Dept Physics & Astron, Rutgers State Univ NJ, Serin W327, New Brunswick, NJ 08903. **E-Mail:** lovelace@physics.rutgers.edu

LOVELACE, RICHARD VAN EVERA, MAGNETOHYDRODYNAMICS THEORY, SIMULATIONS OF ASTROPHYSICAL FLOWS IN JETS & ACCRETION DISKS. **Personal Data:** b St Louis, Mo, October 16, 1941; m 1997, c 2. **Education:** Wash Univ, BS, 1964; Cornell Univ, PhD (physics), 1970. **Honors & Awards:** Fellow American Physical Society 2002. **Professional Experience:** Assoc. Editor, Physics of Plasmas, 2005-6; Orsan Anderson vis scholar, Los Alamos nat Lab, 1999; Overseas Fel, Churchill Col, Cambridge Univ, 1994; Guggenheim Fel, 1990; Vis Prof, Dept Physics, Univ Tex, Austin, 1990; consult, Los Alamos Nat Lab, 1986-; FROM ASST PROF TO PROF APPL PHYSICS, CORNELL UNIV, 1975-; consult, Lawrence Livermore Lab, 1971- & Plasma Physics Lab, Princeton Univ, 1974-1975; Res assoc, Lab Plasma Studies, Cornell Univ, 1970-1973 & Plasma Physics Lab, Princeton Univ, 1973-1974; Vis res assoc, US Naval Res Lab, 1970-1971. **Memberships:** Am Astron Soc; Am Phys Soc; Int Astron Union. **Research Statement & Publications:** Digital search methods for pulsars (the author discovered the period of the crab nebular pulsar); the physics of large-orbit, high current Plasma physics of large-orbit, high current controlled fusion systems; collective phenomena of galaxies and quasars; wave propagation through random media; relativistic magnetohydrodynamics of astrophysical jets, winds and accretion disks; magnetic reconnection in astrophysical jets; plasma accretion to rotating non-aligned magnetized stars. **Mailing Address:** Dept Astron & Dept Applied Physics, Cornell Univ 227 Clark Hall & 412 Space Sci, Ithaca, NY 14853. **Fax:** 607-255-7658. **E-Mail:** RVL1@cornell.edu

LOVELAND, DONALD WILLIAM, MATHEMATICS, COMPUTER SCIENCE. **Personal Data:** b Rochester, NY, December 26, 1934; m 1966, Amy; c Robert & Douglas. **Education:** Oberlin Col, AB, 1956; Mass Inst Technol, SM, 1958; NY Univ, PhD (math), 1964. **Professional Experience:** PROF EMER, DUKE UNIV, 2001-; prof comput sci, Duke Univ, 1973-2001; from asst prof to assoc prof, Carnegie-Mellon Univ, 1967-1973; asst prof, NY Univ, 1964-1967; instr math, NY Univ, 1963-1964; mathematician & programmer, Int Bus Mach Corp, 1958-1959. **Memberships:** Fel Asn Comput Mach; Asn Symbolic Logic; AAAS; fel Am Asn Artificial Intel. **Research Statement & Publications:** Artificial intelligence; theorem proving by computer; logic programming; fast approximation algorithms for computationally hard problems. **Mailing Address:** Duke Univ, PO Box 90129, Durham, NC 27708. **E-Mail:** dwl@cs.duke.edu

LOVELAND, ROBERT EDWARD, BIOLOGY. **Personal Data:** b Camden, NJ, May 3, 1938; m 1962, c 3. **Education:** Rutgers Univ, Camden, AB, 1959; Harvard Univ, MA, 1961, PhD (biol), 1963. **Professional Experience:** ASSOC PROF ECOL, EVOLUTION & NAT RESOURCES, RUTGERS COOK COL & NJ AGR EXP STA, NEW BRUNSWICK, as of 2006; NSF sci fac fel, Univ BC, 1971-1972; assoc prof zoology, Rutgers State Univ NJ, New Brunswick, beginning 1970; asst prof, Rutgers Univ, New Brunswick, 1964-1970; asst prof biol, Long Beach State Col, 1963-1964. **Memberships:** AAAS; Atlantic Estuarine Res Soc. **Research Statement & Publications:** Distribution of marine invertebrates; behavioral modelling; population models of biological systems. **Mailing Address:** Dept Biol Sci, Rutgers Cook Col & NJ Agr Exp Sta, Rutgerts State Univ NJ, Blake 118 93 Lipman Dr, New Brunswick, NJ 08903. **E-Mail:** lovland@biology.rutgers.edu

LOVELAND, WALTER (DAVID), NUCLEAR CHEMISTRY. **Personal Data:** b Chicago, Ill, December 23, 1939; m 1962, Patricia. **Education:** Mass Inst Technol, BS, 1961; Univ Wash, PhD (chem), 1966. **Professional Experience:** PROF CHEM, ORE STATE UNIV, 1981-; Tartar fel, Ore State Univ, 1977; vis scientist, Lawrence Berkeley Lab, 1976, 1977, 1980; US Dept Energy res grant, Ore State Univ, 1968-; from asst prof to assoc prof, Ore State Univ, 1968-1981; res asst prof, Ore State Univ, 1967-1968; res assoc chem, Argonne Nat Lab, 1966-1968. **Memberships:** AAAS; Am Phys Soc; Am Chem Soc. **Research Statement & Publications:** Nuclear reactions, especially heavy ion reactions and fission; activation analysis; use of computers for data acquisition; environmental chemistry. **Mailing Address:** Dept chem, Ore State Univ, Rad Ctr B123 153 Gilbert Hall, Corvallis, OR 97331. **Fax:** 541-737-0480. **E-Mail:** lovland@loveland.chem.orst.edu

LOVELESS, MARILYN D, POPULATION ECOLOGY. **Education:** Albion Col, BA, 1971; Univ Kans, PhD, 1984. **Professional Experience:** ASSOC PROF BIOL, COL WOOSTER, OHIO, 1994-. **Mailing Address:** Col Wooster, Wooster, OH 44691. **Fax:** 330-263-2378. **E-Mail:** mloveless@acs.wooster.edu

LOVELESS, SCOTT E, MACROPHAGE ACTIVATION, ADOPTIVE IMMUNOTHERAPY. **Education:** Va Commonwealth Univ, PhD (pharmacol), 1980. **Professional Experience:** RES IMMUNOTHERAPIST & PHARMACOLOGIST, E I DU PONT Del NEMOURS & CO INC, 1984-. **Mailing Address:** Immunotoxicol Cent Res Dept, E I du Pont de Nemours & Co Inc Haskell Lab Elkton Rd PO Box 50, Newark, DE 19714-0050. **Fax:** 302-366-5207.

LOVELL, ASHLEY C, BUSINESS ANALYSIS & RISK MANAGEMENT, ACCOUNTING. **Personal Data:** b Texon, Tex, November 30, 1944. **Education:** Tarleton State Univ, BS, 1967; Univ Mo, Columbia, MS, 1970, PhD (agr econs), 1971. **Professional Experience:** DIR OF AGRICULTURAL PROGRAMS AND PROF AGR ECON, CENTER FOR AGRIBUSINESS EXCELLENCE, HEAD & PROF AGR ECON, TARLETON STATE UNIV, 1993-; exten specialist & prof, Tex Agr Exten Serv & Dept Agr Econs, Tex A&M Univ, 1978-1993; assoc prof, Tarleton State Univ, 1970-1977. **Memberships:** Am Agr Econ Asn; Southern Agr Econ Assn; Northeastern Agr Econ Assn; Western Agr Econ Assn; TX Soc Certified Pub Accountants. **Research Statement & Publications:** Farm-level management and production economics, especially financial and managerial accounting; tax planning and management; business management and risk management computer applications and simulation, all within the context of public policy development and constraints. **Mailing Address:** Box T-0055, Stephenville, TX 76402. **E-Mail:** lovell@tarleton.edu

LOVELL, BERNARD WENTZEL, COMPUTER SCIENCE, ELECTRICAL ENGINEERING. **Personal Data:** b Greenfield, Mass. **Education:** Mass Inst Technol, BS, 1958, MS, 1958, EE, 1963; Univ Conn, PhD (comput sci), 1969. **Professional Experience:** ASSOC PROF EMER ELEC ENG, UNIV CONN, as of 1998; assoc prof elec eng, Univ Conn, beginning 1969; asst prof, Univ Mass, 1963-1967; instr elec eng, Mass Inst Technol, 1959-1963; Electronic engr, US Naval Ord Lab, 1954-1959. **Memberships:** Inst Elec & Electronics Engrs; Am Phys Soc; Asn Comput Mach. **Research Statement & Publications:** Automata theory; operating systems. **Mailing Address:** Dept Comput Sci & Eng, Univ Conn, U-155 260 Glennbrook, Storrs, CT 06269-0002.

LOVELL, CHARLES W(ILLIAM), CIVIL ENGINEERING, SOIL MECHANICS. **Personal Data:** b Louisville, Ky, November 16, 1922; m 1948, c 2. **Education:** Univ Louisville, BS, 1944; Purdue Univ, MS, 1951, PhD (civil eng), 1957. **Professional Experience:** PROF EMER CIVIL ENG, PURDUE UNIV, 1993-; prof civil eng, Purdue Univ, 1976-1993; vis assoc prof, Mass Inst Technol, 1962-1963; from asst prof to assoc prof, Purdue Univ, 1957-1976; from res asst to res engr & instr, Purdue Univ, 1948-1957; Instr civil eng, Univ Louisville, 1946-1948; mem, Hwy Res Bd, Nat Acad Sci-Nat Res Coun. **Memberships:** Nat Soc Prof Engrs; Am Soc Civil Engrs; Am Soc Eng Educ; Am Soc Testing & Mat. **Research Statement & Publications:** Frost action; load-deformation characteristics of soils; subsurface exploration. **Mailing Address:** Dept Civil Eng, Purdue Eng, CIVL G245, West Lafayette, IN 47907. **Fax:** 317-494-1364. **E-Mail:** lovellc@ecn.purdue.edu

LOVELL, EDWARD GEORGE, ENGINEERING, STRUCTURAL MECHANICS. **Personal Data:** b Windsor, Ont, May 25, 1939; American citizen; c Elise & Ethan. **Education:** Wayne State Univ, BS & MS, 1960; Univ Mich, Ann Arbor, PhD (eng mech), 1967. **Professional Experience:** PROF MECH ENG, UNIV WIS, MADISON, 1995-; chmn eng mech & astronaut, Univ Wis-madison, 1992-1995; NATO sr sci fel, Univ Manchester, Eng, 1973 & Fusion Technol Inst, Wis Ctr Appl Microelectronics, Univ Wis; design engr, Pratt & Whitney Aircraft, Conn, 1970; prof eng mech, Univ Wis-Madison, 1968-1995; Nat Acad Sci-Nat Res Coun res associateship, Langley Res Ctr, NASA, 1967-1968; instr eng mech, Univ Mich, Ann Arbor, 1963-1967; proj engr, Boeing Co, Wash, 1962. **Memberships:** Sigma Xi; Am Soc Mech Engrs; Am Soc Eng Educ. **Research Statement & Publications:** Nonlinear vibrations of structures; structural instability; stress analysis; nuclear reactor structural mechanics; microelectromechanical systems. **Mailing Address:** Dept Mech Eng, Univ Wis, 313 Mech Eng Bldg 1513 Univ Ave, Madison, WI 53706. **E-Mail:** lovell@engr.wisc.edu

LOVELL, HAROLD LEMUEL, fuel science, mineral engineering; deceased, see previous edition for last biography

LOVELL, JAMES A, ASTRONAUTICS. **Personal Data:** b Cleveland, Ohio, March 25, 1928; m Marilyn; c Barbara L, James A, Susan K & Jeffrey C. **Education:** US Naval Acad, BS, 1952. **Honors & Awards:** Robert J Collier Trophy, 1969. **Professional Experience:** RETIRED; exec vpres & bd dir, Centel Corp, ending 1991; sr vpres admin, Centel Corp, beginning 1980; pres, Fisk Tel Systs Inc, 1977-1981; dep dir sci & appln directorate, Manned Spacecraft Ctr, NASA, 1971-1973; astronaut, Apollo 13, 1970; astronaut, Gemini 12, 1966; astronaut, Gemini 6, 1966; astronaut, Manned Spacecraft Ctr, NASA, 1962; test pilot, Navy Air Test Ctr, 1958-1961; astronaut, Gemini 7 flight; flight instr & safety officer, Fighter Squadron 101, Naval Air Sta. **Memberships:** Fel Am Astronaut Soc. **Mailing Address:** 3558 S Union Ave, Chicago, IL 60609.

LOVELL, JAMES BYRON, ENTOMOLOGY. **Personal Data:** b Fallentimber, Pa, March 19, 1927; c 2. **Education:** Pa State Univ, BS, 1950; Univ Ill, MS, 1955, PhD (entom), 1956. **Professional Experience:** RETIRED; prin scientist, Agr Res Div, Am Cyanamid Co, 1956-1991; asst, Univ Ill, 1953-1956; entomologist, US Army Chem Ctr, Md, 1950-1953. **Memberships:** AAAS; Entom Soc Am. **Research Statement & Publications:** Insect physiology and toxicology; mode of action of insecticides; mechanism of resistance in insects. **Mailing Address:** 47 Foster Rd, Pennington, NJ 08534.

LOVELL, MARK A, RADIOCHEMISTRY. **Education:** Berea Col, BA, 1987; Univ Ky, PhD, 1992. **Professional Experience:** ASSOC PROF CHEM, UNIV KY, as of 2006. **Mailing Address:** Dept Chem, Univ Ky, Lexington, KY 40456. **Fax:** 859-323-1069. **E-Mail:** malove2@uky.edu

LOVELL, RICHARD ARLINGTON, NEUROCHEMISTRY. **Personal Data:** b Kentland, Ind, August 4, 1930; m 1965, c 6. **Education:** Xavier Univ, Ohio, BS, 1952, MS, 1953; St Louis Univ, Lic Philos, 1959; McGill Univ, PhD (biochem), 1963. **Professional Experience:** MGR BIOCHEM PHARMACOL, CIBA-GEIGY CORP, SUMMIT, NJ, 1975-; from instr to asst prof neurochem psychiat, Univ Chicago, 1969-1975; Res fel, Schweppe Found, 1968-1971; USPHS Psychopharmacol Res Training Prog fel psychiat, Yale Univ, 1965-1966; Proj assoc physiol, Epilepsy Res Ctr, Univ Wis, 1964-1965. **Memberships:** AAAS; Am Chem Soc; Am Soc Neurochem; Am Epilepsy Soc; Soc Neurosci. **Research Statement & Publications:** Neurochemistry; neuropharmacology; biochemical control mechanisms in the nervous system. **Mailing Address:** 479 Snyder Ave, Berkeley Heights, NJ 07922-2057.

LOVELL, RICHARD THOMAS, FISHERIES, NUTRITION. **Personal Data:** b Lockesburg, Ark, February 21, 1934; m 1963, c 2. **Education:** Okla State Univ, BS, 1956, MS, 1958; La State Univ, PhD (nutrit, biochem), 1963. **Honors & Awards:** Prof Scientist Award, Southern Asn Agr Scientist, 1978; Distinguished Serv Award, Catfish Farmers Am, 1980; Cert Merit, Inst Food Technologists, 1991. **Professional Experience:** PROF EMER FISHERIES & ALLIED AQUACULT, AUBURN UNIV, 1998-; chmn, Comt Fish Nutrit, Nat Res Coun-Nat Acad Sci, 1989-1990; assoc ed, Trans Am Fisheries Soc, beginning 1975; prof fisheries & allied aquacult, Auburn Univ, beginning 1975; mem, Comt Animal Nutrit, Nat Res Coun-Nat Acad Sci, beginning 1974; columnist, Aquacult Mag, beginning 1974; consult fish cult, US AID, 1972-1974; assoc prof, Auburn Univ, 1969-1975; from asst prof to assoc prof food sci, La State Univ, 1963-1969. **Memberships:** Fel Am Inst Chemists; Am Fisheries Soc; Inst Food Technologists; Am Inst Nutrit. **Research Statement & Publications:** Fish nutrition, especially vitamin C requirements and energy metabolism of warm water fish cultured for food; environment-related off-flavors in intensively-cultured food fishes. **Mailing Address:** Dept Fisheries & Allied Aquacult, Auburn Univ, Auburn, AL 36849. **Fax:** 334-844-9208. **E-Mail:** rlovell@ag.auburn.edu

LOVELL, ROBERT GIBSON, internal medicine, allergy; deceased, see previous edition for last biography

LOVELL, ROBERT R(OLAND), SPACE TECHNOLOGY. **Personal Data:** b Gladwin, Mich, February 22, 1937. **Education:** Univ Mich, BS & MS. **Honors & Awards:** Nat Medal Technol, 1991; Yuri Gagarin Medal, USSR Acad Cosmonautics. **Professional Experience:** CORP VPRES & PRES, SPACE SYSTS DIV, ORBITAL SCI CORP, 1987-; dir, Satellite Commun Advan Res & Develop Prog, NASA Hq, 1980-1987; Var tech & tech mgt positions, Lewis Res Ctr, NASA, Cleveland, Ohio, 1962-1980; mgr, Pegasus Prog,

Orbital Sci Corp. **Memberships:** Am Inst Aeronaut & Astronaut. **Research Statement & Publications:** Development of unmanned spacecraft technology; communications systems; rocket propulsion; author of over 50 technical publications; holder of several patents. **Mailing Address:** 21839 Atlantic Blvd, Sterling, VA 20166.

LOVELL, STUART ESTES, computer science; deceased, see previous edition for last biography

LOVELOCK, DAVID, MATHEMATICS, THEORETICAL PHYSICS. **Personal Data:** b Bromley, Eng. **Education:** Univ Natal, BSc, 1959, Hons, 1960, PhD (math), 1962, DSc, 1974. **Professional Experience:** RETIRED; Dept Math, Univ Ariz, as of 2004; Adj prof appl math, Univ Waterloo, 1974-; prof math, Univ Ariz, beginning 1974; prof appl math, Univ Waterloo, Ont, 1974; Nat Res Coun Can grant, Univ Waterloo, 1969-; assoc prof, Univ Waterloo, Ont, 1969-1974; lectr, Bristol Univ, 1963-1969; jr fel, Bristol Univ, 1962-1963; res asst math, Univ Natal, 1960-1961. **Memberships:** Am Math Soc; Tensor Soc. **Research Statement & Publications:** General relativity; calculus of variations; differential geometry. **Mailing Address:** Dept Math, Univ Ariz, 1600 E Univ Blvd, Tucson, AZ 85721-0001. **Fax:** 520-621-8322. **E-Mail:** dsl@math.arizona.edu

LOVELY, RICHARD HERBERT, NEUROBEHAVIORAL TOXICOLOGY, HEALTH PSYCHOLOGY. **Personal Data:** b Santa Monica, Calif, September 20, 1941; m 1988, Anita. **Education:** Calif State Univ, Northridge, BA, 1965; Cent Wash Univ, MS, 1967; Univ Wash, Seattle, PhD (psychol), 1974. **Professional Experience:** PNL SEATTLE RES CTR, BATTELLE MEM INST, 1995-; epidemiol & biomet, Dept Biol, 1989-1994; bd dirs, Bioelectromagnetic Soc, 1985-1988; sr res scientist Neurosci, Dept Biol, 1979-1989; consult & US-USSR exchange scientist, Nat Coun Radiation Protection & Measurements, 1978-1985; consult & US-USSR exchange scientist, Nat Inst Environ Health Sci, 1976-1982; asst prof, Univ Wash, 1975-1979; psychol & rehab med, Univ Wash, 1973-1975; vis prof, Calif State Univ, Chico, 1972-1973; lectr psychol, Univ Wash, 1970-1972; instr psychol, Yakima Valley Col, 1967-1968. **Memberships:** Soc Neuroscience; Psychonomic Soc; Neurobehav Teratol Soc; Bioelectromagnetics Soc. **Research Statement & Publications:** Biopsychological effects of electromagnetic radiation exposure; AIDS in adolescents; in utero determinants of adult behavior; neurobehavioral toxicology; neural substrates of learning and memory, limbic system functions and constraints on animal behavior. **Mailing Address:** PNL Seattle Res Ctr, Battelle Mem Inst, 4000 NE 41st St PO Box C 5395, Seattle, WA 98105-5428. **Fax:** 206-528-3553. **E-Mail:** lovely@battelle.org

LOVENBERG, WALTER MCKAY, BIOCHEMISTRY. **Personal Data:** b Trenton, NJ, August 9, 1934; m 1958, c 2. **Education:** Rutgers Univ, BS, 1956, MS, 1958; George Washington Univ, PhD (biochem), 1962. **Professional Experience:** PRES, LOVENBERG ASSOCS, as of 2004; DIR, MERRIMACK PHARMACEUT, INC, HELICON THERAPEUTICS, INC & PROQUEST PHARMACEUT, INC, as of 2004; MEM BD DIR, SCI ADVI BD, GUILFORD PHARMACEUTICALS, INC, as of 2004; DIR, OSI PHARMACEUT INC, 1994-; pres, Marion Merrell Dow Res Inst, 1989-1993; vpres Strasbourg, France, 1986-1989; dir biochem sci, Merrel Dow Res Inst, 1985-1986; head sect biochem pharmacol, Hypertension-Endocrine Br, 1972-1985; trainee, Nat Heart, Lung & Blood Inst, 1962-1963; Biochemist, Nat Heart, Lung & Blood Inst, 1959-1972; US ed, J Neurochem Int; exec ed, J Analytical Biochem. **Memberships:** Am Soc Biol Chem; Am SocPharmacol & Exp Therapeut; Biochem Soc; Am Soc Neurochem; Am Col Neuropsychopharmacol. **Research Statement & Publications:** Enzymatic mechanisms and the chemistry of proteins involved in neurohumoral amine biosynthesis. **Mailing Address:** OSI Pharmaceuts, Inc, Suite 110, 58 S Service Rd, Melville, NY 11747. **Fax:** 631-752-3880.

LOVER, ROBERT E, MATHEMATICS. **Education:** Kalamazoo Col, BA; Miami Univ, Ohio, MA; Case Western Reserve Univ, PhD. **Professional Experience:** ADJ PROF, PFEIFFER UNIV, as of 2006. **Mailing Address:** Pfeiffer Univ, 4701 Park Rd, Charlotte, NC 28209. **Fax:** 704-563-1272. **E-Mail:** rlover@pfeiffer.edu

LO VERDE, PHILIP THOMAS, PARASITOLOGY, MEDICAL MALACOLOGY. **Personal Data:** b Benton Harbor, Mich, October 5, 1946; m 1965, c 3. **Education:** Univ Mich, BS, 1968, MS, 1971, MS, PhD (epidemiol sci), 1976. **Honors & Awards:** Chester A Herrick Award, Eli Lilly & Co, 1974. **Professional Experience:** PROF MICROBIOL, SCH MED, STATE UNIV NY, BUFFALO, as of 2004; Spec Study Sect, SBIR Study Sect, 1986; Spec Study Sect, Tropical Dis Unit Study Sect, 1984; Spec Study Sect, NIH, 1983; asst prof parasitol, dept micro, sch med, State Univ NY, Buffalo, beginning 1981; asst prof parasitol, dept biol sci, Purdue Univ, 1976-1981; res assoc med malacol, Ain Shams Univ, Cairo, 1974-1975; guest scientist, Naval Med Res Unit No 3, Cairo, Egypt, 1974-1975; curatorial asst, Zool Mus, Univ Mich, 1973-1975; teaching fel, Dept Zoology, 1972-1973; Mus asst, NIH fel, 1970-1975; mus asst, Zool Mus, Univ Mich, 1968-1969. **Memberships:** Am Soc Parasitologists; AAAS; Am Soc Trop Med Hyg. **Research Statement & Publications:** Host-parasite interrelationships; invertebrate defense mechanisms; parasite immunology and molecular biology; parasitology; malacology; schistosomiasis. **Mailing Address:** Dept Microbiol & Immunol, State Univ NY, 619 Biomed Res Bldg, Buffalo, NY 14214-3001. **Fax:** 716-829-2169. **E-Mail:** loverde@buffalo.edu

LOVERING, EDWARD GILBERT, PHARMACEUTICAL CHEMISTRY. **Personal Data:** b Winnipeg, Man, October 15, 1934; m 1958, c 3. **Education:** Univ Man, BSc, 1957, MSc, 1958; Univ Ottawa, PhD (chem), 1961. **Professional Experience:** CONSULT, 1993-; res scientist, Health & Welfare Can, 1971-1993; assoc scientist, Polymer Corp, 1969-1971; res chemist, Polymer Corp Ltd, 1963-1969; Nat Res Coun Can fel, Oxford Univ, 1961-1963; Sci officer radiation chem, Defense Res Bd, 1958-1959. **Memberships:** Am Chem Soc; Chem Inst Can; Sigma Xi. **Research Statement & Publications:** Contaminants in drugs and cosmetics; drug raw material characterization; drug stability; pharmaceutical and cosmetic analysis. **Mailing Address:** 111 Beaver Ridge, Nepean, ON K2E 6E5, Can.

LOVESTEDT, STANLEY ALMER, ORAL SURGERY. **Personal Data:** b Iliff, Colo, June 7, 1913; m 1940, c Priscilla (Strand), Helen (Grant) & Robert A. **Education:** Univ Southern Calif, BS & DDS, 1938; Univ Minn, MS, 1945; Am Bd Oral Surg, dipl. **Professional Experience:** EMER PROF DENT, MAYO MED SCH, 1978-; prof dent, Mayo Grad Sch Med, 1973-1978; prof clin dent, Mayo Grad Sch Med, 1967-1973; mem, dent study sect, NIH, 1964-1968; SR CONSULT, DEPT DENT & ORAL SURG, MAYO CLIN, 1962-; from instr to assoc prof, Mayo Grad Sch Med, 1960-1969; head sect, Mayo Med Sch, 1955-1962; Chief oral diag & roentgenology, US Army Dent Corps, Brooke Army Hosp, Ft Sam Houston, Tex, 1953-1955; mem fac, Mayo Grad Sch Med, 1946-1960; consult, Mayo Med Sch, 1943-1962; Resident oral surg, Mayo Grad Sch Med, 1938-1943. **Memberships:** Fel AAAS; Am Soc Oral Surgeons; Am Dent Asn; fel Am Acad Dent Radiol; fel Am Col Dent (vpres 1965-1966 pres 1968-1969); Sigma Xi; Am Asn Dent Schs; Am Acad Hist Dent; Am Acad Oral Path; Am Acad Hist Med; Am Cancer Soc; Am Acad Oral Med. **Research Statement & Publications:** Radiology; oral medicine. **Mailing Address:** 211 Second St NW Apt 2102, Rochester, MN 55901-3101.

LOVETT, CHARLES MCVEY, DNA REPAIR, GENE REGULATION. **Personal Data:** b Oceanside, NY, November 23, 1951; m Jennifer Gordon; c 4. **Education:** Calif State Polytech Univ, Pomona, BS, 1979, MS, 1980; Cornell Univ, PhD (biochem), 1985. **Professional Experience:** PROF CHEM, WILLIAMS COL, 1995-; from asst prof to assoc prof, Williams Col, 1985-1995. **Research Statement & Publications:** Transcriptional regulation of inducible DNA repair in bacillus subtilis; regulation of competence development in bacillus subtilis. **Mailing Address:** Dept Chem, Williams Col, Williamstown, MA 01267. **Fax:** 413-597-4116. **E-Mail:** clovett@williams.edu

LOVETT, EDMUND J, III, EXPERIMENTAL BIOLOGY. **Professional Experience:** ASSOC VPRES, MAINE MED CTR, as of 2004; CHIEF EXEC OFFICER, MAINE MED CTR, 1986-; DIR, MAINE MED CTR RES INST, 1986-. **Mailing Address:** Maine Med Ctr Res Inst, 125 John Roberts Rd Ste 8, South Portland, ME 04107. **Fax:** 207-761-2190. **E-Mail:** lovete.mmcri@office.mme.org

LOVETT, EVA G, ORGANIC CHEMISTRY. **Personal Data:** b Orange, NJ, August 17, 1940; m 1963. **Education:** Douglass Col, Rutgers Univ, BA, 1962; Univ Rochester, PhD (chem), 1966. **Professional Experience:** INSTR CHEM, FOREST PARK COMMUNITY COL, 1991-; res assoc chem, Victoria Univ, Wellington, NZ, 1989-1990; res chemist, Tretolite Div, Petrolite Corp, St Louis, 1976-1989; res assoc chem, Wash Univ, St Louis, 1969-1976; Sr chemist, Merck, Sharp & Dohme Res Lab, 1966-1967. **Memberships:** AAAS; Am Chem Soc. **Research Statement & Publications:** Synthesis, degradation and mass spectroscopy of natural products, particularly purines, pyrimidines and related heterocyclic compounds; polymer synthesis and characterization. **Mailing Address:** 6807 Pershing Ave, St Louis, MO 63130.

LOVETT, GARY MARTIN, FOREST NUTRIENT CYCLING, ATMOSPHERE-FOREST INTERACTIONS. **Personal Data:** b Albany, NY, July 6, 1953. **Education:** Union Col, BS, 1975; Dartmouth Col, PhD (biol), 1981. **Professional Experience:** SCIENTIST, INST ECOSYSTEM STUDIES, 1995-; assoc mem, Grad Prog Ecol, Rutgers Univ, 1990-; assoc scientist, Inst Ecosyst Studies, 1989-1995; GRAD FAC ECOL, RUTGERS UNIV, 1989-; from asst scientist to assoc scientist, Inst Ecosyst Studies, 1985-1995; res assoc, Oak Ridge Nat Lab, 1983-1985. **Memberships:** Ecol Soc Am; AAAS. **Research Statement & Publications:** Forest nutrient cycling, in particular patterns and mechanisms of atmospheric deposition and atmosphere/canopy interactions; effects of air pollution insects and other stresses on forests. **Mailing Address:** Inst Ecosystem Studies, PO Box AB 65 Sharon Turnpike, Millbrook, NY 12545-0129. **Fax:** 845-677-5976.

LOVETT, JANICE ANN, BIOLOGY. **Education:** Cornell Univ, BS; Ariz State Univ, MS; Ind Univ, PhD. **Professional Experience:** ASSOC PROF BIOL, STATE UNIV NY, as of 2004. **Mailing Address:** Dept Biol, State Univ NY Col, Geneseo, NY 14454.

LOVETT, JOHN ROBERT, ORGANIC CHEMISTRY. **Personal Data:** b Norristown, Pa, June 17, 1931; m 1956, c 3. **Education:** Ursinus Col, BS, 1953; Univ Del, MS, 1955, PhD (chem), 1957. **Professional Experience:** Dir, Amersham Int Plc & Am Chamber Com, UK, 1982-; PRES & MEM BD DIRS, AIR PROD EUROPE, INC, 1981-; adv bd, US Dept Energy, 1978-1981; mem bd dir, Air Prod & Chem Inc, 1977-1981; Bd trustees, Cedar Crest Col, 1977-1981; vpres res, Air Prod & Chem Inc, 1976-1981; worldwide tech mgr, Exxon Chem Co, 1973-1976; vpres paramins dept, Exxon Chem Co, 1970-1973; dir petrol additives lab, Esso Res & Eng Co, 1968-1970; dir govt res lab, Esso Res & Eng Co, 1965-1968; sect head, Esso Res & Eng Co, 1961-1964; sr chemist, Esso Res & Eng Co, 1960-1961; prof leader high energy propellants, Esso Res & Eng Co, 1959-1960; Res chemist polymer processes, Esso Res & Eng Co, 1957-1959. **Memberships:** Am Chem Soc; Indust Res Inst; Mfg Chemists Asn; AAAS. **Research Statement & Publications:** Polymers; chemical additives; industrial gases; catalysts; fossil energy technology. **Mailing Address:** 2830 Liberty St, Allentown, PA 18104-4748.

LOVETT, PAUL SCOTT, MICROBIOLOGY. **Personal Data:** b Philadelphia, Pa, December 14, 1940. **Education:** Delaware Valley Col, BS, 1964; Temple Univ, PhD (microbiol), 1968. **Honors & Awards:** Distinguished Young Scientist Award, Md Acad Sci, 1975. **Professional Experience:** Presidential res prof, Univ MD, Baltimore CO, 1989-1994; PROF BIOL SCI, UNIV MD, BALTIMORE CO, 1978-; mem gen biol study sect, NSF, 1978-1981; career develop award, USPHS, 1976-1981; from asst prof to assoc prof, Univ MD, Baltimore CO, 1970-1978; USPHS fel microbiol, Scripps Clin & Res Found, Calif, 1968-1970. **Memberships:** Am Soc Microbiol; AAAS. **Research Statement & Publications:** Microbial genetics; ribosomes; bacillus plasmids; regulation of inducible cat genes; sporulation converting bacteriophages. **Mailing Address:** Dept Biol Sci, Univ Md Baltimore Co, 1000 Hilltop Circle, Catonsville, MD 21250. **Fax:** 410-455-3875. **E-Mail:** lovett@umbc.edu

LOVETT, SUSAN, GENETICS. **Education:** Univ Calif, Berkeley, PhD. **Professional Experience:** PROF BIOL, BRANDEIS UNIV, as of 2004. **Mailing Address:** Rosenstiel Ctr Brandeis Univ, MS 029 PO Box 549110 415 S St, Waltham, MA 02454-9110. **Fax:** 781-736-2405. **E-Mail:** lovett@brandeis.edu

LOVETT-DOUST, JONATHAN NICOLAS, REPRODUCTIVE ECOLOGY, AQUATIC ECOLOGY & PLANT BIOMONITORING. **Personal Data:** b Croydon, Eng, November 5, 1950; Canadian citizen; m Lesley Clegg; c Henry, Leo & Jack. **Education:** Queens Univ, Kingston, BSc, 1973; Univ Wales, PhD (plant biol), 1978. **Professional Experience:** Assoc ed, Ecosci, 1993-; PROF BIOL, UNIV WINDSOR, 1988-; assoc prof, Hartford Col, 1987-1988; asst prof, Amherst Col, 1981-1987. **Memberships:** Brit Ecol Soc; AAAS; Bot Soc Am; Ecol Soc Am. **Research Statement & Publications:** Population biology and reproductive ecology of plants; problems of sex allocation and the sex ratio; use of plants as biomonitors of organic contaminants in aquatic ecosystems. **Mailing Address:** Dept Biol, Univ Windsor, Windsor, ON N9B 3P4, Can. **Fax:** 519-971-3609. **E-Mail:** jld@uwindsor.ca

LOVICH, JEFFREY EDWARD, MORPHOMETRIC ANALYSIS, EVOLUTIONARY ECOLOGY. **Personal Data:** b Alexandria, Va, m Sharon; c Justin & Ashley. **Education:** George Mason Univ, BS, 1982, MS, 1984; Univ Ga, PhD (ecol), 1990. **Professional Experience:** WILDLIFE BIOLOGIST, PALM SPRINGS FIELD STA, NAT BIOL SURV, 1993-; wildlife biologist, US Bur Land Mgt, 1991-1993; Fac res assoc, Savannah River Ecol Lab, Univ Ga, 1990-1991; bd mem, Calif Exotic Pest Plant Coun. **Memberships:** Am Soc Ichthyologists & Herpetologists; Soc Study Amphibians & Reptiles; Herpetologists' League. **Research Statement & Publications:** Evolutionary ecology, systematics and conservation of North American and Southeast Asian turtles; landscape-level impacts to desert ecosystems; herpetology. **Mailing Address:** Nat Biol Surv, PO Box 2000, 63500 Garnet Ave, Palm Springs Field Sta, North Palm Springs, CA 92258-2000. **Fax:** 619-251-4099. **E-Mail:** jeffrey_lovich@nbs.gov

LOVICK, ROBERT CLYDE, ENGINEERING, ELECTRONIC DEVELOPMENT. **Personal Data:** b Atchison, Kans, August 25, 1921; m 1945, Dorothy Ernst; c Barbara (Bradley).

Education: Univ Nebr, BSc, 1944. **Professional Experience:** PRES, IDEAS FOR INDUST, 1983-; Soc Motion Picture & TV Eng fel, 1963; Sr tech assoc, Eastman Kodak Co, 1944-1983; lectr creativity & innovation. **Memberships:** Fel Soc Motion Picture & TV Eng. **Research Statement & Publications:** Development of proximity fuses for naval ordnance; systems for silver sound records on reversal color films; development of magnetic prestriping on removable backing color films; co-inventor multi-layer digital magnetic recording media; establishment of electronic-optical image evaluation center. **Mailing Address:** 2608 Kanuga Pines Dr, Hendersonville, NC 28739-7014.

LOVINGER, ANDREW JOSEPH, POLYMER & MATERIALS SCIENCE. **Personal Data:** b Athens, Greece, May 15, 1948; American citizen; m 1976, c Michael & Daniel. **Education:** Columbia Univ, BS, 1970, MS, 1971, ScD, 1977. **Honors & Awards:** Dillon Medal, Am Phys Soc, 1985; Welch Found lectr, 1987; Frazer Price Memorial Award, Univ Mass, 1993; Waldo Semon lectr, Univ Akron, 1996; Dow Lectr, Northwestern Univ, 2001. **Professional Experience:** CONSULT, BELL LAB, 2001-; NSF COORDR, ADVANCED MAT PROCESSING, 1997-; POLYMERS PROG DIR, DIV MAT RES, NSF, 1995-; sr staff scientist, div mat res, NSF, 1995-1998; div counc, Am Phys Soc, 1992-; assoc ed, Macromolecules, Am Chem Soc, 1988-; distinguished mem tech staff, Bell Labs, Lucent Technol, 1985-2001; head, Polymer Chem Res Dept, 1985-1994; adj assoc prof, Dept Chem Eng & Appl Chem, Columbia Univ, NY, 1982-1983; adj asst prof, Dept Chem Eng & Appl Chem, Columbia Univ, NY, 1981-1982; mem tech staff, AT&T Bell Labs, 1977-1985; fulbright scholar, 1966-1970. **Memberships:** Am Phys Soc; Am Chem Soc; fel AAAS; Mat Res Soc. **Research Statement & Publications:** Structure and properties of polymeric and organic materials; morphology and phase transitions; high temperature and high strength polymers, electroactive polymers and organics. **Mailing Address:** NSF, 4201 Wilson Blvd, Arlington, VA 22230. **E-Mail:** alovinger@nsf.gov

LOVINGOOD, JUDSON ALLISON, MATHEMATICS, ELECTRICAL ENGINEERING. **Personal Data:** b Birmingham, Ala, July 18, 1936; m 1955, c 4. **Education:** Univ Ala, BSEE, 1958, PhD (math), 1968; Univ Minn, MS, 1963. **Professional Experience:** RETIRED; dir eng & res, Thiokol Corp, 1988-1993; dep mgr, Space Shuttle Prog & Space Shuttle Main Engine, 1979-1987; dir, Systs Dynamics Lab, 1974-1979; chief dynamics & control div, Aero-Astrodyn Lab, 1969-1974; asst prof, Univ Ala, Huntsville, 1968-; dep chief astrodyn guid theory div, Marshall Space Flight Ctr, NASA, 1964-1969; aerospace engr, Marshall Space Flight Ctr, NASA, 1962-1964; res engr, Honeywell Inc, 1959-1962; assoc engr, Martin Co, 1958-1959. **Memberships:** Am Inst Aeronaut & Astronaut. **Research Statement & Publications:** Optimal and adaptive control theory research applications to launch and space vehicles; mathematical research in guidance theory, control theory and celestial mechanics. **Mailing Address:** 108 Hickory Hill Rd, Gurley, AL 35748.

LOVINS, AMORY B, RESOURCE & ENERGY EFFICIENCY, GLOBAL SECURITY. **Personal Data:** b November 13, 1947; m 1979, Hunter. **Education:** Oxford, MA. **Honorary Degrees:** DSc, Bates Col, 1979, Williams Col, 1981, Kalamazoo Col, 1983, Univ Maine, 1985; LLD, Ball State Univ, 1983, Denver Sci Unity Col, 1992. **Honors & Awards:** Grauer lectr, Univ Boston Col, 1979; Nissan Prize; Mitchell Prize; Right Livelihood Award; Onassis Prize. **Professional Experience:** FOUNDER & CHMN, HYPERCAR INC, as of 2002; prin, Lovins Group, 1994; prin tech consult, E Source Inc, 1989-; DIR RES, VPRES & CHIEF EXEC OFFICER, ROCKY MOUNTAIN INST, 1982-; distinguished vis prof, Univ Colo, 1982; Luce vis pof, Dartmouth Col, 1982; distinguished vis scholar, Univ Okla, 1979; regents lectr, Univ Calif, 1978 & 1980; vis scholar, IIASA, 1977; res fel, Merton Col, Oxford, 1969-1971. **Memberships:** Fel AAAS; Am Inst Architects; Soc Automotive Engrs; Int Asn Energy Economists; Am Phys Soc; fel World Acad Arts Sci. **Research Statement & Publications:** Advanced resources and energy efficiency; transforming car, real estate and electricity industries; links to environment, development and security; efficient and sustainable use of resources as a path to global security; author of 24 books. **Mailing Address:** Rocky Mountain Inst, 1739 Snowmass Creek Rd, Snowmass, CO 81654-9199. **Fax:** 970-927-4178. **E-Mail:** ablovins@drmi.org

LOVRIEN, REX EUGENE, physical biochemistry; deceased, see previous edition for last biography

LOVSHIN, LEONARD LOUIS, AQUACULTURE, HATCHERY MANAGEMENT. **Personal Data:** b Rochester, Minn, March 21, 1942; m 1973, c 2. **Education:** Miami Univ, BA, 1964; Univ Wis, MS, 1966; Auburn Univ, PhD (fisheries), 1972. **Professional Experience:** PROF EMER FISHERIES, AUBURN UNIV, as of 2005; prof fisheries, Auburn Univ, 1985-; proj coordr to Govt Panama, small farmer aquacult develop, 1981-1984; from asst prof to assoc prof, Auburn Univ, 1972-1985; USAID-Auburn Univ proj coordr, Tech Asst Prog Fisheries Develop, Ctr Ichthyol Res, Fortaleza, Brazil, 1972-1979. **Memberships:** Am Fisheries Soc; World Aquacult Soc. **Research Statement & Publications:** Fish culture research dealing with Tilapias, all male hybrid tilapias, native species indigenous to Brazil, and the extension of research results to local fish farmers; integrated aquaculture development in rural, tropical Latin America, hatchery management. **Mailing Address:** Dept Fisheries & Allied Aquacult, Auburn Univ, Auburn, AL 36849-3501. **E-Mail:** llovshin@acesag.auburn.edu

LOW, BARBARA WHARTON, PROTEIN STRUCTURE & FUNCTION. **Personal Data:** b Lancaster, Eng, March 23, 1920; American citizen; m 1950, Melchie. **Education:** Oxford Univ, BA, 1942, MA, 1946, DPhil(chem), 1948. **Professional Experience:** PROF EMER & SPEC LECTR, COL PHYSICIANS & SURGEONS, COLUMBIA UNIV, 1990-; Acad Sci, USSR, 1988; prof biochem & molecular biophys, Col Physicians & Surgeons, Columbia Univ, 1985-1990; invited lectr, Chinese Acad Sci, 1981; mem, Biophy & Biophys Chem Study Sect, Div Res Grants, 1966-1969; vis prof, Univ Strasbourg, 1965 & Tohoku Univ, 1975; career develop award, NIH, 1963-1968; sr res fel, NIH, 1959-1963; from assoc prof to prof biochem, Col Physicians & Surgeons, Columbia Univ, 1956-1985; asst prof, Harvard Univ, 1950-1956; assoc mem, Lab Phys Chem, Harvard Univ, 1950-1954; assoc phys chem, Harvard Med Sch, 1948-1950; res assoc, Harvard Med Sch, 1948; spec Rockefeller Found fel, 1947; consult, USPHS. **Memberships:** AAAS; Am Inst Physics; Am Soc Biol Chem; Am Crystallog Asn; Am Acad Arts & Sci; Biophys Soc; Int Soc Toxinology. **Research Statement & Publications:** X-ray crystal structure of non-enzyme proteins and peptides, particularly snake venom post-synaptic neurotoxins; protein-protein interactions; prediction of protein conformation; curaremimetic toxins, interaction with acetylcholine receptors; water band to proteins in H2O. **Mailing Address:** Dept Biochem & Molecular Biophys Col Physicians & Surgeons, Columbia Univ 630 W 168th St, New York, NY 10032. **Fax:** 212-305-7932. **E-Mail:** bwl3@columbia.edu

LOW, BOBBI STIERS, BEHAVIORAL ECOLOGY, ECOLOGICAL DEMOGRAPHY. **Personal Data:** b Louisville, Ky, December 4, 1942; c Michael Muir. **Education:** Univ Louisville, BA, 1962; Univ Tex, Austin, MA, 1964, PhD (evolutionary zool), 1967. **Professional Experience:** PROF NAT RESOURCES, SCH NATURAL RESOURCES, UNIV MICH, ANN ARBOR, 1975-; commonwealth sci & res orgn res assoc ecol, Univ Melbourne & Univ SAustralia, 1969-1972; Can Med Res Coun fel physiol, Univ BC, 1967-1969; fac assoc, Pop Studies Ctr, Univ Mich. **Memberships:** AAAS; Am Soc Naturalists; Sigma Xi; Soc Study Evolution; Human Behav & Evolution Soc(pres, 2002-2005). **Research Statement & Publications:** Evolution of life history strategies; reproductive ecology in arid environments; evolution of sex differences; human resource ecology and sustainability. **Mailing Address:** Dept Nat Resources, Sch Nat Resources & Environ, Univ Mich, G142A Dana Bldg 430 E Univ Ave, Ann Arbor, MI 48109-1115. **E-Mail:** bobbilow@umich.edu

LOW, BOON-CHYE, PLASMA PHYSICS, FLUIDS. **Personal Data:** b Singapore, February 13, 1946; m 1971, Daphne; c Yi-Kai Liu. **Education:** Univ London, UK, BSc, 1968; Univ Chicago, MS, 1969, PhD (physics), 1972. **Professional Experience:** DIR, LONSON ENTERPRISE, as of 2001; SECT HEAD, SOLAR ATMOSPHERE & HELIOSPHERE SECT, NAT CTR ATMOSPHORIC RES, 1997-; mem, Mission Oper Working Group Solar Physics, NASA, 1992-; actg dir, High Altitude Observ, 1989-1990; SR SCIENTIST, HIGH ALTITUDE OBSERV, NAT CTR ATMOSPHERIC RES, 1987-; head coronal interplanetary physics, Nat Ctr Atmospheric Res, 1987-1990; scientist, Nat Ctr Atmospheric Res, 1981-1987; Nat Acad Sci-Nat Res Coun sr res assoc, NASA-Marshall Space Flight Ctr, 1980-1981; Japan Soc Prom Sci fel, Tokyo Astron Observ, Tokyo Univ, 1978-1979; vis scientist, High Altitude Observ, Nat Ctr Atmospheric Res, 1973-1974; res assoc, Enrico Fermi Inst, Univ Chicago, 1972-1973. **Memberships:** Am Phys Soc; Am Astron Soc; Am Geophys Union. **Research Statement & Publications:** Theoretical research in the fluid dynamics and magnetohydrodynamics of solar and astrophysical plasmas. **Mailing Address:** Nat Ctr Atmospheric Res, PO Box 3000, Boulder, CO 80307-3000. **Fax:** 303-497-1589. **E-Mail:** low@hao.ucar.edu

LOW, CHOW-ENG, IMMUNOPATHOLOGY, ORGANIC ANALYTICAL CHEMISTRY. **Personal Data:** b Perak, Malaysia, May 31, 1938; m 1966, c 3. **Education:** Chung Chi Col, Chinese Univ, BS, 1962; Tex Southern Univ, MS, 1966; Univ Tex, Austin, PhD (org chem), 1970. **Professional Experience:** Chmn dept chem, Nat Cheng Kung Univ, Tainan, Taiwan, 1986-1989; Dir, Inst Chem, Nat Chen Kung Univ, Tainan, Taiwan, 1986-1989; PROF CHEM, NAT CHENG KUNG UNIV, TAINAN, TAIWAN, 1984-; asst prof biochem, George Washington Univ Med Ctr, 1978-1984; res assoc, Dept Human Biol Chem & Genetics, Univ Tex Med Br, 1976-1978; res fel, Ind Univ, Bloomington, 1972-1975; Vis asst prof, Dept Chem, La State Univ, 1970-1971. **Memberships:** Am Chem Soc; AAAS; Chem Soc London; Sigma Xi; Chinese Chem Soc. **Research Statement & Publications:** Autoxidation of polyunsaturated fatty acids; lipoxygenase metabolities of polyunsaturated fatty acids; analysis of pollutants; Friedel-Crafts reaction mechanisms; catalytic transfer hydrogenation. **Mailing Address:** Dept Chem, Nat Cheng Kung Univ One Ta-Hsieh Rd, Tainan 70101, Taiwan.

LOW, EMMET FRANCIS, JR, applied mathematics; deceased, see previous edition for last biography

LOW, FRANCIS EUGENE, THEORETICAL PHYSICS. **Personal Data:** b New York, NY, October 27, 1921; m 1948, Natalie; c Julie, Peter & Margaret. **Education:** Harvard Univ, BS, 1942; Columbia Univ, MS, 1947, PhD (physics), 1949. **Honors & Awards:** Loeb lectr, Harvard Univ, 1959 & 1973. **Professional Experience:** INST PROF EMER, DEPT PHYSICS, MASS INST TECHNOL, 1992-; bd mem, Whitehead Inst, 1987-; nat coun, Nat Acad Sci, 1986-1989; inst prof, Lab Nuclear Sci, 1985-1992; provost, Lab Nuclear Sci, 1980-1985; dir, Lab Nuclear Sci, 1979-1985; dir, Ctr Theoret Physics, 1974-1983; Karl Compton prof, Mass Inst Technol, 1968-1985; Guggenheim fel, 1961-1962; Fulbright fel, 1961-1962; prof, Mass Inst Technol, 1957-1968; consult, AEC, 1955-; from asst prof to assoc prof physics, Univ Ill, 1952-1956; mem, Inst Advan Study, 1950-1952; instr physics, Columbia Univ, 1949-1950. **Memberships:** Nat Acad Sci; Am Acad Arts & Sci (vpres, 1986-1987); fel Am Phys Soc; Fedn Am Scientists. **Research Statement & Publications:** Theoretical, atomic and nuclear physics; field theory. **Mailing Address:** Dept Physics, Mass Inst Technol, 77 Mass Ave Rm 6-301, Cambridge, MA 02139. **E-Mail:** low@mitlns.mit.edu

LOW, FRANK JAMES, SOLID STATE PHYSICS. **Personal Data:** b Mobile, Ala, November 23, 1933; m 1956, c 3. **Education:** Yale Univ, BS, 1955; Rice Univ, MA, 1957, PhD (physics), 1959. **Honors & Awards:** Helen B Warner Prize, Am Astron Soc, 1968; Medal Except Sci Achievement, NASA, 1984; Rumford Prize, Am Acad Arts & Sci, 1986. **Professional Experience:** REGENTS RES PROF EMER, STEWARD OBSERV, UNIV ARIZ, 1993-; Regents res prof, Lunar & Planetary Lab, Univ Ariz, 1988-1993; res prof, Lunar & Planetary Lab, Univ Ariz, 1971-1993; adj prof, Rice Univ, 1971-1979; PRES, INFRARED LABS INC, ARIZ, 1967-; Prof space sci, Rice Univ, 1966-1971; res prof, Lunar & Planetary Lab, Univ Ariz, 1965-1979; assoc scientist, Nat Radio Astron Observ, WVa, 1962-1965; mem tech staff, Tex Instruments, Inc, 1959-1962. **Memberships:** Nat Acad Sci; Am Phys Soc; Am Astron Soc; Sigma Xi; fel Am Acad Arts & Sci. **Research Statement & Publications:** Infrared astronomy; solid state physics; low temperature physics. **Mailing Address:** Steward Observ Univ Ariz, Steward 258, Tucson, AZ 85721. **E-Mail:** flow@as.arizona.edu

LOW, G DAVID, AERONAUTICS. **Personal Data:** b February 19, 1956. **Education:** Wash & Lee Univ, BS, 1978; Cornell Univ, (mech eng), 1980; Stanford Univ, MS, (aeronautics & astronautics), 1983. **Honors & Awards:** NASA Space Flight Medals. **Professional Experience:** STAFF, ORBITAL SCI CORP, as of 2006; astronaut, NASA, ending 1996. **Memberships:** Am Inst Aeronaut & Astronaut. **Mailing Address:** Orbital Sci Corp, 21839 Atlantic Blvd, Dulles, VA 20166.

LOW, HANS, ORGANIC CHEMISTRY. **Personal Data:** b Vienna, Austria, October 22, 1921; American citizen; m 1949, c 3. **Education:** Marietta Col, BS, 1950; Purdue Univ, MS, 1952; St Louis Univ, PhD (chem), 1959; Univ Tex, MPH, 1976. **Professional Experience:** SR STAFF TECHNOLOGIST, HEALTH, SAFETY & ENVIRON, SHELL OIL CO, 1978-; staff technologist, Health, Safety & Environ, Shell Oil CO, 1972-1978; group leader lubricant additives, Health, Safety & Environ, Shell Oil CO, 1967-1972; res chemist, Health, Safety & Environ, Shell Oil CO, 1952-1967; Instr German & Latin, Marietta Col, 1947-1950. **Memberships:** Am Chem Soc NY Acad Sci. **Research Statement & Publications:** Petroleum solvents and lubricants; synthetic lubricants; lubricant additives; industrial toxicology; public health. **Mailing Address:** 7855 Cowles Mountain Ct No 19A, San Diego, CA 92119.

LOW, JAMES ALEXANDER, MEDICINE, OBSTETRICS & GYNECOLOGY. **Personal Data:** b Toronto, Ont, September 22, 1925; m 1952, Margery; c Donald, Margaret & Norman. **Education:** Univ Toronto, MD, 1949; FRCS(C), 1955. **Professional Experience:** PROF EMER OBSTET & GYNEC, QUEEN'S UNIV, ONT, as of 2003; prof obstet & gynec, Queen's Univ, ONT, beginning 1985; head dept, Queen's Univ, Ont, 1965-1985; clin teacher obstet & gynec, Univ Toronto, 1955-1965. **Memberships:** Soc Gynec Invest; Can Soc Clin Invest; Soc Obstet & Gynec Can; Am Gynec & Obstet Soc; Am Acad Cerebral Palsy & Develop Med. **Research Statement & Publications:** Perinatal medicine; fetal and newborn cardiorespiratory function mechanism leading to deficits in children; fetal and newborn asphyxia. **Mailing Address:** Dept Obstet, Kingston Gen Hosp, Queen's Univ, Victory Four, Kingston, ON K7L 2V7, Can. **E-Mail:** lowj@kgh.kari.net

LOW, KENNETH BROOKS, GENETICS, DNA RECOMBINATION. **Personal Data:** b New Rochelle, NY, January 19, 1936; m 1960, Elise; c Kennan & David. **Education:** Amherst Col, BA, 1958; Univ Pa, MS, 1960, PhD (molecular biol), 1965. **Professional Experience:** Mem, Prokaryotic Genetics Rev Panel, NSF, 1986-; PROF RES, YALE UNIV, 1984-; sr scientist radiobiol & biol, Yale Univ, 1981-1984; consult, Comn Study Antibiotic Use Animal Feeds, Nat Acad Sci, 1979; mem, Microbiol Genetics Study Sect, NIH, 1978-1982; sr scientist radiobiol, Yale Univ, 1978-1981; assoc prof, Yale Univ, 1973-1978; asst prof radiobiol & microbiol, Yale Univ, 1971-1973; asst prof radiobiol, Yale Univ, 1968-1971; USPHS fel, Med Ctr, NY Univ, 1966-1968. **Memberships:** Am Soc Microbiol. **Research Statement & Publications:** Molecular genetics; genetic recombination and control. **Mailing Address:** 1211 W Lake Ave, Guilfard, CT 06437.

LOW, LAWRENCE J(ACOB), MECHANICAL ENGINEERING, OPERATIONS RESEARCH. **Personal Data:** b New York, NY, June 22, 1921; m 1951, c 1. **Education:** Stevens Inst Technol, ME, 1942. **Professional Experience:** RETIRED; staff scientist, Naval Weapons Res Ctr, SRI Int, 1976-1983; dir, Naval Weapons Res Ctr, SRI Int, 1965-1976; chmn opers anal sect, Advan Surface Missile Assessment Group, 1965; Mem US Marine air defense eval group, Off Naval Res, DC, 1957-1958; sr res engr, Stanford Res Inst, 1955-1965; res aerodynamicist, Cornell Aeronaut Lab, 1946-1950; Aerodynamicist, Curtiss Wright Airplane Div, NY, 1942-1943. **Memberships:** AAAS; Sigma Xi; Am Inst Aeronaut & Astronaut; Opers Res Soc Am; Am Ord Asn. **Research Statement & Publications:** Aerodynamics; fluid mechanics; weapon systems analysis and evaluation. **Mailing Address:** 60 Skywood Way, Woodside, CA 94062.

LOW, LEONE YARBOROUGH, APPLIED STATISTICS, COMPONENTS OF VARIANCE. **Personal Data:** b Cushing, Okla, August 27, 1935; div, c Corbey & David. **Education:** Okla State Univ, BS, 1956, MS, 1958, PhD (math), 1961. **Professional Experience:** Res scientist, Columbus Battelle Labs, 1988-; EMER PROF MATH, WRIGHT STATE UNIV, 1988-; vis assoc prof, Iowa State Univ, 1980-1981; Nat Acad Sci fel, 1967-1968, Nat Res Coun res assoc, Wright-Patterson AFB, 1967-1968; from asst prof to assoc prof, Wright State Univ, 1964-1988; instr math, Univ Ill, 1960-1964; Systs design engr, Chance Vought Aircraft, Dallas, Tex, 1956-1958. **Memberships:** Inst Math Statist; Am Statist Asn; Sigma Xi; fel Royal Statist Soc; Biomet Soc; Am Daffodil Soc Board of dir 1990-2002. **Research Statement & Publications:** Variance component models in the analysis of variance; bootstrapping; experimental design; Taguchi design; inheritance of size and color in narcissus. **Mailing Address:** 381 N Enon Rd, Yellow Springs, OH 45387-9764.

LOW, LOH-LEE, FISHERIES. **Personal Data:** b Kuala Lumpur, Malaysia, January 15, 1948; m 1973, c 2. **Education:** Univ Wash, BS, 1970, MS, 1972, PhD (fisheries), 1974. **Professional Experience:** Affil asst prof, Univ Wash, beginning 1978; consult, Food & Agr Orgn, UN, 1975; FISHERY RES BIOLOGIST & OPERS RES ANALYST, NW FISHERIES CTR, ALASKA FISHERIES SCI CTR, NAT MARINE FISHERIES SERV, NOAA, 1974-; fishery biologist, Univ Wash, 1974. **Research Statement & Publications:** Fisheries population dynamics; computer modelling of fisheries systems; international fisheries management. **Mailing Address:** Alaska Fisheries Sci Ctr, Nat Marine Fisheries Serv, NOAA, 7600 Sandpoint Way NE Bldg 4, Seattle, WA 98115-6349. **Fax:** 206-529-6723. **E-Mail:** loh-lee.low@noaa.gov

LOW, MARC E, MATHEMATICS. **Personal Data:** b Ada, Okla, September 25, 1935; m 1957, c 2. **Education:** Okla State Univ, BS, 1958, MS, 1960; Univ Ill, PhD (math), 1965. **Professional Experience:** ASST DEAN, COL SCI & ENG, 1973-; ASSOC PROF MATH, WRIGHT STATE UNIV, 1971-; asst prof, Wright State Univ, 1965-1971; instr math, Wright State Univ, 1964-1965; EMERITUS. **Memberships:** Math Asn Am; Am Math Soc. **Research Statement & Publications:** Elementary and analytic number theory. **Mailing Address:** Dean Sci Wright State Univ, 3640 Colonel Glenn, Dayton, OH 45435-0001. **E-Mail:** marc.low@wright.edu

LOW, MARY ALICE, NUTRITION. **Personal Data:** b Warren, Ohio, May 15, 1949; m 1971, c 2. **Education:** Univ Mass, BS, 1971; Univ Maine, MS, 1972; Cornell Univ, PhD (nutrit), 1975. **Professional Experience:** Assoc prof nutrit, Syracuse Univ, 1981-; asst prof, Syracuse Univ, 1978-1981; Nutrit res consult, USDA, 1978; asst prof, Syracuse Univ, 1976-1978; Nutrit res consult, Loretto Geriatric Ctr, 1976-1978; Clin instr nutrit, Syracuse Univ, 1974-1976; atty, John B Low, Oxen Hill, Md; ASSOC PROF FOOD NUTRIT & INST ADMIN, AT GRAD SCH UNIV MD. **Memberships:** Am Dietetic Asn; Nutrit Today Soc; Am Pub Health Asn; Soc Nutrit Educ. **Research Statement & Publications:** Socio-cultural correlates of nutritional status. **Mailing Address:** 12401 Hatton Point Rd, Ft Washington, MD 20744.

LOW, MORTON DAVID, NEUROPHYSIOLOGY, SOCIAL ECOLOGY OF HEALTH & PUBLIC HEALTH. **Personal Data:** b Lethbridge, Alta, March 25, 1935; American & Canadian citizen; m 1984, Barbara; c Cecilia A, Sarah E, Peter J & Kelsey A. **Education:** Queen's Univ, Ont, MD & CM, 1960, MSc, 1962; Baylor Univ, PhD (physiol), 1966; FRCP (C), 1973. **Honors & Awards:** Rockwell Chair in Soc & Health, Univ Texas Sch Pub Health, 2000; Tree of Life Award, Jewish Nat Fund, 1995. **Professional Experience:** Advisor to the President on Public Health, University of Calgary, 2005-8; Advisor to the Calgary Regional Health Authority on Community Health, 2005-8; DIR, CTR FOR SOC & POP HEALTH, SCH PUB HEALTH, UNIV TEX, 2000-4; pres, Mickey Leland Nat Urban Air Toxics Res Ctr, 1992-1995; mem, Med Sci Adv Comt, US Info Agency, 1991-1993; dir, Inst Health Policy Res & Educ, 1990-2000; prof, Dept Neurol, Med Sch, Univ Tex Health Sci Ctr, Houston, 1989-2000; PROF NEURAL SCI, GRAD SCH BIOMED SCI, UNIV TEX HEALTH SCI CTR, HOUSTON, 1989-; PROF MGT & POLICY SCI, SCH PUB HEALTH, UNIV TEX HEALTH SCI CTR, HOUSTON, 1989-; pres, Univ Tex Health Sci Ctr, Houston, 1989-2000; mem bd dirs, Health Environ Inst, Univ Houston, 1989-1992; chmn, Coun Univ Teaching Hosps, 1989; attend staff, Univ Hosp, Univ BC Site, 1989; serv staff consult, Dept Diag Neurophysiol, Vancouver Gen Hosp, 1987-1989; dir, Evoked Potential Lab, Univ Hosp, Univ BC Site, 1986-1989; vchmn, Coun Univ Teaching Hosps, 1986-1988; mem, Coun Univ Teaching Hosps, 1985-1989; coordr health sci, Div Neurol, Dept Med, Univ BC, 1985-1989; dir, Vancouver Gen Hosp Res Inst, 1983-1986; interim dir, Vancouver Gen Hosp Res Inst, 1981-1983; actg head, Div Neurol, Dept Med, Univ BC, 1979-1980; actg assoc dean res & grad studies, Fac Med, Dept Med, Univ BC, 1977-1978; clin assoc dean, Fac Med, Dept Med, Univ BC, 1974-1976; vis staff neurol EEG, Shaughnessy Hosp, Vancouver, 1971-1989; consult med staff neurol, Univ Hosp, Univ BC Site, 1970-1989; from assoc prof to prof, Div Neurol, Dept Med, Univ BC, 1968-1989; Dr, Dept Diag Neurophysiol, Vancouver Gen Hosp, 1968-1987; Fom instr to asst prof physiol, Baylor Col Med, 1965-1968; vis prof & lectr, numerous univ, assocs & hosps; consult, Health Protection Br, Health & Welfare Can; health reform consult, Premier of Alberta, Can. **Memberships:** AMA; Am Coun Educ; Int Fedn Socs EEG & Clin Neurophysiol (secy, 1981-1985); fel Am EEG Soc; Can Soc Clin Neurophysiol (secy, 1970-1972, pres, 1972-1974); Can Soc Clin Invest; Can Asn Med Educ; Sigma Xi; AAAS; Can Soc EEG; Am Epilepsy Soc. **Research Statement & Publications:** Electrophysiology of the central nervous system; cognitive neuroscience; sleep disorders; health policy research and development; health services research; social ecology of health. **Mailing Address:** #3196 Professional Faculties Bldg, 2500 Univ Dr NW, Calgary, AB V9P 9B5, Can. **E-Mail:** lowd@ucalgary.ca

LOW, NIELS LEO, MEDICINE. **Personal Data:** b Copenhagen, Denmark, December 16, 1916; American citizen; m 1943, c 2. **Education:** Med Col SC, MD, 1940. **Professional Experience:** PHYSICIAN EMER, BLYTHEDALE CHILDREN'S HOSP, VALHALLA, NY, as of 2003; prof clin neurol & clin pediat, Col Physicians & Surgeons, Columbia Univ, beginning 1975; dir pediat, Blythedale Children's Hosp, Valhalla, Ny, beginning 1967; assoc prof clin neurol, Col Physicians & Surgeons, Columbia Univ, 1967-1975; asst prof neurol, Col Physicians & Surgeons, Columbia Univ, 1960-1967; assoc res prof pediat, Univ Utah, 1956-1958; fel, Columbia Univ, 1955 & 1958-1959; res assoc neurol, Univ Ill, 1954; Clin instr pediat, Marquette Univ, 1946-1953; consult, NIH. **Memberships:** Am EEG Soc; fel Am Acad Neurol; fel Am Acad Pediat; Am Epilepsy Soc; Int Child Neurol Asn (pres) 1975-. **Research Statement & Publications:** Pediatric neurology; metabolic disease affecting brain of children. **Mailing Address:** Blythedale Children's Hosp, Bradhurst Ave, Valhalla, NY 10595. **Fax:** 914-592-0407.

LOW, PHILIP STEWART, MEMBRANE BIOCHEMISTRY, DRUG DESIGN. **Personal Data:** b Ames, Iowa, August 8, 1947; m 1969, Joan; c Philip, Tara, Emily, Justin & Stewart. **Education:** Brigham Young Univ, BS, 1971; Univ Calif, San Diego, PhD (biochem), 1975. **Honors & Awards:** International Union Against Cancer Fellow (1987) Indiana Lions Club Cancer Research Award (1991) Herbert Newby McCoy Award, 1993 Sigma Xi Research Award (1997) Elected Fellow of the American Association for the Advancement of Science (1998). **Professional Experience:** Ralph C. Corley DISTINGUISHED PROF CHEM, DEPT CHEM, PURDUE UNIV, 1995-; Fel Int Union Against Cancer, 1987; PROF BIOCHEM, DEPT CHEM, PURDUE UNIV, 1986-; from asst prof to assoc prof, Dept Chem, Purdue Univ, 1976-1986; res assoc, Dept Chem, Univ Mass, 1975-1976. **Memberships:** Am Soc Hemat; Controlled Release Soc; Am Soc Biochem & Molecular Biol; Am Soc Cell Biol; Am Assoc. Cancer Res. **Research Statement & Publications:** Biochemistry and physical chemistry of biological membranes; Design of receptor-targeted therapeutic and imaging agents. **Mailing Address:** Dept Chem, Purdue Univ, 560 Oval Dr, West Lafayette, IN 47907-2084. **Fax:** 765-494-5272. **E-Mail:** plow@purdue.edu

LOW, ROBERT BURNHAM, PHYSIOLOGY. **Personal Data:** b Greenfield, Mass, September 19, 1940; m 1967, c 2. **Education:** Princeton Univ, BA, 1963; Univ Chicago, PhD (physiol), 1968. **Professional Experience:** Res fel, Dept Pathol, Univ Geneva, Geneva, Switz, 1997-1998 & 1979-1980; provost, Univ Vt, 1994-1996; interim provost, Univ Vt, 1992-1994; interim exec dean, Col Med, 1991-1992; Univ scholar, 1988; assoc dean res, Col Med, 1984-1992; PROF MOLECULAR PHYSIOL & BIOPHYS, COL MED, UNIV VT, 1979-; dir, Vt Pulmonary Specialized Ctr Res, 1976-1992; sr int fogarty fel, 1979; assoc prof, Col Med, Univ VT, 1974-1979; asst prof physiol, Col Med, Univ VT, 1970-1974; NIH fel biol, Mass Inst Technol, 1968-1970; NIH & Muscular Dystrophy res grants, Univ Vt, 1970-. **Memberships:** Am Soc Cell Biol; Am Thoracic Soc. **Research Statement & Publications:** Mammalian protein turnover; physiology and biochemistry of muscle; cytoskeleton; tissue and cell remodeling; lung epithelial cells; smooth muscle. **Mailing Address:** Dept Molecular Physiol & Biophys, Col Med, Univ Vt, Rm D 207 349 Waterman Bldg, Burlington, VT 05405-0068. **Fax:** 802-656-0747. **E-Mail:** Bob.Low@uvm.edu

LOW, TERESA LINGCHUN KAO, PROTEIN CHEMISTRY, THYMIC HORMONES. **Personal Data:** b Hankow, China, February 17, 1941; American citizen; m 1966, c 3. **Education:** Tunghai Univ, Taiwan, BS, 1962; Tex Woman's Univ, MSc, 1966; Univ Tex, Austin, PhD (biochem), 1970. **Professional Experience:** PROF, DEPT BIOCHEM, COL MED, NAT CHENG KUNG UNIV, 1990-; chmn dept, Dept Biochem, Col Med, Nat Cheng Kung Univ, 1984-1990; from asst prof to assoc prof protein chem, Dept Biochem, Med Sch, George Washington Univ, 1981-1984; instr protein chem, Dept Human Biol Chem & Genetics, Univ Tex Med Br, 1977-1978; fel, Dept Human Biol Chem & Genetics, Univ Tex Med Br, 1976-1977; res assoc, Dept Zool, Ind Univ, 1972-1975; Sci res specialist, Dept Biochem, La State Univ, 1970-1971. **Memberships:** Sigma Xi; NY Acad Sci; Am Soc Biochem & Molecular Biol; Protein Soc. **Research Statement & Publications:** Chemical and biological characterization of thymosin, a family of hormones derived from the thymus gland and demonstrated to have potent immunomodulating properties. **Mailing Address:** Dept Biochem Col Med, Nat Cheng Kung Univ, Tainan 70101, Taiwan.

LOW, WALTER CHENEY, NEUROPHYSIOLOGY, NERVE REGENERATION & TRANSPLATION. **Personal Data:** b Madera, Calif, May 11, 1950; m 1983, Margaret; c Matthew & Elizabeth. **Education:** Univ Calif, Santa Barbara, BS, 1972; Univ Mich, MS, 1974, PhD (bioeng), 1979. **Professional Experience:** DIR, RES LAB, DEPT NEUROSURG, UNIV MINN, as of 2004; PROF, NEUROSURG & PHYSIOL, MED SCH, UNIV MINN, 1993-; estab investr award, Am Heart Asn, 1990-; assoc prof, Med Sch, Univ Minn, 1990-1993; prin investr, Minn Med Found, 1990-1991; prin investr, Alzheimer's Dis Asn, 1988-1989; prin investr, Am Heart Asn, 1987-; prin investr, Nat Inst Neurol Cardiol Dis Soc, 1987-1991; dir, Grad Prog Physiol, 1985-1988; prin investr, NIA, 1985-1987; prin investr, NIH, 1984-1985; from asst prof to assoc prof, Ind Med Sch, Ind Univ, 1983-1990; NIH, Nat Heart, Lung & Blood Inst, 1981-1982; res fel, Univ Vt, 1980-1983; fel, Univ Vt, 1980-1981; NIH Fel, Nat Neurol & Commun Dis & Stroke, Univ Mich, 1979; res fel, neurophysiol, Cambridge Univ, 1979-1980; NSF, NATO fel, Cambridge Univ, 1979-1980; res assoc, neurophysiol, Univ Mich, 1978-1979; NIH, Nat Inst Gen Med Sci fel, bioeng, Univ Mich, 1975-1978; founding mem, Am Soc Neural Transplantation. **Memberships:** AAAS; Soc Neuroscience; Am Physiol Soc; NY Acad Sci; Cell Transplant Soc; Am Heart Asn. **Research Statement & Publications:** Central nervous system physiology; neural transplantation and the recovery of function; Parkinson's Disease; Alzheimer's Disease; stroke and cerebral ischemia; neural regeneration; brain tumors. **Mailing Address:** Dept Neurosurg Univ Minn Med Sch, 420 Del St SE, Minneapolis, MN 55455. **E-Mail:** lowwalt@umn.edu

LOW, WILLIAM, PHYSICS. **Personal Data:** b Vienna, Austria, April 25, 1922; Canadian & Israeli citizen; m 1970, Sara Katzburg; c Esther, Nachuh, Abraham, Chava, Shimon, Zipporn, Ayala, Miriam & Rivea. **Education:** Queen's Univ, Ont, BA, 1946; Columbia Univ, MA, 1947, PhD, 1950. **Honorary Degrees:** Dr, Yeshiva Univ, 1989. **Honors & Awards:** Cressy Morrison Award, NY Acad Sci, 1956; Israel Prize Exact Sci, 1961; Rothschild Prize Physics, 1964. **Professional Experience:** EMER PROF PHYSICS, HEBREW UNIV, ISRAEL, 1992-; prof, Univ Toronto, 1990-1992; prof, Tel Aviv, 1988-; prof, Columbia Univ, 1985-1986; chmn bd gov, Jerusalem Col Technol, Israel, 1985; Atomic Energy Estab, Venezuela, 1977; Atomic Energy Lab, France, 1974; chair & Sadie Danciger prof, Hebrew Univ, 1970-1992; pres & rector, Jerusalem Col Technol, Israel, 1969-1981; Weizmann Inst, Mass Inst Technol, 1964-1965 & 1982-1983; Guggenhem fel, 1964-1965; vis scientist, Nat Physics Lab, Ottawa, 1963-1967; vis scientist, Nat Magnet Lab, Mass Inst

Technol, 1959; consult scientist, AEC, Israel, 1963-1966; vis prof, Weizmann Inst, Rehovot, 1962-1964; prof, Hebrew Univ, 1961-1970; vis prof, Inst Technol, 1960-1964; vis prof, Inst Technol, Technion, Israel, 1959-1960; assoc prof, Hebrew Univ, 1959-1960; vis scientist, Lincoln Lab, 1959; vis scientist, Argonne Nat Lab, 1956; sr lectr, Hebrew Univ, Israel, 1955-1958; res assoc, Enrico Fermi Lab, Univ Chicago, 1955-1957; Vis scholar, Oxford Univ, 1954; lectr, Hebrew Univ, Israel, 1950-1954; asst, Columbia Univ, 1946-1950; Tutor physics, Queen's Univ, Ont, 1945-1946; ed, Physics Letters; consult to numerous indust firms; chmn, Israel Comt, Int Union Radio Sci. **Memberships:** Am Phys Soc; NY Acad Sci; Phys Soc Israel (vpres, 1958-1960, pres, 1960-1961 & 1970-1972); Europ Phys Soc; Int Union Pure & Appl Physics. **Research Statement & Publications:** Paramagnetic resonance in solids; microwave spectroscopy in gases; quantum electronics; electron density behind shock waves; light scattering from macromolecules. **Mailing Address:** Microwave Div Racah Inst Physics, Hebrew Univ, Jerusalem, Israel. **E-Mail:** williaml@cc.huit.ac.il

LOWDEN, J ALEXANDER, BIOCHEMICAL GENETICS. **Personal Data:** b Toronto, Ont, February 21, 1933; m 1956, Anne Taylor; c John, Eleanor, Jane & Thomas. **Education:** Univ Toronto, MD, 1957; McGill Univ, PhD (biochem), 1964; CCFMG, 1983. **Professional Experience:** VPRES & CHIEF MED DIR, CROWN LIFE, 1989-; pres, HSC Res & Develop Corp, 1982-1989; Prof pediat & clin biochem, Univ Toronto, 1980-1989; assoc dir, Res Inst, 1975-1989; assoc pediat, Univ Toronto, 1967-1980; res assoc, Univ Toronto, 1965-1967; assoc scientist, Hosp Sick Children, 1964-1974; Helen Hay Whitney Found fel, 1963-1966; Fel neurochem, Montreal Neurol Inst, 1961-1964; Resident pediat, Hosp Sick Children, 1958-1960. **Memberships:** AAAS; Can Biochem Soc; Am Soc Pediat; Soc Pediat Res. **Research Statement & Publications:** Inborn errors of metabolism, especially lysosomal storage disease. **Mailing Address:** 1901 Scarth St, Regina, SK S4P 3B1, Can. **Fax:** 306-751-6041.

LOWDEN, RICHARD MAX, PLANT SYSTEMATICS. **Personal Data:** b Columbus, Ohio, September 27, 1943; m 1970, c 3. **Education:** Ohio State Univ, BA, 1964, MSc, 1967, PhD, 1971. **Professional Experience:** PROF BIOL & BOT, CATH UNIV, SANTIAGO, 1985-; DIR, MOSCOSO HERBARIUM, 1973-; from asst prof to assoc prof, Moscoso Herbarium, 1971-1985; Asst prof bot, Ohio State Univ, 1971. **Memberships:** Sigma Xi; Int Asn Plant Taxon; Asn Trop Biol; Asn Aquatic Vascular Plant Biologists; Acad Ciencias Republica Dominicana. **Research Statement & Publications:** Aquatic freshwater vascular flora of Hispaniola; Latin American botany; botanical collectors; international index compiler. **Mailing Address:** Univ Cath Madre y Maestra, Moscoso Herbarium, Santiago de los Caballeros, Dominican Republic.

LOWDER, J ELBERT, APPLIED PHYSICS. **Personal Data:** b Pinedale, Wyo, March 18, 1940; m 1964, c 3. **Education:** Univ Calif, Berkeley, BS, 1963, MS, 1965; Univ Calif, San Diego, PhD (eng physics), 1971. **Professional Experience:** VPRES, SPARTA INC, 1980-; assoc group leader appl physics, Lincoln Lab, Mass Inst Technol, 1975-1980; mem staff, Lincoln Lab, Mass Inst Technol, 1971-1975; proj engr, Aeronutronic Div, Philco-Ford Corp, 1965-1968; flight test engr, Northrop Aircraft Corp, 1963-1964. **Memberships:** Optical Soc Am; Am Inst Aeronaut & Astronaut; Soc Photo-Optical Instrumentation Engrs. **Research Statement & Publications:** Effects of atmospheric aerosols on propagation of laser radiation; interaction of high power laser radiation with solid surfaces; laser radar applications; passive infrared detection systems. **Mailing Address:** Sparta Inc, 24 Hartwell Ave, Lexington, MA 02173.

LOWDER, JAMES N, HEMATOLOGY, ONCOLOGY. **Personal Data:** b Cleveland, Ohio, August 26, 1950. **Education:** Case Western Res Univ, BS, 1973, MD, 1978. **Professional Experience:** CORP MED DIR, ADVAN DIAGNOSTICS, BECTON DICKINSON, 1989-; assoc med dir, Immunocytometry Systs, 1988-1989; staff, Cleveland Clin Found, 1986-1988. **Memberships:** Am Soc Hemat; AAAS; Am Soc Clin Chemists; Am Soc Clin Oncol; Am Soc Microbiol; Am Soc Immunol. **Mailing Address:** Dept Med, Advan Diag, Becton Dickinson, 7 Loveton Circle PO Box 999, Sparks, MD 21152-5555.

LOWDER, WAYNE MORRIS, radiation physics, dosimetry; deceased, see previous edition for last biography

LOWDIN, PER-OLOV, THEORETICAL PHYSICS, QUANTUM BIOLOGY. **Personal Data:** b Uppsala, Sweden, October 28, 1916; m 1960, Karin Wilhelmina Hook; c Per Erik Assar & Anna Karin Charlotta. **Education:** Univ Uppsala, Fil Kand, 1937, Fil Mag, 1939, Fil Lic, 1942, Fil Dr(theoret physics), 1948. **Honorary Degrees:** Dr, Univ Gent, Belgium, 1975, Univ Paris, 1975, Turku Univ, Finland, 1980. **Honors & Awards:** knight of the Swed Royal Order of North Star; Comdr Swed Royal Order Vasa; St Olaf's Medal, Norway, 1975; Swed-Am Bicentennial Gold Medal, 1979; Lavoisier Medal in Gold, Fr Acad Sci, 1981; Chevalier of Legion of Honour, 1982; Ultrastructure Award, Sanibel Prism, 1985; Niels Bohr Medal, World Asn Theoret Org Chemists, 1987; Oscar Carlson Gold Medal, Swed Chem Soc, 1993. **Professional Experience:** GRAD RES EMER PROF CHEM & PHYSICS, UNIV FLA, 1993-; dir, dir Fla- Latinamerican & Caribbean Basin Exchange Proj, 1985-; sr investr, Nat Found Cancer Res, Washington, DC, 1984-1989; founding dir, Fla Quantum Theory Proj, 1983-; emer prof quantum chem, Univ Uppsala, 1983-; EMER PROF QUANTUM CHEM, UNIV UPPSALA, 1983-; foreign mem Sci Coun Inst Molecular Sci, Okazaki, Japan, 1983-1986; mem Nobel Comt Physics, Swed Royal Acad Sci, 1972-1984; ed-in-chief, Int J Quantum Chem, 1967-; ed-in-chief, Advan in Quantum Chem, 1967-; dir, Uppsala-Fla Exchange Proj, quantum sci, 1960-; grad res prof chem & physics, Univ Fla, 1960-1993; prof quantum chem & head dept, Univ Uppsala, 1960-1982; prof & head, Dept Quantum Chem, 1960-1982; founder & leader, Fla Quantum Theory Proj, 1960-1982; founder & leader, Uppsala Quantum Chem Group, 1955-1982; assoc prof, Univ Uppsala, 1955-1960; assoc prof, Swed Nat Sci Res Coun, 1955-1960; vis prof & consult, Duke Univ, Univ Chicago, Mass Inst Technol & Calif Inst Technol, 1950-1959; H H Wells Phys Lab, Univ Bristol, 1949; asst prof theoret physics, Univ Uppsala, 1948-1955; asst prof theoret physics, Univ Uppsala, 1948-1955; Fel, Swiss Fed Inst Technol, 1946; lectr math & physics, Univ Uppsala, 1942-1948; Lectr mech & math physics, Univ Uppsala, 1942-1948; mem adv bd, Max Planck Soc, Carbon Res, Ruhr, WGer. **Memberships:** Swed Royal Soc Arts & Sci; Swed Royal Soc Sci; Norweg Acad Sci & Lett; Int Soc Quantum Biol (pres, 1971-1972, hon pres); Int Acad Quantum Molecular Sci (vpres, 1968-1979, pres, 1979-1985); Am Chem Soc; fel Am Phys Soc; hon mem Sigma Xi; Brit Phys Soc; Catalonian Quantum Chem Soc; World Asn Theoret Org Chemists (hon pres, 1989-); foreign mem Korean Acad Sci & Technol. **Research Statement & Publications:** Quantum Chem, Solid State Theory and quantum biology; foundations of quantum mechanics and quantum statistics and their reaction to classical mechanics, thermodynamics, etc; theory of chemical reactions, scattering states, and resonances; connection between quantum theory and the special and general theories of relativity; partitioning technique, wave and reaction operators, resolvent methods, rational approximations, etc; author of numerous publications. **Mailing Address:** Quantum Chem Group, Box 518, S-75120 Uppsala, Sweden.

LOWE, CHARLES UPTON, PEDIATRICS. **Personal Data:** b Pelham, NY, August 24, 1921; m 1955, c 4. **Education:** Harvard Univ, BS, 1942; Yale Univ, MD, 1945. **Honors & Awards:** John F Kennedy Mem Lectr, 1966; Grover Powers Mem Lectr, 1969; Clifford G Grulee Award, Am Acad Pediat, 1971; Special Recognition Award, NIH, 1988. **Professional Experience:** ASSOC DIR SPEC PROJ, NAT INST CHILD HEALTH & HUMAN DEVELOP, NIH, as of 1999; spec asst dir, Nat Inst Child Health & Develop, NIH, beginning 1983; actg assoc dir, med appln res, 1980-1982; mem, President's Reorgn Proj Food & Nutrit Study, 1978; spec asst child health affair, Off Asst Secy Health, 1974-1979; exec dir, Nat Comn Protection Human Subjects Biomed & Behav Res, HEW, 1974-1977; exec dir, President's Biomed Res Panel, 1974-1976; sci dir, Nat Inst Child Health & Human Develop, 1968-1974; ed-in-chief, Pediat Res, 1966-1974; dir human develop ctr, Col Med, Univ Fla, 1966-1968; prof, Col Med, Univ Fla, 1965-1968; res prof, Sch Med, State Univ NY Buffalo, 1955-1965; Buswell fel, Sch Med, State Univ NY Buffalo, 1955; assoc prof pediat, Sch Med, State Univ NY Buffalo, 1951-1955; Nat Res Coun fel, Med Sch, Univ Minn, 1948-1951; resident, Mass Gen Hosp, 1947; from intern to asst resident pediat, Children's Hosp, Boston, 1945-1946. **Memberships:** Soc Pediat Res; Soc Exp Biol & Med; Am Soc Exp Path; Am Pediat Soc; Am Soc Clin Invest; Sigma Xi. **Research Statement & Publications:** Clinical and laboratory study of nutritional disease, including celiac and cystic fibrosis of the pancreas; relationship between adrenocortical steroids and nucleic acid metabolism; inborn errors of metabolism and parenteral fluid therapy. **Mailing Address:** Nat Inst Child Health & Human Develop, N, 9000 Rockville Pike, Bethesda, MA 20892. **Fax:** 301-496-4757.

LOWE, DONALD RAY, SEDIMENTOLOGY, PRECAMBRIAN GEOLOGY. **Personal Data:** b Sacramento, Calif, September 22, 1942; American citizen; m 1995, Kathy; c Nina & Deniz. **Education:** Stanford Univ, BS, 1964; Univ Ill, Urbana, PhD (Geol), 1967. **Professional Experience:** Res fel, Japan Soc Prom Sci, 1994; PROF GEOL & ENVIRON SCI, STANFORD UNIV, 1993-; prof geol, Stanford Univ, 1988-1993; consult prof, Dept Earth & space sci, Univ Calif, Los Angeles, 1988; prof, Dept geol, La State Univ, Baton Rouge, La, 1978-1988; actg chmn, Dept geol, La State Univ, Baton Rouge, La, 1982-1983; vis lectr, Dept geol, Carleton Univ, Ottawa, Ont, Can, 1981; vis prof, Dept geol, Univ Ottawa, Ottawa, Ont, Can, 1980-1981; asst prof to prof geol, La State Univ, Baton Rouge, 1970-1978; res assoc, US Geol Surv, Calif, 1968-1970; vis grad fel, Sedimentary Res Lab, Univ Reading, Reading, Eng, 1966-1967; instr geol, Univ Ill, Urbana, 1967-1968; Nat Sci Found Grad fel, 1964-1967. **Memberships:** Int Asn Sedimentologists; Geol Soc Am; Int Soc Study Origin Life; Soc Sedimentary Geol. **Research Statement & Publications:** Archean sedimentology and the application of sedimentological principles to interpreting surface con; composition of the early ocean and atmosphere; paleoecology of Archean life; deep-sea sedimentation and transport systems; archean sedimentology. **Mailing Address:** Dept Geol & Environ Sci, Sch Earth Sci, Standford Univ, Rm 216 320 Stanford Univ Bldg, Stanford, CA 94305. **Fax:** 650-725-0979. **E-Mail:** donald.lowe@stanford.edu

LOWE, FORREST GILBERT, GENERAL MATHEMATICS, ELECTRICAL ENGINEERING. **Personal Data:** b Gilman City, Mo, March 27, 1927; m 1948, Joan B Blaine. **Education:** NW Mo State Univ, BS (sec educ) & BS (physics & math), 1951; Tex Christian Univ, MS, 1962; Nova Univ, EdD, 1989. **Professional Experience:** RETIRED; adj prof mech engr, Univ Mo, Kansas City, 1993-; Instr eng, Univ Mo, Kansas City, 1983-; instr & chmn, Div Physics & Eng, Longview Community Col, 1969-1993; instr physics, Kansas City Jr Col, 1959-1964 & Metrop Community Col Dist, 1964-1969; nuclear engr radiation effects, Convair Div, Gen Dynamics, Ft Worth, Tex, 1956-1959; Teacher physics & math, Kansas City Sch Dist, 1953-1956. **Memberships:** Am Asn Physics Teachers; Nat Soc Prof Engrs; Soc MfgEngrs; Am Soc Eng Educ; Am Inst Physics; Comput & Automated Systs Asn; Robotics Int; Math Asn Am; Nat Asn Indust Technol. **Research Statement & Publications:** Nuclear radiation effects; physics and engineering curriculum. **Mailing Address:** 8412 E 49th St, Kansas City, MO 64129. **Fax:** 816-235-1260.

LOWE, GREGORY ALFRED, PHYSICS. **Education:** Stanford Univ, PhD. **Professional Experience:** PROF, STANFORD LINEAR ACCELERATOR CTR, as of 2005. **Memberships:** Am Phys Soc. **Mailing Address:** MS 33 SLAC Stanford Univ, PO Box 4349, Stanford, CA 94305. **Fax:** 650-926-8793. **E-Mail:** galoew@SLAC.Stanford.EDU

LOWE, IRVING J, SOLID STATE PHYSICS, NUCLEAR MAGNETIC RESONANCE IMAGING. **Personal Data:** b Woonsocket, RI, January 4, 1929; m 1987, Irene; c Marc, Margo & Rachel. **Education:** Cooper Union, BEE, 1951; Wash Univ, St Louis, PhD (physics), 1957. **Professional Experience:** Anderson fel, Lovelace Inst, Albuquerque, NMex, 1993-1994; PROF PHYSICS, UNIV PITTSBURGH, 1966-; assoc prof, Univ Pittsburgh, 1962-1966; asst prof, Univ Minn, 1958-1962; Fel, Sloan Found & res assoc physics, Wash Univ, St Louis, 1956-1958. **Memberships:** Fel Am Phys Soc; Soc Magnetic Resonance. **Research Statement & Publications:** Experimental and theoretical studies of the structure and behavior of solids and biological systems using nuclear magnetic resonance techniques; nuclear magnetic resonance imaging; magnetic resonance in medicine. **Mailing Address:** Dept Physics, Univ Pittsburgh, 105 Allen Hall, Pittsburgh, PA 15260. **Fax:** 412-624-9163. **E-Mail:** ijlowe@andrew.cmu.edu

LOWE, JACK IRA, MARINE ECOLOGY, TOXICOLOGY. **Personal Data:** b Fairmount, Ga, December 8, 1927; m 1957. **Education:** Berea Col, AB, 1950; Univ Ga, MS, 1955. **Professional Experience:** RETIRED; chief exp environ br, Environ Res Lab, 1976-1985; assoc dir tech assistance, Environ Protection Agency, 1975-1976; dep lab dir, Environ Protection Agency, 1971-1975; aquatic biologist, Environ Protection Agency, 1970-1971; Biologist, US Fish & Wildlife Serv, 1957-1961 & US Bur Com Fisheries, 1961-1970. **Memberships:** Am Fisheries Soc; Nat Shellfisheries Asn; Gulf Estuarine Res Soc. **Research Statement & Publications:** Estuarine and coastal ecology; effects of pollutants on marine organisms and their environment. **Mailing Address:** 4461 Sound Side Dr, Gulf Breeze, FL 32561.

LOWE, JAMES, PARTICLE PHYSICS. **Personal Data:** b Birmingham, Eng, June 6, 1935; m 1959, Margaret; c Gerald J. **Education:** Univ Birmingham, BSc, 1956, PhD (physics), 1959. **Professional Experience:** RES PROF, UNIV NMEX, 1989-; lectr physics, Univ Birmingham, 1962-; res assoc, Brookhaven Nat Lab, 1960-1962; res assoc, Columbia Univ, 1959-1960. **Memberships:** Inst Physics; Am Phys Soc. **Research Statement & Publications:** Kaon physics, rare delays; strange particle physics including strange meson, hyperons, H-particles and strange nuclear matter. **Mailing Address:** Physics Dept, Univ NMex, Albuquerque, NM 87131. **Fax:** 505-277-1520. **E-Mail:** lowe@baryon.phys.unm.edu

LOWE, JAMES EDWARD, CARDIAC SURGERY, ELECTROPHYSIOLOGY. **Personal Data:** b Brunswick, Ga, December 27, 1946; m 1969, c 2. **Education:** Stanford Univ, BA, 1969; Univ Calif, Los Angeles, MD, 1973. **Professional Experience:** PROF SURG, DUKE UNIV, 1991-; from asst prof to assoc prof surg & path, Duke Univ, 1986-1990; dir, Surg Electrophysiol Serv, 1983-; investr, Am Heart Asn, 1981-1986. **Memberships:** Am Col Surgeons; Am Col Cardiol; Am Col Chest Physicians; Am Heart Asn; Am Asn Thoracic

Surg; Soc Thoracic Surgeons. **Research Statement & Publications:** Etiology of cardiac arrhythmias; basic pathogenesis of global mycocardial ischemic injury; non-blood contacting biventricular cardiac support devices. **Mailing Address:** Dept Surg, Duke Univ, PO Box 3954, Durham, NC 27710. **Fax:** 919-681-7524. **E-Mail:** lowe0004@mc.duke.edu

LOWE, JAMES HARRY, JR, ENTOMOLOGY. **Personal Data:** b Vonore, Tenn, March 15, 1931; m 1955, c 3. **Education:** Univ Tenn, BA, 1955; Ohio State Univ, MSc, 1957; Yale Univ, PhD (forest entom), 1966. **Professional Experience:** ASSOC PROF FORESTRY & ZOOL, UNIV MONT, 1965-; insect res ecologist, Northeastern Forest Exp Sta, USDA, Conn, 1963-1965; Res entomologist, Northeastern Forest Exp Sta, USDA, Conn, 1959-1962. **Memberships:** Entom Soc Am; Entom Soc Can. **Research Statement & Publications:** Ecology of insects in forest communities; insect dispersal and distribution; alpine entomology; behavioral and meteorological aspects of flight of insects. **Mailing Address:** Sch Forestry, Univ Mont, Missoula, MT 59812-1063.

LOWE, JAMES N, ORGANIC CHEMISTRY. **Personal Data:** b Grand Forks, NDak, May 3, 1936; m 1961, c 3. **Education:** Antioch Col, BS, 1959; Stanford Univ, PhD (chem), 1964. **Professional Experience:** PROF EMER CHEM, UNIV SOUTH, as of 2004; res corp grant, 1980; prof chem, Univ South, beginning 1978; fel Univ Ill, 1977-1978; from asst prof to assoc prof, Univ South, 1971-1978; fel, Univ Calif, Davis, 1970-1971; Am Chem Soc Petrol Res Fund grant, 1964-1966 & 1967-1969; asst prof chem, Smith Col, 1963-1965. **Memberships:** Am Chem Soc; AAAS; Sigma Xi. **Research Statement & Publications:** Coenzyme mechanisms. **Mailing Address:** Dept Chem, Univ South, 735 Univ Ave, Sewanee, TN 37383. **E-Mail:** jlowe@sewanee.edu

LOWE, JAMES URBAN, II, PHYSICAL ORGANIC CHEMISTRY. **Personal Data:** b Durham, NC, June 30, 1921; m Elizabeth; c Joseph K Petway, Meredith Petway, Janet (Thompson) & James U III. **Education:** Va State Col, BS, 1942, MS, 1946; Howard Univ, PhD, 1963; Tenn State Univ, MPA, 1982. **Professional Experience:** RETIRED; interim dir, Acad Develop & Support Serv Div, Grad Sch, Meharry Med Col, 1989-1994; Sch Med, Instnl Res, 1984-1987; dir, Off Instnl Res, 1981-1984; from assoc dean to asst dean admin, Sch Med, Meharry Med Col, 1969-1981; assoc prof biochem, Sch Med, Meharry Med Col, 1968-1987; res chemist, US Govt, Md, 1960-1968; instr, Howard Univ, 1959-1960; fel, Howard Univ, 1956-1959; asst prof chem, Tenn State Col, 1947-1952 & Ft Valley State Col, 1952-1956; co-founder & pres, Lophelps, Inc; consult, Info Serv. **Memberships:** Am Chem Soc; Sigma Xi. **Research Statement & Publications:** Synthesis of 0-nitrobenzoates; aryloxyaliphatic acids; nitroguanidines; physical studies of beta diketones; nuclear magnetic resonance, ultraviolet, infrared spectroscopy of guanidines and perfluoroaromatics; longitudinal study of scholastic performance of Meharry medical students. **Mailing Address:** 4230 Eatons Creek Rd Ste A, Nashville, TN 37218.

LOWE, JOHN III, DAM ENGINEERING, GEOTECHNICAL ENGINEERING. **Personal Data:** b New York, NY, March 14, 1916; m 1943, c 3. **Education:** City Col NY, BS, 1936; Mass Inst Technol, MS, 1937. **Honors & Awards:** Eighth Terzaghi Lect, Soc Soil Mech Mex, 1971, Fourth Nabor Carrillo Lectr, 1978; Second Ann Uscold Lectr, US Comt on Large Dams of Int Comn on Large Dams, 1982; Townsend Harris Medal, City Col New York, 1982; Martin Kapp Lectr, 1986; Mueser-Rutledger Award, 1997. **Professional Experience:** INDEPENDENT CONSULT, DAM ENG & GEOTECH ENG, 1984-; partner, Soil & Rock Eng dept, Tippetts-Abbett-McCarthy-Stratton, 1962-1983; assoc partner, Soil & Rock Eng dept, Tippetts-Abbett-McCarthy-Stratton, 1956-1962; head, Soil & Rock Eng dept, Tippetts-Abbett-McCarthy-Stratton, 1945-1956; physicist, David Taylor Model Basin, US Navy, 1945; Instr civil eng, Univ Md & Mass inst Technol, 1937-1944. **Memberships:** Nat Acad Eng; fel Am Soc Civil Engrs; Int Soc Soil Mech & Found Eng; Int Soc Rock Mech; US Comn Large Dams. **Research Statement & Publications:** Author of chapters in 4 engineering handbooks and of more than 30 technical papers; redam and geotechnical engineering. **Mailing Address:** 26 Grandview Blvd, Yonkers, NY 10710.

LOWE, JOHN EDWARD, VETERINARY SURGERY. **Personal Data:** b Newark, NJ, May 20, 1935; m 1957, Audrey; c William S & Stacy A. **Education:** Cornell Univ, DVM, 1959, MS, 1963. **Professional Experience:** PROF EMER VET SURG, CORNELL UNIV, 1990-; coord mgr, Equine Res Park, 1974-1988; assoc prof vet surg, NY State Col Vet Med, 1968-1990; asst prof vet surg, Cornell Univ, 1963-1968; instr vet path, Cornell Univ, 1961-1963; resident, Cornell Univ, 1960-1961; Intern vet surg, Cornell Univ, 1959-1960. **Memberships:** Am Vet Med Asn; Am Asn Equine Practitioners. **Research Statement & Publications:** Endocrine control of the equine skeletal system; effect of nutrition on equine bone and joint disease; equine gastrointestinal surgery. **Mailing Address:** Dept Vet Med, Cornell Univ, 209 Diag Lab, Upper Tower Rd, Ithaca, NY 14853-6401. **Fax:** 607-253-3943. **E-Mail:** jel23@cornell.edu

LOWE, JOHN PHILIP, QUANTUM CHEMISTRY. **Personal Data:** b Rochester, NY, August 28, 1936; m 1959, c 2. **Education:** Univ Rochester, BS, 1958; Johns Hopkins Univ, MA, 1959; Northwestern Univ, PhD (quantum chem), 1964. **Professional Experience:** PROF EMER CHEM, PA STATE UNIV, UNIV PARK, as of 2005; prof chem, Pa State Univ, Univ Park, beginning 1986; Petrol Res Fund type AC grant, 1969-1971; from asst prof to assoc prof, Pa State Univ, Univ Park, 1966-1986; Petrol Res Fund starter grant, 1966-1968; NIH fel theoret chem, Johns Hopkins Univ, 1964-1966; teacher high sch, NJ, 1959-1960. **Memberships:** AAAS; Am Chem Soc; Am Phys Soc. **Research Statement & Publications:** Chemical carcinogenicity; chemical reactivities; relations between Huckel and ab initio calculations; quantum chemistry of solids. **Mailing Address:** Dept Chem, Pa State Univ, 127 Chem Bldg, Univ Park, PA 16802. **E-Mail:** jl3@psu.edu

LOWE, MARY LORETTE, CONDENSED MATTER. **Education:** Harvard Univ, BA; Univ Pa, PhD. **Professional Experience:** PROF & CHMN PHYSICS, LOYOLA COL, as of 2003. **Mailing Address:** Dept Physics, Loyola Col, 4501 N Charles St, Baltimore, MD 21210-2699. **Fax:** 410-617-2646. **E-Mail:** mlowe@loyola.edu

LOWE, REX LOREN, PHYCOLOGY, LIMNOLOGY. **Personal Data:** b Marshalltown, Iowa, December 28, 1943; m 1964, Sheryn; c Terry & Christopher. **Education:** Iowa State Univ, BS, 1966, PhD (phycol), 1970. **Professional Experience:** Assoc ed, Great Lakes J Res, 1994-; fel, Coopr Inst Limnol & Ecosystems Res, Ann Arbor, MI, 1991-present; vis scientist, Dept Sci & Indust Res, Christchurch, NZ, 1991-1992; vis prof, Univ Mich Biol Sta, 1982- & Va Polytech Inst & State Univ, 1982-1983; PROF BIOL, BOWLING GREEN STATE UNIV, 1980-; vis asst prof, Biol Stat, Col Lit, Sci & Arts, Univ Mich, 1974-1976; collabr, US Nat Park Serv, 1975-1976; consult, Icthyol Assocs, 1971-; asst Prof biol, Ctr Mich Univ, 1971; from asst prof to assoc prof, Bowling Green State Univ, 1970-1981; grad teaching asst, Iowa State Univ, 1966-1969. **Memberships:** Phycol Soc Am; Int Asn Great Lakes Res; NAm Benthological Soc. **Research Statement & Publications:** Community ecology of aquatic ecosystems. **Mailing Address:** Dept Biol, Bowling Green State Univ, Bowling Green, OH 43403. **E-Mail:** lowe@bgsu.opie.edu

LOWE, RICHIE HOWARD, PLANT PHYSIOLOGY, BIOCHEMISTRY. **Personal Data:** b Huff, Ky, April 9, 1935; m 1958, c 2. **Education:** Univ Ky, BS, 1958, MS, 1959; Ore State Univ, PhD (plant physiol), 1963. **Professional Experience:** PLANT PHYSIOLOGIST, AGR RES SERV, USDA, 1974-; res plant physiologist, Agr Res Serv, USDA, 1963-1974. **Memberships:** Am Soc Plant Physiol. **Research Statement & Publications:** Enzymatic activity and biochemical changes associated with plant senescence and post harvest physiology; inorganic nitrogen and phosphorous metabolism. **Mailing Address:** 1077 Spurlock Lane, Nicholasville, KY 40356.

LOWE, ROBERT FRANKLIN, CARDIOVASCULAR PHYSIOLOGY. **Personal Data:** b Chicago, Ill, November 14, 1941. **Education:** Univ Wis, BS, 1964, PhD (physiol), 1969. **Professional Experience:** ASST PROF PHYSIOL, SCH MED, TULANE UNIV, 1970-; NIH fel, Univ Wis-Madison, 1969-1970. **Memberships:** Am Physiol Soc; Am Heart Asn; Am Fedn Clin Res. **Research Statement & Publications:** Autonomic pharmacology. **Mailing Address:** Dept Physiol, Sch Med, Tulane Univ, 1430 Tulane Ave, New Orleans, LA 70112-2699. **Fax:** 504-584-2675.

LOWE, ROBERT PETER, AERONOMY, INFRARED ASTRONOMY. **Personal Data:** b Cambridge, Eng, July 8, 1935; Canadian citizen. **Education:** Univ Western Ont, BSc, 1957, PhD (atomic physics), 1967. **Professional Experience:** PROF EMER PHYSICS, UNIV WESTERN ONT, 2001-; vis prof elect eng, Utah State Univ, 1982; sci officer, Defense Res Bd, Can, 1956-1968. **Memberships:** Am Geophys Union; Can Asn Physicists. **Research Statement & Publications:** Infrared airglow; stratospheric composition; infrared spectroscopy of HII regions and planetary nebulae; electronic, vibrational and rotational excitation in ion-molecular collisions; ground- andspace- based observation of gravity wave effects at the mesopause level. **Mailing Address:** Dept Physics & Astron, Univ Western Ont, London, ON N6A 3K7, Can. **Fax:** 519-661-3129. **E-Mail:** lowe@uwo.ca

LOWE, RONALD EDSEL, REHABILITATION COUNSELING, MENTAL HEALTH. **Personal Data:** b Terre Haute, Ind, January 8, 1935; m 1955, c 6. **Education:** Ohio State Univ, BSc, 1962; Purdue Univ, PhD (entom), 1967; Univ SFla, MA, 1987. **Professional Experience:** CERT PROG COORDR, DEPT REHAB & MENTAL HEALTH COUN, UNIV S FLA, as of 2004; Adj prof, dept rehab & mental coun, Univ S Fla, as of 2003; Adj prof grad fac, Univ SFla, 1993-; environ mgt officer, USDA, Animal & Plant Health Inspection Serv, Vs, Nat Prog Planning Staff, Hyattsville, Md, 1984-; dir, Plant Opers, Animal & Plant Health Inspection Serv, Vet Serv, USDA, Tuxtla Gutierrez, Mex, 1979-1984; proj leader, Cent Am Res, Int Progs Div, Sci & Educ Admin, USDA, 1975-1979; Courtesy prof, Univ Fla, 1966-1976; res entomologist, Cent Am Res, Int Progs Div, Sci & Educ Admin, USDA, 1966-1975; res asst entom, Purdue Univ, 1962-1966; rehab counr, Dept Housing & Urban Develop, New Port Richey; SUPVR, ADULT UNIT & GERIAT PROG, GLENBEIGH HEALTH SOURCES, TAMPA, FLA. **Memberships:** AAAS; Nat Rehab Asn; Am Ment Health Counr Admin; Soc Invert Path; Sigma Xi; Am Bd Med Psychotherapists. **Research Statement & Publications:** Population dynamics of sterile-male release programs; growth regulation compounds for control of medically important insects; pathogenic microorganisms for biological control programs; ecology and epidemiology; agricultural research administration; environmental management; public health; public health and epidemiology. **Mailing Address:** Dept Rehab & Mental Health Coun, Col Arts & Sci, Univ S Fla, SOC-107, Tampa, FL 33620-8100. **Fax:** 813-974-8080.

LOWE, SCOTT ARTHUR, WATER QUALITY MODELING, AIR QUALITY MODELING. **Personal Data:** b Wollongong, NSW, March 23, 1965; m 1996, Mary. **Education:** Univ Wollongong, BE, 1986, PhD (civil eng), 1990. **Professional Experience:** ASSOC PROF ENVIRON ENG, MANHATTAN COL, 1994-; consult, Hydroqual Inc, 1994-; res engr, Commonwealth Sci & Indust res Orgn, 1990-1993. **Memberships:** Am Soc Civil Engrs; Air & Waste Mgt Asn; Sigma Xi. **Research Statement & Publications:** Modeling of water quality within natural and man-made systems from lakes, rivers and estuaries to reservoirs and dams. **Mailing Address:** Dept Environ Eng, Manhattan Col, Riverdale, NY 10471. **Fax:** 718-862-8018. **E-Mail:** slowe@manhattan.edu

LOWE, TERRY CURTIS, THEORETICAL MECHANICAL METALLURGY, NANOSTRUCTURED METALS. **Personal Data:** b Spokane, Wash, November 10, 1955; m 1980, Patrice; c Nicholas Lowe, Mariel Lowe & Beatrice Lowe. **Education:** Univ Calif, Davis, BS, 1978; Stanford Univ, MS, 1979, PhD (mat sci), 1982. **Honors & Awards:** Distinguished Performance Awards, Los Alamos Nat Lab; Award for Distinction in Technology Transfer, Los Alamos Nat Lab. **Professional Experience:** PROGRAM DIRECTOR, SCI & TECH BASE PROGRAMS, LOS ALMOS NAT LAB, 2005-; STAFF, MAT SCI & TECHNOL DIV, LOS ALMOS NAT LAB, as of 2004; CEO, METALLICUM, 2001-2002; CEO, TECHNANOGY, 2000-2001; dep dir, Mat Sci & Technol Div, Los Almos Nat Lab, 1996-2000; MEM STAFF & GROUP LEADER, MAT RES PROCESSING SCI, LOS ALAMOS NAT LABS, 1990-1996; CHMN, INTERAGENCY METAL FORMING WORK GROUP, US DEPT ENERGY, 1985-; vis scholar, Dept Mat Sci, Stanford Univ, 1983-1986; MEM TECH STAFF, SANDIA NAT LABS, LIVERMORE, CALIF, US DEPT ENERGY, 1982-1990; lectr, Div Eng, San Francisco State Univ, 1980-1981. **Memberships:** Am Soc Metals; Am Inst Mining & Metall Engrs; Am Soc Mech Engrs; Sigma Xi. **Research Statement & Publications:** Mathematical modeling of mechanical and physical processes of metals; crystal plasticity modeling of large strain plasticity; finite element analysis of metal forming processes; development of nanostructured materials. **Mailing Address:** Los Alamos Nat Lab, Sci & Technol Base Programs, Mailstop M714, Los Alamos, NM 87545. **Fax:** 505-665-4092. **E-Mail:** tlowe@lanl.gov

LOWE, WILLIAM WEBB, CHEMICAL ENGINEERING. **Personal Data:** b Bartlesville, Okla, December 18, 1920. **Education:** Purdue Univ, BS, 1947. **Professional Experience:** CONSULT MGT & APPL SCI, 1987-; Co-ed, Power Reactor Technol, AEC, 1960; partner, Pickard, Lowe & Garrick Inc, 1956-1986; nuclear engr, Bath Iron Works, Maine, 1954-1956; chief nuclear eng sect, USAEC, 1948-1954; Staff mem radiochem, Los Alamos Sci Lab, 1944-1948. **Memberships:** Am Chem Soc; Am Nuclear Soc. **Research Statement & Publications:** Nuclear engineering; engineering economics. **Mailing Address:** PO Box 595, Rock Hall, MD 21661-0377.

LOWE-KRENTZ, LINDA JEAN, BIOCHEMISTRY. **Personal Data:** b Milwaukee, Wis, 1953; m 1976, c 2. **Education:** Northwestern Univ, BA, 1974, PhD (biochem), 1980. **Professional Experience:** PROF & ASSOC CHMN BIOCHEM, LEHIGH UNIV, as of 2006; assoc prof biochem, Lehigh Univ, as of 2004; asst prof chem, Lehigh Univ, beginning 1986; res asst prof biochem, Chicago Med Sch, Univ Health Sci, 1985-1986. **Memberships:** AAAS; Am Soc Chem Biologists. **Research Statement & Publications:** Endothelial heparan sulfate proteoglycans and their receptors; author of various articles. **Mailing Address:** Depart Biol Sci, Lehigh Univ, 111 Res Dr Rm B217, Bethlehem, PA 18015-4732. **Fax:** 610-758-5851. **E-Mail:** lj10@lehigh.edu

LOWELL, A(RTHUR) I(RWIN), POLYMER CHEMISTRY, EMULSION POLYMERS. **Personal Data:** b New York, NY, November 9, 1925; m Eleanor; c Barbara, Carol & Stewart. **Education:** Brooklyn Col, AB, 1945; Univ Pa, MS, 1948, PhD (chem), 1951. **Professional Experience:** RETIRED; sr res chemist, Sun Chem Corp, 1978-1991; group leader, Norton & Son, 1977-1978; sci teacher pub schs, Edison, NJ, 1973-1976; sect leader, Mobil Chem Co, 1969-1973; group leader, Mobil Chem Co, 1966-1968; sr res chemist, Mobil Chem Co, 1964-1966; res assoc, Heyden Newport Chem Co, 1963; res assoc, Berkeley Chem Corp, 1962; supvr appln res, Lucidol Div, Wallace & Tiernan Inc, 1961-1962; res assoc, Lucidol Div, Wallace & Tiernan Inc, 1959-1960; sect head, Air Reduction Co Inc, 1957-1958; res chemist, Air Reduction Co Inc, 1951-1957. **Memberships:** Am Chem Soc. **Research Statement & Publications:** Polymerization kinetics; organic peroxide initiators; polymer process and product development; emulsion polymerization; coatings; inks in offset printing. **Mailing Address:** 657C Nutley Dr, Monroe Township, NJ 08831.

LOWELL, GARY RICHARD, SKARN PETROLOGY, GREISEN GEOCHEMISTRY. **Personal Data:** b Modesto, Calif, September 26, 1942; m 1968, c 2. **Education:** San Jose State Col, BS, 1965; NMex Inst Mining & Technol, PhD (geol), 1970. **Professional Experience:** Consult, Newmont Explor Ltd, 1985 & 1987; PROF GEOL, SOUTHEAST MO STATE UNIV, 1981-; consult, Houston Int Minerals Corp, Alaska, 1980 & 1981; vis prof geol, Univ Fed do Para, Brazil, 1978-1980; from asst prof to assoc prof, SE MO State Univ, 1969-1981. **Memberships:** Mineral Asn Can. **Research Statement & Publications:** Igneous and metamorphic petrology; tin and tungsten ore deposits. **Mailing Address:** Dept Geol Sci, SE Mo State Univ, 1 Univ Plaza, Cape Girardeau, MO 63701-4710. **E-Mail:** glowell@semovm.semo.edu

LOWELL, JAMES DILLER, PETROLEUM GEOLOGY, STRUCTURAL GEOLOGY. **Personal Data:** b Lincoln, Nebr, August 17, 1933. **Education:** Univ Nebr, BSc, 1955; Columbia Univ, MA, 1957, PhD (geol), 1958. **Professional Experience:** PRES, COLEX-CON INC, 1978-; CONSULT GEOLOGIST, 1976-; assoc, Oil & Gas Consults Int Inc, 1976-; mgr geol, Northwest Explor Co, 1974-1976; explor geologist, Exxon Co, USA, 1973-1974; sr res specialist, Esso Prod Res Co, 1966-1973; asst prof geol, Wash & Lee Univ, 1965-1966; geologist, Am Overseas Petrol Ltd, 1958-1965. **Memberships:** Fel Geol Soc Am; Am Asn Petrol Geologists; Explorer's Club. **Research Statement & Publications:** Structural geology of sedimentary rocks. **Mailing Address:** Ste One 2200 W Berry Ave, Littleton, CO 80120. **Fax:** 303-697-6549. **E-Mail:** lowelljd@aol.com

LOWELL, PHILIP S(IVERLY), CHEMICAL ENGINEERING. **Personal Data:** b Manila, Philippines, July 9, 1931; American citizen; m 1993, Elizabeth Runner; c 3. **Education:** Univ Tex, BS, 1954, MS, 1963, PhD, 1966. **Professional Experience:** CORP FEL, RADIAN CORP, 1991-; prin engr, Radian Corp, 1988-1991; pres, P S Lowell & Co, Inc, 1977-1987; Adj prof, Univ Tex, Austin, 1974 & 1986; proj group mem, Environ Protection Coop Effort, US-USSR, 1974-1979; vpres, Radian Corp, 1969-1977; asst dir chem res, Tracor, Inc, 1964-1969; sr engr, Tex Res Assocs, Inc, 1960-1964; sr process engr, C F Braun & Co, 1959-1960; process engr, C F Braun & Co, 1955-1959; Process engr, Jefferson Chem Co, Inc, 1954-1955. **Memberships:** Am Inst Chem Engrs; Am Chem Soc. **Research Statement & Publications:** Process engineering of chemical plants and refineries; application of thermodynamics to practical problems; research in air pollution control processes; granted 7 patents. **Mailing Address:** Radian Corp, PO Box 201088, Austin, TX 78720-1088.

LOWELL, ROBERT PAUL, GEOPHYSICS, SEA FLOOR HYDROTHERMAL SYSTEMS. **Personal Data:** b Chicago, Ill, April 10, 1943; m 1981, c 5. **Education:** Loyola Univ Chicago, BS, 1965; Ore State Univ, MS, 1967, PhD (geophys), 1972. **Professional Experience:** Grad Coordr, Sch Earth & Atmospheric Sci, 1995-1999; PROF GEOPHYS, GA INST TECHNOL, 1991-; guest investr, Woods Hole Oceanog Inst, 1989; assoc prog dir marine geol & geophys, NSF, 1987-1989; consult, Lawrence Livermore Nat Lab, 1986 1989; from asst prof to assoc prof, Ga Inst Technol, 1971-1991. **Memberships:** Am Geophys Union. **Research Statement & Publications:** Thermal geophysics; modeling of magmatic processes; geothermal energy; hydrothermal systems; fluid flow and chemical reactions in fractured and porous media. **Mailing Address:** Sch Earth & Atmospheric Sci, Ga Inst Technol, ES&T Rm 2248, Atlanta, GA 30332-0340. **Fax:** 404-894-5638. **E-Mail:** bob.lowell@eas.gatech.edu

LOWEN, GERARD G, MECHANICAL ENGINEERING. **Personal Data:** b Munich, Ger, October 25, 1921; American citizen; m 1952, Doris; c Deborah, Nicole & Daniel. **Education:** City Col NY, BME, 1954; Columbia Univ, MSME, 1958; Munich Tech Univ, Dr Ing, 1963. **Honors & Awards:** Mechanism Comt Award, Am Soc Mech Engrs, 1984, Mach Design Award, 1987. **Professional Experience:** EXEC OFFICER PHD PROG, GRAD SCH & UNIV CTR, as of 2003; ASSOC DEAN GRAD STUDIES, CITY COL NEW YORK, 1990-; H KAYSER PROF MECH ENG, CITY COL NEW YORK, 1987-; dept head, City Col New York, 1987-1990; consult, var indust, 1963-; Prof mech eng, City Col New York, 1954-1987; expert witness, Army Armament res & Develop Command res grants; NSF grants, Army res Off. **Memberships:** AAAS; fel Am Soc Mech Engrs; Am Soc Eng Educ; NY Acad Sci; Soc Mfg Engrs; Verein Deutschor Engr. **Research Statement & Publications:** Dynamics of high speed machinery; rigid and elastic body behavior of linkages and mechanisms; kinematic synthesis and analysis; stress and vibration analysis; safety and arming mechanisms. **Mailing Address:** Grad Eng Off, Sch Eng, City Col Rm T152, Convent Ave 138th St, Rm T152, New York, NY 10031. **Fax:** 212-650-8013. **E-Mail:** coming_soon@ccny.cuny.edu

LOWEN, W(ALTER), SYSTEMS SCIENCES & MECHANICAL ENGINEERING, COGNITIVE SCIENCE & BRAIN MODELS. **Personal Data:** b Cologne, Ger, May 17, 1921; m 1943, Sylvia; c Robert G & John G. **Education:** NC State Univ, BME, 1943, MS, 1947; Swiss Fed Inst Technol, DrSc(nuclear eng), 1963. **Professional Experience:** PROF EMER, THOMAS J WATSON SCH, STATE UNIV NY, BINGHAMTON, 1991-; auth, 1982; acad guest, Swiss Fed Inst Technol, Zurich, Switz, 1982; guest sabbaticant, IBM Systs Res Inst, 1978 & 1979; mem charter bd, Vols for Int Tech Assistance, Inc, 1969-; dean, Thomas J Watson Sch, State Univ NY, Binghamton, 1968-1977; prof systs sci, Thomas J Watson Sch, State Univ NY, Binghamton, 1967-1990; dir sch advan technol, Thomas J Watson Sch, State Univ NY, Binghamton, 1967-1968; dir, Vols for Int Tech Assistance, Inc, 1966-1969; vis prof, Swiss Fed Inst Technol, 1965-1966; consult inst appl technol, Nat Bur Stand, 1965-1966; Oak Ridge Nat Lab, 1954-1957 & Gen Elec Co, 1960; actg chmn dept, Union Col, NY, 1959 & 1967; chmn div eng, Union Col, NY, 1956-1959 & 1966-1967; consult, Alco Prod, Inc, 1952-1954; prof, Union Col, NY, 1947-1967; instr mech eng, NC State Col, 1943-1947. **Memberships:** Am Soc Mech Engrs; Am Nuclear Soc; Am Soc Eng Educ; NY Acad Sci; World Acad Arts & Sci; Asn Psychol Types; Int Soc Systs Sci; Sigma Xi. **Research Statement & Publications:** Cognitive models and visual perception; human factors research. **Mailing Address:** 152 Moore Ave, Binghamton, NY 13903-3166.

LOWENGRUB, MORTON, MATHEMATICS. **Personal Data:** b Newark, NJ, March 31, 1935; m 1961, c 1. **Education:** NY Univ, BA, 1956; Calif Inst Technol, MS, 1958; Duke Univ, PhD (math), 1961. **Professional Experience:** EMER PROF MATH, IND UNIV, BLOOMINGTON, as of 2003; ed, Math Reviews, 1981-; ed, Ind Math J, 1977-1981; chmn dept, Ind Univ, Bloomington, 1977-1980; sr res fel, Sci Res Coun, Gt Brit, 1973-1974; prof math, Ind Univ, Bloomington, beginning 1972; assoc prof, Ind Univ, Bloomington, 1967-1972; NSF fel, Glasgow Univ, 1966-1967; asst prof, Wesleyan Univ, 1963-1966; Leverhulme res fel, Glasgow Univ, 1962-1963; asst prof, NC State Col, 1961-1962; instr math, Duke Univ, 1960-1961. **Memberships:** Math Asn Am; Am Math Soc; Soc Indust & Appl Math. **Research Statement & Publications:** Mathematical theory of elasticity. **Mailing Address:** Ind Univ Col Arts & Sci, Kirkwood Hall 104, Bloomington, IN 47405.

LOWENSOHN, HOWARD STANLEY, CORONARY PHYSIOLOGY, EXERCISE. **Personal Data:** b Columbus, Ohio, January 23, 1931; m 1953, c 1. **Education:** Franklin & Marshall Col, BS, 1956; Univ Southern Calif, MS, 1962; Univ Md, PhD (physiol), 1972. **Professional Experience:** Mem, ACE Comt & Grip Comt, Am Physiol Soc, 1988-1991; res adv, Nat Res Coun, 1980-; ASSOC PROF PHYSIOL, UNIFORMED SERV UNIV HEALTH SCI, 1980-; consult, Johns Hopkins Univ, 1977-1985; res physiologist, Walter Reed Army Inst Res, 1963-. **Memberships:** Am Physiol Soc; NY Acad Sci; AAAS; Am Heart Res Coun; Sigma Xi. **Research Statement & Publications:** Hemodynamics of coronary blood flow in chronic conscious dogs at rest, during exercise and with varying degrees of ischemia; hypertrophied hearts, including the initial chronic studies of phasic coronary artery blood flow in the right heart in normal and hypertrophied and dilated hearts; cardiovascular and respiratory research director for pre- clinical drugdevelopment, including cooperative efforts with WHO. **Mailing Address:** 9105 Louis Ave, Silver Spring, MD 20910-2129. **Fax:** 301-427-6589.

LOWENSTEIN, CARL DAVID, APPLIED PHYSICS. **Personal Data:** b New York, NY, September 3, 1934; m 1965, c 1. **Education:** Kent State Univ, BA, 1955; Harvard Univ, SM, 1956, PhD (physics), 1963. **Professional Experience:** ASSOC SPECIALIST, MARINE PHYSICS LAB, UNIV CALIF, SAN DIEGO, 1969-; mem sensors comt, US Navy Deep Submergence Syst Prog, 1964-; asst res physicist, Marine Physics Lab, Univ Calif, San Diego, 1964-1969; res fel, Harvard Univ, 1963-1964. **Memberships:** Acoust Soc Am; Audio Eng Soc; Inst Elec & Electronics Engrs. **Research Statement & Publications:** Synthesis of directive arrays; signal processing; underwater acoustics; computer applications. **Mailing Address:** Marine Physics Lab, Univ Calif San Diego, 0704 9500 Gillman Dr, La Jolla, CA 92093-0704. **E-Mail:** clowenstein@ucsd.edu

LOWENSTEIN, DEREK IRVING, HIGH ENERGY PHYSICS, ACCELERATOR OPERATIONS, NUCLEAR PHYSICS. **Personal Data:** b Hampton Court, Eng, April 26, 1943; m Elaine; c Jessica R Leif & Peter D. **Education:** City Col NY, BS, 1964; Univ Pa, MS, 1965, PhD (physics), 1969. **Honors & Awards:** NASA Recognition Award for the construction of the NASA Space Radiation Laboratory, 2002. **Professional Experience:** Mem, US/Russia Joint Coord Comt Fundamental Properties Matter, Dept Energy, US/Japan Comt High Energy Physics, High Energy Physics Adv Panel, 1993-2003; Chmn. Accelerator Dept.!977-84 Brookhaven National Lab Chmn, AGS Dept, 1984-1999, CHMN. COLLIDER-ACCELERATOR DEPT. 1999- sr physicist 1983-; Principal Investigator NASA Space Radiation Laboratory 2003-; dep chmn, Accelerator Dept, 1981-1984; physicist & head, exp planning & support div, 1977-1984; assoc physicist, Brookhaven Nat Lab, 1975-1977; asst physicist, Brookhaven Nat Lab, 1973-1975; Res assoc, Univ Pa, 1969-1970 & Univ Pittsburgh, 1970-1973. **Memberships:** Fel Am Phys Soc; AAAS; NY Acad Sci. **Research Statement & Publications:** Experimental high energy physics; accelerator operations. **Mailing Address:** Collider-Accelerator Dept, Brookhaven Nat Lab, Mail Stop 0911B, Upton, NY 11973. **Fax:** 631-344-5954. **E-Mail:** lowenstein@bnl.gov

LOWENSTEIN, EDWARD, ANESTHESIOLOGY, CARDIOPULMONARY PHYSIOLOGY. **Personal Data:** b Duisburg, Ger, May 29, 1934; American citizen; m 1959, c 3. **Education:** Univ Mich, MS, 1959; Am Bd Anesthesiol, dipl, Harvard Univ, MA, 1981. **Honors & Awards:** Distinguished Lectr Physiol, Am Col Chest Phys, 1986. **Professional Experience:** HENRY ISAIAH DORR PROF ANESTHESIA, HARVARD MED SCH, as of 2005; chmn, Dept Anesthesia, Beth Israel Hosp, Harvard Med Sch, as of 2004; provost, Dept Anesthesia, Harvard Med Sch, as of 2003; prof anesthesia, Harvard Med Sch, beginning 1981; anesthetist, Mass Gen Hosp, 1971-; from asst prof to assoc prof, Harvard Med Sch, 1970-1981; assoc anesthetist, Mass Gen Hosp, 1968-1971; assoc anesthesia, Harvard Med Sch, 1968-1970. **Memberships:** Am Soc Anesthesiol; Am Physiol Soc; Soc Critical Care Med. **Research Statement & Publications:** Physiological effects of cardiac and pulmonary disease; cardiac anesthesia. **Mailing Address:** Mass Gen Hosp, Dept Anesthesia, Clinics 3 32 Fruit St, Boston, MA 02114. **Fax:** 617-724-8500. **E-Mail:** lowenstein@etherdome.mgh.harvard.edu

LOWENSTEIN, JEROLD MARVIN, NUCLEAR MEDICINE. **Personal Data:** b Danville, Va, February 11, 1926; m 1981, Adrienne Zihlman; c 3. **Education:** Columbia Univ, BS, 1946, MD, 1953. **Professional Experience:** CHAIR, DEPT NUCLEAR MED, CALIF PAC MED CTR, as of 2004; CLIN PROF MED THYROID RES, MED CTR, UNIV CALIF, SAN FRANCISCO, 1981-; partic, Galapagos Int Sci Proj, 1964; from asst clin prof to assoc clin prof, Med Ctr, Univ Calif, San Francisco, 1963-1981; NIH res grant 1960-1966, 1961-1966, 1962-1966; dir nuclear med, Presby Med Ctr, San Francisco, 1959-; instr med & radiol, Sch Med, Stanford Univ, 1957-1958; Nat Found fel radiobiol, 1955-1956; Physicist, Los Alamos Sci Lab, 1946-1948. **Memberships:** AMA; Soc Nuclear Med; fel AAAS. **Research Statement & Publications:** Applications of physics to medicine, especially medical uses of radioactive isotopes; molecular evolution. **Mailing Address:** 2203 Scott, San Francisco, CA 94115.

LOWENSTEIN, JOHN HOOD, QUANTUM FIELD THEORY, NONLINEAR DYNAMICS. **Personal Data:** b Newark, NJ, March 15, 1941; m 1967, Marcia; c Ethan & Alexander. **Education:** Harvard Univ, AB, 1962; Univ Ill, Urbana, MS, 1963, PhD (physics), 1966. **Professional Experience:** Chmn dept, NY Univ, 1985-1988; PROF PHYSICS, NY UNIV, 1981-; assoc prof, NY Univ, 1974-1981; res asst prof, NY Univ, 1972-1974; res assoc, Univ Pittsburgh, 1970-1972; vis asst prof, Univ Sao Paulo, 1968-1970; res assoc physics, Univ Minn, 1966-1968. **Memberships:** Am Phys Soc. **Research Statement & Publications:** Quantum field theory, with emphasis on renormalized perturbation theory and soluble two-dimensional models; nonlinear dynamics. **Mailing Address:** Dept Physics, NY Univ, P O Box 104 4 Wash Pl, New York, NY 10003. **E-Mail:** john.lowenstein@nyu.edu

LOWENSTEIN, JOHN MARTIN, BIOCHEMISTRY. **Personal Data:** b Berlin, Ger, October 28, 1926; m 1954. **Education:** Univ Edinburgh, BS, 1950; Univ London, PhD, 1953. **Professional Experience:** PROF BIOCHEM, BRANDEIS UNIV, as of 2005; lectr, Indian Dept Sci & Indust Res, 1980; ed, J Lipid Res, 1979-; ed, J Biol Chem, 1979-; Helena Rubinstein prof biochem, Brandeis Univ, beginning 1977; mem adv comt, Biochem Study Sect, 1977-1981; mem adv comt, Med Found Res Comt, 1974-1977; ed, Methods Enzymol, Archives Biochem & Biophysics, 1967-1972; prof, Brandeis Univ, 1959-1977; Beit mem fel med res, Oxford Univ, 1955-1958; res assoc biochem, Med Sch, Univ Wis, 1953-1955; demonstr chem & biochem, Med Sch, St Thomas' Hosp, Eng, 1950-1953. **Memberships:** AAAS; Am Chem Soc; Am Soc Biol Chem; Brit Biochem Soc. **Research Statement & Publications:** Regulated enzymes; integration and control of metabolism pathways. **Mailing Address:** Dept Biochem, Brandeis Univ, Waltham, MA 02254-9110. **E-Mail:** lowenstein@brandeis.edu

LOWENSTEIN, MICHAEL ZIMMER, HARMONIC DISTORTION MITIGATION. **Personal Data:** b Hornell, NY, October 4, 1938; m 1962, c 2. **Education:** Oberlin Col, AB, 1960; Ariz State Univ, MS, 1962, PhD (x-ray crystallog), 1965. **Professional Experience:** CHIEF TECHNOL OFFICER, HARMONICS LTD, as of 2003; consult, Consumer's Power Mich, 1995-1997; PRES, HARMONICS LTD, 1993-; lectr, Univ Wis, Milwaukee, 1991-; mgr, Power Qual Systs, Trans-Coil, Inc, 1990-1994; guest lectr, Univ Wis Madison, 1989-1998; dir res & develop, Myron Zucker Inc, 1987-1990; prog mgr, Bio Mass Energy Prog, 1982-1987; educ proj mgr, Joint US-Saudi Prog, Solar Energy Res Inst, 1979-1982; dir, Solar Energy Div, Navarro Community Col, Tex, 1978-1979; consult, Dept Energy, 1976-1978; vis prof, Solar Energy Appln Lab, Colo State Univ, Ft Collins, 1975-1976; consult, Citizen's Workshop, Energy Res & Develop Agency, 1974-1976; prof chem, Adams State Col, 1971-1978; AEC fac res assoc, Ariz State Univ, 1970-1971; asst prof chem, Adams State Col, 1964-1971. **Memberships:** Inst Elec & Electronics Engrs Comput Soc; Power Eng Soc; Indust Appln Soc. **Research Statement & Publications:** Power quality; mitigation of harmonic distortion. **Mailing Address:** Harmonics Ltd, 50 Pocono Rd, Brookfield, CT 06804.

LOWENTHAL, DENNIS DAVID, PLASMA PHYSICS, ELEMENTARY PARTICLE PHYSICS. **Personal Data:** b Yakima, Wash, November 10, 1942; m 1966, c 2. **Education:** Calif State Univ, Northridge, BS, 1965; Univ Calif, Los Angeles, MS, 1966; Univ Calif, Irvine, PhD (physics), 1975. **Professional Experience:** VPRES RES & DEVELOP, ACULIGHT CORP, as of 2005; STAFF MEM, ACULIGHT CORP, 1993-; physicist, Math Sci Northwest, 1975-1980; res & develop engr, Aeronutronic Div, Philco-Ford Corp, 1966-1975. **Memberships:** Am Phys Soc; Optical Soc Am; AAAS. **Research Statement & Publications:** Experimental search for the double beta decay of selenium 1982; geometrical and wave optics; plasma physics diagnostics. **Mailing Address:** Aculight Corp, 11805 N Creek Pkwy S Ste 113, Bothell, WA 98011-8803. **Fax:** 425-482-1101. **E-Mail:** dennis.lowenthal@aculight.com

LOWENTHAL, DOUGLAS H, RECEPTOR MODELLING, ANALYTIC CHEMISTRY. **Personal Data:** b New York, NY, December 19, 1948; m 1982. **Education:** Tufts Univ, BA, 1970; Univ RI, MS, 1976, PhD (oceanog), 1986. **Professional Experience:** ASSOC RES PROF, ATMOSPHERIC SCI CTR, DESERT RES INST, 1996-; asst res prof, Atmospheric Sci Ctr, Desert Res Inst, Reno, Nevada, 1992-1996; asst res prof, Energy Environ Eng Ctr, Desert Res Inst, Reno, 1989-1992; from marine res specialist to assoc marine scientist, Univ RI, 1981-1989; res asst, Univ RI, 1974-1980; teaching asst org chem, Univ RI, 1974; instr, Univ RI, 1973. **Memberships:** Air Pollution Control Asn; Am Geophys Union; Am Asn Aerosol Res; AAAS. **Research Statement & Publications:** Determination of regional sources of air pollution in the Arctic and eastern US; statistical source receptor modelling; published over 100 articles. **Mailing Address:** Div Atmospheric Sci, Desert Res Inst, 2215 Raggio Pkwy, Reno, NV 89512-1095. **E-Mail:** doug.lowenthal@dri.edu

LOWER, STEPHEN K, PHYSICAL CHEMISTRY. **Personal Data:** b Oakland, CA, September 8, 1933; m 1963. **Education:** Univ Calif, Berkeley, BA, 1955; Ore State Univ, MS, 1958; Univ BC, MS, 1960, PhD (phys chem), 1963. **Professional Experience:** RETIRED; mem panel comput assisted instr lang, beginning 1970; assoc prof phys chem, Simon Fraser Univ, 1965-1999; Nat Res Coun Can grants, 1965-1971; fel phys chem, Univ Calif, Los Angeles, 1964-1965; fel phys chem, Polytech Inst Brooklyn, 1963-1964. **Memberships:** Am Chem Soc. **Research Statement & Publications:** Instructional systems design; computer-assisted instruction and instructional technology applied to college science teaching. **Mailing Address:** 7248 Ridge Dr, Burnaby, BC V5A 1B5, Can. **E-Mail:** lower@sfu.ca

LOWER, WILLIAM RUSSELL, GENETICS, ENVIRONMENTAL HEALTH. **Personal Data:** b La Junta, Colo, October 28, 1930; m 1971, c 2. **Education:** Univ Calif, Los Angeles, BA, 1953; Univ Calif, Berkeley, PhD (genetics), 1965. **Professional Experience:** GROUP LEADER, ENVIRON TRACE SUBSTANCES RES CTR, 1972-; ASSOC PROF COMMUNITY HEALTH & MED PRACT & BIOL, UNIV MO-COLUMBIA, 1972-; res assoc biol monitoring, Environ Health Surveillance Ctr, 1970-1972; Fel, Univ Mo, 1969-1970; res assoc, Clin Pharmacol Res Inst, 1967-1969; Res assoc genetics nematodes, Kaiser Found Res Inst, 1964-1966. **Memberships:** Genetics Soc Am; Environ Mutagen Soc; Soc Toxicol; Soc Environ Geochem & Health; Soc Environ Toxicol & Chem; Air Pollution Control Asn; Am Biol Safety Asn. **Research Statement & Publications:** Research and monitoring of genetic, biochemical, and physiological effects of airborne, terrestrial and fresh water environmental pollutants in situ in the real world and under controlled laboratory conditions; mutagenesis of environmental contaminants; development and standardization of new bioassays. **Mailing Address:** 3310 Belle Meade Dr, Columbia, MO 65203.

LOWERY, LEE LEON, STRUCTURAL ENGINEERING, STRUCTURAL FAILURES. **Personal Data:** b Corpus Christi, Tex, December 26, 1938; m 1960, c 2. **Education:** Tex A&M Univ, BS, 1960, MS, 1961, PhD (struct eng), 1967. **Professional Experience:** Shell Oil Corp, 1976-1978 & Marathon Oil Corp, 1977-1978; prod failure analyst, Eng Consult Inc, 1976-1977; prof eng, Tex A&M Univ, beginning 1971; failure analyst, Eng Consult Inc, 1970-1976; res engr, Tex Transp Inst, 1967-; prof struct, Dept Aerospace Eng, 1967-1970; consult engr, Esso Prod Res Corp, 1966-1968; prof construct, Sch Archit, Tex A&M Univ, 1965-1969; res engr, Albritton Eng Corp, 1963-1966; from asst prof to assoc prof, Tex A&M Univ, 1961-1971. **Memberships:** Am Soc Exp Stress Analysis; Am Soc Civil Engrs; Soc Marine Technol; Am Soc Eng Educ; Nat Soc Prof Engrs. **Research Statement & Publications:** Basic research, engineering structures and products; applied research in areas of design and analysis of coastal, offshore structures; product failure analysis, consumer protection; engineering applications of computer analysis. **Mailing Address:** 2905 S Col Ave, Bryan, TX 77801-2510.

LOWERY, RICHARD L, MECHANICAL ENGINEERING. **Personal Data:** b Haven, Kans, July 25, 1935; m 1959, c 2. **Education:** Tex Tech Col, BS, 1956; Okla State Univ, MS, 1957; Purdue Univ, PhD (mech eng), 1961. **Professional Experience:** PROF MECH ENG, OKLA STATE UNIV, as of 2003; HALLIBURTON PROF MECH ENG, OKLA STATE UNIV, 1972-; DIR CTR TEACHING, OKLA STATE UNIV, 1972-; consult, Fed Aviation Agency, 1964-1965; from asst prof to prof, Okla State Univ, 1961-1972; instr mech eng, Tex Tech Col, 1957-1958. **Memberships:** Acoust Soc Am; Am Soc Eng Educ. **Research Statement & Publications:** Acoustics; sonic boom research; ultrasonics; vibrations; instrumentation. **Mailing Address:** Sch Mech & Aerospace eng, Okla State Univ, 218 eng N, Stillwater, OK 74078-5016. **Fax:** 405-744-7873. **E-Mail:** lowery@master.ceat.okstate.edu

LOWES, BRIAN EDWARD, GEOLOGY. **Personal Data:** b Harrow, Eng, September 21, 1935; Canadian citizen; m 1966, c 2. **Education:** Imperial Col, London Univ, BSc, 1957; Queen's Univ, Ont, MSc, 1963; Univ Wash, Seattle, PhD (geol), 1972. **Professional Experience:** PROF, EARTH SCI DEPT, PAC LUTHERAN UNIV, 1982-; chmn, earth sci dept, Pac Lutheran Univ, beginning 1977; from asst prof to assoc prof, Earth Sci Dept, Pac Lutheran Univ, 1968-1982; tech asst, Can Geol Surv, 1963-1964; explor geologist, Hollinger Consol Gold Mines, 1961-1962; mine geologist asst, Opemiska Copper Ventures ltd, 1957-1959. **Memberships:** Geol Soc Am; Geol Asn Can; Mineral Asn Can. **Research Statement & Publications:** Structural geology and metamorphic petrology of crustal basement rocks in Pacific Northwest. **Mailing Address:** Dept Earth Sci, Pac Lutheran Univ, 12180 Park Ave S, Tacoma, WA 98447-0001. **E-Mail:** lowesbe@plu.edu

LOWEY, SUSAN, PROTEIN CHEMISTRY, PHYSICAL CHEMISTRY. **Personal Data:** b Vienna, Austria, January 22, 1933; American citizen. **Education:** Columbia Univ, BA, 1954; Yale Univ, PhD (chem), 1958. **Professional Experience:** PROF, DEPT MOLECULAR PHYSIOL & BIOPHYS, UNIV VT, 1998-; prof biochem, Brandeis Univ, 1974-1998; mem staff, Rosenstiel Basic Med Sci Res Ctr, 1972-1998; assoc prof biochem, Rosenstiel Basic Med Sci Res Ctr, 1972-1974; res assoc, Children's Cancer Res Found, 1959-1972; res fel biol, Harvard Univ, 1957-1959. **Memberships:** Am Chem Soc. **Research Statement & Publications:** Physical chemistry of muscle proteins. **Mailing Address:** Health Sci Res Facil, Univ Vt, Burlington, VT 05405-0068. **Fax:** 802-656-0747. **E-Mail:** lowey@physiology.med.uvm.edu

LOWI, ALVIN JR, THERMAL ENGINEERING & HEAT TRANSFER, ENGINE POWER & FUELS. **Personal Data:** b Gadsden, Ala, July 21, 1929; m 1953, Guillermina G Alverez; c David A, Rosamina, Edna V & Alvin III. **Education:** Ga Inst Technol, BME, 1951, MSME, 1956; Univ Calif, Los Angeles, PhD, 1962. **Professional Experience:** AT ALVIN LOWI & ASSOC, as of 2004; Mem, Reactivity Adv Panel, Calif Air Resources Bd, 1989-; prin investr, Gas Res Inst, 1986-; dir, Southern Calif Tissue Bank, 1983-; VPRES, DAECO FUELS & ENG CO, INC, 1976-; vis lectr eng, Univ Pa, 1972-1974; res assoc, Heather Found, 1966-; fel, Inst Human Studies, 1966-1972; prin, Alvin Louri & Assocs, Consult Engrs, 1962-; Lectr econ, Free Enterprise Inst, 1960-1970; pres, Terraqua, Inc, 1959-1976; mem tech staff eng, TRW Aerospace Corp, 1958-1966; design engr, Air Res Div, Garrett Corp, 1956-1958; Res asst eng exp pract, Ga Inst Technol, 1954-1956; PRES, LION ENG, INC. **Memberships:** Am Soc Mech Engrs; Soc Automotive Engrs; Nat Soc Prof Engrs; Soc Am Inventors. **Research Statement & Publications:** Simultaneous heat and mass transfer applied to novel cooling and distillation apparatus; supplementary fueling of diesel engines by fumigation of alternative volatile fuels; dissolution of natural gas in liquified petroleum materials for application to compact vehicular fuel storage; fire retardation of cellulose fibers for thermal insulation; facultative internal combustion processes; electrohydraulic fuel injection; multicolor pyrometry for particulate measurements; ozone formation of potential of hydrocarbons. **Mailing Address:** Alvin Lowi & Assoc, 2146 Toscanini Dr, San Pedro, CA 90731. **Fax:** 310-548-8457.

LOWINGER, PAUL, PSYCHOTHERAPY & CLINICAL PHARMACOLOGY, PRISON & FORENSIC PSYCHIATRY. **Personal Data:** b Chicago, 1923; m 1948, c Leslie, Wendy & Larry. **Education:** Northwestern Univ, BS, 1945; State Univ Iowa, MD, 1949, MSc, 1953; Am Bd Psychiat & Neurol, dipl, 1956. **Professional Experience:** RETIRED; prof, Dept Psychiat, Sch Med, Univ Calif, San Francisco, 1992; psychiat consult, Fulton Co Jail, Legal Aid, Atlanta, 1988; psychiat consult, Calif Dept Corrections, Brobeck, Phleger & Harrison & Prison Law Off, 1985, 1989; public defender, San Francisco, 1983; med dir, Occupational Stress Clin, Inst Labor & Mental Health, Calif, 1982; mental patients rights, dept mental health, San Francisco, 1982, 1985; Prisoners Legal Serv, State Prison, Salem, Ore, 1981-1982; superior ct, Alameda Co, Oakland, 1980-1986; psychiat consult, San Francisco Co Jail, 1980; assoc clin prof, psychiat, Tulane Univ Sch Med, 1974-1985; grant, Demonstration Proj Health Educ & Welfare, 1974-1979; adj assoc prof psychiat, Tulane Univ Sch Med, 1971-1974; assoc prof, psychiat, Tulane Univ Sch Med, 1962-1971; teaching grant, NIMH, 1959-1971; asst prof, psychiat, Tulane Univ Sch Med, 1959-1962; res grants, NIMH, 1957-1962, 1980-1982; instr, psychiat, Tulane Univ Sch Med, 1955-1959; numerous hosp staff mem & consultancies, 1953; clin instr, psychiat, Tulane Univ Sch Med, 1953-1955. **Memberships:** NY Acad Sci; fel Am Psychiat Asn; Sigma Xi; Am Psychosomat Soc; fel Am Orthopsychiat Asn; Am Asn Advance Sci; Am Asn Univ Profs; Am Psychopath Asn; Nat Med Asn; Am Pub Health Asn; Acad Psychoanal. **Research Statement & Publications:** Psychotherapy; psychosomatic medicine; psychosis; clinical pharmacology; legal medicine and social psychiatry. **Mailing Address:** 77 Belgrave Ave, San Francisco, CA 94117. **E-Mail:** paulow99@yahoo.com

LOWITZ, DAVID AARON, CHEMICAL PHYSICS. **Personal Data:** b Newark, NJ, December 18, 1928; m 1953, Doreen; c Mark A, Judith E, Ronna F (Meister) & Karen A. **Education:** Rutgers Univ, BA, 1950; Pa State Univ, MS, 1953, PhD (physics), 1955. **Honors & Awards:** IR 100 Award, 1972; Philip Morris Jewel Award, 1988, 1990. **Professional Experience:** AFFIL PROF PHYSICS, VA COMMONWEALTH UNIV, 1991-; sr sci, Physics Div, Philip Morris Res Ctr, 1987-1992; asst to dir appl res, Physics Div, Philip Morris Res Ctr, 1982-1987; tech planning coordr appl res, Physics Div, Philip Morris Res Ctr, 1979-1982; mgr, Physics Div, Philip Morris Res Ctr, 1967-1979; res assoc & head cent res physics sect, Lord Corp, 1964-1967; physicist, Gulf Res & Develop Co, 1956-1964; res assoc, Pa State Univ, 1955-1956; Am Petrol Inst fel, 1952-1956; asst physics, Pa State Univ, 1950-1955. **Memberships:** Am Phys Soc; Int Soc Quantum Biol; Sigma Xi. **Research Statement & Publications:** Microwave scattering; quantum mechanics; high pressure liquid viscosity; electromagnetic wave propagation; dielectrics; electron optics; electro-optic technology. **Mailing Address:** 4312 W Franklin St, Richmond, VA 23221. **Fax:** 804-353-4009. **E-Mail:** dlowitz@cabell.vcu.edu

LOWMAN, BERTHA PAULINE, MATHEMATICS. **Personal Data:** b Newton, NC, March 17, 1929. **Education:** Lenoir-Rhyne Col, BS, 1951; Univ Ala, MA, 1952; George Peabody Col, PhD (math), 1976. **Professional Experience:** PROF MATH, WESTERN KY UNIV, 1978-; asst prof, Western KY Univ, 1962-1978; ECarolina Col, 1959-1960 & Elon Col, 1960-1962; asst prof math, Hardin-Simmons Univ, 1955-1959; asst, Univ NC, 1955; instr sci & math, Anderson Col, 1953-1954; Instr math, Campbell Col, 1952-1953. **Memberships:** Math Asn Am; Nat Coun Teachers Math. **Research Statement & Publications:** Number theory and algebra; geometry and history of mathematics; linear algebra. **Mailing Address:** 1025 Roselawn Way, Bowling Green, KY 42104-3158.

LOWMAN, HENRY, CHEMISTRY, PROTEIN ENGINEERING. **Personal Data:** b Columbia, SC, June 14, 1962. **Education:** Johns Hopkins Univ, BA, 1984; Univ Purdue, PhD (chem), 1989. **Professional Experience:** ASSOC DIR, ANTIBODY ENG, GENENTECH, INC, as of 2004; scientist, Genentech Inc, beginning 1992; researcher, Genentech Inc, 1989-1992; NIH fel, 1989. **Memberships:** Am Chem Soc; AAAS. **Mailing Address:** Genentech Inc, One DNA Way, South San Francisco, CA 94080-4990.

LOWMAN, PAUL DANIEL, ASTROGEOLOGY, PHOTOGEOLOGY. **Personal Data:** b Elizabeth, NJ, September 26, 1931; m 1958. **Education:** Rutgers Univ, BS, 1953; Univ Colo, PhD (geol), 1963. **Honors & Awards:** John C Lindsay Mem Award, NASA, 1974. **Professional Experience:** EXPLOR PROG SCIENTIST, NASA, 1988-; GEOPHYSICIST, GEOPHYS BR, LAB TERRESTRIAL PHYSICS, GODDARD SPACE FLIGHT CTR, NASA, 1987-; lectr, Cath Univ, 1963-1966; Univ Calif, Santa Barbara, 1970; vis lectr, US Air Force Inst Technol, 1963-1964; staff, Goddard Space Ctr, 1959-1987. **Memberships:**

Geol Soc Am; AAAS; Am Geophys Union. **Research Statement & Publications:** Planetology; lunar geology; geologic application of orbital photography; remote sensing; comparative planetology. **Mailing Address:** Goddard Space Flight Ctr, Nasa, Code 921, Greenbelt, MD 20771. **E-Mail:** lowman@core2.gsfc.nasa.gov

LOWN, BERNARD, ARRHYTHMOLOGY. **Personal Data:** b Utena, Lithuania, June 7, 1921; American citizen; m 1946, c 3. **Education:** Univ Maine, BS, 1942; Johns Hopkins Univ, MD, 1945. **Honors & Awards:** Nobel Peace Prize, 1985; Nickolay Burdenko Medal, Acad Med Sci USSR, 1983; Andres Bello Medal, Ministry Educ & Ministry Sci, Venezuela, 1986. **Professional Experience:** DIR, LOWN CARDIOVASC CTR, as of 2003; PROF EMER CARDIOL, DEPT NUTRIT, HARVARD SCH PUB HEALTH, 1991-; vis scientist, Mass Inst Technol, beginning 1987; vis scientist, Clin Res Ctr, Mass Inst Technol, beginning 1987; sr physician, Brigham & Womens Hosp, beginning 1984; consult cardiol, HCHP Hosp, 1983-1986; co-pres, Int Physicians Prev Nuclear War, 1980-1993; physician, Brigham & Womens Hosp, 1970-1984; consult cardiol, Childrens Hosp, 1964-1992; consult cardiol, Beth Israel Hosp, 1963-1994; consult cardiol, Newton-Wellesley Hosp, 1963-1985; sr assoc, Brigham & Womens Hosp, 1963-1970; from asst prof to prof cardiol, Dept Nutrit & dir, Cardiovasc Res Lab, 1961-1991; from asst prof to assoc prof cardiol, Sch Pub Health, Harvard Univ, 1961-1974; dir, Samuel Levine Cardiovasc Res Lab, Peter Bent Brigham Hosp, 1956-1958. **Memberships:** Sr mem Inst Med-Nat Acad Sci; Nat Acad Sci Hungary; fel Am Acad Arts & Sci; fel Am Col Cardiol; Am Soc Clin Invest; Am Heart Asn; Asn Am Physicians; AAAS; corresp mem Brit Cardiac Soc; corresp mem Cardiac Soc Australia & NZ; corresp mem Swiss Soc Cardiol; corresp & hon foreign mem Belgian Royal Acad Med; fel Int Col Nutrit; corresp mem Croatia Acad Sci & Arts; foreign mem Russ Acad Med Sci. **Research Statement & Publications:** Sudden cardiac death, identified potential victims and evolved programs for their protection; role of neural and psychologic factors provoking life threatening disturbances of heart rhythms. **Mailing Address:** Lown Cardiovasc Ctr, 21 Longwood Ave, Brookline, MA 02446. **Fax:** 617-734-5763.

LOWN, JAMES WILLIAM, BIOORGANIC CHEMISTRY. **Personal Data:** b Blyth, Eng, December 19, 1934; m 1962, Elizabeth; c Andrew James & Peter Wilslam. **Education:** Univ London, BS, 1956, PhD (org chem), 1959. **Honors & Awards:** Hoffman-La-Roche Award Med Chem, 1996. **Professional Experience:** PROF EMER CHEM, UNIV ALTA, as of 2003; Killam res prof, 1996-; adj prof surg, Univ Alta, 1994-; fel, Int Union Against Cancer, 1992-; mem, UN Educ Sci & Cult Orgn Global Network Molecular & Cellular Biol, 1989-; mem, Nat Cancer Inst, Can, 1977-; prof chem, Univ Alta, beginning 1974; from asst prof to assoc prof, Nat Cancer Inst Can, 1964-1975; asst prof, Univ Alta, 1962-1963; res chemist, Walter Reed Army Inst Res, DC, 1962-1963; fel, Univ Alta, 1961-1962; asst lectr chem, Imp Col, Univ London, 1959-1961. **Memberships:** Am Chem Soc; The Chem Soc; Sigma Xi; Am Asn Cancer Res; Can Soc Chem. **Research Statement & Publications:** Organic reaction mechanisms; heterocyclic synthesis; antibiotics; cancer and viral chemotherapy. **Mailing Address:** Dept Chem, Univ Alta, 11227 Sask Dr, Edmonton, AB T6G 2G2, Can. **Fax:** 780-0492-8231.

LOWNDES, DOUGLAS H, SEMICONDUCTORS, PHOTOVOLTAIC CELL RESEARCH. **Personal Data:** b Pasadena, Calif, January 3, 1940; m 1961, c 2. **Education:** Stanford Univ, BS, 1961; Univ Colo, PhD (physics), 1969. **Professional Experience:** SCI DIR, CTR NANOPHASE MAT SCI, as of 2005; prof mat sci & eng, Univ Tenn, 1986-; sr res staff mem, condensed matter sci div, Oak Ridge Nat Lab, 1979-; guest prof physics, Univ Nijemegen, 1976-1977; assoc, Solar Energy Ctr, 1974-1979; from asst prof to prof physics, Univ Ore, 1970-1979; NSF fel physics, Sch Math & Phys Sci, Univ Sussex, 1968-1970; res asst solid state physics, Hewlett-Packard Assocs, Calif, 1962-1963. **Memberships:** Fel Am Phys Soc; Int Solar Energy Soc; sr mem Inst Elec & Electronics Engrs; Mat Res Soc. **Research Statement & Publications:** Photochemical thin film growth; laser interactions with semiconductors; solar cells; nanosecond and piosecond laser measurements; pulsed laser annealing; superconductivity and magnetism; electronic materials. **Mailing Address:** Oak Ridge Nat Lab, PO Box 2008 Bldg 3150 MS 6056 One Bethel Valley rd, Oak Ridge, TN 37831-6056. **Fax:** 865-576-3676. **E-Mail:** lowndesdh@ornl.gov

LOWNDES, HERBERT EDWARD, NEUROTOXICOLOGY, NEUROPHARMACOLOGY. **Personal Data:** b Barrie, Ont, July 12, 1943; m 1966, c 3. **Education:** Univ Sask, BA, 1964, MSc, 1970; Cornell Univ, PhD (pharmacol), 1972. **Honors & Awards:** Grass Traveling Scientist Award, 1984; Javits Neuroscience Investr Award, NIH, 1985; Merit Award, Rutgers Univ, 1987, 1989, 1990, 1994. **Professional Experience:** PROF PHARMACOL & TOXICOL, STATE UNIV NJ, as of 2005; ASSOC DIR, ENVIRON & OCCUP HEALTH SCI INST, 2003-; DISTINGUISHED PROF, COL PHARM, RUTGERS UNIV, 1985-; consult, Safety & Occup Health Study Sect, NIH, 1985-1988; consult, Health Res, Effects Grants Rev Panel, Environ Protection Agency, 1984-; consult, Toxicol Data Bank, Nat Libr Med, 1981-1985; consult, Toxicol Study Sect, 1980-1984, 1989-1993; from asst prof to prof pharmacol, Col Med & Dent, NJ Med Sch, 1973-1981; fel pharmacol, Univ Western Ont, 1972-1973; vis prof, Univ Paul Sabatier, Toulouse, France, 1966-. **Memberships:** Am Soc Pharmacol & Exp Therapeut; NY Acad Sci; Soc Toxicol; Soc Neuroscience; Am Asn Neuropathologists. **Research Statement & Publications:** Neurotoxicology and neuropharmacology of central and peripheral nervous system, particularly electrophysiological, histochemical and morphological correlates. **Mailing Address:** Toxicol Div, Rutgers Univ, Gordon Rd Rm 208, Rutgers, NJ 08854. **Fax:** 732-445-6905. **E-Mail:** lowndes@eohsi.rutgers.edu

LOWNDES, JOSEPH M, BIOCHEMISTRY, MOLECULAR BIOLOGY. **Personal Data:** b Duluth, Minn, February 28, 1955. **Education:** Univ Notre Dame, BS, 1977; Univ Wis-Madison, MS, 1983, PhD (biochem), 1988. **Professional Experience:** CO-PRIN INVESTR & INSTR, BIOTECHNOLOGY LAB TECHNICIAN PROG, MADISON AREA TECH COL, as of 2003; SR SCIENTIST, DEPT RES & DEVELOP, FIVE PRIME THREE PRIME, 1991-; postdoctoral fel, Dept Pediat, Nat Jewish Ctr Immunol & Resp Med, 1989-1991. **Memberships:** Am Soc Biochem & Molecular Biol; AAAS; Am Chem Soc; Sigma Xi. **Mailing Address:** Madison Area Tech Col, 3550 Anderson St, Madison, WI 53704. **Fax:** 608-246-6955. **E-Mail:** jlowndes@matcmadison.edu

LOWNDES, ROBERT P, PHYSICS. **Personal Data:** b Derby, Eng, December 11, 1939. **Education:** Univ London, BSc, 1962, Queen Mary Col, PhD (exp solid state physics), 1967; Northeastern Univ, MBA, 1976. **Professional Experience:** CHMN, FAC SENATE, NORTHEASTERN UNIV, as of 1999; CHMN, UNIV RES & SCHOLAR COUN, NORTHEASTERN UNIV, as of 1999; interim provost, 1988-1990; dean, Col Arts & Sciences, 1987-1988; chmn dept, Northeastern Univ, 1981-1987; PROF PHYSICS, NORTHEASTERN UNIV, 1978-; assoc prof, Northeastern Univ, 1972-1978; asst prof, Northeastern Univ, 1968-1972; res assoc physics, Mass Inst Technol, 1967-1968. **Memberships:** Am Inst Physics; Brit Inst Physics; fel Sci Res Coun; fel Am Coun Educ; Am Phys Soc. **Research Statement & Publications:** High pressure dielectric and far infrared spectroscopic studies of solids. **Mailing Address:** Col Arts & Sci, Northeastern Univ, Huntington Ave, Boston, MA 02115-5096.

LOWNEY, JEREMIAH RALPH, SEMICONDUCTOR ELECTRONICS, SEMICONDUCTOR PHYSICS. **Personal Data:** b Fall River, Mass, December 16, 1946; m 1980, Anne. **Education:** Mass Inst Technol, Cambridge, BS, 1967, MS, 1968, PhD (elec eng), 1975. **Professional Experience:** Physicist, Nat Inst Stand & Technol, beginning 1979; physicist, Naval Surface Weapons Ctr, 1975-1979; physicist, Naval Ord Lab, 1968-1972. **Memberships:** Am Phys Soc; Inst Elec & Electronics Engrs; AAAS; Sigma Xi. **Research Statement & Publications:** Electronic properties of semiconducting materials, such as band structure, mobility, lifetime, deep-level spectroscopy and impact ionization in silicon and compound semiconductors. **Mailing Address:** Nat Inst Stand & Technol, Bldg 225 Rm A-307, Gaithersburg, MD 20899. **Fax:** 301-948-4081. **E-Mail:** lowney@sed.eeel.nist.gov

LOWRANCE, WILLIAM WILSON, JR, SCIENCE POLICY, RISK ASSESSMENT. **Personal Data:** b El Paso, Tex, May 8, 1943. **Education:** Univ NC, Chapel Hill, AB, 1965; Rockefeller Univ, PhD (biochem), 1970. **Professional Experience:** EXEC DIR, INST MED BENEFIT/RISK FOUND, SWITZ, 1991-; sr fel & dir, Life Sci & Pub Policy Prog, Rockefeller Univ, New York, 1980-1991; vis assoc prof human biol, Stanford Univ, 1978-1980; spec asst to US Secy State, Washington, DC, 1977-1978; res fel, Prog Sci & Int Affairs, Harvard Univ, 1975-1976; resident fel, Nat Acad Sci, Washington, DC, 1973-1975; asst exec ed, J Cell Biol, New York, 1972-1973; res consult, NC Dept Educ, Raleigh, 1971-1972; Res chemist, Tenn Eastman Co, Kingsport, 1970-1971. **Memberships:** AAAS. **Research Statement & Publications:** National and international science policy; decisions regarding public health risks; ethical responsibilities of technical people; nuclear proliferation; synthetic and mechanistic organic photochemistry. **Mailing Address:** Int Med Benefit/Risk Found, 12 rue Jean Calvin Ch-1204, Geneva, Switzerland.

LOWREY, CHARLES BOYCE, PHYSICAL ORGANIC CHEMISTRY. **Personal Data:** b New Orleans, La, March 15, 1941; m 1961, Nita; c Charles II, Barry, Paul & Peyton. **Education:** Centenary Col, BS, 1963; Univ Houston, PhD (heterocyclic chem), 1968. **Professional Experience:** ENVIRONMENT CONSULT, SELF-EMPLOYEED, beginning 1999; sales mgr, Waste Management of Tex, 1995-1998; southern serv region pres, Chem Waste Mgt, 1993-1994; sales mgr, chem waste mgt, 1993-1994; southern regional vpres sales, Chem Waste Mgt, 1982-1992; consult hazardous waste disposal, Price-Curtis & Assoc Inc, 1981-1982; asst gen mgr & tech mgr, Port Arthur, Tex Facil, Chem Water Mgt, Inc, 1979-1981; gen mgr opers & prod, Petrol Assocs of Lafayette, Inc, 1977-1979; asst dean Col, Centenary Col La, 1974-1977; from asst prof to assoc prof chem, Centenary Col La, 1973-1977; water pollution consult, Ford Battery Plant, Shreveport, 1968-1973; water pollution consult, Gould Battery Plant, Shreveport, 1973-1975; consult, Baifield Industs, La, 1966-1970; teaching asst chem, Univ Houston, 1963-1966; sales mgr, Wast Management of Tex, 1995-1998. **Memberships:** Am Chem Soc; sr mem & secy, Apr-La_Tex Sect, 1970-1971; pres, NW La Sect, 1972. **Research Statement & Publications:** Synthesis and study of electronic effects in substituted benzo(b) furans and benzo(b) thiophenes. **Mailing Address:** 17047 Fenny Bridge Lane, Spring, TX 77379. **Fax:** 281-922-1108. **E-Mail:** cblowrey1@earthlink.net

LOWRIE, ALLEN, MARINE GEOLOGY, CONTINENTAL MARGINS. **Personal Data:** b Washington, DC, December 30, 1937; div, c Tanya A. **Education:** Columbia Univ, BA, 1962. **Professional Experience:** Consult geologist, Seagull Int Explor, Houston, Tex, Int Inc, Kenner, La & Bluebonnet Petrol New Orleans, La, 1988-1991; instr, Univ Southern Miss, 1984-1988; MEM STAFF, NAVAL OCEANOG OFF, 1983-; instr, Tulane Univ, New Orleans, La, 1982-1985, 1992; explorationist, Mobil Oil Corp, 1981-1983; invited lectr, Universidad Del Los Andes, Bogota, Colombia, 1978-; consult, St Stanislaus Sch, Bay St Louis, Miss, 1976-1979; guest lectr oceanog & ecol, Calverton Sch, Huntington, Md, 1974-1976; invited lectr, Cath Univ Am, Wash, DC, 1972-1973; oceanogr marine geol, Naval Oceanog Off, 1968-1976, 1978-1981 & Naval Ocean Res & Develop Act, 1976-1978; res asst marine geol, Lamont Geol Observ, 1963-1968. **Memberships:** Soc Econ Paleont & Mineral; Am Asn Petrol Geologists; NY Acad Sci; Am Inst Prof Geologists; Sigma Xi; Geol Soc Am. **Research Statement & Publications:** Subduction zone interaction of North and South America; ocean basin sediment-type and thickness-acoustic response; evolution of passive margins and hydrocarbon traps; prospect developer, promoter and seismic response research; hydrogeology; petroleum exploration. **Mailing Address:** 230 FZ Goss Rd, Picayune, MS 39466-9423.

LOWRIGHT, RICHARD HENRY, SEDIMENTOLOGY. **Personal Data:** b Bethlehem, Pa, August 31, 1940; m 1966. **Education:** Franklin & Marshall Col, AB, 1962; Pa State Univ, PhD (geol), 1971. **Professional Experience:** ASSOC PROF GEOL, SUSQUEHANNA UNIV, 1978-; consult geol, 1973-; asst prof, Susquehanna Univ, 1971-1978; teacher pub sch, NY, 1964-1966. **Memberships:** Nat Water Well Asn. **Research Statement & Publications:** Quantity and quality of ground water in Snyder County, Pa. **Mailing Address:** Dept Geol & Environ Sci, Susquehanna Univ, Selinsgrove, PA 17870.

LOWRY, BRIGHT ANDERSON, III, ASTRONOMY. **Personal Data:** b Newberry, SC, April 6, 1936; m 1965, Judith; c Margaret R & Suzanne B. **Education:** Mass Inst Technol, BS, 1958; Univ Chicago, PhD (phys chem), 1965. **Professional Experience:** YOUNG PROF CHEM & PHYSICS, ERSKINE COL, as of 2001; prof chem, Erskine Col, beginning 1974; from asst prof to assoc prof chem, Southern Methodist Univ, 1966-1974; res assoc, Univ NC, Chapel Hill, 1964-1966; res assoc, Dartmouth Col, 1963-1964. **Memberships:** Am Chem Soc; Am Phys Soc. **Research Statement & Publications:** Physical properties of liquid crystals. **Mailing Address:** Dept Chem & Physics, Erskine Col, Two Wash St, Due West, SC 29639. **E-Mail:** lowry@erskine.edu

LOWRY, CHARLES V, MOLECULAR BIOLOGY. **Education:** Harvard Univ, BA, 1966; Univ Wis, PhD, 1971. **Professional Experience:** ASST PROF, DEPT BIOCHEM & MOLECULAR BIOL, ALBANY MED COL, as of 2004. **Research Statement & Publications:** Mechanisms of regulation of gene expression and the control of cellular differentiation. **Mailing Address:** Dept Biochem & Molecular Biol, Albany Med Col, 47 New Scotland Ave, Albany, NY 12208. **Fax:** 518-262-5689. **E-Mail:** cvlowry@aol.com

LOWRY, ERIC G, PHYSICAL CHEMISTRY. **Personal Data:** b Berlin, Ger, November 23, 1916; American citizen; m 1954, c 1. **Education:** Univ Geneva, PhD (phys chem), 1943. **Professional Experience:** RETIRED; sect supvr, Charles Bruning Co Div, 1977-1981; chief chemist reprography, Addressograph Multigraph Corp, 1965-1977; res chemist, Addressograph Multigraph Corp, 1959-1965; res chemist lithography, Polychrome Corp, 1959; res chemist photog, Remington Rand Div, Sperry Rand Corp, 1951-1958; res chemist fluorochem, Gen Chem Div, Allied Chem Corp, 1947-1949. **Memberships:** AAAS; Am Chem Soc; Soc Photog Sci & Eng; Tech Asn Pulp & Paper Indust. **Research Statement & Publications:** Reprography. **Mailing Address:** 73 Lewis St, Middleton, CT 06457-5226.

LOWRY, GEORGE GORDON, PHYSICAL & POLYMER CHEMISTRY. **Personal Data:** b Chico, Calif, January 12, 1929; m 1953, Janet; c 4. **Education:** Chico State Col, AB, 1950; Stanford Univ, MS, 1952; Mich State Univ, PhD (phys chem), 1963. **Professional Experience:** RETIRED; from assoc prof to prof chem, Western Mich Univ, 1968-1993;

from asst prof to assoc prof chem, Claremont Mens Col, 1963-1968; NSF fel, 1962-1963; res chemist, Dow Chem Co, 1951-1962; res asst, Stanford Res Inst, 1951; independent consult, Environ Safety & Health. **Memberships:** Am Chem Soc; Sigma Xi. **Research Statement & Publications:** Polymerization kinetics and processes; copolymerization; statistical theory of kinetic chain processes; hazardous materials; safety and health. **Mailing Address:** 22 Fairwood Pl, Palmyra, VA 22963-2767.

LOWRY, GERALD LAFAYETTE, FORESTRY, SOIL SCIENCE. **Personal Data:** b Harrisburg, Pa, September 12, 1928; m 1949, c 3. **Education:** Pa State Univ, BS, 1953; Ore State Univ, MS, 1955; Mich State Univ, PhD (forestry), 1961. **Professional Experience:** RETIRED; prof forestry, Stephen F Austin State Univ, beginning 1976; assoc prof, Stephen F Austin State Univ, 1972-1976; chmn, Coun Fertilizer Appln, 1963-1965; res forester, Pulp & Paper Res Inst Can, 1961-1972; vchmn forestry comt, Coun Fertilizer Appln, 1961-1963; spec res asst, Mich State Univ, 1958-1959; asst prof, Ohio State Univ, 1957-1958; instr, Ohio Agr Exp Sta, Wooster, 1955-1961; asst, Ore State Univ, 1953-1955. **Memberships:** Soc Am Foresters; Soil Sci Soc Am; Am Soc Agron; Am Soc Surface Mining & Reclamation. **Research Statement & Publications:** Herbicide effectiveness and usage in the West Gulf region; success of seed-tree regeneration of Loblolly pine; pine site index on major soil types of East Texas; effectiveness of shearing in improving Christmas tree grade; author of numerous publications. **Mailing Address:** Col Forestry, Stephen F Austin State Univ, Nacogdoches, TX 75962-6109.

LOWRY, JAMES LEE, ELECTRICAL ENGINEERING. **Personal Data:** b Birmingham, Ala, February 19, 1931; m 1956, c 3. **Education:** Auburn Univ, BEE, 1955, MS, 1957; Univ Fla, PhD (elec eng), 1963. **Professional Experience:** PROF EMER ELEC ENG, AUBURN UNIV, 1995-; prof elec Eng, Auburn Univ, beginning 1965; assoc prof, Auburn Univ, 1963-1965; teaching assoc, Univ Fla, 1962-1963; from instr to asst prof elec eng, Auburn Univ, 1955-1959; consult, Ala Power Co. **Memberships:** Sr mem Inst Elec & Electronics Engrs; Am Soc Eng Educ; Nat Soc Prof Engrs; Sigma Xi. **Research Statement & Publications:** Circuit analysis and synthesis; power systems. **Mailing Address:** Dept Elec Eng Auburn Univ, 261 Broun Hall, Auburn, AL 36849. **Fax:** 334-844-1809. **E-Mail:** lowry@eng.auburn.edu

LOWRY, JEAN, geology; deceased, see previous edition for last biography

LOWRY, JERALD FRANK, EXPERIMENTAL PHYSICS. **Personal Data:** b Listie, Pa, October 22, 1939; m 1961, Patricia; c Jerald K, Jeffrey K, Brian C & Kristin A. **Education:** Univ Pittsburgh, BS, 1961; Cornell Univ, MS, 1963. **Professional Experience:** SR RES SCIENTIST, WESTINGHOUSE SCI & TECHNOL CTR, 1981-; sr engr appl physics, Westinghouse Sci & Technol Ctr, 1963-1980; teaching asst physics, Cornell Univ, 1961-1963; jr engr, Testing Reactor, Westinghouse Elec Corp, 1961. **Memberships:** Am Phys Soc; AAAS. **Research Statement & Publications:** Low pressure plasmas; fluorescent lamp discharges; generation of high power electron beams; measurement of power density distribution and beam radiance; gas discharge lasers, electron-beam sustained discharges; superconductivity. **Mailing Address:** Westinghouse Res Lab, 1730 Yorktown Pl Beulah Rd, Pittsburgh, PA 15235.

LOWRY, NANCY, PHYSICAL ORGANIC CHEMISTRY. **Personal Data:** b Newburgh, NY, September 4, 1938; m 1961, Thomas; c Kate, Sam & Alex. **Education:** Smith Col, AB, 1960; Mass Inst Technol, PhD (chem), 1965. **Professional Experience:** Dean advising, 2001-2002; dean, nat sci, 1989-1992; PROF CHEM, HAMPSHIRE COL, 1984-; from asst prof to assoc prof, Hampshire Col, 1970-1984; res assoc, Smith Col, 1969-1970; lectr, Smith Col, 1967-1969; res assoc chem, Amherst Col, 1966-1967 & Mass Inst Technol, 1965-1966. **Memberships:** AAAS; Asn Women Sci; Am Chem Soc. **Research Statement & Publications:** Women and science; science education; chemistry in herbs and medicines. **Mailing Address:** Sch Nat Sci, Hampshire Col, Amherst, MA 01002. **Fax:** 413-559-5448. **E-Mail:** nlowry@hampshire.edu

LOWRY, RALPH A(DDISON), ENGINEERING, PHYSICS. **Personal Data:** b Clay County, Mo, August 9, 1926; m 1947, Jean Dunnell; c Stephen R, Margaret J, Cynthia A & John H. **Education:** Iowa State Univ, BS, 1949, PhD (physics), 1955. **Professional Experience:** EMER PROF, UNIV VA, 1991-; assoc dean, Sch Eng & Appl Sci, 1986-1991; dean, Sch Eng & Appl Sci, 1983-1984; John Lloyd Newcomb prof eng & appl sci, Sch Eng & Appl Sci, 1978-1991; prof nuclear eng & eng physics, Sch Eng & Appl Sci, 1977-1991; chmn, Dept Aerospace Eng & Eng Physics, 1965-1972; from assoc prof to prof aerospace eng, Res Labs Eng Sci, Univ Va, 1962-1977; Sr scientist, Res Labs Eng Sci, Univ Va, 1955-1962. **Memberships:** Am Phys Soc; Am emer nissen Soc Eng Educ; emer mem VA Acad sci. **Research Statement & Publications:** Atomic and molecular physics; isotope separation; gas centrifuges; fluid mechanics. **Mailing Address:** 507 Woodchuck Lane, Charlottesville, VA 22902. **E-Mail:** ral@virginia.edu

LOWRY, ROBERT JAMES, BOTANY CELL BIOLOGY. **Personal Data:** b Chelsea, Mich, August 26, 1912; m 1934, Phyllis L lowry; c Mark Ashley Lowry. **Education:** Univ Mich, BS, 1940, MS, 1941, PhD (bot), 1947. **Professional Experience:** EMER PROF BOT, UNIV MICH, ANN ARBOR, 1981-; from asst prof to prof, Univ Mich, Ann Arbor, 1948-1981; asst prof bot, Mich State Univ, 1946-1948; Res assoc, Univ Mich, 1942-1945; (Res assoc in Physics). **Memberships:** AAAS. **Research Statement & Publications:** Cytotaxonomy; electron microscopy. **Mailing Address:** 630 Hampstead Lane, Ann Arbor, MI 48103.

LOWRY, STEPHEN FREDERICK, SURGERY. **Personal Data:** b Colombus, Ohio, November 1, 1947; c 3. **Education:** Ohio, Wesleyan Univ, BA, 1969; Univ Mich Sch Med, MD, 1973. **Professional Experience:** PROF & CHMN, DEPT SURG, ROBERT WOOD JOHNSON MED SCH, as of 1997; ACTING CHIEF, DIV GEN SURG, ROBERT WOOD JOHNSON MED SCH, 2000-2002; ASSOC PROF SURG, NY HOSP-CORNELL MED CTR, 1987-1996; traveling fel, James IV Asn Surgeons, 1987; asst attend surgeon, gastric & mixed tumor serv, 1982 & nutrit, mem, Sloan-Kettering Cancer Ctr, 1985; dir lab surg metab, NY Hosp Cornell Med Ctr, beginning 1982; DIR HYPERALIMENTATION UNIT, NY HOSP-CORNELL MED CTR, 1982-; asst prof surg, NY Hosp-cornell Med Ctr, 1982-1987; vis assoc physician, Rockefeller Univ, 1982. **Memberships:** Am Col Surgeons; Asn Acad Surg; Soc Univ Surgeons; Fed Am Soc Exp Biol; Soc Surg Oncol; Int Soc Surg; Royal College of Surgeons (Edin) Honorary. **Research Statement & Publications:** Identifications mechanisms inducing hypermetabolisms, protein regulation and tissue in trauma, sepsis and cancer; method for restoration of protein homeostasis by nutritional support. **Mailing Address:** UMDNJ-Robert Wood Johnson Med Sch, Clin Acad Bldg, Ste 7300, 125 Paterson St, New Brunswick, NJ 08901-1977. **Fax:** 732-235-6003. **E-Mail:** lowrysf@umdnj.edu

LOWRY, THOMAS HASTINGS, ORGANIC CHEMISTRY. **Personal Data:** b New York, NY, June 16, 1938; m 1961, c 3. **Education:** Princeton Univ, AB, 1960; Harvard Univ, PhD (chem), 1965. **Professional Experience:** Prof chem, Smith Col, 1981-2001; from asst prof to assoc prof, Smith Col, 1966-1981; res assoc, Mass Inst Technol, 1965-1966; NIH fel chem, Mass Inst Technol, 1964-1965. **Memberships:** Am Chem Soc; AAAS. **Research Statement & Publications:** Physical organic chemistry. **Mailing Address:** Dept Chem, Smith Col, Northampton, MA 01063.

LOWRY, WALLACE DEAN, GEOLOGY. **Personal Data:** b Medford, Ore, October 5, 1917; m 1942, Dorothea; c Robert E. **Education:** Ore State Univ, BS, 1939, MS, 1940; Univ Rochester, PhD (geol), 1943. **Professional Experience:** PROF EMER GEOL, VA POLYTECH INST & STATE UNIV, as of 2002; prof geol, Va Polytech Inst & State Univ, 1955-1982; assoc prof, VA Polytech Inst & State Univ, 1949-1955; Texaco, Inc, 1947-1949; geologist, Ore Dept Geol & Mineral Indust, 1942-1947. **Memberships:** Fel Geol Soc Am; Am Asn Petrol Geol; Sigma Xi. **Research Statement & Publications:** Late Cenozoic stratigraphy of the lower Columbia River basin; ferruginous bauxite deposits of Northwestern Oregon; silica sands of Western Virginia; porosity of sandstone reservoir rocks; role of Tertiary volcanism in tectonism; relation of silicification and dolomitization; geology of the Blue Mountains, Oregon; mechanics of Appalachian thrusting; North American geosynclines; exotic Cenozoic gravel deposits of Arizona and southern California. **Mailing Address:** Dept Geosci, VA Polytech Inst & State Univ, 4044 Derring Hall, Blacksburg, VA 24061-0420. **Fax:** 540-231-3386.

LOWRY, WILLIAM THOMAS, OCCUPATIONAL SAFETY & HEALTH. **Personal Data:** b Hobbs, NMex, December 11, 1942; m 1965, c 2. **Education:** E Tex State Univ, BS, 1965, MS, 1967; Colo State Univ, PhD (natural prod chem), 1971; Am Inst Chemists, cert, 1975; Am Bd Forensic Toxicol, cert, 1976. **Professional Experience:** TOXICOLOGIST, PVT PRACT, 1985-; adj asst prof civil eng, Univ Tex, Arlington, 1982-; asst prof path, Univ Tex Southwestern Med Sch, 1977-; from asst prof to assoc prof toxicol, Grad Sch Biomed Sci, Univ Tex Health Sci Ctr, 1977-1985; adj assoc prof, E Tex State Univ, 1977-1980; adj asst prof chem, E Tex State Univ, 1976-1977; instr path & forensic sci, Univ Tex Southwestern Med Sch, 1975-1977; assoc consult, attend staff toxicol, Parkland Mem Hosp, 1973-; toxicologist, Southwestern Inst Forensic Sci, 1973-1985; instr path, Univ Tex Southwestern Med Sch, 1973-1975; spec agent, 1972-1973; res assoc biochem, Va Polytech Inst & State Univ, 1971-1972; chemist, Fed Bur Invest, 1965. **Memberships:** Am Acad Clin Toxicol; Am Acad Forensic Sci; Am Chem Soc; Am Inst Chemists; Am Soc Pharmacog; Sigma Xi. **Research Statement & Publications:** Environmental toxicology; biodegradation of toxic substances; utilizing bacteria; combustion and pulmonary toxicology. **Mailing Address:** 312 W Abram St, Arlington, TX 76010.

LOWTHER, FRANK EUGENE, PETROLEUM ENGINEERING. **Personal Data:** b Orrville, Ohio, February 3, 1929; m 1951, Elizabeth; c 4. **Education:** Ohio State Univ, BS, 1952. **Professional Experience:** CUSTOM TECH CREATIONS INC, BUFFALO, NY, 1993-; CONSULT & TECH Adv, Inc, Buffalo, NY, 1993-; ADV, ENERGY SCI INC, CANADAIGUA, NY, 1993-; res adv, Energy Conversion & Mat Lab, 1985-1993; prin scientist, Energy Conversion & Mat Lab, 1983-1985; chief scientist, Energy Conversion & Mat Lab, 1982-1983; sr res scientist, Atlantic Richfield Co, 1980-1982; sr eng assoc, Union Carbide, 1975-1979; founder dir & vpres, Purification Sci, Inc, 1965-1975; consult, Gen Elec Co, 1957-1965; sr engr, Raytheon Mfg Co, 1952-1957. **Memberships:** Assoc fel Am Inst Aeronaut & Astronaut; Inst Elec & Electronics Engrs; AAAS; NY Acad Sci. **Research Statement & Publications:** Ozone technology; plasma generators; solid state power devices; internal combustion engines; thermoelectrics; virus and bacteria disinfection systems; oil field technology; electric power distribution; nuclear fusion; chemical and physical reactors; exploding bridge wires; weapons. **Mailing Address:** 817 Parkside Ave, Buffalo, NY 14216-2009.

LOWTHER, GERALD EUGENE, CONTACT LENS RESEARCH. **Personal Data:** b September 16, 1943; m 1966, Andrya; c Karen & Daniel. **Education:** Ohio State Univ, BSc, 1966, OD, 1967, MSc, 1969, PhD (physiol optics), 1972. **Honors & Awards:** John Neill Medal, Pa Col Optom, 1985; Max Shapero Mem Lectr Award, Am Acad Optom, 1994. **Professional Experience:** DEAN, IND UNIV SCH OPTOM, 1998-; co-dir, Borish Ctr Ophthal Res, beginning 1995; PROF OPTOM, IND UNIV, 1994-; Univ Ala, Birmingham, 1989-1994; vis prof optom, Univ NSW, 1986; ed, Int Contact Lens Clin J, beginning 1981; prof, Ferris State Univ, 1977-1989; from asst prof to assoc prof optom, Ohio State Univ, 1972-1977. **Memberships:** Fel Am Acad Optom (secy-treas, 1993-1994; pres-elect, 1995-1996; pres, 1997-); Asn Optom Contact Lens Educrs (pres, 1976-1978); Am Optom Asn; Asn Res Vision & Ophthal; Int Soc Contact Lens Res (pres, 1993-1994); Int Asn Contact Lens Educrs. **Research Statement & Publications:** Corneal physiology; tear chemistry; contact lens design and fitting; contact lens solutions; contact lens aftercare problems; contact lens deposits and coatings; dry eye and other ocular conditions. **Mailing Address:** Ind Univ, Bloomington, IN 47405. **Fax:** 812-855-8664. **E-Mail:** glowther@indiana.edu

LOWTHER, JAMES DAVID, MECHANICAL ENGINEERING. **Personal Data:** b Jackson, Miss, June 22, 1939; m 1961, Gayle; c 3. **Education:** Miss State Univ, BS, 1961, MS, 1962; Univ Tex, Austin, PhD (mech eng), 1968. **Professional Experience:** PROF EMER MECH ENG, LA TECH UNIV, as of 2006; univ distinguished prof, La Tech Univ, 1988-1993; Energy Anal & Diag Ctr, La Dept Nat Resources, 1986-1989; Energy Anal & Diag Ctr, US Dept Energy, 1984-1985; prin investr, US Dept Energy, 1980-1981; prin investr, Naval Weapons Eng Suport Activ, 1976-1977; consult, 1973-; prof mech eng, La Tech Univ, beginning 1973; prin investr, NSF res grant, 1970-1971; from asst prof to assoc prof, LA Tech Univ, 1963-1973; mech engr, Baton Rouge refinery, Humble Oil & Refining Co, 1962-1963. **Memberships:** Am Soc Mech Engrs; Am Soc Eng Educ; Sigma Xi. **Research Statement & Publications:** Heat transfer; thermodynamics; energy conservation; computer-based measurement. **Mailing Address:** Dept Mech Eng, Col Eng & Sci, La Tech Univ, PO Box 3178, Ruston, LA 71272. **E-Mail:** lowther@engr.latech.edu

LOWTHER, JOHN LINCOLN, COMPUTER SCIENCE. **Personal Data:** b Burlington, Iowa, September 5, 1943. **Education:** Univ Iowa, BA, 1965, MS, 1967, PhD (comput sci), 1975. **Professional Experience:** Adj assoc prof, Dept Educ, Mich Technol Univ, as of 2004; DIR UNDERGRAD STUDIES, MICH TECHNOL UNIV, as of 2004; ASSOC PROF COMPUT SCI, MICH TECHNOL UNIV, 1977-; from instr to asst prof, Mich Technol Univ, 1974-1977; instr math, Southwest State Univ, 1967-1971. **Memberships:** Asn Comput Mach; Math Asn Am; Sigma Xi; Inst Elec & Electronics Engrs; Am Asn Artificial Intel. **Research Statement & Publications:** Artificial intelligence; programming languages; computer graphics. **Mailing Address:** Dept Comput Sci, Mich Technol Univ, Rekhi Comput Sci Hall 306 Fisher 212 1400 Townsend Dr, Houghton, MI 49931. **Fax:** 906-487-2283. **E-Mail:** john@mtu.edu

LOWTHER, JOHN STEWART, PALEONTOLOGY, PALEOBOTANY. **Personal Data:** b Cochrane, Ont, July 31, 1925; m 1980. **Education:** McGill Univ, BS, 1949, MS, 1950; Univ Mich, PhD (geol), 1957. **Professional Experience:** RETIRED; prof geol, Univ Puget Sound, beginning 1980; from instr to assoc prof, Univ Puget Sound, 1956-1980. **Research Statement & Publications:** Sedimentology; Mesozoic paleobotany and stratigraphy; pollen microstructure; palynology. **Mailing Address:** Dept Geol, Univ Puget Sound, 6229 N Viewmont Dr, Tacoma, WA 98407-1559. **Fax:** 253-756-3352. **E-Mail:** slowther@ups.edu

LOWY, DOUGLAS R, BIOMEDICAL RESEARCH. **Personal Data:** b New York, NY, May 25, 1942; c 5. **Education:** Amherst Col, BA, 1964; NY Univ, MD, 1968. **Honors & Awards:** Sulzberger Award, Am Acad Dermat, 1987; Wallace P Rowe Award Virol, Nat Inst Allergy & Infectious Dis, 1993. **Professional Experience:** HEAD, SIGNALLING & ONCOL SECT, CELLULAR ONCOL LAB, DIV BASIC SCI, NAT CANCER INST, NIH, as of 2005; dep dir, Div Basic Sci, NCI, 1996-; LAB CHIEF & PRIN INVESTR, CELLULAR ONCOL LAB, DIV BASIC SCI, NAT CANCER INST, NIH, 1983-; Lab, NIH, 1975-; res assoc, Lab Viral Dis, Nat Inst Allergy & Infectious Dis, NIH; ed, J Am Soc Microbiol. **Memberships:** Am Acad Dermat; Am Asn Physicians; Am Dermat Asn; Am Soc for Clin Investigational Int; Papillomavirus Soc; Am Soc Microbiol; Soc Invest Dermat. **Research Statement & Publications:** Res interests include Host-parasite relationship, oncogenic viruses, growth regulation, cellular transformation, tumor pathologenesis, oprevention and treatment of tumors and infenction, skin disorders of cell proliferation and differentiation. **Mailing Address:** Nat Cancer Inst, Cellular Oncol Lab Bldg 37 Rm 4106C, Bethesda, MD 20892-4040. **Fax:** 301-480-5322. **E-Mail:** drl@helix.nih.gov

LOWY, R JOEL, PHYSIOLOGY, CELL BIOLOGY. **Personal Data:** b Pittsburgh, Pa, August 24, 1956. **Education:** Col William & Mary, BS, 1974; Va Inst Marine Sci, MA, 1977; Ore State Univ, PhD (zool & biochem), 1982. **Professional Experience:** RES PHYSIOLOGIST, DEPT PHYSIOL, ARMED FORCES RADIOBIOL RES INST, 1988-; sr staff fel, NIH, 1987-1988; Nat res serv award, NIH, 1985-1987. **Memberships:** Sigma Xi; AAAS; Am Physiol Soc; Am Soc Cell Biol. **Mailing Address:** Dept Physiol, Armed Forces Radiobiol Res Inst, 8901 Wis Ave, Bethesda, MD 20889-5603. **E-Mail:** lowy@afrri.usuhs.mil

LOWY, STANLEY H(OWARD), aerospace engineering air & space craft design, air & space craft propulsion; deceased, see previous edition for last biography

LOXLEY, THOMAS EDWARD, EARTH-COUPLED BUILDING SYSTEMS, EDUCATION OUTREACH. **Personal Data:** b Beaver, Pa, January 20, 1940; div. **Education:** Case Western Univ, Cleveland, BS, 1961. **Professional Experience:** World Conf Innovative Housing, Vancouver, 1993; J Bldg Res & Info, London, 1992; SINTEF-NTH, Trondheim, 1991; World Renewable Energy Cong, Reading, 1990; Fraunhofer Bauphysik, Heidenheim, 1990; Int Coun Bldg Res, Paris, 1989; CSTB, Sophia Antipolis, 1989; Tech Univ, Vienna, 1988; N Sun Conf, Borlange, 1988; Royal Inst Tech, Stockholm, 1987; Int Coun Bldg Res, World Cong, Wash, 1986; writer, J Bldg Res & Pract, Paris, 1985; Am Sol Energy Soc, Houston, 1982; lectr, Nat Bur Stand, Denver, 1980; FOUNDER, SR ENG SCIENTIST, INVERTED CAVE EDUC, 1978-; asst prof tech resources, Va Polytech Inst & State Univ, 1975-1978; mech engr, US Naval Surface Weapons Ctr, 1971-1975; pres, Manned Submersible Syst Co, 1969-1971; syst engr, Int Hydrodyn, Ltd, 1968-1969; mech engr, US Naval Weapons Lab, 1961-1965; mech eng, US Army Watervliet Arsenal, 1965-1968. **Memberships:** Int Coun Bldg Res Studies. **Research Statement & Publications:** Developing practical low-rise buildings and equipment systems that are thermally coupled directly to the subsoil under them for ultra low-energy space heating and cooling. **Mailing Address:** 500 Beaver Rd No 601, Ambridge, PA 15003-2013.

LOY, JAMES BRENT, PLANT BREEDING, DEVELOPMENTAL GENETICS. **Personal Data:** b Borger, Tex, February 28, 1941; div, c Reed J, Laura M & James W. **Education:** Okla State Univ, BS, 1963; Colo State Univ, MS, 1965, PhD (genetics), 1967. **Professional Experience:** PROF PLANT BIOL, COL LIFE SCI & AGR, UNIV NH, 1981-; vis scholar bot, Univ Calif, Berkeley, 1974-1975; from asst prof to assoc prof, Univ NH, 1967-1981. **Memberships:** Am Soc Hort Sci; Soc Econ Bot; Nat Agr Plastics Asn. **Research Statement & Publications:** Cucurbit breeding; hormonal and genetic regulation of sex expression in cucumis melo; morpho-physiological investigation of seed and fruit field in cucurbito species. **Mailing Address:** Dept Plant Biol, Col Life Sci & Agr, Univ NH, Taylor Hall 59 Col Rd, Durham, NH 03824. **Fax:** 603-862-4486. **E-Mail:** jbloy@christa.unh.edu

LOY, MICHAEL MING-TAK, PHYSICS TEACHING. **Personal Data:** b China, January 12, 1945; American citizen; m 1970, Ivy; c Michelle & Sharon. **Education:** Univ Calif, Berkeley, BS, 1966, PhD (physics), 1971. **Professional Experience:** ASSOC DEAN SCI, HONG KONG UNIV SCI & TECHNOL, HONG KONG, 1995-; topical ed, J Optical Soc Am, 1993-; PROF PHYSICS, HONG KONG UNIV SCI & TECHNOL, HONG KONG, 1993-; mem steering comt, Laser Sci Topical Group, Am Phys Soc, 1991-1993; dept mgr, Thomas Watson Res Ctr, IBM Corp, 1987-1993; tech planning staff, Thomas Watson Res Ctr, IBM Corp, 1986-1987; Prin investr, Off Naval Res, 1978-1989; mgr, Thomas Watson Res Ctr, IBM Corp, 1978-1986; Res staff mem, Thomas Watson Res Ctr, IBM Corp, 1971-1977. **Memberships:** Fel Am Phys Soc; Optical Soc Am; Int Coun Optics. **Research Statement & Publications:** Laser science; surface science; dynamic properties at or near surfaces; nonlinear optical study techniques. **Mailing Address:** Physics Dept, Hong Kong Univ Sci & Technol Clearwater Bay, Kowloon Hong Kong, China. **Fax:** 852-358-1652. **E-Mail:** phloy@usthk.ust.hk

LOY, REBEKAH, NEURAL ANATOMY, DEVELOPMENT & PLASTICITY. **Personal Data:** b Berkeley, Calif, December 30, 1947; m 1978, c 4. **Education:** Univ Calif, Irvine, BS, 1971, PhD (psychobiol), 1975. **Professional Experience:** RES ASSOC PROF, DEPT NEUROL, UNIV ROCHESTER, as of 1999; sr scientist, Neurol, Univ Rochester, NY, 1991-1996; SCIENTIST, DEPT NEUROL & SURG, UNIV ROCHESTER, 1988-1991; assoc prof, dept Anat, 1983-1988; panel mem, Neurobiology Prog, Subpanel Integrative & Motor Processes, NSF, 1982-1984; prin investr, Nat Inst Neurol & Commun Dis & Stroke, 1978-; asst prof, Neuroscience, Univ Calif, San Diego, 1978-1983; fel, Univ Calif, San Diego, 1975-1978. **Memberships:** AAAS; Soc Neuroscience; Int Soc Develop Neuroscience; Am Asn Anatomists; Asn Neuroscience Dept & Prog. **Research Statement & Publications:** Neuronal reorganization in response to brain injury; sex differences in brain function, development and repair; control of synaptic specificity and plasticity in development, after injury and in response to chronic drug treatment; Alzheimer's disease. **Mailing Address:** Dept Neurol Sch Med & Dent Univ Rochester, 601 Elmwood Ave PO Box 673, Rochester, NY 14642. **Fax:** 585-760-6584. **E-Mail:** becky_loy@urmc.rochester.edu

LOY, ROBERT GRAVES, ANIMAL PHYSIOLOGY. **Personal Data:** b Prescott, Ariz, February 7, 1924; m 1951, c 5. **Education:** Ariz State Univ, BS, 1955; Univ Wis, MS, 1956, PhD, 1959. **Professional Experience:** PROF EMER VET SCI, UNIV KY, 1987-; consult, Equine Reproduction, 1987-; from assoc prof to prof, Univ KY, 1974-1987; agr consult, 1971-1974; from asst to assoc prof vet sci, Univ Ky, 1966-1971; asst prof animal husb, Univ Calif, Davis, 1959-1966; instr genetics, Univ Wis, 1956-1959. **Memberships:** Am Soc Animal Sci. **Research Statement & Publications:** Physiology and endocrinology of reproduction in horses. **Mailing Address:** Dept Vet Sci, Univ Ky, Lexington, KY 40506.

LOYALKA, SUDARSHAN KUMAR, NUCLEAR & MECHANICAL ENGINEERING. **Personal Data:** b Pilani, India, April 11, 1943; m Nirja; c Pranav, Prashant & Shashwat. **Education:** Univ Rajasthan, BEMech, 1964; Stanford Univ, MS, 1965, PhD (nuclear eng), 1967. **Professional Experience:** DIR PARTICULATE SYSTS RES CTR, as of 2005; PROF NUCLEAR ENG, UNIV MO-COLUMBIA, 1989-; CURATOR'S PROF & DIR PSRC, NUCLEAR SCI & ENG INST, UNIV MO, COLUMBIA, 1989-; PROF CHEM & MECH, NUCLEAR SCI & ENG INST, UNIV MO, COLUMBIA, 1989-; Huber O Croft chmn eng, Univ Mo-Columbia, 1983-; vis scientist, Max Planck Inst Aerodyn, Gottingen, 1969-1971; from asst prof to assoc prof, Dept Nuclear Eng, Univ Mo-columbia, 1967-1977. **Memberships:** Sigma Xi; fel Am Nuclear Soc; fel Am Phys Soc; Am Chem Soc. **Research Statement & Publications:** Kinetic theory of gases; neutron transport theory and reactor physics; nuclear reactor safety analysis; mechanics of aerosols. **Mailing Address:** Nuclear Sci & Eng Inst, Univ Mo, E1425C Engr Bldg E, Columbia, MO 65211. **E-Mail:** loyalkas@missouri.edu

LOYD, DAVID HERON, ATOMIC PHYSICS, NUCLEAR PHYSICS. **Personal Data:** b Shreveport, La, July 3, 1941; m 1960, c 2. **Education:** Univ Tex, Austin, BS, 1963, MS, 1964; Univ Wis-Madison, PhD (physics), 1970. **Professional Experience:** PROF PHYSICS, COL SCI, ANGELO STATE UNIV, as of 2003; DEAN COL SCI, ANGELO STATE UNIV, 1996-; asst prof physics, Angelo State Univ, 1969-1996. **Memberships:** Am Phys Soc. **Research Statement & Publications:** Atomic collisions. **Mailing Address:** Dept Physics, Col Sci, Angelo State Univ, 2601 W Ave N, San Angelo, TX 76909. **Fax:** 325-942-2038. **E-Mail:** david.loyd@angelo.edu

LOYNACHAN, THOMAS EUGENE, SOIL MICROBIOLOGY, SOIL FERTILITY. **Personal Data:** b Oskaloosa, Iowa, November 18, 1945; m 1967, Jean; c Mark, Timothy & Alan. **Education:** Iowa State Univ, BS, 1968, MS, 1972; NC State Univ, PhD (soil sci), 1975. **Honors & Awards:** National Association of Colleges and Teachers of Agriculture Teaching Fellow, 1989; National Association of Colleges and Teachers of Agriculture Tressler-AVI Award (teaching and research), 1989; National Association of Colleges and Teachers of Agriculture Ensminger-Interstate Distinguished Teacher Award, 1991; Soil Science Education Award, Soil Science Society of America, 1992; Fellow, American Society of Agronomy, 1993; American Society of Agronomy Agronomic Resident Education Award, 1996; Fellow, Soil Science Society of America, 2000. **Professional Experience:** PROF AGRON, IOWA STATE UNIV; PROF MICROBIOL, IOWA STATE UNIV; ASSOC CHMN & DIR GRAD EDU, DEPT AGRON, IOWA STATE UNIV; MEM TEACHING STAFF SOIL SCI, IOWA STATE UNIV, 1978-; MEM RES STAFF FIXATION & SOIL ECOL, IOWA STATE UNIV, 1978-PRESENT; ASST PROF, UNIV ALASKA, 1975-1978. **Memberships:** AAAS; Soil Sci Soc Am; Am Soc Agron; Coun Agr Sci & Technol. **Research Statement & Publications:** Nitrification inhibitors; oil degradation in Arctic soils; nitrogen fixation of legumes; mycorrhizae of soybean. **Mailing Address:** Dept Agron, Iowa State Univ, 1126H Agron, Ames, IA 50011-1010. **Fax:** 515-294-8146. **E-Mail:** teloynac@iastate.edu

LOZANO, EDGARDO A, BACTERIOLOGY. **Personal Data:** b Tampico, Mex, November 20, 1924; m 1949, c 3. **Education:** Univ Tex, BA, 1948; Univ Wis, MS, 1954; Mont State Univ, PhD (microbiol), 1965. **Professional Experience:** ASSOC PROF MICROBIOL, VET RES LAB, MONT STATE UNIV, 1980-; ASSOC PROF BACT, VET RES LAB, MONT STATE UNIV, 1968-; asst prof bact, Vet Res Lab, Mont State Univ, 1965-1968; dir bioprod, Philips Roxane Inc, 1963-1964; dept head prod & develop, Corn States Labs, 1955-1959; res, Am Sci Labs, 1954-1955; Bacteriologist vaccine prod, Agr Res Serv, 1948-1950. **Research Statement & Publications:** Bacteriological antigens and their purification; bacterial toxins; electrophoresis; telemetry of domestic animals. **Mailing Address:** 1924 Sourdough Rd, Bozeman, MT 59715.

LOZANO, GUILLERMINA, MEDICAL RESEARCH. **Education:** Rutgers Univ, PhD, 1986. **Professional Experience:** PROF, DEPT MOLECULAR GENETICS, UNIV TEX, M. D. ANDERSON CANCER CTR, as of 2005. **Mailing Address:** Dept Molecular Genetics MD Anderson Cancer Ctr, 1515 Holcombe Blvd, Houston, TX 77030-4009. **E-Mail:** gglozano@mdanderson.org

LOZERON, HOMER A, BIOCHEMISTRY. **Personal Data:** b Grande Prairie, Alta, July 24, 1934; m 1967, c 2. **Education:** Univ Alta, BS, 1956, MS, 1959; Univ Wash, PhD (biochem), 1964. **Professional Experience:** ASSOC PROF EMER BIOCHEM, SCH MED, ST LOUIS UNIV, as of 1997; assoc prof biochem, Sch Med, St Louis Univ, beginning 1977; asst prof, Sch Med, St Louis Univ, 1972-1977; instr, McArdle Lab Cancer Res, 1967-1972; proj assoc, McArdle Lab Cancer Res, 1965-1967. **Memberships:** Am Soc Biol Chemists; Am Soc Microbiol. **Research Statement & Publications:** RNA processing pathways and regulation of gene expression in bacterial virus systems. **Mailing Address:** Dept Biochem, St Louis Univ, 1402 S Grand Blvd, St Louis, MO 63104.

LOZIER, DANIEL WILLIAM, NUMERICAL ANALYSIS, MATHEMATICAL SOFTWARE. **Personal Data:** b Portland, Ore, April 10, 1941; m 1966, Elaine; c Daniel W Jr. **Education:** Ore State Univ, BA, math 1962; Am Univ, MA, math 1969; Univ Md, PhD (appl math), 1979. **Professional Experience:** RES MATHEMATICIAN, NAT INST STANDS & TECHNOL, as of 2006; MATHEMATICIAN, NAT BUR STAND, US DEPT COM, 1969-; mathematician, US Army Eng Res & Develop Lab, Ft Belvoir, Va, 1963-1969. **Memberships:** Soc mem Indust Appl Math; Asn mem Comput Mach; Mem Sigma Xi; Am Mem Math soc. **Research Statement & Publications:** Numerical analysis and mathematical software; computation of special functions; forward and backward recurrence methods; floating point and level-index computer arithmetic; numerical aspects of programming languages; vector and parallel computing. **Mailing Address:** Nat Inst Stands & Technol, 100 Bureau Dr Stop 8910, Gaithersburg, MD 20899-8910. **Fax:** 301-990-4127. **E-Mail:** dlozier@nist.gov

LOZZIO, CARMEN BERTUCCI, MEDICAL GENETICS, CELL BIOLOGY. **Personal Data:** b Buenos Aires, Arg, December 20, 1931; American citizen; m 1955, c 1. **Education:** Univ Buenos Aires, physician, 1955, MD, 1960. **Honors & Awards:** Honor Cert, World Cong Obstet & Gynec & Int Cong Internal Med, 1964. **Professional Experience:** Tenn Dept Ment Health, 1974- & Tenn Dept Pub Health, 1978-; PROF MED BIOL, CTR HEALTH SCI, 1978-; US Dept Health, Tenn Dept Human Serv, 1974-; assoc res prof med genetics, Ctr Health Sci, 1972-1978; US Dept Health, Educ & Welfare, 1970-1974; Am Cancer Soc, NIH, 1969-1971 & 1975-1981; Am Cancer Soc, Physicians Med Educ & Res Found, 1969-1970; DIR, BIRTH DEFECTS CTR, MEM RES CTR & HOSP, UNIV TENN, KNOXVILLE, 1966-; Am Cancer Soc, Nat Found-March Dimes, 1966-1980; Am Cancer Soc, Univ Tenn, Knoxville, 1966-1971; from res assoc to asst res prof, Ctr Health Sci, 1965-1972; Pan Am Union, Biol Div, Oak Ridge Nat Lab, 1964; grants, Arg Nat Res Coun, Univ Buenos Aires, 1961-1965; instr genetics, Univ Buenos Aires, 1960-1965; Arg Asn Prog Sci Millet fel & Arg Nat Res Coun fel radiation res, Rivadavia Hosp & Arg AEC, 1957-1960; Physician chg cytol, Rivadavia Hosp, Buenos Aires, 1956-1960. **Memberships:** Genetics Soc Am; Genetics Soc Can; Am Asn Ment Deficiency; Am Soc Human Genetics; NY Acad Sci; Sigma Xi. **Research Statement & Publications:** Studies on human genetics and cytogenetics; genetic counseling and prenatal diagnosis of hereditary disorders; experimental studies on cell culture of human diploid strains with genetic markers and the effect of antimetabolites on mammalian cell cultures. **Mailing Address:** 9709 Tunbridge Lane, Knoxville, TN 37922.

LU, ADOLPH, HIGH ENERGY PHYSICS, DARK MATTER SEARCH. **Personal Data:** b Chengtu, China, February 19, 1942; American citizen; m 1993, Karen. **Education:** Queen's Univ, BSc, 1964; Univ Toronto, MA, 1965; Univ Calif, Berkeley, PhD (physics), 1973. **Professional Experience:** PROF, UNIV CALIF, BERKELEY, as of 2003; RES PHYSICIST, COSMOLOGY GROUP, UNIV CALIF, BERKELEY, 2002-; res physicist high energy physics, Univ Calif, Santa Barbara, 1976-2002; researcher, Univ D'Orsay, Paris, 1973-1975. **Memberships:** Am Phys Soc. **Research Statement & Publications:** Bubble chamber physics; proton storage ring studies; photon cross sections; two photon physics; Z physics; B factory studies; dark matter physics. **Mailing Address:** Univ Calif, Berkeley, CA 94720. **E-Mail:** allu@slac.stanford.edu

LU, ANTHONY Y H, BIOCHEMISTRY. **Personal Data:** b Hupei, China, January 12, 1937; m 1965, c 1. **Education:** Nat Taiwan Univ, BS, 1958; Univ NC, Chapel Hill, PhD (biochem), 1966. **Honors & Awards:** Bernard Brodie Award Drug Metab, Am Soc Pharmacol & Exp Therapeut, 1996. **Professional Experience:** SCI ADV, QUALST INC, as of 2003; adj prof, Susan Lehman Cullman Lab Cancer Res, Dept Chem Biol, State Univ NJ, Rutgers, as of 2003; exec dir, Merck Labs, ending 1999; sr investr, Res Labs, Merck Sharp & Dohme Labs, beginning 1978; res fel, Res Div, Hoffmann-La Roche Inc, 1974-1978; sr biochemist, Res Div, Hoffmann-La Roche Inc, 1970-1974; fel inst sci & technol, Univ Mich, AnnArbor, 1966-1970. **Memberships:** AAAS; Am Chem Soc; Am Soc Pharmacol & Exp Therapeut; Am Soc Biol Chemists; NY Acad Sci. **Research Statement & Publications:** Basic research in biochemistry and biochemical pharmacology. **Mailing Address:** Qualyst Inc, PO Box 12199, Research Triangle Park, NC 27709. **Fax:** 919-313-0163.

LU, BENJAMIN C(HIH) Y(EU), CHEMICAL ENGINEERING. **Personal Data:** b Peking, China, October 20, 1926; Canadian citizen; m Katherine; c Calvin, Joyce & John. **Education:** Nat Cent Univ, China, BASc, 1947; Univ Toronto, MASc, 1951, PhD (chem eng), 1954. **Honorary Degrees:** DSc, Queens Univ, Kingston, Can, 1993. **Honors & Awards:** R S Jane Mem lectr, Can Soc Chem Engrs, 1990. **Professional Experience:** HON CHAIR CHEM ENG, UNIV OTTAWA, 1992-; EMER PROF, UNIV OTTAWA, 1992-; hon prof Inner Mongolia Eng Col, China, 1992; assoced, Can J Chem Eng, 1990-1996; vis prof, Nihon Univ, Japan, 1990; hon prof, Nanjing Inst Chem Technol, China, 1985; hon prof, Beijing Inst Chem Technol, China, 1982; mem, Hazardous Prod Bd Rev, Can Govt, 1980-1982; UNESCO consult, Univ Zulia, Venezuela, 1978; exchange scientist, Japan Soc for Prom Sci, 1977; vis prof, Univ Pittsburgh, 1976; exchange scientist, Inst Chem Process Fundamentals, Czech Acad Sci, 1975; vdean eng, Fac Sci & Eng, 1969-1976; Mem, Grant Selection Comt, Nat Res Coun Can, 1969-1972 & Nat Comt Deans Eng & Appl Sci, 1969-1976; prof chem eng, Univ Ottawa, 1962-1992; chmn dept, Univ Ottawa, 1961-1976; actg chmn dept, Univ Ottawa, 1960; from asst prof to assoc prof, Univ Ottawa, 1956-1962; lectr, Univ Toronto, 1955-1956; res assoc, Ont Res Found, Can, 1954-1955; Asst engr, Chinese Petrol Corp, China, 1947-1950. **Memberships:** Fel Chem Inst Can; Can Soc Chem Engrs; Fel Eng Inst Can. **Research Statement & Publications:** Phase equilibria; thermodynamic properties of solutions; cryogenic research; energy engineering; supercritical fluid extraction; equations of state; interfacial properties. **Mailing Address:** Dept Chem Eng, Univ Ottawa, Ottawa, ON K1N 6N5, Can. **Fax:** 613-562-5172. **E-Mail:** lu@eng.uottawa.ca

LU, BENJAMIN CHI-KO, GENETICS, CELL BIOLOGY. **Personal Data:** b Changchow, China, March 9, 1932; m 1962, Jennie Huang; c Albert & Andrew. **Education:** Taiwan Univ, BS, 1955; Univ Alta, MS, 1962, PhD (bot, genetics), 1965. **Professional Experience:** Mem grant comt (cell biol & genetics), Nat Sci & Eng Res Coun Can, 1985-1988; Univ NC, Chapel Hill, 1983-1984; PROF GENETICS, UNIV GUELPH, 1979-; Natural Sci & Eng Res Coun, Can grant, 1979-; res assoc, Univ Calif, Berkeley, 1973-1974; Nat Res Coun grant, 1968-1978; from asst prof to assoc prof, Univ Guelph, 1967-1979; res grant, Rask-Orsted Found fel & Carlsberg Found grant, 1966-1967; vis fel, Copenhagen Univ, 1966; Nat Res Coun Can overseas fel, 1965-1967; fel fungal genetics, Cambridge Univ, 1965-1967; Instr bot, Taiwan Univ, 1958-1960. **Memberships:** Genetics Soc Can. **Research Statement & Publications:** Meiosis-specific nucleases; cellular programs in meiosis; genetic recombination; synaptonemal complex; light/dark cycle and control of meiosis. **Mailing Address:** Dept Molecular Biol & Genetics, Univ Guelph, Guelph, ON N1G 2W1, Can. **Fax:** 519-837-2075. **E-Mail:** blu@uoguelph.ca

LU, CHENG-YOUN, MATHEMATICS. **Education:** Univ Sci & Technol, Beijing, China, 1982; Stevens Inst Technol, NJ, ME, 1985, PhD, 1991. **Professional Experience:** ADVAN TV LAB, MITSUBISHI ELECTRIC INFO TECHNOL CTR AM INC, 1997-. **Mailing Address:** Mitsubishi Electric Info Technol Ctr Am Inc, 55 Carlston Terr, Cresskill, NJ 07626. **Fax:** 714-229-3854.

LU, CHRISTOPHER D, RUMINANT NUTRITION, INTERNATIONAL AFFAIR. **Personal Data:** b Taipei, Taiwan, China, August 30, 1951; American citizen; c 1. **Education:** Nat Taiwan Univ, BS, 1974; Univ Wis-Madison, MS, 1978, PhD (dairy sci & biochem), 1981. **Professional Experience:** DEAN, COL AGR, SULTON QABOOS UNIV, 1993-; prof & dep dean, Col Agr, Sulton Qaboos Univ, 1992-1993; mem, Mgt Award Comt, Am Soc Animal Sci, 1990-1991; trustee, Bd Southeast Consort Int Develop, 1989-1991; prof & dir, Am Inst Goat Res, 1985-1989 & Int Prog, Langston Univ, 1989-1991; chairperson, Livestock Comt Goats, Am Soc Animal Sci, 1989-1990; Prin rep, Div Int Affairs, Nat Asn State Univs & Land Grant Cols, 1988-1991; res scientist ruminant nutrit, Prairie View A&M Univ, 1982-1985; scientist biochem & nutrit, Int Harvester Co, 1982; from res asst to res assoc ruminant nutrit, Univ Wis-Madison, 1978-1982; hon prof, Independent Univ Azctecas, Mex, Northwestern Agr Univ, China & Independent Univ Nuevo Leon, Mex; ed-in-chief, Sultan Qaboos Univ, Sci Res Agr Sci. **Memberships:** Am Dairy Sci Asn; Am Inst Nutrit; Nutrit Soc UK; Am Soc Animal Sci; Qsn Dirs Int Progs; Int Good Asn (vpres, 1996-). **Research Statement & Publications:** Nutrient requirements for lactation, growth, pregnancy and fiber production in goats; energy and protein utilization; ruminant nutrition; metabolism and physiology. **Mailing Address:** Col Agr, Sultan Qaboos Univ PO Box 34 Al-khod 123, Muscat, Oman. **Fax:** 968513366. **E-Mail:** chrislu@sou.edu

LU, FRANK CHAO, PHARMACOLOGY, SCIENCE COMMUNICATION. **Personal Data:** b Hupeh, China, March 9, 1915. **Education:** Cheeloo Univ, MD, 1939. **Honors & Awards:** Int Achievement Award, Int Soc Regulatory Toxicol, 1987. **Professional Experience:** Vis prof toxicol, Shanghai Med Univ, 1985; lectr, Joint China-WHO Toxicol Course, 1982; CONSULT TOXICOL, 1979-; clin prof pharmacol, Sch Med, Univ Miami, 1977-1979; chief food additives, WHO, 1965-1976; head, Pharmacol & Toxicol Sect, 1960-1965; spec lectr toxicol, Univ Toronoto, 1959-1962; spec lectr pharmacol, Univ Ottawa, 1959-1962; pharmacologist, Food & Drug Labs, Can Dept Nat Health & Welfare, 1951-1960; med res fel pharmacol, McGill Univ, 1948-1951; Res fel exp surg, McGill Univ, 1947-1948; lectr, Cheeloo Univ, 1945-1947; lectr, WChina Union Univ, 1944-1945; sr asst pharmacol, Cheeloo Univ, 1942-1944; Assoc ed, Coun Pub, Chinese Med Asn, 1940-1942; managing ed, Biomed & Environ Sci, Acad Press, Inc; hon prof, Chinese Acad Med Sci, Chinese Acad Prev Med, Shanghai Med Univ, Peking Union Med Col. **Memberships:** Am Col Toxicol; Am Soc Pharmacol & Exp Therapeut; Soc Toxicol; Europ Soc Toxicol; Can Pharmacol Soc; Int Acad Environ Safety; Int Soc Regulatory Toxicol. **Research Statement & Publications:** physiology and pharmacology of coronary circulation; bioassay of drugs; cardiac glycosides; blood dyscrasias; toxicology of drugs, food additives, pesticides and contaminants; principles and procedures for toxicological evaluation of chemicals; assessment of the safety of chemicals, on the basis of toxicological data, by the use of the acceptable daily intake approach. **Mailing Address:** 7452 SW 143rd Ave, Miami, FL 33183. **Fax:** 305-385-1350. **E-Mail:** franklu@webtv.net

LU, FRANK KERPING, AERODYNAMICS & GAS DYNAMICS, EXPERIMENTAL TECHNIQUES. **Personal Data:** b Taipei, Taiwan, October 17, 1954; American citizen; m 1983, Jean; c Richard. **Education:** Cambridge Univ, BA, 1976; Princeton Univ, MSE, 1983; Pa State Univ, PhD (mech eng), 1988. **Honorary Degrees:** MA, Cambridge Univ, 1980. **Professional Experience:** PROF AEROSPACE ENG, UNIV TEX, ARLINGTON, as of 2006; Office Naval Res, beginning 1997; MSE, Inc, Butte, Montana, beginning 1995; prin investr, Tex Advan Res Prog, 1994-1996; co-prin investr, NASA, beginning 1993; dir, Aerodynamics Res Ctr, beginning 1993; assoc prof Aerospace Eng, Univ Tex, Arlington, beginning 1993; prin investr, NASA, 1988-1992; asst prof, Aerodynamics Res Ctr, 1987-1993; res asst, Pa State Univ, 1984-1987; proj engr, ICOS Corp Am, 1982-1983; res asst, Princeton Univ, 1979-1982; admin asst, Singapore Civil Serv, 1979; Eng Officer, Singapore Armed Forces, 1976-1979; lectr, Launchspace, Inc, Falls Church, Va. **Memberships:** Am Inst Aeronaut & Astronaut; Am Soc Mech Engrs; Am Phys Soc; Sigma Xi; Am Soc Eng Educ; Am Helicopter Soc. **Research Statement & Publications:** Experimental supersonic and hypersonic aerodynamics; gas dynamics; turbomachinery and internal flows; unsteady flows and flow-induced vibrations; turbulence. **Mailing Address:** Mech & Aerospace Eng Dept, Univ Tex, Arlington, TX 76019. **Fax:** 817-272-5010. **E-Mail:** franklu@UTA.EDU

LU, FREDERICK MING, MOLECULAR BIOLOGY, MEMBRANE SKELETON PROTEINS. **Personal Data:** b Hing Sua, China, March 29, 1960. **Education:** Quingdao Univ, China, BA; Univ Calif, Santa Barbara, PhD (molecular biol), 1990. **Professional Experience:** RES ASSOC, DEPT HEMAT & ONCOL, CHILDRENS HOSP, BOSTON, 1992-. **Memberships:** Am Soc Cell Biol; AAAS. **Research Statement & Publications:** Molecular biology; membrane skeleton proteins. **Mailing Address:** Dept Hemat & Oncol, Childrens Hosp 300 Longwood Ave, Boston, MA 02115.

LU, GRANT, DIAMOND FILM, OPTICAL FIBERS. **Personal Data:** b Ottawa, Ont, May 9, 1956; American citizen. **Education:** Univ Manchester, Eng, BSc, 1976; Rutgers Univ, MS, 1980, PhD (ceramic eng), 1983. **Honors & Awards:** Mat Res Soc Award, 1981. **Professional Experience:** RES MGR, DIAMOND FILM DIV, NORTON CO, NORTHBOROUGH, MASS, 1994-; sr res engr, Norton CO, Northborough, Mass, 1988-1993; Ed, Am Ceramic Soc, 1985-1987; Mat scientist, Naval Res Lab, Wash, DC, 1983-1988. **Memberships:** Am Ceramic Soc; Int Soc Optical Eng. **Research Statement & Publications:** Thermal and optical applications of diamond film. **Mailing Address:** Diamond Film Div, Norton Co, Northborough, MA 01532.

LU, GUANGQUAN, SPECTROSCOPIC MEASUREMENTS OF CHEMICAL REACTIONS ON SOLID SURFACES, DYNAMICS OF SURFACE PROCESSES DURING THERMAL & PHOTO CHEMICAL VAPOR DEPOSITION OF SEMICONDUCTOR MATERIALS. **Education:** Shandong Univ, China, BS, 1985; Univ Calif, San Diego, MS, 1988, PhD (chem), 1992. **Professional Experience:** RES ASSOC, SURFACE SCI CTR, UNIV PITTSBURGH, 1992-. **Memberships:** Am Chem Soc; Mat Res Soc. **Research Statement & Publications:** Characterizations of the fundamental processes during silicon and germanium chemical vapor depositions; photodestruction of environmentally harmful organic compounds on wide-band semiconductor oxide surfaces. **Mailing Address:** 5533 Fifth Ave No 4, Pittsburgh, PA 15232. **Fax:** 412-624-6003. **E-Mail:** gqlu@vms.cis.pitt.edu

LU, GUO-WEI, SPINAL PROJECTION NEURONS, PLASTICITY OF CENTRAL NERVOUS SYSTEM. **Personal Data:** b Gaixian, China, February 10, 1932; m 1957, c 2. **Education:** China Med Univ, MD, 1955. **Professional Experience:** Vis prof neurol, Univ Wis-Madison, 1987-1988; PROF NEUROBIOL, CHMN DEPT & DIR, INST EXP MED, CAPITAL INST MED, 1983-; int res fel neurosci, Fogarty Int Ctr, NIH, 1980-1982; assoc prof neurophysiol & chmn dept, Chmn Dept & Dir, Inst Exp Med, Capital Inst Med, 1972-1980; asst prof physiol, Chmn Dept & Dir, Inst Exp Med, Capital Inst Med, 1960-1972; Asst prof pathophysiol, Beijing Med Univ, 1955-1960. **Memberships:** Am Physiol Soc; Soc Neurosci; Int Asn Study Pain; Int Brain Res Orgn. **Research Statement & Publications:** Pain physiology and antinociception; anatomico-physiological basis of acupuncture; singly and doubly projecting spinal systems; spinal injuries and stroke; developmental neurobiol of spinal cord and brain; adaptation to and plasticity of hypoxia and pain. **Mailing Address:** Dept Neurobiol Inst Exp Med, Capital Inst Med You An Men St, Beijing 100054, China.

LU, HSIENG S, PROTEIN STRUCTURE. **Personal Data:** b Taiwan, China, July 28, 1947. **Education:** Nat Taiwan Univ, BS, 1970, MS, 1975; NTex State Univ, PhD (biochem), 1981. **Professional Experience:** SR RES SCIENTIST PROTEIN STRUCT, AMGEN, 1988-; res scientist, Protein Develop & Microsequencing Group, 1984-1988; res asst prof, Dept Chem, 1983-1984; Robert A Welch Found fel, 1982-1983; teaching asst biochem, Inst Biochem Sci, Nat Taiwan Univ, Taipei, 1972-1976; Res asst, Pharmacol & Microbiol Group, Panlabs, Inc, Taipei, 1970-1972. **Memberships:** Am Soc Biochem & Molecular Biol; Protein Soc; AAAS. **Research Statement & Publications:** Protein therapeutics; exploration and initial characterization of new therapeutic proteins; protein recovery process and structure-function studies; development of protein analytical methods, QC tests; extensive characterization of therapeutic proteins. **Mailing Address:** Dept Protein Struct, Amgen Inc, Amgen Ctr, Thousand Oaks, CA 91320-1789. **Fax:** 805-499-7464.

LU, HUA, EXPERIMENTAL MECHANICS, PHOTO-MECHANICS. **Personal Data:** m 1971, Guiping; c Yisha. **Education:** Tianjin Univ, BS, 1968, MS, 1982; State Univ NY, Stony Brook, PhD (mech eng), 1989. **Professional Experience:** PROF MECH ENG, RYERSON UNIV, 1995-; vis researcher, Res Div, Ont Hydro, 1990-1992; from asst prof to assoc prof, Ryerson Polytech Univ, 1989-1994; lectr, Tianjin Univ, China, 1978-1982; engr, GCM Inc, China, 1969-1977. **Memberships:** Soc Exp Mech; Soc Photo-Instrumentation Engrs. **Research Statement & Publications:** Research and development of methods in experimental solid mechanics; applications of experimental methods in micro-mechanics; composite mechanics; interfacial mechanics; structure and stress analysis in mechanical engineering and electronic packaging engineering. **Mailing Address:** Dept Mech Eng, Ryerson Univ, 350 Victoria St, Toronto, ON M5B 2K3, Can. **Fax:** 416-979-5265. **E-Mail:** hlu@acs.ryerson.ca

LU, JIANDONG, MATHEMATICS. **Education:** Va Commonwealth Univ, PhD, 1994. **Professional Experience:** ADJ ASST PROF RADIATION, JEFFERSON MED COL, as of 2001. **Mailing Address:** Jefferson Med Col, 1025 Walnut St Suite 100, Philadelphia, PA 19107. **Fax:** 215-955-6000.

LU, JOHN KUEW-HSIUNG, ENDOCRINOLOGY & NEUROENDOCRINOLOGY, REPRODUCTIVE PHYSIOLOGY. **Personal Data:** b Miaoli, Taiwan, China, September 16, 1937; American citizen; m 1969, Marianne; c Judith Maria & John Lawrence. **Education:** Nat Taiwan Normal Univ, BSc, 1961; Nat Taiwan Univ, MSc, 1967; Mich State Univ, PhD (physiol), 1972. **Professional Experience:** PROF OBSTET, GYNEC & ANAT, CELL BIOL, UNIV CALIF, LOS ANGELES, 1988-as of today; health reviewers res, NIH, 1994-1998; mem biochem Endocrinol Study Sect, NIH, 1989-1994; prin investr res grants, Nat Inst Aging, 1980-1991 & 1984-1997; from asst prof to assoc prof, Gynec & Anat, Cell Biol, Univ Calif, Los Angeles, 1977-1988; asst prof endocrinol, Univ Calif, San Diego, 1975-1977; res assoc, Mich State Univ, 1974-1975; postdoctoral fel reproductive endocrinol, Univ Pittsburgh, 1972-1974; teaching asst biol, Mich State Univ, 1968-1972; res asst endocrinol, Purdue Univ, 1967-1968; res asst physiol, Nat Taiwan Univ, 1965-1967; instr biol, Nat Taiwan Normal Univ, 1963-1965; Teacher biol, Hsinchu Sr High Sch, Taiwan, 1961-1962. **Memberships:** Soc Gynec Invest; Am Physiol Soc; NY Acad Sci; Endocrine Soc; Soc Study Reproduction; Sigma Xi; Soc Exp Biol & Med. **Research Statement & Publications:** Animal studies and laboratory investigations to reveal the interactions between ovarian and neuroendocrine functions during reproductive senescence and neuroendocrine aging. **Mailing Address:** Ctr Health Sci, Sch Med, Univ Calif, 10833 Le Conte Ave Rm 22-177, Los Angeles, CA 90095-1740. **Fax:** 310-206-6531. **E-Mail:** jlu@obgyn.medsch.ucla.edu

LU, KEWANG, BIOMATERIALS, DENTAL MATERIALS. **Personal Data:** m May; c Zan Mei, David Luk & Dazhi Lu. **Education:** WChina Univ Med Sci, MDent, 1981. **Professional Experience:** SR RES CHEMIST, DENTSPLY INT, 1993-; res chemist, Denisply Int, 1989-1993; assoc prof, Kumming Med Col, 1982-1989. **Memberships:** Int Asn Dental Res. **Research Statement & Publications:** Develop new dental materials especially bicompatible resin reinforced glass ionomes materials and atraumatic restorative technique materials sponsored by World Health Organization. **Mailing Address:** Caulk L D Div Dentsply Int Inc, 38 W Clarke Ave, Milford, DE 19963.

LU, LE-WU, STRUCTURAL ENGINEERING. **Personal Data:** b Shanghai, China, June 5, 1933; m 1963, c 2. **Education:** Nat Taiwan Univ, BS, 1954; Iowa State Univ, MS, 1956; Lehigh Univ, PhD (civil eng), 1960. **Honors & Awards:** Leon Moisseiff Award, Am Soc Civil Engrs, 1967. **Professional Experience:** PROF EMER CIVIL ENG, LEHIGH UNIV, as of 2005; hon prof, Harbin Civil Eng Inst, 1980; USSR Fulbright-Hays lectureship, Int Coun Exchange Scholars, 1975; prof civil eng, Lehigh Univ, beginning 1969; assoc prof, Lehigh Univ, 1967-1969; res assoc prof, Lehigh Univ, 1965-1967; res asst prof, Lehigh Univ, 1961-1965; res assoc, Lehigh Univ, 1959-1961; res asst civil eng, Lehigh Univ, 1958-1959. **Memberships:** Assoc Am Soc Civil Engrs; Am Concrete Inst; Int Asn Bridge & Struct Engrs; Am Soc Eng Educ; Earthquake Eng Res Inst; Int Asn Struct Safety & Reliability. **Research Statement & Publications:** Behavior of building frames and their components in the elastic and inelastic range; planning and design of tall buildings; response of steel and reinforced concrete building structures to earthquake ground motion. **Mailing Address:** Dept Civil Eng, Lehigh Univ, 13 E Packer Ave Rm A110, Bethlehem, PA 18015-3044. **E-Mail:** lwl0@lehigh.edu

LU, MARY KWANG-RUEY CHAO, ORGANIC CHEMISTRY, MATHEMATICS. **Personal Data:** b Liao-Ning, China, September 6, 1935; American citizen; m 1961, c 2. **Education:** Notre Dame Col, Ohio, BS, 1959; Univ Detroit, MS, 1961; Univ Tenn, Knoxville, PhD (org chem), 1968. **Professional Experience:** PROF CHEM, WALTERS STATE COMMUNITY COL, MORRISTOWN, TENN, 1978-; prof chem & math, Lincoln Mem Univ, 1968-1978; asst prof chem, Morris Col, SC, 1963-1964; chemist, US Testing Co, Inc, 1961-1963; Technician, Chem Lab, NY Hosp, New York, 1959; US Dept Energy res grant. **Memberships:** AAAS; Am Chem Soc. **Research Statement & Publications:** Organometallic chemistry; silicon solar cells. **Mailing Address:** Div Natural Sci, Walters State Comm Col, 500 S Davey Crockett, Morristown, TN 37813. **E-Mail:** mary.lu@wscc.cc.tn.us

LU, MATTHIAS CHI-HWA, PHARMACY, MEDICINAL CHEMISTRY. **Personal Data:** b Fukien, China, January 3, 1940; American citizen; m 1966, Mei; c Daniel & Kathleen. **Education:** Kaohsiung Med Col, Taiwan, BSc, 1963; Ohio State Univ, PhD (med chem), 1969. **Professional Experience:** PROF MED CHEM, COL PHARM, UNIV ILL, CHICAGO, 1996-; ASST HEAD CURRIC AFFAIRS, COL PHARM, UNIV ILL, CHICAGO, 1995-; alt dir grad studies med chem, Grad Col Univ Ill, Chicago, 1994-; coordr curric affairs, Col Pharm, Univ Ill, Chicago, 1992-1995; adj prof, Sch Pharm & Sch Chem, 1990-; vis assoc prof, Grad Inst Pharmaceut Sci, Kaohsiung Col, Kaohsiung, Taiwan, 1990; assoc prof, Col Pharm, Univ Ill, Chicago, 1978-1996; asst prof med chem, Col Pharm, Univ Ill, Chicago, 1973-1978; asst prof, Col Pharm, Univ Mich, Ann Arbor, 1972-1973; instr, Col Pharm, Univ Mich, Ann Arbor, 1971-1972; res assoc, Col Pharm, Univ Mich, Ann Arbor, 1969-1971; res asst med chem, Ohio State Univ, 1967-1969 & Univ Iowa, 1964-1967. **Memberships:** Am Chem Soc; NAm Taiwanese Prof Asn; Am Asn Cols Pharm. **Research Statement & Publications:** Steroidogenesis and metabolisms; drug design; site-directed, endocrine-selective design of antitumor agents; molecular structures as probes for cholinergic receptors; stereochemistry. **Mailing Address:** Dept Med Chem, Col Pharm, Univ Ill-Chicago, Rm 545 Pharm Bldg 833 S Wood, Chicago, IL 60612-7231. **Fax:** 312-996-7107. **E-Mail:** mattlu@uic.edu

LU, NANCY CHAO, NUTRITION, NUTRITION METABOLISM. **Personal Data:** b Sian, China, May 29, 1941; American citizen; m 1966, K; c Richard. **Education:** Nat Taiwan Univ, Taipei, Taiwan, BS, 1963; Univ Wyoming, Laramie, MS, 1965; Univ Calif, Berkeley, PhD (nutrit), 1973. **Honors & Awards:** Ellsworth Dougherty Award, 1976. **Professional Experience:** DIR DIETETIC PROF DIETIETICS, as of 2004; PROF NEMATODE NUTRIT & NUTRIT METAB, DEPT NUTRIT & FOOD SCI, SAN JOSE STATE UNIV, CALIF, 1987-; assoc prof, Dept Nutrit & Food Sci, San Jose State Univ, Calif, 1982-1987; lectr nutrit & metab, Dept Nutrit & Food Sci, San Jose State Univ, Calif, 1980-1982; teaching assoc, Dept Nutrit Sci, Univ Calif, Berkeley, 1979-1980; NIH fel, res assoc & proj coordr NIH nematode grant, 1978-1980; res assoc, Dept Nutrit Sci, Univ Calif, Berkeley, 1976-1978; fel, Dept Nutrit Sci, Univ Calif, Berkeley, 1975-1976; NIH fel, Dept Nutrit Sci, Univ Calif, Berkeley, 1973-1975; res biochemist cardiovasc res, Mt Zion Hosp, San Francisco, Calif, 1966-1968; res biochemist metab res, Highland Hosp, Oakland, Calif, 1965-1966. **Memberships:** Am Inst Nutrit; Am Dietetic Asn; Inst Food Technologist; Soc Exp Biol & Med; Soc Nematol; Sigma Xi; Chinese Am Dietetic Asn. **Research Statement & Publications:** Developing nematodes as a model for food and nutritional research; nutrient requirement and metabolism of vitamins, minerals and growth factors of nematodes; nematode as a screening organism for testing food additives; food toxins. **Mailing Address:** Dept Nutrit & Food Sci, San Jose State Univ, CCB 106, San Jose, CA 95192. **Fax:** 408-924-3114. **E-Mail:** nlu@email.sjsu.edu

LU, PAU-CHANG, MECHANICAL ENGINEERING, AEROSPACE SCIENCE. **Personal Data:** b Kiangsu, China, April 11, 1930; m 1963. **Education:** Nat Taiwan Univ, BS, 1954; Kans State Univ, MS, 1959; Case Western Res Univ, PhD, 1963. **Professional Experience:** EMERITUS, UNIV NEBR, LINCOLN, as of 2002; RETIRED; PROF MECH ENG, UNIV NEBR, LINCOLN, 1972-; assoc prof, Univ Nebr, Lincoln, 1968-1972; asst prof, Kans State Univ, 1957-1959 & Case Western Res Univ, 1963-1968; res assoc, Kans State Univ, 1957-1959 & Case Western Res Univ, 1962-1963; asst eng, Kans State Univ, 1957-1959 & Case Western Res Univ, 1959-1962; asst eng, Cheng Kung Univ, Taiwan, 1956-1957; mech engr, Taiwan Power Co, 1954-1956. **Memberships:** Am Soc Mech Engrs. **Research Statement & Publications:** Viscous flow; magneto-fluid-mechanics; heat exchangers; free convection; integral transforms and other branches of applied mathematics. **Mailing Address:** Mech Eng 255 WSE, Univ Nebr Lincoln PO Box 880656, Lincoln, NE 68588-0656. **E-Mail:** plu2@unl.edu

LU, PHILLIP KEHWA, ASTRONOMY, PHYSICS. **Personal Data:** b Anhui, China, October 11, 1932; m 1959, c 3. **Education:** Maritime Col, Taiwan, BS, 1960; Welsleyan Univ, MA, 1965; Columbia Univ, MPhil, PhD (astron & sci educ), 1970. **Professional Experience:** PROF, DEPT ASTRON, YALE UNIV, as of 2001; carnegie-Mellon fel astron, Yale Univ, 1983-; distinguished prof astron, Western Conn State Univ, beginning 1981; assoc prof astron, Western Conn State Univ, 1977-1981; sci educ scholar, NSF, 1974-1975; consult, Bd Educ, NY, 1974-1975; chem dept, Western Conn State Univ, 1973-1974; asst prof earth & space sci, Western Conn State Univ, 1970-1977; res assoc astron observ, Yale Univ, 1967-1970; instr comput sci, Jefferson Prof Inst, 1965-1967; math analyst inst math, Chinese Acad Sci, 1960-1963; vis prof & consult, Nat Cent Univ, Taiwan. **Memberships:** Fel Royal Astron Soc; Am Astron Soc; Am Phys Soc; Sigma Xi. **Research Statement & Publications:** Primodial helium and stellar chemical abundance of halo and high velocity stars using speckle interferometry; missing mass problem of Milky Way Galaxy using stellar kinematics of faint F-stars to one kiloparsec; photometry and spectroscopy. **Mailing Address:** Dept Astron, Yale Univ, PO Box 208101, New Haven, CT 06520. **E-Mail:** lu@astro.yale.edu

LU, PONZY, MOLECULAR BIOLOGY. **Personal Data:** b Shanghai, China, October 7, 1942; American citizen. **Education:** Calif Inst Technol, BS, 1964; Mass Inst Technol, PhD (biophys), 1970. **Professional Experience:** Med sci study sect, NIH, 1992-1996; Univ Space Res Asn, NASA biotechnol discipline working group, 1986-1991; Biophys chem study sect, NIH, 1982-1986; PROF CHEM, UNIV PA, 1973-; Europ Molecular Biol Orgn fel genetics, Univ Geneva, 1973; Arthritis Found fel biophys, Max Planck Inst Biophys Chem, 1970-1973. **Memberships:** AAAS; Biophys Soc; Sigma Xi; Am Soc Biol Chemists. **Research Statement & Publications:** Molecular components involved in the regulation of gene expression. **Mailing Address:** Dept Chem, Univ Pa, Philadelphia, PA 19104. **E-Mail:** PONZY@SAS.UPENN.EDU

LU, RENNE CHEN, PROTEIN STRUCTURE, CHEMICAL MODIFICATION. **Personal Data:** b China, February 13, 1944; m 1971, c 2. **Education:** Univ Calif, San Diego, PhD (biochem), 1970; Nat Taiwan Univ, BS, 1966. **Professional Experience:** SR SCIENTIST, BOSTON BIOMED RES INST, as of 2004; RES ASSOC, HARVARD MED SCH, as of 2004; prin staff scientist, Boston Biomed Res Inst, beginning 1971. **Memberships:** Am Soc Biochem & Molecular Biol; Am Soc Cell Biol; Biophys Soc; Protein Soc. **Research Statement & Publications:** Myosin V attachment to cargo requires the tight association of two functional subdomains; Two distinct myosin light chain structures are induced by specific variations within the bound IQ motifs-functional implications; author of various articles. **Mailing Address:** Boston Biomed Res Inst, 64 Grove St, Watertown, MA 02472. **E-Mail:** lu@bbri.org

LU, RUNDE, OPEN ARCHITECTED SOFTWARE DEVELOPMENT ENVIRONMENT DESIGN FOR INDUSTRIAL AUTOMATION, INDUSTRIAL AUTOMATION. **Personal Data:** m 1979, Boqiu; c Bo & Maxwell Ray. **Education:** China Univ Mining & Technol, BS, 1977; Bradford Univ, MS, 1981, PhD (control eng), 1983. **Honors & Awards:** Outstanding Young Scientist Award, Hedley Pac Mining Found, 1989; Second Grade Sci & Technol Award, Chinese Govt, 1990. **Professional Experience:** CHIEF ARCHITECT & CHIEF ENG, INTELLUTION INC, 1993-; asst prof res, WVa Univ, 1990-1991; prof automation, China Univ Mining & Technol, 1985-1990. **Research Statement & Publications:** Pioneered soft logic in industrial automation; designed and fully implemented an open architectured software development system. **Mailing Address:** 6417 Woodsbriar Ct, Lisle, IL 60532. **Fax:** 630-357-9394. **E-Mail:** runde@wisdom.com

LU, SHIH-LAI, ORGANIC CHEMISTRY, POLYMER CHEMISTRY. **Personal Data:** b Fukien, China, November 1, 1946; m 1984, Pearl; c 2. **Education:** Fu Jen Univ, BS, 1968; Wright State Univ, MS, 1971; Iowa State Univ, PhD (org chem), 1975. **Professional Experience:** SCIENTIST, 3M CO, as of 2005; SR RES SPECIALIST, 3M CO, 1978-; Res assoc acad res, Iowa State Univ, 1975-1976 & Univ Chicago, 1977-1978. **Memberships:** Am Chem Soc. **Research Statement & Publications:** Synthesis and thermoxidative degradation studies of polymers; mechanistic studies of organic reactions involving carbonium, radical and carbanion intermediates; total synthesis of natural products; polymer characterization; adhesives; radiation curable systems; microreplication; electronic imaging. **Mailing Address:** 3M Co, St Paul, MN 55144-1000. **Fax:** 651-737-3061.

LU, TOH-MING, CONDENSED MATTER PHYSICS. **Personal Data:** b Sibu, Malaysia, June 28, 1943; m 1978, Gwo-Ching; c Victor Lu. **Education:** Cheng Kung Univ, BS, 1968; Worchester Polytech Inst, 1971; Univ Wis-Madison, PhD (physics), 1976. **Honors & Awards:** William H Wiley Distinguished Faculty Award, Rensselaer, 2004; Mat Res Soc Medal Award, 2005. **Professional Experience:** 1999-2005: Director, SRC Center for Advanced Interconnect System and Technology (13 universities, 25 faculty, and 40 graduate students); Associate Director: 1996-1999, Rensselaer 1997- :Associate Director for R&D, Center for Integrated Electronics (CIE), Rensselaer 1992-1997: Chairman, Dept. of Physics, Applied Physics, and Astronomy, Rensselaer 1982- Assistant Professor: 1982-1986; Associate Professor: 1986-1989; Full professor: 1989-, Dept. of Physics, Rensselaer 1979-1982: Research Associate, Materials Science, University of Wisconsin, Madison 1978-1979: Guest Scientist, National Bureau of Standards, Washington, DC 1977-1978: Physics and Math Teacher, Catholic High School, Sibu Malaysia. **Memberships:** Am Phys Soc; Am Vac Soc; Mat Res Soc. **Research Statement & Publications:** Surface, interface, and thin film morphological ordering and roughening; Growth and characterization of metal, ceramic, and polymeric thin films for microelectronics and photonics applications. **Mailing Address:** Dept Physics, Rensselaer Polytech Inst, Troy, NY 12180. **Fax:** 518-276-6680. **E-Mail:** lut@rpi.edu

LU, WEI-KAO, METALLURGY, PHYSICAL CHEMISTRY. **Personal Data:** b Kiangsu, China, April 6, 1933; m 1964. **Education:** Cheng Kung Univ, Taiwan, BS, 1957; Univ Minn, PhD (metall), 1964. **Professional Experience:** PROF EMER, MAT SCI ENG, MCMASTER UNIV, as of 2004; Stelco prof Metall, Mcmaster Univ, 1973-; from asst prof to assoc prof metall, Mcmaster Univ, 1965-1973; Fel, Univ Minn, 1964-1965. **Memberships:**

Am Inst Mining Metall & Petrol Engrs; Iron & Steel Inst Japan; Can Inst Mining & Metall. **Research Statement & Publications:** Theoretical and experimental study of chemical kinetics of gas-solid and slag-metal reactions; heterogeneous kinetics of iron and steelmaking reactions; iron ore agglomeration; coke and carbonization. **Mailing Address:** Dept Mat Sci Eng, McMaster Univ, 1280 Main St W, Hamilton, ON L8S 4L7, Can. **E-Mail:** aboudrea@mcmaster.ca

LU, WEI-YANG, PLASTICITY, EXPERIMENTAL STRESS ANALYSIS. **Personal Data:** b Taiwan, China, March 24, 1950; American citizen; m 1981. **Education:** Nat Taiwan Univ, BS, 1972; Univ NMex, MS, 1976; Yale Univ, PhD (eng & appl sci), 1981. **Professional Experience:** Chmn ed comt, Soc Exp Mech, 1988-; ASSOC PROF MECH, UNIV KY, 1987-; prin investr, NSF, 1986-; consult, Sandia Nat Labs, 1985-; asst prof, Univ KY, 1981-1987; reviewer, NSF, Acta Mech, Exp Mech, J Eng Mat & Technol. **Memberships:** Soc Exp Mech; Am Soc Mech Engrs; Sigma Xi. **Research Statement & Publications:** The effects of inelastic deformation on materials, its application on manufacturing such as machining and forming, and on ultrasonic nondestructive material characterization. **Mailing Address:** Dept Mech Eng Col Eng Univ KY, 151 Ralph G Anderson Bldg, Lexington, KY 40506-0503. **Fax:** 859-257-3304.

LU, WU SHENG, DIGITAL SIGNAL PROCESSING. **Personal Data:** b Shanghai, China, October 5, 1942; Canadian citizen; m 1971, Catherine; c Michael M. **Education:** Fudan Univ, China, BS, 1964; Univ Minn, MS, 1983, PhD (control sci), 1984. **Professional Experience:** PROF ELEC & COMPUT ENG, UNIV VICTORIA, 1991-; assoc ed, Inst Elec & Electronics Engrs Trans Circuits & Syst I 1999-2001; assoc ed, Inst Elec & Electronics Engrs Trans Circuits & Syst Ii, 1993-1995; ed, Can Journal Elec & Comput Eng, 1990-1992; assoc ed, Can Journal Elec & Comput Eng, 1989; assoc prof, Univ Victoria, 1987-1991; vis asst prof, Univ Minn, 1986-1987; Nat Sci & Eng Res Coun fel, 1985. **Memberships:** Fel Eng Inst Can; sr mem Inst Elec & Electronic Engrs; Can Soc Elec & Comput Eng. **Research Statement & Publications:** Robot motion and force control and kinematic control of redundant manipulators; multidimensional digital signal processing, especially one-dimensional and two-dimensional filter design, image restoration and compression; design of analysis-synthesis based filter banks. **Mailing Address:** Dept Elec & Comput Eng, Univ Victoria, PO Box 3055, STN CSC, Victoria, BC V8W 3P6, Can. **Fax:** 250-721-6052. **E-Mail:** wslu@ece.uvic.ca

LU, YEH-PEI, MECHANICAL ENGINEERING. **Personal Data:** American citizen. **Education:** Nat Taiwan Univ, BS, 1958; Univ Houston, MS, 1964, PhD (mech eng), 1967. **Professional Experience:** SR PROJ ENGR, DAVID W TAYLOR NAVAL SHIP RES & DEVELOP CTR, 1972-; mech engr, David W Taylor Naval Ship Res & Develop Ctr, 1968-1972; teaching & res fel, Univ Houston, 1962-1967; customer engr, IBM Corp, Taiwan, 1961; Second Lieutenant eng, Chinese Air Force, 1958-1960. **Memberships:** Am Soc Mech Engrs; Acoust Soc Am; Sigma Xi. **Research Statement & Publications:** Vibration and acoustics; structural dynamics; fluid-structural interaction; numerical analyses. **Mailing Address:** 12713 Hoven Lane, Bowie, MD 20716.

LUBAN, MARSHALL, PHYSICS. **Personal Data:** b Seattle, Wash, May 29, 1936; m 1982, c 2. **Education:** Yeshiva Univ, BA, 1957; Univ Chicago, MSc, 1958, PhD (theoret physics), 1962. **Professional Experience:** SR PHYSICIST, AMES LAB, as of 2006; chmn, Dept Physics & Astron, Iowa State Univ, 1990-1994; vis prof, Wash Univ, St Louis, 1981-1982; mem bd trustees, Jerusalem Inst Technol, 1979-1981; PROF PHYSICS, IOWA STATE UNIV, 1974-; mem bd trustees & exec coun, Bar-Ilan Univ, 1979-1981 & 1971-1974; mem, Israel Coun Res & Develop, 1970-1973; dean fac natural sci, Bar-Ilan Univ, Israel, 1969-1971; assoc prof, Iowa State Univ, 1967-1974; chmn dept, Bar-Ilan Univ, Israel, 1967-1970; Guggenheim Mem Found fel, Bar-Ilan Univ, Israel, 1966-1967; asst prof physics, Univ Pa, 1963-1966; mem, Inst Advan Study, 1962-1963. **Memberships:** Israel Phys Soc (vpres 1978-1979 & pres 1979-1982); Am Phys Soc. **Research Statement & Publications:** Theoretical condensed matter physics. **Mailing Address:** Dept Physics, Iowa State Univ, A523 Physics, Ames, IA 50011. **Fax:** 515-294-0689. **E-Mail:** luban@ameslab.gov

LUBAR, JOEL F, NEUROSCIENCES, PSYCHOPHYSIOLOGY. **Personal Data:** b Washington, DC, November 16, 1938; m 1961, Judith; c So ra ndra & Edward. **Education:** Univ Chicago, BS, 1960, PhD (biopsychol), 1963. **Professional Experience:** Assoc ed, j nuerotherapy, beginning 1998; assoc ed, Biofeedback & Self Regulation, 1991-; dir, Southeastern Biofeedback Inst, 1980-1996; co-dir, Southeastern Biofeedback Inst, 1976-1980; NSF fel, Sch Med, Univ Calif, Los Angeles, 1975-1976; psychol consult, Vet Admin Hosp, 1972-; vis lectr, Inst Physiol, Univ Bergen, Norway, 1972; PROF PSYCHOL, UNIV TENN, 1971-; regional ed, Physiol & Behav J, 1970-; prog dir, 1970-1975; assoc prof, Univ Tenn, 1967-1971; NIH grant, 1965-1973; asst prof psychol, Univ Rochester, 1963-1967. **Memberships:** Am Psychol Asn; Sigma Xi; Soc Neuroscience; Biofeedback Soc Am; fel NY Acad Sci; Asn Appl Psychophysiol & Biofeedback (pres, 1996-1997). **Research Statement & Publications:** Operant control of electroencephalographic and electrophysiological responses with special emphasis on epilepsy, hyperkinesis, learning disabilities and psychophysiological disorders; neuroanatomical substrates of emotional and motivational behavior. **Mailing Address:** Dept Psychol, Univ Tenn, 310 AP, Knoxville, TN 37916.

LUBAROFF, DAVID MARTIN, IMMUNOLOGY. **Personal Data:** b Philadelphia, Pa, February 1, 1938; m 1961, Martha; c Saul, Scoh & Matthew. **Education:** Philadelphia Col Pharm & Sci, BS, 1961; Georgetown Univ, MS, 1964; Yale Univ, PhD (microbiol), 1967. **Professional Experience:** Assoc dir for res infrastruct, Holden comprehensive cancer Ctr, univ Iowa, 1997-; assoc res career scientist, Vet Admin, 1986-; PROF UROL & MICROBIOL & DIR UROL RES, UNIV IOWA, 1982-; from asst prof to assoc prof, Univ Iowa, 1973-1982; asst prof, Univ Pa, 1970-1973; assoc, Univ Pa, 1969-1970; USPHS fel, Univ Pa, 1967-1969. **Memberships:** Am Asn Immunologists; Transplant Soc; AAAS; Int Soc Prev Oncol; Am Asn Cancer Res; Am Urol Asn; soc for Basi urol res. **Research Statement & Publications:** Delayed hypersensitivity reactions; transplantation immunology; tumor immunology; lymphocyte membrane antigens. **Mailing Address:** Dept Urol, Univ Iowa, 375 Newton Rd 3210 MERF, Iowa City, IA 52242-1089. **Fax:** 319-353-4556. **E-Mail:** david-lubaroff@uiowu.edu

LUBATTI, HENRY JOSEPH, PHYSICS. **Personal Data:** b Oakland, Calif, March 16, 1937; m 1968, Catherine; c Karen, Henry Jr & Stephen. **Education:** Univ Calif, Berkeley, AB, 1960, PhD (physics), 1966; Univ Ill, Urbana, MS, 1963. **Honors & Awards:** Alfred P Sloan res fel, 1971-1975; tau beta Pi. **Professional Experience:** Vis, scientist Univ Rome, summer 2001-2005; guest sci fermilab, 1999-2000; ed Physics, fermilab, 1990; guest scientist, SSC Lab, 1991-1993; mem ed adv comt, World Sci Publ Co, Ltd, 1982-; consult & collabr, Los Alamos Nat Lab, 1983-1986; vis scientist, Europ Orgn Nat Res, Geneva, Switz, 1980-1981; PROF PHYSICS, UNIV WASH, 1974-; lectr Herceg-Novi Int Sch, Yugoslavia, 1969 & XII Cracow Sch Theoretical Physics, Zapokane, Poland, 1972; SCI DIR VISUAL TECH LAB, UNIV WASH, 1969-; assoc prof, Univ Wash, 1974-1998; asst prof, Mass Inst Technol, 1968-1969; Vis lectr, Int Sch Physics, Erice, Sicily, 1968; res assoc physics, Linear Accelerator Lab, Univ Paris, 1966-1968; Physicist, Boeing Co, Wash, 1960-1961. **Memberships:** Fel AAAS; fel Am Phys Soc. **Research Statement & Publications:** Elementary particle physics, experimentalist; deep inelastic muon scattering and rare K-decay experiments; design of muon systems for high energy hadron colliders and development of drift cells; new designs of Silicon vertex detectors for high energy collider experiments; search for single top production at the Fermilab collider. **Mailing Address:** Experimental Particle Physics(EPE) group-Physics 351560, Univ Wash, Seattle, WA 98195-1560. **Fax:** 206-685-9242. **E-Mail:** lubatti@u.washington.edu

LUBAWY, WILLIAM CHARLES, PHARMACOLOGY. **Personal Data:** b South Bend, Ind, November 30, 1944; m 1971, Charlotte; c 3. **Education:** Butler Univ, BS, 1967; Ohio State Univ, MS, 1969, PhD (pharmacol), 1972. **Professional Experience:** PROF PHARMACOL & TOXICOL & ASSOC DEAN ACAD AFFAIRS, COL PHARM, UNIV KY, 1983-; assoc prof, pharmacol & Grad Ctr Toxicol, 1977-1982; Asst prof, 1972-1977. **Memberships:** Am Asn Col Pharm; Am Soc P-Col Exp Ther. **Research Statement & Publications:** Factors influencing learning of basic science with the context of application to practice problems. **Mailing Address:** Col Pharm, Univ Ky, 907 Rose St, Lexington, KY 40536-0082. **Fax:** 859-257-7297. **E-Mail:** lubawy@email.uky.edu

LUBBERTS, GERRIT, SOLID STATE ELECTRONICS. **Personal Data:** b Oldemarkt, Neth, September 15, 1935; American citizen; m 1959, Marcia; c Emily & David. **Education:** Univ Rochester, BS, 1962, MS, 1967, PhD, 1971. **Professional Experience:** RETIRED; assoc scientist, Rochester Inst Technol, 1995-1999; res assoc, Eastman Kodak Co, 1978-1992; sr res physicist, Eastman Kodak Co, 1971-1978; res physicist, Eastman Kodak Co, 1962-1971; technician, Eastman Kodak Co, 1958-1962; technician, Case-Hoyt Corp, 1956-1958. **Memberships:** Inst Elec & Electronics Engrs; Am Phys Soc. **Research Statement & Publications:** Semiconductor physics; surface barrier photodetectors, charge coupled devices, high superconducting thin films. **Mailing Address:** 17 Holley Brook Dr, Penfield, NY 14526.

LUBCHENCO, JANE, MARINE ECOLOGY, CONSERVATION BIOLOGY. **Personal Data:** b Denver, Colo, December 4, 1947; m 1971, Bruce A Menge; c Alexei & Duncan. **Education:** Colo Col, BA, 1969; Univ Wash, MS, 1971; Harvard Univ, PhD (ecol), 1975. **Honorary Degrees:** DSc, Drexel Univ, 1992, Colo Col, 1993. **Honors & Awards:** George Mercer Award, Ecol Soc Am, 1979. **Professional Experience:** Trustee, David & Lucile Packard Found, Los Altos, Calif, 2001-; dir, Sea Web, 2000-; dir, Royal Swedish Acad Sci, Beijer Inst Ecol Econs, Sweden, 1999-; bd dirs, Northwest Environ Watch, 1997; mem, Interrain Pac adv coun, 1996-; Int Coun Sci Union's SCA Comt problems Environ, State Oceans Comt, 1996-1999; US deleg, Int Coun Sci Union, 1996; trustee, Monterey Bay Aquarium Bd Trustees & Prog Comt, 1995-; trustee, Environ Defense Fund Bd Trustees & Sci Adv Comt, NY, 1995-; adv ed, Conserv Ecol, 1995-; WAYNE & GLADYS VALLEY PROF MARINE BIOL, ORE STATE UNIV, 1995-; mem, Pew Fels Prog Conserv & Environ Adv Comt, 1995-1998; mem, Sci Steering Comt, 1995-1996; mem, Revelation & Environ, 1995; mem, Int Inst Appl Sys Anal US Adv Group, 1994-; chair, Nat Sci & Tech Coun Nat Forum Environ & Nat Resources Res & Develop, Biodiversity & Ecosystem Dynamics Group, 1994; mem, UN Environ Prog Sci & Tech Adv Panel, 1993-; bd dirs, World Resources Inst, 1993-; adv ed, Ecol Studies, 1993-; DISTINGUISHED PROF ZOOLOGY, ORE STATE UNIV, 1993-; prin investr grants, John D & Catherine T MacArthur Found, 1993-1998; sect coordr, Global Biodiversity Assessment, UN Environ Prog, 1993-1994; prin investr grants, Pew Charitable Trusts, 1992-; Sustainable Biosphere Proj, adv comt, 1992-; coordr substainability cluster, SCOPE exec comt, 1992-1998; Int Coun Sci Union's SCA Comt probs Environ, SCOPE exec comt, 1992-1995; bd mem, Nat Mus Natural Hist, Smithsonian Inst, 1992-1994; mem, US House Rep Comt Sci, Space & Tech, 1992-1993; chair, Comt Environ Res, 1991-1993; chair, Natural Resources & Appl Ecol Working Group II, 1990-1995; mem, Bd Environ Studies & Toxicol, Nat Res Coun, 1989-1995; prin investr grants, Andrew W Mellon Found, 1989-1991, 1993; chmn dept, Ore State Univ, 1989-1992; PROF ZOOLOGY, ORE STATE UNIV, 1988-; nat lectr, Phycol Soc Am, 1987-1989; Inst Oceanol, Qingdao, People's Repub China, 1987; vis assoc prof, Univ Antofagasta, Chile, 1985; from asst prof to assoc prof, Ore State Univ, 1977-1988; prin investr, NSF, 1976-; vis asst prof, Discovery Bay Marine Lab, 1976; asst prof ecol, Harvard Univ, 1975-1977. **Memberships:** Nat Acad Sci; Ecol Soc Am (vpres 1988-1989, pres 1992-1993); Phycol Soc Am; AAAS (pres 1996-1997); Am Acad Arts & Sci; Soc Conserv Biol. **Research Statement & Publications:** Evolutionary population and community ecology, biodiversity, conservation biology, ecological causes and consequences of global change; plant-herbivore and predator-prey interactions; competition; marine ecology; algal ecology; algal life histories; biogeography, chemical ecology; sustainable ecological systems. **Mailing Address:** Dept Zool, Ore State Univ, 3029 Cordley Hall, Corvallis, OR 97331-2914. **Fax:** 541-737-3360. **E-Mail:** lubchenco@oregonstate.edu

LUBECK, MICHAEL D, IMMUNOLOGY. **Professional Experience:** ASSOC DIR, WYETH-AYERST LABS INC, 1985-. **Mailing Address:** Qual Biotech Inc, 1667 Davis St, Camden, NJ 08103.

LUBEGA, SETH GASUZA, EMBRYOLOGY, GENETICS. **Personal Data:** b Mubende, Uganda, December 24, 1936; m 1971, c 2. **Education:** Oakwood Col, BA, 1967; Howard Univ, MS, 1969, PhD (zoology), 1975. **Professional Experience:** PROF BIOL SCI, OAKWOOD COL, as of 2004; assoc prof biol sci, Oakwood Col, 1976-; asst prof, Ft Valley State Col, 1975-1976; instr biol, Oakwood Col, 1971-1972. **Memberships:** Genetic Soc Am; Nat Inst Sci. **Research Statement & Publications:** Isoenzymes of octanol dehydrogenase in populations of Drosophila species, developmental stages, and specific organs. **Mailing Address:** Dept Biol, Oakwood Col, 7000 Adventist Blvd, Huntsville, AL 35896. **Fax:** 256-726-7056.

LUBELL, DAVID, MATHEMATICS. **Personal Data:** b Brooklyn, NY, April 1, 1932; m 1960, c 3. **Education:** Columbia Univ, BS, 1956; NY Univ, PhD (math), 1960. **Professional Experience:** PROF MATH, ADELPHI UNIV, 1975-; assoc prof, Adelphi Univ, 1970-1974; math adv, Nassau Co Med Ctr, 1969-1972; consult, Systs res Group Inc, 1966-1967 & USAF, 1967-1968; asst prof math, NY Univ, 1966-1970; sr mathematician, Systs res Group Inc, 1962-1966; res instr, NY Univ, 1961-1962; Benjamin Peirce instr math, Harvard Univ, 1960-1961. **Memberships:** Am Math Soc. **Research Statement & Publications:** Combinatorics; biomathematics. **Mailing Address:** Dept Math, Adelphi Univ, Rm117, Alumnae Hall, Garden City, NY 11530. **Fax:** 516-877-4499. **E-Mail:** lubell@adelphi.edu

LUBELL, JERRY IRA, ELECTRONICS, NUCLEAR ENGINEERING. **Personal Data:** b New York, NY, October 19, 1943; m 1966, c 2. **Education:** Univ Wash, BS, 1966, MS, 1968. **Professional Experience:** VPRES, ELECTROMAGNETIC & RADIATION EFFECTS SECTOR, MISSION RES CORP, 1987-; from asst to pres, Systs Hardening, 1980-1987; mgr radiation & electromagnetics, Kaman Sci Corp, 1978-1980; Prof nuclear engr, State Calif, 1977-; res scientist, Kaman Sci Corp, 1977-1978; asst mgr, Electronic

Syst & Technol Dept, 1975-1977; head, Response Analysis Sect, 1973-1975; Mem tech staff, TRW Systs Group, 1969-1973. **Memberships:** Am Nuclear Soc. **Research Statement & Publications:** Nuclear weapon effects on electronic systems, subsystems and piece parts; electromagnetic pulse, system generated electromagnetic pulse and transient radiation effects causing both temporary and permanent damage. **Mailing Address:** Mission Res Corp, 102 S Tejon, Colorado Springs, CO 80903.

LUBELL, MARTIN S, SUPERCONDUCTORS, TECHNICAL MANAGEMENT. **Personal Data:** b New York, NY, June 5, 1932. **Education:** Mass Inst Technol, SB, 1954; Univ Calif, Berkeley, MA, 1956. **Professional Experience:** Chmn, standing comt fusion-technol, Inst Elec & Electronics Engrs, Nuclear & Plasma Sci Soc, 1987-1991; mem, Int Magnet Technol Comt, 1983-1988; dep prog mgr, Oak Ridge Nat Lab, 1981-1988; Pres, Appl Superconductors Conf Inc, 1980-1983; adv ed, Cryogenics, 1985 & eng bd, 1979-1985; mem, standing comt fusion-technol, Inst Elec & Electronics Engrs, Nuclear & Plasma Sci Soc, 1977; SECT HEAD, OAK RIDGE NAT LAB, 1976-; asst dept mgr, Oak Ridge Nat Lab, 1974-1976; res physicist, Oak Ridge Nat Lab, 1967-1973; res physicist, Res Labs, Westinghouse Elec Corp, 1956-1967; Asst, Univ Calif, 1955-1956. **Memberships:** Am Phys Soc; Inst Elec & Electronics Engrs; Sigma Xi; Applied Superconductivity Asn; Cryogenic Eng Asn. **Research Statement & Publications:** Low temperature physics; superconductivity; fusion reactor technology; magnets; manage section activities in magnetics and superconductivity; develop superconductivity magnets for fusion machines and conduct research and development on high temperature superconductor magnets and applications. **Mailing Address:** Oak Ridge Nat Lab, PO Box 2008, Oak Ridge, TN 37831. **E-Mail:** lubell@aol.com

LUBELL, MICHAEL S, ELECTRON & POSITRON INTERACTIONS, PHOTON-ATOM INTERACTIONS. **Personal Data:** b New York, NY, March 25, 1943; c Karina. **Education:** Columbia Univ, BA, 1963; Yale Univ, MS, 1965, PhD (physics), 1969. **Professional Experience:** CHMN, PHYSICS DEPT, CITY COL, CITY UNIV, NY, 1998-; mem physics planning comt, Am Physics Soc, 1993-1994; chmn, Cong Liason Comt, Am Physics Soc, 1991-; chmn, Nat Res Coun Army Res, 1990-1991; vis lectr, Inst theoretical physiol, Univ CA, Santa Barbara, 1990; vis prof, Univ Bielefeld, 1991; vis lectr, Univ Tex, Austin, 1990; mem comt pub info, Am Inst Physics, 1988-1992; chmn, Nat Res Coun Army Res, 1988-1990; vice chmn, Nat Res Coun Army Res, 1987-1988; vis sci, Brookhaven Nat Lab, 1986-1987; steering comt, Nat Res Coun Comt Atomic Molecular Sci, 1986; co-chmn, org comt, 1984-1989; org comt, fifth topical Am Physics Soc Conf, 1984-1985; mem panel pub affairs, Am Phys Soc, 1984-1985; chmn, Subcomt Studies, 1984; exec comt, Int Conf Physics Electronic Atomic Collisions, 1983-1991; PROF PHYSICS, CITY COL, CITY UNIV NEW YORK, 1983-; steering comt, Nat Res Coun army res, 1981-1983; org comt, Div Meeting Dir Electron, Atomic Physics, Am Physics Soc, 1981; sci & technol adv, US Sen Christopher J Dodd, Conn, 1980-; Sloan Found fel, City Col, City Univ New York, 1980-1983; assoc prof, City Col, City Univ New York, 1980-1982; AEC fel physics, Sloan Found fel, 1979-1980; prog comt, Div Electron Atomic Physics, Am Physics Soc, 1978; prin investr, Dept Energy & Off Naval Res, NSF, 1974-1994; from instr to assoc prof, Yale Univ, 1971-1980; AEC fel physics, Yale Univ, 1970-1971. **Memberships:** Fel AAAS; fel Am Phys Soc; NY Acad Sci; Sigma Xi. **Research Statement & Publications:** Lepton-atom collisions; laser-atom interactions; polarized particle beams; electro-weak interactions at medium energy; high energy physics with Lepton beams; electron-electron correlation; synchrotron radiation; published 100 articles and 85 conference abstracts. **Mailing Address:** Dept Physics, City Col, City Univ NY, 138th St Convent Ave, New York, NY 10031. **Fax:** 212-650-6940. **E-Mail:** lubell@aps.org

LUBENSKY, TOM C, THEORETICAL CONDENSED MATTER PHYSICS. **Personal Data:** b Kansas City, Mo, May 7, 1943; m 1968, Amy; c David & Ellen. **Education:** Calif Inst Technol, BS, 1964; Harvard Univ, MA, 1965, PhD (physics), 1969. **Honors & Awards:** Oliver E Buckley Prize, Am Phys Soc, 2004; Honored Mem, Int Liquid Crystal Soc, 2004; mem nat acad sci, 2002; fel, AAAS, 2000; fel, Am phys soc, 1985. **Professional Experience:** CHMN, DEPT PHYSICS & ASTRONOMY, UNIV PA, 2001-; Mary Amanda Wood chmn physics, Univ PA, 1998-; consult, Exxon Res & Eng, 1990-1995; Guggenheim fel, 1981-1982; prof, Univ de Paris VI, 1981-1982; Prof Physics, Univ PA, 1980-; res assoc, Harvard Univ, 1976-1980; Sloan Found fel, 1975; from asst prof to assoc prof, Univ PA, 1971-1980; res asst, Brown Univ, 1970-1971; fel, Brown Univ, 1970-1971; NSF fel physics, Fac Sci, Orsay, France, 1969-1970. **Memberships:** Am Phys Soc; AAAS Nat acad sci. **Research Statement & Publications:** Liquid crystals, complex fluids, soft condensed matter physics, phase transitions, cooperative phenomena in random systems, applications of the Wilson renormalization group, quasicrystals. **Mailing Address:** Dept Physics, Univ Pa, Philadelphia, PA 19104. **Fax:** 215-573-3897. **E-Mail:** tom@physics.upenn.edu

LUBEROFF, BENJAMIN JOSEPH, industrial chemistry; deceased, see previous edition for last biography

LUBET, RONALD A, CANCER. **Personal Data:** b New York, NY, July 7, 1946; c 3. **Education:** Univ Tenn, Knoxville, BS, 1969, MS, 1973; Univ Tex Health Sci Ctr, PhD (radiation biol), 1977. **Professional Experience:** NAT CANCER INST SPEC EXPERT, LAB COMP CARCINOGENESIS, NAT CANCER INST, FREDERICK CANCER RES & DEVELOP CTR, 1987-; proj dir, Microbiol Assoc, 1983-1987; asst proj dir, Microbiol Assoc, 1979-1983; fel lab immunodiag, Nat Cancer Inst, 1978-1979; Fel, Dept Biochem, Univ Tex Health Sci Ctr, 1977-1978; reviewer, Arch Environ Toxicol & Contamination, Arch Biochem & Biophys, Carcinogenesis, Biochem Pharm & J Nat Cancer Inst. **Memberships:** Am Col Toxicol; Am Soc Pharm & Exp Therapeut; Am Asn Cancer Res. **Research Statement & Publications:** Mechanisms of tumor promotion; induction of cytochrome P-450 by various xenobiotics; mechanisms of chemical carcinogenesis; mutagenicity of chemical carcinogens and chemotherapeutic compounds; metabolism of a variety of xenobiotics including carcinogens and chemotherapeutic agents; numerous publications. **Mailing Address:** 14221 Woodcrest Dr, Rockville, MD 20853.

LUBIC, RUTH WATSON, NURSE-MIDWIFERY. **Personal Data:** b Bucks County, Pa, January 18, 1927. **Education:** Columbia Univ, BS, 1959, MA, 1961, EdD, 1979. **Honorary Degrees:** LLD, Univ Pa, 1985; DSc, Univ Med & Dent NJ, 1986, State Univ NY, 1993; DHL, Col New Rochelle, Pace Univ, 1992. **Honors & Awards:** Hattie Hemschemeyer Award, Am Col Nurse-Midwives, 1983; Am Acad Nursing, Living Legend Award, 2001; Lievhard Award Inst Med, 2001. **Professional Experience:** Adj prof nursing, Ny Univ, as of 2004; adj prof, Ga Town Univ, as of 2004; PROJ DIR, NACC FOUND, as of 2004; PRES & CEO DC BIRTH CTR, PRES & CEO DC DEVELOP FAMILIES CTR, 1998-; dir clin proj, Maternity Ctr Asn, 1995-1997; vis prof, King Edward Mem Hosp Women, Perth, Australia, 1991; Kate Hanna Harvey prof, Community Health Nursing, Case Western res Univ, 1991; mem, First Off Am Med Deleg to People's Repub China, 1973; gen dir, Downstate Med Ctr, Maternity Ctr Asn, 1970-1995; parent educ & consult, Downstate Med Ctr, Maternity Ctr Asn, 1963-1967; instr clin nurse-midwifery, Downstate Med Ctr, Maternity Ctr Asn, 1962; instr maternal nursing, Sch Nursing, Flower & Fifth Ave Hosp, 1961; expert consult, Off Pub Health & Sci, dept Health & Human Serv. **Memberships:** Inst Med-Nat Acad Sci; fel AAAS; fel Am Acad Nurses; Am Col Nurse-Midwives; Am Pub Health Asn; fel Soc Appl Anthrop; Nat Asn Childbearing Ctrs. **Research Statement & Publications:** Barriers and conflict in maternity care innovation. **Mailing Address:** DC Birth Ctr, 139 W 94th St, New York, NY 10025. **Fax:** 212-749-5286. **E-Mail:** rlubic@aol.com

LUBIN, ARTHUR RICHARD, MATHEMATICAL ANALYSIS. **Personal Data:** b Newark, NJ, March 24, 1947. **Education:** Mich State Univ, BS, 1967; Univ Wis, MA, 1968, PhD (math), 1972. **Professional Experience:** ASSOC PROF APPL MATH, ILL INST TECHNOL, 1981-; asst prof, Ill Inst Technol, 1975-1980; asst prof math, Tulane Univ, 1972-1973 & Northwestern Univ, 1973-1975. **Memberships:** Am Math Soc. **Research Statement & Publications:** Operator theory; functional analysis; Hardy spaces. **Mailing Address:** Dept Appl Math, Ill Inst Technol, Rm 117B Eng One Bldg 10 W 32nd St, Chicago, IL 60616. **Fax:** 312-567-3135. **E-Mail:** lubin@iit.edu

LUBIN, JONATHAN DARBY, NUMBER THEORY, ALGEBRAIC GEOMETRY. **Personal Data:** b Staten Island, NY, August 10, 1936. **Education:** Columbia Univ, AB, 1957; Harvard Univ, AM, 1958, PhD (math), 1963. **Professional Experience:** PROF EMER MATH, BROWN UNIV, as of 2003; lectr, Math Inst, Copenhagen Inst, 1974-1975; prof math, Brown Univ, beginning 1970; assoc prof, Inst Henri Poincare, Univ Paris, 1968-1969; assoc prof, Brown Univ, 1967-1970; from asst to assoc prof, Bowdoin Col, 1963-1967; instr math, Bowdoin Col, 1962-1963. **Memberships:** Am Math Soc. **Research Statement & Publications:** Algebraic geometry; number theory. **Mailing Address:** Dept Math, Brown Univ, PO Box 1917, Providence, RI 02912. **Fax:** 401-863-1122. **E-Mail:** lubinj@math.brown.edu

LUBIN, MARTIN, CELL BIOLOGY. **Personal Data:** b NY, March 30, 1923. **Education:** Harvard Univ, AB, 1942, MD, 1945; Mass Inst Technol, PhD (biophys), 1954. **Professional Experience:** PROF EMER MICROBIOL, DARTMOUTH MED SCH, 1993-; prof, Dartmouth Med Sch, 1968-1993; Guggenheim fel & Commonwealth Fund fel, Lab Molecular Biol, Cambridge Univ, 1965-1967; asst prof, Harvard Med Sch, 1957-1968; Lalor Found fel, 1957-1959; USPHS sr res fel, 1956-1961; assoc pharmacol, Harvard Med Sch, 1954-1957; res assoc biol, Mass Inst Technol, 1953-1954. **Memberships:** Am Soc Biol Chem; Biophys Soc; Am Soc Cell Biol; Soc Gen Physiol. **Research Statement & Publications:** Regulation of cell proliferation. **Mailing Address:** Dept Microbiol, Dartmouth Med Sch, Hanover, NH 03755. **Fax:** 603-643-1864. **E-Mail:** martin.lubin@dartmouth.edu

LUBINIECKI, ANTHONY STANLEY, PROCESS DEVELOPMENT FOR BIOTECHNOLOGY PRODUCTS, MAMMALIAN CELL CULTURE. **Personal Data:** b Greensburg, Pa, October 4, 1946; m 1968, Robin; c Gregory M. **Education:** Carnegie Inst Technol, BS, 1968; Univ Pittsburgh, ScD, 1972. **Honors & Awards:** Hyclone Award, Europ Soc Animal Cell Technol. **Professional Experience:** DIR BIOPHARM DEVELOP, SMITH KLINE BEECHAM, as of 2004; coun mem, Int Asn Biol Stand, 1996-; vchmn, Process Technol Comt, 1993-; secy, Process Technol Comt, 1992-1993; ADJ PROF CHEM & BIOCHEM ENG, UNIV MD, BALTIMORE CO CAMPUS, 1991-; VPRES BIOPHARM DEVELOP, SMITH KLINE BEECHAM, 1988-; vchmn & chmn, Biol & Biotechnol Sect, Pharmaceut Mfrs Asn, Biotechnol Adv Comt, 1988-1992; chmn, Process Technol Comt, 1986-1992; dir process transfers, Genentech Inc, 1986-1988; dir res & demonstration, Genentech Inc, 1983-1986; mgr cell cult oper, Genentech Inc, 1982-1983; Tech Div Biol Prod, Flow Labs Inc, 1980-1982; managing dir, Meloy Labs Inc, 1979-1980; prin investr contract, Nat Inst Child Health & Human Develop, 1975-1977; prin investr contract, Nat Cancer Inst, 1974-1982; prin scientist immunol & virol, Meloy Labs Inc, 1974-1979; prin investr, Nat Inst Allergy & Infectious Dis grant, 1973-1974; prin investr contract, Dengue Task Force, US Army Med Res & Develop Command, 1973-1974; asst res prof, Grad Sch Pub Health, Univ Pittsburgh, 1972-1974; mem, Dengue Task Force, US Army Med Res & Develop Command, 1971-1974; res asst microbiol, Grad Sch Pub Health, Univ Pittsburgh, 1971-1972; mem, Biol & Biotechnol Sect, Pharmaceut Mfrs Asn, Biotechnol Adv Comt, 1986-1988, 1992-. **Memberships:** Am Soc Microbiol; AAAS; Soc Exp Biol & Med; NY Acad Sci; Europ Soc Animal Cell Technol; Int Asn Biol Stand. **Research Statement & Publications:** Cell biology models of human genetic diseases and cancer; interferon; genetic mutants of mammalian cells and their viruses; infectious disease models; carcinogenesis; process development for recombinant; DNA pharmaceuticals and monoclonal antibodies. **Mailing Address:** GlaxoSmithKline, PO Box 13398 5 Moore Dri, Research Triangle Park, NC 27709.

LUBITZ, CECIL ROBERT, NUCLEAR PHYSICS, NEUTRON CROSS SECTIONS. **Personal Data:** b Brooklyn, NY, March 18, 1925; m 1991, Lois; c Faith, Martha & Benjamin. **Education:** US Naval Acad, BS, 1945; Univ Mich, MSEE, 1949, PhD (physics), 1960. **Professional Experience:** PHYSICIST, KNOLLS ATOMIC POWER LAB, LOCKHEED-MARTIN CORP, 1960-; res assoc elec eng, Res Inst, Univ Mich, 1949-1954. **Memberships:** Am Nuclear Soc; Am Phys Soc. **Research Statement & Publications:** Neutron cross sections for technological applications. **Mailing Address:** Knolls Atomic Power Lab, Lockheed-Martin Corp, Schenectady, NY 12301. **Fax:** 518-395-7592. **E-Mail:** lubitz@kapl.gov

LUBKER, ROBERT A(LFRED), METALLURGICAL ENGINEERING. **Personal Data:** b Puyallup, Wash, May 19, 1920; m 1945, Virginia; c Barbara L (Lunding) & Beverly L (Fantini). **Education:** Univ Wash, BS, 1942; Carnegie Mellon Univ, MS, 1946. **Professional Experience:** RETIRED; pres, M&R Refractory Metals Inc, Winslow, NJ, 1980-1983; exec vpres, AVA-Toshin Corp, 1976-1980; vpres, AVA Steel Prod Int, Inc, 1974-1980; vpres technol, Assoc Metals & Minerals Corp, 1972-1974; dir res & develop, Gen Cable Corp, 1970-1972; dir res & develop, CF&I Steel Corp, 1967-1970; vpres res & develop, Alan Wood Steel Co, 1961-1967; dir res & develop, Alan Wood Steel Co, 1958-1961; mgr, Metals Res Dept, Armour Res Found, Ill Inst Technol, 1953-1958; assoc mgr, Metals Res Dept, Armour Res Found, Ill Inst Technol, 1951-1953; asst chmn, Metals Res Dept, Armour Res Found, Ill Inst Technol, 1947-1951; supvr nonferrous metals, Metals Res Dept, Armour Res Found, Ill Inst Technol, 1946-1947; metall engr, Westinghouse Elec Corp, Pa, 1942-1946. **Memberships:** Am Inst Mining, Metall & Petrol Engrs; Am Soc Metals; Am Iron & Steel Inst. **Research Statement & Publications:** General physical metallurgy; welding; foundry; powder metallurgy; extractive metallurgy; mechanical metallurgy; copper, aluminum, titanium, molybdenum, tungsten and alloy steels; supervision and direction of research; engineering problems; wire and cable; steelmaking research and development. **Mailing Address:** 3150 Timberlake Pt, Ponte Vedra Beach, FL 32082.

LUBKIN, ELIHU, THEORETICAL PHYSICS. **Personal Data:** b Brooklyn, NY, October 25, 1933; m 1962, Thelma; c Beta & Irene. **Education:** Columbia Univ, AB, 1954, AM, 1957, PhD (physics), 1960. **Professional Experience:** ASSOC EMER PROF PHYSICS, UNIV WIS-MILWAUKEE, as of 2006; assoc prof physics, UnivWis-Milwaukee, beginning 1966; res asst prof theoret physics, Brown Univ, 1963-1966; res assoc high energy group, Brown Univ, 1961-1963; asst theoret physics radiation lab, Univ Calif, Berkeley, 1959-

1961. **Memberships:** Am Phys Soc. **Research Statement & Publications:** Differential geometry used to interpret the old and for new constructions in physics; interpretation of quantum mechanics; quantum measurement theory; quantum psychology; thermodynamics. **Mailing Address:** Dept Physics, Univ Wis, Rm 422 PO Box 413, Milwaukee, WI 53201. **E-Mail:** eli@uwm.edu

LUBKIN, GLORIA BECKER, PHYSICS, SCIENCE POLICY REPORTING, ED. **Personal Data:** b Philadelphia, Pa, May 16, 1933; div, c David & Sharon. **Education:** Temple Univ, AB, 1953; Boston Univ, MA, 1957. **Honors & Awards:** Gloria Becker Lubkin Professorship of Theoretical Physics Award, Estab in her honor at Univ of Minn, 1990. **Professional Experience:** EDITOR-AT-LARGE, PHYSICS TODAY, 2001-; EDITORIAL DIR, PHYSICS TODAY, 1994-1900; co-chair, Oversight Comt, 1989-; co-chair adv comn, Theoret Physics Inst, Univ Minn, 1987-1988; ED, PHYSICS TODAY, AM INST PHYSICS, 1985-; exec comt, Hist Physics Div, 1983, 1986, 1992, 1995, 1998-; mem, Nieman Adv Comt, Harvard Univ, 1978-1982; mem exec comn, Forum Physics & Soc, 1994 Am Phys Soc, 1977-1978; Nieman fel, Harvard Univ, 1974-1975; sr ed, Physics Today, Am Inst Physics, 1970-1984; Consult, Ctr for Hist & Philos of Physics, Am Inst Physics, 1966-1967; assoc ed, Physics Today, Am Inst Physics, 1963-1969; vpres, Lubkin Assocs, 1962-1963; actg chmn, Dept Physics, Sarah Lawrence Col, 1961-1962; physicist tech res group, Control Data Corp, 1956-1958; Mathematician Aircraft Div, Fairchild Stratos Corp, 1954 & Letterkenny Ord Depot, US Defense Dept, 1955-1956. **Memberships:** COUN MEMBER, PHYSICAL SOC, 1998-; EXEC BOARD, PHYSICAL SOC, 2000-2001; FEL, NY Acad Sci; fel Am Phys Soc; Nat Asn Sci Writers; fel AAAS. **Research Statement & Publications:** Nuclear physics; science policy; physics reporting, writing and editing. **Mailing Address:** Am Inst Physics, 1 Physics Ellipse, College Park, MO 20740. **Fax:** 301-209-0842.

LUBKIN, JAMES LEIGH, STRUCTURAL ENGINEERING, ENGINEERING EDUCATION. **Personal Data:** b New York, NY, March 5, 1925; m 1948, c 2. **Education:** Columbia Univ, BS, 1944, MS, 1947, PhD (appl mech), 1950. **Professional Experience:** PROF EMER CIVIL & ENV ENG, MICH STATE UNIV, as of 2004; Fac fel, Ford Motor Co, 1972-1973; prof civil & sanit eng, mich state univ, beginning 1963; sr res engr & head theoret anal group, Cent Res Lab, Am Mach & Foundry Co, Conn, 1956-1963; sr proj analyst, Appl Physics Div, midwest res inst, 1950-1956; consult, Appl Mech & Eng Probs, Mergenthaler Linotype Co, 1949-1950. **Memberships:** Am Soc Mech Engrs; Soc Exp Stress Analysis; Am Soc Eng Educ; Sigma Xi; Am Asn Univ Prof. **Research Statement & Publications:** Computer-assisted testing and homework; individualized instruction; computer-aided design in engineering; computer applications in engineering education; vibration of vehicles; database management of traffic accident records. **Mailing Address:** Dept Civil Eng, Mich State Univ, 3546 Eng Bldg, East Lansing, MI 48824-1226. **Fax:** 517-432-1827. **E-Mail:** cee@egr.msu.edu

LUBLIN, FRED D, NEUROLOGY, Neuroimmunology. **Personal Data:** b Philadelphia, Pa, September 28, 1946; m 1969. **Education:** Temple Univ, Philadelphia, Pa, AB, 1968; Jefferson Med Col, Philadelphia, Pa, MD, 1972; Am Bd Med Examr, dipl, 1973, Am Bd Psychiat & Neurol, 1977. **Honors & Awards:** Roche Award, Jefferson Med Col, 1970; Henry M Phillips Prize, 1972; William Potter Mem Prize, 1972; Milestone Award, Nat Mult Sclerosis Soc, 1996; Hope Award, Nat Mult Sclerosis Soc, 1999. **Professional Experience:** Mem, Neurol Dis Prog Proj B Comt, Nat Inst Neurol Dis & Stroke, beginning 1990; dir, Div neuroimmunol, Dept Neurol, beginning 1987; VCHMN, DEPT NEUROL, 1987-; chmn, Computer Database Comt, 1986-; prof neurol, Jefferson Med Col, Thomas Jefferson Univ, beginning 1986; co-investr, Triton Bioscience Inc, 1986-1990; examr neurol, Am Bd Psychiat & Neuro, 1986; co-dir, Multiple Sclerosis Comprehensive Clin Ctr, beginning 1984; mem, Comt Drug Develop, Nat Multiple Sclerosis Soc, beginning 1983; assoc prof biochem & molecular biol, Jefferson Med Col, Thomas Jefferson Univ, beginning 1983; prin investr, Nat Multiple Sclerosis Soc res grant, 1981-1993; teacher investr develop award, Nat Inst Neurol & Commun Dis & Stroke, 1978-1983; adj asst prof biochem, Jefferson Med Col, Thomas Jefferson Univ, 1978-1983; attend neurologist, Thomas Jefferson Univ Hosp, beginning 1976; from instr to assoc prof neurol, Dept Neurol, 1976-1986; res assoc biochem, Dept Neurol, 1976-1978; prin investr, Basic Res Support Grant, NIH, 1976-1977; neurologist, NY Hosp, 1975-1976; Instr neurol, Cornell Med Col, 1975-1976; asst neurologist, NY Hosp, 1973-1975. **Memberships:** Am Neurol Asn; Am Acad Neurol; Research Group on Neuroimmunology of the World Federation of Neurology; International Brain Research Organization. **Research Statement & Publications:** Author of various publications. **Mailing Address:** Corinne Goldsmith Dickinson Ctr for MS, Dept Neurol, Mt Sinai Sch Med, New York, NY 10029. **Fax:** 212-423-0440. **E-Mail:** fred.lublin@mssm.edu

LUBLINER, J(ACOB), MECHANICS, BIOPHYSICS. **Personal Data:** b Lodz, Poland, May 5, 1935; American citizen; m 2003, Patricia; c 3. **Education:** Calif Inst Technol, BS, 1957; Columbia Univ, MS, 1958, PhD (eng mech), 1960. **Professional Experience:** RETIRED; Univ Politec Catalunya, Barcelona, Spain, 1986; Univ Costa Rica, San Jose, Costa Rica, 1984; vis prof, Univ Andes, Bogota, Colombia, 1977; NIH spec fel, Weizmann Inst Sci, Israel, 1969-1970; from assoc prof to prof eng sci, Univ Calif, Berkeley, 1968-1994; from asst prof to assoc prof, Univ Calif, Berkeley, 1963-1968; asst prof, Columbia Univ, 1962-1963; preceptor civil eng, Columbia Univ, 1961-1962; NSF fel, Polytech Sch, Paris, 1960-1961; Mem tech staff appl mech, Bell Tel Labs, 1960. **Research Statement & Publications:** Thermomechanics of viscoelastic, viscoplastic and plastic materials; wave propagation in solids; thermodynamics, mechanochemistry; wave propagation in biological systems; high frequency structural dynamics; segmented telescope design; modeling of concrete. **Mailing Address:** 1727 Capistrano Ave, Berkeley, CA 94707-1805. **Fax:** 510643-8928. **E-Mail:** lubliner@ce.berkeley.edu

LUBMAN, DAVID, ACOUSTICS, ELECTRICAL ENGINEERING, ARCHITECTURAL ACOUSTICS & NOISE CONTROL ENGINEERING. **Personal Data:** b Chicago, Ill, August 3, 1934; wid, c Stephen Carl. **Education:** Ill Inst Technol, BS, 1960; Univ Southern Calif, MS, 1962. **Honors & Awards:** Fellow, Acoustical Society of America (1972); Helmholtz-Rayleigh Interdisciplinary Silver Medal in Acoustics, Acoustical Society of America 2002. **Professional Experience:** CHMN, ORANGE COUNTY REGIONAL CHAP, ACOUST SOC AM, 1989-; vis prof acoust, Calif State Univ, Los Angeles, 1976; vis lectr, Univ Calif, Santa Barbara, 1976-1978; sr staff engr, Ground Systs Group, Hughes Aircraft Co, 1976-1994; NAT BUR STANDARDS, WASHINGTON, DC, 1973-1974 & DEPT ARCHIT & CONSTRUCT, STATE OF CALIF, 1976; Aircraft Engine Group, Gen Elec Co, 1971-1973; mem working group, Am Nat Standards Inst, 1970-1974, Co-chair, ANSI WG on classroom acoustics 1998-2002; consult, D Lubman & Assocs, 1969-; consult, Off Naval Res, Washington, DC, 1969-1976; sr scientist, LTV Corp Res Ctr, Anaheim, 1967-1968 & Bolt Beranek & Newman Inc, Van Nuys, 1968-1969; vis prof math, Chapman Col, Orange, 1963-1968; staff engr, Ground Systs Group, Hughes Aircraft Co, 1960-1967; mem, Nat Coun Acoust Consult. **Memberships:** Fel Acoust Soc Am; Inst Noise Control Eng; Am Soc Testing & Mat; Sigma Xi Am Asn for the advan of Sci Acoust Soc of Am; exec councilman, tech comt chair, architectural acoust mem medals of Awards com. **Research Statement & Publications:** Architectural and underwater acoustics; statistics of sound fields over space, time and frequency; reverberation chambers; sound power; noise quality; speech intelligibility; classroom acoust archaeological acoust. **Mailing Address:** 14301 Middletown Lane, Westminster, CA 92683-4514. **Fax:** 714-373-3050. **E-Mail:** dlubman@ix.netcom.com

LUBMAN, DAVID MITCHELL, SEPARATIONS & MASS SPECTROMETRY, PROTEOMICS & CANCER RESEARCH. **Personal Data:** b Brooklyn, NY, April 23, 1954; m 1984, c 6. **Education:** Cornell Univ, AB, 1975; Columbia Univ, MA, 1976; Stanford Univ, PhD (phys chem), 1979. **Honors & Awards:** AP Sloan Fellow Fellow AAAS R&D Research Award. **Professional Experience:** PROF CHEM, UNIV MICH, as of 2003; assoc prof chem, Univ Mich, beginning 1987; Alfred P Sloan fel, 1987-1989; Eli Lilly teaching fel, 1984; asst prof, Univ Mich, 1983-1987; vis scientist chem, Weizman Inst Sci, 1982-1983; staff scientist chem, Quanta-Ray, Inc, 1980-1983. **Memberships:** Am Chem Soc; Am Soc Mass Spectrometry; Am Asn for Cancer Research; CASSS, AAAS. **Research Statement & Publications:** Proteomics of Cancer Cells and Biomarkers. **Mailing Address:** Dept Surgery, Univ Mivh Medical Center, Ann Arbor, MI 48109. **Fax:** 734-615-8108. **E-Mail:** dmlubman@umich.edu

LUBORSKY, FRED EVERETT, PHYSICAL CHEMISTRY. **Personal Data:** b Philadelphia, Pa, May 14, 1923; m 1946, c 3. **Education:** Univ Pa, BS, 1947; Ill Inst Technol, PhD (phys chem), 1952. **Honors & Awards:** Distinguished lectr, Inst Elec & Electronics Engrs, 1979; Centennial Medal, Inst Elec & Electronics Engrs, 1984. **Professional Experience:** PVT CONSULT, 1992-; chmn adv comt, Conf Magnetism & Magnetic Mat, 1980; gen chmn, Second Joint Int Conf Magnetics, Magnetism & Magnetic Mat Conf, 1979; pres, Magnetics Soc, Inst Elec & Electronics Engrs, 1975-1977; ed-in-chief, inst Elec & Electronics Engrs Trans Magnetics, 1972-1975; co-chmn, Tech Prog Comt, Int Conf Magnetism, 1967; phys chemist, res & Develop Ctr, 1958-1992; physicist appl physics unit, Gen Elec Co, 1955-1958; phys chemist instrument dept, Gen Elec Co, 1952-1955; mem, div Eng & Indust res, Nat Acad Sci, 1952-1955; res assoc res lab, Gen Elec Co, 1951-1952; asst chemist, Ill inst Technol, 1947-1951; Coolidge fel, res & Develop, Gen Elec Co. **Memberships:** Nat Acad Eng; Am Chem Soc; Am Phys Soc; fel Inst Elec & Electronics Engrs; NY Acad Sci; Am Inst Chemists; Res Soc; fel Brit Sci Res Coun; AAAS. **Research Statement & Publications:** Nucleation and growth of sub-micron size particles; development of single domain particle permanent magnetic materials; electrochemistry; magnetism; magnetic thin films; amorphous magnetic materials; magnetic separation; magnetic-optic materials; preparation and properties of magnetic materials; superconducting materials. **Mailing Address:** 1162 Lowell Rd, Schenectady, NY 12308.

LUBORSKY, JUDITH LEE, MEMBRANE RECEPTORS, CELL FUNCTIONS. **Education:** State Univ NY, Albany, PhD (biol), 1975. **Professional Experience:** ASSOC PROF & DIR ENDOCRINOL, MED CTR, RUSH UNIV, 1993-; Asst prof obstet & gynec, Yale Univ, 1976-1993. **Research Statement & Publications:** Cellular endocrinology. **Mailing Address:** Med Ctr, Rush Univ, 641 W Oakdale Ave, Chicago, IL 60657.

LUBOWE, ANTHONY G(ARNER), CONNECTORS. **Personal Data:** b New York, NY, December 21, 1937; m 1959, Joan; c David & Jennifer. **Education:** Columbia Univ, AB, 1957, BS, 1958, MS, 1959, EngScD(eng mech), 1961. **Professional Experience:** Dir, Int Electronics Packaging Soc, 1990-1993; TECH MGR, AT&T BELL LABS, 1973-; mem tech staff, AT&T Bell Labs, 1961-1973; Res asst, Sch Eng, Columbia Univ, 1960-1961; corp dir, Int Inst Connector & Interconnection Technol. **Memberships:** Am Soc Mech Engrs; Int Electronics Packaging Soc; Int Inst Connectors Interconnection Technol. **Research Statement & Publications:** Elasticity; orbit prediction; electronic assembly; electronic packaging. **Mailing Address:** Berg Electronics, 67 Whippany Rd Rm 8C-027, Whippany, NJ 07981. **Fax:** 973-386-2084. **E-Mail:** a.g.lubowe@att.com

LUBOWICH, DONALD A, PHYSICS. **Professional Experience:** PROG COORDR, DEPT PHYSICS & ASTRON, HOFSTRA UNIV, as of 2006. **Memberships:** Am Astron Soc. **Mailing Address:** Dept Physics & Astron, Hofstra Univ, Hempstead, NY 11550. **Fax:** 516-463-5146. **E-Mail:** observatory@hofstra.edu

LUBOWSKY, JACK, BIOMATHEMATICS. **Personal Data:** b Brooklyn, NY, July 11, 1940. **Education:** City Col NY, BEE, 1962; Polytech Inst Brooklyn, MSEE, 1966, PhD (elec eng), 1973. **Professional Experience:** PRES, CHIEF CONSULT & JANITOR, SOLUTIONS FIT, as of 2003; dean & assoc vpres, Technol State Univ NY, 1998-2000; congressional sci fel, AAAS & Inst Elec & Electronics Engrs, 1983; assoc prof, Dept Biophys, 1980-; assoc prof, Dept Neurol, 1978-; DIR, SCI COMPUT CTR, STATE UNIV NY HEALTH SCI CTR, BROOKLYN, 1973-; asst prof, Dept Neurol, Down State Med Ctr, 1973-1978; prin investr, Spec Res Resources Div Biomath Comput Ctr, NIH, 1973-1975; Dept Neurol, State Univ NY Health Sci Ctr, 1972-1973; co investr, Spec Res Resources Div Biomath Comput Ctr, NIH, 1972-1973; assoc proc comput sci & biophys, State Univ NY Health Sci Ctr, 1970-1972; instr med comput sci, State Univ NY Health Sci Ctr, 1967-1970; res assoc, State Univ NY Health Sci Ctr, 1966-1967; proj engr, Airborne Instruments Lab, 1962-1966; engr, Brookhaven Nat Labs, 1961-1962; sci adv, Sen Subcomt Energy. **Memberships:** Sr Mem Inst Elec & Electronics Engrs; AAAS; Sigma Xi; Biomed Eng Soc Instrumentation Soc. **Research Statement & Publications:** Application of computers to biomedical research; investigation of adaptive and optimal search techniques to the determination of recognition properties of visual system neurons; Analysis and modeling of Biomedical data. **Mailing Address:** Solutions Fit, 2064 Beverly Way, Merrick, NY 11566-5416. **E-Mail:** j.lubowsky@ieee.org

LUBS, MARIE-LOUISE E, GENETICS. **Education:** Univ Stockholm, BS, PhD. **Professional Experience:** ASSOC PROF PEDIAT, UNIV MIAMI, as of 2005. **Mailing Address:** Dept Pediat Univ Miami, PO Box 016820 Rm 5032 1601 NW 12th Ave, Miami, FL 33101-6820. **E-Mail:** mlubs@med.miami.edu

LUBY, ELLIOT DONALD, PSYCHIATRY, LAW. **Personal Data:** b Detroit, Mich, April 3, 1924; m 1950, c 3. **Education:** Univ Mo-Columbia, BS, 1947; Wash Univ, MD, 1949; Am Bd Psychiat & Neurol, dipl, 1957. **Honors & Awards:** Gold Medal Award, Am Acad Psychosom Med, 1962; Nancy Roeske Med Stud Teaching Award, Am Psychiat Asn, 1993. **Professional Experience:** ADJ PROF LAW, WAYNE STATE UNIV, as of 2004; CHIEF EMER PSYCHIAT, HARPER HOSP, as of 2003; prof law, Wayne State Univ, 1980-; chief psychiat, Harper Hosp, beginning 1978; PROF PSYCHIAT, WAYNE STATE UNIV, 1965-; prof law, Harper Hosp, 1962-1976; assoc dir chg clin serv, Lafayette Clin, Detroit, 1962; chief adult inpatient sect, Lafayette Clin, Detroit, 1957-1962; resident psychiat, Yale Univ, 1952-1954; sr asst surgeon, USPHS, 1951-1952; Resident psychiat, Menninger Found, 1950-1951. **Memberships:** NY Acad Sci; AMA; Am Psychiat Asn; Am Psychosom Soc; fel Am Col Psychiat. **Research Statement & Publications:** Psychopharmacology; drug induced model psychoses and sleep deprivation; law and psychiatry: schizophrenia. **Mailing Address:** Dept Psychiat, Sch Med, Wayne State Univ, 4201 St Antoine, Detroit, MI 48201. **Fax:** 313-577-5900.

LUBY, JAMES P, MEDICAL VIROLOGY. **Education:** Northwestern Univ, BA, 1957, MD, 1961. **Professional Experience:** PROF, DEPT INTERNAL MED, UNIV TEX SOUTHWESTERN, TEX, as of 2006. **Memberships:** AAAS; Am Soc Virol; Am Col Physicians. **Mailing Address:** Univ Tex Southwestern, Dallas, TX 75235-8859.

LUBY, PATRICK JOSEPH, AGRICULTURAL ECONOMICS. **Personal Data:** b Zanesville, Ohio, May 20, 1930; m 1956, Margaret; c James J, Julie M, Mary P & Robert J. **Education:** Univ Dayton, BA, 1952; Purdue Univ, MS, 1954, PhD (agr econ), 1956. **Professional Experience:** ECON & MGT CONSULT, AGR & APPL ECON DEPT & ANIMAL SCI DEPT, UNIV WIS, 1992-; ADJ PROF, AGR & APPL ECON DEPT & ANIMAL SCI DEPT, UNIV WIS, 1992-; corp economist, Oscar Mayer & Co, 1974-1992; vpres, Oscar Mayer & Co, 1972-1992; gen mgr provisions & procurement, Oscar Mayer & Co, 1971-1974; gen mgr provisions, Oscar Mayer & Co, 1966-1971; economist, Oscar Mayer & Co, 1958-1966; asst prof, Purdue Univ, 1956-1958; instr agr econ, Purdue Univ, 1954-1956. **Research Statement & Publications:** Use of statistical methods to analyze and forecast meat and livestock supplies and prices; efficient marketing of livestock and meats. **Mailing Address:** 4506 Woods Ende, Madison, WI 53711. **E-Mail:** pjluby@wisc.edu

LUBY, STEFAN, PHYSICS, SOLID STATE PHYSICS. **Personal Data:** b Bratislava, Slovakia, May 6, 1941; m 1966, Zelmira Kosorinova; c Martina & Barbora. **Education:** Slovak Tech Univ, dipl, 1963, CSc, 1969, PhD, 1969; Slovak Acad Sci, DSc, 1982. **Honorary Degrees:** Doc Habil, Comenius Univ, 1992; Dr(physics), Univ Lecce, Italy. **Honors & Awards:** Science Prize, Slovak Acad Sci, 1983; Humboldt Medal, Ger; Socius Ordinarius, Acad Europaea Sci & Arts, 1996. **Professional Experience:** Hon prof, Slovak Tech Univ, 1996; PRES, SLOVAK ACAD SCI, 1995-; actg pres, Inst Physics, 1994-1995; first vpres, Inst Physics, 1993-1994; Univ Syracuse, 1991 & Univ Chiba, Japan, 1993; mem presidium, Inst Physics, 1992-1993; vis prof, Univ Lecce, 1985-1996; dir, Inst Physics, 1984-1992; Vis scientist, USSR Acad Sci, 1969 & Tech Univ, Ger, 1978; Sci co-worker, Inst Elec Eng, Slovak Acad Sci, 1969-1983. **Memberships:** Am Phys Soc; Slovak Acad Sci; Int Soc Optical Eng. **Research Statement & Publications:** Unipolar integrated circuits; amorphous semiconductors; superconductors; metallic thin films and multilayers; electronics; ration in metallic films; multi-layered mirrors for x-ray optics; patentee in field. **Mailing Address:** Inst Physics-Slovak Acad Sci, Dubravska 9, Bratislava 84228, Slovak Republic. **Fax:** 421-739-5689. **E-Mail:** luby@savba.sk

LUCANSKY, TERRY WAYNE, PLANT ANATOMY, PLANT MORPHOLOGY. **Personal Data:** b Massillon, Ohio, August 21, 1942; c Jimmy David. **Education:** Univ SC, BS, 1964, MS, 1967; Duke Univ, PhD (bot), 1971. **Professional Experience:** UNDER GRAD COORD, UNIV FLA, as of 2005; ASSOC PROF BOT, UNIV FLA, 1976-, asst prof bot, Univ Fla, 1971-1976. **Memberships:** Bot Soc Am; Am Fern Soc; Am Inst Biol Sci; Sigma Xi; Torrey Bot Club. **Research Statement & Publications:** Comparative anatomical and morphological studies of tropical pteridophytes; anatomical studies of aquatic plants and vines in relation to their habit and habitat; pteridology. **Mailing Address:** Dept Bot, Univ Fla, PO Box 118526 3171 McCarty Hall A, Gainesville, FL 32611-8526. **Fax:** 904-392-3993. **E-Mail:** lucansky@botany.ufl.edu

LUCANTONI, DAVID, COMPUTATIONAL PROBABILITY, EXPERT WITNESS. **Education:** Towson State Univ, BS, 1976; Univ Del, MS, 1978, PhD (opers res), 1981. **Honors & Awards:** Mary Hudson Scarborough Award for Excellence in Math, Towson Univ, 1976. **Professional Experience:** Principal Consultant, DLT Consulting, 1998-; VP & CTO, IsoQuantic Technologies, 1994-1998; Distinguished Mem Tech Staff, Bell Labs, 1981-1994. **Memberships:** IEEE, INFORMS, ACM, ICCA. **Research Statement & Publications:** Computationally stable algorithms for the solution of complex stochastic models such as those arising in the theory of queues; Congestion control in networks. **Mailing Address:** DLT Consulting, LLC, 10 Oak Tree Lane, Ocean, NJ 07712. **Fax:** 732-493-4465. **E-Mail:** david.lucantoni@att.net

LUCAS, ALEXANDER RALPH, CHILD PSYCHIATRY. **Personal Data:** b Vienna, Austria, July 30, 1931; American citizen; m 1956, Margaret; c Thomas A, Nance E (Watson), Alexander E & Peter C. **Education:** Mich State Univ, BS, 1953; Univ Mich, MD, 1957. **Professional Experience:** PROF PSYCHIAT, MAYO MED SCH, 1976-; consult, State Minn Dept Pub Welfare, 1972-1980 & NIMH, 1974-1977; assoc prof, May Med Sch, 1973-1976; CONSULT SECT CHILD & ADOLESCENT PSYCHIAT, MAYO CLIN, 1971-; head, Mayo Med Sch, 1971-1981; from asst prof to assoc prof psychiat, Wayne State Univ, 1967-1971; Res child psychiatrist & res coordr, Lafayette Clin, Detroit, 1967-1971; from staff child psychiatrist to sr psychiatrist, Hawthorn Ctr, Northville, Mich, 1962-1967; resident child psychiat, Hawthorn Ctr, Northville, Mich, 1958-1959 & 1961-1962; Rotating intern, Univ Mich Hosp, 1957-1958. **Memberships:** Am Orthop Asn; Am Psychiat Asn; Am Acad Child Psychiat; Soc Prof Child Psychiat; Soc Biol Psychiat. **Research Statement & Publications:** Biologic aspects of child psychiatry; eating disorders. **Mailing Address:** 1135 Plummer Cir SW, Rochester, MN 55902. **Fax:** 507-284-4158.

LUCAS, CAROL N, BIOMEDICAL MATHEMATICS. **Personal Data:** b Aberdeen, SDak, February 13, 1940; m 1961, c 2. **Education:** Dakota Wesleyan Univ, BA, 1961; Univ Ariz, MS, 1967; Univ NC, Chapel Hill, PhD (biomed math, eng), 1973. **Professional Experience:** CHMN BIOMED ENG, UNIV NC, CHAPEL HILL, 1992-; actg chair biomed eng, Div Cardiothoracic Surg, 1990-1992; PROF SURG & BIOMED MATH & ENG, UNIV NC, CHAPEL HILL, 1989-; from asst prof to assoc prof, Div Cardiothoracic Surg, 1977-1989; lectr biomed math & eng, Div Cardiothoracic Surg, 1976-1977; res assoc, Div Cardiothoracic Surg, 1972; res asst biomed math & eng, Univ NC, Chapel Hill, 1967-1968; comput lab asst, Dept Math & Eng, Univ Ariz, 1966-1967; teaching asst, Dept Math & Eng, Univ Ariz, 1965-1967; Jr systs analyst, Cargill, Inc, Minneapolis, 1962-1965; High sch teacher, US Army Educ Ctr, Furth, Ger, 1961-1962; prof surg & prof appl sci. **Memberships:** Am Heart Asn; Sigma Xi; Biomed Eng Soc; Inst Elec & Electronics Engrs; Cardiovasc Systs Dynamics Soc. **Research Statement & Publications:** Mathematical modelling and computer simulation of physiological systems; digital processing of dynamic physiological data. **Mailing Address:** Dept Biomed & Eng, Univ NC, Chapel Hill, NC 27599-7575. **E-Mail:** clucas@bme.unc.edu

LUCAS, COLIN ROBERT, COORDINATION CHEMISTRY. **Personal Data:** b Toronto, Ont, October 11, 1943; American citizen; div, c Neil & Stephen. **Education:** Acadia Univ, BSc, 1968, MSc, 1969; Oxford Univ, PhD (organometallic chem), 1972. **Professional Experience:** DEAN OF SCI, MEM UNIV NFLD, 1999-; head, Dept Chem, 1997-1999; PROF CHEM, MEM UNIV, NFLD, 1993-; from asst prof to assoc prof, Dept Chem, 1974-1993; res fel, Univ Alta, 1973-1974. **Memberships:** Fel Chem Inst Can. **Research Statement & Publications:** Synthesis and properties of organometallic and coordination compounds containing sulphur: catalysis; liquid crystals. **Mailing Address:** Dean Sci, Mem Univ Nfld, St John's, NL A1B 3X7, Can. **E-Mail:** rlucas@mun.ca

LUCAS, DAVID OWEN, IMMUNOLOGY, BUSINESS DEVELOPMENT. **Personal Data:** b Orange, Calif, October 19, 1942; m 1984, Linda Workman; c Philip, Alan & Jason. **Education:** Duke Univ, BA, 1964, PhD (microbiol, immunol), 1969. **Professional Experience:** PRES, CHIEF EXEC OFFICER & DIR, PEDIAPHARM CORP, 1994-; vpres, Children's Hosp Oakland, 1991-1994; vpres, Protein Technol, Petaluma, 1986-1990; actg dept head, Children's Hosp Med Ctr, Harvard Med Sch, 1977-1979; from asst prof to assoc prof microbiol & immunol, Col Med, Univ Ariz, 1970-1986; res fel immunol, Children's Hosp Med Ctr, Harvard Med Sch, 1968-1970; consult, Technol Resources Group, Calif. **Memberships:** AAAS; Am Asn Immunologists; Am Soc Microbiol; Licensing Exec Soc. **Research Statement & Publications:** Cellular immunology; lymphocyte metabolism; interferon; hybridomas; nutritionals and pharmaceuticals development. **Mailing Address:** PediaPharm Corp, CA.

LUCAS, DOUGLAS M, FORENSIC SCIENCE. **Personal Data:** b Windsor, Ont, May 5, 1929; m 1953, Marie Macdonald; c 5. **Education:** Univ Toronto, BSc, 1953, MSc, 1957. **Honors & Awards:** Adelaide Medal, Int Asn Forensic Sci, 1990; Gradwohl Medal, Am Acad Forensic Sci, 1995; Derome Medal, Can Soc Forensic Sci, 1996. **Professional Experience:** RETIRED; vpres, Int Comt Alcohol, Drugs & Traffic Safety, 1984-1986; Chmn, Comt Alcohol & Drugs, Nat Safety Coun, 1977-1979; Dir, Ctr Forensic Sci, 1967-1994. **Memberships:** Can Soc Forensic Sci (pres, 1968-1969); Am Acad Forensic Sci (pres, 1972-1973); Int Asn Forensic Sci (pres, 1967-1969); Am Soc Crime Lab Dirs (pres, 1977-1978). **Research Statement & Publications:** Alcohol, drugs and traffic safety; investigation of fires and explosions; forensic science. **Mailing Address:** 5280 Lakeshore Rd No 1111, Burlington, ON L7L 5R1, Can. **Fax:** 416-314-3225.

LUCAS, EDGAR ARTHUR, ANATOMY, NEUROPHYSIOLOGY. **Personal Data:** b Franklin, Ind, October 28, 1933; m 1960, c 2. **Education:** Ball State Univ, BA, 1961, MS, 1965; Univ Calif, PhD (anat), 1972. **Professional Experience:** DIR, SLEEP CONSULT INC, 1996-; ADJ PROF BIOMED ENG, UNIV TEX, ARLINGTON, 1996-; dir, Sleep Disorders Ctr, All Saints Episcopal Hosp, beginning 1984; CLIN POLYSOMNOGRAPHER, 1978-; mem comt Polysomnography Asn Sleep Disorder Ctrs, 1976-1987; from instr to asst prof anat, Univ Ark Med Ctr, Little Rock, 1972-1984; assoc res engr, Rocketdyne Div, NAm Rockwell Corp, 1964-1965; planner admin, Rocketdyne Div, NAm Rockwell Corp, 1962-1963; teacher, Sch, Town Griffith, 1961-1962. **Memberships:** Inc Soc Chronobiol; Asn Psychophysiol Study Sleep; Am Asn Anat; Sigma Xi; Clin Sleep Soc; Asn Prof Sleep Socs. **Research Statement & Publications:** Biological rhythms; sleep; neurosciences. **Mailing Address:** Sleep Consult Inc, 1521 Cooper St, Ft Worth, TX 76104. **Fax:** 817-336-2159. **E-Mail:** doctors@sleepconsultants.com

LUCAS, FREDERICK VANCE, BLOOD COAGULATION & THROMBOSIS, HEMATOLOGY. **Personal Data:** b Rochester, NY, November 27, 1949; m 1975, Johna; c William & Robert. **Education:** Amherst Col, BA, 1971; Univ Mo, MD, 1975. **Professional Experience:** CHMN DEPT PATH & LAB MED, CLEVELAND CLIN FLA, 1988-; co investr, NIH, 1987-; clin asst prof, Case Western Res Univ, Sch Med, 1984-; coagulation resource comt, Col Am Pathologist, 1983-1985; prin investr, Am Heart Asn, 1983; coun hemat, Am Soc Clin Pathologist, 1982-1987; staff physician, Lab Hemat, 1979-1988; dir, Sch Med Technol, Cleveland Clin Found, 1979-1983; res path, Cleveland Clin Fla, 1975-1979. **Memberships:** Am Heart Asn; Int Acad Path; Am Soc Hemat; AAAS. **Research Statement & Publications:** Clinical coagulation and role of soluble fibrin in cardiovascular disease, specifically the contribution of tissue transglutamivase to crosslinking fibrin; fibrinogen in blood ofpatients with vascular occlusion; development of flowing whole blood model of clotlysis. **Mailing Address:** Cleveland Clin Fla, 3000 W Cypress Creek Rd, Ft Lauderdale, FL 33309.

LUCAS, GENE ALLAN, GENETICS. **Personal Data:** b Des Moines, Iowa, October 15, 1928; m 1948, c 3. **Education:** Drake Univ, BA, 1954, MA, 1958; Iowa State Univ, PhD (genetics), 1968. **Professional Experience:** PROF EMER BIOL, DRAKE UNIV, as of 2005; assoc prof biol, Drake Univ, beginning 1974; asst prof, Drake Univ, 1968-1974; asst genetics, Iowa State Univ, 1961-1966; instr, Drake Univ, 1960-1967; Lab instr biol, Drake Univ, 1954-1959. **Memberships:** AAAS; Genetics Soc Am; Int Oceanog Found. **Research Statement & Publications:** Pigmentation, especially of aquarium fish; pigment genetics of Siamese fighting fish; application of biological principles to world problems; race and population problems; teaching; biology and behavior of Siamese fighting fish. **Mailing Address:** Dept Biol, Drake Univ, 6917 NW 11Ct, Ankeny, IA 50021.

LUCAS, GEORGE BOND, GEOCHEMISTRY. **Personal Data:** b New Orleans, La, December 21, 1924; m 1962, c 1. **Education:** Tulane Univ, BS, 1948; Iowa State Univ, PhD (chem), 1952. **Professional Experience:** RETIRED; from asst prof to prof, Colo Sch Mines, 1956-1987; res chemist, Red Stong Arsenal Res Div, Rohm & Haas Co, 1953-1956; fel, Northwestern Univ, 1952-1953. **Memberships:** Am Chem Soc; Sigma Xi. **Research Statement & Publications:** Reaction mechanisms organic particularly free radical mechanisms. **Mailing Address:** 7925 W Layton Ave No 402, Littleton, CO 80123.

LUCAS, GLENN E, MECHANICAL PROPERTIES OF MATERIALS. **Personal Data:** b Los Angeles, Calif, March 8, 1951; m 1972, c 3. **Education:** Univ Calif, Santa Barbara, BS, 1973; Mass Inst Technol, MS, 1975, ScD(nuclear eng), 1977. **Honors & Awards:** Young Eng Achievement Award, Am Nuclear Soc, 1991. **Professional Experience:** PROF NUCLEAR ENG, UNIV CALIF, SANTA BARBARA, 1987-; vis res prof, Tokyo Univ, 1985; vis res prof, Hokkaido Univ, 1985; consult, govt & private bus, 1978-; Prin investr, numerous res contracts, 1978-; from asst prof to prof, Univ Calif, Santa Barbara, 1978-1987; Engr, Exxon Nuclear, Inc, 1978. **Memberships:** Am Nuclear Soc; Am Soc Metals; AAAS; Sigma Xi; Mat Res Soc; Am Soc Testing & Mat. **Research Statement & Publications:** Effects of environment on microstructural evolution; mechanical properties of structural steels and composite materials. **Mailing Address:** 529 Dorset, Goleta, CA 93117-1643. **Fax:** 805-893-4731. **E-Mail:** gene@engineering.ucsb.edu

LUCAS, HENRY C, JR, INFORMATION TECHNOLOGY. **Personal Data:** b Omaha, Nebr, September 4, 1944; m 1968, Ellen Kuhbach; c Scott & Jonathan. **Education:** Yale Univ, BS, 1966; Mass Inst Technol, MS, 1968, PhD, 1970. **Honors & Awards:** Fel of the asn for info syst. **Professional Experience:** ROBERT H SMITH PROF OF INFO SYST, ROBERT H SMITH SCH OF BUS, UNIV OF MARYLAND, 2000-; Asn Comput Mach Trans on Off, Info & Mgt; vis researcher, Bell Commun Res, NJ, 1991; res prof info systs, Leonard N Stern Sch Bus, NY Univ, 1988-2000; assoc ed, Mgt Sci, 1985-1987; vis prof, INSEAD, Fontainebleau, France, 1985; prof info systs, Grad Sch Bus Admin, 1984-1988; on leave, Europ Systs Res Inst, IBM, La Hulpe, Belgium, 1981; prof & chmn, Schs Bus, NY Univ, 1978-1984; assoc ed, Mis Quarterly, 1978-1983; chmn, Working Group Interaction of Info Systs & the Orgn, Int Fedn Info Processing, 1975-1980; assoc prof computer applications & info systs, Schs Bus, NY Univ, 1974-1978; ed, Performance Eval Rev, 1972-1973; asst prof computer & info systs, Grad Sch Bus, Stanford Univ, 1970-1974; ed, Sloan Mgt Rev, 1967-1968; consult, Arthur D Little, Inc, Cambridge, Mass, 1966-1970. **Memberships:** Asn Comput Mach; Inst Mgt Sci; Inst Elec & Electronics Engrs; Asn Info Syst Ais Uprey publ 1995-1998. **Research Statement & Publications:** Information technology and organizations; information systems implementation; expert systems; value of technology; impact of technology; organization design; Electronic markets, e commerce strategy. **Mailing Address:** 18 Portland Rd, Summit, NJ 07901. **Fax:** 301-405-8655. **E-Mail:** hlucas@rhsmith.umd.edu

LUCAS, J RICHARD, MINING & MINERAL ENGINEERING. **Personal Data:** b Scottdale, Pa, May 3, 1929; m 1952, Joan; c Eric Scott & Jay Hathaway. **Education:** Waynesburg Col, BS, 1951; WVa Univ, BS, 1952; Univ Pittsburgh, MS, 1954; Columbia Univ, PhD (mining eng), 1965. **Honors & Awards:** Donald S Kingery Award. **Professional Experience:** RETIRED; head, Massey prof mining & minerals eng, Va Polytech Inst & State Univ, 1987-1992; dir, Generic Mineral Technol Ctr, Mine Systs Design & Ground Control, beginning 1982; exec comt, Va Mining & Mineral Resources Res Inst, beginning 1979; rev comt, Fel Prog Mining & Minerals Eng & Conserv, Off Educ, HEW, Wash DC, 1979; ad hoc comt coal mine safety, Dept Indust & Resources, 1979; ad hoc comt coal mine safety, Coal Conversion Fac, 1979; prog comt, State Mine Recovery Competition, Div Mines, Va Mining Inst, beginning1978; coordr, Va Ctr Coal & Energy Res, Coal Inst, beginning 1977; Va Polytech Inst & State Univ, head, Dept Mining & Minerals Eng, 1976-1987; consult & reviewer, Ad-Hoc Panel Coal Mining Technol, Nat Res Coun, 1975-1978; consult & reviewer, NSF, 1973-1974, 1976-1977; head, Div Minerals Eng, Va Polytech Inst & State Univ, 1971-1976; mem, Joint Comt Coal Mining Health, Safety & Res, Mining Safety & Health Admin, US Dept Labor & Bur Mines, US Dept Interior, beginning 1970; mem secy's res adv coun coal miner's health, HEW, 1970-1973; consult & reviewer, Prog Comn, Mining Safety & Health Admin, Dept Labor, beginning 1969; actg asst dir, Va Eng Exp Sta, 1963-1964; dir, US Off Coal Res Proj, Va Polytech Inst & State Univ, beginning 1962; head dept, Va Polytech Inst & State Univ, 1961-1971; head div, Ohio State Univ, 1957-1961; mem fac mining eng, Ohio State Univ, 1954-1956; field engr, Joy Mfg Co, 1952-1954; miner, Crucible Steel Co Am, 1948-1952. **Memberships:** Am Inst Mining, Metall & Petrol Engrs; AAAS; Asn Advan Invention & Innovation. **Research Statement & Publications:** Mining systems engineering; mineral property evaluation; mining design and layout; computer applications in underground coal mining systems; coal mining safety research; methane from coal seams; underground coal-mining research. **Mailing Address:** 408 Hemlock Dr SE, Blacksburg, VA 24060.

LUCAS, JAMES M, STATISTICAL METHODOLOGY. **Personal Data:** b Philipsburg, Pa, July 21, 1941. **Education:** Pa State Univ, BS, 1963; Yale Univ, MS, 1965; Tex A&M Univ, PhD (statist), 1972. **Honors & Awards:** Brumbaugh Award, Am Soc Qual Control, 1976. **Professional Experience:** SR CONSULT STATIST, E I DU PONT DEL NEMOURS & CO INC, 1965-; ASSOC ED, J QUAL TECHNOL, 1983-; assoc ed, Chemometrics & Intelligent Lab Systs, 1988; ASSOC ED, TECHNOMETRICS, 1981-; ADJ PROF, UNIV DEL, 1972-; past pres, Del chap, Am Statist Asn. **Memberships:** Fel Am Statist Asn; Am Soc Qual Control. **Research Statement & Publications:** Methods for the control and improvement of industrial processes; cumulative sum techniques; experimental designs. **Mailing Address:** 5120 New Kent Rd, Wilmington, DE 19808. **Fax:** 302-456-4013.

LUCAS, JAMES P, MATERIALS SCIENCE ENGINEERING. **Education:** NC Cent, BS, 1973; Univ Minn, MS, 1978, PhD, 1981. **Professional Experience:** ASSOC PROF, DEPT CHEM ENG & MAT SCI, MICH STATE UNIV, as of 2006. **Research Statement & Publications:** Microstructure evolution/characterization of Pb-free solders alloys and their composites. Nanoindentation characterization of deformation in small-volumes and thin films. Moisture effects in resin matrix composites; Metal matrix composites; Nanoindentation characterization of deformation in small-volumes and thin films; Microstructure evolution / characterization of Pb-free solders alloys and their composites. **Mailing Address:** Dept Chem Eng & Mat Sci, Mich State Univ, 2527 Eng Bldg 3526EB, East Lansing, MI 48824-1226. **E-Mail:** lucas@egr.msu.edu

LUCAS, JAMES P, MATERIALS SCIENCE ENGINEERING. **Education:** NC Central Univ, BS, 1973; Univ Minn, MS, 1978, PhD, 1981. **Professional Experience:** ASSOC PROF, DEPT CHEM ENG & MAT SCI, COLL ENG, MICH STATE UNIV, as of 2006. **Mailing Address:** Dept Chem Eng & Mat Sci, Mich State Univ, 3526EB, East Lansing, MI 48824. **E-Mail:** lucas@egr.msu.edu

LUCAS, JAMES ROBERT, GEOLOGY. **Personal Data:** b Mankato, Minn, April 26, 1947. **Education:** Mankato State Univ, BA, 1969; Univ Iowa, MA, 1973, PhD (geol), 1977. **Professional Experience:** DIR REMOTE SENSING, LOCKHEED STENNIS OPER, MISS, 1994-; adj fac, Univ Tex Permian Basin, 1984-1985 & Univ Nev, Las Vegas, 1991-; mgr, Spatial Analysis Lab, Lockheed Eng & Sci Co, Las Vegas, Nev, 1990-1994; owner, Orion, Ltd, Midland, Tex, 1987-1990; gen partner, Orion, Ltd, Midland, Tex, 1983-1987; vpres, Centaur Explor, Inc, Amarillo, Tex, 1981-1983; prin applns scientist geol, Earth Resources Observ Systs Data Ctr, SDak, 1980-1981; appln scientist water resources, Earth Resources Observ Systs Data Ctr, SDak, 1976-1980; res geologist, Iowa Geol Surv, 1975-1976; prin investr, NASA contract, 1975-1976; Adj instr geol, Univ Iowa, 1975-1976; Instr earth sci, Providence Sch, South St Paul, Minn, 1969-1970. **Memberships:** Am Soc Photogrammetry; Sigma Xi. **Research Statement & Publications:** Remote sensing techniques applied to hydrocarbon, minerals and water resources exploration; Landsat digital image processing for natural resources analysis and interpretation; photographic enhancement of Landsat imagery for geological applications; land classification of Southeast Iowa from computer enhanced Landsat images; glacial geomorphology of Northwest Iowa; semi-quantitative analysis of clay minerals by x-ray diffraction. **Mailing Address:** Lockheed Stennis Oper, Stennis Space Ctr, MS 39529.

LUCAS, JEFFREY ROBERT, OPTIMAL FORAGING THEORY, ENERGY REGULATION. **Personal Data:** b Rockville Center, NY, January 1953; m Denise; c Nicole Alec. **Education:** Fla Inst Technol, BS, 1975; Univ Fla, MS, 1978, PhD (zoology), 1983. **Professional Experience:** PROF BIOL, PURDUE UNIV, 2002-; prin investr, NIMH, 2001; asst prof, Purdue Univ, 1987-1994; assoc prof, 1995-2001; vis asst prof, Univ Redlands, 1986-1987; vis asst prof, Col William & Mary, 1984-1986; NATO fel, Oxford Univ, 1983-1984. **Memberships:** Animal Behav Soc; AAAS; Am Soc Naturalists; Ecol Soc Am; Sigma Xi; Int Soc Behav Ecol Executive Ertin, Animal Behaviour. **Research Statement & Publications:** Ecological implications of energy regulation and food hoarding in birds and mammals; use of dynamic programming to study foraging behavior and life-history tactics. **Mailing Address:** Dept Biol Sci, Purdue Univ, West Lafayette, IN 47907-1392. **E-Mail:** jlucas@bilbo.bio.purdue.edu

LUCAS, JOE NATHAN, CHROMOSOMAL FLOW CYTOMETRY. **Personal Data:** b Lake Providence, La, December 18, 1945; c 1. **Education:** Univ Calif, Los Angeles, BS, 1970, MS, 1972, PhD (biophysics), 1977. **Professional Experience:** PROF EMER, CALIF STATE UNIV, 1996-; SR SCIENTIST, LAWRENCE LIVERMORE NAT LAB, UNIV CALIF, 1978-; chmn bd, Lucas Educ Found Inc, 1978-; instr physics, Calif State Univ, 1978-1979; Fulbright scholar, 1977; scientist & engr, Lawrence Berkeley Nat Lab, Univ Calif, 1977-1978; sci instr, math & sci, Mill Col, 1972-1976. **Memberships:** Soc Anal Cytometry; Radiation Res Soc. **Research Statement & Publications:** Biological dosimetry: rapid image analysis to quantify chromosome aberrations (translocations) in man using chromosome specific probes; slit-scan and fringe-scan flow cytometers to measure the distribution of flourescent dye(s) along isolated chromosomes; flow cytometric devices and procedures for rapid, quantitative classification of chromosomes according to shape and/or flourescent band patterns. **Mailing Address:** Lawrence Livermore Nat Lab, PO Box 808 L 4527, Livermore, CA 94551. **Fax:** 510-422-2282. **E-Mail:** lucas1@llnl.gov

LUCAS, JOHN F, HEURISTIC PROBLEM SOLVING, GRAPHING PROGRAMMABLE CALCULATORS. **Personal Data:** b Chicago, Ill, November 14, 1937; m 1958, Shirley; c Kathryn Lucas March & Christine Ann. **Education:** Univ Wis, Steven's Point, BS, 1960; Univ Ill, MA, 1964; Univ Wis, Madison, PhD (math education), 1972. **Professional Experience:** PROF EMER MATH, UNIV WIS, OSHKOSH, as of 2001; prof math, Univ Wis, Osh Kosh, 1965-1998; teacher Math, Madison, Wis Public Schools, 1960-1963. **Memberships:** emer mem Math Asn of Am; Natl Council of Teachers of Math; Wis Math Council. **Research Statement & Publications:** Heuristic strategies in mathematical problem solving applied to the teaching and learing of single and multivariable calculus; graphing programmable and symbolic manipulation calculators in the teaching and learning of mathematics. **Mailing Address:** Dept Math, Univ Wis, Swart 204 800 Algoma Blvd, Oshkosh, WI 54901-8631. **E-Mail:** lucasj@uwosh.edu

LUCAS, JOHN J, BIOCHEMISTRY, MOLECULAR BIOLOGY. **Professional Experience:** PROF, HEALTH SCI CTR, STATE UNIV NY, as of 2005. **Mailing Address:** Biochem & Molecular Biol Health Sci Ctr, State Univ NY, 4139 Weiskotten Hall, Syracuse, NY 13210-1605. **Fax:** 315-464-8750. **E-Mail:** lucasj@upstate.edu

LUCAS, JOHN PAUL, MICROBIOLOGY. **Personal Data:** b Youngstown, Ohio, November 16, 1945; m 1968. **Education:** Univ Pittsburgh, BS, 1967, MS, 1969. **Honorary Degrees:** ScD (microbiol), Univ Pittsburgh, 1973. **Professional Experience:** MICROBIOLOGIST, FOOD & DRUG ADMIN, 1974-; res assoc virol, Grad Sch Pub Health, Univ Pittsburgh, 1974. **Memberships:** Am Soc Microbiol; Sigma Xi. **Research Statement & Publications:** Develop growing area standards for shellfish. **Mailing Address:** Dept Health Human Serv, Food & Drug Admin, 5600 Fishers Lane Rm 15A16 HFG-1, Rockville, MD 20857. **Fax:** 301-443-0235. **E-Mail:** jlucas@oc.fda.gov

LUCAS, JOHN W, MECHANICAL ENGINEERING, HEAT TRANSFER. **Personal Data:** b Pomona, Calif, March 14, 1923; m 1953, Genevieve; c 3. **Education:** Univ Calif, Berkeley, BS, 1948; Univ Calif, Los Angeles, MS, 1949, PhD (mech eng), 1953. **Professional Experience:** RETIRED; mgr point focus distributed receiver solar energy technol proj, Jet Propulsion Lab, Calif Inst Technol, 1976-1985; exec asst to dir, Jet Propulsion Lab, Calif Inst Technol, 1974-1976; mgr res & planetary quarantine, Jet Propulsion Lab, Calif Inst Technol, 1970-1974; res rep eng mech, Jet Propulsion Lab, Calif Inst Technol, 1966-1970; group supvr, Jet Propulsion Lab, Calif Inst Technol, 1959-1965; sr res engr, Jet Propulsion Lab, Calif Inst Technol, 1954-1959; NSF fel, Fritzhaber Inst, Berlin, Ger, 1953-1954. **Memberships:** Am Inst Aeronaut & Astronaut; Sigma Xi. **Research Statement & Publications:** Ice nucleation in lemons; spacecraft advanced propulsion; radiation, conduction and convection heat transfer as related to spacecraft thermal control in space, on the moon and planets, and in solar thermal energy. **Mailing Address:** 865 Canterbury Rd, San Marino, CA 91108.

LUCAS, KENNETH ROSS, ANALYTICAL CHEMISTRY, POLYMER PHYSICS. **Personal Data:** b Bradford, Pa, June 4, 1939; m 1961, c 4. **Education:** Univ Pittsburgh, BS, 1961; Univ Ill, MS, 1964, PhD (analytical chem), 1966. **Professional Experience:** ASSOC SCIENTIST, FIRESTONE TIRE & RUBBER CO, 1981-; sr res chemist, Firestone Tire & Rubber Co, 1971-1981; res chemist, Firestone Tire & Rubber Co, 1966-1971. **Memberships:** Polymer Chem Div Am Chem Soc Rubber Div; Electron Micros Soc Am. **Research Statement & Publications:** Molten salt and organic electrochemistry; x-ray diffraction; polymer physics; electro-organic synthesis; polymer morphologyanalysis; radiothermoluminescence; scanning electron microscopy; ESCA/Auger spectroscopy. **Mailing Address:** 1464 Gurley Ave, Akron, OH 44310.

LUCAS, LEON THOMAS, PLANT PATHOLOGY, MICROBIOLOGY. **Personal Data:** b Halifax, NC, July 30, 1942; m 1964, c 1. **Education:** NC State Univ, BS, 1964; Univ Calif, Davis, PhD (plant path), 1968. **Professional Experience:** PROF EMER PLANT PATH, NC STATE UNIV, as of 2002; prof plant path, nc state univ, beginning 1980; from asst prof to assoc prof, NC State Univ, 1968-1980; Res asst plant path, Univ Calif, Davis, 1964-1968. **Memberships:** Am Phytopath Soc. **Research Statement & Publications:** Diseases of turfgrasses and forage crops in North Carolina; bacterial diseases of plants. **Mailing Address:** Dept Plant Path, NC State Univ Box 7616, Raleigh, NC 27695-0001. **Fax:** 919-515-7716. **E-Mail:** lt_lucas@ncsu.edu

LUCAS, LINDA C, BIOMEDICAL ENGINEERING, BIOMATERIALS. **Personal Data:** b Waltham, Mass, 1950. **Education:** Univ Ala, BS, 1971, PhD. **Professional Experience:** PROF BIOMED ENG, UNIV ALA, BIRMINGHAM, 1982-; Orthop res asst, Univ Ala, Birmingham, 1978-1982. **Memberships:** Soc Biomat; Acad Dent Mat. **Mailing Address:** Sch Eng Univ Ala, 1717 Seventh Ave S, Birmingham, AL 35294-0001. **E-Mail:** llucas@eng.uab.edu

LUCAS, MARK ALAN, PHOTONUCLEAR REACTIONS, NUCLEON STRUCTURE. **Personal Data:** b Santa Barbara, Calif, April 21, 1964; m 1991, Jodie Gordon; c Ryan. **Education:** Purdue Univ, BS, 1986; Univ Ill, Urbana-Champaign, PhD (physics), 1994. **Professional Experience:** Asst prof, dept of phys and astro, ohio univ, 1999-; visiting asst prof, dept of phs and astro, ohio univ, 1998-1999; POSTDOCTORAL RES ASSOC, PHYSICS DEPT, UNIV SC, 1994-; Guest scientist, Brookhaven Nat Lab, 1994-. **Memberships:** Am Phys Soc. **Research Statement & Publications:** Photopion production and nuclear compton scattering in the region of the delta resonance at the LEGS polarized photon source; studying nucleon structure. **Mailing Address:** Ohio Univ, 252D Clippinger Lab, Athens, OH 45701. **E-Mail:** lucas@ohiou.edu

LUCAS, MYRON CRAN, BIOCHEMICAL GENETICS. **Personal Data:** b Cincinnati, Ohio, November 15, 1946. **Education:** Lewis & Clark Col, BS, 1969; Wash State Univ, PhD (genetics), 1974. **Professional Experience:** PROF BIOL, LA STATE UNIV, SHREVEPORT, 1978-; from asst prof to assoc prof, LA State Univ, Shreveport, 1978-1988; res assoc biochem, Univ Idaho, 1977-1978; adj asst prof biol, Fla State Univ, 1977; res assoc genetics, Univ Ga, 1975-1977; res assoc bot, Univ Ill, Urbana, 1973-1975. **Memberships:** Genetics Soc Am; Am Soc Microbiol; NY Acad Sci; AAAS. **Research Statement & Publications:** Biochemical genetics of Neurospora crassa; structure and function of low molecular weight RNA; gene regulation and synthesis of messenger RNA; characterization of egg jelly glycoproteins in salamanders. **Mailing Address:** Dept Biol Sci La State Univ Shreveport, 1 Univ Pl, Shreveport, LA 71115-2301. **E-Mail:** clucas@pilot.lsus.edu

LUCAS, RICHARD J, MATHEMATICS. **Education:** Univ Ill, BS, MS, PhD. **Professional Experience:** PROF, DEPT MATH & STATIST LOYOLA UNIV CHICAGO, as of 2006.

Mailing Address: Dept Math & Statist, Loyola Univ Chicago, 6525 N Sheridan Rd, Chicago, IL 60626-5311. **Fax:** 773-508-2123. **E-Mail:** rlucas@ luc.edu

LUCAS, ROBERT ALAN, MECHANICAL ENGINEERING. **Personal Data:** b Allentown, Pa, June 13, 1935; m 1957, Joanne A Wetherhold; c Michael J, Elizabeth A, Leslie A & Marya C. **Education:** Lehigh Univ, BS, 1957, MS, 1959, PhD (mech eng), 1964. **Professional Experience:** ASSOC CHMN, DEPT MECH ENG & MECH, LEHIGH UNIV, 1996-; ASSOC PROF MECH ENG, LEHIGH UNIV, 1969-; resident res assoc, Nat Res Coun-Naval Res Lab, DC, 1965-1966; asst prof mech eng, Lehigh Univ, 1964-1969; inst mech eng, Lehigh Univ, 1959-1964; Design engr, Air Prod & Chem, Inc, Pa, 1957-1958. **Memberships:** Am Soc Mech Engrs; Sigma Xi. **Research Statement & Publications:** Machine system simulation and analysis; expert systems; optimization; applied mathematics; dynamics; computer aided design; computer aided instruction; vibrations. **Mailing Address:** Dept Mech Eng & Mech, Lehigh Univ, Packard Lab, 19 Mem Dr W, Bethlehem, PA 18015. **Fax:** 610-758-6224. **E-Mail:** ral1@lehigh.edu

LUCAS, ROBERT ELMER, AGRONOMY, HORTICULTURE. **Personal Data:** b Malolos, Philippines, June 27, 1916; m 1941, Norma; c Richard, Raymond, Milton, Keith & Charles. **Education:** Purdue Univ, BSA, 1939, MS, 1941; Mich State Col, PhD (soil sci), 1947. **Professional Experience:** Vis prof, Univ Fla, 1979-1980; vis prof, Agr Inst, Dublin, Ireland, 1970; PROF EMER, MICH STATE UNIV, 1977-; exten specialist, Mich State Univ, 1953-1977; from assoc prof to prof soil sci, Mich State Univ, 1951-1977; agronomist, Wm Gehring Inc, Ind, 1946-1951, 1977-1978; asst soils, Mich State Col, 1945-1946; asst soils, Va Truck Exp Sta, 1941-1943. **Memberships:** Fel Soil Sci Soc Am; fel Am Soc Agron; Int Peat Soc. **Research Statement & Publications:** Micronutrients in crop production; soil organic matter dynamics and models; physical and chemical properties of organic soils (histosols); comparison of four management systems in vegetable production; plant nutrient requirements. **Mailing Address:** Mich State Univ, East Lansing, MI 48824.

LUCAS, THOMAS RAMSEY, MATHEMATICS. **Personal Data:** b Tampa, Fla, June 9, 1939; m 1970, Barbara; c Sam & John. **Education:** Univ Fla, BS, 1961; Univ Mich, Ann Arbor, MS, 1962; Ga Inst Technol, PhD (math), 1970. **Professional Experience:** PROF MATH, UNIV NC, CHARLOTTE, 1985-; from instr to assoc prof, Univ NC, Charlotte, 1969-1985; Sr engr, Martin Co, 1962-1965. **Memberships:** Am Math Soc; Soc Indust & Appl Math. **Research Statement & Publications:** Numerical analysis; approximation theory; spline theory. **Mailing Address:** 9516 Glenwater Dr, Charlotte, NC 28262-8469. **E-Mail:** trlucas@uncc.edu

LUCAS, WILLIAM FRANKLIN, OPERATIONS RESEARCH, APPLIED MATHEMATICS. **Personal Data:** b Detroit, Mich, April 21, 1933; m 1957, Carolyn; c Robert, Thomas, Joan & Daniel. **Education:** Univ Detroit, BS, 1954, MA, 1956, MS, 1958; Univ Mich, PhD (math), 1963. **Honors & Awards:** Chautaugua Lectr, AAAS, 1975-1979 fel, AAAS. **Professional Experience:** PROF MATH, CLAREMONT GRAD SCH, 1984-; sci exchange with USSR, US Nat Acad Sci, 1976 & 1983; Consult, Rand Corp, 1969-1977 & Educ Develop Ctr, 1975-1979; dir ctr appl math, Cornell Univ, 1971-1974; prof opers res & appl math & math, Cornell Univ, 1970-1984; assoc prof opers res & appl math, Cornell Univ, 1969-1970; mathematician, Rand Corp, 1967-1969; vis assoc prof, Math Res Ctr, Univ Wis-Madison, 1966-1967; Fulbright fel & vis assoc prof econ & statist, Mid East Tech Univ, Ankara, 1965-1966; res instr, Princeton Univ, 1963-1965; asst prof, Univ Detroit, 1962-1963; instr math, Univ Detroit, 1956-1958 & 1961-1962. **Memberships:** Am Math Soc; Math Asn Am; Soc Indust & Appl Math; Asn Women Math; AAAS; Inst Opers Res & Mgt Sci. **Research Statement & Publications:** Elasticity; applied mathematics; game theory. **Mailing Address:** 1598 Beloit, Claremont, CA 91711-3108. **E-Mail:** bill.lucas@cgu.edu

LUCAS, WILLIAM JOHN, PLANT PHYSIOLOGY, PLANT BIOPHYSICS. **Personal Data:** b Adelaide, South Australia, February 23, 1945; m 1967, c 4. **Education:** Univ Adelaide, BSc, 1971, PhD (plant physiol), 1975, DSc(plant physiol), 1990. **Honors & Awards:** Francqui Medal, Belgian Francqui Found, 2001; Martin Gibbs Medal, Am Soc Plant Biologists, 1997; Prof honoris caused, Int Univ Brandy Boissons Spirituenses, Segonzac, France, 1990. **Professional Experience:** PROF BOT, UNIV CALIF, DAVIS, as of 2001; distinguished Prof Lect, Boyce Thompson Inst, Cornell Univ, 1999-2001; Mem, Int Comt Phloem Physiol, 1984-; Guest prof, Univ Gottingen, WGer, 1984-1985; NSF grant, 1978-1994; from asst prof to assoc prof plant physiol, Univ Calif, Davis, 1977-1983; Res assoc, Dept Bot, Univ Toronto, 1975-1977. **Memberships:** Am Soc Plant Physiologists; Australian Soc Plant Physiologists; Can Soc Plant Physiologists; Bot Soc Am; Soc Exp Biol. **Research Statement & Publications:** Biophysical and physiological aspects of transport across plant membranes, in particular the plasmalemma; cell-to-cell communication via plasmodesmata; role of plasmodesmata in virus infection; plasmodesmal trafficking of macromolecules in regulation of developmental and physiological processes. **Mailing Address:** Sect Plant Biol, Univ Calif Div Biol Scis, Davis, CA 95616. **Fax:** 530-752-5410. **E-Mail:** wjlucas@ucdavis.edu

LUCAS, WILLIAM R(AY), INORGANIC CHEMISTRY, MATERIALS SCIENCE & ENGINEERING. **Personal Data:** b Newbern, Tenn, March 1, 1922; m 1948, Polly; c Donna (Watts), William R Jr & Michael L. **Education:** Memphis State Univ, BS, 1943; Vanderbilt Univ, MS, 1950, PhD (chem, metall), 1952. **Honorary Degrees:** DHL, Mobile Col, 1977; DSc, Southeastern Inst Technol, 1980, Univ Ala, Huntsville, 1981. **Honors & Awards:** Except Sci Achievement Medal, NASA, 1964; Oberth Award, Am Inst Aeronaut & Astronaut, 1965; Holger N Toftoy Award, 1976; Space Flight Award, Am Astronaut Soc, 1982; Vet Foreign Wars Space Award, 1983; Elmer A Speery Award, Am Instit Aeronaut & Astronautics, 1986. **Professional Experience:** RETIRED; aerospace consult, 1986-2001; dir, Marshall Space Flight Ctr, NASA, 1974-1986; dep dir, 1971-1974; dir prog develop, 1968-1971; dir Propulsion & Vehicle Eng Lab, 1966-1968; chief Mat Div, 1963-1966; chief eng Mat Br, 1960-1963; chief eng mat br, Army Ballistic Missile Agency, 1956-1960; chief eng mat sect, Army Ballistic Missile Agency, 1955-1956; chief, Chem Sect, 1954-1955; chemist, Guided Missile Develop Div, Redstone Arsenal, 1952-1954; instr chem, Memphis State Univ, 1946-1948. **Memberships:** Nat Acad Eng; fel Am Inst Aeronaut & Astronaut; fel Am Soc Metals; Sigma Xi; Am Chem Soc. **Research Statement & Publications:** Materials engineering, metallurgy and inorganic chemistry; environmental effects on materials, especially space; pioneering work in materials for liquid rockets. **Mailing Address:** 6805 Criner Rd, Huntsville, AL 35802.

LUCAS-LENARD, JEAN MARIAN, MOLECULAR BIOLOGY. **Personal Data:** b Bridgeport, Conn, July 17, 1937; m 1964, John. **Education:** Bryn Mawr Col, AB, 1959; Yale Univ, PhD (protein synthesis), 1963. **Professional Experience:** EMER PROF BIOL, UNIV CONN, 1995-; prof, Univ Conn, 1976-1995; NIH career develop award, 1971-1976; assoc prof biol, Univ Conn, 1970-1976; Estab investr, Am Heart Asn, 1970-1971; asst prof, Rockefeller Univ, 1968-1970; res assoc, Rockefeller Univ, 1965-1968; guest investr protein synthesis, Rockefeller Univ, 1964-1965; USPHS fel enzymol, Inst Physiochem Biol, Paris, 1963-1964. **Memberships:** AAAS; Am Soc Biochem & Molecular Biol; Am Soc Virol. **Research Statement & Publications:** Mechanism of protein biosynthesis in eukaryotes; translational control mechanisms in virus infected cells. **Mailing Address:** 75 N Eagleville Rd, Unit 3044, Storrs, CT 06269-3044. **E-Mail:** lucasl@uconnvm.uconn.edu

LUCAST, DONALD HURRELL, ORGANIC CHEMISTRY. **Personal Data:** b Minneapolis, Minn, July 11, 1946; m 1975, c 3. **Education:** Univ Minn, BS, 1968, PhD (org chem), 1976. **Professional Experience:** RES CHEMIST, 3M, 1983-; res chemist, Ethyl Corp, 1977-1983; fel, Wayne State Univ, 1977 & Univ Detroit, 1975-1976. **Memberships:** Am Chem Soc; Tech Asn Pulp & Paper Indust. **Research Statement & Publications:** Organic synthesis; reaction mechanisms; polymer chemistry. **Mailing Address:** 3M Innovative Properties Co, St Paul, MN 55144-1000.

LUCATORTO, THOMAS B, LASERS. **Personal Data:** b New York, NY, May 9, 1937; m 1979, Linda; c Theresa & Rachael. **Education:** City Univ NY, BS, 1960; Columbia Univ, MA, 1964, PhD (physics), 1968. **Honors & Awards:** IR-100 Award, 1980 & 1984; Silver Medal, Nat Bur Stand, 1980. **Professional Experience:** GROUP LEADER PHYSICIST, NAT INST STAND & TECHNOL, 1972-; Res assoc physics, Columbia Univ, 1968-1969. **Memberships:** Fel Am Phys Soc; Am Optical Soc. **Research Statement & Publications:** Multiphoton ionization; EUV optics; EUV microscopy. **Mailing Address:** 100 Bureau Dr, Bldg 245 Rm B104, Gaithersburg, MD 20899. **Fax:** 301-208-6937. **E-Mail:** thomas.lucatorto@nist.gov

LUCCA, JOHN J, DENTISTRY. **Personal Data:** b Brooklyn, NY, July 12, 1921; m 1946, c 6. **Education:** NY Univ, AB, 1941; Columbia Univ, DDS, 1947; Am Bd Prosthodontics, dipl. **Honors & Awards:** Ewell Medal, 1947. **Professional Experience:** PROF EMER, PROSTHODONTICS, COLUMBIA UNIV, 1987-; hon police surgeon & consult, NY Police Dept, 1964-; prof & dir div, Sch Dent & Oral Surg, 1964-1987; from instr to assoc prof dent, Prosthodontics, Columbia Univ, 1947-1964; consult ed prosthodont, Progreso-Odonto-Stomatologique; attend, Presby Hosp & Westchester County Med Ctr; consult, Vet Admin & USPHS. **Memberships:** fel Am Col Dent; fel Am Col Prosthodont; fel Int Col Dent; fel Int Col Prosthodont. **Research Statement & Publications:** Precision attachment; partial dentures. **Mailing Address:** PO Box 20 P & S, Dept Oral Surg, Colombia Univ, NY, NY 10027-6902.

LUCCHESI, BENEDICT ROBERT, CARDIAC ARRHYTHMIAS, MYOCARDIAL ISCHEMIA. **Education:** Univ Mich, MD, 1964. **Professional Experience:** PROF PHARMACOL, MED SCH, UNIV MICH, 1968-. **Research Statement & Publications:** Cardiovascular pharmacology. **Mailing Address:** Dept Pharmacol, Univ Mich, Med Sci Bldg 1301 C MSRB III, Ann Arbor, MI 48109-0632. **Fax:** 734-647-4782. **E-Mail:** benluc@umich.edu

LUCCHESI, CLAUDE A, ANALYTICAL CHEMISTRY, PHYSICAL CHEMISTRY. **Personal Data:** b Chicago, Ill, April 20, 1929. **Education:** Univ Ill, BS, 1950; Northwestern Univ, PhD, 1954. **Honors & Awards:** Disting Service Award, ALMA, 2002. **Professional Experience:** PROF EMER CHEM & DIR ANAL SERV, NORTHWESTERN UNIV, as of 2006; ed, Bull Anal Lab Mgr Asn, 1984-1987; contrib ed, Analy Chem, 1974-1980; mgr cent coatings lab, Mobil Chem Co, 1967-1968; mgr anal & phys chem dept, Mobil Chem Co, 1961-1967; dir anal res dept, Sherwin-Williams Co, 1956-1961; spectros group leader, Shell Develop Co, Tex, 1954-1956; asst, Northwestern Univ, 1950-1954; consult coatings, healthcare & instrument co; CONSULT DIR, ANALYSIS SERV & SR EMER LECTR; ed, Managing Modern Labs. **Memberships:** Am Chem Soc; Soc Appl Spectros; Instrument Soc Am; Analyt Lab Mgr Asn. **Research Statement & Publications:** General applied spectroscopy; nuclear magnetic resonance spectroscopy; chelate chemistry; plastics and coating characterization and analysis; laboratory management. **Mailing Address:** Dept Chem, Northwestern Univ, Evanston, IL 60208. **Fax:** 847-491-7713. **E-Mail:** c-lucchesi@northwestern.edu

LUCCHESI, JOHN CHARLES, GENETICS. **Personal Data:** b Cairo, Egypt, September 3, 1934; American citizen; m 1955, c 2. **Education:** La Grange Col, AB, 1955; Univ Ga, MS, 1958; Univ Calif, Berkeley, PhD (zoology), 1963. **Professional Experience:** PROF BIO, EMORY UNIV, as of 2003; Aza G Chandler prof biol, beginning 1990; chmn, Genetics Study Sect, Div Res Grants, NIH, 1987-1990; overseas fel, Churchill Col, Eng, beginning 1984; vis investr, Dept Genetics, Univ Cambridge, Eng, 1984; Carry C Boshamer prof biol, 1982-1990; adj prof genetics, Duke Univ, Durham, NC, beginning 1980; prof biol & Genetics, Univ Nc, Chapel Hill, beginning 1980; vis Kenan prof, Dept Genetics, Univ Calif, Berkeley, 1978; NIH res career develop award, 1970-1975; vis investr, Max Planck Inst Biol, Tubingen, Ger, 1969; from asst prof to prof zool & genetics, Univ NC, Chapel Hill, 1965-1980; NIH res assoc biol, Univ Ore, 1963-1965. **Memberships:** Genetics Soc Am (vpres 1990 pres 1991); Am Soc Cell Biol; Soc Develop Biol. **Research Statement & Publications:** Molecular genetics; biochemistry of development; sex differentiation and dosage compensation in Drosophila. **Mailing Address:** Dept Biol, Emory Univ, 1510 Clifton Rd, OWR Res Ctr, Atlanta, GA 30322-1100. **E-Mail:** lucchesi@biology.emory.edu

LUCCHESI, PETER J, PHYSICAL CHEMISTRY. **Personal Data:** b New York, NY, September 23, 1926; m 1949, c 2. **Education:** NY Univ, AB, 1949, MS, 1953, PhD (chem), 1954. **Professional Experience:** RETIRED; vpres corp res, Corp Res Lab, 1975-1985; dir, Corp Res Lab, 1968-1975; res chemist, Exxon Res & Eng Co, 1955-1968; Ill Inst Technol, 1954-1955; NY Univ, 1953-1954; instr chem, Adelphi Col, 1952. **Memberships:** Am Chem Soc; AAAS. **Research Statement & Publications:** Radiation chemistry; heterogeneous catalysis; crystal growth and dissolution. **Mailing Address:** 24 Brearly Rd, Princeton, NJ 08540-6766.

LUCCHITTA, BAERBEL KOESTERS, PLANETARY GEOLOGY, GEOMORPHOLOGY. **Personal Data:** b Muenster, Ger, October 2, 1938; American citizen; m 1964, Ivo; c Maya. **Education:** Kent State Univ, BS, 1961; Pa State Univ, MS, 1963, PhD (geol), 1966. **Honors & Awards:** Spec Recognition Award, NASA, 1979; G K Gilbert Award, Planetary Geol Div, Geol Soc Am, 1995; Antarctic glacier Lucchitta named in honor, 2003; asteroid Baerbel named in honor, 1991. **Professional Experience:** EMER SCIENTIST, US GEOL SURV, 1995-; chmn, Planetary Geol Div, Geol Soc Am, 1991-1992; 1st vchmn, Planetary Geol Div, Geol Soc Am, 1990-1991; lectr, Sigma Xi, 1990-1991; 2nd vchmn, Planetary Geol Div, Geol Soc Am, 1989-1990; planet cartog working group, 1989; secy/treas, Planetary Geol Div, Geol Soc Am, 1987-1989; assoc chief, US Geol Surv, 1986-1991; proj chief, Antarctica, 1982-1995; coordr, Galilean Satellite Geol Mapping Prog, NASA, 1980-1995; assoc ed, J Geophys Res, 1980-1984; mem, Planetary Geol Rev Panel, NASA, 1980-1982; prin investr, martian projs, NASA, 1978-; guest investr, Viking Lander Imaging Team, NASA, 1976; prin investr, 3 lunar projs, NASA, 1974-1978; geologist, Br Astrogeol, US Geol Surv, 1968-1995. **Memberships:** Asn Women Geoscientists; Geol Soc Am; Am Geophys Union; Int Glaciol Soc. **Research Statement & Publications:** Dark mantles, secondary craters, basin formation, plains formation, scarps and ridges, northside and Apollo 17-site geological map of the moon; erosion, landform development, map of Ismenius Lacus, canyons and scarps, landslides, channels, glacial and periglacial features, Valles Marineris geology and structure of Mars; geomorphology and structural geology of earth; geologic map of Jupiter Satellite Europa; structure of Ganymede;

Antarctic investigations with Landsat images, Antarctic coastal changes and glacier velocities. **Mailing Address:** Br Astrogeology, US Geol Surv, 2255 N Gemini Dr, Flagstaff, AZ 86001. **Fax:** 928-556-7014. **E-Mail:** blucchitta@usgs.gov

LUCCHITTA, IVO, GEOLOGY. **Personal Data:** b Budweis, Czech, June 17, 1937; American citizen; m 1964, Baerbel; c Mays. **Education:** Calif Inst Technol, BSc, 1961; Pa State Univ, PhD (geol), 1966. **Honors & Awards:** Spec commendation, geol training astronauts, Geol Soc Am, 1970; Group Achievement Award, Earth Resources Technol Satellite geol anal & image processing, NASA, 1975; Super Serv Award, US Dept Int, 1989. **Professional Experience:** GEOLOGIST EMER, US GEOL SURV, 1995-; proj chief Quaternary Grand Canyon, Shivwits-Grand Wash Wilderness Area, 1990; dep asst chief geologist, proj chief & coordr Apollo geol methods, US Geol Surv, 1985-1987; ADJ PROF, NORTHERN ARIZ UNIV, 1985-; res grant, Nat Geog Soc, 1984; res fel, Univ Rome, Italy, 1984; geologist, Shivwits-Grand Wash Wilderness Area, 1980-1995; geologist & proj chief, Wariz Tectonics, 1973-1995; geologist nat landslide overview map, proj chief & coordr Apollo geol methods, US Geol Surv, 1973-1974; geologist & proj chief earth resources technol satellite appln & anal, proj chief & coordr Apollo geol methods, US Geol Surv, 1970-1973; Geologist, proj chief & coordr Apollo geol methods, US Geol Surv, 1966-1970; RES GEOLOGIST, US GEOL SURV, 1966-; Museum NAriz grants, 1963, 1964; Penrose Bequest grant, Geol Soc Am, 1963. **Memberships:** Fel Geol Soc Am. **Research Statement & Publications:** Tectonic history of southwestern Colorado plateau and of plateau basin and range transition; basement control of structure; tectonic heredity; history of Colorado river and Grand Canyon; Cenozoic continental rocks; quatenory chronology and processes; Quaternary of the Grand Canyon; structure and tectonics of Cordilleran core complexes. **Mailing Address:** US Geol Surv, Northern Ariz Univ, 2255 N Gemini Dr, Flagstaff, AZ 86001. **E-Mail:** ivo@lucchitta.com

LUCCI, ROBERT DOMINICK, ANALYTICAL CHEMISTRY. **Personal Data:** b Norwalk, Conn, July 11, 1950; m 1971, c 2. **Education:** Univ Conn, BA, 1972; Cornell Univ, PhD (org chem), 1977. **Professional Experience:** DIR, TECH DEVELOP, MOLECULAR BIO SYSTEMS INC, SAN DIEGO, 1992-; Sr scientist, Abbott Lab, 1987-1992; Sr scientist, Hoffmann-Laroche, Inc, 1977-1987. **Memberships:** Am Chem Soc; Sigma Xi. **Research Statement & Publications:** Safe, economic and environmentally sound industrial chemical processes from research synthesis. **Mailing Address:** 6364 St Therese Way, San Diego, CA 92120.

LUCE, JAMES EDWARD, PAPER CHEMISTRY, PHYSICS. **Personal Data:** b Toronto, Ont, August 24, 1935; American citizen. **Education:** Univ Toronto, BASc, 1956; McGill Univ, PhD (chem), 1960; NY Inst Tech, MBA, 1980. **Professional Experience:** CONSULT, PAPER PERFORMANCE & PAPERMAKING, 1995-; mgr paper sci & technol, Int Paper Co, 1987-1995; mgr papermaking technol, Int Paper Co, 1984-1987; assoc dir advan develop, Int Paper Co, 1981-1984; sr mgr oper systs develop, Int Paper Co, 1972-1981; sci admin officer, Atomic Energy Can, Ltd, 1971; asst mgr basic res, CIP res Ltd, 1960-1971. **Memberships:** Fel Tech Asn Pulp & Paper Indust; Can Pulp & Paper Asn; Int Asn Sci Papermakers. **Research Statement & Publications:** Application of modern instrumental techniques to control of pulp and paper processes; development of papermaking processes; paper structure and properties. **Mailing Address:** 38 Jefferson St, Troy, NY 12180. **Fax:** 914-987-2152. **E-Mail:** luce@warwick.net

LUCE, R(OBERT) DUNCAN, MATHEMATICAL PSYCHOLOGY, THEORY MEASUREMENT. **Personal Data:** b Scranton, Pa, May 16, 1925; m 1988, Carolyn; c Aurora Luce Prowell. **Education:** Mass Inst Technol, BS, 1945, PhD (math), 1950. **Honorary Degrees:** MS, Harvard Univ, 1976. **Honors & Awards:** Distinguished Sci Contrib Award, Am Psychol Asn, 1970; Gold Medal Lifetime Achievement Psychol Sci, 2001; UCI Medal, 2001; UCI Daniel G Aldrich, Jr Award Serv, 2003; Frank P Ramsay Medal Decision Anal Soc, 2003; Nat Medal Sci, 2003; Norman Anderson Award Lifetime Contribs Psychol, 2004. **Professional Experience:** DISTINGUISHED RES PROF COGNITIVE SCI & ECON, UNIV CALIF, IRVINE, 1992-; VICTOR S THOMAS PROF EMER, HARVARD UNIV, 1988-; distinguished prof & dir, math behav sci, Uni Calif, Irvine, 1988-1992; Victor S Thomas prof psychol, Harvard Univ, 1983-1988; Guggenheim Found fel, 1980-1981; Alfred North Whitehead prof psychol & math psychol, Harvard Univ, 1976-1981; prof soc sci, Univ Calif, Irvine, 1972-1975; vis prof social sci, Inst Advan Study, Princeton, 1969-1972; vis prof psychol, Cath Univ Rio Del Janeiro, 1968-1969; prof psychol, Benjamin Franklin prof, 1967-1968; prof psychol, Univ Pa, 1959-1967; Lectr social rels, Harvard Univ, 1957-1959; asst prof sociol & math statist, Columbia Univ, 1954-1957; fel, Ctr Advan Study Behav Sci, 1954-1955, 1966-1967, 1987-1988; managing dir, Behav Models Proj, Columbia Univ, 1953-1957; Mem staff, Res Lab Electronics, Mass Inst Technol, 1950-1953. **Memberships:** Nat Acad Sci; fel Am Acad Arts & Sci; Soc Math Psychol (pres 1979); Psychometric Soc (pres 1976-1977); fel Soc Exp Psychologists; Am Math Soc; fel Am Psychol Asn; Fedn Behav Psychol & Cognitive Sci (pres 1988-1990); Am Philos Soc; fel Am Psychol Soc. **Research Statement & Publications:** Theoretical work on measurement and structures, especially conjoint and utility ones; theoretical and experimental work in psychophysics, including absolute identification, detection and recognition, magnitude estimation and reaction time. **Mailing Address:** Social Sci Plz, Univ Calif, Irvine, CA 92697-5100. **Fax:** 949-824-3733. **E-Mail:** rdluce@uci.edu

LUCE, ROBERT JAMES, ROCK MAGNETISM. **Personal Data:** b Boston, Mass, August 7, 1921; m 1981. **Education:** Drexel Univ, BS, 1973; Univ Pittsburgh, MS, 1975, PhD (geophysics), 1980. **Professional Experience:** ASSOC PROF EMER PHYSICS & GEOL, WASH & JEFFERSON COL, as of 2003; assoc prof physics & geol, Wash & Jefferson Col, beginning 1980. **Memberships:** Am Phys Soc; Am Asn Physics Teachers. **Research Statement & Publications:** Theoretical models of hadronic atoms. **Mailing Address:** Dept Physics, Wash & Jefferson Col, Washington, PA 15301.

LUCE, WILLIAM GLENN, ANIMAL NUTRITION. **Personal Data:** b Beaver Dam, Ky, March 21, 1936; m 1970, Nancy; c William Glenn Jr & Bryan Ward. **Education:** Univ Ky, BS, 1958; Univ Nebr, MS, 1964, PhD (animal nutrit), 1965. **Honors & Awards:** Extension Award, Am Soc Animal Sci. **Professional Experience:** PROF SWINE EXTEN, OKLA STATE UNIV, 1968-; asst prof swine exten, Univ Ga, 1965-1968; asst nutrit res, Univ Nebr, 1962-1965; co-mgr grocery & meat merchandising, Kroger Co, Ky, 1960-1962; mgt trainee grocery & meat merchandising, Kroger Co, Ky, 1958-1960. **Memberships:** Sigma Xi; Am Soc Animal Sci; Am Registry Prof Animal Scientists; Coun Agr Sci & Technol. **Research Statement & Publications:** Swine nutrition; cereal grain utilization and amino acid requirements. **Mailing Address:** Dept Animal Sci, Okla State Univ, Stillwater, OK 74078-1828. **Fax:** 405-744-7390. **E-Mail:** billuce@ionet.net

LUCEY, CAROL ANN, THEORETICAL PHYSICS, PHILOSOPHY OF SCIENCE. **Personal Data:** b Johnstown, NY, September 16, 1943; m 1964, c 1. **Education:** Harpur Col, BA, 1965; State Univ NY, Binghamton, MA, 1968; Brown Univ, PhD (physics), 1972. **Professional Experience:** PRES, WESTERN NEV COMMUNITY COL, as of 2002; Nat Endowment Humanities fel, 1979-1980; Actg assoc dean instr, Jamestown Community Col, 1976-1978; PROF PHYSICS, A, 1973-. **Memberships:** Am Phys Soc; Philos Sci Asn. **Research Statement & Publications:** Study of cosmological implications for elementary particle physics; gauge theories and general relativity; scientific methodology. **Mailing Address:** Western Nev Community Col, 2201 W Col Pkwy, Carson City, NV 89703. **Fax:** 775-887-3051.

LUCEY, EDGAR C, PULMONARY. **Personal Data:** b February 27, 1945; m 1970, Lore; c Mark & Jennifer. **Education:** Morningside Col, Iowa, BS, 1967; Idaho State Univ, Pocatello, MS, 1971, PhD (physiol), 1975. **Professional Experience:** ASSOC RES PROF, SCH MED, BOSTON UNIV, as of 2003; mem, Animal Studies Subcomt, Vet Admin Med Ctr, 1986- & chair, Res Safety Subcomt, 1991-1992; res physiologist, Boston Vet Admin Med Ctr, beginning 1979; asst res prof med, Dept Physiol, 1979-1987; instr respiratory syst, Dept Physiol, 1976-1978; lectr physiol & instr human physiol & advan physiol, Humboldt State Univ, 1974-1976. **Memberships:** Am Physiol Soc; NY Acad Sci. **Research Statement & Publications:** Pathogeneses of pulmonary emphysema, fibrosis and airway secretory cell metaplasia; author of various publications. **Mailing Address:** Boston Vet Admin Med Ctr, 150 S Huntington Ave, Boston, MA 02130. **Fax:** 617-278-4540. **E-Mail:** edlucey@bu.edu

LUCEY, JEROLD FRANCIS, PEDIATRICS. **Personal Data:** b Holyoke, Mass, March 26, 1926; m 1950, c 3. **Education:** Dartmouth Col, AB, 1948; NY Univ, MD, 1952. **Honors & Awards:** Goulee Award, Am Asn Pediatrics, 1981; United Cerebral Palsy Prize, 1984; McDonald Award, 1990. **Professional Experience:** ENDOWED CHMN, HARRY WALLACE PROFESSORSHIP NEONATOL, 1995-; Humboldt Found fel, 1978; Litchfield lectr, Oxford Univ, 1978; ed-in-chief, Pediatrics, 1973-; mem, Am Bd Pediat Exam, 1970; chmn, Nat Bd Med Exam, 1968-1972; PROF PEDIAT, COL MED, UNIV VT, 1967-; res fel biochem, Harvard Med Sch, 1960-1961; Markle scholar, 1959-1964; consult, Vt State Health Dept, 1956-1981; from instr to assoc prof, Col Med, Univ VT, 1956-1966; Nat Found Infantile Paralysis res fel, Harvard Med Sch, 1955-1956; Mead Johnson fel, Columbia-Presby Med Ctr, 1954-1955; Bowen Brooks scholar, NY Acad Med, Bellevue Hosp, New York, 1954; asst resident, Columbia-Presby Med Ctr, 1953-1955; Intern pediat, Bellevue Hosp, New York, 1952-1953. **Memberships:** Soc Pediat Res; fel Am Acad Pediat; Am Pediat Soc; Am Soc Photobiol; Royal Soc Med; Sigma Xi. **Research Statement & Publications:** Neonatal physiology; transcutaneous oxygen. bilirubin metabolism; surfactant. **Mailing Address:** Dept Pediat, Fletcher Allen Health Care, Burlington, VT 05401.

LUCEY, JOHN WILLIAM, NUCLEAR ENGINEERING, INDUSTRIAL ENERGY CONSERVATION. **Personal Data:** b Winthrop, Mass, August 21, 1935; m 1957, Nancy Brozovich; c Josephine, John M, Thomas & Christopher. **Education:** Univ Notre Dame, BS, 1957; Mass Inst Technol, SM, 1963, PhD (nuclear eng), 1965. **Professional Experience:** PROF EMER, UNIV NOTRE DAME, as of 2006; dir, Notre Dame Indust Assessment Ctr, 1990- 2001; dir, Notre Dame Summer Eng Prog London, beginning 1988; dir, Ind Civil Defense Prof Adv Serv, 1969-1973; assoc prof nuclear eng, Univ Notre Dame, beginning 1968; asst prof, Univ Notre Dame, 1965-1968. **Memberships:** Am Nuclear Soc; Am Soc Eng Educ; Health Physics Soc; Sigma Xi; Soc Radiol Protection. **Research Statement & Publications:** Numerical methods for nuclear reactor calculations; radiation shielding; transport calculations; energy conservation for small and medium sized industry. **Mailing Address:** Dept Aerospace & Mech Eng, 365 Fitzpatrick Hall, Notre Dame, IN 46556. **Fax:** 574-631-8341. **E-Mail:** jlucey@nd.edu

LUCEY, ROBERT FRANCIS, agronomy; deceased, see previous edition for last biography

LUCHANSKY, JOHN B, MICROBIOLOGY. **Education:** PA State Univ, BS, 1980; Iowa State Univ, MS, 1983, PhD (microbiol), 1987. **Professional Experience:** RES LEADER, EASTERN REGIONAL RES CTR, ARS, USDA, WYNDMOOR, PA, 1999-. **Mailing Address:** Eastern Regional Res Ctr, ARS, USDA, 600 E Mermaid Lane, Wyndmoor, PA 19038. **Fax:** 215-233-6581. **E-Mail:** jluchansky@errc.ars.usda.gov

LUCHER, LYNNE ANNETTE, VIROLOGY, PROTEIN CHEMISTRY. **Personal Data:** b Houston, Tex, June 18, 1954. **Education:** Lindenwood Cols, St Charles, Mo, BA, 1976; Rice Univ, Houston, PhD (biochem), 1983. **Professional Experience:** DEPT BIOL SCI, UNIV ALASKA, 1994-; from asst prof to assoc prof virol & microbiol, Ill State Univ, Normal, 1985-1994; res assoc, Med Sch, St Louis Univ, 1982-1985. **Memberships:** Am Soc Microbiol; Am Soc Virol; AAAS. **Research Statement & Publications:** Biochemistry of adenovirus interaction with a host cell; reactions which determine whether a lytic infection or transformation occurs. **Mailing Address:** Dept Biol Sci, Univ Alaska, Sci Bldg Rm 128 3211 Providence Dr, Anchorage, AK 99508. **Fax:** 907-334-2161. **E-Mail:** lynne_lucher@health.state.ak.us

LUCHSINGER, WAYNE WESLEY, BIOCHEMISTRY. **Personal Data:** b Milaca, Minn, May 8, 1924; m 1943, Sadie; c Sharon K, Jerry W, Susan W & David W. **Education:** Univ Minn, BS, 1951, MS, 1954, PhD (biochem), 1956. **Professional Experience:** PROF EMER CHEM & BIOCHEM, ARIZ STATE UNIV, 1984-; from assoc prof to prof, Ariz State Univ, 1966-1984; assoc prof biochem, WVa Univ, 1960-1966; asst dir res, Kurth Malting Co, 1958-1960; sr chemist, Kurth Malting Co, 1956-1958; asst biochem, Univ Minn, 1951-1955. **Memberships:** AAAS; Am Chem Soc; Am Soc Brewing Chem; Am Asn Cereal Chem. **Research Statement & Publications:** Enzymes; barley carbohydrates; chemistry and mechanism of action of enzymes; carbohydrate structure. **Mailing Address:** Dept Chem & Biochem, Ariz State Univ, Tempe, AZ 85287-1604. **Fax:** 480-965-2747.

LUCHTEL, DANIEL LEE, ELECTRON MICROSCOPY, CELL BIOLOGY. **Personal Data:** b Carroll, Iowa, January 13, 1942. **Education:** St Benedict's Col, Kans, BS, 1963; Univ Wash, PhD (zoology), 1969. **Professional Experience:** PROF ENVIRON OCCUP HEALTH SCI, UNIV WASH, as of 2003; assoc prof environ health, Univ Wash, beginning 1983; asst prof, Univ Wash, 1975-1982; res assoc environ health, Univ Wash, 1973-1975; Res fel, Hubrecht Lab, Utrecht, Neth, 1972; res assoc biol struct, Univ Wash, 1971-1973; NIH fel, Univ Wash, 1969-1971. **Memberships:** AAAS; Sigma Xi; Am Soc Cell Biol; Am Inst Biol Sci; Electron Micros Soc Am. **Research Statement & Publications:** Lung ultrastructure and effects of gaseous and particulate air pollutants; respiratory tract mucus and mechanisms of mucous cell secretion; lung development; mechanisms of pulmonary edema; tracheal organ cultures. **Mailing Address:** Dept Environ & Occup Health Sci Univ Wash, Health Sci Bldg F-561B PO Box 357234, Seattle, WA 98195-7234. **Fax:** 206-685-3990. **E-Mail:** dluchtel@u.washington.edu

LUCIA, ANGELO, CHEMICAL ENGINEERING. **Education:** Univ Conn, PhD (chem eng), 1981. **Professional Experience:** CHESTER H KIRK PROF, CHEM ENG, UNIV RI, as of 2004. **Mailing Address:** Univ RI, Dept Chem Eng, Kingston, RI 02881. **Fax:** 401-874-4689. **E-Mail:** lucia@egr.uri.edu

LUCIANO, DENNIS, MATHEMATICS. **Education:** LeMoyne Col, BS, 1967; Syracuse Univ, MS, 1969, PhD, 1974. **Honors & Awards:** 12th George Polya Award, Math Asn Am;

Sears-Roebuck Found Award, 1991. **Professional Experience:** DEPT CHAIR & PROF MATH, WESTERN NEW ENGLAND COL, 1989-. **Mailing Address:** Dept Math & Comput Sci, Western New England Col, 129 Longview Dr, Longmeadow, MA 01106. **Fax:** 413-782-1275. **E-Mail:** dluciano@wnec.edu

LUCID, MICHAEL FRANCIS, INORGANIC CHEMISTRY. **Personal Data:** b Indianapolis, Ind, February 23, 1937; m 1967, c 3. **Education:** Ind Univ, Bloomington, BS, 1961; Purdue Univ, Lafayette, MS, 1965. **Professional Experience:** SR STAFF MINING ENGR, SHELL MINING CO, 1987-; proj mgr, Shell Mining Co, 1985-1987; staff mining engr, Shell Mining Co, 1983-1984; mgr mining develop, Shell Mining Co, 1980-1983; staff engr, Shell Mining Co, 1978-1980; res proj chemist, Kerr McGee Corp, 1975-1978; sr res chemist, Kerr McGee Corp, 1967-1975; Res chemist, Kerr McGee Corp, 1965-1967. **Memberships:** Am Chem Soc. **Research Statement & Publications:** Hydrometallurgy; solvent extraction; ion exchange; solution chemistry; geochemistry; solution mining, uranium, vanadium, copper, gold; oil shale. **Mailing Address:** 1622 Gunwale, Houston, TX 77062-4538.

LUCID, SHANNON W, BIOCHEMISTRY, ASTRONAUTICS. **Personal Data:** b Shanghai, China, January 14, 1943; m Michael; c Kawai D, ShandaraM & Michael K. **Education:** Univ Okla, BS, 6, MS, 1970, PhD (biochem), 1973. **Professional Experience:** ASTRONAUT, LYNDON B JOHNSON SPACE CTR, NASA, 1979-; res assoc, Okla Med Res Found, beginning 1974; chemist, Kerr-McGee, 1966-1968; sr lab technician, Okla Med Res Found, 1964-1966. **Research Statement & Publications:** Chemistry. **Mailing Address:** Johnson Space Ctr, NASA, 2101 NASA Rd one, Houston, TX 77058. **E-Mail:** shannon.w.lucid@nasa.gov

LUCIER, GEORGE W, TOXICOLOGY. **Personal Data:** b Southbridge, Mass, June 23, 1943. **Education:** Univ Md, PhD (entom), 1970. **Professional Experience:** RES CHEMIST, NAT INST ENVIRON HEALTH SCI, NIH, as of 2004; DIR, ENVIRON TOXICOL PROGS, as of 1998; CHIEF, LAB BIOCHEM RISK ANALYSIS, NAT INST ENVIRON HEALTH SCI, NIH, 1983-; ED, ENVIRON HEALTH PERSPECTIVES, 1973-. **Memberships:** Am Soc Toxicol; Endocrine Soc; Teratology Soc. **Research Statement & Publications:** Applications of biochemical data to human risk assessment. **Mailing Address:** Nat Inst Environ Health Sci, NIH, PO Box 12233, Research Triangle Park, NC 27709. **Fax:** 919-541-3647. **E-Mail:** lucier@niehs.nih.gov

LUCIER, JOHN J, ORGANIC CHEMISTRY. **Personal Data:** b Detroit, Mich, August 10, 1917. **Education:** Univ Dayton, BS, 1937; Western Res Univ, MS, 1950, PhD (org chem), 1951. **Professional Experience:** Distinguished serv prof, Univ Dayton, 1988; chmn dept, Univ Dayton, 1964-1979; PROF CHEM, UNIV DAYTON, 1963-; from asst prof to assoc prof, Univ Dayton, 1952-1963; instr chem, Univ Dayton, 1945-1947 & 1951-1952. **Memberships:** Fel AAAS; Am Chem Soc; Soc Appl Spectros; NY Acad Sci; Chem Soc. **Research Statement & Publications:** Organic synthesis; infrared spectroscopy; history of science. **Mailing Address:** Dept Chem, Univ Dayton, Dayton, OH 45469-2357.

LUCIS, RUTA, COMPARATIVE ENDOCRINOLOGY. **Personal Data:** b Rujiena, Latvia, April 9, 1925; Canadian citizen; m 1949, c 2. **Education:** Sir George Williams Univ, BSc, 1957; McGill Univ, MS, 1964, PhD (invest med), 1966. **Professional Experience:** RETIRED; clin chemist, Animal Res Inst, Ottawa, 1972-1990; res asst, Path Inst, 1966-1971; res asst endocrinol, McGill Univ, 1962-1965. **Memberships:** NY Acad Sci. **Research Statement & Publications:** Biochemistry of steroids; immunochemical assays and metabolism of hormones; environmental health. **Mailing Address:** 1512 Caverley St, Ottawa, ON K1G 0Y1, Can.

LUCK, DENNIS NOEL, MOLECULAR BIOLOGY. **Personal Data:** b Durban, SAfrica, December 8, 1939. **Education:** Univ Natal, BSc, 1961, MSc, 1963; Oxford Univ, DPhil (molecular biol), 1966. **Professional Experience:** RETIRED; chmn biol, Oberlin Col, 1995-1998; vis prof, Dept Biochem, Univ BC, Vancouver, Can, 1984-1985, 1986-1987, 1990-1991; prof biol, Oberlin Col, 1982-2005; foreign expert, Shanxi Agr Univ, Taigu, Shanxi, People's Repub China, 1982; consult biochemist, Gilford Instrument Lab, Oberlin, Ohio, 1980-1982; Eleanor Roosevelt Int Cancer fel, Univ Oxford, 1978-1979; from asst prof to assoc prof, Oberlin Col, 1972-1982; asst prof zoology, Univ Tex, Austin, 1970-1972; vis asst prof pharmacol, Baylor Col Med, 1969; lectr biochem, Univ Natal, 1966-1968. **Memberships:** Brit Biochem Soc; Am Soc Biochem & Molecular Biol; Am Soc Cell Biol; Am Soc Microbiol; fel, Ohio Acad Sci. **Research Statement & Publications:** Structure-function studies on growth hormone and prolactin. **Mailing Address:** Dept Biol, Oberlin Col, Sci Ctr K200C, Oberlin, OH 44074. **Fax:** 440-775-8960. **E-Mail:** dennis.n.luck@oberlin.edu

LUCK, GEORGE E, AERONAUTICS. **Professional Experience:** AVIATION CONSULTANT, as of 2005. **Memberships:** Am Inst Aeronaut & Astronaut. **Mailing Address:** Boeing Co Airplane Grp 777 Div, PO Box 3707 MS 02-78, Seattle, WA 98124. **Fax:** 206-294-1689. **E-Mail:** George.Luck@verizon.net

LUCK, LEON D(AN), CIVIL ENGINEERING. **Personal Data:** b Spokane, Wash, April 25, 1921; m 1941, c 2. **Education:** Wash State Univ, BS, 1943; Univ Minn, MS, 1951; Stanford Univ, CE, 1960. **Honors & Awards:** Western Elec Award, Am Soc Eng Educ, 1982. **Professional Experience:** PROF EMER CIVIL ENG, WASH STATE UNIV, 1983-; fulbright lectr, Chungbuk Nat Univ, Rep Korea, 1983-1984; chmn dept civil & environ eng, Wash State Univ, 1972-1976; from assoc prof to prof, Wash State Univ, 1959-1983; lectr, Stanford Univ, 1957-1959; consult engr, Potlatch Forests, Inc, 1956-1960; from instr to assoc prof civil eng, Wash State Univ, 1947-1957; mine engr, Pend Oreille Mines & Metals Co, 1943 & 1946-1947. **Memberships:** Am Soc Civil Engrs; Am Soc Eng Educ; Nat Soc Prof Engrs. **Research Statement & Publications:** Shear characteristics of Palouse clay; seepage flow through porous soil media; rigid frame analysis by matrix methods with the aid of a digital computer. **Mailing Address:** Dept Civil Eng, Wash State Univ, PO Box 642910, Pullman, WA 99164-2910. **Fax:** 509-335-2576.

LUCK, LINDA A, BIOCHEMISTRY. **Education:** Univ Vt, PhD (Chem), 1989. **Honors & Awards:** Am Chem Soc; Nat Cancer Inst. **Professional Experience:** PROF CHEM & PRE MED ADV, CLARKSON UNIV, 2005; SR SCIENTIST, NAT INST ENVIRON SCI, as of 2005; from asst prof to assoc prof, Dept Chem, Clarkson Univ, 1996-200. **Research Statement & Publications:** Structure relates to function in biological molecules; fluorescence; NMR; mass spectrometry; X-ray crystallography; electrochemistry; molecular graphics; site-directed mutagenesis; DNA sequencing; gene cloning; and protein purification. **Mailing Address:** Dept Chem & Biol, Clarkson Univ, 263 Sci Ctr POBox 5810, Potsdam, NY 13699-5810. **Fax:** 315-268-6610. **E-Mail:** luckla@clarkson.edu

LUCK, MICHAEL S, BIOTECHNOLOGY, GASTROINTESTINAL PHARMACOLOGY & INFECTIOUS DISEASE. **Personal Data:** b Milwaukee, Wis, May 1954. **Education:** Marquette Univ, BS, 1976; Univ Wis, PhD (pharmacol), 1994. **Professional Experience:** SR SCIENTIST, IMMUCELL CORP, 1996-; postdoctoral trainee toxicol, Univ Wis, 1994-1995; Med technologist, Milwaukee County med Complex, 1977-1989. **Research Statement & Publications:** Research and development of therapies for the treatment and prevention of gastrointestinal infectious disease; clinical development of vaccines and oral passive antibody treatment of gastrointestinal infectious disease; development of specific vaccines that produce high titer specific immunity against select antigens of infectious agents. **Mailing Address:** ImmuCell Corp, 56 Evergren Dr, Portland, ME 04103-1066. **Fax:** 207-878-2117. **E-Mail:** luckimcell@aol.com

LUCK, RICHARD EARLE, ASTROPHYSICS, ASTRONOMY. **Personal Data:** b Roanoke, Va, March 9, 1950; m 1978. **Education:** Univ Va, BA, 1972; Univ Tex, MA, 1975, PhD (astron), 1977. **Professional Experience:** PROF PHYSICS, CASE WESTERN RESERVE UNIV, as of 2003; WARNER PROF & CHMN ASTRON, DEPT ASTRON, CASE WESTERN RESERVE UNIV, 1994-; DIR, WARNER & SWAYZE OBSERV, CASE WESTERN RESERVE UNIV, 1994-; RES ASSOC, DEPT PHYSICS & ASTRON, LA STATE UNIV, 1977-. **Memberships:** Am Astron Soc; Royal Astron Soc. **Research Statement & Publications:** Chemical composition of late-type stars to determine the effects of stellar and galactic chemical evolution on such objects. **Mailing Address:** Dept Astron, Case Western Reserve Univ, 422 AW Smith Bldg, 10900 Euclid Ave, Cleveland, OH 44106. **Fax:** 216-368-5406. **E-Mail:** luck@fafnir.astr.cwru.edu

LUCK, RUSSELL M, POLYMER CHEMISTRY, ORGANIC CHEMISTRY. **Personal Data:** b Reading, Pa, May 11, 1926; m 1963, c 2. **Education:** Albright Col, BSc, 1947; Bucknell Univ, MSc, 1948. **Professional Experience:** RETIRED; adv scientist, Res & Develop Ctr, 1983-1987; fel scientist, Res & Develop Ctr, 1971-1983; sr engr, Res & Develop Ctr, 1960-1971; engr, Mat Eng Dept, Westinghouse Elec Corp, 1953-1960; asst prod mgr, Wyomissing Glazed Papers Inc, 1948-1951; asst chem, Bucknell Univ, 1947-1948. **Memberships:** Am Chem Soc. **Research Statement & Publications:** Organic and inorganic polymers for application as lubricants and electrical insulations with high temperature capabilities. **Mailing Address:** 1241 Harvest Dr, Monroeville, PA 15146.

LUCK, STANLEY D, BIOPHYSICAL CHEMISTRY. **Personal Data:** b Kingston, Jamaica, December 13, 1957. **Education:** Univ Waterloo, Can, BS, 1981; Univ BC, Can, PhD (chem), 1987. **Professional Experience:** Res assoc, Fox Chase Cancer Ctr, beginning 1991; res assoc, Protein Dynamics, 1987-1991. **Memberships:** Biophys Soc. **Research Statement & Publications:** Biophysical chemistry. **Mailing Address:** Inst Cancer Res, Fox Chase Cancer Ctr, 7701 Burholme Ave, Philadelphia, PA 19111.

LUCKE, ROBERT LANCASTER, ATMOSPHERIC CHEMISTRY & PHYSICS. **Personal Data:** b Norfolk, Va, July 22, 1945. **Education:** Johns Hopkins Univ, BA, 1968, MA, 1972, PhD (physics), 1975. **Professional Experience:** PRES, NAVAL RES LAB, as of 2004; RES PHYSICIST, US NAVAL RES LAB, WASH, 1982-; asst prof physics & astron, Univ Toledo, Ohio, 1979-1981; Nat Res Coun fel, Goddard Space Flight Ctr, NASA, 1976-1978; assoc res scientist physics, Johns Hopkins Univ, 1975-1976. **Memberships:** Am Astron Soc. **Research Statement & Publications:** Far ultraviolet albedo of the moon; coronal line emmission in supernova remnants; x-ray astronomy; astronomical instrumentation. **Mailing Address:** US Naval Res Lab, Code 7218 4555 Overlook Ave SW, Washington, DC 20735. **E-Mail:** lucke@wvms.nrl.navy.mil

LUCKE, WILLIAM E, ANALYTICAL CHEMISTRY. **Personal Data:** b Grand Island, Nebr, July 31, 1936; m 1959, c 5. **Education:** Univ Nebr, BS, 1958; Ohio State Univ, PhD (chem), 1963. **Professional Experience:** RETIRED; mgr regulatory affairs, Cincinnati Milacron Inc, as of 1996; sr anal chemist, cimcool div, Cincinnati Milacron Inc, beginning 1974; supvr, Cimcool Customer Lab Serv, Cincinnati Milacron Inc, 1971-1974; res assoc, Cincinnati Milling Mach Co, 1969-1971; res chemist, Olympic Res Div, Rayonier Inc, 1963-1969. **Memberships:** AAAS; Am Chem Soc. **Research Statement & Publications:** Carbohydrate, cellulose and wood chemistry; analytical chemistry of industrial metal working products. **Mailing Address:** 959 Nordyke Rd, Cincinnati, OH 45255.

LUCKENBACH, MARK WAYNE, MARINE BENTHIC ECOLOGY, SHELLFISH AQUACULTURE. **Personal Data:** b Houston, Tex, May 10, 1955; m 1979, Michelle; c Joshua D & Patrick J. **Education:** Univ NC, BS, 1977; Univ SC, PhD (biol), 1985. **Professional Experience:** PROF, VA INST MARINE SCI, COL WILLIAM & MARY, as of 1995; assoc prof, Va Inst Marine Sci, Col William & Mary, beginning 1990; DIR, OYSTER AQUACULT PROG & SCIENTIST-IN-CHARGE, EASTERN SHORE LAB, 1990-; asst prof, Col William & Mary, 1985-1990. **Memberships:** AAAS; Estuarine Res Fedn; Nat Shellfisheries Asn. **Research Statement & Publications:** Marine benthic ecology with emphasis on hydrodynamic effects on recruitment, feeding and growth of invertebrates; shellfish aquaculture. **Mailing Address:** Dept Biol Sci, VA Ist Marine Sci, Gloucester Pt PO Box 1346, Parksley, VA 23062-1346. **Fax:** 757-787-5831. **E-Mail:** luck@vims.edu

LUCKENBILL-EDDS, LOUISE, DEVELOPMENTAL BIOLOGY, NEUROBIOLOGY. **Personal Data:** b Lebanon, Pa, November 19, 1936; m 1986. **Education:** Oberlin Col, BA, 1958; Brown Univ, PhD (biol), 1964. **Professional Experience:** Sr int fel, NIH, Fogarty Ctr, 1989-1990; sci fel, Max Planck Inst Biochem, Ger, 1989-1990; Guest scientist, Nat Inst Dent Res, NIH, Bethesda, Md, 1985-1986; ASSOC PROF ZOOL & BIOMED SCI, OHIO UNIV, ATHENS, 1977-; instr, Dept Neuropath, Harvard Med Sch, 1975-1977; asst prof biol sci, Smith Col, 1969-1975; sci fel, Hubrecht Lab, Royal Netherlands Acad Sci & Letters, 1968-1969; instr res dermat, Sch Med, Boston Univ, 1966-1968; Arthritis Found res fel arthritis & connective tissue dis, Sch Med, Boston Univ, 1965-1966. **Memberships:** AAAS; Am Soc Zool; Soc Develop Biol; Soc Neuroscience; Sigma Xi. **Research Statement & Publications:** Laminin-mediated neurite outgrowth; histogenesis of sympathetic neurons; migration and differentiation of neural crest cells. **Mailing Address:** Dept Biol Sci, Ohio Univ, Athens, OH 45701. **Fax:** 740-593-0300. **E-Mail:** luckenbill@ouvaxa.cats.ohiou.edu

LUCKENS, MARK MANFRED, PHARMACOLOGY, TOXICOLOGY. **Personal Data:** b Kiev, Russia, April 7, 1912; American citizen; m 1943, c 2. **Education:** Columbia Univ, BS, 1935; NY Univ, MS, 1950; Univ Conn, PhD (pharmacol, toxicol), 1963; Polytech Inst NY, MSES, 1972; Am Bd Indust Hyg, dipl. **Professional Experience:** RETIRED; pvt pract, beginning 1977; consult, Nat Inst Occup Health & Safety, 1977; consult, Spindletop Res Ctr, 1965-; mem fac & co-dir interdisciplinary grad prog toxicol, Univ Ky, 1973-1977; Fulbright travel grant, 1965-1966; award, Partners-in-the-Americas, 1965-1966; consult, Lab Serv, Childrens's Hosp, Louisville, Ky, 1963-; dir, Inst Environ Toxicol & Occup Hyg, Univ Ky, 1962-1977; consult, Lexington-Fayette County Dept Health, Ky Poison Info & Environ Health Control Prog, 1961-; consult, Ky State Dept Human Resources, 1961-; from asst prof to assoc prof toxicol & pharmacol, Col Pharm, Univ Ky, 1961-1977; toxicologist, Conn State Dept Health, 1954-1961; dir, Emmet Tech Assocs, 1948-1954; inspector, Chem Warfare Serv, 1941-1943; chief chemist, Technichem Labs, 1937-1941; chemist, Wilkow Food Prod, 1933-1936; jr chemist, Wilkow Food Prod, 1928-1933; dir, Hemispheric Prog Poison Info & Control; mem, adv comt pesticides, Ky Dept Agr vis prof, Polytech Inst Guayaquil; vis dir, Oceano vis prof, Polytech Inst of Guayaquil. **Memberships:** Fel AAAS; fel Am Inst Chem; fel Am Acad Indust Hyg; fel Am Acad Forensic Sci; Am Chem Soc;

Sigma Xi. **Research Statement & Publications:** Toxicodynamics; comparative toxicology and pharmacology; environmental, occupational, clinical, analytical, food and forensic toxicology; chemical pathology; drug action in hibernation; biorhythms; effects of psychosocial parameters on toxicity and pharmacologic action. **Mailing Address:** 4609 Edgemont Dr, Austin, TX 78731.

LUCKERT, H(ANS) J(OACHIM), AERODYNAMICS, APPLIED MATHEMATICS. **Personal Data:** b Ger, August 26, 1905; Canadian citizen; m 1953, Ilse Schwabedissen; c Doris. **Education:** Harvard Univ, AM, 1929; Univ Berlin, Dr Phil, 1933. **Professional Experience:** RETIRED; Phoenix Eng, Space Res Corp, 1983-1989; Phoenix Eng, Inc, Newport, Vt, 1982-1983; consult, Potton Tech Indust, Inc, 1980-1981; chief aerodynamicist, Space Res Corp, 1969-1980; chief aerodynamicist, Space Res Inst, Inc, 1968-1969; hon res assoc, McGill Univ, 1967-1985; chief aerodynamicist, Space Res Inst, McGill Univ, 1965-1968; mem assoc comt space res, Nat Res Coun Res Coord Group, Upper Atmosphere Res Vehicles, 1964-1967; staff scientist res & develop, Missiles & Systs Div, 1964-1965; Chmn, Nat Res Coun Res Coord Group, Upper Atmosphere Res Vehicles, 1964-1965; mem assoc comt aerodyn, Nat Res Coun Res Coord Group, Upper Atmosphere Res Vehicles, 1963-1966; sect chief missiles & space res, Missiles & Systs Div, 1963-1964; chief tech sect, Missiles & Systs Div, 1957-1963; design specialist, Canadair, Ltd, 1954-1957; engr, Canadair, Ltd, 1952-1954; consult aerodyn, Control Comn for Ger, 1947-1952; scientist transl & aero res, Brit Ministry Supply, 1945-1947; sr group leader aerodyn, Arado Aircraft Co, 1937-1945; aerodynamicist, Henschel Aircraft Co, 1935-1937; Asst to prof math, Mining Acad Freiberg, Ger, 1929-1934. **Memberships:** Assoc fel Am Inst Aeronaut & Astronaut; fel Can Aeronaut & Space Inst; Ger Soc Aeronaut & Astronaut. **Research Statement & Publications:** Aerodynamics and physics; astronautics; aircraft and missiles. **Mailing Address:** 197 58th Ave, Laval des Rapides, PQ H7V 2A5, Can.

LUCKETT, WINTER PATRICK, EVOLUTIONARY BILOGY, SYSTEMATICS. **Personal Data:** b Atlanta, Ga, March 23, 1937. **Education:** Univ Mo, AB, 1961, MA, 1963; Univ Wis-Madison, PhD (anat), 1967. **Professional Experience:** Assoc prof anat, Sch Med, Creighton Univ, 1975-; asst prof anat, Col Physicians & Surgeons, Columbia Univ, 1969-1975; instr, Col Physicians & Surgeons, Columbia Univ, 1968-1969; DEPT ANAT, UNIV PR, SAN JUAN. **Memberships:** AAAS; Am Asn Anat; Soc Study Reproduction; Int Primatol Soc. **Research Statement & Publications:** Comparative morphogenesis of the placenta and fetal membranes; endocrinology of reproduction; evolution of mammals; dental development and evolution in mammals. **Mailing Address:** Dept Anat, Univ PR, Campus G PO Box 365067, San Juan, PR 00936-0567.

LUCKEY, GEORGE WILLIAM, PHYSICAL CHEMISTRY, DIAGNOSTIC IMAGING. **Personal Data:** b Dayton, Ohio, April 17, 1925; m 1958, Doris J Waring; c George R, Jana E & John A. **Education:** Oberlin Col, BA, 1947; Rochester Univ, PhD (chem), 1950. **Professional Experience:** RETIRED; res fel & lab head, Spec Res Lab, 1977-1986; Appl Photog Div, 1956-1960 & Spec Res Dept, 1961-1977; Mem staff, Photog Theory Dept, Eastman Kodak Co, 1950-1956. **Memberships:** Am Chem Soc; Am Phys Soc; Royal Soc Chem; Soc The soc for imaging sci technol(15 & T) Electrochem Soc; Sigma Xi. **Research Statement & Publications:** Photochemistry; photographic theory; luminescence; photographic processing chemistry; photographic and radiographic systems. **Mailing Address:** 240 Weymouth Dr, Rochester, NY 14625-1917.

LUCKEY, PAUL DAVID, JR, ELECTROMAGNETISM. **Personal Data:** b Pittsburgh, Pa, May 18, 1928; wid, c 3. **Education:** Carnegie Inst Technol, BS, 1949; Cornell Univ, PhD (physics), 1954. **Professional Experience:** SR RES SCIENTIST PHYSICS, MASS INST TECHNOL, 1970-; mem sci res staff, Mass Inst Technol, 1956-1970; Res assoc physics, Cornell Univ, 1953-1956. **Memberships:** Am Phys Soc. **Research Statement & Publications:** Meson physics; photoproduction of Pi mesons; electron synchrotrons. **Mailing Address:** CERN EP Div CH-1211, Geneva 23, Switzerland.

LUCKEY, THOMAS DONNELL, BIOCHEMISTRY, NUTRITION. **Personal Data:** b Casper, Wyo, May 15, 1919; m 1943, Pauline; c Jane, Mary & Donna. **Education:** Colo Agr Col, BS, 1941; Univ Wis, MS, 1944, PhD (biochem), 1946. **Honors & Awards:** Knighted, Greifenstein Castle, 1984. **Professional Experience:** RETIRED; bd dir, Radiation Sci & Health Inc, beginning 1996; chief exec officer, Oralu Corp, beginning 1991; vis prof, Univ Qatar, 1983; Av Humboldt Sr Sci Award, 1978-1980; mem, Subcomt Interaction Infection & Nutrit, Nat Acad Sci, 1972-1974; moderator symp gnotobiol, Int Meeting Microbiol, Moscow, 1966; dir, W Cent States Biochem Conf, beginning 1964; Am Inst Nutrit traveling fel, Cong, 1963; Commonwealth res fel, 1961-1962; Univ Mo fel, Stockholm Microbiol Cong, 1958; NSF traveling fel, Paris Nutrit Cong, 1957; prof biochem, Sch Med, Univ Mo, Columbia, 1954-1984; asst res prof biochem, Univ Notre Dame, 1946-1954; asst, Univ Wis, 1942-1946; asst, Agr & Mech Col, Tex, 1941-1942; nutrit consult, NASA Johnson Space Ctr, Houston; consult, McDonnell Aircraft Corp, Mygrodol Prod Inc & Gen Elec Co. **Memberships:** AAAS; Am Chem Soc; Soc Exp Biol & Med; Am Soc Microbiol; Am Inst Nutrit; Sigma Xi. **Research Statement & Publications:** Nutrition and metabolism of germ-free vertebrates; folic acid and related compounds in chick nutrition; comparative nutrition; modes of action of antibiotics; gnotobiology; thymic hormones; hormesis; low level radiation effects; biochemistry and nutrition; author. **Mailing Address:** 1719 Brandon Woods Dr, Lawrence, KS 66047. **Fax:** 970-669-0186.

LUCKHAM, DAVID COMPTOM, COMPUTER SCIENCE. **Personal Data:** b Kingston, Jamaica, September 7, 1936. **Education:** Univ London, BSc, 1956, MSc, 1957; Mass Inst Technol, PhD (math logic), 1963. **Professional Experience:** PROF EMER ELEC ENG, STANFORD UNIV, 2002-; Systs Control Inc, 1978; res prof elec eng, 1977-1999; Vinton Hayes sr res fel, Harvard Univ, 1976; sr res assoc, Stanford Artificial Intel Lab, 1972-1977; res comput scientist, Stanford Univ, 1972-1976; Jet Propulsion Lab, 1971; from asst prof to assoc prof, Univ Calif, Los Angeles, 1970-1972; res assoc comput sci, Stanford Univ, 1968-1970; lectr, Ctr Comput & Automation, Imp Col, Univ London, 1967-1968; lectr math, Univ Manchester, 1965-1968; Sci Coun res grant, Univ Manchester, 1965-1968; res assoc comput sci, Mass Inst Technol, 1963-1965; consult, Bolt, Beranek & Newman Inc, 1963-1965. **Memberships:** Am Math Soc; Asn Comput Mach; Asn Symbolic Logic. **Research Statement & Publications:** Theory of computation; automated proof procedures and applications to computer-aided programming, verification of programs; semantics of programming languages; parallel programs; microprocessor systems; artificial intelligence; published four books and over 100 technical papers. **Mailing Address:** Comput Systs Lab, Stanford Univ, Gates Comput Sci Bldg 353 Serra Mall, Stanford, CA 94305. **Fax:** 650-323-1422. **E-Mail:** luckham@stanford.edu

LUCKMANN, WILLIAM HENRY, ENTOMOLOGY. **Personal Data:** b Cape Girardeau, Mo, January 15, 1926; m 1949, c 5. **Education:** Univ Mo, BS, 1949; Univ Ill, MS, 1951, PhD, 1956. **Professional Experience:** PROF EMER, OFF AGR ENTOM, COL AGR, UNIV ILL, 1984-; prof & head, Off Agr Entom, Col Agr, Univ Ill, 1965-1984; head sect econ entom, State Natural Hist Surv, Ill, 1965-1984; entomologist, State Natural Hist Surv, Ill, 1959-1984; assoc entomologist, State Natural Hist Surv, Ill, 1954-1959; tech develop, Shell Chem Corp, Colo, 1953-1954; asst entomologist, State Natural Hist Surv, Ill, 1951-1953. **Memberships:** Entom Soc Am. **Research Statement & Publications:** Ecology; biology; applied control. **Mailing Address:** Univ Ill, 607 E Peabody, Champaign, IL 61820.

LUCKOCK, ARLENE SUZANNE, NEUROPHYSIOLOGY, ENDOCRINOLOGY. **Personal Data:** b Oakland, Calif, November 23, 1948; m 1976, c 2. **Education:** Univ Calif, Berkeley, BA, 1969, PhD (physiol), 1974. **Professional Experience:** PROF PHYSIOL, PALMER COL CHIROPRACTIC W, as of 2004; assoc prof physiol, Palmer Col Chiropractic W, beginning 1979; instr physiol, West Valley Col, Saratoga, Calif, 1978-1979; fel, Dept Psychiat, Med Sch, Stanford Univ, 1974-1976 & Dept Genetics, 1976-1978. **Research Statement & Publications:** Effects of thyroid hormones on mammalian brain development; genetic differences in testosterone synthesis in two strains of mice; genetic polymorphisms in testosterone estradiol binding globulin in human populations. **Mailing Address:** Dept Physiol, Palmer Col Chiropractic W, Rm 139 90 E Tasman Dr, San Jose, CA 95134. **Fax:** 408-944-6032. **E-Mail:** arlene.luckock@palmer.edu

LUCKRING, JAMES MICHAEL, AERODYNAMICS. **Personal Data:** b Canton, Ohio, August 5, 1951; c Ellen, Diane & Jeff. **Education:** Purdue Univ, BS, 1973, MS, 1974; NC State Univ, PhD (aerospace eng), 1985. **Professional Experience:** FULL PROF LECTR AERODYN, GEORGE WASH UNIV, 1986-; SR RES ENGR, LANGLEY RES CTR, NASA, 1974-. **Memberships:** Assoc fel Am Inst Aeronaut & Astronaut. **Research Statement & Publications:** Experimental and applied computational aerodynamics for advanced configurations. **Mailing Address:** Langley Res Ctr NASA, MS 286, Hampton, VA 23681.

LUCKRING, R(ICHARD) M(ICHAEL), TECHNICAL MANAGEMENT. **Personal Data:** b Canton, Ohio, February 3, 1917; m 1954, Viola; c Mimi, Paula, Michael, Eve, Abby & Andrea. **Education:** Heidelberg Col, BS, 1940; Lehigh Univ, BS, 1942. **Professional Experience:** RETIRED; planning assoc, Chem, Dyes & Pigments Dept, 1978-1981; environ mgr, Pigments Dept, 1975-1978; tech mgr inorg fibers, Pigments Dept, 1971-1975; res mgr, Pigments Dept, 1955-1971; res supvr, Pigments Dept, 1953-1955; res engr, Pigments Dept, 1952-1953; field engr, Eng Dept, E I Du Pont de Nemours & Co, 1942-1952. **Memberships:** Am Chem Soc; Am Inst Chem Engrs. **Research Statement & Publications:** Process development; extractive metallurgy; refractory metals; titanate and titanium dioxide products and processes. **Mailing Address:** 108 Meriden Dr, Hockessin, DE 19707.

LUCKY, ROBERT W, ELECTRICAL ENGINEERING. **Personal Data:** b Pittsburgh, Pa, January 9, 1936; m 1961, Joan; c 2. **Education:** Purdue Univ, BS, 1957, MS, 1959, PhD (elec eng), 1961. **Honorary Degrees:** DEng, Purdue Univ, 1988; DSc, NJ Inst Technol, 1991. **Honors & Awards:** Edwin Armstrong Award, Inst Elec & Electronics Engrs Commun Soc, 1975; Centennial Medal, Inst Elec & Electronics Engrs, 1984, Edison Medal, 1995; Marconi Int Prize, Marconi Found, 1986. **Professional Experience:** CONSULT, as of 2004; CHAIR TELECOM RES COUN, NAT RES COUN, as of 2004; CHAIR, TECHNOL ADVISORY COUN, FED COMMUNICATION COMN, as of 2004; vpres appl res, Bellcore, 1992-2002; exec dir, Communications Sci Res Div, 1992-2002; Off Sci & Technol Policy Nat Crit Technol Panel, 1990- & vis Comt Advan Technol, Nat Inst Stand & Technol, 1991-1992; Comput Sci & Technol Bd, Nat Res Coun, 1986-; mem, Strategic Defense Initiative Adv Comt, 1986-1989; chmn, Sci Adv Bd, USAF, 1986-1989; vchmn, Sci Adv Bd, USAF, 1983-1986; exec dir, Res Commun Sci Div, 1982-1992; consult ed, J Telecommun Networks, 1978-1986; dir elec & comput systs, Digital-Switching Processing Res Dept, 1978-1982; vpres, Inst Elec & Electronics Engrs, Commun Soc, 1978; asst dir elec comput, Digital-Switching Processing Res Dept, 1977-1978; dept head, Digital-Switching Processing Res Dept, 1976-1977; ed, Proc Inst Elec & Electronics Engrs, 1974-1976; assoc ed, Trans Info Theory, 1971-1974; asst ed, Trans Commun, Inst Elec & Electronics Engrs, 1970-1973; head, Data Theory Dept, 1965-1976; supvr, Signal Theory Group, 1964-1965; mem tech staff, Bell Labs, Holmdel, NJ, 1961-1964. **Memberships:** Nat Acad Eng; fel Inst Elec & Electronics Engrs (vpres 1978-1979 & 1981-1982). **Research Statement & Publications:** Communication theory; information theory; data transmission; author of over 50 publications; awarded 11 patents. **Mailing Address:** 48 Gillespie Ave, Fair Haven, NJ 07704. **E-Mail:** rlucky@telcordia.com

LUCOVSKY, GERALD, SOLID STATE PHYSICS. **Personal Data:** b New York, NY, February 28, 1935; m 1957, c 5. **Education:** Univ Rochester, BS, 1956, MA, 1958; Temple Univ, PhD (physics), 1960. **Professional Experience:** UNIV PROF PHYSICS, NC STATE UNIV, RALEIGH, 1980-; sr res fel, Gen Sci Lab, Palo Alto Res Ctr, 1974-1980; assoc lab mgr, Gen Sci Lab, 1973-1974; solid state sci br, Palo Alto Res Ctr, 1970-1973; solid state res br, Photoconductor Res Br, Xerox Corp, 1969-1970; mgr, Photoconductor Res Br, Xerox Corp, 1968-1969; assoc prof eng, Case Western Res Univ, 1967-1968; sr scientist, Xerox Corp, 1965-1967; mem staff solid state physics, Philco Corp, Pa, 1958-1965. **Memberships:** Fel Am Phys Soc. **Research Statement & Publications:** Optical properties of solids; lattice dynamics; amorphous semiconductors. **Mailing Address:** Dept Physics, NC State Univ, PO Box 8202, Raleigh, NC 27695. **Fax:** 919-515-6538. **E-Mail:** gerry lucovsky@ncsu.edu

LUCZAK, RICHARD, PARALLEL PROGRAMMING, NUMERICAL GRID GENERATION. **Personal Data:** b Lodz, Poland, April 8, 1957; American citizen. **Education:** Tech Univ Lodz, MS, 1981, PhD (appl math), 1988. **Professional Experience:** COMPUT MATHEMATICIAN, NUMERICAL ALGORITHMS GROUP INC, 1991-; res & develop engr, Unotech Corp, 1989; appl mathematician, Tech Univ, Lodz, Poland, 1981-1988. **Memberships:** Soc Indust & Appl Math; Asn Comput Mach. **Research Statement & Publications:** Design, implementation, testing of algorithms for numerical solution of partial differential equations on parallel computers; design of a new computational technique applicable to finite element analysis resulting in a great speedup and better accuracy of coefficients of global stiffness matrix and load vector. **Mailing Address:** 2388 Patrick Blvd, Fairborn, OH 45431. **E-Mail:** luczak@hotmail.com

LUDDEN, GERALD D, MATHEMATICS. **Personal Data:** b Quincy, Ill, September 6, 1937; m 1961, c 3. **Education:** St Ambrose Col, BA, 1959; Univ Notre Dame, MS, 1961, PhD (math), 1966. **Professional Experience:** PROF MATH, MICH STATE UNIV, 1977-; from asst prof to assoc prof, Mich State Univ, 1966-1977; lectr math, Ind Univ, 1965-1966. **Memberships:** Math Asn Am; Am Math Soc; Tensor Soc. **Research Statement & Publications:** Hypersurfaces of manifolds with an f-structure; submanifolds of real and complex space forms. **Mailing Address:** Mich State Univ, East Lansing, MI 48824-0001. **E-Mail:** ludden@msu.edu

LUDDEN, PAUL W, BIOCHEMISTRY. **Personal Data:** b Omaha, Nebr, November 7, 1950; m 1974. **Education:** Univ Nebr, Lincoln, BS, 1972; Univ Wis-Madison, PhD (biochem), 1977. **Professional Experience:** ASSOC DEAN BIOCHEM, UNIV WIS, MADISON, 2002-; asst prof, Univ Wis-Madison, 1981-1985; asst prof biochem & asst biochemist, Univ Calif, Riverside, 1978-1981; res assoc, Mich State Univ, 1977-1978; fel, Rockefeller Found, 1977-1978; res asst, Univ Wis-Madison, 1972-1977. **Memberships:**

Am Soc Plant Physiol; Am Soc Microbiol. **Research Statement & Publications:** Plant biochemistry; nitrogen metabolism in plants and bacteria; carbon monoxide oxidation. **Mailing Address:** Dept Biochem, Univ Wis, 420 Henry Mall, 433 Babcock Dr, Madison, WI 53706-1569. **Fax:** 608-262-3453. **E-Mail:** pludden@cals.wisc.edu

LUDDEN, THOMAS MARCELLUS, BIOPHARMACEUTICS, DRUG METABOLISM. **Personal Data:** b Kansas City, Mo, January 16, 1946; m 1979, c 4. **Education:** Univ Mo, Kansas City, BS, 1969, PhD (pharmacol), 1973. **Professional Experience:** VPRES, PHARMACOMETRIC RES & DEVELOP, GLOBOMAX LLC, as of 2005; PROF PHARMACOL, FOOD & DRUG ADMIN, 1991-; prof, Univ Tex, Austin, 1985-1991; Southwestern Drug Centennial fel pharm, 1985-1987; prof pharmacol, Univ Tex Health Sci Ctr, San Antonio, 1985-1986; tech consult, Audie Murphy Vet Hosp, San Antonio, 1977-1983; from asst prof to assoc prof, Univ Tex Health Sci Ctr, San Antonio, 1976-1985; from asst prof to assoc prof pharmacol, Univ Tex, Austin, 1975-1985; sis res assoc pharmaceut, Ohio State Univ, 1974-1975. **Memberships:** Am Pharmaceut Asn; Am Asn Pharmaceut Sci; Sigma Xi; NY Acad Sci; fel Am Col Clin Pharm. **Research Statement & Publications:** Applied pharmacokinetics and new drug development. **Mailing Address:** GloboMax LLC, 7250 Pkwy Dr Ste 430, Hanover, MD 21076. **Fax:** 410-712-0737. **E-Mail:** luddent@globomax.com

LUDEKE, RUDOLF, SOLID STATE PHYSICS, MATERIAL SCIENCE. **Personal Data:** b Hannover, Ger, May 6, 1937; m 1964, c 2. **Education:** Univ Cincinnati, BS, 1961; Harvard Univ, MA, 1962, PhD (appl physics), 1968. **Professional Experience:** Prog chmn & conf chmn, Conf Physics & Chem Semi-conductor Interfaces, 1987; comt mem, Elec Mat & Processing Div, Am Vacuum Soc, 1986-; vis scholar, Dept Physics, Univ Utah, 1986-1987; assoc ed, J Vacuum Sci & Tech, 1982-1984; vis scientist, Max Planck Inst, Stuttgart, Ger, 1977-1978; Alexander Von Humboldt Found fel, 1977; RES STAFF MEM, T J WATSON RES CTR, IBM CORP, 1968-. **Memberships:** Am Phys Soc; Sigma Xi; Mat Res Soc; Am Vacuum Soc. **Research Statement & Publications:** Semiconductor physics; surface and interface physics; thin film technology; structure and electronic properties of semiconductor interfaces, growth and characterization of semiconductor thin films and structures by molecular beum epitary, co-investor of the man-made semiconductor super lattice, optial properties of solids. **Mailing Address:** Int Bus Mach, T J Watson Res Ctr, PO Box 218, Yorktown Heights, NY 10598. **E-Mail:** ludeke@us.ibm.com

LUDEL, JACQUELINE, BIOPSYCHOLOGY, SENSORY SYSTEM. **Personal Data:** b Boston, Mass, 17, 1945. **Education:** Queens Col, NY, BA, 1966; Ind Univ, PhD (psychol), 1971. **Professional Experience:** PROF EMER BIOL & PSYCHOL, GUILFORD COL, 1997-; trustee, Marine Mammal Strandin Ctr, 1979-1986; Danforth assoc, 1979-1985; kenan grant, Guilford Col, 1977-1978; prof biol & psychol, Guilford Col, 1976-1997; asst prof psychol, Jacksonville Univ, 1971-1973 & Stockton State Col, 1973-1976; assoc instr, Ind Univ, 1967-1971; grad fel, NSF, 1966-1971. **Memberships:** Psychol Social Responsibility. **Research Statement & Publications:** Sensory anatomy and physiology; stranded and beached cetaceans; science writing. **Mailing Address:** Depts Biol & Psychol, Guilford Col, 5800 W Friendly Ave, Greensboro, NC 27410. **Fax:** 910-316-2951. **E-Mail:** ludelj@rascal.guilford.edu

LUDEMA, KENNETH C, MECHANICAL ENGINEERING, SURFACE PHYSICS. **Personal Data:** b Dorr, Mich, April 30, 1928; m 1955, c 5. **Education:** Calvin Col, BS, 1955; Univ Mich, BS, 1955, MS, 1956, PhD (mech eng), 1963; Cambridge Univ, PhD (physics), 1965. **Professional Experience:** PROF EMER MECH ENG, UNIV MICH, ANN ARBOR, as of 2003; prof mech eng, Univ Mich, Ann Arbor, beginning 1972; from asst prof to assoc prof, Univ Mich, Ann Arbor, 1964-1972; Ford Found & Univ Mich Inst Sci & Technol fac develop grant, Cambridge Univ, 1962-1964; instr mech eng, Univ Mich, 1955-1962. **Memberships:** Am Soc Mech Engrs; Am Soc Testing & Math. **Research Statement & Publications:** Sliding friction and wear behavior of solids, steels, plastics and rubbers; fundamental adhesion mechanisms between dissimilar materials; skid resistance properties of tires and roads. **Mailing Address:** Dept Mech Eng, Univ Mich, 2026 GG Brown Lab, Ann Arbor, MI 48109-2125. **Fax:** 734-647-3170. **E-Mail:** kenlud@umich.edu

LUDEMAN, LONNIE C, ENGINEERING. **Education:** SDak Sch Mines & Technol, BS (elec eng), 1963, MS, 1964; Ariz State Univ, PhD, 1968. **Professional Experience:** PROF EMER, DEPT ELEC & COMPUT ENG, NMEX STATE UNIV, as of 2006. **Mailing Address:** Dept Elec Comput Eng, NMex State Univ, Las Cruces, NM 88003. **Fax:** 505-646-1435. **E-Mail:** lludeman@nmsu.edu

LUDEMANN, CARL ARNOLD, ACCELERATOR DESIGN & CONTROL. **Personal Data:** b Brooklyn, NY, June 21, 1934; m 1956, c 2. **Education:** Brooklyn Col, BS, 1956; Univ Md, PhD (nuclear physics, elec eng), 1964. **Professional Experience:** RETIRED; physicist, Electronuclear Div, 1971-1993; physicist, Electronuclear Div, 1965-1971; vis scientist, Oak Ridge Nat Lab, 1964-1965; Res assoc physics, Univ Md, 1964-1965. **Memberships:** Am Phys Soc; Am Asn Physics Teachers. **Research Statement & Publications:** Neutron threshold measurements; gamma ray spectroscopy; angular correlation and nuclear reaction mechanism; nuclear structure studies; accelerator control, accelerator design. **Mailing Address:** 130 Newhaven Rd, Oak Ridge, TN 37830.

LUDERS, RICHARD CHRISTIAN, ANALYTICAL CHEMISTRY. **Personal Data:** b Staten Island, NY, July 23, 1934; m 1957, c 2. **Education:** Wagner Col, BS, 1956. **Professional Experience:** SR CHEMIST, DRUG METAB DIV, CIBA-GEIGY CORP, 1972-; head bioanal studies, Drug Metab Sect, 1970-1972; supvr, Ciba Pharmaceut Co, 1967-1970; group supvr anal res, Ciba Pharmaceut Co, 1966-1967; chemist, Ciba Pharmaceut Co, 1958-1966; Chemist, S B Penick & Co, 1956-1957. **Memberships:** Am Chem Soc. **Research Statement & Publications:** Gas liquid chromatographic analysis and methods development for pharmaceutical compounds, preparations and raw materials; blood level determinations of pharmaceutical compounds. **Mailing Address:** RD 2, Katonah, NY 10536-9802.

LUDIN, ROGER LOUIS, NUCLEAR PHYSICS, SOLID MODLING. **Personal Data:** b Jersey City, NJ, June 13, 1944; m 1966, Diane; c Stephen & Joyce. **Education:** Brown Univ, ScB, 1966; Worcester Polytech Inst, MS, 1968, PhD (physics), 1969. **Professional Experience:** LECTR MECH ENG, CALIF POLYTECH STATE UNIV, SAN LUIS OBISPO, 1984-; prof physics, Burlington Co Col, NJ, 1971-1986; Fel, Worcester Polytech Inst, 1969-1971. **Memberships:** AAAS; Am Asn Mech Engr; Am Asn Engineeringr Education; Sigma Xi. **Research Statement & Publications:** Neutron-deuteron scattering. **Mailing Address:** Dept Mech Eng, Calif Polytech State Univ, San Luis Obispo, CA 93407-0358. **E-Mail:** rludin@calpoly.edu

LUDINGTON, MARTIN A, NUCLEAR PHYSICS. **Personal Data:** b Detroit, Mich, March 7, 1943; m 1979, Kathryn; c Elizabeth & Andrew. **Education:** Albion Col, AB, 1964; Univ Mich, MS, 1965, PhD (physics), 1969. **Professional Experience:** CHMN PHYSICS, ALBION COL, as of 2003; chmn, Physics Dept, Albion Col, 1980-1983 & 1989-1992; PROF PHYSICS, ALBION COL, 1969-; from assist to assoc prof physics, Albion Col, 1969-1985; mem, Coun Undergrad Res, Am Asn Physics Teachers & Am Phys Soc; Adj res scientist, Phoenix Mem Lab 1991-. **Memberships:** Am Phys Soc; Am Asn Physics Teachers. **Research Statement & Publications:** High accuracy efficiency calib of gamma detectors; low level counting. **Mailing Address:** Dept Physics, Albion Col, 111 Epworth Hall, Albion, MI 49224. **E-Mail:** mludington@albion.edu

LUDKE, JAMES LARRY, ENVIRONMENTAL BIOLOGY. **Personal Data:** b Vicksburg, Miss, January 11, 1942. **Education:** Millsaps Col, BS, 1964; Miss State Univ, MS, 1967, PhD (physiol), 1970. **Professional Experience:** REGIONAL CHIEF BIOLOGIST, US GEOL SURVEY, as of 2003; res physiologist, Patuxent Wildlife Res Ctr, US Fish & Wildlife Serv, beginning 1971; res asst physiol, Miss State Univ, 1970-1971; dir, sci ctr-leetown, Nat Biol Surv; dep chief, off res supp. **Memberships:** Am Soc Zoologists; Sigma Xi; AAAS. **Research Statement & Publications:** Study of the chronic or lethal effects of pollutants on nontarget species; emphasis on fate of chemicals, diagnostic methods and chemical interactions. **Mailing Address:** Cent Regional Off, Biol Resources, US Geol Survey, Denver Federal Ctr Bldg 20 P O Box 25046 MS 300, Denver, CO 80225-0046. **Fax:** 303-236-2733. **E-Mail:** larry_ludke@usgs.gov

LUDLOW, CHRISTY L, NEUROPHYSIOLOGY, INTEGRATED SYSTEMS RESEARCH. **Personal Data:** b Montreal, Que, June 7, 1944; American citizen; m 1968, Gregory. **Education:** McGill Univ, BSc, 1965, MSc, 1967; NY Univ, PhD (psycholing, speech path), 1973. **Honors & Awards:** Dir Award, NIH, 1977; Hons, MD Speech-Language-Hearing Asn, 1995; Hons, Am Acad Otolaryngol-Head & Neck Surg, 1997. **Professional Experience:** CHIEF, LARYNGEAL & SPEECH SECT, DIV INTRAMURAL RES NAT INST NEUROL DIS & STROKE, 1998-; res speech pathologist, Nat Inst Deafness & Other Commun Dis, 1988-1998; res speech path nat inst neurol & communicative disorders & stroke, 1975-1988; vis lectr speech & hearing sci, Univ Md, 1973-1974; proj mgr, Am Speech & Hearing Asn, 1973-1974; res speech pathologist, W A Anderson fel, 1970-1972; res speech pathologist, Med Ctr, NY Univ, 1967-1970; res asst, McGill Univ, 1966-1967. **Memberships:** Acoust Soc Am; Soc Neuroscience; Asn Res Otolaryngol; fel Am Speech-Lang-Hearing Asn; Acad Aphasia; fel Am Laryngol Asn. **Research Statement & Publications:** vocal pathologies; neurological disorders affecting speech and language functioning; neurophysiology of laryngeal movement control during speech in disorders of spasmodic dysphonia and stuttering; pathophysiology and pathogenesis idiopathic voice, speech and swallowing disorders. **Mailing Address:** Bldg 10 Rm 5D38 Laryngeal & Speech Sect MNB NINDS, 10 Ctr Dr MSC 1416, Bethesda, MD 20892-1416. **Fax:** 301-480-0803. **E-Mail:** ludlow@ninds.nih.gov

LUDLOW, DOUGLAS KENT, CHARACTERIZATION OF SURFACE PROPERTIES OF COAL & FLYASH, ACTIVATED CARBON & COMPOSITE ADSORBENTS & CATALYSTS. **Personal Data:** b Spanish Fork, Utah, March 19, 1957; m 1979, Sherryl; c Chalise, Allison, Leslie, Katherine & Megan. **Education:** Brigham Young Univ, BS, 1982; Ariz State Univ, PhD (chem eng), 1986. **Honors & Awards:** Res Initiation Award, Eng Found, 1989; Fulbright Sr Scholar, Hebrew Univ Jerusalem 1992. **Professional Experience:** Acting chmn, Univ Mo, Rolla, 2006-; chmn, Univ Mo, Rolla, 1996-2003; PROF CHEM ENG, UNIV MO, ROLLA, 1996-; dept chair, Univ NDak, 1994-1996; vis prof chem, Hebrew Univ Jerusalem, Israel, 1992-1993; vis prof chem, Fulbright sr scholar, 1992-1993; Fulbright sr scholar, Coun Int Exchange Scholars, 1992-1993; from asst prof to assoc prof chem eng, Univ NDak, 1986-1996; Process engr, Monsanto Inorg Chem, 1979-1980. **Memberships:** Am Inst Chem Engrs; Am Chem Soc; Am Soc Eng Educ; Sigma Xi. **Research Statement & Publications:** Characterization of surfaces including coal, char, composite adsorbents and catalysts; hydrogen storage on carbon nanotube and nanoparticile composites, tapplication of fractal geometry to determine surface morphology from physisorption measurements; inorganic transformations during coal combustion; nitrous oxide selective catalytic reduction using fabric filters for simultaneous nitrous oxide and particulate removal. **Mailing Address:** Chem Eng, Univ Mo, 143 Schrenk Hall, Rolla, MO 65409. **Fax:** 573-341-4377. **E-Mail:** dludlow@umr.edu

LUDLUM, KENNETH HILLS, PHYSICAL CHEMISTRY. **Personal Data:** b Albany, NY, November 16, 1929; m 1953, c 4. **Education:** Col Educ Albany, BA, 1951, MA, 1952; Rensselaer Polytech Inst, PhD (phys chem), 1961. **Professional Experience:** RETIRED; coordr, Texaco BNV Cons & Toxicol, 1987-1992; res assoc, Beacon Res Lab, 1980-1992; sr res chemist, Beacon Res Lab, 1973-1980; res chemist, Beacon Res Lab, 1965-1973; sr chemist, Beacon Res Lab, 1962-1965; Chemist, Texaco Inc, 1961-1962; Chemist, Beacon Res Lab, 1961-1962. **Memberships:** Am Chem Soc; Catalysis Soc; Air Pollution Control Asn. **Research Statement & Publications:** Reaction kinetics; air pollution studies and related environmental science; catalysis and surface chemistry. **Mailing Address:** 117 N Elm St, Beacon, NY 12508.

LUDMAN, ALLAN, GEOLOGY, TECTONICS. **Personal Data:** b Brooklyn, NY, March 7, 1943; m Elaine. **Education:** Brooklyn Col, BS, 1963; Ind Univ, Bloomington, AM, 1965; Univ Pa, PhD (geol), 1969. **Professional Experience:** Interim provost, Queens Col, 2000-2001; dir, Queens Col, Globe NY Metro Program, 1999; PROF EARTH & ENVIRON SCI, QUEEN COL, NY, 1982-; from asst to prof, Queen Col, NY, 1975-1982; asst prof geol, Smith Col, 1969-1975; field geologist, Maine Geol Surv, 1966-; mem fac, PhD Prog Earth & Environ Sci, Grad Sch, City Col NY. **Memberships:** Geol Soc Am; Sigma Xi; Geol Asn Can; Geol Soc Am (Chairman, Northeastern Section); Sigma Xi; Geol Am Can; Atlantic Geoscience Soc. **Research Statement & Publications:** Regional geologic mapping in central and eastern Maine; low-temperature metamorphism of pelitic and calcareous rocks; tectonic evolution of northeastern New England; application of geographic information system to geologic mapping. **Mailing Address:** Sch Earth & Environ Sci, Queens Col, SB E206, Flushing, NY 11367-0904. **Fax:** 718-997-3300. **E-Mail:** allan_ludman@qc.edu

LUDMAN, JACQUES ERNEST, SOLID STATE PHYSICS. **Personal Data:** b Chicago, Ill, November 26, 1934; m 1970, c 1. **Education:** Middlebury Col, BA, 1956; Northeastern Univ, PhD (solid state physics), 1973. **Professional Experience:** PRES, NORTHEAST PHOTOSCI INC, 1990-; chief, Optical Processing Sect, 1975-1989; res physicist, Air Force Cambridge Res Lab, 1959-1975. **Memberships:** Sigma Xi. **Research Statement & Publications:** Injection laser development; radiation damage effects on semiconductor devices; infrared sensor physics. **Mailing Address:** Northeast Photosci Inc, 18 Flagg Rd, Hollis, NH 03049. **Fax:** 603-465-2859. **E-Mail:** jacques@mciworld.com

LUDTKA, GERALD M, MATERIAL SCIENCE. **Education:** Carnegie Mellon Univ, PhD (Metall & Mat Sci); Drexel Univ, BS, MS. **Honors & Awards:** E O Lawrence Mem Award, US Dept Energy, 1994. **Professional Experience:** DISTINGUISHED RES & DEVELOP STAFF MEM, METALS & CERAMICS DIV, OAK RIDGE NAT LAB, as of 2004. **Mailing Address:** Metals & Ceramics Div, Oak Ridge Nat Lab, PO Box 2008 MS 6064 Bldg 4515, Oak Ridge, TN 37831-6064. **Fax:** 865-574-3940. **E-Mail:** ludtkagm1@ornl.gov

LUDUENA, RICHARD FROILAN, BIOCHEMISTRY. **Personal Data:** b San Francisco, Calif, February 9, 1946; m 1981, Linda; c Sara Diana. **Education:** Harvard Univ, BA,

1967; Stanford Univ, PhD (biol), 1973. **Professional Experience:** PROF BIOCHEM, UNIV TEX HEALTH SCI CTR, SAN ANTONIO, 1988-; from asst prof to assoc prof, Univ Tex Health Sci Ctr, San Antonio, 1976-1988; fel genetics, Sch Med, Stanford Univ, 1975-1976; Jane Coffin Childs Mem Fund Med Res fel, 1973-1975; fel pharmacol, Sch Med, Stanford Univ, 1973-1975. **Memberships:** Am Soc Cell Biol; Int Soc Neurochem; Am Soc Biochem & Molecular Biol. **Research Statement & Publications:** Regulation of microtubule assembly; structure and evolution of tubulin; pharmacology of microtubule proteins; tubulin isotypes. **Mailing Address:** Dept Biochem, Univ Tex Health Sci Ctr, MED Rm 438D 7703 Floyd Curl Dr, San Antonio, TX 78229-3900. **Fax:** 210-567-6595. **E-Mail:** luduena@uthscsa.edu

LUDVIGSEN, CARL W, PATHOLOGY. **Personal Data:** b Palo Alto, Calif. **Education:** Univ Colo, Boulder, BA, 1974; Wash Univ, St Louis, Mo, MD & PhD, 1980; Am Bd Path, cert, 1985; Creighton Univ, JD, 1988. **Professional Experience:** SR VPRES, ATHENA DIAG, WORCESTER, MASS, as of 2003; CHIEF FINANCIAL OFFICER, LAB ONE, 1997-; chief managing officer, Evp Corp, beginning 1997; chief oper officer, Evp Corp, 1993-1996; clin assoc prof, Dept Path, Sch Med, Med Ctr, Univ Kans, Kansas City, 1990-1993; assoc med dir, Bus Mens Assurance Co, Kansas City, Mo, 1989-; chief pathologist & sr vpres, Home Off Res Lab, Lenexa, Kans, 1989-1990; dir, Emergency Rm & Labs, Sandstone Area Hosp, Minn, 1988-1989; consult, Ariel Answer Prizes, 1986-; emergency rm physician, Lutheran Hosp, Omaha, Nebr & Bryan Mem Hosp, Lincoln, Nebr, 1986-1988; dir chem, spec chem & toxicol, Med Ctr, Univ Nebr, 1983-1986; mem, Prod Eval & Stand Comt, 1983-1985; clin chem fel, Univ Minn, Minneapolis, 1982-1983; Young investr award, Acad Clin Lab Physicians & Scientists, Seattle, Wash, 1982; clin path resident, Univ Minn, Minneapolis, 1980-1982; tutor physiol, path & pharmacol, 1976-1977; teaching asst, Dept Anat, Sch Med, Wash Univ, St Louis, Mo, 1976. **Memberships:** Fel Am Col Legal Med; Am Med Asn; fel Clin Asn Path; Am Soc Clin Pathologists; Am Soc Law & Med; AAAS; Am Asn Clin Chemists; Am Diabetes Asn; Acad Clin Lab Physicians & Scientists; Asn Clin Scientists. **Research Statement & Publications:** Validation, verification and correlation of various toxicologic measurement modalities; aspects of lipid measurements as related to coronary artery dosage risk; general population studies; development of alcohol abuse markers suitable for population screening; author of various publications. **Mailing Address:** Athena Diag Inc, 377 Plantation St, Worcester, MA 01605-2300.

LUDVIGSEN, F J BERNHARD T, MEDICAL TECHNOLOGY, CLINICAL CHEMISTRY. **Personal Data:** b Copenhagen, Denmark, October 3, 1923; American citizen; m 1944, Ellon; c Lise-Lotte & Stig Michael. **Education:** Copenhagen Univ, Denmark, PhD, 1954. **Professional Experience:** ADJ ASSOC PROF MED TECHNOL, UNIV S ALA, as of 1997; ASSOC PROF ANESTHESIOL, UNIV S ALA, 1984-; assoc prof med technol, Univ S Ala, beginning 1982; pres, Blue Ridge Med Lab, 1976-1981; Tech Corp, Tarrytown, NY, 1969-1971; consult, Path Assoc, Greenville, SC, 1967-1976; head, Dept Chem, Greenville Hosp Syst, 1963-1976; dir biochem, Muscular Dystrophy Res Lab, Univ Alta Hosp, 1960-1963; asst prof & head, Anethesia Res Lab, Univ Sask, 1959; chief, Clin Serv Lab, Sask Cancer & Med Res Inst, 1958-1959; res chief clin chem, Med Lab, Copenhagen, 1954-1958. **Memberships:** Am Asn Clin Chemists. **Research Statement & Publications:** Fibrogen and heavy metals; hypothermia; enzymes in muscle; tissue homogenization; lead poisoning; laboratory administration; automation and computers; blood loss monitoring; electrolyte monitoring; lactate monitoring, urea monitoring, instrumentation; several patents. **Mailing Address:** Dept Med Technol, Univ S Ala, 1504 Springhill Ave, Mobile, AL 36604. **Fax:** 334-434-3403. **E-Mail:** bludvigs@jaguar1.usouthal.edu

LUDWICK, ADRIANE GURAK, PHYSICAL ORGANIC CHEMISTRY. **Personal Data:** b Passaic, NJ, June 16, 1941; wid Larry (deceased); c Michael & Douglas. **Education:** Rutgers Univ, New Brunswick, AB, 1963; Univ Ill, Urbana, MS, 1965, PhD (chem), 1967. **Professional Experience:** Ceraming eng, Naval Air Develop Ctr, 1990-1991; NIH fac fel, Macromolecular Res Ctr, Univ Mich, 1978-1980; mem Chem Div, Lawrence Livermore Lab, 1978; AT&T Bell Labs, 1982-1985; NSF fac fel, Macromolecular Res Ctr, Univ Mich, 1979-1980; PROF CHEM, COL AGR, ENVIRON & NAT SCI, TUSKEGEE UNIV, 1977-; res assoc, Environ Sci Div, Oak Ridge Nat Lab, 1974; from asst prof to assoc prof, Tuskegee Univ, 1969-1977; vis asst prof & res assoc, Univ Ill, Urbana, 1968-1969; asst prof chem, Tuskegee Univ, 1967-1968. **Memberships:** AAAS; Am Chem Soc; Sigma Xi; Am Soc Eng Educ. **Research Statement & Publications:** Synthetic macromolecules and simpler organic molecules with potential engineering and health-related applications. **Mailing Address:** Dept Chem, Tuskegee Univ, Armstrong Hall, Tuskegee, AL 36088. **E-Mail:** aludwick@tusk.edu

LUDWIG, ALLEN CLARENCE, ASPHALT-EMULSION TECHNOLOGY, PLASTICS TECHNIQUE. **Personal Data:** b San Antonio, Tex, November 3, 1938; m 1960, Mary; c 4. **Education:** Tex A&M Univ, BS, 1960, Reg & Lic Professional Eng-Tex State. **Honors & Awards:** IR 100 Award, 1979. **Professional Experience:** OWNER, ALLEN C LUDWIG, PE CONSULT, 1986-; process res & eng, dept Energy Conversion & Combustion Technol, Fuels & Lubricants Res Div, 1982-1986; sr res engr, process res & eng dept, Vehicle & raffic Safety, 1974-1982; sr res engr, Systs Develop, div Automotive Res, 1969-1974; res develop, Southwest Res Inst, 1963-1969; nuclear res chemist, ASAF, 1960-1963; chem engr, Tech Serv Div, Monsanto Chem Co, 1960. **Research Statement & Publications:** Sulfur product and process development have been principal areas of interest; numerous US and foreign patents; many technical publications; three Foreign lic. **Mailing Address:** 5914 Brenda Ln, San Antonio, TX 78240. **Fax:** 210-684-2747.

LUDWIG, CHARLES HEBERLE, WOOD CHEMISTRY. **Personal Data:** b Minneapolis, Minn, May 1, 1920; m 1956, c 2. **Education:** Macalester Col, BA, 1942; Univ Wash, PhD (chem), 1961. **Professional Experience:** RETIRED; mem res staff, Ga Pac Corp, 1961-1982; mfg chemist, Univ Wash, 1956-1961; chemist, D A Dodd, Mfg Chemist, 1947-1955. **Memberships:** Am Chem Soc; Sigma Xi. **Research Statement & Publications:** Nuclear magnetic resonance spectroscopy of lignins and lignin models; chemistry of lignosulfonates and other lignins; nuclear magnetic resonance studies of lignin; model compounds and related materials; product development of lignosulfonates. **Mailing Address:** PO Box 999, Waldron, WA 98297.

LUDWIG, CLAUS BERTHOLD, molecular spectroscopy, environmental physics; deceased, see previous edition for last biography

LUDWIG, DONALD A, MATHEMATICS, APPLIED MATHEMATICS. **Personal Data:** b New York, NY, November 14, 1933; m 1953, c 2. **Education:** NY Univ, BA, 1954, MS, 1957, PhD (math), 1959. **Professional Experience:** PROF EMER MATH, UNIV BC, as of 1997; prof Math, Univ Bc, beginning 1974; Guggenheim fel, Tel Aviv, Rehovot, Dundee, 1970-1971; from assoc prof to prof, NY Univ, 1964-1974; asst prof, Univ Calif, Berkeley, 1961-1964; fine instr, Princeton Univ, 1960-1961; res assoc math, Inst Math Sci, NY Univ, 1959-1960. **Memberships:** Am Math Soc; Soc Indust & Appl Math; fel Royal Soc Can. **Research Statement & Publications:** Partial differential equations; mathematical methods for population biology. **Mailing Address:** Dept Math, Univ BC, Ecology Hut B8 Rm 120H, Vancouver, BC V6T 1Z2, Can. **Fax:** 604-822-6074. **E-Mail:** ludwig@math.ubc.ca

LUDWIG, EDWARD JAMES, NUCLEAR PHYSICS. **Personal Data:** b New York, NY, April 13, 1937; m 1958, Helen; c Kenneth, Janet, Joanne & Carolyn. **Education:** Fordham Univ, BS, 1958; Ind Univ, MS, 1960, PhD (physics), 1963. **Professional Experience:** Assoc dir, Steering Comt Mem & Collabr, Triangle Univ Nuclear Lab, 1992-; vis prof, Univ Munich, 1989; vis prof, Lawrence Berkeley Lab, 1980; PROF PHYSICS, UNIV NC, CHAPEL HILL, 1976-; vis prof, Univ Birmingham, 1973; from asst prof to assoc prof, Univ NC, Chapel Hill, 1966-1971; res fel physics, Rutgers Univ, 1963-1966; prin investr, DOE res contract. **Memberships:** Am Phys Soc. **Research Statement & Publications:** Nuclear reactions and scattering cross sections and polarization effects; reaction mechanisms; resonance studies; studies of few-nucleon systems. **Mailing Address:** Dept Physics & Astron, Univ NC, 106 Philips, Chapel Hill, NC 27599-3255. **Fax:** 919-962-0480. **E-Mail:** ludwig@tunl.duke.edu

LUDWIG, FRANK ARNO, ELECTROCHEMICAL OR THERMAL REGENERATIVE FUEL CELLS, ELECTROCHEMICAL SENSORS. **Personal Data:** b West Reading, Pa, January 17, 1931; m 1973, Joann; c David, Annemarie, Heidi, Tom, Peter, Henry & Julianne. **Education:** Calif Inst Technol, BS, 1953; Case Western Reserve Univ, MS, 1965, PhD (phys chem), 1968. **Honors & Awards:** Hughes Electro-optical & Data Syst Group Pat Award. **Professional Experience:** CONSULT, 1994-; chief scientist, Mat Technol Lab, Hughes Aircraft Co, 1982-1994; prin engr corrosion, mat develop, Ford Aerospace & Commun Corp, 1979-1982; mgr, Near-Term Elec Vehicle Battery Contracts, Argonne Nat Lab, 1978-1979; supvr, Res Lab, Ford Motor Co, 1969-1978; dept mgr org electrolyte batteries, electrochem trace gas sensors, Whittaker Corp, 1968-1969; dept mgr fuel cells, thermogalvanics, Electro-Optical Systs, Inc, 1958-1962; res engr, Hughes Aircraft Co, 1956-1957; vpres, Tech Commun, Inc, 1955-1958; Proj engr, Carter Labs, Inc, 1953-1956. **Research Statement & Publications:** Materials, corrosion, chemical and electrochemical kinetics, ac impedance techniques; development of new batteries and fuel cells; electroanalytical device inventions; improvements in batteries for electric vehicles; energy storage and conversion device inventions; electrochemical sensors inventions; thermodynamics; electroplating and surface finishing innovations. **Mailing Address:** 29443 Whitley Collins Dr, Rancho Palos Verdes, CA 90275. **Fax:** 310-377-4989. **E-Mail:** joladwig@aol.com

LUDWIG, FREDERIC C, EXPERIMENTAL PATHOLOGY. **Personal Data:** b Bad Nauheim, WGer, January 22, 1924; American citizen; m 1958, c 4. **Education:** Univ T bingen, MD, 1949; Univ Paris, ScD(radiobiol), 1958. **Honors & Awards:** Award, Nat Inst Hyg, France, 1959. **Professional Experience:** RETIRED; prof path & radiol sci, Col Med, Univ Calif, Irvine, 1971-1993; Consult, Stanford Res Inst, 1965-; assoc prof in residence, Med Ctr, Univ Calif, San Francisco, 1965-1971; lectr path, Med Ctr, Univ Calif, San Francisco, 1962-1965; assoc res pathologist, Med Ctr, Univ Calif, San Francisco, 1958-1962; Sect chief radiation path, AEC, France, 1955-1959; vis fel, St John's Col, Cambridge. **Memberships:** Radiation Res Soc Am; Am Soc Exp Path; NY Acad Sci; Fr Asn Anat; Ger Path Soc. **Research Statement & Publications:** Abscopal effects of radiation; radiation injury in blood forming organs; pathogenesis of radiation leukemia; homeostasis of white blood cells; gerontology. **Mailing Address:** Schneidhainerstr 34, 61462 Koenigstein Ts, Ger.

LUDWIG, FREDERICK JOHN, ANALYTICAL CHEMISTRY, ORGANIC CHEMISTRY. **Personal Data:** b St Louis, Mo, June 20, 1928; m 1956, c Frederick John Jr & Lawrence Charles. **Education:** Wash Univ, AB, 1950; St Louis Univ, PhD (chem), 1953. **Professional Experience:** ANALYSIS RES SPECIALIST, PETROLITE CORP, 1992-; res scientist, Tretolite Div, 1973-1992; group leader, Petrolite Corp, 1959-1973; res chemist, Uranium Div, Mallinckrodt Chem Corp, 1955-1959; lab asst chem, St Louis Univ, 1950-1953. **Memberships:** Am Chem Soc; Sigma Xi. **Research Statement & Publications:** Gas-liquid and liquid-solid chromatography; infrared spectroscopy; wax-polymers; water-treatment chemicals; nuclear magnetic resonance spectroscopy. **Mailing Address:** Res Lab Petrolite Corp, 369 Marshall Ave, St Louis, MO 63119.

LUDWIG, GARRY (GERHARD ADOLF), GENERAL RELATIVITY. **Personal Data:** b Mannheim, Ger, September 4, 1940; Canadian & German citizen; m 1968, Roberta. **Education:** Univ Toronto, BS, 1962; Brown Univ, PhD (physics), 1966. **Professional Experience:** PROF EMER, UNIV ALTA, 2003-; prof math, Univ Alta, 1982-2003; Nat Res Coun grants, 1967-1997; From asst prof to assoc prof, Univ Alta, 1966-1982. **Memberships:** Am Math Soc; Am Phys Soc; Can Math Soc; Int Soc Gen Relativity & Gravitation. **Research Statement & Publications:** General relativity and gravitation; asymptotically flat spacetimes, H-space, exact solutions, spin-coefficient formalisms. **Mailing Address:** Dept Math & Statist Sci, Univ Alta, 632 Cent Acad Bldg, Edmonton, AB T6G 2G1, Can. **Fax:** 780-492-6826. **E-Mail:** gludwig@math.ualberta.ca

LUDWIG, GEORGE H, SPACE SYSTEMS DESIGN, SPACE SCIENCES. **Personal Data:** b Johnson Co, Iowa, November 13, 1927; m 1950, Rosalie F; c Barbara R, George V, Sharon L & Kathy A. **Education:** Univ Iowa, BA, 1956, MS (physics), 1959, PhD (elec eng), 1960. **Honors & Awards:** Golden Plate Award, Acad Achievement, 1962; NOAA Prog & Mgt Award, Nat Oceanic & Atmospheric Admin, 1977; Except Sci Achievement Medal, NASA, 1984; Except Serv Medal, NASA, 1969. **Professional Experience:** Vis sr scientist, Calif Inst Technol, 1989-1991; vis sr scientist, Calif Inst Tech, NASA Hq, 1989-1991; sr res assoc, Univ Colo, 1985-1991; consult, Data Mgt & Space Sta, 1984-1992; asst chief scientist, NASA, 1983-1984; dir, Environ Res Labs, 1981-1983; sr scientist, Environ Res Labs, 1980-1981; tech dir, Nat Environ Satellite Serv, Nat Oceanic & Atmospheric Admin, 1980; dir opers, Nat Environ Satellite Serv, Nat Oceanic & Atmospheric Admin, 1975-1980; dir systs integration, Nat Environ Satellite Serv, Nat Oceanic & Atmospheric Admin, 1972-1975; assoc dir data opers, Goddard Space Flight Ctr, NASA, 1971-1972; chief, Info Processing Div, 1965-1971; head, Instrumentation Sect, Goddard Space Flight Ctr, NASA, 1960-1965; res assoc space res, Univ Iowa, 1960. **Memberships:** Sigma Xi; sr mem Am Geophys Union; sr mem Inst Elec & Electronics Engrs; Interna Torch Club. **Research Statement & Publications:** Cosmic rays; development of space instrumentation; on board and ground data processing; co-discovery and investigation of Van Allen radiation belts; atmospheric, oceanic, hydrologic remote sensing and forecasting; direction of space, atmospheric and oceanic environmental research. **Mailing Address:** 215 Aspen Trail, Winchester, VA 22602. **E-Mail:** ludwiggh@visuallink.com

LUDWIG, GERALD W, POWER ELECTRONICS, SIMULATION. **Personal Data:** b New York, NY, January 7, 1930; m 1951, c 3. **Education:** Harvard Univ, AB, 1950, AM, 1951, PhD (chem physics), 1955; Rensselaer Polytech Inst, MA, 1987. **Professional Experience:** RETIRED; mgr, Integrated Circuits Br, 1971-1974; physicist, Res & Develop Ctr, Gen Elec Corp, 1965-1971; liaison scientist, Res & Develop Ctr, Gen Elec Corp, 1963-1965; physicist, Res & Develop Ctr, Gen Elec Corp, 1955-1963. **Memberships:** Fel Am

Phys Soc; sr mem Inst Elec & Electronics Engrs; Electrochem Soc. **Research Statement & Publications:** Transport properties of semiconductors; electron paramagnetic resonance; Gunn effect; x-ray and cathode ray phosphors; semiconductor materials and processing; charge transfer devices; integrated circuits; modelling and simulation of power electronic circuits and systems. **Mailing Address:** 112 Glenhill Dr, Scotia, NY 12302.

LUDWIG, HARVEY F, ENVIRONMENTAL & SANITARY ENGINEERING. **Personal Data:** b Saskatoon, Sask, December 4, 1916. **Education:** Univ Calif, Berkeley, BS, 1938, MS, 1942; Clemsen Univ, DEng, 1965. **Professional Experience:** DISTINGUISHED ENVIRON ENG, SEATEC INT CONSULT ENGS, as of 2001; PRES, SOUTHEAST ASIA TECHNOL, BANGKOK, THAILAND, 1973-; chmn & pres, Eng Sci, Inc, 1956-1972; assoc prof eng, Univ Calif, Berkeley, 1949-1951; Sanit engr, USPHS, 1943-1946. **Memberships:** Nat Acad Eng; Sigma Xi. **Mailing Address:** SEATEC Int Consult Engs, 972/1, Vorasubin Bldg, PO Box 8-101, Bangkok, Thailand. **E-Mail:** ludwig@mozart.inet.co.th

LUDWIG, HUBERT JOSEPH, MATHEMATICS. **Personal Data:** b Lincoln, Ill, July 27, 1934; m 1965, Sharon; c Jonathan & Jennifer. **Education:** Univ Ill, Urbana, BS, 1956; St Louis Univ, MS, 1964, PhD (math), 1968. **Professional Experience:** PROF EMER MATH, BALL STATE UNIV, 2000-; prof math, Ball State Univ, 1981-2000; from asst prof to assoc prof, Ball State Univ, 1968-1981; teaching asst math, St Louis Univ, 1965-1968; instr math, chem & eng mech, Springfield Col, Ill, 1956-1965. **Memberships:** Math Asn Am; Nat Coun Teachers Math; Sigma Xi. **Research Statement & Publications:** Chaotic dynamics; 2-metric spaces; logo and fractals; computers in secondary mathematics education. **Mailing Address:** Dept Math Sci, Ball State Univ, Muncie, IN 47306-0490. **Fax:** 317-285-1721. **E-Mail:** hjludwig7@cswebmail.com

LUDWIG, MARTHA LOUISE, BIOCHEMISTRY. **Personal Data:** b Pittsburgh, Pa, August 16, 1931; m. **Education:** Cornell Univ, BA, 1952, PhD (biochem), 1956; Univ Calif, Berkeley, MA, 1955. **Honors & Awards:** Garvan Medal, American Chemical Society, 1983. **Professional Experience:** PROF, DEPT BIOL CHEM & RES SCIENTIST, BIOPHYS RES DIV, UNIV MICH, ANN ARBOR, 1975-; from asst prof to assoc prof, Biophys Res Div, Univ Mich, Ann Arbor, 1967-1975; res fel chem, Harvard Univ, 1962-1967; res assoc biol, Mass Inst Technol, 1959-1962; res fel biochem, Harvard Med Sch, 1956-1959. **Memberships:** Nat Acad Sci; AAAS; Am Chem Soc; Am Soc Biol Chemists; Biophys Soc; Am Crystallog Asn. **Research Statement & Publications:** Protein crystallography; protein structure and function. **Mailing Address:** Dept Biological Chem, Univ Mich, Ann Arbor, MI 48109. **E-Mail:** mlludwig@umich.edu

LUDWIG, MATTHIAS HEINZ, SEMICONDUCTOR TECHNOLOGY, POROUS SILICON. **Personal Data:** b Leipzig, Ger, July 13, 1954; m 1980, Angelika; c Kaj. **Education:** Humboldt Univ, Berlin, Ger, BS, 1980, MS, 1981, PhD (physics), 1987. **Professional Experience:** ADJ PROF MAT SCI, UNIV FLA, 1994-; consult, AME Labormessanlagen Berlin, 1993-; vis scientist, Univ Fla, 1992-1994; prin investr, Ger NSF, 1991-1994; res assoc semiconductor technol, Humboldt Univ, Ger, 1989-1992; vis scientist, Tech Univ Nowgorod/Univ Petersburg, Russia, 1989; prin investr infrared detectors, Werk fuer Fernsehelektronik, Ger, 1987-1989. **Memberships:** Ger Asn Teachers; Mat Res Soc. **Research Statement & Publications:** Luminescence of spark-processed porous silicon; infrared detectors made from III/V semiconductors; surface and interface properties of semiconductors. **Mailing Address:** Dept Mat Sci & Eng Univ Fla, PO Box 116400 Rhines Hall, Gainesville, FL 32611. **Fax:** 352-846-0326. **E-Mail:** mludw@mail.mse.ufc.edu

LUDWIG, OLIVER GEORGE, PHYSICAL CHEMISTRY. **Personal Data:** b Philadelphia, Pa, November 15, 1935. **Education:** Villanova Univ, BS, 1957; Carnegie Inst Technol, MS, 1960, PhD (quantum chem), 1961. **Professional Experience:** PROF CHEM, VILLANOVA UNIV, as of 2004; actg chmn, Dept Chem, Villanova Univ, 1969-1970; assoc prof Chem, Villanova Univ, beginning 1968; asst prof chem & fac assoc, Comput Ctr, Univ Notre Dame, 1963-1968; NSF fel, 1961-1963; mem math lab & sr res worker theoret chem, Cambridge Univ, 1961-1963. **Memberships:** Am Chem Soc; Am Phys Soc; Asn Comput Mach. **Research Statement & Publications:** Quantum chemistry; chemical applications of digital computers; development of methods for scientific computing. **Mailing Address:** Dept Chem, Villanova Univ, Mendel Hall Rm 214E 800 E Lancaster Ave, Villanova, PA 19805. **Fax:** 610-519-7167. **E-Mail:** oliver.ludwig@villanova.edu

LUDWIG, THEODORE FREDERICK, PROSTHODONTICS. **Personal Data:** b Castlewood, SDak, July 8, 1924; m 1945, c 1. **Education:** Cent Col, Iowa, AB, 1945; Ohio State DDS, 1959, MSc, 1963. **Professional Experience:** RETIRED; assoc prof prosthodontics, Col Dent Med, Med Univ SC, 1969-1986; asst prof, Sch Dent, Univ Iowa, 1967-1969; mem, Carl O Boucher Prosthodontic Conf, 1966-; Asst prof dent, Sch Dent, WVa Univ, 1963-1967; NIH grant, 1962-1963. **Memberships:** Am Dent Asn. **Research Statement & Publications:** Esthetics in complete dentures; design and metals in removable partial dentures. **Mailing Address:** 523 N Third, Livingston, MT 59047.

LUDWIG, WILLIAM E, NUTRITION. **Education:** La State Univ, BS; La Inst Technol, MBA. **Professional Experience:** ADMINR, FOOD & NUTRIT SERV, 1993-. **Mailing Address:** Food & Nutrit Serv, USDA, 1244 Speer Blvd, Suite 903, Denver, CO 80204.

LUEBBE, RAY HENRY, PHYSICAL CHEMISTRY. **Personal Data:** b Schenectady, NY, March 31, 1931; m 1959, Dorothy; c Elizabeth, Karen & Melissa. **Education:** Dartmouth Col, AB, 1953; Univ Wis, PhD (phys chem), 1958. **Professional Experience:** RETIRED; mgr electrophotog mat & process develop, Am Graphics, Am Int, 1986-1992; sr process develop engr, Harris Graphics Co, 1985-1986; dir process technol, Environ Technol Inc, 1982-1985; unit mgr, Qwip Systs, Exxon Enterprises, 1979-1982; scientist, Xerox Corp, 1964-1979; chemist, Photo Prod Dept, E I du Pont de Nemours & Co, 1958-1964; asst phys chem, Univ Wis, 1953-1955. **Memberships:** Am Chem Soc; Soc Photo Sci & Eng. **Research Statement & Publications:** Hot atom and photo chemistry; photographic science; photopolymerization; electrophotography. **Mailing Address:** 305 Blackstone Dr, Centerville, OH 45459.

LUEBKE, EMMETH AUGUST, physics, nuclear safety law; deceased, see previous edition for last biography

LUEBS, RALPH EDWARD, SOIL & WATER MANAGEMENT, SOIL FERTILITY. **Personal Data:** b WoodRiver, Nebr, March 21, 1922; m 1951, c 4. **Education:** Univ Nebr, BS, 1948, MS, 1952; Iowa State Univ, PhD (soil fertil), 1954. **Professional Experience:** RETIRED; int consult agronomist, beginning 1982; sr proj scientist, Environ Systs Div, 1981-1982; chief, agron div, Woodward-Clyde Consults, 1975-1981; Univ Calif, Riverside, 1959-1975; Ft Hays Exp Sta, Kans, 1956-1959; soil scientist, Agr Res Serv, Univ Nebr, USDA, 1955-1956; asst agron, Univ Nebr, 1948-1949. **Memberships:** Am Soc Agron; Soil Sci Soc Am; Sigma Xi; Soil Conserv Soc Am. **Research Statement & Publications:** Nitrogen availability and rainfall use efficiency for dryland crops; mined land reclamation; diagnosis of low crop production. **Mailing Address:** 13347 W Exposition Dr, Lakewood, CO 80228-3037.

LUECK, CHARLES HENRY, ANALYTICAL CHEMISTRY. **Personal Data:** b St Paul, Minn, October 1, 1928; m 1955, c 6. **Education:** Col St Thomas, BS, 1950; Univ Detroit, MS, 1953; Wayne State Univ, PhD, 1956. **Professional Experience:** Res assoc & anal res supvr, Textile Fibers Dept, E I du Pont Del Nemours & Co, 1956-1985; CHEM INSTR, BEAUFORT COMMUNITY COL, Wash, NC. **Memberships:** Am Chem Soc; Am Soc Qual Control. **Research Statement & Publications:** Spectrophotometric analysis; chemical degradation studies; quality systems; test method uniformity & control. **Mailing Address:** 113 Hills Creek Rd, Blounts Creek, NC 27814.

LUECKE, DONALD H, MEDICAL RESEARCH. **Personal Data:** b St Paul, Minn, August 29, 1936; c 2. **Education:** Macalester Col, BA, 1959; Univ Ill, MS, 1961; Univ NDak, BS, 1973; Mich State Univ, MD, 1975. **Professional Experience:** DEP DIR, NAT INST DEAFNESS & OTHER COMMUN DISORDERS, NIH, as of 2004; dep dir, Div Res Grants, NIH, beginning 1987; MED OFFICER, DIV RES GRANTS, NIH, 1987-; med officer & dep dir, Extramural Activ Prog, 1982-1987; med officer & dep dir, Stroke & Trauma Prog, Nat Inst Neurol & Commun Dis & Stroke, 1981-1982; med officer & chief, Spec Prog Br, Div Cancer Cause & Prev, Nat Cancer Inst, 1979-1981; med officer, Prog Admin & actg head, Physiol Sci Sect, Physiol & Biomed Eng Prog, Nat Inst Gen Med Sci, 1977-1978; med officer & head, Clin Studies Sect, Collab Res Br, Viral Oncol Prog, Div Cancer Cause & Prev, Nat Cancer Inst, NIH, 1976; grad teaching & res asst, Dept Human Develop, Col Human Med, Mich State Univ, 1974-1975; virologist & dep proj dir, Spec Virus Cancer Prog, Nat Cancer Inst, 1969-1973; virologist & res supvr, Dept Microbiol, Univ NDak, 1965-1969; microbiologist, Dept Health, NDak State, 1962-1964; teaching asst, Dept Microbiol, Med Ctr, Univ Ill, 1959-1962. **Memberships:** Am Soc Microbiol; AMA; NY Acad Sci. **Research Statement & Publications:** Medicine; cancer. **Mailing Address:** Nat Inst Deafness & Other Commun Disorders NIH, Rm 3C-02 Bldg 31 9000 Rockville Pike, Bethesda, MD 20892.

LUECKE, FRANK, OPTICAL ENGINEERING. **Education:** Creighton Univ, BS; Marquette Univ, BSME. **Honors & Awards:** Eng Excellence Award, Optical Soc Am, 1995. **Professional Experience:** CONSULT, FRANKDESIGN LLC, as of 2001; founder & sr vpres, New Focus Inc, 1990-1998; Sr Engr, Div IBM Res, Almaden, Calif, 1986-1990; Engr, IBM Systs Develop Div, Rochester, Minnesota, 1967-1986. **Mailing Address:** FrankDesign LLC, 1815 Mayfield Dr, Crestwood, KY 40014-9604. **Fax:** 502-225-9394. **E-Mail:** frank@frankdesignllc.com

LUECKE, GLENN RICHARD, Parallel Algorithm & Tools. **Personal Data:** b Bryan, Texas, 1944; m 1967, Christine; c Paul Glenn & Elizabeth Christine. **Education:** Mich State Univ, BS; Calif Inst Tech, PhD. **Professional Experience:** PROF MATH & DIR, HIGH PERFORMANCE COMP, IOWA STATE UNIV, as of 2005; DIR, HIGH PERFORMANCE COMP, ITS, as of 2005; mem exec adv comt, Cornell Nat Supercomputing Facil, 1994-1997; mem, IBM Tech Adv comt, 1990-1996. **Memberships:** SIAM, ACM, IEEE. **Research Statement & Publications:** Cluster Efficiency; MPI Programs; Cluster Parallel Computers. **Mailing Address:** Iowa State Univ, 271 Durham Center, Ames, IA 50011-2251. **Fax:** 515-294-1717. **E-Mail:** grl@iastate.edu

LUECKE, GREG R, MECHANICAL ENGINEERING, ROBOTICS. **Personal Data:** b Orange, Tex, December 2, 1956. **Education:** Univ Mo, BS, 1979; Yale Univ, MS, 1986; Pa State Univ, PhD, 1992. **Honors & Awards:** Ralph R Teetor Educ Award, Soc Automotive Engrs, 1996. **Professional Experience:** ASSOC PROF MECH ENG, IOWA STATE UNIV, as of 2004; asst prof mech eng, Iowa State Univ, beginning 1992; fac fel, Iowa Ctr Emerging Mfg & Technol, 1992; Mech design consult, Dept Mech Eng, Pa State Univ, 1990; VAX comput syst mgr, Dept Mech Eng, Pa State Univ, 1988-1992; design engr, Mech Flight Controls, Sikorsky Aircraft, Conn, 1981-1988; Assoc engr/scientist, McDonnell-Douglass Corp, Calif, 1980-1981; instr mech eng, Bridgeport Eng Inst, Conn. **Memberships:** Inst Elec & Electronics Engrs; Am Soc Mech Engrs; Soc Automotive Engrs; Am Helicopter Soc. **Research Statement & Publications:** Dynamic system analysis and robot applications in virtual reality for interactive force feedback. **Mailing Address:** Dept Mech Eng, Iowa State Univ, 1620 F Howe Hall, Ames, IA 50011. **Fax:** 515-299-3261. **E-Mail:** grluecke@iastate.edu

LUECKE, RICHARD H, CHEMICAL ENGINEERING, MATHEMATICAL & BIOLOGICAL MODELING. **Personal Data:** b Cincinnati, Ohio, March 27, 1930; m 1953, c Brad, Greg, Mark, Genise & Connie. **Education:** Univ Cincinnati, BChE, 1953; Univ Okla, MChE, 1963, PhD (chem eng), 1966. **Professional Experience:** PROF EMER CHEM, UNIV MO, as of 2004; CONSULT, DOT PROD CORP, 1994-; fac res fel, Oak Ridge Assoc Univ, 1990; consult, Dynamic Matrix Co, 1988-1990; consult, Chemshare Corp, Okla, beginning 1969; prof chem eng, Univ mo, columbia, beginning 1980; assoc prof, Dot Prod Corp, 1967-1980; res engr, Monsanto Co, 1966-1967; engr, E I du Pont Del Nemours & Co, Inc, 1953-1962. **Memberships:** Am Inst Chem Eng. **Research Statement & Publications:** Process control; optimization; mathematical methods; bioengineering; biological modeling (200 publications including more than 50 refereed publications); authored 200 publications. **Mailing Address:** 408 Spring Valley Rd, Columbia, MO 65203. **E-Mail:** luecke@ecvaxz.ecn.missouri.edu

LUECKE, RICHARD WILLIAM, BIOCHEMISTRY, NUTRITION. **Personal Data:** b St Paul, Minn, July 12, 1917; m 1941, c 3. **Education:** Macalester Col, BA, 1939; Univ Minn, MS, 1941, PhD (biochem), 1943. **Professional Experience:** RETIRED; consult, Merck Sharp & Dohme Res Labs, 1962-1969; mem food & nutrit bd, Food & Agr Orgn, UN, 1960-1965; consult, Armour Res Labs, Chicago, 1955-1966; mem comt animal nutrit, Nat Res Coun, 1955-1965; prof biochem, Mich State Univ, 1945-1987; assoc prof biochem, Tex A & M Univ, 1943-1945. **Memberships:** Am Chem Soc; Am Inst Nutrit; Am Soc Biol Chemists. **Research Statement & Publications:** Trace element metabolism in animals. **Mailing Address:** 1893 Birchwood Dr, Okemos, MI 48864-2766.

LUEDECKE, LLOYD O, DAIRY BACTERIOLOGY. **Personal Data:** b Hamilton, Mont, July 28, 1934; m 1957, c 2. **Education:** Mont State Col, BS, 1956; Mich State Univ, MS, 1958, PhD (food sci), 1962. **Professional Experience:** PROF EMER FOOD SCI, WASH STATE UNIV, as of 2003; prof food sci, Wash State Univ, 1977-2000; assoc prof, Wash State Univ, 1973-1977; assoc prof & assoc dairy scientist, Wash State Univ, 1970-1973; Asst prof dairy sci, Wash State Univ, 1962-1970. **Memberships:** Am Dairy Sci Asn; Inst Food Technol. **Research Statement & Publications:** Heat resistance of psychrophiles; bacteriological aspects of mastitis. **Mailing Address:** Dept Food Sci, Wash State Univ, Pullman, WA 99164-0001.

LUEDEMAN, JOHN KEITH, ALGEBRA, MATHEMATICS EDUCATION. **Personal Data:** b Ft Wayne, Ind, April 27, 1941; div, c Keith, Eric, Jody & Cathy. **Education:** Valparaiso Univ, BA, 1963; Southern Ill Univ, Carbondale, MA, 1965; State Univ NY, Buffalo, PhD (math), 1969. **Professional Experience:** PROF EMER MATH, CLEMSON UNIV, as of 2005; prof educ, Clemson Univ, 1988-; dir, Ctr Ex Math Sci Educ, Clemson Univ, 1984-; prof math, Clemson Univ, 1980-; consult math, Oconee Co Sch Syst, SC, 1974-; from asst prof to assoc prof, Clemson Univ, 1968-1980; Instr math, State Univ NY, Buffalo, 1967-1968. **Memberships:** Am Math Soc; Math Asn Am; Sigma Xi; Nat Coun Teachers Math; Asn Math Teacher Educr. **Research Statement & Publications:** Mathematics education; mathematical biology; semigroups; graph theory; computing on graphs. **Mailing Address:** Dept Math, Clemson Univ, Clemson, SC 29634-1907. **E-Mail:** lued@clemson.clemson.edu

LUEDER, ERNST H, DIGITAL SIGNAL PROCESSING, OPTIMIZATION OF SYSTEMS. **Personal Data:** b Schiltach, Ger, February 20, 1932; m Helen Abramson; c Tilmon & Christoph. **Education:** Univ Stuttgart, Dipl Ing, 1958, Dr Ing(elec commun), 1962, Dr Ing habil, 1966. **Honors & Awards:** Order of Merit 1st Class Fed Repub Ger, 1991. **Professional Experience:** FULL PROF & DIR, INST NETWORK & SYSTS THEORY, UNIV STUTTGART, 1971-; Mem tech staff, Bell Tel Labs, NJ, 1968-1971; privat-dozent, Inst Network & Systs Theory, Univ Stuttgart, 1966-1968; Consult, Fed Ministry Sci & Technol, Bonn; Heinrich-Hertz-Inst, Berlin. **Memberships:** Fel Inst Elec & Electronics Engrs; Soc Info Display (vpres); Int Soc Hybrid Microelectronics; Int Soc Optical Eng; Soc Info Technol Ger; NY Acad Sci. **Research Statement & Publications:** Design of passive, RC-active, switched capacitor, digital and saw filters; digital and optical signal processing; optimization of systems; realization of flat panel liquid crystal displays; thin film sensors. **Mailing Address:** Univ Stuttgart, Pfaffenwaldring 47, 70550 Stuttgart, Ger.

LUEG, RUSSELL E, ELECTRICAL ENGINEERING. **Personal Data:** b Chicago, Ill, November 24, 1929; m 1956, c 5. **Education:** Univ Ark, BS, 1951; Univ Tex, MS, 1956, PhD (elec eng), 1961. **Professional Experience:** PROF EMER ELEC ENG, UNIV ALA, as of 2004; assoc dean admin, Univ Ala, beginning 1988; actg head dept, Univ Ala, 1966-1968; prof elec eng, Univ Ala, beginning 1964; consult, Army Missile Command, Ala, 1964-1965; assoc prof, Univ Ala, 1960-1964; radio engr & instr elec eng, Univ Tex, 1954-1960; prog engr, Gen Elec Co, NY, 1953-1954. **Memberships:** Inst Elec & Electronics Engrs; Am Soc Eng Educ. **Research Statement & Publications:** Nonlinear control systems. **Mailing Address:** Univ Ala, Tuscaloosa, AL 35406.

LUE-HING, CECIL, CIVIL & ENVIRONMENTAL ENGINEERING. **Personal Data:** b Jamaica, WI, November 3, 1930; m 1952, c 2. **Education:** Marquette Univ, BCE, 1961; Case Inst Technol, MS, 1963; Wash Univ, St Louis, DSc(sanit eng), 1966. **Professional Experience:** PRES, CECIL LUE-HING & ASSOC INC, as of 2005; dir res & develop, Metrop Water Reclamation Dist, Greater Chicago, beginning 1977; sr assoc, Ryckman, Edgerley, Tomlinson & Assocs, 1968-1977; assoc, Ryckman, Edgerley, Tomlinson & Assocs, 1966-1968; asst prof, Wash Univ, St Louis, 1965-1966; res assoc environ eng, Wash Univ, St Louis, 1963-1965; res assoc clin biochem, Huron Rd Hosp, Ohio, 1961-1963; instr histol & cytol chem & lab supvr, Sch Med Technol, Mt Sinai Hosp, Wis, 1955-1961; chief technician, Col Med, Univ Wis, 1950-1955; fel, Wash Univ, Mo. **Memberships:** AAAS; Am Soc Civil Engrs; Am Pub Health Asn; Water Pollution Control Fedn; Am Water Works Asn. **Research Statement & Publications:** Pesticide pollution of water supplies; significance of enzyme response in pesticide detection in water supplies; phosphorus and nutrient removal from water supplies; industrial wastes detoxification and biodegradation. **Mailing Address:** Cecil Lue-Hing & Associates, Inc, 6815 County Line Lane, Ste 40B-E, Burr Ridge, IL 60527-5724. **Fax:** 630-986-0607. **E-Mail:** clhai@aol.com

LUEHR, CHARLES POLING, APPLIED MATHEMATICS, MATHEMATICAL PHYSICS. **Personal Data:** b Plentywood, Mont, September 27, 1930. **Education:** Ore State Univ, BS, 1953, MS, 1956; Univ Calif, Berkeley, PhD (appl math), 1962. **Professional Experience:** RETIRED; sr res scientist, NMex Eng Res Inst, Univ NMex, 1985-1995; intergovt personnel act USAF Phillips Lab, Kirtland AFB 1990-1993; res scholar, Air Force Weapons Lab, Kirtland AFB, 1983-1984; vis assoc prof, Math, Ore State Univ, 1980-1982; res visitor, Inst Nuclear Sci, Nat Univ Mex, 1973-1988; mem prof staff, Tempo Ctr Adv Studies, Gen Elec Co, Calif, 1962-1968; res asst, Los Alamos Sci Lab, Summers 1955-1958. **Memberships:** Math Asn Am; Am Math Soc; AmPhys Soc; Soc Indust & Appl Math; Sigma Xi. **Research Statement & Publications:** Methods of mathematical physics; tensor analysis; abstract theory of spinors with applications in quantum mechanics and relativity theory; modern differential geometry applied to physics; scientific computing. **Mailing Address:** 920 Continental Lp SE Apt 27, Albuquerque, NM 87101.

LUEHRMANN, ARTHUR WILLETT, JR, COMPUTER SCIENCE, SCIENCE EDUCATION. **Personal Data:** b New Orleans, La, March 8, 1931; m 1961, Martha Ramirez; c Mia & Nils. **Education:** Univ Chicago, AB, 1955, SB, 1957, SM, 1961, PhD (physics), 1966. **Honors & Awards:** Fulbright lect, Fulbright Comn, Colombia, 1969. **Professional Experience:** FOUNDING PARTNER, COMPUT LITERACY PRESS, 1981-; assoc dir, Lawrence Hall Sci, Univ Calif, Berkeley, 1977-1980; adj assoc prof physics & dir, Off Acad Comput, 1970-1977; From instr to asst prof, Dartmouth Col, 1965-1970. **Memberships:** AAAS. **Research Statement & Publications:** Solid state theory; band structure; computational physics; computer graphics; computer-based instruction; solid state physics. **Mailing Address:** Compu Literacy Press Inc, 15, Triangle Park, Cincinnati, OH 45246. **Fax:** 513-530-0110.

LUEHRS, DEAN C, INORGANIC CHEMISTRY. **Personal Data:** b Fremont, Nebr, April 20, 1939; m 1969, c 1. **Education:** Mich State Univ, BS, 1961; Univ Kans, PhD (chem), 1965. **Professional Experience:** PROF EMER CHEM, MICH STATE TECHNOL UNIV, as of 2004; assoc prof chem, Mich State Technol Univ, beginning 1969; asst prof, Mich State Technol Univ, 1965-1969. **Memberships:** Am Chem Soc. **Research Statement & Publications:** Nonaqueous solvents; electrochemistry; QSAR. **Mailing Address:** Dept Chem, Mich Technol Univ, Houghton, MI 49931.

LUEKING, DONALD ROBERT, MICROBIAL BIOCHEMISTRY. **Personal Data:** b Cincinnati, Ohio, November 24, 1946; m 1973. **Education:** Ind Univ, Bloomington, BS, 1969, PhD (microbiol), 1973. **Professional Experience:** ASSOC PROF, DEPT BIOL SCI, MICH TECHNOL UNIV, as of 2004; DIR GRAD STUDIES, MICH TECHNOL UNIV, as of 2004; asst prof, Tex A&M Univ, 1978-; fel, Univ Ill, Urbana, 1975-1978; fel, Univ Pa, 1974-1975; Trainee microbiol, Univ Pa, 1973-1974. **Memberships:** Am Soc Microbiol; AAAS; Sigma Xi. **Research Statement & Publications:** The use of the photosynthetic bacteria as a model system for the study of the factors involved in the regulation of membrane biosynthesis and differentiation. **Mailing Address:** Dept Biol Sci, Mich Technol Univ, 1400 Townsend Dr, Houghton, MI 49931. **Fax:** 877-883-9508. **E-Mail:** drluekin@mtu.edu

LUENBERGER, DAVID GILBERT, SYSTEMS ENGINEERING, INVESTMENT SCIENCE. **Personal Data:** b Los Angeles, Calif, September 16, 1937; m 1962, Nancy; c Susan, Robert, Jill & Jenna. **Education:** Calif Inst Technol, BS, 1959; Stanford Univ, MS, 1961, PhD (elec eng), 1963. **Honors & Awards:** Hendrik W Bode Lectr Prize, Control Systs Soc, Inst Elec & Electronics Engrs, 1990; Oldenburger Medal, Amer Soc Mech Engineers, 1998. **Professional Experience:** Vis prof, Mass Inst Technol, 1976 & Tech Univ Denmark, 1986; Time& Space Processing, 1981 & Optimization Technol Inc, 1983-; chmn, eng-econ systs, Stanford Univ, 1980-1991; Intasa, Systs Control Inc, 1974-1983; PROF, DEPT ENG-ECON SYSTS & ELEC ENG, STANFORD UNIV, 1971-; tech asst to dir, Off Sci & Technol, Exec Off Pres, 1971-1972; Intasa, Systs Control Inc, 1970-1972; assoc prof, dept eng-econ systs & elec eng, Stanford Univ, 1967-1971; consult, Stanford Res Inst, 1966-; asst prof elec eng, Eng-econ Systs, Stanford Univ, 1963-1967; engr, Westinghouse Elec Corp, 1961-1963. **Memberships:** Inst Mgt Sci; Am Asn Univ Prof; Inst Elec & Electronics Engrs; Economet Soc; Am Soc Eng Educ; Am Finance Asn; Soc Econ Dynamics & Control (pres 1987-); Soc Prom Econ Theory; Soc Advan Econ Theory. **Research Statement & Publications:** Control systems, particularly multivariable systems; optimization, including control, operations research and estimation; economic systems; finance; business strategy. **Mailing Address:** Dept Mgt Sci & Eng, Standford Univ, Terman 410, Stanford, CA 94305-4025. **Fax:** 650-723-1614. **E-Mail:** luen@leland.stanford.edu

LUEPKER, RUSSELL VINCENT, EPIDEMIOLOGY, CARDIOLOGY. **Personal Data:** b Chicago, Ill, October 1, 1942; m 1966, Ellen L Thompson; c Ian & Carl. **Education:** Grinnell Col, BA, 1964; Univ Rochester, MD, 1969; Harvard Univ, MS, 1976. **Honorary Degrees:** PhD, Univ Lund, Swed, 1996. **Professional Experience:** HEAD, DIV EPIDEMIOL, UNIV MINN, as of 2002; PRIN INVESTR, EPI RES PROJ, UNIV MINN, as of 2002; CHMN, COUN EPIDEMIOL, AM HEART ASN, 1992-; dir, div epidemiol, Univ Minn, beginning 1991; bush leadership fel, 1990; PROF EPIDEMIOL & MED, UNIV MINN, MINNEAPOLIS, 1987-; assoc dir, Div Epidemiol, 1986-1991; vis prof, Univ Goteborg, Sweden, 1986; Univ Southern Calif, Los Angeles, 1985-; consult, NIH, 1980-; from asst prof to assoc prof, Div Epidemiol, 1976-1987; nat res serv award, Nat Heart, Lung & Blood Inst, 1975-1977; dir, Lipid Clin, 1975-1976; from res asst to asst resident, Peter Bent Brigham Hosp/Med Ctr, 1973-1976; intern, Univ Hosp, San Diego Co & Univ Calif, San Diego, 1969-1970. **Memberships:** Fel Am Col Physicians; fel Am Col Cardiol; Am Heart Asn; fel Am Col Epidemiol; Am Epidemiol Soc. **Research Statement & Publications:** Epidemiology and medicine; epidemiology and prevention of cardiovascular diseases at the individual and community levels. **Mailing Address:** Div Epidemiol, Univ Minn, 1300 S Second St, Suite 300, Minneapolis, MN 55454. **Fax:** 612-624-0315. **E-Mail:** luepker@epi.umn.edu

LUER, CARL A, BIOCHEMISTRY, IMMUNOLOGY. **Personal Data:** b St Louis, Mo, November 9, 1948. **Education:** Duke Univ, BA, 1970; Univ SFla, MS, 1974; Univ Kans, PhD (biochem), 1978. **Professional Experience:** MGR, MARINE BIOMED RES PROG, MOTE MARINE LAB, as of 2002; Adj asst prof, Dept Med, Brown Univ, 1991-; SR SCIENTIST, MOTE MARINE LAB, 1985-; Staff scientist, Mote Marine Lab, 1979-1985. **Memberships:** Am Soc Biochem & Molecular Biol; Sigma Xi. **Mailing Address:** Mote Marine Lab, 1600 Thompson Pkwy, Sarasota, FL 34236-1096. **Fax:** 941-388-4312. **E-Mail:** caluer@mote.org

LUERSSEN, FRANK W, METALLURGY, PHYSICAL CHEMISTRY. **Personal Data:** b Reading, Pa, August 14, 1927; m 1950, c 5. **Education:** Pa State Univ, BS, 1950; Lehigh Univ, MS, 1951; Xavier Univ, PhD, 1956. **Honorary Degrees:** LLD, Calumet Col; DPS, Xavier Univ, 1992. **Honors & Awards:** Howe Mem Lectr, Am Inst Mining, Metall & Petrol Engrs, 1984, Benjamin Fairless Award, 1985. **Professional Experience:** RETIRED; mem, Indust Policy Adv Comt, US Dept Com, 1988 & bd trustees, Mus Sci & Indust; chmn & chief exec officer, Res Dept, 1983-; pres & chief exec officer, Res Dept, 1982-1983; exec vpres & pres, Res Dept, 1978-1982; vpres steel mfg, Res Dept, 1977-1978; vpres res, Res Dept, 1968-1977; mgr, Res Dept, 1964-1968; assoc mgr, Res Dept, 1963-1964; asst mgr, Res Dept, 1962-1963; chief res engr, Inland Steel Co, 1957-1961; chief reduction & ref, Inland Steel Co, 1954-1957; metallurgist, Inland Steel Co, 1952-1954; Jr res engr, Bethlehem Steel Corp, 1951-1952; chmn, Phys Chem Steelmaking Group, Am Iron & Steel Inst, Gen Res Comt & Comt Mfg; Trustee, Northwestern Univ. **Memberships:** Nat Acad Eng; hon mem Am Iron & Steel Inst; fel Am Soc Metals; Am Inst Mining, Metall & Petrol Engrs. **Research Statement & Publications:** Physical chemistry of slag metal systems in steel refining; process research in ironmaking and steelmaking; physical metallurgy of iron base alloy systems. **Mailing Address:** 8226 Park View Ave, Munster, IN 46321.

LUESCHEN, WILLIAM EVERETT, AGRONOMY. **Personal Data:** b Springfield, Ill, January 29, 1942; m 1965, c 2. **Education:** Southern Ill Univ, BS, 1964; Univ Ill, MS, 1966, PhD (agron), 1968. **Professional Experience:** PROF AGRON, SOUTHERN EXP STA, UNIV MINN, beginning 1968. **Memberships:** Am Soc Agron; Crop Sci Soc Am; Weed Sci Soc Am; Coun Agr Sci & Tech; Am Reg Cert Prof Agron Crops & Soils; Am Forage & Grassland Coun. **Research Statement & Publications:** Crop production, management and weed science. **Mailing Address:** Dept Agron & Plant Genetics, Univ Minn, 411 Borlaug Hall 1991 Buford Circle, St Paul, MN 55108-6026. **Fax:** 612-625-1268. **E-Mail:** luesc001@umn.edu

LUESSENHOP, ALFRED JOHN, MEDICINE, NEUROSURGERY. **Personal Data:** b Chicago, Ill, February 6, 1926; m 1952, c 4. **Education:** Yale Univ, BS, 1949; Harvard Med Sch, MD, 1952. **Professional Experience:** RETIRED; prof surg, Sch Med, Georgetown Univ, beginning 1973; consult, Fed Aviation Agency, 1967 & Nat Naval Med Ctr, 1967-; head, Neurosurg Prog, Sch Med, Georgetown Univ, 1966-1993; clin consult, Vet Admin Hosp, 1965-; clin consult, Nat Inst Neurol Dis & Stroke, 1965-; chief div neurosurg, Sch Med, Georgetown Univ, beginning 1965; from instr to assoc prof neurosurg, Sch Med, Georgetown Univ, 1960-1973; res consult, Nat Inst Neurol Dis & Stroke, 1960-1965; vis scientist, Nat Inst Neurol Dis & Blindness, 1959-1960; Teaching fel, Harvard Med Sch, 1957-1958; resident neurosurg, Mass Gen Hosp, 1953-1958; res fel neurosurg, Harvard Med Sch, 1953-1954; Intern surg, Univ Chicago, 1952-1953. **Memberships:** Cong Neurol Surg; Am Asn Neurol Surg; Soc Neurol Surg; Am Acad Neurosurg. **Research Statement & Publications:** Cerebrovascular disease. **Mailing Address:** Dept Neurosurg, Georgetown Univ Hosp, 3800 Reservoir Rd NW, Washington, DC 20007.

LUETJE, ROBERT E, METALLURGY. **Professional Experience:** RETIRED; vpres technol, Kolene Corp, Detroit, 1986-2002; pres, Heat Treating Soc, Am Soc Metals, 1998-1999. **Memberships:** Am Soc Metals; fel Eng Soc Detroit. **Mailing Address:** Kolene Corp, 12890 Westwood Ave, Detroit, MI 48223.

LUETZELSCHWAB, JOHN WILLIAM, HEALTH PHYSICS. **Personal Data:** b Hammond, Ind, September 8, 1940; m 1963, Marcia; c Dana & Mark. **Education:** Earlham Col, BA, 1962; Wash Univ, MA & PhD (physics), 1968; cert Am Bd Health Physics. **Professional Experience:** RETIRED; prof physics & astron, Dickinson Col, 1983-2003; from asst prof to assoc prof, Dickinson Col, 1968-1983. **Memberships:** Am Asn Physics Teachers; Health Physics Soc. **Research Statement & Publications:** Environmental radioactivity; radon in the environment and in homes. **Mailing Address:** 1750 Valley Rd, Etters, PA 17319. **E-Mail:** luetzelj@dickinson.edu

LUFKIN, DANIEL HARLOW, SOLAR PHYSICS. **Personal Data:** b Philadelphia, Pa, September 26, 1930; m 1951, Patricia; c 3. **Education:** Mass Inst Technol, BS, 1952,

MS, 1958; Univ Stockholm, Fil lic meteorol, 1964. **Professional Experience:** RETIRED; dir, Off Systs & Advan Technol, Nat Oceanic & Atmospheric Admin, 1976-1986; asst prof astron, Hood Col, 1975-1987; consult, Solar Energy Sci Serv, 1974-1987; dir solar forecast facil, Air Weather Serv, USAF, DC, 1969-1973; meteorol officer, Air Weather Serv, USAF, DC, 1953-1969. **Memberships:** Am Meteorol Soc. **Research Statement & Publications:** Optical instrumentation for satellite remote sensing. **Mailing Address:** 303 W Col Terrace, Frederick, MD 21701. **E-Mail:** dlufkin@fred.net

LUFT, HAROLD STEPHEN, HEALTH ECONOMICS, HEALTH SERVICES RESEARCH. **Personal Data:** b Newark, NJ, January 6, 1947; m 1970, Lorraine; c Shira Luft Gallagher & Jana Levinson Luft. **Education:** Harvard Univ, AB, 1968, MA, 1970, PhD (econ), 1973. **Honors & Awards:** Distinguished Article of the Year Award, Association for Health Services Research, 1988; Distinguished Fellow, Association for Health Services Research, 1997; Baxter Health Services Research Prize, AUPHA, 1998; Distinguished Investigator of the Year, Association for Health Services Research, 1999; Flinn Distinguished Scholar in Healthcare Management and Policy, University of Arizona and Arizona State University, 1986. **Professional Experience:** Director and Caldwell B. Esselstyn Professor of Health Policy and Health Economics, INST HEALTH POLICY STUDIES, UNIV CALIF, SAN FRANCISCO, 1995-; actg dir, Univ Calif, San Francisco, 1993-1995; Associate Director, 1986-1993; Professor of Health Economics, 1982-; Associate Professor of Health Economics. Health Services Research journal, Co-Editor in Chief, 2000-, Senior Associate Editor, 1996-2000. **Memberships:** Institute of Medicine-National Academy of Sciences, elected 1985; IOM Council 1989-1994; AcademyHealth, formerly Asn for Health Services Research, member of board, 1995-2005; American Public Health Asn; American Economics Asn; International Health Economics Association; Western Economics Asn. **Research Statement & Publications:** health maintenance organizations; restructuring incentive systems in health care; measuring quality of care; competition in health care; interdisciplinary research and policy applications. **Mailing Address:** Inst for Health Policy Studies, 3333 Calif St, Laurel Heights, Ste 265, San Francisco, CA 94118. **Fax:** 415-476-0705. **E-Mail:** hal.luft@ucsf.edu

LUFT, JOHN HERMAN, HISTOLOGY. **Personal Data:** b Portland, Ore, February 6, 1927; m 1949, c 3. **Education:** Univ Wash, BS, 1949, MD, 1953. **Professional Experience:** PROF BIOL STRUCT, MED MED SCH, UNIV WASH, 1967-; USPHS sr fel, 1957-1965; from asst prof anat to assoc prof, Med Med Sch, Univ Wash, 1956-1967; Nat Res Coun Rockefeller fel, Harvard Med Sch, 1954-1956; intern, Peter Bent Brigham Hosp, Boston, Mass, 1953-1954. **Memberships:** AAAS. **Research Statement & Publications:** Microscopy and electron microscopy; fixatives; basic cellular structure and function; external cell coats; ultrastructure; biomechanics. **Mailing Address:** Dept Biol Struct, Univ Wash Med Sch, SM-20, Seattle, WA 98195.

LUFT, LUDWIG, PHYSICAL CHEMISTRY. **Personal Data:** b Lvov, Poland, November 9, 1926; American citizen; m 1952, Anne; c Frederick J & Naomi M (Cameron). **Education:** Univ Frankfurt, dipl, 1951; Univ Kans, PhD (phys chem), 1956. **Professional Experience:** RETIRED; lectr & adj prof chem eng, Tufts Univ, Medford, Mass, 1982-1985; pres, Luft Instruments, Inc, 1963-1997; dir res, Instrumentation Lab Inc, 1963; sr scientist, Allied Res Assocs, 1962-1963; tech & managerial mem staff, Gen Elec Co, 1958-1962; res supvr, MSA Res Corp, 1957-1958; asst prof chem, Univ Miami, 1955-1957. **Memberships:** AAAS; Am Chem Soc; Instrument Soc Am. **Research Statement & Publications:** Chemical engineering; automatic controls; methods development; electrochemistry. **Mailing Address:** 3 Hillside Rd, Lincoln, MA 01773-0214.

LUFT, STANLEY JEREMIE, GEOLOGY. **Personal Data:** b Turin, Italy, September 26, 1927; American citizen; m 1991, Eleanor J Shearer; c Andrew, Anthony, Stephen & Edmund. **Education:** Syracuse Univ, AB, 1949; Pa State Col, MS, 1951. **Honors & Awards:** Gerard Gilbert Award. **Professional Experience:** RETIRED; geologist, Northern Pac Rwy Co, 1956-1958 & US Geol Surv, 1961-1988; proj geologist, Callahan Mining Corp, 1961; prof geol & mineral & head dept, Oriente Univ, 1959-1960; geologist mineral deposits, US Geol Surv, 1954-1956; explor geologist, NJ Zinc Co, 1951-1954; Asst geol, Pa State Col, 1949-1951. **Memberships:** Fel Geol Soc Am. **Research Statement & Publications:** Petrography and petrology of volcanic rocks; drainage evolution of Kentucky; geology of uranium in Tertiary intermontaine basins; basin analysis; Northern Powder River Basin; geologic hazards mitigation. **Mailing Address:** 16291 W 56th Pl, Golden, CO 80403.

LUFTIG, RONALD BERNARD, MICROBIOLOGY, BIOPHYSICS. **Personal Data:** b Brooklyn, NY, December 8, 1939; m 1961, c 4. **Education:** City Col NY, BS, 1960; NY Univ, MS, 1962; Univ Chicago, PhD (biophys), 1967. **Professional Experience:** PROF & HEAD DEPT, MICROBIOL, MED SCH, LA STATE UNIV, 1983-; Univ SC Med Sch, 1979-1983 & La State Univ, beginning 1983; prof microbiol, Med Sch, Univ SC, 1979-1983; sr scientist, Worcester Found Exp Biol, 1974-1979; res grants, Worcester Found, 1974-1979; NIH res grant, Med Ctr, Duke Univ, 1970-1973; asst prof microbiol, Med Ctr, Duke Univ, 1969-1973; NSF fel, Calif Inst Technol, 1967-1969. **Memberships:** AAAS; Am Soc Biol Chem; Am Soc Microbiol; Am Soc Cell Biol; Sigma Xi; Am Soc Virol. **Research Statement & Publications:** Leukemia virus morphogenesis; acquired immune deficiency syndrome virus proteinase inhibitors; enteric adenovirus structure. **Mailing Address:** Dept Microbiol, La State Univ Med Ctr 1901 Perdido St, New Orleans, LA 70112-1393. **E-Mail:** rlufti@lsuhsc.edu

LUGASSY, ARMAND AMRAM, MATERIALS SCIENCE, PROSTHODONTICS. **Personal Data:** b Kenitra, Morocco, July 23, 1933; m 1966, c 2. **Education:** Toulouse Fac Med & Pharm, France, Chirurgien-Dentiste, 1959; Univ Pa, DDS, 1962, PhD (metall, mat sci), 1968. **Professional Experience:** Vet Admin Hosp, Livermore, 1980-; PROF FIXED PROSTHODONT, SCH DENT, UNIV PAC, 1977-; consult, USPHS Hosp, San Francisco, Calif, 1971-; assoc prof, Sch Dent, Univ Pac, 1971-1977; asst prof biol mat, Dent-Med Sch, Northwestern Univ, 1968-1971; Nat Inst Dent res traineeship, Sch Metall & Mat Sci, Univ Pa, 1963-1968; instr, Sch Dent Med, Univ Pa, 1962-1963; Monitor oper dent, Toulouse Fac Med & Pharm, France, 1958-1959. **Memberships:** Am Soc Metals; Int Asn Dent Res. **Research Statement & Publications:** Physical properties of calcified tissues; behavior of materials and devices in clinical applications in living vertebrates. **Mailing Address:** Dept Fixed Prosthodont, Univ Pac Sch Dent 2155 Webster St, San Francisco, CA 94115. **E-Mail:** alugassy@pacific.edu

LUGAY, JOAQUIN CASTRO, BIOCHEMISTRY, FOOD SCIENCE. **Personal Data:** b Manila, Philippines, April 3, 1938; American citizen; m 1962, c 3. **Education:** Univ Santo Thomas, Manila, BS, 1960; State Univ NY, PhD (chem), 1969. **Professional Experience:** SR LAB MGR PROTEIN BIOTECHNOL COFFEE, GEN FOODS CORP, 1978-; sr res specialist protein, Gen Foods Corp, 1973-1977; res specialist, Gen Foods Corp, 1971-1973; sr chemist biotechnol, Gen Foods Corp, 1969-1971; chemist rice lipids, Int Rice Res Inst, 1962-1963; chemist brewing, San Miguel Brewery Inc, 1960-1962; PRIN SCIENTIST, KRAFT GEN FOOD CORP. **Memberships:** AAAS; Am Chem Soc; Sigma Xi. **Research Statement & Publications:** Isolation and characterization of enzymes; utilization of enzymes in foods; protein texturization; meat analogs; pet food palatability; functional properties of proteins; protein modification; alternate sources of proteins. **Mailing Address:** Kraft Gen Foods Corp, 555 S Broadway, Glenview, IL 60025.

LUGER, GEORGE F, COMPUTER SCIENCE, INTELLIGENT SYSTEMS & COGNITIVE SCIENCE. **Personal Data:** b Spokane, Wash, December 1, 1940; m 1969, Kathleen Kelly; c Sara L, David & Peter. **Education:** Gonzaga Univ, MS, 1966; Univ Notre Dame, MS, 1969; Univ Pa, PhD (artificial intel), 1973. **Professional Experience:** Consult, Learning Tree Int, 1984-; PROF COMPUT SCI & PSYCHOL, DEPT COMPUT SCI, UNIV NMEX, ALBUQUERQUE, 1979-; res fel, Dept Artificial Intel, Univ Edinburgh, Scotland, UK, 1974-1979. **Memberships:** Inst Elec & Electronics Engrs; Am Asn Artificial Intel; Asn Comput Mach; Cognitive Sci Soc. **Research Statement & Publications:** Artificial intelligence, especially related to modelling human problem solving, machine learning and expert system design; cognitive science. **Mailing Address:** Dept Comput Sci, Univ NMex, Albuquerque, NM 87106. **Fax:** 505-277-6927. **E-Mail:** luger@cs.unm.edu

LUGINBUHL, DAVID R, MATHEMATICS. **Education:** Univ Ill, PhD (comput sci). **Professional Experience:** STAFF, AIR FORCE OFF SCI RES, as of 2006; ASSOC PROF, DEPT MATH & COMPUT SCI, WESTERN CAROLINA UNIV, as of 2006. **Mailing Address:** Air Force Off Sci Res, 875 N Randolph St, Arlington, VA 22203. **Fax:** 202-404-7496. **E-Mail:** luginbuh@afosr.af.mil

LUGINBUHL, GERALDINE HOBSON, MICROBIOLOGY. **Personal Data:** b Los Angeles, Calif, February 27, 1944; m 1965, c 1. **Education:** Stanford Univ, BS, 1965; Univ NC, Chapel Hill, PhD (bact, immunol), 1971. **Professional Experience:** PROF MICROBIOL & DIR UNDERGRAD PROGS, NC STATE UNIV, as of 2001; assoc prof microbiol, NC state univ, 1980-; asst prof, NC State Univ, 1974-1980; NIH fel bact, Duke Univ, 1971-1974. **Memberships:** Am Soc Microbiol; Sigma Xi. **Research Statement & Publications:** Genetics and physiology of virulence; alcaligenes. **Mailing Address:** Dept Microbiol Box 7615, NC State Univ, Raleigh, NC 27695-0001. **Fax:** 919-515-7867. **E-Mail:** geraldine_luginbuhl@ncsu.edu

LUGINBUHL, WILLIAM HOSSFELD, PATHOLOGY. **Personal Data:** b Des Moines, Iowa, March 11, 1929; m 1955, c 5. **Education:** Iowa State Univ, BS, 1949; Northwestern Univ, MD, 1953. **Professional Experience:** RETIRED; dean health sci & col, Col Med, Univ Vt, beginnning 1970; PROF PATH, COL MED, UNIV VT, 1967-; assoc dean col, Col Med, Univ VT, 1967-1970; from asst prof to assoc prof, Col Med, Univ VT, 1960-1967; Fel, Col Med, Univ Vt, 1959-1960; resident, Univ Hosps Cleveland, Ohio, 1955-1957; resident path, Children's Mem Hosp, 1954-1955; Intern, Wesley Mem Hosp, Chicago, Ill, 1953-1954. **Memberships:** Col Am Path; Am Soc Clin Path; Sigma Xi. **Research Statement & Publications:** Gynecologic and obstetrical pathology; endometrial anatomy and physiology. **Mailing Address:** Dept Path, Obstet-Gynec Col Med Alumni Bldg, Univ Vt, Burlington, VT 05401.

LUGMAIR, GUENTER WILHELM, COSMOCHEMISTRY, GEOCHRONOLOGY. **Personal Data:** b Wels, Austria, February 5, 1940; m 1965, Rosemarie; c Claus & Claudia. **Education:** Univ Vienna, Austria, PhD (physics), 1968. **Honors & Awards:** Fel, Meteoritical Soc, 1980; G P Merrill Award, Nat Acad Sci, 1987; Mem, Max-Planck-Soc, Ger, 1996; Fel, Am Geochemical Soc, 1997; Hon Fel, European Union Geosciences (EUG), 1998; Mem, Academia Europaea, 2000; Fel, Am Geophys Union, 2000; Leonard Medal, Meteoritical Soc, 2000; UCSD Distinguished Res Scientist, 2005. **Professional Experience:** RES CHEMIST, UNIV CALIF, SAN DIEGO, 1984-; DIR, MAX PLANCK INST CHEM & COSMOCHEM, MAINZ, GER, Emeritus 2005; lunar & planetary sci rev panel, NASA, 1985-1987; prin investr, NASA & NSF, 1981-; assoc ed, J Geophys Res, 1981-1984; assoc res geochem, Scripps Inst Oceanog, 1979-1984; mem-consult, Rev Panel, 1978-1980; assoc res chem, Univ Calif, San Diego, 1977-1984; asst res chemist, Univ Calif, San Diego, 1971-1977; co-investr, Lunar & Planetary Sci Prog, NASA, 1969-1981; Consult, Jet Propulsion Lab, Calif Inst Technol, 1969-1971; chemist, Univ Calif, San Diego, 1968-1971; Fel nuclear physics, Max Planck Inst, Mainz, Ger, 1965-1968. **Memberships:** Am Geophys Union; Meteoritical Soc; AAAS; Max Planck Soc, Ger; Am Geochemical Soc; European Geophys Soc. **Research Statement & Publications:** Origin and history of the solar system; nucleosynthesis; extinct radioactivities; geo dating of terrestial and extraterrestial materials; cosmic ray effects. **Mailing Address:** SIO-GRD 0212, Univ Calif San Diego 9500 Gilman Dr, La Jolla, CA 92093-0212. **Fax:** 858-822-4945. **E-Mail:** glugmair@ucsd.edu

LUGO, ARIEL E, BOTANY, ECOLOGY. **Personal Data:** b Mayaguez, PR, April 28, 1943; m 1984, Helen; c Ariel A & Alma V. **Education:** Univ PR, BS, 1963, MS, 1965; Univ NC, Chapel Hill, PhD (ecol), 1969. **Honors & Awards:** Distinguished Scientist Award, USDA Forest Serv, 1990. **Professional Experience:** DIR, INT INST TROP FORESTRY, USDA FOREST SERV, 1995-; actg dir, USDA, 1995; actg dir & supvry res ecologist, Rio Piedras, PR, 1992-1994; pres, Asn Trop Biol, 1990; dir, Int Inst Trop Forestry, 1986-1992; coun, Asn Trop Biol, 1985-1987; pres, Sci Teachers Asn, PR, 1981; proj leader, Int Inst Trop Forestry, 1980-1992; head div, Ctr Energy & Environ Res, Univ PR, 1980-1988; consult, Collier Co Nature Conserv, 1980; consult, Orgn Am States, 1979-1980; staff mem, Coun Environ Qual Exec Off Pres, Wash, 1978-1979; consult, Nat Wildlife Fedn & World Bank, 1978; co-chmn, Fed Comt Ecol Reserves, 1977-1979; actg dir, Ctr Wetlands, Univ Fla, Gainesville, 1977-1978; consult, Nat Audubon Soc & County Lee, Fla, 1977; assoc prof, Dept Bot, Univ Fla, Gainesville, 1976-1979; consult, SWFla Regional Planning Coun, 1976-1977; consult, Environ Qual Bd, 1976-1977; consult, Rockefeller Found, 1976; consult, Fla Dept Natural Resources, 1976; consult, Unesco, 1975-1976, 1978, 1983, 1985-1986; consult, PR Dept Natural Resources, 1975-1976; hon prof & lectr, Univ PR, 1974-1976, 1980-; consult, US Justice Dept, 1974, 1978; sci & technol, PR Dept Natural Resources, Puerta Del Tierra, 1974-1975; consult, US Environ Protection Agency, 1974; asst secy planning & resource anal, PR Dept Natural Resources, Puerta Del Tierra, 1973-1974; consult, US Dept Interior, 1972, 1973, 1976, 1977; consult, Am Oil Co, HW Lochner, Inc, US Postal Serv & US Forest Serv, 1972; consult, Save Our Bays Asn, 1970; asst prof, Dept Bot, Univ Fla, Gainesville, 1969-1973, 1975-1976. **Memberships:** Sigma Xi; Ecol Soc Am; Asn Trop Biol; Int Soc Trop Ecol; Int Asn Ecol; Nat Wetlands Tech Coun; Soc Restoration Ecol. **Research Statement & Publications:** Subtropical wet forestry and dry forestry; mangrove forests; granite outcrops; hardwood forests; sandpine forest; farm ponds; fresh water praire; lab microcosms; assessment of the role of tropical forests in the carbon; cycle of the world; tropical tree plantations in Puerto Rico. **Mailing Address:** Int Inst Trop Forestry USDA Forestry Serv, 1201 Calle Ceiba, Rio Piedras, PR 00926-1119. **Fax:** 787-766-6263. **E-Mail:** alugo@fs.fed.us

LUGO, HERMINIO LUGO, PLANT PHYSIOLOGY. **Personal Data:** b San German, PR, June 6, 1918; m 1941, c 2. **Education:** Polytech Inst, PR, BA, 1939; Cornell Univ, MS, 1948, PhD, 1954. **Professional Experience:** DIR CAYEY UNIV COL, UNIV PR, 1978-; DIR PREMED STUDIES, UNIV PR, 1971-; PROF ECOL, UNIV PR, 1969-; Fel, Inst Ecol, Univ Ga, 1968-1969; acad coord, Rio Piedras Campus, 1966-1969; prof biol, Univ PR,

1960-1969; asst dean studies, Univ PR, 1960-1966; from asst prof to prof biol, bot & plant physiol, Col Agr, Mayaguez, 1948-1960; instr biol & bot, Polytech Inst PR, 1946-1947; Teacher pub sch, PR, 1941-1946. **Memberships:** Bot Soc Am; Am Soc Agr Sci; Sigma Xi. **Research Statement & Publications:** Germination of vanilla seeds. **Mailing Address:** 162 Calla Ganges, Paraiso, Rio Piedras, PR 00926.

LUGO-LOPEZ, MIGUEL ANGEL, soil science; deceased, see previous edition for last biography

LUGT, HANS JOSEF, FLUID DYNAMICS, VORTEX THEORY. **Personal Data:** b Bonn, Ger, September 12, 1930; American citizen; m 1957, Anneliese; c Christian & Brigitte. **Education:** Univ Bonn, Vordiplom, 1952; Aachen Tech Univ, Diplom, 1954; Stuttgart Tech Univ, PhD (eng), 1960. **Honors & Awards:** David W Taylor Award 1974, US Navy, 1975; Sigma Xi Award, 1980; Alexander von Humboldt US Sr Scientist Award, Ger Govt, 1981; Distinguished Civilian Serv Award, USN, 1982. **Professional Experience:** RETIRED; prof lectr, George Wash Univ, beginning 1988; sr res scientist, Numerical Mech Div, 1978-1995; head, Numerical Mech Div, 1974-1978; prof lectr, George Wash Univ, 1968-1969; scientist consult, Naval Surface Warfare Ctr, 1967-1974; lectr, Am Univ, 1962-1966; res physicist hydrodyn, US Naval Weapons Lab, Va, 1960-1966; head, Physics Lab, 1957-1960; asst hydraul, Ruhrgas AG, Essen, Ger, 1954-1957. **Memberships:** Fel Am Phys Soc; Sigma Xi; Asn Appl Math & Mech Ger; Am Hist Soc. **Research Statement & Publications:** Mathematical fluid dynamics; vortex motion; rotating fluids; numerical solution of Navier-Stokes equations. **Mailing Address:** 10317 Crown Point Ct, Potomac, MD 20854-3901. **Fax:** 301-983-3843.

LUGTHART, GARRIT JOHN, ENTOMOLOGY, GENETICS. **Personal Data:** b Los Angeles, Calif, February 11, 1923; m 1955, Joan; c 3. **Education:** Mich State Univ, BS, 1950, MS, 1951; Univ Wis, PhD (entom), 1959. **Professional Experience:** PROF EMER BIOL, LE MOYNE COL, NY, 1991-; chmn dept, Le Moyne Col, NY, 1979-1991; assoc prof biol, Le Moyne Col, NY, 1961-1991; assoc prof biol, Adrian Col, 1956-1961. **Memberships:** Entom Soc Am; Am Genetic Asn; Sigma Xi. **Research Statement & Publications:** Biology and control of insects injurious to humans and human genetics. **Mailing Address:** Dept Biol, Le Moyne Col, 1419 Salt Springs Rd, Syracuse, NY 13214.

LUH, JIANG, ALGEBRA. **Personal Data:** b Haining, Chekiang, China, June 24, 1932; m 1956, Tsu-Yunn; c Albert, Ellice & Michael. **Education:** Taiwan Normal Univ, BS, 1956; Univ Nebr, MS, 1959; Univ Mich, PhD (math), 1963. **Professional Experience:** PROF EMER MATH, NC STATE UNIV, as of 2003; prof math, nc state univ, beginning 1971; assoc prof, NC State Univ, 1968-1971; assoc prof math, Wright State Univ, 1966-1968; assoc prof math, Ind State Univ, 1963-1966. **Memberships:** Am Math Soc; Math Asn Am. **Research Statement & Publications:** Ring theory; semi-group theory; linear algebra. **Mailing Address:** 8908 Oodvine Ct, Raleigh, NC 27613. **E-Mail:** luh@math.ncsu.edu

LUH, JOHNSON YANG-SENG, ELECTRICAL ENGINEERING, APPLIED MATHEMATICS. **Personal Data:** b Shanghai, China, April 9, 1925; American citizen; m 1957, c 2. **Education:** Utopia Univ, China, BS, 1947; Harvard Univ, MS, 1950; Univ Minn, PhD (elec eng), 1963. **Professional Experience:** MCQUEEN QUATTLEBAUM PROF ELEC & COMPUT ENG, CLEMSON UNIV, as of 2004; prof elec eng, Purdue Univ, 1972-1973; prin investr, NASA res grant, Jet Propulsion Lab, 1965-; assoc prof, Purdue Univ, 1965-1971; sr res scientist, Honeywell, Inc, 1963-1965; Lectr, Univ Minn, 1963-1965; staff engr, Int Bus Mach Corp, 1962-1963; instr elec eng, Univ Minn, 1958-1960; assoc engr, Int Bus Mach Corp, 1957-1958; engr, Nat Pneumatic Co, 1951-1956 & Curtiss-Wright Corp, 1956-1957; Teaching fel elec eng, Harvard Univ, 1950-1951. **Memberships:** Soc Indust & Appl Math; sr mem Inst Elec & Electronics Engrs; sr mem Am Astronaut Soc; Sigma Xi. **Research Statement & Publications:** Control and information systems and computer aided engineering design, especially bounded-state, stochastic control, learning and communication, and data reduction systems. **Mailing Address:** Dept Elec & Comput Eng, Clemson Univ, 221E Riggs Hall, Clemson, SC 29634. **Fax:** 864-656-5910. **E-Mail:** johnson.luh@ces.clemson.edu

LUH, YUHSHI, SPECIALTY CHEMICALS & MATERIALS, ADHESIVES. **Personal Data:** b Kaohsiung, Taiwan, February 14, 1949; c 2. **Education:** Nat Taiwan Univ, BS, 1971; Rice Univ, PhD (chem), 1976. **Honors & Awards:** Welch Fund Award, 1974. **Professional Experience:** Spec lectr, Univ New Haven, 1989-1990; SR RES CHEMIST, AM CYANAMID CO, 1984-; res chemist, Mine Safety & Appliances Co, 1983-1984; res scientist, Gulf Oil Co, Gulf Sci & Technol Co, 1981-1983; res chemist, Mobil Oil Corp, Mobil Res & Develop Co, 1979-1981; NIH postdoctoral fel, Mass Inst Technol, 1978-1979; Proj investr, M D Anderson Hosp & Tumor Inst, 1977-1978. **Memberships:** Am Chem Soc. **Research Statement & Publications:** Biomaterials; ultraviolet stabilizers; photochromics; adhesives; crosslinking chemistry; specialty chemicals; enhanced oil recovery; chemotherapy; pharmaceuticals; petrochemicals; process development; organic and polymer synthesis; product formulation and testing; product development; structure-property relationships. **Mailing Address:** 948 Red Fox Rd, Orange, CT 06477-1035.

LUHMAN, JANET G, PLANETARY PHYSICS. **Education:** Carnegie-Mellon Univ, BS, 1968; Univ Md, MS, 1971, PhD, 1974. **Professional Experience:** SR FEL, SPACE SCI LAB, UNIV CALIF, BERKELEY, as of 2004; res geophysicist, Space Sci Lab, Univ Calif, Berkeley, as of 1998. **Memberships:** Am Astron Soc; Am Geophys Union. **Mailing Address:** Space Sci Lab Univ Calif Berkeley, Grizzly Peak Blvd, Berkeley, CA 94720. **Fax:** 510-643-8302. **E-Mail:** jgluhmann@sunspot.ssl.berkeley.edu

LUHMANN, N C, JR, PHYSICS. **Education:** Univ Md, Col Park, PhD (physics), 1972. **Professional Experience:** DISTINGUISHED PROF PHYSICS, UNIV CALIF, DAVIS, as of 2006. **Mailing Address:** Dept Physics, Univ Calif, 228 Walker Hall, Davis, CA 95616. **Fax:** 530-754-9070. **E-Mail:** ncluhmann@ucdavis.edu

LUI, YIU-KWAN, PHYSICAL CHEMISTRY. **Personal Data:** b Hong Kong, March 24, 1937; American citizen; m 1967, c 1. **Education:** Chung Chi Col, Hong Kong, BS, 1959; Lehigh Univ, MS, 1961, PhD (phys chem), 1966. **Professional Experience:** RES ASSOC, ENGELHARD INDUST DIV, ENGELHARD CORP, 1981-; sr res chemist, Engelhard Indust Div, Engelhard Corp, 1978-1981; res chemist, Engelhard Indust Div, Engelhard Corp, 1976-1978; res chemist, Indust Chem Div, 1975; res chemist, Titanium Pigment Div, NL Indust, 1965-1974. **Memberships:** Am Chem Soc. **Research Statement & Publications:** Heterogeneous catalysis; preparation and characterization of precious metal catalysts; colloid and surface properties of silica and alumina; physical properties of rheological additives; dispersion stability; physical and surface properties of titanium dioxide pigments. **Mailing Address:** Engelhard Corp, 101 Wood Ave P O Box 770, Iselin, NJ 08830-0770.

LUIBRAND, RICHARD THOMAS, ORGANIC CHEMISTRY. **Personal Data:** b Detroit, Mich, April 13, 1945. **Education:** Wayne State Univ, BS, 1966; Univ Wis, PhD (org chem), 1971. **Professional Experience:** CHMN & PROF ORG CHEM, CALIF STATE UNIV, EAST BAY, as of 2005; Cottrell res grant, Res Corp, 1973; from asst prof to assoc prof, Calif State Univ, Hayward, 1972-1981; Fel, Alexander von Humboldt Found, WGer, 1971-1972. **Memberships:** Am Chem Soc. **Research Statement & Publications:** Reaction mechanisms in organic chemistry; natural products chemistry; computational chemistry. **Mailing Address:** Dept Chem & Biochem, Calif State Univ, E Bay, Hayward, CA 94542. **E-Mail:** rich.luibrand@csueastbay.edu

LUINE, VICTORIA NALL, NEUROSCIENCES. **Personal Data:** b Pine Bluff, Ark, April 22, 1945; m 1976, David; c Richard. **Education:** Allegheny Col, BS, 1967; State Univ NY, Buffalo, PhD (pharmacol), 1971. **Honors & Awards:** Gold citation, Allegheny Col, 2001. **Professional Experience:** PROF, DEPT PSYCHOL, HUNTER COL & PROG BIOPSYCHOL & BIOL, CITY UNIV NEW YORK, 1987-; adj prof, Rockefeller Univ, 1987-; assoc prof, Dept Physiol, 1977-1987; asst prof neurochem, Rockefeller Univ, 1975-1977; res assoc, Rockefeller Univ, 1972-1975. **Memberships:** AAAS; Soc Neuroscience; Endocrine Soc; NY Acad Sci. **Research Statement & Publications:** Steroid hormone regulation of central neurotransmitters and their role in behavior, memory and aging. **Mailing Address:** Hunter Col CUNY, Dept Psychol 695 Park Ave, New York, NY 10021-5024. **Fax:** 212-650-3546. **E-Mail:** vluine@hunter.cuny.edu

LUISKUTTY, CHERIYAKALTHIL THOMAS, MOSSBAUER SPECTROSCOPY, HYDRAULIC FRACTURE MODELING. **Personal Data:** b Kangazha, India, October 18, 1944; m 1966, Celia; c Tom, Sara & George. **Education:** Univ Kerala, India, BS, 1965, MS, 1969; Univ Louisville, PhD (physics), 1974. **Professional Experience:** PROF PHYSICS & ENG, ORAL ROBERTS UNIV, 1989-; consult, Amoco Res Ctr, 1987-1988; res fel, Mech Eng Dept, Univ Tulsa, 1986-1987; res fel & consult, Nat Inst Petrol & Energy Res, 1985-1986; consult, John Zink Co, 1981; from asst prof to assoc prof, Oral Roberts Univ, 1980-1989; teacher & supt, Evangel Schs, Louisville, 1974-1980; sci officer trainee, Bhabha Atomic Res Ctr, India, 1969; sci asst, Bhabha Atomic Res Ctr, India, 1965-1967. **Memberships:** Am Phys Soc; Am Soc Eng Educ. **Research Statement & Publications:** Mossbauer spectroscopy and hydraulic fracture modeling; engineering and science education and the need for ethics and spirituality in society. **Mailing Address:** 8177 S Harvard Ave, PMB 426, Tulsa, OK 74137. **Fax:** 918-495-7648. **E-Mail:** tluiskutty@oru.edu

LUK, FRANKLIN T, PARALLEL COMPUTING, SIGNAL PROCESSING. **Personal Data:** b Hong Kong, China, March 23, 1950; American citizen; m 1986, Vivian; c Jessica & David. **Education:** Calif Inst Technol, BS, 1972; Stanford Univ, MS, 1974 PhD (comput sci), 1978. **Professional Experience:** Vis prof, Chinese Univ, Hong Kong, 1993-1994; PROF COMPUT SCI, RENSSELAER POLYTECH INST, 1992-; chair, Dept Comput Sci, Rensselaer Polytech Inst, beginning 1992; prof, Cornell Univ, 1988-1991; assoc prof elec eng, Cornell Univ, 1984-1988; asst prof comput sci, Cornell Univ, 1978-1984. **Memberships:** Am Comput Mech; Inst Elec & Electronics Engrs; Soc Indust & Appl Math. **Research Statement & Publications:** Numerical Analysis; scientific computation; parallel processing; matrix algorithms. **Mailing Address:** Rensselaer Polytech Inst, 110 Eigth St, Troy, NY 12180-3590. **Fax:** 518-276-4033.

LUK, GORDON DAVID, POLYAMINES, GASTROENTEROLOGY. **Personal Data:** b Shanghai, China, November 15, 1950; American citizen; m 1973, c 2. **Education:** Univ Pa, BA, 1971; Harvard Med Sch, MD, 1975; Am Bd Internal Med, cert med, 1978, cert gastroenterol, 1979. **Professional Experience:** PROF, DALLAS VET ADMIN MED CTR, 1991-; asst prof med & oncol, Johns Hopkins Univ, 1980-1991; PHYSICIAN, JOHNS HOPKINS HOSP, 1979-; instr med, John Hopkins Univ, 1979-1980; fel gastroenterol, Dallas Vet Admin Med Ctr, 1977-1979; resident med, Dallas Vet Admin Med Ctr, 1975-1977. **Memberships:** Am Fedn Clin Res; Am Col Physician; Am Gastroenterol Asn; Am Soc Gastrointestinal Endoscopy; Am Asn Study Liver Dis. **Research Statement & Publications:** Cell proliferation and differentiation with special emphasis on the potential regulatory role of polyamines; diseases of gastrointestinal epithelia and neoplastic diseases. **Mailing Address:** S Western Med Ctr, Univ Tex, 4500 S Lancaster Rd, Dallas, TX 75216-7191.

LUK, KIN-CHUN C, DESIGN & SYNTHESIS OF COMPOUNDS FOR USE AS DRUGS, CORPORATE CHEMICAL & BIOLOGICAL DATABASES. **Personal Data:** b Hong Kong, March 11, 1950. **Education:** Univ Wis-Eau Claire, BS, 1973; Mass Inst Technol, PhD (org chem), 1977. **Professional Experience:** RES LEADER, HOFFMANN-LA ROCHE INC, 1996-; res investr, 1988-1996; Sr scientist, 1977-1988. **Memberships:** Am Chem Soc; Sigma Xi; AAAS. **Research Statement & Publications:** Design and synthesis of small organic molecules for use as drug, especially in the area of anti-bacterial, anti-viral and anti-inflammatory diseases; design and implementation of corporate chemical and biological databases. **Mailing Address:** Dept Chem Res, Hoffmann-La Roche, Inc, 340 Kingsland St, Nutley, NJ 07110.

LUK, KING SING, STRUCTURAL ENGINEERING. **Personal Data:** b Canton, China, September 1, 1932; American citizen; m 1957, Kit Ming Wong; c Doris, Steven, Eric & Marcus. **Education:** Calif State Univ, BS, 1957; Univ Southern Calif, MSCE, 1960; Univ Calif, Los Angeles, PhD (dynamics, soils & struct eng), 1971. **Professional Experience:** Dir, Mech Nat Bank, 1982-; EMER PROF CIVIL ENG, CALIF STATE UNIV, LOS ANGELES, 1982-; comnr, Calif Seismic Safety Comn, 1979-1983; pres, Cathay Pac Inc, 1974-; prof, Calif State Univ, Los Angeles, 1970-1983; from assoc chmn to chmn dept, Calif State Univ, Los Angeles, 1966-1972; Pres, King S Luk & Assoc, Calif, 1960-; from asst prof to assoc prof, Calif State Univ, Los Angeles, 1960-1965; Chief engr, R E Rule, Inc, Calif, 1958-1960. **Memberships:** Fel Am Soc Civil Engrs. **Research Statement & Publications:** Engineering education; structural and earthquake engineering in design and practice of reinforced concrete and steel structures; foundations; time dependent soil and foundation engineering; reinforced concretes; author of numerous publications. **Mailing Address:** Luk & Luk Inc, 55 S Raymond Ave Suite 302, Alhambra, CA 91801-7106.

LUKACH, CARL ANDREW, ORGANIC CHEMISTRY, POLYMER CHEMISTRY. **Personal Data:** b Wilkes-Barre, Pa, December 18, 1930; m 1953, Joan Wojcik; c Carl, Theodor, & Marianna. **Education:** Lehigh Univ, BS, 1952, MS, 1953; Univ Notre Dame, PhD (org chem), 1957. **Honors & Awards:** Coauthor of chapter in book Copolymerization, 1960; Awarded 13 US patents from 1964 to 1995. **Professional Experience:** Ret 1992; res & develop mgr, France, 1990-1992; world-wide mgr, petrol appln, 1987-1989; petrol recovery appln, Chem Sci Div, 1982-1985; proj mgr cellulose derivatives, Chem Sci Div, 1980-1981; mgr, Chem Sci Div, 1978-1979; res mgr, Org Div, 1973-1978; res supvr, Hercules Inc, 1969-1973; Res chemist, Hercules Inc, 1956-1969; Res mgr, Hercules Inc, Aqualon Div. **Memberships:** Emer mem Am Chem Soc; Sigma Xi; Soc Petrol Engrs; Am Petrol Inst. **Research Statement & Publications:** Polymerization and copolymerization of olefins and olefin oxides; polymerization kinetics; conformational analysis; reverse osmosis; cross-linking agents; paper chemistry; cellulose chemistry; oil and gas drilling fluids, fracturing fluids and completion fluids; casing cement; cosmetics, toothpaste and shampoo; low fat substitutes in food. **Mailing Address:** 109 Downs Dr, Limerick, Wilmington, DE 19807-2556. **E-Mail:** cluka@aol.com

LUKACSKO, ALISON B, PHARMACEUTICAL PRODUCT DEVELOPMENT. **Personal Data:** b Utica, NY, January 30, 1951; m 1979, Peter; c Jeffrey & Michael. **Education:** NY Med Col, MS, 1978, PhD (pharmacol), 1979. **Professional Experience:** MGR PHARMACOL & TOXICOL, BRISTOL MYERS PRODS, as of 2002; DIR RES & DEVELOP, BRISTOL MYERS PRODS, 1991-; dir prod develop, 1990-1991; mgr pharmacol/toxicol, 1985-1990. **Memberships:** Fel Am Col Nutrit; Soc Toxicol; Prod Develop Mgt Asn. **Research Statement & Publications:** Direct research and development and support activities associated with over the counter health care pharmaceutical development by integrating technology with consumer/patient needs. **Mailing Address:** Bristol-Myers Squibb Co, 345 Park Ave, Newyork, NY 10154-0037. **Fax:** 212-546-4020.

LUKAS, GEORGE, INDUSTRIAL PHARMACY. **Personal Data:** b Budapest, Hungary, March 16, 1931; m 1956, c 2. **Education:** Univ Budapest, BS, 1954; Polytech Inst Brooklyn, MS, 1960; Mass Inst Technol, PhD (org chem), 1963; NY Univ, MBA, 1972. **Professional Experience:** CHEM CONSULT, GEORGE LUCAS ASSOCIATES, INC, 1995-; exec dir, pharmaceut & pharm technol, Ciba-Geigy Corp, beginning 1991; adj prof, Col Pharm, Univ RI, beginning 1989; dir pharmaceut & pharm technol, Biochem Dept, 1981-1990; adj assoc prof, Dept Pharmacol, NY Med Col, 1980-1990; assoc dir, Biochem Dept, 1980-1981; mgr drug metabol, Biochem Dept, 1971-1980; group leader, Biochem Dept, 1967-1971; res biochemist, Ciba-Geigy Corp, 1965-1967; res chemist, Ciba-Geigy Corp, 1964-1965; NIH fel, Inst Chem Natural Substances, Gif-Sur-Yvette, France, 1963-1964; develop engr, Chas Pfizer & Co, 1957-1959; chemist, Avery Industs, Calif, 1957; Develop engr, United Pharmaceut Works, Hungary, 1954-1956. **Memberships:** Am Asn Pharmaceut Sci. **Research Statement & Publications:** Chemistry of natural products; pharmacodynamics; absorption and disposition of drugs. **Mailing Address:** George Lucas Associates, Inc, 91 Woodland Ave, Summit, NJ 07901. **Fax:** 908-2737534. **E-Mail:** george@glukas.com

LUKAS, JOAN DONALDSON, LOGIC, PROGRAMMING LANGUAGES & COMPILERS. **Personal Data:** b New Haven, Conn, June 19, 1942; m 1990, Seamus; c David & Jon. **Education:** Columbia Univ, AB, 1963; Mass Inst Technol, PhD (math), 1967. **Professional Experience:** PROF EMERITA, DEPT MATH, UNIV MASS, BOSTAN, as of 2005; prof comput sci, Univ Mass, Boston, as of 2004; PROF MATH, UNIV MASS, BOSTON, 1993-; consult, 1981-; vis lectr, Brandeis Univ, 1971 & 1979, 1994; From asst prof to assoc prof, Univ Mass, Boston, 1967-1993. **Memberships:** Am Math Soc; Math Asn Am; Asn Symbolic Logic; Asn Comput Mach; Inst Elec & Electronics Engrs Comput Soc. **Research Statement & Publications:** Mathematical logic; recursive function theory; compiler optimization for parallel architectures. **Mailing Address:** Dept Math & Comput Sci, Univ Mass, 100 Morrissey Blvd, Boston, MA 02125-3393. **Fax:** 617-287-6433. **E-Mail:** joan@cs.umb.edu

LUKAS, RONALD JOHN, NEUROCHEMISTRY. **Personal Data:** b Syracuse, NY, August 22, 1949; m 1972, Julie; c Eric T. **Education:** State Univ NY, Cortland, BS, 1971; State Univ NY, Downstate Med Ctr, PhD (biophys), 1976. **Professional Experience:** SR RES SCIENTIST, BARROW NEUROL INST, PHOENIX, as of 2004; PROF PHARAMACOL, UNIV ARIZ, TUSCON, as of 2004; SR STAFF SCIENTIST, DIV NEUROBIOLOGY, 1990-; grant rev, Nat Sci Found, 1990-1991; res assoc prof, Univ Ariz, Tucson, 1989-; adj prof, chem & biochem, Ariz State Univ, Tempe, beginning 1989; vice chmn, Div Neurobiology, 1987-1994; DIR, CLINICAL ASSAY DEVELOP LAB, PHOENIX, ARIZ, 1985-; DIR, LAB NEUROCHEMISTRY, BARROW NEUROL INST, PHOENIX, ARIZ, 1980-; res asst prof, pharmacol, Univ Ariz, Tucson, 1980-1988; fel neurobiology, Stanford Univ, 1979-1980; res assoc, Lab Chem Biodynamics, 1978-1979; fel, Univ Calif, Berkeley, 1976-1978. **Memberships:** Soc Neuroscience; Am Soc Neurochemistry; Biophys Soc; Sigma Xi; Am Soc Pharmacol & Exp Therapeut; Int Soc Neurochemistry; Am Cancer Soc. **Research Statement & Publications:** Neurotransmitters, neurotoxins and synaptic receptors, nervous system hormone, tropic factors and molecular aspects of developmental neurobiology; Published over 25 artilces. **Mailing Address:** Barrow Neurol Inst, 350 W Thomas Rd, Phoenix, AZ 85013. **Fax:** 602-406-4172. **E-Mail:** rlukas@chw.edu

LUKASEWYCZ, OMELAN ALEXANDER, IMMUNOBIOLOGY, ACADEMIC ADMINISTRATION. **Personal Data:** b 1942; American citizen; m 1968, c 2. **Education:** St Joseph's Col, Pa, AB, 1964; Villanova Univ, MS, 1968; Bryn Mawr Col, PhD (microbiol), 1972. **Professional Experience:** HEAD, DEPT MED MICROBIOL & IMMUNOL, SCH MED, UNIV MINN, DULUTH, as of 2005; fel, Bush Found, Minn, 1983; ASSOC PROF MED MICROBIOL & IMMUNOL, SCH MED, UNIV MINN, DULUTH, 1978-; ASST DEAN CURRICULAR AFFAIRS, SCH MED, UNIV MINN, DULUTH, 1977-; asst prof, Sch Med, Univ Minn, Duluth, 1975-1978; lectr microbiol, Med Sch, Univ Mich, Ann Arbor, 1973-1975; res scholar tumor immunol, Sch Med, Univ Mich, Ann Arbor, 1973-1975; res asst microbiol, Univ Tex, Austin, 1970-1972. **Memberships:** Am Soc Microbiol; AAAS; Am Asn Immunologists; Fedn Am Socs Exp Med; Sigma Xi. **Research Statement & Publications:** Evaluation of immunocompetent cell populations in immune mechanisms of leukemia; contribution of B and T cell subsets; role of macrophage; role of histocompatibility antigens; role of copper in the immune response; effects of copper deficiency on tumor immunity. **Mailing Address:** Dept Med Microbiol & Immunol, Sch Med, Univ Minn, 336 1035 Univ Dr, Duluth, MN 55812-2487. **Fax:** 218-726-7937. **E-Mail:** olukasew@d.umn.edu

LUKASIEWICZ, JULIUS, AEROSPACE ENGINEERING. **Personal Data:** b Warsaw, Poland, November 7, 1919; American citizen; m 1941, c 2. **Education:** Univ London, BSc, 1943, DIC, 1945, DSc(eng), 1966; Polish Tech Univ, Eng, dipl, 1944. **Professional Experience:** Mgr transp study, Sci Coun Can, 1977-1978; PROF ENG, CARLETON UNIV, 1971-; prof aerospace eng & assoc dean grad studies & res, Whittemore prof eng, 1970-1971; consult adv comt, US Air Force Systs Command, Nat Acad Sci, 1969-1971; prof aerospace eng & assoc dean grad studies & res, Col Eng, Va Polytech Inst & State Univ, 1968-1970; mem, Adv Group Aeronaut Res & Develop, NATO, 1962-1968; Chmn, Aeroballistic Range Asn, 1961-1962 & Supersonic Tunnel Asn, 1961-1962; chief Von Karman Gas Dynamics Facil, Arnold Eng Develop Ctr, ARO, Inc, Tenn, 1958-1968; head high speed aerodyn lab, Nat Res Coun Can, 1949-1957; Sr sci officer, Aerodyn Dept, Royal Aircraft Estab, Eng, 1945- 1948. **Memberships:** Fel Am Inst Aeronaut & Astronaut; fel Can Aeronaut & Space Inst; fel Brit Inst Mech Engrs; NY Acad Sci. **Research Statement & Publications:** High speed aerodynamics; test facilities; energy and transportation; technology-society interaction. **Mailing Address:** 46 Whippoorwill Dr, Ottawa, ON K1J 7H9, Can.

LUKASIK, STEPHEN JOSEPH, PHYSICS. **Personal Data:** b Staten Island, NY, March 19, 1931; m 1983, c 6. **Education:** Rensselaer Polytech Inst, BS, 1951; Mass Inst Technol, SM, 1953, PhD (physics), 1956. **Honorary Degrees:** DEng, Stevens Inst Technol, 1987. **Honors & Awards:** Ottens Res Award, 1963. **Professional Experience:** CONSULT SAIC CORP, as of 2002; VIS PROF, GA INST TECHNOL, as of 2002; Mem, Harvey Mudd Col, 1987-; mem bd trustees, Nat Security Indust Asn, 1986-; mem, bd dirs, Software Productivity Consortium, 1985-; corp vpres technol, Northrop Corp, beginning 1985; vpres & mgr, Northrop Res & Technol Ctr, 1982-1985; chief scientist, Fed Commun Comn, 1979-1982; ed, Info Soc, 1978-; chief scientist, Rand Corp, 1978-1979; vpres nat security res, Rand Corp, 1977-1978; mem, Comput Sci Adv Comt, Stanford Univ, 1976-1982; mem, Bd Trustees, Stevens Inst Technol, 1975-; vpres, Systs Develop Div, Xerox Corp, 1975-1976; dir, Advan Res Projs Agency, 1971-1974; dept dir, Advan Res Projs Agency, 1968-1971; dir nuclear test detection, Advan Res Projs Agency, 1966-1968; consult, Vitro labs, Vitro Corp Am, 1959-1966; assoc res prof physics, Fluid Physics Div, Davidson Lab, Stevens Inst Technol, 1959-1966; chief, Fluid Physics Div, Davidson Lab, Stevens Inst Technol, 1957-1966; scientist, Westinghouse Elec Corp, 1955-1957; Acoust engr, Bolt, Beranek & Newman Co, 1952-1955; Asst physics, Mass Inst Technol, 1951-1955. **Memberships:** AAAS; Am Phys Soc; Sigma Xi. **Research Statement & Publications:** Relaxation processes in gases and liquids; viscous boundary layer phenomena; energy dissipation processes in water waves; interaction of explosives with magnetic fields.

LUKASKI, HENRY CHARLES, TRACE ELEMENT METABOLISM, BODY COMPOSITION ASSESSMENT. **Personal Data:** b Dearborn, Mich, September 28, 1947; m 1977, c 2. **Education:** Eastern Mich Univ, BS, 1973; Pa State Univ, MS, 1976, PhD (physiol & nutrit), 1979. **Professional Experience:** ANIMAL GENETIST, NAT CTR GENETICS RES, AGR RES SERV, USDA, as of 2005; ASST DIR, AGR RES SERV, USDA, as of 2005; RES LEADER, GRAND FORKS HUMAN NUTRIT CTR, AGR RES SERV, USDA, 1990-; Consult, NIH, 1987- & Nat Sci& Eng Res Coun, Can, 1989-; INSTR MED, UNIV NDAK SCH MED, 1988-; res physiologist, Grand Forks Human Nutrit Ctr, Univ NDak, 1983-1990; biologist, Grand Forks Human Nutrit Ctr, Univ NDak, 1980-1982; USDA Agr Res Serv postdoctoral fel nutrit, Grand Forks Human Nutrit Ctr, Univ NDak, 1979-1980; res collabr, Brookhaven Nat Lab, 1978-1979. **Memberships:** Am Physiol Soc; Am Inst Nutrit; Am Soc Clin Nutrit; fel Am Col Sports Med; fel Human Biol Coun; NY Acad Sci. **Research Statement & Publications:** Human nutritional requirements for trace minerals and the physiologic and functional effects of graded trace element deficiencies in humans; human body composition assessment. **Mailing Address:** Nat Ctr Genetics Res, Agr Res Serv, USDA, 2420 2nd Ave, Grand Forks, ND 58202-0000. **Fax:** 701-795-8230. **E-Mail:** hlukaski@gfhnrc.ars.usda.gov

LUKE, BRIAN, THEORETICAL CHEMISTRY. **Personal Data:** b Montreal, Que, October 12, 1953. **Education:** Calif Inst Technol, BS, 1975, NSF, 1976; Univ Southern Calif, PhD (theoret chem), 1980. **Professional Experience:** SR SCIENTIST, ADVAN BIOMED COMPUT CTR, NAT CANCER INST, FREDERICK, 1995-; sr scientist, Appl Enrichment Ctr, Ibm, Kingston, 1987-1995; staff scientist, Life Sci Div, SRI Int & Molecular Res Inst, 1983-1987; fel, Carnegie-Mellon Univ, 1981-1983. **Memberships:** Am Chem Soc; NY Acad Sci; AAAS; fel Am Inst Chemists. **Research Statement & Publications:** Calibration and efficient usage of current theoretical methods; protein structure determination. **Mailing Address:** Advan Biomed Comput Ctr, Nat Cancer Inst, Ste 3036A 6116 Exec Blvd MSC8322, Bethesda, MD 20892-8322. **E-Mail:** lukeb@ncifcrf.gov

LUKE, HERBERT HODGES, PLANT PATHOLOGY. **Personal Data:** b Pavo, Ga, February 2, 1923; m 1946, c 2. **Education:** Univ Ga, BS, 1950; La State Univ, MS, 1952, PhD, 1954. **Professional Experience:** RETIRED; prof plant path, Univ Fla, 1970-1986; Plant pathologist, Agr Exp Sta, 1955-1986; Plant pathologist, Delta Br Exp Sta, USDA, Miss, 1954-1955. **Memberships:** Am Phytopath Soc. **Research Statement & Publications:** Chemical nature of disease resistance in plants, particularly isolation and identification of host metabolites that inhibit pathogenesis of pathogen; chemical and genetic control of small grain diseases. **Mailing Address:** 1401 NW 61st Terr, Gainesville, FL 32605.

LUKE, JAMES LINDSAY, FORENSIC PATHOLOGY. **Personal Data:** b Cleveland, Ohio, August 29, 1932; m 1957, c 3. **Education:** Columbia Univ, BS, 1956; Western Res Univ, MD, 1960. **Professional Experience:** DIR ENVIRON PATH, ARMED FORCES INST PATH, 1993-; chief med examr, Univ Conn Health Ctr, 1987-1989; FORENSIC PATH, FBI ACAD, 1984-; dist scientist, Armed Forces Inst Path, 1983-1986; prof forensic path, Sch Med, Univ Okla & chief med examr, 1971-1983; clin prof path, Georgetown Univ, George Wash Univ & Howard Univ, 1971-1983, 1989-; chief med examr, Wash, DC, 1971-1983; State med examr, Okla, 1967-1971; assoc med examr forensic path, OffChief Med Examr, NY, 1965-1967; staff researcher, Lab Exp Path, Nat Inst Arthritis & Metab Dis, 1963-1965; chief resident, Inst Path, Western Res Univ, 1961-1963; Intern Path, Yale-New Haven Hosp, 1960-1961. **Memberships:** fel Am Acad Forensic Sci; Nat Asn Med Examr. **Research Statement & Publications:** Epidemiological research in legal medicine; pathology of asphyxia, strangulation, hanging and sudden natural death; aspects of forensic pathology as related to pediatrics; pathology of silicone implant capsular tissues. **Mailing Address:** Off Armed Forces Med Examr, Armed Forces Inst Path, Washington, DC 20306. **Fax:** 301-319-0635.

LUKE, JON CHRISTIAN, APPLIED MATHEMATICS. **Personal Data:** b Minneapolis, Minn, August 10, 1940; m 1983, Jeanne; c Amanda K & Rosa E. **Education:** Mass Inst Technol, SB, 1962, SM, 1963; Calif Inst Technol, PhD (appl math), 1966. **Professional Experience:** ASSOC PROF EMERITUS, DEPT MATH SCI, IND UNIV-PURDUE UNIV, INDIANAPOLIS, beginning 1979-; assoc prof, dept math sci, Ind Univ-purdue Univ, Indianapolis, 1979-; asst prof, Ind Univ-purdue Univ, Indianapolis, 1975-1979; vis assoc, Calif Inst Technol, 1974-1975; postdoctoral assoc, Univ Minn, 1973-1974; asst prof math, Univ Calif, San Diego, 1966-1973; NSF fel, 1966-1968. **Memberships:** Sigma Xi; Soc Indust & Appl Math; NY Acad Sci. **Research Statement & Publications:** Nonlinear methods in applied mathematics; applications in nonlinear wave problems, geomorphology, economics, biophysics and acoustics. **Mailing Address:** Dept Math Ind Univ-Purdue Univ Indpolis, 402 N Blackford St, Indianapolis, IN 46202. **E-Mail:** jluke@math.iupui.edu

LUKE, ROBERT A, PARTICLE PHYSICS. **Personal Data:** b Rigby, Idaho, January 5, 1938; m 1964, c 6. **Education:** Utah State Univ, BS, 1962, MS, 1966, PhD (physics), 1968. **Professional Experience:** PROF EMER PHYSICS, BOISE STATE UNIV, as of 2004; dept chmn, Boise State Univ, beginning 1983; prof physics, Boise State Univ, beginning 1977; from asst prof to assoc prof, 1968-1977. **Memberships:** Am Asn Physics Teachers; Am Nuclear Soc. **Research Statement & Publications:** X-ray investigation of clay mixtures; multi-pion production in pion proton interactions. **Mailing Address:** Dept Physics, Boise State Univ, 1910 Univ Dr, Boise, ID 83725-1570. **Fax:** 208-426-4330. **E-Mail:** rluke@mac.boisestate.edu

LUKE, STANLEY D, MATHEMATICS. **Personal Data:** b Sialkot, West Pakistan, January 1, 1928; m 1952, c 5. **Education:** Univ Panjab, WPakistan, BA, 1947, MA, 1949; Carnegie-Mellon Univ, MS, 1954; Univ Pittsburgh, PhD (math), 1968. **Professional Experience:** PROF EMER, DEPT MATH, SEATTLE PAC COL, 1993-; prof math, Nebr Wesleyan Univ, beginning 1968; instr, Univ Pittsburgh, 1967-1968; prof math, Gordon Col, W Pakistan, 1949-1964. **Memberships:** Math Asn Am. **Research Statement & Publications:** Mathematical analysis with special interest in summability. **Mailing Address:** Dept Math, Seattle Pac Col, 3307 Third Ave W, Seattle, WA 98119-1997.

LUKE, SUNNY, GENETICS. **Education:** Kariyavattam, India; Adelphi Univ, US; Inst of Biol, UK. **Professional Experience:** DIR EDUC. **Mailing Address:** 14 Mountain View Dr, West Paterson, NJ 07424.

LUKEHART, CHARLES MARTIN, ORGANOMETALLIC CHEMISTRY, NANOCOMPOSITES. **Personal Data:** b DuBois, Pa, December 21, 1946; m 1973, c 3. **Education:** Pa State Univ, BS, 1968; Mass Inst Technol, PhD (inorg chem), 1972. **Professional Experience:** PROF CHEM, VANDERBILT UNIV, 1982-; Alfred P Sloan res fel, 1979-1983; from asst prof to assoc prof, Vanderbilt Univ, 1973-1982; res assoc chem, Tex A&M Univ, 1972-1973. **Memberships:** Am Chem Soc; Mats Res Soc. **Research Statement & Publications:** Synthesis, characterization and chemical reactivity of organometallic and coordination complexes containing transition metals; new synthetic routes to nanocomposite materials. **Mailing Address:** Dept Chem, Vanderbilt Univ, 7862 Stevenson Ctr, VU Sta B 351822, Nashville, TN 37235-1822. **Fax:** 615-322-4936. **E-Mail:** charles.m.lukehart@vanderbilt.edu

LUKEHART, SHEILA A, MEDICAL RESEARCH. **Education:** Univ Calif, PhD, 1978. **Professional Experience:** ADJ RES PROF PATHOBIOLOGY, SCHL PUB HEALTH & COMMUNITY MED, UNIV WASH, 1998-; ADJ RES PROF PERIODONT, SCH DENT, UNIV WASH, 1995-; RES PROF ALLERGY & INFECTIOUS DIS, SCH MED, UNIV WASH, 1980-. **Mailing Address:** Dept Med Harborview Med Ctr Univ Wash, 325 Ninth Ave Box 359779, Seattle, WA 98104-2499. **Fax:** 206-341-5363. **E-Mail:** lukehart@u.washington.edu

LUKEN, JAMES O, BOTANY. **Education:** Southern Ill Univ, BS, 1977; Western Wash Univ, MS, 1979; Duke Univ, PhD (Botany), 1984. **Professional Experience:** PROF, DEPT BIOL, COASTAL CAROLINA UNIV, 2001-; chair, Dept Biol, Coastal Carolina Univ, 2001-2005; prof, Dept Biol Sci, Northern Ky Univ, 1997-2001; assoc dean, Col Arts & Sci, Northern Ky Univ, 1999-2000; actn chair person, Dept Biol Sci, Northern Ky Univ, 1999; dir, Environ Sci Prog, Northern Ky Univ, 1999-2001; from asst to assoc prof, Dept Biol Sci, Northern Ky Univ, 1984-1997. **Memberships:** Exec Comt, Southern Appalachian Bot Soc, 2003-; Chair, S E Chapter, Ecol Soc Am, 2004-. **Research Statement & Publications:** Carolina bay ecotones; long-term community change in salt marsh; venus' fly trap restoration; wetland integrity; powerline corridors. **Mailing Address:** Dept Biol, Coastal Carolina Univ, POBox 261954, Conway, SC 29528-6054. **Fax:** 843-349-2201. **E-Mail:** JoLuken@coastal.edu

LUKENS, HERBERT RICHARD, JR, CHEMISTRY, PSYCHOPHYSIOLOGY. **Personal Data:** b Coquille, Ore, May 19, 1921; m 1945, Eleanor; c 2. **Education:** Univ Calif, Berkeley, BA, 1945; US Int Univ, San Diego, MA, 1975, PhD (human behav), 1978. **Professional Experience:** Dianletry Detectore, 1991-1999; CONSULT, SAN DIEGO YOUTH SERV, 1977-; family counsr, San Diego Youth Serv, 1975-1977; chemist, IRT Corp, 1973-1991; Shell Develop Co, 1955-1962 & Gen Atomic, 1962-1973; chemist, Tracerlab Inc, 1948-1955; chemist, Consumers Yeast Co, 1946-1948; chemist, Albers Milling Co, 1945-1946. **Memberships:** Am Chem Soc; Planetary Soc. **Research Statement & Publications:** Anxiety, its psychophysiology and existential aspects; biochemistry, immunochemical applications; nucleonics, nuclear fuel cycle. **Mailing Address:** 5616 Abalone Pl, La Jolla, CA 92037-7501.

LUKENS, LEWIS NELSON, BIOCHEMISTRY. **Personal Data:** b Philadelphia, Pa, January 21, 1927; m 1964, c 4. **Education:** Harvard Univ, BA, 1949; Univ Pa, PhD (biochem), 1958. **Professional Experience:** PROF EMER MOLECULAR BIOL & BIOCHEM, WESLEYAN UNIV, as of 2003; chmn biol dept, Wesleyan Univ, 1978-1981; prof molecular biol & biochem, Wesleyan Univ, beginning 1973; assoc prof, Wesleyan Univ, 1966-1973; asst prof biochem, Yale Univ, 1964-1966; Nat Res Coun res fel chem, USPHS res fel, 1959-1960; Nat Res Coun res fel chem, Columbia Univ, 1958-1959; instr biochem, Mass Inst Technol, 1956-1958. **Memberships:** Am Soc Biol Chem. **Research Statement & Publications:** Protein synthesis and its control in eukaryotes, especially collagen. **Mailing Address:** Dept Molecular Biol & Biochem, Wesleyan Univ, Hall-Atwater Lab, Middletown, CT 06459. **Fax:** 860-685-2141. **E-Mail:** llukens@wesleyan.edu

LUKENS, PAUL W, JR, MAMMALOGY. **Personal Data:** b Hibbing, Minn, April 24, 1928; m 1960, c 2. **Education:** Univ Minn, BS, 1952, PhD (zool), 1963; Tex A&M Univ, MS, 1956. **Professional Experience:** RETIRED; prof zool, Univ Wis-Superior, 1970-1991; Bd regents res grant, Univ Wis, 1965-1966; From instr to assoc prof, Univ Wis-Superior, 1961-1970. **Memberships:** Am Soc Mammal. **Research Statement & Publications:** Identification, interpretation and paleoecology of vertebrate faunas from archaeological sites; paleozoology; environmental conservation. **Mailing Address:** 810 11th Ave, Superior, MN 55616.

LUKENS, RAYMOND JAMES, PLANT PATHOLOGY. **Personal Data:** b Beverly, NJ, February 25, 1930; m 1954, c 5. **Education:** Rutgers Univ, BS, 1954, MS, 1955; Univ Md, PhD (bot), 1958. **Professional Experience:** RETIRED; Lectr plant path, Univ Calif, Berkeley, 1977-1978; sr plant pathologist, Ortho Div, Chevron Chem Co, 1975-1986; plant pathologist, Conn Agr Exp Sta, 1970-1975; assoc plant pathologist, Conn Agr Exp Sta, 1960-1969; Asst plant pathologist, Conn Agr Exp Sta, 1957-1960. **Memberships:** Soc Indust Microbiol; Am Phytopath Soc; Bot Soc Am; Sigma Xi. **Research Statement & Publications:** Chemistry of fungicides; correlation between structure and activity of fungicides; fungicide screening and plant disease control. **Mailing Address:** 2009 Westview Ct, Modesto, CA 95350.

LUKERT, MICHAEL T, GEOLOGY, GEOCHEMISTRY. **Personal Data:** b Kansas City, Mo, June 28, 1937; m 1961, c 3. **Education:** Univ Ill, BS, 1960; Northern Ill Univ, MS, 1962; Case Western Reserve Univ, PhD (geol), 1973. **Professional Experience:** RETIRED; adj prof, Thiel Col, 1975-1976 & Mercyhurst Col, 1979 & 1981; geologist C, Va Div Mineral Resources, 1976-1977; consult, Pa Geol Surv, 1975; prof geol, Edinboro Univ Pa, 1974-1996; from asst prof to assoc prof, Edinboro Univ PA, 1967-1974; instr geol, Northern Ill Univ, 1962-1964. **Memberships:** Geol Soc Am. **Research Statement & Publications:** Geochronology; igneous and metamorphic petrology; Precambrian geology; geostatistics. **Mailing Address:** 12081 Angling Rd, Edinboro, PA 16412.

LUKERT, PHIL DEAN, MICROBIOLOGY. **Personal Data:** b Topeka, Kans, November 1, 1931; m 1956, c 4. **Education:** Kans State Univ, BS, 1953, DVM, 1960, MS, 1961; Iowa State Univ, PhD (microbiol), 1967. **Professional Experience:** PROF MED MICROBIOL, UNIV GA, as of 1997; MEM FAC, COL VET MED, UNIV GA, 1967-; res vet, Nat Animal Dis Lab, Agr Res Serv, USDA, Iowa, 1961-1967; res assoc microbiol, Kans State Univ, 1960-1961. **Memberships:** Am Vet Med Asn; AmSoc Microbiol; Am Asn Avian Path. **Research Statement & Publications:** Animal virology, particularly pathogenesis of viral infections, identification of new pathogenic viruses and the development of new diagnostic methods for viral diseases. **Mailing Address:** Dept Med Microbiol, Col Vet Med Univ Ga, Athens, GA 30602. **E-Mail:** plukert@vet.uga.edu

LUKES, ROBERT MICHAEL, ORGANIC CHEMISTRY. **Personal Data:** b San Francisco, Calif, March 27, 1923; m 1949, Mary; c 6. **Education:** Univ San Francisco, BS, 1943; Univ Calif, MS, 1947; Univ Notre Dame, PhD (org chem), 1949. **Professional Experience:** RETIRED; mgr, Finish Systs Lab, Major Appliance Labs, 1964-1985; supvr, Insulation Lab, Locomotive & Car Equip Dept, 1958-1964; res assoc, Res Labs, Gen Elec Co, 1954-1958; res chemist, Merck & Co, Inc, 1949-1953. **Memberships:** Am Chem Soc; fel Am Inst Chemists. **Research Statement & Publications:** Hydrogenation; steroid synthesis; plastics; resins; electrical insulation; surface coatings; paint; surface chemistry; electroless plating. **Mailing Address:** 223 Bramton Rd, Louisville, KY 40207-3419.

LUKES, THOMAS MARK, FOOD SCIENCE. **Personal Data:** b San Jose, Calif, March 28, 1920; m 1952, c 4. **Education:** San Jose State Col, BS, 1947; Univ Calif, Berkeley, MS, 1949. **Professional Experience:** RETIRED; prof food processing, Calif Polytech State Univ, San Luis Obispo, 1973-1985; head dept food indust, Calif Polytech State Univ, San Luis Obispo, beginning 1973; assoc prof, Calif Polytech State Univ, San Luis Obispo, 1962-1973; head lab qual control, Gentry Div, Consol Food Corp, 1951-1962; microbiologist, Real Gold Citrus, Mutual Orange Distributor, 1949-1951. **Memberships:** AAAS; Inst Food Technol; Am Chem Soc. **Research Statement & Publications:** Application of evolutionary operations to the food processing industry; development of chemical methods of flavor evaluation and application of new developments in food dehydration to the industrial scale. **Mailing Address:** 176, Del Norte, San Luis Obispo, CA 93401-1508.

LUKEZIC, FELIX LEE, PLANT PATHOLOGY. **Personal Data:** b Florence, Colo, May 27, 1933; m 1955, c 2. **Education:** Colo State Univ, BS, 1956, MS, 1958; Univ Calif, PhD (plant path), 1963. **Professional Experience:** PROF EMER PLANT PATH, PA STATE UNIV, 1975-; from asst prof to assoc prof, PA State Univ, 1965-1975; plant pathologist, Div Trop Res, United Fruit Co, Honduras, 1963-1965; lab technician, Univ Calif, 1958-1963; Asst plant path, Colo State Univ, 1956-1958. **Memberships:** Am Phytopath Soc; Am Soc Microbiol. **Research Statement & Publications:** Physiology of plant parasitism, especially bacterial caused diseases. **Mailing Address:** Dept Plant Path 121 Buckhout Lab, Pa State Univ, University Park, PA 16802-4506. **E-Mail:** fll1@psu.edu

LUKIN, MARVIN, ORGANIC CHEMISTRY, BIOCHEMISTRY. **Personal Data:** b Cleveland, Ohio, February 12, 1928; m 1962, Judith; c Jonathan & Joshua. **Education:** Ohio Univ, BS, 1949; Case Western Res Univ, MS, 1954, PhD (org chem), 1956. **Professional Experience:** EMER PROF CHEM, YOUNGSTOWN STATE UNIV, 1996-; from asst prof to prof, Youngstown State Univ, 1975-1996; fel antibiotics, Case Western Res Univ, 1966-1967; staff asst, Cleveland Clin, 1963-1965; res assoc immunochem, St Lukes Hosp, 1961-1963; fel protein chem, Albert Einstein Col Med, 1957-1961; Fel org synthesis, Mellon Inst, 1956-1957. **Memberships:** Am Chem Soc; Sigma Xi; emer mem Am assoc for the advan of sci. **Research Statement & Publications:** Organic synthesis; peptide synthesis. **Mailing Address:** 3411 Heritage Court, Canfield, OH 44406. **E-Mail:** jlukin01@sceinet.com

LUKOW, ODEAN MICHELIN, CEREAL CHEMISTRY, CEREAL QUALITY. **Personal Data:** b Winnipeg, Man. **Education:** Univ Man, BSc, 1974, MSC, 1977, PhD (cereal chem), 1982. **Professional Experience:** CHMN MEM, PROTIEN DIV, CEREAL RES CTR, AGR & AGRI-FOOD CAN, as of 2006; RES SCIENTIST CEREAL CHEM, AGR CAN, 1982-; lectr microbiol, Univ Man, 1977-1978. **Memberships:** Am Asn Cereal Chemists; Inst Food Technologists; Sigma Xi. **Research Statement & Publications:** Annual cereal quality evaluation of Western Canadian breeders' lines of wheat; the biochemical basis of cereal quality as related to the protein component. **Mailing Address:** Cereal Res Ctr, Agr & Agri-Food Can, 195 Dafoe Rd, Winnipeg, MB R3T 2M9, Can. **Fax:** 204-983-4604. **E-Mail:** olukow@agr.gc.ca

LUKOWIAK, KENNETH DANIEL, NEUROPHYSIOLOGY, NEUROETHOLOGY. **Personal Data:** b Newark, NJ, January 10, 1947; m 1990, Kim; c Kai & Bryn. **Education:** Iona Col, BSc, 1969; State Univ NY, Albany, PhD (neurophysiol), 1973. **Professional Experience:** PROF MED PHYSIOL, UNIV CALGARY, 1985-; vis prof med, Tribuhyan Univ, Kathmandu, Nepal, 1981-; from asst prof to assoc prof, Univ Calgary, 1978-1985; asst prof physiol, McGill Univ, 1975-1978; CIHR funding since 1974 to 2008; NIH fel, 1973-1975; Fel neurophysiol, Univ Ky, 1973-1975. **Memberships:** Am Physiol Soc; Can Physiol Soc; AAAS; Soc Neuroscience. **Research Statement & Publications:** Causal mechanisms of learning, memory, and forgetting; Effects of environmental toxins on behaviour; natural predation, stress, and memory; central pattern generations and behavior. **Mailing Address:** Hotchkiss Brain Inst Univ Calgary, Calgary, AB T2N 4N1, Can. **Fax:** 403-283-2700. **E-Mail:** lukowiak@ucalgary.ca

LUKS, EUGENE M, COMPUTER SCIENCES, GENERAL. **Education:** City Col NY, BS, 1960; Mass Inst Technol, PhD, 1966. **Professional Experience:** PROF, DEPT COMPUT & INFO SCI, ORE UNIV, as of 2004. **Mailing Address:** Dept Comput & Info Sci, Univ Ore, 120 Deschutes Hall, Eugene, OR 97403-1202. **Fax:** 541-346-5373. **E-Mail:** luks@cs.uoregon.edu

LULLA, JACK D, FLEXIBLE DIELECTRICS. **Education:** City Col NY, BS, 1950. **Professional Experience:** SR VPRES, TECHNICAL TAPE, 1986-. **Memberships:** Am Chem Soc. **Research Statement & Publications:** Polymer coatings and adhesives. **Mailing Address:** 40 E 88th St, New York, NY 10128.

LULLA, KAMLESH P, AERONAUTICS. **Honors & Awards:** Manned Flight Awareness Award, NASA, 1993. **Professional Experience:** CHIEF SCIENTIST EARTH OBSERVATION, NASA JOHNSON SPACE CTR, as of 2006. **Mailing Address:** Human Exploration Sci Off, Space & Life Sci Directorate, NASA Johnson Space Ctr, KX3, Houston, TX 77058. **Fax:** 281-483-2911. **E-Mail:** kamlesh.p.lulla1@jsc.nasa.gov

LUM, BERT K B, PHARMACOLOGY. **Personal Data:** b Honolulu, Hawaii, May 9, 1929; m 1952, Annie; c 4. **Education:** Univ Mich, BS, 1951, PhD (pharmacol), 1956; Univ Kans, MD, 1960. **Professional Experience:** PROF EMER MED, SCH MED, UNIV HAWAII, MANOA, as of 2004; prof pharmacol & chmn dept, sch med, Univ Hawaii, Manoa, beginning 1969; asst chmn dept, sch med, Marquette Univ, 1964-1969; from asst prof to prof, sch med, Marquette Univ, 1962-1969; from instr to asst prof pharmacol, Med Ctr, Univ Kans, 1956-1962. **Memberships:** Am Soc Pharmacol & Exp Therapeut; Cardiac Muscle Soc; Asn Med Sch Pharmacol. **Research Statement & Publications:** Cardiovascular and autonomic pharmacology. **Mailing Address:** Dept Pharmacol, Univ Hawaii Sch Med, 3675 Kilauea Ave, Honolulu, HI 96816. **Fax:** 808-956-3165. **E-Mail:** bertl@hawaii.edu

LUM, HENRY JR, AERONAUTICS. **Education:** Purdue Univ & Stanford Univ, PhD (elec eng). **Professional Experience:** CHIEF, INFO SCI DIV, AMES RES CTR, as of 2006. **Mailing Address:** NASA Ames Research Ctr, MS/269-1, Moffett Field, CA 94035. **Fax:** 415-604-6544. **E-Mail:** hlum@mail.arc.nasa.gov

LUM, KIN K, PHOTOGRAPHIC CHEMISTRY. **Personal Data:** b Ipoh, Malaya, September 4, 1940; American citizen; m 1965, c 2. **Education:** Hong Kong Baptist Col, BSc, 1962;

Baylor Univ, PhD (org chem), 1966. **Professional Experience:** RETIRED; res fel, Eastman Kodak Co Res Labs, 1994-2002; sr res assoc, Eastman Kodak CO Res Labs, 1968-1994; Res fel, Utah State Univ, 1966-1968. **Memberships:** Am Chem Soc; Soc Photog Sci & Eng. **Research Statement & Publications:** Application of novel imaging chemistry into color image transfer systems. **Mailing Address:** 633, Chatelaine Dr, Webster, NY 14580.

LUM, LAWRENCE, EXPERIMENTAL BIOLOGY. **Professional Experience:** PROF INTERNAL MED, WAYNE STATE UNIV, 1989-. **Mailing Address:** Hemat & Oncol Div, Wayne State Univ PO Box 02188, Detroit, MI 48202-0188. **Fax:** 313-745-9113. **E-Mail:** llum@mail.jhmi.edu

LUM, LEWIS, MATHEMATICS. **Education:** Ore State Univ, BS, 1968; Univ Ore, PhD, 1973. **Professional Experience:** CHAIR, DEPT MATH, UNIV PORTLAND, as of 2006. **Mailing Address:** Math Dept, Univ Portland, 5000 N Willamette Blvd, Portland, OR 97203-5798. **Fax:** 503-725-3661.

LUM, PATRICK TUNG MOON, ENTOMOLOGY. **Personal Data:** b Honolulu, Hawaii, November 6, 1928; div, c 2. **Education:** Earlham Col, BA, 1950; Univ Ill, MS, 1952, PhD (entom), 1956. **Professional Experience:** RETIRED; res entomologist, Stored Prod Insect Res & Develop, USDA, beginning 1965; res biologist, Entom Res Ctr, Fla State Bd Health, 1957-1965; asst entom, USPHS res fel, 1957; res assoc, Univ Ill, 1956; asst entom, Univ Ill, 1954-1956. **Memberships:** Int Mgt Coun; Entom Soc Am. **Research Statement & Publications:** Pathogenecity of micro-organisms to insects; photoperiodism and circadian rhythms in insects; physiology, behavior and morphology of reproduction in moths. **Mailing Address:** 1252 Silver Prospect Dr, Las Vegas, NV 89108.

LUMB, ALAN M, WATER RESEARCH ENGINEERING, WATER SHED MODELING. **Personal Data:** b Kansas, Mo, February 1942. **Education:** Univ Kans, BS, 1964, MS, 1966; Stanford Univ, PhD (civil eng), 1970. **Professional Experience:** HYDROLOGIST, NAT WATER INFO SYSTS, US GEOL SURV, as of 1999; CHIEF, NAT WATER INFO SYSTS, 1995-. **Memberships:** Am Soc Civil Engrs; Am Geophys Union; Am Water Resource Asn. **Mailing Address:** Nat Water Info Systs, US Geol Surv, MS 437 Nat Ctr, Reston, VA 20192. **Fax:** 703-648-5295.

LUMB, JUDITH RAE M, IMMUNOLOGY. **Personal Data:** b Bridgeport, Conn, March 19, 1943; m 1964, c Timothy Alan & Jeffrey Thomas. **Education:** Univ Kans, BA, 1965, MA, 1966; Stanford Univ, PhD (med microbiol), 1969. **Professional Experience:** RETIRED; actg chmn, Atlanta Univ, 1983-1985; NIH career develop award, 1975-1980; From asst prof to prof biol, Atlanta Univ, 1969-1987. **Memberships:** AAAS; Reticuloendothelial Soc; Am Soc Microbiol; Am Soc Cell Biol; Cellular Kinetics Soc. **Research Statement & Publications:** Biochemistry of alkaline phosphatase of C57BL lymphomas; derepression of embryo functions in C57BL lymphomas; computer simulation of the development of the thymus; early lymphocyte differentiation. **Mailing Address:** Caye Caulker, Belize.

LUMB, RALPH F, PHYSICAL CHEMISTRY, NUCLEAR SCIENCES. **Personal Data:** b Worcester, Mass, May 27, 1921; m 1941, c 8. **Education:** Clark Univ, AB, 1947, PhD (phys chem), 1951. **Professional Experience:** PRES, ALLIANCE PRESERVE SOMERS CTR INC, as of 2004; PROP, RALPH LUMB ASSOCS, 1986-; sr consult, Wackenhut Advan Technol, 1984-1986; pres, Nusac Inc, 1971-1984; pres, Advan Technol Consult Corp, 1968-1971; consult, Univ Buffalo Nuclear Reactor Proj, 1956-1960 & Safeguards Br, Int Atomic Energy Agency, 1963-; dir, Western NY Nuclear Res Ctr, Inc, 1960-1968; vpres, Quantum Inc, 1959-1960; proj leader, Quantum Inc, 1956-1959; Secy, adv comt uranium standards, AEC, 1953-1956; chief, Chem-Physics Br, Div Nuclear Mat Mgt, US AEC, 1951-1956; instr chem, Assumption Col, 1947-1948 & Northeastern Univ, 1949-1951. **Memberships:** Fel AAAS; fel Am Inst Chemists; Am Nuclear Soc; fel Inst Nuclear Mat Mgt. **Research Statement & Publications:** Applications of nuclear energy; nuclear research; reactor design, operation and utilization. **Mailing Address:** Alliance Preserv Somers Ctr Inc, 8 Salem Dr, Somers, CT 06071. **Fax:** 860-749-5879.

LUMB, ROGER H, BIOCHEMISTRY. **Personal Data:** b Union, NJ, June 29, 1940; m 1962, c 3. **Education:** Alfred Univ, BA, 1962; Univ SC, MS, 1965, PhD (biol), 1967. **Professional Experience:** RETIRED; res, Utrecht, Neth, 1975-1976; prof biol, Western Carolina Univ, beginning 1974; Damon Runyon fel, 1971-1973; from asst prof to assoc prof, Western Carolina Univ, 1967-1974; instr biol, Univ SC, 1965-1967. **Memberships:** Sigma Xi. **Research Statement & Publications:** Lipid metabolism in lung; lipid metabolism in cancer cells; membrane biochemistry; lipid mediator mechanisms in fish. **Mailing Address:** Dept Biol, Western Carolina Univ, 132 Nat Sci Bldg, Cullowhee, NC 28723. **Fax:** 828-227-7647. **E-Mail:** lumb@wcu.edu

LUMB, WILLIAM VALJEAN, VETERINARY SURGERY & ANESTHESIOLOGY. **Personal Data:** b Sioux City, Iowa, November 26, 1921; m 1949, Lilly Carlson; c John W. **Education:** Kans State Univ, DVM, 1943; Tex A&M Univ, MS, 1953; Univ Minn, PhD (vet med), 1957; Am Col Vet Anethesiologists, dipl; Am Col Vet Surgeons, dipl. **Honorary Degrees:** DSc, Ohio State Univ, 1999. **Honors & Awards:** Gaines Award, 1965; Ralston-Purina Res Award, 1980; Jakob Markowitz Award, Am Acad Surg Res, 1987. **Professional Experience:** EMER PROF, COL VET MED, COLO STATE UNIV, 1981-; prof surg, Colo State Univ, 1963-1981; dir surg lab, Colo State Univ, 1963-1979; assoc prof med, Colo State Univ, 1960-1963; assoc prof clin & surg, Colo State Univ, 1954-1958 & surg & med, Mich State Univ, 1958-1960; from instr to assoc prof med & surg, Tex A&M Univ, 1949-1952; from intern to resident, Angell Mem Animal Hosp, Boston, 1946-1948; Pres, Lubra Co. **Memberships:** Nat Acad Sci; NY Acad Sci; Am Asn Vet Clinicians; pres, 1979-; Am Col Vet Surg; AAAS; Am Vet Med Asn; Am Col Vet Anesthesiologists. **Research Statement & Publications:** Experimental surgery and anesthesiology; published 2 books and small animal auesthesia, vetermory anesthesia (with w.ejones 1 over 150 articles. **Mailing Address:** 1905 Mohawk, Ft Collins, CO 80525.

LUMBERS, SYDNEY BLAKE, geology, petrology, mineral deposits; deceased, see previous edition for last biography

LUMENG, LAWRENCE, MEDICINE & BIOCHEMISTRY, GASTROENTEROLOGY & HEPATOLOGY. **Personal Data:** b Manila, Philippines, August 10, 1939; American citizen; m 1966, c 2. **Education:** Ind Univ, Bloomington, BS, 1960; Ind Univ, Indianapolis, MD, 1964, MS, 1969; Am Bd Internal Med, dipl, 1970. **Professional Experience:** Dir, gastroenterol & hepatol, Ind Univ Med Ctr, 1984-; PROF MED BIOCHEM, SCH MED, IND UNIV, INDIANAPOLIS, 1979-; chief gastroenterol, Vet Admin Hosp, Indianapolis, 1977-; clin investr, Vet Admin Hosp, Indianapolis, 1973-1976; From asst prof to assoc prof, Sch Med, Ind Univ, Indianapolis, 1971-1979; Res & educ associateship, Vet Admin Hosp, Indianapolis, 1971-1973. **Memberships:** Am Soc Clin Investr; Am Col Phys; Am Soc Biol Chemists; Am Gastroenterol Asn; Am Asn Study Liver Dis; Res Soc Alcoholism. **Research Statement & Publications:** Regulation of metabolic pathways; ethanol metabolism; pyridoxine and thiamine metabolism; clinical liver diseases; Genetic aspects and risk fectors in alcholism and alcoholic liver disease. **Mailing Address:** Med Res & Libr Bldg, Ind Univ Med Ctr 975 W Walnut st Rm 327, Indianapolis, IN 46202-5121. **Fax:** 317-274-3106. **E-Mail:** llumeng@iupui.edu

LUMLEY, JOHN L(EASK), FLUID MECHANICS, TURBULENCE. **Personal Data:** b Detroit, Mich, November 4, 1930; m 1953, Jane; c Katherine L, Jennifer F & John C. **Education:** Harvard Univ, AB, 1952; Johns Hopkins Univ, MSE, 1954, PhD (aeronaut), 1957. **Honorary Degrees:** Haute Distinction Hon Causa, Ecole Centrale Lyon, 1987. **Honors & Awards:** Medallion, Univ Liege, 1971; Fluid & Plasmadynamics Prize & Dryden Lectr, Am Inst Aeronaut & Astronaut, 1982; Fluid Dynamics Prize, Am Phys Soc, 1990; Timoshenko Medal, Am Soc Mech Engrs, 1993. **Professional Experience:** PROF EMER ENG, SIBLEY SCH MECH & AEROSPACE ENG, CORNELL UNIV, as of 2005; chmn, Stanford/NASA Ames Ctr Turbulence Res, 1995 & 1997; chmn, peer rev comt, NASA Lewis Ctr Modeling Turbulence & Transition, 1993; chmn, Stanford/NASA Ames Ctr Turbulence Res, 1990 & 1991; mem adv comt, Stanford/NASA Ames Ctr Turbulence Res, 1989; coordr, Grad Exchange Prog Cornell Univ/Ecole Centrale de Lyon, 1984-; Willis H Carrier prof eng, Sibley Sch Mech & Aerospace Eng, Cornell Univ, beginning 1977; vis prof, Univ Louvain-la-Neuve, Belg & Fulbright sr lectr, Univ Liege, 1973-1974; Guggenheim fel, Mech Fluids Lab, Sch Cent Lyon & Inst Mech Statist Turbulence, Univ d'Aix-Marseille II, France, 1973-1974; exchange prof, Univ Aix-Marseille, 1966-1967; Evan Pugh prof, Penn State Univ, 1974-1977; from assoc prof to prof aerospace eng, Penn State Univ, 1961-1974; from asst prof to assoc prof eng res, Penn State Univ, 1959-1961; fel, Johns Hopkins Univ, 1958-1959; res assoc mech eng, Johns Hopkins Univ, 1957-1959; courtesy fel, Johns Hopkins Univ, 1957-1958; instr, McCoy Col, 1956-1959; asst aeronaut, Johns Hopkins Univ, 1954-1957; asst & jr instr mech eng, Johns Hopkins Univ, 1953-1954. **Memberships:** Nat Acad Eng; Soc Natural Philos; NY Acad Sci; fel Am Acad Mech; Am Inst Aeronaut & Astronaut; fel Am Acad Arts & Sci; fel Am Phys Soc. **Research Statement & Publications:** Turbulence; stochastic processes; electronic instrumentation. **Mailing Address:** Cornell Univ, 256 Upson Hall, Ithaca, NY 14853. **Fax:** 607-255-1222. **E-Mail:** jll4@cornell.edu

LUMMA, WILLIAM CARL, ORGANIC CHEMISTRY, MEDICINAL CHEMISTRY. **Personal Data:** b Detroit, Mich, April 21, 1941; m 1975, Patricia; c Keith & Carl. **Education:** Wayne State Univ, BS, 1963; Mass Inst Technol, PhD (org chem), 1966. **Professional Experience:** SR SCIENTIST, MERCK, SHARP & DOHME RES LABS, W POINT, PA, 1990-; DIR MED CHEM, BERLEX LAB, CEDAR KNOLLS, NJ, 1982-; sr res fel med chem, Rahway, NJ, 1981-1982; res fel, Rahway, NJ, 1972-1981; sr res chemist process develop, Rahway, NJ, 1970-1972; asst prof chem, St Louis Univ, 1966-1970. **Memberships:** Am Chem Soc; NY Acad Sci; AAAS. **Research Statement & Publications:** Heterocyclic and organic synthetic chemistry. **Mailing Address:** Merck Res Labs, 770 Sumneytown Pike, West Point, PA 19486. **E-Mail:** wlummahome@netsape.net

LUMPKIN, MICHAEL DIRKSEN, NEUROENDOCRINOLOGY, NEUROIMMUNOLOGY. **Personal Data:** b Dallas, Tex, February 2, 1953. **Education:** Univ Tex, Austin, BA, 1975; Univ Tex Sothwestern Med Ctr, PhD (physiol), 1981. **Professional Experience:** PROF & CHMN, PHYSIOL, MED SCH, GEORGETOWN UNIV, 1993-; lectureship award, Univ Modena, Italy, 1990; VA, NIH, 1989-; consult, NSF, 1988-; consult, Adamha, 1988-; VA, 1988-; March Dimes, 1988-; prin investr, NIH grants, 1986-1994; from asst prof to assoc prof, Med Sch, Georgetown Univ, 1984-1993; res assoc, neuroendocrinol, Univ Tex Health Sci Ctr, Dallas, 1981-1983; lectr, Univ Tex Health Sci Ctr, Dallas, 1978-1982; teaching asst physiol, NIH fel, 1976-1981; teaching asst physiol, Univ Tex Health Sci Ctr, Dallas, 1975-1976. **Memberships:** Endocrine Soc; Soc Neuroscience; Soc Neuroimmunomodulation. **Research Statement & Publications:** Neuropeptide control of anterior pituitary stress hormones; hypothalamic and pituitary hormone regulation of male and female gonadal function; cytokine regulation of neuroendocrine function and growth. **Mailing Address:** Dept Physiol Sch Med, Georgetown Univ, 3900 Reservoir Rd NW, Washington, DC 20007. **Fax:** 202-687-7407. **E-Mail:** mlumpk01@georgetown.edu

LUMRY, RUFUSWORTH II, BIOCHEMISTRY. **Personal Data:** b Bismarck, NDak, November 3, div, c 3. **Education:** Harvard Univ, AB, 1942, MS, 1948, PhD (chem physics), 1948. **Professional Experience:** PROF EMER CHEM, UNIV MINN, MINNEAPOLIS, as of 2004; Univ Calif, San Diego, 1977-1978 & Univ Granada, Spain, 1985; dir, Lab Biophys Chem, 1963-1986; vis prof, Inst Biol Chem Rome, 1963; vis prof, Inst Protein Res, Osaka, Japan, 1961; NSF sr fel & vis prof, Lab Carlsberg, Copenhagen, 1959-1960; prof phys chem, Univ Minn, Minneapolis, beginning 1957; assoc prof, Univ Minn, Minneapolis, 1953-1957; asst res prof biochem, Univ Utah, 1951-1953; asst prof phys chem, Univ Utah, 1950-1953; Merck fel, Univ Utah, 1948-1950; res assoc, Div Eight, Nat Defense Res Comt, 1942-1945. **Memberships:** Am Chem Soc; Soc Biol Chem; Sigma Xi; Biophys Soc. **Research Statement & Publications:** Biophysical chemistry; enzymes, proteins; fast reactions; water and water solutions. **Mailing Address:** Dept Chem, Univ Minn, Smith Hall 1, Minneapolis, MN 55455-0431. **Fax:** 612-626-7541. **E-Mail:** lumry@umn.edu

LUMSDAINE, EDWARD, EDUCATION, ENTREPRENEURSHIP. **Personal Data:** b Hong Kong, September 30, 1937; American citizen; m 1959, Monika; c Andrew, Anne J, Alfred & Arnold. **Education:** NMex State Univ, BSME, 1963, MSME, 1964, ScD(eng), 1966. **Honorary Degrees:** DSc, New Mex State Univ. **Honors & Awards:** chester l carlson award for innovation in engr edu, ASEE, 1994. **Professional Experience:** DEAN & PROF MECH ENG, MICH TECHNOL UNIV, 2002-; SPEC PROF OF BUS, UNIV NOTTINGHAM, 1999-; dean & prof mech eng, Univ Mich, Dearborn, 1982-1988 & Univ Toledo, 1988-1993; consult & bd mem, Am Supplies Inst, beginning 1986; bd mem, Am Solar Energy Soc, 1985-1989; consult, Ford Motor Co, beginning 1984; Tatung Inst Technol, Taipei, Repub of China, 1978 & Qatar Univ, Doha, 1983; dir & prof mech & aerospace eng, Univ Tenn, Knoxville, 1981-1983; lectr, US Info Serv, 1981; UNESCO expert consult, Cairo Univ, 1979-1980; dir, NMex Solar Energy Inst, 1978-1981; prof mech eng, Phys Sci Lab, NMex State Univ, 1977-1981; sr res engr, Phys Sci Lab, NMex State Univ, 1977-1978; vis prof, Cairo Univ, Egypt, 1974; from assoc prof to prof fluid flow & aeroacoust, Univ Tenn, Knoxville, 1972-1977; from asst prof to assoc prof mech eng, SDak State Univ, 1967-1972; res engr, Boeing Co, 1966-1967; prin investr, NSF, Am Soc Heating, Refrig & Air Conditioning Engrs, NASA, Dept Energy, HEW & others. **Memberships:** Fel Am Soc Mech Engrs; Am Soc Eng Educ; assoc fel Am Inst Aeronaut & Astronaut. **Research Statement & Publications:** Heat transfer; fluid mechanics; turbomachinery; aeroacoustics; solar energy applications in photovoltaics, desalineation and irrigation; energy conservation; teaching with microcomputers; product quality; noise-harshness vibrations; author on software in engineering mathematics and of books on creativity problem solving; engr design and entrepreneurship. **Mailing Address:** Col Eng, Mich Technol Univ, 1400 Townsend Dr, Hancock, MI 49931-1295. **Fax:** 906-487-2822. **E-Mail:** lumsdain@mtu.edu

LUMSDEN, CHARLES JOHN, THEORETICAL PHYSICS. **Personal Data:** b Hamilton, Ont, April 9, 1949. **Education:** Univ Toronto, BSc, 1972, MSc, 1974, PhD (theoret physics), PhD, 1978. **Honors & Awards:** Sir John Cunningham McLennan Award Physics, 1972; E C Stevens Award Physics, 1977. **Professional Experience:** PROF, DEPT MED, UNIV TORONTO, as of 2003; Scientist, Med Res Coun Can, 1988; assoc prof, Dept Med, Univ Toronto, 1983-1990; Scholar, Med Res Coun Can, 1983-1988; fel, Dept Biol, Harvard Univ, 1979-1982; Spec lectr biophys, Univ Toronto, 1975-1978. **Memberships:** Am Phys Soc; Soc Math Biol; Biophys Soc. **Research Statement & Publications:** Published numerous articles on sociobiology, physiology, statistical mechanics and mathematical biology. **Mailing Address:** Inst Med Sci, Toronto Univ, Rm 7317 One King's Col Cir, Toronto, ON M5S 1A8, Can. **Fax:** 416-978-3701. **E-Mail:** charles.lumsden@utoronto.ca

LUMSDEN, DAVID NORMAN, GEOLOGY. **Personal Data:** b Buffalo, NY, August 29, 1935; m 1963, c 2. **Education:** State Univ NY, Buffalo, BA, 1958, MA, 1960; Univ Ill, PhD (geol), 1965. **Professional Experience:** PROF GEOL, MEMPHIS STATE UNIV, 1977-; from asst prof to assoc prof, Memphis State Univ, 1967-1977; sr geologist, Pan Am Petrol Corp, 1965-1967; Res engr, Carborundum Co, 1960-1962. **Memberships:** Geol Soc Am; Am Asn Petrol Geol; Soc Econ Paleont & Mineral; Sigma Xi. **Research Statement & Publications:** Study of carbonate and quartzose sedimentary rocks. **Mailing Address:** Dept Geol, Memphis State Univ, Memphis, TN 38152. **Fax:** 901-678-2178. **E-Mail:** dlumsden@cc.memphis.edu

LUMSDEN, JESSIE B, SURFACE PHYSICS. **Personal Data:** b Louisa, Va, October 29, 1942. **Education:** Univ Richmond, BS, 1965; Ohio State Univ, PhD (physics), 1970. **Professional Experience:** SR SCIENTIST, ROCKWELL INT SCI CTR, 1978-; staff mem dept metall eng, Ohio State Univ, 1970-1978. **Memberships:** Am Phys Soc; Electrochem Soc. **Mailing Address:** Rockwell Int Sci Ctr, PO Box 1085, Thousand Oaks, CA 91360.

LUMSDEN, ROBERT DOUGLAS, PLANT PATHOLOGY. **Personal Data:** b Washington, DC, June 21, 1938; m 1960, Valerie; c 2. **Education:** NC State Univ, BS, 1961, MS, 1963; Cornell Univ, PhD (plant path), 1967. **Professional Experience:** RETIRED; supvry res plant pathologist, biocontrol plant dis lab, plant sci inst, Beltsville, Agr Res Serv, USDA, Beltsville, Md, ending 2001; fel, USDA Agr Res Serv, 1987; res plant pathologist, Agr Res Ctr W, 1966-1992. **Memberships:** Fel Am Phytopath Soc. **Research Statement & Publications:** Physiology of plant diseases, including the physiology of pathogenesis and disease resistance; pathology and biological control of plant pathogens, especially soilborne plant pathogens; soil ecology; mechanism of action of biological control agents. **Mailing Address:** 13437 Yorktown Dr, Bowie, MD 20715. **E-Mail:** rlumsden@asrr.arsusda.gov

LUNA, ELIZABETH J, CELL BIOLOGY, MEMBRANE BIOCHEMISTRY. **Personal Data:** b Poplar Bluff, Mo, October 18, 1951; m 1974, Alonzo. **Education:** Southern Ill Univ-Carbondale, BA, 1972; Stanford Univ, PhD (chem), 1977. **Honors & Awards:** Robert A Bensley Award, Am Asn Anat, 1993. **Professional Experience:** PROF, DEPT CELL BIOL, UNIV MASS, 1997-; prin scientist, Worcester Found Exp Biol, 1993-1997; sr scientist, Worcester Found Exp Biol, 1988-1993; asst prof biol, Princeton Univ, 1981-1988; res assoc, dept cell biol & develop biol, Harvard Univ, 1977-1981. **Memberships:** AAAS; Am Chem Soc; Am Soc Cell Biol; Biophys Soc; Protein Soc; Am Asn Cancer Res. **Research Statement & Publications:** Cytoskeleton membrane interaction and regulation. **Mailing Address:** Dept Cell Biol, Univ Mass, 55 Lake Ave N Biotech 4 Ste 306, Worcester, MA 01655. **Fax:** 508-856-8774. **E-Mail:** Elizabeth.Luna@umassmed.edu

LUNARDINI, VIRGIL J(OSEPH), JR, MECHANICAL & ARCTIC ENGINEERING, HEAT TRANSFER. **Personal Data:** b Holyoke, Mass, May 10, 1935; m 1960, c 3. **Education:** Univ Notre Dame, BS, 1957; Ohio State Univ, MS, 1960, PhD (mech eng), 1963. **Honors & Awards:** Eugene Jacob Award, Petroleum Div, Am Soc Mech Engrs, 1981; Ralph James Award, 1985; Am Soc Mech Engrs Award, 1987. **Professional Experience:** Chisolm-Ryder, Pace Consults, 1983-1985; Chisolm-Ryder, Gulf Interstate, 1983; adj prof Thayer Sch, Dartmouth, 1979-; RES ENGR, US COLD REGIONS LAB, 1979-; Chisolm-Ryder, NY, 1968- & Govt Can, 1978-1979; from assoc prof to prof mech eng, Univ Ottawa, 1969-1979; State Univ NY Buffalo fac fel, 1967; assoc prof, State Univ NY, Buffalo, 1966-1969; Pratt & Whitney Aircraft Div, United Aircraft Corp, 1966-1967; Consult, NASA Lewis Labs, Ohio, 1964; asst prof, Clarkson Col Technol, 1963-1966; Instr eng, Ohio State Univ, 1958-1963. **Memberships:** Am Soc Mech Engrs; Sigma Xi. **Research Statement & Publications:** Permafrost heat transfer; cold regions engineering; energy conservation; global climate change. **Mailing Address:** US Cold Regions Lab, 72 Lyme Rd, Hanover, NH 03755-1290.

LUNCHICK, CURT, FARM WORKER PROTECTION, HUMAN EXPOSURE TO PESTICIDES. **Personal Data:** b New York, NY, June 28, 1953; m 1985, c 2. **Education:** Univ Md, Col Park, BS, 1974; NC State Univ, MS, 1977. **Professional Experience:** HEAD, NONDIETARY EXPOSURE & RISK ASSESSMENT, BAYER CORP SCI, 1998-; supvry chemist, Occup & Residential Exposure, US Environ Protection Agency, 1991-1992; chemist, Occup & Residential Exposure, Off Pesticide Progs, US Environ Protection Agency, 1984-1991; sect supvr, Toxicol Lab, Litton Bionetics, Inc, 1978-1980 & Dynamac Corp, 1981-1984. **Research Statement & Publications:** Exposure of humans to pesticides applied in residential settings; use of immunoassay and protective clothing to protect agricultural workers from pesticides; regulatory guidelines concerning human exposure to pesticides and hazard reduction options. **Mailing Address:** Bayer Crop Sci, 2 T W Alexander Dr, Research Triangle Park, NC 27709.

LUND, ANDERS EDWARD, wood science & technology; deceased, see previous edition for last biography

LUND, CHARLES EDWARD, STRUCTURAL & THERMAL ANALYSIS, FINITE ELEMENT METHODS. **Personal Data:** b Fremont, Mich, April 4, 1946; m 1994, Shirley; c Deanna. **Education:** Univ Mich, BSE, 1968, MSE, 1970. **Professional Experience:** STRUCT METHODS SPECIALIST, PARKER ABEX NWL AEROSPACE, 2002-; OWNER, LUND & LUND, 1995-; lectr, Dept Mech Eng, Western Mich Univ, 1984, 1985; struct methods specialist, Parker Abex Nwl Aerospace, 1977-2000; struct engr, Lockheed Missiles & Space Co, 1970-1977; assoc engr, McDonnell-Douglas Astro Co, 1968-1969. **Memberships:** Am Inst Aeronaut & Astronaut; Am Soc Mech Engr. **Research Statement & Publications:** Carbon fiber-epoxy composite hydraulic actuaters; granted two patents. **Mailing Address:** Parker Abex NWL Aerospace, 217 E Orleans St, Otsego, MI 49078. **E-Mail:** chuck@lundandlund.net

LUND, DARYL B, FOOD ENGINEERING, FOOD PROCESSING. **Personal Data:** b San Bernardino, Calif, November 4, 1941; m 1963, Dawn; c Kristine & Eric. **Education:** Univ Wis-Madison, BS, 1963, MS, 1965, PhD (food sci, chem eng), 1968. **Honors & Awards:** Howard Lectr, Dept Food Sci, Univ Ill, 1985; Food Eng Award, Dairy & Food Industs Supply Asn/Am Soc Agr Eng, 1987; Int Award, Inst Food Technol, 1995; Carl Fellers Award, Inst Food Technol, 2003; Irving Award Serv, Am Distance Educ Consortium, 2001; WR Woodroof Lectr, Univ Ga, March 2003. **Professional Experience:** EXEC DIR, N CENT ASN AGR EXP STA DIRS, UNIV WIS, as of 2005; PROF FOOD ENG, UNIV WIS, MADISON, as of 2005; dean, Col Agr Life Sci, Cornell Univ, 1995-2000; exec dean agr & nat resources, Rutgers Univ, 1989-1995; chmn, Dept Food Sci, Rutgers Univ, 1988-1989; assoc dir, NJ Agr Exp Sta, 1988-1989; chmn, Food Sci Dept, 1984-1987; invited vis prof, Agr Univ, Wageningen, Holland, 1979; prof food sci & agr eng, Univ Wis-Madison, 1977-1987; vis expert, Bogor Agr Univ, Indonesia, 1973, 1990, 1992; from instr to assoc prof food sci, Univ Wis-Madison, 1967-1977. **Memberships:** fel, Inst Food Technol; Am Soc Agr Bio Eng; Am Inst Chem Engrs; Sigma Xi; Am Inst Nutrit; Amer Assoc Advan Sci; Phi Tau Sigma; Gamma Sigma Delta; Inst Food Sci Technol (UK); charter mem, Int Acad Food Sci Technol. **Research Statement & Publications:** Food engineering; fouling of heat exchangers; nutrient retention in processing; starch gelatinization; water movement in foods; microwave heat transfer. **Mailing Address:** Dept Food Sci, Univ Wis, 212D Agr Hall 1450 Linden Dr, Madison, WI 53706. **Fax:** 608-265-6434. **E-Mail:** dlund@cals.wisc.edu

LUND, DOUGLAS E, GENETICS, EMBRYOLOGY. **Personal Data:** b Newcastle, Nebr, December 12, 1933; m 1958, c 2. **Education:** Nebr Wesleyan Univ, BA, 1958; Univ Nebr, MS, 1960, PhD (zoology), 1962. **Professional Experience:** PROF EMER BIOL, KEARNEY STATE COL, UNIV NEBR, 1999-; asst prof zool, Univ Nebr, 1962-1968. **Memberships:** AAAS; Sigma Xi. **Research Statement & Publications:** Temperature effects on early developmental stages of mammalian embryos; carbon dioxide sensitivity in Drosophila. **Mailing Address:** Dept Biol, Kearney State Col, Univ Nebr, 905 W 25th St, Kearney, NE 68849.

LUND, FREDERICK H(ENRY), AEROSPACE & ELECTRONICS ENGINEERING. **Personal Data:** b Seattle, Wash, June 2, 1929; m 1950, Joyce P Monpleasure; c Frederick B, Christopher M, Peter A & A Leslie. **Education:** Univ Wash, BSEE, 1951; Mass Inst Technol, SM, 1957. **Professional Experience:** RETIRED; mem, Missile Systs Tech Comt, Am Inst Aeronaut & Astronaut, 1987-1991; mem prof staff, Martin Marietta Corp, Orlando, 1969-1993; consult, 1994-1995; sr res engr, Stanford Res Inst, 1965-1969; Mem exec comt, Mil Opers Res Symp, Off Naval Res, 1962-1966; sect chmn, Inst Elec & Electronics Engrs, 1962-1963; Combat engr, unit commander, US Army Corps Engrs, 1951-1953. **Memberships:** Inst Elec & Electronics Engrs; Sigma Xi; Asn Old Crows; Am Inst Aeronaut & Astronaut; Mil Opers Res Soc. **Research Statement & Publications:** Conduct of system analyses; operations research studies; analysis of electronic and optical countermeasures systems; development, test and evaluation of missile weapon systems; development of electronic instrumentation for guided missile systems; military requirements analyses; ballistic missile defense studies; strategic defense initiative architecture studies; pershing II/intermediate range nuclear force (INF) studies. **Mailing Address:** 610 S Lake Sybelia Dr, Maitland, FL 32751.

LUND, HARTVIG ROALD, AGRONOMY. **Personal Data:** b Fargo, NDak, May 15, 1933; m Janet; c Jeffrey, Susan, Anders & Adrian. **Education:** NDak State Univ, BS, 1955, MS, 1958; Purdue Univ, PhD (agron, plant breeding), 1965. **Professional Experience:** RETIRED; prof emer, Dean, Col Agr & Dir, Agr Exp Sta, 1979-1992; prof agron, NDak State Univ, 1974-; assoc dean, Col Agr & assoc dir, 1974-1979; asst dean, Col Agr & asst dir, Agr Exp Sta, NDak State Univ, 1971-1974; assoc prof, Col Agr & Dir, Agr Exp Sta, 1965-1974; res asst, Purdue Univ, 1962-1965; asst prof, NDak State Univ, 1959-1962; res asst agron, NDak State Univ, 1955-1958. **Research Statement & Publications:** Rust genetics of durum wheat; chemical mutagenesis in corn; corn breeding and corn endosperm genetics. **Mailing Address:** 23299 Pelican Bass Lane, Pelican Rapids, MN 56572. **E-Mail:** hrlund@loretel.net

LUND, J KENNETH, CHEMICAL ENGINEERING. **Personal Data:** b Brooklyn, NY, February 11, 1933; m 1960, c 2. **Education:** Polytech Inst Brooklyn, BChE, 1955; Princeton Univ, MSE, 1958, PhD (chem eng), 1963. **Professional Experience:** SR VPRES, EXEC TECH RES, VARO CORP, 1978-; asst to pres, Occidental Res Corp, 1974-1978; dir res & develop, Polyester Div, Olin Corp, 1971-1973; prod develop mgr, NJ, 1969-1971; res group leader, Hydrocarbons & Polymers Div, Tex, 1965-1969; sr res engr, Plastics Div, Monsanto Co, Mass, 1961-1965. **Memberships:** Am Chem Soc; Soc Plastics Engrs; Am Inst Chem Engrs. **Research Statement & Publications:** Polymer melt rheology; shear degradation of polymer melts; polymer fatigue failure; high speed tensile studies; extrusion processing of polyolefins and foamed polystyrene polyolefins. **Mailing Address:** Lund & Assoc Inc, 1300 Hollencrest Dr, West Covina, CA 91791-3711.

LUND, JOHN EDWARD, VETERINARY PATHOLOGY. **Personal Data:** b Detroit, Mich, March 16, 1939; m 1959, Carol E; c Mark A & Anne E. **Education:** Mich State Univ, BS, 1962, MS & DVM, 1964; Wash State Univ, PhD (vet sci), 1969; Am Cl Vet Pathologists, dipl. **Honors & Awards:** am course of verryary pathology. **Professional Experience:** Sr res advisr in pathology, pharmacia, 2000-; DISTINGUISHED RES SCIENTIST, UPJOHN CO, 1992-; dir, Tsukusa Lab, 1990-1992; assoc dir, Upjohn Co, 1985-1990; res head, Upjohn Co, 1980-1985; sr res scientist, Upjohn Co, 1977-1980; mgr & res assoc, Exp Path Sect, Biol Dept, 1974-1977; sr scientist, Battelle Northwest Labs, Wash, 1973-1974; from asst prof to assoc prof, Sch Vet Sci & Med, Purdue Univ, 1970-1973; Consult & vet pathologist, Inst Chem Biol, Univ San Francisco, 1969-1972; Instr path, Med Sch, Stanford Univ, 1968-1970. **Memberships:** Am Vet Med Asn; Am Soc Vet Clin Path; Soc Toxicol Pathologists; amer col of vet pathol. **Research Statement & Publications:** Hematologic diseases of animals; toxicologic pathology; chemical carcinogenesis. **Mailing Address:** Pharmacia, 301 Henrietta st, Kalamazoo, MI 49007.

LUND, JOHN R, MATHEMATICS. **Education:** Univ Tenn, BS, 1971; Univ Utah, MS, 1973, PhD (math), 1978. **Professional Experience:** PROF, DEPT MATH SCI, MONT STATE UNIV, as of 2006. **Mailing Address:** Math Dept, Mont State Univ, Bozeman, MT 59715. **Fax:** 406-994-6879. **E-Mail:** umsfjlun@math.montana.edu

LUND, JOHN TURNER, PHYSICAL CHEMISTRY, INTELLIGENT SYSTEMS. **Personal Data:** b Brooklyn, NY, November 3, 1929; m 1955, c 2. **Education:** Brown Univ, AB, 1951; Univ Wash, PhD (phys chem), 1954; Univ Del, MS, 1985. **Professional Experience:** EXEC DIR EDUC AID, E I DU PONT DEL NEMOURS & CO, INC, 1986-; res chemist, E I Du Pont Del Nemours & CO, Inc, 1955-1986; Fel, Univ Wash, 1954-1955. **Memberships:** Am Chem Soc; Am Phys Soc. **Research Statement & Publications:** Industrial research on textile fibers; intelligent computer systems for problem solving. **Mailing Address:** 901 Centre Rd, Westover Hills, Wilmington, DE 19807-2801.

LUND, LANNY JACK, SOIL MORPHOLOGY & CLASSIFICATION. **Personal Data:** b Dalton, Nebr, May 1, 1943; m 1964, c 2. **Education:** Univ Nebr, BS, 1965, MS, 1968; Purdue Univ, PhD, 1971. **Professional Experience:** PROF EMERITUS, DEPT SOIL & ENVIRON SCI, UNIV CALIF, as of 2006; asst vpres prog UC div agr & natural resources, Univ Calif, Riverside, 1999-; Assoc dean, Agr Exp Sta, 1990-1996; chmn, Dept Soil & Environ Sci, Univ Calif, Riverside, 1985-1990 & 1997-1999; PROF SOIL SCI & SOIL SCIENTIST, UNIV CALIF, RIVERSIDE, 1983-; assoc prof & assoc soil scientist, Univ Calif, Riverside, 1977-1983; Asst prof & asst soil scientist, Univ Calif, Riverside, 1971-1977. **Memberships:** Am Soc Agron; Soil Sci Soc Am. **Research Statement & Publica-**

tions: Soil morphology, genesis and classification; soil and the environment. **Mailing Address:** Dept Soil & Environ Sci Univ Calif, 300 Lakeside Dr 6 Floor, Oakland, CA 94612-3550. **E-Mail:** lanny.lund@ucop.edu

LUND, MARK WYLIE, LENS DESIGN, X-RAY OPTICS. **Personal Data:** b Santa Rosa, Calif, September 9, 1952; m 1977, Barbara Novakovich; c Ellen, Audrey, Andrea & Samuel. **Education:** Brigham Young Univ, BS, 1977; San Diego State Univ, MS, 1979; Ariz State Univ, PhD (physics), 1989. **Professional Experience:** DIR, MOXTEK INC, 1990-; prin engr, Optical Disk Div, Honeywell, 1986-1989; sr electronic engr, Govt Electronics Div, Motorola, 1983-1986; proj engr, Night Vision Div, Litton Industs, 1981-1983; mem tech staff, Hughes Aircraft Co, 1979-1981. **Memberships:** Optical Soc Am; Int Soc Optical Eng; Microbeam Anal Soc; Micros Soc Am; Mat Res Soc. **Research Statement & Publications:** Developing products for the analytical x-ray market: energy dispersive detectors, ultra-low noise fets, x-ray multilayer optics, crystal growth of wide bandgap semiconductors; display systems; night vision; lens design; unconventional optical system design from far infrared through x-rays; x-ray spectrometry; coherent bremsstrahlung. **Mailing Address:** Moxtek, Inc, 969 E 200 N, Orem, UT 84057. **Fax:** 801-221-1121. **E-Mail:** mlund@moxtek.com

LUND, MELVIN ROBERT, DENTISTRY. **Personal Data:** b Siren, Wis, October 17, 1922; m 1946, c 3. **Education:** Univ Ore, DMD, 1946; Univ Mich, MS, 1954. **Professional Experience:** PROF EMER DENT, IND UNIV, 1991-; prof oper dent & chmn dept, Ind Univ, Purdue Univ, Indianapolis, 1971-1991; fel, Claremont Grad Sch, 1969-1970; from instr to prof restorative dent, Loma Linda Univ, 1953-1971. **Memberships:** Int Asn Dent Res; Acad Oper Dent; Am Acad Gold Foil Opers (pres, 1979-1980). **Research Statement & Publications:** Physical research in dental materials; biologic research in dental procedures. **Mailing Address:** Sch Dent, Ind Univ, 1121 W Mich St, Indianapolis, IN 46202. **Fax:** 317-274-241.

LUND, PAULINE KAY, GROWTH FACTORS, GASTROENTEROLOGY. **Personal Data:** b Golborne, Lancashire, April 20, 1955; m 1980, Mark; c Emma & Alice. **Education:** Univ Newcastle, UK, BSc Hons, 1975, PhD (gastrointestinal endocrinol), 1979. **Professional Experience:** PROF PHYSIOL, UNIV NC SCH MED, as of 2006; PROF NUTRIT, UNIV NC, CHAPEL HILL, 1998-; distinguished prof univ teaching, Dept Physiol, Univ NC, 1995-1998; assoc prof pediat, Dept Pediat, Univ Nc, 1995-; PROF CELL & MOLECULAR PHYSIOL & PEDIAT, UNIV NC, CHAPEL HILL, 1993-; mem endocrinol study sect, NIH, 1989-1993; assoc dir, Ctr Gastrointestinal Biol & Dis, 1989-1992; assoc prof physiol & pediat, Univ NC, 1988-1993; asst prof physiol, Univ NC, 1982-1988; res fel, Lab Molecular Endocrinol, Harvard Med Sch, Mass Gen Hosp, 1979-1988; demonstr physiol, Univ Newcastle, UK, 1977-1979. **Memberships:** Endocrine soc. **Research Statement & Publications:** Insulin-like growth factors biosynthesis and action; role of growth factorsand peptide hormones in intestinal growth and development; molecular correlation of neuronal function; inflammatory bowel disease and fibrosis. **Mailing Address:** Dept Physiol, Univ Nc Sch Med, CB 7545 Med Sci Res Bldg, Chapel Hill, NC 27599-7545. **Fax:** 919-966-6927. **E-Mail:** empk@med.unc.edu

LUND, RICHARD, VERTEBRATE PALEONTOLOGY. **Personal Data:** b New York, NY, September 17, 1939; m 1978, c 3. **Education:** Univ Mich, Ann Arbor, BS, 1961, MS, 1963; Columbia Univ, PhD (zoology), 1968. **Professional Experience:** PROF EMER BIOL, ADELPHI UNIV, 2002-; DIR EMER, PROG ENVIRON STUDIES, 2002-; dir, prog environ studies, 1996-2002; res assoc Ichthyology, Am Mus Natural Hist, 1982-; prof biol, Adelphi Univ, 1981-2002; prin investr, NSF, Mississippian fishes from Montana, 1974-1985; from asst prof to assoc prof, Adelphi Univ, 1974-1981; res assoc, WVa Geol Surv, 1974; Pittsburgh Found fel, Univ Pittsburgh, 1971-1974; res assoc, Carnegie Mus, 1969-; asst prof earth & plant sci, Univ Pittsburgh, 1969-1974; Pittsburgh Found fel, Carnegie Mus, 1967-1969; asst cur fossil fish, Sect Vert Fossils, Carnegie Mus, 1966-1969. **Memberships:** AAAS; Soc Vert Paleont; Am Soc Icthyol & Herpet; Am Soc Zoologists; Ecol Soc Am; Am Elasmobranch Soc (secy, 1984). **Research Statement & Publications:** Fossil fish; late Paleozoic biostratigraphy; morphology and relationship of early osteichthyan and chondrichthyan fishes with emphasis on the fishes of the Mississippian Bear Gulch Limestone. **Mailing Address:** Dept Biol, Adelphia Univ, Sci Bldg 103 One S Ave, Garden City, NY 11530. **Fax:** 516-877-4209. **E-Mail:** lund@adelphi.edu

LUND, STEVE, AGRONOMY ADMINISTRATOR. **Personal Data:** b Wis, December 3, 1923; m Grace Mary B; c Steve, John, Thomas, Cynthia & Lisa. **Education:** Clemson Col, BS, 1949; Univ Wis, MS, 1951, PhD (agron), 1953. **Professional Experience:** EMER PROF, ORE STATE UNIV, 1985-; EMER PROF, RUTGERS UNIV, 1975-; supt & prof, Columbia Basin Agr Res Ctr, 1975-1985; Chmn dept soils & crops, Rutgers Univ, New Brunswick, 1971-1975; res prof, Rutgers Univ, New Brunswick, 1962-1975; from asst res specialist to assoc res specialist farm crops, Rutgers Univ, New Brunswick, 1954-1962; Exten agronomist, Clemson Col, 1953-1954. **Memberships:** Am Soc Agron; Crop Sci Soc Am; Sigma XI emer mem. **Research Statement & Publications:** Cereal breeding. **Mailing Address:** 1201 SW 23rd St, Pendleton, OR 97801-4404. **E-Mail:** sqtlund@uci.net

LUNDBERG, BRUCE N, MATHEMATICS. **Education:** Grand Canyon Univ, BA; Ariz State Univ, MA; Fuller Theol Seminary, MA; Colo State Univ, PhD. **Professional Experience:** ASSOC PROF, DEPT MATH, COLO STATE UNIV, 1993-. **Mailing Address:** Math Dept, Colo State Univ, 2200 Bonforte Blvd, Pueblo, CO 81001-4901. **Fax:** 719-549-2732. **E-Mail:** lundberg@meteor.uscolo.edu

LUNDBERG, GEORGE DAVID, PATHOLOGY. **Personal Data:** b Pensacola, Fla, March 21, 1933; m 1983, Patricia; c George, Charles, Carol, Christopher & Melinda. **Education:** Univ Ala, BS, 1952; Med Col Ala, MD, 1957; Am Bd Path, dipl anat & clin path, 1962; Baylor Univ, MS, 1964. **Honorary Degrees:** ScD, State Univ NY, Syracuse, 1988, Eleanor Jefferson Univ, Phila, 1993, Univ Ala, 1994, Med Col Ohio, 1995. **Honors & Awards:** Am Soc Clin Path, 1996, Col Am Path, 1996; mem bd dirs, Am Soc Clin Path. **Professional Experience:** Adj prof health policy, Inst Health Serv Res, Harvard Sch Pub Health, Harvard Univ, 1992-; vpres sci info & ed-in-chief jour, AMA, 1982-; CLIN PROF PATH, NORTHWESTERN & HARVARD UNIV, 1982-; clin prof path, Georgetown & Northwestern, 1982-1992; prof & chmn path, Sch Med, Univ Calif, Davis & dir path & labs, Med Ctr, Sacramento, 1977-1982; vis prof forensic med, Lund Univ, Sweden, 1976 & Univ London, 1976-1977; from asst dir to assoc dir labs, Los Angeles Co/Univ Southern Calif Med Ctr, 1968-1977; from assoc prof to prof path, Sch Med, Univ Southern Calif, 1967-1977; chief path, William Beaumont Gen Hosp, El Paso, Tex, 1964-1967; US Army Med Res & Develop Command res grants, 1963-1964 & 1965-1967; res officer, Letterman Gen Hosp, San Francisco, Calif, 1963-1964; chief anat path, Letterman Gen Hosp, San Francisco, Calif, 1962-1963; resident path, Brooke Gen Hosp, San Antonio, Tex, 1958-1962; intern, Tripler Gen Hosp, Honolulu, Hawaii, 1957-1958. **Memberships:** Inst Med-Nat Acad Sci; Am Soc Clin Path (pres); Am Asn Path & Bact; Int Acad Path; Am Acad Forensic Sci; Col Am Path. **Research Statement & Publications:** Laboratory computer applications; diseases produced by drugs; toxicology; drug abuse; laboratory management; boxing and brain damage; methods of education; strategic planning; biomedical communication; violence. **Mailing Address:** Inst Health Serv Res, Harvard Sch Pub Health, Harvard Univ, Rm 710 339 E Chicago Ave, Chicago, IL 60611. **E-Mail:** george_lundberg@mail.medscape.com

LUNDBERG, JOHN L(AUREN), POLYMER SCIENCE, TEXTILE ENGINEERING. **Personal Data:** b St Paul, Minn, October 8, 1924; m 1955, c 4. **Education:** Univ Minn, BChE, 1948; Univ Calif, PhD (chem), 1952. **Professional Experience:** PROF EMER TEXTILE & FIBRE ENG, GA INST TECHNOL, as of 2004; callaway prof textile chem, Ga Inst Technol, beginning 1972; chmn dept, Clemson Univ, 1970-1971; assoc prof textile chem, Clemson Univ, 1968-1971; adj prof, Polytech Inst Brooklyn, 1964-1968; lectr, Polytech Inst Brooklyn, 1963; Vis assoc prof, Polytech Inst Brooklyn, 1961-1962; Mem tech staff, Bell Tel Labs, Inc, 1952-1968. **Memberships:** AAAS; Am Asn Textile Chem & Colorists; Am Asn Textile Technol; Am Chem Soc; Am Inst Chem; Sigma Xi. **Research Statement & Publications:** Physical chemistry and physics of polymers, fibers and textiles; solution chemistry, diffusion and physical properties of polymer solutions; light scattering by fibers, liquids and solutions. **Mailing Address:** Sch Polymer, Textile & Fibre Eng, Ga Inst technol, MRDC 1, 801 Ferst Drive, NW, Atlanta, GA 30332-0295. **Fax:** 404-894-2490.

LUNDBERG, ROBERT DEAN, POLYMER CHEMISTRY. **Personal Data:** b Valley City, NDak, May 30, 1928; m 1953, Patricia E Goeschel; c Michael & Barbara. **Education:** Harvard Univ, BA, 1952, MA & PhD (phys chem), 1957. **Honors & Awards:** Chem Pioneer, Am Inst Chem, 1986. **Professional Experience:** RETIRED; Consult, Exxon Res & Eng Co, 1990-; chief scientist, Exxon Res & Eng Res Lab, 1984-1990; sci adv, Exxon Res & Eng Res Lab, 1976-1984; sr res assoc, Exxon Chem Co, 1971-1976; res assoc, Exxon Chem Co, 1970-1971; vpres res, Inter-Polymer Res Corp, 1969-1970; group leader, Res & Develop Dept, Union Carbide Chem & Plastic Co, 1962-1969; chemist, Union Carbide Corp, 1957-1962; Chemist, Eastman Kodak Co, 1952-1953. **Memberships:** Am Chem Soc; NY Acad Sci; Am Inst Chemists. **Research Statement & Publications:** Synthesis of synthetic polypeptides; polymer interactions; ionic polymers; block copolymers; thermoplastic elastomers; polymer blends; dilute polymer solution behavior. **Mailing Address:** 3017 Travis Close, Williamsburg, VA 23185-7666. **Fax:** 908-730-2536.

LUNDBLAD, ROGER LAUREN, BIOCHEMISTRY, BIOTECHNOLOGY. **Personal Data:** b San Francisco, Calif, October 31, 1939; div. **Education:** Pac Lutheran Univ, BS, 1961; Univ Wash, PhD (biochem), 1965. **Professional Experience:** CONSULT BIOTECHNOLOGY & BIOTECHNOLOGY EDUC, 2000-; Ed Chief, Internet Journal Genomics Proteomics, as of 2005; dir sci & tech develop, Baxter Hyland Immuno, CA, 1998-2000; ed in chief, Biotechnology & Appl Biochem, 1996-2002; dir sci & tech develop, Baxter Healthcare-Hyland div, CA, 1993-1998; dir Sci & Tech Develop, Baxter Healthcare-Immunotherapy Div, Duarte, CA, 1992-1993; Dir Tech Develop, Baxter Healthcare-Hyland Biotechnology, Hayward, CA, 1991-1992; Consult, Baxter Healthcare-Hyland Div, Glendale, CA, 1988-1991; dir, Protein Fractionation/Struct Anal Core Facil, Depart Path, Univ NC, Chapel Hill, NC, 1985-1988; ADDJ PROF PATH, UNIV NC, CHAPEL HILL, 1991-; Assoc dir admin, dent res ctr, Univ NC, Chapel Hill, 1978-1984; Assoc Dir Prog Develop, Ctr Thrombosis Hemostasis, Univ NC, Chapel Hill, NC, 1978-1991; from asst prof to assoc prof, Path, biochem & periodontics, Univ NC, Chapel Hill, NC, 1968-1977; res assoc, Rockefeller Univ, NY, 1966-1968; Res assoc, Dept biochem, Univ Wash, 1965-1966; res assist, dept biochem, Univ Wash, 1961-1965; Mem, Coun Basic Sci & Coun Thrombosis, Am Heart Asn. **Memberships:** AAAS; Am Chem Soc; Am Soc Biol Chem; Am Soc Microbiol; Sigma Xi. **Research Statement & Publications:** Mechanism of blood coagulation; protein chemistry; salivary proteins; oral microbiology; Thrombosis and Hemostasis. **Mailing Address:** Dept Path Univ NC, Chapel Hill, NC 27516-6695. **E-Mail:** lundbladr@bellsouth.net

LUNDBLAD, VICTORIA JOAN, GENETICS. **Education:** Univ Calif, BA, 1976; Harvard Univ, PhD, 1983. **Professional Experience:** GRADUATE FAC & PROF MOLECULAR & HUMAN GENETICS, BAYLOR COL MED, as of 2005. **Mailing Address:** Inst Molecular Genetics Baylor Col Med, One Baylor Plaza, Houston, TX 77030-3498. **Fax:** 713-798-5931. **E-Mail:** lundblad@bcm.tmc.edu

LUNDE, BARBARA KEGERREIS, ELECTRICAL & RADIO ENGINEERING, HEALTH PHYSICS. **Personal Data:** b Oak Park, Ill, August 10, 1937; wid, c Karen R, Thomas R, Yvonne (Friday), Julie A (Allen), Eugene (Carpino), John (Carpino) & Martin (Carpino). **Education:** Northwestern Univ, Ill, BA, 1957; Iowa State Univ, PhD (condensed matter physics), 1970. **Professional Experience:** Mem, Des Moines Elec Exam Bd, 1993-; PRES, SILVER LINING, 1987-; assoc prof archit, Iowa State Univ, 1987-1988; asst prof physics, Iowa State Univ, 1986-1987; mem, Iowa Bldg Code Coun, 1984-; ENGR, US WEST, 1980-; assoc prof civil eng, Ames Lab, 1980-1981; vpres & chief engr, Radio Sta KJJY, 1976-1980; solar & elec engr, Brooks Borg & Skiles, Engrs-Architects, 1976-1980; assoc engr, Ames Lab, 1974-1976; asst prof aerospace eng, Iowa State Univ, 1971-1976; assoc biophys, Iowa State Univ, 1971-1972; mem, Nat Adv Comn Foods, Food & Drug Admin, 1971-1972; asst prof food & nutrit, Iowa State Univ, 1970-1971; vpres & chief engr, Radio Sta KEZT, 1967-1975; aerospace engr, Goddard Space Flight Ctr, NASA, 1961-1965; res engr, Charles Stark Draper Lab, Mass Inst Technol, 1959-1961. **Memberships:** Asn Energy Engrs; Am Soc Heating Refrig & Air Conditioning Engrs; Am Inst Aeronaut & Astronaut; Nat Soc Prof Engrs; sr mem Inst Elec & Electronic Engrs; Sigma Xi. **Research Statement & Publications:** Nuclear magnetic resonance of metals; solar energy for heating and cooling; electrical design of buildings; energy management in buildings; planning communication networks; protection of people from electromagnetic fields; health physics. **Mailing Address:** 2209 Park Ave, Des Moines, IA 50321-1503.

LUNDE, MILFORD NORMAN, PARASITOLOGY. **Personal Data:** b Dodgeville, Wis, April 17, 1924; m 1950, c 2. **Education:** Luther Col, AB, 1947; Univ NC, MPH, 1948. **Professional Experience:** RETIRED; res parasitologist, Lab Parasitic Dis, Nat Inst Allergy & Infectious Dis, NIH, 1955-1989; bacteriologist, Army Med Ctr, Ft Detrick, Md, 1953-1955; parasitologist, Inst Trop Med, Bowman-Gray Sch Med, 1951-1952 & Am Found Trop Med, 1952-1953; Bacteriologist, WVa State Hyg Lab, 1948-1951. **Memberships:** Am Soc Parasitologists; Am Soc Trop Med & Hyg. **Research Statement & Publications:** Immunodiagnosis of parasitic diseases; application of enzyme immunoassay for detection of antigens and characterization of antibodies; toxoplasmosis; amebiasis and schistosomiasis. **Mailing Address:** North 985, Sarona, WI 54870-9747.

LUNDE, PETER J, chemical & solar engineering; deceased, see previous edition for last biography

LUNDEEN, ALLAN JAY, ORGANIC CHEMISTRY. **Personal Data:** b New York, NY, August 24, 1932; m 1954, c 4. **Education:** Southwestern Col, Kans, AB, 1954; Rice Univ, PhD (chem), 1957. **Professional Experience:** RETIRED; dir plastics res, Continental Oil Co, 1978-1993; dir explor res, Continental Oil Co, 1970-1978; res group leader, Continental Oil Co, 1962-1970; sr res chemist, Continental Oil Co, 1960-1962; res chemist org chem, Continental Oil Co, 1957-1960. **Memberships:** Am Chem Soc. **Research Statement & Publications:** Chemistry of mustard oil glucosides; reactions of carbonium ions; heterogenous catalysis; chemistry of organoaluminum compounds; hydrocarbon oxidation; polymer chemistry. **Mailing Address:** 8501 Navidad Dr, Austin, TX 78735.

LUNDEEN, CARL VICTOR, BIOCHEMISTRY. **Personal Data:** b Baltimore, Md, January 20, 1943; m 1965, c 3. **Education:** Univ NC, Chapel Hill, AB, 1965; Rockefeller Univ, PhD (life sci), 1972. **Professional Experience:** ASSOC PROF BIOL, UNIV NC, WILMINGTON, 1977-; asst prof biol, Univ NC, Wilmington, 1974-1977; asst prof chem, Univ NC, Wilmington, 1972-1974; res assoc plant biol, Rockefeller Univ, 1971-1972. **Memberships:** Sigma Xi. **Research Statement & Publications:** Attempting to elucidate the mechanisms by which autonomous cells attain the capability for rapid growth. **Mailing Address:** Dept Biol, Univ NC, 601 S Col Rd, Wilmington, NC 28401. **E-Mail:** lundeenc@uncw.edu

LUNDEEN, STEPHEN ROLF, PHYSICS. **Education:** Trinity Col, BS, 1969; Harvard Univ, 1975. **Professional Experience:** PROF PHYSICS, COLO STATE UNIV, as of 2005. **Memberships:** Am Phys Soc. **Mailing Address:** Dept Physics, Colo State Univ, Ft Collins, CO 80523. **Fax:** 970-491-7947. **E-Mail:** lundeen@lamar.colostate.edu

LUNDEGARD, ROBERT JAMES, SCIENCE POLICY, TECHNICAL MANAGEMENT. **Personal Data:** b Youngstown, Ohio, February 22, 1927; m 1951, c 1. **Education:** Ohio Univ, BS, 1950; Purdue Univ, MS, 1952, PhD (math), 1956. **Honors & Awards:** Fleming award, US Govt, 1967. **Professional Experience:** RETIRED; chief, Statist Eng Div, Nat Inst Stand & Technol, beginning 1987; dir, naval cost analysis, Dept Navy, 1981-1987; dep dir, Math Sci Div, Dept Naval Res, 1978-1981; dir, Math Sci Div, Dept Naval Res, 1968-1978. **Memberships:** Fel Am Statist Asn. **Research Statement & Publications:** Develop statistical methods for engineering, with emphasis on achieving quality goals through the design of processes and products. **Mailing Address:** Nat Inst Stand & Technol, Rm 353, Gaithersburg, MD 20899. **Fax:** 301-990-4127. **E-Mail:** robert.lundegard@nist.gov

LUNDELIUS, ERNEST LUTHER, VERTEBRATE PALEONTOLOGY. **Personal Data:** b Austin, Tex, December 2, 1927; m 1953, Judith; c Jennifer (Welch) & Rolf E. **Education:** Univ Tex, BS, 1950; Univ Chicago, PhD (paleozool), 1954. **Honors & Awards:** Honorary mem, soc of Vertebrate paleontology, 2001. **Professional Experience:** PROF EMER VERT PALEONT, UNIV TEX, as of 2005; John A Wilson prof vert paleont, univ tex, austin, 1978-1998; Fulbright scholar vert paleont, Fulbright sr scholar, 1976; prof geol, Univ Tex, Austin, 1969-1998; from asst prof to assoc prof, Univ Tex, Austin, 1957-1969; res fel paleoecol, Calif Inst Technol, 1956-1957; Fulbright scholar vert paleont, Univ Western Australia, 1954-1955. **Memberships:** Soc Vert Paleont (secy-treas, 1975-, pres, 1981); Soc Study Evolution; Am Soc Mammalogists; Geol Soc Am; Am Soc Naturalists. **Research Statement & Publications:** Pleistocene vertebrates; paleoecology; adaptive morphology; Australian marsupials. **Mailing Address:** 7310 Running Rope, Austin, TX 78731-2132. **Fax:** 512-232-5518. **E-Mail:** erniel@mail.utexas.edu

LUNDELL, ALBERT THOMAS, MATHEMATICS. **Personal Data:** b Riverside, Calif, December 23, 1931; m 1952, Virginia Owen; c John, Martha & David. **Education:** Univ Utah, AB, 1952, AM, 1955; Brown Univ, PhD (math), 1960. **Professional Experience:** PROF EMER, MATHS UNIV COLO, BOULDER, as of 2003; prof math, Univ Colo, Boulder, beginning 1970; chmn dept, Univ Colo, Boulder, 1970-1972; assoc prof, Univ Colo, Boulder, 1966-1969; asst prof, Purdue Univ, 1962-1966; lectr, Univ Calif, Berkeley, 1960-1962; Instr math, Brown Univ, 1959-1960. **Memberships:** Am Math Soc. **Research Statement & Publications:** Algebraic topology. **Mailing Address:** Dept Math, Box 395, Univ Colo, Boulder, CO 80309. **Fax:** 303-492-7707. **E-Mail:** lundell@euclid.colorado.edu

LUNDEN, ALLYN OSCAR, PLANT BREEDING, PLANT GENETICS. **Personal Data:** b Toronto, SDak, February 5, 1931; m 1955, c 3. **Education:** SDak State Col, BS, 1952, MS, 1956; Univ Fla, PhD (plant genetics), 1960. **Professional Experience:** RETIRED; seed researcher, Seed Lab, 1981-1986; head, Seed Lab, 1976-1980; assoc prof agron, SDak State Univ, 1964-1976; assoc prof agron, Univ Tenn-AEC Agr Res Lab, 1962-1964; asst scientist plant genetics, Univ Tenn-AEC Agr Res Lab, 1959-1962; Asst agronomist, SDak State Col, 1955-1956. **Memberships:** Am Soc Agron; Asn Off Seed Anal. **Research Statement & Publications:** Irradiation sensitivity of plant tissues; genetic effects of ionizing and ultraviolet irradiation of plant tissues; seed testing techniques; seed vigor testing; seed germination; seed technology; seed storage research. **Mailing Address:** 614 Seven Ave S, Brookings, SD 57006.

LUNDERGAN, CHARLES DONALD, SYSTEMS RESEARCH, REMOTE SENSORS. **Personal Data:** b Washington, Ind, September 24, 1923; m 1972, Elaine M Prusha; c Michael, Timothy, Donal & Dan. **Education:** Univ Notre Dame, BSc, 1947, MSc, 1951. **Professional Experience:** RETIRED; consult, 1973-1975 & mgt staff, 1989-1995; mem staff systs res, 1973-1975 & mgt staff, 1978-1989; reactor safety res, 1973-1975 & mgt staff, 1975-1978; mem staff mat res, Sandia Lab, 1967-1973; div supvr, Sandia Lab, 1962-1967; Res consult George Mallinckrodt Res, 1953-1954 & Ohio State, Wright-Patterson AFB, 1962-1963; sect supvr, Sandia Lab, 1961-1962; physicist mat sci, Sandia Lab, 1956-1961; instr physics, Agr & Mech Col, Tex, 1954-1956; actg dir aeronaut eng, St Louis Univ, 1952-1954; Instr math, St Louis Univ, 1951-1954. **Research Statement & Publications:** Equations of state of solids, propagation of shock waves in solids, dynamic stress-strain relations of metals; dynamic behavior of composites; effects of nuclear explosions; remote detection of nuclear effects. **Mailing Address:** 140 Beaver Cir, Pagosa Spgs, CO 81147.

LUNDGREN, CLAES ERIK GUNNAR, PHYSIOLOGY. **Personal Data:** b Stockholm, Sweden, January 21, 1931. **Education:** Univ Lund, MD, 1959, PhD (physiol), 1967. **Professional Experience:** PROF PHYSIOL, SCH MED, STATE UNIV NY, BUFFALO, 1999-; DIR, CTR RES & EDUC SPEC ENVIRON, STATE UNIV NY, BUFFALO, 1977-; vis assoc prof physiol, Univ Lund, Sweden, 1974-1977; assoc prof physiol, Fac Med, Univ Lund, Sweden, 1967-1977; consult aviation med, Royal Swed Air Force, 1959-1977. **Mailing Address:** State Univ NY, Sch Med & Biomed Sci, CRESE, 24 Sherman Hall 3435 Main St, Buffalo, NY 14214. **Fax:** 716-829-2384. **E-Mail:** clundgre@acsu.buffalo.edu

LUNDGREN, DALE A(LLEN), AIR POLLUTION, INDUSTRIAL HYGIENE. **Personal Data:** b Duluth, Minn, April 26, 1932; m 1954, c 6. **Education:** Univ Minn, BS, 1958, MS, 1962, PhD (environ health), 1973. **Professional Experience:** PROF EMER ENVIRON ENG, UNIV FLA, as of 2003; prof environ eng, Univ Fla, beginning 1972; consult, Dale A Lundgren Assoc, 1972- & various indust; chief engr-dir, Air Pollution Control Equipment Sect, Environ Res Corp, St Paul, Minn, 1969-1972; specialist & head aerosol lab, Statewide Air Pollution Res Ctr, Univ Calif, Riverside, 1967-1969; head air & particle anal lab, Ctr Air Environ Studies & instr mech eng & air pollution, Pa State Univ, 1965-1967; prin scientist, Appl Sci Div, Litton Industs, Inc, 1963-1965; scientist, Electronics Div, Gen Mills, Inc, 1961-1963; asst mech eng, Univ Minn, 1958-1961; engr, Link-Belt Co, Minn, 1955-1958. **Memberships:** Air Pollution Control Asn; Am Indust Hyg Asn; Am Soc Mech Engrs; Am Asn Aerosol Res; Soc Aerosol Res Germany. **Research Statement & Publications:** Aerosol physics; air pollution; industrial hygiene; air sampling instrumentation; air pollution control equipment. **Mailing Address:** Dept Environ Eng Univ Fla, 408 Black Hall PO Box 116450, Gainesville, FL 32611-6450. **E-Mail:** dalund@ufl.edu

LUNDGREN, DAVID L(EE), RADIOBIOLOGY, INHALATION TOXICOLOGY. **Personal Data:** b Aberdeen, Wash, September 28, 1931; wid, c 5. **Education:** Ore State Univ, BS, 1954; Univ Utah, MS, 1961, PhD (microbiol), 1968. **Professional Experience:** RADIOBIOLOGIST, LOVELACE INHALATION TOXICOL RES INST, 1966-; microbiologist, Biol Div, Dugway Proving Ground, 1964-1966; chief infectious disease lab, Univ Utah, 1961-1964; chief epizool diag lab, Univ Utah, 1959-1962; Bacteriologist, Univ Utah, 1954-1959. **Memberships:** Radiation Res Soc; Am Soc Microbiol; Health Physics Soc; Soc Exp Biol & Med; Sigma Xi; AAAS; Am Pub Health Asn. **Research Statement & Publications:** Toxicity of inhaled radionuclides from nuclear energy generation; biological effects of internally deposited radionuclides in experimental animals; extrapolation of data from laboratory animals to man. **Mailing Address:** ITRI, PO Box 5890, Albuquerque, NM 87115.

LUNDGREN, DAVID WAYNE, MEDICAL RESEARCH. **Education:** Southern Ill Univ, PhD. **Professional Experience:** ASSOC PROF, DEPT NEUROL, CASE WESTERN RES UNIV, as of 2004. **Mailing Address:** Dept Neurol Metro Health Med Ctr Case Western Res Univ, 3395 Scranton Rd, Cleveland, OH 44109-1998.

LUNDGREN, HARRY RICHARD, STRUCTURAL ENGINEERING. **Personal Data:** b Chicago, Ill, May 2, 1928; m 1955, Joyce E Boller. **Education:** Purdue Univ, BSCE, 1950; Ariz State Univ, MSE, 1962; Okla State Univ, PhD (struct eng), 1967. **Professional Experience:** PROF EMER CIVIL & ENVIRON ENG, ARIZ STATE UNIV, 1989-; from instr to prof, Ariz State Univ, 1962-1989; sr civil engr, Salt River Proj, 1959-1961; vpres eng, R B Feffer & Sons, Ariz, 1958-1959; Proj engr, Kawneer Co, Mich, 1953-1958; Pres, Comt Acad Sci & Eng. **Memberships:** Am Soc Civil Engrs; Sigma Xi. **Research Statement & Publications:** Finite element applications to structural engineering problems; structural stability; light gauge steel structures; wind engineering; software development. **Mailing Address:** Dept Civil & Environ Eng, Ariz State Univ, PO Box 875306, Tempe, AZ 85287-5306. **Fax:** 480-965-0557.

LUNDGREN, J RICHARD, APPLICATIONS OF GRAPH THEORY. **Personal Data:** b Springfield, Mass, October 1, 1942; m 1964, c 2. **Education:** Worcester Polytech Inst, BS, 1964; Ohio State Univ, MS, 1969, PhD (math), 1971. **Professional Experience:** PROF MATH, UNIV COLO, DENVER, 1986-; Chmn, Dept Math, Univ Colo, 2001-2003; chmn dept, Univ Colo, Denver, 1984-1990; assoc prof, Univ Colo, Denver, 1981-1986; assoc prof math, Allegheny Col, 1977-1981; from asst to assoc prof math, Allegheny Col, 1971-1981; Teaching assoc, depart Math, Ohio State Univ, 1967-1971; Proj engr, New Eng Tel Co, 1964-1967; Res grant, Off Naval Res, 1996-1999; Res grant, Off Naval Res, 1993-1996; Res grant, Off Naval Res 1990-1993; Res grant, Off Naval Res, 1987-1990. **Memberships:** Am Math Soc; Math Asn Am; Soc Indust & Appl Math; fel Inst Combinatorics & Its Appln. **Research Statement & Publications:** Applications of graphs and matrices; mathematical modeling. **Mailing Address:** Dept Math Univ COLO, 1250 14th St 6 Floor, Lakewood, CO 80217-3364. **Fax:** 303-556-8550. **E-Mail:** Richard.Lundgren@cudenver.edu

LUNDGREN, LAWRENCE WILLIAM, JR, ENVIRONMENTAL GEOLOGY, RISK COMMUNICATION. **Personal Data:** b Attleboro, Mass, March 17, 1932; m 1981, Ann Frodi; c Gary, Julie & Annika. **Education:** Brown Univ, AB, 1953; Yale Univ, PhD (geol), 1958. **Professional Experience:** PROF EMER GEOL, UNIV ROCHESTER, as of 2003; Vis researcher, Dept Water & Environ Studies, Univ Linkoping, Sweden, 1991-; mem staff, US Geol Surv, Menlo Park, 1977; NSF fac fel geog & environ eng, Johns Hopkins Univ, 1976; chmn, Dept Geol Sci, 1971-1974 & 1976-1986; prof geol, Univ Rochester, beginning 1967; Fulbright lectr, Finland, 1967-1968; from instr to assoc prof geol, Univ Rochester, 1956-1967. **Memberships:** AAAS; Geol Soc Am; Sigma Xi; Am Geophys Union. **Research Statement & Publications:** Impact of Chernobyl on Sweden; geology and public policy. **Mailing Address:** Dept Geol, Univ Rochester 500 Joseph C Wilson, Rochester, NY 14627-9000. **Fax:** 585-244-5689. **E-Mail:** urlarry@att.net

LUNDGREN, T S, PHYSICS. **Education:** Univ Minn, BS, 1954, MS, 1956, PhD (fluid dynamics), 1960. **Professional Experience:** PROF EMER AEROSPACE ENG & MECH, UNIV MINN, as of 2004. **Memberships:** Am Phys Soc. **Mailing Address:** Dept Aerospace Eng & Mech, Univ Minn, 205b Akerman Hall, Minneapolis, MN 55455. **Fax:** 612-626-1558. **E-Mail:** lundgren@aem.umn.edu

LUNDHOLM, J(OSEPH) G(IDEON), APPLIED PHYSICS, ENGINEERING PHYSICS. **Personal Data:** b Emporia, Kans, February 19, 1925; m 1956, c 2. **Education:** Kans State Univ, BS, 1946, MS, 1948; NC State Univ, PhD (eng physics), 1956. **Professional Experience:** CONSULT, 1986-; study mgr, Adv Missions Anal Off, Goddard Space Flight Ctr, NASA, 1983-1986; adv technol mgr, adv land observations systs off, 1981-1983; res assoc, Mat Sci Dept, Univ Md, 1978-1979; Mem, Comt on Radioactive Waste Mgt, Nat Acad Sci, 1976-1978; res prog mgr, Off Aeronaut & Space Technol Res Div, 1974-1981; mgr exp prog, Skylab Prog, Hq, 1965-1974; dir adv res & tech, Space Systs Div, Fairchild-Hiller Corp, 1964-1965; proj mgr, Adv Space Systs, 1962-1964; mem tech staff, Res & Adv Develop Div, Avco Co, Mass, 1960-1962; supvr syst control & safety, Compact Power Plants, 1959-1960; staff res specialist, Reactor Develop Dept, Atomics Int Div, NAm Aviation, Inc, 1957-1959; supvr, Raleigh Res Reactor, 1952-1957; res assoc physics, NC State Univ, 1952-1956; instrumentation develop engr, Oak Ridge Nat Lab, 1948-1952; instr math, Kans State Univ, 1947-1948. **Memberships:** Assoc fel Am Inst Aeronaut & Astronaut; sr mem Am Astronaut Soc. **Research Statement & Publications:** Space research and technology, especially space payloads, laser systems, advance energy conversion methods, ultra low temperature coolers; nuclear systems technology and safety; ultra high pressure research; instrumentation and control systems; earth remote sensing technology. **Mailing Address:** 8106 Postoak Rd, Rockville, MD 20854.

LUNDIN, CARL D, PHYSICAL METALLURGY. **Personal Data:** b Yonkers, NY, December 16, 1934; m 1957, c 3. **Education:** Rensselaer Polytech Inst, BMetEng, 1957, PhD (mat sci), 1966. **Honors & Awards:** Adams Mem Award, Am Welding Soc, 1968 & 1973, Sparager Award, 1978; McKay-Helm Award, 1981; Adams Mem lectr, Am Welding Soc, 1981. **Professional Experience:** MAGNAVOX PROF ENG, TENN TOMORROW PROF & DIR WELDING RES, UNIV TENN, KNOXVILLE, 1977-; welding sect mgr, Babcock & Wilcox Co, 1975-1977; from assoc prof to prof metall & dir welding res, Univ Tenn, 1968-1975; consult, Oak Ridge Nat Labs, 1967-; NSF res initiation grant, 1967-1968; from instr to asst prof, Rensselaer Polytech Inst, 1962-1968; Supvr welding res mat div, Rensselaer Polytech Inst, 1960-1968; Res asst metall, Rensselaer Polytech Inst, 1960-1962; mem, Welding Res Coun & Pressure Vessel Res Comt. **Memberships:** Am Welding Soc; Am Soc Metals. **Research Statement & Publications:** Physical metallurgy associated with welding and joining-solid state transformations, solidification, diffusion, fissuring, arc physics; process development in welding industry. **Mailing Address:** Dept Mat Sci, Univ Tenn 1345 Circle Park, Knoxville, TN 37996-0001. **E-Mail:** lundin@utk.edu

LUNDIN, FRANK E, JR, EPIDEMIOLOGY. **Personal Data:** b Chicago, Ill, August 25, 1928; m 1979, c 4. **Education:** Manchester Col, BA, 1949; Ind Univ, MD, 1953; Johns Hopkins Univ, MPH, 1959, DrPH, 1962. **Professional Experience:** RETIRED; Consult, Food & Drugs Admin, 1988-1993; sr epidemiologist, Epidemiol Stuides Br, Bur Radiol Health, Food & Drugs Admin, USPHS, 1980-1988; chief, Epidemiol Br, Epidemiol & Biomet Div, Nat Inst Child Health & Human Develop, 1975- 1980; dep chief, Epidemiol Br, Epidemiol & Biomet Div, Nat Inst Child Health & Human Develop, 1974-1975; sr epidemiologist, Epidemiol Br, Epidemiol & Biomet Div, Nat Inst Child Health & Human Develop, 1971-1974; sr epidemiologist, Occup Stuides, Nat Inst Environ Health Sci, NIH, 1967-1971; head special studies section, Epidemiol Br, Nat Cancer Inst, 1962-1967; res assoc, Johns Hopkins Univ, 1961-1962; instr, Johns Hopkins Univ, 1960-1961; epidemiologist, Cancer Invest, Nat Cancer Inst, Univ Tenn, 1956-1958; staff physician, Hosp, Carville, La, 1954-1956; USPHS, Norfolk, Va, 1953-; intern, Hosp, 1953-1954. **Memberships:** Soc Epidemiol Res; Am Pub Health Asn; Soc Occup & Environ Health; Am Med Asn. **Research Statement & Publications:** Epidemiology of cancer, especially of the cervix; lung cancer; leukemia and lymphoma; occupational cancer, infant and fetal mortality and parental smoking; health effects of radiation. **Mailing Address:** 7212 Maple Ave, Takoma Park, MD 20912.

LUNDIN, ROBERT ENOR, NUCLEAR MAGNETIC RESONANCE. **Personal Data:** b Boston, Mass, March 19, 1927; m 1952, Jane; c Rebecca & Susan. **Education:** Harvard Univ, AB, 1950; Univ Calif, Berkeley, PhD (chem), 1955. **Honors & Awards:** Petersen Award, Am Chem Soc, 2002. **Professional Experience:** COLLAB, WESTERN REGIONAL RES CTR, USDA, 1987-; res leader, Western Regional Res Ctr, USDA, 1981-1987; res chemist, Western Regional Res Ctr, USDA, 1958-1981; res chemist, Res Ctr, Texaco Inc, 1955-1958. **Memberships:** AAAS; Am Chem Soc. **Research Statement & Publications:** High resolution nuclear magnetic resonance spectroscopy; catalysis; radiation chemistry; gaseous thermodynamics. **Mailing Address:** Western Regional Res Ctr USDA, 800 Buchanan St, Albany, CA 94710. **Fax:** 510-559-5777. **E-Mail:** lundin@pw.usda.gov

LUNDIN, ROBERT FOLKE, GEOLOGY, PALEONTOLOGY. **Personal Data:** b Rockford, Ill, July 20, 1936; m 1958. **Education:** Augustana Col, Ill, AB, 1958; Univ Ill, MS, 1961, PhD (geol), 1962. **Professional Experience:** PROF EMER GEOL SCI, ARIZ STATE UNIV, as of 2004; assoc chmn Dept, Ariz State Univ, 1978-; prof geol, Ariz State Univ, 1974-; co-ed, J Paleont, 1974-1980; Swed Natural Sci Res Coun res grant, 1973-1974 & 1981; distinguished vis prof, Univ Uppsala, 1973-1974 & 1981; Res Corp res grant, 1970; guest scientist, Univ Uppsala, 1970; res comt res grants, Ariz State Univ, 1966-1967, 1970-1974 & 1976; Petrol Res Fund res grants, 1963-1965, 1966-1968 & 1970-1972; from asst prof to assoc prof, Ariz State Univ, 1962-1974. **Memberships:** Soc Econ Paleont & Mineral; Am Asn Petrol Geol; Geol Soc Am; Paleont Soc; Int Paleont Asn. **Research Statement & Publications:** Siluro, Devonian and Mississippi ostracodes, conodonts and stratigraphy; Cenozoic stratigraphy; freshwater ostracodes. **Mailing Address:** Dept Geol, Ariz State Univ, BOX 871404, Tempe, AZ 85287-1404. **E-Mail:** airfl@asuvm.inre.asu.edu

LUNDQUIST, CHARLES ARTHUR, SPACE SCIENCES. **Personal Data:** b Webster, SDak, March 26, 1928; m 1951, Patricia; c Clara, Dawn, Eric, Frances & Gary. **Education:** SDak State Univ, BS, 1949; Univ Kans, PhD (physics), 1953. **Honorary Degrees:** DSc, SDak State Univ, Brookings, 1979. **Honors & Awards:** Herman Oberth Award, Am Inst Aeronaut & Astronaut, 1978. **Professional Experience:** RETIRED; dir, Interactive Proj Off, Marshall Space Flight Ctr, beginning 1999; assoc vpres res, Univ Ala, Huntsville, 1990-1998; dir, Consortium Mat Develop Space, 1985-1999; dir res, Univ Ala, Huntsville, 1982-1990; dir, Space Sci Lab, Marshall Space Flight Ctr, NASA, 1973-1982; vis prof physics, Univ Ala, Huntsville, 1973-1981; asst dir sci, Smithsonian Astrophys Observ, 1962-1973; assoc, Harvard Col Observ, 1962-1973; chief, Physics & Astrophys Br, Marshall Space Flight Ctr, NASA, 1960-1962; chief physics & astrophys sect, Army Ballistic Missile Agency, 1956-1960; physicist, Tech Feasibility Study Off, Redstone Arsenal, 1954-1956; asst prof eng res, Pa State Univ, 1953-1954. **Memberships:** AAAS; Int Astron Union; Am Astron Soc; Am Geophys Union; Am Phys Soc; NY Acad Sci; Nat Speleol Soc; Meteoritic Soc; Sigma Xi. **Research Statement & Publications:** Spacecraft orbital mechanics and orbit determination; space technology; classical mechanics; radiative transfer. **Mailing Address:** 214 Jones Valley Dr S W, Huntsville, AL 35802-1724. **E-Mail:** lundquc@enail.uah.edu

LUNDRY, JERRY LEE, SUPERSONIC WING DESIGN, WAKE VORTICES. **Personal Data:** b Canton, Ill, January 18, 1937. **Education:** Univ Ill, BS, 1958, MS, 1959. **Honors & Awards:** Outstanding Performance Tech Mgt, Am Inst Aeronaut & Astronaut, 1988. **Professional Experience:** Supvr aerodyn design processes & technol, Boeing Com Airplanes, 1996-1999; chief engr, NWTC, 1994-1996; supvr aerodyn, Boeing Com Airplanes, 1977-1994; aerodyn engr, Boeing Com Airplanes, 1970-1977; aerodynamicist, Douglas Aircraft Co, 1959-1970. **Memberships:** Assoc fel Am Inst Aeronaut & Astronaut. **Research Statement & Publications:** Induced drag; winglets; supersonic wing design; wake vortices. **Mailing Address:** 1000 Sunset Way, Bellevue, WA 98004-4023.

LUNDSAGER, C(HRISTIAN) BENT, ENGINEERING, PLASTICS. **Personal Data:** b Denmark, February 27, 1925; American citizen; m 1947, Else; c Soren, Meg, Hanne & Eva. **Education:** Tech Univ Denmark, MSc, 1950. **Professional Experience:** CONSULT, 1990-; res assoc, res div, W R Grace & Co, Columbia, Md, 1962-1990; engr, Tech Univ Denmark, 1947-1952; E I du Pont Del Nemours & Co, Inc, 1952-1962. **Memberships:** emer mem Soc Plastics Engrs; Pres Balto-Wash. Section 1967. **Research Statement & Publications:** Thermoplastics processing; concept development of novel products and processes including ceramics. **Mailing Address:** 1308 Patuxent Dr, Ashton, MD 20861.

LUNDSTROM, JERRY E, SEPARATION PROCESSES, WATER TREATMENT. **Personal Data:** b Waupun, Wis, August 23, 1937; div, c Amy B. **Education:** Univ Wisconsin, Madison, BS, 1960; Stanford Univ, MS, 1965; Univ Kansas, PhD (phys chem), 1970; Babson Col, MBA, 1979. **Honors & Awards:** Freedman Foundation Award, NY Academy of Sciences, 1972. **Professional Experience:** PRINCIPAL, LUNDSTROM ASSOC, 1987-; Profit Ctr Mgr, Contat Res & New Bus Devel, Ionics Inc, 1976-1986; Proj Mgr, New Bus Devel, Brunswick Corp, 1972-1976; Devel Engr Med Ventrures, General Electric Co, 1969-1972; Res & Teaching Asst, Univ Kans, 1965-1969; Sr Res Asst, Stanford Univ, 1962-1965; Res Asst, Phys Chem Lab, Univ Wis, 1961.; Instructor, General Chem, Univ Wis, 1960-1962. **Memberships:** Am Chem Soc; NY Academy of Sci; Am Asn for the Adv of Sci; North Am Membrane Soc. **Mailing Address:** PO Box 267, Andover, MA 01810. **Fax:** 978-474-0991. **E-Mail:** jlund@mathbox.com

LUNDSTROM, LOUIS C, AUTOMOTIVE ENGINEERING, HIGHWAY SAFETY. **Personal Data:** b Tekamah, Nebr, June 7, 1915; m 1995, Phyllis B. **Education:** Univ Nebr, BS & MS, 1939. **Honorary Degrees:** Univ Nebr, PhD (eng), 1962. **Professional Experience:** RETIRED; exec dir environ activ, Gen Motors Corp, 1973-1980; dir auto safety, Gen Motors Corp, 1965-1973; Dir proving ground, Gen Motors Corp, 1956-1965. **Memberships:** affil Nat Acad Eng; fel Soc Automotive Engrs. **Research Statement & Publications:** Vehicle and highway safety; Vehicle Testing & Instrumentation. **Mailing Address:** 10015 W Royal Oak Rd Apt 225, Sun City, AZ 85351-3117.

LUNDSTROM, MARK STEVEN, SEMICONDUCTOR DEVICES, NANOELECTRONICS, COMPUTATIONAL ELECTRONICS. **Personal Data:** b Alexandria, Minn, June 8, 1951; m 1972, Mary; c Will & Nicholas. **Education:** Univ Minn, BEE, 1973, MSEE, 1974; Purdue Univ, PhD (elec eng), 1980. **Honors & Awards:** Frederick Emmons Termon Award, Am Soc Elec Engrs, 1993; Inst Elec & Electronics Engrs Cledo Brunetti Award 2002; Tech Excellence Award, Semiconductor Res Corp, 2002. **Professional Experience:** DIR, NETWORK COMPUTATIONAL NANOTECHNOLOGY, 2002-; asst dean eng, 1991-1993; dir, Opto Electronics Res Ctr, 1989-1993; DON & CAROL SCIFRES DISTINGUISHED PROF ELEC ENG, PURDUE UNIV, 1988-; from asst prof to assoc prof, Purdue Univ, 1980-1988; mem tech staff, Hewlett-Packard Corp, 1974-1977. **Memberships:** Fel Inst Elec & Electronics Engrs; Sigma Xi; fel Am Phys Soc; AAAS; Am Soc Eng Educ. **Research Statement & Publications:** nanoscale electronic devices, carrier transport in semiconductor, computational electronics. **Mailing Address:** Purdue Univ, 465 Northwestern Ave Rm 310 EE Bldg, West Lafayette, IN 47907-2035. **Fax:** 765-494-6441. **E-Mail:** lundstro@purdue.edu

LUNDSTROM, RONALD CHARLES, BIOTECHNOLOGY, SEAFOOD TECHNOLOGY, MARINE FORENSICS. **Personal Data:** b Lynn, Mass, March 15, 1952; m 1977, Martha; c Karin E & Kenneth C. **Education:** Northeastern Univ, BA, 1975. **Honors & Awards:** Silver Medal, US Dept Com, 1989. **Professional Experience:** Forensic Biologist, National Ocean Service 2004 - present; Res. Food Technologist, NAT MARINE FISHERIES SERV, 1975-2004; Assoc referee, AOAC, 1978-1993. **Memberships:** Electrophoresis Soc. **Research Statement & Publications:** Seafood quality and safety; development of biochemical species identification methods; Marine Forensics. **Mailing Address:** National Ocean Service, NOAA, 219 Ft Johnson Rd, Charleston, SC 29412. **E-Mail:** ron.lundstrom@noaa.gov

LUNDY, JOHN KENT, FORENSIC ANTHROPOLOGY. **Personal Data:** b Vancouver, Wash, January 21, 1946; m 1968, c 1. **Education:** Western Wash Univ, Bellingham, BA, 1976, MA, 1977; Univ Witwatersrand, Johannesburg, SAfrica, PhD (anat), 1984; Am Bd Forensic Anthropol, dipl, 1988. **Professional Experience:** PROF CLARK COL, as of 2005; consult, USN, 1987; FORENSIC ANTHROPOLOGIST, CENT INDENTIFICATION LAB, US ARMY, HAWAII, 1986-; adj asst prof & former dir, forensic studies, Dent Sch, Ore Health Sci Univ, 1984-1986; consult forensic anthrop, 1982-; adj asst prof, Dept Anthrop, Portland State Univ, 1982-; med examr & forensic anthropologist, Multnomah Co Med Examr, Portland, Ore, 1982-1986; asst prof, Nat Col Naturopathic Med, 1981-1982; asst lectr anat, Univ Witwatersrand, 1980. **Memberships:** Am Acad Forensic Sci; Am Asn Phys Anthropologists; Am Anthrop Asn; Sigma Xi. **Research Statement & Publications:** Human variation and evolution; morphometric analysis; forensic anthropology; physical anthropology of Southern Africa; Pacific Northwest. **Mailing Address:** Dept Soc Sci, Clark Col, 1800 E McLoughlin Blvd Foster Hall, Vancouver, WA 98663-3598. **E-Mail:** jlundy@clark.edu

LUNDY, RICHARD ALAN, HIGH ENERGY PHYSICS. **Personal Data:** b Sullivan, Ind, August 20, 1934; m 1960, c 2. **Education:** Univ Chicago, PhD (physics), 1962. **Honors & Awards:** Nat Medal Technol, US Govt, 1989. **Professional Experience:** RETIRED; Assoc dir, Fermi Nat Accelerator Lab, 1984-1989. **Research Statement & Publications:** High energy physics; large superconducting magnet systems. **Mailing Address:** PO Box 506, White Salmon, WA 98672.

LUNDY, TED SADLER, RESEARCH ADMINISTRATION, METALS & CERAMICS. **Personal Data:** b Sumner Co, Tenn, April 24, 1933; m 1955, c Tina M. **Education:** Univ Tenn, BS, 1954, MS, 1957, PhD (metall), 1964; Oak Ridge Sch Reactor Technol, Dr Pile Eng, 1958. **Professional Experience:** PART TIME PROF, UNIV TENN, as of 2006; DIR, CTR MFG RES, TENN TECHNOL UNIV, 1990-; assoc prof mech eng, Mfg Ctr, Tenn Technol Univ, 1988-1990; mgr, Energy Conversion & Utilization Technologies, 1985-1988; nat prog mgr, Building Thermal Envelope Systs & Insulating Mat, 1977-1985; metallurgist, Prog Planning & Analysis, 1975-1976; group leader diffusion studies, Metals & Ceramics Div, Oak Ridge Nat Lab, 1972-1975; supvr corrosion res, Metals & Ceramics Div, Oak Ridge Nat Lab, 1971-1972; lectr, Univ Tenn, 1966-; group leader diffusion studies, Metals & Ceramics Div, Oak Ridge Nat Lab, 1959-1971; metallurgist, Metals & Ceramics Div, Oak Ridge Nat Lab, 1957-1959; instr eng drawing, Univ Tenn, 1955-1957; mem, Knox Co Conn; mem bd dirs, Knoxville Urban League; consultative coun, Nat Inst Bldg Sci. **Memberships:** Sigma Xi; Am Inst Mining Metall & Petrol Engrs; Am Soc Metals; Am Soc Testing & Mat; Am Soc Heating Refrig & Air-Conditioning Engrs; Soc Mfg Engrs. **Research Statement & Publications:** Solid state reactions; diffusion in metals and ceramics; building sciences; heat transfer and moisture flow; materials sciences. **Mailing Address:** Ctr Mfg Res, Tenn Technol Univ, Brown Hall 222 PO Box 5077, Cookeville, TN 38505. **Fax:** 615-372-6345. **E-Mail:** tlundy@tennessee.edu

LUNER, PHILIP, PHYSICAL CHEMISTRY. **Personal Data:** b Vilno, Poland, June 1, 1925; American citizen; m 1951, c 2. **Education:** Loyola Col, BSc, 1947; McGill Univ, PhD (phys chem), 1951. **Professional Experience:** Prof pulp & paper res, State Univ NY, as of 2002; PROF EMER PAPER SCI & ENG, STATE UNIV NY, 1995-; prof pulp & paper res, State Univ NY, beginning 1964; from res assoc to assoc prof, Empire State Paper res Inst, 1957-1964; group leader, Sulfite Pulp Mfrs League, 1954-1957; Res chemist, Pulp & Paper res Inst Can, 1951-1954. **Memberships:** Am Chem Soc; Tech Asn Pulp & Paper Indust; Can Pulp & Paper Asn; Sigma Xi. **Research Statement & Publications:** Diffusion and penetration studies of pulping; chromophores in model lignin compounds; mechanical properties of fibers and paper; surface chemical properties of wood polymers. **Mailing Address:** Dept Paper Sci & Eng, State Univ NY, Walters Hall, One Forestry dr, Syracuse, NY 13210-2778. **E-Mail:** pluner@syr.edu

LUNER, STEPHEN JAY, IMMUNOCHEMISTRY, PATHOLOGY. **Personal Data:** b New York, NY, October 2, 1940; m 1965, Evelyn; c Sean, Beth & Susan. **Education:** Calif Inst Technol, BS, 1961; Univ Calif, Los Angeles, PhD (biophys), 1969. **Professional Experience:** ASSOC PROF PATH, DALHOUSIE UNIV, 1991-; vis assoc prof biol chem, Univ Calif, Los Angeles, 1991-1992; asst prof, Dalhousie Univ, 1977-1991; asst prof residence pediat, Biophys Lab, 1972-1977; asst resbiophysicist, Biophys Lab, 1971; NIMH trainee, Univ Calif, Los Angeles, 1969-1971; res biophysicist, Univ Calif, Los Angeles, 1968-1971. **Memberships:** Am Soc Cell Biol. **Research Statement & Publications:** Electrophoresis; cell surface antigens; effects of enzymes on cell interactions. **Mailing Address:** Dept Path, Dalhousie Univ, Tupper Bldg, Halifax, NS B3H 4H7, Can. **Fax:** 902-494-2519. **E-Mail:** sjluner@ac.dal.ca

LUNINE, JONATHAN IRVING, PLANETARY SCIENCES. **Personal Data:** b New York, NY, June 26, 1959; m Cynthia; c Joseph. **Education:** Univ Rochester, BS, 1980; Calif Inst Technol, MS, 1983, PhD (planetary sci), 1985. **Honors & Awards:** Harold C Urey Prize, Div Planetary Sci, Am Astron Soc, 1988; Zeldovich Prize, Comt Space Res, Int Coun Sci Unions, 1990; James Macelwane Medal, Am Geophys Union, 1995; Authur Adel Award, Northern Ariz Univ, 2000. **Professional Experience:** PROF PLANETARY SCI & PHYSICS, UNIV ARIZ, 2001-; DISTINGUISHED VIS SCIENTIST, NASA JET PROPULSION LAB, 2000-; CHAIR, THEORETICAL ASTROPHYSICS PROG, UNIV ARIZ, 2000-; prof planetary sci, Univ Ariz, beginning 1995; from asst prof to assoc prof, Univ Ariz, 1986-1995; vis asst prof, Univ Calif, Los Angeles, 1986; res assoc, Univ Ariz, 1984-1986. **Memberships:** Sigma Xi; Am Astron Soc; fel Am Geophys Union; Int Acad Astronauts; fel AAAS. **Research Statement & Publications:** Theoretical studies of outer solar system satellites, comets, their present nature and evolution, emphasizing physical chemistry of ices and volatiles; modeling of the evolution of substellar mass objects, brown dwarfs; terrestrial photochemical processes; autra solar planets; published over 160 articles. **Mailing Address:** Lunar Planetary Lab Univ Ariz, 1629 E Univ Blvd, Tucson, AZ 85721-0092. **Fax:** 520-626-8250. **E-Mail:** jlunine@lpl.arizona.edu

LUNING, CHARLES D, MATHEMATICS. **Education:** Math Univ Colo, BS, 1963, MS, 1965; Math Purdue Univ, PhD, 1971. **Professional Experience:** PROF, DEPT MATH & STATIST, SAM HOUSTON STATE UNIV, as of 2006. **Mailing Address:** Math Dept, Sam Houston State Univ, PO Box 2206, Huntsville, TX 77341-2206. **Fax:** 936-294-1882. **E-Mail:** dluning@shsu.edu

LUNK, WILLIAM ALLAN, ORNITHOLOGY. **Personal Data:** b Johnstown, Pa, May 6, 1919; m 1947, c 4. **Education:** Univ WVa, AB, 1941, MS, 1946; Univ Mich, PhD (zoology), 1955. **Professional Experience:** RETIRED; assoc cur exhibits & lectr zoology, 1985-1988; actg dir, 1964-1988; cur exhibits, 1964-1989; consult, Kalamazoo Nature Ctr, Mich, 1963-1977; preparator, Exhibit Mus, Univ Mich, Ann Arbor, 1949-1959; instr biol, Univ WVa, 1946-1947. **Memberships:** Cooper Ornith Soc; Wilson Ornith Soc; Am Ornith Union. **Research Statement & Publications:** Ornithological life history; taxonomy and distribution; fossil birds; exhibit techniques. **Mailing Address:** 865 N Wagner Rd, Ann Arbor, MI 48103-2146.

LUNN, ANTHONY CROWTHER, BIOMATERIALS, POLYMER PHYSICS. **Personal Data:** b Huddersfield, Eng, September 25, 1946; American citizen; m 1972, Phyllis. **Education:** Cambridge Univ, Eng, BA, 1967; Harvard Univ, MS, 1968. **Honorary Degrees:** DSc, Mass Inst Technol, 1972. **Professional Experience:** MGR ADVAN TECHNOL, JOHNSON & JOHNSON INTERVENTIONAL SYSTS, 1990-; sect mgr, Ethicon Inc, Johnson & Johnson Co, 1981-1990; proj leader, Chem Res Div, Am Cyanamid Co, 1973-1981; res assoc, Mass Inst Technol, 1972-1973; res scientist, Pioneering Res Lab, Du Pont Co, 1969. **Memberships:** Am Chem Soc; Fiber Soc; Int Soc Endovascular Surg; Sigma Xi; AAAS; Soc Biomat. **Research Statement & Publications:** Development of novel products for use in angioplasty and minimally invasive surgery; implantable stents and other devices. **Mailing Address:** Johnson & Johnson Interventional Systs, PO Box 4917, Warren, NJ 07059-0917.

LUNN, CHARLES ALBERT, PROTEIN ENGINEERING OF CYTOKINES-LYMPHOKINES, RATIONAL DRUG DESIGN. **Personal Data:** b Audubon, NJ, December 2, 1953; m Kathleen S Morgan; c Forrest H & K Danielle. **Education:** Johns Hopkins Univ, BA, 1976, PhD (biochem), 84. **Honors & Awards:** President's Award, Schering-Plough Corp, 1988. **Professional Experience:** SR PRIN SCIENTIST, DEPT MOLECULAR BIOL, SCHERING-PLOUGH RES INST, 1993-; Fel, Dept Biochem, State Univ NY, Stony Brook, 1984-1986. **Research Statement & Publications:** Used protein mutagenesis and biochemical approaches to probe the importance of protein structure in biological function; results will be used to attempt to rationally design novel immunomodulatory drugs. **Mailing Address:** Schering-Plough Res Inst, 2015 Galloping Hill Rd, Kenilworth, NJ 07033. **Fax:** 908-298-3083. **E-Mail:** charles.lunn@spcorp.com

LUNNEY, GLYNN S, AERONAUTICS. **Professional Experience:** VPRES & GEN MGR, ROCKWELL INT SPACE SYSTS DIV, as of 2006. **Memberships:** Am Astronaut Soc; Am Inst Aeronaut & Astronaut. **Mailing Address:** Rockwell Int Corp, 600 Gemini St, Houston, TX 77058-2754. **Fax:** 713-232-4000.

LUNNEY, JOAN K, ANIMAL INFECTIOUS DISEASES, ANIMAL GENOME. **Personal Data:** b Philadelphia, Pa, July 19, 1946; m 1979. **Education:** Chestnut Hill Col, Philadelphia, Pa, BS, 1968; Johns Hopkins Univ, Baltimore, Md, PhD (biochem), 1976. **Professional Experience:** RES SCIENTIST, BARC, USDA, as of 2003; ACT NAT PROG LEADER, ANIMAL HEALTH, NAT PROG STAF, AGR RES SERV, USDA, 2001-; Secy, Swine Genome Comt, 1993-; comt mem, Nat Animal Genetic Resources Comt, USDA, 1991-; mem, Vet Immunol Comt, Am Asn Immunologists, 1990-1993; chairperson, Swine CD Workshop, Int Union Immunol Sci, 1990-1992; comt mem, Comt Res Animal Genome, US Exp Stas Comt Orgn & Policy, 1990; adv coun mem, Portuguese NSF, 1987-1990; RES IMMUNOLOGIST SWINE IMMUNOGENETICS, HELMINTHIC DIS LAB, AGR RES SERV, USDA, 1983-; panel mem, Cellular Physiol Panel, NSF, 1983-1987; sr staff fel, Immunol Br, Nat Cancer Inst, 1979-1983; postdoctoral fel swine immunogenetics & biochem, Immunol Br, Nat Cancer Inst, 1976-1979; chemist cell surface receptors, Lab Biochem Pharmacol, Nat Inst Arthritis, Metab Digestive Dis, NIH, 1973-1976. **Memberships:** Am Asn Immunologists; Transplantation Soc; Asn Women Sci; Int Soc Animal Genetics; Am Asn Vet Parisitologists; Am Asn Vet Immunologists. **Research Statement & Publications:** Analyses of immunologic mechanisms and genetic control of swine responses to infectious diseases; understanding of basic swine immune responses and of complexity of swine genome. **Mailing Address:** APDL, BARC, ARS, USDA, Bldg 1040 Rm 104, Beltsville, MD 20705-2350. **Fax:** 301-504-5306. **E-Mail:** jlunney@anri.barc.usda.gov

LUNSFORD, CARL DALTON, PHARMACEUTICAL CHEMISTRY. **Personal Data:** b Richmond, Va, February 11, 1927; m 1947, c 3. **Education:** Univ Richmond, BS, 1949, MS, 1950; Univ Va, PhD (chem), 1953. **Professional Experience:** SR VPRES, A H ROBINS CO, INC, 1980-; vpres, A H Robins Co, Inc, 1973-1980; asst vpres, A H Robins Co, Inc, 1966-1974; dir res, A H Robins Co, Inc, 1964-1966; dir labs, A H Robins Co, Inc, 1962-1964; dir, A H Robins Co, Inc, 1959-1964; assoc dir chem res, A H Robins Co, Inc, 1958; res chemist, A H Robins Co, Inc, 1953-1957; Instr chem, Univ Va, 1952-1953. **Memberships:** AAAS; Am Chem Soc; Am Inst Chemists. **Research Statement & Publications:** Medicinal and organic chemistry and development. **Mailing Address:** PO Box 590, Irvington, VA 22480.

LUNSFORD, JACK HORNER, HETEROGENEOUS CATALYSIS, SURFACE CHEMISTRY. **Personal Data:** b Houston, Tex, February 6, 1936; m 1960, c 7. **Education:** Tex A&M Univ, BS, 1957; Rice Univ, PhD (chem eng), 1962. **Honors & Awards:** Paul H Emmett Award, Catalysis Soc, 1975; Catalysis Soc Metropolitan NY Award, Excellence Catalysis, 1986. **Professional Experience:** DISTINGUISHED PROF EMER CHEM, TEX A&M UNIV, as of 2004; PROF CHEM, TEX A&M UNIV, 1971-; from asst prof to assoc prof, Tex A&M Univ, 1966-1971; asst prof chem, Sam Houston State Col, 1965-1966; Asst prof chem eng, Univ Idaho, 1961-1962. **Memberships:** Am Chem Soc. **Research Statement & Publications:** Surface chemistry and heterogeneous catalysis, using modern spectroscopic techniques; Catalytic Oxidative Coupling Of Methane. **Mailing Address:** Dept chem, Univ Tex A&M, Col Sta, Bryan, TX 77842. **Fax:** 979-845-4719. **E-Mail:** iunsford@mail.tamu.edu

LUNSFORD, JESSE V(ERNON), CIVIL & SANITARY ENGINEERING. **Personal Data:** b Ninnekah, Okla, September 4, 1923; m 1948, c 5. **Education:** Univ NMex, BS, 1953; Univ Calif, MS, 1954. **Professional Experience:** PROF CIVIL ENG, NMEX STATE UNIV, 1958-; assoc prof, Rensselaer Polytech Inst, 1957-1958; Asst prof & asst res engr, Wash State Univ, 1954-1957. **Memberships:** Am Soc Civil Engrs; Nat Soc Prof Engrs; Am Soc Eng Educ; Am Pub Health Asn; Am Water Works Asn. **Research Statement & Publications:** Anaerobic digestion; stream sanitation; algae production; water reclamation and utilization. **Mailing Address:** 2035 Corley Dr, Las Cruces, NM 88001.

LUNSFORD, MATT D, MATHEMATICS. **Education:** La Tech Univ, BS, 1987; Univ Nebr, MS, 1989; Tulane Univ, PhD (math), 1993. **Professional Experience:** PROF MATH, UNION UNIV, 2004-. **Mailing Address:** Dept Math & Comput Sci, Union Univ, 1050 Union Univ Dr, Jackson, TN 38305. **Fax:** 731-661-5175. **E-Mail:** mlunsfor@uu.edu

LUNSFORD, RALPH D, AUDIO-VIDEO EQUIPMENT & TAPES REGARDING CONSUMER PRODUCTS, LINEAR SOLID STATE APPLICATIONS ENGINEERING. **Personal Data:** b Ninety Six, SC, January 7, 1934; m 1957, Antoinette M; c Mark A. **Education:** Clemson Univ, BS (industrial physics), 1956; Penn State Univ, MSEE Level Counsis 1977; Univ WI, Battery Selection Product Design Cert 1991. **Professional Experience:** RETIRED; mem, Camcorder Battery Stand Comt, Electronic Industs Asn, 1990-; Liaison officer UL/CSA matters, Thomson Consumer Electronics, Inc, 1985-; mgr prod eng & qual or solid state appln engr, Thomson Consumer Electronics, Inc, 1979-1994; sr engr audio for auto radios, Ford Motor Co, 1976-1979; sr proj engr, Audio Amplifiers Design, Dynaco, Inc, Div Tyco Labs, 1973-1976; proj mgr, Audio & FM Receivers & Amplifiers, Brit Industs, Div Avnet, 1971-1973; vpres eng, Audio Tape Duplication, Nat Tape Serv, Inc, 1968-1971; proj engr audio & acoust, CBS TV Network, 1966-1968; Elec engr audio electronics acoust, RCA Corp, 1956-1966. **Memberships:** life mem Audio Eng Soc; mem Am Inst Physics. **Research Statement & Publications:** Microphones used in space program; designer of audio electronic systems used in Ford auto radio; developed state of the art audio tape duplicating system; developed state of the art battery cycling equipment; camcorder battery sid (EIA) Audio/Acoustic Standards (CAS, RCA, Thomson, Ford). **Mailing Address:** 3002 Raymond Ave, Abington, PA 19001.

LUNT, HARRY EDWARD, FAILURE ANALYSIS, STANDARDS DEVELOPMENT. **Personal Data:** b New York, NY, April 30, 1924; m 1950, c 5. **Education:** Syracuse Univ, AB, 1948; Iowa State Univ, MS, 1953. **Honors & Awards:** Award of Merit, Am Soc Testing & Mat, 1981; Robert J Painter Award, Standards Eng Soc, 1989. **Professional Experience:** Mem bd dirs, Comt A-1 Steel, Am Soc Testing & Mat, beginning 1991; chmn, Comt A-1 Steel, Am Soc Testing & Mat, 1986-1991; CORP CONSULT ENGR, BURNS & ROE ENTERPRISES, INC, 1974-; corp metallurgist, Worthington Corp, 1967-1974; sr engr, Westinghouse Res Labs, 1963-1966; develop metallurgist, US Steel Corp, 1953-1963; Res asst, Ames Lab, US Atomic Energy Comn, 1950-1953. **Memberships:** Fel Am Soc Testing & Mat; fel Am Soc Metals; Nat Asn Corrosion Engrs; Am Welding Soc. **Research Statement & Publications:** Development of standards for steel and liason among national and international standards organizations; metallurgy and failure analysis, particularly for power generation equipment. **Mailing Address:** 13 Brockden Dr, Mendham, NJ 07945. **Fax:** 973-543-2229. **E-Mail:** helunt@aol.com

LUNT, OWEN RAYNAL, SOIL FERTILITY. **Personal Data:** b El Paso, Tex, April 8, 1921; m 1953, c 3. **Education:** Brigham Young Univ, AB, 1947; NC State Univ, PhD (agron), 1951. **Professional Experience:** Tech Expert, Malaysia, 1985; Tech Expert, Kenya, 1983; Tech Expert, Int Atomic Energy Agency, Columbia, 1971; DIR, LAB NUCLEAR MED & RADIATION BIOL, 1968-; actg chmn dept biophys, Univ Calif, Los Angeles, 1965-1970; actg dir lab nuclear med & radiation biol, Univ Calif, Los Angeles, 1965-1968; PROF BIOL, UNIV CALIF, LOS ANGELES, 1963-; from instr to assoc prof soil sci, Univ Calif, Los Angeles, 1951-1963; Lectr soil chem, NC State Univ, 1950. **Memberships:** Fel Soil Sci Soc Am; fel Am Soc Agron; Am Soc Hort Sci; Am Nuclear Soc. **Research Statement & Publications:** Soil chemistry; environmental pollution. **Mailing Address:** 1200 Roberto Lane, Los Angeles, CA 90077-2334.

LUNT, STEELE RAY, medical entomology; deceased, see previous edition for last biography

LUNT, TERESA F, COMPUTER SCIENCE. **Education:** Princeton Univ, AB; Ind Univ, MA (Appl Math). **Professional Experience:** MGR COMPUT SCI LAB, & RES SCIENTIST, PALO ALTO RES CTR, as of 2006. **Mailing Address:** Palo Alto Res Ctr, 3333 Coyote Hill Rd, Palo Alto, CA 94304.

LUNTE, CRAIG EDWARD, BIOANALYTICAL CHEMISTRY. **Personal Data:** b August 6, 1957; m 1983, Susan; c Alyson & Kathryn. **Education:** Univ Mo, Rolla, BS, 1979; Purdue Univ, PhD (analytical chem), 1984. **Professional Experience:** PROF, DEPT CHEM, UNIV KANS, 1997-; Adj prof, Dept Pharmaceut Chem, Univ Kans, 1990-; Chairman Dept Chem from 2001-2005; from asst to assoc prof, Dept Chem, Univ Kans, 1987-1997; res assoc, Univ Cincinnati, 1986-1987; Res scientist, Procter & Gamble, 1984-1986. **Memberships:** Am Chem Soc; Am Asn Pharmaceut Scientists; Soc Electroanal Chem; Int Soc Study Xenobiotics; Sigma Xi; AAAS. **Research Statement & Publications:** Bioanalytical chemistry; development of microdialysis sampling for in vivo monitoring; developing microanalytical techniques such as capillary electrophoresis and microbone; liquid chromatography; detector development. **Mailing Address:** Dept Chem, Univ Kans, 2010 Malott Hall, 1251 Wescoe Hall Dr, Lawrence, KS 66045. **Fax:** 785-864-5396. **E-Mail:** clunte@ku.edu

LUNTZ, MAURICE HAROLD, GLAUCOMA SURGERY, CATARACT SURGERY. **Personal Data:** b Cape Town, SAfrica, July 27, 1930; American citizen; m 1957, Angela; c Melvyn, Caryn & David. **Education:** Univ Cape Town, MB ChB, 1952; Univ Witwatersrand, MD, 1974; FRCS Ed, 1958, FACS, 1978. **Honors & Awards:** Sam & Dora Cohen Medal, Univ Capetown, 1984; Honor Award, Am Acad Ophthal, 1986; Gold Medal, Univ Rome, 1987. **Professional Experience:** CLIN PROF OPTHAL, SCH MED, NY UNIV, as of 2000; pres bd surgeon dir, Manhattan Eye Ear & Throat Hosp, 1991-1995; dir emer, Beth Israel Med Ctr, 1989-; chmn, Ophthal Sect, NY Acad Med, 1989-1990; CLIN PROF OPHTHAL, MT SINAI SCH MED, 1978-; dir ophthal, Beth Israel Med Ctr, 1978-1979; consult, Corneal Disease Hip, NY, 1978; Academia, Ophthalmologica Int, 1975-; prof & chmn ophthal, Univ Witwatersrand, Johannesburg, 1964-1978. **Memberships:** Int Coun Ophthal; Int Glaucoma Cong. **Research Statement & Publications:** Surgical procedures for glaucoma; new techniques for glaucoma surgery and evaluation of existing techniques. **Mailing Address:** Sch Med, NY Univ, 121 E 60th St, New York, NY 10022. **Fax:** 212-223-2881.

LUNTZ, MYRON, RADIATION PHYSICS. **Personal Data:** b New York, NY, January 16, 1940; m 1964, Susan; c Barbara & Jonathan. **Education:** City Col NY, BS, 1962; Univ Conn, MS, 1964, PhD (physics), 1968. **Professional Experience:** PROF PHYSICS, STATE UNIV NY COL FREDONIA, 1982-; chmn dept, State Univ NY Col Fredonia, 1978-1984; Vis assoc prof physics, Univ Del, 1975-1976; from asst prof to assoc prof, State Univ NY Col Fredonia, 1969-1982; vis scientist, Inst Physics, Univ Aarhus, 1968-1969; fel, Univ Conn, 1968; Res asst physics, Univ Conn, 1964-1968. **Memberships:** Am Phys Soc; Am Asn Physics Teachers; Sigma Xi; Soc Physics Students. **Research Statement & Publications:** Theoretical study of the penetration of matter by energetic charged particles, with emphasis on effects associated with the spatial distribution of energy desposition about particle tracks; experimental study of surface alteration of metal substrates by ion beam irradiation. **Mailing Address:** Prof Emer Physics, 9 Holland Ct, Glenmont, NY 12077. **E-Mail:** luntzm@fredonia.edu

LUO, PEILIN, ELECTRONICS CIRCUIT & SYSTEM, MANUFACTURE METHODS. **Personal Data:** b Tianjin, China, December 30, 1913; m 1941, c 3. **Education:** Nat Chiaotung Univ, BS, 1935; Calif Inst Technol, PhD (elec eng, physics & math), 1952. **Honors & Awards:** Centennial Medal, Inst Elec & Electronics Engrs, 1984. **Professional Experience:** CONSULT, SCI & TECH ADV COMT, MINISTRY MACH & ELECTRONICS INDUST, 1988-; dep dir, Sci & Tech Admin, 1993-1982 & Sci & Tech Comt, Ministry Electronics Indust, 1980-1988; Mem, Nat Natural Sci Award Comt, 1965-1990; dep chief engr, Admin Electronics Indust, 1956-1962; chief engr, NChina Combine Radio & Component Mfg, 1953-1956; dept dir, Technol Dept, Admin Telecom Indust, 1950-1953; Var tech positions, Chinese factories, 1935-1948; guest prof, Peking Univ, Chinese Electronic Sci & Univ, Xi-Dian Electronics Sci & Tech Univ; hon prof, Beijing Inst Technol. **Memberships:** Sigma Xi; fel Inst Elec & Electronics Engrs; fel Chinese Inst Electronics. **Research Statement & Publications:** Electronic circuit, transmitters and receivers, radar system and decision theory; computer arithmatics; policy of science and especially electronics development; application of mathematics to national economics. **Mailing Address:** Sci & Tech Consult Comt Ministry Mach & Electronics, Nanshagon 2 Entrance Bldg 11, Beijing Sarlihe 100823, China.

LUO, STEVEN X, CATALYSIS, POLYMERIZATION. **Personal Data:** b Longchuan, China, November 27, 1962; American citizen. **Education:** Sun Yatsen Univ, BS, 1982; Yale Univ, MS, 1986, MPhil, 1987, PhD (chem), 1990. **Professional Experience:** SR RES SCIENTIST, BRIDGESTONE-FIRESTONE RES, 2000-; res scientist, Bridgestone-Firestone Res, 1995-2000; postdoctoral res fel, Los Alamos Nat Lab, 1992-1995; postdoctoral res assoc, Yale Univ, 1990-1992; res assoc, Leather Indust Res Inst, 1982-1984. **Memberships:** Am Chem Soc. **Research Statement & Publications:** Transition metal organometallic chemistry and inorganic chemisty; coordination chemistry; Ziegler-Natta polymerization; homogeneous catalysis; polymer chemistry and design of new ligards for catalysis. **Mailing Address:** Bridgestone/Firestone Res, 1200 Firestone Parwy, Akron, OH 44317. **Fax:** 330-379-7530.

LUOMA, ERNIE VICTOR, INDUSTRIAL CHEMISTRY. **Personal Data:** b Sault Ste Marie, Mich, September 1, 1932; m 1954, c 5. **Education:** Mich Technol Univ, BS, 1954; Univ Calif, Berkeley, MS, 1956; Mich State Univ, PhD (phys inorg chem), 1966. **Professional Experience:** DIR ANALYTICAL SCI, CORP RES & DEVELOP, DOW CHEM CO, 1980-; dir, Analytical Labs, 1978-1980; tech dir, Dow Chem Co, 1977-1978; res mgr, Dow Chem Co, 1970-1977; group leader, Dow Chem Co, 1962-1970; chemist, Dow Chem Co, 1957-1962; Instr chem, Mich Technol Univ, 1956-1957. **Memberships:** Am Chem Soc; Am Inst Chem Engrs. **Research Statement & Publications:** Industrial research. **Mailing Address:** 1030 Allen Ave, Ashtabula, OH 44092-2298.

LUONGO, CESAR AUGUSTO, SUPERCONDUCTING MAGNETS & POWER DEVICES, THERMAL-FLUID SCIENCES & TEAM-BASED ENGINEERING DESIGN. **Personal Data:** b Montevideo, Uruguay, October 5, 1954; m 1985, Maria; c Francisco & Julia. **Education:** Univ Uruguay, Montevideo, Ing, 1979; Stanford Univ, Palo Alto, MS, 1981, PhD (mech eng), 1986. **Professional Experience:** PROF MECH ENG, FAMU-FSU COL ENG, as of 2006; mgr, Supercond Technol, Bechtel, beginning 1992; mgr, Develop Gas Pipelines software, Stoner Assocs Inc, 1989-1992; Sr engr, R&D Div, Bechtel, 1986-1989. **Memberships:** Inst Elec & Electronics Engrs. **Research Statement & Publications:** Superconducting magnetic energy storage; magnet design; superconducting (HTS) electric motors; thermal and fluid dynamics analyses; electromagnetics; system studies. **Mailing Address:** Dept Mech Eng, FAMU-FSU Col Eng, Rm 229, 2525 Pottsdamer St, Tallahassee, FL 32310-6046. **Fax:** 850-410-6337. **E-Mail:** luongo@magnet.fsu.edu

LUPAN, DAVID MARTIN, MEDICAL MYCOLOGY. **Personal Data:** b Cleveland, Ohio, October 23, 1945; m 1968, Joyce; c Michael & Nicole. **Education:** Univ Ariz, BS, 1967; Univ Iowa, MS, 1970, PhD (microbiol), 1973. **Professional Experience:** INTERIM DEAN RES & DEVELOP, UNIV NEVADA, as of 2003; SR ASSOC DEAN BASIC SCI & RES, UNIV NV, 1997-; Prof Microbiol, Sch Med Sci, Univ Nev, Reno, 1987-1997; From asst prof to assoc prof, 1973-1987. **Memberships:** Sigma Xi; Am Soc Microbiol; Int Soc Human & Animal Mycol; Med Mycol Soc Am. **Research Statement & Publications:** The mechanism of pathogenesis of fungi; Regulation of iron transport in pathogenic fungi. **Mailing Address:** Dept Microbiol & Immunol Sch Med Sci, Univ Nev, Reno, NV 89557-0046. **Fax:** 775-327-2332. **E-Mail:** dmlupan@med.unr.edu

LUPASH, LAWRENCE O, KALMAN FILTER, NUMERICAL METHODS IN CONTROL THEORY. **Personal Data:** b Bucharest, Romania, May 29, 1942; American citizen; div. **Education:** Polytech Inst Bucharest, Romania, MSc, 1965, PhD (control & comput eng), 1972. **Professional Experience:** INTERMETRICS INC, as of 1993; SR ANALYST, INTERMETRICS INC, 1980-; lectr informatics & math, Univ Bucharest, Romania, 1973-1978; vis lectr, Univ Tirana, Albania, 1973; sr analyst & sr researcher control & comput appln, Univ Bucharest Comput Ctr, 1972-1979; sr researcher & control eng, Inst Automation, Bucharest, Romania, 1971-1972; asst prof, Fac Automation, Polytech Inst Bucharest, 1966-1968, 1971-1972; researcher-engr & control eng, Inst Automation, Bucharest, Romania, 1965-1968. **Memberships:** Inst Elec & Electronics Engrs; Asn Comput Mach; Soc Indust & Appl Math. **Research Statement & Publications:** Numerical techniques for software applications in technical-scientific problems; applied mathematics; optimization; numerical methods in control theory; estimation; stability and control of multivariable systems. **Mailing Address:** Intermetrics Inc, 733 Concord Ave, Cambridge, MA 02138. **Fax:** 617-868-2843.

LUPINSKI, JOHN HENRY, POLYMER CHEMISTRY. **Personal Data:** b Schenectady, NY, February 28, 1927; m 1954, c 3. **Education:** State Univ Leyden, BS, 1949, MS, 1953, PhD (chem), 1959. **Professional Experience:** CONSULT, POLYMERIC MAT, as of 2003; unit mgr corp res & develop, Gen Elec Co, beginning 1979; proj mgr, Corp Res & Develop Ctr, 1972-1979; res chemist, Res & Develop Ctr, 1960-1972. **Memberships:** AAAS; Am Chem Soc; Fedn Am Scientist. **Research Statement & Publications:** Organic conductors; polymer electro-chemistry; electrical insulation and polymer application processes; electrostatics. **Mailing Address:** 44465 Chamberlain Terrace 307, Ashburn, VA 20147. **E-Mail:** j.lupinski@att.net

LUPLOW, WAYNE CHARLES, DEVELOPMENT OF HIGH DEFINITION TELEVISION FOR TERRESTRIAL BROADCAST, QUALITY & RELIABILITY OF SEMICONDUCTOR COMPONENTS. **Personal Data:** b Milwaukee, Wis, January 16, 1940; m 1960, c 4. **Education:** Univ Wis, BS, 1962; Univ Pa, MS, 1964. **Professional Experience:** BD DIRS, ADV TV SYSTS COMT, as of 2005; CHAIR, CEA VIDEO SYSTS COMT, as of 2005; VPRES, HDTV STANDARDS & PROM, ZENITH ELECTRONICS CORP, as of 2005; exec dir Res & Develop HDTV, Zanith Electronics Corp, beginning 1987; publ chmn, Transactions ed, beginning 1980; publ chmn, Consumer Electronics Soc, Inst Elec & Electronics Engrs, beginning 1976; admin comt, Consumer Electronics Soc, 1975-; eng dir components & reliability, Zenith Electronics Corp, 1974-1987; engr & leader, Tv Res, Zenith Electronics Corp, 1964-1974; engr Tv Res, RCA, 1962-1964. **Memberships:** Sr mem Inst Elec & Electronics Engrs. **Research Statement & Publications:** High definition television and other comunications systems relating to consumer electronics. **Mailing Address:** Zenith Electronics Corp, 2000 Millbrook Dr, Lincolnshire, IL 60069. **Fax:** 847-941-8555. **E-Mail:** wayne.luplow@zenith.com

LUPO, ANTHONY ROCCO, SYNOPTIC SCALE DYNAMICS, CLIMATE DYNAMICS. **Personal Data:** b Auburn, NY, March 13, 1966; m Allison A Wood; c Mary E & Grace A. **Education:** State Univ NY, Oswego, BS, 1988; Purdue Univ, MS, 1991, PhD (atmospheric sci), 1995. **Professional Experience:** ASSOC PROF, DEPT ATMOSPHERIC SCI, UNIV MO, 2003-; asst prof, Dept Soil & Atmospheric Sci, Univ Mo, 1997-2003; postdoctoral res assoc, State Univ Ny, Albany, 1995-1997. **Memberships:** Am Meteorol Soc; Royal Meteorol Soc; Sigma Xi; Am Geophys Union; Nat Weather Asn. **Research Statement & Publications:** Large and synoptic-scale atmospheric dynamics; structure and maintenance of blocking anticyclones and transient cyclones. **Mailing Address:** Dept Atmospheric Sci, 389 Mc Reynolds Hall, Univ Mo, Columbia, MO 65211. **Fax:** 573-884-5133. **E-Mail:** lupoa@missouri.edu

LUPSKI, JAMES RICHARD, HUMAN GENETICS, GENETIC ENGINEERING. **Personal Data:** b RockvilleCenter, NY, February 22, 1957; m 1986, Gabriella; c Alessandra M & Marcella D. **Education:** NY Univ, BA, 1979, MS, 1983, PhD (molecular biol), 1984; NY Univ Med Ctr, MD, 1985. **Honors & Awards:** Young Investr Award, Abbott Labs, 1989 & Southern Sect, Am Fedn Clin Res, 1991. **Professional Experience:** PROF PEDIAT, MED SCIENTIST TRAINING PROG, BAYLOR COL MED, 1995-; CULLEN PROF MOLECULAR & HUMAN GENETICS, MED SCIENTIST TRAINING PROG, BAYLOR COL MED, 1995-; DIR, MED SCIENTIST TRAINING PROG, BAYLOR COL MED, 1993-; assoc prof, Dept Molecular & Human Genetics & Dept Pediat, 1992-1995; fel med genetics, Baylor Col Med, 1991; PEW scholar, Human Genetics, 1990-1994; res asst prof, Inst Molecular Genetics, 1987-1992; res asst prof pediat, Baylor Col Med, 1986-1987; guest prof, Ctr Advan Molecular Biol, Punjab Univ, Lahore, Pakistan, 1986; res asst prof biochem, Dept Biochem, NY Univ Med Ctr, 1985-1986; co-founder, Bacterial Barcodes, Inc; Am ed, Neurogenetics. **Memberships:** AMA; fel AAAS; NY Acad Sci; Am Soc Microbiol; Genetics Soc Am; Am Soc Human Genetics; fel Am Acad Pediat; Soc Pediat Res; Am Fedn Clin Res; fel Am Col Med Genetics. **Research Statement & Publications:** Regulation of complex gene systems in E coli and mechanisms of DNA rearrangements; mechanisms for disease causing mutations in humans; DNA fingerprinting of infectious disease agents; published over 20 articles. **Mailing Address:** Dept Molecular Human Genetics Baylor Col Med, One Baylor Plaza, Houston, TX 77030. **Fax:** 713-798-5073. **E-Mail:** jlupski@bcm.tmc.edu

LUPTON, JOHN EDWARD, CHEMICAL OCEANOGRAPHY, ISOTOPE GEOLOGY. **Personal Data:** b Bakersfield, Calif, July 30, 1944. **Education:** Princeton Univ, BA, 1966; Calif Inst Technol, PhD (physics), 1972. **Professional Experience:** CHEM OCEANOGR, PAC MARINE ENVIRON LAB, HATFIELD MARINE SCI CTR, NAT OCEANIC & ATMOSPHERIC ADMIN, as of 2004; Adj prof, Univ Calif, Santa Barbara, 1989-; RES OCEANOGR, MARINE SCI INST, UNIV CALIF, SANTA BARBARA, 1989-; assoc res oceanogr, Marine Sci Inst, Univ Calif, Santa Barbara, 1981-1989; adj assoc prof geol, Univ Calif, Santa Barbara, 1981-1989; cruise coordr res vessel, Melville Vulcan Exped, Scripps Inst Oceanog, 1980-1981; asst res physicist, Scripps Inst Oceanog, 1973-1981. **Memberships:** Am Geophys Union. **Research Statement & Publications:** Application of helium and rare gas isotopes to ocean circulation studies; geothermal and volcanic gases; outgassing of mantle volatiles; numerical modeling of ocean tracer distributions. **Mailing Address:** Pac Marine Environ Lab, Hatfield Marine Sci Ctr, Nat Oceanic Atmospheric Admin, 2115 S E OSU Dr, Newport, OR 97365. **Fax:** 541-867-3907. **E-Mail:** john.e.lupton@noaa.gov

LUPTON, WILLIAM HAMILTON, PLASMA PHYSICS, ELECTRICAL ENGINEERING. **Personal Data:** b Charlottesville, Va, July 25, 1930. **Education:** Univ Va, BA, 1950; Univ Md, PhD (physics), 1960. **Professional Experience:** RETIRED; sr scientist, Jaycor, 1985-1992; Physicist, Radio Div, Nat Bur Stand, 1952-1955 & Plasma Physics Div, US Naval Res Lab, 1960-1985. **Memberships:** Sigma Xi. **Research Statement & Publications:** Plasma spectroscopy; high voltage and high current pulse technology; high power laser development. **Mailing Address:** 16509 Montecrest Lane, Gaithersburg, MD 20878-2163.

LUQI,, RAPID PROTOTYPING, REAL-TIME SYSTEMS. **Personal Data:** b Shanghai, China, May 4, 1949; m 1985, c 1. **Education:** Jilin Univ, China, BS, 1975; Univ Minn, MS, 1984, PhD (computer sci), 1986. **Honors & Awards:** Menneken Fac Award Excellence, 1991. **Professional Experience:** PROF, COMPUT SCI DEPT, NAVAL POSTGRAD SCH, 1995-; NSF presidential young investr award, 1990; mem, Prog Comt Syst Design & Network Conf, Inst Elec & Electronics Engrs, 1989 & 1990; from asst prof to assoc prof, Comput Sci Dept, Naval Postgrad Sch, 1986-1995; adj asst prof, Comput Sci Dept, Univ Minn, 1986-1990; mem tech staff, Int Software Systs, Inc, 1984-1985; teaching res & proj asst, Comput Sci Dept, Univ Minn, 1981-1986; Asst researcher, Sci Acad China, Peking, 1975-1980; assoc ed, J Systs Integration & Software Design & Process World, Inst Elec & Electronics Engrs; first & second Int Conf Systs Integration, Inst Elec & Electronics Engrs/Asn Comput Mach; tech consult, Int Software Systs, Inc & Honeywell Res Ctr; prin investr, NSF, Dept Navy, Army & Air Force Off Scientific Res. **Memberships:** Inst Elec & Electronics Engrs; Inst Elec & Electronics Engrs Comput Soc; Asn Comput Mach. **Research Statement & Publications:** Computer aided software engineering; designs computer languages and computer support for software automation; rapid prototyping methodology and tools; author of numerous publications and books. **Mailing Address:** Dept Comput Sci, Naval Postgrad Sch, 833 Dyer Rd, Monterey, CA 93943. **Fax:** 831-656-2189. **E-Mail:** luqi@nps.edu

LUQUET, LIDIA R, MATHEMATICS. **Education:** Cornell Univ, PhD, 1972. **Professional Experience:** FAC, DEPT MATH & COMPUT SCI, ST MARY'S COL, CA, as of 2006. **Mailing Address:** St Mary's Col, PO Box 3556, Moraga, CA 94575-3556. **Fax:** 925-376-4027. **E-Mail:** lluquet@stmarys-ca.edu

LURA, RICHARD DEAN, PHYSICAL ORGANIC CHEMISTRY. **Personal Data:** b Kenosha, Wis, August 21, 1945; m 1968. **Education:** Univ Wis, BS, 1967; Iowa State Univ, PhD (chem), 1971. **Professional Experience:** PROF CHEM, MILLIGAN COL, as of 2003; CHMN SCI LEARNING, MILLIGAN COL, as of 2003; assoc prof chem, Milligan Col, beginning 1980; consult, R I Schattner Co, 1972-1979; asst prof, Milligan Col, 1971-1980. **Research Statement & Publications:** Research and devleopment of germicidal and sporicidal solutions for hospital and home use. **Mailing Address:** Dept Chem Milligan Col Univ, PO Box 500, Milligan Col, TN 37682. **E-Mail:** rdlura@milligan.edu

LURAIN, JOHN ROBERT, III, GYNECOLOGIC ONCOLOGY. **Personal Data:** b Princeton, Ill, October 27, 1946; m 1969, Nell; c Alice & Kathryn. **Education:** Oberlin Col, AB, 1968; Univ NC, MD, 1972. **Honors & Awards:** Purdue-Frederick Award, Am Col Obstet Gynec, 1983. **Professional Experience:** PROF OBSTET-GYNEC, SCH MED, NORTHWESTERN UNIV, 1989-; dir, Div Gynec Oncol, Prentice Women's Hosp, Sch Med, Northwestern Univ, 1985-; jr fac fel, Am Cancer Soc, 1980-1983; dir, John I Brewer Trophoblastic Dis Ctr, 1979-; from asst prof to assoc prof, Sch Med, Northwestern Univ, 1979-1988; fel gynec oncol, Roswell Park Cancer Inst, 1977-1979; clin fel, Am Cancer Soc, 1977-1979; lieutenant comdr, med corps, USNR, Naval Regional Med Ctr, Portsmouth, Va, 1975-1977; galloway fel, Mem Sloan Kettering Cancer Ctr, 1975; resident obstet-gynec, Magee Womens Hosp, Univ Pittsburgh, 1972-1975. **Memberships:** Soc Gynec Oncologists; Am Soc Clin Oncol; Am Soc Colposcopy & Cervical Path; Am Col Obstetricians & Gynecologists. **Research Statement & Publications:** Gestational trophoblasic disease; endometrial cancer; cervical cancer; laser therapy; hormone receptors; chemotherapy and surgery; ovarian cancer. **Mailing Address:** Northwestern Univ Med Sch, Practice Womens Hosp, 333 E Superior St, Chicago, IL 60611. **Fax:** 312-695-6870. **E-Mail:** jlurain@nmh.org

LURCH, E(DWARD) NORMAN, ELECTRICAL ENGINEERING. **Personal Data:** b Morristown, NJ, December 23, 1919; m 1941, c 4. **Education:** NY Univ, BEE, 1940, MEE, 1943. **Professional Experience:** PROF ELECTRONICS, STATE UNIV NY AGR & TECH COL, FARMINGDALE, 1966-; assoc prof, State Univ NY Agr & Tech Col, Farmingdale, 1965-1966; aerospace technologist, Goddard Space Flight Ctr, NASA, 1962-1965; chief engr, Chemtronics, Inc, 1960-1961; Lectr grad div, State Univ NY Col, New Paltz, 1958-1961; consult engr, Oil Heat Inst, Long Island, 1957-1959; assoc prof electronics, State Univ NY Agr & Tech Col, Farmingdale, 1949-1960; asst prof, Clarkson Col Technol, 1948-1949; asst prof, Univ Fla, 1947; instr, Manhattan Col, 1943-1947; Tutor elec eng, City Col New York, 1941-1943. **Research Statement & Publications:** Fundamentals of electronics; electric circuits. **Mailing Address:** 11 Black Duck Dr, Stony Brook, NY 11790.

LURIA, S(AUL) M(ARTIN), PHYSIOLOGICAL PSYCHOLOGY. **Personal Data:** b Athol, Mass, December 24, 1929; m 1963, c 2. **Education:** Univ Richmond, BS, 1949; Univ Pa, MA, 1951, PhD (psychol), 1955. **Professional Experience:** HEAD, DEPT VISION, US NAVAL SUBMARINE MED CTR, 1983-; Univ Conn, 1968-1970 & Univ New Haven, 1971-1990; lectr, Univ RI, beginning 1966; res psychologist, Vision Dept, US Naval Submarine Med Ctr, 1957-1983. **Memberships:** Fel AAAS; fel Am Psychol Asn; fel Optical Soc Am; Psychonomic Soc; fel NY Acad Sci. **Research Statement & Publications:** Vision. **Mailing Address:** Naval Submarine Med Res Lab, PO Box 900, Groton, CT 06349-5900. **Fax:** 860-694-4809.

LURIE, ALAN GORDON, RADIATION BIOLOGY, CARCINOGENESIS. **Personal Data:** b Los Angeles, Calif, April 23, 1946; m 1969, c 2. **Education:** Univ Calif, Los Angeles, DDS, 1970; Univ Rochester, PhD (radiation biol, biophys), 1974. **Honors & Awards:** E H Hatton Award, Int Asn Dent Res, 1969. **Professional Experience:** PROF & HEAD ORAL & MAXILLOFACIAL RADIOL, UNIV CONN HEALTH CTR, as of 2005; assoc prof oral diag, Univ Conn Health Ctr, beginning 1977; asst prof oral diag, Univ Conn Health Ctr, 1977; HEW/NIH grants, Am Cancer Soc, 1975-; Consult oral radiol, Newington Vet Admin Hosp, 1975-; Asst prof oral radiol, Univ Conn Health Ctr, 1973-1977. **Memberships:** Am Asn Cancer Res; Radiation Res Soc; Int Asn Dent Res. **Research Statement & Publications:** Radiation pathophysiology; radiation carcinogenesis and cocarcinogenesis at low doses; chemical carcinogenesis; mechanistic roles of vascular changes during carcinogenesis. **Mailing Address:** Dept Oral Radiol, Univ Conn Health Ctr, 263 Farmington Ave, Farmington, CT 06030-1605. **E-Mail:** lurie@nso.uchc.edu

LURIE, ARNOLD PAUL, ORGANIC CHEMISTRY. **Personal Data:** b Brooklyn, NY, July 22, 1932; m 1954, c 3. **Education:** NY Univ, BA, 1954; Purdue Univ, PhD (org chem), 1958. **Professional Experience:** RETIRED; res assoc, Res Lab, 1966-1989; info scientist, Res Lab, 1965-1989; sr res chemist, Eastman Kodak Co, 1961-1966; res chemist, Eastman Kodak Co, 1958-1961; fel, Purdue Univ, 1958; lab asst org chem, Purdue Univ, 1954-1956. **Memberships:** Am Chem Soc. **Research Statement & Publications:** Synthetic and theoretical organic chemistry related to photographic systems; computerized handling of information. **Mailing Address:** 4380 Camrose Lane, West Palm Beach, FL 33417.

LURIE, FRED MARCUS, PHYSICS. **Personal Data:** b Boston, Mass, November 16, 1930. **Education:** Univ NC, ChapelHill, BS, 1952; Univ Ill, Urbana, MS, 1957, PhD, 1963. **Professional Experience:** ASSOC PROF EMER PHYSICS, IND UNIV, as of 2005; assoc prof physics, Ind Univ, Bloomington, beginning 1970; asst prof, Ind Univ, Bloomington, 1967-1970; from instr to asst prof, Univ Pa, 1963-1967; teaching asst physics, Univ Ill, Urbana, 1957-1959. **Memberships:** Am Phys Soc. **Mailing Address:** Dept Physics, Ind Univ, 727 E Third St, Bloomington, IN 47405-7105. **Fax:** 812-855-5533.

LURIE, JOAN B, THEORETICAL SOLID STATE PHYSICS. **Personal Data:** b New York, NY, January 21, 1941; m 1961, c 2. **Education:** Brooklyn Col, BS, 1961; Rutgers Univ, MS, 1962, PhD (physics), 1967. **Professional Experience:** ADVAN SYSTS MGR, SPACE & TECHNOL GROUP, TRW, 1991-; prin scientist, Mitre Corp, 1989-1990; dept mgr, Hughes, 1984-1989; mem res staff, IDA, NJ, 1981-1984; from asst prof to assoc prof physics, Rider Col, 1972-1981; fel solid state physics, Rutgers Univ, 1970-1972; syst programmer comput sci, Appl Data Res, 1969-1970; fel appl math, Univ Col, Univ London, 1967-1968; Mem tech staff physics res, RCA Labs, 1962-1966; Am Phys Soc indust fel, Colgate Palmolive Res Lab. **Memberships:** Am Phys Soc; Inst Elec & Electronics Engrs. **Research Statement & Publications:** Theoretical research in lattice dynamics of solid state of rare gases; computer assisted instruction, particularly in physics and mathematics; image analysis. **Mailing Address:** Div Space & Technol, TRW Inc, Hermosa Beach, CA 90254.

LURIE, NORMAN A(LAN), NUCLEAR PHYSICS & ENGINEERING, ELECTROOPTICS. **Personal Data:** b Detroit, Mich, December 2, 1940; m 1967, c 2. **Education:** Univ Mich, BSE, 1963, MSE, 1965, PhD (nuclear eng), 1969. **Professional Experience:** VPRES & DIV MGR, ELECTRONIC VISION SYST DIV, SCI APPLICATIONS INT CORP, 1989-; SR SCIENTIST, SCI APPLICATIONS INT CORP, 1987-; mgr tech pers, Nuclear Systs Div, 1981-1986; prog mgr res, Nuclear Systs Div, 1978-1981; prin physicist, Nuclear Systs Div, 1976-1986; staff physicist, IRT Corp, 1975-1976; sr physicist, IRT Corp, 1974-1975; sr res assoc, Brandeis Univ, 1971-1974; res collabr, Brookhaven Nat Lab, 1971-1974; fel physics, Univ Mo-Columbia, 1969-1971. **Memberships:** Sigma Xi. **Research Statement & Publications:** Applied nuclear physics; electrooptics. **Mailing Address:** Sci Appl Int Corp, 10436 El Comal Dr, San Diego, CA 92124-1005.

LURIE, ROBERT MANDEL, CHEMICAL ENGINEERING, COLLOIDAL CHEMISTRY. **Personal Data:** b Boston, Mass, February 24, 1931; m 1953, c 3. **Education:** Mass Inst Technol, SB, 1952, ScD(chem eng), 1955. **Professional Experience:** RETIRED; pres, Nyacol Prod Inc, 1970-1989; dir mats, Systs Div, 1965-1970; mgr mat develop, Res & Adv Develop Div, Avco Corp, 1963-1965; sr chem engr, Ionics Inc, 1960-1963; chem engr & prod res mgr, Dewey & Almy Chem Co Div, W R Grace & Co, 1955-1960. **Memberships:** Am Chem Soc; Am Inst Chem Engrs; Sigma Xi; AAAS. **Research Statement & Publications:** Polymer synthesis; adhesion of polymers; unit operations of polymer manufacture and polymer fabrications; electrochemistry; fuel cells; ablation phenomena; physics of reinforced plastics; reentry vehicle design; organic dyes; colloidal chemicals. **Mailing Address:** Four Tufts Rd, Lexington, MA 02173.

LURIX, PAUL LESLIE, INFRARED SPECTROSCOPY, DATA BASE APPLICATIONS. **Personal Data:** b Bridgeport, Conn, April 6, 1949; m 1970, Cynthia; c Paul Christopher, Alexander Tristan & Einar Gabrielson. **Education:** Drew Univ, BA, 1971; Purdue Univ, MS, 1973. **Professional Experience:** Baylor Col med 2000-; consult, Phillips 1966, 1986-; Compaq Comput, 1996-; consult, Conoco Inc, 1987-; PRES, LURIX CORP, 1982-; vpres, Tex Labs Inc, 1980-1982; vpres, Diesel King Corp, 1980-1982; Consult, 1977-1982; chief chemist, Caleb Brett USA Inc, 1977-1980; tech dir, Analysts Inc, 1976-1977; Phillips, 1966. **Memberships:** Fel Am Inst Chemists; Am Chem Soc; Am Soc Testing & Mat; Soc Appl Spectros; NY Acad Sci; AAAS. **Research Statement & Publications:** Design and implementation of multi user information systems; studies of liquid structure through infrared spectroscopy; granted one patent. **Mailing Address:** PO Box 148, Fulshear, TX 77441. **Fax:** 281-346-1607. **E-Mail:** paul@lurix.com

LURKIS, ALEXANDER, ENGINEERING EXPERT IN POWER & LIGHTING. **Personal Data:** b New York, NY, October 1, 1908; m 1930, c Jeffrey Lowell Lurkis (deceased). **Education:** Cooper Union, BSEE, 1930; NY Univ, BSEE, 1934; Univ State NY, Tech Teacher Cert, 1936. **Honors & Awards:** Design Excellence, Fifth Biennial Am Iron & Steel Inst, 1972; Design Excellence, Fifth Biennial HUD Award, 1972. **Professional Experience:** Pres, Icare Press, 1981-1985; secy-treas, Glimmer Security Systs, 1976-1981; chmn, Illuminating Eng Soc Energy Comt, 1974-1977; CONSULT ENGR, ALEXANDER LURKIS, PE, 1964-; arbitrator, Am Arbitration Asn, 1964-; pres consult engrs, Alexander Lurkis, Pe, 1964-1990; act comm, Bur Gas & Elec, New York City Dept Water, Gas & Elec, 1961; chief eng, Bur Gas & Elec, New York City Dept Water, Gas & Elec, 1959-1964; Vpres, Peak Tech Asn, 1951-1959; sr elec engr, New York City Bd Transp & Transit Authority, 1942-1958; elec engr, F R Harris, Inc, consult engrs, 1940-1941; Jr elec engr, New York City Bd Transp & Transit Authority, 1930-1940. **Memberships:** Fel Illuminating Eng Soc; sr mem Inst Elec & Electronics Engrs; fel NY Acad Sci. **Research Statement & Publications:** Ten utility standard US patents; 1 Canadian standard patent; 1 traffic signal US patent; 1 US patent for museum security; Non-Fiction Book, "The Power Brink"' Novel "A Serpent At Her Breast". **Mailing Address:** 193-12 Nero Ave, Jamaica, NY 11423.

LURYI, SERGE, PHYSICS OF SEMICONDUCTOR DEVICES. **Personal Data:** b Leningrad, USSR, October 9, 1947; Canadian & American citizen; m 1982, Nadia; c Helen, Nathan & Alex. **Education:** Univ Leningrad, USSR, dipl physics, 1971; Univ Toronto, Can, MS, 1975, PhD (physics), 1978. **Professional Experience:** DIR, CTR ADVAN TECHNOL SENSOR SYSTS, 1998-; DISTINGUISHED PROF & CHMN, DEPT ELEC & COMPUT ENG, STATE UNIV NY, STONY BROOK, 1994-; distinguished mem tech staff 1990-1994; ed, Inst Elec & Electronic Engrs Trans Elec Devices, 1986-1990; supvr, AT&T Bell Labs, 1985-1990; mem tech staff, AT&T Bell Labs, 1980-1985; fel, Univ Toronto, 1978-1980; res engr, VNIIG, Leningrad, 1971-1973. **Memberships:** Fel Inst Elec & Electronic Engrs; fel Am Phys Soc; fel Inst Elec & Electronics Engrs. **Research Statement & Publications:** Physics of exploratory semiconductor devices; Inventor of new semiconductor devices and technologies. **Mailing Address:** Dept Elec & Comput Eng State Univ NY, Stony Brook, NY 11794-2350. **Fax:** 63-632-8494. **E-Mail:** Serge.Luryi@StonyBrook.edu

LUSAS, EDMUND W, FOOD SCIENCE, FOOD TECHNOLOGY & FEEDS PROCESSING. **Personal Data:** b Woodbury, Conn, November 25, 1931; m 1957, c 3. **Education:** Univ Conn, BS, 1954; Iowa State Univ, MS, 1955; Univ Wis, PhD (food technol), 1958; Univ Chicago, MBA, 1972. **Professional Experience:** RETIRED; head Fats, Oils & Extrusion Progs, Tex A&M Univ, beginning 1993; dir, Food Protein Res & Develop Ctr, 1978-1993; mgr sci serv, Res Labs, Quaker Oats Co, 1972-1977; mgr pet foods res, Res Labs, Quaker Oats Co, 1966-1972; mgr canned foods res, Res Labs, Quaker Oats Co, 1964-1966; proj leader, Res Labs, Quaker Oats Co, 1958-1964. **Memberships:** Sigma Xi; Inst Food Technol; Am Chem Soc; Am Oil Chemists Soc; Am Cereal Chem Asn; Am Soc Agr Engr. **Research Statement & Publications:** Protein and oil utilization from cottonseed, peanuts, soy, sunflower and sesame; development of processes for converting crops into food, feed and industrial ingredients; human and pet food development; research and development administration; technical staff services management. **Mailing Address:** Food Protein Res & Develop Ctr, Tex A&M Univ, Col Sta, TX 77843-2476. **Fax:** 979-845-2744.

LUSCHER, ULRICH, ARCTIC ENGINEERING, HAZARDOUS WASTE ENGINEERING. **Personal Data:** b Oftringen, Switz, July 18, 1932; m 1983, Joanne; c Mark E & Dan R. **Education:** Swiss Fed Inst Technol, BS, 1956; Mass Inst Technol, SM, 1959, ScD(civil eng & soil mech), 1963. **Professional Experience:** BD DIRS, VICE CHMN, ALAMEDA CTR ENVIRON TECHNOLOGIES, as of 2004; SR CONSULT, WOODWARD-CLYDE CONSULTS, as of 2004; prin mem, Woodward-Clyde Consults, beginning 1975; mem staff, Woodward-clyde Consults, 1967-1974; asst prof civil eng, Mass Inst Technol, 1963-1967; res engr, Mass Inst Technol, 1959-1960; Designer, Vevey Metal Works, Switz, 1957 & Stone & Webster Eng Corp, 1958-1959. **Memberships:** Am Soc Civil Engrs; Int Soc Soil Mech & Found Eng; Am Consult Engrs; Soc Am Mil Engrs. **Research Statement & Publications:** Soil mechanics and foundation engineering; research in soil mechanics; underground structures; permafrost and arctic engineering; remediation technologies. **Mailing Address:** Alameda Ctr Environ Technologies Corp, 851, W Midway Ave, Bldg 7, Alameda Pt, Alameda, CA 94501-5085. **Fax:** 510-749-6862.

LUSCINSKAS, FRANCIS W, MEDICAL RESEARCH. **Education:** Boston Univ Sch Med, PhD (biochem), 1986. **Professional Experience:** RES ASSOC, DEPT PATH, BRIGHAM & WOMEN'S HOSP, as of 2005; ASSOC PROF PATH, HARVARD MED SCH, as of 2005. **Mailing Address:** Dept Pathol Brigham & Women's Hosp, LMRC Bldg Rm 401a 221 Longwood Ave, Boston, MA 02115. **Fax:** 617-732-5933. **E-Mail:** fluscinskas@rics.bwh.harvard.edu

LUSHBOUGH, CHANNING HARDEN, NUTRITION, RESOURCE MANAGEMENT. **Personal Data:** b Watertown, SDak, August 11, 1929; m 1952, Eloise H Turner; c 4. **Education:** Univ Chicago, AB, 1948, AM, 1952, PhD (nutrit, biochem), 1956. **Professional Experience:** DIR, MHJ TRUST, 1997-; mkt rep, Round Hill Asset Mgt Inc, 1986-1994; mkt rep, Tweedy, Browne Inc, 1981-1984; vpres qual assurance, Kraft Inc, 1975-1981; dir & exec secy, Citizens Comn on Science, Law & Food Supply, Rockefeller Univ, 1973-1975; assoc dir, Consumers Union US, 1971-1973; vpres planning & develop, Blue Cross, NY, 1967-1971; dir prod info, Res Ctr, Mead Johnson & Co, Ind, 1959-1967; lectr, Univ Chicago, 1957-1959 & Northwestern Univ, 1958-1959; assoc biochemist & actg chief, Div Biochem & Nutrit, Am Meat Inst Found, Ill, 1956-1959; Instr grad nutrit, Ill Inst Technol, 1956; Res chemist, Res Lab, Carnation Co, Wis, 1950-1951. **Memberships:** AAAS; NY Acad Sci; Sigma Xi. **Research Statement & Publications:** Nutritional quality of natural proteins; effects of processing on vitamin retention; relations of dietary fat, protein and carbohydrate to atherosclerosis. **Mailing Address:** 420 Elm St, Glenview, IL 60025-4949.

LUSHER, JEANNE MARIE, BLOOD COAGULATION, PLATELET DISORDERS. **Personal Data:** b Toledo, Ohio, June 9, 1935. **Education:** Univ Cincinnati, BS, 1956, MD, 1960. **Honors & Awards:** Marion I Barnhart Hemostasis Res Prof, Wayne State Univ, 1988; Lawrence Weiner Award, Wayne State Univ, Sch Med, 1990; Kenneth Brinkhous Award, Nat Hemophilia Found, 1993. **Professional Experience:** PRES ACAD & DISTINGUISHED PROF PEDIAT, WAYNE STATE UNIV, as of 2003; chmn, Int Soc Thrombosis & Hemostasis Sci & Stand Comt, beginning 1996; chmn, med sci adv coun, Nat Hemmophilia Found, beginning 1994; med dir, Nat Hemophilia Found, 1987-1994; mem res manpower comt, NIH, 1987-1991; DIR, DIV HEMAT & ONCOL, CHILDREN'S HOSP MICH, 1984-; mem hemat study sect, NIH, 1981-1986; prof pediat, Wayne state Univ, beginning 1974; fel hemat-oncol, Child Res Ctr Mich & Wash Univ Sch Med, 1964-1966; residency pediat, Tulane Univ Charity Hosp La, 1961-1964; internship, George Wash Univ Hosp, 1960-1961. **Memberships:** Int Soc Thrombois Hemostasis; Am Soc Hemat; Soc Pediat Res; Am Soc Pediat Hemat-Oncol. **Research Statement & Publications:** Hemostasis and in blood product safety; studying mechanism of inhibitor antibody development against clotting factors; alternatives to use of blood products for control of bleeding, role of DDAVP formulations. **Mailing Address:** Childrens Hosp Mich, 3901 Beaubien Blvd, Detroit, MI 48201. **Fax:** 313-745-5237. **E-Mail:** jlusher@med.wayne.edu

LUSIGNAN, BRUCE BURR, ELECTRICAL ENGINEERING. **Personal Data:** b San Francisco, Calif, December 22, 1936; m 1985, Eleanor; c Jeanne, Kerry, Anne (Hausch), Coleen Curtin, Noreen Curtin & Stephanie Curtin. **Education:** Stanford Univ, BS, 1958, MS, 1959, PhD (elec eng), 1963. **Professional Experience:** DIR, COMMUN SATELLITE PLANNING CTR & CTR INT COOP SPACE COMMUN & NETWORKS, GROUND STA ENG & DIGITAL & PHOTONIC SWITCH SYST, STANFORD UNIV, as of 2005; ASSOC PROF ELEC ENG, STANFORD UNIV, 1968-; asst prof, Stanford Univ, 1965-1968; actg asst prof, Stanford Univ, 1963-1965; res asst, Stanford Univ, 1962-1964; Instr, Stanford Univ, 1962-1963. **Research Statement & Publications:** Applications of satellite, radio, fiber optics and digital technology to communications; transfer of planning and manufacturing knowledge to developing countries; Mars exploration; international space exploration policy. **Mailing Address:** Dept Elect, Stanford Univ, 237 Packard Elec Eng Bldg, 350 Serra Mall, Stanford, CA 94305-9510. **Fax:** 650-724-4798. **E-Mail:** lusignan@ee.stanford.edu

LUSIS, ALDONS JEKABS, MOLECULAR BIOLOGY. **Personal Data:** b Esslingen, Ger, June 22, 1947; American citizen. **Education:** Wash State Univ, BS, 1969; Ore State Univ, PhD (biochem), 1973. **Professional Experience:** PROF, DEPT MED, MICROBIOL & MOLECULAR GENETICS, UNIV CALIF, as of 2003; NIH fel, 1974-; Res assoc molecular biol, Roswell Park Mem Inst, 1973-1980. **Memberships:** Sigma Xi. **Research Statement & Publications:** Mechanisms controlling developmental expression of enzymes in mammals; processing of mouse lysosomal enzymes; Molecular genetics of atherosclerosis. **Mailing Address:** Dept Med Sch Med Univ Calif, 10833 LeConte Ave 47-123 Ctr Health Sci, Los Angeles, CA 90095-1679. **Fax:** 310-794-7345. **E-Mail:** jlusis@mednet.ucla.edu

LUSK, JOAN EDITH, BIOCHEMISTRY. **Personal Data:** b Teaneck, NJ, July 29, 1942. **Education:** Radcliffe Col, BA, 1964; Harvard Univ, PhD (biol chem), 1970. **Professional Experience:** ASSOC DEAN, GRAD SCH, BROWN UNIV, as of 2002; Assoc Prof Chem, Brown Univ, beginning 1977; NIH career develop award, 1976; Prin investr, NIH res grant, 1973- & NSF grant, beginning 1974; asst prof, Brown Univ, 1972-1977; Nat Cystic Fibrosis Res Found fel biol, NIH fel biol, 1971-1972; Nat Cystic Fibrosis Res Found fel biol, Mass Inst Technol, 1970-1971. **Memberships:** Am Soc Microbiol; AAAS. **Research Statement & Publications:** Membrane structure and function; colicin action; transport. **Mailing Address:** Assoc Dean Grad Sch, Brown Univ, Box 1867 42 Charlesfield St, Providence, RI 02912. **Fax:** 401-863-7341. **E-Mail:** joan_lusk@brown.edu

LUSK, MARK THOMAS, PHASE TRANSITION KINETICS, EVOLVING MICROSTRUCTURES. **Education:** US Naval Acad, BS, 1982; Colo State Univ, MS, 1988; Calif Inst Technol, PhD (appl mech), 1992. **Honors & Awards:** Career award, NSF, 1995. **Professional Experience:** CHMN, DEPT MECH ENG, COLO SCH MINES, as of 2004; HEAD, ENG SYST GRAD PROG, COLO SCH MINES, as of 2004; ASSOC PROF MECH & MAT, COLO SCH MINES, 1998-; Career award, NSF, 1995; asst prof eng, Colo Sch Mines, 1994-1997; Asst prof elec eng, Iowa State Univ, 1992-1994; nuclear eng, US Navy, 1984-1987. **Mailing Address:** Div Eng, Colo Sch Mines, BB326/328D, Golden, CO 80401. **Fax:** 303-273-3602. **E-Mail:** mlusk@mines.edu

LUSKEY, KENNETH L, DIABETES. **Professional Experience:** VPRES MED AFFAIRS, METABOLEX INC, 2000-. **Mailing Address:** Metabolex, Inc, 3876 Bay Ctr Pl, Hayward, CA 94545. **Fax:** 510-293-9090.

LUSKIN, MITCHELL B, NUMERICAL ANALYSIS, PARTIAL DIFFERENTIAL EQUATIONS. **Personal Data:** b Pasadena, Calif, November 13, 1951; m 1976, Barbara Roth; c Jonathan, Marlise & Benjamin. **Education:** Yale Univ, BS, 1973; Univ Chicago, MS, 1974, PhD (math), 1977. **Honors & Awards:** Presidential Young Investr Award, 1984; Invited Lect, Intnl Congress of Maths, 2002. **Professional Experience:** Ed, J Comp Physics, 1997-1999-; PROF MATH, UNIV MINN, 1990-; ed-in-chief, Soc Indust & Appl Math J Numerical Anal, 1990-1995; prof appl math, Calif Inst Technol, 1989-1990; ed, Dynamics & Differential Equations, 1988-; mem grad fac, Dept Aerospace Eng & Mech, 1987-; fel, Minn Supercomputer Inst, 1985-; ed, Soc Indust & Appl Math J Numerical Anal, 1982-1990; from asst prof to prof, Univ Minn, 1981-1989; vis mem, Courant Inst, NY Univ, 1980-1981; Vis prof, Ecole Polytechnique Federale, Lausanne, Switz, 1980; asst prof, Univ Mich, 1979-1981; Hildebrandt asst prof math, Univ Mich, 1977-1979. **Memberships:** Soc Indust & Appl Math. **Research Statement & Publications:** Scientific computing; numerical analysis; applied mathematics; partial differential equations; computational mechanics. **Mailing Address:** Sch Math, Univ Minn 206 Church St SE, Minneapolis, MN 55455. **Fax:** 612-626-2017. **E-Mail:** luskin@math.umn.edu

LUSS, DAN, CHEMICAL REACTION ENGINEERING. **Personal Data:** b Tel Aviv, Israel, May 5, 1938; American citizen; m 1966, Amalia; c Noya & Limor. **Education:** Israel Inst Technol, BSc, 1960, MSc, 1963; Univ Minn, Minneapolis, PhD (chem eng), 1966. **Honors & Awards:** Honor Scroll Award, Indust & Eng Div, Am Chem Soc, 1969; A P Colburn Award, Am Inst Chem Engrs, 1972; Curtis W McGraw Res Award, Am Soc Eng Educ, 1977; Prof Progress Award, Am Inst Chem Engrs, 1979; Wilhelm Award, Am Inst Chem Engrs, 1986. **Professional Experience:** INTERIM CHAIR, DEPT CHEM ENG, UNIV HOUSTON, as of 2006; Dir, Am Inst Chem Engrs, 1986-1988; chmn, dept chem eng, Univ Houston, 1975-1985; PROF CHEM ENG, UNIV HOUSTON, 1972-; from asst prof to assoc prof, Univ Houston, 1967-1972; Asst prof chem eng, Univ Minn, 1966-1967. **Memberships:** Nat Acad Eng; Am Chem Soc; fel Am Inst Chem Engrs. **Research Statement & Publications:** Dynamics of chemical reactors; diffusional effects in catalysts; lumping of complex reactions networks; synthesis of superconducting ceramics; production of synthesis gas in membrane reactors. **Mailing Address:** Dept Chem Eng, Univ Houston, 4800 Calhoun Ave S224, Houston, TX 77204-4004. **Fax:** 713-743-4323. **E-Mail:** dluss@uh.edu

LUSSIER, ANDRE (JOSEPH ALFRED), INTERNAL MEDICINE, RHEUMATOLOGY. **Personal Data:** b Sherbrooke, Que, May 27, 1933; m 1961, c 3. **Education:** Univ Montreal, BA, 1954, MD, 1959; Col Med, Que, cert internal med, 1964 & cert rheumatology, 1970; Royal Col Physicians & Surgeons, cert internal med, 1965; FCRCP(C), 1972. **Honors & Awards:** Basic Res Prize, Asn Fr Lang Physicians Can. **Professional Experience:** Mem, Med Res Coun Can, beginning 1988; dir, Clin Res Ctr, 1980-1984; PROF MED, UNIV SHERBROOKE & UNIV HOSP CTR, 1975-; dir, Rheumatic Dis Unit, Univ Sherbrooke, 1969-1984; Assoc clin res, Can Arthritis Soc, 1969-1979; assoc prof med, Rheumatic Dis Unit, Univ Sherbrooke, 1969-1975. **Memberships:** Am Rheumatism Asn; Royal Col Med; Can Rheumatism Asn (secy 1981-1984 & vpres 1984-1986 pres 1986-1988); Pan Am League Against Rheumatism (vpres 1982-1986); Can Soc Clin Invest; hon mem Fr Soc Rheumatology. **Research Statement & Publications:** Etiopathogenesis and pathological ossification of the spine; mechanism of microcrystal arthritides; normalization of terminology used in semiology of musculoskeletal system; efficacy and toxicity of non steroidal antiinflammatory drugs, especially of the consecutive gastro-intestinal microbleeding; hyperostotic disease: basic and clin research (pathogenesis). **Mailing Address:** Dept Med Rheumatol, Univ Sherbrooke, Sherbrooke, PQ J1H 5N4, Can. **Fax:** 819-564-5265.

LUSSIER, GILLES L, VETERINARY PATHOLOGY, VIROLOGY. **Personal Data:** b St Charles, Que, October 5, 1934; m 1957, c 2. **Education:** Univ Montreal, BA, 1955, DVM, 1959; Univ Toronto, MSc, 1961, Univ Sask, PhD (path), 1973. **Professional Experience:** RETIRED; prof path & virol, Res Ctr, 1983-1990; head virol, Res Ctr, 1975-1983; from res asst to res assoc, Armand-Frappier Inst, 1961-1974. **Memberships:** Can Vet Med Asn; Can Soc Microbiologists; Can Asn Lab Animal Sci; Can Asn Vet Pathologists; Am Asn Lab Animal Sci. **Research Statement & Publications:** Comparative pathology of viral diseases and viral vaccines; diagnosis of viral diseases of laboratory animals. **Mailing Address:** 10145 Fabre, Montreal, PQ H3C 3E1, Can.

LUSSIER, ROGER JEAN, SYNTHETIC INORGANIC & ORGANOMETALLIC CHEMISTRY. **Personal Data:** b Newport, RI, April 29, 1943. **Education:** Univ Mass, Amherst, BS, 1965; Brown Univ, PhD (inorg chem), 1969; Johns Hopkins Univ, MA, 1975. **Professional Experience:** R & D fel, 2002; sen res assoc, 1994-2001; ENG SPECIALIST, DAVISON DIV, W R GRACE & CO, 1985-; res assoc, Davison Div, W R Grace & CO, 1981-1984; sr res chemist, Davison Div, W R Grace & CO, 1980-1982; res chemist, Davison Div, W R Grace & CO, 1970-1980; NSF grant, Cath Univ Am, 1969-1970. **Memberships:** Am Chem Soc. **Research Statement & Publications:** Heterogeneous catalysis; reaction mechanisms; homogeneous catalysis; transition metal chemistry; surface chemistry; mineral synthesis and chemistry; zeolite synthesis and characterization. **Mailing Address:** Davison Tech Ctr, W R Grace & Co, 7500 Grace Dr 5603 Chem Rd, Columbia, MD 21044-4098. **Fax:** 410-531-4695. **E-Mail:** roger.lussier@grace.com

LUSSKIN, ROBERT MILLER, ORGANIC CHEMISTRY. **Personal Data:** b December 14, 1921; m 1947, c 2. **Education:** Harvard Univ, AB, 1943; NY Univ, MS, 1946, PhD (chem), 1950. **Professional Experience:** RETIRED; adj prof chem, Univ Mo, St Louis, 1987; dir, Cent Res & Develop, Ralston Purina Co, 1982-1986; dir tech serv, Raltech Sci Serv, 1977-1982; tech dir, Resource Planning Assocs, 1975-1977; mgr new concepts res, Kimberly-Clark Corp, Wis, 1972-1975; mgr basic & explor res, Kimberly-Clark Corp, Wis, 1968-1972; supt nonwoven lab, Kimberly-Clark Corp, Wis, 1967-1968; dir chem res, UOP Chem Co, Universal Oil Prod Co, 1960-1967; res dir, Trubek Labs, 1956-1960, chemist, 1947-1955; chemist, Grosvenor Labs, 1945-1946; chemist, Spencer Kellogg & Sons, 1943. **Memberships:** AAAS; Am Chem Soc. **Research Statement & Publications:** Business strategy development; consumer new products; polymer and fiber research; chemical intermediates; energy and materials management; analytical and environmental chemistry management. **Mailing Address:** 12856 Hawthicket Lane, Des Peres, MO 63131.

LUSTER, MICHAEL I, IMMUNOTOXICOLOGY. **Personal Data:** b Malden, Mass, September 18, 1947. **Education:** Loyola Univ, PhD (microbiol & immunol), 1974. **Professional Experience:** CHIEF, TOXICOL & MOLECULAR BIOL, HEALTH EFFECTS LAB DIV, NAT INST OCCUP SAFETY & HEALTH, as of 2004; ADJ PROF MICROBIOL, IMMUNOL & CELL BIOL, HEALTH SCI CTR, SCH MED, as of 2004; group leader, Immuno-Toxicol Group, Nat Inst Environ Health, NIH, beginning 1976. **Memberships:** Soc Toxicol; Am Asn Immunol; Int Soc Immunopharmacol. **Research Statement & Publications:** Risk assessment in immunotoxicology. II. Relationship between immune and host resistance tests; Interleukin 8 production by human pulmonary epithelial cells following exposure to asbestos; Arsenic mediates skin neoplasia by chronic stimulation of keratinocyte derived growth factors. **Mailing Address:** Toxicol & Moleculat Biol Branch, Nat Inst Occup Safety & Health, 1095 Willowdale Rd, Morgantown, WV 26505. **E-Mail:** myl@niords1.em.cdc.gov

LUSTGARTEN, RONALD KRISSES, SOLVOLYSIS, PATENTS. **Personal Data:** b New York, NY, February 24, 1942. **Education:** Columbia Univ, AB, 1962; Pa State Univ, PhD (chem), 1966. **Professional Experience:** MKT STAFF, COLUMBIA INNOVATION ENTERPRISE, 1994-; assoc dir, Columbia Innovation Enterprise, ending 1994; secy, Am Chem Soc, Kalamazoo Sect, 1983-1985; RES/STAFF SCIENTIST, UPJOHN CO, 1972-; res assoc & Mellon fel chem, Carnegie-Mellon Univ, 1968-1972; NIH fel, Univ Calif, Los Angeles, 1966-1968; NSF fel, 1965. **Memberships:** AAAS; Am Chem Soc; Fedn Am Scientists; Sigma Xi. **Research Statement & Publications:** Organic mechanisms; reactive intermediates; kinetics. **Mailing Address:** 11 Kim Hunter Rd, Englewood Cliffs, NJ 07632.

LUSTICK, SHELDON IRVING, ENVIRONMENTAL PHYSIOLOGY, VERTEBRATE ZOOLOGY. **Personal Data:** b Syracuse, NY, August 16, 1934; m 1970, c Danielle & Erica. **Education:** San Fernando Valley State Col, BA, 1963; Syracuse Univ, MS, 1965; Univ

Calif, Los Angeles, PhD (zool), 1968. **Professional Experience:** EMER PROF ZOOL, ENVIRON BIOL GRAD PROG, OHIO STATE UNIV, 1991-; DIR, ENVIRON BIOL GRAD PROG, OHIO STATE UNIV, 1977-; NSF grant, 1976-1978 & 1980-1983 & Air Force Off Sci Res grant, 1978-1980; Dept Interior res grant, 1969-1972 & 1973-1975; from asst prof to prof, Environ Biol Grad Prog, Ohio State Univ, 1968-1991. **Memberships:** AAAS; Cooper Ornith Soc; Am Ornith Soc; Ecol Soc Am; Sigma Xi. **Research Statement & Publications:** How animals adapt physiologically to environmental stress. **Mailing Address:** 6939 Riverside Dr, Powell, OH 43065.

LUSTIG, ARTHUR J, BIOLOGY. **Education:** Univ Chicago, BA, 1975, PhD (biochem), 1981. **Professional Experience:** PROF BIOCHEM, TULANE CANCER CTR, TULANE UNIV HEALTH SCI CTR, 2005-. **Mailing Address:** Tulane Cancer Ctr, 1430 Tulane Ave Box SL-43, New Orleans, LA 70112-2699. **Fax:** 504-988-2739. **E-Mail:** alustig@tulane.edu

LUSTIG, HARRY, SOLAR ENERGY. **Personal Data:** b Vienna, Austria, September 23, 1925; American citizen; m 1980, Rosalind Wells; c Lawrence J. **Education:** City Col N Y, BS, 1948; Univ Ill, MS, 1949, PhD (physics), 1953. **Honors & Awards:** Townsend Horris Medal for Notable Achievement, City Col NY Alumni Asn Medal, 1985. **Professional Experience:** RETIRED; treas, Am Phys Soc, 1985-1996; resident prof, City Col, City Univ NY, 1985-1993; consult, NJ Dept Higher Educ, 1983-1985; consult, Univ Mass, 1983; provost & vpres acad affairs, City Col, City Univ NY, 1982-1985; consult, Univ S Fla, 1981; consult, Univ SDak, 1980; consult, US Int Commun Agency, 1978; dean sci, City Col, City Univ NY, 1975-1982; dean col lib arts & sci, City Col, City Univ NY, 1973-1974; consult, UNESCO, 1972-1975; assoc dean sci, City Col, City Univ NY, 1972-1975; sr officer, UNESCO, 1970-1972; exec off doctoral prog physics, City Col, City Univ NY, 1968-1970; vis prof, Univ Wash, 1967, 1969; chmn dept physics, City Col, City Univ NY, 1965-1970; Fulbright prof, Univ Col, Dublin, 1964-1965; fel & visiting prof, Univ Colo, 1962, 1966; vis res asst prof, Univ Ill, 1959-1960; principal scientist, Nuclear Develop Corp Am, 1955-1960; from instr to professor physics, City Col, City Univ NY, 1953-1985; teaching & res asst, Physics, Univ Ill 1949-1953; fel, Univ Ill, 1948-1949. **Memberships:** Fel Am Phys Soc (treas, 1985-1996); Emer Mem fel NY Acad Sci (vpres, 1984); sr Mem Sigma Xi; Am Asn Physics Teachers; sen mem Am Asn Univ Prof. **Research Statement & Publications:** Theoretical nuclear physics; Mossbauer effect; solar energy; science education; economics of scientific publishing; hist of phys. **Mailing Address:** 304 Chula Vista St, Santa Fe, NM 57801. **Fax:** 505-989-1939. **E-Mail:** lustig@aps.org

LUSTIG, HOWARD E(RIC), ELECTRONICS, SYSTEMS ENGINEERING. **Personal Data:** b Vienna, Austria, October 23, 1925; American citizen; m 1950, c 3. **Education:** Columbia Univ, BS, 1949, MSEE, 1951, EE, 1956. **Professional Experience:** VPRES, MGT INFO SYSTS TELEPHONICS CORP, 1980-; prog mgr, Mgt Info Systs Telephonics Corp, 1976-1980; asst vpres, Citibank, 1974-1976; vpres eng, Am Comput Commun Co, Inc, 1970-1971 & Phonplex Corp, 1971-1974; corp dir eng, Superior Mfg & Instrument Corp, 1967-1970; prod area mgr eng mgt, Radio Receptor Div, Gen Instrument Corp, 1959-1967; proj supvr electronic eng, Ford Instrument Co, Sperry Rand Corp, 1951-1959; Instr electronics, Sch Eng, Cooper Union, 1949-1951. **Memberships:** Sr mem Inst Elec & Electronics Engrs; AmSoc Photogram; Marine Technol Soc. **Research Statement & Publications:** Military reconnaissance systems; digital interface and processing systems; oceanographic sensors; engineering management. **Mailing Address:** 4127 Primrose Dr, Allentown, PA 18104.

LUSTIG, MAX, INORGANIC CHEMISTRY, AIR POLLUTION. **Personal Data:** b Chicago, Ill, April 9, 1932; m 1954, c 1. **Education:** Univ Calif, Los Angeles, BS, 1957; Univ Wash, PhD (inorg chem), 1962. **Professional Experience:** RETIRED; consult, 1980-1985; consult environ effects & chem hazards, IIT Res Inst, 1978-1980; res chemist, IIT Res Inst, 1973-1978; asst prof chem, Memphis State Univ, 1968-1973; eve instr, Univ Ala, 1963-1968; res chemist, Redstone Arsenal Res Div, Rohm& Haas Co, Ala, 1962-1968; chemist, Olin Mathieson Chem Corp, 1957-1958. **Memberships:** Am Chem Soc; fel Am Inst Chemists. **Research Statement & Publications:** Physical and chemical studies of boron hydrides; chemistry of non-metal compounds with oxygen and fluorine, especially peroxides and hypofluorites; free radical chemistry; organometallic compounds; air pollution studies; high vacuum techniques; reaction kinetics involving air pollutants in the troposphere and stratosphere. **Mailing Address:** 8303 Steven Lane, West Hills, CA 91304.

LUSTIG, STANLEY, research administration, plastics engineering; deceased, see previous edition for last biography

LUSTMAN, BENJAMIN, metallurgy, nuclear materials; deceased, see previous edition for last biography

LUSTY, CAROL JEAN, MOLECULAR GENETICS. **Personal Data:** b Chicago, Ill, September 25, 1936. **Education:** Univ Mich, BS, 1958; Wayne State Univ, PhD (biochem), 1963. **Professional Experience:** Mem, Phys Biochem Study Sect, 1990-1994; mem, Dept Molecular Genetics, Pub Health Res Inst, beginning 1986; mem, Nat Adv Comt, 1985-1988; Dept Molecular Genetics, Dept Biochem, 1981-1986; assoc mem, Dept Biochem, 1978-1981; prin investr, PIR, 1974-; assoc, Pub Health Res Inst, 1968-1978. **Memberships:** Am Chem Soc; Am Soc Biol Chemists; AAAS; NY Acad Sci; Harvey Soc. **Research Statement & Publications:** Structure and evolution of carbamyl phosphate synthetases; regulatory mechanisms of mammalian arginine biosynthesis; protein structure and function. **Mailing Address:** Pub Health Res Inst, 455 First Ave, New York, NY 10016. **Fax:** 212-578-0804. **E-Mail:** lusty@phri.nyu.edu

LUSZTIG, GEORGE, THEORY OF GROUP REPRESENTATIONS. **Personal Data:** b Timisoara, Romania, May 20, 1946; American citizen; c Irene & Tamar. **Education:** Princeton Univ, MA, 1971, PhD (math), 1971. **Honorary Degrees:** Dr Honoris causa, Universite Paris VII, 1997. **Honors & Awards:** Cole Prize, Am Math Soc, 1985; Brouwer Medal, Dutch Math Soc, 1999. **Professional Experience:** PROF MATH, MASS INST TECHNOL, 1978-; from res fel to prof math, Univ Warwick, UK, 1971-1977; mem, Inst Advan Study, Princeton, NJ, 1969-1971. **Memberships:** Nat Acad Sci; London Math Soc; fel Royal Soc; Am Math Soc; fel Am Acad Arts & Sci. **Mailing Address:** Dept Math, Mass Inst Technol, 77 Mass Ave Rm 2-276, Cambridge, MA 02139. **Fax:** 617-253-4358. **E-Mail:** gyuri@math.mit.edu

LUTCHEN, KENNETH R, BIOMEDICAL ENGINEERING. **Personal Data:** b New York, NY, 1955. **Education:** Univ Va, BS, 1977; Case Western Res Univ, MS, 1980, PhD (biomed eng), 1983. **Professional Experience:** CHAIR BIOMED ENG, BOSTON UNIV, 1998-; PROF BIOMED ENG, BOSTON UNIV, 1998-; assoc chmn, Boston Univ, 1992-1997; from asst prof to assoc prof biomed eng, 1985-1998. **Memberships:** Sr mem Biomed Eng Soc; Am Physiol Soc. **Mailing Address:** Dept Biomed Eng, Boston Univ, 44 Cummington St Ste 107, Boston, MA 02215. **Fax:** 617-353-6766. **E-Mail:** klutch@bu.edu

LUTES, CHARLENE MCCLANAHAN, GENETICS, DEVELOPMENTAL BIOLOGY. **Personal Data:** b Grundy, Va, February 4, 1938; div. **Education:** Radford Col, BS, 1959; Ohio State Univ, MSc, 1962, PhD (genetics), 1968. **Professional Experience:** PROF EMER BIOL SCI, RADFORD UNIV, as of 2001; dean, Col Arts & Sci, 1987-1991; chmn, Dept Biol, 1981-1987; prof biol, Radford Univ, beginning 1980; from instr to prof, Radford Col, 1964-1980. **Memberships:** Nat Asn Biol Teachers; Soc Col Sci Teaching; Am Inst Biol Sci. **Research Statement & Publications:** Developmental genetics of wing venation patterns in Drosophila melanogaster. **Mailing Address:** Dept Biol, Radford Univ, Box 6931, Radford, VA 24142-6931. **E-Mail:** clutes@qmail.biology.runet.edu

LUTES, DALLAS D, PLANT PATHOLOGY. **Personal Data:** b St Louis, Mo, July 12, 1925; m 1945, c 2. **Education:** La Polytech Inst, BS, 1949; Univ Mo, PhD (bot), 1954. **Professional Experience:** RETIRED; prof bot & bact, La Tech Univ, 1974-1990; head dept, La Tech Univ, 1963-1973; from assoc prof to prof, La Tech Univ, 1955-1974; Instr bot, ETex State Col, 1954-1955. **Memberships:** AAAS. **Research Statement & Publications:** Disease resistance by breeding; virus transmission; seed germination affected by light; mistletoe seed germination; fern taxonomy and distribution. **Mailing Address:** Box 3052 Tech Sta, Ruston, LA 71272.

LUTES, LOREN DANIEL, ENGINEERING MECHANICS. **Personal Data:** b Stapleton, Nebr, December 1, 1939; m 1982, c 4. **Education:** Univ Nebr, BSc, 1960, MSc, 1961; Calif Inst Technol, PhD (appl mech), 1967. **Honors & Awards:** Wason Res Medal, Am Concrete Inst, 1964; State-of-the-Art Award, Am Soc Civil Engrs, 1983. **Professional Experience:** PROF EMER AND ADJ PROF, TEX A&M UNIV, 2002-; prof & head civil eng, Auburn Univ, 1992-1993; prof civil eng, TEX A&M UNIV, 1988-2002; vis assoc prof civil eng, Univ Waterloo, 1974-1975; vis prof, Univ Chile, 1971; from asst prof to prof & chair civil eng, Rice Univ, 1967-1987; res engr, Jet Propulsion Lab, 1967. **Memberships:** Am Soc Civil Engrs; Int Asn Struct Safety & Reliability; Soc Eng Sci; Am Asn Wind Eng. **Research Statement & Publications:** Response of linear and nonlinear systems to random excitations; first-passage probabilities for stochastic processes; fatigue damage caused by stochastic loadings. **Mailing Address:** 69 Thunder Mountain Rd, Edgewood, NM 87015.

LUTEYN, JAMES LEONARD, SYSTEMATIC BOTANY. **Personal Data:** b Kalamazoo, Mich, June 23, 1948. **Education:** Western Mich Univ, BA, 1970; Duke Univ, MA, 1972, PhD (bot), 1975. **Professional Experience:** MARY FLAGLER CARY CUR BOT, NY BOT GARDENS, 1998-; SR CUR BOT, NY BOT GARDENS, 1989-; co-ed, Flora Neotropica, 1984-; assoc ed, Taxon, 1987-1982; cur bot, NY Bot Gardens, 1981-1989; Assoc ed, Flora Neotropica, 1979-1983; Co-ed, Flora Neotropica, 1984-1990; ed, Proceedings Int Rhododendron Conf, 1978; Cur, NY Bot Gardens, 1981-1989; Assoc ed, BRITTONIA, 1976-1981; Adj Assoc Prof, Lehman Col, City Univ NY, 1976-; Assoc cur, NY Bot Gardens, 1975-1981. **Memberships:** Am Soc Plant Taxonomists; Int Asn Plant Taxon; Bot Soc Am. **Research Statement & Publications:** Evolution and systematics of the neotropical Ericaceae, Plumbaginaceae, and Companulaceae-Lobelioideae; Tropical forest: Botanical dynamics, speciation and diversity. **Mailing Address:** Dept Bot NY Bot Garden, Bronx River Pathway Fordham Rd, Bronx, NY 10458. **E-Mail:** jluteyn@nybg.org

LUTH, VERA G, ELEMENTARY PARTICLE PHYSICS. **Personal Data:** b Ger, December 15, 1943; m 1977, Karl L Brown. **Education:** Univ Heidelberg, MS, 1969, PhD (physics), 1974. **Professional Experience:** RES PROF, STANDFORD LINEAR ACCELERATOR CTR, as of 2004; SSC Lab, 1992-1994; SCIENTIST, DEPT PHYSICS RES CTR, STANFORD UNIV, 1974-. **Memberships:** Am Phys Soc; Europ Phys Soc. **Research Statement & Publications:** Experiments on CP violation in K and B decay weak interactions of heavy flavor particles; E plus E minus annihilation. **Mailing Address:** Stanford Linear Accelerator Ctr, 2575 Sand Hill Rd, Menlo Park, CA 94025.

LUTH, WILLIAM CLAIR, GEOLOGY, GEOCHEMISTRY. **Personal Data:** b Winterset, Iowa, June 28, 1934; m 1953, Betty L Heubrock; c Linda D, Robert W & Sharon J. **Education:** Univ Iowa, BA, 1958, MS, 1960; Pa State Univ, PhD (geochem), 1963. **Professional Experience:** ADJ PROF, DEPT GEOL, ARIZ STATE UNIV, TEMPE, 1996-; dir, Eng & Geoscience Div, 1995-1996; mgr, Geoscience Res Prog, US Dept Energy, 1990-1995; mgr, environ technol dept, 1989-1990; mgr, Geoscience dept, 1982-1989; supvr, Geophys Res Div, Sandia Nat Labs, 1979-1982; vis staff mem, Los Alamos Nat Lab, 1978; geoscientist, Off Basic Energy Sci, Dept Energy, Wash, DC, 1976-1978; from assoc prof to prof geol, Stanford Univ, 1968-1979; Alfred P Sloan Found res fel, Mass Inst Technol, 1966-1967; asst prof, Mass Inst Technol, 1965-1968; Res assoc geochem, Pa State Univ, 1963-1965. **Memberships:** Am Geophys Union; Geol Soc Am; Mineral Soc Am; Geochem Soc; Sigma Xi. **Research Statement & Publications:** Experimental petrology; physical chemistry of the igneous and metamorphic rocks; phase equilibria in silicate-volatile systems at high pressure and temperature; disposal radioactive wastes. **Mailing Address:** 6532 E June St, Mesa, AZ 85205. **E-Mail:** bluth@xroads.com

LUTHARDT, FRED W, GENETICS. **Education:** Ind Univ, PhD (med genetics), 1971. **Professional Experience:** LAB DIR, DYNAGENE CYTOGENETICS LAB, as of 2005. **Mailing Address:** Dynagene Cytogenetics Lab, 819 Boylston Ave Second Floor, Seattle, WA 98104. **Fax:** 206-386-2631. **E-Mail:** fluthardt@dynagene.com

LUTHER, EDWARD TURNER, GEOLOGY. **Personal Data:** b Nashville, Tenn, February 11, 1928; m 1955, c 2. **Education:** Vanderbilt Univ, BA, 1950, MS, 1951. **Professional Experience:** ASST STATE GEOLOGIST, TENN DIV GEOL, 1967-; fuels engr, Tenn Valley Authority, 1957; instr, Univ Tenn, Nashville, 1955-1957 & 1976-1978; from geologist to chief geologist, Tenn Div Geol, 1951-1977. **Memberships:** Fel Geol Soc Am; Sigma Xi. **Research Statement & Publications:** Areal and economic geology of various areas in Tennessee, particularly the stratigraphy and structural geology of the Cumberland Plateau; coal resources, particularly in Eastern United States. **Mailing Address:** Tn Div Geol, 701 Broadway, Nashville, TN 37203.

LUTHER, GEORGE WILLIAM, III, INORGANIC & MARINE CHEMISTRY. **Personal Data:** b Philadelphia, Pa, February 17, 1947; m 1971, Betty; c Gregory & Stephanie. **Education:** LaSalle Col, BA, 1968; Univ Pittsburgh, PhD (chem), 1972. **Professional Experience:** PROF MARINE STUDIES, UNIV DEL, 1986-; assoc dean, Col Marine Studies, 1986-1988; Investr, Nat Sci Found, 1983-; From asst prof to prof chem, Kean Col, NJ, 1972-1986 & chmn, dept physics, 1976-1984; Investr, Nat Oceanic & Atmospheric Admin grant, 1976-1980; chmn, N Jersey Am Chem Soc. **Memberships:** Am Chem Soc; AAAS; Microbeam Anal Soc; Sigma Xi; Am Geophys Union; Am Soc Limnol & Oceanog. **Research Statement & Publications:** Sulphur, iodine, metal speciation in seawater and sediments; mineral dissolution and formation; x-ray microanalysis of particulates; chemical oceanography-ocean, estuaries Hydrothermal jents and anoxic basins; Sensor develop; Environ Electrochem; Geochemical Transactions. **Mailing Address:** Col Marine Studies Univ Del, 700 Pilottown Rd, Lewes, DE 19958. **E-Mail:** luther@udel.edu

LUTHER, HERBERT GEORGE, BIOENGINEERING & BIOMEDICAL ENGINEERING. **Personal Data:** b Brooklyn, NY, October 1, 1914; m 1938, c 4. **Education:** Cooper Union, New York, BChE, 1940; NY Univ, MS, 1944; Polytech Inst Brooklyn, DChE, 1957. **Professional Experience:** Dir animal health res, Hoffman-La-Roche Inc, Nutley, NJ, 1974-1982; PRES, LUTHER ASSOCS INC, 1969-1974 & 1982-; sci dir agr, Chas Pfizer & Co, 1959-1969; dir agr res & develop, Chas Pfizer & Co, 1952-1959; asst dir tech serv, Chas Pfizer & Co, 1945-1952; Dir biochem labs, 1941-1944; Expert, Comn Food Additives, WHO/Food Agr Orgn; consult res & develop. **Memberships:** Am Chem Soc; Am Inst Chem Engrs; Am Asn Animal Sci; Poultry Sci Asn; Am Inst Chemists; Am Asn Agr Eng; Asn Consult Chemists & Chem Engrs; Am Asn Indust Vet; Inst Food Technol; NY Acad Sci; Math Asn Am; Animal Nutrit Res Coun; Sigma Xi; Int Union Pure & Appl Chem; AAAS. **Research Statement & Publications:** Antibiotics; antibacterials; vitamins; steroids; tranquilizers; unidentified growth factors; enzymes; antioxidants; nutrition; animal health; pharmacokinetics; operations research; food and feed technology; bioengineering; biotechnology; agricultural engineering; clearance and approval of drugs through Food and Drug Administration and other regulatory agencies. **Mailing Address:** The Mill, Head of the River, Smithtown, NY 11787-2699.

LUTHER, HOLGER MARTIN, MASS SPECTROMETRY, ELECTRON OPTICS. **Personal Data:** b Gdynia, Poland, February 4, 1940; American citizen; m 1969. **Education:** Marietta Col, BScL, 1963; Pa State Univ, MS, 1966, PhD (physics), 1970. **Professional Experience:** CHIEF SCIENTIST, SENSOR SYSTS GROUP, C S DRAPER LABS, 1987-; staff mem, Sensor Systs Group, C S Draper Labs, 1980-1987; staff mem, Avco Everett Corp, 1977-1980; Electron Sci & Tech Ctr, Div Carson Alexiou Corp, 1976-1977; EPSCO Labs, 1975-1976; Fac mem, Bridgeport Eng Inst, 1971-1977; sr res physicist, CBS Labs, 1969-1975. **Memberships:** Soc Photo-Optical Instumentation Engrs. **Research Statement & Publications:** Electron-optical and elctro-optical instrumentation; compact radio frequency mass spectrometers; electron beam recorders and storage tubes; high speed tracking cameras for charged particle beams and ultra high resolution angle sensors. **Mailing Address:** 294 Perkins Row, Topsfield, MA 01983.

LUTHER, LESTER CHARLES, INDUSTRIAL ENGINEERING. **Personal Data:** b Joliet, Ill, April 19, 1931; m 1954, c 4. **Education:** Univ Ill, Urbana, BS, 1953, 1958; Univ Nebr, Lincoln, MS, 1960; Ariz State Univ, PhD (indust eng), 1968. **Professional Experience:** PROF EMER MECH ENG, CALIF STATE UNIV, SACRAMENTO, 1994-; NSF fel, Sacramento State Col, 1971-1972; indust engr, McClellan AFB, Calif, 1969-1970; from assoc prof to prof, Calif State Univ, Sacramento, 1968-1986; qual assurance engr, Motorola, Inc, 1962-1968; indust engr, Reynolds Metals Co, Ariz, 1961-1962; indust engr, Cushman Motor Works, Nebr, 1959-1961; instr mech eng, Univ Nebr, 1958-1961. **Memberships:** Am Inst Indust Engr; Am Soc Eng Educ. **Research Statement & Publications:** Economic interactions between quality assurance and inventory control. **Mailing Address:** 3516 Chelsea Rd, Shingle Springs, CA 95682.

LUTHER, LONNIE W, REGULATORY POLICY DEVELOPMENT FOR NEW ANIMAL DRUG PRODUCTS, QUALITY CONTROL OF NEW ANIMAL DRUG APPROVAL PROCESS. **Personal Data:** b Fayetteville, Ark, April 16, 1945; m 1970, Mina; c Lonette W, Margaret A, Londell W & Marla W. **Education:** Univ Ark, BS, MS; Tex A & M Univ, PhD (poultry nutrit). **Professional Experience:** CHIEF, GENETIC ANIMAL DRUG & QUAL CONTROL STAFF, CTR VET MED, 1989-; chief, Swine & Poultry Drugs Br, 1986-1989; chief, Poultry Drug Br, 1976-1986; sci reviewer, Bur Vet Med, 1974-1976; grad res asst, Tex A&M Univ, 1971-1974; mgr, Turkey Exp Sta, Univ Ark, 1969-1971. **Memberships:** Poultry Sci Asn; Am Registry Prof Animal Scientists. **Mailing Address:** Ctr Vet Med, Food & Drug Admin, 7519 Standish Pl, Rockville, MD 20855. **E-Mail:** lluther@cvm.fda.gov

LUTHER, MARK E, OCEANOGRAPHY. **Education:** Univ NC, BA, 1976, MS, 1980, PhD (Phys oceanog), 1982. **Professional Experience:** ASSOC PROF, UNIV S FLA, as of 2006. **Mailing Address:** Dept Marine Sci, Univ S Fla, 140 Seventh Ave S, St Petersburg, FL 33701-5016. **Fax:** 727-873-1240. **E-Mail:** mluther@marine.usf.edu

LUTHER, NORMAN Y, MATHEMATICAL DEMOGRAPHY. **Personal Data:** b Palo Alto, Calif, June 3, 1936; m 1958, Rosalind; c Gregory, Gordon, Melissa & Marnie. **Education:** Stanford Univ, BS, 1958; Univ Iowa, MS, 1960, PhD (math), 1963. **Professional Experience:** PROF MATH, HAWAII PAC COL, 1987-; vis assoc prof, Univ Hawaii, 1982-1983; sr fel, E W Prog Pop, 1978-; danforth assoc, 1972-; assoc prof, Albany State Col, Ga, 1971-1972; from asst prof to assoc prof math, Wash State Univ, 1964-1987; NSF fel, 1963-1964; instr math, Univ Iowa, 1963. **Memberships:** Am Math Soc; Math Asn Am; Pop Asn Am. **Research Statement & Publications:** Probability and statistics; measure theory; mathematical demography. **Mailing Address:** Hawaii Pac Univ, Rm 242 1188 Fr St Mall, Honolulu, HI 96813-2713. **Fax:** 808-944-7490. **E-Mail:** nluther@hawaii.edu

LUTHERER, LORENZ O, PHYSIOLOGY, INTERNAL MEDICINE. **Personal Data:** b Cleveland, Ohio, January 20, 1936. **Education:** Haverford Col, AB, 1958; Univ Iowa, MS, 1964; Univ Fla, PhD (physiol), 1969; Tex Tech Univ, MD, 1977. **Professional Experience:** Secy & mem bd sci dirs, Tex Soc Biomed Res, 1989-; PROF, DEPT PHYSIOL & DEPT INTERNAL MED, HEALTH SCI CTR, SCH MED, TEX TECH UNIV, LUBBOCK, 1986-; chmn, InstnlAnimal Care & Use Comt, 1985-1989; chmn, Hypertension Task Force, 1985-1987; coordr, Grad Prog, Dept Physiol, 1982-1986; mem, Radiation Safety Comt, Health Sci Ctr, Sch Med, Tex Tech Univ, 1981-; asst prof, Dept Internal Med, 1981-1986; asst dean curric, Health Sci Ctr, Sch Med, Tex Tech Univ, Lubbock, 1979-1981; chmn, Prog Comt, 1978 & 1991; coordr curric, Health Sci Ctr, Sch Med, Tex Tech Univ, Lubbock, 1978-1979; mem, Hypertension Screening Comt, 1976-1977; mem, bd dirs, Lubbock Chap, Tex Affil, Am Heart Asn, 1975-1979, 1985-1988; mem, Prof Educ Comt, 1975-1976; from asst prof to assoc prof, Dept Physiol, 1972-1986; Div Genetics, Endocrinol & Med, 1971-1972; postdoctoral fel, Dept Physiol, 1969-1971; NIH trainee fel, Col Med, Univ Fla, Gainesville, 1966-1969; res physiologist, US Army Res Inst Environ Med, Natick, Mass, 1964-1965; Grad res asst, NIH trainee fel, 1963-1964; grad teaching asst, Col Med, Univ Iowa, Iowa City, 1962-1963; Grad res asst, Col Med, Univ Iowa, Iowa City, 1961-1962; Res assoc, Arctic Inst NAm, Point Barrow, Alaska, 1961. **Memberships:** Am Physiol Soc; Shock Soc. **Research Statement & Publications:** Author of various publications. **Mailing Address:** Dept Physiol, Tex Tech Univ, 3601 Fourth St, Lubbock, TX 79430-6551. **E-Mail:** lorenz.lutherer@ttuhsc.edu

LUTHEY, JOE LEE, SPACE PHYSICS. **Personal Data:** b Winslow, Ariz, September 21, 1943. **Education:** Univ Calif, Berkeley, AB, 1965; Univ Kans, Lawrence, PhD (physics), 1970. **Professional Experience:** MARKET ANALYSIS, COMPUT CONSULT, CALIF INST TECHNOL, 1993-; mem tech staff, New Earth Probe, Jet Propulsion Lab, 1977-1993; consult radiation physics, Calif Inst Technol, 1975-1977; resident res assoc, Nat Res Coun, Jet Propulsion Lab, 1973-1975; resident res assoc space physics, Calif Inst Technol, 1973-1975; consult, Physics Dept, Univ Iowa, 1973-1974; res assoc space physics, Univ Iowa, Iowa City, 1970-1973. **Memberships:** Am Geophys Union; Am Phys Soc. **Research Statement & Publications:** Test/create Jovian radiation belt models; determine x-ray and gamma-ray emission from natural and artificial satellites in the Jovian trapped electron proton belts. **Mailing Address:** 80 Marion Ave, Pasadena, CA 91106.

LUTHRA, HARVINDER SINGH, RHEUMATOLOGY, IMMUNOLOGY. **Personal Data:** b Amritsar, Punjab India, March 14, 1945; m 1975, Annu Duggal; c Payal, Gauri & Sonaar. **Education:** Christian Med Col, India, MB & BS, 1967; Am Bd Internal Med, 1973; Am Bd Internal Med & Rheumatology, 1974. **Honors & Awards:** 5, 969, 787 issued Oct 12th HLA-DRBI, 1999; elec mem, Nat Soc Clin Rheumatologists, 2000; Am top doctors, 2001, 2002. **Professional Experience:** Chair, Div Rheumatology, Mayo Clin & Mayo Med Sch, Rochester, Minn, 1996-; prof med, John F Finn Minn Arthritis Found 1995-; vice chair res, Dept Med, Mayo Clin, Rochester, Minn, 1993-1996; CONSULT RHEUMATOLOGY, MAYO CLIN, ROCHESTER, MINN, 1975-; assoc consult, Mayo Grad Sch, 1974-1975; trainee rheumatology, Mayo Grad Sch, 1972-1974; resident internal med, Mt Sinai Hosp, Chicago, Ill, 1970-1972; intern, Middlesex Gen Hosp New Brunswick, NJ, 1969; resident, Christian Med Col, India, 1968; Intern, Christian Med Col, India, 1967. **Memberships:** Int Med Acad Sci; fel Am Rheumatism Asn; Sigma Xi; Am Fedn Clin Res; AAAS; fel Am Col Physicians; Am Asn Immunologists Am Bd Internal Med; Subspecialty Bd Rheumatology; Sci Prog Comt 48th, 49th, 50th, 51th; mem-membership comt 59th, 60th, Cahir-Crystalline Atrhopathies Subsection; Strategic Planning Comt, 200 Chari-Abstact Selection Comt. **Research Statement & Publications:** To understand genetic mechanisms involved in development of rheumatic dis like reumatoid arthritis, spondyloarthropathies. **Mailing Address:** Div Rheumatology & Internal Med, Mayo clin & Mayo found, 200 First St SW, Rochester, MN 55905-000 1. **Fax:** 507-266-6518. **E-Mail:** luthra@mayo.edu

LUTHRA, KRISHAN LAL, HIGH TEMPERATURE & METALLURGICAL CHEMISTRY. **Personal Data:** b Jaipur, India, September 28, 1949; m 1981, Sudipti. **Education:** Univ Rajasthan, BEng, 1970; Indian Inst Technol, Kanpur, MTech, 1972; Univ Pa, PhD (metall & mat sci), 1976. **Professional Experience:** MGR, THERMAL & STRUCT CERAMICS, CERAMICS LAB, GEN ELEC CO, as of 2003; MGR, COMPOSITES & STRUCT CERAMICS PROG, GEN ELEC CO, 1989-; Metallurgist, Corp Res & Develop, 1976-1989; res fel, Dept Metall & Mat Sci, Univ Pa, 1972-1976; Sr res asst, Dept Metall Eng, Indian Inst Technol, Kanpur, 1971-1972. **Memberships:** Electrochem Soc; Metall Soc; Am Ceramic Soc; Am Soc Metals; Am Inst Mining, Metall & Petrol Engs. **Research Statement & Publications:** Thermodynamics and kinetics of high temperature reactions; corrosion at elevated temperatures; gas-liquid-solid reactions; high temperature materials; ceramic composites. **Mailing Address:** Ceramics Lab GE Global Res, PO Box 8, Schenectady, NY 12301. **Fax:** 518-387-6016. **E-Mail:** luthra@crd.ge.com

LUTHY, JAKOB WILHELM, chemistry; deceased, see previous edition for last biography

LUTHY, RICHARD GODFREY, ENVIRONMENTAL & CIVIL ENGINEERING. **Personal Data:** b June 11, 1945; m 1969, Mary; c Matthew, Mara & Jessica. **Education:** Univ Calif, Berkeley, BS, 1967, MS (Ocean Eng), 1974, PhD (civil eng), 1976; Univ Hawaii, MS (civil Eng), 1969. **Honors & Awards:** G Tallman Ladd Award, Carnegie Inst Technol, 1977; Nalco Award, Asn Environ Eng Prof, 1978 & 1982; Eddy Medal, Water Pollution Control Fedn, 1980; Founders Award, US Nat Comn Int Asn Water Qual Res & Control, 1986 & 1993; Eng Sci Award, Asn Environ Eng Prof, 1988; Chair, Gordon Res Conf Environ Sci; Water, 1994; Prof Res Award Pa Water Environ Asn, 1996; Shimizu Co Visiting Prof, Dept Civil Eng, Stanford Univ, 1996-1997; Cleanup Proj Yr, US Dept Defense, Strategic Environ Res & Develop Prog, 1999. **Professional Experience:** SILAS H PALMER PROF, DEPT CIVIL & ENVIRON ENG, STANFORD UNIV, 2000-; thomas lord prof, Dept Environ Eng, Carnegie Mellon Univ, 1996-1999; Chair, Comt Bioavailability Contaminants Soils, Sediments & Ground Water, Nat Res Coun, 2000-; head, Dept Civil Eng & Environ Eng, Carnegie Inst Technol, 1989-1996; deleg, Water Sci & Technol Bd, Nat Acad Eng, Wash, Beijing, 1988; chmn, Conf Fundamental Res Directions Environ Eng, NSF/Asn Environ Eng Prof, 1988; assoc dean, Carnegie Inst Technol, 1986-1988; actg head, Carnegie Inst Technol, 1985-1986; act dean, Carnegie Inst Technol, 1988; prof, Dept Civil Eng, Carnegie Inst Technol, 1983-1999; Fac Chmn-Chmn/Elect, Carnegie Inst Technol, 1984-1986 & 1997-1999; from asst prof to assoc prof, Dept Civil Eng, Carnegie Inst Technol, 1975-1983; res asst, Div Sanit Eng, Univ Calif, Berkeley, 1973-1975; asst officer-in-charge, underwater construct team, Naval Civil Eng Lab, Civil Eng Corps, US Navy, 1971-1972; res proj officer, Naval Civil Eng Lab, Civil Eng Corps, US Navy, 1970-1971; Res asst, Dept Civil Eng, Univ Hawaii, 1968-1969; Consult, Allied-Signal, Environ Res & Technol Inc, IT Corp, Baker Chem Co, Koppers Co, Inc, US Steel, Alcoa, SmithKline-Beckman, FMC Corp, Exxon, Aetna Casualty & Ins, Remediation Technol Inc, US Dept Energy & US Environ Protection Agency, Texaco, Baltimo. **Memberships:** Water Environ Fedn; Am Soc Civil Engrs; Am Chem Soc; Int Asn Water Qual; vpres, Asn Environ Eng Prof, 1986-1987; pres, Asn Environ Eng Prof, 1987-1988; Am Water Works Asn; Am Acad Environ Engrs. **Research Statement & Publications:** Hazardous substances in wastewaters and ground waters; wastewater treatment and industrial wastewater treatment; chemistry of diluteaqueous systems; treatment of wastewaters from petroleum refining, chemical manufacturing, coal conversion, and iron and steel making; Underwater Construction Survey; Coal Gasification Process. **Mailing Address:** Dept Civil & Environ Eng Stanford univ, Rm M-52 Terman Bldg, Stanford, CA 94305-4020. **Fax:** 650-725-8662. **E-Mail:** luthy@stanford.edu

LUTON, EDGAR FRANK, internal medicine; deceased, see previous edition for last biography

LUTSCH, EDWARD F, ZOOLOGY. **Personal Data:** b Chicago, Ill, November 23, 1930; m 1965, c 2. **Education:** Northern Ill Univ, BS, 1952; Northwestern Univ, MS, 1957, PhD (biol), 1962. **Professional Experience:** PROF BIOL, NORTHEASTERN ILL UNIV, 1974-; lectr, Northwestern Univ, 1969-; from asst prof to assoc prof, Northeastern Ill Univ, 1968-1974; asst prof zool, Univ Ill, Chicago, 1962-1968. **Memberships:** AAAS; Am Inst Biol Sci; Am Soc Zoologists. **Research Statement & Publications:** Biological rhythms and clocks; rhythmic response of animals to pharmacological drugs; comparative physiology; animal behavior. **Mailing Address:** Dept Biol, Northeastern Ill Univ, 5500 N St Louis Ave, Chicago, IL 60625-4625.

LUTSKY, IRVING, LABORATORY ANIMAL MEDICINE. **Personal Data:** b Paterson, NJ, June 12, 1926; m 1948, c 4. **Education:** Rutgers Univ, BS, 1948; Purdue Univ, MS, 1951; Univ Pa, VMD, 1955; Am Col Lab Animal Med, dipl, 1965. **Honors & Awards:** Res Award, Am Asn Lab Animal Sci, 1977. **Professional Experience:** PROF & CHMN, DEPT COMP MED, SCH MED, HEBREW UNIV, 1972-; Vis prof comp med, Sch Med, Hebrew Univ, 1971-1972; assoc prof comp med, Med ColWis, 1966-1972; adminr surg res lab, Allen Bradley Med Sci Lab, 1960-1972; asst prof vet sci, Med ColWis, 1960-1966; staff vet, Fromm Labs, 1955-1958; Res asst poultry diseases, Purdue Univ, 1949-1951. **Memberships:** Am Soc Microbiol; Am Asn Lab Animal Sci; Am Vet Med Asn; Asn Gnotobiotics; Am Soc Lab Animal Pract; fel Am Acad Allergy & Immunol. **Research Statement & Publications:** Infectious diseases; natural disease resistance; applied gnotobiology; occupational allergies; occupationally related hypersensitivity; lung disease in laboratory animal workers, veterinarians and poultry workers. **Mailing Address:** Dept Comp Med Sch Med, Hebrew Univ POB 12272, Jerusalem 91120, Israel.

LUTTER, LEONARD C, MOLECULAR BIOLOGY. **Education:** Wis Univ, PhD, 1973. **Professional Experience:** DIR, DEPT MOLECULAR BIOL, HENRY FORD HOSP, beginning 1988. **Research Statement & Publications:** Characterization of cellular and viral transcription complexes. **Mailing Address:** Henry Ford Hosp, Sch Med, Wayne State Univ, Detroit, MI 48202-3450. **E-Mail:** llutter@genetics.wayne.edu

LUTTMANN, FREDERICK WILLIAM, IV, MATHEMATICS. **Personal Data:** b New Brunswick, NJ, August 9, 1940; div. **Education:** Amherst Col, AB, 1961; Stanford Univ, MS, 1964; Univ Ariz, PhD (math), 1967; Col Financial Planning, CFP, 1984. **Professional Experience:** PROF MATH, SONOMA STATE UNIV, 1970-; assoc prof math, Alaska Methodist Univ, 1967-1970; assoc, Univ Ariz, 1963-1967. **Memberships:** Math Asn Am; Assoc Editor Amer Math Month. **Research Statement & Publications:** Steiner symmetrization of convex bodies; polynomial interpolation; symmerty in plane ormanution. **Mailing Address:** Dept Math, Sonoma State Univ, Rohnert Park, CA 94928. **E-Mail:** rick.marks@sonoma.edu

LUTTON, JOHN D, EXPERIMENTAL HEMATOLOGY/IMMUNOLOGY. **Personal Data:** b Sioux City, Iowa, February 3, 1937; m Melody; c Marguerite & Laura. **Education:** Univ Nebr, BS, 1961, MS, 1963; NY Univ, PhD (cell biol & physiol), 1969. **Professional Experience:** INST HUMAN GENETICS AND BIOCHEM, 2000-; adj prof cell biol& anat, NY Med Col, 1978-; res prof & adj prof pharmacol, NY Med Col, 1997-; adj fac immunology & infectious dis, Rockefeller Univ, 2000-; guest investr, Rockefeller Univ, 1994-1999; prof med, NY Med Col, 1989-1997; assoc prof med, NY Med Col, 1977-1988; asst prof med, SUNY Downstate Med Ctr, 1977; res asst prof physiol & biophysics, Mt Sinai Sch Med, 1973-1977; instructor & sci anatomy & cell biol, NY Univ Sch Med, 1971-1973; asst prof biol, NY Univ Wash Square Col, 1970-1971. **Memberships:** Am Soc Hemat; Int Soc Exp Hemat; Reticulo Endothelial Soc; AAAS. **Research Statement & Publications:** Innate immune factors in normal and diseased states.Growth factors and the regulation of hematopoiesis: bone marrow growth and in vitro aspects on the regulation of erythropoiesis including regulatory aspects of hemebiosynthesis and degradation; in vitro characteristics of disorders such as anemia, polycythemins, neoplastic states and disorders of iron metabolism; granulopoiesis; differentiation of leukemic cells. **Mailing Address:** 42 Redwood Dr, Highland Mills, NY 10930. **E-Mail:** luttonj@mail.rockefeller.edu

LUTTON, JOHN KAZUO, NEUROPHARMACOLOGY, ENZYMOLOGY. **Personal Data:** b Tokyo, Japan, July 11, 1949; American citizen; m 1971, c 1. **Education:** Pac Lutheran Univ, BS, 1971; Purdue Univ, PhD (biochem), 1976. **Professional Experience:** PROF CHEM, KENYON COL, as of 2001; vis prof chem, Ohio State Univ, 1995-1996; asst prof chem, Kenyon Col, beginning 1980; res assoc, Univ NC, 1977-1980; res assoc pharmacol, Med Sch, Univ Colo, 1976-1977; chem anal, Ind State Chem Off, 1972-1973; grad student, Dept Biochem, Purdue Univ, 1971-1976. **Memberships:** Am Chem Soc; AAAS; Sigma Xi. **Research Statement & Publications:** Molecular mechanisms of hormone action especially the role of cyclic nucleotides in brain function and cell growth; enzymatic mechanisms of redox enzymes especially flavin-containing dehydrogenases. **Mailing Address:** Dept Chem Kenyon Col, 212 Tomsich Hall, Gambier, OH 43022. **E-Mail:** lutton@kenyon.edu

LUTTON, LEWIS MONTFORT, CIRCADIAN RHYTHMS, EXERCISE PHYSIOLOGY. **Personal Data:** b Cincinnati, Ohio, July 14, 1945; m 1982, Marianne; c Wolf, Bram, Richard, Janine, Robert & Beth. **Education:** Swarthmore Col, BA, 1968; Cornell Univ, PhD (environ physiol), 1976. **Professional Experience:** PROF BIOL, MERCYHURST COL, 1993-; chmn, Sci Div, 1985-1990; pres, Col Senate, 1985-1986; dir, Biol Dept, 1983-; dir, Hon Prog, 1983-1990; Pre med adv, Mercyhurst Col, 1980-1996; from asst prof to assoc prof, Mercyhurst Col, 1980-1993; asst prof, Allegheny Col, 1976-1980; Inst, Allegheny Col, 1974-1976. **Memberships:** Am Soc Mammalogists; Nat Asn Biol Teachers; AAAS; Inst Religion & Sci; Soc Res Biol Rhythms. **Research Statement & Publications:** Behavioral pharmacology of the Circadian rhythm of hamsters; elucidate the biochemical mechanisms underlying photic entrainment. **Mailing Address:** Dept Biol Mercyhurst Col, Glenwood Hills, Erie, PA 16546. **Fax:** 814-824-2188. **E-Mail:** lutton@utopia.mercy.edu

LUTTRELL, ERIC MARTIN, PETROLEUM GEOLOGY. **Personal Data:** b Wheeling, WVa, May 12, 1941; m 1963, Janet; c Dawn (Christilles) & Brooke (Calender). **Education:** Univ Wis-Madison, BS, 1962, MS, 1965; Princeton Univ, PhD (geol), 1968. **Professional Experience:** VPRES EXPLOR & NEW DEVELOP, BPX-ALASKA, 1991-; explor mgr, Latin Am, BP Explor, 1989-1990; onshore explor mgr, Anadarko, 1986-1989; proj mgr, Anadarko, 1984-1986; asst explor mgr, Stand Oil Prof Co, 1982-1984; regional geologist, Stand Oil Prof Co, 1980-1982; consult explor geologist, Res & Tech Dept, 1979-1980; asst supvr geol res, Res & Tech Dept, 1976-1979; res geologist, Res & Tech Dept, 1973-1976; sr geologist, Producing Dept, Texaco Inc, 1969-1973; geologist, Producing Dept, Texaco Inc, 1968-1969. **Memberships:** Geol Soc Am; Soc Econ Paleontologists & Mineralogists; Am Asn Petrol Geologists. **Research Statement & Publications:** Applications of seismic stratigraphy clastic sedimentology; organic geochemistry and geologic thermometry to petroleum exploration. **Mailing Address:** 4690 Southpark Bluff Dr, Anchorage, AK 99516.

LUTTRELL, GEORGE HOWARD, ANALYTICAL CHEMISTRY. **Personal Data:** b Glendale, Calif, December 23, 1941; m 1964. **Education:** Univ Tex, BS, 1965; Southern Methodist Univ, MS, 1969; Univ Ga, PhD (chem), 1975. **Professional Experience:** MEM STAFF, ALCON LABS, PR, 1977-; ctr Labs, Alcon Labs, 1975-1977; res chemist anal, Alcon Labs, 1969-1972. **Memberships:** Am Chem Soc; Sigma Xi. **Research Statement & Publications:** Preconcentration of trace metal cations and oxyanions for analysis by x-ray fluorescence using immobilized complexing and chelating reagents. **Mailing Address:** Luttrell Consult Inc, 3619 Lake Powell Dr, Arlington, TX 76016.

LUTTS, JOHN A, LIE GROUPS, HISTORY OF MATH, APPROXIMATION THEORY. **Personal Data:** b Baltimore, Md, February 26, 1932; m 1967, Ruth; c Judith, John, Eric, Irene, Claire, Paul & Laetitia. **Education:** Spring Hill Col, BS, 1957; Univ Pa, MA, 1959, PhD (math), 1961; Woodstock Col, Md, STL, 1965. **Professional Experience:** ASSOC PROF MATH, UNIV MASS, HARBOR CAMPUS, 1970-; fac res grant, Univ Mass, Harbor Campus, 1970-1971; fac growth fel, Univ Mass, Harbor Campus, 1967; asst prof, Univ Mass, Harbor Campus, 1966-1970; from instr to asst prof math, Loyola Col, Md, 1965-1966. **Memberships:** Math Asn Am. **Research Statement & Publications:** Cultural history of mathematics; approximation theory. **Mailing Address:** Univ Mass Harbor Campus, Dept Math/Comput Sci, Rm S-3-178, Boston, MA 02125-3393. **Fax:** 617-287-6433. **E-Mail:** lutts@math.umb.edu

LUTWAK, ERWIN, MATHEMATICS. **Personal Data:** b USSR, February 9, 1946; American citizen; m 1968. **Education:** Polytech Inst Brooklyn, BS, 1968, MS, 1972, PhD (math), 1974. **Professional Experience:** HEAD, DEPT MATH, POLYTECH UNIV, as of 2002; Chair, Math Sect, NY Acad Sci, 1988-1990; PROF MATH, POLYTECH UNIV, 1986-; from asst prof to assoc prof, Polytech Univ, 1975-1986; Asst prof math, Col Pharmaceut Sci, Columbia Univ, 1970-1975. **Memberships:** Am Math Soc; London Math Soc; Math Asn Am; Sigma Xi; NY Acad Sci. **Research Statement & Publications:** Convexity; integral geometry; analytic and geometric inequalities. **Mailing Address:** Dept Math, Polytech Univ, Rogers Hall 305G 6 Metrotech Ctr, Brooklyn, NY 11201-2990. **Fax:** 718-260-3660. **E-Mail:** elutwak@poly.edu

LUTWAK, LEO, endocrinology, nutrition; deceased, see previous edition for last biography

LUTY, FRITZ, SOLID STATE PHYSICS. **Personal Data:** b Essen, Ger, April 12, 1928; m 1960, c 2. **Education:** Univ Gottingen, dipl physics, 1953; Stuttgart Univ, Dr rer nat(physics), 1956. **Professional Experience:** DISTINGUISHED PROF EMER PHYSICS, UNIV UTAH, as of 2004; distinguished res award, Univ Utah, 1984; vis prof, Soc Advan Sci, Japan, 1973; prof physics, Univ Utah, beginning 1965; dozent, Physics Inst, 1964-1965; vis assoc prof, Univ Ill, Urbana, 1963; asst physics, Stuttgart Univ, 1953-1962. **Memberships:** Fel Am Phys Soc; Ger Phys Soc. **Research Statement & Publications:** Defects in ionic crystals; radiation damage; absorption and emission spectroscopy; field emission; magneto-optics, paraelectric and paraelastic effects; low temperature dielectric and electro-caloric studies; raman-scattering; phase transitions; material development for tunable laser application. **Mailing Address:** Dept Physics, Univ Utah, Salt Lake City, UT 84112.

LUTZ, ALBERT WILLIAM, AGRICULTURAL CHEMISTRY. **Personal Data:** b Baltimore, Md, September 26, 1924; m 1951, c 2. **Education:** Johns Hopkins Univ, AB, 1949, MA, 1950, PhD (chem), 1953. **Honors & Awards:** J Shelton Horsley Award. **Professional Experience:** GROUP LEADER CHEM DISCOVERY, AGR DIV, AM CYANAMID CO, 1985-; group leaeer herbicides, Am Cyanamid Co, 1969-1985; sr res chemist, Am Cyanamid Co, 1959-1969; res chemist, Am Cyanamid Co, 1957-1959; res chemist, Chemagro Corp, 1956-1957; Assoc prof chem, Col William & Mary, 1953-1956. **Memberships:** Am Chem Soc. **Research Statement & Publications:** Pesticides, particularly growth regulants and herbicides. **Mailing Address:** 873 Cherry Hill Rd, Princeton, NJ 08540.

LUTZ, BARRY LAFEAN, PLANETARY & COMETARY ATMOSPHERES, MOLECULAR SPECTROSCOPY. **Personal Data:** b Windsor, Pa, January 2, 1944; American citizen; m 1981, Mary. **Education:** Lebanon Valley Col, BS, 1965; Princeton Univ, AM, 1967, PhD (astrophys sci), 1968. **Professional Experience:** CHAIR, DEPT PHYSICS & ASTRON, NORTHERN ARIZ UNIV, 1992-; PROF PHYSICS & ASTRON, NORTHERN ARIZ UNIV, 1991-; vis scholar, Dept Physics & Astron, Univ Calif, Berkeley, 1990; adj prof, Northern Ariz Univ, 1988-1991; consult, NASA Planetary Astron Mgt Oper Working Group, 1985-; adj prof, Ariz State Univ, 1983-1986; adj assoc prof, Ariz State Univ, 1981-1983; vis astronr, Univ Dijon, 1980; vis astronr, Observ Paris, 1979; astronr, Lowell Observ, 1977-1991; prin investr, NASA, 1975-; consult, Kitt Peak Nat Observ, 1973; prin investr, NSF, 1972-1988; from adj asst prof to adj assoc prof, State Univ NY, Stony Brook, 1971-1981; sr res assoc, Dept Earth & Space Sci, State Univ NY, Stony Brook, 1971-1977; res astronr, Lick Observ, Univ Calif, 1970-1971; fel physics, Nat Res Coun Can, 1968-1970. **Memberships:** Int Astron Union; Am Astron Soc; Sigma Xi; Am Geophys Union; Am Assoc physics teachers; Nat Sci teachers assoc Coun undergrad res. **Research Statement & Publications:** High resolution spectroscopy of the interstellar medium, of comets and of stellar and planetary atmospheres; laboratory astrophysics; intensity measurements and long path length planetary atmospheres simulations; absolute spectrophotometry of planetary atmospheres and of comets and narrow band photopolarimetric imaging of planets; science education. **Mailing Address:** Dept Physics & Astron, Northern Ariz Univ, Flagstaff, AZ 86011-6010. **Fax:** 928-523-8688. **E-Mail:** barry.lutz@nau.edu

LUTZ, CHRIS P, PHYSICS. **Honors & Awards:** Newcomb Cleveland Prize, AAAS, 1993 & 1994. **Professional Experience:** RES SCIENTIST, IBM ALMADEN RES CTR, SAN JOSE, CALIF, as of 1996. **Mailing Address:** Almaden Res Ctr, IBM, 650 Harry Rd, San Jose, CA 95120-6099. **Fax:** 408-927-2100. **E-Mail:** lutz@almaden.ibm.com

LUTZ, DONALD ALEXANDER, MATHEMATICS, DIFFERENTIAL EQUATIONS. **Personal Data:** b Syracuse, NY, April 2, 1940; m 1968, Margaret; c Catherine, Elizabeth & Christopher. **Education:** Syracuse Univ, BS, 1961, MS, 1963, PhD (math), 1965. **Professional Experience:** PROF MATH, SAN DIEGO STATE UNIV, 1986-2000; Humboldt fel, Univ Ulm, WGer, 1975-1976; vis assoc prof math, Univ Southern Calif, 1973; vis asst prof, Math Res Ctr, Univ Wis-Madison, 1969-1970; lectr, Univ Md, 1967-1969; from asst prof to prof math, Univ Wis-Milwaukee, 1965-1986; instr math, Syracuse Univ, 1965. **Memberships:** Am Math Soc; German Math Union. **Research Statement & Publications:** Systems of linear ordinary differential equations with meromorphic coefficients; systems of linear difference equations. **Mailing Address:** Dept Math Sci, San Diego State Univ, 5500 Campanile Dr, San Diego, CA 92182-0314. **E-Mail:** lutz@math.sdsu.edu

LUTZ, HARRY FRANK, NUCLEAR PHYSICS. **Personal Data:** b Philadelphia, Pa, January 30, 1936; m 1960, c 2. **Education:** Univ Pa, AB, 1957; Mass Inst Technol, PhD (physics), 1961. **Professional Experience:** RETIRED; physicist, Lawrence Livermore Lab, 1961-1996. **Memberships:** Am Phys Soc. **Research Statement & Publications:** Nuclear reactions and nuclear spectroscopy. **Mailing Address:** 4545 Entrada St, Pleasanton, CA 94566. **Fax:** 510-424-6889.

LUTZ, JULIE HAYNES, ASTRONOMY. **Personal Data:** b Mt Vernon, Ohio, December 17, 1944; wid, c Melissa & Clea. **Education:** San Diego State Univ, BA, 1965; Univ Ill, MS, 1968, PhD (astron), 1972. **Professional Experience:** DIR, NASA REGIONAL EDUCR RESOURCE CTR, as of 2000; ASSOC DIR, WASH NASA SPACE GRANT CONSTRIUM, as of 2000; Dir, NASA Space Network, NW, as of 2000; Dir, UW Manastash Ridge Observ, as of 2000; Res Prof astron, Univ WA, as of 2000; Prog comm, AAAS, 1997-; dir, Prog Astron, 1996-; Astron Sect, AAAS, 1993-1995; chair, Math & Astron, Wash State Univ, 1992-1996; dir, Div Astron Sci, NSF, 1990-1992; Prof Astron & Math, Wash State Univ, 1984-; assoc provost, Wash State Univ, 1981-1982; asst dean sci, Wash State Univ, 1978-1979; From asst prof to assoc prof, Wash State Univ, 1972-1984. **Memberships:** Int Astron Union; Royal Astron Soc; Am Astron Soc; pres, Astron Soc Pac, 1990-1990; AAAS. **Research Statement & Publications:** Planetary nebulae; stellar evolution. **Mailing Address:** Prof Astron, Wash State Univ, PO Box 351310, Seattle, WA 98195-1310. **Fax:** 206-685-0403. **E-Mail:** nasaerc@u.washington.edu

LUTZ, MICHAEL W, SCIENTIFIC COMPUTING, MATHEMATICAL MODELING OF BIOLOGICAL SYSTEMS. **Personal Data:** b New York, NY, July 3, 1960. **Education:** Duke Univ, BS, 1981, PhD (biomed eng), 1986. **Professional Experience:** HEAD, BIOINFORMATIC SCI, GLAXOSMITHKLINE, as of 2004; MGR RES DATA SYSTS, GLAXO INC, 1988-. **Memberships:** Am Statist Asn; Biomed Eng Soc. **Mailing Address:** GlaxoSmithKline, PO Box 13398, 5 Moore Dr, Res Triangle Park, NC 27709.

LUTZ, PAUL E, INVERTEBRATE ZOOLOGY, ECOLOGY & ENVIRONMENTAL SCIENCE. **Personal Data:** b Hickory, NC, June 25, 1934; c Carol S. **Education:** Lenoir-Rhyne Col, AB, 1956; Univ Miami, MS, 1958; Univ NC, PhD (zoology), 1962. **Honorary Degrees:** LHD, Lenoir-Rhyne Col, 1983. **Honors & Awards:** Fac Marshal, Univ Nc, Greensboro, 1992. **Professional Experience:** PROF EMER BIOL, UNIV NC, GREENSBORO, as of 2005; pres, NC Acad Sci, 1993-1994; prof biol, Univ Nc, Greensboro, beginning 1970; NSF, 1965-1967; grantee, Am Philos Soc, 1964; from instr to assoc prof, Univ NC, Greensboro, 1961-1970; grad asst, Univ NC, 1958-1961; grad asst, Univ Miami, 1956-1958. **Memberships:** AAAS; Ecol Soc Am; Sigma Xi; Am Inst Biol Sci. **Research Statement & Publications:** Ecology and physiology of aquatic insects, especially effects of temperature and photoperiod as they affect seasonal regulation of developmental patterns in the Odonata. **Mailing Address:** Dept Biol, Univ NC, Greensboro, NC 27412-5001. **Fax:** 910-334-5839. **E-Mail:** pelutz@goodall.uncq.edu

LUTZ, PETER LOUIS, RESPIRATION, OSMOREGULATION. **Personal Data:** b Glasgow, Scotland, September 29, 1939. **Education:** Glasgow Univ, Scotland, BSc, 1964, PhD (zool), 1970. **Professional Experience:** MCGINTY CHAIR MARINE BIOL, FLA ATLANTIC UNIV, 1990-; prof physiol & chmn, Marine Sch, 1982-1990; assoc prof, Miami Univ, Fla, 1976-1982; lectr biol, Bath Univ, Eng, 1972-1976; asst prof biol, Duke Univ, NC, 1970-1972; biol, Univ Glasgow, Scotland, 1969-1970; Lectr physiol, Univ Ife, Nigeria, 1964-1966. **Memberships:** Soc Exp Biol; Am Physiol Soc. **Research Statement & Publications:** Animal physiology, particularly respiration and osmoregulation; an ae robic brain metabolism. **Mailing Address:** Fla Atlantic Univ, Boca Raton, FL 33431-0991. **E-Mail:** lntz@fau.edu

LUTZ, RAYMOND, OPERATIONS MANAGEMENT. **Personal Data:** b Oak Park, Ill, February 27, 1935; American citizen; m Nancy C. Lutz. **Education:** Univ NMex, BSME, 1958, MBA, 1962; Iowa State Univ, PhD (eng valuation), 1964. **Honors & Awards:** E L Grant Award, Am Soc Eng Educ, 1972; Fred Crane Distinguished Serv Award, Inst Indust Engrs, 1987. **Professional Experience:** Ed, Indust Mgt, 1983-1987; exec dean grad studies & res, Sch Mgt, 1979-1991; prof opers mgt, Univ Tex, Dallas, 1973-2001; dean, Sch Mgt, 1973-1978; ed, Eng Economist, 1972-1977; from assoc prof to prof indust eng, Univ Okla, 1968-1972; asst prof mech eng, NMex State Univ, 1964-1967; asst indust eng, Iowa State Univ, 1961-1964; instr mech eng, Univ NMex, 1958-1961; bd dirs, Sigma Xi. **Memberships:** Fel AAAS; fel Am Inst Indust Engrs; Sigma Xi. **Research Statement & Publications:** Operations management; industrial management; shipbuilding technology. **Mailing Address:** 1230 Turquoise Trail, Cerrillos, NM 87010. **Fax:** 505-424-8955. **E-Mail:** rplutz@att.net

LUTZ, RAYMOND PAUL, PHYSICAL ORGANIC CHEMISTRY. **Personal Data:** b Cleveland, Ohio, May 31, 1932. **Education:** Univ Fla, BS, 1953, MS, 1955; Calif Inst Technol, PhD (org chem), 1962. **Professional Experience:** PROF EMER CHEM, PORTLAND STATE UNIV, 1983-; from asst prof to assoc prof, Portland State Univ, 1968-1983; asst prof, Univ Ill, Chicago, 1965-1968; lectr, Harvard Univ, 1964-1965; instr chem, Harvard Univ, 1961-1964; Res chemist, E I du Pont Del Nemours & Co, Ky & Mich, 1955-1957. **Memberships:** Am Chem Soc. **Research Statement & Publications:** Reaction mechanisms, including displacement reactions and thermal isomerizations. **Mailing Address:** Dept Chem, Portland State Univ, PO Box 751, Portland, OR 97207. **E-Mail:** lutzr@pdx.edu

LUTZ, RICHARD ARTHUR, BIOLOGICAL OCEANOGRAPHY, MARINE ECOLOGY. **Personal Data:** b New York, NY, June 8, 1949; m 1981, c 3. **Education:** Univ Va, BA, 1971; Univ Maine, PhD (oceanog), 1975. **Honors & Awards:** Thurlow C Nelson Award, Nat Shellfisheries Asn, 1973; Excellence Res Award, Cook Col, Rutgers Univ, 1995; 2005 Sci Literacy Achievement Award, NJ Asn Biomed Res contributions Sci Dir IMAX Film, Volcanoes of the Deep Sea. **Professional Experience:** PROF, INST MARINE & COASTAL SCI, RUTGERS UNIV, 1987-; dir, Fish & Aquacult Tex Ctr, 1986-1997; prin investr NSF grants, 1981-; from asst prof to assoc prof, Rutgers Univ, 1979-1987; co-prin investr NSF grants, 1978-; assoc investr, Nat Oceanic & Atmospheric Admin sea grant, Yale Univ, 1978-; res assoc, Dept geol & geophys, Yale Univ, 1977-1979; biol consult, Blue Gold Sea Farms, 1976-; res assoc, Darling Ctr, 1975-1978; prin investr, Nat Oceanic & Atmospheric Admin sea grants, 1975-1978; res asst, dept oceanog, Univ Maine, 1971-1975. **Memberships:** World Mariculture Soc; Nat Shellfisheries Asn (vpres 1981-1982; pres-elect 1982-1983; pres 1983-1984); Am Soc Zoologists; Estuarine Res Fedn; AAAS; Sigma Xi. **Research Statement & Publications:** Shellfish biology; molluscan shell structure and mineralogy; shellfish aquaculture; bivalve larval ecology; marine ecology and paleoecology; malacology; paleoclimatology; deep-sea hydrothermal vents, ecology. **Mailing Address:** Inst Marine & Coastal Sci, Rutgers Univ, 71 Dudley Rd, New Brunswick, NJ 08901-8521. **Fax:** 732-932-6557. **E-Mail:** rlutz@imcs.rutgers.edu

LUTZ, ROBERT WILLIAM, CHEMICAL PHYSICS, COMPUTER SCIENCE. **Personal Data:** b Mason City, Iowa, September 14, 1937; m Joe; c 4. **Education:** Drake Univ, BA, 1962; Univ NMex, MS, 1966; Ill Inst Technol, PhD (physics), 1969. **Professional Experience:** EMER ASSOC PROF, DRAKE UNIV, 2002-; from asst provost info technol to assoc provost info technol, Drake Univ, 1993-1998; mem, EDUCOM bd trustees, 1989-1992; mem bd dir, Drake Univ Instnl Rep, 1991-1996; dir comput & telecom, Drake Univ, 1986-1993; chair, am comput Mach-Spec Int Group Univ Col Comput Serv, 1983-1985; dir comput serv, Drake Univ, 1974-1986; from asst prof to assoc prof, Drake Univ, 1969-2002; Nat Sci Found Trainee, Ill Inst Tech, Ill, 1966-1969; staff mem, los alamos sci lab, 1962-1966; res asst physics, los alamos sci lab, 1962-1964. **Memberships:** Sigma Xi; Asn Comput Mach; Spec Interest Group Comput Uses Educ; Spec Interest Group Univ& Col Comput. **Research Statement & Publications:** Computer assisted instruction; computers in undergraduate curriculum. **Mailing Address:** Dept Physics Drake Univ, Harvey Ingham 31B, Des Moines, IA 50311-4505. **Fax:** 515-271-1943. **E-Mail:** robert.lutz@drake.edu

LUTZ, WILSON BOYD, BIOCHEMISTRY, ORGANIC CHEMISTRY. **Personal Data:** b Mogadore, Ohio, May 12, 1927; m 1950, Mary; c 2. **Education:** Manchester Col, BA, 1950; Ohio State Univ, PhD (org chem), 1955. **Professional Experience:** PROF EMER CHEM, MANCHESTER COL, 1992-; consult, Miles Lab, Elkhart, Ind, 1982; res assoc & dir, Inst Biomed Res, Univ Tex, Austin, 1981; prof chem, Manchester Col, 1972-1992; guest worker, NIH, 1971; consult, Warner-Lambert Res Inst, 1963-1966; from asst prof to assoc prof, Manchester Col, 1962-1972; sr scientist, Warner-Lambert Res Inst, 1960-1962; scientist, Warner-Lambert Res Inst, 1957-1960; fel biochem, Med Col, Cornell Univ, 1955-1957. **Memberships:** Am Chem Soc. **Research Statement & Publications:** Synthesis of new derivatives of hydroxylamine and substances of biological interest including melanogenic indoles. **Mailing Address:** Dept Chem, Manchester Col, 604 E Col Ave, North Manchester, IN 46962. **E-Mail:** wblutz@manchester.edu

LUTZE, MARGARET, GENETICS. **Education:** Univ Chicago, BA, 1973, PhD, 1988. **Professional Experience:** SR LECTR, SCH CONTINUING STUDIES, NORTHWESTERN UNIV, 1993-; ADJ PROF, DEPT NATURAL SCI, LOYOLA UNIV, 1993-; ADJ FAC, DEPT BIOL, DEPAUL UNIV, 1992 -. **Mailing Address:** Loyola Univ Chicago, 6525 N Sheridan Rd, Chicago, IL 60626. **Fax:** 773-508-3514. **E-Mail:** mlutze@luc.edu

LUTZER, DAVID JOHN, MATHEMATICS. **Personal Data:** b Sioux Falls, SDak, March 27, 1943; m 1982, c 4. **Education:** Creighton Univ, Omaha, NE, BS, 1964, Oxford Univ, Eng, dipl advan math, 1966; Univ Wash, Seattle, PhD (math), 1970. **Honors & Awards:** Jefferson Award, Col William & Mary, 1995. **Professional Experience:** CHANCELLOR PROF, DEPT MATH, COL WILLIAM & MARY, 2001-; PROF MATH, COL WILLIAM & MARY, 1995-; actg provost, Col William & Mary, 1993; dean, Dept Math, Col William & Mary, 1987-1995; prof & chair, Miami Univ, Oxford Ohio, 1982-1987; prof math, Tex Tech Univ, 1976-1982; NSF grants, 1971-1972, 1974, 1975-1976, 1977-1978, & 1980-1982; from asst prof to assoc prof math, Univ Pittsburgh, 1970-1978; NSF fel, 1964 & 1966. **Memberships:** Am Math Soc; Math Asn Am; Soc Indust & Appl Math. **Research Statement & Publications:** Self-theoretic topology in ordered spaces and function spaces. **Mailing Address:** Dept Math, Col William & Mary, Jones Hall 129 PO Box 8795, Williamsburg, VA 23187-8795. **Fax:** 757-221-7400. **E-Mail:** lutzer@math.wm.edu

LUU, JANE, COMETS, SMALL SOLAR SYSTEM OBJECTS. **Personal Data:** b Saigon, Vietnam, July 15, 1963; American citizen. **Education:** Stanford Univ, BS, 1984; Mass Inst Technol, PhD (planetary astron), 1990. **Honors & Awards:** Annie J Cannon Award, Am Asn Univ Women, 1991. **Professional Experience:** HUBBLE FEL, DEPT PHYSICS, STANFORD UNIV, 1992-; Harvard-Smithsonian fel, Ctr Astrophys, Harvard Univ, 1990-1992. **Memberships:** Am Astron Soc. **Research Statement & Publications:** Origin of small bodies in the solar system and their interrelations; comet nuclei-their physical properties and their implications on the early solar system eg the origin and evolution of the Kuiper belt of comets. **Mailing Address:** Dept Physics, Stanford Univ, Stanford, CA 94305-4060. **Fax:** 650-725-6544. **E-Mail:** luu@blinky.stanford.edu

LUUS, R(EIN), CHEMICAL ENGINEERING. **Personal Data:** b Tartu, Estonia, March 8, 1939; Canadian citizen; m 1973, c Brian & Kristina. **Education:** Univ Toronto, BASc, 1961, MASc, 1962; Princeton Univ, AM, 1963, PhD (chem eng), 1964. **Honors & Awards:** Steacie Prize, Nat Res Coun Can, 1976; ERCO Award, Can Soc Chem Eng, 1980. **Professional Experience:** PROF EMER, CHEM ENG, UNIV TORONTO, as of 2005; Vis assoc, Calif Inst Technol, 1979-1980; PROF CHEM ENG, UNIV TORONTO, 1974-; Milltronics Ltd, 1967-1971 & Imperial Oil Ltd, 1974-1977; Nat Res Coun Can sr indust fel, 1972-1973; dir, Chem Eng Res Consults Ltd, 1966-; Consult, Shell Oil Co Can, 1966-1970 & 1978-1979; from asst prof to assoc prof, Univ Toronto, 1965-1974; Consult, Can Gen Elec Co, Ltd, 1965-1966; Fel optimal control, Princeton Univ, 1964-1965. **Memberships:** Can Soc Chem Eng (secy, 1967-1968, vchmn, 1968-1969, chmn, 1969-1970, past chmn 1970-1971); fel Chem Inst Can; Am Inst Chem Eng. **Research Statement & Publications:** Development of optimization procedures suitable for optimal and suboptimal control of nonlinear systems; nonlinear analysis; optimal control of time delay systems; parameter estimation; model reduction; dynamic programming. **Mailing Address:** Dept Chem Eng Univ Toronto, 200 Col St Wallberg Bldg, Toronto, ON M5S 1A4, Can. **Fax:** 416-978-8605. **E-Mail:** luus@chem-eng.utoronto.ca

LUX, SAMUEL E, IV, ONCOLOGY. **Education:** Kansas Univ Sch Med, MD, 1967. **Professional Experience:** ROBERT A STRANAHAN PROF PEDIAT, HARVARD MED SCH, as of 2004; CHIEF, DIV HEMAT & ONCOL, CHILDREN'S HOSP, 1985-. **Mailing Address:** Div Hemat & Oncol, Children's Hosp Boston, 300 Longwood Ave Enders 761, Boston, MA 02115-5737. **Fax:** 617-738-5922. **E-Mail:** lux@enders.tch.harvard.edu

LUXEMBURG, WILHELMUS ANTHONIUS JOSEPHUS, MATHEMATICAL ANALYSIS. **Personal Data:** b Delft, Neth, April 11, 1929; m 1955, c 2. **Education:** State Univ Leiden, BSc, 1950, MSc, 1953; Delft Univ Technol, PhD, 1955. **Honors & Awards:** Humboldt award, 1980. **Professional Experience:** PROF EMER MATH, CALIF INST TECHNOL, 2000-; exec officer, Calif Inst Technol, 1970-1985; prof math, Calif Inst Technol, 1962-2000; from asst prof to assoc prof, Calif Inst Technol, 1958-1962; asst prof, Univ Toronto, 1956-1958; Fel math, Queen's Univ, Can, 1955-1956. **Memberships:** Am Math Soc; Can Math Cong; Neth Math Soc; corresp mem Royal Acad Sci Amsterdam. **Research Statement & Publications:** Functional analysis, particularly measure and integration theory, Banach function space theory and theory of locally convex spaces; Riesz spaces; nonstandard analysis. **Mailing Address:** Dept Math, Calif Inst Technol, Pasadena, CA 91125. **Fax:** 626-585-1728. **E-Mail:** lux@its.caltech.edu

LUXENBERG, HAROLD RICHARD, COMPUTER VOICE INPUT & OUTPUT, COMPUTER GRAPHICS. **Personal Data:** b Chicago, Ill, February 2, 1921; m 1942, Jean Weisskopf; c Susan K, James R & Robert C. **Education:** Univ Calif, Los Angeles, BA, 1942, MA, 1948, PhD (math), 1950. **Honors & Awards:** Beatrice Winner Mem Award, Soc Info Display, 1987. **Professional Experience:** PROF COMPUT SCI, CALIF STATE UNIV, CHICO, 1970-; consult, Lux Assocs, 1964-1970; vpres eng & asst gen mgr, Houston Fearless Corp, 1961-1963; mgr, Display Dept, Thompson-Ramo-Wooldridge Corp, 1959-1960; proj consult, Litton Industs, 1956-1958; consult engr, Remington Rand, Inc, 1953-1955; Lectr & instr, Univ Calif, Los Angeles, 1952-1969; res physicist, Hughes Res & Develop Labs, 1951-1953; Mathematician, Nat Bur Stand, 1950-1951. **Memberships:** Fel Soc Info Display (pres 1960-1962); Sigma Xi. **Research Statement & Publications:** Data display; document storage and retrieval; photo-optical systems; digital computers in command and control applications. **Mailing Address:** Comput Sci Calif State Univ, 101 Orange St, Chico, CA 95929-0001. **Fax:** 530-898-5995. **E-Mail:** hluxenberg@oavax.csuchico.edu

LUXHOJ, JAMES THOMAS, LOGISTICS, DECISION SUPPORT SYSTEMS, LOGISTIC, AVIATION SAFETY AND RISK ANALYSIS. **Personal Data:** b Staten Island, NY, January 13, 1956; m 1987, Catherine Anne; c 2. **Education:** Va Polytech Inst & State Univ, BS, 1984, MS, 1985, PhD (indust eng & opers res), 1986. **Honors & Awards:** Ralph R Teetor Award Eng Educ Excellence, Soc Automotive Engrs, 1989. **Professional Experience:** EXEC OFFICER, DEPT INDUST ENG, RUTGERS UNIV, as of 2004; PROF, DEPT INDUST ENG, RUTGERS UNIV, as of 2004; prin investr, Fed Aviation Admin, 1997- 2002; vis prof, Aalborg Univ, Denmark, 1994-2001; fel, Danish Res Acad, 1994; dept ed, Inst Indust Engrs Trans, beginning 1993; assoc prof indust eng, Rutgers State Univ Nj, beginning 1992; chmn, Eng Econ Div, Am Soc Eng Educ, 1991-1992; hackensack Water Co, 1988 & NSF, 1991-1992; vchmn & prog chmn, Eng Econ Div, Am Soc Eng Educ, 1990-1991; assoc ed, Inst Indust Engrs Trans, 1989-1992; treas-secy, Eng Econ Div, Am Soc Eng Educ, 1989; co-prin investr, Fed Aviation Admin, 1989; prin investr, NASA Langley Res Ctr, 1988; chief fac adv, Rutgers Univ Chap Inst Indust Engrs, 1987- 1998; Co-investr, USDA, 1987-1989; asst prof, Rutgers State Univ NJ, 1986-1992. **Memberships:** Sigma Xi; sr mem Inst Indust Engrs; sr mem Soc Logistics Engrs; Am Soc Eng Educ. **Research Statement & Publications:** Aviation safty & rick analysis; production and operations management; logistics; decision support and expert systems. **Mailing Ad-**

dress: Dept Indust Eng, Rutgers Univ, Rm 210, Busch Campus, Core Bldg, Piscataway, NJ 08854-8018. **E-Mail:** jluxhoj@rci.rutgers.edu

LUXMOORE, ROBERT JOHN, SOIL PHYSICS, WHOLE PLANT PHYSIOLOGY. **Personal Data:** b Adelaide, Australia, November 7, 1940; m 1975, Annetta P Watson. **Education:** Univ Adelaide, BS, 1962, BS, 1963; Univ Calif, Riverside, PhD (soil physics), 1969. **Professional Experience:** AT ENVIRON SCI DIV, OAK RIDGE NAT LAB, as of 2004; Adj prof, Univ Tenn, 1992-; ed-chief, Soil Sci Soc Am, 1991-1993; mem, Rural Abandoned Mines Prog, Tenn, 1980-1981; consult, Ctr Law & Social Policy, Wash, DC, 1979; Vis scientist, Commonwealth Sci & Indust Res Orgn, Australia, 1976; SOIL & PLANT SCIENTIST, OAK RIDGE NAT LAB, 1973-; res assoc, Univ Wis-Madison, 1971-1972; fel, Univ Calif, Riverside, 1970-1971; res assoc, Univ Ill, 1969-1970; res asst, Univ Calif, Riverside, 1966-1969; Agronomist, Dept Agr, SAustralia, 1963-1966. **Memberships:** Am Soc Agron; fel Soil Sci Soc Am; Crop Sci Soc Am; Am Geophys Union; fel AAAS; Int Soc Soil Sci. **Research Statement & Publications:** Experimental and computer modeling research on the relationships between environmental variables and whole plant physiological processes including disruptions induced by pollutant stress and soil variability effects on hydrologic transport processes. **Mailing Address:** Environ Sci Div, Oak Ridge Nat Lab, PO Box 2008, Oak Ridge, TN 37831-6038. **Fax:** 865-435-7397. **E-Mail:** rjl@ornl.gov

LUXON, BRUCE ARLIE, ANIMAL PHYSIOLOGY, MEDICINE. **Personal Data:** b Ft Dodge, Iowa, March 8, 1955; American citizen; m 1985. **Education:** Univ Iowa, BS, 1976; Univ Mo, Columbia, PhD (math), 1983, MD, 1985. **Professional Experience:** ASSOC PROF INTERNAL MED, ST LOUIS UNIV SCH MED, 1997-; asst prof internel med, St Louis Univ, 1992-1997; CLIN STAFF, ST LOUIS UNIV HOSP, 1992-; CLIN STAFF, JOHN COCHRAN VA HOSP, 1992-; CLIN STAFF, ST MARY'S HEALTH CTR, 1992-; clin staff, Marshall Browning Hosp, 1992-2000; fel gastroenterol, Univ Calif, San Francisco, 1989-; asst prof, Dept Med, Univ Mo, 1985-1989. **Memberships:** Soc Indust & Appl Math; Soc Math Biol. **Research Statement & Publications:** Biomathematics of hepatic transport; biophysics of bile formation; hepatic drug metabolism; removal of albumin-bound substances by liver cells; author of various article. **Mailing Address:** St Louis Univ Sch Med, 3660 Vista Ave Grand Blvd PO Box 15250, St Louis, MO 63110-0250. **Fax:** 314-577-8125. **E-Mail:** luxonba@slu.edu

LUXON, JAMES THOMAS, LASER SURFACE MODIFICATION, BEAM PROPAGATION. **Personal Data:** b Norwalk, Ohio, November 12, 1934; m 1961, c 2. **Education:** Wabash Col, BA, 1958; Mich State Univ, MS, 1964, PhD (eng), 1969. **Professional Experience:** PROF EMER MAT SCI, KETTERING COL, as of 2004; DEAN ACAD PROGS & RES, kettering col, as of 2004; dean, grad studies, Exten Serv & Res, begijnning 1993; dept head sci math, Gen Motors Inst, 1988-1989; Rhodes prof, Eng & Mgt Inst, Gen Motors Inst alumni grant, 1983; allied distinguished prof & dir laser lab, eng & mgt Inst, Gen Motors Inst, beginning 1981; prof mat sci, Gen Motors Inst, 1981-1985; vis prof laser, Univ Lulea, Sweden, 1981; assoc prof elec eng, Gen Motors Inst, 1969-1980; instr physics, Gen Motors Inst, 1961-1967; analytical engr, New Departure Div, Gen Motors Corp, 1959-1961. **Memberships:** Optical Soc Am; Laser Inst Am (pres, 1986); Soc Mfg Engrs. **Research Statement & Publications:** Mathematical description of focusing and beam propagation for high-order mode laser beams; laser surface modification. **Mailing Address:** 11365 Grand Oak Dr, Grand Blanc, MI 48439.

LUYBEN, WILLIAM LANDES, CHEMICAL ENGINEERING. **Personal Data:** b Omaha, Nebr, October 17, 1933; m 1963, c 2. **Education:** Pa State Univ, BS, 1955; Rutgers Univ, MBA, 1958; Univ Del, MSChE, 1962, PhD (chem eng), 1963. **Professional Experience:** PROF CHEM ENG, LEHIGH UNIV, 1973-; consult, E I du Pont Del Nemours & Co, Inc & Sun Oil Co, 1967-; assoc prof, Lehigh Univ, 1967-1973; tech serv engr, E I du Pont Del Nemours & Co, Inc, 1963-1967; Lectr, Univ Del, 1963-1966; Process engr, Humble Oil & Refining Co, 1955-1958 & Iranian Oil & Refining Co, 1958-1960. **Memberships:** Am Inst Chem Eng. **Research Statement & Publications:** Process dynamics, control and simulation, particularly in distillation columns and chemical reactors. **Mailing Address:** Dept Chem Eng, Lehigh Univ, 27 Memorial Dr W, Bethlehem, PA 18015-3044. **E-Mail:** wll0@lehigh.edu

LUYENDYK, BRUCE PETER, MARINE GEOPHYSICS, MARINE SCIENCES. **Personal Data:** b Freeport, NY, February 23, 1943; m 1967, Taylor; c Loren T. **Education:** San Diego State Col, BS, 1965; Scripps Inst Oceanog, Univ Calif, San Diego, PhD (oceanog), 1969. **Honors & Awards:** Fel, Geological Soc of Amer, 1975; Newcomb Cleveland Prize, AAAS, 1980; Antarctic Serv Medal, NSG, 1990; Fel, Amer Geophysical Union, 2002. **Professional Experience:** Assoc ed, J Geophys Res, 1982-1984; PROF GEOL SCI, UNIV CALIF, SANTA BARBARA, 1981-; ASSOC DEAN, MATH, LIFE & PHYS SCI, UCSB, 2005-; Tectonophysics, 1988-1992; Chair, Dept Geol Sci, UCSB, 1997-2003; Dir, Inst Crustal Studies, UCSB, 1988-1997; actg dir, Inst Crustal Studies, UCSB, 1987-1988; mem ed bd, PAGEOPH, 1988-1995; assoc ed, Marine Geophys Researchers, 1976-1992; ed adv, Geol Mag, 1975-1979; from asst prof to assoc prof, Univ Calif, Santa Barbara, 1973-1981; mem working group Mid-Atlantic Ridge, US Geodyn Comn, 1971; Mem working group marine geophys data, Comn Oceanog, Nat Acad Sci, 1971; asst scientist, Woods Hole Oceanog Inst, 1970-1973; fel, Woods Hole Oceanog Inst, 1969-1970; res asst oceanog, Scripps Inst Oceanog, Univ Calif, San Diego, 1965-1969; Geophysicist, US Navy Electronics Lab ctr, 1965-1966. **Memberships:** fel Am Geophys Union; fel Geol Soc Am. **Research Statement & Publications:** Geotectonics; paleomagnetism; paleoceanography; Marine geophysics. **Mailing Address:** Dept Geol Sci Univ Calif, Webb 2036, Santa Barbara, CA 93106. **E-Mail:** luyendyk@geol.ucsb.edu

LUYKX, PETER (VAN OOSTERZEE), CYTOGENETICS, HUMAN GENETICS. **Personal Data:** b Detroit, Mich, December 14, 1937; m 1978, c 4. **Education:** Harvard Univ, AB, 1959; Univ Calif, Berkeley, PhD (zoology), 1964. **Professional Experience:** PROF BIOL, UNIV MIAMI, 1982-; NSF res grants, 1978-1988; from asst prof to assoc prof, dept biol, Univ Miami, 1967-1982; NIH res grants, 1965-1973; Asst prof zool, Univ Minn, Minneapolis, 1964-1967. **Memberships:** AAAS; Genetics Soc Am; Am Soc Cell Biol; Entom Soc Am; Am Soc Human Genetics. **Research Statement & Publications:** Meiosis and mitosis; cytogenetics of termites; sex chromosome evolution. **Mailing Address:** Dept Biol, Univ Miami, PO Box 248106, Miami, FL 33124-8106. **Fax:** 305-284-3039. **E-Mail:** pluykx@bio.miami.edu

LUYTEN, JAMES REINDERT, PHYSICAL OCEANOGRAPHY. **Personal Data:** b Minneapolis, Minn, December 26, 1941; m 1967, Meredith; c 3. **Education:** Reed Col, AB, 1963; Harvard Univ, AM, 1965, PhD (chem physics), 1969. **Professional Experience:** EXEC VPRES & DIR RES, WOODS HOLE OCEANOG INST, 2002-; sr assoc dir & dir res, Woods Hole Oceanog Inst, 1996-2002; mem, naval res adv comt, 1997-2003; assoc dir res, Woods Hole Oceanog Inst, 1994-1996; chmn, dept Physical Oceanog, Woods Hole Oceanog Inst, 1990-1994; SR SCIENTIST, WOODS HOLE OCEANOG INST, 1986-; vis sci, NCAR, 1983-1984; assoc scientist, Woods Hole Oceanog Inst, 1975-1986; asst scientist, Woods Hole Oceanog Inst, 1971-1975; Lectr, geophys fluid dynamics, Harvard Univ, 1971-; Summer Fel, Geophys Fluid Dynamics, Woods Hole Oceanog Inst, 1968; res fel, geophys fluid dynamics, Harvard Univ, 1969-1971. **Memberships:** Am Geophys Union; Award comt mem, Am Meteorol Soc, 1998-2003; mem, Am Meteorol soc, 2002-. **Research Statement & Publications:** Theoretical and observational study of the dynamics of low frequency variability of ocean circulation; moored current meter arrays; observations of the Gulf Stream system; equatorial current systems in Pacific and Indian Oceans; models of the thermocline in the subtropical gyres. **Mailing Address:** Woods Hole Oceanog Inst, 221 Oyster Pond Rd Bell House MS 39, Woods Hole, MA 02543. **Fax:** 508-457-2189. **E-Mail:** jluyten@whoi.edu

LUZZI, THEODORE E, ENGINEERING SCIENCE. **Personal Data:** b Floral Park, NY, June 15, 1927; m 1955, c 2. **Education:** Stevens Inst Technol, ME, 1951; Mass Inst Technol, MS, 1953; Columbia Univ, Eng ScD, 1963. **Professional Experience:** RETIRED; sr staff scientist, Grumman Aerospace Corp, 1982-1990; staff scientist, Grumman Aerospace Corp, 1973-1982; res scientist plasma physics, Grumman Aerospace Corp, 1963-1973; res engr, Grumman Aerospace Corp, 1958-1961; engr, M W Kellogg Co, NY, 1953-1958. **Memberships:** Am Phys Soc; Am Inst Aeronaut & Astronaut; Am Soc Mech Eng; Sigma Xi. **Research Statement & Publications:** Gas dynamics; plasma physics; heat transfer. **Mailing Address:** 4489 Terra Lane, St Joseph, MI 49085-9319.

LUZZIO, ANTHONY JOSEPH, immunology; deceased, see previous edition for last biography

LUZZIO, FREDERICK ANTHONY, SYNTHETIC ORGANIC CHEMISTRY. **Personal Data:** b Lawrence, Mass, September 17, 1953. **Education:** Vanderbilt Univ, BS, 1976; Tufts Univ, MS, 1979, PhD (chem), 1982. **Professional Experience:** ASSOC PROF, UNIV LOUISVILLE, 1995-; asst prof, Univ Louisville, 1988-1995; sr develop chemist, E I du Pont Del Nemours, 1985-1988; fel, Harvard Univ, 1982-1985; consult, Arthur D Little, Inc, 1978-1985; res chemist, Arthur D Little, Inc, 1976-1978. **Memberships:** Am Chem Soc. **Research Statement & Publications:** Synthetic organic chemistry; synthesis of natural products, nucleosides, carbohydrates; synthetic methods, chiral oxidation, ultrasound-promoted reactions; isolation and structural elucidation of marine natural products. **Mailing Address:** Dept Chem, Univ Louisville, Louisville, KY 40292. **Fax:** 502-852-8149. **E-Mail:** faluzz01@athena.louisville.edu

LWOWSKI, WALTER WILHELM GUSTAV, ORGANIC CHEMISTRY. **Personal Data:** b Garmisch, Ger, December 28, 1928; American citizen. **Education:** Univ Heidelberg, dipl, 1954, Dr rer nat, 1955. **Professional Experience:** PROF EMER CHEM, NMEX UNIV, as of 2003; res prof chem, NMex State Univ, beginning 1966; asst prof, Yale Univ, 1960-1966; res fel chem, Harvard Univ, 1959-1960; asst, Univ Heidelberg, 1957-1959; fel, Univ Calif, Los Angeles, 1955-1957; mem bd dirs, Boehringer-Mannheim Corp, Indianapolis. **Memberships:** Fel AAAS; Am Chem Soc; fel NY Acad Sci; Ger Chem Soc; Royal Soc Chem. **Research Statement & Publications:** Reactions mechanisms; electron-deficient nitrogen intermediates; photochemistry; heterocyclic chemistry; heteroatom rearrangements. **Mailing Address:** Dept Chem & Biochem, NMex State Univ, PO Box 30001, 1175 N Horseshoe Dr, Las Cruces, NM 88003-8001. **E-Mail:** wlwowski@nmsu.edu

LYBECK, A(LVIN) H(IGGINS), INDUSTRIAL CHEMISTRY. **Personal Data:** b Trenton, NJ, February 28, 1919; m 1945, c 1. **Education:** Polytech Inst, Brooklyn, BS, 1941. **Professional Experience:** TECH MGR, CERRO WIRE & CABLE CO, 1967-; develop mgr, Brand-Rex Div, Am Enka Corp, Conn, 1960-1967; lab dir, William Brand & Co, Inc, 1950-1959; sr res chemist, Congoleum-Nairn, Inc, 1947-1950; res chemist, Gen Cable Co, 1944-1947; Asst develop engr, US Rubber Co, 1941-1944. **Memberships:** Am Chem Soc; Inst Elec & Electronics Eng; Am Inst Chem. **Research Statement & Publications:** Development of electrical insulation systems for wire and cables. **Mailing Address:** 31 Surrey Lane, Branford, CT 06405.

LYBRAND, TERRY PAUL, MOLECULAR BIOPHYSICS, MOLECULAR SIMULATION & MODELING. **Personal Data:** b Augusta, Ga, October 8, 1957; m 1984, c 2. **Education:** Univ SC, BS, 1980; Univ Calif, San Francisco, PhD (pharmaceut chem), 1984. **Professional Experience:** PROF DEPT CHEM, VANDERBILT UNIV, as of 2004; PROF DEPT PHARMACOL, VANDERBILT UNIV, as of 2004; PROF CTR STRUCT BIOL, VANDERBILT UNIV, as of 2004; assoc prof Bioeng & adj assoc prof chem, Univ Wash, beginning 1996; Sci Med New Investr Lectr, 1992; asst prof, Univ Wash, 1990-1996; Searle scholar, 1988-1992; asst prof med chem, Univ Minn, 1988-1990; McKnight-Land Grant Prof, Univ Minn, 1988-1990; NSF presidential young investr, 1987-1992; postdoctoral molecular biophys, Univ Houston, 1985-1987; affil staff scientist, Pac Northwest Nat Lab, Richland, Wash. **Memberships:** Am Chem Soc. **Research Statement & Publications:** Computer simulation of biological molecules to gain an understanding of their properties and behavior in atomic detail; atomic motions in large biological molecules and the relationship of these motions to biological function. **Mailing Address:** Ctr Struct Biol Vanderbilt Univ, 5154C Biosci MRB III, Nashville, TN 37232-8725. **Fax:** 615-936-2211. **E-Mail:** terry.p.lybrand@vanderbilt.edu

LYCETTE, R(ICHARD) (MILTON), PHYSIOLOGY, MICROBIOLOGY. **Personal Data:** b Houlton, Maine, September 20, 1926; m 1952, c 5. **Education:** Univ Maine, Orono, BS, 1950; Ill Inst Technol, MS, 1963, PhD (physiol), 1968. **Professional Experience:** Trustee, CCEE Soc, NY, 1990; LAB DIR & VPRES RES & DEVELOP, AFFIL MARINE PROD CO, BIOMED SYST CO, MAINE, 1984-; lab dir & consult, SNP Chem Co, Saginaw, Mich, 1982-1984; adj & res liaison, Detroit Polymer Inst & Indust Labs, 1980-1983; lab dir, World Wide Chem Corp, 1980-1982; res assoc physiol, Med Sch, Wayne State Univ, 1976-1979; sr chemist polymers, Fuller/OBrien Corp, South Bend, Ind, 1974-1976; dir blood prod res & develop, Parke-Davis Co, Detroit, 1973-1974; dir white cell res sect, Blood Res Ctr, Am Nat Red Cross, Bethesda, Md, 1972-1973; consult biochemist, Togus Vet Admin Hosp, Maine, 1971-1972; sci adv to gov, Off Res & Develop, Maine, 1970-1973; consult, Ind Biomed Systs Co, Mich, 1969-; vis lectr & prof, Univ Maine, Augusta, 1969-1973; res assoc blood physiol, Presby St Luke's Hosp & Med Sch, Univ Ill, Chicago, 1962-1969; NIH fels, Nat Heart Inst & Off Surgeon Gen, US Army, 1962-1969; res scientist, Continental Can Co, Chicago, 1952-1962; Food technologist bacteriol & foods chem, Gen Foods Corp, Albion, NY, 1950-1952. **Memberships:** Am Soc Microbiol; Am Chem Soc; fel Royal Microbiol Soc. **Research Statement & Publications:** Cell physiology and microbiology; influence of cell membranes and lipids on aggregation; bioenergetics in cancer; degradation polymers; blood coagulation process; immunology; Limulus substances for wide scale bacterial/viral diagnosis cures including AIDS, herpes, pioneering new device for study live membranes at angstrom levels. **Mailing Address:** 104 Worth St, Houlton, ME 04730.

LYDA, STUART D, PLANT PATHOLOGY. **Personal Data:** b Bridger, Mont, June 6, 1930; m 1953, JoAnne Koeneke; c Harriette A, Thomas D, Sonja J, Karen K & Timothy S. **Education:** Mont State Col, BS, 1956, MS, 1958; Univ Calif, PhD (plant path), 1963. **Professional Experience:** EMER PROF PLANT PATH, TEX A&M UNIV, 1994-; from assoc prof to prof, Tex A&M Univ, 1967-1994; assoc prof plant path, Univ Nev, Reno, 1962-1967; Lab technician, Univ Calif, 1959-1962. **Memberships:** AAAS; Mycol Soc Am; Am Phytopath Soc. **Research Statement & Publications:** Fungus and plant physiology; mycology; ecology and physiology of plant pathogenic, soilborne fungi. **Mailing Address:** PO Box 3507, Tex A&M Univ, Bryan, TX 77805-3507. **Fax:** 979-845-6483. **E-Mail:** 2lazy2@prodigy.net

LYDING, ARTHUR R, RHEOLOGICAL ADDITIVES, POLYURETHANES. **Personal Data:** b New York, NY, May 12, 1925; m 1957, c 1. **Education:** Cornell Univ, BA, 1945; Univ Pa, MS, 1948, PhD (chem), 1951. **Professional Experience:** Sci Ger translr, 1979-; SECT LEADER NL CHEM, NL INDUSTS, INC, HIGHTSTOWN, 1975-; sr res scientist, FMC Corp, 1969-1975; tech asst to vpres res & develop, Pkg Div, 1964-1969; Asst prof, Southern Conn State Col, 1964-1969; group leader polymers div, Olin Mathieson Chem Corp, Conn, 1957-1964; sr res chemist, Olin Industs, 1952-1956; res chemist, Heyden Chem Corp, 1950-1952; control chemist, Gen Baking Co, 1946; Instr, Cornell Univ, 1944-1945. **Memberships:** Am Chem Soc; Sigma Xi. **Research Statement & Publications:** Agricultural chemicals; vinyl monomers and polymers; polyurethanes; oil additives; cellulose chemistry; textile stain repellents and flame retardants; fluorochemicals; emulsion polymerization; synthesis of polymers and plastics additives; coatings; rheological additives. **Mailing Address:** 24 Broadripple Dr, Princeton, NJ 08540-4012.

LYE, ROBERT J, GENETICS. **Personal Data:** b St Paul, Minn, May 30, 1955. **Education:** Johns Hopkins Univ, BA, 1977; Univ Colo, Boulder, PhD (cell biol), 1989. **Professional Experience:** RES ASSOC, DEPT CELL BIOL, UNIV VA HEALTH SYST, as of 2006; postdoctoral res fel, Health Sci Ctr, Univ Va, beginning 1995; postdoctoral res fel, Sch Med, Wash Univ, 1989-1995. **Memberships:** Genetics Soc Am; Am Soc Cell Biol. **Mailing Address:** Dept Cell Biol, Univ Va Health Syst, Box 439 Jordan Hall, Charlottesville, VA 22908.

LYE, STEPHEN J, PHYSIOLOGY. **Education:** Univ Bristol, PhD (reproductive biol), 1980. **Professional Experience:** SR INVESTR & VPRES RES, MT SINAI HOSP, as of 2006; ASSOC DIR, SAMUEL LUNENFELD RES INST, as of 2006. **Mailing Address:** Samuel Lunenfeld Res Inst, Mt Sinai Hosp, Rm 870 982 600 Univ Ave, Toronto, ON M5G 1X5, Can. **Fax:** 416-586-8857. **E-Mail:** lye@mshri.on.ca

LYEL, MARGARET, FLUID MECHANICS. **Professional Experience:** AT, DEPT MECH & AEROSPACE ENG, W VA UNIV, as of 2004; RES, NAT INST STAND & TECHNOL, as of 2004. **Mailing Address:** Mech & Aerospace Eng, W Va Univ, Morgantown, WV 26506-6101.

LYERLA, JO ANN HARDING, BIOLOGY, ECOLOGICAL GENETICS. **Personal Data:** b Long Beach, Calif, September 28, 1940; m 1964, c 1. **Education:** Univ Calif, Davis, BS, 1962; San Diego State Univ, MA, 1967; Clark Univ, PhD (biol), 1978. **Professional Experience:** PROF BIOL, BECKER JR COL, LEICESTER, as of 1999; assoc prof biol, Becker Jr Col, Leicester, beginning 1976; Pa State Univ, 1967-1970 & Rockefeller Univ, 1966-1967; Gen Atomics Div, Gen Dynamics Corp, 1963-1964; lab technician, Univ Calif, Davis, 1962-1963. **Memberships:** Genetics Soc; Am Soc Zoologists. **Research Statement & Publications:** Ecological genetics of terrestial isopods; isozyme studies in animal population. **Mailing Address:** Dept Biol Sci, Becker Col, Leicester Campus Acad Bldg 61 Sever St, Worcester, MA 01609.

LYERLA, TIMOTHY ARDEN, DEVELOPMENTAL GENETICS. **Personal Data:** b Long Beach, Calif, March 5, 1940; m 1964, Jo; c 1. **Education:** Univ Calif, Davis, BA, 1963; San Diego State Col, MA, 1967; Pa State Univ, Univ Park, PhD (zoology), 1970. **Professional Experience:** PROF BIOL, CLARK UNIV, 1989-; ASSOC BIOCHEM, SHRIVER CTR MENT RETARDATION, WALTHAM, MASS, 1980-; NSF sci fac fel, 1978-1979; from asst prof to assoc prof, Shriver Ctr Ment Retardation, Waltham, Mass, 1971-1988; NIH fel, Northwestern Univ, Ill, 1970-1971. **Memberships:** Fel AAAS; Soc Integrative & Comp Biol; Soc Develop Biol; Sigma Xi; Am Soc Cell Biol; Soc Vitro Biol. **Research Statement & Publications:** Pigment genetics in vertebrates; cell differentiation in amphibian development; lysosomal storage diseases in humans. **Mailing Address:** Dept Biol, Clark Univ, 950 Main St, Worcester, MA 01610. **Fax:** 508-793-8861. **E-Mail:** tlyerla@clarku.edu

LYERLY, HERBERT KIM, HIV ASSOCIATED MALIGNANCIES, GENE THERAPY. **Personal Data:** b San Diego, Calif, August 26, 1958. **Education:** Univ Calif, Riverside, BS, 1980; Univ Calif, Los Angeles, MD, 1983. **Honors & Awards:** Achievement Award, Am Col Surgeons, 1989. **Professional Experience:** GEORGE BARTH GELLER PROF, DUKE UNIV, as of 2002; ASST PROF IMMUNOL, DUKE UNIV MED CTR, as of 2003; ASSOC PROF PATH, DUKE UNIV MED CTR, as of 2003; mem, Sci Adv Comt, Am Found AIDS Res, 1991-; investr, Ctr AIDS Res & mem, Comprehensive Cancer Ctr, Duke Univ Med Ctr, 1991-; asst prof path, Duke Univ Med Ctr, beginning 1991; ASST PROF SURG, DUKE UNIV MED CTR, 1990-. **Memberships:** Sigma Xi. **Research Statement & Publications:** Surgical oncology. **Mailing Address:** Dept Surgery, Duke Univ Med Ctr, Box 2606, Durham, NC 27710. **Fax:** 919-684-5653. **E-Mail:** lyerl001@mc.duke.edu

LYFORD, JOHN H, JR, ECOLOGY. **Personal Data:** b Chicago, Ill, July 10, 1928; div, c 6. **Education:** Carleton Col, BA, 1950; Ore State Univ, MS, 1962, PhD (bot), 1966. **Professional Experience:** EMER PROF BIOL, ORE STATE UNIV, 1992-; from asst prof to assoc prof, Ore State Univ, 1965-1992; res biologist, Ore State Game Comn, 1963-1965; Pub sch teacher, Wash, 1955-1962. **Memberships:** AAAS; Ecol Soc Am; Am Bryol Soc. **Research Statement & Publications:** Trophic structure of aquatic communities; ecology and distribution of mosses. **Mailing Address:** 342 NW 21st St, Corvallis, OR 97330. **E-Mail:** lyfordjo@onid.orst.edu

LYFORD, SIDNEY JOHN, ANIMAL NUTRITION, BIOCHEMISTRY. **Personal Data:** b Exeter, NH, January 20, 1937; m 1961, Sheila; c John N, Glenn S & Lisa K. **Education:** Univ NH, BS, 1958; NC State Univ, MS, 1960, PhD (animal nutrit), 1964. **Professional Experience:** PROF EMER ANIMAL NUTRIT, UNIV MASS, AMHERST, as of 2001; DIR, DEPARTMENTAL UNDERGRAD PROG, 1992-; consult animal nutrit. **Memberships:** Am Dairy Sci Asn; Am Soc Animal Sci; Sigma Xi. **Research Statement & Publications:** Nutrition and feeding of dairy calves; nutritive evaluation of byproduct materials as animal feedstuffs. **Mailing Address:** Dept Vet & Animal Sci, Univ Mass, 303 Stockbridge Hall, Amherst, MA 01003. **Fax:** 413-545-6326. **E-Mail:** lyford@vasci.umass.edu

LYGRE, DAVID GERALD, BIOCHEMISTRY. **Personal Data:** b Minot, NDak, August 10, 1942; m 1966, Laurae; c Jedd & Lindsay. **Education:** Concordia Col, Moorhead, Minn, BA, 1964; Univ ND, PhD (biochem), 1968. **Professional Experience:** PROF BIOCHEM, CENT WASH UNIV, as of 2003; Assoc dean, res corp grant, Cent Wash Univ, 1983-1989; asst dean, res corp grant, Cent Wash Univ, 1980-1983; prof chem, Cent Wash Univ, beginning 1979; from asst prof to assoc prof, res corp grant, Cent Wash Univ, 1970-1979; Am Cancer Soc fel, Case Western Res Univ, 1968-1970; Lectr, Am Inst Chem Engrs. **Memberships:** Am Chem Soc; Sigma Xi; AAAS. **Research Statement & Publications:** Enzymology of carbohydrate metabolism; biochemistry of aging; authored chemistry textbooks. **Mailing Address:** Dept Chem Cent Wash Univ, 400 E Univ Way, Ellensburg, WA 98926-7539. **Fax:** 509-963-1050. **E-Mail:** lygred@cwu.edu

LYJAK, ROBERT FRED, MATHEMATICS. **Personal Data:** b Detroit, Mich. **Education:** Wayne State Univ, BS, 1951; Univ Mich, Ann Arbor, MA, 1953, PhD (math), 1960. **Professional Experience:** PROF EMER MATH & COMPUTER SCI, UNIV MICH, DEARBORN, 1984-; prof math, Univ Mich, Dearborn, 1969-1984; chmn dept, Univ Mich, Dearborn, 1967-1970; assoc prof, Univ Mich, Dearborn, 1966-1969; res mathematician, Conduction Corp, 1962-1963 & Res Inst, Univ Mich, 1963-1966; mathematician, Res Inst, 1959-1962; instr math, Univ, 1956-1958; assoc mathematician, Res Inst, Univ Mich, 1953-1956. **Memberships:** Am Math Soc. **Research Statement & Publications:** Transformation groups; mathematical models of stochastic systems. **Mailing Address:** 21410 Waterloo Rd, Chelsea, MI 48118.

LYKE, EDWARD BONSTEEL, CYTOLOGY, INVERTEBRATE ZOOLOGY. **Personal Data:** b Boston, Mass, November 9, 1937; m 1962, c 2. **Education:** Miami Univ, BA, 1959; Univ Wis, MS, 1962, PhD (zoology), 1965. **Professional Experience:** PROF EMER, BIOL SCI, CALIF STATE UNIV, as of 2000; PROF BIOL SCI, CALIF STATE UNIV, HAYWARD, 1973-; from asst prof to assoc prof, 1965-1973. **Memberships:** AAAS; Am Soc Zoologists; Am Inst Biol Sci; Marine Biol Asn UK; Sigma Xi. **Research Statement & Publications:** Invertebrate cytology and histology; spermatogenesis and oogenesis; ecology of estuarine invertebrates; Investigations on the structure of adult and larval lower invertebrate animals. **Mailing Address:** Dept Biol Sci, Calif State Univ, Hayward, CA 94542. **E-Mail:** elyke@csuhayward.edu

LYKKEN, DAVID THORESON, GENETICS, PSYCHIATRY. **Personal Data:** b Minneapolis, Minn, June 18, 1928; wid Harriet; c Jesse H, Joseph D & Matthew A. **Education:** Univ Minn, BA, 1949, MA, 1952, PhD (psychol), 1955. **Honors & Awards:** Distinguished Contrib to Psychol Award, Am Psychol Asn, 1990; Distinguished Contrib to Psychophysiol, Soc Psychophysiol Res, 1998; Distinguished Sci Contrib to Applns Psychol, Am Psychol Asn, 2001. **Professional Experience:** EMER PROF PSYCHOL, UNIV MINN, 1998-; prof psychol, Univ Minn, 1965-1998; fel, Ctr Advan Study Behav Sci, 1959-1960; from asst prof to assoc prof, Univ Minn, 1957-1965. **Memberships:** Fel Am Psychol Asn; fel AAAS; Soc Psychophysiol Res (pres, 1980); Behav Genetics Soc. **Research Statement & Publications:** Psychological studies of twins, reared together or apart, and their families; study of emergenic traits which are genetic but do not run in families; studies of polygraphic interrogation (lie detection). **Mailing Address:** Dept Psychol N-218 Elliott Hall, Univ Minn 75 E River Rd SE, Minneapolis, MN 55455-0280. **Fax:** 612-626-2079. **E-Mail:** dlykken@tfs.psych.umn.edu

LYKKEN, GLENNIRVEN, PHYSICS, NUTRITION. **Personal Data:** b Grafton, NDak, January 27, 1939; m 1964, Dacon; c Timothy, Mark, Christopher & Jennifer. **Education:** Univ NDak, BSEE, 1961; Univ NC, MS, 1964, PhD (physics), 1966. **Professional Experience:** Health physicist, Grand Forks Human Nutrit Res Ctr, USDA, Grand Forks, NDak, 1988-; res physicist, Grand Forks Human Nutrit Res Ctr, USDA, Grand Forks, NDak, 1977-1988; PROF PHYSICS, UNIV NDAK, 1976-; vis prof, Univ NC, 1969-1970; from asst prof to assoc prof, Univ NDak, 1965-1976; asst physics, Univ NDak, 1961-1962 & Univ NC, 1962-1965. **Memberships:** Sigma Xi; Am Phys Soc; Am Inst Nutrit. **Research Statement & Publications:** Whole body counting of low level gamma emissions from humans; environmental radon uptake and distribution in the body; health effects in humans; bioavailability of essential trace elements; alpha particle spectroscopy-emissions from lead. **Mailing Address:** Dept Physics, Univ NDak, 219 Witmer Hall Box 7129, Grand Forks, ND 58202. **E-Mail:** glenn_lykken@und.nodak.edu

LYKOS, PETER GEORGE, PHYSICAL CHEMISTRY. **Personal Data:** b Chicago, Ill, January 22, 1927; m 1950, Marie; c George, Kristina & Andrew. **Education:** Northwestern Univ, BS, 1950; Carnegie Inst Technol, PhD (chem), 1955. **Professional Experience:** Assoc dean planning, Ill Inst Technol, beginning 1993; assoc dean planning, Beijing, 1987 assoc dean planning, Italy, 1989; assoc dean planning, WGer, Fed Repub Ger, 1985; assoc dean planning, Wash, DC, 1982; originator series int conferences comput chem res & educ, Japan, 1980; originator series int conferences comput chem res & educ, USSR, 1978; mem comt prof training, beginning 1977; adv comt, Chem & Eng News, 1977-1980; mem bd, Asn Media-based Continuing Eng Educ, 1976-1978; dir, Interactive Instr TV Network, 1976-1978; originator series int conferences comput chem res & educ, Venezuela, 1976; co-chmn, Nat Resource Comput Chem Proposal Develop Team, Argonne Univs Asn-Argonne Nat Lab, 1974-1977; chmn, Comput Chem Div, Am Chem Soc, 1973-1977; originator series int conferences comput chem res & educ, Yugoslavia, 1973; prog dir, Off Comput Activities, NSF, 1971-1973; originator series int conferences comput chem res & educ, Ill, 1971; mem-at-large & chmn comt comput chem, Nat Acad Sci-Nat Res Coun, 1968-1974; pres, Four Pi, Inc, 1966-; consult, Dept Radiation Ther, Michael Reese Hosp, 1966-1970; PROF CHEM, ILL INST TECHNOL, 1964-; dir, Comput Ctr & Comput Sci Dept, 1964-1971; consult, Solid State Sci Div, Argonne Nat Lab, 1958-1967; from instr to assoc prof chem, Ill Inst Technol, 1955-1964; Instr chem, Carnegie Inst Technol, 1954-1955; sci consult, Video Satellite Delivery, Nat Tech Univ. **Memberships:** Asn Comput Mach; Am Chem Soc; Sigma Xi. **Research Statement & Publications:** Semiempirical Quantum chemistry; computational chemistry; computers in chemical education. **Mailing Address:** Dept Chem, Ill Inst Technol, 3101 S Dearborn St Life Sci Bldg, Chicago, IL 60616-3793. **Fax:** 312-567-3480. **E-Mail:** lykos@iit.edu

LYKOUDIS, PAUL S, AERONAUTICAL ENGINEERING. **Personal Data:** m 1953, c 1. **Education:** Nat Tech Univ, Greece, Mech & Elec Engr, 1950; Purdue Univ, MS, 1954, PhD, 1956. **Honors & Awards:** Res Award, Sigma Xi, 1987. **Professional Experience:** PROF EMER NUCLEAR ENG, PURDUE UNIV, as of 2004; prof Nuclear Eng, Astronautics & Eng Sci, Purdue Univ, beginning 1985; head dept nuclear eng, Purdue Univ, 1973-1985; dir aerospace sci lab, Purdue Univ, 1968-1973; NSF grant, beginning 1960; prof aerospace, Astronautics & Eng Sci, Purdue Univ, beginning 1960; consult, Rand Corp, beginning 1960; from asst prof to assoc prof, Purdue Univ, 1956-1960. **Memberships:** Assoc fel Am Inst Aeronaut & Astronaut; Am Phys Soc; Am Astron Soc; Am Nuclear Soc; Sigma Xi. **Research Statement & Publications:** Contributor of numerous papers in field of fluid mechanics, magneto-fluid-mechanics, astrophysics, and fluid mechanics of physiological systems. **Mailing Address:** Dept Nuc Eng, Purdue Univ, 1290 Nuc Eng Bldg, West Lafayette, IN 47907-1290. **Fax:** 765-494-9570. **E-Mail:** lykoudis@ecn.purdue.edu

LYLE, BENJAMIN FRANKLIN, INDUSTRIAL ENGINEERING, SYSTEMS ANALYSIS. **Personal Data:** b Johnson City, Tenn, August 14, 1933; m 1957, c 3. **Education:** Univ Tenn, Knoxville, BS, 1955, MS, 1956; E Tenn State Univ, MA, 1962; NMex State Univ, ScD(indust eng), 1969. **Professional Experience:** PROF MATH, E TENN STATE UNIV, 1976-; assoc prof, E Tenn State Univ, 1970-1976; from instr to asst prof indust eng, NMex State Univ, 1966-1970; instr math, E Tenn State Univ, 1961-1966; pres, Lyle Furniture Co, Tenn, 1955-1961; Engr artist, Fisher Body Div, Gen Motors Corp, Mich, 1955. **Member-**

ships: Am Inst Indust Eng; Am Soc Eng Educ; Nat Soc Prof Engrs. **Research Statement & Publications:** Decision theory; economic evaluation; mathematical modeling. **Mailing Address:** Dept Technol, E Tenn State Univ PO Box 10001, Johnson City, TN 37614-0002.

LYLE, EVERETT SAMUEL, JR, FORESTRY, SOIL SCIENCE. **Personal Data:** b Dyersburg, Tenn, March 17, 1927; m 1947, c 2. **Education:** Univ Ga, BSF, 1951; Duke Univ, MF, 1952; Auburn Univ, PhD (soil sci), 1969. **Professional Experience:** PVT CONSULT, 1987-; land reclamation consult, Auburn Univ, 1986-1987; state comnr, Ala Surface Mining Reclamation Comn, 1976-1980; Researcher, Ala Surface Mine Reclamation Coun, 1973-1977; researcher, Auburn Univ, 1957-1986; Staff asst, Union Camp Corp, 1952-1957. **Memberships:** Soc Am Foresters; Am Soc Agron; Soil Sci Soc Am; Can Land Reclamation Asn. **Research Statement & Publications:** Coal surface mine reclamation; tree nutrition; forest soils. **Mailing Address:** Tate Rd, Jasper, AL 35501.

LYLE, LEON RICHARDS, TECHNICAL MANAGEMENT. **Personal Data:** b Ottumwa, Iowa, November 28, 1941; m 1972, Mary; c Elizabeth & Daniel. **Education:** Drake Univ, BA, 1963, MA, 1967; Mont State Univ, PhD (microbiol), 1969. **Professional Experience:** DIR TECH PLANNING, MALLINCKRODT INC, 1996-; dir tech planning, Hybridoma Lab, 1991-1996; assoc dir tech planning, Hybridoma Lab, 1989-1991; sci prog chmn, Nat Meeting St Louis, Clin Ligand Assay Soc, 1986-1987; assoc dir nuclear med, Hybridoma Lab, 1985-1989; Indust rep, Immunol Devices Adv Panel, Off Med Devices, Food & Drug Admin, 1981-1988; asst dir, Hybridoma Lab, 1980-1985; group leader immunol, Mallinckrodt Med Inc, 1975-1980; chemist immunol, Mallinckrodt Med Inc, 1973-1975; postdoctoral fel immunol, Sch Med, Wash Univ, 1970-1973. **Memberships:** Am Asn Immunologists; AAAS. **Research Statement & Publications:** Identification, implementation and administration of extramural research programs in medical and chemical divisions. **Mailing Address:** Mallinckrodt Inc, 675 McDonnell Blvd PO Box 5840, St Louis, MO 63134. **Fax:** 314-895-8992. **E-Mail:** lrlyle@mkg.com

LYLE, ROBERT EDWARD, JR, PHARMACEUTICAL CHEMISTRY, STRUCTURAL CHEMISTRY. **Personal Data:** b Atlanta, Ga, January 26, 1926; m 1997. **Education:** Emory Univ, BA, 1945, MS, 1946; Univ Wis-Madison, PhD (org chem), 1949. **Honors & Awards:** Harry-Carol Mosher Award, Am Chem Soc, 1987 Kuebler Award, AXE, 1998. **Professional Experience:** VPRES & TREAS, GRL CONSULTS, 1991-; Adj prof, Univ Tex, San Antonio, 1982-; vpres chem & chem eng, SW Res Inst, 1979-1991; prof & chair chem, Univ NTex, 1976-1979; prof chem, Univ NH, 1951-1976; Asst prof chem, Oberlin Col, 1949-1951; vis prof, Univ Va. **Memberships:** Am Chem Soc; Royal Soc Chem; AAAS. **Research Statement & Publications:** Stereochemistry of nitrogen heterocycles; organic synthesis of heterocyclic compounds; microencapsulation and drug delivery systems. **Mailing Address:** 12814 Kings Forest, San Antonio, TX 78230. **Fax:** 210-492-5330. **E-Mail:** geegeel@aol.com

LYLE, WILLIAM MONTGOMERY, OPTOMETRY. **Personal Data:** b Summerside, PEI, October 4, 1913; m 1956, c 3. **Education:** Col Optom Ont, dipl, 1938, OD, 1958; Ind Univ, Bloomington, MS, 1963, PhD (physiol optics), 1965. **Honors & Awards:** President's Award, Can Asn Optom. **Professional Experience:** Ed, Optom & Vision Sci, beginning 1989; DISTINGUISHED PROF EMER OPTOM, UNIV WATERLOO, 1989-; adj prof, Univ Waterloo, 1984-1989; ed, Am J Optom & Physiol Optics, 1979-1988; dir clins, Univ Waterloo, 1974-1977; pres, Asn Schs Optom Can, 1971-1973; from assoc prof to prof optom, Univ Waterloo, 1967-1984; chief path sect, Univ Waterloo, 1967-1974; asst prof optom, Col Optom Ont, 1965-1967; lectr, Ind Univ, 1962-1965; res assoc physiol optics, Ind Univ, 1960-1962; pvt pract optom, 1938-1960. **Memberships:** Can Asn Optom (pres 1955-1957); AAAS; Am Acad Optom; Am Soc Human Genetics; Am Optom Asn; Sigma Xi. **Research Statement & Publications:** Side effects of drugs; inheritance of astigmatism; intraracial differences in refraction; lasers. **Mailing Address:** Sch Optom, Univ Waterloo, Waterloo, ON N2L 3G1, Can. **Fax:** 519-746-7937. **E-Mail:** optjourn@sciborg.uwaterloo.ca

LYLES, LEON, AGRICULTURAL ENGINEERING, RESEARCH ADMINISTRATION. **Personal Data:** b Wetumka, Okla, January 18, 1932; m Jerry. **Education:** Okla State Univ, BS, 1955; Kans State Univ, MS, 1959, PhD (mech eng), 1970. **Professional Experience:** RETIRED; res leader, Wind Erosion Res Unit, 1975-1988; wind erosion res, Agr Res Serv, USDA, 1964-1975; water mgt res, Agr Res Serv, USDA, 1960-1964; agr engr erosion res, Agr Res Serv, USDA, 1957-1960. **Memberships:** Am Soc Agr Engrs; Soil Sci Soc Am. **Research Statement & Publications:** Wind erosion and water management (dryland) research. **Mailing Address:** 1801 Va Dr, Manhattan, KS 66502.

LYLES, LESTER L, AERONAUTICAL & ASTRONAUTICAL ENGINEERING. **Professional Experience:** RETIRED; dir, Ballistic Missile Defense Orgn, Dept Defense, as of 1999. **Mailing Address:** Ballistic Missile Defense Orgn, Dept Defense, 7100 Defense Pentagon, Washington, DC 20301.

LYMAN, BEVERLY ANN, BIOCHEMISTRY, TOXICOLOGY. **Personal Data:** b Philadelphia, Pa, August 22, 1956; m 1981, Henry M Laboda; c Alex & Elizabeth. **Education:** Thomas Jefferson Univ, BS, 1978; Univ Pa, MS, 1982; Hahnemann Med Col, PhD (biochem), 1986. **Professional Experience:** FAC, PATENT RESOURCES GROUP, INC, as of 2004; WITH WOOD HERRON & EVANS, 1993-; assoc prof, Clin Lab Sci & Med Chem, Univ Tenn, Memphis, 1989-1993; Fel, Chem Indust Inst Toxicol, 1987-1988. **Memberships:** Am Soc Biochem & Molecular Biol; AAAS; Sigma Xi; Am Soc Med Technol; Soc Toxicol. **Research Statement & Publications:** Biochemical toxicology of anticancer drugs; biochemistry of surface-active antithrombotic agents for prostheses. **Mailing Address:** Wood Herron & Evans, 2700 Carew Tower, Cincinnati, OH 45202.

LYMAN, DONALD JOSEPH, POLYMER CHEMISTRY, BIOMATERIALS. **Personal Data:** b Chicago, Ill, November 5, 1926; m 1978, c 2. **Education:** Univ Nev, BS, 1949; Univ Del, MS, 1951, PhD (chem), 1952. **Honors & Awards:** Am Soc Artificial Internal Organs Award, 1969; Clemson Award Basic Res, Soc Biomaterials, 1982; Distinguished Res Award, Univ Utah, 1982; biomed sci & eng, world biomed lang, 1994. **Professional Experience:** EMER PROF MAT SCI & BIOENG, UNIV UTAH, 1989-; pres, Vascular Int Inc, 1983-1986; prof bioeng, Univ Utah, 1974-1989; mem, eval panel polymer div, Nat Bur Stand, 1973-1976; prof mat sci; res assoc prof surg, adj prof chan Univ Utah, 1969-1989; head biomed polymer res, Stanford Res Int, 1964-1969; Lectr, Dept Mat Sci, Stanford Univ, 1964-1968; sr polymer chemist, Stanford Res Int, 1961-1964; res chemist high polymers, E I du Pont de Nemours & Co, 1952-1961; Asst chem, Univ Del, 1950-1952; chmn, Gordon Conf Sci & Technol Biomat; mem, comt surv mat sci & eng, Nat Acad Sci. **Memberships:** AAAS; emer mem, Am Chem Soc; Am Soc Artificial Internal Organs; Soc Biomat; Int Soc Artificial Organs; appl spectros. **Research Statement & Publications:** Synthetic polymers and polymer intermediates; mechanisms of polymerization; structure-property relationships of polymers; biomedical polymers; implants for artificial organs and reconstruction surgery; infrared spectroscopy. **Mailing Address:** PO Box 5314, Lacey, WA 98509-5314.

LYMAN, FRANK LEWIS, TOXICOLOGY. **Personal Data:** b Springfield, Ill, November 6, 1921; m 1947, Julia; c Patty, Frank III, Richard, Robert, Jon & Don. **Education:** Swarthmore Col, AB, 1943; Hahnemann Med Col, MD, 1946; Bd Toxicol Sci, dipl. **Professional Experience:** RETIRED; assoc prof, Sch Med, Temple Univ, beginning 1977; consult toxicol, 1976-1987; mem var comts, Nat Acad Sci, 1975-1981; dir indust med, Ciba Geigy Corp, 1963-1976; asst to med dir, Med Dept, Geigy Chem Corp, 1961-1963; instr, Seton Hall Col, 1960-1962; assoc dir, Med Dept, Geigy Chem Corp, 1960-1961; assoc med dir, Mead Johnson & Co, 1957-1960; staff pediatrician, US Naval Hosp, Beaufort, SC, 1955-1957; pvt pract, Iowa, 1948-1955; physician, coach & instr biol, William Penn Col, 1947-1948; W Jersey Hosp, Camden, NJ, 1947. **Memberships:** AMA; Am Col Toxicol; Soc Toxicol; fel Am Acad Clin Toxicol. **Research Statement & Publications:** Dietary management of phenylketonuria; toxicology of fluorescent whitening agents; pesticide toxicology. **Mailing Address:** 1068 F Long Beach Blvd, North Beach, NJ 08008.

LYMAN, FREDERIC A, MECHANICAL ENGINEERING. **Personal Data:** b Syracuse, NY, September 4, 1934; m 1954, Marilyn Mawson; c Ruth, Martha & Sarah. **Education:** Syracuse Univ, BME, 1955, MME, 1957; Rensselaer Polytech Inst, PhD (eng mech), 1961. **Professional Experience:** PROF EMER, SYRACUSE UNIV, 1995-; prin res engr, Case Western Res Univ/NASA Lewis Inst Computational Mech Propulsion, 1985-1986; prof mech & aerospace eng, Syracuse Univ, 1978-1995; vis res engr, Princeton Univ, 1977-1978; assoc prof, Syracuse Univ, 1970-1978; assoc prof eng, Case Western Res Univ, 1967-1970; head plasma flow sect, Lewis Res Ctr, NASA, 1966-1967; aerospace res engr, Lewis Res Ctr, NASA, 1962-1966; preceptor eng mech, Columbia Univ, 1961-1962. **Memberships:** AAAS; Am Phys Soc; Am Soc Mech Engrs. **Research Statement & Publications:** Fluid mechanics; heat transfer; plasma dynamics; acoustics; combustion; Turbomachinary. **Mailing Address:** 323 Scott Ave, Syracuse, NY 13224-1725.

LYMAN, GARY HERBERT, PUBLIC HEALTH & EPIDEMIOLOGY, BIOMATHEMATICS. **Personal Data:** b Buffalo, NY, February 24, 1946; m 1978, Carolyn; c Stephen & Christopher. **Education:** State Univ NY, BA, 1968, MD, 1972; Harvard Univ, MPH, 1982. **Professional Experience:** CHIEF EPIDEMIOL & BIOSTATIST, UNIV SOUTH FLA, 1993-; PROF MED & BIOSTATIST, UNIV SOUTH FLA, 1977-; prof med, Rochester Sch Med & Dent, 2002; prof Biochem & Satist, Albany Sch Pub Health, 2000-2002; head hemat oncol, Dept Med, Albany Med Col, 2000-2002; vis prof, Med Satist Unit, London Sch Hyg Trop Med, 1997-1998; prof epidemiol & biostatist, Univ South Fla, Col Pub health, 1986-2000; prof med, Univ South Fla, Col Med, 1986-2000; chief med oncol, 1979-1983; from asst prof to assoc prof, Univ South Fla, 1977-1986; chief med, H Lee Moffitt Cancer Ctr & Res Inst, 1985-1993; res instr med, State Univ NY, 1974-1977. **Memberships:** AAAS; Am Soc Hemat; Am Soc Clin Oncol; Am Asn Cancer Res; Am Col Physicians. **Research Statement & Publications:** Cancer epidemiology; clinical decision making; mathematical modeling; design and analysis of clincial trials; clinical pharmacology. **Mailing Address:** H Lee Moffitt Cancer Ctr & Res Inst, 601 Elmwood Ave, PO Box 704, Rochester, NY 14642-8704. **Fax:** 585-276-1885. **E-Mail:** lyman@aarlo.moffitt.usf.edu

LYMAN, HARVARD, PLANT PHYSIOLOGY, MOLECULAR BIOLOGY. **Personal Data:** b San Francisco, Calif, September 25, 1931. **Education:** Univ Calif, Berkeley, BA, 1953; Univ Wash, MS, 1957; Brandeis Univ, PhD (biol), 1960. **Professional Experience:** ASSOC PROF BIOCHEM & CELL BIOL, STATE UNIV NY, STONY BROOK, as of 1999; NSF travel grant, 1970-1972, grant, 1964; assoc scientist, Med Dept, 1967-1968; asst scientist microbiol, Brookhaven Nat Lab, NY, 1965-1967; NIH res grant, 1963-1965; asst prof biol, Brooklyn Col, 1963-1965; vis scientist biochem, Brookhaven Nat Lab, 1962-1963; instr, Brooklyn Col, 1960-1962; asst biol, Univ Wash, 1955-1957. **Memberships:** AAAS; Am Soc Plant Physiologists; Soc Protozoologists; Am Soc Cell Biologists; Biophys Soc. **Research Statement & Publications:** Biosynthesis and inheritance of cellular organelles; development, physiology and differentiation of algae and fleshy and unicellular fungi. **Mailing Address:** Dept Biol, State Univ NY, 310 Life Sci Bldg, Stony Brook, NY 11794-5215. **Fax:** 516-632-9730. **E-Mail:** hlyman@allinl.cc.sunysb.edu

LYMAN, JOHN L, LASER PHOTOCHEMISTRY, THERMODYNAMICS. **Personal Data:** b Delta, Utah, June 16, 1944; m 1968, c 5. **Education:** Brigham Young Univ, BS, 1968, PhD (phys chem), 1973. **Professional Experience:** Vis prof, Univ NewSWales, Kensington, Australia, 1987; FEL, LOS ALAMOS NAT LAB, 1983-; vis scientist, Max Planck Inst Quantum-Optics, Garching, WGer, 1982, 1984 & 1990; asst group leader, Los Alamos Nat Lab, 1981-1982; Guest prof, Ctr Interdisciplinary Res, Univ Bielefeld, WGer, 1980; mem staff, Los Alamos Nat Lab, 1973-1981; Phys scientist asst, US Army Dugway Proving Ground, 1969-1970. **Memberships:** Am Chem Soc; Optical Soc Am; fel Am Inst Chem. **Research Statement & Publications:** Chemical kinetics; interaction of laser radiation with polyatomic molecules, including laser photochemistry, laser istope separation, infrared excitation of polyatomic molecules, and vibrational energy dynamics. **Mailing Address:** Los Alamos Nat Lab, Los Alamos, NM 87544. **Fax:** 505-667-0440. **E-Mail:** lyman@lanl.gov

LYMAN, JOHN TOMPKINS, BIOPHYSICS. **Personal Data:** b Berkeley, Calif, May 25, 1932; m 1980, c 3. **Education:** Univ Calif, AB, 1954 & 1958, PhD (biophys), 1965. **Professional Experience:** STAFF SR SCIENTIST, LAWRENCE BERKELEY LAB, 1979-; biophysicist, 1965-1979; Res asst, 1959-1965. **Memberships:** Am Asn Physicists in Med; AAAS; Sigma Xi. **Research Statement & Publications:** Radiation physics; radiation therapy; radiobiology; heavy charged-particle radiation dosimetry; radiobiology and radiotherapy. **Mailing Address:** 10 Tanglewood Rd, MS 55-121, Berkeley, CA 94705-1421.

LYMAN, ONA RUFUS, PHYSICS. **Personal Data:** b Jamaica, Vt, November 18, 1930; m 1954, c 3. **Education:** Univ Vt, BA, 1952. **Professional Experience:** RETIRED; physicist, Terminal Ballistics Lab, Ballistics Res Lab, Aberdeen Proving Groun, 1956-1995; jr engr, Sprague Elec Co, 1952-1954. **Research Statement & Publications:** Neutron shielding; combustion; interaction of laser beams with materials; blast and fragment protection for industrial workers; initiation mechanisms of explosives; explosive safety in storage and transport; vulnerability of gun propellants to hostile threats. **Mailing Address:** 303 Carter St, Aberdeen, MD 21001.

LYMAN, W(ILKES) STUART, PHYSICAL METALLURGY. **Personal Data:** b Mt Vernon, SDak, April 13, 1924; m 1948, Martha; c Mary C (Onkka), Richard F & Barbara L (Varangis). **Education:** Univ Notre Dame, BS, 1944; Univ Calif, MS, 1952. **Professional Experience:** RETIRED; sr adv, Copper Develop Asn Inc, 1994-2000; sr vpres, Copper Develop Asn Inc, 1981-1994; vpres, Copper Develop Asn Inc, 1979-1981; mgr tech serv & mkt res, Copper Develop Asn Inc, 1964-1979; div chief, Battelle Mem Inst, 1962-1964; div consult ferrous metall, Battelle Mem Inst, 1957-1962; asst dept consult, Battelle Mem Inst, 1955-1957; staff metallurgist, Mat Adv Bd, Nat Res Coun, 1951-1954; res engr, Inst Eng Res, 1950-1951; asst, Univ Calif, 1949-1950; engr, Spec Assignment, Heidelberg, 1948-1949; head adv planning unit, Off Chief Engr, US Forces Frankfurt, Ger, 1946-1947; jr metallurgist, Nat Adv Comt Aeronaut, Ohio, 1944. **Memberships:** Am Soc Metals; Inst

Mat. **Research Statement & Publications:** Metal fabrication; materials application; alloy selection. **Mailing Address:** N Bridge Terr, Mt Kisco, NY 10549.

LYMAN, WILLIAM RAY, CHEMISTRY, RADIOISOTOPES IN RESEARCH. **Personal Data:** b Stratton, Vt, May 30, 1920; m 1944, Vera; c William Ray Jr, Richard Christian, Vera Ellen (Lane) & Philip Carl. **Education:** Univ Vt, BS, 1941; Mass Inst Technol, PhD (org chem), 1947; Columbia Univ, AM, 1947. **Professional Experience:** RETIRED; consult, Rohm & Haas Co, 1985-1987; spec assignment, Rohm & Haas Co, 1984-1985; res sect mgr, Rohm & Haas Co, 1981-1984; proj leader, Rohm & Haas Co, 1973-1981; lab head, Rohm & Haas Co, 1966-1973; res chemist, Rohm & Haas Co, 1948-1966; res chemist, Resinous Prod & Chem Co, 1947-1948; jr chemist, Tenn Eastman Corp Div, Eastman Kodak Co, 1944-1946; asst chem, Columbia Univ, 1941-1944. **Memberships:** Am Chem Soc. **Research Statement & Publications:** Pesticide residue analysis; fate of pesticides in plant and animal systems and in the environment. **Mailing Address:** 728 Norristown Rd, Apt G 209, Ambler, PA 19002.

LYMANGROVER, JOHN R, ENDOCRINOLOGY, ELECTROPHYISOLOGY. **Personal Data:** b Ft Wayne, Ind, July 24, 1944. **Education:** Xavier Univ, BS, 1966; Univ Ky, MS, 1968; Univ Cincinnati, PhD (physiol), 1972. **Professional Experience:** RETIRED; chmn, Sci Rev Adminr, Nat Inst Arthritis & Musculoskeletal & Skin Dis, as of 2003; adj assoc prof, Dept Elec Eng, Tulane Univ, 1980-; assoc prof, Dept Physiol & Pharmacol, 1980-; dir, Med Physiol, Bowman-Gray Med Sch, 1980-; consult & grants reviewer, NIH, 1979-1981; asst prof, Dept Physiol, Tulane Univ, 1975-1980; fel res, Dept Biochem, Med Col Ohio, 1972-1975. **Memberships:** AAAS; Sigma Xi; Bioelectromagnetics Soc; Endocrine Soc; Am Heart Asn. **Research Statement & Publications:** Neuroendocrinology; biological effects of electric fields; mechanism of peptide hormone action on adrenal cortical hormone release; role of endogenous opioids on adrenal steroid secretion and regulation of blood pressure. **Mailing Address:** 12909 Turkey Branch Pkwy, Rockville, MD 20853. **E-Mail:** lymangrj@mail.nih.gov

LYMN, RICHARD WESLEY, BIOPHYSICS, BIOCHEMISTRY. **Personal Data:** b Flushing, NY, July 26, 1944; m 1970, c 2. **Education:** Johns Hopkins Univ, BA, 1964; Univ Chicago, PhD (biophys), 1970. **Professional Experience:** Chmn, Biophys Soc, 1990-1991; treas, Publ Comt, 1987-1991; DIR MUSCLE BIOL PROG, NIH, 1984-; treas, Biophys Soc, 1982-1987; asst assoc dir, Arthritis, Musculoskeletal & Skin Dis, Nat Inst Arthritis, Diabetes, Digestive & Kidney Dis, 1979-1983; grants assoc, Div Res Grants, 1978-1979; sr staff fel biophys, Phys Biol Lab, Nat Inst Arthritis Metab & Digestive Dis, 1974-1978; Brit-Am fel, Am Heart Asn, MRC Lab Molecular Biol, Cambridge, Eng, 1971-1974; USPHS fel biophys, Univ Chicago, 1970-1971. **Memberships:** Biophys Soc; Am Soc Biol Chemists; AAAS. **Research Statement & Publications:** Enzyme kinetics; cellular and morphological movement; mathematical modelling; molecular mechanism of muscle contraction and tension development; science administration. **Mailing Address:** Nat Inst Arthritis & Musculoskeletal & Skin Dis, Nat Inst Health, 6701 Democracy Blvd One Democracy Plaza Rm 860 Ste 800, Bethesda, MD 20892. **Fax:** 301-480-4543. **E-Mail:** lymnr@mail.nih.gov

LYNCH, BENJAMIN LEO, ORAL SURGERY. **Personal Data:** b Omaha, Nebr, December 29, 1923; m 1956, Colleen; c Kathleen, Mary Beth, Patrick, George, Martha & Estelle. **Education:** Creighton Univ, BS, 1945, DDS, 1947, MA, 1953; Northwestern Univ, MSD, 1954; Am Bd Oral Surg, dipl. **Professional Experience:** PROF EMER ORAL SURG, CREIGHTON UNIV, 1986-; secy staff, Omaha Surg Ctr, 1981-1983; staff mem & exec comt, Omaha Surg Ctr, 1979-1983; treas, Children's Mem Hosp Med-Dent Staff, 1979-1981; pres, Nebr Dental Serv Corp, 1974-1978; exec comt, bd dir, Nebr Blue Cross-Blue Shield, 1973-1981; mem bd dirs, Nebr Dental Serv Corp, 1972-1978; mem, bd dir, Nebr Blue Cross-Blue Shield, 1968-1989; pres, Omaha-Douglas County Health Bd, 1968; vpres, Omaha-Douglas County Health Bd, 1967; coordr, Dent Sch Grad & Post-grad Prog, 1967; mem, Omaha-Douglas County Health Bd, 1966-1968; prof oral surg, Creighton Univ, beginning 1957; guest lectr, Ft Sam Houston, 1957-1958; Med Field Sch, Walter Reed Army Post-grad Sch Med, 1956-1957; Med Field Sch, Ft Sam Houston, 1955-1956; fac mem, San Antonio Jr Col, 1955; dir, Oral Surg Dept, 1954-1967; dean, Sch Dent, 1954-1961; pres dent staff, Children's Mem Hosp, 1952-1953 & 1959-1960; staff mem, Children's Mem Hosp Med-Dent Staff, 1950-1988; from asst instr to assoc prof oral surg, Creighton Univ, 1948-1957; consult, Vet Hosp & Strategic Air Command Hq, Omaha, Nebr & Jenny Edmundson Hosp, Council Bluffs, Iowa. **Memberships:** Am Soc Oral & Maxillofacial Surgeons; Am Dent Asn; fel Am Col Dent. **Research Statement & Publications:** Dental education. **Mailing Address:** Dept Oral Surg, Creighton Univ, 2500 Calif Plaza, Omaha, NE 68178.

LYNCH, BRIAN MAURICE, PHYSICAL ORGANIC CHEMISTRY, CHEMICAL INFORMATION. **Personal Data:** b Melbourne, Australia, January 20, 1930; m 1956, Elizabeth; c Alexandra Helen & Martin James. **Education:** Univ Melbourne, BSc, 1952, MSc, 1954, PhD (chem), 1956. **Professional Experience:** Mem, educ comt, chem info div, Am Chem Soc, beginning 1996; SR RES PROF, CHEM MED INFO, ST FRANCIS XAVIER UNIV, 1995-; proj Seraphim fel, Eastern Mich Univ, 1988; natural sci & eng res coun sr indust fel, NS Res Found, 1981-1982; chmn dept, St Francis Xavier Univ, 1980-1986 & 1972-1979; prof org chem, St Francis Xavier Univ, 1968-1995; nat res coun can sr res fel, Australian Nat Univ, 1968-1969; assoc prof, St Francis Xavier Univ, 1962-1968; asst prof phys chem, Mem Univ Nfld, 1959-1962; res officer chem, Div Coal Res, Commonwealth Sci & Indust Res Orgn, Australia, 1958-1959; asst prof org chem, St Francis Xavier Univ, Can, 1957-1958; fel & vis prof cancer chemother, NMex Highlands Univ, 1956-1957. **Memberships:** Am Chem Soc; fel Can Soc Chem; fel Royal Soc Chem London; Soc Appl Spectros; fel Chem Inst Can. **Research Statement & Publications:** Nuclear magnetic resonance; infrared spectra by Fourier transform techniques; internet resources for chemistry and health. **Mailing Address:** Dept Chem, St Francis Xavier Univ, PO Box 5000, Antigonish, NS B2G 2W5, Can. **Fax:** 902-867-2414. **E-Mail:** blynch@juliet.stfsc.ca

LYNCH, CAROL BECKER, BEHAVIORAL GENETICS, EVOLUTIONARY GENETICS. **Personal Data:** b New York, NY, December 3, 1942; m 1967, Robert. **Education:** Mt Holyoke Col, AB, 1964; Univ Mich, MA, 1965; Univ Iowa, PhD (zoology), 1971. **Honors & Awards:** Fel AAAS; Res Career Develop Award, NIH. **Professional Experience:** DEAN GRAD SCH & ASSOC VICE CHANCELLOR RES, UNIV COLO, BOULDER, 1992-; Prog dir, Pop Biol & Physiol Ecol, NSF, 1990-1992; dean sci, Wesleyan Univ, 1988-1991; prof biol, Wesleyan Univ, 1985-1992; from asst prof to prof, Wesleyan Univ, 1973-1985; NSF fel, Inst Behav Genetics, Univ Colo, 1972-1973. **Memberships:** Behav Genetics Asn; AAAS; Soc Study Evolution; Am Soc Naturalists. **Research Statement & Publications:** Genetic and environmental influences on behavioral and physiological thermoregulation in mice; empirical tests of quantitative; genetic theory; genetic influence on circadian rhythms. **Mailing Address:** Univ Colo Boulder, 26 UCB, Boulder, CO 80309-0026. **Fax:** 303-492-5777. **E-Mail:** carol.lynch@colorado.edu

LYNCH, CHARLES ANDREW, SYNTHETIC FAT SUBSTITUTES, SYNTHETIC LUBRICANTS. **Personal Data:** b Brooklyn, NY, January 6, 1935; m 1960, Marilyn A Monaco; c Nancy & Cara. **Education:** Manhattan Col, BS, 1956; Univ Notre Dame, PhD (org chem), 1960. **Professional Experience:** VPRES TECHNOL, HATCO CORP, 1991-; tech dir, Dir Sales & Mkt/New Bus Develop, 1981-1990; exec vpres & tech dir, Am Oil & Supply Co, 1974-1980; mgr org appln res, FMC Corp, 1965-1974; Res chemist, Esso Res & Eng Co, 1960-1965. **Memberships:** Am Chem Soc; Am Oil Chemists Soc; Soc Tribologists & Lubrication Engrs; Soc Automotive Engrs; Chem Mgt & Resources Asn; Com Develop Asn. **Research Statement & Publications:** Advanced high temperature liquid lubricant development; advanced dielectric fluids; fat substitutes; product and process research. **Mailing Address:** 19 Gordon Way, Princeton, NJ 08540-3925.

LYNCH, DANIEL ROGER, COMPUTATION, APPLIED MATHEMATICS. **Personal Data:** b Glens Falls, NY, 1950. **Education:** Mass Inst Technol, BS & MS, 1972; Princeton Univ, MS, 1976, PhD (civil eng), 1978. **Professional Experience:** MACLEAN PROF ENG, DARTMOUTH COL, 1993-; exec dir, Regional Asn Res Gulf Maine, 1992-1994; prof, Dartmouth Col, 1989-1993; assoc dean eng, Dartmouth Col, 1985-1989; prin young investr, NSF, 1984; hydrologist, US Geol Surv, 1977-1979; qual assurance engr, C R Bard Inc, 1973-1975; engr, Stone & Webster, 1972-1973. **Memberships:** Am Geophys Union; Am Soc Civil Engrs. **Research Statement & Publications:** Advanced computational methods for environmental simulation; coastal ocean. **Mailing Address:** Thayer Sch Eng, Dartmouth Col, 8000 Cummings Hall, Hanover, NH 03755-8000. **E-Mail:** daniel.r.lynch@dartmouth.edu

LYNCH, DARREL LUVENE, ORGANIC CHEMISTRY, SOIL MICROBIOLOGY. **Personal Data:** b Dewey, Okla, February 6, 1921; m 1949, Dorothy; c Alan, Francis, Alice & Margaret. **Education:** Univ Ill, PhD (agron), 1953; Univ Del, MS, 1957. **Professional Experience:** PROF EMER BIOL SCI, NORTHERN ILL UNIV, 1982-; from assoc prof to prof, Northern Ill Univ, 1966-1982; assoc prof chem, Ga Southern Col, 1960-1962; asst prof soil sci, Univ Alta, 1958-1960; asst prof agron, Univ Del, 1952-1958; instr & asst soil biol, Univ Ill, 1948-1952. **Memberships:** Am Soc Microbiol. **Research Statement & Publications:** Nitrogen fixation of Rhizobia and nodulation; soil organic matter; soil polysaccharides; morphology and nutrition studies with algae; ultrastructure studies with the Actinoplanaceae; pigment production in bacteria. **Mailing Address:** Dept Biol Sci, Northern Ill Univ, De Kalb, IL 60115.

LYNCH, DAVID DEXTER, THEORY OF INERTIAL INSTRUMENTS, MODELING & SIMULATION OF AUTOMOTIVE CRASH SENSORS. **Personal Data:** b Brooklyn, NY, May 22, 1934; m 1954, Lorene; c M Coleen (Barker), Christopher S, Kimberly A & Jonathan J. **Education:** Tufts Univ, BS, 1956; Harvard Univ, Am, 1957, PhD (theoret physics), 1967; Univ Calif, Santa Barbara, BA, 1986. **Professional Experience:** RETIRED, 1999; consult, Navig Syst Div, Northrop Grumman beginning 2001; chief scientist, Guidance & Control Systs Div, Litton Systs INC, beginning 1995; prin tech fel, Advan Instrument Technol Sect, 1992-1995; staff engr, Advan Instrument Technol Sect, 1980-1991; mem, Task Group Design Marine Risers, Am Petrol Inst, 1974-1975; head, Advan Instrument Technol Sect, 1969-1980; head physics group, Delco Systs Opers, Delco Electronics Corp, 1967-1969; engr, Delco Systs Opers, Delco Electronics Corp, 1963-1967; instr physics, Tufts Univ, 1959-1963. **Research Statement & Publications:** Theory and design analysis of inertial instruments including the laser gyroscope, the fiber-optic gyroscope, and the hemispherical-resonator gyroscope; math modeling and simulation of crash sensors for automotive air-cushion restraint systems. **Mailing Address:** 5442 Berkeley Rd, Santa Barbara, CA 93111-1614. **Fax:** 805-961-6726. **E-Mail:** lynch@littongcs.com

LYNCH, DAVID H, IMMUNOLOGY. **Personal Data:** b San Francisco, Calif, August 5, 1950. **Education:** Univ Calif, Santa Cruz, BS, 1974; Univ Utah, PhD (exp path), 1979. **Professional Experience:** SR STAFF SCIENTIST IMMUNOL, IMMUNEX CORP, as of 2002; STAFF SCIENTIST IMMUNOL, IMMUNEX CORP, 1988-; res asst prof, Dept Obstet-Gynec, 1985-1988; IPA investr, Immunol Br, Nat Cancer Inst, 1982-1985; res instr, Dept Obstet-Gynec, 1981-1982; Post doctoral fel, Dept Path, Sch Med, Univ Utah, 1979-1981. **Memberships:** Sigma Xi; Am Asn Immunologists. **Mailing Address:** Dept Immunobiology, Immunex Corp, 51 Univ St, Seattle, WA 98101-2977. **Fax:** 206-623-4572.

LYNCH, DAVID WILLIAM, SOLID STATE PHYSICS, OPTICAL PROPERTIES OF SOLIDS. **Personal Data:** b Rochester, NY, July 14, 1932; m 1992, Glenys; c Jean, Richard & David. **Education:** Rensselaer Polytech Inst, BS, 1954; Univ Ill, MS, 1955, PhD (physics), 1958. **Professional Experience:** Dir, Microelectronics Res Ctr, 1995-1999; DISTINGUISHED PROF PHYSICS, IOWA STATE UNIV, 1985-; chmn dept, 1985-1990; actg assoc dir, Synchrotron Radiation Lab, Stoughton, Wis, 1984; vis prof, Univ Physics Hamburg, 1974; sr physicist, Ames Lab, US Dept Energy, 1966-; from asst prof to prof, 1959-1985; Fulbright fel, Pavia, Italy, 1958-1959. **Memberships:** AAAS; fel Am Phys Soc. **Research Statement & Publications:** Optical properties of solids, including use of synchrotron radiation and modulation-spectroscopy; photoelectron spectroscopy. **Mailing Address:** Dept Physics & Astron, Iowa State Univ, Ames, IA 50011. **Fax:** 515-294-0689. **E-Mail:** dwl@ameslab.gov

LYNCH, DENIS PATRICK, ORAL PATHOLOGY, ORAL MEDICINE. **Personal Data:** b Kansas City, Kans, October 5, 1951; m 1973, Monica; c Sydney A & Shannon M. **Education:** Univ Calif, San Francisco, DDS, 1976; Univ Ala, PhD, 1986. **Honors & Awards:** Gabbs Award, Am Acad Oral Path Award, & Am Acad Oral Med Award, Univ Calif, San Francisco, 1976; Golden Pen Award, Int Col Dent, 1985; Award, Am Col Dent, 1987; Award, Pierre Fauchard Acad, 1987. **Professional Experience:** PROF ORAL & MAXILLOFACIAL PATH & ASSOC DEAN ACAD AFFAIRS, MARQUETTE UNIV, 2002-; PROF DERMAT, MED COL WIS, as of 2002; Chair, Parameters Comt, Am Acad Oral Maxillofacial Path, 1995-; prof med, Div Dermat, Col Med, 1994-2002; prof biologic & diag sci, Univ Tenn Col Dent, 1993-2002; exec assoc dean, Univ Tenn Col Dent, 1993-; pres, Exp Path Group, Int Asn Dent Res, 1992-1993; curric consult, Comn Dent Accreditation, 1990-1996; adj assoc prof, Col Med, Tex A&M Univ, 1989-1993; adj assoc prof community med, Baylor Col Med, 1989-1993; exec assoc dean, Univ Tex Dent Br, 1989-1992; assoc prof, Univ Tex Dent Br, 1988-1993; consult, Bering Clin, 1987-1993; assoc dean acad affairs, Univ Tex Dent Br, 1987-1989; vpres dent res & develop, Pearce Sci & Tech Assocs, 1986-1993; mem, Janssen Res Coun, Janssen Pharmaceut, 1986-1993; mem, Pres Task Force on AIDS, Univ Tex Health Sci Ctr, Houston, 1986; chmn, Sect Path, Am Asn Dent Schs, 1984-1985; adj asst prof path & lab med, Col Med, Tex A&M Univ, 1983-1989; asst prof path, Univ Tex Dent Br, 1981-1987; mem, Comn Accreditation, Am Dent Asn, 1975-1979. **Memberships:** Am Asn Dent Schs; Int Asn Dent Res; Am Acad Oral Maxillofacial Path; Am Dent Asn; Sigma Xi. **Research Statement & Publications:** Oral manifestations of Acquired Immune Deficiency Syndrome; opportunistic fungal infections; oral candidasis, mucocutaneous disease; recurrent oral ulcerations; infectious hazards in dentistry. **Mailing Address:** Dean Sch Dent, Marquette Univ, Milwaukee, WI 53202. **E-Mail:** denis.lynch@marquette.edu

LYNCH, DERMOT ROBORG, PLANT BREEDING, PLANT PHYSIOLOGY. **Personal Data:** b Johannesburg, SAfrica, February 9, 1940; Canadian citizen; m 1965, c 2. **Educa-**

tion: Univ Natal, SAfrica, BSc, 1963, MSc, 1969; Univ Guelph, Can, PhD (plant physiol), 1974. **Professional Experience:** SR RES SCIENTIST, POTATO BREEDING & GENETICS, LETHBRIDGE RES CTR, AGR & AGRI-FOOD CAN RES CTR, 2003-; ASST PROF POTATO & VEGETABLE CROPS, NS AGR COL, res scientist potato breeding, Lethbridge res sta, agr Can, 1978-; res scientist, McCain Foods Ltd, 1974-1975; res scientist potato mgt & physiol, Tech Servs, Dept Agr, 1968-1971; Crop specialist, Tech Servs, Dept Agr, 1965-1966. **Memberships:** Agr Inst Can; Potato Asn Am; Europ Asn Potato Res. **Research Statement & Publications:** Potato breeding and Genetics; physiology of the potato and development of superior management options. **Mailing Address:** Lethbridge Res Ctr AAFC, 5403 One Ave S PO Box 3000, Lethbridge, AB T1J 4B1, Can. **Fax:** 403-382-3156. **E-Mail:** lynchd@agr.gc.ca

LYNCH, DON MURL, ORGANIC CHEMISTRY, MEDICAL DEVICES & DIAGNOSTICS. **Personal Data:** b Delano, Calif, February 19, 1934. **Education:** Fresno State Col, AB, 1960; Univ Calif, Berkeley, PhD (org chem), 1964. **Professional Experience:** CLIN PROJ MGR, ABBOTT LABS, 1984-; clin monitor, Abbott Labs, 1981-1984; sr clin res assoc, Abbott Labs, 1978-1981; sr res chemist, Abbott Labs, 1968-1978; sr res chemist, Cutter Labs, 1967-1968; sr res chemist, Abbott Labs, 1964-1967. **Research Statement & Publications:** Synthesis of potential pharmaceuticals and agricultural chemicals; isolation, structure and synthesis of natural products; clinical investigation of IV nutritionals and diagnostic medical devices. **Mailing Address:** Abbott Labs D7B5 AP8B, Abbott Park, IL 60064.

LYNCH, EDWARD CONOVER, INTERNAL MEDICINE, HEMATOLOGY. **Personal Data:** b Fayette, Mo, February 24, 1933; m 1955, Nell R Robinson; c Edward D, David R, Deborah R & Stephen R. **Education:** Wash Univ, BA, 1953, MD, 1956. **Honors & Awards:** Master Amn College of Physicians, 1999. **Professional Experience:** DISTINGUISHED SERV PROF, BAYLOR COL MED, 1995-; assoc chmn dept, Baylor Col Med, 1977-2000; dean student affairs, Med Sch, 1974-1976; adj prof, Rice Univ, 1973-1999; PROF MED, BAYLOR COL MED, 1972-; assoc dean, Med Sch, 1971-1974; adj assoc prof biomed eng, Rice Univ, 1971-1973; from instr to assoc prof, Baylor Col Med, 1962-1972; from assoc resident to chief resident, Strong Mem Hosp, Rochester, NY, 1958-1960; from intern to asst resident med, Barnes Hosp, St Louis, Mo, 1956-1958. **Memberships:** Am Col Physicians; Am Fedn Clin Res; Am Soc Hemat; So Soc Clin Invest. **Research Statement & Publications:** Effects of physical forces on erythrocytes and blood rheology; internal distribution of iron in various anemias. **Mailing Address:** 311 Wilchester Blvd, Houston, TX 77079-7326.

LYNCH, FRANK W, ENGINEERING & ELECTRONICS, AERONAUTICS & AEROSPACE. **Personal Data:** b San Francisco, Calif, November 26, 1921; m 1950, Marilyn H; c Molly L & Kathryn L. **Education:** Stanford Univ, AB, 1943; Univ Calif, AB, 1996. **Honorary Degrees:** JD, Northrop Univ, 1984. **Professional Experience:** RETIRED; vchmn, Tactical & Electronic Systs Group, Northrop Corp, 1987-1989; pres & chief operating officer, Tactical & Electronic Systs Group, Northrop Corp, 1980-1987; sr vpres, Tactical & Electronic Systs Group, Northrop Corp, 1979-1980; sr vpres opers, Electro-Mech Div, 1976-1979; vpres & mgr, Electro-Mech Div, 1969-1975; vpres eng, Hallamore Electronics, 1957-1959; chief flight controls, Northrop Aircraft Inc, 1954-1955; asst chief guid & controls, Northrop Aircraft Inc, 1952-1954 & 1955-1957; gen supvr component develop, Northrop Aircraft Inc, 1951-1952; supvr dynamic anal, Northrop Aircraft Inc, 1950-1951; res engr, Northrop Aircraft Inc, 1950; Res lab analyst, Boeing Airplane Co, Seattle, 1948-1950. **Memberships:** Aerospace Indust Asn Am; sr mem Inst Elec & Electronics Engrs; Am Ord Asn. **Research Statement & Publications:** Analog computers and flight simulators; autopilots; guidance sensor systems; astroinertial guidance systems; aeronaptics & aerospace. **Mailing Address:** 1933 Altura Dr, Corona Del Mar, CA 92625.

LYNCH, GEORGE ROBERT, PHYSIOLOGICAL ECOLOGY, COMPARATIVE PHYSIOLOGY. **Personal Data:** b Pittsburgh, Pa, October 5, 1941; m 1967, Carol. **Education:** Grove City Col, BS, 1964; Univ Mich, MS, 1966; Univ Iowa, PhD (zoology), 1973. **Professional Experience:** PROF, DEPT INTEGRATIVE PHYSIOL, UNIV COLO; 2003-; PROF ENVIRON POP & ORGANISMIC BIOL, UNIV COLO, 1993-2003; Von Humbodlt fel, 1984; from asst prof to prof biol, Wesleyan Univ, 1975-1992; asst prof zool, Univ Maine, Orono, 1974-1975; NIH fel, Inst Behav Genetics, Univ Colo, 1972-1973; instr biol, Augustana Col, Ill, 1967-1969; Instr zool, Ohio Wesleyan Univ, 1966-1967. **Memberships:** Am Physiol Soc; Soc Neuroscience; Soc Res Biol Rhythms. **Research Statement & Publications:** Animal photoperiodism and the role that the neural clock plays in photoperiod time measurement. **Mailing Address:** Dept Environ Pop & Organismic Biol, Univ Colo, Boulder, CO 80309-0334. **Fax:** 303-492-4009. **E-Mail:** robert.lynch@colorado.edu

LYNCH, GERARD FRANCIS, PHYSICS, ENGINEERING PHYSICS. **Personal Data:** b Glascow, Scotland, October 10, 1945; Canadian citizen; m 1967, c 2. **Education:** Glasgow Univ, BSc, 1967; Queen's Univ, Can, PhD (physics), 1971. **Honors & Awards:** Des Cunningham award, Ottawa ctr res innovation, 2003. **Professional Experience:** VICE CHMN, CAN PHOTONICS CONSORTIUM, as of 2004; PRES & CHIEF EXEC OFFICER, PHOTONICS RES ONT, 1997-; vpres mkt & sales, Atomic Energy Can Ltd, beginning 1991; gen mgr, local energy systs bus unit, chalk river nuclear labs, 1985-1991; exec asst, Electronics Br, 1984-1985; head, Electronics Br, 1981-1984; spec lectr, Queen's Univ, 1979-; mem working group, Int Electrotech Comn, 1976-; scientist, Atomic Energy Can Ltd, 1973-1981; Lectr physics, Queen's Univ, 1971-1973; Fel, Queen's Univ, 1971. **Memberships:** Instrument Soc Am; Optical soc Am; Optoelectronic indust develop asn. **Research Statement & Publications:** Instrumentation development for nuclear reactor applications; infrared spectroscopy; radiation detection and measurement and analytical techniques. **Mailing Address:** Photonics Res Ont, Ste 129 60 St-Georges St, Toronto, ON M5S 1A7, Can. **Fax:** 416-971-2117. **E-Mail:** glynch@pro.on.ca

LYNCH, HARRY JAMES, NEUROENDOCRINOLOGY. **Personal Data:** b Glenfield, Pa, January 18, 1929; m 1963. **Education:** Geneva Col, BS, 1957; Univ Pittsburgh, PhD (biol), 1971. **Professional Experience:** RETIRED; res affil, Mass Inst Technol, beginning 1992; res scientist, Lab Neuroendocrine Regulation, Dept Appl Biol Sci, 1981-1992; res assoc, Lab Richard Wurtman, 1974-1975; NIH fel, Mass Inst Technol, 1971-1973; sr tech fel res asst, Univ Pittsburgh, 1966-1971; clin chemist, Western Pa Hosp, Pittsburgh, 1955-1966. **Memberships:** Endocrine Soc; Am Asn Clin Chemists; AAAS; Am Soc Zoologists. **Research Statement & Publications:** Neuroendocrine regulation exemplified by the pineal gland of vertebrate animals; pineal gland function as evidenced by melatonin biosynthesis and excretion; physiological, pharmacological, and environmental factors that influence pineal function. **Mailing Address:** 42 Marivista Ave, Waltham, MA 02451.

LYNCH, HENRY T, MEDICAL GENETICS, MEDICAL ONCOLOGY. **Personal Data:** b Lawrence, Mass, January 4, 1928; m 1951, Jane; c Patrick, Kathleen & Ann. **Education:** Univ Okla, BS, 1951; Univ Denver, MA, 1952; Univ Tex, MD, 1960. **Honors & Awards:** Billings Silver Medal, AMA, 1966; Ungerman-Lubin lectr Cancer Res, 1987. **Professional Experience:** DIR CANCER CTR, SCH MED, CREIGHTON UNIV, 1994-; prof prev med & pub health, Sch Med, Creighton Univ, beginning 1971; chmn dept, Sch Med, Creighton Univ, beginning 1967; assoc prof, Sch Med, Creighton Univ, 1967-1971; asst prof biol & asst internist, M D Anderson Hosp & Tumor Inst, Tex, 1966-1967; USPHS sr clin cancer trainee, Eppley Cancer Inst, Nebr, 1964-1966; resident internal med, Col Med, Univ Nebr, 1961-1964; intern, St Mary's Hosp, Evansville, Ind, 1960-1961. **Memberships:** Am Soc Clin Oncol. **Research Statement & Publications:** Cancer genetics; Study of families with excess of certain cancers, associated with other cancers; identification of natual history; screening based on identified matuared genes. **Mailing Address:** Dept Prev Med & Pub Health, Creighton Univ Sch Med 2500 Calif Plaza, Omaha, NE 68178. **Fax:** 402-280-1734. **E-Mail:** htlynch@creighton.edu

LYNCH, JAMES CARLYLE, NEUROPHYSIOLOGY, NEUROANATOMY. **Personal Data:** b Clifton Hill, Mo, March 1, 1942; m 1965, c 2. **Education:** Univ Mo, AB, 1964; Stanford Univ, MA & PhD (neurol sci), 1971. **Honors & Awards:** Andrew Mellon career develop award, 1974. **Professional Experience:** PROF ANAT & ASST PROF RES OPHTHAL, UNIV MISS MED CTR, 1987-; assoc prof, Univ Miss Med Ctr, 1982-; asst prof anat, Univ Miss Med Ctr, 1981-1982; asst prof physiol, Mayo Med Sch, 1976-1981; assoc consult physiol, Mayo Found, 1976-1981; Instr physiol, Sch Med, Johns Hopkins Univ, 1974-1976; Nat Inst Neurol Dis & Stroke neurophysiol training grant, Dept Physiol, Sch Med, Johns Hopkins Univ, 1971-1973. **Memberships:** AAAS; Europ Neuroscience Asn; Soc Neuroscience; Asn Res Vision & Ophthal. **Research Statement & Publications:** Central neural mechanisms of sensation, perception and motor control; eye movement control in subhuman primates. **Mailing Address:** Dept Anat, Univ Miss Sch Med, 2500 N State St, Jackson, MS 39216-4505. **Fax:** 601-984-1655. **E-Mail:** jclynch@anatomy.umsmed.edu

LYNCH, JOHN AUGUST, ANALYTICAL CHEMISTRY. **Personal Data:** b January 29, 1947; American citizen; m 1982. **Education:** StPeter's Col, NJ, BS, 1970; Pa State Univ, PhD (chem), 1976. **Professional Experience:** PROF CHEM, UNIV TENN, CHATTANOOGA, as of 2003; Fel, Univ Chattanooga Found, 1984 & 1988; assoc prof chem, Univ Tenn, Chattanooga, beginning 1980; NSF/URP grants, 1980, 1981; Res Corp grant, 1977-; Univ Chattanooga Found grant, 1976-1978; asst prof, Univ Tenn, Chattanooga, 1975-1980; NSF teaching asst chem, PHS res fel, 1971-1975; NSF teaching asst chem, Pa State Univ, 1970-1971. **Memberships:** Am Chem Soc. **Research Statement & Publications:** Thermometric methods of analysis used in conjunction with computer interpretation of data; automated titrations; development of instructional microcomputer software; Analytical Chemistry; kinetic methods of analysis. **Mailing Address:** Dept Chem, Univ Tenn, 437 Grote Hall, Chattanooga, TN 37403. **E-Mail:** john-lynch@utc.edu

LYNCH, JOHN BROWN, PLASTIC SURGERY. **Personal Data:** b Akron, Ohio, February 5, 1929; m 1950, c 2. **Education:** Vanderbilt Univ, BS, 1949; Univ Tenn, MD, 1952; Am Bd Surg & Am Bd Plastic Surg, dipl. **Professional Experience:** PROF EMER PLASTIC SURG, SCH MED, VANDERBILT UNIV, as of 2000; pres, Southern Med Assoc, 1985; mem, food & drug admin adv panel, HHS, Gen Surg & Plastic Surg Devices, beginning 1974; nat consult plastic surg to surgeon gen, USAF, beginning 1974; prof plastic surg, Sch Med, Vanderbilt Univ, beginning 1973; chmn dept, Vanderbilt Univ Sch Med, beginning 1973; from instr to assoc prof, Univ Tex Med Br, Galveston, 1962-1973; res plastic surg, Univ Tex Med Br, Galveston, 1959-1962; resident surg, Univ Tex Med Br, Galveston, 1956-1959; internship, john gaston hosp, Tenn, 1953-1954. **Memberships:** AMA; Am Soc Plastic & Reconstructive Surgeons; Am Asn Plastic Surg; fel Am Col Surg; Plastic Surg Res Coun. **Research Statement & Publications:** Pathophysiological aspects of burns and laboratory projects related to congenital anomalies. **Mailing Address:** Plastic Surg Med Ctr, Vanderbilt Univ Hosp, N Rm S-2221, Nashville, TN 37232.

LYNCH, JOHN DOUGLAS, ZOOLOGY, HERPETOLOGY. **Personal Data:** b Collins, Iowa, July 30, 1942; c Jennifer (Anders) & Douglas. **Education:** Univ Ill, Urbana, BA, 1964, MS, 1965; Univ Kans, PhD (zoology), 1969. **Professional Experience:** RETIRED; prof life sci, Univ Nebr, Lincoln, 1980-1998; vis prof, Nat Univ Colombia, Inst Natural Sci, 1996, 1992 & 1985; assoc prof, Univ Nebr, Lincoln, 1973-1980; asst prof zoology, Univ Nebr, Lincoln, 1969-1973. **Memberships:** Am Soc Ichthyol & Herpet; Soc Syst Biol; Soc Study Amphibians & Reptiles; Herpetologist's League; Willi Hennig Soc. **Research Statement & Publications:** Systematics and zoogeography of leptodactyloid frogs especially of neotropical genus Eleutherodactylus; evolution in tropical ecosystems; conservation biology of cyprinodont fishes. **Mailing Address:** Sch Biol Sci, Univ Nebr, Lincoln, NE 68588. **Fax:** 402-472-2083. **E-Mail:** jlynch@unlinfo.unl.edu

LYNCH, JOHN THOMAS, SPACE PLASMA PHYSICS. **Personal Data:** b Washington, DC, March 21, 1938; m 1980, Carol; c John T III & Michael G. **Education:** Va Polytech Inst, BS, 1963; Univ Wis, MS, 1965, PhD (physics), 1972. **Professional Experience:** RETIRED; prog dir, NSF, as of 2005; prog scientist, NASA Hq, 1981-1985; staff mem, Los Alamos Nat Lab, 1979-1981; vis staff mem, Los Alamos Nat Lab, 1978-1979; assoc scientist physics, Univ Wis-Madison, 1978-1979; asst scientist, Univ Wis-Madison, 1975-1978; lectr physics, Univ Wis-Madison, 1972-1978; res assoc, Univ Wis-Madison, 1972-1975; prog dir, Antarctic Aeronomy & Astrophys. **Memberships:** Am Geophys Union; AAAS; Astron Soc Pac. **Research Statement & Publications:** Aeronomy and astrophysics. **Mailing Address:** 4505 Argyte Terr, Washington, DC 20011.

LYNCH, JOSEPH J, CARDIOVASCULAR PHARMACOLOGY. **Personal Data:** b Baltimore, Md, April 18, 1956. **Education:** Loyola Col, BA, 1978; Ohio State Univ, PhD (pharmacol), 1982. **Professional Experience:** SR DIR, DEPT PHARMACOL, MERCK RES LABS, as of 2003; assoc dir, Dept Pharmacol, Merck, Sharp & Dohme Res Labs, beginning 1991; sr res pharmacologist, 1988-1991. **Memberships:** Am Soc Therapeut. **Mailing Address:** Dept Pharmacol, Merck Res Labs, WP 46 300, West Point, PA 19486-0004. **E-Mail:** joseph_lynch@merck.com

LYNCH, MAURICE PATRICK, BIOLOGICAL OCEANOGRAPHY, PHYSIOLOGICAL ECOLOGY. **Personal Data:** b Boston, Mass, February 24, 1936; m 1965, c 2. **Education:** Harvard Col, AB, 1957; Col William & Mary, MA, 1965, PhD (marine sci), 1972. **Professional Experience:** Assoc grad dean, Sch Marine Sci, 1987-1989; chmn, Sci & Tech Adv Comt, Chesapeake Bay Prog, 1985-1989; dir, Va Sea Grant Prog & Chesapeake Res Chesapeake Res Consortium, 1984-1988; asst dir & head, Div Marine Resource Mgt, Col William & Mary, Univ Va, 1981-1986; asst dir & head, Div Spec Progs & Sci Serv, Va Inst Marine Sci, 1977-1982; assoc prof, Div Marine Resource Mgt, Col William & Mary, Univ Va, 1976-1979; PROF, SCH MARINE SCI & HEAD, OFF SPEC PROGS, SCH MARINE SCI, VA INST MARINE SCI, COL WILLIAM & MARY, VA UNIV, 1975-; asst dir & head, Div Biol Oceanog, 1975-1977; vpres, Coastal Eviron Assoc Inc, 1974-; adj prof earth sci, Va State Col, 1974; sr marine scientist & head, Dept Spec Progs, 1973-1975; assoc marine scientist, Col William & Mary, 1971-1973; USN, 1957-1988. **Memberships:** Am Inst Biol Sci; Marine Technol Soc; Am Soc Zoologists; Am Fisheries Soc; Am Soc Limnol & Oceanog; Coastal Soc (pres-elect, 1981-1983, pres, 1983-1985); Atlantic Estuarine Res Soc; AAAS. **Research Statement & Publications:** Management of marine and estuarine resources with special emphasis on management-research interactions and communications; physiology of marine and estuarine organisms with special emphasis on development of physiological condition indices. **Mailing Address:** Brown House 204, William & Mary Sch Marine Sci, Gloucester Point, VA 23062. **E-Mail:** mlynch@vims.edu

LYNCH, NANCY ANN, MATHEMATICS. **Personal Data:** b Brooklyn, NY, January 19, 1958; m 1969, Dennis; c Patrick, Kathleen (deceased) & Mary. **Education:** Brooklyn Col, BS, 1968; Mass Inst Technol, PhD, 1972. **Professional Experience:** NEC PROF SOFTWARE SCI & ENG, MASS INST TECHNOL, as of 2003; Apollo Comp, Chelmsford & AT&T Bell Labs, Murray Hill, NJ, 1986-1989 & Digital Equip Corp, 1990; PROF ELEC ENG & COMPUT SCI, MASS INST TECHNOL, CAMBRIDGE, 1986-; consult, Comput Corp Am, Cambridge, 1984-1986; Ellen Swallow Richards chair, Mass Inst Technol, 1982-1987; assoc prof, Mass Inst Technol, Cambridge, 1982-1986; assoc prof comput sci, Ga Tech Univ, Atlanta, 1977-1982; Fla Int, Univ Miami, 1976-1977; Univ Southern Calif, Los Angeles, 1973-1976; asst prof math, Tufts Univ, Medford, Mass, 1972-1973. **Memberships:** Asn Comput Mach. **Research Statement & Publications:** Computer science; mathematics; author of numerous articles. **Mailing Address:** Dept Elec Eng & Comput Sci, Mass Inst Technol, 77 Mass Ave, Cambridge, MA 02139-4307. **Fax:** 617-258-8682. **E-Mail:** lynch@theory.lcs.mit.edu

LYNCH, PETER JOHN, DERMATOLOGY. **Personal Data:** b Minneapolis, Minn, October 22, 1936; m 1964, c 2. **Education:** Univ Minn, Minneapolis, BS, 1959, MD, 1961. **Professional Experience:** RETIRED; prof dermat & chair, Dept Dermat, Univ Calif, Davis, 1995-2000; assoc head, Dept Internal Med, 1977-1995; prof dermat & chief div, Univ Ariz, 1975-1995; vet admin hosp, Tucson, Ariz & Kino Community Hosp, Tucson, Ariz, 1974-; assoc prof, Univ Ariz, 1973-1975; Vet Admin Hosp, Ann Arbor, Mich, 1971-1973; from asst prof to assoc prof, Univ Mich, Ann Arbor, 1970-1973; consult, Wayne Co Gen Hosp, Eloise, Mich, 1968-1973; clin instr dermat, Univ Minn, Minneapolis, 1965-1966. **Memberships:** AAAS; Am Acad Dermat; Soc Invest Dermat; Am Dermat Asn; Asn Am Med Cols. **Research Statement & Publications:** Clinical subjects in diseases of the skin. **Mailing Address:** Dept Dermat, Univ Calif, 1605 Alhambra Blvd No 2300, Sacramento, CA 95816.

LYNCH, PETER ROBIN, PHYSIOLOGY. **Personal Data:** b Philadelphia, Pa, July 18, 1927; m 1953, c 3. **Education:** Univ Miami, BS, 1950; Temple Univ, MS, 1954, PhD (physiol), 1958. **Professional Experience:** RETIRED; PROF EMER INTERNAL MED, SCH MED, TEMPLE UNIV, as of 2003; chmn, physiol dept, beginning 1987; prof internal med, Sch Med, Temple Univ, beginning 1986; adj prof, Druckkhammer laboratorium, Kantonsppital, Zurich, Switz, 1977-1978; prof physiol & radiol, Sch Med, Temple Univ, beginning 1970; from instr to assoc prof physiol, Physiol Dept, 1958-1970. **Memberships:** Am Physiol Soc; Sigma Xi; Am Heart Asn; AAAS; N Am Soc Cardiac Radiol. **Research Statement & Publications:** Cardiovascular and radiologic physiology; rheology. **Mailing Address:** Dept Physiol, Med Sch, Temple Univ, Philadelphia, PA 19140.

LYNCH, RICHARD G, PATHOLOGY. **Personal Data:** b April 9, 1934. **Education:** Univ Mo, BA, 1961; Univ Rochester, MD, 1966. **Professional Experience:** Mem, 1982 & Bd Sci Counr, Div Cancer Biol & Diag, Nat Cancer Inst, 1987-1991; block chmn, Tumor Immunol Prog, 1985 & Meetings, Am Asn Immunologists, 1986; Chmn, Path B Study Sect, NIH, 1983-1986; PROF MICROBIOL, DEPT PATH, COL MED, UNIV IOWA, IOWA CITY, 1982-; dir, NIH Training Prog Membranes & Immunol, Sch Med, 1980-1981; from asst prof to assoc prof path, Wash Univ, St Louis, Mo, 1972-1980; postdoctoral immunol res fel, Wash Univ, St Louis, Mo, 1969-1972; Path resident, Wash Univ, St Louis, Mo, 1966-1969. **Research Statement & Publications:** Pathology; immunology. **Mailing Address:** Dept Path Col Med, Univ Iowa Health Care, 357 Med Res Ctr, Iowa City, IA 52242-1182. **Fax:** 319-335-8348. **E-Mail:** richard-lynch@uiowa.edu

LYNCH, RICHARD WALLACE, CHEMICAL PHYSICS, CHEMICAL ENGINEERING. **Personal Data:** b Ft Leavenworth, Kans, June 17, 1939; m 1962, Myra; c Susan, Sara & Andrew. **Education:** Univ Calif, Berkeley, BS, 1962; Univ Ill, MS, 1964, PhD (chem eng), 1966. **Professional Experience:** DIR, GEOSCI & GEOTECHNOL, SANDIA LABS, 1992-; dir environ safety & health, Waste Mgt & Environ Progs, 1990-1992; dir nuclear waste mgt & transp, Waste Mgt & Environ Progs, 1983-1990; mgr, Waste Mgt & Environ Progs, 1976-1983; supvr, Chem Technol Div, 1973-1976; supvr, Appl Mat Sci Div, 1971-1973; tech staff mem chem physics, Sandia Labs, 1968-1971 & 1966. **Memberships:** AAAS; Am Inst Chem Engrs; Am Phys Soc; Sigma Xi. **Research Statement & Publications:** Nuclear waste solidification; geologic isolation of nuclear wastes; exploration and production of gas, oil and geothermal resources. **Mailing Address:** 7500 Osuna Rd NE, Albuquerque, NM 87109.

LYNCH, ROBERT D, ENGINEERING. **Professional Experience:** DEAN, COL ENG, VILLANOVA UNIV, as of 1999. **Mailing Address:** Col Eng, Villanova Univ, 800 Lancaster Ave, Villanova, PA 19085. **Fax:** 610-519-4941. **E-Mail:** rlynch@email.vill.edu

LYNCH, ROBERT EARL, ENTOMOLOGY. **Personal Data:** b Luxora, Ark, October 4, 1943; m 1961, Nita; c Robert Jr & Robin. **Education:** Ark State Univ, BS, 1965; Iowa State Univ, MS, 1969, PhD (entom), 1974. **Professional Experience:** RETIRED; res entomologist, crop protection & mgt res unit, USDA, as of 2004; supvry res entomologist, USDA, beginning 1983; res entomologist, USDA, 1969-1983; entomologist, USDA, 1968-1969; Agr res technician, USDA, 1966-1968. **Memberships:** Entom Soc Am; Am Peanut Res & Educ Asn. **Research Statement & Publications:** Population distributions and economic thresholds of insects on forage grasses and peanuts; resistance in peanuts and forage grasses to insects. **Mailing Address:** Crop Protection & Mgt Res Unit USDA Agr Res Serv, PO Box 748, Tifton, GA 31793-0748. **Fax:** 229-387-2321. **E-Mail:** rlynch@tifton.usda.gov

LYNCH, ROBERT EMMETT, NUMERICAL ANALYSIS. **Personal Data:** b Chicago, Ill, February 5, 1932; m 1955, Martha B Hacker; c Barbara A, William R & Pamela E. **Education:** Cornell Univ, BEngPhys, 1954; Harvard Univ, MA, 1959, PhD (appl math), 1963. **Professional Experience:** Prof Emeritus 1996-; PROF COMPUT SCI & MATH, PURDUE UNIV, 1985-; 1996 assoc prof, Purdue Univ, 1967-1984; assoc prof, Univ Tex, Austin, 1966-1967; asst prof math & res mathematician, Univ Tex, Austin, 1964-1966; Sr res mathematician, Res Labs, Gen Motors Corp, 1961-1964. **Memberships:** Sigma Xi. **Research Statement & Publications:** Numerical analysis, particularly numerical solution of partial differential equations, applied mathematics and computational biology. **Mailing Address:** 41843 Baintree Cir, Northville, MI 48167.

LYNCH, ROBERT MICHAEL, STATISTICS, INFORMATION SYSTEMS. **Personal Data:** b Brooklyn, NY, May 30, 1944; m 1969, c 2. **Education:** State Univ NY, Brockport, BSc, 1966; Univ Northern Colo, PhD (statist), 1971. **Professional Experience:** Dean, Kenneth W Monfort Col Bus, Univ Northern Colo, 1995-2001; ed, IBS Comput Quart, 1989-; reviewer, Australian Comput J, 1987-; vis prof, Info Systs, Cowen Univ, Perth, Australia, 1986-1987; assoc dean, Univ Northern Colo, 1984-1994; labor & policies group, Oak Ridge Assoc Univs, Tenn, 1982-; consult, Weiss & Assoc, Aurora Co, 1982-1989, Health Care Financing, State Wyo; vis prof, Col VI, 1981-1982; consult ed, J Exp Educ, 1978-1982; Fulbright prof, Thammasat Univ, Bangkok, 1978-1979; ed collabr & reviewer, Current Index Statist, J Comput Reviews, 1973-; PROF STATIST, UNIV NORTHERN COLO, 1973-; fel WIE, Inst Educ Leadership, George Wash Univ, 1972-1973; asst prof mgt, Eastern Ill Univ, 1971-1973. **Memberships:** Royal Statist Soc; Am Statist Asn; Asn Comput Mach; Inst Elec & Electronics Engrs. **Research Statement & Publications:** Linear models; data base management systems. **Mailing Address:** Comput Info Dept, Monfort Col Bus, Univ Northern Colo, Kepner Hall 2053 B, PO Box 128, Greeley, CO 80639. **Fax:** 970-351-2500. **E-Mail:** robert.lynch@unco.edu

LYNCH, STEVEN PAUL, SYSTEMATIC BOTANY, POLLINATION ECOLOGY. **Personal Data:** b Los Angeles, Calif, August 19, 1946; m 1967, c 1. **Education:** Calif Polytech State Univ, San Luis Obispo, BS, 1969, MA, 1971; Univ Calif, Davis, PhD (bot), 1977. **Professional Experience:** PROF BIOL, LA STATE UNIV, as of 2004; Environ consult, Demopulos & Ferguson Inc Assoc Engrs, 1978-; asst prof biol, la state univ, beginning 1977; Researcher, Univ Calif, Davis, 1977. **Memberships:** Bot Soc Am; Am Soc Plant Taxonomists; Int Soc Plant Taxonomists; Sigma Xi. **Research Statement & Publications:** Plant-animal coevolution; floral biology of Asclepias; Monarch Butterfly migratory and feeding behavior; systematics of the Asclepiadaceae and Euphorbiaceae; pollen morphology and Angiosperm Phylogeny; scanning electron microscopy techniques. **Mailing Address:** Dept Biol Sci, La State Univ One Univ Pl, Shreveport, LA 71115-2399. **Fax:** 318-797-5230. **E-Mail:** slynch@pilot.lsus.edu

LYNCH, T(HOMAS) E(LWIN), ENGINEERING. **Personal Data:** b Mexico, Maine, August 7, 1914; m 1944, Mary. **Education:** Univ Maine, BS, 1938. **Professional Experience:** CHMN, DESIGN & MFG CO, 1982-; CHMN, CLEVELAND CRYSTALS INC, 1972-; vpres, Gould Inc, 1969-1975; vpres, Ord Prod Div, 1965-1969; gen mgt, Ord Prod Div, 1957-1959; head, Dept Electronics Eng, 1943-1952 & Clevite Corp, 1952-1957; Engr, Brush Develop Co, 1939-1943. **Memberships:** Audio Eng Soc; Am Defense Prep Asn; Nat Security Indust Asn; Inst Elec & Electronics Engrs. **Research Statement & Publications:** Underwater sound; disc and magnetic recording; underwater ordnance; government contracting; energy technology. **Mailing Address:** Old Mill Rd, Gates Mills, OH 44040.

LYNCH, THOMAS JOHN, POLYMER PROCESSING, APPLICATION OF ENGINEERING POLYMERS. **Personal Data:** b Quincy, Mass, March 3, 1941; m 1969. **Education:** Boston Col, BS, 1962; Mass Inst Tech, PhD (org chem), 1966. **Professional Experience:** CHIEF EXEC OFFICER & PRES, ELECTRONICS DIV, TYCO ENGINEERED PROD & SERV DIV, as of 2006; DIR, POLYMER PROCESS TECHNOL, AMP INC, 1990-; prog mgt, Environ Progs, 1987-1990; dir, Environ Progs, 1983-1987; mgr polystyrene prodres, 1971-1975 & Gulf Oil Chem Co, 1978-1983; res assoc, Gulf Oil Chem Co, 1978 & 1971-1975; sr res chemist, Gulf Oil Chem Co, 1975-1978; res chemist, Gulf Res & Develop Co, 1966-1971; fel NSF, 1962-1966; Woodrow Wilson fel, 1958-1962. **Memberships:** AAAS; Am Chem Soc; Chem Soc. **Research Statement & Publications:** Application and modification of engineering polymer for electrical/electronic connectors; solid state polymerization and polymer recycling; program and production management. **Mailing Address:** Amp Inc, MS 128 063 PO Box 3608, Harrisburg, PA 17105-3608.

LYNCH, WESLEY CLYDE, NEUROPSYCHOLOGY. **Personal Data:** b Vancouver, Wash, February 28, 1944; m 1965. **Education:** Univ Hawaii, BA, 1967; Hollins Col, MA, 1968; Univ NMex, PhD (exp psychol), 1972. **Professional Experience:** PROF PSYCHOL, MONT STATE UNIV, 1997-; head, dept psyhol, Mont State Univ, 1993-1998; from asst prof to assoc prof psychol, Mont State Univ, 1980-1997; lect, dept psychol, Mont State Univ, 1979-1980; Asst Res Behav Biologist, Calif Primate Res Ctr, Davis, CA, 1978-1979; res assoc psychol, Yale Univ, 1975-1976; Adj asst prof, Rockefeller Univ, 1975-1976; vis asst fel physiol psychol, John B Pierce Found Lab, 1975-1977; asst prof, Rockefeller Univ, 1973-1975; Fel physiol psychol, Rockefeller Univ, 1971-1973; Fel, Dept Psychol, Univ NMex, Albuquerque, NM, 1970-1971; Grad Res Asst, Dept Psychol, Hollins Col, VA, 1967-1968; Undergrad Res Asst, Dept Psychol, Univ Hawaii, 1966-1967. **Memberships:** Am Psychol Asn; AAAS; Sigma Xi; mem, Acad eating dis; mem, Soc Neuroscience; mem, Soc study ingestive behav. **Research Statement & Publications:** Psychological and physiological bases of motivation, reward and learning. **Mailing Address:** Dept Psychol, Mont State Univ, 328 Traphagen Hall, Bozeman, MT 59717-0001. **Fax:** 406-994-3804. **E-Mail:** wlynch@montana.edu

LYNCH, WILLIAM C, MATHEMATICS, COMPUTER SCIENCE. **Personal Data:** b Cleveland, Ohio, April 27, 1937; div, c John H, Michael W, Timothy P & Brian K. **Education:** Case Univ, BS, 1959; Univ Wis, MS, 1960, PhD (math), 1963. **Professional Experience:** RETIRED; chief Technical officer, Poprlet technol inc, 2000-2002; chair, Interval Res Corp, 1993-2000; Am Super Comput Inc, 1985; prin scientist, Xerox Corp, 1976-1985, 1986-1993; vis prof, Univ Fed Rio de Janeiro, 1975; vis prof, Comput Lab, Univ Newcastle, 1970-1971; from asst prof to prof comput eng, Case Western Res Univ, 1963-1976; asst prof, Univ Wis, 1963; actg instr numerical anal, Univ Wis, 1962-1963. **Memberships:** AAAS; Asn Comput Mach; Am Math Soc; Sigma Xi. **Research Statement & Publications:** Mathematical linguistics; design, construction, measurement and modelling of operating systems; signal processing. **Mailing Address:** 3331 Thomas Dr, Palo Alto, CA 94303. **E-Mail:** lynchw@acm.org

LYNCH, WILLIAM GREGORY, NUCLEAR PHYSICS. **Personal Data:** m, c 2. **Education:** Univ Colo, BS, 1973; Univ Wash, MS, 1975, PhD (physics), 1980. **Honors & Awards:** Pres Young Investr Award, 1985. **Professional Experience:** PROF, DEPT PHYS & ASTRON & NAT SUPERCONDUCTING CYCLOTRON LAB, MICH STATE UNIV, as of 2004; RESEARCHER, CYCLOTRON LAB, MICH STATE UNIV, 1980-. **Memberships:** Am Phys Soc. **Research Statement & Publications:** Understanding the properties of excited nuclear matter, including the relationship between the pressure, density, temperature and proton concentration in dense, strongly interacting systems; low density phase transition in such systems, between a fermi liquid state typical of the interiors of nuclei and a gas of nucleons. **Mailing Address:** Cyclotron Lab, Mich State Univ, East Lansing, MI 48824. **Fax:** 517-353-5967. **E-Mail:** lynch@nscl.msu.edu

LYN-COOK, BEVERLY D, MEDICAL RESEARCH. **Education:** Ft Valley State Univ, BS, 1977; Atlanta Univ, MS, 1979, PhD (cell biol), 1981. **Professional Experience:** SR RES SCIENTIST, DIV MOLECULAR EPIDEMIOL, NAT CTR TOXICOL RES, 1997-. **Mailing Address:** Nat Ctr Toxicol Res, HFT-140, Jefferson, AR 72079.

LYND, JULIAN QUENTIN, SOIL SCIENCE. **Personal Data:** b Joplin, Mo, February 11, 1922; wid, c Donna & Joel. **Education:** Univ Ark, BS, 1943; Mich State Univ, MS, 1947, PhD (soil sci), 1948. **Professional Experience:** PROF AGRON, OKLA STATE UNIV, as of 1993; assoc prof, Okla State Univ, 1952-1957; asst prof soil sci, Mich State Univ, 1948-1951. **Memberships:** Fel Am Soc Agron; fel Soil Sci Soc Am; Int Soc Soil Sci; Am Soc Microbiol; Mycol Soc Am. **Research Statement & Publications:** Soil microbiology; induced antibiosis to carcinogenic mycotoxins and biopathway of biotoxin degradation;

n-fixation. **Mailing Address:** Dept Agron, Okla State Univ, Stillwater, OK 74078-0507. **Fax:** 405-744-5269. **E-Mail:** jql@gis.agr.okstate.edu

LYNDE, RICHARD ARTHUR, INORGANIC CHEMISTRY. **Personal Data:** b Orange, NJ, April 12, 1942; m 1961, c 2. **Education:** Hamilton Col, BA, 1964; Iowa State Univ, PhD (inorg chem), 1970. **Professional Experience:** PROVOST & VPRES, ACAD AFFAIRS, MONTCLAIR STATE UNIV, as of 2004; PROF & DEAN, SCH MATH & NATURAL SCI, MONTCLAIR STATE COL, 1980-; actg dean, Dept Chem, 1976-1980; assoc prof, Dept Chem, 1975-1980; chmn, Dept Chem, 1973-1976; Asst prof, Montclair State Col, 1970-1975. **Memberships:** Am Chem Soc; AAAS; Sigma Xi. **Research Statement & Publications:** Elucidation of the stoichiometry, structure and bonding of compounds formed by the post-transition and transition metals in unusual oxidation states. **Mailing Address:** Off Provost, Montclair State Univ, 1 Normal Ave, Montclair, NJ 07043. **Fax:** 973-655-7647. **E-Mail:** lynder@mail.montclair.edu

LYNDEN-BELL, DONALD, ASTRONOMY. **Personal Data:** b Dover, Eng, April 5, 1935; m 1961, Ruth Marion Truscott; c Marion & Edward. **Education:** Univ Cambridge, BA, 1956, PhD, 1960. **Honorary Degrees:** DSc, Univ Sussex, 1987. **Honors & Awards:** Schwarzsch Medal, Ger Astron Asn; Dirk Brouwer Prize, Am Astron Soc, 1990; Eddington Medal, Royal Astron Soc, 1984, Gold Medal, 1993. **Professional Experience:** Dir, Inst Astron, Univ Cambridge, 1992-1994, 1982-1987 & 1972-1977; vis Oort prof, Leiden Univ, Neth, 1992; Einstein fel, Israeli Acad, 1990; PROF ASTROPHYS, UNIV CAMBRIDGE & CLARE COL, 1972-; vis prof, Univ Sussex, 1970-1972; prin sci officer, Royal Greenwich Observ, 1965-1972; asst lectr math, Clare Col, Cambridge, 1962-1965; Res fel, Clare Col, 1960-1965; Harkness fel, Calif Inst Technol, 1960-1962. **Memberships:** Foreign assoc Nat Acad Sci; fel Royal Soc; fel Royal Astron Soc (pres). **Mailing Address:** Inst Astron Observ, Madingley Rd, Cambridge CB3 OHA, UK.

LYNDS, BEVERLY T, ASTRONOMY. **Personal Data:** b Shreveport, La, August 19, 1929; wid Leo (Deceased); c 1. **Education:** Centenary Col, BS, 1949; Univ Calif, PhD (astron), 1955. **Professional Experience:** RETIRED; asn Univ Res Astronomers, 1987, Univ Hawaii, 1988; consult, Astron Adv Panel, NSF, 1975-1977; consult, NSF Sci & Technol Policy Off, Adv Group Sci Progs, 1975-1977; astronr, Kitt Peak Nat Observ, 1974-1986; asst dir, Kitt Peak Nat Observ, 1971-1978; from asst prof & asst astronr to assoc prof astron & assoc astronr, Steward Observ, Univ Ariz, 1962-1971; res assoc astron, Nat Radio Astron Observ, Green Bank, WVa, 1960-1962. **Memberships:** Am Astron Soc; Int Astron Union. **Research Statement & Publications:** Interstellar medium; galactic structure; composition of galaxies. **Mailing Address:** 3244 Sixth St, Boulder, CO 80304.

LYNDS, CLARENCE ROGER, OBSERVATION COSMOLOGY. **Personal Data:** b Kirkwood, Mo, July 28, 1928; m 1954, c 1. **Education:** Univ Calif, AB, 1952, PhD (astron), 1955. **Professional Experience:** Astronr, Kitt Peak Nat Observ, beginning 1968; from asst to assoc astronr, Kitt Peak Nat Observ, 1961-1968; asst astronr, Nat Radio Astron Observ, 1959-1961; Nat Res Coun Can fel, Dom Astrophys Observ, Can, 1958-1959; jr res astronr & assoc astronr, Univ Calif, 1955-1958; astronr, Univ Calif, 1953-1954; Asst, Lick Observ, 1952. **Memberships:** Nat Acad Sci; Am Astron Soc; Royal Astron Soc; Int Astron Union. **Research Statement & Publications:** Photometry and spectroscopy of quasi-stellar objects and galaxies; observational cosmology; optical interferometry. **Mailing Address:** Kitt Peak Nat Observ, PO Box 26732, Tucson, AZ 85726.

LYNE, LEONARD MURRAY, PAPER CHEMISTRY. **Personal Data:** b Riverhurst, Sask, August 20, 1919; m 1946, c 1. **Education:** Queen's Univ Ont, BSc, 1942, MSc, 1946. **Professional Experience:** RETIRED; dir qual assurance, Ont Paper Co, 1967-1983; asst res dir pulp & paper, Ont Paper Co, 1965-1967; head printability, Pulp & Paper Res Inst, 1962-1965; res mgr, E B Eddy Co, 1956-1962; res chemist, E B Eddy Co, 1946-1956; res chemist, Dom Plywoods, Ltd, 1945-1946; chemist, Int Nickel Co, 1942-1943. **Memberships:** Tech Asn Pulp & Paper Indust; Can Pulp & Paper Asn. **Research Statement & Publications:** Fundamental and applied research of pulp and paper. **Mailing Address:** 128 William St, Box 402, Niagara-on-the-Lake, ON L0S 1J0, Can.

LYNK, EDGAR THOMAS, LASERS. **Personal Data:** b Kansas City, Mo, August 26, 1941. **Education:** Yale Univ, BS, 1963, MS, 1965, PhD (physics), 1970. **Professional Experience:** STAFF PHYSICIST, CORP RES & DEVELOP CTR, GEN ELEC CO, 1974-; assoc prof physics, Southern Univ, 1969-1974. **Memberships:** AAAS; Am Phys Soc; Inst Elec & Electronics Engrs. **Research Statement & Publications:** Atomic excitation cross sections; computerized tomography; ultrasound for medical imaging. **Mailing Address:** 70 Park Terr Apt 2G, New York, NY 10001.

LYNN, D JOANNE, ETHICS, GERIATRICS. **Personal Data:** b Oakland, Md, July 2, 1951. **Education:** Dickinson Col, BS, 1970; Boston Univ, MD, 1974; Am Bd Internal Med cert, 1977; George Wash Univ, MA, 1984; Dartmouth Col, MS, 1995. **Honorary Degrees:** MA, Dartmouth Col, 1991. **Professional Experience:** Mem, Comt Care End Life, 1996-; adj prof med community & family med, Dartmouth Med Sch, 1995-; PROF HEALTH CARE SCI & MED, GEORGE WASH MED CTR, 1995-; DIR, CTR IMPROVE CARE DYING, GEORGE WASH UNIV, 1995-; mem, Comt Eval NIH Women's Health Initiative, 1993; sr assoc, Ctr Evaluative Clin Sci, Dartmouth Med Sch, 1992-1995; assoc dir, Ctr Aging, Dartmouth-Hitchcock Med Ctr, 1992-1995; mem, Comt Social & Ethical Impacts Develop Biomed, Inst Med-Nat Acad Sci, 1992-1994; assoc chmn, Ctr Improve Care Dying, George Wash Univ, 1990-1992; asst dir med studies, President's Comn Study Ethical Prob Med Biomed Behav Res, 1981-1983; staff physician, Wash Home, 1979-1992; private pract, Clinton, Md, 1978-1981; assoc med & humanities, Div Exp Prog, George Wash Univ, 1978-1981; emergency room & triage physician, Wash Vet Admin Hosp, 1977-1978; resident, Robert Wood Johnson clin scholar, 1977-1978; from instr to prof, Ctr Improve Care Dying, George Wash Univ, 1976-1992; resident, Geo Wash Univ Med Ctr, 1974-1977. **Memberships:** Inst Med-Nat Acad Sci; fel Am Geriatrics Soc; Am Hosp Asn; fel Am Col Physicians. **Research Statement & Publications:** Care of the dying; continuous quality improvement; geriatrics; managed care; measurement of quality; medical decision-making; medical ethics; outcomes research; palliative medicine; public policy; contributor of numerous publications. **Mailing Address:** Ctr Improve Care Dying, George Wash Univ, 1001 22nd St N W Ste 820, Washington, DC 20037.

LYNN, DENIS HEWARD, CILIATOLOGY, ELECTRON MICROSCOPY. **Personal Data:** b Kingston, Ont, April 20, 1947; m 1973, Portia; c Francis C & Robin P. **Education:** Univ Guelph, BSc, 1969; Univ Toronto, PhD (zoology), 1975. **Professional Experience:** PROF ZOOL & PROTISTOL, UNIV GUELPH, 1992-; actg chair, Univ Guelph, 1995-1996; asst dean, Univ Guelph, 1994-2001; from asst prof to assoc prof, Univ Guelph, 1977-1993; fel cell biol, Dept Zool, Univ St Andrews, Scotland, 1975-1977; Res assoc protozool, Dept Zool, Univ Md, College Park, 1972-1973. **Memberships:** Mem Am Micros Soc; The Journal of Eukaryotic Microbiol; Soc Protozoologists; Can Soc Cell Mol Biol Biochem; Can Soc Zool; Int Soc Evolutionary Protistology. **Research Statement & Publications:** Form and function of ciliated protists as unicellular organisms using techniques of light and electron microscopy; ecology and systematics of protists, especially ciliates; using techniques of cytology, molecular biology (electrophoresis, DNA) and numerical taxonomy. **Mailing Address:** Dept Zool, Univ Guelph, Guelph, ON N1G 2W1, Can.

LYNN, HUGH BAILEY, SURGERY. **Personal Data:** b Verona, NJ, August 13, 1914; m 1940, c 3. **Education:** Princeton Univ, AB, 1936; Columbia Univ, MD, 1940. **Professional Experience:** PROF SURG, UNIV ALA, BIRMINGHAM, 1978-; prof surg, Mayo Grad Sch Med, Univ Minn, 1971-1978; head sect pediat surg, Mayo Clin, 1961-1978; surgeon-in-chief, Children's Hosp, Louisville, Ky, 1953-1960; assoc prof surg & chief sect pediat surg, Sch Med, Univ Louisville, 1953-1960; assoc surg, Newark Babies Hosp, 1952-1953; Teaching fel, Harvard Univ, 1951-1952. **Memberships:** Fel Am Col Surg; Am Acad Pediat. **Mailing Address:** Stonehedge Farm, PO Box 1040, Middleburg, VA 22117-1040.

LYNN, JEFFREY WHIDDEN, CONDENSED MATTER PHYSICS, NEUTRON SCATTERING, SUPERCONDUCTIVITY. **Personal Data:** b Hackensack, NJ, March 2, 1947; m 1964, Linda; c Robert & Heather. **Education:** Ga Inst Technol, BS, 1969, MS, 1970, PhD (physics), 1974. **Professional Experience:** PHYSICIST & TEAM LEADER, NAT INST STAN & TECHNOL CTR NEUTRON RES, as of 2005; PROF PHYSICS, CTR SUPERCONDUCTIVITY RES, UNIV MD, as of 2005; Adj Prof Physics, Univ Md, 1997-present; Chr, Topical Group Magnetism-Am Phys Soc, 1999-2003; Founder, Actg dir, Ctr Superconductivity Res, 1988-1989; Inst Laue Langevin, Grenoble, France, 1983-1984; Res Corp grant, 1977-1980; prof physics, univ Md, 1976-1997; NSF grants, 1976-; res physicist, Nat Bur Stand/Nat Inst Stand & Technol, 1976-1992; res assoc, Brookhaven Nat Lab, 1974-1976; Res asst physics, Oak Ridge Nat Lab, 1972-1974; Oak Ridge Assoc Univ Fell, 1972-1974. **Memberships:** Fel Am Phys Soc; Fel Wash Acad Sci; AAAS; Mat Res Soc.; Neutron Scattering Soc Am. **Research Statement & Publications:** Neutron scattering-condensed matter physics; magnetic properties of solids; spin dynamics; magnetic and structural phase transitions; structurally amorphous solids; magnetic superconductors; CMR materials; fundamental physics of neutrons; magnetic order and flux lattice in superconductors. **Mailing Address:** Ctr Neutron Res, Nat Inst Stand & Technol, Gaithersburg, MD 20899-8562. **Fax:** 301-921-9847. **E-Mail:** jeff.lynn@nist.gov

LYNN, JOHN R, OPHTHALMOLOGY. **Personal Data:** b Dallas, Tex, March 8, 1930; m 1954, c 5. **Education:** Rice Univ, BA, 1951; Univ Tex, MD, 1955. **Professional Experience:** PROF SURG, UNIV TEX HEALTH SCI CTR DALLAS, 1970-; CHMN, DEPT OPHTHAL, 1963-; from asst prof to assoc prof, Dept Ophthal, 1963-1970; Nat Inst Neurol Dis & Blindness spec fel, Univ Iowa Hosps, 1961-1963 & Eye Clin, Univ Tu bingen, 1962-1963; Res assoc, Univ Iowa Hosps, 1961-1963. **Memberships:** AMA; Am Acad Ophthal & Otolaryngol; Asn Res Vision & Ophthal. **Research Statement & Publications:** Methods of clinical perimetry; acute visual function effects by raising the intraocular pressure; threshold, summation and visual acuity of accentric scotomatous areas during phototopic, mesopic and scotopic adaptations. **Mailing Address:** 7150 Greenville Ave Suite 300, Dallas, TX 75231-5185.

LYNN, JOHN WENDELL, ORGANIC CHEMISTRY. **Personal Data:** b New York, NY, March 23, 1925; m 1946, c 3. **Education:** Yale Univ, BS, 1948, PhD (chem), 1951. **Professional Experience:** STAFF, NEUTRON CONDENSED MATTER SCI, CTR NEUTRON RES, NAT INST STAND & TECHNOL, as of 2004; CONSULT, 1985-; assoc dir res & develop, Fibers & Fabrics, 1973-1985; new venture mgr chem & plastics, Fibers & Fabrics, 1972-1973; dir technol, Fibers & Fabrics, 1969-1972; mgr new mkt develop, Org Chem Res Dept, Union Carbide Corp, 1969-1970; asst dir res & develop, Org Chem Res Dept, Union Carbide Corp, 1961-1969; res assoc, Org Chem Res Dept, Union Carbide Corp, 1960-1961; group leader, Org Chem Res Dept, Union Carbide Corp, 1955-1960; res chemist & proj leader, Org Chem Res Dept, Union Carbide Corp, 1951-1955. **Memberships:** Am Chem Soc; Electrochem Soc; AAAS. **Research Statement & Publications:** Nitrogenous substances; vinyl monomers; organic synthesis; synthetic fibers; vinyl fabrics; nonwovens; thermoplastic M and E resins; phenolic resins, water-soluble polymers. **Mailing Address:** Ctr Neutron Res, Nat Inst Stand & Technol, 100 Bur Dr, Gaithersburg, MD 20899-8562.

LYNN, KELVIN G, SOLID STATE PHYSICS, MATERIALS SCIENCE. **Personal Data:** b Rapid City, SDak, February 2, 1948; m Cindy; c Molly & Adam. **Education:** Univ Utah, BS, 1971, BS, 1972, PhD (mat sci), 1974. **Honors & Awards:** Garner Doe Award, Solid State Physicists. **Professional Experience:** PROF PHYSICS, WASH STATE UNIV, as of 2003; DIR, CTR MAT RES, WASH STATE UNIV, as of 2003; vis prof, State Univ NY, Stony Brook, 1977-; physicist, Brookhaven Nat Lab, beginning 1974; Res vis, Bell Labs, 1974-1977; Res assoc, Dept Mat Sci, Univ Utah, 1973-1974; adj prof, Univ Guelph, Ont; mem adv bd, Int Positron Annihilation; head, Mat Sci Div. **Memberships:** Fel Am Phys Soc; Am Inst Metall Engrs; Am Soc Metals; Mat Res Soc; Nat Acad Sci. **Research Statement & Publications:** Defects in semiconductors and metals, photovoltaics materials, room temperature radiation detectors, electronic structure, optical memories, microelectrical and mechanical systems, coatings. **Mailing Address:** Dept Physics, Wash State Univ, Rm Webster 625, Pullman, WA 99164-2711. **Fax:** 509-335-4145. **E-Mail:** kgl@mrc.wsu.edu

LYNN, LARRY, PHYSICS. **Personal Data:** b September 5, 1930. **Education:** Tufts Univ, BS, 1951. **Professional Experience:** DIR DEFENSE ADVAN RES PROJ AGENCY, DEPT DEFENSE, 1995-. **Mailing Address:** Dept Defense, 3701 N Fairfax Dr, Arlington, VA 22203.

LYNN, MERRILL, POLYMER CHEMISTRY. **Personal Data:** b New Columbia, Pa, November 20, 1930; m 1957, Lydia; c Alexander & Katherine. **Education:** Bucknell Univ, BS, 1956; Univ Fla, PhD (chem), 1961. **Professional Experience:** CONSULT, 1970-; sr develop assoc chem, Corning Inc, 1970-1995; res chemist, Esso res & Eng Co, 1961-1969. **Memberships:** Am Chem Soc; Am Inst Chem; Am Ceramic Soc. **Research Statement & Publications:** Bonding to glass surfaces; glass reinforced plastics; polymer modifications; coating resins; immobilized enzymes; ceramic binders. **Mailing Address:** 16 Olcott Rd N, Big Flats, NY 14814.

LYNN, RALPH BEVERLEY, CARDIOVASCULAR & THORACIC SURGERY. **Personal Data:** b Penetanguishene, Ont, August 24, 1921; m 1944, Blanche Wellman; c 4. **Education:** Queen's Univ, Ont, MD, CM, 1945; FRCS(E), 1948; FRCS, 1949; Royal Col Physicians & Surgeons Can, cert, 1957; FRCS, 1958; FRCS(C), 1965. **Professional Experience:** EMER PROF, KINGSTON GEN HOSP, 1980-; fel coun clin cardiol, Am Heart Asn, 1965; prof surg, Sch Med, Queen's Univ, Ont, 1962; consult, Hotel Dieu & Can Forces Hosp, 1958- & Dept Vet Affairs, 1958-; HEAD CARDIOTHORACIC UNIT, KINGSTON GEN HOSP, 1958-; assoc prof, Kingston Gen Hosp, 1958-1962; from asst prof to assoc prof surg, Univ Sask, 1955-1958; Markle scholar, Univ Sask, 1955-1957; sr registr, Southampton Chest Hosp, Eng, 1954-1955; traveling fel, Post-Grad Med Fedn, Johns Hopkins Univ, 1951-1952; surgeon, Cleveland City Hosp, Ohio, 1950-1951; Nat Res Coun Can scholar, Western Res Univ, 1950-1951; asst lectr surg, Post-Grad Med Sch, Univ London, 1949-1950 & 1952-1954; clin tutor, Royal Infirmary, Edinburgh, Scotland, 1948-1949; sr registr, Post-Grad Med Sch, Univ London, 1947-1948; sr intern surg, Royal Victoria Hosp, Montreal, Que, 1946-1947; Jr intern, Kingston Gen Hosp, 1944-1946. **Memberships:** NY Acad Sci; Can Thoracic Soc; Royal Soc Med; Asn Thoracic Surg; fel Am Col Surg; fel Am Col Chest Physicians. **Research Statement & Publications:** Thoracic, cardiovascular and peripheral vascular surgery. **Mailing Address:** Dept Surg, Queen's Univ Sch Med, Kingston, ON K7L 3N6, Can.

LYNN, R(ALPH) EMERSON, CHEMICAL ENGINEERING. **Personal Data:** b Elkhart, Ind, March 17, 1920; m 1946. **Education:** Purdue Univ, BS, 1942; Univ Tex, MS, 1949, PhD (chem eng), 1953. **Professional Experience:** RETIRED; alcoa prof chem eng, Ohio State Univ, 1967-1982; mgr, E P Rubber Develop, B F Goodrich Chem Co, Ohio, 1966-1967; prog planning, B F Goodrich Chem Co Div, 1960-1966; mgr chem eng res, B F Goodrich Co, 1956-1960; res scientist, B F Goodrich Co, 1956; sr res engr, B F Goodrich Co, 1952-1956; tech serv supvr, US Rubber Co, 1943-1946. **Memberships:** AAAS; Am Chem Soc; fel Am Inst Chem Engrs; Soc Plastics Engrs; Am Soc Eng Educ. **Research Statement & Publications:** Economics; thermodynamics; kinetics; polymerization and polymer processing. **Mailing Address:** 9221 W Broward Blvd No 2510, Ft Lauderdale, FL 33324-2415.

LYNN, RAYMOND J, MEDICAL MICROBIOLOGY, HOST-PARASITE INTERACTION. **Personal Data:** b Bitner, Pa, October 23, 1928; m 1958, c 3. **Education:** Univ Pittsburgh, BS, 1952, MS, 1953; Univ Pa, PhD (med microbiol), 1956. **Professional Experience:** ASSOC DEAN, SCH MED, UNIV SDAK, VERMILLION, 1983-; rep Dak Affil, regional rev comt, Am Heart Asn, 1975-1978; Secy-treas, SDak Bd Examr Basic Sci, 1971-1979; PROF MICROBIOL, SCH MED, UNIV SDAK, VERMILLION, 1970-; from asst prof to assoc prof, Sch Med, Univ Sdak, Vermillion, 1961-1970; instr, Sch Med, Univ Pittsburgh, 1960-1961; res assoc microbiol, Sch Med, Univ Pittsburgh, 1958-1960; res microbiologist, Univ Pa, 1956-1957; res investr microbiol, Univ Pa, 1953-1956; Asst biol, Univ Pittsburgh, 1952-1953. **Memberships:** AAAS; Am Pub Health Asn; Am Soc Microbiol; Soc Exp Biol & Med; NY Acad Sci. **Research Statement & Publications:** Immunology of the Mycoplasmataceae; role of L-forms in sequelae disease states; immunochemistry of streptococcal L-forms and relation of such antigens to rheumatic fever and acute glomerular nephritis; cell-wall defective microorganisms as agents of immunoregulation. **Mailing Address:** Dept Microbiol, Med Sch, Univ SDak, 414 E Clark, Vermillion, SD 57069-2307.

LYNN, ROBERT K, DRUG METABOLISM. **Personal Data:** b Ky, October 29, 1947. **Education:** Murray State Univ, BA, 1969; Australian Nat Univ, PhD (chem), 1974. **Professional Experience:** DIR & VPRES DRUG METAB & PHARMACOKINETICS, SMITHKLINE BEECHAM PHARMACEUT, WELWYN, ENG, 1991-; group dir drug metab, SmithKline Beecham Pharmaceuticals, King Prussia, Pa, 1989-1990; group dir drug metab & pharmacokinetics, Welwyn, Eng, 1987-1989; dir, King Prussia, Pa, 1986-1987; asst dir drug metab, Smith Kline & French Labs, Philadelphia, 1982-1986; res asst prof, Clin Pharmacol Div, 1978-1982; young environ health scientist award, Nat Inst Environ Health Sci, 1978-1981; Prin investr, Nat Inst Environ Health Sci, 1977-1983; res instr, Clin Pharmacol Div, 1977-1978; res assoc, Dept Pharmacol, Sch Med, Ore Health Sci Univ, Portland, 1974-1977; res scholar, Med Chem Group, Australian Nat Univ, Canberra, 1971-1974; Res asst, Dept Pharmacol, Sch Med, Vanderbilt Univ, Nashville, 1969-1971. **Memberships:** Am Soc Pharmacol & Exp Therapeut; Am Soc Mass Spectrometry; Am Chem Soc; AAAS. **Research Statement & Publications:** Drug metabolism; pharmacokinetics; analytical chemistry; environmental chemical metabolism. **Mailing Address:** SmithKline Beecham Pharmaceut, PO Box 1539 UW2730, King of Prussia, PA 19406-0939. **Fax:** 610-270-6037. **E-Mail:** bob_lynn@sbphrd.com

LYNN, ROBERT THOMAS, ANIMAL BEHAVIOR, ECOLOGY. **Personal Data:** b Coleman, Tex, January 15, 1931; m 1954, c 2. **Education:** Fla State Univ, BA, 1956, MA, 1957; Univ Okla, PhD (zool), 1963. **Professional Experience:** PROF BIOL SCI, SOUTHWESTERN OKLA STATE UNIV, 1967-; assoc prof, Presby Col, SC, 1964-1967; asst prof, Emory & Henry Col, 1963-1964; Instr biol, Austin Col, 1957-1959. **Memberships:** AAAS; Ecol Soc Am; Am Inst Biol Sci; Am Ornith Union; Wilson Ornith Soc. **Research Statement & Publications:** Ecology and behavior of birds and lizards. **Mailing Address:** 1208 N Indiana, Weatherford, OK 73096-2223.

LYNN, ROGER YEN SHEN, COMPUTER SCIENCE, OPERATIONS RESEARCH. **Personal Data:** b Shanghai, China, January 18, 1941; c 1. **Education:** Cheng Kung Univ, Taiwan, BS, 1961; Brown Univ, MS, 1964; Courant, NY Univ, PhD (math), 1968. **Professional Experience:** ASSOC PROF MATH, VILLANOVA UNIV, as of 2005; asst prof Math, Villanova Univ, beginning 1971; asst prof, Univ Ind, Bloomington, 1969-1971; Lectr math, Univ Ind, Bloomington, 1968-1969. **Memberships:** Am Math Soc; Soc Indust & Appl Math; NY Acad Sci; Asn Comput Mach. **Research Statement & Publications:** Asymptotic solutions of differential equations; operations research; computer graphics. **Mailing Address:** Dept Math Sci, Villanova Univ, St Augustine Ctr 381 800 Lanchester Ave, Villanova, PA 19085. **Fax:** 610-519-6928. **E-Mail:** roger.lynn@villanova.edu

LYNN, SCOTT, CHEMICAL ENGINEERING. **Personal Data:** b Iola, Kans, June 18, 1928; m, c 4. **Education:** Calif Inst Technol, BS, 1950, MS, 1951, PhD (chem eng), 1954. **Honors & Awards:** Fulbright lectr, Delft Tech Univ, Neth, 1973. **Professional Experience:** PROF EMER CHEM ENG, UNIV CALIF, BERKELEY, as of 2004; ASSOC DEAN, COL CHEM, 1986-1994; prof chem eng, Univ Calif, Berkeley, beginning 1969; actg prof, Col Chem, 1967-1969; Ed, Indust Electrolytic Div, J Electrochem Soc, 1960-1990; res engr, Dow Chem Co, Calif, 1954-1967; Asst, Tech Hogesch, Holland, 1953-1954. **Memberships:** Am Chem Soc; fel Am Inst Chem Engrs. **Research Statement & Publications:** Separation processes; gas absorption; electrochemistry and electrochemical engineering; process synthesis and development; sulfur recovery processes. **Mailing Address:** Chem Engr, Univ Calif, 316 Gilman, Berkeley, CA 94720-1462. **Fax:** 510-642-4778. **E-Mail:** lynn@cchem.berkeley.edu

LYNN, THOMAS NEIL, JR, MEDICINE, PREVENTIVE MEDICINE. **Personal Data:** b Ft Worth, Tex, February 14, 1930; m 1952, c 3. **Education:** Univ Okla, BS, 1951, MD, 1955. **Professional Experience:** RETIRED; vpres, Baptist Med Ctr, Oklahoma City, 1980; dean, Col Med, 1976-1980; actg dean, Col Med, 1974-1976; prof family pract, community med & dent & chmn dept, 1969-1980; assoc prof prev med & pub health, Med Ctr, Univ Okla, 1964-1969; vchmn dept, Med Ctr, Univ Okla, 1963-1969; asst prof med, Med Ctr, Univ Okla, 1963-1969; asst prof prev med, Med Ctr, Univ Okla, 1961-1964; instr, Med Ctr, Univ Okla, 1961-1963; chief res, Med Ctr, Univ Okla, 1959-1961; clin assoc, Nat Heart Inst, Md, 1957-1959; From intern to asst resident med, Barnes Hosp, St Louis, 1955-1957. **Memberships:** AMA. **Research Statement & Publications:** Epidemiology of coronary artery disease; psycho-social aspects of dependence and rehabilitation; ballistocardiography and electrocardiography. **Mailing Address:** 3300 Northwest Exp, Oklahoma City, OK 75112.

LYNN, WALTER R(OYAL), CIVIL & ENVIRONMENTAL ENGINEERING. **Personal Data:** b New York, NY, October 1, 1928; m 1960, c 1. **Education:** Univ Miami, Fla, BSCE, 1950; Univ NC, MSSE, 1954; Northwestern Univ, PhD, 1963. **Professional Experience:** PROF EMER CIVIL & ENVIRON ENG, CORNELL UNIV, as of 2004; US Nat Comt Nat Disaster Reduction, Nat Res Coun, 1993-; chmn, Bd Nat Disaster, 1992; dean Univ fac, Ctr Environ Qual Mgt, 1988-1993; chmn, Comn Water Res, 1987-1991; chmn, NY State Water Res Planning Coun, brginning 1986; chmn, Water Sci & Technol bd, Nat Res Coun, 1982-1985; dir, Prog Sci, Tech & Soc, beginning 1980; Sci Tech & Soc Prog, Ctr Environ Qual Mgt, 1980-1988; bd trustees, Cornell Univ, 1980-1985; mem bd dir, Cornell Res Found, 1978-; assoc ed, J Environ Econs & Mgt, 1978-; mem, Rockefeller Fdn, 1976-1980; adj prof pub health, Med Col, Cornell Univ, 1971-1980; Sch Civil & Environ Eng, Ctr Environ Qual Mgt, 1970-1978; mem, WHO, beginning 1969; assoc ed, J Oper Res, 1968-1976; prof civil & environ eng, Cornell Univ, beginning 1967; dir, Ctr Environ Qual Mgt, 1966-1976; assoc prof, Cornell Univ, 1961-1967; assoc prof, Univ Miami, 1958-1961; consult, Reeder & Lynn, Consult Engrs, 1957-1961; dir res, Ralph B Carter Co, 1955-1957; asst prof civil eng, Univ Miami, 1954-1958. **Memberships:** AAAS; Am Soc Civil Engrs; Sigma Xi. **Research Statement & Publications:** Systems analysis and operations research applications in civil and environmental engineering and public health; environmental control; science, technology policy, science and technology for development. **Mailing Address:** Sch Civil & Environ Eng, Cornell Univ, 423 Hillister Hall, Ithaca, NY 14853-3501. **E-Mail:** wrl1@cornell.edu

LYNN, WARREN CLARK, SOIL SCIENCE. **Personal Data:** b Satanta, Kans, December 4, 1935; m 1960, c 3. **Education:** Kans State Univ, BS, 1957, MS, 1958; Univ Calif, PhD (soil sci), 1964. **Professional Experience:** RES SOIL SCIENTIST, NAT SOIL SURV LAB, USDA, as of 2004; soil scientist, Nat Soil Surv Lab, USDA, beginning 1963. **Memberships:** Int Soc Soil Sci; Soil Sci Soc Am; Clay Minerals Soc; Int Peat Soc. **Research Statement & Publications:** Properties of cat clays or acid sulfate soils; clay minerals in relation to soil properties; organic soils. **Mailing Address:** Nat Soil Surv, USDA, 100 Centennial Mall N, Rm 152, Lincoln, NE 68508-2849. **Fax:** 402-437-5760. **E-Mail:** warren.lynn@nssc.nrcs.usda.gov

LYNN, WILLIAM SANFORD, MEDICINE. **Personal Data:** b June 14, 1922. **Education:** Ala Polytech Inst, BS, 1943; Columbia Univ, MD, 1946. **Professional Experience:** RES PROF, DIV HUMAN NUTRIT, MED BR, UNIV TEX, 1987-; Dir, Toxicol Prog, 1981-1986; chief, Pulmonary Serv, Durham Vet Admin Hosp, 1974-1982; prof med & assoc prof biochem, Med Ctr, Duke Univ, 1972-1987; Markle scholar, Duke Univ, 1956-1961; assoc med & biochem, Med Ctr, Duke Univ, 1955-1972; Dir, Diabetic Clin, 1955-1958; fel, Dept Biochem, Univ Pa, 1953-1955; resident physician, Raybrook, NY State Tuberc Sanitarium, NY, 1953; resident, Dept Med, 1951-1952; fel, Dept Endocrinol, Med Ctr, Duke Univ, 1950; Fel pulmonary physiol, Trudeau Sanitarium, Saranac Lake, NY, 1946-1949; mem, Duke Comprehensive Cancer Ctr; ed, Arch Environ Health. **Memberships:** Am Soc Biol Chemists; Am Soc Clin Investigators; Biophys Soc; Am Thoracic Soc; Asn Am Physicians; Soc Toxicol. **Research Statement & Publications:** Pathogenesis of HIV, TNF and dexamethasone and cotton dust; role of lean beef in lipid metabolism in man; mechanism of cytotoxicity of oxidized sterols; cholesterol and cell growth; numerous publications. **Mailing Address:** 1104 NE Ninth St Apt 201, Smithfield, TX 78957.

LYNN, YEN-MOW, APPLIED MATHEMATICS. **Personal Data:** b Shanghai, China, January 17, 1935; c Edward, Kirk & Genevieve. **Education:** Nat Taiwan Univ, BS, 1955; Calif Inst Technol, MS, 1957, PhD, 1961. **Professional Experience:** Chmn dept, Univ MD, Baltimore CO, 1976-1982; PROF MATH, UNIV MD, BALTIMORE CO, 1972-; consult, Ames Res Ctr, NASA, 1966; Ballistic Res Lab, US Army, 1969-1975; assoc prof, Univ MD, Baltimore CO, 1967-1972; assoc prof, Ill Inst Technol, 1964-1967; from asst res scientist to assoc res scientist, Courant Inst Math Sci, NY Univ, 1960-1964. **Memberships:** Am Math Soc; Soc Indust & Appl Math; Am Phys Soc. **Research Statement & Publications:** Magneto-gasdynamics; plasma physics; partial differential equations; rotating fluids. **Mailing Address:** Univ Md, Dept Math & Statist, Rm MP411, Baltimore, MD 21250. **Fax:** 410-455-1066. **E-Mail:** lynn@math.umbc.edu

LYNNE-DAVIES, PATRICIA, RESPIRATORY PHYSIOLOGY. **Personal Data:** b Swansa, Wales, July 4, 1933. **Education:** Conjoint Bd, London, MRCS-LRCP, 1961; McGill Univ, PhD (physiol), 1969. **Professional Experience:** PROF, DEPT INTERNAL MED, WAYNE STATE UNIV, 1980-; assoc prof, Stanford Univ, 1974-1980; asst prof, Dept Med, Univ Alta, 1969-1974. **Memberships:** Am Fedn Clin Res; Am Physiol Soc. **Mailing Address:** 15801 Windmill Pointe Dr, Grosse Pointe Park, MI 48230-1841.

LYO, IN-WHAN, PHYSICS. **Education:** Seoul Nat Univ, BS, 1980; Univ Pa, PhD (Physics), 1988. **Professional Experience:** ASSOC PROF, PHYSICS DEPT, YONSEI UNIV, 1996-; res staff, IBM T J watson Res Ctr, 1991-1996; fel, IBM T J watson Res Ctr, 1988-1991. **Mailing Address:** Yonsei Univ, Seoul, Korea. **Fax:** 82-2-2123-7090. **E-Mail:** lyo@phya.yonsei.ac.kr

LYO, SUNGKWUN KENNETH, SEMICONDUCTOR PHYSICS, QUANTUM TRANSPORT & MANY-BODY THEORY. **Personal Data:** b Pyongnam, Korea, July 3, 1941; American citizen; m 1971, Nahmyoung; c John, Grace & Christopher. **Education:** Seoul Nat Univ, Korea, BA, 1964; Univ Calif, Los Angeles, PhD (physics), 1972. **Honors & Awards:** Award of Excellence, sandia nat labs, 1994, 1999; Basic Energy Sci Award, US Dept Energy, 1993; except contribr Award, Sandia nat labs, 1988. **Professional Experience:** PRES, SANDIA NAT LABS, 1992-; vis scholar, Seoul Nat Univ, 1991; sr mem tech staff physics, Sandia Nat Labs, 1988-1992; vis prof, Korea Advan Inst Sci, 1980; mem tech staff, Sandia Nat Labs, 1977-1988; adj asst prof, Univ Calif, Los Angeles, 1974-1977; res assoc physics, Univ Chicago, 1973-1974; asst res physicist, Univ Calif, Los Angeles, 1972-1973. **Memberships:** Am Phys Soc; Mat Res Soc. **Research Statement & Publications:** Ferromagnetic Hall effect; spin-lattice relaxation; hopping transport in disordered solids; quantum transport and many-body effects in metals, semiconductors and organic conductors; optical properties of quantum wells. **Mailing Address:** Sandia Nat Labs, PO Box 5800 MS 1415, Albuquerque, NM 87185-5800. **Fax:** 505-844-1197. **E-Mail:** sklyo@sandia.gov

LYON, BETTY C, MATHEMATICS. **Professional Experience:** PROF EMER, MATH DEPT, EASTERN NMEX UNIV, as of 2006. **Memberships:** Am Math Soc. **Mailing Address:** Math Sci Dept, Eastern NMex Univ, Sta 18, Portales, NM 88130. **Fax:** 505-562-2362.

LYON, CAMERON KIRBY, ORGANIC CHEMISTRY. **Personal Data:** b Islampur, India, July 23, 1923; American citizen; m 1948, c 3. **Education:** Col Wooster, BA, 1947; Northwestern Univ, PhD (chem), 1952. **Professional Experience:** RETIRED; chemist, Western Regional Res Lab, USDA, Albany, 1959-1986; chemist, Jackson Lab, E I du Pont de Nemours & Co, 1951-1959. **Memberships:** Emer mem Am Chem Soc. **Research Statement & Publications:** Polymers; urethanes; fats and oils; oilseed and leaf proteins. **Mailing Address:** Five N Lane, Orinda, CA 94563-2204.

LYON, DAVID LOUIS, ECOLOGY, ORNITHOLOGY. **Personal Data:** b Oshkosh, Wis, January 20, 1935; m 1957, c 3. **Education:** Beloit Col, BA, 1956; Univ Mo, MA, 1959;

Iowa State Univ, PhD (wildlife ecol), 1965. **Professional Experience:** PROF BIOL, CORNELL COL, as of 1998; assoc prof biol, Cornell Col, beginning 1973; asst prof, Cornell Col, 1965-1973; Wildlife biologist, Nebr Game & Parks Comn, 1959-1961. **Memberships:** AAAS; Ecol Soc Am; Am Ornithologists' Union. **Research Statement & Publications:** Competition ecology, particularly territoriality and its relation to resource utilization; pollination ecology. **Mailing Address:** Dept Biol, Cornell Col, 600 First Ave W, Mt Vernon, IA 52314.

LYON, DAVID N, PHYSICAL CHEMISTRY. **Personal Data:** b Altoona, Kans, April 15, 1942; m 1942, c 2. **Education:** Univ Mo, MA, 1942; Univ Calif, PhD (chem), 1948. **Professional Experience:** PROF EMER CHEM ENG, COL CHEM, UNIV CALIF, BERKELEY, as of 2005; Asst dean, Col Chem, Univ Calif, Berkeley, 1969-1972; prof chem eng, Col Chem, Univ Calif, Berkeley, beginning 1965; res chem engr, Univ Calif, Berkeley, 1959-1965; lectr chem eng, Univ Calif, Berkeley, 1957-1965; assoc res chemist, Univ Calif, Berkeley, 1953-1959; asst res chemist, Univ Calif, Berkeley, 1951-1953; Res assoc, Univ Calif, Berkeley, 1948-1951. **Memberships:** NY Acad Sci; AAAS; Am Chem Soc; Am Inst Chem Eng; Sigma Xi. **Research Statement & Publications:** Chemical thermodynamics; cryogenic engineering; chemical process design. **Mailing Address:** Dept Chem eng, Univ Calif, 201 Gilman, Berkeley, CA 94556-1313. **E-Mail:** lyon@cchem.berkeley.edu

LYON, DONALD WILKINSON, INORGANIC CHEMISTRY. **Personal Data:** b Manchester, Eng, August 6, 1916; American citizen; m 1942, Martha Crane; c Richard, Evelyn (Brownlee) & David. **Education:** Ohio Wesleyan Univ, BA, 1937; Ohio State Univ, PhD (inorg chem), 1941. **Honors & Awards:** Borman Award, Am Soc Eng Educ, 1981, Freund Award, 1993. **Professional Experience:** RETIRED; personnel coordr, Chem Dyes & Pigments Dept, 1977-1981; admin supvr, Pigments Dept, 1962-1977; tech supvr, E I du Pont de Nemours & Co, Inc, 1954-1962; Res chemist, E I du Pont de Nemours & Co, Inc, 1941-1954. **Memberships:** Am Chem Soc; Am Soc Eng Educ. **Research Statement & Publications:** Titanium dioxide. **Mailing Address:** 110 Banbury Dr, Windsor Hills, Wilmington, DE 19803-2602.

LYON, DUANE EDGAR, FOREST PRODUCTS, WOOD SCIENCE WOOD COMPOSITE MATERIALS. **Personal Data:** b Muskegon, Mich, March 12, 1939; m 1961, Diana; c Karla & Keith. **Education:** Univ Mich, BS, 1962, MS, 1963; Univ Calif, Berkeley, PhD (forest prod), 1975. **Professional Experience:** PROF EMER, MISS STATE UNIV, as of 2005; vis prof, MOI Univ, Kenya, 1988; PROF FOREST PROD, MISS FOREST PROD LAB, MISS STATE UNIV, 1985-; Vis Scientist, USDA Forest Prod Lab, 1980; from asst prof to assoc prof, Miss Forest Prod Lab, Miss State Univ, 1973-1985; asst specialist, Forest Prod Lab, Univ Calif, 1966-1973; Asst technologist, Dept Wood Technol, Wash State Univ, 1963-1966. **Memberships:** Forest Prod Res Soc; Soc Wood Sci & Technol (pres, 1996-1997). **Research Statement & Publications:** Development and characterization of compositeEngineering materials made wholly or in part from wood; wood performance; effect of adverse environments on wood performance; wood sidingand and furniture construction. **Mailing Address:** Miss State Univ, 111 Grand Ridge Rd, Starkville, MS 39759. **Fax:** 662-325-8126. **E-Mail:** dlyon@up.net

LYON, EDWARD SPAFFORD, GENITOURINARY SURGERY, ENDOUROLOGY. **Personal Data:** b Chicago, Ill, February 26, 1926; m 1951, Valerie Traut; c Nancy, Susan, Ross, Janice, Roger, Alice, Paul, Steven, Sally, John, Valerie & Mark. **Education:** Univ Chicago, PhB, 1948, SB, 1950, MD, 1953. **Honors & Awards:** Pro Meritate Medal, Int Soc Urol Endoscopy. **Professional Experience:** EMER PROF UROL, UNIV CHICAGO, 1996-; from asst prof to prof, Univ Hosps, 1959-1996; resident urol, Univ Hosps, 1956-1959; resident surg, Univ Hosps, 1954-1956; Intern, Univ Hosps, 1953-1954. **Memberships:** Am Urol Asn; Soc Univ Urologists; Int Soc Urol Endoscopy; Endourology Soc; Soc Urol & Eng. **Research Statement & Publications:** Urolithiasis. **Mailing Address:** 11246 Longwood Dr, Chicago, IL 60643. **Fax:** 773-702-1001. **E-Mail:** e_lyon@uchicago.edu

LYON, GORDON EDWARD, PROGRAMMING TECHNIQUES, SOFTWARE ARCHITECTURE. **Personal Data:** b New London, Wis, June 8, 1942; m 1971, Carla; c Merritt & Adrienne. **Education:** Mich Technol Univ, BS (physics w/honor) 1964; Univ Mich, MS (applied math), 1966, MS (comp sci), 1967, PhD (comput sci), 1972. **Honors & Awards:** Silver Medal Award, US Dept Com, 1978; R&D Magazine RD-100 (team) Award, 1997. **Professional Experience:** ACTG DIV CHIEF, CONVERGENT INFO SYS DIV & GROUP LEADER, DISTRIBUTED SYS TECHNOL GROUP, NAT INST STAND & TECHNOL, as of 2002; res, Software Diagnostics & Conform Testing Div, beginning 2003; mgr, Parallel Processing Group, 1992-2003; adj prof lectr, Dept Decision Sci, George Mason Univ, 1984-1985; Assoc prof lectr, Dept Elec Eng & Comput Sci, George Wash Univ, 1978-1979; mgr, Programming Lang Group, 1978-1982; COMPUT SCIENTIST, NAT INST SCI & TECHNOL, 1972-; res assoc, Dept Psychiat, Ment Health Res Inst, Univ Mich, 1970-1972; Mathematician, Comput Sci Dept, Gen Motors Res Labs, 1967-1968. **Memberships:** Asn Comput Mach; Soc Indust Appl Math; Comput Soc Inst Elec & Electronics Engrs. **Research Statement & Publications:** Primarily interested in software programming techniques; contributions in the areas of syntactic pattern recognition; scatter storage; programming language tools; performance measurement for parallel systems; software testing. **Mailing Address:** Nat Inst Stand & Technol, 100 Bur Dr STOP 8951, Gaithersburg, MD 20899. **Fax:** 301-926-9675. **E-Mail:** lyon@nist.gov

LYON, GORDON FREDERICK, PHYSICS. **Personal Data:** b London, Eng, May 10, 1922; Canadian citizen; m 1943, c 1. **Education:** Univ Sask, BA, 1956, MA, 1958, PhD (physics), 1961. **Professional Experience:** RETIRED; prof physics, Univ Western Ont, 1969-1988; mem subcomt aeronomy, Nat Res Coun Can, 1966-; Mem comn 6, Int Union Geod & Geophys-Int Asn Geomag & Aeronomy, 1963-; from asst prof to assoc prof, Univ Western Ont, 1962-1969; Instr physics, Univ Sask, 1956-1962. **Memberships:** Am Geophys Union; Am Asn Physics Teachers; Can Asn Physicists. **Research Statement & Publications:** Radio physics of the upper atmosphere; scattering of radio waves by ionospheric inhomogeneities; ionospheric absorption; travelling ionospheric disturbances; ionospheric electron content utilizing beacon satellites; associated geophysical phenomena; aurora. **Mailing Address:** Apt 114 Gainesborough Rd, London, ON N6G 1Z8, Can.

LYON, IRVING, HEPATIC GLUTATHIONE HOMEOSTASIS. **Personal Data:** b Los Angeles, Calif, May 10, 1921; m 1948, Harriette; c David, Charles & Lawrence. **Education:** Univ Calif, Los Angeles, AB, 1942, MA, 1949; Univ Calif, Berkeley, PhD (physiol), 1952. **Professional Experience:** RETIRED; res biochemist hepatol, US Vet Admin Wadsworth Hosp Ctr, Los Angeles, 1981-1989; res physiologist tumor-lipid biochem, Univ Calif, Los Angeles, 1979-1981; consult, environ health & nutrit, beginning 1975; spec consult energy resources & conserv, Calif State Comn, Los Angeles, 1975; sr visitor, Inst Biol Chem A, Univ Copenhagen, Denmark, 1972-1974; vis investr, Jackson Lab, Bar Harbor, Maine, 1971; NSF res fel, dept physiol & biophys, Univ Ill, Urbana, 1970; Inst Med Res, Putnam Mem Hosp, Bennington, Vt, Dept Biochem, Physiol & Oncol, Univ Wis-Madison, Will Rogers Mem Hosp, Saranac Lake, NY & Lab Pharmacol, Baltimore Cancer Res Ctr, Nat Cancer Inst, 1968; prof biol, sci fac, Bennington Col, Vt, 1967-1972; lectr, Soc Gen Physiologists, Woods Hole, Mass, 1963; assoc prof biochem, Chicago Med Sch, Ill, 1962-1967; res assoc physiol & biochem bone, orthop surg, Presby-St Luke's Hosp, Chicago, 1958-1962; asst prof biol chem, Univ Ill, Chicago, 1958-1962; res biochemist physiol & biochem skin, med dept, Toni Co, Chicago, 1954-1958; res & teaching fel, Rockefeller Found-Med Sci Dept Nutrit, Harvard Sch Pub Health, 1952-1954; researcher & gen lab asst mammalian physiol, Univ Calif, Berkeley, 1949-1952; lab & teaching asst mammalian anat & gen embryol, Univ Southern Calif, Los Angeles, 1947-1949. **Memberships:** Fel AAAS; fel Int Col Appl Nutrit; Am Physiol Soc; NY Acad Sci. **Research Statement & Publications:** Liver transplantation studies; prevention of post-ischemic injury; hepatic enzymes and oxidant injury; consultant on EIR's for development projects proposed in environmentally-sensitive areas. **Mailing Address:** 3529 Greenfield Ave, Los Angeles, CA 90034.

LYON, JAMES F, INTERNATIONAL PHYSICS. **Education:** Mass Inst Technol, BS, 1960, MS, 1962; Univ Tenn, PhD (physics), 1969. **Professional Experience:** EXEC OFFICER, OAK RIDGE NAT LAB, as of 2002; RES SCIENTIST, OAK RIDGE NAT LAB, 1964-. **Memberships:** Am Phys Soc. **Mailing Address:** Fusion Energy Div Oak Ridge Nat Lab, PO Box 2008, Oak Ridge, TN 37831-6062. **Fax:** 615-576-7926. **E-Mail:** lyonjf@fed.ornl.gov

LYON, JEFFREY A, IMMUNOLOGY. **Personal Data:** c 2. **Education:** Va Mil Inst, BS, 1970; Univ SC, PhD (biochem), 1974. **Professional Experience:** RES CHEMIST, DEPT IMMUNOL, WALTER REED ARMY INST RES, 1980-; res chemist, Div Biochem, 1975-1980. **Memberships:** Am Asn Immunologists; Am Soc Trop Med & Hyg; Sigma Xi. **Mailing Address:** Dept Immunol, Walter Reed Army Inst Res, 503 Robert Grant Ave, Silver Spring, MD 20910.

LYON, JOHN B(ENNETT), CHEMICAL ENGINEERING. **Personal Data:** b Washington, DC, March 13, 1927; m 1957, c 1. **Education:** Catholic Univ, BChE, 1950; Univ Del, PhD (chem eng), 1953. **Professional Experience:** SR TECH ASSOC, E I DU PONT DEL NEMOURS & CO, INC, 1986-; staff engr, Sabine River Works, 1980-1985; sr engr, Richmond, Va, 1976-1980; Spruance Film Plant, Richmond, Va, 1965-1976; process develop supvr, Clinton Film Plant, Iowa, 1962-1965; engr res supvr, Yerkes Res Lab, 1960-1962; res engr, Film Dept, 1958-1959; tech investr, Film Dept, 1957-1958; Res engr, Polychem Dept, E I du Pont Del Nemours & Co Inc, 1953-1957. **Memberships:** Am Chem Soc; Am Inst Chem Engrs; Sigma Xi. **Research Statement & Publications:** Heat and mass transfer; application of reaction kinetics. **Mailing Address:** 1824 Lindenwood Dr, Orange, TX 77630.

LYON, JOHN BLAKESLEE, BIOCHEMISTRY. **Personal Data:** b Auburn, NY, March 17, 1925; m 1948, c 2. **Education:** Hamilton Col, AB, 1950; Brown Univ, ScM, 1952, PhD (biol), 1954. **Honors & Awards:** Lederle Med Fac award, Emory Univ, 1956-1959; Lederle Med Fac award, USPHS sr res fel, 1959. **Professional Experience:** RETIRED; from instr to prof biochem, Emory Univ, 1956-1992; Life Inst Med Res Fund fel biochem, Emory Univ, 1954-1956; asst biol, Brown Univ, 1950-1952. **Memberships:** Am Soc Biol Chem. **Research Statement & Publications:** Regulatory mechanisms of metabolism; glycogen metabolism; vitamin B-6. **Mailing Address:** 6278 Leeward Lane, Flowery Branch, GA 30542. **Fax:** 404-727-2738.

LYON, JOHN GRIMSON, REMOTE SENSOR & GLOBAL IONOSPHERIC STUDIES TECHNOLOGIES, ENVIRONMENTAL SCIENCE & ENGINEERING. **Personal Data:** b Berkeley, Calif, February 1954; m 1986, Lynn Krise; c Sarah F. **Education:** Reed Col, Portland, Ore, BA, 1977; Univ Mich, Ann Arbor, MS, 1979, PhD (natural resources), 1981. **Professional Experience:** DIR, ENVIRON SCI DIV, NAT EXPOSURE RES LAB, 1999-; Vis scientist, US Environ Protection Agency, Environ Monitoring Systs Lab, 1991-1994; assoc ed, Photogram Eng & Remote Sensing, 1988-; chair, Aerospace Div Remote Sensing Comt, Am Soc Civil Engrs, 1987-1989; Civil engr, US Army Corps Engrs, Dist Detroit, 1985-1988; assoc prof natural resources, Ohio State Univ, 1981-1999; assoc prof civil eng, Ohio State Univ, 1981-1999; Res assoc, Sch Natural Resources, Univ Mich, 1977-1981; res assoc, NASA Ames Res Ctr, 1976-1977; ed-in-chief, Lewis Publ. **Memberships:** Am Soc Photogram & Remote Sensing; Am Soc Civil Engrs; Inst Elec & Electronics Engrs; Am Cong Surveying & Mapping; Am Soc Agr; Soil & Water Conserv Soc. **Research Statement & Publications:** Application of remote sensor and geographic information system technologies to natural resource and engineering problems including wetlands, water quality, vegetation, soils, and landscape ecology; author of over 30 refereed journals. **Mailing Address:** Dept Civil Eng, Ohio State Univ, 2070 Neil Ave, Columbus, OH 43210-1226.

LYON, LEONARD JACK, WILDLIFE ECOLOGY, FOREST ECOLOGY. **Personal Data:** b Sterling, Colo, October 31, 1929; m 1956, c 2. **Education:** Colo State Univ, BS, 1951, MS, 1953; Univ Mich, PhD (wildlife mgt), 1960. **Professional Experience:** RETIRED; scientist emer, 1996; res assoc, Univ Idaho, 1989-; res assoc, Univ Mont, 1965-; Wildlife Biologist & Proj Leader Forest Wildlife Habitat, Forestry Sci Lab, Intermountain Res Sta, US Forest Serv, 1962-; res biologist & proj leader pheasant habitat, Colo Game & Fish Dept, 1955-1962. **Memberships:** Wildlife Soc. **Research Statement & Publications:** Forest seral ecology; wildlife habitat. **Mailing Address:** Forestry Sci Lab US Forest Serv, Rocy Mountian Research Station, Missoula, MT 59807-8089. **E-Mail:** ljack@micromania.net

LYON, RICHARD H, MECHANICAL ENGINEERING, ACOUSTICS. **Personal Data:** b Evansville, Ind, August 24, 1929; m 1965, Jean; c Katherine Lyon Davis, Geoffrey Cleveland & Suzanne Lyon Riggle. **Education:** Evansville Col, AB, 1952; Mass Inst Technol, PhD (physics), 1955. **Honorary Degrees:** DEng, Univ Evansville, 1976. **Honors & Awards:** Rayleigh Medal, Inst Acoust, 1995; Gold Medal Acoustical Soc of Am 2002. **Professional Experience:** PROF EMER MECH ENG, MASS INST TECHNOL, 1995-; PRES, R H LYON CORP, 1976-; founder & prin, Cambridge Collaborative Inc, 1970-1990; prof, 1970-1995; BBN corp vpres & dir, Phys Sci Div, 1967-1970; dept head, Bolt Beranek & Newman Inc, 1964-1970; researcher, Bolt Beranek & Newman Inc, 1960-1964; NSF post doctoral fel, Univ Manchester, 1959; from asst prof to assoc prof, Elec Eng Dept, Univ Minn, 1956-1959. **Memberships:** Nat Acad Eng; fel Acoust Soc Am (pres 1993-1994); fel AAAS; Sigma Xi; Inst Noise Control Eng; Am Soc Mech Engrs. **Research Statement & Publications:** Machine dynamics; random vibration; sound generation; interaction of sound and structures; application of statistics to engineering analysis; propogation of environmental noise; active noise and vibration control. **Mailing Address:** R H Lyon Corp, 691 Concord Ave, Cambridge, MA 02138. **Fax:** 617-864-0779. **E-Mail:** rhlyon@lyoncorp.com

LYON, RICHARD KENNETH, PHYSICAL CHEMISTRY. **Personal Data:** b Cleveland, Ohio, December 22, 1933; m 1968, c John & David. **Education:** Col William & Mary, BS, 1955; Harvard Univ, PhD (phys chem), 1960. **Honors & Awards:** Indust Res 100 Award;

Chem Award, Am Chem Soc. **Professional Experience:** SR SCIENTIST ENERGY & ENVIRON RES, EXXON RES & ENG CO, 1986-; sci adv, Cent Basic Res Lab, 1980-1986; sr res assoc, Cent Basic Res Lab, 1975-1980; res assoc, Cent Basic Res Lab, 1967-1975; sr chemist, Cent Basic Res Lab, 1964-1967; chemist, Exxon Res & Eng Co, 1960-1964. **Memberships:** Am Chem Soc; Combustion Inst. **Research Statement & Publications:** Chemical reaction kinetics; combustion science; cage effect in solution and gas phase; gas phase detonations and shock waves; radiation and high pressure chemistry; laser isotope separation; nox control. **Mailing Address:** 20 Finn Rd, Pittstown, MD 08867. **E-Mail:** rlyonheart@worldnet.alt.net

LYON, ROBERT LYNDON, FOREST ENTOMOLOGY, INSECT TOXICOLOGY. **Personal Data:** b Dolgeville, NY, April 17, 1927; m 1984, c 7. **Education:** Syracuse Univ, BS, 1953, MS, 1954; Univ Calif, Berkeley, PhD (insect toxicol), 1961. **Professional Experience:** RETIRED; mem nat staff, Forest Insect & Dis Res, US Forest Serv, beginning 1976; staff res forest entomologist, Forest Insect & Dis Res, US Forest Serv, 1976-1992; supvry res entomologist & proj leader, Insecticide Eval Proj, 1972-1976; res entomologist, Pac SW Forest & Range Exp Sta, 1953-1972. **Memberships:** Entom Soc Am. **Research Statement & Publications:** Development of safe, selective, nonpersistent and effective chemical insecticides and techniques to manage forest insect populations and protect forest resource values with minimal adverse effects on the environment. **Mailing Address:** 900 N Stafford St, Arlington, VA 22203.

LYON, RONALD JAMES PEARSON, GEOLOGY, MINERALOGY. **Personal Data:** b Northam, Western Australia, January 15, 1928; American citizen; m 1961, c 4. **Education:** Univ Western Australia, BS, 1948, Hons, 1949; Univ Calif, Berkeley, PhD (geol), 1954. **Honors & Awards:** Photog Interpretation Award, Am Soc Photogram, 1972. **Professional Experience:** PROF EMER, DEPT GEOL & ENVIRON SCI, STANFORD UNIV, 1993-; assoc chmn, dept appl earth sci, Stanford Univ, 1990-1993; mem remote sensing group, Int Hydrol Decade, Nat Acad Sci, 1972-; prof appl earth sci, Stanford Univ, 1972-1993; CONSULT & PRIN ASSOC, EARTH SATELLITE CORP, 1970-; consult planetary atmosphere, NASA, 1968-1970; chmn geol panel, Nat Acad Sci, Woods Hole, Mass, 1967-1969; assoc prof appl earth sci, Stanford Univ, 1965-1972; Nat Acad Sci sr fel geol, Ames Res Ctr, NASA, 1963-1965; sr geochemist, Stanford Res Inst, 1959-1963; geochemist, Kennecott Res Ctr, Utah, 1956-1959; res off mining, Commonwealth Sci Res Orgn, Australia, 1954-1956; Fulbright travel grant, 1951-1954 & 1978-1979; Goewey res fel geol, Univ Calif, Berkeley, 1951-1954; geologist, Lake George Mines, Captains Flat, NSW, 1949-1951. **Memberships:** AAAS; Soc Econ Geol; Am Soc Photogram. **Research Statement & Publications:** Use of airborne geophysical techniques and remote sensing in exploration for mineral deposits; recognition of rock and soil materials using land satellite and Skylab spectral data; airborne scanners. **Mailing Address:** Dept Geol & Environ Scis, Sch Earth Scis, Stanford Univ, Mitchell Bldg B05, Stanford, CA 94305-2210. **Fax:** 650-725-0979. **E-Mail:** lyon@pangea.stanford.edu

LYON, WILLIAM FRANCIS, ECONOMIC ENTOMOLOGY. **Personal Data:** b Mt Gilead, Ohio, January 24, 1937; m 1995, Joann; c Cynthia, Kara, Fred & Jim. **Education:** Ohio State Univ, BSc, 1959, MSc, 1962, PhD (entom), 1969. **Professional Experience:** Vols Overseas Coop Assistance Entom consult, Egypt, 1993-; USAID entom consult, Guinea Bissau, 1988; PROF ENTOM, OHIO STATE UNIV, 1982-; assoc prof, Afgoi Agr Res Sta, Mogdiscio, Somalia, 1976-1978; asst & assoc, Ohio State Univ, 1974-1976; asst prof & pest mgt entomologist, Univ Nairobi, Kenya, 1973-1974; asst prof entom & plant protection entomologist, Makerere Univ, Uganda, 1972-1973; exten entomologist, Ohio Coop Exten Serv, 1966-1972; surv entomologist, Ohio Agr Res & Develop Ctr, 1962-1964; County exten agent, Ohio Coop Exten Serv, 1959-1961; res fel, Ohio State Univ Ctr African Studies. **Memberships:** Entom Soc Am; Am Inst Biol Sci; E African Acad. **Research Statement & Publications:** Identification and control of household/structural, livestock, poultry and pet pests, mosquito insects; 4-H youth projects. **Mailing Address:** Dept Entom, Exten Entom Bldg, Ohio State Univ 1991 Kenny Rd, Columbus, OH 43210-1090. **Fax:** 419-292-9783. **E-Mail:** lyon.2@osu.edu

LYON, WILLIAM GRAHAM, PHYSICAL CHEMISTRY, ENVIRONMENTAL GEOCHEMISTRY. **Personal Data:** b Chelsea, Mass, April 29, 1944; m 1965, Jean; c Laura & Steven. **Education:** Univ Mich, BS, 1966, MS, 1968, PhD (chem), 1973. **Professional Experience:** TECH SERV MGR, SHAW ENVIRON & INFRASTRUCTURE INC, as of 2003; ENVIRON PHYS CHEMIST, MAN TECH ENVIRON TECHNOL INC, 1988-; fel, Phillips Petroleum Co, 1976-1988 & Argonne Nat Lab, 1974-1976; Fel phys chem, Univ Mich, 1973-1974. **Memberships:** Am Chem Soc; Sigma Xi; Soc Appl Spectros. **Research Statement & Publications:** Environmental geochemistry; studies of the distribution and characterization of natural organic matter in the subsurface. **Mailing Address:** Sect Res, Shaw Environ & Infrastructure, Inc, PO Box 1198, Ada, OK 74821-1198. **Fax:** 580-436-8501. **E-Mail:** lyon.william@epa.gov

LYON, WILLIAM SOUTHERN, JR, RADIOCHEMISTRY. **Personal Data:** b Pulaski, Va, January 25, 1922; wid Carey Greer (deceased); c 2. **Education:** Univ Va, BS, 1943; Univ Tenn, MS, 1968. **Honors & Awards:** Radiation Indust Award, Am Nuclear Soc, 1980; Hevesy Medal, 1981. **Professional Experience:** CONSULT, 1985-; head, analytical methodol, 1977-1985; regional ed, J Radioanal Chem, 1971-; assoc ed, Radiochem-Radioanal Lett, 1970-; Nat Coun Radiation Protection, 1967-; Consult, Thai Atomic Energy for Peace Lab, Bangkok, 1966-; group leader radiochem, Oak Ridge Nat Lab, 1962-1977; chemist, Oak Ridge Nat Lab, 1947-1962; lab foreman, Tenn Eastman Corp, 1945-1947; Chemist, E I du Pont de Nemours & Co, WVa, 1943-1944 & Wash, 1944-1945; mem sci comt 1925. **Memberships:** Am Chem Soc; Am Nuclear Soc emer mem. **Research Statement & Publications:** Trace element analysis; new energy sources; nuclear decay schemes; specialized radioactivity measurements; scientometrics. **Mailing Address:** 638 Chapel Point Lane, Knoxville, TN 37922.

LYONS, ANTHONY VINCENT, FLUID MECHANICS, PULP & PAPER TECHNOLOGY. **Personal Data:** b Buffalo, NY, February 25, 1955; m 1987, Debra M Stillo; c Michael, Christine, Stephanie & John. **Education:** Univ Buffalo, BS, 1973, MS, 1981; Lehigh Univ, PhD (chem eng), 1985. **Professional Experience:** ASST LEADER, IMERYS PIGMENTS PAPER, as of 2003; LEADER PAPER TECHNOL, ECCI AM/PAC, 1994-; Dir coatings & finishings res, Repap Technol Inc, 1989-1994. **Memberships:** Tech Asn Pulp & Paper Industs; Can Pulp & Paper Asn; Paper Indust Mgt Asn. **Research Statement & Publications:** Kinetics of yeast fermentations and the hydrodynamics of bubble columns; mechanics of calendering; the fluid mechanics of coating; the rheology of coatings; the interactions of papermaking materials and their influence on paper properties. **Mailing Address:** Imerys, Inc, Turn Maine Montparnasse, 33 Ave Maine, F-75755, Paris, France. **E-Mail:** tonylyons@imerys.com

LYONS, CARL J(OHN), CHEMICAL ENGINEERING. **Personal Data:** b Chicago, Ill, April 20, 1924; m 1947, c 3. **Education:** Pa State Univ, BSc, 1947; Ohio State Univ, MSc, 1950. **Professional Experience:** RETIRED; assoc dir, proj mgt & prog develop, 1980-1986; assoc dir, proj mgt & prog develop, 1976-1980; assoc dir, Res Opers, 1973-1976; from asst div chief fuels & phys chem to mgr biol, environ & chem dept, Intellectual Property Develop, Battelle Columbus Labs, 1947-1973. **Memberships:** AAAS; Am Chem Soc; Am Ord Asn. **Research Statement & Publications:** Physical chemistry of fuel reactions; surface chemistry; environmental effects of combustion; solid waste technology; application of physical sciences to medical sciences; circulating fluid bed boiler. **Mailing Address:** 3550 Schirtzinger Rd, Hilliard, OH 43026.

LYONS, DONALD HERBERT, PHYSICS. **Personal Data:** b Buffalo, NY, February 28, 1929; m 1951, Rosalyn; c Russell, Barry & David. **Education:** Univ Buffalo, BA, 1949; Univ Pa, MA, 1951, PhD (physics), 1954. **Professional Experience:** PROF EMER, THEORETICAL SOLID STATE PHYSICS, UNIV MASS, BOSTON, as of 2006; chmn dept, Univ Mass, Boston, 1967-1968 & 1970-1972; from assoc prof to prof physics, Univ Mass, Boston, 1966-1994; staff scientist, Sperry Rand Res Ctr, Mass, 1964-1966; Fulbright grant, 1963-1964; res prof physics, Inst Solid State Physics, Univ Tokyo, 1963-1964; staff scientist, Lincoln Lab, Mass Inst Technol, 1956-1961 & Sperry Rand Res Ctr, 1961-1963. **Memberships:** Am Phys Soc. **Research Statement & Publications:** Theoretical magnetism; communication theory; theoretical nuclear physics. **Mailing Address:** Univ Mass Boston, 100 Morrissey Boulevard, Boston, MA 02125-3393. **E-Mail:** lyons-d@rcn.com

LYONS, EDWARD ARTHUR, RADIOLOGY, ULTRASOUND. **Personal Data:** b Halifax, NS, March 15, 1943; Canadian citizen; m 1967, c 2. **Education:** Univ Man, BSc, 1963, MD, 1968. **Honors & Awards:** Presidential Recognition Award, Am Inst Ultrasound Med, 1981. **Professional Experience:** Head & prof, dept radiol, Health Sci Ctr, Winnipeg, St Boniface Hosp, 1990-1995; assoc prof anat, Univ Man, beginning 1990; PROF RADIOL, UNIV MAN, 1996-; STAFF RADIOL, ULTRASOUND SEC, HEALTH SCI CTR, 1996-; prof obstet & gynec, beginning 1989; head, Ultrasound Sect, Health Sci Ctr, Winnipeg, St Boniface Hosp, 1973-1991. **Memberships:** Am Inst Ultrasound Med; Can Asn Radiologists; Soc Radiol Ultrasound; Am Col Radiol; Man & Can Med Asn; Am Roentgen Soc; Am Inst Ultrasound Med; Asn Univ Radiologist; Radiol Soc NAm; Am Fertil Soc. **Research Statement & Publications:** Long term effects of ultrasound; immunological effects of ultrasound; early pregnancy failure; Therapy in Pediatrics. **Mailing Address:** Health Sci Ctr, Univ Man, Ultrasound Sect GE342 820 Sherbrook St, Winnipeg, MB R3A 1R9, Can. **Fax:** 204-787-3355. **E-Mail:** lyons@cc.umanitoba.ca

LYONS, EUGENE T, PARASITOLOGY. **Personal Data:** b Yankton, SDak, May 6, 1931. **Education:** SDak State Univ, BS, 1956; Kans State Univ, MS, 1958; Colo State Univ, PhD (parasitol), 1963. **Professional Experience:** PROF PARASITOL, UNIV KY, 1977-; assoc prof, 1970-1977; Asst prof, 1958-1960 & 1963-1970. **Memberships:** Am Soc Parasitol; Wildlife Dis Asn. **Research Statement & Publications:** Parasites of jackrabbits, fur seals, horses, sheep and cattle. **Mailing Address:** 1149 E Cooper Dr, Lexington, KY 40502.

LYONS, GEORGE D, OTOLARYNGOLOGY. **Personal Data:** b New Orleans, La, January 19, 1928; m 1954, Agnes; c Geo III, Michael, Shelley, Timothy & Pamela. **Education:** Southeastern La Col, BS, 1950; La State Univ, New Orleans, MD, 1954. **Honors & Awards:** Recognition Award, AMA. **Professional Experience:** PROF BIOCOMMUN, SCH MED, LA STATE UNIV, NEW ORLEANS, 1977-; mem, Soc Acad Chmn Otolaryngol, 1972-; PROF OTOLARYNGOL & HEAD DEPT, SCH MED, LA STATE UNIV, NEW ORLEANS, 1971-; assoc prof, Sch Med, LA State Univ, New Orleans, 1970-1971; from clin instr to clin assoc prof, Sch Med, LA State Univ, New Orleans, 1958-1970. **Memberships:** Fel Am Laryngol Rhinol & Otol Soc; fel Am Acad Facial Plastic & Reconstruct Surg; fel Am Col Surg; fel Pan-Am Soc Otolaryngol; fel Am Broncho-Esophag Soc; fel Am Laryngol Soc. **Research Statement & Publications:** Regional plastic surgery; otology; laryngology & voice. **Mailing Address:** La State Univ, Med Ctr 2020 Gravier Suite A, New Orleans, LA 70112-2234. **Fax:** 504-568-4460.

LYONS, JAMES EDWARD, ORGANIC CHEMISTRY, ORGANOMETALLIC CHEMISTRY. **Personal Data:** b Montpelier, Vt, October 20, 1937; m Marlyne; c Deborah & Cheryl. **Education:** Boston Col, BS, 1959; Purdue Univ, MS, 1961; Univ Calif, Davis, PhD (org chem), 1968. **Honors & Awards:** Philadelphia Catalysis Soc Award, 1987; Schuitt Award for Excellence in Catalysis (Univ Del), 1991; E V Murphree Award in Industrial and Engineering Chemistry, American Chemical Society, 2004. **Professional Experience:** Adjunct Professor of Chemistry, Dept of Chemical Engineering, University of Delaware, 2002-, SCI ADV, CATALYST GROUP, 1999-2004, Dialog Consultant 2004-; chem fel, Sunoco, 1994-1999; group leader, Sun Co, 1977-1994; sr res chemist, Sun Co, 1974-1977; res chemist, Sun Co, 1968-1974; chemist, Res & Develop Ctr, Gen Elec Co, 1962-1964. **Memberships:** AAAS; Am Chem Soc; NY Acad Sci (sect chair 1980-1983); North Am Catalysis Soc. **Research Statement & Publications:** Mechanisms and synthetic applications of transition metal catalyzed reactions in organic and organometallic systems. **Mailing Address:** Catalyst Group, 714 N Bethlehem Pike, Spring House, PA 19477. **Fax:** 215-628-2267. **E-Mail:** lyonscat@aol.com

LYONS, JAMES MARTIN, PLANT PHYSIOLOGY. **Personal Data:** b Livermore, Calif, October 9, 1929; m 1956, c 2. **Education:** Univ Calif, Berkeley, BS, 1951; Univ Calif, Davis, MS, 1958, PhD (plant physiol), 1962. **Honors & Awards:** Campbell Award, Am Inst Biol Sci, 1971. **Professional Experience:** ASST DIR, EXP STA, EMER PROF VEG CROPS, UNIV CALIF, DAVIS, 1991-; assoc dean, Col Agr & Environ, 1973-1981; prof veg crops & plant physiologist, Col Agr & Environ, 1970-1991; chmn, Dept Veg Crops, Univ Calif, Davis, 1970-1973; assoc prof, chmn dept & assoc plant physiologist, 1966-1970; asst prof, Dept Veg Crops, 1965-1966; vchmn, Dept Veg Crops, 1964-1966; asst plant physiologist, Univ Calif, Riverside, 1962-1966. **Memberships:** Am Soc Hort Sci; Am Soc Plant Physiol; Int Soc Hort Sci. **Research Statement & Publications:** Biochemistry and physiology of fruit ripening; low temperature biology and chilling injury in vegetable crops. **Mailing Address:** Dept Vegetable Crops, Univ Calif, Davis, CA 95616.

LYONS, JERRY L, FLUID MECHANICS FOR COMPONENTS, SYSTEMS DESIGNS. **Personal Data:** b St Louis, Mo, April 2, 1939; c Karen S (Andershock). **Education:** Southwest Univ, MSME, 1983, PhD (engr mgt), 1984. **Honors & Awards:** Winston Churchhill Medal, 1988; Dwight D Eisenhower Achievement Award, 1990 Engr of the year 1983, sme Award of merit, St Louis Engrs Club Award of merit. **Professional Experience:** PRES & CHIEF EXEC OFFICER, INNOVATIVE CONTROLS INC, 1991-; pres, Lyons Pub Co, 1983-; consult fluids control, Wis Univ, 1977-1990; Vpres & gen mgr, Engr Res & Develop, Fluid Control Div, Essex Indust Inc, 1977-1990; PRES & CHIEF EXEC OFFICER, YANKEE INGENUITY INC, 1974-; mgr engr res, Chemetron Corp, 1973-1977; Proj engr, Essex Cryogenics Indust, 1970-1973; Proj engr, Harris Mfg Co, 1965-1970. **Memberships:** Winston Churchhill Wisdom Soc; sr mem Soc Mfg Engrs; sr mem Instrument Soc Am; Comput & Automated Systs Asn; Nat Soc Prof Engrs; fel Am Soc Mech Engrs; Am Security Coun St Louis exec comm for Continuing engr edu, univ Missouri Columbia, and was its first chairman in 1980-1981; He was bestowed with the St Louis engrs Club "Award of Merit" for res and for the Design develop of Fluid Components in the fields of Manufacturing & mech eng; He also served as chairman and the founder of the PVP-OAC valve comm for ASME and served as its chairman for three (two-three)terms; In 1982 he was invited as a guest speaker at the United States naval acad & numerous other universities; Dr Lyons was a founder of the St Louis CASA(Computer and Automated sys asn chapter and was its first Chairman in 1980-1981; St Louis soc of Manufacturing engr; He served as an int dir of the soc for two terma in 1982-1984 and 1985-1987. **Research Statement & Publications:** Control systems engineering; author of numerous publications. **Mailing Address:** 1719 Wisteria Pl, Ft Wayne, IN 46818.

LYONS, JOHN WINSHIP, PHYSICAL CHEMISTRY. **Personal Data:** b Reading, Mass, November 5, 1930; m 1953, Grace; c Margaret, Maryann, John H & Louis M. **Education:** Harvard Univ, AB, 1952; Wash Univ, AM, 1963, PhD (phys chem), 1964. **Honors & Awards:** Gold Medal Award, US Dept Com, 1977; Pres Mgt Improvement Award, White House, 1977, Distinguished Exec Rank Award, 1981. **Professional Experience:** FAC EMER, BIOTECHNOLOGY INT, UNIV MD as of 2005; dir, Army Res Lab, beginning 1993; dir, Nat Inst Stand & Technol, 1990-1993; mem adv com eng, NSF & adv coun, Col Eng, Univ Md, 1979-1990; mem bd dir, Nat Fire Protection Agency, 1978-1984; dir, Nat Eng Lab, 1977-1990; Chmn, Prod Res Comt, 1974-1979; dir, Ctr Fire Res, Nat Bur Stand, 1973-1977; Prof chemist, Monsanto Co, 1955-1973; mem, Comt Superconductivity, Fed Fed Adv Comm, Consol & Conversion Defense Res & Develop Labs & Blue Ribbon Comt, Res & Pub Serv, Univ Md. **Memberships:** Nat Acad Eng; fel AAAS; Am Chem Soc; Am Inst Chem Engrs; Sigma Xi. **Research Statement & Publications:** Phosphorus compounds; rheology; fire and fire retardants; surface chemistry; polyelectrolytes; solution behavior of DNA. **Mailing Address:** Univ Md, Biotechnol Inst, Baltimore, MD 21202.

LYONS, JOSEPH PAUL, OPERATIONS RESEARCH, PUBLIC HEALTH. **Personal Data:** b Ardmore, Pa, December 9, 1947; m 1970, c 1. **Education:** Bloomsburg State Col, BA, 1970; Johns Hopkins Univ, ScD, 1975. **Professional Experience:** Asst clin prof, dept Psychiat, Sch Med & adj asst prof, dept Indust Eng, Sch Eng, State Univ NY Buffalo, 1975-; SCIENTIST ALCOHOLISM, RES INST ALCOHOLISM, 1975-; admin consult, Md Dept Ment Hyg, 1973; Nat inst Ment Health trainee, Johns Hopkins Univ, 1971-1975; assoc consult, Elliott assocs, 1971-1974; Syst analyst ment health, Pa Off Ment Health, 1970-1971. **Memberships:** Oper Res Soc Am; AAAS; Asn Ment Health Admin. **Research Statement & Publications:** Problem oriented record and its application to alcoholism service delivery; treatment planning in both in-patient and out-patient settings and systems design for delivery of alcoholism services. **Mailing Address:** Dept Indust Eng Bell Hall, State Univ NY Buffalo, Buffalo, NY 14260-0001.

LYONS, KENNETH BRENT, SOLID STATE PHYSICS. **Personal Data:** b St Louis, Mo, August 31, 1946; m 1968, c 2. **Education:** Univ Okla, BS, 1968; Univ Colo, MS, 1969, PhD (physics), 1973. **Professional Experience:** TECH CHAIR, UNDERGRAD RES PROG, AT&T LABS, as of 2003; res mem, AT & T Labs, as of 2005; vpres, AT & T Bell Labs, 1988; distinguished mem staff, At&T Bell Labs, beginning 1987; mem res staff, 1973-1987. **Memberships:** Am Phys Soc. **Research Statement & Publications:** Raman and Brillouin light scattering in solids, with emphasis on non-equilibrium phenomena, phase transitions, and magnetic scattering in oxide superconductors; magnetooptics. **Mailing Address:** AT & T Labs, 180 Park Ave PO Box 971, Florham Park, NJ 07932-0971. **Fax:** 908-582-4113. **E-Mail:** kbl@research.att.com

LYONS, MICHAEL JOSEPH, VIROLOGY, IMMUNOLOGY. **Personal Data:** b Cork, Ireland, September 16, 1930; American citizen; m 1960, Yvonne Barnett; c Fiona, Conor, Patricia & Desmond. **Education:** Nat Univ Ireland, BS, 1953, MS, 1954; Univ Glasgow, PhD (biochem), 1959. **Professional Experience:** Adj prof, Rockefeller Univ, 1992-; Adj assoc prof, Rockefeller Univ, 1978-1992; PROF LIFE SCI, NY INST TECHNOL, 1976-; asst prof microbiol, Cornell Univ Sch Med, 1969-1976; asst prof microbiol, Univ Pa, 1966-1969; Res assoc, Rockefeller Univ, 1961-1966. **Memberships:** Harvey Soc. **Research Statement & Publications:** Virology and immunology; author of numerous publications. **Mailing Address:** 53 Eiler Lane, Irvington, NY 10533.

LYONS, NANCY I, ECOLOGICAL STATISTICS. **Personal Data:** b Akron, Ohio, September 17, 1946. **Education:** Kent State Univ, BS, 1968, MA, 1970; NC State Univ, PhD (statist), 1975. **Professional Experience:** ASSOC PROF STATIST, UNIV GA, 1981-; asst prof, Univ Ga, 1975-1981; statistician, Res Triangle Inst, 1974-1975. **Memberships:** Am Statist Asn; Biomet Soc. **Research Statement & Publications:** Statistical inference with applications to ecology; computer simulation techniques; sample surveys. **Mailing Address:** Dept Statist Univ Ga, 226 Statist Bldg, Athens, GA 30601-3040. **Fax:** 706-542-3391. **E-Mail:** nancy@stat.uga.edu

LYONS, PAUL CHRISTOPHER, PALEOBOTANY, COAL GEOLOGY. **Personal Data:** b Cambridge, Mass, October 1, 1938; m 1963, c Sheryl, Russell, Crystal, Sandra & Jennifer. **Education:** Boston Univ, AB, 1963, AM, 1964, PhD (geol), 1969. **Professional Experience:** RETIRED; res geologist, beginning 1991; adj prof chem, Univ Pittsburgh, 1985-1991; lectr, Lowell Technol Inst, 1972; lectr, Boston Univ Metrop Col, 1972-1973; res grants, Boston Univ, 1971-1972 & Mineral Soc Gt Brit; asst prof phys sci, Boston Univ, 1969-1975; instr, Boston Univ, 1968-1969; pub sch teacher, Mass, 1964-1968. **Memberships:** NY Acad Sci; fel Geol Soc Am; Am Asn Petrol Geologist; Bot Soc Am; Int Comn Coal Petrol. **Research Statement & Publications:** Pennsylvanian stratigraphy, coal geology. **Mailing Address:** US Geol Surv Nat Ctr, 12201 Sunrise Valley Dr, Reston, VA 20192-1834.

LYONS, PETER BRUCE, PLASMA PHYSICS. **Personal Data:** b Hammond, Ind, February 23, 1943; m 1963, Lois; c 3. **Education:** Univ Ariz, BS, 1964; Calif Inst Technol, PhD (physics), 1969. **Professional Experience:** COMNR, US NUCLEAR COMN, as of 2005; DIR INDUST PARTNERSHIPS, LOS ALAMOS NAT LAB, 1993-; dep assoc dir, Los Alamos Nat Lab, 1985-1993; prog mgr, Los Alamos Nat Lab, 1984-1985; group leader, Los Alamos Nat Lab, 1979-1984; alt group leader, Los Alamos Nat Lab, 1977-1979; assoc group leader, Los Alamos Nat Lab, 1976-1977; staff mem, Los Alamos Nat Lab, 1969-1976. **Memberships:** Am Phys Soc; Optical Soc Am; Inst Elec & Electronics Engrs. **Research Statement & Publications:** X-ray interactions and dosimetry; high intensity monoenergetic x-ray generation; x-ray and nuclear detectors and instrumentation; low energy nuclear physics; fiber optic technology; plasma diagnostics; accelerator technology; plastic scintillators; technology transfer. **Mailing Address:** Group IPO MS K571, Los Alamos Nat Lab, Los Alamos, NM 87545. **E-Mail:** plyons@lanl.gov

LYONS, PETER FRANCIS, PHYSICAL CHEMISTRY, POLYMER SCIENCE. **Personal Data:** b Philadelphia, Pa, November 29, 1942; m 1968, c 3. **Education:** Villanova Univ, BS, 1964; Princeton Univ, MA, 1967, PhD (chem), 1970. **Professional Experience:** PRIN, DU PONT CONSULT SOLUTIONS, WILMINGTON, as of 2002; CHMN & CHIEF EXEC OFFICER, NAT POSTAL FORUM, 2001-; strategic planning mgr, E I Du Pont Del Nemours & Co, Inc, beginning 1989; int marketing mgr, E I Du Pont Del Nemours & Co, Inc, 1987-1989; bus develop mgr, E I Du Pont Del Nemours & Co, Inc, 1984-1986; tech marketing mgr, E I Du Pont Del Nemours & Co, Inc, 1984; sr planning consult, E I Du Pont Del Nemours & Co, Inc, 1982-1983; bus strategist, E I Du Pont Del Nemours & Co, Inc, 1980-1981; mkt supvr, E I Du Pont Del Nemours & Co, Inc, 1978-1980; mkt rep, E I Du Pont Del Nemours & Co, Inc, 1973-1978; sr res chemist, E I Du Pont Del Nemours & Co, Inc, 1971-1973; res chemist, E I Du Pont Del Nemours & Co, Inc, 1968-1971. **Memberships:** Am Chem Soc. **Research Statement & Publications:** Physical chemistry of polymeric systems including work on degradation, strength mechanisms and viscosity theory. **Mailing Address:** DuPont Consult Solutions, 1007 Market St, Wilmington, DE 19898.

LYONS, PHILIP AUGUSTINE, PHYSICAL CHEMISTRY. **Personal Data:** b Lancashire, Eng, May 26, 1916; American citizen; m 1949, Margaret; c Catherine, Ellen, Janet & Wiliam. **Education:** La Salle Col, BA, 1937; Univ Wis, PhD (chem), 1948. **Professional Experience:** PROF EMER CHEM, YALE UNIV, 1987-; consult, Audiotape Corp, Robertshaw Fulton Corp, Bendin Aviation Corp, Pratt & Whitney Corp, TVA, Conn Comn Higher Educ, 1973-1976; vis prof, Univ Islamabad, WPakistan, 1971; chmn, Yale Univ, 1966-1970, 1978-1979; from instr to prof, Yale Univ, 1948-1987; chemist, US Chem Warfare Serv, 1940-1945; Spectroscopist, NAm Smelting Corp, 1936-1939. **Memberships:** Am Chem Soc; Sigma Xi. **Research Statement & Publications:** Raman spectra; nonaqueous solutions; diffusion in liquids; Soret effect; reversible thermodynamics. **Mailing Address:** Dept Chem, Yale Univ, PO Box 208107, 225 Prospect St, New Haven, CT 06520-8107. **Fax:** 203-432-6144.

LYONS, RUSSELL DAVID, STOCHASTIC PROCESSES ON GRAPHS. **Personal Data:** b Stoneham, Mass, September 6, 1957. **Education:** Case Western Reserve Univ, BA, 1979; Univ Mich, PhD (math), 1983. **Professional Experience:** PROF MATH, GEORGIA INST TECH, 2000-; PROF MATH, INDIANA UNIV, 1994-; assoc prof math, Indiana Univ, 1990-1994; asst prof math, Stanford Univ, 1985-1990. **Memberships:** Am Math Soc; Math Asn Am Inst; Sigma Xi. **Research Statement & Publications:** Research combines harmonic analysis, functional analysis, erg otic theory and probability factors; random walks and percolation. **Mailing Address:** Dept Math, Ind Univ, Bloomington, IN 47405-5701. **Fax:** 812-855-0046. **E-Mail:** rdlyons@indiana.edu

LYONS, RUSSETTE M, CELL BIOLOGY. **Personal Data:** b Smithtown, NY, February 13, 1953. **Education:** State Univ NY, BA, 1975; Univ Nebr, MS, 1978, PhD (life sci), 1985. **Professional Experience:** DIR, PRECLIN SAFETY & CORE TECHNOL, GENETIC THER INC, as of 2001; CELL BIOL GROUP LEADER & RES SCIENTIST, GENETIC THER INC, 1990-; asst res prof, Dept Cell Biol, 1988-1990; postdoctoral cancer biol, Vanderbilt Med Ctr, 1985-1988. **Memberships:** Am Asn Cancer Res; Am Soc Cell Biol. **Mailing Address:** Genetic Therapy Inc, 938 Clopper Rd, Gaithersburg, MD 20878. **Fax:** 301-590-2626.

LYONS, WILLIAM BERRY, GEOCHEMISTRY. **Personal Data:** b Gainesville, Fla, February 8, 1947. **Education:** Brown Univ, BA, 1969; Univ Conn, MSc, 1972 & PhD (oceanog), 1979. **Professional Experience:** DIR, BYRD POLAR RES CTR, as of 2005; PROF GEOL SCI, OHIO STATE UNIV, as of 2004; assoc prof geochem, Univ NH, beginning 1985; asst prof, geochem, Univ NH, 1980-1985; res scientist, geochem, Univ NH, 1979-1980; fel geochem, Univ NH, 1976-1979. **Memberships:** Am Geophys Union; Geochem Soc; Am Soc Immunol & Oceanog; Soc Econ Paleontologists & Mineralogists; Int Glaciol Soc; Int Asn Geochem & Cosmochem. **Research Statement & Publications:** Chemistry of glacial ice and snow; geochemistry of lakes and lacustrine sediments as well as paleoclimatic studies. **Mailing Address:** Dept Geol Sci, Ohio State Univ, 1090 Carmack Rd, Columbus, OH 43210-1002. **Fax:** 614-292-7688. **E-Mail:** lyons.142@osu.edu

LYONS, WILLIAM GREGORY, MICROWAVE ENGINEERING, SUPERCONDUCTIVE ELECTRONICS. **Personal Data:** b Amarillo, Tex, July 30, 1960; m 1993. **Education:** Univ Ill, BS, 1982, MS, 1983, PhD (elec eng), 1989. **Professional Experience:** STAFF MEM, LINCOLN LAB, MASS INST TECHNOL, 1989-; res asst, Electro-Physics Lab, 1983-1989; res asst, MBE Group, Univ Ill, 1982-1983; summer assoc, Circuit Packaging Div, IBM, Austin, Tex, 1981; eng asst, Bryerton Inc, 1979. **Memberships:** Inst Elec & Electronics Engrs; Am Phys Soc; Sigma Xi. **Research Statement & Publications:** Fundamental properties of superconductors; development of superconducting microwave devices and system prototypes and rf circuits for communication, radar, remote sensing and instrumentation; built superconductive devices for two space experiments and microwave devices for the consortium for superconducting electronics; III-V microwave and optoelectronic devices and studies of collective quantum mechanical effects. **Mailing Address:** 244 Wood St, Lexington, MA 02420-9108. **E-Mail:** lyons@ll.mit.edu

LYRENE, PAUL MAGNUS, PLANT BREEDING. **Personal Data:** b Ala, April 16, 1946. **Education:** Auburn Univ, BS, 1968; Univ Wis, MS, 1970, PhD (plant breeding), 1974. **Professional Experience:** PROF PLANT BREEDING & GENETICS, DEPT HORT SCI, UNIV FLA, as of 2004; asst prof hort, Univ Fla Exp Sta, beginning 1977; DIR, FLA AGR EXP STA, 1977-; asst prof agron, 1974-1977. **Memberships:** Am Soc Hort Sci; Fla Plant Soc. **Research Statement & Publications:** Blueberry variety improvement; blueberry interspecific hybridization; blueberry cytogenetics and polyploidy; Zizyphus (Chinese date) investigations. **Mailing Address:** Dept Hort Sci, Univ Fla, 2135 Fifield Hall, Gainesville, FL 32606. **E-Mail:** pml@mail.ifas.ufl.edu

LYS, JEREMY EION ALLEYNE, HIGH ENERGY PHYSICS. **Personal Data:** b Dannevirke, NZ, April 17, 1938; m 1968, c 2. **Education:** Univ Canterbury, BS, 1958, MS, 1960; Oxford Univ, PhD (physics), 1964; Mitchell Col, NSW, DipEd, 1974. **Professional Experience:** RETIRED; physicist, Lawrence Berkeley Nat Lab, as of 2002; physicist, Univ Calif, Berkeley, 1982-; physicist, Lawrence Berkeley Nat Lab, 1977-1981; res assoc physics, Fermi Nat Accelerator Lab, 1975-1977; sch teacher sci, Del la Salle Col, NSW, 1972-1974; res assoc physics, Univ Mich, 1966-1972; res fel physics, Univ Liverpool, 1963-1965. **Memberships:** Am Phys Soc. **Research Statement & Publications:** High energy physics. **Mailing Address:** Lawrence Berkeley Nat Lab, Bldg 50B5239 One Cyclotron Rd, Berkeley, CA 94720-8156. **Fax:** 510-486-4047. **E-Mail:** lys@lbl.gov

LYSAK, ROBERT LOUIS, SPACE PLASMA PHYSICS, MAGNETOSPHERIC PHYSICS. **Personal Data:** b Chicago, Ill, January 18, 1955. **Education:** Mich State Univ, BS, 1975; Univ Calif, Berkeley, PhD (physics), 1980. **Professional Experience:** PROF PHYSICS, UNIV MINN, as of 2005; assoc prof Physics, Univ Minn, beginning 1987; asst prof, Univ Minn, 1982-1987; stipendiat, Max-Planch Inst fur Extraterrestrische Physik, 1981; asst researcher, Univ Calif, 1980-1982; res asst, Univ Calif, 1976-1980; teaching asst physics, Univ Calif, 1975-1977. **Memberships:** Am Geophys Union; Am Phys Soc. **Research Statement & Publications:** Theoretical and numerical investigations of auroral current dynamics, particle accelerations, plasma instabilities, magnetic reconnection and MHD waves and turbulance. **Mailing Address:** Dept Physics, Univ Minn, 375 Tate Lab Physics, Minneapolis, MN 55406. **Fax:** 612-626-2029. **E-Mail:** bob@aurora.space.umn.edu

LYSER, KATHERINE MAY, NEUROEMBRYOLOGY. **Personal Data:** b Berkeley, Calif, May 11, 1933; m 1965. **Education:** Oberlin Col, AB, 1955, Radcliffe Col, MA, 1957, PhD (biol), 1960. **Professional Experience:** PROF EMER BIOL SCI, HUNTER COL CITY, UNIV NY, beginning 1976; fac res award, City Univ NY, 1976-1982, 1987-1989; guest investr, P A Weiss Lab, Rockefeller Univ, 1967-1970; from asst prof to assoc prof, Hunter Col City Univ New York, 1965-1976; USPHS res grants, Med Col, Cornell Univ, 1963 & Hunter Col, 1965-1970; asst prof, Sch Med & Dent, Georgetown Univ, 1964-1965; united Cerebral Palsy Res & Educ Found grant, Cornell Univ & Georgetown Univ, 1964-1965; instr anat, Med Col, Cornell Univ, 1962-1964; res fel, Med Col, Cornell Univ, 1961-1962; part-time fac mem, Sarah Lawrence Col, 1961-1962; NSF fel exp embryol, Col France, 1960-1961; instr zool, Oberlin Col, 1957-1958. **Memberships:** Int Soc Develop Neuroscience; Am Soc Zool; Soc Neuroscience; Soc Develop Biol. **Research Statement & Publications:** Factors controlling development in the embryonic nervous system, especially cytological differentiation and cellular morphogenesis in retinal and other neurons and in neuronal tumors. **Mailing Address:** Dept Biol Sci, Hunter Col, City Univ NY, Rm 927 Hunter N, 695 Park Ave, New York, NY 10021. **Fax:** 212-772-5227.

LYSIAK, RICHARD JOHN, physics; deceased, see previous edition for last biography

LYSNE, PETER C, APPLIED PHYSICS. **Personal Data:** b Milwaukee, Wis, July 20, 1939; m 1962, c 2. **Education:** Grinnell Col, BA, 1961; Ariz State Univ, PhD (physics), 1966. **Professional Experience:** Vchmn bd, Dosecc, Inc, 1993-; chmn, Joides Downhole Measurements Panel, 1993-; DISTINGUISHED MEM TECH STAFF, GEOTHERMAL RES, GEOSCIENCE RES DRILLING OFF, SANDIA NAT LABS, 1989-; staff mem, Geothermal Res, 1977-1989; staff mem, Shock Physics Res, 1966-1977. **Memberships:** Am Geophys Union; Soc Prof Well Log Analysts. **Research Statement & Publications:** Thermodynamics and its relation to shock physics; shock propagation in solid, liquid and porous media; shock-wave induced depolarization of ferroelectrics; neutron log analysis. **Mailing Address:** Sandia Nat Lab, PO Box 5800, Albuquerque, NM 87185. **E-Mail:** pclysne@sandia.gov

LYSTER, MARK ALLAN, ORGANIC CHEMISTRY. **Personal Data:** b Kalamazoo, Mich, January 5, 1953; m 1975, c 4. **Education:** Albion Col, BA, 1975; Univ Calif, Los Angeles, PhD (org chem), 1979. **Professional Experience:** RES CHEMIST, UPJOHN CO, 1979-. **Memberships:** Am Chem Soc. **Research Statement & Publications:** Developing processes to produce bulk quantities of prospective new drugs. **Mailing Address:** Upjohn Co 1510-91-1, Kalamazoo, MI 49001-0199.

LYSYJ, IHOR, ENVIRONMENTAL ENGINEERING. **Personal Data:** b Tarnow, Poland, April 13, 1929; American citizen; m 1957, Natalie Bilonok; c Oleg & Roxanna. **Education:** Ukrainian Tech Inst, Ger, MS, 1950. **Professional Experience:** Sr engr, Comput Sci Corp, Air Force Flight Test Ctr, 1992-1996; CONSULT ENGR, I LYSYJ CONSULTS, 1991-; sr scientist, Furgo-McClelland, 1989-1991; prog mgr, Combustion Eng, 1984-1989; prin scientist, Rocketdyne Div, Rockwell Int Corp, 1961-1984; res scientist, Ethicon, Inc, 1960-1961; analytical chemist, Cent Res Lab, Food Mach & Chem Corp, 1956-1960; dir res, Gaston Johnston Corp, 1954-1956; Analytical chemist, Ex-Lax, Inc, NY, 1952-1954; Consulting Environ Engr; sr prin engr, Comput Sci Corp, Air Force Flight Test Ctr. **Memberships:** Am Chem Soc. **Research Statement & Publications:** Waste water and hazardous materials treatment; chemical detection and sensing technology; environmental quality monitoring systems and networks; regulatory analysis and pollution assessments; environmental engineering. **Mailing Address:** 8917 Hachita Dr, Austin, TX 78749.

LYSYK, TIMOTHY JAMES, MODELLING PEST POPULATION DYNAMICS & BIOLOGICAL PROCESSES, MEDICAL-VETERINARY ENTOMOLOGY. **Personal Data:** b Ottawa, Ont, August 6, 1959; m 1992, Sophia; c Emily. **Education:** Univ Alta, BS (Hons), 1980; SDak State Univ, MS, 1982; NC State Univ, PhD (entom), 1985. **Honors & Awards:** C Gordon Hewitt Award, Entom Soc Can, 1996. **Professional Experience:** Adj prof, Univ Lethbridge, beginning 1993; RES SCIENTIST, LETHBRIDGE RES CTR, AGR CAN, 1989-; guest instr livestock pest mgt, Simon Frazer Univ, beginning 1989; Res scientist, Forestry Can, 1985-1989. **Memberships:** Entom Soc Can; Entom Soc Am. **Research Statement & Publications:** Biology and ecology of Diptera affecting livestock, development of population dynamics models and developing integrated pest management strategies. **Mailing Address:** Lethbridge Res Ctr, Agr & Agr-Food Can, PO Box 3000 Main, Lethbridge, AB T1J 4B1, Can. **Fax:** 403-382-3156. **E-Mail:** lysyk@abrsle.agr.ca

LYTLE, CARL DAVID, BIOPHYSICS. **Personal Data:** b Millersburg, Ohio, January 28, 1941; c 2. **Education:** Kent State Univ, BS, 1963; Cornell Univ, MS, 1965; Pa State Univ, PhD (biophys), 1968. **Professional Experience:** RES BIOPHYSICIST, FOOD & DRUG ADMIN, as of 2006; biophysicist ctr devices & radiol health, beginning 1989; dir, Div Life Sci, 1985-1989; assoc ed, Photochem & Photobiol, 1978-1983; res biophysicist, Multi Environ Stresses Br, 1974-1985; chief, Multi Environ Stresses Br, 1971-1974; adj prof, George Wash Univ, 1971-1972; chief, Path Studies Sect, Environ Protection Agency, 1970-1971; chief, Path Studies Sect, 1970; res biophysicist, Bur Radiol Health, USPHS, 1968-1970. **Memberships:** AAAS; Am Soc Photobiol; Am Soc Microbiol Planetary Soc. **Research Statement & Publications:** Radiation virology; photodynamic virus inactivation; virus penetration of barrier materials. **Mailing Address:** Ctr Devices & Radiol Health, Food & Drug Admin, 5600 Fishers Lane, Rockville, MD 20857. **E-Mail:** cdl@cdrh.fda.gov

LYTLE, CHARLES FRANKLIN, INVERTEBRATE ZOOLOGY. **Personal Data:** b Crawfordsville, Ind, May 13, 1932; m 1955, c 5. **Education:** Wabash Col, AB, 1953; Ind Univ, MA, 1958, PhD (zoology), 1959. **Professional Experience:** Pres sci, NC State Univ, beginning 1989; exec dir, NC Student Acad Sci, 1985-1990; Educ Testing Serv, beginning 1969; Col Bd, beginning 1980; res assoc, NC Mus Natural Hist, beginning 1977; PROF ZOOL, NC STATE UNIV, 1972-; COORDR BIOL SCI PROG, NC STATE UNIV, 1969-; assoc prof, NC State Univ, 1969-1972; from asst prof to assoc prof zool, Pa State Univ, 1964-1969; res analyst, US Govt, 1962-1964; consult, US Dept Army, 1962-1963; asst prof, Tulane Univ, 1960-1962; res assoc, Ind Univ, 1959-1960; fel embryol, Ind Univ, 1959; asst zool, Ind Univ, 1953-1955, 1957-1958; vis prof, Duke Univ, Univ Ala, Fla Atlantic Univ. **Memberships:** Fel AAAS; Am Soc Zool; Am Inst Biol Sci; Sigma Xi; Soc Col Sci Teachers; Nat Asn Sci Teachers; Nat Asn Biol Teachers. **Research Statement & Publications:** Invertebrate zoology; cell biology; cellular structure and function in invertebrate development; differentiation and regulation of cellular organelles; systematics and ecology of Hydrozoa; biological education; instructional television; academic computing. **Mailing Address:** 102 Carmel Ct, Cary, NC 27511-5560. **Fax:** 919-515-1172. **E-Mail:** lytle_bio@ncsu.edu

LYTLE, FARREL WAYNE, SOLID STATE PHYSICS, STRUCTURAL CHEMISTRY. **Personal Data:** b Cedar City, Utah, November 10, 1934; m 1954, Manetta; c Nelson W, W Reed, C Mel & Drew B. **Education:** Univ Nev, BS, 1956, MS, 1958. **Honors & Awards:** Warren Diffraction Physics Award, Am Crystallog Asn, 1979. **Professional Experience:** Prin res scientist, Boeing Sci Res Labs, Boeing Co, 1974-1990; PRES, EXAFS CO, 1974-; sr basic res scientist, Boeing Sci Res Labs, Boeing Co, 1960-1974; Grad Study, Univ Wash, 1960-1963; chemist, US Bur Mines, 1955-1958. **Memberships:** Fel AAAS; fel Am Phys Soc; Am Chem Soc; Mat Res Soc. **Research Statement & Publications:** X-ray physics, x-ray absorbtion fine structure spectroscopy and x-ray diffraction; materials science; structural inorganic chemistry; amorphous structures; structure of catalysts. **Mailing Address:** EXAFS Company, Pioche, NV 89043. **Fax:** 775-962-5571. **E-Mail:** FWLytle@pioche.igate.com

LYTLE, FRED EDWARD, CHEMISTRY. **Personal Data:** b Lewisburg, Pa, January 13, 1943; m 1988, Joyce; c Bradley & Megan. **Education:** Juniata Col, BS, 1964; Mass Inst Technol, PhD (Anal chem), 1968. **Honors & Awards:** Merck Co Found Fac Develop Award, 1969; Am Chem Instrumentation Award, 1986; Analytical Chem Award, Am Chem Soc Award, 1988. **Professional Experience:** PROF CHEM, PURDUE UNIV, WEST LAFAYETTE, 1979-; from asst Prof to assoc prof chem, Purdue Univ, West Lafayette, 1968-1979. **Memberships:** Am Chem Soc; Soc Appl Spectros. **Research Statement & Publications:** Time resolved spectroscopy; trace analysis; use of lasers in applied spectroscopy; two-photon spectroscopy. **Mailing Address:** Dept Chem, Purdue Univ, 1393 Brwn Bldg, West Lafayette, IN 47907-1393. **E-Mail:** flytle@purdue.edu

LYTLE, LOY DENHAM, PSYCHOPHARMACOLOGY, NEUROSCIENCES. **Personal Data:** b Glendale, Calif, April 8, 1943; m 1974, c 2. **Education:** Univ Calif, Santa Barbara, BA, 1966; Princeton Univ, PhD (psychol), 1970. **Professional Experience:** Dir, Off Summer Sessions, Univ Calif, Santa Barbara, as of 2003; dean extended learning Ser, Univ Calif, Santa Barbara, as of 2003; ASSOC PROF PSYCHOPHARMACOL, UNIV CALIF, SANTA BARBARA, 1977-; Alfred P Sloan fel Neuroscience, 1975; asst prof psychopharmacol, Mass Inst Technol, 1972-1977; NIMH fel neuropharmacol, Mass Inst Technol, 1970-1972. **Memberships:** Am Soc Pharmacol & Exp Therapeut; Nutrit Soc; Int Soc Develop Psychobiol; Neuroscience Soc; AAAS; Sigma Xi. **Research Statement & Publications:** Effects of drugs on physiological and behavioral development; diet and drug induced changes in behavior; effects of drugs on brain and peripheral neurotransmitters. **Mailing Address:** Dept Psychol, Univ Calif, Rm 3316A, Santa Barbara, CA 93106-9660. **Fax:** 805-893-4303. **E-Mail:** lytle@psych.ucsb.edu

LYTLE, MICHAEL ALLEN, TECHNOLOGY TRANSFER, ACADEMIC GOVERNMENT RELATIONS. **Personal Data:** b Salina, Kans, October 22, 1946; c Eric A. **Education:** Ind Univ, AB, 1973; Tex A&M Univ, MEd, 1978. **Professional Experience:** Adj lecturer, Criminal Justice Marymount Univ, 1999-; SR LECTR, CRIMINAL JUSTICE, 1995-1997; exec dir inst develop, Univ Tex, Brownsville, 1993-1995; prin & sr counsel, Erik/Alexander Group, 1992-1993; Sci Freedom & Responsibility Award, AAAS, 1990-1995; adj asst prof, Int Bus Trade, 1989-1992; chair, Nat Security Defense Admin, Am Soc Pub Admin, 1989-1991; dir fed rels, Syracuse Univ, 1987-1993; sr res assoc, Technol & Info Policy, Syracuse Univ, 1987-1992; dir res develop, Syracuse Univ, 1987; mem, Mil Critical Technologies Adv Panel, US Dept Com, 1985-1990; mem, Tex Technol Ind Legis Task Force, State Tex, 1985-1987; spec asst to chancellor, Tex A&M Univ Syst, 1984-1987; asst dir govt rels, Tex A&M Univ Syst, 1983-1984; asst to chancellor, Tex A&M Univ Syst, 1981-1983; staff assoc, Tex A&M Univ Syst, 1980-1981. **Memberships:** AAAS; Sigma Xi; Am College Forensic Examiners; Forensic Sci Soc; Acad Criminal Justice Sci. **Research Statement & Publications:** Enabler, facilitator and gatekeeper for science, technology and innovation in the policymaking and political arenas. **Mailing Address:** 260 S Reynolds St No 403, Alexandria, VA 22304-9568. **Fax:** 703-841-4762. **E-Mail:** lytle@saic.com

LYTTON, BERNARD, UROLOGY. **Personal Data:** b London, Eng, June 28, 1926; American citizen; m 1963, Norma; c Sharon, Susan, Timothy & Jennifer. **Education:** Univ London, MB, BS, 1948; FRCS, 1955; Yale Univ, MA. **Honors & Awards:** Hugh H Young Award, Am Urol Asn, 1985. **Professional Experience:** DONALD GUTHRIE PROF EMER SURG, SCH MED, YALE UNIV, as of 2002; Donald Guthrie prof surg, Sch Med, Yale Univ, 1988-2000; PROF UROL, DEPT SURG, SCH MED, YALE UNIV, 1971-; consult, West Haven Vet Admin Hosp, beginning 1962; Hartford Hosp & Hosp St Raphael, 1968-; chief sect urol, Sch Med, Yale Univ, 1967-1987; attend, Yale-New Haven Hosp, 1962-; from asst prof to assoc prof, Sch Med, Yale Univ, 1962-1971; Brit Empire Cancer res fel surg, Univ Hosp, King's Col, Univ London, 1961-1962; resident surg, Royal Victoria Hosp, McGill Univ, 1957-1958; house officer med & surg, London Hosp, 1955-1961; USPHS grant. **Memberships:** AAAS; fel Am Col Surg; Soc Pelvic Surg; Am Asn Genito-Urinary Surg; Clin Soc Genito-Urinary Surgeons; Am Urol Asn. **Research Statement & Publications:** Immunologic aspects of cancer; delayed hypersensitivity response to autogenous tumor extracts; problems of renal ischemia; renal responses to alterations in bladder pressure; compensatory renal growth in parabiotic animals and effects of hemodialysis; endoscopic treatment of urinary calculi; orthotopic bladder replacement. **Mailing Address:** Dept Surg, Yale Univ, PO Box 208062, New Haven, CT 06520-8062. **Fax:** 203-785-4043. **E-Mail:** bernard.lytton@yale.edu

LYTTON, JACK L(ESTER), MATERIALS SCIENCE, METALLURGY. **Personal Data:** b Los Angeles, Calif, August 4, 1933; m 1954, c 4. **Education:** Univ Calif, Berkeley, BS, 1956, MS, 1957; Stanford Univ, PhD (mat sci), 1962. **Professional Experience:** PROF EMER, DEPT MAT SCI & ENG, VA POLYTECH INST & STATE UNIV, 1992-; prof, VA Polytech Inst & State Univ, 1965-1992; res scientist, Lockheed Missiles & Space Co, 1960-1965; res engr, Inst Eng Res, Univ Calif, Berkeley, 1956-1957. **Memberships:** Am Soc Metals; Am Inst Mining Metall & Petrol Engrs. **Research Statement & Publications:** Mechanical behavior of solids, recovery and creep at high temperatures; plastic flow and fracture; failure analysis; structure-property relationships; electronmicroscopy. **Mailing Address:** Dept Mat Sci & Eng, VA Polytech Inst State Univ, 213 Holden Hall, Blacksburg, FL 24061. **Fax:** 540-231-8919.

LYTTON, ROBERT LEONARD, PAVEMENTS, EXPANSIVE SOILS. **Personal Data:** b Port Arthur, Tex, October 23, 1937; m 1961, Marilyn; c Lynn Elizabeth, Robert Douglas & John Kirby. **Education:** Univ Tex, Austin, BS, 1960, MS, 1961, PhD (civil eng), 1967. **Honors & Awards:** John B Hawley Award, Tex Sect, Am Soc Civil Engrs, 1966; Everite Bursary Award, Coun Sci & Indust Res, S Africa, 1984; Zachry Sr Researcher Award, Tex Transp Inst, 1996. **Professional Experience:** Dir MLA Labs, Inc, 1986-; dir, Geostruct Tool Kit Inc, 1992-; dir, Lyric Technol Lic, 1997-; F J BENSON CHAIR PROF, TEX A & M UNIV, 1995-; head, Infrastruct & Transp Div, Dept Civil Eng, 1993-1995; A P & Florence Wiley chair prof, Tex A&M Univ, 1990-1995; US Rep, Comt TC-6, Int Soc Soil Mech & Geotechnical Engrs, 1987-; consult, Strategic Hwy Res Prog, 1985-1987; bd consult, US Army CEngr, 1984-1987; head, Mat, Pavements & Construct Div, Tex Transp Inst, 1982-1991; ERES Consults, Inc, 1981-1995; dir, Meyer, Lytton, Allen, Whitaker Inc, 1980-; mem tech adv bd, Post-Tensioning Inst, 1978-; Mem pub adv bd, Int J Analysis & Numerical Methods Geo Mech, 1977-; prof soils & pavements, Tex A&M Univ, 1976; assoc prof, Tex A&M Univ, 1971-1976; asst prof mat & soils, Univ Tex, Austin, 1967-1968; fel NSF, Australian Commonwealth Sci Inst Res Orgn, 1963-1965; assoc, Dannenbaum Eng Corp, 1969-1970; engr officer, 35th Eng Construct Group, US Army, 1961-1963; civil engr, Naval Civil Eng Lab, Calif, 1960; prin investr, Strategic Highway Res Prog, Proj A005, 1990-1992. **Memberships:** Am Soc Civil Engrs; Transp Res Bd; Asn Asphalt Paving Technologists; Post-Tensioning Inst; Am Concrete Inst; Int Soc Soil Mech & Geotechnical Eng; fel Am Soc Civil Engrs; life mem Am Soc Civil Engrs. **Research Statement & Publications:** Non destructive testing of pavements; analysis and design of pavement evaluation, foundations and pavements on expansive clays; fracture mechanics; probabilistic design; operations research; pavement network optimization; climatic and environmental effects. **Mailing Address:** 2108 Barak Lane, Bryan, TX 77802-4628.

LYUBSKY, SERGEY, PATHOLOGY. **Personal Data:** b Moscow, USSR, June 2, 1945; American citizen; c 1. **Education:** Moscow Univ, MD, 1968; Inst Human Morphol, Moscow, PhD (cell biol), 1975; Am Bd Path, dipl, 1985. **Professional Experience:** STAFF PATHOLOGIST, ELECTRON MICROS LAB, VET ADMIN MED CTR, NORTHPORT, NY, 1985-; ASST PROF PATH, STATE UNIV NY, STONY BROOK, 1985-; assoc dir, Electron Micros Lab, Vet Admin Med Ctr, Northport, NY, beginning 1985; chief resident path, Yale-New Haven Hosp, Conn, 1984; resident anat & clin path, George Wash Univ, 1980-1983; vis assoc, Lab Path, Nat Cancer Inst, NIH, 1979; prin investr, Lab Cell Biol, Inst Human Morphol, Moscow, 1975-1978; postdoctoral fel cytogenetics, Soviet Nat Cancer Inst, Moscow, 1968-1970; mem, Res & Develop Comt, Cancer Comt & Tumor Bd, Vet Admin Hosp. **Research Statement & Publications:** Author of numerous papers and abstracts. **Mailing Address:** State Univ NY, Dept Path, Nicolls Rd, Stony Brook, NY 11794.